Look what people are saying...

"The range is amazing -- it's gigantic!"
  - CNN

"I can do so much with this!"
  - Perez Hilton

"Many small businesses, publicists and marketers want to get their products in celebrities' hands. This book is the solution."
  - Entrepreneur Magazine

"Of all the resources for celebrity addresses, this book is far and away the most useful. It is essential for any serious autograph collector."
  - Autograph Magazine

"Similar titles do not boast as many entries. If your library needs a current celebrity address book, this would be good. Recommended for all libraries."
  - Library Journal

"A superb, quick and easy-to-use reference for entertainment industry professionals and fans alike."
  - Midwest Book Review

"This guide offers priceless information that would otherwise take hours to research. Owning this book is like cutting six degrees of separation down to one simple degree."
  - Curled Up With a Good Book

"The time saved by already having the celebrity's contact information rather than Googling and cold-calling will certainly pay for the book in the long run."
  - Absolute Write

"Some of the best money you'll ever spend. This book is an excellent value and provides you (and me) with great publicity opportunities."
  - Paul Hartunian, Paul Hartunian's Publicity Letter, Hartunian.com

"If you opt to pursue a celebrity or celebrities on your own to use in your advertising, or get a 'blurb' from for your book, etc., this is the place to get contact information."
  - Dan Kennedy, Glazer-Kennedy Inner Circle, DanKennedyPresents.com

"The most helpful book I have ever owned. Worth every penny."
  - Jill Jackson, Syndicated Columnist, Jill Jackson's Hollywood

Visit CelebrityBlackBook.com for more testimonials and success stories!

the celebrity black book

2008 deluxe edition

Over 55,000 Accurate Celebrity Addresses

Edited by Jordan McAuley
Completely Revised & Updated
18th Annual Edition

Visit Us Online
www.ContactAnyCelebrity.com

Editorial Director, Mega Niche Media: Jordan McAuley
Research Director, Contact Any Celebrity: Kyle Burkhalter

Celebrity Black Book Web site: CelebrityBlackBook.com
Contact Any Celebrity Web site: ContactAnyCelebrity.com
Mega Niche Media Web site: MegaNiche.com

The Celebrity Black Book 2008: Over 55,000 Accurate Celebrity Addresses.

Quantity discounts are available on bulk purchases of this book for educational training purposes, fundraising or gift giving. Special books, booklets or book excerpts can also be created to fit your specific needs. Contact Mega Niche Media LLC, 8721 Santa Monica Blvd. #431, West Hollywood, CA 90069-4507 for more information.

ISBN-10: 1-60487-002-8
ISBN-13: 978-1-60487-002-2

Library of Congress Control Number 2004115012

Cover design by Matt Burkhalter Design - matt.burkhalter.com
Interior design by Data Management, Inc. - DBMan.com

Visit ContactAnyCelebrity.com for more information on our products and services.

About the Editor

Jordan McAuley is the Founder and President of Contact Any Celebrity (www.ContactAnyCelebrity.com) located in West Hollywood, California, a service that helps fans, businesses, nonprofits, authors and the media get in touch with over 54,565 celebrities worldwide.

After majoring in both Motion Picture Business and English Literature at the University of Miami, Jordan moved to Hollywood. In Los Angeles, he worked at a movie production company and a large Beverly Hills talent agency as an agent's assistant. These experiences -- combined with working at Wilhelmina Models in South Beach during college plus internships at CNN and Turner Entertainment -- have provided him with insider knowledge on the best ways to contact celebrities.

Today, Contact Any Celebrity is known internationally as the most accurate source of celebrity contact information due to Jordan's extensive experience and personal entertainment industry contacts. Jordan's online database contains the best contact information for over 54,565 celebrities worldwide (including mailing address, agent, manager, publicist, production company and charitable cause) plus info for over 7,000 celebrity representatives and over 4,000 entertainment companies (with phone, fax and email addresses).

Jordan and his services have been featured on CNN and by such national media as *USA Today*, *Us Weekly*, *Entrepreneur*, *The Village Voice*, and Sirius Satellite Radio. He is also recommended in several bestselling books including Timothy Ferris' instant New York Times best-seller *The 4-Hour Workweek*, Dan Kennedy's *The Ultimate Marketing Plan*, Dan Poynter's *Self-Publishing Manual* and John Kremer's *1001 Ways to Market Your Books* (which includes a chapter by Jordan on how to get celebrity book endorsements).

Along with the Celebrity Black Book, Jordan is also the author of *Celebrity Leverage*, *Secrets to Contacting Celebrities* and *Help from Hollywood*.

For more information on Jordan's books and resources, visit his official Web site at www.JordanMcAuley.com.

Activate Your Free 60-Day Online Membership:
www.contactanycelebrity.com/activate

Introduction

Welcome to the *Celebrity Black Book 2008!* Whether you're a fan, business person, nonprofit, author or a member of the media, you're bound to find this book useful. It contains the best mailing addresses for over 55,000 celebrities and public figures. Everyone who is anyone is inside: actors, athletes, musicians, politicians, world leaders, artists, authors... even reality TV stars! The list goes on and on as you'll see once you start flipping through the following pages.

This book is a staple for fans who want to request autographs, nonprofits who want to do the same so they can hold an autograph auction to raise money for their cause, businesses who want to get their products and services in the hands of celebrities, authors who want to get celebrity endorsements for their books, and members of the media who want to get an interview or a quote. There are so many uses, the possibilities are endless!

Of course, with over 55,000 celebrities who move and change representation on a daily basis, this book cannot possibly be 100% accurate. That's why you also get a free 60-day Membership to Contact Any Celebrity's online database so you can get automatic updates. This database contains the best mailing address, agent, manager, publicist, production company and charitable cause for each celebrity, plus contact information for over 4,000 celebrity representatives and over 7,000 entertainment companies with phone, fax and emails.

To activate your free 60-day Membership, visit www.contactanycelebrity.com/activate/.

You may be wondering exactly how to write a fan letter so you have the best chance of getting a response. Or you may be wondering how to approach celebrities for signed memorabilia donations so you can hold a successful celebrity autograph auction. Or you may be wondering how to get a celebrity book endorsement or how to get your products in the hands of celebrities. Don't worry, all of this is easy to accomplish!

Visit the Article Archives section of Contact Any Celebrity for my free special reports, insider secrets and expert interviews at www.contactanycelebrity.com/articles/.

Enjoy your *Celebrity Black Book 2008* -- I'd love to hear your success stories!

Sincerely,

Jordan McAuley
Founder & President
Contact Any Celebrity
www.ContactAnyCelebrity.com
jordan@contactanycelebrity.com

112 (Music Group)
c/o Staff Member *Da Twelve Music Inc*
3060 Peachtree Rd NW Ste 1420
Atlanta, GA 30305-2241, USA

12 Stones (Music Group)
c/o Staff Member *Wind-up Records*
72 Madison Ave Fl 8
New York, NY 10016-8731, USA

3 (Three) Doors Down (Music Group)
c/o Staff Member *In De Goot Entertainment*
119 W 23rd St Ste 609
New York, NY 10011-2594, USA

30 Seconds To Mars (Music Group)
c/o Staff Member *Virgin Records (NY)*
304 Park Ave S Fl 5
New York, NY 10010-4316, USA

311 (Music Group)
311 Touring Inc
946 N Croft Ave
Los Angeles, CA 90069-4204, USA

3LW (Music Group)
1211 S Highland Ave
Los Angeles, CA 90019-1734, USA

3T (Music Group)
To The Tee
15445 Ventura Blvd # 316
Sherman Oaks, CA 91403-3005, USA

5th (Fifth) Dimension, The (Music Group)
c/o Staff Member *Paradise Artists*
108 E Matilija St
Ojai, CA 93023-2639, USA

A

A R S (Actor)
15 Sarangapani Street
T Nagar
Chennai, TN 600 017, INDIA

A1 (Music Group)
c/o Staff Member *Concorde Intl Artists Ltd*
101 Shepherds Bush Rd
London W6 7LP, UNITED KINGDOM (UK)

A3 (Music Group)
c/o Staff Member *Paradigm (Monterey)*
509 Hartnell St
Monterey, CA 93940-2825, USA

Aadland, Beverly (Actor)
27617 Ennismore Ave
Canyon Country, CA 91351-3414, USA

Aaker, Lee (Actor)
PO Box 8013
Mammoth Lakes, CA 93546-8013, USA

Aalto, Antti (Hockey Player)
Mighty Ducks of Anaheim
300 Ocean Ave
Seal Beach, CA 90740-6031, USA

Aames, Willie (Actor)
10209 SE Division St
Portland, OR 97266-1327, USA

Aamni (Actor, Bollywood)
6 Parthasarathi Puram Extension
Chennai, TN 600017, INDIA

Aaron, Caroline (Actor)
c/o Staff Member *Kass & Stokes Management*
9229 W Sunset Blvd Ste 504
Los Angeles, CA 90069-3405, USA

Aaron, Chester (Writer)
PO Box 388
Occidental, CA 95465-0388, USA

Aaron, Hank (Baseball Player)
1611 Adams Dr SW
Atlanta, GA 30311-3625, USA

Aaron, Henry J (Economist)
1326 Hemlock St NW
Washington, DC 20012-1551, USA

Aaron, Paul (Director)
1604 Courtney Ave
Los Angeles, CA 90046-2708, USA

Aaron, Tommy (Golfer)
440 E Lake Dr
Gainesville, GA 30506-1740, USA

Aarthi (Actor, Bollywood)
18 Senthil Andavar Koil Street
Dhanalakshmi Colony Saligramam
Chennai, TN 600079, INDIA

Aas, Roald (Speed Skater)
Enebakkvn 252
Oslo 11 1187, NORWAY

Aase, Donald W (Don) (Baseball Player)
Boston Red Sox
5055 Via Ricardo
Yorba Linda, CA 92886-4526, USA

Abad, Andy (Baseball Player)
c/o Staff Member *Cincinnati Reds*
100 Cinergy Fld
Cinergy Field
Cincinnati, OH 45202, USA

Abair, Mindy (Musician)
PO Box 931513
Los Angeles, CA 90093-1513, USA

Abakanowicz, Magdalena (Artist)
Ul Bzowa 1
Warsaw 02-708, POLAND

Abalkin, Leonid I (Economist)
Academy of Scienes
Nakhimovsky Prospekt 32
Moscow 117218, RUSSIA

Abams, John N (General)
Commanding General
US Training/Doctrine Command
Fort Monroe, VA 23651, USA

ABBA (Music Group)
Postbus 3079
Roosendaal NL-4700 GB, THE NETHERLANDS

Abbado, Claudio (Conductor)
Piazzetta Bossi 1
Milan 20121, ITALY

Abbas (Actor, Bollywood)
C-24 1702 BBA QTRS AUSTIN TOWN
Bangalore, KA, INDIA

Abbatiello, Carmine (Athlete)
176 Stone Hill Rd
Colts Neck, NJ 07722-1730, USA

Abbe, Elfriede M (Artist)
Applewood
Manchester Center, VT 05255, USA

Abbey, Joe (Football Player)
Chicago Bears
1814 N Bonnie Brae St
Denton, TX 76207, USA

Abbott, Bruce (Actor)
c/o Staff Member *Metropolitan*
4500 Wilshire Blvd Fl 2
Los Angeles, CA 90010-3858, USA

Abbott, D Thomas (Business Person)
Salvin Corp
333 Ludlow St
Stamford, CT 06902-6987, USA

Abbott, Diahnne (Actor)
460 W Avenue 46
Los Angeles, CA 90065-5006, USA

Abbott, Glenn (Baseball Player)
Oakland A's
4413 Dawson Dr
North Little Rock, AR 72116-7037, USA

Abbott, Gregory
PO Box 68
Bergenfield, NJ 07621-0068, USA

Abbott, Jeff (Baseball Player)
Chicago White Sox
6403 Chastain Dr NE
Atlanta, GA 30342-4181, USA

Abbott, Kurt (Baseball Player)
Oakland A's
613 Howard Creek Ln
Stuart, FL 34994-9114, USA

Abbott, Paul (Baseball Player)
Minnesota Twins
1945 Dana Pl
Fullerton, CA 92831-1216, USA

Abbott, Preston S (Doctor)
1305 Namassin Rd
Alexandria, VA 22308-1043, USA

Abbott, Reg (Hockey Player)
Montreal Canadiens
5239 Hanover Pl
Victoria, BC V8Y 2C7, CANADA

Abbott, Vince (Football Player)
San Diego Chargers
121 Via Waziers
Newport Beach, CA 92663-5517, USA

Abboud, A Robert (Business Person)
A Robert Abboud Co
212 Stone Hill Center
Lake Zurich, IL 60047, USA

Abboud, Joseph M (Designer, Fashion Designer)
650 5th Ave # 2700
New York, NY 10019-6108, USA

Abdnor, James (Politician, Senator)
PO Box 217
Kennebec, SD 57544-0217, USA

Abdrashitov, Vadim Y (Director)
3D Frunzenskaya 8 #211
Moscow 119270, RUSSIA

Abdul, Paula (Musician, Reality TV Star)
c/o Staff Member *American Idol*
7800 Beverly Blvd # 251
Los Angeles, CA 90036-2112, USA

Abdul-Aziz, Zaid (Basketball Player)
Cincinnati Royals
11300 3rd Ave NE Apt 131
Seattle, WA 98125-6040, USA

Abdul-Jabbar, Kareem (Basketball Player)
PO Box 5220
Playa Del Rey, CA 90296-5220, USA

Abdul-Jabbar, Karim (Football Player)
c/o Harlan Werner *Sports Placement Service*
6671 W Sunset Blvd Ste 1521
Los Angeles, CA 90028-7123, USA

Abdul-Saboor, Mikal (Football Player)
Pittsburgh Steelers
5465 Derby Chase Ct
Alpharetta, GA 30005-7882, USA

Abdulov, Aleksandr G (Actor)
Peschanaya Str 4 #3
Moscow 125252, RUSSIA

Abdur-Rahim, Shareef (Basketball Player)
c/o Staff Member *Atlanta Hawks*
101 Marietta St NW Ste 1900
Centennial Tower
Atlanta, GA 30303-2771, USA

Abed, Rodrigo (Actor)
c/o Gabriel Blanco *Gabriel Blanco Iglesias (Mexico)*
Rio Balsas 35-32
Colonia Cuauhtemoc
DF 06500, MEXICO

Abeernethy, Tom (Basketball Player)
Los Angeles Lakers
5905 William Conner Way
Carmel, IN 46033-8826, USA

Abel (DJ)
c/o Len Evans *Project Publicity*
312 W 53rd St
New York, NY 10019-5743, USA

Abel, Gerald (Hockey Player)
Detroit Red Wings
26850 Halsted Rd
Farmington Hills, MI 48331-3557, USA

Abel, Jessica (Artist)
c/o Staff Member *Fantagraphics Books*
7563 Lake City Way NE
Seattle, WA 98115-4218, USA

Abel, Joy (Bowler)
PO Box 296
Lansing, IL 60438, USA

Abell, Bud (Football Player)
Kansas City Chiefs
118 Ridgecest Ct
Panama City, FL 32405, USA

Abell, Tim (Actor)
c/o Tammy Rosen *Melanie Greene Management & Productions*
425 N Robertson Blvd
West Hollywood, CA 90048-1735, USA

Abelson, Alan (Writer)
Barron's Magazine - Editorial Dept
200 Liberty St
New York, NY 10281-1003, USA

Abelson, Robert P (Doctor)
1155 Whitney Ave
Hamden, CT 06517-3434, USA

Abercrombie, Ian (Actor)
c/o Staff Member *Cunningham Escott Slevin & Doherty (NY)*
257 Park Ave S Rm 950
New York, NY 10010-7304, USA

Abercrombie, John L (Musician)
Joel Chriss
300 Mercer St Apt 3J
New York, NY 10003-6732, USA

Abercrombie, Neil (Government Official)
1050 Ala Moana Blvd Ste 2680
Honolulu, HI 96814-4933, USA

Abercrombie, Walter (Coach, Football Coach, Football Player)
Pittsburgh Steelers
100 Legend Ln
American Football Coaches Association
Waco, TX 76706-1243, USA

Abernathie, Bill (Baseball Player)
Cleveland Indians
35808 Avenue E
Yucaipa, CA 92399-4935, USA

Abernathy, Brent (Baseball Player)
Tampa Bay Devil Rays
508 Cascade Cir
Palm Harbor, FL 34684-3505, USA

Abernathy, Robert (Baseball Player)
Kansas City Monarchs
2491 Walker Ln
Nashville, TN 37207-4213, USA

Abernathy, Robert (Correspondent)
c/o Staff Member *Public Broadcasting
Service (PBS)*
1320 Braddock Pl
Alexandria, VA 22314-1692, USA

Abernathy, Tal (Baseball Player)
Philadelphia Athletics
1621 Fairfield Dr
Gastonia, NC 28054-5171, USA

Abert, Donald B (Publisher)
Milwaukee Journal
333 W State St
Milwaukee, WI 53203-1309, USA

Abgrall, Dennis (Hockey Player)
Los Angeles Kings
16607 S 12th Pl
Phoenix, AZ 85048-4703, USA

Abhishek, Bachchan (Actor, Bollywood)
Prateeksha
10th Rd Juhu Scheme
Mumbai, MS 400049, INDIA

Abhishek, V B (Actor)
10 ALS Garden 83 A
Natarajan Salai Dhanalakshmi Colony
Chennai, TN 600 026, INDIA

Abigail (Musician)
c/o Staff Member *Diva Central Inc*
7510 W Sunset Blvd Ste 1445
Los Angeles, CA 90046-3408, USA

Abiodun, Oyewole (Musician)
c/o Staff Member *Agency Group Ltd, The
(UK)*
361-373 City Road
London EC1V 1PQ, UNITED KINGDOM
(UK)

Abizaid, John P (General)
Commander
US Central Command
Macdill Air Force Base, FL 33621, USA

Able, Forest (Basketball Player)
Syracuse Nationals
11102 Mitchell Hill Rd
Fairdale, KY 40118-9425, USA

Ablon, Ralph E (Business Person)
Ogden Corp
PO Box 2615
Fairfield, NJ 07004-0216, USA

Ablow, Keith (Doctor)
c/o Greg Lipstone *William Morris Agency
(WMA-LA)*
1 William Morris Pl
Beverly Hills, CA 90212-4261, USA

Aboud, John (Writer)
Modern Humorist
335 Court St
Pmb 177
Brooklyn, NY 11231-4335, USA

Aboulhosn, Hassan (Football Player)
Washington Redskins
2703 Oaklawn Blvd
Hopewell, VA 23860-4934, USA

Abourezk, James G (Politician, Senator)
21 Dupont Cir NW Ste 400
Washington, DC 20036-1547, USA

Abragam, Anatole (Scientist)
33 Rue Croulebarbe
Paris 75013, FRANCE

Abraham, F Murray (Actor)
c/o Staff Member *William Morris Agency
(WMA-LA)*
1 William Morris Pl
Beverly Hills, CA 90212-4261, USA

Abraham, John (Football Player)
New York Jets
1944 Weaver St
Timmonsville, SC 29161-9083, USA

Abraham, Nate (Football Player)
Tampa Bay Buccaneers
3038 Wentworth Way
Tarpon Springs, FL 34688-8445, USA

Abraham, Robert (Football Player)
Houston Oilers
1106 Hemingway St
Myrtle Beach, SC 29577-3321, USA

Abraham, Spencer E (Politician, Senator)
Energy Dept
1000 Independence Ave SW
Washington, DC 20585-0001, USA

Abrahamian, Emil (Cartoonist)
147 Woodleaf Dr
Winter Springs, FL 32708-6159, USA

Abrahams, Jim S (Director)
c/o Steve Rabineau *William Morris
Agency (WMA-LA)*
9601 Wilshire Blvd Fl 3
Beverly Hills, CA 90210-5204, USA

Abrahams, Jonathan (Jon) (Actor)
c/o Beth Holden-Garland *Untitled
Entertainment (LA)*
331 N Maple Dr Fl 3
Beverly Hills, CA 90210-3827, USA

Abrahamse, Taylor
Rockyz Kidz
146 Shuter St
Studio B
Toronto, ON M5A 1V9, CANADA

Abrahamson, James A (Business Person,
General)
3557 Havercamp Rd
Hibbing, MN 55746-8142, USA

Abram, Norm (Entertainer)
c/o Staff Member *This Old House*
PO Box 130
Concord, MA 01742-0130, USA

Abramovich, Roman (Business Person)
Millhouse Capital UK Ltd
Hill House
1 Little New St
London EC4A 3TR, UNITED KINGDOM
(UK)

Abramowicz, Daniel (Danny) (Football
Player)
New Orleans Saints
143 Parkdale Rd
Steubenville, OH 43952-3609, USA

Abramowicz, Sidney (Football Player)
Baltimore Colts
3341 Thomashire Ct
Marietta, GA 30066-4786, USA

Abrams, Bobby (Football Player)
New York Giants
1470 Pampas Dr
Montgomery, AL 36117-2310, USA

Abrams, Dan (Television Host)
c/o Staff Member *MSNBC (NJ)*
Nbc/One Microsoft Corporation
1 Msnc Plaza
Secaucus, NJ 07094, USA

Abrams, Eliot
Dogwood Farm Lane 10607
Great Falls, VA 22066, USA

Abrams, Elliott (Government Official)
10607 Dogwood Farm Ln
Great Falls, VA 22066-2937, USA

Abrams, Jeffrey (JJ) (Actor, Producer,
Writer)
c/o Staff Member *Bad Robot*
500 S Buena Vista St Bldg 23 Rm 26
Burbank, CA 91521-0001, USA

Abrams, JJ (Director)
c/o Staff Member *William Morris Agency
(WMA-LA)*
1 William Morris Pl
Beverly Hills, CA 90212-4261, USA

Abramson, Leslie (Actor)
4929 Wilshire Blvd
Los Angeles, CA 90010-3808, USA

Abramson, Neil (Director, Writer)
c/o Staff Member *United Talent Agency
(UTA)*
9560 Wilshire Blvd Ste 500
Beverly Hills, CA 90212-2401, USA

Abreu, Aldo (Musician)
Concert Artists Guild
850 7th Ave Ste 1205
New York, NY 10019-5230, USA

Abreu, Bobby (Baseball Player)
Houston Astros
2611 W Mimi Cir
Philadelphia, PA 19131-2839, USA

Abreu, Irina (Actor)
c/o Staff Member *Televisa*
Blvd Adolfo Lopez Mateos 232
Colonia San Angel INN
DF CP 01060, MEXICO

Abrikosov, Alexei A (Nobel Prize
Laureate)
804 Houston St
Lemont, IL 60439-4338, USA

Abroms, Edward M (Director)
EMA Enterprises
1866 Marlowe St
Thousand Oaks, CA 91360-3331, USA

Abronzino, Umberto (Soccer Player)
1336 Settle Ave
San Jose, CA 95125-2363, USA

Abrunhosa, Pedro (Musician)
Polygram Records
825 8th Ave
Worldwide Plaza
New York, NY 10019-7416, USA

Abruzzese, Ray (Football Player)
Buffalo Bills
3031 N Ocean Blvd Apt 1906
Fort Lauderdale, FL 33308-7331, USA

Abruzzo, Ray (Actor)
c/o Staff Member *Peter Strain &
Associates Inc (LA)*
5455 Wilshire Blvd Ste 1812
Los Angeles, CA 90036-4268, USA

Absher, Dick (Football Player)
Washington Redskins
511 Small Reward Rd
Huntingtown, MD 20639-3408, USA

Abshire, David M (Diplomat)
Strategic/International Studies Center
1800 K St NW Ste 400
Washington, DC 20006-2230, USA

abtahi, omid (Actor)
c/o Michael Greene *Greene & Associates*
190 N Canon Dr Ste 200
Beverly Hills, CA 90210-5319, USA

Abul-Ragheb, Ali (Prime Minister)
Prime Minister's Office
PO Box 80
Amman 35215, JORDAN

Accola, Paul (Skier)
Bolgenstr 17
Davos Platz 7270, SWITZERLAND

Acconci, Vito (Artist)
20 Jay St Ste 215
Brooklyn, NY 11201-8319, USA

AC/DC (Music Group)
c/o Alvin Handwerker *Prager & Fenton*
12424 Wilshire Blvd Ste 1000
Los Angeles, CA 90025-1071, USA

Ace, Buddy (Musician)
Rodgers Redding
1048 Tattnall St
Macon, GA 31201-1537, USA

Ace of Base (Music Group)
Indiakaj 1
Copenhagen DK-2100 OE, DENMARK

Acevedo, Hernan F (Scientist)
Allegheny-Singer Research Institute
320 E North Ave
Pittsburgh, PA 15212-4756, USA

Acevedo, Juan (Baseball Player)
c/o Staff Member *Arizona Diamondbacks*
401 E Jefferson St
Bank One Ballpark
Phoenix, AZ 85004-2438, USA

Acevedo, Kirk (Actor)
c/o Chris Schmidt *Paradigm (LA)*
360 N Crescent Dr
North Bldg
Beverly Hills, CA 90210-6820, USA

Achebe, Chinua (Writer)
Bard College
Language & Literature Dept
PO Box 41
Annandale, NY 12504, USA

Achica, George (Football Player)
Indianapolis Colts
3165 Lone Bluff Way
San Jose, CA 95111-1264, USA

Achtymichuk, Gene (Hockey Player)
Montreal Canadiens
9985 93 Ave
Fort Saskatchewan, AB T8L 1N5,
CANADA

Acid Test (Music Group)
83 Riverside Dr
New York, NY 10024-5713, USA

Ackeman, Leslie (Actor)
950 2nd St Apt 201
Santa Monica, CA 90403-2439, USA

Acker, Amy (Actor)
c/o Matthew Lesher *Lesher Entertainment
Inc*
1134 S Cloverdale Ave
Los Angeles, CA 90019-6737, USA

Acker, Bill (Football Player)
St Louis Cardinals
1505 Delwood Ln
Alice, TX 78332-4073, USA

Acker, Jim (Baseball Player)
Toronto Blue Jays
PO Box Aa
Freer, TX 78357-2027, USA

Acker, Joseph E (Doctor)
1307 Old Weisgarber Rd
Knoxville, TN 37909, USA

Acker, Tom (Baseball Player)
Cincinnati Reds
118 Gloucester Rd
Stuarts Draft, VA 24477-3328, USA

Ackeren, Robert V (Director)
Kurfurstendamm 132A
Berlin 10711, GERMANY

Ackerman, Andrew (Andy) (Director, Editor, Producer)
c/o Staff Member *Kaplan-Stahler-Gumer Agency*
8383 Wilshire Blvd Ste 923
Beverly Hills, CA 90211-2408, USA

Ackerman, Buddy (Basketball Player)
New York Knicks
27 Nassau Rd
Oceanside, NY 11572-3016, USA

Ackerman, F Duane (Business Person)
BellSouth Corp
1155 Peachtree St NE Ste P1
Atlanta, GA 30309-7698, USA

Ackerman, Joshua (Actor)
c/o Staff Member *Burstein Company, The*
15304 W Sunset Blvd Ste 208
Pacific Palisades, CA 90272-3656, USA

Ackerman, Leslie (Actor)
4439 Worster Ave
Studio City, CA 91604, USA

Ackerman, Michael W (General)
Pentagon
Hqusa - Inspector General
Washington, DC 20310-0001, USA

Ackerman, Roger G (Business Person)
Coming Inc
Houghton Park
Coming, NY 14831, USA

Ackerman, Thomas E (Cinematographer)
1644 San Leandro Ln
Montecito, CA 93108-2638, USA

Ackerman, Tom (Football Player)
17511 N Greenbluff Rd
Colbert, WA 99005-9505, USA

Ackerman, William (Composer)
Drake Assoc
177 Woodland Ave
Westwood, NJ 07675-3218, USA

Ackermann, Rosemarie (Athlete, Track Athlete)
Str der Jugend 72
Cottbus 03050, GERMANY

Ackland, Joss (Actor)
c/o Staff Member *Jonathan Altaras Assoc Ltd*
13 Shorts Gardens
London WC2H 9AT, UNITED KINGDOM (UK)

Ackles, Jensen (Actor)
c/o Rachel Shapiro *Jeff Morrone Management*
9350 Wilshire Blvd Ste 224
Beverly Hills, CA 90212-3204, USA

Ackroyd, David (Actor)
273 N Many Lakes Dr
Kalispell, MT 59901-8344, USA

Ackroyd, Peter (Writer)
Anthony Shell Assoc
43 Doughty St
London WC1N 2LF, UNITED KINGDOM (UK)

Acks, Ron (Football Player)
Atlanta Falcons
563 Licklog Rdg
Hayesville, NC 28904-4879, USA

Acohido, Byron (Journalist)
Seattle Times Editorial Dept
1120 John St
Seattle, WA 98109-5321, USA

Acomb, Doug (Hockey Player)
Toronto Maple Leafs
18 Millstone Crt
Markham, ON L3R 7M4, CANADA

Acorah, Derek (Actor, Misc)
PO Box 32
Ormskirk
Lancashire L40 9SN, UNITED KINGDOM (UK)

Acord, Lance (Cinematographer)
c/o Staff Member *Dattner Dispoto and Associates*
10635 Santa Monica Blvd Ste 165
Los Angeles, CA 90025-8306, USA

Acorn, Fred (Football Player)
Tampa Bay Buccaneers
8805 N Plaza Ct Apt 1175
Austin, TX 78753-4891, USA

Acosta, Eduardo (Baseball Player)
Pittsburgh Pirates
22822 Boltana
Mission Viejo, CA 92691-1717, USA

Acovone, Jay (Actor)
c/o Staff Member *GVA Talent Agency Inc*
9229 W Sunset Blvd Ste 320
Los Angeles, CA 90069-3403, USA

Acrivos, Andreas (Scientist)
145 W 67th St
New York, NY 10023-5923, USA

Acton, Bud (Basketball Player)
San Diego Rockets
PO Box 87
Empire, MI 49630-0087, USA

Acton, Keith (Coach, Hockey Player)
Montreal Canadiens
Toronto Maple Leafs 300-40 Bay Street
Attn Coaching Staff
Toronto, ON M5J 2X2, CANADA

Acton, Loren W (Astronaut)
PO Box 1857
Bozeman, MT 59771-1857, USA

Acuba, Jason 'Wee Man' (Actor)
c/o Staff Member *LW 1 Inc*
7257 Beverly Blvd Fl 2
Los Angeles, CA 90036-2503, USA

Acuff, Amy
1 Rca Dome Ste 120
Indianapolis, IN 46225-1023, USA

Adade, Manohar (Actor, Bollywood)
199 Vellala Street
Purasawakkam
Chennai, TN 600 084, INDIA

Adair, Deborah (Actor)
c/o Staff Member *Cast Images*
2530 J St Ste 330
Sacramento, CA 95816-4849, USA

Adair, Tatum (Actor)
Mission Talent Agency
10929 Vanowen St Ste 138
Atten: Goro Hamasaki
North Hollywood, CA 91605-6435, USA

Adam, Robert (Architect)
Winchester Design
9 Upper High St
Winchester
Hants S023 8UT, UNITED KINGDOM (UK)

Adam, Russ (Hockey Player)
Toronto Maple Leafs
69 Old Petty Harbour Rd
St. John's, NL A1G 1H6, CANADA

Adam, Theo (Opera Singer)
Schillerstr 14
Dresden 01326, GERMANY

Adamchik, Ed (Football Player)
New York Giants
234 Princeton Ave
Pittsburgh, PA 15229-1516, USA

Adamkus, Valdas (Politician, President)
c/o Staff Member *Presidential Office (Lithuania)*
Gediminas 53
Vilnius 232026, LITHUANIA

Adams, Ace (Baseball Player)
New York Giants
PO Box 72046
Albany, GA 31708-2046, USA

Adams, Alvan (Basketball Player)
5617 N Palo Cristi Rd
Paradise Valley, AZ 85253-7544, USA

Adams, Amy (Actor)
c/o Stacy Boniello *The Firm*
9465 Wilshire Blvd Fl 6
Beverly Hills, CA 90212-2605, USA

Adams, Bob (Baseball Player)
Detroit Tigers
31713 157th St E
Llano, CA 93544-1222, USA

Adams, Brent (Football Player)
Atlanta Falcons
3615 Parkmont Ct
Norcross, GA 30092-4521, USA

Adams, Brooke (Actor)
248 S Van Ness Ave
Los Angeles, CA 90004-3921, USA

Adams, Bryan (Hockey Player)
c/o Staff Member *Atlanta Thrashers*
101 Marietta St NW Ste 1900
Centennial Tower
Atlanta, GA 30303-2771, USA

Adams, Bryan (Musician)
c/o Bruce Allen *SL Feldman & Associates*
1505 W 2nd Ave #200
Vancouver, BC V6H 3Y4, CANADA

Adams, Charles (Baseball Player)
Chicago Cubs
6058 Puerto Dr
Rancho Murieta, CA 95683-9314, USA

Adams, Charles J (Religious Leader)
Progressive National Baptist Convention
601 50th St NE
Washington, DC 20019-5498, USA

Adams, David (Football Player)
7456 E Rio Verde Dr
Tucson, AZ 85715-3535, USA

Adams, Dick (Baseball Player)
Philadelphia Athletics
4650 Dulin Rd Spc 136
Fallbrook, CA 92028-9362, USA

Adams, Doug (Baseball Player)
Chicago White Sox
1129 Harmony Cir NE
Janesville, WI 53545-2072, USA

Adams, Edie (Actor)
8040 Ocean Ave
Los Angeles, CA 90046, USA

Adams, Evan (Actor)
c/o Staff Member *Characters Talent Agency, The (Toronto)*
8 Elm St 3rd FL
Toronto, ON M5G 1G7, CANADA

Adams, Flozell (Football Player)
Dallas Cowboys
5201 Reflection Ct
Flower Mound, TX 75022-8144, USA

Adams, George (Basketball Player)
San Diego Conqoistadors
508 Watergate Cir
Gastonia, NC 28052-7718, USA

Adams, George (Football Player)
New York Giants
2410 Damsel Katie Dr
Lewisville, TX 75056-5801, USA

Adams, George R (Musician)
Joel Chriss
300 Mercer St Apt 3J
New York, NY 10003-6732, USA

Adams, Gerard (Gerry) (Politician)
Sinn Fein/IRA
51/55 Falls Road
Belfast, Northern Ireland BT 12, UNITED KINGDOM (UK)

Adams, Glenn (Baseball Player)
San Francisco Giants
RR 1
Sedan, NM 88436, USA

Adams, Greg (Hockey Player)
Philadelphia Flyers
GRECA Construction Management
33 Lois Lane
Duncan, BC V9L 5H4, CANADA

Adams, Henry (Football Player)
Chicago Cardinals
53 4th St
California, PA 15419-1109, USA

Adams, Herb (Baseball Player)
Chicago White Sox
4021 E 84th St
Tulsa, OK 74137-1724, USA

Adams, Jane (Actor)
c/o Staff Member *Framework Entertainment (LA)*
9057 Nemo St # C
W Hollywood, CA 90069-5511, USA

Adams, Joey Lauren (Actor)
c/o Chris Andrews *Creative Artists Agency LCC (CAA-LA)*
2000 Avenue Of The Stars
Los Angeles, CA 90067-4700, USA

Adams, John (Golfer)
4610 County Road 42200
Paris, TX 75462-1391, USA

Adams, John (Hockey Player)
Boston Bruins
109 Nottingham Cres
Thunder Bay, ON P7G 1B4, CANADA

Adams, John C (Musician)
c/o Staff Member *Elektra Records*
75 Rockefeller Plz Fl 17
New York, NY 10019-6927, USA

Adams, John H (Religious Leader)
African Methodist Church
1134 11th St NW
Washington, DC 20001-4316, USA

Adams, Julie (Actor)
Sutton Barth Vennari
145 S Fairfax Ave Ste 310
Los Angeles, CA 90036-2176, USA

Adams, Julius (Football Player)
New England Patriots
2135 Jefferson Davis St
Macon, GA 31201, USA

Adams, Keith (Football Player)
Dallas Cowboys
404 Baker Cir NW
Atlanta, GA 30318-6318, USA

Adams, Kenneth S (Bud) (Football Player)
c/o Team Member *Tennessee Titans*
460 Great Circle Rd
Baptist Sports Park
Nashville, TN 37228-1404, USA

Adams, Kevyn (Hockey Player)
Toronto Maple Leafs
3837 Route 430
Bemus Point, NY 14712-9535, USA

Adams, Linda
c/o Staff Member *Crews*
828 Clemont Dr NE
Atlanta, GA 30306-3694, USA

Adams, Lorraine (Journalist)
Washington Post - Editorial Dept
1150 15th St NW
Washington, DC 20071-0001, USA

Adams, Mark (Artist)
1400 Geary Blvd Rm 218
San Francisco, CA 94109-6565, USA

Adams, Mary Kay (Actor)
Roe Enterprises
PO Box 2023
Fairfield, IA 52556-0034, USA

Adams, Maud (Actor)
PO Box 10838
Beverly Hills, CA 90213-3838, USA

Adams, Michael F (Educator)
University of Georgia
President's Office
Athens, GA 30602, USA

Adams, Mike (Baseball Player)
Minnesota Twins
13205 Jo Ln NE
Albuquerque, NM 87111-7112, USA

Adams, Noah (Correspondent)
National Public Radio
635 Massachusetts Ave NW
Washington, DC 20001-3753, USA

Adams, Oleta (Music Group)
Engine Entertainment
940 Gale Ln Apt 117
Nashville, TN 37204-3096, USA

Adams, Pat (Artist)
370 Elm St
Bennington, VT 05201-2214, USA

Adams, Patch (Doctor)
6855 Washington Blvd
Arlington, VA 22213-1120, USA

Adams, Pete (Football Player)
Cleveland Browns
1443 Hygeia Ave
Encinitas, CA 92024-1624, USA

Adams, Ranald T Jr (General)
1002 Emerald Dr
Alexandria, VA 22308-2626, USA

Adams, Richard G (Writer)
Benwell's
26 Church St
Whitechurch
Hants RG28 7AR, UNITED KINGDOM
(UK)

Adams, Richard N (Doctor, Misc)
PO Box Zz
Basalt, CO 81621-0800, USA

Adams, Ricky (Baseball Player)
California Angels
6437 Garnet St
Alta Loma, CA 91701-4009, USA

Adams, Ryan (Music Group, Songwriter, Writer)
High Road
751 Bridgeway # 300
Sausalito, CA 94965-2165, USA

Adams, Sam (Football Player)
Seattle Seahawks
12010 Holly Stone Dr
Houston, TX 77070-5420, USA

Adams, Sassoon Beverly (Model)
1923 Selby Ave Apt 203
Los Angeles, CA 90025-5867, USA

Adams, Scott (Cartoonist)
Harper Business Publishers
10 E 53rd St
New York, NY 10022-5244, USA

Adams, Scott (Football Player)
Minnesota Vikings
1171 Middlebrooks Rd
Watkinsville, GA 30677-3820, USA

Adams, Tag (Adult Film Star)
c/o Staff Member *Diva Central Inc*
7510 W Sunset Blvd Ste 1445
Los Angeles, CA 90046-3408, USA

Adams, Tom (Football Player)
Minnesota Vikings
20606 Crystal Springs Loop
Grand Rapids, MN 55744-5183, USA

Adams, Tony (Football Player)
Kansas City Chiefs
14012 Juniper St
Overland Park, KS 66224-3578, USA

Adams, Trace (Music Group)
Borman
1222 16th Ave S Ste 23
Nashville, TN 37212-2926, USA

Adams, Vashone (Football Player)
Cleveland Browns
2940 S Parker Ct
Aurora, CO 80014-3018, USA

Adams, William J (Football Player)
Buffalo Bills
12 Willowby Way
Lynnfield, MA 01940-1022, USA

Adams, Willie (Baseball Player)
Oakland A's
11903 Kibbee Ave
La Mirada, CA 90638-1518, USA

Adams, Willie J (Football Player)
Washington Redskins
2513 Forest Creek Dr
Fort Worth, TX 76123-1145, USA

Adams, Willis (Football Player)
Cleveland Browns
7831 Quail Meadow Dr
Houston, TX 77071-2337, USA

Adams, Yolanda (Music Group, Musician)
Mahogany Entertainment
PO Box 4367
Upper Marlboro, MD 20775-0367, USA

Adams, Yolonda (Musician)
Elektra Records
75 Rockefeller Plz
New York, NY 10019-6908, USA

Adams Jr, Robert McCornick (Misc)
PO Box Zz
Basalt, CO 81621-0800, USA

Adamson, Andrew (Director)
c/o Jeremy Zimmer *United Talent Agency (UTA)*
9560 Wilshire Blvd Ste 500
Beverly Hills, CA 90212-2401, USA

Adamson, Joel (Baseball Player)
Florida Marlins
14832 S 46th Pl
Phoenix, AZ 85044-6872, USA

Adamson, Ken (Football Player)
Denver Broncos
2424 Del Monte St
West Sacramento, CA 95691-3808, USA

Adamson, Mike (Baseball Player)
Baltimore Orioles
17610 Canterbury Dr
Monument, CO 80132-8310, USA

Adamson, Robert (Actor)
c/o Theo Asweissen *Koopman Management*
PO Box 1317
Pacific Palisades, CA 90272-1317, USA

Adamson, Robert E Jr (Admiral)
1709 Bohnhoff Ct
Virginia Beach, VA 23454-2520, USA

Aday, Marvin Lee (Meat Loaf / Meatloaf) (Musician)
c/o Miles Levy *James/Levy/Jacobson Management*
3500 W Olive Ave Ste 1470
Burbank, CA 91505-5514, USA

ADC Band
17397 Santa Barbara Dr
Detroit, MI 48221-2526, USA

Addabbo, Anthony (Actor)
c/o Staff Member *SDB Partners Inc*
1801 Avenue Of The Stars Ste 902
Los Angeles, CA 90067-5981, USA

Addams, Abe (Football Player)
Detroit Lions
477 Colesburg Rd
Elizabethtown, KY 42701-6144, USA

Adderley, Herb (Football Player)
Green Bay Packers
1058 Tristram Cir
Mantua, NJ 08051-2204, USA

Adderly, Herb
PO Box 219
Mantua, NJ 08051-0219, USA

Addiction, Jane's (Musician)
c/o Staff Member *Creative Artists Agency LCC (CAA-LA)*
2000 Avenue Of The Stars
Los Angeles, CA 90067-4700, USA

Addis, Bob (Baseball Player)
Boston Braves
7466 Hollycroft Ln
Mentor, OH 44060-5611, USA

Addison, Rafael (Basketball Player)
Phoenix Suns
12 Elmridge Rd
Jamesville, NY 13078-9743, USA

Addison, Tom (Football Player)
Boston Patriots
1799 County Line Pl
Douglasville, GA 30135-1187, USA

Adduci, Jim (Baseball Player)
St Louis Cardinals
16314 Crescent Lake Dr
Crest Hill, IL 60403-1643, USA

Adduci, Nick (Football Player)
Washington Redskins
717 Birchwood Rd
Frankfort, IL 60423-1031, USA

Adduono, Rick (Hockey Player)
Boston Bruins
153 Donald St W
Thunder Bay, ON P7E 5X8, CANADA

Addy, Mark (Actor)
c/o Andy Cohen *International Creative Management (ICM-LA)*
10250 Constellation Blvd
Los Angeles, CA 90067-6200, USA

Ade, King Sunny (Music Group)
Monterey International
200 W Superior St Ste 202
Chicago, IL 60610-3554, USA

Adelman, Kenneth L (Government Official)
Int'l Contemporary Studies Institute
4018 27th St N
Arlington, VA 22207-5207, USA

Adelman, Rick (Basketball Player, Coach)
San Diego Rockets
11919 SW Breyman Ave
Portland, OR 97219-8412, USA

Adelson, Sheldon (Business Person)
The Venetian Resort Hotel Casino
3355 Las Vegas Blvd S
Las Vegas, NV 89109-8941, USA

Adelstein, Paul (Actor)
c/o Marsha McManus *Principal Entertainment (LA)*
1964 Westwood Blvd Ste 400
Los Angeles, CA 90025-4695, USA

Adem (Music Group)
c/o Staff Member *Paradigm (Monterey)*
509 Hartnell St
Monterey, CA 93940-2825, USA

Adey, Christopher
137 Anson Road
Willesden Green NW2 4AH, UNITED KINGDOM (UK)

Adickes, John M (Football Player)
Chicago Bears
205 W Fair Oaks Pl
San Antonio, TX 78209-3710, USA

Adickes, Mark (Football Player)
Kansas City Chiefs
5226 Holly St
Bellaire, TX 77401-4804, USA

Adie, Kate (Journalist)
c/o Staff Member *BBC Television Centre*
Incoming Mail
Wood Lane
London W12 7RJ, UNITED KINGDOM
(UK)

Adjani, Isabelle (Actor)
c/o Staff Member *ArtMedia*
20 av Rapp
Paris 75007, FRANCE

Adjodhia, Jules (Prime Minister)
Prime Minister's Office
Kleine Combeweg 1
Paramaribo, SURINAME

Adkins, James (Football Player)
Kansas City Chiefs
209 Redwood Dr
Coppell, TX 75019-5422, USA

Adkins, John
28208 Village 28
Camarillo, CA 93012-7619, USA

Adkins, Jon (Baseball Player)
Chicago White Sox
RR 2 Box 2306
Wayne, WV 25570, USA

Adkins, Margene (Football Player)
Dallas Cowboys
2312 Donnyville Ct
Fort Worth, TX 76119-3111, USA

Adkins, Sam (Football Player)
Seattle Seahawks
15912 NE 160th St
Woodinville, WA 98072-8910, USA

Adkins, Seth (Actor)
c/o Staff Member *Paradigm (LA)*
360 N Crescent Dr
North Bldg
Beverly Hills, CA 90210-6820, USA

Adkins, Steve (Baseball Player)
New York Yankees
5001 Derry Way
Tampa, FL 33647-1338, USA

Adkins, Trace (Music Group, Musician)
c/o Rick Shipp *William Morris Agency
(WMA-TN)*
1600 Division St Ste 300
Nashville, TN 37203-2755, USA

Adkisson, Perry L (Educator, Misc)
9211 Lake Forest Ct N
College Station, TX 77845-8757, USA

Adleman, Leonard (Scientist)
University of Southern California
Computer Math Dept
Los Angeles, CA 90089-0001, USA

Adler, Brian (Composer)
Gorfaine/Schwartz
4111 W Alameda Ave Ste 509
Burbank, CA 91505-4171, USA

Adler, Charles (Actor)
c/o Luanne Salandy-Regis *Innovative
Artists (LA)*
1505 10th St
Santa Monica, CA 90401-2805, USA

Adler, Jerry (Actor)
Paradigm Agency
10100 Santa Monica Blvd Ste 2500
Los Angeles, CA 90067-4116, USA

Adler, Lee (Artist)
Lime Kiln Farm
Climax, NY 12042, USA

Adler, Lou (Actor, Director, Producer)
Ode Sounds & Visuals
3969 Villa Costera
Malibu, CA 90265-5151, USA

Adler, Matt
PO Box 1866
Studio City, CA 91614-0866, USA

Adler, Richard (Composer, Songwriter,
Writer)
PO Box 1151
Southampton, NY 11969-1151, USA

Adler, Stephen L (Physicist)
Institute for Advanced Study
Einstein Lane
Princeton, NJ 08540, USA

Adler, Steven (Music Group)
Big FD Entertainment
301 Arizona Ave Ste 200
Santa Monica, CA 90401-1364, USA

Adlesh, Dave (Baseball Player)
Houston Colt 45's
9770 Avenida Monterey
Cypress, CA 90630-3446, USA

Adlon, Pamela (Actor, Voice Over Artist)
c/o Dan Baron *Agency for the Performing
Arts (APA-LA)*
405 S Beverly Dr
Beverly Hills, CA 90212-4416, USA

Adni, Daniel (Musician)
64A Menelik Road
London NW2 3RH, UNITED KINGDOM
(UK)

Adoboli, Koffi Eugene (Prime Minister)
Prime Minister's Office
BP 5618
Lome, TOGO

Adoor, Gopalkrishnan (Director)
Darsanam
Trivandrum, Kerala 695017, INDIA

Adorf, Mario (Actor)
Perlacher Str 28
Grunwald D-82031, GERMANY

Adoti, Rasaaq (Actor)
c/o Staff Member *Coast to Coast Talent
Group*
3350 Barham Blvd
Los Angeles, CA 90068-1404, USA

Adotta, Kip (Actor, Comedian)
PO Box 5734
Santa Rosa, CA 95402-5734, USA

Adria, Ferran (Chef)
El Bulli
En Cala Montjoi Roses
Girona 17480, SPAIN

Adulyadey, King (King, Politician)
BhumibolVilla Chitralada
Bangkok, THAILAND

Adway, Dwayne (Actor)
c/o Mark Schumacher *Schumacher
Management*
9255 W Sunset Blvd Ste 727
Los Angeles, CA 90069-3304, USA

Adyrkhayeva, Svetlana D (Ballerina)
1 Smolensky Pereulor 9
#74
Moscow 121099, RUSSIA

Aedo, Daniela (Actor)
c/o Staff Member *Televisa*
Blvd Adolfo Lopez Mateos 232
Colonia San Angel INN
DF CP 01060, MEXICO

Aerle, Taree (Artist, Music Group)
William Morris Agency
1325 Avenue Of The Americas
New York, NY 10019-6091, USA

Aerosmith (Music Group)
c/o Staff Member *Paradigm (Monterey)*
509 Hartnell St
Monterey, CA 93940-2825, USA

Afanasiyev, Viktor M (Cosmonaut)
Potchta Kosmonavtov
Moskovskoi Oblasti
Syvisdny Goroduk 141160, RUSSIA

Afenir, Troy (Baseball Player)
Houston Astros
459 Old Via Rancho Dr
Escondido, CA 92029-7959, USA

Affeldt, Jeremy (Baseball Player)
Kansas City Royals
969 Crestwood Rd
Englewood, FL 34223-3905, USA

Affholter, Erik (Football Player)
Green Bay Packers
638 Lindero Canyon Rd # 331
Agoura Hills, CA 91377-5457, USA

Affleck, Ben (Actor)
c/o Staff Member *LivePlanet*
2644 30th St
Santa Monica, CA 90405-3060, USA

Affleck, Bruce (Hockey Player)
St Louis Blues
1847 Oxborough Ct
Chesterfield, MO 63017-8037, USA

Affleck, Casey (Actor, Producer, Writer)
c/o Sean Elliott *Endeavor Agency LLC (LA)*
9601 Wilshire Blvd Fl 3
Beverly Hills, CA 90210-5204, USA

Affleck, James G (Business Person)
American Cyanamid
5 Giralda Farms
Madison, NJ 07940-1027, USA

AFI (Music Group)
c/o Staff Member *Leave Home Booking*
1216 California St
Huntington Beach, CA 92648-4104, USA

Afinogenov, Maxim (Hockey Player)
Buffalo Sabres
878 Ridge View Way
International Sports Advisors
Franklin Lakes, NJ 07417-1524, USA

Afrika, Bambaataa (Artist, Musician)
KLB Productions
70A Greenwich Ave # 441
New York, NY 10011-8300, USA

Afroman (Artist, Music Group)
Crescent Moon
20 Music Sq W Frnt
Nashville, TN 37203-3220, USA

Aftermath (Music Group)
c/o Tom Workman *Starcrest Entertainment
Corp*
4585 N River Rd
Zanesville, OH 43701-7768, USA

Aga Khan IV, Prince Karim (Religious
Leader)
Aiglemont
Gouvieux 60270, FRANCE

Agajanian, Benjamin (Ben) (Football
Player)
Philadelphia Eagles
4381 Green Ave Apt C
Los Alamitos, CA 90720-3532, USA

Agam, Yaacov (Artist)
26 Rue Boulard
Paris 75014, FRANCE

Agarwal, Anu (Actor, Bollywood)
503 Godavari
Khan Pochkhawala Road Worli
Mumbai, MS 400025, INDIA

Agase, Alexander G (Alex) (Coach,
Football Coach, Football Player)
1281 Pine Ridge Cir E Apt C2
Tarpon Springs, FL 34688-6409, USA

Agassi, Andre (Tennis Player)
8921 Andre Dr
Las Vegas, NV 89148-1405, USA

Agbayani, Benny (Baseball Player)
New York Mets
66-948 Kolu Pl
Waialua, HI 96791-9743, USA

Age, Louis (Football Player)
Chicago Bears
712 N Dupre St
New Orleans, LA 70119-4109, USA

Agee, Sam (Football Player)
Chicago Cardinals
508 Mose Dr Apt 506
Sparta, TN 38583-1213, USA

Agee, Tommie (Football Player)
Seattle Seahawks
1505 Blackhawk Dr
Opelika, AL 36801-3513, USA

Agena, Keiko (Actor)
c/oGilmore Girls
4000 Warner Blvd Bldg 2222
Burbank, CA 91522-0001, USA

Ager, Nikita (Actor)
c/o Paul Santana *Agency for the
Performing Arts (APA-LA)*
405 S Beverly Dr
Beverly Hills, CA 90212-4416, USA

Aghayan, Ray (Designer)
431 S Fairfax Ave # 3
Los Angeles, CA 90036-3123, USA

Aghdashloo, Shohreh (Actor)
c/o Michael Katcher *Creative Artists
Agency LCC (CAA-LA)*
2000 Avenue Of The Stars
Los Angeles, CA 90067-4700, USA

Agler, Bob (Football Player)
Los Angeles Rams
2150 Shawbury Ct E
Columbus, OH 43229-3934, USA

Agna, Tom (Actor, Producer, Writer)
c/o Lisa Harrison *Endeavor Agency LLC
(LA)*
9601 Wilshire Blvd Fl 3
Beverly Hills, CA 90210-5204, USA

Agnelo, Geraldo Majella Cardinal
(Religious Leader)
Rue Martin Alfanso de Souza 270
Salvador, BA 40100-050, BRAZIL

Agnew, Harold M (Physicist)
322 Punta Baja Dr
Solana Beach, CA 92075-1720, USA

Agnew, Jim (Hockey Player)
Vancouver Canucks
2805 Terrace Dr
Missoula, MT 59803-9603, USA

Agnew Jr, Ray (Football Player)
New England Patriots
2215 Cline St
Winston Salem, NC 27107-2411, USA

Agnihotri, Atul (Actor, Bollywood)
Ashwini
Pali Mala Road Bandra
Mumbai, MS 400050, INDIA

Agnus, Michael (Business Person)
Whitbread PLC
Chiswell St
London EC1Y 4SD, UNITED KINGDOM
(UK)

Agoos, Jeff (Soccer Player)
235 Pascack Rd
Park Ridge, NJ 07656-1125, USA

Agostini, Didier (Actor)
Cineart
36 Rue de Ponthieu
Paris 75008, FRANCE

Agosto, Ben (Figure Skater)
c/o Staff Member *Champions on Ice*
3500 W 80th St
Tom Collins Enterprises Inc
Minneapolis, MN 55431-1068, USA

Agosto, Juan (Baseball Player)
Chicago White Sox
3815 65th St E # 175
Bradenton, FL 34208-6613, USA

Agre, Bernard Cardinal (Religious Leader)
Archeveche
Ave Jean-Paul II
Abidjan 01 BP 1287, IVORY COAST

Agre, Peter (Nobel Prize Laureate)
7033 Lenleigh Road
Baltimore, MD 21212, USA

Agt, Andries A M Van (Prime Minister)
Europa House
9-15 Sambancho Chiyodaku
Tokyo 102, JAPAN

Aguilar, Pepe (Music Group)
Agency Group Ltd
1775 Broadway Ste 515
New York, NY 10019-1903, USA

Aguilera, Christina (Musician, Songwriter, Writer)
c/o Irving Azoff *Azoffmusic Management*
1100 Glendon Ave Ste 2000
Los Angeles, CA 90024-3524, USA

Aguilera, Hellweg Max (Photographer)
PO Box 289
White Plains, NY 10605-0289, USA

Aguilera, Richard W (Rick) (Baseball Player)
New York Mets
PO Box 174
Rancho Santa Fe, CA 92067-0174, USA

Aguirre, Beatriz (Actor)
c/o Staff Member *Televisa*
Blvd Adolfo Lopez Mateos 232
Colonia San Angel INN
DF CP 01060, MEXICO

Aguirre, Mark (Athlete)
125 S Pennsylvania St
Indianapolis, IN 46204-3610, USA

Aguirre, Mark A (Basketball Player, Misc)
Dallas Mavericks
10281 Highland Ct
Frisco, TX 75034-2415, USA

Agustoni, Gilberto Cardinal (Religious Leader)
Piazzi della Citla Leorina 9
Rome 00193, ITALY

Agutter, Jenny (Actor)
c/o Staff Member *Marmont Management*
Langham House
308 Regent St
London W1B 3AT, UNITED KINGDOM
(UK)

Ahana (Actor, Bollywood)
26-B-17 Elegant Apts
Hindi Prachara Sabha Road
Chennai, TN 600017, INDIA

Ahanotu, Chidi (Football Player)
Tampa Bay Buccaneers
1036 Royal Pass Rd
Tampa, FL 33602-5708, USA

Ahdout, Jonathan (Actor)
c/o Andrew Rogers *Paradigm (LA)*
360 N Crescent Dr
North Bldg
Beverly Hills, CA 90210-6820, USA

Aheam, Kevin (Hockey Player)
174 Marlborough St
Boston, MA 02116-1822, USA

Ahearne, Pat (Baseball Player)
Detroit Tigers
246 Milam Ln
Bastrop, TX 78602-3108, USA

Ahem, Jim (Golfer)
314 E Wagon Wheel Dr
Phoenix, AZ 85020-4066, USA

A'Hern, Basia (Actor)
c/o Staff Member *Nickelodeon UK*
PO Box 6425
LONDON W1A 6UR, UNITED
KINGDOM (UK)

Ahern, Bertie (Prime Minister)
Prime Minister's Office
Upper Merrion St
Dublin, IRELAND

Ahern, Fred (Hockey Player)
California Golden Seals
21 Crescent St
Plympton, MA 02367-1410, USA

Ahern, Neal (Producer)
c/o Staff Member *William Morris Agency (WMA-LA)*
1 William Morris Pl
Beverly Hills, CA 90212-4261, USA

Ahith, Kumar (Actor)
8/10 Norton Apartment
I Floor Mandavelli
Chennai, TN 600 028, INDIA

Ahmed, Kazi Zafar (Prime Minister)
Jatiya Sangsad
Dhaka, BANGLADESH

Aho, Esko (Prime Minister)
Centre Party
Pursimiehenkatu 15
Helsinki 00150, FINLAND

Ahrens, David (Football Player)
St Louis Cardinals
5864 Manchester Ct
Pittsboro, IN 46167-9064, USA

Ahrens, Lynn (Musician)
Willaim Morris Agency
151 El Camino Dr
Beverly Hills, CA 90212-2775, USA

Ahrens, Thomas J (Geophysicist, Physicist)
California Institute of Technology
Seismology Laboratory
Pasadena, CA 91125-0001, USA

Ahronovitch, Yuri
Stockholm Philharmonic
Hotorget 8
Stockholm, SWEDEN

Aida, Takefumi (Architect)
1-3-2 Okubo
Shinjukuku
Tokyo 169, JAPAN

Aiello, Anthony (Football Player)
Detroit Lions
9 Taylor Ave
Norwalk, OH 44857-1645, USA

Aiello, Danny (Actor)
c/o Johnnie Planco *Untitled Entertainment (NY)*
322 8th Ave Ste 601
New York, NY 10001-6715, USA

Aiken, Clay (Musician)
c/o Simon Renshaw *Strategics Artist Management*
1100 Glendon Ave Ste 1000
Los Angeles, CA 90024-3514, USA

Aiken, John (Hockey Player)
Montreal Canadiens
18 Pinetree Rd
Billerica, MA 01821-3446, USA

Aiken, Kimberly
PO Box 119
Atlantic City, NJ 08404, USA

Aiken, Liam (Actor)
c/o Ellen Gilbert *Abrams Artists Agency (NY)*
275 7th Ave Fl 26
New York, NY 10001-6708, USA

Aiken, Linda H (Activist)
2209 Lombard St
Philadelphia, PA 19146-1107, USA

Aikens, Carl (Football Player)
Los Angeles Raiders
931 W Arquilla Dr Apt 114
Glenwood, IL 60425-1143, USA

Aikens, Curtis (Chef)
68 Baca Vis
Novato, CA 94947-2102, USA

Aikens, Willie (Baseball Player)
California Angels
PO Box 01732-031 A3-611
Atlanta, GA 30315, USA

Aikman, Laura Holly (Actor)
551 Green Lanes
Palmers Green
London N13 3DR, UNITED KINGDOM
(UK)

Aikman, Troy K (Athlete, Football Player)
c/o Staff Member *Troy Aikman Foundation, The*
PO Box 3427
Coppell, TX 75019-9427, USA

Ailes, Roger E (Business Person)
c/o Staff Member *Fox News Channel (NY)*
1211 Avenue Of The Americas
Level C1
New York, NY 10036-8701, USA

Ailsby, Lloyd (Hockey Player)
New York Rangers
RR 1 Box 1
Weymark, SK S0N 2V0, CANADA

Aimee, Anouk (Actor)
c/o Staff Member *ArtMedia*
20 av Rapp
Paris 75007, FRANCE

Aimi, Milton (Soccer Player)
19927 Stonelodge St
Katy, TX 77450-5201, USA

Ainge, Daniel R (Danny) (Basketball Player)
Boston Celtics
140 Wellesley Ave
Wellesley Hills, MA 02481-7209, USA

Ainsleigh, H Gordon (Athlete, Track Athlete)
17119 Placer Hills Rd
Meadow Vista, CA 95722-9508, USA

Ainsworth, Kurt (Baseball Player)
San Francisco Giants
15220 Memorial Tower Dr
Baton Rouge, LA 70810-0301, USA

Airborne Toxic Event, The (Music Group)
c/o Staff Member *Paradigm (Monterey)*
509 Hartnell St
Monterey, CA 93940-2825, USA

Airpushers (Music Group)
c/o Staff Member *Paradigm (Monterey)*
509 Hartnell St
Monterey, CA 93940-2825, USA

Aitay, Victor (Musician)
800 Deerfield Rd Apt 203
Highland Park, IL 60035-3548, USA

Aitch, Matt (Basketball Player)
Indiana Pacers
1525 Bentbrook Cir
Lansing, MI 48917-1402, USA

Aitken, Brad (Hockey Player)
Pittsburgh Penguins
825 Royal Orchard Dr
Oshawa, ON L1K 1Z8, CANADA

Aitken, John (Artist)
University College
Slade Art School
London WC1E 6BT, UNITED KINGDOM
(UK)

Aitmatov, Chingiz T (Writer)
Ulitsa Toklogulstz 98
#9
Bishkek 720003, KYRGYZSTAN

Aivazoff, Micah (Hockey Player)
New York Islanders
6916 Hammond St
Powell River, BC V8A 1R4, CANADA

Aizenberg Selove, Fay (Physicist)
118 Cherry Ln
Wynnewood, PA 19096-1209, USA

Ajayrathnam (Actor)
78 Gajapathy Street
Shenoy Nagar
Chennai, TN 600 030, INDIA

Akayev, Askar (President)
President's Office
Government House
Bishkek 720003, KYRGYZSTAN

Akbar, Taufik (Astronaut)
Jalan Simp
Pahlawan III/24
Bandung 40124, INDONESIA

Akebono (Wrestler)
Azumazeki Stable
4-6-4 Higashi Komagala
Ryogoku
Tokyo, JAPAN

Akens, Jewell
5228 Marburn Ave
Los Angeles, CA 90043-2103, USA

Aker, Jack (Baseball Player)
Kansas City A's
44 Slayback Dr
Princeton Junction, NJ 08550-1912, USA

Akerfelds, Darrel (Baseball Player)
Oakland A's
12834 W Rosewood Dr
El Mirage, AZ 85335-7209, USA

Akerlof, George A (Nobel Prize Laureate)
University of California
Economics Dept
Evans Hall
Berkeley, CA 94720-0001, USA

Akerlund, Jonas (Director)
c/o Staff Member *International Creative
Management (ICM-LA)*
10250 Constellation Blvd
Los Angeles, CA 90067-6200, USA

Akerman, Malin (Actor)
c/o Staff Member *Alan Siegel
Entertainment*
345 N Maple Dr Ste 375
Beverly Hills, CA 90210-5942, USA

Akers, Fred (Coach, Football Coach)
Purdue University
Athletic Dept
West Lafayette, IN 47907, USA

Akers, John F (Business Person)
PO Box 194
Pebble Beach, CA 93953-0194, USA

Akers, Michelle (Soccer Player)
c/o Staff Member *US Soccer Federation*
1801 S Prairie Ave
Chicago, IL 60616-1319, USA

Akhtar, Javed (Songwriter, Writer)
702 Sagar Samrat Green Field Road
Near Juhu P O Juhu
Bombay, MS 400 049, INDIA

Akihito (King)
Imperial Palace
1-1 Chiyoda
Chiyodaku
Tokyo 100, JAPAN

Akihoto, EmperorThe Palace
1-1 ChiyodaChiyoda-Ku
Tokyo, JAPAN

Akil, Salim (Director)
c/o Staff Member *International Creative
Management (ICM-LA)*
10250 Constellation Blvd
Los Angeles, CA 90067-6200, USA

Akin, Harold (Football Player)
St Louis Cardinals
8216 NW 99th St
Oklahoma City, OK 73162-5002, USA

Akin, Henry (Basketball Player)
New York Knicks
18924 40th Pi NE
Lake Forest Park, WA 98155, USA

Akinnuoye-Agbaje, Adewale (Actor)
c/o Joshua Pollack *Agency for the
Performing Arts (APA-NY)*
888 7th Ave
New York, NY 10106-0001, USA

Akins, Rhett (Musician)
RPM Mgmt
209 10th Ave S Ste 229
Nashville, TN 37203-0721, USA

Akiu, Mike (Football Player)
Houston Oilers
PO Box 1845
Kailua, HI 96734-8845, USA

Akiyama, Kazuyoshi (Conductor)
Columbia Artists Mgmt Inc
1790 Broadway Fl 6
New York, NY 10019-1412, USA

Akiyama, Toyohiro (Astronaut, Journalist)
Tokyo Broadcasting Systems
3-6-5 Akasaka
Minaloku
Tokyo 107, JAPAN

Akiyoshi, Toshiko (Composer, Musician)
Berkeley Agency
2608 9th St
Berkeley, CA 94710-2550, USA

Akon (Musician)
c/o Staff Member *Universal Records*
825 8th Ave
New York, NY 10019-7472, USA

Akoshino (Royalty)
Imperial Palace
Tokyo, JAPAN

Akroyd, Dan (Actor, Musician, Producer,
Writer)
c/o Fred Specktor *Creative Artists Agency
LCC (CAA-LA)*
2000 Avenue Of The Stars
Los Angeles, CA 90067-4700, USA

Aksyonov, Vassily P (Writer)
Random House
1745 Broadway # B1
New York, NY 10019-4305, USA

Aksyonov, Vladimir V (Cosmonaut)
Astrakhansky Per 5
Kv 100
Moscow 129010, RUSSIA

Al and the Transamericans (Music Group)
c/o Staff Member *Paradigm (Monterey)*
509 Hartnell St
Monterey, CA 93940-2825, USA

Al-Assad, Bashar (Politician, President)
c/o Staff Member *Presidential Office
(Syria)*
Muharreem Abu Rumanch
Al-Rashid Street
Damascas, SYRIA

al-Aziz, Abdullah Ibn Abdul (Prince)
Council of Ministers
Murabba
Riyadh 11121, SAUDI ARABIA

Al Fayed, Mohammed
The Ritz Hotel Place Vendome
Paris, FRANCE

Al-Hoss, Selim (Prime Minister)
Premier's Office
Serail
Place de l'Eloile
Beirut, LEBANON

Al-Yawer, Sheik Ghazi Mashal Ajll
(President)
President's Office
Al-Sijound Majalis
Karradat Mariam
Baghdad, IRAQ

al-Zubi, Mahmoud (Prime Minister)
Premier's Office
Damascas
SYRIA

Alabama (Music Group)
c/o Greg Oswald *William Morris Agency
(WMA-TN)*
1600 Division St Ste 300
Nashville, TN 37203-2755, USA

Alagna, Roberto (Opera Singer)
Levon Sayan
2 Rue du Prieure
Nyon 1260, SWITZERLAND

Alagu, K (Actor)
17 T N H B Staff Quarter Dr Ramaswamy
Road
Chennai, TN 600 078, INDIA

Alaia, Azzedine (Designer, Fashion
Designer)
18 Rue de la Verrerie
Paris 75008, FRANCE

Alaigal, Selvakumar (Actor)
9A Pari St
Avvai Nagar Choolaimedu
Chennai, TN 600 094, INDIA

Alan, Buddy (Musician)
600 E Gilbert Dr
Tempe, AZ 85281-2021, USA

Alarcon, Arthur L (Judge)
US Court of Appeals
312 N Spring St Ste G33
Los Angeles, CA 90012-4711, USA

Alatorre, Javier (Actor)
c/o Staff Member *TV Azteca*
Periferico Sur 4121
Colonia Fuentes del Pedregal
DF CP 14141, MEXICO

Alazraqui, Carlos (Actor)
c/o Heidi Rotbart *Heidi Rotbart
Management*
4000 Warner Blvd Bldg 160 Rm 716
Burbank, CA 91522-0001, USA

Alba, Jessica (Actor)
c/o Chris Henze *Thruline Entertainment*
9250 Wilshire Blvd Ground Fl
Beverly Hills, CA 90210, USA

Alban, Richard (Football Player)
Washington Redskins
306 Belpaire Ct
Newtown Square, PA 19073-2128, USA

Albanese, Licia (Opera Singer)
Nathan Hale Dr
Wilson Point
South Norwalk, CT 06854, USA

Albano, Lou (Wrestler)
16 Mechanic St
Carmel, NY 10512-2212, USA

Albarn, Damon (Musician, Songwriter,
Writer)
CMO Mgmt
Ransomes Dock
35 Parkgale Road #32
London SW11 4NP, UNITED KINGDOM
(UK)

Albea, Troy (Football Player)
Indianapolis Colts
1070 L And N Rd
Lincolnton, GA 30817-4724, USA

Albeck, Stan (Basketball Player, Coach)
Toronto Raptors
Air Canada Center
40 Bay St
Toronto, ON M5J 2NB, CANADA

Albee, Edward
PO Box 697
Montauk, NY 11954-0503, USA

Albee, Edward F (Writer)
14 Harrison St
New York, NY 10013-2842, USA

Alberghetti, Anna Maria (Actor, Musician)
10333 Chrysanthemum Ln
Los Angeles, CA 90077-2812, USA

Albers, Hans (Business Person)
BASF AG
Carl-Bosch-Str 38
Ludwigshafen 78351, GERMANY

Albers, Kristi (Golfer)
5872 Via Cuesta Dr
El Paso, TX 79912-6608, USA

Alberstein, Chara (Musician)
DL Media
PO Box 2728
Bala Cynwyd, PA 19004-6728, USA

Albert, Calvin (Artist)
6525 Brandywine Dr S
Margate, FL 33063-5538, USA

Albert, John G (General)
Albert Farms
Rr2
Monroe, VA 24574, USA

Albert, Marv (Sportscaster)
TNT-TV
1050 Techwood Dr NW
Sports Department
Atlanta, GA 30318-5604, USA

Albert II (King)
Koninklijk Palais
Rue de Brederode
Brussels 1000, BELGIUM

Albert (Prince) (Royalty)
Palais de Monaco
Boite Postale 518
Monacode Cedex 98015, MONACO

Alberti, Micah (Actor)
c/o Abby Bluestone *Innovative Artists (LA)*
1505 10th St
Santa Monica, CA 90401-2805, USA

Alberto, Padre (Actor)
c/o Staff Member *Telemundo*
2470 W 8th Ave
Hialeah, FL 33010-2000, USA

Alberts, Butch (Baseball Player)
Toronto Blue Jays
3063 Amberlea Ln
Baldwinsville, NY 13027-1613, USA

Alberts, Trev (Football Player)
Indianapolis Colts
10430 E Hickory Ridge Dr
Rochelle, IL 61068-9790, USA

Albita (Musician)
Estefan Enterprises
6205 SW 40th St
Miami, FL 33155-4823, USA

Albom, Mitch (Writer)
25600 Franklin Park Dr
Franklin, MI 48025-1211, USA

Albrecht, A Chim (Wrestler)
Physique Promotions
9668 Moss Glen Ave
Fountain Valley, CA 92708-1053, USA

Albrecht, Art (Football Player)
Pittsburgh Steelers
1216 S 12th St
Manitowoc, WI 54220-5224, USA

Albrecht, Gerd
Mariedi Anders Artists
535 El Camino Del Mar
San Francisco, CA 94121-1099, USA

Albrecht, Karl (Business Person)
ALDI Corporate
1200 N Kirk Rd
Batavia, IL 60510-1443, USA

Albrecht, Ted (Football Player)
Chicago Bears
1314 W Fork Dr
Lake Forest, IL 60045-3539, USA

Albrecht, Theo (Business Person)
ALDI Corporate
1200 N Kirk Rd
Batavia, IL 60510-1443, USA

Albright, Ethan (Football Player)
Miami Dolphins
19181 Ferry Field Ter
Leesburg, VA 20176-1276, USA

Albright, Gerald (Musician)
c/o Ron Moss *Chapman Management*
14011 Ventura Blvd
Sherman Oaks, CA 91423-3533, USA

Albright, Ira (Football Player)
Buffalo Bills
1613 Panama Pl
Dallas, TX 75215-3349, USA

Albright, Lola (Actor)
213 N Valley St # 136
Burbank, CA 91505, USA

Albright, Madeleine K (Politician, Secretary)
1318 34th St NW
Washington, DC 20007-2801, USA

Albright, Tenley E (Doctor)
186 Windswept Way
Osterville, MA 02655, USA

Albright, William (Football Player)
New York Giants
315 Bolands Private Dr
Shell Lake, WI 54871-8723, USA

Albuquerque, Lita (Artist)
305 Boyd St
Los Angeles, CA 90013-1509, USA

Albury, Victor (Baseball Player)
Minnesota Twins
926 Truman Ave Apt D
Key West, FL 33040-6431, USA

Albus, Jim (Golfer)
3972 Somerset Dr Unit 1
Sarasota, FL 34242-1110, USA

Alcala, Santo (Baseball Player)
Cincinnati Reds
Ramon Mota #18
San Pedro de Macoris, DOMINICAN REPUBLIC

Alcantara, Izzy (Baseball Player)
Boston Red Sox
125 N Bend St Apt 1
Pawtucket, RI 02860-3136, USA

Alcaraz, Lalo (Cartoonist, Editor)
PO Box 63052
Los Angeles, CA 90063-0052, USA

Alcock, Charles (Physicist)
Lawrence Livermore Laboratory
7000 East Ave
Livermore, CA 94550-9698, USA

Alcorn, Gary (Basketball Player)
Detroit Pistons
2552 Trenton Ave
Clovis, CA 93619-4249, USA

Alcott, Amy S (Golfer)
Golf HOF
323 Amalfi Dr
Santa Monica, CA 90402-1127, USA

Alda, Alan (Actor)
Scientific American Frontiers
70 Coolidge Hill Rd
Chedd-Angier Production Co
Watertown, MA 02472-5003, USA

Alda, Rutanya (Actor)
363 Manhattan Ave # 2
New York, NY 10026-2318, USA

Aldcorn, Gary (Hockey Player)
Toronto Maple Leafs
PO Box 5072 RPO Claremont
Claremont, ON L1Y 1Z8, CANADA

Alden, Bruce (Producer)
c/o Staff Member *Vision Art Management*
9200 W Sunset Blvd Ph 1
Los Angeles, CA 90069-3601, USA

Alden, Ginger (Actor, Model, Musician)
Ron Leyser
25 Rolling Hill Ct W
Sag Harbor, NY 11963-2012, USA

Alden, Norman (Actor)
c/o Staff Member *Twentieth Century Artists*
15760 Ventura Blvd Ste 700
Encino, CA 91436-3016, USA

Alden Robinson, Phil (Director)
Creative Artists Agency
9830 Wilshire Blvd
Beverly Hills, CA 90212-1804, USA

Alderete, Loretta (Golfer)
43750 Salpare Pl
Indio, CA 92203-2941, USA

Alderfer-Benner, Gertrude (Baseball Player)
2191 County Line Rd
East Greenville, PA 18041-2700, USA

Alderman, Darrell (Race Car Driver)
D A Construction Co
8145 Flemingsburg Rd
Morehead, KY 40351, USA

Alderman, Grady (Football Player)
Detroit Lions
1990 Elk Valley Dr
Evergreen, CO 80439-4943, USA

Alderton, John (Football Player)
Pittsburgh Steelers
12314 Williams Rd SE
Cumberland, MD 21502-7961, USA

Aldisert, Ruggero J (Judge)
120 Cremona Dr # 0
Goleta, CA 93117-5511, USA

Aldiss, Brian W (Writer)
Hambledon
39 Saint Andrews Road
Old Headington
Oxford OX3 9DL, UNITED KINGDOM (UK)

Aldred, Scott (Baseball Player)
Detroit Tigers
3508 Malachite Dr
Zephyrhills, FL 33540-7422, USA

Aldred, Sophie (Actor)
1 Duchess St
#1
London S1N 3EE, UNITED KINGDOM (UK)

Aldredge, Theoni V (Designer)
425 Lafayette St
New York, NY 10003-7021, USA

Aldrete, Mike (Baseball Player)
San Francisco Giants
231 Via Del Pinar
Monterey, CA 93940-2504, USA

Aldrich, Jay (Baseball Player)
Milwaukee Brewers
9209 S 51st St
Franklin, WI 53132-9275, USA

Aldrich, John H (Politician, Scientist)
Duke University
Political Science Dept
Durham, NC 27708-0001, USA

Aldrich, Lance (Cartoonist)
University Press Syndicate
4520 Main St
Kansas City, MO 64111-1876, USA

Aldridge, Donald O (General)
1004 Incol Road #168
Bellevue, NE 68005, USA

Aldridge, Edward C (pete) Jr (Government Official)
Aerospace Corp
2350 E El Segundo Blvd
El Segundo, CA 90245-4691, USA

Aldridge, Melvin (Football Player)
Houston Oilers
14618 Braden Dr E
Houston, TX 77047-6752, USA

Aldridge, Sabrina (Actor)
c/o Allee Newhoff *Irene Marie Management Group*
728 Ocean Dr
Miami Beach, FL 33139-6220, USA

Aldridge Jr, Allen (Football Player)
Denver Broncos
2111 Hammerwood Dr
Missouri City, TX 77489-4137, USA

Aldrin, Edwin (Buzz) (Astronaut)
c/o Staff Member *Cunningham Escott Slevin & Doherty (LA)*
10635 Santa Monica Blvd Ste 130
Los Angeles, CA 90025-8306, USA

Aleandro, Norma (Actor)
Blanco Encalada 1150
Buenos Aires 1428, ARGENTINA

Alechinsky, Pierre (Artist)
2 Bis Rue Henri Barbusse
Bougival 78380, FRANCE

Alejandro, Kevin (Actor)
c/o Staff Member *Main Title Entertainment*
5225 Wilshire Blvd Ste 500
Los Angeles, CA 90036-4349, USA

Aleksander, Grant (Actor)
c/o Robert Attermann *Abrams Artists Agency (LA)*
9200 W Sunset Blvd Ph 11
Los Angeles, CA 90069-3601, USA

Aleksinas, Charles (Basketball Player)
Golden State Warriors
16 Litchfield Rd
Morris, CT 06763-1522, USA

Aleksiy II (Religious Leader)
Moscow Patriarchy
Chisty Per 5
Moscow 119034, RUSSIA

Aleno, Charles
601 Marion Ct
Deland, FL 32720-3217, USA

Alerlol, George (Nobel Prize Laureate)
University of California
Economics Dept
Berkeley, CA 94720-0001, USA

Alesi, Jean (Race Car Driver)
HWA GmbH
Benzstr 8
Affalterbach 71563, GERMANY

Alessi, Raquel (Actor)
c/o Rhonda Price *Gersh Agency, The (NY)*
41 Madison Ave Fl 33
New York, NY 10010-2202, USA

Aletter, Frank (Actor)
5430 Corbin Ave
Tarzana, CA 91356-2927, USA

Alex (Actor)
2 Rajaji North Street
Pushpa Nagar Nungambakkam
Chennai, TN, INDIA

Alex, Keith (Football Player)
Atlanta Falcons
6985 Reno Cir
Beaumont, TX 77708-3594, USA

Alexakis, Art (Musician)
Pinnacle Entertainment
30 Glenn St
White Plains, NY 10603-3254, USA

Alexakos, Steve (Football Player)
Denver Broncos
22300 Hathaway Ave Apt A
Hayward, CA 94541-4861, USA

Alexander, A Lamar (Educator, Governor, Secretary, Senator)
2233 Blue Springs Rd
Ashland City, TN 37015-3816, USA

Alexander, Brooke (Actor)
c/o Staff Member *Abrams Artists Agency (LA)*
9200 W Sunset Blvd Ph 11
Los Angeles, CA 90069-3601, USA

Alexander, Bruce (Football Player)
508 Englewood Dr
Lufkin, TX 75901-5844, USA

Alexander, Christopher W J (Architect)
2701 Shasta Rd
Berkeley, CA 94708-1923, USA

Alexander, Claire (Hockey Player)
Toronto Maple Leafs
11 Tammy Cir
St Catharines, ON L1Y 1R2, CANADA

Alexander, Clifford L Jr (Government Official)
412 A St SE
Washington, DC 20003-3807, USA

Alexander, Corey (Basketball Player)
440 Alpha St
Waynesboro, VA 22980-3904, USA

Alexander, Dan (Football Player)
New York Jets
57925 Canal St
Plaquemine, LA 70764-3730, USA

Alexander, Dan (Football Player)
Tennessee Titans
407 Knob Ct
Franklin, TN 37064-2390, USA

Alexander, David (Football Player)
Philadelphia Eagles
11420 S Granite Pl
Tulsa, OK 74137-8113, USA

Alexander, Denise (Actor)
270 N Canon Dr # 1919
Beverly Hills, CA 90210-5323, USA

Alexander, Derrick S (Football Player)
Cleveland Browns
25381 W 149th Ct
Olathe, KS 66061-8531, USA

Alexander, Doyle
Los Angeles Dodgers
5416 Hunter Park Ct
Arlington, TX 76017-3557, USA

Alexander, Eric (Musician)
Joel Chriss
300 Mercer St Apt 3J
New York, NY 10003-6732, USA

Alexander, Erika (Actor)
c/o Craig Shapiro *Innovative Artists (LA)*
1505 10th St
Santa Monica, CA 90401-2805, USA

Alexander, Flex (Actor)
c/o David Goldman *Power Entertainment*
9100 Wilshire Blvd # 700
Beverly Hills, CA 90212-3401, USA

Alexander, Gary (Baseball Player)
San Francisco Giants
5420 Senford Ave
Los Angeles, CA 90056-1029, USA

Alexander, Gerald (Baseball Player)
Texas Rangers
307 Woodland Dr
Donaldsonville, LA 70346-9752, USA

Alexander, Harold (Football Player)
Denver Broncos
590 J D Dr
Pickens, SC 29671-9035, USA

Alexander, Jamie (Game Show Host)
c/o Staff Member *William Morris Agency (WMA-LA)*
1 William Morris Pl
Beverly Hills, CA 90212-4261, USA

Alexander, Jane (Actor, Government Official)
William Morris Agency
1325 Avenue Of The Americas
New York, NY 10019-6091, USA

Alexander, Jason (Actor, Comedian, Producer)
c/o Staff Member *Angel Ark Productions*
5042 Wilshire Blvd # 592
Los Angeles, CA 90036-4305, USA

Alexander, Jeff (Football Player)
Denver Broncos
5283 Elkhart St
Denver, CO 80239-6042, USA

Alexander, John (Football Player)
Miami Dolphins
312 Lee Pl
Plainfield, NJ 07063-1337, USA

Alexander, Jules (Musician)
Variety Artists
793 Higuera St Ste 6
San Luis Obispo, CA 93401-0500, USA

Alexander, Keith (Actor)
c/o Staff Member *Cunningham Escott Slevin & Doherty (LA)*
10635 Santa Monica Blvd Ste 130
Los Angeles, CA 90025-8306, USA

Alexander, Kermit (Football Player)
San Francisco 49ers
13428 Maxella Ave # 120
Marina Del Rey, CA 90292-5620, USA

Alexander, Khandi (Actor)
c/o Staff Member *Innovative Artists (LA)*
1505 10th St
Santa Monica, CA 90401-2805, USA

Alexander, Lloyd (Writer)
c/o Staff Member *Random House Publicity*
1745 Broadway
New York, NY 10019-4343, USA

Alexander, Manny (Baseball Player)
Baltimore Orioles
3660 N Lake Drive Apt 2664
Chicago, IL 60613, USA

Alexander, Matt (Baseball Player)
Chicago Cubs
2419 Stonewall St
Shreveport, LA 71103-3451, USA

alexander, maximillian (Actor)
c/o Staff Member *Schumacher Management*
9255 W Sunset Blvd Ste 727
Los Angeles, CA 90069-3304, USA

Alexander, Monty (Musician)
Bennett Morgan
RR 376 Box 1282
Wappingers Falls, NY 12590, USA

Alexander, R Minter (General)
824 Eden Ct
Alexandria, VA 22308-2034, USA

Alexander, Ray (Football Player)
Denver Broncos
933 NE 199th St Apt 206
Miami, FL 33179-3029, USA

Alexander, Robert M (Misc)
14 Moor Park Mount
Leeds LS6 4BU, UNITED KINGDOM (UK)

Alexander, Rogers (Football Player)
New York Jets
6935 Westmoreland Rd
Falls Church, VA 22042-2657, USA

Alexander, Sarah (Actor)
c/o Mimi DiTrani *Untitled Entertainment (LA)*
331 N Maple Dr Fl 3
Beverly Hills, CA 90210-3827, USA

Alexander, Sasha (Actor)
c/o Staff Member *William Morris Agency (WMA-LA)*
1 William Morris Pl
Beverly Hills, CA 90212-4261, USA

Alexander, Shasha (Actor)
Endeavor Talent Agency
9701 Wilshire Blvd Ste 1000
Beverly Hills, CA 90212-2010, USA

Alexander, Shaun (Football Player)
c/o Staff Member *Seattle Seahawks*
11220 NE 53rd St
Kirkland, WA 98033-7595, USA

Alexander, Stephen (Football Player)
Washington Redskins
2914 Lacey Dr
Chickasha, OK 73018-7342, USA

Alexander, Susana (Actor)
c/o Staff Member *TV Azteca*
Periferico Sur 4121
Colonia Fuentes del Pedregal
DF CP 14141, MEXICO

Alexander, Victor (Basketball Player)
8405 Holcomb Bridge Rd
Alpharetta, GA 30022, USA

Alexander, Willie (Football Player)
Houston Oilers
7219 Holder Forest Cir
Houston, TX 77088-7431, USA

Alexander, Willie (Musician)
Tournmaline Music Group
894 Mayville Rd
Bethel, ME 04217-4605, USA

Alexander of Weedon, Robert S (Financier)
National Westminster Bank
41 Lothbury
London EC2P 2BP, UNITED KINGDOM (UK)

Alexander (Prince Yogoslavia) (Prince)
36 Park Lane
London W1Y 3LE, UNITED KINGDOM (UK)

Alexandre, Boniface (Judge, President)
President's Office
Palacio Nacional
Port-au-Prince, HAITI

Alexandrov, Alexander P (Cosmonaut)
Hovanskaya Ul 3
#27
Moscow 129515, RUSSIA

Alexie, Sherman (Writer)
PO Box 376
Wellpinit, WA 99040-0376, USA

Alfaro, Victor (Designer, Fashion Designer)
130 Barrow St
New York, NY 10014-2856, USA

Alferov, Zhores (Nobel Prize Laureate)
Ioffe Institute
26 Polytekhnicheskaya
Saint Petersburg 194021, RUSSIA

Alfieri, Janet (Cartoonist)
15 Bumpus Rd
Plymouth, MA 02360-3511, USA

Alfonseca, Antonio (Baseball Player)
Florida Marlins
3020 SW 189th Ter
Miramar, FL 33029-5861, USA

Alfonso, Kristian (Actor)
c/o Jack Gilardi *International Creative Management (ICM-LA)*
10250 Constellation Blvd
Los Angeles, CA 90067-6200, USA

Alfonzo, Edgardo (Baseball Player)
New York Mets
65 Wensley Dr
Great Neck, NY 11020-1834, USA

Alford, Brian (Football Player)
New York Giants
21011 Kenosha St
Oak Park, MI 48237-3813, USA

Alford, Bruce (Football Player)
New York Yankees
4916 Arborlawn Dr
Fort Worth, TX 76109-3204, USA

Alford, Darnell (Football Player)
Kansas City Chiefs
5806 Danielle Dr
Fredericksburg, VA 22407-6485, USA

Alford, Steve (Basketball Player)
Dallas Mavericks
11804 Beringer Ave NE
Albuquerque, NM 87122-7102, USA

Alford, William (Writer)
150 Federal St # 2600
Boston, MA 02110-1713, USA

Alfredsson, Daniel (Hockey Player)
Ottawa Senators
I M G Attn J P Barry 801 6th Street SW
Ste 235
Calgary, AB T2P 3V8, CANADA

Alfredsson, Helen (Golfer)
6043 Jamestown Park
Orlando, FL 32819-4435, USA

Algabid, Hamid (President)
National Assembly
Vice President's Office
Niamey, NIGER

Ali, Laila (Athlete, Boxer)
c/o Staff Member *Sports Placement Service*
6671 W Sunset Blvd Ste 1521
Los Angeles, CA 90028-7123, USA

Ali, May May (Actor)
c/o Kristene Wallis *Wallis Agency*
210 N Pass Ave Ste 205
Burbank, CA 91505-3936, USA

Ali, Muhammad (Athlete, Boxer)
Ali Farm
PO Box 160
Berrien Springs, MI 49103-0160, USA

Ali, Somy (Actor, Bollywood)
208 Vindhyachal 22 Mount Mary Road
Bandra
Bombay, MS 400 050, INDIA

Ali, Tatyana (Actor)
c/o Staff Member *Kohner Agency, The*
9300 Wilshire Blvd Ste 555
Beverly Hills, CA 90212-3211, USA

Ali Khan, Saif (Actor, Bollywood)
Bungalow 5, Belscot Tower
Lokhandwala Complex Andheri Link Road
Mumbai, MS 400058, INDIA

Alice In Chains (Music Group)
The Plaza
535 Kings Rd
London SW10 OSZ, UNITED KINGDOM (UK)

Alicea, Luis (Baseball Player)
St Louis Cardinals
2140 C Rd
Loxahatchee, FL 33470-3837, USA

Alicia, Karen (Actor)
c/o Staff Member *Televisa*
Blvd Adolfo Lopez Mateos 232
Colonia San Angel INN
DF CP 01060, MEXICO

Alien Ant Farm (Music Group)
c/o Staff Member *Creative Artists Agency LCC (CAA-LA)*
2000 Avenue Of The Stars
Los Angeles, CA 90067-4700, USA

Aliens, The (Music Group)
c/o Staff Member *Paradigm (Monterey)*
509 Hartnell St
Monterey, CA 93940-2825, USA

Alikhan, Anwar (Actor)
Parkavi Apartments Phase IV No 15-F 18
Mariamman Koil Street
West K K Nagar
Chennai, TN 600 078, INDIA

Alington, William H (Architect)
60 Homewood Crescent
Wellington, NEW ZEALAND

Alis, Robert (Cinematographer)
13920 72nd Rd
Flushing, NY 11367-2319, USA

Alisha (Musician)
Famous Artists Agency
250 W 57th St
New York, NY 10107-0001, USA

Alison, Jane (Writer)
FarrarStraus Giroux
19 Union Sq W
New York, NY 10003-3304, USA

Alito, Samuel A Jr (Judge)
US Court of Appeals
50 Walnut St Rm 5040
US Courthouse
Newark, NJ 07102-3571, USA

Aliyev, Ilham (President)
President's Office
Baku 370066, AZERBAIJAN

All-American Rejects, The (Music Group)
c/o Jenna Adler *Creative Artists Agency LCC (CAA-LA)*
2000 Avenue Of The Stars
Los Angeles, CA 90067-4700, USA

All For One / All-4-One (Music Group)
c/o Staff Member *Performers Of the World/ Management Interests Associates (POW/MIA)*
8901 Melrose Ave
2nd Floor
West Hollywood, CA 90069-5605, USA

All Saints (Music Group)
72 Chancellors Rd
London W6 9SG, UNITED KINGDOM (UK)

Allain, William A (Governor)
970 Momingside St
Jackson, MS 39202, USA

Allais, Emile (Skier)
Imeuble Cassiopee
Cluses 7430, FRANCE

Allais, Maurice (Nobel Prize Laureate)
60 Blvd Saint-Michel
Paris 75006, FRANCE

Allan, Gabrielle (Producer)
c/o Staff Member *United Talent Agency (UTA)*
9560 Wilshire Blvd Ste 500
Beverly Hills, CA 90212-2401, USA

Allan, Gary (Musician)
c/o *Texas Sounds*
PO Box 1644
Dickinson, TX 77539-1644, USA

Allan, Jed (Actor)
c/o Monique Moss *Warren Cowan & Associates PR*
8899 Beverly Blvd Ste 919
Los Angeles, CA 90048-2436, USA

Allan, Stephen D (Steve) (Golfer)
c/o Staff Member *Pro-Sport Management*
7373 E Doubletree Ranch Rd Ste 170
Scottsdale, AZ 85258-2036, USA

Allanson, Andy (Baseball Player)
Cleveland Indians
43850 20th St E
Lancaster, CA 93535-4290, USA

Allard, Beatrice (Baseball Player)
1040 Ridgewood Dr
Lillian, AL 36549-5334, USA

Allard, Brian (Baseball Player)
Texas Rangers
22102 N Perry Rd
Colbert, WA 99005-9488, USA

Allard, Linda M (Designer, Fashion Designer)
Ellen Tracy Corp
575 Fashion Ave
New York, NY 10018-2095, USA

Allawi, Iyad (Prime Minister)
Prime Minister's Office
Karradat Mariam
Baghdad, IRAQ

Allbaugh, Joseph (Government Official)
Federal Emergency Management Agency
500 C St SW
Washington, DC 20472-0001, USA

Allegre, Claude J (Misc)
Recherce/Technologie Institute
110 Rue Grenelle
Paris 75700, FRANCE

Allegre, Raul (Football Player)
Baltimore Colts
6500 Rain Creek Pkwy
Austin, TX 78759-6147, USA

Allem, Fulton (Golfer)
6876 Hidden Glade Pl
Sanford, FL 32771-6429, USA

Allen, Agnes (Baseball Player)
48226 232nd St
Flandreau, SD 57028-6651, USA

Allen, Aleisha (Actor)
c/o Jan Jarrett *Jordan Gill & Dornbaum Talent Agency*
1133 Broadway Ste 623
New York, NY 10010-8021, USA

allen, andrew james (Actor)
c/o Staff Member *Curtis Talent Management*
9607 Arby Dr
Beverly Hills, CA 90210-1202, USA

Allen, Anthony (Football Player)
Atlanta Falcons
956 20th Ave
Seattle, WA 98122-4736, USA

Allen, Bernie (Baseball Player)
Minnesota Twins
3725 Coventry Way
Carmel, IN 46033-3026, USA

Allen, Betty (Opera Singer)
Harlem School of Arts
645 Saint Nicholas Ave
New York, NY 10030-1098, USA

Allen, Bob (Baseball Player)
Philadelphia Phillies
1888 Arnes Cir W
Chesapeake, VA 23321, USA

Allen, Bob (Baseball Player)
Cleveland Indians
PO Box 667
Tatum, TX 75691, USA

Allen, Bob (Basketball Player)
San Francisco Warriors
104 Hidden Ct
Russell, KY 41169, USA

Allen, Bobby (Hockey Player)
Edmonton Oilers
9 Park Ave Apt 705
Hull, MA 02045-3191, USA

Allen, Bruce (Race Car Driver)
Reger-Morrison Racing Engines
1120 Enterprise Pl
Arlington, TX 76001-7138, USA

Allen, Byron (Comedian)
c/o Eric Schwartzman *Schwartzman & Associates PR*
1925 Century Park E Ste 2300
Los Angeles, CA 90067-2724, USA

Allen, C Keith (Hockey Player)
Detroit Red Wings
10000 Highland Ave
Long Beach Township, NJ 08008-3166, USA

Allen, Carl (Football Player)
St Louis Cardinals
1614 Hornsby Ave
Saint Louis, MO 63147-1410, USA

Allen, Chad (Actor)
c/o Staff Member *Mythgarden*
11026 Ventura Blvd Ste 8
Studio City, CA 91604-3570, USA

Allen, Chad (Baseball Player)
Minnesota Twins
7152 Blackwood Dr
Dallas, TX 75231-5604, USA

Allen, Chuck (Athlete, Football Player)
San Diego Chargers
192 Victoria Loop
Port Townsend, WA 98368-9400, USA

Allen, Clarence R (Misc, Scientist)
1763 Royal Oaks Dr Apt F306
Duarte, CA 91010-1987, USA

Allen, Corey (Actor, Director)
8642 Hollywood Blvd
Los Angeles, CA 90069-1416, USA

Allen, Danielle Sherie (Actor)
c/o Staff Member *Privilege Talent Agency*
PO Box 260860
Encino, CA 91426-0860, USA

Allen, Debbie (Actor, Choreographer)
c/o Staff Member *Red Bird Productions*
3623 Hayden Ave
Culver City, CA 90232-2458, USA

Allen, Dick (Baseball Player)
Philadelphia Phillies
PO Box 254
Wampum, PA 16157-0254, USA

Allen, Doug (Artist)
c/o Staff Member *Fantagraphics Books*
7563 Lake City Way NE
Seattle, WA 98115-4218, USA

Allen, Doug (Football Player)
Buffalo Bills
542 N Gardner St
Los Angeles, CA 90036-5709, USA

Allen, Duane D (Musician)
88 New Shackle Island Rd
Hendersonville, TN 37075-2393, USA

Allen, Egypt (Football Player)
Chicago Bears
2115 Rubens Dr
Dallas, TX 75224-4146, USA

Allen, Frances E (Scientist)
Finney Farm
Croton On Hudson, NY 10520, USA

Allen, George F (Governor, Senator)
PO Box 17704
Richmond, VA 23226-7704, USA

Allen, Geri (Composer, Musician)
Clayton Ross Productions
508 Shoreline Hwy
Mill Valley, CA 94941-3738, USA

Allen, Grady (Football Player)
Atlanta Falcons
317 Circleview Dr N
Hurst, TX 76054-3518, USA

Allen, Greg (Football Player)
Cleveland Browns
4993 Canal St
Milton, FL 32570-5900, USA

Allen, Hank (Baseball Player)
Washington Senators
PO Box 4612
Upper Marlboro, MD 20775-0612, USA

Allen, Henry (Critic)
Washington Post
Editorial Dept 1150 15th St NW
Washington, DC 20071-0001, USA

Allen, Herb (Business Person)
Allen & Co
711 5th Ave Fl 10
New York, NY 10022-3168, USA

Allen, J Presson (Producer, Writer)
Lewis Allen Productions
1501 Broadway Ste 1614
New York, NY 10036-5600, USA

Allen, Jackie (Football Player)
Oakland Raiders
7152 Blackwood Dr
Dallas, TX 75231-5604, USA

Allen, Jamie (Baseball Player)
Seattle Mariners
1920 E Belmont Dr
Tempe, AZ 85284-1719, USA

Allen, Jeff (Football Player)
Miami Dolphins
7808 State Route 177
Camden, OH 45311-9680, USA

Allen, Jerry (Football Player)
Baltimore Colts
14 Washinton Valley Rd
Morristown, NJ 07960, USA

Allen, Jimmy (Football Player)
Pittsburgh Steelers
3437 S La Brea Ave Apt 201
Los Angeles, CA 90016-5234, USA

Allen, Joan (Actor)
c/o Staff Member *International Creative Management (ICM-LA)*
10250 Constellation Blvd
Los Angeles, CA 90067-6200, USA

Allen, Jonelle (Actor)
c/o Staff Member *SMS Talent Inc*
8730 W Sunset Blvd Ste 440
Los Angeles, CA 90069-2277, USA

Allen, Joseph P (Astronaut)
LBJ Sapce Center
2101 Nasa Pkwy
C/O Astronaut Office
Houston, TX 77058-3607, USA

Allen, Karen (Actor)
c/o Chris Schmidt *Paradigm (LA)*
360 N Crescent Dr
North Bldg
Beverly Hills, CA 90210-6820, USA

Allen, Kevin (Director)
William Morris Agency
52/53 Poland Place
London W1F 7LX, UNITED KINGDOM (UK)

Allen, Kevin (Football Player)
Philadelphia Eagles
2422 Hazelcrest Ln
Cincinnati, OH 45231-1132, USA

Allen, Kim (Baseball Player)
Seattle Mariners
2705 La Praix St
Highland, CA 92346-1928, USA

Allen, Krista (Actor)
Stone Manners
6500 Wilshire Blvd Ste 550
Los Angeles, CA 90048-4950, USA

Allen, Larry C (Football Player)
Dallas Cowboys
6290 Old Redwood Hwy
Santa Rosa, CA 95403-1123, USA

Allen, Leo (Writer)
c/o Staff Member *Saturday Night Live*
30 Rockefeller Plz Fl 17
New York, NY 10112-0015, USA

Allen, Lew Jr (General)
Draper Laboratory
555 Technology Sq
Cambridge, MA 02139-3563, USA

Allen, Lily (Musician)
c/o Staff Member *Paradigm (Monterey)*
509 Hartnell St
Monterey, CA 93940-2825, USA

Allen, Lloyd (Baseball Player)
California Angels
2340 Castlewood Dr
Toledo, OH 43613-3923, USA

Allen, Lou (Football Player)
Pittsburgh Steelers
1309 Hobbs Rd
Greensboro, NC 27410-4823, USA

Allen, Loy Jr (Race Car Driver)
3197 Steamboat Ridge Rd
Port Orange, FL 32128-6917, USA

Allen, Lucius (Basketball Player)
Seattle SuperSonics
1915 Buckingham Rd
Los Angeles, CA 90016-1701, USA

Allen, Marcus (Actor, Producer)
c/o Jack Gilardi *International Creative Management (ICM-LA)*
10250 Constellation Blvd
Los Angeles, CA 90067-6200, USA

Allen, Marty (Actor, Comedian)
3847 Tropical Vine St
Las Vegas, NV 89147-8079, USA

Allen, Marvin (Football Player)
New England Patriots
1806 Las Cruces Ln
Wichita Falls, TX 76306-5205, USA

Allen, Maryon P (Senator)
1551 Creekstone Cir
Birmingham, AL 35243-2827, USA

Allen, Michael (Football Player)
Seattle Seahawks
8839 NE 147th St
Kenmore, WA 98028-4727, USA

Allen, Michael (Golfer)
5827 E Anderson Dr
Scottsdale, AZ 85254-5941, USA

Allen, Nancy (Actor)
c/o Staff Member *Sneak Preview Entertainment*
PO Box 3238
Hollywood, CA 90078-3238, USA

Allen, Natalie (Correspondent)
Cable News Network
1050 Techwood Dr NW
News Dept
Atlanta, GA 30318-5604, USA

Allen, Neil (Baseball Player)
New York Mets
3619 Torrey Pines Blvd
Sarasota, FL 34238-2828, USA

Allen, Pam (Golfer)
809 Delphinium Dr
Billings, MT 59102-3409, USA

Allen, Patrick (Football Player)
Houston Oilers
427 20th Ave E
Seattle, WA 98112-5313, USA

Allen, Paul (Business Person)
The Paul G Allen Family Foundation
505 5th Ave S Ste 900
Seattle, WA 98104-3821, USA

Allen, Rae (Actor)
c/o Staff Member *Kyle Fritz Management*
6325 Heather Dr
Los Angeles, CA 90068-1633, USA

Allen, Randy (Basketball Player)
Sacramento Kings
10185 Nichols Lake Rd
Milton, FL 32583-9267, USA

Allen, Rax Jr (Music Group)
209 10th Ave S Ste 527
Nashville, TN 37203-7103, USA

Allen, Ray (Actor, Basketball Player)
c/o Staff Member *3 Arts Entertainment Inc*
9460 Wilshire Blvd Fl 7
Beverly Hills, CA 90212-2713, USA

Allen, Richard (Actor)
89 Saltergate
Chesterfield S40 IUS, UNITED KINGDOM (UK)

Allen, Richard A (Richie) (Baseball Player)
RR 2
Wampum, PA 16157, USA

Allen, Richard J (Rick) (Music Group)
Q Prime Mgmt
729 7th Ave Rm 1400
New York, NY 10019-6889, USA

Allen, Richard V (Government Official)
905 16th St NW
Washington, DC 20006-1703, USA

Allen, Robert (Business Person, Writer)
Instant Income Inc
PO Box 1450
Orem, UT 84059-1450, USA

Allen, Rod (Baseball Player)
Seattle Mariners
3150 E Woodland Dr
Phoenix, AZ 85048-7702, USA

Allen, Ron (Baseball Player)
St Louis Cardinals
917 Winona Dr
Youngstown, OH 44511-1404, USA

Allen, Rosalind (Actor)
c/o John Carrabino *John Carrabino Management*
5900 Wilshire Blvd Ste 406
Los Angeles, CA 90036-5015, USA

Allen, Sam (Baseball Player)
Kansas City Monarchs
2734 Gate House Rd Apt 108
Norfolk, VA 23504-4057, USA

Allen, Scott (Figure Skater)
40 Brayton St
Englewood, NJ 07631-3116, USA

Allen, Sian Barbara (Actor)
1411 N Alberta St Apt 7
Portland, OR 97217-3761, USA

Allen, Sin Barbara (Actor)
732 S Plymouth Blvd # E
Los Angeles, CA 90005-4814, USA

Allen, Ted (Television Host)
c/o Staff Member *Queer Eye for the Straight Guy*
119 Braintree St
Boston, MA 02134-1628, USA

Allen, Terry (Football Player)
Cincinnati Bengals
3670 Highway 334
Commerce, GA 30530-5098, USA

Allen, Thomas B (Opera Singer)
I C M Artists
40 W 57th St
New York, NY 10019-4001, USA

Allen, Tim (Actor, Comedian, Producer, Writer)
c/o Rick Messina *Messina Baker/ Entertainment*
955 Carrillo Dr Ste 100
Los Angeles, CA 90048-5400, USA

Allen, Will (Football Player)
New York Giants
2325 SW 105th Ter
Davie, FL 33324-7608, USA

Allen, Willard M (Doctor)
211 Key Haighway
Baltimore, MD 21230, USA

Allen, William L (Editor)
National Geographic Magazine
17th & M NW
Washington, DC 20036, USA

Allen, Woody (Actor, Comedian, Director)
c/o Staff Member *Perdido Productions*
140 W 57th St Ste 4B
New York, NY 10019-3326, USA

Allen-Moritt, Krista (Actor)
c/o Staff Member *Brillstein-Grey Entertainment*
9150 Wilshire Blvd Ste 350
Beverly Hills, CA 90212-3453, USA

Allen-Mullins, Doreen (Baseball Player)
1104 Somonauk St
Sycamore, IL 60178-2521, USA

Allenby, Robert (Golfer)
Master's Int'l Hurst Grove
Sanford Lane
Hurts
Berkshire RG10 0SQ, UNITED KINGDOM (UK)

Allende, Fernando (Actor)
c/o Staff Member *El Dorado Pictures*
725 Arizona Ave Ste 100
Santa Monica, CA 90401-1734, USA

Allende, Isabel (Writer)
92 Fernwood Dr
San Rafael, CA 94901-1533, USA

Allenson, Gary (Baseball Player)
Boston Red Sox
711 SE 34th St
Cape Coral, FL 33904-4900, USA

Allensworth, Jermaine (Baseball Player)
Pittsburgh Pirates
1824 Euclid Dr
Anderson, IN 46011-3937, USA

Allerman, Kurt (Football Player)
St Louis Cardinals
2511 Blue Heron Dr
Hudson, OH 44236-1866, USA

Allert, Ty (Football Player)
San Diego Chargers
1504 County Road 308
Lexington, TX 78947-4113, USA

Allesandro, Nivola
ICM
9830 Wilshire Blvd
Beverly Hills, CA 90212-1804, USA

Alley, Alphonse (President)
Carre 181-182
BP 48
Cotonou, BENIN

Alley, Donald (Football Player)
Baltimore Colts
3258 Parade Cir W
Colorado Springs, CO 80917-2931, USA

Alley, Gene (Baseball Player)
Pittsburgh Pirates
10236 Steuben Dr
Glen Allen, VA 23060-3072, USA

Alley, Kirstie (Actor, Producer)
c/o Jason Weinberg *Untitled Entertainment (LA)*
331 N Maple Dr Fl 3
Beverly Hills, CA 90210-3827, USA

Alley, Kristie (Actor)
c/o Staff Member *True BlueProductions*
PO Box 27127
Los Angeles, CA 90027-0127, USA

Alley, Steve (Hockey Player)
Hartford Whalers
545 College Rd
Lake Forest, IL 60045-2319, USA

Alley Cats
PO Box 1031
Montrose, CA 91021-1031, USA

Allfrey, Vincent G (Misc)
24 Winthrop Ct
Tenafly, NJ 07670-1616, USA

Allgood, Lonnie (Football Player)
Cincinnati Bengals
12 Drake Rd
Somerset, NJ 08873-2369, USA

Allie, Gair (Baseball Player)
Pittsburgh Pirates
11818 Button Willow Cv
San Antonio, TX 78213-1220, USA

Allietta, Bob (Baseball Player)
California Angels
25 Robinson Rd
Falmouth, MA 02540-3840, USA

Allimadi, E Otema (Prime Minister)
PO Box Gulu
Gulu District, UGANDA

Allinson, Michael
112 Knollwood Dr
Larchmont, NY 10538, USA

Allione, Tsultrim (Religious Leader)
Tara Mandala Retreat Center
PO Box 3040
Pagosa Springs, CO 81147-3040, USA

Allison, Dana (Baseball Player)
Oakland A's
1337 Robinhood Ln
Front Royal, VA 22630-4535, USA

Allison, Dave (Coach, Hockey Player)
PO Box 1416
International Falls, MN 56649-1416, USA

Allison, Donnie (Race Car Driver)
355 Quail Dr
Salisbury, NC 28147-8860, USA

Allison, Glenn (Bowler)
1844 S Haster St Spc 138
Anaheim, CA 92802-3750, USA

Allison, Henry (Football Player)
Philadelphia Eagles
458 W Ellis Ave
Inglewood, CA 90302-1109, USA

Allison, Herbert M (Business Person)
TIAA-CREF
730 3rd Ave
New York, NY 10017-3207, USA

Allison, Jerry (Musician, Songwriter, Writer)
8455 New Bethel Rd
Lyles, TN 37098-1909, USA

Allison, Jim (Football Player)
San Diego Chargers
5706 Laramie Way
San Diego, CA 92120-1426, USA

Allison, John A IV (Financier)
BB&T Corp
200 W 2nd St
Winston Salem, NC 27101-4019, USA

Allison, John V (War Hero)
2007 Banshore Rd
Niceville, FL 32578, USA

Allison, Mike (Hockey Player)
New York Rangers
7204 Birchmont Ct NE
Bemidji, MN 56601-8615, USA

Allison, Mose J Jr (Composer, Musician)
82 Ballad Ct
Eastport, NY 11941-1602, USA

Allison, Odis (Basketball Player)
Golden State Warriors
2163 Sawtooth Mountain Dr
Henderson, NV 89044-0107, USA

Allison, Ray (Hockey Player)
Hartford Whalers
106 N Valleybrook Rd
Cherry Hill, NJ 08034-3809, USA

Allison, Richard C (Judge)
24 Circle Dr
Manhasset, NY 11030-1121, USA

Allison, Robert J Jr
Anadarko Petroleum Corp
1201 Lake Robbins Dr
Spring, TX 77380-1176, USA

Allison, Stacy (Mountaineer)
6633 SE 29th Ave
Portland, OR 97202-8721, USA

Allison Jr, Graham T (Educator)
69 Pinehurst Rd
Belmont, MA 02478-1502, USA

Alliss, Peter (Sportscaster)
Int'l Mgmt Group
1 Erieview Plz
1360 E 9th St #1300
Cleveland, OH 44114-1738, USA

Alliston, Vaughn (Football Player)
Denver Broncos
7493 Apple Yard Ln
Cordova, TN 38016-8770, USA

Allman, Greg (Musician)
Allman Brothers Band Inc
18 Tamworth Rd
Waban, MA 02468-2220, USA

Allor, Kristin
11940 Willow Ridge Dr
Willow Springs, IL 60480-1187, USA

Allouache, Merzak (Director)
Cite des Asphodeles Bt D15
183 Ben Aknoun
Algiers, ALGERIA

Allport, Chris M (Actor)
1324 Pine St
Santa Monica, CA 90405-2612, USA

Allport, Christopher (Actor)
c/o Staff Member *Pakula/King & Associates*
9229 W Sunset Blvd Ste 315
Los Angeles, CA 90069-3403, USA

Allred, Beau (Baseball Player)
Cleveland Indians
2094 S Shannon Rd
Safford, AZ 85546-9344, USA

Allred, Brian (Football Player)
Seattle Seahawks
16470 Ed Warfield Rd
Woodbine, MD 21797-7806, USA

Allred, Gloria R (Attorney, Attorney General, General, Lawyer)
Allred Maroko Goldberg
6300 Wilshire Blvd Ste 1500
Los Angeles, CA 90048-5217, USA

Allred, John (Football Player)
Chicago Bears
PO Box 748
Del Mar, CA 92014-0748, USA

Allsopp, Kirstie (Actor)
c/o Staff Member *Arlington Enterprises Ltd*
1-3 Charlotte St
London W1P 1HD, UNITED KINGDOM (UK)

Allsup, Mike (Music Group, Musician)
Mckenzie Accountancy
5171 Caliente St Unit 134
Las Vegas, NV 89119-2198, USA

Allsup, Tommy (Music Group)
Tophands Talent
PO Box 1547
Arlington, TX 76004-1547, USA

Allums, Darrell (Basketball Player)
3584 Brenton Ave Apt B
Lynwood, CA 90262-2031, USA

Almanza, Armando (Baseball Player)
Florida Marlins
11601 SW 52nd St
Cooper City, FL 33330-4250, USA

Almanzar, Carlos (Athlete, Baseball Player)
c/o Staff Member *San Diego Padres*
100 Park Blvd
San Diego, CA 92101-7405, USA

Almeda, Alex
5067 Woodley Ave
Encino, CA 91436-1472, USA

Almee, Anouk (Actor)
ICM France
37 Rue de Acacias
Paris 75017, FRANCE

Almen, Lowell G (Religious Leader)
Evangelical Lutheran Church
8765 W Higgins Rd
Chicago, IL 60631-4192, USA

Almodovar, Pedro (Director)
El Deseo SA
Ruiz Perello 25
Madrid 28028, SPAIN

Almon, Bill (Baseball Player)
San Diego Padres
42 Channel Vw Unit 4
Warwick, RI 02889-6544, USA

Almond, David (Writer)
c/o Staff Member *Doubleday/ RandomHouse*
1745 Broadway
New York, NY 10019-4305, USA

Almond, Marc (Music Group)
Take Out Productions
630 9th Ave Ste 603
New York, NY 10036-3748, USA

Almunia, Amann Joaquin (Government Official)
Piaza de las Cortes #9
4A Planta
Madrid 28014, SPAIN

Almy, Brook (Actor)
c/o Jerald Silverhardt *Saffron Management*
9171 Wilshire Blvd Ste 441
Beverly Hills, CA 90210-5516, USA

Alois (Prince)
Schloss Vaduz
Vaduz 9490, LIECHTENSTEIN

Alomar, Roberto (Baseball Player)
c/o Staff Member *Tampa Bay Devil Rays*
1 Tropicana Dr
Tropicana Field
Saint Petersburg, FL 33705-1703, USA

Alomar Jr, Sandy (Baseball Player)
San Diego Padres
4635 Prestwick Xing
Westlake, OH 44145-5073, USA

Alomar Sr, Sandy (Baseball Player)
Milwaukee Braves
PO Box 367
Salinas, PR 00751-0367, USA

Alonsa, Alicia (Ballerina)
Calzada 510 Entre D & E
El Vedada, Havana CP 10400, CUBA

Alonso, Anabel (Actor)
GRPC SL
Calles Fuencarral 17
Madrid 28004, SPAIN

Alonso, Daniella (Actor)
c/o Staff Member *Gersh Agency, The (LA)*
232 N Canon Dr
Beverly Hills, CA 90210-5302, USA

Alonso, Fernando (Race Car Driver)
Villamiana, 67
Limanes 33199, SPAIN

Alonso, Laz (Actor)
c/o Evan Hainey *Untitled Entertainment (LA)*
331 N Maple Dr Fl 3
Beverly Hills, CA 90210-3827, USA

Alonso, Maria Conchita (Actor, Music Group)
118 S Beverly Dr Ste 201
Beverly Hills, CA 90212-3016, USA

Alosio, Ryan (Actor)
c/o Staff Member *Marshak/Zachary Company, The*
8840 Wilshire Blvd Fl 1
Beverly Hills, CA 90211-2606, USA

Alou, Felipe (Baseball Player)
San Francisco Giants
7263 Davit Cir
Lake Worth, FL 33467-7782, USA

Alou, Jesus (Baseball Player)
San Francisco Giants
Apartado Postal 539/2 Lafaria
Santo Domingo, DOMINICAN REPUBLIC

Alou, Mateo (Baseball Player)
San Francisco Giants
PO Box 30063 MDJ Troncuso #16
Paraiso
Santo Domingo, DOMINICAN REPUBLIC

Alou, Moises (Baseball Player)
Pittsburgh Pirates
13095 NW 13th St
Pembroke Pines, FL 33028-2711, USA

Alpert, Herb (Musician)
31930 Pacific Coast Hwy
Malibu, CA 90265-2524, USA

Alpert, Hollis
PO Box 142
Shelter Island, NY 11964-0142, USA

Alpert, Joseph S (Doctor)
3440 E Cathedral Rock Cir
Tucson, AZ 85718-1379, USA

Alphand, Luc (Skier)
Chalet Le Balme Chantemarie
Sierra Chavalier 05330, FRANCE

Alpher, Ralph A (Physicist)
253 Ascot Ln
Schenectady, NY 12309-4964, USA

Alsgaard, Thomas (Skier)
Cathinka Guldbergsveg 16
Holter 2034, NORWAY

Alsop, Marin (Musician)
c/o Staff Member *International Creative Management (ICM-LA)*
10250 Constellation Blvd
Los Angeles, CA 90067-6200, USA

Alsop, Will (Architect)
Bishop's Wharf
39-49 Parkgate Road
London SW11 4NP, UNITED KINGDOM (UK)

Alston, Alyce Carolyn (Publisher)
Oprah Magazine
224 W 57th St # 900
New York, NY 10019-3200, USA

Alston, Barbara (Music Group)
Superstars Unlimited
PO Box 371371
Las Vegas, NV 89137-1371, USA

Alston, Del (Baseball Player)
New York Yankees
3608 Fairview Ave Apt 3
Baltimore, MD 21216-1338, USA

Alston, Garvin (Baseball Player)
Colorado Rockies
4705 E Thunderhill Pl
Phoenix, AZ 85044-4905, USA

Alston, Mack (Football Player)
Washington Redskins
5421 Echols Ave
Alexandria, VA 22311-1344, USA

Alston, Rafer (Basketball Player)
c/o Staff Member *Toronto Raptors*
20 Bay St #1702
Toronto, ON M5J 2N8, CANADA

Alston, Reeves Shirley (Music Group)
GHR Entertainment
6014 N Pointe Pl
Woodland Hills, CA 91367-5500, USA

Alstott, Mike (Football Player)
Tampa Bay Buccaneers
7800 9th Ave S
Saint Petersburg, FL 33707-2731, USA

Alt, Carol (Actor)
c/o Scott Hart *Nanas/Hart Entertainment*
14622 Ventura Blvd Ste 746
Sherman Oaks, CA 91403-3600, USA

Alt, John M (Football Player)
Kansas City Chiefs
1 Scotch Pine Rd
Saint Paul, MN 55127-2033, USA

Altenberg, Wolfgang (General)
Birkenhof 44
Brenen-Saint-Magnus 28759, GERMANY

Alter, Hobie (Designer, Misc, Yachtsman)
PO Box 1008
Oceanside, CA 92051-1008, USA

Alter Bridge (Music Group)
c/o Staff Member *Wind-up Records*
72 Madison Ave Fl 8
New York, NY 10016-8731, USA

Alther, Lisa (Writer)
1086 Silver St
Hinesburg, VT 05461-9450, USA

Althoff, James (Football Player)
Chicago Bears
201 Lake Ct
Crystal Lake, IL 60014-5203, USA

Altman, Chelsea (Actor)
c/o Staff Member *Innovative Artists (LA)*
1505 10th St
Santa Monica, CA 90401-2805, USA

Altman, George (Baseball Player)
Kansas City Monarchs
915 Midpoint Dr
O Fallon, MO 63366-5906, USA

Altman, Jeff (Actor)
c/o Staff Member *Richard De La Font Agency*
4845 S Sheridan Rd Ste 505
Tulsa, OK 74145-5719, USA

Altman, Scott D (Astronaut)
3011 Harvest Hill Dr
Friendswood, TX 77546-5047, USA

Altman, Sidney (Nobel Prize Laureate)
71 Blake Rd
Hamden, CT 06517-3404, USA

Altman, Stuart H (Educator)
11 Bakers Hill Rd
Weston, MA 02493-1708, USA

Altmeyer, Jeannine T (Opera Singer)
Im Muhlader
Herrliberg 8709, SWITZERLAND

Altobelli, Joseph (Joe) (Baseball Player)
Cleveland Indians
10 Stowell Dr Apt 3
Rochester, NY 14616-1889, USA

Altomar, Tony
44 Norvel Ln
Stamford, CT 06905-1316, USA

Alusik, George (Baseball Player)
Detroit Tigers
PO Box 454
Woodbridge, NJ 07095-0454, USA

Alva, Luigi
via Moscova 46/3
Mailand 20121, ITALY

Alvarado, Natividad (Naty) (Misc)
Equitable of Iowa
2700 N Main St
Santa Ana, CA 92705-6634, USA

Alvarez, Barry (Coach, Football Coach)
University of Wisconsin
Athletic Dept
Medison, WI 53711, USA

Alvarez, Gabe (Baseball Player)
Detroit Tigers
4401 La Madera Ave
El Monte, CA 91732-2009, USA

Alvarez, Isabel (Baseball Player)
2402 Monmouth Ave
Fort Wayne, IN 46809-1732, USA

Alvarez, Jose (Baseball Player)
Minnesota Twins
210 Murphy Ln
Greenville, SC 29607-4934, USA

Alvarez, Mario Roberto (Architect)
Marlo Roberto Alvarez Assoc
Solis 370
Buenos Aires, ARGENTINA

Alvarez, Orlando (Baseball Player)
Los Angeles Dodgers
Cummunidad Dolores 37
Rio Grande, PR 00745, USA

Alvarez, Rogelio (Baseball Player)
Cincinnati Reds
5010 NW 183rd St
Miami Gardens, FL 33055-2929, USA

Alvarez, Victor (Baseball Player)
c/o Staff Member *Los Angeles Dodgers (LA Dodgers)*
1000 Elysian Park Ave
Los Angeles, CA 90012-1112, USA

Alvarez, Wilson (Baseball Player)
Texas Rangers
6927 Westchester Cir
Bradenton, FL 34202-2584, USA

Alvarez Martinez, Francisco Cardinal (Religious Leader)
Arco de Palacio 3
Toledo 45002, SPAIN

Alvers, Steve (Football Player)
Buffalo Bills
9751 SW 115th Ave
Miami, FL 33176-2553, USA

Alves, Joe (Director)
4176 Rosario Rd
Woodland Hills, CA 91364-6025, USA

Alvim, Anna (Actor)
c/o Jean Fox *Fox-Albert Management*
88 Central Park W
New York, NY 10023-5209, USA

Alvin, Dave (Musician, Songwriter, Writer)
Mark Pucci
5000 Oak Bluff Ct
Atlanta, GA 30350-1069, USA

Alvina, Anicee (Actor)
41 Rue de l'Echese
Le Visinet 75008, FRANCE

Alvis, Max (Baseball Player)
Cleveland Indians
806 Hunterwood Dr
Jasper, TX 75951-2820, USA

Alvord, Steve (Football Player)
St Louis Cardinals
2907 Cherrywood Ave
Bellingham, WA 98225-1210, USA

Alward, Tom (Football Player)
Tampa Bay Buccaneers
5051 Bensett Trl
Davison, MI 48423-8781, USA

Alwin, Robert (Basketball Player)
Oshkosh All Stars
1120 Turnberry Ln
York, PA 17403-9115, USA

Alworth, Lance (Football Player)
San Diego Chargers
990 Highland Dr Ste 300
Solana Beach, CA 92075-2438, USA

Alyea, Brant (Baseball Player)
Washington Senators
119 Lockhardt Rd
Tryon, NC 28782, USA

Alyson, Jocelyn E (Musician)
c/o Staff Member *Diva Central Inc*
7510 W Sunset Blvd Ste 1445
Los Angeles, CA 90046-3408, USA

Ama, Shola (Musician)
12 One Mgmt
Executive Suite
20 Damien St
London E1 2HX, UNITED KINGDOM (UK)

Amaechi, John (Basketball Player)
Cleveland Cavaliers
5747 E Aire Libre Ave
Scottsdale, AZ 85254-1206, USA

Amaker, Tommy (Basketball Player, Coach)
University of Michigan
Athletic Dept
Ann Arbor, MI 48109, USA

Amalfitano, J Joseph (Joe) (Baseball Player)
265 Bowstring Dr
Sedona, AZ 86336-6523, USA

Amalfitano, Joey (Baseball Player)
New York Giants
265 Bowstring Dr
Sedona, AZ 86336-6523, USA

Amalou, J K (Director)
William Morris Agency
52/53 Poland Space
London W1F 7LX, UNITED KINGDOM (UK)

Aman, Zeenat (Actor, Bollywood)
Neelam Apartments 3rd Floor
Mount Mary Road Bandra
Bombay, MS 400 050, INDIA

Amanar, Simona (Gymnast)
Gymnastic Federation
Str Vasile Conta 16
Budapest 70139, ROMANIA

Amandes, Tom (Actor)
Writers & Artists
360 N Crescent Dr Bldg North
Beverly Hills, CA 90210-6818, USA

Amanpour, Christiane (Correspondent, Journalist)
Cable News Network
2 Stephen St
#100
London W1P 1PL, UNITED KINGDOM (UK)

Amara, Lucine (Opera Singer)
260 W End Ave Apt 7A
New York, NY 10023-3659, USA

Amaral, Bob
14643 Hamlin St
Van Nuys, CA 91411-1610, USA

Amaral, Richard L (Rich) (Baseball Player)
Seattle Mariners
6525 Silverspur Ln
Huntington Beach, CA 92648-1516, USA

Amarjargal, Rinchinnyamiyn (Prime Minister)
Prime Minister's Office
Ulan Bator, Great Hural 12, MONGOLIA

Amaro Jr, Ruben (Baseball Player)
California Angels
1063 Country Hills Rd
Yardley, PA 19067-6024, USA

Amaro Sr, Ruben (Baseball Player)
St Louis Cardinals
4098 Cinnamon Way
Weston, FL 33331-3810, USA

Amato, Giuliano (Prime Minister)
Carmera dei Deputati
Piazza di Montecitorio
Rome 00186, ITALY

Amato, Joe (Race Car Driver)
Amato Racing
1 Amato Dr
Moosic, PA 18507-1788, USA

Amaya, Armando (Artist)
Lopex 137
Depto 1
Mexico City 06070 CP, MEXICO

Amazing Jonathan, The (Actor)
c/o Staff Member *International Creative Management (ICM-LA)*
10250 Constellation Blvd
Los Angeles, CA 90067-6200, USA

Amazing Rhythm Aces (Music Group)
c/o Staff Member *Fat City Artists*
1906 Chet Atkins Blvd Apt 502
Nashville, TN 37212-2122, USA

Ambani, Anil
Reliance Capital
'H' Block 1st Floor
Dhirubhai Ambani Knowledge City, Navi Mumbai 400 710, INDIA

Ambani, Mukesh (Business Person)
Reliance Industries Limited
Makers Chambers - IV
Nariman Point
Mumbai 400 021, INDIA

Ambasz, Emilio (Architect)
200 W 90th St Apt 11A
New York, NY 10024-1236, USA

Amber (Musician)
Artists & Audience Entertainment
PO Box 35
Pawling, NY 12564-0035, USA

Ambler, Wayne
305 Tournament Rd
Ponte Vedra, FL 32082-3646, USA

Ambro, Thomas L (Judge)
US Court of Appeals
844 N King St
Federal Building
Wilmington, DE 19801-3519, USA

Ambrose, Ashley (Football Player)
Indianapolis Colts
2877 Major Ridge Trl
Duluth, GA 30097-4986, USA

Ambrose, Lauren (Actor)
c/o Billy Lazarus *United Talent Agency (UTA)*
9560 Wilshire Blvd Ste 500
Beverly Hills, CA 90212-2401, USA

Ambrose, Richard (Football Player)
Cleveland Browns
24049 Stonehedge Dr
Cleveland, OH 44145-4864, USA

Ambrosio, Alessandra (Model)
c/o Staff Member *Elite Model Management (NY)*
111 E 22nd St
New York, NY 10010-5400, USA

Ambroziak, Peter (Hockey Player)
Buffalo Sabres
608 Noble Cres
Ottawa, ON K1V 7H9, CANADA

Ambrozic, Aloysius Matthew Cardinal (Religious Leader)
Archdiocese
1155 Yonge St
Toronto, ON M4T 1W2, CANADA

Ambuehl, Clindy (Actor)
Paul Kohner
9300 Wilshire Blvd Ste 555
Beverly Hills, CA 90212-3211, USA

Ambulance Ltd (Music Group)
c/o Staff Member *Paradigm (Monterey)*
509 Hartnell St
Monterey, CA 93940-2825, USA

Amedori, John Patrick (Actor)
c/o Rodney Omanoff *Creative Management Group (CMG)*
8522 National Blvd Ste 108
Culver City, CA 90232-2454, USA

Ameling, Elly (Music Group, Musician)
Hubstein Artist Services
65 W 90th St Apt 13F
New York, NY 10024-1510, USA

Amelio, Gilbert F (Business Person)
13416 Middle Fork Ln
Los Altos, CA 94022-2420, USA

Amelung, Ed (Baseball Player)
Los Angeles Dodgers
16681 Cedar Cir
Fountain Valley, CA 92708-2310, USA

Amen, Irving (Artist)
PO Box 812365
Boca Raton, FL 33481-2365, USA

Amenabar, Alejandro (Director, Musician, Writer)
c/o Sunmin Park *Maxmedia*
1620 Broadway
Santa Monica, CA 90404-2776, USA

Amend, Bill (Artist, Cartoonist)
Universal Press Syndicate
4520 Main St
Kansas City, MO 64111-1876, USA

Amendola, Tony (Actor)
c/o Staff Member *Marc Bass Agency Inc*
9255 W Sunset Blvd Ste 727
West Hollywood, CA 90069-3304, USA

Ament, Jeff (Musician)
Annie Ohayon Media Relations
525 Broadway # 600
New York, NY 10012-4411, USA

Amer, Nicolas
14 Great Russell St
London, ENGLAND WC1B 3NH, UNITED KINGDOM (UK)

America (Musician)
c/o Staff Member *William Morris Agency (WMA-LA)*
1 William Morris Pl
Beverly Hills, CA 90212-4261, USA

Amerie (Musician)
c/o Richard Murphy *International Creative Management (ICM-NY)*
40 W 57th St
New York, NY 10019-4001, USA

Amerson, Glenn (Football Player)
Philadelphia Eagles
4857 Mustang Rd
Brenham, TX 77833-8746, USA

Ames, Aldrich
PO Box 3000
White Deer, PA 17887-3000, USA

Ames, Bruce N (Misc)
1324 Spruce St
Berkeley, CA 94709-1435, USA

Ames, David (Football Player)
New York Titans
7909 Alvarado Rd
Richmond, VA 23229-4208, USA

Ames, Denise (Actor)
Studio Talent Group
1328 12th St
Santa Monica, CA 90401-2051, USA

Ames, Ed (Actor, Musician)
c/o Staff Member *Paradise Artists*
108 E Matilija St
Ojai, CA 93023-2639, USA

Ames, Frank Anthony (Musician)
1235 Potomac St NW
Washington, DC 20007-3230, USA

Ames, Rachel (Actor)
Atkins Assoc
8040 Ventura Canyon Ave
Panorama City, CA 91402-6313, USA

Amick, Madchen (Actor)
c/o Kesha Williams *Melanie Greene Management & Productions*
425 N Robertson Blvd
West Hollywood, CA 90048-1735, USA

Amiez, Sebastien (Skier)
Ave Chasse-Foret
Pralognan, FRANCE

Amigo Vallejo, Carlos Cardinal (Religious Leader)
Archdiocese
Piaza Virgin de los Reyes S/N
Seville 41004, SPAIN

Amiina (Musician)
c/o Staff Member *Paradigm (Monterey)*
509 Hartnell St
Monterey, CA 93940-2825, USA

Amin, Idi
Box 8948
Jidda 21492, SAUDI ARABIA

Amini (Actor, Bollywood)
6 Parthasarathipuram
T Nagar
Chennai, TN 600017, INDIA

Amis, Martin (Journalist, Writer)
P F D
Drury House
34-43 Russell St
London WC2B 5HA, UNITED KINGDOM (UK)

Amis, Suzy (Actor, Model)
c/o Davien Littlefield *Davien Littlefield Management*
33 W 67th St Ph
New York, NY 10023-6224, USA

Amlong, Joe (Athlete)
HC 36 Box 73
Sand Coulee, MT 59472, USA

Amlong, Thomas (Athlete)
166 Four Mile River Rd
Old Lyme, CT 06371-1325, USA

Ammaccapane, Danielle (Golfer)
13214 N 13th St
Phoenix, AZ 85022, USA

Ammaccapane, Dina (Golfer)
4407 E Blanche Dr
Phoenix, AZ 85032-4881, USA

Ammachi (Religious Leader)
Amrita IInstitutions
Ettimadai
Coimbatore, Tamil Nadu 641105, INDIA

Amman, Richard (Football Player)
Baltimore Colts
2907 Lake Joanna Dr
Eustis, FL 32726-7824, USA

Ammann, Simon (Speed Skater)
Ski Verband
Worbstr 52
Muri 3074, SWITZERLAND

Amodeo, Mike (Hockey Player)
Winnipeg Jets
16 Coulton Crt
Whitby, ON L1N 7A9, CANADA

Amor, Vincente (Baseball Player)
Chicago Cubs
13871 SW 52nd St
Miramar, FL 33027-5945, USA

Amorosi, Vanessa (Musician)
Mar Jac Productions
PO Box 51
Caulfield South, VIC, AUSTRALIA

Amos, John (Actor)
c/o Nicole Cataldo *Diverse Talent Group*
1875 Century Park E Ste 2250
Los Angeles, CA 90067-2563, USA

Amos, Paul S (Business Person)
AFLAC Inc
1932 Wynnton Rd
Columbus, GA 31999-0002, USA

Amos, Tori (Musician, Songwriter, Writer)
c/o Carole Kinzel *Creative Artists Agency LCC (CAA-LA)*
2000 Avenue Of The Stars
Los Angeles, CA 90067-4700, USA

Amos, Wally (Famous) (Business Person)
PO Box 897
Kailua, HI 96734-0897, USA

Amoyal, Pierre A W (Musician)
Jacques Thelen
252 Rue de Faubourg Saint-Honore
Paris 75008, FRANCE

Amplas, John (Actor)
443 Meridian Dr
Pittsburgh, PA 15228-2613, USA

Amram, David W III (Composer, Musician)
Peekskill Hollow Farm
Peekskill Hollow Road
Putnam Valley, NY 10579, USA

Amrapurkar, Sadashiv (Actor, Bollywood, Comedian)
A/201 Panchdhara Off Yari Road
Versova Andheri
Bombay, MS 400 058, INDIA

Amritraj, Vijay (Tennis Player)
First Serve Entertainment
7277 Hayvenhurst Ave
Van Nuys, CA 91406-2860, USA

Amsler, Marty (Football Player)
Chicago Bears
4009 Fairfax Rd
Evansville, IN 47710-3718, USA

Amsterdam, Anthony G (Attorney, Attorney General, Educator, General)
68 Middle Line Hwy
Southampton, NY 11968-1645, USA

Amstrong, Otis (Football Player)
Denver Broncos
7183 S Newport Way
Centennial, CO 80112-1613, USA

Amstutz, Joe (Football Player)
Cleveland Browns
24840 Arrow Ct Apt 29
Tehachapi, CA 93561-7124, USA

Amte, Baba (Religious Leader)
Maharogi Sewa Samiti
Waora Anandwan
Dist Chandrapur, Maharashtra 442914, INDIA

Amundsen, Norman (Football Player)
Green Bay Packers
3901 Hemlock Dr
Valparaiso, IN 46383-1813, USA

Amurri, Eva (Actor)
c/o Staff Member *United Talent Agency (UTA)*
9560 Wilshire Blvd Ste 500
Beverly Hills, CA 90212-2401, USA

Ana-Alicia (Actor)
S D B Partners
1801 Avenue Of Stars Ste 902
Los Angeles, CA 90067-5981, USA

Anagarano, Michael (Actor)
c/o Staff Member *Coast to Coast Talent Group*
3350 Barham Blvd
Los Angeles, CA 90068-1404, USA

Anagnostopoulos, Constantine E (Doctor)
3959 Mount Vernon Dr
Bloomfield Hills, MI 48301-3227, USA

Anahi (Actor)
c/o Staff Member *Televisa*
Blvd Adolfo Lopez Mateos 232
Colonia San Angel INN
DF CP 01060, MEXICO

Anakin, Douglas (Athlete)
PO Box 27
Windermere, BC V0B 2L, CANADA

Anand, Babu N (Actor)
1 A Officers Defence Colony St
Thomas Mount
Chennai, TN 600 097, INDIA

Anand, Dev (Actor, Bollywood)
2 Iris Park
Juhu
Mumbai, MS 400049, INDIA

Anand, J N (Actor)
No 8 B N Reddy Road
T Nagar
Chennai, TN 600 017, INDIA

Anand, Sabita (Actor, Bollywood)
61 Sivan Koil Ist Cross Street
Kodambakkam
Chennai, TN 600024, INDIA

Anand, Tinnu (Actor, Bollywood,
Director, Filmmaker)
101 Lakshadeep Glmohar Cross Road No
4
JVPD Scheme
Bombay, MS 400 049, INDIA

Anand, Tinu (Actor, Bollywood, Director)
101 Lakshyadeep 4th X Road
Juhu Scheme
Mumbai, MS 400049, INDIA

Anand, Vijay (Actor, Bollywood, Director,
Filmmaker, Producer)
Ketnav 17 Union Park Pali Hill
Khar
Bombay, MS 400 052, INDIA

Ananiashvill, Nina G (Ballerina)
Bolshoi Theatre
1 Ploschad Sverdlove
Moscow 103009, RUSSIA

Anantha, Raaj (Actor)
25 2nd Cross Street
Lake Area
Chennai, TN 600 034, INDIA

Anapau, Kristina (Actor)
c/o Staff Member *One Entertainment (LA)*
12 W 57th St Ph
New York, NY 10019-3900, USA

Anastasio, Trey (Musician)
c/o Staff Member *Paradigm (Monterey)*
509 Hartnell St
Monterey, CA 93940-2825, USA

Anaya, Rudolfo (Writer)
5324 Canada Vista Pl NW
Albuquerque, NM 87120-2412, USA

Anaya, Toney (Governor)
711 E May Ave
Las Cruces, NM 88001-2833, USA

Anbusrinivas (Actor)
12 Ramanajum Street
Nungambakkam
Chennai, TN 600 034, INDIA

Ancheta, Bernie (Director, Writer)
c/o Staff Member *Lenhoff & Lenhoff*
830 Palm Ave
West Hollywood, CA 90069-4009, USA

Anchia, Juan-Ruiz (Cinematographer)
Stanford-Beckett-Skouras
1015 Gayley Ave
Los Angeles, CA 90024-3413, USA

Ancker-Johnson, Betsy (Physicist)
222 Harbour Dr Apt 311
Naples, FL 34103-4087, USA

Andabaker, Rudy (Football Player)
Pittsburgh Steelers
450 8th St
Donora, PA 15033-2108, USA

Anddrson, Rebecca Moesta
PO Box 767
Monument, CO 80132-0767, USA

Andere, Jacqueline (Actor)
c/o Staff Member *Televisa*
Blvd Adolfo Lopez Mateos 232
Colonia San Angel INN
DF CP 01060, MEXICO

Anderegg, Bob (Basketball Player)
New York Knicks
11708 E Onyx Ave
Scottsdale, AZ 85259-5017, USA

Anders, Andrea (Actor)
c/o Wendi Green *Abrams Artists Agency
(LA)*
9200 W Sunset Blvd Ph 11
Los Angeles, CA 90069-3601, USA

Anders, David (Actor)
c/o Lenore Zerman *Liberman/Zerman
Management*
252 N Larchmont Blvd Ste 200
Los Angeles, CA 90004-3754, USA

Anders, Kimble (Football Player)
Kansas City Chiefs
8631 Fairhaven St Apt 9811
San Antonio, TX 78229-2058, USA

Anders, William A (Astronaut, General)
c/o Staff Member *NASA*
2101 Nasa Pkwy
Johnson Space Center
Houston, TX 77058-3691, USA

Andersen, Anthony (Actor)
1619 Broadway # 900
New York, NY 10019-7412, USA

Andersen, Barbara (Actor)
PO Box 10118
Santa Fe, NM 87504, USA

Andersen, Elmer L (Governor)
1483 Bussard Ct
Arden Hills, MN 55112-3628, USA

Andersen, Eric (Musician, Songwriter,
Writer)
Drake
177 Woodland Ave
Westwood, NJ 07675-3218, USA

Andersen, Greta (Swimmer)
19332 Brooktrail Ln
Huntington Beach, CA 92648-5578, USA

Andersen, Hjalmar (Hjallis) (Speed Skater)
Velferden for Handelsflaten
Trondheimsvn 2
Oslo 5 0560, NORWAY

Andersen, Jason (Football Player)
New England Patriots
1845 W Canyon View Dr Apt 410
Saint George, UT 84770-5832, USA

Andersen, Larry (Baseball Player)
Cleveland Indians
2043 Sunray Cir
West Linn, OR 97068-4802, USA

Andersen, Mogens (Football Player)
Strandagervej 28
Hellerup, Copenhagen 2900, DENMARK

Andersen, Morten (Football Player)
New Orleans Saints
6501 Old Shadburn Ferry Rd
Buford, GA 30518-1137, USA

Andersen, Reidar (Skier)
National Ski Hall of Fame
PO Box 191
Ishpeming, MI 49849-0191, USA

Andersen, Watts Teresa (Swimmer)
2582 Marsha Way
San Jose, CA 95125-4029, USA

Andersion, Robert P (Football Player)
New York Giants
244 Carmel Dr
Melbourne, FL 32940-7782, USA

Anderson, Alfred (Football Player)
Minnesota Vikings
2805 Chesterwood Ct
Mansfield, TX 76063-8809, USA

Anderson, Allan (Baseball Player)
Minnesota Twins
1491 Lancaster Kirkersville Rd NW
Lancaster, OH 43130-8969, USA

Anderson, Anthony (Actor, Producer)
c/o E Brian Dobbins *Principato/Young
Management*
9665 Wilshire Blvd Ste 500
Beverly Hills, CA 90212-2312, USA

Anderson, Antonio (Football Player)
Dallas Cowboys
657 E 26th St Apt 4C
Brooklyn, NY 11210-2134, USA

Anderson, Aric (Football Player)
Green Bay Packers
16306 Rolling View Trl
Cypress, TX 77433-5856, USA

Anderson, Audrey Marie (Actor)
c/o Staff Member *Untitled Entertainment
(NY)*
322 8th Ave Ste 601
New York, NY 10001-6715, USA

Anderson, Bill (Football Player)
Washington Redskins
6924 Lark Ln
Knoxville, TN 37919-5928, USA

Anderson, Bill (Musician, Songwriter,
Writer)
8222 N 19th Ave Apt 308
Phoenix, AZ 85021-5202, USA

Anderson, Bob (Baseball Player)
Chicago Cubs
4209 E 104th St
Tulsa, OK 74137-6216, USA

Anderson, Bobby (Football Player)
Denver Broncos
79125 Big Horn Trl
La Quinta, CA 92253-4523, USA

Anderson, Brad (Director)
422 Santa Monica Court
Escondido, CA 92029, USA

Anderson, Brad (Football Player)
Chicago Bears
13730 E Gary Rd
Scottsdale, AZ 85259-4644, USA

Anderson, Brad (Race Car Driver)
1240 S Cucamonga Ave
Ontario, CA 91761-4505, USA

Anderson, Bradley J (Brad) (Cartoonist)
13022 Wood Harbour Dr
Montgomery, TX 77356-8046, USA

Anderson, Brady (Baseball Player)
c/o Staff Member *San Diego Padres*
100 Park Blvd
San Diego, CA 92101-7405, USA

Anderson, Brett (Musician)
c/o Molly Neuman *Lookout! Records*
PO Box 11374
Berkeley, CA 94712-2374, USA

Anderson, Brian (Baseball Player)
California Angels
80 Park Ln
Chagrin Falls, OH 44022-2427, USA

Anderson, Bruce A (Football Player)
Los Angeles Rams
1224 NE Walnut St
Roseburg, OR 97470-2026, USA

Anderson, Bruford
44 Oswald Close Fetcham
Leatherhead, ENGLAND KT22 9UG,
UNITED KINGDOM (UK)

Anderson, Bud (Baseball Player)
Cleveland Indians
240 Twin Ln E
Wantagh, NY 11793-1963, USA

Anderson, Camille (Actor)
c/o Jerry Shandrew *Shandrew Public
Relations*
1050 S Stanley Ave
Los Angeles, CA 90019-6634, USA

Anderson, Chantelle (Basketball Player)
Cleveland Rockers
1 Center Ct
Gund Arena
Cleveland, OH 44115-4001, USA

Anderson, Charlie (Football Player)
Chicago Cardinals
2323 Melrose Ave
Bossier City, LA 71111-5952, USA

Anderson, Chris (Business Person, Writer)
The Long Tail
1165 Miller Ave
Berkeley, CA 94708-1754, USA

Anderson, Clayton C (Astronaut)
1909 Summer Reef Dr
League City, TX 77573-6659, USA

Anderson, Clifford (Basketball Player)
Los Angeles Lakers
2096A S John Russell Cir
Elkins Park, PA 19027-1017, USA

Anderson, Craig (Baseball Player)
St Louis Cardinals
19217 SW 96th Loop
Dunnellon, FL 34432-4201, USA

Anderson, Curtis (Football Player)
Kansas City Chiefs
967 Kemper Meadow Dr
Cincinnati, OH 45240-1463, USA

Anderson, Dale (Hockey Player)
Detroit Red Wings
2217 Haultain Ave
Saskatoon, SK S7J 1P7, CANADA

Anderson, Dan (Basketball Player)
New Jercy Americans
423 River St
Minneapolis, MN 55401-2515, USA

Anderson, Dan (Basketball Player)
Portland Trail Blazers
20558 SW Gracie St
Beaverton, OR 97006-1623, USA

Anderson, Darren (Football Player)
New England Patriots
7328 Overland Park Ct
West Chester, OH 45069-5560, USA

Anderson, Daryl (Actor)
24136 Friar St
Woodland Hills, CA 91367-1240, USA

Anderson, Dave
8 Inness Rd
Tenafly, NJ 07670-2715, USA

Anderson, David (Baseball Player)
Los Angeles Dodgers
207 Athletic Office Bldg
Memphis, TN 38152-3730, USA

Anderson, Derek (Basketball Player)
c/o Staff Member *Miami Heat*
601 Biscayne Blvd
American Airlines Arena
Miami, FL 33132-1801, USA

Anderson, Dion (Actor)
S D B Partners
1801 Avenue Of Stars Ste 902
Los Angeles, CA 90067-5981, USA

Anderson, Don (Football Player)
Indianapolis Colts
10090 Beechdale St
Detroit, MI 48204-2567, USA

Anderson, Don L (Misc)
669 Alameda St # E
Altadena, CA 91001-3001, USA

Anderson, Donny (Football Player)
Green Bay Packers
4516 Lovers Ln # 133
Dallas, TX 75225-6925, USA

Anderson, Duwayne M (Scientist)
PO Box 468
Hamilton, WA 98255-0468, USA

Anderson, Dwain (Baseball Player)
Oakland A's
1807 Fallbrook Dr
Alamo, CA 94507-2810, USA

Anderson, Earl (Hockey Player)
Detroit Red Wings
602 3rd Ave NE
Roseau, MN 56751-1809, USA

Anderson, Eddie Lee (Football Player)
Seattle Seahawks
209 Shenandoah Trl
Warner Robins, GA 31088-6284, USA

Anderson, Edward G (Ed) III (General)
Senior Representative
United Nations Military Committee
Washington, DC 20318-0001, USA

Anderson, Eric (Basketball Player)
New York Knicks
14 Nathan Dr
Valparaiso, IN 46383-9309, USA

Anderson, Erich (Actor)
Paradigm Agency
10100 Santa Monica Blvd Ste 2500
Los Angeles, CA 90067-4116, USA

Anderson, Erick (Football Player)
Kansas City Chiefs
2919 Attleboro Rd
Cleveland, OH 44120-1815, USA

Anderson, Erriestine I (Musician)
Thomas Cassidy
11761 E Speedway Blvd
Tucson, AZ 85748-2017, USA

Anderson, Flipper (Football Player)
Los Angeles Rams
190 Abbey Hill Rd
Suwanee, GA 30024-1976, USA

Anderson, Fred (Football Player)
Pittsburgh Steelers
11810 NE 48th Pl
Kirkland, WA 98033-8750, USA

Anderson, Garret J (Baseball Player)
California Angels
34 Vernal Spg
Irvine, CA 92603-0405, USA

Anderson, Gary L (Writer)
National Rifle Assn
11250 Waples Mill Rd
Fairfax, VA 22030-9400, USA

Anderson, Gary W (Football Player)
San Diego Chargers
1 Ridgefield Ct
Little Rock, AR 72223-4608, USA

Anderson, George L (Sparky) (Baseball Player)
Philadelphia Phillies
PO Box 6415
Thousand Oaks, CA 91359-6415, USA

Anderson, Gerry (Director, Entertainer)
Gerry Anderson Magazine
332 Lytham Road
Blackpool FY4 1DW, UNITED KINGDOM (UK)

Anderson, Gillian (Actor)
Creative Artists Agency
9830 Wilshire Blvd
Beverly Hills, CA 90212-1804, USA

Anderson, Glenn (Hockey Player)
Edmonton Oilers
42 W 69th St Apt 2A
New York, NY 10023-5265, USA

Anderson, H George (Religious Leader)
Evangelical Lutheran Church
8765 W Higgins Rd
Chicago, IL 60631-4192, USA

Anderson, Hans Christian (Scientist)
Stanford University
Chemistry Dept
Stanford, CA 94305, USA

Anderson, Harry (Actor, Magician)
c/o Glenn Bickel *Creative Artists Agency LCC (CAA-LA)*
2000 Avenue Of The Stars
Los Angeles, CA 90067-4700, USA

Anderson, Ho Che (Artist)
c/o Staff Member *Fantagraphics Books*
7563 Lake City Way NE
Seattle, WA 98115-4218, USA

Anderson, Howard A (Actor)
PO Box 2230
Los Angeles, CA 90028, USA

Anderson, Howard A Jr (Cinematographer)
c/o Staff Member *Howard Anderson Company*
5161 Lankershim Blvd
North Hollywood, CA 91601-4962, USA

Anderson, Ian (Musician, Songwriter, Writer)
43 Brook Green
London W6 7ER, UNITED KINGDOM (UK)

Anderson, J C (Golfer)
c/o Staff Member *Pro Golfers Association (PGA) Tour*
112 Tpc Blvd
Ponte Vedra Beach, FL 32082, USA

Anderson, Jamal (Football Player)
Atlanta Falcons
3301 N Morino St
Chandler, AZ 85224-1130, USA

Anderson, James (Cricketer)
c/o Staff Member *International Sports Management Ltd (ISM UK)*
Cherry Tree Farm
Cherry Tree Lane
Rostherne, Cheshire WA14 3RZ, UNITED KINGDOM (UK)

Anderson, James (Football Player)
San Diego Chargers
5706 Laramie Way
San Diego, CA 92120-1426, USA

Anderson, James F (Religious Leader)
12 Surf Ave
Ocean Grove, NJ 07756-1629, USA

Anderson, James G (Misc)
Harvard Unviversity
Eatrh-Planetary Physics Center
Cambridge, MA 02138, USA

Anderson, James W (Doctor)
University of Kentucky
Medical Center
Endocrinology Dept
Lexington, KY 40506-0001, USA

Anderson, Jamie (Actor)
c/o Craig Wyckoff *Epstein Wyckoff & Assoc (LA)*
11350 Ventura Blvd Ste 100
Studio City, CA 91604-3140, USA

Anderson, Janet (Golfer)
4311 W Ardmore Rd
Laveen, AZ 85339-2112, USA

Anderson, Jim (Baseball Player)
California Angels
21301 Bottletree Ln Unit 1128
Newhall, CA 91321-4451, USA

Anderson, Jimmy (Hockey Player)
Los Angeles Kings
4H Castle Hill Rd
Agawam, MA 01001-2460, USA

Anderson, Jo
1505 10th St
Santa Monica, CA 90401-2805, USA

Anderson, John (Football Player)
Green Bay Packers
14730 Crestwood Ct
Elm Grove, WI 53122-1603, USA

Anderson, John (Hockey Player)
Toronto Maple Leafs
724 Butterfield Rd Apt 112
Oakbrook Terrace, IL 60181-4222, USA

Anderson, John (Musician, Songwriter, Writer)
Bobby Roberts
PO Box 1547
Goodlettsville, TN 37070-1547, USA

Anderson, John B (Misc)
3300 NE 36th St Apt 1016
Fort Lauderdale, FL 33308-6734, USA

Anderson, John E (Attorney, Attorney General, General)
Kindel & Anderson
555 S Flower St # 2601
Los Angeles, CA 90071-2300, USA

Anderson, John Jr (Governor)
16609 W 133rd St
Olathe, KS 66062-1575, USA

Anderson, Jon (Musician)
Sun Artists
9 Hillgate St
London W8 7SP, UNITED KINGDOM (UK)

Anderson, June (Opera Singer)
Herbert Breslin
119 W 57th St Ste 1505
New York, NY 10019-2401, USA

Anderson, Kenneth A (Ken) (Coach, Football Coach, Football Player)
Cincinnati Bengals
1707 Waterleaf Dr
Sewickley, PA 15143-2452, USA

Anderson, Kenny (Basketball Player)
270 N Canon Dr # 1289
Beverly Hills, CA 90210-5323, USA

Anderson, Kent (Baseball Player)
California Angels
925 E Twin Church Rd
Timmonsville, SC 29161-8528, USA

Anderson, Kevin (Actor)
Writers & Artists
360 N Crescent Dr Bldg North
Beverly Hills, CA 90210-6818, USA

Anderson, Kevin C (Actor)
c/o Mel McKeon *McKeon-Valeo-Myones Management*
9100 Wilshire Blvd Ste 350W
Beverly Hills, CA 90212-3437, USA

Anderson, Kevin J (Writer)
c/o Robert Gottlieb *Trident Media Group LLC*
41 Madison Ave Fl 36
New York, NY 10010-2257, USA

Anderson, Kim (Basketball Player)
Portland Trail Blazers
602 Somerset Dr
Warrensburg, MO 64093-1674, USA

Anderson, Kim S (Football Player)
Baltimore Colts
6709 La Tijera Blvd # 222
Los Angeles, CA 90045-2017, USA

Anderson, Laurie (Musician)
Maine Road
195 Chrystie St # 501F
New York, NY 10002-1214, USA

Anderson, Lawrence A (Football Player)
Pittsburgh Steelers
3170 Blanchard Rd
Shreveport, LA 71103-2142, USA

Anderson, Loni (Actor)
c/o Staff Member *Innovative Artists (LA)*
1505 10th St
Santa Monica, CA 90401-2805, USA

Anderson, Louie (Actor, Comedian, Producer, Writer)
c/o Barry Katz *New Wave Entertainment (LA)*
2660 W Olive Ave
Burbank, CA 91505-4525, USA

Anderson, Loule (Actor, Comedian)
8033 W Sunset Blvd # 605
West Hollywood, CA 90046-2401, USA

Anderson, Lynn (Musician)
Anders Productions
4925 Tyne Valley Blvd
Nashville, TN 37220-1500, USA

Anderson, Marlon (Baseball Player)
Philadelphia Phillies
1603 Turning Leaf Ct
Sugar Land, TX 77479-6489, USA

Anderson, Mary (Actor)
1127 N Norman Pl
Los Angeles, CA 90049-1538, USA

Anderson, Matt (Baseball Player)
Detroit Tigers
4115 Woodmont Park Ln
Louisville, KY 40245-8431, USA

Anderson, May (Model)
Jim Paris
10880 Wilshire Blvd Ste 520
C/O Lewis, Joffe & Company
Los Angeles, CA 90024-4114, USA

Anderson, Melody (Actor)
PO Box 350
New York, NY 10028-0017, USA

Anderson, Michael (Musician, Songwriter, Writer)
Brock Assoc
7106 Moores Ln # 200
Brentwood, TN 37027-2903, USA

Anderson, Michael H (Physicist)
University of Colorado
Physics Dept
Boulder, CO 80309-0001, USA

Anderson, Michael J (Director)
Paul Burford
52 Yorkminster Road
North York, ON M2P 1M3, CANADA

Anderson, Mike (Baseball Player)
Cincinnati Reds
407 Prairie Grass Ct
Hartland, WI 53029-8562, USA

Anderson, Mike (Baseball Player)
Philadelphia Phillies
RR 1
Timmonsville, SC 29161, USA

Anderson, Mike (Football Player)
Denver Broncos
PO Box 260887
Littleton, CO 80163-0887, USA

Anderson, Mitchell (Actor)
c/o David Cohn *David Cohn Management*
14431 Ventura Blvd # 139
Sherman Oaks, CA 91423-2606, USA

Anderson, Murray (Hockey Player)
Washington Capitals
38 Head Ave PO Box 38 Stn Main
The Pas, MB R9A 1K3, CANADA

Anderson, Neal (Football Player)
Chicago Bears
Community Bank Of Marion County
1603 SW 19th Ave Attn Board Of
Directors
Ocala, FL 34474, USA

Anderson, Neilson (Basketball Player)
Orlando Magic
163 Harbor Isle Cir N
Memphis, TN 38103-0841, USA

Anderson, Nick (Basketball Player)
9163 Port Cypress Dr
Orlando, FL 32836, USA

Anderson, Nick (Cartoonist, Editor)
Courier Journal
525 W Broadway
Editorial Dept
Louisville, KY 40202-2137, USA

Anderson, Ottis J (O J) (Football Player)
St Louis Cardinals
PO Box 399
Orange, NJ 07051-0399, USA

Anderson, Pamela (Actor)
c/o Nick Stevens *United Talent Agency
(UTA)*
9560 Wilshire Blvd Ste 500
Beverly Hills, CA 90212-2401, USA

Anderson, Paul Thomas (Director, Writer)
c/o Staff Member *Ghoulardi Film
Company*
4133 Lankership Blvd
N Hollywood, CA 91602, USA

Anderson, Paul W S (Director)
c/o Staff Member *Impact Pictures*
11 Naples Court
72 St. James Dr.
London SW12 8SX, UNITED KINGDOM
(UK)

Anderson, Philip W (Nobel Prize
Laureate)
Princeton University
Physics Dept
Princeton, NJ 08544-0001, USA

Anderson, Poul
3 Las Palomas
Orinda, CA 94563-1915, USA

Anderson, R Lanier III (Judge)
US Court of Appeals
56 Forsyth St NW
Atlanta, GA 30303-2295, USA

Anderson, Ralph (Football Player)
Pittsburgh Steelers
908 Hilltop Dr Apt C
Irving, TX 75060-3925, USA

Anderson, Randy (Race Car Driver)
Brad Anderson Enterprises
1240 S Cucamonga Ave
Ontario, CA 91761-4505, USA

Anderson, Rashard (Football Player)
Carolina Panthers
676 N First Ave
Forest, MS 39074-3637, USA

Anderson, Ray (Musician)
James faith Entertainment
318 Wynn Ln
Port Jefferson, NY 11777-1670, USA

Anderson, Reid B (Dancer, Director)
Stuttgart Ballet
Ober Schlossgarten 6
Stuttgart 70173, GERMANY

Anderson, Renee (Actor)
2818 Laurel Canyon Blvd
Los Angeles, CA 90046, USA

Anderson, Richard (Actor)
10120 Cielo Dr
Beverly Hills, CA 90210-2037, USA

Anderson, Richard Dean (Actor)
c/o Leigh Brillstein *International Creative
Management (ICM-LA)*
10250 Constellation Blvd
Los Angeles, CA 90067-6200, USA

Anderson, Richard J (Football Player)
New Orleans Saints
206 Baker St
Lodi, OH 44254-1407, USA

Anderson, Richard P (Dick) (Football
Player)
Miami Dolphins
4603 Santa Maria St
Coral Gables, FL 33146-1132, USA

Anderson, Rick (Baseball Player)
New York Mets
3929 Benjamin Dr
Saint Paul, MN 55125-3396, USA

Anderson, Robert G W (Misc)
British Museum
Great Russell St
London WC1B 3DG, UNITED KINGDOM
(UK)

Anderson, Robert W (Writer)
14 Sutton Pl S
New York, NY 10022-3071, USA

Anderson, Ron (Hockey Player)
Washington Capitals
11 Wallace Rd
Lynn, MA 01902-2011, USA

Anderson, Ron (Hockey Player)
Detroit Red Wings
72 Woodside Close
Airdrie, AB T4B 2C7, CANADA

Anderson, Ross (Journalist)
Seattle Times
1120 John St
Editorial Dept
Seattle, WA 98109-5321, USA

Anderson, Russ (Hockey Player)
Pittsburgh Penguins
76 Fern Dr
Plantsville, CT 06479-1810, USA

Anderson, Sam (Actor)
c/o Staff Member *TalentWorks (LA)*
3500 W Olive Ave Ste 1400
Burbank, CA 91505-5512, USA

Anderson, Scott (Baseball Player)
Texas Rangers
13061 Amber Pl
Lake Oswego, OR 97034-1524, USA

Anderson, Shandon (Basketball Player)
c/o Staff Member *Miami Heat*
601 Biscayne Blvd
American Airlines Arena
Miami, FL 33132-1801, USA

Anderson, Shelly (Race Car Driver)
1240 S Cucamonga Ave
Ontario, CA 91761-4505, USA

Anderson, Stephen H (Judge)
US Court of Appeals
125 S State St
Federal Building
Salt Lake City, UT 84138-1102, USA

Anderson, Stuart (Football Player)
Washington Redskins
7800 George W Watkins Rd
Quinton, VA 23141-2633, USA

Anderson, Taz (Football Player)
St Louis Cardinals
3690 Northside Dr NW
Atlanta, GA 30305-1037, USA

Anderson, Terence (Terry) (Journalist)
17 Sunlight Hl
Yonkers, NY 10704-2903, USA

Anderson, Terry (Producer)
Pinewood Studios
Iverheath
Iver
Bucks SL0 0NH, UNITED KINGDOM
(UK)

Anderson, Theodore W (Economist,
Mathematician)
746 Santa Ynez St
Stanford, CA 94305-8441, USA

Anderson, Tom (Actor, Producer, Writer)
c/o Staff Member *Gersh Agency, The (LA)*
232 N Canon Dr
Beverly Hills, CA 90210-5302, USA

Anderson, Vickey Ray (Athlete, Football
Player)
Green Bay Packers
1145 SW 132nd St
Oklahoma City, OK 73170-6957, USA

Anderson, W French (Misc)
USC Medical School
144 E Lake View Terrace
Los Angeles, CA 90039, USA

Anderson, W William (Football Player)
Washington Redskins
6924 Lark Ln
Knoxville, TN 37919-5928, USA

Anderson, Warren M (Business Person)
270 Park Ave
New York, NY 10017-2014, USA

Anderson, Webster (War Hero)
3044 US Highway 321 N
Winnsboro, SC 29180-8346, USA

Anderson, Wendell R (Governor, Senator)
Larkin & Hoffman
1700 First Bank Plaza W
Minneapolis, MN 55402, USA

Anderson, Wes (Director, Writer)
United Talent Agency
9560 Wilshire Blvd Ste 500
Beverly Hills, CA 90212-2401, USA

Anderson, Wessell (Musician)
Fat City Artists
1906 Chet Atkins Blvd Apt 502
Nashville, TN 37212-2122, USA

Anderson, Weston (Physicist)
Varian Assoc
611 Hansen Way
Palo Alto, CA 94304-1078, USA

Anderson, Wilford C (War Hero)
3585 Round Barn Blvd
Santa Rosa, CA 95403-0134, USA

Anderson, William R (Misc)
10505 Miller Rd
Oakton, VA 22124-1709, USA

Anderson, Willie (Basketball Player)
Toronto Raptors
Air Canada Center
40 Bay St
Toronto, ON M5J 2N8, CANADA

Anderson, Willie (Football Player)
Cincinnati Bengals
577 Greentree Ln
Auburn, AL 36832-2942, USA

Anderson III, N Christian (Editor,
Publisher)
Gazette Telegraph
30 S Prospect St
Colorado Springs, CO 80903-3671, USA

Anderson-Perkin, Janet (Baseball Player)
244 Ottawa Street N
Regina, SK S4R 2V3, CANADA

Anderson-Sheriffs, Vivian (Baseball
Player)
2654 N 117th St
Wauwatosa, WI 53226-1124, USA

Andersson, Benny (Composer, Musician)
Mono Music
Sodra Brobaeken 41-A
Stockholm 111 49, SWEDEN

Andersson, Bibi (Actor)
Agents Associes Beaume
201 Faubourg Saint Honore
Paris 75008, FRANCE

Andersson, Harriet (Actor)
Roslagsgatan 15
Stockholm 113 55, SWEDEN

Andersson, Henrik (Musician)
MOB Agency
6404 Wilshire Blvd Ste 505
Los Angeles, CA 90048-5507, USA

Andersson, Kent-Erik (Hockey Player)
Minnesota North Stars
Persiljav-9
Karlstad S-65351, SWEDEN

Anderszewski, Piotr (Conductor,
Musician)
Virgin Classics Records
90 University Pl
New York, NY 10003-4506, USA

Anderzunas, Wally (Basketball Player)
Cincinnati Royals
3609 F St
Omaha, NE 68107-1345, USA

Andes, Karen (Misc)
G P Putnam's Sons
375 Hudson St
New York, NY 10014-3658, USA

Ando, Tadao (Architect)
Tadao Ando Architect
5-23-2 Toyosaki
Kitaku, Osaka 531, JAPAN

Andov, Stojan (President)
Sobranje
11 Oktombri Blvd
Skopje 91000, MACEDONIA

Andrade, Sergio (Musician)
DreamWorks Records
9268 W 3rd St
Beverly Hills, CA 90210-3713, USA

Andrade, William T (Billy) (Golfer)
4429 E Brookhaven Dr NE
Atlanta, GA 30319-1007, USA

Andrascik, Steve (Hockey Player)
New York Rangers
32 Early Ln
Annville, PA 17003-8623, USA

Andre, Carl (Artist)
689 Crown St
Brooklyn, NY 11213-5303, USA

Andre, Maurice (Musician)
Presles-en-Brie
Tournan-en-Brie 77220, FRANCE

Andre, Peter (Musician)
55 Drury Ln
London 4217, UNITED KINGDOM (UK)

Andre-Deshays, Claudie (Misc)
Hopital Cochin
Rhumatologie Dept
Paris 75000, FRANCE

Andrea, Paul (Hockey Player)
New York Rangers
22 Melissa Cres
Sydney, NS B1P 6X2, CANADA

Andreas, Dwayne O (Business Person)
181 Southmoreland Pl
Decatur, IL 62521-3738, USA

Andreas, G Allen (Business Person)
Archer-Daniels-Midland
4666 E Faries Pkwy
Decatur, IL 62526-5666, USA

Andreasen, Nancy C (Doctor)
200 Hawkings Dr
Iowa City, IA 52242, USA

Andreeff, Starr (Actor)
C N A Assoc
1875 Century Park E Ste 2250
Los Angeles, CA 90067-2563, USA

Andreessen, Marc (Designer)
Opsware
599 N Mathilda Ave
Sunnyvale, CA 94085-3505, USA

Andrei, Alessandro (Athlete, Track Athlete)
Via V Bellini 1
Scandicci, Firenze 50018, ITALY

Andreotti, Giulio
Piazza Montecitorio 13
Rome I-00186, ITALY

Andres, Ernie (Baseball Player)
Boston Red Sox
5714 Garden Lakes Dr
Bradenton, FL 34203-7226, USA

Andress, Tuck (Musician)
Windham Hill Records
PO Box 5501
Beverly Hills, CA 90209-5501, USA

Andress, Ursula (Actor)
Via Francesco Siacci 38
Rome 00186, ITALY

Andretti, John (Race Car Driver)
107 Keats Rd
Mooresville, NC 28117-8769, USA

Andretti, Mario (Race Car Driver)
457 Rose Inn Ave
Nazareth, PA 18064-9234, USA

Andretti, Michael M (Race Car Driver)
471 Rose Inn Ave
Nazareth, PA 18064-9234, USA

Andrew, C Robert (Rob) (Athlete, Misc)
Newcastle RFC
Newcastle-upon-Tyne NE3 2DT, UNITED KINGDOM (UK)

Andrew, HRH
PrinceSunninghill Park
Windsor, ENGLAND, UNITED KINGDOM (UK)

Andrew, Kim (Baseball Player)
Boston Red Sox
10052 Densmore Ave
Sepulveda, CA 91343-1454, USA

Andrew, Phillip (Actor)
c/o Bonnie Liedtke *William Morris Agency (WMA-LA)*
3500 W Olive Ave Ste 1400
Burbank, CA 91505-5512, USA

Andrew, Prince (Prince, Royalty)
Buckingham Palace
London SW1A 1AA, UNITED KINGDOM (UK)

Andrews, Al (Boxer)
1119 River St
Rhinelander, WI 54501-2404, USA

Andrews, Al (Football Player)
Buffalo Bills
PO Box 82256
Atlanta, GA 30354-0256, USA

Andrews, Andy (Actor, Comedian)
PO Box 17321
Nashville, TN 37217-0321, USA

Andrews, Anthony (Actor)
13 Manor Place
Oxford, Oxon, UNITED KINGDOM (UK)

Andrews, Billy (Football Player)
Cleveland Browns
PO Box 703
Highway 10 E
Clinton, LA 70722-0703, USA

Andrews, Donna (Golfer)
2301 Hawthorne Rd
Lynchburg, VA 24503-2903, USA

Andrews, Fred (Baseball Player)
c/o Staff Member *Philadelphia Phillies*
3501 S Broad St
Veterans Stadium
Philadelphia, PA 19148, USA

Andrews, Giuseppe (Actor)
PO Box 24561
Ventura, CA 93002-4561, USA

Andrews, Hub (Baseball Player)
New York Giants
2305 N 2nd Ave
Dodge City, KS 67801-2534, USA

Andrews, Inez (Musician)
Subrena Artists
330 W 56th St Apt 18M
New York, NY 10019-4222, USA

Andrews, James (Doctor)
American Sports Medicine Institute
2660 10th Ave S Ste 505
Birmingham, AL 35205-1626, USA

Andrews, James E (Misc)
Presbyterian Church (USA)
100 Witherspoon St
Louisville, KY 40202-6300, USA

Andrews, Jessica (Musician)
c/o Rodney (Rod) Essig *Creative Artists Agency (CAA-Nashville)*
3310 W End Ave Fl 5
Nashville, TN 37203-1028, USA

Andrews, John (Baseball Player)
St Louis Cardinals
9292 Gordon Ave
La Habra, CA 90631-2452, USA

Andrews, John H (Architect)
John Andrews Int'l
PO Box 7087
McMahon's Point, NSW 2060, AUSTRALIA

Andrews, John M (Football Player)
San Diego Chargers
7306 Summer Trail Dr
Sugar Land, TX 77479-6233, USA

Andrews, Julie (Dame) (Actor, Musician)
c/o Steve Sauer *Media Four*
8840 Wilshire Blvd Fl 2
Beverly Hills, CA 90211-2606, USA

Andrews, Ken (Musician)
c/o Staff Member *Paradigm (Monterey)*
509 Hartnell St
Monterey, CA 93940-2825, USA

Andrews, Lee (Musician)
Mars Talent
27 L Ambiance Ct
Bardonia, NY 10954-1421, USA

Andrews, Mark (Senator)
3354 165th Ave SE
Mapleton, ND 58059-9746, USA

Andrews, Mike (Baseball Player)
Boston Red Sox
375 Longwood Ave
Boston, MA 02215-5395, USA

Andrews, Mitch (Football Player)
Denver Broncos
129 Grand Ave
Lafayette, LA 70503-4636, USA

Andrews, Naveen (Actor)
c/o Renee Jennett *Renee Jennett Management*
10028 Farragut Dr
Culver City, CA 90232-3228, USA

Andrews, Patricia (Patt) (Musician)
9823 Aldea Ave
Northridge, CA 91325-1915, USA

Andrews, Patty (Musician)
9823 Aldea Ave
Northridge, CA 91325-1915, USA

Andrews, Rob (Baseball Player)
Houston Astros
1280 Mountbatten Ct
Concord, CA 94518-3927, USA

Andrews, Robert (Writer)
G P Putnam's Sons
375 Hudson St
New York, NY 10014-3658, USA

Andrews, Robert F (Misc)
5879 Beulah Land
Lakeland, FL 33810, USA

Andrews, Russell (Actor)
c/o Jenny Delaney *Forster-Delaney Entertainment*
12533 Woodgreen St
Los Angeles, CA 90066-2723, USA

Andrews, Shane (Baseball Player)
Montreal Expos
807 Dennis Way
Carlsbad, NM 88220-3072, USA

Andrews, Theresa (Swimmer)
2004 Homewood Rd
Annapolis, MD 21409-5970, USA

Andrews, Thomas (Football Player)
Chicago Bears
1918 Wickham Way
Louisville, KY 40223-1059, USA

Andrews, Tina (Actor)
c/o Staff Member *William Morris Agency (WMA-LA)*
1 William Morris Pl
Beverly Hills, CA 90212-4261, USA

Andrews, William L (Football Player)
Atlanta Falcons
628 Bartow Dr
Dacula, GA 30019-5064, USA

Andrews II, George E (Football Player)
Los Angeles Rams
10195 Overhill Dr
Santa Ana, CA 92705-1515, USA

Andreychuck, Dave (Hockey Player)
38 Bishopsgate Ave
Hamilton, ON L8V 3K4, CANADA

Andreychuk, Dave (Hockey Player)
Buffalo Sabres
18130 Longwater Run Dr
Tampa, FL 33647-2211, USA

Andrianarivo, Tantely (Prime Minister)
Prime Minister's Office
Mahazoarivo, Antananarivo, MADAGASCAR

Andrie, George J (Football Player)
Dallas Cowboys
26536 E Zeerip
Drummond Island, MI 49726, USA

Andriessen, Louis (Composer)
Nonesuch Records
75 Rockefeller Plz
New York, NY 10019-6908, USA

Andrieu, Sebastien (Actor, Model)
c/o Staff Member *Creature Entertainment*
11766 Wilshire Blvd Ste 1610
Los Angeles, CA 90025-6565, USA

Andros, Plato (Football Player)
Chicago Cardinals
1707 Crown Point Ave
Norman, OK 73072-5865, USA

Androsky, Carol (Actor)
Henderson/Hogan
8285 W Sunset Blvd Ste 1
West Hollywood, CA 90046-2420, USA

Andruff, Ron (Hockey Player)
Montreal Canadiens
72 1/2 Irving Pl Apt 1F
New York, NY 10003-2223, USA

Andrulis, Greg (Coach, Football Coach)
Columbus Crew
2121 Velman Ave
Columbus, OH 43211, USA

Andrus, Cecil (Governor, Senator)
1280 Candleridge Dr
Boise, ID 83712-6504, USA

Andrus, Lou
Denver Broncos
739 W 550 S
Orem, UT 84058-6070, USA

Andrus, Sheldon (Football Player)
New Orleans Saints
210 Belle Meade Blvd
Thibodaux, LA 70301-4908, USA

Andrusak, Greg (Hockey Player)
Pittsburgh Penguins
5244 Hwy 3A
Nelson, BC V1L 6N6, CANADA

Andrusyshsyn, Zenon (Football Player)
Kansas City Chiefs
2823 Lake Saxon Dr
Land O Lakes, FL 34639-6620, USA

Andruzzi, Joe (Football Player)
Green Bay Packers
640 Sheldon Ave
Staten Island, NY 10312-2645, USA

Andujar, Joaquin (Baseball Player)
Houston Astros
Ave Lamiama Tio #47
San Pedro de Macoris, DOMINICAN
REPUBLIC

Ane, Charles T (Charlie) III (Football
Player)
Kansas City Chiefs
749 16th Ave
Honolulu, HI 96816-4121, USA

Ane Jr, Charlie (Football Player)
Detroit Lions
741 16th Ave
Honolulu, HI 96816-4121, USA

Anemone
82 rue Bonaparte
Paris 75006, FRANCE

Angarano, Michael (Actor)
Coast to Coast Talent
3350 Barham Blvd
Los Angeles, CA 90068-1404, USA

Angel, Ashley Parker (Musician)
c/o Chuck James *Gersh Agency, The (LA)*
232 N Canon Dr
Beverly Hills, CA 90210-5302, USA

Angel, Criss (Magician, Musician)
Criss Angel Production Office
3900 Las Vegas Blvd S
Luxor Hotel & Casino
Las Vegas, NV 89119-1004, USA

Angel, Heather H (Photographer)
Highways
6 Vicarage Hill
Farnham, Surrey GU9 8HJ, UNITED
KINGDOM (UK)

Angel, Joe (Baseball Player, Sportscaster)
San Francisco Giants
2767 Pinehurst
Weston, FL 33332-1807, USA

Angel, Ryland (Musician)
c/o Staff Member *Paradigm (Monterey)*
509 Hartnell St
Monterey, CA 93940-2825, USA

Angel, Vanessa (Actor)
c/o Staff Member *Marsala/Tappan
Management*
8324 Fountain Ave Apt B
Los Angeles, CA 90069-2916, USA

Angelil, Rene (Actor, Writer)
c/o Staff Member *United Talent Agency
(UTA)*
9560 Wilshire Blvd Ste 500
Beverly Hills, CA 90212-2401, USA

Angelini, Florenzo Cardinal (Religious
Leader)
Via Anneo Lucano 47
Rome 00136, ITALY

Angelini, Norm (Baseball Player)
Kansas City Royals
15063 E Chenango Pl
Aurora, CO 80015-2136, USA

Angell, Wayne D (Financier, Government
Official)
Bear Steams Co
383 Madison Ave
New York, NY 10017, USA

Angelopoulos, Theodoros (Theo) (Actor,
Director, Producer, Writer)
Solmou 18
106 82
Athens, GREECE

Angelos, Peter (Baseball Player)
Baltimore Orioles
100 N Charles St
Baltimore, MD 21201-3805, USA

Angelou, Maya (Writer)
c/o Helen Brann *Helen Brann Agency*
94 Curtis Rd
Bridgewater, CT 06752-1204, USA

Angels, Anaheim
2000 E Gene Autry Way
Edison Field
Anaheim, CA 92806-6143, USA

Angels & Airwaves (Music Group)
c/o Staff Member *Geffen Records*
2220 Colorado Ave
Santa Monica, CA 90404-3506, USA

Angelycal Musical (Music Group)
c/o Staff Member *Sony Music Miami*
605 Lincoln Rd Fl 7
Miami Beach, FL 33139-2900, USA

Angelyne (Actor, Artist, Model)
c/o Staff Member *Angelyne Management*
5670 Wilshire Blvd Fl 22
Los Angeles, CA 90036-5679, USA

Angerer, Paul (Composer)
Esteplatz 3/26
Vienna 1030, AUSTRIA

Angerer, Peter (Athlete)
Wagenau 2
Hammer 17326, GERMANY

Angle, Kurt (Wrestler)
Hawk & Co
PO Box 97007
Pittsburgh, PA 15229-0007, USA

Angler, Natalie M (Journalist)
New York Times
229 W 43rd St
Editorial Dept
New York, NY 10036-3959, USA

Anglim, Philip (Actor)
2404 Grand Canal
Venice, CA 90291-4508, USA

Anglin, Jennifer (Actor)
651 N Kilkea Dr
Los Angeles, CA 90048-2213, USA

Angotti, Lou (Hockey Player)
New York Rangers
2850 NE 14th Street Cswy Apt 401B
Pompano Beach, FL 33062-3640, USA

Anguiano, Raul (Artist)
Anaxagoras 1326
Colonia Narvate
Mexico City 13 DF, MEXICO

Anhalt, Edward (Actor)
13906 Fiji Way Apt 148
Marina Del Rey, CA 90292-6930, USA

Anholt, Christien (Actor)
Covington International
4237 Morro Dr
Woodland Hills, CA 91364-5521, USA

Anholt, Darrell (Hockey Player)
Chicago Blackhawks
4935-49th Street
Hughen Den, AB T0B 2E0, CANADA

Anikulap-Kuti, Femi (Musician,
Songwriter, Writer)
MCA Records
70 Universal City Plz
Universal City, CA 91608-1011, USA

Animals, The (Music Group)
PO Box 1821
Ojai, CA 93024-1821, USA

Anissina, Marina (Figure Skater)
c/o Staff Member *Champions on Ice*
3500 W 80th St
Tom Collins Enterprises Inc
Minneapolis, MN 55431-1068, USA

Aniston, Jennifer (Actor)
c/o Marc Gurvitz *Brillstein-Grey
Entertainment*
9150 Wilshire Blvd Ste 350
Beverly Hills, CA 90212-3453, USA

Aniston, John (Actor)
PO Box 514
5520 Platt Ave
West Hills, CA 91307, USA

Anjali (Actor, Bollywood)
14 Ganapathi Colony
1 Street Gopalpuram
Chennai, TN 600006, INDIA

Anjali, Devi (Actor, Bollywood)
6 Bags Road
Raja Annamalai Puram
Chennai, TN 600028, INDIA

Anjard Sr, Ronald P (Business Person)
10942 Montego Dr
San Diego, CA 92124-1423, USA

Anju (Actor, Bollywood)
37 Nagarathanammal Nagar
Janaki Nagar
Chennai, TN 600017, INDIA

Anka, Paul (Actor, Musician, Songwriter,
Writer)
Paul Anka Productions
5706 Corsa Ave Ste 200
Westlake Village, CA 91362-4057, USA

Ankiel, Rick (Baseball Player)
St Louis Cardinals
126 Sandpiper Cir
Jupiter, FL 33477-8433, USA

Ankrom, Scott (Football Player)
Dallas Cowboys
1206 Harvest Cyn
San Antonio, TX 78258-3836, USA

Anlyan, William G (Doctor)
Duke Medical Center
100 Seeley Mudd Building #109
Durham, NC 27710-0001, USA

Annable, Dave (Actor)
c/o Sue Leibman *Barking Dog
Entertainment*
9 Desbrosses St Fl 2
New York, NY 10013-1701, USA

Annakin, Kenneth (Ken) (Director)
Denise Denny
9233 Swallow Dr
Los Angeles, CA 90069-1145, USA

Annan, Kofi A (General)
Secretary General's Ofc
1 United Nations Plz
New York, NY 10017-3514, USA

Annaud, Jean-Jacques (Director)
Reperage
16 Rue Saint-Vincent
Paris 75018, FRANCE

Anne (Royalty)
Gatecombe Park
Gloucestershire, UNITED KINGDOM
(UK)

Anne of Bourbon-Palma (Royalty)
Villa Serena
77 Chemin Louis-Degallier
Versoix-Geneva 1290, SWITZERLAND

Annenberg, Wallis (Publisher)
10273 Century Woods Dr
Los Angeles, CA 90067-6312, USA

Annett, Chloe (Actor)
c/o Staff Member *Innovative Artists (LA)*
1505 10th St
Santa Monica, CA 90401-2805, USA

Annis, Francesca (Actor)
International Creative Mgmt
76 Oxford St
London W1N 0AX, UNITED KINGDOM
(UK)

Anno, Sam (Football Player)
Los Angeles Rams
12934 Ferndale Ave
Los Angeles, CA 90066-3520, USA

Annu, Kapoor (Actor, Bollywood)
F-19 Flat No. 504 Green Crest Yamuna
Nagar
Opp Parasrampuria Tower Andheri(W)
Mumbai, MS 400053, INDIA

Annunziata, Robert (Business Person)
Global Crossing Ltd
Wessex House
45 Reid St
Hamilton, HM 12, BERMUDA

Ansa, Tina McElroy (Writer)
William Morris Agency
151 El Camino Dr
Beverly Hills, CA 90212-2775, USA

Ansara, Edward (Actor)
Jack Scagnetti
5118 Vineland Ave # 102
North Hollywood, CA 91601-3814, USA

Ansara, Michael (Actor)
4624 Park Mirasol
Calabasas, CA 91302-1731, USA

Ansari, Anousheh (Astronaut)
6101 W Plano Prkwy #210
Plano, TX 75093, USA

Anschutz, Philip F (Business Person)
c/o Staff Member *Anschutz Film Group*
1888 Century Park E Fl 14
Century City, CA 90067-1702, USA

Anselmo, Philip (Musician)
Concrete Mgmt
361 W Broadway # 200
New York, NY 10013-2209, USA

Anslow, Hub (Hockey Player)
New York Rangers
118-721 Chapel Cres
Ottawa, ON K1N 9P6, CANADA

Anspach, Susan (Actor)
PO Box 5605
Santa Monica, CA 90409-5605, USA

Anspaugh, David (Director, Producer)
Creative Artists Agency
9830 Wilshire Blvd
Beverly Hills, CA 90212-1804, USA

Ant, Adam (Musician)
c/o Staff Member *Peters Fraser & Dunlop (PFD - UK)*
Drury House
34-43 Russell St
London WC2B 5HA, UNITED KINGDOM (UK)

Antes, Horst (Artist)
Hohenbergstr 11
Karlsruhe (Wolfartsweier 76228, GERMANY

Anthony, Barbara Cox (Business Person)
Cox Enterprises
1400 Lake Hearn Dr NE
Atlanta, GA 30319-1418, USA

Anthony, Carl (Misc)
Harvard University
Kennedy Government School
Cambridge, MA 02138, USA

Anthony, Carmelo (Basketball Player)
Denver Nuggets
1000 Chopper Cir
Pepsi Center
Denver, CO 80204-5805, USA

Anthony, Charles (Football Player)
San Diego Chargers
38709 Farwell Dr
Fremont, CA 94536-7218, USA

Anthony, Edward (Football Player)
New Orleans Saints
3433 Mill Run Ln
Pfafftown, NC 27040-9478, USA

Anthony, Eric (Baseball Player)
Houston Astros
42 Fosters Ct
Sugar Land, TX 77479, USA

Anthony, Greg (Basketball Player)
520 S 4th St
Las Vegas, NV 89101-6520, USA

Anthony, Jasmine Jessica (Actor)
c/o Staff Member *Gem Entertainment Group*
2530 Wilshire Blvd Fl 3
Santa Monica, CA 90403-4643, USA

Anthony, Jason (Model)
Boss Models
80 8th Ave
New York, NY 10011-5126, USA

Anthony, Lysette (Actor)
46 Old Compton St
London WV 5PB, UNITED KINGDOM (UK)

Anthony, Marc (Actor, Musician, Songwriter, Writer)
c/o Bryan Lourd *Creative Artists Agency LCC (CAA-LA)*
2000 Avenue Of The Stars
Los Angeles, CA 90067-4700, USA

Anthony, Michael (Musician)
Van Halen
10100 Santa Monica Blvd Ste 1300
Los Angeles, CA 90067-4114, USA

Anthony, Piers
PO Box 2289
Inverness, FL 34451-2289, USA

Anthony, Ray (Musician)
9288 Kinglet Dr
Los Angeles, CA 90069-1114, USA

Anthony, Reidel (Football Player)
Tampa Bay Buccaneers
PO Box 23
South Bay, FL 33493-0023, USA

Anthony, Terry (Football Player)
Tampa Bay Buccaneers
1200 Beville Rd Apt 91
Daytona Beach, FL 32114-5778, USA

Anthrax (Music Group)
c/o Dave Kirby *Agency Group Ltd, The (LA)*
1880 Century Park E Ste 711
Los Angeles, CA 90067-1618, USA

Antin, Jonathan (Reality TV Star, Stylist)
Jonathan Salon
901 Westbourne Dr
West Hollywood, CA 90069-4113, USA

Antin, Robin (Actor, Choreographer)
c/o Staff Member *McDonald/Selznick Assoc (MSA)*
1611A N El Centro Ave
Hollywood, CA 90028, USA

Antin, Steve (Actor, Writer)
c/o Doug MacLaren *International Creative Management (ICM-LA)*
10250 Constellation Blvd
Los Angeles, CA 90067-6200, USA

Antoine, Lionel (Football Player)
Chicago Bears
627 Murray St
Biloxi, MS 39530-3234, USA

Antoine, Timlin (Football Player)
Philadelphia Eagles
5452 New Grange Garth
Columbia, MD 21045-2422, USA

Anton, Alan (Musician)
Macklam Feldman Mgmt
1505 W 2nd Ave #200
Vancouver, BC V6H 3Y4, CANADA

Anton, Craig (Actor)
United Talent Agency
9560 Wilshire Blvd Ste 500
Beverly Hills, CA 90212-2401, USA

Anton, Susan (Actor, Live Show)
Susan Anton Inc
10300 W Charleston Blvd Ste 13
Las Vegas, NV 89135-5008, USA

Antonakakis, Dimitris (Architect)
Atelier 66
Emm Benaki 118
Athens 114-73, GREECE

Antonakakis, Suzana M (Architect)
Atelier 66
Emm Benaki 118
Athens 114-73, GREECE

Antonelli, Dominic A (Astronaut)
4106 Oak Blossom Ct
Houston, TX 77059-3264, USA

Antonelli, Ennio Cardinal (Religious Leader)
Archdiocese
Piazza S Giovanni 3
Florence 50129, ITALY

Antonelli, Johnny (Baseball Player)
Boston Braves
18 Tobey Ct
Pittsford, NY 14534-1854, USA

Antonelli, Laura (Actor)
Pietrovalle
Via B Buozzi 51
Rome 00197, ITALY

Antonetti, Lorenzo Cardinal (Religious Leader)
Patrimony of the Holy See
Palazzo Apostolico
Vatican City 00120, VATICAN CITY

Antonio (Dancer)
Caslada 7
Madrid, SPAIN

Antonio, Jim (Actor)
Epstein-Wyckoff
280 S Beverly Dr Ste 400
Beverly Hills, CA 90212-3904, USA

Antonio, Lou (Actor)
530 S Gaylord Dr
Burbank, CA 91505-4714, USA

Antonio dos Santos R, Eanes (General, President)
Partido Renovador Democratico
Travessa do Falo 9
Lisbon 1200, PORTUGAL

Antonioni, Michelangelo (Director)
Via Vincenzo Tiberio 18
Rome 00191, ITALY

Antonovich, Mike (Hockey Player)
Minnesota North Stars
PO Box 224
Coleraine, MN 55722-0224, USA

Antosky, Shawn (Hockey Player)
Vancouver Canucks
359 Brantwood Park Rd
Brantford, ON N3P 1G8, CANADA

Antoun (Khouri), Bishop (Religious Leader)
Antiochian Orthodox Christian Archdiocese
358 Mountain Rd
Englewood, NJ 07631-3798, USA

Antrobus, Charles (Governor)
Governor General's Office
Kingstown
SAINT VINCENT & GRENADINES

Antuofermo, Vito (Boxer)
16019 81st St
Howard Beach, NY 11414-2924, USA

Antwine, Houston (Football Player)
Boston Patriots
6627 Laurel Valley Dr
Memphis, TN 38135-1576, USA

Anu, Christine (Musician)
Robert Bamham Mgmt
432 Tyagarah Road
Myocum, NSW 2481, AUSTRALIA

Anuja (Actor, Bollywood)
4-B Periyar Street Happee Home Apts
Gandhi Nagar Saligram
Chennai, TN 600093, INDIA

Anusha (Actor, Bollywood)
Flat Non 202 II Floor
167 Eldams Road
Chennai, TN 600018, INDIA

Anuszkiewicz, Richard J (Artist)
76 Chestnut St
Englewood, NJ 07631-3045, USA

Anwar, Gabrielle (Actor)
United Talent Agency
9560 Wilshire Blvd Ste 500
Beverly Hills, CA 90212-2401, USA

Aoki, Chieko N (Business Person)
Westin Hotels Co
777 Westchester Ave
Westin Building
White Plains, NY 10604-3520, USA

Aoki, Devon (Actor)
c/o Mimi DiTrani *Untitled Entertainment (LA)*
331 N Maple Dr Fl 3
Beverly Hills, CA 90210-3827, USA

Aoki, Rocky (Athlete, Business Person)
Benihana of Tokyo
8685 NW 53rd Ter Ste 201
Miami, FL 33166-4591, USA

Aoloo Sunshine (Music Group)
c/o Staff Member *Paradigm (Monterey)*
509 Hartnell St
Monterey, CA 93940-2825, USA

Aouita, Said (Athlete, Track Athlete)
Abdejil Bencheikh
9 Rue Soivissi
Loubira
Rabat, MOROCCO

Apap, Gilles (Musician)
Columbia Artists Mgmt Inc
1790 Broadway Fl 6
New York, NY 10019-1412, USA

Aparicio, Luis E (Baseball Player)
Chicago White Sox
Calle 67 #26-82
Maracalbo, VENEZUELA

Apatow, Judd (Director, Producer, Writer)
Apatow Productions
11788 W Pico Blvd
Los Angeles, CA 90064-1309, USA

Apel, Katrin (Athlete)
Suedlung 9
Grafenroda 99330, GERMANY

Apodaca, Bob (Baseball Player)
New York Mets
2999 SW Van Buren Ter
Port Saint Lucie, FL 34953-4262, USA

Apodaca, Raymond S (Jerry) (Governor)
6223 Utah Ave NW
Washington, DC 20015-2431, USA

Apodaka, Bob
PO Box 7845
Columbia, SC 29202-7845, USA

Apollonia (Actor, Model)
c/o Siri Garber *Platform Public Relations*
2133 Holly Dr
Los Angeles, CA 90068-2851, USA

Aponte Martinez, Luis Cardinal (Misc)
Arzobispado
201 Calle San Jorge
Apatado S-1967
Santurce, PR 00912-3405, USA

Appel, Deena (Designer)
c/o Jon Furie *Montana Artists Agency*
7715 W Sunset Blvd Fl 3
Los Angeles, CA 90046-3912, USA

Appel, Fiona (Musician, Songwriter, Writer)
H K Mgmt
9200 W Sunset Blvd Ste 530
Los Angeles, CA 90069-3509, USA

Appice, Carmine (Musician)
Long Distance Entertainment
568 SE Woodbright #234
Boynton Beach, FL 33435, USA

Appier, Kevin
Kansas City Royals
24761 Goldcrest Dr
Bonita Springs, FL 34134-0945, USA

Apple, Fiona (Musician)
c/o Staff Member *Paradigm (Monterey)*
509 Hartnell St
Monterey, CA 93940-2825, USA

Appleby, Shiri (Actor)
c/o Tracey Jacobs *United Talent Agency (UTA)*
9560 Wilshire Blvd Ste 500
Beverly Hills, CA 90212-2401, USA

Appleby, Stuart (Golfer)
9724 Chestnut Ridge Dr
Windermere, FL 34786-8943, USA

Applegate, Christina (Actor)
c/o Rick Kurtzman *Creative Artists Agency LCC (CAA-LA)*
2000 Avenue Of The Stars
Los Angeles, CA 90067-4700, USA

Applegate, Eddie (Actor)
Studio Talent Group
1328 12th St
Santa Monica, CA 90401-2051, USA

Applegate, Gideon (Baseball Player)
New York Cubans
7 Jenness Dr
South Newfane, VT 05351-9753, USA

Applegate, Jodi (Correspondent)
WNYW
205 E 67th St
New York, NY 10065-6050, USA

Applegren, Amy (Baseball Player)
1245 Sunset Dr
East Peoria, IL 61611-1169, USA

Applen, Henry E (Misc)
Plant Guard Workers Union
25510 Kelly Rd
Roseville, MI 48066-4932, USA

Appleton, James R (Educator)
University of Redlands
President's Office
Redlands, CA 92373, USA

Appleton, Myra (Editor)
Cosmopolitan Magazine
224 W 57th St
Editorial Dept
New York, NY 10019-3200, USA

Appleton, Steven R (Business Person)
Micron Technology
PO Box 6
Boise, ID 83707-0006, USA

Appolonia (Kotero) (Actor)
c/o Staff Member *TalentWorks (LA)*
3500 W Olive Ave Ste 1400
Burbank, CA 91505-5512, USA

Apps Jr, Syl (Hockey Player)
New York Rangers
36 Pennock Cres
Markham, ON L3R 3M4, CANADA

Aprea, John (Actor)
401 S Detroit St Apt 113
Los Angeles, CA 90036-3618, USA

April, Johnny (Musician)
c/o Staff Member *Mitch Schneider Organization, The*
14724 Ventura Blvd Ste 710
Sherman Oaks, CA 91403-3520, USA

April Wine (Music Group)
c/o Staff Member *Mascioli Entertainment Corp*
2202 Curry Ford Rd Ste E
Orlando, FL 32806-2478, USA

Apt, Jerome (Jay) (Astronaut)
4 Shadycourt Dr
Pittsburgh, PA 15232-2914, USA

Apted, Michael (Actor)
c/o Staff Member *Creative Artists Agency LCC (CAA-LA)*
2000 Avenue Of The Stars
Los Angeles, CA 90067-4700, USA

Apted, Michael D (Director)
360 N Saltair Ave
Los Angeles, CA 90049-2915, USA

Apuna, Ben (Football Player)
New York Giants
950 Lehua Ave Apt 804
Pearl City, HI 96782-3338, USA

Aqua (Music Group)
c/o John Aagaard *TG Management Productions & Publishing*
Badehusvej 1
2 sal tv
Aalborg 9000, DENMARK

Aqualung (Music Group)
c/o Staff Member *Paradigm (Monterey)*
509 Hartnell St
Monterey, CA 93940-2825, USA

Aquilino, Thomas J Jr (Judge)
US Court of International Trade
1 Federal Plz
New York, NY 10278-0001, USA

Aquino, Amy
PO Box 5617
Beverly Hills, CA 90209-5617, USA

Aquino, Amy (Actor)
9615 Brighton Way Ste 300
Beverly Hills, CA 90210-5118, USA

Aquino, Corazon C (Nobel Prize Laureate, President)
119 de la Rosa Comer
Castro St
Makati City, Manila, PHILIPPINES

Arad, Avi (Producer, Writer)
c/o Staff Member *Marvel Studios Inc*
9242 Beverly Blvd Ste 350
Beverly Hills, CA 90210-3721, USA

Aragall Garriga, Glacomo (Opera Singer)
Stafford Law Assoc
6 Barham Close
Weybridge
Surrey KT1 9PR, UNITED KINGDOM (UK)

Aragon, Art (Boxer)
19050 Wells Dr
Tarzana, CA 91356-3937, USA

Aragones, Sergio (Cartoonist)
PO Box 696
Ojai, CA 93024-0696, USA

Araguz, Leo (Football Player)
Oakland Raiders
3201 Araguz St
Harlingen, TX 78552-7835, USA

Araiza, Armando (Actor)
c/o Staff Member *Televisa*
Blvd Adolfo Lopez Mateos 232
Colonia San Angel INN
DF CP 01060, MEXICO

Araiza, Francisco (Opera Singer)
Columbia Artists Mgmt Inc
1790 Broadway Fl 6
New York, NY 10019-1412, USA

Arakawa, Toyozo (Artist)
4-101 O-Hatacho
Tokyo, JAPAN

Araki, Greg (Director)
c/o Staff Member *United Talent Agency (UTA)*
9560 Wilshire Blvd Ste 500
Beverly Hills, CA 90212-2401, USA

Arambula, Aracely (Actor)
c/o Staff Member *Televisa*
Blvd Adolfo Lopez Mateos 232
Colonia San Angel INN
DF CP 01060, MEXICO

Aramburu, Juan Carlos Cardinal (Religious Leader)
Arzobispado
Suipacha 1034
Buenos Aires 1008, ARGENTINA

Arana, Facundo (Actor)
c/o Staff Member *Telefe - Argentina*
Pavon 2444 (C1248AAT)
Buenos Aires, ARGENTINA

Arana, Tomas (Actor)
c/o Melanie Greene *Melanie Greene Management & Productions*
425 N Robertson Blvd
West Hollywood, CA 90048-1735, USA

Arango, Juan Carlos (Actor)
c/o Gabriel Blanco *Gabriel Blanco Iglesias (Mexico)*
Rio Balsas 35-32
Colonia Cuauhtemoc
DF 06500, MEXICO

Arapostathis, Evan (Football Player)
St Louis Cardinals
5353 W Falls View Dr
San Diego, CA 92115-1427, USA

Ararktsyan, Babken G (Government Official)
National Assembly
Marshal Bagzamyan Prosp 26
Yerevan 375019, ARMENIA

Arashi, Qadi Abdul Karim al
Constituent People's Assembly
Sana'a, YEMEN

Arau, Alfonso (Director)
Productions AA
Privada Rafael Oliva 8
Coyoacan 04120, MEXICO

Arau, Fernando (Actor)
c/o Staff Member *Univision*
605 3rd Ave Fl 12
New York, NY 10158-1299, USA

Araujo, Serafim Fernandes de Cardinal (Religious Leader)
Curia Metropolitana
Av Brasil 2079
Belo Horizonte, MG 30240-002, BRAZIL

Aravind, Ramesh (Actor, Bollywood)
F1 4th Block
Bajaj Apartments Nandanam Extn
Chennai, TN 600035, INDIA

Araya, Zeudy (Actor)
Carol Levi Co
Via Giuseppe Pisanelli
Rome 00196, ITALY

Arbaaz, Ali Khan (Actor, Bollywood)
602 Sea King Apts
Band Stand Bandra (W)
Mumbai, MS 400050, INDIA

Arbanas, Frederick V (Fred) (Football Player)
Dallas Cowboys
3350 SW Hook Rd
Lees Summit, MO 64082-1524, USA

Arbeid, Murray (Designer, Fashion Designer)
202 Ebury St
London SW1W 8UN, UNITED KINGDOM (UK)

Arber, Werner (Nobel Prize Laureate)
70 Klingelbergstr
Basel 4056, SWITZERLAND

Arbour, Al (Hockey Player)
Detroit Red Wings
2071 Harbour Links Dr
Longboat Key, FL 34228-4281, USA

Arbour, John (Hockey Player)
Boston Bruins
125 Waterloo St
Fort Erie, ON L2A 3K1, CANADA

Arbour, Louise (Government Official)
UN Human Rights Commision
1 United Nations Plz
New York, NY 10017-3515, USA

Arbour-Parrott, Beatrice (Baseball Player)
691 Elm St
Somerset, MA 02726-4034, USA

Arbuckle, Charles (Football Player)
Indianapolis Colts
805 Oak Park Dr
Round Rock, TX 78681-4077, USA

Arbulu Galliani, Guillermo (Prime Minister)
Prime Minister's Office
Urb Corpac
Calle 1 Oesta S/N
Lima 27, PERU

Arbus, Alan (Actor)
2208 N Beverly Glen Blvd
Los Angeles, CA 90077-2502, USA

Arbus, Loreen
8841 Appian Way
Los Angeles, CA 90046-7734, USA

Arcain, Janeth (Basketball Player)
c/o Staff Member *Houston Comets*
1510 Polk St
Houston, TX 77002-1099, USA

Archambault, Lee J (Astronaut)
4318 Sweet Cicely Ct
Houston, TX 77059-3126, USA

Archambeau, Lester (Football Player)
Green Bay Packers
10520 Montclair Way
Duluth, GA 30097-1840, USA

Archana (Actor, Bollywood)
8 North Cresent Road
T Nagar
Chennai, TN 600017, INDIA

Archer, Anne (Actor)
c/o Steven Fenton *Fenton-Kritzer Entertainment*
8840 Wilshire Blvd Fl 3
Beverly Hills, CA 90211-2606, USA

Archer, Bernard
Holt Barton
Witham Frairy Somerset, ENGLAND, UNITED KINGDOM (UK)

Archer, Beverly (Actor)
Judy Schoen
606 N Larchmont Blvd Ste 309
Los Angeles, CA 90004-1309, USA

Archer, Dan (Football Player)
Oakland Raiders
65 Sunnyside Ave
Mill Valley, CA 94941-1924, USA

Archer, Glenn L Jr (Judge)
US Court of Appeals
717 Madison Pl NW
Washington, DC 20439-0001, USA

Archer, Jeffrey (Actor, Writer)
c/o Staff Member *Curtis Brown Ltd*
Hay Market House 28/29
Hay Market Fl 4
London SW1 Y45, UNITED KINGDOM (UK)

Archer, Jim (Baseball Player)
Kansas City A's
1414 Oleander Dr
Tarpon Springs, FL 34689-2308, USA

Archer, John (Writer)
10901 176th Cir NE # 3601
Redmond, WA 98052-7218, USA

Archer, Tasmin
20 Manchester Sq
London, ENGLAND W1M 5AE, UNITED KINGDOM (UK)

Archer of Weston-Super-Mare, Jeffrey H (Government Official, Writer)
93 Albert Embankment
London SE1 7TY, UNITED KINGDOM (UK)

Archerd, Army (Journalist)
Variety Magazine - Editorial Dept
5700 Wilshire Blvd
Los Angeles, CA 90036-3659, USA

Archibaid, Nathaniel (Nate) (Basketball Player)
2920 Holland Ave
Bronx, NY 10467-8304, USA

Archibald, Dave (Hockey Player)
Minnesota North Stars
6792 Henry St
Chillwack, BC V2R 2W1, CANADA

Archibald, Nate (Basketball Player)
Cincinnati Royals
6495 Broadway
Bronx, NY 10471-2704, USA

Archibald, Nolan D (Business Person)
Black & Decker Corp
701 E Joppa Rd
Towson, MD 21286-5502, USA

Archie, Mike (Football Player)
Houston Oilers
631 Hamilton Ave
Farrell, PA 16121-1937, USA

Archipoeski, Ken (Musician)
PO Box 656507
Fresh Meadows, NY 11365-6507, USA

Architecture in Helsinki (Music Group)
c/o Staff Member *Paradigm (Monterey)*
509 Hartnell St
Monterey, CA 93940-2825, USA

Archuleta, Adam (Football Player)
St Louis Rams
1237 W Galveston St
Chandler, AZ 85224-4335, USA

Arcia, Jose (Baseball Player)
Chicago Cubs
7325 NW 3rd St
Miami, FL 33126-4211, USA

Arcieri, Leila (Actor)
c/o Staff Member *Paradigm (LA)*
360 N Crescent Dr
North Bldg
Beverly Hills, CA 90210-6820, USA

Arcineiga, Tomas A (Educator)
California State College
President's Office
Bakersfield, CA, USA

Arctic Monkeys (Music Group)
c/o Staff Member *Paradigm (Monterey)*
509 Hartnell St
Monterey, CA 93940-2825, USA

Ard, Johnny (Baseball Player)
Bowman
3815 Edinburg Cir
Valdosta, GA 31605-7858, USA

Ard, William D (Bill) (Football Player)
New York Giants
41 Vail Ln
Watchung, NJ 07069-6149, USA

Ardalan, Nader (Architect)
KEO International Consultants
PO Box 3679
Safat 13037, KUWAIT

Ardant, Fanny (Actor)
Artmedia
20 Ave Rapp
Paris 75007, FRANCE

Ardell, Dan (Baseball Player)
Los Angeles Angels
554 Hazel Dr Apt 177
Corona Del Mar, CA 92625-2535, USA

Ardell, Donald B (Doctor)
288 Beach Dr NE Apt 11C
Saint Petersburg, FL 33701-3481, USA

Arden, Jann (Musician, Songwriter, Writer)
Macklam Feldman Mgmt
1505 W 2nd Ave
#200
Vancouver, BC V6H 3Y4, CANADA

Arden, John (Writer)
Cassarotto
60/66 Wardour St
London W1V 4ND, UNITED KINGDOM (UK)

Arden, Michael (Actor)
c/o Biff Liff *William Morris Agency (WMA-NY)*
1325 Avenue Of The Americas
New York, NY 10019-6026, USA

Arden, Toni (Musician)
3434 75th St
Jackson Heights, NY 11372-1150, USA

Arditi, Pierre
6-8 rue Lalande
Paris 75014, FRANCE

Ardito Barletta, Nicolas (President)
PO Box 7737
Panama City 9, PANAMA

Arditti, Irvine (Musician)
Lattidue Arts
109 Boul Saint-Joseph Quest
Montreal, PA H2T 2P7, CANADA

Ardizoia, Rinaldo (Baseball Player)
New York Yankees
130 Santa Rosa Ave
San Francisco, CA 94112-1930, USA

Ardizzone, Anthony (Football Player)
New York Giants
27 S Farview Ave
Paramus, NJ 07652-2629, USA

Ardolino, Todd (Director)
Creative Artists Agency
9830 Wilshire Blvd
Beverly Hills, CA 90212-1804, USA

Ardolino, Tom (Musician)
Skyline Music
PO Box 38
Jefferson, NH 03583-0038, USA

Aregood, Richards L (Journalist)
Philadelphia Daily News
400 N Broad St
Editorial Dept
Philadelphia, PA 19130-4015, USA

Arellano, Stephanie (Actor)
c/o Ken Jacobson *James/Levy/Jacobson Management*
3500 W Olive Ave Ste 1470
Burbank, CA 91505-5514, USA

Arena, Anthony (Football Player)
Detroit Lions
2013 Western Ave
Mattoon, IL 61938-2854, USA

Arena, Tina (Musician)
Magnus Entertainment
5 Darley St
Neutral Bay, NSW 2089, AUSTRALIA

Arenas, Gilbert (Basketball Player)
c/o Staff Member *Washington Wizards*
601 F St NW
Mci Center
Washington, DC 20004-1605, USA

Arenas, Joe (Football Player)
San Francisco 49ers
12508 E Ventura Dr
Galveston, TX 77554-9719, USA

Arenberg, Lee (Actor)
c/o Staff Member *Gage Group, The (LA)*
14724 Ventura Blvd Ste 505
Sherman Oaks, CA 91403-3505, USA

Arens, Moshe (Government Official)
Ministry of Defence
Rehov Kapian
Hakirya, Tel-Aviv 67695, ISRAEL

Arent, Eddi
Am Postplatz 5
Titisee-Neustadt 79822, GERMANY

Areshenkoff, Ron (Hockey Player)
Edmonton Oilers
329 12th Ave
Estevan, SK S4A 1E3, CANADA

Aretsky, Ken (Business Person)
21 Club
21 W 52nd St
New York, NY 10019-6181, USA

Arfons, Arthur E (Art) (Race Car Driver)
PO Box 1409
Saint Charles, MO 63302-1409, USA

Argento, Asia (Actor)
Moviement
Via P Cavallini 24
Rome 00193, ITALY

Argento, Dario (Director)
ADC
Via Balemonti 2
Rome, ITALY

Argento, Dominick (Composer)
Universit of Minnesota
Music Dept
Ferguson Hall
Minneapolis, MN 55455, USA

Argenziano, Carmen (Actor)
c/o Staff Member *TalentWorks (LA)*
3500 W Olive Ave Ste 1400
Burbank, CA 91505-5512, USA

Argerich, Martha (Musician)
Jacques Thelen Agence
252 Rue Faubourg
Saint Honore
Paris 75008, FRANCE

Argott, Don (Director, Producer)
c/o David Gersh *Gersh Agency, The (LA)*
232 N Canon Dr
Beverly Hills, CA 90210-5302, USA

Arguello, Alexis
1 Hall Of Fame Dr
Canastota, NY 13032-1175, USA

Ariail, David (Football Player)
Brooklyn Dodgers
5620 Sheraton Dr
Fayetteville, NC 28303-2624, USA

Arian, David (Misc)
International Longshoremen's Union
1188 Franklin St
San Francisco, CA 94109-6898, USA

Arias, Alex (Baseball Player)
Chicago Cubs
37 Edmund Rd
West Park, FL 33023-5231, USA

Arias, Mariana (Actor)
c/o Staff Member *Telefe - Argentina*
Pavon 2444 (C1248AAT)
Buenos Aires, ARGENTINA

Arias, Ricardo M (President)
Apdo 4549
Panama City, PANAMA

Arias, Rudy (Baseball Player)
Chicago White Sox
3911 NW 11th St
Miami, FL 33126-3614, USA

Arias, Silvana (Actor)
Diane Perez Entertainment
838 N Fairfax Ave
Los Angeles, CA 90046-7208, USA

Arias, Yancey (Actor)
c/o Chris Henze *Thruline Entertainment*
9250 Wilshire Blvd Ground Fl
Beverly Hills, CA 90210, USA

Arias-Sanchez, Oscar (Nobel Prize Laureate, Politician, President)
Arias Foundation for Peace
Apdo 8-6410-1000
San Jose, COSTA RICA

Arie, India (Musician, Songwriter)
c/o Staff Member *Tracey Miller & Associates*
2610 Fire Rd
Egg Harbor Township, NJ 08234-9551, USA

Aries, Jacqueline (Actor)
c/o Tracy Quinn *Himber Entertainment Inc*
15760 Ventura Blvd Ste 700
Encino, CA 91436-3016, USA

Ariey, Mike (Football Player)
Green Bay Packers
PO Box 708
Bakersfield, CA 93302-0708, USA

Arigoni, Dulio (Misc)
Im Glockenacker 42
Zurich 8053, SWITZERLAND

Arima, Akito (Physicist)
Physical Research Institute
Hirosawa 2-1
Wakoshi, Saltarna 351-01, JAPAN

Arinze, Francis Cardinal (Religious Leader)
Pontifical Council for Inter-Religious Dialogue
Vatican City 00120, VATICAN CITY

Aris, Ben
47 West Sq
London, ENGLAND SE11 4SP, UNITED KINGDOM (UK)

Arison, M Micky (Business Person)
Camivai Corp
3655 NW 87th Ave
Doral, FL 33178-2418, USA

Aristide, Jean-Bertrand (President)
President's Office
Palace du Gouvernement
Port-Au-Prince, HAITI

Ariyoshi, George R (Governor)
745 Fort St Ste 500
Honolulu, HI 96813-3805, USA

Arizin, Paul J (Basketball Player)
Philadelphia Warriors
117 Crosspointe Dr
West Chester, PA 19380-4165, USA

Arjun (Actor)
B3-C Block
109 G N Chetty Road T Nagar
Chennai, TN 600 017, INDIA

Ark, The (Music Group)
c/o Staff Member *Paradigm (Monterey)*
509 Hartnell St
Monterey, CA 93940-2825, USA

Arkadius (Designer, Fashion Designer)
c/o Staff Member *Arkadius*
41 Brondesbury Road
London, England NW6 6BP, UNITED KINGDOM (UK)

Arkangel R-15 (Music Group)
c/o Staff Member *Sony Music Miami*
605 Lincoln Rd Fl 7
Miami Beach, FL 33139-2900, USA

Arkhipov, Denis (Hockey Player)
Nashville Predators
716 Sweet Cherry Ct
Nashville, TN 37215-6174, USA

Arkhipova, Irina K (Opera Singer)
Bryusov Per 2/14
#27
Moscow 103009, RUSSIA

Arkin, Adam (Actor)
c/o Marsha McManus *Principal Entertainment (LA)*
1964 Westwood Blvd Ste 400
Los Angeles, CA 90025-4695, USA

Arkin, Alan (Actor)
c/o Estelle Lasher *Principal Entertainment (LA)*
1964 Westwood Blvd Ste 400
Los Angeles, CA 90025-4695, USA

Arlauckas, Joe (Basketball Player)
Sacramento Kings
272 E Henrietta Rd
Rochester, NY 14620-4626, USA

Arlich, Don (Baseball Player)
Houston Astros
7877 73rd St S
Cottage Grove, MN 55016-1919, USA

Arlin, Steve (Baseball Player)
San Diego Padres
6819 Claremore Ave
San Diego, CA 92120-3125, USA

Arm, Mark (Musician)
Legends of 21st Century
7 Trinity Row
Florence, MA 01062-1931, USA

Armacost, Michael H (Diplomat)
State Department
2201 C St NW
Washington, DC 20520-0099, USA

Arman (Artist)
Arman Studios
430 Washington St
New York, NY 10013-1721, USA

Armani, Giorgio (Designer, Fashion Designer)
Via Borgonuovo 21
Milan 20121, ITALY

Armaou, Lindsay (Musician)
Clintons
55 Drury Lane
Covent Garden
London WC2B 5SQ, UNITED KINGDOM (UK)

Armas, Antonio R (Tony) (Baseball Player)
Los Mercedes #37
P Piruto-Edo
Anzoategui, VENEZUELA

Armas, Chris (Soccer Player)
Chicago Fire
7000 S Harlem Ave
Bridgeview, IL 60455-1160, USA

Armas, Marcos (Baseball Player)
Oakland A's
Calle Las Mercedes #37
Puerto Piritu, VENEZUELA

Armas, Tony (Baseball Player)
c/o Staff Member *Washington Nationals*
2400 East Capitol Street SE
Rfk Stadium
Washington, DC 20003, USA

Armato, Ange (Baseball Player)
5082 Valley Pines Dr
Rockford, IL 61109-3774, USA

Armatrading, Joan (Musician, Songwriter, Writer)
21 Ramilles St
London W1V 1DF, UNITED KINGDOM (UK)

Armbrister, Ed (Baseball Player)
Cincinnati Reds
McQuay St Box 2003
Nassau
Bahamas, WEST INDIES

Armdt-Proefrock, Ellen (Baseball Player)
905 Alpine St
Brodhead, WI 53520-1052, USA

Armedariz, Pedro Jr (Actor)
Diamond Artists
9200 W Sunset Blvd Ste 701
West Hollywood, CA 90069-3602, USA

Armenante, Jilian (Actor)
Susan Smith
121A N San Vincente Blvd
Beverly Hills, CA 90211, USA

Armenante, Jillian (Actor)
c/o Staff Member *Metropolitan*
4500 Wilshire Blvd Fl 2
Los Angeles, CA 90010-3858, USA

Armitage, Alison (Actor, Model)
c/o Staff Member *Schiowitz/Clay/Ankrum & Ross FKA Talent Syndicate, The*
1680 Vine St Ste 614
Los Angeles, CA 90028-8833, USA

Armitage, Karole (Choreographer, Dancer)
350 W 21st St
New York, NY 10011-3318, USA

Armour, Thomas D (Tommy) III (Golfer)
4211 Saint Andrews Blvd
Irving, TX 75038-6445, USA

Arms, Russell (Actor, Musician)
312 Hillcrest Dr
Hamilton, IL 62341-1106, USA

Armstead, Jessie (Football Player)
New York Giants
1316 Mill Stream Dr
Dallas, TX 75232-4604, USA

Armstead, Jimmie (Baseball Player)
Indianapolis ABC's
81 Vaughn Ave
New Rochelle, NY 10801-3122, USA

Armstrong, A James (Misc)
Broadway Methodist Church
1100 W 42nd St Ste 210
Indianapolis, IN 46208-3300, USA

Armstrong, Adger (Football Player)
Houston Oilers
6403 Paddington St
Houston, TX 77085-3000, USA

Armstrong, Alan (Actor)
Markham & Froggatt
Julian House
4 Windmill St
London W1P 1HF, UNITED KINGDOM (UK)

Armstrong, Anne
Armstrong Ranch
Armstrong, TX 78338, USA

Armstrong, Antonio (Football Player)
Miami Dolphins
6218 Hirsch Rd
Houston, TX 77026-1524, USA

Armstrong, B J (Basketball Player)
1220 Boden Pl
Fort Washington, PA 19034-1504, USA

Armstrong, Bess (Actor)
William Morris Agency
151 El Camino Dr
Beverly Hills, CA 90212-2775, USA

Armstrong, Billie Joe (Musician, Songwriter, Writer)
Warner Bros Records
3300 Warner Blvd
Burbank, CA 91505-4694, USA

Armstrong, BJ (Basketball Player)
Chicago Bulls
1220 Boden Pl
Fort Washington, PA 19034-1504, USA

Armstrong, Bruce (Football Player)
New England Patriots
12543 Brookwood Ct
Davie, FL 33330-1207, USA

Armstrong, Charlotte (Baseball Player)
5838 N 81st St
Scottsdale, AZ 85250-6208, USA

Armstrong, Clay M (Scientist)
University of Pennsylvania
Medical School 3400 Spruce
Philadelphia, PA 19104, USA

Armstrong, Curtis (Actor)
3867 Shannon Rd
Los Angeles, CA 90027-1441, USA

Armstrong, Darrell (Basketball Player)
Orlando Magic
337 Broadmoor Way
McDonough, GA 30253-4290, USA

Armstrong, Debbie
Box 710 Taos Sky Valley
Taos, NM 87525, USA

Armstrong, Deborah (Debbie) (Skier)
PO Box 770925
Steamboat Springs, CO 80477-0925, USA

Armstrong, Dwight (Actor)
c/o Paul Greenstone *Paul Greenstone Entertainment*
1227 Union St
San Francisco, CA 94109-1922, USA

Armstrong, Garner Ted
PO Box 2525
Tyler, TX 75710-2525, USA

Armstrong, George (Hockey Player)
Toronto Maple Leafs
22 St Cuthbert's Rd
Toronto, ON M4G 1V1, CANADA

Armstrong, Gillian (Director)
Harry Linstead
500 Oxford St
Bondi Junction, NSW 2022, AUSTRALIA

Armstrong, Harvey (Football Player)
Philadelphia Eagles
7514 Centenary Dr
Rowlett, TX 75089-3068, USA

Armstrong, Jack (Baseball Player)
Cincinnati Reds
272 E River Park Dr
Jupiter, FL 33477-9381, USA

Armstrong, Jonas (Actor)
c/o Staff Member *Artists Rights Group Talent (ARG)*
4 Great Portland St
London W1W 8PA, UNITED KINGDOM (UK)

Armstrong, Karen (Writer)
c/o Staff Member *Random House*
1540 Broadway
New York, NY 10036-4039, USA

Armstrong, Kerry (Actor)
Barbara Leane Mgmt
261 Miller St
North Sydney, NSW 2060, AUSTRALIA

Armstrong, Lance (Athlete)
Lance Armstrong Foundation
PO Box 161150
Austin, TX 78716-1150, USA

Armstrong, Michael (Director)
114 N Doheny Dr
West Hollywood, CA 90048-2013, USA

Armstrong, Mike (Baseball Player)
San Diego Padres
525 Ashbrook Ct
Athens, GA 30605-3985, USA

Armstrong, Murray A (Coach, Hockey Player)
Toronto Maple Leafs
104 Augusta Cir
Saint Augustine, FL 32086-8819, USA

Armstrong, Neil (Astronaut)
CTA Inc
PO Box 436
Rt 123
Lebanon, OH 45036-0436, USA

Armstrong, Neil (Referee)
1169 Sherwood Trail
Sarnia, ON N7V 2H3, CANADA

Armstrong, Neill (Football Player)
Philadelphia Eagles
109 Forest Hill Dr
Roanoke, TX 76262-5535, USA

Armstrong, Quincy (Football Player)
Cleveland Browns
5801 E Fm 4
Grandview, TX 76050-3005, USA

Armstrong, RG (Actor)
3856 Reklaw Dr
Studio City, CA 91604-3831, USA

Armstrong, Robb (Cartoonist)
United Feature Syndicate
200 Madison Ave
New York, NY 10016-3911, USA

Armstrong, Robert (Basketball Player)
Philadelphia 76ers
1527 Widdicomb Ave NW
Grand Rapids, MI 49504-3048, USA

Armstrong, Russell P (War Hero)
425 Bench Rd
Fallon, NV 89406-6334, USA

Armstrong, Samaire (Actor)
c/o Loch Powell *Leverage Management*
1610 Broadway
Santa Monica, CA 90404-2792, USA

Armstrong, Scotty (Basketball Player)
Indianapolis Kauskys
8635 Winchester Rd
Fort Wayne, IN 46819-2249, USA

Armstrong, Sheila A (Musician, Opera Singer)
Harvesters Tilford Road
Hindhead
Surrey GU26 6SQ, UNITED KINGDOM (UK)

Armstrong, Spence M (General)
9714 Bluedale St
Alexandria, VA 22308, USA

Armstrong, Tate (Basketball Player)
Chicago Bulls
14704 Westbury Rd
Rockville, MD 20853-1610, USA

Armstrong, Thomas (Race Car Driver)
PacWest Racing Group
150 Gasoline Aly
Indianapolis, IN 46222-3965, USA

Armstrong, Thomas H W (Misc)
1 East St
Olney
Bucks MK46 4AP, UNITED KINGDOM (UK)

Armstrong, Tom (Cartoonist)
North American Syndicate
235 E 45th St
New York, NY 10017-3305, USA

Armstrong, Trace (Football Player)
10191 Winding Ridge Rd
Saint Louis, MO 63124-1157, USA

Armstrong, Ty (Golfer)
11529 Kensington Dr
Eden Prairie, MN 55347-4943, USA

Armstrong, Valorie (Actor)
Contemporary Artists
610 Santa Monica Blvd Ste 202
Santa Monica, CA 90401-1645, USA

Armstrong, Vaughn (Actor)
1903 Apex Ave
Los Angeles, CA 90039-3115, USA

Armstrong, Wally (Golfer)
Signature Sports Group
4150 Olson Memorial Hwy Ste 110
Minneapolis, MN 55422-4804, USA

Armstrong, William (Writer)
6 Roland St
Newton, MA 02461-1920, USA

Armstrong, William L (Senator)
1900 E Girard Pl Apt 1004
Englewood, CO 80113-3113, USA

Army of Lovers
78 Stanley Gardens
London, ENGLAND W3 7SN, UNITED KINGDOM (UK)

Arnason, Chuck (Hockey Player)
Montreal Canadiens
39 Grimston Rd
Winnipeg, MB R3T 3T2, CANADA

Arnatt, John
3 Warren Cottage Woodland Way
Surrey, ENGLAND KT20 6NN, UNITED KINGDOM (UK)

Arnaud, Jean-Loup (Government Official)
55 Rue de Seine
Paris 75006, FRANCE

Arnault, Bernard (Business Person)
Moet Hennessy Louis Vuitton
30 Ave Hoche
Paris 75008, FRANCE

Arnaz, Lucie (Actor)
c/o Staff Member *Scott Stander & Associates*
13701 Riverside Dr Ste 201
Sherman Oaks, CA 91423-2447, USA

Arnaz, Lusie (Actor)
PO Box 330
Georgetown, CT 06829-0330, USA

Arndt, Denis (Actor)
c/o Staff Member *Artist Group International (NY)*
150 E 58th St Fl 19
New York, NY 10155-1900, USA

Arndt, Larry (Baseball Player)
Oakland A's
5970 E West Miramar Dr
Tucson, AZ 85715-3024, USA

Arndt, Michael (Writer)
c/o Tom Strickler *Endeavor Agency LLC (LA)*
9601 Wilshire Blvd Fl 3
Beverly Hills, CA 90210-5204, USA

Arndt, Richard (Football Player)
Pittsburgh Steelers
2130 Parkdale Dr
Kingwood, TX 77339-2351, USA

Arneil, Richard A S (Composer)
Benhall Lodge
Benhall
Suffolk IP17 1DJ, UNITED KINGDOM (UK)

Arnelle
c/o Staff Member *Dion Peronneau Agency*
5170 Veronica St
Los Angeles, CA 90008-1123, USA

Arnelle, Jesse (Basketball Player)
Fort Wayne Pistons
400 Urbano Dr
San Francisco, CA 94127-2827, USA

Arnesen, Lasse
Fagerborggata 34
Oslo N-0360, NORWAY

Arnesen, Liv (Skier)
119 N 4th St Ste 406
Yourexpidition
Minneapolis, MN 55401-1790, USA

Arneson, Jim (Football Player)
Dallas Cowboys
12649 S 71st St
Tempe, AZ 85284-3105, USA

Arness, James (Actor)
PO Box 49599
Los Angeles, CA 90049-0599, USA

Arnett, Jon D (Football Player)
Los Angeles Rams
PO Box 4077
Palos Verdes Estates, CA 90274-9558, USA

Arnett, Will (Actor)
c/o Peter Principato *Principato/Young Management*
9665 Wilshire Blvd Ste 500
Beverly Hills, CA 90212-2312, USA

Arnette, Jay (Basketball Player)
Cincinnati Royals
2 Hillside Ct
Austin, TX 78746-6436, USA

Arnette, Jeanetta (Actor)
466 N Harper Ave
Los Angeles, CA 90048-2221, USA

Arngrim, Alison (Actor)
PO Box 98
Tujunga, CA 91043-0098, USA

Arning, Lisa (Actor)
c/o Julie Wolff *The Morgan Agency*
1200 N Doheny Dr
Los Angeles, CA 90069-1723, USA

Arno, Ed
11220 72nd Dr
Flushing, NY 11375-5661, USA

Arnold, Anna Bing (Philanthropist)
Anna Bing Arnold Foundation
9700 W Pico Blvd
Los Angeles, CA 90035-4711, USA

Arnold, Ben (Musician)
Golden Guru
227 Pine St
Philadelphia, PA 19106-4326, USA

Arnold, Brian A (General)
Commander Space & Missile Systems Center
Los Angeles Air Force Base, CA 90245, USA

Arnold, Charles (Baseball Player)
Memphis Red Sox
19537 Beaverland St
Detroit, MI 48219-5507, USA

Arnold, Charlotte (Actor)
c/o Norbert Abrams *Noble Kaplan Agency*
1260 Yonge St Fl 2
Toronto, ON M4T 1W6, CANADA

Arnold, Chris (Baseball Player)
San Francisco Giants
2219 El Capitan Ave
Arcadia, CA 91006-5110, USA

Arnold, David (Football Player)
Pittsburgh Steelers
1615 Stanley St
New Britain, CT 06053-2439, USA

Arnold, Debbie (Actor)
M Arnold Mgmt
12 Cambridge Park
Ease Twickenham
Middx TW1 2PF, UNITED KINGDOM (UK)

Arnold, Eddy (Actor)
PO Box 97
Brentwood, TN 37024-0097, USA

Arnold, Edward (Eddy) (Music Group)
PO Box 97
Franklin Road
Brentwood, TN 37024-0097, USA

Arnold, Eve (Photographer)
Magnum Photographic Agency
5 Old St
London EC1V 9HL, UNITED KINGDOM (UK)

Arnold, Gary H (Critic)
5133 1st St N
Arlington, VA 22203-1207, USA

Arnold, Jackson D (Admiral, War Hero)
Los Pinos Box 185
Rancho Santa Fe, CA 92067, USA

Arnold, Jahine (Football Player)
Pittsburgh Steelers
9119 Whispering Willow Way
Tampa, FL 33614-4913, USA

Arnold, James E (Football Player)
Kansas City Chiefs
223 Boxwood Dr
Franklin, TN 37069-6979, USA

Arnold, James R (Misc)
University of California
Chemistry Dept
Code 0524
La Jolla, CA 92093, USA

Arnold, Jamie (Baseball Player)
Los Angeles Dodgers
11716 Meredith Drive
Temple, AZ 76502, USA

Arnold, Kristine (Music Group)
Monty Hitchcock Mgmt
5101 Overton Rd
Nashville, TN 37220-1920, USA

Arnold, Lefrancis (Football Player)
Denver Broncos
3312 W 80th St
Inglewood, CA 90305-1354, USA

Arnold, Lenna (Baseball Player)
4312 Dodge Ave
Fort Wayne, IN 46815-6925, USA

Arnold, Louise (Baseball Player)
52806 Brandel Ave
South Bend, IN 46635-1250, USA

Arnold, Monica (Actor, Musician)
c/o Staff Member *Handprint Entertainment*
1100 Glendon Ave Ste 1000
Los Angeles, CA 90024-3514, USA

Arnold, Murray (Basketball Player, Coach)
Western Kentucky University
Athletic Dept
Bowling Green, KY 42101, USA

Arnold, Scott (Baseball Player)
St Louis Cardinals
2936 Runnymede Way
Lexington, KY 40503-2813, USA

Arnold, Stuart (Publisher)
Fortune Magazine
Rockefeller Center
New York, NY 10020, USA

Arnold, Tichina (Actor)
c/o Geoff Cheddy *Brillstein-Grey
Entertainment*
9150 Wilshire Blvd Ste 350
Beverly Hills, CA 90212-3453, USA

Arnold, Tom (Actor, Comedian)
c/o Staff Member *Brillstein-Grey
Entertainment*
9150 Wilshire Blvd Ste 350
Beverly Hills, CA 90212-3453, USA

Arnold, Tony (Baseball Player)
Baltimore Orioles
5708 Vineyard Ln
Mc Kinney, TX 75070-9569, USA

Arnold, Walt (Football Player)
Los Angeles Rams
8503 La Sala Grande NE
Albuquerque, NM 87111-4564, USA

Arnold Jr, Harry L (Doctor, Writer)
250 Laurel St Apt 301
San Francisco, CA 94118-2045, USA

Arnoldi, Charles A (Artist)
721 Hampton Dr
Venice, CA 90291-3018, USA

Arnott, Jason (Hockey Player)
Edmonton Oilers
47 Governors Way
Brentwood, TN 37027-8926, USA

Arnott, Jason (Hockey Player)
Budget Rent-a-Car
412 Dunlop St W
Barrie, ON L4N 1C1, CANADA

Arnoul, Francoise (Actor)
53 Rue Censier
Paris 75005, FRANCE

Arns, Paulo E Cardinal (Religious Leader)
Alvenida Higienopolos 890
CP 6778
Sao Paulo, SP 01064, BRAZIL

Arnsberg, Brad (Baseball Player)
New York Yankees
706 Chaffee Ct
Arlington, TX 76006-2001, USA

Arnstein, Rolly (Music Group)
Bad Boy Entertainment
1540 Broadway # 3000
New York, NY 10036-4039, USA

Arnsten, Stefan
1017 Laurel Way
Beverly Hills, CA 90210-2304, USA

Arntz, Jason (Athlete)
95A Finnegan Ln
Kendall Park, NJ 08824-1644, USA

Arnzen, Robert (Basketball Player)
New York Nets
8 Grand Lake Dr
Fort Thomas, KY 41075-4100, USA

Arocha, Rene (Baseball Player)
St Louis Cardinals
14273 SW 24th St
Miami, FL 33175-8001, USA

Aronofsky, Darren (Director)
c/o Staff Member *Amoeba Proteus*
438 W 37th St Rm 5G
New York, NY 10018-9557, USA

Arons, Arnold B (Physicist)
10313 Lake Shord Blvd NE
Seattle, WA 98125, USA

Aronson, Judie (Actor)
c/o Staff Member *ATA Management*
292 5th Ave Fl 4
New York, NY 10001-4513, USA

Arora, Amrita (Actor, Bollywood)
Amrita Arora Plot No198 Poojakunj Apts
Sher-e-Punjab Colony Plot No. 195
Andheri (E)
Mumbai, MS 400093, INDIA

Arpel, Adrien (Beauty Pageant Winner)
Adrien Arpel Cosmetics
400 Hackensack Ave
Hackensack, NJ 07601-6310, USA

Arpey, Gerard (Business Person)
AMR Corp
433 Amon Carter Blvd
Forth Worth, TX 76155, USA

Arpino, Gerald P (Choreographer)
City Center Joffrey Ballet
70 E Lake St Ste 1300
Chicago, IL 60601-7458, USA

Arquette, Alexis (Actor)
c/o Staff Member *Innovative Artists (LA)*
1505 10th St
Santa Monica, CA 90401-2805, USA

Arquette, David (Actor)
c/o Cindy Guagenti *BWR (BWR-LA)*
9100 Wilshire Blvd Fl 6
West Tower
Beverly Hills, CA 90212-3401, USA

Arquette, Patricia (Actor)
c/o Molly Madden *3 Arts Entertainment
Inc*
9460 Wilshire Blvd Fl 7
Beverly Hills, CA 90212-2713, USA

Arquette, Rosanna (Actor)
c/o Steve Tellez *Creative Artists Agency
LCC (CAA-LA)*
2000 Avenue Of The Stars
Los Angeles, CA 90067-4700, USA

Arrants, Rod (Actor)
1173 Regent St
Alameda, CA 94501-5330, USA

Arras, Maria Celeste (Actor)
c/o Staff Member *Telemundo*
2470 W 8th Ave
Hialeah, FL 33010-2000, USA

Arredondo, Rosa (Actor)
c/o Suzanne (Sue) Wohl *TalentWorks (LA)*
3500 W Olive Ave Ste 1400
Burbank, CA 91505-5512, USA

Arrigo, Gerry (Baseball Player)
Minnesota Twins
3740 Redthome Dr
Amelia, OH 45102, USA

Arrindell, Clement A (Governor)
Lark
Bird Rock, SAINT KITTS & NEVIS

Arrington, Buddy (Race Car Driver)
2620 Kings Mountain Rd
Martinsville, VA 24112, USA

Arrington, Jill (Sportscaster)
CBS-TV
51 W 52nd St
Sports Dept
New York, NY 10019-6119, USA

Arrington, LaVar (Football Player)
Washington Redskins
1514 Cedar Lane Farm Rd
Annapolis, MD 21409-5625, USA

Arrington, Richard (Football Player)
Philadelphia Eagles
2585 King Cir SE
Conyers, GA 30013-1981, USA

Arriola, Dante (Director)
c/o David Flynn *Chaos Management*
1680 Vine St
Taft Building #310
Hollywood, CA 90028-8851, USA

Arriola, Gus
PO Box 3275
Carmel, CA 93921-3275, USA

Arrobio, Charles (Football Player)
Minnesota Vikings
481 Linda Vista Ave
Pasadena, CA 91105-1119, USA

Arrojo, Luis (Baseball Player)
Tampa Bay Devil Rays
5684 36th Ave N
Saint Petersburg, FL 33710-1914, USA

Arrow, Kenneth J (Nobel Prize Laureate)
620 Sand Hill Rd Apt 406C
Palo Alto, CA 94304-2093, USA

Arroyo, Bronson (Baseball Player)
Pittsburgh Pirates
47 Olive St
Brooksville, FL 34601-2125, USA

Arroyo, Carlos (Basketball Player)
c/o Staff Member *Utah Jazz*
301 W South Temple
Delta Center
Salt Lake City, UT 84101-1216, USA

Arroyo, Fernando (Baseball Player)
Detroit Tigers
5232 E Ingram St
Mesa, AZ 85205-3434, USA

Arroyo, Jose (Writer)
c/o Staff Member *Kaplan-Stahler-Gumer
Agency*
8383 Wilshire Blvd Ste 923
Beverly Hills, CA 90211-2408, USA

Arroyo, Luis E (Baseball Player)
St Louis Cardinals
PO Box 354
Penuelas, PR 00624-0354, USA

Arroyo, Martina (Opera Singer)
Berkshire Corsert Artists
20 Alfred Dr
Pittsfield, MA 01201-8430, USA

Arroyo, Rudolph (Baseball Player)
St Louis Cardinals
828 Sierra Vista Ave
Mountain View, CA 94043-1706, USA

Art of Noise, The (Music Group)
PO Box 199
London W11 4AN, UNITED KINGDOM
(UK)

Arteage, Rosalia (President)
Vice President's Office
Gobiemo Palacio
Garcia Morena, Quito, ECUADOR

Artemas, Cole (Cartoonist)
15 Regency Mnr Apt 15-8
Rutland, VT 05701-5310, USA

Artemis, Cole
1050 Colonial Dr
Rutland, VT 05701-9575, USA

Arterburn, Elmer (Football Player)
Chicago Cardinals
3819 29th St
Lubbock, TX 79410-2508, USA

Artest, Ron (Basketball Player)
c/o Staff Member *Sacramento Kings*
1 Sports Pkwy
Arco Arena
Sacramento, CA 95834-2301, USA

Arteta, Miguel (Director)
c/o David Lubliner *William Morris
Agency (WMA-LA)*
1 William Morris Pl
Beverly Hills, CA 90212-4261, USA

Arthur, Beatrice (Bea) (Actor)
c/o Matthew (Matt) Del Piano *Creative
Artists Agency LCC (CAA-LA)*
2000 Avenue Of The Stars
Los Angeles, CA 90067-4700, USA

Arthur, Fred (Hockey Player)
Hartford Whalers
203-1408 Ernest Ave
London, ON N6E 3B2, CANADA

Arthur, Joseph (Musician)
c/o Staff Member *Paradigm (Monterey)*
509 Hartnell St
Monterey, CA 93940-2825, USA

Arthur, Maureen (Actor)
9171 Wilshire Blvd # 530
Beverly Hills, CA 90210-5530, USA

Arthur, Mike (Football Player)
Cincinnati Bengals
10445 Sharondale Rd
Cincinnati, OH 45241-3077, USA

Arthur, Owen (Prime Minister)
Prime Minister's Office
Bay St
Saint Michael
Bridgetown, BARBADOS

Arthur, Perry (Golfer)
7513 Zurich Dr
Plano, TX 75025-3118, USA

Arthur, Rebeca (Actor)
Epstein-Wyckoff
280 S Beverly Dr Ste 400
Beverly Hills, CA 90212-3904, USA

Arthurs, John (Basketball Player)
Milwaukee Bucks
1429 Henry Clay Ave
New Orleans, LA 70118-6059, USA

Arthurs, Paul (Bonehead) (Musician)
Ignition Mgmt
54 Linhope St
London NW1 6HL, UNITED KINGDOM
(UK)

Artoe, Mike (Football Player)
Chicago Bears
17 Canterbury Ct
Wilmette, IL 60091-2822, USA

Artschwager, Richard E (Artist)
PO Box 12
Hudson, NY 12534-0012, USA

Artsebarsky, Anatoli P (Cosmonaut)
Potchta Kosmonavtov
Moskovskoi Oblasti
Syvisdny Goroduk 141160, RUSSIA

Artzt, Alice J (Musician)
51 Hawthorne Ave
Princeton, NJ 08540-3803, USA

Artzt, Edwin L (Business Person)
3849 Hedgewood Dr
Lawrenceburg, IN 47025-8047, USA

Arulmani (Actor)
15 Pookara Street
Saidapet
Chennai, TN 600 015, INDIA

Arum, Robert (Bob) (Boxer)
36 Gulf Stream Ct
Las Vegas, NV 89113-1354, USA

Arun, Ila (Actor, Bollywood)
401 Paradise Apartments
7th Road Santacruz East
Bombay, MS 400055, INDIA

Arvesen, Nina (Actor)
412 Culver Blvd Apt 9
Playa Del Rey, CA 90293-7765, USA

Arvie, Herman (Football Player)
Cleveland Browns
1046 Highway 3043
Opelousas, LA 70570-2117, USA

Arvind, V (Actor)
1 65th Street 12th Avenue
Ashok Nagar
Chennai, TN 600 083, INDIA

Arvindasamy (Actor)
29A Muthiah Street
Cathedral Road
Chennai, TN 600 086, INDIA

Arzu Irigoyen, Alvaro E (President)
President's Office
Palacio Nacional
Guatemala City, GUATEMALA

As Tall as Lions (Music Group)
c/o Staff Member *Paradigm (Monterey)*
509 Hartnell St
Monterey, CA 93940-2825, USA

Asadoor, Randy (Baseball Player)
San Diego Padres
4857 E Richmond Ave
Clovis, CA 93619-8673, USA

Asay, Chuck (Cartoonist)
Colorada Springs Gazette
303 S Prospect St
Colorado Springs, CO 80903-3748, USA

Asbury, Bill (Football Player)
Pittsburgh Steelers
119 Wildernest Ln
Port Matilda, PA 16870-7107, USA

Asbury, Kelly (Actor)
c/o Staff Member *Creative Artists Agency
LCC (CAA-LA)*
2000 Avenue Of The Stars
Los Angeles, CA 90067-4700, USA

Asbury, Martin (Cartoonist)
Stoneworld
Pitch Green
Princes Risborough, Bucks HP27 9QG,
UNITED KINGDOM (UK)

Ascencio, Nelson (Actor)
c/o Heidi Rotbart *Heidi Rotbart
Management*
4000 Warner Blvd Bldg 160 Rm 716
Burbank, CA 91522-0001, USA

Aschbacher, Darrel (Football Player)
Philadelphia Eagles
915 NE Wyoming Dr
Prineville, OR 97754-7905, USA

Aschenbrener, Frank (Football Player)
16372 E Jacklin Dr
Fountain Hills, AZ 85268-5608, USA

Ash, Mary Kay (Business Person)
Mary Kay Ash Charitable Foundation
PO Box 799044
Dallas, TX 75379-9044, USA

Ash, Nadine (Golfer)
Quantum Sports Management
5625 E Wethersfield Rd
Scottsdale, AZ 85254-4317, USA

Ash, Roy L (Business Person, Government
Official)
655 Funchal Rd
Los Angeles, CA 90077-3211, USA

Asham, Arron (Hockey Player)
Montreal Canadiens
Pro-Rep Entertainment Consulting
Attn Art Breeze 113-276 Midpark Way SE
Calgary, AB T2X 1J6, CANADA

Ashanti (Musician)
c/o Harry Gold *TalentWorks (LA)*
3500 W Olive Ave Ste 1400
Burbank, CA 91505-5512, USA

Ashbery, John L (Writer)
326 Belmont Ave
Buffalo, NY 14223-1550, USA

Ashbrook, Dana (Actor)
Rigberg Roberts Rugolo
1180 S Beverly Dr Ste 601
Los Angeles, CA 90035-1158, USA

Ashbrook, Daphne (Actor)
Innovative Atrists
1505 10th St
Santa Monica, CA 90401-2805, USA

Ashbrook, Stephen (Musician)
Green Room
2280 NW Thurman St
Portland, OR 97210-2519, USA

Ashby, Alan (Baseball Player)
Cleveland Indians
12011 Cypress Creek Lakes Dr
Cypress, TX 77433-1872, USA

Ashby, Andy (Baseball Player)
Philadelphia Phillies
2 Osborne Dr
Pittston, PA 18640-3751, USA

Ashby, Jeffrey S (Astronaut)
NASA
2101 Nasa Pkwy
Johnson Space Center
Houston, TX 77058-3691, USA

Ashby, Linden (Actor)
639 N Larchmont Blvd Ste 207
Los Angeles, CA 90004-1323, USA

Ashcroft, John D (Attorney, Attorney
General, General, Governor, Senator)
Justice Department
10th St & Constitution Ave NW
Washington, DC 20530-0001, USA

Ashcroft, Richard (Musician, Songwriter)
c/o Staff Member *Paradigm (NY)*
360 Park Ave S Fl 16
New York, NY 10010-1716, USA

Ashdown, J J D (Paddy) (Government
Official)
Vane Cottage
Norton Sub Hamdon
Somerset TA14 6SG, UNITED KINGDOM
(UK)

Ashdown, Paddy
House of Commons
London, ENGLAND SW1A 0AA, UNITED
KINGDOM (UK)

Ashe, Chrstopher (Actor)
c/o Paul Greenstone *Paul Greenstone
Entertainment*
1227 Union St
San Francisco, CA 94109-1922, USA

Ashe, Danni (Adult Film Star, Business
Person)
Video Bliss
520 Washington Blvd # 445
Marina Del Rey, CA 90292, USA

Ashenfelter III, Horace (Athlete, Track
Athlete)
100 Hawthome Ave
Glen Ridge, NJ 07028, USA

Asher, Barry (Bowler)
Professional Bowlers Assn
719 2nd Ave Ste 701
Seattle, WA 98104-1747, USA

Asher, Jane (Actor)
24 Cale St
London SW3 3QU, UNITED KINGDOM
(UK)

Asher, Robert (Football Player)
Dallas Cowboys
4800 S Chicago Beach Dr Apt 612S
Chicago, IL 60615-3569, USA

Asherson, Renee (Actor)
28 Elsworthy Road
London NW3, UNITED KINGDOM (UK)

Ashford, David
53 Moat Dr Harrow
Middlesex, ENGLAND, UNITED
KINGDOM (UK)

Ashford, Mandy (Music Group)
Evolution Talent
1776 Broadway Ste 1500
New York, NY 10019-2002, USA

Ashford, Matthew (Actor)
c/o Staff Member *David Shapira &
Associates*
193 N Robertson Blvd
Beverly Hills, CA 90211-2103, USA

Ashford, Michelle (Producer, Writer)
c/o Staff Member *William Morris Agency
(WMA-LA)*
1 William Morris Pl
Beverly Hills, CA 90212-4261, USA

Ashford, Roslyn (Music Group)
Thomas Cassidy
11761 E Speedway Blvd
Tucson, AZ 85748-2017, USA

Ashford, Tucker (Baseball Player)
San Diego Padres
502 S Maple St
Covington, TN 38019-2830, USA

Ashford, Washington Evelyn (Athlete,
Track Athlete)
38997 Cherry Point Ln
Murrieta, CA 92563-8814, USA

Ashida, Jun (Designer, Fashion Designer)
1-3-3 Aobadai
Meguroku
Tokyo 153, JAPAN

Ashihara, Yoshinobu (Architect)
Ashihara Architects
31-15 Sakuragaokacho
Shibuyaku
Tokyo 150, JAPAN

Ashkenasi, Shmuel (Musician)
3800 N Lake Shore Dr
Chicago, IL 60613-3301, USA

Ashkenazy, Vladimir D (Musician)
Savinka
Kappelistr 15
Meggen 6045, SWITZERLAND

Ashley, Billy (Baseball Player)
Los Angeles Dodgers
4331 W Mariposa Grande
Glendale, AZ 85310-3947, USA

Ashley, Elizabeth (Actor)
1223 N Ogden Dr
West Hollywood, CA 90046-4706, USA

Ashley, Jennifer (Actor)
129 W Wilson St Ste 202
Costa Mesa, CA 92627-1586, USA

Ashley, John (Hockey Player, Referee)
Hockey Hall of Fame
BCE Place
30 Yonge St
Toronto, ON M5E 1X8, CANADA

Ashley, Laurence (Actor)
Cineart
36 Rue de Ponthieu
Paris 75008, FRANCE

Ashley, Leon (Musician)
PO Box 567
Hendersonville, TN 37077-0567, USA

Ashley, Merrill (Ballerina)
New York City Ballet
Lincoln Center Plaza
New York, NY 10023, USA

Ashman, Duane (Football Player)
Kansas City Chiefs
2625 Antler Ct
Silver Spring, MD 20904-7157, USA

Ashmore, Aaron (Actor)
KG Talent
55 1/2 Sumach Street
Toronto, ON M5A 3J6, CANADA

Ashmore, Darryl (Football Player)
Los Angeles Rams
8695 Thornbrook Terrace Pt
Boynton Beach, FL 33473-4882, USA

Ashmore, Edward B (Admiral)
Naval Secretary
Victor Bldg
HM Naval Base
Portsmouth, Hants, UNITED KINGDOM
(UK)

Ashmore, Frank (Actor)
c/o Staff Member *Howard Talent West*
10657 Riverside Dr
Toluca Lake, CA 91602-2341, USA

Ashmore, Shawn (Actor)
c/o Chuck James *Gersh Agency, The (LA)*
232 N Canon Dr
Beverly Hills, CA 90210-5302, USA

Ashrawl, Hanan (Politician)
Higher Education Ministry
PO Box 17360
Jerusalem, West Bank, ISRAEL

Ashton, Brent (Hockey Player)
Vancouver Canucks
311 Brabant Cres
Saskatoon, SK S7J 3Y9, CANADA

Ashton, Dean (Actor)
c/o Staff Member *Laine Management*
Laine House
131 victoria road
salford M6 8LF, UNITED KINGDOM (UK)

Ashton, John (Actor)
PO Box 272489
Fort Collins, CO 80527-2489, USA

Ashton, Peter S (Scientist)
233 Herald Road
Carlisle, MA 01741, USA

Ashton, Susan (Music Group)
Bob Doyle Assoc
713 18th Ave S
Nashville, TN 37203-3214, USA

Ashton-Griffiths, Roger
16 Chelmsford Rd
London, ENGLAND E11 1BS, UNITED
KINGDOM (UK)

Ashworth, Frank (Hockey Player)
Chicago Blackhawks
PO Box 144
Fairmont Hot Springs, BC V0B 1L0,
CANADA

Ashworth, Gerald (Gerry) (Athlete, Track
Athlete)
PO Box 2
Ogunquit, ME 03907-0002, USA

Ashworth, Jeanne C (Speed Skater)
Whiteface Highway
Wilmington, NY 12997, USA

Asia (Music Group)
%Michael Rosen
7715 W Sunset Blvd Fl 3
Los Angeles, CA 90046-3912, USA

Asian Dub Foundation (Music Group)
c/o Staff Member *Paradigm (Monterey)*
509 Hartnell St
Monterey, CA 93940-2825, USA

Askea, Mike (Football Player)
Denver Broncos
PO Box 2391
Ooltewah, TN 37363-2391, USA

Askew, Desmond (Actor)
c/o Staff Member *Envision Entertainment*
9255 W Sunset Blvd Ste 500
West Hollywood, CA 90069-3301, USA

Askew, Luke (Actor)
Media Artists Group
6300 Wilshire Blvd Ste 1470
Los Angeles, CA 90048-5200, USA

Askew, Reubin O (Governor)
PO Box 12487
Tallahassee, FL 32317-2487, USA

Askson, Bert (Football Player)
Pittsburgh Steelers
7713 Charlesmont St
Houston, TX 77016-3927, USA

Asleep At The Wheel
PO Box 463
Austin, TX 78767-0463, USA

Aslyn (Musician)
c/o Staff Member *Paradigm (Monterey)*
509 Hartnell St
Monterey, CA 93940-2825, USA

Asmonga, Don (Basketball Player)
Baltimore Bullets
124 Naylor Dr
Belle Vernon, PA 15012-4729, USA

Asner, Ed (Actor)
c/o Michael Greene *Greene & Associates*
190 N Canon Dr Ste 200
Beverly Hills, CA 90210-5319, USA

Asomugha, Nnamdi (Football Player)
Oakland Raiders
1220 Harbor Bay Pkwy
Alameda, CA 94502-6570, USA

Aspen, Jennifer (Actor)
c/o Joel Stevens *Joel Stevens
Entertainment*
206 S Brand Blvd
Glendale, CA 91204-1310, USA

Asplin, Edward W (Business Person)
601 Carlson Pkwy Ste 1050
Hopkins, MN 55305-5219, USA

Aspromonte, Bob
Brooklyn Dodgers
1000 Uptown Park Blvd Apt 241
Houston, TX 77056-3243, USA

Aspromonte, Kenneth J (Ken) (Baseball
Player)
Boston Red Sox
2 Derham Parc St
Houston, TX 77024-5200, USA

Asrani (Actor, Bollywood)
B3 Beach House Apartments
Gandhigram Rd Juhu
Mumbai, MS 400049, INDIA

Assante, Armand (Actor)
RR 1 Box 561
Campbell Hall, NY 10916, USA

Asselstine, Brian (Baseball Player)
Atlanta Braves
1488 Country Ct
Santa Ynez, CA 93460-9754, USA

Assenmacher, Ivan (Doctor)
419 Ave d'Occitanie
Montpellier 34090, FRANCE

Assenmacher, Paul (Baseball Player)
Atlanta Braves
500 Covington Cv
Alpharetta, GA 30022-5574, USA

Assuras, Thalia (Television Host)
c/o Staff Member *CBS Weekend Evening
News*
524 W 57th St Fl 8
New York, NY 10019-2930, USA

Astacio, Pedro (Baseball Player)
Los Angeles Dodgers
666 Dundee Rd Ste 704
Northbrook, IL 60062-2734, USA

Astanova, Lola (Musician)
c/o Gail Parenteau *Parenteau Guidance*
132 E 35th St # 3J
New York, NY 10016-3892, USA

Astin, John (Actor, Director)
3801 Canterbury Rd Unit 505
Baltimore, MD 21218-2374, USA

Astin, Mackenzie (Actor)
c/o Staff Member *William Morris Agency
(WMA-LA)*
1 William Morris Pl
Beverly Hills, CA 90212-4261, USA

Astin, Sean (Actor)
c/o Aron Giannini *The Collective*
9100 Wilshire Blvd # 700 W
Beverly Hills, CA 90212-3401, USA

Astley, Rick (Musician)
Unit 4 Plato St
72-74 Saint Dionis Road
London SW6 4UT, UNITED KINGDOM
(UK)

Aston, Lottie (Athlete, Model)
PO Box 9272
Truckee, CA 96162-7272, USA

Astor, Brooke (Misc)
Vincent Astor Foundations
405 Park Ave Ste 1702
New York, NY 10022-9403, USA

Astrom, Hardy (Hockey Player)
New York Rangers
Satervagen 9A
Samsjo S-89208, SWEDEN

Astroth, Joe C (Baseball Player)
Philadelphia Athletics
151 Moyer Rd
Chalfont, PA 18914-3128, USA

Asturaga, Nova (Government Official)
Permanent Mission of Nicaragua
820 2nd Ave Rm 801
New York, NY 10017-4526, USA

Asuma, Linda (Actor)
c/o Tom Chasin *Chasin Agency, The*
8899 Beverly Blvd Ste 716
Los Angeles, CA 90048-2449, USA

Aswanikumar, G (Actor)
Plot 780 29th Street
T N H B Korattur
Chennai, TN 600 080, INDIA

Atchison, David W (Religious Leader)
Southern Baptist Convention
5452 Granny White Pike
Brentwood, TN 37027, USA

Atchison, Michael (Cartoonist)
Associated Press
450 W 33rd St Fl 7
New York, NY 10001-2606, USA

Atchison, Scott
3112 Olympic Dr
Bakersfield, CA 93308-1533, USA

Atchley, Justin (Baseball Player)
Cincinnati Reds
17958 Cove Ln
Mount Vernon, WA 98274-8126, USA

Aterciopelados (Musician)
c/o Staff Member *BMG*
1540 Broadway
New York, NY 10036-4074, USA

Atessis, Bill (Football Player)
New England Patriots
PO Box 616
Phoenix, AZ 85001-0616, USA

Atha, Richard (Basketball Player)
New York Knicks
PO Box 256
402 N Justus
Ruskin, FL 33575-0256, USA

Athas, Pete (Football Player)
New York Giants
11390 NE 8th Ave
Biscayne Park, FL 33161-6318, USA

Atherton, Keith (Baseball Player)
Oakland A's
PO Box 571
Cobbs Creek, VA 23035-0571, USA

Atherton, William (Actor)
5102 San Feliciano Dr
Woodland Hills, CA 91364-1624, USA

Athfield, Ian C (Architect)
105 Amritser St
Khandallah
Wellington, NEW ZEALAND

Athlete (Music Group)
c/o Staff Member *Paradigm (Monterey)*
509 Hartnell St
Monterey, CA 93940-2825, USA

Athow, Kirk L (Misc)
2104 Crestview Ct
Lafayette, IN 47905-2152, USA

Atilla
2350 Benedict Canyon Dr
Beverly Hills, CA 90210-1409, USA

Atiyeh, Victor (Governor)
Victor Atiyeh Co
509 SW Park Ave # 205
Portland, OR 97205, USA

Atkeson, Dale
Washington Redskins
4308 Crest Dr
Manhattan Beach, CA 90266-3082, USA

Atkin, Harvey (Actor)
527 S Curson Ave
Los Angeles, CA 90036-3252, USA

Atkins, Bob (Football Player)
St Louis Cardinals
15871 Misty Loch Ln
Houston, TX 77084-6795, USA

Atkins, Christopher
c/o Melanie Sharp-Snyder *Sharp Talent*
117 N Orlando Ave
Los Angeles, CA 90048-3403, USA

Atkins, Dave (Football Player)
San Francisco 49ers
38140 Windy Hill Ln
Solon, OH 44139-3186, USA

Atkins, Doug (Football Player)
Cleveland Browns
PO Box 14007
Knoxville, TN 37914-1007, USA

Atkins, Essence (Actor)
c/o Marni Goldman *Abrams Artists
Agency (LA)*
9200 W Sunset Blvd Ph 11
Los Angeles, CA 90069-3601, USA

Atkins, Garrett (Baseball Player)
Colorado Rockies
31 Cezanne
Irvine, CA 92603-0207, USA

Atkins, Gene (Football Player)
New Orleans Saints
1111 Southcreek Dr Apt 1012
Round Rock, TX 78664-7171, USA

Atkins, George (Football Player)
Detroit Lions
3445 Polo Downs
Birmingham, AL 35226-3371, USA

Atkins, Jeffrey (Ja Rule) (Actor, Artist,
Musician)
c/o Staff Member *Handprint Entertainment*
1100 Glendon Ave Ste 1000
Los Angeles, CA 90024-3514, USA

Atkins, Jim (Baseball Player)
Boston Red Sox
1030 County Road 1518
Cullman, AL 35058-0910, USA

Atkins, Kelvin (Football Player)
Chicago Bears
4978 Timber Ridge Trl
Ocoee, FL 34761-8460, USA

Atkins, Larry (Football Player)
Kansas City Chiefs
911 Broadway St
Venice, CA 90291-3409, USA

Atkins, Rodney (Musician)
c/o Staff Member *Creative Artists Agency (CAA-Nashville)*
3310 W End Ave Fl 5
Nashville, TN 37203-1028, USA

Atkins, Sharif (Actor)
c/o Christopher (Chris) Wright *Christopher Wright Management*
3207 Winnie Dr
Los Angeles, CA 90068-1439, USA

Atkins, Tom (Actor)
Paradigm Agency
10100 Santa Monica Blvd Ste 2500
Los Angeles, CA 90067-4116, USA

Atkinson, Al (Football Player)
New York Jets
218 Wells Ln
Springfield, PA 19064-3038, USA

Atkinson, Bill (Baseball Player)
Montreal Expos
15 Argyle Cres
Chatham, ON N7L 4T7, CANADA

Atkinson, Frank (Football Player)
Pittsburgh Steelers
7 Franciscan Rdg
Portola Valley, CA 94028-8043, USA

Atkinson, George (Football Player)
Oakland Raiders
3570 Caldeira Dr
Livermore, CA 94550-6563, USA

Atkinson, Jayne (Actor)
Innovative Artists
1505 10th St
Santa Monica, CA 90401-2805, USA

Atkinson, Jess (Football Player)
New York Giants
2913 Southaven Dr
Annapolis, MD 21401-7125, USA

Atkinson, Ray N (Business Person)
Guy F Atkinson Co
1001 Bayhill Dr
San Bruno, CA 94066-3062, USA

Atkinson, Rick (Journalist, Writer)
Kansas City Times
1729 Grand Blvd
Editorial Dept
Kansas City, MO 64108-1458, USA

Atkinson, Ron (Soccer Player)
Nottingham Forest
Pavillion Road
Bridgeford
Nottingham N62 5JF, UNITED KINGDOM (UK)

Atkinson, Rowan (Actor)
c/o Peter Bennett-Jones *Tiger Aspect Pictures (UK)*
7 Soho Square
London W1D 3DQ, UNITED KINGDOM (UK)

Atkisson, Sharyl (Correspondent)
Cable News Network
1051 Techwood Dr NW
News Dept
Atlanta, GA 30318, USA

Atkov, Oleg Y (Cosmonaut)
Potchta Kosmonavtov
Moskovskoi Oblasti
Syvisdny Goroduk 141160, RUSSIA

Atler, Vanessa
PO Box 860847
Plano, TX 75086-0847, USA

Atomic Kitten (Music Group)
c/o Staff Member *Concorde Intl Artists Ltd*
101 Shepherds Bush Rd
London W6 7LP, UNITED KINGDOM (UK)

Atopare, Silas (Governor)
Governor General's Office
Konedobu
Port Moresby, PAPUA NEW GUINEA

Attack, Massive (Music Group)
c/o Staff Member *Paradigm (Monterey)*
509 Hartnell St
Monterey, CA 93940-2825, USA

Attal, Yvan (Actor, Director)
Artmedia
20 Ave Rapp
Paris 75007, FRANCE

Attanasio, Paul (Producer, Writer)
c/o David O'Connor *Creative Artists Agency LCC (CAA-LA)*
2000 Avenue Of The Stars
Los Angeles, CA 90067-4700, USA

Attardi, Michael (Football Player)
Los Angeles Rams
11 Walada Ave
Port Monmouth, NJ 07758-1325, USA

Attell, Dave (Comedian)
c/o Staff Member *Gersh Agency, The (NY)*
41 Madison Ave Fl 33
New York, NY 10010-2202, USA

Attenborough, David (Actor, Writer)
5 Park Road
Richmond Surrey, ENGLAND TW10 6NS, UNITED KINGDOM (UK)

Attenborough, Richard S (Actor, Director)
Old Farms
Beaver Lodge
Richmond Green, Surrey TW9 1NQ, UNITED KINGDOM (UK)

Atterton, Edward (Actor)
PFD
Drury House
34-43 Russell St
London WC2B 5HA, UNITED KINGDOM (UK)

Attlee, Frank III (Business Person)
Monsanto Co
800 N Lindbergh Blvd
Saint Louis, MO 63167-0001, USA

Attles, Al (Basketball Player, Coach)
Philadelphia Warriors
195 Villanova Dr
Oakland, CA 94611-1108, USA

Attwell, Bob (Hockey Player)
Colorado Rockies
270 Whitehead Cres
Bolton, ON L7E 3Y2, CANADA

Attwell, Ron (Hockey Player)
St Louis Blues
PO Box 292
Sundridge, ON P0A 1Z0, CANADA

Atun, Hakki (Prime Minister)
Gov't Assembly
North Cyprus Republic
Via Mersin 10
Lefkosa, TURKEY

Atwater, H Brewster Jr (Business Person)
IDS Center
80 S 8th St
Minneapolis, MN 55402-2100, USA

Atwater, Stephen D (Steve) (Football Player)
Denver Broncos
2510 Sugarloaf Club Dr
Duluth, GA 30097-7407, USA

Atwater Rhodes, Amelia (Writer)
c/o Staff Member *Random House Publicity*
1745 Broadway
New York, NY 10019-4343, USA

Atwell, Alfred (Astronaut)
3253 Ennis Ct
Las Vegas, NV 89121-5761, USA

Atwood, Casey (Race Car Driver)
Ultra/Evemham Motorsports
160 Munday Rd
Statesville, NC 28677-9665, USA

Atwood, Jensen (Actor)
c/o Staff Member *Noah's Arc*
75 Charles Rowen House
Merlin Street
London WC1X OEJ, UNITED KINGDOM (UK)

Atwood, Margaret E (Writer)
McClelland/Stewart
481 University Ave
#900
Toronto, ON M5G 2E9, CANADA

Atwood, Susie (Sue) (Swimmer)
5624 E 2nd St
Long Beach, CA 90803-3904, USA

Atzmon, Moshe
Marignanostr 12
Basel 4059, SWITZERLAND

Auber, Brigitte
56 rue Guy-Moquet
Paris F-75017, FRANCE

Auberjonois, Rene (Actor)
c/o Staff Member *Cunningham Escott Slevin & Doherty (LA)*
10635 Santa Monica Blvd Ste 130
Los Angeles, CA 90025-8306, USA

Aubert, KD (Actor)
c/o Andrew Weitz *Endeavor Agency LLC (LA)*
9601 Wilshire Blvd Fl 3
Beverly Hills, CA 90210-5204, USA

Aubin, Serge (Hockey Player)
Colorado Avalanche
6040 Greensbury Drive
New Albany, OH 43504, USA

Auboin, Jean A (Misc)
27 Ave des Baumettes
Nice 06000, FRANCE

Aubrey, Emlyn (Golfer)
2013 Surrey Ln
Bossier City, LA 71111-5534, USA

Aubrey, James (Actor)
Van Gelder
18-21 Jermyn St #300
London SW1Y 6HP, UNITED KINGDOM (UK)

Aubry, Cecile (Actor)
Le Moulin Bleu
6 Chemin Moulin Bleu
Sant-Cyr-sous-Dourdan 91410, FRANCE

Aubry, Cristina (Actor)
Carol Levi Co
Via Giuseppe Pisanelli
Rome 00196, ITALY

Aubry, Eugene E (Architect)
8021 Marina Isles Ln
Holmes Beach, FL 34217-1063, USA

Aubry, Pierre (Hockey Player)
Quebec Nordiques
110 Rue Buisson
Cap-De-La-Madeleine, PQ G8V 1K4, CANADA

Aubuchon, Chet (Basketball Player)
107 2nd St NW
Ruskin, FL 33570-3929, USA

Aubuchon, Remi (Producer)
c/o Staff Member *International Creative Management (ICM-LA)*
10250 Constellation Blvd
Los Angeles, CA 90067-6200, USA

Auburn, David (Writer)
97 W Elmwood Ave
Clawson, MI 48017-1228, USA

Auchincloss, Louis S (Writer)
1111 Park Ave # 14D
New York, NY 10128-1234, USA

Aucoin, Adrian (Hockey Player)
Vancouver Canucks
19101 Mandarin Grove Pl
Tampa, FL 33647-3095, USA

AuCoin, Les (Misc)
Bogle & Gates
601 13th St NW # 370
Washington, DC 20005-3807, USA

Aude, Rich (Baseball Player)
Pittsburgh Pirates
4817 Natoma Ave
Woodland Hills, CA 91364-3416, USA

Audet, Earl (Football Player)
Washington Redskins
3015 Thatcher Ave
Marina Del Rey, CA 90292-5532, USA

Audette, Donald (Hockey Player)
Buffalo Sabres
2605 Pecan Meadow Dr
Garland, TX 75040-3982, USA

Audick, Daniel (Football Player)
St Louis Cardinals
13253 Sparren Ave
San Diego, CA 92129-2324, USA

Audioslave (Music Group)
c/o Staff Member *Creative Artists Agency LCC (CAA-LA)*
2000 Avenue Of The Stars
Los Angeles, CA 90067-4700, USA

Audran, Stephane (Actor)
2F De Marthod
11 Rue Chanez 70016E, FRANCE

Auel, Jean M (Writer)
PO Box 8278
Portland, OR 97207-8278, USA

Auer, Barbara (Actor)
Agentur Carola Studlar
Neurieder Str 1C
Planegg 82152, GERMANY

Auer, Joe (Football Player)
Buffalo Bills
1138 Washington Ave
Winter Park, FL 32789-5657, USA

Auer, Scott (Football Player)
Kansas City Chiefs
2921 Burge Dr
Crown Point, IN 46307-8172, USA

Auerbach, Frank (Artist)
Marlborough Fine Art Gallery
6 Albermarle St
London W1X 4BY, UNITED KINGDOM (UK)

Auerbach, Rick (Baseball Player)
Milwaukee Brewers
2139 Stunt Rd
Calabasas, CA 91302-2358, USA

Auerbach, Stanley I (Misc)
3314 W End Ave Apt 202
Nashville, TN 37203-0916, USA

Auermann, Nadia (Model)
Elite Models
4 Rue de la Paiz
Paris 75002, FRANCE

Auermann, Nadja
Via San Vittore 40
Milan I-20123, ITALY

AufDerMaur, Melissa (Music Group, Musician)
Artist Group International
9560 Wilshire Blvd Ste 400
Beverly Hills, CA 90212-2416, USA

Auger, Brian (Music Group, Musician)
Earthtone
8306 Wilshire Blvd # 981
Beverly Hills, CA 90211-2304, USA

Auger, Claudine (Actor)
Artmedia
20 Ave Rapp
Paris 75007, FRANCE

Auger, Pierre V (Physicist)
12 Rue Emile Faguet
Paris 75014, FRANCE

Aughtman, Dowe (Football Player)
Dallas Cowboys
2 Buckhead Ln
Opelika, AL 36804-7645, USA

Augmon, Stacey (Basketball Player)
4212 Kessler Ridge Dr
Marietta, GA 30062, USA

August, Bille (Director)
2800 Lyngby
DENMARK

August, Don (Baseball Player)
Milwaukee Brewers
28372 Lorente
Mission Viejo, CA 92692-2240, USA

August, John (Director, Musician, Producer, Writer)
c/o David Kramer *United Talent Agency (UTA)*
9560 Wilshire Blvd Ste 500
Beverly Hills, CA 90212-2401, USA

August, Pernilla (Actor)
Royal Dramatic Theater
Box 5037
Stockholm 102 41, SWEDEN

August, Steve (Football Player)
Seattle Seahawks
7704 E 86th St
Tulsa, OK 74133-6651, USA

Augusta, Kim (Golfer)
16 Rachela Ct
East Providence, RI 02914-3063, USA

Augustain, Ira (Actor)
Diamond Artists
9200 W Sunset Blvd Ste 701
West Hollywood, CA 90069-3602, USA

Augustana (Musician)
c/o Staff Member *Paradigm (Monterey)*
509 Hartnell St
Monterey, CA 93940-2825, USA

Augustine, Dave (Baseball Player)
Pittsburgh Pirates
PO Box 1114
Saint Albans, WV 25177-1114, USA

Augustine, Jerry (Baseball Player)
Milwaukee Brewers
S74W13490 Courtland Ln
Muskego, WI 53150-3937, USA

Augustine, Norman R (Business Person)
24131 Doreen Dr
Gaithersburg, MD 20882-3001, USA

Augustnyiak, Jerry (Music Group, Musician)
Agency for Performing Arts
405 S Beverly Dr Ste 500
Beverly Hills, CA 90212-4425, USA

Augustus, Seimone (Basketball Player)
Matheny Sears Linkert & Long, LLP
3638 American River Dr
C/O Eric Wiesel
Sacramento, CA 95864-5901, USA

Augustus, Sherman (Actor)
c/o Nadja Koglin *Richard Schwartz Management*
2934 1/2 N Beverly Glen Cir # 107
Los Angeles, CA 90077-1724, USA

Augustyniak, Mike (Football Player)
New York Jets
1305 Silver Lake Dr
Melbourne, FL 32940-1953, USA

Auker, Eldon L (Baseball Player)
Detroit Tigers
29675 Bristol Ln
Bingham Farms, MI 48025-4620, USA

Aulby, Mike
1591 Springmill Ponds Cir
Carmel, IN 46032-8552, USA

Aulenti, Gae (Architect)
4 Piazza San Marco
Milan 20121, ITALY

Ault, Chris (Coach, Football Coach)
University of Nevada
Athletic Dept
Reno, NV 89557-0001, USA

Ault, James M (Religious Leader)
1 Amoskegan Dr
Brunswick, ME 04011-9524, USA

Aumont, Michel
8 rue Herold
Paris 75001, FRANCE

Aurel, Jean
40 rue Lauriston
Paris F-75116, FRANCE

Auriemma, Geno (Basketball Player, Coach)
University of Connecticut
2095 Hillside Rd
Storrs Mansfield, CT 06269-9017, USA

Aurilla, Rich (Baseball Player)
San Francisco Giants
5448 E Mariposa St
Phoenix, AZ 85018-3124, USA

Ausanio, Joe (Baseball Player)
New York Yankees
646 Delaware Ave
Kingston, NY 12401-5141, USA

Ausbie, Hubert (Basketball Player)
Harlem Globetrotters
902 Arthur Dr
Little Rock, AR 72204-1524, USA

Ausmus, Brad (Baseball Player)
San Diego Padres
1644 Stratford Way
Del Mar, CA 92014-2444, USA

Ausoin, Derek (Baseball Player)
Montreal Expos
233 W 77th St Apt 5E
New York, NY 10024-6809, USA

Aust, Dennis (Baseball Player)
St Louis Cardinals
16252 Estuary Ct
Bokeelia, FL 33922-1535, USA

Auster, Paul (Director, Writer)
c/o Ron Bernstein *International Creative Management (ICM-LA)*
10250 Constellation Blvd
Los Angeles, CA 90067-6200, USA

Austin, A Woody (Golfer)
705B SE Melody Ln
Lees Summit, MO 64063-4380, USA

Austin, Alana (Actor)
c/o Lena Roklin *Roklin Management*
8530 Wilshire Blvd Ste 550
Beverly Hills, CA 90211-3133, USA

Austin, Bill (Football Player)
New York Giants
9412 Shellfish Ct
Las Vegas, NV 89117-0267, USA

Austin, Billy (Football Player)
Indianapolis Colts
3435 Westheimer Rd Apt 711
Houston, TX 77027-5359, USA

Austin, Charles (Athlete, Track Athlete)
514 Duncan Dr
San Marcos, TX 78666-4900, USA

Austin, Cliff (Football Player)
New Orleans Saints
1652 Valencia Rd
Decatur, GA 30032-5263, USA

Austin, Dallas (Actor)
c/o Tracy Christian *Don Buchwald & Associates Inc (LA)*
18000 Coastline Dr Apt 8
Malibu, CA 90265-5727, USA

Austin, Darlene
PO Box 171143
Nashville, TN 37217-8143, USA

Austin, Darrell (Football Player)
New York Jets
268 Austin Rd
Union, SC 29379-7658, USA

Austin, Debbie (Golfer)
6733 Bittersweet Ln
Orlando, FL 32819-4635, USA

Austin, Denise (Fitness Expert)
PrimeCare Systems, Inc
610 Thimble Shoals Blvd Ste 402A
Newport News, VA 23606-4509, USA

Austin, Hise (Football Player)
Green Bay Packers
31522 Crestwood Park
Conroe, TX 77385-7501, USA

Austin, Jeff (Baseball Player)
c/o Staff Member *Cincinnati Reds*
100 Cinergy Fld
Cinergy Field
Cincinnati, OH 45202, USA

Austin, Jeff (Musician)
c/o Staff Member *Paradigm (Monterey)*
509 Hartnell St
Monterey, CA 93940-2825, USA

Austin, Jim (Baseball Player)
Milwaukee Brewers
20974 Rootstown Ter
Ashburn, VA 20147-4839, USA

Austin, John (Basketball Player)
Baltimore Bullets
1330 Riggs St NW
Washington, DC 20009-4325, USA

Austin, Kent (Football Player)
St Louis Cardinals
704 Legends Crest Dr
Franklin, TN 37069-4659, USA

Austin, Ocie (Football Player)
Baltimore Colts
1531 Jefferson St
Oakland, CA 94612, USA

Austin, Patti (Music Group)
3 Loudon Dr Unit 8
Fishkill, NY 12524-1870, USA

Austin, Reggie (Football Player)
Chicago Bears
3339 Deerwood Ln
Rex, GA 30273-2475, USA

Austin, Rick (Baseball Player)
Cleveland Indians
6509 Claret Ct
Kansas City, MO 64152-6084, USA

Austin, Sherrie (Musician)
c/o Staff Member *William Morris Agency (WMA-TN)*
1600 Division St Ste 300
Nashville, TN 37203-2755, USA

Austin, Steve (Stone Cold) (Wrestler)
c/o Staff Member *World Wrestling Entertainment (WWE)*
1241 E Main St
Stamford, CT 06902-3520, USA

Austin, Teri (Actor)
4245 Laurelgrove Ave
Studio City, CA 91604-1624, USA

Austin, Thomas (Football Player)
Buffalo Bills
489 S El Camino Real
San Mateo, CA 94402-1727, USA

Austin, Tracy (Tennis Player)
1751 Pinnacle Dr Ste 1500
McLean, VA 22102-3833, USA

Austin-Grow, Vivian
140 W Via Lola
Palm Springs, CA 92262-4339, USA

Austin Jr, M P (Business Person)
BMC Software
2101 Citywest Blvd
Houston, TX 77042-2829, USA

Auston, Jim
c/o Staff Member *Curb Records (Nashville)*
48 Music Sq E
Nashville, TN 37203-4639, USA

Austregesilo de Athayde, Belarmino M (Journalist)
Rua Cosme Velho 599
Rio de Janeiro RJ, BRAZIL

The Celebrity Black Book 2008

Austrian, Robert (Physicist)
Univ of Pennsylvania
36 Hamilton Cir
Med Center
Philadelphia, PA 19130, USA

Auteuil, Daniel (Actor)
Artmedia
20 Ave Rapp
Paris 75007, FRANCE

Auth, Tony (Cartoonist, Editor)
Philadelphia Inquirer
Editorial Dept
1830 Town Center Dr
Langhome, PA 19047, USA

Autolitano, Astrid (Business Person)
Mattel Inc
333 Continental Blvd
El Segundo, CA 90245-5032, USA

Autrey, Billy (Football Player)
Chicago Bears
9810 Knoboak Dr
Houston, TX 77080-6432, USA

Autry, Alan (Actor)
David Shapira
193 N Robertson Blvd
Beverly Hills, CA 90211-2103, USA

Autry, Albert (Baseball Player)
Atlanta Braves
319 Hogans Valley Way
Cary, NC 27513-5682, USA

Autry, Jim (Golfer, Misc)
Professional Golfer's Assn
PO Box 109601
Palm Beach Gardens, FL 33410-9601,
USA

Auyeung, Jin (Musician)
c/o Staff Member Virgin Records (NY)
304 Park Ave S Fl 5
New York, NY 10010-4316, USA

Auzenne, Troy (Football Player)
Chicago Bears
1501 Bluff Ct
Diamond Bar, CA 91765-4301, USA

Avalon (Music Group)
PO Box 150867
Nashville, TN 37215-0867, USA

Avalon, Frankie (Actor, Music Group)
4303 Spring Forest Ln
Westlake Village, CA 91362-5605, USA

Avari, Erick (Actor)
c/o James Suskin James Suskin
Management
2 Charlton St Apt 5K
New York, NY 10014-4917, USA

Avary, Roger (Director)
c/o Staff Member Creative Artists Agency
LCC (CAA-LA)
2000 Avenue Of The Stars
Los Angeles, CA 90067-4700, USA

Avdelsayed, Gabriel (Religious Leader)
Coptic Orthodox Curch
427 W Side Ave
Jersey City, NJ 07304-1403, USA

Avdeyev, Sergei V (Cosmonaut)
Potchta Kosmonavtov
Moskovskoi Oblasti
Syvisdny Goroduk 141160, RUSSIA

Avedon, Doe
4333 Hayvenhurst Ave
Encino, CA 91436-3537, USA

Avellan, Elizabeth (Producer)
c/o Staff Member International Creative
Management (ICM-LA)
10250 Constellation Blvd
Los Angeles, CA 90067-6200, USA

Avellini, Bob (Football Player)
Chicago Bears
1085 Flamingo Dr
Roselle, IL 60172-4731, USA

Aven, Bruce (Baseball Player)
Cleveland Indians
1097 NW 167th Ave
Pembroke Pines, FL 33028-1479, USA

Averell, Tom (Football Player)
New York Titans
100 Highland Pines Ct Apt 32
Pittsburgh, PA 15237-2038, USA

Averitt, William (Basketball Player)
San Antonio Spurs
PO Box 1371
Hopkinsville, KY 42241-1371, USA

Averno, Sisto (Football Player)
Baltimore Colts
4759 Bonnie Brae Rd
Baltimore, MD 21208-2017, USA

Averre, Berton (Music Group, Musician)
17510 Posetano Rd
Pacific Palisades, CA 90272-4175, USA

Avery, Don (Football Player)
Washington Redskins
179 Rivo Alto Canal
Long Beach, CA 90803-4063, USA

Avery, Eric (Actor, Musician)
c/o Jeff Frasco Creative Artists Agency
LCC (CAA-LA)
2000 Avenue Of The Stars
Los Angeles, CA 90067-4700, USA

Avery, James (Actor)
c/o Joel King Pakula/King & Associates
9229 W Sunset Blvd Ste 315
Los Angeles, CA 90069-3403, USA

Avery, John (Football Player)
Miami Dolphins
12 Ballantree Dr
Asheville, NC 28803-2018, USA

Avery, Ken (Football Player)
New York Giants
625 Indian Ridge Dr
Nashville, TN 37221-4035, USA

Avery, Margaret (Actor)
Artists Agency
1180 S Beverly Dr Ste 301
Los Angeles, CA 90035-1154, USA

Avery, Mary Ellen (Doctor, Physicist)
52 Liberty St
Plymouth, MA 02360-4176, USA

Avery, Phyllis (Actor)
609 Sterling Pl
South Pasadena, CA 91030-1621, USA

Avery, Sean (Hockey Player)
c/o Staff Member Los Angeles Kings
1111 S Figueroa St
Los Angeles, CA 90015-1300, USA

Avery, Steve (Football Player)
Houston Oilers
34825 Lake Drive
Oconomow, WI 53066, USA

Avery, Steven T (Steve) (Baseball Player)
Atlanta Braves
22721 Coachlight Cir
Taylor, MI 48180-6381, USA

Avery, Val (Actor)
84 Grove St Apt 19
New York, NY 10014-3567, USA

Avery, William H (Governor)
509 Grove St # 109
Wakefield, KS 67487-9159, USA

Avery, William J (Business Person)
Crown Cork & Seal
1 Crown Way
Philadelphia, PA 19154-4599, USA

Avezzano, Joe (Football Player)
Boston Patriots
1208 Lakeridge Ln
Irving, TX 75063-5080, USA

Aviance, Kevin (Musician)
Kevin Aviance World
115 E 57th St Fl 11
New York, NY 10022-2120, USA

Avila, Alejandro (Actor)
c/o Staff Member Televisa
Blvd Adolfo Lopez Mateos 232
Colonia San Angel INN
DF CP 01060, MEXICO

Avila, Mariana (Actor)
c/o Staff Member Televisa
Blvd Adolfo Lopez Mateos 232
Colonia San Angel INN
DF CP 01060, MEXICO

Avildsen, John G (Director)
2423 Briarcrest Rd
Beverly Hills, CA 90210-1819, USA

Aviles, Ramon (Baseball Player)
Boston Red Sox
2 Calle E # C19
Manati, PR 00674-4028, USA

Avinger, Clarence (Football Player)
New York Giants
3901 W Rogers Ave
Tampa, FL 33611-3526, USA

Avital, Mili (Actor)
Creative Artists Agency
9830 Wilshire Blvd
Beverly Hills, CA 90212-1804, USA

Avnet, Jon (Director, Producer)
c/o Staff Member Brooklyn Films
3815 Hughes Ave
Culver City, CA 90232-2715, USA

Avnet, Jonathan M (Jon) (Director,
Producer)
3815 Hughes Ave
Culver City, CA 90232-2715, USA

Avni, Aki
c/o Neil Bagg Don Buchwald &
Associates Inc (LA)
6500 Wilshire Blvd Ste 2200
Los Angeles, CA 90048-4942, USA

Avory, Mike (Musician)
Larry Page
29 Rushton Mews
London W11 1RB, UNITED KINGDOM
(UK)

Awalt, Rob (Football Player)
St Louis Cardinals
5011 Highgrove Ct
Granite Bay, CA 95746-7101, USA

Awrey, Donald W (Don) (Hockey Player)
Boston Bruins
14960 Collier Blvd # 1036
Naples, FL 34119-7713, USA

Awsome
10 Bourlit Close
London, ENGLAND W1T 7PJ, UNITED
KINGDOM (UK)

Awtrey, Dennis (Basketball Player)
520 W Clarendon Ave Unit D4
Phoenix, AZ 85013-3430, USA

Ax, Emmanuel (Music Group, Musician)
c/o Staff Member Askonas Holt Ltd
Lonsdale Chambers
27 Chancery St
WC2A 1PF, UNITED KINGDOM (UK)

Axelsson, P J (Hockey Player)
Boston Bruins
121 Mount Vernon St
Boston, MA 02108-1104, USA

Axtell, George C (War Hero)
615 Laurel Lake Dr Unit A103
Columbus, NC 28722-7425, USA

Ay-O (Artist)
2-6-38 Matsuyama
Kiyoseshi
Tokyo, JAPAN

Ayala, Alexis (Actor)
c/o Staff Member Televisa
Blvd Adolfo Lopez Mateos 232
Colonia San Angel INN
DF CP 01060, MEXICO

Ayala, Paul (Boxer)
7524 Creek Meadow Dr
Fort Worth, TX 76123-1980, USA

Ayanna, Charlotte (Actor)
Industry Entertainment
955 Carrillo Dr Ste 300
Los Angeles, CA 90048-5400, USA

Aybar, Manny (Athlete)
401 E Jefferson St
Phoenix, AZ 85004-2438, USA

Aybar, Manuel (Baseball Player)
St Louis Cardinals
3020 SW 189th Ter
Miramar, FL 33029-5861, USA

Ayckbourn, Alan (Director, Writer)
M Ramsay
14A Goodwins Ct
Saint Martin's Lane
London WC2N 4LL, UNITED KINGDOM
(UK)

Aycock, Alice (Artist)
62 Greene St
New York, NY 10012-4346, USA

Aycock, H David (Business Person)
Nucor Corp
2100 Rexford Rd
Charlotte, NC 28211-3589, USA

Aycock, Thomas (Golfer)
2124 Glendale Ave
Texarkana, AR 71854-3564, USA

Aycox, Nicki (Actor)
c/o Erik Kritzer Fenton-Kritzer
Entertainment
8840 Wilshire Blvd Fl 3
Beverly Hills, CA 90211-2606, USA

Aydelette, William (Football Player)
Green Bay Packers
115 Woodward Rd
Trussville, AL 35173-1251, USA

Ayer, David (Producer, Writer)
Crave Films
3312 W Sunset Blvd
Los Angeles, CA 90026-2118, USA

Ayers, Chuck (Cartoonist)
Unversal Press Syndicate
4520 Main St
Kansas City, MO 64111-1876, USA

Ayers, Dick (Cartoonist)
64 Beech St W
White Plains, NY 10604-2230, USA

Ayers, Randy (Basketball Player, Coach)
Philadelphia 76ers
1st Union Center 3601 S Broad St
Philadelphia, PA 19148, USA

Ayers, Roy E Jr (Music Group, Musician)
Associated Booking Corp
PO Box 2055
New York, NY 10021-0051, USA

Ayers, Sam (Actor)
c/o Staff Member *Bobby Ball Talent Agency*
4605 Lankershim Blvd Ste 721
North Hollywood, CA 91602-1878, USA

Aykroyd, Dan (Actor, Comedian)
c/o Staff Member *Creative Artists Agency LCC (CAA-LA)*
2000 Avenue Of The Stars
Los Angeles, CA 90067-4700, USA

Aylesworth, Reiko (Actor)
c/o Staff Member *Innovative Artists (LA)*
1505 10th St
Santa Monica, CA 90401-2805, USA

Aylward, John (Actor)
c/o Staff Member *Mitchell K Stubbs & Assoc (MKS)*
8695 Washington Blvd Ste 204
Culver City, CA 90232-7419, USA

Aylwin Azocar, Patricio (President)
Teresa Salas 786
Providencia, Santiago, CHILE

Ayrault, Bob (Baseball Player)
Philadelphia Phillies
3012 Green Dr
Carson City, NV 89701-3363, USA

Ayrault, Joe (Baseball Player)
Atlanta Braves
2338 Vintage St
Sarasota, FL 34240-8317, USA

Ayre, Calvin (Business Person)
Bodog
Oficentro Ejecutivo Sabana Sur
Edificio 7, 5 Piso
San Jose 00000, COSTA RICA

Ayres, Leah
15718 Milbank St
Encino, CA 91436-1637, USA

Ayres, Rosalind (Actor)
c/o Staff Member *Lou Coulson Agency*
37 Berwick St Fl 1
London WIV 3RF, UNITED KINGDOM (UK)

Aytes, Rochelle (Actor)
c/o Seth Greenky *Green Key Mgmt (NY)*
251 W 89th St Apt 4A
New York, NY 10024-1713, USA

AZ, Martyo (Reality TV Star)
c/o Staff Member *Creative Artists Agency LCC (CAA-LA)*
2000 Avenue Of The Stars
Los Angeles, CA 90067-4700, USA

Azar, Steve (Music Group)
Gold Mountain
2 Music Cir S Ste 212
Nashville, TN 37203-5708, USA

Azaria, Hank (Actor)
15030 Ventura Blvd # 710
Sherman Oaks, CA 91403-5470, USA

Azcue, Jose (Baseball Player)
Cincinnati Reds
7609 W 115th St
Overland Park, KS 66210-2614, USA

Azelby, Joe (Football Player)
Buffalo Bills
14 Pierce Ave
Cresskill, NJ 07626-1126, USA

Azimov, Yakhyo (Prime Minister)
Prime Minister's Office
Rudaki Prosp 42
Dushaube 743051, TAJIKISTAN

Azinger, Paul (Golfer)
7847 Chick Evans Pl
Sarasota, FL 34240-8752, USA

Aziz, Tariq (Prime Minister)
Prime Minister's Office
Karadat Mariam
Baghdad, IRAQ

Azizi, Anthony (Actor)
c/o Staff Member *Geddes Agency, The*
8430 Santa Monica Blvd Ste 200
Los Angeles, CA 90069-4253, USA

Azlan, Muhibuddin Shah (King)
Sultan's Palace
Istana Bukit Serene
Kuala Lumpur, MALAYSIA

Azlynn, Valerie (Actor)
c/o Devon Jackson *Trademark Talent*
4758 Allott Ave
Sherman Oaks, CA 91423-2403, USA

Azmi, Shabana (Actor, Bollywood)
702 Sagar Samrat
Greenfields Juhu
Mumbai, MS 400049, INDIA

Aznar, Jose Maria (Prime Minister)
Prime Minister's Office
Complejo de las Moncloa
Madrid 28071, SPAIN

Aznavour, Charles (Actor, Musician, Songwriter, Writer)
Agents Associes (AA)
210 rue du Faubourg st
Honore, PARIS, FRANCE

Azria, Max (Designer, Fashion Designer)
BCBG/Max Azaria
2761 Fruitland Ave
Los Angeles, CA 90058-3607, USA

Azul Azul (Music Group)
c/o Staff Member *Sony Music Miami*
605 Lincoln Rd Fl 7
Miami Beach, FL 33139-2900, USA

Azuma, Norio (Artist)
276 Riverside Dr
New York, NY 10025-5204, USA

Azuma, Takamitsu (Architect)
Azuma Architects
3-6-1 Minami-Aoyama
Minatoku
Tokyo 107, JAPAN

Azumah, Jerry (Football Player)
39 King St
Worcester, MA 01610-2454, USA

Azzara, Candice (Actor)
Meridian Artists
20720 Ventura Blvd Ste 300
Woodland Hills, CA 91364-6266, USA

Azzaro, Chrissy (Designer, Fashion Designer)
c/o Staff Member *Perception Public Relations LLC*
3940 Laurel Cyn
Pmb 169
Studio City, CA 91604-3709, USA

Azzi, Jennifer (Basketball Player)
San Antonio Silver Stars
1 Sbc Center Pkwy
San Antonio, TX 78219-3604, USA

B

B, Jon (Musician, Songwriter, Writer)
Devour Mgmt
6399 Wilshire Blvd Ste 426
Los Angeles, CA 90048-5714, USA

B-52's, The (Music Group)
c/o Staff Member *Direct Management Group*
947 N La Cienega Blvd Ste G
Los Angeles, CA 90069-4700, USA

B-Real (Artist, Musician)
William Morris Agency
151 El Camino Dr
Beverly Hills, CA 90212-2775, USA

B2K (Music Group)
c/o Chris Stokes *Ultimate Group, The*
848 N La Cienega Blvd Ste 201
West Hollywood, CA 90069-6600, USA

Baab, Mike (Football Player)
Cleveland Browns
1705 Windlea Dr
Euless, TX 76040-4016, USA

Baack, Steve (Football Player)
Detroit Lions
15335 SW Turnagain Dr
Portland, OR 97224-2579, USA

Baba, Enclik Abdul Ghafar Bin (Prime Minister)
Rural Development Ministry
Jalan Raja Laut
Kuala Lumpur 50606, MALAYSIA

Babando, Pete (Hockey Player)
Boston Bruins
50 Golden Ave W
Timmins, ON P4N 3K3, CANADA

Babashoff, Jack (Swimmer)
4859 Monroe Ave
San Diego, CA 92115-3246, USA

Babashoff, Shirley (Swimmer)
17254 Santa Clara St
Fountain Valley, CA 92708-3337, USA

Babatunde, Obba (Actor)
Stone Manners
6500 Wilshire Blvd Ste 550
Los Angeles, CA 90048-4950, USA

Babb, Charlie (Football Player)
Miami Dolphins
371 Heron Ave
Naples, FL 34108-2115, USA

Babb, Eugene (Football Player)
5110 W 9th Ave
Stillwater, OK 74074-1465, USA

Babb-Sprague, Kristen (Swimmer)
4677 Pine Valley Cir
Stockton, CA 95219-1881, USA

Babbar, Raj (Actor, Bollywood)
Nepathaya Plot 20
Gulmohar Road JVPD Scheme
Mumbai, MS 400049, INDIA

Babbidge, Homes D Jr (Educator)
3 Diving St
Stonington, CT 06378-1405, USA

Babbit, Jamie (Director, Producer, Writer)
c/o Staff Member *Innovative Artists (LA)*
1505 10th St
Santa Monica, CA 90401-2805, USA

Babbitt, Bruce E (Governor, Secretary)
5169 Watson St NW
Washington, DC 20016-5330, USA

Babbitt, Milton B (Composer)
222 Western Way
Princeton, NJ 08540-5306, USA

Babbitt, Natalie (Writer)
Farrar Strous Giroux
19 Union Sq W
New York, NY 10003-3304, USA

Babcock, Barbara (Actor)
PO Box 222271
Carmel, CA 93922-2271, USA

Babcock, Bob (Baseball Player)
Texas Rangers
1192 Johns Ln
New Castle, PA 16101-6774, USA

Babcock, Mike (Coach, Hockey Player)
c/o Staff Member *Detroit Red Wings*
600 Civic Center Dr
Joe Luis Arena
Detroit, MI 48226-4419, USA

Babcock, Tim M (Governor)
Ox Bow Ranch
PO Box 877
Helena, MT 59624-0877, USA

Babcock, Todd (Actor)
c/o Staff Member *Gage Group, The (LA)*
14724 Ventura Blvd Ste 505
Sherman Oaks, CA 91403-3505, USA

Babe, Warren (Hockey Player)
Minnesota North Stars
601 6 Ave SW
Medicine Hat, AB T1A 5B3, CANADA

Babenco, Hector E (Director)
c/o Johnnie Planco *Untitled Entertainment (NY)*
322 8th Ave Ste 601
New York, NY 10001-6715, USA

Babich, Bob (Football Player)
San Diego Chargers
4994 Mount Ashmun Dr
San Diego, CA 92111-3930, USA

Babilonia, Tai (Figure Skater)
13889 Valley Vista Blvd
Sherman Oaks, CA 91423-4662, USA

Babin, Rex (Cartoonist, Editor)
Sacramento Bee
21st & Q Sts
Editorial Dept
Sacramento, CA 95816, USA

Babinecz, John (Football Player)
Dallas Cowboys
810 Trout Run Dr
Malvern, PA 19355-3148, USA

Babitt, Shooty (Baseball Player)
Oakland A's
4912 Plaza Way
Richmond, CA 94804-4346, USA

Babu, Ganesh (Actor)
No 1 Janaki Avenue
Abhiramapuram
Chennai, TN 600 028, INDIA

Baby, John (Hockey Player)
Cleveland Barons
3232 Eden Township Rd
Sudbury, ON P3G 1G1, CANADA

Baby, Peggy (Actor)
2219 Canyon Brook Ln
Newman, CA 95360-2407, USA

Babych, Dave (Hockey Player)
Winnipeg Jets
1315 Wellington Cres
Winnipeg, MB R3N 0A9, CANADA

Babych, Wayne (Hockey Player)
St Louis Blues
1315 Wellington Cres
Winnipeg, MB R3N 0A9, CANADA

Baby's
1545 Archer Rd
Bronx, NY 10462-5817, USA

Baca, John P (War Hero)
PO Box 9203
San Diego, CA 92169-0203, USA

Bacall, Lauren (Actor)
Dakota Hotel
1 W 72nd St Apt 43
New York, NY 10023-3418, USA

Baccarin, Morena (Actor)
c/o Scott Wexler *3 Arts Entertainment Inc*
9460 Wilshire Blvd Fl 7
Beverly Hills, CA 90212-2713, USA

Bach, Barbara (Actor)
2 Glynde Mews
London SW3 1SB, UNITED KINGDOM (UK)

Bach, Catherine (Actor)
c/o Steve Rohr *Rohr Talent Public Relations*
1901 Avenue Of The Stars Ste 365
Los Angeles, CA 90067-6025, USA

Bach, Emmanuelle (Actor)
Artmedia
20 Ave Rapp
Paris 75007, FRANCE

Bach, Jillian (Actor)
c/o Staff Member *Metropolitan*
4500 Wilshire Blvd Fl 2
Los Angeles, CA 90010-3858, USA

Bach, Pamela (Actor)
William Morris Agence
151 El Camino Dr
Beverly Hills, CA 90212-2775, USA

Bach, Richard (Writer)
Dell Publishing
1540 Broadway
New York, NY 10036-4039, USA

Bach, Sebastian (Actor, Music Group)
Premier Talent
3 E 54th St # 1100
New York, NY 10022-3108, USA

Bach, Steven K (Producer)
101 Park Ave # 4300
New York, NY 10178-0002, USA

Bachan, Abhishek (Bollywood)
Pratiksha, 10th Rd
JVPD Scheme
Mumbai 400049, INDIA

Bachan, Jaya (Actor, Bollywood)
Pratiksha 10th Road
JVPD Scheme
Mumbai 400049, INDIA

Bachans (Actor)
Pratiksha 10th Rd
JVPD Scheme
Mumbai 400049, INDIA

Bacharach, Burt (Composer, Musician)
681 Amalfi Dr
Pacific Palisades, CA 90272-4507, USA

Bachardy, Don (Writer)
145 Adelaide Dr
Santa Monica, CA 90402-1223, USA

Bachchan, Amitabh (Actor, Bollywood)
Pratiksha
10th Road Juhu Scheme
Mumbai, MS 400049, INDIA

Bachchan, Jaya (Actor, Bollywood)
Pratiksha 10rh Road
JVPD Scheme
Mumbai, MS 400049, INDIA

Bacher, Avron (Ali) (Cricketer, Misc)
United Cricket Board
PO Box 55009
Northlands 2116, SOUTH AFRICA

Bachleda-Curus, Alicja (Actor)
c/o Sarah Lum *Leverage Management*
1610 Broadway
Santa Monica, CA 90404-2792, USA

Bachman, Jay (Football Player)
Denver Broncos
4602 Delphene Cir
Louisville, KY 40241-6109, USA

Bachman, Randy (Music Group, Songwriter, Writer)
Entertainment Services
6400 Pleasant Park Dr
Chanhassen, MN 55317-8804, USA

Bachman, Tal (Music Group, Musician, Songwriter, Writer)
Q Prime
729 7th Ave Rm 1600
New York, NY 10019-6880, USA

Bachman, Ted (Football Player)
Seattle Seahawks
2890 Huntington Blvd Apt 110
Fresno, CA 93721-2346, USA

Bachmann, Maria (Music Group, Musician)
Columbia Artists Mgmt Inc
1790 Broadway Fl 6
New York, NY 10019-1412, USA

Bachrach, Louis F Jr (Photographer)
Bachrach Inc
647 Boylston St # 2
Boston, MA 02116-2804, USA

Bachtol, Hubert (Football Player)
Baltimore Colts
7917 Taranto Dr
Austin, TX 78729-7440, USA

Bacic, Steve (Actor)
c/o Staff Member *Progressive Artists Agency*
400 S Beverly Dr Ste 216
Beverly Hills, CA 90212-4404, USA

Baciocco, Albert Juozas Cardinal (Admiral)
747 Pitt St
Mount Pleasant, SC 29464-5022, USA

Backe, Brandon (Baseball Player)
Tampa Bay Devil Rays
2550 Quaker Dr
Texas City, TX 77590-3740, USA

Backe, John D (Business Person)
Backe Group
83 General Warren Blvd Ste 100
Malvern, PA 19355-1252, USA

Backis, Audrys Juozas Cardinal (Religious Leader)
Sventaragio 4
Vilnius, LITHUANIA

Backley, Stephen (Steve) (Athlete, Track Athlete)
Cambridge Harriers
56A-60 Glenhurst Ave
Bexley, Kent DA5 3QN, UNITED KINGDOM (UK)

Backman, Jules (Economist, Writer)
59 Crane Rd
Scarsdale, NY 10583-4347, USA

Backman, Mike (Hockey Player)
New York Rangers
50 Pond Pl
Cos Cob, CT 06807-2220, USA

Backman, Walter W (Wally) (Baseball Player)
New York Mets
241 SE Mercury Ln
Prineville, OR 97754-2803, USA

Backstreet Boys (Music Group)
c/o Johnny Wright *Wright-Crear Management*
3815 Hughes Ave
Culver City, CA 90232-2715, USA

Backstrom, Ralph (Hockey Player)
Montreal Canadiens
220 Habitat Cir
Windsor, CO 80550-6196, USA

Backus, Billy (Boxer)
308 N Main St
Canastota, NY 13032-1070, USA

Backus, George E (Geophysicist, Physicist)
9362 La Jolla Farms Rd
La Jolla, CA 92037-1125, USA

Backus, Gus (Musician)
Lustig Talent
PO Box 770850
Orlando, FL 32877-0850, USA

Backus, Jeff (Football Player)
Detroit Lions
4624 Fitzpatrick Way
Norcross, GA 30092-1004, USA

Backus, Sharon (Coach)
University of California
Athletic Dept
Los Angeles, CA 90024, USA

Bacon, Coy (Football Player)
Los Angeles Rams
1017 S 8th St
Ironton, OH 45638-1944, USA

Bacon, Edmund N (Architect)
1025 N 4th St Apt D
Philadelphia, PA 19123-1533, USA

Bacon, James (Writer)
10982 Topeka Dr
Northridge, CA 91326-2322, USA

Bacon, Kelvin (Actor)
PO Box 668
Sharon, CT 06069-0668, USA

Bacon, Kevin (Actor)
15030 Ventura Blvd # 710
Sherman Oaks, CA 91403-5470, USA

Bacon, Michael (Actor)
c/o Jennifer Lee Garland *Circle Talent Associates*
433 N Camden Dr Ste 400
Beverly Hills, CA 90210-4408, USA

Bacon, Nicky D (War Hero)
Medal of Honor Society
40 Patriots Point Rd
Mount Pleasant, SC 29464-4377, USA

Bacon, Roger F (Admiral)
24285 Johnson Rd NW
Poulsbo, WA 98370-9606, USA

Bacon Brothers, The (Music Group)
c/o Staff Member *Paradigm (Monterey)*
509 Hartnell St
Monterey, CA 93940-2825, USA

Bacot, J Carter (Financier)
48 Porter Pl
Montclair, NJ 07042-2036, USA

Bacs, Ludovic (Composer)
31 D Golescu
Sc III E7 V Ap 87
Bucharest 1, ROMANIA

Bacsik, Mike (Baseball Player)
Texas Rangers
4014 Falcon Lake Dr
Arlington, TX 76016-4126, USA

Bacuicchi, Antonello (Misc)
Co-Regent's Office
Government Palace
San Marino 47031, SAN MARINO

Bad Company (Music Group)
c/o Staff Member *Creative Artists Agency LCC (CAA-LA)*
2000 Avenue Of The Stars
Los Angeles, CA 90067-4700, USA

Bada, Jeffrey (Misc)
Scripps Institute of Oceanography
Chemistry Dept
La Jolla, CA 92093, USA

Badalamenti, Angelo (Composer)
11 Fidelian Way
Lincoln Park, NJ 07035-1534, USA

Badalucco, Michael (Actor)
Manhattan Beach Studios
1600 Rosecrans Ave # 1A
Manhattan Beach, CA 90266-3708, USA

Badawi, Abdullah Ahamad (Prime Minister)
Prime Minister's Office
Jalan Dato Onn
Kuala Lumpur 50502, MALAYSIA

Baddeley, Aaron (Golfer)
c/o Staff Member *Pro-Sport Management*
7373 E Doubletree Ranch Rd Ste 170
Scottsdale, AZ 85258-2036, USA

Badel, Sarah
4 Ovington Gardens
London, ENGLAND SW3 1LS, UNITED KINGDOM (UK)

Badelt, Klaus (Musician)
Gorfaine/Schwartz
4111 W Alameda Ave Ste 509
Burbank, CA 91505-4171, USA

Bader, Diedrich (Actor)
c/o Joel Rudnick *Paradigm (LA)*
360 N Crescent Dr
North Bldg
Beverly Hills, CA 90210-6820, USA

Badger, Brad (Football Player)
c/o Team Member *Oakland Raiders*
1220 Harbor Bay Pkwy
Alameda, CA 94502-6570, USA

Badgley, Mark (Designer, Fashion Designer)
Badgley Mischka
525 Fashion Ave
New York, NY 10018-4901, USA

Badgley, Mark (Fashion Designer)
c/o Staff Member *Badgley Mischka*
215 W 40th St Fl 9
New York, NY 10018-1575, USA

Badgley, Penn (Actor)
c/o Jeff Kolodny *William Morris Agency (WMA-LA)*
1 William Morris Pl
Beverly Hills, CA 90212-4261, USA

Badham, John M (Director)
Badham Company
344 Clerendon Road
Beverly Hills, CA 90210, USA

Badham, Mary (Actor)
3344 Clerendon Rd
Beverly Hills, CA 90210-1059, USA

Badie, Mina (Actor)
c/o Staff Member *Rigberg-Rugolo Entertainment*
1180 S Beverly Dr Ste 601
Los Angeles, CA 90035-1158, USA

Badly Drawn Boy (Music Group)
c/o Staff Member *Paradigm (Monterey)*
509 Hartnell St
Monterey, CA 93940-2825, USA

Badnarik, Michael (Politician)
Badnarik Campaign Headquarters
6633 E Highway 290 E
Austin, TX 78723-1172, USA

Badu, Erykah (Musician, Songwriter, Writer)
c/o Cara Lewis *William Morris Agency (WMA-NY)*
1325 Avenue Of The Americas
New York, NY 10019-6026, USA

Badura-Skoda, Paul (Composer, Musician)
Zuckerkandlgass 14
Vienna 1190, AUSTRIA

Baechtold, James (Basketball Player)
Baltimore Bullets
104 Pleasant Ridge Dr
Richmond, KY 40475-3529, USA

Baeling, Becky (Musician)
c/o Staff Member *Diva Central Inc*
7510 W Sunset Blvd Ste 1445
Los Angeles, CA 90046-3408, USA

Baer, Amy (Business Person)
c/o Staff Member *Columbia Pictures*
10202 Washington Blvd
Culver City, CA 90232-3119, USA

Baer, Gordy (Bowler)
8577 Tullamore Dr
Tinley Park, IL 60487-4774, USA

Baer, Parley
4967 Bilmoor Ave
Tarzana, CA 91356-4412, USA

Baer, Robert J (Jacob) (General)
6213 Militia Ct
Fairfax Station, VA 22039-1325, USA

Baerga, Carlos (Baseball Player)
c/o Staff Member *Washington Nationals*
2400 East Capitol Street SE
Rfk Stadium
Washington, DC 20003, USA

Baez, Eddie (DJ)
c/o Staff Member *Diva Central Inc*
7510 W Sunset Blvd Ste 1445
Los Angeles, CA 90046-3408, USA

Baez, Joan (Musician, Songwriter, Writer)
c/o Staff Member *Vanguard Records*
2700 Pennsylvania Ave
Santa Monica, CA 90404-4066, USA

Baez, Jose (Baseball Player)
Seattle Mariners
153 Lexington Ave
Jersey City, NJ 07304-1203, USA

Baeza, Braulio (Jockey)
Janice Blake
204 Raven Dr
Trail Creek, IN 46360-5730, USA

Baeza, Paloma (Actor)
PFD
Drury House
34-43 Russell St
London WC2B 5HA, UNITED KINGDOM (UK)

Bafaro, Michael (Director, Writer)
c/o Staff Member *Lenhoff & Lenhoff*
830 Palm Ave
West Hollywood, CA 90069-4009, USA

Bagabandi, Ntsaagiyn (President)
President's Office
Great Hural
Ulan Bator, MONGOLIA

Bagdasarian Jr, Ross (Actor, Producer)
c/o Staff Member *Bagdasarian Productions*
1192 E Mountain Dr
Montecito, CA 93108-1119, USA

Bagge, Peter (Artist)
c/o Staff Member *Fantagraphics Books*
7563 Lake City Way NE
Seattle, WA 98115-4218, USA

Baggetta, Vincent (Actor)
3928 Madelia Ave
Sherman Oaks, CA 91403-4624, USA

Baggio, Roberto (Soccer Player)
Bologna FC
Via Casteldebole 10
Bologna 40132, ITALY

Baggott, Julianna (Writer)
Pocket Books
1230 Avenue Of The Americas
New York, NY 10020-1586, USA

Bagian, James P (Astronaut)
21537 Holmbury Rd
Northville, MI 48167-1021, USA

Bagley, John (Basketball Player)
90 Harral Ave
Bridgeport, CT 06604-3001, USA

Bagnal, Charles W (General)
Ratchford Assoc
221 W Springs Rd
Columbia, SC 29223-6948, USA

Bagwell, Jeffrey R (Jeff) (Baseball Player)
Houston Astros
4 Saddle Crk
Houston, TX 77024-6834, USA

Bagwell, Marcus (Buff) (Wrestler)
213 Morning Mist Way
Woodstock, GA 30189-8194, USA

Bagwell, Marcus (Buff) (Wrestler)
c/o Staff Member *Ultimate Pros*
3412 S Moonflower Ave
Sioux Falls, SD 57110-4420, USA

Baham, Curtis (Football Player)
Seattle Seahawks
5936 Oxford Pl
New Orleans, LA 70131-3908, USA

Bahns, Maxine (Actor)
c/o Jerry Shandrew *Shandrew Public Relations*
1050 S Stanley Ave
Los Angeles, CA 90019-6634, USA

Bahouth, Peter (Misc)
Greenpeace
702 H St NW Ste 300
Washington, DC 20001-3876, USA

Bahr, Chris (Football Player)
Cincinnati Bengals
122 Kaywood Dr
Boalsburg, PA 16827-1686, USA

Bahr, Ed (Baseball Player)
Pittsburgh Pirates
326 217th Pl SW
Bothell, WA 98021-8228, USA

Bahr, Egon (Government Official)
Ollenhauerster 1
Bonn 53113, GERMANY

Bahr, Matthew D (Matt) (Football Player)
Pittsburgh Steelers
53 Parkridge Ln
Pittsburgh, PA 15228-1105, USA

Bahr, Morton (Misc)
Communications Workers Union
501 3rd St NW
Washington, DC 20001-2760, USA

Bahr, Walter (Soccer Player)
250 Elks Road
Boalsburg, PA 16827, USA

Bai, Pandari (Actor, Bollywood)
54 Pillayar Koil Street
Vadapalani
Chennai, TN 600026, INDIA

Bai, Yang (Actor)
978 Huashan Road
Shanghai 200050, CHINA

Bailar, Benjamin F (Educator, Government Official)
410 Walnut Rd
Lake Forest, IL 60045-2254, USA

Bailes, Scott (Baseball Player)
Cleveland Indians
2415 E Edgewood St
Springfield, MO 65804-3905, USA

Bailey, Cory (Baseball Player)
Boston Red Sox
3822 2nd Dr NE
Bradenton, FL 34208-5074, USA

Bailey, Damon (Basketball Player)
Indiana Pacers
723 Diamond Rd
Heltonville, IN 47436-8559, USA

Bailey, Don (Football Player)
Indianapolis Colts
14831 NW 7th Ave
North Miami, FL 33168-3105, USA

Bailey, Ed (Baseball Player)
Cincinnati Reds
642 Broome Rd
Knoxville, TN 37909-2107, USA

Bailey, Eion (Actor)
c/o Staff Member *I/D PR (LA)*
8409 Santa Monica Blvd
West Hollywood, CA 90069-4209, USA

Bailey, Elmer (Football Player)
Miami Dolphins
PO Box 551991
Opa Locka, FL 33055-0991, USA

Bailey, F Lee (Attorney, Attorney General, General)
Beverly & Freeman
823 N Olive Ave
West Palm Beach, FL 33401-3709, USA

Bailey, G W (Actor)
c/o Staff Member *Leavitt Talent Group*
6404 Wilshire Blvd Ste 950
Los Angeles, CA 90048-5529, USA

Bailey, Harold (Football Player)
Houston Oilers
22502 Prince George Ln
Katy, TX 77449-2723, USA

Bailey, Howard (Baseball Player)
Detroit Tigers
11674 156th Ave
West Olive, MI 49460-9388, USA

Bailey, Jim (Football Player)
Baltimore Colts
5219 Stone Creek Ct
Lawrence, KS 66049-4792, USA

Bailey, Joel
6550 Murietta Ave
Van Nuys, CA 91401-1511, USA

Bailey, John (Cinematographer)
United Talent Agency
9560 Wilshire Blvd Ste 500
Beverly Hills, CA 90212-2401, USA

Bailey, Johnny L (Football Player)
Chicago Bears
7225 Bellerive Dr Apt 123
Houston, TX 77036-3116, USA

Bailey, Karsten (Football Player)
Seattle Seahawks
16 Salbide Ave
Newnan, GA 30263-2501, USA

Bailey, Keith E (Business Person)
Williams Companies
1 One Williams Ctr
Tulsa, OK 74172-0140, USA

Bailey, Leonard L (Doctor)
Loma Linda University
Medical School
Loma Linda, CA 92350-0001, USA

Bailey, Mark (Baseball Player)
Houston Astros
32703 Waltham Xing
Fulshear, TX 77441-4203, USA

Bailey, Mark (Football Player)
Kansas City Chiefs
3229 Corniche Ln
Roseville, CA 95661-3970, USA

Bailey, Maxwell C (General)
306 2nd St
Paris, KY 40361-1641, USA

Bailey, Michael (Doctor)
Northwestern University
Psychology Dept
Evanston, IL 60208-0001, USA

Bailey, Norman S (Opera Singer)
84 Warham Road
South Croydon, Surrey CR2 6LB, UNITED KINGDOM (UK)

Bailey, Paul (Writer)
79 Davisville Road
London W12 9SH, UNITED KINGDOM
(UK)

Bailey, Philip (Musician)
Covenant Agency
123 California Ave Apt 116
Santa Monica, CA 90403-3560, USA

Bailey, Razzy (Musician, Songwriter, Writer)
Doc Sedelmeier
PO Box 62
Geneva, NE 68361-0062, USA

Bailey, Robert M (Football Player)
Los Angeles Rams
15325 SW 99th Ave
Miami, FL 33157-1708, USA

Bailey, Roger (Baseball Player)
Colorado Rockies
11045 Puma Run
Littleton, CO 80124-9420, USA

Bailey, Scott (Actor)
c/o Staff Member *Stone Manners Talent & Literary (LA)*
6500 Wilshire Blvd Ste 550
Los Angeles, CA 90048-4950, USA

Bailey, Stacey (Football Player)
Atlanta Falcons
3400 Lakewind Way
Alpharetta, GA 30005-6943, USA

Bailey, Steve (Baseball Player)
Cleveland Indians
4600 Queen Anne Ave
Lorain, OH 44052-5648, USA

Bailey, Steven W (Reality TV Star)
c/o Scott Fedro *Lone Star Entertainment*
139 S Beverly Dr Ste 314
Beverly Hills, CA 90212-3040, USA

Bailey, T Wayne (Activist, Politician)
Stetson University
Political Science Dept
Stetson, FL 32720, USA

Bailey, Teddy (Football Player)
Buffalo Bills
7825 Elbrook Ave
Cincinnati, OH 45237-2207, USA

Bailey, Thomas H (Financier)
Janus Capital Corp
100 Fillmore St
Denver, CO 80206-4916, USA

Bailey II, Irving W (Business Person)
Providian Corp
400 W Market St
Louisville, KY 40202-3346, USA

Bailey Rae, Corinne (Musician)
Running Media Group
14 Victoria Road
Douglas, Isle of Man IM2 4ER, UNITED KINGDOM

Baillargeon, Joel (Hockey Player)
Winnipeg Jets
165b Rue du Coutelier
Saint-Augustin-De-Desmaures, PQ G3A 2J7, CANADA

Bailor, Bob (Baseball Player)
Baltimore Orioles
1950 Swan Ln
Palm Harbor, FL 34683-6275, USA

Bailyn, Bernard (Historian)
170 Clifton St
Belmont, MA 02478-2604, USA

Bain, Anthony (Actor)
c/o TJ Stein *Stein Entertainment Group*
11271 Ventura Blvd # 477
Studio City, CA 91604-3136, USA

Bain, Barbara (Actor)
831 S Dunsmuir Ave
Los Angeles, CA 90036-4731, USA

Bain, Conrad (Actor)
1230 Chickory Ln
Los Angeles, CA 90049-1403, USA

Bain, Michael (Actor)
c/o TJ Stein *Stein Entertainment Group*
11271 Ventura Blvd # 477
Studio City, CA 91604-3136, USA

Bain, William E (Bill) (Football Player)
Green Bay Packers
27661 Paseo Barona
San Juan Capistrano, CA 92675-2851, USA

Bainbridge, Beryl (Actor, Writer)
42 Albert St
London NW1 7NU, UNITED KINGDOM (UK)

Bainbridge, Merril (Musician, Songwriter, Writer)
001 Productions
PO Box 1760
Collingswood, VIC 3068, AUSTRALIA

Baines, Harold D (Baseball Player)
Chicago White Sox
PO Box 335
Saint Michaels, MD 21663-0335, USA

Baio, Scott (Actor)
c/o Chuck Binder *Binder & Associates*
1465 Lindacrest Dr
Beverly Hills, CA 90210-2519, USA

Baiocchi, Hugh (Golfer)
3656 Half Moon Dr
Orlando, FL 32812-3816, USA

Bair, Doug (Baseball Player)
Pittsburgh Pirates
560 Ohio Pike
Cincinnati, OH 45255-3315, USA

Baird, Bill (Football Player)
New York Jets
6050 E Heaton Ave
Fresno, CA 93727-5606, USA

Baird, Briny (Golfer)
c/o Staff Member *Pro Golfers Assoc of America (PGA)*
100 Avenue Of The Champions
Palm Beach Gardens, FL 33418-3653, USA

Baird, Butch (Golfer)
PO Box 2633
Carefree, AZ 85377-2633, USA

Baird, Diora (Actor)
c/o Joel King *Pakula/King & Associates*
9229 W Sunset Blvd Ste 315
Los Angeles, CA 90069-3403, USA

Baird, Frank
Indianapolis Kauskys
1725 Juniper Pi Apt 208
Goshen, IN 46526, USA

Baird, James M (Religious Leader)
Presbyterian Church
PO Box 1428
Decatur, GA 30031-1428, USA

baird, jenni (Actor)
c/o Michael P Levine *Levine Management*
9028 W Sunset Blvd # Ph1
Los Angeles, CA 90069-1846, USA

Baird, Stuart (Director)
William Morris Agency
151 El Camino Dr
Beverly Hills, CA 90212-2775, USA

Bairstow, Scott H (Actor)
c/o Andrea Pett-Joseph *Brillstein-Grey Entertainment*
9150 Wilshire Blvd Ste 350
Beverly Hills, CA 90212-3453, USA

Baisi, Al (Football Player)
Chicago Bears
1636 Garden Ave
Saint Paul, MN 55113-5724, USA

Baiul, Oksana (Figure Skater)
The Viardo Agency
832 N La Brea Ave
Los Angeles, CA 90038-3341, USA

Bajanowsky, Louis J (Architect)
Cambridge Seven Assoc
1050 Massachusetts Ave
Cambridge, MA 02138-5359, USA

Bajardi, Lane (Television Host)
c/o Staff Member *Bloomberg Television*
731 Lexington Ave
New York, NY 10022-1331, USA

Bajpai, Manoj (Actor, Bollywood)
304 Victoria Shastrinagar
Lokhandwala Complex Andheri(W)
Mumbai, MS 4000593, INDIA

Bakalyan, Richard (Actor)
1070 S Bedford St
Los Angeles, CA 90035-2102, USA

Bakatin, Vadim V (Government Official)
Kotelnicheskaya Nab 17
Moscow 103240, RUSSIA

Bakay, Nick (Actor)
c/o Staff Member *United Talent Agency (UTA)*
9560 Wilshire Blvd Ste 500
Beverly Hills, CA 90212-2401, USA

Bakenhaster, Dave (Baseball Player)
St Louis Cardinals
3710 Rome Corners Rd
Galena, OH 43021-9490, USA

Baker, Al (Football Player)
Detroit Lions
2784 Trinity Ct
Avon, OH 44011-1951, USA

Baker, Art (Football Player)
Buffalo Bills
247 Main St # B
Buzzards Bay, MA 02532-3232, USA

Baker, Bill (Baseball Player)
Cincinnati Reds
250 Manor Cir
Myrtle Beach, SC 29588-7202, USA

Baker, Bill (Hockey Player)
Montreal Canadiens
605 Sugarbush Trl
Brainerd, MN 56401, USA

Baker, Blanche (Actor)
2501 Palisade Ave Apt B2
Bronx, NY 10463-6104, USA

Baker, Brenda (Actor)
Agency for Performing Arts
405 S Beverly Dr Ste 500
Beverly Hills, CA 90212-4425, USA

Baker, Buddy (Race Car Driver)
4860 Moonlite Bay Dr
Sherrills Ford, NC 28673-9242, USA

Baker, Carroll (Actor)
Abrams Artists
9200 W Sunset Blvd Ste 1125
Los Angeles, CA 90069-3610, USA

Baker, Charles (Football Player)
St Louis Cardinals
3026 Tres Logos Ln
Dallas, TX 75228-1730, USA

Baker, Chuck (Baseball Player)
San Diego Padres
3035 Mescalero Dr
Lake Havasu City, AZ 86404-9605, USA

Baker, Colin (Actor)
Evans & Reiss
100 Fawe Park Road
London SW15 2EA, UNITED KINGDOM (UK)

Baker, Dave (Baseball Player)
Toronto Blue Jays
22234 S23 Hwy
Lacona, IA 50139-6669, USA

Baker, Diane (Actor)
2733 Outpost Dr
Los Angeles, CA 90068-2061, USA

Baker, Donald K (Cinematographer)
11789 Lakeshore N
Auburn, CA 95602-8326, USA

Baker, Doug (Baseball Player)
Detroit Tigers
2454 Heyneman Holw
Fallbrook, CA 92028-3666, USA

Baker, Dylan (Actor)
Paradigm Agency
10100 Santa Monica Blvd Ste 2500
Los Angeles, CA 90067-4116, USA

Baker, Earl P Jr (War Hero)
10100 Cypress Cove Dr
Fort Myers, FL 33908-7638, USA

Baker, Edward (Football Player)
Houston Oilers
74 Page Hill Rd
Far Hills, NJ 07931-2400, USA

Baker, Ellen Shulman (Astronaut)
2207 Garden Stream Ct
Houston, TX 77062-3650, USA

Baker, Floyd (Baseball Player)
St Louis Browns
3855 Edinburgh Dr
Youngstown, OH 44511-1127, USA

Baker, Frank (Baseball Player)
New York Yankees
4105 A Pl
Meridian, MS 39301-1038, USA

Baker, Ginger (Musician)
Twist Mgmt
4230 Del Rey Ave # 621
Marina Del Rey, CA 90292-5603, USA

Baker, Graham (Director)
10 Buckingham St
London WC2, UNITED KINGDOM (UK)

Baker, Jack (Baseball Player)
Boston Red Sox
5513 Hunters Hill Rd
Irondale, AL 35210-3011, USA

Baker, James A (Football Player)
Detroit Lions
2784 Trinity Ct
Avon, OH 44011-1951, USA

Baker, Jamie (Hockey Player)
Quebec Nordiques
3417 San Pasqual St
Pasadena, CA 91107-5416, USA

Baker, Janet A (Musician, Opera Singer)
Transart Ltd
8 Bristol Gardens
London W9 2JG, UNITED KINGDOM
(UK)

Baker, Joe Don (Actor)
c/o Staff Member *The Artists Agency (LA)*
1180 S Beverly Dr Ste 301
Los Angeles, CA 90035-1154, USA

Baker, John (Football Player)
Detroit Lions
1616 Battery Dr
Raleigh, NC 27610-3365, USA

Baker, John F Jr (War Hero)
Medal of Honor Society
40 Patriots Point Rd
Mount Pleasant, SC 29464-4377, USA

Baker, John R (General)
Vice Commander
Air Mobility Command
Scott Air Force Base, IL 62225, USA

Baker, John W (Football Player)
New York Giants
72 Oak Village Blvd S
Homosassa, FL 34446-5945, USA

Baker, Johnnie B (Dusty) (Baseball Player)
Minnesota Twins
40 Livingston Terrace Dr
San Bruno, CA 94066-2800, USA

Baker, Kathy (Actor)
1146 N Central Ave # 163
Glendale, CA 91202-2506, USA

Baker, Keith (Football Player)
Philadelphia Eagles
3203 S Marsalis Ave
Dallas, TX 75216-5203, USA

Baker, Kendall L (Educator)
University of North Dakota
525 S Main St
Lehr Memorial 201A
Ada, OH 45810-6000, USA

Baker, Kenny (Actor)
51 Mulgrave Ave
Ashton
Preston, Lancashire PR2 1HJ, UNITED
KINGDOM (UK)

Baker, Kitana (Actor)
c/o Jason Newman *Untitled Entertainment
(LA)*
331 N Maple Dr Fl 3
Beverly Hills, CA 90210-3827, USA

Baker, Laurie (Hockey Player)
67 Prairie St
Concord, MA 01742-2924, USA

Baker, Leslie M Jr (Financier)
Wachovia Corp
301 N Main St
Winston Salem, NC 27150-0002, USA

Baker, Lewis (Musician)
Joe Terry Mgmt
PO Box 279
Williamstown, NJ 08094-0279, USA

Baker, Loris (Football Player)
Washington Redskins
1009 Brentwood Pl
Fircrest, WA 98466-5922, USA

Baker, Michael A (Mike) (Astronaut)
NASA
2101 Nasa Pkwy
Johnson Space Center
Houston, TX 77058-3691, USA

Baker, Myron (Football Player)
Chicago Bears
297 Peart Rd
Alexandria, LA 71302-9344, USA

Baker, Paul T (Misc)
1000 Escalon Ave Apt A3005
Sunnyvale, CA 94085-1638, USA

Baker, Peter (Golfer)
I M G
1360 E 9th St Ste 100
Cleveland, OH 44114-1730, USA

Baker, Rae (Actor)
c/o Staff Member *Marmont Management*
Langham House
308 Regent St
London W1B 3AT, UNITED KINGDOM
(UK)

Baker, Ralph (Football Player)
New York Jets
36 Sunshine Cir
Lewistown, PA 17044-9264, USA

Baker, Raymond (Actor)
253A 26th St # 312
Santa Monica, CA 90402-2523, USA

Baker, Robby (Musician)
Management Trust
219 Dufferin St #309B
Toronto, ON M5K 3J1, CANADA

Baker, Robert (Actor)
c/o Ben Levine *Evolution Entertainment
(LA)*
10585 Santa Monica Blvd Ste 120
Los Angeles, CA 90025-4984, USA

Baker, Robert (Attorney, Attorney
General, General)
Baker Silberberg Keener
2850 Ocean Park Blvd
Santa Monica, CA 90405-2955, USA

Baker, Ron (Football Player)
Baltimore Colts
1253 E Willham Dr
Stillwater, OK 74075, USA

Baker, Roy Ward
125 Gloucester Rd
London, ENGLAND SW7 4TE, UNITED
KINGDOM (UK)

Baker, Russell W (Writer)
New York Times
229 W 43rd St
Editorial Dept
New York, NY 10036-3959, USA

Baker, Sam (Football Player)
Washington Redskins
1009 Brentwood Pl
Fircrest, WA 98466-5922, USA

Baker, Scott (Baseball Player)
Oakland A's
327 Lingering Ln
Henderson, NV 89012-3262, USA

Baker, Scott Thompson (Actor)
17651 Sidwell St
Granada Hills, CA 91344-1054, USA

Baker, Simon (Actor)
c/o Beth Holden-Garland *Untitled
Entertainment (LA)*
331 N Maple Dr Fl 3
Beverly Hills, CA 90210-3827, USA

Baker, Steve (Baseball Player)
Detroit Tigers
27527 Easy Acres Dr
Eugene, OR 97405-4500, USA

Baker, Steve (Hockey Player)
New York Rangers
32 Riverview Dr
Cohasset, MA 02025-1539, USA

Baker, Terry (Football Player)
Los Angeles Rams
3208 SW Fairmount Blvd
Portland, OR 97239-1443, USA

Baker, Tom (Actor)
JM Associates
77 Beak St
London W1R 3LE, UNITED KINGDOM
(UK)

Baker, Tyler Christopher (Actor)
c/o Staff Member *Beddingfield Company,
The*
9255 W Sunset Blvd Ste 920
Los Angeles, CA 90069-3306, USA

Baker, Vernon J (War Hero)
650 Vernon Lane
Saint Maries, ID 83861, USA

Baker, Vin (Basketball Player)
PO Box 179
Old Saybrook, CT 06475-0179, USA

Baker, W Thane (Athlete, Track Athlete)
6704 Saint John Ct
Granbury, TX 76049-4520, USA

Baker, Wayne (Football Player)
San Francisco 49ers
30753 US Highway 2 S
Libby, MT 59923-9517, USA

Baker, William (Bill) (Hockey Player)
6005 Sugarbush Trl
Brainerd, MN 56401-7055, USA

Baker, William O (Misc)
AT&T Bell Lucent Laboratory
600 Mountain Ave
New Providence, NJ 07974-2008, USA

Baker-Finch, Ian (Golfer)
788 Harbour Isle Pl
West Palm Beach, FL 33410-4408, USA

Baker III, James A (Politician)
910 Louisiana St
1 Shell Plz
Houston, TX 77002-4916, USA

Baker Jr, Howard H (Diplomat, Politician,
Senator)
US Embassy
10-1-1 Akasaka
Minatoku
Tokyo 1-7, JAPAN

Baker-Wise, Phyllis (Baseball Player)
20390 Partello Rd
Marshall, MI 49068-9394, USA

Bakhtair, Rudi (Correspondent)
Cable News Network
1050 Techwood Dr NW
News Dept
Atlanta, GA 30318-5604, USA

Bakke, Brenda (Actor)
c/o Staff Member *The House of
Representatives*
211 S Beverly Dr Ste 208
Beverly Hills, CA 90212-3879, USA

Bakken, Earl (Doctor, Inventor)
68-1399 Mauna Lani Dr
Kamuela, HI 96743-9777, USA

Bakken, James L (Jim) (Football Player)
St Louis Cardinals
230 Glen Hollow Rd
Madison, WI 53705-1166, USA

Bakker, James O (Jim) (Religious Leader)
123 E End Rd
Branson, MO 65616-3701, USA

Bako, Brigitte (Actor)
Kritzer
12200 W Olympic Blvd Ste 400
Los Angeles, CA 90064-1047, USA

Bako, Paul (Baseball Player)
Detroit Tigers
110 Coventry St
Lafayette, LA 70506-6149, USA

Bakovic, Pete (Hockey Player)
Vancouver Canucks
7991 S 47th St
Franklin, WI 53132-8468, USA

Bakula, Scott (Actor)
c/o Chris Andrews *Creative Artists Agency
LCC (CAA-LA)*
2000 Avenue Of The Stars
Los Angeles, CA 90067-4700, USA

Balaban, Bob (Director, Producer, Writer)
c/o Staff Member *Chicago Films*
101 5th Ave Fl 8
New York, NY 10003-1008, USA

Balaban, Liane (Actor)
c/o Ralph Zimmerman *Great North Artists
Management Inc (Canada)*
350 Duponte
Tononto, ON M5R 1V9, CANADA

Baladmenti, Angelo (Composer)
4146 Lankershim Blvd Ste 401
North Hollywood, CA 91602-2832, USA

Balambika (Actor, Bollywood)
3 Indira Gandhi Street
Chennai, TN 600093, INDIA

Balandin, Aleksandr N (Cosmonaut)
Potcha Kosmonavtov
Moskovskoi Oblasti
Syvisdny Goroduk 141160, RUSSIA

Balas, Mike (Baseball Player)
Boston Bees
12 Mary Shepherd Rd
Littleton, MA 01460-2261, USA

Balaski, Belinda (Actor)
Epstein-Wyckoff
280 S Beverly Dr Ste 400
Beverly Hills, CA 90212-3904, USA

Balassa, Sandor (Composer)
18 Sumegvar Str
Budapest 1118, HUNGARY

Balasubramaniyam, S P (Actor, Musician)
16 Kamdar Nagar
Nungambakkam
Chennai, TN 600 034, INDIA

Balaz, John (Baseball Player)
California Angels
3757 Udall St Unit 301
San Diego, CA 92107-2448, USA

Balazs, Andre (Business Person)
Andre Balazs Properties
295 Lafayette St Fl 7
The Puck Bldg
New York, NY 10012-2701, USA

Balboa, Marcelo (Soccer Player)
13139 Hedda Dr
Cerritos, CA 90703-6146, USA

Balboni, Steve (Baseball Player)
New York Yankees
117 Burlington Rd
New Providence, NJ 07974-2709, USA

Balcer, Rene (Producer, Writer)
c/o Adam Berkowitz *Creative Artists
Agency LCC (CAA-LA)*
2000 Avenue Of The Stars
Los Angeles, CA 90067-4700, USA

Baldacci, Lou (Football Player)
Pittsburgh Steelers
983 Coral Dr
Pebble Beach, CA 93953-2538, USA

Baldassin, Mike (Football Player)
San Francisco 49ers
13634 Bandix Rd SE
Olalla, WA 98359, USA

Baldavin, Barbara (Actor)
228 17th St
Manhattan Beach, CA 90266-4634, USA

Balderstone, James S (Business Person)
115 Mont Albert Road
Canterbuy, VIC 3126, AUSTRALIA

Baldeschwieler, John D (Misc)
PO Box 50065
Pasadena, CA 91115-0065, USA

Baldessari, John (Artist)
2001 1/2 Main St
Santa Monica, CA 90405-1021, USA

Balding, Rebecca (Actor)
2001 Winnetka Place
Woodland Hills, CA 91364, USA

Baldinger, Brian (Football Player,
Sportscaster)
Fox-TV
21 S Elmwood Rd
Marlton, NJ 08053-2562, USA

Baldinger, Gary (Football Player)
Kansas City Chiefs
114 Adam Rd
Massapequa, NY 11758-8102, USA

Baldinger, Rich (Football Player)
New York Giants
5401 Phelps Rd
Kansas City, MO 64136-1224, USA

Baldischwiler, Karl (Football Player)
Detroit Lions
3033 N Willow Dr
Newcastle, OK 73065-6456, USA

Baldissin, Mike (Football Player)
San Francisco 49ers
13634 Bandix Dr
Olalla, WA 98359-9467, USA

Baldock, Bobby R (Judge)
US Court of Appeals
PO Box 2388
Roswell, NM 88202-2388, USA

Baldridge, Letitia (Business Person,
Writer)
2339 Massachusetts Ave NW
Washington, DC 20008-2803, USA

Baldry, Long John (Musician)
Macklam Feidman Mgmt
1505 W 2nd Ave #200
Vancouver, BC V6H 3Y4, CANADA

Baldschun, Jack E (Baseball Player)
Philadelphia Phillies
311 Erie Rd
Green Bay, WI 54311-7706, USA

Baldwin, Adam (Actor)
c/o Steven Siebert *Lighthouse
Entertainment*
409 N Camden Dr Ste 202
Beverly Hills, CA 90210-4423, USA

Baldwin, Alec (Actor)
15030 Ventura Blvd # 710
Sherman Oaks, CA 91403-5470, USA

Baldwin, Billy (Baseball Player)
Detroit Tigers
878 Packard Dr
Akron, OH 44320-2816, USA

Baldwin, Burr (Football Player)
219 S Plateau Dr
West Covina, CA 91791-2230, USA

Baldwin, Daniel (Actor)
c/o Daniel (Dan) Spilo *Artistry
Management*
525 Westbourne Dr
West Hollywood, CA 90048-1913, USA

Baldwin, Dave (Baseball Player)
Washington Senators
PO Box 190
Yachats, OR 97498-0190, USA

Baldwin, Don (Football Player)
New York Jets
3624 Wind Chime Ln
Saint Charles, MO 63301-7405, USA

Baldwin, Doug (Hockey Player)
Toronto Maple Leafs
Gimli Golf Club 180 Cook Avenue
Gimli, MB R0C 1B0, CANADA

Baldwin, Frank (Baseball Player)
Cincinnati Reds
6359 Beaver Pike
Beaver, OH 45613-9318, USA

Baldwin, Jack (Race Car Driver)
4748 Balmoral Way NE
Marietta, GA 30068-1604, USA

Baldwin, Jack E (Misc)
Oxford University
Dyson Perrins Lab
S Park Rd
Oxford OX1 3QY, UNITED KINGDOM
(UK)

Baldwin, James (Baseball Player)
Chicago White Sox
18 Monteith Pl
Pinehurst, NC 28374-8542, USA

Baldwin, Jeff (Baseball Player)
Houston Astros
807 15th St
Kenova, WV 25530-1711, USA

Baldwin, John A (Jack) Jr (Admiral)
1371 Millersville Rd
Millersville, MD 21108-2120, USA

Baldwin, John W (Historian)
Johns Hopkins University
History Dept
Baltimore, MD 21218, USA

Baldwin, Judy (Actor)
12518 Addison St
Valley Village, CA 91607-2925, USA

Baldwin, Keith M (Football Player)
Cleveland Browns
124 Leonardville Rd
Belford, NJ 07718-1131, USA

Baldwin, Margaret (Writer)
PO Box 1106
Williams Bay, WI 53191-1106, USA

Baldwin, Randy (Football Player)
Minnesota Vikings
862 S 9th St
Griffin, GA 30224-4823, USA

Baldwin, Reggie (Baseball Player)
Houston Astros
763 S Liebold St
Detroit, MI 48217-1219, USA

Baldwin, Robert E (Economist)
125 Nautilus Dr
Madison, WI 53705-4329, USA

Baldwin, Stephen (Actor)
c/o Alex D'Andrea *Edmonds Management*
1635 N Cahuenga Blvd Fl 5
Los Angeles, CA 90028-6201, USA

Baldwin, Tom (Football Player)
New York Jets
2991 190th Pl
Lansing, IL 60438-3475, USA

Baldwin, William (Editor)
Forbes Magazine
60 5th Ave
Editorial Dept
New York, NY 10011-8868, USA

Baldwin, William (Billy) (Actor)
c/o JoAnne Colonna *Brillstein-Grey
Entertainment*
9150 Wilshire Blvd Ste 350
Beverly Hills, CA 90212-3453, USA

Bale, Christian (Actor)
c/o Patrick Whitesell *Endeavor Agency
LLC (LA)*
9601 Wilshire Blvd Fl 3
Beverly Hills, CA 90210-5204, USA

Bale, John (Baseball Player)
Toronto Blue Jays
PO Box 806
Crestview, FL 32536-0806, USA

Balenda, Carla
15848 Woodvale Rd
Encino, CA 91436-3443, USA

Bales, Lee (Baseball Player)
Atlanta Braves
7422 Greatwood Lake Dr
Sugar Land, TX 77479-6302, USA

Bales, Michael (Hockey Player)
Boston Bruins
470 Brunswick Ave
Toronto, ON M5R 2Z5, CANADA

Balfour, Earl (Hockey Player)
Toronto Maple Leafs
230 Portview Road RR3 Stn Main
Port Perry, ON L9L 1B4, CANADA

Balfour, Eric (Actor)
United Talent Agency
9560 Wilshire Blvd Ste 500
Beverly Hills, CA 90212-2401, USA

Balgimbayev, Nurlan (Prime Minister)
Dom Pravieelstva
Pl im VI Lenina
Astana 148008, KAZAKHSTAN

Baliani, Marco (Actor)
Carol Levi Co
Via Giuseppe Pisanelli
Rome 00196, ITALY

Baliles, Gerald L (Governor)
951 E Byrd St
Riverfront Plaza East Tower
Richmond, VA 23219-4040, USA

Balitran, Celine (Model)
Ford Model Agency
142 Greene St # 400
New York, NY 10012-3236, USA

Balk, Fairuza (Actor)
Rigberg Roberts Rugolo
1180 S Beverly Dr Ste 601
Los Angeles, CA 90035-1158, USA

Balkenende, Jan-Peter (Prime Minister)
Premier's Office
Binnenhof 20
Postbus 20001
EA Hague, THE NETHERLANDS

Balkenhol, Klaus (Athlete)
Narzissenweg 11A
Hilden 40723, GERMANY

Ball, Alan (Producer)
c/o Andrew Cannava *United Talent
Agency (UTA)*
9560 Wilshire Blvd Ste 500
Beverly Hills, CA 90212-2401, USA

Ball, David (Musician)
Buddy Lee
38 Music Sq E Ste 200
Nashville, TN 37203-4304, USA

Ball, Edward (Writer)
Farrar Straus Giroux
19 Union Sq W Fl 11
New York, NY 10003-3304, USA

Ball, Eric C (Football Player)
Cincinnati Bengals
10614 Margate Ter
Cincinnati, OH 45241-3000, USA

Ball, Ian (Musician)
c/o Staff Member *Paradigm (Monterey)*
509 Hartnell St
Monterey, CA 93940-2825, USA

Ball, Jason (Football Player)
San Diego Chargers
325 S Jessie Doe
Durham, NH 03824, USA

Ball, Jeff (Baseball Player)
San Francisco Giants
740 18th Pl
Vero Beach, FL 32960-5408, USA

Ball, Jerry L (Football Player)
Detroit Lions
3311 Meadowside Dr
Sugar Land, TX 77478-4051, USA

Ball, Larry (Football Player)
Miami Dolphins
8830 SW 57th St
Cooper City, FL 33328-5100, USA

Ball, Michael A (Actor, Musician)
PO Box 2073
Colchester, Essex CO4 3WS, UNITED
KINGDOM (UK)

Ball, Robert (Football Player)
Cleveland Browns
35 Summit Rd
Clifton, NJ 07012-2008, USA

Ball, Robert M (Government Official)
1776 Massachusetts Ave NW
Washington, DC 20036-1904, USA

Ball, Sam (Actor)
Gersh Agency
232 N Canon Dr
Beverly Hills, CA 90210-5302, USA

Ball, Sam (Football Player)
Baltimore Colts
1220 Glenshield Way
Henderson, KY 42420-2530, USA

Ball, Taylor (Actor)
c/o Jeff Kolodny *William Morris Agency (WMA-LA)*
1 William Morris Pl
Beverly Hills, CA 90212-4261, USA

Ball, Terry (Hockey Player)
Philadelphia Flyers
239 Emerson Ave
Winnipeg, MB R2G 1G1, CANADA

Balladur, Edouard (Prime Minister)
5 Rue Jean Formige
Paris 75015, FRANCE

Ballantine, Carl (Actor)
2575 N Beachwood Dr
Los Angeles, CA 90068-2341, USA

Ballantine, Sara (Actor)
Talent Group
5670 Wilshire Blvd Ste 820
Los Angeles, CA 90036-5613, USA

Ballantyne (Designer, Fashion Designer)
c/o Staff Member *Ballantyne*
4-6 Savile Road
London, England W1S 3PD, UNITED KINGDOM (UK)

Ballard, Carroll (Director)
PO Box 556
Saint Helena, CA 94574-5056, USA

Ballard, Del Jr (Bowler)
Ebonite International
PO Box 746
Hopkinsville, KY 42241-0746, USA

Ballard, Donald E (War Hero)
PO Box 34593
North Kansas City, MO 64116-0993, USA

Ballard, Florence (Musician)
c/o Staff Member *Diva Central Inc*
7510 W Sunset Blvd Ste 1445
Los Angeles, CA 90046-3408, USA

Ballard, Greg (Basketball Player)
4440 Harbor Ln N
Minneapolis, MN 55446-2765, USA

Ballard, Howard (Football Player)
Buffalo Bills
PO Box 584
Ashland, AL 36251-0584, USA

Ballard, James Graham (JG) (Writer)
36 Old Charlton Rd
Shepperton
Middx TW17 8AT, UNITED KINGDOM (UK)

Ballard, Jeff (Baseball Player)
Baltimore Orioles
4828 Rimrock Rd
Billings, MT 59106-1317, USA

Ballard, Kaye (Actor)
PO Box 922
Rancho Mirage, CA 92270-0922, USA

Ballard, Quinton (Football Player)
Baltimore Colts
4005 Saint Patrick Dr
Greensboro, NC 27406-6420, USA

Ballard, Robert D (Oceanographer)
Institute for Exploration
55 Coogan Blvd
Mystic, CT 06355-1927, USA

Baller, Jay (Baseball Player)
Philadelphia Phillies
303 Spring Valley Rd
Reading, PA 19605-2747, USA

Ballerini, Edoardo (Actor)
c/o JB Roberts *Thruline Entertainment*
9250 Wilshire Blvd Ground Fl
Beverly Hills, CA 90210, USA

Ballesteros, Roberto (Actor)
c/o Staff Member *Televisa*
Blvd Adolfo Lopez Mateos 232
Colonia San Angel INN
DF CP 01060, MEXICO

Ballesteros, Seveiano (Seve) (Golfer)
Fareway SA
C/Padaje del Pena no 2
Curata Planta
Santander E-39008, SPAIN

Ballestros, Anderson (Actor)
c/o J R Heermans *LatinActors*
39 Brussels St
San Francisco, CA 94134-1236, USA

Balley, Otha (Baseball Player)
Birmingham Black Barons
937 6th Pl SW
Birmingham, AL 35211-1743, USA

Ballhaus, Florian M (Cinematographer)
115 Berkeley Pl
Brooklyn, NY 11217-3603, USA

Ballhaus, Michael (Cinematographer)
11 Elm Pl
Rye, NY 10580-2918, USA

Ballingall, Chris (Baseball Player)
52879 25th St
Mattawan, MI 49071-8803, USA

Ballinger, Mark (Baseball Player)
Cleveland Indians
101 Glenwood Ave
Woodside, CA 94062-3512, USA

Ballmer, Steven A (Business Person)
Microsoft Corp
1 Microsoft Way
Redmond, WA 98052-8300, USA

Ballon, Adrienne (Actor)
c/o Staff Member *International Creative Management (ICM-LA)*
10250 Constellation Blvd
Los Angeles, CA 90067-6200, USA

Ballou, Mark (Actor)
c/o Staff Member *Imperium 7 Talent Agency*
9911 W Pico Blvd Ste 1290
Los Angeles, CA 90035-2726, USA

Ballou, Tyson (Model)
c/o Staff Member *IMG Models*
304 Park Ave S Fl 12
New York, NY 10010-4301, USA

Balmaseda, Liz (Journalist)
Miami Herald
1 Herald Plz
Editorial Dept
Miami, FL 33132-1693, USA

Balmer, Jean Francois (Actor)
c/o Staff Member *ArtMedia*
20 av Rapp
Paris 75007, FRANCE

Balmer, Jean-Francois (Actor)
Artmedia
20 Ave Rapp
Paris 75007, FRANCE

Balog, Bob (Football Player)
Pittsburgh Steelers
331 Monongahela Ave
Glassport, PA 15045-1439, USA

Balraaj, Anand (Actor, Bollywood)
72/1 AV Villa, Kakori Camp
Aram Nagar, Seven Bungalows Versova
Andheri
Mumbai, MS 400058, INDIA

Balsam, Talia (Actor)
304 Spring St Apt 3W
New York, NY 10013-1387, USA

Balsamo, Tony (Baseball Player)
Chicago Cubs
15 Doral Ln
Bay Shore, NY 11706-8840, USA

Balser, Glennon (Religious Leader)
Advent Christian Church
6315 Studley Rd
Mechanicsville, VA 23116, USA

Balsley, Philip E (Musician)
191 Abbington Rd
Swoope, VA 24479-2217, USA

Baltes, Jameson (Actor)
Hervey/Grimes
PO Box 64249
Los Angeles, CA 90064-0249, USA

Baltica, Kremerata (Musician)
c/o Staff Member *International Creative Management (ICM-LA)*
10250 Constellation Blvd
Los Angeles, CA 90067-6200, USA

Baltimore, Bryon (Hockey Player)
Edmonton Oilers
McCauig Desrochers
2401-10088 Ave NW
Edmonton, AB T5J 2Z1, CANADA

Baltimore, David (Educator, Nobel Prize Laureate)
31460 Beach Park Road
Malibu, CA 90265, USA

Baltron, Donna (Actor)
C N A Assoc
1925 Century Park E Ste 750
Los Angeles, CA 90067-2708, USA

Baltsa, Agnes (Opera Singer)
Manuela Kursidem
Wasagasse 12/1/3
Vienna 1090, AUSTRIA

Baltz, Lewis (Photographer)
11693 San Vincente Blvd #527
Los Angeles, CA 90049, USA

Baluik, Stan (Hockey Player)
Boston Bruins
46 Kent St
Cumberland, RI 02864-7032, USA

Balul, Oksana (Figure Skater)
Bob Young
PO Box 988
Niantic, CT 06357-0988, USA

Balzary, Michael (Flea) (Actor, Musician)
c/o Staff Member *Innovative Artists (LA)*
1505 10th St
Santa Monica, CA 90401-2805, USA

Bama, Jim (Artist)
PO Box 148
Wapiti, WY 82450-0148, USA

Bamber, Jamie
c/o Alan Siegel *Alan Siegel Entertainment*
345 N Maple Dr Ste 375
Beverly Hills, CA 90210-5942, USA

Bamberger, George (Baseball Player)
New York Giants
455 Bath Club Blvd N
North Redington Beach, FL 33708-1529, USA

Bamberger, Hal (Baseball Player)
New York Giants
480 Mountz Rd
Birdsboro, PA 19508-8011, USA

Bamford, Maria (Actor)
c/o Bob Read *ReBar Management*
10061 Riverside Dr # 722
Toluca Lake, CA 91602-2560, USA

Bamman, Gerry (Actor)
Writers & Artists
360 N Crescent Dr Bldg North
Beverly Hills, CA 90210-6818, USA

Bana, Eric (Actor, Comedian)
c/o John Fogelman *William Morris Agency (WMA-LA)*
1 William Morris Pl
Beverly Hills, CA 90212-4261, USA

Banach, Edward (Ed) (Wrestler)
2128 Country Club Blvd
Ames, IA 50014-7061, USA

Banach, Louis (Lou) (Wrestler)
3276 E Fairfax Rd
Cleveland Heights, OH 44118-4206, USA

Banachowski, Andy (Coach, Volleyball Player)
University of California
Athletic Dept
Los Angeles, CA 90024, USA

Banaszak, John A (Football Player)
Pittsburgh Steelers
420 Robinhood Ln
McMurray, PA 15317-2717, USA

Banaszak, Pete (Football Player)
Oakland Raiders
1021 Inverness Dr
Saint Augustine, FL 32092-2787, USA

Banaszek, Cas (Football Player)
San Francisco 49ers
1018 Cohen Ct
Petaluma, CA 94952-5263, USA

Banaszynski, Jacqui (Journalist)
Saint Paul Pioneer Press
345 Cedar St
Editorial Dept
Saint Paul, MN 55101-1057, USA

Banbury, F H Frith (Director)
18 Park Saint James
Prince Albert Road
London NW8 7LE, UNITED KINGDOM (UK)

Bancroft, Cameron (Actor)
c/o Staff Member *Gersh Agency, The (LA)*
232 N Canon Dr
Beverly Hills, CA 90210-5302, USA

Band, Richard H (Composer)
24053 Bessemer St
Woodland Hills, CA 91367-2919, USA

Band of Bees, A (Music Group)
c/o Staff Member *Paradigm (Monterey)*
509 Hartnell St
Monterey, CA 93940-2825, USA

Banda El Limon, Arrolladora (Music Group)
c/o Staff Member *Sony Music Miami*
605 Lincoln Rd Fl 7
Miami Beach, FL 33139-2900, USA

Banda Pachuco (Music Group)
c/o Staff Member *Sony Music Miami*
605 Lincoln Rd Fl 7
Miami Beach, FL 33139-2900, USA

Bandar, Prince Sultan-al-saud
601 New Hampshire Ave NW
Washington, DC 20037-2405, USA

Banderas, Antonio (Actor, Director, Musician, Producer)
c/o Emanuel Nunez *Creative Artists Agency LCC (CAA-LA)*
2000 Avenue Of The Stars
Los Angeles, CA 90067-4700, USA

Bandholz, Antonio (Misc)
Sohnholm 92
Westerholz 24977, GERMANY

Bando, Chris (Baseball Player)
Cleveland Indians
6930 Woodlands Ln
Solon, OH 44139-4664, USA

Bando, Salvatore L (Sal) (Baseball Player)
Kansas City A's
W308N6225 Shore Acres Rd
Hartland, WI 53029-8723, USA

Bandura, Jeff (Hockey Player)
New York Rangers
1306 Cambria Dr
Joliet, IL 60431-7542, USA

Bandy, Don (Football Player)
Washington Redskins
215 E Calvin St
Taft, CA 93268-2915, USA

Bandy, Moe (Musician, Songwriter, Writer)
Blackwood Mgmt
PO Box 5331
Sevierville, TN 37864-5331, USA

Bane, Eddie (Baseball Player)
Minnesota Twins
598 Paloma Ct
Encinitas, CA 92024-2392, USA

Banes, Lisa (Actor)
c/o Tim Angle *Don Buchwald & Associates Inc (LA)*
6500 Wilshire Blvd Ste 2200
Los Angeles, CA 90048-4942, USA

Banet, Herbert (Football Player)
Green Bay Packers
6050 S 800 E-92 # 217
Fort Wayne, IN 46814-9201, USA

Baney, Dick (Baseball Player)
Seattle Pilots
2231 Northup Dr
Tustin, CA 92782-1028, USA

Banfield, Ashleigh (Correspondent)
NBC-TV
30 Rockefeller Plz Ste 270E
News Dept
New York, NY 10112-0299, USA

Banfield, Ashliegh (Actor)
c/o Staff Member *William Morris Agency (WMA-LA)*
1 William Morris Pl
Beverly Hills, CA 90212-4261, USA

Bang, Molly (Writer)
43 Drumlin Rd
Falmouth, MA 02540-2505, USA

Bang Lime (Music Group)
c/o Staff Member *Paradigm (Monterey)*
509 Hartnell St
Monterey, CA 93940-2825, USA

Bangemann, Martin (Government Official)
European Commission
200 Rue de la Loi
Brussels 1049, BELGIUM

Bangerter, Norman H (Governor)
603 E South Temple
Salt Lake City, UT 84102-1101, USA

Bangles, The (Music Group)
c/o Brett Steinberg *Creative Artists Agency LCC (CAA-LA)*
2000 Avenue Of The Stars
Los Angeles, CA 90067-4700, USA

Banham, Frank (Hockey Player)
Mighty Ducks of Anaheim
139 W Grayling Ln
Suffield, CT 06078-1960, USA

Bani, John (President)
President's Office
Port Vila, VANUATU

Banister, Jeff (Baseball Player)
Pittsburgh Pirates
5228 Hidden Brook Ln
League City, TX 77573-5783, USA

Bank, Frank (Actor)
PO Box 902
North Palm Springs, CA 92258, USA

Bank, Melissa (Producer, Writer)
c/o Sylvie Rabineau *Rabineau Wachter and Sanford Literary Agency*
522 Wilshire Blvd Ste L
Santa Monica, CA 90401-1445, USA

Banke, Paul (Boxer)
1926 Bobolink Way
Pomona, CA 91767-2828, USA

Banker, Ted (Football Player)
New York Jets
1862 Park Ave
East Meadow, NY 11554-4007, USA

Bankhead, Scott (Baseball Player)
Kansas City Royals
1236 Idlewood Dr
Asheboro, NC 27205-4119, USA

Banks, Brian (Baseball Player)
Milwaukee Brewers
1053 N Alba
Mesa, AZ 85213-5462, USA

Banks, Brianna (Adult Film Star)
c/o Staff Member *Atlas Multimedia Inc*
9035 Independence Ave
Canoga Park, CA 91304-1743, USA

Banks, Carl (Football Player)
New York Giants
7 Glenview Dr
Warren, NJ 07059-5476, USA

Banks, Chip (Football Player)
55 Fair Haven Way SE
Smyrna, GA 30080-8087, USA

Banks, Chuck (Football Player)
Houston Oilers
3705 Valley Hill Dr
Randallstown, MD 21133-4822, USA

Banks, Darren (Hockey Player)
Boston Bruins
30 Piedmont Ave
Waltham, MA 02451-3013, USA

Banks, David (Actor)
Shane Collins Assoc
2-5 Stedham Pl
Bloomsbury
London WC1A 1BU, ENGLAND

Banks, Dennis (Misc)
General Delivery
Oglala, SD 57764-9999, USA

Banks, Elizabeth (Actor)
c/o Alissa Vradenburg *Untitled Entertainment (LA)*
331 N Maple Dr Fl 3
Beverly Hills, CA 90210-3827, USA

Banks, Ernie (Baseball Player)
c/o Staff Member *Chicago Cubs*
1060 W Addison St
Wrigley Field
Chicago, IL 60613-4397, USA

Banks, Fred (Football Player)
Cleveland Browns
PO Box 1571
Mableton, GA 30126-1009, USA

Banks, Gene (Basketball Player)
Bluefield State College
219 Rock St
Athletic Dept
Bluefield, WV 24701-2198, USA

Banks, Gene (Basketball Player)
San Antonio Spurs
1210 Sloan St
Greensboro, NC 27401-3442, USA

Banks, Gordon (Football Player)
New Orleans Saints
2644 E Trinity Mills Rd
Carrollton, TX 75006-2136, USA

Banks, Jonathan (Actor)
909 Euclid St Apt 8
Santa Monica, CA 90403-3097, USA

Banks, Lloyd (Musician)
c/o Staff Member *Interscope Records (LA) - Main*
2220 Colorado Ave
Santa Monica, CA 90404-3506, USA

Banks, Morwenna (Actor, Writer)
c/o Staff Member *International Creative Management (ICM-LA)*
10250 Constellation Blvd
Los Angeles, CA 90067-6200, USA

Banks, Robert (Football Player)
Houston Oilers
2412 Laguard Dr
Hampton, VA 23661-2418, USA

Banks, Russell (Writer)
Princeton University
English Debt
Princeton, NJ 08544-0001, USA

Banks, Steven (Actor, Comedian)
Gersh Agency
232 N Canon Dr
Beverly Hills, CA 90210-5302, USA

Banks, Steven Gary (Producer, Writer)
c/o Staff Member *Evolution Entertainment (LA)*
901 N Highland Ave
Los Angeles, CA 90038-2412, USA

Banks, Ted (Coach)
Riverside Community College
Athletic Dept
Riverside, CA 92506, USA

Banks, Tom (Football Player)
St Louis Cardinals
358 Wisteria St
Fairhope, AL 36532-1729, USA

Banks, Tony (Football Player)
St Louis Rams
2211 Vaquero Club Dr
Westlake, TX 76262-9080, USA

Banks, Tyra (Actor, Model, Producer)
c/o Staff Member *Bankable Productions*
6310 San Vicente Blvd Ste 505
Los Angeles, CA 90048-5421, USA

Banks, Walker (Basketball Player)
Pittsburgh Condors
3207 Brentwood Dr
Champaign, IL 61821-3482, USA

Banks, Willie (Baseball Player)
Minnesota Twins
2115 NW 56th St
Miami, FL 33142-3011, USA

Bankston, Michael (Football Player)
Phoenix Cardinals
938 Kingwood Dr Apt 220
Humble, TX 77339-4446, USA

Bankston, Warren (Football Player)
Pittsburgh Steelers
4201 Bordeaux Dr
Kenner, LA 70065-1739, USA

Banner, Bob (Director, Producer)
17132 Palisades Cir
Pacific Palisades, CA 90272-2144, USA

Banner, David (Musician)
c/o Staff Member *Universal Records*
825 8th Ave
New York, NY 10019-7472, USA

Banner, Penny
6810 Cabot Cir
Charlotte, NC 28226-3928, USA

Bannerman, Bill (Director, Producer)
Mirisch Agency
1875 Century Park E Ste 2025
C/O Lawrence Mirisch
Los Angeles, CA 90067-2501, USA

Bannerman, Isabella (Cartoonist)
41 South Dr
Hastings On Hudson, NY 10706-1813, USA

Bannerman, Murray (Hockey Player)
Vancouver Canucks
826 Raintree Dr
Naperville, IL 60540-6381, USA

Bannister, Alan (Baseball Player)
Philadelphia Phillies
405 48th St NW
Bradenton, FL 34209-1921, USA

Bannister, Floyd F (Baseball Player)
Houston Astros
6701E E Caballo Dr
Paradise Valley, AZ 85253, USA

Bannister, Reggie (Actor, Musician)
Magic Inc
4450 California Pl
Box 315
Long Beach, CA 90807-2209, USA

Bannister, Roger G (Athlete, Scientist, Track Athlete)
21 Bardwell Road
Oxford OX2 6SV, UNITED KINGDOM (UK)

Bannister, Trevor (Actor)
David Daly
68 Old Brompton Road
London SW7 3LQ, UNITED KINGDOM (UK)

Bannon, Bruce (Football Player)
Miami Dolphins
5845 Hickory Hollow Ln
Doylestown, PA 18902-9414, USA

Bannon, Jack (Actor)
6470 E Sunnyside Rd
Coeur D Alene, ID 83814-9503, USA

Bannon, Shaun (Musician)
Artist Group International
9560 Wilshire Blvd Ste 400
Beverly Hills, CA 90212-2416, USA

Bano, Al
I-72020 Cellino San Marco
(Brindise), ITALY

Banois, Vincent J (Football Player)
24256J Tamarack Trl
Southfield, MI 48075, USA

Banowsky, William S (Business Person, Educator)
Gaylord Broadcasting Co
PO Box 25125
Oklahoma City, OK 73125-0125, USA

Bansavage, Al (Football Player)
Los Angeles Chargers
PO Box 1172
Jensen Beach, FL 34958-1172, USA

Banta, Brad (Football Player)
Indianapolis Colts
626 N River Rd
Denham Springs, LA 70726-2817, USA

Banta, Jack (Baseball Player)
Brooklyn Dodgers
3215 E 30th Ave
Hutchinson, KS 67502-1511, USA

Bantock, Nick (Misc, Writer)
Chronicle Books
85 2nd St
San Francisco, CA 94105-3459, USA

Bantom, Mike (Basketball Player)
Phoenix Suns
418 Egret Ln
Secaucus, NJ 07094-2219, USA

Banuchandar (Actor)
26 B N Reddy Road
Chennai, TN 600 017, INDIA

Bao, Joseph Y (Doctor)
17436 Terry Lyn Ln
Cerritos, CA 90703-8522, USA

Bapitha (Actor, Bollywood)
7 Ayyappan Nagar 2nd Street
Cinmaya Nagar
Chennai, TN 600111, INDIA

Baptist, Travis (Baseball Player)
Minnesota Twins
21405 SW Rock Rd
Beaverton, OR 97006-1505, USA

Baptista, Juan Alfonso (Actor)
c/o Gabriel Blanco *Gabriel Blanco Iglesias (Mexico)*
Rio Balsas 35-32
Colonia Cuauhtemoc
DF 06500, MEXICO

Baquero, Ivana (Actor)
c/o Peter Safran *The Safran Company*
2000 Avenue Of The Stars Ste 600N
Los Angeles, CA 90067-4708, USA

Baquet, Dean P (Journalist)
New York Times
229 W 43rd St
Editorial Dept
New York, NY 10036-3959, USA

Bar, Olaf (Opera Singer)
Organisation of Int'l Artistique
16 Ave FD Roosevelt
Paris 75008, FRANCE

Bar-Josef, Ofer (Archaeologist)
Harvard University
Archaeology Dept
Cambridge, MA 02138, USA

Barahona, Ralph (Hockey Player)
Boston Bruins
4608 Bellflower Blvd
Lakewood, CA 90713-2502, USA

Barajas, Rod (Baseball Player)
Arizona Diamondbacks
8533 N 50th Pl
Paradise Valley, AZ 85253-2006, USA

Barak, Ehud (General, Prime Minister)
Israel Labor Party
16 Hayarkon St
Tel-Aviv 63571, ISRAEL

Baran, Paul (Inventor)
Com21 Inc
PO Box 36308
San Jose, CA 95158-6308, USA

Baranova, Anastasia (Actor)
c/o Staff Member *Gersh Agency, The (LA)*
232 N Canon Dr
Beverly Hills, CA 90210-5302, USA

Baranski, Christine (Actor)
c/o Lisa Loosemore *Viking Entertainment*
445 W 23rd St Ste 1A
New York, NY 10011-1445, USA

Barany, Istvan (Swimmer)
I Attila Utca 87
Budapest 01012, HUNGARY

Baratta, Adam (Actor)
c/o Larry Shapiro *Nine Yards Entertainment*
8530 Wilshire Blvd Fl 5
Beverly Hills, CA 90211-3102, USA

Barbacid, Mariano (Misc)
CNIO
Melchor Fernandez Almagro 3
Madrid 28029, SPAIN

Barbara, Kingsolver E (Writer)
c/o Staff Member *HarperCollins Publishers*
10 E 53rd St Fl 17
New York, NY 10022-5244, USA

Barbarin, Phillipe X I Cardinal (Religious Leader)
Archdiocese
1 Place de Fouriere
Lyon Cedex 05 69321, FRANCE

Barbaro, Gary W (Football Player)
Kansas City Chiefs
1000 Giuffrias Ave
Metairie, LA 70001-3649, USA

Barbat, Roxanne (Director, Producer, Writer)
c/o Staff Member *Fantastic Films*
3854 Clayton Ave
Los Angeles, CA 90027-4720, USA

Barbay, Roland (Football Player)
Seattle Seahawks
1025 Breckenridge Dr
Slidell, LA 70461-5313, USA

Barbe, Andy (Hockey Player)
Toronto Maple Leafs
837 Fisher Heights
Monongahela, PA 15063, USA

Barbeau, Adrienne (Actor, Musician)
c/o Staff Member *Metropolitan*
4500 Wilshire Blvd Fl 2
Los Angeles, CA 90010-3858, USA

Barber, Andrea (Actor)
Savage Agency
6212 Banner Ave
Los Angeles, CA 90038-2802, USA

Barber, Bill (Hockey Player)
105 Harmon Dr
Blackwood, NJ 08012-5198, USA

Barber, Brian (Baseball Player)
St Louis Cardinals
7123 Yacht Basin Ave Apt 327
Orlando, FL 32835-6611, USA

Barber, Chris (Musician)
Cromwell Mgmt
45 High St
Huntington
Cambridgeshire PE29 3TE, UNITED KINGDOM (UK)

Barber, Christopher E (Football Player)
Cincinnati Bengals
2621 Monaco Cove Cir
Orlando, FL 32825-8442, USA

Barber, Glynis (Actor)
Susan Sharper
Queen's House
1 Leicester
London WC2H 7BP, UNITED KINGDOM (UK)

Barber, John (Basketball Player)
St Louis Hawks
1554 Mahan St
Orangeburg, SC 29118-3546, USA

Barber, Kurt (Football Player)
New York Jets
17940 E Payson St
Azusa, CA 91702-5748, USA

Barber, Marion (Football Player)
New York Jets
3825 Harbor Ln N
Minneapolis, MN 55446-3319, USA

Barber, Michael (Football Player)
Seattle Seahawks
3020 Prosperity Church Rd Ste 1
Charlotte, NC 28269-8100, USA

Barber, Mike (Football Player)
Houston Oilers
PO Box 1086
Desoto, TX 75123-1086, USA

Barber, Miller (Golfer)
2627 Rivercrest Dr
Sherman, TX 75092, USA

Barber, Paul (Actor, Producer, Writer)
c/o Staff Member *Paradigm (LA)*
360 N Crescent Dr
North Bldg
Beverly Hills, CA 90210-6820, USA

Barber, Ronder (Football Player)
Tampa Bay Buccaneers
17119 Journeys End Dr
Odessa, FL 33556-2442, USA

Barber, Rudy (Football Player)
Miami Dolphins
1411 NW 175th St
Miami, FL 33169-4660, USA

Barber, Shawn (Football Player)
Washington Redskins
15073 Sherwood Rd
Overland Park, KS 66224-3846, USA

Barber, Steve (Baseball Player)
Minnesota Twins
1517 Cushman Dr
Sierra Vista, AZ 85635-2144, USA

Barber, Steve (Baseball Player)
Baltimore Orioles
1997 Joy View Ln
Henderson, NV 89012-4553, USA

Barber, Stewart C (Stew) (Football Player)
Buffalo Bills
2138 Country Manor Dr
Mount Pleasant, SC 29466-7448, USA

Barber, Tiki (Football Player)
c/o Staff Member *NBC Sports (NY)*
30 Rockefeller Plz
New York, NY 10112-0015, USA

Barber, William (Cinematographer)
2509 Whitechapel Pl
Thousand Oaks, CA 91362-5356, USA

Barberie, Bret (Baseball Player)
Montreal Expos
28758 Bruin Pl
Santa Clarita, CA 91390-5285, USA

Barberie, Jillian (Actor, Television Host)
c/o John Ferriter *William Morris Agency (WMA-LA)*
1 William Morris Pl
Beverly Hills, CA 90212-4261, USA

Barberos, Alessandro (Business Person)
Fiat Spa
Corso G Marconi 10/20
Turin 10125, ITALY

Barbi, Shane (Model)
c/o Jeffery LeBeau *Peacock & LeBeau*
3741 E 4th St
Long Beach, CA 90814-1628, USA

Barbi, Sia (Model)
c/o Jeffery LeBeau *Peacock & LeBeau*
3741 E 4th St
Long Beach, CA 90814-1628, USA

Barbieri, Gato (Musician)
Central Entertainment Services
123 Harvard Ave
Staten Island, NY 10301-1312, USA

Barbieri, Jim (Baseball Player)
Los Angeles Dodgers
13619 E 5th Ave
Spokane Valley, WA 99216-0600, USA

Barbolak, Pete (Football Player)
Pittsburgh Steelers
200 Olive Ave Spc B1
Vista, CA 92083-4968, USA

Barbon, Roberto (Baseball Player)
New York Cubans
Gabukun Dencho-2-Chome 6-Ban 460
Nishinomiya City
Hyogok, JAPAN

Barbot, Ivan (Lawyer)
4 Rue Marguerite
Paris 75017, FRANCE

Barbour, Ian (Physicist, Scientist)
Carleton College
Theology Dept
Northfield, MN 55057, USA

Barbour, John (Actor, Comedian, Writer)
54 Pine Isle Ct
Henderson, NV 89074-0681, USA

Barbour, Ross (Musician)
Four Freshmen
PO Box 93534
Las Vegas, NV 89193-3534, USA

Barbutti, Pete (Musician)
Thomas Cassidy
11761 E Speedway Blvd
Tucson, AZ 85748-2017, USA

Barcelona, Custo (Designer, Fashion Designer)
c/o Staff Member *Custo Barcelona*
2 Michael Road
1927 Bldg, North Entrance
London, England SW6 2AD, UNITED KINGDOM (UK)

Barclay, Paris (Actor)
c/o Steve Lovett *Lovett Management*
1327 Brinkley Ave
Los Angeles, CA 90049-3619, USA

Bard, Allen J (Misc)
6202 Mountainclimb Dr
Austin, TX 78731-3906, USA

Bard, Josh (Baseball Player)
Cleveland Indians
2505 Akron St
Denver, CO 80238-2764, USA

Bardem, Javier E (Actor, Producer)
c/o Elyse Scherz *Endeavor Agency LLC (LA)*
9601 Wilshire Blvd Fl 3
Beverly Hills, CA 90210-5204, USA

Bardot, Brigitte (Actor)
c/o Ghyslaire Calmels Boch
Fondation Brigitte Bardot
45 rue Vineuse
Paris 75116, FRANCE

Bare, Bobby (Musician)
c/o Staff Member *The Bobby Roberts Company Inc*
PO Box 1547
Goodlettsville, TN 37070-1547, USA

Bare, Robert J (Bobby) (Musician, Songwriter, Writer)
2401 Music Valley Dr
Nashville, TN 37214-1002, USA

Barefoot, Ken (Football Player)
Washington Redskins
1204 Lawrence Grey Dr
Virginia Beach, VA 23455-5605, USA

Bareikis, Arija (Actor)
c/o Rhonda Price *Gersh Agency, The (NY)*
41 Madison Ave Fl 33
New York, NY 10010-2202, USA

Bareikis, Arlia (Actor)
360 W 23rd St
New York, NY 10011-2258, USA

Bareilles, Sara (Musician)
c/o Staff Member *Paradigm (Monterey)*
509 Hartnell St
Monterey, CA 93940-2825, USA

Barenaked Ladies, Barenaked Ladies (Music Group)
c/o Staff Member *Paradigm (NY)*
360 Park Ave S Fl 16
New York, NY 10010-1716, USA

Barenboim, Daniel (Conductor, Musician)
29 Rue de la Coulouvreeniere
Geneva 1206, SWITZERLAND

Baretto, Ray (Musician)
Creative Music Consultants
181 Chrystie St # 300
New York, NY 10002-1275, USA

Barfield, Jesse L (Baseball Player)
Toronto Blue Jays
5814 Spanish Moss Ct
Spring, TX 77379-6482, USA

Barfield, John (Baseball Player)
Texas Rangers
13027 Childress Rd
Bauxite, AR 72011-9189, USA

Barfoot, Van T (War Hero)
4801 Namozine Rd
Leaning Oaks Farm
Ford, VA 23850-2828, USA

Bargar, Greg (Baseball Player)
Montreal Expos
902 Felbar Ave
Torrance, CA 90503-5128, USA

Bargnani, Andrea (Basketball Player)
c/o Leon Rose *Creative Artists Agency LCC (CAA-LA)*
2000 Avenue Of The Stars
Los Angeles, CA 90067-4700, USA

Barhorst, Barney (Basketball Player)
Chicago Stags
8004 River Bay Dr E
Indianapolis, IN 46240-2994, USA

Barierre, Tony (Actor)
c/o TJ Stein *Stein Entertainment Group*
11271 Ventura Blvd # 477
Studio City, CA 91604-3136, USA

Barinholtz, Ike (Comedian)
c/o Jai Khanna *Brillstein-Grey Entertainment*
9150 Wilshire Blvd Ste 350
Beverly Hills, CA 90212-3453, USA

Barisich, Carl J (Football Player)
Cleveland Browns
10747 McGregor Dr
Columbia, MD 21044-4956, USA

Barjatya, Sooraj (Bollywood, Director, Producer)
Bhana 1st Floor
422 Veer Sawarkar Road Prabhadevi
Dadar
Mumbai, MS 400025, INDIA

Barkauskas, Antanas S (President)
Akmenu 71
Vilnus, LITHUANIA

Barkely, Douglas (Doug) (Coach, Hockey Player)
523-3131 63 Ave NE
Calgary, AB T3E 6N4, CANADA

Barker, Bryan (Football Player)
Kansas City Chiefs
1225 Selva Marina Cir
Atlantic Beach, FL 32233-5525, USA

Barker, Clive (Director, Writer)
c/o Staff Member *Seraphim Films*
1606 Argyle Ave
Hollywood, CA 90028-6408, USA

Barker, Clyde F (Doctor)
3 Coopertown Rd
Haverford, PA 19041-1012, USA

Barker, Ed (Football Player)
Pittsburgh Steelers
12002 Clover Creek Dr SW
Lakewood, WA 98499-5210, USA

Barker, Glen (Baseball Player)
Houston Astros
18222 Thicket Grove Rd
Houston, TX 77084-7598, USA

Barker, Jordan (Actor)
c/o Staff Member *Select Artists Ltd (CA-Westside Office)*
1138 12th St Apt 1
Santa Monica, CA 90403-5459, USA

Barker, Len (Baseball Player)
Texas Rangers
445 Amberidge Trl NW
Atlanta, GA 30328-2806, USA

Barker, Lois (Baseball Player)
195 W Main St Apt 6
Chester, NJ 07930-2451, USA

Barker, Pat (Writer)
Gillion Aitken
29 Fernshaw Road
London SW10 0TG, UNITED KINGDOM (UK)

Barker, Ray (Baseball Player)
Baltimore Orioles
303 Greenbriar Rd
Martinsburg, WV 25401-2827, USA

Barker, Rich (Baseball Player)
Chicago Cubs
17 Landers Rd
Stoneham, MA 02180-1409, USA

Barker, Richard A (Religious Leader)
Orthodox Presbyterian Church
PO Box P
Willow Grove, PA 19090, USA

Barker, Roy (Football Player)
Minnesota Vikings
23 Saint Marks Cir
Central Islip, NY 11749-1728, USA

Barker, Tom (Actor)
London Mgmt
2-4 Noel St
London W1V 3RB, UNITED KINGDOM (UK)

Barker, Travis (Musician)
c/o Dvora Vener Englefield *BWR (BWR-LA)*
9100 Wilshire Blvd Fl 6
West Tower
Beverly Hills, CA 90212-3401, USA

Barker-Lequia, Joan (Baseball Player)
3236 34th St SW
Grandville, MI 49418-1905, USA

Barkett, Andy (Baseball Player)
US Olympic Team
820 Old Rucker Rd
Alpharetta, GA 30004-6373, USA

Barkin, Ellen (Actor)
Baker/Winokur/Ryder
9100 Wilshire Blvd # 600
Beverly Hills, CA 90212-3401, USA

Barkley, Brian (Baseball Player)
Boston Red Sox
9208 Spring Ridge Cir
Woodway, TX 76712-8764, USA

Barkley, Charles W (Basketball Player, Television Host)
c/o Staff Member *Turner Network Television (TNT-ATL)*
1050 Techwood Dr NW
Atlanta, GA 30318-5604, USA

Barkley, Dean M (Politician)
1300 W Medicine Lake Dr Apt 101
Minneapolis, MN 55441-4854, USA

Barkley, Iran (Boxer)
2645 3rd Ave
Bronx, NY 10451-6329, USA

Barkley, Jeff (Baseball Player)
Cleveland Indians
264 3rd Ave NE
Hickory, NC 28601-5016, USA

Barkman, Tyler Jane (Janie) (Swimmer)
Princeton University
Athletic Dept
Princeton, NJ 08544-0001, USA

Barksdale, James (Jim) (Business Person)
Barksdale Group
2730 Sand Hill Rd
Menlo Park, CA 94025-7071, USA

Barksdale, LaQuanda (Basketball Player)
San Antonio Silver Stars
1 Sbc Center Pkwy
San Antonio, TX 78219-3604, USA

Barksdale, Rhesa H (Judge)
US Court of Appeals
245 E Capitol St
Jackson, MS 39201-2409, USA

Barkum, Jerome P (Football Player)
New York Jets
2720 Palmer Dr Apt J5
Gulfport, MS 39507-2854, USA

Barkworth, Peter
47 Flask Walk
London, ENGLAND NW3 1HH, UNITED KINGDOM (UK)

Barletta, Joseph (Publisher)
TV Guide Magazine
100 Matsonford Road
Wayne, PA 19080-0001, USA

Barlow, Bob (Hockey Player)
Minnesota North Stars
4912 Wesley Rd
Victoria, BC V8Y 1Y5, CANADA

Barlow, Corey (Football Player)
Philadelphia Eagles
1258 Inverness Cove Pl
Birmingham, AL 35242-4255, USA

Barlow, Craig (Golfer)
PO Box 90040
Henderson, NV 89009-0040, USA

Barlow, Gary (Musician, Songwriter, Writer)
c/o Staff Member *Arista Records (NY)*
6 W 57th St
New York, NY 10019-3901, USA

Barlow, Mike (Baseball Player)
St Louis Cardinals
4524 Francis Rd
Cazenovia, NY 13035-8470, USA

Barlow, Perry (Cartoonist)
New Yorker Magazine
4 Times Sq
Editorial Dept
New York, NY 10036-6592, USA

Barlow, Reggie (Football Player)
Jacksonville Jaguars
3319 Woodley Rd
Montgomery, AL 36116-3154, USA

Barmes, Bruce (Baseball Player)
Washington Senators
509 McDonald Ave
Charlotte, NC 28203-5321, USA

Barmore, Leon (Baseball Player)
1100 Brookhaven Ave
Ruston, LA 71270-8505, USA

Barnaby, Matthew (Hockey Player)
Buffalo Sabres
134 King Anthony Way
Getzville, NY 14068-1414, USA

Barndt, Tom (Football Player)
Kansas City Chiefs
11041 Romola St
Las Vegas, NV 89141-3410, USA

Barnes, Al (Football Player)
Detroit Lions
5635 Criollo Dr
Las Vegas, NV 89122-3454, USA

Barnes, Benny J (Football Player)
Dallas Cowboys
5003 Fleming Ave
Richmond, CA 94804-4718, USA

Barnes, Billy Ray (Football Player)
Philadelphia Eagles
501 W Ryder Ave
Landis, NC 28088-1238, USA

Barnes, Blair (Hockey Player)
Los Angeles Kings
McIntosh Point
Christopher Lake, SK S0J 0N0, CANADA

Barnes, Brian (Baseball Player)
Montreal Expos
860 River Cove Dr
Dacula, GA 30019-2090, USA

Barnes, Bruce (Football Player)
New England Patriots
7129 Alexandria Pl
Stockton, CA 95207-1503, USA

Barnes, Christopher Daniel (Actor)
3824 Fairway Ave
Studio City, CA 91604-2303, USA

Barnes, Clive A (Critic)
New York Post
1211 Avenue Of The Americas
New York, NY 10036-8790, USA

Barnes, Erich (Football Player)
Chicago Bears
712 Warburton Ave
Yonkers, NY 10701-1501, USA

Barnes, Ernest E (Football Player)
New York Titans
4435 Camellia Ave
North Hollywood, CA 91602-1905, USA

Barnes, Frank (Baseball Player)
Kansas City Monarchs
1508 Brazil St
Greenville, MS 38701-2622, USA

Barnes, Gary (Football Player)
Green Bay Packers
172 Falling Springs Rd
Central, SC 29630-9406, USA

Barnes, Jeff (Football Player)
Oakland Raiders
3158 Kelly St
Hayward, CA 94541-3524, USA

Barnes, Jhane (Designer, Fashion
Designer)
Jhane Barnes Inc
140 W 57th St Ste 5B
New York, NY 10019-3326, USA

Barnes, Jimmy (Musician)
Harbour Agency
135 Forbes St
Wooloomooloo, NSW 2011, AUSTRALIA

Barnes, Joanna (Actor)
PO Box 1103
Gualala, CA 95445-1103, USA

Barnes, John (Baseball Player)
Minnesota Twins
9860 E Lindner Ave
Mesa, AZ 85209-2569, USA

Barnes, Johnnie (Football Player)
San Diego Chargers
212 Charlemagne Dr
Suffolk, VA 23435-1453, USA

Barnes, Julian P (Writer)
P F D Drury House
34-43 Russell St
London WC2B 5HA, UNITED KINGDOM
(UK)

Barnes, Larry (Football Player)
San Francisco 49ers
410 Navajo Street
Simla, CO 80835, USA

Barnes, Linda (Writer)
56 Seaver St
Brookline, MA 02445-5749, USA

Barnes, Lute (Baseball Player)
New York Mets
35911 Donny Cir
Palm Desert, CA 92211-2657, USA

Barnes, Mike H (Football Player)
St Louis Cardinals
205 Cindy St S
Keller, TX 76248-2341, USA

Barnes, Mike J (Football Player)
Baltimore Colts
27474 Plank Rd
Guys Mills, PA 16327-5434, USA

Barnes, Norm (Hockey Player)
Philadelphia Flyers
17 Meadow Xing
Simsbury, CT 06070-1006, USA

Barnes, Pat (Football Player)
Kansas City Chiefs
5 Willowglade
Dove Canyon, CA 92679-3813, USA

Barnes, Pricilla (Actor)
c/o Staff Member *GVA Talent Agency Inc*
9229 W Sunset Blvd Ste 320
Los Angeles, CA 90069-3403, USA

Barnes, Rashidi (Football Player)
Cleveland Browns
1720 E 2nd St Apt 12
Long Beach, CA 90802-8409, USA

Barnes, Reggie (Football Player)
Pittsburgh Steelers
505 W Springdale Ln
Grand Prairie, TX 75052-5122, USA

Barnes, Rich (Baseball Player)
Chicago White Sox
2845 Wilderness Rd
West Palm Beach, FL 33409-2030, USA

Barnes, Rick (Basketball Player)
Texas University
Athletic Dept
Austin, TX 78713, USA

Barnes, Robert H (Psychic)
Texas Tech University
PO Box 4349
Medical School
Lubbock, TX 79409-0007, USA

Barnes, Rod (Basketball Player)
Mississippi State University
Athletic Dept
Mississippi State, MS 39762, USA

Barnes, Rodrigo (Football Player)
Dallas Cowboys
PO Box 302
Waco, TX 76703-0302, USA

Barnes, Roosevelt Jr (Football Player)
Detroit Lions
3128 Covington Manor Rd
Fort Wayne, IN 46814-9126, USA

Barnes, Skeeter (Baseball Player)
Cincinnati Reds
11544 Winding Wood Dr
Indianapolis, IN 46235-9731, USA

Barnes, Stu (Hockey Player)
Winnipeg Jets
5069 Royal Creek Ln
Plano, TX 75093-4069, USA

Barnes, Tomur (Football Player)
Houston Oilers
PO Box 744
Highlands, TX 77562-0744, USA

Barnes, Wallace (Business Person)
Barnes Group
123 Main St
Bristol, CT 06010-6376, USA

Barnes, Walt (Football Player)
Washington Redskins
839 Broad St
PO Box 1383
Steamboat Springs, CO 80487, USA

Barnes, William (Baseball Player)
Baltimore Elite Giants
19792 Ardmore St
Detroit, MI 48235-1503, USA

Barnes Jr, Harry G (Diplomat)
Hapenny Road
Peacham, VT 05862, USA

Barnes-McCoy, Joyce (Baseball Player)
1313 E 19th Ave
Hutchinson, KS 67502-5061, USA

Barnet, Will (Artist, Educator)
National Arts Club
15 Gramercy Park S
New York, NY 10003-1796, USA

Barnett, Dick (Basketball Player)
St Johns University
College Of Professional Studies
8000 Utopia Parkway
Queens, NY 11439, USA

Barnett, Douglas (Football Player)
Los Angeles Rams
651 Park Ln
Billings, MT 59102-1930, USA

Barnett, Fred (Football Player)
Philadelphia Eagles
428 N 13th St Apt 5F
Philadelphia, PA 19123-3629, USA

Barnett, Gary (Coach, Football Coach)
Colorado University
Athletic Dept
Boulder, CO 80309-0001, USA

Barnett, Jim (Basketball Player)
7 Kittiwake Rd
Orinda, CA 94563-1716, USA

Barnett, Jonathan (Architect)
4501 Connecticut Ave NW
Washington, DC 20008-3710, USA

Barnett, Mandy (Musician)
c/o Staff Member *Paradigm (Nashville)*
124 12th Ave S Ste 410
Nashville, TN 37203-3170, USA

Barnett, Nate (Basketball Player)
Indiana Pacers
PO Box 242
Wilmington, DE 19899-0242, USA

Barnett, Oliver (Football Player)
Atlanta Falcons
1133 Autumn Ridge Dr
Lexington, KY 40509-2055, USA

Barnett, Sabrina (Model)
Next Model Mgmt
23 Watts St
New York, NY 10013, USA

Barnett, Steven (Steve) (Football Player)
Chicago Bears
308 Romae Ct
Danville, CA 94526-1863, USA

Barnette, Curtis H (Business Person)
Bethlehem Steel
1 E Broad St Ste 210
Bethlehem, PA 18018-5951, USA

Barney, Edith (Baseball Player)
329 Blackburn Blvd
Venice, FL 34287-1507, USA

Barney, Eppie (Football Player)
Cleveland Browns
24570 Lincoln Ct
Farmington Hills, MI 48335-1638, USA

Barney, Matthew (Artist, Entertainer)
515 W 24th St
Barbara Gladstone Gallery
New York, NY 10011-1104, USA

Barney Jr, Lemuel J (Lem) (Football
Player)
Detroit Lions
775 Kentbrook Dr
Commerce Township, MI 48382-5013,
USA

Barnhardt, Tom (Football Player)
Chicago Bears
1115 Edgedale Dr
Salisbury, NC 28144-2118, USA

Barnhart, Vic (Baseball Player)
Pittsburgh Pirates
13102 Unger Rd
Hagerstown, MD 21742-1428, USA

Barnhill, Norton (Basketball Player)
Seattle SuperSonics
1718 Park Terrace Ln
Winston Salem, NC 27127-4794, USA

Barnhill, Scott (Model)
c/o Staff Member *IMG Models*
304 Park Ave S Fl 12
New York, NY 10010-4301, USA

Barnowski, Ed (Baseball Player)
Baltimore Orioles
2380 Lake Lucy Rd
Chanhassen, MN 55317-7561, USA

Barnwell, Ysaye (Musician)
Sweet Honey Agency
PO Box 600099
Newtonville, MA 02460-0001, USA

Barocco, Rocco (Designer, Fashion
Designer)
Via Occhio Marion
Capri/Napoli 80773, ITALY

Baron, Crespo Enrique (Government
Official)
European Parliament
97/113 Rue Velliard
Brussels 1040, BELGIUM

Baron, Jimmy (Baseball Player)
19402 Texas Laurel Trl
Humble, TX 77346-3309, USA

Baron, Lita
1508 S La Verne Way
Palm Springs, CA 92264-9253, USA

Baron, Martin D (Editor)
Boston Globe
Editorial Dept
135 Wt Morrissey Blvd
Dorchester, MA 02125, USA

Baron, Murray (Hockey Player)
Philadelphia Flyers
8400 E Dixileta Dr Unit 118
Scottsdale, AZ 85266-2268, USA

Baron, Natalia (Actor)
c/o Tiffany Kuzon *Evolution Entertainment* (LA)
901 N Highland Ave
Los Angeles, CA 90038-2412, USA

Barone, Dick (Baseball Player)
Pittsburgh Pirates
1220 Heather Glen Cir
Hollister, CA 95023-5153, USA

Barr, Bob (Business Person, Politician)
Office of Bob Barr
900 Circle 75 Pkwy SE Ste 1280
Atlanta, GA 30339-6016, USA

Barr, Dave (Golfer)
Duncan MacKenzie
10620 Southdale Rd
Richmond, BC V7A 2W7, CANADA

Barr, Doris (Baseball Player)
312-1712 Portage Avenue
Winnipeg, MB R3J 0E3, CANADA

Barr, Doug (Actor)
PO Box 63
Rutherford, CA 94573-0063, USA

Barr, Jim (Baseball Player)
San Francisco Giants
6335 Oak Hill Dr
Granite Bay, CA 95746-8908, USA

Barr, Julia (Actor)
Saint Laurent Assoc
Cherokee Station
PO Box 20191
New York, NY 10075, USA

Barr, Nevada (Writer)
G P Putnam's Sons
375 Hudson St
New York, NY 10014-3658, USA

Barr, Roseanne (Actor, Comedian, Producer, Writer)
c/o Ruthanne Secunda *United Talent Agency* (UTA)
9560 Wilshire Blvd Ste 500
Beverly Hills, CA 90212-2401, USA

Barr, Steve (Baseball Player)
Boston Red Sox
470 Village Cir SW
Winter Haven, FL 33880-1668, USA

Barr, Terry (Football Player)
Detroit Lions
1546 Indianwood Ct
Bloomfield Hills, MI 48302-0729, USA

Barragan, Cuno (Baseball Player)
Chicago Cubs
1824 Saint Ann Ct
Carmichael, CA 95608-5643, USA

Barranca, German (Baseball Player)
Kansas City Royals
199 Kreidler Ave
York, PA 17402-4976, USA

Barrasso, Thomas (Tom) (Hockey Player)
Buffalo Sabres
12820 Rosalie St
Raleigh, NC 27614-7970, USA

Barratt, Michael R (Astronaut)
2102 Pleasant Palm Cir
League City, TX 77573-6670, USA

Barrault, Doug (Hockey Player)
RE/MAX of Golden
Box 20033
420D 9th Avenue North
Golden, BC V0A 1H0, CANADA

Barrault, Marie-Christine (Actor)
Cineart
36 Rue de Ponthlieu
Paris 75008, FRANCE

Barraza, Adriana (Actor)
Paramount Vantage
5555 Melrose Ave
Chevalier Bldg
Los Angeles, CA 90038-3197, USA

Barraza, Maria (Actor)
c/o Staff Member *TV Caracol*
Calle 76 #11 - 35
Piso 10AA
Bogota DC 26484, COLOMBIA

Barre, Raymond (Prime Minister)
4-6 Ave Emile-Acollas
Paris 75007, FRANCE

Barrese, Sasha (Actor)
c/o Todd Eisner *Agency for the Performing Arts* (APA-LA)
405 S Beverly Dr
Beverly Hills, CA 90212-4416, USA

Barreto, Bruno (Director)
30 W 61st St Apt 15B
New York, NY 10023-7612, USA

Barrett, Alice (Actor)
Alliance Talent
9171 Wilshire Blvd Ste 441
Beverly Hills, CA 90210-5516, USA

Barrett, Brendan Ryan (Actor)
c/o Staff Member *Stone Manners Talent & Literary* (LA)
6500 Wilshire Blvd Ste 550
Los Angeles, CA 90048-4950, USA

Barrett, Brendon Ryan (Actor)
9255 W Sunset Blvd Ste 1010
West Hollywood, CA 90069-3307, USA

Barrett, Colleen (Business Person)
Southwest Airlines
PO Box 36611
2702 Love Field Dr
Dallas, TX 75235-1611, USA

Barrett, Craig R (Business Person)
Intel Corp
2200 Mission College Blvd
Santa Clara, CA 95054-1549, USA

Barrett, David (Football Player)
Arizona Cardinals
PO Box 342442
Memphis, TN 38184-2442, USA

Barrett, Emmett (Football Player)
New York Giants
11520 SE Sunnyside Rd Apt 304
Clackamas, OR 97015-4309, USA

Barrett, Ernie (Basketball Player)
Boston Celtics
2105 Grand Ridge Ct
Manhattan, KS 66503-8695, USA

Barrett, Fred (Hockey Player)
Minnesota North Stars
3016 Leitrim Rd
Gloucester, ON K1T 3V9, CANADA

Barrett, Jacinda (Actor)
c/o Joan Green *Joan Green Management*
1836 Courtney Ter
Los Angeles, CA 90046-2106, USA

Barrett, James E (Judge)
US Court of Appeals
2120 Capitol Ave Ste 2131
Cheyenne, WY 82001-3658, USA

Barrett, Jean (Football Player)
San Francisco 49ers
7494 S Sleepy Hollow Dr
Tulsa, OK 74136-5919, USA

Barrett, Malcolm (Actor)
c/o Craig Dorfman *Blueprint Management*
5670 Wilshire Blvd Ste 2525
Los Angeles, CA 90036-5647, USA

Barrett, Mario
c/o Staff Member *Richard De La Font Agency*
4845 S Sheridan Rd Ste 505
Tulsa, OK 74145-5719, USA

Barrett, Martin G (Marty) (Baseball Player)
Boston Red Sox
3552 Ridge Meadow St
Las Vegas, NV 89135-7811, USA

Barrett, Michael (Mike) (Basketball Player)
5721 Templegate Dr
Nashville, TN 37221-4108, USA

Barrett, Stephen (Activist, Doctor)
PO Box 1747
Allentown, PA 18105-1747, USA

Barrett, Thomas J (Admiral)
Vice Commandant US Court Guard
2100 2nd St SW
Washington, DC 20593-0001, USA

Barrett, Tim (Baseball Player)
Montreal Expos
5588 Jandel Dr
Aurora, IN 47001-3010, USA

Barrett, Tina (Actor, Musician)
c/o Staff Member *S Club 7*
9830 Wilshire Blvd
Creative Artists Agency Lcc (Caa-La)
Beverly Hills, CA 90212-1804, USA

Barrett, Tom (Baseball Player)
Philadelphia Phillies
5306 W Jupiter Way
Chandler, AZ 85226-8622, USA

Barrett, Wade (Soccer Player)
Fredrikstad Fotballklubb Sport ASA
Mads Stangs gate 20
Fredrikstad N-1610, NORWAY

Barrett, William (Misc)
34 Harwood Ave
Sleepy Hollow, NY 10591-1309, USA

Barretto, Amber (Actor)
c/o Suzanne Bennett *Diverse Talent Group*
1875 Century Park E Ste 2250
Los Angeles, CA 90067-2563, USA

Barrichello, Rubens (Race Car Driver)
c/o Staff Member *Jaguar Racing Ltd*
Bradbourne Drive
Tilbrook
Milton Keynes MK7 8BJ, UNITED KINGDOM (UK)

Barrie, Barbara (Actor)
c/o Staff Member *Innovative Artists* (LA)
1505 10th St
Santa Monica, CA 90401-2805, USA

Barrie, Chris (Actor, Comedian)
International Creative Mgmt
76 Oxford St
London W1N 0AX, UNITED KINGDOM (UK)

Barrie, Doug (Hockey Player)
Pittsburgh Penguins
11203 79 St NW
Edmonton, AB T5B 2J8, CANADA

Barrie, Sebastian (Football Player)
Green Bay Packers
870 Astaire Ave
Duncanville, TX 75137-4720, USA

Barrile, Anthony (Actor)
Alliance Talent
9171 Wilshire Blvd Ste 441
Beverly Hills, CA 90210-5516, USA

Barrileaux, James (Misc)
Dryden Flight Research Center
PO Box 273
Edwards, CA 93523-0273, USA

Barringer, Patricia (Baseball Player)
16608 N 51st St
Scottsdale, AZ 85254-1063, USA

Barrino, Fantasia (Musician)
c/o Staff Member *American Idol*
7800 Beverly Blvd # 251
Los Angeles, CA 90036-2112, USA

Barrios, Jose (Baseball Player)
San Francisco Giants
6484 SW 25th St
Miami, FL 33155-2958, USA

Barris, Chuck (Television Host)
c/o Staff Member *Hyperion Books*
77 W 66th St
11th Floor
New York, NY 10023-6201, USA

Barris, George (Designer, Misc)
Barris Kustom Industries
10811 Riverside Dr
North Hollywood, CA 91602-2308, USA

Barriw, Barbara (Actor)
15 W 72nd St Apt 2A
New York, NY 10023-3419, USA

Barron, Alex (Race Car Driver)
Gurney Racing
2334 S Broadway
Santa Ana, CA 92707-3250, USA

Barron, Dana (Actor)
c/o Kevin Turner *Coast to Coast Talent Group*
3350 Barham Blvd
Los Angeles, CA 90068-1404, USA

Barron, Doug (Golfer)
5080 Peg Ln
Memphis, TN 38117-2147, USA

Barron, Kenneth (Kenny) (Composer, Musician)
Joel Chriss
300 Mercer St Apt 3J
New York, NY 10003-6732, USA

Barron, Tony (Baseball Player)
Montreal Expos
16014 123rd Avenue Ct E
Puyallup, WA 98374-9649, USA

Barros, Dana (Basketball Player)
c/o Staff Member *Boston Celtics*
151 Merrimac St # 1
Boston, MA 02114-4714, USA

Barrow, Geoff (Musician)
Fruit
Saga Center
326 Kensal Road
London W10 5BZ, UNITED KINGDOM (UK)

Barrow, Michael C (Football Player)
Houston Oilers
1717 N Bayshore Dr Apt 3255
Miami, FL 33132-1167, USA

Barrowman, John (Actor)
c/o Staff Member *Innovative Artists (LA)*
1505 10th St
Santa Monica, CA 90401-2805, USA

Barrowman, Mike (Swimmer)
706 N Wamer St
Bay City, MI 48706, USA

Barrows, Scott (Football Player)
Detroit Lions
3600 Kern Rd
Lake Orion, MI 48360-2351, USA

Barrows, Sydney Biddle (Business Person, Writer)
210 W 70th St Apt 209
New York, NY 10023-4363, USA

Barrs, Jay (Athlete)
6395 Senoma Dr
Salt Lake City, UT 84121-2264, USA

Barrueco, Manuel (Musician)
Columbia Artists Mgmt Inc
1790 Broadway Fl 6
New York, NY 10019-1412, USA

Barry, A L (Religious Leader)
Lutheran Church Missouri Synod
1333 S Kirkwood Rd
Saint Louis, MO 63122-7295, USA

Barry, Allan (Football Player)
Green Bay Packers
3760 Edgeview Dr
Pasadena, CA 91107-1309, USA

Barry, Brent (Basketball Player)
712 The Strand
Hermosa Beach, CA 90254-4457, USA

Barry, Claudia (Musician)
Talent Consultants Int'l
1560 Broadway # 1308
New York, NY 10036-1518, USA

Barry, Claudja (Musician)
Talent Consultants International
105 Shad Row Ste B
Piermont, NY 10968-3001, USA

Barry, Daniel T (Dan) (Astronaut)
46 Ashton Ln
South Hadley, MA 01075-2143, USA

Barry, Dave (Journalist, Writer)
Miami Herald
1 Herald Plz
Editorial Dept
Miami, FL 33132-1693, USA

Barry, Ed (Hockey Player)
Boston Bruins
61 Pleasant St
Needham, MA 02492-2950, USA

Barry, Gene (Actor)
12178 Ventura Blvd Ste 205
Studio City, CA 91604-2540, USA

Barry, Jeff (Baseball Player)
New York Mets
2156 Duncan Dr
Medford, OR 97504-8670, USA

Barry, Jeff (Composer)
BMI
8730 W Sunset Blvd # 300W
Los Angeles, CA 90069-2210, USA

Barry, John (Composer)
540 Centre Island Rd
Oyster Bay, NY 11771-5016, USA

Barry, John J (Misc)
Int'l Brotherhood of Electrical Workers
1125 15th St NW
Washington, DC 20005-2702, USA

Barry, Jon (Basketball Player)
Milwaukee Bucks
5030 Paces Station Dr
Atlanta, GA 30339-4055, USA

Barry, Jon (Basketball Player)
Detroit Pistons
2 Championship Dr
Palace
Auburn Hills, MI 48326-1753, USA

Barry, Len (Musician)
Cape Entertainment
8432 NW 31st Ct
Sunrise, FL 33351-8901, USA

Barry, Lynda (Cartoonist)
PO Box 447
Footville, WI 53537-0447, USA

Barry, Marion S (Politician)
161 Raleigh St SE
Washington, DC 20032-1528, USA

Barry, Maryanne Trump (Judge)
US Court of Appeals
50 Walnut St Rm 5040
US Courthouse
Newark, NJ 07102-3571, USA

Barry, Odell (Football Player)
Denver Broncos
2561 Ranch Reserve Rdg
Denver, CO 80234-2695, USA

Barry, Patricia (Actor)
12742 Highwood St
Los Angeles, CA 90049-2624, USA

Barry, Paul (Football Player)
Los Angeles Rams
409 Kingswood Dr
El Paso, TX 79932-2217, USA

Barry, Randy (Reality TV Star)
c/o Michael (Mike) Esterman *Esterman Entertainment*
214 Park Rd
Riva, MD 21140-1224, USA

Barry, Raymond J (Actor)
Metropolitan Talent Agency
4500 Wilshire Blvd Fl 2
Los Angeles, CA 90010-3858, USA

Barry, Rich (Baseball Player)
Philadelphia Phillies
12020 Hoffman St Apt C
Studio City, CA 91604-2075, USA

Barry, Rick (Basketball Player)
San Francisco Warriors
5240 Broadmoor Bluffs Dr
Colorado Springs, CO 80906-7912, USA

Barry, Rod (Adult Film Star)
c/o Staff Member *Diva Central Inc*
7510 W Sunset Blvd Ste 1445
Los Angeles, CA 90046-3408, USA

Barry, Seymour (Sy) (Cartoonist)
225 Fairfield Dr E
Holbrook, NY 11741-2866, USA

Barry, Todd (Comedian)
c/o David (Dave) Becky *3 Arts Entertainment Inc*
9460 Wilshire Blvd Fl 7
Beverly Hills, CA 90212-2713, USA

Barry III, Richard F D (Rick) (Basketball Player)
KNBR Radio
55 Hawthorne #1100
San Francisco, CA 94106-0001, USA

Barrymore, Drew (Actor, Producer)
c/o Staff Member *Flower Films Inc*
4000 Warner Blvd
Bungalow 3
Burbank, CA 91522-0001, USA

Barsh, Gregory S (Doctor)
Stanford University
Medical Center
Pediatrics Dept
Stanford, CA 94305, USA

Barsotti, Charles (Cartoonist)
419 E 55th St
Kansas City, MO 64110-2453, USA

Bart, Peter (Writer)
c/o Daniel A (Dan) Strone *Trident Media Group LLC*
41 Madison Ave Fl 36
New York, NY 10010-2257, USA

Bart, Roger (Actor)
c/o Michael Baum *Handprint Entertainment*
1100 Glendon Ave Ste 1000
Los Angeles, CA 90024-3514, USA

Bartecko, Lubos (Hockey Player)
St Louis Blues
121 Windy Acres Estates Dr
Ballwin, MO 63021-4232, USA

Bartee, Kimera (Baseball Player)
c/o Staff Member *Chicago Cubs*
1060 W Addison St
Wrigley Field
Chicago, IL 60613-4397, USA

Bartee, William (Football Player)
Kansas City Chiefs
17 Talaquah Blvd
Ormond Beach, FL 32174-3705, USA

Bartek, Steve (Musician)
c/o Staff Member *Kraft-Engel Management*
15233 Ventura Blvd Ste 200
Sherman Oaks, CA 91403-2244, USA

Bartel, Jean
229 Bronwood Ave
Los Angeles, CA 90049-3103, USA

Bartel, Robin (Hockey Player)
Calgary Flames
367 Nordstrum Rd
Saskatoon, SK S7K 6P9, CANADA

Bartels, Wolfgang (Skier)
Womdihof Hintersee
Ransau 83486, GERMANY

Barth, Robert (Religious Leader)
Churches of Christ in Christian Union
PO Box 30
Circleville, OH 43113-0030, USA

Bartha, Justin (Actor)
c/o Toni Howard *International Creative Management (ICM-LA)*
10250 Constellation Blvd
Los Angeles, CA 90067-6200, USA

Bartholomay, William C (Baseball Player)
Atlanta Braves
180 E Pearson St Apt 3307
Chicago, IL 60611-6730, USA

Bartholomew, Brent (Football Player)
Miami Dolphins
809 N Lake Pleasant Rd
Apopka, FL 32712-3219, USA

Bartholomew, Logan (Actor)
c/o Beverly Strong *Anonymous Content (CA)*
9350 Wilshire Blvd Ste 224
Beverly Hills, CA 90212-3204, USA

Bartholomew, Reginald (Diplomat)
State Department
2201 C St NW
Washington, DC 20520-0099, USA

Bartilson, Lynsey (Actor)
c/o Neil Bagg *Don Buchwald & Associates Inc (LA)*
6500 Wilshire Blvd Ste 2200
Los Angeles, CA 90048-4942, USA

Bartirome, Tony (Baseball Player)
Pittsburgh Pirates
1104 Palma Sola Blvd
Bradenton, FL 34209-3342, USA

Bartiromo, Maria (Correspondent)
c/o Staff Member *CNBC (DC)*
1025 Connecticut Ave NW Ste 800
Washington, DC 20036-5419, USA

Bartkowski, Steven J (Steve) (Football Player)
Atlanta Falcons
10745 Bell Rd
Duluth, GA 30097-1801, USA

Bartle, Cheryl (Actor)
8281 Melrose Ave Ste 200
Los Angeles, CA 90046-6890, USA

Bartles, Edward (Basketball Player)
Washinton Capitals
105 Hemlock Dr
Killingworth, CT 06419-2225, USA

Bartlett, Bonnie (Actor, Musician)
12805 Hortense St
Studio City, CA 91604-1124, USA

Bartlett, Doug (Football Player)
Philadelphia Eagles
9133 26th St
Brookfield, IL 60513-1006, USA

Bartlett, Erinn (Actor)
c/o Randy James *James/Levy/Jacobson Management*
3500 W Olive Ave Ste 1470
Burbank, CA 91505-5514, USA

Bartlett, Jennifer L (Artist)
Paula Cooper Gallery
534 W 21st St
New York, NY 10011-2812, USA

Bartlett, Jim (Hockey Player)
Montreal Canadiens
8718 Chadwick Dr
Tampa, FL 33635-6212, USA

Bartlett, Neil (Misc)
6 Oak Dr
Orinda, CA 94563-3912, USA

Bartlett, Robin (Actor)
c/o Staff Member *Gersh Agency, The (LA)*
232 N Canon Dr
Beverly Hills, CA 90210-5302, USA

Bartlett, Thomas A (Educator)
1209 SW 6th Ave Unit 904
Portland, OR 97204-1031, USA

Bartletti, Don (Journalist)
Los Angeles Times
202 W 1st St
Editorial Dept
Los Angeles, CA 90012-4105, USA

Bartley, Boyd (Baseball Player)
Brooklyn Dodgers
7500 Noreast Dr
Fort Worth, TX 76180-6736, USA

Bartley, Ephesians (Football Player)
Philadelphia Eagles
3552 Kittery Dr
Snellville, GA 30039-6033, USA

Bartoe, John-David F (Astronaut)
2724 Lighthouse Dr
Houston, TX 77058-4318, USA

Bartoletti, Bruno (Conductor)
Chicago Lyric Opera
20 N Wacker Dr
Chicago, IL 60606-2806, USA

Bartoli, Cecilia (Musician)
Decca Music Group Limited
8 St James's Square
London SW1Y 4JU, UNITED KINGDOM
(UK)

Bartolome, Victor (Basketball Player)
Golden State Warriors
1025A Rinconada Rd
Santa Barbara, CA 93101-1424, USA

Bartolomew, Ken (Speed Skater)
4820 Bryant Ave S
Minneapolis, MN 55419-5359, USA

Barton, Austin (Artist)
100 N Lake
Joseph, OR 97846, USA

Barton, Bob (Baseball Player)
San Francisco Giants
37193 Stardust Way
Murrieta, CA 92563-5076, USA

Barton, Don (Football Player)
Green Bay Packers
706 Trenton Dr
Tyler, TX 75703-1110, USA

Barton, Dorie (Actor)
c/o Daniel (Dan) Spilo *Artistry
Management*
525 Westbourne Dr
West Hollywood, CA 90048-1913, USA

Barton, Eileen (Musician)
4 Lackawanna Dr
Newton, NJ 07860-5508, USA

Barton, Eric (Football Player)
Oakland Raiders
9902 Lee Dr
Eden Prairie, MN 55347-4802, USA

Barton, Glenys (Artist)
Angela Flowers Gallery
199-205 Richmond Road
London E8 3NJ, UNITED KINGDOM (UK)

Barton, Gregory (Greg) (Football Player)
Detroit Lions
13965 SW Barlow Ct
Beaverton, OR 97008-5525, USA

Barton, Harris S (Football Player)
The Nat Org of Pro Athletes
1806 Watermere Ln
Windermere, FL 34786-6121, USA

Barton, Jacqueline K (Misc)
California Institute of Technology
Chemistry Dept
Pasadena, CA 91125-0001, USA

Barton, James (Football Player)
Dallas Cowboys
2126 Taylor Ln
Newark, OH 43055-6091, USA

Barton, Lou Ann (Musician)
2010 Kinney Ave
Austin, TX 78704-4008, USA

Barton, Mischa (Actor)
c/o Patti Felker *Nelson/Felker LLP*
10880 Wilshire Blvd # 2070
Los Angeles, CA 90024-4101, USA

Barton, Rachel (Musician)
I C M Artists
40 W 57th St
New York, NY 10019-4001, USA

Barton, Shawn (Baseball Player)
Seattle Mariners
4012 Hilltop Ave
Reading, PA 19605-1123, USA

Bartosch, Dave (Baseball Player)
St Louis Cardinals
6437 Riverplace Dr
Nashville, TN 37221-6549, USA

Bartosik, Alison (Swimmer)
c/o Staff Member *Premier Management
Group*
700 Evanvale Ct
Cary, NC 27518-2806, USA

Bartucelli, Jean-Louis
9 rue Benard
Paris F-75014, FRANCE

Bartz, Carol A (Business Person)
Autodesk Inc
111 McLnnis Parkway
San Rafael, CA 94903, USA

Bartz, Gary L (Composer, Musician)
Joel Chriss
300 Mercer St Apt 3J
New York, NY 10003-6732, USA

Baruchel, Jay (Actor)
c/o Staff Member *Glenn Talent
Management*
3981 St Laurent #730
Montreal, PQ H2W 1Y5, CANADA

Baryshnikov, Mikhail (Actor, Dancer)
c/o Staff Member *Creative Artists Agency
LCC (CAA-LA)*
2000 Avenue Of The Stars
Los Angeles, CA 90067-4700, USA

Barzilauskas, Carl (Football Player)
New York Jets
4444 Lower Schooner Rd
Nashville, IN 47448-9476, USA

Basapez, Sergio (Actor)
c/o Staff Member *TV Azteca*
Periferico Sur 4121
Colonia Fuentes del Pedregal
DF CP 14141, MEXICO

Basaraba, Gary (Actor)
26 Rue Albus
Toulouse 31300, FRANCE

Basch, Harry (Actor)
920 1/2 S Serrano Ave
Los Angeles, CA 90006-1108, USA

Basche, David Alan (Actor)
c/o Lainie Sorkin Stolhanske *Management
360*
9111 Wilshire Blvd
Beverly Hills, CA 90210-5508, USA

Baschnagel, Brian D (Football Player)
1823 Ridgewood Ln W
Glenview, IL 60025, USA

Basco, Dante (Actor)
Don Buchwald
6500 Wilshire Blvd Ste 2200
Los Angeles, CA 90048-4942, USA

Basco, Derek (Actor)
c/o Staff Member *GVA Talent Agency Inc*
9229 W Sunset Blvd Ste 320
Los Angeles, CA 90069-3403, USA

Basco, Dion (Actor)
Schiowitz/Clay/Rose
1680 Vine St Ste 1016
Los Angeles, CA 90028-8800, USA

Basgall, Monty (Baseball Player)
Pittsburgh Pirates
1321 Buckhorn Cir
Sierra Vista, AZ 85635-0902, USA

Bashir, Martin (Correspondent, Journalist,
Television Host)
c/o Staff Member *Nightline*
1717 Desales St NW
Washington, DC 20036-4401, USA

Bashkirov, Dmitri A (Musician)
25 Martirez Oblatos
Pozuelo
Madrid, SPAIN

Basia (Music Group)
c/o Staff Member *Creative Artists Agency
LCC (CAA-LA)*
2000 Avenue Of The Stars
Los Angeles, CA 90067-4700, USA

Basilio, Carmen (Boxer)
67 Boxwood Dr
Rochester, NY 14617-4002, USA

Basinger, Kim (Actor)
c/o Rick Nicita *Creative Artists Agency
LCC (CAA-LA)*
2000 Avenue Of The Stars
Los Angeles, CA 90067-4700, USA

Basinski, Ed (Baseball Player)
Brooklyn Dodgers
4110 SE Jackson St
Milwaukie, OR 97222-5936, USA

Baska, Richard (Football Player)
Denver Broncos
PO Box 5322
Central Point, OR 97502-0053, USA

Bass, Bob (Basketball Player, Coach,
Misc)
2266 Deerfield Dr
Fort Mill, SC 29715-6941, USA

Bass, Fontella (Music Group, Musician)
Cape Entertainment
1181 NW 76th Ave
Plantation, FL 33322-5120, USA

Bass, George F (Archaeologist)
1600 Dominik Dr
College Station, TX 77840-3623, USA

Bass, Glenn (Football Player)
Buffalo Bills
2601 Armstrong Rd
Tallahassee, FL 32308-0803, USA

Bass, Jules (Director, Musician, Producer,
Writer)
c/o Staff Member *Rankin/Bass Productions*
24 W 55th St
New York, NY 10019-5320, USA

Bass, Kevin (Baseball Player)
Houston Astros
3630 Maranatha Dr
Sugar Land, TX 77479-9665, USA

Bass, Lance (Musician)
c/o Katie Rhodes *Untitled Entertainment
(LA)*
331 N Maple Dr Fl 3
Beverly Hills, CA 90210-3827, USA

Bass, Michael T (Football Player)
Detroit Lions
4703 NW 36th St
Gainesville, FL 32605-1017, USA

Bass, Randy (Baseball Player)
Minnesota Twins
2709 SW Coombs Rd
Lawton, OK 73505-0809, USA

Bass, Ronald (Writer)
c/o Staff Member *Creative Artists Agency
LCC (CAA-LA)*
2000 Avenue Of The Stars
Los Angeles, CA 90067-4700, USA

Bass, Ronald (Ron) (Writer)
Creative Artists Agency
9830 Wilshire Blvd
Beverly Hills, CA 90212-1804, USA

Bassen, Bob (Coach, Hockey Player)
New York Islanders
Utah Grizzlies 3200 Decker Lake Dr
Attn Coaching Staff
Salt Lake City, UT 84119, USA

Bassen, Hank (Hockey Player)
Chicago Blackhawks
8808 48 Ave NW
Calgary, AB T3B 2B2, CANADA

Bassett, Angela (Actor)
c/o Jason Weinberg *Untitled
Entertainment (LA)*
331 N Maple Dr Fl 3
Beverly Hills, CA 90210-3827, USA

Bassett, Brian (Cartoonist, Editor)
Seattle Times
1120 John St
Editorial Dept
Seattle, WA 98109-5321, USA

Bassett, Leslie R (Composer)
5433 Ashmoore Ln
Flowery Branch, GA 30542-2777, USA

Bassett, Tim (Basketball Player)
San Diego Conqistadors
2222 Encino Loop
San Antonio, TX 78259-1903, USA

Bassey, Dame Shirley (Musician)
c/o Staff Member *William Morris Agency
(WMA-LA)*
1 William Morris Pl
Beverly Hills, CA 90212-4261, USA

Bassey, Jennifer (Actor)
12 E 86th St Apt 1728
New York, NY 10028-0517, USA

Basslitz, Georg (Artist)
Schloss Demeberg
Holle 31188, GERMANY

Bassman, Herman (Football Player)
Philadelphia Eagles
910 Sunset Ave
Petersburg, VA 23805-2824, USA

Bast, William
6691 Whitley Ter
Los Angeles, CA 90068-3220, USA

Bastedo, Alexandra (Actor)
Charlesworth
68 Old Brompton Rd #280
London SW7 3LQ, UNITED KINGDOM
(UK)

Bastian, Noah (Actor, Musician)
c/o Staff Member *Amsel Eisenstadt &
Frazier Inc*
5055 Wilshire Blvd Ste 865
Los Angeles, CA 90036-6109, USA

Bat for Lashes (Music Group)
c/o Staff Member *Paradigm (Monterey)*
509 Hartnell St
Monterey, CA 93940-2825, USA

Batali, Dean (Writer)
c/o Michael Van Dyck *Genesis*
360 N Crescent Dr Bldg North
Beverly Hills, CA 90210-6818, USA

Batali, Mario (Chef, Television Host)
c/o Staff Member *Food Network, The*
75 9th Ave
New York, NY 10011-7006, USA

Batch, Charlie (Football Player)
Detroit Lions
1322 N Huron River Dr
Ypsilanti, MI 48197-1615, USA

Batchelor, Amelia
14811 Mulholland Dr
Los Angeles, CA 90077-1731, USA

Batchelor, Rich (Baseball Player)
St Louis Cardinals
1004 Pineneedle Rd
Hartsville, SC 29550-8452, USA

Bateman, Brian (Golfer)
2910 River Oaks Dr
Monroe, LA 71201-2028, USA

Bateman, Jason (Actor)
c/o Michael Rotenberg *3 Arts Entertainment Inc*
9460 Wilshire Blvd Fl 7
Beverly Hills, CA 90212-2713, USA

Bateman, Justine (Actor)
11288 Ventura Blvd # 190
Studio City, CA 91604-3187, USA

Bateman, Marv (Football Player)
Dallas Cowboys
1189 E Pinion St
Washington, UT 84780-8865, USA

Bates, Alfred (Athlete, Track Athlete)
4506 Mulberry St
Philadelphia, PA 19124-3724, USA

Bates, Bill (Football Player)
Dallas Cowboys
1252 Neck Rd
Ponte Vedra, FL 32082-4112, USA

Bates, Charles C (Oceanographer)
501 S La Posada Cir Apt 388
Green Valley, AZ 85614-5109, USA

Bates, Del (Baseball Player)
Philadelphia Phillies
8213 NE 115th Way
Kirkland, WA 98034-3506, USA

Bates, Dick (Baseball Player)
Seattle Pilots
5859 W Cielo Grande
Glendale, AZ 85310-3631, USA

Bates, Dwayne (Football Player)
Chicago Bears
76 Houston Loop
Jackson, SC 29831-3119, USA

Bates, Jason (Baseball Player)
Colorado Rockies
9856 W Freiburg Dr Unit F
Littleton, CO 80127-5949, USA

Bates, Kathy (Actor)
c/o Susan Smith *Susan Smith Company, The*
1344 N Wetherly Dr
Los Angeles, CA 90069-1817, USA

Bates, Mario (Football Player)
New Orleans Saints
7249 E Del Acero Dr
Scottsdale, AZ 85258-2068, USA

Bates, Michael (Football Player)
Seattle Seahawks
14222 S 5th St
Phoenix, AZ 85048-1812, USA

Bates, Pat (Golfer)
215 Ward Cir Ste 200
Brentwood, TN 37027-2306, USA

Bates, Patrick J (Football Player)
Oakland Raiders
2745 N Collins St Apt 11123
Arlington, TX 76006-7108, USA

Bates, Robert T (Misc)
Railroad Signalman Brotherhood
601 W Golf Rd
Mount Prospect, IL 60056-4276, USA

Bates, Shawn (Hockey Player)
Boston Bruins
35 Bradshaw St
Medford, MA 02155-4819, USA

Bates, Ted (Football Player)
Chicago Cardinals
4036 Paige St
Los Angeles, CA 90031-1437, USA

Bathe, Frank (Hockey Player)
Detroit Red Wings
2 Meadowood Dr
Scarborough, ME 04074-9421, USA

Bathe, Ryan Michelle (Actor)
c/o Nick Campbell *Commonwealth Talent Group*
5225 Wilshire Blvd Ste 509
Los Angeles, CA 90036-4349, USA

Bathgate, Andy (Hockey Player)
New York Rangers
43 Brentwood Dr
Brampton, ON L6T 1R1, CANADA

Bathgate, Frank (Hockey Player)
New York Rangers
602-330 Mill St S
Brampton, ON L6Y 3V3, CANADA

Batikis, Annastasia (Baseball Player)
1023 Crab Tree Ln
Racine, WI 53406-4109, USA

Batinkoff, Randall (Actor)
1330 4th St
Santa Monica, CA 90401-1302, USA

Batista, Dave (Wrestler)
Demon Wrestling Inc
2020 Penn Ave NW # 179
Washington, DC 20006-1811, USA

Batista, Tony (Athlete)
333 W Camden St
Baltimore, MD 21201-2435, USA

Batiste, Kevin (Baseball Player)
Toronto Blue Jays
3624 Avenue M
Galveston, TX 77550-4145, USA

Batiste, Kim (Baseball Player)
Philadelphia Phillies
16163 Aikens Rd
Prairieville, LA 70769-4903, USA

Batiste, Michael (Football Player)
Dallas Cowboys
2720 Edmonds St
Beaumont, TX 77705-1437, USA

Batiuk, Thomas M (Tom) (Cartoonist)
Universal Press Syndicate
4520 Main St
Kansas City, MO 64111-1876, USA

Batra, Pooja (Actor, Bollywood)
403H Gokul Vihar II
Thakur Complex Kandivli (E)
Mumbai, MS 400068, INDIA

Battaglia, Bates (Hockey Player)
Carolina Hurricanes
510 Glenwood Ave Apt 512
Raleigh, NC 27603-1263, USA

Battaglia, Marco (Football Player)
Cincinnati Bengals
15832 79th St
Howard Beach, NY 11414-2907, USA

Battaglia, Matt (Actor)
c/o Stew Strunk *Main Title Entertainment*
5225 Wilshire Blvd Ste 500
Los Angeles, CA 90036-4349, USA

Battaglia, Rik (Actor)
Viale Montegrappa 10
Colle Verde Guidonia
Rome 00012, ITALY

Batten, Patrick (Football Player)
Detroit Lions
4202 Noble Creek Dr NW
Atlanta, GA 30327-5129, USA

Battista, Bobbie
c/o Staff Member *Atamira*
3400 Peachtree Rd NE Ste 300
Atlanta, GA 30326-1107, USA

Battle, Allen (Baseball Player)
St Louis Cardinals
106 Donette Loop
Daphne, AL 36526-7764, USA

Battle, Howard (Baseball Player)
Toronto Blue Jays
420 Fayard St
Biloxi, MS 39530-2070, USA

Battle, James (Football Player)
Minnesota Vikings
5 Oasis Crt
St Albert, AB T8N 6X2, CANADA

Battle, John (Basketball Player)
Atlanta Hawks
Genral Delivery
Riverdale, GA 30274, USA

Battle, Kathleen D (Opera Singer)
Columbia Artists Mgmt Inc
1790 Broadway Fl 6
New York, NY 10019-1412, USA

Battle, Lois (Writer)
Viking Press
375 Hudson St
New York, NY 10014-3658, USA

Battle, Mike (Football Player)
New York Jets
PO Box 1156
Amherst, VA 24521-1156, USA

Battle, Ralph (Football Player)
Cincinnati Bengals
184 Timber Oak Rd
Huntsville, AL 35806-4110, USA

Battle, Terry (Football Player)
Arizona Cardinals
37678 Rushing Wind Ct
Murrieta, CA 92563-2734, USA

Batts, Lloyd (Basketball Player)
Virginia Squires
500 S Dante Ave
Glenwood, IL 60425-2137, USA

Batts, Matt (Baseball Player)
Boston Red Sox
17927 Silver Creek Ct
Baton Rouge, LA 70810-8918, USA

Batts, Warren L (Business Person)
Premark International
3600 W Lake Ave
Glenview, IL 60026-1215, USA

Bauchau, Patrick (Actor)
c/o Richard Schwartz *Richard Schwartz Management*
2934 1/2 N Beverly Glen Cir # 107
Los Angeles, CA 90077-1724, USA

Baudry, Patrick
305 Ave Mairie
Eaunas 31600, FRANCE

Bauer, Alice (Golfer)
LPGA Pioneer
77165 Avenida Arteaga
La Quinta, CA 92253-2552, USA

Bauer, Belinda (Actor)
410 Wilshire Blvd # 54
Santa Monica, CA 90401-1410, USA

Bauer, Chris (Actor)
c/o Staff Member *Framework Entertainment (LA)*
9057 Nemo St # C
W Hollywood, CA 90069-5511, USA

Bauer, Erwin A (Photographer)
8880 SE 19th Avenue Rd
Ocala, FL 34480-5711, USA

Bauer, Hank (Football Player)
San Diego Chargers
11150 Alejo Pl
San Diego, CA 92124-1521, USA

Bauer, Henry A (Hank) (Baseball Player)
Hank Bauer, Inc
243 Elkwood Ave
Imperial Beach, CA 91932-2413, USA

Bauer, Jaime Lyn (Actor)
Tyler Kjar
5116 Lankershim Blvd
North Hollywood, CA 91601-3717, USA

Bauer, John (Football Player)
New York Giants
9764 Cambridge Cir
Mokena, IL 60448-7726, USA

Bauer, Kristen (Actor)
c/o Arthur Toretsky *Paradigm (LA)*
360 N Crescent Dr
North Bldg
Beverly Hills, CA 90210-6820, USA

Bauer, Kristin (Actor)
c/o Ben Levine *Evolution Entertainment (LA)*
10585 Santa Monica Blvd Ste 120
Los Angeles, CA 90025-4984, USA

Bauer, Linda Susan
2476 Glendale Cir SE
Smyrna, GA 30080-1830, USA

Bauer, Peggy (Photographer)
8880 SE 19th Avenue Rd
Ocala, FL 34480-5711, USA

Bauer, Peter (Publisher)
People Magazine
Rockefeller Center
Time-Life Building
New York, NY 10020, USA

Bauer, Rick (Baseball Player)
Baltimore Orioles
6643 W Limelight Dr
Boise, ID 83714-6109, USA

Bauer, Steven (Actor)
Innovative Artists
1505 10th Ave St
Santa Monica, CA 90401, USA

Bauer, William J (Judge)
US Court of Appeals
111 N Canal St
Chicago, IL 60606-7206, USA

Baugh, Gavin (Baseball Player)
3605 Pasadena Dr
San Mateo, CA 94403-2947, USA

Baugh, Laura (Golfer)
5225 Timberview Ter
Orlando, FL 32819-3924, USA

Baugh, Samuel A (Sammy) (Coach, Football Player)
Washington Redskins
General Delivery
Rotan, TX 79546-9999, USA

Baugh, Tom (Football Player)
Kansas City Chiefs
14716 S Bynum Rd
Lone Jack, MO 64070-9286, USA

Baughan, Maxie C (Coach, Football Player)
Philadelphia Eagles
3355 Lawndale Rd
Reisterstown, MD 21136-4026, USA

Baughman, J Ross (Journalist, Misc, Photographer)
203 S Payne St
Alexandria, VA 22314-3529, USA

Baughman, Justin (Baseball Player)
Anaheim Angels
4052 NE 21st Ave
Portland, OR 97212-1433, USA

Baum, Herbert M (Business Person)
Quarker State Corp
700 Milam St
Houston, TX 77002-2806, USA

Bauman, Gary (Hockey Player)
Montreal Canadiens
191 Southampton Dr SW
Calgary, AB T2W 0V5, CANADA

Bauman, John Bowzer
3168 Oakshire Dr
Los Angeles, CA 90068-1743, USA

Bauman, Jon (Bowzer) (Music Group)
Cape Entertainment
1161 NW 76th St Ave
Plantation, FL 33322, USA

Bauman, Rashad (Football Player)
Washington Redskins
1150 Darlene Ln
Eugene, OR 97401-1551, USA

Baumann, Frank M (Baseball Player)
Boston Red Sox
7712 Sunray Ln
Saint Louis, MO 63123-1938, USA

Baumann, Herbert K W (Composer)
Franziskaserster 16 #1419
Munich 81669, GERMANY

Baumbach, Noah (Actor)
c/o Brad Gross *Brad Gross Agency, The*
6715 Hollywood Blvd # 236
Los Angeles, CA 90028-4627, USA

Baumgardner, Larry (Football Player)
Baltimore Colts
1125 Loma Ave # 143
Coronado, CA 92118-2835, USA

Baumgarten, Ross (Baseball Player)
Chicago White Sox
1020 Bluff Rd
Glencoe, IL 60022-1152, USA

Baumgartner, Bruce (Motivational Speaker, Wrestler)
12765 Forrest Dr
Edinboro, PA 16412-1281, USA

Baumgartner, John (Baseball Player)
Detroit Tigers
1215 Oxford Ct
Birmingham, AL 35242-4676, USA

Baumgartner, Mary (Baseball Player)
60 Lane 440 Jimmerson Lk
Fremont, IN 46737-9634, USA

Baumgartner, Steve (Football Player)
New Orleans Saints
144 Brookside Dr
Mandeville, LA 70471-3202, USA

Baumgartner, William (Doctor)
Johns Hopkins Hospital
600 N Wolfe St
Baltimore, MD 21287-0005, USA

Baumhower, Robert G (Bob) (Football Player)
Miami Dolphins
21201 Ayrshire Ln
Fairhope, AL 36532-4479, USA

Baumler, Hans-Jurgen
18 chemin du Casteller
Le Rouret 06650, FRANCE

Baun, Bob (Hockey Player)
Toronto Maple Leafs
35 Pittman Cres
Ajax, ON L1S 3G4, CANADA

Bauta, Ed (Baseball Player)
St Louis Cardinals
4820 Bitterbrush Dr
Boise, ID 83703-3804, USA

Baute, Joseph A (Business Person)
Nashua Corp
11 Trafalgar Sq # 200
Nashua, NH 03063-4902, USA

Bautista, Danny (Baseball Player)
Detroit Tigers
901 E Van Buren St Apt 1063
Phoenix, AZ 85006-4014, USA

Bautista, Franciso Javier Jr (Frankie J) (Musician)
c/o Staff Member *BMG*
1540 Broadway
New York, NY 10036-4074, USA

Bautista, Jose (Baseball Player)
Baltimore Orioles
4241 SW 149th Ter
Miramar, FL 33027-3339, USA

Bavaro, David (Football Player)
Phoenix Cardinals
55 Ash St Unit 14
Danvers, MA 01923-2710, USA

Bavaro, Mark (Football Player)
New York Giants
17 Long Hl
Boxford, MA 01921-2453, USA

Bawel, Edward (Football Player)
Philadelphia Eagles
1169 2nd Ave
Jasper, IN 47546-3411, USA

Bax, Kylie (Actor, Model)
c/o Staff Member *Storm Model Management Limited*
5 Jubilee Place Fl 5
London SW3 3TD, UNITED KINGDOM (UK)

Baxendale, Helen (Actor)
c/o Staff Member *Yakety Yak*
8 Bloomsbury Sq
London WC1A 2UA, UNITED KINGDOM (UK)

Baxes, Mike (Baseball Player)
Kansas City A's
303 Wickham Dr
Mill Valley, CA 94941-3443, USA

Baxley, Rob (Football Player)
Phoenix Cardinals
39 Oak Creek Dr
Yorkville, IL 60560-9779, USA

Baxter, Fred (Football Player)
New York Jets
PO Box 14
Brundidge, AL 36010-0014, USA

Baxter, James (Animator)
Dream Works SKG
100 University City Plaza
University City, CA 91608, USA

Baxter, Jeff (Skunk) (Music Group, Musician)
Monterey Peninsula Artists
509 Hartnell St
Monterey, CA 93940-2825, USA

Baxter, Lloyd (Football Player)
Green Bay Packers
2500 Homedale Dr
Austin, TX 78704-3837, USA

Baxter, Meredith (Actor)
9229 W Sunset Blvd Ste 710
West Hollywood, CA 90069-3407, USA

Baxter, Paul (Hockey Player)
Quebec Nordiques
452 NW 120th Dr
Coral Springs, FL 33071-4025, USA

Bay, Frances (Actor)
Henderson/Hogan
8285 W Sunset Blvd Ste 1
West Hollywood, CA 90046-2420, USA

Bay, Michael (Actor, Director, Producer)
c/o Staff Member *Bay Films*
631 Colorado Ave
Santa Monica, CA 90401-2507, USA

Bay, Susan (Actor)
801 Stone Canyon Rd
Los Angeles, CA 90077-2911, USA

Bay, Willow
1050 Techwood Dr NW
Atlanta, GA 30318-5604, USA

Bay City Rollers (Music Group)
297 Kinderkamack Rd Ste 101
Oradell, NJ 07649-1535, USA

Baye, Nathalie
10 avenue George V
Paris F-75008, FRANCE

Bayes, G E (Religious Leader)
Free Methodist Church
PO Box 535002
Winona Lake, IN 46590, USA

Bayle, Silvia (Actor)
c/o Staff Member *Telefe - Argentina*
Pavon 2444 (C1248AAT)
Buenos Aires, ARGENTINA

Bayless, Martin (Football Player)
St Louis Cardinals
757 Ernroe Dr
Dayton, OH 45408-1507, USA

Bayless, Rick (Football Player)
Minnesota Vikings
885 Dawn Ave
Shoreview, MN 55126-6403, USA

Bayley, Aaron (Musician)
c/o Staff Member *Pop Idol (Fremantle Media)*
2700 Colorado Ave Ste 450
Santa Monica, CA 90404-3599, USA

Bayliss, Rachel
Somerset Park Farm
Congelton Chelshire, ENGLAND, UNITED KINGDOM (UK)

Baylon, Noah (Writer)
c/o James (Jamie) Feldman *Lichter Grossman Nichols Adler & Goodman*
9200 W Sunset Blvd Ste 1200
Los Angeles, CA 90069-3607, USA

Baylor, Don (Baseball Player)
Baltimore Orioles
56325 Riviera
La Quinta, CA 92253-5008, USA

Baylor, Elgin (Basketball Player)
Minneapolis Lakers
2480 Briarcrest Rd
Beverly Hills, CA 90210-1820, USA

Baylor, John (Football Player)
Indianapolis Colts
211 Oak St
Hattiesburg, MS 39401-2372, USA

Baylor, Raymond (Football Player)
San Diego Chargers
5302 Heathercrest St
Houston, TX 77045-5230, USA

Baylor, Tim (Football Player)
Baltimore Colts
1302 Douglas Ave
Minneapolis, MN 55403-2904, USA

Bayne, Howard (Basketball Player)
Kentucky Colonels
8809 Stoney Point Dr
Las Vegas, NV 89134-8615, USA

Baynham, Craig (Football Player)
Dallas Cowboys
1 7th St Apt 1102
Augusta, GA 30901-1397, USA

Bayo, Maria (Opera Singer)
Opera et Concert
Maxifilianstr 22
Munich 80539, GERMANY

Bayona, Alvaro (Actor)
c/o Gabriel Blanco *Gabriel Blanco Iglesias (Mexico)*
Rio Balsas 35-32
Colonia Cuauhtemoc
DF 06500, MEXICO

Baz, Farouk El- (Geophysicist, Physicist)
Boston University
Remot Sensing Center
Boston, MA 02215, USA

Baze, Winiford (Football Player)
Philadelphia Eagles
5317 New Copeland Rd Apt 119
Tyler, TX 75703-3964, USA

Bazell, Robert J (Correspondent)
NBC-TV News Dept
4001 Nebraska Ave NW
Washington, DC 20016-2733, USA

Bazer, Fuller W (Scientist)
8600 Creekview Ct
College Station, TX 77845-5560, USA

BB Mak (Music Group)
c/o Staff Member *Hollywood Records*
500 S Buena Vista St
Burbank, CA 91521-0002, USA

Beach, Adam (Actor)
c/o Robert Lange *Kleinberg, Lopez, Lange,
Cuddy, & Edel*
2049 Century Park E Ste 3180
Los Angeles, CA 90067-3205, USA

Beach, Bill (Bowler)
435 Koehler Dr
Sharpsville, PA 16150-1839, USA

Beach, Ed (Football Player)
Washington Redskins
938 Sedgewick Ave
Westfield, NJ 07090, USA

Beach, Edward (Basketball Player)
Minneapolis Lakers
10114 Lawyers Rd
Vienna, VA 22181-2940, USA

Beach, Gary (Actor)
62 W 62nd St Apt 6F
New York, NY 10023-7007, USA

Beach, Michael (Actor)
1823 Virginia Rd
Los Angeles, CA 90019-5938, USA

Beach, Pat (Football Player)
Baltimore Colts
2523 West Beach Rd
Oak Harbor, WA 98277-8865, USA

Beach, Roger C (Business Person)
Unocal Corp
2141 Rosecrans Ave
El Segundo, CA 90245-4747, USA

Beach, Sanjay (Football Player)
New York Jets
2989 Riviera Ln
Westlake, OH 44145-6844, USA

Beacham, Stephanie (Actor)
c/o Staff Member *Peters Fraser & Dunlop
(PFD - UK)*
Drury House
34-43 Russell St
London WC2B 5HA, UNITED KINGDOM
(UK)

Beacher, Jeff (Producer, Television Host)
5275 Arville St Ste 348
Las Vegas, NV 89118-4948, USA

Beachy, Roger N (Scientist)
526 W Polo Dr
Saint Louis, MO 63105, USA

Beadle, Jeremy (Actor)
c/o Staff Member *MPC Entertainment*
MPC House
15-16 Maple Mews
London NW6 5UZ, UNITED KINGDOM
(UK)

Beagle, Ronald G (Ron) (Football Player)
3830 San Ysidro Way
Sacramento, CA 95864-5260, USA

Beahan, Kate (Actor)
c/o Suzan Bymel *Management 360*
9111 Wilshire Blvd
Beverly Hills, CA 90210-5508, USA

Beal, Jack (Artist)
80 Epps Rd
Oneonta, NY 13820-6440, USA

Beal, Jeff (Composer)
c/o Staff Member *Gorfaine/Schwartz
Agency Inc*
4111 W Alameda Ave Ste 509
Burbank, CA 91505-4171, USA

Beal, Norm (Football Player)
St Louis Cardinals
21246 Jade Dr
Rocky Mount, MO 65072-2953, USA

Beale, Betty (Writer)
2926 Garfield St NW
Washington, DC 20008-3536, USA

Beall, Bob (Baseball Player)
Atlanta Braves
513 NE Birchwood Rd
Hillsboro, OR 97124-3374, USA

Beals, Jennifer (Actor)
1503 Ventura Blvd #710
Sherman Oaks, CA 91403, USA

Beals, Shawn (Football Player)
Philadelphia Eagles
250 Edward Ave
Pittsburg, CA 94565-4107, USA

Beals, Vaughn L Jr (Business Person)
Harley-Davidson Inc
3700 W Juneau Ave
Milwaukee, WI 53208-2865, USA

Beam, C Arien (Judge)
US Court of Appeals
Federal Building
100 Centennial Mall N
Lincoln, NE 68508-3859, USA

Beaman, Lee Anne (Actor)
Cavaleri Assoc
178 S Victory Blvd Ste 205
Burbank, CA 91502-2881, USA

Beamer, Frank (Coach, Football Coach)
Virginia Polytechnic Institute
Athletic Dept
Blacksburg, VA 24061-0001, USA

Beamer, Lisa (Writer)
The Todd M Beamer Foundation
PO Box 32
Cranbury, NJ 08512-0032, USA

Beamon, Autry Jr (Football Player)
Minnesota Vikings
12200 River Ridge Blvd
Burnsville, MN 55337-1608, USA

Beamon, Trey (Baseball Player)
Pittsburgh Pirates
9730 Whitehurst Dr Apt 51
Dallas, TX 75243-8756, USA

Beamon Jr, Charlie (Baseball Player)
Seattle Mariners
2019 89th Ave Apt A
Oakland, CA 94621-1032, USA

Beamon Sr, Charlie (Baseball Player)
Baltimore Orioles
1717 Woodland Ave Apt 313
East Palo Alto, CA 94303-2313, USA

Bean, Alan L (Astronaut)
9173 Briar Forest Dr
Houston, TX 77024-7222, USA

Bean, Andy (Golfer)
2912 Grasslands Dr
Lakeland, FL 33803-5418, USA

Bean, Bill (Baseball Player)
Detroit Tigers
5601 N Bay Rd
Miami Beach, FL 33140-2033, USA

Bean, Bubba (Football Player)
Atlanta Falcons
1117 Todd Trl
College Station, TX 77845-5145, USA

Bean, Dawn Pawson (Swimmer)
11902 Red Hill Ave
Santa Ana, CA 92705-3106, USA

Bean, Henry (Director)
William Moris Agency
151 El Camino Dr
Beverly Hills, CA 90212-2775, USA

Bean, Orson (Actor, Comedian)
444 Carroll Canal
Venice, CA 90291-4682, USA

Bean, Robert (Football Player)
Cincinnati Bengals
4197 Summit Crossing Dr
Decatur, GA 30034-3544, USA

Bean, Sean (Actor)
c/o Sarah Jackson *Seven Summits Pictures
& Management*
8906 W Olympic Blvd Ground Floor
Beverly Hills, CA 90211, USA

Bean, William Bennett (Doctor)
11 Rowland Ct
Iowa City, IA 52246-2439, USA

Beane, Billy (Baseball Player)
New York Mets
1720 Knollfield Way
Encinitas, CA 92024-1974, USA

Bear, Greg
c/o Vince Gerardis *Created By*
1041 N Formosa Ave
Formosa Bldg, Room 10
West Hollywood, CA 90046-6703, USA

Bearak, Barry (Journalist)
New York Times
229 W 43rd St
Editorial Dept
New York, NY 10036-3959, USA

Beard, Al (Basketball Player)
New Jercy Americans
615 Hardeman Ave
Fort Valley, GA 31030-3439, USA

Beard, Alana (Basketball Player)
Washington Mystics
601 F St NW
Mcl Center
Washington, DC 20004-1605, USA

Beard, Alfred (Butch) (Basketball Player,
Coach)
Atlanta Hawks
3834 Berleigh Hill Ct
Burtonsville, MD 20866-1392, USA

Beard, Amanda (Swimmer)
c/o Staff Member *PMG Sports*
700 Evanvale Ct
Cary, NC 27518-2806, USA

Beard, Dave (Baseball Player)
Oakland A's
5325 Derby Chase Ct
Alpharetta, GA 30005-7883, USA

Beard, Ed (Football Player)
San Francisco 49ers
4861 Strand Dr
Virginia Beach, VA 23462-6449, USA

Beard, Frank (Golfer)
70 Rocio Ct
Palm Desert, CA 92260-3160, USA

Beard, Frank (Musician)
Lone Wolf Mgmt
PO Box 163690
Austin, TX 78716-3690, USA

Beard, Mike (Baseball Player)
Atlanta Braves
400 Walnut St
Little Rock, AR 72205-4042, USA

Beard, Ralph (Basketball Player)
Indianapolis Jets
7805 McCarthy Ln
Louisville, KY 40222-4326, USA

Beard, Ted (Baseball Player)
Pittsburgh Pirates
10517 Stetor Ct
Fishers, IN 46038, USA

Beard, Tom (Football Player)
Buffalo Bills
164 Gale Rd
Mason, MI 48854-9735, USA

Beare, Gary (Baseball Player)
Milwaukee Brewers
12718 Shadowline St
Poway, CA 92064-6416, USA

Bearse, Amanda (Actor)
c/o Staff Member *Genesis*
8530 Wilshire Blvd Fl 3
Beverly Hills, CA 90211-3114, USA

Bearse, Kevin (Baseball Player)
Cleveland Indians
36 Sarah Ln
Howell, NJ 07731-9055, USA

Beart, Emmanuelle
10 avenue George V
Paris F-75008, FRANCE

Beart, Guy (Musician, Songwriter, Writer)
Editions Temporel
2 Rue du Marquis de Mores
Garches 92380, FRANCE

Beasley, Aaron (Football Player)
Jacksonville Jaguars
514 Lincoln Ave
Pottstown, PA 19464-4726, USA

Beasley, Allyce (Actor)
SBV
145 S Fairfax Ave Ste 310
Los Angeles, CA 90036-2176, USA

Beasley, Alyce (Actor)
c/o Staff Member *TalentWorks (LA)*
3500 W Olive Ave Ste 1400
Burbank, CA 91505-5512, USA

Beasley, Bruce M (Artist)
322 Lewis St
Oakland, CA 94607-1236, USA

Beasley, Charles (Basketball Player)
Dallas Chaparrals
6164 Marquira Ave
Dallas, TX 75214, USA

Beasley, Chris (Baseball Player)
California Angels
1013 W Cooley Dr
Gilbert, AZ 85233-2540, USA

Beasley, Derrick (Football Player)
New England Patriots
141 North St
Andover, MA 01810-1131, USA

Beasley, Fred (Football Player)
San Francisco 49ers
PO Box 210931
Montgomery, AL 36121-0931, USA

Beasley, John (Actor)
c/o Staff Member *Bauman Redanty & Shaul Agency*
5757 Wilshire Blvd Ste 473
Los Angeles, CA 90036-3632, USA

Beasley, John (Basketball Player)
Dallas Chaparrals
RR 1 Box 1699
Malakoff, TX 75148, USA

Beasley, Lew (Baseball Player)
Texas Rangers
24671 Newtown Rd
Bowling Green, VA 22427-2725, USA

Beasley, Terry P (Football Player)
San Francisco 49ers
1725 Roanoke Ln
Auburn, AL 36830-1916, USA

Beasley, Tom (Football Player)
Pittsburgh Steelers
301 Riding Ridge Rd
Annapolis, MD 21403-1653, USA

Beastie Boys (Music Group)
c/o Staff Member *Nasty Little Man*
110 Greene St Ste 605
New York, NY 10012-3838, USA

Beathard, Pete (Football Player)
Kansas City Chiefs
3770 Drake St
Houston, TX 77005-1118, USA

Beaton, Frank (Hockey Player)
New York Rangers
4042 Water Willow Ln
Birmingham, AL 35244-6407, USA

Beatrix, HM Queen
Kasteel Drakesteijn
Lage Vuursche 3744 BA, THE NETHERLANDS

Beattie, Joseph (Actor)
Ken McReddie Associates
36 - 40 Glasshouse St
London W1B 5DL, UNITED KINGDOM (UK)

Beattle, Ann (Writer)
Janklow & Nesbit
445 Park Ave # 1300
New York, NY 10022-2606, USA

Beattle, Bob (Skier)
210 Aabc Ste N
Aspen, CO 81611-3537, USA

Beattle, Bruce (Cartoonist)
Daytona Beach News-Journal
901 6th St
Editorial Dept
Daytona Beach, FL 32117-8099, USA

Beattle, Jim (Baseball Player)
New York Yankees
1 Kenwood Rd
Baltimore, MD 21210-2533, USA

Beatty, Blaine (Baseball Player)
New York Mets
867 Kolodzey Rd
Victoria, TX 77905-2520, USA

Beatty, Charles (Football Player)
Pittsburgh Steelers
PO Box 2634
Waxahachie, TX 75168-8634, USA

Beatty, Ed (Football Player)
San Francisco 49ers
108 Mariners Is
Mandeville, LA 70448-6800, USA

Beatty, Jim
1516 Larochelle Ln
Charlotte, NC 28226-6868, USA

Beatty, Ned (Actor)
2706 N Beachwood Dr
Los Angeles, CA 90068-1922, USA

Beatty, Warren (Actor, Director, Producer)
c/o Richard Lovett *Creative Artists Agency LCC (CAA-LA)*
2000 Avenue Of The Stars
Los Angeles, CA 90067-4700, USA

Beaty, Zelmo (Basketball Player)
St Louis Hawks
2808 120th Ave NE
Bellevue, WA 98005-1515, USA

Beau Brummels
PO Box 53664
Indianapolis, IN 46253-0664, USA

Beauchamp, Jim (Baseball Player)
St Louis Cardinals
105 Paula Dr
Tyrone, GA 30290-2612, USA

Beauchamp, Joe (Football Player)
San Diego Chargers
4805 N 24th Pl
Milwaukee, WI 53209-5630, USA

Beaudin, Norm (Hockey Player)
St Louis Blues
255 Forest Lake Blvd N
Attn Hockey Shop
Oldsmar, FL 34677-5515, USA

Beaudoin, Doug (Football Player)
New England Patriots
15143 Springview St
Tampa, FL 33624-2374, USA

Beaufit, Mark (Hockey Player)
San Jose Sharks
443 Blemhuber Ave
Marquette, MI 49855-4803, USA

Beauford, Carter (Musician)
Red Light Mgmt
PO Box 520
Crozet, VA 22932-0520, USA

Beaufoy, Simon (Writer)
Creative Artists Agency
9830 Wilshire Blvd
Beverly Hills, CA 90212-1804, USA

Beaumont, Jimmy
2002 Duquesne Ave
McKeesport, PA 15132-5103, USA

Beaumont, Thomas (Actor)
c/o Staff Member *Scott Stander & Associates*
13701 Riverside Dr Ste 201
Sherman Oaks, CA 91423-2447, USA

Beaupre, Don (Hockey Player)
Minnesota North Stars
5020 Scriver Rd
Edina, MN 55436-1158, USA

Beauregard, Stephane (Hockey Player)
Winnipeg Jets
175 Rue Des Plaines
Cowansville, PQ J2K 3T8, CANADA

Beauvais-Nilon, Garcelle (Actor)
c/o Chuck James *Gersh Agency, The (LA)*
232 N Canon Dr
Beverly Hills, CA 90210-5302, USA

Beauvais-Nilon, Garcelle (Actor, Model)
Nina Blanchard
8826 Burton Way
Beverly Hills, CA 90211-1715, USA

Beaver, Jim (Actor)
Artists Agency
1180 S Beverly Dr Ste 301
Los Angeles, CA 90035-1154, USA

Beaver, Joe (Rodeo Rider)
PO Box 1595
Huntsville, TX 77342-1595, USA

Beaver, Terry (Actor)
Paradigm Agency
10100 Santa Monica Blvd Ste 2500
Los Angeles, CA 90067-4116, USA

Beavers, Scott (Football Player)
Denver Broncos
4030 Pittman Rd
College Park, GA 30349-1439, USA

Beban, Gary J (Football Player)
Washington Redskins
20 Timber Ln
Northbrook, IL 60062-3716, USA

Bebout, Nick (Football Player)
Atlanta Falcons
1606 Major Ave
Riverton, WY 82501-8900, USA

Bech, Debra (Actor)
Minnesota Public Radio
480 Cedar St
Saint Paul, MN 55101-2230, USA

Becherer, Hans W (Business Person)
Deere Co
1 John Deere Pl
Moline, IL 61265-8098, USA

Becht, Anthony (Football Player)
New York Jets
911 Morgan Ave
Drexel Hill, PA 19026-3316, USA

Bechtel, Riley P (Business Person)
Bechtel Group
50 Beale St
San Francisco, CA 94105-1895, USA

Bechtel, Stephen D Jr (Business Person)
Bechtel Group
50 Beale St
San Francisco, CA 94105-1895, USA

Beck, Aaron T (Doctor)
3600 Market St Ste 700
Philadelphia, PA 19104-2652, USA

Beck, Braden (Football Player)
Houston Oilers
691 Milverton Rd
Los Altos, CA 94022-3928, USA

Beck, Byron (Basketball Player)
Denver Nuggets
1909 S Williams St
Kennewick, WA 99338-1820, USA

Beck, Chip (Golfer)
11 Pembroke Dr
Lake Forest, IL 60045-2147, USA

Beck, Ernest (Basketball Player)
Philadelphia Warriors
1523 Brierwood Rd
Havertown, PA 19083-2910, USA

Beck, Glen
c/o Staff Member *CNN (NY)*
1 Time Warner Ctr
New York, NY 10019-6038, USA

Beck, Jeff (Musician)
c/o Staff Member *Creative Artists Agency LCC (CAA-LA)*
2000 Avenue Of The Stars
Los Angeles, CA 90067-4700, USA

Beck, John E (Football Player)
New Orleans Saints
PO Box 530930
San Diego, CA 92153-0930, USA

Beck, Maria (Actor)
c/o Staff Member *Lichtman/Salners Company*
15865 Royal Haven Pl
Sherman Oaks, CA 91403-4724, USA

Beck, Martha (Writer)
18011 N 14th Pl
Phoenix, AZ 85022-7201, USA

Beck, Martin (Actor)
Lichtman/Salners
15865 Royal Haven Pl
Sherman Oaks, CA 91403-4724, USA

Beck, Mat (Cinematographer)
621 Via De La Paz
Pacific Palisades, CA 90272-4365, USA

Beck, Michael (Actor)
c/o Staff Member *Paradigm (LA)*
360 N Crescent Dr
North Bldg
Beverly Hills, CA 90210-6820, USA

Beck, Ray M (Football Player)
New York Giants
745 N College St
Cedartown, GA 30125-2260, USA

Beck, Rick (Baseball Player)
New York Yankees
8218 N Sumter Ct
Spokane, WA 99208-5749, USA

Beck, Robin (Musician)
Cavaricci & White
156 W 56th St Ste 1803
New York, NY 10019-3878, USA

Beck, Rod (Baseball Player)
San Francisco Giants
8623 E Mescal St
Scottsdale, AZ 85260-6632, USA

Beck Hilton, Kimberly (Actor)
Badgley Connor Talent
1680 Vine St Ste 1016
Los Angeles, CA 90028-8800, USA

Beckel, Robert D (General)
New Mexico Military Institute
Superintendent's Office
Roswell, NM 88201, USA

Becker, Arthur (Basketball Player)
Houston Mavericks
2027 E Rancho Dr
Phoenix, AZ 85016-2702, USA

Becker, Boris (Tennis Player)
Grafenau
Grafenauweg, Zug 6300, SWITZERLAND

Becker, Donna (Baseball Player)
5316 40th Ave
Kenosha, WI 53144-2707, USA

Becker, Doug (Football Player)
Chicago Bears
7525 Baywind Dr
Cincinnati, OH 45242-5907, USA

Becker, Edward R (Judge)
US Court of Appeals
601 Market St
US Couthouse
Philadelphia, PA 19106-1790, USA

Becker, Gary S (Nobel Prize Laureate)
1308 E 58th St
Chicago, IL 60637-1717, USA

Becker, George (Misc)
United Steelworkers of America
5 Gateway Ctr
Pittsburgh, PA 15222, USA

Becker, Gerry (Actor)
c/o Oliver Mossi *Paradigm (LA)*
360 N Crescent Dr
North Bldg
Beverly Hills, CA 90210-6820, USA

Becker, Gretchen (Actor)
Acme Talent
4727 Wilshire Blvd Ste 333
Los Angeles, CA 90010-3874, USA

Becker, Harold (Director)
Creative Artists Agency
9830 Wilshire Blvd
Beverly Hills, CA 90212-1804, USA

Becker, Isaura (Actor)
c/o Staff Member *Televisa*
Blvd Adolfo Lopez Mateos 232
Colonia San Angel INN
DF CP 01060, MEXICO

Becker, Kuno (Actor)
c/o Ivan De Paz *Arenas Entertainment*
100 N Crescent Dr
Garden Level
Beverly Hills, CA 90210-5408, USA

Becker, Kurt (Football Player)
Chicago Bears
49W412 Scott Rd
Big Rock, IL 60511-9489, USA

Becker, Margaret (Musician)
Sparrow Communications
101 Winners Cir N
Brentwood, TN 37027-5017, USA

Becker, Quinn H (Doctor, General)
2111 Peninsula Dr
San Antonio, TX 78239-3077, USA

Becker, Rich (Baseball Player)
Minnesota Twins
210 Mary Senica Ct
La Salle, IL 61301-9676, USA

Becker, Rob (Actor, Comedian)
William Moris Agency
151 El Camino Dr
Beverly Hills, CA 90212-2775, USA

Becker, Robert J (Misc)
6 Oak Brook Club Dr Apt J101
Oak Brook, IL 60523-1323, USA

Becker, Thomas (Athlete)
Hagedomweg 6A
Solingen 42697, GERMANY

Becker, Tony (Actor)
Howard Talent West
10657 Riverside Dr
C/O Bonnie Howard
Toluca Lake, CA 91602-2341, USA

Beckert, Glenn (Baseball Player)
Chicago Cubs
1953 Arkansas Ave
Englewood, FL 34224-5505, USA

Becket, MacDonald G (Architect)
Becket Group
2501 Colorado Ave
Santa Monica, CA 90404-3500, USA

Beckett, Bob (Hockey Player)
Boston Bruins
38 Fonthill Blvd
Markham, ON L3R 1V7, CANADA

Beckett, Josh (Baseball Player)
c/o Staff Member *Boston Red Sox*
Fenway Park
4 Yawkey Way
Boston, MA 02215-3496, USA

Beckett, Robbie (Baseball Player)
Colorado Rockies
15625 Harry Lind Rd
Elgin, TX 78621, USA

Beckett, Rogers (Football Player)
San Diego Chargers
635 Gaelic Ct
Apopka, FL 32712-4724, USA

Beckett, Wendy (Sister)
BBC-TV
Center Wood Ln
London, ENGLAND W12 7R3, UNITED
KINGDOM (UK)

Beckford, Roxanne (Actor)
9255 W Sunset Blvd Ste 401
Los Angeles, CA 90069-3302, USA

Beckford, Tyson (Actor, Model)
Bethann Entertainment
345 E 18th St # 229
New York, NY 10003-2808, USA

Beckham, Brice (Actor)
6561 E Espanita St
Long Beach, CA 90815-4635, USA

Beckham, David (Athlete, Soccer Player)
c/o Staff Member *Nineteen (19)
Entertainment*
Unit 32, Ransomes Dock
35-37 Parkgate Road
London SW11 4NP, UNITED KINGDOM
(UK)

Beckham, Victoria Adams (Actor,
Musician)
c/o Jeff Frasco *Creative Artists Agency
LCC (CAA-LA)*
2000 Avenue Of The Stars
Los Angeles, CA 90067-4700, USA

Beckinsale, Kate (Actor)
c/o Tracy Brennan *Creative Artists Agency
LCC (CAA-LA)*
2000 Avenue Of The Stars
Los Angeles, CA 90067-4700, USA

Beckless, Ian (Football Player)
Tampa Bay Buccaneers
4915 Andros Dr
Tampa, FL 33629-4801, USA

Beckley, Gerry (Music Group, Musician)
Agency for Performing Arts
405 S Beverly Dr Ste 500
Beverly Hills, CA 90212-4425, USA

Beckman, Cameron (Golfer)
415 Bentley Mnr
Shavano Park, TX 78249-2062, USA

Beckman, Ed (Football Player)
Kansas City Chiefs
4295 18th St NE
Naples, FL 34120-6409, USA

Beckman, Thomas (Football Player)
St Louis Cardinals
3672 Cedar Shake Dr
Rochester Hills, MI 48309-1013, USA

Beckwith, Alan (Actor)
3928 Carpenter Ave
Studio City, CA 91604-3764, USA

Beckwith, Joe (Baseball Player)
Los Angeles Dodgers
2057 Country Squire Rd
Auburn, AL 36830, USA

Becquer, Julio (Baseball Player)
Washington Senators
2237 Noble Ave N
Minneapolis, MN 55422-3661, USA

Becton, C W (Religious Leader)
*United Pentacostal Free Will Baptist
Church*
8855 Dunn Rd
Hazelwood, MO 63042-2212, USA

Becton, Julius W Jr (Educator, General)
Prairie View A & M University
President's Office
Prairie View, TX 77446, USA

Bedard, Irene (Actor)
Don Buchwald
6500 Wilshire Blvd Ste 2200
Los Angeles, CA 90048-4942, USA

Bedard, James A (Hockey Player)
Washington Capitals
7039 Garden St
Niagara Falls, ON L2G 1H8, CANADA

Bedard, James L (Hockey Player)
Chicago Blackhawks
317 Crawford Avenue E
Melfort, SK S0E 1A0, CANADA

Bedard, Myriam (Athlete)
3329 Pinecourt
Neufchatel, PQ G2B 2E4, CANADA

Bedelia, Bonnie (Actor)
c/o Lee Brillstein *International Creative
Management (ICM-LA)*
10250 Constellation Blvd
Los Angeles, CA 90067-6200, USA

Bedell, Bob (Basketball Player)
Anaheim Amigos
3107 Kipling Way
Louisville, KY 40205-3005, USA

Bedell, Brad (Football Player)
Cleveland Browns
545 N Altura Rd
Arcadia, CA 91007-6059, USA

BeDell, Chad Ryan
PO Box 699
Clark, CO 80428-0699, USA

Bedell, Howie (Baseball Player)
Milwaukee Braves
1187 Crestwood Dr
Pottstown, PA 19464-2931, USA

Bedford, Brian (Actor)
Arts Management Group
1133 Broadway Ste 1025
New York, NY 10010-7985, USA

Bedford, Steuart J R
Harrison/Parrott
12 Penzance Place
London W11 4PA, UNITED KINGDOM
(UK)

Bedford, Vance (Football Player)
St Louis Cardinals
1711 Cypress Pointe Ct
Ann Arbor, MI 48108-8505, USA

Bedi, Kabir (Actor, Bollywood)
B4 Beach House Apt
Gandhigram Road
Mumbai, MS 400054, INDIA

Bedingfield, Daniel (Musician)
Island Def Jam Music Group, The
825 8th Ave
New York, NY 10019-7416, USA

Bedingfield, Natasha (Musician)
c/o Staff Member *RCA Records (LA)*
8750 Wilshire Blvd Fl 2
Beverly Hills, CA 90211-2715, USA

Bednarik, Charles P (Chuck) (Football
Player)
Philadelphia Eagles
6379 Winding Rd
Coopersburg, PA 18036-9410, USA

Bednarski, John (Hockey Player)
New York Rangers
18706 Peninsula Cove Ln
Cornelius, NC 28031-7753, USA

Bedore, Thomas (Football Player)
Washington Redskins
211 73rd St
Niagara Falls, NY 14304-4028, USA

Bedrosian, Stephen W (Steve) (Baseball
Player)
Atlanta Braves
3915 Gordon Rd
Senoia, GA 30276, USA

Bedsole, Harold (Hal) (Football Player)
Minnesota Vikings
78661 Rainswept Way
Palm Desert, CA 92211-3035, USA

Beebe, Dion (Cinematographer)
International Creative Mgmt
8942 Wilshire Blvd # 219
Beverly Hills, CA 90211-1908, USA

Beebe, Don (Football Player)
Buffalo Bills
House Of Speed Inc 301 Snow St
Sugar Grove, IL 60554, USA

Beeby, Thomas H (Architect)
Hammond Beeby Babka
440 N Wells St Ste 630
Chicago, IL 60610-4546, USA

Beech, Matt (Baseball Player)
Philadelphia Phillies
2950 W Bay Dr Apt B4
Belleair Bluffs, FL 33770-2640, USA

Beechen, Adam (Writer)
c/o Staff Member *Natural Talent Inc*
3331 Ocean Park Blvd Ste 203
Santa Monica, CA 90405-3225, USA

Beede, Frank (Football Player)
Seattle Seahawks
1645 Somerset Pl
Antioch, CA 94509-2183, USA

Beekley, Bruce (Football Player)
Green Bay Packers
1351 Eaton Ave
San Carlos, CA 94070-4940, USA

Beeman, Greg (Actor, Director, Producer,
Writer)
c/o Jay Sures *United Talent Agency (UTA)*
9560 Wilshire Blvd Ste 500
Beverly Hills, CA 90212-2401, USA

Beene, Andy (Baseball Player)
Milwaukee Brewers
HC 1 Box 859
Center Point, TX 78010, USA

Beene, Fred (Baseball Player)
Baltimore Orioles
PO Box 143
Oakhurst, TX 77359-0143, USA

Beer, A M (Editor)
Spectator
Editorial Dept
44 Frid St
Hamilton, ON L8N 3G3, CANADA

Beer, Tom (Football Player)
Denver Broncos
292 Changebridge Rd Apt 3
Pine Brook, NJ 07058-9543, USA

Beering, Steven C (Educator)
Purdue University
President's Office
West Lafayette, IN 47907, USA

Beers, Bob (Hockey Player)
Boston Bruins
97 Blake Rd
Lexington, MA 02420-3212, USA

Beers, Clarence (Baseball Player)
St Louis Cardinals
2430 N Dodge Blvd Apt 118
Tucson, AZ 85716-2631, USA

Beesley, Max (Actor)
c/o Beth Holden-Garland *Untitled Entertainment (LA)*
331 N Maple Dr Fl 3
Beverly Hills, CA 90210-3827, USA

Beeson, Jack H (Composer)
404 Riverside Dr # 1C
New York, NY 10025-1861, USA

Beeson, Paul B (Doctor, Physicist)
7 Riverwoods Dr Apt F125
Exeter, NH 03833-4385, USA

Beeson, Terry (Football Player)
Seattle Seahawks
1302 Hibbard St
Coffeyville, KS 67337-1412, USA

Beezer, Robert R (Judge)
US Court of Appeals
1010 5th Ave
US Courthouse
Seattle, WA 98104-1195, USA

Bega, Leslie (Actor)
31 1/2 Buccaneer St
Marina Del Rey, CA 90292-5103, USA

Bega, Lou
Postfach 80 01 49
Munich D-81601, GERMANY

Begala, Paul (Television Host)
c/o Staff Member *Crossfire*
820 1st St NE Fl 10
Washington, DC 20002-4243, USA

Begay, Notah (Golfer)
3620 Vista Del Sur St NW
Albuquerque, NM 87120-1583, USA

Begert, William J (General)
Commander Pacific Air Force
Hickam Air Force Base, HI 96853, USA

Begg, Varyl (Admiral)
Copyhold Cottage Chilbotton
Stockbridge
Hants, UNITED KINGDOM (UK)

Beggs, James M (Government Official, Misc)
1177 N Great Southwest Pkwy
Grand Prairie, TX 75050-2629, USA

Beghe, Jason (Actor)
c/o Steven Fenton *Fenton-Kritzer Entertainment*
8840 Wilshire Blvd Fl 3
Beverly Hills, CA 90211-2606, USA

Beghe, Renato (Judge)
US Tax Court
400 2nt St NW
Washington, DC 20217-0001, USA

Begler, Michael (Producer)
c/o Staff Member *William Morris Agency (WMA-LA)*
1 William Morris Pl
Beverly Hills, CA 90212-4261, USA

Begley Jr, Ed (Actor, Director)
c/o Steve Rosenblum *Sterling/Winters Company, The*
10900 Wilshire Blvd Ste 1550
Los Angeles, CA 90024-6525, USA

Begovich, Mike (Actor)
c/o Beverly Strong *Anonymous Content (CA)*
3532 Hayden Ave
Culver City, CA 90232-2413, USA

Behagen, Ron (Basketball Player)
kansas City-Omaha Kings
1101 Juniper St NE Apt 401
Atlanta, GA 30309-7655, USA

Behanna, Rick (Baseball Player)
Cleveland Indians
164 Bradford Station Dr
Sharpsburg, GA 30277-2035, USA

Behar, Joy (Actor)
c/o Staff Member *View, The*
320 W 66th St
New York, NY 10023-6304, USA

Behe, Michael (Misc, Writer)
Lehigh University
Biochemistry Dept
Bethlehem, PA 18015, USA

Behl, Mohnish (Actor, Bollywood)
Sagar Sangeet 30th Floor
Opp Colaba Post Office
Bombay, MS 400 005, INDIA

Behle, Jochen (Skier)
Sonnenhof 1
Willingen 34508, GERMANY

Behm, Forrest E (Football Player)
3 Briarcliff Dr
Corning, NY 14830-3328, USA

Behney, Mel (Baseball Player)
Cincinnati Reds
4711 Elkwood Ln
Arlington, TX 76016-1826, USA

Behnken, Robert L (Astronaut)
43708 Dejay St
Lancaster, CA 93536-5781, USA

Behr, Aaron (Actor)
c/o Staff Member *Acme Talent & Literary (LA)*
4727 Wilshire Blvd Ste 333
Los Angeles, CA 90010-3874, USA

Behr, Dani
195 March Wall #24 Norex
London, ENGLAND E14 9SG, UNITED KINGDOM (UK)

Behr, Jason (Actor)
c/o Robert Stein *Robert Stein Management*
345 N Maple Dr Ste 317
Beverly Hills, CA 90210-3856, USA

Behrend, Marc (Hockey Player)
Winnipeg Jets
1808 Savannah Way
Waunakee, WI 53597-2307, USA

Behrendt, Greg (Comedian, Radio Personality)
The Greg Behrendt Show
9336 Washington Blvd
Culver City, CA 90232-2628, USA

Behrens, Hildegard (Opera Singer)
Herbert Breslin
119 W 57th St Ste 1505
New York, NY 10019-2401, USA

Behrens, Sam (Actor)
530 Bryant Dr
Canoga Park, CA 91304-1019, USA

Behrman, Dave (Football Player)
Buffalo Bills
10187 25 1/2 Mile Rd
Albion, MI 49224-9751, USA

Beier, Thomas (Football Player)
Miami Dolphins
5055 Hammock Lake Dr
Coral Gables, FL 33156-2221, USA

Beilina, Nina (Musician)
400 W 43rd St Apt 7D
New York, NY 10036-6304, USA

Beimel, Joe (Baseball Player)
Pittsburgh Pirates
107 Beacon Hill Dr
Cranberry Twp, PA 16066-6801, USA

Beirne, Jim (Football Player)
Houston Oilers
2 Cedar Chase Pl
Spring, TX 77381-3030, USA

Beirne, Kevin (Baseball Player)
Chicago White Sox
2 Cedar Chase Pl
Spring, TX 77381-3030, USA

Beisel, Monty (Football Player)
Kansas City Chiefs
608 Herkimer St
Oskaloosa, KS 66066-5014, USA

Beisler, Randy (Football Player)
Philadelphia Eagles
899 Northgate Dr Ste 500
San Rafael, CA 94903-3667, USA

Bel Biv Devoe
8942 Wilshire Blvd
Beverly Hills, CA 90211-1908, USA

Belafonte, Harry (Actor, Musician)
c/o Owen Laster *William Morris Agency (WMA-NY)*
1325 Avenue Of The Americas
New York, NY 10019-6026, USA

Belafonte, Shari (Actor, Musician)
c/o Rick Hersh *Celebrity Consultants LLC*
3340 Ocean Park Blvd Ste 3030
Santa Monica, CA 90405-3217, USA

Belaga, Julie (Financier)
Export-Import Bank
811 Vermont Ave NW
Washington, DC 20571-0002, USA

Belak, Wade (Hockey Player)
Colorado Avalanche
PO Box 1167
Battleford, SK S0M 0E0, CANADA

Belbin, Tanith (Figure Skater)
c/o Staff Member *Champions on Ice*
3500 W 80th St
Tom Collins Enterprises Inc
Minneapolis, MN 55431-1068, USA

Belcher, Kevin (Baseball Player)
Texas Rangers
2208 Highway 121
Bedford, TX 76021-5981, USA

Belchlavek, Jiri (Conductor)
Czechoslovakia Philharmonic
Alsovo Nabr 12
Prague 11001, CZECH REPUBLIC

Belden, Bob (Football Player)
Dallas Cowboys
6701 Militia Hill St NW
Canton, OH 44718-1391, USA

Belen, Ana (Actor, Musician)
Rompeolas Productions
1761 Calle Alabama
Rio Piedras, PR 00926-3451, USA

Belew, Adrian (Musician)
Umbrella Artists Mgmt
2612 Erie Ave
Cincinnati, OH 45208-2002, USA

Belford, Christina (Actor)
10635 Santa Monica Blvd Ste 130
Los Angeles, CA 90025-8306, USA

Belfour, Edward (Ed) (Hockey Player)
Chicago Blackhawks
9830 Sarle Rd
Freeland, MI 48623, USA

Belhumeur, Michel (Hockey Player)
Washington Capitals
58 Little Falls Ln
Rockville, VA 23146-2123, USA

Belichick, Bill (Coach, Football Coach)
c/o Staff Member *New England Patriots*
60 Washington St
Gillette Stadium - RR 1
Foxboro, MA 02035-1388, USA

Belichick, Steve (Football Player)
Detroit Lions
3035 Aberdeen Rd
Annapolis, MD 21403-1301, USA

Belin, Gaspard D (Attorney, Attorney General, General)
4 Willard St
Cambridge, MA 02138-4837, USA

Belinda, Stan (Baseball Player)
Pittsburgh Pirates
454 Sylvan Dr
State College, PA 16803-1514, USA

Belisle, Danny (Hockey Player)
New York Rangers
3967 Glen Oaks Manor Dr
Sarasota, FL 34232-1045, USA

Belisle, Matt (Baseball Player)
Cincinnati Reds
4009 Sierra Dr
Austin, TX 78731-3913, USA

Belita
44 Crabtree Lane
London, ENGLAND SW6 6LW, UNITED KINGDOM (UK)

Belitz, Todd (Baseball Player)
Oakland A's
17901 N Colton Ct
Colbert, WA 99005-9174, USA

Beliveau, Jean (Hockey Player)
Montreal Canadiens
155 Rue Victoria
Longueuil, PQ J4H 2J4, CANADA

Belk, Anthony (Football Player)
Cleveland Browns
1207 Park Rd NW Apt 201
Washington, DC 20010-2027, USA

Belk, Bill (Football Player)
San Francisco 49ers
12 Ricemill Ferry
Columbia, SC 29229-9034, USA

Belka, Marek (Prime Minister)
Ul Ursad Rady Ministrow
Ul Wiejska 4/8
Warsaw 00-583, POLAND

Belkirch, Gary B (War Hero)
68 South Ave
Hilton, NY 14468-1310, USA

Belknap, Anna (Actor)
c/o Steve Stone *Cornerstone Talent Agency*
37 W 20th St Ste 1108
New York, NY 10011-3713, USA

Bell, Albert (Football Player)
Green Bay Packers
16222 Hunsaker Ave
Paramount, CA 90723-4762, USA

Bell, Anthony D (Football Player)
St Louis Cardinals
232 Agate Way
Hercules, CA 94547-1749, USA

Bell, Archie (Musician)
Speer Entertainment Services
PO Box 2620
McDonough, GA 30253-1738, USA

Bell, Art (Business Person)
c/o Staff Member *Court TV*
600 3rd Ave Frnt 2
New York, NY 10016-1901, USA

Bell, Bill (Baseball Player)
Kansas City Monarchs
3401 Urbandale Ave
Des Moines, IA 50310-4006, USA

Bell, Billy Ray (Football Player)
Houston Oilers
4006 Mossy Grove Ct
Humble, TX 77346-2498, USA

Bell, Bob (Football Player)
Detroit Lions
7415 N 12th St
Elkins Park, PA 19027-3052, USA

Bell, Bobby (Football Player)
Kansas City Chiefs
208 NW Shagbark St
Lees Summit, MO 64064-1445, USA

Bell, Byron (Basketball Player)
Oshkosh All Stars
1141 Williams St
Lake Geneva, WI 53147-1260, USA

Bell, C Gordon (Scientist)
Microsoft Corp
1 Microsoft Way
Redmond, WA 98052-8300, USA

Bell, Carlos (Football Player)
New Orleans Saints
14411 Hartshill Dr
Houston, TX 77044-4925, USA

Bell, Catherine (Actor)
c/o Daniel (Danny) Sussman *Brillstein-Grey Entertainment*
9150 Wilshire Blvd Ste 350
Beverly Hills, CA 90212-3453, USA

Bell, Charles (Business Person)
McDonald's Corp
1 McDonalds Plz
1 Kroc Dr
Oak Brook, IL 60523-1911, USA

Bell, Clyde R (Bob) (Admiral)
1301 Harney St
Omaha, NE 68102-1832, USA

Bell, Coby
c/o Staff Member *Vincent Cirrincione Associates*
1516 N Fairfax Ave
Los Angeles, CA 90046-2608, USA

Bell, Coleman (Football Player)
Washington Redskins
4426 Hidden Shadow Dr
Tampa, FL 33614-1470, USA

Bell, David (Baseball Player)
Cleveland Indians
9710 E La Posada Cir
Scottsdale, AZ 85255-3716, USA

Bell, David G (Buddy) (Baseball Player)
Cleveland Indians
PO Box 11718
Chandler, AZ 85248-0012, USA

Bell, Dennis (Basketball Player)
New York Knicks
RR 2
Lucasville, OH 45648, USA

Bell, Derek N (Baseball Player)
c/o Staff Member *Pittsburgh Pirates*
115 Federal St
Pnc Park
Pittsburgh, PA 15212-5740, USA

Bell, Drake (Actor)
c/o Theresa Peters *William Morris Agency (WMA-LA)*
1 William Morris Pl
Beverly Hills, CA 90212-4261, USA

Bell, Drew Tyler (Actor, Director, Producer, Writer)
c/o Beverly Strong *Anonymous Content (CA)*
9350 Wilshire Blvd Ste 224
Beverly Hills, CA 90212-3204, USA

Bell, Eddie A (Football Player)
New York Jets
4529 Tacoma Ter
Fort Worth, TX 76123-4005, USA

Bell, Eddie B (Football Player)
Philadelphia Eagles
515 W Chelten Ave Apt 1308
Philadelphia, PA 19144-4427, USA

Bell, Eric (Baseball Player)
Baltimore Orioles
1140 S 124th St
Chandler, AZ 85286-1121, USA

Bell, Gerard (Football Player)
Tampa Bay Buccaneers
1347 Deerbourne Dr
Zephyrhills, FL 33543-6754, USA

Bell, Grantis (Football Player)
Washington Redskins
3049 La Mirage Dr
Lauderhill, FL 33319-4246, USA

Bell, Greg (Football Player)
Buffalo Bills
5849 Azalea Way
Goleta, CA 93117-2158, USA

Bell, Gregory (Gerg) (Athlete, Track Athlete)
5983 E Division Rd
Logansport, IN 46947-7972, USA

Bell, Harry (Hockey Player)
New York Rangers
7711 N Invergordon Rd
Paradise Valley, AZ 85253-3169, USA

Bell, Hilari (Writer)
PO Box 877
Chestertown, MD 21620-0877, USA

Bell, Jaime (Actor)
c/o Staff Member *Endeavor Agency LLC (LA)*
9601 Wilshire Blvd Fl 3
Beverly Hills, CA 90210-5204, USA

Bell, James D (Diplomat)
154 Zinfandel Cir
Scotts Valley, CA 95066-3259, USA

Bell, Jason (Football Player)
Dallas Cowboys
2903 Sierra Dr
Carrollton, TX 75007-5626, USA

Bell, Jay S (Baseball Player)
Cleveland Indians
PO Box 50249
Phoenix, AZ 85076-0249, USA

Bell, Jerry (Baseball Player)
Milwaukee Brewers
631 Audrey Rd
Mount Juliet, TN 37122-3844, USA

Bell, Jerry (Football Player)
Tampa Bay Buccaneers
1347 Deerbourne Dr
Zephyrhills, FL 33543-6754, USA

Bell, Joe (Hockey Player)
New York Rangers
10522 11th Ave NE
Seattle, WA 98125-7506, USA

Bell, John (Musician)
Brown Cat Inc
400 Foundry St
Athens, GA 30601-2623, USA

Bell, John Anthony (Actor, Director)
Bell Shakespeare Co
88 George St
Level 1
Rocks, NSW 200, AUSTRALIA

Bell, Jorge A M (George) (Athlete, Baseball Player)
Lamiama #14
Bell 2nd Planto
San Pedro de Macoris, DOMINICAN REPUBLIC

Bell, Joshua (Musician)
I M G Artists
3 Burlington Lane
Chiswick
London W4 2TH, UNITED KINGDOM (UK)

Bell, Judie
PO Box 121626
Nashville, TN 37212-1626, USA

Bell, Kendrell (Football Player)
Pittsburgh Steelers
423 Delaware St Ste 103
Kansas City, MO 64105-1278, USA

Bell, Kerwin (Football Player)
Indianapolis Colts
525 3rd St N Apt 508
Jacksonville Beach, FL 32250-7039, USA

Bell, Kevin (Baseball Player)
Chicago White Sox
621 Sue St
Little Chute, WI 54140-2424, USA

Bell, Kevin (Football Player)
New York Jets
5780 Phyllis Ln
Beaumont, TX 77713-9539, USA

Bell, Kristen (Actor)
c/o Tracy Brennan *Creative Artists Agency LCC (CAA-LA)*
2000 Avenue Of The Stars
Los Angeles, CA 90067-4700, USA

Bell, Lake (Actor)
c/o Staff Member *Burstein Company, The*
15304 W Sunset Blvd Ste 208
Pacific Palisades, CA 90272-3656, USA

Bell, Larry S (Artist)
PO Box 4101
Taos, NM 87571, USA

Bell, Lauralee (Actor)
C/O Nancy Schmidt
10 Universal City Plz Ste 2000
Boutique Talent Agency
Universal City, CA 91608-1074, USA

Bell, Lynette (Swimmer)
149 Henry St
Merwether NSW 22, AUSTRALIA

Bell, Madison Smartt (Writer)
Random House
1745 Broadway # B1
New York, NY 10019-4305, USA

Bell, Marcus (Football Player)
Seattle Seahawks
PO Box 1375
Saint Johns, AZ 85936-1375, USA

Bell, Mark E (Football Player)
Seattle Seahawks
2701 Wild Rose St
Wichita, KS 67205-1607, USA

Bell, Marshall (Actor)
IFA Talent Agency
8730 W Sunset Blvd Ste 490
Los Angeles, CA 90069-2248, USA

Bell, Michael (Actor)
Dade/Schulz
6442 Coldwater Canyon Ave Ste 206
North Hollywood, CA 91606-1137, USA

Bell, Mike (Baseball Player)
Atlanta Braves
1331 Noah Ave
Spring Hill, FL 34608-5767, USA

Bell, Mike (Race Car Driver)
American Motorcycle Assn
13515 Yarmouth Dr
Pickerington, OH 43147-8273, USA

Bell, Mike J (Football Player)
Kansas City Chiefs
7405 Lakewood Cir
Wichita, KS 67205-1608, USA

Bell, Myron (Football Player)
Pittsburgh Steelers
1012 Kinder Rd
Toledo, OH 43615-6814, USA

Bell, Nick (Football Player)
Los Angeles Raiders
19958 Bushard St
Huntington Beach, CA 92646-4012, USA

Bell, Richard T (Football Player)
Minnesota Vikings
12106 City View Ln SE
Chatfield, MN 55923-1719, USA

Bell, Ricky (Football Player)
Jacksonville Jaguars
4805 Barrington Dr
Columbia, SC 29203-3413, USA

Bell, Rini (Actor)
c/o Staff Member *Creative Management Group (CMG)*
8522 National Blvd Ste 108
Culver City, CA 90232-2454, USA

Bell, Robert (Musician)
c/o Staff Member *J Bird Entertainment Agency*
4905 S Atlantic Ave
Ponce Inlet, FL 32127-7311, USA

Bell, Sam (Coach)
2310 E Woodstock Pl
Bloomington, IN 47401-6179, USA

Bell, Sean (Actor)
c/o Daniel Sladek *Daniel Sladek Entertainment Corporation*
8306 Wilshire Blvd # 510
Beverly Hills, CA 90211-2304, USA

Bell, Terry (Baseball Player)
Kansas City Royals
8352 Normandy Creek Dr
Dayton, OH 45458-3284, USA

Bell, Theo (Football Player)
San Diego Chargers
12412 Windmill Cove Dr
Riverview, FL 33569-8216, USA

Bell, Tobin (Actor)
c/o Staff Member *Saffron Management*
9171 Wilshire Blvd Ste 441
Beverly Hills, CA 90210-5516, USA

Bell, Tom (Actor)
Shepherd & Ford
13 Randor Walk
London SW3 4BP, UNITED KINGDOM (UK)

Bell, Tommy (Astronaut)
205 S Redondo Ave
Manhattan Beach, CA 90266-7039, USA

Bell Calloway, Vanessa (Actor)
c/o Staff Member *Nine Yards Entertainment*
8530 Wilshire Blvd Fl 5
Beverly Hills, CA 90211-3102, USA

Bell-Lundy, Sandra (Cartoonist)
255 Northwood Dr
Welland, ON L3C 6V1, CANADA

Bell X1 (Music Group)
c/o Staff Member *Paradigm (Monterey)*
509 Hartnell St
Monterey, CA 93940-2825, USA

Bella, Ivan (Cosmonaut)
Potchta Kosmonavtov
Moskovskoi Oblasti
Syvisdny Goroduk 141160, RUSSIA

Bella, John (Baseball Player)
New York Yankees
409 N Cypress Dr Apt 7
Tequesta, FL 33469-2656, USA

Bella, Rachael (Actor)
c/o Leonard Torgan *Leverage Management*
1610 Broadway
Santa Monica, CA 90404-2792, USA

Bellamy, Bill (Actor, Comedian)
Talent Entertainment Group
9111 Wilshire Blvd
Beverly Hills, CA 90210-5508, USA

Bellamy, Carol (Misc)
United Nations Children's Fund
3 United Nations Plz
New York, NY 10017-4414, USA

Bellamy, David J (Writer)
Mill House Bedbum
Bishop Auckland
County Durham DL13 3NN, UNITED KINGDOM (UK)

Bellamy, Ned (Actor)
c/o Laina Cohn *Relativity Management*
8899 Beverly Blvd Ste 510
Los Angeles, CA 90048-2449, USA

Bellamy, Walt (Basketball Player)
Chicago Packers
2884 Lakeshore Dr
College Park, GA 30337-4420, USA

Belland, Neil (Hockey Player)
Vancouver Canucks
868 Renaissance Dr
Oshawa, ON L1J 8K9, CANADA

Bellar, Clara (Actor)
c/o Staff Member *IFA Talent Agency*
8730 W Sunset Blvd Ste 490
Los Angeles, CA 90069-2248, USA

Belle, Albert J (Baseball Player)
Cleveland Indians
9574 E Ann Way
Scottsdale, AZ 85260-5016, USA

Belle, Camilla (Actor)
c/o Nick Styne *Creative Artists Agency LCC (CAA-LA)*
2000 Avenue Of The Stars
Los Angeles, CA 90067-4700, USA

Belle, Regina (Musician)
Green Light
PO Box 3172
Beverly Hills, CA 90212-0172, USA

Bellecourt, Vernon (Activist)
American Indian Vovement
1209 4th St SE
Minneapolis, MN 55414-2026, USA

Bellefeuille, Blake (Hockey Player)
Columbus Blue Jackets
20 Glen Rd
Harwich, MA 02645-3339, USA

Beller, Kathleen (Actor)
PO Box 806
Half Moon Bay, CA 94019-0806, USA

Bellflower, Nellie (Actor, Producer)
c/o Staff Member *Keylight Entertainment Group*
425 Park Ave S Apt 19D
New York, NY 10016-8019, USA

Bellhorn, Mark (Basketball Player)
Oakland A's
1447 Palomino Way
Oviedo, FL 32765-9304, USA

Belliard, Rafael (Baseball Player)
Pittsburgh Pirates
10846 King Bay Dr
Boca Raton, FL 33498-4548, USA

Belliard, Ronnie (Baseball Player)
c/o Staff Member *Cleveland Indians*
2401 Ontario St
Jacobs Field
Cleveland, OH 44115-4003, USA

Bellinger, Clay (Baseball Player)
New York Yankees
1390 E Horseshoe Dr
Chandler, AZ 85249-4761, USA

Bellinger, Rodney (Football Player)
Buffalo Bills
7913 SW 104th St Apt G107
Miami, FL 33156-3656, USA

Bellingham, Lynda (Actor)
c/o Staff Member *Yakety Yak*
8 Bloomsbury Sq
London WC1A 2UA, UNITED KINGDOM (UK)

Bellingham, Norman (Misc)
208 Morgan St NW
Washington, DC 20001-1292, USA

Bellini, Mario (Architect)
Architecture Center
66 Portland Place
London W1, UNITED KINGDOM (UK)

Bellino, Joe (Football Player)
Boston Patriots
45 Hayden Ln
Bedford, MA 01730-1140, USA

Bellisario, Donald P (Actor, Director, Producer, Writer)
Broder Kurland Webb Uffner
10250 Constellation Blvd
Los Angeles, CA 90067-6200, USA

Bellman-Balchunas, Lois (Baseball Player)
5200 Westview Ln
Lisle, IL 60532-2420, USA

Bellmon, Henry (Governor, Senator)
RR 1
Red Rock, OK 74651, USA

Bello, Maria (Actor)
Creative Artists Agency
9830 Wilshire Blvd
Beverly Hills, CA 90212-1804, USA

Belloir, Bob (Baseball Player)
PO Box 2933
Savannah, GA 31402-2933, USA

Bellotti, Mike (Coach, Football Coach)
University of Oregon
Athletic Dept
Eugen, OR 97403, USA

Bellovin, Steven M (Scientist)
AT & T Research Labs
180 Park Ave
PO Box 971
Florham Park, NJ 07932-1049, USA

Bellows, Brian (Hockey Player)
Minnesota North Stars
5205 Mirror Lakes Dr
Minneapolis, MN 55436-2050, USA

Bellows, Gil (Actor)
c/o Scott Henderson *William Morris Agency (WMA-LA)*
1 William Morris Pl
Beverly Hills, CA 90212-4261, USA

Bellson, Louie
901 Winding River Rd
Vero Beach, FL 32963-2548, USA

Bellucci, Monica (Actor, Model)
c/o Nick Styne *Creative Artists Agency LCC (CAA-LA)*
2000 Avenue Of The Stars
Los Angeles, CA 90067-4700, USA

Bellugi, Piero
50027 Strada In Chianti
Florence, ITALY

Bellwood, Pamela (Actor)
c/o Richard Murphy *Personal Management Company*
425 N Robertson Blvd
West Hollywood, CA 90048-1735, USA

Belm, Michaela (Model)
Agentur Talents
Ohmstr 5
Munich 80802, GERMANY

Belmares, Roland (DJ)
c/o Staff Member *Diva Central Inc*
7510 W Sunset Blvd Ste 1445
Los Angeles, CA 90046-3408, USA

Belmondo, Jean-Paul (Actor)
9 Rue des Saint Peres
Paris 75007, FRANCE

Belo, Carlos Filipe Ximenes (Nobel Prize Laureate, Religious Leader)
Catholic Bishop Dili
EAST TIMOR

Belote Hamlin, Melissa (Swimmer)
7311 Exmore St
Springfield, VA 22150-4025, USA

Belotti, George (Football Player)
Houston Oilers
330 E Algrove St
Covina, CA 91723-2608, USA

Belousova, Ludmila (Figure Skater)
Chalet Hubel
Grindelwald 3818, SWITZERLAND

Belov, Sergei (Basketball Player)
Basket Cassino
Vis Appia Nuova
Cassino
Rome, ITALY

Belser, Ceaser (Football Player)
Kansas City Chiefs
6309 Fox Hunt Dr
Arlington, TX 76001-5655, USA

Beltrami, Marco (Composer)
Air-Edel
9255 W Sunset Blvd # 200
West Hollywood, CA 90069-3309, USA

Beltran, Carlos (Baseball Player)
Kansas City Royals
18 Paseo Alcala
Manati, PR 00674-5766, USA

Beltran, Rigoberto (Baseball Player)
St Louis Cardinals
4612 Fairhope Dr
La Mirada, CA 90638-6120, USA

Beltran, Robert (Actor)
2210 Talmadge St
Los Angeles, CA 90027-2918, USA

Beltre, Adrian (Athlete, Baseball Player)
c/o Staff Member *Los Angeles Dodgers (LA Dodgers)*
1000 Elysian Park Ave
Los Angeles, CA 90012-1112, USA

Belushi, James (Jim) (Actor)
c/o Marc Gurvitz *Brillstein-Grey Entertainment*
9150 Wilshire Blvd Ste 350
Beverly Hills, CA 90212-3453, USA

Belvin, Art (Football Player)
Dallas Cowboys
6506 Centre Place Cir
Spring, TX 77379-2937, USA

Belzer, Richard (Actor, Comedian)
c/o Chris Smith *International Creative Management (ICM-LA)*
10250 Constellation Blvd
Los Angeles, CA 90067-6200, USA

Beman, Deane R (Golfer)
Golf HOF
255 Deer Haven Dr
Ponte Vedra Beach, FL 32082-2108, USA

Bemhard (Prince)
Soestdijk Palace
Baarn, THE NETHERLANDS

Bemiller, Al
Buffalo Bills
5002 Armor Rd
Orchard Park, NY 14127-4401, USA

Bemis, Cliff (Actor)
Beartooth Productions
11271 Ventura Blvd
Pmb 366
Studio City, CA 91604-3136, USA

Bemoras, Irving (Basketball Player)
Milwaukee Hawks
416 Satinwood Ter
Buffalo Grove, IL 60089-6614, USA

Bemvenuti, Luciana (Golfer)
3673 Wickford Ln
Duluth, GA 30096-2409, USA

Ben Ali, Zine al-Abidine (General, President)
President's Office
Palais Presidentiel
Tunis, TUNISIA

Ben-Victor, Paul (Actor)
c/o Michael Garnett *Leverage Management*
1610 Broadway
Santa Monica, CA 90404-2792, USA

Benacerraf, Baruj (Nobel Prize Laureate)
111 Perkins St
Boston, MA 02130-4313, USA

Benackova, Gabriela (Opera Singer)
Oper et Concert
Maximilianstr 22
Munich 80539, GERMANY

Benade Leo, Edward (General)
417 Pine Ridge Road #A
Carthage, NC 28327, USA

Benanti, Laura (Actor)
c/o Staff Member *Creative Artists Agency LCC (CAA-LA)*
2000 Avenue Of The Stars
Los Angeles, CA 90067-4700, USA

Benard, Marvin (Baseball Player)
San Francisco Giants
30405 S 903 Pr SE
Kennewick, WA 99338-7346, USA

Benard, Maurice (Actor)
c/o Staff Member *Stone Manners Talent & Literary (LA)*
6500 Wilshire Blvd Ste 550
Los Angeles, CA 90048-4950, USA

Benatar, Pat (Musician, Songwriter, Writer)
c/o Bradley Goodman *William Morris Agency (WMA-LA)*
1 William Morris Pl
Beverly Hills, CA 90212-4261, USA

Benavides, Fortunato P (Pete) (Judge)
US Court of Appeals
903 San Jacinto Blvd
Austin, TX 78701-2449, USA

Benavides, Freddie (Baseball Player)
Cincinnati Reds
2502 Garfield St
Laredo, TX 78043-3030, USA

Benavides, Osvaldo (Actor)
c/o Staff Member *Televisa*
Blvd Adolfo Lopez Mateos 232
Colonia San Angel INN
DF CP 01060, MEXICO

Benben, Brian (Actor)
c/o Staff Member *Gersh Agency, The (LA)*
232 N Canon Dr
Beverly Hills, CA 90210-5302, USA

Benchoff, Dennis L (Den) (General)
380 Arbor Rd
Lancaster, PA 17601-3204, USA

Bender, Candace
PO Box 341489
Los Angeles, CA 90034-9489, USA

Bender, Carey (Football Player)
Buffalo Bills
840 S 15th St
Marion, IA 52302-5001, USA

Bender, Gary N (Sportscaster)
TNT-TV
1050 Techwood Dr NW
Sports Dept
Atlanta, GA 30318-5604, USA

Bender, Thomas (Historian)
54 Washington Mews
New York, NY 10003-6608, USA

Bender, Wes (Football Player)
Los Angeles Raiders
150 S Glenoaks Blvd # 9127
Burbank, CA 91502-1314, USA

Bendix, Simone (Actor)
Joy Jameson
2/19 Plaza
535 Kings Road
London SW10 0SZ, UNITED KINGDOM (UK)

Bendlin, Kurt (Athlete, Track Athlete)
DLV
Asfelder Str 27
Leverkusen 64289, GERMANY

Bendre, Sonali (Actor, Bollywood)
A/203 43 Paradise Apts
Swami Samarth Nagar 1st Cross Lane
Andheri(W)
Mumbai, MS 400053, INDIA

Bendross, Jesse (Football Player)
San Diego Chargers
5226 SW 22nd St
West Park, FL 33023-3118, USA

Bene, Bill (Baseball Player)
1063 Bella Vista Ave
Pasadena, CA 91107-1860, USA

Benedek, George B (Physicist)
Massachusetts Institute of Technology
Physics Dept
Cambridge, MA 02139, USA

Benedek, Joana (Actor)
c/o Staff Member *Televisa*
Blvd Adolfo Lopez Mateos 232
Colonia San Angel INN
DF CP 01060, MEXICO

Benedeti, Paulo (Actor)
1560 NW 13th Ave
Boca Raton, FL 33486-1217, USA

Benedict, Bruce (Baseball Player)
Minnesota Twins
335 Quiet Water Ln
Atlanta, GA 30350-3724, USA

Benedict, Dirk (Actor, Director, Writer)
c/o Staff Member *Acme Talent & Literary (LA)*
4727 Wilshire Blvd Ste 333
Los Angeles, CA 90010-3874, USA

Benedict, Dirk (Actor, Director, Writer)
PO Box 634
Bigfork, MT 59911-0634, USA

Benedict, Paul (Actor)
84 Rockland Pl
Newton, MA 02464-1234, USA

Benedict, Robert Patrick (Actor)
c/o Charles Silver *SMS Talent Inc*
8730 W Sunset Blvd Ste 440
Los Angeles, CA 90069-2277, USA

Benedict XVI, Pope (Religious Leader)
Apostolic Palace
Vatican City 00120, ITALY

Benedicto, Lourdes (Actor)
c/o Bob McGowan *McGowan Management*
8733 W Sunset Blvd Ste 103
W Hollywood, CA 90069-2241, USA

Benefield, Daved (Football Player)
San Francisco 49ers
420 N Rodeo Dr # 15281
Beverly Hills, CA 90210-4502, USA

Benepe, Jim (Golfer)
1955 1/2 Frackelton St
Sheridan, WY 82801-2526, USA

Benes, Alan (Baseball Player)
St Louis Cardinals
13005 Wheatfield Farm Rd
Saint Louis, MO 63141-8546, USA

Benes, Andrew C (Andy) (Baseball Player)
San Diego Padres
1127 Highland Point Dr
Saint Louis, MO 63131-1420, USA

Benetton, Giuliana (Business Person)
Benetton Group SpA
Via Minelli
Ponzano Treviso 31050, ITALY

Benetton, Luciano (Business Person)
Benetton Group SpA
Via Minelli
Ponzano Treviso 31050, ITALY

Benfatti, Lou (Football Player)
New York Jets
19 Pleasant Ln
Newfoundland, NJ 07435-1105, USA

Benflis, Ali (Prime Minister)
Prime Minister's Office
Palais du Gouvernement
Algiers, ALGERIA

Benford, Gregory (Writer)
c/o Vince Gerardis *Created By*
1041 N Formosa Ave
Formosa Bldg, Room 10
West Hollywood, CA 90046-6703, USA

Bengis, Fred (Baseball Player)
546 Quail Ct
Longs, SC 29568-8638, USA

Benglis, Lynda (Artist)
222 Bowery
New York, NY 10012-4216, USA

Bengoechea, Fernando (Photographer)
1345 Hymettus Ave
Encinitas, CA 92024-1748, USA

Bengston, Billy Al (Artist)
805 Hampton Dr
Venice, CA 90291-3020, USA

Benhima, Mohamed (Prime Minister)
Km 5.5
Route des Zaers
Rabat, MOROCCO

Benigni, Roberto (Actor)
c/o Nancy Seltzer *Nancy Seltzer & Associates*
6220 Del Valle Dr
Los Angeles, CA 90048-5306, USA

Benignl, Roberto (Actor, Director)
Via Traversa 44
Vergaglio
Provinz di Prato, ITALY

Bening, Annette (Actor)
c/o Kevin Huvane *Creative Artists Agency LCC (CAA-LA)*
2000 Avenue Of The Stars
Los Angeles, CA 90067-4700, USA

Benioff, David (Producer, Writer)
c/o Guymon Casady *Management 360*
9111 Wilshire Blvd
Beverly Hills, CA 90210-5508, USA

Benirschke, Rolf J (Football Player)
San Diego Chargers
PO Box 9922
Rancho Santa Fe, CA 92067-4922, USA

Benish, Dan (Football Player)
Atlanta Falcons
1158 Trailblazer Way NW
Lilburn, GA 30047-3575, USA

Benitez, Armando G (Baseball Player)
Batey El Soco
Ramon Santana, DOMINICAN REPUBLIC

Benitez, John (Jellybean)
William Morris Agency
151 El Camino Dr
Beverly Hills, CA 90212-2775, USA

Benitez, Yamil (Baseball Player)
San Francisco Giants
13 Calle Rev Francisco Colon B
Rio Piedres, PR 00925, USA

Benitz, Max (Actor)
c/o Michael Baum *Handprint Entertainment*
1100 Glendon Ave Ste 1000
Los Angeles, CA 90024-3514, USA

Benjamin, Andre (Andre 3000) (Artist, Musician)
c/o Charles King *William Morris Agency (WMA-LA)*
1 William Morris Pl
Beverly Hills, CA 90212-4261, USA

Benjamin, Guy (Football Player)
Miami Dolphins
1337 Lower Campus Rd
Honolulu, HI 96822-2312, USA

Benjamin, Jill (Actor)
c/o Staff Member *Power Entertainment*
9100 Wilshire Blvd # 700
Beverly Hills, CA 90212-3401, USA

Benjamin, Richard (Actor, Director)
c/o Staff Member *Gersh Agency, The (LA)*
232 N Canon Dr
Beverly Hills, CA 90210-5302, USA

Benjamin, Ryan (Football Player)
Cincinnati Bengals
PO Box 289
Pixley, CA 93256-0289, USA

Benjamin, Stan (Baseball Player)
Philadelphia Phillies
15 Speak Way
Harwich, MA 02645-2324, USA

Benkovic, Stephen J (Misc)
771 Teaberry Ln
State College, PA 16803-3183, USA

Benmosche, Robert H (Business Person)
Metropolitan Life Insurance
1 Madison Ave
New York, NY 10010-3681, USA

Benn, Anthony N W (Tony) (Government Official)
House of Commons
Westminster
London SW1A 0AA, UNITED KINGDOM (UK)

Benn, Nigel (Boxer)
Matchroom Boxing
10 Western Road
Romford Essex RM1 3JT, UNITED KINGDOM (UK)

Bennack Jr, Frank A (Publisher)
Hearst Corp
300 W 57th St Fl 42
New York, NY 10019-3790, USA

Benners, Fred (Football Player)
New York Giants
5211 Shadywood Ln
Dallas, TX 75209-2207, USA

Bennett, A L (Basketball Player)
523 N Willow Pl
Jenks, OK 74037-3489, USA

Bennett, Barry (Football Player)
New Orleans Saints
22047 Ginseng Rd
Long Prairie, MN 56347-4754, USA

Bennett, Bill (DJ)
c/o Staff Member *Diva Central Inc.*
7510 W Sunset Blvd Ste 1445
Los Angeles, CA 90046-3408, USA

Bennett, Bill (Hockey Player)
Boston Bruins
465C Middlebridge Rd
Wakefield, RI 02879-7116, USA

Bennett, Bob (Musician, Songwriter, Writer)
c/o Vicki Jennette *The Benjamin Artist Agency*
PO Box 92348
Nashville, TN 37209-8348, USA

Bennett, Brooke (Swimmer)
2585 Rowe Rd
Milford, MI 48380-2337, USA

Bennett, Bruce
2518 Beverwil Dr
Los Angeles, CA 90034-1063, USA

Bennett, Carl (Basketball Player)
Fort Wayne Zollner Pistons
2834 Little River Run
Fort Wayne, IN 46804-2573, USA

Bennett, Charles A (Football Player)
Miami Dolphins
19804 Bobolink Dr
Hialeah, FL 33015-2112, USA

Bennett, Clay (Cartoonist)
Christian Science Monitor
1 Norway St
Editorial Dept
Boston, MA 02115-3195, USA

Bennett, Curt (Hockey Player)
St Louis Blues
44 Polale St
Kihei, HI 96753-8283, USA

Bennett, Darren (Football Player)
San Diego Chargers
5299 Soledad Mountain Rd
San Diego, CA 92109, USA

Bennett, Dave (Baseball Player)
Philadelphia Phillies
408 N Fairchild St
Yreka, CA 96097-2219, USA

Bennett, Dennis (Baseball Player)
Philadelphia Phillies
630 N 5th St
Klamath Falls, OR 97601-3028, USA

Bennett, Donnell (Football Player)
Kansas City Chiefs
8055 W Leitner Dr
Coral Springs, FL 33067-2013, USA

Bennett, Edgar (Football Player)
Green Bay Packers
1880 Horseshoe Ln
De Pere, WI 54115-7947, USA

Bennett, Elmer (Basketball Player)
Cleveland Cavaliers
RR 1
Greencastle, IN 46135, USA

Bennett, Erik (Baseball Player)
California Angels
517 3rd St Apt 884
Yreka, CA 96097-2437, USA

Bennett, Fleur
25 Whitehall
London, ENGLAND SW1A 2BS, UNITED KINGDOM (UK)

Bennett, Fran (Actor)
749 N La Fayette Park Pl
Los Angeles, CA 90026-2917, USA

Bennett, Gary (Baseball Player)
Philadelphia Phillies
39895 N Delany Rd
Wadsworth, IL 60083-9516, USA

Bennett, Hywel (Actor)
Gavin Barker
45 S Molton St
London W1Y 3RD, UNITED KINGDOM (UK)

Bennett, Jeff (Baseball Player)
c/o Staff Member *Nashville Sounds*
534 Chestnut St
Nashville, TN 37203-4800, USA

Bennett, Jimmy (Actor)
c/o Jason Newman *Untitled Entertainment (LA)*
331 N Maple Dr Fl 3
Beverly Hills, CA 90210-3827, USA

Bennett, Joe C (Educator)
4101 Altamont Rd
Birmingham, AL 35213-2813, USA

Bennett, Joel (Baseball Player)
Baltimore Orioles
401 Riley Rd
Windsor, NY 13865-1043, USA

Bennett, John (Governor)
New Jersy State Senate
125 W State St
Trenton, NJ 08608-1101, USA

Bennett, Jonathan (Actor)
c/o Staff Member *Amplitude Entertainment*
8033 W Sunset Blvd # 823
West Hollywood, CA 90046-2401, USA

Bennett, Michael (Football Player)
Minnesota Vikings
9520 Viking Dr
Eden Prairie, MN 55344-3898, USA

Bennett, Monte (Football Player)
New Orleans Saints
2075 Avenue U
Sterling, KS 67579-8917, USA

Bennett, Nelson (Skier)
807 S 20th Ave
Yakima, WA 98902-4228, USA

Bennett, Nigel (Actor)
c/o Larry Goldhar *Characters Talent Agency, The (Toronto)*
8 Elm St 3rd FL
Toronto, ON M5G 1G7, CANADA

Bennett, Paris (Musician)
c/o Staff Member *American Idol*
7800 Beverly Blvd # 251
Los Angeles, CA 90036-2112, USA

Bennett, Richard Rodney (Composer)
Novello Co
8-9 Firth St
London W1V 5TZ, UNITED KINGDOM (UK)

Bennett, Rick (Hockey Player)
22 Brown St
Providence, RI 02918-0001, USA

Bennett, Robert (Bob) (Swimmer)
70 Rivo Alto Canal
Long Beach, CA 90803-4047, USA

Bennett, Robert R (Business Person)
Home Shopping Network
2501 118th Ave N
Saint Petersburg, FL 33716-1900, USA

Bennett, Robert S (Attorney, Attorney General, General)
1840 24th St NW
Washington, DC 20008-4024, USA

Bennett, Roy (Football Player)
San Diego Chargers
455 Wynbrooke Pkwy
Stone Mountain, GA 30087-4765, USA

Bennett, Sean (Football Player)
New York Giants
12163 E State Road 62
Saint Meinrad, IN 47577-9673, USA

Bennett, Tony (Basketball Player)
Charlotte Hornets
1530 NW Nicole Ct
Pullman, WA 99163-8882, USA

Bennett, Tony (Musician)
c/o Jeff Frasco *Creative Artists Agency LCC (CAA-LA)*
2000 Avenue Of The Stars
Los Angeles, CA 90067-4700, USA

Bennett, Tracie (Actor)
Annette Stone
9 Newburgh St
London W1V 1LA, UNITED KINGDOM (UK)

Bennett, William (Politician, Secretary)
862 Venable Pl NW
Washington, DC 20012-2612, USA

Bennett Jr, Harvey (Hockey Player)
Pittsburgh Penguins
1096 Warwick Neck Ave
Warwick, RI 02889-6815, USA

Bennett Sr, Harvey (Hockey Player)
Boston Bruins
63 Bayview Ave
East Greenwich, RI 02818-4103, USA

Bennie, Dan
22121 Cleveland St
Dearborn, MI 48124-3462, USA

Benning, Brian (Hockey Player)
St Louis Blues
Interstate Batteries of Northern Alberta
11404 156 St NW
Edmonton, AB T5M 3N2, CANADA

Benning, Jim (Hockey Player)
Toronto Maple Leafs
PO Box 1264
Sherwood, OR 97140-1264, USA

Bennington, Chester (Musician)
c/o Staff Member *Warner Bros Records (LA)*
3300 Warner Blvd
Burbank, CA 91505-4694, USA

Benny, Joan
1131 Coldwater Canyon Dr
Beverly Hills, CA 90210-2402, USA

Benoit, David (Musician)
Fitzgerald-Hartley
34 N Palm St # 100
Ventura, CA 93001-2635, USA

Benoit-Samuelson, Joan (Athlete, Track Athlete)
95 Lower Flying Point Rd
Freeport, ME 04032-6305, USA

Benrubi, Abraham (Actor)
c/o Staff Member *Stone Manners Talent & Literary (LA)*
6500 Wilshire Blvd Ste 550
Los Angeles, CA 90048-4950, USA

Benson, Amber (Actor)
c/o Staff Member *United Talent Agency (UTA)*
9560 Wilshire Blvd Ste 500
Beverly Hills, CA 90212-2401, USA

Benson, Andrew A (Misc)
6044 Folsom Dr
La Jolla, CA 92037-6711, USA

Benson, Anna (Model)
6025 Sandy Springs Cir NE # 313
Atlanta, GA 30328-3863, USA

Benson, Brad (Football Player)
New York Giants
Brad Benson Mitsubishi
3905 Route 1 South
Monmouth Junction, NJ 08852, USA

Benson, Charles (Football Player)
Miami Dolphins
9440 Gross St
Beaumont, TX 77707-1147, USA

Benson, Cliff (Football Player)
Atlanta Falcons
6520 Tennessee Ave
Willowbrook, IL 60527-1861, USA

Benson, Darren (Football Player)
Dallas Cowboys
PO Box 742614
Dallas, TX 75374-2614, USA

Benson, Doug (Comedian)
c/o Staff Member *OmniPop Inc (LA)*
4605 Lankershim Blvd Ste 201
North Hollywood, CA 91602-1874, USA

Benson, George (Musician)
9200 W Sunset Blvd Ste 600
West Hollywood, CA 90069-3196, USA

Benson, Harry (Photographer)
181 E 73rd St Apt 18A
New York, NY 10021-3566, USA

Benson, Herbert (Doctor)
Mind/Body Medical Institute
Beth Israel Hospital
Brookline, MA 02146, USA

Benson, Kent (Basketball Player)
3003 E Daniel St
Bloomington, IN 47401-4391, USA

Benson, Kris (Baseball Player)
Pittsburgh Pirates
5550 Claire Rose Ln NW
Atlanta, GA 30327-4829, USA

Benson, Robby (Actor)
c/o Rob Rothman *Rothman Brecher Agency*
9250 Wilshire Blvd Ph B
Beverly Hills, CA 90212-3346, USA

Benson, Stephen R (Steve) (Cartoonist)
Arizona Republic
200 E Van Buren St
Editorial Dept
Phoenix, AZ 85004-2238, USA

Benson, Sydney W (Misc)
1110 N Bundy Dr
Los Angeles, CA 90049-1513, USA

Benson, Thomas (Football Player)
Atlanta Falcons
PO Box 701341
Dallas, TX 75370-1341, USA

Benson, Troy (Football Player)
New York Jets
1038 Victoria Pl
Gibsonia, PA 15044-9200, USA

Benson, Vern (Baseball Player)
Philadelphia Athletics
PO Box 127
Granite Quarry, NC 28072-0127, USA

Benson Jr, Johnny (Race Car Driver)
PO Box 150619
Grand Rapids, MI 49515-0619, USA

Benson-Landes, Wendy (Actor)
c/o Staff Member *Northern Exposure
Talent Management*
1077 Marinaside Cresc #2502
Vancouver, BC V6Z 2Z5, CANADA

Bentley, Albert (Football Player)
Indianapolis Colts
5312 17th Ave SW
Naples, FL 34116-5611, USA

Bentley, Dierks (Musician)
Rogue Music Group
346 21st Ave N
Nashville, TN 37203-1848, USA

Bentley, Eric (Writer)
194 Riverside Dr
New York, NY 10025-7259, USA

Bentley, John (Actor)
Wedgewood House
Peterworth
Sussex, UNITED KINGDOM (UK)

Bentley, Lecharles (Football Player)
New Orleans Saints
5350 Harvestwood Ln
Columbus, OH 43230-4064, USA

Bentley, Ray (Football Player,
Sportscaster)
Buffalo Bills
4050 Redbush Dr SW
Grandville, MI 49418-3041, USA

Bentley, Stacey (Misc)
PO Box 26
Santa Monica, CA 90406-0026, USA

Bentley, Wes (Actor)
c/o Scott Lambert *William Morris Agency
(WMA-LA)*
1 William Morris Pl
Beverly Hills, CA 90212-4261, USA

Benton, Andrew K (Educator)
Pepperdine University
President's Office
Malibu, CA 90265, USA

Benton, Barbi (Actor, Model)
40 N 4th St
Carbondale, CO 81623-2012, USA

Benton, Brad (Adult Film Star)
c/o Staff Member *Diva Central Inc*
7510 W Sunset Blvd Ste 1445
Los Angeles, CA 90046-3408, USA

Benton, Butch (Baseball Player)
New York Mets
12314 SE 60th Ave
Belleview, FL 34420-5200, USA

Benton, Fletcher (Artist)
250 Dore St
San Francisco, CA 94103-4308, USA

Benton, Robert (Director)
International Creative Mgmt
40 W 57th St Ste 1800
New York, NY 10019-4001, USA

Benvenuti, Giovanni (Nino) (Boxer)
FPI Viaie Tiziano 70
Rome 00196, ITALY

Benvenuti, Nino
Via Giuseppe Ferrari 35
Rome 00127, ITALY

Benymon, Chico (Actor)
c/o Staff Member *Gersh Agency, The (LA)*
232 N Canon Dr
Beverly Hills, CA 90210-5302, USA

Benz, Julia (Actor)
Innovative Artists
1505 10th St
Santa Monica, CA 90401-2805, USA

Benz, Julie (Actor)
c/o Vincent Cirrincione *Vincent
Cirrincione Associates*
1516 N Fairfax Ave
Los Angeles, CA 90046-2608, USA

Benz, Julie (Actor)
c/o Staff Member *William Morris Agency
(WMA-LA)*
1 William Morris Pl
Beverly Hills, CA 90212-4261, USA

Benz, Larry (Football Player)
Cleveland Browns
1526 Brummel St
Evanston, IL 60202-3708, USA

Benz, Sepp (Athlete)
Kiefernweg 37
Zurich 8057, SWITZERLAND

Benza, AJ (Actor)
5670 Wilshire Blvd # 400W
Los Angeles, CA 90036-5679, USA

Benzali, Daniel (Actor)
c/o Staff Member *Diverse Talent Group*
1875 Century Park E Ste 2250
Los Angeles, CA 90067-2563, USA

Benzi, Roberto
12 Villa Sainte Foy
Neuilly-sur-Seine 92200, FRANCE

Beotti, Valentina (Actor)
Carol Levi Co
Via Giuseppe Pisanelli
Rome 00196, ITALY

Beranek, Josef (Hockey Player)
Pittsburgh Penguins
66 Mario Lemieux Pl
Melton Arena
Pittsburgh, PA 15219-3504, USA

Berard, Bryan (Hockey Player)
New York Islanders
9 Holly Ln
Cumberland, RI 02864-3328, USA

Berberet, Lou (Baseball Player)
New York Yankees
2500 Keppel Sands Dr
Las Vegas, NV 89134-7586, USA

Berblinger, Jeff (Baseball Player)
St Louis Cardinals
102 Swanee Dr
Goddard, KS 67052-9420, USA

Bercaw, John E (Misc)
California Institute of Technology
Chemistry Dept
Pasadena, CA 91125-0001, USA

Berce, Gene (Basketball Player)
Oshkosh All Stars
1119 Hawthorne Pl Apt G
Pewaukee, WI 53072-6576, USA

Bercich, Bob (Football Player)
Dallas Cowboys
19017 Edward Pkwy
Mokena, IL 60448-8565, USA

Bercich, Pete (Football Player)
Minnesota Vikings
RR 1 Box 369
New Lenox, IL 60451, USA

Bercu, Michaeala
Habaal-Shem Tov #10--#93
Herzelia 46342l, ISRAEL

Berdahl, Robert M (Educator)
University of California
Chancellor's Office
Berkeley, CA 94720-0001, USA

Bere, Jason (Baseball Player)
Chicago White Sox
101 Lowell St
Reading, MA 01867-2112, USA

Berenblum, Isaac (Doctor)
Weizmann Institute of Science
Pathology Dept
Rehovot, ISRAEL

Berendzen, Richard E (Educator)
1300 Crystal Dr
Arlington, VA 22202-3234, USA

Berenger, Tom (Actor)
c/o Colton Gramm *Brillstein-Grey
Entertainment*
9150 Wilshire Blvd Ste 350
Beverly Hills, CA 90212-3453, USA

Berenguer, Juan (Baseball Player)
New York Mets
8616 Alisa Ct
Chanhassen, MN 55317-9373, USA

Berenson, Ken (Red) (Coach, Hockey
Player)
Montreal Canadiens
3555 Daleview Dr
Ann Arbor, MI 48105-9686, USA

Berenzweig, Andrew (Hockey Player)
Nashville Predators
4504 Dovewood Ln
Sylvania, OH 43560-4315, USA

Beresford, Bruce (Director)
c/o Steve Kenis *Steve Kenis & Company*
72 Dean St
London W1D 3SG, UNITED KINGDOM
(UK)

Beresford, Meg (Activist)
Wiston Lodge
Wiston
Biggar ML12 6HT, SCOTLAND

Berezhnaya, Yelena (Figure Skater)
Ice House Skating Rink
111 Midtown Bridge Approac
Hackensack, NJ 07601-7505, USA

Berezin, Sergei (Hockey Player)
Toronto Maple Leafs
1645 SW 4th Ave
Boca Raton, FL 33432-7232, USA

Berezney, Peter (Football Player)
Los Angeles Dons
PO Box Cc
Saint Bonaventure, NY 14778-2358, USA

Berezovsky, Boris V (Musician)
IMG Artists
3 Burlington Lane
Chiswick
London W4 2TH, UNITED KINGDOM
(UK)

Berezovy, Anatoli N (Cosmonaut)
Potchia Kosmonavtov
Moskovskoi Oblasti
Syvisdny Goroduk 141160, RUSSIA

Berfield, Justin (Actor)
c/o Elissa Leeds-Fickman *Reel Talent
Management*
438 Tuallitan Rd
Los Angeles, CA 90049-1941, USA

Berg, Aki (Hockey Player)
Los Angeles Kings
7400 Metro Blvd Ste 280
Ocatagon Sports Representation
Minneapolis, MN 55439-2363, USA

Berg, Aki-Petteri (Hockey Player)
Octagon
1751 Pinnacle Dr Ste 1500
McLean, VA 22102-3833, USA

Berg, Dave (Baseball Player)
Florida Marlins
1917 Stonecastle Dr
Roanoke, TX 76262-4912, USA

Berg, Matraca (Musician)
Joe's Garage
4405 Belmont Park Ter
Nashville, TN 37215-3609, USA

Berg, Paul (Nobel Prize Laureate)
Stanford University
Medical School
Beckman Center
Stanford, CA 94305, USA

Berg, Peter (Actor)
H S I Productions
3630 Eastham Dr
Culver City, CA 90232-2411, USA

Berg, Yehuda (Religious Leader)
Kabbalah Center International
1066 S La Cienega Blvd
Los Angeles, CA 90035-2508, USA

Berganio, David Jr (Golfer)
17811 Lahey St
Granada Hills, CA 91344-4030, USA

Berganza, Teresa (Opera Singer)
La Rossinlana Archanda 5
28200 San Lorenzo del Escorial
Madrid, SPAIN

Berge, Francine (Actor)
Cineart
36 Rue de Ponthiew
Paris 75008, FRANCE

Berge, Ole M (Misc)
Maintenance of Way Brotherhood
12050 Woodward Ave
Detroit, MI 48203-3578, USA

Berge, Pierre V G (Business Person)
Yves Saint Laurent SA
5 Ave Marceau
Paris 75116, FRANCE

Bergen, Candice (Actor)
c/o Heidi Schaeffer *PMK/HBH Public Relations (PMK-LA)*
700 N San Vicente Blvd Ste G910
West Hollywood, CA 90069-5061, USA

Bergen, Danny (Actor)
c/o Staff Member *Paul Lane Entertainment*
468 N Camden Dr
Beverly Hills, CA 90210-4507, USA

Bergen, Gary (Basketball Player)
New York Knicks
11601 Paris St
Henderson, CO 80640-7616, USA

Bergen, Polly (Actor, Musician, Producer, Writer)
Jan McCormack
1746 S Britain Rd
Southbury, CT 06488-3200, USA

Berger, Brandon (Baseball Player)
Kansas City Royals
99 W Orchard Rd
Ft Mitchell, KY 41011-2633, USA

Berger, Gerhard (Race Car Driver)
Berger Motorsport
Postfach 1121
Vaduz 9490, AUSTRIA

Berger, Helmut (Actor)
Viale Parioli 50
Rome 00197, ITALY

Berger, John (Writer)
Quincy
Mieussy
Taninges 74440, FRANCE

Berger, Lee (Actor)
57 Fellows Dr
Brentwood, NH 03833-6130, USA

Berger, Ronald (Football Player)
Boston Patriots
6000 Lagorce Dr
Miami Beach, FL 33140-2117, USA

Berger, Senta (Actor)
Sentana Films
Gebsattelstr 30
Munich 81541, GERMANY

Berger, Thomas L (Writer)
PO Box 11
Palisades, NY 10964-0011, USA

Berger-Brown, Barbara (Baseball Player)
1633 Farmer Ave
Murray, KY 42071-2234, USA

Berger-Knebl, Joan (Baseball Player)
16 Home Pl
Lodi, NJ 07644-1512, USA

Berger-Taylor, Norma (Baseball Player)
529 N Blerman Ave
Villa Park, IL 60181, USA

Bergeron, Michel (Coach)
CHL T630
25 Rue Bryant
Sherbrooke, PQ J1J 3Z5, CANADA

Bergeron, Peter (Baseball Player)
Montreal Expos
13 Arnold Ln
Greenfield, MA 01301-9743, USA

Bergeron, Tom (Actor, Producer)
c/o Staff Member *IMG Artists Worldwide (NY)*
825 7th Ave
8th Floor
New York, NY 10019-6014, USA

Bergeron, Yves (Hockey Player)
Pittsburgh Penguins
1035 Clearwater Ave
Bathurst, NB E2A 4H5, CANADA

Bergeson, Eric (Football Player)
Los Angeles Rams
2579 Sherwood Dr
Salt Lake City, UT 84108-2457, USA

Bergevin, Marc (Hockey Player)
Chicago Blackhawks
6707 Barberry Pl
Carlsbad, CA 92011-3418, USA

Bergey, Bruce (Football Player)
Kansas City Cheifs
7700 SW River Rd
Hillsboro, OR 97123-9108, USA

Bergey, John (Inventor)
1807 Mayflower Cir
Lancaster, PA 17603-6039, USA

Bergey, William E (Bill) (Football Player)
Cincinatti Bengals
2 Hickory Ln
Chadds Ford, PA 19317-9715, USA

Berggren, Jenny (Musician)
Basic Music Mgmt
Norrtullsgatan 51
Stockholm 113 45, SWEDEN

Berggren, Jonas (Musician)
Basic Music Mgmt
Norrtullsgatan 51
Stockholm 11345, SWEDEN

Berggren, Malin (Musician)
Basic Music Mgmt
Norrtullsgatan 51
Stockholm 11345, SWEDEN

Berggren, Thommy (Actor)
Swedish Film Institute
PO Box 27126
Stockholm 102 52, SWEDEN

Bergh, Larry (Basketball Player)
Pittsburgh Condors
1840 Bent Pine Hl
Fogelsville, PA 18051-1501, USA

Bergi, Emily (Actor)
Innovative Artists
1505 10th St
Santa Monica, CA 90401-2805, USA

Bergin, Michael (Actor, Model)
c/o Tom Chasin *Chasin Agency, The*
8899 Beverly Blvd Ste 716
Los Angeles, CA 90048-2449, USA

Bergin, Patrick (Actor)
Hyler Mgmt
25 Sea Colony Dr
Santa Monica, CA 90405-5495, USA

Bergkamp, Dennis (Soccer Player)
Arsenal FC
Arsenal Stadium
Avenell Road
London N5 1BU, UNITED KINGDOM (UK)

Bergland, Robert S (Bob) (Secretary)
1104 7th Ave SE
Roseau, MN 56751-2313, USA

Bergland, Tim (Hockey Player)
Washington Capitals
721 Labree Ave N
Thief River Falls, MN 56701-1632, USA

Berglind (Icey) (Television Host)
c/o Staff Member *E! Entertainment Television (LA)*
5750 Wilshire Blvd
Los Angeles, CA 90036-3697, USA

Bergloff, Bob (Hockey Player)
Minnesota North Stars
10200 Harriet Ave S
Minneapolis, MN 55420-5233, USA

Berglund, Bo (Hockey Player)
Quebec Nordiques
1 Seymour H Knox III Plz Ste 1
Buffalo Sabres Attn Scouting Dept
Buffalo, NY 14203-3007, USA

Berglund, Paavo A E (Conductor)
Munkkiniemenranta 41
Helsinki 33 00330, FINLAND

Bergman, Alan (Musician)
714 N Maple Dr
Beverly Hills, CA 90210-3411, USA

Bergman, Andrew C (Director, Writer)
555 W 57th St Ste 1230
New York, NY 10019-2925, USA

Bergman, Arnfinn (Skier)
Nils Collett Vogtsv 58
Oslo 7 0765, NORWAY

Bergman, Dave (Baseball Player)
New York Yankees
728 Canterbury Ct
Grosse Pointe Woods, MI 48236-1294, USA

Bergman, Ingmar (Director)
Box 73
Farosund 62036, SWEDEN

Bergman, Jaime
Writers & Artists Agency
360 N Crescent Dr Bldg North
Beverly Hills, CA 90210-6818, USA

Bergman, Jamie (Actor, Model)
c/o Staff Member *Special Artists Agency*
9465 Wilshire Blvd Ste 890
Beverly Hills, CA 90212-2607, USA

Bergman, Marilyn K (Musician)
714 N Maple Dr
Beverly Hills, CA 90210-3411, USA

Bergman, Martin (Producer)
641 Lexington Ave
New York, NY 10022-4503, USA

Bergman, Peter (Actor)
c/o Staff Member *Young and the Restless, The*
7800 Beverly Blvd # 3305
Los Angeles, CA 90036-2112, USA

Bergman, Robert G (Misc)
501 Coventry Rd
Kensington, CA 94707-1316, USA

Bergman, Sean (Baseball Player)
Detroit Tigers
18540 Jw Donohue Rd
Wilmington, IL 60481, USA

Bergman, Thommie (Hockey Player)
Detroit Red Wings
Toronto Maple Leafs
300-40 Bay Street Attn Scouting Dept
Toront, ON M5J 2X2, CANADA

Bergmann, Erma (Baseball Player)
6613 Morganford Rd
Saint Louis, MO 63116-2835, USA

Bergoglio, Jose Mario Cardinal (Religious Leader)
Arzobispado
Rivadavia 415
Buenos Aires 1002, ARGENTINA

Bergomi, Giuseppe
via Trento 1
Settala (MI) 20090, ITALY

Bergonzi, Cario (Opera Singer)
I C M Artists
40 W 57th St
New York, NY 10019-4001, USA

Bergoust, Eric (Skier)
228 W Main St
Missoula, MT 59802-4345, USA

Bergquist, Curt (Doctor)
Allergon AB
Valinge 2090
Angelhoim 262 92, SWEDEN

Bergstein, Eleanor (Director, Producer, Writer)
c/o Staff Member *Creative Artists Agency LCC (CAA-LA)*
2000 Avenue Of The Stars
Los Angeles, CA 90067-4700, USA

Bergsten, C Fred (Economist)
4106 Sleepy Hollow Rd
Annandale, VA 22003-2042, USA

Berio, Luciano
11 Colombaig Radiocobdoli
Siena 53100, ITALY

Beristain, Gabriel L (Cinematographer)
United Talent Agency
9560 Wilshire Blvd Ste 500
Beverly Hills, CA 90212-2401, USA

Berkeley, Elizabeth (Actor, Model)
c/o Staff Member *Innovative Artists (LA)*
1505 10th St
Santa Monica, CA 90401-2805, USA

Berkeley, Michael F (Composer)
Rogers Coleridge White
20 Powis Mews
London W11 1JN, UNITED KINGDOM (UK)

Berkeley, Xander (Actor)
Abrams Artists
9200 W Sunset Blvd Ste 1125
Los Angeles, CA 90069-3610, USA

Berkley, Elizabeth (Actor)
c/o Craig Shapiro *Innovative Artists (LA)*
1505 10th St
Santa Monica, CA 90401-2805, USA

Berkman, Lance (Baseball Player)
Houston Astros
285 Bryn Mawr Cir
Houston, TX 77024-6811, USA

Berkner, Laurie (Musician)
PO Box 250774
Columbia University Station
New York, NY 10025-1529, USA

Berkoff, David (Swimmer)
Harvard University
Athletic Dept
Cambridge, MA 02138, USA

Berkowitz, Bob (Entertainer)
CNBC-TV
2200 Fletcher Ave
Fort Lee, NJ 07024-5005, USA

Berkus, Nate ((Designer)
Nate Berkus Associates
406 N Wood St
Chicago, IL 60622-6260, USA

Berlant, Anthony (Tony) (Artist)
Los Angeles Louver Gallery
55 N Venice Blvd
Venice, CA 90291-8907, USA

Berlanti, Greg (Producer)
c/o Staff Member *Everwood*
1000 W 2610 S
Salt Lake City, UT 84119-2434, USA

Berlin, Clay (Publisher)
2935 Franciscan Way
Carmel, CA 93923-9216, USA

Berlin, Eddie (Football Player)
Tennesse Titans
604 44th St
Des Moines, IA 50312-2302, USA

Berlin, Mike (Bowler)
12 Coventry Ln
Muscatine, IA 52761-5659, USA

Berlin, Steve (Musician)
c/o Staff Member *Paradigm (Monterey)*
509 Hartnell St
Monterey, CA 93940-2825, USA

Berliner, Alain (Director)
United Talent Agency
9560 Wilshire Blvd Ste 500
Beverly Hills, CA 90212-2401, USA

Berlinger, Warren (Actor)
10642 Arnel Pl
Chatsworth, CA 91311-2501, USA

Berlinsky, Dmitri (Musician)
35 W 64th St Apt 7F
New York, NY 10023-6757, USA

Berlioux, Daniel (Actor)
Cineart
36 Rue de Ponthieu
Paris 75008, FRANCE

Berlusconi, Silvio (Prime Minister)
Premier's Office
Palazzo Chigi
Piazza Colonna
Rome 00187, ITALY

Berman, Andy (Actor)
c/o Staff Member *Gersh Agency, The (LA)*
232 N Canon Dr
Beverly Hills, CA 90210-5302, USA

Berman, Boris (Musician)
Columbia Artists Mgmt Inc
1790 Broadway Fl 6
New York, NY 10019-1412, USA

Berman, Chris (Sportscaster)
c/o Staff Member *ESPN (Main)*
935 Middle St
Espn Plaza
Bristol, CT 06010-1000, USA

Berman, Jennifer (Doctor)
University of California
Women's Sexual Health Center
Los Angeles, CA 90024, USA

Berman, Josh (Producer)
c/o Staff Member *Jackoway Tyerman Wertheimer Austen Mandelbaum & Morris*
1888 Century Park E Fl 18
Los Angeles, CA 90067-1702, USA

Berman, Laura (Doctor)
University of California
Women's Sexual Health Center
Los Angeles, CA 90024, USA

Berman, Lazar N (Musician)
World Touring Productions
12 Nicola Ln
Nesconset, NY 11767-1550, USA

Berman, Rick (Producer, Writer)
c/o Staff Member *Rick Berman Productions*
5555 Melrose Ave
Cooper Bldg #232
Los Angeles, CA 90038-3989, USA

Berman, Shari Springer (Director)
c/o Staff Member *Creative Artists Agency LCC (CAA-LA)*
2000 Avenue Of The Stars
Los Angeles, CA 90067-4700, USA

Berman, Shelley (Actor, Comedian)
268 Bell Canyon Rd
Bell Canyon, CA 91307-1112, USA

Bermudez, Gustavo (Actor)
c/o Staff Member *Telefe - Argentina*
Pavon 2444 (C1248AAT)
Buenos Aires, ARGENTINA

Bermudez, Joe (DJ)
c/o Staff Member *Diva Central Inc*
7510 W Sunset Blvd Ste 1445
Los Angeles, CA 90046-3408, USA

Bernabei, Ray (Soccer Player)
541 Woodview Dr
Longwood, FL 32779-2614, USA

Bernadotte, Princess Marianne
Villagatan 10
Stockholm S-11432, SWEDEN

Bernadotte af Wisborg, Count Lennart
Insel Mainau
Konstanz D-78465, GERMANY

Bernal, Gael Garcia (Actor)
c/o Elyse Scherz *Endeavor Agency LLC (LA)*
9601 Wilshire Blvd Fl 3
Beverly Hills, CA 90210-5204, USA

Bernal, Vic (Baseball Player)
San Diego Padres
4632 Abner St
Los Angeles, CA 90032-3847, USA

Bernard, Betsy (Business Person)
American Telephone & Telegraph Corp
32 Avenue Of The Americas
New York, NY 10013-2473, USA

Bernard, Carlos (Actor)
CunninghamEscottDipene
10635 Santa Monica Blvd Ste 130
Los Angeles, CA 90025-8306, USA

Bernard, Claire M A (Musician)
53 Rue Rabelais
Lyon 69003, FRANCE

Bernard, Crystal (Actor, Musician, Songwriter, Writer)
Creative Artists Agency
9830 Wilshire Blvd
Beverly Hills, CA 90212-1804, USA

Bernard, Dwight (Baseball Player)
New York Mets
5120 N Norwich Ln
Belle Rive, IL 62810-2703, USA

Bernard, Ed (Actor)
PO Box 7965
Northridge, CA 91327-7965, USA

Bernard, Henry (Architect)
44 Av D'Ilena
Paris 75116, FRANCE

Bernard, James
#1 Oakley Gardens Chelsea
London, ENGLAND SW3 5QH, UNITED KINGDOM (UK)

Bernard, Robyn
3227 Cardiff Ave
Los Angeles, CA 90034-2811, USA

Bernardi, Frank (Football Player)
Chicago Cardinals
PO Box 1015
Broomfield, CO 80038-1015, USA

Bernazard, Tony (Baseball Player)
Montreal Expos
Santa Av D-25 Urb Santa Elvira
Caguas, PR 00625, USA

Berner, Robert A (Misc)
15 Hickory Hill Rd
North Haven, CT 06473-2916, USA

Bernero, Adam (Baseball Player)
Detroit Tigers
1231 Sibley Rd
Toledo, OH 43615-4660, USA

Bernero, Edward Allen (Writer)
c/o Staff Member *Endeavor Agency LLC (LA)*
9601 Wilshire Blvd Fl 3
Beverly Hills, CA 90210-5204, USA

Berners-Lee, Timothy J (Scientist)
Massachusetts Institute of Technology
Computer Sci Lab
Cambridge, MA 02139, USA

Bernet, Ed (Football Player)
Pittsburgh Steelers
7967 Caruth Ct
Dallas, TX 75225-8135, USA

Bernet, Lee (Football Player)
Denver Broncos
4689 Stoddart Ln
Saint Paul, MN 55127-2334, USA

Berney, Bob (President)
c/o Staff Member *Newmarket Films*
597 5th Ave Fl 7
New York, NY 10017-8264, USA

Bernhard, Ruth (Photographer)
1826 Loyola Dr
Burlingame, CA 94010-5749, USA

Bernhard, Sandra (Actor, Comedian, Musician)
c/o Tim Curtis *William Morris Agency (WMA-LA)*
1 William Morris Pl
Beverly Hills, CA 90212-4261, USA

Bernhardt, Daniel (Actor)
6500 Wilshire Blvd Ste 2200
Los Angeles, CA 90048-4942, USA

Bernhardt, Juan (Baseball Player)
New York Yankees
Eduardo Brito 13
San Pedro de Macoris, DOMINICAN REPUBLIC

Bernhardt, Kevin (Writer)
c/o Staff Member *Lichter Grossman Nichols Adler & Goodman*
9200 W Sunset Blvd Ste 1200
Los Angeles, CA 90069-3607, USA

Bernhardt, Roger (Football Player)
New York Jets
PO Box 4631
Lawrence, KS 66046-1631, USA

Bernhardt, Tim (Hockey Player)
Toronto Maple Leafs
RR 1
Schomberg, ON L0G 1T0, CANADA

Bernheimer, Martin (Musician)
17350 W Sunset Blvd Apt 702C
Pacific Palisades, CA 90272-4109, USA

Bernich, Ken (Football Player)
New York Jets
504 Woodland Park Cir
Mary Esther, FL 32569-1577, USA

Bernier, Serge (Hockey Player)
Philadelphia Flyers
534 Rue Elisabeth
Rimouski, PQ G5L 3M9, CANADA

Bernier, Sylvie (Race Car Driver)
Olympic Assn
Cite du Harve
Montreal, PQ H3C 3R4, CANADA

Berns, Rick (Football Player)
Tampa Bay Buccaneers
632 Canyon Springs Dr
Canyon Lake, TX 78133-4301, USA

Bernsen, Corbin (Actor)
c/o Randy James *James/Levy/Jacobson Management*
3500 W Olive Ave Ste 1470
Burbank, CA 91505-5514, USA

Bernstein, Besil (Misc)
90 Farquhar Road
Dulwich SE19 1LT, UNITED KINGDOM (UK)

Bernstein, Bonnie (Television Host)
c/o Staff Member *CBS Television*
51 W 52nd St
New York, NY 10019-6119, USA

Bernstein, Carl (Journalist)
William Moris Agency
151 El Camino Dr
Beverly Hills, CA 90212-2775, USA

Bernstein, Charles (Composer)
FMA
6525 W Sunset Blvd Ste 300
Los Angeles, CA 90028-7200, USA

Bernstein, Josh (Television Host)
c/o Jim Ornstein *William Morris Agency (WMA-NY)*
1325 Avenue Of The Americas
New York, NY 10019-6026, USA

Bernstein, Kenny (Race Car Driver)
King Racing
26231 Dimension Dr
Lake Forest, CA 92630-7805, USA

Bernstine, Rod (Football Player)
San Diego Chargers
15635 E Prentice Ln
Centennial, CO 80015-4262, USA

Berov, Lyuben (Prime Minister)
Rights & Freedom Movement
Tzarigradsko Shosse 47/1
Sofia 1408, BULGARIA

Berra, Dale (Baseball Player)
Pittsburgh Pirates
19 Highland Ave
Montclair, NJ 07042-1909, USA

Berra, Lawrence P (Yogi) (Baseball Player)
New York Yankees
19 Highland Ave
Montclair, NJ 07042-1909, USA

Berra, Tim (Football Player)
Baltimore Colts
23 Wilson Ter
West Caldwell, NJ 07006-7953, USA

Berres, Ray (Baseball Player)
Brooklyn Dodgers
5522 6th Ave
Kenosha, WI 53140-3710, USA

Berresford, Susan V (Misc)
Ford Foundation
320 E 43rd St
New York, NY 10017-4890, USA

Berri, Claude (Director, Producer)
Renn Espace d'Art Contemporain
7 Rue de Lille
Paris 75007, FRANCE

Berridge, Elizabeth (Actor)
Judy Schoen
606 N Larchmont Blvd Ste 309
Los Angeles, CA 90004-1309, USA

Berrigan, Daniel (Activist)
220 W 98th St Apt 11L
New York, NY 10025-5677, USA

Berroa, Geronimo (Baseball Player)
Atlanta Braves
3681 Broadway Apt 23
New York, NY 10031-1539, USA

Berruti, Livio (Activist)
Via Avigliana 45
Torino 10138, ITALY

Berry, Bert (Football Player)
Indianapolis Colts
1402 E Coral Cove Dr
Gilbert, AZ 85234-2600, USA

Berry, Bill (Baseball Player)
Negro Baseball Leagues
2231 Dickinson St
Philadelphia, PA 19146-4204, USA

Berry, Bill (Musician)
REM/Athens Ltd
170 College Ave
Athens, GA 30601-2805, USA

Berry, Bob (Football Player)
Minnesota Vikings
1351 Wilson Cir
Gardnerville, NV 89410-6022, USA

Berry, Brad (Hockey Player)
Winnipeg Jets
1005 S 20th St
Grand Forks, ND 58201-4132, USA

Berry, Charles E (Chuck) (Musician, Songwriter, Writer)
691 Buckner Rd
Berry Park
Wentzville, MO 63385-5442, USA

Berry, David (Actor)
5903 Winton St
Dallas, TX 75206-5536, USA

Berry, Ed (Football Player)
Green Bay Packers
4215 Skymont Dr
Belmont, CA 94002-1245, USA

Berry, Glen (Actor)
c/o Staff Member *Peters Fraser & Dunlop (PFD - UK)*
Drury House
34-43 Russell St
London WC2B 5HA, UNITED KINGDOM (UK)

Berry, Halle (Actor, Model)
c/o Vincent Cirrincione *Vincent Cirrincione Associates*
1516 N Fairfax Ave
Los Angeles, CA 90046-2608, USA

Berry, Jennifer (Beauty Pageant Winner)
c/o Staff Member *The Miss America Organization*
2 Miss America Way Ste 1000
Atlantic City, NJ 08401-4142, USA

Berry, Jim (Cartoonist)
United Feature Syndicate
200 Madison Ave
New York, NY 10016-3911, USA

Berry, John (Musician)
Firstars Mgmt
14724 Ventura Blvd Ph
Sherman Oaks, CA 91403-3513, USA

Berry, Ken (Actor)
13911 Fenton Ave
Sylmar, CA 91342, USA

Berry, Ken (Baseball Player)
Chicago White Sox
1131 SW Camden Ln
Topeka, KS 66604-1980, USA

Berry, Kevin (Swimmer)
28 George St
Manly, NSW 2295, AUSTRALIA

Berry, Michael J (Misc)
PO Box 1421
Pebble Beach, CA 93953-1421, USA

Berry, Neil (Baseball Player)
Detroit Tigers
407 Inkster Ave
Kalamazoo, MI 49001-4220, USA

Berry, R Stephen (Misc)
5317 S University Ave
Chicago, IL 60615-5105, USA

Berry, Raymond E (Coach, Football Coach, Football Player)
Baltimore Colts
1110 SE Broad St
Murfreesboro, TN 37130-5027, USA

Berry, Reggie (Football Player)
San Diego Chargers
564 E Bradenhall Dr
Carson, CA 90746-1127, USA

Berry, Rex (Football Player)
San Fransisco 49ers
55 Marrcrest S
Provo, UT 84604-3800, USA

Berry, Robert V (Bob) (Coach, Hockey Player)
Montreal Canadiens
640 3rd St
Hermosa Beach, CA 90254-4710, USA

Berry, Royce (Football Player)
Cincinatti Bengals
2100 Tanglewilde St Apt 9
Houston, TX 77063-1209, USA

Berry, Sean (Baseball Player)
Kansas City Royals
PO Box 3829
Paso Robles, CA 93447-3829, USA

Berry, Vincent (Actor)
Academy Kids Mgmt
4942 Vineland Ave Ste 103
North Hollywood, CA 91601-5639, USA

Berry, Walter (Basketball Player)
Portland Trail Blazers
23 Cameron Rd
Saddle River, NJ 07458-2935, USA

Berry, Wendell E (Writer)
River Road
Port Royal, KY 40058, USA

Berryhill, Damon (Baseball Player)
Chicago Cubs
11 Springbrook Rd
Laguna Niguel, CA 92677-5719, USA

Berryman, Michael (Actor)
PO Box 697
Clearlake, CA 95422-0697, USA

Berschet, Marv (Football Player)
Washington Redskins
8396 Clifton Rd
South Charleston, OH 45368-8653, USA

Bersia, John (Journalist)
Orlando Sentinel
633 N Orange Ave
Editorial Dept
Orlando, FL 32801-1349, USA

Bertaina, Frank (Baseball Player)
Baltimore Orioles
PO Box 232
Napa, CA 94559-0232, USA

Bertelmann, Fred
Am Hohenberg 9
Berg/Starnberger -See D-82335, GERMANY

Bertelsen, Jim (Football Player)
Pittsburgh Steelers
1001 Golds Rd
Wimberley, TX 78676-6053, USA

Berteotti, Missie (Golfer)
300 Ocean Trail Way Apt 1304
Jupiter, FL 33477-5522, USA

Berteotti, Missy (Golfer)
3221 Annandale Dr
Presto, PA 15142-1055, USA

Berthiaume, Daniel (Hockey Player)
Winnipeg Jets
140 Rue Coulonge
Longueuil, PQ J4G 1H6, CANADA

Berthiaume-Wicken, Elizabeth (Baseball Player)
52 E 20th Ave
Vancouver, BC V5V 1L6, CANADA

Berthold, Helmut (Misc)
Meyerstr 21
Hamburg 21075, GERMANY

Berti, Joel (Actor)
c/o Melissa Hirschenson *Innovative Artists (LA)*
1505 10th St
Santa Monica, CA 90401-2805, USA

Bertie, Diego (Musician)
c/o Gabriel Blanco *Gabriel Blanco Iglesias (Mexico)*
Rio Balsas 35-32
Colonia Cuauhtemoc
DF 06500, MEXICO

Bertil (Prince)
Hert Av Halland
Kungl Slottel
Stockholm 1130, SWEDEN

Bertinelli, Valerie (Actor)
c/o Wes Stevens *VOX Inc*
5670 Wilshire Blvd Ste 820
Los Angeles, CA 90036-5613, USA

Bertini, Catherine (Misc)
United Nations
1 United Nations Plz
New York, NY 10017-3515, USA

Bertoia, Reno (Baseball Player)
Detroit Tigers
705-5125 Riverside Dr E
Windsor, ON N8S 4L8, CANADA

Bertolucci, Bernardo (Actor)
Via Della Lungara 3
Rome 00165, ITALY

Bertone, Tarcisco Cardinal (Religious Leader)
Archdiocese Piazza Matteotti 4
Genoa 16123, ITALY

Bertotti, Mike (Baseball Player)
Chicago White Sox
14 Jupiter Rd
Highland Mls, NY 10930-2916, USA

Bertram, Laura (Actor)
c/o Staff Member *Lucas Talent Inc*
Sun Tower Floor 7
100 W Pender St
Vancouver, BC V6B 1R8, CANADA

Bertuca, Tony (Football Player)
Baltimore Colts
2014 N Newcastle Ave
Chicago, IL 60707-3332, USA

Bertuzzi, Todd (Hockey Player)
New York Islanders
Newport Sports Management Inc
Attn Donald Meehan 601-201 City Centre Dr
Mississauga, ON L5B 1T4, CANADA

Berube, Craig (Hockey Player)
Philadelphia Flyers
1341 Durham Rd
New Hope, PA 18938-9479, USA

Berumen, Andres (Baseball Player)
San Diego Padres
PO Box 1436
Banning, CA 92220-0010, USA

Berzon, Marsha S (Judge)
US Court of Appeals
95 7th St
Court Building
San Francisco, CA 94103-1518, USA

Besana, Fred (Baseball Player)
Baltimore Orioles
222 Diamond Oaks Rd
Roseville, CA 95678-1007, USA

Beschorner-Baskovich, Mary (Baseball Player)
211 Sandy Ln
Plano, IL 60545-2054, USA

Besedin, Vladimir (Figure Skater)
c/o Staff Member *Champions on Ice*
3500 W 80th St
Tom Collins Enterprises Inc
Minneapolis, MN 55431-1068, USA

Bess, Daniel (Actor)
c/o Raelle Koota *Anonymous Content (NY)*
8522 National Blvd Ste 101
Culver City, CA 90232-2454, USA

Bess, Rufus (Football Player)
Oakland Raiders
8685 Magnolia Trl Apt 214
Eden Prairie, MN 55344-7664, USA

Bessey, Joe
c/o Joe Bessey Motorsport
PO Box 525
Scarborough, ME 04070-0525, USA

Bessillieu, Donald A (Don) (Football Player)
Miami Dolphins
4787 Gardiner Dr
Columbus, GA 31907-3441, USA

Bessmertnova, Natalia (Ballerina)
Sretenskii Blvd 6/1
#9
Moscow 101000, RUSSIA

Bessmertnykh, Aleksandr (Government Official)
Yelizarova Str 10
Moscow 103064, RUSSIA

Besson, Luc (Director)
CBC
11 Rue de la Croix Boissee
Mennecy 91540, FRANCE

Best, Art (Football Player)
Chicago Bears
420 Lockville Rd
Pickerington, OH 43147-1360, USA

Best, Greg (Football Player)
Pittsburgh Steelers
2859 Darlington Rd
Beaver Falls, PA 15010-1054, USA

Best, James (Actor)
PO Box 621027
Oviedo, FL 32762-1027, USA

Best, John O (Soccer Player)
1065 Lomita Blvd
Harbor City, CA 90710-1901, USA

Best, Karl (Baseball Player)
Seattle Mariners
PO Box 1790
Snohomish, WA 98291-1790, USA

Best, Kevin
PO Box 1164
Hesperia, CA 92345, USA

Best, Pete (Musician)
8 Hymans Green
W Derby
Liverpool 12, UNITED KINGDOM (UK)

Best, Travis (Basketball Player)
Indiana Pacers
703 Bradley Rd
Springfield, MA 01109-1424, USA

Bestar, Maria (Musician)
c/o Staff Member Sony Music Miami
605 Lincoln Rd Fl 7
Miami Beach, FL 33139-2900, USA

Bester, Allan (Hockey Player)
Toronto Maple Leafs
12527 Crayford Ave
Orlando, FL 32837-8536, USA

Bestwicke, Martine (Actor)
Goldey Co
1156 S Carmelia Ave #B
Los Angeles, CA 90049, USA

Beswick, Jim (Baseball Player)
San Diego Padres
6911 Buckhorn Dr
Columbus, GA 31904-3212, USA

Betancourt, Jeff (Director)
c/o Staff Member Broder Webb Chervin
Silbermann Agency, The (BWCS)
10250 Constellation Blvd Ste P
Los Angeles, CA 90067-6213, USA

Betancurt, Natalia (Actor)
c/o Staff Member TV Caracol
Calle 76 #11 - 35
Piso 10AA
Bogota DC 26484, COLOMBIA

Bethea, Bill (Baseball Player)
Minnesota Twins
PO Box 1000 Attn Athletic Dept
Arkansas State University
Jonesboro, AR 72403, USA

Bethea, Ellen (Actor)
Independent Artists
505 8th Ave Rm 2208
New York, NY 10018-4519, USA

Bethea, Elvin L (Football Player)
Houston Oilers
16211 Leslie Ln
Missouri City, TX 77489-1012, USA

Bethke, Jim (Baseball Player)
New York Mets
6209 N Robinhood Ln
Kansas City, MO 64151-2849, USA

Bethune, Bobby (Football Player)
San Diego Chargers
PO Box 692
Leeds, AL 35094-0011, USA

Bethune, George (Football Player)
Los Angeles Rams
2817 Gaslight Ln W
Mobile, AL 36695-3130, USA

Bethune, Patricia (Actor)
c/o Peter Kluge Impact Artists Group LLC
244 N California St
Burbank, CA 91505-3505, USA

Bethune, Zina (Actor)
3096 Lake Hollywood Dr
Los Angeles, CA 90068-1565, USA

Bets, Maxim (Hockey Player)
Mighty Ducks of Anaheim
600 Main St
Worcester, MA 01608-2061, USA

Bettany, Paul (Actor)
c/o Melanie Greene Melanie Greene
Management & Productions
425 N Robertson Blvd
West Hollywood, CA 90048-1735, USA

Bettencourt, Liliane (Business Person)
L'Oreal
575 5th Ave
New York, NY 10017-2446, USA

Bettendorf, Jeff (Baseball Player)
Oakland A's
210 W Rainey St
Ozark, MO 65721-9012, USA

Bettenhausen, Gary (Race Car Driver)
2741 Chesterfield Dr
Bettendorf, IA 52722-6251, USA

Betters, Doug L (Football Player)
Miami Dolphins
3352 E Lakeshore Dr
Whitefish, MT 59937-8009, USA

Betterson, Doug (Football Player)
Philadelphia Eagles
2442 46th St
Pennsauken, NJ 08110-2018, USA

Betterson, James (Football Player)
Philadelphia Eagles
234 Allens Ln
Mullica Hill, NJ 08062-2005, USA

Bettiga, Mike (Football Player)
San Fransisco 49ers
1165 Vista Dr
Fortuna, CA 95540-1514, USA

Bettio, Silvio (Hockey Player)
Boston Bruins
1405 Wedgewood Dr
Sudbury, ON P3A 3E3, CANADA

Bettis, Angela (Actor)
1122 Roxbury Dr
Los Angeles, CA 90035-1031, USA

Bettis, Tom (Football Player)
Green Bay Packers
3523 N Peach Hollow Cir
Pearland, TX 77584-4007, USA

Bettman, Gary B (Misc)
National Hockey League
1251 Avenue Of The Americas
New York, NY 10020-1192, USA

Bettridge, Ed (Football Player)
Cleveland Browns
200 Seaward Way
Avon Lake, OH 44012-2414, USA

Betts, Austin W (General)
8003 North Holw Ste 204
San Antonio, TX 78240-2360, USA

Betts, Dickey (Musician)
c/o Staff Member Intrepid Artists
1300 Baxter St Ste 405
Midtown Plz
Charlotte, NC 28204-3081, USA

Betts, Dickie (Musician)
FreeFalls
PO Box 604
Chagrin Falls, OH 44022-0604, USA

Betts, Katherine (Editor)
Harper's Bazaar
1770 Broadway
Editorial Dept
New York, NY 10019, USA

Betts, Ladell (Football Player)
c/o Staff Member Washington Redskins
21300 Redskin Park Dr
Ashburn, VA 20147-6100, USA

Beuchel, Ted (Musician)
Variety Artists
793 Higuera St Ste 6
San Luis Obispo, CA 93401-0500, USA

Beueriein, Stephen T (Steve) (Football Player)
15624 McCullers Ct
Charlotte, NC 28277-1478, USA

Beuerlein, Steve (Football Player)
Los Angeles Raiders
15624 McCullers Ct
Charlotte, NC 28277-1478, USA

Beukeboom, Jeff (Hockey Player)
Edmonton Oilers
464 Wagg Rd RR 4
Uxbridge, ON L9P 1R4, CANADA

Beutler, Ernest (Doctor)
2707 Costebelle Dr
La Jolla, CA 92037-3518, USA

Beutler, Tom (Football Player)
Cleveland Browns
7218 Longwater Dr
Maumee, OH 43537-8663, USA

Bevacqua, Kurt (Baseball Player)
Cleveland Indians
2607 Pirineos Way Unit 101
Carlsbad, CA 92009-7333, USA

Bevan, Tim (Actor, Producer)
c/o Staff Member Working Title Films
9720 Wilshire Blvd Fl 4
Beverly Hills, CA 90212-2000, USA

Bevan, Timothy H (Financier)
Barclay's Bank
54 Lombard St
London EC3P 3AH, UNITED KINGDOM
(UK)

Beverley, Frankie (Musician)
115 Cherokee Rose Ln
Fairburn, GA 30213-3459, USA

Beverley, Nick (Coach, Hockey Player)
Boston Bruins
Blairhampton Road 00
Minden, ON K0M 2K0, CANADA

Beverley Sisters (Actor, Music Group)
Adam Nolan
80 Highcroft Ave Bispham
Blackpool, Lancashire FY20BW, UNITED
KINGDOM (UK)

Beverlin, Jason (Baseball Player)
Cleveland Indians
1128 Old Shire Way
Statesboro, GA 30461-2994, USA

Beverly, David (Football Player)
Houston Oilers
15 Wood Cove Dr
The Woodlands, TX 77381-3312, USA

Beverly, Eric (Football Player)
Detroit Lions
PO Box 492433
Lawrenceville, GA 30049-0041, USA

Beverly, Randy (Football Player)
New York Jets
PO Box 425
Westbury, NY 11590-0130, USA

Beverly Jr, Ed (Football Player)
San Fransisco 49ers
13051 Golansville Rd
Ruther Glen, VA 22546-4029, USA

Bevill, Lisa (Musician)
Jeff Roberts
3050 Business Park Cir Ste 301
Goodlettsville, TN 37072-3588, USA

Bevington, Terry P (Baseball Player, Misc)
2600 Halle Pkwy
Collierville, TN 38017-8888, USA

Bevis, Leslie (Actor)
Epstein-Wyckoff
280 S Beverly Dr Ste 400
Beverly Hills, CA 90212-3904, USA

Bevis, Muriel (Baseball Player)
538 Idlewood Dr
Mount Juliet, TN 37122-2118, USA

Bewkes, Jeff (Business Person)
Time Warner
75 Rockefeller Plz
New York, NY 10019-6990, USA

Bey, Andy (Musician)
Megaforce Entertainment
PO Box 779
New Hope, PA 18938-0779, USA

Bey, Richard (Entertainer)
445 Park Ave # 1000
New York, NY 10022-2606, USA

Bey, Turhan (Actor)
Paradisgasse Ave 47
Vienna, XIX 1190, AUSTRIA

Beyer, Brad (Actor)
c/o Jeff Hunter William Morris Agency
(WMA-NY)
1325 Avenue Of The Americas
New York, NY 10019-6026, USA

Beyer, Troy (Actor)
c/o David Saunders Agency for the
Performing Arts (APA-LA)
405 S Beverly Dr
Beverly Hills, CA 90212-4416, USA

Beymer, Richard (Actor)
1818 N Fuller Ave
Los Angeles, CA 90046-2306, USA

Bezic, Sandra (Figure Skater, Sportscaster)
c/o Staff Member NBC Sports (NY)
30 Rockefeller Plz
New York, NY 10112-0015, USA

Bezos, Jeff (Business Person)
Amazon.com
PO Box 81226
Seattle, WA 98108-1300, USA

BG (Musician)
c/o Staff Member *JL Entertainment Inc*
18653 Ventura Blvd # 340
Tarzana, CA 91356-4103, USA

Bhagwan (Actor, Bollywood)
25 Lallubhai Mansion Shankarrao Palav
Marg
Mumbai, MS 400014, INDIA

Bhagwati, Jagdish N (Economist)
Columbia University
Economics Dept
New York, NY 10027, USA

Bhagyashree (Actor, Bollywood)
96/B Hirak Society
SV Rd Vile Parle
Mumbai, MS 400056, INDIA

Bhan Bhagta Gurung (War Hero)
Victoria Cross Assn
Old Admiralty Building
London SW1A 2BL, UNITED KINGDOM
(UK)

Bhanu, Prakash (Bharathan) (Actor)
12/2 Circular Road United India Colony
Kodambakkam
Chennai, TN 600 024, INDIA

Bhanupriya (Actor, Bollywood)
4 1st Cross Street
Vijayaraghava Road
Chennai, TN 600017, INDIA

Bhaskar, Sanjeev (Actor)
c/o Staff Member *BBC Artist Mail*
PO Box 1116
Belfast BT2 7AJ, UNITED KINGDOM
(UK)

Bhatnagar, Deepti (Actor, Bollywood)
42 Ashok Apts
Gandhigram Road Juhu
Mumbai, MS 400049, INDIA

Bhatnagar, Dipti (Actor, Bollywood)
42 Ashoka Apts
Gandhigram Rd Juhu
Mumbai, MS 400049, INDIA

Bhatt, Mahesh (Bollywood, Director, Filmmaker)
205 Silver Beach Apartments
Near Sun-N-Sand Hotel Juhu
Bombay, MS 400049, INDIA

Bhatt, Mukesh (Bollywood, Director, Filmmaker, Producer)
10 Shubh Jeevan Co-op Society
JVPD Scheme
Bombay, MS 400 049, INDIA

Bhattacharya, Basu (Actor, Bollywood, Director)
36 Carter Road Bandra
Mumbai, MS 400050, INDIA

Bhattarai, Krishna Prasad (Prime Minister)
Nepali Congress Central Office
Baneshwar
Kathmandu, NEPAL

Bhave, Ashwini (Actor, Bollywood)
A-9 Green View
Suburban Soc Shiv Shrushti
Mumbai, MS 400024, INDIA

Bhumibol, Adulyadej (King)
Royal Residence
Chirtalad a Villa
Bangkok, THAILAND

Biafra, Jello
PO Box 419092
San Francisco, CA 94141-9092, USA

Biagiotti, Laura (Designer, Fashion Designer)
Studio Biagiotti
Via Borgopesco 19
Milan 20121, ITALY

Biakabutuka, Tshimanga (Tim) (Football Player)
Carolina Panthers
110 Sonnys Way
Fort Mill, SC 29708-6415, USA

Bialik, Mayim (Actor)
Coppage Co
5411 Camellia Ave
North Hollywood, CA 91601-2615, USA

Bialosuknia, Wesley (Basketball Player)
Oakland Oaks
29 Bayberry Dr
Bristol, CT 06010-7604, USA

Bialowas, Dwight (Hockey Player)
Atlanta Flames
15616 Park Terrace Dr
Eden Prairie, MN 55346-2429, USA

Biancalana, Buddy (Baseball Player)
Kansas City Royals
7901 30th Ave N
Saint Petersburg, FL 33710-1151, USA

Bianchi, Rosa Maria (Actor)
c/o Staff Member *Televisa*
Blvd Adolfo Lopez Mateos 232
Colonia San Angel INN
DF CP 01060, MEXICO

Bianchin, Wayne (Hockey Player)
Pittsburgh Penguins
5060 Lost Terrace Dr
Nanaimo, BC V9T 5E4, CANADA

Bianchl, Alfred (Al) (Basketball Player, Coach)
Miami Heat
601 Biscayne Blvd
American Airlines Arena
Miami, FL 33132-1801, USA

Bianco, Tom (Baseball Player)
Milwaukee Brewers
12 Knolltop Dr
Nesconset, NY 11767-2222, USA

Bibb, John (Writer)
Nashville Tennessean
1100 Broadway
Editorial Dept
Nashville, TN 37203-3116, USA

Bibb, Laslie (Actor)
9615 Brighton Way Ste 300
Beverly Hills, CA 90210-5118, USA

Bibb, Leslie (Actor)
c/o Edward (Eddie) Yablans *International Creative Management (ICM-LA)*
10250 Constellation Blvd
Los Angeles, CA 90067-6200, USA

Bibby, Henry (Basketball Player)
New York Knicks
University Of Southern California Athletic
Los Angeles, CA 90089-0001, USA

Bibby, Jim (Baseball Player)
St Louis Cardinals
1826 S Coolwell Rd
Madison Heights, VA 24572-4567, USA

Bibby, Mike (Basketball Player)
Sacramento Kings
1 Sports Pkwy
Arco Arena
Sacramento, CA 95834-2301, USA

Bice, Bo (Musician)
c/o Staff Member *Creative Artists Agency LCC (CAA-LA)*
2000 Avenue Of The Stars
Los Angeles, CA 90067-4700, USA

Bichette, Dante (Baseball Player)
California Angels
1830 Gipson Green Ln
Winter Park, FL 32789-1480, USA

Bickerstaff, Bernard T (Bernie) (Coach)
Charlotte Bobcats
333 E Trade St
Charlotte, NC 28202-2331, USA

Bickett, Duane (Football Player)
Indianapolis Colts
508 Van Dyke Ave
Del Mar, CA 92014-2545, USA

Bickford, Valerie (Actor)
c/o Staff Member *The Learning Channel (TLC)*
7700 Wisconsin Ave
Bethesda, MD 20814-3578, USA

Bickle, Rich (Race Car Driver)
3700 Teaberry Ct
Charlotte, NC 28227-8656, USA

Bicknell, Charlie (Baseball Player)
Philadelphia Phillies
109 Creekside Ln
Chapel Hill, TN 37034-7049, USA

Bidart, Frank (Writer)
Wellesley College
106 Central St
English Dept
Wellesley, MA 02481-8204, USA

Biddle, Dennis (Baseball Player)
Chicago American Giants
9418 N Green Bay Rd Apt 241
Milwaukee, WI 53209-1070, USA

Biddle, Martin (Archaeologist)
19 Hamilton Road
Oxford OX2 7OY, UNITED KINGDOM
(UK)

Biddle, Melvin E (War Hero)
918 Essex Dr
Anderson, IN 46013-1613, USA

Biddle, Rocky (Baseball Player)
Chicago White Sox
1620 Calle Clervos
San Dimas, CA 91773, USA

Bidner, Todd (Hockey Player)
Washington Capitals
434 Oozloffsky
Petrolia, ON N0N 1R0, CANADA

Bidwell, Charles E (Misc)
5835 S Kimbark Ave
Chicago, IL 60637-1635, USA

Bidwell, Josh (Football Player)
Green Bay Packers
1380 W 40th Ave
Eugene, OR 97405-2001, USA

Bieber, Owen F (Misc)
United Auto Workers Union
8000 E Jefferson Ave
Detroit, MI 48214-3963, USA

Biebl-Prelevic, Heidi (Skier)
Haus Olympia
Oberstaufen 87534, GERMANY

Biedenbach, Edward (Basketball Player)
Phoenix Suns
92 Kimberly Ave
Asheville, NC 28804-3607, USA

Biederman, Charles J (Artist)
5840 Collischan Rd
Red Wing, MN 55066-1113, USA

Biedermann, Leo (Football Player)
Cleveland Browns
11640 Evergreen Creek Ln
Las Vegas, NV 89135-1650, USA

Biegler, David W (Business Person)
Texas Utilities Co
1601 Bryan St
Energy Plaza
Dallas, TX 75201-3430, USA

Biehn, Michael (Actor)
11220 Valley Spring Ln
North Hollywood, CA 91602-2611, USA

Bieka, Silverstre Siale (Prime Minister)
Prime Minister's Office
Malabo, EQUATORIAL GUINEA

Biekert, Gregory (Football Player)
Los Angeles Raiders
2360 Fish Creek Pl
Danville, CA 94506-2063, USA

Biel, Jessica (Actor)
c/o Kim Hodgert *Creative Artists Agency LCC (CAA-LA)*
2000 Avenue Of The Stars
Los Angeles, CA 90067-4700, USA

Bielec, Frank (Television Host)
c/o Staff Member *Trading Spaces*
7700 Wisconsin Ave
The Learning Channel
Bethesda, MD 20814-3578, USA

Bielecki, J Krzysztof (Prime Minister)
Urzad Rady Ministrow
Al Ujazdowskie 9
Warsaw 00-918, POLAND

Bielecki, Mike (Baseball Player)
Pittsburgh Pirates
1505 Habersham Pl
Crownsville, MD 21032-2230, USA

Bielke, Don (Basketball Player)
Fort Wayne Pistons
3769 Corte Cancion
Thousand Oaks, CA 91360, USA

Biellmann, Denise (Figure Skater)
Im Brachli 25
Zurich 8053, SWITZERLAND

Bielski, Dick (Football Player)
Philadelphia Eagles
27 Malibu Ct
Towson, MD 21204-2047, USA

Bien, Fijate (Musician)
c/o Staff Member *William Morris Agency (WMA-LA)*
1 William Morris Pl
Beverly Hills, CA 90212-4261, USA

Bienen, Andy (Writer)
c/o Staff Member *United Talent Agency (UTA)*
9560 Wilshire Blvd Ste 500
Beverly Hills, CA 90212-2401, USA

Bieniemy, Eric (Football Player)
San Diego Chargers
3314 Fox Tail Trl NW
Prior Lake, MN 55372-1684, USA

Bierbrodt, Nick (Baseball Player)
Arizona Diamondbacks
1741 W Laredo St
Chandler, AZ 85224-8219, USA

Biercevicz, Greg (Baseball Player)
21 Mead Farm Rd
Seymour, CT 06483-2453, USA

Bierko, Craig (Actor, Musician)
Talent Entertainment Group
9111 Wilshire Blvd
Beverly Hills, CA 90210-5508, USA

Bies, Don (Golfer)
1262 NW Blakely Ct
Seattle, WA 98177-4340, USA

Bies Susan, Schmidt (Government
Official)
Federal Reserve Board
20th St & Constitution Ave
Washington, DC 20551-0001, USA

Bieser, Steve (Baseball Player)
New York Mets
11770 Royal Oak Ct
Sainte Genevieve, MO 63670-8690, USA

Bieshu, Mariya L (Opera Singer)
24 Pushkin Str
Chisinau 2012, MOLDOVA

Bietila, Walter (Skier)
General Delivery
Iron Mountain, MI 49801-9999, USA

Biffen, John (Government Official)
Tanat House
Llanyblodwel Oswestry
Shropshire SY10 8NQ, UNITED
KINGDOM (UK)

Biffi, Giacomo Cardinal (Religious Leader)
Archdiocese of Bologna
Via Altabella 6
Bologna 40126, ITALY

Biffle, Greg (Race Car Driver)
122 Knob Hill Rd
Mooresville, NC 28117-6847, USA

Biffle, Jerome (Athlete, Track Athlete)
3205 Monaco Pkwy
Denver, CO 80207-2203, USA

Big & Rich (Music Group)
c/o Keith Miller *William Morris Agency
(WMA-TN)*
1600 Division St Ste 300
Nashville, TN 37203-2755, USA

Big Bad Voodoo Daddy
c/o Staff Member *Creative Artists Agency
LCC (CAA-LA)*
2000 Avenue Of The Stars
Los Angeles, CA 90067-4700, USA

Big Blue, The (Music Group)
c/o Staff Member *Pop Idol (Fremantle
Media)*
2700 Colorado Ave Ste 450
Santa Monica, CA 90404-3599, USA

Big Dismal (Music Group)
c/o Staff Member *Wind-up Records*
72 Madison Ave Fl 8
New York, NY 10016-8731, USA

Big Preach (Musician)
c/o Staff Member *UGF Entertainment Inc*
3105 S Mlk Jr Blvd #313
Lansing, MI 48910, USA

Big Tigger (Television Host)
c/o Michael (Mike) Esterman *Esterman
Entertainment*
214 Park Rd
Riva, MD 21140-1224, USA

Big Tymers (Music Group)
c/o Staff Member *International Creative
Management (ICM-LA)*
10250 Constellation Blvd
Los Angeles, CA 90067-6200, USA

Bigbie, Larry (Baseball Player)
Baltimore Orioles
2250 E 61st Ave
Hobart, IN 46342-6820, USA

Bigeleisen, Jacob (Misc)
900 N Taylor St Apt 1817
Arlington, VA 22203-1893, USA

Bigelow, Kathryn (Director)
Creative Artists Agency
9830 Wilshire Blvd
Beverly Hills, CA 90212-1804, USA

Bigelow, Tom
4944 W 50 S
Winchester, IN 47394-8537, USA

Biggerstaff, Sean (Actor)
c/o Staff Member *International Creative
Management (ICM-UK)*
Oxford House
76 Oxford St
London W1N OAX, UNITED KINGDOM
(UK)

Biggins, Al-Mela (Reality TV Star)
c/o Staff Member *Trading Spouses*
3151 Cahuenga Blvd W Ste 300
Rocket Science Laboratories
Los Angeles, CA 90068-1768, USA

Biggio, Craig (Baseball Player)
Houston Astros
6520 Belmont St
Houston, TX 77005-3804, USA

Biggs, Don (Hockey Player)
Minnesota North Stars
10050 Somerset Dr
Loveland, OH 45140-1863, USA

Biggs, Jason (Actor)
c/o Peter Kiernan *Management 360*
9111 Wilshire Blvd
Beverly Hills, CA 90210-5508, USA

Biggs, John H (Business Person)
240 E 47th St # 47D
New York, NY 10017-2131, USA

Biggs, Peter M
Willows
London Road
Saint Ives, Huntingdon Cam PE17 4ES,
UNITED KINGDOM (UK)

Biggs, Ronald
201 rue Monte Alegre Santa Teresa
Rio de Janeiro, BRAZIL

Biggs-Dawson, Rozann
c/o Staff Member *Innovative Artists (LA)*
1505 10th St
Santa Monica, CA 90401-2805, USA

Bigley, Thomas J (Admiral)
1329 Carpers Farm Way
Vienna, VA 22182-1348, USA

Bignotti, George (Race Car Driver)
9413 Steeplehill Dr
Las Vegas, NV 89117-7271, USA

Bijan (Designer, Fashion Designer)
420 N Rodeo Dr
Beverly Hills, CA 90210-4502, USA

Bikel, Theodore (Actor)
94 Honey Hill Rd
Wilton, CT 06897-5008, USA

Bila, Lucie (Actor, Musician)
Theate Ta Fantastika
Karlova UI 8
Prague 1 110 00, CZECH REPUBLIC

Bilal (Musician)
Creative Artists Agency
9830 Wilshire Blvd
Beverly Hills, CA 90212-1804, USA

Bilardello, Dann (Baseball Player)
Cincinnati Reds
560 Alexandra Ave SW
Vero Beach, FL 32968-4032, USA

Bilderback, Nicole (Actor)
c/o Matt Luber *Nine Yards Entertainment*
8530 Wilshire Blvd Fl 5
Beverly Hills, CA 90211-3102, USA

Bildt, Carl (Prime Minister)
Svenges Riksdag
Stockholm 10012, SWEDEN

Biletnikoff, Frederick (Fred) (Coach,
Football Player)
Oakland Raiders
1736 Avondale Dr
Roseville, CA 95747-8389, USA

Bilheimer, Robert S (Religious Leader)
15256 Knightwood Rd
Cold Spring, MN 56320-9649, USA

Bill, Tony (Actor, Director, Producer)
Barnstorm Films
73 Market St
Venice, CA 90291-3603, USA

Billick, Brian (Football Player)
c/o Staff Member *Baltimore Ravens*
1 Winning Dr
Owings Mills, MD 21117-4776, USA

Billie (Musician)
CIA
Concorde House
101 Sherpherds Bush Road
London W6 7LP, UNITED KINGDOM
(UK)

Billingham, John E (Jack) (Baseball Player)
loq
625 Faulkner St
New Smyrna Beach, FL 32168-6421, USA

Billings, Dick (Baseball Player)
Washington Senators
1917 Creek Wood Dr
Arlington, TX 76006-6611, USA

Billings, Earl (Actor)
c/o Staff Member *The Artists Group Ltd
(LA)*
1650 Broadway Ste 610
New York, NY 10019-6833, USA

Billings, Marland P (Misc)
Westside Road
Rfd
North Conway, NH 03860, USA

Billingslea, Beau (Actor)
6025 Sepulveda Blvd Ste 201
Van Nuys, CA 91411-2513, USA

Billingslea, Shavonda
c/o Michael (Mike) Esterman *Esterman
Entertainment*
214 Park Rd
Riva, MD 21140-1224, USA

Billingsley, Barbara (Actor, Model)
c/o Randy Rubenstein *Commercials
Unlimited*
190 N Canon Dr Ste 302
Beverly Hills, CA 90210-5314, USA

Billingsley, Brett (Baseball Player)
Florida Marlins
16112 Medlar Ln
Chino Hills, CA 91709-3625, USA

Billingsley, Hobie (Coach)
746 Pepperridge Dr
Bloomington, IN 47401-9884, USA

Billingsley, John (Actor)
c/o Michael Greenwald *Don Buchwald &
Associates Inc (LA)*
6500 Wilshire Blvd Ste 2200
Los Angeles, CA 90048-4942, USA

Billingsley, John (Actor)
c/o Doug Ealy *AKA Talent Agency*
6310 San Vicente Blvd Ste 200
Los Angeles, CA 90048-5488, USA

Billingsley, John (Baseball Player)
Memphis Red Sox
3614 N 24th Pl
Milwaukee, WI 53206-1325, USA

Billingsley, Peter
9028 W Sunset Blvd Ph 1
Los Angeles, CA 90069-1830, USA

Billingsley, Ray (Cartoonist)
King Features Syndicate
888 7th Ave Ste 201
New York, NY 10106-0201, USA

Billingsley, Ron (Football Player)
San Diego Chargers
PO Box 2455
Gadsden, AL 35903-0455, USA

Billingsley, Sam (Baseball Player)
Memphis Red Sox
1426 W State St
Milwaukee, WI 53233-1249, USA

Billington, Kevin (Director)
33 Courtnell St
London W2 5BU, UNITED KINGDOM
(UK)

Billman, John (Football Player)
Brooklyn Dodgers
7500 York Ave S Apt 618
Minneapolis, MN 55435-4737, USA

Billups, Chauncey (Basketball Player)
Detroit Pistons
Palace
2 Championship Dr
Aubum Hills, CA 91604, USA

Billups, Terry (Football Player)
Dallas Cowboys
1127 Euclid Ave Apt 212
Cleveland, OH 44115-1607, USA

Billy Talent (Music Group)
Nettwerk Productions
1650 West 2nd Ave
Vancouver, BC V6J 4R3, CANADA

Billy Vera and the Beaters (Music Group)
c/o Troy Blakely *Agency for the
Performing Arts (APA-LA)*
405 S Beverly Dr
Beverly Hills, CA 90212-4416, USA

Bilson, Bruce (Director)
Downwind Enterprices
12505 Sarah St
Studio City, CA 91604-1113, USA

Bilson, Malcolm (Musician)
132 N Sunset Dr
Ithaca, NY 14850-1460, USA

Bilson, Rachel (Actor)
c/o Jim Toth *Creative Artists Agency LCC (CAA-LA)*
2000 Avenue Of The Stars
Los Angeles, CA 90067-4700, USA

Binchy, Maeve (Writer)
Irish Times
11-15 D'Olier St
Dublin 2, IRELAND

Binder, John (Religious Leader)
North American Baptist Conference
1S210 Summit Ave
Oakbrook Terrace, IL 60181-3994, USA

Binder, Mike (Actor, Director, Writer)
Three Arts Entertainment
9460 Wishire Blvd #700
Beverly Hills, CA 90212, USA

Binder, Theodor (Physicist)
Taos Canyon
Taos, NM 87571, USA

Bindu (Actor, Bollywood)
C1-2 Eden Hall Opp Lotus Cinema
Worli
Mumbai, MS 400018, INDIA

Bindugosh (Actor, Bollywood)
76A 1st Cross Street
Ventatesa Nagar
Chennai, TN 600093, INDIA

Bing, David (Dave) (Basketball Player)
New York Knicks
1111 Rosedale Ct
Detroit, MI 48211-1076, USA

Bing, Jonathan
c/o Daniel A (Dan) Strone *Trident Media Group LLC*
41 Madison Ave Fl 36
New York, NY 10010-2257, USA

Bingham, Craig (Football Player)
Pittsburgh Steelers
179 Black Oak Dr
Pittsburgh, PA 15220-2007, USA

Bingham, Gregory R (Greg) (Football Player)
Houston Oilers
3710 W Valley Dr
Missouri City, TX 77459-4320, USA

Bingham, Guy (Football Player)
New York Jets
9214 Keegan Trl
Missoula, MT 59808-9382, USA

Bingham, Traci (Actor, Model)
c/o Rob D'Avola *Identity Talent Agency (ID)*
9107 Wilshire Blvd Ste 450
Beverly Hills, CA 90210-5535, USA

Binkley, Gregg (Actor)
c/o Staff Member *The Artists Group Ltd (LA)*
1650 Broadway Ste 610
New York, NY 10019-6833, USA

Binkley, Leslie J (Les) (Hockey Player)
Pittsburgh Penguins
RR 3
Main Station
Hanover, ON N4N 3B9, CANADA

Binks, George (Baseball Player)
Washington Senators
4803 Belmont Rd
Downers Grove, IL 60515-3219, USA

Binmore, Kenneth G (Economist)
Newsmills
Whitebrooks
Monmouth, Gwent NP5 4TY, UNITED KINGDOM (UK)

Binn, Dave (Football Player)
San Diego Chargers
2005 Loring St
San Diego, CA 92109-1407, USA

Binnig, Gerd K (Nobel Prize Laureate)
IBM Research Laboratory
Saumerstr 4
Ruschlikon 8803, SWITZERLAND

Binns, Malcolm (Musician)
233 Court Road
Orpington, Kent BR6 9BY, UNITED KINGDOM (UK)

Binoche, Juliette (Actor)
Artmedia
20 Ave Rapp
Paris 75007, FRANCE

Binoche, Juliette (Actor)
c/o Staff Member *United Talent Agency (UTA)*
9560 Wilshire Blvd Ste 500
Beverly Hills, CA 90212-2401, USA

Binotto, John (Football Player)
Pittsburgh Steelers
277 E McMurray Rd
Canonsburg, PA 15317-2929, USA

Bintley, David (Choreographer)
Royal Ballet
Covent Garden
Bow St
London WC2E 9DD, UNITED KINGDOM (UK)

Biodrowski, Denny (Football Player)
Kansas City Cheifs
2305 Grizzly Run Ln
Euless, TX 76039-6073, USA

Biondi, Frank J Jr (Business Person)
Seagram Co
1430 Peel St
Monstreal, PQ H3A 1S9, CANADA

Biondi, Matthew N (Matt) (Swimmer)
Nicholas A Biondi
1404 Rimer Dr
Moraga, CA 94556-2555, USA

Birch, L Charles (Misc)
5A/73 Yarranabbe Road
Darling Point, NSW 2027, AUSTRALIA

Birch, Stanley F Jr (Judge)
US Court of Appeals
56 Forsyth St NW
Atlanta, GA 30303-2295, USA

Birch, Thora (Actor)
c/o Brett Norensberg *Gersh Agency, The (LA)*
232 N Canon Dr
Beverly Hills, CA 90210-5302, USA

Birchard, Bruce (Religious Leader)
Friends General Conference
1216 Arch St Ste 2A
Philadelphia, PA 19107-2835, USA

Birck, Michael J (Business Person)
Tellabs Inc
1415 W Diehl Rd
Naperville, IL 60563-2349, USA

Bird, Antonia (Director)
International Creative Mgmt
76 Oxford St
London W1N 0AX, UNITED KINGDOM (UK)

Bird, Brad (Director, Writer)
c/o Staff Member *Pixar Animation Studios*
1200 Park Ave
Emeryville, CA 94608-3677, USA

Bird, Cory (Football Player)
Indianapolis Colts
4618 Harding Hwy
Mays Landing, NJ 08330-2736, USA

Bird, Doug (Baseball Player)
Kansas City Royals
11821 Lady Anne Cir
Cape Coral, FL 33991-7548, USA

Bird, Forrest M (Inventor)
212 N Cerritos Dr
Palm Springs, CA 92262, USA

Bird, Jerry Lee (Basketball Player)
New York Knicks
114 Scenic View Dr
Corbin, KY 40701, USA

Bird, Larry J (Basketball Player, Coach)
c/o Staff Member *Indiana Pacers*
125 S Pennsylvania St
Conseco Fieldhouse
Indianapolis, IN 46204-3610, USA

Bird, Lester B (Prime Minister)
Prime Minister's Office
Factory Road
Saint John's, ANTIGUA & BARBUDA

Bird, Rodger (Football Player)
Oakland Raiders
215 S Elm St
Henderson, KY 42420-3510, USA

Bird, Sue (Basketball Player)
Seatle Storm
351 Elliott Ave W Ste 500
Seattle, WA 98119-4153, USA

Bird, Thora (Actor)
Old Loft 21 Leinster Mews
Lancaster Gate
London W2, UNITED KINGDOM (UK)

Bird, Vicki
PO Box 428
Portland, TN 37148-0428, USA

Bird-Phillips, Nalda (Baseball Player)
2033 Honeydew Ln NW
Kennesaw, GA 30152-5852, USA

Birdsell, Lilli (Actor)
c/o John Crosby *John Crosby Management*
1310 N Spaulding Ave
Los Angeles, CA 90046-4010, USA

Birdsong, Carl (Football Player)
St Louis Cardinals
1807 Clubview Dr
Amarillo, TX 79124-1731, USA

Birdsong, Cindy (Musician)
c/o Staff Member *Diva Central Inc*
7510 W Sunset Blvd Ste 1445
Los Angeles, CA 90046-3408, USA

Birk, Matt (Football Player)
Minnesota Vikings
2145 Stanford Ave
Saint Paul, MN 55105-1222, USA

Birk, Roger E (Business Person)
Federal National Mortgage Assn
3900 Wilconsin Ave NW
Washington, DC 20016, USA

Birkavs, Valdis (Prime Minister)
Foreign Affairs Ministry
Brivbas Blvd 36
Riga 1395, LATVIA

Birkbeck, Mike (Baseball Player)
Milwaukee Brewers
1705 W Hill Dr
Orrville, OH 44667-1331, USA

Birkell, Lauren (Actor)
c/o Tiffany Kuzon *Evolution Entertainment (LA)*
901 N Highland Ave
Los Angeles, CA 90038-2412, USA

Birkerts, Gunnar (Architect)
Gunnar Birkets Assoc
28105 Greenfield Rd
Southfield, MI 48076-3046, USA

Birkett, Zoe (Musician)
c/o Staff Member *Pop Idol (Fremantle Media)*
2700 Colorado Ave Ste 450
Santa Monica, CA 90404-3599, USA

Birkin, Jane (Actor)
Cineart
36 Rue de Ponthieu
Paris 75008, FRANCE

Birman, Len (Actor)
Michael Mann talent
977 Lake St
Venice, CA 90291-2853, USA

Birmingham, Stephen (Writer)
Brandt & Brandt
1501 Broadway
New York, NY 10036-5689, USA

Birney, David (Actor)
20 Ocean Park Blvd # 118
Santa Monica, CA 90405-3589, USA

Birney, Earle (Writer)
1204-130 Carlton St
Toronto, ON M5A 4K3, CANADA

Birney, Frank (Actor)
c/o Staff Member *Bauman Redanty & Shaul Agency*
5757 Wilshire Blvd Ste 473
Los Angeles, CA 90036-3632, USA

Biron, Martin (Hockey Player)
Buffalo Sabres
5161 Kraus Rd
Clarence, NY 14031-1567, USA

Birren, James E (Misc)
University of California
Borun Gerontology Center
Los Angeles, CA 90024, USA

Birrer, Babe (Baseball Player)
Detroit Tigers
115 Ranch Trl W
Williamsville, NY 14221-2214, USA

Birthistle, Eva (Actor)
c/o Staff Member *Endeavor Agency LLC (LA)*
9601 Wilshire Blvd Fl 3
Beverly Hills, CA 90210-5204, USA

Birtsas, Tim (Baseball Player)
Oakland A's
43 Robertson Ct
Clarkston, MI 48346-1547, USA

Birtwistle, Harrison (Composer)
Allied Artists
42 Montpelier Square
London SW7 1JZ, UNITED KINGDOM (UK)

Biscaha, Joe (Football Player)
New York Giants
700 N Delaware Ave Apt 3
Beach Haven, NJ 08008-2056, USA

Bisher, J Furman (Writer)
431 Lester Rd
Fayetteville, GA 30215-4930, USA

Bishop, Elvin (Musician)
DeLeon Artists
4031 Panama Ct
Piedmont, CA 94611-4930, USA

Bishop, Greg (Football Player)
New York Giants
PO Box 2263
Lodi, CA 95241-2263, USA

Bishop, Harold (Football Player)
Tampa Bay Buccaneers
4113 Woodland Hills Dr
Tuscaloosa, AL 35405-2777, USA

Bishop, J Michael (Nobel Prize Laureate)
University of California
Hooper Foundation
San Francisco, CA 94143-0001, USA

Bishop, Keith (Football Player)
Denver Broncos
PO Box 133111
Spring, TX 77393-3111, USA

Bishop, Kelly (Actor)
c/o Robert Attermann *Abrams Artists Agency (LA)*
9200 W Sunset Blvd Ph 11
Los Angeles, CA 90069-3601, USA

Bishop, Kevin (Actor)
c/o Staff Member *Gavin Barker Assoc*
2D Wimpole St
London W1G 0EB, UNITED KINGDOM (UK)

Bishop, Michael (Football Player)
New England Patriots
113 Philpot St
Willis, TX 77378, USA

Bishop, Mike (Football Player)
c/o Staff Member *Green Bay Packers*
PO Box 10628
Green Bay, WI 54307-0628, USA

Bishop, Robert R (Business Person)
Silicon Graphics
1600 Amphitheatre Pkwy
Mountain View, CA 94043-1351, USA

Bishop, Sonny (Football Player)
Dallas Texans
22843 Hale Rd
Land O Lakes, FL 34639-4030, USA

Bisoglio, Val (Actor)
House of Representatives
211 S Beverly Dr Ste 208
Beverly Hills, CA 90212-3879, USA

Bissant, John (Baseball Player)
Chicago American Giants
2762 Marengo St
New Orleans, LA 70115-6214, USA

Bissell, Charles O (Cartoonist, Editor)
1006 Tower Pl
Nashville, TN 37204-4135, USA

Bissell, Charles P (Phil) (Cartoonist)
Cartoon Corner
4 Cross Hill Cir
Forestdale, MA 02644-1630, USA

Bissell, Jean G (Judge)
US Court of Appeals
717 Madison Pl NW
Washington, DC 20439-0001, USA

Bissell, Mina J (Physicist)
Lawrence Berkeley Laboratory
1 Cyclotron Rd
Berkeley, CA 94720-8099, USA

Bisset, Jacqueline (Actor)
1815 Benedict Canyon Dr
Beverly Hills, CA 90210-2006, USA

Bissett, Josie (Actor)
c/o Ron West *Thruline Entertainment*
9250 Wilshire Blvd Ground Fl
Beverly Hills, CA 90210, USA

Bissinger, Buzz (Writer)
c/o *Houghton Mifflin Company Trade Division*
222 Berkeley St
Adult Editorial 8th Fl
Boston, MA 02116-3748, USA

Bisson, Yannick (Actor)
c/o Robyn Friedman *Artist Management Inc*
464 King St E
Toronto, ON M5A 1L7, CANADA

Bista, Kirti Nidhi (Prime Minister)
Gyaneshawor
Kathmandu, NEPAL

Bitker, Joe (Baseball Player)
Oakland A's
39 Blackstone Ct
Chico, CA 95928-9428, USA

Bitterlich, Don (Football Player)
Seattle Seahawks
101 Medinah Dr
Blue Bell, PA 19422-3213, USA

Bittiger, Jeff (Baseball Player)
Philadelphia Phillies
695 3rd St
Secaucus, NJ 07094-3113, USA

Bittinger, Ned (Designer)
16 Camino De Vecinos
Santa Fe, NM 87507-7901, USA

Bittle, Ryan (Actor)
Hollander Talent
3518 Cahuenga Blvd W # 103
Los Angeles, CA 90068, USA

Bittner, Armin (Skier)
Rauchbergstr 30
Izell 83334, GERMANY

Bittner, Dick (Hockey Player)
Boston Bruins
244 Wolf Willow Rd NW
Edmonton, AB T5T 6N3, CANADA

Bittner, Jayne (Baseball Player)
15536 Northville Forest Dr Apt U250
Plymouth, MI 48170, USA

Bittner, Lauren (Actor)
c/o Jill McGrath *Abrams Artists Agency (NY)*
275 7th Ave Fl 26
New York, NY 10001-6708, USA

Biya, Paul (President)
Palais Presidentiel
Rue de L'Exploration
Yaounde, CAMEROON

Bizkit, Limp (Music Group)
c/o Staff Member *Creative Artists Agency LCC (CAA-LA)*
2000 Avenue Of The Stars
Los Angeles, CA 90067-4700, USA

Bizzy, Bone (Artist, Musician)
Creatice Artists Agency
9830 Wilshire Blvd
Beverly Hills, CA 90212-1804, USA

Bjarni V, Tryggvason (Astronaut)
Space Agency
6767 Route de Aeroport
Saint Hubert, PQ J3Y 8Y9, CANADA

Bjedov-Gabrilo, Djurdjica (Swimmer)
Brace Santini 33
5800 Split
Serbia & Montenegro, SERBIA-MONTENEGRO

Bjorge, Jamie (Actor)
10061 Riverside Dr
Box 113
Toluca Lake, CA 91602-2560, USA

Bjork (Actor, Musician, Songwriter, Writer)
c/o Sam Kirby *William Morris Agency (WMA-NY)*
1325 Avenue Of The Americas
New York, NY 10019-6026, USA

Bjork, Anita (Actor)
AB Baggensgatan 9
Stockholm 111 31, SWEDEN

Bjorklund, Anders (Doctor)
University of Lund
Neurology Dept
Lund, SWEDEN

Bjorkman, George (Baseball Player)
Houston Astros
3525 Teakwood Ln
Plano, TX 75075-1783, USA

Bjorkman, Jonas (Tennis Player)
Octagon
1751 Pinnacle Dr Ste 1500
McLean, VA 22102-3833, USA

Bjorlin, Nadia (Actor)
c/o Staff Member *Days of Our Lives*
3000 W Alameda Ave
Burbank, CA 91523-0001, USA

Bjornson, Eric (Football Player)
Dallas Cowboys
14755 Preston Rd Ste 830
Dallas, TX 75254-7864, USA

Bjugstad, Scott (Hockey Player)
Minnesota North Stars
2874 Lisbon Ave N
Lake Elmo, MN 55042-8554, USA

Blab, Uwe (Basketball Player)
Dallas Mavericks
5993 Mount Gainor
Wimberley, TX 78676-4278, USA

Blachnik, Gabriele (Designer, Fashion Designer)
Blachnik Gabriele KG
Marstallstr 8
Munich 80539, GERMANY

Black, Alex (Actor)
c/o Staff Member *Innovative Artists (LA)*
1505 10th St
Santa Monica, CA 90401-2805, USA

Black, Barbara A (Attorney, Attorney General, Educator, General)
Columbia University
435 W 116th St
Law School
New York, NY 10027-7237, USA

Black, Bibi (Musician)
Columbia Artists Mgmt Inc
1790 Broadway Fl 6
New York, NY 10019-1412, USA

Black, BiBi (Musician)
c/o Staff Member *EMI Recorded Music (EMI Group - NY)*
150 5th Ave
New York, NY 10011-4311, USA

Black, Bill (Baseball Player)
Detroit Tigers
264 Braeshire Dr
Ballwin, MO 63021-5659, USA

Black, Brantley (Actor)
c/o Taylor Jacobs *Cinema Talent Agency*
468 N Camden Dr # 200
Beverly Hills, CA 90210-4507, USA

Black, Bud (Baseball Player)
Seattle Mariners
PO Box 2133
Rancho Santa Fe, CA 92067-2133, USA

Black, Carole (Business Person)
c/o Staff Member *Lifetime Entertainment Services*
309 W 49th St
New York, NY 10019-7316, USA

Black, Cathleen P (Publisher)
Hearst Corp
300 W 57th St Fl 42
Magazine Division
New York, NY 10019-3790, USA

Black, Cilla (Actor, Musician)
Bobsons Productions
10 Abbet Orchard St
London SW1P 2JP, UNITED KINGDOM (UK)

Black, Claudia (Actor)
c/o Staff Member *Artists Independent Management (LA)*
825 Nowita Pl
Venice, CA 90291-3836, USA

Black, Clint (Actor, Musician, Songwriter, Writer)
c/o Staff Member *William Morris Agency (WMA-LA)*
1 William Morris Pl
Beverly Hills, CA 90212-4261, USA

Black, Conrad M (Publisher)
1 Canada Square
Canary Wharf
London E14 5DT, UNITED KINGDOM (UK)

Black, David (Producer, Writer)
c/o Johnnie Planco *Untitled Entertainment (NY)*
322 8th Ave Ste 601
New York, NY 10001-6715, USA

Black, Frank (Musician)
c/o Staff Member *Paradigm (Monterey)*
509 Hartnell St
Monterey, CA 93940-2825, USA

Black, Holly (Writer)
10 Pleasant Ct
Amherst, MA 01002-1513, USA

Black, Jack (Actor, Comedian, Musician)
c/o Sharon Sheinwold *United Talent Agency (UTA)*
9560 Wilshire Blvd Ste 500
Beverly Hills, CA 90212-2401, USA

Black, James W (Nobel Prize Laureate)
3 Ferrings
Dulwich
London SE21 7LU, UNITED KINGDOM (UK)

Black, Jay (Musician)
Charles Rapp
1650 Broadway Ste 1410
New York, NY 10019-6882, USA

Black, Karen (Actor, Director, Producer, Writer)
c/o Gabrielle Allabashi *Ellis Talent Group*
4705 Laurel Canyon Blvd Ste 300
Valley Village, CA 91607-5901, USA

Black, Leonard (Football Player)
Washington Redskins
2705 Preston Woods Ln Apt 12
Fayetteville, NC 28304-3629, USA

Black, Lewis (Actor, Comedian)
Agency for Performing Arts
405 S Beverly Dr Ste 500
Beverly Hills, CA 90212-4425, USA

Black, Lisa Hartman (Actor)
c/o Marnie Sparer *Innovative Artists (LA)*
1505 10th St
Santa Monica, CA 90401-2805, USA

Black, Lucas (Actor)
c/o Chris Fenton *H2F*
9000 W Sunset Blvd Ste 710
West Hollywood, CA 90069-5807, USA

Black, Marina (Actor)
c/o Lewis Kay *Bragman/Nyman/Cafarelli (BNC)*
8687 Melrose Ave Fl 8
Pacific Design Center
Los Angeles, CA 90069-5701, USA

Black, Mary (Musician)
International Music Network
278 S Main St #400
Gloucester, MA 01930, USA

Black, Michael Ian (Actor, Architect)
United Talent Agency
9560 Wilshire Blvd Ste 500
Beverly Hills, CA 90212-2401, USA

Black, Mike (Football Player)
Detroit Lions
5690 Stonekirk Pl NW
Acworth, GA 30101-6915, USA

Black, Mike D (Football Player)
Philadelphia Eagles
609 Grider Dr
Roseville, CA 95678-1244, USA

Black, Robert P (Financier, Government Official)
2133 Cedarfield Ln
Richmond, VA 23233-1937, USA

Black, Ronnie (Golfer)
5118 N Ocean Ave
Tucson, AZ 85704-2545, USA

Black, Shane (Writer)
c/o Staff Member *Endeavor Agency LLC (LA)*
9601 Wilshire Blvd Fl 3
Beverly Hills, CA 90210-5204, USA

Black, Stan (Football Player)
San Fransisco 49ers
470 Johnstone Dr
Madison, MS 39110-7586, USA

Black, Steve (Hockey Player)
Detroit Red Wings
417 Amethyst Cres
Thunder Bay, ON P7C 1T2, CANADA

Black, Thought (Musician)
William Morris Agency
1325 Avenue Of The Americas
New York, NY 10019-6091, USA

Black, Tim (Football Player)
St Louis Cardinals
10520 Kilo Rd
Clarendon, TX 79226-5100, USA

Black, Todd (Producer)
c/o Staff Member *International Creative Management (ICM-LA)*
10250 Constellation Blvd
Los Angeles, CA 90067-6200, USA

Black Box Recorder (Music Group)
c/o Staff Member *Paradigm (Monterey)*
509 Hartnell St
Monterey, CA 93940-2825, USA

Black Crowes, The (Music Group)
c/o Staff Member *Paradigm (Monterey)*
509 Hartnell St
Monterey, CA 93940-2825, USA

Black Eyed Peas, The (Music Group)
c/o Staff Member *DAS Communications*
83 Riverside Dr
New York, NY 10024-5713, USA

Black Mambazo, Ladysmith (Actor, Musician)
c/o Staff Member *William Morris Agency (WMA-LA)*
1 William Morris Pl
Beverly Hills, CA 90212-4261, USA

Black Oak Arkansas
6400 Pleasant Park Dr
Chanhassen, MN 55317-8804, USA

Black Sabbath (Music Group)
c/o Rob Light *Creative Artists Agency LCC (CAA-LA)*
2000 Avenue Of The Stars
Los Angeles, CA 90067-4700, USA

Blackaby, Ethan (Baseball Player)
Milwaukee Braves
2308 E Orangewood Ave
Phoenix, AZ 85020-4730, USA

Blackburn, Bill (Football Player)
Chicago Cardinals
1902 Laurel Oaks Dr
Richmond, TX 77469-4839, USA

Blackburn, Bob (Hockey Player)
New York Rangers
141 Robert Street
PO Box 1761
New Liskeard, ON P0J 1P0, CANADA

Blackburn, Dan (Hockey Player)
New York Rangers
12 Carey Dr
Bedford, NY 10506-2025, USA

Blackburn, Don (Hockey Player)
Boston Bruins
50 Ramstein Rd
New Hartford, CT 06057-3202, USA

Blackburn, Elizabeth (Misc)
294 Yerba Buena Ave
San Francisco, CA 94127-1638, USA

Blackburn, Greta (Actor)
Dade/Schultz
6442 Coldwater Canyon Ave Ste 206
North Hollywood, CA 91606-1137, USA

Blackburn, Woody (Golfer)
PO Box 215
Orange Park, FL 32067-0215, USA

Blackiston, Caroline (Actor)
Caroline Dawson
125 Gloucester Road
London SW7 4IE, UNITED KINGDOM (UK)

Blackjack
35 Brentwood Ave
Farmingville, NY 11738-1942, USA

Blackledge, Todd (Football Player)
Kansas City Cheifs
2711 Glenmont Rd NW
Canton, OH 44708-1345, USA

Blackman, Don (Football Player)
New England Patriots
48 Shire Dr S
East Amherst, NY 14051-1814, USA

Blackman, Honor (Actor)
Michael Ladkin Mgmt
1 Duchess St
#1
London W1N 3DE, UNITED KINGDOM (UK)

Blackman, Robert (Football Player)
Seattle Seahawks
70 Glenwood N
Van Vleck, TX 77482-6292, USA

Blackman, Robert R Jr (General)
Commanding General
III Expeditionary Force Okinawa
FPO, AP 96602, USA

Blackman, Rolando (Basketball Player, Sportscaster)
CBS-TV
51 W 52nd St
Sports Dept
New York, NY 10019-6119, USA

Blackmar, Phil (Golfer)
4420 Janssen Dr
Corpus Christi, TX 78411-2817, USA

Blackmore, Ritchie (Musician)
Performers of the World
8901 Melrose Ave # 200
West Hollywood, CA 90069-5605, USA

Blackshear, Jeff (Football Player)
Seattle Seahawks
9229 Christo Ct
Owings Mills, MD 21117-3596, USA

Blackthorne, Paul (Actor)
c/o Staff Member *Seven Summits Pictures & Management*
8906 W Olympic Blvd Ground Floor
Beverly Hills, CA 90211, USA

Blackwelder, Myra (Golfer)
2009 Hill Gail Way
Versailles, KY 40383-9132, USA

Blackwell, Alois (Football Player)
Dallas Cowboys
1617 Fannin St Apt 2310
Houston, TX 77002-7654, USA

Blackwell, Chris (Business Person, Musician)
6 Hadley Gardens
C F Blackwell
London W4 4NX, UNITED KINGDOM (UK)

Blackwell, Harolyn (Opera Singer)
Columbia Artists Mgmt Inc
1790 Broadway Fl 6
New York, NY 10019-1412, USA

Blackwell, Nathaniel (Basketball Player)
San Antonio Spurs
1926 S 22nd St
Philadelphia, PA 19145-2724, USA

Blackwell, Tim (Baseball Player)
Boston Red Sox
8854 Whiteport Ln
San Diego, CA 92119-2135, USA

Blackwell, Will (Football Player)
Pittsburgh Steelers
2528 Goldenmoon St
Las Vegas, NV 89108-4480, USA

Blackwell, Willie (Football Player)
Washington Redskins
3363 Flat Shoals Rd
Atlanta, GA 30349, USA

Blackwood, Glenn (Football Player)
Minnesota Vikings
3480 Ambassador Dr
Wellington, FL 33414-6815, USA

Blackwood, Lyle (Football Player)
Cincinatti Bengals
18020 Windtop Ln
Dallas, TX 75287-6658, USA

Blackwood, Nina (Entertainer)
c/o Danny Sheridan *Crisis Management & Associates*
16161 Ventura Blvd # 714
Encino, CA 91436-2522, USA

Blackwood, Sarah (Musician)
Primary Talent Int'l
2-12 Petonville Road
London N1 9PL, UNITED KINGDOM (UK)

Blacque, Taurean (Actor)
5049 Rock Springs Rd
Lithonia, GA 30038-2239, USA

Bladd, Stephen Jo (Musician)
Nick Ben-Meir
652 N Doheny Dr
Los Angeles, CA 90069-5526, USA

Blade, Brian (Musician)
Ted Kurland
173 Brighton Ave
Boston, MA 02134-2003, USA

Blade, Willie (Football Player)
Dallas Cowboys
331 Cobblestone Rd
Auburn, GA 30011-3022, USA

Blades, Brian K (Football Player)
Seattle Seahawks
1900 SW 70th Ter
Plantation, FL 33317-5010, USA

Blades, H Benedict (Bennie) (Football Player)
Detroit Lions
1900 SW 70th Ter
Plantation, FL 33317-5010, USA

Bladt, Rick (Baseball Player)
Chicago Cubs
525 Maple St
Mount Angel, OR 97362-9616, USA

Blaese, R Michael (Doctor)
National Cancer Institute
9000 Rockville Pike
Bethesda, MD 20892-0001, USA

Blaha, John E (Astronaut)
18219 Indian Row
San Antonio, TX 78259, USA

Blahak, Joseph (Football Player)
Houston Oilers
4040 N 21st St
Lincoln, NE 68521-1203, USA

Blahnik, Manolo (Designer, Fashion Designer)
49-51 Old Church St
London SW3 5BS, UNITED KINGDOM (UK)

Blahoski, Alana (Hockey Player)
76 Charles St Apt H
New York, NY 10014-2676, USA

Blaine, David (Magician)
c/o Alan Berger *Creative Artists Agency LCC (CAA-LA)*
2000 Avenue Of The Stars
Los Angeles, CA 90067-4700, USA

Blaine, Ed (Football Player)
Green Bay Packers
4 E Clarkson Rd
Columbia, MO 65203-3520, USA

Blair, Anthony C L (Tony) (Politician, Prime Minister)
c/o Staff Member *Prime Minister's Office (England, UK)*
10 Downing Street
London, England SW1 2AA, UNITED KINGDOM (UK)

Blair, Barry (Cartoonist)
PO Box 612
Murray Hill Station
New York, NY 10156-0612, USA

Blair, Betsy (Actor)
11 Chalcot Gardens
Englands Lane
London NW3 4YB, UNITED KINGDOM (UK)

Blair, Bonnie (Speed Skater)
1223 Aspen Ct
Delafield, WI 53018-1300, USA

Blair, Charles (Hockey Player)
Toronto Maple Leafs
869 Niagara Pky
Fort Erie, ON L2A 5M4, CANADA

Blair, George (Hockey Player)
Toronto Maple Leafs
61 Kingsmill St
Fort Erie, ON L2A 4E5, CANADA

Blair, George L (Football Player)
San Diego Chargers
1233 Karen Dr
Laurel, MS 39440-2186, USA

Blair, Isla (Actor)
Mayer & Eden
Grafton House
2/3 Golden House
London W1R 3AD, UNITED KINGDOM (UK)

Blair, Ken (Football Player)
Philadelphia Eagles
1837 NE 51st St
Oklahoma City, OK 73111-7005, USA

Blair, Linda (Actor)
4727 Wilshire Blvd Ste 333
Los Angeles, CA 90010-3874, USA

Blair, Lionel (Dancer)
68 Old Brompton Road #200
London, England SW7 3LQ, UNITED KINGDOM (UK)

Blair, Maybelle (Baseball Player)
39220 Palm Greens Pkwy
Palm Desert, CA 92260-1362, USA

Blair, Paul (Baseball Player)
Baltimore Orioles
10829 Sherwood Hill Rd
Owings Mills, MD 21117-5826, USA

Blair, Paul (Football Player)
Chicago Bears
345 Abilene Ave
Edmond, OK 73003-6313, USA

Blair, Selma (Actor)
c/o Peter Levine *Creative Artists Agency LCC (CAA-LA)*
2000 Avenue Of The Stars
Los Angeles, CA 90067-4700, USA

Blair, Stanley (Football Player)
Phoenix Cardinals
901 Deer Run N
Pine Bluff, AR 71603-8158, USA

Blair, William (Baseball Player)
Birmingham Black Barons
3906 S Lancaster Rd
Dallas, TX 75216-5635, USA

Blair, William (Director)
c/o Staff Member *New Star Entertainment*
PO Box 84172
San Diego, CA 92138-4172, USA

Blair, William Draper Jr (Attorney, Attorney General, Diplomat, General)
435 E 52nd St # 6B
New York, NY 10022-6445, USA

Blair, Willie (Baseball Player)
Toronto Blue Jays
62 Elder Ln
Pikeville, KY 41501-3119, USA

Blais, Madeleine H (Journalist)
Miami Herald
1 Herald Plz
Editorial Dept
Miami, FL 33132-1693, USA

Blaise, Kerlin (Football Player)
Detroit Lions
37026 Aspen Dr
Farmington Hills, MI 48335-5482, USA

Blake, Andre (Actor)
c/o Staff Member *Kerin-Goldberg Associates*
155 E 55th St Ste 5D
New York, NY 10022-4038, USA

Blake, Asha (Correspondent)
NBC-TV
30 Rockefeller Plz Ste 270E
News Dept
New York, NY 10112-0299, USA

Blake, Bob (Hockey Player)
Boston Bruins
801 Hat Trick Ave
US Hockey Hall Of Fame
Eveleth, MN 55734-8640, USA

Blake, Bud
PO Box 146
Damariscotta, ME 04543-0146, USA

Blake, Casey (Baseball Player)
Toronto Blue Jays
208 W Kentucky Ave
Indianola, IA 50125-1112, USA

Blake, Ed (Baseball Player)
Cincinnati Reds
208 Willow Creek Ct
Belleville, IL 62223-4207, USA

Blake, Geoffrey (Writer)
c/o Staff Member *Creative Artists Agency LCC (CAA-LA)*
2000 Avenue Of The Stars
Los Angeles, CA 90067-4700, USA

Blake, George R (Editor)
Cincinnati Enquirer
617 Vine St
Editorial Dept
Cincinnati, OH 45202-2433, USA

Blake, James (Tennis Player)
c/o Staff Member *ATP Tour*
201 Atp Tour Blvd
Ponte Vedra Beach, FL 32082-3211, USA

Blake, Jason (Hockey Player)
Los Angeles Kings
10 Meadow Ln
Glen Head, NY 11545-1123, USA

Blake, Jay Don (Golfer)
2859 Calle Del Sol
Saint George, UT 84790-7968, USA

Blake, Jeff (Football Player)
Philadelphia Eagles
1 Novacare Way
Philadelphia, PA 19145-5996, USA

Blake, John C (Artist)
Oz Voorburgwal 131
Amsterdam 1012 ER, THE NETHERLANDS

Blake, Josh (Actor)
c/o Staff Member *Pakula/King & Associates*
9229 W Sunset Blvd Ste 315
Los Angeles, CA 90069-3403, USA

Blake, Julian W (Bud) (Cartoonist)
PO Box 146
Damariscotta, ME 04543-0146, USA

Blake, Marcia (Writer)
c/o Staff Member *Creative Artists Agency LCC (CAA-LA)*
2000 Avenue Of The Stars
Los Angeles, CA 90067-4700, USA

Blake, Norman (Musician)
Scott O'Malley Assoc
433 E Cucharras St
Colorado Springs, CO 80903-3609, USA

Blake, Peter (Architect)
1377 Walnut St
Newton Highlands, MA 02461-1851, USA

Blake, Peter T (Artist)
Waddington Galleries
11 Cork St
London W1X 1PD, UNITED KINGDOM (UK)

Blake, Quentin (Artist, Philanthropist)
The Roald Dahl Foundation
92 High Street
Great Missenden
Buckinghamshire HP16 0AN, UNITED KINGDOM (UK)

Blake, Ricky (Football Player)
Dallas Cowboys
210 S Vine St Apt A
Winchester, TN 37398-1762, USA

Blake, Rockwell (Opera Singer)
1 Onondaga Ln
Plattsburgh, NY 12901-1130, USA

Blake, Stephanie (Actor)
First Artists
1631 N Bristol St # 820
Santa Ana, CA 92706-3342, USA

Blake, Susan (Correspondent)
News Center 4
1001 Van Ness Ave
San Francisco, CA 94109-6913, USA

Blake, Tchad (Musician)
Monterey International
200 W Superior St Ste 202
Chicago, IL 60610-3554, USA

Blake, Teresa (Actor)
Stone Manners
6500 Wilshire Blvd Ste 550
Los Angeles, CA 90048-4950, USA

Blake, Theo (Adult Film Star)
c/o Staff Member *Diva Central Inc*
7510 W Sunset Blvd Ste 1445
Los Angeles, CA 90046-3408, USA

Blake, Tom (Football Player)
New York Bulldogs
2017 Tullis Dr
Middletown, OH 45042-2962, USA

Blakeley, Ronee (Actor, Musician)
8033 W Sunset Blvd # 693
West Hollywood, CA 90046-2401, USA

Blakely, Rachel (Actor)
c/o Staff Member *Morrissey Management*
77 Glebe Point Road
Sydney NSW 2037, AUSTRALIA

Blakely, Susan (Actor, Model)
Jaffe Co
9663 Santa Monica Blvd # 214
Beverly Hills, CA 90210-4303, USA

Blakemore, Colin B (Doctor)
University Laboratory of Physiology
Parks Road
Oxford OX1 3PT, UNITED KINGDOM (UK)

Blakemore, Michael (Actor, Director, Writer)
18 Upper Park Rd
London NW3 2UP, UNITED KINGDOM (UK)

Blakemore, Sean (Actor)
c/o Steven Jang *SDB Partners Inc*
1801 Avenue Of The Stars Ste 902
Los Angeles, CA 90067-5981, USA

Blaker, Clay (Musician, Songwriter, Writer)
Texas Sounds Entertainment
PO Box 1644
Dickinson, TX 77539-1644, USA

Blakey, Marion (Government Official)
Federal Aviation Agency
800 Independence Ave SW
Washington, DC 20591-0004, USA

Blalack, Robert (Cinematographer)
12251 Huston St
North Hollywood, CA 91607-3616, USA

Blalock, Jane (Golfer)
43 Thorndike St #10
Cambridge, MA 02141, USA

Blamire, Larry (Actor, Director, Writer)
10878 Bloomfield St
Toluca Lake, CA 91602-2213, USA

Blanc, Georges (Chef)
Le Mere Blanc
Vonnas, Ain 01540, FRANCE

Blanc, Jennifer (Actor)
Writers & Artists
360 N Crescent Dr Bldg North
Beverly Hills, CA 90210-6818, USA

Blanc, Michel (Actor)
c/o Dominique Besnehard *ArtMedia*
20 av Rapp
Paris 75007, FRANCE

Blanc, Raymond R A (Chef)
Le Manoir
Church Road
Great Milton, Oxford OX44 7PD, UNITED KINGDOM (UK)

Blancas, Homero (Golfer)
6826 Queensclub Dr
Houston, TX 77069-1216, USA

Blanchard, Cary (Football Player)
New Orleans Saints
7208 NW 131st St
Oklahoma City, OK 73142-2540, USA

Blanchard, Felix Doc
30395 Olympus
Bulverde, TX 78163-2726, USA

Blanchard, George S (General)
9160 Belvoir Woods Pkwy
Fort Belvoir, VA 22060-2703, USA

Blanchard, James H (Financier)
Synovus Financial Corp
PO Box 120
901 Front Ave
Columbus, GA 31902-0120, USA

Blanchard, James J (Diplomat, Governor)
426 4th St NE
Washington, DC 20002-4902, USA

Blanchard, John (Baseball Player)
New York Yankees
230 Central Ave N Apt 306
Wayzata, MN 55391-1215, USA

Blanchard, John A (Business Person)
Delux Corp
3680 Victoria St N
Shoreview, MN 55126-2906, USA

Blanchard, Nina (Misc)
3610 Wrightwood Dr
Studio City, CA 91604-3946, USA

Blanchard, Rachel (Actor)
c/o Christian Donatelli *Benderspink*
110 S Fairfax Ave Ste 350
Los Angeles, CA 90036-2179, USA

Blanchard, Tammy (Actor)
c/o Carol Bodie *International Creative Management (ICM-LA)*
10250 Constellation Blvd
Los Angeles, CA 90067-6200, USA

Blanchard, Terence (Composer, Musician)
BMI
8730 W Sunset Blvd # 300W
Los Angeles, CA 90069-2210, USA

Blanchard, Tim (Religious Leader)
Conservative Baptist Assn
1501 W Mineral Ave # B
Littleton, CO 80120-5612, USA

Blanchard, Tom (Football Player)
New York Giants
1410 NE Heritage Dr
Grants Pass, OR 97526-3534, USA

Blanchett, Cate (Actor)
c/o Robyn Gardiner *RGM Associates (Australia)*
PO Box 128
Surry Hills NSW 2010, AUSTRALIA

Blanco, Gil (Baseball Player)
New York Yankees
18403 N 16th Pl
Phoenix, AZ 85022-1355, USA

Blanco-Cervantes, Raul (President)
Apdo 918
San Jose, COSTA RICA

Bland, Bobby Blue
1995 Broadway Ste 501
New York, NY 10023-5882, USA

Bland, Bobby (Blue) (Musician)
It's Happening Presents
PO Box 8073
Pittsburg, CA 94565-8073, USA

Bland, Carl (Football Player)
Detroit Lions
445 Coventry Trail Ln
Maryland Heights, MO 63043-5135, USA

Bland, John (Golfer)
PO Box 451436
Westlake, OH 44145-0638, USA

Bland, Nate (Baseball Player)
Houston Astros
1342 W Esplanade Ave
Kenner, LA 70065-6237, USA

Blanda, George (Football Player)
Chicago Bears
18 Forest Gate Cir
Oak Brook, IL 60523-2129, USA

Blandon, Roberto (Actor)
c/o Staff Member *TV Azteca*
Periferico Sur 4121
Colonia Fuentes del Pedregal
DF CP 14141, MEXICO

Blaney, Dave (Race Car Driver)
1751 W Lexington Ave
High Point, NC 27262-7115, USA

Blaney, George (Basketball Player)
New York Knicks
1633 Main St
Glastonbury, CT 06033-3133, USA

Blank, Matt (Baseball Player)
Montreal Expos
5226 Overridge Dr
Arlington, TX 76017-1211, USA

Blankenship, Greg (Football Player)
Oakland Raiders
2067 La Con Ct Apt 1
Campbell, CA 95008-4315, USA

Blankenship, Kevin (Baseball Player)
Chicago Cubs
5014 Regency Dr
Rocklin, CA 95677-4420, USA

Blankenship, Lance (Baseball Player)
Oakland A's
340 Kimberwicke Ct
Alamo, CA 94507-2703, USA

Blankers-Koen, Fanny (Athlete, Track Athlete)
Olympic Committee
Surinamestraat 33
La Harve 2585, THE NETHERLANDS

Blankfield, Mark 5 (Actor)
c/o Staff Member *The Artists Group Ltd (LA)*
1650 Broadway Ste 610
New York, NY 10019-6833, USA

Blanks, Billy (Actor, Athlete)
c/o Staff Member *William Morris Agency (WMA-LA)*
1 William Morris Pl
Beverly Hills, CA 90212-4261, USA

Blanks, Larvell (Baseball Player)
Atlanta Braves
3825 E Carson Rd
Phoenix, AZ 85042-6217, USA

Blanks, Sid (Football Player)
Houston Oilers
PO Box 130551
Spring, TX 77393-0551, USA

Blanton, Jerry (Football Player)
Kansas City Cheifs
1942 Calumet Ave
Toledo, OH 43607-1605, USA

Blarikfield, Mark (Actor)
Artists Group
10 100 Santa Monica Blvd #2490
Los Angeles, CA 90067, USA

Blasco, Chuck (Musician)
Media Promotion Enterprises
423 6th Ave
Huntington, WV 25701-1935, USA

Blashford-Snell, John N (Misc)
Exploration Society
Motcome
Shaftesbury
Dorset SP7 9PB, UNITED KINGDOM (UK)

Blasi, Rosa (Actor)
8060 Melrose Ave
Los Angeles, CA 90046-7017, USA

Blasingame, Wade (Baseball Player)
Milwaukee Braves
5207 Riverhill Rd NE
Marietta, GA 30068-4865, USA

Blass, Stephen R (Steve) (Baseball Player)
Pittsburgh Pirates
1756 Quigg Dr
Pittsburgh, PA 15241-2023, USA

Blasucci, Dick (Producer)
c/o Staff Member *Kaplan-Stahler-Gumer Agency*
8383 Wilshire Blvd Ste 923
Beverly Hills, CA 90211-2408, USA

Blateric, Steve (Baseball Player)
Cincinnati Reds
2855 S Monaco Pkwy Apt 2-304
Denver, CO 80222-7191, USA

Blatnick, Jeff (Actor)
848 Whitney Dr
Schenectady, NY 12309-3020, USA

Blatnik, Johnny (Baseball Player)
Philadelphia Phillies
68615 Chermont Rd
Bridgeport, OH 43912, USA

Blatny, Zdenek (Hockey Player)
Atlanta Thrashers
878 Ridge View Way
International Sports Advisors
Franklin Lakes, NJ 07417-1524, USA

Blatt, Melanie (Musician)
c/o Staff Member *Concorde Intl Artists Ltd*
101 Shepherds Bush Rd
London W6 7LP, UNITED KINGDOM (UK)

Blatter, Joseph (Sepp) (Football Executive)
Federation Int'l Football Assn
PO Box 85
Zurich 8030, SWITZERLAND

Blattner, Buddy (Baseball Player)
St Louis Cardinals
576 E Highway 42
Lake Ozark, MO 65049, USA

Blatty, William Peter (Writer)
7018 Longwood Dr
Bethesda, MD 20817-2118, USA

Blau, Daniel (Artist)
Belgradstr 26
Munich 80796, GERMANY

Blauser, Jeff (Baseball Player)
Atlanta Braves
3005 Compton Ct
Alpharetta, GA 30022-7127, USA

Blaylock, Anthony (Football Player)
Cleveland Browns
88 Brighton Dr
Garner, NC 27529-6872, USA

Blaylock, Bob (Baseball Player)
St Louis Cardinals
472933 E 1122 Rd
Muldrow, OK 74948-5589, USA

Blaylock, Gary (Baseball Player)
St Louis Cardinals
PO Box 241
Malden, MO 63863-0241, USA

Blaylock, Mookie (Basketball Player)
c/o Staff Member *Golden State Warriors*
1001 Broadway
Oakland, CA 94607-4019, USA

Blazelowski, Carol A (Basketball Player)
New York Liberty
2 Penn Plz
Madison Square Garden
New York, NY 10121-1703, USA

Blazier, Ron (Baseball Player)
Philadelphia Phillies
610 N 9th St
Bellwood, PA 16617-1524, USA

Blazitz, Micael (Football Player)
Chicago Bears
27100 Bunert Rd
Warren, MI 48088-6013, USA

Bleak, David B (War Hero)
355 Louise Dr
Arco, ID 83213-8743, USA

Bleaney, Brebis (Physicist)
Garford House
Garford Road
Oxford OX1 3PU, UNITED KINGDOM (UK)

Bledel, Alexis (Actor, Model)
c/o Megan Silverman *Endeavor Agency LLC (LA)*
9601 Wilshire Blvd Fl 3
Beverly Hills, CA 90210-5204, USA

Bledsoe, Curtis (Football Player)
Kansas City Cheifs
1012 Red Oak Pl
Chula Vista, CA 91910-6750, USA

Bledsoe, Drew (Football Player)
New England Patriots
845 Delrey Rd
Whitefish, MT 59937-8020, USA

Bledsoe, Tempestt (Actor)
c/o Staff Member *GVA Talent Agency Inc*
9229 W Sunset Blvd Ste 320
Los Angeles, CA 90069-3403, USA

Bleek (Cox), Memphis (Malik) (Artist, Musician)
Green Light Talent Agency
PO Box 3172
Beverly Hills, CA 90212-0172, USA

Bleeth, Yasmine (Actor)
Creatice Artists Agency
9830 Wilshire Blvd
Beverly Hills, CA 90212-1804, USA

Blegen, Judith (Opera Singer)
91 Central Park W # 1B
New York, NY 10023-4600, USA

Bleick, Tom (Football Player)
Baltimore Colts
PO Box 187
Talladega, AL 35161-0187, USA

Bleier, Robert P (Rocky) (Football Player)
Pittsburgh Steelers
929 Osage Rd
Pittsburgh, PA 15243-1011, USA

Bleiler, Gretchen (Snowboarder)
USOC Headquarters
1 Olympic Plz
Colorado Springs, CO 80909-5780, USA

Blessed, Brian (Actor)
Associated International Mgmt
5 Denmark St
London WC2H 8LP, UNITED KINGDOM
(UK)

Blessen, Karen A (Journalist)
Karen Blessen Illustration
6327 Vickery Blvd
Dallas, TX 75214-3348, USA

Blessitt, Ike (Baseball Player)
Detroit Tigers
19712 Anglin St
Detroit, MI 48234-1469, USA

Blethen, Frank A (Publisher)
Seatle Times Publisher's Office
1120 John St
Seattle, WA 98109-5321, USA

Blethyn, Brenda A (Actor)
61-63 Portobello Road
London W1N OAX, UNITED KINGDOM
(UK)

Bleu, Corbin (Actor)
c/o Bonnie Liedtke *William Morris
Agency (WMA-LA)*
3500 W Olive Ave Ste 1400
Burbank, CA 91505-5512, USA

Blevins, Michael (Actor)
13 W 100th St Apt 2C
New York, NY 10025-4815, USA

Bley, Carla B (Composer, Musician)
Watt Works
PO Box 67
Willow, NY 12495-0218, USA

Bley, Paul (Composer, Musician)
Legacy Records
550 Madison Ave # 1700
New York, NY 10022-3211, USA

Blick, Richard (Dick) (Swimmer)
1602 N Nye Ave
Fremont, NE 68025-3328, USA

Blier, Bertrand (Director)
11 Rue Margueritte
Paris 75017, FRANCE

Blige, Mary J (Musician)
c/o Jill Littman *Handprint Entertainment*
1100 Glendon Ave Ste 1000
Los Angeles, CA 90024-3514, USA

Bligen, Dennis (Football Player)
New York Jets
PO Box 101
West Hempstead, NY 11552-0101, USA

Blim, Richard D (Doctor)
304 W 172nd St
Belton, MO 64012, USA

Blinder, Alan S (Financier, Government
Official)
Princeton University
Economics Dept
Princeton, NJ 08544-0001, USA

Blink 182 (Music Group)
c/o Darryl Eaton *Creative Artists Agency
LCC (CAA-LA)*
2000 Avenue Of The Stars
Los Angeles, CA 90067-4700, USA

Blinka, Stan (Football Player)
New York Jets
3304 Carriage Cir
Export, PA 15632-9213, USA

Bliss, Boti Anne (Actor)
Chase/Goldberg Management
3400 San Marino St # A
Los Angeles, CA 90006-1106, USA

Bliss, Caroline
34-43 Russell
London, ENGLAND WC2B 5HA, UNITED
KINGDOM (UK)

Blitt, Ricky (Writer)
c/o Nick Reed *International Creative
Management (ICM-LA)*
10250 Constellation Blvd
Los Angeles, CA 90067-6200, USA

Blittner, Larry (Baseball Player)
Washington Senators
915 3rd Ave NW
Pocahontas, IA 50574-1413, USA

Blitz, Andy (Writer)
c/o Staff Member *3 Arts Entertainment Inc*
9460 Wilshire Blvd Fl 7
Beverly Hills, CA 90212-2713, USA

Blitzer, Wolf (Correspondent, Television
Host)
Late Edition with Wolf Blitzer
820 1st St NE
Cnn
Washington, DC 20002-4243, USA

Blobel, Gunter K J (Nobel Prize Laureate)
Rockefeller University
1230 York Ave
Cell Biology Dept
New York, NY 10065-6399, USA

Bloch, Erich (Engineer, Scientist)
National Science Foundation
1800 C St NE
Washington, DC 20002-6604, USA

Blochwitz, Hans-Peter (Opera Singer)
Matthew Sprizzo
18 Allison Ave
Staten Island, NY 10306-2806, USA

Block, Cy (Baseball Player)
Chicago Cubs
10 S Middle Neck Rd
Great Neck, NY 11021-3463, USA

Block, Francesca Lia (Writer)
c/o Angela Cheng Caplan *Cheng Caplan
Co*
1680 Vine St Ste 808
Hollywood, CA 90028-8834, USA

Block, Hunt
PO Box 462
Greens Farms, CT 06838-0462, USA

Block, John (Basketball Player)
Los Angeles Lakers
3900 Lomaland Dr
Point Loma Nazarene College Attn
Athletic Dept
San Diego, CA 92106-2810, USA

Block, John R (Secretary)
National Wholesale Grocers Assn
201 Park Washington Ct
Falls Church, VA 22046-4527, USA

Block, Ken (Hockey Player)
Vancouver Canucks
4901 Windrift Way
Carmel, IN 46033-9510, USA

Block, Lawrence (Writer)
299 W 12th St Apt 12D
New York, NY 10014-1829, USA

Block, Ned J (Misc)
29 Washington Sq W
New York, NY 10011-9180, USA

Blocker, Dirk (Actor)
5063 La Ramada Dr
Santa Barbara, CA 93111-1846, USA

Blocker, Terry (Baseball Player)
New York Mets
745 Guide Post Ln
Stone Mountain, GA 30088-1943, USA

Bloemberg, Jeff (Hockey Player)
New York Rangers
170 Diagonal Road
Wingham, ON N0G 1W0, CANADA

Bloemstedt, Herbert T
Kunstleragentur Raab & Bohm
Plankengasse 7
Vienna 1010, AUSTRIA

Blomberg, Ron (Baseball Player)
New York Yankees
11660 Mountain Laurel Dr
Roswell, GA 30075-1329, USA

Blombergen, Nicolaas (Nobel Prize
Laureate)
13835 E Langtree Ln
Tucson, AZ 85747-9637, USA

Blomdahl, Ben (Baseball Player)
Detroit Tigers
5370 Nottingham Rd
Riverside, CA 92506-1511, USA

Blomgren, Michael (Actor)
c/o Staff Member *Select Artists Ltd (CA-
Westside Office)*
1138 12th St Apt 1
Santa Monica, CA 90403-5459, USA

Blomquist, Rich (Actor)
c/o Staff Member *Creative Artists Agency
LCC (CAA-LA)*
2000 Avenue Of The Stars
Los Angeles, CA 90067-4700, USA

Blomqvist, Timo (Hockey Player)
Washington Capitals
HIFK Helsinki Ligaforeningen HIFK rd
Mantytie 23
Helsinki 00270, FINLAND

Blonde streak (Music Group)
c/o John Elias *Three Twins Entertainment,
Inc*
PO Box 100210
Staten Island, NY 10310-0210, USA

Blondie (Musician)
c/o Staff Member *Paradigm (Monterey)*
509 Hartnell St
Monterey, CA 93940-2825, USA

Blong, Jenni (Actor)
c/o Susan Smith *Susan Smith Company,
The*
1344 N Wetherly Dr
Los Angeles, CA 90069-1817, USA

Blonsky, Nikki (Actor)
c/o Staff Member *William Morris Agency
(WMA-LA)*
1 William Morris Pl
Beverly Hills, CA 90212-4261, USA

Blood, Edward J (Skier)
2 Beech Hill Rd
Durham, NH 03824-1803, USA

Bloodgood, Moon (Actor)
c/o Jack Heller *Schiff Company*
9465 Wilshire Blvd Ste 480
Beverly Hills, CA 90212-2603, USA

Bloodworth-Thomason, Linda (Producer,
Writer)
c/o Staff Member *Mozark Productions*
4024 Radford Ave Bldg 5 # 104
Studio City, CA 91604-2101, USA

Bloom, Alfred H (Educator)
Swarthmore College
President's Office
Swarthmore, PA 19081, USA

Bloom, Anne (Actor)
Abrams Artists
9200 W Sunset Blvd Ste 1125
Los Angeles, CA 90069-3610, USA

Bloom, Brian (Actor)
c/o Joel Dean *TalentWorks (LA)*
9200 W Sunset Blvd Ste 900
Los Angeles, CA 90069-3604, USA

Bloom, Claire (Actor)
c/o Staff Member *Conway Van Gelder Ltd*
18-21 Jermyn St Fl 3
London SW1Y 6HP, UNITED KINGDOM
(UK)

Bloom, Floyd E (Physicist)
628 Pacific View Dr
San Diego, CA 92109-1768, USA

Bloom, Jeremy (Actor, Athlete, Football
Player, Skier)
c/o Staff Member *Agency Group Ltd, The
(UK)*
361-373 City Road
London EC1V 1PQ, UNITED KINGDOM
(UK)

Bloom, Lindsay (Actor)
PO Box 412
Weldon, CA 93283-0412, USA

Bloom, Lisa (Television Host)
c/o Staff Member *Court TV*
600 3rd Ave Frnt 2
New York, NY 10016-1901, USA

Bloom, Luka (Music Group)
Mattie Fox Mgmt
Derryneel Ballinalee
Longford, IRELAND

Bloom, Mike (Hockey Player)
Washington Capitals
139 Peppertree Pl
Marina, CA 93933-2139, USA

Bloom, Orlando (Actor)
c/o Aleen Keshishian *Brillstein-Grey
Entertainment*
9150 Wilshire Blvd Ste 350
Beverly Hills, CA 90212-3453, USA

Bloom, Samantha (Actor)
c/o Paul Lyon-Maris *International Creative
Management (ICM-UK)*
Oxford House
76 Oxford St
London W1N OAX, UNITED KINGDOM
(UK)

Bloom, Ursula (Writer)
Newton House Walls Dr Ravenglass
Cumbria, UNITED KINGDOM (UK)

Bloom, Verna (Actor)
327 E 82nd St
New York, NY 10028-4103, USA

Bloomberg, Michael R (Politician)
Mayor's Office
Gracie Mansion
New York, NY 10007, USA

Bloomfield, Clyde (Baseball Player)
St Louis Cardinals
14250 State Highway 180
Gulf Shores, AL 36542-8222, USA

Bloomfield, Michael J (Mike) (Astronaut)
14302 Autumn Canyon Trce
Houston, TX 77062-2193, USA

Bloomfield, Sara (Director, Misc)
Holocaust Memorial Museum
100 Wallenberg Place SW
Washington, DC 20024, USA

Blosser, Greg (Baseball Player)
Boston Red Sox
5525 47th Ct E
Bradenton, FL 34203-5655, USA

Blount, Alvin (Football Player)
Dallas Cowboys
11102 Belton St
Upper Marlboro, MD 20774-1404, USA

Blount, Corie (Basketball Player)
Chicago Bulls
662 W Huntington Dr
Monrovia, CA 91016, USA

Blount, Eric (Football Player)
Phoenix Cardinals
202 King St
Ayden, NC 28513, USA

Blount, John E (Football Player)
Tampa Bay Buccaneers
1212 Daffodil Ln
Longview, TX 75604-2834, USA

Blount, Lamar (Football Player)
Miami Seahawks
5174 McCoy Dr
Jackson, MS 39211-4546, USA

Blount, Lisa (Actor)
c/o Staff Member *William Morris Agency (WMA-LA)*
1 William Morris Pl
Beverly Hills, CA 90212-4261, USA

Blount, Melvin C (Mel) (Football Executive, Football Player)
Pittsburgh Steelers
6 Mel Blount Dr
Claysville, PA 15323-1329, USA

Blount, Winton M III (Business Person)
Blount Inc
4909 SE International Way
Portland, OR 97222-4679, USA

Blout, Elkan R (Misc)
1010 Memorial Dr Apt 12A
Cambridge, MA 02138-4856, USA

Blow, Kurtis (Music Group)
Entertainment Artists
2409 21st Ave S Ste 100
Nashville, TN 37212-5317, USA

Blowers, Mike (Baseball Player)
New York Yankees
22211 42nd Ave E
Spanaway, WA 98387-6889, USA

Blu, D K (Musician)
c/o Mike Rosen *Working Artists Agency*
13525 Ventura Blvd
Sherman Oaks, CA 91423-3801, USA

Blucas, Marc (Actor)
c/o Staff Member *Endeavor Agency LLC (LA)*
9601 Wilshire Blvd Fl 3
Beverly Hills, CA 90210-5204, USA

Blucker, Sara (Actor)
c/o TJ Stein *Stein Entertainment Group*
11271 Ventura Blvd # 477
Studio City, CA 91604-3136, USA

Blue (Musician)
c/o Staff Member *Concorde Intl Artists Ltd*
101 Shepherds Bush Rd
London W6 7LP, UNITED KINGDOM (UK)

Blue, Callum (Actor)
c/o Staff Member *Untitled Entertainment (LA)*
331 N Maple Dr Fl 3
Beverly Hills, CA 90210-3827, USA

Blue, Forrest (Football Player)
San Fransisco 49ers
5350 Butler Rd
Penryn, CA 95663-9661, USA

Blue, John (Hockey Player)
Boston Bruins
2301 Half Moon Ln
Costa Mesa, CA 92627-6738, USA

Blue, Luther (Football Player)
Detroit Lions
6952 Ravines Cir
West Bloomfield, MI 48322-2757, USA

Blue, Vida (Baseball Player)
Oakland A's
PO Box 1449
Pleasanton, CA 94566-0349, USA

Blue Man Group (Music Group)
c/o Staff Member *Paradigm (Monterey)*
509 Hartnell St
Monterey, CA 93940-2825, USA

Blues Traveler (Music Group)
c/o Keith Sarkisian *William Morris Agency (WMA-LA)*
1 William Morris Pl
Beverly Hills, CA 90212-4261, USA

Bluford Jr, Guion S (Guy) (Astronaut)
PO Box 549
North Olmsted, OH 44070-0549, USA

Bluhm, Kay (Athlete)
Bahnorstr 104
Potsdam 14480, GERMANY

Blum, Arlene (Mountaineer)
University of California
Biochemistry Dept
Berkeley, CA 94720-0001, USA

Blum, Geoff (Baseball Player)
Montreal Expos
414 E Hawthorne St
Ontario, CA 91764-1751, USA

Blum, H Steven (General)
Chief National Guard Bureau
Hqusa Pentagon
Washington, DC 20310-0001, USA

Blum, John (Coach, Hockey Player)
Edmonton Oilers
Belle Tire Detroit Lightning
34400 Utica Rd Attn Coaching Staff
Fraser, MI 48026, USA

Blum, Stephanie (Comedian)
c/o Staff Member *Don Buchwald & Associates Inc (LA)*
6500 Wilshire Blvd Ste 2200
Los Angeles, CA 90048-4942, USA

Bluma, Jaime (Baseball Player)
Kansas City Royals
15219 Reeds St
Overland Park, KS 66223-3241, USA

Blumas, Trevor (Actor)
c/o Staff Member *Premier Artists Management Ltd*
1502 Stoneybrook Cresc
London, ON N5X 1C5, CANADA

Blumberg, Baruch S (Nobel Prize Laureate)
324 Lawrence Ct
Philadelphia, PA 19106-4211, USA

Blume, Bernard (Basketball Player)
Chicago Bulls
29248 SE Powell Valley Rd
Gresham, OR 97080-9040, USA

Blume, Judy (Writer)
JB Props Inc
C/O Tashmoo Productions 244 Fifth Ave 11th Fl
New York, NY 10001, USA

Blume, Martin (Physicist)
Brookhaven National Laboratory
2 Center St
Upton, NY 11973-9700, USA

Blumenthal, W Michael (Financier, Misc, Secretary)
227 Ridgeview Rd
Princeton, NJ 08540-7666, USA

Blundell, Mark (Race Car Driver)
4001 Methanol Ln
Indianapolis, IN 46268-4855, USA

Blundell, Pamela (Designer, Fashion Designer)
Copperwheat Blundell
14 Cheshire St
London E2 6EH, UNITED KINGDOM (UK)

Blundin, Matt (Football Player)
Kansas City Cheifs
731 Milmont Ave
Swarthmore, PA 19081-2519, USA

Blunstone, Colin (Music Group)
Barry Collins
21A Cliftown Southend-on-Sea
Sussex SS1 1AB, UNITED KINGDOM (UK)

Blunt, Emily (Actor)
c/o Chris Andrews *Creative Artists Agency LCC (CAA-LA)*
2000 Avenue Of The Stars
Los Angeles, CA 90067-4700, USA

Blunt, James (Musician)
c/o Staff Member *Twenty-First Artists Ltd (UK)*
1 Blythe Rd
London W14 OHG, UNITED KINGDOM (UK)

Blunt, Matt (Governor)
Office of the Governor
State Capitol Building #216
Jefferson City, MO 65101, USA

Blur (Music Group)
c/o Staff Member *United Talent Agency (UTA)*
9560 Wilshire Blvd Ste 500
Beverly Hills, CA 90212-2401, USA

Blurth, Ray (Bowler)
569 Beauford Dr
Saint Louis, MO 63122-1413, USA

Bly, Dre' (Football Player)
St Louis Rams
4312 Topsail Lndg
Chesapeake, VA 23321-6601, USA

Bly, Robert (Misc, Writer)
1904 Girard Ave S
Minneapolis, MN 55403-2945, USA

Blyleven, Bert (Baseball Player)
Minnesota Twins
1501 McGregor Reserve Dr
Fort Myers, FL 33901-9658, USA

Blyth, Ann (Actor, Music Group)
PO Box 9754
Rancho Santa Fe, CA 92067-4754, USA

Blyth, Chay (Misc, Yachtsman)
Inmans House 12 London Road Sheet Petersfield
Hamps GU31 4BE, UNITED KINGDOM (UK)

Blythe, Jamie (Reality TV Star)
c/o Michael (Mike) Esterman *Esterman Entertainment*
214 Park Rd
Riva, MD 21140-1224, USA

Blyzka, Mike (Baseball Player)
St Louis Browns
2816 E 7th St
Cheyenne, WY 82001-5612, USA

Boal, Mark (Writer)
c/o Staff Member *Creative Artists Agency LCC (CAA-LA)*
2000 Avenue Of The Stars
Los Angeles, CA 90067-4700, USA

Board, Dwaine (Football Player)
San Fransisco 49ers
1850 9th St W
Kirkland, WA 98033-4837, USA

Boath, Freddie (Actor)
c/o Staff Member *Sasha Leslie Management*
34 Pember Rd
London NW10 5LS, UNITED KINGDOM (UK)

Boatman, Michael (Actor)
c/o Nancy Sanders *Sanders/Armstrong Management*
2120 Colorado Ave Ste 120
Santa Monica, CA 90404-3561, USA

Boatswain, Harry (Football Player)
San Fransisco 49ers
2650 Bedford Ave
Brooklyn, NY 11210-1236, USA

Boatwright, Ron (Football Player)
San Diego Chargers
1801 E Main St
Henderson, TX 75652-3324, USA

Bob, Tim (Music Group, Musician)
ArtistDirect
1601 Cloverfield Blvd # 400
Santa Monica, CA 90404-4082, USA

Bobb, Nelson (Basketball Player)
Philadelphia Warriors
8 Concord Cir
Bala Cynwyd, PA 19004-2607, USA

Bobby Chacon, Bobby Chacon (Boxer)
Main Street III Gym
752 S Main St
Huntington Hotel
Los Angeles, CA 90014-2013, USA

Bobek, Nicole (Figure Skater)
19220 Seaview Rd # 100
Jupiter, FL 33469-2402, USA

Bobko, Karol J (Astronaut)
32 Mansion Ct
Menlo Park, CA 94025-6658, USA

Bobo, DJ (Music Group)
Postfach
Wauwil 6242, SWITZERLAND

Bobo, Jonah (Actor)
c/o Ellen Gilbert *Abrams Artists Agency (LA)*
9200 W Sunset Blvd Ph 11
Los Angeles, CA 90069-3601, USA

Boccabella, John (Baseball Player)
Chicago Cubs
1035 Lea Dr
San Rafael, CA 94903-3747, USA

Bocek, Milt (Baseball Player)
Chicago White Sox
3000 McCormick Ave
Brookfield, IL 60513-1058, USA

Bocelli, Andrea (Music Group, Musician)
Galleria del Corso 4
Milan 201122, ITALY

Bochco, Steven (Producer, Writer)
c/o Staff Member *Steven Bochco Productions*
3000 Olympic Blvd # 1310
Santa Monica, CA 90404-5073, USA

Bochner, Hart (Actor)
Gersh Agency
232 N Canon Dr
Beverly Hills, CA 90210-5302, USA

Bochte, Bruce (Baseball Player)
California Angels
311 Rydal Ave
Mill Valley, CA 94941-3441, USA

Bochtler, Doug (Baseball Player)
San Diego Padres
154 Narrow Gate Rd
Maryville, TN 37801-1077, USA

Bochy, Bruce (Baseball Player)
Houston Astros
16144 Brittany Park Ln
Poway, CA 92064-2069, USA

Bock, Charles
PO Box 4197
Incline Village, NV 89450-4197, USA

Bock, Edward J (Business Person, Football Player)
2232 Clifton Forge Dr
Saint Louis, MO 63131-3107, USA

Bock, Jerrold L (Jerry) (Composer)
145 Wellington Rd
New Rochelle, NY 10804-3705, USA

Bock, John (Football Player)
New York Jets
627 Cambridge Ter
Weston, FL 33326-3568, USA

Bock, Joseph (Football Player)
St Louis Cardinals
319 E Elm St
East Rochester, NY 14445-1509, USA

Bockhorn, Arlen (Basketball Player)
Cincinnati Royals
3540 Big Tree Rd
Bellbrook, OH 45305-1971, USA

Bockman, Eddie (Baseball Player)
New York Yankees
1400 Millbrae Ave # 2
Millbrae, CA 94030-2831, USA

Bockus, Randy (Baseball Player)
San Francisco Giants
560 Helena Dr
Tallmadge, OH 44278-2667, USA

Bocuse, Paul (Business Person, Misc)
40 Rue de la Plage
Collonges-au-Mont d'Or 69660, FRANCE

Bodden, Alonzo (Actor, Comedian)
c/o Staff Member *Rozon/Mercer Management*
9250 Wilshire Blvd Ste 100
Beverly Hills, CA 90212-3343, USA

Boddicker, Michael J (Mike) (Basketball Player)
Baltimore Orioles
11324 W 121st Ter
Overland Park, KS 66213-1978, USA

Boddy, Gregg (Hockey Player)
Vancouver Canucks
2271 Sorrento Dr
Coquitlam, BC V3K 6P4, CANADA

Bode, John R (War Hero)
1100 Warm Sands Dr SE
Albuquerque, NM 87123-4329, USA

Bode, Ken (Correspondent, Educator)
Northwestern University
Journalism School
Evanston, IL 60206, USA

Bodemann, Joe
Meinholz 1
Meine D-38527, GERMANY

Boden, Lynn (Football Player)
Detroit Lions
417 S 78th St Apt 7
Omaha, NE 68114-4540, USA

Boden, Margaret A (Misc)
Brighton University
Cognitive Science School
Brighton BN1 9QH, UNITED KINGDOM (UK)

Bodett, Tom (Entertainer, Writer)
PO Box 268
Putney, VT 05346-0268, USA

Bodine, Geoff
PO Box 1790
Monroe, NC 28111-1790, USA

Bodine, Geoffrey (Geoff) (Race Car Driver)
Brett Bodine Racing
158 Bluffton Rd
Mooresville, NC 28115-5773, USA

Bodine, Todd (Race Car Driver)
PO Box 419
Mooresville, NC 28115-0419, USA

Bodison, Wolfgang (Actor)
J Michael Bloom
9255 W Sunset Blvd Ste 710
Los Angeles, CA 90069-3304, USA

Bodmer, Walter F (Misc, Scientist)
Oxford University
Hertford College
Oxford OX1 3BW, UNITED KINGDOM (UK)

Bodnar, Gus (Hockey Player)
Toronto Maple Leafs
436 Jane Ave
Oshawa, ON L1J 3L4, CANADA

Boede, Marvin J (Misc)
Plumbing & Pipe Fitting Union
901 Massachusetts Ave NW
Washington, DC 20001-4307, USA

Boedeker, Bill (Football Player)
Green Bay Packers
1321 Traders Xing
Fort Wayne, IN 46845-1527, USA

Boeheim, James A (Jim) Jr (Basketball Player, Coach)
Syracuse University
Manley Field House
Syracuse, NY 13244-0001, USA

Boehm, Gottfried K (Architect, Historian)
Sevogelplatz 1
Basel 4052, SWITZERLAND

Boehm, Ron (Hockey Player)
Oakland Seals
235 Simons Rd NW
Calgary, AB T2K 2X4, CANADA

Boehmer, Len (Baseball Player)
Cincinnati Reds
206 Townview Ct
Wentzville, MO 63385-2925, USA

Boehne, Edward G (Financier)
Federal Reserve Bank
Independance Mall
100 N 6th St
Philadelphia, PA 19106, USA

Boehringer, Brian (Baseball Player)
New York Yankees
7 Sunset
Festus, MO 63028, USA

Boehrs, Jessica (Actor)
Jondral Kunstlermanagement
Am Kliepesch 13a 50859
Cologne, GERMANY

Boeke, Jim (Football Player)
Los Angeles Rams
18914 San Blas St
Fountain Valley, CA 92708-7430, USA

Boen, Earl
PO Box 11086
Beverly Hills, CA 90213-4586, USA

Boerner, Jacqueline (Speed Skater)
Bemhard-Bastlein-Str 55
Berlin 10367, GERMANY

Boerwinkle, Tom (Basketball Player)
Chicago Bulls
8524 Walredon Ave
Burr Ridge, IL 60527-8344, USA

Boeschenstein, William W (Business Person)
10617 Cardiff Rd
Perrysburg, OH 43551-3404, USA

Boesel, Raul (Race Car Driver)
R. Pe. Guilherme Pompeo
1 centro
Santana do Parnaiba 01000, SPAIN

Boesel, Raul (Race Car Driver)
150 SE 25th Rd Apt 4E
Miami, FL 33129-2403, USA

Boesen, Dannis L (Astronaut)
6613 Sandra Ave NE
Albuquerque, NM 87109-3639, USA

Boever, Joe (Baseball Player)
St Louis Cardinals
13085 Morris Rd Unit 11112
Alpharetta, GA 30004-4113, USA

Boff, Leonardo G D (Misc)
Pr M Leao 12/204 Alto Vale Encantado
Rio de Janeiro 20531-350, BRAZIL

Boffill, Angela (Music Group)
1385 York Ave Apt 6B
New York, NY 10021-3906, USA

Bofill, Ricardo (Architect)
Taller de Arguitectura
14 Ave de la Indurstria
Barcelona 08960, SPAIN

Bofinger, Heinz (Architect)
Beibricher Allee 49
Wiesbaden 65187, GERMANY

Bogar, Tim (Baseball Player)
New York Mets
0N032 Pauley Sq
Geneva, IL 60134-4442, USA

Bogart, Andrea (Actor)
c/o Staff Member *Kazarian/Spencer & Assoc (LA)*
11969 Ventura Blvd
Box 7409 Fl 3
Studio City, CA 91604-2630, USA

Bogart, Paul (Director, Television Host)
1801 Century Park E Ste 2160
Los Angeles, CA 90067-2343, USA

Bogdanovich, Peter (Director)
c/o Johnnie Planco *Untitled Entertainment (NY)*
322 8th Ave Ste 601
New York, NY 10001-6715, USA

Bogeberg, J B (Misc)
Bandana Mgmt
11 Elvaston Place #300
London SW7 5QC, UNITED KINGDOM (UK)

Bogener, Terry (Baseball Player)
Texas Rangers
411 E McCabe Ave
Palmyra, MO 63461-2012, USA

Boggs, Haskell (Cinematographer)
3710 Goodland Ave
Studio City, CA 91604-2312, USA

Boggs, Tommy (Baseball Player)
Texas Rangers
1450 Long Mdw
Salado, TX 76571-5367, USA

Boggs, Wade A (Baseball Player)
Boston Red Sox
6006 Windham Pl
Tampa, FL 33647-1149, USA

Bogguss, Suzy (Music Group, Songwriter, Writer)
c/o John Huie *Creative Artists Agency (CAA-Nashville)*
3310 W End Ave Fl 5
Nashville, TN 37203-1028, USA

Bogle, John C (Financier)
612 Shipton Ln
Bryn Mawr, PA 19010-3647, USA

Bogle, Warren (Baseball Player)
Oakland A's
11605 SW 103rd Ave
Miami, FL 33176-4001, USA

Bogner, Willy (Designer, Fashion Designer)
Bogner Film GmbH
Saint-Veit-Str 4
Munich 81673, GERMANY

Bogosian, Eric (Actor, Artist)
c/o Michael Cardonick *Creative Artists Agency LCC (CAA-LA)*
2000 Avenue Of The Stars
Los Angeles, CA 90067-4700, USA

Bogues, Muggsy (Basketball Player)
Washinton Bullets
2318 Houston Branch Rd
Charlotte, NC 28270-0795, USA

Boguniecki, Eric (Hockey Player)
Florida Panthers
58 Hine St
West Haven, CT 06516-4707, USA

Bogush, Elizabeth (Actor)
c/o Craig Shapiro *Innovative Artists (LA)*
1505 10th St
Santa Monica, CA 90401-2805, USA

Bohan, Justin (Actor)
c/o Staff Member *Don Buchwald &*
Associates Inc (LA)
6500 Wilshire Blvd Ste 2200
Los Angeles, CA 90048-4942, USA

Bohan, Marc (Designer, Fashion Designer)
35 Rue du Bourg a Mont
Chatillon Sur Seine 21400, FRANCE

Bohannon, Fred (Football Player)
Pittsburgh Steelers
5312 Goldmar Dr
Birmingham, AL 35210-2812, USA

Bohanon, Brian (Baseball Player)
Texas Rangers
243 W Thorn Way
Houston, TX 77015-2069, USA

Bohay, Heidi (Actor)
48 Main St
South Bound Brook, NJ 08880-1448, USA

Bohem, Les (Producer, Writer)
c/o Staff Member *United Talent Agency*
(UTA)
9560 Wilshire Blvd Ste 500
Beverly Hills, CA 90212-2401, USA

Bohigas, Guardiola Oriol (Architect)
Calle Calvert 71
Barcelona 21, SPAIN

Bohlen, Dieter
Carla Fornells Peguera
(Mallorca) 35E-07160, SPAIN

Bohling, Dewey (Football Player)
New York Titans
5705 Cambria Rd NW
Albuquerque, NM 87120-2317, USA

Bohlinger, Rob (Football Player)
Carolina Panthers
12650 69th Ave N
Maple Grove, MN 55369-5438, USA

Bohlke, Sanders (Musician)
c/o Staff Member *Paradigm (Monterey)*
509 Hartnell St
Monterey, CA 93940-2825, USA

Bohlmann, Ralph A (Religious Leader)
Lutheran Church Missouri Synod
1333 S Kirkwood Rd
Saint Louis, MO 63122-7295, USA

Bohn, Jason (Golfer)
161 Graves Rd
Acworth, GA 30101-6117, USA

Bohn, Parker III (Bowler)
25 Pitney Ln
Jackson, NJ 08527-2933, USA

Bohnet, John (Baseball Player)
Cleveland Indians
224 Panorama Dr
Benicia, CA 94510-1523, USA

Bohovich, Reed (Football Player)
New York Giants
11574 SE Plandome Dr
Hobe Sound, FL 33455-7901, USA

Bohr, Aage N (Nobel Prize Laureate)
Strangade 34 1-Sal
Copenhagen 1401, DENMARK

Bohrer, Thomas (Athlete)
77 Crest St
Concord, MA 01742-3006, USA

Bohringer, Romaine
5 rue Clement-Marot
Paris F-75008, FRANCE

Boikov, Alexandre (Hockey Player)
Nashville Predators
2138 Charleys Creek Rd
Culloden, WV 25510, USA

Boileau, Linda (Cartoonist, Editor)
Frankfort State Journal
321 W Main St
Editorial Dept
Frankfort, KY 40601-1890, USA

Boimistruck, Fred (Hockey Player)
Toronto Maple Leafs
PO Box 92
Hornepayne, ON P0M 1Z0, CANADA

Boireau, Michael (Football Player)
Minnesota Vikings
11421 Azalea Trl
Hampton, GA 30228-3231, USA

Boisclair, Bruce (Baseball Player)
New York Mets
5532 Jon Dodson Dr
Agoura, CA 91301-2063, USA

Boisson, Christine (Actor)
Artmedia
21 Ave Rapp
Paris 75007, FRANCE

Boisvert, Gilles (Hockey Player)
Detroit Red Wings
10213 Greenside Dr
Cockeysville, MD 21030-3332, USA

Boitano, Brian (Figure Skater)
Brian Boitano Enterprises
101 1st St # 370
Los Altos Hills, CA 94022-2750, USA

Boitano, Danny (Baseball Player)
Philadelphia Phillies
15400 Winchester Blvd Apt 43
Los Gatos, CA 95030-2346, USA

Boiteux, Jean (Swimmer)
51 Ave de Merignac
Bordeaux, Cauderan 33200, FRANCE

Boivin, Leo J (Hockey Player)
Toronto Maple Leafs
PO Box 406
Prescott, ON K0E 1T0, CANADA

Bojovic, Novo (Football Player)
St Louis Cardinals
22097 Worcester Dr
Novi, MI 48374-3956, USA

Bok, Arthur (Football Player)
Baltimore Colts
540 Lake Drive Clear Lk
Fremont, IN 46737-9559, USA

Bok, Bart J (Astronomer, Educator)
200 N Sierra Vista Dr
Tucson, AZ 85719-3841, USA

Bok, Chip (Cartoonist, Editor)
709 Castle Blvd
Akron, OH 44313-5709, USA

Bok, Derek C (Educator)
Harvard University
Kennedy Government School
Cambridge, MA 02138, USA

Bok, Sissela (Misc)
75 Cambridge Pkwy # 610
Cambridge, MA 02142-1229, USA

Bokadia, K C (Bollywood, Director, Filmmaker, Producer)
A12 Neha Apartments Juhu Tara Road
Juhu
Bombay, MS 400 049, INDIA

Bokamper, Kim (Football Player)
Miami Dolphins
301 NW 127th Ave
Plantation, FL 33325-2318, USA

Bokelmann, Dick (Baseball Player)
St Louis Cardinals
629 N Belmont Ave
Arlington Heights, IL 60004-5601, USA

Bol, Manute (Basketball Player)
Washinton Bullets
106 Union Wharf
Boston, MA 02109-1281, USA

Bolaşos, Enrique (President)
President's Office
Casa de Gobierno #2398
Managua, NICARAGUA

Bolcom, William E (Composer)
3080 Whitmore Lake Rd
Ann Arbor, MI 48105-9649, USA

Bolden, Charles F Jr (Astronaut, General)
14111 Lake Scene Trl
Houston, TX 77059-4406, USA

Bolden, Rickey (Football Player)
Cleveland Browns
301 High Pointe Dr
Lagrange, GA 30240-9718, USA

Boldirev, Ivan (Hockey Player)
Boston Bruins
2003 Woodmere Dr
Valparaiso, IN 46383-6680, USA

Boldon, Ato (Athlete, Track Athlete)
PO Box 3703
Santa Cruz, Trinidad, TRINIDAD &
TOBAGO

Bolduc, Dan (Hockey Player)
Detroit Red Wings
27 Daisy Ln
Sidney, ME 04330-1809, USA

Boles, Carl (Baseball Player)
San Francisco Giants
5618 Pine Bay Dr
Tampa, FL 33625-4025, USA

Boles, John E (Baseball Player, Misc)
7901 Timberlake Dr
West Melbourne, FL 32904-2151, USA

Bolger, Bill (Basketball Player)
Baltimore Bullets
525 Ahlstrand Rd
Glen Ellyn, IL 60137-6980, USA

Bolger, Emma (Actor)
c/o Abby Bluestone *Innovative Artists (LA)*
1505 10th St
Santa Monica, CA 90401-2805, USA

Bolger, James B (Jim) (Prime Minister)
New Zealand Embassy
37 Observatory Cir NW
Washington, DC 20008-3627, USA

Bolger, Jim (Baseball Player)
Cincinnati Reds
5524 Sidney Rd
Cincinnati, OH 45238-3215, USA

Bolick, Frank (Baseball Player)
Montreal Expos
841 Airport Rd
Paxinos, PA 17860-7205, USA

Bolin, Bobby D (Baseball Player)
San Francisco Giants
PO Box 1948
Easley, SC 29641-1948, USA

Bolkiah, Mu'izuddin Waddaulah (Misc)
Istana Darul Hana, BRUNEI
DARUSSALAM

Bolkovac, Nick (Football Player)
Pittsburgh Steelers
1418 Humbolt Ave
Youngstown, OH 44502-2755, USA

Boll, Don (Football Player)
Washington Redskins
PO Box 131
Scribner, NE 68057-0131, USA

Bollen, Roger (Cartoonist)
Tribune Media Services
435 N Michigan Ave Ste 1500
Chicago, IL 60611-4012, USA

Bolles, Richard N (Writer)
10 Stirling Dr
Danville, CA 94526-2921, USA

Bollettieri, Nick (Coach, Tennis Player)
Nick Bollettieri Tennis Academy
5500 34th St W
Bradenton, FL 34210-3506, USA

Bolling, Claude (Composer, Music Group)
20 Ave de Lorrainne
Garches, FRANCE

Bolling, Frank (Baseball Player)
Detroit Tigers
171 Fenwick Rd
Mobile, AL 36608-1743, USA

Bolling, Milt (Baseball Player)
Boston Red Sox
4009 Old Shell Rd Apt E11
Mobile, AL 36608-1385, USA

Bolling, Tiffany (Actor)
12483 Braddock Dr
Los Angeles, CA 90066-6813, USA

Bollinger, Brian (Football Player)
San Fransisco 49ers
763 Malibu Ln
Indialantic, FL 32903-3617, USA

Bollinger, Brooks (Football Player)
c/o Team Member *New York Jets*
1000 Fulton Ave
Hempstead, NY 11550-1030, USA

Bollinger, Danielle (Musician)
c/o Len Evans *Project Publicity*
312 W 53rd St
New York, NY 10019-5743, USA

Bollinger, Lee C (Educator)
Columbia University
President's Office
New York, NY 10027, USA

Bollman, Ryan (Actor)
c/o Staff Member *Lichtman/Salners*
Company
15865 Royal Haven Pl
Sherman Oaks, CA 91403-4724, USA

Bollo, Greg (Baseball Player)
Chicago White Sox
31032 Birchlawn St
Garden City, MI 48135-1957, USA

Bologna, Joseph (Actor)
16830 Ventura Blvd Ste 326
Encino, CA 91436-1725, USA

Bolonchuk, Larry (Hockey Player)
Vancouver Canucks
385 Woodlawn St
Winnipeg, MB R3J 2J2, CANADA

Bolstorff, Douglas (Basketball Player)
Detroit Pistons
1553 Skyline Ct
Saint Paul, MN 55121-1148, USA

Bolt, Jeremy (Producer)
c/o Ken Kamins *Key Creatives*
9595 Wilshire Blvd Ste 800
Beverly Hills, CA 90212-2508, USA

Bolt, Mae (Bowler)
1516 Robinhood Ln
La Grange Park, IL 60526-1129, USA

Bolt, Tommy (Golfer)
3690 W Treyburn Path
Lecanto, FL 34461-7805, USA

Bolten, Joshua (Government Official)
Office of Management/Budget
Executive Office Building
Washington, DC 20503-0001, USA

Bolton, Michael (Musician, Songwriter, Writer)
c/o Louis Levin *Levin/Nelson Entertainment*
130 W 57th St Apt 7B
New York, NY 10019-3311, USA

Bolton, Rodney (Baseball Player)
Chicago White Sox
2195 Ooltewah Ringgold Rd
Ooltewah, TN 37363-9392, USA

Bolton, Ron (Football Player)
New England Patriots
408 Maiden Ln
Chesapeake, VA 23325-4607, USA

Bolton, Ruthie (Basketball Player)
c/o Staff Member *Sacramento Monarchs*
1 Sports Pkwy
Arco Arena
Sacramento, CA 95834-2300, USA

Bolton, Scott (Football Player)
Green Bay Packers
1635 Ashmoor Dr E
Mobile, AL 36695-4345, USA

Bolton, Tom (Baseball Player)
Boston Red Sox
2288 Rolling Hills Dr
Nolensville, TN 37135-9483, USA

Bolton-Holifield, Ruthie (Basketball Player)
Sacramento Monarchs
1 Sports Pkwy
Arco Arena
Sacramento, CA 95834-2300, USA

Bolyard, Bob (Basketball Player)
Anderson Duffy Packers
10607 Wild Flower Pl
Fort Wayne, IN 46845-1687, USA

Bolzan, Scott (Football Player)
Cleveland Browns
1417 Ashford Ln
Aurora, IL 60502-1363, USA

Bomback, Mark (Baseball Player)
Milwaukee Brewers
2482 Riverside Ave
Somerset, MA 02726-5149, USA

Bombardir, Brad (Hockey Player)
New Jersey Devils
8959 Baywatch Trl NW
Walker, MN 56484-2063, USA

Bomer, Matthew (Actor)
c/o Bonnie Bernstein *Endeavor Agency LLC (NY)*
152 W 57th St Fl 25
New York, NY 10019-3310, USA

Bon Jovi, Jon (Actor, Music Group, Songwriter, Writer)
c/o Chuck James *Gersh Agency, The (LA)*
232 N Canon Dr
Beverly Hills, CA 90210-5302, USA

Bonaduce, Danny (Actor, Music Group)
c/o Paul Nagle *William Morris Agency (WMA-LA)*
1 William Morris Pl
Beverly Hills, CA 90212-4261, USA

Bonaly, Surya (Figure Skater)
c/o Staff Member *Champions on Ice*
3500 W 80th St
Tom Collins Enterprises Inc
Minneapolis, MN 55431-1068, USA

Bonamy, James (Musician)
Hallmark Direction
713 18th Ave S
Nashville, TN 37203-3214, USA

Bonanno, Louie
PO Box 583
Laguna Beach, CA 92652-0583, USA

Bond, Alan (Business Person, Yachtsman)
89 Watkins Road
Dalkeith, WA 6069, AUSTRALIA

Bond, Christopher S (Kit) (Governor, Senator)
308 E High St Ste 202
Jefferson City, MO 65101-3237, USA

Bond, Edward (Writer)
Orchard Way
Great Wilbraham, Cambridge CB1 5KA, UNITED KINGDOM (UK)

Bond, H Julian (Activist)
54435 41st Place NW
Washington, DC 20015, USA

Bond, J Max Jr (Architect)
Davis Broder Assoc
100 E 42nd St
New York, NY 10017, USA

Bond, Larry (Writer)
c/o Robert Gottlieb *Trident Media Group LLC*
41 Madison Ave Fl 36
New York, NY 10010-2257, USA

Bond, Phillip (Basketball Player)
Houston Rockets
208 Northwestern Pkwy
Louisville, KY 40212-2732, USA

Bond, Samantha (Actor)
Conway Van Gelder Robinson
18-21 Jermyn St
London SW1Y 6NB, UNITED KINGDOM (UK)

Bond, Samatha (Actor)
c/o Staff Member *Innovative Artists (LA)*
1505 10th St
Santa Monica, CA 90401-2805, USA

Bond, Victoria A (Composer)
Roanoke Symphony
541 Luck Ave SW Ste 200
Roanoke, VA 24016-5055, USA

Bondar, Roberta L (Astronaut)
Space Agency
P O Box 7014 Station V
Vanier, ON K1L 8E2, CANADA

Bondevik, Kjell Magne (Prime Minister)
Statsministerens Kontor
Postboks 8001 Dep
Oslo 0030, NORWAY

Bondra, Peter (Hockey Player)
Washington Capitals
372 Carriage Park Way
Annapolis, MD 21401-7709, USA

Bonds, Barry (Baseball Player)
c/o Team Member *San Francisco Giants*
24 Willie Mays Plz
Sbc Park
San Francisco, CA 94107-2199, USA

Bonds, Gary U S (Music Group)
Entity Communications
875 Avenue Of The Americas Rm 1908
New York, NY 10001-3507, USA

Bone Thugs-N-Harmony (Music Group)
c/o Staff Member *Sony Music Entertainment*
555 Madison Ave
New York, NY 10022-3301, USA

Boneham, Rupert (Reality TV Star)
c/o Staff Member *Abrams Artists Agency (NY)*
275 7th Ave Fl 26
New York, NY 10001-6708, USA

Bonehman, Rupert (Actor)
c/o Staff Member *Ruth Webb Enterprises*
10580 Des Moines Ave
Northridge, CA 91326-2926, USA

Bonell, Carlos A (Composer, Music Group)
Upbeat Mgmt
Sutton Business Centre
Wallington, Surrey SM6 7AH, UNITED KINGDOM (UK)

Bonelli, Ernest (Football Player)
Chicago Cardinals
1200 E Peppertree Ln Apt 602
Sarasota, FL 34242-8712, USA

Bonerz, Peter (Actor, Comedian, Director)
3637 Lowry Rd
Los Angeles, CA 90027-1435, USA

Bones, Ricky (Baseball Player)
San Diego Padres
Villa Rosa 2 A19
Guayama, PR 00654, USA

Bonet, Lisa (Actor)
c/o Staff Member *Don Buchwald & Associates Inc (NY)*
10 E 44th St
New York, NY 10017-3601, USA

Bonet, Pep (Architect)
C/Pujades 62
Barcelona 08005, SPAIN

Bong, Jung (Baseball Player)
Atlanta Braves
2917 Asteria Pointe
Duluth, GA 30097-5221, USA

Bongiovanni, Nino (Baseball Player)
Cincinnati Reds
416 Rosewood Ave
San Jose, CA 95117-1649, USA

Bongo, Albert-Bernard Omar (President)
President's Office
Blvd de Independence
Libreville BP 546, GABON

Bonham, Bill (Baseball Player)
Chicago Cubs
2135 Holly Ln
Solvang, CA 93463-2207, USA

Bonham, Ron (Basketball Player)
Boston Celtics
8020 S County Road 700 E
Selma, IN 47383-9621, USA

Bonham, Shane (Football Player)
Detroit Lions
3431 Ardennes Dr
Maryville, TN 37801-9591, USA

Bonham, Tracy (Music Group, Songwriter)
c/o Staff Member *Paradigm (Monterey)*
509 Hartnell St
Monterey, CA 93940-2825, USA

Bonham Carter, Helena (Actor)
c/o Adam Isaacs *United Talent Agency (UTA)*
9560 Wilshire Blvd Ste 500
Beverly Hills, CA 90212-2401, USA

Bonifant, J Evan (Actor)
c/o Staff Member *Pacific Artists Management*
1404-510 W Hastings St
Vancouver, BC V6B 1L8, CANADA

Bonikowski, Joe (Baseball Player)
Minnesota Twins
6701 Old Reid Rd
Charlotte, NC 28210-4622, USA

Bonilla, Hector (Actor)
c/o Staff Member *TV Azteca*
Periferico Sur 4121
Colonia Fuentes del Pedregal
DF CP 14141, MEXICO

Bonilla, Juan (Baseball Player)
San Diego Padres
2902 Orchidcrest Dr
Crestview, FL 32539-8528, USA

Bonilla, Roberto M A (Bobby) (Baseball Player)
Pittsburgh Pirates
390 Round Hill Rd
Greenwich, CT 06831-2637, USA

Bonin, Gordie (Race Car Driver)
12471 Stanford St
Los Angeles, CA 90066, USA

Bonin, Marcel (Hockey Player)
Detroit Red Wings
408 Rue Precieux-Sang
Joliette, PQ J6E 2M5, CANADA

Bonington, Christian J S (Mountaineer)
Badger Hill Nether Row Hesket
Newmarket
Cumbria, UNITED KINGDON (UK)

Bonk, Radek (Hockey Player)
Ottawa Senators
I M G Attn J P Barry
801 6th Street SW Ste 235
Calgary, AB T2P 3V8, CANADA

Bonnaire, Sandrine
36 rue de Ponthieu
Paris F-75008, FRANCE

Bonnell, Barry (Baseball Player)
Atlanta Braves
2102 179th Ct NE
Redmond, WA 98052-6064, USA

Bonner, Anthony (Basketball Player)
Sacramento Kings
5854 Elmbank Ave
Saint Louis, MO 63120-1116, USA

Bonner, Bobby (Baseball Player)
Baltimore Orioles
990 Manitou Rd
Hilton, NY 14468-9367, USA

Bonner, Elayna
Uliza Tschakalowa 48
Moscow, RUSSIA

Bonner, Frank (Actor)
Stone Manners
6500 Wilshire Blvd Ste 550
Los Angeles, CA 90048-4950, USA

Bonner, Melvin (Football Player)
Denver Broncos
PO Box 474
Bay City, TX 77404-0474, USA

Bonness, Rik (Football Player)
Oakland Raiders
1650 Farnam St
Omaha, NE 68102-2104, USA

Bonneville, Hugh (Actor)
c/o Staff Member Paradigm (LA)
360 N Crescent Dr
North Bldg
Beverly Hills, CA 90210-6820, USA

Bonney, Barbara (Opera Singer)
Gunnarsbyn
Edane 671 94, SWEDEN

Bono (Music Group, Songwriter, Writer)
Edun Apparel Ltd
30-32 Sir John Rogerson's Quay
Dublin 2, IRELAND

Bono, Mary (Politician)
Mary Bono
1555 S Palm Canyon Dr Ste D105
Palm Springs, CA 92264-8303, USA

Bono, Steven C (Steve) (Football Player)
Minnesota Vikings
1100 Hamilton Ave
Palo Alto, CA 94301-2216, USA

Bonoff, Karla (Music Group, Songwriter, Writer)
2122 E Valley Rd
Santa Barbara, CA 93108-1513, USA

Bonsall, Joseph S (Joe) Jr (Music Group)
New Leaf Press
PO Box 726
Green Forest, AR 72638-0726, USA

Bonsalle, George (Basketball Player)
Chicago Packers
11804 Del Rey Ave NE
Albuquerque, NM 87122-2417, USA

Bonsignore, Jason (Hockey Player)
Edmonton Oilers
2152 Edgemere Dr
Rochester, NY 14612-1102, USA

Bontemps, Ronald (Ron) (Basketball Player)
Olympics
133 S Illinois Ave
Morton, IL 61550-2683, USA

Bonvicini, Joan (Basketball Player, Coach)
University of Arizona
Atheletic Dept McKale Memorial Center
Memorial
Tucson, AZ 85721-0001, USA

Bonynge, Richard A
Chale Monet Rte de Sonloup
Les Avants 1833, SWITZERLAND

Boo, Jim (Hockey Player)
Minnesota North Stars
431 Park Ave
Mahtomedi, MN 55115-1661, USA

Boo, Katherine (Journalist)
Washington Post
Editorial Dept 1150 15th St NW
Washington, DC 20071-0001, USA

Boochever, Robert (Judge)
US Court of Appeals
125 S Grand Ave
Pasadena, CA 91105-1652, USA

Booker, Buddy (Baseball Player)
Cleveland Indians
PO Box 59
Brookneal, VA 24528-0059, USA

Booker, Butch (Basketball Player)
Miami Floridians
305 Barker Ave
Lansdowne, PA 19050-1215, USA

Booker, Chris (Correspondent)
c/o Staff Member Entertainment Tonight (ET)
5555 Melrose Ave
Mae West Bldg Fl 2
Los Angeles, CA 90038-3989, USA

Booker, Greg (Baseball Player)
San Diego Padres
1535 Charleigh Ct
Elon College, NC 27244-9770, USA

Booker, Rod (Baseball Player)
St Louis Cardinals
526 W Altadena Dr
Altadena, CA 91001-4204, USA

Booker, Vaughn (Football Player)
Kansas City Cheifs
1620 Powers St
Cincinnati, OH 45223-2658, USA

Bookout, Billy (Football Player)
Green Bay Packers
11 Page St
Hurst, TX 76053-8048, USA

Bookwalter, J R (Director)
PO Box 6573
Akron, OH 44312-0573, USA

Boom, Benn (Actor)
c/o Staff Member William Morris Agency (WMA-LA)
1 William Morris Pl
Beverly Hills, CA 90212-4261, USA

Boomer, Linwood (Producer, Writer)
c/o Philip Raskind Endeavor Agency LLC (LA)
9601 Wilshire Blvd Fl 3
Beverly Hills, CA 90210-5204, USA

Boon, David C (Cricketer)
Durham Cricket Club
Chester-le-Street
County Durham DH3 3QR, UNITED KINGDON (UK)

Boone, Aaron (Baseball Player)
Cincinnati Reds
9701 E Happy Valley Rd Unit 5
Scottsdale, AZ 85255-2323, USA

Boone, Bob (Baseball Player)
Philadelphia Phillies
1432 Misty Sea Way
San Marcos, CA 92078-1010, USA

Boone, Bret (Baseball Player)
Seattle Mariners
18305 Calle Stellina
Rancho Santa Fe, CA 92091-0165, USA

Boone, Danny (Baseball Player)
San Diego Padres
320 Minnesota Ave
El Cajon, CA 92020-6118, USA

Boone, Debby (Actor, Musician)
4334 Kester Ave
Sherman Oaks, CA 91403-4135, USA

Boone, J R (Football Player)
Chicago Bears
3731 Allan St
Selma, CA 93662-2203, USA

Boone, James (Football Player)
Cleveland Browns
2529 Butler Bay Dr N
Windermere, FL 34786-6111, USA

Boone, Pat (Actor, Musician)
904 N Beverly Dr
Beverly Hills, CA 90210-2913, USA

Boone, Randy (Actor)
4150 Arch Dr Apt 223
Studio City, CA 91604-3236, USA

Boone, Ron (Basketball Player)
Dallas Chaparrals
3877 Pheasant Ridge Rd
Salt Lake City, UT 84109-3835, USA

Boone, Steve (Music Group, Musician)
Pipeline Artists Mgmt
620 16th Ave S
Hopkins, MN 55343-7833, USA

Boorman, John (Director)
Merlin Films
16 Upper Pembroke St
Dublin 2, IRELAND

Booros, James (Golfer)
2615 W Pennsylvania St
Allentown, PA 18104-2921, USA

Boortz, Neal (Radio Personality)
1601 W Peachtree St NE
Atlanta, GA 30309-2641, USA

Boose, Dorian (Football Player)
New York Jets
4448 Oakdale Crescent Ct Apt 221
Fairfax, VA 22030-6739, USA

Boosler, Elayne (Actor, Comedian)
c/o Bill Siddons Core Entertainment Organization
14724 Ventura Blvd Ph
Sherman Oaks, CA 91403-3513, USA

Bootcheck, Chris (Baseball Player)
Anaheim Angels
4433 N Vintage Hills Trl
La Porte, IN 46350-7419, USA

Booth, Adrian (Actor)
3922 Glenridge Dr
Sherman Oaks, CA 91423-4645, USA

Booth, Brad (Football Player)
Philadelphia Eagles
529 S Bandini St
San Pedro, CA 90731-2328, USA

Booth, Clarence (Football Player)
Chicago Cardinals
33 Cor Dale Ct
Lafayette, IN 47904-1043, USA

Booth, Connie (Actor)
Kate Feast
Primrose Hill Studios
Fitzroy Rd
London NW1 8TR, UNITED KINGDOM (UK)

Booth, George (Cartoonist)
PO Box 1539
Stony Brook, NY 11790-0830, USA

Booth, Kellee (Golfer)
4804 Goldeneyes Ln
McKinney, TX 75070-9037, USA

Booth, Lindy (Actor)
c/o Ronda Cooper Characters Talent Agency, The (Toronto)
8 Elm St 3rd FL
Toronto, ON M5G 1G7, CANADA

Boothe, Powers (Actor)
23629 Long Valley Rd
Hidden Hills, CA 91302-2406, USA

Boothroyd, Betty (Government Official)
House of Commons
Westminster
London SW1A 0AA, UNITED KINGDOM (UK)

Booty, John (Football Player)
New York Jets
16401 Governor Bridge Rd Apt 407
Bowie, MD 20716-3717, USA

Booty, Josh (Football Player)
Cleveland Browns
9335 S Highway A1A
Melbourne Beach, FL 32951-4104, USA

Boozer, Carlos (Basketball Player)
Cleveland Cavaliers
1 Center Ct
Gund Arena
Cleveland, OH 44115-4001, USA

Boozer, Emerson (Football Player)
New York Jets
25 Windham Dr
Huntington Station, NY 11746-4541, USA

Boozer, Robert (Bob) (Basketball Player)
Cincinnati Royals
PO Box 94754
Nebraska Board Of Parole
Lincoln, NE 68509-4754, USA

Borbon, Pedro (Baseball Player)
Atlanta Braves
5505 Lakota Dr
Edinburg, TX 78539-7526, USA

Borboni, Paola
Via degli Artisti 23
Rome I-000187, ITALY

Borchard, Joe (Baseball Player)
Chicago White Sox
1942 Bancroft St
Camarillo, CA 93010-4510, USA

Borchardt, Jon (Football Player)
Buffalo Bills
3336 Burks Ln
Austin, TX 78732-2118, USA

Borcky, Dennis (Football Player)
New York Giants
18 Weathervane Rd
Aston, PA 19014-2616, USA

Bordaberry, Arocena Juan M (President)
Juaquin Suarez 2868
Montevideo, URUGUAY

Bordano, Chris (Football Player)
New Orleans Saints
2788 Morning Moon
New Braunfels, TX 78132-4785, USA

Bordeleau, Christian (Hockey Player)
Montreal Canadiens
2538 Boul Rene-Laennec
Laval, PQ H7K 3R8, CANADA

Bordeleau, J P (Hockey Player)
Chicago Blackhawks
91 Regal Drive
Dartmouth, NS B2W 4E9, CANADA

Bordeleau, Paulin (Hockey Player)
Vancouver Canucks
281a Rue Principale
la Sarre, PQ J9Z 1Z1, CANADA

Bordelon, Kenneth (Football Player)
New Orleans Saints
1224 Octavia St
New Orleans, LA 70115-4223, USA

Borden, Amanda (Gymnast)
Cincinnati Gymnastics Acadamy
3536 Woodridge Blvd
Fairfield, OH 45014, USA

Borden, Lynn (Actor)
Associated Artists
6399 Wilshire Blvd Ste 211
Los Angeles, CA 90048-5705, USA

Borden, Robert (Producer)
c/o Staff Member *United Talent Agency
(UTA)*
9560 Wilshire Blvd Ste 500
Beverly Hills, CA 90212-2401, USA

Borden, Scott (Actor)
c/o Staff Member *Progressive Artists
Agency*
400 S Beverly Dr Ste 216
Beverly Hills, CA 90212-4404, USA

Borden, Steve (Sting) (Wrestler)
16654 Soledad Canyon Rd # 315
Canyon Country, CA 91387-3217, USA

Border, Allan R (Cricketer)
Cricket Board
90 Jolimont St
Jolimont VIC 3002, AUSTRALIA

Borders, Pat (Baseball Player)
Toronto Blue Jays
1135 S Lakeshore Blvd
Lake Wales, FL 33853-4244, USA

Bordi, Rich (Baseball Player)
Oakland A's
979 Golf Course Dr # 187
Rohnert Park, CA 94928-1892, USA

Bordick, Mike (Baseball Player)
Oakland A's
1302 Locust Ave
Towson, MD 21204-6619, USA

Bordley, Bill (Baseball Player)
San Francisco Giants
39 Moccasin Ln
Rolling Hills Estates, CA 90274-2506,
USA

Boreanaz, David (Actor)
c/o Michael Katcher *Creative Artists
Agency LCC (CAA-LA)*
2000 Avenue Of The Stars
Los Angeles, CA 90067-4700, USA

Boren, David L (Educator, Governor,
Senator)
705 W Boyd
Norman, OK 73019-0001, USA

Borg, Bjorn R (Tennis Player)
International Management Group
Pier House Chiswick
London W4M 3NN, UNITED KINGDON
(UK)

Borg, Kim (Opera Singer)
Osterbrogade 158
Copenhagen 2100, DENMARK

Borg-Aplin, Lorraine (Baseball Player)
3611 Laverne Cir Apt 2
Baxter, MN 56425, USA

Borges, YamilRaimundtheatre
Wallgasse 18-20
Vienna 1060, AUSTRIA

Borghi, Frank (Soccer Player)
4123 Poepping St
Saint Louis, MO 63123-7726, USA

Borgman, James A (Jim) (Cartoonist,
Editor)
Cincinnati Enquirer
617 Vine St
Editorial Dept
Cincinnati, OH 45202-2433, USA

Borgmann, Glenn (Baseball Player)
Minnesota Twins
16 Lundy Ter
Butler, NJ 07405-1926, USA

Borgnine, Ernest (Actor)
c/o Linda Bensky *Bensky Entertainment*
15030 Ventura Blvd # 343
Sherman Oaks, CA 91403-5470, USA

Borgognone, Dirk (Football Player)
Green Bay Packers
220 Rae Ct
Sparks, NV 89436-7900, USA

Boris, Angel (Actor)
c/o Staff Member *Acme Talent & Literary
(LA)*
4727 Wilshire Blvd Ste 333
Los Angeles, CA 90010-3874, USA

Boris, Paul (Baseball Player)
Minnesota Twins
28 Sunnyside Ln
Hillsborough, NJ 08844-4738, USA

Boris, Ruthanna (Ballerina,
Choreographer)
Center for Dance
6510 Gladys Ave
El Cerrito, CA 94530-2210, USA

Bork, Erik (Writer)
CAA
9830 Wilshire Blvd
Beverly Hills, CA 90212-1804, USA

Bork, Frank (Baseball Player)
Pittsburgh Pirates
8488 Dunsinane Dr
Dublin, OH 43017-9420, USA

Bork, George (Football Player)
7316 Conventry Dr S
Spring Grove, IL 60081, USA

Bork, Judge Robert
5171 Palisade Ln NW
Washington, DC 20016-5337, USA

Bork, Robert H (Judge)
6520 Ridge St
McLean, VA 22101-2237, USA

Borkh, Inge (Opera Singer)
Haus Weitblick
Wienacht 9405, SWITZERLAND

Borkowski, Bob (Baseball Player)
Chicago Cubs
1031 Gerhard St
Dayton, OH 45404-2052, USA

Borkowski, David (Baseball Player)
Detroit Tigers
35308 Monza Ct
Sterling Heights, MI 48312-4060, USA

Borland, Toby (Baseball Player)
Philadelphia Phillies
8642 Quitman Hwy
Quitman, LA 71268-1282, USA

Borland, Tom (Baseball Player)
Boston Red Sox
624 W Cherokee Ave
Stillwater, OK 74075-1405, USA

Borlaug, Norman E (Nobel Prize Laureate)
P O Box 6-641
Mexico City DF SP 06600, MEXICO

Borlenghi, Matt (Actor)
c/o Staff Member *Don Buchwald &
Associates Inc (LA)*
6500 Wilshire Blvd Ste 2200
Los Angeles, CA 90048-4942, USA

Borman, Frank (Astronaut, Business
Person)
Patlex Corp
PO Box 1139
Fairacres, NM 88033-1139, USA

Born, Ruth (Baseball Player)
4205 Meridian Woods Dr
Valparaiso, IN 46385-7014, USA

Borntrager, Mary Christner (Writer)
c/o Staff Member *Herald Press*
616 Walnut Ave
Scottdale, PA 15683-1992, USA

Borodina, Olga V (Opera Singer)
Lies Askonas
6 Henrietta St
London WC2E 8LA, UNITED KINGDON
(UK)

Borofsky, Jonathan (Artist)
57 Market St
Venice, CA 90291-3603, USA

Borom, Red (Baseball Player)
Detroit Tigers
827 Highland Oaks Dr
Dallas, TX 75232-1211, USA

Boron, Kathrin (Athlete)
Potsdamer RG
An Der Pirschheide
Potsdam 14471, GERMANY

Boros, Guy (Golfer)
2540 SE 8th St
Pompano Beach, FL 33062-6738, USA

Boros, Steve (Baseball Player)
Detroit Tigers
3102 N Himes Ave
Tampa, FL 33607-1834, USA

Boross, Peter (Prime Minister)
Kossouth Lajos Ter 1-3
Budapest 1055, HUNGARY

Borotsik, Jack (Hockey Player)
St Louis Blues
Lot 17 1st Street N
Wasagaming, MB R0J 2H0, CANADA

Borowiak, Tony (Music Group)
MPI Talent
9255 W Sunset Blvd Ste 407
Los Angeles, CA 90069-3302, USA

Borowski, Joe (Baseball Player)
Baltimore Orioles
120 E Curtis St
Linden, NJ 07036-2930, USA

Borrego, Jesse (Actor)
c/o Kay Liberman *Liberman/Zerman
Management*
252 N Larchmont Blvd Ste 200
Los Angeles, CA 90004-3754, USA

Borrero, Alejandra (Actor)
c/o Gabriel Blanco *Gabriel Blanco
Iglesias (Mexico)*
Rio Balsas 35-32
Colonia Cuauhtemoc
DF 06500, MEXICO

Borresen, Richard (Football Player)
Dallas Cowboys
2291 Jefferson St
East Meadow, NY 11554-1907, USA

Borris, Angel (Actor)
c/o Lara Rosenstock *Lara Rosenstock
Management*
8371 Blackburn Ave Apt 1
Los Angeles, CA 90048-4245, USA

Borsavage, Ike (Basketball Player)
Philadelphia Warriors
219 Doris Ave
Southampton, PA 18966-2771, USA

Borschevsky, Nikolai (Hockey Player)
Toronto Maple Leafs
3 Geranium Crt
Richmond Hill, ON L4C 7M7, CANADA

Borschman, Laurie (Hockey Player)
Toronto Maple Leafs
27 Delamere Drive
Stittsville, ON K2S 1G7, CANADA

Borst, Plet (Misc)
Meentweg 87
Bussum 1406 KE, THE NETHERLANDS

Borstein, Alex (Actor)
c/o Judy Wixon-Darmody *Mosaic Media
Group*
24 Music Sq W Fl 1
Nashville, TN 37203-6661, USA

Borth, Michelle (Actor)
c/o Mark Rousso *New Wave
Entertainment (LA)*
2660 W Olive Ave
Burbank, CA 91505-4525, USA

Borton, Della (D B) (Writer)
Ohio Wesleyan University
Dept Of English
Delaware, OH 43015, USA

Bortz, Mark (Football Player)
Chicago Bears
1640 Old Barn Cir
Libertyville, IL 60048-1295, USA

Boryla, Mike (Football Player)
Philadelphia Eagles
7781 Oakview Pl
Castle Rock, CO 80108-8868, USA

Boryla, Vince (Basketball Player, Misc)
New York Knicks
5577 S Emporia Cir
Greenwood Village, CO 80111-3543,
USA

Borysenko, Joan (Doctor, Writer)
Mind-Body Health Sciences Inc
393 Dixon Rd
Boulder, CO 80302-9769, USA

Borzov, Valeri F (Athlete, Track Athlete)
Sport & Youth Ministry
Esplanadna St 42
Kiev 23 252023, UKRAINE

Bosa, John (Football Player)
Miami Dolphins
12605 Biscayne Bay Dr
North Miami, FL 33181-2413, USA

Bosarge, Wade (Football Player)
Miami Dolphins
7463 Tara Dr N
Mobile, AL 36619-1113, USA

Bosch, Don (Baseball Player)
Pittsburgh Pirates
14446 N State Highway 3
Fort Jones, CA 96032, USA

Bosch, Francisco (Actor)
Re.Animator Management
c/o Suzanne Gielgud
Victoria House 125 Queens Rd
Brighton BN1 3WB, UNITED KINGDOM
(UK)

Boschman, Ed (Religious Leader)
*Mennonite Brethren Churches General
Conference*
PO Box 347
Newton, KS 67114-0347, USA

Bosco, Philip (Actor)
Judy Schoen
606 N Larchmont Blvd Ste 309
Los Angeles, CA 90004-1309, USA

Bose, Amar G (Inventor)
Bose Corp Mountain
Framington, MA 01701, USA

Bose, Eleanora (Model)
I M G Models
304 Park Ave S # 1200
New York, NY 10010-4301, USA

Bose, Miguel (Actor, Music Group,
Songwriter, Writer)
RLM Producciones
Puerto Santa Maria 65
Madrid 28043, SPAIN

Boselll, Tony (Football Player)
6 Glendenning Ln
Houston, TX 77024-6827, USA

Boselli, Tony (Football Player)
Jacksonville Jaguars
12400 W Highway 71 # 350-170
Bee Cave, TX 78738-6517, USA

Bosetti, Rick (Baseball Player)
Philadelphia Phillies
1471 Arroyo Manor Dr
Redding, CA 96003-9215, USA

Bosio, Chris (Baseball Player)
Milwaukee Brewers
10425 Ambassador Dr
Rancho Cordova, CA 95670-2203, USA

Boskie, Shawn (Baseball Player)
Chicago Cubs
10220 N 55th St
Paradise Valley, AZ 85253-1168, USA

Boskin, Michael J (Government Official)
Stanford University
Hoover Instution
Stanford, CA 94305, USA

Bosley, Thad (Baseball Player)
California Angels
19440 Amhurst Ct
Cerritos, CA 90703-6787, USA

Bosley, Tom (Actor)
Burton Moss
8827 Beverly Blvd # L
Los Angeles, CA 90048-2405, USA

Bosman, Dick (Baseball Player)
Washington Senators
3511 Landmark Trl
Palm Harbor, FL 34684-5015, USA

Boso, Casper (Football Player)
St Louis Cardinals
8811 Calumet Dr
Indianapolis, IN 46236-9031, USA

Bossard, Andre (Judge, Lawyer, Misc)
228 Rue de la Convention
Paris 75015, FRANCE

Bosseler, Don J (Football Player)
Washington Redskins
7636 SW 102nd St # 214
Miami, FL 33156-3165, USA

Bossidy, Lawrence A (Larry) (Business
Person)
Honeywell Inc
Honeywell Plaza
Minneapolis, MN 55408, USA

Bosson, Barbara (Actor)
694 Amalfi Dr
Pacific Palisades, CA 90272-4506, USA

Bossy, Michael (Mike) (Hockey Player)
New York Islanders
136 Place Ducharne
Rosemere, PQ J7A 4H8, CANADA

Bostelle, Tom (Artist)
Aeolian Palace Gallery
267 Spring Run Ln
Downingtown, PA 19335-4410, USA

Bostic, Jeff (Football Player)
Washington Redskins
8250 Royal Saint Georges Ln
Duluth, GA 30097-1649, USA

Bostic, Jim (Basketball Player)
Detroit Pistons
111 Valentine Ln Apt 2D
Yonkers, NY 10705-3426, USA

Bostic, Joe (Football Player)
St Louis Cardinals
3507 Bromley Wood Ln
Greensboro, NC 27410-2182, USA

Bostic, John (Football Player)
Detroit Lions
611 Canaveral Ave
Titusville, FL 32796-7615, USA

Bostic, Keith (Football Player)
Houston Oilers
2419 Duchess Way
Stafford, TX 77477-6227, USA

Bostock, Lyman Sr (Baseball Player)
Brooklyn Royal Giants
305 17th Ave SW
Birmingham, AL 35211-3837, USA

Boston (Music Group)
c/o Staff Member *Sanctuary Music
Management (LA)*
301 Arizona Ave Ste 200
Santa Monica, CA 90401-1364, USA

Boston, Daryl (Baseball Player)
Chicago White Sox
1016 Valley Ln
Cincinnati, OH 45229-1932, USA

Boston, David (Football Player)
Arizona Cardinals
3738 Mykonos Ln Unit 127
San Diego, CA 92130-5543, USA

Boston, Lawrence (Basketball Player)
Washington Bullets
6362 Holiday Hills Ct
Bedford, OH 44146-3159, USA

Boston, McKinley (Football Player)
New York Giants
1986 Coyote Ridge Dr
Las Cruces, NM 88011-4042, USA

Boston, Rachel (Actor)
c/o Vera Mihailovich *Forward
Entertainment*
9171 Wilshire Blvd Ste 406
Beverly Hills, CA 90210-5516, USA

Bostridge, Ian (Musician)
c/o Staff Member *International Creative
Management (ICM-LA)*
10250 Constellation Blvd
Los Angeles, CA 90067-6200, USA

Bostrom, Zachary (Actor)
Kazarian/Spencer
11365 Ventura Blvd Ste 100
Box 7403
Studio City, CA 91604-3148, USA

Bostwick, Dunbar (Race Car Driver)
1623 Dewey Ave
Pompano Beach, FL 33060, USA

Bostwick, Jackson
Shazam!
PO Box 1452
Mount Juliet, TN 37121-1452, USA

Boswell, David W (Dave) (Baseball
Player)
Minnesota Twins
309 Roxbury Ct
Joppa, MD 21085-4744, USA

Boswell, Ken (Baseball Player)
New York Mets
PO Box 1244
Johnson City, TX 78636-1244, USA

Boswell, Thomas M (Writer)
Washington Post
Sports Dept 1150 15th St NW
Washington, DC 20071-0001, USA

Boswell, Tom (Basketball Player)
Boston Celtics
341 N Anton Dr
Montgomery, AL 36105-2112, USA

Bosworth, Brian (Actor, Football Player)
Seattle Seahawks
6375 Meadows Ct
Malibu, CA 90265-1706, USA

Bosworth, Kate (Actor)
c/o Billy Lazarus *United Talent Agency
(UTA)*
9560 Wilshire Blvd Ste 500
Beverly Hills, CA 90212-2401, USA

Botchan, Ron (Football Player)
Los Angeles Chargers
55 Toscana Way E
Rancho Mirage, CA 92270-1977, USA

Boteach, Rabbi Shmuley (Activist, Writer)
c/o Robert Gottlieb *Trident Media Group
LLC*
41 Madison Ave Fl 36
New York, NY 10010-2257, USA

Botehho, Joao (Director)
Assicuacai de Realizadores
Rua de Palmeira 7 R/C
Lisbon 1200, PORTUGAL

Botelho, Derek (Baseball Player)
Kansas City Royals
PO Box 470517
Kissimmee, FL 34747-0517, USA

Botero, Fernando (Artist)
Nohra Haime Gallery
41 E 57th St # 600
New York, NY 10022, USA

Botha, Francois (Frans) (Boxer)
White Buffalo
PO Box 3982
Clearwater, FL 33767-8982, USA

Botha, Pieter W (President)
Die Anker
Wildemess, 6560, SOUTH AFRICA

Botha, Roelof F (Government Official)
P O Box 16176
Pretoria North 0116, SOUTH AFRICA

Botham, Ian T (Cricketer)
Ludorum Mgmt
33 Tooley St
London SE1 2QF, UNITED KINGDOM
(UK)

Bothwell, Tim (Coach, Hockey Player)
New York Rangers
Atlanta Thrashers PO Box 1053766
Attn Coaching Staff
Atlanta, GA 30310-0537, USA

Botkin, Kirk (Football Player)
New Orleans Saints
9018 Augusta St
Beach City, TX 77520-9767, USA

Botsford, Beth (Swimmer)
2210 River Bend Ct
White Hall, MD 21161-9214, USA

Botsford, Sara (Actor)
Kordek Agency
8490 W Sunset Blvd Ste 403
West Hollywood, CA 90069-1926, USA

Botta, Mario (Architect)
Via Ciani 16
Lugano 6904, SWITZERLAND

Bottalico, Ricky (Baseball Player)
Philadelphia Phillies
71 Murphy Dr
Rocky Hill, CT 06067-1865, USA

Bottcher, Martin
Via Longhena 3
Lugano CH-6900, SWITZERLAND

Bottenfield, Kent (Baseball Player)
Montreal Expos
1323 Cottingham Dr
Franklin, TN 37067-8660, USA

Botterill, Jason (Hockey Player)
Dallas Stars
236 Sunnyside Dr
Toledo, OH 43612-3625, USA

Botting, Ralph (Baseball Player)
California Angels
7 Somerset
Dove Canyon, CA 92679-3701, USA

Bottom, Joe (Swimmer)
PO Box 3840
Chico, CA 95927-3840, USA

Bottomley, Virginia (Government Official)
House of Commons
Westminster
London SW1A 0AA, UNITED KINGDOM
(UK)

Bottoms, Joseph (Actor)
c/o Belle Zwerdling *Progressive Artists
Agency*
400 S Beverly Dr Ste 216
Beverly Hills, CA 90212-4404, USA

Bottoms, Sam (Actor)
4719 Willowcrest Ave
North Hollywood, CA 91602-1417, USA

Bottoms, Timothy (Actor)
532 Hot Springs Rd
Santa Barbara, CA 93108-2014, USA

Botz, Bob
Los Angeles Angels
14229 Desert Fire Ct
Horizon City, TX 79928-6422, USA

Boublil, Alain A (Songwriter, Writer)
Cameron Mackintosh Ltd
1 Bedford Square
London WC1B 3RA, UNITED KINGDOM
(UK)

Boucha, Henry (Hockey Player)
Detroit Red Wings
PO Box 757
Warroad, MN 56763-0757, USA

Bouchard, Dan (Hockey Player)
Atlanta Flames
3111 Hillsdale Ct SE
Marietta, GA 30067-5431, USA

Bouchard, Emile (Hockey Player)
Montreal Canadians
213 Marie-Victoria Blvd
Vercheres, PQ J0L 2R0, CANADA

Bouchard, Emile J (Butch) (Hockey
Player)
CSAS
P O Box 60036 RPO Glen Abbey
Oakville, ON L6M 3H2, CANADA

Bouchard, Marc (Producer)
c/o Staff Member *Cirque du Soleil Inc*
8400 2e Avenue
Montreal, PQ H1Z 4M6, CANADA

Bouchard, Pierre (Hockey Player)
Montreal Canadians
208 Marie-Victorian
Vercheres, PQ J0L 2R0, CANADA

Bouchee, Ed
Philadelphia Phillies
1621 E Tremaine Ave
Gilbert, AZ 85234-8140, USA

Boucher, Brian (Hockey Player)
Philadelphia Flyers
9 Ridge View Ct
Smithfield, RI 02917-2507, USA

Boucher, Gaetan (Speed Skater)
Center Sportif
3850 Edger
Saint Hubert, PQ J4T 368, CANADA

Boucher, Pierre (Photographer)
L'Ermitage 7th Ave Massoul
Faremountiers
Coulomiers 77120, FRANCE

Boucher, Savannah (Actor)
H W A Talent
3500 W Olive Ave Ste 1400
Burbank, CA 91505-5512, USA

Bouchez, Elodie (Actor)
c/o Scott Zimmerman *Untitled
Entertainment (LA)*
331 N Maple Dr Fl 3
Beverly Hills, CA 90210-3827, USA

Bouck, Brittany Page (Actor)
c/o Henry Penner *Penner PR*
8225 Santa Monica Blvd
West Hollywood, CA 90046-5912, USA

Boudart, Michel (Engineer, Misc)
512 Gerona Rd
Stanford, CA 94305-8449, USA

Boudin, Michael (Judge)
US Appeals Court
McCormack Federal Building
Boston, MA 02109, USA

Boudreau, Bruce (Hockey Player)
Toronto Maple Leafs
6297 Harvest Field Ln
Harrisburg, PA 17111-7063, USA

Boudrias, Andre (Hockey Player)
Montreal Canadians
1008-4300 Place des Cageux
Laval, PQ H7W 423, CANADA

Bouggess, Lee (Football Player)
Philadelphia Eagles
171 Villa Knoll Ct
Sicklerville, NJ 08081-2923, USA

Boughner, Barry (Hockey Player)
Oaklands Seals
52 Locke Ave
St Thomas, ON N5P 3X7, CANADA

Boughner, Bob (Hockey Player)
Buffalo Sabres
5541 Puerta Del Sol Blvd S Apt 414
Saint Petersburg, FL 33715-1448, USA

Bouillon, Jean-Christophe
Wildbacher 9
Hinwil CH 8340, SWITZERLAND

Boujenah, Michael
35 rue de Rivoli
Paris 75004, FRANCE

Bouldin, Carl (Baseball Player)
Washington Senators
53 Wesley Dr
Wilder, KY 41076-1472, USA

Boulerice, Jesse (Hockey Player)
St Louis Blues
152 McClellan Ave
West Berlin, NJ 08091-1652, USA

Bouley, Gilbert (Football Player)
Cleveland Rams
459 Commercial St
Weymouth, MA 02188-3724, USA

Boulez, Pierre (Composer, Conductor)
IRCAM
1 Place Igor Stravinsky
Paris 75004, FRANCE

Boulos, Frenchy (Soccer Player)
20 Elvin St
Staten Island, NY 10314-4049, USA

Boulud, David (Chef)
Daniel Restaurant
60 E 65th St
New York, NY 10065-7056, USA

Boulware, Peter (Football Player)
Baltimore Ravens
305 Leaning Tree Rd
Columbia, SC 29223-3010, USA

Bouman, Todd (Football Player)
Minnesota Vikings
7136 Harrison Hill Trl
Chanhassen, MN 55317-7581, USA

Bouquet, Carole (Actor, Model)
Agents Associes Beaume
201 Faubourg Saint Honore
Paris 75008, FRANCE

Bourbonnais, Rick (Hockey Player)
St Louis Blues
643 E Parkway Ct
Boise, ID 83706-6526, USA

Bourcier, Jean-Louis (Hockey Player)
Montreal Canadians
623 RG St Laurent
St-Etienne-Beauharnois, PQ J0S 1S0,
CANADA

Bourdeaux, Brandy (Actor)
c/o Staff Member *Coralie Jr Theatrical
Agency*
907 S Victory Blvd
Burbank, CA 91502-2430, USA

Bourdeaux, Michael (Religious Leader)
Keston College
Heathfield Road Keston
Kent BR2 6BA, UNITED KINGDOM (UK)

Bourdian, Anthony (Chef)
Food Network
1180 Avenue Of The Americas Ste 1200
New York, NY 10036-8401, USA

Boures, Emil (Football Player)
Pittsburgh Steelers
426 W Swissvale Ave
Pittsburgh, PA 15218-1637, USA

Bourgeois, Charles (Hockey Player)
Calgary Flames
PO Box 1481 Stn Main
Moncton, NB E1C 8T6, CANADA

Bourgeois, Louise (Misc)
347 W 20th St
New York, NY 10011-3300, USA

Bourgeois, Steve (Baseball Player)
San Francisco Giants
PO Box 143
Paulina, LA 70763-0143, USA

Bourgignon, Serge (Director)
18 Rue de General-Malterre
Paris 75016, FRANCE

Bourjaily, Vance (Writer)
Redbird Farm RR 3
Iowa City, IA 52240, USA

Bourjos, Chris (Baseball Player)
San Francisco Giants
10345 E Dreyfus Ave
Scottsdale, AZ 85260-9006, USA

Bourne, Bob (Hockey Player)
New York Islanders
17 Darius Ct
Dix Hills, NY 11746-5341, USA

Bourne, Judith
707 Crestmoore Pl
Venice, CA 90291-4816, USA

Bourne, Shae-Lynn (Figure Skater)
Connecticut Skating Center
300 Alumni Rd
Newington, CT 06111-1865, USA

Bournigal, Rafael (Baseball Player)
Los Angeles Dodgers
630 Crescent Hills Dr
Lakeland, FL 33813-4667, USA

Bournissen, Chantal (Skier)
1983 Evolene
SWITZERLAND

Bourque, Pat (Baseball Player)
Chicago Cubs
2350 N Augusta Dr
Flagstaff, AZ 86004-7536, USA

Bourque, Phil (Hockey Player)
207 Moody Rd
Clinton, PA 15026-1738, USA

Bourque, Pierre (Misc)
Hotel de Ville
275 Rue Notre Dame Est
Montreal, PQ H2Y 1C6, CANADA

Bourque, Raymond J (Ray) (Hockey
Player)
Boston Bruins
47C Dana Rd
Boxford, MA 01921-2661, USA

Bourret, Caprice (Actor)
c/o Nadja Koglin *Richard Schwartz
Management*
2934 1/2 N Beverly Glen Cir # 107
Los Angeles, CA 90077-1724, USA

Boushka, Richard (Dick) (Basketball
Player)
Olympics
5414 W 145th St
Overland Park, KS 66224-3756, USA

Bouteflika, Abdul Aziz (President)
President's Office
Al-Mouradia
Algiers, ALGERIA

Boutette, Pat (Hockey Player)
Toronto Maple Leafs
The Doctors House Restaurant
PO Box 460
Kleinburg, ON L0J 1C0, CANADA

Boutilier, Paul (Hockey Player)
New York Islanders
35 Elgin Lane
Bedford, NS B4A 2K2, CANADA

Bouton, Jim (Baseball Player)
New York Yankees
PO Box 188
North Egremont, MA 01252-0188, USA

Boutros-Ghali, Boutros (Secretary)
Inter'l Francophonie Org
28 Rue de Bourgogne
Paris 75007, FRANCE

Boutwell, Thomas (Football Player)
Miami Dolphins
32353 Oaken Wood St
Denham Springs, LA 70726-1666, USA

Bouvet, Didier (Skier)
Bouvet-Sports
Abondance 74360, FRANCE

Bouvia, Gloria (Bowler)
658 NE 23rd Pl
Gresham, OR 97030, USA

Bouwmeester, Jay (Hockey Player)
Florida Panthers
28 Greenoch Cres NW
Edmonton, AB T6L 1B4, CANADA

Bouyer, Willie (Football Player)
Seattle Seahawks
6560 Chesterbrook Dr
Elk Grove, CA 95758-6326, USA

Bouza, Matt (Football Player)
Baltimore Colts
1042 Via Nueva
Lafayette, CA 94549-2726, USA

Bouzeos, Phil (Football Player)
Chicago Rockets
10 Pembroke Ln
Oak Brook, IL 60523-1727, USA

Bova, Raoul (Actor)
c/o Alan Siegel *Alan Siegel Entertainment*
345 N Maple Dr Ste 375
Beverly Hills, CA 90210-5942, USA

Bovee, Mike (Baseball Player)
Anaheim Angels
11173 Kelowa Rd Apt 35
San Diego, CA 92126, USA

Boven, Don (Basketball Player)
Waterloo Hawks
218 Pretty Lake Dr
Mattawan, MI 49071-9467, USA

Bowa, Lawrence R (Larry) (Baseball
Player, Misc)
Philadelphia Phillies
129 Upper Gulph Rd
Radnor, PA 19087-4625, USA

Bowab, John
2598 Greenvalley Rd
Los Angeles, CA 90046-1438, USA

Bowdell III, Gordon (Football Player)
Denver Broncos
10929 Stoney Point Dr
South Lyon, MI 48178-9296, USA

Bowden, Craig (Golfer)
4651 S Amber Dr
Bloomington, IN 47401-8359, USA

Bowden, Mark (Director, Writer)
c/o Ron Bernstein *International Creative
Management (ICM-LA)*
10250 Constellation Blvd
Los Angeles, CA 90067-6200, USA

Bowden, Robert (Bobby) (Coach, Football
Coach)
Florida State University
Athletic Dept
Tallahassee, FL 32306, USA

Bowden, Terry (Coach, Football Coach,
Sportscaster)
ABC-TV
77 W 66th St
Sports Dept
New York, NY 10023-6201, USA

Bowden, Tommy (Coach, Football Coach)
Clemson University
Athletic Dept
Clemson, SC 29364, USA

Bowdler, William G (Diplomat)
State Department
2201 C St NW
Washington, DC 20520-0099, USA

Bowe, David (Actor)
Karg/Weissenbach
329 N Wetherly Dr Ste 101
Beverly Hills, CA 90211-1674, USA

Bowe, Riddick L (Boxer)
714 Ahmer Dr
Fort Washington, MD 20744, USA

Bowe, Rosemarie (Actor)
321 St Pierre Rd
Los Angeles, CA 90077-3432, USA

Bowen, Andrea (Actor)
c/o Staff Member *Terrific Talent
Associates*
419 Park Ave # 1009
New York, NY 10022-4402, USA

Bowen, Jason (Hockey Player)
Philadelphia Flyers
6031 Main St
Voorhees, NJ 08043-4653, USA

Bowen, Jimmy (Music Group, Musician)
PO Box 454
Lebanon, TN 37088-0454, USA

Bowen, Julie (Actor)
c/o Kay Liberman *Liberman/Zerman
Management*
252 N Larchmont Blvd Ste 200
Los Angeles, CA 90004-3754, USA

Bowen, Michael (Actor)
Diverse Talent Agency
1875 Century Park E Ste 2250
Los Angeles, CA 90067-2563, USA

Bowen, Nanci (Golfer)
193 Tucker Rd
Macon, GA 31210-4423, USA

Bowen, Otis R (Secretary)
PO Box 348
Bremen, IN 46506-0348, USA

Bowen, Pamela
1140 Avenue Of The Americas # 500
New York, NY 10036-5803, USA

Bowen, Ryan (Baseball Player)
Houston Astros
2806 Maryland Avenue
Fort Worth, TX 76162, USA

Bowen, Sam (Baseball Player)
Boston Red Sox
8219 Victory Trl
Brentwood, TN 37027-7374, USA

Bowen, William G (Educator, Misc)
Andrew Mellon Foundation
140 E 62nd St
New York, NY 10065-8124, USA

Bowens, Tim (Football Player)
Miami Dolphins
PO Box 93
Okolona, MS 38860-0093, USA

Bowens, Tom (Basketball Player)
Denver Rockets
304 Martin Luther King St
Okolona, MS 38860-1330, USA

Bower, Antoinette (Actor)
1529 N Beverly Glen Blvd
Los Angeles, CA 90077-3129, USA

Bower, John W (Johny) (Hockey Player)
3937 Parkgate Dr
Mississauga, ON L5N 7B4, CANADA

Bower, Robert W (Inventor)
University of California
Microelectronics Dept
Davis, CA 95616, USA

Bowers, Brent (Baseball Player)
Baltimore Orioles
19257 Manchester Dr
Mokena, IL 60448-7747, USA

Bowers, Chris (Actor)
c/o Staff Member *Gersh Agency, The (LA)*
232 N Canon Dr
Beverly Hills, CA 90210-5302, USA

Bowers, Dane (Actor, Musician)
Penshurst Place
90-92 SouthBridge Rd
Croydon, Surrey CRO 1AF, UNITED
KINGDOM (UK)

Bowers, John (Misc)
International Longshoremen's Assn
17 Battery Pl
New York, NY 10004-1207, USA

Bowers, John W (Religious Leader)
Foursquare Gospel Int'l Church
1100 Glendale Blvd
Los Angeles, CA 90026-3203, USA

Bowers, Stew (Baseball Player)
Boston Red Sox
1620 Ridgeway Rd
Havertown, PA 19083-2513, USA

Bowers, William (Football Player)
Los Angeles Rams
43295 Lacovia Dr
Bermuda Dunes, CA 92203-8016, USA

Bowersox, Kenneth D (Astronaut)
16907 Soaring Forest Dr
Houston, TX 77059-4003, USA

Bowick, Vantonio (Football Player)
Atlanta Falcons
PO Box 234
Slocomb, AL 36375-0234, USA

Bowie, David (Actor, Music Group)
c/o Mitch Schneider *Mitch Schneider
Organization, The*
14724 Ventura Blvd Ste 710
Sherman Oaks, CA 91403-3520, USA

Bowie, Heather (Golfer)
4200 Oak Park Ct
Fort Worth, TX 76109-9552, USA

Bowie, Jim (Baseball Player)
Oakland A's
620 Suisun St
Suisun City, CA 94585-2438, USA

Bowie, Larry D (Football Player)
Washington Redskins
1609 Parkwin Ave
Anniston, AL 36201-3460, USA

Bowie, Larry G (Football Player)
Minnesota Vikings
260 Clarence St
Saint Paul, MN 55106-6572, USA

Bowie, Micah (Baseball Player)
Atlanta Braves
2039 Small Town Dr
New Braunfels, TX 78130-9063, USA

Bowie, Sam (Basketball Player)
901 Curtilage
Lexington, KY 40502, USA

Bowker, Albert H (Educator)
1523 New Hampshire Ave NW
Washington, DC 20036-1203, USA

Bowker, Judi (Actor)
66 Berkeley House 5 Hay Hill
London W1X 7LH, UNITED KINGDOM
(UK)

Bowles, Brian (Baseball Player)
Toronto Blue Jays
2001 Flournoy Rd
Manhattan Beach, CA 90266-2534, USA

Bowles, Charlie (Baseball Player)
Philadelphia Athletics
2309 24th Ave NE
Hickory, NC 28601-7931, USA

Bowles, Crandall C (Business Person)
Springs Industries
205 N White St
Fort Mill, SC 29715-1654, USA

Bowles, Erskine B (Government Official)
6725 Old Providence Rd
Charlotte, NC 28226-7735, USA

Bowles, Lauren (Actor)
c/o Staff Member *Endeavor Agency LLC
(LA)*
9601 Wilshire Blvd Fl 3
Beverly Hills, CA 90210-5204, USA

Bowles, Peter
125 Gloucester Rd
London, ENGLAND SW7, UNITED
KINGDOM (UK)

Bowlin, Hoss (Baseball Player)
Kansas City A's
PO Box 1026
Livingston, AL 35470-1026, USA

Bowling, Andy (Football Player)
Atlanta Falcons
7421 Straightstone Rd
Long Island, VA 24569-2945, USA

Bowling, Orbie (Basketball Player)
Kentucky Colonels
10179 Frank Rd
Collierville, TN 38017-3623, USA

Bowling, Steve (Baseball Player)
Milwaukee Brewers
524 E 117th St S
Jenks, OK 74037-3618, USA

Bowling for Soup (Music Group)
c/o Staff Member *Agency Group Ltd, The
(UK)*
361-373 City Road
London EC1V 1PQ, UNITED KINGDOM
(UK)

Bowman, Bob (Baseball Player)
Philadelphia Phillies
702 W Mountain Ridge Rd
Lake Almanor, CA 96137-9585, USA

Bowman, Christopher (Figure Skater)
5653 Kester Ave
Van Nuys, CA 91411-3310, USA

Bowman, Elizabeth (Golfer)
82 Davidson St
Chula Vista, CA 91910-3002, USA

Bowman, Harry W (Business Person)
Outboard Marine
1325 Remington Rd Ste H
Schaumburg, IL 60173-4815, USA

Bowman, Jim (Football Player)
New England Patriots
12 Stony Field Rd
Norton, MA 02766-1143, USA

Bowman, Ken (Football Player)
Green Bay Packers
2278 E Celosia Way
Oro Valley, AZ 85755-7166, USA

Bowman, Kirk (Hockey Player)
Chicago Blackhawks
740 Point Pelee Drive RR 1
Leamington, ON N8H 3V4, CANADA

Bowman, Pasco M II (Judge)
US Court of Appeals
US Courthouse
811 Grand Ave
Kansas City, MO 64106, USA

Bowman, W Scott (Scotty) (Coach,
Hockey Player, Misc)
56 Halston Pkwy
East Amherst, NY 14051-1842, USA

Bownass, Jack (Hockey Player)
Montreal Canadians
PO Box 117 GD
Belair, MB R0E 0E0, CANADA

Bownes, Fabien (Football Player)
Chicago Bears
8127 149th Pl NE Unit B112
Redmond, WA 98052-6582, USA

Bowsfield, Ted (Baseball Player)
Boston Red Sox
PO Box 1492
Nipomo, CA 93444-1492, USA

Bowyer, William (Artist)
12 Cleveland Ave Chiswick
London W4 1SN, UNITED KINGDOM
(UK)

Bowyer Jr, Walter (Football Player)
Denver Broncos
75 Avalon Ave
Oakville, CT 06779-2001, USA

Boxberger, Loa (Bowler)
PO Box 708
Russell, KS 67665-0708, USA

Boxleitner, Bruce (Actor)
23679 Calabasas Rd # 181
Calabasas, CA 91302-1502, USA

Boy Hits Car (Music Group)
c/o Staff Member *Wind-up Records*
72 Madison Ave Fl 8
New York, NY 10016-8731, USA

Boyar, Lombardo (Actor)
Greene & Associates
526 N Larchmont Blvd Ste 201
Los Angeles, CA 90004-1300, USA

Boyarsky, Jerry (Football Player)
New Orleans Saints
RR 1 Box 357
Olyphant, PA 18447-9735, USA

Boyce, Kim (Music Group)
200 Nathan Dr
Hollister, MO 65672-6123, USA

Boycott, Geoffrey (Cricketer)
Cricket Club
Headingley Cricket Ground Leeds
Yorks LS6 3BY, UNITED KINGDOM (UK)

Boyd, Alan S (Misc, Secretary)
437 5th Ave S Apt 3D
Edmonds, WA 98020-3460, USA

Boyd, Billy (Actor)
c/o Sarah Jackson *Seven Summits Pictures
& Management*
8906 W Olympic Blvd Ground Floor
Beverly Hills, CA 90211, USA

Boyd, Bob (Baseball Player)
Memphis Red Sox
2811 N Vassar St
Wichita, KS 67220-2437, USA

Boyd, Bob (Football Player)
Los Angeles Rams
2105 Lansdowne Dr
Garland, TX 75040-3343, USA

Boyd, Brandon (Musician)
c/o Marlene Tsuchii *Creative Artists
Agency LCC (CAA-LA)*
2000 Avenue Of The Stars
Los Angeles, CA 90067-4700, USA

Boyd, Brent (Football Player)
Minnesota Vikings
948 N Coast Highway 101 Apt 185
Encinitas, CA 92024-2078, USA

Boyd, Cayden (Actor)
c/o Ellen Drantch-Billet *James/Levy/
Jacobson Management*
3500 W Olive Ave Ste 1470
Burbank, CA 91505-5514, USA

Boyd, Cletis L (Clete) (Baseball Player)
2034 20th Avenue Pkwy
Indian Rocks Beach, FL 33785-2967, USA

Boyd, Davis (Oil Can) (Baseball Player)
PO Box 8058
Meridian, MS 39303-8058, USA

Boyd, Dennis (Baseball Player)
Boston Red Sox
903 23rd St
Meridian, MS 39301-2530, USA

Boyd, Fred (Basketball Player)
Philadelphia 76ers
10915 Open Trail Rd
Bakersfield, CA 93311-2892, USA

Boyd, Gary (Baseball Player)
Cleveland Indians
15308 Haas Ave
Gardena, CA 90249-4239, USA

Boyd, Greg (Baseball Player)
9 Inez Way
Stafford, VA 22554-5515, USA

Boyd, Greg P (Football Player)
New England Patriots
4021 N 59th St
Phoenix, AZ 85018-4614, USA

Boyd, Herbert W (Inventor, Misc)
PO Box 7318
Rancho Santa Fe, CA 92067-7318, USA

Boyd, James (Football Player)
Jacksonville Jaguars
3711 Breeze Port Arch
Chesapeake, VA 23321-3184, USA

Boyd, Jason (Baseball Player)
Pittsburgh Pirates
412 Hillsboro Ave
Edwardsville, IL 62025-1730, USA

Boyd, Jenna (Actor)
c/o Ellen Drantch-Billet *James/Levy/
Jacobson Management*
3500 W Olive Ave Ste 1470
Burbank, CA 91505-5514, USA

Boyd, Malcolm (Religious Leader, Writer)
Saint Augustine-by-Sea Episcpal Church
1227 4th St
Santa Monica, CA 90401-1303, USA

Boyd, Malik (Football Player)
Minnesota Vikings
5815 Fairway Manor Ln
Spring, TX 77373-4988, USA

Boyd, Paul D (Nobel Prize Laureate)
1033 Somera Rd
Los Angeles, CA 90077-2625, USA

Boyd, Randy (Hockey Player)
Pittsburgh Penguins
1769 Blackwillow Dr
Marietta, GA 30066-1954, USA

Boyd, Richard A (Misc)
Fraternal Order of Police
2100 Gardiner Ln
Louisville, KY 40205-2962, USA

Boyd, Robert (Golfer)
828 Robert E Lee Dr
Wilmington, NC 28412-7138, USA

Boyd, Stephen (Football Player)
Detroit Lions
1805 Golf Ridge Dr
Bloomfield Hills, MI 48302-1721, USA

Boyd, Tanya (Actor)
Amsel Eisenstadt Frazier
5055 Wilshire Blvd Ste 860
Los Angeles, CA 90036-6108, USA

Boyens, Philippa (Writer)
c/o Nick Reed *International Creative
Management (ICM-LA)*
10250 Constellation Blvd
Los Angeles, CA 90067-6200, USA

Boyer, Brant (Football Player)
Miami Dolphins
5375 W 4680 S
Hooper, UT 84315, USA

Boyer, Clete (Baseball Player)
Kansas City A's
2034 20th Avenue Pkwy
Indian Rocks Beach, FL 33785-2967, USA

Boyer, Cloyd (Baseball Player)
St Louis Cardinals
14528 County Road 210
Jasper, MO 64755, USA

Boyer, Jacqueline
162 rue Perronet
Neuilly s/s 92200, FRANCE

Boyer, Mark (Football Player)
Indianapolis Colts
21942 Kaneohe Ln
Huntington Beach, CA 92646-7828, USA

Boyer, Verdi (Football Player)
Brooklyn Dodgers
300 N Lake Ave Ste 930
Pasadena, CA 91101-4106, USA

Boyer, Wally (Hockey Player)
Toronto Maple Leafs
400 Manly St
Midland, ON L4R 3E3, CANADA

Boyet, William
PO Box 1805
Studio City, CA 91614-0805, USA

Boyett, Lon (Football Player)
San Fransisco 49ers
44361 Nolina Cir
Lancaster, CA 93536-6252, USA

Boyette, Garland (Football Player)
St Louis Cardinals
4003 E Valley Dr
Missouri City, TX 77459-4322, USA

Boykin, Deral (Football Player)
Los Angeles Rams
350 Silver Oaks Dr Apt 7
Kent, OH 44240-4165, USA

Boykin, William G (General)
DepUndersecretary Intelligence
Defense Dept Pentagon
Washington, DC 20301-0001, USA

Boyko, Darren (Hockey Player)
Winnipeg Jets
1099 Aberdeen Ave
Winnipeg, MB R2X 0X1, CANADA

Boylan, Eileen (Actor)
c/o Staff Member *Stone Manners Talent &
Literary (LA)*
6500 Wilshire Blvd Ste 550
Los Angeles, CA 90048-4950, USA

Boylan, Jeanne
c/o Staff Member *William Morris Agency
(WMA-LA)*
1 William Morris Pl
Beverly Hills, CA 90212-4261, USA

Boylan, Jim (Football Player)
Minnesota Vikings
13155 Portofino Dr
Del Mar, CA 92014-3827, USA

Boyland, Dorian (Baseball Player)
Pittsburgh Pirates
15570 SW Cynthia Ln
Beaverton, OR 97007-6867, USA

Boyle, Clune Charlotte (Swimmer)
50 Browns Grv # 31
Scottsville, NY 14546-1302, USA

Boyle, Dan (Hockey Player)
Florida Panthers
4703 W Heron Ln
Tampa, FL 33629-5557, USA

Boyle, Danny (Director)
International Creative Management
76 Oxford St
London W1N 0AX, UNITED KINGDOM
(UK)

Boyle, Jim (Football Player)
5411 Style Ln
Cincinnati, OH 45238-4236, USA

Boyle, Lara Flynn (Actor)
c/o Gina Rugolo-Judd *Rigberg-Rugolo
Entertainment*
1180 S Beverly Dr Ste 601
Los Angeles, CA 90035-1158, USA

Boyle, Lisa (Actor, Model)
7336 Santa Monica Blvd # 776
W Hollywood, CA 90046-6616, USA

Boyle, T Coraghessan (Writer)
University of Southern California
English Dept
Los Angeles, CA 90089-0001, USA

Boyles, Harry (Baseball Player)
Chicago White Sox
RR 6 Box 17
Eufaula, OK 74432-9153, USA

Boynes, Winford (Basketball Player)
New Jersey Nets
8979 Haflinger Way
Elk Grove, CA 95757-3262, USA

Boynton, George (Football Player)
Oakland Raiders
917 Sartain Dr
Andrews, TX 79714-3817, USA

Boynton, John (Football Player)
Miami Dolphins
203 Pratt St
Pikeville, TN 37367, USA

Boynton, Robert M (Doctor, Misc)
376 Bellaire St
Del Mar, CA 92014-2207, USA

Boynton, Sandra (Artist, Misc)
Recycled Paper Products
3636 N Broadway St
Chicago, IL 60613-4568, USA

Boysaw, Gregory (Football Player)
New York Giants
3421 Derby Dr
Jonesboro, AR 72404-7796, USA

Boysen, Sarah (Misc)
Ohio State University
Psychology Dept
Columbus, OH 43210, USA

boysetsfire (Music Group)
c/o Staff Member *Wind-up Records*
72 Madison Ave Fl 8
New York, NY 10016-8731, USA

Bozarth, Marci (Golfer)
6510A Hart Ln
Austin, TX 78731-3139, USA

Boze, Marshall (Baseball Player)
Milwaukee Brewers
3210 Breckenridge Dr
Springfield, IL 62704-5508, USA

Bozek, Steve (Hockey Player)
Los Angeles Kings
8410 E Whispering Wind Dr
Scottsdale, AZ 85255-2863, USA

Bozilovic, Ivana (Actor)
c/o Jon Orlando *Xposure Public Relations*
8271 Melrose Ave Ste 110
Los Angeles, CA 90046-6800, USA

Boznic, Josip Cardinal (Religious Leader)
Zagreb Archdiocese
Kaptol 31 PP 553
Zagreb Hrvatska 10001, CROATIA

Bozo, Laura (Actor)
c/o Staff Member *Telemundo*
2470 W 8th Ave
Hialeah, FL 33010-2000, USA

BR5-49
9830 Wilshire Blvd
Beverly Hills, CA 90212-1804, USA

Braase, Ordeil (Football Player)
15549 W Clear Canyon Dr
Surprise, AZ 85374-4563, USA

Braase, Ordell (Football Player)
Baltimore Colts
204 3rd St W Apt 201
Bradenton, FL 34205-8857, USA

Brabham, Daniel (Football Player)
Houston Oilers
16378 Pailette St
Prairieville, LA 70769-6230, USA

Brabham, John A (Jack) (Race Car Driver)
5 Ruxley Lane Ewell
Surrey KT19 0JB, UNITED KINGDOM
(UK)

Brabham, Sir Jack
Box 654
Miranda NSW 2228, AUSTRALIA

Bracco, Lorraine (Actor)
c/o Heather Reynolds *One Entertainment*
(NY)
12 W 57th St Ph
New York, NY 10019-3900, USA

Brace, William F (Geophysicist, Misc,
Physicist)
49 Liberty St
Concord, MA 01742-1715, USA

Bracelin, Greg (Football Player)
Denver Broncos
5465 Calumet Ave
La Jolla, CA 92037-7604, USA

Bracey, Steve (Basketball Player)
Atlanata Hawks
142 Van Buren St
Brooklyn, NY 11221-1319, USA

Bracher, Karl D (Historian, Misc,
Politician)
Unversitat Bonn
Stationsweg 17
Bonn 53127, GERMANY

Bracht, Stephanie (Golfer)
2004 Delancey Dr
Norman, OK 73071-3872, USA

Brack, Kenny (Race Car Driver)
Team Rahal
4601 Lyman Dr
Hilliard, OH 43026-1249, USA

Brack, Reginald K Jr (Publisher)
12 Huntzinger Dr
Greenwich, CT 06831-4110, USA

Bracken, Don (Football Player)
Green Bay Packers
107 1/2 Malaga Ave
Birmingham, AL 35209-2024, USA

Brackenburry, Curt (Hockey Player)
Quebec Nordiques
76212 Evergreen Bluff Dr
South Haven, MI 49090-1662, USA

Brackens, Tony (Football Player)
Jacksonville Jaguars
193 Private Road 407
Fairfield, TX 75840-6022, USA

Brackett, Griffin (Model)
860 NE 73rd St
Miami, FL 33138-5228, USA

Brackett, M L (Football Player)
Chicago Bears
1216 Monte Vista Dr
Gadsden, AL 35904-3643, USA

Brackins, Charles (Football Player)
Green Bay Packers
6423 Hanley Ln
Houston, TX 77016-2015, USA

Bradberry, Gary (Race Car Driver)
c/o Tri Star Motorsports
6006 Ball Park Rd
Thomasville, NC 27360-7942, USA

Bradbury, Janette Lane (Actor)
10817 King St
Toluca Lake, CA 91602, USA

Bradbury, Ray D (Writer)
10265 Cheviot Dr
Los Angeles, CA 90064-4737, USA

Brademas, John (Educator)
New York University
Presindent's Emeritus Office
New York, NY 10012, USA

Braden, Vic (Coach, Tennis Player)
22000 Trabuco Canyon Road
Trabuco Canyon, CA 92678, USA

Bradford, Barbara Taylor (Writer)
Bradford Enterprises
450 Park Ave Ste 2303
New York, NY 10022-2688, USA

Bradford, Buddy (Baseball Player)
Chicago White Sox
6440 Springpark Ave
Los Angeles, CA 90056-2222, USA

Bradford, Chad (Baseball Player)
Chicago White Sox
3867 Bill Downing Rd
Raymond, MS 39154-8097, USA

Bradford, Jesse (Actor)
c/o Jason Barrett *Alchemy Entertainment*
1401 Ocean Ave # 301
Santa Monica, CA 90401-2106, USA

Bradford, Paul (Football Player)
San Diego Chargers
2239 Pulgas Ave
Palo Alto, CA 94303-1755, USA

Bradford, Richard (Actor)
2511 Canyon Dr
Los Angeles, CA 90068-2415, USA

Bradford, Ronnie (Football Player)
Denver Broncos
965 Allen Lake Ln
Suwanee, GA 30024-4179, USA

Bradford, William (Business Person)
Halliburton Co
500 N Akard St
Lincoln Plaza
Dallas, TX 75201-3302, USA

Bradfute, Byron (Football Player)
Dallas Texans
939 Moonglow Ave
New Braunfels, TX 78130-6081, USA

Bradlee, Benjamin C (Editor)
3014 N St NW
Washington, DC 20007-3404, USA

Bradley, Alonzo (Basketball Player)
Houston Rockets
1713 Briaroaks Dr
Flower Mound, TX 75028-3482, USA

Bradley, Bert (Baseball Player)
Oakland A's
RR 1
Toledo, IL 62468, USA

Bradley, Bill (Basketball Player)
New York Knicks
10 Crestmont Rd Apt 6M
Montclair, NJ 07042-1933, USA

Bradley, Bob (Coach, Soccer Player)
Chicago Fire
7000 S Harlem Ave
Bridgeview, IL 60455-1160, USA

Bradley, Brian (Hockey Player)
Calgary Flames
6417 E Maclaurin Dr
Tampa, FL 33647-1171, USA

Bradley, Bruce (Athlete, Misc)
262 Saint Joseph Ave
Long Beach, CA 90803-1720, USA

Bradley, Carlos (Football Player)
San Diego Chargers
1316 E Cliveden St
Philadelphia, PA 19119-3948, USA

Bradley, Dave (Football Player)
Green Bay Packers
30 Hillside Dr
Lewistown, PA 17044-9307, USA

Bradley, Dick (Cartoonist, Misc)
10176 Corporate Square Dr Ste 200
Saint Louis, MO 63132-2924, USA

Bradley, Dudley (Basketball Player)
Indiana Pacers
9830 Clanford Rd
Randallstown, MD 21133-2508, USA

Bradley, Ed (Football Player)
Chicago Bears
PO Box 1313
Winston Salem, NC 27102-1313, USA

Bradley, Ed (Football Player)
Pittsburgh Steelers
187 Fryes Creek Ln
Clemmons, NC 27012-6838, USA

Bradley, Frank (Baseball Player)
Kansas City Monarchs
PO Box 516
Benton, LA 71006-0516, USA

Bradley, Fred (Baseball Player)
Chicago White Sox
4540 Layman Ave
Pico Rivera, CA 90660-2022, USA

Bradley, Freddie (Football Player)
San Diego Chargers
229 S Ventura Rd
Port Hueneme, CA 93041-3368, USA

Bradley, Gordon (Coach, Soccer Player)
14300 Bakerwood Pl
Haymarket, VA 20169-2638, USA

Bradley, James (Actor)
1565 Riverside Dr # 4
Glendale, CA 91201, USA

Bradley, Kathleen (Actor)
Kazarian/Spencer
11365 Ventura Blvd Ste 100
Studio City, CA 91604-3148, USA

Bradley, Luther (Football Player)
Detroit Lions
19575 Stratford Rd
Detroit, MI 48221-1848, USA

Bradley, Marion Zimmer (Writer)
c/o Russell Galen *Scovil-Chichak-Galen*
Literary Agency
276 5th Ave Rm 708
New York, NY 10001-4509, USA

Bradley, Mark (Baseball Player)
Los Angeles Dodgers
515 Savannah Ave Apt C
Elizabethtown, KY 42701-2386, USA

Bradley, Michael (Basketball Player)
6150 Blackjack Ct N
Punta Gorda, FL 33982-9606, USA

Bradley, Michael (Mike) (Golfer)
17914 Burnt Oak Ln
Lithia, FL 33547-4802, USA

Bradley, Milton (Baseball Player)
Montreal Expos
801 N Maria Ave
Redondo Beach, CA 90277-2243, USA

Bradley, Otha (Football Player)
San Diego Chargers
PO Box 59071
Los Angeles, CA 90059-0071, USA

Bradley, Patricia E (Pat) (Golfer)
Opus
PO Box 116
Cheboygan, MI 49721-0116, USA

Bradley, Phil (Baseball Player)
Seattle Mariners
6950 Seminole Ct
Columbia, MO 65203-9669, USA

Bradley, Rebecca (Golfer)
14443 W Lee Shore Dr
Willis, TX 77318-7407, USA

Bradley, Robert A (Physicist)
2465 S Downing St
Denver, CO 80210-5822, USA

Bradley, Ryan (Baseball Player)
New York Yankees
3454 Alder Pl
Chino Hills, CA 91709-2005, USA

Bradley, Scott (Baseball Player)
New York Yankees
43 Chicory Ln
Pennington, NJ 08534-1926, USA

Bradley, Shawn (Basketball Player)
Philadelphia 76ers
PO Box 744
Highway 10
Castle Dale, UT 84513-0744, USA

Bradley, Tom (Baseball Player)
California Angels
4104 Woodberry St
University Park, MD 20782-1169, USA

Bradley, William W (Bill) (Basketball Player, Senator)
711 5th Ave Fl 9
New York, NY 10022-3111, USA

Bradley-Boyd, Grace
23872 Marmara Bay
Monarch Beach, CA 92629-4411, USA

Bradley Jr, Harold (Football Player)
Cleveland Browns
1302 Asbury Ave
Evanston, IL 60201-4108, USA

Bradshaw (Wrestler)
139 Denny Ln
Athens, TX 75751, USA

Bradshaw, James A (Football Player)
Pittsburgh Steelers
449 Tresham Rd
Gahanna, OH 43230-2224, USA

Bradshaw, John E (Actor, Director, Writer)
c/o Victoria Wisdom *Becsey/Wisdom/Kalajian*
849 S Wooster St Apt 7
Los Angeles, CA 90035-1792, USA

Bradshaw, Morris (Football Player)
Oakland Raiders
82 Steuben Bay
Alameda, CA 94502-6406, USA

Bradshaw, Terry (Baseball Player)
St Louis Cardinals
6605 Snow Geese Ln
Prince George, VA 23875-4620, USA

Bradshaw, Terry (Football Player, Sportscaster)
RR 1 Box 1033
Thackerville, OK 73459-9742, USA

Brady, Beau (Actor)
c/o Staff Member *Darren Gray Management*
2 Marston Lane
Portsmouth, Hampshire
PO3 5T, ENGLAND

Brady, Brian (Baseball Player)
California Angels
48 Gables Way
Jackson, NJ 08527-6310, USA

Brady, Charles E (Astronaut)
92 Red Wing Ln
Eastsound, WA 98245-8517, USA

Brady, Doug (Baseball Player)
Chicago White Sox
800 W Douglas Ave
Jacksonville, IL 62650-1826, USA

Brady, Ed (Football Player)
Los Angeles Rams
5755 White Path Ln
Liberty Twp, OH 45011-1273, USA

Brady, Jeff (Football Player)
Pittsburgh Steelers
16411 Burniston Dr
Tampa, FL 33647-2790, USA

Brady, Jim (Baseball Player)
Detroit Tigers
1072 Meadow View Ln
Saint Augustine, FL 32092-1055, USA

Brady, Kyle (Football Player)
New York Jets
2221 Alicia Ln
Atlantic Beach, FL 32233-5975, USA

Brady, Nicholas F (Misc, Secretary, Senator)
Darby Overseas Investments
1133 Connecticut Ave NW Ste 400
Washington, DC 20036-4361, USA

Brady, Pat (Cartoonist)
United Feature Syndicate
200 Madison Ave
New York, NY 10016-3911, USA

Brady, Patrick (Football Player)
Pittsburgh Steelers
8990 Lombardi Rd
Reno, NV 89511-9537, USA

Brady, Patrick H (War Hero)
2809 179th Ave E
Lake Tapps, WA 98391-6419, USA

Brady, Ray (Correspondent)
CBS-TV
524 W 57th St
News Dept
New York, NY 10019-2924, USA

Brady, Roscoe O (Misc)
6026 Valerian Ln
Rockville, MD 20852-3410, USA

Brady, Sarah (Activist)
Handgun Control
1225 I St NW Ste 1100
Washington, DC 20005-3991, USA

Brady, Tom (Actor)
c/o Stuart Fry *Endeavor Agency LLC (LA)*
9601 Wilshire Blvd Fl 3
Beverly Hills, CA 90210-5204, USA

Brady, Tom (Football Player)
c/o Staff Member *New England Patriots*
60 Washington St
Gillette Stadium - RR 1
Foxboro, MA 02035-1388, USA

Brady, Wayne (Actor, Comedian)
c/o Bernie Brillstein *Brillstein-Grey Entertainment*
9150 Wilshire Blvd Ste 350
Beverly Hills, CA 90212-3453, USA

Braeden, Eric (Actor)
c/o Staff Member *Diverse Talent Group*
1875 Century Park E Ste 2250
Los Angeles, CA 90067-2563, USA

Braff, Zach (Actor, Writer)
c/o Sandra Chang *Industry Entertainment*
955 Carrillo Dr Ste 300
Los Angeles, CA 90048-5400, USA

Braga, Alice (Actor)
c/o Will Ward *ROAR LLC*
9701 Wilshire Blvd Fl 8
Beverly Hills, CA 90212-2008, USA

Braga, Brannon (Writer)
c/o Staff Member *Endeavor Agency LLC (LA)*
9601 Wilshire Blvd Fl 3
Beverly Hills, CA 90210-5204, USA

Braga, Sonia (Actor)
41 River Ter Apt 1403
New York, NY 10282-1118, USA

Bragan, Bobby (Baseball Player)
Philadelphia Phillies
3116 W 6th St
Fort Worth, TX 76107-2712, USA

Bragg, Billy (Musician)
Sincere Mgmt
6 Bravington Road
#6
London W9 3AH, UNITED KINGDOM (UK)

Bragg, Darrell B (Misc)
University of British Columbia
Vancouver, BC V6T 2AZ, CANADA

Bragg, Darren (Baseball Player)
Seattle Mariners
163 Patriot Rd
Southbury, CT 06488-1274, USA

Bragg, Don
PO Box 171
New Gretna, NJ 08224-0171, USA

Bragg, Donald G (Don) (Athlete, Track Athlete)
554 Mt Dell Dr
Clayton, CA 94517-1503, USA

Bragg, Melvyn (Writer)
12 Hampstead Hill Gardens
London NW3 2PL, UNITED KINGDOM (UK)

Bragg, Mike (Football Player)
Washington Redskins
212 Park Terrace Ct SE Apt 78
Vienna, VA 22180-5886, USA

Braggs, Byron (Football Player)
Green Bay Packers
19469 Mill Dam Pl
Leesburg, VA 20176-8428, USA

Braggs, Glenn (Baseball Player)
Milwaukee Brewers
4827 Azucena Rd
Woodland Hills, CA 91364-4039, USA

Braggs, Stephen (Football Player)
Cleveland Browns
120 Power House Rd
Lawndale, NC 28090-7407, USA

Bragin, Rob (Writer)
c/o Staff Member *William Morris Agency (WMA-LA)*
1 William Morris Pl
Beverly Hills, CA 90212-4261, USA

Bragnalo, Rick (Hockey Player)
Washington Capitals
515 Christine St E
Thunder Bay, ON P7E 4P3, CANADA

Bragonier, Dennis (Football Player)
San Fransisco 49ers
PO Box 1206
Roseville, CA 95678-8206, USA

Braham, Rich (Football Player)
Cincinatti Bengals
2522 Thirs Dr
Villa Hills, KY 41017-1165, USA

Brahaney, Thomas F (Tom) (Football Player)
St Louis Cardinals
17 Winchester Ct
Midland, TX 79705-6360, USA

Brainin, Nobert (Musician)
19 Prowse Ave
Busbey Heath
Herts WD2 1JS, UNITED KINGDOM (UK)

Brainville, Ives
34 Cours de Vincennes
Paris 75012, FRANCE

Brakes, The (Music Group)
c/o Staff Member *Paradigm (Monterey)*
509 Hartnell St
Monterey, CA 93940-2825, USA

Bramall of Busfield, Edwin N W (Misc)
House of Lords
Westminster
London SW1A 0PW, UNITED KINGDOM (UK)

Bramhall, Mark (Actor)
c/o Alexandra Karrys *Divine Management*
3822 Latrobe St
Los Angeles, CA 90031-1446, USA

Bramlett, Delaney (Musician)
PO Box 177
Sunland, CA 91041-0177, USA

Bramlett, John (Football Player)
Denver Broncos
159 Cotton Ridge Cv S
Cordova, TN 38018-7409, USA

Brammer, Mark (Football Player)
Buffalo Bills
1 Orchard Hill Dr
Orchard Park, NY 14127-3535, USA

Branagh, Kenneth (Actor, Director)
c/o Staff Member *Endeavor Agency LLC (LA)*
9601 Wilshire Blvd Fl 3
Beverly Hills, CA 90210-5204, USA

Branca, John G (Attorney, Attorney General, General)
Ziffren Brittenham Branca
1801 Century Park W
Los Angeles, CA 90067-6409, USA

Branca, Ralph (Baseball Player)
Brooklyn Dodgers
800 Westchester Ave Ste N409
Rye Brook, NY 10573-1328, USA

Brancato, Al (Baseball Player)
Philadelphia Athletics
108 Green Valley Rd
Upper Darby, PA 19082-1308, USA

Brancato, John D (JD) (Producer, Writer)
c/o Staff Member *Broder Webb Chervin Silbermann Agency, The (BWCS)*
10250 Constellation Blvd Ste P
Los Angeles, CA 90067-6213, USA

Brancato Jr, Lillo (Actor)
c/o Craig Shapiro *Innovative Artists (LA)*
1505 10th St
Santa Monica, CA 90401-2805, USA

Branch, Adrian (Basketball Player)
Los Angeles Lakers
18008 Fence Post Ct
Gaithersburg, MD 20877-3794, USA

Branch, Clifford (Cliff) (Coach, Football Coach, Football Player)
Oakland Raiders
2071 Stonefield Ln
Santa Rosa, CA 95403-0952, USA

Branch, Harvey (Baseball Player)
St Louis Cardinals
4995 Jolly Dr
Memphis, TN 38109-7123, USA

Branch, Michelle (Musician, Songwriter, Writer)
50 Indian Ruin Rd
Sedona, AZ 86351-7341, USA

Branch, Reggie (Football Player)
Washington Redskins
515 San Lanta Cir
Sanford, FL 32771-5903, USA

Branch, Roy (Baseball Player)
Seattle Mariners
5322 Terry Ave
Saint Louis, MO 63120-2021, USA

Branch, Vanessa (Actor)
c/o Staff Member *3 Arts Entertainment Inc*
9460 Wilshire Blvd Fl 7
Beverly Hills, CA 90212-2713, USA

Branch, William B (Writer)
53 Cortlandt Ave
New Rochelle, NY 10801-2032, USA

Brand, Colette (Skier)
Rigistr 24
Baar 6340, SWITZERLAND

Brand, Daniel (Dan) (Wrestler)
4321 Bridgeview Dr
Oakland, CA 94602-1910, USA

Brand, Elton (Basketball Player)
Los Angeles Clippers
1111 S Figueroa St
Staples Center
Los Angeles, CA 90015-1300, USA

Brand, Glen (Wrestler)
PO Box 6069
Omaha, NE 68106-0069, USA

Brand, Jolene
8321 Beverly Blvd
Los Angeles, CA 90048-2607, USA

Brand, Joshua (Producer)
c/o Staff Member *William Morris Agency (WMA-LA)*
1 William Morris Pl
Beverly Hills, CA 90212-4261, USA

Brand, Julie (Golfer)
6 Emerald Way
Ocala, FL 34472-2333, USA

Brand, Myles (Educator)
Indiana University
President's Office
Bloomington, IN 47405, USA

Brand, Neville (Actor)
c/o Staff Member *International Creative Management (ICM-LA)*
10250 Constellation Blvd
Los Angeles, CA 90067-6200, USA

Brand, Oscar (Musician, Songwriter, Writer)
Gypsy Hill Music
141 Baker Hill Rd
Great Neck, NY 11023-1715, USA

Brand, Robert (Designer)
508 W End Ave
New York, NY 10024-4328, USA

Brand, Ron (Baseball Player)
Pittsburgh Pirates
4421 Staten Island Dr
Plano, TX 75024-3867, USA

Brand, Steven (Actor)
c/o Benjamin Tappan *Bauer Company, The*
9300 Wilshire Blvd Ph
Beverly Hills, CA 90212-3213, USA

Brand, Vance D (Astronaut)
NASA Dryden Flight Center
PO Box 273
Edwards, CA 93523-0273, USA

Brandauer, Klaus Maria (Actor)
Novapool Gmbh
Paul Lincke Ufer 42-43
Berlin 10999, GERMANY

Brandenburg, Mark (Baseball Player)
Texas Rangers
9801 Cantertrot Dr
Humble, TX 77338, USA

Brandenstein, Daniel C (Astronaut)
12802 Tri City Beach Rd
Baytown, TX 77520-9216, USA

Brandes, John (Football Player)
Indianapolis Colts
905 Ashland Ct
Mansfield, TX 76063-3802, USA

Brandi (Model)
Next Model Mgmt
23 Watts St
New York, NY 10013, USA

Brandon, Barbara (Cartoonist)
Universal Press Syndicate
4520 Main St
Kansas City, MO 64111-1876, USA

Brandon, Clark (Actor)
Jennings Assoc
28035 Dorothy Dr Ste 210A
Agoura, CA 91301-2685, USA

Brandon, Darrell (Baseball Player)
Boston Red Sox
12 Southcliff Dr
Plymouth, MA 02360-1463, USA

Brandon, Jeb (Actor)
c/o Staff Member *Endeavor Agency LLC (LA)*
9601 Wilshire Blvd Fl 3
Beverly Hills, CA 90210-5204, USA

Brandon, John (Actor)
Coast to Coast Talent
3350 Barham Blvd
Los Angeles, CA 90068-1404, USA

Brandon, Michael (Actor)
Epstein-Wyckoff
280 S Beverly Dr Ste 400
Beverly Hills, CA 90212-3904, USA

Brandon, Michael (Football Player)
Indianapolis Colts
910 E Green St
Perry, FL 32347-3514, USA

Brands, Tom (Wrestler)
4494 Taft Ave SE
Iowa City, IA 52240-8166, USA

Brands, X (Actor)
17171 Roscoe Blvd # 104
Northridge, CA 91325-4060, USA

Brandt, Hank (Actor)
Contemporary Artists
610 Santa Monica Blvd Ste 202
Santa Monica, CA 90401-1645, USA

Brandt, Jackie (Baseball Player)
New York Giants
611 Osage Dr
Papillion, NE 68046-2432, USA

Brandt, Jim (Football Player)
Pittsburgh Steelers
714 Zumbro Dr NW
Rochester, MN 55901-2379, USA

Brandt, Jon (Musician)
Monterey Peninsula Artists
509 Hartnell St
Monterey, CA 93940-2825, USA

Brandt, Paul (Musician)
c/o Staff Member *William Morris Agency (WMA-LA)*
1 William Morris Pl
Beverly Hills, CA 90212-4261, USA

Brandt, Victor (Actor)
H David Moss
733 Seward St Ph
Los Angeles, CA 90038-3503, USA

Branduardi, Angelo
Viale di Trastevere 1-108
Rome I-00153, ITALY

Brandy, J C (Actor)
Henderson/Hogan
8285 W Sunset Blvd Ste 1
West Hollywood, CA 90046-2420, USA

Brandywine, Marcia (Correspondent)
743 Huntley Dr
Los Angeles, CA 90069-5008, USA

Brannagh, Brigid (Actor)
c/o Adam Levine *Anthem Entertainment*
6100 Wilshire Blvd Ste 1170
Los Angeles, CA 90048-5116, USA

Brannan, Charles F (Secretary)
3131 E Alameda Ave
Denver, CO 80209-3409, USA

Brannan, Solomon (Football Player)
Kansas City Cheifs
2500 Cascade Rd SW
Atlanta, GA 30311-3228, USA

Brannon, Ronald (Religious Leader)
Wesleyan Church
PO Box 50434
Indianapolis, IN 46250-0434, USA

Brannum, Bob (Basketball Player)
Sheboygan Redskins
331 Furnace St
Marshfield, MA 02050-2324, USA

Branson, Brad (Basketball Player)
Cleavland Cavaliers
10714 Meadow Lake Ln
Houston, TX 77042-2815, USA

Branson, Jeff (Baseball Player)
Cincinnati Reds
10749 Spokane Ct
Union, KY 41091-7160, USA

Branson, Jeff Branson (Actor)
c/o Robert Attermann *Abrams Artists Agency (LA)*
9200 W Sunset Blvd Ph 11
Los Angeles, CA 90069-3601, USA

Branson, Jesse (Basketball Player)
Philadelphia 76ers
309 Forest Dr
Graham, NC 27253-4405, USA

Branson, Richard (Business Person)
Virgin Group
120 Campden Hill Rd
London W8 7AR, UNITED KINGDOM (UK)

Brant, Marshall (Baseball Player)
New York Yankees
604 Scotland Dr
Santa Rosa, CA 95409-4419, USA

Brant, Tim (Sportscaster)
ABC-TV
77 W 66th St
Sports Dept
New York, NY 10023-6201, USA

Brantley, Betsy (Actor)
c/o Staff Member *Mitchell K Stubbs & Assoc (MKS)*
8695 Washington Blvd Ste 204
Culver City, CA 90232-7419, USA

Brantley, Chris (Football Player)
Los Angeles Rams
257 Hamilton Rd
Teaneck, NJ 07666-6367, USA

Brantley, Cliff (Baseball Player)
Philadelphia Phillies
42 Morningstar Rd
Staten Island, NY 10303-2809, USA

Brantley, Jeff (Baseball Player)
San Francisco Giants
2 Saint Charles Pl
Clinton, MS 39056-9301, USA

Brantley, John (Football Player)
Houston Oilers
1300 Pimlico Ln
Bishop, GA 30621-6215, USA

Brantley, Mickey (Baseball Player)
Seattle Mariners
3089 SW Ventura St
Port Saint Lucie, FL 34953-4220, USA

Brantley, Ollie (Baseball Player)
Memphis Red Sox
215 S Alabama St
Marianna, AR 72360-2578, USA

Brantley, Rick (Musician)
c/o Staff Member *Paradigm (Monterey)*
509 Hartnell St
Monterey, CA 93940-2825, USA

Brantley, Scot (Football Player)
Tampa Bay Buccaneers
11309 Galleria Dr
Tampa, FL 33618-8748, USA

Branton, Gene (Football Player)
Tampa Bay Buccaneers
7008 Hazelhurst Ct
Tampa, FL 33615-2945, USA

Branyan, Russ (Baseball Player)
Cleveland Indians
13400 Osmond Rd
Burton, OH 44021-9519, USA

Brasar, Per-Olov (Hockey Player)
Minnesota North Stars
Heden 99
Leksland 793 92, SWEDEN

Brasco, Jim (Basketball Player)
Syracuse Nationals
225 W Neck Rd
Huntington, NY 11743-2458, USA

Brashares, Ann (Writer)
c/o Jennifer Rudolph Walsh *William Morris Agency (WMA-LA)*
1 William Morris Pl
Beverly Hills, CA 90212-4261, USA

Brashear, Carl (Misc)
3 Stuttaford Dr
Sandston, VA 23150-1434, USA

Brasi, TinoVia Ferraioli
Isola Farnesi
Rome I-00123, ITALY

Braslow, Paul (Artist)
118 Saint Thomas Way
Belvedere Tiburon, CA 94920-1032, USA

Brassette, Amy (Actor)
c/o Marv Dauer *Marv Dauer Management*
11661 San Vicente Blvd Ste 104
Los Angeles, CA 90049-5150, USA

Brasseur, Claude (Actor)
Artmedia
20 Ave Rapp
Paris 75007, FRANCE

Brathwaite, Nicholas (Prime Minister)
House of Representatives
Saint George's, GRENADA

Bratkowski, Edmund R (Zeke) (Coach, Football Player)
Chicago Bears
224 Anchors Lake Dr N
Santa Rosa Beach, FL 32459-4106, USA

Bratt, Benjamin (Actor)
c/o Nina Nisenholtz *N2N Entertainment*
1230 Montana Ave Apt 203
Santa Monica, CA 90403-5987, USA

Bratton, Creed (Musician)
Thomas Cassidy
11761 E Speedway Blvd
Tucson, AZ 85748-2017, USA

Bratton, Jason (Football Player)
Buffalo Bills
1104 Regal Oak Dr
Longview, TX 75604-2141, USA

Bratton, Joseph K (General)
5902 Blakeford Dr
Windermere, FL 34786-5601, USA

Bratton, William J (Lawyer)
Los Angeles Police Dept
150 S Los Angeles St
Los Angeles, CA 90012, USA

Bratz, Mike (Basketball Player)
7503 Tillman Hill Rd
Colleyville, TX 76034-6929, USA

Bratzke, Chad (Football Player)
New York Giants
237 S Washington Dr
Sarasota, FL 34236-1720, USA

Brauer, Arik (Artist)
Academy of Fine Arts
Schillerplatz 3
Vienna 1010, AUSTRIA

Braugher, Andre (Actor)
361 Charlton Ave
South Orange, NJ 07079, USA

Brauman, John (Misc)
849 Tolman Dr
Palo Alto, CA 94305-1025, USA

Braun, Allen (Scientist)
National Institute on Deafness
9000 Rockville Pike
Bethesda, MD 20892-0001, USA

Braun, Carl (Basketball Player, Coach)
5603 SE Foxcross Pl
Stuart, FL 34997-8044, USA

Braun, John (Baseball Player)
Milwaukee Braves
4711 Westerly Ct
Oceanside, CA 92056-3001, USA

Braun, Lillian Jackson (Writer)
Blanche Gregory Inc
2 Tudor Place
New York, NY 10017, USA

Braun, Pinkas (Actor, Director)
Unterdorf
8261
Hemishofen/SH, SWITZERLAND

Braun, Richard L (War Hero)
1912 Whittle Wood Road
Williamsburg, VA 23185, USA

Braun, Steve (Actor)
c/o Tiffany Kuzon *Evolution Entertainment (LA)*
901 N Highland Ave
Los Angeles, CA 90038-2412, USA

Braun, Steve (Baseball Player)
Minnesota Twins
14300 Hickory Links Ct Apt 181
Fort Myers, FL 33912-7887, USA

Braun, Tamara (Actor)
c/o Staff Member *General Hospital*
500 S Buena Vista St
Burbank, CA 91521-0001, USA

Braun, Wendy (Actor)
c/o Staff Member *The House of Representatives*
211 S Beverly Dr Ste 208
Beverly Hills, CA 90212-3879, USA

Braunduardi, Angelo
Viale Travestere
Rome 1-10800153, ITALY

Braunwald, Eugene (Physicist)
Partners Healthcare
800 Boylston St
Boston, MA 02199-8001, USA

Braver, Rita (Correspondent)
CBS-TV
2020 M St NW
News Dept
Washington, DC 20036-3304, USA

Braverman, Bart (Actor)
House of Representatives
211 S Beverly Dr Ste 208
Beverly Hills, CA 90212-3879, USA

Braverman, Chuck (Director, Producer)
Braverman Productions Inc
3000 Olympic Blvd
Santa Monica, CA 90404-5073, USA

Bravo, Alex (Football Player)
Los Angeles Rams
2316 Pine Ave
Manhattan Beach, CA 90266-2835, USA

Bravo, Tony (Actor)
c/o Staff Member *Televisa*
Blvd Adolfo Lopez Mateos 232
Colonia San Angel INN
DF CP 01060, MEXICO

Braxton, Anthony (Composer)
Berkeley Agency
2608 9th St
Berkeley, CA 94710-2550, USA

Braxton, David (Football Player)
Minnesota Vikings
26898 Primrose Ln
Westlake, OH 44145-5487, USA

Braxton, Toni (Musician, Songwriter, Writer)
c/o Brad Cafarelli *Bragman/Nyman/ Cafarelli (BNC)*
8687 Melrose Ave Fl 8
Pacific Design Center
Los Angeles, CA 90069-5701, USA

Braxton, Tyrone S (Football Player)
Denver Broncos
455 Keamey St
Denver, CO 80220, USA

Braxton III, Hezekiah (Football Player)
San Diego Chargers
12715 Norwood Ln
Fort Washington, MD 20744-6312, USA

Bray, Deanne (Actor)
c/o Sid Craig *Craig Management*
2240 Miramonte Cir E Unit C
Palm Springs, CA 92264-5734, USA

Brayton, Tyler (Football Player)
Oakland Raiders
1220 Harbor Bay Pkwy
Alameda, CA 94502-6570, USA

Brazadskas, Algirdas (President)
Tumiskiu 30
Vilnius 2016, LITHUANIA

Brazelton, Dewon (Baseball Player)
Tampa Bay Devil Rays
107 Scenic Dr
Tullahoma, TN 37388-5422, USA

Brazelton, T Berry (Doctor)
23 Hawthorne St
Cambridge, MA 02138-4829, USA

Brazen, Randi
10138 Main St
Bellevue, WA 98004-6022, USA

Braziel, Larry (Football Player)
Baltimore Colts
831 Netherland Dr
Arlington, TX 76017-6019, USA

Brazil, Jeff (Journalist)
Orlando Sentinel
633 N Orange Ave
Editorial Dept
Orlando, FL 32801-1349, USA

Brazil, John R (Educator)
Bradley University
President's Office
Peoria, IL 61625-0001, USA

Brazile, Robert L Jr (Football Player)
Houston Oilers
263 Woodland Ave
Satsuma, AL 36572-2202, USA

Brazinsky, Sam (Football Player)
Buffalo Bisons
12 South St
Manville, NJ 08835-1861, USA

Brazzell, Chris (Football Player)
Dallas Cowboys
1205 Las Palmas Cir
Alice, TX 78332-3169, USA

Bready, Richard L (Business Person)
166 President Ave
Providence, RI 02906-4616, USA

Breaking Benjamin (Music Group)
c/o Staff Member *Hollywood Records*
500 S Buena Vista St
Burbank, CA 91521-0002, USA

Breaking Point (Music Group)
c/o Staff Member *Wind-up Records*
72 Madison Ave Fl 8
New York, NY 10016-8731, USA

Bream, Julian (Musician)
Hazard Chase
Richmond House
16-20 Regent St
Cambridge CB2 1DB, UNITED KINGDOM (UK)

Bream, Sid (Baseball Player)
Los Angeles Dodgers
115 Sabie Run
Zelienople, PA 16063, USA

Breathed, Berkeley (Cartoonist)
Washington Post Writers Group
1150 15th St NW
Washington, DC 20071-0001, USA

Breathwaite, Edward (Writer)
University of West Indies
History Dept
Mona
Kingston 7, JAMAICA

Breaux, Don (Football Player)
Denver Broncos
19027 Southport Dr
Cornelius, NC 28031-6478, USA

Breazeale, Jim (Baseball Player)
Atlanta Braves
1812 Sunset Ave
Bay City, TX 77414-4655, USA

Breck, Jonathan (Actor)
c/o Staff Member *Vanguard Management Group*
8060 Melrose Ave Fl 4th
Los Angeles, CA 90046-7038, USA

Breck, Peter (Actor)
c/o Karin Christopher *Sterling Artists Management Inc*
1836 West 5th Ave #207
Vancouver, BC V6J 1P3, CANADA

Breckenridge, Alex (Actor)
c/o Staff Member *Kohner Agency, The*
9300 Wilshire Blvd Ste 555
Beverly Hills, CA 90212-3211, USA

Breckenridge, Laura (Actor)
c/o Glenn Rigberg *Rigberg-Rugolo Entertainment*
1180 S Beverly Dr Ste 601
Los Angeles, CA 90035-1158, USA

Brecker, Randy (Musician)
Tropix International
163 3rd Ave # 206
New York, NY 10003-2523, USA

Brede, Brent (Baseball Player)
Minnesota Twins
1891 J Rock Rd
Trenton, IL 62293-2924, USA

Breder, Charles M (Misc)
6275 Manasola Key Road
Englewood, FL 34223, USA

Breding, Ed (Football Player)
Washington Redskins
126 NW Pritchard
Harlowton, MT 59036, USA

Bredsen, Espen (Skier)
Hellerud Gardsvei 18
Oslo 0671, NORWAY

Breech, Jim (Football Player)
Oakland Raiders
5155 Grandin Ridge Dr
Liberty Twp, OH 45011-8312, USA

Breeden, Danny (Baseball Player)
Cincinnati Reds
5111 B Ave
Loxley, AL 36551-4537, USA

Breeden, Hal (Baseball Player)
Chicago Cubs
665 Middle Rd S
Leesburg, GA 31763-3442, USA

Breeden, Louis (Football Player)
11264 Grooms Rd Ste E
Cincinnati, OH 45242-1418, USA

Breeden, Richard C (Government Official)
Coopers & Lybrand
1800 M St NW
Washington, DC 20036-5802, USA

Breeding, Marv (Baseball Player)
Baltimore Orioles
1800 Old Moulton Rd
Decatur, AL 35601-2146, USA

Breedlove, N Craig (Race Car Driver)
200 N Front St
Rio Vista, CA 94571-1420, USA

Breedlove, Rod (Football Player)
Pittsburgh Steelers
1664 Carlyle Dr Apt H
Crofton, MD 21114-1430, USA

Breen, Adrian (Football Player)
Cincinatti Bengals
6899 Longview Dr
Liberty Twp, OH 45011-7270, USA

Breen, Bobby (Actor)
10550 NW 71st Pl
Tamarac, FL 33321-2210, USA

Breen, Edward D (Business Person)
Tyco International
273 Corporate Dr # 100
Portsmouth, NH 03801-6807, USA

Breen, George (Swimmer)
425 Pepper Mill Ct
Sewell, NJ 08080-2963, USA

Breen, John G (Business Person)
18800 N Park Blvd
Shaker Heights, OH 44122-1809, USA

Breen, Monica (Writer)
c/o Staff Member *Endeavor Agency LLC
(LA)*
9601 Wilshire Blvd Fl 3
Beverly Hills, CA 90210-5204, USA

Breen, Patrick (Actor)
Gersh Agency
232 N Canon Dr
Beverly Hills, CA 90210-5302, USA

Breen, Shelley (Musician)
TBA Artists Mgmt
300 10th Ave S
Nashville, TN 37203-4125, USA

Breen, Stephen (Steve) (Cartoonist)
San Diego Union-Telegram
PO Box 120191
San Diego, CA 92112-0191, USA

Brees, Drew (Football Player)
c/o Staff Member *New Orleans Saints*
5800 Airline Dr
Metairie, LA 70003-3876, USA

Bregel, Jeff (Football Player)
San Fransisco 49ers
15431 Tulsa St Spc 33
Mission Hills, CA 91345-1349, USA

Bregman, Buddy (Actor)
c/o Staff Member *Paul Lane Entertainment*
468 N Camden Dr
Beverly Hills, CA 90210-4507, USA

Bregman Recht, Tracey (Actor)
Bell-Phillip Productions
7800 Beverly Blvd # 3371
Los Angeles, CA 90036-2112, USA

Brehaut, Jeff (Golfer)
1085 Leonello Ave
Los Altos, CA 94024-4914, USA

Breidenbach, Warren (Doctor)
Jewish Hospital
217 E Chestnut St
Surgery Dept
Louisville, KY 40202-1821, USA

Breiman, Valerie (Director)
c/o Staff Member *Industry Entertainment*
955 Carrillo Dr Ste 300
Los Angeles, CA 90048-5400, USA

Breining, Fred (Baseball Player)
San Francisco Giants
2120 Ticonderoga Dr
San Mateo, CA 94402-4045, USA

Breitenbach, Ken (Hockey Player)
Buffalo Sabres
12 Catherine St
St Catharines, ON L2R 5E5, CANADA

Breitenstien, Robert (Football Player)
Denver Broncos
8524 S Winston Ave
Tulsa, OK 74137-1914, USA

Breitner, Paul
Kuckucksweg 4
Brunnthal D-85649, GERMANY

Breitschwerdt, Werner (Business Person)
Daimler-Benz AG
Mercedesstr 136
Stuttgart 70322, GERMANY

Breland, Mark (Boxer)
PO Box 980
Denmark, SC 29042-0980, USA

Bremmer, Paul L (Politician, Writer)
c/o Staff Member *Simon & Schuster*
1230 6th Ave
New York, NY 10020-1586, USA

Bremmer, Rory
c/o Staff Member *BBC Artist Mail*
PO Box 1116
Belfast BT2 7AJ, UNITED KINGDOM
(UK)

Bremner, Ewen (Actor)
International Creative Mgmt
76 Oxford St
London W1N 0AX, UNITED KINGDOM
(UK)

Brenan, Gerald (Writer)
Alhaurin El Grande
Malaga, SPAIN

Brendel, Alfred (Musician)
Vanguard/Omega Classics
27 W 72nd St
New York, NY 10023-3498, USA

Brendel, Wolfgang (Opera Singer)
Manuela Kursiden
Wasagasse 12/1/3
Vienna 1090, AUSTRIA

Brenden, Hallgeir (Skier)
2417 Torberget
NORWAY

Brendi, Pavel (Hockey Player)
Philadelphia Flyers
1400 Edwards Mill Rd
Raleigh, NC 27607-3624, USA

Brendon, Nicholas (Actor)
Platform
2666 N Beachwood Dr
Los Angeles, CA 90068-2308, USA

Breneman, Curtis E (Misc)
38 Cartyle Ave
Troy, NY 12180, USA

Brenley, Bob (Baseball Player)
San Francisco Giants
9726 E Laurel Ln
Scottsdale, AZ 85260-5959, USA

Brennaman, Marty (Baseball Player,
Sportscaster)
Cincinnati Reds
2363 Heather Hill Blvd N
Cincinnati, OH 45244-2666, USA

Brennaman, Thom (Baseball Player,
Sportscaster)
Arizona Diamondbacks
738 Park Ave
Terrace Park, OH 45174-1021, USA

Brennan, Amy (Actor)
Creative Artists Agency
9830 Wilshire Blvd
Beverly Hills, CA 90212-1804, USA

Brennan, Bernard F (Business Person)
Montgomery Ward
822 Montgomery Ave Ste 204
Narberth, PA 19072-1946, USA

Brennan, Brian (Football Player)
Cleveland Browns
2961 Edgewood Rd
Cleveland, OH 44124-5101, USA

Brennan, Christine (Writer)
Washington Post
Sports Dept
1150 15th Ave NW
Washington, DC 20071-0001, USA

Brennan, Dan (Hockey Player)
Los Angeles Kings
1912 108 Ave
Dawson Creek, BC V1G 2T8, CANADA

Brennan, Edward A (Business Person)
AMR Corp
433 Amon Carter Blvd
Fort Worth, TX 76155, USA

Brennan, Joseph E (Governor)
104 Frances St
Portland, ME 04102-2512, USA

Brennan, Kevin (Actor, Comedian)
United Talent Agency
9560 Wilshire Blvd Ste 500
Beverly Hills, CA 90212-2401, USA

Brennan, Leo (Football Player)
Philadelphia Eagles
PO Box 1272
Marlborough, MA 01752-9272, USA

Brennan, Maire (Musician, Songwriter,
Writer)
Soho Agency
55 Fulham High St
London SW6 3JJ, UNITED KINGDOM
(UK)

Brennan, Melissa (Actor)
6520 Platt Ave # 634
West Hills, CA 91307-3218, USA

Brennan, Mike (Football Player)
Cincinnati Bengals
33660 Fox Rd
Easton, MD 21601-6746, USA

Brennan, Pete (Basketball Player)
New York Knicks
288-1 Route 23C
Jeweet, NY 12444, USA

Brennan, Rich (Hockey Player)
Colorado Avalanche
14 Reflection Way
South Yarmouth, MA 02664-2045, USA

Brennan, Terrance P (Terry) (Coach,
Football Player)
1731 Wildberry Dr Unit C
Glenview, IL 60025-1742, USA

Brennan, Tom (Baseball Player)
Cleveland Indians
10701 S Keating Ave Apt 2C
Oak Lawn, IL 60453-5465, USA

Brennan, William (Baseball Player)
Los Angeles Dodgers
802 Cottage Hill Dr
Macon, GA 31210-7628, USA

Brenneman, Amy (Actor, Producer,
Writer)
c/o Connie Tavel *Forward Entertainment*
9255 W Sunset Blvd Ste 805
Los Angeles, CA 90069-3305, USA

Brenneman, Jim (Baseball Player)
New York Yankees
16800 Pfeifer Way
Perris, CA 92570-8404, USA

Brenneman, John (Hockey Player)
Chicago Blackhawks
247 Radley Rd
Mississauga, ON L5G 2R6, CANADA

Brenner, Al (Football Player)
New York Giants
748 Maple St
Niles, MI 49120-3255, USA

Brenner, David (Actor, Comedian)
3749 Amber Lantern Cir
Las Vegas, NV 89147-6813, USA

Brenner, Dori (Actor)
210 W 101st St Apt 15C
New York, NY 10025-5040, USA

Brenner, Hoby (Football Player)
New Orleans Saints
40 Calle Ameno
San Clemente, CA 92672-2367, USA

Brenner, Lisa (Actor)
7729 W Sunset Blvd
Los Angeles, CA 90046, USA

Brenner, Sydney (Nobel Prize Laureate)
Salk Institute
10100 N Torrey Pines Rd
La Jolla, CA 92037, USA

Brenner, Teddy (Boxer)
24 W 55th St # 9C
New York, NY 10019-5320, USA

Brent, Eve (Actor)
Craig Mgmt
125 S Sycamore Ave
Los Angeles, CA 90036-2938, USA

Bresee, Bobbie (Actor)
PO Box 1222
Hollywood, CA 90078-1222, USA

Breslawsky, Marc C (Business Person)
Pitney Bowes Inc
1 Elmcroft Rd
Stamford, CT 06926-0700, USA

Breslin, Abigail (Actor)
c/o Staff Member *Coast to Coast Talent
Group*
3350 Barham Blvd
Los Angeles, CA 90068-1404, USA

Breslin, Jimmy (Journalist)
Newsday
235 Pinelawn Rd
Editorial Dept
Melville, NY 11747-4250, USA

Breslin, Spencer (Actor)
Cunningham/EscottDipene
10635 Santa Monica Blvd Ste 130
Los Angeles, CA 90025-8306, USA

Breslow, Lester (Physicist)
10926 Verano Rd
Los Angeles, CA 90077-2224, USA

Breslow, Ronald C (Misc)
295 Three Mile Harbor Rd
East Hampton, NY 11937-2014, USA

Bress, Eric (Director, Producer, Writer)
c/o Staff Member *Endeavor Agency LLC
(LA)*
9601 Wilshire Blvd Fl 3
Beverly Hills, CA 90210-5204, USA

Bressoud, Eddie (Baseball Player)
New York Giants
515 Marble Canyon Ln
San Ramon, CA 94582-4830, USA

Brest, Martin (Director, Producer)
831 Paseo Miramar
Pacific Palisades, CA 90272-3028, USA

Brett, George (Baseball Player)
Bayer Advantage Classic Tournament Office
4707 W 135th St
The Pride Of Kansas City Foundation
Leawood, KS 66224-9732, USA

Brett, Grorge (Baseball Player)
6512 Granada Dr
Prairie Village, KS 66208-1540, USA

Brett, Jonathan (Actor)
Agency for Performing Arts
405 S Beverly Dr Ste 500
Beverly Hills, CA 90212-4425, USA

Bretto, Joe (Hockey Player)
Philadelphia Flyers
10681 W Hacky Rd
Hibbing, MN 55746-8102, USA

Brettschneider, Carl (Football Player)
Chicago Cardinals
4649 Bird View Ct
Las Vegas, NV 89129-5326, USA

Breuer, Grit (Athlete, Track Athlete)
Konrad-Adenauer-Str 16
Garbsen 30823, GERMANY

Breuer, Jim (Comedian)
c/o Lee Kernis *Brillstein-Grey Entertainment*
9150 Wilshire Blvd Ste 350
Beverly Hills, CA 90212-3453, USA

Breunig, Robert P (Bob) (Football Player)
Dallas Cowboys
9215 Westview Cir
Dallas, TX 75231-2502, USA

Brew, Dorian (Football Player)
Baltimore Ravens
3965 Nara Dr
Florissant, MO 63033-3222, USA

Brewer, Albert P (Governor)
2520 Ashford Pl
Birmingham, AL 35243-2241, USA

Brewer, Billy (Baseball Player)
Kansas City Royals
7405 Woodway Dr
Waco, TX 76712-6153, USA

Brewer, Craig (Director, Producer, Writer)
c/o Staff Member *William Morris Agency (WMA-LA)*
1 William Morris Pl
Beverly Hills, CA 90212-4261, USA

Brewer, Derek Stanley (Educator)
Emmanuel College
English Dept
Cambridge CB2 3AP, UNITED KINGDOM (UK)

Brewer, Dewell (Football Player)
Indianapolis Colts
950 E Paces Ferry Rd NE Ste 2700
Dean Witter
Atlanta, GA 30326-1386, USA

Brewer, Donald (Musician)
Lustig Talent
PO Box 770850
Orlando, FL 32877-0850, USA

Brewer, Gay Jr (Golfer)
6606 Arbor Ridge Dr
Crestwood, KY 40014-7744, USA

Brewer, Jack (Baseball Player)
New York Giants
28271 W Worcester Rd
Sun City, CA 92586-2653, USA

Brewer, Jim T (Basketball Player, Coach)
1814 S 23rd Ave
Maywood, IL 60153-2810, USA

Brewer, Leo (Misc)
5739 SW Downs View Ct
Portland, OR 97221-1201, USA

Brewer, Mike (Baseball Player)
Kansas City Royals
40 Amherst Ave
Menlo Park, CA 94025-3802, USA

Brewer, Richard G (Physicist)
730 De Soto Dr
Palo Alto, CA 94303-2806, USA

Brewer, Rodney (Baseball Player)
St Louis Cardinals
1201 Lavanham Ct
Apopka, FL 32712-3069, USA

Brewer, Sean (Football Player)
Cincinatti Bengals
20042 Dayton St
Riverside, CA 92508-6300, USA

Brewer, Tony
Los Angeles Dodgers
839 Golden Poppy St
Las Vegas, NV 89110-2858, USA

Brewington, Jamie (Baseball Player)
San Francisco Giants
3370 S Roger Ct
Chandler, AZ 85286-2481, USA

Brewster, Jordana (Actor)
c/o Peter Levine *Creative Artists Agency LCC (CAA-LA)*
2000 Avenue Of The Stars
Los Angeles, CA 90067-4700, USA

Brewster, Paget (Actor)
c/o Staff Member *Burstein Company, The*
15304 W Sunset Blvd Ste 208
Pacific Palisades, CA 90272-3656, USA

Brewster, Pete (Football Player)
Cleveland Browns
PO Box 183
Peculiar, MO 64078-0183, USA

Brewton, Maia (Actor)
c/o Paul Bennett *PB Management*
6523 W 6th St
Los Angeles, CA 90048-4715, USA

Brey, Mike (Coach)
Notre Dame University
Athletic Dept
Notre Dame, IN 46556, USA

Breyer, Stephen G (Judge)
US Supreme Court
1 1st St NE
Washington, DC 20543-0002, USA

Brezina, Bobby (Football Player)
Houston Oilers
1204 Pine Hollow Dr
Friendswood, TX 77546-4634, USA

Brezina, Greg (Football Player)
Atlanta Falcons
2360 Leach Rd
Greensboro, GA 30642, USA

Breziner, Salome
PO Box 5617
Beverly Hills, CA 90209-5617, USA

Brezner, Larry (Producer)
c/o Larry Brezner *MBST Entertainment*
345 N Maple Dr Ste 200
Beverly Hills, CA 90210-3860, USA

Brian, Earl W (Publisher)
United Press International
1400 L St NW
Washington, DC 20005-3509, USA

Brice, Alan (Baseball Player)
Chicago White Sox
6726 71st St E
Bradenton, FL 34203-71.73, USA

Brice, William J (Artist)
427 Beloit Ave
Los Angeles, CA 90049-3405, USA

Bricekel, James R (General)
4798 Hanging Moss Ln
Sarasota, FL 34238-4301, USA

Brickell, Beth (Director)
PO Box 119
Paron, AR 72122-0119, USA

Brickell, Edie (Musician, Songwriter, Writer)
88 Central Park W
New York, NY 10023-5209, USA

Brickell, Beth
PO Box 26
Paron, AR 72122-0026, USA

Brickell, Edie (Musician)
88 Central Park W
New York, NY 10023-5209, USA

Bricker, Neal S (Physicist)
4240 Piedmont Mesa Rd
Claremont, CA 91711-2332, USA

Brickhouse, Smith N (Religious Leader)
Church of Christ
PO Box 472
Independence, MO 64051-0472, USA

Brickley, Andy (Hockey Player)
Philadelphia Flyers
5 Mill River Ln
Hingham, MA 02043-3455, USA

Bricklin, Daniel S (Designer)
Trellix Corp
300 Bahr Ave
Concord, MA 01742, USA

Brickman, Jim (Actor)
Brickman Music
4651 Cahuenga Blvd Apt 204
Toluca Lake, CA 91602-1561, USA

Brickman, Paul (Director)
4116 Holly Knoll Dr
Los Angeles, CA 90027-3222, USA

Brickowski, Frank (Basketball Player)
Seattle SuperSonics
534 NW 23rd Ave
Portland, OR 97210, USA

Bricusse, Leslie (Composer, Musician)
8730 W Sunset Blvd # 300W
Los Angeles, CA 90069-2210, USA

Bridgeforth, William (Baseball Player)
Baltimore Elite Giants
4766 Drakes Branch Rd
Nashville, TN 37218-1436, USA

Bridgeman, Ulysses (Basketball Player)
Milwaukee Bucks
14610 Woodlake Trce
Louisville, KY 40245-5134, USA

Bridgers, Sean (Actor)
c/o Darris Hatch *Daris Hatch Management*
9538 Brighton Way Ste 308
Beverly Hills, CA 90210-4516, USA

Bridges, Alan J S (Director)
28 High St
Shepperton
Middx TW7 9AW, UNITED KINGDOM (UK)

Bridges, Alicia
1560 Broadway # 1308
New York, NY 10036-1518, USA

Bridges, Allcia (Musician, Songwriter, Writer)
Talent Consultants International
105 Shad Row Ste B
Piermont, NY 10968-3001, USA

Bridges, Angelica (Actor, Model)
c/o Marv Dauer *Marv Dauer Management*
11661 San Vicente Blvd Ste 104
Los Angeles, CA 90049-5150, USA

Bridges, Beau (Actor)
c/o Steve Tellez *Creative Artists Agency LCC (CAA-LA)*
2000 Avenue Of The Stars
Los Angeles, CA 90067-4700, USA

Bridges, Chris (Ludacris) (Actor, Musician, Producer)
c/o Dana Sims *William Morris Agency (WMA-LA)*
1 William Morris Pl
Beverly Hills, CA 90212-4261, USA

Bridges, Jeff (Actor, Producer)
988 Hot Springs Rd
Montecito, CA 93108, USA

Bridges, Rocky (Baseball Player)
Brooklyn Dodgers
2927 N Julia St Unit 59
Coeur D Alene, ID 83815, USA

Bridges, Todd A (Actor)
16002 Nordhoff St
North Hills, CA 91343-3042, USA

Bridges Jr, Roy D (Astronaut, General)
113 William Barksdale
Williamsburg, VA 23185-8211, USA

Bridgewater, Dee Dee (Musician)
B H Hopper Mgmt
Elvirastr 25
Munich 80636, GERMANY

Bridgman, Mel (Hockey Player)
Philadelphia Flyers
2121 Farrell Ave
Redondo Beach, CA 90278-1818, USA

Bridwell, Norman (Writer)
PO Box 869
Edgartown, MA 02539-0869, USA

Brief Smile, A (Music Group)
c/o Staff Member *Paradigm (Monterey)*
509 Hartnell St
Monterey, CA 93940-2825, USA

Briehl, Tom (Football Player)
Houston Oilers
7752 N Via De La Montana
Scottsdale, AZ 85258-3320, USA

Briere, Daniel (Hockey Player)
Phoenix Coyotes
16000 Ventura Blvd Ste 212
Encino, CA 91436-2748, USA

Brierley, Ronald A (Business Person)
Guinness Peat Group
21-26 Garlick Hill
London EC4 2AU, UNITED KINGDOM (UK)

Briers, Richard (Actor, Comedian)
c/o Christian Hodell *Hamilton Hodell Ltd*
66 - 68 Margaret St 5th Fl
London W1W 8SR, UNITED KINGDOM
(UK)

Brigati, Eddie (Musician, Songwriter, Writer)
Dassinger Creative
172 2nd Ave
Little Falls, NJ 07424-2237, USA

Briggs, Dan (Baseball Player)
California Angels
231 France St
Sonoma, CA 95476-7141, USA

Briggs, Danny (Golfer)
3730 Ravens Trace Ln
Franklin, TN 37064-4710, USA

Briggs, Edward S (Admiral)
3648 Lago Sereno
Escondido, CA 92029-7902, USA

Briggs, John (Baseball Player)
Philadelphia Phillies
238 Wall Ave
Paterson, NJ 07504-1016, USA

Briggs, Johnny T (Baseball Player)
Chicago Cubs
PO Box 4025
Camp Connell, CA 95223-4025, USA

Briggs, Paul (Football Player)
Detroit Lions
521 W Curie Ave
Santa Ana, CA 92707-3917, USA

Briggs, Raymond R (Cartoonist, Writer)
Weston
Underhill Lane
Westmeston near Hassocks
Sussex, UNITED KINGDOM (UK)

Briggs, Wilma (Baseball Player)
111 Summit Ave
Wakefield, RI 02879-2228, USA

Briggs of Lewes, Asa (Historian)
Caprons Keere St
Lewes
Sussex, UNITED KINGDOM (UK)

Brigham, Jeremy (Football Player)
Oakland Raiders
1141 Catalina Dr
Livermore, CA 94550-5928, USA

Bright, Cameron (Actor)
c/o Stephanie Comer *United Talent Agency (UTA)*
9560 Wilshire Blvd Ste 500
Beverly Hills, CA 90212-2401, USA

Bright, Kevin S (Director, Producer, Writer)
c/o Staff Member *International Creative Management (ICM-LA)*
10250 Constellation Blvd
Los Angeles, CA 90067-6200, USA

Bright, Leon (Football Player)
New York Giants
1183 Dutton Ave
Deland, FL 32720-5011, USA

Bright, Myron H (Judge)
655 1st Ave N Ste 340
Fargo, ND 58102-4952, USA

Brightman, Sarah (Actor, Musician)
The Mill
Mill Lane
Cookham SL6 9QT, UNITED KINGDOM
(UK)

Briley, Greg (Baseball Player)
Seattle Mariners
2170 Sunnybrook Rd
Greenville, NC 27834-1164, USA

Briley, John (Actor, Producer, Writer)
c/o Jack Gilardi *International Creative Management (ICM-LA)*
10250 Constellation Blvd
Los Angeles, CA 90067-6200, USA

Brill, Charlie (Actor)
3635 Wrightwood Dr
Studio City, CA 91604-3947, USA

Brill, Francesca (Actor)
Kate Feast Primrose Hill Studios
Fitzroy Road
London NW1 8TR, UNITED KINGDOM
(UK)

Brill, Winston J (Misc)
12529 237th Way NE
Redmond, WA 98053-5618, USA

Brillstein, Bernie (Producer)
c/o Staff Member *Brillstein-Grey Entertainment*
9150 Wilshire Blvd Ste 350
Beverly Hills, CA 90212-3453, USA

Brilz, Darrick (Football Player)
Washington Redskins
3020 Issaquah Pine Lake Rd SE # 525
Issaquah, WA 98075-7253, USA

Brim, Michael (Football Player)
Phoenix Cardinals
14499 Three Oaks Ct
Montpelier, VA 23192-2814, USA

Brimanis, Aris (Hockey Player)
Philadelphia Flyers
5200 Secluded Cir
Anchorage, AK 99516-3061, USA

Brimley, Wilford (Actor)
B7 Ranch
10000 North
Lehi, UT 84043, USA

Brimmer, Andrew F (Economist, Government Official)
Brimmer Co
4400 Macarthur Blvd NW
Washington, DC 20007-2589, USA

Brin, Sergey (Business Person, Engineer)
Google Inc
1600 Amphitheatre Pkwy # 41
Mountain View, CA 94043-1351, USA

Brind'amour, Rod (Hockey Player)
St Louis Blues
12304 Birchfalls Dr
Raleigh, NC 27614-7900, USA

Brindley, Doug (Hockey Player)
Toronto Maple Leafs
Caledon Village Ontario Provincial Police
18473 Hurontario Street
Caledon Village, ON L0N 1C0, CANADA

Brinegar, Claude S (Business Person, Secretary)
PO Box 4346
Stanford, CA 94309, USA

Bring, Murray H (Business Person)
Altria Group
120 Park Ave
New York, NY 10017-5577, USA

Brink, Andre P (Writer)
University of Cape Town
English Dept
Rondebosch 7700, SOUTH AFRICA

Brink, Brad (Baseball Player)
Philadelphia Phillies
2628 Surrey Ave
Modesto, CA 95355-4668, USA

Brink, Frank Jr (Physicist)
Pine Run
#E1 Ferry & Iron Roads
Doylestown, PA 18901, USA

Brink, K Robert (Publisher)
Town & Country Megazine
1700 Broadway
New York, NY 10019-5905, USA

Brink, Larry (Football Player)
Los Angeles Rams
13310 Tierra Heights Rd
Redding, CA 96003-7489, USA

Brink, R Alexander (Misc)
8301 Old Sauk Rd Apt 326
Middleton, WI 53562-4394, USA

Brinker, Bob (Business Person, Radio Personality)
AdPad Inc
5226 E Wagoner Rd
Scottsdale, AZ 85254-7636, USA

Brinker, Nancy (Business Person)
The Susan G. Komen Breast Cancer Foundation, Inc
5005 Lbj Fwy Ste 250
Dallas, TX 75244-6125, USA

Brinkley, Christie (Model)
c/o Brian Dubin *William Morris Agency (WMA-NY)*
1325 Avenue Of The Americas
New York, NY 10019-6026, USA

Brinkman, Chuck (Baseball Player)
Chicago White Sox
11849 County Road C
Bryan, OH 43506-8524, USA

Brinkman, Ed (Baseball Player)
Washington Senators
4510 Clearwater Pl Unit 7
Cincinnati, OH 45248-1715, USA

Brinkman, John A (Historian)
1321 E 56th St Apt 4
Chicago, IL 60637-1762, USA

Brinkman, William F (Physicist)
20 Constitution Hl W
Princeton, NJ 08540-6748, USA

Brinkmann, Robert S (Cinematographer)
Spyros Skouras
631 Wilshire Blvd # 2C
Santa Monica, CA 90401-1510, USA

Brinson, Larry (Football Player)
Dallas Cowboys
300 Catawbah Rd
Clemson, SC 29631-2829, USA

Brion, Francoise
11 rue de Seine
Paris 75006, FRANCE

Brion, John (Composer)
Gortaine/Schwartz
13245 Riverside Dr Ste 450
Sherman Oaks, CA 91423-2172, USA

Brisco, Jack (Wrestler)
19018 Blake Rd
Odessa, FL 33556-4402, USA

Brisco, Marlin (Football Player)
379 Newport Ave Apt 107
Long Beach, CA 90814-7011, USA

Brisco, Valerie (Athlete, Track Athlete)
USA Track & Field
4341 Starlight Dr
Indianapolis, IN 46239-1473, USA

Briscoe, Brent (Actor)
c/o Staff Member *United Talent Agency (UTA)*
9560 Wilshire Blvd Ste 500
Beverly Hills, CA 90212-2401, USA

Briscoe, Dolph Jr (Governor)
338 Pecan St
Uvalde, TX 78801-3941, USA

Briscoe, John (Baseball Player)
Oakland A's
6815 Casa Loma Ave
Dallas, TX 75214-4003, USA

Briscoe, Mary Beck (Judge)
US Appeals Court
4839 W 15th St
Lawrence, KS 66049, USA

Brisebois, Danielle (Actor, Musician)
c/o Staff Member *McDaniel Entertainment*
2021 S Westgate Ave
Los Angeles, CA 90025-6118, USA

Brissie, Leland V (Lou) (Baseball Player)
Philadelphia Athletics
1908 White Pine Dr
North Augusta, SC 29841-2147, USA

Brisson, Lance
4570 Noeline Way
Encino, CA 91436-2108, USA

Brister, Walter A (Bubby) III (Football Player)
Pittsburgh Steelers
139 Fontainbleau Dr
Mandeville, LA 70471-6434, USA

Bristor, John (Football Player)
San Fransisco 49ers
70 Rinehart Ln
Waynesburg, PA 15370-3412, USA

Bristow, Allan (Basketball Player)
Philadelphia 76ers
510 Sand Hill Ct
Marco Island, FL 34145-5859, USA

Bristow, Allan M (Basketball Player, Coach)
PO Box 635
Gloucester Point, VA 23062-0635, USA

Britain, Radie (Composer)
PO Box 17
Smithville, IN 47458-0017, USA

Brito, Jorge (Baseball Player)
Colorado Rockies
308 Mark St SW
Decatur, AL 35601-6420, USA

Britt, Chris (Cartoonist)
State Journal-Register
1 Copley Plz
Editorial Dept
Springfield, IL 62701-1927, USA

Britt, James (Football Player)
Atlanta Falcons
PO Box 371202
Decatur, GA 30037-1202, USA

Britt, Jessie (Football Player)
Pittsburgh Steelers
4003 Coltrain Rd
Greensboro, NC 27455-2631, USA

Britt, Michael (Musician)
Borman Entertainment
1222 16th Ave S Ste 23
Nashville, TN 37212-2926, USA

Britt, Tyrone (Basketball Player)
San Diego Rockes
100 S Broad St Apt 102C
Philadelphia, PA 19110-1023, USA

Britt, Wayman (Basketball Player)
Detroit Pistons
973 Paradise Lake Dr SE
Grand Rapids, MI 49546-3828, USA

Brittain, Machael (Basketball Player)
San Antonio Spurs
2314 Gables Dr NE
Atlanta, GA 30319-4189, USA

Brittany, Morgan (Actor, Model)
3434 Cornell Rd
Agoura Hills, CA 91301-2714, USA

Britten, Roy J (Misc)
Kerckhoff Marine Laboratory
101 Dahlia Ave
Corona Del Mar, CA 92625-2814, USA

Brittenham, Harry (Attorney, Attorney General, General)
Ziffren Brittenham Branca
1801 Century Park W
Los Angeles, CA 90067-6409, USA

Brittenum, John (Football Player)
San Diego Chargers
PO Box 3773
Fayetteville, AR 72702-3773, USA

Britton, Benjamin (Inventor)
University of Cincinnati
Fine Arts Dept
Cincinnati, OH 45221-0001, USA

Britton, Connie (Actor)
c/o Staff Member *Handprint Entertainment*
1100 Glendon Ave Ste 1000
Los Angeles, CA 90024-3514, USA

Britton, Dave (Basketball Player)
Washington Bullets
6321 Old Ox Rd
Dallas, TX 75241-2733, USA

Britton, Jim (Baseball Player)
Minnesota Twins
825 Forestwalk Dr
Suwanee, GA 30024-4243, USA

Britton, Tony (Actor)
International Creative Mgmt
76 Oxford St
London W1N 0AX, UNITED KINGDOM (UK)

Britz, Greg (Hockey Player)
Toronto Maple Leafs
245 Ocean Ave
Marblehead, MA 01945-3700, USA

Britz, Jerilyn (Golfer)
415 E Lincoln St Apt 7
Luverne, MN 56156-1643, USA

Brizan, George (Prime Minister)
Prime Minister's Office
Botanical Gardens
Saint George's, GRENADA

Brizzolara, Tony (Baseball Player)
Atlanta Braves
1638 Princess Cir NE
Atlanta, GA 30345-4160, USA

Broadbent, Jim (Actor)
International Creative Mgmt
76 Oxford St
London, ENGLAND W1N 0AX, UNITED KINGDOM (UK)

Broadbent, John Edward (Government Official)
1386 Nicola
#30
Vancouver, BC V6G 2G2, CANADA

Broaddus, J Alfred Jr (Financier)
Federal Reserve Bank
PO Box 27622
Richmond, VA 23261-7622, USA

Broadhead, James L (Business Person)
FPL Group
700 Universe Blvd
Juno Beach, FL 33408-2657, USA

Broadnax, Jerry (Football Player)
Houston Oilers
2631 Nina Cir
Grand Prairie, TX 75052-5325, USA

Broadus, Calvin (Snoop Dogg) (Artist, Musician)
c/o Staff Member *Doggy Style Records*
1142 S Diamond Bar Blvd # 504
Diamond Bar, CA 91765-2203, USA

Brobeck, John R (Physicist)
224 Vassar Ave
Swarthmore, PA 19081-1634, USA

Broberg, Gus (Basketball Player)
208 El Pueblo Way
Palm Beach, FL 33480-3218, USA

Broberg, Pete (Baseball Player)
Washington Senators
220 Monterey Rd
Palm Beach, FL 33480-3228, USA

Brocail, Doug (Baseball Player)
San Diego Padres
8011 Meadow Vista Dr
Missouri City, TX 77459-5734, USA

Broccoli, Barbara (Producer)
c/o Staff Member *Creative Artists Agency LCC (CAA-LA)*
2000 Avenue Of The Stars
Los Angeles, CA 90067-4700, USA

Broches, Aron (Attorney, Attorney General, General)
44 Pond St
Wakefield, RI 02879-4009, USA

Brochtrup, William (Bill) (Actor)
S D B Partners
1801 Avenue Of Stars Ste 902
Los Angeles, CA 90067-5981, USA

Brochu, Stephane (Hockey Player)
Montreal Canadiens
13759 Olsen Rd
Posen, MI 49776-9208, USA

Brock, Chris (Baseball Player)
Atlanta Braves
7684 Markham Bend Pl
Sanford, FL 32771-8107, USA

Brock, Clyde (Football Player)
Dallas Cowboys
3105 SW 98th Ave
Portland, OR 97225-2924, USA

Brock, Dieter (Football Player)
Los Angeles Rams
Tusculum College 60 Shiloh Rd
Attn Atheletic Dept
Greeneville, TN 37745, USA

Brock, Greg (Baseball Player)
Los Angeles Dodgers
3727 Valley Oak Dr
Loveland, CO 80538-8930, USA

Brock, Lou (Baseball Player)
Chicago Cubs
61 Barkley Pl
Saint Charles, MO 63301-4569, USA

Brock, Matt (Football Player)
Green Bay Packers
3105 SW 98th Ave
Portland, OR 97225-2924, USA

Brock, Peter (Football Player)
New England Patriots
12 Stonefield Ct
North Attleboro, MA 02760-4771, USA

Brock, Stanley J (Stan) (Football Player)
New Orleans Saints
2555 SW 81st Ave
Portland, OR 97225-3839, USA

Brock, Stevie (Actor)
Official International Fan Club
PO Box 5308
Bellingham, WA 98227-5308, USA

Brock, Willie (Football Player)
Detroit Lions
2778 SE Irwin Ct
Hillsboro, OR 97123-6232, USA

Brock III, William E (Bill) (Secretary, Senator)
16 Revell St
Annapolis, MD 21401-2611, USA

Brock Jr, Lou (Football Player)
San Diego Chargers
1015 Sandstone Dr
Saint Louis, MO 63146-5031, USA

Brockermeyer, Blake (Football Player)
Carolina Panthers
PO Box 789
Wilson, WY 83014-0789, USA

Brockert, Richard C (Misc)
United Telegraph Workers
701 E Gude Dr
Rockville, MD 20850-1329, USA

Brockington, John (Football Player)
Green Bay Packers
701 B St Ste 1500
San Diego, CA 92101-8170, USA

Brockovich, Erin (Writer)
5707 Corsa Ave
Westlake Village, CA 91362-4058, USA

Brodbin, Kevin (Writer)
Creative Artists Agency
9830 Wilshire Blvd
Beverly Hills, CA 90212-1804, USA

Broden, Connie (Hockey Player)
Montreal Canadiens
88 Valecrest Dr
Etobicoke, ON M9A 4P6, CANADA

Broder, David S (Writer)
900 N Taylor St Apt 922
Arlington, VA 22203-1866, USA

Broder, Samuel (Misc)
IVAX Corp
4400 Biscayne Blvd
Miami, FL 33137-3204, USA

Broderick, Beth (Actor)
Innovative Artists
1505 10th St
Santa Monica, CA 90401-2805, USA

Broderick, Ken (Hockey Player)
Minnesota North Stars
20 Harrogate Sq
Williamsville, NY 14221-4051, USA

Broderick, Len (Hockey Player)
Minnesota Canadiens
216 Inverness Way
Easley, SC 29642-3116, USA

Broderick, Matthew (Actor)
c/o Matthew (Matt) Del Piano *Creative Artists Agency LCC (CAA-LA)*
2000 Avenue Of The Stars
Los Angeles, CA 90067-4700, USA

Broderson, Morris (Artist)
5707 Costello Ave
Van Nuys, CA 91401-4329, USA

Brodeur, Martin (Hockey Player)
c/o Staff Member *New Jersey Devils*
50 Route 120
Continental Arena
E Rutherford, NJ 07073-2131, USA

Brodeur, Richard (Hockey Player)
Vancouver Canucks
33536 Hawthorne Ave
Abbotsford, BC V2S 1B8, CANADA

Brodie, H Keith H (Misc)
63 Beverly Dr
Durham, NC 27707-2223, USA

Brodie, John (Football Player, Golfer)
San Francisco 49ers
49350 Avenida Fernando
La Quinta, CA 92253-2742, USA

Brodie, Kevin (Actor)
3925 Big Oak Dr Apt 5
Studio City, CA 91604-3800, USA

Brodnax, J W (Football Player)
Denver Broncos
3190 1st St
Berwick, LA 70342-2704, USA

Brodowski, Dick (Baseball Player)
Boston Red Sox
120 Pine St
Manchester, MA 01944-1022, USA

Brodsky, Julian A (Business Person)
Comcast Corp
1500 Market St
Philadelphia, PA 19102-2196, USA

Brody, Adam (Actor)
c/o Doug Wald *Raw Talent Management*
9615 Brighton Way Ste 300
Beverly Hills, CA 90210-5118, USA

Brody, Adrien (Actor)
c/o Bryan Lourd *Creative Artists Agency LCC (CAA-LA)*
2000 Avenue Of The Stars
Los Angeles, CA 90067-4700, USA

Brody, Jane E (Journalist)
New York Times
229 W 43rd St
Editorial Dept
New York, NY 10036-3959, USA

Brody, Kenneth D (Financier)
Export-Import Bank
811 Vermont Ave NW
Washington, DC 20571-0002, USA

Brody, Lane (Music Group)
Black Stallion Country Productions
PO Box 368
Tujunga, CA 91043-0368, USA

Broecker, Wallace S (Geophysicist, Misc, Physicist)
Lamont-Doherty Earth Observatory
PO Box 1000
Palisades, NY 10964-8000, USA

Broelsch, Christopher E (Doctor, Misc)
University of Chicago
Medical Center Surgery Dept Box 259
Chicago, IL 60690, USA

Brogan, James (Basketball Player)
San Antonio Spurs
6631 Hollycrest Ct
San Diego, CA 92121-4137, USA

Brogdon, Cindy (Basketball Player)
4932 Shadowood Pkwy SE
Atlanta, GA 30339-2346, USA

Broglio, Ernie (Baseball Player)
St Louis Cardinals
2838 Via Carmen
San Jose, CA 95124-1442, USA

Brogna, Rico (Baseball Player)
Detroit Tigers
110 Woodbury Rd
Watertown, CT 06795-2130, USA

Brohamer, Jack (Baseball Player)
Cleveland Indians
39017 Narcissus Dr
Palm Desert, CA 92211-1882, USA

Brohawn, Troy (Baseball Player)
Arizona Diamondbacks
1619 Taylors Island Rd
Woolford, MD 21677-1328, USA

Brokaw, Gary (Basketball Player, Coach, Misc)
Milwaukee Bucks
3829 Nancy Creek Rd
Charlotte, NC 28270-4437, USA

Brokaw, Tom (Journalist, Television Host)
c/o Staff Member *NBC Nightly News*
30 Rockefeller Plz # 300S
New York, NY 10112-0015, USA

Broken Lizard (Comedian)
c/o Staff Member *United Talent Agency (UTA)*
9560 Wilshire Blvd Ste 500
Beverly Hills, CA 90212-2401, USA

Brolin, James (Actor)
c/o Christopher Barrett *Metropolitan*
4500 Wilshire Blvd Fl 2
Los Angeles, CA 90010-3858, USA

Brolin, Josh (Actor)
c/o Michael Cooper *William Morris Agency (WMA-LA)*
1 William Morris Pl
Beverly Hills, CA 90212-4261, USA

Brolly, Shane (Actor)
c/o Staff Member *Marsh Entertainment*
12444 Ventura Blvd Ste 203
Studio City, CA 91604-2409, USA

Bromberg, David (Musician)
c/o Staff Member *Agency Group Ltd, The (LA)*
1880 Century Park E Ste 711
Los Angeles, CA 90067-1618, USA

Bromell, Loranzo (Football Player)
Miami Dolphins
13800 Crowne Hill Ln
Hopkins, MN 55305-2255, USA

Bromley, D Allan (Government Official, Physicist)
3102 23rd St
Lubbock, TX 79410-2123, USA

Bromley, Gary (Hockey Player)
Buffalo Sabres
380 Dartmoor Dr
Coquitlam, BC V3K 5V2, CANADA

Bron, Eleanor (Actor)
c/o Rebecca Blond *Rebecca Blond Associates*
69a Kings Rd
London SW3 4NX, UNITED KINGDOM (UK)

Bronars, Edward J (General)
3354 Rose Ln
Falls Church, VA 22042-4031, USA

Brondell, Ken (Baseball Player)
New York Giants
7029 De Celis Pl
Van Nuys, CA 91406-3702, USA

Bronfman, Charles (Baseball Player, Business Person)
Montreal Expos
501 N Lake Way
Palm Beach, FL 33480-3520, USA

Bronfman, Yefin (Musician)
I C M Artists
40 W 57th St
New York, NY 10019-4001, USA

Bronkey, Jeff (Baseball Player)
Texas Rangers
622 Sunny Brook Dr
Edmond, OK 73034-4224, USA

Bronleewe, Matt (Musician)
Flood Burnstead McCready McCarthy
1700 Hayes St Ste 304
Nashville, TN 37203-3014, USA

Bronson, Ben (Football Player)
Indianapolis Colts
13333 West Rd Apt 1717
Houston, TX 77041-6153, USA

Bronson, Oswald P Sr (Educator)
Bethune-Cookman College
President's Office
Daytona Beach, FL 32114, USA

Bronson, Po (Writer)
Random House
1745 Broadway # B1
New York, NY 10019-4305, USA

Bronstad, Jim (Baseball Player)
New York Yankees
63 One Main Pl
Benbrook, TX 76126-2206, USA

Bronstein, Elizabeth (Producer)
c/o Staff Member *Creative Artists Agency LCC (CAA-LA)*
2000 Avenue Of The Stars
Los Angeles, CA 90067-4700, USA

Brook, Holly (Musician)
c/o Staff Member *Paradigm (Monterey)*
509 Hartnell St
Monterey, CA 93940-2825, USA

Brook, Jayne (Actor)
c/o Staff Member *Brillstein-Grey Entertainment*
9150 Wilshire Blvd Ste 350
Beverly Hills, CA 90212-3453, USA

Brook, Kelly (Actor)
c/o Joan Hyler *Hyler Management*
3000 Olympic Blvd Bldg 5 Ste 2250
Santa Monica, CA 90404-5073, USA

Brook, Peter S P (Director)
CICT
13 Blvd de Rochechouart
Paris 75009, FRANCE

Brooke, Allison (Music Group, Songwriter, Writer)
2-K/EMI Records
6920 W Sunset Blvd
Los Angeles, CA 90028-7010, USA

Brooke, Bob (Hockey Player)
New York Rangers
15496 Stanbury Curv
Eden Prairie, MN 55347-2433, USA

Brooke, Edward W III (Senator)
O'Connor & Hannan
1919 Pennsylvania Ave NW Ste 800
Washington, DC 20006-3401, USA

Brooke, Jonatha (Musician, Songwriter, Writer)
Brooke
1255 5th Ave Apt 7J
New York, NY 10029-3848, USA

Brooke, Paul
19 Sydney Mews
London, ENGLAND SW3 6HL, UNITED KINGDOM (UK)

Brooke-Taylor, Tim (Actor, Comedian)
Jill Foster Ltd
3 Lonsdale Road
London SW13 9ED, UNITED KINGDOM (UK)

Brookens, Ike (Baseball Player)
Detroit Tigers
1053 Brookens Rd
Fayetteville, PA 17222-9314, USA

Brookens, Tom (Baseball Player)
Detroit Tigers
488 Black Gap Rd
Fayetteville, PA 17222-9717, USA

Brooker, Gary (Musician, Songwriter, Writer)
5 Cranley Gardens
London SW7, UNITED KINGDOM (UK)

Brooker, Tommy (Football Player)
Dallas Cowboys
306 Woodbridge Dr
Tuscaloosa, AL 35406, USA

Brookes, Harvey (Physicist)
Harvard University
Aiken Computation Laboratory
Cambridge, MA 02138, USA

Brookes, Jacqueline (Actor)
William Morris Agency
151 El Camino Dr
Beverly Hills, CA 90212-2775, USA

Brookes, Peter (Cartoonist)
London Times
Editorial Dept
1 Pennington St
London E98 1SS, UNITED KINGDOM (UK)

Brookfield, Price (Basketball Player)
Chicago American Gears
90 Fox Run Rd HC 57
Pinehurst, NC 28374-8043, USA

Brookhart, Maurice S (Misc)
University of North Carolina
Chemistry Dept
Chapel Hill, NC 27514, USA

Brookins, Clarence (Basketball Player)
Miami Floridians
8266 Fayette St
Philadelphia, PA 19150-2002, USA

Brookins, Gary (Cartoonist)
Richmond Newspapers
Editorial Dept
PO Box 85333
Richmond, VA 23293-0001, USA

Brooklyn Bridge
PO Box 309M
Bay Shore, NY 11706, USA

Brookner, Anita (Writer)
68 Elm Park Gardens
#6
London SW10 9PB, UNITED KINGDOM (UK)

Brooks, Aaron (Football Player)
Green Bay Packers
6 Viper Ct
Hampton, VA 23666-2277, USA

Brooks, Albert (Actor, Director, Writer)
c/o Herb Nanas *Nanas/Hart Entertainment*
14945 Ventura Blvd # 746
Sherman Oaks, CA 91403-5955, USA

Brooks, Amanda (Actor)
c/o Staff Member *Nine Yards Entertainment*
8530 Wilshire Blvd Fl 5
Beverly Hills, CA 90211-3102, USA

Brooks, Angelle (Actor)
c/o Staff Member *Pakula/King & Associates*
9229 W Sunset Blvd Ste 315
Los Angeles, CA 90069-3403, USA

Brooks, Avery (Actor)
c/o Staff Member *Innovative Artists (LA)*
1505 10th St
Santa Monica, CA 90401-2805, USA

Brooks, Barrett (Football Player)
Philadelphia Eagles
11 Berkshire Dr Apt 25
Voorhees, NJ 08043-3448, USA

Brooks, Bill (Football Player)
Indianapolis Colts
1088 Laurelwood
Carmel, IN 46032-8742, USA

Brooks, Bobby D (Football Player)
New York Giants
7416 Red Osier Rd
Dallas, TX 75249-1349, USA

Brooks, Bucky (Football Player)
Buffalo Bills
5124 Casland Dr
Raleigh, NC 27604-5449, USA

Brooks, Chet (Football Player)
San Francisco 49ers
655 Shadyway Dr
Dallas, TX 75232-4821, USA

Brooks, Conrad (Actor)
PO Box 264
Inwood, WV 25428-0264, USA

Brooks, Danny (Musician)
American Promotions
2011 Ferry Ave Apt U19
Camden, NJ 08104-1900, USA

Brooks, David Allen (David A) (Actor)
c/o Staff Member *Candy Entertainment Management*
8981 W Sunset Blvd Ste 310
West Hollywood, CA 90069-1848, USA

Brooks, Derrick (Football Player)
Tampa Bay Buccaneers
1713 Cedrus Ln
Pensacola, FL 32514-1909, USA

Brooks, Donnie (Musician)
Al Lampkin Entertainment
1817 W Verdugo Ave
Burbank, CA 91506-2149, USA

Brooks, E R (Business Person)
Central & South West Corp
1616 Woodall Rogers Freeway
Dallas, TX 75202, USA

Brooks, Ed (Golfer)
6604 Augusta Rd
Fort Worth, TX 76132-4564, USA

Brooks, Ethan (Football Player)
Atlanta Falcons
8 Gatewood
Avon, CT 06001-3949, USA

Brooks, Garth (Musician, Songwriter, Writer)
c/o Staff Member Red Strokes Entertainment
9465 Wilshire Blvd Ste 319
Beverly Hills, CA 90212-2602, USA

Brooks, Geraldine (Writer)
Viking Press
375 Hudson St
New York, NY 10014-3658, USA

Brooks, Golden (Actor)
c/o Staff Member Nine Yards Entertainment
8530 Wilshire Blvd Fl 5
Beverly Hills, CA 90211-3102, USA

Brooks, Herb (Athlete)
180 Birchwood Ave
Saint Paul, MN 55110-1612, USA

Brooks, Hubert (Hubie) (Baseball Player)
New York Mets
15001 Olive St
Hesperia, CA 92345-3306, USA

Brooks, James (Football Player)
San Diego Chargers
5398 Harbourwatch Way
Mason, OH 45040-8393, USA

Brooks, James L (Actor)
c/o Jeff Berg International Creative Management (ICM-LA)
10250 Constellation Blvd
Los Angeles, CA 90067-6200, USA

Brooks, Jason (Actor)
289 S Robertson Blvd # 424
Beverly Hills, CA 90211-2810, USA

Brooks, Jerry (Baseball Player)
Los Angeles Dodgers
15152 Mountain View Ln
Frisco, TX 75035-6882, USA

Brooks, Joel (Actor)
c/o Martin Gage Gage Group, The (LA)
14724 Ventura Blvd Ste 505
Sherman Oaks, CA 91403-3505, USA

Brooks, John E (Educator)
College of Holy Cross
President's Office
Worcester, MA 01610, USA

Brooks, Jon (Football Player)
Detroit Lions
104 Carver St
Saluda, SC 29138-1514, USA

Brooks, Karen (Musician)
5408 Clearview Ln
Waterford, WI 53185-2950, USA

Brooks, Kevin (Football Player)
Dallas Cowboys
13410 Preston Rd # 360
Dallas, TX 75240-5299, USA

Brooks, Kimberly A (Actor)
c/o Kevin Turner Coast to Coast Talent Group
3350 Barham Blvd
Los Angeles, CA 90068-1404, USA

Brooks, Kix (Musician, Songwriter, Writer)
Brooks & Dunn
PO Box 120669
Nashville, TN 37212-0669, USA

Brooks, Lala (Misc)
Superstars Unlimited
PO Box 371371
Las Vegas, NV 89137-1371, USA

Brooks, Larry (Coach, Football Player)
Los Angeles Rams
1730 Winder St
Richmond, VA 23220-6422, USA

Brooks, Lee (Football Player)
Houston Oilers
4206 Bamford Dr
Austin, TX 78731-1355, USA

Brooks, Mark (Golfer)
4215 Pershing Ave
Fort Worth, TX 76107-4314, USA

Brooks, Mehcad (Actor)
c/o David (Dave) Fleming Mosaic Media Group
24 Music Sq W Fl 1
Nashville, TN 37203-6661, USA

Brooks, Mel (Actor, Director)
c/o Staff Member BrooksFilms Ltd
9336 Washington Blvd
Culver City, CA 90232-2628, USA

Brooks, Meredith (Musician)
Capitol Records
1750 Vine St
Los Angeles, CA 90028-5274, USA

Brooks, Michael (Basketball Player)
San Diego Clippers
495 Bethany St
San Diego, CA 92114-5539, USA

Brooks, Michael (Football Player)
Denver Broncos
30 Pine Tree Dr
Honey Brook, PA 19344-1254, USA

Brooks, Michael (Football Player)
San Diego Chargers
5002 Weatherstone Dr
Greensboro, NC 27406-8724, USA

Brooks, Nathan (Boxer)
21274 Ellacott Pkwy Apt M208
Cleveland, OH 44128-4431, USA

Brooks, Perry (Football Player)
Washington Redskins
15010 Plastron Ct
Woodbridge, VA 22193-5846, USA

Brooks, Randi (Actor, Model)
3205 Evergreen Point Rd
Medina, WA 98039-1029, USA

Brooks, Reggie (Football Player)
Washington Redskins
1701 Portage Ave
South Bend, IN 46616-1919, USA

Brooks, Rich (Coach, Football Coach)
University of Kentucky
Athletic Dept
Lexington, KY 40506-0001, USA

Brooks, Richard (Actor)
333 Washington Blvd # 102
Marina Del Rey, CA 90292-5136, USA

Brooks, Robert (Football Player)
Green Bay Packers
8611 N 17th Pl
Phoenix, AZ 85020-3320, USA

Brooks, Ross (Hockey Player)
Boston Bruins
196 Old River Rd Apt 215
Lincoln, RI 02865-1133, USA

Brooks, Steve (Football Player)
Detroit Lions
8306 Wilshire Blvd Apt 154
Beverly Hills, CA 90211-2304, USA

Brooks, Terry (Writer)
c/o Staff Member Doubleday/ RandomHouse
1745 Broadway
New York, NY 10019-4305, USA

Brooks, Tony (Football Player)
Philadelphia Eagles
19626 Northrop St
Cassopolis, MI 49031-9328, USA

Brooks, William (Bud) (Football Player)
Detroit Lions
302 Doubloon Cir
Hot Springs, AR 71913, USA

Brooks & Dunn (Music Group)
PO Box 120669
Nashville, TN 37212-0669, USA

Brooks Jr, Cliff (Football Player)
Cleveland Browns
12023 Briar Forest Dr
Houston, TX 77077-3027, USA

Brookshier, Thomas (Tom) (Football Player, Sportscaster)
Philadelphia Eagles
1130 Riverview Ln
West Conshohocken, PA 19428-2964, USA

Brophy, Jay (Football Player)
Miami Dolphins
2117 Prestwick Dr
Uniontown, OH 44685-8847, USA

Brophy, Kevin (Actor)
15010 Hamlin St
Van Nuys, CA 91411-1408, USA

Brophy, Theodore F (Business Person)
60 Arch St
Greenwich, CT 06830-2507, USA

Brorby, Wade (Judge)
US Court of Appeals
2120 Capitol Ave Ste 2131
Cheyenne, WY 82001-3658, USA

Broshears, Robert (Artist)
Robert Broshears Studio
8020 NW Holly Rd
Bremerton, WA 98312-9536, USA

Brosius, Scott D (Baseball Player)
Oakland A's
3207 NW Westside Rd
McMinnville, OR 97128, USA

Broski, David C (Educator)
University of Illinois
President's Office
Chicago, IL 60607, USA

Brosky, Albert (Al) (Football Player)
Chicago Cardinals
2031 Yellow Daisy Ct
Naperville, IL 60563-0234, USA

Brosnan, Jim (Baseball Player)
Chicago Cubs
7742 Churchill St
Morton Grove, IL 60053-1805, USA

Brosnan, Pierce (Actor, Producer)
c/o Staff Member Irish Dreamtime
3110 Main St Ste 200
Santa Monica, CA 90405-5353, USA

Bross, Terry (Baseball Player)
New York Mets
7952 E Camino Real
Scottsdale, AZ 85255-6136, USA

Brossart, Willie (Hockey Player)
Philadelphia Flyers
9318 Susquehanna Trl
Ashland, VA 23005-3382, USA

Brosseau, Frank (Baseball Player)
Pittsburgh Pirates
41 Island Rd
Saint Paul, MN 55127-2635, USA

Brostek, Bern (Football Player)
Saint Louis Rarns
901 N Broadway
Saint Louis, MO 63101-2800, USA

Broten, Aaron (Hockey Player)
Colorado Rockies
307 3rd Ave SE
Roseau, MN 56751-1526, USA

Broten, Neal (Hockey Player)
Minnesota North Stars
N8216 690th St
River Falls, WI 54022-4535, USA

Broth, Ed
c/o Daniel A (Dan) Strone Trident Media Group LLC
41 Madison Ave Fl 36
New York, NY 10010-2257, USA

Brotherhood of Man, Rochdale
PO Box 106
ENGLAND 0L16 4HW, UNITED KINGDOM (UK)

Brothers, Bellamy, The (Musician)
c/o Staff Member Agency for the Performing Arts (APA-LA)
405 S Beverly Dr
Beverly Hills, CA 90212-4416, USA

Brothers, Dr Joyce (Actor, Doctor)
c/o Brian Dubin William Morris Agency (WMA-NY)
1325 Avenue Of The Americas
New York, NY 10019-6026, USA

Brothers, Joyce D (Physicist)
NBC Westwood One Radio Network
524 W 57th St
New York, NY 10019-2930, USA

Brotman, Jeffrey (Business Person)
Costco Wholesale Corp
999 Lake Dr Ste 200
Issaquah, WA 98027-8982, USA

Brough, Randi (Actor)
11684 Ventura Blvd # 476
Studio City, CA 91604-2699, USA

Brough Clapp, A Louise (Tennis Player)
1808 Voluntary Rd
Vista, CA 92084-3112, USA

Broughton, Bruce (Composer)
Air-Edel
9255 W Sunset Blvd # 200
West Hollywood, CA 90069-3309, USA

Broughton, Luther (Football Player)
Philadelphia Eagles
PO Box 371
Huger, SC 29450-0371, USA

Broughton, Willie (Football Player)
Indianapolis Colts
1724 Lacy Ln
Mesquite, TX 75181-1560, USA

Brouhard, Mark (Baseball Player)
Milwaukee Brewers
6289 Jackie Ave
Woodland Hills, CA 91367-1424, USA

Broussard, Ben (Baseball Player)
Cleveland Indians
9170 Mapes St
Beaumont, TX 77707-1250, USA

Broussard, Fred (Football Player)
Pittsburgh Steelers
9750 False River Rd
New Roads, LA 70760, USA

Broussard, Marc (Musician)
c/o Staff Member *Paradigm (Monterey)*
509 Hartnell St
Monterey, CA 93940-2825, USA

Broussard, Rebecca (Actor)
9911 W Pico Blvd Ph A
Los Angeles, CA 90035-2713, USA

Broussard, Steve (Football Player)
Green Bay Packers
3017 E Big Range Ct
Ontario, CA 91761-9107, USA

Brouwenstyn, Gerada
Bachplein 3
Amsterdam NL-1077 GH, THE
NETHERLANDS

Brouwenstyn, Gerarda (Opera Singer)
3 Bachpiein
Armsterdam, THE NETHERLANDS

Brow, Scott (Baseball Player)
Toronto Blue Jays
1194 W Remington Dr
Chandler, AZ 85286-6385, USA

Browder, Ben (Actor)
McCann - Knotek Associates
1321 Londonderry Pl
C/O Hank McCann
Los Angeles, CA 90069-1352, USA

Brower, Bob (Baseball Player)
Texas Rangers
2703 N Van Buren St
Hutchinson, KS 67502-2017, USA

Brower, James (Baseball Player)
Cleveland Indians
4947 Green Valley Rd
Minnetonka, MN 55345-3318, USA

Brower, Jordan
9100 Wilshire Blvd Ste 503E
Beverly Hills, CA 90212-3419, USA

Brower, Jordan Lloyd (Actor)
c/o Beverly Strong *Anonymous Content (CA)*
9350 Wilshire Blvd Ste 224
Beverly Hills, CA 90212-3204, USA

Brower, Laurie (Golfer)
19231 Valley Dr
Villa Park, CA 92861-2343, USA

Brown, A B (Football Player)
New York Jets
224 Wesley St
Salem, NJ 08079-1714, USA

Brown, Aaron (Correspondent)
c/o Staff Member *NS Bienstock Inc*
1740 Broadway Fl 24
New York, NY 10019-4382, USA

Brown, Aaron C (Football Player)
Tampa Bay Buccaneers
3312 Russett Dr
Tampa, FL 33618-1308, USA

Brown, Adrian (Baseball Player)
Pittsburgh Pirates
706 Palmetto St
Summit, MS 39666, USA

Brown, Alison (Musician, Songwriter, Writer)
SRO Artists
6629 University Ave Ste 206
Middleton, WI 53562-3037, USA

Brown, Allen (Football Player)
Green Bay Packers
PO Box 18076
Natchez, MS 39122-8076, USA

Brown, Alton (Baseball Player)
Washington Senators
253 Consul Ave
Virginia Beach, VA 23462-3511, USA

Brown, Alton (Chef, Television Host)
c/o Staff Member *Food Network, The*
75 9th Ave
New York, NY 10011-7006, USA

Brown, Andre (Football Player)
Miami Dolphins
11245 S Emerald Ave
Chicago, IL 60628-4706, USA

Brown, Andy (Hockey Player)
Detroit Red Wings
6175 S 125 W
Trafalgar, IN 46181, USA

Brown, Arnie (Hockey Player)
Toronto Maple Leafs
827 W Peninsula Ct
Oxford, MI 48371-6725, USA

Brown, Arnold (Football Player)
Detroit Lions
8763 Stephens Church Rd
Wilmington, NC 28411-7985, USA

Brown, Arthur E Jr (General)
35 Fairway Winds Pl
Hilton Head Island, SC 29928-5547, USA

Brown, Ashley Nicole (Actor)
Hervey/Grimes
PO Box 64249
Los Angeles, CA 90064-0249, USA

Brown, Bailey (Judge)
US Court of Appeals
167 N Main St
Federal Building
Memphis, TN 38103-1816, USA

Brown, Bill (Football Player)
Chicago Bears
9365 Libby Ln
Eden Prairie, MN 55347-4282, USA

Brown, Bill (Football Player)
Los Angeles Rams
PO Box 8533
Victorville, CA 92392, USA

Brown, Billy Aaron (Actor)
c/o Staff Member *Stone Manners Talent & Literary (LA)*
6500 Wilshire Blvd Ste 550
Los Angeles, CA 90048-4950, USA

Brown, Billy Ray (Golfer)
4110 Woodlake Ln
Missouri City, TX 77459-4330, USA

Brown, Blair (Actor)
18 E 53rd St # 140
New York, NY 10022-5202, USA

Brown, Bo (Cartoonist)
3500 West Chester Pike # A210
Newtown Square, PA 19073-4101, USA

Brown, Bob (Basketball Player)
Providence Steamrollers
7 Charleston St S
Sugar Land, TX 77478-3656, USA

Brown, Bobby (Baseball Player)
Toronto Blue Jays
700 Pleasant Ridge Ct
Chesapeake, VA 23322-2747, USA

Brown, Bobby (Baseball Player)
New York Yankees
4100 Clarke Ave
Fort Worth, TX 76107-2407, USA

Brown, Booker (Football Player)
San Diego Chargers
15946 Koch St # B
Mojave, CA 93501-1395, USA

Brown, Brant (Baseball Player)
Chicago Cubs
1612 Fieldspring Dr
Bakersfield, CA 93311-3542, USA

Brown, Bruce (Photographer)
15550 Calle Real
Gaviota, CA 93117-9729, USA

Brown, Bryan (Actor)
June Cann Mgmt
110 Queen St
Woollahra, NSW 2025, AUSTRALIA

Brown, C Edward (Eddie) (Football Player)
Cleveland Browns
3465 Commodore Pt
Knoxville, TN 37922-6566, USA

Brown, Campbell (Correspondent)
NBC-TV
30 Rockefeller Plz Ste 270E
News Dept
New York, NY 10112-0299, USA

Brown, Carlos (Football Player)
Green Bay Packers
1106 E Newhall Dr
Fresno, CA 93720-4084, USA

Brown, Cedrick (Football Player)
Philadelphia Eagles
74 Arbor Meadow Dr
Sicklerville, NJ 08081-1754, USA

Brown, Chad (Actor)
c/o Staff Member *Sterling/Winters Company, The*
1900 Avenue Of The Stars Fl 5
Los Angeles, CA 90067-4301, USA

Brown, Chadwick (Chad) (Football Player)
Phoenix Cardinals
2827 Holliston Ave
Altadena, CA 91001-2009, USA

Brown, Charles (Football Player)
Washington Redskins
2942 River Rd
Johns Island, SC 29455-8814, USA

Brown, Charles E (Football Player)
Chicago Bears
7317 S Merrill Ave
Chicago, IL 60649-3208, USA

Brown, Charlie (Football Player)
Detroit Lions
3113 Cherry Valley Cir
Fairfield, CA 94534-7510, USA

Brown, Charlie R (Football Player)
New Orleans Saints
5226 Washington Pl
Saint Louis, MO 63108-1117, USA

Brown, Chris (Baseball Player)
San Francisco Giants
5015 Brighton Ave
Los Angeles, CA 90062-2434, USA

Brown, Chris (Football Player)
Pittsburgh Steelers
7161 Cypress Dr
Westerville, OH 43082-8111, USA

Brown, Chris (Musician)
c/o Staff Member *Jive Records*
137 W 25th St
New York, NY 10001-7216, USA

Brown, Chucky (Basketball Player)
Cleveland Cavaliers
102 Balsamwood Ct
Cary, NC 27513-3456, USA

Brown, Cindy (Basketball Player)
Detroit Shock
2 Championship Dr
Palace
Auburn Hills, MI 48326-1753, USA

Brown, Clancy (Actor)
3141 Oakdell Ln
Studio City, CA 91604-4218, USA

Brown, Cleophus (Baseball Player)
Louisville Clippers
3912 Sharon Church Rd
Pinson, AL 35126-2660, USA

Brown, Clifford (Baseball Player)
Indianapolis Clowns
5104 N 37th St
Tampa, FL 33610-6421, USA

Brown, Cornell (Football Player)
Baltimore Ravens
1107 Early St
Lynchburg, VA 24503-4508, USA

Brown, Corwin (Football Player)
New England Patriots
1124 E 90th St
Chicago, IL 60619-7936, USA

Brown, Courtney (Football Player)
Cleveland Browns
1133
Berea, OH 44017, USA

Brown, Curt (Baseball Player)
California Angels
821 SW 49th Ter
Margate, FL 33068-3123, USA

Brown, Curtis (Baseball Player)
Montreal Expos
3200 Cloudview Dr
Sacramento, CA 95833-2700, USA

Brown, Curtis (Football Player)
Buffalo Bills
1035 Lindenwood Ave
Saint Charles, MO 63301-0801, USA

Brown, Curtis (Hockey Player)
Buffalo Sabres
1856 Emory St
San Jose, CA 95126-1912, USA

Brown, Curtis L Jr (Astronaut)
204 Starrwood
Hudson, WI 54016-7174, USA

Brown, Dale (Writer)
c/o Robert Gottlieb *Trident Media Group LLC*
41 Madison Ave Fl 36
New York, NY 10010-2257, USA

Brown, Dale D (Coach, Sportscaster)
ESPN-TV
935 Middle St
Sports Dept Espn Plaza
Bristol, CT 06010-1000, USA

Brown, Dan (Writer)
c/o Staff Member *Doubleday/ RandomHouse*
1745 Broadway
New York, NY 10019-4305, USA

Brown, Daniel G (General)
Deputy Cinc
US Transportation Command
Scott Air Force Base, IL 62225, USA

Brown, Darrell (Baseball Player)
Detroit Tigers
1323 N Blackwelder Ave
Oklahoma City, OK 73106-2215, USA

Brown, Dave (Hockey Player)
Philadelphia Flyers
Corestates Complex Ste 2
Philadelphia Flyers 1
Philadelphia, PA 19148, USA

Brown, David (Producer)
Zanuck/Brown Co
200 W 57th St
New York, NY 10019-3211, USA

Brown, David P (Athlete)
345 Willow Springs Dr
Talent, OR 97540-9682, USA

Brown, Dee (Basketball Player)
1232 Lake Whitney Dr
Windermere, FL 34786-6070, USA

Brown, Denise
PO Box 3777
Monarch Bay, CA 92629-8777, USA

Brown, Derek (Football Player)
New York Giants
13 Four Leaf Mnr
Rexford, NY 12148-1490, USA

Brown, Dermal (Baseball Player)
Kansas City Royals
2626 Balmoral Ct
Kissimmee, FL 34744-8442, USA

Brown, Donald C (Football Player)
San Diego Chargers
2797 Union Ave
San Jose, CA 95124-1433, USA

Brown, Doug (Football Player)
Los Angeles Rams
PO Box 688
Keno, OR 97627-0688, USA

Brown, Doug (Hockey Player)
New Jersey Devils
3188 Bradway Blvd
Bloomfield Hills, MI 48301-2504, USA

Brown, Dwier (Actor)
c/o Billy Miller *Billy Miller Management*
8730 W Sunset Blvd Ste 270
Los Angeles, CA 90069-2247, USA

Brown, Eddie (Football Player)
Cincinnati Bengals
628 Cedar Park Dr
Daytona Beach, FL 32114-5112, USA

Brown, Edmund G (Jerry) Jr (Governor)
Mayor's Office
City Hall
Frank Ogawa Plaza
Oakland, CA 94612, USA

Brown, Edward (Ed) (Football Player)
3395 S Higuera St Spc 61
San Luis Obispo, CA 93401-6936, USA

Brown, Edward R (Cinematographer)
3925 S Jones Blvd Apt 1011
Las Vegas, NV 89103-7101, USA

Brown, Eric (Football Player)
Denver Broncos
7566 Lincoln Village Dr
San Antonio, TX 78244-1517, USA

Brown, Errol
PO Box 106
Rochdale, ENGLAND OL16 4HW,
UNITED KINGDOM (UK)

Brown, Faith (Actor)
Million Dollar Music Co
12 Praed Mews
London W2 1QY, UNITED KINGDOM
(UK)

Brown, Foxy (Musician)
c/o Lee Daniels *Lee Daniels Entertainment*
39 W 131st St
New York, NY 10037-3502, USA

Brown, Fred (Basketball Player, Coach)
3696 72nd Pl SE
Mercer Island, WA 98040-3353, USA

Brown, Fred (Football Player)
Buffalo Bills
1050 Riverbend Club Dr SE
Atlanta, GA 30339-2805, USA

Brown, Fred R (Football Player)
Los Angeles Rams
4128 Rigel Ave
Lompoc, CA 93436-1248, USA

Brown, G Hanks (Hank) (Senator)
Daniels Fund
55 Madison St Ste 255
Denver, CO 80206-5420, USA

Brown, Gary (Football Player)
Green Bay Packers
5 Crystal Ln
Brentwood, NY 11717-1114, USA

Brown, Gary (Football Player)
Houston Oilers
198 Starr Rd
Montoursville, PA 17754-9340, USA

Brown, Gates (Baseball Player)
Detroit Tigers
17206 Santa Barbara Dr
Detroit, MI 48221-2525, USA

Brown, Georg Stanford (Actor)
2565 Greenvalley Rd
Los Angeles, CA 90046-1437, USA

Brown, George (Basketball Player)
Minneapolis Lakers
24652 Santa Barbara St
Southfield, MI 48075-2526, USA

Brown, George (Football Player)
Washington Redskins
4401 Flower Valley Dr
Rockville, MD 20853-1813, USA

Brown, Gordie (Comedian)
c/o Staff Member *William Morris Agency (WMA-LA)*
1 William Morris Pl
Beverly Hills, CA 90212-4261, USA

Brown, Greg (Football Player)
Philadelphia Eagles
1016 Hartley Ct
Sicklerville, NJ 08081-1109, USA

Brown, Greg (Hockey Player)
Buffalo Sabres
45 Marlboro Rd
Southborough, MA 01772-1207, USA

Brown, Hal (Baseball Player)
Chicago White Sox
4216 Henderson Rd
Greensboro, NC 27410-4305, USA

Brown, Harold (Secretary)
Strategic/International Studies Center
1800 K St NW Ste 400
Washington, DC 20006-2230, USA

Brown, Helen Gurley (Editor, Writer)
1 W 81st St # 22D
New York, NY 10024-6048, USA

Brown, Henry (Actor)
1101 E Pike St Ste 300
Seattle, WA 98122-3938, USA

Brown, Henry (Baseball Player)
Kansas City Monarchs
3056 N 26th St
Milwaukee, WI 53206-1123, USA

Brown, Henry W (War Hero)
2825 Carter Rd Unit 117
Sumter, SC 29150-1733, USA

Brown, Heritage Doris (Athlete, Track Athlete)
Seattle Pacific College
Athletic Dept
Seattle, WA 98119, USA

Brown, Himan (Director)
285 Central Park W
New York, NY 10024-3006, USA

Brown, Hubie (Coach)
120 Foxridge Rd NW
Atlanta, GA 30327-4310, USA

Brown, Ivory Lee (Football Player)
Phoenix Cardinals
9931 Brockbank Dr
Dallas, TX 75220-1647, USA

Brown, J B (Football Player)
Miami Dolphins
12520 Woodsong Ln
Mitchellville, MD 20721-4224, USA

Brown, J Cristopher (Cris) (Baseball Player)
5015 Brighton Ave
Los Angeles, CA 90062-2434, USA

Brown, J Gordon (Government Official)
House of Commons
Westminister
London SW1A 0AA, UNITED KINGDOM (UK)

Brown, Jackie (Baseball Player)
Washington Senators
RR 3 Box 508
Holdenville, OK 74848, USA

Brown, James (Baseball Player)
Newark Eagles
10715 Inwood St
Jamaica, NY 11435-5305, USA

Brown, James (Football Player)
Cleveland Browns
4911 Knox St
Philadelphia, PA 19144-3617, USA

Brown, James (Musician)
c/o Rob Heller *William Morris Agency (WMA-LA)*
1 William Morris Pl
Beverly Hills, CA 90212-4261, USA

Brown, James (Sportscaster)
Fox-TV
205 W 67th St
Sports Dept
New York, NY 10021, USA

Brown, James (Jim) (Actor)
c/o Harlan Werner *Sports Placement Service*
6671 W Sunset Blvd Ste 1521
Los Angeles, CA 90028-7123, USA

Brown, James R (General)
18286 Buccaneer Ter
Leesburg, VA 20176-8479, USA

Brown, Jamie (Actor)
c/o Melisa Spamer *Domain*
9229 W Sunset Blvd Ste 415
West Hollywood, CA 90069-3404, USA

Brown, Jarvis (Baseball Player)
Minnesota Twins
1412 85th St
Kenosha, WI 53143-6420, USA

Brown, Jay W Jr (Financier)
MBIA Inc
113 King St
Armonk, NY 10504-1610, USA

Brown, Jeff (Hockey Player)
Quebec Nordiques
1136 Cabinview Ct
Chesterfield, MO 63017-2471, USA

Brown, Jim (Actor, Football Player)
Cleveland Browns
1851 Sunset Plaza Dr
Los Angeles, CA 90069-1313, USA

Brown, Jim Ed (Musician)
Billy Deaton Talent
5811 Still Hollow Rd
Nashville, TN 37215-4819, USA

Brown, John (Basketball Player)
Atlanta Hawks
1329 N Florissant Rd
Saint Louis, MO 63135-1153, USA

Brown, John (Football Player)
Cleveland Browns
101 Gadshill Pl
Pittsburgh, PA 15237-2341, USA

Brown, John Y Jr (Governor)
3928 Weber Way
Lexington, KY 40514-1008, USA

Brown, Jophrey (Baseball Player)
Chicago Cubs
3008 W 81st St
Inglewood, CA 90305-1425, USA

Brown, Judge Joe (Judge)
c/o Staff Member *Judge Joe Brown*
125 W 55th St
New York, NY 10019-5369, USA

Brown, Julie (Actor, Comedian)
11288 Ventura Blvd # 728
Studio City, CA 91604-3187, USA

Brown, Junior (Musician)
c/o Staff Member *Paradigm (Monterey)*
509 Hartnell St
Monterey, CA 93940-2825, USA

Brown, Kaci (Musician)
c/o Staff Member *Interscope Records (LA) - Main*
2220 Colorado Ave
Santa Monica, CA 90404-3506, USA

Brown, Kale (Actor)
c/o Staff Member *Gage Group, The (LA)*
14724 Ventura Blvd Ste 505
Sherman Oaks, CA 91403-3505, USA

Brown, Katie (Designer, Television Host)
c/o Staff Member *Style Network*
5750 Wilshire Blvd
Los Angeles, CA 90036-3697, USA

Brown, Kedrick (Basketball Player)
Boston Celtics
151 Merrimac St # 1
Boston, MA 02114-4714, USA

Brown, Keith (Baseball Player)
Cincinnati Reds
6313 Willow Oak Dr
Nashville, TN 37221-3980, USA

Brown, Keith (Hockey Player)
Chicago Blackhawks
4615 Sloan Rdg
Cumming, GA 30028-6932, USA

Brown, Ken (Hockey Player)
Chicago Blackhawks
Edmonton Sun 9300 47 St NW
Edmonton, AB T6B 2P6, CANADA

Brown, Ken A (Football Player)
Denver Broncos
1106 Johanna Bay Dr
Midlothian, VA 23114-7116, USA

Brown, Ken J (Football Player)
Cleveland Browns
2004 Miramar Blvd
Oklahoma City, OK 73111-1808, USA

Brown, Kenneth J (Misc)
Graphic Communications Int'l Union
1900 L St NW
Washington, DC 20036-5007, USA

Brown, Kevin (Baseball Player)
c/o Team Member *New York Yankees*
Yankee Stadium
161st St & River Ave
Bronx, NY 10451, USA

Brown, Kimberlin Ann (Actor)
c/o Staff Member *Pakula/King &
Associates*
9229 W Sunset Blvd Ste 315
Los Angeles, CA 90069-3403, USA

Brown, Kimberly J (Actor)
2069 Troon Dr
Henderson, NV 89074-0669, USA

Brown, Koffee (Musician)
Red Entertainment Group
481 8th Ave # 1750
New York, NY 10001-1809, USA

Brown, Kwarne (Basketball Player)
Washington Wizards MCI Centre
601 F St NW
Washington, DC 20004-1605, USA

Brown, Larry (Baseball Player)
Cleveland Indians
13158 La Mirada Cir
Wellington, FL 33414-3997, USA

Brown, Larry (Football Player)
Pittsburgh Steelers
1377 Glencoe Ave
Pittsburgh, PA 15205-4342, USA

Brown, Larry (Football Player)
Washington Redskins
12004 Piney Glen Ln
Potomac, MD 20854-1417, USA

Brown, Larry (Hockey Player)
New York Rangers
21 Landing Dr
Dobbs Ferry, NY 10522-1181, USA

Brown, Larry (Hockey Player)
5781 Eucalyptus Dr
Garden Valley, CA 95633-9622, USA

Brown, Lawrence H (Larry) (Basketball
Player, Coach)
Detroit Pistons
2 Championship Dr
Palace
Auburn Hills, MI 48326-1753, USA

Brown, Lee P (Government Official)
Mayor's Office
901 Bagby St # 300
City Hall
Houston, TX 77002-2526, USA

Brown, Leon (Baseball Player)
New York Mets
7537 S La Rosa Dr
Tempe, AZ 85283-4627, USA

Brown, Leonard (Baseball Player)
Homestead Grays
4411 19th St NE
Washington, DC 20018-3305, USA

Brown, Les (Motivational Speaker)
PO Box 806217
Chicago, IL 60680-4123, USA

Brown, Lester R (Misc)
Worldwatch Institute
1776 Massachusetts Ave NW
Washington, DC 20036-1995, USA

Brown, Lewis (Basketball Player)
Washington Bullets
902 E Imperial Hwy
Los Angeles, CA 90059-1622, USA

Brown, Lomas (Football Player)
Detroit Lions
11360 SW 164th St
Miami, FL 33157-2712, USA

Brown, Mack (Coach)
University of Texas
Athletic Dept
Austin, TX 78712, USA

Brown, Marc (Writer)
PO Box 873
West Tisbury, MA 02575-0873, USA

Brown, Mark (Baseball Player)
Baltimore Orioles
108 NE 1st Street Ter
Blue Springs, MO 64014-2814, USA

Brown, Mark (Football Player)
Miami Dolphins
2761 SW 81st Way
Davie, FL 33328-1617, USA

Brown, Mark N (Astronaut)
80 Earlsgate Rd
Dayton, OH 45440-3664, USA

Brown, Marty (Baseball Player)
Cincinnati Reds
4425 Bent Tree Blvd
Sarasota, FL 34241-6013, USA

Brown, Marty (Musician)
Mitchell Fox Mgmt
212 3rd Ave N
Nashville, TN 37201-1626, USA

Brown, Marv (Football Player)
Detroit Lions
1807 Surry Oaks Dr
New Caney, TX 77357-2938, USA

Brown, Matt (Director)
c/o Kenny Goodman *William Morris
Agency (WMA-NY)*
1325 Avenue Of The Americas
New York, NY 10019-6026, USA

Brown, Melanie (Musician)
c/o Wes Stevens *VOX Inc*
5670 Wilshire Blvd Ste 820
Los Angeles, CA 90036-5613, USA

Brown, Michael (Basketball Player)
Chicago Bulls
5095 N Chieftain St
Las Vegas, NV 89149-2513, USA

Brown, Michael S (Nobel Prize Laureate)
5719 Redwood Ln
Dallas, TX 75209-2421, USA

Brown, Mike (Baseball Player)
Boston Red Sox
8712 Pine Needles Ct
Vienna, VA 22182-2337, USA

Brown, Mike (Coach)
c/o Staff Member *Cleveland Cavaliers*
1 Center Ct
Gund Arena
Cleveland, OH 44115-4001, USA

Brown, Myron (Basketball Player)
Minnesota Timberwolves
10382 Grubbs Rd
Wexford, PA 15090-9420, USA

Brown, Na (Football Player)
Philadelphia Eagles
PO Box 853
Fletcher, NC 28732-0853, USA

Brown, Napoleon (Nappy) (Musician)
1023 Moretz Ave
Charlotte, NC 28206-2128, USA

Brown, Norman W (Business Person)
Foote Cone Belding
101 E Erie St
Chicago, IL 60611-2850, USA

Brown, Norris (Football Player)
Minnesota Vikings
320 Pinehaven Street Ext
Laurens, SC 29360, USA

Brown, Olivia (Actor)
David Shapira
193 N Robertson Blvd
Beverly Hills, CA 90211-2103, USA

Brown, Ollie (Baseball Player)
San Francisco Giants
8462 Country Club Dr
Buena Park, CA 90621-1421, USA

Brown, Orlando (Actor)
c/o Wendi Green *Abrams Artists Agency
(LA)*
9200 W Sunset Blvd Ph 11
Los Angeles, CA 90069-3601, USA

Brown, Oscar (Baseball Player)
Atlanta Braves
19113 Gunlock Ave
Carson, CA 90746-2825, USA

Brown, Otto (Football Player)
Dallas Cowboys
456 Alcorn Ave
Dallas, TX 75217-5833, USA

Brown, Owsley II (Business Person)
Brown-Forman Corp
850 Dixie Hwy
Louisville, KY 40210-1038, USA

Brown, P J (Basketball Player)
New Jersey Nets
903 N Cypress St
Carthage, TX 75633-1375, USA

Brown, Patricia (Baseball Player)
1100 Governors Dr Apt 26
Winthrop, MA 02152-3254, USA

Brown, Patrick (Misc)
Stanford University
Medical School
Biochemistry Dept
Stanford, CA 94305, USA

Brown, Paul (Baseball Player)
Philadelphia Phillies
RR 4 Box 244
Holdenville, OK 74848, USA

Brown, Paul (Musician)
c/o Staff Member *Verve Music Group*
1755 Broadway Frnt 3
New York, NY 10019-3743, USA

Brown, Peter (Actor)
5328 Alhama Dr
Woodland Hills, CA 91364-2013, USA

Brown, Philip (Actor)
8721 W Sunset Blvd Ste 200
Los Angeles, CA 90069-2272, USA

Brown, Preston (Football Player)
New England Patriots
6804 Jones Valley Dr SE
Huntsville, AL 35802-1920, USA

Brown, Ralph (Football Player)
New York Giants
9395 Old Post Dr
Rancho Cucamonga, CA 91730-5765,
USA

Brown, Randy (Baseball Player)
California Angels
PO Box 326
Plymouth, FL 32768-0326, USA

Brown, Ray (Football Player)
Detroit Lions
222 Republic Dr
Allen Park, MI 48101-3650, USA

Brown, Raymond (Football Player)
Atlanta Falcons
4936 Lake Fjord Pass
Marietta, GA 30068-1639, USA

Brown, Reb (Actor)
5454 Virgenes Rd
Calabasas, CA 91302-1080, USA

Brown, Reggie (Football Player)
Houston Oilers
2242 NW 93rd Ter
Miami, FL 33147-3068, USA

Brown, Reggie D (Football Player)
Detroit Lions
20101 Bentler St
Detroit, MI 48219-1387, USA

Brown, Reggie V (Football Player)
Atlanta Falcons
1325 Oxford Ln
Union, NJ 07083-5447, USA

Brown, Richard (Football Player)
Los Angeles Rams
5652 Alfred Ave
Westminster, CA 92683-2810, USA

Brown, Richard E (Tex) III (General)
Deputy Cofs For Personnel
Hqusaf Pentagon
Washington, DC 20330-0001, USA

Brown, Rob (Actor)
c/o Gabrielle (Gaby) Morgerman *William
Morris Agency (WMA-LA)*
1 William Morris Pl
Beverly Hills, CA 90212-4261, USA

Brown, Robert (Football Player)
Green Bay Packers
30 Upper Curry Rd N
Cynthiana, KY 41031-4763, USA

Brown, Robert (Football Player)
St Louis Cardinals
PO Box 3
Merigold, MS 38759-0003, USA

Brown, Robert D (Business Person)
Milacron Inc
2090 Florence Ave
Cincinnati, OH 45206-2455, USA

Brown, Robert S (Bob) (Football Player)
Philadelphia Eagles
1628 Fairmont Dr
San Leandro, CA 94578-1929, USA

Brown, Roger L (Football Player)
Detroit Lions
9 N Point Dr
Portsmouth, VA 23703-3644, USA

Brown, Ron (Football Player)
Los Angeles Rams
3961 Via Marisol Apt 331
Los Angeles, CA 90042-4973, USA

Brown, Roosevelt (Baseball Player)
Chicago Cubs
6551 Thea Ln Apt S17
Columbus, GA 31907-0822, USA

Brown, Ruben (Football Player)
Buffalo Bills
170 Fox Meadow Ln
Orchard Park, NY 14127-2866, USA

Brown, Rush (Football Player)
St Louis Cardinals
2425 Cartertown Rd
Clinton, NC 28328-7467, USA

Brown, Samantha (Actor)
c/o Mark Turner *Abrams Artists Agency
(LA)*
9200 W Sunset Blvd Ph 11
Los Angeles, CA 90069-3601, USA

Brown, Samuel M (Football Player)
San Francisco 49ers
25 Franklin Creek Rd N
Savannah, GA 31411-2826, USA

Brown, Sandra (Writer)
1306 W Abram St
Arlington, TX 76013-1703, USA

Brown, Sara (Actor)
Media Artists Group
6300 Wilshire Blvd Ste 1470
Los Angeles, CA 90048-5200, USA

Brown, Sarah (Actor)
c/o Staff Member *McKeon-Valeo-Myones
Management*
9100 Wilshire Blvd Ste 350W
Beverly Hills, CA 90212-3437, USA

Brown, Scott (Baseball Player)
Cincinnati Reds
1238 Alton Pierce Rd
Dequincy, LA 70633-4501, USA

Brown, Selwyn (Football Player)
Tampa Bay Buccaneers
3533 Inverrary Blvd W
Lauderhill, FL 33319-7114, USA

Brown, Shay
499 Erin Dr
Knoxville, TN 37919, USA

Brown, Sonny (Football Player)
Houston Oilers
825 Shadow Wood Dr
Edmond, OK 73034-7061, USA

Brown, Stan (Basketball Player)
Philadelphia Warriors
2201 Tremont St
Philadelphia, PA 19115-5041, USA

Brown, Stan (Football Player)
Cleveland Browns
PO Box 533
Benicia, CA 94510-0533, USA

Brown, Susan (Actor)
11931 Addison St
N Hollywood, CA 91607-3106, USA

Brown, Sylvia
Sylvia Browne Corporation
1700 Winchester Blvd Ste 100
Campbell, CA 95008-1163, USA

Brown, Sylvia (Psychic)
PO Box 5100
Carlsbad, CA 92018-5100, USA

Brown, T Graham (Musician)
Bobby Roberts
3050 Business Park Cir Ste 303
Goodlettsville, TN 37072-3588, USA

Brown, Tarrick (Baseball Player)
Chicago Cubs
18631 Collins St Apt 33
Tarzana, CA 91356-2178, USA

Brown, Terry (Football Player)
St Louis Cardinals
401 N 6th St
Marlow, OK 73055-1813, USA

Brown, Theotis J (Football Player)
St Louis Cardinals
9604 W 121st Ter
Overland Park, KS 66213-1691, USA

Brown, Thomas M (Football Player)
Pittsburgh Steelers
6024 Approach Rd
Sarasota, FL 34238-5721, USA

Brown, Thomas Wilson
3033 Vista Crest Dr
Los Angeles, CA 90068-1824, USA

Brown, Tim (Football Player)
c/o Team Member *Tampa Bay Buccaneers*
1 Bucanner Place
Tampa, FL 33607, USA

Brown, Timmy (Football Player)
Green Bay Packers
3574 E Bogert Trl
Palm Springs, CA 92264-9623, USA

Brown, Timothy D (Tim) (Football Player)
Los Angeles Raiders
1340 Thistlewood Dr
Desoto, TX 75115-7700, USA

Brown, Tina (Talk Show Host, Writer)
c/o Staff Member *Topic A With Tina
Brown*
900 Sylvan Ave
Cnbc
Englewood Cliffs, NJ 07632-3312, USA

Brown, Tom (Baseball Player)
Washington Senators
27981 Nanticoke Rd
Salisbury, MD 21801-1645, USA

Brown, Tom (Baseball Player)
Seattle Mariners
600 Valencia Rd
Venice, FL 34285-2538, USA

Brown, Tom (Football Player)
Miami Dolphins
702 Placid Ct
Gibsonia, PA 15044-8016, USA

Brown, Tom W (Football Player)
Philadelphia Eagles
201 High Point Dr
Waco, TX 76705-1750, USA

Brown, Tommy (Baseball Player)
Brooklyn Dodgers
8119 Shady Pl
Brentwood, TN 37027-7344, USA

Brown, Tony (Football Player)
Houston Oilers
11629 Garrick Ave
Sylmar, CA 91342-6533, USA

Brown, Tracy (Ballerina)
Royal Ballet
Convent Garden
Bow St
London WC2E 9DD, UNITED KINGDOM
(UK)

Brown, Trisha (Choreographer, Dancer)
Trisha Brown Dance Co
211 W 61st St
New York, NY 10023-7832, USA

Brown, Troy (Football Player)
New England Patriots
124 Pine Hvn
Barnwell, SC 29812-2817, USA

Brown, Vincent B (Football Player)
New England Patriots
1615 Thoreau Dr
Suwanee, GA 30024-2090, USA

Brown, W Earl (Actor)
c/o Staff Member *The Artists Group Ltd
(LA)*
1650 Broadway Ste 610
New York, NY 10019-6833, USA

Brown, Wayne (Hockey Player)
Boston Bruins
50 Montgomerry Blvd
Belleville, ON K8N 1H9, CANADA

Brown, Wes (Actor)
c/o Stacy Abrams *Abrams Artists Agency
(LA)*
9200 W Sunset Blvd Ph 11
Los Angeles, CA 90069-3601, USA

Brown, William D (Bill) (Coach, Football
Player)
Bromley Printing
514 Northdale Blvd NW
Minneapolis, MN 55448-3357, USA

Brown, William F (Willie) (Coach,
Football Player)
New England Patriots
27138 Lillegard Ct
Tracy, CA 95304-8866, USA

Brown, Willie (Baseball Player)
3430 John Hancock Dr
Tallahassee, FL 32312-1536, USA

Brown, Winston (Baseball Player)
12144 SW 50th St
Cooper City, FL 33330-4476, USA

Brown, Woody
11844 Otsego St
Valley Village, CA 91607-3223, USA

Brown, Wren (Actor)
c/o Sara Schedeen
36550 SE Boitano Rd
Sarabeth Schedeen Management
Sandy, OR 97055-6658, USA

Brown III, Guy (Football Player)
Dallas Cowboys
1015 Briar Hill Cir
Duncanville, TX 75137-3733, USA

Brown Jr, Larry (Football Player)
Dallas Cowboys
5603 Sycamore Dr
Colleyville, TX 76034-5063, USA

Browne, Byron (Baseball Player)
Chicago Cubs
7369 W Sanna St
Peoria, AZ 85345-7193, USA

Browne, Chris (Cartoonist)
King Features Syndicate
888 7th Ave Ste 201
New York, NY 10106-0201, USA

Browne, E John P (Business Person)
BP Exploration Co
1 Finsbury Circus
London EC2M 7BA, UNITED KINGDOM
(UK)

Browne, Gordon (Football Player)
New York Jets
25 Harbourside Rd
North Quincy, MA 02171-1555, USA

Browne, Jackson (Musician, Songwriter,
Writer)
c/o Donald Miller *Donald Miller
Management*
12746 Kling St
Studio City, CA 91604-1125, USA

Browne, James C (Football Player)
Los Angeles Raiders
6265 Crest Forest Ct E
Clarkston, MI 48348-4581, USA

Browne, Jerry (Baseball Player)
Texas Rangers
2A Prince St
Christiansted, VI 00820, USA

Browne, Kathy
PO Box 2939
Beverly Hills, CA 90213-2939, USA

Browne, Leslie (Actor, Ballerina)
2025 Broadway Apt 6F
New York, NY 10023-5038, USA

Browne, Olin (Golfer)
PO Box 2066
Hobe Sound, FL 33475-2066, USA

Browne, Secor D (Engineer, Government
Official)
2101 L St NW # 207
Washington, DC 20037-1526, USA

Browne, Victor (Actor)
c/o Lara Rosenstock *Lara Rosenstock
Management*
8371 Blackburn Ave Apt 1
Los Angeles, CA 90048-4245, USA

Browne, Zachary (Actor)
c/o Staff Member *Iris Burton Agency*
8916 Ashcroft Ave
West Hollywood, CA 90048-2404, USA

Browner, Jim (Football Player)
Cincinnati Bengals
508 E Sedgwick St
Philadelphia, PA 19119-1326, USA

Browner, Joey (Football Player)
PO Box 571
Pierz, MN 56364-0571, USA

Browner, Keith (Football Player)
Tampa Bay Buccaneers
1015 Sandoval Ct
Stockton, CA 95206-1896, USA

Browner, Ross (Football Player)
Cincinnati Bengals
7900 Indian Springs Dr
Nashville, TN 37221-1147, USA

Browning, Cal (Baseball Player)
St Louis Cardinals
111 Buckner Dr
Ruidoso, NM 88345-6913, USA

Browning, Edmond L (Religious Leader)
5164 Imai Rd
Hood River, OR 97031-9442, USA

Browning, Emily Jane (Actor)
c/o Theresa Peters *William Morris Agency (WMA-LA)*
1 William Morris Pl
Beverly Hills, CA 90212-4261, USA

Browning, Gregg (Football Player)
New York Giants
2282 S Madison St
Denver, CO 80210-4921, USA

Browning, James R (Judge)
US Court of Appeals
95 7th St
Court Building
San Francisco, CA 94103-1518, USA

Browning, Kurt (Figure Skater)
Int'l Management Group
175 Bloor St E #400
Toronto, ON M4W 3R8, CANADA

Browning, Ricou (Actor)
5221 SW 196th Ln
Southwest Ranches, FL 33332-1111, USA

Browning, Ryan (Actor)
United Talent Agency
9560 Wilshire Blvd Ste 500
Beverly Hills, CA 90212-2401, USA

Browning, Thomas L (Tom) (Baseball Player)
Cincinnati Reds
3094 Friars Ln
Edgewood, KY 41017-8126, USA

Brownlee, Claude (Football Player)
Miami Dolphins
2711 Hood St
Columbus, GA 31906-3251, USA

Brownlow, Kevin (Producer)
Photoplay Productions
21 Princess Road
London NW1, UNITED KINGDOM (UK)

Brownmiller, Susan (Activist)
61 Jane St
New York, NY 10014-5107, USA

Brownschidle, Jack (Hockey Player)
St Louis Blues
8673 Millcreek Dr
East Amherst, NY 14051-2085, USA

Brownschidle, Jeff (Hockey Player)
Hartford Whalers
35 Hidden Pines Ct
East Amherst, NY 14051-1688, USA

Brownson, Mark (Baseball Player)
Colorado Rockies
13992 Aster Ave
Wellington, FL 33414-8509, USA

Brownstein, Carrie (Music Group, Musician)
Legends of 21st Century
7 Trinity Row
Florence, MA 01062-1931, USA

Brownstein, Michael L (Publisher)
Ladies Home Journal
125 Park Ave Fl 20
New York, NY 10017-8501, USA

Browny, Jann (Musician)
Tracy Gershon Mgmt
PO Box 158400
Nashville, TN 37215-8400, USA

Broyles, Frank F (Coach, Football Player, Sportscaster)
University of Arkansas
Broyles Athletic Complex
Fayetteville, AR 72701, USA

Brubaker, Bruce (Baseball Player)
Los Angeles Dodgers
140 Southtown Blvd
Champion Ford
Owensboro, KY 42303-7759, USA

Brubaker, Jeff (Hockey Player)
Hartford Whalers
1715 W Market St
Greensboro, NC 27403-1710, USA

Brubeck, David W (Dave) (Music Group, Musician)
221 Millstone Rd
Wilton, CT 06897-1218, USA

Brubeck, William H (Government Official)
7 Linden St
Cambridge, MA 02138-5004, USA

Bruce, Aundray (Football Player)
Atlanta Falcons
1730 Wentworth Dr
Montgomery, AL 36106-2639, USA

Bruce, Bob (Baseball Player)
Detroit Tigers
633 Mission Cir
Irving, TX 75063-6617, USA

Bruce, Bruce (Comedian)
c/o Staff Member *Agency for the Performing Arts (APA-LA)*
405 S Beverly Dr
Beverly Hills, CA 90212-4416, USA

Bruce, Christopher (Choreographer)
Rambert Dance Co
94 Chiswick High Road
London W4 1SH, UNITED KINGDOM (UK)

Bruce, David (Hockey Player)
Vancouver Canucks
5137 Willrod Rd
Thunder Bay, ON P7B 5E3, CANADA

Bruce, Ed
1022 16th Ave S
Nashville, TN 37212-2303, USA

Bruce, George
3 rue de Plaisance
Paris F-75014, FRANCE

Bruce, Isaac I (Football Player)
Los Angeles Rams
14241 Appalachian Trl
Davie, FL 33325-6506, USA

Bruce, Jack (Music Group, Songwriter, Writer)
International Creative Mgmt
40 W 57th St Ste 1800
New York, NY 10019-4001, USA

Bruce, Richard Francis (Editor)
Mirisch Agency
1801 Century Park E Ste 1801
Los Angeles, CA 90067-2320, USA

Bruce, Robert V (Historian)
606 13th Ave SE
Olympia, WA 98501-2313, USA

Bruce, Tom
122 Sea Terrace Way
Aptos, CA 95003-4521, USA

Brucie, Cousin
PO Box 50
New York, NY 10101-0050, USA

Bruckbauer, Fred (Baseball Player)
Minnesota Twins
7673 Colonial Ct
Naples, FL 34112-7755, USA

Brucker, Earle (Baseball Player)
Philadelphia Athletics
629 Mundy Ter
El Cajon, CA 92020-2310, USA

Bruckheimer, Jerry (Director, Producer)
c/o Staff Member *Jerry Bruckheimer Films*
1631 10th St
Santa Monica, CA 90404-3705, USA

Bruckner, Agnes (Actor)
c/o Susan Curtis *Curtis Talent Management*
9607 Arby Dr
Beverly Hills, CA 90210-1202, USA

Bruckner, Amy (Actor)
c/o Susan Curtis *Curtis Talent Management*
9607 Arby Dr
Beverly Hills, CA 90210-1202, USA

Bruckner, Greg (Golfer)
3906 E Potter Dr
Phoenix, AZ 85050-4837, USA

Bruckner, Les (Football Player)
Chicago Cardinals
1325 Valley View Rd Apt 307
Glendale, CA 91202-4420, USA

Brudzinski, Robert L (Bob) (Athlete)
1057 Lido Ct
Weston, FL 33326-2903, USA

Brue, Bob (Golfer)
4316 N Sheffield Ave
Milwaukee, WI 53211-1432, USA

Brueckman, Charlie (Football Player)
Washington Redskins
7439 Plott Rd
Charlotte, NC 28215-9440, USA

Bruel, Patrick (Music Group)
Artmedia
20 Ave Rapp
Paris 75007, FRANCE

Brueland, Lowell K (Misc)
420 La Z Acres Rd
Westminster, SC 29693-5109, USA

Bruen, John D (Business Person, General)
6104 Greenlawn Ct
Springfield, VA 22152-1314, USA

Bruener, Mark (Football Player)
Pittsburgh Steelers
26 Commanders Pt
Missouri City, TX 77459-6643, USA

Bruett, J T (Baseball Player)
Minnesota Twins
214 N Oak Park Ave Apt 3bb
Oak Park, IL 60302-2166, USA

Bruggink, Eric G (Judge)
US Claims Court
717 Madison Pl NW
Washington, DC 20439-0001, USA

Bruguera, Sergi (Tennis Player)
C'Escipion 42
Barcelona 08023, SPAIN

Bruhert, Mike (Baseball Player)
New York Mets
907 Center Dr
Franklin Square, NY 11010-2005, USA

Bruhin, John (Football Player)
Tampa Bay Buccaneers
6960 Taylors View Ln
Knoxville, TN 37921-2843, USA

Brumback, Charles T (Publisher)
435 N Michigan Ave Fl 7
Chicago, IL 60611-4027, USA

Brumbly, Charlie (Actor)
c/o Staff Member *DDO Artist Agency*
8322 Beverly Blvd Ste 301
Los Angeles, CA 90048-2665, USA

Brumel, Valeryi
Louknetzkaya Nab 8
Moscow, RUSSIA

Brumfield, Jackson (Football Player)
San Francisco 49ers
25644 Highway 25
Franklinton, LA 70438-5126, USA

Brumfield, Jacob D (Baseball Player)
Cincinnati Reds
43275 Tillman Dr
Hammond, LA 70403-2811, USA

Brumfield, Scott (Football Player)
Cincinnati Bengals
1150 E 900 S
Spanish Fork, UT 84660-2629, USA

Brumfield-White, Dolores (Baseball Player)
1604 Millcreek Dr
Arkadelphia, AR 71923-3024, USA

Brumley, Duff (Baseball Player)
Texas Rangers
230 Cg Earnest Rd NW
Charleston, TN 37310-6625, USA

Brumley, Mike (Baseball Player)
Chicago Cubs
1020 Western Trl
Keller, TX 76248-4924, USA

Brumley, Robert L (Football Player)
Detroit Lions
256 E Sunset Rd
San Antonio, TX 78209-2760, USA

Brumm, Donald D (Don) (Football Player)
St Louis Cardinals
511 County Road 442
New Franklin, MO 65274-9704, USA

Brummer, Glenn (Baseball Player)
St Louis Cardinals
1830 Dalton Dr
Belleville, IL 62226-8207, USA

Brummer, Renate (Astronaut)
NOAA/FSL
325 Broadway St
Boulder, CO 80305-3337, USA

Brummett, Greg (Baseball Player)
San Francisco Giants
605 W 10th St
Concordia, KS 66901-4011, USA

Brumwell, Murray (Hockey Player)
Minnesota North Stars
727 Tabriz Dr
Billings, MT 59105-2809, USA

Brunansky, Thomas A (Tom) (Baseball Player)
California Angels
13411 Summit Cir
Poway, CA 92064-2169, USA

Brundage, Dewey (Football Player)
Pittsburgh Steelers
220 S 400 W
Orem, UT 84058-5329, USA

Brundage, Howard D (Publisher)
RR 2 Box 332-47
Old Lyme, CT 06371, USA

Brundy, Stan (Basketball Player)
New Jersey Nets
4644 Stephen Girard Ave
New Orleans, LA 70126-4756, USA

Brunell, Mark (Football Player)
Green Bay Packers
1519 Marilyn Way
Santa Maria, CA 93454-5946, USA

Brunelli, Sam (Football Player)
Denver Broncos
1080 Wisconsin Ave NW Apt 104
Washington, DC 20007-6052, USA

Bruner, Jerome S (Misc)
200 Mercer St
New York, NY 10012-1546, USA

Bruner, Michael L (Mike) (Swimmer)
718 Belden Dr
Los Altos, CA 94022-1673, USA

Brunet, Andree Joly (Figure Skater)
2805 Boyne City Rd
Boyne City, MI 49712, USA

Brunet, Bob (Football Player)
Washington Redskins
25001 La Highway 1032
Denham Springs, LA 70726, USA

Brunette, Andrew (Hockey Player)
Washington Capitals
1018 W Morgan St
Duluth, MN 55811-4425, USA

Brunettes, The (Music Group)
c/o Staff Member *Paradigm (Monterey)*
509 Hartnell St
Monterey, CA 93940-2825, USA

Brunetti, Melvin T (Judge)
US Court of Appeals
40 W Liberty St
Reno, NV 89501, USA

Brunetti, Wayne H (Business Person)
New Century Energies
1225 17th St Ste 100
Denver, CO 80202-5518, USA

Bruney, Fred (Football Player)
San Francisco 49ers
13160 Village Chase Cir
Tampa, FL 33618-8330, USA

Brungardt, Kurt
c/o Daniel A (Dan) Strone *Trident Media Group LLC*
41 Madison Ave Fl 36
New York, NY 10010-2257, USA

Bruni, Carla (Model, Music Group, Songwriter, Writer)
Marilyn Gauthier Agency
4 Rue de la Paix
Paris 75002, FRANCE

Brunkhorst, Brian (Basketball Player)
Los Angeles Stars
6182 Brumder Rd
Hartland, WI 53029-9709, USA

Brunner, J Terrance (Misc)
Better Government Assn
230 N Michigan Ave
Chicago, IL 60601-5906, USA

Brunner, Scott (Football Player)
New York Giants
734 14th Ave
Prospect Park, PA 19076-1206, USA

Bruno, Chris (Actor)
Stone Manners
6500 Wilshire Blvd Ste 550
Los Angeles, CA 90048-4950, USA

Bruno, Corbucci
Via dei Colli della Farnesina 144
Rome I-00194, ITALY

Bruno, Dylan (Actor)
Gersh Agency
223 N Canon Dr
Beverly Hills, CA 90210, USA

Bruno, Frank
Box 2266
Brentwood Essex, ENGLAND CM1S 0AQ, UNITED KINGDOM (UK)

Bruno, Franklin R (Frank) (Boxer)
P O Box 2266 Brentwood
Essex CM15 0AQ, UNITED KINGDOM (UK)

Bruno, Tom (Baseball Player)
Kansas City Royals
19196 Sd Highway 1804
Pierre, SD 57501-7401, USA

Bruns, Breck (Actor)
c/o TJ Stein *Stein Entertainment Group*
11271 Ventura Blvd # 477
Studio City, CA 91604-3136, USA

Brunsberg, Ario (Baseball Player)
Detroit Tigers
883 104th Ln NW
Coon Rapids, MN 55433-6542, USA

Brunson, Larry (Football Player)
Kansas City Chiefs
6104 E Peakview Pl
Centennial, CO 80111-4326, USA

Brunson, Mike (Football Player)
Atlanta Falcons
4602 E Fremont St
Phoenix, AZ 85042-6425, USA

Brunson, Will (Baseball Player)
Los Angeles Dodgers
13992 Aster Ave
Wellington, FL 33414-8509, USA

Bruntlett, Eric (Baseball Player)
Houston Astros
3903 E 200 N
Lafayette, IN 47905-7855, USA

Brupbacher, Ross (Football Player)
Chicago Bears
200 Pembroke Ln
Lafayette, LA 70508-5616, USA

Bruschi, Tedy (Football Player)
New England Patriots
31 Jeffrey Dr
North Attleboro, MA 02760-2761, USA

Bruske, Jim (Baseball Player)
Los Angeles Dodgers
5242 N Quail Run Pl
Paradise Valley, AZ 85253-7051, USA

Bruskin, Grisha (Artist)
236 W 26th St Rm 705
New York, NY 10001-6736, USA

Bruson, Renato (Opera Singer)
Columbia Artists Mgmt Inc
1790 Broadway Fl 6
New York, NY 10019-1412, USA

Brusstar, Warren (Baseball Player)
Philadelphia Phillies
3320 Redwood Rd
Napa, CA 94558-9544, USA

Brusteln, Robert S (Critic, Educator, Producer)
Harvard University
64 Brattle St
Loeb Drama Center
Cambridge, MA 02138-3443, USA

Brutcher, Len (Baseball Player)
4510 Hallam Hill Ln
Lakeland, FL 33813-1808, USA

Bruton, John G (Prime Minister)
Qomelstown
Dunboyne, County Meath, IRELAND

Bry, Ellen (Actor)
Media Artists Group
6300 Wilshire Blvd Ste 1470
Los Angeles, CA 90048-5200, USA

Bryan, Alan (Archaeologist)
University of Alberta
Archaeology Dept
Edmonton, AB T6G 2J8, CANADA

Bryan, Billy (Baseball Player)
Kansas City A's
3001 Hickory Ln
Opelika, AL 36801-2221, USA

Bryan, Billy (Football Player)
Denver Broncos
3408 Creekwood Drive
Tuscaloosa, AL 35453, USA

Bryan, David (Misc)
Bon Jovi Mgmt
248 W 17th St Apt 501
New York, NY 10011-5330, USA

Bryan, Donald S (Misc)
702 Melba St
Adel, GA 31620-1626, USA

Bryan, Dora (Actor)
11 Marine Parade Brighton
Sussex, UNITED KINGDOM (UK)

Bryan, Mark (Music Group, Musician)
FishCo Mgmt
2519 Devine St
Columbia, SC 29205-2435, USA

Bryan, Rick D (Football Player)
Atlanta Falcons
15526 S 295th East Ave
Coweta, OK 74429-5550, USA

Bryan, Sabrina (Actor)
c/o Staff Member *Abrams Artists Agency (LA)*
9200 W Sunset Blvd Ph 11
Los Angeles, CA 90069-3601, USA

Bryan, Steve (Football Player)
Denver Broncos
RR 2 Box 332-38
Coweta, OK 74429, USA

Bryan, Walter (Football Player)
Baltimore Colts
757 Kenwood Dr
Abilene, TX 79601-5539, USA

Bryan, Wright (Journalist)
3747 Peachtree Rd NE Apt 516
Atlanta, GA 30319-1361, USA

Bryan, Zachery Ty (Actor)
c/o Samantha Crisp *Kohner Agency, The*
9300 Wilshire Blvd Ste 555
Beverly Hills, CA 90212-3211, USA

Bryant, Anita (Activist, Music Group)
Blackwood Mgmt
PO Box 5331
Sevierville, TN 37864-5331, USA

Bryant, Antonio (Football Player)
c/o Staff Member *Dallas Cowboys*
1 Cowboys Pkwy
Irving, TX 75063-4999, USA

Bryant, Bart (Golfer)
1233 Lake Whitney Dr
Windermere, FL 34786-6069, USA

Bryant, Brad (Golfer)
3407 Bridgefield Dr
Lakeland, FL 33803-5914, USA

Bryant, Charles (Football Player)
St Louis Cardinals
3110 Lincoln St
Lorain, OH 44052-2715, USA

Bryant, Clark Rosalyn (Athlete, Track Athlete)
3901 Somerset Dr
Los Angeles, CA 90008-1704, USA

Bryant, Derek (Baseball Player)
Oakland A's
1047 Redwood Dr
Lexington, KY 40511-1133, USA

Bryant, Domingo (Football Player)
Houston Oilers
19703 Campfield Dr
Katy, TX 77449-6691, USA

Bryant, Don (Baseball Player)
Chicago Cubs
1844 Swiss Oaks St
Jacksonville, FL 32259-8954, USA

Bryant, Edward (Football Player)
San Francisco 49ers
1824 NW Radial Hwy
Omaha, NE 68104-5176, USA

Bryant, Fernando (Football Player)
Jacksonville Jaguars
2336 Emerald Dr
Jonesboro, GA 30236-5226, USA

Bryant, Gray (Editor)
34 Horatio St
New York, NY 10014-1622, USA

Bryant, Gyude (President)
President's Office
Executive Mansion Capitol Hill
Monrovia, LIBERIA

Bryant, Hubie (Football Player)
Pittsburgh Steelers
PO Box 488
Lawrenceville, VA 23868-0488, USA

Bryant, Jeff (Football Player)
Seattle Seahawks
PO Box 362240
Decatur, GA 30036-2240, USA

Bryant, Joe (Basketball Player)
Philadelphia 76ers
1835 N 72nd St
Philadelphia, PA 19151-2311, USA

Bryant, Joshua (Actor)
216 Paseo Del Pueblo Norte Ste M
Taos, NM 87571-5912, USA

Bryant, Joy (Actor)
c/o Staff Member *Creative Artists Agency LCC (CAA-LA)*
2000 Avenue Of The Stars
Los Angeles, CA 90067-4700, USA

Bryant, Kelvin (Football Player)
Washington Redskins
1803 Chiles Higgins Ct
Greensboro, NC 27406-9456, USA

Bryant, Kobe (Basketball Player)
Los Angeles Lakers
1224 Remington Rd
Wynnewood, PA 19096-2330, USA

Bryant, Mark (Basketball Player)
Portland Trail Blazers
7 Paradise Point Dr
Sugar Land, TX 77478-3176, USA

Bryant, Ralph (Baseball Player)
Los Angeles Dodgers
367 Spruill Bridge Rd
Temple, GA 30179-4568, USA

Bryant, Ray (Music Group, Musician)
Maxine Harvard Unlimited
7942 W Bell Rd
Glendale, AZ 85308-8708, USA

Bryant, Steve (Football Player)
Houston Oilers
12618 Laleu Ln
Houston, TX 77071-3735, USA

Bryant, Taman (Football Player)
New York Giants
2742 Bryant St
Vineland, NJ 08361-3021, USA

Bryant, Todd (Actor)
9150 Wilshire Blvd Ste 175
Beverly Hills, CA 90212-3450, USA

Bryant, Tony (Football Player)
Oakland Raiders
2351 Sombrero Blvd
Marathon, FL 33050-2468, USA

Bryant, Trent (Football Player)
Washington Redskins
4801 S Tiemey Dr
Independence, MO 64055, USA

Bryant, W Cullen (Football Player)
Los Angeles Rams
6495 Timber Bluff Pt
Colorado Springs, CO 80918-6237, USA

Bryant, Walter (Football Player)
Minnesota Vikings
509 Nottingham Rd
Columbia, SC 29210-3719, USA

Bryant, Waymond (Football Player)
Chicago Bears
2440 Covington Dr
Flower Mound, TX 75028-4666, USA

Bryant, Wendell (Football Player)
Arizona Cardinals
PO Box 888
Phoenix, AZ 85001-0888, USA

Bryars, R Gavin (Composer)
Bolton-Quinn Ltd
8 Pottery Lane
London W11 4LZ, UNITED KINGDOM
(UK)

Bryden, T R (Baseball Player)
California Angels
412 22nd St SE Apt C
Auburn, WA 98002-6837, USA

Brye, Steve (Baseball Player)
Minnesota Twins
621 S Spring St Apt 603
Los Angeles, CA 90014-3918, USA

Brylin, Sergei (Hockey Player)
New Jersey Devils
32 Robert Dr
Short Hills, NJ 07078-1507, USA

Bryniarski, Andrew (Actor)
c/o Staff Member *Flutie Entertainment (NY)*
270 Lafayette St Ste 1400
New York, NY 10012-3364, USA

Bryson, Bill (Writer)
c/o Staff Member *Random House Publicity*
1745 Broadway
New York, NY 10019-4343, USA

Bryson, Peabo (Music Group, Musician, Songwriter, Writer)
Agency for the Performing Arts
405 S Beverly Dr Ste 500
Beverly Hills, CA 90212-4425, USA

Bryson, Shawn (Football Player)
Buffalo Bills
418 Heatherstone Dr
Franklin, NC 28734-0274, USA

Bryson, William C (Judge)
US Appeals Court
717 Madison Pl NW
Washington, DC 20439-0001, USA

Brzeska, Magdalena (Gymnast)
Vitesse Karcher GmbH
Porschestr 6
Fellbach 70736, GERMANY

Brzezinski, Zbigniew (Educator, Government Official)
Strategic/International Studies Center
1800 K St NW Ste 400
Washington, DC 20006-2230, USA

Buanne, Patrizio (Musician)
PO Box 293
Tadworth KT20 5SX, UNITED KINGDOM
(UK)

Buatta, Mario (Designer)
120 E 80th St
New York, NY 10075-0306, USA

Bubas, Vic (Basketball Player, Coach)
133 Robert E Lane
Bluffton, SC 29909, USA

Bubka, Sergie N (Athlete, Track Athlete)
Andresi Kulikowski
Vasavagen 13
Solna 171 39, SWEDEN

Bubka, Surgei N (Athlete, Track Athlete)
Andresi Kulikowski
Vasavagen 13
Solna 171 39, SWEDEN

Buble, Michael (Musician)
3048 Cardinal Drive
Burnaby, BC V5A 2T6, CANADA

Bubna, P F (Religious Leader)
Christian & Missionary Alliance
PO Box 3500
Colorado Springs, CO 80935, USA

Bucatinsky, Dan (Actor, Producer, Writer)
c/o Staff Member *Endeavor Agency LLC (LA)*
9601 Wilshire Blvd Fl 3
Beverly Hills, CA 90210-5204, USA

Buccellati, Giorgio (Misc)
University of California
Near Eastern Languages Dept
Los Angeles, CA 90024, USA

Buccellato, Benedetta (Actor)
Carlo Levi Co
Via Giuseppe Pisanelli
Rome 00196, ITALY

Bucci, George (Basketball Player)
New York Nets
15 Peter Ave
Newburgh, NY 12550-8812, USA

Bucha, Paul W (War Hero)
601 N Salem Rd
Ridgefield, CT 06877-1926, USA

Buchanan, Bob (Baseball Player)
Cincinnati Reds
2035 Bever Ave SE
Cedar Rapids, IA 52403-2716, USA

Buchanan, Brian (Baseball Player)
Minnesota Twins
8600 El Mirasol Ct
Fort Myers, FL 33967-0521, USA

Buchanan, Charles (Football Player)
Cleveland Browns
1715 Windover Dr
Nashville, TN 37218-2410, USA

Buchanan, Edna (Journalist)
PO Box 403556
Miami Beach, FL 33140-1556, USA

Buchanan, Ian (Actor, Model)
Gold Marshak Liedtke
3500 W Olive Ave Ste 1400
Burbank, CA 91505-5512, USA

Buchanan, Isobel (Opera Singer)
Marks Mgmt
14 New Burlington St
London W1X 1FF, UNITED KINGDOM
(UK)

Buchanan, James M (Nobel Prize Laureate)
George Mason University
Study Of Public Choice Center
Fairfax, VA 22030, USA

Buchanan, Jensen (Actor)
Paradigm Agency
10100 Santa Monica Blvd Ste 2500
Los Angeles, CA 90067-4116, USA

Buchanan, John M (Misc)
56 Meriam St
Lexington, MA 02420-3622, USA

Buchanan, John M (Religious Leader)
Presbyterian Church USA
100 Witherspoon St
Louisville, KY 40202-6300, USA

Buchanan, Ken (Boxer)
45 Marmion Road Greenfaulds
Cumbemaul G67 4AN, SCOTLAND

Buchanan, Phillip (Football Player)
Oakland Raiders
6185 Meadowview Cir
Fort Myers, FL 33916-4906, USA

Buchanan, Ray (Football Player)
Indianapolis Colts
2888 Major Ridge Trl
Duluth, GA 30097-4987, USA

Buchanan, Richard (Football Player)
Los Angeles Rams
216 Brookwood Ln W
Bolingbrook, IL 60440-5511, USA

Buchanan, Robert S (Astronaut)
3 Lariat Ln
Rolling Hills Estates, CA 90274-4119, USA

Buchanan, Ron (Hockey Player)
Boston Bruins
2007 Harris Road #911
Clyde, TX 79510, USA

Buchanan, Tim (Football Player)
Cincinnati Bengals
888 Magnolia Ave Apt 1
Pasadena, CA 91106-3700, USA

Buchanan, Tom (Reality TV Star)
3130 Valley Rd
Saltville, VA 24370-4373, USA

Buchanan, Willie J (Football Player)
Green Bay Packers
2742 Mesa Dr
Oceanside, CA 92054-3717, USA

Buchbinder, Rudolf (Music Group, Musician)
Columbia Artists Mgmt Inc
1790 Broadway Fl 6
New York, NY 10019-1412, USA

Buchek, Jerry (Baseball Player)
St Louis Cardinals
349 Port Dr Unit 1
Kimberling City, MO 65686-8726, USA

Buchel, Lloyd M (Misc)
16296 Rostrata Hill Rd
Poway, CA 92064-1720, USA

Buchel, Marco (Skier)
Ramschwagweg 55
Balzers 9496, SWITZERLAND

Bucher, Jim (Baseball Player)
Brooklyn Dodgers
4837 E Trindle Rd
Mechanicsburg, PA 17050-3680, USA

Buchheim, Lothar-Gunther (Writer)
Johann-Biersack-Str 23
Feldafing 82340, GERMANY

Buchholz, Christopher
17 rue Pierre Lescot
Paris F-75001, FRANCE

Buchli, James F (Jim) (Astronaut)
1602 Fairoaks St
Seabrook, TX 77586-5921, USA

Buchmann, Ralner (Misc, Race Car Driver)
Project Indy
434 E Main St
Brownsburg, IN 46112-1419, USA

Buchwald, Art (Misc, Writer)
4327 Hawthorne St NW # W
Washington, DC 20016-3570, USA

Buck, Craig (Volleyball Player)
PO Box 603
Goleta, CA 93116-0603, USA

Buck, Detlev (Director)
Agentur Sigrid Narjes
Goethestr 17
Munich 80336, GERMANY

Buck, John E (Artist)
11229 Cottonwood Rd
Bozeman, MT 59718-9576, USA

Buck, Mike E (Football Player)
New Orleans Saints
321 Fox Den Ct
Destin, FL 32541-4317, USA

Buck, Peter (Music Group, Musician)
Rem/Athens Ltd
170 College Ave
Athens, GA 30601-2805, USA

Buck, Robert T Jr (Director, Misc)
Brooklyn Museum
200 Eastern Pkwy
Brooklyn, NY 11238-6099, USA

Buck, Samantha (Actor)
c/o Staff Member *Red Wall Management*
9255 W Sunset Blvd Ste 727
Los Angeles, CA 90069-3304, USA

Buck, Scott (Producer)
c/o Staff Member *William Morris Agency (WMA-LA)*
1 William Morris Pl
Beverly Hills, CA 90212-4261, USA

Buckbee, Ed (Misc, Scientist)
47 Revere Way
Huntsville, AL 35801-2847, USA

Buckels, Gary (Baseball Player)
St Louis Cardinals
3510 E Longridge Dr
Orange, CA 92867-2021, USA

Buckey, Don (Football Player)
New York Jets
8809 Audley Cir
Raleigh, NC 27615-3801, USA

Buckey, Jay C Jr (Astronaut)
14 Valley Rd
Hanover, NH 03755-2228, USA

Buckhalter, Joe (Basketball Player)
Cincinnati Royals
3900 Rose Hill Ave
201 A
Cincinnati, OH 45229-1478, USA

Buckingham, Gregory (Greg) (Swimmer)
338 Ridge Rd
San Carlos, CA 94070-4423, USA

Buckingham, Jane (Television Host)
c/o Staff Member *Style Network*
5750 Wilshire Blvd
Los Angeles, CA 90036-3697, USA

Buckingham, Lindsay
299 N Saltair Ave
Los Angeles, CA 90049-2912, USA

Buckingham, Lindsey (Music Group, Musician)
c/o Brett Steinberg *Creative Artists Agency LCC (CAA-LA)*
2000 Avenue Of The Stars
Los Angeles, CA 90067-4700, USA

Buckingham, Marcus (Writer)
Simon & Schuster/Pocket/Summit
1230 Avenue Of The Americas
New York, NY 10020-1513, USA

Buckinghams, The (Music Group)
Paradise Artists
PO Box 1821
Ojai, CA 93024-1821, USA

Buckland, Jonny (Music Group, Musician)
Nettwerk Mgmt
1650 W 2nd Ave
Vancouver, BC V6J 4R3, CANADA

Buckles, Bradley (Government Official, Misc)
Alcohol Tobacco Firearms Agency
650 Massachusetts Ave NW
Washington, DC 20001-3796, USA

Bucklew, Neil S (Educator)
West Virginia University
President's Office
Morgantown, WV 26506, USA

Buckley, A J (Actor)
Innovative Artists
1505 10th St
Santa Monica, CA 90401-2805, USA

Buckley, Barry (Football Player)
Miami Dolphins
26 Forest Notch
Cohasset, MA 02025-1133, USA

Buckley, Betty (Actor, Director, Musician)
Park Ave Talent
404 Park Ave S Ste 1000
New York, NY 10016-8412, USA

Buckley, Carol (Misc)
Elephant Sanctuary
PO Box 393
Hohenwald, TN 38462-0393, USA

Buckley, Curtis (Football Player)
Tampa Bay Buccaneers
2208 Cantura Dr
Mesquite, TX 75181-4653, USA

Buckley, D Terrell (Football Player)
Green Bay Packers
4215 Palmetto Trl
Weston, FL 33331-3823, USA

Buckley, James L (Judge, Senator)
PO Box 597
Sharon, CT 06069-0597, USA

Buckley, Jean (Baseball Player)
143 Monarch Dr
Fortuna, CA 95540-3451, USA

Buckley, Kathy (Actor)
c/o Staff Member *GVA Talent Agency Inc*
9229 W Sunset Blvd Ste 320
Los Angeles, CA 90069-3403, USA

Buckley, Kevin (Baseball Player)
Texas Rangers
34 Calvin St
Braintree, MA 02184-3814, USA

Buckley, Marcus W (Football Player)
New York Giants
7100 Monterrey Dr
Fort Worth, TX 76112-4234, USA

Buckley, Richard E (Conductor)
310 W 55th St Apt 1K
New York, NY 10019-5107, USA

Buckley, Robert (Actor)
c/o Patricia (Patty) Woo *TalentWorks (LA)*
3500 W Olive Ave Ste 1400
Burbank, CA 91505-5512, USA

Buckley, Travis (Baseball Player)
10020 England Dr
Overland Park, KS 66212-4138, USA

Buckley, William F Jr (Correspondent, Editor)
215 Lexington Ave
New York, NY 10016-6023, USA

Buckman, James E (Business Person)
Cendant Corp
9 W 57th St
New York, NY 10019-2701, USA

Buckman, Tom (Football Player)
Denver Broncos
2806 Springbranch Ct
Grapevine, TX 76051-2677, USA

Buckner, Betty
10643 Riverside Dr
Toluca Lake, CA 91602-2341, USA

Buckner, Bill (Baseball Player)
Los Angeles Dodgers
4405 E Wild Horse Ln
Boise, ID 83712-7593, USA

Buckner, Brentson (Football Player)
Pittsburgh Steelers
423 Leary Ct
Columbus, GA 31907-5403, USA

Buckner, Cleveland (Basketball Player)
New York Knicks
19227 S Grandee Ave
Carson, CA 90746-2805, USA

Buckner, Pam (Bowler)
645 Utah St
Reno, NV 89506-8979, USA

Buckner, Shelley (Actor)
c/o Staff Member *Cunningham Escott Slevin & Doherty (LA)*
10635 Santa Monica Blvd Ste 130
Los Angeles, CA 90025-8306, USA

Buckner, William (Quinn) (Basketball Player, Coach)
Milwaukee Bucks
857 Valencia Blvd
Irving, TX 75039-3057, USA

Buckson, David P (Governor)
60 Exchange Dr
Camden Wyoming, DE 19934-4311, USA

Bucyk, John (Hockey Player)
Detroit Red Wings
Hockey Hall of Fame
BCE Place 30 Yonge Street
Toronto, ON M5E 1X8, CANADA

Buczkowski, Bob (Football Player)
Los Angeles Raiders
4515 Northern Pike
Monroeville, PA 15146-2915, USA

Budarin, Nikolai M (Cosmonaut)
Potchta Kosmonavtov
Moskovskoi Oblasti
Syvisdny Goroduk 141160, RUSSIA

Budaska, Mark (Baseball Player)
Oakland A's
15025 W Buttonwood Dr
Sun City West, AZ 85375-5750, USA

Budd, David (Basketball Player)
New York Knicks
40 N Woodland Ave
Woodbury, NJ 08096-2517, USA

Budd, Frank (Athlete, Football Player, Track Athlete)
Philadelphia Eagles
138 Dorchester Rd
Mount Laurel, NJ 08054-1408, USA

Budd, Harold (Composer, Misc)
Opal/Warner Bros Records
6834 Camrose Dr
Los Angeles, CA 90068-3162, USA

Budd, Julie (Actor, Music Group)
Julie Budd Productions
163 Amsterdam Ave # 224
New York, NY 10023-5001, USA

Budd, Pieterse Zola (Athlete, Track Athlete)
General Delivery
Bloemfontein, SOUTH AFRICA

Budd, Zola
1 Church Row Wandsworth Plain
London, ENGLAND SW18, UNITED KINGDOM (UK)

Budde, Brad E (Football Player)
Kansas City Chiefs
5121 W 159th Ter
Stilwell, KS 66085-8956, USA

Budde, Ed (Football Player)
Kansas City Chiefs
5121 W 159th Ter
Stilwell, KS 66085-8956, USA

Budden, Joe (Actor)
c/o Mark Cheatham *International Creative Management (ICM-NY)*
40 W 57th St
New York, NY 10019-4001, USA

Buddie, Mike (Baseball Player)
New York Yankees
11169 Blodgett Creek Trl
Strongsville, OH 44149-3102, USA

Buddin, Don (Baseball Player)
Boston Red Sox
27 Harvest Ct
Greenville, SC 29601-4409, USA

Buddy, Brandon (Actor)
c/o Jon Simmons *Simmons & Scott Entertainment*
4110 W Burbank Blvd
Burbank, CA 91505-2121, USA

Budig, Gene (Baseball Player, Educator, President)
5 Sandwedge Ln
Isle Of Palms, SC 29451-2820, USA

Budig, Rebecca
13576 Cheltenham Dr
Sherman Oaks, CA 91423-4818, USA

Budka, Frank (Football Player)
Los Angeles Rams
2637 SW Abel St
Port Saint Lucie, FL 34953-2834, USA

Budko, Walter (Basketball Player, Coach)
Baltimore Bullets
2525 Pot Spring Rd Unit L703
Lutherville Timonium, MD 21093-2852, USA

Budness, Bill (Football Player)
Oakland Raiders
401 Huckle Hill Rd
Bernardston, MA 01337-9423, USA

Budney, Albert J Jr (Business Person)
Niagara Mohawk Holdings
300 Erie Blvd W
Syracuse, NY 13202-4250, USA

Budnick, Neil G (Financier)
MBIA Inc
113 King St
Armonk, NY 10504-1610, USA

Budrewicz, Tom (Football Player)
New York Titans
13 Olde Farms Rd
Boxford, MA 01921-1915, USA

Budzinski, Mark (Baseball Player)
Cincinnati Reds
4919 Packard Rd
Glen Allen, VA 23060-3536, USA

Bueche, Wendell F (Business Person)
IMC Global
2100 Sanders Rd
Northbrook, IL 60062-6139, USA

Buechele, Steve (Baseball Player)
Texas Rangers
2600 Royal Glen Dr
Arlington, TX 76012-5553, USA

Buechler, John Carl (Director)
12031 Vose St # 19-21
North Hollywood, CA 91605-5752, USA

Buechler, Jud (Basketball Player)
1515 West Ln
Del Mar, CA 92014-4137, USA

Buechrle, James (Baseball Player)
Chicago White Sox
333 W 35th St
Comiskey Park
Chicago, IL 60616-3651, USA

Buehler, George (Football Player)
Oakland Raiders
63 Tara Rd
Orinda, CA 94563-3116, USA

Buehler, Jud (Basketball Player)
New Jersey Knicks
4576 South Ln
Del Mar, CA 92014-4139, USA

Buehrie, Mark (Baseball Player)
Chicago White Sox
1837 Prescott Rdg
Saint Charles, MO 63303-5345, USA

Buell, Bebe (Actor)
c/o Ivan Bart *International Management
Group (IMG NY)*
26 Riverside Dr
Rumson, NJ 07760-1048, USA

Bueno, Maria (Tennis Player)
Rua Consolagao 3414 #10 Edificio
Agustus
Sao Paulo 1001, BRAZIL

Buerge, Aaron (Reality TV Star)
c/o Staff Member *Maximum Talent*
1873 S Bellaire St Ste 915
Denver, CO 80222-4356, USA

Buerger, Martin J (Misc)
Weston Road
Lincoln, MA 01773, USA

Buetow, Bart (Football Player)
New York Giants
4152 Kipling St
Wheat Ridge, CO 80033-4147, USA

Buffenbarger, R Thomas (Misc)
International Machinists Assn
9000 Machinists Pl
Upper Marlboro, MD 20772-2675, USA

Buffett, Jimmy (Music Group, Songwriter,
Writer)
c/o Rand Holston *Creative Artists Agency
LCC (CAA-LA)*
2000 Avenue Of The Stars
Los Angeles, CA 90067-4700, USA

Buffett, Peter (Musician)
c/o Staff Member *Paradigm (Monterey)*
509 Hartnell St
Monterey, CA 93940-2825, USA

Buffett, Warren E (Business Person)
Berkshire Hathaway
3555 Farnam St Ste 1440
Omaha, NE 68131-3378, USA

Buffington, Harry (Football Player)
New York Giants
3306 38th St
Lubbock, TX 79413-2714, USA

Buffkins, Archie Lee (Misc)
Kennedy Center
Executive Suite
Washington, DC 20566-0001, USA

Buffone, Douglas J (Doug) (Football
Player)
Chicago Bears
1272 W Lexington St
Chicago, IL 60607-4110, USA

Bufi, Ylli (Prime Minister)
Privatization Ministry
Keshilli i Ministrave
Tirana, ALBANIA

Bufman, Zev (Producer)
520 Brickett Key Dr #612
Miami, FL 33131, USA

Buford, Damon J (Baseball Player)
Baltimore Orioles
4509 E Woodland Dr
Phoenix, AZ 85048-7640, USA

Buford, Don (Baseball Player)
Chicago White Sox
15412 Valley Vista Blvd
Sherman Oaks, CA 91403-3812, USA

Buford, Maury (Football Player)
San Diego Chargers
2901 Sweet Briar St
Grapevine, TX 76051-2651, USA

Bugenhagen, Gary (Football Player)
Buffalo Bills
4337 Henneberry Rd
Manlius, NY 13104-8425, USA

Buggs, Dany (Football Player)
New York Giants
3186 Evans Mill Rd
Lithonia, GA 30038-2420, USA

Buggs, Wamon (Football Player)
Green Bay Packers
5700 Sonoma Trce
Antioch, TN 37013-4273, USA

Bugliosi, Vincent T (Writer)
3699 Wilshire Blvd Ste 850
Los Angeles, CA 90010-2737, USA

Bugner, Joe (Boxer)
22 Buckingham St
Surrey Hills, NSW 2010, AUSTRALIA

Buhari, Muhammadu (General, President)
GRA
Daura
Katsina State, NIGERIA

Buhr, Doug (Hockey Player)
Kansas City Scouts
1-1568 12th Ave E
Vancouver, BC V5N 2A3, CANADA

Buhrmaster, Robert C (Business Person)
Jostens Inc
3601 Minnesota Dr Ste 400
Minneapolis, MN 55435-6008, USA

Buice, Dewayne (Baseball Player)
California Angels
PO Box 5185
Incline Village, NV 89450-5185, USA

Buie, Drew (Football Player)
Oakland Raiders
2815 Eland Dr
Winston Salem, NC 27127-7284, USA

Buitenhuis, Penelope (Director, Writer)
c/o Carl Lieberman *Characters Talent
Agency, The (Toronto)*
8 Elm St 3rd FL
Toronto, ON M5G 1G7, CANADA

Bujnoch, Glenn (Football Player)
Cincinnati Bengals
7598 Fairwayglen Dr
Cincinnati, OH 45248-2800, USA

Bujold, Genevieve (Actor)
1327 Ocean Ave Ste J
Blake Agency
Santa Monica, CA 90401-1033, USA

Bukant, Joseph (Football Player)
Philadelphia Eagles
PO Box 311
Portage, MI 49081-0311, USA

Bukaty, Fred (Football Player)
Denver Broncos
10930 Glen Arbor Rd
Kansas City, MO 64114-4959, USA

Buker, Cy (Baseball Player)
Brooklyn Dodgers
108 W Central Ave
Greenwood, WI 54437-9468, USA

Bukich, Rudy (Football Player)
Los Angeles Rams
7910 Ivanhoe Ave # 333
La Jolla, CA 92037-4511, USA

Bukovich, Tony (Hockey Player)
Detroit Red Wings
517 Shelden Ave Apt 208
Houghton, MI 49931-2161, USA

Buksar, George (Football Player)
Baltimore Colts
33400 N Burr Oak Dr
Solon, OH 44139-5550, USA

Buktenica, Raymond (Actor)
Special Artists Agency
9465 Wilshire Blvd Ste 880
Beverly Hills, CA 90212-2607, USA

Bukvich, Ryan (Baseball Player)
Kansas City Royals
200 Apple Blossom Cir
Brandon, MS 39047-7691, USA

Bulaich, Norman B (Norm) (Football
Player)
Baltimore Colts
421 Lynndale Ct
Hurst, TX 76054-2725, USA

Bulatovic, Momir (President)
Vlada Savezne Republike
Lenina 2
Belgrade 11070, SERBIA-MONTENEGRO

Bulger, Chet (Football Player)
Chicago Cardinals
4317 Majestic Ln
Fairfax, VA 22033-3500, USA

Bulifant, Joyce (Actor)
James/Levy/Jacobson
3500 W Olive Ave Ste 1470
Burbank, CA 91505-5514, USA

Bull, John S (Astronaut)
PO Box 1106
South Lake Tahoe, CA 96156-1106, USA

Bull, Richard (Actor)
750 N Rush St Apt 1903
Chicago, IL 60611-2581, USA

Bull, Ronald D (Ronnie) (Football Player)
Chicago Bears
15 Redspire Ct
Bolingbrook, IL 60490-3175, USA

Bull, Scott (Football Player)
San Francisco 49ers
3660 N Front St Ste 3
Fayetteville, AR 72703-5177, USA

Bullard, Kendricke (Football Player)
Jacksonville Jaguars
3624 Burdyshaw Dr
Jonesboro, AR 72401-8735, USA

Bullard, Louis E (Football Player)
Seattle Seahawks
3129 Friars Bridge Pass
Franklin, TN 37064-2169, USA

Bullard, Matt (Basketball Player)
Houston Rockets
10 Balmoral Pi
Spring, TX 77382, USA

Bullard, Mike (Hockey Player)
Pittsburgh Penguins
1170 Shillington Ave
Ottawa, ON K1Z 7Z4, CANADA

Bullen, Voy M (Religious Leader)
Church of God
1207 Willowbrook Dr SE
Huntsville, AL 35802-3826, USA

Bullet, Scott (Baseball Player)
Pittsburgh Pirates
218 Vicky Bullett St
Martinsburg, WV 25404-4511, USA

Bulling, Bud (Baseball Player)
Minnesota Twins
4805 Yellowstone Ct NE
Salem, OR 97305-3066, USA

Bullinger, Jim (Baseball Player)
Chicago Cubs
2504 Elise Ave
Metairie, LA 70003-1931, USA

Bullinger, Kirk (Baseball Player)
Montreal Expos
1245 Wyndham N
Gretna, LA 70056-8365, USA

Bullins, Ed (Writer)
425 Lafayette St
New York, NY 10003-7021, USA

Bullitt, John C (Attorney, Attorney
General, General, Government Official)
Shearman Sterling
53 Wall St
New York, NY 10005, USA

Bullmann, Maik (Wrestler)
AC Bavaria Goldbach
Postfach 1112
Goldbach 63769, GERMANY

Bulloch, Jeremy (Actor)
Fett Photos
10 Birchwood Rd
London SW17 9BQ, UNITED KINGDOM
(UK)

Bullock, Dona (Actor)
Writers & Artists
360 N Crescent Dr Bldg North
Beverly Hills, CA 90210-6818, USA

Bullock, Donna (Actor)
10000 Santa Monica Blvd # 305
Los Angeles, CA 90067, USA

Bullock, Eric (Baseball Player)
Houston Astros
17503 Harwick Ct
Carson, CA 90746-1617, USA

Bullock, J R (Business Person)
Laidlaw Inc
3221 N Service Road
Burlington, ON L7R 3Y8, CANADA

Bullock, Jim J (Actor)
612 Lighthouse Ave # 200
Pacific Grove, CA 93950-2615, USA

Bullock, Jim J (Actor)
c/o Staff Member *Bohemia Entertainment
Group*
8170 Beverly Blvd Ste 102
Los Angeles, CA 90048-4533, USA

Bullock, Sandra (Actor, Producer)
c/o Elizabeth (Beth) Swofford *Creative
Artists Agency LCC (CAA-LA)*
2000 Avenue Of The Stars
Los Angeles, CA 90067-4700, USA

Bullock, Vicki (Basketball Player)
Charlotte Sting
333 E Trade St
Charlotte, NC 28202-2331, USA

Bullocks, Amos (Football Player)
Dallas Cowboys
17209 Dobson Ave
South Holland, IL 60473-3535, USA

Bullough, Hank (Football Player)
Green Bay Packers
4439 Copperhill Dr
Okemos, MI 48864-2067, USA

Bulluck, Keith (Football Player)
874 Nialta Ln
Brentwood, TN 37027-8232, USA

Bulriss, Mark P (Business Person)
Great Lakes Chemical
199 Benson Rd
Waterbury, CT 06749-0001, USA

Bumbeck, David (Artist)
Drew Lane Rd 3
Middleburry, VT 05753, USA

Bumbry, Alonzo B (Al) (Baseball Player)
Baltimore Orioles
28 Tremblant Ct
Lutherville Timonium, MD 21093-3748, USA

Bumbry, Grace (Opera Singer)
Opera et Concert
Maximilianstr 22
Munich 80539, GERMANY

Bumgardner, Max (Football Player)
Detroit Lions
6243 State Highway 34 S
Quinlan, TX 75474-3054, USA

Bumgarner, Wayne
PO Box 208
Claremont, NC 28610-0208, USA

Bumiller, William
9255 W Sunset Blvd Ste 515
Los Angeles, CA 90069-3301, USA

Bump, Nate (Baseball Player)
Florida Marlins
653 Valerie Dr
Newtown Square, PA 19073-1502, USA

Bumpers, Dale (Governor, Senator)
7613 Honesty Way
Bethesda, MD 20817-5519, USA

Bunce, Gregory (Basketball Player)
New York Knicks
1710 Redwood Way
Upland, CA 91784-1767, USA

Bunce, Larry (Basketball Player)
Anaheim Amigos
210 Wall St Apt 906
Seattle, WA 98121-3449, USA

Bunch, Jarrod (Football Player)
New York Giants
1580 Hemlock Dr
Ashtabula, OH 44004-9360, USA

Bunch, Jimmy Castor (Musician)
Universal Attractions
145 W 57th St
New York, NY 10019-2220, USA

Bunch, Melvin (Baseball Player)
Kansas City Royals
12 Tyler Ln
Hooks, TX 75561-7013, USA

Bunch, Sidney (Baseball Player)
Birmingham Black Barons
2313 Elliott Ave Apt M4
Nashville, TN 37204, USA

Bund, Karlheinz (Business Person)
Huyssenallee 82-84
Essen Ruhr 45128, GERMANY

Bundchen, Gisele (Model)
c/o Staff Member *IMG Models*
304 Park Ave S Fl 12
New York, NY 10010-4301, USA

Bundy, Brooke (Actor)
833 N Martel Ave
Los Angeles, CA 90046-7508, USA

Bunim, Mary-Ellis (Producer)
c/o Staff Member *Bunim/Murray Productions Inc*
6007 Sepulveda Blvd
Van Nuys, CA 91411-2502, USA

Bunker, Wallace E (Wally) (Baseball Player)
330 Coosaw Way Unit 38
Ridgeland, SC 29936-4968, USA

Bunker, Wally (Baseball Player)
Baltimore Orioles
330 Coosaw Way Unit 38
Ridgeland, SC 29936-4968, USA

Bunkowsky-Scherbak, Barb (Golfer)
8725 Marlamoor Ln
West Palm Beach, FL 33412-1614, USA

Bunnell, Dewey (Music Group, Musician)
Agency for Performing Arts
405 S Beverly Dr Ste 500
Beverly Hills, CA 90212-4425, USA

Bunnell, John (Actor, Television Host)
c/o Greg Horangic *Endeavor Agency LLC (LA)*
9601 Wilshire Blvd Fl 3
Beverly Hills, CA 90210-5204, USA

Bunnett, Joseph F (Misc)
608 Arroyo Seco
Santa Cruz, CA 95060-3148, USA

Bunnetta, Bill (Bowler)
1176 E San Bruno Ave
Fresno, CA 93710-7109, USA

Bunning, James P D (Jim) (Baseball Player, Senator)
Detroit Tigers
4 Fairway Dr
Southgate, KY 41071-3022, USA

Bunning, Jim (Politician, Senator)
c/o Staff Member *United States Senate (Hart Office)*
316 Hart Senate Office Building
Washington, DC 20510-0001, USA

Bunny, Lady (Comedian, DJ)
c/o Staff Member *Diva Central Inc*
7510 W Sunset Blvd Ste 1445
Los Angeles, CA 90046-3408, USA

Bunt, Dick
11 Irving Pl
Greenlawn, NY 11740-3113, USA

Bunt, Richard (Basketball Player)
New York Knicks
Reeback Dr
Ossining, NY 10562, USA

Bunting, Eve (Writer)
Harper Collins Publishers
10 E 53rd St Fl Cellar2
New York, NY 10022-5076, USA

Bunting, John (Football Player)
Philadelphia Eagles
PO Box 250
Hampstead, NC 28443-0250, USA

Bunting, William (Basketball Player)
Carolina Cougars
11000 Pacer Ct
Raleigh, NC 27614-9604, USA

Bunton, Emma (Music Group, Musician)
c/o Jeff Frasco *Creative Artists Agency LCC (CAA-LA)*
2000 Avenue Of The Stars
Los Angeles, CA 90067-4700, USA

Bunyan, John (Football Player)
Staten Island Stapletons
92 Radburn Rd
Glen Rock, NJ 07452-3417, USA

Bunz, Dan (Football Player)
San Francisco 49ers
4230 Rocklin Rd Apt 2
Rocklin, CA 95677-2832, USA

Buoniconti, Nicholas A (Nick) (Business Person, Football Player)
Boston Patriots
445 Grand Bay Dr Apt 803
Key Biscayne, FL 33149-1907, USA

Buono, Cara (Actor)
c/o Peter Benedek *United Talent Agency (UTA)*
9560 Wilshire Blvd Ste 500
Beverly Hills, CA 90212-2401, USA

Buono, Carla
25 Sea Colony Dr
Santa Monica, CA 90405-5495, USA

Buraas, Hans-Peter (Skier)
Norges Skiforbund
Postboks 3853
Ulleval Hageby, Oslo 0805, NORWAY

Burba, Dave (Baseball Player)
Seattle Mariners
378 N Shore Ln
Gilbert, AZ 85233-4702, USA

Burba, Edwin H Jr (General)
256 Montrose Dr
McDonough, GA 30253-4242, USA

Burbach, Bill (Baseball Player)
New York Yankees
147 Shenandoah Dr
Johnson City, TN 37601-5459, USA

Burbank, Daniel C (Dan) (Astronaut)
3210 Water Elm Way
Houston, TX 77059, USA

Burbules, Peter G (General)
8287 Chestnut Point Ln
Hayes, VA 23072-3835, USA

Burch, Elliot (Misc, Race Car Driver)
402 Corey Ln
Middletown, RI 02842-5664, USA

Burch, Jerry (Football Player)
Oakland Raiders
3100 Cleburne St
Houston, TX 77004-4501, USA

Burchart, Larry (Baseball Player)
Cleveland Indians
5310 E 94th St
Tulsa, OK 74137-4417, USA

Burchfiel, Burrell C (Geophysicist, Misc, Physicist)
9 Robinson Park
Winchester, MA 01890-3717, USA

Burchfield, Don (Football Player)
New Orleans Saints
26450 Summer Greens Dr
Bonita Springs, FL 34135-2328, USA

Burchuladze, Paata (Opera Singer)
Raab & Bohm
Piankengasse 7
Vienna 1010, AUSTRIA

Burckhalter, Joseph H (Inventor)
705 Valley Brook Rd
Wilmington, NC 28412-3243, USA

Burd, Steven A (Business Person)
Safeway Inc
5918 Stoneridge Mall Rd
Pleasanton, CA 94588-3229, USA

Burda, Bob (Baseball Player)
St Louis Cardinals
4502 E Carol Ave Unit 14
Mesa, AZ 85206-2077, USA

Burden, Ross (Chef)
c/o Staff Member *Roseman Organisation, The*
51 Queen Anne St
London W1G 9HS, UNITED KINGDOM (UK)

Burden, Ticky (Basketball Player)
Virginia Squires
4332 Grove Ave Apt C
Winston Salem, NC 27105-2837, USA

Burden, William A M (Diplomat, Financier)
820 5th Ave
New York, NY 10065-7267, USA

Burdette, Freddie (Baseball Player)
Chicago Cubs
1200 Kingstown Ct Apt G5
Albany, GA 31707-3581, USA

Burdette, Lou
2019 Beveva Rd.
Sarasota, FL 34232, USA

Burdette, S Lewis (Lew) (Baseball Player)
New York Yankees
17709 Deer Isle Cirlce
Winter Garden, FL 34787, USA

Burditt, Joyce (Writer)
Knopf
201 E 50th St
New York, NY 10022-7703, USA

Burdon, Eric (Music Group, Songwriter, Writer)
Lustig Talent
PO Box 770850
Orlando, FL 32877-0850, USA

Bure, Paval
V100 N. Renfrew St.
Vancouver, BC V5K 3N7, CANADA

Bure, Pavel (Hockey Player)
Vancouver Canucks
11091 Redhawk St
Plantation, FL 33324-2167, USA

Bure, Valeri (Hockey Player)
Montreal Canadians
10371 Golden Eagle Ct
Plantation, FL 33324-2161, USA

Burega, Bill (Hockey Player)
Toronto Maple Leafs
RR 1
Elginburgh, ON K0H 1M0, CANADA

Bureker-Stopper, Geraldine (Baseball Player)
2006 SE 41st Ave
Portland, OR 97214-5966, USA

Burford, Christopher W (Chris) (Football Player)
Dallas Texans
1215 Broken Feather Ct
Reno, NV 89511-5350, USA

Burg, Mark (Producer)
c/o Staff Member *Evolution Entertainment (LA)*
901 N Highland Ave
Los Angeles, CA 90038-2412, USA

Burge, Gregg
420 Madison Ave # 1400
New York, NY 10017-1107, USA

Burgee, John H (Architect)
Perelanda Farm Skunks Misery Road
Millerton, NY 12546, USA

Burger, Michael (Actor)
c/o Staff Member *Richard De La Font Agency*
4845 S Sheridan Rd Ste 505
Tulsa, OK 74145-5719, USA

Burger, Neil (Director)
c/o Staff Member *Endeavor Agency LLC (LA)*
9601 Wilshire Blvd Fl 3
Beverly Hills, CA 90210-5204, USA

Burgere, Andre
67 quai d'Orsay
Paris F-75007, FRANCE

Burgess, Adrian (Mountaineer)
324 G St
Anderson, SC 29625-4147, USA

Burgess, Annie (Athlete)
601 F St NW
Washington, DC 20004-1605, USA

Burgess, Bobby
11684 Ventura Blvd # 691
Studio City, CA 91604-2699, USA

Burgess, Christian
33 Gastein Rd
London W6 8LT, ENGLAND

Burgess, Don (Cinematographer)
Gersh Agency
232 N Canon Dr
Beverly Hills, CA 90210-5302, USA

Burgess, Greg
1144 Holly Oaks Ct
Jacksonville, FL 32259-2804, USA

Burgess, Mitchell (Writer)
c/o Staff Member *Broder Webb Chervin Silbermann Agency, The (BWCS)*
10250 Constellation Blvd Ste P
Los Angeles, CA 90067-6213, USA

Burgess, Robert K (Business Person)
Pulte Corp
33 Bloomfield Hills Pkwy
Bloomfield Hills, MI 48304-2944, USA

Burgess, Ronnie (Football Player)
Green Bay Packers
303 Brandymill Blvd
Myrtle Beach, SC 29588-7227, USA

Burgess, Tom (Baseball Player)
St Louis Cardinals
97 Sunray Ave
London, ON N6P 1C6, CANADA

Burgess, Tony (Misc)
US Geological Survey
119 National Center
Reston, VA, USA

Burgess, Warren D (Religious Leader)
Reformed Church in America
475 Riverside Dr
New York, NY 10115-0101, USA

Burghardt, Raymond F (Diplomat)
US Embassy
7 Lang Ha St
Ba Dinh
Hanoi, VIETNAM

Burghardt, Walter J (Misc)
19 L St NW
Washington, DC 20001, USA

Burghoff, Gary (Actor)
Scott Stander
13701 Riverside Dr Ste 201
Sherman Oaks, CA 91423-2447, USA

Burgi, Richard (Actor)
124 Sunset Ter
Laguna Beach, CA 92651-3967, USA

Burgin, C David (Editor)
Oakland Tribune
409 13th St
Editorial Dept
Oakland, CA 94612-2605, USA

Burgmeier, Ted (Football Player)
Kansas City Chiefs
861 Scenic Hts
East Dubuque, IL 61025-1041, USA

Burgmeler, Tom (Baseball Player)
California Angels
13118 Walmer St
Overland Park, KS 66209-3618, USA

Burgon, Geoffrey (Composer)
Chester Music
8-9 Firth St
London W1V 5TZ, UNITED KINGDOM (UK)

Burham, Daniel (Business Person)
Raytheon Co
141 Spring St
Lexington, MA 02421, USA

Burham, James B (Financier)
Mellon Bank
1 Mellon Bank Ctr # 400
Pittsburgh, PA 15258-0001, USA

Burhoe, Ralph Wendell (Misc)
Montgomery Place
5550 S South Shore Dr #715
Chicago, IL 60637, USA

Burich, Bill (Baseball Player)
Philadelphia Phillies
1175 La Moree Rd Spc 62
San Marcos, CA 92078-4519, USA

Burk, Mack (Baseball Player)
Philadelphia Phillies
5710 Glen Pines Dr
Houston, TX 77069-1852, USA

Burk, Scott (Football Player)
Cincinnati Bengals
10076 E Caley Pl
Englewood, CO 80111-5604, USA

Burka, Vern (Football Player)
San Francisco 49ers
580 Riviera Cir
Nipomo, CA 93444-8866, USA

Burke, Alfred (Actor)
Jameson
219 The Plaza
535 Kings St
London SW10 0SZ, UNITED KINGDOM (UK)

Burke, Bernard F (Physicist)
10 Bloomfield St
Lexington, MA 02421-5608, USA

Burke, Billy (Actor)
c/o Ellen Meyer *Ellen Meyer Entertainment*
8899 Beverly Blvd Ste 612
Los Angeles, CA 90048-2429, USA

Burke, Brooke (Actor, Model)
c/o Jeff Kolodny *William Morris Agency (WMA-LA)*
1 William Morris Pl
Beverly Hills, CA 90212-4261, USA

Burke, Chris (Actor)
426 S Orange Grove Ave
Los Angeles, CA 90036-3102, USA

Burke, Clement (Clem) (Musician)
Shore Fire Media
32 Court St Ste 1600
Brooklyn, NY 11201-4441, USA

Burke, David (Actor)
c/o Doug Wald *Raw Talent Management*
9615 Brighton Way Ste 300
Beverly Hills, CA 90210-5118, USA

Burke, David (Actor)
Writers & Artists
360 N Crescent Dr Bldg North
Beverly Hills, CA 90210-6818, USA

Burke, Delta (Actor)
4270 Farmdale Ave
Studio City, CA 91604-2733, USA

Burke, Don (Football Player)
San Francisco 49ers
518 Island Ave
Reno, NV 89501-1714, USA

Burke, Ed
285 E Main St
Los Gatos, CA 95030-6106, USA

Burke, Ernest (Baseball Player)
Baltimore Elite Giants
9451 Common Brook Rd Apt 302
Owings Mills, MD 21117-7582, USA

Burke, Hederman Lynn (Swimmer)
26 White Oak Tree Rd
Syosset, NY 11791-1210, USA

Burke, Jack Sr (Golfer)
Champions Golf Club
13722 Champions Dr
Houston, TX 77069-1399, USA

Burke, James (Correspondent)
Henley House
Terrace Bames
London SW13 0NP, UNITED KINGDOM (UK)

Burke, James D (Director)
Saint Louis Art Museum
Forest Park
Saint Louis, MO 63110-1380, USA

Burke, James E (Business Person)
Johnson & Johnson
317 George St # 200
New Brunswick, NJ 08901-2008, USA

Burke, James Lee
114 5th Ave
New York, NY 10011-5604, USA

Burke, James Lee (Writer)
Boubleday Press
1540 Broadway
New York, NY 10036-4039, USA

Burke, Joe (Football Player)
New York Jets
7 Maplewood St
Albany, NY 12208-2413, USA

Burke, John (Baseball Player)
Colorado Rockies
3490 Westbrook Ln
Littleton, CO 80129-1527, USA

Burke, John (Football Player)
New England Patriots
44 Chestnut Ridge Rd
Holmdel, NJ 07733-1437, USA

Burke, John F (Doctor, Educator)
984 Memorial Dr Apt 503
Cambridge, MA 02138-5747, USA

Burke, Joseph C (Educator)
Rockefeller Institute
411 State St
Albany, NY 12203-1085, USA

Burke, Kathy (Actor)
Stephen Halton Mgmt
83 Shepperton Road
London N1 3DF, UNITED KINGDOM (UK)

Burke, Kelly H (General)
Stafford Burke Hecker
1006 Cameron St
Alexandria, VA 22314-2427, USA

Burke, Leo (Baseball Player)
Baltimore Orioles
1729 Woodburn Drive
Hagerstown, MD 21742, USA

Burke, Michael Reilly
10100 Santa Monica Blvd Ste 2500
Los Angeles, CA 90067-4116, USA

Burke, Mike (Football Player)
Los Angeles Rams
1296 E Gibson Rd
Woodland, CA 95776-6378, USA

Burke, Patrick (Golfer)
24 Saint Georges Ct
Coto De Caza, CA 92679-4926, USA

Burke, Paul
2217 N Avenida Caballeros
Palm Springs, CA 92262-3301, USA

Burke, Philip (Artist)
L.B. Madison Fine Art
335 Buffalo Ave
Niagara Falls, NY 14303-1232, USA

Burke, Randall (Football Player)
Baltimore Colts
3420 Chestnut Hill Ln
Lexington, KY 40509-1916, USA

Burke, Robert John (Actor)
Gersh Agency
232 N Canon Dr
Beverly Hills, CA 90210-5302, USA

Burke, Sarah (Reality TV Star)
c/o Michael (Mike) Esterman *Esterman Entertainment*
214 Park Rd
Riva, MD 21140-1224, USA

Burke, Soloman
1048 Tattnall St
Macon, GA 31201-1537, USA

Burke, Steve (Football Player)
New England Patriots
RR 3 Box 553-F
Austin, TX 78754, USA

Burket, Harriet (Editor)
700 John Ringling Blvd
Sarasota, FL 34236-1542, USA

Burkett, Chris (Football Player)
Buffalo Bills
296 Dover Ln
Madison, MS 39110-9726, USA

Burkett, Jackie (Football Player)
Baltimore Colts
895 Santa Rosa Blvd Apt 709
Fort Walton Beach, FL 32548-1913, USA

Burkett, John D (Baseball Player)
San Francisco Giants
1404 Laurel Ln
Southlake, TX 76092-3573, USA

Burkhalter, Correll (Football Player)
Philadelphia Eagles
221 Robert Owens Rd
Mount Olive, MS 39119-4651, USA

Burkhalter, Edward A Jr (Admiral)
4128 Fort Washington Place
Alexandria, VA 22304, USA

Burkhardt, Francois (Architect)
3 Rue de Venise
Paris 75004, FRANCE

Burkhardt, Lisa (Sportscaster)
Madison Square Garden Network
4 Pennsylvania Plaza
New York, NY 10001, USA

Burkhart, Ken (Baseball Player)
St Louis Cardinals
3708 Splendor Dr
Knoxville, TN 37918-5610, USA

Burkholder, JoAnn (Physicist)
North Carolina State University
Botany Dept
Raleigh, NC 27695-0001, USA

Burkholder, Owen E (Religious Leader)
421 S 2nd St Ste 600
Elkhart, IN 46516-3243, USA

Burkl, Fred A (Misc)
United Retail Workers Union
9865 W Roosevelt Rd
Westchester, IL 60154-2767, USA

Burkley, Dennis (Actor)
5145 Costello Ave
Sherman Oaks, CA 91423-1207, USA

Burkman, Roger (Basketball Player)
Chicago Bulls
3242 Beals Branch Dr
Louisville, KY 40206-3049, USA

Burkovich, Shirley (Baseball Player)
67430 Ovante Rd
Cathedral City, CA 92234-8402, USA

Burks, Audra (Golfer)
1210 N 8th St
Rogers, AR 72756-2818, USA

Burks, Ellis R (Baseball Player)
Boston Red Sox
115 South Ln
Chagrin Falls, OH 44022-1145, USA

Burks, Randy (Football Player)
Chicago Bears
300 Moyer Dr
Broken Bow, OK 74728-1519, USA

Burks, Shawn (Football Player)
Washington Redskins
5752 Nottaway Dr
Baton Rouge, LA 70820-5415, USA

Burks, Steve (Football Player)
New England Patriots
2568 Mount Tabor Rd
Cabot, AR 72023-9596, USA

Burl, Alex (Football Player)
Chicago Cardinals
2949 Monaco Pkwy
Denver, CO 80207-2850, USA

Burleson, Richard P (Rick) (Baseball Player)
Boston Red Sox
241 E Country Hills Dr
La Habra, CA 90631-7623, USA

Burleson, Tom (Basketball Player)
Seattle SuperSonics
PO Box 861
Newland, NC 28657-0861, USA

Burley, Gary (Football Player)
Cincinnati Bengals
514 Bristol Ln
Birmingham, AL 35226-1947, USA

Burlinson, Tom (Actor)
c/o Staff Member *June Cann Management*
73 Jersey Rd
Woollahra 2025, AUSTRALIA

Burman, George (Football Player)
Chicago Bears
1646 James St
Syracuse, NY 13203-2816, USA

Burmaster, Jack (Basketball Player)
Oshkosh All Stars
840 Echo Ln
Glenview, IL 60025-3369, USA

Burn, Scott (Writer)
c/o Staff Member *Creative Artists Agency LCC (CAA-LA)*
2000 Avenue Of The Stars
Los Angeles, CA 90067-4700, USA

Burnell, Max (Football Player)
Chicago Bears
PO Box 1076
Rockwall, TX 75087-1076, USA

Burner, David L (Business Person)
B F Goodrich Co
2550 W Tyvola Rd
3 Coliseum Centre
Charlotte, NC 28217-4574, USA

Burnes, Karen (Correspondent)
CBS-TV
51 W 52nd St
News Dept
New York, NY 10019-6119, USA

Burnett, A J (Baseball Player)
Florida Marlins
15208 Jarrettsvl Pike
Monkton, MD 21111-2423, USA

Burnett, Bobby (Football Player)
Buffalo Bills
5321 Gould Cir
Castle Rock, CO 80109-7726, USA

Burnett, Carol (Actor, Comedian)
c/o Brian Mann *International Creative Management (ICM-LA)*
10250 Constellation Blvd
Los Angeles, CA 90067-6200, USA

Burnett, Chester (Football Player)
Washington Redskins
2610 Ivanhoe St
Denver, CO 80207-3409, USA

Burnett, Erin (Correspondent)
c/o Staff Member *CNBC (DC)*
1025 Connecticut Ave NW Ste 800
Washington, DC 20036-5419, USA

Burnett, Howard J (Educator)
Washington & Jefferson College
President's Office
Washington, PA 15301, USA

Burnett, James E (Government Official)
Transportations Safety Board
800 Independence Ave SW
Washington, DC 20594-0004, USA

Burnett, Mark (Producer)
c/o Staff Member *Mark Burnett Productions*
640 N Sepulveda Blvd
Los Angeles, CA 90049-2108, USA

Burnett, Nancy
7800 Beverly Blvd # 3305
Los Angeles, CA 90036-2112, USA

Burnett, T-Bone (Musician, Producer, Songwriter)
c/o Staff Member *Paradigm (Monterey)*
509 Hartnell St
Monterey, CA 93940-2825, USA

Burnett, Webbie D (Football Player)
New Orleans Saints
5305 San Antonio Ave Apt 128
Orlando, FL 32839-2222, USA

Burnette, Dave (Football Player)
Dallas Cowboys
4201 Senator St
Texarkana, AR 71854-1528, USA

Burnette, Olivia
121 N San Vicente Blvd
Beverly Hills, CA 90211-2303, USA

Burnette, Reggie (Football Player)
Green Bay Packers
7803 Chasewood Dr
Missouri City, TX 77489-1836, USA

Burnette, Rocky (Musician)
1900 Avenue Of Stars # 2530
Los Angeles, CA 90067-4301, USA

Burnette, Thomas N Jr (General)
Deputy Cinc
US Joint Forces Command
Norfolk, VA 23551-0001, USA

Burnin' Daylight
PO Box 150245
Nashville, TN 37215-0245, USA

Burnine, Hank (Football Player)
New York Giants
709 W Rieck Rd
Tyler, TX 75703-3559, USA

Burning, Spear (Musician)
13034 231st St
Springfield Gardens, NY 11413-1832, USA

Burnitz, Jeromy (Baseball Player)
New York Mets
12259 Berea Ct
Poway, CA 92064-6131, USA

Burnley, James H IV (Secretary)
Shaw Pittman Potts Trowbridge
2300 N St NW
Washington, DC 20037-1172, USA

Burns, Annie (Musician, Songwriter, Writer)
Drake Assoc
177 Woodland Ave
Westwood, NJ 07675-3218, USA

Burns, Bob (Musician)
12512 Fraser Ave
Granada Hills, CA 91344-1321, USA

Burns, Britt (Baseball Player)
Chicago White Sox
847 Black Bird Ct
Rockledge, FL 32955-6304, USA

Burns, Brooke (Actor, Model)
c/o Jonathan Bluman *Paradigm (LA)*
360 N Crescent Dr
North Bldg
Beverly Hills, CA 90210-6820, USA

Burns, Charles (Artist)
c/o Staff Member *Fantagraphics Books*
7563 Lake City Way NE
Seattle, WA 98115-4218, USA

Burns, Christian (Musician)
Day Time
Crown House
225 Kensington High St
London W8 8SA, UNITED KINGDOM (UK)

Burns, David (Basketball Player)
New York Nets
2623 Bainbride Dr
Dallas, TX 75237, USA

Burns, Edward (Actor, Director)
c/o Rick Yorn *The Firm*
9465 Wilshire Blvd Fl 6
Beverly Hills, CA 90212-2605, USA

Burns, Eileen
4000 W. 43rd St.
New York, NY 10036, USA

Burns, Evers (Basketball Player)
Sacramento Kings
13024 Silver Maple Ct
Bowie, MD 20715-1932, USA

Burns, George (Basketball Player)
New York Nets
16 E Poplar St
Floral Park, NY 11001-3145, USA

Burns, George (Golfer)
10459 Prestwick Rd
Boynton Beach, FL 33436-4418, USA

Burns, Heather (Actor)
c/o Courtney Kivowitz *Benderspink*
110 S Fairfax Ave Ste 350
Los Angeles, CA 90036-2179, USA

Burns, James MacGregor (Historian, Scientist)
Bee Hill Road
High Mowing
Williamstown, MA 01267, USA

Burns, Jason (Football Player)
Cincinnati Bengals
8923 S Marshfield Ave
Chicago, IL 60620-4955, USA

Burns, Jeannie (Musician, Songwriter, Writer)
Drake Assoc
177 Woodland Ave
Westwood, NJ 07675-3218, USA

Burns, Jere
1465 Lindacrest Dr
Beverly Hills, CA 90210-2519, USA

Burns, Jerry
9520 Viking Dr
Eden Prairie, MN 55344-3825, USA

Burns, Jim
2706 Lincoln St
Evanston, IL 60201-2043, USA

Burns, John F (Journalist)
New York Times
229 W 43rd St
Editorial Dept
New York, NY 10036-3959, USA

Burns, Keith (Football Player)
Denver Broncos
7991 S Kittredge Way
Englewood, CO 80112-4631, USA

Burns, Ken (Director, Producer)
c/o Staff Member *Florentine Films*
59 Maple Grove Rd
PO Box 613
Walpole, NH 03608, USA

Burns, Kenneth L (Ken) (Director)
Florentine Films
Maple Grove Road
Walpole, NH 03608, USA

Burns, Lamont (Football Player)
New York Jets
104 Northwood Street
Greensboro, NC 27401, USA

Burns, M Anthony (Business Person)
Ryder System Inc
11690 NW 105th St
Medley, FL 33178-1103, USA

Burns, Marie (Musician, Songwriter, Writer)
Drake Assoc
177 Woodland Ave
Westwood, NJ 07675-3218, USA

Burns, Megan (Actor)
c/o Kathryn Fleming *Peters Fraser & Dunlop (PFD - UK)*
Drury House
34-43 Russell St
London WC2B 5HA, UNITED KINGDOM (UK)

Burns, Mike (Football Player)
San Francisco 49ers
540 Stege Ave
Richmond, CA 94804-4133, USA

Burns, Pat (Coach)
New Jersey Devils
Continental Arena
50 RR 120 N
East Rutherford, NJ 07073, USA

Burns, Regan (Actor)
c/o Staff Member *OmniPop Inc (LA)*
4605 Lankershim Blvd Ste 201
North Hollywood, CA 91602-1874, USA

Burns, Robert (Football Player)
New York Jets
4170 Ashford Dunwoody Rd NE Ste 300
Atlanta, GA 30319-1457, USA

Burns, Robert H (Misc)
1015 University Bay Dr
Madison, WI 53705-2250, USA

Burns, Steven (Actor)
c/o Staff Member *Davis Spylios Management*
244 W 54th St # 707
New York, NY 10019, USA

Burns, Todd (Baseball Player)
Oakland A's
PO Box 111
Princeton, AL 35766-0111, USA

Burnside, Pete (Baseball Player)
New York Giants
1945 Chestnut Ave
Wilmette, IL 60091-1509, USA

Burnside, Sheldon (Baseball Player)
Detroit Tigers
7519 Wynford Cir
Montgomery, AL 36117-7483, USA

Burpo, George (Baseball Player)
Cincinnati Reds
8981 E Palms Park Dr
Tucson, AZ 85715-5644, USA

Burr, Bill (Comedian)
c/o Staff Member *William Morris Agency (WMA-LA)*
1 William Morris Pl
Beverly Hills, CA 90212-4261, USA

Burrell, Garland L Jr (Judge)
US District Court
5011 St
Sacramento, CA 95814, USA

Burrell, George R (Football Player)
Denver Broncos
129 W Upsal St
Philadelphia, PA 19119-4003, USA

Burrell, John (Football Player)
Pittsburgh Steelers
376 Park Lake Dr
Mead, OK 73449-6352, USA

Burrell, Kenny
163 3rd Ave # 206
New York, NY 10003-2523, USA

Burrell, Leroy (Athlete, Track Athlete)
University of Houston
Athletic Dept
Houston, TX 77023, USA

Burrell, Ode (Football Player)
Houston Oilers
8600 Bayou Castelle Dr
Gautier, MS 39553-1802, USA

Burrell, Pat (Baseball Player)
c/o Staff Member *Philadelphia Phillies*
3501 S Broad St
Veterans Stadium
Philadelphia, PA 19148, USA

Burrell, Scott (Basketball Player)
Charlotte Hornets
331 Evergreen Ave
Hamden, CT 06518-2745, USA

Burress, Hedy (Actor)
c/o Jeri Scott *Jeri Scott Management*
211 S Beverly Dr
Beverly Hills, CA 90212-3828, USA

Burress, Plaxico (Football Player)
Pittsburgh Steelers
47 Huntington Ter
Totowa, NJ 07512-2181, USA

Burright, Larry (Baseball Player)
Los Angeles Dodgers
1239 E Palm Dr
Glendora, CA 91741-2347, USA

Burrino, Fantasia (Musician, Reality TV Star)
c/o Staff Member *J Records (Division of BMG Entertainment)*
745 5th Ave Fl 6
New York, NY 10151-0099, USA

Burris, Arthur (Basketball Player)
Fort Wayne Pistons
1606 Edgewood Dr
Lebanon, TN 37087-3110, USA

Burris, Jeffrey L (Jeff) (Football Player)
Buffalo Bills
77 Reynolds St
Rock Hill, SC 29730-4368, USA

Burris, Kurt (Buddy) (Football Player)
2617 Fairfield Dr
Norman, OK 73072-7024, USA

Burris, Ray (Baseball Player)
Chicago Cubs
2708 Golden Creek Ln Apt 1208
Arlington, TX 76006-3557, USA

Burris, Robert H (Misc)
6225 Mineral Point Rd Apt 96
Madison, WI 53705-4574, USA

Burriss, Bo (Football Player)
New Orleans Saints
818 Pinemont Dr Apt 38
Houston, TX 77018-1529, USA

Burriss, Buddy (Football Player)
Green Bay Packers
2617 Fairfield Dr
Norman, OK 73072-7024, USA

Burrough, Junior (Basketball Player)
Boston Celtics
2138 Syracuse Dr
Charlotte, NC 28216-4423, USA

Burrough, Kenneth O (Ken) (Football Player)
New Orleans Saints
206 Sweetgum Dr
Haughton, LA 71037-8829, USA

Burroughs, Augusten (Writer)
Ralph M Vicinanza Ltd
303 W 18th St
New York, NY 10011-4440, USA

Burroughs, Don (Football Player)
Los Angeles Rams
1074 Stillwater Ct
Ventura, CA 93004-2451, USA

Burroughs, Jeffrey A (Jeff) (Baseball Player)
Washington Senators
6155 Laguna Ct
Long Beach, CA 90803-4812, USA

Burroughs, Sean (Baseball Player)
San Diego Padres
6155 Laguna Ct
Long Beach, CA 90803-4812, USA

Burroughs, William S (Musician)
PO Box 147
Lawrence, KS 66044-0147, USA

Burrow, Bob
520 W Crocus Dr
Radcliff, KY 40160-2308, USA

Burrow, Curtis (Football Player)
Green Bay Packers
51 W Cadron Ridge Rd
Greenbrier, AR 72058-9102, USA

Burrow, Ken (Football Player)
Atlanta Falcons
5371 Dunwoody Club Crk
Atlanta, GA 30360-1363, USA

Burrow, Robert (Basketball Player)
Rochester Royals
2228 Oakbranch Cir
Franklin, TN 37064-7407, USA

Burrowes, Norma E (Opera Singer)
56 Rochester Road
London NW1 9JG, UNITED KINGDOM (UK)

Burrows, Darren E (Actor)
Writers & Artists
360 N Crescent Dr Bldg North
Beverly Hills, CA 90210-6818, USA

Burrows, Edwin G (Writer)
Oxford University Press
198 Madison Ave Fl 9
New York, NY 10016-4308, USA

Burrows, Eva (Religious Leader)
102 Domain Park
193 Domain Road
South Yarra, VIC 3141, AUSTRALIA

Burrows, J Stuart (Opera Singer)
Nirvana
35 Saint Fagans Dr Saint Fagans
Cardiff, Wales CF5 6EF, UNITED KINGDOM (UK)

Burrows, James (Director)
c/o Staff Member *Broder Webb Chervin Silbermann Agency, The (BWCS)*
10250 Constellation Blvd Ste P
Los Angeles, CA 90067-6213, USA

Burrows, Stephen (Designer, Fashion Designer)
10 W 57th St
New York, NY 10019-3901, USA

Burrows, Terry (Baseball Player)
Texas Rangers
7019 Burgandy Dr
Lake Charles, LA 70605-0252, USA

Burrus, Harry (Football Player)
New York Yankees
508 Avenue D SE
Winter Haven, FL 33880-3532, USA

Burrus, William (Misc)
American Postal Workers Union
1300 L St NW
Washington, DC 20005-4128, USA

Bursch, Daniel W (Astronaut)
1305 Buena Vista Ave
Pacific Grove, CA 93950-5505, USA

Burshnick, Anthony J (General)
7715 Carrleigh Pkwy
Springfield, VA 22152-1305, USA

Burson, Jim (Football Player)
St Louis Cardinals
351 Heath Rd
Dawsonville, GA 30534-5603, USA

Burstyn, Ellen (Actor)
Matrix Movies
PO Box 217
Washington Springs Road
Palisades, NY 10964-0217, USA

Burt, James M (War Hero)
PO Box 744
Colony Park
Bowling Green, VA 22427-0744, USA

Burt, Jim (Football Player)
New York Giants
10 River Farms Ln
Saddle River, NJ 07458-3028, USA

Burt, Robert N (Business Person)
FMC Corp
200 E Randolph St
Chicago, IL 60601-6801, USA

Burtnett, Wellington (Hockey Player)
1703 Pouliot Pl
Wilmington, MA 01887-4558, USA

Burton, Albert (Football Player)
Houston Oilers
339 S Martin Luther King Blvd
Daytona Beach, FL 32114, USA

Burton, Amanda (Actor)
International Creative Mgmt
8942 Wilshire Blvd # 219
Beverly Hills, CA 90211-1908, USA

Burton, Brandie (Golfer)
3480 Pleasant Hill Dr
Highland, CA 92346-7214, USA

Burton, Ed
660 W Hile Rd
Norton Shores, MI 49441-5467, USA

Burton, Ellis (Baseball Player)
St Louis Cardinals
15621 Beach Blvd Spc 7
Westminster, CA 92683-7120, USA

Burton, Gary (Musician)
Berklee College of Music
1140 Boylston St
Boston, MA 02215-3693, USA

Burton, Glenn W (Misc)
PO Box 472
Clayton, GA 30525-0012, USA

Burton, Hilarie (Actor)
c/o Meg Mortimer *Principal Entertainment*
(LA)
1964 Westwood Blvd Ste 400
Los Angeles, CA 90025-4695, USA

Burton, Jake (Skier)
Burton Snowboards
80 Industrial Pkwy
Burlington, VT 05401-5434, USA

Burton, James (Football Player)
Chicago Bears
458 W Altadena Dr
Altadena, CA 91001-4202, USA

Burton, Jeff (Race Car Driver)
15555 Huntersville Concord Rd
Huntersville, NC 28078-6642, USA

Burton, Jim (Baseball Player)
Boston Red Sox
6540 Shaftesbury Rd
Charlotte, NC 28270-2839, USA

Burton, Kate (Actor, Musician)
Gersh Agency
232 N Canon Dr
Beverly Hills, CA 90210-5302, USA

Burton, Lance (Misc)
Monte Carlo Resort & Casino
3770 Las Vegas Blvd S
Las Vegas, NV 89109-4323, USA

Burton, Lawrence (Football Player)
New Orleans Saints
41 San Gabriel
Rancho Santa Margarita, CA 92688-3127,
USA

Burton, Leonard (Football Player)
Buffalo Bills
7728 Evening Shade Cv
Memphis, TN 38125-3103, USA

Burton, LeVar (Actor)
c/o Dino Carlaftes *Metropolitan*
4500 Wilshire Blvd Fl 2
Los Angeles, CA 90010-3858, USA

Burton, Nelson Jr (Bowler)
9359 SW Eagles Lndg
Stuart, FL 34997-7969, USA

Burton, Norman (Actor)
3641 Meadville Dr
Sherman Oaks, CA 91403-4312, USA

Burton, Robert G (Publisher)
World Color Press
101 Park Ave
New York, NY 10178-0002, USA

Burton, Ron L (Football Player)
Dallas Cowboys
5707 Cross Creek Dr
Colorado Springs, CO 80924-8119, USA

Burton, Samantha (Actor)
c/o Rob Woodburn *Jet Set Talent Agency*
2160 Alzanida De La Playa
La Jolla, CA 92037, USA

Burton, Shane (Football Player)
Miami Dolphins
PO Box 522
Hewitt Road
Catawba, NC 28609-0522, USA

Burton, Steve (Actor)
4814 Lemore Ave
Sherman Oaks, CA 91403, USA

Burton, Tim (Director, Producer)
c/o Staff Member *Tim Burton Productions*
8033 W Sunset Blvd # 7500
West Hollywood, CA 90046-2401, USA

Burton, Tony (Actor)
3500 W Olive Ave Ste 1400
Burbank, CA 91505-5512, USA

Burton, Ward (Race Car Driver)
The Ward Burton Wildlife Foundation
PO Box 519
Halifax, VA 24558-0519, USA

Burton, Warren
280 S Beverly Dr Ste 400
Beverly Hills, CA 90212-3904, USA

Burton, Willie (Basketball Player)
Miami Heat
18900 Fleming St
Detroit, MI 48234-1392, USA

Burton Jr, John (Actor)
12711 Ventura Blvd Ste 490
Studio City, CA 91604-2477, USA

Burton-Woody, Patty (Baseball Player)
918 N Walnut St
Steele, MO 63877-1316, USA

Burtschy, Moe (Baseball Player)
Philadelphia Athletics
519 Montview Ct
Cincinnati, OH 45238-4618, USA

Burtt, Dennis (Baseball Player)
Minnesota Twins
135 W Stadium Dr
Stockton, CA 95204-3117, USA

Burtt, Steve (Basketball Player)
Golden State Warriors
PO Box 700
New York, NY 10039-0661, USA

Burum, Stephen H (Cinematographer)
Mirisch Agency
1801 Century Park E Ste 1801
Los Angeles, CA 90067-2320, USA

Burwell, Barbara
1100 Millston Rd
Wayzata, MN 55391-9411, USA

Burwell, Carter (Composer)
Creative Artists Agency
9830 Wilshire Blvd
Beverly Hills, CA 90212-1804, USA

Burwell, Dick (Baseball Player)
Chicago Cubs
PO Box 1825
Twin Falls, ID 83303-1825, USA

Bury, Pol (Artist)
12 Vallee da la Taupe-Perdreauville
Mantes-La-Jolie 78200, FRANCE

Busby, Mike (Baseball Player)
St Louis Cardinals
18115 N 113th Ave
Surprise, AZ 85374-6955, USA

Busby, Paul (Baseball Player)
Philadelphia Phillies
2011 35th Ave
Meridian, MS 39301-2831, USA

Busby, Steve (Baseball Player)
Kansas City Royals
2701 Brittany Ln
Grapevine, TX 76051-4302, USA

Busby, Wayne
287 S Tampa Ave
Orlando, FL 32805-2157, USA

Buscemi, Steve (Actor, Director)
c/o Lee Stollman *Endeavor Agency LLC*
(LA)
9601 Wilshire Blvd Fl 3
Beverly Hills, CA 90210-5204, USA

Busch, Adam (Actor)
c/o Ryan Revel *Imparato Fay Management*
1126 Roxbury Dr
Los Angeles, CA 90035-1031, USA

Busch, August A III (Business Person)
Anheuser-Busch Cos
1 Busch Pl
Saint Louis, MO 63118-1852, USA

Busch, Charles (Actor, Writer)
c/o Jeff Melnick *Eighth Square*
Entertainment
606 N Larchmont Blvd Ste 307
Los Angeles, CA 90004-1309, USA

Busch, Kurt (Race Car Driver)
c/o Staff Member *National Association of*
Stock Car Racing (NASCAR)
1801 Speedway Blvd
Daytona Beach, FL 32114-1215, USA

Busch, Mike (Baseball Player)
Los Angeles Dodgers
PO Box 273
Eldon, IA 52554-0273, USA

Buschhorn, Don (Baseball Player)
Kansas City A's
17804 E 26th St S
Independence, MO 64057-1350, USA

Buse, Don (Basketball Player)
Indiana Pacers
7300 W State Road 64
Huntingburg, IN 47542-9781, USA

Busemann, Frank (Athlete, Track Athlete)
Borkumstr 13A
Recklinghausen 45665, GERMANY

Buser, Martin (Race Car Driver)
PO Box 520997
Big Lake, AK 99652-0997, USA

Busey, Gary (Actor)
c/o Vicki Roberts *Vicki M Roberts*
PO Box 642326
Los Angeles, CA 90064-7169, USA

Busey, Jake (Actor)
c/o Michael McConnell *Innovative Artists*
(LA)
1505 10th St
Santa Monica, CA 90401-2805, USA

Busfield, Timothy (Actor)
2416 G St Apt D
Sacramento, CA 95816-3635, USA

Bush
c/o Staff Member *William Morris Agency*
(WMA-LA)
1 William Morris Pl
Beverly Hills, CA 90212-4261, USA

Bush, Barbara P (First Lady)
PO Box 79798
Houston, TX 77279-9798, USA

Bush, Billy (Television Host)
c/o Staff Member *Access Hollywood*
Nbc
3000 W Alameda Ave Trailer E
Burbank, CA 91523-0001, USA

Bush, Blair (Football Player)
Cincinnati Bengals
1223 Spring St Apt 601
Seattle, WA 98104-3573, USA

Bush, Dave (Musician)
CMO Mgmt
Ransomes Dock
35-37 Parkgate Road
London SW11 4NP, UNITED KINGDOM
(UK)

Bush, Dick
8 Grande Parade #16 Plymouth
Devon PL1 3DF, ENGLAND

Bush, Frank (Football Player)
Houston Oilers
1126 W Armstrong Way
Chandler, AZ 85286-6306, USA

Bush, George W (Politician, President)
White House
1600 Pennsylvania Ave NW
Washington, DC 20500-0004, USA

Bush, Homer (Baseball Player)
New York Yankees
1402 Exeter Ct
Southlake, TX 76092-4219, USA

Bush, Jeb (Governor)
36 W Pine St
Orlando, FL 32801-2612, USA

Bush, Jim (Coach)
5106 Bounty Ln
Culver City, CA 90230-4302, USA

Bush, Kate (Musician, Songwriter, Writer)
PO Box 120 Welling
Kent DA16 3DS, UNITED KINGDOM
(UK)

Bush, Kristian (Musician)
c/o Staff Member *Gail Gellman*
Management
23852 Pch #920
Malibu, CA 90265, USA

Bush, Laura (First Lady, Politician)
c/o Staff Member *White House, The*
1600 Pennsylvania Ave NW
Washington, DC 20500-0003, USA

Bush, Lesley L (Misc)
93 Featherbed Ln
Hopewell, NJ 08525-1001, USA

Bush, Randy (Baseball Player)
Minnesota Twins
37 Kings Canyon Dr
New Orleans, LA 70131-8611, USA

Bush, Reggie (Football Player)
c/o Staff Member *New Orleans Saints*
5800 Airline Dr
Metairie, LA 70003-3876, USA

Bush, Sophia (Actor)
c/o Joan Green *Joan Green Management*
1836 Courtney Ter
Los Angeles, CA 90046-2106, USA

Bush, Walter L (Misc)
5200 Malibu Dr
Minneapolis, MN 55436-1030, USA

Bush, William Green (Actor)
Gold Marshak Liedtke
3500 W Olive Ave Ste 1400
Burbank, CA 91505-5512, USA

Bush Sr, George (Ex-President, President)
The Office of George Bush
PO Box 79798
Houston, TX 77279-9798, USA

Bushing, Chris (Baseball Player)
Cincinnati Reds
12830 NW 21st St
Pembroke Pines, FL 33028-2534, USA

Bushinsky, Joseph M (Jay)
(Correspondent)
Rehov Hatsafon 5
Savyon 56540, ISRAEL

Bushland, Raymond C (Misc)
200 Concord Plaza Dr
San Antonio, TX 78216-6943, USA

Bushnell, Bill (Director)
2751 Pelham Pl
Los Angeles, CA 90068-2326, USA

Bushnell, Candace (Writer)
c/o Rosalie Swedlin *Industry
Entertainment*
955 Carrillo Dr Ste 300
Los Angeles, CA 90048-5400, USA

Bushy, Ronald (Ron) (Musician)
Entertainment Services Int'l
6400 Pleasant Park Dr
Chanhassen, MN 55317-8804, USA

Busick, Steve (Football Player)
Denver Broncos
585 Osage St
Denver, CO 80204-4911, USA

Busino, Orlando (Cartoonist)
12 Shadblow Hill Rd
Ridgefield, CT 06877-5221, USA

Buskey, Mike (Baseball Player)
Philadelphia Phillies
117 Cedar Woods Trl
Canton, GA 30114-7769, USA

Buss, Jerry H (Business Person)
Los Angeles Lakers
1111 S Figueroa St
Staples Center
Los Angeles, CA 90015-1300, USA

Bussard, Robert W (Physicist)
9705 Carroll Centre Rd Ste 103
San Diego, CA 92126-6505, USA

Busse, Ray (Baseball Player)
Houston Astros
4265 Lemon St
Cocoa, FL 32926-2148, USA

Bussell, Darcey A (Ballerina)
155 New King's Road
London SW6 4SJ, UNITED KINGDOM
(UK)

Bussell, Gerry (Football Player)
Denver Broncos
29 Lockhart Ln
Saint Augustine, FL 32080-6530, USA

Bussey, Barney (Football Player)
Cincinnati Bengals
5059 Park Ridge Ct
West Chester, OH 45069-5552, USA

Bustamante, Carlos (Scientist)
University of California
Howard Hughes Medical Institute
Berkeley, CA 94720-0001, USA

Busted (Music Group)
c/o Staff Member *Helter Skelter (UK)*
535 Kings Rd
The Plaza
London SW10 0SZ, UNITED KINGDOM
(UK)

Buster, Dolly
Am Schornacker 66
Wesel D-46485, GERMANY

Buster, John E (Misc)
Harbor-UCLA Medical Center
PO Box 2910
Torrance, CA 90509-2910, USA

Butala, Tony (Musician)
PO Box 151
Mc Kees Rocks, PA 15136-0151, USA

Butcher, Clyde (Photographer)
52388 Tamiami Trail E
Chokoloskee, FL 34138, USA

Butcher, Donnie (Basketball Player)
New York Knicks
1725 Burns Rd
Milford, MI 48381-1215, USA

Butcher, John (Baseball Player)
Texas Rangers
820 Woodridge Dr S
Chaska, MN 55318-1266, USA

Butcher, Mike (Baseball Player)
California Angels
324 33rd Ave
East Moline, IL 61244-3124, USA

Butcher, Paul (Football Player)
Detroit Lions
2239 Topanga Skyline Dr
Topanga, CA 90290-4051, USA

Butcher, Rodney (Golfer)
7333 Hideaway Trl
New Port Richey, FL 34655-4006, USA

Butcher, Willard C (Financier)
101 Park Ave
New York, NY 10178-0002, USA

Butcher-Marsh, Mary (Baseball Player)
1119 Cedar St
Carson City, NV 89701-5025, USA

Butera, Sal (Baseball Player)
Minnesota Twins
324 Tersas Ct
Lake Mary, FL 32746-5143, USA

Butera, Sam
PO Box 43295
L
Las Vegas, NV 89116-1295, USA

Buthelezi, Chief Mangosuthu G
(Politician)
Home Affairs Ministry
Private Bag x741
Pretoria 0001, SOUTH AFRICA

Buthelezi, Minister Mangosuthu
Union Bldg
Pretoria 0001, SOUTH AFRICA

Butka, Ed (Baseball Player)
Washington Senators
131 W College St
Canonsburg, PA 15317-1150, USA

Butkus, Richard J (Dick) (Actor, Football
Player)
Chicago Bears
21647 Rambla Vis
Malibu, CA 90265, USA

Butler, Adam (Baseball Player)
Atlanta Braves
815 Providence Rd
Towson, MD 21286-2964, USA

Butler, Bernard (Musician)
Interceptor Enterprises
98 White Lion St
London N1 9PF, UNITED KINGDOM
(UK)

Butler, Bill (Baseball Player)
Kansas City Royals
141 Buckskin Ln
Berkeley Springs, WV 25411-5519, USA

Butler, Bill C (Cinematographer)
1097 Aviation Blvd
Hermosa Beach, CA 90254-4023, USA

Butler, Bob (Football Player)
Philadelphia Eagles
120 Holly Hills Dr
Mount Sterling, KY 40353-9738, USA

Butler, Brett (Actor, Comedian)
William Morris Agency
151 El Camino Dr
Beverly Hills, CA 90212-2775, USA

Butler, Brett M (Baseball Player)
2286 Flowering Crab Dr E
Lafayette, IN 47905-7729, USA

Butler, Caron (Basketball Player)
Miami Heat
601 Biscayne Blvd
American Airlines Arena
Miami, FL 33132-1801, USA

Butler, Cecil (Baseball Player)
Milwaukee Braves
5126 Hickory Gap Trail
Dallas, GA 30132, USA

Butler, Charles (Basketball Player)
Syracuse Nationals
453 Arbor Cir
Youngstown, OH 44505-1915, USA

Butler, Charles W (Football Player)
Seattle Seahawks
5496 Celestial Dr
Atwater, CA 95301-3165, USA

Butler, Conrad (Actor)
Paradigm Agency
10100 Santa Monica Blvd Ste 2500
Los Angeles, CA 90067-4116, USA

Butler, Dan
8730 W Sunset Blvd Ste 480
Los Angeles, CA 90069-2277, USA

Butler, David
10 Highgate West Hill
London, ENGLAND NW 6JR, UNITED
KINGDOM (UK)

Butler, Dean (Actor)
1310 Westholme Ave
Los Angeles, CA 90024-5016, USA

Butler, Elbert (Basketball Player)
New Jersey Knicks
153 Willow Ave
Rochester, NY 14609-1244, USA

Butler, Floyd (Football Player)
Chicago Bears
7354 S Merrill Ave
Chicago, IL 60649-3209, USA

Butler, Gary (Football Player)
Kansas City Chiefs
6660 S Piney Creek Cir
Centennial, CO 80016, USA

Butler, Gary C (Business Person)
Automatic Data Processing
1 Adp Blvd Ste 1
Roseland, NJ 07068-1728, USA

Butler, George L (General)
Peter Kiewit & Sons
11122 William Plz
Omaha, NE 68144-1873, USA

Butler, Gerard (Actor)
c/o Alan Siegel *Alan Siegel Entertainment*
345 N Maple Dr Ste 375
Beverly Hills, CA 90210-5942, USA

Butler, Greg (Basketball Player)
New Jersey Knicks
1 Oakridge Dr
Port Chester, NY 10573-5311, USA

Butler, Jack (Football Player)
Pittsburgh Steelers
510 E 11th Ave
Munhall, PA 15120-2004, USA

Butler, James (Football Player)
Pittsburgh Steelers
3181 Spring St
Atlanta, GA 30349-2345, USA

Butler, Jerry (Iceman) (Musician,
Songwriter, Writer)
c/o Jeremy Plager *Creative Artists Agency
LCC (CAA-LA)*
2000 Avenue Of The Stars
Los Angeles, CA 90067-4700, USA

Butler, Jerry O (Football Player)
Buffalo Bills
17117 Shaker Blvd
Cleveland, OH 44120-1635, USA

Butler, Joe (Musician)
Pipeline Artists Mgmt
620 16th Ave S
Hopkins, MN 55343-7833, USA

Butler, John (Musician)
c/o Staff Member *Paradigm (Monterey)*
509 Hartnell St
Monterey, CA 93940-2825, USA

Butler, Keith (Football Player)
Seattle Seahawks
805 Cavan Dr
Cranberry Twp, PA 16066-2333, USA

Butler, Kevin (Football Player)
Chicago Bears
3256 Bagley Psge
Duluth, GA 30097-3788, USA

Butler, LeRoy (Football Player)
Green Bay Packers
4119 Westloop Ln
Jacksonville, FL 32277-1729, USA

Butler, Martin (Composer)
Princeton University
Music Dept
Princeton, NJ 08544-0001, USA

Butler, Michael (Football Player)
Green Bay Packers
3107 Magalene Forest Ct
Tampa, FL 33618, USA

Butler, Mike (Basketball Player)
New Orleans Buccaneers
9900 Woodland Fern Drive Apt D
Memphis, TN 38138, USA

Butler, Mitchell (Basketball Player)
Washington Bullets
1468 Paseo De Oro
Pacific Palisades, CA 90272-1961, USA

Butler, Ray (Football Player)
Baltimore Colts
9700 Leawood Blvd Apt 1307
Houston, TX 77099-2661, USA

Butler, Robert (Director)
650 Club View Dr
Los Angeles, CA 90024-2624, USA

Butler, Robert (Football Player)
Atlanta Falcons
5567 Naylor Ct
Norcross, GA 30092-2072, USA

Butler, Robert N (Misc)
Mount Sinai Medical Center
Geriatrics Dept
1 Levy Plaza
New York, NY 10029, USA

Butler, Robert Olen (Writer)
1009 Concord Rd Apt 230
Tallahassee, FL 32308-6294, USA

Butler, Samuel C (Attorney, Attorney
General, General)
Cravath Swain Moore
825 8th Ave
New York, NY 10019-7475, USA

Butler, Skip (Football Player)
New Orleans Saints
1427 Danbury Dr
Mansfield, TX 76063-3847, USA

Butler, William D (Football Player)
Green Bay Packers
200 E Liberty St
Berlin, WI 54923-1223, USA

Butler, William E (Business Person)
Eaton Corp
1111 Superior Ave E
Eaton Center
Cleveland, OH 44114-2535, USA

Butler, William E (Football Player)
New Orleans Saints
3030 Cherry Hl
Manhattan, KS 66503-3011, USA

Butler, Yancy (Actor)
c/o Peg Donegan *Framework
Entertainment (LA)*
9057 Nemo St # C
W Hollywood, CA 90069-5511, USA

Butler-Henderson, Vicki (Actor)
c/o Staff Member *Princess Productions*
Whiteley's Centre
151 Queensway
London W2 4SB, UNITED KINGDOM
(UK)

Butor, Michael (Writer)
A L'Ecart
Lucinges
Bonne 74380, FRANCE

Butsko, Harry (Football Player)
Washington Redskins
4 Milo Cir
Duncannon, PA 17020-9647, USA

Butt, Yondani
Gurtman & Murtha
450 Fashion Ave Ste 603
New York, NY 10123-0691, USA

Buttafuoco, Joey (Actor)
c/o Staff Member *Ruth Webb Enterprises*
10580 Des Moines Ave
Northridge, CA 91326-2926, USA

Butterfield, Alexander P (Government
Official)
3410 Brookwood Dr
Fairfax, VA 22030-2009, USA

Butterfield, Betty (Comedian)
c/o Staff Member *Diva Central Inc*
7510 W Sunset Blvd Ste 1445
Los Angeles, CA 90046-3408, USA

Butterfield, Deborah K (Artist)
11229 Cottonwood Rd
Bozeman, MT 59718-9576, USA

Butterfield, Jack (Misc)
55 Pineridge Dr
Westfield, MA 01085-4544, USA

Butterfly Boucher (Music Group)
c/o Staff Member *Paradigm (Monterey)*
509 Hartnell St
Monterey, CA 93940-2825, USA

Butters, Tom (Baseball Player)
Pittsburgh Pirates
4 Turnberry Ct
Durham, NC 27712-9465, USA

Butthole Surfers
315 S Coast Hwy # 100
Encinitas, CA 92024-3543, USA

Buttle, Gregory E (Greg) (Football Player)
New York Jets
5 Hollacher Dr
Northport, NY 11768-1552, USA

Button, Richard T (Dick) (Figure Skater,
Producer)
Candio Productions
765 Park Ave # 6B
New York, NY 10021-4254, USA

Butts, Earl
2741 N Salisbury St # 2116
W Lafayette, IN 47906-1431, USA

Butts, James (Athlete, Track Athlete)
16950 Belforest Dr
Carson, CA 90746-1113, USA

Butts, Robert (Football Player)
New York Jets
108 Circle Dr
Flushing, OH 43977-9738, USA

Butz, David E (Dave) (Football Player)
St Louis Cardinals
300 Britanna Dr
Swansea, IL 62226-2439, USA

Butz, Earl (Secretary)
2741 N Salisbury St
West Lafayette, IN 47906-1431, USA

Butzer, Hans E (Architect)
University of Oklahoma
Architecture Division
Gould Hall
Norman, OK 73019-0001, USA

Butzner, John D Jr (Judge)
US Court of Appeals
PO Box 2188
Richmond, VA 23218-2188, USA

Buxbaum, Richard M (Attorney, Attorney
General, Educator, General)
University of California
Boalt Hall
Berkeley, CA 94720-0001, USA

Buxton, Sarah (Actor)
c/o Staff Member *Origin Talent Agency*
4705 Laurel Canyon Blvd Ste 306
Studio City, CA 91607-5940, USA

Buzek, Jerzy (Prime Minister)
Kancelária Prezesa Ministrow
Al Ujazdowskie
1/3
Warsaw 00-583, POLAND

Buzhardt, Johnny (Baseball Player)
Chicago Cubs
37 Brinton Hite Rd
Prosperity, SC 29127-8237, USA

Buzin, Rich (Football Player)
New York Giants
23004 Mastick Rd Apt 216
North Olmsted, OH 44070-3770, USA

Buzzi, Ruth (Actor, Comedian)
c/o Staff Member *Amsel Eisenstadt &
Frazier Inc*
5055 Wilshire Blvd Ste 865
Los Angeles, CA 90036-6109, USA

B*Witched (Music Group)
c/o Staff Member *Concorde Intl Artists Ltd*
101 Shepherds Bush Rd
London W6 7LP, UNITED KINGDOM
(UK)

Byars, Betsy C (Writer)
401 Rudder Rdg
Seneca, SC 29678-2035, USA

Byas, Rick (Football Player)
Atlanta Falcons
807 Gregory St
Normal, IL 61761-2448, USA

Byatt, Antonia Susan (A S) (Writer)
37 Rusholme Road
London SW15 3LF, UNITED KINGDOM
(UK)

Bychkov, Semyon
Buffalo Symphony Orchestra
499 Franklin St
Buffalo, NY 14202-1121, USA

Bye, Karyn (Hockey Player)
322 Gandy Dancer Cir
Hudson, WI 54016-8186, USA

Bye, Kermit E (Judge)
US Court of Appeals
657 2nd Ave N
Fargo, ND 58102-4727, USA

Byerly, Bud (Baseball Player)
St Louis Cardinals
8611 Old Sappington Rd
Sappington, MO 63126-2009, USA

Byers, Clinton (Basketball Player)
Akron Goodyear Wingfoots
4257 Leewood Rd
Stow, OH 44224-2555, USA

Byers, Ken (Football Player)
New York Giants
4650 Willow Hills Ln
Cincinnati, OH 45243-4228, USA

Byers, Nina (Physicist)
University of California
Physics Dept
Los Angeles, CA 90024, USA

Byers, Scott (Football Player)
San Diego Chargers
6060 Buckingham Pkwy Apt 314
Culver City, CA 90230-6825, USA

Byers, Steve (Actor)
c/o Robyn Friedman *Artist Management
Inc*
464 King St E
Toronto, ON M5A 1L7, CANADA

Byers, Walter (Misc)
25707 Aiken Switch Rd
Emmett, KS 66422-9719, USA

Bykovsky, Valeri F (Cosmonaut)
Potchta Kosmonavtov
Moskovskoi Oblasti
Syvisdny Goroduk 141160, RUSSIA

Byner, Earnest A (Football Player)
Cleveland Browns
850 Stembridge Rd SE
Milledgeville, GA 31061-9527, USA

Byner, John (Actor)
American Mgmt
19948 Mayall St
Chatsworth, CA 91311-3522, USA

Bynes, Amanda (Actor, Comedian)
c/o Jason Heyman *Creative Artists Agency
LCC (CAA-LA)*
2000 Avenue Of The Stars
Los Angeles, CA 90067-4700, USA

Bynoe, Peter C B (Misc)
Denver Nuggets
1000 Chopper Cir
Pepsi Center
Denver, CO 80204-5805, USA

Bynum, Mike (Baseball Player)
San Diego Padres
1830 Denver West Dr Apt 2412
Golden, CO 80401-3151, USA

Byrd, Benjamin F Jr (Doctor)
4220 Hardling Pike #380
Nashville, TN 37205, USA

Byrd, Boris (Football Player)
New York Giants
1376 Richpond Rockfield Rd
Bowling Green, KY 42101-7407, USA

Byrd, Dan (Actor)
c/o Daniel (Dan) Spilo *Artistry
Management*
525 Westbourne Dr
West Hollywood, CA 90048-1913, USA

Byrd, Darryl (Football Player)
Los Angeles Raiders
138 Mission Dr
Palo Alto, CA 94303-2752, USA

Byrd, Dennis (Football Player)
New York Jets
10306 N 143rd East Ave
Owasso, OK 74055-5930, USA

Byrd, Dennis W (Football Player)
Boston Patriots
105 Gaston Dr
Elizabeth City, NC 27909-8412, USA

Byrd, Donald (Musician)
DL Media
PO Box 2728
Bala Cynwyd, PA 19004-6728, USA

Byrd, Eugene (Actor)
c/o Rodney Omanoff *Creative
Management Group (CMG)*
8522 National Blvd Ste 108
Culver City, CA 90232-2454, USA

Byrd, George (Football Player)
Buffalo Bills
23 Wayside Rd
Westborough, MA 01581-3620, USA

Byrd, Harry F Jr (Senator)
Rockingham Publishing Co
2 N Kent St
Winchester, VA 22601-5038, USA

Byrd, Isaac (Football Player)
Tennessee Titans
5712 Astra Ave
Saint Louis, MO 63147-1012, USA

Byrd, Israel (Football Player)
New Orleans Saints
5712 Astra Ave
Saint Louis, MO 63147-1012, USA

Byrd, Jeff (Baseball Player)
Toronto Blue Jays
PO Box 2652
Lakeside, CA 92040-0932, USA

Byrd, Jim (Baseball Player)
Boston Red Sox
511 NW Woodridge Dr
Lawton, OK 73507-2265, USA

Byrd, Jonathan (Golfer)
110 Meadow Brk
Saint Simons Island, GA 31522-2459,
USA

Byrd, McArthur (Football Player)
Los Angeles Rams
10291 Sheldon Rd
Elk Grove, CA 95624-9341, USA

Byrd, Paul (Baseball Player)
New York Mets
910 Foxhollow Run
Alpharetta, GA 30004-0977, USA

Byrd, Richard (Football Player)
Houston Oilers
2230 Haley Rd
Terry, MS 39170-8820, USA

Byrd, Robin
Box 305 Lenox Hill Sta.
New York, NY 10021, USA

Byrd, Tom (Actor)
United Talent Agency
14011 Ventura Blvd # 213
Sherman Oaks, CA 91423-3533, USA

Byrd, Tracy (Musician)
Carter & Co Artist Management
PO Box 128195
Nashville, TN 37212-8195, USA

Byrdak, Tim (Baseball Player)
Kansas City Royals
16721 W Seneca Dr
Lockport, IL 60441-4269, USA

Byrds, The
PO Box 1333
Manomet, MA 02345-1333, USA

Byrne, Brendan T (Governor)
6 Becker Farm Rd
Roseland, NJ 07068-1738, USA

Byrne, Chris (Actor)
Central Artists
3310 W Burbank Blvd # A
Burbank, CA 91505-2230, USA

Byrne, David (Musician, Songwriter,
Writer)
195 Chrystie St Rm 901F
Maine Road Management
New York, NY 10002-1230, USA

Byrne, Gabriel (Actor)
Industry Entertainment
955 Carrillo Dr Ste 300
Los Angeles, CA 90048-5400, USA

Byrne, Garry (Publisher)
Variety Inc
5700 Wilshire Blvd Ste 120
Los Angeles, CA 90036-3644, USA

Byrne, John (Cartoonist)
DC Comics
1700 Broadway Ste 700
New York, NY 10019-5905, USA

Byrne, Josh (Actor)
Hervey/Grimes
PO Box 64249
Los Angeles, CA 90064-0249, USA

Byrne, Martha
c/o Staff Member *Innovative Artists (LA)*
1505 10th St
Santa Monica, CA 90401-2805, USA

Byrne, Michael (Actor)
Conway Van Gelder Robinson
18-21 Jermyn St
London SW1Y 6NB, UNITED KINGDOM
(UK)

Byrne, Nicky (Musician)
c/o Staff Member *Solo Agency Ltd (UK)*
55 Fulham High St
London SW6 3JJ, UNITED KINGDOM
(UK)

Byrne, Rose (Actor)
c/o Robyn Gardiner *RGM Associates
(Australia)*
PO Box 128
Surry Hills NSW 2010, AUSTRALIA

Byrne, Steve (Musician)
c/o Staff Member *Paradigm (Monterey)*
509 Hartnell St
Monterey, CA 93940-2825, USA

Byrne, Thomas J (Tommy) (Baseball
Player)
New York Yankees
1108 Fairway Villas Dr
Wake Forest, NC 27587-5179, USA

Byrnes, Edd (Actor)
PO Box 1623
Beverly Hills, CA 90213-1623, USA

Byrnes, Eric (Baseball Player)
Oakland A's
35 Skywood Way
Woodside, CA 94062-4839, USA

Byrnes, Jim (Actor)
c/o Staff Member *Characters Talent
Agency, The (Toronto)*
8 Elm St 3rd FL
Toronto, ON M5G 1G7, CANADA

Byrnes, Kevin P (General)
Assistant Vice Chief of Staff
Hqusa
Pentagon
Washington, DC 20310-0001, USA

Byrnes, Marty (Basketball Player)
Phoenix Suns
8739 3rd Ave
Pleasant Pr, WI 53158-4709, USA

Byron, Jeffrey (Actor)
Shapiro-Lichtman
1333 Beverly Green Dr
Los Angeles, CA 90035-1018, USA

Byron, Jeffrey (Actor)
8827 Beverly Blvd
Los Angeles, CA 90048-2405, USA

Byrorn, Don (Musician)
Hans Wendl Productions
2220 California St
Berkeley, CA 94703-1608, USA

Byrorn, Monty (Musician, Songwriter,
Writer)
Gurley Co
1204B Cedar Ln
Nashville, TN 37212-5910, USA

Byrum, Curt (Golfer)
12441 N 86th St
Scottsdale, AZ 85260-5343, USA

Byrum, John W (Director)
7435 Woodrow Wilson Dr
Los Angeles, CA 90046-1322, USA

Byrum, Tom (Golfer)
70 Sierra Oaks Dr
Sugar Land, TX 77479-5724, USA

Bystrom, Marty (Baseball Player)
Philadelphia Phillies
PO Box 26
Geigertown, PA 19523-0026, USA

Bywater, William H (Misc)
International Electronic Workers
1126 16th St NW
Washington, DC 20036-4804, USA

Bzdelik, Jeff (Coach)
Denver Nuggets
1000 Chopper Cir
Pepsi Center
Denver, CO 80204-5805, USA

Caan, James (Actor, Director)
c/o Jim Berkus *United Talent Agency
(UTA)*
9560 Wilshire Blvd Ste 500
Beverly Hills, CA 90212-2401, USA

Caan, Scott (Actor)
United Talent Agency
6560 Wilshire Blvd #500
Beverly Hills, CA 90212, USA

Caballe, Monserrat
Avenida Madronos 27
Madrid 28043, SPAIN

Caballe, Montserrat (Opera Singer)
Opera Carlos Caballe
Via Augusta 59
Barcelona 08006, SPAIN

Caballero, Ralph (Baseball Player)
Philadelphia Phillies
6770 Milne Blvd
New Orleans, LA 70124, USA

Cabana, Robert D (Astronaut)
18315 Cape Bahamas Ln
Houston, TX 77058-3406, USA

Cabas (Musician)
c/o Staff Member *Creative Artists Agency
LCC (CAA-LA)*
2000 Avenue Of The Stars
Los Angeles, CA 90067-4700, USA

Cabel, Barney (Basketball Player)
Detroit Pistons
1134 S Main St
Hampstead, MD 21074-2255, USA

Cabell, Enos M (Baseball Player)
Baltimore Orioles
4103 Frost Court
Missouri City, TX 77549, USA

Cabibbo, Nicola (Physicist)
ENEA
Viale Regina Margherita 125
Rome 00198, ITALY

Cable Guy, The, Larry (Comedian)
c/o Nick Nuciforo *Creative Artists Agency
LCC (CAA-LA)*
2000 Avenue Of The Stars
Los Angeles, CA 90067-4700, USA

Cabot, Louis W (Business Person)
Brookings Institution
1775 Massachusetts Ave NW
Washington, DC 20036-2103, USA

Cabral, Brian (Football Player)
Atlanta Falcons
5008 Ellsworth Pl
Boulder, CO 80303-1210, USA

Cabral, Sam A (Misc)
Police Associations International Union
1421 Prince St
Alexandria, VA 22314-2867, USA

Cabranes, Jose A (Judge)
US District Court
141 Church St Ste 214
New Haven, CT 06510-2030, USA

Cabrera, Jolbert (Baseball Player)
c/o Staff Member *Los Angeles Dodgers
(LA Dodgers)*
1000 Elysian Park Ave
Los Angeles, CA 90012-1112, USA

Cabrera, Ryan (Musician)
c/o Ruth Gonzalez *Creative Artists
Agency LCC (CAA-LA)*
2000 Avenue Of The Stars
Los Angeles, CA 90067-4700, USA

Cabrera, Santiago (Actor)
c/o Suzan Bymel *Management 360*
9111 Wilshire Blvd
Beverly Hills, CA 90210-5508, USA

Caccialanza, Lorenzo (Actor)
Ambrosio/Mortimer
PO Box 16758
Beverly Hills, CA 90209-2758, USA

Cacciavillan, Agnostino Cardinal
(Religious Leader)
Patrimony of Holy See
Palazzo Apostolico
Vatican City 00120, VATICAN CITY

Cacek, Craig (Baseball Player)
Houston Astros
909 6th St Apt 3
Santa Monica, CA 90403-2700, USA

Caceres, Edgar (Baseball Player)
Kansas City Royals
2300 El Jobean Rd
Port Charlotte, FL 33948-1120, USA

Caceres, Kurt (Actor)
c/o Kathy Atkinson *Washington Square
Arts (LA)*
1041 N Formosa Ave
Writers Bldg #305
West Hollywood, CA 90046-6703, USA

Cackowski, Liz (Actor, Comedian)
c/o Staff Member *Creative Artists Agency
LCC (CAA-LA)*
2000 Avenue Of The Stars
Los Angeles, CA 90067-4700, USA

Cacoyannis, Michael (Director)
15 Mouson St
Athens 117-41, GREECE

Cadall, Ava
8484 Wilshire Blvd Ste 745
Beverly Hills, CA 90211-3235, USA

Cadaret, Greg (Baseball Player)
Oakland A's
22636 Bridlewood Ln
Palo Cedro, CA 96073-9524, USA

Cadbury, Adrian (Business Person)
Bank of England
Threadneedle St
London EC2R 8AH, UNITED KINGDOM
(UK)

Cade, Eddie (Football Player)
New England Patriots
501 W 4th St
Eloy, AZ 85231-2206, USA

Cade, J Robert (Inventor, Misc)
University of Florida
Medical School Physiology Dept
Gainesville, FL 32610, USA

Cadile, Jim (Football Player)
Chicago Bears
1738 Spring St
Medford, OR 97504-6351, USA

Cadillacs, The
PO Box 8406
Santa Cruz, CA 95061-8406, USA

Cadogan, William J (Business Person)
ADC Communications
PO Box 1101
Minneapolis, MN 55440-1101, USA

Cadrez, Glenn (Football Player)
New York Jets
299 S Haskell Dr
El Centro, CA 92243-5548, USA

Cady, Sherry (Scientist)
Portland State University
Geology Dept
Portland, OR 97207, USA

Caesar, Shirley (Music Group)
Shirley Caesar Outreach Ministries
3310 Croasdaile Dr Ste 902
Durham, NC 27705-6806, USA

Caesar, Sid (Actor, Comedian)
1910 Loma Vista Dr
Beverly Hills, CA 90210-1840, USA

Caesars, The (Music Group)
c/o Staff Member *Paradigm (Monterey)*
509 Hartnell St
Monterey, CA 93940-2825, USA

Cafagna-Tesoro, Ashley (Actor)
c/o Staff Member *Tesoro Entertainment*
205D N Stephanie St # No115
Henderson, NV 89074-8060, USA

Cafego, George
10121 El Pinar Dr
Knoxville, TN 37922-4158, USA

Cafferata, Hector A Jr (War Hero)
1807 Plum Ln
Venice, FL 34293-2040, USA

Caffey, Charlotte (Music Group,
Musician)
4800 Bryn Mawr Rd
Los Angeles, CA 90027-1109, USA

Caffey, Jason (Basketball Player)
c/o Staff Member *Milwaukee Bucks*
1001 N 4th St
Bradley Center
Milwaukee, WI 53203-1312, USA

Caffie, Joe (Baseball Player)
Cleveland Buckeyes
PO Box 1932
Warren, OH 44482-1932, USA

Cagatay, Mustafa (Prime Minister)
60 Cumhuriyet Caddesi
Kyrenia, CYPRUS

Cage, Nicolas (Actor)
c/o Staff Member *Saturn Films*
9000 W Sunset Blvd Ste 911
W Hollywood, CA 90069-5809, USA

Cage, Wayne (Baseball Player)
Cleveland Indians
1305 Davis Blvd
Ruston, LA 71270-6405, USA

Cagle, Chris (Musician)
c/o Staff Member *William Morris Agency
(WMA-TN)*
1600 Division St Ste 300
Nashville, TN 37203-2755, USA

Cagle, J Douglas (Business Person)
Cagle's Inc
2000 Hills Ave NW
Atlanta, GA 30318-2817, USA

Cagle, Jim (Football Player)
Philadelphia Eagles
745 Sharpshooters Rdg NW
Marietta, GA 30064-4731, USA

Cagle, Johnny (Football Player)
Boston Patriots
1645 Citation Dr
Aiken, SC 29803-5223, USA

Cagle, Yvonne D (Astronaut)
c/o Staff Member *NASA*
2101 Nasa Pkwy
Johnson Space Center
Houston, TX 77058-3691, USA

Caglini, Umperto
via Don Crocetti #3
Fabriano (Ancona) 60044, ITALY

Cahill, Eddie (Actor)
c/o David Seltzer *Management 360*
9111 Wilshire Blvd
Beverly Hills, CA 90210-5508, USA

Cahill, James (Actor)
31 Chambers St Ste 311
New York, NY 10007-4030, USA

Cahill, Laura (Writer)
c/o Staff Member *Broder Webb Chervin
Silbermann Agency, The (BWCS)*
10250 Constellation Blvd Ste P
Los Angeles, CA 90067-6213, USA

Cahill, Teresa M (Opera Singer)
65 Leyland Road
London SE12 8DW, UNITED KINGDOM
(UK)

Cahill, Thomas (Writer)
Doubleday Press
1540 Broadway
New York, NY 10036-4039, USA

Cahill, William (Football Player)
Buffalo Bills
24204 Crystal Lake Rd
Woodinville, WA 98077-9596, USA

Cahn, John W (Misc)
2032 43rd Ave E Apt 18
Seattle, WA 98112-2764, USA

Cahoon, Todd (Actor)
c/o Laura Pallas *Pallas Management*
12535 Chandler Blvd Apt 1
Valley Village, CA 91607-1934, USA

Cahouet, Frank V (Financier)
Mellon Bank Corp
1 Mellon Bank Center 500 Grant St
Pittsburgh, PA 15219, USA

Caifanes (Music Group)
c/o Staff Member *BMG*
1540 Broadway
New York, NY 10036-4074, USA

Cain, Carl (Basketball Player)
Olympics
3045 Sun Valley Dr
Pickerington, OH 43147-9090, USA

Cain, Dean (Actor)
c/o Stephen (Steve) Small *Paradigm (LA)*
360 N Crescent Dr
North Bldg
Beverly Hills, CA 90210-6820, USA

Cain, James (Football Player)
Chicago Cardinals
348 Holly St
Eudora, AR 71640-2223, USA

Cain, John Paul (Golfer)
1404 Avondale St
Sweetwater, TX 79556-2614, USA

Cain, Jonathan (Musician)
Hemming Morse
160 Spear St Ste 1900
San Francisco, CA 94105-1548, USA

Cain, Les (Baseball Player)
Detroit Tigers
31 Cutting Ct
Richmond, CA 94804-4217, USA

Cain, Lynn (Football Player)
Atlanta Falcons
5740 W Centinela Ave Apt 403
Los Angeles, CA 90045-8819, USA

Cain, Mick
7800 Beverly Blvd # 3371
Los Angeles, CA 90036-2112, USA

Caine, Michael (Actor)
c/o Duncan Heath *International Creative
Management (ICM-UK)*
Oxford House
76 Oxford St
London W1N OAX, UNITED KINGDOM
(UK)

Caio, Francesco (Business Person)
Ing C Olivetti Co
Via G Jervos 77
Ivrea/Truin 10015, ITALY

Calabrese, Gerry (Basketball Player)
Syracuse Nationals
351 Esplanade Pl
Cliffside Park, NJ 07010-2708, USA

Calabresi, Guido (Judge)
US Appeals Court
157 Church St
New Haven, CT 06510-2109, USA

Calabro, Thomas (Actor)
12400 Ventura Blvd # 369
Studio City, CA 91604-2406, USA

Calacurcio-Thomas, Aldine (Baseball
Player)
5438 Nottingham Dr
Loves Park, IL 61111-3605, USA

Calatrava, Santiago (Architect, Engineer)
Santiago Calatrava SA
Hoschgasse 5
Zurich 8008, SWITZERLAND

Caldeiro, Fernando (Frank) (Astronaut)
2211 Summer Reef Dr
League City, TX 77573-6657, USA

Calder, David
1 Winterwell Rd.
London, ENGLAND SW2 5TB, UNITED
KINGDOM (UK)

Calder, Nigel
8 The Chase Furnace Green
Crawley W. Sussex, ENGLAND RH10
6HW, UNITED KINGDOM (UK)

Caldera, Rodriguez Rafael (President)
Ave Urdaneta 33-2 Apdo 2060
Caracas 1010, VENEZUELA

Calderon, Leticia (Actor)
c/o Staff Member *Televisa*
Blvd Adolfo Lopez Mateos 232
Colonia San Angel INN
DF CP 01060, MEXICO

Calderon, Sila Maria (Governor)
Governer's Office
PO Box 9020082
La Fortaleza
San Juan, PR 00902-0082, USA

Calderon, Wilmer (Actor)
c/o Lena Roklin *Roklin Management*
8530 Wilshire Blvd Ste 550
Beverly Hills, CA 90211-3133, USA

Calderon Fournier, Rafael A (President)
Partido Unidad Social Cristiana
San Jose, COSTA RICA

Calderone, Sammy (Baseball Player)
New York Giants
1000 Cooper St
Beverly, NJ 08010-1708, USA

Caldicott, Helen (Activist, Doctor, Misc)
Physicians for Responsibility
4423 Lehigh Rd # 337
College Park, MD 20740-3127, USA

Caldwell, Adrian (Basketball Player)
Houston Rockets
10606 Brooklet Pi
Houston, TX 77099, USA

Caldwell, Alan (Football Player)
New York Giants
1370 Kerner Rd
Kernersville, NC 27284-8943, USA

Caldwell, Bobby (Musician, Songwriter,
Writer)
Public Relations Partners
12702 Landale St
Studio City, CA 91604-1349, USA

Caldwell, Darryl (Football Player)
Buffalo Bills
4604 Malinta Ln
Chattanooga, TN 37416-3728, USA

Caldwell, Gail (Journalist)
Boston Globe
Editorial Dept
135 W T Morrissey Blvd
Dorchester, MA 02139, USA

Caldwell, Jim (Basketball Player)
New York Knicks
705 Freedom Ln
Roswell, GA 30075-7911, USA

Caldwell, Joe (Basketball Player)
Detroit Pistons
15 E Pebble Beach Dr
Tempe, AZ 85282-5127, USA

Caldwell, John (Cartoonist)
King Features Syndicate
888 7th Ave Ste 201
New York, NY 10106-0201, USA

Caldwell, Joseph (Joe) (Basketball Player)
1750 Boulder St
Colorado Springs, CO 80890, USA

Caldwell, Kimberly (Musician, Reality TV Star)
c/o Michael (Mike) Esterman *Esterman Entertainment*
214 Park Rd
Riva, MD 21140-1224, USA

Caldwell, Matt (Musician)
c/o Staff Member *Paradigm (Monterey)*
509 Hartnell St
Monterey, CA 93940-2825, USA

Caldwell, Mike (Baseball Player)
San Diego Padres
1645 Brook Run Dr
Raleigh, NC 27614-9732, USA

Caldwell, Mike (Football Player)
Cleveland Browns
646 Robertsville Rd
Oak Ridge, TN 37830-4724, USA

Caldwell, Mike T (Football Player)
San Francisco 49ers
41621 N Bent Creek Ct
Phoenix, AZ 85086-1903, USA

Caldwell, Philip (Business Person)
Smith Barney Shearson
200 Vesey St
New York, NY 10285-1000, USA

Caldwell, Ralph W (Football Player)
San Diego Chargers
4054 Charlene Dr
Los Angeles, CA 90043-1510, USA

Caldwell, Ravin (Football Player)
Washington Redskins
4415 Johnson St
Fort Smith, AR 72904-4531, USA

Caldwell, Rex (Golfer)
260 El Dorado Blvd Apt 3006
Webster, TX 77598-2251, USA

Caldwell, William A (Editor)
Vineyard Gazette
S Summer St
Editorial Dept
Edgartown, MA 02539, USA

Caldwell, Zoe (Actor)
Whitehead-Stevens
1501 Broadway
New York, NY 10036-5601, USA

Cale, J J (Music Group, Musician)
Rosebud Agency
PO Box 170429
San Francisco, CA 94117-0429, USA

Cale, John (Music Group, Musician)
Firebrand Mgmt
12 Rickett St
West Brompton
London SW6 1RU, UNITED KINGDOM (UK)

Cale, Paula
345 N Maple Dr Ste 200
Beverly Hills, CA 90210-3860, USA

Cale, Puala (Actor)
Gersh Agency
232 N Canon Dr
Beverly Hills, CA 90210-5302, USA

Calegari, Maria (Ballerina)
New York City Ballet
Lincoln Center Plaza
New York, NY 10023, USA

Calero, Kiko (Baseball Player)
St Louis Cardinals
1954 Calle Francisco Zuniga
San Juan, PR 00926-7638, USA

Calfa, Don (Actor)
Richard Sundel
1910 Holmby Ave Apt 1
Los Angeles, CA 90025-5936, USA

Calfa, Marian (Prime Minister)
Calfa Pravni Kancelar Premyslovska 28
Prague 3 130 00, CZECH REPUBLIC

Calhoon, Jesse M (Misc)
Marine Engineers Union
17 Battery Pl
New York, NY 10004-1207, USA

Calhoun, Bill (Basketball Player)
Rochester Royals
3740 El Cerro View Cir
Reno, NV 89509-5610, USA

Calhoun, Corky (Misc, Yachtsman)
Surfer Magazine
PO Box 1028
Dana Point, CA 92629-5028, USA

Calhoun, David (Basketball Player)
Phoenix Suns
17912 Lafayette Dr
Olney, MD 20832-2129, USA

Calhoun, Donald C (Don) (Football Player)
Buffalo Bills
1308 N Crestway St
Wichita, KS 67208-2810, USA

Calhoun, Jeff (Baseball Player)
Houston Astros
10002 Springwood Forest Dr
Houston, TX 77080-6419, USA

Calhoun, Jim (Basketball Player, Coach)
Connecticut University
2111 Hillside Rd
Storrs Mansfield, CT 06269-9002, USA

Calhoun, Mike (Football Player)
Tampa Bay Buccaneers
325 Mineola Ave
Akron, OH 44313-7860, USA

Calhoun, Monica (Actor)
Innovative Artists
1505 10th St
Santa Monica, CA 90401-2805, USA

Cali, Joseph (Actor)
25630 Edenwild Rd
Monte Nido, CA 91302-2265, USA

Caliendo, Frank (Actor)
c/o Steve Smooke *Creative Artists Agency LCC (CAA-LA)*
2000 Avenue Of The Stars
Los Angeles, CA 90067-4700, USA

Califano, Joseph
3551 Springfield Lane
Washington, DC 20008, USA

Califano, Joseph A Jr (Secretary)
Casa at Columbia
633 3rd Ave # 1900
New York, NY 10017-6706, USA

Caligiuri, Fred (Baseball Player)
Philadelphia Athletics
100 Baker St
Rimersburg, PA 16248-4324, USA

Calip, Demetrius (Basketball Player)
Los Angeles Lakers
9955 Wish Ave
Northridge, CA 91325-1655, USA

Calipari, John (Basketball Player, Coach)
University of Memphis
Athletic Dept
Memphis, TN 38152-0001, USA

Calisher, Hortense (Writer)
Marion Boyars
365 5th Ave # 5406
New York, NY 10016-4309, USA

Call, Anthony (Actor)
Michael Thomas Agency
134 E 10th St
New York, NY 10003, USA

Call, Brandon (Actor)
5918 Van Nuys Blvd
Van Nuys, CA 91401-3623, USA

Call, Jack (Football Player)
Baltimore Colts
3321 Cool Branch Rd
Churchville, MD 21028-1107, USA

Call, Kevin (Football Player)
Indianapolis Colts
839 Carey Rd
Carmel, IN 46033-9324, USA

Callaghan-Maxwell, Marge (Baseball Player)
203-5748 Rupert St
Vancouver, BC V5R 2K6, CANADA

Callahan, Ben (Baseball Player)
Oakland A's
1140 Asheford Green Ave
Concord, NC 28027-8185, USA

Callahan, Bill (Coach, Football Coach)
University of Nebraska
Athletic Dept
Lincoln, NE 68588, USA

Callahan, Bob (Football Player)
Buffalo Bills
5448 Alta Vis
Laguna Woods, CA 92637-2709, USA

Callahan, James (Actor)
1159 Via Estrellada
Fallbrook, CA 92028-1747, USA

Callahan, John (Actor)
Levin Representatives
2402 4th St Apt 6
Santa Monica, CA 90405-3664, USA

Callahan, John (Cartoonist)
Viking Press
375 Hudson St
New York, NY 10014-3658, USA

Callan, Cecile (Actor)
SMZ
8730 W Sunset Blvd Ste 480
Los Angeles, CA 90069-2277, USA

Callan, K (Actor)
4957 Matilija Ave
Sherman Oaks, CA 91423-1921, USA

Callan, Michael (Actor)
1651 Camden Ave Apt 3
Los Angeles, CA 90025-3537, USA

Calland, Lee (Football Player)
Minnesota Vikings
6624 Windwood Cir
Douglasville, GA 30135-1647, USA

Callaway, Howard H (Bo) (Government Official)
Callaway Gardens
Pine Mountain, GA 31822, USA

Callaway, Liz (Actor, Artist, Voice Over Artist)
c/o Staff Member *Gage Group, The (NY)*
450 Fashion Ave Ste 1809
New York, NY 10123-1890, USA

Callaway, Mark (The Undertaker) (Wrestler)
c/o Staff Member *World Wrestling Entertainment (WWE)*
1241 E Main St
Stamford, CT 06902-3520, USA

Callaway, Mickey (Baseball Player)
Tampa Bay Devil Rays
8061 Stonewyck Rd
Germantown, TN 38138-2351, USA

Callaway, Paul Smith (Music Group, Musician)
Washington Cathedral
Mount Saint Alban
Washington, DC 20016, USA

Callaway, Thomas (Actor)
House of Representatives
211 S Beverly Dr Ste 208
Beverly Hills, CA 90212-3879, USA

Callen, Bryan (Actor, Musician)
c/o Staff Member *Paradigm (Monterey)*
509 Hartnell St
Monterey, CA 93940-2825, USA

Callen, Jones Gloria (Swimmer)
1508 Chafton Rd
Charleston, WV 25314-1603, USA

Callery, Sean (Composer)
Gorfaine/Schwartz
4111 W Alameda Ave Ste 509
Burbank, CA 91505-4171, USA

Callicutt, Ken (Football Player)
Detroit Lions
6644 Longworth Dr
Waterford, MI 48329-1343, USA

Callies, Sarah Wayne (Actor)
c/o Staff Member *William Morris Agency (WMA-LA)*
1 William Morris Pl
Beverly Hills, CA 90212-4261, USA

Calligaro, Len (Football Player)
New York Giants
208 Oak St
Hurley, WI 54534-1071, USA

Calling, The (Music Group)
c/o Staff Member *William Morris Agency (WMA-LA)*
1 William Morris Pl
Beverly Hills, CA 90212-4261, USA

Callis, James (Actor, Director)
c/o Staff Member *Alan Siegel Entertainment*
345 N Maple Dr Ste 375
Beverly Hills, CA 90210-5942, USA

Callow, Simon (Actor)
Marina Martin
12/13 Poland St
London W1V 3DE, UNITED KINGDOM (UK)

Calloway, AJ (Television Host)
c/o Michael (Mike) Esterman *Esterman Entertainment*
214 Park Rd
Riva, MD 21140-1224, USA

Calloway, Chris (Football Player)
New York Giants
280 Willow Glade Pt
Alpharetta, GA 30022-1024, USA

Calloway, Ernie (Football Player)
Philadelphia Eagles
104 Keeter Center Dr
Raleigh, NC 27601-2667, USA

Calloway, Ron (Baseball Player)
Montreal Expos
3868 Las Colinas Dr
Las Cruces, NM 88012-0693, USA

Callum, Keith Rene
525 Seymour St. #500
Vancouver, BC V6B 3H7, CANADA

Calmus, Dick (Baseball Player)
Los Angeles Dodgers
3823 S 28th West Ave
Tulsa, OK 74107-5452, USA

Calne, Roy Y (Doctor)
Addenbrooke's Hospital
Hills Road
Cambridge CB2 2QQ, UNITED
KINGDOM (UK)

Caltabiano, Tom (Comedian)
c/o Staff Member *United Talent Agency
(UTA)*
9560 Wilshire Blvd Ste 500
Beverly Hills, CA 90212-2401, USA

Calvert, James F (Admiral, Writer)
PO Box 787
Saint Michaels, MD 21663-0787, USA

Calvert, Mark (Baseball Player)
San Francisco Giants
908 W Waco St
Broken Arrow, OK 74011-2819, USA

Calvet, Jacques (Financier)
31 Ave Victor Hugo
Paris 75116, FRANCE

Calvin, John (Actor)
2503 Ware Rd
Austin, TX 78741-5720, USA

Calvin, Mack (Basketball Player)
Los Angeles Stars
930 Figueroa Ter Apt 602
Los Angeles, CA 90012-3076, USA

Calvin, Thomas (Football Player)
Pittsburgh Steelers
2712 McTavish Ave SW
Decatur, AL 35603-1106, USA

Calvo, Paul M (Governor)
Governor's Office
Capitol Building
Agana, GU 96910, USA

Calvo-Sotelo, Bustelo Leopoldo (Prime
Minister)
Buho 1 Somosaguas
Madrid, SPAIN

Camacho, Andy
4545 Encino Ave
Encino, CA 91316-3834, USA

Camacho, Ernie (Baseball Player)
Oakland A's
746 Saint Regis Way
Salinas, CA 93905-1642, USA

Camacho, Hector (Macho) (Boxer)
8034 Solitaire Ct
Orlando, FL 32836-6044, USA

Camarata, Toodie (Conductor, Musician)
3515 Berry Dr
Studio City, CA 91604-3882, USA

Camarda, Charles J (Astronaut)
PO Box 58603
Houston, TX 77258-8603, USA

Camarillo, Rich (Football Player)
New England Patriots
1941 E Clubhouse Dr
Phoenix, AZ 85048-4061, USA

Camastra, Danielle (Actor)
c/o Staff Member *David Shapira &
Associates*
193 N Robertson Blvd
Beverly Hills, CA 90211-2103, USA

Cambal, Dennis (Football Player)
New York Jets
24 Hedge Row
West Yarmouth, MA 02673-5813, USA

Cambre, Ronald C (Business Person)
Newmont Mining
9903 W Laurel Pl
Littleton, CO 80127-3900, USA

Cambria, Fred (Baseball Player)
Pittsburgh Pirates
12 Iris Ct
Northport, NY 11768-3207, USA

Cambria, John (Cinematographer)
6910 Mayall St
North Hills, CA 91343, USA

Camby, Marcus (Basketball Player)
Toronto Raptors
925 Lincoln St Apt 14G
Denver, CO 80203-2768, USA

Camden, John (Business Person)
RMC Group
Coldgarbour Lane
Thorpe
Egham, Surrey TW20 8TD, UNITED
KINGDOM (UK)

Camdessus, Michel J (Financier)
International Monetary Fund
700 19th St NW
Washington, DC 20431-0002, USA

Cameletti, Rob
643 N La Cienega Blvd
Los Angeles, CA 90069-5201, USA

Camelia-Romer, Susanne (Misc, Prime
Minister)
Primier's Office
Fort Amsterdam 17
Willemstad, NETHERLANDS ANTILLES

Cameron, Candance (Actor)
Barbara Camaron Assoc
8369 Sausalito Ave # A
Canoga Park, CA 91304-3342, USA

Cameron, Dallas (Football Player)
Denver Broncos
7977 W 12th Ave
Hialeah-Miami Lakes High School
Hialeah, FL 33014-3534, USA

Cameron, David (Designer, Fashion
Designer)
Schauspielschule Krauss
Weihburggasse 19
Vienna 1010, AUSTRIA

Cameron, Dean (Actor)
Landmark Artists Mgmt
4116 W Magnolia Blvd
Burbank, CA 91505-2782, USA

Cameron, Don R (Educator, Misc)
National Education Association
1201 16th St NW
Washington, DC 20036-3290, USA

Cameron, Duncan (Music Group,
Musician)
Sawyer Brown Inc
5200 Old Harding Rd
Franklin, TN 37064-9406, USA

Cameron, Dwayne (Actor)
The Syndicate
100 Universal City Plz # 6148
C/O Scott Karp
Universal City, CA 91608-1002, USA

Cameron, Glenn S (Football Player)
Cincinnati Bengals
8082 Steeplechase Dr
Palm Beach Gardens, FL 33418-7703,
USA

Cameron, James (Director, Producer)
LightStorm Entertainment
919 Santa Monica Blvd
Santa Monica, CA 90401-2704, USA

Cameron, Joanna (Actor)
Cameron Productions
PO Box 1011
Pebble Beach, CA 93953-1011, USA

Cameron, John
. 35 Ragged Hall Lane
St. Albans Herts, ENGLAND AL2 3LB,
UNITED KINGDOM (UK)

Cameron, Kenneth D (Astronaut)
Austvagen 13
Vastra Frotunda 42676, SWEDEN

Cameron, Kirk (Actor)
Mark Craig Productions
1383 Callens Rd
Ventura, CA 93003-5602, USA

Cameron, Laura (Actor)
8383 Wilshire Blvd # 954
Beverly Hills, CA 90211-2412, USA

Cameron, Mat (Music Group, Musician)
Susan Silver Mgmt
6523 California Ave SW # 348
Seattle, WA 98136-1833, USA

Cameron, Mechelle (Swimmer)
Box 2 Site 1SS3
Calgary, AL T3C 3N9, CANADA

Cameron, Mike (Baseball Player)
c/o Staff Member *New York Mets*
12301 Roosevelt Ave
Shea Stadium
Flushing, NY 11368-1699, USA

Cameron, Paul (Football Player)
Pittsburgh Steelers
1931 Bush St Apt 149
Oceanside, CA 92058-9105, USA

Cameron, Rhona (Actor)
c/o Staff Member *Jeremy Hicks Associates*
11-12 Tottenham News
London W1T 4AG, UNITED KINGDOM
(UK)

Cameron, Scotty (Golfer)
Acushnet Company
333 Bridge St
C/O Gordon Sanborn
Fairhaven, MA 02719-4900, USA

Cameron-Bure, Candace (Actor)
Redrock Entertainment Development
118 S Cordova St Fl 3
Burbank, CA 91505-4610, USA

Camilleri, Louis C (Business Person)
Altria Group
120 Park Ave
New York, NY 10017-5577, USA

Camilleri, Terry (Actor)
c/o Sheryl Abrams *PTI Talent Agency*
14724 Ventura Blvd Ph
Sherman Oaks, CA 91403-3513, USA

Camilli, Doug (Baseball Player)
Los Angeles Dodgers
4245 61st St
Vero Beach, FL 32967-8807, USA

Camilli, Lou (Baseball Player)
Cleveland Indians
4700 Oahu Dr NE
Albuquerque, NM 87111-2820, USA

Camilo, Michael (Musician)
Joel Chriss
300 Mercer St Apt 3J
New York, NY 10003-6732, USA

Camilo, Michel (Music Group, Musician)
Redondo Music
590 W End Ave # 6
New York, NY 10024-1722, USA

Caminito, Jerry (Race Car Driver)
Blue Thunder Racing
480 Hyson Rd
Jackson, NJ 08527-4442, USA

Cammack, Eric (Baseball Player)
New York Mets
2136 Walker Ln
Nederland, TX 77627-4729, USA

Cammermeyer, Margarethe
4632 Tompkins Rd
Langley, WA 98260-9695, USA

Cammuso, Frank (Cartoonist)
1725 James St # 1
Syracuse, NY 13206-3201, USA

Camoy, Martin (Economist)
Stanford University
Economic Studies Center
Stanford, CA 94305, USA

Camp, Colleen (Actor)
473 N Tigertail Rd
Los Angeles, CA 90049-2807, USA

Camp, Greg (Musician)
Creative Artists Agency
9830 Wilshire Blvd
Beverly Hills, CA 90212-1804, USA

Camp, Jeremy (Musician)
c/o Staff Member *Third Coast Artists
Agency*
2021 21st Ave S Ste 220
Nashville, TN 37212-4348, USA

Camp, Jim (Football Player)
Brooklyn Dodgers
117 Dover Ct
Hurdle Mills, NC 27541-7520, USA

Camp, John (Journalist)
Saint Paul Pioneer Press
345 Cedar St
Editorial Dept
Saint Paul, MN 55101-1057, USA

Camp, Rick (Baseball Player)
Atlanta Braves
20 Green Meadow Dr
Trion, GA 30753-1131, USA

Camp, Shawn
PO Box 121972
Nashville, TN 37212-1972, USA

Camp, Steve (Music Group)
Third Coast Artists
2021 21st Ave S Ste 220
Nashville, TN 37212-4348, USA

Campana, Al (Football Player)
Chicago Bears
509 Sexton St
Struthers, OH 44471-1148, USA

Campanella, Joseph (Actor)
4196 Colfax Ave
Studio City, CA 91604-2165, USA

Campaneris, Bert (Baseball Player)
Kansas City A's
PO Box 5096
Scottsdale, AZ 85261-5096, USA

Campanis, Jim (Baseball Player)
US Olympic Team
62 Deer Creek Rd
Pomona, CA 91766-4934, USA

Campau, Thomas E (Cinematographer)
2000 S Hammond Lake Rd
West Bloomfield, MI 48324-1816, USA

Campbell, A Kim (Prime Minister)
Harvard University
Kennedy School Of Government
Cambridge, MA 02138, USA

Campbell, Alan (Actor)
Gersh Agency
41 Madison Ave Ste 3301
New York, NY 10010-2210, USA

Campbell, Ben Nighthorse
456 New Jersey Ave SE
Washington, DC 20003-4038, USA

Campbell, Bill (Baseball Player)
Minnesota Twins
133 S Hale St
Palatine, IL 60067-6211, USA

Campbell, Billy (Actor)
c/o Sean Fay *Imparato Fay Management*
1126 Roxbury Dr
Los Angeles, CA 90035-1031, USA

Campbell, Bruce (Actor)
c/o Barry McPherson *Agency for the Performing Arts (APA-LA)*
405 S Beverly Dr
Beverly Hills, CA 90212-4416, USA

Campbell, Carol
Agt. Uschi Drews Droysenstr. 2
Berlin D-10629, GERMANY

Campbell, Carter (Football Player)
San Francisco 49ers
24834 Winterberry Ln
Plainfield, IL 60585-5685, USA

Campbell, Chad (Golfer)
1309 NW 12th St
Andrews, TX 79714-2711, USA

Campbell, Cheryl (Actor)
Michael Whitehall
125 Gloucester Road
London SW7 4TE, UNITED KINGDOM
(UK)

Campbell, Christa (Actor)
c/o Frank Gonzales *The Agency (CA)*
3711 Ocean Front Walk # 1
Marina Del Rey, CA 90292-5705, USA

Campbell, Christian (Actor)
12533 Woodgreen St
Los Angeles, CA 90066-2723, USA

Campbell, Colin (Soupy) (Coach, Hockey Player)
New York Rangers
2 Penn Plz
Madison Square Garden
New York, NY 10121-1703, USA

Campbell, Dan (Football Player)
New York Giants
PO Box 97
County Road 2111
Meridian, TX 76665-0097, USA

Campbell, Darian
1 Wandsworth Plain
London, ENGLAND SW17 1EH, UNITED
KINGDOM (UK)

Campbell, Dave (Baseball Player)
Detroit Tigers
726 N Dundee Dr
Post Falls, ID 83854-8886, USA

Campbell, Dave (Baseball Player)
Atlanta Braves
878 Amidon St
Deltona, FL 32725-7206, USA

Campbell, Dick (Football Player)
Pittsburgh Steelers
2557 Nicolet Dr
Green Bay, WI 54311-7225, USA

Campbell, Earl C (Football Player)
Houston Oilers
2937 Thousand Oaks Dr
Austin, TX 78746-7661, USA

Campbell, Elden (Basketball Player)
Los Angeles Lakers
17252 Hawthorne Blvd # 493
Torrance, CA 90504-1032, USA

Campbell, Garry (Producer, Writer)
c/o Staff Member *Creative Artists Agency LCC (CAA-LA)*
2000 Avenue Of The Stars
Los Angeles, CA 90067-4700, USA

Campbell, Gary (Football Player)
Chicago Bears
PO Box 775353
Steamboat Springs, CO 80477-5353, USA

Campbell, Gene (Hockey Player)
1554 Wilshire Dr NE
Rochester, MN 55906-4363, USA

Campbell, Glen (Music Group)
Glen Campbell Enterprises
1888 Century Park E Fl 9th
Los Angeles, CA 90067-1735, USA

Campbell, Helen Hannah (Baseball Player)
17077 San Mateo St
Fountain Valley, CA 92708-7658, USA

Campbell, Isobel (Music Group, Musician)
Legends of 21st Century
7 Trinity Row
Florence, MA 01062-1931, USA

Campbell, James (Baseball Player)
St Louis Cardinals
209 W Seven Pines St
Lamar, SC 29069-8964, USA

Campbell, Jeff (Baseball Player)
Homestead Grays
4194 San Miguel Ave
San Diego, CA 92113-1842, USA

Campbell, Jeff (Football Player)
Detroit Lions
120 Weston Ln
Southlake, TX 76092-2304, USA

Campbell, Jennifer
9200 W Sunset Blvd Ste 1130
Los Angeles, CA 90069-3606, USA

Campbell, Jessica (Actor)
Somers Teitelbaum David
8840 Wilshire Blvd # 200
Beverly Hills, CA 90211-2606, USA

Campbell, Jim (Baseball Player)
Houston Colt 45's
1924 Knollwood Ln
Los Altos, CA 94024-6720, USA

Campbell, Jim (Baseball Player)
Kansas City Royals
1671 6th St
Oroville, CA 95965-4057, USA

Campbell, Joe (Baseball Player)
Chicago Cubs
330 Legends Ct
Bowling Green, KY 42103-2550, USA

Campbell, John (Race Car Driver)
John D Campbell Stable
823 Allison Dr
Rivervale, NJ 07675-6602, USA

Campbell, John W (Football Player)
Minnesota Vikings
12908 Welcome Ln
Burnsville, MN 55337-3626, USA

Campbell, Joshua (Actor)
c/o Staff Member *Select Artists Ltd (CA-Westside Office)*
1138 12th St Apt 1
Santa Monica, CA 90403-5459, USA

Campbell, Julia (Actor)
Innovative Artists
1505 10th St
Santa Monica, CA 90401-2805, USA

Campbell, Ken (Actor)
c/o Staff Member *Marathon Entertainment*
8060 Melrose Ave Fl 4th
Los Angeles, CA 90046-7038, USA

Campbell, Kevin (Baseball Player)
Oakland A's
207 Ridout Dr
Des Arc, AR 72040-3335, USA

Campbell, Kim (Prime Minister)
Canadian Consulate
550 S Hope St Ste 900
Los Angeles, CA 90071-2654, USA

Campbell, L Arthur (Misc, Scientist)
Rockefeller University
1230 York Ave
Medical Center
New York, NY 10065-6399, USA

Campbell, Lamar (Football Player)
Detroit Lions
2511 W 7th St
Chester, PA 19013-2109, USA

Campbell, Larry Joe (Actor)
c/o Staff Member *Brillstein-Grey Entertainment*
9150 Wilshire Blvd Ste 350
Beverly Hills, CA 90212-3453, USA

Campbell, Lewis B (Business Person)
Textron Inc
40 Westminster St
Providence, RI 02903-2503, USA

Campbell, Luther
8400 NE 2nd Ave
Miami, FL 33138-3804, USA

Campbell, Luther (Skywalker) (Music Group)
Famous Artists Agency
250 W 57th St
New York, NY 10107-0001, USA

Campbell, Marion (Football Player)
San Francisco 49ers
351 Marsh Point Cir
Saint Augustine, FL 32080-5864, USA

Campbell, Martin (Director)
International Creative Mgmt
8942 Wilshire Blvd # 219
Beverly Hills, CA 90211-1908, USA

Campbell, Matthew (Football Player)
Carolina Panthers
9 Timberidge Dr
North Augusta, SC 29860-9725, USA

Campbell, Michael (Golfer)
Masters International Hurst Grove
Sanford Lane
Hurst Berkshire RG10 0SQ, UNITED
KINGDOM (UK)

Campbell, Mike (Baseball Player)
Seattle Mariners
4500 36th Ave SW Apt 12
Seattle, WA 98126-2750, USA

Campbell, Mike (Football Player)
Detroit Lions
383 Inverness Dr
Winston Salem, NC 27107-6030, USA

Campbell, Milton (Milt) (Athlete, Football Player, Track Athlete)
Cleveland Browns
1132 Saint Marks Pl
Plainfield, NJ 07062-1410, USA

Campbell, Naomi (Actor, Model, Music Group)
c/o Vanessa Pereira *Artists Independent Management (LA)*
825 Nowita Pl
Venice, CA 90291-3836, USA

Campbell, Nell (Actor)
246 W 14th St
New York, NY 10011-7201, USA

Campbell, Neve (Actor)
12533 Woodgreen St
Los Angeles, CA 90066-2723, USA

Campbell, Nicholas (Actor)
1206 N Orange Grove Ave
West Hollywood, CA 90046-5351, USA

Campbell, Patrick J (Misc)
Carpenter & Joiners Union
101 Constitution Ave NW
Washington, DC 20001-2133, USA

Campbell, Paul (Actor)
c/o Staff Member *ROAR LLC*
9701 Wilshire Blvd Ste 850
Beverly Hills, CA 90212-2032, USA

Campbell, Paul (Baseball Player)
c/o Staff Member *Boston Red Sox*
Fenway Park
4 Yawkey Way
Boston, MA 02215-3496, USA

Campbell, Robert (Architect, Critic, Misc)
54 Antrim St
Cambridge, MA 02139-1102, USA

Campbell, Robert H (Business Person)
Sunoco Inc
10 Penn Center 1801 Market St
Philadelphia, PA 19103, USA

Campbell, Ron (Baseball Player)
Chicago Cubs
1104 Sweetbriar Ave NW
Cleveland, TN 37311-1657, USA

Campbell, Scott (Football Player)
Pittsburgh Steelers
123 Oak Ln
Hershey, PA 17033-1748, USA

Campbell, Scott Michael (Actor)
c/o Danielle Allman *Allman/Rea Management*
141 S Barrington Ave Ste E
Los Angeles, CA 90049-3314, USA

Campbell, Sonny (Football Player)
Atlanta Falcons
6250 N Desert Willow Dr
Tucson, AZ 85743-8701, USA

Campbell, Stacy Dean
1105 16th Ave S Ste C
Nashville, TN 37212-2327, USA

Campbell, Tevin (Actor, Musician)
c/o Staff Member *Pyramid Entertainment Group*
377 Rector Pl Apt 21A
New York, NY 10280-1439, USA

Campbell, Vivian (Music Group, Musician)
Int'l Talent Booking
27A Floral St #300
London WC2E 9DQ, UNITED KINGDOM (UK)

Campbell, William (Actor)
21502 Velicata St
Woodland Hills, CA 91364-1905, USA

Campbell, William J (General)
3267 Alex Findlay Pl
Sarasota, FL 34240-8701, USA

Campbell, Woodrow (Football Player)
Houston Oilers
9122 Weymouth Dr
Houston, TX 77031-3034, USA

Campbell-Martin, Tisha (Actor)
c/o Pearl Wexler *Kohner Agency, The*
9300 Wilshire Blvd Ste 555
Beverly Hills, CA 90212-3211, USA

Campen, James (Football Player)
New Orleans Saints
2789 Ichabod Ln
Green Bay, WI 54313-3209, USA

Camper, Cardell (Baseball Player)
Cleveland Indians
1611 Washington Ave
San Jacinto, CA 92583-5729, USA

Campese, David I (Athlete, Misc)
D C Management Group
870 Pacific Highway #4
Gordon, NSW 2072, AUSTRALIA

Campfield, William (Football Player)
Philadelphia Eagles
532 Radcliff Dr
Westerville, OH 43082-6338, USA

Campion, Jane (Director)
Hilary Linstead
500 Oxford St
Bondi Junction, NSW 2022, AUSTRALIA

Campisi, Sal (Baseball Player)
St Louis Cardinals
644 77th Ave
St Pete Beach, FL 33706-1708, USA

Campo, Dave (Coach, Football Coach)
Celveland Browns
76 Lou Groza Blvd
Berea, OH 44017-1269, USA

Campos, Arsenio (Actor)
c/o Staff Member *Televisa*
Blvd Adolfo Lopez Mateos 232
Colonia San Angel INN
DF CP 01060, MEXICO

Campos, Bruno (Actor)
SDB Partners
1801 Avenue Of Stars Ste 902
Los Angeles, CA 90067-5981, USA

Campos, Francisco (Baseball Player)
Washington Senators
201 W Park Dr Apt 103
Miami, FL 33172-5426, USA

Campos, Jorge (Soccer Player)
Federacion de Futbol Assn
Col Juarez
Mexico City 6, DF CP 06600, MEXICO

Cam'ron (Musician)
c/o Staff Member *International Creative Management (ICM-LA)*
10250 Constellation Blvd
Los Angeles, CA 90067-6200, USA

Canada, Larry (Football Player)
Denver Broncos
3793 W 78th St
Chicago, IL 60652-1855, USA

Canada, Ron (Actor)
c/o Christopher (Chris) Wright *Christopher Wright Management*
3207 Winnie Dr
Los Angeles, CA 90068-1439, USA

Canadas, Esther (Actor, Model)
Wilhelmina Models
300 Park Ave S Fl 2
New York, NY 10010-5398, USA

Canadec, Tony
1746 Carriage Ct
Green Bay, WI 54304-2812, USA

Canadian Brass
450 7th Ave Ste 603
New York, NY 10123-0691, USA

Canady, James (Jim) (Football Player)
Chicago Bears
303 Sunset Dr
Burnet, TX 78611-9737, USA

Canagata, Bill (Baseball Player)
Indianapolis Clowns
25 W 132nd St Apt 10R
New York, NY 10037-3205, USA

Canale, George (Baseball Player)
Milwaukee Brewers
7333 Old Mill Rd
Roanoke, VA 24018-6712, USA

Canale, Gianna Maria
8 via A. Richelmy
Rome I-00165, ITALY

Canale, Justin (Football Player)
Boston Patriots
2889 Sky Ridge Dr
Memphis, TN 38127-7415, USA

Canale, Whit (Football Player)
Miami Dolphins
2166 Thomas Rd
Memphis, TN 38134-5616, USA

Canals, Maria (Actor)
c/o Staff Member *Agency for the Performing Arts (APA-LA)*
405 S Beverly Dr
Beverly Hills, CA 90212-4416, USA

Canary, David (Actor)
c/o Staff Member *All My Children*
500 S Buena Vista St
Burbank, CA 91521-0001, USA

Candaele, Casey (Baseball Player)
Montreal Expos
251 Broad St
San Luis Obispo, CA 93405-2303, USA

Candelaria, John (Baseball Player)
Pittsburgh Pirates
606 Wingspread
Peachtree City, GA 30269-3363, USA

Candeloro, Philippe (Figure Skater)
Federation des Sports de Glace
35 Rue Felicien David
Paris 75016, FRANCE

Candills, Georges (Architect)
17 Rue Campagne-Premiere
Paris 75014, FRANCE

Candiotti, Thomas C (Tom) (Baseball Player)
Milwaukee Brewers
6061 E Jenan Dr
Scottsdale, AZ 85254-4972, USA

Candlebox (Music Group)
c/o Staff Member *Maverick Recording Co (LA)*
3300 Warner Blvd
Burbank, CA 91505-4632, USA

Cane, Mark A (Misc, Oceanographer)
Lamont Doherty Earth Observatory
Route 9W
Palisades, NY 10964, USA

Caneira, John (Baseball Player)
California Angels
18 Spruce Dr
Naugatuck, CT 06770-4231, USA

Canella, Guldo (Architect)
Via Revere 7
Milan 20123, ITALY

Canerday, Natalie (Actor)
c/o Staff Member *Bauman Redanty & Shaul Agency*
5757 Wilshire Blvd Ste 473
Los Angeles, CA 90036-3632, USA

Canete, Ariel (Golfer)
Advantage International
1751 Pinnacle Dr Ste 1500
Mc Lean, VA 22102-3833, USA

Canfield, Jack (Writer)
The Jack Canfield Companies
PO Box 30880
Santa Barbara, CA 93130-0880, USA

Canfield, Mary Grace (Actor)
Shelly & Pierce
13775A Mono Way # 220
Sonora, CA 95370-8813, USA

Canfield, Paul (Physicist)
Iowa State University
Physics Dept
Arnes, IA 50011, USA

Canfield, William L (Bill) (Cartoonist, Editor)
Star Ledger
1 Star Ledger Plz
Editorial Dept
Newark, NJ 07102-1291, USA

Cangelosi, John (Baseball Player)
Chicago White Sox
6201 US Highway 41 N Lot 2080
Palmetto, FL 34221-9337, USA

Cangemi, Joseph P (Misc)
1409 Mount Ayr Cir
Bowling Green, KY 42103-4708, USA

Canibus (Musician)
c/o Staff Member *Famous Artists Agency*
250 W 57th St # 821
New York, NY 10107-0001, USA

Canidate, Trung (Football Player)
St Louis Rams
1707 W Clarendon Ave
Phoenix, AZ 85015-5502, USA

Canizales, Gaby (Boxer)
2205 Saint Maria Ave
Laredo, TX 78040, USA

Canizaro, Jay (Baseball Player)
San Francisco Giants
19523 Piney Lake Dr
Spring, TX 77388-3060, USA

Canley, Sheldon (Football Player)
New York Jets
264 Altair Ave
Lompoc, CA 93436-1424, USA

Cannatella, Trishelle (Reality TV Star)
c/o Staff Member *Bunim/Murray Productions Inc*
6007 Sepulveda Blvd
Van Nuys, CA 91411-2502, USA

Cannava, Anthony (Football Player)
Green Bay Packers
26 Royall St
Medford, MA 02155-4512, USA

Cannavale, Bobby (Actor)
c/o Aleen Keshishian *Brillstein-Grey Entertainment*
9150 Wilshire Blvd Ste 350
Beverly Hills, CA 90212-3453, USA

Cannavino, Joe (Football Player)
Oakland Raiders
1600 Brittain Rd Apt 626
Akron, OH 44310-2774, USA

Canned Heat
PO Box 3773
San Rafael, CA 94912-3773, USA

Cannell, Stephen J (Producer, Writer)
1220 Hillcrest Ave
Pasadena, CA 91106-4435, USA

Cannizzaro, Chris (Baseball Player)
St Louis Cardinals
13597 Grain Ln
San Diego, CA 92129-2851, USA

Cannon, Ace (Musician)
American Mgmt
19948 Mayall St
Chatsworth, CA 91311-3522, USA

Cannon, Billy (Football Player)
Houston Oilers
1640 Sherwood Forest Blvd
Baton Rouge, LA 70815-5458, USA

Cannon, Carey (Actor)
c/o Staff Member *Geddes Agency, The*
8430 Santa Monica Blvd Ste 200
Los Angeles, CA 90069-4253, USA

Cannon, Danny (Producer)
c/o Staff Member *International Creative Management (ICM-LA)*
10250 Constellation Blvd
Los Angeles, CA 90067-6200, USA

Cannon, Dyan (Actor)
1100 Alta Loma Rd Apt 808
West Hollywood, CA 90069-2438, USA

Cannon, Freddy
18641 Cassandra St
Tarzana, CA 91356-4509, USA

Cannon, Freddy (Boom Boom) (Music Group, Songwriter, Writer)
Rick Levy Mgmt
4250 A1A S Unit D11
Saint Augustine, FL 32080-7431, USA

Cannon, Glenn
1717 Mott-Smith Dr
Honolulu, HI 96822-2873, USA

Cannon, Harold (Actor)
c/o Staff Member *Select Artists Ltd (CA-Valley Office)*
PO Box 4359
Burbank, CA 91503-4359, USA

Cannon, J J (Baseball Player)
Houston Astros
3017 Cedarwood Village Ln
Pensacola, FL 32514-6251, USA

Cannon, Joe (Soccer Player)
c/o Staff Member *Colorado Rapids Soccer Club*
1000 Chopper Cir
Pepsi Center
Denver, CO 80204-5805, USA

Cannon, John (Football Player)
Tampa Bay Buccaneers
2911 W Bay Vista Ave
Tampa, FL 33611-1609, USA

Cannon, Katherine (Actor)
1310 Westholme Ave
Los Angeles, CA 90024-5016, USA

Cannon, Mark (Football Player)
Green Bay Packers
2604 Riveroaks Dr
Arlington, TX 76006-3638, USA

Cannon, Nick (Actor, Producer)
c/o Michael Goldman *Michael Goldman Management*
11818 Laurel Hills Rd
Studio City, CA 91604-3723, USA

Cannon, William A (Billy) (Football Player)
176 Shirley Cir
Monterey, LA 71354-4124, USA

Cano, Roberto (Actor)
c/o Staff Member *TV Caracol*
Calle 76 #11 - 35
Piso 10AA
Bogota DC 26484, COLOMBIA

Canova, Diana (Actor)
Grand View Management
578 Washington Blvd Ste 688
Marina Del Rey, CA 90292-5442, USA

Canseco, Jose (Baseball Player, Reality TV Star)
c/o Michael (Mike) Esterman *Esterman Entertainment*
214 Park Rd
Riva, MD 21140-1224, USA

Canseco, Ozzie (Baseball Player)
Oakland A's
10131 N Lake Vista Cir
Davie, FL 33328-1101, USA

Cansino, Athena (Actor)
c/o Victor (Viktor) Kruglov *Victor Kruglov Talent Management*
7461 Beverly Blvd Ste 403
Los Angeles, CA 90036-2774, USA

Cantaline, Anita (Bowler)
31455 Pinto Dr
Warren, MI 48093-7624, USA

Cantey, Charisie (Sportscaster)
ABC-TV
77 W 66th St
Sports Dept
New York, NY 10023-6201, USA

Cantillo, Jose Pablo (Actor)
c/o Paul Brown *Flutie Entertainment (NY)*
270 Lafayette St Ste 1400
New York, NY 10012-3364, USA

Canton, Denio (Baseball Player)
New York Cubans
1330 NW 5th St Apt 5
Miami, FL 33125-4734, USA

Canton, Joanna (Actor)
c/o Staff Member *Liberman/Zerman Management*
252 N Larchmont Blvd Ste 200
Los Angeles, CA 90004-3754, USA

Cantona, Eric (Soccer Player)
French Federation de Football
60 Bis Ave D'Ilena
Paris 75783, FRANCE

Cantone, Vic (Cartoonist, Editor)
238 Blackpool Ct
Ridge, NY 11961-8115, USA

Cantoral, Itati (Actor)
c/o Gabriel Blanco *Gabriel Blanco Iglesias (Mexico)*
Rio Balsas 35-32
Colonia Cuauhtemoc
DF 06500, MEXICO

Cantrell, Barry (Football Player)
Dallas Cowboys
142 Underwood Dr
Palatka, FL 32177-8166, USA

Cantrell, Blu (Music Group)
Arista Records
8750 Wilshire Blvd # 300
Beverly Hills, CA 90211-2713, USA

Cantrell, Jerry (Actor)
c/o Staff Member *Core Entertainment Organization*
14724 Ventura Blvd Ph
Sherman Oaks, CA 91403-3513, USA

Cantrell, Jerry (Musician)
c/o Staff Member *William Morris Agency (WMA-LA)*
1 William Morris Pl
Beverly Hills, CA 90212-4261, USA

Cantrell, Lana (Music Group)
300 E 71st St
New York, NY 10021-5234, USA

Cantrell, Wayne
18265 Wakecrest Dr
Malibu, CA 90265-5600, USA

Canyon, George (Musician)
c/o Staff Member *Paradigm (Monterey)*
509 Hartnell St
Monterey, CA 93940-2825, USA

Capa, Cornell (Photographer)
275 5th Ave
New York, NY 10016-6514, USA

Capalbo, Carmen C (Director, Producer)
500 2nd Ave
New York, NY 10016-8606, USA

Caparulo, John (Comedian)
c/o Staff Member *Brillstein-Grey Entertainment*
9150 Wilshire Blvd Ste 350
Beverly Hills, CA 90212-3453, USA

Capasso, Federico (Physicist)
Lucent Technologies
600 Mountain Ave
Bell Labs
New Providence, NJ 07974-2008, USA

Capece, Bill (Football Player)
Tampa Bay Buccaneers
867 Hill Roost Rd
Tallahassee, FL 32312-6716, USA

Capek, Frantisek (Athlete)
Michelangelova 4
Prague 10 100 00, CZECH REPUBLIC

Capel, Jon
PO Box 120
Indianapolis, IN 46206, USA

Capel, Mike (Baseball Player)
Chicago Cubs
3901 Northshore Dr
Montgomery, TX 77356-5369, USA

Capellas, Michael (Business Person)
MCI
500 Clinton Center Dr
Clinton, MS 39056-5630, USA

Capellino, Ally (Designer, Fashion Designer)
N1R Metropolitan Wharf
Wapping Wall
London E1 9SS, UNITED KINGDOM (UK)

Capers, Dom (Coach, Football Coach)
Houston Texans
4400 Post Oak Pkwy Ste 1400
Houston, TX 77027-3440, USA

Capers, Wayne (Football Player)
Pittsburgh Steelers
28 Greenlawn Dr
Pittsburgh, PA 15220-2503, USA

Caperton, W Gaston III (Governor, Misc)
College Board
45 Columbus Ave
Presiden's Office
New York, NY 10023-6992, USA

Capilla, Doug (Baseball Player)
St Louis Cardinals
PO Box 54053
San Jose, CA 95154-0053, USA

Capilla, Perez Joaquin (Misc)
Torres de Mixcoac
Lomas de Platerce
Mexico City 19, DF, MEXICO

Caplan, Lizzy (Actor)
c/o Ryan Revel *Imparato Fay Management*
1126 Roxbury Dr
Los Angeles, CA 90035-1031, USA

Capleton (Musician)
Agency Group Ltd
1775 Broadway Ste 515
New York, NY 10019-1903, USA

Caplin, Mortimer M (Government Official)
5610 Wisconsin Ave Ph 18E
Bethesda, MD 20815-4442, USA

Capoblanco, Tito (Director, Opera Singer)
Pittsburgh Opera Co
711 Penn Ave # 800
Pittsburgh, PA 15222-3402, USA

Capodice, John (Actor)
c/o Staff Member *Sharp Talent*
117 N Orlando Ave
Los Angeles, CA 90048-3403, USA

Capon, Edwin G (Religious Leader)
Swedenborgian Church
11 Highland Ave
Newtonville, MA 02460-1852, USA

Capone, Warren (Football Player)
Dallas Cowboys
11999 Longridge Ave Apt 602
Baton Rouge, LA 70816-3923, USA

Caponera, John (Actor, Comedian)
Messina Baker Entertainment
955 Carrillo Dr Ste 100
Los Angeles, CA 90048-5400, USA

Caponi, Donna M (Golfer)
11 Bedford St
Burlington, MA 01803-3771, USA

Capp, Dick (Football Player)
Green Bay Packers
PO Box 2193
Cary, NC 27512-2193, USA

Cappadona, Robert (Football Player)
Boston Patriots
25 Summer St
Watertown, MA 02472-3457, USA

Cappelletti, Gino R M (Football Player)
Boston Patriots
19 Louis Dr
Wellesley, MA 02481-1164, USA

Cappelletti, John (Football Player)
Los Angeles Rams
28791 Brant Lane
Laguna Beach, CA 92677, USA

Cappleman, William (Football Player)
Minnesota Vikings
1506 Sydney Ln
Lynn Haven, FL 32444-2928, USA

Capps, Steve (Designer, Misc)
Microsoft Corp
1 Microsoft Way
Redmond, WA 98052-8300, USA

Capps, Thomas E (Business Person)
Dominion Resources
120 Tredegar St
Richmond, VA 23219-4306, USA

Cappuzzello, George (Baseball Player)
Detroit Tigers
2024 Stillwood Pl
Windermere, FL 34786-8329, USA

Capra, Buzz (Baseball Player)
New York Mets
2061 E Parkview Cir
Hoffman Estates, IL 60169-2644, USA

Capra, Francis (Actor)
c/o Staff Member *Melissa Prophet Management*
4321 Matilija Ave Apt 21
Sherman Oaks, CA 91423-3672, USA

Capra, Nick (Baseball Player)
Texas Rangers
300 Town Park Rd
Norman, OK 73072-4538, USA

Capri, Ahna
16547 Vanowen St Apt 209
Van Nuys, CA 91406-4710, USA

Capri, Sophia
5124 Mayfield Rd
Lyndhurst, OH 44124-2406, USA

Capria, Carl (Football Player)
Detroit Lions
35 S Gladstone Ave
Indianapolis, IN 46201-4513, USA

Capriati, Jennifer (Tennis Player)
c/o Caroline Smith *Women's Tennis Association (WTA (UK))*
Bank Lane
Roehampton
London SW15 5XZ, UNITED KINGDOM (UK)

Caprice (Model, Music Group, Songwriter, Writer)
Mission Control
Business Center Lower Road
London SE16 2XB, UNITED KINGDOM (UK)

Capshaw, Jessica (Actor)
c/o Raelle Koota Anonymous Content (NY)
588 Broadway Rm 1005
New York, NY 10012-5239, USA

Capshaw, Kate (Actor)
c/o Kevin Huvane Creative Artists Agency LCC (CAA-LA)
2000 Avenue Of The Stars
Los Angeles, CA 90067-4700, USA

Captain, Raj (Actor)
951 Munuswamy Salai
K K Nagar
Chennai, TN 600 078, INDIA

Capuano, Chris (Baseball Player)
Arizona Diamondbacks
35 Woodbrook Ter
West Springfield, MA 01089-4441, USA

Capucill, Terese (Dancer)
Martha Graham dance Center
440 Lafayette St
New York, NY 10003-6919, USA

Cara, Irene (Actor, Music Group)
c/o Betty McCormick Midwest Talent Management Inc
4821 Lankershim Blvd Ste F
Pmb 149
N Hollywood, CA 91601-4572, USA

Carafotes, Paul (Actor)
8033 W Sunset Blvd # 3554
West Hollywood, CA 90046-2401, USA

Caramanlis, Costas (Prime Minister)
Premier's Office
17 Stissichoros St
King George V Ave
Athens, GREECE

Carano, Glenn (Football Player)
Dallas Cowboys
2551 E Lake Ridge Shrs
Reno, NV 89519-5787, USA

Carapella, Alfred (Football Player)
San Francisco 49ers
10 Woodlot Rd
Eastchester, NY 10709-1204, USA

Carasco, Joe (King) (Music Group)
Texas Sounds
2317 Pecan St
Dickinson, TX 77539-4949, USA

Caravello, Joe (Football Player)
Washington Redskins
633 W Palm Ave
El Segundo, CA 90245-2065, USA

Caray, Skip (Baseball Player, Sportscaster)
Atlanta Braves
4745 Riverview Rd NW
Atlanta, GA 30327-4231, USA

Carazo, Odio Rodrigo (Educator, President)
University for Peace
Apdo 199
San Jose, COSTA RICA

Carbajal, Michael (Boxer)
PO Box 510
Phoenix, AZ 85001-0510, USA

Carberry, Deirdre (Ballerina)
American Ballet Theater
890 Broadway
New York, NY 10003-1278, USA

Carbo, Bernie (Baseball Player)
Cincinnati Reds
6352 Woodside Dr S
Theodore, AL 36582-3992, USA

Carbonara, David (Composer)
Gorfaine/Schwartz
4111 W Alameda Ave Ste 509
Burbank, CA 91505-4171, USA

Carbonell, Nestor (Actor)
c/o JB Roberts Thruline Entertainment
9250 Wilshire Blvd Ground Fl
Beverly Hills, CA 90210, USA

Carbonneau, Guy (Hockey Player, Misc)
Dallas Stars
Starcenter 211 Cowboys Parkway
Irving, TX 75063, USA

Carcaterra, Lorenzo (Writer)
William Morris Agency
151 El Camino Dr
Beverly Hills, CA 90212-2775, USA

Card, Andrew H Jr (Misc, Secretary)
White House
1600 Pennsylvania Ave NW
Washington, DC 20500-0004, USA

Card, Michael (Music Group, Musician)
1143 Dora Whitley Rd
Franklin, TN 37064-4788, USA

Cardamone, Richard J (Judge)
US Court of Appeals
10 Broad St Ste 322
Utica, NY 13501-1259, USA

Cardellini, Linda (Actor)
Gersh Agency
232 N Canon Dr
Beverly Hills, CA 90210-5302, USA

Carden, Joan M (Opera Singer)
Jennifer Eddy
596 Saint Kilda Road #11
Melbourne, VIC 3004, AUSTRALIA

Cardenal, Jose D (Baseball Player)
San Francisco Giants
118 Bridgewater Ct
Bradenton, FL 34212-9302, USA

Cardenas, Elsa
Altamirano 126
Mexico DF, MEXICO

Cardenas, Leo (Baseball Player)
Cincinnati Reds
5412 Ravenna St
Cincinnati, OH 45227-1718, USA

Cardich, Augusto (Archaeologist)
University of La Plata
Archaeology Dept
La Plata, ARGENTINA

Cardiff, Jack (Cinematographer)
32 Woodland Rise
London N10, UNITED KINGDOM (UK)

Cardigans, The (Music Group)
c/o Staff Member International Talent Booking (ITB - UK)
27A Floral St Fl 3
Covent Garden
London WC2E 9, UNITED KINGDOM (UK)

Cardin, Pierre (Designer, Fashion Designer)
59 Rue du Foubourg-St-Honore
Paris 75008, FRANCE

Cardinahl, Jessika
Vogelbeerenweg 4
Hamburg D-22299, GERMANY

Cardinal, Douglas J (Architect)
7011A Manchester Blvd # 315
Alexandria, VA 22310-3202, USA

Cardinal, Fred (Football Player)
New York Yankees
1457 Maple St
Barberton, OH 44203-7615, USA

Cardinal, Randy (Baseball Player)
Houston Colt 45's
3810 W Verde Way
North Las Vegas, NV 89031-4812, USA

Cardinale, Claudia (Actor)
Via Flaminia Km 77
Prima Porta
Rome 00188, ITALY

Cardinalem, Lindsey (Musician)
c/o Staff Member American Idol
7800 Beverly Blvd # 251
Los Angeles, CA 90036-2112, USA

Cardona, Manolo (Actor)
c/o Nina Shaw Del, Shaw, Moonves, Tanaka & Finkelstein
2120 Colorado Ave Ste 200
Santa Monica, CA 90404-3561, USA

Cardone, Vivien (Actor)
c/o Staff Member Everwood
1000 W 2610 S
Salt Lake City, UT 84119-2434, USA

Cardos, John Bud
PO Box 7430
Burbank, CA 91510-7430, USA

Cardosa, Patricia (Director)
c/o Staff Member International Creative Management (ICM-LA)
10250 Constellation Blvd
Los Angeles, CA 90067-6200, USA

Cardoso, Fernando
Palacio do Planalto
Brasilia DF 70150-900, BRAZIL

Cardoso, Patricia (Director)
c/o Rosalie Swedlin Industry Entertainment
955 Carrillo Dr Ste 300
Los Angeles, CA 90048-5400, USA

Cardwell, Donald E (Don) (Baseball Player)
Philadelphia Phillies
PO Box 454
Clemmons, NC 27012-0454, USA

Care, Peter (Director)
c/o Staff Member Creative Artists Agency LCC (CAA-LA)
2000 Avenue Of The Stars
Los Angeles, CA 90067-4700, USA

Carell, Steve (Actor)
c/o Steve Sauer Media Four
8840 Wilshire Blvd Fl 2
Beverly Hills, CA 90211-2606, USA

Carelli, Rick (Race Car Driver)
PO Box 1000
Arvada, CO 80001-1000, USA

Caretto-Brown, Patty (Swimmer)
16079 Mesquite Cir
Santa Ana, CA 92708-1513, USA

Carew, Drew (Actor, Comedian)
Messina Baker Entertainment
955 Carrillo Dr Ste 100
Los Angeles, CA 90048-5400, USA

Carew, Rod (Baseball Player)
Minnesota Twins
40 Tanglewood
Aliso Viejo, CA 92656-1821, USA

Carey, Andrew A (Andy) (Baseball Player)
New York Yankees
PO Box 8708
Dept 434
Newport Beach, CA 92658-8708, USA

Carey, Duane G (Astronaut)
5938 Instone Cir
Colorado Springs, CO 80922-1716, USA

Carey, Ezekiel (Music Group)
509 E Ridgecrest Blvd Apt A
Ridgecrest, CA 93555-3959, USA

Carey, Hugh L (Governor)
WR Grace Co
1114 Avenue Of The Americas
New York, NY 10036-7703, USA

Carey, Jim (Hockey) (Hockey Player)
4848 Hanging Moss Ln
Sarasota, FL 34238-3313, USA

Carey, Mariah (Music Group, Musician, Songwriter, Writer)
c/o Benny Medina Handprint Entertainment
1100 Glendon Ave Ste 1000
Los Angeles, CA 90024-3514, USA

Carey, Matthew Thomas (Actor)
c/o Abby Bluestone Innovative Artists (LA)
1505 10th St
Santa Monica, CA 90401-2805, USA

Carey, Michelle (Actor)
H David Moss
733 Seward St Ph
Los Angeles, CA 90038-3503, USA

Carey, Paul (Baseball Player)
Baltimore Orioles
47 Kingman St
Weymouth, MA 02188-2215, USA

Carey, Peter (Writer)
International Creative Mgmt
40 W 57th St Ste 1800
New York, NY 10019-4001, USA

Carey, Philip
56 W 66th St
New York, NY 10023-6225, USA

Carey, Rick
119 Rockland Ave
Larchmont, NY 10538-1430, USA

Carey, Tony
BMG Postfach 800149
Munich D-81601, GERMANY

Carey Jr, Harry (Actor)
PO Box 1388
Goleta, CA 93116-1388, USA

Cargo, David F (Governor)
6422 Concordia Rd NE
Albuquerque, NM 87111-1228, USA

Carides, Gia (Actor)
Robyn Gardiner Mgmt
397 Riley St
Surrey Hills, NSW 2010, AUSTRALIA

Caridis, Miltiades (Conductor)
Himmelhofgasse 10
Vienna 1130, AUSTRIA

Carille, Lori
1065 Lyndhurst Dr
Pittsburgh, PA 15206-4535, USA

Carillo, Mary (Sportscaster)
822 Boylston St Ste 203
Chestnut Hill, MA 02467-2504, USA

Cariou, Len (Actor)
Paradigm Agency
10100 Santa Monica Blvd Ste 2500
Los Angeles, CA 90067-4116, USA

Carithers, William Jr (Physicist)
Fermi Net Acceleration Lab
PO Box 500
D-Zero Collaboration
Batavia, IL 60510-5011, USA

Carl, Harland (Football Player)
Chicago Bears
1419 N Douglas St
Appleton, WI 54914-2517, USA

Carl, Jann (Television Host)
c/o Staff Member *Entertainment Tonight (ET)*
5555 Melrose Ave
Mae West Bldg Fl 2
Los Angeles, CA 90038-3989, USA

Carl XVI, Gustaf (King)
Kungliga Slottet
Slottsbacken
Stockholm 111 30, SWEDEN

Carle, Eric (Artist)
PO Box 485
Northampton, MA 01061-0485, USA

Carlei, Carlo (Director)
Creative Artists Agency
9830 Wilshire Blvd
Beverly Hills, CA 90212-1804, USA

Carles Gordo, Ricardo M Cardinal (Religious Leader)
Carrer del Bisbe 5
Barcelona 08002, SPAIN

Carlesimo, Pete J (P J) (Basketball Player, Coach, Sportscaster)
San Antonio Spurs
Alamodome 1 Sbc Center
San Antonio, TX 78219, USA

Carlile, Brandi (Musician)
c/o Staff Member *Paradigm (Monterey)*
509 Hartnell St
Monterey, CA 93940-2825, USA

Carlile, Forbes (Coach, Swimmer)
16 Cross St
Ryde, NSW 2112, AUSTRALIA

Carlin, George (Actor, Comedian)
c/o Staff Member *Richard De La Font Agency*
4845 S Sheridan Rd Ste 505
Tulsa, OK 74145-5719, USA

Carlin, Jim (Baseball Player)
Philadelphia Phillies
816 4th Ct
Pleasant Grove, AL 35127-1825, USA

Carlin, John W (Governor)
1208 Wyndham Heights Dr
Manhattan, KS 66503-8676, USA

Carlin, Thomas R (Publisher)
Saint Paul Pioneer Press
Publisher's Office
345 Cdear
Saint Paul, MN 55101, USA

Carlin, Vidal (Football Player)
St Louis Cardinals
634 Baker St
San Francisco, CA 94117-1456, USA

Carling, William D C (Athlete, Misc, Sportscaster)
Insights Ltd
22 Suffolk St
London SW1Y 4HG, UNITED KINGDOM (UK)

Carlino, Lewis John (Director, Writer)
991 Oakmont St
Los Angeles, CA 90049-2228, USA

Carlisie, Rick (Basketball Player)
Boston Celtics
RR 4
Ogdensburg, NY 13669, USA

Carlisle, Belinda (Model, Music Group, Songwriter, Writer)
c/o Staff Member *William Morris Agency (WMA-LA)*
1 William Morris Pl
Beverly Hills, CA 90212-4261, USA

Carlisle, Cooper (Football Player)
Denver Broncos
2032 Sorrelwood Ct
San Ramon, CA 94582-5004, USA

Carlisle, James B (General, Governor)
Governer General's Office
Government House
Saint John's, ANTIGUA & BARBUDA

Carlisle, Jodi (Actor, Comedian)
c/o Staff Member *International Creative Management (ICM-LA)*
10250 Constellation Blvd
Los Angeles, CA 90067-6200, USA

Carlisle, Mary (Actor)
517 N Rodeo Dr
Beverly Hills, CA 90210-3206, USA

Carlisle Hart, Kitty (Actor, Music Group)
32 E 64th St
New York, NY 10065-7359, USA

Carlos, Francisco (Baseball Player)
Chicago White Sox
6027 N 7th St
Phoenix, AZ 85014-1802, USA

Carlos, John (Athlete, Track Athlete)
68640 Tortuga Rd
Cathedral City, CA 92234-3874, USA

Carlos, Jordan (Musician)
c/o Staff Member *Paradigm (Monterey)*
509 Hartnell St
Monterey, CA 93940-2825, USA

Carlos I, Juan (King)
Palacio de la Zarzuela
Madrid 28671, SPAIN

Carlos Moco, Marcolino Jose (Prime Minister)
Movimento Popular de Libertacao de Angola
Luanda, ANGOLA

Carlot, Maxime (Prime Minister)
P O Box 698
Port Vila, VANUATU

Carlson, Amy (Actor)
c/o Darris Hatch *Daris Hatch Management*
9538 Brighton Way Ste 308
Beverly Hills, CA 90210-4516, USA

Carlson, Arne H (Governor)
145 Holly Ln N
Minneapolis, MN 55447-3547, USA

Carlson, Cody (Football Player)
Houston Oilers
3417 Foothill Ter
Austin, TX 78731-5826, USA

Carlson, Dan (Baseball Player)
San Francisco Giants
334 N Wickford Cir
Shreveport, LA 71115-2935, USA

Carlson, Don (Basketball Player)
Chicago Stags
41 Island Rd
Saint Paul, MN 55127-2635, USA

Carlson, Dudley L (Admiral)
Navy League
2300 Wilson Blvd Ste 210
Arlington, VA 22201-5426, USA

Carlson, Gretchen (Television Host)
c/o Staff Member *CBS Weekend Evening News*
524 W 57th St Fl 8
New York, NY 10019-2930, USA

Carlson, Jack W (Misc)
American Assn of Retired Persons
1901 K St NW
Washington, DC 20006, USA

Carlson, Jeff (Football Player)
Tampa Bay Buccaneers
12105 Lexington Park Dr Apt 308
Tampa, FL 33626-2720, USA

Carlson, John A (Business Person)
Cray Research
655 Lone Oak Dr Bldg A
Eagan, MN 55121-1652, USA

Carlson, K C (Cartoonist)
DC Comics
1700 Broadway
New York, NY 10019-5914, USA

Carlson, Karen (Actor)
3700 Ventura Canyon Ave
Sherman Oaks, CA 91423-4709, USA

Carlson, Katrina (Actor)
c/o Staff Member *Sara Bennett Agency*
6404 Hollywood Blvd Ste 316
Los Angeles, CA 90028-6244, USA

Carlson, Kelly (Actor)
c/o Margot Klar *Cunningham Escott Slevin & Doherty (LA)*
10635 Santa Monica Blvd Ste 130
Los Angeles, CA 90025-8306, USA

Carlson, Lane (Model)
c/o Staff Member *WARNING Models*
449 S Beverly Dr Ste 101
Beverly Hills, CA 90212-4428, USA

Carlson, Paulette (Music Group)
Mark Sonder Music
250 W 57th St Ste 1830
Fisk Building
New York, NY 10107-1804, USA

Carlson, Richard (Writer)
Pennsylvania State Univ
613 Moore Bldg
University Park, PA 16802-3106, USA

Carlson, Shane (Model)
c/o Staff Member *WARNING Models*
449 S Beverly Dr Ste 101
Beverly Hills, CA 90212-4428, USA

Carlson, Stuart (Cartoonist)
Universal Press Syndicate
4520 Main St
Kansas City, MO 64111-1876, USA

Carlson, Tucker (Television Host)
c/o Staff Member *MSNBC (NJ)*
Nbc/One Microsoft Corporation
1 Msnc Plaza
Secaucus, NJ 07094, USA

Carlson, Veronica (Actor)
7844 Kavanagh Ct
Sarasota, FL 34240-7906, USA

Carlsson, Arvid (Nobel Prize Laureate)
Gotheburg University
P O Box 100
Gotheburg 405 30, SWEDEN

Carlsson, Ingvar G (Prime Minister)
Riksdagen
Stockholm 100 12, SWEDEN

Carlton, Carl (Musician)
Randolph Enterprises
Oakland
Inkster, MI 48141, USA

Carlton, Larry (Musician)
c/o Staff Member *Paradigm (Monterey)*
509 Hartnell St
Monterey, CA 93940-2825, USA

Carlton, Paul K (General)
1716 Briescrest Dr # 702
Bryan, TX 77802, USA

Carlton, Steven N (Steve) (Baseball Player)
St Louis Cardinals
555 S Camino Del Rio Ste B2
Durango, CO 81303-6852, USA

Carlton, Vanessa (Musician)
c/o Mitch Rose *Creative Artists Agency LCC (CAA-LA)*
2000 Avenue Of The Stars
Los Angeles, CA 90067-4700, USA

Carlton, Venessa (Music Group)
Peter Malkin Mgmt
410 Park Ave Ste 420
New York, NY 10022-9459, USA

Carlton, Wray (Football Player)
Buffalo Bills
29 Pine Ter
Orchard Park, NY 14127-3929, USA

Carlucci, Dave (Music Group)
Joe Terry Mgmt
PO Box 279
Williamstown, NJ 08094-0279, USA

Carlucci, Frank C
1001 Pennsylvania Ave NW
Washington, DC 20004-2505, USA

Carlyle, Joan H (Opera Singer)
Laundry Cottage Hammer
North Wales SY13 4QX, UNITED KINGDOM (UK)

Carlyle, Randy (Coach, Hockey Player)
Washington Capitals
601 F St NW
Mcl Center
Washington, DC 20004-1605, USA

Carmack, Chris (Actor)
c/o Theodore B Gekis *Gekis Management*
4217 Verdugo View Dr
Los Angeles, CA 90065-4317, USA

Carman (Music Group)
Carman Ministries
PO Box 5093
Brentwood, TN 37024-5093, USA

Carman, Don (Baseball Player)
Philadelphia Phillies
555 Murex Dr
Naples, FL 34102-5141, USA

Carman, Gregory W (Judge)
US Court of International Trade
1 Federal Plz
New York, NY 10278-0001, USA

Carman, Patrick (Writer)
1247 Studebaker Dr
Walla Walla, WA 99362-8845, USA

Carmazzi, Giovanni (Football Player)
San Francisco 49ers
1501 Secret Ravine Pkwy Unit 1925
Roseville, CA 95661-6022, USA

Carmel, Leon (Baseball Player)
St Louis Cardinals
10 Pheasant Valley Dr
Coram, NY 11727-2320, USA

Carmen, Eric (Music Group, Songwriter, Writer)
David Spero Mgmt
1679 S Belvoir Blvd
South Euclid, OH 44121-3773, USA

Carmen, Jean
PO Box 3367
Laguna Hills, CA 92654-3367, USA

Carmen, Jeanne (Actor, Model)
Brandon James
PO Box 11812
Newport Beach, CA 92658-5042, USA

Carmen, Julie (Actor)
Metropolitan Talent Agency
4500 Wilshire Blvd Fl 2
Los Angeles, CA 90010-3858, USA

Carmichael, Al (Football Player)
Green Bay Packers
78641 Hampshire Ave
Palm Desert, CA 92211-1960, USA

Carmichael, Greg (Musician)
Monterey International
200 W Superior St Ste 202
Chicago, IL 60610-3554, USA

Carmichael, Ian (Actor)
London Mgmt
2-4 Noel St
London W1V 3RB, UNITED KINGDOM (UK)

Carmichael, L Harold (Football Player)
Philadelphia Eagles
38 Birch Ln
Glassboro, NJ 08028-2821, USA

Carmichael, Paul (Football Player)
Denver Broncos
550 Orange Ave Unit 335
Long Beach, CA 90802-7011, USA

Carmindy (Stylist, Television Host)
Jay at Kramer + Kramer
156 5th Ave Ste 420
New York, NY 10010-7794, USA

Carmine, Michael (Cinematographer)
3615 West Dr
Douglaston, NY 11363-1243, USA

Carmine, Robert (Musician)
c/o Staff Member *Geffen Records*
2220 Colorado Ave
Santa Monica, CA 90404-3506, USA

Carmody, Steve (Football Player)
Denver Broncos
PO Box 119
Jackson, MS 39205-0119, USA

Carmona, Richard H (Government Official, Misc, Physicist)
Surgeon General's Office
200 Independence Ave SW
Washington, DC 20201-0004, USA

Carn, Jean
PO Box 27641
Philadelphia, PA 19118-0641, USA

Carnahan, Joe (Director)
c/o Staff Member *Endeavor Agency LLC (LA)*
9601 Wilshire Blvd Fl 3
Beverly Hills, CA 90210-5204, USA

Carne, Judy (Actor, Comedian)
2 Horatio St Apt 10N
New York, NY 10014-1632, USA

Carnelly, Ray (Football Player)
Brooklyn Dodgers
4650 Collier St Apt 135
Beaumont, TX 77706-6999, USA

Carner, JoAnne (Golfer)
3030 S Ocean Blvd Apt 325
Palm Beach, FL 33480-6610, USA

Carner, Randall
11043 Kling St
N Hollywood, CA 91602-1721, USA

Carnes, Kim (Music Group, Songwriter, Writer)
1829 Tyne Blvd
Nashville, TN 37215-4701, USA

Carnes, Ryan (Actor)
c/o Carl Scott *Simmons & Scott Entertainment*
4110 W Burbank Blvd
Burbank, CA 91505-2121, USA

Carnesale, Albert (Educator)
University of California
Chancellor's Office
Los Angeles, CA 90024, USA

Carnett, Eddie (Baseball Player)
Boston Braves
2639 Ridgeview Dr
Lebanon, MO 65536-5178, USA

Carnevale, Bernard L (Ben) (Basketball Player, Coach)
5109 Dorset Mews
Williamsburg, VA 23188-8511, USA

Carnevale, Mark (Golfer)
24 Loggerhead Ln
Ponte Vedra Beach, FL 32082-2581, USA

Carney, John M (Football Player)
Tampa Bay Buccaneers
2950 Wishbone Way
Encinitas, CA 92024-7235, USA

Carney, Reeve (Musician)
c/o Staff Member *Paradigm (Monterey)*
509 Hartnell St
Monterey, CA 93940-2825, USA

Carney, Robert (Basketball Player)
Minneapolis Lakers
2 Cypress Pt
Pekin, IL 61554-2620, USA

Carney, Thomas P (General)
9806 Kirktree Ct
Fairfax, VA 22032-1059, USA

Carns, Michael P C (Mike) (General)
966 Coral Dr
Pebble Beach, CA 93953-2503, USA

Caro, Anthony A (Artist, Misc)
111 Frognal Hampstead
London NW3, UNITED KINGDOM (UK)

Caro, Niki (Director, Writer)
c/o Staff Member *Broder Webb Chervin Silbermann Agency, The (BWCS)*
10250 Constellation Blvd Ste P
Los Angeles, CA 90067-6213, USA

Caro, Robert A (Writer)
Robert A Caro Assoc
250 W 57th St
New York, NY 10107-0001, USA

Carolan, Brett (Football Player)
San Francisco 49ers
3218 43rd Ave W
Seattle, WA 98199-2437, USA

Caroline (Misc, Prince)
Villa Le Clos Saint Pierre
Ave San-Martin
Monte Carlo, MONACO

Caroline, James C (J C) (Football Player)
Chicago Bears
2501 Stanford Dr
Champaign, IL 61820-7634, USA

Caroline, Princess
Villa Le Clos St. Pierre ave. Saint Martin
Monte Carlo, MONACO

Carolla, Adam (Radio Personality, Talk Show Host)
c/o James Dixon *Dixon Talent*
436 W 45th St Fl 3
New York, NY 10036-3501, USA

Carollo, Joe (Football Player)
Los Angeles Rams
4634 Meyer Way
Carmichael, CA 95608-1144, USA

Caron, Leslie (Actor, Dancer)
6 Rue De Bellechalsse
Paris 75007, FRANCE

Caron, Roger (Football Player)
Indianapolis Colts
71 School St
Williamstown, MA 01267-2411, USA

Carothers, Don (Football Player)
Denver Broncos
1405 Cedar Dr
Traverse City, MI 49684-8104, USA

Carothers, Robert L (Educator)
University of Rhode Island
President's Office
Kingston, RI 02881, USA

Carothers, Veronica (Actor)
535 N Heatherstone Dr
Orange, CA 92869-2648, USA

Carp, Daniel A (Dan) (Business Person)
Eastman Kodak Co
343 State St
Rochester, NY 14650-0001, USA

Carpendale, Howard
200 Admirals Cove Blvd
Jupiter, FL 33477-4046, USA

Carpenter, Bob (Baseball Player)
New York Giants
205 S Princeton Ave
Arlington Heights, IL 60005-1666, USA

Carpenter, Bob (Basketball Player)
Oshkosh All Stars
401 Ashwood Ln
McKinney, TX 75069-8547, USA

Carpenter, Bob (Hockey Player)
PO Box 451
Alton Bay, NH 03810-0451, USA

Carpenter, Carleton (Actor)
RR 2
Warwick, NY 10990, USA

Carpenter, Chad (Football Player)
Arizona Cardinals
21311 S 187th Way
Queen Creek, AZ 85242-3668, USA

Carpenter, Charisma (Actor, Model)
c/o John Carrabino *John Carrabino Management*
5900 Wilshire Blvd Ste 406
Los Angeles, CA 90036-5015, USA

Carpenter, Chris (Baseball Player)
Toronto Blue Jays
2 Donna Ln
Raymond, NH 03077-1537, USA

Carpenter, Cris (Baseball Player)
St Louis Cardinals
1484 Heritage Pl
Gainesville, GA 30501-1249, USA

Carpenter, Dave (Cartoonist, Editor)
PO Box 520
Emmetsburg, IA 50536-0520, USA

Carpenter, George (War Hero)
1010 Green Hill Dr
Paris, TN 38242-5226, USA

Carpenter, Jennifer (Actor)
c/o Staff Member *Endeavor Agency LLC (LA)*
9601 Wilshire Blvd Fl 3
Beverly Hills, CA 90210-5204, USA

Carpenter, John (Director)
c/o Jim Wiatt *William Morris Agency (WMA-LA)*
1 William Morris Pl
Beverly Hills, CA 90212-4261, USA

Carpenter, John M (Opera Singer)
Maurel Enterprises
225 W 34th St Ste 1012
New York, NY 10122-1012, USA

Carpenter, Ken (Football Player)
Cleveland Browns
PO Box 172
Seaside, OR 97138-0172, USA

Carpenter, Kip (Speed Skater)
W375S10897 Prairie Ln
Eagle, WI 53119-1742, USA

Carpenter, Lewis (Football Player)
Detroit Lions
1743 Rolling Rapids Dr
New Braunfels, TX 78130-3056, USA

Carpenter, Liz (Activist)
116 Skyline Dr
West Lake Hills, TX 78746-3643, USA

Carpenter, M Scott (Astronaut)
PO Box 3161
Vail, CO 81658-3161, USA

Carpenter, Marj C (Religious Leader)
Presbyterian Church USA
100 Witherspoon St
Louisville, KY 40202-6300, USA

Carpenter, Mary Chapin (Musician)
c/o Staff Member *Paradigm (Monterey)*
509 Hartnell St
Monterey, CA 93940-2825, USA

Carpenter, Patrick (Race Car Driver)
Team Players
2015 Peel
#500
Montreal, PQ H3A 1T8, CANADA

Carpenter, Preston (Football Player)
Cleveland Browns
2205 W Memphis St
Broken Arrow, OK 74012-4626, USA

Carpenter, Richard (Musician, Songwriter, Writer)
960 Country Valley Rd
Westlake Village, CA 91362-5631, USA

Carpenter, Rob (Football Player)
Houston Oilers
1601 Wheeling Rd NE
Lancaster, OH 43130-8706, USA

Carpenter, Ron (Football Player)
San Diego Chargers
1500 Wade Haven Ct
McKinney, TX 75071-5985, USA

Carpenter, Ron (Football Player)
Cincinnati Bengals
1181 Chersonese Round
Mount Pleasant, SC 29464-9544, USA

Carpenter, Russell P (Cinematographer)
Gersh Agency
232 N Canon Dr
Beverly Hills, CA 90210-5302, USA

Carpenter, Teresa (Journalist)
Village Voice
36 Cooper Sq
Editorial Dept
New York, NY 10003-7149, USA

Carpenter, W M (Business Person)
Bausch & Lomb
1 Bausch And Lomb Pl
Rochester, NY 14604-2799, USA

Carpenter, William S (Bill) Jr (Football Player)
PO Box 4067
Whitefish, MT 59937-4067, USA

Carpin, Frank (Baseball Player)
Pittsburgh Pirates
4014 Park Ave
Richmond, VA 23221-1120, USA

Carr, Antoine (Basketball Player)
Atlanta Hawks
5724 Croyden Cir
Wichita, KS 67220-3119, USA

Carr, Austin (Basketball Player)
Cleveland Cavaliers
32659 Allenbury Dr
Solon, OH 44139-6018, USA

Carr, Caleb (Writer)
Don Buchwald
6500 Wilshire Blvd Ste 2200
Los Angeles, CA 90048-4942, USA

Carr, Catherine (Cathy) (Swimmer)
409 10th St
Davis, CA 95616-1941, USA

Carr, Charmain
4150 Hayvenhurst Ave
Encino, CA 91436-3852, USA

Carr, Charmian (Actor, Musician)
Arete Publishing Co
636 Pomello Dr
Claremont, CA 91711-2043, USA

Carr, Chuck (Baseball Player)
New York Mets
5419 E Greenway St
Mesa, AZ 85205-4360, USA

Carr, Darleen (Actor)
Abrams Artists
9200 W Sunset Blvd Ste 1125
Los Angeles, CA 90069-3610, USA

Carr, David (Football Player)
Houston Texans
4400 Post Oak Pkwy Ste 1400
Houston, TX 77027-3440, USA

Carr, Edwin (Football Player)
San Francisco 49ers
1908 Scott Rd
Oreland, PA 19075-1519, USA

Carr, Fred (Football Player)
Green Bay Packers
6274 S 17th Pl
Phoenix, AZ 85042-4568, USA

Carr, Gregg (Football Player)
Pittsburgh Steelers
4314 Kennesaw Dr
Birmingham, AL 35213-3312, USA

Carr, Henry (Athlete, Football Player, Track Athlete)
New York Giants
1612 Pinebrook Dr
Griffin, GA 30224-3957, USA

Carr, James H (Football Player)
Chicago Cardinals
13718 Indigo Ln
Fishers, IN 46038-8307, USA

Carr, Jane (Actor)
6200 Mount Angelus Dr
Los Angeles, CA 90042-3526, USA

Carr, Jimmy (Actor)
c/o Staff Member William Morris Agency (WMA-LA)
1 William Morris Pl
Beverly Hills, CA 90212-4261, USA

Carr, Kenneth M (Admiral)
2322 Fort Scott Dr
Arlington, VA 22202-2207, USA

Carr, Kenny (Baseball Player)
Los Angeles Lakers
24421 SW Valley View Rd
West Linn, OR 97068-9632, USA

Carr, Levart (Football Player)
San Diego Chargers
16 Birnamwood Dr
Burnsville, MN 55337-2933, USA

Carr, Lloyd (Coach)
University of Michigan
Athletic Dept
Ann Arbor, MI 48109, USA

Carr, Lydell (Football Player)
Phoenix Cardinals
2217 Harrisburg Ln
Plano, TX 75025-5515, USA

Carr, M L (Basketball Player)
St Louis Spirits
168 Beaver Rd
Weston, MA 02493-1036, USA

Carr, Michael L (M L) (Basketball Player, Coach)
Boston Celtics
151 Merrimac St # 1
Boston, MA 02114-4714, USA

Carr, Roger D (Football Player)
Baltimore Colts
101 Green Forest Dr
Monroe, LA 71203-8860, USA

Carr, Steve (Musician)
c/o Staff Member Creative Artists Agency LCC (CAA-LA)
2000 Avenue Of The Stars
Los Angeles, CA 90067-4700, USA

Carr, Vikki (Actor, Musician)
c/o Mary O'Brien
10370 Michael Todd Ter
Glenview, IL 60025-3747, USA

Carr of Hadley, L Robert (Government Official)
14 North Court
Great Peter St
London SW1 3LL, UNITED KINGDOM (UK)

Carra, Raffella
Via Nemea 21
Rome I-00194, ITALY

Carrabba, Chris (Musician)
c/o Richard Egan Hard 8 Management
2118 Wilshire Blvd # 361
Santa Monica, CA 90403-5784, USA

Carrack, Paul (Musician, Songwriter, Writer)
Firstars Mgmt
14724 Ventura Blvd Ph
Sherman Oaks, CA 91403-3513, USA

Carradine, David (Actor)
c/o Chuck Binder Binder & Associates
1465 Lindacrest Dr
Beverly Hills, CA 90210-2519, USA

Carradine, Ever (Actor)
c/o Lainie Sorkin Stolhanske Management 360
9111 Wilshire Blvd
Beverly Hills, CA 90210-5508, USA

Carradine, Keith (Actor, Musician, Songwriter, Writer)
c/o John Bauer John Bauer Management
1420 NW Gilman Blvd # 2335
Issaquah, WA 98027-5394, USA

Carradine, Robert (Actor)
c/o Staff Member Marshak/Zachary Company, The
8840 Wilshire Blvd Fl 1
Beverly Hills, CA 90211-2606, USA

Carragher, Jamie (Soccer Player)
The FA
25 Soho Square
London W1D 4FA, UNITED KINGDOM (UK)

Carraher, Harlen
2832 Abenel St. #1
Los Angeles, CA 90039, USA

Carrasco, D J (Baseball Player)
Kansas City Royals
642 W Fargo Ave Apt C
Hanford, CA 93230-1375, USA

Carre, Isabelle
8 rue de Duras
Paris F-75008, FRANCE

Carreker, Alphonso (Football Player)
Green Bay Packers
5599 Asheforde Ln
Marietta, GA 30068-1851, USA

Carrell, Duane (Football Player)
Dallas Cowboys
6525 Willow Springs Rd
Springfield, IL 62712-9501, USA

Carrell, John (Football Player)
Houston Oilers
2303 Cliffs Edge Dr
Austin, TX 78733-6031, USA

Carreno, J Manuel (Ballerina)
Royal Ballet
Covent Garden
Bow St
London WC2E 9DD, UNITED KINGDOM (UK)

Carreon, Mark (Baseball Player)
New York Mets
1034 Hutson Cir
Summit, MS 39666-9152, USA

Carrera, Asia (Adult Film Star)
c/o Staff Member Atlas Multimedia Inc
9035 Independence Ave
Canoga Park, CA 91304-1743, USA

Carrera, Barbara (Actor, Model)
c/o Staff Member Cunningham Escott Slevin & Doherty (LA)
10635 Santa Monica Blvd Ste 130
Los Angeles, CA 90025-8306, USA

Carrera, Carlos (Director)
c/o Staff Member Creative Artists Agency LCC (CAA-LA)
2000 Avenue Of The Stars
Los Angeles, CA 90067-4700, USA

Carreras, Jose (Opera Singer)
Foundacion Jose Carreras
Calle Muntaner 283
Barcelona 08021, SPAIN

Carrere, Tia (Actor, Model)
c/o Staff Member Phoenician Films Entertainment
6630 W Sunset Blvd
Los Angeles, CA 90028-7104, USA

Carretto, Joseph A Jr (Astronaut)
4534 E 85th St
Tulsa, OK 74137-1918, USA

Carrey, Jim (Actor, Comedian)
c/o Eric Gold Mosaic Media Group
24 Music Sq W Fl 1
Nashville, TN 37203-6661, USA

Carrick, Michael (Soccer Player)
The FA
25 Soho Square
London W1D 4FA, UNITED KINGDOM (UK)

Carrier, Darel (Basketball Player)
Kentucky Colonels
4224 Glasgow Rd
Oakland, KY 42159-6836, USA

Carrier, J Mark (Football Player)
4115 Highland Park Cir
Lutz, FL 33558-5314, USA

Carrier, Mark A (Football Player)
Chicago Bears
3061 Katherine Pl
Ellicott City, MD 21042-2188, USA

Carriere, Jean P J (Writer)
Les Broussanes Domessargues
Ledignan 30350, FRANCE

Carriere, Mathieu (Actor)
Agentur Schafer
Friesenstr 53
Cologne 50670, GERMANY

Carril, Pete (Coach)
Sacramento Kings
1 Sports Pkwy
Arco Arena
Sacramento, CA 95834-2301, USA

Carrillo, Elpidia (Actor)
Bresler Kelly Assoc
11500 W Olympic Blvd Ste 510
Los Angeles, CA 90064-1527, USA

Carrillo, Erick (Actor)
c/o Staff Member Three Moons Entertainment Inc
7040F W Sunset Blvd # 206
Los Angeles, CA 90028-7521, USA

Carrillo, Yadhira (Actor)
c/o Staff Member Televisa
Blvd Adolfo Lopez Mateos 232
Colonia San Angel INN
DF CP 01060, MEXICO

Carrington, Alan (Misc)
46 Lakewood Road
Chandler's Ford
Hants SO53 1EX, UNITED KINGDOM
(UK)

Carrington, Bob (Basketball Player)
New York Nets
PO Box 131301
Carlsbad, CA 92013-1301, USA

Carrington, Chuck (Actor)
c/o Darryl Taja *Epidemic Pictures and Management*
301 N Canon Dr Ste 207
Beverly Hills, CA 90210-4726, USA

Carrington, Darren (Football Player)
Denver Broncos
14097 Montfort Ct
San Diego, CA 92128-4283, USA

Carrington, Debbie Lee (Actor)
Jonis
8147 Tunney Ave
Reseda, CA 91335-1042, USA

Carrington, Lord
Bledlow Aylesbury
Bucks, ENGLAND HP17 9PE, UNITED
KINGDOM (UK)

Carrington, Paul (Attorney, Educator)
Duke University
Law School
Durham, NC 27708-0001, USA

Carrington, Peter A R (Government Official)
Manor House
Bledlow near Aylesbury
Bucks HP17 9PE, UNITED KINGDOM
(UK)

Carrithers, Don (Baseball Player)
San Francisco Giants
9367 Sunny Glade Ct
Elk Grove, CA 95758-4208, USA

Carroll, Bruce (Musician, Songwriter, Writer)
William Morris Agency
1600 Division St Ste 300
Nashville, TN 37203-2755, USA

Carroll, Clay P (Baseball Player)
Milwaukee Braves
3052 22nd St
Sarasota, FL 34234-8742, USA

Carroll, Diahann (Actor, Musician)
c/o Staff Member *Cunningham Escott Slevin & Doherty (LA)*
10635 Santa Monica Blvd Ste 130
Los Angeles, CA 90025-8306, USA

Carroll, Earl (Speedo) (Musician)
PS #87
180 W 78th St
New York, NY 10024, USA

Carroll, Earl W (Misc)
United Garment Workers of America
PO Box 239
Hermitage, TN 37076-0239, USA

Carroll, Georgia (Actor, Musician)
504 E Franklin St
Chapel Hill, NC 27514-3708, USA

Carroll, James (Football Player)
New York Giants
13880 Stirling Rd
Southwest Ranches, FL 33330-3019, USA

Carroll, Jamey (Baseball Player)
Montreal Expos
503 Dogwood Dr
Wylie, TX 75098-3851, USA

Carroll, Jay (Football Player)
Tampa Bay Buccaneers
117 Homedale Rd
Hopkins, MN 55343-8519, USA

Carroll, Joe (Football Player)
Oakland Raiders
4541 Fairfield St
Pittsburgh, PA 15201-2031, USA

Carroll, Joe Barry (Basketball Player)
Denver Nuggets
1000 Chopper Cir
Pepsi Center
Denver, CO 80204-5805, USA

Carroll, John B (Misc)
2158 Penrose Ln
Fairbanks, AK 99709-6213, USA

Carroll, Julian M (Governor)
Carroll Assoc
PO Box 1491
Frankfort, KY 40602-1491, USA

Carroll, Kent J (Admiral)
Country Club of North Carolina
1600 Morganton Rd Unit 30X
Pinehurst, NC 28374-6890, USA

Carroll, Leo (Football Player)
Green Bay Packers
34448 Agua Dulce Canyon Rd
Santa Clarita, CA 91390-4668, USA

Carroll, Lester (Les) (Cartoonist)
1715 Ivyhill Loop N
Columbus, OH 43229-5223, USA

Carroll, Mickey
7225 Saint Charles Rock Rd
Saint Louis, MO 63133-1735, USA

Carroll, Pat (Actor)
14 Old Tavern Ln
Harwich Port, MA 02646-1519, USA

Carroll, Pete (Coach, Football Coach)
University of Southern California
Heritage Hall
Los Angeles, CA 90089-0001, USA

Carroll, Rocky (Actor)
c/o Staff Member *Innovative Artists (LA)*
1505 10th St
Santa Monica, CA 90401-2805, USA

Carroll, Ron (Football Player)
Houston Oilers
3320 La Vista Ave
Bay City, TX 77414-2793, USA

Carroll, Tom (Baseball Player)
Cincinnati Reds
38572 Pheasant Hill Ln
Hamilton, VA 20158-3302, USA

Carroll, Tommy (Baseball Player)
New York Yankees
304 Sonnet Ct
Peachtree City, GA 30269-3357, USA

Carroll, Wesley (Football Player)
New Orleans Saints
11740 SW 102nd St
Miami, FL 33186-2734, USA

Carroll, Willard (Director, Producer, Writer)
c/o Staff Member *Hyperion Pictures*
111 N Maryland Ave # 300
Glendale, CA 91206-4238, USA

Carruth, Paul (Football Player)
Green Bay Packers
373 Brentwood Ave
Trussville, AL 35173-1103, USA

Carruth, Rae (Football Player)
Carolina Panthers
12653 Tucker Crossing Ln
Charlotte, NC 28273-4746, USA

Carruthers, Garrey E (Governor)
4405 Echo Canyon Rd
Las Cruces, NM 88011-7523, USA

Carruthers, James H (Red) (Skier)
8 Malone Ave
Garnerville, NY 10923-1812, USA

Carruthers, Peter (Figure Skater)
22 E 71st St
New York, NY 10021-4975, USA

Carry, Jerry
PO Box 919
Huntsville, AR 72740-0919, USA

Carry, Julius
4091 Farmdale Ave
Studio City, CA 91604-3013, USA

Carsey, Marcy
4024 Radford Ave # 3
Studio City, CA 91604-2101, USA

Carson, Benjamin S (Doctor)
Johns Hopkins University Medical Center
Baltimore, MD 21218, USA

Carson, Bud (Football Player)
Saint Louis Rams
901 N Broadway
Saint Louis, MO 63101-2800, USA

Carson, Carlos A (Football Player)
Kansas City Chief
4747 W 150th Ter
Overland Park, KS 66224-3410, USA

Carson, David (Director)
10474 Santa Monica Blvd
Los Angeles, CA 90025-6929, USA

Carson, Harold D (Harry) (Football Player)
New York Giants
732 Barrister Ct
Franklin Lakes, NJ 07417-2711, USA

Carson, Hunter
8730 W Sunset Blvd Ste 490
Los Angeles, CA 90069-2248, USA

Carson, James (Jimmy) (Hockey Player)
1154 Ridgeway Dr
Rochester, MI 48307-1771, USA

Carson, Jeff (Musician)
Shipley Biddy Entertainment
1104 Hunting Creek Rd
Franklin, TN 37069-4754, USA

Carson, Joanna
400 St Cloud Rd
Los Angeles, CA 90077-3425, USA

Carson, Joanne
11001 W Sunset Blvd
Los Angeles, CA 90049-3224, USA

Carson, Kern (Football Player)
San Diego Chargers
6358 Antioch Ave
Riverside, CA 92504-1624, USA

Carson, Lisa Nicole (Actor)
c/o Scott Zimmerman *Untitled Entertainment (LA)*
331 N Maple Dr Fl 3
Beverly Hills, CA 90210-3827, USA

Carson, Malcolm (Football Player)
Minnesota Vikings
PO Box 11847
Birmingham, AL 35202-1847, USA

Carson, T C
1505 10th St
Santa Monica, CA 90401-2805, USA

Carson, William H (Willie) (Jockey)
Minster House
Bamsley
Cirencester, Glos, UNITED KINGDOM
(UK)

Carsten, Peter
Via Garibaldi 11
SVN-Piran, Istrien, SLOVAKIA

Carstens, Christiane
Kielortallee 65
Hamburg D-20144, GERMANY

Carswell, Dwayne (Football Player)
Denver Broncos
1305 Ivyhedge Ave
Saint Augustine, FL 32092-5020, USA

Carswell, Robert (Football Player)
San Diego Chargers
709 Stonebridge Ter
Lithonia, GA 30058-9060, USA

Cartagena, Victoria (Actor)
c/o Larry Taube *Principal Entertainment (LA)*
1964 Westwood Blvd Ste 400
Los Angeles, CA 90025-4695, USA

Carter, Aaron (Actor, Musician)
c/o Frederick Levy *Management 101*
5527 1/2 Cahuenga Blvd
North Hollywood, CA 91601, USA

Carter, Alex (Actor)
c/o Richard Caplan *Gilbertson-Kincaid Management*
1334 3rd Street Promenade Ste 201
Santa Monica, CA 90401-1320, USA

Carter, Allen (Football Player)
New England Patriots
2400 Ridgeview Dr Apt 404
Chino Hills, CA 91709-4378, USA

Carter, Amy
1 Woodland Dr.
Plains, GA 31780, USA

Carter, Andy (Baseball Player)
Philadelphia Phillies
106 Montgomery Ave
Glenside, PA 19038-8228, USA

Carter, Anthony (Football Player)
Minnesota Vikings
4314 Danielson Dr
Lake Worth, FL 33467-3628, USA

Carter, Antonio (Football Player)
Chicago Bears
7839 Maple Grove Dr
Lewis Center, OH 43035-9350, USA

Carter, Bernard (Football Player)
Jacksonville Jaguars
261 Pinestraw Cir
Altamonte Springs, FL 32714-5416, USA

Carter, Betsy (Musician)
4356 Briarwood Dr
Urbana, OH 43078-8217, USA

Carter, Carl (Football Player)
St Louis Cardinals
3256 Centennial Rd
Forest Hill, TX 76119-7103, USA

Carter, Cheryl (Actor)
CunninghamEscottDipene
10635 Santa Monica Blvd Ste 130
Los Angeles, CA 90025-8306, USA

Carter, Chris (Football Player)
New England Patriots
1500 Mill Creek Dr
Desoto, TX 75115-1705, USA

Carter, Chris (Producer)
Broder Kurland Webb Uffner
10250 Constellation Blvd
Los Angeles, CA 90067-6200, USA

Carter, Clarence (Basketball Player)
Baltimore Bullets
5108 Fairway Oaks Dr
Windermere, FL 34786-8933, USA

Carter, Clarence (Musician)
Rodgers Redding
1048 Tattnall St
Macon, GA 31201-1537, USA

Carter, Cris (Football Player)
Philadelphia Eagles
2493 NW 46th St
Boca Raton, FL 33431-8432, USA

Carter, Dale (Football Player)
Kansas City Chiefs
10416 Magnolia Heights Cir
Covington, GA 30014-4102, USA

Carter, Darren (Comedian)
c/o Staff Member *William Morris Agency
(WMA-LA)*
1 William Morris Pl
Beverly Hills, CA 90212-4261, USA

Carter, David (Football Player)
Houston Oilers
2401 Long Reach Dr
Sugar Land, TX 77478-4127, USA

Carter, Deanna (Actor, Musician)
c/o John Huie *Creative Artists Agency
(CAA-Nashville)*
3310 W End Ave Fl 5
Nashville, TN 37203-1028, USA

Carter, Dexter A (Football Player)
San Francisco 49ers
7130 Nesters Dr
Tallahassee, FL 32312-6740, USA

Carter, Dixie (Actor)
9100 Hazen Dr
Beverly Hills, CA 90210-1843, USA

Carter, Donald J (Don) (Bowler)
9895 SW 96th St
Miami, FL 33176-2802, USA

Carter, Elliott C Jr (Composer)
31 W 12th St
New York, NY 10011-8500, USA

Carter, Finn (Actor)
c/o Craig Dorfman *Blueprint Management*
5670 Wilshire Blvd Ste 2525
Los Angeles, CA 90036-5647, USA

Carter, Frank (Misc)
Glass Molders Pottery Plastics Union
608 E Baltimore Pike
Media, PA 19063-1735, USA

Carter, Fred (Basketball Player)
Baltimore Bullets
2979 W School House Ln Apt 703K
Philadelphia, PA 19144-5319, USA

Carter, Frederick J (Fred) (Baseball
Player, Coach)
5070 Parkside Ave # 3500
Philadelphia, PA 19131-4747, USA

Carter, Gary E (Baseball Player)
Montreal Expos
560 Village Blvd Ste 260
The Gary Carter Foundation
West Palm Beach, FL 33409-1963, USA

Carter, Gaylord
555 E Ocean Blvd Ste 810
Long Beach, CA 90802-5056, USA

Carter, Gerald (Football Player)
New York Jets
3917 Cheshire Ct
Bryan, TX 77802-4905, USA

Carter, Hodding III
211 S Saint Asaph St
Alexandria, VA 22314-3743, USA

Carter, Howard (Basketball Player)
Denver Nuggets
7572 Hanks Dr
Baton Rouge, LA 70812-3707, USA

Carter, Jack (Actor, Comedian)
1023 Chevy Chase Dr
Beverly Hills, CA 90210-2707, USA

Carter, Jake (Basketball Player)
Hammond Calumet Buccaneers
1648 Hanging Cliff Dr
Dallas, TX 75224, USA

Carter, Jay (Musician)
Brothers Mgmt
141 Dunbar Ave
Fords, NJ 08863-1551, USA

Carter, Jeff (Baseball Player)
Chicago White Sox
4625 River Overlook Dr
Valrico, FL 33596-7878, USA

Carter, Jim (Football Player)
Green Bay Packers
1500 Morning Glory Ln
Wausau, WI 54401-7686, USA

Carter, Jim (Golfer)
12575 N 130th Way
Scottsdale, AZ 85259-3542, USA

Carter, Jodie (Football Player)
Miami Dolphins
5921 Timberview Rd
Little Rock, AR 72204-8559, USA

Carter, Joe (Baseball Player)
Chicago Cubs
3000 W 117th St
Leawood, KS 66211-2923, USA

Carter, John (Musician)
Resort Attractions
2375 E Tropicana Ave Ste 304
Las Vegas, NV 89119-9808, USA

Carter, John Mack (Editor)
Good Housekeeping Magazine
959 8th Ave
Editorial Dept
New York, NY 10019-3737, USA

Carter, Kent (Football Player)
New England Patriots
18657 Klum Pl
Rowland Heights, CA 91748-4851, USA

Carter, Kevin (Football Player)
St Louis Rams
1070 Vaughn Crest Dr
Franklin, TN 37069-7211, USA

Carter, Ki-Jana (Football Player)
Cincinnati Bengals
1293 NW 121st Ave
Plantation, FL 33323-2441, USA

Carter, Lance (Baseball Player)
Kansas City Royals
306 74th Street Ct NW
Bradenton, FL 34209-2220, USA

Carter, Larry (Baseball Player)
San Francisco Giants
801 S Madison St
Wilmington, DE 19801-5121, USA

Carter, Laverne (Bowler)
4750 Madrigal Way
Las Vegas, NV 89122-6133, USA

Carter, Louis (Football Player)
Oakland Raiders
8209 Swamp Rose Pl
Laurel, MD 20724-1963, USA

Carter, Lynda (Actor)
c/o Melissa Prophet *Melissa Prophet
Management*
4321 Matilija Ave Apt 21
Sherman Oaks, CA 91423-3672, USA

Carter, M L (Football Player)
Kansas City Chiefs
5020 Adobe Rd
Twentynine Palms, CA 92277-1802, USA

Carter, Marshall N (Financier)
State Street Corp
225 Franklin St
Boston, MA 02110-2875, USA

Carter, Mel (Musician)
Cape Entertainment
8432 NW 31st Ct
Sunrise, FL 33351-8901, USA

Carter, Michael (Actor)
London Mgmt
2-4 Noel St
London W1V 3RB, UNITED KINGDOM
(UK)

Carter, Michael D (Football Player)
San Francisco 49ers
901 Red Oak Creek Dr
Ovilla, TX 75154-3615, USA

Carter, Mike (Baseball Player)
Atlanta Braves
12215 Magnolia Crescent Dr Apt D
Roswell, GA 30075-5568, USA

Carter, Mike (Football Player)
Green Bay Packers
2257 Summerton Dr
San Jose, CA 95122-3381, USA

Carter, Nathan (Actor)
c/o Norbert Abrams *Noble Kaplan Agency*
1260 Yonge St Fl 2
Toronto, ON M4T 1W6, CANADA

Carter, Nick (Musician, Songwriter,
Writer)
c/o Kenneth Crear *Wright-Crear
Management*
3815 Hughes Ave
Culver City, CA 90232-2715, USA

Carter, Pat (Football Player)
Detroit Lions
4511 Misty Hollow Dr
Missouri City, TX 77459-4473, USA

Carter, Paula (Bowler)
9895 SW 96th St
Miami, FL 33176-2802, USA

Carter, Perry (Football Player)
Kansas City Chiefs
639 NE Newport Dr
Lees Summit, MO 64064-2043, USA

Carter, Powell F Jr (Admiral)
699 Fillmore St
Harpers Ferry, WV 25425, USA

Carter, Rachel
PO Box 1663
Julian, CA 92036-1663, USA

Carter, Rodney (Football Player)
Pittsburgh Steelers
4490 Jasmine Dr
Bethlehem, PA 18020-8840, USA

Carter, Ron (Basketball Player)
Los Angeles Stars
6245 Bristol Pkwy Ste 201
Culver City, CA 90230-6903, USA

Carter, Ronald L (Ron) (Composer,
Musician)
Bridge Agency
35 Clark St Apt A5
Brooklyn, NY 11201-2374, USA

Carter, Rosalynn (First Lady)
Carter Center
451 Freedom Pkwy NE
Atlanta, GA 30307, USA

Carter, Rosana (Opera Singer)
Angel Records
150 5th Ave
New York, NY 10011-4311, USA

Carter, Roy
PO Box 204
Goodlettsville, TN 37070-0204, USA

Carter, Rubin (Coach, Football Player)
Florida A&M University
Athletic Dept
Tallahassee, FL 32307, USA

Carter, Rubin (Hurricane) (Boxer)
*Assoc in Defense of the Wrongly
Convicted*
85 King St E #318
Toronto, ON M5C 1G3, CANADA

Carter, Rublin (Football Player)
1793 Vineyard Way
Tallahassee, FL 32317-7915, USA

Carter, Russell (Football Player)
New York Jets
216 Lilac Ln
Douglassville, PA 19518-1121, USA

Carter, Sarah (Actor)
c/o Steve Caserta *Sanders/Armstrong
Management*
2120 Colorado Ave Ste 120
Santa Monica, CA 90404-3561, USA

Carter, Shawn (Jay-Z) (Musician,
Producer)
c/o Staff Member *Island Def Jam Music
Group*
825 8th Ave Fl 28
New York, NY 10019-7416, USA

Carter, Sol (Baseball Player)
Philadelphia Athletics
2402 Gale Pl
El Dorado, AR 71730-3034, USA

Carter, Stephen L (Attorney, Attorney
General, General, Writer)
Yale University
Law School
New Haven, CT 06520, USA

Carter, Steve (Baseball Player)
Pittsburgh Pirates
13006 Innisbrook Dr
Beltsville, MD 20705-1196, USA

Carter, Terry (Actor)
244 Madison Ave # 332
New York, NY 10016-2817, USA

Carter, Thomas (Director)
140 N Tigertail Rd
Los Angeles, CA 90049-2706, USA

Carter, Tim (Football Player)
New York Giants
4860 26th Ct S
Saint Petersburg, FL 33712-4322, USA

Carter, Tom (Football Player)
Washington Redskins
4548 Bristol Ln
Cincinnati, OH 45229-1214, USA

Carter, Tom (Golfer)
3787 County Line Rd
Quakertown, PA 18951-2085, USA

Carter, Vince (Basketball Player)
c/o Staff Member *New Jersey Nets*
390 Murray Hill Pkwy
E Rutherford, NJ 07073-2109, USA

Carter, Virgil (Football Player)
Chicago Bears
2010 Whitebluff Dr
San Dimas, CA 91773-1337, USA

Carter III, W Hodding (Government Official)
214 N Columbus St
Alexandria, VA 22314-2412, USA

Carter Jr, James E (Jimmy) (Ex-President, Nobel Prize Laureate, Politician, President)
Carter Center
453 Freedom Pkwy NE
Atlanta, GA 30307-1406, USA

Carteris, Gabrielle (Actor)
c/o Jeff Danis *International Creative Management (ICM-LA)*
10250 Constellation Blvd
Los Angeles, CA 90067-6200, USA

Carter's Chord (Music Group)
c/o Staff Member *Paradigm (Monterey)*
509 Hartnell St
Monterey, CA 93940-2825, USA

Carthen, Jason (Football Player)
New England Patriots
3978 Jeanne Dr
Cleveland, OH 44134, USA

Carthon, Maurice (Football Player)
New York Giants
910 S Pecan St
Osceola, AR 72370-3637, USA

Carthy, Eliza (Musician, Songwriter, Writer)
Agency Group Ltd
1775 Broadway Ste 515
New York, NY 10019-1903, USA

Cartwright, Angela (Actor)
Rubber Boots
11333 Moor Park St # 433
Toluca Lake, CA 91602-2618, USA

Cartwright, Bill (Basketball Player, Coach)
New York Knicks
711 Jennifer Ct
Lake Forest, IL 60045-4312, USA

Cartwright, Bill (Basketball Player, Coach)
2222 Francisco Dr Ste 510
El Dorado Hills, CA 95762-3766, USA

Cartwright, James F (General)
Director Structure Resources Assessment
Hqusmc Navy Station
Washington, DC 20380-0001, USA

Cartwright, Nancy (Actor)
c/o Marcia Hurwitz *Innovative Artists (LA)*
1505 10th St
Santa Monica, CA 90401-2805, USA

Cartwright, Veronica (Actor)
12754 Sarah St
Studio City, CA 91604-1135, USA

Carty, Jay (Basketball Player)
Los Angeles Lakers
1033 Newton Rd
Santa Barbara, CA 93103-2023, USA

Carty, Ricardo A J (Rico) (Baseball Player)
Milwaukee Braves
5 Ens Enriquillo
San Pedro de Macoris, DOMINICAN REPUBLIC

Caruana, Patrick P (Sat) (General)
1922 Havemeyer Ln
Redondo Beach, CA 90278-4830, USA

Caruana, Peter R (Politician)
Chief Minister's Office
10/3 Irish Town
GIBRALTAR

Caruso, David (Actor)
c/o Jason Weinberg *Untitled Entertainment (LA)*
331 N Maple Dr Fl 3
Beverly Hills, CA 90210-3827, USA

Caruso, Mike (Baseball Player)
Cleveland Indians
10763 NW 21st Pl
Coral Springs, FL 33071-4219, USA

Carvel, Elbert N (Governor)
1100 N Market St
Wilmington, DE 19801-1243, USA

Carver, Brent (Actor, Musician)
Live Entertainment
1500 Broadway Ste 902
New York, NY 10036-4055, USA

Carver, Dale (Football Player)
Cleveland Browns
1328 Vista Ter
Titusville, FL 32780-4343, USA

Carver, Dana (Actor, Comedian)
775 E Blithedale Ave # 501
Mill Valley, CA 94941-1554, USA

Carver, Johnny (Musician)
House of Talent
9 Lucy Ln
Sherwood, AR 72120-3612, USA

Carver, Melvin (Football Player)
Tampa Bay Buccaneers
6256 Kingbird Manor Dr
Lithia, FL 33547-5049, USA

Carver, Randall (Actor)
Tyler Kjar
5144 Vineland Ave
North Hollywood, CA 91601-3849, USA

Carver, Shante (Football Player)
Dallas Cowboys
929 Sugarberry Dr
Coppell, TX 75019-3503, USA

Carveth-Dunn, Betty (Baseball Player)
11531 77th Avenue
Edmonton, AB T6G 0M2, CANADA

Carvey, Dana (Actor)
c/o Ron Hofmann *BWR (BWR-LA)*
9100 Wilshire Blvd Fl 6
West Tower
Beverly Hills, CA 90212-3401, USA

Carvilie, C James Jr (Politician)
209 Pennsylvania Ave SE # 800
Washington, DC 20003-1107, USA

Carville, James (Television Host)
424 S Washington St
Alexandria, VA 22314-3630, USA

Cary, Chuck (Baseball Player)
Detroit Tigers
484 Bayshore Dr
Miramar Beach, FL 32550-4063, USA

Cary, Scott (Baseball Player)
Washington Senators
PO Box 205
Bronson, MI 49028-0205, USA

Cary, W Sterling (Religious Leader)
2344 Vardon Ln
Flossmoor, IL 60422-1363, USA

Cary Brothers (Music Group)
c/o Staff Member *Paradigm (Monterey)*
509 Hartnell St
Monterey, CA 93940-2825, USA

Casablancas, John (Model)
Elite Model Mgmt
111 E 22nd St Rm 200
New York, NY 10010-5414, USA

Casablancas, Julian (Musician, Songwriter, Writer)
MVO Ltd
370 7th Ave # 807
New York, NY 10001-3912, USA

Casadesus, Jean-Claude (Conductor)
23 Blvd de la Liberte
Lille 59800, FRANCE

Casados, Eloy (Actor)
Epstein/Wyckoff
280 S Beverly Dr Ste 400
Beverly Hills, CA 90212-3904, USA

Casados, Rene (Actor)
c/o Staff Member *Televisa*
Blvd Adolfo Lopez Mateos 232
Colonia San Angel INN
DF CP 01060, MEXICO

Casady, Jack (Musician)
Ron Rainey Mgmt
315 S Beverly Dr Ste 407
Beverly Hills, CA 90212-4301, USA

Casale, Jerry (Baseball Player)
Boston Red Sox
600 County Ave Apt 408
Secaucus, NJ 07094-2610, USA

Casali, Kim (Cartoonist)
Times-Mirror Syndicate
Times-Mirror Square
Los Angeles, CA 90053, USA

Casals, Rosemary (Rosie) (Tennis Player)
Sportswoman Inc
PO Box 537
Sausalito, CA 94966-0537, USA

Casals, Rosie
PO Box 537
Sausalito, CA 94966-0537, USA

Casanega, Ken (Football Player)
San Francisco 49ers
480 Donald Dr
Hollister, CA 95023-6364, USA

Casanova, Paul (Baseball Player)
Indianapolis Clowns
5370 NW 183rd St
Miami Gardens, FL 33055-2304, USA

Casanova, Raul (Baseball Player)
Detroit Tigers
2180 S Sanctuary Dr
New Berlin, WI 53151-1923, USA

Casanova, Thomas H (Tommy) (Football Player)
141 Gardinia Ln
Crowley, LA 70526-3107, USA

Casares, Adolfo Bioy
Posadas 1650-5
(1112) Buenos Aires, ARGENTINA

Casares, Ricardo (Rick) (Football Player)
Chicago Bears
4107 Starfish Ln
Tampa, FL 33615-5428, USA

Casbarian, John (Architect)
Taft Architects
2370 Rice Blvd Ste 112
Houston, TX 77005-2644, USA

Cascada (Musician)
Blue Art Event GmbH
c/o Frank Ehrlich
Varlar 41
D- 48720, Rosendahl, GERMANY

Cascadden, Chad (Football Player)
New York Jets
2611 Winsor Dr
Eau Claire, WI 54703-1778, USA

Case, Harold
34 Cunningham Park Harrow
Middlesex, ENGLAND HA1 4AL, UNITED KINGDOM (UK)

Case, J Scott (Football Player)
4930 Price Dr
Suwanee, GA 30024-4186, USA

Case, John (Writer)
Random House
1745 Broadway # B1
New York, NY 10019-4305, USA

Case, Pete (Football Player)
Philadelphia Eagles
6960 Driskell Cir
Cumming, GA 30041-4714, USA

Case, Ronald (Football Player)
Philadelphia Eagles
6960 Driskell Cir
Cumming, GA 30041-4714, USA

Case, Sharon (Actor)
c/o Jerry Shandrew *Shandrew Public Relations*
1050 S Stanley Ave
Los Angeles, CA 90019-6634, USA

Case, Stephen M (Steve) (Business Person)
1717 Rhode Island Ave NW
7th Fl
Washington, DC 20036-3023, USA

Case, Stoney (Football Player)
Arizona Cardinals
1813 E 49th St
Odessa, TX 79762-4524, USA

Case, Walter Jr (Race Car Driver)
60 Edgecomb Rd
Lisbon Falls, ME 04252-9740, USA

Casel, Nitanju Bolade (Musician)
Sweet Honey Agency
PO Box 600099
Newtonville, MA 02460-0001, USA

Casella, Max
1505 10th St
Santa Monica, CA 90401-2805, USA

Casely-Hayford, Joe (Designer, Fashion Designer)
c/o Staff Member *Joe Casely-Hayford*
128 Shoreditch High Street
London, England E1 6JE, UNITED KINGDOM (UK)

Casey, Bernie (Football Player)
San Francisco 49ers
6145 Flight Ave
Los Angeles, CA 90056-1509, USA

Casey, Dillon (Actor)
c/o Norbert Abrams *Noble Kaplan Agency*
1260 Yonge St Fl 2
Toronto, ON M4T 1W6, CANADA

Casey, Harry W (Musician)
7530 Loch Ness Dr
Miami Lakes, FL 33014-6014, USA

Casey, John D (Writer)
University of Virginia
English Dept
Charlottesville, VA 22903, USA

Casey, Jon (Hockey Player)
Saint Louis Blues
1401 Clark Ave
Sawis Center
Saint Louis, MO 63103-2700, USA

Casey, Lawrence
4139 Vanetta Pl
N Hollywood, CA 91604-2342, USA

Casey, Lee
Paul Kohner Agency Inc
9300 Wilshire Blvd Ste 555
Beverly Hills, CA 90212-3211, USA

Casey, Maurice F (General)
7017 Union Mill Rd
Clifton, VA 20124-1122, USA

Casey, Paddy (Musician)
c/o Staff Member *Helter Skelter (UK)*
535 Kings Rd
The Plaza
London SW10 0SZ, UNITED KINGDOM (UK)

Casey, Peter (Director)
Jim Preminger Agency
10866 Wilshire Blvd Fl 10
Los Angeles, CA 90024-4350, USA

Casey, Sean (Baseball Player)
Cleveland Indians
2423 Maryland Dr
Pittsburgh, PA 15241-2415, USA

Casey, Tim (Football Player)
Chicago Bears
4285 NW Malheur Ave
Portland, OR 97229-2880, USA

Cash, Bill (Baseball Player)
Philadelphia Stars
1715 W Cheltenham Ave
Elkins Park, PA 19027-1048, USA

Cash, Cornelius (Basketball Player)
Detroit Pistons
1661 Miami Chapel Rd
Dayton, OH 45408-2527, USA

Cash, David (Baseball Player)
Pittsburgh Pirates
16308 Birkdale Dr
Odessa, FL 33556-2802, USA

Cash, Gerald C (Governor)
4 Bristol St
PO Box N476
Nassau, BAHAMAS

Cash, Keith L (Football Player)
Pittsburgh Steelers
9839 Heritage Farm Rd
San Antonio, TX 78245-1217, USA

Cash, Kerry (Football Player)
Indianapolis Colts
9839 Heritage Farm Rd
San Antonio, TX 78245-1217, USA

Cash, Kevin (Baseball Player)
Toront Blue Jays
1160 Kenly Ave Apt 1
Hagerstown, MD 21740-7467, USA

Cash, Pat (Tennis Player)
281 Clarence St
Sydney NSW 2000, AUSTRALIA

Cash, Rick (Football Player)
Atlanta Falcons
203 E Benton St
Savannah, MO 64485-1720, USA

Cash, Ron (Baseball Player)
Detroit Tigers
820 Green Forest Dr SE
Smyrna, GA 30082-3438, USA

Cash, Rosanne (Musician, Songwriter, Writer)
Danny Kahn
45 W 11th St Apt 7B
New York, NY 10011-8633, USA

Cash, Sam (Basketball Player)
Memphis Tams
25825 Karisa Cir
Moreno Valley, CA 92551-1968, USA

Cash, Swin (Basketball Player)
Detroit Shock
2 Championship Dr
Palace
Auburn Hills, MI 48326-1753, USA

Cash, Tommy (Musician, Songwriter, Writer)
PO Box 1230
Hendersonville, TN 37077-1230, USA

Cashen, Frank (Baseball Player)
New York Mets
7600 Mahogany Run
Port Saint Lucie, FL 34986-3213, USA

Cashion, Red (Football Player)
NFL Referee
PO Box 3889
Bryan, TX 77805-3889, USA

Cashman, John Jr (Misc)
PO Box 11889
Lexington, KY 40578-1889, USA

Cashman, Terry (Musician)
15 Engle St
Englewood, NJ 07631-2936, USA

Casian, Larry (Baseball Player)
Minnesota Twins
1939 Popcorn St NW
Salem, OR 97304-2841, USA

Casiavska, Vera (Gymnast)
SVS Sparta Prague
Korunovacni 29
Prague 7, CZECH REPUBLIC

Casida, John E (Misc)
1570 La Vereda Rd
Berkeley, CA 94708-2036, USA

Casillas, Tony (Football Player)
Atlanta Falcons
6201 Bay Valley Ct
Flower Mound, TX 75022-5573, USA

Casiraghi, Pierlulgi (Soccer Player)
Lazio Rorna
Via Novaro 32
Rome 00197, ITALY

Caskey, Craig (Baseball Player)
Montreal Expos
17422 Palomino Dr
Bothell, WA 98012-6419, USA

Casner, Ken (Football Player)
Los Angeles Rams
1808 Laurel Lake Dr
Waco, TX 76710-2829, USA

Casnoff, Philip (Actor)
c/o Darris Hatch *Daris Hatch Management*
9538 Brighton Way Ste 308
Beverly Hills, CA 90210-4516, USA

Casnoff, Phillip (Actor)
216 S Plymouth Blvd
Los Angeles, CA 90004-3814, USA

Caso, Mark
1252 S Ogden Dr Apt 8
Los Angeles, CA 90019-2435, USA

Cason, James (Football Player)
San Francisco 49ers
1802 E Washington Ave Apt 29
Harlingen, TX 78550-5711, USA

Caspar, Donald L D (Physicist)
2605 Lotus Dr
Tallahassee, FL 32312-3009, USA

Caspary, Tina (Actor)
11350 Ventura Blvd Ste 206
Studio City, CA 91604-3140, USA

Casper, David J (Dave) (Football Player)
Oakland Raiders
1525 Alamo Way
Alamo, CA 94507-1502, USA

Casper, Gerhard (Attorney, Educator)
Stanford University
Law School
Abbott Way
Stanford, CT 94305, USA

Casper, John H (Astronaut)
4414 Village Corner Dr
Houston, TX 77059-4025, USA

Casper, Robert (Actor)
CunninghamEscottDipene
10635 Santa Monica Blvd Ste 130
Los Angeles, CA 90025-8306, USA

Caspersson, Tobjorn O (Doctor)
Emanuel Birkes Vag 2
Ronninge 14400, SWEDEN

Cass, Christopher (Actor)
Halpern Assoc
PO Box 5597
Santa Monica, CA 90409-5597, USA

Cassady, Craig (Football Player)
New Orleans Saints
4091 Nottinghill Gate Rd
Columbus, OH 43220-3940, USA

Cassady, Howard (Hopalong) (Football Player)
Detroit Lions
539 Severn Ave
Tampa, FL 33606-4045, USA

Cassar, Jon (Producer)
c/o Staff Member *Roklin Management*
8530 Wilshire Blvd Ste 550
Beverly Hills, CA 90211-3133, USA

Cassara, Frank (Football Player)
San Francisco 49ers
9113 Brookshire Ave
Downey, CA 90240-2910, USA

Cassaveters, Nick (Actor, Director)
22223 Buena Ventura St
Woodland Hills, CA 91364-5007, USA

Cassavetes, Nick (Actor)
c/o Staff Member *William Morris Agency (WMA-LA)*
1 William Morris Pl
Beverly Hills, CA 90212-4261, USA

Cassel, Seymour (Actor)
c/o Harry Abrams *Abrams Artists Agency (LA)*
9200 W Sunset Blvd Ph 11
Los Angeles, CA 90069-3601, USA

Cassel, Vincent (Actor)
United Talent Agency
9560 Wilshire Blvd Ste 500
Beverly Hills, CA 90212-2401, USA

Cassell, Sam (Basketball Player)
Houston Rockets
6000 Reirns Road Apt 3402
Houston, TX 77036, USA

Cassels, A James H (Misc)
Hamble End Higham Road
Barrow Bury Saint Edmunds
Suffolk, UNITED KINGDOM (UK)

Casserino, Lt Col Frank J
2407 Willow Glen Dr
Colorado Springs, CO 80920-1200, USA

Cassese, Tom (Football Player)
Denver Broncos
80 Van Buren St
Port Jefferson Station, NY 11776-3173, USA

Casseus, Gabriel (Actor)
Metropolitan Talent Agency
4500 Wilshire Blvd Fl 2
Los Angeles, CA 90010-3858, USA

Cassidy (Musician)
c/o Staff Member *J Records (Division of BMG Entertainment)*
745 5th Ave Fl 6
New York, NY 10151-0099, USA

Cassidy, Bruce (Coach, Hockey Player)
1810 Winella Dr SE
Grand Rapids, MI 49506, USA

Cassidy, David (Actor, Musician)
c/o Jo-Ann Geffen *JAG Entertainment*
4265 Hazeltine Ave
Sherman Oaks, CA 91423-4245, USA

Cassidy, Ed
PO Box 1508
Arroyo Grande, CA 93421-1508, USA

Cassidy, Edward I Cardinal (Religious Leader)
Council for Christian Unity
Piazza del S Uffizio 11
Rome 00193, ITALY

Cassidy, Elaine (Actor)
c/o Staff Member *International Creative Management (ICM-LA)*
10250 Constellation Blvd
Los Angeles, CA 90067-6200, USA

Cassidy, Joanna (Actor)
c/o Bette Smith *Bette Smith Management*
499 N Canon Dr
Beverly Hills, CA 90210-4842, USA

Cassidy, Katie (Actor)
c/o Doreen Wilcox *Blue Train Entertainment*
798 Brooktree Rd
Pacific Palisades, CA 90272-3901, USA

Cassidy, Michael (Actor)
c/o Vic Ramos *Vic Ramos Management*
49 W 9th St Apt 5B
New York, NY 10011-9202, USA

Cassidy, Patrick (Actor)
Innovative Artists
1505 10th St
Santa Monica, CA 90401-2805, USA

Cassidy, Ron (Football Player)
Green Bay Packers
2214 W 171st St
Torrance, CA 90504-2925, USA

Cassidy, Ryan
4949 Strohm Ave
N Hollywood, CA 91601-4843, USA

Cassidy, Scott (Baseball Player)
Toront Blue Jays
4203 Hunting Creek Dr
Clay, NY 13041-8718, USA

Cassidy, Shaun (Actor, Musician)
c/o Staff Member *Shaun Cassidy Productions*
4000 Warner Blvd Bldg 191 # 205
Burbank, CA 91522-0001, USA

Cassie (Musician)
c/o Staff Member *Maverick Recording Co (LA)*
3300 Warner Blvd
Burbank, CA 91505-4632, USA

Cassini, Jack (Baseball Player)
Pittsburgh Pirates
2498 Leisure World
Mesa, AZ 85206-5416, USA

Casson, Mel (Cartoonist)
King Features Syndicate
888 7th Ave Ste 201
New York, NY 10106-0201, USA

Cast, Edward
4 Bankside Dr Thames Ditton
Surrey, ENGLAND KT7 0AQ, UNITED KINGDOM (UK)

Cast, Tricia (Actor)
20 Georgette Road
Rolling Hills Estates, CA 90274, USA

Casta, Laetitia (Actor)
c/o Staff Member *ArtMedia*
20 av Rapp
Paris 75007, FRANCE

Castaneda, Jorge A (Government Official)
Anillo Periferico Sur 3180 #1120
Jardines del Pedregal 01900, MEXICO

Castel, Nico (Opera Singer)
RPA Mgmt
4 Adelaide Ln
Washingtonville, NY 10992-1816, USA

Castellaneta, Dan (Actor, Musician, Writer)
c/o Arlene Forster *Forster-Delaney Entertainment*
12533 Woodgreen St
Los Angeles, CA 90066-2723, USA

Castellini, Clateo (Business Person)
Becton Dickinson Co
1 Becton Dr
Franklin Lakes, NJ 07417-1880, USA

Castelluccio, Frederico (Actor)
c/o Nicole Nassar *Nicole Nassar PR*
1111 10th St Unit 104
Santa Monica, CA 90403-5363, USA

Caster, Rich (Football Player)
New York Jets
41 Lincoln Ct
Rockville Centre, NY 11570-5744, USA

Casteres, Rick
4107 Starfish Ln
Tampa, FL 33615-5428, USA

Castete, Jesse (Football Player)
Chicago Bears
302 W Lee St
Sulphur, LA 70663-5440, USA

Castiglia, Jim (Baseball Player)
Philadelphia Athletics
5301 Westbard Cir Apt 313
Bethesda, MD 20816-1427, USA

Castiglione, Joe (Baseball Player, Sportscaster)
Boston Red Sox
100 King Phillips Pathe
Marshfield, MA 02050-5714, USA

Castiglione, Pete (Baseball Player)
Pittsburgh Pirates
1320 NE 26th Ter
Pompano Beach, FL 33062-3806, USA

Castilla, Vinny (Baseball Player)
Atlanta Braves
7680 Polo Ridge Dr
Littleton, CO 80128-2502, USA

Castille, Jeremiah (Football Player)
Tampa Bay Buccaneers
2904 Kirkcaldy Ln
Birmingham, AL 35242-4117, USA

Castillio, Susie (Actor, Beauty Pageant Winner)
c/o Vincent Cirrincione *Vincent Cirrincione Associates*
1516 N Fairfax Ave
Los Angeles, CA 90046-2608, USA

Castillo, Alberto (Baseball Player)
New York Mets
10059 Perfect Dr
Port Saint Lucie, FL 34986-3062, USA

Castillo, Bobby (Baseball Player)
Los Angeles Dodgers
316 Calle Amarillo SW
Albuquerque, NM 87121-9300, USA

Castillo, Frank (Baseball Player)
Chicago Cubs
9333 N 129th Pl
Scottsdale, AZ 85259-6231, USA

Castillo, Luis (Baseball Player)
Florida Marlins
1900 Purdy Ave Apt 1903
Miami Beach, FL 33139-1437, USA

Castillo, Marty (Baseball Player)
Detroit Tigers
2710 Del Prado Blvd S Apt 214
Cape Coral, FL 33904-5788, USA

Castillo, Patricio (Actor)
c/o Staff Member *Televisa*
Blvd Adolfo Lopez Mateos 232
Colonia San Angel INN
DF CP 01060, MEXICO

Castillo, Vinicio (Athlete, Baseball Player)
c/o Staff Member *Atlanta Braves*
PO Box 4064
Turner Field
Atlanta, GA 30302-4064, USA

Castillo Lara, Rosalio Jose Cardinal (Religious Leader)
Palazzo del Governatorato
00120, VATICAN CITY

Castino, John (Baseball Player)
Minnesota Twins
6290 Bluestem Rd S
Hamel, MN 55340-4546, USA

Castle, Don (Baseball Player)
Texas Rangers
24 Country Club Ln
Senatobia, MS 38668, USA

Castle, Eric (Football Player)
San Diego Chargers
41984 Cut Off Dr
Lebanon, OR 97355-9120, USA

Castle, Jo Ann (Musician)
Welk Resort Center
1984 State Highway 165
Branson, MO 65616-8936, USA

Castle, John (Actor)
Larry Dalzell
91 Regent St
London W1R 7TB, UNITED KINGDOM (UK)

Castle, Michael N (Governor)
300 S New St
Dover, DE 19904-6726, USA

Castle, Nick (Director)
Creative Artists Agency
9830 Wilshire Blvd
Beverly Hills, CA 90212-1804, USA

Castle-Hughes, Keisha (Actor)
Auckland Actors
PO Box 56460
Dominion Road
Auckland 1030, NEW ZEALAND

Castle of Blackbum, Barbara A (Government Official)
House of Lords
Westminster
London SW1A 0PW, UNITED KINGDOM (UK)

Castleman, Albert W Jr (Misc)
425 Hillcrest Ave
State College, PA 16803-3419, USA

Castleman, E Riva (Misc)
Museum of Modern Art
11 W 53rd St
New York, NY 10019-5497, USA

Castleman, Foster (Baseball Player)
New York Giants
8250 Graves Rd
Cincinnati, OH 45243-3633, USA

Castor, Chris (Football Player)
Seattle Seahawks
206 Connors Cir
Cary, NC 27511-6100, USA

Castrillon Hoyos, Dario Cardinal (Religious Leader)
Arzobispado
Calle 33 N 21-18
Bucaramanga
Santander, COLOMBIA

Castro, Bill (Baseball Player)
Milwaukee Brewers
5217 W Harvard Dr
Franklin, WI 53132-8192, USA

Castro, Cristian (Musician)
c/o Staff Member *BMG*
1540 Broadway
New York, NY 10036-4074, USA

Castro, Daniela (Actor)
c/o Staff Member *Televisa*
Blvd Adolfo Lopez Mateos 232
Colonia San Angel INN
DF CP 01060, MEXICO

Castro, Emilio (Religious Leader)
World Council of Churches
475 Riverside Dr
New York, NY 10115-0697, USA

Castro, Juan (Baseball Player)
Cincinnati Reds
19402 N 62nd Ave
Glendale, AZ 85308-7666, USA

Castro, Ramon (Baseball Player)
Florida Marlins
19801 E Country Club Dr Apt 602E
Miami, FL 33180-4811, USA

Castro, Raquel (Actor)
c/o Staff Member *Endeavor Agency LLC (LA)*
9601 Wilshire Blvd Fl 3
Beverly Hills, CA 90210-5204, USA

Castro, Raul H (Diplomat, Governor)
429 W Crawford St
Nogales, AZ 85621-2507, USA

Castro Ruz, Fidel (President)
Palacio del Gobierno
Plaza de Revolucion
Havana, CUBA

Castro Ruz, Raul (Prime Minister)
First Vice President's Office
Plaza de la Revolucion
Havana, CUBA

Castroneves, Helio (Race Car Driver)
3138 Commodore Plz Ste 307
Miami, FL 33133-5814, USA

Catalano, Eduardo F (Architect)
44 Grozier Rd
Cambridge, MA 02138-3315, USA

Catalanotto, Frank (Baseball Player)
Detroit Tigers
4 Muffins Mdws
Saint James, NY 11780-1233, USA

Catalino, Ken (Cartoonist, Editor)
Creators Syndicate
5777 W Century Blvd Ste 700
Los Angeles, CA 90045-9023, USA

Catalona, William J (Misc)
Washington University
Medical School
Urology Division
Saint Louis, MO 63110, USA

Catanho, Alcides (Football Player)
New England Patriots
931 Pennington St # 1
Elizabeth, NJ 07202-1584, USA

Catanzaro, Tony (Dancer)
3496 NW 7th St
Miami, FL 33125-4014, USA

Catchings, Harvey (Basketball Player)
Philadelphia 76ers
18034 Saint Emilion Ct
Spring, TX 77379-2808, USA

Catchings, Tamika (Athlete)
125 S Pennsylvania Ave
Indianapolis, IN 46204-3610, USA

Cater, Danny (Baseball Player)
Philadelphia Phillies
3268 Candlewood Trl
Plano, TX 75023-1320, USA

Cater, Greg (Football Player)
Buffalo Bills
19 Warwick Way SE
Rome, GA 30161-4058, USA

Cates, Dariene (Actor)
13340 Fm 740
Forney, TX 75126-6802, USA

Cates, Gilbert (Director, Producer)
Gilbert Cates Productions
10920 Wilshire Blvd # 600
Los Angeles, CA 90024-6502, USA

Cates, Phoebe (Actor)
1636 3rd Ave # 309
New York, NY 10128-3622, USA

Cathcard, Patti (Musician)
Windham Hill Records
PO Box 5501
Beverly Hills, CA 90209-5501, USA

Cathcart, Royal (Football Player)
San Francisco 49ers
4585 Green Tree Ln
Irvine, CA 92612-2239, USA

Cathcart, Sam (Football Player)
San Francisco 49ers
1127 Sunnyslope Ln
Santa Maria, CA 93455-3442, USA

Catledge, Terry (Basketball Player)
Philadelphia 76ers
4667 Market St
Tupelo, MS 38801-8432, USA

Catlett, Mary Jo (Actor)
4375 Farmdale Ave
Studio City, CA 91604-2737, USA

Catlett, Sid (Basketball Player)
Cincinnati Royals
3110 Scottish Ave
Suitland, MD 20746-3136, USA

Catlin, Thomas (Tom) (Coach, Football Player)
Cleveland Browns
22621 NE 25th Way
Redmond, WA 98074-6413, USA

Cato, Keefe (Baseball Player)
Cincinnati Reds
98 Maryton Rd
White Plains, NY 10603-2016, USA

Cato, Kelvin (Basketball Player)
Portland Trail Blazers
13607 Winter Creek Ct
Houston, TX 77077-1550, USA

Cato, Robert Milton (Prime Minister)
PO Box 138
Ratho Mill
SAINT VINCENT & GRENADINES

Caton, Jack Joseph (General)
17230 Citronia St
Northridge, CA 91325-1934, USA

Caton Jones, Michael (Director)
William Moris Agency
52/53 Poland Place
London W1F 7LX, UNITED KINGDOM
(UK)

Catrow, David (Cartoonist, Editor)
Springfield News-Sun
202 N Limestone St
Editorial Dept
Springfield, OH 45503-4246, USA

Cattage, Bobby (Basketball Player)
Utah Jazz
4838 US Highway 29 S
Auburn, AL 36830-8184, USA

Cattaneo, Peter (Director)
International Creative Mgmt
76 Oxford St
London W1N OAX, UNITED KINGDOM
(UK)

Cattell, Christine (Actor)
Epstein-Wyckoff
280 S Beverly Dr Ste 400
Beverly Hills, CA 90212-3904, USA

Cattermole, Paul (Actor)
c/o Staff Member *S Club 7*
9830 Wilshire Blvd
Creative Artists Agency Lcc (Caa-La)
Beverly Hills, CA 90212-1804, USA

Catto, Henry E Jr (Diplomat)
110 E Crockett St
San Antonio, TX 78205-2612, USA

Cattrail, Kim (Actor)
c/o Carol Bodie *International Creative
Management (ICM-LA)*
10250 Constellation Blvd
Los Angeles, CA 90067-6200, USA

Caubere, Philippe
10 passage du Charolais
Paris F-75012, FRANCE

Caudill, Bill (Baseball Player)
Chicago Cubs
11605 NE 41st St
Kirkland, WA 98033-8742, USA

Cauduro, Eugenia (Actor)
c/o Staff Member *Televisa*
Blvd Adolfo Lopez Mateos 232
Colonia San Angel INN
DF CP 01060, MEXICO

Cauffiel, Jessica (Actor)
c/o Trice Koopman *Koopman
Management*
PO Box 1317
Pacific Palisades, CA 90272-1317, USA

Caulfield, Emma (Actor)
c/o Ellen Drantch-Billet *James/Levy/
Jacobson Management*
3500 W Olive Ave Ste 1470
Burbank, CA 91505-5514, USA

Caulfield, Lore (Designer, Fashion
Designer)
2228 Cotner Ave
Los Angeles, CA 90064-1802, USA

Caulfield, Maxwell (Actor)
PO Box 56987
Sherman Oaks, CA 91413-1987, USA

Caulkins, Tracy
511 Oman St
Nashville, TN 37203-1234, USA

Cause in Effect
4707 N. Maiden
Chicago, IL 60640, USA

Causey, Wayne (Baseball Player)
Baltimore Orioles
2905 Paynter Dr
Ruston, LA 71270-5242, USA

Causwell, Duane (Basketball Player)
Sacramento Kings
3 Pierce Dr
Stony Point, NY 10980-3701, USA

Cauterize (Music Group)
c/o Staff Member *Wind-up Records*
72 Madison Ave Fl 8
New York, NY 10016-8731, USA

Cauthen, Stephen M (Steve) (Misc)
Cauthen Ranch
167 S Main St
Rfd Boone County
Walton, KY 41094, USA

Cauthen, Steve
167 S Main St
Walton, KY 41094, USA

Cava, Cassandra
911 N Kings Rd Apt 301
Los Angeles, CA 90069-6215, USA

Cavadini, Catherine (Cathy) (Actor)
c/o Staff Member *International Creative
Management (ICM-LA)*
10250 Constellation Blvd
Los Angeles, CA 90067-6200, USA

Cavaiani, Jon R (War Hero)
10956 Green St Unit 230
Columbia, CA 95310-9742, USA

Cavalera, Max (Musician)
Variety Artists
793 Higuera St Ste 6
San Luis Obispo, CA 93401-0500, USA

Cavalier, Carrie
3200 W Wyoming Ave
Burbank, CA 91505-1923, USA

Cavaliere, Felix (Composer, Musician)
Primo Productions
PO Box 253
Audubon, NJ 08106-0253, USA

Cavallari, Kristin (Reality TV Star)
c/o Staff Member *MTV Films*
5555 Melrose Ave
Modular Bldg #213
Los Angeles, CA 90038-3989, USA

Cavalli, Carmen (Football Player)
Oakland Raiders
6221 Madison Ct
Bensalem, PA 19020-1802, USA

Cavalli, Constanza (Actor)
c/o Gabriel Blanco *Gabriel Blanco
Iglesias (Mexico)*
Rio Balsas 35-32
Colonia Cuauhtemoc
DF 06500, MEXICO

Cavalli, Roberto (Designer, Fashion
Designer)
Via del Cantone 29
Osmannoro Sesto Florentino
Firenze 50019, ITALY

Cavanagh, Megan (Actor)
c/o Steven Levy *The Firm*
9465 Wilshire Blvd Fl 6
Beverly Hills, CA 90212-2605, USA

Cavanagh, Tom (Actor)
c/o Brian Swardstrom *Endeavor Agency
LLC (LA)*
9601 Wilshire Blvd Fl 3
Beverly Hills, CA 90210-5204, USA

Cavanaugh, Christine (Actor)
Allman
342 S Cochran Ave # 30
Los Angeles, CA 90036-3320, USA

Cavanaugh, Joe (Hockey Player)
25 Nathaniel Greene Dr
East Greenwich, RI 02818-2019, USA

Cavanaugh, Matthew A (Matt) (Football
Player)
New England Patriots
8 Barstad Ct
Lutherville Timonium, MD 21093-3501,
USA

Cavanaugh, Michael (Actor)
Ambrosio/Mortimer
165 W 46th St
New York, NY 10036-2501, USA

Cavanaugh, Page (Musician)
5442 Woodman Ave
Sherman Oaks, CA 91401-5831, USA

Cavaretta, Philip J (Phil) (Baseball Player)
Chicago Cubs
4637 Kellogg Dr SW
Lilburn, GA 30047-4407, USA

Cavazos, Lauro F (Secretary)
173 Annursnac Hill Rd
Concord, MA 01742-5402, USA

Cavazos, Lumi (Actor)
Visionary Entertainment
8265 W Sunset Blvd Ste 203
West Hollywood, CA 90046-2470, USA

Cave, Nick (Musician, Songwriter, Writer)
Billions Corp
833 W Chicago Ave Ste 101
Chicago, IL 60622-8408, USA

Caven, Ingrid
91 rue Faubourg St. Honore
Paris F-75008, FRANCE

Cavenall, Ron (Basketball Player)
New York Knicks
PO Box 450983
Houston, TX 77245-0983, USA

Caver, James (Football Player)
Detroit Lions
10722 Mersington Ave
Kansas City, MO 64137-1870, USA

Caver, Quinton (Football Player)
Philadelphia Eagles
PO Box 4371
Anniston, AL 36204-4371, USA

Cavett, Dick (Actor, Writer)
c/o Staff Member *Don Buchwald &
Associates Inc (LA)*
6500 Wilshire Blvd Ste 2200
Los Angeles, CA 90048-4942, USA

Cavic, Milorad (Mike) (Swimmer)
Cal Bears Athletics
Swimming
Haas Pavilion #4422
Berkeley, CA 94720-4422, USA

Caviezel, James (Jim) (Actor)
c/o Beverlee Dean *Beverlee Dean
Management*
8924 Clifton Way Apt 103
Beverly Hills, CA 90211-1779, USA

Cavill, Henry (Actor)
c/o Staff Member *Peters Fraser & Dunlop
(PFD - UK)*
Drury House
34-43 Russell St
London WC2B 5HA, UNITED KINGDOM
(UK)

Cavuto, Neil (Television Host)
c/o Staff Member *Fox News Channel (NY)*
1211 Avenue Of The Americas
Level C1
New York, NY 10036-8701, USA

Cawley, Tucker (Actor)
c/o Adam Berkowitz *Creative Artists
Agency LCC (CAA-LA)*
2000 Avenue Of The Stars
Los Angeles, CA 90067-4700, USA

Cawley, Warren (Rex) (Athlete, Track Athlete)
1655 San Rafael Dr
Corona, CA 92882-6410, USA

Cawley, Yvonne Goolagong
1360 E 9th St Ste 100
Cleveland, OH 44114-1730, USA

Caylor, Lowell (Football Player)
Cleveland Browns
403 Woodway Dr
Greer, SC 29651-6869, USA

Cazenove, Christopher (Actor)
32 Bolingbroke Grove
London SW11, UNITED KINGDOM (UK)

Ce Marco, Cardinal (Religious Leader)
S Marco 318
Venice 30124, ITALY

Ceasor, Curtis (Football Player)
New York Jets
4805 Corley St
Beaumont, TX 77707-4224, USA

Ceballos, Cedric (Basketball Player)
Phoenix Suns
1560 W Augusta Ave
Phoenix, AZ 85021-7099, USA

Ceberano, Kate (Musician)
Richard East Productions
Kildean Lane
Winchelsea, VIC 3241, AUSTRALIA

Ceccarelli, Art (Baseball Player)
Kansas City A's
63 Hall Dr
Orange, CT 06477-2545, USA

Ceccato, Aldo (Conductor)
Chaunt da Crusch
Zuoz 7524, SWITZERLAND

Cech, Thomas R (Nobel Prize Laureate)
PO Box 215
Boulder, CO 80309-0001, USA

Cechmanek, Roman (Hockey Player)
Los Angeles Kings
1111 S Figueroa St
Staples Center
Los Angeles, CA 90015-1300, USA

Cedano, Cesar (Baseball Player)
Houston Astros
2112 Marisol Loop
Kissimmee, FL 34743-3232, USA

Cedano, Roger (Baseball Player)
Los Angeles Dodgers
7004 Portmarnock Pl
Bradenton, FL 34202-2593, USA

Cedeno, Matt (Actor)
c/o Ryan Daly *Kazarian/Spencer & Assoc (LA)*
11969 Ventura Blvd
Box 7409 Fl 3
Studio City, CA 91604-2630, USA

Cedras, Raoul (General)
Continental Riande Hotel
Panama City, PANAMA

Cee-Lo (Artist, Musician)
William Morris Agency
1325 Avenue Of The Americas
New York, NY 10019-6091, USA

Cefalo, Jimmy (Football Player)
Miami Dolphins
6675 Roxbury Ln
Miami Beach, FL 33141-4532, USA

Ceglarski, Leonard (Len) (Coach, Hockey Player)
61 Lantern Ln
Duxbury, MA 02332-4915, USA

Celant, Gerwano (Misc)
Solomon Guggenheim Museum
1971 5th Ave
New York, NY 10128, USA

Celeda (Musician)
c/o Staff Member *Diva Central Inc*
7510 W Sunset Blvd Ste 1445
Los Angeles, CA 90046-3408, USA

Celi, Ari (Actor)
c/o Staff Member *SMS Talent Inc*
8730 W Sunset Blvd Ste 440
Los Angeles, CA 90069-2277, USA

Cellins, Art (Basketball Player)
Atlanta Hawks
4915 NW 15th Ct
Miami, FL 33142-4122, USA

Cellucci, A Paul (Diplomat, Governor)
State Department
2201 C St NW
Washington, DC 20520-0099, USA

Celmins, Vija (Artist)
49 Crosby St
New York, NY 10012-4464, USA

Celotto, Mario (Football Player)
Buffalo Bills
47 Evirel Pl
Oakland, CA 94611-1323, USA

Cena, John (Actor, Wrestler)
c/o Dan Baime *International Creative Management (ICM-LA)*
10250 Constellation Blvd
Los Angeles, CA 90067-6200, USA

Cenac, Winston Francis (Prime Minister)
7 High St
Box 629
Castries, SAINT LUCIA

Cenker, Robert J (Astronaut)
GORCA Inc
155 Hickory Corner Rd
East Windsor, NJ 08520-2417, USA

Cennamo, Ralph (Misc)
Leather Plastics & Novelty Workers Union
265 W 14th St
New York, NY 10011-7103, USA

Center, Pete (Baseball Player)
Cleveland Indians
PO Box 64
Campton, KY 41301-0064, USA

Centers, Larry (Football Player)
Phoenix Cardinals
1204 Strathmore Dr
Southlake, TX 76092-9519, USA

Cepeda, Angie (Actor)
c/o Katrina Bayonis *Kuranda Management Intl*
Santo Angel, 84
Madrid 28043, SPAIN

Cepeda, Oriando M (Baseball Player)
2305 Palmer Ct
Fairfield, CA 94534-7550, USA

Cepicky, Matt (Baseball Player)
Montreal Expos
201 Pinecrest Cir Apt D
Jupiter, FL 33458-7685, USA

Cepicky, Scott (Baseball Player)
Bowman
5957 Hitching Post Ln
Nashville, TN 37211-6933, USA

Cera, Michael
9 Sultan St. #200
Toronto, ON M5S 1, CANADA

Cerami, Anthony (Misc)
Ram Island Dr
Shelter Island, NY 11964, USA

Cerbone, Jason (Actor)
c/o Vera Mihailovich *Forward Entertainment*
9255 W Sunset Blvd Ste 805
Los Angeles, CA 90069-3305, USA

Cerda, Jalme (Baseball Player)
New York Mets
1308 Grove St
Selma, CA 93662-3705, USA

Ceresino, Gordy (Football Player)
San Francisco 49ers
PO Box 675515
Rancho Santa Fe, CA 92067-5515, USA

Cerezo, Arevalo M Vincio (President)
Partido Democracia Cristiana
Avda Elena 20-66
Guatemala City, GUATEMALA

Cerf, Vinton G (Scientist)
3614 Camelot Dr
Annandale, VA 22003-1302, USA

Cerha, Friedrich (Composer, Conductor)
Doblinger Music
Dorotheergasse 10
PO Box 882
Vienna 1011, AUSTRIA

Cerlan, Paul G (General)
3524 Old Course Ln
Valrico, FL 33596-9219, USA

Cernadas, Segundo (Actor)
c/o Staff Member *Telefe - Argentina*
Pavon 2444 (C1248AAT)
Buenos Aires, ARGENTINA

Cerne, Joseph (Football Player)
San Francisco 49ers
536 Valley West Ct
West Des Moines, IA 50265-3900, USA

Cerny, Jobe (Artist, Voice Over Artist)
259 Hazel Ave
Highland Park, IL 60035-3359, USA

Ceron, Laura (Actor)
c/o Michael Greenwald *Don Buchwald & Associates Inc (LA)*
6500 Wilshire Blvd Ste 2200
Los Angeles, CA 90048-4942, USA

Cerqua, Marq (Football Player)
Tampa Bay Buccaneers
14050 Biscayne Blvd Apt 906
North Miami Beach, FL 33181-1557, USA

Cerrone, Rick (Athlete)
100 Old Palisade Rd Apt 3509
Fort Lee, NJ 07024-7027, USA

Cerruda, Ron (Golfer)
c/o Staff Member *Pro Golfers Association (PGA) Tour*
112 Tpc Blvd
Ponte Vedra Beach, FL 32082, USA

Cerruti, Nino (Designer, Fashion Designer)
3 Place de la Madeleine
Paris 75008, FRANCE

Certo, Tish (Golfer)
1302 NW Bentley Cir Apt A
Port Saint Lucie, FL 34986-1867, USA

Cerv, Robert H (Bob) (Baseball Player)
New York Yankees
1620 Avenue M
Hawarden, IA 51023-1612, USA

Cervantes, Gary (Actor)
2240 Mardel Ave
Whittier, CA 90601-1532, USA

Cervenka, Exene (Musician)
Performers of the World
8901 Melrose Ave # 200
West Hollywood, CA 90069-5605, USA

Cerveris, Michael
465 S Detroit St Apt 403
Los Angeles, CA 90036-3560, USA

Cervi, Al (Basketball Player)
Buffalo Bisons
177 Dunrovin Ln
Rochester, NY 14618-4815, USA

Cervl, Valentina (Actor)
Artmedia
20 Ave Rapp
Paris 75007, FRANCE

Cesaire, Aime Ferdinand (Writer)
La Mairie
Fort-de-France
Martinique 97200, WEST INDIES

Cesarani, Sai (Designer, Fashion Designer)
SJC Concepts
40 E 80th St
New York, NY 10075-0230, USA

Cesare, Billy (Football Player)
Tampa Bay Buccaneers
1655 Hendry Isles Blvd
Clewiston, FL 33440-5825, USA

Cestaro, Alexander (Football Player)
New York Giants
289 Devoe Ave
Yonkers, NY 10705-2709, USA

Cetara, Pete
8900 Wilshire Blvd Ste 300
Beverly Hills, CA 90211-1959, USA

Cetera, Peter (Musician, Songwriter, Writer)
c/o Staff Member *Monterey Peninsula Artists (Chicago)*
200 W Superior St Ste 202
Chicago, IL 60610-3554, USA

Cetlinski, Matthew (Matt) (Swimmer)
13121 SE 93rd Terrace Rd
Summerfield, FL 34491-9347, USA

Ceulemans, Raymond
Mister 100
Grote Markt 28
Lier BE-2500, BELGIUM

Cey, Ron (Baseball Player)
Los Angeles Dodgers
22714 Creole Rd
Woodland Hills, CA 91364-3925, USA

Chabat, Alain (Actor)
c/o Staff Member *Endeavor Agency LLC (LA)*
9601 Wilshire Blvd Fl 3
Beverly Hills, CA 90210-5204, USA

Chaber, Madelyn J (Attorney, Attorney General, General)
101 California St
San Francisco, CA 94111-5802, USA

Chabert, Lacey (Actor)
c/o Aron Giannini *The Collective*
9100 Wilshire Blvd # 700 W
Beverly Hills, CA 90212-3401, USA

Chabon, Michael (Writer)
Random House
1745 Broadway # B1
New York, NY 10019-4305, USA

Chabot, Herbert L (Judge)
US Tax Court
400 2nd St NW
Washington, DC 20217-0002, USA

Chabraja, Nicholas D (Business Person)
General Dynamics
3190 Fairview Park Dr Ste 100
Falls Church, VA 22042-4545, USA

Chabria, Renee (Director)
c/o Staff Member *Management 360*
9111 Wilshire Blvd
Beverly Hills, CA 90210-5508, USA

Chabrol, Claude (Director, Producer)
VMA
40 Rue Francois 1er
Paris 75008, FRANCE

Chace, William E (Educator)
Emory University
Prisident's Office
Atlanta, GA 30322-0001, USA

Chacon, Alex Pineda (Soccer Player)
Los Angeles Galaxy
1010 Rose Bowl Dr
Pasadena, CA 91103, USA

Chacurian, Chico (Soccer Player)
96 Stratford Rd
Stratford, CT 06615-7760, USA

Chad & Jake
PO Box 1160
Whitney, TX 76692-1160, USA

Chadha, Gurinder (Director)
c/o Staff Member *International Creative Management (ICM-LA)*
10250 Constellation Blvd
Los Angeles, CA 90067-6200, USA

Chadirji, Rifat Kamil (Architect)
28 Troy Court
Kensington High St
London W8, UNITED KINGDOM (UK)

Chadli, Bendjedid (President)
Palace Emir Abedelkader
Algiers, ALGERIA

Chadnois, Lynn (Football Player)
Pittsburgh Steelers
2048 Walden Ct
Flint, MI 48532-2419, USA

Chadwick, J Leslie (Les) (Musician)
Barry Collins
21A Cliftown Road
Southend-on-Sea
Essex SS1 1AB, UNITED KINGDOM (UK)

Chadwick, June (Actor)
Contemporary Artists
610 Santa Monica Blvd Ste 202
Santa Monica, CA 90401-1645, USA

Chadwick, Ray (Baseball Player)
California Angels
607 Gattis St
Durham, NC 27701-2831, USA

Chadwick, William L (Bill) (Misc)
PO Box 501
Country Club Dr
Cutchogue, NY 11935-0501, USA

Chafetz, Sidney (Artist)
Ohio State University
Art Dept
Columbus, OH 43210, USA

Chaffee, Don (Director)
7020 La Presa Dr
Los Angeles, CA 90068-3105, USA

Chaffee, Susan (Suzy) (Skier)
5106 E Woodwind Ln
Anaheim, CA 92807-1239, USA

Chaffey, Pat (Football Player)
Atlanta Falcons
10415 SW Gardner Ct
Tualatin, OR 97062-7208, USA

Chafin, Brian
4107 Medical Pkwy Ste 210
Austin, TX 78756-3738, USA

Chaiken, Ilene (Producer, Writer)
c/o Cori Wellins *William Morris Agency (WMA-LA)*
1 William Morris Pl
Beverly Hills, CA 90212-4261, USA

Chailly, Riccardo (Conductor)
Royal Concertgebrew
Jacob Obrechtstraat 51
Armsterdam, 1071 KJ 41, THE NETHERLANDS

Chairmen of the Board
11320 Pine Valley Club Dr
Charlotte, NC 28277-4051, USA

Chakales, Bob (Baseball Player)
Cleveland Indians
8916 River Rd
Richmond, VA 23229-7718, USA

Chakiris, George (Actor, Dancer, Musician)
7266 Clinton St
Los Angeles, CA 90036-1969, USA

Chakraborty, Pramod (Bollywood, Director, Filmmaker, Producer)
Natraj Studios 194 M V Road
Andheri (E)
Bombay, MS 400 069, INDIA

Chakravarthi, Vinu (Actor, Bollywood)
63 Apusali Street
Chennai, TN 600093, INDIA

Chakravarthy, Dheephan (Actor)
Auroammaa 5/17 Royal Villa 4th Main Road Extn
Kottur Gardens
Chennai, TN 600 085, INDIA

Chalayan, Hussein (Designer, Fashion Designer)
71 Endell Road
London WC2 9AJ, UNITED KINGDOM (UK)

Chalenski, Mike (Football Player)
Philadelphia Eagles
225 S Michigan Ave
Kenilworth, NJ 07033-1727, USA

Chalfont, A G (Arthur) (Government Official)
House of Lords
Westminster
London SW1A 0PW, UNITED KINGDOM (UK)

Chalk, Dave (Baseball Player)
California Angels
137 Cross Timbers Trl
Coppell, TX 75019-3731, USA

Chalke, Sarah (Actor)
c/o John Carrabino *John Carrabino Management*
5900 Wilshire Blvd Ste 406
Los Angeles, CA 90036-5015, USA

Chalker, Will (Model)
c/o Staff Member *New York Model Management*
596 Broadway # 701
New York, NY 10012-3210, USA

Challis, Christopher
18 Middle Roy
London, ENGLAND W10 5AT, UNITED KINGDOM (UK)

Chalmers, Judith
23 Eyot Gardens
London, ENGLAND W10 5AT, UNITED KINGDOM (UK)

Chaloner, William G (Misc)
20 Parke Road
London SW13 9NG, UNITED KINGDOM (UK)

Chamberlain, Bill (Basketball Player)
Kentucky Coloneis
1527 Terrace Cir Apt B
Laurinburg, NC 28352-6002, USA

Chamberlain, Byron (Football Player)
Denver Broncos
7777 E Yale Ave Apt N 108
Denver, CO 80231-6055, USA

Chamberlain, Craig (Baseball Player)
Kansas City Royals
PO Box 473
Surfside, CA 90743-0473, USA

Chamberlain, Dan (Football Player)
Buffalo Bills
6356 Puerto Dr
Rancho Murieta, CA 95683-9357, USA

Chamberlain, Jimmy (Musician)
Creative Artists Agency
9830 Wilshire Blvd
Beverly Hills, CA 90212-1804, USA

Chamberlain, John A (Artist)
Ten Coconut Inc
1315 10th St
Sarasota, FL 34236-3302, USA

Chamberlain, Owen (Nobel Prize Laureate)
882 Santa Barbara Rd
Berkeley, CA 94707-2018, USA

Chamberlain, Richard (Actor)
Panacea Entertainment
13587 Andalusia Dr
C/O Eric Gardner
Santa Rosa Valley, CA 93012-9226, USA

Chamberlain, Wes (Baseball Player)
Philadelphia Phillies
PO Box 1358
Homewood, IL 60430-0358, USA

Chambers, Al (Baseball Player)
Seattle Mariners
1303 N 14th St
Harrisburg, PA 17103-1206, USA

Chambers, Anne Cox (Business Person, Diplomat)
Cox Enterprises
1440 Lake Hearn Dr NE
Atlanta, GA 30319, USA

Chambers, Christina (Actor)
c/o Lena Roklin *Roklin Management*
8530 Wilshire Blvd Ste 550
Beverly Hills, CA 90211-3133, USA

Chambers, Cliff (Baseball Player)
Chicago Cubs
749 N Eagle Rd
Eagle, ID 83616-6909, USA

Chambers, Emma (Actor)
c/o Staff Member *Conway Van Gelder Ltd*
18-21 Jermyn St Fl 3
London SW1Y 6HP, UNITED KINGDOM (UK)

Chambers, Erin (Actor)
c/o Ted Schachter *Schachter Entertainment*
1157 S Beverly Dr Fl 2
Los Angeles, CA 90035-1119, USA

Chambers, Faune (Actor)
c/o Mara Santino *Kazarian/Spencer & Assoc (LA)*
11969 Ventura Blvd
Box 7409 Fl 3
Studio City, CA 91604-2630, USA

Chambers, Faune (Actor)
c/o Staff Member *Roklin Management*
8530 Wilshire Blvd Ste 550
Beverly Hills, CA 90211-3133, USA

Chambers, Jerry (Basketball Player)
Los Angeles Lakers
4135 Don Diablo Dr
Los Angeles, CA 90008-4305, USA

Chambers, John
433 S Fairview St
Burbank, CA 91505-4713, USA

Chambers, Justin (Actor)
c/o Sandra Chang *Industry Entertainment*
955 Carrillo Dr Ste 300
Los Angeles, CA 90048-5400, USA

Chambers, Kasey (Musician)
c/o Staff Member *Paradigm (Monterey)*
509 Hartnell St
Monterey, CA 93940-2825, USA

Chambers, Lester (Musician)
Lustig Talent
PO Box 770850
Orlando, FL 32877-0850, USA

Chambers, Marilyn (Actor, Adult Film Star)
Five K Sales
1122 White Rock Dr
Dixon, IL 61021-9049, USA

Chambers, Rebecca (Actor)
Writers & Artists
360 N Crescent Dr Bldg North
Beverly Hills, CA 90210-6818, USA

Chambers, Tom (Basketball Player)
San Diego Clippers
153 E 2550 N
Ogden, UT 84414, USA

Chambers, Wallace (Wally) (Football Player)
Chicago Bears
1838 Joslin St
Saginaw, MI 48602-1123, USA

Chambers, Willie (Musician)
Noga Mgmt
PO Box 1428
Studio City, CA 91614-0428, USA

Chambers Brothers, The
1601 S Rainbow Blvd Ste 210
Las Vegas, NV 89146-0030, USA

Chamblee, Al (Football Player)
Tampa Bay Buccaneers
845 Garrow Rd
Newport News, VA 23608-3387, USA

Chamblee, Brandel (Golfer)
10800 E Cactus Rd Unit 32
Scottsdale, AZ 85259-2505, USA

Chamblee, Jim (Baseball Player)
Cincinnati Reds
1408 Broadway St
Denton, TX 76201-2714, USA

Chambon, Pierre H (Misc)
Institute Genetique Moleculaire/Cellulaire
BP 163
Illkirch 67404, FRANCE

Champagne, Ed (Football Player)
Los Angeles Rams
7320 Old Hundred Rd
Raleigh, NC 27613-3529, USA

Champion, Billy (Baseball Player)
Philadelphia Phillies
240 Triple H Farm Rd
Inman, SC 29349, USA

Champion, Marge (Actor, Dancer)
484 W 43rd St
New York, NY 10036-6319, USA

Champion, Mike (Baseball Player)
San Diego Padres
28952 Modjeska Canyon Rd
Silverado, CA 92676-9779, USA

Champion, Will (Musician)
Nettwerk Mgmt
1650 W 2nd Ave
Vancouver, BC V6J 4R3, CANADA

Champlin, Charles (Critic)
2169 Linda Flora Dr
Los Angeles, CA 90077-1408, USA

Chan, Ernie (Cartoonist)
4131 Vale Ave
Oakland, CA 94619-2223, USA

Chan, Jackie (Actor)
c/o Fred Specktor *Creative Artists Agency LCC (CAA-LA)*
2000 Avenue Of The Stars
Los Angeles, CA 90067-4700, USA

Chan, Johnny (Misc)
PO Box 3247
C/O Mark Karowe
Manhattan Beach, CA 90266-1247, USA

Chan, Jullus (Prime Minister)
PO Box 6030
Boroto
PAPUA NEW GUINEA

Chan, Sy (Misc)
Premier's Office
Phnorn-Penh
PEOPLE'S REPUBLIC OF KAMPUCHEA

Chance, Bob (Baseball Player)
Cleveland Indians
2258 Oakridge Dr
Charleston, WV 25311-1723, USA

Chance, Britton (Misc, Yachtsman)
4014 Pine St
Philadelphia, PA 19104-4132, USA

Chance, Dean (Baseball Player)
Los Angeles Angels
9505 W Smithville Western Rd
Wooster, OH 44691-9209, USA

Chance, Jeff
PO Box 2977
Hendersonville, TN 37077-2977, USA

Chance, Larry (Musician)
Brothers Mgmt
141 Dunbar Ave
Fords, NJ 08863-1551, USA

Chancellor, Van (Coach)
Houston Comets
2 Greenway Plz Ste 400
Houston, TX 77046-0202, USA

Chancey, Robert (Football Player)
San Diego Chargers
5780 Airport Rd
Coosada, AL 36020-3022, USA

Chandler, Al (Football Player)
Cincinnati Bengals
PO Box 21733
Oklahoma City, OK 73156-1733, USA

Chandler, Christopher M (Chris) (Football Player)
2529 12th Ave W
Seattle, WA 98119-2116, USA

Chandler, Colby H (Business Person)
Ford Motor Co
American Road
Dearborn, MI 48126, USA

Chandler, Donald G (Don) (Football Player)
New York Giants
3248 E 93rd St
Tulsa, OK 74137-3639, USA

Chandler, Gene (Football Player)
New York Yankees
550 Southmoor Cir
Stockbridge, GA 30281-4974, USA

Chandler, Gene (Musician)
Entertainment Consultants
1207 Penshurst Ct
Abingdon, MD 21009-1268, USA

Chandler, Jeff (Boxer)
6242 Horner St
Philadelphia, PA 19144, USA

Chandler, John (Baseball Player)
New York Black Yankees
5108 US Highway 220 N
Summerfield, NC 27358-9762, USA

Chandler, Karl (Football Player)
New York Giants
5 Plymouth Rd
Newtown Square, PA 19073-1409, USA

Chandler, Kyle (Actor)
c/o Leslie Siebert *Gersh Agency, The (LA)*
232 N Canon Dr
Beverly Hills, CA 90210-5302, USA

Chandler, Thornton (Football Player)
Dallas Cowboys
8646 Guinevere St
Houston, TX 77029-3357, USA

Chandler, Tyson (Basketball Player)
59 English Turn Dr
New Orleans, LA 70131-3308, USA

Chandler, Wesley S (Wes) (Football Player)
New Orleans Saints
207 Howard Ave
New Smyrna Beach, FL 32168-8195, USA

Chandola, Walter (Photographer)
50 Spring Hill Rd
Annandale, NJ 08801-3505, USA

Chandra, Asha (Actor, Bollywood)
C6/6 Sangeeta Apartments
Juhu Santacruz
Mumbai, MS 400049, INDIA

Chandran, S S (Actor)
34A Asumpon Muthuramalingum Street
Rajaji Colony
Chennai, TN 600 092, INDIA

Chandran, Sudha (Actor, Bollywood)
4, Mahant Road Extension 6141250
Vile Parkel (E)
Mumbai, MS 400057, INDIA

Chandran, T K S (Actor)
D25 Amutham Colony
South Boag Road
Chennai, TN 600 017, INDIA

Chandrasekar (Actor)
34 Senthil Nagar Main Road Chinna
Porur
Near Valasaravakkam
Chennai, TN 600 116, INDIA

Chandrasekhar, Bhagwat S (Cricketer)
571 31st Cross
4th Block Jayanagar
Bangalore 56011, INDIA

Chandrasekhar, Jay (Comedian)
c/o Staff Member *United Talent Agency (UTA)*
9560 Wilshire Blvd Ste 500
Beverly Hills, CA 90212-2401, USA

Chanel, Patrice
12001 Ventura Blvd # 331
Studio City, CA 91604, USA

Chanel, Tally (Actor, Model)
Don Gerler
3349 Cahuenga Blvd W Ste 1
Los Angeles, CA 90068-1379, USA

Chaney, Darrel (Baseball Player)
Cincinnati Reds
906 Woodbrier
Saute Nacoche, GA 30571-5106, USA

Chaney, Don (Basketball Player)
Boston Celtics
20711 Park Pine Dr
Katy, TX 77450-2811, USA

Chaney, John (Basketball Player)
Syracuse Nationals
1639 Sharp Rd
Baton Rouge, LA 70815-4879, USA

Chaney, John (Coach)
Temple University
Athletic Dept
Philadelphia, PA 19122, USA

Chang, Christina (Actor)
c/o Staff Member *TalentWorks (LA)*
3500 W Olive Ave Ste 1400
Burbank, CA 91505-5512, USA

Chang, Chun-hsiung (Prime Minister)
Premier's Office
1 Chunghsiao East Road
Section 1
Taipei, TAIWAN

Chang, Jeannette (Publisher)
Harper's Bazaar Magazine
1700 Broadway
New York, NY 10019-5905, USA

Chang, Michael (Tennis Player)
PO Box 6080
Mission Viejo, CA 92690-6080, USA

Chang, Sarah (Musician)
I C M Artists
40 W 57th St
New York, NY 10019-4001, USA

Chang-Diaz, Franklin R (Astronaut)
NASA
2101 Nasa Pkwy
Johnson Space Center
Houston, TX 77058-3691, USA

Channing, Carol (Actor, Musician)
c/o Staff Member *William Morris Agency (WMA-LA)*
1 William Morris Pl
Beverly Hills, CA 90212-4261, USA

Channing, Stockard (Actor)
c/o Barbara Gale *Envoy Entertainment*
3656 Dellvale Pl
Encino, CA 91436-4144, USA

Chant, Charlie (Baseball Player)
Oakland A's
7831 Sycamore Ave
Riverside, CA 92504-2632, USA

Chantels, The (Music Group)
c/o Staff Member *Creative Entertainment Associates Inc*
6 Esterbrook Ln
Cherry Hill, NJ 08003-4002, USA

Chanticleer (Musician)
c/o Staff Member *International Creative Management (ICM-LA)*
10250 Constellation Blvd
Los Angeles, CA 90067-6200, USA

Chantres, Carlos (Baseball Player)
67 Amherst St
Nashua, NH 03064-2561, USA

Chao, Elaine L (Secretary)
Labor Department
200 Constitution Ave NW
Washington, DC 20216-0002, USA

Chao, Rosalind (Actor)
Don Buchwald
6500 Wilshire Blvd Ste 2200
Los Angeles, CA 90048-4942, USA

Chao, Vic (Actor)
c/o Staff Member *Osbrink Talent Agency*
4343 Lankershim Blvd # 100
North Hollywood, CA 91602-2705, USA

Chapelle, Dave (Actor)
c/o Matthew (Matt) Labov *BWR (BWR-LA)*
9100 Wilshire Blvd Fl 6
West Tower
Beverly Hills, CA 90212-3401, USA

Chapin, Darrin (Baseball Player)
New York Yankees
328 Portage Easterly Rd
Cortland, OH 44410-9510, USA

Chapin, Doug
9911 W Pico Blvd Ph 1
Los Angeles, CA 90035-2703, USA

Chapin, Dwight L (Government Official, Publisher)
San Francisco Examiner
110 5th St
San Francisco, CA 94103-2972, USA

Chapin, Lauren (Actor)
11940 Reedy Creek Dr Apt 207
Orlando, FL 32836-6834, USA

Chapin, Miles
9200 W Sunset Blvd Ste 1130
Los Angeles, CA 90069-3606, USA

Chapin, Schuyler G (Misc)
650 Park Ave
New York, NY 10065-6115, USA

Chapin, Tom (Musician, Songwriter, Writer)
57 Piermont Pl
Piermont, NY 10968-1128, USA

Chaplin, Alexander (Actor)
c/o Tammy Rosen *Melanie Greene Management & Productions*
425 N Robertson Blvd
West Hollywood, CA 90048-1735, USA

Chaplin, Ben (Actor)
London Mgmt
2-4 Noel St
London W1V 3RB, UNITED KINGDOM (UK)

Chaplin, Brit (Actor)
345 N Maple Dr Ste 300
Beverly Hills, CA 90210-6116, USA

Chaplin, Geraldine (Actor, Writer)
c/o Staff Member *William Morris Agency (WMA-LA)*
1 William Morris Pl
Beverly Hills, CA 90212-4261, USA

Chaplin, Greg (Baseball Player)
Anaheim Angels
12426 Glenfield Ave
Tampa, FL 33626-2606, USA

Chaplin, Josephine
10 av. George V.
Paris F-75008, FRANCE

Chaplin, Kiera (Actor, Producer)
c/o Staff Member *Creative Artists Agency LCC (CAA-LA)*
2000 Avenue Of The Stars
Los Angeles, CA 90067-4700, USA

Chapman, Alvah H Jr (Publisher)
Grove Harbour
1690 S Bayshore Ln Apt 10A
Miami, FL 33133-4067, USA

Chapman, Beth Nielsen (Musician, Songwriter, Writer)
Sussman Assoc
1222 16th Ave S Fl 3
Nashville, TN 37212-2926, USA

Chapman, Bruce K (Government Official)
Discovery Institute
1201 3rd Ave # 4000
Seattle, WA 98101-3029, USA

Chapman, Clarence (Football Player)
New Orleans Saints
14820 Parkside St
Detroit, MI 48238-2155, USA

Chapman, David S (Football Player)
New England Patriots
789 N Main St
New Martinsville, WV 26155-1414, USA

Chapman, Doug (Football Player)
Minnesota Vikings
6215 Chesterfield Meadows Dr
Chesterfield, VA 23832-6597, USA

Chapman, Dr Philip K (Astronaut)
416 Ives Ter
Sunnyvale, CA 94087-1944, USA

Chapman, Duane (Dog) (Actor, Reality TV Star)
c/o Staff Member *Dog the Bounty Hunter*
235 E 45th St
New York, NY 10017-3305, USA

Chapman, Gil (Football Player)
New Orleans Saints
771 Cranford Ave
Westfield, NJ 07090-1308, USA

Chapman, Judith (Actor)
11670 W Sunset Blvd Apt 312
Los Angeles, CA 90049-2069, USA

Chapman, Kelvin (Baseball Player)
New York Mets
9301 Laughlin Way
Redwood Valley, CA 95470-6425, USA

Chapman, Kevin (Actor)
c/o Ellen Meyer *Ellen Meyer Entertainment*
8899 Beverly Blvd Ste 612
Los Angeles, CA 90048-2429, USA

Chapman, Lanel (Actor)
Susan Smith
1344 N Wetherly Dr
Los Angeles, CA 90069-1817, USA

Chapman, Leland (Actor, Reality TV Star)
c/o Staff Member *Dog the Bounty Hunter*
235 E 45th St
New York, NY 10017-3305, USA

Chapman, Mark David
#81 A 3860 Box 149
Attica Corr. Facility
Attica, NY 14011, USA

Chapman, Max C Jr (Financier)
Normura Securities
2 World Financial Ctr
200 Liberty St
New York, NY 10281-1705, USA

Chapman, Michael J (Cinematographer, Director)
501 S Beverly Dr # 300
Beverly Hills, CA 90212-4562, USA

Chapman, Mike (Football Player)
Atlanta Falcons
8731 Avator Cir
Boerne, TX 78015-4424, USA

Chapman, Nicki (Actor)
c/o Staff Member *Pop Idol (Fremantle Media)*
2700 Colorado Ave Ste 450
Santa Monica, CA 90404-3599, USA

Chapman, Paul
63 Oakwood Rd.
London, ENGLAND NW11 6RJ, UNITED KINGDOM (UK)

Chapman, Rex (Basketball Player)
Charlotte Hornets
6014 E Jenan Dr
Scottsdale, AZ 85254-4907, USA

Chapman, Robert F (Judge)
PO Box 253
Linville, NC 28646-0253, USA

Chapman, Samuel B (Sam) (Baseball Player)
Philadelphia Athletics
PO Box 688
Kentfield, CA 94914-0688, USA

Chapman, Steven Curtis (Musician, Songwriter, Writer)
c/o Sparrow Records
PO Box 5010
Brentwood, TN 37024-5010, USA

Chapman, Thomas F (Business Person)
Equifax Inc
1550 Peachtree St NE
Atlanta, GA 30309-2468, USA

Chapman, Tracy (Musician, Songwriter, Writer)
c/o Steven Jensen *The Independent Group LLC*
947 N La Cienega Blvd Ste G
Los Angeles, CA 90069-4700, USA

Chapman, Travis (Baseball Player)
Philadelphia Phillies
5215 Hickson Rd
Jacksonville, FL 32207-5856, USA

Chapman, Wayne (Basketball Player)
Kentucky Coloneis
3593 Salisbury Dr
Lexington, KY 40510-9742, USA

Chapman, Wes (Ballerina)
American Ballet Theater
890 Broadway
New York, NY 10003-1278, USA

Chapot, Frank (Horse Racer)
1 Ople Road
Neshanic Station, NJ 08853, USA

Chapoy, Pati (Actor)
c/o Staff Member *TV Azteca*
Periferico Sur 4121
Colonia Fuentes del Pedregal
DF CP 14141, MEXICO

Chappas, Harry (Baseball Player)
Chicago White Sox
22 SE 1st Ave
Dania, FL 33004-3611, USA

Chappell, Crystal (Actor)
235 Newport Ave
Grover Beach, CA 93433-1512, USA

Chappell, Fred D (Writer)
305 Kensington Rd
Greensboro, NC 27403-1732, USA

Chappell, Gregory S (Greg) (Cricketer)
S A Cricket Assn
Andelaide Oval
North Adelaide, SA 5006, AUSTRALIA

Chappell, Len (Basketball Player)
Syracuse Nationals
7624 Chestnut Ln
Waterford, WI 53185-1707, USA

Chappelle, Dave (Actor)
c/o Staff Member *Gersh Agency, The (LA)*
232 N Canon Dr
Beverly Hills, CA 90210-5302, USA

Chappelle, David (Actor, Comedian)
Creative Artists Agency
9830 Wilshire Blvd
Beverly Hills, CA 90212-1804, USA

Chapple, Dave (Football Player)
Buffalo Bills
5 Kara E
Irvine, CA 92620-1855, USA

Chappuis, Bob (Football Player)
Brooklyn Dodgers
4054 Glacier Hills Cir
Ann Arbor, MI 48105-3646, USA

Chapuisat, Stephane (Soccer Player)
Borussia Dortmund Soccer Club
Strobeialle
Dortmund 44139, GERMANY

Chapura, Richard (Football Player)
Chicago Bears
1835 Caribbean Dr
Sarasota, FL 34231-5411, USA

Charan, Raaj N (Actor)
Shri Renuka Mandir 154
Vasudevan Nagar Jaffarkhanpet
Chennai, TN 600 095, INDIA

Charboneau, Joe (Baseball Player)
22700 Shore Center Dr
Cleveland, OH 44123-1637, USA

Charbonneau, Patricia (Actor)
749 1/2 N La Fayette Park Pl
Los Angeles, CA 90026-6559, USA

Charette, William R (Doc) (War Hero)
5237 Limberlost Ln
Lake Wales, FL 33898-8866, USA

Charisse, Cyd (Actor, Dancer)
PO Box 1029
Frazier Park, CA 93225-1029, USA

Charland, Colin (Baseball Player)
Fleer
5303 Alta Vista Ln
Arlington, TX 76017-1735, USA

Charlap, Bill (Musician)
Abby Hoffer
223 1/2 E 48th St
New York, NY 10017, USA

Charles, Bob (Golfer)
5329 Sea Biscuit Rd
Palm Beach Gardens, FL 33418-7818, USA

Charles, Bradley (Basketball Player)
Boston Celtics
10086 Wyecliff Dr
Littleton, CO 80126-4563, USA

Charles, Caroline (Designer, Fashion Designer)
56/57 Beauchamp Place
London SW3, UNITED KINGDOM (UK)

Charles, Craig (Actor)
PFD
Drury House
34-43 Russell St
London WC2B 5HA, UNITED KINGDOM (UK)

Charles, Daedra (Basketball Player)
Los Angeles Sparks
111 S Figueroa St
Staples Center
Los Angeles, CA 90012, USA

Charles, Ed (Baseball Player)
Kansas City A's
57 Park Ter E Apt B58
New York, NY 10034-1449, USA

Charles, Gaius (Actor)
c/o Stephen Hirsh *Gersh Agency, The (LA)*
232 N Canon Dr
Beverly Hills, CA 90210-5302, USA

Charles, John (Football Player)
Boston Patriots
5644 Westheimer Rd # 164
Houston, TX 77056-4002, USA

Charles, Josh (Actor)
International Creative Mgmt
8942 Wilshire Blvd # 219
Beverly Hills, CA 90211-1908, USA

Charles, Ken (Basketball Player)
Buffalo Bisons
621 Putnam Ava
Brooklyn, NY 11221, USA

Charles, Lorenzo (Basketball Player)
Atlanta Hawks
1460 Pennsylvania Ave Apt 7B
Brooklyn, NY 11239-2503, USA

Charles, Nick (Sportscaster)
Cable News Network
1050 Techwood Dr NW
News Dept
Atlanta, GA 30318-5604, USA

Charles, Prince (Prince, Royalty)
Clarence House
Stable Tard Gate
London SW1, UNITED KINGDOM (UK)

Charles, Suzette
2705 Cricket Hollow Ct
Hendersonville, NV 89014, USA

Charleson, Leslie (Actor)
4851 Cromwell Ave
Los Angeles, CA 90027-1141, USA

Charlesworth, James H (Misc)
Princeton Theological Seminary
Theology Dept
Princeton, NJ 08540, USA

Charlton, Janet
7560 Hollywood Blvd Apt 310
Los Angeles, CA 90046-2863, USA

Charlton, Norm (Baseball Player)
Cincinnati Reds
312 Estes Dr
Rockport, TX 78382-9758, USA

Charlton, Robert (Bobby) (Soccer Player)
Garthollerton
Cleford Road
Ollerton near Knutsford, Cheshire,
UNITED KINGDOM (UK)

Charmila (Actor, Bollywood)
27/1 Habibullah Road
T Nagar
Chennai, TN 600017, INDIA

Charmoli, Tony (Choreographer, Director)
1271 Sunset Plaza Dr
Los Angeles, CA 90069-1256, USA

Charney, Jordan (Actor)
Epstein-Wyckoff
280 S Beverly Dr Ste 400
Beverly Hills, CA 90212-3904, USA

Charo (Musician)
c/o Staff Member *William Morris Agency (WMA-LA)*
1 William Morris Pl
Beverly Hills, CA 90212-4261, USA

Charpak, Georges (Nobel Prize Laureate)
2 Rue de Poissy
Paris 75005, FRANCE

Charren, Peggy (Activist)
Action for Children's Television
PO Box 383090
Cambridge, MA 02238, USA

Charron, Paul R (Business Person)
Liz Claiborne Inc
1441 Broadway
New York, NY 10018-2088, USA

Chartoff, Melanie (Actor)
Artists Agency
1180 S Beverly Dr Ste 301
Los Angeles, CA 90035-1154, USA

Chartoff, Robert (Producer)
PO Box 3628
Granada Hills, CA 91394-0628, USA

Charton, Pete (Baseball Player)
Boston Red Sox
27 Vincinda Ln
Harriman, TN 37748-3014, USA

Charuhasan (Actor)
37 Maharani Chinnamani Road
Chennai, TN 600 018, INDIA

Charvet, David (Actor)
510 18th Ave
Honolulu, HI 96816-4442, USA

Charyk, Joseph V (Business Person)
790 Andrews Ave Apt A302
Delray Beach, FL 33483-7257, USA

Chase, Alison (Director)
Pilolobus Dance Theater
PO Box 388
Washington Depot, CT 06794-0388, USA

Chase, Alston (Writer)
c/o Deborah Clarke Grosvenor *The Bohrman Agency*
8899 Beverly Blvd Ste 811
Los Angeles, CA 90048-2452, USA

Chase, Bailey (Actor)
c/o Staff Member *Don Buchwald & Associates Inc (LA)*
6500 Wilshire Blvd Ste 2200
Los Angeles, CA 90048-4942, USA

Chase, Barrie (Actor, Dancer)
446 Carroll Canal
Venice, CA 90291-4682, USA

Chase, Chevy (Actor, Comedian, Producer, Writer)
c/o Staff Member *Innovative Artists (NY)*
235 Park Ave S Fl 7
New York, NY 10003-1405, USA

Chase, Daveigh (Actor)
c/o Susan Curtis *Curtis Talent Management*
9607 Arby Dr
Beverly Hills, CA 90210-1202, USA

Chase, David (Producer)
c/o Staff Member *United Talent Agency (UTA)*
9560 Wilshire Blvd Ste 500
Beverly Hills, CA 90212-2401, USA

Chase, Hayley (Actor)
c/o Staff Member *Bobby Ball Talent Agency*
4605 Lankershim Blvd Ste 721
North Hollywood, CA 91602-1878, USA

Chase, John (Hockey Player)
170 Broadway Rm 609
New York, NY 10038-4462, USA

Chase, Lorraine
68 Old Brompton Rd.
London, ENGLAND SW7, UNITED KINGDOM (UK)

Chase, Sylvia B (Correspondent)
ABC-TV
77 W 66th St
News Dept
New York, NY 10023-6201, USA

Chasez, Joshua Scott (JC) (Musician)
Podwall Entertainment
10635 Santa Monica Blvd Ste 340
Los Angeles, CA 90025-8316, USA

Chass, Murray (Writer)
New York Times
229 W 43rd St
Editorial Dept
New York, NY 10036-3959, USA

Chast, Roz (Comedian)
New Yorker Magazine
4 Times Sq
Editorial Dept
New York, NY 10036-6592, USA

Chastain, Brandi (Model, Soccer Player)
1661 University Way
San Jose, CA 95126-1555, USA

Chastel, Andre (Writer)
30 Rue de Lubeck
Paris 75116, FRANCE

Chatham, Russell (Artist)
Deep Creek
General Delivery
Livingston, MT 59047-9999, USA

Chatman, Charles (Baseball Player)
Detroit Clowns
2024 Clarksdale Ave
Memphis, TN 38108-1313, USA

Chatterjee, Moushumi (Actor, Bollywood)
Nibbana annexe 1st Floor
Pali Hill Bandra
Bombay, MS 400 050, INDIA

Chatterji, Basu (Actor, Bollywood, Director, Filmmaker)
Violete Villa 1st Floor West Avenue
Santacruz
Mumbai, MS 400054, INDIA

Chatwin, Justin (Actor)
c/o Lainie Sorkin Stolhanske *Management 360*
9111 Wilshire Blvd
Beverly Hills, CA 90210-5508, USA

Chaudhari, Mahima (Actor)
D5 4th Floor Silver View
Versova Andheri
Bombay, MS 400 061, INDIA

Chauvire, Yvette (Ballerina)
21 Place du Commerce
Paris 75015, FRANCE

Chavarria, Ossle (Baseball Player)
Kansas City A's
201-9061 Home St
Burnaby, BC V3N 4L2, CANADA

Chaves, Richard J (Actor)
c/o Staff Member *Media Artists Group*
6300 Wilshire Blvd Ste 1470
Los Angeles, CA 90048-5200, USA

Chavez, Eric (Baseball Player)
c/o Staff Member *Oakland Athletics*
7000 Coliseum Way
Oakland, CA 94621-1992, USA

Chavez, Frias Hugo R (President)
Palacio de Miraflores
Avenida Urdaneta
Caracas 1010, VENEZUELA

Chavez, Julio Cesar
1 Hall Of Fame Dr
Canastota, NY 13032-1175, USA

Chavez, Marga (Actor)
c/o Staff Member *Select Artists Ltd (CA-Valley Office)*
PO Box 4359
Burbank, CA 91503-4359, USA

Chavira, Ricardo Antonio (Actor)
c/o Steven Jang *SDB Partners Inc*
1801 Avenue Of The Stars Ste 902
Los Angeles, CA 90067-5981, USA

Chavis, Benjamin
PO Box 1661
Ellicott City, MD 21041-1661, USA

Chavous, Barney L (Coach, Football Coach, Football Player)
Denver Broncos
601 Chavous Rd
Aiken, SC 29803-5031, USA

Chavous, Corey (Football Player)
Arizona Cardinals
267 N Kenneth Pl
Chandler, AZ 85226-2944, USA

Chawla, Juhi (Actor, Bollywood)
153 Oxford Tower Yamuna Nagar
Oshiwara Complex Andheri (W)
Mumbai, MS 400058, INDIA

Chayanne (Actor, Musician)
c/o Steve Chasman *Ace Media*
1411 5th St Ste 405
Santa Monica, CA 90401-2417, USA

Chaykin, Maury (Actor)
c/o Dan Baron *Agency for the Performing Arts (APA-LA)*
405 S Beverly Dr
Beverly Hills, CA 90212-4416, USA

Chazov, Yevgeny I (Doctor)
Cardiology Research Center
Cherepkovskaya Ul 15-A
Moscow 121552, RUSSIA

Cheadle, Don (Actor)
c/o Kay Liberman *Liberman/Zerman Management*
252 N Larchmont Blvd Ste 200
Los Angeles, CA 90004-3754, USA

Cheaney, Calbert N (Basketball Player)
Golden State Warriors
1001 Broadway
Oakland, CA 94607-4019, USA

Cheatham, Ernie (Football Player)
Pittsburgh Steelers
400 Ashton St
Pittsburgh, PA 15207-1786, USA

Cheatham, Maree (Actor)
Yvette Schumer
8787 Shoreham Dr
West Hollywood, CA 90069-2231, USA

Chechi, Yuri
Viale Tiziano 70
Rome 00196, ITALY

Checker, Chubby (Musician, Songwriter, Writer)
Twisted Ent
320 Fayette St # 200
Conshohocken, PA 19428-1902, USA

Checo, Robinson (Baseball Player)
Boston Red Sox
Romulo Bentan Cul #04
Santiago, DOMINICAN REPUBLIC

Cheek, James E (Educator)
1201 S Benbow Rd
Greensboro, NC 27406-2115, USA

Cheek, John (Opera Singer)
ICM Artists
40 W 57th St
New York, NY 10019-4001, USA

Cheek, Louis (Football Player)
Miami Dolphins
1807 Worsham Pl
Greensboro, NC 27408-3113, USA

Cheek, Molly (Actor)
c/o Staff Member *Pakula/King & Associates*
9229 W Sunset Blvd Ste 315
Los Angeles, CA 90069-3403, USA

Cheeks, Danyel
8033 W Sunset Blvd # 851
West Hollywood, CA 90046-2401, USA

Cheeks, Judy
49-50 New Bond St.
London, ENGLAND W1, UNITED KINGDOM (UK)

Cheeks, Maurica E (Mo) (Basketball Player, Coach)
7325 SW Childs Rd
Portland, OR 97224-7713, USA

Cheeks, Maurice (Basketball Player)
Philadelphia 76ers
709 Broad Acres Rd
Penn Valley, PA 19072-1512, USA

Cheena, Manager (Actor)
No 8 Vivekanandapuram Ist Street
West Mambalam
Chennai, TN 600 033, INDIA

Cheetwood, Derk (Actor)
c/o Staff Member *Bohemia Entertainment Group*
8170 Beverly Blvd Ste 102
Los Angeles, CA 90048-4533, USA

Cheever, Eddie (Race Car Driver)
Cheever Racing
8266 Zionsville Rd
Indianapolis, IN 46268-1627, USA

Cheever, Michael (Football Player)
Jacksonville Jaguars
27 Sherwood Dr
Newnan, GA 30263-1134, USA

Cheevers, Gary
905 Lewis O Gray Dr
Saugus, MA 01906-4406, USA

Chekamauskas, Vitautas (Architect)
State Arts Academy
Maironio 6
Vilnius 2600, LITHUANIA

Chelberg, Robert D (General)
Cubic Applications
Unit 30400 Box R
APO, AE 09131-0400, USA

Chelf, Donald (Football Player)
Buffalo Bills
7329 Bottle Brush Dr
Spring Hill, FL 34606-7023, USA

Cheli, Giovanni Cardinal (Religious Leader)
Pastoral Care of Migrants Council
Piazza Calisto 16
Rome 00153, ITALY

Cheli, Maurizio (Astronaut)
c/o Staff Member *NASA*
2101 Nasa Pkwy
Johnson Space Center
Houston, TX 77058-3691, USA

Cheli-Merchez, Marianne (Astronaut)
132 Rue Van Aliard
Bruxelles 1180, BELGIUM

Chelios, Christos K (Chris) (Hockey Player)
790 Falmouth Dr
Bloomfield Hills, MI 48304-3308, USA

Chellgren, Paul W (Business Person)
Ashland Inc
PO Box 391
Covington, KY 41015, USA

Chelsom, Peter (Actor)
c/o John Burnham *International Creative Management (ICM-LA)*
10250 Constellation Blvd
Los Angeles, CA 90067-6200, USA

Chemiakin, Mihail
Rt 9H Box 0079
Claverack, NY 12513, USA

Chen, Bruce (Athlete, Baseball Player)
c/o Staff Member *Cincinnati Reds*
100 Cinergy Fld
Cinergy Field
Cincinnati, OH 45202, USA

Chen, Da (Writer)
c/o Staff Member *Writers and Artists Group Intl (NY)*
19 W 44th St Ste 1000
New York, NY 10036-6101, USA

Chen, Edith (Musician)
Columbia Artists Mgmt Inc
1790 Broadway Fl 6
New York, NY 10019-1412, USA

Chen, Irvin S Y (Scientist)
University of California
Med Center
Hematology Dept
Los Angeles, CA 90024, USA

Chen, Joan (Actor, Director)
2601 Filbert St
San Francisco, CA 94123-3215, USA

Chen, Joie (Correspondent)
Cable News Network
1050 Techwood Dr NW
News Dept
Atlanta, GA 30318-5604, USA

Chen, Julie (Television Host)
c/o Staff Member *CBS News*
524 W 57th St
Viacom Inc
New York, NY 10019-2924, USA

Chen, Kaige (Director)
International Creative Mgmt
8942 Wilshire Blvd # 219
Beverly Hills, CA 90211-1908, USA

Chen, Lincoln C (Doctor)
302 Dean Rd
Brookline, MA 02445-4141, USA

Chen, Lu (Figure Skater)
Skating Assn
54 Baishiqiao Road
Haidian District
Beijing 10044, CHINA

Chen, Lynn (Actor)
c/o Staff Member *International Creative Management (ICM-LA)*
10250 Constellation Blvd
Los Angeles, CA 90067-6200, USA

Chen, Robert (Musician)
Columbia Artists Mgmt Inc
1790 Broadway Fl 6
New York, NY 10019-1412, USA

Chen, Shui-bian (President)
President's Office
Chieshshou Hall
Chung-King Road
Taipei 100, TAIWAN

Chen, Xieyang
Shanghai Symphony Orchestra
105 Hunan Road
Shanghai 200031, CHINA

Chen, Yi (Composer)
University of Missouri
Music Dept
Kansas City, MO 64110, USA

Chen, Zuohuang (Conductor)
Wichita Symphony Orchestra
225 W Douglas Ave Ste 207
Concert Hall
Wichita, KS 67202-3100, USA

Chenery, Penny (Misc)
20 Roberts Ln
Saratoga Springs, NY 12866-2814, USA

Cheney, Lynne V (Government Official)
American Enterprise Institute
1150 17th St NW
Washington, DC 20036-4670, USA

Cheney, Richad B (Dick) (Politician, President, Vice President)
c/o Staff Member *White House, The*
1600 Pennsylvania Ave NW
Washington, DC 20500-0003, USA

Cheney, Richard B (President, Secretary, Vice President)
6613 Madison Dr
McLean, VA 22101, USA

Cheng, Olivia (Actor)
c/o Elena Kirschner *Lucas Talent Inc*
Sun Tower Floor 7
100 W Pender St
Vancouver, BC V6B 1R8, CANADA

Chenier, Phil (Basketball Player)
Baltimore Bullets
12121 Blue Flag Way
Columbia, MD 21044-2753, USA

Chennault, Anna (Business Person)
TAC International
1049 30th St NW
Chennault Building
Washington, DC 20007-3823, USA

Chenoweth, Kristin (Actor, Musician)
c/o Tony Lipp *Creative Artists Agency LCC (CAA-LA)*
2000 Avenue Of The Stars
Los Angeles, CA 90067-4700, USA

Cher (Actor, Director, Musician, Producer)
c/o Roger Davies *RD Worldwide Management*
1158 26th St # 564
Santa Monica, CA 90403-4698, USA

Chereau, Patrice (Director)
Nanterre-Amandiers
7 Ave Pablo Picasso
Nanterre 9200, FRANCE

Cherestal, Jean-Marie (Prime Minister)
Prime Minister's Office
Palais Ministeres
Port-au-Prince, HAITI

Cherilyn (Cher) (Actor, Musician)
c/o Lindsay Scott *Lindsay Scott Management*
8899 Beverly Blvd Ste 609
Los Angeles, CA 90048-2429, USA

Chermayeff, Peter (Architect)
15 E 26th St
New York, NY 10010-1505, USA

Chernin, Peter (Business Person)
News Corp
1211 Avenue Of The Americas
New York, NY 10036-8701, USA

Chernobrovkina, Tatyana A (Ballerina)
Moscow Musical Theater
B Dimitrovka Str 17
Moscow 103009, RUSSIA

Chernov, Vladimir K (Opera Singer)
Columbia Artists Mgmt Inc
1790 Broadway Fl 6
New York, NY 10019-1412, USA

Chernow, Ron (Writer)
63 Joralemon St
Brooklyn, NY 11201-4003, USA

Cherrelle (Musician)
Associated Booking Corp
PO Box 2055
New York, NY 10021-0051, USA

Cherri, Agustina (Actor)
c/o Staff Member *Telefe - Argentina*
Pavon 2444 (C1248AAT)
Buenos Aires, ARGENTINA

Cherry, Deron (Football Player)
Kansas City Chiefs
4320 NE Courtney Dr
Lees Summit, MO 64064-1638, USA

Cherry, Don S (Coach, Hockey Player)
Cherry's Grapevine
1233 Queensway
Etobicoke, ON M8Z 1S1, CANADA

Cherry, Eagle Eye (Musician)
39A Gramercy Park N Apt 1C
New York, NY 10010-6312, USA

Cherry, Fred V (War Hero)
720 Dale Dr
Silver Spring, MD 20910-4267, USA

Cherry, Jonathan (Actor)
c/o Jim Sheasgreen *Look Management*
1529 W 6th Ave #110
Vancouver, BC V6J 1R, CANADA

Cherry, Mike (Football Player)
New York Giants
4106 Central Pl
Texarkana, AR 71854-1617, USA

Cherry, Nena (Musician)
c/o Staff Member *Paradigm (Monterey)*
509 Hartnell St
Monterey, CA 93940-2825, USA

Cherry, Neneh (Musician)
PO Box 1622
London NW10 5TF, UNITED KINGDOM (UK)

Cherry Poppin' Daddies
83 Riverside Dr
New York, NY 10024-5713, USA

Chertoff, Michael (Attorney, Attorney General, General, Government Official)
Justice Department
10th St & Constitution Ave NW
Washington, DC 20530-0001, USA

Chertok, Jack (Producer)
515 Ocean Ave # 305
Santa Monica, CA 90402-2609, USA

Cherundolo, Charles (Football Player)
Cleveland Rams
601 Church St
Moscow, PA 18444-9068, USA

Chesley, Al (Football Player)
Philadelphia Eagles
11713 Bishops Content Rd
Bowie, MD 20721-2583, USA

Chesney, Kenny (Musician)
PO Box 128529
Nashville, TN 37212-8529, USA

Chesnutt, Mark
1106 16th Ave S
Nashville, TN 37212-2305, USA

Chesser, George (Football Player)
Miami Dolphins
18 Hialeah St
Starkville, MS 39759-2751, USA

Chesson 3rd, Wes (Football Player)
Atlanta Falcons
326 Transylvania Ave
Raleigh, NC 27609-6952, USA

Chester, Colby (Actor)
Talent Group
5670 Wilshire Blvd Ste 820
Los Angeles, CA 90036-5613, USA

Chester, Larry (Football Player)
Indianapolis Colts
6359 Celtic Dr SW
Atlanta, GA 30331-9414, USA

Chester, Raymond T (Football Player)
Oakland Raiders
4722 Grass Valley Rd
Oakland, CA 94605-5622, USA

Chestnut, Cyrus (Musician)
Avenue Management Group
250 W 57th St # 407
New York, NY 10107-0001, USA

Chestnut, Mary Boykin (Educator)
Sweet Briar College
President's Office
Sweet Briar, VA 24595, USA

Chestnut, Morris (Actor)
c/o Michael Nilon *Creative Artists Agency
LCC (CAA-LA)*
2000 Avenue Of The Stars
Los Angeles, CA 90067-4700, USA

Chetry, Kiran (Anchor)
c/o Staff Member *CNN (NY)*
1 Time Warner Ctr
New York, NY 10019-6038, USA

Chetti, Joseph (Football Player)
Buffalo Bills
7 Baur St
Babylon, NY 11704-3320, USA

Chetwynd, Lionel (Producer, Writer)
c/o Bruce Vinokour *Creative Artists
Agency LCC (CAA-LA)*
2000 Avenue Of The Stars
Los Angeles, CA 90067-4700, USA

Cheung, Maggie (Actor)
c/o Ted Schachter *Schachter
Entertainment*
1157 S Beverly Dr Fl 2
Los Angeles, CA 90035-1119, USA

Cheung, Tim (Animator)
c/o Staff Member *DreamWorks SKG*
100 Universal City Plz
Universal City, CA 91608-1002, USA

Chevalier, Tracy (Writer)
EP Dutton
375 Hudson St
New York, NY 10014-3658, USA

Chevelle (Music Group)
c/o Staff Member *Creative Artists Agency
LCC (CAA-LA)*
2000 Avenue Of The Stars
Los Angeles, CA 90067-4700, USA

Chew, Geoffrey F (Physicist)
10 Maybeck Twin Dr
Berkeley, CA 94708-2037, USA

Chew Jr, Sam
8075 W 3rd St # 303
Los Angeles, CA 90048-4318, USA

Cheyne, Hank (Actor)
c/o Staff Member *Jillian Neal
Management*
8455 Beverly Blvd Ste 303
Los Angeles, CA 90048-3421, USA

Cheyunski, Jim (Football Player)
Boston Patriots
10386 Fox Glen Dr
Bridgeville, DE 19933-4564, USA

Chi, Haotian (General)
National Defense Ministry
Jingshanqiq Jie
Beijing, CHINA

Chi-Lites, The (Music Group)
c/o Staff Member *Universal Attractions*
145 W 57th St Fl 15
New York, NY 10019-2220, USA

Chia, Sandro (Artist)
Castello Romitorio
Montalcino, Siena, ITALY

Chiadel, Dana (Athlete)
5302 Flanders Ave
Kensington, MD 20895-1139, USA

Chiamparino, Scott (Baseball Player)
Texas Rangers
179 Ortega Ave
Mountain View, CA 94040-1439, USA

Chianese, Dominic (Actor)
c/o Brian Liebman *Liebman Entertainment*
25 E 21st St Ph
New York, NY 10010-6226, USA

Chiao, Dr Leroy (Astronaut)
2108 Butler Dr
Friendswood, TX 77546-5514, USA

Chiara, Maria (Opera Singer)
Columbia Artists Mgmt Inc
1790 Broadway Fl 6
New York, NY 10019-1412, USA

Chiasson, Scott (Baseball Player)
Chicago Cubs
498 Canterbury Tpke # A
Norwich, CT 06360-1373, USA

Chicago (Music Group)
Howard Rose Agency, The
9460 Wilshire Blvd Ste 310
Beverly Hills, CA 90212-2710, USA

Chickillo, Anthony (Football Player)
San Diego Chargers
6920 Spanish Moss Cir
Tampa, FL 33625-6556, USA

Chickillo, Nick (Football Player)
Chicago Bears
19025 E Saint Andrews Dr
Hialeah, FL 33015-2314, USA

Chiechi, Carolyn P (Judge)
US Tax Court
400 2nd St NW
Washington, DC 20217-0002, USA

Chieftans, The (Music Group)
c/o Staff Member *International Creative
Management (ICM-LA)*
10250 Constellation Blvd
Los Angeles, CA 90067-6200, USA

Chievous, Derrick (Basketball Player)
Houston Rockets
2300 Cherry Ridge Ln
Columbia, MO 65203-5744, USA

Chiffer, Floyd (Baseball Player)
San Diego Padres
4325 Levelside Ave
Lakewood, CA 90712-3752, USA

Chiffons, The
PO Box 770850
Orlando, FL 32877-0850, USA

Chihara, Charles S (Misc)
567 Cragmont Ave
Berkeley, CA 94708-1205, USA

Chihara, Paul (Composer)
3815 W Olive Ave Ste 202
Burbank, CA 91505-4676, USA

Chihuly, Dale P (Artist)
Chihuly Inc
1111 NW 50th St
Seattle, WA 98107-5120, USA

Chikezie, Caroline (Actor)
c/o Jane Lehrer *Jane Lehrer Associates*
100A Chalk Farm Road
London NW1 8EH, UNITED KINGDOM
(UK)

Chiklis, Michael (Actor)
c/o Brian Swardstrom *Endeavor Agency
LLC (LA)*
9601 Wilshire Blvd Fl 3
Beverly Hills, CA 90210-5204, USA

Child, Jane (Musician)
7095 Hollywood Blvd Ste 747
Los Angeles, CA 90028-8912, USA

Childers, Ernest (War Hero)
13681 S 308th East Ave
Coweta, OK 74429-5728, USA

Childress, Kallie Flynn (Actor)
c/o TJ Stein *Stein Entertainment Group*
11271 Ventura Blvd # 477
Studio City, CA 91604-3136, USA

Childress, Raymond C (Ray) Jr (Football
Player)
Houston Oilers
639 Shady Hollow St
Houston, TX 77056-1635, USA

Childress, Richard (R C) (Misc)
Childress Racing
PO Box 1189
Industrial Dr
Welcome, NC 27374-1189, USA

Childress, Rocky (Baseball Player)
Philadelphia Phillies
5 Meadow Glen Ct
Santa Rosa, CA 95404-1845, USA

Childs, Barton (Physicist)
1019 Winding Way
Baltimore, MD 21210-1232, USA

Childs, Brevard S (Misc)
508 Amity Rd
Bethany, CT 06524-3015, USA

Childs, Charissa (Golfer)
811 Mallet Hill Rd Apt 1409
Columbia, SC 29223-4416, USA

Childs, Clarence (Football Player)
New York Giants
1652 Lawrence Cir
Daytona Beach, FL 32117-3942, USA

Childs, David M (Architect)
Skidmore Owings Merrill
14 Wall St
New York, NY 10005-2105, USA

Childs, Henry (Football Player)
Atlanta Falcons
8304 Allman Rd
Shawnee Mission, KS 66219-2705, USA

Chiles, Henry G (Hank) Jr (Admiral)
6436 Pima St
Alexandria, VA 22312-2043, USA

Chiles, Linden (Actor)
2521 Skyline Dr
Topanga, CA 90290, USA

Chiles, Rich (Baseball Player)
Houston Astros
18147 Mallard St
Woodland, CA 95695-6038, USA

Chilies, Lois (Actor)
c/o Staff Member *Abrams Artists Agency
(LA)*
9200 W Sunset Blvd Ph 11
Los Angeles, CA 90069-3601, USA

Chillemi, Connie (Golfer)
2701 NE 10th St Apt 705
Ocala, FL 34470-5689, USA

Chilstrom, Ken (Misc)
9120 Belvoir Woods Pkwy Apt 211
Fort Belvoir, VA 22060-2723, USA

Chilton, Alex (Musician)
Rick Levy Mgmt
4250 A1A S Unit D11
Saint Augustine, FL 32080-7431, USA

Chilton, Gene (Football Player)
St Louis Cardinals
RR 2 Box 2542
Jacksonville, TX 75766, USA

Chilton, Kevin P (Astronaut)
16 Custer Dr
Offutt A F B, NE 68113-1018, USA

Chiminello, Bianca (Actor)
c/o Staff Member *Matt Sherman
Management*
7510 W Sunset Blvd # 1413
Los Angeles, CA 90046-3408, USA

Chin, Tsai (Actor)
Writers & Artists
360 N Crescent Dr Bldg North
Beverly Hills, CA 90210-6818, USA

Chinaglia, Giorgio (Soccer Player)
3-9-1 Via Quartara
Genoa 16148, ITALY

Chinese, Dominic
9150 Wilshire Blvd Ste 350
Beverly Hills, CA 90212-3453, USA

Chingy (Musician)
c/o Johnny Wright *Wright-Crear
Management*
3815 Hughes Ave
Culver City, CA 90232-2715, USA

Chinlund, Nick (Actor)
c/o Davien Littlefield *Davien Littlefield
Management*
33 W 67th St Ph
New York, NY 10023-6224, USA

Chinny, Jayanth (Actor)
67 1st Main Road
R A Puram
Chennai, TN 600 028, INDIA

Chipley, William (Football Player)
Boston Yankees
504 Fleetwood Dr
Lookout Mountain, TN 37350-1469, USA

Chirac, Jacques R (President)
Patals de L'Elysee
55-57 Faubourg Saint Honore
Paris 75008, FRANCE

Chiranjeevi (Actor, Bollywood)
No. 4 Porur Somasundaram Street T
Nagar
Chennai, TN 600017, INDIA

Chishholm-Carrillo, Linda (Volleyball
Player)
17213 Vose St
Van Nuys, CA 91406-3633, USA

Chisholm, Ashleigh (Actor)
c/o Staff Member *Nickelodeon UK*
PO Box 6425
LONDON W1A 6UR, UNITED
KINGDOM (UK)

Chisholm, Melanie (Musician)
c/o Staff Member *Solo Agency Ltd (UK)*
55 Fulham High St
London SW6 3JJ, UNITED KINGDOM
(UK)

Chism, Tom (Baseball Player)
Baltimore Orioles
532 W Brookhaven Rd Apt F1
Brookhaven, PA 19015-1824, USA

Chissano, Joaquim A (President)
President's Office
Avda Julius Nyerere 2000
Maputo, MOZAMBIQUE

Chitalada, Sot (Boxer)
Home Express Co
242/19 Moo 10
Sukhumvit Road
Cholburi 20210, THAILAND

Chitren, Steve (Baseball Player)
Oakland A's
10417 Smokemont Ct
Las Vegas, NV 89129-4515, USA

Chittister, Joan D (Misc)
Saint Scholastica Priory
335 E 9th St
Erie, PA 16503, USA

Chittum, Nels (Baseball Player)
St Louis Cardinals
616 Bonita Pkwy
Hendersonville, TN 37075-4632, USA

Chitty, Sir Thomas
Bow Cottage W. Hoathly
Sussex, ENGLAND RH19 4QF, UNITED
KINGDOM (UK)

Chitwood, Joey
4410 W Alva St
Tampa, FL 33614-7639, USA

Chitwood, Joey Jr (Race Car Driver)
863 Seddon Cove Way
Tampa, FL 33602-5704, USA

Chitwood, Joey, Jr. (Race Car Driver)
Chicagoland Speedway
800 Speedway Blvd
Joliet, IL 60431, USA

Chivers, Warren (Skier)
Vermont Academy
Saxtons River, VT 05154, USA

Chlumsky, Anna (Actor)
David S Lee
641 W Lake St Ste 402
Chicago, IL 60661-1049, USA

Chlupsa, Bob (Baseball Player)
St Louis Cardinals
55 Willow St
Garden City, NY 11530-6316, USA

Chmura, Mark W (Football Player)
Green Bay Packers
S18W28948 Price Ct
Waukesha, WI 53188-9551, USA

Cho (Actor)
26-A Raja Annamataipuram
2nd Main Road
Chennai, TN 600 028, INDIA

Cho, Catherine (Musician)
Columbia Artists Mgmt Inc
1790 Broadway Fl 6
New York, NY 10019-1412, USA

Cho, Frank (Cartoonist)
Creators Syndicate
5777 W Century Blvd Ste 700
Los Angeles, CA 90045-9023, USA

Cho, Fujio (Business Person)
Toyota Motor Corp
1 Toyotacho
Toyota City, Aicji Prefecture 471, JAPAN

Cho, John (Actor)
c/o Staff Member *William Morris Agency
(WMA-LA)*
1 William Morris Pl
Beverly Hills, CA 90212-4261, USA

Cho, Margaret (Actor, Comedian)
c/o Stacey Mark *William Morris Agency
(WMA-LA)*
1 William Morris Pl
Beverly Hills, CA 90212-4261, USA

Cho, Paul (Misc)
Full Gospel Central Church
Yoida Plaza
Seoul, SOUTH KOREA

Choate, Don (Baseball Player)
San Francisco Giants
9506 Maryann Dr
Fairview Heights, IL 62208-1625, USA

Choate, Jerry D (Business Person)
Allstate Insurance
2775 Sanders Rd
Allstate Plaza
Northbrook, IL 60062-6127, USA

Choate, Randy (Baseball Player)
New York Yankees
20818 Lake Vienna Dr
Land O Lakes, FL 34638-8321, USA

Chodorow, Marvin (Engineer, Physicist)
81 Pearce Mitchell Pl
Stanford, CA 94305-8535, USA

Choi, K J (Golfer)
1360 E 9th St
Cleveland, OH 44114-1737, USA

Choi, Yun (Actor)
c/o Staff Member *Select Artists Ltd (CA-
Westside Office)*
1138 12th St Apt 1
Santa Monica, CA 90403-5459, USA

Chokachi, David (Actor)
c/o Sean Fay *Imparato Fay Management*
1126 Roxbury Dr
Los Angeles, CA 90035-1031, USA

Chokkalinga, Bhavadhar (Actor)
10 Thiruvalluvar Street
M G R Nagar
Chennai, TN 600 078, INDIA

Chol, Hee Seop (Baseball Player)
Chicago Cubs
14310 SE 29th Cir
Vancouver, WA 98683-7691, USA

Cholodenko, Lisa (Director, Editor,
Producer, Writer)
c/o Bart Walker *Creative Artists Agency
(CAA-NY)*
162 5th Ave Fl 6
New York, NY 10010-6047, USA

Choma, John (Football Player)
San Francisco 49ers
1544 Carol Ave
Burlingame, CA 94010-5231, USA

Chomet, Sylvain (Director, Writer)
c/o Robert Newman *International Creative
Management (ICM-LA)*
10250 Constellation Blvd
Los Angeles, CA 90067-6200, USA

Chomsky, Marvin J (Director)
15200 W Sunset Blvd Ste 209
Pacific Palisades, CA 90272-3621, USA

Chonacas, Katie (Actor, Model)
c/o Staff Member *Axiom Management*
16302 Crowne Brook Cir
Franklin, TN 37067-1673, USA

Chones, James (Jim) (Basketball Player)
735 Beacon Hill Dr
Chagrin Falls, OH 44022-2188, USA

Chones, Jim (Basketball Player)
New York Nets
23511 Chagrin Blvd Apt 515E
Beachwood, OH 44122-5539, USA

Chong, Rae Dawn (Actor)
c/o David Fox *Myman Abell Fineman
Greenspan & Light LLP*
11601 Wilshire Blvd Fl 22
Los Angeles, CA 90025-0509, USA

Chong, Thomas
1625 Casale Rd
Pacific Palisades, CA 90272-2717, USA

Chong, Thomas (Tommy) (Actor,
Comedian)
c/o Rick Greenstein *Gersh Agency, The
(LA)*
232 N Canon Dr
Beverly Hills, CA 90210-5302, USA

Chopra, B R (Bollywood, Director)
B R House Juhu Tara Road
Santacruz
Mumbai, MS 400049, INDIA

Chopra, Deepak (Doctor, Writer)
c/o Robert Gottlieb *Trident Media Group
LLC*
41 Madison Ave Fl 36
New York, NY 10010-2257, USA

Chopra, Prem (Actor, Bollywood)
144A Nibbana Pali Hill
Bandra
Bombay, MS 400 050, INDIA

Chopra, Priyanka (Actor)
Rajesh Chopra
1826 Amar Nath Bldg #2
Bhagirath Palace
Delhi 110006, INDIA

Chopra, Ravi (Bollywood, Director,
Filmmaker, Producer)
B R House
Juhu Tara Road Santacruz
Bombay, MS 400 049, INDIA

Chopra, Uday (Actor)
c/o Staff Member *Yash Raj Films Private
Ltd (India)*
17 Vkas Park
Jalpankhi Society, Juhu
Mumbai 400 049, INDIA

Chopra, Vidhu Vinod (Bollywood,
Director, Filmmaker, Producer)
B-30 Kalpana Apartments
Sheley Ranjan Road Bandra
Mumbai, MS 400050, INDIA

Chopra, Yash (Bollywood, Director,
Filmmaker, Producer)
Yashraj Films
Bungalow No. 17
Jalpankhi Soc Vikas Park Juhu Tara Road
Mumbai, MS 400049, INDIA

Chorvat, Scarlett (Actor)
Innovative Artists
1505 10th St
Santa Monica, CA 90401-2805, USA

Chorzempa, Daniel W (Misc)
Kunstleragentur Raab & Bohm
Plankengasse 7
Vienna 1010, AUSTRIA

Chou, Jay (Musician)
c/o Staff Member *BMG*
1540 Broadway
New York, NY 10036-4074, USA

Choudhury, Sarita (Actor)
c/o Kathy Atkinson *Washington Square
Arts (LA)*
1041 N Formosa Ave
Writers Bldg #305
West Hollywood, CA 90046-6703, USA

Chouinard, Josee (Figure Skater)
c/o Staff Member *International
Management Group (IMG Canada)*
175 Bloor St E
S Tower #400
Toronto, CA M4W 3R8, CANADA

Chouinard, Marie (Choreographer,
Dancer)
Compagnie Chouinard
3981 Boul Saint-Laurent
Montreal, PQ H2W 1Y5, CANADA

Choureau, Etchika
9 rue du Docteur Blanche
Paris F-75016, FRANCE

Chow, Amy (Gymnast)
West Valley Gymnastics School
1190 Dell Ave # 1
Campbell, CA 95008-6614, USA

Chow, China (Actor)
c/o Darren Goldberg *1 Management*
9000 W Sunset Blvd Ph 1550
West Hollywood, CA 90069-1838, USA

Chow, Gregory C (Economist)
30 Hardy Dr
Princeton, NJ 08540-1211, USA

Chow, Raymond
23 Barker Rd. Craigside Mansion #5B
HONG KONG

Chow, Stephen (Actor)
c/o Alan Grodin *Weissman Wolff
Bergman Coleman Silverman Holmes*
9665 Wilshire Blvd Ste 900
Beverly Hills, CA 90212-2345, USA

Chow, Steven (Actor)
c/o Alan Grodin *Weissman Wolff
Bergman Coleman Silverman Holmes*
9665 Wilshire Blvd Ste 900
Beverly Hills, CA 90212-2345, USA

Chrebet, Wayne (Football Player)
New York Jets
19 Swallow Tail Ct
Jackson, NJ 08527-2872, USA

Chretien, J J Jean (Prime Minister)
Prime Minister's Office
24 Sussex Dr
Ottawa, ON K1M 0MS, CANADA

Chretien, Jean-Loup (Astronaut, General)
Astronautes Direction
2 Place Maurice Quentin
Paris 75029, FRANCE

Chrique, Emanuelle (Actor)
c/o Jaime Misher *Endeavor Agency LLC
(LA)*
9601 Wilshire Blvd Fl 3
Beverly Hills, CA 90210-5204, USA

Chris, Mike (Baseball Player)
Detroit Tigers
12437 Woodgreen St
Los Angeles, CA 90066-2721, USA

Chrisley, Neil (Baseball Player)
Washington Senators
280 Myrtle Green Dr Apt B
Conway, SC 29526-9040, USA

Christ, Chad
9200 W Sunset Blvd Ste 900
Los Angeles, CA 90069-3604, USA

Christ, Dorothy (Baseball Player)
120 E Battell St Apt 108
Mishawaka, IN 46545-6660, USA

Christ, Fred (Basketball Player)
New York Knicks
1606 Atlantic St Apt B
Melbourne Beach, FL 32951-2339, USA

Christensen, Bruce (Baseball Player)
California Angels
PO Box 178
Moroni, UT 84646-0178, USA

Christensen, Cal (Basketball Player)
Tri-Cities Blackhawks
395 Canal Rd
Waterville, OH 43566-1338, USA

Christensen, Erika (Actor)
c/o Jeff Golenberg *The Collective*
9100 Wilshire Blvd # 700 W
Beverly Hills, CA 90212-3401, USA

Christensen, Hayden (Actor)
c/o Staff Member *Forest Park Pictures*
450 N Roxbury Dr Fl 8
Beverly Hills, CA 90210-4222, USA

Christensen, Helena (Model)
c/o Duncan Heath *International Creative Management (ICM-UK)*
Oxford House
76 Oxford St
London W1N OAX, UNITED KINGDOM (UK)

Christensen, John (Baseball Player)
New York Mets
2931 Yuma Dr
Lake Havasu City, AZ 86406-8568, USA

Christensen, Kai (Architect)
100 Vester Voldgade
Copenhagen V 1552, DENMARK

Christensen, McKay (Baseball Player)
Chicago White Sox
2288 New Harvest Ln
Lehi, UT 84043-4774, USA

Christensen, Todd (Football Player)
New York Giants
991 Sunburst Ln
Alpine, UT 84004-1203, USA

Christensen Jr, Erik (Football Player)
Washington Redskins
2643 Brintons Bridge Rd
West Chester, PA 19382-7084, USA

Christenson, Gary (Baseball Player)
Kansas City Royals
436 E Tremaine Ave
Gilbert, AZ 85234-4624, USA

Christenson, Larry (Baseball Player)
Philadelphia Phillies
1465 Le Boutillier Rd
Malvern, PA 19355-8741, USA

Christenson, Ryan (Baseball Player)
Oakland A's
4021 Canario St Unit 136
Carlsbad, CA 92008-6102, USA

Christian, Bob (Football Player)
Chicago Bears
1475 Buford Dr # 403-102
Lawrenceville, GA 30043-3798, USA

Christian, Christina (Musician)
c/o Staff Member *Fox Television Studios*
10201 W Pico Blvd Bldg 41
Los Angeles, CA 90064-2606, USA

Christian, Claudia (Actor)
c/o Staff Member *Abrams Artists Agency (LA)*
9200 W Sunset Blvd Ph 11
Los Angeles, CA 90069-3601, USA

Christian, David W (Dave) (Hockey Player)
3501 Rivershore Dr
Moorhead, MN 56560-5554, USA

Christian, Eddie (Baseball Player)
1126 NE Lija Loop
Portland, OR 97211-1318, USA

Christian, Gabrielle (Actor)
c/o Robert Haas *Innovative Artists (LA)*
4343 Lankershim Blvd # 100
North Hollywood, CA 91602-2705, USA

Christian, Gordon (Hockey Player)
604 Lake St NW
Warroad, MN 56763-2123, USA

Christian, Richard (Actor)
c/o Staff Member *Select Artists Ltd (CA-Westside Office)*
1138 12th St Apt 1
Santa Monica, CA 90403-5459, USA

Christian, Roger (Hockey Player)
508 Carrol St NW
Warroad, MN 56763, USA

Christian, Shawn (Actor)
c/o Staff Member *Burstein Company, The*
15304 W Sunset Blvd Ste 208
Pacific Palisades, CA 90272-3656, USA

Christian, William (Bill) (Hockey Player)
502 Carrol St NW
Warroad, MN 56763, USA

Christian-Jacque (Director, Writer)
42 Bis Rue de paris
Boulogne, Billancourt 92100, FRANCE

Christians, F Wilhelm (Financier)
Kobigsallee 51
Dusseldorf, GERMANY

Christians, The
370 City Rd.
London, ENGLAND EC1V 2QA, UNITED KINGDOM (UK)

Christiansen, Clay (Baseball Player)
New York Yankees
RR 3
Columbus, KS 66725, USA

Christiansen, Helena (Actor)
62 Blvd Sebastopol
Paris 75003, FRANCE

Christiansen, Jason (Baseball Player)
Philadelphia Phillies
311 4th Street
Herman, NE 68029, USA

Christiansen, Robert S (Football Player)
Buffalo Bills
2022 Thornhill Dr
Roseville, CA 95746-7144, USA

Christianson, Bob (Musician)
c/o Mike Rosen *Working Artists Agency*
13525 Ventura Blvd
Sherman Oaks, CA 91423-3801, USA

Christie, Doug (Basketball Player)
c/o Team Member *Orlando Magic*
8701 Maitland Summit Blvd
Orlando, FL 32810-5915, USA

Christie, Doug (Basketball Player)
Los Angeles Lakers
851 S Cloverdale Ave
Los Angeles, CA 90036-4818, USA

Christie, Julianna
252 N Larchmont Blvd Ste 200
Los Angeles, CA 90004-3754, USA

Christie, Julie (Actor, Model)
c/o Brian Swardstrom *Endeavor Agency LLC (LA)*
9601 Wilshire Blvd Fl 3
Beverly Hills, CA 90210-5204, USA

Christie, Karen
PO Box 111011
Nashville, TN 37222-1011, USA

Christie, Linford (Athlete, Track Athlete)
Nuff Respect
107 Sherland Road
Twickenham
Middx TW9 4HB, UNITED KINGDOM (UK)

Christie, Lou (Musician)
Lightning Strikes Music
2417 Jericho Tpke # 219
New Hyde Park, NY 11040-4710, USA

Christie, Mike (Golfer)
211 Imperial Dr
Greenville, SC 29615-2316, USA

Christie, Steve (Football Player)
Tampa Bay Buccaneers
12362 Carmel Country Rd Unit 108
San Diego, CA 92130-4508, USA

Christie, Tony
C.P. 162 Les Barzette
Montana-Vermala CH-3962, SWITZERLAND

Christie, Warren (Actor)
c/o Trina Allen *Pacific Artists Management*
1404-510 W Hastings St
Vancouver, BC V6B 1L8, CANADA

Christie, William (Musician)
Les Arts Florissants
2 Rue de Saint-Petersbourg
Paris 75008, FRANCE

Christine, Andrew (Andy) (Cartoonist)
King Features Syndicate
888 7th Ave Ste 201
New York, NY 10106-0201, USA

Christlieb, Peter (Pete) (Musician)
Thomas Cassidy
11761 E Speedway Blvd
Tucson, AZ 85748-2017, USA

Christmas, Steve (Baseball Player)
Cincinnati Reds
600 Bentley St
Oviedo, FL 32765-8169, USA

Christo (Javacheff) (Artist)
48 Howard St
New York, NY 10013-2514, USA

Christon, Shameka (Basketball Player)
New York Liberty
2 Penn Plz
Madison Square Garden
New York, NY 10121-1703, USA

Christopher, Dennis (Actor)
BR&S
5757 Wilshire Blvd Ste 473
Los Angeles, CA 90036-3632, USA

Christopher, Gerard
11900 Goshen Ave Apt 203
Los Angeles, CA 90049-6380, USA

Christopher, Gretchen (Musician)
509 E Ridgecrest Blvd # 1A
Ridgecrest, CA 93555-3959, USA

Christopher, Herb (Football Player)
Kansas City Chiefs
1031 King Way Dr
Lithonia, GA 30058-6113, USA

Christopher, Joe (Baseball Player)
Pittsburgh Pirates
PO Box 65240
Baltimore, MD 21209-0240, USA

Christopher, Matt (Writer)
c/o Dale Christopher
PO Box 2511
Wilton, NY 12831-5511, USA

Christopher, Mike (Baseball Player)
Los Angeles Dodgers
RR 1 Box 445
Church Road, VA 23833, USA

Christopher, Thom (Actor)
Ambrosio/Mortimer
PO Box 16758
Beverly Hills, CA 90209-2758, USA

Christopher, Tyler
10100 Santa Monica Blvd Ste 2500
Los Angeles, CA 90067-4116, USA

Christopher, Warren M (Secretary)
1701 Coldwater Canyon Dr
Beverly Hills, CA 90210, USA

Christopher, William (Actor)
Artists Group
1650 Broadway Ste 610
New York, NY 10019-6833, USA

Christopherson, James (Football Player)
Minnesota Vikings
526 Queens Ct
Moorhead, MN 56560-6777, USA

Christy, Earl (Football Player)
New York Jets
10825 S Prairie Ave
Chicago, IL 60628-3620, USA

Christy, George
170 N Carmelina Ave
Los Angeles, CA 90049-2737, USA

Christy, Greg (Football Player)
Buffalo Bills
3 Concord St
Natrona Heights, PA 15065-9732, USA

Christy, Jeff (Football Player)
Minnesota Vikings
138 Horseshoe Dr
Freeport, PA 16229-1712, USA

Christy, Robert F (Physicist)
1230 Arden Rd
Pasadena, CA 91106-4146, USA

Chryplewicz, Pete (Football Player)
Detroit Lions
11473 Claymont Cir
Windermere, FL 34786-5312, USA

Chrysostom, Bishop (Religious Leader)
Serbian Orthodox Church
PO Box 519
St Sava Monastery
Libertyville, IL 60048-0519, USA

Chryssa (Artist)
565 Broadway
Soho
New York, NY 10012-3925, USA

Chu, Paul C W (Physicist)
University of Houston
Center For Superconductivity
Houston, TX 77204-0001, USA

Chu, Steven (Nobel Prize Laureate)
6231 Contra Costa Rd
Oakland, CA 94618-2142, USA

Chubais, Anatoly B (Government Official)
United Power Grids
Kitaigorodsky Proyezd 7
Moscow 103074, RUSSIA

Chubin, Steve (Basketball Player)
Anaheim Amigos
10213 Ramblewood Dr
Coral Springs, FL 33071-6511, USA

Chuck, D (Musician)
Richard Walters
1800 Argyle Ave # 408
Los Angeles, CA 90028-5253, USA

Chuck, Wendy (Designer)
c/o Heather Parker *Innovative Artists (LA)*
1505 10th St
Santa Monica, CA 90401-2805, USA

Chuck Wagon Gang
4408 Buffalo Ln
Joshua, TX 76058-5521, USA

Chulack, Christopher (Director, Producer, Writer)
c/o Staff Member *Creative Artists Agency LCC (CAA-LA)*
2000 Avenue Of The Stars
Los Angeles, CA 90067-4700, USA

Chulk, Vinnie (Baseball Player)
Toront Blue Jays
10062 SW 223rd Ter
Cutler Bay, FL 33190-1584, USA

Chung, Constance Y (Connie)
(Correspondent)
c/o Alan Berger *Creative Artists Agency LCC (CAA-LA)*
2000 Avenue Of The Stars
Los Angeles, CA 90067-4700, USA

Chung, Eugene (Football Player)
New England Patriots
109 Surrey Ln
Ponte Vedra Beach, FL 32082-3942, USA

Chung, Mark (Soccer Player)
Columbus Crew
2121 Velman Ave
Columbus, OH 43211, USA

Chung, Myung-Whun (Musician)
Hans Ulrich Schmid
Postfach 1617
Hanover 30016, GERMANY

Chupack, Cindy
c/o Daniel A (Dan) Strone *Trident Media Group LLC*
41 Madison Ave Fl 36
New York, NY 10010-2257, USA

Church, Charlotte (Musician)
7 Dials Cambridge Bridge
Covent Garden
London WC2H 9HU, UNITED KINGDOM (UK)

Church, Sam (Misc)
United Mine Workers of America
8315 Lee Hwy Fl 5
Fairfax, VA 22031-2215, USA

Church Lane, North Stoke Wallingford
ENGLAND
OX10 6BQ, UNITED KINGDOM (UK)

Churches, Brady J (Business Person)
Consolidated Stores
1105 N Market St
Wilmington, DE 19801-1216, USA

Churchill, Caryl (Writer)
Cassarotto
60/66 Wardour St
London W1V 4ND, UNITED KINGDOM (UK)

Churchman, Ricky (Football Player)
San Francisco 49ers
445 Cherry Blossom Loop
Richland, WA 99352-7851, USA

Churchwell, Donnis (Football Player)
Washington Redskins
PO Box 520
Leakesville, MS 39451-0520, USA

Churn, Chuck (Baseball Player)
Pittsburgh Pirates
733 Trevino Dr
Lady Lake, FL 32159-5575, USA

Chuy, Don (Football Player)
Los Angeles Rams
11690 Oxnard St
North Hollywood, CA 91606-4878, USA

Chvatal, Cynthia (Producer)
c/o Staff Member *United Talent Agency (UTA)*
9560 Wilshire Blvd Ste 500
Beverly Hills, CA 90212-2401, USA

Chwast, Seymour (Artist)
Push Pin Group
55 E 9th St Apt 1G
New York, NY 10003-6312, USA

Ciaffa, Chris
627 N Las Palmas Ave
Los Angeles, CA 90004-1019, USA

Cialini, Julie (Artist, Model)
PO Box 55536
Valencia, CA 91385-0536, USA

Ciampi, Joe (Coach)
Auburn University
Athletic Dept
Auburn, AL 36831, USA

Cianfrocco, Archi (Baseball Player)
Montreal Expos
12424 Addax Ct
San Diego, CA 92129-4141, USA

Ciara (Musician)
c/o David Wirtschafter *William Morris Agency (WMA-LA)*
1 William Morris Pl
Beverly Hills, CA 90212-4261, USA

Ciardi, Mark (Baseball Player)
Milwaukee Brewers
21 Mitchell Ave
Piscataway, NJ 08854-5560, USA

Cias, Darryl (Baseball Player)
Oakland A's
12330 Lithuania Dr
Granada Hills, CA 91344-1637, USA

Cibrian, Eddie (Actor)
c/o Steve Sauer *Media Four*
8840 Wilshire Blvd Fl 2
Beverly Hills, CA 90211-2606, USA

Ciccarelli, Dino (Hockey Player)
1872 Clarence St
Sarnia, ON N7X 1C7, CANADA

Cicciolina
Via Cassia 1818
Rome I-00123, ITALY

Ciccippio, Joseph
2107 3rd St
Norristown, PA 19401-1930, USA

Ciccolella, Jude (Actor)
c/o Staff Member *McKeon-Valeo-Myones Management*
9100 Wilshire Blvd Ste 350W
Beverly Hills, CA 90212-3437, USA

Ciccolella, Mike (Football Player)
New York Giants
8145 Station House Rd
Dayton, OH 45458-2931, USA

Ciccone, Christopher (Designer)
Bernhardt Design/Pacific Design Center
8687 Melrose Ave Ste B230
West Hollywood, CA 90069-5786, USA

Cicerone, Aldo (Musician)
Gerhild Baron Mgmt
Dombacher Str 41/III/3
Vienna 1170, AUSTRIA

Cicerone, Ralph J (Scientist)
University of California
Earth Science Dept
Rowland Hall
Irvine, CA 92717, USA

Cichowski, Chick (Football Player)
Pittsburgh Steelers
3903 Oak Ave
Northbrook, IL 60062-4922, USA

Cichowski, Tom (Football Player)
Denver Broncos
3903 Oak Ave
Northbrook, IL 60062-4922, USA

Cichy, Joe J (Football Player)
9806 Isiand Road
Bismarck, ND 58503, USA

Cid, Celeste (Actor)
c/o Staff Member *Telefe - Argentina*
Pavon 2444 (C1248AAT)
Buenos Aires, ARGENTINA

Cienfuegos, Mauricio (Soccer Player)
Los Angeles Galaxy
1010 Rose Bowl Dr
Pasadena, CA 91103, USA

Cifelli, Gus (Football Player)
Detroit Lions
377 Kendry
Bloomfield Township, MI 48302-0442, USA

Cifers, Ed (Football Player)
Washington Redskins
5600 Meadow Glen Dr
Knoxville, TN 37919-8623, USA

Cigliuti, Natalia (Actor)
c/o Felicia Sager *Art Work Entertainment*
5900 Wilshire Blvd Ste 2150
Los Angeles, CA 90036-5021, USA

Cihocki, Al (Baseball Player)
Cleveland Indians
43 Cochise Cir
Medford Lakes, NJ 08055-9769, USA

Cilento, Diane (Actor)
Box 600
Spring Hill, Queensland 4004, AUSTRALIA

Cilla
5 Moorland Ave. Sale
Cheshire, ENGLAND M33 3FL, UNITED KINGDOM (UK)

Ciller, Tansu (Prime Minister)
True Path Party
Selanik Cod 40
Kizilay, Ankara, TURKEY

Cimarro, Mario (Actor)
c/o Staff Member *Televisa*
Blvd Adolfo Lopez Mateos 232
Colonia San Angel INN
DF CP 01060, MEXICO

Cimber, Matt (Director, Producer, Writer)
Cimero Enterprises
3620 Beverly Glen Blvd # 1A
Sherman Oaks, CA 91423-4403, USA

Cimino, Leonardo (Actor)
Michael Hartig Agency
156 5th Ave Ste 820
New York, NY 10010-7767, USA

Cimino, Michael (Director)
9015 Alto Cedro Dr
Beverly Hills, CA 90210-1804, USA

Cimino, Pete (Baseball Player)
Minnesota Twins
14 Fillmore St
Bristol, PA 19007-5415, USA

Cimmo, Leonardo (Actor)
Michael Hartig Agency
156 5th Ave Ste 820
New York, NY 10010-7767, USA

Cimoll, Gino (Baseball Player)
Brooklyn Dodgers
39 Mooring Ln
Daly City, CA 94014-2847, USA

Cimorelli, Frank (Baseball Player)
St Louis Cardinals
3770 N 97th Pl
Milwaukee, WI 53222-2635, USA

Cincotti, Peter (Musician)
Vector Mgmt
113 E 55th St
New York, NY 10022-3502, USA

Cinderella (Music Group, Musician)
Tom Keifer
6129 S Riverbend Dr
Nashville, TN 37221-3937, USA

Cindric, Ann (Baseball Player)
210 Greenside Ave Apt 4
Canonsburg, PA 15317-3862, USA

Cindrich, Joe (Football Player)
Dallas Cowboys
1310 Trinity Dr
Menlo Park, CA 94025-6680, USA

Cindrich, Ralph (Football Player)
New England Patriots
1160 Harvard Rd
Pittsburgh, PA 15205-1713, USA

Cineson All-Stars (Music Group)
c/o Staff Member *Paradigm (Monterey)*
509 Hartnell St
Monterey, CA 93940-2825, USA

Cink, Stewart (Golfer)
2195 Lockett Ct
Duluth, GA 30097-5012, USA

Cintron, Alex (Baseball Player)
Arizona Diamondbacks
HC 2 Box 8575
Yabucoa, PR 00767-9599, USA

Cioffi, Charles (Actor)
Paradigm Agency
10100 Santa Monica Blvd Ste 2500
Los Angeles, CA 90067-4116, USA

Ciokey, Janna (Actor)
J Michael Bloom
9255 W Sunset Blvd Ste 710
Los Angeles, CA 90069-3304, USA

Cipa, Larry (Football Player)
New Orleans Saints
250 Torrent Ct
Rochester Hills, MI 48307-3871, USA

Cipriani, Frank (Baseball Player)
Kansas City A's
14 Oakhill Dr
Buffalo, NY 14224-4214, USA

Cipriani Thorne, Juan Luis Cardinal
(Religious Leader)
Arzobispado
Plaza de Armas S/N
Apartado 1512
Lima 100, PERU

Circi, Cristian (Architect)
Cirici Arquitecte
Carrer de Pujades 63 2-N
Barcelona 08005, SPAIN

Ciriani, Henri (Architect)
61 Rue Pascal
Paris 75013, FRANCE

Cirillo, Jeff (Baseball Player)
Milwaukee Brewers
PO Box 233
Medina, WA 98039-0233, USA

Cirrincione, Vincent
151 El Camino Dr
Beverly Hills, CA 90212-2704, USA

Cisar, George (Baseball Player)
Brooklyn Dodgers
9026 W 24th St
Riverside, IL 60546-1027, USA

Cisco, Galen (Baseball Player)
Boston Red Sox
604 Elmwood Ln
Celina, OH 45822-2966, USA

Cisneros, Evelyn (Ballerina)
San Francisco Ballet
455 Franklin St
San Francisco, CA 94102-4471, USA

Cisneros, Henry G (Secretary)
2002 W Houslon St
San Antonio, TX 78207, USA

Cisowski, Steve (Football Player)
Dallas Cowboys
1543 Vista Club Cir Apt 304
Santa Clara, CA 95054-3747, USA

Citarella, Ralph (Baseball Player)
St Louis Cardinals
29 E Sherman Ave
Colonia, NJ 07067-1412, USA

Citro, Ralph (Boxer)
32 N Black Horse Pike
Blackwood, NJ 08012-3093, USA

Citterio, Antonio (Architect)
Antonio Citterio Partners
Via Cerva 4
Milan 20122, ITALY

Citti, Christine (Actor)
Artmedia
20 Ave Rapp
Paris 75007, FRANCE

City High (Music Group)
c/o Staff Member *William Morris Agency (WMA-LA)*
1 William Morris Pl
Beverly Hills, CA 90212-4261, USA

Civiletti, Benjamin R (Attorney, Attorney General, General)
14 Meadow Rd
Baltimore, MD 21212-1021, USA

Cizik, Robert (Business Person)
8839 Hamess Creek Lane
Houston, TX 77024, USA

CK, Louis (Actor, Comedian)
c/o Staff Member *United Talent Agency (UTA)*
9560 Wilshire Blvd Ste 500
Beverly Hills, CA 90212-2401, USA

Claar, Brian (Golfer)
27 Bentgrass Pl
The Woodlands, TX 77381-6122, USA

Clabo, Neal (Football Player)
1100 Beaverton Rd
Knoxville, TN 37919-7089, USA

Clack, Darryl (Football Player)
Dallas Cowboys
2806 Pierce Ave
El Paso, TX 79930-4234, USA

Clack, James T (Jim) (Football Player)
Pittsburgh Steelers
3631 Cherry Hill Dr
Greensboro, NC 27410-9141, USA

Claes, Willy (Government Official)
Berkenlaan 23
Hasselt 3500, BELGIUM

Claiborne, Chris (Football Player)
Detroit Lions
33 Olympia Hills Cir
Las Vegas, NV 89141-6046, USA

Claiborne, Craig
30 Park Pl
East Hampton, NY 11937-2407, USA

Clairmont, Patsy (Writer)
Milk n Honey Inc
PO Box 36
Brighton, MI 48116-0036, USA

Claitt, Rickey (Football Player)
Washington Redskins
5830 Grand Canyon Dr
Orlando, FL 32810-3232, USA

Clampi, Cario A (President, Prime Minister)
President's Office
Palazzo del Quirinale
Rome 00187, ITALY

Clampi, Joe (Coach)
Auburn University
Athletic Dept
Aubum, AL 36831, USA

Clancy, Edward B Cardinal (Religious Leader)
Sydney Archdiocese
Polding House 276 Pitt St
Sydney, NSW 2000, AUSTRALIA

Clancy, Gil (Boxer)
47 Morris Ave W
Malverne, NY 11565-1025, USA

Clancy, Jim (Baseball Player)
PO Box 148
Twin Lakes, WI 53181-0148, USA

Clancy, Sam (Football Player)
Seattle Seahawks
6522 Llewellyn Pl
Pittsburgh, PA 15206-3308, USA

Clancy, Thomas J (Tom) (Writer)
PO Box 800
PO Box 800
Huntingtown, MD 20639-0800, USA

Clancy Brothers
177 Woodland Ave
Westwood, NJ 07675-3218, USA

Clanton, Jimmy (Musician)
4425 Kingwood Dr
Kingwood, TX 77339-3701, USA

Clap Your Hands Say Yeah (Music Group)
c/o Staff Member *Paradigm (Monterey)*
509 Hartnell St
Monterey, CA 93940-2825, USA

Claphan, Sam (Football Player)
San Diego Chargers
RR 1 Box 2245
Stilwell, OK 74960-9774, USA

Clapp, Gordon (Actor)
Paul Kohner
9300 Wilshire Blvd Ste 555
Beverly Hills, CA 90212-3211, USA

Clapp, Nicholas R (Producer)
PO Box 1019
Borrego Springs, CA 92004-1019, USA

Clapp, Thomas (Football Player)
Tampa Bay Buccaneers
804 Live Oak St
Metairie, LA 70005-1216, USA

Clapton, Eric (Musician)
46 Kensington Court
London WE8 5DT, UNITED KINGDOM (UK)

Clardy, Jon C (Misc)
Cornell University
Chemistry Dept
Ithaca, NY 14853, USA

Clarey, Doug (Baseball Player)
St Louis Cardinals
2116 Hillhurst Ave
Los Angeles, CA 90027-2004, USA

Claridge, Dennis (Football Player)
Green Bay Packers
2621 Calvert St
Lincoln, NE 68502-4935, USA

Clarin, Hans Joachim
Zellerhornstr. 75
Aschau D-83229, GERMANY

Clarizio, Louis (Baseball Player)
Chicago American Giants
133 Lela Ln
Schaumburg, IL 60193-1339, USA

Clark, Al (Football Player)
Detroit Lions
PO Box 971
Bogalusa, LA 70429-0971, USA

Clark, Alan (Musician)
Damage Mgmt
16 Lambton Place
London W11 2SH, UNITED KINGDOM (UK)

Clark, Allie (Baseball Player)
New York Yankees
250 N Stevens Ave
South Amboy, NJ 08879, USA

Clark, Anthiony (Actor)
c/o Jennifer Pinto *Pinnacle PR*
8265 W Sunset Blvd Ste 201
West Hollywood, CA 90046-2470, USA

Clark, Anthony (Actor, Comedian)
c/o Jennifer Craig *Gersh Agency, The (LA)*
232 N Canon Dr
Beverly Hills, CA 90210-5302, USA

Clark, Archie (Basketball Player)
Los Angeles Lakers
4268 10th St
Ecorse, MI 48229-1219, USA

Clark, Archie (Basketball Player)
600 Randolph St Ste 323
Wayne County Building
Detroit, MI 48226-2831, USA

Clark, Bernard (Football Player)
Cincinnati Bengals
1506 W Spruce St
Tampa, FL 33607-3513, USA

Clark, Blake
18735 Hillsboro Rd
Northridge, CA 91326-3916, USA

Clark, Bob (Correspondent)
ABC-TV
5010 Creston St
News Dept
Hyattsville, MD 20781-1216, USA

Clark, Bobby (Baseball Player)
California Angels
1030 Perrisito St
Perris, CA 92570-2345, USA

Clark, Brady (Baseball Player)
Cincinnati Reds
PO Box 638
Walterville, OR 97489-0638, USA

Clark, Bruce (Football Player)
New Orleans Saints
366 Clark Loop
Robeline, LA 71469, USA

Clark, Bryan (Actor)
Epstein-Wyckoff
280 S Beverly Dr Ste 400
Beverly Hills, CA 90212-3904, USA

Clark, Bryan (Baseball Player)
Seattle Mariners
508 Clark St
Madera, CA 93638-1662, USA

Clark, Bryan (Football Player)
Cincinnati Bengals
1482 Lochridge Rd
Bloomfield Hills, MI 48302-0733, USA

Clark, C Joseph (Joe) (Prime Minister)
707 7th Ave SW
#1300
Calgary, AB T2P 3H6, CANADA

Clark, Candy (Actor)
13935 Hatteras St
Van Nuys, CA 91401-4342, USA

Clark, Carol Hiqgins (Writer)
300 E 56th St
New York, NY 10022-4136, USA

Clark, Corinne (Baseball Player)
7224 Hawthorn Ave NE
Albuquerque, NM 87113-2084, USA

Clark, Dallas (Football Player)
Indianapolis Colts
7001 W 56th St
Indianapolis, IN 46254-9698, USA

Clark, Daniel (Actor)
c/o Staff Member *Schachter Entertainment*
1157 S Beverly Dr Fl 2
Los Angeles, CA 90035-1119, USA

Clark, Danny (Football Player)
Jacksonville Jaguars
213 Seneca Trl
Bloomingdale, IL 60108-2432, USA

Clark, Dave (Baseball Player)
Cleveland Indians
106 Road 686
Tupelo, MS 38801-0625, USA

Clark, Dick (Producer)
c/o Staff Member *Dick Clark Productions*
2900 Olympic Blvd
Santa Monica, CA 90404-4127, USA

Clark, Doran
6399 Wilshire Blvd Ste 414
Los Angeles, CA 90048-5716, USA

Clark, Dwight (Football Player)
San Francisco 49ers
2511 Sedley Rd
Charlotte, NC 28211-3658, USA

Clark, Earl (Swimmer)
1145 NE 126th St Apt 4
North Miami, FL 33161-5027, USA

Clark, Gail (Football Player)
Chicago Bears
411 Miami Ave
Bellefontaine, OH 43311-2322, USA

Clark, Gary (Football Player)
PO Box 202
Dublin, VA 24084-0202, USA

Clark, Gene (Musician)
Artists International Mgmt
9850 Sandaltoot Road #458
Boca Raton, FL 33428, USA

Clark, George W (Physicist)
Massachusetts Institute of Technology
Physics Dept
Cambridge, MA 02139, USA

Clark, Glen (Baseball Player)
Atlanta Braves
5605 Marblehead Dr
Dallas, TX 75232-2356, USA

Clark, Guy (Musician, Songwriter, Writer)
Keith Case Assoc
1025 17th Ave S Fl 2
Nashville, TN 37212-2211, USA

Clark, Harry (Football Player)
Los Angeles Dons
1121 Patton Dr
Morgantown, WV 26505-3756, USA

Clark, Helen (Prime Minister)
Prime Minister's Office
Parliament Buildings
Wellington, NEW ZEALAND

Clark, Howie (Baseball Player)
Baltimore Orioles
14204 439th Ave SE
North Bend, WA 98045-9209, USA

Clark, Jack (Baseball Player)
San Diego Padres
6541 Scottsdale Way
Frisco, TX 75034-4015, USA

Clark, James (Jim) (Business Person)
Neoteris
940 Stewart Dr
Sunnyvale, CA 94085-3912, USA

Clark, Jerald (Baseball Player)
San Diego Padres
200 E Pecan Dr
Crockett, TX 75835-4018, USA

Clark, Jessie (Football Player)
Green Bay Packers
5343 E Taylor St Apt 104
Phoenix, AZ 85008-7902, USA

Clark, Jim (Baseball Player)
Cleveland Indians
659 S Indian Hill Blvd Apt C
Claremont, CA 91711-5486, USA

Clark, Joe
PO Box 96848
Washington, DC 20090-6848, USA

Clark, Joe (Educator)
Essex County Detention Center
208 Essex Ave
Newark, NJ 07103, USA

Clark, Kelly (Skier)
PO Box 725
178 Route 100
West Dover, VT 05356-0725, USA

Clark, Kelvin (Football Player)
Denver Broncos
3812 Evesham Dr
Plano, TX 75025-3818, USA

Clark, Kenneth B (Psychic)
PO Box 126
Hastings On Hudson, NY 10706-0126, USA

Clark, Keon (Basketball Player)
Utah Jazz Delta Center
301 W South Temple
Salt Lake City, UT 84101-1216, USA

Clark, Kevin (Football Player)
Denver Broncos
3962 S Chase Way
Denver, CO 80235-3133, USA

Clark, Kevin Alexander (Actor)
c/o Ann Geddes *Geddes Agency, The*
8430 Santa Monica Blvd Ste 200
Los Angeles, CA 90069-4253, USA

Clark, L Hill (Business Person)
Crane Co
100 Stamford Pl
Stamford, CT 06902-6784, USA

Clark, Larry (Filmmaker)
c/o Staff Member *International Creative Management (ICM-LA)*
10250 Constellation Blvd
Los Angeles, CA 90067-6200, USA

Clark, Laurel B (Doctor)
305 Harborside Cir
Kemah, TX 77565-2991, USA

Clark, Leroy (Football Player)
Houston Oilers
5458 Osprey Dr
Houston, TX 77048-1109, USA

Clark, Louis S (Football Player)
Seattle Seahawks
PO Box 2118
Jacksonville, FL 32203-2118, USA

Clark, Marcia (Lawyer)
c/o Staff Member *William Morris Agency (WMA-LA)*
1 William Morris Pl
Beverly Hills, CA 90212-4261, USA

Clark, Mario (Football Player)
Buffalo Bills
695 Palisade St Apt 695
Pasadena, CA 91103-2059, USA

Clark, Mark (Baseball Player)
St Louis Cardinals
316 Sebring Rd
Springfield, IL 62707-9375, USA

Clark, Mary Ellen (Swimmer)
213 Lauderdale Trl
Fort Lauderdale, FL 33312-7126, USA

Clark, Mary Higgins (Writer)
Werimus Brook Road
Saddle River, NJ 07458, USA

Clark, Matt (Actor)
1199 Park Ave Apt 15D
New York, NY 10128-1791, USA

Clark, Mel (Baseball Player)
Philadelphia Phillies
RR 1 Box 97
West Columbia, WV 25287-9721, USA

Clark, Micheal (Choreographer, Dancer)
Barbican Centre
Silk St
London EC2Y 8DS, UNITED KINGDOM (UK)

Clark, Monte D (Football Player)
San Francisco 49ers
1482 Lochridge Rd
Bloomfield Township, MI 48302-0733, USA

Clark, Mystro (Actor, Comedian)
c/o Staff Member *International Creative Management (ICM-LA)*
10250 Constellation Blvd
Los Angeles, CA 90067-6200, USA

Clark, Oliver (Actor)
House of Representatives
211 S Beverly Dr Ste 208
Beverly Hills, CA 90212-3879, USA

Clark, Perry (Coach)
Miami University
Athletic Dept
Coral Gables, FL 33124, USA

Clark, Peter B (Publisher)
7675 La Jolla Blvd Unit 203
La Jolla, CA 92037-4747, USA

Clark, Petula (Musician)
15 chemin Rieu Colign
Geneva, SWITZERLAND

Clark, Phil (Baseball Player)
St Louis Cardinals
228 Pineknoll Rd
Sylvester, GA 31791-7625, USA

Clark, Phil (Baseball Player)
Detroit Tigers
9062 Dancy Tree Ct
Orlando, FL 32836-5059, USA

Clark, Phil (Football Player)
Dallas Cowboys
760 Essington Ln
Buffalo Grove, IL 60089-1417, USA

Clark, Ramsey
37 W 12th St Apt 2B
New York, NY 10011-8503, USA

Clark, Richard C (Dick) (Senator)
4424 Edmunds St NW # 1070
Washington, DC 20007-1117, USA

Clark, Rickey (Baseball Player)
California Angels
8953 Emerald Waters Ct
Las Vegas, NV 89147-6501, USA

Clark, Robert C (Artist)
34 Monterey Ct
Manhattan Beach, CA 90266-7237, USA

Clark, Ron (Baseball Player)
Minnesota Twins
700 Starkey Rd Apt 511
Largo, FL 33771-2344, USA

Clark, Roy (Musician)
Roy Clark Productions
3225 S Norwood Ave
Tulsa, OK 74135-5493, USA

Clark, Ryan (Football Player)
New York Giants
768 Goucher St
Gretna, LA 70056-4434, USA

Clark, Sedric (Football Player)
Baltimore Ravens
7819 Chasewood Dr
Missouri City, TX 77489-1836, USA

Clark, Spencer Treat (Actor)
c/o Michael Greenwald *Don Buchwald & Associates Inc (LA)*
6500 Wilshire Blvd Ste 2200
Los Angeles, CA 90048-4942, USA

Clark, Stephen E (Steve) (Swimmer)
29 Martling Rd
San Anselmo, CA 94960-1172, USA

Clark, Susan (Actor)
13400 Riverside Dr Ste 308
Sherman Oaks, CA 91423-2541, USA

Clark, Terri (Musician)
c/o Keith Miller *William Morris Agency (WMA-TN)*
1600 Division St Ste 300
Nashville, TN 37203-2755, USA

Clark, Terry (Baseball Player)
California Angels
7100 Santa Barbara Ct
Fontana, CA 92336-2909, USA

Clark, Tony (Baseball Player)
Detroit Tigers
7916 W Villa Lindo Dr
Peoria, AZ 85383-1022, USA

Clark, Vernon E (Admiral)
Chief Of Naval Operations
Hqusn Pentagon
Washington, DC 20350-0001, USA

Clark, W G (Architect)
Clark & Menefee Architects
4048 E Main St
Charlottesville, VA 22902, USA

Clark, W Ramsey (General)
37 W 12th St
New York, NY 10011-8502, USA

Clark, Wayne (Football Player)
San Diego Chargers
12512 Brighton Pl
Tustin, CA 92780-2875, USA

Clark, Wendel (Hockey Player)
Toronto Maple Leafs
40 Bay St
Toronto, ON M5J 2K2, CANADA

Clark, Wesley K (Wes) (General)
Stephens Group
111 Center St
Little Rock, AR 72201-4425, USA

Clark, Will (Adult Film Star)
c/o Staff Member *Diva Central Inc*
7510 W Sunset Blvd Ste 1445
Los Angeles, CA 90046-3408, USA

Clark, William (Baseball Player)
Boston Red Sox
601 Labelle St
Boscobel, WI 53805-1426, USA

Clark, William P (Secretary)
4424 Edmunds St NW # 1070
Washington, DC 20007-1117, USA

Clark-Cole, Dorinda (Musician)
c/o Staff Member *Gospocentric*
421 E Beach Ave
Inglewood, CA 90302-3103, USA

Clark-Sheard, Karen (Musician)
c/o Staff Member *Elektra Records*
75 Rockefeller Plz Fl 17
New York, NY 10019-6927, USA

Clarke, Allan (Music Group, Musician)
Hill Farm Hackleton
Northantshire NN7 2DH, UNITED
KINGDOM (UK)

Clarke, Angela (Actor)
3930 Weeping Willow Dr
Moorpark, CA 93021-2842, USA

Clarke, Bob (Cartoonist)
7480 Rivershore Dr
Seaford, DE 19973-4328, USA

Clarke, Brian Patrick (Actor)
2102 Clubside Dr
Longwood, FL 32779-6211, USA

Clarke, Elis E I (President)
16 Frederick St
Port of Spain, TRINIDAD & TOBAGO

Clarke, Emily (Actor)
c/o Darren Goldberg *1 Management*
9000 W Sunset Blvd Ph 1550
West Hollywood, CA 90069-1838, USA

Clarke, Emmy (Actor)
c/o Darren Goldberg *1 Management*
9000 W Sunset Blvd Ph 1550
West Hollywood, CA 90069-1838, USA

Clarke, Frank (Football Player)
Cleveland Browns
1753 Sixty Street
Beloit, WI 53511, USA

Clarke, Gilby (Music Group, Musician)
Sammy Boyd Entertainment
212 Allen Ave
Allenhurst, NJ 07711-1006, USA

Clarke, Gilmore D (Architect)
480 Park Ave
New York, NY 10022-1613, USA

Clarke, Hagood (Football Player)
Buffalo Bills
2500 NE 37th Dr
Fort Lauderdale, FL 33308-6323, USA

Clarke, Horace (Baseball Player)
New York Yankees
PO Box 891
Frederiksted, VI 00841-0891, USA

Clarke, John (Actor)
Days of Our Lives Show
Knbc-Tv 3000W Alameda Ave
Burbank, CA 91523-0001, USA

Clarke, Ken (Football Player)
Philadelphia Eagles
1700 Stoney Brook Way
Alpharetta, GA 30005-3999, USA

Clarke, Kenneth H (Government Official)
House of Commons
Westminster
London SW1A 0AA, UNITED KINGDOM
(UK)

Clarke, Lenny (Actor)
8383 Wilshire Blvd Ste 550
Beverly Hills, CA 90211-2417, USA

Clarke, Leon T (Football Player)
Los Angeles Rams
13330 Saint Andrews Dr
Seal Beach, CA 90740-4196, USA

Clarke, Martha (Choreographer, Dancer)
Sheldon Soffer Mgmt
130 W 56th St
New York, NY 10019-3866, USA

Clarke, Melinda (Actor)
c/o David Brownstein *Art Work
Entertainment*
5900 Wilshire Blvd Ste 2150
Los Angeles, CA 90036-5021, USA

Clarke, Michael (Music Group, Musician)
Artists International Mgmt
9850 Sandalfoot Blvd # 458
Boca Raton, FL 33428-6645, USA

Clarke, Richard (Lawyer, Misc)
National Security Council
1600 Pennsylvania Ave NW
Washington, DC 20500-0003, USA

Clarke, Robert L (Government Official)
Bracewell & Patterson
711 Louisiana St Ste 2900
Houston, TX 77002-2770, USA

Clarke, Ronald (Ron) (Athlete, Track
Athlete)
1 Bay St
Brighton, VIC 3186, AUSTRALIA

Clarke, Sarah (Actor)
c/o Lainie Sorkin Stolhanske *Management
360*
9111 Wilshire Blvd
Beverly Hills, CA 90210-5508, USA

Clarke, Sir Arthur C (Misc, Writer)
Leslie's House 25 Barnes Place
Colombo 07, SRI LANKA

Clarke, Stan (Baseball Player)
Toronto Blue Jays
5333 Sanders Dr
Toledo, OH 43615-6860, USA

Clarke, Stanley (Musician)
c/o Brice Gaeta *Broder Webb Chervin
Silbermann Agency, The (BWCS)*
10250 Constellation Blvd Ste P
Los Angeles, CA 90067-6213, USA

Clarke, Thomas E (Business Person)
Nice Inc
1 Bowerman Dr
Beaverton, OR 97005-0979, USA

Clarkson, Adrienne (General, Governor)
Governor General's Office
1 Sussex Dr
Ottawa, ON K1A 0A2, CANADA

Clarkson, Jeremy (Television Host)
c/o Staff Member *XS Promotions*
57 Fonthill Rd
Aberdeen AB11 6UQ, UNITED
KINGDOM (UK)

Clarkson, Patricia (Actor)
c/o Scott Bankston *Jeff Morrone
Management*
9350 Wilshire Blvd Ste 224
Beverly Hills, CA 90212-3204, USA

Clary, Julian (Actor)
PO Box 976
Swindon
SN5 7HN, UNITED KINGDOM (UK)

Clary, Marty (Baseball Player)
Atlanta Braves
205 Torktown Ct
Easley, SC 29642, USA

Clary, Robert (Actor)
10001 Sundial Ln
Beverly Hills, CA 90210-2719, USA

Clasby, Bob (Football Player)
St Louis Cardinals
8180 E Shea Blvd Unit 1090
Scottsdale, AZ 85260-6572, USA

Clash, Kevin (Artist, Voice Over Artist)
c/o Staff Member *Sesame Workshop*
1 Lincoln Plz
New York, NY 10023-7163, USA

Clash, The
268 Camden Rd.
London, ENGLAND NW1, UNITED
KINGDOM (UK)

Clatterbuck, Bob (Football Player)
New York Giants
454 W 100 N
Hurricane, UT 84737-2010, USA

Clatterbuck, Tamara (Actor)
House of Representatives
211 S Beverly Dr Ste 208
Beverly Hills, CA 90212-3879, USA

Clatworthy, Robert (Artist, Misc)
Moelfre Cynghordy
Landovery Dyfed
Wales SA20 0UW, UNITED KINGDOM
(UK)

Clatyon, Barry (Artist, Voice Over Artist)
Talking Heads
88-90 Crawford St
London W1H 2BS, UNITED KINGDOM
(UK)

Claudel, Aurelie (Model)
c/o Staff Member *IMG Models*
304 Park Ave S Fl 12
New York, NY 10010-4301, USA

Clauser, Francis H (Educator, Engineer)
4072 Chevy Chase Dr
Flintridge, CA 91011-3923, USA

Claussen, Brandon (Baseball Player)
New York Yankees
2611 N Kentucky Ave Apt 116
Roswell, NM 88201-5870, USA

Clavel, Bernard (Writer)
Albin Michel 22 Rue Huyghens
Paris 75014, FRANCE

Clavier, Christian (Actor)
Agents Associes Beaume
201 Faubourg Saint Honore
Paris 75008, FRANCE

Clawhammer
Box 1519
Nijnegen 6501 BM, THE NETHERLANDS

Clawson, John (Basketball Player)
102 Danvilla Ct
Danville, CA 94526-2402, USA

Claxton, Craig (Speedy) (Basketball
Player)
Golden State Warriors
1001 Broadway
Oakland, CA 94607-4019, USA

Clay, Andrew (Actor, Comedian)
Artist Group International
9560 Wilshire Blvd Ste 400
Beverly Hills, CA 90212-2416, USA

Clay, Andrew Dice
c/o Scott Hart *Nanas/Hart Entertainment*
14622 Ventura Blvd Ste 746
Sherman Oaks, CA 91403-3600, USA

Clay, Danny (Baseball Player)
Philadelphia Phillies
1060 Lilley Ave
Columbus, OH 43206-1734, USA

Clay, Hayward (Football Player)
St Louis Rams
PO Box 234
Snyder, TX 79550-0234, USA

Clay, John (Football Player)
Los Angeles Raiders
1425 Leroy Ave
Saint Louis, MO 63133-1723, USA

Clay, Ken (Baseball Player)
New York Yankees
4523 60th Street Ct W
Bradenton, FL 34210-2729, USA

Clay, Nicholas
15 Golden Sq. #315
London, ENGLAND W1R 3AG, UNITED
KINGDOM (UK)

Clay, Randy (Football Player)
New York Giants
2771 Whisper Path St
San Antonio, TX 78230-3720, USA

Clay, Walter (Football Player)
Chicago Rockets
2827 Arlington Ave
Pueblo, CO 81003-1315, USA

Clayborn, Raymond D (Ray) (Football
Player)
New England Patriots
20610 Aspen Canyon Dr
Katy, TX 77450-7091, USA

Clayburgh, Jill (Actor)
PO Box 432
Lakeville, CT 06039-0432, USA

Clayderman, Richard (Musician)
Denis Vaughan Management
P O Box 28286
London N21 3WT, UNITED KINGDOM
(UK)

Clayman, Ralph V (Doctor, Misc)
Bames Hospital
416 S Kingshighway Blvd
Surgery Dept
Saint Louis, MO 63110, USA

Claypool, Lee (Music Group, Musician)
Figurehead Mgmt
3470 19th St
San Francisco, CA 94110-1740, USA

Claypool, Les (Musician)
c/o Staff Member *Paradigm (Monterey)*
509 Hartnell St
Monterey, CA 93940-2825, USA

Clayson, Jane (Correspondent)
CBS-TV
51 W 52nd St
News Dept
New York, NY 10019-6119, USA

Clayton, Adam (Music Group, Musician)
Principle Mgmt
30-32 Sir John Rogersons Quay
Dublin @, IRELAND

Clayton, Donald D (Misc)
Clemson University
Physic/Astrophysics Dept
Clemson, SC 29634-0001, USA

Clayton, Harvey (Football Player)
Pittsburgh Steelers
15303 SW 143rd St
Miami, FL 33196-2879, USA

Clayton, Ralph (Football Player)
St Louis Cardinals
16174 Normandy St
Detroit, MI 48221-3136, USA

Clayton, Robert N (Geophysicist, Misc, Physicist)
5201 S Comell Ave
Chicago, IL 60615, USA

Clayton, Royce (Baseball Player)
San Francisco Giants
7425 N Ironwood Dr
Paradise Valley, AZ 85253-3153, USA

Clayton, Thomas David (Music Group, Musician)
Music Avenue Inc
43 Washington St
Groveland, MA 01834-1142, USA

Cleamons, Jim (Basketball Player)
Los Angeles Lakers
3067 Oak Spring St
Columbus, OH 43219-3020, USA

Cleamons, Jim (Basketball Player, Coach)
1601 1st St
Manhattan Beach, CA 90266-7003, USA

Clear, Mark (Baseball Player)
California Angels
3229 Armsley Dr
Chino Hills, CA 91709-3862, USA

Clearwater, Keith (Golfer)
1077 E Bretonwoods Ln
Orem, UT 84097-8200, USA

Cleary, Joe (Baseball Player)
Washington Senators
135 W 225th St Apt 1H
Bronx, NY 10463-6841, USA

Cleary, Jon Stephen (Writer)
HarperCollins
23 Ryde Road
Pymble, NSW 2073, AUSTRALIA

Cleary, Robert (Bob) (Hockey Player)
680 South Ave Unit 8
Weston, MA 02493-1192, USA

Cleary, Thomas (Writer)
c/o Staff Member *Random House*
1540 Broadway
New York, NY 10036-4039, USA

Cleary, William J (Bill) Jr (Coach, Hockey Player)
27 Kingwood Road
Auburndale, MA 02466, USA

Cleave, Mary L (Astronaut)
NASA
Earth Science Office
Code As Room 7R86
Washington, DC 20546-0001, USA

Cleaver, Alan (Designer, Fashion Designer)
Via Vallone 11
Monte Conero
Sirolo, ITALY

Cledwyn of Penrhos (Government Official)
Penmorfa Trearddur
Holyhead Gwynedd
Wales, UNITED KINGDOM (UK)

Cleese, John (Actor, Comedian, Writer)
c/o Tony Lipp *Creative Artists Agency LCC (CAA-LA)*
2000 Avenue Of The Stars
Los Angeles, CA 90067-4700, USA

Clef (Music Group, Musician)
DAS Communications
83 Riverside Dr
New York, NY 10024-5713, USA

Clegg, Johnny (Music Group, Musician)
Monterey International
200 W Superior St Ste 202
Chicago, IL 60610-3554, USA

Cleghorn, Ellen
9200 W Sunset Blvd Ste 900
Los Angeles, CA 90069-3604, USA

Cleghorne, Ellen (Actor, Comedian)
c/o Frederick Levy *Management 101*
5527 1/2 Cahuenga Blvd
North Hollywood, CA 91601, USA

Cleland, J Maxwell (Max) (Senator)
340 Mockingbird Ln SE
Smyrna, GA 30082-3729, USA

Clemens, Barry (Basketball Player)
New York Knicks
18500 Lake Rd Ste 300
Rocky River, OH 44116-1751, USA

Clemens, Clarence
c/o Neil Vineberg *Vineberg Communications*
PO Box 205
Westhampton
Westhampton, NY 11977-0205, USA

Clemens, Donella (Religious Leader)
Monnonite Church
722 N Main St
Newton, KS 67114-1819, USA

Clemens, Doug (Baseball Player)
St Louis Cardinals
4799 Lower Mountain Rd
New Hope, PA 18938-9454, USA

Clemens, Robert (Football Player)
Green Bay Packers
689 Big Foot Rd
Scottsboro, AL 35768-7304, USA

Clemens, Roger (Baseball Player)
c/o Team Member *New York Yankees*
Yankee Stadium
161st St & River Ave
Bronx, NY 10451, USA

Clement, Anthony (Football Player)
Arizona Cardinals
141 Navajo Ln
Opelousas, LA 70570-0324, USA

Clement, Aurore (Actor)
Artmedia
20 Ave Rapp
Paris 75007, FRANCE

Clement, Matt (Baseball Player)
San Diego Padres
425 Vista Dr
Butler, PA 16001-3221, USA

Clement F, Haynsworth Jr (Judge)
111 Boxwood Ln
Greenville, SC 29601-3812, USA

Clemente, Carmine D (Misc, Physicist)
11737 Bellagio Rd
Los Angeles, CA 90049-2158, USA

Clemente, Fransesco (Artist)
684 Broadway
New York, NY 10012-1125, USA

Clements, Dick (Director, Producer, Writer)
c/o Bruce Kaufman *Broder Webb Chervin Silbermann Agency, The (BWCS)*
10250 Constellation Blvd Ste P
Los Angeles, CA 90067-6213, USA

Clements, John A (Misc, Physicist)
University of California
Cardiovascular Institute
San Francisco, CA 94143-0001, USA

Clements, Kim (Writer)
c/o Staff Member *Creative Artists Agency LCC (CAA-LA)*
2000 Avenue Of The Stars
Los Angeles, CA 90067-4700, USA

Clements, Lennie (Golfer)
PO Box 182197
Coronado, CA 92178-2197, USA

Clements, Nate (Football Player)
Buffalo Bills
1 Bills Dr
Orchard Park, NY 14127-2237, USA

Clements, Pat (Baseball Player)
California Angels
166 Lazy S Ln
Chico, CA 95928-9112, USA

Clements, Ronald (Ron) (Director, Producer, Writer)
c/o Staff Member *Ziffren Brittenham Branca Fischer Gilbert-Lurie, Stiffman & Cook*
1801 Century Park W
Los Angeles, CA 90067-6409, USA

Clements, Ronalds F (Animator, Director)
Disney Animation
P O Box 10200
Burbank, CA 91521-0001, USA

Clements, Suzanne (Designer, Fashion Designer)
Clements Ribeiro Ltd
48 S Molton St
London W1X 1HE, UNITED KINGDOM (UK)

Clements, Tom (Football Player)
Kansas City Chiefs
403 Landon Gate
Pittsburgh, PA 15238-1539, USA

Clements, Vincent (Football Player)
New York Giants
62 Chatham Rd
Kensington, CT 06037-1104, USA

Clements, William P Jr (Governor)
1901 N Adard St
Dallas, TX 75201, USA

Clemons, Chris (Baseball Player)
Chicago White Sox
503 Lux Dr
Robinson, TX 76706-6225, USA

Clemons, Clarence (Music Group, Musician)
Long Distance Enter
568 E Woodbright Road #234
Boynton Beach, FL 33435, USA

Clemons, Craig (Football Player)
Chicago Bears
1517 D Ave NE
Cedar Rapids, IA 52402-5148, USA

Clemons, Duane (Football Player)
Minnesota Vikings
7512 Dr Phillips Blvd Ste 50-908
Orlando, FL 32819-5420, USA

Clemons, Lance (Baseball Player)
Kansas City Royals
4516 Golf Club Ln
Brooksville, FL 34609-0303, USA

Clemons, Ray (Football Player)
Green Bay Packers
PO Box 276493
Sacramento, CA 95827-6493, USA

Clendenin, Bob (Actor)
c/o Staff Member *Origin Talent Agency*
4705 Laurel Canyon Blvd Ste 306
Studio City, CA 91607-5940, USA

Clennon, David (Actor)
c/o Michael Greene *Greene & Associates*
190 N Canon Dr Ste 200
Beverly Hills, CA 90210-5319, USA

Cleopatra
c/o Staff Member *20th Century Fox*
10201 W Pico Blvd
Los Angeles, CA 90064-2651, USA

Clerico, Christian (Business Person, Misc)
Lido-Normandie
116 Bis Ave des Champs Elyees
Paris 75008, FRANCE

Clervoy, Jean-Francois (Misc)
NASA
2101 Nasa Pkwy
Johnson Space Flight Center
Houston, TX 77058-3691, USA

Cleveland, J Harlan (Diplomat, Educator)
46891 Grissom St
Sterling, VA 20165-3593, USA

Cleveland, Patience (Actor)
PO Box 490
Richland, MO 65556-0490, USA

Cleveland, Paul M (Diplomat)
808 Crooked Crow Ln
Great Falls, VA 22066-2409, USA

Cleveland, Reggie (Baseball Player)
St Louis Cardinals
202 Creekview Dr
Anna, TX 75409-3577, USA

Clevenger, Raymond C III (Judge)
US Court of Appeals
717 Madison Pl NW
Washington, DC 20439-0001, USA

Clevenger, Tex (Baseball Player)
Boston Red Sox
31727 Country Club Dr
Porterville, CA 93257-9610, USA

Clexton, Edward W Jr (Admiral)
1000 Bobolink Dr
Virginia Beach, VA 23451-4906, USA

Cliburn, Stan (Baseball Player)
California Angels
4807 Highway 80 W
Jackson, MS 39209-4704, USA

Cliburn, Stewart (Baseball Player)
California Angels
727 Nimitz St
Jackson, MS 39209-6118, USA

Cliburn, Van (Musician)
PO Box 470219
Fort Worth, TX 76147-0219, USA

Cliche, Karen (Actor)
c/o Sandy Martinez *Martinez Creative Management*
7012 St Laurent Blvd #200
Montreal, PQ H2S 3E2, CANADA

Click, Cash Money (Music Group)
c/o Staff Member *JL Entertainment Inc*
18653 Ventura Blvd # 340
Tarzana, CA 91356-4103, USA

Cliff, Jimmy (Music Group, Songwriter, Writer)
51 Lady Musgrave Rd
Kingston, JAMAICA

Clifford, Linda (Music Group)
c/o Staff Member *Diva Central Inc*
7510 W Sunset Blvd Ste 1445
Los Angeles, CA 90046-3408, USA

Clifford, M Richard (Rich) (Astronaut)
3700 Bay Area Blvd
Houston, TX 77058-1160, USA

Clift, Eleanor
1750 Pennsylvania Ave NW Ste 1220
Washington, DC 20006-4504, USA

Clift, William B III (Photographer)
PO Box 6035
Santa Fe, NM 87502-6035, USA

Clifton, Greg (Football Player)
Washington Redskins
2717 Botany St
Charlotte, NC 28216-4431, USA

Clifton, Kyle (Football Player)
Washington Redskins
777 South Point Ct
Aledo, TX 76008-4134, USA

Cliks, The (Music Group)
c/o Staff Member *Paradigm (Monterey)*
509 Hartnell St
Monterey, CA 93940-2825, USA

Cline, Jackie (Football Player)
Pittsburgh Steelers
5935 High Forrest Dr
Mc Calla, AL 35111-4205, USA

Cline, Martin J (Educator, Misc)
University of California
Med Center Hematology Dept
Los Angeles, CA 90024, USA

Cline, Richard (Cartoonist)
New Yorker Magazine
4 Times Sq
Editorial Dept
New York, NY 10036-6592, USA

Cline, Ty (Baseball Player)
Cleveland Indians
37 Wappoo Creek Pl
Charleston, SC 29412-2121, USA

Cline Sr, Tony (Football Player)
Buffalo Bills
59 Chestnut Pl
Danville, CA 94506-4542, USA

Clines, Gene (Baseball Player)
Pittsburgh Pirates
5303 9th Avenue Dr W
Bradenton, FL 34209-4205, USA

Clinkscale, F Dextor (Football Player)
Dallas Cowboys
206 Michaux Dr
Greenville, SC 29605-3156, USA

Clinkscales, Joey (Football Player)
Pittsburgh Steelers
4295 Willow Pond Cv
Memphis, TN 38125-3132, USA

Clinkscales, Sherard (Baseball Player)
5725 Town Center Dr Apt 8
Granger, IN 46530-4426, USA

Clinton, Chelsea
15 Old House Ln
Chappaqua, NY 10514, USA

Clinton, George (Music Group, Musician, Songwriter, Writer)
c/o Bruce Solar *Agency Group Ltd, The (LA)*
1880 Century Park E Ste 711
Los Angeles, CA 90067-1618, USA

Clinton, Hillary Rodham (Ex-First Lady, First Lady, Politician)
United States Senate
476 Russell Senate Office Building
Washington, DC 20510-0001, USA

Clinton, William J (Bill) (Ex-President, Politician, President)
55 W 125th St
New York, NY 10027-4516, USA

Clinton-Davis of Hackney, Stanley C (Government Official)
House of Lords
Westminster
London SW1A 0PW, UNITED KINGDOM (UK)

Clisters, Kim (Tennis Player)
Assn of Tennis Professionals
200 Tournament Rd
Ponte Vedra Beach, FL 32082, USA

Clive, John
4 Court Lodge Chelsea
London, ENGLAND SW3 AJA, UNITED KINGDOM (UK)

Cloepfil, Brad (Architect)
Allied Works Architecture
910 NW Hoyt St Ste 200
Portland, OR 97209-3208, USA

Clohessy, Robert (Actor)
Don Buchwald
6500 Wilshire Blvd Ste 2200
Los Angeles, CA 90048-4942, USA

Cloke, Kristen (Actor)
c/o Staff Member *Mitchell K Stubbs & Assoc (MKS)*
8695 Washington Blvd Ste 204
Culver City, CA 90232-7419, USA

Clokey, Art (Cartoonist)
359 Los Osos Valley Rd
Los Osos, CA 93402-3119, USA

Clone, Jean (Baseball Player)
2661 Kid Curry Dr
Bozeman, MT 59718-8726, USA

Cloninger, Tony (Baseball Player)
Milwaukee Braves
PO Box 1500
Denver, NC 28037-2006, USA

Clontz, Brad (Baseball Player)
Atlanta Braves
735 Eider Down Ct
Alpharetta, GA 30022-6198, USA

Clooney, George (Actor, Producer)
c/o Staff Member *Smoke House*
4000 Warner Blvd Bldg 15
Burbank, CA 91522-0001, USA

Clooney, Nick (Actor, Writer)
The Cincinnati Post
125 E Court St
Cincinnati, OH 45202-1214, USA

Close, Bill (Basketball Player)
555 Byron St Apt 409
Palo Alto, CA 94301-2038, USA

Close, Charles T (Chuck) (Artist)
20 Bond St
New York, NY 10012-2406, USA

Close, Eric (Actor)
c/o Robert Goodman *Robert Goodman Management*
100 S Alameda St Unit 416
Los Angeles, CA 90012-3948, USA

Close, Glenn (Actor)
c/o Kevin Huvane *Creative Artists Agency LCC (CAA-LA)*
2000 Avenue Of The Stars
Los Angeles, CA 90067-4700, USA

Close, Joshua (Actor)
c/o Graciella Sanchez *One Entertainment (LA)*
12 W 57th St Ph
New York, NY 10019-3900, USA

Closs, Bill (Basketball Player)
Indianapolis Kautskys
10320 W Loyola Dr # 201
Los Altos, CA 94024-6510, USA

Closter, Al (Baseball Player)
Washington Senators
4103 Hickory Rd
Richmond, VA 23235-1437, USA

Clotet, Lluis (Architect)
Studio PER
Caspe 151
Barcelona 08013, SPAIN

Clotworthy, Robert (Actor)
c/o Staff Member *Amsel Eisenstadt & Frazier Inc*
5055 Wilshire Blvd Ste 865
Los Angeles, CA 90036-6109, USA

Clotworthy, Robert L (Bob) (Coach, Misc, Swimmer)
HC 74 Box 22313
El Prado, NM 87529-9523, USA

Cloud, Jack M (Football Player)
Green Bay Packers
805 Janice Dr
Annapolis, MD 21403-2801, USA

Cloud, Mike (Football Player)
Kansas City Chiefs
508 Turnpike Ave
Portsmouth, RI 02871-1515, USA

Cloude, Ken (Baseball Player)
Seattle Mariners
8126 Del Haven Rd
Dundalk, MD 21222-3425, USA

Clough, Gerald W (Educator)
Georgia Institute of Techonlogy
President's Office
Atlanta, GA 30332-0001, USA

Clougherty, Pat (Baseball Player)
US Olympic Team
3160 Arden Dr
Saint Paul, MN 55129-7782, USA

Clovers, The
1607 Belvidere Rd
Belvidere, NC 27919-9615, USA

Clowes, Dan (Artist)
c/o Staff Member *Fantagraphics Books*
7563 Lake City Way NE
Seattle, WA 98115-4218, USA

Cloyd, Paul (Basketball Player)
Sheboygan Redskins
508 Skyview Dr
Waunakee, WI 53597-3123, USA

Club, Culture (Musician)
c/o Staff Member *William Morris Agency (WMA-LA)*
1 William Morris Pl
Beverly Hills, CA 90212-4261, USA

Cluggish, Bob (Basketball Player)
New York Knicks
270 Lake Seminary Cir
Maitland, FL 32751-3311, USA

Clune, Don (Football Player)
New York Giants
322 N Orange St
Media, PA 19063-2308, USA

Clutterbuck, Bryan (Baseball Player)
Milwaukee Brewers
1986 Lovell Ct
Milford, MI 48381-4171, USA

Clwson, John (Basketball Player)
Oakland Oaks
33 San Ysidro Ct
Danville, CA 94526-1545, USA

Clyburn, Danny (Baseball Player)
Baltimore Orioles
148 E Brooklyn Ave
Lancaster, SC 29720-3326, USA

Clyde, Ben (Basketball Player)
Bosten Celtics
8356 A Street Apt #1
Saint Petersburg, FL 33701, USA

Clyde, David (Baseball Player)
Texas Rangers
18802 S Roselake Dr
Tomball, TX 77377-3504, USA

Clyde, Tom (Baseball Player)
Philadelphia Athletics
210 Chestnut Ln
Coppell, TX 75019-5390, USA

Clyne, Patricia (Designer, Fashion Designer)
353 W 39th St
New York, NY 10018-1417, USA

Coachman, Bobby (Baseball Player)
California Angels
PO Box 44
Cottonwood, AL 36320-0044, USA

Coachman, Davis Alice (Athlete, Track Athlete)
811 Gibson St
Tuskegee, AL 36083-7253, USA

Coady, Richard (Football Player)
Chicago Bears
17106 Spanky Pl
Dallas, TX 75248-1533, USA

Coakley, Dexter (Football Player)
Dallas Cowboys
408 Maggie St
Mount Pleasant, SC 29464-9256, USA

Coan, Bert (Football Player)
Kansas City Chiefs
14517 N US Highway 59
Nacogdoches, TX 75965-9004, USA

Coan, Gil (Baseball Player)
Washington Senators
PO Box 558
Brevard, NC 28712, USA

Coase, Ronald H (Nobel Prize Laureate)
University of Chicago
1111 E 60th St
Law School
Chicago, IL 60637-2776, USA

Coasters, The
2756 N Green Valley Pkwy # 449
Henderson, NV 89014-2120, USA

Coates, Ben (Football Player)
New England Patriots
5940 Londonberry Court
Concord, NC 28027, USA

Coates, Jim (Baseball Player)
New York Yankees
1098 Oak Hill Rd
Lancaster, VA 22503-4009, USA

Coates, Kim (Actor)
Paradigm Agency
10100 Santa Monica Blvd Ste 2500
Los Angeles, CA 90067-4116, USA

Coates, Phyllis (Actor)
PO Box 1969
Boyes Hot Springs, CA 95416-1969, USA

Coates, Ray (Football Player)
Detroit Lions
3402 Arlington St
New Orleans, LA 70121-3607, USA

Coats, Dan (Senator)
1300 S Harrison St Rm 3158
Fort Wayne, IN 46802-3446, USA

Coats, Kristi (Golfer)
185 Wildwood Trl
Petal, MS 39465-2681, USA

Coats, Michael L (Astronaut)
3203 Acorn Wood Way
Houston, TX 77059-3175, USA

Cobb, Charles (Football Player)
Detroit Lions
6075 N Forkner Ave
Fresno, CA 93711-1827, USA

Cobb, David (Politician)
c/o Staff Member *The Green Party of the United States*
PO Box 57065
Washington, DC 20037-0065, USA

Cobb, Garry (Football Player)
Detroit Lions
1258 Chanticleer
Cherry Hill, NJ 08003-4817, USA

Cobb, Geraldyn M (Jerrie) (Astronaut)
1008 Beach Blvd
Sun City Center, FL 33573-5405, USA

Cobb, Henry N (Architect)
Pei Cobb Freed Partners
88 Pine St Lbby 1
New York, NY 10005-1841, USA

Cobb, Julie (Actor)
S D B Partners
1801 Avenue Of The Stars Ste 902
Los Angeles, CA 90067-5981, USA

Cobb, Keith Hamilton (Actor)
c/o Lee Dintsman *Agency for the Performing Arts (APA-LA)*
405 S Beverly Dr
Beverly Hills, CA 90212-4416, USA

Cobb, Marvin (Football Player)
Cincinnati Bengals
830 19th St
Manhattan Beach, CA 90266-2678, USA

Cobb, Reggie (Football Player)
Tampa Bay Buccaneers
5942 Aruba Ln
Knoxville, TN 37921-5187, USA

Cobb, Terrie
PO Box 5508
Sun City Center, FL 33571-5508, USA

Cobb, Trevor (Football Player)
Chicago Bears
351 Tuscany Way Apt 206
Melbourne, FL 32940-8191, USA

Cobbin, James (Baseball Player)
New York Black Yankees
121 E Rayen Ave
Youngstown, OH 44503-1620, USA

Cobbs, Bill (Actor)
c/o Staff Member *TalentWorks (LA)*
3500 W Olive Ave Ste 1400
Burbank, CA 91505-5512, USA

Cobert, Bob (Composer)
B M I
8730 W Sunset Blvd Ste 300
Los Angeles, CA 90069-2276, USA

Cobham, William C (Billy) (Music Group, Musician)
Joel Chriss
300 Mercer St Apt 3J
New York, NY 10003-6732, USA

Coblenz, Walter (Director, Producer)
4310 Cahuenga Blvd Unit 401
Toluca Lake, CA 91602-2713, USA

Cobos, Jesus Lopez (Conductor)
Cincinnati Symphony
1241 Elm St
Cincinnati, OH 45202-7531, USA

Cobum, Cindy C (Bowler)
Ladies Professional Bowling Tour
7200 Harrison Ave # 7171
Rockford, IL 61112-1017, USA

Cobum, Doris (Bowler)
130 Dalton Dr
Buffalo, NY 14223-2221, USA

Coburn, John G (General)
Commanding General Army Material Command
Alexandria, VA 22333-0001, USA

Cocanower, James S (Jaime) (Baseball Player)
Milwaukee Brewers
10777 Gram B Cir
Lowell, AR 72745-8446, USA

Coccioletti, Philip (Actor)
c/o Carmen Lavia *Fifi Oscard Agency*
110 W 40th St Rm 1601
New York, NY 10018-8512, USA

Cochereau, Pierre (Music Group, Musician)
15 Bis des Ursins
Paris 75004, FRANCE

Cochran, Antonio (Football Player)
Seattle Seahawks
421 Travelers Rest Rd
Montezuma, GA 31063-2032, USA

Cochran, Barbara Ann (Skier)
213 Brown Hill W
El Prado, NM 87529, USA

Cochran, Hank (Music Group, Songwriter, Writer)
Hunter's Lake
RR 2 Box 438
Hendersonville, TN 37075, USA

Cochran, John (Correspondent)
ABC-TV
5010 Creston St
News Dept
Hyattsville, MD 20781-1216, USA

Cochran, John (Football Player)
Chicago Cardinals
1249 Driftwood Dr
De Pere, WI 54115-1813, USA

Cochran, Leslie H (Educator)
Youngstown State University
President's Office
Youngstown, OH 44555-0001, USA

Cochran, Robert (Producer, Writer)
c/o Lee Dintsman *Agency for the Performing Arts (APA-LA)*
405 S Beverly Dr
Beverly Hills, CA 90212-4416, USA

Cochran, Russ (Golfer)
3 Circle Lake Dr
Paducah, KY 42001-9753, USA

Cochran, Shannon (Actor)
Stubbs
1450 S Robertson Blvd
Los Angeles, CA 90035-3402, USA

Cochrane, Dave (Baseball Player)
Chicago White Sox
11 Muirfield
Trabuco Canyon, CA 92679-3427, USA

Cochrane, Rory (Actor)
c/o Beth Holden-Garland *Untitled Entertainment (LA)*
331 N Maple Dr Fl 3
Beverly Hills, CA 90210-3827, USA

Cockburn, Bruce (Music Group, Musician, Songwriter, Writer)
Agency Group Ltd
1775 Broadway Ste 515
New York, NY 10019-1903, USA

Cocker, Jarvis (Musician, Songwriter)
c/o Staff Member *Paradigm (Monterey)*
509 Hartnell St
Monterey, CA 93940-2825, USA

Cocker, Joe (Music Group)
15030 Ventura Blvd # 710
Sherman Oaks, CA 91403-5470, USA

Cockerill, Kay (Golfer)
1345 Arroyo Ave
San Carlos, CA 94070-3912, USA

Cockrell, Alan (Baseball Player)
Colorado Rockies
306 Millstream Ter
Colorado Springs, CO 80904-4217, USA

Cockrell, Kenneth D (Astronaut)
2030 Hillside Oak Ln
Houston, TX 77062-3642, USA

Cockroft, Donald L (Don) (Football Player)
Cleveland Browns
2377 Thornhill Dr
Colorado Springs, CO 80920-5326, USA

Cockroft, Sherman (Football Player)
Kansas City Chiefs
18707 Vanderlip Ave
Santa Ana, CA 92705-3255, USA

Coder, Ron (Football Player)
Seattle Seahawks
25 N Bryant Ave
Pittsburgh, PA 15202-3346, USA

Codey, Lawrence R (Business Person)
Public Service Enterprise
PO Box 1171
80 Park Plaza
Newark, NJ 07101-1171, USA

Codiroli, Chris (Baseball Player)
Oakland A's
2700 Hillcrest Dr
Cameron Park, CA 95682-9279, USA

Codrescu, Andrei (Writer)
Louisiana State University
English Dept
Baton Rouge, LA 70803-0001, USA

Coduri, Camille (Actor)
International Creative Mgmt
76 Oxford St
London W1N 0AX, UNITED KINGDOM (UK)

Cody, Bill (Football Player)
Detroit Lions
209 Orleans Dr
Fairhope, AL 36532-4218, USA

Cody, Commander (Musician)
Skyline Music
Old Cherry Mountain Road
Jefferson, NH 03583, USA

Coe, Barry
PO Box 100
Sun Valley, ID 83353-0100, USA

Coe, David Allan (Music Group, Musician, Songwriter, Writer)
783 Rippling Creek Rd
Nixa, MO 65714-6716, USA

Coe, George (Actor)
c/o Martin Gage *Gage Group, The (LA)*
14724 Ventura Blvd Ste 505
Sherman Oaks, CA 91403-3505, USA

Coe, Sabastian N (Athlete, Track Athlete)
Starswood High Barn Road
Effingham
Surrey KT24 5PW, UNITED KINGDOM (UK)

Coe, Sebastian
Jarvis Hotels Ltd
Castle House
Desborough Road
High Wycombe, Bucks HP11 2PR, UNITED KINGDOM (UK)

Coe, Sue (Artist)
Galerie Saint Etienne
24 W 57th St
New York, NY 10019-3918, USA

Coe-Jones, Dawn (Golfer)
17319 Emerald Chase Dr
Tampa, FL 33647-3516, USA

Coelen, Chris (Director, Producer, Writer)
c/o Chris Coelen *United Talent Agency (UTA)*
9560 Wilshire Blvd Ste 500
Beverly Hills, CA 90212-2401, USA

Coelho, Paulo (Writer)
Instituto Paulo Coelho
Henrique Pechman
Av Copacabana 1133 salas 601 / 602
Rio de Janeiro 22070-010, BRAZIL

Coelho, Susie (Actor)
1347 Rossmoyne Ave
Glendale, CA 91207-1852, USA

Coen, Ethan (Director, Writer)
United Talent Agency
9560 Wilshire Blvd Ste 500
Beverly Hills, CA 90212-2401, USA

Coen, Joel (Director, Writer)
United Talent Agency
9560 Wilshire Blvd Ste 500
Beverly Hills, CA 90212-2401, USA

Coetzee, Gerrie (Boxer)
22 Sydney Road
Ravenswood, Boksburg 1460, SOUTH AFRICA

Coetzee, John M (Nobel Prize Laureate)
P O Box 92
Rondebosch, Cape Province 7700, SOUTH AFRICA

Coetzer, Amanda (Tennis Player)
Octagon
1751 Pinnacle Dr Ste 1500
McLean, VA 22102-3833, USA

Cofer, J Michael (Mike) (Football Player)
New England Patriots
2688 Hollowvale Ln
Henderson, NV 89052-2846, USA

Coffey, Don (Football Player)
Green Bay Packers
231 Redfield Dr
Jackson, TN 38305-8534, USA

Coffey, John L (Judge)
US Court Appeals
517 E Wisconsin Ave
US Courthouse
Milwaukee, WI 53202-4500, USA

Coffey, Junior L (Football Player)
Green Bay Packers
17228 32nd Ave S Apt E-12
Seatac, WA 98188-4402, USA

Coffey, Kellie (Musician)
c/o Staff Member *William Morris Agency (WMA-TN)*
1600 Division St Ste 300
Nashville, TN 37203-2755, USA

Coffey, Ken (Football Player)
Washington Redskins
3322 Medinah Ct
Sugar Land, TX 77479-2459, USA

Coffey, Paul
633 Hawthorne St
Birmingham, MI 48009-1650, USA

Coffey, Paul D (Hockey Player)
Phoenix Coyotes
9375 E Bell Rd
Alltel Ice Den
Scottsdale, AZ 85260-1540, USA

Coffey, Richard (Basketball Player)
Minnesota Timberwolves
10330 Quail Ave N
Minneapolis, MN 55443-5413, USA

Coffey, Scott
143 Wadsworth Ave
Santa Monica, CA 90405-3509, USA

Coffield, Kelly (Actor)
c/o Staff Member *Innovative Artists (NY)*
235 Park Ave S Fl 7
New York, NY 10003-1405, USA

Coffield, Randy (Football Player)
Seattle Seahawks
7110 Lake Basin Rd
Tallahassee, FL 32312-6708, USA

Coffin, Edmund (Tad) (Horse Racer)
General Delivery
Strafford, VT 05072-9999, USA

Coffin, Fredrick (Actor)
Susan Smith
1344 N Wetherly Dr
Los Angeles, CA 90069-1817, USA

Coffman, Kevin (Baseball Player)
Atlanta Braves
313 Kelly Dr
Victoria, TX 77904-1503, USA

Coffman, Paul (Football Player)
Green Bay Packers
14103 E 195th St
Peculiar, MO 64078-9199, USA

Coffman, Vance D (Business Person)
Lockheed Martin Corp
6801 Rockledge Dr
Bethesda, MD 20817-1877, USA

Cofield, Fred (Basketball Player)
New York Knicks
833 Frederick St
Ypsilanti, MI 48197-5270, USA

Cofield, Tim (Football Player)
Kansas City Chiefs
312 NE Warrington Ct
Lees Summit, MO 64064-1603, USA

Cogan, Kevin (Race Car Driver)
205 Rocky Point Rd
Palos Verdes Estates, CA 90274-2621, USA

Cogdill, Gail (Football Player)
Detroit Lions
12922 E 36th Ave
Spokane Valley, WA 99206-8405, USA

Coggin, David (Baseball Player)
Philadelphia Phillies
1090 W 20th St
Upland, CA 91784-1532, USA

Coggins, Frank (Baseball Player)
Washington Senators
106 Armstead Cir
Griffin, GA 30223-1502, USA

Coghlan, Eamon (Athlete, Track Athlete)
Int'l Mgmt Group
1 Erieview Plz
1360 E 9th St #1300
Cleveland, OH 44114-1738, USA

Coghlan, Frank Junior
12522 Argyle Dr
Los Alamitos, CA 90720-4734, USA

Coghlan, Frank (Junior) Jr (Actor)
28506 Ray Ct
Saugus, CA 91350-1244, USA

Cohan, Chris (Basketball Player, Misc)
Goldan State Warriors
1001 Broadway
Oakland, CA 94607-4019, USA

Cohan, Lauren (Actor)
c/o Lenore Zerman *Liberman/Zerman Management*
252 N Larchmont Blvd Ste 200
Los Angeles, CA 90004-3754, USA

Cohan, Robert P (Choreographer)
The Place 17 Dukes Road
London WC1H 9AB, UNITED KINGDOM (UK)

Coheleach, Guy J (Artist)
Pandion Art
PO Box 96
Bernardsville, NJ 07924-0096, USA

Cohen, Aaron (Astronaut, Misc)
1310 Essex Grn
College Station, TX 77845-9355, USA

Cohen, Avishai (Music Group, Musician)
Ron Moss Mgmt
2635 Griffith Park Blvd
Los Angeles, CA 90039-2519, USA

Cohen, Hy (Baseball Player)
Chicago Cubs
35734 Donny Cir
Palm Desert, CA 92211-2695, USA

Cohen, Larry (Director)
2111 Coldwater Canyon Dr
Beverly Hills, CA 90210-1734, USA

Cohen, Leonard N (Music Group, Songwriter, Writer)
c/o Staff Member *Sony Music Canada*
1121 Leslie St
Toronto, ON M3C 2J9, CANADA

Cohen, Marvin L (Physicist)
10 Forest Ln
Berkeley, CA 94708-1447, USA

Cohen, Mary Ann (Judge)
US Tax Court
400 2nd St NW
Washington, DC 20217-0002, USA

Cohen, Matt (Actor)
c/o Sharon Lane *Lane Management Group*
13017 Woodbridge St
Studio City, CA 91604-1431, USA

Cohen, Rob (Director)
United Talent Agency
9560 Wilshire Blvd Ste 500
Beverly Hills, CA 90212-2401, USA

Cohen, Robert (Music Group, Musician)
Intermusica Artists
16 Duncan Terrace
London N1 8BZ, UNITED KINGDOM (UK)

Cohen, Sacha Baron (Ali G, Borat) (Actor, Producer, Writer)
c/o Jimmy Miller *Mosaic Media Group*
24 Music Sq W Fl 1
Nashville, TN 37203-6661, USA

Cohen, Sarah (Journalist)
Washington Post
Editorial Dept 1150 15th St NW
Washington, DC 20071-0001, USA

Cohen, Sasha (Figure Skater)
c/o Staff Member *Champions on Ice*
3500 W 80th St
Tom Collins Enterprises Inc
Minneapolis, MN 55431-1068, USA

Cohen, Scott (Actor)
Shelley Jefrey Assoc
12400 Ventura Blvd
Studio City, CA 91604-2406, USA

Cohen, Sheldon S (Government Official)
5518 Trent St
Chevy Chase, MD 20815-5512, USA

Cohen, Stanley (Nobel Prize Laureate)
Vanderbilt University
Medical Center 1161 21st Ave
Nashville, TN 37232-0001, USA

Cohen, Steve (Business Person)
SAC Capital Advisors
72 Cummings Ave
Stamford, CT 06902, USA

Cohen-Tannoudji, Claude K (Nobel Prize Laureate)
38 Rue des Cordelieres
Paris 75013, FRANCE

Cohn, Alfred (Al) (Bowler)
13918 S Clark St
Riverdale, IL 60827-2058, USA

Cohn, Ethan (Actor)
c/o Darren Goldberg *1 Management*
9000 W Sunset Blvd Ph 1550
West Hollywood, CA 90069-1838, USA

Cohn, Gary (Journalist)
Balitmore Sun
501 N Calvert St
Editorial Dept
Baltimore, MD 21202-3604, USA

Cohn, Marc (Music Group, Songwriter, Writer)
Creative Artists Agency
9830 Wilshire Blvd
Beverly Hills, CA 90212-1804, USA

Cohn, Mindy (Actor)
Osbrink Talent Agency
4343 Lankershim Blvd # 100
North Hollywood, CA 91602-2705, USA

Cohner, Danny (Musician)
Nine Inch Nails
63 Main St
Cold Spring, NY 10516-3014, USA

Coia, Angelo (Football Player)
Chicago Bears
231 Hagen Rd
Brigantine, NJ 08203-3043, USA

Coia, Arthur A (Misc)
Laborers' International Uinon
905 16th St NW
Washington, DC 20006-1703, USA

Coifman, Ronald R (Scientist)
11 Hickory Road
North Haven, CT 06473, USA

Cojocaru, Steven (Correspondent)
c/o Staff Member *Entertainment Tonight (ET)*
5555 Melrose Ave
Mae West Bldg Fl 2
Los Angeles, CA 90038-3989, USA

Coker, Larry (Coach, Football Coach)
Miami University
Athletic Dept
Coral Gables, FL 33124, USA

Cokes, Curtis (Boxer)
618 Calcutta Dr
Dallas, TX 75241-1001, USA

Colalillo, Mike (War Hero)
5703 Nicollet St Apt 6
Duluth, MN 55807-2477, USA

Colalucci, Gianluigi (Artist, Misc)
Office of Restoration
Vatican City 00120, VATICAN CITY

Colangelo, Jerry (Basketball Player)
Arizona Diamondbacks
70 E Country Club Dr
Phoenix, AZ 85014-5435, USA

Colangelo, Mike (Baseball Player)
Anaheim Angels
4303 Candlestick Ct
Dumfries, VA 22025-1606, USA

Colantoni, Enrico (Actor)
11931 Hesby St
Valley Village, CA 91607-3113, USA

Colasuonno, Louis C (Editor)
New York Daily News
220 E 42nd St
Editorial Dept
New York, NY 10017-5806, USA

Colavito, Rocky (Baseball Player)
Cleveland Indians
656 Scenic Dr
Bernville, PA 19506-8257, USA

Colavito, Steve (Football Player)
Philadelphia Eagles
57 Fairview Ct
Nanuet, NY 10954-3230, USA

Colbern, Mike (Baseball Player)
Chicago White Sox
5120 E Tano St
Phoenix, AZ 85044-4121, USA

Colbert, Craig (Baseball Player)
San Francisco Giants
1616 E Coliseum Blvd
Fort Wayne, IN 46805-1450, USA

Colbert, Darrell (Football Player)
Kansas City Chiefs
6514 River Bluff Dr
Houston, TX 77085-1306, USA

Colbert, Jim (Golfer)
118 Wanish Pl
Palm Desert, CA 92260-7316, USA

Colbert, Nate (Baseball Player)
Houston Astros
2756 N Green Valley Pkwy
Henderson, NV 89014-2120, USA

Colbert, Rondy (Football Player)
New York Giants
5622 Cedarburg Dr
Houston, TX 77048-1821, USA

Colbert, Stephen (Actor, Producer, Writer)
c/o James Dixon Dixon Talent
436 W 45th St Fl 3
New York, NY 10036-3501, USA

Colbert, Vine (Baseball Player)
Cleveland Indians
7516 Catone Ct
Oxon Hill, MD 20745-1760, USA

Colborn, James W (Jim) (Baseball Player)
Chicago Cubs
2932 Solimar Beach Dr
Ventura, CA 93001-9754, USA

Colborn, Richard (Musician)
Legends of 21st Century
7 Trinity Row
Florence, MA 01062-1931, USA

Colbrunn, Greg (Baseball Player)
Montreal Expos
3196 Pignatelli Cres
Mount Pleasant, SC 29466-8060, USA

Colchico, Dan (Football Player)
San Francisco 49ers
5160 Paul Scarlet Dr
Concord, CA 94521-3134, USA

Cold (Music Group)
c/o Darryl Eaton Creative Artists Agency
LCC (CAA-LA)
2000 Avenue Of The Stars
Los Angeles, CA 90067-4700, USA

Cold War Kids (Music Group)
c/o Staff Member Paradigm (Monterey)
509 Hartnell St
Monterey, CA 93940-2825, USA

Coldplay (Music Group)
c/o Staff Member Paradigm (NY)
360 Park Ave S Fl 16
New York, NY 10010-1716, USA

Cole, Alex (Baseball Player)
Cleveland Indians
2654 N McMullen Booth Rd Apt 115
Clearwater, FL 33761-4074, USA

Cole, Anne (Designer, Fashion Designer)
Cole of California
6040 Bandini Blvd
Los Angeles, CA 90040-2905, USA

Cole, Ashley (Soccer Player)
Arsenal London
Avenell Road Highbury
London N5 1BU, UNITED KINGDOM
(UK)

Cole, Bob (Sportscaster)
Molstar Communications
250 Bloor St E #805
Toronto, ON M4W 1E6, CANADA

Cole, Bradley (Actor)
c/o Staff Member Peters Fraser & Dunlop
(PFD - UK)
Drury House
34-43 Russell St
London WC2B 5HA, UNITED KINGDOM
(UK)

Cole, Cecil (Baseball Player)
Newark Eagles
201 N 12th St
Connellsville, PA 15425-2422, USA

Cole, Christina (Actor)
c/o Staff Member Conway Van Gelder Ltd
18-21 Jermyn St Fl 3
London SW1Y 6HP, UNITED KINGDOM
(UK)

Cole, Dave (Baseball Player)
Boston Barves
2072 Pebble Beach Blvd
Orlando, FL 32826-5255, USA

Cole, Dennis (Actor)
c/o Staff Member Hartig Hilepo Agency
Ltd
54 W 21st St Rm 610
New York, NY 10010-7344, USA

Cole, Dick (Baseball Player)
Pittsburgh Pirates
3149 Madeira Ave
Costa Mesa, CA 92626-2323, USA

Cole, Emerson (Football Player)
Cleveland Browns
2142 Riverdale Sq W
Columbus, OH 43232-4063, USA

Cole, Eunice (Misc)
American Nurses Assn
2420 Pershing Rd
Kansas City, MO 64108-2501, USA

Cole, Ford (Football Player)
Oakland Raiders
8500 E Woodland Rd
Tucson, AZ 85749-8141, USA

Cole, Fred (Football Player)
Los Angeles Chargers
10 Tuscan Rd
Livingston, NJ 07039-2919, USA

Cole, Freddy (Music Group)
Producers Inc
11806 N 56th St
Tampa, FL 33617-1652, USA

Cole, Gary (Actor)
3855 Berry Dr
Studio City, CA 91604-3887, USA

Cole, George (Actor)
Joy Jameson Ltd
2-19 The Plaza
535 Kings Road
London SW10 0SZ, UNITED KINGDOM
(UK)

Cole, Holly (Musician)
Alert Music
41 Britain St
#305
Toronto, ON M5A 1R7, CANADA

Cole, Joanna (Writer)
c/o Staff Member Scholastic Entertainment
557 Broadway
New York, NY 10012-3999, USA

Cole, John (Cartoonist)
Durham Herald-Sun
2828 Pickett Rd
Durham, NC 27705-5613, USA

Cole, Julie Dawn (Actor)
Barry Burnett
31 Coventry St
London W1V 8AS, UNITED KINGDOM
(UK)

Cole, Kenneth (Designer)
Kenneth Cole Productions Inc
601 W 50th St
New York, NY 10019, USA

Cole, Keyshia (Musician)
c/o John Marx William Morris Agency
(WMA-LA)
1 William Morris Pl
Beverly Hills, CA 90212-4261, USA

Cole, Kimberly Lynn (Actor)
36 Longview Ct
Montgomery, AL 36108-2018, USA

Cole, Kyla (Adult Film Star)
Adrian Daskalov
Nabrezi SPB 446
Ostrava 70800, CZECH REPUBLIC

Cole, Larry R (Football Player)
Dallas Cowboys
400 Country Pl
Colleyville, TX 76034-7598, USA

Cole, Lily (Actor, Model)
c/o Staff Member Storm Model
Management Limited
5 Jubilee Place Fl 5
London SW3 3TD, UNITED KINGDOM
(UK)

Cole, Lloyd (Musician)
Supervision Mgmt
109B Regents Park Road
London NW1 8UR, UNITED KINGDOM
(UK)

Cole, Michael (Actor)
5121 Varna Ave
Sherman Oaks, CA 91423-1526, USA

Cole, Natalie (Actor, Musician)
c/o Scott Henderson William Morris
Agency (WMA-LA)
1 William Morris Pl
Beverly Hills, CA 90212-4261, USA

Cole, Nigel (Director, Writer)
c/o Rosalie Swedlin Industry
Entertainment
955 Carrillo Dr Ste 300
Los Angeles, CA 90048-5400, USA

Cole, Olivia (Actor)
Century Artists
PO Box 59747
Santa Barbara, CA 93150, USA

Cole, P K
32522 Bowman Knoll Dr
Westlake Village, CA 91361-5520, USA

Cole, Paula (Musician)
Monterey Peninsula Artists
509 Hartnell St
Monterey, CA 93940-2825, USA

Cole, Robin (Football Player)
9 Brook Ln
Eighty Four, PA 15330-2603, USA

Cole, Stu (Baseball Player)
Montreal Expos
6527 Willow Gate Ln
Charlotte, NC 28215-4014, USA

Cole, Taylor (Actor)
c/o Staff Member Spelling Television Inc
5700 Wilshire Blvd
Los Angeles, CA 90036-3659, USA

Cole, Terry (Football Player)
743 Sanders St
Indianapolis, IN 46203-1856, USA

Cole, Tina (Actor)
778 University Ave
Junior League Of Sacramento
Sacramento, CA 95825-6703, USA

Cole, Victor (Baseball Player)
Pittsburgh Pirates
138 Estonallie Rd
Mercer, TN 38392-7102, USA

Colella, Richard (Rick) (Swimmer)
217 19th Pl
Kirkland, WA 98033-4903, USA

Coleman, Andre (Football Player)
San Diego Chargers
5975 Corte Playa Cartagena
San Diego, CA 92124-1179, USA

Coleman, Catherine G (Cady) (Astronaut)
13619 Willow Heights Ct
Houston, TX 77059-3583, USA

Coleman, Cosey (Football Player)
Tampa Bay Buccaneers
11901 Northumberland Dr
Tampa, FL 33626-1327, USA

Coleman, Dabney (Actor)
360 N Kenter Ave
Los Angeles, CA 90049-2336, USA

Coleman, Daniel J (Publisher)
Popular Mechanics Magazine
224 W 57th St
New York, NY 10019-3200, USA

Coleman, Dave (Baseball Player)
Boston Red Sox
4303 Delhi Dr
Dayton, OH 45432-3411, USA

Coleman, Derrick D (Basketball Player)
Philadelphia 76ers
3601 S Broad St
1st Union Center
Philadelphia, PA 19148-5287, USA

Coleman, Don E (Football Player)
424 McPherson Ave
Lansing, MI 48915-1158, USA

Coleman, Durell
800 S Robertson Blvd Ste 5
Los Angeles, CA 90035-1634, USA

Coleman, E C (Basketball Player)
Houston Rockets
370 E Harmon Ave
Las Vegas, NV 89169-7003, USA

Coleman, Eric (Football Player)
New England Patriots
2933 Elm St
Denver, CO 80207-2658, USA

Coleman, Gary (Actor)
c/o Staff Member Tisherman Agency Inc
6767 Forest Lawn Dr Ste 101
Los Angeles, CA 90068-1050, USA

Coleman, George E (Musician)
63 E 9th St
New York, NY 10003-6302, USA

Coleman, Greg (Football Player)
Cleveland Browns
2313 River Pointe Cir
Minneapolis, MN 55411-4279, USA

Coleman, Holly
3579 E Foothill Blvd # 520
Pasadena, CA 91107-3119, USA

Coleman, Jack (Actor)
c/o Staff Member *Bauman Redanty & Shaul Agency*
5757 Wilshire Blvd Ste 473
Los Angeles, CA 90036-3632, USA

Coleman, Jerry (Baseball Player)
New York Yankees
1004 Havenhurst Dr
La Jolla, CA 92037-6803, USA

Coleman, Jospeh H (Joe) (Baseball Player)
Washington Senators
17851 Eagle View Ln
Cape Coral, FL 33909-3019, USA

Coleman, Karon (Football Player)
Denver Broncos
5006 Brannon Hill Ct
Sugar Land, TX 77479-3843, USA

Coleman, Leonard (Football Player)
Indianapolis Colts
125 NE 13th Ave
Boynton Beach, FL 33435-3124, USA

Coleman, Lincoln (Football Player)
Dallas Cowboys
PO Box 496
Seguin, TX 78156-0496, USA

Coleman, Lisa
3575 Cahuenga Blvd W Ste 450
Los Angeles, CA 90068-1364, USA

Coleman, Marco D (Football Player)
Miami Dolphins
11036 Turnbridge Dr
Jacksonville, FL 32256-2328, USA

Coleman, Marcus (Football Player)
New York Jets
1736 Mapleleaf Dr
Wylie, TX 75098-8166, USA

Coleman, Mary Sue (Educator)
University of Michigan
President's Office
Ann Arbor, MI 48109, USA

Coleman, Mike (Baseball Player)
Boston Red Sox
PO Box 1962
Madison, TN 37116-1962, USA

Coleman, Monique (Actor)
c/o Gabrielle Allabashi *Ellis Talent Group*
4705 Laurel Canyon Blvd Ste 300
Valley Village, CA 91607-5901, USA

Coleman, Ornette (Composer, Musician)
Monterey International
200 W Superior St Ste 202
Chicago, IL 60610-3554, USA

Coleman, Paul (Baseball Player)
2704 Brentwood Dr
Tyler, TX 75701-5902, USA

Coleman, Ray (Baseball Player)
St Louis Browns
PO Box 8
Hornbrook, CA 96044-0008, USA

Coleman, Roderick (Football Player)
Oakland Raiders
35 Netherwood Dr
Coatesville, PA 19320-1469, USA

Coleman, Ronnie (Football Player)
Denver Broncos
16039 Williwaw Dr
Houston, TX 77083-5375, USA

Coleman, Sidney (Football Player)
Tampa Bay Buccaneers
299 Highway 39 N Apt A25
De Kalb, MS 39328-9465, USA

Coleman, Sidney R (Physicist)
1 Richdale Ave Unit 12
Cambridge, MA 02140-2610, USA

Coleman, Signy (Actor)
9200 W Sunset Blvd Ste 625
Los Angeles, CA 90069-3609, USA

Coleman, Steve (Football Player)
Denver Broncos
81 W Johnson St
Philadelphia, PA 19144-1937, USA

Coleman, Vincent M (Vince) (Baseball Player)
St Louis Cardinals
7825 Highland Village Pl
San Diego, CA 92129-5182, USA

Coleman, Walter (Baseball Player)
New York Yankees
HC 1 Box 236
New Russia, NY 12964, USA

Coleman, William T Jr (Secretary)
O'Melveny & Myers
555 13th St NW # 500
Washington, DC 20004-1109, USA

Coleman Jr, Leonard (Baseball Player)
283 3rd St
Beach Haven, NJ 08008, USA

Colemane, Norris (Basketball Player)
Baltimore Bullets
20676 Seneca Ave
Brownstown Twp, MI 48183-5040, USA

Coles, Bimbo (Basketball Player)
Miami Heat
PO Box 1063
Lewisburg, WV 24901-4063, USA

Coles, Darnell (Baseball Player)
Seattle Mariners
306 Signature Ter
Safety Harbor, FL 34695-5425, USA

Coles, Kim (Actor, Comedian)
9000 Cynthia St Apt 403
West Hollywood, CA 90069-4871, USA

Coles, Laveranues (Football Player)
c/o Team Member *New York Jets*
1000 Fulton Ave
Hempstead, NY 11550-1030, USA

Coles, Robert M (Psychic)
Harvard University
75 Mount Auburn St
Health Services
Cambridge, MA 02138-4960, USA

Colescott, Warrington W (Artist)
RR 1
Hollandale, WI 53544, USA

Coletta, Chris (Baseball Player)
California Angels
206 SW 45th St
Cape Coral, FL 33914-5906, USA

Coley, Daryl (Musician)
Daryl Coley Ministries
417 E Regent St
Inglewood, CA 90301-1315, USA

Coley, James (Football Player)
Chicago Bears
111 Pebble Park Rd
Starr, SC 29684-9259, USA

Coley, John Ford (Musician, Songwriter, Writer)
Earthtone
8306 Wilshire Blvd # 981
Beverly Hills, CA 90211-2304, USA

Colgate, Stirling A (Physicist)
422 Estante Way
Los Alamos, NM 87544-3812, USA

Colgrass, Michael C (Composer)
583 Palmerston Ave
Toronto, ON M6G 2P6, CANADA

Colier, Jason (Basketball Player)
Houston Rockets
19318 Kristen Pine Dr
Humble, TX 77346-2084, USA

Colin, Charlie (Musician)
Jon Landau
80 Main St
Greenwich, CT 06830, USA

Colin, Margaret (Actor)
41 Bradford Ave
Montclair, NJ 07043-1024, USA

Colinet, Stalin (Football Player)
Minnesota Vikings
1541 Brickell Ave Apt A 1001
Miami, FL 33129-1213, USA

C'Oliveira, Damon (Actor)
c/o Staff Member *LeFeaver Talent Management Ltd*
2 College St #202
Toronto, ON M5G 1K3, CANADA

Coll, Stephen W (Journalist)
Washington Post
Editorial Dept
1150 15th St NW
Washington, DC 20071-0001, USA

Colladay, Martin G (General)
409 Dowding Ct
Bellevue, NE 68005-2464, USA

Collard, Jean-Philippe (Musician)
Boite Postal 210
Paris Cedex 09 75426, FRANCE

Collective Soul (Music Group)
c/o Staff Member *Creative Artists Agency LCC (CAA-LA)*
2000 Avenue Of The Stars
Los Angeles, CA 90067-4700, USA

Collen, Phil (Musician)
Q Prime Mgmt
729 7th Ave Rm 1400
New York, NY 10019-6889, USA

Collet, Christopher
8730 W Sunset Blvd Ste 480
Los Angeles, CA 90069-2277, USA

Collett, Elmer (Football Player)
San Francisco 49ers
PO Box 522
10 Avenida Farralone
Stinson Beach, CA 94970-0522, USA

Collette, Buddy (Musician)
5532 S Corning Ave
Los Angeles, CA 90056-1303, USA

Collette, Toni (Actor)
Shanahan Mgmt
Berman House
91 Campbell Street
Berman House 2010, AUSTRALIA

Colletti, Stephen (Reality TV Star)
c/o Tyler Grasham *Agency for the Performing Arts (APA-LA)*
405 S Beverly Dr
Beverly Hills, CA 90212-4416, USA

Colley, Dana (Musician)
Creative Performance Group
48 Laight St
New York, NY 10013-2016, USA

Colley, Ed (Cartoonist)
11 Blaisdell Ter
Ipswich, MA 01938-1706, USA

Colley, Kenneth (Actor)
Kenneth McReddie
91 Regent St
London W1R 7TB, UNITED KINGDOM (UK)

Colley, Michael C (Admiral)
444 Magnolia Dr
Gulf Shores, AL 36542-4408, USA

Collie, Bruce (Football Player)
San Francisco 49ers
9595 Ranch Road 12 Ste 13
Wimberley, TX 78676-5248, USA

Collie, Mark (Actor, Musician, Songwriter, Writer)
Dreamcatcher Artist Mgmt
2908 Poston Ave
Nashville, TN 37203-1312, USA

Collier, Don
PO Box 1269
Benson, AZ 85602-1269, USA

Collier, Floyd (Football Player)
San Francisco 49ers
2081 Ronda Granada Unit D
Laguna Woods, CA 92637-0728, USA

Collier, James (Football Player)
New York Giants
922 Bromley Dr
Baton Rouge, LA 70808-5814, USA

Collier, Lesley F (Ballerina)
Royal Ballet
Convent Garden
Bow St
London WC2E 9DD, UNITED KINGDOM (UK)

Collier, Mark (Actor)
c/o John Crosby *John Crosby Management*
1310 N Spaulding Ave
Los Angeles, CA 90046-4010, USA

Collier, Mike (Football Player)
Pittsburgh Steelers
528 W Church St Apt B
Hagerstown, MD 21740-4630, USA

Collier, Steve (Football Player)
Green Bay Packers
637 E Woodland Park Ave Apt 704
Chicago, IL 60616-4287, USA

Collier, Timothy (Tim) (Football Player)
Kansas City Chiefs
3116 50th St
Dallas, TX 75216-7343, USA

Collingwood, Chris (Musician, Songwriter, Writer)
MOB Agency
6404 Wilshire Blvd Ste 505
Los Angeles, CA 90048-5507, USA

Collins, Albin (Football Player)
Baltimore Colts
1006 N Bonnie St
Gonzales, LA 70737-4502, USA

Collins, Alfred (Football Player)
Atlanta Falcons
2455 Cedar Canyon Ct SE
Marietta, GA 30067-6617, USA

Collins, Arthur D Jr (Business Person)
7000 Central Ave NE
Medtronic Inc
Minneapolis, MN 55432-3568, USA

Collins, Bill (Hockey Player)
5000 Town Ctr Apt 505
Southfield, MI 48075-1112, USA

Collins, Billy (Writer)
City College of New York
English Dept
New York, NY 10031, USA

Collins, Blake Jeremy
4942 Vineland Ave Ste 200
N Hollywood, CA 91601-5646, USA

Collins, Bobby (Football Player)
Buffalo Bills
PO Box 920384
Norcross, GA 30010-0384, USA

Collins, Bootsy (Musician)
Performers of the World
8901 Melrose Ave # 200
West Hollywood, CA 90069-5605, USA

Collins, Brett W (Football Player)
Green Bay Packers
21275 NW Rock Creek Blvd
Portland, OR 97229-1041, USA

Collins, Bud (Sportscaster)
822 Boylston St Ste 203
Chestnut Hill, MA 02467-2504, USA

Collins, C F (Football Player)
Detroit Lions
10065 Garden St
Livonia, MI 48150-3110, USA

Collins, Clifton (Actor)
c/o Alex Schaffel *United Talent Agency
(UTA)*
9560 Wilshire Blvd Ste 500
Beverly Hills, CA 90212-2401, USA

Collins, David S (Dave) (Baseball Player)
California Angels
632 Race St # 4
Cincinnati, OH 45202-2323, USA

Collins, Donald E (Don) (Baseball Player)
127 Deerwood Trl
Sharpsburg, GA 30277-2002, USA

Collins, Douglas (Doug) (Basketball
Player, Coach, Sportscaster)
Philadelphia 76ers
10040 E Happy Valley Rd Unit 617
Scottsdale, AZ 85255-2355, USA

Collins, Duane E (Business Person)
Parker Hannifin Corp
6035 Parkland Blvd
Cleveland, OH 44124-4141, USA

Collins, Dwight (Football Player)
Minnesota Vikings
821 12th St
Beaver Falls, PA 15010-4416, USA

Collins, Eileen M (Astronaut)
2024 Pebble Beach Dr
League City, TX 77573-6403, USA

Collins, Francis S (Misc)
*National Human Genome Research
Institute*
31 Center St
Bethesda, MD 20892-0001, USA

Collins, Gary (Actor)
William Morris Agency
151 El Camino Dr
Beverly Hills, CA 90212-2775, USA

Collins, Gary J (Football Player)
Cleveland Browns
221 Lamp Post Ln
Hershey, PA 17033-1881, USA

Collins, George (Football Player)
St Louis Cardinals
2043 Northside Rd
Perry, GA 31069-2224, USA

Collins, Glen L (Football Player)
Cincinnati Bengals
817 E River Pl
Jackson, MS 39202-3403, USA

Collins, Jack (Actor)
Contemporary Artists
610 Santa Monica Blvd Ste 202
Santa Monica, CA 90401-1645, USA

Collins, Jackie (Writer)
c/o Amy Schiffman *Gersh Agency, The
(LA)*
232 N Canon Dr
Beverly Hills, CA 90210-5302, USA

Collins, Jason (Basketball Player)
13120 Constable Ave
Granada Hills, CA 91344-1105, USA

Collins, Jessica
c/o Rick Ax *Gold Coast Management*
1023 1/2 Abbot Kinney Blvd
Venice, CA 90291-5536, USA

Collins, Jim (Football Player)
Los Angeles Rams
2140 E Oceanfront
Newport Beach, CA 92661-1525, USA

Collins, Joan (Actor)
c/o Joel Dean *TalentWorks (LA)*
3500 W Olive Ave Ste 1400
Burbank, CA 91505-5512, USA

Collins, Joely (Actor)
c/o Staff Member *TalentWorks (LA)*
3500 W Olive Ave Ste 1400
Burbank, CA 91505-5512, USA

Collins, John G (Financier)
Summit Bancorp
PO Box 2066
Carnegie Center
Princeton, NJ 08543-2066, USA

Collins, John W (Business Person)
Clorox Co
1221 Broadway
Oakland, CA 94612-1888, USA

Collins, Judy (Musician, Songwriter,
Writer)
Rocky Mountains Production
PO Box 1296
New York, NY 10025-1296, USA

Collins, Kate (Actor)
1410 York Ave Apt 4D
New York, NY 10021-3401, USA

Collins, Kerry (Football Player)
c/o Team Member *Oakland Raiders*
1220 Harbor Bay Pkwy
Alameda, CA 94502-6570, USA

Collins, Lauren (Actor)
c/o Staff Member *Talent Vision*
30 Glen Cameron Rd #100
Thornhill, ON L3T 1N7, CANADA

Collins, Lewis
22 Westbere Rd
London, ENGLAND NW2 3SR, UNITED
KINGDOM (UK)

Collins, Lynn (Actor)
c/o Stephanie Ritz *Endeavor Agency LLC
(NY)*
23 Watts St Fl 6
New York, NY 10013, USA

Collins, Mark (Football Player)
New York Giants
2568 Baseline St Apt 155
Highland, CA 92346-2840, USA

Collins, Martha Layne (Educator,
Governor)
Saint Catheine College
President's Office
Saint Catherine, KY 40061, USA

Collins, Marva (Educator)
Westside Preparatory School
8035 S Honore St
Chicago, IL 60620-4562, USA

Collins, Misha (Actor)
S M S Talent
8730 W Sunset Blvd Ste 440
Los Angeles, CA 90069-2277, USA

Collins, Mo (Comedian)
c/o Leland LaBarre *Diverse Talent Group*
1875 Century Park E Ste 2250
Los Angeles, CA 90067-2563, USA

Collins, Patrick (Actor)
c/o Staff Member *Tisherman Agency Inc*
6767 Forest Lawn Dr Ste 101
Los Angeles, CA 90068-1050, USA

Collins, Paul (Football Player)
New England Patriots
1441 Bayshore Dr
Kemah, TX 77565-3045, USA

Collins, Pauline (Actor)
Michael Whitehall
125 Gloucester Road
London SW7 4TE, UNITED KINGDOM
(UK)

Collins, Phil (Musician, Songwriter,
Writer)
c/o Mara Buxbaum *I/D PR (NY)*
155 Spring St Fl 6
New York, NY 10012-5208, USA

Collins, Roosevelt (Football Player)
Miami Dolphins
3600 Holly St
Denison, TX 75020-3714, USA

Collins, Shane (Football Player)
Washington Redskins
PO Box 11090
Bozeman, MT 59719-1090, USA

Collins, Shawn (Football Player)
Atlanta Falcons
2744 Preece St
San Diego, CA 92111-5416, USA

Collins, Stephen (Actor)
c/o Constance Freiberg *Envision
Entertainment*
9255 W Sunset Blvd Ste 500
West Hollywood, CA 90069-3301, USA

Collins, Terry L (Misc)
PO Box 508
Okemos, MI 48805-0508, USA

Collins, Thomas H (Admiral)
Commandant US Coast Guard
2100 2nd St SW
Washington, DC 20593-0002, USA

Collins, Todd F (Football Player)
New England Patriots
1279 Collins Rd
New Market, TN 37820-3837, USA

Collins, Todd S (Football Player)
Buffalo Bills
26 Cambridge Cir
Victor, NY 14564-1503, USA

Collins, Tony (Football Player)
New England Patriots
PO Box 260062
Pembroke Pines, FL 33026-7062, USA

Collinsworth, Cris (Football Player,
Sportscaster)
Cincinnati Bengals
1211 Avenue Of The Americas Ste 302
Fox Sports
New York, NY 10036-8701, USA

Collis, Shannon (Actor)
c/o Meredith Fine *Coast to Coast Talent
Group*
3350 Barham Blvd
Los Angeles, CA 90068-1404, USA

Collison, Nick (Basketball Player)
Seattle SuperSonics
1201 3rd Ave Ste 1000
Seattle, WA 98101-3038, USA

Collman, James P (Misc)
794 Tolman Dr
Stanford, CA 94305-1045, USA

Collum, Jackie (Baseball Player)
St Louis Cardinals
523 11th Ave
Grinnell, IA 50112-2612, USA

Colman, Booth (Actor)
2160 Century Park E Apt 603
Los Angeles, CA 90067-2214, USA

Colman, Wayne (Football Player)
Philadelphia Eagles
604 N Somerset Ave
Ventnor City, NJ 08406-1551, USA

Colmenares, Grecia (Actor)
c/o Staff Member *Telefe - Argentina*
Pavon 2444 (C1248AAT)
Buenos Aires, ARGENTINA

Colmes, Alan (Correspondent)
c/o Staff Member *Hannity & Colmes*
1211 Avenue Of The Americas
New York, NY 10036-8701, USA

Colo, Don (Football Player)
Baltimore Colts
7355 E Claremont St
Scottsdale, AZ 85250-5526, USA

Coloma, Marcus (Actor)
c/o Paul Rosicker *Gersh Agency, The (LA)*
232 N Canon Dr
Beverly Hills, CA 90210-5302, USA

Colombini, Aldo
PO Box 829
Newbury Park, CA 91319-0829, USA

Colombo, Emilio (Prime Minister)
Via Aurelia
Rome 239, ITALY

Colomby, Bobby
1423 Holmby Ave
Los Angeles, CA 90024-5104, USA

Colomby, Scott (Actor)
Borinstein Oreck Bogart
3172 Dona Susana Dr
Studio City, CA 91604-4356, USA

Colon, Bartolo (Baseball Player)
Cleveland Indians
3308 Islewood Ave
Weston, FL 33332-2517, USA

Colon, Miriam (Actor)
51 W 52nd St
New York, NY 10019-6119, USA

Colone, Joe (Basketball Player)
New York Knicks
534 Carter Ave
West Deptford, NJ 08096, USA

Color Me Badd
PO Box 552113
Carol City, FL 33055-0113, USA

Colorito, Tony (Football Player)
Denver Broncos
17805 SW Cicero Ct
Beaverton, OR 97007-9036, USA

Colosi, Nicholas (Nick) (Misc)
2220 Applewood Dr
Freehold, NJ 07728-3982, USA

Colpaert, Dick (Baseball Player)
Pittsburgh Pirates
47412 Eldon Dr
Shelby Township, MI 48317-2912, USA

Colquitt, Craig (Football Player)
Pittsburgh Steelers
1905 Pitts Field Ln
Knoxville, TN 37922-6197, USA

Colquitt, Jimmy (Football Player)
Seattle Seahawks
11722 Hardin Valley Rd
Knoxville, TN 37932-2319, USA

Colson, Elizabeth F (Misc)
University of California
Anthropology Dept
Berkeley, CA 94720-0001, USA

Colson, Lloyd A (Baseball Player)
New York Yankees
PO Box 128
Hollis, OK 73550-0128, USA

Colson, William (Bill) (Editor)
Sports Illustrated
Editorial Dept
Time-Life Building
New York, NY 10020, USA

Colston, Tim (Football Player)
Carolina Panthers
6804 N 47th St
Tampa, FL 33610-1808, USA

Colt, Marshall (Actor)
1150 Anchorage Ln Unit 612
San Diego, CA 92106-3124, USA

Colter, Jessie (Musician)
Shout Factory
2042A Armacost Ave
Los Angeles, CA 90025, USA

Colteryahn, Lloyd (Football Player)
Baltimore Colts
General Delivery
Taylors Island, MD 21669-9999, USA

Colton, Frank B (Inventor)
6402 N 27th St
Phoenix, AZ 85016-8938, USA

Colton, Graham (Musician)
c/o Staff Member *More Music Group*
397 Little Neck Rd Ste 305
Virginia Beach, VA 23452-5764, USA

Colton, Lawrence R (Larry) (Baseball Player)
Philadelphia Phillies
3027 NE 68th Ave
Portland, OR 97213-5215, USA

Colton, Michael (Writer)
c/o Tony Etz *Creative Artists Agency LCC (CAA-LA)*
2000 Avenue Of The Stars
Los Angeles, CA 90067-4700, USA

Coltraine, Robbie (Actor)
19 Sydney Mews
London SW3 6HL, UNITED KINGDOM (UK)

Coltrane, Chi
5955 Tuxedo Ter
Los Angeles, CA 90068-2461, USA

Coltrane, Robbie (Actor)
Caroline Dawson & Associates
125 Gloucester Road
2nd Fl
London SW7 4TE, UNITED KINGDOM (UK)

Coluccio, Bob (Baseball Player)
Milwaukee Brewers
369 Flower St
Costa Mesa, CA 92627-2352, USA

Columbu, Franco (Misc)
2265 Westwood Blvd Ste A
Los Angeles, CA 90064-2050, USA

Columbus, Chris (Director, Producer)
c/o Staff Member *1492 Pictures*
4000 Warner Blvd
Producers Bldg 3 #18
Burbank, CA 91522-0001, USA

Columbus, Christopher J (Chris) (Director, Writer)
Leavensden Studios
PO Box 3000
Leavesden WD2 7LT, UNITED KINGDOM (UK)

Colunga, Fernando (Actor)
c/o Staff Member *Televisa*
Blvd Adolfo Lopez Mateos 232
Colonia San Angel INN
DF CP 01060, MEXICO

Colussy, Dan A (Business Person)
20 Saint Thomas Dr
West Palm Beach, FL 33418-4598, USA

Colville, Alex (Artist)
408 Main St
Wolfville, NS B0P 1XP, CANADA

Colvin, James (Football Player)
Baltimore Colts
1310 Rancho Vista Dr
Mc Kinney, TX 75070-5485, USA

Colvin, John O (Judge)
US Tax Court
400 2nd St NW
Washington, DC 20217-0002, USA

Colvin, Les (Hockey Player)
62 Foxhunt Trail
Courtice, ON L1E 2E4, CANADA

Colvin, Rossevelt (Football Player)
Chicago Bears
12521 Old Stone Dr
Indianapolis, IN 46236-9225, USA

Colvin, Shawn (Musician, Songwriter)
c/o Staff Member *Paradigm (Monterey)*
509 Hartnell St
Monterey, CA 93940-2825, USA

Colwell, John A (Physicist)
American Diabetes Assn
1701 N Beauregard St
Alexandria, VA 22311-1733, USA

Colyar, Michael (Actor, Comedian)
Mysterie Talent Management
1301 S Ogden Dr
Los Angeles, CA 90019-2438, USA

Colyer, Steve (Baseball Player)
Los Angeles Dodgers
104 Laura Hill Rd
Saint Peters, MO 63376-3619, USA

Colzie, Jim (Baseball Player)
Indianapolis Clowns
3140 Day Ave
Coconut Grove, FL 33133-5111, USA

Comaneci, Nadia (Gymnast)
4421 Hidden Hill Rd
Norman, OK 73072-2899, USA

Combe, Jeff (Baseball Player)
Cincinnati Reds
743 Tudor Cir
Thousand Oaks, CA 91360-5246, USA

Combes, Willard W (Cartoonist)
1266 Oakridge Dr
Cleveland, OH 44121-1623, USA

Combs, Chris (Football Player)
Pittsburgh Steelers
3627 Dogwood Ln SW
Roanoke, VA 24015-4503, USA

Combs, Glenn (Basketball Player)
Dallas Chaparrals
3627 Dogwood Ln SW
Roanoke, VA 24015-4503, USA

Combs, Holly Marie (Actor)
c/o Ken Kaplan *Gersh Agency, The (LA)*
232 N Canon Dr
Beverly Hills, CA 90210-5302, USA

Combs, Jeffrey (Actor)
1875 Century Park E Ste 2250
Los Angeles, CA 90067-2563, USA

Combs, Patrick D (Pat) (Baseball Player)
Philadelphia Phillies
203 Timber Lake Way
Southlake, TX 76092-7217, USA

Combs, Sean John (P Diddy) (Musician, Producer)
c/o Peter Safran *The Safran Company*
2000 Avenue Of The Stars Ste 600N
Los Angeles, CA 90067-4708, USA

Comeau, Andy (Actor)
c/o Staff Member *Rigberg-Rugolo Entertainment*
1180 S Beverly Dr Ste 601
Los Angeles, CA 90035-1158, USA

Comeaux, Darren (Football Player)
Denver Broncos
6313 Kristle Ln
Brusly, LA 70719, USA

Comeaux, John (Basketball Player)
New Orleans Buccaneers
PO Box 327
Carencro, LA 70520-0327, USA

Comegys, Dallas (Basketball Player)
73 Water St
Park Forest, IL 60466-1416, USA

Comegys, Dallas (Basketball Player)
New Jersey Nets
4330 Wayne Ave
Philadelphia, PA 19140-1745, USA

Comella, Greg (Football Player)
New York Giants
2222 Maroneal St Unit 1617
Houston, TX 77030-3254, USA

Comer, Anjanette (Actor)
Dade/Schultz
6442 Coldwater Canyon Ave Ste 206
North Hollywood, CA 91606-1137, USA

Comer, James P (Psychic)
Yale University
230 S Frontage Rd
Child Study Center
New Haven, CT 06519-1124, USA

Comer, Steve (Baseball Player)
Texas Rangers
1321 Lake Dr W Apt 314
Chanhassen, MN 55317-3512, USA

Comer, Wayne (Baseball Player)
Detroit Tigers
145 Marcus St
Shenandoah, VA 22849-3917, USA

Comess, Aaron (Musician)
DAS Communications
83 Riverside Dr
New York, NY 10024-5713, USA

Comfort, Brad
PO Box 715
Mercer Island, WA 98040-0715, USA

Comi, Paul (Actor)
2395 Ridgeway Rd
San Marino, CA 91108-2116, USA

Comiskey, Chuck (Football Player)
New Orleans Saints
2502 Convent Ave
Pascagoula, MS 39567-4517, USA

Comissiona, Sergiu (Conductor)
Helsinki Philharmonic
Karamzininkatu 4
Helsinki 00100, FINLAND

Comley, Larry (Basketball Player)
Baltimore Bullets
5230 E 66th Way
Commerce City, CO 80022-2442, USA

Command, Jim (Baseball Player)
Philadelphia Phillies
2136 Cranbrook Dr NE
Grand Rapids, MI 49505-5721, USA

Commodores, The
1920 Benson Ave
Saint Paul, MN 55116-3214, USA

Common (Artist, Music Group)
c/o Derek Dudley *Artistic Control Management Inc*
685 Lambert Dr NE
Atlanta, GA 30324-4125, USA

Commoner, Barry (Misc)
Queens College
Biology Of Natural Systems Center
Flushing, NY 11367, USA

Compagnonl, Deborah (Skier)
Via Frodonfo 3
Santa Catarina Valfurna 2303, ITALY

Compaore, Blaise (President)
President's Office
Boile Postale 7031
Ouagadougou, BURKINA FASO

Compte, Maurice (Actor)
c/o Brit Reece *PMK/HBH Public Relations (PMK-LA)*
700 N San Vicente Blvd Ste G910
West Hollywood, CA 90069-5061, USA

Compton, Ann Woodruff (Correspondent)
ABC-TV
5010 Creston St
News Dept
Hyattsville, MD 20781-1216, USA

Compton, Clint (Baseball Player)
Chicago Cubs
PO Box 574
Harlowton, MT 59036-0574, USA

Compton, Denis C S (Cricketer)
Sunday Express
245 Blackfriars Road
London SE1 9UX, UNITED KINGDOM
(UK)

Compton, Dick (Football Player)
Detroit Lions
3408 Briarcliff Ct S
Irving, TX 75062-3206, USA

Compton, Forrest (Actor)
CunninghamEscottDipene
257 Park Ave S Rm 900
New York, NY 10010-7304, USA

Compton, John G M (Prime Minister)
PO Box 149
Castries, SAINT LUCIA

Compton, Mike (Baseball Player)
Philadelphia Phillies
8624 Leighton Dr
Tampa, FL 33614-1723, USA

Compton, Ogden (Football Player)
Chicago Cardinals
13918 Preston Valley Pl
Dallas, TX 75240-4769, USA

Compton, Richard (Actor)
Agency for Performing Arts
405 S Beverly Dr Ste 500
Beverly Hills, CA 90212-4425, USA

Comstock, Keith (Baseball Player)
Minnesota Twins
9615 E Desert Trl
Scottsdale, AZ 85260-4624, USA

Conacher, Brian (Hockey Player)
120-10 Walder Ave
Toronto, ON M4V 1G2, CANADA

Conant, Kenneth J (Archaeologist)
3 Carlton Village #T105
Bedford, MA 01730, USA

Conant, Sean (Actor)
c/o Staff Member *Rising Picture*
PO Box 2
North Hampton, NH 03862-0002, USA

Conatsor, Clint (Baseball Player)
Boston Braves
26701 Quail Crk Apt 191
Laguna Hills, CA 92656-3010, USA

Conaty, William (Football Player)
Buffalo Bills
203 Country Club Dr
Moorestown, NJ 08057-3977, USA

Conaway, Christi
334 Huntley Dr
West Hollywood, CA 90048-1919, USA

Conaway, Cristi (Actor)
443 14th St
Santa Monica, CA 90402-2131, USA

Conaway, Jeff (Actor)
c/o Alexandra Karrys *Divine Management*
117 N Orlando Ave
Los Angeles, CA 90048-3403, USA

Concepcion, David I (Davey) (Athlete,
Baseball Player)
Urbanizacion Los Caobos Botalon 5D
5 Piso
Maracay, VENEZUELA

Concepion, David I (Davey) (Baseball
Player)
Urb Los Caobos Botalon 5D
5-Piso-Maracay, VENEZUELA

Concrete Blonde (Music Group)
Concrete Blonde Touring Company Inc
16830 Ventura Blvd Ste 501
Encino, CA 91436-1717, USA

Concretes, The (Music Group)
c/o Staff Member *Paradigm (Monterey)*
509 Hartnell St
Monterey, CA 93940-2825, USA

Conde, Ninel (Actor)
c/o Gabriel Blanco *Gabriel Blanco
Iglesias (Mexico)*
Rio Balsas 35-32
Colonia Cuauhtemoc
DF 06500, MEXICO

Conde, Ramon (Baseball Player)
Chicago White Sox
PO Box 57
Juana Diaz, PR 00795-0057, USA

Condit, Philip M (Business Person)
Boeing Co
PO Box 3707
Seattle, WA 98124-2207, USA

Condon, Bill (Director, Writer)
c/o Staff Member *William Morris Agency
(WMA-LA)*
1 William Morris Pl
Beverly Hills, CA 90212-4261, USA

Condon, Jill (Producer, Writer)
c/o Staff Member *United Talent Agency
(UTA)*
9560 Wilshire Blvd Ste 500
Beverly Hills, CA 90212-2401, USA

Condon, Paul (Lawyer)
Metropolitan Police
New Scottland Yard Broadway
London SW1H 0BG, UNITED KINGDOM
(UK)

Condon, Tom (Football Player)
Kansas City Chiefs
700 W 47th St Ste 800
Kansas City, MO 64112-1922, USA

Condra, Julie (Actor)
c/o Staff Member *Gold Coast
Management*
1023 1/2 Abbot Kinney Blvd
Venice, CA 90291-5536, USA

Condren, Glen (Football Player)
New York Giants
8557 N 175th East Ave
Owasso, OK 74055-5638, USA

Condrey, Clay (Baseball Player)
San Diego Padres
412 N 8th St
Navasota, TX 77868-2927, USA

Condron, Christopher M (Financier)
Melton Financial Corp
Mellon Bank Center
500 Grant St
Pittsburgh, PA 15258-0001, USA

Cone, David B (Baseball Player)
Kansas City Royals
376 Westover Rd
Stamford, CT 06902-1929, USA

Cone, Fred (Football Player)
Green Bay Packers
PO Box 1819
Blairsville, GA 30514-1819, USA

Cone Vanderbush, Carin (Swimmer)
116 Washington Rd # B
West Point, NY 10996-1403, USA

Confederate Railroad (Music Group)
The Bobby Roberts Company Inc
PO Box 1547
Goodlettsville, TN 37070-1547, USA

Confessional, Dashboard (Musician)
Ellis Industries Inc.
234 Shoreward Dr
Great Neck, NY 11021-2734, USA

Conforti, Gino (Actor)
Orange Gove Group
12178 Ventura Blvd Ste 205
Studio City, CA 91604-2540, USA

Congdon, Jeff (Basketball Player)
Anaheim Amigos
505 Highland View Ct
Mesquite, NV 89027-8844, USA

Conger, Harry M (Business Person)
Homestake Mining Co
650 California St
San Francisco, CA 94108-2702, USA

Conigliaro, Billy (Baseball Player)
Boston Red Sox
501 Cabot St Unit 2
Beverly, MA 01915-2580, USA

Conine, Jeff (Baseball Player)
3166 Inverness
Weston, FL 33332-1816, USA

Conjar, Larry (Football Player)
Cleveland Browns
542 Sheridan Rd
Evanston, IL 60202-3124, USA

Conkey, Margaret (Archaeologist)
University of California
Archaeological Research Facility
Berkeley, CA 94720-0001, USA

Conlan, Shane P (Football Player)
Buffalo Bills
521 East Dr
Sewickley, PA 15143-1114, USA

Conlee, Gerald (Football Player)
Cleveland Rams
11588 Via Rancho San Diego # D3048
El Cajon, CA 92019-5277, USA

Conlee, John (Musician)
John Conlee Enterprises
38 Music Sq E Ste 117
Nashville, TN 37203-4334, USA

Conley, Bob (Baseball Player)
Philadelphia Phillies
16A Canton Dr
Whiting, NJ 08759-1725, USA

Conley, Clare D (Editor)
Hemlock Farms
Hawley, PA 18428, USA

Conley, D Eugene (Gene) (Baseball
Player, Basketball Player)
Boston Celtics
2105 Grafton Ave
Clermont, FL 34711-5241, USA

Conley, Earl Thomas (Musician,
Songwriter, Writer)
657 Baker Rd
Smyrna, TN 37167-4777, USA

Conley, Jack (Actor)
c/o Julia Buchwald *Don Buchwald &
Associates Inc (LA)*
6500 Wilshire Blvd Ste 2200
Los Angeles, CA 90048-4942, USA

Conley, Jill
10332 Christine Pl
Chatsworth, CA 91311-1917, USA

Conley, Joe (Actor)
PO Box 6487
Thousand Oaks, CA 91359-6487, USA

Conley, Larry (Basketball Player)
Kentucky Colonels
5422 Forest Springs Dr
Dunwoody, GA 30338-3606, USA

Conley, Michael (Mike) (Athlete, Track
Athlete)
University of Arkansas
Athletic Dept
Fayetteville, AR 72701, USA

Conlin, Chris (Football Player)
Miami Dolphins
4864 Tropicana Ave
Cooper City, FL 33330-4428, USA

Conlin, Edward (Basketball Player)
Syracuse Nationals
153 N Mountain Ave
Montclair, NJ 07042-2347, USA

Conlin, Michaela (Actor)
c/o Amanda Glazer *Kohner Agency, The*
9300 Wilshire Blvd Ste 555
Beverly Hills, CA 90212-3211, USA

Conlon, James J
Shuman Assoc
120 W 58th St Apt 8D
New York, NY 10019-2126, USA

Conn, Didi (Actor, Musician)
1901 Avenue Of The Stars Ste 1450
Los Angeles, CA 90067-6087, USA

Conn, Richard (Football Player)
Pittsburgh Steelers
144 Sugarmill Ln
Moore, SC 29369-9497, USA

Conn, Terri (Actor)
1268 E 14th St
Brooklyn, NY 11230-5241, USA

Conneff, Kevin (Musician)
Macklam Feldman Mgmt
1505 W 2nd Ave
#200
Vancouver, BC V6H 3Y4, CANADA

Connell, Desmond Cardinal (Religious
Leader)
Archbishop's House
Drumcondra
Dublin 9, IRELAND

Connell, Elizabeth (Opera Singer)
I M G Artists
3 Burlingtone Lane
Chiswick
London W4 2TH, UNITED KINGDOM
(UK)

Connell, Evan S Jr (Writer)
320 Artist Rd
Fort Macy 13
Santa Fe, NM 87501-2079, USA

Connell, Jane
905 W End Ave
New York, NY 10025-3530, USA

Connell, Thurman C (Financier)
Federal Home Loan Bank
907 Walnut St
Des Moines, IA 50309-3501, USA

Connelly, Billy (Actor, Musician,
Producer, Writer)
c/o Gene Parseghian *Untitled
Entertainment (NY)*
322 8th Ave Ste 601
New York, NY 10001-6715, USA

Connelly, Jennifer (Actor)
c/o Risa Shapiro *International Creative Management (ICM-LA)*
10250 Constellation Blvd
Los Angeles, CA 90067-6200, USA

Connelly, Michael (Writer)
Little Brown
3 Center Plz
Boston, MA 02108-2084, USA

Connelly, Mike (Football Player)
Dallas Cowboys
9352 Creel Creek Dr
Dallas, TX 75228-4132, USA

Connelly, Steve (Baseball Player)
Oakland A's
1863 Litchfield Ave
Long Beach, CA 90815-3037, USA

Conner, Bart (Gymnast)
4421 Hidden Hill Rd
Norman, OK 73072-2899, USA

Conner, Bruce (Artist)
45 Sussex St
San Francisco, CA 94131-3011, USA

Conner, Chris (Actor)
c/o Staff Member *Nine Yards Entertainment*
8530 Wilshire Blvd Fl 5
Beverly Hills, CA 90211-3102, USA

Conner, Clyde (Football Player)
San Francisco 49ers
510 Valencia Dr
Los Altos, CA 94022-1761, USA

Conner, Darion (Football Player)
Atlanta Falcons
18001 Allison Park Pl Apt 105
Tampa, FL 33647-2896, USA

Conner, Dennis
1011 Anchorage Ln
San Diego, CA 92106-3005, USA

Conner, Frank (Golfer)
c/o Staff Member *Pro Golfers Association (PGA) Tour*
112 Tpc Blvd
Ponte Vedra Beach, FL 32082, USA

Conner, Jimmy Dan (Basketball Player)
Kentucky Colonels
5009 Old Federal Rd
Louisville, KY 40207-1200, USA

Conner, Lester (Basketball Player)
Golden State Warriors
13836 Coldwater Dr
Carmel, IN 46032-8562, USA

Conners, Dan (Football Player)
Oakland Raiders
1032 Chorro St
San Luis Obispo, CA 93401-3223, USA

Connery, Jason (Actor)
David Shapira
193 N Robertson Blvd
Beverly Hills, CA 90211-2103, USA

Connery, Sean (Actor)
c/o Nancy Seltzer *Nancy Seltzer & Associates*
6220 Del Valle Dr
Los Angeles, CA 90048-5306, USA

Connery, Vincent L (Misc)
National Treasury Employees Union
1730 K St NW
Washington, DC 20006, USA

Connick Jr, Harry (Actor, Musician)
c/o Ann Marie Wilkins *Wilkins Management*
323 Broadway
Cambridge, MA 02139-1801, USA

Conniff, Cal (Skier)
157 Pleasantview Ave
Longmeadow, MA 01106-1021, USA

Connolly, Billy (Actor)
Tickety-Boo Ltd
Boathouse
Crabtree Lane
London SW6 6LU, UNITED KINGDOM (UK)

Connolly, Kevin (Actor)
c/o Troy Zien *William Morris Agency (WMA-LA)*
1 William Morris Pl
Beverly Hills, CA 90212-4261, USA

Connolly, Olga Fikotova (Athlete, Track Athlete)
606 Narcissus Ave
Corona Del Mar, CA 92625-2417, USA

Connolly, Ted (Football Player)
San Francisco 49ers
2790 Wrondel Way Apt 23
Reno, NV 89502-4359, USA

Connor, Chris (Musician)
Maxine Harvard Unlimited
7942 W Bell Rd Ste C5
Glendale, AZ 85308-8710, USA

Connor, Christopher M (Business Person)
Sherwin-Williams Co
101 W Prospect Ave
Cleveland, OH 44115-1075, USA

Connor, Joseph E (Business Person, Government Official)
Under-Secretary General's Office
United Nations
Un Plaza
New York, NY 10017, USA

Connor, Patrick
3 Spring Bank
New Mills nr. Stockport, ENGLAND SK12 4AS, UNITED KINGDOM (UK)

Connor, Ralph (Misc)
9866 W Highwood Ct
Sun City, AZ 85373-1771, USA

Connor, Richard L (Publisher)
Fort Worth Star-Telegram
400 W 7th St
Fort Worth, TX 76102-4793, USA

Connor, Shannon (Model)
4 Rockage Rd
Warren, NJ 07059-5506, USA

Connors, Bill (Baseball Player)
Chicago Cubs
3329 Enterprise Rd E
Safety Harbor, FL 34695-5307, USA

Connors, Carol (Songwriter, Writer)
1709 Ferrari Dr
Beverly Hills, CA 90210-1603, USA

Connors, James S (Jimmy) (Tennis Player)
1962 E Valley Rd
Santa Barbara, CA 93108-1428, USA

Connors, Merv (Baseball Player)
Chicago White Sox
1131 Addison St
Berkeley, CA 94702-1607, USA

Connors, Mike (Actor, Producer)
c/o Jack Gilardi *International Creative Management (ICM-LA)*
10250 Constellation Blvd
Los Angeles, CA 90067-6200, USA

Connway, Craig (Business Person)
PeopleSoft Inc
4460 Hacienda Dr
Pleasanton, CA 94588-2761, USA

Conoly, Zuehl (Football Player)
Chicago Cardinals
PO Box 35
Brackettville, TX 78832-0035, USA

Conombo, Joseph I (Prime Minister)
2003 Ave de la Liberte
BP 613
Dadoya, Ouagadougou, BURKINA FASO

Conover, Lloyd H (Inventor)
5200 Brittany Dr S Apt 304
Saint Petersburg, FL 33715-1523, USA

Conover, Scott (Football Player)
Detroit Lions
118 Amberly Dr Unit D
Manalapan, NJ 07726-2307, USA

Conoway, Christi
PO Box 46515
Los Angeles, CA 90046-0515, USA

Conrad, Barnaby
3530 Pine Valley Dr
Sarasota, FL 34239-4335, USA

Conrad, Bobby Joe (Football Player)
St Louis Cardinals
148 County Road 3270
Clifton, TX 76634-4678, USA

Conrad, Chris (Football Player)
Pittsburgh Steelers
984 Orangewood Dr
Brea, CA 92821-2514, USA

Conrad, David (Actor)
c/o Stephen Hirsh *Gersh Agency, The (LA)*
232 N Canon Dr
Beverly Hills, CA 90210-5302, USA

Conrad, Eve Burch
23388 Mulholland Dr
Woodland Hills, CA 91364-2733, USA

Conrad, Fred (Photographer)
New York Times
229 W 43rd St
Editorial Dept
New York, NY 10036-3959, USA

Conrad, James A (Financier)
Source One Mortgage
27555 Famington Road
Famington Hills, MI 48334, USA

Conrad, Kimberly
10236 Charing Cross Rd
Los Angeles, CA 90024-1815, USA

Conrad, Lauren (Reality TV Star)
29 Vista Del Sol
Laguna Beach, CA 92651-6745, USA

Conrad, Paul
28649 Crestridge Rd
Palos Verdes, CA 90274, USA

Conrad, Paul F (Cartoonist)
28649 Crestridge Rd
Palos Verdes Estates, CA 90275-5068, USA

Conrad, Robert (Actor)
444 Saddle Trl
Thousand Oaks, CA 91361-5219, USA

Conrad, Shane
9255 W Sunset Blvd Ste 620
Los Angeles, CA 90069-3303, USA

Conradt, Jody (Coach)
9614 Leaning Rock Cir
Austin, TX 78730-2725, USA

Conran, Jasper A T (Designer, Fashion Designer)
Jasper Conran Ltd
2 Munden St
London W14 0RH, UNITED KINGDOM (UK)

Conran, Philip J (War Hero)
4706 Calle Reina
Santa Barbara, CA 93110-2018, USA

Conran, Terence O (Designer)
22 SHad Thames
London SE1 2YU, UNITED KINGDOM (UK)

Conroy, D Patrick (Pat) (Writer)
Houghton Mifflin
222 Berkeley St # 700
Boston, MA 02116-3748, USA

Conroy, Frances (Actor)
International Creative Mgmt
8942 Wilshire Blvd # 219
Beverly Hills, CA 90211-1908, USA

Conroy, Kevin
c/o Staff Member *Imperium 7 Talent Agency*
9911 W Pico Blvd Ste 1290
Los Angeles, CA 90035-2726, USA

Conroy, Pat (Writer)
5053 Ocean Blvd # 134
Sarasota, FL 34242-1607, USA

Conroy, Tim (Baseball Player)
Oakland A's
109 Moonlight Dr
Monroeville, PA 15146-2028, USA

Considine, John (Actor)
16 1/2 Red Coal Lane
Greenwich, CT 06830, USA

Considine, Paddy (Actor, Writer)
c/o Staff Member *Creative Artists Agency LCC (CAA-LA)*
2000 Avenue Of The Stars
Los Angeles, CA 90067-4700, USA

Considine, Tim (Actor)
3708 Mountain View Ave
Los Angeles, CA 90066-3112, USA

Consolo, Billy (Baseball Player)
Boston Red Sox
1266 Willsbrook Ct
Westlake Village, CA 91361-1423, USA

Conspirator (Music Group)
c/o Staff Member *Paradigm (Monterey)*
509 Hartnell St
Monterey, CA 93940-2825, USA

Constable, Jim (Baseball Player)
New York Giants
818 Allison Dr
Jonesborough, TN 37659-5143, USA

Constantin, Michel
17 blvd. Bartole Beauvallon
St. Maxime 83120, FRANCE

Constantine, ex-King
4 Linnell Dr.Hampstead Way
London, ENGLAND NW11, UNITED KINGDOM (UK)

Constantine, Kevin
5928 Jenny Lind Ct
San Jose, CA 95120-1789, USA

Constantine, Michael (Actor)
1604 Bern St
Reading, PA 19604-1630, USA

Constantine II (King)
4 Linnell Dr
Hampstead Way
London NW11, UNITED KINGDOM (UK)

Consuegra, Sandalio S C (Sandy)
(Baseball Player)
Washington Senators
10847 NW 7th St Apt 21
Miami, FL 33172-3763, USA

Consuelos, Mark (Actor)
c/o Heidi Slan *PMK/HBH Public Relations (PMK-LA)*
700 N San Vicente Blvd Ste G910
West Hollywood, CA 90069-5061, USA

Conte, Dino
2325 Fox Hills Dr
Los Angeles, CA 90064-2603, USA

Conte, Lansana (President)
President's Office
Conakry, GUINEA

Conte, Lou (Choreographer)
Hubbard Street Dance Co
1147 W Jackson Blvd
Chicago, IL 60607-2905, USA

Conti, Al
PO Box 701
Portsmouth, RI 02871-0701, USA

Conti, Bill (Composer)
117 Fremont Pl
Los Angeles, CA 90005-3868, USA

Conti, Jason (Baseball Player)
Arizona Diamondbacks
740 N April Dr
Chandler, AZ 85226-1632, USA

Conti, Tom (Actor)
Chatto & Linnit
Prince of Wales Coventry St
London W1V 7FE, UNITED KINGDOM (UK)

Contino, Dick (Music Group, Musician)
3355 Nahatan Way
Las Vegas, NV 89169-3119, USA

Contner, James A (Cinematographer)
4146 Ventura Canyon Ave
Sherman Oaks, CA 91423-4328, USA

Contoulis, John (Football Player)
New York Giants
686 Groton Long Point Rd
Groton, CT 06340-5503, USA

Contours, The
1161 NW 76th Ave
Plantation, FL 33322-5120, USA

Contreras, Jose (Athlete, Baseball Player)
c/o Staff Member *Chicago White Sox*
333 W 35th St
Comiskey Park
Chicago, IL 60616-3651, USA

Contreras, Nardi (Baseball Player)
Chicago White Sox
17546 Willow Pond Dr
Lutz, FL 33549-5602, USA

Contz, Bill (Football Player)
Cleveland Browns
106 Grace Dr
Cranberry Twp, PA 16066-2308, USA

Converse, Frank (Actor)
Artists Group
1650 Broadway Ste 610
New York, NY 10019-6833, USA

Converse, Jim (Baseball Player)
Seattle Mariners
11865 Cobble Brook Dr
Rancho Cordova, CA 95742-8008, USA

Converse-Roberts, William (Actor)
Innovative Artists
1505 10th St
Santa Monica, CA 90401-2805, USA

Conway, Billy (Music Group, Musician)
Creative Performance Group
48 Laight St
New York, NY 10013-2016, USA

Conway, Brett (Football Player)
Washington Redskins
1422 Kensington Ct
Southlake, TX 76092-9512, USA

Conway, Curtis (Football Player)
Chicago Bears
446 E Phelps St
Gilbert, AZ 85295-2091, USA

Conway, Dave (Football Player)
Green Bay Packers
6402 Wolfcreek Pass
Austin, TX 78749-1824, USA

Conway, Gary (Actor)
11240 Chimney Rock Rd
Paso Robles, CA 93446-9792, USA

Conway, James (General)
Commanding General I Marine
Expeditionary Force
Camp Pendleton, CA 92055, USA

Conway, James L (Director)
Creative Artists Agency
9830 Wilshire Blvd
Beverly Hills, CA 90212-1804, USA

Conway, Jill K (Historian)
65 Commonwealth Ave # 8B
Boston, MA 02116-2304, USA

Conway, John W (Business Person)
Crown Cork & Seal
1 Crown Way
Philadelphia, PA 19154-4599, USA

Conway, Kevin (Actor)
25 Centurypark W
New York, NY 10023, USA

Conway, Rob (Wrestler)
c/o Staff Member *World Wrestling Entertainment (WWE)*
1241 E Main St
Stamford, CT 06902-3520, USA

Conway, Tim (Actor, Comedian, Writer)
c/o Steve Tellez *Creative Artists Agency LCC (CAA-LA)*
2000 Avenue Of The Stars
Los Angeles, CA 90067-4700, USA

Conwell, Angell (Actor)
c/o Melanie Greene *Melanie Greene Management & Productions*
425 N Robertson Blvd
West Hollywood, CA 90048-1735, USA

Conwell, Easther M (Physicist)
800 Phillips Rd
Webster, NY 14580-9720, USA

Conwell, Ernie (Football Player)
St Louis Rams
13527 SE 268th St
Kent, WA 98042-8033, USA

Conwell, Joseph (Football Player)
Philadelphia Eagles
1301 Stoney River Dr
Ambler, PA 19002-1159, USA

Conwell, Tommy (Music Group, Musician)
Brothers Mgmt
141 Dunbar Ave
Fords, NJ 08863-1551, USA

Coobar, Abdulmegid (Prime Minister)
Asadu El-Furat St 29
Garden City
Tripoli, LIBYA

Cooder, Ry (Composer, Music Group, Musician)
326 Entrada Dr
Santa Monica, CA 90402-1202, USA

Coody, Charles (Golfer)
1555 Oldham Ln
Abilene, TX 79602-4143, USA

Coogan, Dodie
PO Box 413
Palm Springs, CA 92263-0413, USA

Coogan, Keith (Actor)
1640 S Sepulveda Blvd Ste 218
Los Angeles, CA 90025-7535, USA

Coogan, Richard
5805 Whitsett Ave Apt 103
N Hollywood, CA 91607-1146, USA

Cook, A J (Actor)
c/o David Guillod *United Talent Agency (UTA)*
9560 Wilshire Blvd Ste 500
Beverly Hills, CA 90212-2401, USA

Cook, Aaron (Baseball Player)
Colorado Rockies
707 Schultz Dr
Hamilton, OH 45013, USA

Cook, Andy (Baseball Player)
New York Yankees
3312 Central Ave
Memphis, TN 38111-4402, USA

Cook, Ann T
5412 Riverhills Dr
Temple Terrace, FL 33617-7136, USA

Cook, Anthony (Football Player)
Houston Oilers
203 Grace Hts
Bennettsville, SC 29512-3732, USA

Cook, Barbara (Actor, Music Group)
c/o Staff Member *Cunningham Escott Slevin & Doherty (LA)*
10635 Santa Monica Blvd Ste 130
Los Angeles, CA 90025-8306, USA

Cook, Bert (Basketball Player)
New York Knicks
2571 W 5725 S
Roy, UT 84067-1326, USA

Cook, Beryl (Artist)
Coach House 1A Camp Road Clifton
Bristol BS8 3LW, UNITED KINGDOM (UK)

Cook, Bob (Football Player)
Oakland Raiders
100 Sioux Ct
Hendersonville, TN 37075-4634, USA

Cook, Brian (Basketball Player)
Los Angeles Lakers
1111 S Figueroa St
Staples Center
Los Angeles, CA 90015-1300, USA

Cook, Carole (Actor, Comedian)
8829 Ashcroft Ave
West Hollywood, CA 90048-2401, USA

Cook, Cliff (Baseball Player)
Cincinnati Reds
605 E Williamsburg Mnr
Arlington, TX 76014-1145, USA

Cook, Dane (Actor)
c/o Staff Member *Creative Artists Agency LCC (CAA-LA)*
2000 Avenue Of The Stars
Los Angeles, CA 90067-4700, USA

Cook, Darwin (Basketball Player)
New Jersey Nets
7361 Ojai Dr
Palmdale, CA 93551-4722, USA

Cook, Dennis (Baseball Player)
San Francisco Giants
3413 Serene Hills Ct
Austin, TX 78738-1230, USA

Cook, Donald G (General)
Commander Air Education/Training
Command
Randolph Air Force Base, TX 78155, USA

Cook, Doris (Baseball Player)
1059 Airport Rd
Muskegon, MI 49441-5101, USA

Cook, Edward J (Football Player)
Chicago Cardinals
902 Briarwood Ct
Sewell, NJ 08080-3508, USA

Cook, Fielder
180 Central Park S
New York, NY 10019-1562, USA

Cook, Fred (Football Player)
Baltimore Colts
4402 Market St
Pascagoula, MS 39567-2224, USA

Cook, Glen (Baseball Player)
Texas Rangers
424 Scarlet Sage Dr
League City, TX 77573-6426, USA

Cook, Jason (Actor)
c/o Meredith Fine *Coast to Coast Talent Group*
3350 Barham Blvd
Los Angeles, CA 90068-1404, USA

Cook, Jeff (Basketball Player)
Phoenix Suns
4908 E Doubletree Ranch Rd
Paradise Valley, AZ 85253-1556, USA

Cook, Jeffrey A (Jeff) (Music Group, Musician)
PO Box 35967
Fort Payne, AL 35967, USA

Cook, John (Golfer)
8815 Conroy Windermere Rd # 40
Orlando, FL 32835-3129, USA

Cook, Judy (Bowler)
Ladies Professional Bowling Tour
7200 Harrison Ave # 7171
Rockford, IL 61112-1017, USA

Cook, Leigh
9560 Wilshire Blvd # 516
Beverly Hills, CA 90212-2427, USA

Cook, Marv (Football Player)
New England Patriots
425 Butternut Ln
Iowa City, IA 52246-2782, USA

Cook, Mike (Baseball Player)
California Angels
216 Harlech Way
Charleston, SC 29414-6876, USA

Cook, Norm (Basketball Player)
Bosten Celtics
1003 N Logan St
Lincoln, IL 62656-1746, USA

Cook, Paul (Music Group, Musician)
Solo Agency
55 Fulham High St
London SW6 3JJ, UNITED KINGDOM
(UK)

Cook, Paul M (Business Person)
SRI International
333 Ravenswood Ave
Menlo Park, CA 94025-3493, USA

Cook, Peter F C (Architect)
54 Compayne Gardens
London NW6 3RY, UNITED KINGDOM
(UK)

Cook, Rachael Leigh (Lee) (Actor)
c/o Randy James *James/Levy/Jacobson Management*
3500 W Olive Ave Ste 1470
Burbank, CA 91505-5514, USA

Cook, Rachel Leigh (Actor)
Moongate Mgmt
4570 Van Nuys Blvd # 171
Sherman Oaks, CA 91403-2913, USA

Cook, Rashard (Football Player)
Philadelphia Eagles
7882 Gribble St
San Diego, CA 92114-6019, USA

Cook, Richard (Scientist)
Jet Propulsion Laboratory
4800 Oak Grove Dr
Pasadena, CA 91109-8001, USA

Cook, Robert (Basketball Player)
Sheboygan Redskins
RR 4 Box 354
Lake Geneva, WI 53147, USA

Cook, Robert (Opera Singer)
Quavers 53 Friars Ave
Fiem Barnet
London N2O OXG, UNITED KINGDOM
(UK)

Cook, Robert F (Robin) (Government Official)
House of Commons
Westminster
London SW1A 0AA, UNITED KINGDOM
(UK)

Cook, Robin (Writer)
4601 Gulf Shore Blvd N # P4
Naples, FL 34103-2221, USA

Cook, Ron (Baseball Player)
Houston Astros
1918 Franklin Dr
Longview, TX 75601-4111, USA

Cook, Stanton R (Publisher)
224 Raleigh Rd
Kenilworth, IL 60043-1209, USA

Cook, Steve (Baseball Player)
Pittsburgh Pirates
1 SW Bowerman Dr # M53
Beaverton, OR 97005-0979, USA

Cook, Steve (Bowler)
1209 Devonshire Ct
Roseville, CA 95661-5470, USA

Cook, Thomas A (Writer)
Bantam Books
1540 Broadway
New York, NY 10036-4039, USA

Cook, Toi (Football Player)
New Orleans Saints
11718 Barrington Ct # 805
Los Angeles, CA 90049-2930, USA

Cooke, Amelia (Actor)
c/o Darren Goldberg *1 Management*
9000 W Sunset Blvd Ph 1550
West Hollywood, CA 90069-1838, USA

Cooke, David (Basketball Player)
Sacramento Kings
PO Box 270591
San Diego, CA 92198-2591, USA

Cooke, Howard F H (General, Governor)
King's House Hope Road
Kingston 10, JAMAICA

Cooke, Janis (Journalist)
Washington Post
1150 15th St NW
Washington, DC 20071-0002, USA

Cooke, Joe (Basketball Player)
Cleveland Cavaliers
1 W Campbell Ave Apt 2035
Phoenix, AZ 85013-4911, USA

Cooke, John P (Misc)
290 Branchville Rd
Ridgefield, CT 06877, USA

Cooke, Josh (Actor)
c/o Adam Griffin *The Collective*
331 N Maple Dr Fl 2
Beverly Hills, CA 90210-3827, USA

Cooke, William (Football Player)
Green Bay Packers
1851 Hillside Rd
Fairfield, CT 06824-2017, USA

Cooks, Johnie (Football Player)
Baltimore Colts
1839 New Light Road
Merigold, MS 38759, USA

Cooks, Kerry (Football Player)
Green Bay Packers
1305 Meadow Creek Dr Apt 111
Irving, TX 75038-7202, USA

Cooks, Rayford (Football Player)
Houston Oilers
1839 Nomans St
Dallas, TX 75212, USA

Cooksey, Danny
9300 Wilshire Blvd # 410
Beverly Hills, CA 90212-3213, USA

Cooksey, Dave (Religious Leader)
Brethren Church
524 College Ave
Ashland, OH 44805-3703, USA

Cooksey, Patty (Athlete)
c/oChurchill Downs
700 Central Ave
Race Office
Louisville, KY 40208-1200, USA

Cookson, Brent (Baseball Player)
Kansas City Royals
1232 Manzanita Dr
Santa Paula, CA 93060-1239, USA

Cookson, Peter
30 Norfolk Rd.
Southfield, MA 01259, USA

Cool Breeze
PO Box 470642
San Francisco, CA 94147-0642, USA

Coolbaugh, Mike (Baseball Player)
Milwaukee Brewers
12146 Apricot Dr
San Antonio, TX 78247-4352, USA

Coolbaugh, Scott (Baseball Player)
Texas Rangers
6708 Carriage Ln
Colleyville, TX 76034-5771, USA

Cooley, Denton (Doctor, Misc)
3014 Del Monte Dr
Houston, TX 77019-3214, USA

Cooley, Ryan (Actor)
c/o Norbert Abrams *Noble Kaplan Agency*
1260 Yonge St Fl 2
Toronto, ON M4T 1W6, CANADA

Cooley, Tonya (Reality TV Star)
c/o Staff Member *Bunim/Murray Productions Inc*
6007 Sepulveda Blvd
Van Nuys, CA 91411-2502, USA

Cooleyb, Chelsea (Beauty Pageant Winner)
c/o Staff Member *Miss Universe Organization, The*
1370 Avenue Of The Americas Fl 16
New York, NY 10019-4602, USA

Coolidge, Charles H (War Hero)
1054 Balmoral Dr
Signal Mountain, TN 37377-2904, USA

Coolidge, Charles H Jr (General)
Vice Cinc Air Force Material Command
Wright-Patterson Air Force, OH 45433, USA

Coolidge, Harold J (Misc)
38 Standley St
Beverly, MA 01915-2020, USA

Coolidge, Jennifer (Actor, Writer)
c/o Lisa Gallant *International Creative Management (ICM-LA)*
10250 Constellation Blvd
Los Angeles, CA 90067-6200, USA

Coolidge, Martha (Director)
760 N La Cienega Blvd
Los Angeles, CA 90069-5204, USA

Coolidge, Rita (Music Group)
PO Box 571
Gwynedd Valley, PA 19437-0571, USA

Coolio (Actor, Musician)
c/o Staff Member *Don Buchwald & Associates Inc (LA)*
6500 Wilshire Blvd Ste 2200
Los Angeles, CA 90048-4942, USA

Coombe, George W (Attorney, Attorney General, General)
Graham & James
1 Maritime Plz
San Francisco, CA 94111-3492, USA

Coombs, Danny (Baseball Player)
Houston Colt 45's
14130 Cleobrook Dr
Houston, TX 77070-3744, USA

Coombs, Pat
5 Wendela Ct Harrow-On-The-Hill
Middlesex, ENGLAND, UNITED KINGDOM (UK)

Coombs, Philip H (Economist)
617 W Main St
Chester, CT 06412, USA

Coombs-Mueller, Carol
772 Tyrol Ct.
Crestline, CA 92325, USA

Coomer, Ron (Baseball Player)
Minnesota Twins
7021 Howard Ln
Eden Prairie, MN 55346-3053, USA

Coonce, Ricky (Music Group, Musician)
Thomas Cassidy
11761 E Speedway Blvd
Tucson, AZ 85748-2017, USA

Cooney, Gerry (Boxer)
FIST
265 W 14th St Ste 200
New York, NY 10011-7188, USA

Cooney, Joan Ganz (Educator, Misc, Television Host)
Children's TV Workshop
1 Lincoln Plz
New York, NY 10023-7163, USA

Cooney, Mark (Football Player)
Green Bay Packers
8005 Flower Ct
Arvada, CO 80005-2445, USA

Coonts, Stephen (Writer)
40 Upland Rd
Colorado Springs, CO 80906-4246, USA

Cooper, Adrian (Football Player)
Pittsburgh Steelers
3120 Saint Paul St
Denver, CO 80205-4840, USA

Cooper, Alexander (Architect)
Cooper Robertson & Partners
311 W 43rd St
New York, NY 10036-6415, USA

Cooper, Alice (Music Group, Songwriter, Writer)
c/o Jonny (Jon) Podell *Podell Talent Agency LLC*
22 W 21st St Fl 9
New York, NY 10010-7095, USA

Cooper, Amy Levin (Editor)
60 Sutton Pl S # 16C
New York, NY 10022-4168, USA

Cooper, Anderson (Correspondent, Journalist, Television Host)
Anderson Cooper 360
1 Time Warner Ctr Fl 4
Cnn
New York, NY 10019-8012, USA

Cooper, Artis (Basketball Player)
Golden State Warriors
5013 Millstone Way
Granite Bay, CA 95746-6126, USA

Cooper, Ashley
194 Bellevue Ave
Newport, RI 02840-3515, USA

Cooper, Bill (Football Player)
San Francisco 49ers
16056 Greenwood Rd
Monte Sereno, CA 95030-3018, USA

Cooper, Bonnie (Baseball Player)
PO Box 26
119 Sampson Street
Tremont, IL 61568-0026, USA

Cooper, Bradley (Actor)
c/o Susan Calogerakis *Thruline Entertainment*
9250 Wilshire Blvd Ground Fl
Beverly Hills, CA 90210, USA

Cooper, Brian (Baseball Player)
Anaheim Angels
346 W Ada Ave
Glendora, CA 91741-4248, USA

Cooper, Camille (Basketball Player)
New York Liberty
2 Penn Plz
Madison Square Garden
New York, NY 10121-1703, USA

Cooper, Carl (Golfer)
4823 Scenic Woods Trl
Kingwood, TX 77345-2323, USA

Cooper, Cecil C (Baseball Player)
Boston Red Sox
24802 Boulder Lakes Ct
Katy, TX 77494-3900, USA

Cooper, Charles (Actor)
c/o Joel Kleinman *Baier/Kleinman International*
3575 Cahuenga Blvd W Ste 500
Los Angeles, CA 90068-1344, USA

Cooper, Charles G (General)
3410 Barger Dr
Falls Church, VA 22044-1201, USA

Cooper, Chris (Actor)
c/o Julie Silverman-Yorn *The Firm*
9465 Wilshire Blvd Fl 6
Beverly Hills, CA 90212-2605, USA

Cooper, Christian
General Delivery
Sun Valley, ID 83353-9999, USA

Cooper, Christin (Skier)
1001 E Hyman Ave
Aspen, CO 81611-2612, USA

Cooper, Cortz (Religious Leader)
Presbyterian Church in America
1852 Century Plaza
Atlanta, GA 30345, USA

Cooper, Cynthia (Basketball Player, Coach)
3910 Chatfield Ct
Sugar Land, TX 77479-4101, USA

Cooper, Daniel L (Admiral)
121 Leisure Ct
Wyomissing, PA 19610-1969, USA

Cooper, Dave (Artist)
c/o Staff Member *Fantagraphics Books*
7563 Lake City Way NE
Seattle, WA 98115-4218, USA

Cooper, Dominic (Actor)
c/o Joel Lubin *Creative Artists Agency LCC (CAA-LA)*
2000 Avenue Of The Stars
Los Angeles, CA 90067-4700, USA

Cooper, Don (Baseball Player)
Minnesota Twins
2320 Arborfield Ln
Sarasota, FL 34235-1807, USA

Cooper, Duane (Basketball Player)
Los Angeles Lakers
13813 Ocana Ave
Bellflower, CA 90706-2528, USA

Cooper, Earl (Football Player)
San Francisco 49ers
2224 E Highway 21
Lincoln, TX 78948-6496, USA

Cooper, Gary (Baseball Player)
Houston Astros
1136 Birch Cir
Alpine, UT 84004-1212, USA

Cooper, Gary (Baseball Player)
Atlanta Braves
402 E Victory Dr
Savannah, GA 31405-2254, USA

Cooper, George (Football Player)
San Francisco 49ers
1616 Bloomfield Place Dr Apt 141B
Bloomfield Hills, MI 48302-0859, USA

Cooper, Hal (Director)
2651 Hutton Dr
Beverly Hills, CA 90210-1213, USA

Cooper, Henry (Boxer)
16 Barley House Hildonbroom Farm
Ridings Lane
Kent TN11 9JN, UNITED KINGDOM (UK)

Cooper, Imogen (Music Group, Musician)
Van Walsum Mgmt
4 Addison Bridge Place
London W14 8XP, UNITED KINGDOM (UK)

Cooper, Jackie (Actor, Director)
10430 Wilshire Blvd Apt 1603
Los Angeles, CA 90024-4680, USA

Cooper, James P (Football Player)
Brooklyn Dodgers
2713 Eastover Dr
Odessa, TX 79762-7830, USA

Cooper, Jeanne (Actor)
8401 Edwin Dr
Los Angeles, CA 90046-1025, USA

Cooper, Jilly (Writer)
Desmond Elliott
38 Bury St
London SW1Y 6AU, UNITED KINGDOM (UK)

Cooper, Joel D (Doctor)
Washington University
Medical School Surgery Dept
Saint Louis, MO 63110, USA

Cooper, John M (Misc)
182 Western Way
Princeton, NJ 08540-7208, USA

Cooper, Justin (Actor)
c/o Staff Member *Cunningham Escott Slevin & Doherty (LA)*
10635 Santa Monica Blvd Ste 130
Los Angeles, CA 90025-8306, USA

Cooper, Lattie F (Educator)
Arizona State University
President's Office
Tempe, AZ 85287-0001, USA

Cooper, Leon N (Nobel Prize Laureate)
49 Intervale Rd
Providence, RI 02906-4843, USA

Cooper, Lester I (Producer)
45 Morningside Dr S
Westport, CT 06880-5414, USA

Cooper, Louis (Football Player)
Kansas City Chiefs
200 Gregg Ave
Marion, SC 29571-3824, USA

Cooper, Marilyn (Actor)
Gage Group
315 W 57th St Frnt 4H
New York, NY 10019-3158, USA

Cooper, Mark S (Football Player)
Denver Broncos
6598 S Telluride St
Aurora, CO 80016-3158, USA

Cooper, Matthew T (General)
9326 Fairfax St
Alexandria, VA 22309-3016, USA

Cooper, Namrata (Actor)
c/o Staff Member *Amsel Eisenstadt & Frazier Inc*
5055 Wilshire Blvd Ste 865
Los Angeles, CA 90036-6109, USA

Cooper, Paula (Misc)
Paula Cooper Gallery
534 W 21st St
New York, NY 10011-2812, USA

Cooper, Ray (Producer)
c/o Staff Member *@Radical.Media (NY)*
435 Hudson St Fl 6
New York, NY 10014-3947, USA

Cooper, Roxanne (Musician)
c/o Staff Member *Pop Idol (Fremantle Media)*
2700 Colorado Ave Ste 450
Santa Monica, CA 90404-3599, USA

Cooper, Scott (Actor)
c/o Leland LaBarre *Diverse Talent Group*
1875 Century Park E Ste 2250
Los Angeles, CA 90067-2563, USA

Cooper, Scott (Baseball Player)
Boston Red Sox
7 Fairways Cir Apt F
Saint Charles, MO 63303-3353, USA

Cooper, Stephen (Business Person)
Enron Corp
1331 Lamar St Ste 1600
Houston, TX 77010-3118, USA

Cooper, Thurlow (Football Player)
New York Titans
21 Andrews Ave
Falmouth, ME 04105-1901, USA

Cooper, Wayne (Artist)
PO Box 106
Depew, OK 74028-0106, USA

Cooper, Wayne (Basketball Player)
Golden State Warriors
Millstone Way
Granite Bay, CA 95746, USA

Cooper, Wilma Lee (Musician)
Charles Rapp Enterprises
1650 Broadway Ste 1410
New York, NY 10019-6833, USA

Cooperfield, David (Misc)
2000 West Loop S Ste 1300
Houston, TX 77027-3512, USA

Cooperwheat, Lee (Designer, Fashion Designer)
Cooperwheat Blundell
14 Cheshire St
London E2 6EH, UNITED KINGDOM (UK)

Coors, William K (Business Person)
Adolph Coors Co
1221 Ford St
Golden, CO 80401-1132, USA

Coover, Robert (Writer)
Brown University
Linden Press
49 George St
Providence, RI 02912-0001, USA

Cope, Derrike (Race Car Driver)
CLR Racing
1900 Spanish River Rd
Boca Raton, FL 33432-8064, USA

Cope, Jonathan (Dancer)
Royal Ballet
Covent Garden
Bow St
London WC2E 9DD, UNITED KINGDOM (UK)

Cope, Julian (Musician, Songwriter, Writer)
International Talent Group
729 7th Ave Rm 1600
New York, NY 10019-6880, USA

Cope, Kenneth
61-63 Kent House 87 Regent St.
London, ENGLAND W1R 7HF, UNITED KINGDOM (UK)

Copeland, Adam (Edge) (Wrestler)
c/o Staff Member *World Wrestling Entertainment (WWE)*
1241 E Main St
Stamford, CT 06902-3520, USA

Copeland, Al (Business Person, Race Car Driver)
5001 Folse Dr
Metairie, LA 70006-1020, USA

Copeland, Cyrus
c/o Daniel A (Dan) Strone *Trident Media Group LLC*
41 Madison Ave Fl 36
New York, NY 10010-2257, USA

Copeland, Danny (Football Player)
Washington Redskins
186 Old Newton Rd
Pelham, GA 31779-4043, USA

Copeland, Hollis (Basketball Player)
New York Knicks
257 Upland Ave
Trenton, NJ 08638-2331, USA

Copeland, Horace (Football Player)
Tampa Bay Buccaneers
4195 Blakemore Pl
Spring Hill, FL 34609-0694, USA

Copeland, Jim (Football Player)
Cleveland Browns
1935 Blue Ridge Rd
Charlottesville, VA 22903-1215, USA

Copeland, Joan (Actor)
88 Central Park W
New York, NY 10023-5209, USA

Copeland, Kenneth (Misc)
Kenneth Copeland Ministries
PO Box 2908
Fort Worth, TX 76113, USA

Copeland, Lanard (Basketball Player)
Philadelphia 76ers
4115 Pierce Rd
Atlanta, GA 30349-3648, USA

Copeland, Stewart (Composer)
2420 Arbutus Dr
Los Angeles, CA 90049-1209, USA

Copley, Jeff E
687 State Hwy 194
Kimper, KY 41539, USA

Copley, Teri (Actor, Model)
13351 Riverside Dr # D513
Sherman Oaks, CA 91423-2542, USA

Copon, Michael (Actor)
c/o Staff Member *Kazarian/Spencer & Assoc (LA)*
11969 Ventura Blvd
Box 7409 Fl 3
Studio City, CA 91604-2630, USA

Copp, D Harold (Misc)
4755 Belmont Ave
Vancouver, BC V6T 1A8, CANADA

Coppenbarger, Ron (Football Player)
Atlanta Falcons
7890 James Island Trl
Jacksonville, FL 32256-7355, USA

Coppens, Yves (Misc)
4 Rue du Pont-aux-Choux
Paris 75003, FRANCE

Copperfield, David (Entertainer)
c/o Jason Weinberg *Untitled Entertainment (LA)*
331 N Maple Dr Fl 3
Beverly Hills, CA 90210-3827, USA

Copping, Allen A (Educator)
Louisiana State University System
President's Office
Baton Rouge, LA 70817, USA

Coppinger, Rocky (Baseball Player)
Baltimore Orioles
7208 Alto Rey Ave
El Paso, TX 79912-2100, USA

Coppola, Alicia (Actor)
William Morris Agency
151 El Camino Dr
Beverly Hills, CA 90212-2775, USA

Coppola, Chris (Actor)
c/o Staff Member *Independent Management Group (IMG)*
717 N Alta Vista Blvd
Los Angeles, CA 90046-7601, USA

Coppola, Francis Ford (Director)
c/o Staff Member *American Zoetrope*
916 Kearny St
San Francisco, CA 94133-5107, USA

Coppola, Sofia (Actor, Director, Writer)
c/o Bart Walker *Creative Artists Agency (CAA-NY)*
162 5th Ave Fl 6
New York, NY 10010-6047, USA

Coppolla, Alicia (Actor)
c/o Jeff Witjas *Agency for the Performing Arts (APA-NY)*
888 7th Ave
New York, NY 10106-0001, USA

Coquillette, Trace (Baseball Player)
Montreal Expos
5200 Mississippi Bar Dr
Orangevale, CA 95662-5717, USA

Cora, Alex (Baseball Player)
Los Angeles Dodgers
F12 Calle 14
Caguas, PR 00727-6935, USA

Cora, Jose M (Joey) (Baseball Player)
San Diego Padres
Calle 17
F12 Villa Nueva
Caguas, PR 00725, USA

Corabi, John (Musician)
Union Entertainment Group
1323 Newbury Rd Ste 104
Newbury Park, CA 91320-3679, USA

Coraci, Frank
9701 Wilshire Blvd Ste 1000
Beverly Hills, CA 90212-2010, USA

Coral, The (Music Group)
c/o Staff Member *Paradigm (Monterey)*
509 Hartnell St
Monterey, CA 93940-2825, USA

Corbet, Brady (Actor)
c/o Brian Young *Untitled Entertainment (LA)*
331 N Maple Dr Fl 3
Beverly Hills, CA 90210-3827, USA

Corbett, Doug (Baseball Player)
Minnesota Twins
861214 N Hampton Club Way
Fernandina Beach, FL 32034-8700, USA

Corbett, Gene (Baseball Player)
Philadelphia Phillies
1109 S Schumaker Dr Apt 204
Salisbury, MD 21804-9259, USA

Corbett, Gretchen (Actor)
S D B Partners
1801 Avenue Of Stars Ste 902
Los Angeles, CA 90067-5981, USA

Corbett, James (Football Player)
Cincinnati Bengals
2723 Marlo Way
Lakeside Park, KY 41017-2121, USA

Corbett, John (Actor)
c/o Steve Lovett *Lovett Management*
1327 Brinkley Ave
Los Angeles, CA 90049-3619, USA

Corbett, Luke R (Business Person)
Kerr-McGee Corp
Kerr-Mcgee Center
Oklahoma City, OK 73125, USA

Corbett, Michael (Actor)
2665 Chart Place
Los Angeles, CA 90046, USA

Corbett, Mike (Athlete)
PO Box 2809
Oakhurst, CA 93644-2809, USA

Corbett, Ronnie (Actor, Comedian)
International Artistes
235 Regent St
London W1R 8AX, UNITED KINGDOM (UK)

Corbett, Sherman (Baseball Player)
California Angels
7031 Washita Way
San Antonio, TX 78256-2310, USA

Corbett, Steve (Football Player)
New England Patriots
3 Wake Robin Rd
Sudbury, MA 01776-1726, USA

Corbin, Archie (Baseball Player)
Kansas City Royals
7525 Tram Rd
Beaumont, TX 77713-8723, USA

Corbin, Barry (Actor)
2113 Greta Ln
Fort Worth, TX 76120-5201, USA

Corbin, Ray (Baseball Player)
Minnesota Twins
922 Liberty St SW
Live Oak, FL 32064-3619, USA

Corbin, Tyrone (Basketball Player)
San Antonio Spurs
301 Oakbrook Dr
Columbia, SC 29223-8119, USA

Corbin, Tyrone (Basketball Player)
New York Knicks
2 Penn Plz
Madison Square Garden
New York, NY 10121-1703, USA

Corbo, Vincent J (Business Person)
Hercules Inc
Hercules Plaza
1313 N Market St
Wilmington, DE 19894-0001, USA

Corbucci, Bruno
via dei Colli della Farnesia 144
Rome, ITALY

Corbus, William (Football Player)
1100 Union St # 1100
San Francisco, CA 94109-2019, USA

Corchiani, Chris (Basketball Player)
Orlando Magic
720 Latta St
Raleigh, NC 27607-7204, USA

Corcoran, Barbara (Business Person)
226 W 26th St Fl 8
New York, NY 10001-6700, USA

Corcoran, Kevin (Actor)
8617 Balcom Ave
Northridge, CA 91325-3101, USA

Corcoran, Roy (Baseball Player)
Montreal Expos
3305 E Main St
Slaughter, LA 70777, USA

Corcoran, Tim (Baseball Player)
Detroit Tigers
4349 Friar Cir
La Verne, CA 91750-2718, USA

Cord, Alex (Actor)
c/o Staff Member *Coast to Coast Talent Group*
3350 Barham Blvd
Los Angeles, CA 90068-1404, USA

Cordalis, Costa
Rippoldsauer Str. 32
Freudenstadt D-72250, GERMANY

Corday, Barbara (Business Person)
2011 Cummings Dr
Los Angeles, CA 90027-1728, USA

Corday, Mara
PO Box 800393
Valencia, CA 91380-0393, USA

Corddry, Nate (Actor)
c/o Jill McGrath *Abrams Artists Agency (NY)*
275 7th Ave Fl 26
New York, NY 10001-6708, USA

Corder, Roger (Inventor)
Queen Mary Medical School
Turner St
London E1 2AD, UNITED KINGDOM (UK)

Cordero, Angel T Jr (Jockey)
New York Racing Assn
PO Box 170090
Ozone Park, NY 11417-0090, USA

Cordero, Angelo
PO Box 110090
Jamaica, NY 11411-0090, USA

Cordero, Chad (Baseball Player)
Montreal Expos
13305 Noble Pl
Chino, CA 91710-4742, USA

Cordero, Joaquin (Actor)
c/o Staff Member *Televisa*
Blvd Adolfo Lopez Mateos 232
Colonia San Angel INN
DF CP 01060, MEXICO

Cordero, Wilfredo N (Wil) (Baseball Player)
Montreal Expos
25844 Kensington Dr
Westlake, OH 44145-1472, USA

Cordes-Elliott, Gloria (Baseball Player)
86 Malone Ave
Staten Island, NY 10306-4110, USA

Cordileone, Lou (Football Player)
New York Giants
5312 Mark Ct
Agoura Hills, CA 91301-5200, USA

Cordova, Francisco (Athlete, Baseball Player)
c/o Staff Member *San Diego Padres*
100 Park Blvd
San Diego, CA 92101-7405, USA

Cordova, Marty (Baseball Player)
Montreal Expos
47 Club Vista Dr
Henderson, NV 89052-6603, USA

Cordovez, Zegers Diego (Educator, Government Official)
Foreign Affairs Ministry
Avda 10 Agosta y Carrion
Quito, ECUADOR

Corduner, Allan (Actor)
c/o Staff Member *Innovative Artists (LA)*
1505 10th St
Santa Monica, CA 90401-2805, USA

Corea, Armando (Chick) (Composer, Musician)
Chick Corea Productions
10400 Samoa Ave
Tujunga, CA 91042-1921, USA

Corella, Angel
890 Broadway
New York, NY 10003-1211, USA

Corey, Bryan (Baseball Player)
Arizona Diamondbacks
3060 N Ridgecrest Unit 171
Mesa, AZ 85207-1081, USA

Corey, Elias J (Nobel Prize Laureate)
20 Avon Hill St
Cambridge, MA 02140-3608, USA

Corey, Irwin (Professor) (Actor, Comedian)
c/o Richard Corey *Worlds Foremost Management*
165 W 21st St
New York, NY 10011-3218, USA

Corey, Jill (Musician)
64 Division Ave
Levittown, NY 11756-2999, USA

Corey, Mark (Baseball Player)
Baltimore Orioles
9321 Cornell Cir
Highlands Ranch, CO 80130-4143, USA

Corey, Mark (Baseball Player)
New York Mets
6811 Sterrettania Rd
Fairview, PA 16415-2918, USA

Corey, Walt (Football Player)
Dallas Texans
26007 Timber Meadow Dr
Lees Summit, MO 64086-9528, USA

Corgan, Billy (Musician, Songwriter, Writer)
c/o Sam Kirby *William Morris Agency (WMA-NY)*
1325 Avenue Of The Americas
New York, NY 10019-6026, USA

Cori, Carl T (Business Person)
Sigma-Aldrich Corp
3050 Spruce St
Saint Louis, MO 63103-2530, USA

Cori, Yarckin (Musician)
GreeneHouse Management, Inc
PO Box 151234
Altamonte Springs, FL 32715-1234, USA

Corigliano, John P (Composer)
365 W End Ave
New York, NY 10024-6511, USA

Corker, John (Football Player)
Houston Oilers
6401 SW 57th Pl
South Miami, FL 33143-3605, USA

Corkins, Mike (Baseball Player)
San Diego Padres
3760 Chemehuevi Blvd
Lake Havasu City, AZ 86406-6449, USA

Corley, Al (Actor)
Code Entertainment
9229 W Sunset Blvd Ste 615
Los Angeles, CA 90069-3406, USA

Corley, Annie (Actor)
c/o Renee Jennett *Renee Jennett Management*
5757 Wilshire Blvd Ste 473
Los Angeles, CA 90036-3632, USA

Corley, Kenneth (Basketball Player)
Cleveland Rebels
915 W 5th St
Pawhuska, OK 74056-4007, USA

Corley, Ray (Basketball Player)
Syracuse Nationals
590 Elwood Rd
East Northport, NY 11731-5629, USA

Corman, Avery (Writer)
International Creative Mgmt
40 W 57th St Ste 1800
New York, NY 10019-4001, USA

Corman, Roger W (Actor, Director, Producer, Writer)
c/o Staff Member *New Concorde International*
11600 San Vincente Blvd
Los Angeles, CA 90049, USA

Cormier, Joe (Football Player)
Los Angeles Raiders
9110 La Salle Ave
Los Angeles, CA 90047-3608, USA

Cormier, Rheal (Baseball Player)
St Louis Cardinals
15711 Cedar Grove Ln
Wellington, FL 33414-6312, USA

Corneille (Artist)
Society of Independent Artists
Cours la Reine
Paris 75008, FRANCE

Corneisen, Rufus (Religious Leader)
415 S Chester Rd
Swarthmore, PA 19081-2303, USA

Cornejo, Mardie (Baseball Player)
New York Mets
321 E 3rd St
Wellington, KS 67152-2706, USA

Cornejo, Nate (Baseball Player)
Detroit Tigers
1600 N B St
Wellington, KS 67152-4405, USA

Cornelison, Jerry (Football Player)
Dallas Texans
12713 Cedar St
Leawood, KS 66209-1873, USA

Cornelius, Charles (Football Player)
Miami Dolphins
8865 Okeechobee Blvd Apt 306
West Palm Beach, FL 33411-5125, USA

Cornelius, Don (Producer)
12685 Mulholland Dr
Beverly Hills, CA 90210-1332, USA

Cornelius, Helen (Musician, Songwriter, Writer)
PO Box 121089
Nashville, TN 37212-1089, USA

Cornelius, James (Business Person)
Guidant Corp
111 Monument Cir
Indianapolis, IN 46204-5129, USA

Cornelius, Reid (Baseball Player)
Montreal Expos
10117 Hunt Club Ln
West Palm Beach, FL 33418-4568, USA

Cornell, Chris (Musician)
c/o Staff Member *The Firm*
9465 Wilshire Blvd Fl 6
Beverly Hills, CA 90212-2605, USA

Cornell, Eric A (Nobel Prize Laureate)
University of Colorado
PO Box 440
Boulder, CO 80309-0001, USA

Cornell, Harry M Jr (Business Person)
leggett & Platt Inc
1 Leggett Rd
Carthage, MO 64836-9649, USA

Cornell, Jeff (Baseball Player)
San Francisco Giants
1644 SW Jeffrey Cir
Lees Summit, MO 64081-4115, USA

Cornell, Lydia (Actor)
269 S Beverly Dr
Beverly Hills, CA 90212-3851, USA

Cornell, Robert (Football Player)
Cleveland Browns
2605 239th Ave SE
Issaquah, WA 98075-9442, USA

Cornett, Betty Jane (Baseball Player)
99 Corbett Ct Apt 410
Pittsburgh, PA 15237-3030, USA

Cornett, Brad (Baseball Player)
Toronto Blue Jays
1704 N Avenue I
Lamesa, TX 79331-3140, USA

Cornett, Leanza (Actor)
c/o Staff Member *Endeavor Agency LLC (LA)*
9601 Wilshire Blvd Fl 3
Beverly Hills, CA 90210-5204, USA

Cornforth, John W (Nobel Prize Laureate)
Saxon Down
Cuilfail Lewes
East Sussex BN7 2BE, UNITED KINGDOM (UK)

Cornish, Frank E (Football Player)
San Diego Chargers
305 Sheffield Dr
Southlake, TX 76092-7142, USA

Cornish, Nick (Actor)
c/o Robert Stein *Robert Stein Management*
345 N Maple Dr Ste 317
Beverly Hills, CA 90210-3856, USA

Cornog, Robert A (Business Person)
Snap-On Corp
PO Box 1410
Kenosha, WI 53141-1410, USA

Cornthwaite, Robert (Actor)
23388 Mulholland Dr # 12
Woodland Hills, CA 91364-2733, USA

Cornutt, Terry (Baseball Player)
San Francisco Giants
179 W Hazel St
Roseburg, OR 97470-2211, USA

Cornwell, Fred (Football Player)
Dallas Cowboys
2107 Windward Ln
Newport Beach, CA 92660-3820, USA

Cornwell, Johnny (Musician)
Overland Productions
156 W 56th St # 500
New York, NY 10019-3800, USA

Cornwell, Patricia (Actor, Producer, Writer)
c/o Ron Bernstein *International Creative Management (ICM-LA)*
10250 Constellation Blvd
Los Angeles, CA 90067-6200, USA

Corolla, Adam (Actor, Producer, Writer)
c/o Staff Member *Dixon Talent*
436 W 45th St Fl 3
New York, NY 10036-3501, USA

Corone, Antoni (Actor)
c/o Staff Member *Miller & Company Management*
427 N Canon Dr Ste 215
Beverly Hills, CA 90210-4840, USA

Corr, Andrea (Music Group)
c/o Jamie Freed *The Collective*
8530 Wilshire Blvd Fl 5
Beverly Hills, CA 90211-3102, USA

Corr, Caroline (Music Group)
John Hughes
6 Martello Terr Sandycove
Dunlaoughaire
Dublin, IRELAND

Corr, Edwin G (Diplomat)
1617 Jenkins Ave
Norman, OK 73072-6508, USA

Corr, Jim (Music Group)
John Hughes
6 Martello Terr Sandycove
Dunlaoughaire
Dublin, IRELAND

Corr, Ryan (Actor)
c/o Staff Member *Nickelodeon UK*
PO Box 6425
LONDON W1A 6UR, UNITED KINGDOM (UK)

Corr, Sharon (Music Group)
John Hughes
6 Martello Terr Sandycove
Dunlaoughaire
Dublin, IRELAND

Corrado, Fred (Business Person)
Great A & P Tea Co
2 Paragon Dr
Montvale, NJ 07645-1718, USA

Corrado, Gabriel (Actor)
c/o Staff Member *Telefe - Argentina*
Pavon 2444 (C1248AAT)
Buenos Aires, ARGENTINA

Corral, Frank (Football Player)
Los Angeles Rams
Riverside Municipal Bldg 3900 Main St
3900 Main
Attn Graffiti Control Coordinator
Riverside, CA 92522-0001, USA

Corrales, Pat (Baseball Player)
Philadelphia Phillies
571 Big Canoe
Big Canoe, GA 30143-5128, USA

Correa, Charles M (Architect)
Sonmarg Napean Sea Road
Bombay 40006, INDIA

Correa, Edwin (Baseball Player)
Chicago White Sox
A2 Calle Milagros Cabezas
Carolina, PR 00987-7101, USA

Correal, Charles (Football Player)
Atlanta Falcons
110 Springbrooke Dr
Venetia, PA 15367-1054, USA

Correale, Pete (Musician)
c/o Staff Member *Monterey Peninsula Artists (Chicago)*
200 W Superior St Ste 202
Chicago, IL 60610-3554, USA

Correia, Kevin (Baseball Player)
San Francisco Giants
5844 Riley St Apt 1
San Diego, CA 92110-1789, USA

Correia, Rod (Baseball Player)
California Angels
24 S Bulfinch St Unit 102
North Attleboro, MA 02760-3154, USA

Correll, Alston D (Pete) (Business Person)
Georgia-Pacific Corp
133 Peachtree St NE
Atlanta, GA 30303-1847, USA

Correll, Vic (Baseball Player)
Boston Red Sox
119 Kentucky Downs
Perry, GA 31069-8514, USA

Correnti, John D (Business Person)
Nucor Corp
2100 Rexford Rd
Charlotte, NC 28211-3589, USA

Corretja, Alex (Tennis Player)
Assn of Tennis Professionals
200 Tournament Rd
Ponte Vedra Beach, FL 32082, USA

Corri, Adrienne
2-4 Noel St.
London, ENGLAND W1V 3RB, UNITED KINGDOM (UK)

Corridon-Mortell, Marie (Swimmer)
13 Heritage Vlg # A
Southbury, CT 06488-1601, USA

Corrie, Emily (Actor)
c/o Kathryn Fleming *Peters Fraser & Dunlop (PFD - UK)*
Drury House
34-43 Russell St
London WC2B 5HA, UNITED KINGDOM (UK)

Corrigan, E Gerald (Financier, Government Official)
Goldman Sanchs Co
85 Broad St
New York, NY 10004-2456, USA

Corrigan, Kevin (Actor)
c/o Leslie Siebert *Gersh Agency, The (LA)*
232 N Canon Dr
Beverly Hills, CA 90210-5302, USA

Corrigan, Patrick (Cartoonist, Editor)
Toronto Star
Editorial Dept 1 Yonge St
Toronto, ON M5E 1E5, CANADA

Corrigan, Robert A (Educator)
San Fransisco State University
President's Office
San Fransisco, CA 94123, USA

Corrigan, Wilfred J (Business Person)
LSI Logic
1621 Barber Ln
Milpitas, CA 95035-7458, USA

Corrigan-Maguire, Mairead (Nobel Prize Laureate)
Peace People
224 Lisbum Road
Belfast BT9 6GB, NORTHERN IRELAND

Corrington, Kip (Football Player)
Denver Broncos
6407 Olympic Ct
Greensboro, NC 27410-8412, USA

Corripio Ahumada, Ernesto Cardinal (Religious Leader)
Apotinar Nieto 40 Col Tetlameyer
Mexico City 04730, MEXICO

Corroface, Georges
1 rue Guenegaud
Paris F-75006, FRANCE

Corsaro, Frank A (Director)
33 Riverside Dr
New York, NY 10023-8012, USA

Corsi, Jim (Baseball Player)
Oakland A's
48 Eastview Rd
Hopkinton, MA 01748-1853, USA

Corso, John A (Cinematographer)
241 W 13th St Apt 21
New York, NY 10011-7738, USA

Corson, Dale R (Educator, Physicist)
401 Savage Farm Dr
Ithaca, NY 14850-6506, USA

Corson, Keith D (Business Person)
Coachmen Industries
PO Box 3300
Elkhart, IN 46515-3300, USA

Corson, Shayne (Hockey Player)
Richard Curran
411 Timber Ln
Devon, PA 19333-1232, USA

Cort, Barry (Baseball Player)
Milwaukee Brewers
13106 N Florida Ave # 116
Tampa, FL 33612-3474, USA

Cort, Bud (Actor)
c/o Staff Member *Don Buchwald & Associates Inc (NY)*
10 E 44th St
New York, NY 10017-3601, USA

Cortazar, Esteban (Designer, Fashion Designer)
Esteban Cortazar Inc
9th Fl
11 1 NE 1st St
Miami, FL 33132, USA

Cortes, Joaquin (Choreographer, Dancer)
c/o Jorge Pinos *William Morris Agency (WMA-LA)*
1 William Morris Pl
Beverly Hills, CA 90212-4261, USA

Cortes, Ron (Journalist)
Philadelphia Inquirer
400 N Broad St
Editorial Dept
Philadelphia, PA 19130-4099, USA

Cortese, Dan (Actor)
28873 Via Venezia
Malibu, CA 90265-4061, USA

Cortese, Joe (Actor)
2065 Coldwater Canyon Dr
Beverly Hills, CA 90210-1732, USA

Cortese, Valentina (Actor)
Pretta S Erasmo 6
Milan 20121, ITALY

Cortez, Alfonso (Actor)
CunninghamEscottDipene
10635 Santa Monica Blvd Ste 130
Los Angeles, CA 90025-8306, USA

Cortright, Edgar M Jr (Astronaut, Engineer, Misc)
9701 Calvin Ave
Northridge, CA 91324-1617, USA

Corvino, Anthony (Football Player)
New York Jets
PO Box 57
North Haven, CT 06473-0057, USA

Corvo (Musician)
c/o Staff Member *Sony Music Miami*
605 Lincoln Rd Fl 7
Miami Beach, FL 33139-2900, USA

Corwin, Jeff (Actor)
Jeff Corwin Experience
PO Box 2904
Toluca Lake, CA 91610-0904, USA

Corwin, Lola (Reality TV Star)
c/o Cindy Osbrink *Osbrink Talent Agency*
4343 Lankershim Blvd # 100
North Hollywood, CA 91602-2705, USA

Corwin, Norman (Writer)
USC
3551 Ironsdale Parkway
Los Angeles, CA 90089-0001, USA

Coryatt, Quentin J (Football Player)
Indianapolis Colts
611 Cannon Ln
Sugar Land, TX 77479-5846, USA

Coryell, Donald D (Don) (Coach, Football Coach)
PO Box 1576
Friday Harbor, WA 98250-1576, USA

Coryell, Larry (Music Group, Musician)
Tedd Kurland
173 Brighton Ave
Boston, MA 02134-2003, USA

Corzine, Dave (Basketball Player)
Washington Bullets
1161 W Hunting Dr
Palatine, IL 60067-6673, USA

Corzine, Lester (Football Player)
Cincinnati Reds
4685 Barcelona Way
Oceanside, CA 92056-5107, USA

Cosbie, Douglas D (Doug) (Football Player)
Dallas Cowboys
4241 Val Verde Rd
Loomis, CA 95650-9474, USA

Cosby, Bill (Actor, Comedian)
c/o David Brokaw *Brokaw Company, The*
9255 W Sunset Blvd Ste 804
Los Angeles, CA 90069-3305, USA

Cosby, Rita (Television Host)
c/o Staff Member *MSNBC (NJ)*
Nbc/One Microsoft Corporation
1 Msnc Plaza
Secaucus, NJ 07094, USA

Coscarelli, Don (Director, Producer, Writer)
c/o Staff Member *Starway International*
12021 Wilshire Blvd # 661
Los Angeles, CA 90025-1206, USA

Coscina, Dennis (Golfer)
211 Main St
East Windsor, CT 06088-9518, USA

Cose, Ellis (Activist, Misc)
Harper Collins Publisher
10 E 53rd St Fl Cellar2
New York, NY 10022-5076, USA

Cosey, Ray (Baseball Player)
Oakland A's
139 Byxbee St
San Francisco, CA 94132-2602, USA

Cosgrave, Liam (Prime Minister)
Beachperk Templeogue County
Dublin, IRELAND

Cosgrove, Daniel (Actor)
c/o Staff Member *James/Levy/Jacobson Management*
3500 W Olive Ave Ste 1470
Burbank, CA 91505-5514, USA

Cosgrove, Mike (Baseball Player)
Houston Astros
8813 W Corrine Dr
Peoria, AZ 85381-8166, USA

Cosgrove, Miranda (Actor)
c/o Staff Member *Cunningham Escott Slevin & Doherty (LA)*
10635 Santa Monica Blvd Ste 130
Los Angeles, CA 90025-8306, USA

Cosic, Dobrica (President)
Sciences/Arts Academy
Knez Mikallove 35
Belgrade, SERBIA-MONTENEGRO

Cosiga, Fransesco (President)
Palazzo Giustiniani
Via Della Dogana Vecchia 29
Rome 00186, ITALY

Coslet, Bruce N (Coach, Football Coach, Football Player)
Cincinnati Bengals
1778 Ivy Pointe Ct
Naples, FL 34109-3375, USA

Cosman, Jim (Baseball Player)
St Louis Cardinals
3676 Oakley Ave
Memphis, TN 38111-6166, USA

Cosmovici, Cristiano B (Astronaut)
Istituto Fisica Spazio Interplanetario
CP 27
Frascati 00044, ITALY

Cosner, Don (Football Player)
Chicago Cardinals
141 NW Carter Farms Ct
Bremerton, WA 98310-2090, USA

Cosper, Kina (Music Group)
Green Light Talent Agency
PO Box 3172
Beverly Hills, CA 90212-0172, USA

Cosso, Pierre
13 rue Madeleine Michelis
Neuilly 92200, FRANCE

Cossotto, Fiorenza (Opera Singer)
IUMA
Via E Filiberto 125
Rome 00185, ITALY

Costa, David J (Dave) (Football Player)
Oakland Raiders
40 Halili Ln Apt 4M
Kihei, HI 96753-6070, USA

Costa, Don
7920 W Sunset Blvd Ste 300
Los Angeles, CA 90046-3300, USA

Costa, Gal (Music Group)
Bridge Agency
35 Clark St Apt A5
Brooklyn, NY 11201-2374, USA

Costa, Mary (Opera Singer)
3340 Kingston Pike Unit 1
Knoxville, TN 37919-4674, USA

Costa, Paul (Football Player)
Buffalo Bills
8017 Kristina Ln
North Richland Hills, TX 76180-1747, USA

Costa-Gavras, Constantin
244 rue Saint-Jacques
Paris 75005, FRANCE

Costa-Gavras, Konstaninos (Director)
Artmedia
20 Ave Rapp
Paris 75007, FRANCE

Costanza, Margaret (Midge) (Government Official)
4518 Agnes Ave
Studio City, CA 91607-4105, USA

Costanzo, Paulo (Actor)
United Talent Agency
9560 Wilshire Blvd Ste 500
Beverly Hills, CA 90212-2401, USA

Costanzo, Robert (Actor)
Gold Marshak Liedtke
3500 W Olive Ave Ste 1400
Burbank, CA 91505-5512, USA

Costas, Bob (Baseball Player, Sportscaster)
c/o Staff Member *Endeavor Agency LLC (LA)*
9601 Wilshire Blvd Fl 3
Beverly Hills, CA 90210-5204, USA

Costas, Carlos
Entenze 332-334 Atico 2a
Barcelona E-08029, SPAIN

Costello, Billy (Boxer)
17 2nd Ave
Kingston, NY 12401-3225, USA

Costello, Brad (Football Player)
Cincinnati Bengals
1098A Long Beach Blvd
Beach Haven, NJ 08008-5626, USA

Costello, Elvis (Music Group, Musician, Songwriter, Writer)
c/o Tony Goldring *William Morris Agency (WMA-LA)*
1 William Morris Pl
Beverly Hills, CA 90212-4261, USA

Costello, John (Baseball Player)
St Louis Cardinals
68 Royal Oak Dr Apt 206
Vero Beach, FL 32962-3755, USA

Costello, Mariclare (Actor)
Borinstein Oreck Bogart
3172 Dona Susana Dr
Studio City, CA 91604-4356, USA

Costello, Mark (Writer)
Fordham Univesity
Law School
New York, NY 10458, USA

Costello, Murray (Hockey Player)
105 Kenilworth St
Ottawa, ON K1Y 3Y8, CANADA

Costello, Patty (Bowler)
2405 Pittston Ave
Scranton, PA 18505-3213, USA

Costello, Sue (Actor)
United Talent Agency
9560 Wilshire Blvd Ste 500
Beverly Hills, CA 90212-2401, USA

Costello, Thomas (Football Player)
New York Giants
PO Box 611
Pelham, NY 10803-0611, USA

Costello, Vince (Football Player)
Cleveland Browns
12300 Perry St
Overland Park, KS 66213-1811, USA

Costelloe, Paul (Designer, Fashion
Designer)
Moygashel Mills
Dungannon BT71 7PB, NORTHERN
IRELAND

Coster, Nicolas (Actor)
1624 N Vista St
Los Angeles, CA 90046-2818, USA

Coster, Ritchie (Actor)
*c/o Glenn Daniels Glenn Daniels Arts
Management*
56 Warren St Apt 5E
New York, NY 10007-1097, USA

Costle, Douglas M (Educator, Government
Official)
Harvard University
Public Health School
Cambridge, MA 02138, USA

Costner, Kevin (Actor, Director)
*c/o Rick Nicita Creative Artists Agency
LCC (CAA-LA)*
2000 Avenue Of The Stars
Los Angeles, CA 90067-4700, USA

Costo, Tim (Baseball Player)
Cincinnati Reds
3107 Pintail Ln
Signal Mountain, TN 37377-1439, USA

Coston, Fred (Football Player)
Philadelphia Eagles
4200 Shorecrest Dr
Dallas, TX 75209-1722, USA

Coston, Zed (Football Player)
Philadelphia Eagles
4200 Shorecrest Dr
Dallas, TX 75209-1722, USA

Cota, Chad (Football Player)
Carolina Panthers
216 Island Pointe Dr
Medford, OR 97504-9453, USA

Cota, Humberto (Baseball Player)
c/o Staff Member Pittsburgh Pirates
115 Federal St
Pnc Park
Pittsburgh, PA 15212-5740, USA

Cotchett, Joseph W (Attorney, Attorney
General, General)
840 Malcolm Rd
Burlingame, CA 94010-1401, USA

Cote, David (Business Person)
TRW Inc
1900 Richmond Rd
Cleveland, OH 44124, USA

Cothran, Jeff (Football Player)
Cincinnati Bengals
5671 Oakview Ter
Liberty Twp, OH 45011-2494, USA

Cothran, Sherry (Music Group)
Turner Management Group
9200 W Sunset Blvd Ste 600
West Hollywood, CA 90069-3196, USA

Cothren, Paige (Football Player)
Los Angeles Rams
1332 Highway 15 S
Woodland, MS 39776-9741, USA

Cotlow, Lewis N (Misc)
132 Lakeshore Dr
North Palm Beach, FL 33408-3687, USA

Cotney, Mark (Football Player)
Houston Oilers
4809 Cheval Blvd
Lutz, FL 33558-5338, USA

Cotorna, D (Actor)
c/o Jeff Golenberg The Collective
9100 Wilshire Blvd # 700 W
Beverly Hills, CA 90212-3401, USA

Cotrona, DJ (Actor)
c/o Aron Giannini The Collective
9100 Wilshire Blvd # 700 W
Beverly Hills, CA 90212-3401, USA

Cotrubas, Ileana (Opera Singer)
Royal Opera House
Convent Garden Bow St
London WC2, UNITED KINGDOM (UK)

Cottet, Mia (Actor)
Metropolitan Talent Agency
4500 Wilshire Blvd Fl 2
Los Angeles, CA 90010-3858, USA

Cotti, Flavio (President)
Christian Democratic Party
Klaraweg 6
Bem 3001, SWITZERLAND

Cottier, Chuck (Baseball Player)
Milwaukee Braves
7129 Lake Ballinger Way
Edmonds, WA 98026-8545, USA

Cottier, George Cardinal (Religious
Leader)
Convento Santa Sabina
Piazza Pierro d'Illiria
Rome 00193, ITALY

Cottingham, Robert (Artist)
PO Box 604
Blackman Road
Newtown, CT 06470-0604, USA

Cotto, Delilah (Actor)
c/o Ivan De Paz Arenas Entertainment
100 N Crescent Dr
Garden Level
Beverly Hills, CA 90210-5408, USA

Cotto, Henry (Baseball Player)
Chicago Cubs
1141 W Thomas Rd
Phoenix, AZ 85013-4206, USA

Cotton, Barney (Football Player)
Cincinnati Bengals
2402 Sundown Dr
Ames, IA 50014-8220, USA

Cotton, Blaine (Actor)
Jack Scagnetti Talent
5118 Vineland Ave # 102
North Hollywood, CA 91601-3814, USA

Cotton, Fest (Football Player)
Cleveland Browns
5101 Coulson Dr
Dayton, OH 45418-2034, USA

Cotton, Frank A (Misc)
RR 2 Box 230
Twaycliffe Ranch
Bryan, TX 77808, USA

Cotton, James (Music Group, Musician)
James Cotton Mgmt
235 W Eugenie St # G 10
Chicago, IL 60614-5774, USA

Cotton, John (Basketball Player)
Denver Nuggets
11426 County Road 4 S
Alamosa, CO 81101-9630, USA

Cotton, Joseph F (Misc)
20 Linda Vista Ave
Atherton, CA 94027-5429, USA

Cotton, Josie (Music Group)
2794 Hume Rd
Malibu, CA 90265-3435, USA

Cotton, Marcus (Football Player)
Atlanta Falcons
484 Lake Park Ave Apt 280
Oakland, CA 94610-2730, USA

Cotton, Robin (Doctor)
20271 Goldenrod Ln Ste 120
Germantown, MD 20876-4064, USA

Cottrell, Dana (Football Player)
New England Patriots
4185 129th Pl SE Apt D103
Bellevue, WA 98006-1389, USA

Cottrell, Ted (Football Player)
Atlanta Falcons
135 Spring Meadow Dr Apt 5
Buffalo, NY 14221-8436, USA

Cottrell, William (Football Player)
Detroit Lions
39675 Patterson Ln
Cleveland, OH 44139-6705, USA

Cotts, Neal (Baseball Player)
Chicago White Sox
1 McKendree Park Rd
Lebanon, IL 62254-1266, USA

Couch, Chris (Golfer)
307 Johns Creek Pkwy
Saint Augustine, FL 32092-5064, USA

Couch, Tim (Football Player)
Cleveland Browns
2110 N Ocean Blvd Apt 2802
Fort Lauderdale, FL 33305-1946, USA

Couchee, Mike (Baseball Player)
San Diego Padres
3060 N Ridgecrest Unit 155
Mesa, AZ 85207-1080, USA

Couffer, Jack (Cinematographer)
c/o Jordan Bayer Original Artists (LA)
9465 Wilshire Blvd Ste 324
Beverly Hills, CA 90212-2602, USA

Coughlan, Marisa (Actor)
*c/o Alissa Vradenburg Untitled
Entertainment (LA)*
331 N Maple Dr Fl 3
Beverly Hills, CA 90210-3827, USA

Coughlin, Bernard J (Educator)
Gonzaga University
Chancellor's Office
Spokane, WA 99258-0001, USA

Coughlin, Kevin
1090 N Euclid Ave
Sarasota, FL 34237-3013, USA

Coughlin, Tom (Coach, Football Coach)
New York Giants
Giants Stadium
East Rutherford, NJ 07073, USA

Coughran, John (Basketball Player)
Golden State Warriors
5476 Morningside Dr
San Jose, CA 95138-2244, USA

Coughtry, Marian (Baseball Player)
Boston Red Sox
9113 NE 65th St
Vancouver, WA 98662-4412, USA

Coulier, Dave
9150 Wilshire Blvd Ste 350
Beverly Hills, CA 90212-3453, USA

Coulier, David (Actor)
International Creative Mgmt
8942 Wilshire Blvd # 219
Beverly Hills, CA 90211-1908, USA

Coulson, Catherine E (Actor)
1115 Terra Ave
Ashland, OR 97520-3565, USA

Coulson, Christian (Actor)
*c/o Staff Member Artists Rights Group
(ARG London)*
4 Great Portland St
London W1W 8PA, UNITED KINGDOM
(UK)

Coulter, Art
500 Spanish Fort Blvd Apt 203
Spanish Fort, AL 36527-5008, USA

Coulter, Brian (Music Group, Musician)
Ashley Talent
2002 Hogback Rd Ste 20
Ann Arbor, MI 48105-9736, USA

Coulter, Catherine (Writer)
PO Box 17
Mill Valley, CA 94942-0017, USA

Coulter, DeWitt E (Tex) (Football Player)
New York Giants
5001 Convict Hill Rd Apt 503
Austin, TX 78749-2220, USA

Coulter, Michael (Cinematographer)
35 Carlton Mansions Randolph Ave
London W9 1NP, UNITED KINGDOM
(UK)

Coulter, Phil (Music Group)
87th Street Ltd
24 Upper Mount St
Dublin, IRELAND

Coulter, Tom (Baseball Player)
St Louis Cardinals
718 Trenton St
Toronto, OH 43964-1269, USA

Coulthard, David (Race Car Driver)
Martin Brundle
Kings Lynn
Tottenhill
Norfolk PE32 0PX, UNITED KINGDOM
(UK)

Council, Keith (Football Player)
New York Giants
4418 Lenox Blvd
Orlando, FL 32811-4541, USA

Counsell, Craig (Baseball Player)
Colorado Rockies
5301 Blue Lagoon Dr Ste 900
Miami, FL 33126-7007, USA

Counting Crows (Music Group)
c/o Staff Member *Creative Artists Agency
LCC (CAA-LA)*
2000 Avenue Of The Stars
Los Angeles, CA 90067-4700, USA

Counts, Mel (Basketball Player)
Bosten Celtics
1581 Matheny Rd NE
Gervais, OR 97026-8762, USA

Coupland, Douglas (Writer)
c/o Michael Siegel *Michael Siegel &
Assoc*
8330 W 3rd St
Los Angeles, CA 90048-4311, USA

Courant, Ernest D (Physicist)
40 W 72nd St # 4l
New York, NY 10023-4119, USA

Couric, Katie (Journalist, Television Host)
c/o Alan Berger *Creative Artists Agency
LCC (CAA-LA)*
2000 Avenue Of The Stars
Los Angeles, CA 90067-4700, USA

Courier, James S (Jim) Jr (Tennis Player)
9533 Blandford Rd
Orlando, FL 32827-7008, USA

Courier, Jim
1 Erieview Plz # 1300
Cleveland, OH 44114-1738, USA

Courreges, Andre (Designer, Fashion
Designer)
27 Rue Delabordere
Neuilly-Sur-Seine 92, FRANCE

Courtemanche, Michael (Actor)
c/o Staff Member *Encore Management*
6300 Avenue du Parc bur406
Montreal, PQ H2V 4H8, CANADA

Courtenay, Ed (Hockey Player)
San Jose Sharks
3107 Firestone Rd
North Charleston, SC 29418, USA

Courtenay, Tom (Actor)
Jonathan Altaras
13 Shorts Gardens
London WC2H 9AT, UNITED KINGDOM
(UK)

Courtin, Steve (Basketball Player)
Philadelphia 76ers
1109 Grinnell Rd
Wilmington, DE 19803-5125, USA

Courtland, Jerome
1837 Westleigh Dr
Glenview, IL 60025-7611, USA

Courtney, Patricia (Baseball Player)
8 Eagle Loop Ln
Freedom, NH 03836-5311, USA

Courtney, Thomas W (Tom) (Athlete,
Track Athlete)
PO Box 215
Sewickley, PA 15143-0215, USA

Courtright, John (Baseball Player)
Cincinnati Reds
316 S Roosevelt Ave
Columbus, OH 43209-1829, USA

Courville, Vince (Football Player)
Pittsburgh Steelers
5123 Avenue R
Galveston, TX 77551-5282, USA

Cousin, Philip R (Religious Leader)
Episcopal Church
PO Box 2970
District Headquarters
Jacksonville, FL 32203-2970, USA

Cousin, Terry (Football Player)
Atlanta Falcons
11143 Waxberry Dr
Charlotte, NC 28277-2862, USA

Cousineau, Tom (Football Player)
Cleveland Browns
910 Eaton Ave
Akron, OH 44303-1312, USA

Cousins, Christopher (Actor)
c/o Deborah Miller *Deborah Miller &
Company Management*
427 N Canon Dr Ste 215
Beverly Hills, CA 90210-4840, USA

Cousins, Jomo (Football Player)
Arizona Cardinals
12425 Bramfield Dr
Riverview, FL 33579-7771, USA

Cousins, Ralph W (Admiral)
Leconfield House Curzon St
London W1Y 8JR, UNITED KINGDOM
(UK)

Cousins, Robin (Figure Skater)
Billy Marsh
174-8 N Gower St
London NW1 2NB, UNITED KINGDOM
(UK)

Cousteau, Jean-Michel (Oceanographer)
Ocean Futures Society
325 Chapala St
Santa Barbara, CA 93101-3407, USA

Cousy, Bob
459 Salisbury St
Worcester, MA 01609, USA

Cousy, Robert J (Bob) (Basketball Player)
Bosten Celtics
427 Salisbury St
Worcester, MA 01609-1266, USA

Coutre, Larry (Football Player)
Green Bay Packers
11848 Sunchase Ct
Boca Raton, FL 33498-6814, USA

Coutteure, Ronny
28 rue Basfroi
Paris 75011, FRANCE

Couture, Randy (Actor)
c/o Jeremy Lappen *Triumph Entertainment*
7920 W Sunset Blvd Fl 2
Los Angeles, CA 90046-3300, USA

Covay, Don (Music Group, Songwriter,
Writer)
Rawstock
PO Box 110002
Cambria Heights, NY 11411-0002, USA

Cover Girls
141 Dunbar Ave
Fords, NJ 08863-1551, USA

Coverdale, David (Music Group,
Musician)
c/o Staff Member *Agency for the
Performing Arts (APA-LA)*
405 S Beverly Dr
Beverly Hills, CA 90212-4416, USA

Coverly, Dave (Cartoonist, Editor)
Bloomington Herald-Times
Editorial Dept 1900 Walnut
Bloomington, IN 47401, USA

Covert, Allen (Actor)
c/o Adam Venit *Endeavor Agency LLC
(LA)*
9601 Wilshire Blvd Fl 3
Beverly Hills, CA 90210-5204, USA

Covert, James (Jimbo) (Football Player)
Chicago Bears
450 Hunter Ln
Lake Forest, IL 60045-2778, USA

Covey, Richard O (Astronaut)
1155 High Lake Vw
Colorado Springs, CO 80906-8717, USA

Covic, Nebojsa (Prime Minister)
Prime Minister's Office
Nemanjina 11
Belgrade 11000, SERBIA

Coville, Bruce
PO Box 6110
Syracuse, NY 13217-6110, USA

Covington, John (Football Player)
Indianapolis Colts
10901 Valley Forge Cir
Carmel, IN 46032-8667, USA

Covington, Scott (Football Player)
Cincinnati Bengals
24 Ashburton Pl
Laguna Niguel, CA 92677-4745, USA

Covington, Tony (Football Player)
Tampa Bay Buccaneers
11160C1 South Lakes Dr
Reston, VA 20191-4327, USA

Covington, Warren (Music Group)
1627 Open Field Loop
Brandon, FL 33510-2096, USA

Covington, Wes (Baseball Player)
Milwaukee Braves
905-10145 119 St NW
Edmonton, AB T5K 1Z2, CANADA

Cowan, Billy (Baseball Player)
Chicago Cubs
1539 Via Coronel
Palos Verdes Estates, CA 90274-1941,
USA

Cowan, Elliot (Actor)
c/o Laura Berwick *Hofflund/Polone*
9465 Wilshire Blvd Ste 890
Beverly Hills, CA 90212-2607, USA

Cowan, George A (Misc)
Santa Fe Institute
1399 Hyde Park Rd
Santa Fe, NM 87501-8943, USA

Cowan, Lawrence (Football Player)
Los Angeles Rams
63 Oakland Hills Pl
Rotonda West, FL 33947-2257, USA

Cowan, Ralph Wolfe (Artist)
243 29th St
West Palm Beach, FL 33407-5207, USA

Cowart, Sam (Football Player)
Buffalo Bills
11110 Fallgate Point Ct
Jacksonville, FL 32256-4833, USA

Cowboy Junkies
c/o Staff Member *Paradigm (Monterey)*
509 Hartnell St
Monterey, CA 93940-2825, USA

Cowell, Simon (Producer, Reality TV Star,
Writer)
c/o Staff Member *American Idol*
7800 Beverly Blvd # 251
Los Angeles, CA 90036-2112, USA

Cowen, Robert E (Judge)
US Court of Appeals
402 E State St
Judicial Complex
Trenton, NJ 08608-1507, USA

Cowen, Scott (Educator)
Tulane University
President's Office
New Orleans, LA 70118, USA

Cowen, Wilson (Judge)
US Court of Appeals
717 Madison Pl NW
Washington, DC 20439-0001, USA

Cowen, Zelman (Attorney, Attorney
General, Educator, General)
4 Treasury Place
East Melbourne, VIC 3002, AUSTRALIA

Cowhill, William J (Admiral)
9428 Vernon Dr
Great Falls, VA 22066-2227, USA

Cowick, Bruce (Hockey Player)
Philadelphia Flyers
2953 Cressida Cres
Victoria, BC V9B 5W7, CANADA

Cowley, Joe (Baseball Player)
Atlanta Braves
102 Summertree Dr
Nicholasville, KY 40356-9185, USA

Cowlings, Al (Football Player)
Buffalo Bills
PO Box 1064
Pacific Palisades, CA 90272-1064, USA

Cowper, Nicola (Actor)
Brunskill Mgmt
169 Queens Gate #A8
London SW7 5EH, UNITED KINGDOM
(UK)

Cowper, Stephen C (Steve) (Governor)
PO Box A
Juneau, AK 99811, USA

Cowsill, Susan (Musician)
c/o Valerie Turner Polishook *V Public
Relations LLC*
PO Box 341810
Bethesda, MD 20827-1810, USA

Cox, Alex (Actor, Director)
United Talent Agency
9560 Wilshire Blvd Ste 500
Beverly Hills, CA 90212-2401, USA

Cox, Billy (Football Player)
Washington Redskins
5192 Marsh Field Ln
Sarasota, FL 34235-7029, USA

Cox, Bobby (Baseball Player)
New York Yankees
2938 Windstone Cir
Marietta, GA 30062-5685, USA

Cox, Brian (Actor)
Conway Van Gelder Robinson
18-21 Jermyn St
London SW1Y 6NB, UNITED KINGDOM
(UK)

Cox, Bryan (Football Player)
Miami Dolphins
3040 Peachtree Rd NW Unit 1206
Atlanta, GA 30305-2290, USA

Cox, C Jay (Director, Producer, Writer)
c/o Scott Zimmerman *Untitled Entertainment (LA)*
331 N Maple Dr Fl 3
Beverly Hills, CA 90210-3827, USA

Cox, Casey (Athlete, Baseball Player)
Washington Senators
2840 La Concha Dr
Clearwater, FL 33762-2203, USA

Cox, Charles C (Government Official)
Lexecon Inc
332 S Michigan Ave
Chicago, IL 60604-4397, USA

Cox, Chris (Musician)
c/o Staff Member *Diva Central Inc*
7510 W Sunset Blvd Ste 1445
Los Angeles, CA 90046-3408, USA

Cox, Christina (Actor)
Rysher Entertainment
3400 W Riverside Dr # 600
Burbank, CA 91505-4669, USA

Cox, Danny (Motivational Speaker, Writer)
17381 Bonner Dr
Tustin, CA 92780-1837, USA

Cox, Danny B (Baseball Player)
St Louis Cardinals
306 Feagin Mill Rd
Warner Robins, GA 31088-6208, USA

Cox, David R (Doctor, Misc)
Stanford University
Human Genome Center
Stanford, CA 94305, USA

Cox, Deborah (Musician, Songwriter)
c/o John Dukakis *Overbrook Entertainment*
450 N Roxbury Dr Fl 4
Beverly Hills, CA 90210-4232, USA

Cox, Emmett R (Judge)
US Court of Appeals
113 Saint Joseph St Ste 127
Mobile, AL 36602-3621, USA

Cox, Frederick W (Fred) (Football Player)
Minnesota Vikings
401 E River St
Monticello, MN 55362-9397, USA

Cox, G David (Religious Leader)
Church of God
PO Box 2420
Anderson, IN 46018-2420, USA

Cox, Glenn (Baseball Player)
Kansas City A's
PO Box 432
Los Molinos, CA 96055-0432, USA

Cox, Harvey G Jr (Educator, Misc)
Harvard University
Divinity School
Cambridge, MA 02140, USA

Cox, Jeff (Baseball Player)
Oakland A's
2727 E Vanderhoof Dr
West Covina, CA 91791-2247, USA

Cox, Jennifer Elise (Actor)
Metropolitan Talent Agency
4500 Wilshire Blvd Fl 2
Los Angeles, CA 90010-3858, USA

Cox, Jim (Baseball Player)
Montreal Expos
8370 E Charter Oak Rd
Scottsdale, AZ 85260-5256, USA

Cox, John (Football Player)
Washington Redskins
5192 Marsh Field Ln
Sarasota, FL 34235-7029, USA

Cox, Johnny (Basketball Player, Coach)
Chicago Zephyrs
849 N Main St
Hazard, KY 41701-1345, USA

Cox, Kris (Golfer)
5350 Richard Ave
Dallas, TX 75206-6712, USA

Cox, Larry (Football Player)
Denver Broncos
10326 Catlett Ln
La Porte, TX 77571-4218, USA

Cox, Lynne (Swimmer)
Advanced Sport Research
4141 Ball Rd # 142
Cypress, CA 90630-3465, USA

Cox, Mark (Tennis Player)
Oaks Astead Woods
Astead
Surrey KT21 2ER, UNITED KINGDOM (UK)

Cox, Nikki (Actor)
United Talent Agency
9560 Wilshire Blvd Ste 500
Beverly Hills, CA 90212-2401, USA

Cox, Paul (Director)
Illumination Films
1 Victoria Ave
Albert Park, VIC 3208, AUSTRALIA

Cox, Philip S (Architect)
Cox Richardson Architects
469 Kent St
Sydney, NSW 2000, AUSTRALIA

Cox, Ralph (Hockey Player)
Massport
1 Harborside Dr Ste 200S
East Boston, MA 02128-2909, USA

Cox, Richard
9200 W Sunset Blvd Ste 900
Los Angeles, CA 90069-3604, USA

Cox, Richard Ian
8730 W Sunset Blvd Ste 480
Los Angeles, CA 90069-2277, USA

Cox, Robert G (Financier)
Summit Bancorp
PO Box 2066
Princeton, NJ 08543-2066, USA

Cox, Ronny (Actor)
13948 Magnolia Blvd
Sherman Oaks, CA 91423-1230, USA

Cox, Stephen J (Artist)
154 Barnsbury Road
Islington
London N1 0ER, UNITED KINGDOM (UK)

Cox, Steve (Baseball Player)
Tampa Bay Devil Rays
1351 Cottage Cir
Porterville, CA 93257-8892, USA

Cox, Steve (Football Player)
Cleveland Browns
1001 E Lakeshore Dr
Jonesboro, AR 72401-4352, USA

Cox, Ted (Baseball Player)
Boston Red Sox
5117 Kennington Ln
Oklahoma City, OK 73150-4415, USA

Cox, Terry (Baseball Player)
California Angels
PO Box 577
Capitan, NM 88316-0577, USA

Cox, Tom (Football Player)
Los Angeles Rams
2121 S Mill Ave # 231
Tempe, AZ 85282-2138, USA

Cox, Tony (Actor)
c/o Staff Member *New Wave Entertainment (LA)*
2660 W Olive Ave
Burbank, CA 91505-4525, USA

Cox, Vera
345 N Maple Dr Ste 397
Beverly Hills, CA 90210-3856, USA

Cox, Warren J (Architect)
Hartman Cox Architects
1025 Thomas Jefferson St NW
Washington, DC 20007-5201, USA

Cox Arquette, Courteney (Actor)
c/o Staff Member *Coquette Productions*
8105 W 3rd St
West Hollywood, CA 90048-4308, USA

Coxe, Craig (Hockey Player)
Vancouver Canucks
45 Rollins Pl
Laguna Niguel, CA 92677-4137, USA

Coyle, Eric (Football Player)
Washington Redskins
397 County Road 26
Longmont, CO 80504-9515, USA

Coyle, Ross (Football Player)
Los Angeles Rams
PO Box 68
Blanchard, OK 73010-0068, USA

Coyne, Colleen (Hockey Player)
267 Lake Shore Dr
East Falmouth, MA 02536-2701, USA

Coyote, Peter (Actor)
c/o Stephanie Simon *Untitled Entertainment (LA)*
331 N Maple Dr Fl 3
Beverly Hills, CA 90210-3827, USA

Cozart, Charlie
Boston Braves
605 8th Ave SW Apt C1
Conover, NC 28613-2957, USA

Cozler, Jimmy (Musician, Songwriter, Writer)
J Racords
745 5th Ave # 600
New York, NY 10151-0099, USA

Crabb, Claude (Football Player)
Washington Redskins
49581 Wayne St
Indio, CA 92201-9752, USA

Crabbe, Cuffy
2140 E 5th St Ste 4
Tempe, AZ 85281-3043, USA

Crable, Bob (Football Player)
New York Jets
564 Miami Trace Ct
Loveland, OH 45140-8021, USA

Crabtree, Eric (Football Player)
Denver Broncos
3342 Arapahoe St
Denver, CO 80205-2741, USA

Crabtree, Tim (Baseball Player)
Toronto Blue Jays
1503 Kingswood Ln
Colleyville, TX 76034-5580, USA

Craddock, Bantz (General)
Commander
US Southern Command Miami
APO, AA 34001, USA

Craddock, Billy Crash
PO Box 428
Portland, TN 37148-0428, USA

Craddock, Billy (Crash) (Musician, Songwriter, Writer)
3007 Old Martinsville Road
Greensboro, NC 27455, USA

Cradle, Rickey (Baseball Player)
Seattle Mariners
PO Box 1661
Brea, CA 92822-1661, USA

Craft, Chris
14919 Village Elm St
Houston, TX 77062-2914, USA

Craft, Christine (Correspondent)
KRBK-TV
500 Media Pl
News Dept
Sacramento, CA 95815-3733, USA

Craft, Jason (Football Player)
Jacksonville Jaguars
11688 Amistad Ct
Jacksonville, FL 32256-2925, USA

Craft, Russ (Football Player)
Philadelphia Eagles
800 High St
Wellsburg, WV 26070-1548, USA

Craft, Sammi (Actor)
c/o Staff Member *Paradigm (LA)*
360 N Crescent Dr
North Bldg
Beverly Hills, CA 90210-6820, USA

Crafter, Jane (Golfer)
317 W Almeria Rd
Phoenix, AZ 85003-1140, USA

Crafts, Hannah (Writer)
c/o Staff Member *Creative Artists Agency LCC (CAA-LA)*
2000 Avenue Of The Stars
Los Angeles, CA 90067-4700, USA

Cragg, Anthony D (Tony) (Artist)
Adolf-Vorwerk-Str 24
Wuppertal 42287, GERMANY

Craggs, George (Soccer Player)
6223 6th Ave NW
Seattle, WA 98107-2131, USA

Craig, Daniel (Actor)
c/o Rick Kurtzman *Creative Artists Agency LCC (CAA-LA)*
2000 Avenue Of The Stars
Los Angeles, CA 90067-4700, USA

Craig, Elijah (Actor)
Agency for Performing Arts
405 S Beverly Dr Ste 500
Beverly Hills, CA 90212-4425, USA

Craig, James D (Jim) (Hockey Player)
Atlanta Flames
15 Jyra Ln
North Easton, MA 02356-2739, USA

Craig, Jenny (Doctor, Misc)
5770 Fleet St
Carlsbad, CA 92008-4700, USA

Craig, Michael (Actor)
Chatto & Linnit
Prince of Wales
Coventry St
London W1V 7FE, UNITED KINGDOM (UK)

Craig, Mike (Hockey Player)
Minnesota North Stars
29907 County Road 3
Merrifield, MN 56465-4402, USA

Craig, Neal (Football Player)
Cincinnati Bengals
2231 Crane Ave
Cincinnati, OH 45207-1322, USA

Craig, Pete (Baseball Player)
Washington Senators
5915 Carmel Ln
Raleigh, NC 27609-3953, USA

Craig, Richard (Inventor)
Pacific Northwest National Laboratory
902 Battelle Blvd
Richland, WA 99354-1793, USA

Craig, Roger (Baseball Player)
Brooklyn Dodgers
PO Box 2174
Borrego Springs, CA 92004-2174, USA

Craig, Roger T (Football Player)
San Francisco 49ers
271 Vista Verde Way
Portola Valley, CA 94028-8149, USA

Craig, Wendy
29 Roehampton Gate
London, ENGLAND SW15 5JR, UNITED
KINGDOM (UK)

Craig, William (Government Official)
23 Annadale Ave
Belfast BT7 3JJ, NORTHERN IRELAND

Craig, William (Bill) (Swimmer)
PO Box 629
Newport Beach, CA 92661-0629, USA

Craig, Yvonne (Actor)
YC/MC Ltd
PO Box 827
Pacific Palisades, CA 90272-0827, USA

Craig of Radley, David B (Misc)
House of Lords
Westminster
London SW1A 0PW, UNITED KINGDOM
(UK)

Craighead, John J (Misc)
5125 Orchard Ave
Missoula, MT 59803-2524, USA

Crain, Keith E (Publisher)
Crain Communications
1400 Woodbridge St
Detroit, MI 48207-3187, USA

Crain, Rance (Publisher)
Crain Communications
360 N Michigan Ave
Chicago, IL 60601-3814, USA

Crain, William (Director)
Contemporary Artists
610 Santa Monica Blvd Ste 202
Santa Monica, CA 90401-1645, USA

Crais, Robert (Writer)
12829 Landale St
Studio City, CA 91604-1352, USA

Cram, Jerry (Baseball Player)
Kansas City Royals
2 Castletree
Rancho Santa Margarita, CA 92688-5550,
USA

Cram, Stephen (Steve) (Athlete, Track
Athlete)
General Delivery
Jarrow, UNITED KINGDOM (UK)

Cramer, Douglas
738 Sarbonne Rd
Los Angeles, CA 90077-3302, USA

Cramer, Grant (Actor)
Richard Sindell
1910 Holmby Ave Apt 1
Los Angeles, CA 90025-5936, USA

Cramer, Peggy (Baseball Player)
1160 E Old Andrew Johnson Hwy
Talbott, TN 37877-3103, USA

Cramer, Richard Ben (Journalist, Writer)
Philadelphia Inquirer
400 N Broad St
Editorial Dept
Philadelphia, PA 19130-4099, USA

Cramps, The
1775 Broadway Ste 433
New York, NY 10019-1903, USA

Crampton, Barbara (Actor)
Stone Manners
6500 Wilshire Blvd Ste 550
Los Angeles, CA 90048-4950, USA

Crampton, Bruce (Golfer)
225 Winter Crest Ln
Severna Park, MD 21146-3104, USA

Cramsey, Denise (Producer)
c/o Staff Member *Trading Spaces*
7700 Wisconsin Ave
The Learning Channel
Bethesda, MD 20814-3578, USA

Cramton, Roger C (Attorney, Attorney
General, General)
49 Highgate Cir
Ithaca, NY 14850-1486, USA

Cranberries, The (Music Group)
c/o Staff Member *Creative Artists Agency
LCC (CAA-LA)*
2000 Avenue Of The Stars
Los Angeles, CA 90067-4700, USA

Crandall, Delmar W (Del) (Baseball
Player)
Boston Braves
1355 Clear Lake Pl
Brea, CA 92821-2807, USA

Crane, Ben (Golfer)
2223 Cedar Elm Ter
Westlake, TX 76262-9028, USA

Crane, Brian
PO Box 51771
Sparks, NV 89435-1771, USA

Crane, David (Director, Producer, Writer)
c/o Staff Member *Bright Kauffman Crane
Productions*
4000 Warner Blvd Bldg 160 # 750
Burbank, CA 91522-0001, USA

Crane, Fred
PO Box 937
Barnesville, GA 30204-0937, USA

Crane, Gary (Football Player)
Denver Broncos
6 Greystone
Bentonville, AR 72712-4098, USA

Crane, Horace R (Physicist)
66 Cavanaugh Lake Rd
Chelsea, MI 48118-9732, USA

Crane, John (Writer)
c/o Staff Member *Agency for the
Performing Arts (APA-LA)*
405 S Beverly Dr
Beverly Hills, CA 90212-4416, USA

Crane, Kenneth G (Director)
6627 Lindenhurst Ave
Los Angeles, CA 90048-4611, USA

Crane, Paul (Football Player)
New York Jets
12 N Monterey St
Mobile, AL 36604-1317, USA

Crane, Tony (Actor)
Abrams Artists
9200 W Sunset Blvd Ste 1125
Los Angeles, CA 90069-3610, USA

Cranston, Bryan (Actor)
c/o Staff Member *United Talent Agency
(UTA)*
9560 Wilshire Blvd Ste 500
Beverly Hills, CA 90212-2401, USA

Cranston, Toller (Figure Skater)
Int'l Management Grp
1st Clair Ave E
#700
Toronto, ON M4T 2V7, CANADA

Crash Test Dummies
c/o Sandy Rogers *Deep Fried Records*
1146 Lakeshore Rd
PO Box 195
Selkirk, ON N0A 1P0, CANADA

Craven, Bill (Football Player)
Cleveland Browns
4363 N Buckhead Dr NE
Atlanta, GA 30342-3451, USA

Craven, Gemma
42 Hazelbury Rd.
London, ENGLAND SW6 2ND, UNITED
KINGDOM (UK)

Craven, Matt (Actor)
11445 Tongareva St
Malibu, CA 90265-2224, USA

Craven, Ricky (Race Car Driver)
5918 Moray Ct NW
Concord, NC 28027-6438, USA

Craven, Wes (Director)
2419 Solar Dr
Los Angeles, CA 90046-1740, USA

Craver, Aaron (Football Player)
Miami Dolphins
821 W Maple St
Compton, CA 90220-1829, USA

Crawford, Bennie (Hank) Jr (Composer,
Musician)
Maxine Harvard
7942 W Bell Rd Ste C5 Pmb 51
Glendale, AZ 85308-8710, USA

Crawford, Bob (Hockey Player)
St Louis Blues
6 Progress Dr
Cromwell, CT 06416-1034, USA

Crawford, Brad (Football Player)
RR 2
Winamac, IL 46996, USA

Crawford, Bryce L Jr (Misc)
3220 Lake Johanna Blvd # 58
Saint Paul, MN 55112-7944, USA

Crawford, Chace (Actor)
c/o Staff Member *International Creative
Management (ICM-LA)*
10250 Constellation Blvd
Los Angeles, CA 90067-6200, USA

Crawford, Cheyne (Actor)
c/o Amy Slomovits *Joan Green
Management*
1836 Courtney Ter
Los Angeles, CA 90046-2106, USA

Crawford, Christina (Writer)
7 Springs Farm Sanders Road
Tensed, ID 83870, USA

Crawford, Cindy (Actor, Model)
c/o Steve Laschever *Creative Artists
Agency LCC (CAA-LA)*
2000 Avenue Of The Stars
Los Angeles, CA 90067-4700, USA

Crawford, Clayne (Actor)
c/o Paul Nelson *Mosaic Media Group*
24 Music Sq W Fl 1
Nashville, TN 37203-6661, USA

Crawford, Denver (Football Player)
New York Yankees
817 Colonial Heights Rd
Kingsport, TN 37663-2148, USA

Crawford, Ed (Football Player)
New York Giants
204 Country Club Rd
Oxford, MS 38655-2606, USA

Crawford, Fred (Basketball Player)
New York Knicks
24 W Lawn Dr
Teaneck, NJ 07666-5612, USA

Crawford, Henry C (Shag) (Misc)
568 Reed Rd Apt D2
Broomall, PA 19008-3645, USA

Crawford, Hilton (Football Player)
Buffalo Bills
262 Hagen St
Buffalo, NY 14215-3959, USA

Crawford, Jamal (Basketball Player)
Chicago Bulls United Center
1901 W Madison St
Chicago, IL 60612-2459, USA

Crawford, Jim (Baseball Player)
Houston Astros
4370 E Gemini Pl
Chandler, AZ 85249-5829, USA

Crawford, Joan (Basketball Player)
4734 S Harvard Ave Apt 22
Tulsa, OK 74135-3036, USA

Crawford, Johnny (Actor, Musician)
Johnny Crawford Entertainment
PO Box 1851
Los Angeles, CA 90078-1851, USA

Crawford, Keith (Football Player)
New York Giants
RR 5 Box 5008
Palestine, TX 75801, USA

Crawford, Kirsty (Musician)
c/o Staff Member *Pop Idol (Fremantle
Media)*
2700 Colorado Ave Ste 450
Santa Monica, CA 90404-3599, USA

Crawford, Lou (Hockey Player)
Boston Bruins
St John's Maple Leafs
50 New Gower St
St. John's, NL A1C 1J3, CANADA

Crawford, Marc (Hockey Player)
Vancouver Canucks
Vancouver Canucks
800 Griffiths Way Attn Hockey Program
Vancouver, BC V6B 6G1, CANADA

Crawford, Michael (Actor, Musician)
c/o Steve Levine *International Creative
Management (ICM-LA)*
10250 Constellation Blvd
Los Angeles, CA 90067-6200, USA

Crawford, Paxton (Baseball Player)
Boston Red Sox
PO Box 445
Plumerville, AR 72127-0445, USA

Crawford, Rachael (Actor)
c/o Staff Member *Coast to Coast Talent Group*
3350 Barham Blvd
Los Angeles, CA 90068-1404, USA

Crawford, Randy (Musician)
911 Park St SW
Grand Rapids, MI 49504-6241, USA

Crawford, Rufus (Baseball Player)
St Louis Browns
7800 Mockingbird Ln Lot 52
North Richland Hills, TX 76180-5568, USA

Crawford, Steve (Baseball Player)
Boston Red Sox
PO Box 828
Salina, OK 74365-0828, USA

Crawford, Vernon (Football Player)
New England Patriots
2001 Gemini St Apt 1305
Houston, TX 77058-2062, USA

Crawford, William J (War Hero)
28520 County Road 14
Rocky Ford, CO 81067-9637, USA

Crawley, Pauline (Baseball Player)
68670 Raposa Rd
Cathedral City, CA 92234-8148, USA

Cray, Robert (Musician)
Rosebud Agency
PO Box 170429
San Francisco, CA 94117-0429, USA

Crazy Mohan (Actor)
5 Chokkalingam Street
Mandavelli
Chennai, TN 600 028, INDIA

Creamer, Paula (Golfer)
c/o Staff Member *Ladies Pro Golf Association (LPGA)*
100 International Golf Dr
Daytona Beach, FL 32124-1082, USA

Creamer, Roger W (Writer)
180 E Hartsdale Ave Apt 2E
Hartsdale, NY 10530-3540, USA

Creamer, Timothy J (Astronaut)
5103 Carefree Dr
League City, TX 77573-3195, USA

Crear, Mark (Athlete, Track Athlete)
Octagon
1751 Pinnacle Dr Ste 1500
McLean, VA 22102-3833, USA

Creavalle, Laura (Misc)
Club Creavalle
230 Danforth Ave
Toronto, ON M4K 1N4, CANADA

Creber, William
140 Hollister Ave Apt 3
Santa Monica, CA 90405-3534, USA

Crede, Joe (Baseball Player)
Chicago White Sox
PO Box 62
Westphalia, MO 65085-0062, USA

Creech, Bob (Football Player)
Philadelphia Eagles
6323 Park Ln
Dallas, TX 75225-2108, USA

Creech, Sharon (Writer)
Harper Collins Publishers
10 E 53rd St Fl Cellar2
New York, NY 10022-5076, USA

Creech, Wilbur L (General)
20 Quail Run Rd
Henderson, NV 89014-2147, USA

Creed (Music Group)
c/o Staff Member *Wind-up Records*
72 Madison Ave Fl 8
New York, NY 10016-8731, USA

Creedence Clearwater Revisited
40 W 57th St
New York, NY 10019-4001, USA

Creeggan, Jim (Musician)
Nettwerk Mgmt
8730 Wilshire Blvd # 304
Beverly Hills, CA 90211-2716, USA

Creek, Doug (Baseball Player)
St Louis Cardinals
117 Gabriel Dr
Martinsburg, WV 25405-6185, USA

Creek, Luther (Actor)
c/o Staff Member *International Creative Management (ICM-LA)*
10250 Constellation Blvd
Los Angeles, CA 90067-6200, USA

Creekmur, Louis (Lou) (Football Player)
Detroit Lions
7521 SW 1st St
Plantation, FL 33317-3201, USA

Creel, Keith (Baseball Player)
Kansas City Royals
527 Trail Ridge Dr
Duncanville, TX 75116-2433, USA

Creel, Monica
4526 Wilshire Blvd
Los Angeles, CA 90010-3801, USA

Cregar, Bill (Football Player)
Pittsburgh Steelers
22 Locust Ct
Spring Lake, NJ 07762-2109, USA

Creighton, Jim (Basketball Player)
Atlanta Hawks
5297 S Geneva St
Englewood, CO 80111-6210, USA

Creighton, Joanne V (Educator)
Mount Holyoke College
President's Office
South Hadley, MA 01075, USA

Creighton, John D (Publisher)
Toronto Sun
333 King St E
Toronto, ON M5A 3X5, CANADA

Creighton, John O (Astronaut)
2111 SW 174th St
Burien, WA 98166-3259, USA

Creighton Sr, David T (Coach, Hockey Player)
5202 Spectacular Bid Dr
Wesley Chapel, FL 33544-1576, USA

Creme, Lol (Musician)
Heronden Hall
Tenferden
Kent, UNITED KINGDOM (UK)

Cremins, Bob (Baseball Player)
Boston Red Sox
415 Manor Ridge Rd
Pelham, NY 10803-2315, USA

Cremins, Bobby (Coach)
150 Bobby John Road
Atlanta, GA 30332-0001, USA

Crenkovski, Branko (Prime Minister)
Prime Minister's Office
Dame Grueva 6
Skopje 9100, MACEDONIA

Crenshaw, Leon (Football Player)
Green Bay Packers
4700 Velpoe Dr
Columbus, GA 31907-6515, USA

Crenshaw, Willis (Football Player)
St Louis Cardinals
1 New Ballas Pl Apt 216
Saint Louis, MO 63146-8705, USA

Creole, Kid (Musician)
Ron Rainey Mgmt
315 S Beverly Dr Ste 407
Beverly Hills, CA 90212-4301, USA

Creskoff, Rebecca (Actor)
c/o Staff Member *Innovative Artists (LA)*
1505 10th St
Santa Monica, CA 90401-2805, USA

Crespin, Regine (Opera Singer)
Musicaglotz
3 Ave Frochet
Paris 75009, FRANCE

Crespino, Robert (Football Player)
Cleveland Browns
4 Glen Eagles Dr
Jackson, MS 39211-2512, USA

Crespo, Elvis (Musician)
c/o Staff Member *Sony Music Miami*
605 Lincoln Rd Fl 7
Miami Beach, FL 33139-2900, USA

Crespo, Felipe (Baseball Player)
Toronto Blue Jays
80 Calle Arboleda Del Rio
Gurabo, PR 00778-5013, USA

Cressend, Jack (Baseball Player)
Minnesota Twins
105 Donovan Dr
Scott, LA 70583-5666, USA

Cressman, Dave (Hockey Player)
Minnesota North Stars
University of Waterloo 200 University Avenue W
Attn Hockey Program
Waterloo, ON N2L 3G1, CANADA

Cresson, Edith (Prime Minister)
Mairie
Chatellerault Cedex 86018, FRANCE

Creswell, Smiley (Football Player)
Philadelphia Eagles
1 Academy Way
Monroe, WA 98272-2006, USA

Cretler, Jean-Luc (Skier)
153 Ave du Marechal Lereic
BP 20
Bourq Saint Maurice 73700, FRANCE

Creutz, Edward C (Physicist)
PO Box 2757
Rancho Santa Fe, CA 92067-2757, USA

Crew-Cuts, The
29 Cedar St
Cresskill, NJ 07626-2508, USA

Crewdson, John M (Journalist)
Chicago Tribune
435 N Michigan Ave
Editorial Dept
Chicago, IL 60611-4024, USA

Crewe, Albert V (Physicist)
8 Summitt Dr
Chesterton, IN 46304-1024, USA

Crews, Gina (Reality TV Star)
10211 W State Road 235
Alachua, FL 32615-4947, USA

Crews, Harry E (Writer)
University of Florida
English Dept
Gainesville, FL 32611, USA

Crews, Philip (Misc)
University of California
Chemistry Dept
Santa Cruz, CA 99504, USA

Crews, Terry (Actor)
c/o Staff Member *William Morris Agency (WMA-LA)*
1 William Morris Pl
Beverly Hills, CA 90212-4261, USA

Crewson, Wendy (Actor)
438 Queen St E
Toronto, ON M5A 1T4, CANADA

Crha, Jiri (Hockey Player)
Toronto Maple Leafs
8023 Laurel Ridge Ct
Delray Beach, FL 33446-9537, USA

Crialese, Emanuele (Director)
c/o Staff Member *Endeavor Agency LLC (LA)*
9601 Wilshire Blvd Fl 3
Beverly Hills, CA 90210-5204, USA

Cribbins, Barnard (Actor)
Hamm Court
Weybridge, Surrey, UNITED KINGDOM (UK)

Cribbs, Joe S (Football Player)
Buffalo Bills
6131 Eagle Point Cir
Birmingham, AL 35242-6938, USA

Crichton, Dr Michael (Actor, Director, Producer, Writer)
c/o Lynn Nesbit *Janklow & Nesbit*
445 Park Ave
New York, NY 10022-2606, USA

Cricketts, The
3322 W End Ave # 520
Nashville, TN 37203-1031, USA

Crickhowell of Pont Esgob, Nicholas E (Politician)
4 Henning St
London SW11 3DR, UNITED KINGDOM (UK)

Crider, Jerry (Baseball Player)
Minnesota Twins
Apartado Postal 321 Cuidad Obregon
Sonora, MEXICO

Crider, Melissa (Actor)
c/o Daniel (Dan) Spilo *Artistry Management*
525 Westbourne Dr
West Hollywood, CA 90048-1913, USA

Crider, Melissa (Actor)
Paradigm Agency
10100 Santa Monica Blvd Ste 2500
Los Angeles, CA 90067-4116, USA

Crier, Catherine (Correspondent, Television Host)
Catherine Crier Live
600 3rd Ave Fl 17
Courtroom Television Network
New York, NY 10016-1900, USA

Crile, Susan (Artist)
168 W 86th St
New York, NY 10024-4022, USA

Crilley, Mark (Writer)
Delacorte Press
1540 Broadway
New York, NY 10036-4039, USA

Crim, Chuck (Baseball Player)
Milwaukee Brewers
951 S Copper Key Ct
Gilbert, AZ 85233-7402, USA

Crimian, Jack (Baseball Player)
St Louis Cardinals
3012 Green St
Claymont, DE 19703-2026, USA

Cripe, Dave (Baseball Player)
Kansas City Royals
1835 Montara Way
San Jacinto, CA 92583-5832, USA

Crippen, Robert L (Astronaut)
781 Harbour Isle Pl
West Palm Beach, FL 33410-4408, USA

Criqui, Don (Sportscaster)
CBS-TV
51 W 52nd St
Sports Dept
New York, NY 10019-6119, USA

Criscione, Dave (Baseball Player)
Baltimore Orioles
87 Hamlet St
Fredonia, NY 14063-2143, USA

Crisman, Joel (Football Player)
Tampa Bay Buccaneers
8823 Creekside Way Apt 1836
Littleton, CO 80129-1593, USA

Crisostomo, Manny (Journalist, Photographer)
Pacific Daily News
PO Box Dn
Hagatna, GU 96932-7508, USA

Crisp, Covelli (Baseball Player)
Cleveland Indians
9949 Warwick Dr
Desert Hot Springs, CA 92240-1307, USA

Crisp, Terry A (Coach, Hockey Player)
Boston Bruins
805 Cherry Laurel Ct
Nashville, TN 37215-6173, USA

Criss, Charles (Basketball Player)
Atlanta Hawks
4310 Melanie Ln
Atlanta, GA 30349-2849, USA

Criss, Peter (Musician)
McGhee Entertainment
8730 W Sunset Blvd Ste 200
West Hollywood, CA 90069-2275, USA

Crist, Charlie (Attorney)
Charlie Crist for Governor
PO Box 311
Tallahassee, FL 32302-0311, USA

Crist, George B (General)
CBS-TV
51 W 52nd St
News Dept
New York, NY 10019-6119, USA

Crist, Joel (Football Player)
New York Giants
PO Box 369
Greenhurst, NY 14742-0369, USA

Crist, Judith (Journalist)
180 Riverside Dr
New York, NY 10024-1021, USA

Cristal, Linda (Actor)
9129 Hazen Dr
Beverly Hills, CA 90210-1825, USA

Cristofer, Michael (Director, Writer)
c/o Geyer Kosinski *Media Talent Group*
9200 W Sunset Blvd Ste 810
W Hollywood, CA 90069-3603, USA

Cristol, Stanley J (Misc)
1638 W 3rd Ave
Durango, CO 81301-4912, USA

Critchfield, Charles L (Physicist)
PO Box 993
Los Alamos, NM 87544-0993, USA

Critchfield, Russell (Basketball Player)
Oakland Oaks
7 Patches Dr
Chico, CA 95928-4353, USA

Crite, Winston (Basketball Player)
Phoenix Suns
8812 Heely Ct
Bakersfield, CA 93311-1923, USA

Critelli, Michael (Business Person)
Pitney Bowes Inc
1 Elmcroft Rd
Stamford, CT 06926-0700, USA

Criter, Ken (Football Player)
Denver Broncos
PO Box 441343
Aurora, CO 80044-1343, USA

Crittenden, Ray (Football Player)
New England Patriots
8915 Garden Gate Dr
Fairfax, VA 22031-1475, USA

Croce, A J
1027 Meade Ave
San Diego, CA 92116-1038, USA

Croce, Stefania (Golfer)
Vantage Sports Management
222 W Commack Avenue #203
Winter Park, FL 32789, USA

Crocicchia, James (Football Player)
New York Giants
11 Lanesboro Rd
Ladera Ranch, CA 92694-0712, USA

Crocker, Dillard (Basketball Player)
Detroit Vagabond Kings
1710 Cedar St
Niles, MI 49120-2135, USA

Crockett, Bobby (Football Player)
Buffalo Bills
PO Box 26
Harriet, AR 72639-0026, USA

Crockett, Gibson (Cartoonist)
4713 Great Oak Rd
Rockville, MD 20853-1607, USA

Crockett, Monte (Football Player)
Buffalo Bills
General Delivery
Pence Springs, WV 24962-9999, USA

Crockett, Willis (Football Player)
Dallas Cowboys
1307 Coffee Ave S
Douglas, GA 31533-4516, USA

Crockett, Zack (Football Player)
Indianapolis Colts
6136 NW 120th Ter
Coral Springs, FL 33076-1913, USA

Croel, Mike (Football Player)
Denver Broncos
8305 Lookout Mountain Ave
Los Angeles, CA 90046-1548, USA

Croft, Dwayne (Opera Singer)
Columbia Artists Mgmt Inc
1790 Broadway Fl 6
New York, NY 10019-1412, USA

Crofts, Dash (Musician, Songwriter, Writer)
Nationwide Entertainment
2756 N Green Valley Pkwy
Henderson, NV 89014-2120, USA

Croghan, Emma-Kate (Director)
Hilary Linstead
500 Oxford St
Bondi Junction, NSW 2022, AUSTRALIA

Croker, Stephen B (Steve) (General)
2 Byford Ct
Chestertown, MD 21620-1642, USA

Croll, Jimmy (Misc)
Thoroughbred Racing Assn
420 Fair Hill Dr # 1
Elkton, MD 21921-2573, USA

Cromartie, Warren (Baseball Player)
c/o Staff Member *Montreal Expos*
4549 Avenue Pierre de Coubertin
Montreal, PQ H1V 3N7, CANADA

Crombeen, Mike (Hockey Player)
Cleveland Barons
817 Foxcroft Blvd
Newmarket, ON L3X 1M8, CANADA

Crombie, Jonathan (Actor)
Sullivan Entertainment
111 Davenport Road
Toronto, ON M5R 3R3, CANADA

Cromer, D T (Baseball Player)
Cincinnati Reds
5057 Highway 17 Business
Murrells Inlt, SC 29576-5653, USA

Cromer, Tripp (Baseball Player)
St Louis Cardinals
32 W Tombee Ln
Columbia, SC 29209-0844, USA

Cromwell, James (Actor)
c/o Pippa Markham *Markham and Froggatt Agency*
4 Windmill St
London W1T 1HF, UNITED KINGDOM (UK)

Cromwell, Nolan (Coach, Football Coach, Football Player)
Los Angeles Rams
2624 140th Ave NE
Bellevue, WA 98005-1824, USA

Cron, Chris (Baseball Player)
California Angels
14879 S 43rd Pl
Phoenix, AZ 85044-6788, USA

Cronan, Pete (Football Player)
Seattle Seahawks
13 Saddle Hill Rd
Hopkinton, MA 01748-1151, USA

Cronbach, Lee J (Educator)
2614 Oregon St
Union City, CA 94587-4320, USA

Crone, Ray (Baseball Player)
Milwaukee Braves
508 Panorama
Waxahachie, TX 75165-5919, USA

Cronenberg, David (Actor)
David Cronenberg Productions
217 Avenue Road
Toronto, ON M5R 2J3, CANADA

Cronenweth, Regina
5410 Wilshire Blvd # 227
Los Angeles, CA 90036-4216, USA

Cronin, Eugene (Football Player)
Detroit Lions
2445 37th Ave
Sacramento, CA 95822-3613, USA

Cronin, James W (Nobel Prize Laureate)
5825 S Dorchester Ave
Chicago, IL 60637-1764, USA

Cronin, Kevin (Musician)
Shapiro Co
9229 W Sunset Blvd Ste 607
Los Angeles, CA 90069-3406, USA

Cronin, Rachel (Actor)
c/o Lisa King *King Talent*
303-228 E 4th Ave
Vancouver, BC V5T 1G5, CANADA

Cronin, Rich (Musician)
c/o Staff Member *Gersh Agency, The (LA)*
232 N Canon Dr
Beverly Hills, CA 90210-5302, USA

Cronkite, Walter
51 W 52nd St # 1934
New York, NY 10019-6119, USA

Cronnenberg, David (Director)
Toronto Antenna
244 DuPont St #200
Toronto, ON M5R 1V7, CANADA

Cronyn, Christopher (Producer)
c/o Staff Member *Lichter Grossman Nichols Adler & Goodman*
9200 W Sunset Blvd Ste 1200
Los Angeles, CA 90069-3607, USA

Cronyn, Susan Cooper (Producer, Writer)
c/o Ron Bernstein *International Creative Management (ICM-LA)*
10250 Constellation Blvd
Los Angeles, CA 90067-6200, USA

Crook, Edward Jr (Boxer)
4512 Moline Ave
Columbus, GA 31907-6625, USA

Crook & Chase
3201 Dickerson Pike
Nashville, TN 37207-2905, USA

Crooke, Edward A (Business Person)
Constellation Energy Group
39 W Lexington St
Baltimore, MD 21201-3979, USA

Crooke, Leland (Actor)
c/o Staff Member *Badgley-Connor Agency*
1680 Vine St Ste 1016
Los Angeles, CA 90028-8800, USA

Croom, Sylvester (Coach, Football Player)
New Orleans Saints
3909 12th St NE
Tuscaloosa, AL 35404-2004, USA

Cropper, Marshall (Football Player)
Pittsburgh Steelers
2932 Fort Baker Dr SE
Washington, DC 20020-7222, USA

Crosbie, Annette
68 St. James's St.
London, ENGLAND SW1A 1PH, UNITED KINGDOM (UK)

Crosbie, John C (Politician)
235 Water St
Saint John's, NF A1C 5L3, CANADA

Crosby, Alfred W (Historian)
2506 Bowman Ave
Austin, TX 78703-2314, USA

Crosby, Bobby (Baseball Player)
Oakland A's
11463 Anticost Way
Cypress, CA 90630-5429, USA

Crosby, Bubba (Baseball Player)
Los Angeles Dodgers
4512 Magnolia St
Bellaire, TX 77401-4211, USA

Crosby, Cathy Lee (Actor)
c/o Staff Member *CLC Productions*
1223 Santa Monica Blvd # 404
Santa Monica, CA 90404, USA

Crosby, Cleveland (Football Player)
Baltimore Colts
2703 Sandal Walk
Pearland, TX 77584-3365, USA

Crosby, David (Musician)
1460 4th St Ste 300
Santa Monica, CA 90401-3415, USA

Crosby, Denise (Actor, Model)
8242 Blackburn Ave
Los Angeles, CA 90048-4216, USA

Crosby, Ed (Baseball Player)
St Louis Cardinals
6952 Brightwood Ln Apt 9
Garden Grove, CA 92845-2976, USA

Crosby, Elaine (Golfer)
2580 Meadowbrook Ln
Jackson, MI 49201-7702, USA

Crosby, Kathryn
PO Box 85
Genoa, NV 89411-0085, USA

Crosby, Ken (Baseball Player)
Chicago Cubs
PO Box 680306
Park City, UT 84068-0306, USA

Crosby, Lucinda (Actor)
4942 Vineland Ave Ste 200
North Hollywood, CA 91601-5646, USA

Crosby, Mark
3500 W Olive Ave Ste 1400
Burbank, CA 91505-5512, USA

Crosby, Norm (Actor, Comedian)
c/o Bernie Brillstein *Brillstein-Grey Entertainment*
9150 Wilshire Blvd Ste 350
Beverly Hills, CA 90212-3453, USA

Crosby, Paul (Musician)
Helter Skelter
Plaza
535 Kings Road
London SW10 0S, UNITED KINGDOM (UK)

Crosby, Phil (Actor)
800 S Figueroa St Ste 1200
Los Angeles, CA 90017-2581, USA

Crosby, Rob
PO Box 121551
Nashville, TN 37212-1551, USA

Crosby, Robbin
8250 Grand View Dr
Los Angeles, CA 90046-1916, USA

Crosby, Sidney (Athlete, Hockey Player)
c/o Staff Member *Pittsburgh Penguins*
66 Mario Lemieux Pl
Mellon Arena
Pittsburgh, PA 15219-3504, USA

Crosby, Steve (Coach, Football Coach, Football Player)
New York Giants
Vanderbitt University 2201 W End Ave
Attn Football Coaching Staff
Nashville, TN 37235-0001, USA

Crosby Stills Nash & Young (Music Group)
c/o Staff Member *William Morris Agency (WMA-LA)*
1 William Morris Pl
Beverly Hills, CA 90212-4261, USA

Croshere, Austin (Basketball Player)
Indiana Pacers
125 S Pennsylvania St
Conseco Fieldhouse
Indianapolis, IN 46204-3610, USA

Cross, Ben (Actor)
Shepherd & Ford
13 Radnor Walk
London SW3 4BP, UNITED KINGDOM (UK)

Cross, Christopher (Musician, Songwriter, Writer)
568 Radcliffe Ave
Pacific Palisades, CA 90272-4329, USA

Cross, Cory (Hockey Player)
Tampa Bay Lightning
2963 W Bayshore Ct
Tampa, FL 33611, USA

Cross, David (Actor)
c/o Staff Member *International Creative Management (ICM-LA)*
10250 Constellation Blvd
Los Angeles, CA 90067-6200, USA

Cross, Howard (Football Player)
New York Giants
399 Berkley Rd
Gurley, AL 35748-9524, USA

Cross, Irv (Football Player, Sportscaster)
Philadelphia Eagles
2196 Marison Road
Roseville, MN 55113, USA

Cross, Jeff (Basketball Player)
Los Angeles Clippers
1 Holmes Rd
Dovr Foxcroft, ME 04426, USA

Cross, Jeff (Football Player)
Miami Dolphins
2715 Walkers Way
Weston, FL 33331-3021, USA

Cross, Joseph (Actor)
Innovative Artists
1505 10th St
Santa Monica, CA 90401-2805, USA

Cross, Justin (Football Player)
Buffalo Bills
10 Longwood Dr
Hampton, NH 03842-1122, USA

Cross, Marcia (Actor)
c/o Staff Member *Desperate Housewives*
2300 W Riverside Dr
Abc Television
Burbank, CA 91506-2976, USA

Cross, Randall L (Randy) (Football Player, Sportscaster)
San Francisco 49ers
155 Travertine Trl
Alpharetta, GA 30022-5196, USA

Cross, Roger (Actor)
c/o Staff Member *SMS Talent Inc*
8730 W Sunset Blvd Ste 440
Los Angeles, CA 90069-2277, USA

Cross, Russell (Basketball Player)
Elmhurst College
190 S Prospect Ave
Athletic Dept
Elmhurst, IL 60126-3296, USA

Cross, Terry M (Admiral)
Coast Guard Island
Commander US Coast Guard Pacific
Alameda, CA 94501, USA

Crossan, Dave (Football Player)
Washington Redskins
727 Cloverfields Dr
Stevensville, MD 21666-2437, USA

Crosse, Liris (Actor, Model)
Wilhelmina Creative Mgmt
300 Park Ave S # 200
New York, NY 10010-5313, USA

Crossfade (Music Group)
Ed Sloan
216 Lincoln St
West Columbia, SC 29170-1812, USA

Crossley, Charlotte (Actor, Musician)
Stone Manners Agency
6500 Wilshire Blvd Ste 550
Los Angeles, CA 90048-4950, USA

Crosswhite, Leon (Football Player)
Detroit Lions
11089 Folkstone Dr
Yukon, OK 73099-8051, USA

Croston, Dave (Football Player)
Green Bay Packers
17 Dorchester Rd
Sioux City, IA 51106-9750, USA

Croteau, Gary (Hockey Player)
Los Angeles Kings
8380 E Hindsdale Ave
Centennial, CO 80112, USA

Crotty, Jim (Football Player)
Washington Redskins
215 S 195th St
Des Moines, WA 98148-2137, USA

Crotty, John (Basketball Player)
Utah Jazz
120 Brighton Ave
Spring Lake, NJ 07762-1511, USA

Crouch, Andrae (Musician, Songwriter, Writer)
c/o Staff Member *William Morris Agency (WMA-LA)*
1 William Morris Pl
Beverly Hills, CA 90212-4261, USA

Crouch, Eric (Football Player)
St Louis Rams
14870 Jaynes St
Omaha, NE 68116-4353, USA

Crouch, Lindsay (Actor)
15115 1/2 W Sunset Blvd Ste A
Pacific Palisades, CA 90272-3751, USA

Crouch, Paul (Misc)
Trinity Broadcasting Network
PO Box A
Santa Ana, CA 92711-2101, USA

Crouch, Roger K (Astronaut)
Carriage Hill Dr
Laurel, MD 20707, USA

Crouch, Sandra (Musician, Songwriter, Writer)
Sparrow Communications Group
101 Winners Cir N
Brentwood, TN 37027-5017, USA

Crouch, William T (Bill) (Journalist, Photographer)
5660 Valley Oaks Ct
Placerville, CA 95667-9363, USA

Crouch, Zach (Baseball Player)
Boston Red Sox
3122 Tory Ln
Sacramento, CA 95827-1915, USA

Croucher, Juan
45 Cayuse Ln
Rancho Palos Verdes, CA 90275-5155, USA

Crouse, Lindsay
c/o Wendy Hurst *Global Business Management Inc*
15250 Ventura Blvd Ste 710
Sherman Oaks, CA 91403-3219, USA

Crouthamel, Jake (Football Player)
Boston Patriots
385 Elliott Rd
Centerville, MA 02632-3666, USA

Crouther, Lance (Actor, Producer, Writer)
c/o Ari Greenburg *Endeavor Agency LLC (LA)*
9601 Wilshire Blvd Fl 3
Beverly Hills, CA 90210-5204, USA

Crow, Al (Football Player)
Boston Patriots
6191 Occoquan Forest Dr
Manassas, VA 20112-3034, USA

Crow, Bill (Basketball Player)
Anaheim Amigos
21300 River Rd # 15
Perris, CA 92570-8390, USA

Crow, Dean (Baseball Player)
Detroit Tigers
11507 Wickchester Ln
Houston, TX 77043-4521, USA

Crow, Don (Baseball Player)
Los Angeles Dodgers
1554 Brook Dr
Fort Mill, SC 29708-7291, USA

Crow, F Trammell (Business Person)
Trammell Crow Co
2001 Ross Ave
Trammell Crow Center
Dallas, TX 75201-2998, USA

Crow, Harian R (Business Person)
Trammell Crow Co
2001 Ross Ave
Trammell Crow Center
Dallas, TX 75201-2998, USA

Crow, James F (Misc)
24 Glenway St
Madison, WI 53705-5206, USA

Crow, John David (Coach, Football Coach, Football Player)
Chicago Cardinals
5004 Augusta Cir
College Station, TX 77845-8983, USA

Crow, Lindon (Football Player)
Chicago Cardinals
6800 S Strand Ave # 481
Yuma, AZ 85364-9727, USA

Crow, Mark (Basketball Player)
New Jersey Nets
501 W Bay St
Jacksonville, FL 32202-4428, USA

Crow, Martin D (Cricketer)
PO Box 109302
New Market
Auckland, NEW ZEALAND

Crow, Sheryl (Actor, Musician, Songwriter, Writer)
c/o John Marx *William Morris Agency (WMA-LA)*
1 William Morris Pl
Beverly Hills, CA 90212-4261, USA

Crow, Wayne (Football Player)
Oakland Raiders
39471 Manorgate Rd
Palm Desert, CA 92211-1918, USA

Crowded House, 3 Mitchell Rd
Rose Bay
Sydney NSW 2929, AUSTRALIA

Crowder, Bruce (Hockey Player)
Boston Bruins
7 Nashua Dr
Nashua, NH 03064, USA

Crowder, Corey (Basketball Player)
Utah Jazz
725 Ballard Bridge Rd
Carrollton, GA 30117-9104, USA

Crowder, Keith (Hockey Player)
Boston Bruins
PO Box 95 Stn Main
Essex, ON N8M 2Y1, CANADA

Crowe, Cameron (Director, Writer)
117 E Louisa St # 506
Seattle, WA 98102-3203, USA

Crowe, George (Baseball Player)
New York Black Yankees
1955 D O Mills Ct
Gold River, CA 95670-7843, USA

Crowe, Mia (Actor, Model)
Mia Crowe Official Fan Club
7336 Santa Monica Blvd # 633
West Hollywood, CA 90046-6616, USA

Crowe, Phil (Hockey Player)
Los Angeles Kings
PO Box 115
Willow Grove, PA 19090-0115, USA

Crowe, Russell (Actor)
c/o George Freeman *William Morris Agency (WMA-LA)*
1 William Morris Pl
Beverly Hills, CA 90212-4261, USA

Crowe, Sara
13 Shorts Garden
London, ENGLAND WC2H 9AT, UNITED KINGDOM (UK)

Crowe, Tonya (Actor)
13030 Mindanao Way Apt 4
Marina Del Rey, CA 90292-6456, USA

Crowe, William J Jr (Admiral, Diplomat)
Global Options
1615 L St NW Ste 300
Washington, DC 20036-5655, USA

Crowell, Craven H Jr (Government Official)
Tennessee Valley Authority
400 W Summit Hill Dr
Knoxville, TN 37902-1419, USA

Crowell, Germane (Football Player)
Detroit Lions
200 Luzelle Dr
Winston Salem, NC 27103-6464, USA

Crowell, James (Baseball Player)
Cincinnati Reds
4003 Sleighbell Ln
Valparaiso, IN 46383-1943, USA

Crowell, John C (Misc)
300 Hot Springs Rd
Montecito, CA 93108-2038, USA

Crowell, Rodney
2 Music Cir S Ste 212
Nashville, TN 37203-5708, USA

Crowell, Rodney J (Musician, Songwriter, Writer)
Joe's Garage
4405 Belmont Park Ter
Nashville, TN 37215-3609, USA

Crowley, Ben (Actor)
c/o Staff Member *Kass & Stokes Management*
9229 W Sunset Blvd Ste 504
Los Angeles, CA 90069-3405, USA

Crowley, Joseph N (Educator)
University of Nevada
President's Office
Reno, NV 89557-0001, USA

Crowley, Monica (Television Host)
c/o Staff Member *MSNBC (NJ)*
Nbc/One Microsoft Corporation
1 Msnc Plaza
Secaucus, NJ 07094, USA

Crowley, Patricia (Actor)
TMCE
270 N Canon Dr # 1064
Beverly Hills, CA 90210-5323, USA

Crowley, Terry (Baseball Player)
Baltimore Orioles
10626 Anglo Hill Rd
Cockeysville, MD 21030-2929, USA

Crown, David A (Misc)
3344 Twin Lakes Ln
Sanibel, FL 33957-5528, USA

Crown, Lester (Business Person)
Henry Crown & Co
222 N Lasalle St
Chicago, IL 60601-1120, USA

Crowson, Richard (Cartoonist, Editor)
Wichita Eagle-Beacon
825 E Douglas Ave
Editorial Dept
Wichita, KS 67202-3512, USA

Crowton, Gary (Coach, Football Coach)
Brigham Young University
Athletic Dept
Provo, UT 84602, USA

Croyle, Philip (Football Player)
Houston Oilers
5883 Treetop Ct
San Jose, CA 95123-4346, USA

Crozier, Joseph R (Joe) (Coach, Hockey Player)
Toronto Maple Leafs
1 Seymour H Knox III Plz Ste 1
Buffalo Sabres
Buffalo, NY 14203-3007, USA

Crudale, Mike (Baseball Player)
St Louis Cardinals
2319 Tree Creek Pl
Danville, CA 94506-2065, USA

Crudup, Billy (Actor)
c/o Jimmy Darmody *Creative Artists Agency LCC (CAA-LA)*
2000 Avenue Of The Stars
Los Angeles, CA 90067-4700, USA

Cruikshank, Thomas H (Business Person)
5949 Sherry Ln Ste 1035
Dallas, TX 75225-6521, USA

Cruise, Tom (Actor, Director, Producer)
c/o Staff Member *Cruise/Wagner Productions (C/W)*
10250 Constellation Blvd # 11007
Los Angeles, CA 90067-6200, USA

Cruisie, Jennifer (Writer)
c/o *Argh Ink LLC*
285 5th Ave # 470
Brooklyn, NY 11215-2425, USA

Crum, E Denzel (Denny) (Coach)
12038 Hunting Crest Dr
Prospect, KY 40059-8405, USA

Crumb, George H (Composer)
240 Kirk Ln
Media, PA 19063-2216, USA

Crumb, Robert (Artist, Cartoonist)
c/o Staff Member *Fantagraphics Books*
7563 Lake City Way NE
Seattle, WA 98115-4218, USA

Crumb, Robert (R) (Cartoonist)
20 Rue du Pont Vieux
Sauve 30610, FRANCE

Crumley, James R Jr (Religious Leader)
108 Castle Church Rd
Chapin, SC 29036-7853, USA

Crumling, Gene (Baseball Player)
St Louis Cardinals
135 Lisa Cir
York, PA 17406-9323, USA

Crumm, Denny
12038 Hunting Crest Dr
Prospect, KY 40059-8405, USA

Crump, Dwayne (Football Player)
St Louis Cardinals
35708 Marciel Ave
Madera, CA 93636-8414, USA

Crump, Harry (Football Player)
Boston Patriots
50 Park Row W Apt 809
Providence, RI 02903-1151, USA

Crusan, Doug (Football Player)
Miami Dolphins
6263 Hanover Ct
Fishers, IN 46038-1799, USA

Crutcher, Chris
3405 E Marion Ct
Spokane, WA 99223-7215, USA

Crutcher, Lawrence M (Publisher)
Book-of-the-Month Club
Rockefeller Center
New York, NY 10020, USA

Crutchfield, Dwayne (Football Player)
New York Jets
6936 Rebecca Dr
Niagara Falls, NY 14304-3053, USA

Crutchfield, Edward E (Financier)
First Union Corp
1 First Union Center
Charlotte, NC 28288-0001, USA

Crutzen, Paul J (Nobel Prize Laureate)
Max Planck Chemistry Institute
J J Becher-Weg 27
Mainz 55128, GERMANY

Cruyff, Johan (Coach, Soccer Player)
Koninklike Nederk Voetbalbod
Postbus 515
Zeist, AM 3700, THE NETHERLANDS

Cruz, Alexis (Actor)
c/o Staff Member *Abrams Artists Agency (LA)*
9200 W Sunset Blvd Ph 11
Los Angeles, CA 90069-3601, USA

Cruz, Cirilio (Baseball Player)
St Louis Cardinals
E8 Calle H
Arroyo, PR 00714-2236, USA

Cruz, Deivi (Baseball Player)
Detroit Tigers
611 Woodward Ave
Detroit, MI 48226-3408, USA

Cruz, Henry (Baseball Player)
Los Angeles Dodgers
16 Calle Un W
Fajardo, PR 00738, USA

Cruz, Jacob (Baseball Player)
San Francisco Giants
1582 W Commerce Ave
Gilbert, AZ 85233-4103, USA

Cruz, Jose D (Baseball Player)
St Louis Cardinals
2309 Delta Bridge Dr
Pearland, TX 77584-1566, USA

Cruz, Juan (Athlete, Baseball Player)
c/o Staff Member *Chicago Cubs*
1060 W Addison St
Wrigley Field
Chicago, IL 60613-4397, USA

Cruz, Julio (Baseball Player)
Seattle Mariners
6599 170th Pl SE
Bellevue, WA 98006-6012, USA

Cruz, Mike (DJ)
c/o Staff Member *Diva Central Inc*
7510 W Sunset Blvd Ste 1445
Los Angeles, CA 90046-3408, USA

Cruz, Penelope (Actor, Model)
c/o Brandt Joel *Creative Artists Agency LCC (CAA-LA)*
2000 Avenue Of The Stars
Los Angeles, CA 90067-4700, USA

Cruz, Raymond
8383 Wilshire Blvd # 954
Beverly Hills, CA 90211-2412, USA

Cruz, Smith Martin (Writer)
Random House
1745 Broadway # B1
New York, NY 10019-4305, USA

Cruz, Todd (Baseball Player)
Philadelphia Phillies
15655 Reed Dr
Fontana, CA 92336-8710, USA

Cruz, Valerie (Actor)
c/o Staff Member *Innovative Artists (LA)*
1505 10th St
Santa Monica, CA 90401-2805, USA

Cruz, Wilson
Latin Hollywood Films
153 San Vicente Blvd Apt 2G
Santa Monica, CA 90402-1507, USA

Cruz-Romo, Gilda (Opera Singer)
1315 Lockhill Selma Rd
San Antonio, TX 78213-1915, USA

Crvenkovski, Branko (President)
President's Office
Skopje, MACEDONIA

Cryder, Robert (Football Player)
New England Patriots
17411 NE 129th St
Redmond, WA 98052-1323, USA

Cryer, Gretchen (Actor, Songwriter, Writer)
885 W End Ave
New York, NY 10025-3501, USA

Cryer, Jon (Actor)
Media Artists Group
6300 Wilshire Blvd Ste 1470
Los Angeles, CA 90048-5200, USA

Cryer, Suzanne (Actor)
c/o Chris Schmidt *Paradigm (LA)*
360 N Crescent Dr
North Bldg
Beverly Hills, CA 90210-6820, USA

Cryner, Bobby
PO Box 2147
Hendersonville, TN 37077-2147, USA

Crystal, Billy (Actor, Comedian)
c/o Larry Brezner *MBST Entertainment*
345 N Maple Dr Ste 200
Beverly Hills, CA 90210-3860, USA

Crystals (Music Group)
27-L Ambiance Ct
Bardonia, NY 10954, USA

Csikszentmihalyi, Mihaly (Misc)
5848 S University Ave
Chicago, IL 60637-1554, USA

Csokas, Marton (Actor)
c/o George Freeman *William Morris Agency (WMA-LA)*
1 William Morris Pl
Beverly Hills, CA 90212-4261, USA

Csonka, Lawrence R (Larry) (Football Player)
Miami Dolphins
37256 Hunter Camp Rd
Lisbon, OH 44432-9464, USA

Cua, Rick (Musician)
Greg Menza
1086 Rip Steele Rd
Columbia, TN 38401-7745, USA

Cuaron, Alfonso (Director)
Endeavor Talent Agency
9701 Wilshire Blvd Ste 1000
Beverly Hills, CA 90212-2010, USA

Cuban, Mark (Actor, Director)
2929 Entertainment
9100 Wilshire Blvd Ste 500 W
Beverly Hills, CA 90212-3401, USA

Cuban, Mark (Business Person)
c/o Staff Member *Dallas Mavericks*
2909 Taylor St
Dallas, TX 75226-1909, USA

Cubbage, Mike (Baseball Player)
Texas Rangers
3349 Carroll Creek Rd
Keswick, VA 22947-9156, USA

Cubitt, David (Actor)
c/o Jimmy Cundiff *United Talent Agency (UTA)*
9560 Wilshire Blvd Ste 500
Beverly Hills, CA 90212-2401, USA

Cuccinello, Al (Baseball Player)
New York Giants
180 Park Ave
Hauppauge, NY 11788-2924, USA

Cuccurullo, Waren (Musician)
DD Productions
93A Westbourne Park Villas
London W2 5ED, UNITED KINGDOM
(UK)

Cuche, Didier (Skier)
Les Bugnenets
Le Paquier 2058, SWITZERLAND

Cucinotta, Maria Grazia (Actor)
Cucchini Mgmt
Lundolevere del Melini 10
Rome 00192, ITALY

Cuckney, John G (Financier)
1 Cornhill
London EC3V 3QR, UNITED KINGDOM
(UK)

Cudahy, Richard D (Judge)
US Court of Appeals
219 S Dearborn St
Chicago, IL 60604-1874, USA

Cuddy, Jim (Musician)
Agency Group Ltd
1775 Broadway Ste 515
New York, NY 10019-1903, USA

Cuddyer, Michael (Baseball Player)
Minnesota Twins
10240 Washingtonia Palm Way
Fort Myers, FL 33966-6915, USA

Cudlitz, Michael (Actor)
c/o Karen Goldberg *Metropolitan*
4500 Wilshire Blvd Fl 2
Los Angeles, CA 90010-3858, USA

Cudmore, Daniel (Actor)
c/o Murray Gibson *Characters Talent Agency, The (Toronto)*
8 Elm St 3rd FL
Toronto, ON M5G 1G7, CANADA

Cueliar, Miguel S (Mike) (Baseball Player)
1002 Chesterfield Cir
Winter Springs, FL 32708-4707, USA

Cuellar, Bobby (Baseball Player)
Texas Rangers
705 E 6th St
Alice, TX 78332-4651, USA

Cueto, Al (Basketball Player)
Miami Floridians
5714 Riviera Dr
Coral Gables, FL 33146-2751, USA

Cuevas, Alberto (Writer)
c/o Staff Member *Creative Artists Agency LCC (CAA-LA)*
2000 Avenue Of The Stars
Los Angeles, CA 90067-4700, USA

Cuevas, Beto (Actor, Musician)
c/o David Guillod *United Talent Agency (UTA)*
9560 Wilshire Blvd Ste 500
Beverly Hills, CA 90212-2401, USA

Cuevas, Jose Luis
Galeana 109
Col. San Angel Inn (01000) Mexico DF,
MEXICO

Culbertson, Frank L Jr (Astronaut)
15500 Meherrin Dr
Centreville, VA 20120-3733, USA

Culbreath, Jim (Football Player)
Green Bay Packers
212 Elder Ave
Yeadon, PA 19050-3028, USA

Culbreath, Joshua (Josh) (Athlete, Track Athlete)
Central State University
Athletic Dept
Wilberforce, OH 45384, USA

Culhane, Jim (Hockey Player)
Hartford Whalers
General Delivery
Soldotna, AK 99669-9999, USA

Culkin, Kieran (Actor)
c/o Emily Gerson Saines *Overbrook Entertainment*
450 N Roxbury Dr Fl 4
Beverly Hills, CA 90210-4232, USA

Culkin, Macaulay (Actor)
c/o Emily Gerson Saines *Overbrook Entertainment*
450 N Roxbury Dr Fl 4
Beverly Hills, CA 90210-4232, USA

Culkin, Rory (Actor)
c/o Emily Gerson Saines *Overbrook Entertainment*
450 N Roxbury Dr Fl 4
Beverly Hills, CA 90210-4232, USA

Cullares, Willie (Football Player)
Philadelphia Eagles
3721 Bryant Cir # 3721
Kansas City, KS 66102-3703, USA

Cullen, Barry (Hockey Player)
Toronto Maple Leafs
RR 1
Puslinch, ON N0B 2J0, CANADA

Cullen, Brett (Actor)
c/o Miles Levy *James/Levy/Jacobson Management*
3500 W Olive Ave Ste 1470
Burbank, CA 91505-5514, USA

Cullen, Brian (Hockey Player)
Toronto Maple Leafs
Brian Cullen Motors
PO Box 187 Station Main
St Catharines, ON L2R 6S8, CANADA

Cullen, Jack (Baseball Player)
New York Yankees
164 Alexander Ave
Nutley, NJ 07110-1002, USA

Cullen, John (Hockey Player)
Pittsburgh Penguins
223 Hawick Ln
McDonough, GA 30253-4236, USA

Cullen, Kimberly (Actor)
8916 Ashcroft Ave
West Hollywood, CA 90048-2404, USA

Cullen, Matt (Hockey Player)
Mighty Ducks of Anaheim
5109 2nd St E
West Fargo, ND 58078-8211, USA

Cullen, Peter (Actor, Voice Over Artist)
c/o Staff Member *Tisherman Agency Inc*
6767 Forest Lawn Dr Ste 101
Los Angeles, CA 90068-1050, USA

Cullen, Ray (Hockey Player)
New York Rangers
20 Sydenham Dr RR 2
Ilderton, ON N0M 2A0, CANADA

Cullen, Sean M
10100 Santa Monica Blvd Ste 2500
Los Angeles, CA 90067-4116, USA

Cullen, Tim (Baseball Player)
Washington Senators
159 W G St
Benicia, CA 94510-3114, USA

Cullens, E Van (Business Person)
Harris Corp
1025 W Nasa Blvd
Melbourne, FL 32919-0001, USA

Culler, Glen (Scientist)
Culler Scientific Systems Corp
100 Burns Pl
Goleta, CA 93117, USA

Culligan, Joe (Writer)
Research Investigative Services
650 NE 126th St
North Miami, FL 33161-4821, USA

Cullinan, Edward H (Architect)
Wharf
1 Baldwin Terrace
London N1 7RU, UNITED KINGDOM
(UK)

Cullity, Dave (Football Player)
San Francisco 49ers
5420 Jarman St
Colorado Springs, CO 80906-8210, USA

Cullum, Jamie (Musician)
c/o Christopher Dalston *Creative Artists Agency LCC (CAA-LA)*
2000 Avenue Of The Stars
Los Angeles, CA 90067-4700, USA

Cullum, John (Actor, Musician)
Writers & Artists
360 Park Ave # 16
New York, NY 10022-5909, USA

Cullum, Kaitlin (Actor)
c/o Sheila Wenzel *Innovative Artists (LA)*
1505 10th St
Santa Monica, CA 90401-2805, USA

Cullum, Kimberly
8916 Ashcroft Ave
West Hollywood, CA 90048-2404, USA

Cullum, Leo (Cartoonist)
2900 Valmere Dr
Malibu, CA 90265-2970, USA

Cullum, Mark E (Cartoonist, Editor)
5401 Forest Acres Dr
Nashville, TN 37220-2100, USA

Culp, Curley (Football Player)
Kansas City Chiefs
12405 Alameda Trace Cir Apt 1213
Austin, TX 78727-6444, USA

Culp, Ray (Baseball Player)
Philadelphia Phillies
7400 Waterline Rd
Austin, TX 78731-2055, USA

Culp, Robert (Actor)
1840 El Cerrito Pl # 1
Los Angeles, CA 90068-3739, USA

Culp, Stephen (Actor)
c/o Miriam Milgrom *Berkman Henoch Peterson & Peddy*
100 Garden City Plz
Garden City, NY 11530-3203, USA

Culp, Steven (Actor)
c/o Miriam Milgrom *Berkman Henoch Peterson & Peddy*
100 Garden City Plz
Garden City, NY 11530-3203, USA

Culpepper, Daunte (Football Player)
c/o Staff Member *Minnesota Vikings*
9520 Viking Dr
Eden Prairie, MN 55344-3898, USA

Culpepper, Robert E (Football Player)
Chicago Cardinals
1535 45th Ave E
Ellenton, FL 34222-2643, USA

Cult, The
c/o Staff Member *Immortal Entertainment*
11965 Venice Blvd Ste 204
Los Angeles, CA 90066-3954, USA

Cult Jam
PO Box 30284
Brooklyn, NY 11203-0284, USA

Culture Beat
Schleiermacher Str. 2
Darmstadt D-64283, GERMANY

Culver, Curt S (Financier)
MGIC Investment Corp
250 E Kilbourn Ave
Milwaukee, WI 53202-3102, USA

Culver, George (Baseball Player)
Cleveland Indians
5409 Rustic Canyon St
Bakersfield, CA 93306-7315, USA

Culver, John C (Senator)
5409 Spangler Ave
Bethesda, MD 20816-1847, USA

Culver, Michael
77 Beak St.
London, ENGLAND W1F 9ST, UNITED
KINGDOM (UK)

Culver, Molly (Actor)
c/o Staff Member *Stone Manners Talent &
Literary (LA)*
6500 Wilshire Blvd Ste 550
Los Angeles, CA 90048-4950, USA

Cumberland, John (Baseball Player)
New York Yankees
19417 Golden Slipper Pl
Lutz, FL 33558-9209, USA

Cumberland Gap
159 Madison Ave Apt 2G
New York, NY 10016-5434, USA

Cumby, George E (Football Player)
Green Bay Packers
12090 Cross Fence Trl
Tyler, TX 75706-4239, USA

Cumming, Alan (Actor, Musician)
c/o Tracy Brennan *Creative Artists Agency
LCC (CAA-LA)*
2000 Avenue Of The Stars
Los Angeles, CA 90067-4700, USA

Cummings, Burton (Musician, Songwriter,
Writer)
Lustig Talent
PO Box 770850
Orlando, FL 32877-0850, USA

Cummings, Dave
4130 La Village Dr. #107
La Jolla, CA 92037, USA

Cummings, Ed (Football Player)
New York Jets
237 Schearbrook Ln
Stevensville, MT 59870-6405, USA

Cummings, Jim (Actor)
c/o Tom Parziale *Visionary Entertainment*
1558 N Stanley Ave
West Hollywood, CA 90046-2711, USA

Cummings, John (Baseball Player)
Seattle Mariners
21 Park Paseo
Laguna Beach, CA 92677-5317, USA

Cummings, Midre (Baseball Player)
Pittsburgh Pirates
408 Denise St
Tarpon Springs, FL 34689-1967, USA

Cummings, Pat (Basketball Player)
Milwaukee Bucks
9024 Symmes Knoll Ct
Loveland, OH 45140-9330, USA

Cummings, Ralph W (Misc)
106 Darcy Dr
Clarksville, VA 23927-3524, USA

Cummings, Steve (Baseball Player)
Toronto Blue Jays
11010 Sagecrest Ln
Houston, TX 77089-3904, USA

Cummings, Terry (Basketball Player)
San Diego Clippers
1092 Jimson Cir SE
Conyers, GA 30013-2086, USA

Cummins, Barry (Hockey Player)
California Golden Seals
155 Marsden St
Kimberley, BC V1A 1G8, CANADA

Cummins, Gregory Scott (Actor)
Schiowitz/Clay/Rose
1680 Vine St Ste 1016
Los Angeles, CA 90028-8800, USA

Cummins, Peggy (Actor)
17 Brockley Road
Bexhill-on-Sea
Sussex TN39 4TT, UNITED KINGDOM
(UK)

Cumpsty, Michael (Actor)
c/o Staff Member *Innovative Artists (LA)*
1505 10th St
Santa Monica, CA 90401-2805, USA

Cundey, Dean R (Cinematographer)
344 Georgian Rd
La Canada, CA 91011-3519, USA

Cundieff, Rusty (Actor)
c/o Norman Aladjem *Paradigm (LA)*
360 N Crescent Dr
North Bldg
Beverly Hills, CA 90210-6820, USA

Cunnane, Will (Baseball Player)
San Diego Padres
24636 George Washington Dr
Plainfield, IL 60544-4421, USA

Cunneyworth, Randy (Coach, Hockey
Player)
Buffalo Sabres
1 War Memorial Sq Ste 2
Rochester Americans Attn Coaching Staff
Rochester, NY 14614-2109, USA

Cunniff, Jill (Musician)
Metropolitan Entertainment
2 Penn Plz # 2600
New York, NY 10121-0101, USA

Cunningham, Bennie L (Football Player)
Pittsburgh Steelers
PO Box 1086
Seneca, SC 29679-1086, USA

Cunningham, Bill (Musician)
Horizon Mgmt
PO Box 8770
Endwell, NY 13762-8770, USA

Cunningham, Bill (Radio Personality)
8044 Montgomery Rd Ste 650
Cincinnati, OH 45236-2959, USA

Cunningham, Doug (Football Player)
San Francisco 49ers
5060 Harling Pl
Jackson, MS 39211-4731, USA

Cunningham, Earl (Baseball Player)
7645 Garners Ferry Rd Apt 1009C
Columbia, SC 29209-3830, USA

Cunningham, Gunther (Coach, Football
Coach, Football Player)
Tennessee Titan
460 Great Circle Rd
Nashville, TN 37228-1404, USA

Cunningham, Jay (Football Player)
Boston Patriots
3617 Farland Rd
University Heights, OH 44118-3016, USA

Cunningham, Jeffrey M (Publisher)
Forbes Magazine
60 5th Ave
New York, NY 10011-8868, USA

Cunningham, Joe (Baseball Player)
St Louis Cardinals
RR 1 Box 80A
Koshkonong, MO 65692-9526, USA

Cunningham, Katherine (Actor)
c/o Jean-Pierre (JP) Henraux *Shelter
Entertainment*
9255 W Sunset Blvd Ste 1010
Los Angeles, CA 90069-3307, USA

Cunningham, Liam (Actor)
Marina Martin
12/13 Poland St
London W1V 3DE, UNITED KINGDOM
(UK)

Cunningham, Merce (Choreographer,
Dancer)
Cunningham Dance Foundation
55 Bethune St
New York, NY 10014-1791, USA

Cunningham, Michael (Writer)
Farrar Straus Giroux
19 Union Sq W Fl 11
New York, NY 10003-3304, USA

Cunningham, Randall (Football Player)
Philadelphia Eagles
365 E Robindale Rd
Las Vegas, NV 89123-1823, USA

Cunningham, Richard (Football Player)
Buffalo Bills
100 Rosewood Ct
Peachtree City, GA 30269-2237, USA

Cunningham, Richie (Football Player)
Dallas Cowboys
610 Cheyenne Dr
Houma, LA 70360-6060, USA

Cunningham, Sean (Director, Producer)
4420 Hayvenhurst Ave
Encino, CA 91436-3248, USA

Cunningham, Walter (Astronaut)
AVD
PO Box 604
Glenn Dale, MD 20769-0604, USA

Cunningham, William J (Billy) (Basketball
Player, Coach)
Philadelphia 76ers
31 Front St # 33
Conshohocken, PA 19428-2867, USA

Cuoco, Kaley (Actor)
c/o Steven Jang *SDB Partners Inc*
1801 Avenue Of The Stars Ste 902
Los Angeles, CA 90067-5981, USA

Cuomo, Christopher (Chris)
(Correspondent)
c/o Staff Member *Primetime*
147 Columbus Ave
New York, NY 10023-6503, USA

Cuomo, Jerome J (Inventor)
IBM T J Watson Research Center
PO Box 218
Yorktown Heights, NY 10598-0218, USA

Cuomo, Mario (Governor)
50 Sutton Pl S Apt 11G
New York, NY 10022-4130, USA

Cuomo, Secy Andrew
4571 7th St SW
Washington, DC 20024, USA

Cuozzo, Gary S (Football Player)
Baltimore Colts
4 Swimming River Rd
Lincroft, NJ 07738-1727, USA

Cupolo, Bill (Hockey Player)
Boston Bruins
5982 Dorchester Rd
Niagara Falls, ON L2G 5T1, CANADA

Cupp, James N (War Hero)
4904 Aspen Hill Rd
Rockville, MD 20853-3710, USA

Cura, Francesco (Actor)
c/o Staff Member *Origin Talent Agency*
4705 Laurel Canyon Blvd Ste 306
Studio City, CA 91607-5940, USA

Cura, Jose (Opera Singer)
Columbia Artists Mgmt Inc
1790 Broadway Fl 6
New York, NY 10019-1412, USA

Curatola, Vincent (Actor)
c/o Howard Axel *TMT Entertainment
Group*
648 Broadway # 1002
New York, NY 10012-2301, USA

Curb, Mike
3907 W Alameda Ave
Burbank, CA 91505-4359, USA

Curbeam, Robert L Jr (Astronaut)
15806 Virginia Fern Way
Houston, TX 77059-3002, USA

Curci, Francis (Football Player)
Dallas Cowboys
14707 Croydon Pl
Tampa, FL 33618-2160, USA

Curcillo, Anthony (Football Player)
Chicago Cardinals
23887 Corte Emerado
Murrieta, CA 92562-3539, USA

Curcio, Michael (Football Player)
Philadelphia Eagles
6035 Ken Scull Ave
Mays Landing, NJ 08330-1853, USA

Cure, Armand (Basketball Player, Football
Player)
Providence Steamrollers
4303 Petit Ave
Encino, CA 91436-3516, USA

Cure, Robert (Football Player)
Los Angeles Rams
145 Main St
Los Altos, CA 94022-2912, USA

Cure, The (Music Group)
c/o Rick Roskin *Creative Artists Agency
LCC (CAA-LA)*
2000 Avenue Of The Stars
Los Angeles, CA 90067-4700, USA

Cureton, Earl (Basketball Player)
Philadelphia 76ers
7306 Balsam Ct
West Bloomfield, MI 48322-2821, USA

Cureton, Thomas K (Misc)
501 E Washington St
Urbana, IL 61801-4320, USA

Curfman, Shannon (Musician)
Monterey International
200 W Superior St Ste 202
Chicago, IL 60610-3554, USA

Curie-Good, Louise
1317 Delresto Dr
Beverly Hills, CA 90210-2100, USA

Curl, Carolyn (Skier)
Robert U Curt
405 N Westridge Dr
Idaho Falls, ID 83402-5447, USA

Curl, Robert F Jr (Nobel Prize Laureate)
1824 Bolsover St
Houston, TX 77005-1728, USA

Curlander, Paul J (Business Person)
Lexmark International
740 W New Circle Road
Lexington, KY 40550-0001, USA

Curler, James (Business Person)
Bernis Co
222 S 9th St
Minneapolis, MN 55402-3904, USA

Curley, Bill (Basketball Player)
Detroit Pistons
377 Autumn Ave
Duxbury, MA 02332-4614, USA

Curley, Edwin M (Misc)
2645 Pin Oak Dr
Ann Arbor, MI 48103-2370, USA

Curley, John J (Publisher)
Gannett Co
1100 Wilson Blvd
Arlington, VA 22209-2249, USA

Curley, Marianne (Writer)
43 Nariah Cres
Toormina NSW 2452, AUSTRALIA

Curley, Thomas (Tom) (Publisher)
Associated Press
450 W 33rd St Fl 7
New York, NY 10001-2606, USA

Curley, Walter J P Jr (Diplomat, Financier)
885 3rd Ave # 1200
New York, NY 10022-4834, USA

Curnin, Thomas F (Attorney, Attorney General, General)
Cahill Gordon Reindel
80 Pine St
New York, NY 10005-1790, USA

Curran, Brian (Hockey Player)
Boston Bruins
3100 Deborah Dr Apt 103
Monroe, LA 71201-2092, USA

Curran, Charles E (Misc)
Southern Methodist University
Dallas Hall
Dallas, TX 75275-0001, USA

Curran, Francis (Basketball Player)
Toledo Jeeps
3 Grotto Dr
Danville, PA 17821-8112, USA

Curran, Kevin (Tennis Player)
5808 Back Ct
Austin, TX 78731-3301, USA

Curran, Mike (Hockey Player)
7615 Lanewood Ln N
Maple Grove, MN 55311-2608, USA

Curran, Pat (Football Player)
Los Angeles Rams
3195 Avenida Magoria
Escondido, CA 92029-7422, USA

Curran, Tony (Actor)
c/o Tammy Rosen *Melanie Greene Management & Productions*
425 N Robertson Blvd
West Hollywood, CA 90048-1735, USA

Currence, Lafayette (Baseball Player)
Milwaukee Brewers
1238 Stanley Dr
Rock Hill, SC 29730-5068, USA

Current, Mike (Football Player)
Miami Dolphins
593 Lone Oak Loop
Silverton, OR 97381-1472, USA

Currey, Francis S (War Hero)
106 Catfish Landing Cir
Bonneau, SC 29431-8604, USA

Currie, Bill (Baseball Player)
Washington Senators
125 Lakeside Dr SW
Arlington, GA 39813, USA

Currie, Cherie (Actor, Musician)
Times Productions
520 Washington Blvd # 199
Marina Del Rey, CA 90292, USA

Currie, Daniel (Dan) (Football Player)
Green Bay Packers
2801 Wyandotte St Apt 15
Las Vegas, NV 89102-6413, USA

Currie, Gordon (Actor)
c/o Jennifer Goldhar *Characters Talent Agency, The (Toronto)*
8 Elm St 3rd FL
Toronto, ON M5G 1G7, CANADA

Currie, Louise (Actor)
1317 Delresto Dr
Beverly Hills, CA 90210-2100, USA

Currie, Malcolm R (Business Person)
Hughes Aircraft Co
PO Box 956
El Segundo, CA 90245-0956, USA

Currie, Nancy J (Astronaut)
1863 Bending Stream Dr
League City, TX 77573-3699, USA

Currie, Sondra (Actor)
3951 Longridge Ave
Sherman Oaks, CA 91423-4923, USA

Currier, William (Football Player)
Houston Oilers
8661 Monticello Rd
Columbia, SC 29203-9706, USA

Currin, James A (Football Player)
Baltimore Colts
383 Cedarbrook Ct
Venice, FL 34292-4623, USA

Currin, Perry (Baseball Player)
St Louis Browns
818 Amberstone Dr
San Antonio, TX 78258-2345, USA

Currington, Billy (Musician)
c/o Staff Member *Universal Music Group (TN)*
60 Music Sq E
Nashville, TN 37203-4325, USA

Curris, Constantine W (Educator)
Clemson University
President's Office
Sikes Hall
Clemson, SC 29634-0001, USA

Curry, Adrianna (Actor, Model)
c/o Phil Viardo *The Viardo Agency*
6740 Franklin Pl Apt 206
Los Angeles, CA 90028-4516, USA

Curry, Alana (Actor)
PO Box 1852
Burbank, CA 91507-1852, USA

Curry, Anne (Anchor, Correspondent)
c/o Staff Member *Today Show, The*
30 Rockefeller Plz # 374E
New York, NY 10112-0015, USA

Curry, Bill (Coach, Football Coach, Football Player)
Green Bay Packers
4007 Penhurst Dr
Marietta, GA 30062-6162, USA

Curry, Buddy (Football Player)
Atlanta Falcons
4407 Trestle Way
Buford, GA 30518-6055, USA

Curry, Craig (Football Player)
Tampa Bay Buccaneers
3210 Amber Forest Dr
Houston, TX 77068-2005, USA

Curry, Dell (Basketball Player)
8381 Providence Rd
Charlotte, NC 28277-9753, USA

Curry, Dell (Basketball Player)
Utah Jazz
Paine Run Rd
Grottoes, VA 24441, USA

Curry, Denise (Basketball Player, Coach)
San Jose Lasers
230 California St Ste 510
San Francisco, CA 94111-4331, USA

Curry, Don 'DC' (Actor)
c/o Staff Member *Gersh Agency, The (LA)*
232 N Canon Dr
Beverly Hills, CA 90210-5302, USA

Curry, Donald (Boxer)
3621 Vancouver Dr
Fort Worth, TX 76119-2277, USA

Curry, Eddy (Basketball Player)
Chicago Bulls
1901 W Madison St
United Center
Chicago, IL 60612-2459, USA

Curry, Eric F (Football Player)
Tampa Bay Buccaneers
4555 Swilcan Bridge Ln N
Jacksonville, FL 32224-5618, USA

Curry, Floyd (Hockey Player)
Montreal Canadiens
Too III To Sign Autographs
Montreal, PQ H3X 2P6, CANADA

Curry, Mark (Actor)
c/o Ben Feigin *Nine Yards Entertainment*
8530 Wilshire Blvd Fl 5
Beverly Hills, CA 90211-3102, USA

Curry, Mike (Basketball Player)
Philadelphia 76ers
2880 Wells Dr
Augusta, GA 30906-5373, USA

Curry, Stephen (Actor)
c/o Robyn Gardiner *RGM Associates (Australia)*
PO Box 128
Surry Hills NSW 2010, AUSTRALIA

Curry, Steve (Baseball Player)
Boston Red Sox
10725 Obee Rd
Whitehouse, OH 43571-9250, USA

Curry, Tim (Actor)
c/o Ben Press *Innovative Artists (LA)*
1505 10th St
Santa Monica, CA 90401-2805, USA

Curry, Tony (Baseball Player)
Philadelphia Phillies
PO Box 7054
Nassau, BAHAMAS

Curtin, David S (Journalist)
Colorado Springs Gazette Telegraph
30 S Prospect St
Colorado Springs, CO 80903-3638, USA

Curtin, David Y (Misc)
12114 Lakewood Ct
Fort Myers, FL 33908-2833, USA

Curtin, Jane T (Actor)
International Creative Mgmt
8942 Wilshire Blvd # 219
Beverly Hills, CA 90211-1908, USA

Curtin, John J Jr (Attorney, Attorney General, General)
Bingham Dana Gould
150 Federal St Fl 15
Boston, MA 02110-1726, USA

Curtin, Valeria (Actor)
Writers & Artists
360 N Crescent Dr Bldg North
Beverly Hills, CA 90210-6818, USA

Curtin, Valerie
15622 Meadowgate Rd
Encino, CA 91436-3431, USA

Curtis, Ben (Actor)
c/o Staff Member *Abrams Artists Agency (NY)*
275 7th Ave Fl 26
New York, NY 10001-6708, USA

Curtis, Ben (Golfer)
26 N Main St
Ostrander, OH 43061-9660, USA

Curtis, Chad (Baseball Player)
California Angels
1400 Buttrick Ave SE
Ada, MI 49301-9614, USA

Curtis, Cuneo Ann E (Swimmer)
35 Golden Hinde Blvd
San Rafael, CA 94903-3816, USA

Curtis, Don (Wrestler)
920 Middleton Rd
Jacksonville, FL 32211-6273, USA

Curtis, Isaac F (Football Player)
Cincinnati Bengals
711 Clinton Springs Ave
Cincinnati, OH 45229-1300, USA

Curtis, J Michael (Mike) (Football Player)
Baltimore Colts
7917 Rivers Fall Dr
Potomac, MD 20854, USA

Curtis, Jack (Baseball Player)
Chicago Cubs
4949 Ike Starnes Rd
Granite Falls, NC 28630-8631, USA

Curtis, Jamie Lee (Actor)
c/o Rick Kurtzman *Creative Artists Agency LCC (CAA-LA)*
2000 Avenue Of The Stars
Los Angeles, CA 90067-4700, USA

Curtis, John (Baseball Player)
Boston Red Sox
1800 Roundhill Rd Apt 1207
Charleston, WV 25314-1559, USA

Curtis, Kelly (Actor)
651 N Kilkea Dr
Los Angeles, CA 90048-2213, USA

Curtis, Kenneth M (Diplomat, Governor)
Curtis Thaxter
1 Canal Plz Ste 1000
Portland, ME 04101-6407, USA

Curtis, King (Baseball Player)
St Louis Cardinals
2538 Beechwood Dr
Vineland, NJ 08361-2932, USA

Curtis, Richard (Writer)
c/o Staff Member *Peters Fraser & Dunlop
(PFD - UK)*
Drury House
34-43 Russell St
London WC2B 5HA, UNITED KINGDOM
(UK)

Curtis, Robert (Actor)
c/o Staff Member *Bauman Redanty &
Shaul Agency*
5757 Wilshire Blvd Ste 473
Los Angeles, CA 90036-3632, USA

Curtis, Robin (Actor)
1147 Beverly Hill Dr
Cincinnati, OH 45208-4323, USA

Curtis, Todd (Actor)
2046 14th St Apt 10
Santa Monica, CA 90405-1641, USA

Curtis, Tony (Actor)
c/o Susan Weaving *William Morris
Agency (WMA-LA)*
1 William Morris Pl
Beverly Hills, CA 90212-4261, USA

Curtola, Bobby (Musician)
ESP Productions
720 Spadina Ave
#PH2
Toronto, ON M5S 2T9, CANADA

Cusack, Ann (Actor)
Innovative Artists
1505 10th St
Santa Monica, CA 90401-2805, USA

Cusack, Joan (Actor, Comedian)
c/o Tracey Jacobs *United Talent Agency
(UTA)*
9560 Wilshire Blvd Ste 500
Beverly Hills, CA 90212-2401, USA

Cusack, John (Actor)
c/o Staff Member *New Crime Productions*
555 Rose Ave
Venice, CA 90291-8656, USA

Cusack, Sinead (Actor)
Markham & Froggatt Julian House
4 Windmill St.
London W1P 1HF, UNITED KINGDOM
(UK)

Cushenan, Ian (Hockey Player)
Chicago Blackhawks
4014 Dryden Dr
North Olmsted, OH 44070-1928, USA

Cushing, Matt (Football Player)
Pittsburgh Steelers
1027 Adelia St
Downers Grove, IL 60516-2832, USA

Cushman, David W (Misc)
20 Lake Shore Dr
Princeton Junction, NJ 08550-4906, USA

Cushman, Karen (Writer)
Clarion Books
215 Park Ave S
New York, NY 10003-1603, USA

Cussler, Clive (Writer)
c/o Staff Member *Peter Lampack Agency*
551 5th Ave Rm 1613
New York, NY 10176-0187, USA

Cust, Jack (Baseball Player)
Arizona Diamondbacks
145 Route 31 N
Pennington, NJ 08534-3615, USA

Custom (Musician)
ArtistDirect
1601 Cloverfield Blvd # 400
Santa Monica, CA 90404-4082, USA

Cutcliffe, David (Coach, Football Coach)
University of Mississippi
Athletic Dept
University, MS 38677, USA

Cuthbert, Elisha (Actor)
c/o John Carrabino *John Carrabino
Management*
5900 Wilshire Blvd Ste 406
Los Angeles, CA 90036-5015, USA

Cuthbert, Randy (Football Player)
Pittsburgh Steelers
406 Longleaf Dr
Perkasie, PA 18944-5413, USA

Cuthbeth, Elizabeth (Betty) (Athlete,
Track Athlete)
4/7 Karara Close
Halls Head
Mandurah, WA 6210, AUSTRALIA

Cutler, Alexander M (Business Person)
Eaton Corp
1111 Superior Ave E
Eaton Center
Cleveland, OH 44114-2535, USA

Cutler, Bruce (Attorney, Attorney General,
General)
41 Madison Ave
New York, NY 10010-2202, USA

Cutler, Walter L (Diplomat)
Meridian International Center
1630 Crescent Pl NW
Washington, DC 20009-4004, USA

Cutliffe, Molly (Actor)
Herney/Grimes
PO Box 64249
Los Angeles, CA 90064-0249, USA

Cutrufello, Mary (Musician, Songwriter,
Writer)
Joe's Garage
4405 Belmont Park Ter
Nashville, TN 37215-3609, USA

Cutsinger, Gary (Football Player)
Houston Oilers
210 N River Hills Rd
Austin, TX 78733-3403, USA

Cutter, Kiki (Skier)
PO Box 1317
Carbondale, CO 81623-1317, USA

Cutter, Lise (Actor)
PO Box 2665
Sag Harbor, NY 11963-0119, USA

Cutter, Slade D (Football Player)
9214 River Crescent Dr
Annapolis, MD 21401-7770, USA

Cutts, Don (Hockey Player)
Edmonton Oilers
19966 Sommette Dr
Sonora, CA 95370, USA

Cuviello, Peter M (General)
Director
Defence Information Systems Agency
Alington, VA 22204, USA

Cuyler, Milt (Baseball Player)
Detroit Tigers
962 Lamar Rd
Macon, GA 31210-7109, USA

Cverko, Andy (Football Player)
Green Bay Packers
6018 N Winthrop Ave
Chicago, IL 60660-2624, USA

Cwiklinski, Stanley (Athlete)
2840 Maple St
San Diego, CA 92104-4940, USA

Cypher, John
9229 W Sunset Blvd Ste 315
Los Angeles, CA 90069-3403, USA

Cypher, Jon (Actor)
498 Manzanita Ave
Ventura, CA 93001-2227, USA

Cyphers, Charles
324 E 1st St Ste 300
Los Angeles, CA 90012-3850, USA

Cypress, Tawny
c/o Staff Member *Abrams Artists Agency
(NY)*
275 7th Ave Fl 26
New York, NY 10001-6708, USA

Cypress Hill (Music Group)
c/o Staff Member *William Morris Agency
(WMA-LA)*
1 William Morris Pl
Beverly Hills, CA 90212-4261, USA

Cyr, Conrad K (Judge)
US Courts of Appeals
PO Box 635
Bangor, ME 04402-0635, USA

Cyr, Denis (Hockey Player)
Calgary Flames
9816 N Townsend Dr
Peoria, IL 61615-1388, USA

Cyr, Paul (Hockey Player)
Buffalo Sabres
5064 Richardson Rd
Port Alberni, BC V9Y 5R8, CANADA

Cyrus, Billy Ray (Musician, Songwriter,
Writer)
c/o Staff Member *Cunningham Escott
Slevin & Doherty (LA)*
10635 Santa Monica Blvd Ste 130
Los Angeles, CA 90025-8306, USA

Cyrus, Miley (Actor, Musician)
c/o Meghan Prophet *PMK/HBH Public
Relations (PMK-LA)*
700 N San Vicente Blvd Ste G910
West Hollywood, CA 90069-5061, USA

Czajkowski, Jim (Baseball Player)
Colorado Rockies
1648 Rivergate Dr
Sevierville, TN 37862-9321, USA

Czapsky, Stefan (Cinematographer)
RR 3 Box 278
Unadilla, NY 13849, USA

Czerny, Henry (Actor)
c/o Perry Zimel *Oscars Abrams Zimel &
Associates*
438 Queen St E
Toronto, ON M5A 1T4, CANADA

Czrongursky, Jan (Prime Minister)
Prime Minister's Office
Nam Slobody 1
Bratislava 81370, SLOVAKIA

Czuchry, Matt (Actor)
c/o Jeff Golenberg *The Collective*
9100 Wilshire Blvd # 700 W
Beverly Hills, CA 90212-3401, USA

Czyz, Bobby (Boxer)
110 Pennsylvania Ave
Flemington, NJ 08822-1202, USA

D, Deezer (Actor)
c/o Staff Member *Acme Talent & Literary
(LA)*
4727 Wilshire Blvd Ste 333
Los Angeles, CA 90010-3874, USA

D-12 (Musician)
Evolution Talent Agency
1776 Broadway Fl 15
New York, NY 10019-2002, USA

D12 (Music Group)
c/o Staff Member *William Morris Agency
(WMA-NY)*
1325 Avenue Of The Americas
New York, NY 10019-6026, USA

Da Band (Music Group)
c/o Staff Member *Bad Boy Worldwide
Entertainment*
1710 Broadway
New York, NY 10019-5254, USA

Da Brat (Musician)
c/o Staff Member *William Morris Agency
(WMA-LA)*
1 William Morris Pl
Beverly Hills, CA 90212-4261, USA

Daal, Omar (Baseball Player)
Los Angeles Dodgers
2458 Provence Ct
Weston, FL 33327-1304, USA

Daanen, Jerome (Football Player)
St Louis Cardinals
1011 S Erie St
De Pere, WI 54115-3109, USA

D'Abaldo, Chris (Musician)
Helter Skelter Plaza
535 Kings Road
London SW10 0S, UNITED KINGDOM
(UK)

Daberko, David A (Financier)
National City Corp
1900 E 9th St
National City Center
Cleveland, OH 44114-3484, USA

Dabich, Mike (Basketball Player)
Oakland Oaks
464 S Indiana Ave
Hudson, WY 82515, USA

Dabney, Carlton (Football Player)
Atlanta Falcons
2522 Northumberland Ave
Richmond, VA 23220-1504, USA

D'Abo, Maryam (Actor)
Artist Independent
32 Tavistock St
London WC2E 7PB, UNITED KINGDOM
(UK)

D'Abo, Olivia (Actor)
c/o Sam Maydew *The Collective*
9100 Wilshire Blvd # 700 W
Beverly Hills, CA 90212-3401, USA

Dacascos, Mark (Actor)
c/o Eric Nelson *Jaymes & Company*
12444 Ventura Blvd Ste 103
Studio City, CA 91604-2409, USA

D'Acquisto, John F (Baseball Player)
1441 Santa Lucia Rd Unit 615
Chula Vista, CA 91913-3600, USA

Dacruz Policarpo, Jose Cardinal
(Religious Leader)
Curia Patriarcal
Camo dos Martires da Patria 45
Lisbon 1150, PORTUGAL

Dacus, Don (Actor)
8455 Fountain Ave Apt 512
Los Angeles, CA 90069-2543, USA

Daddario, Alex (Actor)
c/o Jerry Shandrew *Shandrew Public Relations*
1050 S Stanley Ave
Los Angeles, CA 90019-6634, USA

Dade, Paul (Baseball Player)
c/o Staff Member *Anaheim Angels*
2000 E Gene Autry Way
Edison Field
Anaheim, CA 92806-6143, USA

Dadswell, Doug (Hockey Player)
Calgary Flames
Box 13 Site 7 RR 1
De Winton, AB T0L 0X0, CANADA

Daehlie, Bjorn (Skier)
Cathinka Guldbergs Veg 64
Holler 2034, NORWAY

Daetweiler, Louella (Baseball Player)
415 S Poplar Ave
Brea, CA 92821-6650, USA

Daffer, Ted (Football Player)
Chicago Bears
2176 McCurdy Rd
Stone Mountain, GA 30087-1324, USA

Dafoe, Willem (Actor)
c/o Frank Frattaroli *Widescreen Management*
270 Lafayette St Ste 402
New York, NY 10012-3327, USA

Daft, Douglas (Business Person)
Coca Cola Co
310 North Ave NW
1 Coca Cola Plaza
Atlanta, GA 30313-2499, USA

Daft, Kevin (Football Player)
Tennessee Titans
13781 Grovesite Dr
Santa Ana, CA 92705, USA

Daggett, Timothy (Tim) (Gymnast)
134 Country Club Dr
East Longmeadow, MA 01028-5807, USA

D'Agosto, Nicholas (Actor)
c/o Faras Rabadi *Emerald Talent Group*
6464 W Sunset Blvd
Los Angeles, CA 90028-8001, USA

Dagres, Angie (Baseball Player)
Baltimore Orioles
PO Box 27
Rowley, MA 01969-0027, USA

Dagworthy Prew, Wendy A (Designer, Fashion Designer)
18 Melrose Terrace
London W6, UNITED KINGDOM (UK)

Dahl, Arlene
PO Box 116
Sparkill, NY 10976-0116, USA

Dahl, Christopher (Educator)
State University of New York College
President's Office
Genesco, NY 14454, USA

Dahl, John (Director, Writer)
c/o Jason Spitz *Endeavor Agency LLC (LA)*
9601 Wilshire Blvd Fl 3
Beverly Hills, CA 90210-5204, USA

Dahl, Lawrence F (Misc)
4817 Woodburn Dr
Madison, WI 53711-1345, USA

Dahl, Sophie (Actor, Model)
Storm Model Mgmt
5 Jubilee Place
London SW3, UNITED KINGDOM (UK)

Dahlbeck, Eva
Box 27126
Stockholm 102 52, SWEDEN

Dahlberg, A William (Business Person)
Southern Co
270 Peachtree St NW
Atlanta, GA 30303-1283, USA

Dahlberg, Kenneth H (Ken) (War Hero)
19360 Walden Trl
Wayzata, MN 55391-3548, USA

Dahlen, Ulf (Hockey Player)
New York Rangers
Vinbarsvagen 17
Ostersund, SWEDEN

Dahler, Ed (Basketball Player)
Philadelphia Warriors
511 E Tremont St
Hillsboro, IL 62049-1801, USA

Dahlke, Jerry (Baseball Player)
Chicago White Sox
201 S Pine Lake Dr
Batesville, MS 38606, USA

Dahlquist, Chris (Hockey Player)
Pittsburgh Penguins
10859 Purdey Rd
Eden Prairie, MN 55347-5236, USA

Dahm, Jaclyn (Actor)
c/o Amy Godsick *Candy Entertainment Management*
8981 W Sunset Blvd Ste 310
West Hollywood, CA 90069-1848, USA

Dahm, Nicole (Actor, Model)
c/o Amy Godsick *Candy Entertainment Management*
8981 W Sunset Blvd Ste 310
West Hollywood, CA 90069-1848, USA

Dahm, Werner K (Misc)
106 Sadie Spring Ct NW
Huntsville, AL 35806-6000, USA

Dahrendorf, Ralf Gustav
Postfach 5560
Konstanz D-78434, GERMANY

Dai, Ailian (Choreographer, Dancer)
Hua Qiao Gong Yu #2-16
Hua Yuan Cun
Hai Dian, Beijing 100044, CHINA

Dai, Sijie (Writer)
c/o Staff Member *Knopf Publishing Group*
1745 Broadway
New York, NY 10019-4305, USA

Daiches, David (Writer)
22 Belgrave Crescent
Edinburgh EH4 3AL, SCOTLAND

Daigle, Alain (Hockey Player)
Chicago Blackhawks
3510 Rue de Bordeaux
Trois-Rivieres-Ouest, PQ G8Y 3P7, CANADA

Daigle, Alexander (Hockey Player)
3510 Rue Bordeaux
Trois-Rivieres-Quest, PQ G8Y 3P7, CANADA

Daigneault, J J (Hockey Player)
Minnesota Wild
175 Kellogg Blvd W
Xcel Energy Arena
Saint Paul, MN 55102-1206, USA

Dailey, Bill (Baseball Player)
Cleveland Indians
5019 Meadow Way
Dublin, VA 24084-5721, USA

Dailey, Bob (Hockey Player)
Vancouver Canucks
130 7th Ave # A
Haddon Heights, NJ 08035-1622, USA

Dailey, Peter H (Diplomat)
State Department
2201 C St NW
Washington, DC 20520-0099, USA

Dailey, Quintin (Basketball Player)
22808 Hilton Head Dr Unit 28
Diamond Bar, CA 91765-2264, USA

Dailey, Quintin (Basketball Player)
Chicago Bulls
2678 S Decatur Blvd Apt 108
Las Vegas, NV 89102-8941, USA

Daily, Bill (Actor)
1331 Park Ave SW Unit 802
Albuquerque, NM 87102-2855, USA

Daily, Gretchen (Misc)
Stanford University
Ecology Dept
Stanford, CA 94305, USA

Daily, Parker (Religious Leader)
Baptist Bible Fellowship International
PO Box 191
Springfield, MO 65801-0191, USA

Daingerfield, Michael (Actor)
c/o Staff Member *Kirk Talent Agencies Inc*
1006 Beach Ave 8th Floor
Vancouver, BC V6E 1T7, CANADA

Dainton, Frederick S (Misc)
Fieldside
Water Eaton Lane
Kidlington, Oxford OX5 2PR, UNITED KINGDOM (UK)

Daio, Norberto J D C A (Prime Minister)
Prime Minister's Office
CP 38
Sao Tome, SAO TOME & PRINCIPE

Dajani, Nadia (Actor)
Innovative Artists
1505 10th St
Santa Monica, CA 90401-2805, USA

Dal Canton, Bruce (Baseball Player)
Pittsburgh Pirates
624 Ray Dr
Carnegie, PA 15106-1808, USA

Daland, Peter (Coach)
PO Box 2443
Aquebogue, NY 11931-2443, USA

Dalbavie, Andre (Composer)
Van Walsum Mgmt
4 Addison Bridge Place
London W14 8XP, UNITED KINGDOM (UK)

Dalberto, Michel (Musician)
13 Blvd Henri Plumof
Vevey 1800, SWITZERLAND

Daldry, Stephen (Director)
Royal Court Theater
Sloane Square
London SW1, UNITED KINGDOM (UK)

Dale, Alan (Actor)
c/o Holly Lebed *Himber Entertainment Inc*
15760 Ventura Blvd Ste 700
Encino, CA 91436-3016, USA

Dale, Bruce (Photographer)
National Geographic Magazine
1145 17th St NW
Washington, DC 20036-4688, USA

Dale, Carroll W (Football Player)
Los Angeles Rams
1 College Ave
Wise, VA 24293-4400, USA

Dale, Dick
PO Box 1713
Twentynine Palms, CA 92277-1000, USA

Dale, James Badge (Actor)
c/o Chris Schmidt *Paradigm (LA)*
360 N Crescent Dr
North Bldg
Beverly Hills, CA 90210-6820, USA

Dale, Jim (Actor)
Mark Sendroff
230 W 56th St # 63B
New York, NY 10019-4306, USA

Dale, Roland (Football Player)
Washington Redskins
128 Bridlewood Dr
Brandon, MS 39047-8410, USA

Dale, William B (Economist, Government Official)
9707 Old Georgetown Rd Apt 2201
Bethesda, MD 20814-1755, USA

Dale & Grace (Music Group)
Sea Cruise Productions
PO Box 1875
Gretna, LA 70054-1875, USA

D'Alema, Massima (Prime Minister)
Prime Minister's Office
Piazza Colomma 370
Rome 00187, ITALY

Dalembert, Samuel (Basketball Player)
Philadelphia 76ers
3601 S Broad St
1st Union Center
Philadelphia, PA 19148-5287, USA

Dalena, Pete (Baseball Player)
Cleveland Indians
4951 N Thorne Ave
Fresno, CA 93704-2935, USA

D'Aleo, Angelo (Musician)
Paramount Entertainment
PO Box 12
Far Hills, NJ 07931-0012, USA

Dales-Schuman, Stacey (Basketball Player)
Washington Mystics
601 F St NW
Mci Center
Washington, DC 20004-1605, USA

Dalesandro, Mark (Baseball Player)
California Angels
1908 Arbor Fields Dr
Plainfield, IL 60586-5729, USA

D'Alessio, Diana (Golfer)
6955 Nunn Rd
Lakeland, FL 33813-3821, USA

Daley, Joe (Hockey Player)
Pittsburgh Penguins
Joe Daley's Cards 666 St James St
Winnipeg, MB R3G 3J6, CANADA

Daley, John (Golfer)
c/o Staff Member *Pro Golfers Assoc of America (PGA)*
100 Avenue Of The Champions
Palm Beach Gardens, FL 33418-3653, USA

Daley, John Francis (Actor)
c/o Ruth Young *Peters Fraser & Dunlop (PFD - UK)*
Drury House
34-43 Russell St
London WC2B 5HA, UNITED KINGDOM (UK)

Daley, Patrick (Hockey Player)
Winnipeg Jets
118 Mount Olive Dr
Toronto, ON M9V 2E2, CANADA

Daley, Pete (Baseball Player)
Boston Red Sox
4019 Calle Mira Monte
Newbury Park, CA 91320-1932, USA

Daley, Richard M (Politician)
Mayor's Office
121 N Lasalle St
City Hall
Chicago, IL 60602-1279, USA

Daley, Rosle (Chef, Writer)
Harpo Productions
110 N Carpenter St
Chicago, IL 60607-2146, USA

Daley, William N (Bill) (Secretary)
SBC Communications
175 E Houston
San Antonio, TX 78205-2255, USA

Dalgarno, Brad (Hockey Player)
New York Islanders
1146 Fairfield Pl
Oakville, ON L6M 2L9, CANADA

Dalgilsh, Kenneth M (Kenny) (Soccer Player)
FC Newcastle United
Saint James Park
Newcastle-on-Tyne NE1 4ST, UNITED KINGDOM (UK)

Dalheimer, Patrick (Musician)
Freedman & Smith
350 W End Ave Apt 1
New York, NY 10024-6818, USA

Dalhousie, Simon R (Government Official)
Brechin Castle
Brechin DD9 6SH, SCOTLAND

Dali, Bobby (Musician)
H K Mgmt
9200 W Sunset Blvd Ste 530
Los Angeles, CA 90069-3509, USA

Dali, Tracy (Actor, Model)
PO Box 69541
Los Angeles, CA 90069-0541, USA

Dalian, Susan (Actor)
c/o Staff Member *GVA Talent Agency Inc*
9229 W Sunset Blvd Ste 320
Los Angeles, CA 90069-3403, USA

Dalie, Beatrice (Actor)
Artmedia
20 Ave Rapp
Paris 75007, FRANCE

Dalis, Irene (Opera Singer)
1731 Cherry Grove Dr
San Jose, CA 95125-5512, USA

Dalkas, Nicole (Golfer)
288 Green Mountain Dr
Palm Desert, CA 92211-3246, USA

Dalkowski, Steve (Baseball Player)
55 Grand St
Walnut Hill Care Center
New Britain, CT 06052-2021, USA

Dallafior, Ken (Football Player)
San Diego Chargers
721 Harry Paul Dr
Lake Orion, MI 48362-2840, USA

Dallas, Matt (Actor)
c/o Jason Weinberg *Untitled Entertainment (LA)*
331 N Maple Dr Fl 3
Beverly Hills, CA 90210-3827, USA

Dallas Cowboys Cheerleaders
1 Cowboys Pkwy
Irving, TX 75063-4924, USA

Dallesandro, Joe (Actor)
521 W Briar Pl Apt 505
Chicago, IL 60657-4655, USA

Dallman, Marty (Hockey Player)
Toronto Maple Leafs
3843 Main St
Niagara Falls, ON L2G 6B4, CANADA

Dalm, Jan
DALM
Dv de Merwedestraat
HI Ambacht
GB 3341, THE NETHERLANDS

Dalmacci, Ricardo (Actor)
c/o Gabriel Blanco *Gabriel Blanco Iglesias (Mexico)*
Rio Balsas 35-32
Colonia Cuauhtemoc
DF 06500, MEXICO

Dalrymple, Clay (Baseball Player)
Philadelphia Phillies
28248 Mateer Rd
Gold Beach, OR 97444-9618, USA

Dalrymple, Gary B (Misc)
1847 NW Hillcrest Dr
Corvallis, OR 97330-1859, USA

Dalton, Audrey (Actor)
2241 Labrusca
Mission Viejo, CA 92692, USA

Dalton, James E (General)
61 Misty Acres Rd
Rolling Hills Estates, CA 90274-5749, USA

Dalton, John H (Government Official)
3710 University Ave NW
Washington, DC 20016-5618, USA

Dalton, Kristin (Actor)
c/o Bob McGowan *McGowan Management*
8733 W Sunset Blvd Ste 103
W Hollywood, CA 90069-2241, USA

Dalton, Lacy J (Musician)
820 Cartwright Rd
Reno, NV 89521-7134, USA

Dalton, Lional (Football Player)
Baltimore Ravens
11907 Hunting Tweed Dr
Owings Mills, MD 21117-1528, USA

Dalton, Mike (Baseball Player)
Detroit Tigers
354 Flynn Ave
Mountain View, CA 94043-3923, USA

Dalton, Nic (Musician)
Agency Group Ltd
1775 Broadway Ste 515
New York, NY 10019-1903, USA

Dalton, Nicole (Actor)
c/o Staff Member *McKeon-Valeo-Myones Management*
9100 Wilshire Blvd Ste 350W
Beverly Hills, CA 90212-3437, USA

Dalton, Oakley (Football Player)
New Orleans Saints
715 Harpertown Ln
Tunnel Hill, IL 62972-3329, USA

Dalton, Timothy (Actor)
c/o Michael Black *Michael Black Management*
9701 Wilshire Blvd Ste 1000
Beverly Hills, CA 90212-2010, USA

Daltrey, Roger (Actor)
c/o Darryl Marshak *Marshak/Zachary Company, The*
8840 Wilshire Blvd Fl 1
Beverly Hills, CA 90211-2606, USA

Daltry, Roger (Actor, Musician)
Conway Van Gelder Robinson
18-21 Jermyn St
London SW1Y 6NB, UNITED KINGDOM (UK)

Daluiso, Brad (Football Player)
Atlanta Falcons
13258 Glencliff Way
San Diego, CA 92130-1309, USA

Daly, Cahal Brendan Cardinal (Religious Leader)
Ard Mhacha
23 Rosetta Ave
Belfast BT7 3HG, NORTHERN IRELAND

Daly, Carson (Television Host)
Last Call with Carson Daly
3000 W Alameda Ave
Bungalow 1600
Burbank, CA 91523-0001, USA

Daly, Charles J (Chuck) (Coach)
18586 SE Village Cir
Tequesta, FL 33469-1724, USA

Daly, John (Golfer)
10093 Par St
Dardanelle, AR 72834-8793, USA

Daly, John (Producer)
Hemdale
7960 Beverly Blvd
Los Angeles, CA 90048, USA

Daly, Michael J (War Hero)
155 Redding Rd
Fairfield, CT 06824-1932, USA

Daly, Rad (Actor)
c/o Staff Member *Brady Brannon & Rich*
5670 Wilshire Blvd Ste 820
Los Angeles, CA 90036-5613, USA

Daly, Robert (Baseball Player)
Los Angeles Dodgers
10779 Bellagio Rd
Los Angeles, CA 90077-3731, USA

Daly, Tess (Television Host)
c/o Staff Member *John Noel Management*
10A Belmont St
Floor 2
London NW1 8HH, UNITED KINGDOM (UK)

Daly, Tim (Actor, Producer)
c/o Staff Member *Red House Entertainment*
22287 Mulholland Hwy # 129
Calabasas, CA 91302-5157, USA

Daly, Timothy (Actor)
Industry Entertainment
955 Carrillo Dr Ste 300
Los Angeles, CA 90048-5400, USA

Daly, Tyne (Actor)
c/o Doug Wald *Raw Talent Management*
9615 Brighton Way Ste 300
Beverly Hills, CA 90210-5118, USA

Daly-Donofrio, Heather (Golfer)
1524 Bronson Rd
Fairfield, CT 06824-2828, USA

Dam, Kenneth W (Attorney, Attorney General, General, Government Official)
University of Chicago
1111 E 60th St
Law School
Chicago, IL 60637-2776, USA

Damadian, Raymond V (Inventor)
FONAR Corp
110 Marcus Dr
Melville, NY 11747-4292, USA

Damageplan (Music Group)
2706 Monterrey St
Arlington, TX 76015-1323, USA

Damanchiah, Godfrey (Actor, Comedian)
c/o Brian Stern *William Morris Agency (WMA-NY)*
1325 Avenue Of The Americas
New York, NY 10019-6026, USA

Damas, Bertila (Actor)
PO Box 17193
Beverly Hills, CA 90209-3193, USA

Damasio, Antonio R (Doctor)
University of Iowa Hospital
Neurology Dept
Iowa City, IA 52242, USA

Damaska, Jack (Baseball Player)
St Louis Cardinals
252 Blackhawk Rd
Beaver Falls, PA 15010-1404, USA

D'Amato, Mike (Football Player)
New York Jets
7 Lansing Ln
East Northport, NY 11731-5325, USA

DaMatta, Cristiano (Race Car Driver)
Newman-Haas Racing
50 Tower Parkway
Lincolnshire, IL 60069, USA

D'Amboise, Jacques (Choreographer, Dancer)
National Dance Institute
594 Broadway Rm 805
New York, NY 10012-3257, USA

D'Ambrosio, Dominick (Misc)
Allied Industrial Workers Union
3520 W Oklahoma Ave
Milwaukee, WI 53215-4175, USA

Dameshek, David (Actor, Writer)
c/o Staff Member *Creative Artists Agency LCC (CAA-LA)*
2000 Avenue Of The Stars
Los Angeles, CA 90067-4700, USA

Damian, Alexa (Actor)
c/o Staff Member *Televisa*
Blvd Adolfo Lopez Mateos 232
Colonia San Angel INN
DF CP 01060, MEXICO

Damian, Michael (Actor, Musician)
Gold Marshak Liedtke
3500 W Olive Ave Ste 1400
Burbank, CA 91505-5512, USA

Damiani, Damiano (Director)
Via Delle Terme Deciane 2
Rome 00153, ITALY

D'Amico, Jeff (Baseball Player)
6903 Cedar Ridge Dr
Pinellas Park, FL 33781-4904, USA

D'Amico, William D (Athlete)
30 Greenwood St
Lake Placid, NY 12946-1214, USA

Damkroger, Maury (Football Player)
New England Patriots
1722 S 166th Cir
Omaha, NE 68108-1502, USA

Dammerman, Dennis D (Business Person)
General Electric Co
3135 Easton Tumpike
Fairfield, CT 06828-0001, USA

Damon, Johnny D (Baseball Player)
c/o Team Member *New York Yankees*
Yankee Stadium
161st St & River Ave
Bronx, NY 10451, USA

Damon, Mark (Actor)
2781 Benedict Canyon Dr
Beverly Hills, CA 90210-1024, USA

Damon, Matt (Actor)
c/o Patrick Whitesell *Endeavor Agency LLC (LA)*
9601 Wilshire Blvd Fl 3
Beverly Hills, CA 90210-5204, USA

Damon, Stuart (Actor)
387 N Van Ness Ave
Los Angeles, CA 90004, USA

Damon, Una (Actor)
Writer's & Artists
360 N Crescent Dr Bldg North
Beverly Hills, CA 90210-6818, USA

Damone, Vic (Actor, Musician)
c/o Staff Member *International Ventures*
25864 Tournament Rd Ste L
Valencia, CA 91355-2375, USA

Damore, John (Football Player)
Chicago Bears
332 Gatesby Rd
Riverside, IL 60546-1616, USA

Dampier, Erick (Basketball Player)
Indiana Pacers
18724 Wainsborough Ln
Dallas, TX 75287-5525, USA

Dampier, Louie (Basketball Player)
Kentucky Colonels
2808 New Moody Ln
La Grange, KY 40031-9453, USA

Dampler, Erick (Basketball Player)
2635 Sea View Parkway
Alameda, CA 94502, USA

Damron, Robert (Golfer)
6001 Masters Blvd
Orlando, FL 32819-4303, USA

Damus, Mike (Actor)
c/o Staff Member *United Talent Agency (UTA)*
9560 Wilshire Blvd Ste 500
Beverly Hills, CA 90212-2401, USA

Dan-Jumbo, Andrew (Reality TV Star)
c/o Staff Member *The Learning Channel (TLC)*
7700 Wisconsin Ave
Bethesda, MD 20814-3578, USA

Dana, Bill (Actor, Comedian)
5965 Peacock Ridge Rd # 563
Rancho Palos Verdes, CA 90275-3479, USA

Dana, Justin (Actor)
13111 Ventura Blvd Ste 102
Studio City, CA 91604-2218, USA

Dana, William (Bill) (Misc)
21400 Grand Oaks Ave
Tehachapi, CA 93561-8848, USA

Danare, Malcolm (Actor)
c/o Monique Moss *Warren Cowan & Associates PR*
8899 Beverly Blvd Ste 919
Los Angeles, CA 90048-2436, USA

Danby, Gordon T (Inventor)
126 Sound Rd
Wading River, NY 11792, USA

Dance, Bill (Fisherman)
Bill Dance's Fishing
PO Box 198
Brownsville, TN 38012-0198, USA

Dance, Charies (Actor)
7812 Forsythe St
Sunland, CA 91040-2502, USA

Dance, Charles (Actor)
c/o Paul Lyon-Maris *International Creative Management (ICM-UK)*
Oxford House
76 Oxford St
London W1N OAX, UNITED KINGDOM (UK)

Dancer, Stanley F (Race Car Driver)
1624 E Atlantic Blvd
Pompano Beach, FL 33060-6751, USA

Dancy, Hugh (Actor)
c/o Gene Parseghian *Untitled Entertainment (NY)*
322 8th Ave Ste 601
New York, NY 10001-6715, USA

Dancy, John (Correspondent)
Harvard University
Kennedy Government School
Cambridge, MA 02138, USA

Dandenault, Mathieu (Hockey Player)
Detroit Red Wings
2615 Dorchester Rd
Birmingham, MI 48009-5990, USA

Dando, Evan (Musician)
Agency Group Ltd
1775 Broadway Ste 515
New York, NY 10019-1903, USA

Dandridge, Bob (Basketball Player)
Milwaukee Bucks
1708 Saint Denis Ave
Norfolk, VA 23509-1004, USA

Dandy Warholds, The (Music Group)
c/o Staff Member *Tsunami Entertainment*
2525 Hyperion Ave
Los Angeles, CA 90027-3316, USA

Dane, Alexandra (Actor)
Rolf Kruger Mgmt
205 Chudliegh Road
London SE4 1EG, UNITED KINGDOM (UK)

Dane, Eric (Actor)
c/o William Choi *Management 360*
9111 Wilshire Blvd
Beverly Hills, CA 90210-5508, USA

Dane, Paul (Misc)
12105 Ambassador Dr Apt 515
Colorado Springs, CO 80921-3629, USA

Daneker, Pat (Baseball Player)
Chicago White Sox
1419 Ritchey St
Williamsport, PA 17701-2640, USA

Danelli, Dino (Musician)
Rascals Cassidy
11761 E Speedway Blvd
Tucson, AZ 85748-2017, USA

Danelo, Joe (Football Player)
Green Bay Packers
3601 Roxbury St
San Pedro, CA 90731-6440, USA

Danenhauer, Bill (Football Player)
Denver Broncos
10 Kirkby Cir
Bella Vista, AR 72715-2349, USA

Danes, Claire (Actor)
c/o Michael D Aglion *Michael Aglion Management*
205 S Beverly Dr Ste 208
Beverly Hills, CA 90212-3867, USA

Danesh, Darius (Musician)
c/o Staff Member *Pop Idol (Fremantle Media)*
2700 Colorado Ave Ste 450
Santa Monica, CA 90404-3599, USA

Daneyko, Ken (Hockey Player)
New Jersey Devils
11 Combs Hollow Rd
Mendham, NJ 07945-2204, USA

Danforth, Douglas D (Baseball Player, Business Person)
8787 Bay Colony Dr Apt 1002
Naples, FL 34108-0784, USA

Danforth, Fred (Artist)
PO Box 828
Middlebury, VT 05753-0828, USA

Danforth, John C (Jack) (Senator)
US Permanent Mission
799 Union Plz
United Nations
New York, NY 10017-3505, USA

D'Angelo (Musician, Songwriter, Writer)
c/o Staff Member *William Morris Agency (WMA-LA)*
1 William Morris Pl
Beverly Hills, CA 90212-4261, USA

D'Angelo, Beverly (Actor)
c/o Brian Mann *International Creative Management (ICM-LA)*
10250 Constellation Blvd
Los Angeles, CA 90067-6200, USA

D'Angelo, Josephine (Baseball Player)
6141 W Higgins Ave Apt 5A
Chicago, IL 60630-1853, USA

D'Angio, Giulio J (Misc)
Children's Hospital
34th & Civic Center Blvd
Philadelphia, PA 19104, USA

Daniel, Brittany (Actor)
c/o Sean Elliott *Endeavor Agency LLC (LA)*
9601 Wilshire Blvd Fl 3
Beverly Hills, CA 90210-5204, USA

Daniel, Chuck (Baseball Player)
Detroit Tigers
59 Jilguero Way
Hot Springs Village, AR 71909-6928, USA

Daniel, Elizabeth A (Beth) (Golfer)
1350 Echo Dr
Jupiter, FL 33458-7728, USA

Daniel, Eugene (Football Player)
Indianapolis Colts
6708 Pikes Ln
Baton Rouge, LA 70808-4274, USA

Daniel, Kenny (Football Player)
New York Giants
2911 Center Ave
Richmond, CA 94804-3022, USA

Daniel, Margaret Truman (Writer)
c/o Staff Member *Random House*
1540 Broadway
New York, NY 10036-4039, USA

Daniel, Robert (Football Player)
Carolina Panthers
9860 Scyene Rd Apt 518
Dallas, TX 75227-1951, USA

Daniel, Willie (Football Player)
Pittsburgh Steelers
1711 Oktoc Rd
Starkville, MS 39759-7901, USA

Danielpour, Richard (Composer)
Sony Classics Records
2100 Colorado Ave
Santa Monica, CA 90404-3504, USA

Daniels, Anthony (Actor)
c/o Fifi Oscard *Fifi Oscard Agency*
110 W 40th St Rm 1601
New York, NY 10018-8512, USA

Daniels, Antonio (Basketball Player)
Seatle SuperSonics
1201 3rd Ave Ste 1000
Seattle, WA 98101-3038, USA

Daniels, Bennie (Baseball Player)
Pittsburgh Pirates
938 W 156th St
Compton, CA 90220-3504, USA

Daniels, Charlie (Musician, Songwriter, Writer)
CDB Mgmt
14410 Central Pike
Mount Juliet, TN 37122-5800, USA

Daniels, Cheryl (Bowler)
6574 Crest Top Dr
West Bloomfield, MI 48322-2656, USA

Daniels, Clem (Football Player)
Dallas Texans
1614 102nd Ave Apt 1
Oakland, CA 94603-3247, USA

Daniels, Erin (Actor)
c/o Andrew Rogers *Paradigm (LA)*
360 N Crescent Dr
North Bldg
Beverly Hills, CA 90210-6820, USA

Daniels, Fred (Baseball Player)
Philadelphia Phillies
PO Box 6208
Statesville, NC 28687-6208, USA

Daniels, Greg (Actor)
c/o Staff Member *Endeavor Agency LLC (LA)*
9601 Wilshire Blvd Fl 3
Beverly Hills, CA 90210-5204, USA

Daniels, Jack (Baseball Player)
Boston Braves
3715 Elmridge Dr
Evansville, IN 47711-3059, USA

Daniels, Jeff (Actor)
701 Glazier Rd
Chelsea, MI 48118-9781, USA

Daniels, Jeff (Hockey Player)
Pittsburgh Penguins
108 Delaplane Ct
Morrisville, NC 27560-6987, USA

Daniels, Jerome (Football Player)
Arizona Cardinals
21831 S 218th St
Queen Creek, AZ 85242-4110, USA

Daniels, Kal (Baseball Player)
Cincinnati Reds
100 Echo Ln
Warner Robins, GA 31088-7458, USA

Daniels, Kevin (Actor)
c/o Staff Member *Lesher Entertainment Inc*
1134 S Cloverdale Ave
Los Angeles, CA 90019-6737, USA

Daniels, Marquis
c/o Staff Member *Dallas Mavericks*
2909 Taylor St
Dallas, TX 75226-1909, USA

Daniels, Melvin (Mel) (Basketball Player)
Minnesota Muskies
19789 Centennial Rd
Sheridan, IN 46069-9789, USA

Daniels, William (Actor)
12805 Hortense St
Studio City, CA 91604-1124, USA

Daniels, William B (Physicist)
283 Dallam Rd
Newark, DE 19711-3620, USA

Danielsen, Egil (Athlete, Track Athlete)
Roreks Gate 9
Hamar 2300, NORWAY

Danielson, Gary D (Football Player)
Detroit Lions
10112 Magnolia Bnd
Bonita Springs, FL 34135-8109, USA

Danielsson, Bengt F (Misc)
Box 558
Papette, TAHITI

Daniloff, Nicholas (Journalist)
PO Box 892
Chester, VT 05143-0892, USA

Danity Kane (Music Group)
c/o Staff Member *Bad Boy Worldwide Entertainment*
1440 Broadway Fl 16
New York, NY 10018-2320, USA

Dankworth, John
The Old Rectory Wavendon
Milton Keynes, ENGLAND MK17 8LT, UNITED KINGDOM (UK)

Dankworth, John P W (Composer, Musician)
Old Rectory
Wavendon, Milton Kenyes MK17 8LT, UNITED KINGDOM (UK)

Danmeier, Rick (Football Player)
4917 Ridge Rd
Minneapolis, MN 55436-1012, USA

Danneels, Godfried Cardinal (Religious Leader)
Aartsbisdom
Wollemarkt 15
Mechelen 2800, BELGIUM

Danner, Blythe (Actor)
c/o Tony Lipp *Creative Artists Agency LCC (CAA-LA)*
2000 Avenue Of The Stars
Los Angeles, CA 90067-4700, USA

Danner, Christian (Misc)
JAS Engineering
Viale Europa
72 Strada Bn 1
Cusago 20090, ITALY

Danning, Harry (Baseball Player)
New York Giants
212 Fox Chapel Ct
Valparaiso, IN 46385-8001, USA

Danning, Sybil (Actor, Model)
Adventures Production
1438 N Gower St Ste 35
Los Angeles, CA 90028-8362, USA

Danny & The Juniors
PO Box 279
Williamstown, NJ 08094-0279, USA

Dano, Paul Franklin (Actor)
c/o Sandra Chang *Industry Entertainment*
955 Carrillo Dr Ste 300
Los Angeles, CA 90048-5400, USA

Danoff, Bettye (Golfer)
2908 Roper Dr
Plano, TX 75025-2413, USA

Danson, Ted (Actor)
c/o Keith Addis *Industry Entertainment*
955 Carrillo Dr Ste 300
Los Angeles, CA 90048-5400, USA

Dante, Joe (Director)
2321 Holly Dr
Los Angeles, CA 90068-2711, USA

Dante, Michael (Actor)
3349 Cahuenga Blvd W Ste 1
Los Angeles, CA 90068-1379, USA

Dantine, Nikki (Actor)
707 N Palm Dr
Beverly Hills, CA 90210-3416, USA

Danto, Arthur C (Misc)
Columbia University
Philosophy Dept
New York, NY 10024, USA

Dantoni, Mike (Basketball Player)
KC-Omaha Kings
22634 SE 44th Pi
Issaquah, WA 98029, USA

D'Antoni, Mike (Basketball Player, Coach)
Phoenix Suns
201 E Jefferson St
Phoenix, AZ 85004-2412, USA

Dantzig, George B (Scientist)
2509 Tamalpais Ave
El Cerrito, CA 94530-1561, USA

Dantzig, Rudi Van (Choreographer)
Emma-Straat 27
Amsterdam, THE NETHERLANDS

Danz, Shirley (Baseball Player)
PO Box 280
Hendersonville, NC 28793-0280, USA

Danza, Tony (Actor)
c/o Staff Member *Katie Face Productions*
13351 Riverside Dr # 610
Sherman Oaks, CA 91423-2542, USA

Danzig
PO Box 884563
San Francisco, CA 94188-4563, USA

Danzig, Frederick P (Editor)
Advertising Age
220 E 42nd St
Editorial Dept
New York, NY 10017-5806, USA

Danziger, Jeff (Cartoonist, Editor)
RFD
Plainfield, VT 05667, USA

Daoud, Ignace Moussa I Cardinal (Religious Leader)
Palazzo del Bramante
Via della Conciliazione 34
Rome 00193, ITALY

Daoust, Dan (Hockey Player)
Montreal Canadiens
55 John Stiver Cres
Markham, ON L3R 9B6, CANADA

Daphnis, Nassos (Artist)
362 W Broadway
New York, NY 10013-5303, USA

Dapkus-Wolf, Eleanor (Baseball Player)
9150 Mallard Cv
Saint John, IN 46373-9019, USA

Dapper, Cliff (Baseball Player)
Brooklyn Dodgers
733 Burma Rd
Fallbrook, CA 92028-9424, USA

Dar Dar, Kirby (Football Player)
Miami Dolphins
120 W Baybridge Dr
Weston, FL 33326, USA

Dara, Olu (Actor)
c/o Staff Member *Monterey Peninsula Artists (Chicago)*
200 W Superior St Ste 202
Chicago, IL 60610-3554, USA

Darabont, Frank (Director, Writer)
William Morris Agency
151 El Camino Dr
Beverly Hills, CA 90212-2775, USA

D'Arbanville, Patti (Actor)
c/o Staff Member *Moskowit Agency*
10440 Queens Blvd Apt 15V
Forest Hills, NY 11375-8145, USA

Darboven, Hanne (Artist)
Am Burgberg 26
Hamburg 21079, GERMANY

Darby, Kim (Actor)
Michael Slessinger
8730 W Sunset Blvd Ste 220W
Los Angeles, CA 90069-2275, USA

D'Arby, Terence Trent (Musician)
Boulevard Mgmt
21731 Ventura Blvd Ste 300
Woodland Hills, CA 91364-1851, USA

D'Arby, Terence Trent (Sananda Maitreya) (Musician)
Sananda Records
Sempione 38
Milan 20154, ITALY

Darc, Mireille (Actor)
Agents Associes Beaume
201 Faubourg Saint Honore
Paris 75008, FRANCE

D'Arcangelo, Ildebrando (Opera Singer)
Lies Askonas
6 Henrietta St
London WC2E 8LA, UNITED KINGDOM (UK)

Darcey, Pete (Basketball Player)
Milwaukee Hawks
17600 N Anderson Rd
Arcadia, OK 73007-7113, USA

Darcum, Max (Skier)
PO Box 189
Dillon, CO 80435-0189, USA

D'Arcy (Musician)
Cohen Brothers Mgmt
500 Molino St Ste 104
Los Angeles, CA 90013-2264, USA

Darcy, Dame (Artist)
c/o Staff Member *Fantagraphics Books*
7563 Lake City Way NE
Seattle, WA 98115-4218, USA

D'Arcy, James (Actor)
c/o Staff Member *Markham and Froggatt Agency*
4 Windmill St
London W1T 1HF, UNITED KINGDOM (UK)

D'Arcy, Margaretta (Writer)
Cassarotto
60/66 Wardour St
London W1V 4ND, UNITED KINGDOM (UK)

Darcy, Pat (Baseball Player)
Cincinnati Reds
515 S Columbus Blvd
Tucson, AZ 85711-4753, USA

Darden, Christopher
c/o Staff Member *William Morris Agency (WMA-LA)*
1 William Morris Pl
Beverly Hills, CA 90212-4261, USA

Darden, Thom (Football Player)
Cleveland Browns
637 20th Ave SW
Cedar Rapids, IA 52404-5520, USA

Dare, Yinka (Basketball Player)
New Jersey Nets
PO Box 523
Redding Ridge, CT 06876-0523, USA

Daredevil (Music Group)
c/o Staff Member *Wind-up Records*
72 Madison Ave Fl 8
New York, NY 10016-8731, USA

Darego, Agbani (Model)
c/o Staff Member *Miss World Ltd*
21 Golden Sq
London W1R 3PA, UNITED KINGDOM (UK)

Darehshori, Nader F (Publisher)
Houghton Mifflin Co
222 Berkeley St
Boston, MA 02116-3760, USA

Darensbourg, Vic (Baseball Player)
Florida Marlins
4151 Abernethy Forest Pl
Las Vegas, NV 89141-4336, USA

Darius, Donovin (Football Player)
Jacksonville Jaguars
9839 Old Baymeadows Rd # 111
Jacksonville, FL 32256, USA

Dark, Al (Baseball Player)
Boston Braves
103 Cranberry Way
Easley, SC 29642-3200, USA

Dark, Mike (Hockey Player)
St Louis Blues
741 Wellington St
Sarina, ON N7T 1J3, CANADA

Dark Star Orchestra (Music Group)
PO Box 1282
Evanston, IL 60204-1282, USA

Darling, Charles (Chuck) (Basketball Player)
Olympics
8066 S Krameria Way
Centennial, CO 80112-3040, USA

Darling, Jennifer (Actor)
13351 Riverside Dr # 427
Sherman Oaks, CA 91423-2542, USA

Darling, Joan (Actor)
PO Box 6700
Tesuque, NM 87574-6700, USA

Darling, Ron (Baseball Player)
19 Woodland St
Millbury, MA 01527-3155, USA

Darmaatmadja, Julius Riyadi Cardinal (Religious Leader)
Keuskupan Agung
Jl Katedral 7
Jakarta 10710, INDONESIA

Darman, Richard G (Government Official)
1137 Crest Ln
McLean, VA 22101-1805, USA

Darnton, John (Journalist, Writer)
New York Times
229 W 43rd St
Editorial Dept
New York, NY 10036-3959, USA

Darnton, Robert C (Historian)
975 Memorial Dr Apt 411
Cambridge, MA 02138-5793, USA

Darr, Mike (Baseball Player)
Toronto Blue Jays
1461 Maplebrook Ln
Corona, CA 92881-0704, USA

Darragh, Dan (Football Player)
Buffalo Bills
201 Sewickley Ridge Ct
Sewickley, PA 15143-8973, USA

Darren, James (Actor, Musician)
PO Box 1088
Beverly Hills, CA 90213-1088, USA

Darrian, Raquel (Adult Film Star)
49 Eaton Ct
Manhasset, NY 11030-4052, USA

Darrieux, Danielle (Actor)
Nicole Cann
1 Rue Alfred de Vigny
Paris 75008, FRANCE

Darrow, Barry (Football Player)
Cleveland Browns
1599 1/2 Sleeping Child Rd
Hamilton, MT 59840-9775, USA

Darwin, Bobby (Baseball Player)
Los Angeles Angels
17509 Alora Ave
Cerritos, CA 90703-5524, USA

Darwin, Danny (Baseball Player)
Texas Rangers
1300 N Saint James Cir
Pilot Point, TX 76258-2725, USA

Darwin, Jeff (Baseball Player)
Seattle Mariners
1010 W Russell Ave
Bonham, TX 75418-2332, USA

Darwin, Matt (Football Player)
Philadelphia Eagles
1103 N Waddill St
Mc Kinney, TX 75069-2963, USA

Darwitz, Natalie (Hockey Player)
c/o Staff Member *US Olympic Committee*
1750 E Boulder St
Alumni Relations
Colorado Springs, CO 80909-5724, USA

Das, Alisha (Actor)
19583 Bowers Dr
Topanga, CA 90290-3102, USA

Das, Nandita (Actor)
c/o Aude Powell *Brunskill Management*
Suite 8A
169 Queen's Gate
London SW7 5HE, UNITED KINGDOM (UK)

Dascascos, Marc (Actor)
PO Box 1549
Studio City, CA 91614-0549, USA

Dascenzo, Doug (Baseball Player)
Chicago Cubs
PO Box 7
Hiller, PA 15444-0007, USA

Daschle, Tom (Politician)
New Leadership For America
821 N Maple
Watertown, SD 57201-1681, USA

D'Ascoli, Bernard (Musician)
Clarion/Seven Muses
47 Whitehall Park
London N19 3TW, UNITED KINGDOM (UK)

Dash, Damon (Actor, Director, Producer, Writer)
c/o Staff Member *Dash Films*
825 8th Ave Fl 29
New York, NY 10019-7416, USA

Dash, Julie (Actor, Director, Producer, Writer)
c/o Kimber Wheeler *TalentWorks (LA)*
3500 W Olive Ave Ste 1400
Burbank, CA 91505-5512, USA

Dash, Leon O Jr (Journalist)
Washington Post
Editorial Dept
1150 15th Ave NW
Washington, DC 20071-0001, USA

Dash, Sam
110 Newlands St
Chevy Chase, MD 20815-3333, USA

Dash, Sarah (Musician)
Talent Consultants International
105 Shad Row Ste B
Piermont, NY 10968-3001, USA

Dash, Stacey (Actor)
c/o Erik Kritzer *Fenton-Kritzer Entertainment*
8840 Wilshire Blvd Fl 3
Beverly Hills, CA 90211-2606, USA

Daskalakis, Cleon (Hockey Player)
Boston Bruins
752 Main St
Boxford, MA 01921-1127, USA

Dassier, Uwe (Swimmer)
Stolze-Schrey-Str 6
Wilday 15745, GREECE

Dassin, Jules (Director)
c/o Staff Member *Foundation Melina Mercouri*
9-11 Polygnotou Str
Athens 11521, GREECE

Dasso, Frank (Baseball Player)
Cincinnati Reds
1413 Madison St
Wenatchee, WA 98801-1729, USA

Dater, Judy L (Photographer)
2430 5th St Ste J
Berkeley, CA 94710-2452, USA

Datsyuk, Pavel (Hockey Player)
1958 Maplewood Ave
Bloomfield Hills, MI 48302-0209, USA

Dattilo, Bryan (Actor)
c/o Staff Member *Cohen/Thomas Agency*
1888 N Crescent Heights Blvd
Los Angeles, CA 90069-1647, USA

Dattilo, Kristin (Actor)
c/o Jim Hess *Paradigm (LA)*
360 N Crescent Dr
North Bldg
Beverly Hills, CA 90210-6820, USA

Datz, Jeff (Baseball Player)
Detroit Tigers
867 Longbrook Dr
Wadsworth, OH 44281-8815, USA

Daubach, Brian (Baseball Player)
Florida Marlins
2059 Bowler Rd
O Fallon, IL 62269-7008, USA

Dauben, William G (Misc)
20 Eagle Hl
Kensington, CA 94707-1408, USA

Dauer, Rich (Baseball Player)
Baltimore Orioles
2510 Brook Haven Ln
Hinckley, OH 44233-9672, USA

Daugherty, Bradley L (Brad) (Basketball Player)
Cleveland Cavaliers
1239 Cane Creek Rd
Fletcher, NC 28732-9474, USA

Daugherty, Dick (Football Player)
Los Angeles Rams
5600 E Paseo Lomas
Tucson, AZ 85750-1026, USA

Daugherty, Doc (Baseball Player)
Detroit Tigers
195 Lakeview Dr
Russell Springs, KY 42642, USA

Daugherty, Jack (Baseball Player)
Montreal Expos
20360 N 95th Pl
Scottsdale, AZ 85255-6646, USA

Daugherty, Martha Craig (Judge)
US Court of Appeals
701 Broadway
Nashville, TN 37203-3944, USA

Daugherty, Michael (Composer)
Argo London Records
810 7th Ave
New York, NY 10019-5818, USA

Daughtry, Chris (Musician)
c/o Deanna Daughtry
2205 Oak Ridge Rd Ste K
Pmb 179
Oak Ridge, NC 27310-8729, USA

Daukas, Lou (Football Player)
Brooklyn Dodgers
120 Boulder Cir
Glastonbury, CT 06033-4116, USA

Daukas, Nick (Football Player)
Brooklyn Dodgers
1 City Pl
Hartford, CT 06103-3432, USA

Dauline, Marie (Musician)
Todo Mundo
PO Box 652
Cooper Station
New York, NY 10276-0652, USA

Daulton, Darren A (Baseball Player)
Philadelphia Phillies
643 Woodbridge Dr
Melbourne, FL 32940-1738, USA

Dauplaise, Norman (Jockey)
29 W 36th St # 1000
New York, NY 10018-7907, USA

Daurey, Dana (Actor)
S M S Talent
8730 W Sunset Blvd Ste 440
Los Angeles, CA 90069-2277, USA

Dausset, Jean B G (Nobel Prize Laureate)
9 Rue de Villersexel
Paris 75007, FRANCE

Davalillo, Vic (Baseball Player)
Cleveland Indians
Calle Trujillo 7 Mariperez Q V
Caracas, VENEZUELA

Davalos, Alexa (Actor)
c/o Scott Wexler *3 Arts Entertainment Inc*
9460 Wilshire Blvd Fl 7
Beverly Hills, CA 90212-2713, USA

Davalos, Elyssa
2934 1/2 N Beverly Glen Cir # 53
Los Angeles, CA 90077-1724, USA

Davalos, Richard (Actor)
2311 Vista Gordo Dr
Los Angeles, CA 90026-2021, USA

Davanon, Jeff (Baseball Player)
Anaheim Angels
731 E Buena Vista Dr
Chandler, AZ 85249-3975, USA

Davanon, Jerry (Baseball Player)
San Diego Padres
5323 Hidalgo St
Houston, TX 77056-6208, USA

Dave, Al (Football Player)
Dallas Cowboys
5173 Waring Rd # 441
San Diego, CA 92120-2705, USA

Davenport, A Nigel (Actor)
5 Ann's Close
Kinnerton Street
London SW1, UNITED KINGDOM (UK)

Davenport, Adell (Baseball Player)
Topps
1764 Belt Line Rd Apt 155
Garland, TX 75044-6824, USA

Davenport, Charles (Football Player)
Pittsburgh Steelers
5706 Edmeston Dr
Fayetteville, NC 28311-0423, USA

Davenport, Jack (Actor)
c/o Lorraine Hamilton *Hamilton Hodell Ltd*
66 - 68 Margaret St 5th Fl
London W1W 8SR, UNITED KINGDOM (UK)

Davenport, Jim (Baseball Player)
San Francisco Giants
1016 Hewitt Dr
San Carlos, CA 94070-3601, USA

Davenport, Joe (Baseball Player)
Chicago White Sox
10102 Wycliffe St
Santee, CA 92071-1176, USA

Davenport, Lindsay
PO Box 10179
Newport Beach, CA 92658-0179, USA

Davenport, Nigel (Actor)
Green & Underwood
2 Conduit St
London W1R9TG, UNITED KINGDOM
(UK)

Davenport Jr, Guy M (Writer)
128 Owsley Ave
Lexington, KY 40502-1526, USA

Davey, Don (Football Player)
Green Bay Packers
212 Ocean Front
Neptune Beach, FL 32266-6113, USA

Davey, Mike (Baseball Player)
Atlanta Braves
902 W Melinda Ln
Spokane, WA 99203-1363, USA

Davey, Tom (Baseball Player)
c/o Staff Member *Toronto Blue Jays*
Skydome
1 Blue Jay Way #3200
Toronto, ON M5V 1J1, CANADA

Davi, Robert (Actor)
c/o Staff Member *Paradigm (LA)*
360 N Crescent Dr
North Bldg
Beverly Hills, CA 90210-6820, USA

Daviau, Allen (Cinematographer)
2249 Bronson Hill Dr
Los Angeles, CA 90068-2407, USA

Davich, Jacob (Actor)
c/o Staff Member *Paradigm (LA)*
360 N Crescent Dr
North Bldg
Beverly Hills, CA 90210-6820, USA

Davich, Marty (Composer)
530 S Greenwood Ave
Pasadena, CA 91107-5101, USA

David, Andre (Baseball Player)
Minnesota Twins
17341 W Banff Ln
Surprise, AZ 85388-7712, USA

David, Charlie (Actor)
CTM International
205-309 W Cordova St
Vancouver, BC V6B 1E5, CANADA

David, Craig (Musician)
c/o Cara Lewis *William Morris Agency (WMA-NY)*
1325 Avenue Of The Americas
New York, NY 10019-6026, USA

David, George A L (Business Person)
United Technologies Corp
United Technologies Building
Hartford, CT 06101, USA

David, Hal (Musician)
10430 Wilshire Blvd
Los Angeles, CA 90024-4651, USA

David, Jim (Football Player)
Detroit Lions
2570 Aspen Ln
Bloomfield Township, MI 48302-1006,
USA

David, John R (Misc)
Harvard Public Health School
665 Huntington Ave
Boston, MA 02115-6021, USA

David, Keith (Actor)
c/o Josh Silver *Sneak Preview Entertainment*
PO Box 3238
Hollywood, CA 90078-3238, USA

David, Larry (Actor, Producer, Writer)
c/o Ariel (Ari) Emanuel *Endeavor Agency LLC (LA)*
9601 Wilshire Blvd Fl 3
Beverly Hills, CA 90210-5204, USA

David, Mack
1575 Toledo Cir
Palm Springs, CA 92264-9535, USA

David, Mohato (Prince)
Royal Palace
PO Box 524
Maseru, LESOTHO

David, Peter (Actor)
PO Box 239
Bayport, NY 11705-0239, USA

David Bossert, David Bossert (Director,
Producer)
c/o Staff Member *Walt Disney Television Animation*
500 S Buena Vista St
Burbank, CA 91521-0001, USA

Davidovich, Bella (Musician)
Columbia Artists Mgmt Inc
1790 Broadway Fl 6
New York, NY 10019-1412, USA

Davidovich, Lolita (Actor)
1503 Ventura Blvd #710
Sherman Oaks, CA 91403, USA

Davidovsky, Mario (Composer)
Harvard University
Music Dept
Cambridge, MA 02138, USA

Davids, Hollace (Producer)
c/o Staff Member *Universal Pictures*
100 Universal City Plz
Universal City, CA 91608-1002, USA

Davidson, Amy (Actor)
c/o Staff Member *Paradigm (LA)*
360 N Crescent Dr
North Bldg
Beverly Hills, CA 90210-6820, USA

Davidson, Ben E (Football Player)
Green Bay Packers
4737 Angels Pt
La Mesa, CA 91941-6899, USA

Davidson, Bruce O (Misc)
RR 842
Unionville, PA 19375, USA

Davidson, Cleatus (Baseball Player)
Minnesota Twins
2560 Possum Trot Ave
Haines City, FL 33844-8855, USA

Davidson, Cotton (Football Player)
Baltimore Colts
435 Old Osage Rd
Gatesville, TX 76528-3362, USA

Davidson, Diane Mott (Writer)
c/o Author Mail *Bantam-Dell Publishing (NY)*
1745 Broadway
New York, NY 10019-4343, USA

Davidson, Eileen (Actor)
11300 W Olympic Blvd Ste 610
Los Angeles, CA 90064-1643, USA

Davidson, Ernest R (Misc)
18514 36th Ave W Apt A
Lynnwood, WA 98037-7623, USA

Davidson, George A Jr (Business Person)
Consolidated Natural Gas
625 Liberty Ave
Pittsburgh, PA 15222-3110, USA

Davidson, Gordon (Director, Producer)
Center Theatre Group
135 N Grand Ave
Mark Taper Forum
Los Angeles, CA 90012-3013, USA

Davidson, Jeff (Football Player)
Denver Broncos
11216 Waightstill Way
Charlotte, NC 28277-3725, USA

Davidson, Jeff (Motivational Speaker)
Breathing Space Institute
2417 Honeysuckle Rd
Chapel Hill, NC 27514-6819, USA

Davidson, Jim (Actor)
William Morris Agency
151 El Camino Dr
Beverly Hills, CA 90212-2775, USA

Davidson, John (Actor, Musician)
16551 Kettler Ln
Huntington Beach, CA 92647-4328, USA

Davidson, John (Hockey Player)
St Louis Blues
240 Conway Hill Rd
Saint Louis, MO 63141-7238, USA

Davidson, Ken (Football Player)
Pittsburgh Steelers
1922 Thompson Crossing Dr
Richmond, TX 77469-6707, USA

Davidson, Mark (Baseball Player)
Minnesota Twins
996 Old Mountain Rd
Statesville, NC 28677-2082, USA

Davidson, Owen (Tennis Player)
39 N Lakemist Harbour Pl
Spring, TX 77381-3344, USA

Davidson, Ralph P (Publisher)
494 Harbor Rd
Southport, CT 06890-1319, USA

Davidson, Ronald C (Physicist)
Princeton University
Plasma Physics Laboratory
Princeton, NJ 08544-0001, USA

Davidson, Ted (Baseball Player)
Cincinnati Reds
515 De Armond Pl
Santa Maria, CA 93454-6714, USA

Davidson, Tommy (Actor, Comedian)
c/o Karynne Tencer *Tencer & Associates PR*
9777 Wilshire Blvd Ste 1005
Beverly Hills, CA 90212-1901, USA

Davie, Alan (Artist)
Gamels Studio
Rush Green
Hertford SG13 7SB, UNITED KINGDOM
(UK)

Davie, Donald A (Writer)
4 High St
Silverton
Exeter EX5 4JB, UNITED KINGDOM (UK)

Davie, Jerry (Baseball Player)
Detroit Tigers
2800 US Highway 17 92 W Lot 1
Haines City, FL 33844-7375, USA

Davies, Colin Rex
7A Fitzroy Park
London, ENGLAND N6 6HS, UNITED
KINGDOM (UK)

Davies, Dave (Musician)
Larry Page
29 Ruston Mews
London W11 1RB, UNITED KINGDOM
(UK)

Davies, Dennis Russell
Am Wichelshof 24
Bonn 53111, GERMANY

Davies, Gail (Musician)
246 Cherokee Rd
Nashville, TN 37205-1818, USA

Davies, Geralnt Wyn (Actor)
Oscars Abrams Zimel
438 Queen St W
Toronto, ON M5A 1T4, CANADA

Davies, Jeremy (Actor)
United Talent Agency
9560 Wilshire Blvd Ste 500
Beverly Hills, CA 90212-2401, USA

Davies, Kenneth (Hockey Player)
New York Rangers
370 Williston Way
Pawtucket, RI 02861-4114, USA

Davies, Lane (Actor)
PO Box 20531
Thousand Oaks, CA 91358, USA

Davies, Laura (Golfer)
c/o Tony Davies
21 Addlestone Park
Addleston KT15 1RZ, UNITED
KINGDOM (UK)

Davies, Linda (Writer)
Calle Once 286
La Molona
Lima, PERU

Davies, Matt (Artist, Cartoonist, Editor)
Journal News
1 Gannett Dr
Editorial Dept
White Plains, NY 10604-3402, USA

Davies, Mike (Architect)
Rogers Partnership
Thames Wharf
Rainville Road
London N6 94A, UNITED KINGDOM
(UK)

Davies, Peter (Misc)
Albert Einstein Medical College
Biochemistry Dept
Bronx, NY 10461, USA

Davies, Peter Maxwell (Composer)
Judy Arnold
50 Hogarth Road
London SW5 0PU, UNITED KINGDOM
(UK)

Davies, Raymond D (Ray) (Musician, Songwriter, Writer)
Larry Page
29 Ruston Mews
London W11 1RB, UNITED KINGDOM
(UK)

Davies, Raymond Douglas (Ray) (Actor, Director, Musician, Writer)
c/o Sheldon (Shelly) Schultz *Trident Media Group LLC*
41 Madison Ave Fl 36
New York, NY 10010-2257, USA

Davies, Russel T (Writer)
c/o Lisa Harrison *Endeavor Agency LLC (LA)*
9601 Wilshire Blvd Fl 3
Beverly Hills, CA 90210-5204, USA

Davies, Ryland (Opera Singer)
71 Fairmile Lane
Cobham
Surrey KT11 2DG, UNITED KINGDOM
(UK)

Davies, Tamara (Actor)
c/o Staff Member *Bauman Redanty & Shaul Agency*
5757 Wilshire Blvd Ste 473
Los Angeles, CA 90036-3632, USA

Davies, Terence (Director)
Nigel Britton Mgmt
11-15 Betterton St
London WC2H 9BP, UNITED KINGDOM
(UK)

Davies, Warrick (Actor)
International Creative Mgmt
76 Oxford St
London W1N 0AX, UNITED KINGDOM
(UK)

Davies, Wyn (Actor)
c/o Staff Member *Screen Actors Guild (SAG-LA)*
5757 Wilshire Blvd
Los Angeles, CA 90036-5810, USA

Davis, A Dano (Business Person)
Winn-Dixie Stores
5050 Edgewood Ct
Jacksonville, FL 32254-1665, USA

Davis, Al
1220 Harbor Bay Pkwy
Alameda, CA 94502-6501, USA

Davis, Alvin (Baseball Player)
Seattle Mariners
7983 Armagosa Dr
Riverside, CA 92508-8713, USA

Davis, Andrew (Director)
The Agency
1800 Avenue Of Stars Ste 400
Los Angeles, CA 90067-4206, USA

Davis, Andrew (Football Player)
Washington Redskins
14500 Fiske Dr
Silver Spring, MD 20906-1737, USA

Davis, Andrew F
Askonas Holt
27 Chancerty Lane
London WC2A 1PF, UNITED KINGDOM
(UK)

Davis, Angela Y (Activist, Educator, Politician)
Speakout
PO Box 99096
Emeryville, CA 94662-9096, USA

Davis, Ann B (Actor)
23315 Eagle Gap
San Antonio, TX 78255-2103, USA

Davis, Anne B (Actor)
c/o Leanna Levy *Cassell-Levy Inc*
843 N Sycamore Ave
Los Angeles, CA 90038-3391, USA

Davis, Anthony (Composer, Musician)
Andriolo Communications
115 E 9th St
New York, NY 10003-5414, USA

Davis, Anthony (Football Player)
696 Cardiff
Irvine, CA 92606-0876, USA

Davis, Antone (Football Player)
Philadelphia Eagles
4016 Norwood Ave
Chattanooga, TN 37415-7112, USA

Davis, Antonio (Basketball Player)
625 Willow Glen Dr
El Paso, TX 79922-2210, USA

Davis, Aree (Actor)
c/o Myrna Lieberman *Myrna Lieberman Management*
3001 Hollyridge Dr
Hollywood, CA 90068-1951, USA

Davis, Arthur (Football Player)
Pittsburgh Steelers
8260 SW Woodbridge Ct
Wilsonville, OR 97070-7458, USA

Davis, Aubrey (Basketball Player)
St Louis Bombers
118 Glen Cove Pi
Ponte Vedra Beach, FL 32082, USA

Davis, Bard (Basketball Player)
Los Angeles Lakers
2703 Ridge Top Ln
Arlington, TX 76006-2729, USA

Davis, Baron (Basketball Player)
New Orleans Hornets
1250 Poydras St # 19
New Orleans Arena
New Orleans, LA 70113-1804, USA

Davis, Ben (Baseball Player)
San Diego Padres
416 Homestead Dr
West Chester, PA 19382-8242, USA

Davis, Ben (Football Player)
Cleveland Browns
16600 Parkland Dr
Shaker Heights, OH 44120-2540, USA

Davis, Bennie L (General)
101 Goldenrod Way
Georgetown, TX 78633-4573, USA

Davis, Beryl
1870 Caminito Del Cielo
Glendale, CA 91208-3049, USA

Davis, Bill (Baseball Player)
Cleveland Indians
6638 Knox Ave S
Minneapolis, MN 55423-2161, USA

Davis, Billy (Football Player)
Dallas Cowboys
1717 E Belt Line Rd Apt 1418
Coppell, TX 75019-4242, USA

Davis, Bob (Baseball Player)
San Diego Padres
PO Box 198
Locust Grove, OK 74352-0198, USA

Davis, Brandy (Baseball Player)
Pittsburgh Pirates
56 Union School Rd
Elkton, MD 21921-2198, USA

Davis, Brianne (Actor)
c/o Staff Member *Art Work Entertainment*
5900 Wilshire Blvd Ste 2150
Los Angeles, CA 90036-5021, USA

Davis, Brock (Baseball Player)
Houston Colt 45's
2080 W Ontario Ave
Corona, CA 92882-5627, USA

Davis, Buddy (Basketball Player)
Philadelphia Warriors
6582 Fm 841
Lufkin, TX 75901-4633, USA

Davis, Butch (Baseball Player)
Kansas City Royals
1108 Brucemont Dr
Garner, NC 27529-4505, USA

Davis, Carl (Composer)
99 Church Road
Barnes
London SW13 9HL, UNITED KINGDOM
(UK)

Davis, Charles (Basketball Player)
Washington Bullets
6261 Hillsboro Pike
Nashville, TN 37215-5501, USA

Davis, Charles D (Football Player)
Cincinnati Bengals
8935 Aspen Eadow Dr
Houston, TX 77071, USA

Davis, Charles M (Football Player)
Pittsburgh Steelers
PO Box 772011
Houston, TX 77215-2011, USA

Davis, Chili (Baseball Player)
c/o Team Member *San Francisco Giants*
24 Willie Mays Plz
Sbc Park
San Francisco, CA 94107-2199, USA

Davis, Chip (Musician)
c/o Staff Member *Brokaw Company, The*
9255 W Sunset Blvd Ste 804
Los Angeles, CA 90069-3305, USA

Davis, Christopher W (Football Player)
New York Giants
PO Box 493
Washington, DC 20044-0493, USA

Davis, Clarence (Football Player)
Oakland Raiders
PO Box 452
Brice, OH 43109-0452, USA

Davis, Clifton (Actor)
9200 W Sunset Blvd Ste 900
Los Angeles, CA 90069-3604, USA

Davis, Clive J (Business Person)
c/o Staff Member *BMG Entertainment*
1540 Broadway
New York, NY 10036-4039, USA

Davis, Colin R
Alison Glaster
39 Huntingdon St
London N1 1BP, UNITED KINGDOM
(UK)

Davis, Dale (Baseball Player)
Indiana Pacers
7945 Beaumont Green Pl
Indianapolis, NC 27455, USA

Davis, Dana (Actor)
c/o Darryl Marshak *Marshak/Zachary Company, The*
8840 Wilshire Blvd Fl 1
Beverly Hills, CA 90211-2606, USA

Davis, Daniel (Actor)
c/o Staff Member *Innovative Artists (NY)*
235 Park Ave S Fl 7
New York, NY 10003-1405, USA

Davis, Danny (Musician)
Danny Davis Productions
PO Box 210317
Nashville, TN 37221-0317, USA

Davis, David Brion (Historian, Writer)
783 Lambert Rd
Orange, CT 06477, USA

Davis, David (Dave) (Bowler)
DeStasio
710 Shore Rd
Spring Lake, NJ 07762-1855, USA

Davis, DeRay (Actor)
c/o April Lim *Global Artists Agency*
1648 Wilcox Ave Ste 3
Los Angeles, CA 90028-6898, USA

Davis, Dexter (Football Player)
Phoenix Cardinals
724 White Pine Way
Sumter, SC 29154-6209, USA

Davis, Don (Golfer)
15910 Fm 529 Rd Apt 219
Houston, TX 77095-2579, USA

Davis, Don H Jr (Business Person)
Rockwell International
1201 S 2nd St
Milwaukee, WI 53204-2498, USA

Davis, Don S (Actor)
Gold Marshak Liedtke
3500 W Olive Ave Ste 1400
Burbank, CA 91505-5512, USA

Davis, Donald (Football Player)
New York Giants
739 E 48th St
Los Angeles, CA 90011-4008, USA

Davis, Donnie (Football Player)
Dallas Texans
5323 Trail Lake Dr
Houston, TX 77045-4038, USA

Davis, Doug (Baseball Player)
California Angels
279 Whites Church Rd
Bloomsburg, PA 17815-7156, USA

Davis, Doug (Baseball Player)
Texas Rangers
1524 Fieldcrest Dr
Pleasant Hill, CA 94523-1016, USA

Davis, Douglas S (Football Player)
Minnesota Vikings
613 Hitching Post Dr
Brandon, FL 33511-7808, USA

Davis, Dwight (Basketball Player)
Cleveland Cavaliers
PO Box 324
Newfields, NH 03856-0324, USA

Davis, Ed (Basketball Player)
Pittsburgh Condors
36750 US Highway 19 N # 26-3437
Palm Harbor, FL 34684-1239, USA

Davis, Elizabeth (Musician)
Rave Booking
PO Box 310780
Jamaica, NY 11431-0780, USA

Davis, Elliot M (Cinematographer)
1328 Arch St
Berkeley, CA 94708-1825, USA

Davis, Emanuel (Basketball Player)
Atlanta Hawks
190 Marietta St NW
Atlanta, GA 30303-2717, USA

Davis, Eric (Baseball Player)
Cincinnati Reds
5334 Collingwood Cir
Calabasas, CA 91302-3137, USA

Davis, Eric W (Football Player)
San Francisco 49ers
3737 Coyote Cyn
Soquel, CA 95073-3034, USA

Davis, Eugene (Actor)
c/o Jimmy Cota *The Artists Agency (LA)*
1180 S Beverly Dr Ste 301
Los Angeles, CA 90035-1154, USA

Davis, Franchell 'Frenchie'
c/o Staff Member *American Idol*
7800 Beverly Blvd # 251
Los Angeles, CA 90036-2112, USA

Davis, Gary (Football Player)
Miami Dolphins
10750 San Marcos Rd
Atascadero, CA 93422-2126, USA

Davis, Geena (Actor)
c/o Kevin Huvane *Creative Artists Agency LCC (CAA-LA)*
2000 Avenue Of The Stars
Los Angeles, CA 90067-4700, USA

Davis, George (Baseball Player)
Kansas City Monarchs
3092 Kimball Ave
Memphis, TN 38114-4070, USA

Davis, Glenn
627 Llewelyn Rd
Berwyn, PA 19312-2012, USA

Davis, Glenn A (Football Player)
Detroit Lions
801 Robinson Ave
Barberton, OH 44203-3763, USA

Davis, Glenn E (Baseball Player)
Houston Astros
1448 Grove Park Dr Apt 1407
Columbus, GA 31904-1598, USA

Davis, Gray (Ex-Governor)
State Capitol Building
Sacramento, CA 95814, USA

Davis, Greg (Football Player)
Atlanta Falcons
1418 W Mountain Sky Ave
Phoenix, AZ 85045-1952, USA

Davis, H Thomas (Tommy) (Baseball Player)
Los Angeles Dodgers
9767 Whirlaway St
Alta Loma, CA 91737-1643, USA

Davis, Harper (Football Player)
Los Angeles Dons
1224 Springdale Dr
Jackson, MS 39211-3130, USA

Davis, Harrison (Football Player)
San Diego Chargers
6409 Lesser Dr
Greeley, CO 80634-9595, USA

Davis, Hope (Actor)
United Talent Agency
9560 Wilshire Blvd Ste 500
Beverly Hills, CA 90212-2401, USA

Davis, Hubert (Basketball Player)
New York Knicks
204 Lancaster Dr
Chapel Hill, NC 27517-3429, USA

Davis, J J (Baseball Player)
Pittsburgh Pirates
7302 Forrest Rader Dr
Charlotte, NC 28227-9830, USA

Davis, Jack (Football Player)
Boston Patriots
2751 Challenger Dr
Palm Harbor, FL 34683-7233, USA

Davis, Jacke (Baseball Player)
Philadelphia Phillies
1109 W Panola St
Carthage, TX 75633-2341, USA

Davis, James (Basketball Player)
Rochesster Royals
44 Van Ter
Sparkill, NY 10976-1406, USA

Davis, James (Football Player)
Oakland Raiders
5701 S St Andrews Pl
Los Angeles, CA 90062-2649, USA

Davis, James B (General)
3600 Wimber Blvd
Palm Harbor, FL 34685, USA

Davis, James O (Doctor)
546 Warren Ave
Saint Louis, MO 63130-4154, USA

Davis, James R (Jim) (Cartoonist)
5440 E County Road 450 N
Albany, IN 47320-9728, USA

Davis, Jason (Baseball Player)
Cleveland Indians
345 Carriage Ln NE
Cleveland, TN 37312-6708, USA

Davis, Jay (Golfer)
c/o Staff Member *Pro Golfers Association (PGA) Tour*
112 Tpc Blvd
Ponte Vedra Beach, FL 32082, USA

Davis, Jeff (Actor)
c/o Staff Member *United Talent Agency (UTA)*
9560 Wilshire Blvd Ste 500
Beverly Hills, CA 90212-2401, USA

Davis, Jerome (Football Player)
Chicago Cardinals
515 N 4th St
Palatka, FL 32177-3523, USA

Davis, Jerry (Baseball Player)
San Diego Padres
72 Theresa St
Trenton, NJ 08618-1531, USA

Davis, Jesse (Musician)
Concord Records
100 N Crescent Dr Ste 275
Beverly Hills, CA 90210-5412, USA

Davis, Jill A (Writer)
Random House
1745 Broadway # B1
New York, NY 10019-4305, USA

Davis, Jody (Baseball Player)
Chicago Cubs
4445 Shirley Rd
Gainesville, GA 30506-5104, USA

Davis, John (Baseball Player)
Kansas City Royals
76871 Castle Ct
Palm Desert, CA 92211-7100, USA

Davis, John (Football Player)
Houston Oilers
901 Forest Pond Dr
Marietta, GA 30068-4420, USA

Davis, John A. (Actor, Composer, Director, Producer, Writer)
c/o Rob Carlson *William Morris Agency (WMA-LA)*
1 William Morris Pl
Beverly Hills, CA 90212-4261, USA

Davis, John A (Actor, Director, Producer, Writer)
c/o Staff Member *DNA Productions*
PO Box 630024
Irving, TX 75063-0110, USA

Davis, Johnny (Basketball Player, Coach)
Portland Trail Blazers
135 W Market St Apt 2D
Indianapolis, IN 46204-2817, USA

Davis, Jonathan (Musician)
c/o Staff Member *Kraft-Engel Management*
15233 Ventura Blvd Ste 200
Sherman Oaks, CA 91403-2244, USA

Davis, Jonathan Houseman (Musician)
c/o Staff Member *William Morris Agency (WMA-LA)*
1 William Morris Pl
Beverly Hills, CA 90212-4261, USA

Davis, Josie (Actor)
CunninghamEscottDipene
10635 Santa Monica Blvd Ste 130
Los Angeles, CA 90025-8306, USA

Davis, Judy (Actor)
Shanahan Mgmt
PO Box 1509
Darlinghurst, NSW 1300, AUSTRALIA

Davis, Kane (Baseball Player)
Cleveland Indians
4794 Ripley Rd
Reedy, WV 25270-9504, USA

Davis, Keith B (Football Player)
New York Giants
PO Box 112214
Carrollton, TX 75011-2214, USA

Davis, Kenneth E (Football Player)
Green Bay Packers
1224 Blooklawn Dr
Arlington, TX 76018, USA

Davis, Kim (Hockey Player)
Pittsburgh Penguins
14 Shorecrest Dr
Winnipeg, MB R3P 1N2, CANADA

Davis, Kristin (Actor)
c/o David (Dave) Fleming *Mosaic Media Group*
24 Music Sq W Fl 1
Nashville, TN 37203-6661, USA

Davis, Kyle (Football Player)
Dallas Cowboys
104 Futurity Ln
Weatherford, TX 76087-4606, USA

Davis, L Edward (Religious Leader)
Evangelical Presbyterian Church
26049 5 Mile Rd
Detroit, MI 48239-3235, USA

Davis, Lamar (Football Player)
Miami Seahawks
502 Ashantilly Ave
Saint Simons Island, GA 31522-3609, USA

Davis, Lee (Basketball Player)
New Orleans Buccaneers
5024 Fieldgreen Xing Apt B2
Stone Mountain, GA 30088-3103, USA

Davis, Lee (Director)
Gersh Agency
232 N Canon Dr
Beverly Hills, CA 90210-5302, USA

Davis, Leonard (Football Player)
Arizona Cardinals
PO Box 888
Phoenix, AZ 85001-0888, USA

Davis, Linda (Musician)
5548 W Shady Trl
Old Hickory, TN 37138-1321, USA

Davis, Lorenzo (Football Player)
Pittsburgh Steelers
2501 NW 11th St
Dillard High School
Fort Lauderdale, FL 33311-5702, USA

Davis, Lorne (Hockey Player)
Montreal Canadiens
236 Frontenac Dr
Regina, SK S4S 4L3, CANADA

Davis, Lucy (Actor)
c/o Staff Member *Water Street Management*
5225 Wilshire Blvd Ste 615
Los Angeles, CA 90036-4350, USA

Davis, Mac (Actor, Musician, Songwriter, Writer)
Grant & Tani
9100 Wilshire Blvd Ste 1000W
Beverly Hills, CA 90212-3463, USA

Davis, Mark (Baseball Player)
California Angels
1672 E Mountain St
Pasadena, CA 91104-3935, USA

Davis, Mark A (Basketball Player)
Minnesota Timberwolves
108 Government Cir # A
Thibodaux, LA 70301-6615, USA

Davis, Mark G (Basketball Player)
Milwaukee Bucks
3120 Aaron Dr
Chesapeake, VA 23323-2600, USA

Davis, Mark W (Baseball Player)
8867 E Sierra Pinta Dr
Scottsdale, AZ 85255-9174, USA

Davis, Martha (Musician)
Paradise Artists
108 E Matilija St
Ojai, CA 93023-2639, USA

Davis, Matt (Actor)
c/o Staff Member *McKeon-Valeo-Myones Management*
9100 Wilshire Blvd Ste 350W
Beverly Hills, CA 90212-3437, USA

Davis, Matthew (Actor)
Lynda Goodfriend
338 S Beachwood Dr
Burbank, CA 91506-2713, USA

Davis, Melvyn (Basketball Player)
New York Knicks
PO Box 29
Suffern, NY 10901-0029, USA

Davis, Mia Amber (Actor, Model)
c/o Staff Member *Ikon Model Management*
140 W 22nd St
New York, NY 10011-2420, USA

Davis, Michael (Basketball Player)
New York Knicks
110 W Clay St
Richmond, VA 23220-3913, USA

Davis, Michael A (Football Player)
Houston Oilers
PO Box 23025
Belleville, IL 62223-0025, USA

Davis, Michael L (Football Player)
Oakland Raiders
PO Box 614
Pro Athlete Marketing
Beaver Falls, PA 15010-0614, USA

Davis, Mike (Baseball Player)
c/o Staff Member *Oakland Athletics*
7000 Coliseum Way
Oakland, CA 94621-1992, USA

Davis, Mike (Basketball Player)
Baltimore Bullets
100 W 92nd St Apt 29E
New York, NY 10025-7546, USA

Davis, Milton (Composer)
c/o Staff Member *Windswept (LA)*
9320 Wilshire Blvd Ste 200
Beverly Hills, CA 90212-3217, USA

Davis, Monti (Basketball Player)
Philadelphia 76ers
328 Tod Ln
Youngstown, OH 44504-1403, USA

Davis, Musiello
200 Wyndemere Way
Janette
Naples, FL 34105-7125, USA

Davis, N Jan (Astronaut)
4105 Cumberland Pass Apt 814
Fort Worth, TX 76116-0753, USA

Davis, Nathaniel (Diplomat)
1783 Longwood Ave
Claremont, CA 91711-3129, USA

Davis, Neriah (Actor, Model)
c/o Jon Orlando *Xposure Public Relations*
8271 Melrose Ave Ste 110
Los Angeles, CA 90046-6800, USA

Davis, Nick (Basketball Player)
Baltimore Bullets
512 Lamp Post Ln
Camp Hill, PA 17011-1429, USA

Davis, Odie (Baseball Player)
Texas Rangers
1014 Montana St
San Antonio, TX 78203-1117, USA

Davis, Oliver (Football Player)
Cleveland Browns
1527 Evanston Ct
Marietta, GA 30062-2148, USA

Davis, Otis (Baseball Player)
Brooklyn Dodgers
1115 Royal Troon Ct
Tarpon Springs, FL 34688-6327, USA

Davis, Paige (Television Host)
ID Public Relations
8409 Santa Monica Blvd
West Hollywood, CA 90069-4209, USA

Davis, Pascall (Football Player)
St Louis Rams
937 Plumeria Dr
Arlington, TX 76002-2402, USA

Davis, Paul H (Butch) (Coach)
Clveland Browns
76 Lou Groza Blvd
Berea, OH 44017-1269, USA

Davis, Phyllis (Actor)
29330 SE Hillyard Dr # D14
Boring, OR 97009-8502, USA

Davis, Preston (Football Player)
Indianapolis Colts
1282 W 100th Pl
Northglenn, CO 80260-6208, USA

Davis, Ralph (Basketball Player)
Cincinnati Royals
2624 S Kathwood Cir
Cincinnati, OH 45236-1026, USA

Davis, Rennie (Politician)
Birth of a New Nation
905 S Gilpin St
Denver, CO 80209-4520, USA

Davis, Reuben (Football Player)
Tampa Bay Buccaneers
4424 Lystra Rd
Chapel Hill, NC 27517-8854, USA

Davis, Richard (Musician)
SRO Artists
6629 University Ave Ste 206
Middleton, WI 53562-3037, USA

Davis, Robert T (Bobby) Jr (Football Player)
Boston Yanks
3721 Eaglebrook Dr
Gastonia, NC 28056-8832, USA

Davis, Roger (Actor)
Janette Anderson Talent Agency
9682 Via Torino
Burbank, CA 91504-1410, USA

Davis, Roger (Football Player)
Chicago Bears
17522 Harvard Ave
Cleveland, OH 44128-1718, USA

Davis, Ron (Baseball Player)
New York Yankees
11748 N 90th Pl
Scottsdale, AZ 85260-6841, USA

Davis, Ron (Basketball Player)
Atlanta Hawks
316 E Keogh Dr
Phoenix, AZ 85022-1836, USA

Davis, Ronald (Football Player)
St Louis Cardinals
44 Mariner Green Dr
Corte Madera, CA 94925-2042, USA

Davis, Ronald (Ron) (Artist)
PO Box 293
Arroyo Hondo, NM 87513-0293, USA

Davis, Ross (Baseball Player)
Baltimore Elite Giants
3799 E Willow St Apt 405
Long Beach, CA 90815-1769, USA

Davis, Russ (Baseball Player)
New York Yankees
3351 Crescent Dr
Hueytown, AL 35023-2919, USA

Davis, Russell (Football Player)
Chicago Bears
309 N Reilly Rd
Fayetteville, NC 28303-2001, USA

Davis, Russell (Football Player)
Pittsburgh Steelers
1208 Tanbark Ln E
Jackson, MI 49203-1275, USA

Davis, Russell A (Football Player)
Buffalo Bills
4236 Crosswood Dr
Burtonsville, MD 20866-1350, USA

Davis, Russell C (General)
Chief National Guard Bureau
Hqusaf
Pentagon
Washington, DC 20310-0001, USA

Davis, Ruth (Baseball Player)
1917 Park Ave
Cheyenne, WY 82007-3395, USA

Davis, Sam (Football Player)
Pittsburgh Steelers
423 Edgemont St
Mt Washington, PA 15211-2405, USA

Davis, Sammy (Football Player)
San Diego Chargers
4020 Murphy Canyon Rd
San Diego, CA 92123-4407, USA

Davis, Sammy L (War Hero)
3376 N 100th St
Flat Rock, IL 62427, USA

Davis, Scott (Figure Skater)
5308 Worthington Dr
Bethesda, MD 20816-1620, USA

Davis, Spencer
PO Box 1821
Ojai, CA 93024-1821, USA

Davis, Stephen H (Engineer, Mathematician)
2735 Simpson St
Evanston, IL 60201-2029, USA

Davis, Steve (Baseball Player)
Chicago Cubs
6717 Westbury Ct
Benbrook, TX 76132-2700, USA

Davis, Steve (Football Player)
Pittsburgh Steelers
812 McCorkie Dr
Lexington, VA 24450, USA

Davis, Steve (Misc)
Matchroom Snooker Ltd
10 Western Road
Romford
Essex RM1 3JT, UNITED KINGDOM (UK)

Davis, Storm (Baseball Player)
Baltimore Orioles
8469 Mizner Cir E
Jacksonville, FL 32217-4326, USA

Davis, Ted (Football Player)
Baltimore Colts
5401 Riverbend Dr
Knoxville, TN 37919-8953, USA

Davis, Terrell (Athlete)
Denver Broncos
13655 Broncos Pkwy
Englewood, CO 80112-4150, USA

Davis, Tim (Baseball Player)
Seattle Mariners
19867 NW County Road 67
Bristol, FL 32321-3713, USA

Davis, Todd (Actor)
245 S Keystone St
Burbank, CA 91506-2727, USA

Davis, Tommy (Baseball Player)
Baltimore Orioles
4685 Cavalier Dr
Semmes, AL 36575-4467, USA

Davis, Trench (Baseball Player)
Pittsburgh Pirates
306 40th Street Cir W
Palmetto, FL 34221-9516, USA

Davis, Troy (Football Player)
New Orleans Saints
11861 SW 190th St
Miami, FL 33177-3940, USA

Davis, Truman A (Misc)
Congress of Industrial Unions
303 Ridge St
Alton, IL 62002-6492, USA

Davis, Vicki (Actor)
c/o Staff Member *Handprint Entertainment*
1100 Glendon Ave Ste 1000
Los Angeles, CA 90024-3514, USA

Davis, Viola (Actor)
Agency for Performing Arts
405 S Beverly Dr Ste 500
Beverly Hills, CA 90212-4425, USA

Davis, W Eugene (Judge)
US Court of Appeals
556 Jefferson St
Lafayette, LA 70501-6950, USA

Davis, Walter (Basketball Player)
c/o Staff Member *Washington Wizards*
601 F St NW
Mcl Center
Washington, DC 20004-1605, USA

Davis, Walter (Basketball Player)
6549 E Euclid Pi
Centennial, CO 80111, USA

Davis, Warren (Basketball Player)
Anaheim Amigos
4865 Alexander Rd
Fort Washington, MD 20744, USA

Davis, Warwick
c/o Staff Member *Willow Personal Management*
151 Main Street
Yaxley PE7 3LD, UNITED KINGDOM (UK)

Davis, Wendell (Football Player)
Chicago Bears
25797 N Arrowhead Dr
Mundelein, IL 60060-4040, USA

Davis, Wendell (Football Player)
San Diego Chargers
PO Box 76384
Washington, DC 20013-6384, USA

Davis, Wendell (Football Player)
Dallas Cowboys
6831 Kennon St
Shreveport, LA 71119-7519, USA

Davis, William (Actor)
c/o Staff Member *Lucas Talent Inc*
Sun Tower Floor 7
100 W Pender St
Vancouver, BC V6B 1R8, CANADA

Davis, William (Baseball Player)
Philadelphia Stars
605 Harden St
Reidsville, NC 27320-2811, USA

Davis, William D (Willie) (Football Player)
Cleveland Browns
7352 Vista Del Mar
Venice, CA 90293, USA

Davis, William E (Business Person)
Niagara Mohawk Holdings
300 Erie Blvd W
Syracuse, NY 13202-4250, USA

Davis, William G (Government Official)
Tory Tory DesLauries
Aetna Tower
#3000
Toronto, ON M5K 1N2, CANADA

Davis, William L (Business Person)
R R Donnelley & Sons
77 W Wacker Dr
Chicago, IL 60601-1604, USA

Davis, Willie (Baseball Player)
Los Angeles Dodgers
1916 W Victory Blvd
Burbank, CA 91506-1150, USA

Davis, Woody (Baseball Player)
Detroit Tigers
PO Box 97
Odum, GA 31555-0097, USA

Davis-Wrightsil, Clarissa (Basketball Player)
Phoenix Mercury
201 E Jefferson St
American West Arena
Phoenix, AZ 85004-2412, USA

Davison, Beverly C (Religious Leader)
American Baptist Churches
PO Box 851
Valley Forge, PA 19482-0851, USA

Davison, Bruce (Actor)
Gersh Agency
232 N Canon Dr
Beverly Hills, CA 90210-5302, USA

Davison, Fred C (Educator)
National Science Foundation
1 7th St Ste 502
Augusta, GA 30901-1341, USA

Davison, Michelle
1830 Grace Ave Apt 7
Los Angeles, CA 90028-4881, USA

Davison, Mike (Baseball Player)
San Francisco Giants
578 Prospect St NE
Hutchinson, MN 55350-1715, USA

Davison, Peter (Actor)
18-21 Jermyn St
#300
London SW1Y 6NB, UNITED KINGDOM
(UK)

Davison, Sam (Religious Leader)
International Baptist Bible Fellowship
720 E Kearnet St
Springfield, MO 65803, USA

Davison, Scott (Baseball Player)
c/o Staff Member *Houston Astros*
501 Crawford St
Astros Field
Houston, TX 77002-2113, USA

Davoli, Andrew (Actor)
c/o Greg Clark *Untitled Entertainment (LA)*
331 N Maple Dr Fl 3
Beverly Hills, CA 90210-3827, USA

Dawber, Pam (Actor)
c/o Staff Member *Wings Productions Inc*
2236 Encinitas Blvd Ste A
Encinitas, CA 92024-4353, USA

Dawe, Jason (Hockey Player)
Buffalo Sabres
5695 Field Brook Dr # F
East Amherst, NY 14051-2508, USA

Dawes, Joseph (Cartoonist)
20 Church Ct
Closter, NJ 07624-2803, USA

Dawkins, Brian (Football Player)
c/o Staff Member *Philadelphia Eagles*
1 Novacare Way
Philadelphia, PA 19145-5996, USA

Dawkins, Dale (Football Player)
New York Jets
388 Woodman Dr
Belgrade, MT 59714-7242, USA

Dawkins, Darryl (Basketball Player)
Philadelphia 76ers
Alexander Rd
Atwater, OH 44201, USA

Dawkins, Johnny (Basketball Player)
Duke University
Cameron Indoor Stadium
Athletic Dept
Durham, NC 27708-0001, USA

Dawkins, Johnny (Basketball Player)
San Antonio Spurs
2604 Vintage Hill Ct
Durham, NC 27712-9492, USA

Dawkins, Peter M (Pete) (Business Person, Football Player)
80 W River Rd
Rumson, NJ 07760-1139, USA

Dawkins, Sean (Football Player)
Indianapolis Colts
826 Weichert Dr
Morgan Hill, CA 95037-3785, USA

Dawkins, Travis (Gookie) (Baseball Player)
Cincinnati Reds
PO Box 81325
Conyers, GA 30013-9325, USA

Dawley, Bill (Baseball Player)
Houston Astros
RR 2
Jewett City, CT 06351, USA

Dawley, Joey (Baseball Player)
Atlanta Braves
14767 Big Bear Dr
Moreno Valley, CA 92555-7054, USA

Dawley, Joseph W (Joe) (Artist)
13 Wholly St
Cranford, NJ 07016, USA

Dawsey, Lawrence (Football Player)
Tampa Bay Buccaneers
2801 Chancellorsville Dr Apt 922
Tallahassee, FL 32312-4822, USA

Dawson, Andre (Baseball Player)
Montreal Expos
10601 SW 74th Ave
Miami, FL 33156-3829, USA

Dawson, Anthony
Via Riccione 6 Fregene
Fiumicino RM 00050, ITALY

Dawson, Ashley Taylor (Actor)
c/o Staff Member *Blackburn Sachs Associates*
88-90 Crawford St
London W1H 2BS, UNITED KINGDOM
(UK)

Dawson, Buck (Swimmer)
Swimming Hall of Fame
1 Hall Of Fame Dr
Fort Lauderdale, FL 33316-1694, USA

Dawson, Dale (Football Player)
Minnesota Vikings
4487 Gardenia Dr
Palm Beach Gardens, FL 33410-5438, USA

Dawson, Dermontti (Football Player)
Pittsburgh Steelers
24 Avenue Of Champions
Nicholasville, KY 40356-9721, USA

Dawson, Douglas A (Doug) (Football Player)
St Louis Cardinals
1 Riverway Ste 900
Dawson Financial Services
Houston, TX 77056-1906, USA

Dawson, eonard R (Lenny/Len) (Athlete, Correspondent, Football Player)
Pittsburgh Steelers
4950 Central St Apt 606
Kansas City, MO 64112-2588, USA

Dawson, Gib (Football Player)
Green Bay Packers
135 E Mariette Ave
Phoenix, AZ 85012, USA

Dawson, J Cutler Jr (Admiral)
Commander
Striking Fleet Atlantic/2Nd Fleet
FPO, AE 08506, USA

Dawson, Jim (Basketball Player)
Indiana Pacers
61 Glendale Ave
Rye, NY 10580-1547, USA

Dawson, Kim (Actor, Producer, Writer)
c/o Staff Member *Skydog Productions*
1000 Universal Studios Plz Bldg 22A
Orlando, FL 32819-7601, USA

Dawson, Lake (Football Player)
Kansas City Chiefs
33228 37th Pl SW
Federal Way, WA 98023-2959, USA

Dawson, Marco (Golfer)
3053 Shoal Creek Village Dr
Lakeland, FL 33803-5425, USA

Dawson, Mike (Football Player)
St Louis Cardinals
8070 N Highcountry Ave
Tucson, AZ 85741-4624, USA

Dawson, Rhett (Football Player)
Houston Oilers
1717 W 6th St Ste 260
Austin, TX 78703-4777, USA

Dawson, Richard (Actor)
1117 Angelo Dr
Beverly Hills, CA 90210-2703, USA

Dawson, Rosario (Actor)
c/o Evan Hainey *Untitled Entertainment (LA)*
331 N Maple Dr Fl 3
Beverly Hills, CA 90210-3827, USA

Dawson, Roxann (Actor)
Innovative Artists
1505 10th St
Santa Monica, CA 90401-2805, USA

Day, Bill (Cartoonist)
Memphis Commercial-Appeal
495 Union Ave
Editorial Dept
Memphis, TN 38103-3217, USA

Day, Boots (Baseball Player)
St Louis Cardinals
1154 Vespasian Way
Chesterfield, MO 63017-3016, USA

Day, Charlie (Actor)
c/o Bonnie Bernstein *Endeavor Agency LLC (NY)*
23 Watts St Fl 6
New York, NY 10013, USA

Day, Chon (Cartoonist)
127 Main St
Ashaway, RI 02804-2239, USA

Day, Doris (Actor)
c/o Linda Dozoretz *Linda Dozoretz Communications*
8033 W Sunset Blvd # 996
West Hollywood, CA 90046-2401, USA

Day, Eagle (Football Player)
Washington Redskins
262 Eastbrooke St
Jackson, MS 39216-4716, USA

Day, EJay (Musician)
c/o Staff Member *Fox Television Studios*
10201 W Pico Blvd Bldg 41
Los Angeles, CA 90064-2606, USA

Day, Felicia (Actor)
c/o Staff Member *Lighthouse Entertainment*
409 N Camden Dr Ste 202
Beverly Hills, CA 90210-4423, USA

Day, Gail (Publisher)
Plaboy Magazine
680 N Lake Shore Dr
Chicago, IL 60611-4546, USA

Day, Glen (Golfer)
PO Box 25620
Little Rock, AR 72221-5620, USA

Day, Howie (Musician)
c/o Staff Member *Paradigm (Monterey)*
509 Hartnell St
Monterey, CA 93940-2825, USA

Day, Inaya (Musician)
c/o Staff Member *Diva Central Inc*
7510 W Sunset Blvd Ste 1445
Los Angeles, CA 90046-3408, USA

Day, Jennifer
PO Box 120479
Nashville, TN 37212-0479, USA

Day, Joe (Hockey Player)
Hartford Whalers
805 Shoreline Rd
Lake Barrington, IL 60010-3878, USA

Day, Julian (Business Person)
Kmart
PO Box 8073
Royal Oak, MI 48068-8073, USA

Day, Laraine
10313 Lauriston Ave
Los Angeles, CA 90025-6010, USA

Day, Larraine (Actor)
71 Sand Rio
Ivins, UT 84738-6004, USA

Day, Mary (Misc)
Washington Ballet
3515 Wisconsin Ave NW
Washington, DC 20016-3085, USA

Day, Matt (Actor)
Robyn Gardiner Mgmt
397 Riley St
Surrey Hills, NSW 2010, AUSTRALIA

Day, Patrick (Jockey)
c/o Staff Member *Jockeys Guild*
PO Box 150
Forward
Monrovia, CA 91017-0150, USA

Day, Peter R (Scientist)
8200 Tarsier Ave
New Port Richey, FL 34653-6559, USA

Day, Robert (Director)
Creative Artists Agency
9830 Wilshire Blvd
Beverly Hills, CA 90212-1804, USA

Day, Terry (Football Player)
New York Jets
PO Box 85
Pickens, MS 39146-0085, USA

Day, Thomas B (Educator)
San Diego State University
President's Office
San Diego, CA 92182, USA

Day, Zach (Baseball Player)
Montreal Expos
7133 Glenellyn Dr
Cincinnati, OH 45236-3709, USA

Day-George, Lynda (Actor)
10310 Riverside Dr Apt 104
Toluca Lake, CA 91602-2457, USA

Day-Lewis, Daniel (Actor)
c/o Gene Parseghian *Untitled
Entertainment (NY)*
322 8th Ave Ste 601
New York, NY 10001-6715, USA

Dayan, Isaac (Actor)
c/o Staff Member *TV Caracol*
Calle 76 #11 - 35
Piso 10AA
Bogota DC 26484, COLOMBIA

Daye, Darren (Basketball Player)
Washington Bullets
41 Carriage Dr
Irvine, CA 92602-0776, USA

Dayett, Brian (Baseball Player)
New York Yankees
10 Hemlock Terrace Ext
Deep River, CT 06417-1606, USA

Daykin, Anthony (Football Player)
Detroit Lions
5204 Cross Ridge Cir
Woodstock, GA 30188-4381, USA

Dayley, Ken (Baseball Player)
Atlanta Braves
2115 E 12th St
The Dalles, OR 97058-3913, USA

Dayne, Ron (Football Player)
New York Giants
211 Harbor View Ter
Edgewater, NJ 07020-1190, USA

Dayne, Taylor (Actor, Musician)
c/o Staff Member *Innovative Artists (LA)*
1505 10th St
Santa Monica, CA 90401-2805, USA

Days, Drews S III (Educator, Government
Official)
Yale University
Law School
New Haven, CT 06520, USA

Dayton, Jonathan (Director)
Bob Industries
1313 5th St
Santa Monica, CA 90401-1414, USA

Dayton, June (Actor)
Abrams Artists
9200 W Sunset Blvd Ste 1125
Los Angeles, CA 90069-3610, USA

Daze, Eric (Hockey Player)
Chicago Blackhawks
213 W 3rd St
Hinsdale, IL 60521-4021, USA

dc Talk (Musician)
c/o Staff Member *Creative Artists Agency
LCC (CAA-LA)*
2000 Avenue Of The Stars
Los Angeles, CA 90067-4700, USA

De Angelis, Rosemary
817 W End Ave
New York, NY 10025-5370, USA

de Aragow, Maria
1159 10th Ave
San Diego, CA 92101-5509, USA

De Benning, Burr (Actor)
4235 Kingfisher Rd
Calabasas, CA 91302-1842, USA

De Blanc, Jefferson J (Misc)
321 Saint Martin St
Saint Martinville, LA 70582-4531, USA

De Bont, Jan (Director, Producer)
c/o Staff Member *Blue Tulip Productions*
2202 Main St
Santa Monica, CA 90405-2218, USA

De Bruijn, Inge (Athlete, Olympic Athlete,
Swimmer)
Top voor Talent
Van Ostadestraat 368-2
Amsterdam 1074 XA, THE
NETHERLANDS

de Cordova, Fred (Actor, Director,
Producer)
1875 Carla Rdg
Beverly Hills, CA 90210-1936, USA

de Dios, Silvia (Actor)
c/o Staff Member *TV Caracol*
Calle 76 #11 - 35
Piso 10AA
Bogota DC 26484, COLOMBIA

De Eugenia, Coco (Actor)
c/o Nancy Harding *Powerhouse Talent*
PO Box 1748
Studio City, CA 91614-0748, USA

de Gruiin, Inge
PO Box 302
Arnhem 6800 AH, THE NETHERLANDS

De Heer, Rolf (Director, Producer, Writer)
c/o Staff Member *Vertigo Productions Pty
Ltd*
3 Butler Dr
Hendon SA 5014, AUSTRALIA

De Jesus, Wanda (Actor)
c/o Staff Member *Abrams Artists Agency
(LA)*
9200 W Sunset Blvd Ph 11
Los Angeles, CA 90069-3601, USA

De Jong, Michael
c/o Staff Member *Mark Edward Inc*
325 W 8th St #1011
New York, NY 10018, USA

De La Cruz, Veronica (Television Host)
c/o Staff Member *CNN (Atlanta)*
1 Cnn Ctr NW
PO Box 105366
Atlanta, GA 30303-2762, USA

de la Fuente, Marian (Actor)
c/o Staff Member *Telemundo*
2470 W 8th Ave
Hialeah, FL 33010-2000, USA

De La Garza, Alana (Actor)
c/o Staff Member *SDB Partners Inc*
1801 Avenue Of The Stars Ste 902
Los Angeles, CA 90067-5981, USA

De La Hoya, Oscar (Athlete, Boxer)
c/o Staff Member *Creative Artists Agency
LCC (CAA-LA)*
2000 Avenue Of The Stars
Los Angeles, CA 90067-4700, USA

de la Reguera, Ana (Actor)
c/o Staff Member *TV Azteca*
Periferico Sur 4121
Colonia Fuentes del Pedregal
DF CP 14141, MEXICO

De La Renta, Oscar (Fashion Designer)
550 7th Ave Fl 8
New York, NY 10018-3229, USA

De La Soul (Music Group)
2697 Heath Ave
Bronx, NY 10463-7546, USA

De La Tour, Frances (Actor)
Kate Feast
Primrose Hill Studios
Fitzroy Road
London, England NW18TR, UNITED
KINGDOM (UK)

De Laurentiis, Giada (Chef)
c/o Staff Member *Food Network, The*
75 9th Ave
New York, NY 10011-7006, USA

De Laurentiis, Raffaella (Actor, Producer)
Rafaella Productions
100 Universal City Plz
Bungalow 5162
Universal City, CA 91608-1002, USA

De Laurentis, Dino (Producer)
c/o Staff Member *Dino De Laurentis
Company*
100 Universal City Plz
Bungalow 5195
Universal City, CA 91608-1002, USA

de Leon, Miguel (Actor)
c/o Staff Member *Televisa*
Blvd Adolfo Lopez Mateos 232
Colonia San Angel INN
DF CP 01060, MEXICO

de Lint, Derek
Features Creative Management
Entrepotdok 76-A
Amsterdam AD, THE NETHERLANDS

De Longis, Anthony
PO Box 323
Burbank, CA 91503-0323, USA

De Los Angeles, Victoria (Opera Singer)
Avenida de Pedralbes 57
Barcelona 08034, SPAIN

de Mol, John (Producer)
c/o Staff Member *William Morris Agency
(WMA-LA)*
1 William Morris Pl
Beverly Hills, CA 90212-4261, USA

de Molina, Raul (Actor)
c/o Staff Member *Univision*
605 3rd Ave Fl 12
New York, NY 10158-1299, USA

De Munn, Jeffrey (Jeff) (Actor)
c/o Larry Taube *Principal Entertainment
(LA)*
1964 Westwood Blvd Ste 400
Los Angeles, CA 90025-4695, USA

de Pablo, Cote (Actor)
c/o Jason Spire *Inspire Entertainment*
252 7th Ave Apt 7Z
New York, NY 10001-7336, USA

De Paul, Lynsey
21A Clifftown Rd
Southend-on-Sea Essex, ENGLAND SSI
1AB, UNITED KINGDOM (UK)

de Ravin, Emilie (Actor)
c/o Darren Goldberg *1 Management*
9000 W Sunset Blvd Ph 1550
West Hollywood, CA 90069-1838, USA

De Rossi, Portia (Actor)
c/o Nancy Josephson *Endeavor Agency
LLC (LA)*
9601 Wilshire Blvd Fl 3
Beverly Hills, CA 90210-5204, USA

de Silva, Jorge (Actor)
c/o Staff Member *Televisa*
Blvd Adolfo Lopez Mateos 232
Colonia San Angel INN
DF CP 01060, MEXICO

de Vasconcelos, Tasha (Actor)
c/o Samira Higham *International Creative
Management (ICM-UK)*
Oxford House
76 Oxford St
London W1N OAX, UNITED KINGDOM
(UK)

De Vries, Peter
170 Cross Hwy
Westport, CT 06880-2841, USA

Dea, Bill (Hockey Player)
New York Rangers
2636 W Bartlett Way
Queen Creek, AZ 85242-6611, USA

Deacon, Brian
85 Gladstone Rd.
London, ENGLAND SW19, UNITED
KINGDOM (UK)

Deacon, John (Musician)
The Mill Mill Lane
367 Windsor Hwy
New Windsor, NY 12553-7900, USA

Deacon, Richard (Artist)
Lisson Gallery
67 Lisson St
London NW1 5DA, UNITED KINGDOM
(UK)

Deacon, Terrence (Misc)
Harvard University
Neuroanatomy Dept
Cambridge, MA 02138, USA

Dead Can Dance (Music Group)
c/o Staff Member *William Morris Agency
(WMA-LA)*
1 William Morris Pl
Beverly Hills, CA 90212-4261, USA

Dead, The (Music Group)
c/o Staff Member *Paradigm (Monterey)*
509 Hartnell St
Monterey, CA 93940-2825, USA

Deadmarsh, Adam (Hockey Player)
Quebec Nordiques
PO Box 262
Metaline Falls, WA 99153-0262, USA

Deadmarsh, Butch (Hockey Player)
Buffalo Sabres
282 Diamond Dr SE
Calgary, AB T2J 7E2, CANADA

Deadsy (Music Group)
c/o Jenna Adler *Creative Artists Agency
LCC (CAA-LA)*
2000 Avenue Of The Stars
Los Angeles, CA 90067-4700, USA

DeAgostini, Doris (Skier)
6780 Airolo
SWITZERLAND

Deakin, Paul (Musician)
AristoMedia
1620 16th Ave S
Nashville, TN 37212-2908, USA

Deakins, Roger (Cinematographer)
International Creative Mgmt
8942 Wilshire Blvd # 219
Beverly Hills, CA 90211-1908, USA

Deal, Ellis (Baseball Player)
Boston Red Sox
9009 N May Ave Apt 164
Oklahoma City, OK 73120-4464, USA

Deal, Kim (Musician)
William Morris Agency
151 El Camino Dr
Beverly Hills, CA 90212-2775, USA

Deal, Lance (Athlete, Track Athlete)
911 Elkay Dr
Eugene, OR 97404-6512, USA

Deal, Rufus (Football Player)
Washington Redskins
5309 10th Ave E
Tuscaloosa, AL 35405-5111, USA

DeAlmeida, Joaquin
2372 Veteran Ave # 102
Los Angeles, CA 90064-2147, USA

Dean, Barry (Hockey Player)
Colorado Rockies
315 Marsh Street
Maple Creek, SK S0N 1N0, CANADA

Dean, Christopher (Dancer)
124 Ladies Mile Road
Brighton
East Sussex BN1 8TE, UNITED
KINGDOM (UK)

Dean, Eddie (Actor, Musician)
32161 Sailview Ln
Westlake Village, CA 91361-3620, USA

Dean, Fred (Football Player)
Washington Redskins
Howard University
601 Fairmont St NW Cook Hall
Washington, DC 20001, USA

Dean, Hazel
7 Kentish Town Rd.
London, ENGLAND NW1 8N4, UNITED
KINGDOM (UK)

Dean, Howard (Politician)
Democratic National Committee
430 S Capitol St SE
Washington, DC 20003-4095, USA

Dean, Ira (Musician)
Creative Artists Agency
9830 Wilshire Blvd
Beverly Hills, CA 90212-1804, USA

Dean, Jimmy (Musician)
10151 Carver Rd
Cincinnati, OH 45242-4758, USA

Dean, John G (Diplomat)
29 Blvd Jules Sandeau
Paris 75116, FRANCE

Dean, Kevin (Hockey Player)
New Jersey Devils
1905 Wayzata Blvd
Sports Personnel Services
Wayzata, MN 55391-5001, USA

Dean, Kiley (Musician)
c/o Staff Member *Interscope Records (LA)*
- Main
2220 Colorado Ave
Santa Monica, CA 90404-3506, USA

Dean, Laura (Choreographer, Composer)
Dean Dance & Music Foundation
552 Broadway # 400
New York, NY 10012-3922, USA

Dean, Loren (Actor)
c/o Staff Member *Thruline Entertainment*
9250 Wilshire Blvd Ground Fl
Beverly Hills, CA 90210, USA

Dean, Paula (Actor)
The Lady and Sons
102 W Congress St
Savannah, GA 31401-2508, USA

Dean, Paula (Chef, Television Host)
The Lady and Son's Restaurant
311 W Congress St
Savannah, GA 31401-2408, USA

Dean, Randy (Football Player)
New York Giants
1310 E Bay Point Rd
Bayside, WI 53217-1405, USA

Dean, Stafford R (Opera Singer)
I C M Artists
40 W 57th St
New York, NY 10019-4001, USA

Dean, Ted (Football Player)
Philadelphia Eagles
16474 W Lava Dr
Surprise, AZ 85374-6250, USA

Dean, Tommy (Baseball Player)
c/o Staff Member *Los Angeles Dodgers*
(LA Dodgers)
1000 Elysian Park Ave
Los Angeles, CA 90012-1112, USA

Dean, Vernon (Football Player)
Washington Redskins
9639 W Withers Way Cir
Houston, TX 77065-4905, USA

Dean III, John W (Misc)
9496 Rembert Ln
Beverly Hills, CA 90210-1720, USA

DeAnda, Paula (Musician)
c/o Staff Member *J Records (Division of*
BMG Entertainment)
745 5th Ave Fl 6
New York, NY 10151-0099, USA

Deane, William Patrick (General)
Government House
Canberra, ACT 26000, AUSTRALIA

DeAngelis, Beverly (Psychic)
505 S Beverly Dr # 1017
Beverly Hills, CA 90212, USA

Deangelis, Billy (Basketball Player)
New Jersey Nets
14 Pickering Dr
Trenton, NJ 08691-2332, USA

Deardan, Robin (Actor)
c/o Staff Member *Commercial Talent*
Agency
9255 W Sunset Blvd Ste 505
West Hollywood, CA 90069-3301, USA

Dearden, James (Director)
International Creative Mgmt
8942 Wilshire Blvd # 219
Beverly Hills, CA 90211-1908, USA

Deardorff, Jeff (Baseball Player)
Milwaukee Brewers
16823 Rockwell Heights Ln
Clermont, FL 34711-7907, USA

Deardurff-Schmidt, Deena (Swimmer)
742 Murray Dr
El Cajon, CA 92020-5640, USA

Dearie, Blossom (Musician, Songwriter,
Writer)
F Sharp Productions
PO Box 2040
New York, NY 10101-2040, USA

DeArmond, Frank (Astronaut)
3086 Ravencrest Cir
Prescott, AZ 86303-5790, USA

Deas, Justin (Actor)
Paradigm Agency
10100 Santa Monica Blvd Ste 2500
Los Angeles, CA 90067-4116, USA

D'Eath, Tom (Misc)
PO Box 350437
Grand Island, FL 32735-0437, USA

Deavenport, Earnest Jr (Business Person)
Eastman Chemical Co
100 N Eastman Rd
Kingsport, TN 37660-5299, USA

Deaver, Jeffrey (Writer)
Pocket Star Books
1230 Avenue Of The Americas
New York, NY 10020-1513, USA

Deaver, Michael K (Government Official)
Deaver Assoc
1025 Thomas Jefferson St NW
Washington, DC 20007-5201, USA

Deb, Debbie (Musician)
c/o Staff Member *Green Light Talent*
Agency
PO Box 3172
Beverly Hills, CA 90212-0172, USA

DeBakey, Michael E (Doctor)
Baylor Medical Center
1200 Moursund St
Houston, TX 77030-3404, USA

DeBarge, Eldra (El) (Music Group,
Musician)
c/o Staff Member *Pyramid Entertainment*
Group
377 Rector Pl Apt 21A
New York, NY 10280-1439, USA

Debarr, Denny (Baseball Player)
Toronto Blue Jays
33843 Juliet Cir
Fremont, CA 94555-3452, USA

Debela, Kingsford (General, Governor)
PO Box 113
Port Moresby, PAPUA NEW GUINEA

DeBellevue, Charles B (War Hero)
916 Huntsman Rd
Edmond, OK 73003-3520, USA

DeBello, James (Actor)
c/o Craig Shapiro *Innovative Artists (LA)*
1505 10th St
Santa Monica, CA 90401-2805, USA

Debenedet, Nelson (Hockey Player)
Detroit Red Wings
21637 Welch Rd
Northville, MI 48167-2101, USA

DeBerg, Steve (Coach, Football Player)
San Francisco 49ers
17920 Simms Rd
Odessa, FL 33556-4751, USA

Deblois, Lucien (Hockey Player)
New York Rangers
407-350 Boul Graham
Mont-Royal, PQ H3P-2C8, CANADA

Debney, John (Composer)
Kraft-Benjamin-Engel
15233 Ventura Blvd Ste 200
Sherman Oaks, CA 91403-2244, USA

DeBoer, Harm E (Business Person)
Russell Corp
755 Lee St
Alexander City, AL 35010-2638, USA

DeBoer, Nicole (Actor)
c/o Steven Fenton *Fenton-Kritzer*
Entertainment
8840 Wilshire Blvd Fl 3
Beverly Hills, CA 90211-2606, USA

DeBoer, Rick (Actor)
Pacific Artists
510 W Hastings St
#1404
Vancouver, BC V6B 1L8, CANADA

Debol, Dave (Hockey Player)
Hartford Whalers
3133 Textile Rd
Saline, MI 48176-9789, USA

DeBold, Adolfo J (Doctor, Physicist)
Ottawa Civic Hospital
1053 Carling Ave
Ottawa, ON K1Y 4E9, CANADA

DeBorba, Dorothy (Actor)
PO Box 2723
Livermore, CA 94551-2723, USA

DeBorchgrave, Arnaud (Editor)
2141 Wyoming Ave NW
Washington, DC 20008-3916, USA

Debre, Michael (Prime Minister)
20 Rue Jacob
Paris 75006, FRANCE

DeBrunhoff, Laurent (Writer)
Mary Ryan Gallery
527 W 26th St
New York, NY 10001-5503, USA

DeBurgh, Chris (Musician, Songwriter,
Writer)
Kenny Thomson Mgmt
754 Fulham Road
London SW6 5SW, UNITED KINGDOM
(UK)

Deby, Idriss (General, President)
President's Office
N'Djamena
CHAD

Decambra-Kelley, Lillian (Baseball Player)
250 South St
Somerset, MA 02726-5616, USA

DeCarava, Roy (Photographer)
81 Halsey St
Brooklyn, NY 11216-1902, USA

DeCario, Yvonne (Actor)
1483 Golf Course Ln
Nipomo, CA 93444-9307, USA

DeCarl, Nancy
4615 Winnetka
Woodland Hills, CA 91364, USA

Decarlo, Arthur (Football Player)
Pittsburgh Steelers
9030 Manordale Ln
Ellicott City, MD 21042-5327, USA

DeCarlo, Mark (Actor)
c/o Staff Member *Lapides Entertainment*
1724 Venture Blvd Penthouse
Sherman Oaks, CA 92403, USA

DeCasabianca, Carnille (Actor)
Artmedia
20 Ave Rapp
Paris 75007, FRANCE

DeCastelia, F Robert (Athlete, Track
Athlete)
Australian Institute of Sport
PO Box 176
Belconnen, ACT 2616, AUSTRALIA

DeCesare, Carmella (Actor, Model)
c/o Staff Member *Playboy Enterprises Inc*
680 N Lake Shore Dr Ste 1500
Chicago, IL 60611-4455, USA

DeCinces, Douglas V (Doug) (Baseball
Player)
Baltimore Orioles
124 Riviera Way
Laguna Beach, CA 92651-1012, USA

Decker, Franz-Paul (Conductor)
Herbert Barrett
266 W 37th St Fl 20
New York, NY 10018-6648, USA

Decker, Marty (Baseball Player)
San Diego Padres
1630 Youngs Ln
Yuba City, CA 95991-1925, USA

Decker, Scott (Business Person)
HEALTHvision
6330 Commerce Dr Ste 100
Irving, TX 75063-6010, USA

Decker, Steve (Baseball Player)
San Francisco Giants
1024 Laurelridge St NE
Keizer, OR 97303-7208, USA

Deckers, Daphne (Actor)
Nagtzaan
Hoge Naardenweg 44
Hilversum, AG 1217, THE
NETHERLANDS

DeConcini, Dennis (Senator)
6014 Chesterbrook Rd
McLean, VA 22101-3210, USA

DeCosta, Sara (Hockey Player)
200 Cowesett Green Dr
Warwick, RI 02886-8570, USA

DeCoster, Roger (Race Car Driver)
MC Sports
1919 Torrance Blvd
Torrance, CA 90501-2722, USA

Decter, Midge (Writer)
120 E 81st St
New York, NY 10028-1428, USA

Dedkov, Anatoli I (Cosmonaut)
Potchta Kosmonavtov
Moskovskoi Oblasti
Syvisdny, Goroduk 141160, RUSSIA

Dedler, Karin
Hohenegg 21
Dietmannsried D-87463, GERMANY

Dedmon, Jeff (Baseball Player)
Atlanta Braves
21102 Broadwell Ave
Torrance, CA 90502-1636, USA

Dedrick, Jim (Baseball Player)
Baltimore Orioles
2929 NW Kennedy Ct
Portland, OR 97229-8099, USA

DeDuve, Christian R (Nobel Prize
Laureate)
80 Central Park W
New York, NY 10023-5204, USA

Dee, Donald (Don) (Basketball Player)
7924 N Pennsylvania Ave
Kansas City, MO 64118-1416, USA

Dee, Donnie (Football Player)
Indianapolis Colts
4927 Lassen Dr
Oceanside, CA 92056-5478, USA

Dee, Joey (Musician)
Horizon Mgmt
PO Box 8770
Endwell, NY 13762-8770, USA

Dee, Ruby (Actor)
44 Cortlandt Ave
New Rochelle, NY 10801-2006, USA

Dee, Sally (Golfer)
3508 W Barcelona St
Tampa, FL 33629-7010, USA

Dee-Lite (Musician)
428 Cedar St NW
Washington, DC 20012, USA

Deeb, Gary (Critic)
Chicago Sun-Times
350 N Orleans St Ste 1270
Editorial Dept
Chicago, IL 60654-2148, USA

Deedes of Aldington, William F
(Government Official)
New Hayters
Aldington, Kent TN25 7DT, UNITED
KINGDOM (UK)

Deedle, Nelson
PO Box 5358
Scottsdale, AZ 85261-5358, USA

Deeds, Lord Bill (Journalist)
c/o Staff Member *UNICEF*
Africa House
64-78 Kingsway
London WC2B 6NB, UNITED KINGDOM
(UK)

Deeley, Cat (Actor)
c/o Staff Member *Sue Terry Voices*
18 Broadwick St Fl 5
London W1F 8HS, UNITED KINGDOM
(UK)

Deen, Paula (Chef, Television Host,
Writer)
c/o Barry Weiner *The Artists Agency (LA)*
1180 S Beverly Dr Ste 301
Los Angeles, CA 90035-1154, USA

Deep Purple (Music Group)
c/o Staff Member *Agency Group Ltd, The
(UK)*
361-373 City Road
London EC1V 1PQ, UNITED KINGDOM
(UK)

Deependra Bir, Bikaram Shah Dev
(Prince)
Narayanhiti Royal Palace
Durbeg Marg
Kathmandu, NEPAL

Deer, Ada E (Government Official)
2537 Mutchler Rd
Fitchburg, WI 53711-7011, USA

Deering, John (Cartoonist)
6701 Westover Dr
Little Rock, AR 72207-3447, USA

Dees, Archie (Basketball Player)
Cincinnati Royals
4405 N Hillview Dr
Bloomington, IN 47408-9770, USA

Dees, Bowen C (Scientist)
29059 Meadow Glen Way W
Escondido, CA 92026-6502, USA

Dees, Charlie (Baseball Player)
Los Angeles Angels
1064 Allison Woods Ct
Lawrenceville, GA 30043-5383, USA

Dees, Morris S Jr (Activist)
Southern Poverty Law Center
PO Box 548
Montgomery, AL 36101-0548, USA

Dees, Rick (Entertainer, Musician)
KIIS-Radio
3400 W Riverside Dr Ste 800
Burbank, CA 91505-4671, USA

Deese, Derrick (Football Player)
San Francisco 49ers
PO Box 3356
Cerritos, CA 90703-3356, USA

Def Leppard
72 Chancellor's Rd
London, ENGLAND W6 9QB, UNITED
KINGDOM (UK)

DeFanti, Tom (Inventor)
University of Illinois
Electronic Visualization Labe
Chicago, IL 60607, USA

Default (Music Group)
c/o Staff Member *Agency Group Ltd, The
(NY)*
1775 Broadway Ste 515
New York, NY 10019-1903, USA

Defazio, Dean (Hockey Player)
Pittsburgh Penguins
2475 Logan Ave
Oakville, ON L6H 6P3, CANADA

DeFelitta, Raymond (Director, Writer)
c/o Gary Ungar *Exile Entertainment*
732 El Medio Ave
Pacific Palisades, CA 90272-3451, USA

DeFer, Kaylee (Actor)
c/o Staff Member *Abrams Artists Agency
(LA)*
9200 W Sunset Blvd Ph 11
Los Angeles, CA 90069-3601, USA

DeFerran, Gil (Race Car Driver)
524 Royal Plaza Dr
Fort Lauderdale, FL 33301-2518, USA

DeFleur, Lois B (Educator)
State University of New York
President's Office
Binghamton, NY 13902, USA

Deford, Frank (Writer)
PO Box 1109
Greens Farms, CT 06838-1109, USA

DeForest, Roy (Artist)
PO Box 47
Port Costa, CA 94569-0047, USA

DeForrest, Jeff (Sportscaster)
5211 NE 14th Ter
Fort Lauderdale, FL 33334-4907, USA

DeFrancisco, Joseph E (Joe) (General)
7754 Chars Ln
Springfield, VA 22153-1841, USA

DeFranco, Buddy (Musician)
22525 Coral Ave
Panama City, FL 32413-3047, USA

DeFrank, Joe (Race Car Driver)
PO Box 655
Lake Pleasant, NY 12108-0655, USA

DeFrantz, Anita (Misc)
US Olympic Committee
1 Olympic Plz
Colorado Springs, CO 80909-5760, USA

DeFreitas, Eric (Bowler)
175 W 12th St
New York, NY 10011-8275, USA

Deftones, The (Music Group)
c/o Jenna Adler *Creative Artists Agency
LCC (CAA-LA)*
2000 Avenue Of The Stars
Los Angeles, CA 90067-4700, USA

Deganhardt, Johannes J Cardinal
(Religious Leader)
Erzbischofliches Generalvikariat
Domplatz 3
Paderborn 33098, GERMANY

DeGarmo, Diana (Musician)
c/o Staff Member *American Idol*
7800 Beverly Blvd # 251
Los Angeles, CA 90036-2112, USA

DeGaspa, Philippe (Publisher)
Canadian Living Magazine
50 Holly St
Toronto, ON M4S 3B3, CANADA

Degeneres, Betty (Activist, Writer)
PlanetOut Partners USA Inc
PO Box 500
Attn: Ask Betty
San Francisco, CA 94104-0500, USA

Degeneres, Ellen (Actor, Comedian, Talk
Show Host)
The Ellen DeGeneres Show
Telepictures Productions
3000 W Alameda Ave #2700
Burbank, CA 91523-0001, USA

DeGennes, Pierre-Gilles (Nobel Prize
Laureate)
11 Place Marcelin-Berthelot
Paris 75005, FRANCE

Degerick, Mike (Baseball Player)
Chicago White Sox
2702 Lake Osborne Dr
Lake Worth, FL 33461-5665, USA

Degg, Jakki (Actor, Model)
c/o Staff Member *Jakki Degg.net*
PO Box 3673
Cannock WS12 1WD, UNITED
KINGDOM (UK)

DeGioia, John (Educator)
Georgetown University
President's Office
Washington, DC 20057-0001, USA

DeGiorgi, Salvatore Cardinal (Religious
Leader)
Curia Archivescovile
Corso Vittorio Emanuele 461
Palermo 90134, ITALY

DeGivenchy, Hubert (Designer, Fashion
Designer)
3 Avenue George V
Paris 75008, FRANCE

Degler, Carl N (Historian, Writer)
907 Mears Ct
Stanford, CA 94305-1041, USA

DeGlvenchy, Hubert T (Designer, Fashion
Designer)
3 Ave George V
Paris 75008, FRANCE

Degnan, John J (Business Person)
Chubb Corp
15 Mountain View Rd
Warren, NJ 07059-6795, USA

DeGrate, Tony (Football Player)
Green Bay Packers
13007 Heinerman Dr #901
Austin, TX 78727, USA

DeGraw, Gavin (Musician)
c/o Jonny (Jon) Podell *Podell Talent Agency LLC*
22 W 21st St Fl 9
New York, NY 10010-7095, USA

Degray, Dale (Hockey Player)
Calgary Flames
120-400 Grenfell St
Oshawa, ON L1J 4W7, CANADA

Dehaan, Kory (Baseball Player)
San Diego Padres
216 E 12th St
Pella, IA 50219-2218, USA

DeHaan, Richard W (Religious Leader)
3000 Kraft Ave SE
Grand Rapids, MI 49512-2024, USA

Dehaene, Jean-Luc (Prime Minister)
Berkendallaan 52
Vilvoorde 1800, BELGIUM

Dehart, Rick (Baseball Player)
Montreal Expos
811 NE Wabash Ave
Topeka, KS 66616-1443, USA

DeHaven, Gloria (Actor)
9232 Sunnyfield Dr
Las Vegas, NV 89134-6348, USA

DeHaven, Penny
PO Box 83
Brentwood, TN 37024-0083, USA

DeHavilland, Olivia (Actor)
c/o Staff Member *Douglas Gorman Rothacker & Wilhelm Inc*
1501 Broadway Ste 703
New York, NY 10036-5505, USA

Dehere, Terry (Basketball Player)
Los Angeles Clippers
120 Wayne St
Jersey City, NJ 07302-3406, USA

Dehmelt, Hans G (Nobel Prize Laureate)
1600 43rd Ave E
Seattle, WA 98112-3205, USA

Deighton, Len
10 Iron Bridge House Bridge Approach
London, ENGLAND NW1 8BD, UNITED KINGDOM (UK)

Deighton, Leonard C (Len) (Writer)
Fairymount Blackrock
Dundalk
County Louth, IRELAND

Deisenhofer, Johann (Nobel Prize Laureate)
3860 Echo Brook Ln
Dallas, TX 75229-5221, USA

Deitch, Donna (Director)
International Creative Mgmt
8942 Wilshire Blvd # 219
Beverly Hills, CA 90211-1908, USA

Deja, Andreas (Animator)
Disney Animation
PO Box 10200
Lake Buena Vista, FL 32830-0200, USA

Deja Vu
1 Touchstone Lane Chard
Somerset, ENGLAND TA20 1RF, UNITED KINGDOM (UK)

Dejdel, Jim (Baseball Player)
New York Yankees
14312 Wright Way
Broomfield, CO 80023-4045, USA

Dejean, Mike (Baseball Player)
Colorado Rockies
107 Yellowood Dr
West Monroe, LA 71291-9532, USA

Dejesus, Ivan (Baseball Player)
Los Angeles Dodgers
14608 Velleux Dr
Orlando, FL 32837-5467, USA

Dejesus, Jose (Baseball Player)
Kansas City Royals
7E6 Villa Del Carmen
Cidra, PR 00639, USA

Dejohn, Mark (Baseball Player)
Detroit Tigers
21 Bunker Hill Rd
New Britain, CT 06053-2206, USA

DeJohnette, Jack (Composer)
Silver Hollow Road
Willow, NY 12495, USA

DeJong, Pierre (Misc)
Laerence Livermore Laboratory
7000 East Ave
Livermore, CA 94550-9698, USA

DeJordy, Denis E (Hockey Player)
Chicago Blackhawks
472 Cherrin Des-Patriotes
Saint Charles, PQ J0L 2G0, CANADA

Dejurnett, Charles (Football Player)
San Diego Chargers
1355 Heritage Ct
Escondido, CA 92027-3972, USA

Dekdebrun, Allen (Football Player)
Buffalo Bisons
26 Hampton Hill Dr
Williamsville, NY 14221-5840, USA

DeKierk, Albert (Composer)
Crayenesterlaan
Haarlem 22, THE NETHERLANDS

DeKierk, Frederik W (Nobel Prize Laureate)
7 Eaton Square
London SW1, UNITED KINGDOM (UK)

DeKieweit, Cornelis W (Historian)
22 Berkeley St
Rochester, NY 14607-2209, USA

Dekker, Thomas (Actor)
c/o Staff Member *TalentWorks (LA)*
3500 W Olive Ave Ste 1400
Burbank, CA 91505-5512, USA

Del Amitri (Music Group, Songwriter, Writer)
c/o Scott Clayton *Creative Artists Agency (CAA-Nashville)*
3310 W End Ave Fl 5
Nashville, TN 37203-1028, USA

Del Arco, Jonathan (Actor)
c/o Kyle Fritz *Kyle Fritz Management*
6325 Heather Dr
Los Angeles, CA 90068-1633, USA

Del Bello, Jack (Football Player)
Baltimore Colts
391 Belfast Ter
Sebastian, FL 32958-5509, USA

del Boca, Andrea (Actor)
c/o Staff Member *Telefe - Argentina*
Pavon 2444 (C1248AAT)
Buenos Aires, ARGENTINA

del Castillo, Eric (Actor)
c/o Staff Member *Televisa*
Blvd Adolfo Lopez Mateos 232
Colonia San Angel INN
DF CP 01060, MEXICO

Del Castillo-Kinney, Ysora (Baseball Player)
1555 W 44th Pl Apt 216C
Hialeah, FL 33012-7837, USA

Del Gaizo, Jim (Football Player)
Miami Dolphins
9581 NW 13th St
Plantation, FL 33322-4809, USA

Del Greco, Al (Football Player)
Green Bay Packers
1012 Little Turtle Cir
Birmingham, AL 35242-3282, USA

Del Greco, Bobby (Baseball Player)
Pittsburgh Pirates
625 Southview Dr
Pittsburgh, PA 15226-2540, USA

Del Negro, Matthew (Actor)
c/o Adam Lazarus *Bauman Redanty & Shaul Agency*
5757 Wilshire Blvd Ste 473
Los Angeles, CA 90036-3632, USA

Del Negro, Vinny (Basketball Player)
Sacramento Kings
4719 N 65th St
Scottsdale, AZ 85251-1042, USA

Del Piero, Alessandro (Soccer Player)
Juventus FC
Piazza Crimea 7
Turin 10131, ITALY

Del Regil, Estrellita
PO Box 2004
Beverly Hills, CA 90213-2004, USA

del Rincon, Fernando (Actor)
c/o Staff Member *Univision*
605 3rd Ave Fl 12
New York, NY 10158-1299, USA

Del Rio, Jack (Coach, Football Player)
New Orleans Saints
4466 Glen Kernan Pkwy E
Jacksonville, FL 32224-5626, USA

Del Rio, Rebekah (Musician)
2280 Grass Valley Hwy # 138
Auburn, CA 95603-2536, USA

Del Rubio, Millie
PO Box 6923
San Pedro, CA 90734-6923, USA

Del Savio, Garton (Baseball Player)
Philadelphia Phillies
10417 Stream Park Ct
Dayton, OH 45458-9569, USA

del Solar, Fernando (Actor)
c/o Staff Member *TV Azteca*
Periferico Sur 4121
Colonia Fuentes del Pedregal
DF CP 14141, MEXICO

Del Toro, Benicio (Actor)
c/o Rick Yorn *The Firm*
9465 Wilshire Blvd Fl 6
Beverly Hills, CA 90212-2605, USA

Del Toro, Guillermo (Director, Writer)
c/o Gary Ungar *Exile Entertainment*
732 El Medio Ave
Pacific Palisades, CA 90272-3451, USA

Del-Vikings, The (Music Group)
PO Box 770850
Orlando, FL 32877-0850, USA

DeLaBilliere, Peter (General)
Robert Fleming Holdings
25 Copthall Ave
London EC2R 7DR, UNITED KINGDOM (UK)

Delacote, Jacques
Dr Hilbert Maximilianstr 22
Munich 80539, GERMANY

DeLaCruz, Rosie (Model)
Willhelmina Models
300 Park Ave S # 200
New York, NY 10010-5313, USA

DeLaFuente, Cristian (Actor)
Stubbs Agency
1450 S Robertson Blvd
Los Angeles, CA 90035-3402, USA

DeLaFuente, Joel (Actor)
LMRK
130 W 42nd St Ste 1906
New York, NY 10036-7902, USA

Delahoussaye, Eddie
c/o Staff Member *Jockeys Guild*
PO Box 150
Forward
Monrovia, CA 91017-0150, USA

Delahoussaye, Ryan (Musician)
Ashley Talent
2002 Hogback Rd Ste 20
Ann Arbor, MI 48105-9736, USA

Delahoz, Mike (Baseball Player)
Cleveland Indians
PO Box 441233
Miami, FL 33144-1233, USA

Delain, Moneca (Actor)
c/o Staff Member *Pacific Artists Management*
1404-510 W Hastings St
Vancouver, BC V6B 1L8, CANADA

Delaire, Suzy
46 rue de Varenne
Paris 75007, FRANCE

Delamaza, Roland (Baseball Player)
Kansas City Royals
28533 Silverking Trl
Santa Clarita, CA 91390-5248, USA

DeLamielleure, Joseph M (Joe) (Football Player)
Buffalo Bills
7818 Ridgeloch Pl
Charlotte, NC 28226-3008, USA

DeLancie, John (Actor)
1313 Brunswick Ave
South Pasadena, CA 91030-3509, USA

Delaney, F James (Jim) (Athlete, Track Athlete)
3787 Skyfarm Dr
Santa Rosa, CA 95403-0993, USA

Delaney, Kim (Actor, Model)
c/o Staff Member *Gersh Agency, The (LA)*
232 N Canon Dr
Beverly Hills, CA 90210-5302, USA

Delaney, Pat
PO Box 273
Tamworth, NH 03886-0273, USA

Delaney, Shelagh (Writer)
Tess Sayle
11 Jubilee Place
London SW3 3TE, UNITED KINGDOM (UK)

Delano, Diane (Actor)
Gold Marshak Liedtke
3500 W Olive Ave Ste 1400
Burbank, CA 91505-5512, USA

Delano, Robert B (Misc)
American Farm Bureau Federation
1501 E Woodfield Rd Ste 300W
Schaumburg, IL 60173-5422, USA

Delany, Dana (Actor)
Brillstein/Grey
9150 Wilshire Blvd Ste 350
Beverly Hills, CA 90212-3453, USA

DeLap, Tony (Artist)
225 Jasmine Ave
Corona Del Mar, CA 92625-3035, USA

DeLaPuente, Raygada Oscar (Prime Minister)
Prime Minister's Office
Urb Corpac
Calle 1 Oeste
Lima, S/N, PERU

DelArco, Jonathan (Actor)
Michael Slessinger
8730 W Sunset Blvd Ste 220W
Los Angeles, CA 90069-2275, USA

DeLaria, Lea (Actor)
c/o Diana Doussant *TalentWorks (LA)*
3500 W Olive Ave Ste 1400
Burbank, CA 91505-5512, USA

DeLaRocha, Zack (Musician)
GAS Entertainment
8935 Lindblade St
Culver City, CA 90232-2438, USA

DeLaRosa, Evelyn (Opera Singer)
Dorothy Cone Artists
150 W 55th St
New York, NY 10019-5305, USA

DeLaRosa, Yvonne (Actor)
c/o Staff Member *Heidi Rotbart Management*
4000 Warner Blvd Bldg 160 Rm 716
Burbank, CA 91522-0001, USA

DeLarrocha, Alicia (Musician)
Farmaceutic Carbonell
46-48 Atic
Barcelona 34, SPAIN

DeLatour, David (Actor)
c/o Staff Member *Kass & Stokes Management*
9229 W Sunset Blvd Ste 504
Los Angeles, CA 90069-3405, USA

DeLatour, Frances (Actor)
Kate Feast
Primrose Hill Studios
Fitzroy Road
London NW1 8TR, UNITED KINGDOM (UK)

DeLaurentiis, Dino (Producer)
Via Poutina Ku
Rome 23270, ITALY

Delay, Tom (Ex-Congressman)
242 Cannon Hob
Washington, DC 20515-4322, USA

Delays Delirium (Music Group)
c/o Staff Member *Paradigm (Monterey)*
509 Hartnell St
Monterey, CA 93940-2825, USA

DeLeeuw, Ton (Composer)
Costerusiaan 4
Hilversum, THE NETHERLANDS

Delehanty, Hugh (Editor)
AARP Publications
Editorial Dept
601 E St NW
Washington, DC 20049-0001, USA

DeLeo, Dean (Musician)
Q Prime
729 7th Ave Rm 1600
New York, NY 10019-6880, USA

DeLeo, Robert (Composer)
Q Prime
729 7th Ave Rm 1600
New York, NY 10019-6880, USA

Deleon, Jose (Baseball Player)
Pittsburgh Pirates
7021 NW 70th St
Parkland, FL 33067-1486, USA

Deleone, Tom (Football Player)
Cincinnati Bengals
3104 Mountain Ridge Ct # 68147
Park City, UT 84060, USA

Delfino, Carlos Francisco (Basketball Player)
Detroit Pistons
2 Championship Dr
Palace
Auburn Hills, MI 48326-1753, USA

Delfino, Majandra (Actor)
c/o Lewis Kay *Bragman/Nyman/Cafarelli (BNC)*
8687 Melrose Ave Fl 8
Pacific Design Center
Los Angeles, CA 90069-5701, USA

Delfino, Marieh (Actor)
c/o Lewis Kay *Bragman/Nyman/Cafarelli (BNC)*
8687 Melrose Ave Fl 8
Pacific Design Center
Los Angeles, CA 90069-5701, USA

Delfs, Andreas (Conductor)
Saint Paul Chamber Orchestra
408 Saint Peter St
Saint Paul, MN 55102-1497, USA

Delgado, Carlos J (Baseball Player)
c/o Staff Member *New York Mets*
12301 Roosevelt Ave
Shea Stadium
Flushing, NY 11368-1699, USA

Delgado, Chiquinquira (Actor)
c/o Gabriel Blanco *Gabriel Blanco Iglesias (Mexico)*
Rio Balsas 35-32
Colonia Cuauhtemoc
DF 06500, MEXICO

Delgado, Emilio (Actor)
c/o Staff Member *Sesame Workshop*
1 Lincoln Plz
New York, NY 10023-7163, USA

Delgado, Issac (Musician)
Ralph Mercado Mgmt
568 Broadway # 806
New York, NY 10012-3225, USA

Delguidice, Matt (Hockey Player)
Boston Bruins
25 Church St
North Branford, CT 06471-1418, USA

Delhaven, Robert M (War Hero)
3716 Terrace View Dr
Encino, CA 91436, USA

Delhi, Ganesh (Actor)
No12 62nd Street
Ashok Nagar
Chennai, TN 600 083, INDIA

Delhomme, Jake (Football Player)
Carolina Panthers
800 S Mint St
Ericsson Stadium
Charlotte, NC 28202-1640, USA

Delhoyo, George (Actor)
c/o Staff Member *TalentWorks (LA)*
3500 W Olive Ave Ste 1400
Burbank, CA 91505-5512, USA

D'Elia, Chris (Actor, Writer)
c/o Stephanie Davis *3 Arts Entertainment Inc*
9460 Wilshire Blvd Fl 7
Beverly Hills, CA 90212-2713, USA

D'Elia, Federico (Actor)
c/o Staff Member *Telefe - Argentina*
Pavon 2444 (C1248AAT)
Buenos Aires, ARGENTINA

Delia, Joseph (Football Player)
San Francisco 49ers
PO Box 19654
Irvine, CA 92623-9654, USA

Delilah (Radio Personality)
Radio Delilah Media Group
15260 Ventura Blvd Ste 400
Sherman Oaks, CA 91403-5300, USA

DeLillo, Don (Writer)
57 Rossmore Ave
Bronxville, NY 10708-5615, USA

Delisle, Jim (Football Player)
Green Bay Packers
S34W32228 Journeys Way
Waukesha, WI 53189-9494, USA

DeLislt, Paul (Musician)
Creative Artists Agency
9830 Wilshire Blvd
Beverly Hills, CA 90212-1804, USA

Delizia, Cara (Actor)
c/o Staff Member *Abrams Artists Agency (LA)*
9200 W Sunset Blvd Ph 11
Los Angeles, CA 90069-3601, USA

Delk, Joan (Golfer)
830 Forest Path Ln
Alpharetta, GA 30022-6468, USA

Delk, Tony (Basketball Player)
c/o Staff Member *Atlanta Hawks*
101 Marietta St NW Ste 1900
Centennial Tower
Atlanta, GA 30303-2771, USA

Dell, Michael S (Business Person)
Dell Inc
1 Dell Way
Round Rock, TX 78682-7000, USA

DellaCasa-Debeljevic, Lisa (Opera Singer)
Schloss Gottlieben
Thurgau, SWITZERLAND

Dellaero, Jason (Baseball Player)
Chicago White Sox
3313 SE 10th Ave
Cape Coral, FL 33904-4714, USA

DellaMalva, Joseph (Actor)
William Morris Agency
151 El Camino Dr
Beverly Hills, CA 90212-2775, USA

Dellanos, Myrka (Actor)
c/o Staff Member *Univision*
605 3rd Ave Fl 12
New York, NY 10158-1299, USA

Dellenbach, Jeff (Football Player)
Miami Dolphins
1002 Pine Branch Dr
Weston, FL 33326-2840, USA

Delli Colli, Tomino
Via Pietro Micheli 78
Rome I-00197, ITALY

Dellinger, Walter (Educator)
Duke University
Law School
Durham, NC 27706, USA

DelloJolo, Norman (Composer)
PO Box 154
East Hampton, NY 11937-0154, USA

Dellucci, Dave (Baseball Player)
Baltimore Orioles
18489 Lake Tulip Ave
Baton Rouge, LA 70817-9502, USA

DelNegro, Vinny (Basketball Player)
c/o Staff Member *San Antonio Spurs*
100 Montana St
Alamodome
San Antonio, TX 78203-1031, USA

Delo, Ken (Actor)
161 Avondale Dr # 93-8
Branson, MO 65616-3646, USA

Delock, Ivan M (Ike) (Baseball Player)
Boston Red Sox
433 Cypress Way E
Naples, FL 34110-1107, USA

Delon, Alain (Actor)
Alain Delon Diffusion
12 Rue Saint-Victor
Geneva 1206, SWITZERLAND

Delon, Anthony (Actor)
Intertalent
5 Rue Clement-Marot
Paris 75008, FRANCE

Delon, Nathalie
3 Quai Malaquais
Paris 75006, FRANCE

DeLong, Keith A (Football Player)
San Francisco 49ers
1850 Greywell Rd
Knoxville, TN 37922-9454, USA

DeLong, Michael P (General)
Deputy Commander
US Central Command
Macdill Air Force Base, FL 33621, USA

Delong, Nate (Basketball Player)
Milwaukee Hawks
PO Box 485
Hayward, WI 54843-0485, USA

DeLong, Steve C (Football Player)
San Diego Chargers
4103 Dyanax St
Chesapeake, VA 23324-1419, USA

DeLongis, Anthony (Actor)
PO Box 2445
Canyon Country, CA 91386-2445, USA

Deloplaine, Jack (Football Player)
Pittsburgh Steelers
215 Montana St
Pittsburgh, PA 15214-1630, USA

Delora, Jennifer (Actor)
Gilla Roos
9744 Wilshire Blvd Ste 203
Beverly Hills, CA 90212-1812, USA

DeLorenzo, Michael (Actor)
c/o Staff Member *The Artists Group Ltd*
(LA)
1650 Broadway Ste 610
New York, NY 10019-6833, USA

Delorme, Daniele
16 rue de Marignan
Paris 75008, FRANCE

Delorme, Gilbert (Hockey Player)
Montreal Canadiens
Le Rocket de Montreal Attn: Coaching
Staff 2800 Rue Viau
Montreal, PQ H1V 3J3, CANADA

Delors, Jacques L J (Government Official)
19 Blvd de Bercy
Paris 75012, FRANCE

Delparte, Guy (Hockey Player)
Colorado Rockies
173 Sandy Hill Rd
South Portland, ME 04106-4029, USA

Delpino, Robert L (Football Player)
Los Angeles Rams
632 Shadybrook Ln Apt 115
Corona, CA 92879-6547, USA

Delpy, Julie (Actor)
c/o Glenn Rigberg *Rigberg-Rugolo*
Entertainment
1180 S Beverly Dr Ste 601
Los Angeles, CA 90035-1158, USA

Delsing, Jay (Golfer)
1833 Aston Way
Chesterfield, MO 63005-4579, USA

Delson, Brad (Musician)
c/o Staff Member *Artist Group*
International (NY)
150 E 58th St Fl 19
New York, NY 10155-1900, USA

Delta Spirit (Music Group)
c/o Staff Member *Paradigm (Monterey)*
509 Hartnell St
Monterey, CA 93940-2825, USA

DelTredici, David (Composer)
463 West St Apt G121
New York, NY 10014-2029, USA

Deluca, Annette (Golfer)
7 Turtle Creek Dr Apt D
Jupiter, FL 33469-1530, USA

DeLuca, Mike (Producer)
Michael De Luca Productions
10202 Washington Blvd
Astaire Bldg Ste 3028
Culver City, CA 90232-3119, USA

Deluca, Sam (Football Player)
Los Angeles Chargers
42 Shore Rd
Pelham, NY 10803-3612, USA

Deluca, Tony (Football Player)
Green Bay Packers
57 Cognewaugh Rd
Cos Cob, CT 06807-1735, USA

DeLucas, Lawrence J (Astronaut)
909 19th St S
Birmingham, AL 35205, USA

Delucca, Jerry (Football Player)
Philadelphia Eagles
27 Pulaski St
Peabody, MA 01960-1831, USA

DeLucchi, Michele (Architect)
Via Cenisio 40
Milan 20154, ITALY

DeLucia, Paco (Musician)
International Music Network
278 S Main St #400
Gloucester, MA 01930, USA

Delucia, Rich (Baseball Player)
Seattle Mariners
3 Muirfield Dr
Reading, PA 19607-3348, USA

Delugg, Milton (Musician)
2740 Claray Dr
Los Angeles, CA 90077-2018, USA

DeLuise, David (Actor)
c/o Ted Schachter *Schachter*
Entertainment
1157 S Beverly Dr Fl 2
Los Angeles, CA 90035-1119, USA

Deluise, Dom (Actor, Comedian)
1186 Corsica Dr
Pacific Palisades, CA 90272-4014, USA

Deluise, Michael (Actor)
1186 Corsica Dr
Pacific Palisades, CA 90272-4014, USA

Deluise, Peter (Actor)
c/o Lee Dinstman *Agency for the*
Performing Arts (APA-LA)
405 S Beverly Dr
Beverly Hills, CA 90212-4416, USA

Delvecchio, Alexander P (Alex) (Hockey
Player)
Detroit Red Wings
PO Box 526
Delvecchio Enterprises
Southfield, MI 48037-0526, USA

Demaestri, Joe (Baseball Player)
Chicago White Sox
50 Fairway Dr
Novato, CA 94949-5904, USA

DeMaiziere, Lothar (Prime Minister)
Am Kupfergraben 6/6A
Berlin 10117, GERMANY

Demao, Albert (Football Player)
Washington Redskins
16206 Atlantis Dr
Bowie, MD 20716-3839, USA

Demarchelier, Patrick (Photographer)
162 W 21st St
New York, NY 10011-3202, USA

Demarco, Ab Jr (Hockey Player)
New York Rangers
211 Regal Rd
North Bay, ON P1B 8G4, CANADA

Demarco, Brian (Football Player)
Jacksonville Jaguars
503 E 200th St Ste 200
Demarco Mortgage Association
Cleveland, OH 44119-1562, USA

DeMarco, Guido (President)
President's Office
Palace
Valletta, MALTA

DeMarco, Jean (Artist)
Cervaro
Prov-Frosinore 03044, ITALY

Demarco, Robert (Football Player)
St Louis Cardinals
PO Box 37118
Saint Louis, MO 63141-1618, USA

DeMarco, Tony (Boxer)
PO Box 53664
Indianapolis, IN 46253-0664, USA

DeMarcus, Jay (Musician)
LGB Media
1228 Pineview Ln
Nashville, TN 37211-7422, USA

Demarest, Arthur A (Archaeologist)
Vanderbilt University
Anthropology Dept
Nashville, TN 37235-0001, USA

Demarie, John (Football Player)
Cleveland Browns
2019 Choupique Rd
Sulphur, LA 70663-8430, USA

Demars, Billy (Baseball Player)
Philadelphia Athletics
770 Island Way Apt 305
Clearwater, FL 33767-1824, USA

Demars, Bruce (Admiral)
41 Manters Pt
Plymouth, MA 02360-2412, USA

DeMatteo, Drea (Actor)
c/o Amanda Silverman *42West*
220 W 42nd St Fl 12
New York, NY 10036-7200, USA

Dembo, Fennis (Basketball Player)
Detroit Pistons
5404 Cornell Dr
Irondale, AL 35210-2930, USA

DeMedeiros, Maria (Actor)
William Morris Agency
151 El Camino Dr
Beverly Hills, CA 90212-2775, USA

DeMenezes, Fradique (President)
President's Office
Pargo do Povo
Sao Tome, SAO TOME & PRINCIPE

DeMent, Iris (Songwriter, Writer)
c/o Staff Member *Paradigm (Monterey)*
509 Hartnell St
Monterey, CA 93940-2825, USA

DeMent, Jack (Misc)
Oregon Health Care Center
11325 NE Weidler St # 44
Portland, OR 97220-1950, USA

Dement, Kenneth (Football Player)
316 S Kingshighway St
Sikeston, MO 63801-2948, USA

Dementieva, Elena (Tennis Player)
c/o Staff Member *Octagon (VA)*
1751 Pinnacle Dr Ste 1500
McLean, VA 22102-3833, USA

DeMerchant, Paul (Religious Leader)
Missionary Church
PO Box 9127
Fort Wayne, IN 46899-9127, USA

Demerit, John (Baseball Player)
Milwaukee Braves
550 W Walters St
Port Washington, WI 53074-1430, USA

Demery, Larry (Baseball Player)
Pittsburgh Pirates
10719 Petalo Dr
Bakersfield, CA 93311-2289, USA

Demeter, Don (Baseball Player)
Brooklyn Dodgers
6240 S Country Club Dr
Oklahoma City, OK 73159-1844, USA

Demeter, Steve (Baseball Player)
Detroit Tigers
6032 Ravine Blvd
Cleveland, OH 44134-3047, USA

Demetral, Chris (Actor)
c/o Jamie Gold *JMG Management*
18000 Coastline Dr Apt 8
Malibu, CA 90265-5727, USA

Demetriadis, Phoklon (Cartoonist)
3rd September St 174
Athens, GREECE

Demetrios (Religious Leader)
Greek Orthodox Church
89 E 79th St # 19
New York, NY 10075, USA

Demeulemeester, Ann (Designer, Fashion
Designer)
c/o Staff Member *Ann Demeulemeester*
6 Rue Milne Edwards
Paris 75017, FRANCE

Demic, Larry (Basketball Player)
New York Knicks
680 S Lassen Ct
Anaheim, CA 92804-3123, USA

DeMille, Nelson (Writer)
61 Hilton Ave Ste 23
Garden City, NY 11530-2813, USA

Demin, Lev S (Cosmonaut)
Potchta Kosmonavtov
Moskovskol Oblasti
Syvisdny Goroduk 141160, RUSSIA

Deming, Peter (Cinematographer)
Sandra Marsh Mgmt
9150 Wilshire Blvd Ste 220
Beverly Hills, CA 90212-3429, USA

DeMita, L Ciriaco (Prime Minister)
Partito Democrazia Cristiana
Piazza de Gesu 46
Rome 00186, ITALY

Demitra, Pavol (Hockey Player)
Ottawa Senators
16514 Midway Drive
Chesterfield, MO 63005, USA

Demme, Jonathan (Director)
c/o Staff Member *International Creative*
Management (ICM-LA)
10250 Constellation Blvd
Los Angeles, CA 90067-6200, USA

Demola, Don (Baseball Player)
Montreal Expos
352 Village Dr
Hauppauge, NY 11788-3225, USA

DeMont, Rick (Swimmer)
84-596 Upena St
Waianae, HI 96792-1933, USA

DeMontebello, Philippe L (Misc)
Metropolitan Museum of Art
82nd St & 5th Ave
New York, NY 10028, USA

DeMornay, Rebecca (Actor)
c/o Staff Member *Gersh Agency, The (LA)*
232 N Canon Dr
Beverly Hills, CA 90210-5302, USA

Demoss, Bob (Football Player)
New York Bulldogs
117 Knox Dr
West Lafayette, IN 47906-2147, USA

**DeMott, William (Bill, Hugh Morris,
Crash the Terminator)** (Wrestler)
c/o Staff Member *World Wrestling*
Entertainment (WWE)
1241 E Main St
Stamford, CT 06902-3520, USA

Dempsey, Cedric (Misc)
National Collegiate Athletic Assn
70 W Washington St
Indianapolis, IN 46204, USA

Dempsey, Con (Baseball Player)
Montreal Expos
1530 Cordilleras Rd
Redwood City, CA 94062-3208, USA

Dempsey, George (Basketball Player)
Philadelphia Warriors
6945 Cedar Ave
Pennsauken, NJ 08109-2713, USA

Dempsey, J Rikard (Rick) (Baseball Player)
Los Angeles Dodgers
1000 Elysian Park Ave
Stadium
Los Angeles, CA 90012-1199, USA

Dempsey, Mark (Baseball Player)
San Francisco Giants
673 W Martindale Rd
Union, OH 45322-3043, USA

Dempsey, Nathan (Hockey Player)
Toronto Maple Leafs
Pro-Rep Entertainment Consulting Attn:
Art Breeze
113-276 Midpark Way SE
Calgary, AB T2X 1J6, CANADA

Dempsey, Pat (Baseball Player)
10116 Oro Vista Ave
Sunland, CA 91040-3238, USA

Dempsey, Patrick (Actor)
c/o Staff Member *Grey's Anatomy*
500 S Buena Vista St
Burbank, CA 91521-0001, USA

Dempsey, Rick (Baseball Player)
Minnesota Twins
1673 Crown Ridge Ct
Westlake Village, CA 91362-4731, USA

Dempsey, Thomas (Tom) (Football Player)
New Orleans Saints
4922 York St
Metairie, LA 70001-1036, USA

Dempster, Ryan (Baseball Player)
Florida Marlins
21050 NE 38th Ave Apt 2606
Miami, FL 33180-4082, USA

Demsetz, Harold (Economist)
University of California
Economics Dept
Los Angeles, CA 90024, USA

Demsey, Todd (Golfer)
8140 E Arroyo Seco Rd
Scottsdale, AZ 85266-1056, USA

DeMunn, Jeffrey (Actor)
Gersh Agency
232 N Canon Dr
Beverly Hills, CA 90210-5302, USA

DeMuron, Pierre (Architect)
Herzog & De Meuron Architekten
Rheinschanze 6
Basel 4056, SWITZERLAND

Demus, Jorg (Musician)
LYRA
Doblinger Hauptstr 77-A/10
Vienna 1190, AUSTRIA

Demuth, Richard H (Attorney, Attorney General, Financier, General)
7 Eliot Rd
Lexington, MA 02421-5649, USA

Den, Tagayasu (Choreographer)
Ondekoza
Koda Performing Arts Co
Sado Island, JAPAN

Den Herder, Vern W (Football Player)
Miami Dolphins
1277 S Main Ave
Sioux Center, IA 51250-1229, USA

Denard, Michael (Dancer)
Paris Opera Ballet
Place de l'Opera
Paris 75009, FRANCE

Denberg, Lori Beth (Actor)
c/o Staff Member *Acme Talent & Literary (LA)*
4727 Wilshire Blvd Ste 333
Los Angeles, CA 90010-3874, USA

Dench, Judi (Actor)
c/o Victoria Belfrage *Julian Belfrage & Associates*
Adam House
14 New Burlington St
London W1S 3BQ, UNITED KINGDOM (UK)

Denehy, Bill (Baseball Player)
New York Mets
5096 Eastwinds Dr
Orlando, FL 32819-3517, USA

Denes, Agnes C (Artist)
595 Broadway
New York, NY 10012-3222, USA

Deneuve, Catherine (Actor)
c/o Claire Blondel *ArtMedia*
20 av Rapp
Paris 75007, FRANCE

Deng, Luol (Basketball Player)
Phoenix Suns
201 E Jefferson St
Phoenix, AZ 85004-2412, USA

Denicourt, Marianne (Actor)
Artmedia
20 Ave Rapp
Paris 75007, FRANCE

DeNiro, Robert (Actor)
TriBeCa Productions
375 Greenwich St
Tribeca Film Center
New York, NY 10013-2379, USA

Denis, Louis (Hockey Player)
Montreal Canadiens
20051 Country Road 17
Lancaster, ON K0C 1N0, CANADA

Denis, Marc (Hockey Player)
c/o Staff Member *Tampa Bay Lightning*
401 Channelside Dr
Ice Palace
Tampa, FL 33602-5400, USA

Denisof, Alexis (Actor)
c/o Daniel (Dan) Spilo *Artistry Management*
525 Westbourne Dr
West Hollywood, CA 90048-1913, USA

Denison, Anthony (Actor)
10100 Santa Monica Blvd Ste 1060
Los Angeles, CA 90067-4151, USA

Denisov, Edison V (Composer)
Studentcheskaia 44/28
#35
Moscow 121165, RUSSIA

Denker, Henry (Writer)
241 Central Park W
New York, NY 10024-4530, USA

Denman, Brian (Baseball Player)
Boston Red Sox
16 Cindy Dr
Buffalo, NY 14221-3002, USA

Denman, David (Actor)
c/o Rebecca (Becca) Kovacik *Hofflund/Polone*
9465 Wilshire Blvd Ste 890
Beverly Hills, CA 90212-2607, USA

Denman, Tony (Actor)
c/o Beverly Strong *Anonymous Content (CA)*
9350 Wilshire Blvd Ste 224
Beverly Hills, CA 90212-3204, USA

Dennard, Kenny (Basketball Player)
Kansas City Kings
6641 Westchester Ave
Houston, TX 77005-3755, USA

Dennard, Mark (Football Player)
Miami Dolphins
1008 Muirfield Vlg
College Station, TX 77845-8936, USA

Dennard, Preston (Football Player)
Los Angeles Rams
4545 Greene Ave NW
Albuquerque, NM 87114-4296, USA

Dennard, Robert H (Inventor)
2054 Quaker Ridge Rd
Croton On Hudson, NY 10520-3514, USA

Dennehy, Brian (Actor)
c/o Susan Smith *Susan Smith Company, The*
1344 N Wetherly Dr
Los Angeles, CA 90069-1817, USA

Dennehy, Kathleen (Actor)
Susan Nathe
8281 Melrose Ave Ste 200
Los Angeles, CA 90046-6890, USA

Denneriein, Barbara (Musician)
Tsingtauer Str 66
Munich 81827, GERMANY

Dennert-Hill, Pauline (Baseball Player)
415 Clinton St
Owosso, MI 48867-2718, USA

Dennett, Daniel C (Misc)
20 Ironwood Rd
North Andover, MA 01845-2103, USA

Denney, Austin (Football Player)
Chicago Bears
6933 Riverwood Dr
Knoxville, TN 37920-6025, USA

Denning, Blaine (Basketball Player)
Baltimore Bullets
3577 Highland Blvd
Highland, MI 48356-1827, USA

Denning, Hazel M (Writer)
Llewellyn Worldwide
2143 Wooddale Dr
Saint Paul, MN 55125-2989, USA

Dennings, Kat (Actor)
c/o Staff Member *Creative Management Group*
3815 Hughes Ave Fl 3
Culver City, CA 90232-2715, USA

Dennis, Cathy (Musician)
19 Music
Ransomes Gate #32
35-37 Parkgate
London SW11 4NP, UNITED KINGDOM (UK)

Dennis, Clark (Golfer)
4117 Sarita Dr
Fort Worth, TX 76109-4743, USA

Dennis, Don (Baseball Player)
St Louis Cardinals
RR 2
Stanton, NE 68779, USA

Dennis, Donna F (Artist)
131 Duane St
New York, NY 10013-3850, USA

Dennis, Guy (Football Player)
Cincinnati Bengals
PO Box 142846
Gainesville, FL 32614-2846, USA

Dennis, Jim (Race Car Driver)
1810 Little Mastens Corner Rd
Harrington, DE 19952-3219, USA

Dennis, Mark (Football Player)
Miami Dolphins
52 Cambridge Ln
Lincolnshire, IL 60069-3101, USA

Dennis, Mike (Football Player)
Los Angeles Rams
5 Sandalwood Dr
Madison, MS 39110-9249, USA

Dennis, Mike (Musician)
American Promotions
2011 Ferry Ave Apt U19
Camden, NJ 08104-1900, USA

Dennis, Norm (Hockey Player)
St Louis Blues
1531 Highway 3-B
Fruitvale, BC V0G 1L0, CANADA

Dennis, Pamela (Designer, Fashion Designer)
c/o Jerry Shandrew *Shandrew Public Relations*
1050 S Stanley Ave
Los Angeles, CA 90019-6634, USA

Dennison, Bonnie (Actor)
c/o Staff Member *Terrific Talent Associates*
419 Park Ave # 1009
New York, NY 10022-4402, USA

Dennison, Doug (Football Player)
Dallas Cowboys
10032 Royal Ln
Dallas, TX 75238-1204, USA

Dennison, Glenn (Football Player)
New York Jets
1104 Tucker Ln
Ashton, MD 20861-9766, USA

Dennison, Rick (Football Player)
Denver Broncos
PO Box 999
Suffield, CT 06078-0999, USA

Denny, Christopher (Musician)
c/o Staff Member *Paradigm (Monterey)*
509 Hartnell St
Monterey, CA 93940-2825, USA

Denny, Dorothy
15707 La Verida Dr
Victorville, CA 92395-3413, USA

Denny, Floyd W Jr (Misc)
1 Carolina Mdws Apt 308
Chapel Hill, NC 27517-8508, USA

Denny, John (Baseball Player)
St Louis Cardinals
13430 E Camino La Cebadilla
Tucson, AZ 85749-8611, USA

Denny, Robyn (Artist)
20/30 Wilds Rents
#4B
London SE14QG, UNITED KINGDOM
(UK)

Denny, Simone (Musician)
c/o Staff Member *Diva Central Inc*
7510 W Sunset Blvd Ste 1445
Los Angeles, CA 90046-3408, USA

DenOuden, Wilerninintie (Willy)
(Swimmer)
Goudsewagenstraat 23B
Rotterdam, THE NETHERLANDS

Densham, Pen (Director)
International Creative Mgmt
8942 Wilshire Blvd # 219
Beverly Hills, CA 90211-1908, USA

Densmore, Elizabeth (Actor)
c/o Sharon Lane *Lane Management Group*
13017 Woodbridge St
Studio City, CA 91604-1431, USA

Densmore, John (Musician)
49 Halderman Road
Santa Monica, CA 90402, USA

Denson, Al (Football Player)
Denver Broncos
6019 Bart Rd
Jacksonville, FL 32209-1809, USA

Denson, Autry (Football Player)
Miami Dolphins
2585 SW Calder St
Port Saint Lucie, FL 34953-7310, USA

Denson, Drew (Baseball Player)
Atlanta Braves
1718 Avonlea Ave
Cincinnati, OH 45237-6110, USA

Denson, Keith (Football Player)
New York Jets
28024 Eagle Peak Ave
Canyon Country, CA 91387-3105, USA

Denson, Moses (Football Player)
Washington Redskins
14005 Drake Dr
Rockville, MD 20853-2641, USA

Dent, Burnell (Football Player)
Green Bay Packers
2904 Essex Ave
La Place, LA 70068-2241, USA

Dent, Catherine (Actor)
c/o Staff Member *Shield, The*
4151 Prospect Ave Bldg A # 200
Los Angeles, CA 90027-4524, USA

Dent, Frederick B (Secretary)
221 Montgornery St
Spartanburg, SC 29302, USA

Dent, Jim (Golfer)
PO Box 290656
Tampa, FL 33687-0656, USA

Dent, Richard L (Coach, Football Coach,
Football Player)
Chicago Bears
4453 Rfd
Long Grove, IL 60047-6900, USA

Dent, Robert (Football Player)
Cleveland Browns
8106 Arroyo Way
Stockton, CA 95209-2904, USA

Dent, Russell E 'Bucky' (Athlete)
8895 Indian River Run
Boynton Beach, FL 33472-2445, USA

Denton, Derek A (Physicist)
816 Irring Road
Toorak, VIC 3142, AUSTRALIA

Denton, James (Actor)
c/o John Crosby *John Crosby Management*
1310 N Spaulding Ave
Los Angeles, CA 90046-4010, USA

Denton, Mona (Baseball Player)
1880 S Newton St
Denver, CO 80219-4503, USA

Denton, Randy (Basketball Player)
Carolina Cougars
515 Sunnybrook Rd
Raleigh, NC 27610-2850, USA

Denton, Sandi (Pepa) (Musician)
Famous Artists Agency
250 W 57th St
New York, NY 10107-0001, USA

Denton Jr, Jeremiah A (Senator)
531 Thomas Bransby
Williamsburg, VA 23185-8245, USA

Denzongapa, Danny (Actor, Bollywood)
Dzongrilla 11th Road
Juhu
Mumbai, MS, INDIA

Deol, Bobby (Actor, Bollywood)
Plot No 22, 11th Road
JVPD Scheme Juhu
Mumbai, MS 400049, INDIA

Deol, Dharmendra (Actor, Bollywood)
Plot No 22 11th Rd
Juhu
Mumbai, MS 400049, INDIA

Deol, Sunny (Actor, Bollywood)
Plot No 22
11th Road JVPD Scheme
Mumbai, MS 400026, INDIA

DeOre, Bill (Cartoonist)
Dallas News
Communications Center
Editorial Dept
Dallas, TX 75211, USA

Deossie, Steve (Football Player)
Dallas Cowboys
835 Chestnut St
North Andover, MA 01845-6010, USA

DePalma, Brian R (Director)
c/o Jeff Berg *International Creative
Management (ICM-LA)*
10250 Constellation Blvd
Los Angeles, CA 90067-6200, USA

Depalo, Jim (Baseball Player)
TCMA
4727 7th Ave SW
Naples, FL 34119-4039, USA

DePandi, Giuliana (Actor)
c/o Staff Member *William Morris Agency
(WMA-LA)*
1 William Morris Pl
Beverly Hills, CA 90212-4261, USA

DePandi, Giuliana (Actor)
c/o Pamela Kohl *3 Arts Entertainment Inc*
9460 Wilshire Blvd Fl 7
Beverly Hills, CA 90212-2713, USA

Depardieu, Gerard (Actor)
c/o John Ptak *Creative Artists Agency LCC
(CAA-LA)*
2000 Avenue Of The Stars
Los Angeles, CA 90067-4700, USA

Depardon, Raymond (Photographer)
18 Bis Rue Henri Barbusse
Paris 75005, FRANCE

Departure, Themm (Music Group)
c/o Staff Member *Paradigm (Monterey)*
509 Hartnell St
Monterey, CA 93940-2825, USA

Depaso, Tom (Football Player)
Cincinnati Bengals
2108 Polo Pointe Dr
Vienna, VA 22181-2804, USA

Depastino, Joe (Baseball Player)
New York Mets
4142 Center Pointe Cir Apt 62A
Sarasota, FL 34233-1681, USA

Depaula, Sean (Baseball Player)
Cleveland Indians
2 Thomas St
Derry, NH 03038-2988, USA

DePavia, James
PO Box 11152
Greenwich, CT 06831-1152, USA

Depeche Mode (Music Group)
c/o Carole Kinzel *Creative Artists Agency
LCC (CAA-LA)*
2000 Avenue Of The Stars
Los Angeles, CA 90067-4700, USA

DePeyer, Gervase
1250 S Washington St
Porto Vecchio 109
Alexandria, VA 22314-4411, USA

DePortzamparc, Christian (Architect)
Architecte DPLG
1 Rue de L'Aude
Paris 75014, FRANCE

DePoyster, Jerry D (Football Player)
Detroit Lions
657 Barlow Cir
Rock Springs, WY 82901-3201, USA

Depp, Johnny (Actor, Director)
c/o Staff Member *Infinitum Nihil*
3000 Olympic Blvd # 1550
C/O leg
Santa Monica, CA 90404-5073, USA

Depre, Joe (Basketball Player)
New York Nets
59 Oneida St
Rochester, NY 14621-4027, USA

DePree, Hopwood (Actor)
c/o Staff Member *ROAR LLC*
9701 Wilshire Blvd Ste 850
Beverly Hills, CA 90212-2032, USA

DePreist, James A (Conductor)
Konsert AB
Kungsgatan 32
Stockholm 11135, SWEDEN

DePrume, Cathryn (Actor)
c/o Staff Member *Flick East West Talents
Inc*
9057 Nemo St Ste A
West Hollywood, CA 90069-5511, USA

Dequenne, Emilie (Actor)
Cineart
36 Rue de Ponthieu
Paris 75008, FRANCE

Dequenne, Emilie (Cartoonist)
Houston Post
Editorial Dept
4888 Loop Central Dr #390
Houston, TX 77081, USA

Derbez, Silvia (Actor)
c/o Staff Member *Televisa*
Blvd Adolfo Lopez Mateos 232
Colonia San Angel INN
DF CP 01060, MEXICO

Derby, Dean (Football Player)
Pittsburgh Steelers
1682 Corkrum Rd
Walla Walla, WA 99362-8628, USA

Derbyshire, Andrew G (Architect)
4 Sunnyfield
Hatfield
Herts AL9 5DX, UNITED KINGDOM (UK)

Derek, Bo (Actor, Model)
c/o Chuck Binder *Binder & Associates*
1465 Lindacrest Dr
Beverly Hills, CA 90210-2519, USA

Dereuck, Colleen (Athlete)
4172 Saint Croix St
Boulder, CO 80301, USA

Dergan, Lisa (Actor, Model, Television
Host)
c/o Ken Lindner *Ken Lindner & Associates*
2049 Century Park E Ste 3050
Los Angeles, CA 90067-3136, USA

Deriso, Walter M Jr (Financier)
Synovus Financial Corp
PO Box 120
901 Front Ave
Columbus, GA 31902-0120, USA

Derlago, Bill (Hockey Player)
Vancouver Canucks
Seven View Chrysler 2685 Highway 7
Concord, ON L4K 1V8, CANADA

Derline, Rodney (Basketball Player)
Seattle SuperSonics
12612 SE 215th St
Kent, WA 98031-2287, USA

Dern, Bruce (Actor)
PO Box 1581
Santa Monica, CA 90406-1581, USA

Dern, Laura (Actor)
c/o Jason Weinberg *Untitled
Entertainment (LA)*
331 N Maple Dr Fl 3
Beverly Hills, CA 90210-3827, USA

Dernesch, Helga (Opera Singer)
Neutorgasse 2/22
Vienna 1013, AUSTRIA

Dernier, Bob (Baseball Player)
Cleveland Indians
13153 Carter St
Overland Park, KS 66213-4655, USA

Deroo, Brian (Football Player)
Baltimore Colts
49224 Escalante St
Indio, CA 92201-8850, USA

DeRosa, Mark (Athlete, Baseball Player)
Atlanta Braves
626 8th St
Carlstadt, NJ 07072-1702, USA

DeRosa, William (Misc)
Columbia Artists Mgmt Inc
1790 Broadway Fl 6
New York, NY 10019-1412, USA

DeRosier, David (Physicist)
27 Chesterfield Rd
Newton, MA 02465-2343, USA

Derosier, Michael (Musician)
Borman Entertainment
1250 6th St Ste 401
Santa Monica, CA 90401-1638, USA

Derow, Peter A (Publisher)
PO Box 534
Bedford, NY 10506-0534, USA

Derr, Kenneth T (Business Person)
Chevron Corp
6001 Bollinger Canyon Rd
San Ramon, CA 94583-2398, USA

Derrick, Edward (Baseball Player)
Baltimore Elite Giants
PO Box 158473
Nashville, TN 37215-8473, USA

Derrick, Jim (Baseball Player)
Boston Red Sox
340 Cedar Vale Dr
Lexington, SC 29073-9463, USA

Derricks, Cleavant (Actor)
480 Burano Ct
Agoura Hills, CA 91377, USA

Derringer, Rick (Musician)
c/o Steve Peck *Fantasma Productions Inc*
854 Conniston Rd
West Palm Beach, FL 33405-2131, USA

Derrington, Jim (Baseball Player)
Chicago White Sox
711 Sandlewood Ave
La Habra, CA 90631-7248, USA

Derry, Kathy (Physicist)
PO Box 1656
Laguna Beach, CA 92652-1656, USA

Derry, Russ (Baseball Player)
New York Yankees
8619 N Myrtle Ave
Kansas City, MO 64156-1298, USA

Dersch, Hans (Swimmer)
7217 E 55th Pl
Tulsa, OK 74145-7704, USA

Dershowitz, Alan M (Educator, Lawyer)
1563 Massachusetts Ave
Cambridge, MA 02138-2903, USA

Dervan, Peter B (Misc)
California Institute of Technology
Chemistry Dept
Pasadena, CA 91125-0001, USA

Derwin, Mark (Actor)
Stone Manners
6500 Wilshire Blvd Ste 550
Los Angeles, CA 90048-4950, USA

Derwinski, Edward J (Secretary)
Derwinski Assoc
1800 Diagonal Rd Ste 600
Alexandria, VA 22314-2840, USA

Des Barres, Michael (Actor)
c/o Pam Ellis *Ellis Talent Group*
4705 Laurel Canyon Blvd Ste 300
Valley Village, CA 91607-5901, USA

Desai, Anita (Writer)
Deborah Rogers Ltd
20 Powis Mews
London W11 1JN, UNITED KINGDOM
(UK)

Desai, Ketan (Bollywood, Director,
Producer)
3C Swapnalok Jagmohandas Marg
Bombay, MS 400 026, INDIA

Desailly, Jean (Actor)
Babette Pouget
9 Square Villaret de Joyeuse
Paris 75017, FRANCE

Desailly, Marcel (Soccer Player)
FC Chelsea Stamford Bridge
Fulham Road
London SW6 1HS, UNITED KINGDOM
(UK)

deSando, Anthony
PO Box 5617
Beverly Hills, CA 90209-5617, USA

deSantis, Guiseppe
Fiano Romano Via del Commercio 1
Rome I-00154, ITALY

DeSantis, Jaclyn (Actor)
c/o Sarah Fargo *Paradigm (NY)*
360 Park Ave S Fl 16
New York, NY 10010-1716, USA

deSantis, Luigi
Via della Villa di Lucina 72
Rome I-00145, ITALY

Desanto, Tom (Producer)
c/o Renee Kurtz *William Morris Agency
(WMA-LA)*
1 William Morris Pl
Beverly Hills, CA 90212-4261, USA

Descendants, The
4230 Del Rey Ave # 621
Marina Del Rey, CA 90292-5603, USA

Deschaine, Dick (Football Player)
Green Bay Packers
205 Cavil Way
De Pere, WI 54115-3775, USA

Deschanel, Caleb (Cinematographer)
Dark Light Pictures
812 N Highland Ave
Los Angeles, CA 90038-3417, USA

Deschanel, Emily (Actor)
c/o Rachel Shapiro *Jeff Morrone
Management*
9350 Wilshire Blvd Ste 224
Beverly Hills, CA 90212-3204, USA

Deschanel, Mary Jo (Actor)
844 Chautauqua Blvd
Pacific Palisades, CA 90272-3801, USA

Deschanel, Zooey (Actor)
844 Chautauqua Blvd
Pacific Palisades, CA 90272-3801, USA

Descombes-Dinehart, Nancy (Baseball
Player)
59607 County Road 11
Elkhart, IN 46517-9178, USA

Descombes-Lesko, Jeanie (Baseball
Player)
4401 145th Ave NE Apt J5
Bellevue, WA 98007-3160, USA

Desert, Alex (Actor)
c/o Staff Member *Pakula/King &
Associates*
9229 W Sunset Blvd Ste 315
Los Angeles, CA 90069-3403, USA

Desfor, Max (Journalist)
15115 Interlachen Dr Apt 1018
Silver Spring, MD 20906-5644, USA

Deshales, Jim (Baseball Player)
New York Yankees
151 N Taylor Point Dr
Spring, TX 77382-1240, USA

Deshane, Charles (Football Player)
Detroit Lions
8622 David Dr
Tampa, FL 33635-9707, USA

DeShields, Delino L (Baseball Player)
720 Marcus Nyah Ct
Atlanta, GA 30349-4048, USA

Desiderio, Robert (Actor)
1475 Sierra Vista Dr
Aspen, CO 81611-1044, USA

Desilva, John (Baseball Player)
Montreal Expos
32750 Airport Rd
Fort Bragg, CA 95437-9514, USA

DeSimone, Livio D (Desi) (Business
Person)
Minnesota Mining & Manufacturing
3M Center
Saint Paul, MN 55144-0002, USA

Deskins, Donald (Football Player)
Oakland Raiders
3240 Pittsview Dr
Ann Arbor, MI 48108-1946, USA

Deskur, Andrzej Maria Cardinal
(Religious Leader)
Palazzo S Carlo
00120, VATICAN CITY

Deslongchamps, Pierre (Misc)
1884 Rue des Orioles
Laval, PQ H7L 5T8, CANADA

Desman, Shawn (Musician)
c/o Staff Member *BMG*
1540 Broadway
New York, NY 10036-4074, USA

Desmormeaux, Kent (Jockey)
Desmormeaux Racing Stable
385 W Huntington Dr
Arcadia, CA 91007, USA

Desny, Ivan (Actor)
Casa al Sole
Ascona-Collina 6612, SWITZERLAND

Desormeaux, Kent (Jockey)
c/o Staff Member *Jockeys Guild*
PO Box 150
Forward
Monrovia, CA 91017-0150, USA

Despadovich, Nada
6500 Wilshire Blvd Ste 2200
Los Angeles, CA 90048-4942, USA

Despotopoulos, Johannes (Jan) (Architect)
Anapiron Polemou 7
Athens 11521, GREECE

Des'ree (Musician)
Solo Agency
55 Fulham High St
London SW6 3JJ, UNITED KINGDOM
(UK)

Dess, Darrell (Football Player)
Pittsburgh Steelers
224 Summer Ave
New Castle, PA 16105, USA

Dessay, Natalie (Opera Singer)
Herbert Breslin
119 W 57th St Ste 1505
New York, NY 10019-2401, USA

Dessens, Elmer (Baseball Player)
Pittsburgh Pirates
PO Box 312
Leipsic, OH 45856-0312, USA

DeStefano, Mike (Musician)
c/o Staff Member *Paradigm (Monterey)*
509 Hartnell St
Monterey, CA 93940-2825, USA

Destiny's Child (Music Group)
c/o Dennis Ashley *Creative Artists Agency
LCC (CAA-LA)*
2000 Avenue Of The Stars
Los Angeles, CA 90067-4700, USA

Destrade, Orestes (Baseball Player)
New York Yankees
9218 Sydney Rd
Brentwood, TN 37027-8152, USA

Destri, Jimmy (Misc)
Shore Fire Media
32 Court St Ste 1600
Brooklyn, NY 11201-4441, USA

Desutter, Wayne (Football Player)
Buffalo Bills
4450 Antietam Creek Trl
Leesburg, FL 34748-1203, USA

DeTar, Dean E (War Hero)
7785 Portwood Rd
Azle, TX 76020-5839, USA

Deters, Harold (Football Player)
Dallas Cowboys
1602 Woods Creek Dr
Garner, NC 27529-4761, USA

Detherage, Bob (Baseball Player)
Kansas City Royals
322 Turf Ln
Carl Junction, MO 64834-9575, USA

Detmer, Amanda (Actor)
c/o John Carrabino *John Carrabino
Management*
5900 Wilshire Blvd Ste 406
Los Angeles, CA 90036-5015, USA

Detmer, Ty H (Football Player)
PO Box 942
Jourdanton, TX 78026-0942, USA

Detmer, Ty (Football Player)
Green Bay Packers
PO Box 942
Jourdanton, TX 78026-0942, USA

Detmers, Maruschka (Actor)
Myriam Bru
80 Avenue Charles de Gaulle
Neuilly Sur Seine 92200, FRANCE

Detorie, Rick (Cartoonist)
Creators Syndicate
5777 W Century Blvd Ste 700
Los Angeles, CA 90045-9023, USA

Detroit, Marcella (Musician, Songwriter,
Writer)
MCM Mgmt
40 Langham St
#300
London W1N 5RG, UNITED KINGDOM
(UK)

Dettlaff, Bill (Golfer)
133 Clearlake Dr
Ponte Vedra Beach, FL 32082-2178, USA

Dettmer, John (Baseball Player)
Texas Rangers
549 Hickory View Ln
Ballwin, MO 63011-1500, USA

Dettore, Tom (Baseball Player)
Pittsburgh Pirates
1120 McEwen Ave
Canonsburg, PA 15317-1928, USA

Detweiler, David K (Physicist)
Waverty Heights
1400 Waverty Road #A212
Gladwyne, PA 19035, USA

Detweiler, Ducky (Baseball Player)
Boston Braves
312 Holt St
Federalsburg, MD 21632-1403, USA

Detweiler, Robert C (Educator)
1450 Ellis Ave
Cambria, CA 93428-5960, USA

Detwiler, Chuck (Football Player)
San Diego Chargers
21 Windsong
Irvine, CA 92614-5455, USA

Deukmejian, C George (Ex-Governor, Governor)
Sidley & Austin
555 W 5th St
Los Angeles, CA 90013-1010, USA

Deutch, Howard (Director)
International Creative Mgmt
8942 Wilshire Blvd # 219
Beverly Hills, CA 90211-1908, USA

Deutch, Howie (Actor, Director, Producer, Writer)
c/o Andrew Hersh *Lovett Management*
1327 Brinkley Ave
Los Angeles, CA 90049-3619, USA

Deutch, John M (Government Official)
51 Clifton St
Belmont, MA 02478-3353, USA

Deutekom, Cristina (Opera Singer)
Lancasterdreet 41
Dronten, TG 8251, THE NETHERLANDS

Deutsch, Dave (Basketball Player)
New York Knicks
315 Fairmount Rd
Long Valley, NJ 07853-3012, USA

Deutsch, Donny (Television Host)
Open City Films
122 Hudson St Fl 5
New York, NY 10013-2355, USA

Deutsch, Patti (Actor)
Yvette Bikoff
1040 1st Ave # 1126
New York, NY 10022-2991, USA

Dev, Mukul (Actor, Bollywood)
Karan Apts 5th Floor
Yari Road Versova
Mumbai, MS 40061, INDIA

Deva, Prabhu (Actor, Choreographer, Comedian, Dancer, Musician)
68 T T K Road
Alwarpet
Chennai, TN 600 018, INDIA

DeValeria, Dennis (Writer)
213 Hillendale Rd
Pittsburgh, PA 15237-1803, USA

Devane, William (Actor)
Innovative Artists
1505 10th St
Santa Monica, CA 90401-2805, USA

DeVarona, Donna (Sportscaster, Swimmer)
TWI
420 W 45th St # 500
New York, NY 10036-3503, USA

Devault, Calvin (Actor)
Amset Eisenstadt Frazier
5055 Wilshire Blvd Ste 860
Los Angeles, CA 90036-6108, USA

Devayani (Actor, Bollywood)
51 Indira Gandhi Street
Saligramam
Chennai, TN 600093, INDIA

Devenzio, Dick (Basketball Player)
Syracuse Nationals
1116 Home Pi
Matthews, NC 28105, USA

Dever, Barbara (Opera Singer)
Wolf Artists Mgmt
13 E 69th St Apt 3R
New York, NY 10021-4968, USA

Deveraux, Jude (Writer)
Pocket Books
1230 Avenue Of The Americas
New York, NY 10020-1586, USA

Devereaux, Mike (Baseball Player)
Los Angeles Dodgers
2236 W Doublegrove St
West Covina, CA 91790-5607, USA

Devgan, Ajay (Actor, Bollywood)
5/6 Sheetal Apt
Opp. Chandan Cinema Juhu
Mumbai, MS 400049, INDIA

DeVicenzo, Roberto (Golfer)
Nonl Lann
5025 Veloz Ave
Tarzana, CA 91356-4514, USA

Devicq, Paula (Actor, Model)
William Morris Agency
151 El Camino Dr
Beverly Hills, CA 90212-2775, USA

Deville, CC (Musician)
H K Mgmt
9200 W Sunset Blvd Ste 530
Los Angeles, CA 90069-3509, USA

Deville, Michael (Director)
36 Rue Reinhardt
Boulogne 92100, FRANCE

Devine, Adrian (Baseball Player)
Atlanta Braves
271 Timber Laurel Ln
Lawrenceville, GA 30043-6504, USA

Devine, Harold (Boxer)
595 Wyckoff Ave
Wyckoff, NJ 07481-1337, USA

Devine, Loretta (Actor)
c/o Don Spradlin *Essential Talent Management*
6464 W Sunset Blvd Ste 760
Los Angeles, CA 90028-8006, USA

DeVink, Lodewijk J R (Business Person)
Warner-Lambert Co
201 Tabor Rd
Morris Plains, NJ 07950-2614, USA

Devisree (Actor, Bollywood)
1 Bharathi Apts
Bharathi Nagar 3rd Street T Nagar
Chennai, TN 600017, INDIA

DeVita, Vincent T Jr (Misc)
Yale Comprehensive Cancer Center
333 Cedar St
New Haven, CT 06510-3206, USA

DeVito, Danny (Actor, Comedian, Director)
c/o Kevin Huvane *Creative Artists Agency LCC (CAA-LA)*
2000 Avenue Of The Stars
Los Angeles, CA 90067-4700, USA

Devito, Louie (Director)
c/o Len Evans *Project Publicity*
312 W 53rd St
New York, NY 10019-5743, USA

Devitt, John (Swimmer)
46 Beacon Ave
Beacon Hill, NSW 2100, AUSTRALIA

DeVitto, Torrey (Actor)
c/o Josh Pollack *Agency for the Performing Arts (APA-LA)*
405 S Beverly Dr
Beverly Hills, CA 90212-4416, USA

Devliegher, Charles (Football Player)
Buffalo Bills
RR 6 Box 339
Byhalia, MS 38611, USA

Devlin, Barry (Director, Writer)
c/o Michael Peretzian *Creative Artists Agency LCC (CAA-LA)*
2000 Avenue Of The Stars
Los Angeles, CA 90067-4700, USA

Devlin, Bruce (Golfer)
HC 7 Box 305l
Payson, AZ 85541-9761, USA

Devlin, Chris (Football Player)
Cincinnati Bengals
100 Meadow Lark Ln
Boalsburg, PA 16827-1800, USA

Devlin, Dean (Actor, Director, Producer)
Electric Entertainment
1438 N Gower St Ste 24
Los Angeles, CA 90028-8306, USA

Devlin, Jim (Baseball Player)
Cleveland Indians
2227 Snyder Ave
Bloomsburg, PA 17815-3106, USA

Devlin, Joseph (Football Player)
Buffalo Bills
3715 Schintzius Rd
Eden, NY 14057-9790, USA

Devlin, Mike (Football Player)
Arizona Cardinals
48 Shore Rd
Mount Sinai, NY 11766-1420, USA

Devlin, Robert M (Business Person)
American General Corp
2929 Allen Pkwy
Houston, TX 77019-2155, USA

Devlins, The (Music Group)
c/o Staff Member *Paradigm (Monterey)*
509 Hartnell St
Monterey, CA 93940-2825, USA

Devo
PO Box 6868
Burbank, CA 91510-6868, USA

Devoll, Hal (Baseball Player)
Detroit Vegabond Kings
8928 Fox Ave
Allen Park, MI 48101-1502, USA

Devon (Adult Film Star)
c/o Staff Member *Atlas Entertainment*
6100 Wilshire Blvd Ste 1170
Los Angeles, CA 90048-5116, USA

Devon, Dayna (Television Host)
c/o Staff Member *Extra (LA)*
1840 Victory Blvd
Telepictures Productions
Glendale, CA 91201-2558, USA

Devries, Jared (Football Player)
Detroit Lions
1272 Edgewood Rd
Birmingham, MI 48009-3633, USA

DeVries, William C (Doctor)
DeVries Associates
7 Snowmound Ct
Rockville, MD 20850-2850, USA

deVry, William (Actor)
c/o Staff Member *The House of Representatives*
211 S Beverly Dr Ste 208
Beverly Hills, CA 90212-3879, USA

DeWaart, Edo (Conductor)
Essenlaan 68
Rotterdam 3016, THE NETHERLANDS

Dewan, Jenna (Actor)
c/o Joanne Wiles *William Morris Agency (WMA-LA)*
1 William Morris Pl
Beverly Hills, CA 90212-4261, USA

Dewar, Faber (Designer)
c/o Staff Member *Trading Spaces*
7700 Wisconsin Ave
The Learning Channel
Bethesda, MD 20814-3578, USA

Dewar, Jane E (Editor)
Legion Magazine
359 Kent St
#504
Ottawa, ON K2P 0R6, CANADA

Dewar, Susan (Cartoonist)
Universal Press Syndicate
4520 Main St
Kansas City, MO 64111-1876, USA

Dewberry, Michelle (Reality TV Star)
Taylor Herring
11 Westway Centre
69 St Marks Road
London W10 6JG, UNITED KINGDOM
(UK)

DeWet, Shaun (Model)
c/o Staff Member *Elite Model Management (NY)*
111 E 22nd St
New York, NY 10010-5400, USA

Dewey, Duane E (War Hero)
RR 1 Box 494
Irons, MI 49644, USA

Dewey, Mark (Baseball Player)
San Francisco Giants
PO Box 14
New Era, MI 49446-0014, USA

DeWilde, Edy (Director)
Stedelijk Museum
Amsterdam, THE NETHERLANDS

Dewillis, Jeff (Baseball Player)
Toronto Blue Jays
8918 Wind Side Dr
Houston, TX 77040-3460, USA

DeWinne, Frank (Cosmonaut)
349 Squadron
Vilegbaiss
Kleine Brogel
Peer, 10W TAC 3990, BELGIUM

DeWitt, Bryce S (Physicist)
University of Texas
Physics Dept
Austin, TX 78712, USA

DeWitt, Doug (Boxer)
2035 Central Ave
Yonkers, NY 10710, USA

DeWitt, Joyce (Actor)
c/o Staff Member *JG Business Management Inc*
PO Box 7309
Santa Monica, CA 90406-7309, USA

Dewitt, Matt (Baseball Player)
Toronto Blue Jays
7177 Sixshooter Dr
Las Vegas, NV 89119-4517, USA

DeWitt, Rosemary (Actor)
c/o Staff Member *Gersh Agency, The (NY)*
41 Madison Ave Fl 33
New York, NY 10010-2202, USA

Dewitt, William O (Baseball Player)
St Louis Cardinals
5825 Drewry Farm Ln
Cincinnati, OH 45243-3441, USA

DeWitt, Willie (Boxer)
605 N Water St
Burnet, TX 78611-1742, USA

DeWitt-Morette, Cecile (Physicist)
2411 Vista Ln
Austin, TX 78703-2343, USA

Dews, Peter B (Psychic)
280 Newtonville Ave Apt 221
Newtonville, MA 02460-2098, USA

DeWulf, Noureen (Actor)
c/o Tiffany Kuzon *Evolution Entertainment (LA)*
901 N Highland Ave
Los Angeles, CA 90038-2412, USA

Dewveall, Willard (Football Player)
Chicago Bears
14211 Bonney Brier Dr
Houston, TX 77069-1325, USA

Dexter, Mary (Director)
Hank Tani
14542 Delaware Dr
Moorpark, CA 93021-3560, USA

Dexter, Pete (Writer)
c/o Author Mail *Doubleday*
1745 Broadway
New York, NY 10019-4305, USA

Dexter, Peter W (Writer)
Sacramento Bee
21st & Q Sts
Editorial Dept
Sacramento, CA 95816, USA

Dey, Susan (Actor)
1640 S Sepulveda Blvd Ste 530
Los Angeles, CA 90025-7538, USA

DeYoung, Cliff (Actor)
481 Savona Way
Oak Park, CA 91377-4842, USA

DeYoung, Dennis (Musician)
15941 Harlem Ave
Tinley Park, IL 60477-1609, USA

Dezhurov, Vladimir N (Cosmonaut)
Potchta Kosmonavtov
Moskovskoi Oblasti
Syvisdny Goroduk 141160, RUSSIA

Dezonie, Hank (Basketball Player)
Tri-Cities Blackhawks
700 Lenox Ave Apt 17D
New York, NY 10039-4518, USA

Dhabhara, Firdaus S (Scientist)
Rockefeller University
1230 York Ave
Neurology Dept
New York, NY 10065-6399, USA

Dhamu (Actor)
84 Pycrofts Road 36 ADK Mansion
Triplicane
Chennai, TN 600 005, INDIA

Dhanapal (Actor)
8 A G Block
Pallaku Maa Nagar Luz
Chennai, TN 600 004, INDIA

Dhanoa, Guddu (Actor)
8A My Little Home
10th Road JVPD Scheme
Bombay, MS 400 049, INDIA

Dharmasakti, Sanya (Prime Minister)
15 Saukhumvit Road
Soi 41
Bangkok, THAILAND

D'Harnoncourt, Anne (Director)
Philadelphia Museum of Art
25th & Franklin Parkway
Philadelphia, PA 19101, USA

Dhavernas, Caroline (Actor)
c/o Rhonda Price *Gersh Agency, The (NY)*
41 Madison Ave Fl 3
New York, NY 10010-2202, USA

Dhawan, David (Director, Filmmaker)
A-15 Sagar Darshan
Carter Road Khar
Mumbai, MS 400052, INDIA

Dhue, Laurie (Anchor)
c/o Staff Member *Fox News Channel (NY)*
1211 Avenue Of The Americas
Level C1
New York, NY 10036-8701, USA

Di Maggio, Dominic P (Dom) (Athlete, Baseball Player)
162 Point Rd
Marion, MA 02738-1931, USA

Di Meola, Al (Musician)
Entourage Talent
133 W 25th St
5th Floor
New York, NY 10001-7206, USA

Di Montezemolo, Luca (Business Person, Race Car Driver)
c/o Staff Member *Jaguar Racing Ltd*
Bradbourne Drive
Tilbrook
Milton Keynes MK7 8BJ, UNITED KINGDOM (UK)

Dial, Leroy (Buddy) (Football Player)
Pittsburgh Steelers
115 Anna St
Tomball, TX 77375-6609, USA

Diallo, Mmadou (Soccer Player)
New England Revolution
1 Patriot Pl
Cmgi Field
Foxboro, MA 02035-1388, USA

Diamandis, Peter G (Publisher)
Diamandis Communications
1515 Broadway
New York, NY 10036-8901, USA

Diamandopoulos, Peter (Educator)
530 E 76th St Apt 32G
New York, NY 10021-3174, USA

Diamantopoulos, Chris (Actor)
c/o Patricia (Patty) Woo *TalentWorks (LA)*
3500 W Olive Ave Ste 1400
Burbank, CA 91505-5512, USA

Diamini, Barnabas S (Prime Minister)
Prime Minister's Office
PO Box 395
Mbabane, SWAZILAND

Diamond, Abel J (Architect)
Diamond Schmitz Co
2 Berkeley St
#600
Toronto, ON M5A 2W3, CANADA

Diamond, Bobby
5309 Comercio Way
Woodland Hills, CA 91364-2030, USA

Diamond, Charles (Football Player)
Dallas Texans
7300 SW 69th Ct
Miami, FL 33143-4420, USA

Diamond, Diane (Television Host)
c/o Staff Member *Court TV*
600 3rd Ave Frnt 2
New York, NY 10016-1901, USA

Diamond, Dustin (Actor)
c/o Staff Member *Jack Koshick Presents*
1626 N Prospect Ave Apt 1801
Milwaukee, WI 53202-2435, USA

Diamond, Joel (Producer)
Joel Diamond Entertainment
3940 Laurel Canyon Blvd Ste 441
Studio City, CA 91604-3709, USA

Diamond, Marian C (Misc)
2583 Virginia St
Berkeley, CA 94709-1108, USA

Diamond, Michael (Mike D) (Musician)
GAS Entertainment
8935 Lindblade St
Culver City, CA 90232-2438, USA

Diamond, Michael T (DJ)
c/o Staff Member *Diva Central Inc*
7510 W Sunset Blvd Ste 1445
Los Angeles, CA 90046-3408, USA

Diamond, Neil (Musician)
c/o Staff Member *Sony Records*
2100 Colorado Ave
Santa Monica, CA 90404-3504, USA

Diamond, Reed (Actor)
William Morris Agency
151 El Camino Dr
Beverly Hills, CA 90212-2775, USA

Diamond, Seymour (Doctor)
Diamond Headache Clinic
467 W Deming Pl Ste 500
Chicago, IL 60614-2970, USA

Diamond Rio (Musician)
c/o Staff Member *William Morris Agency (WMA-LA)*
1 William Morris Pl
Beverly Hills, CA 90212-4261, USA

Diamonds, The (Music Group)
561 Keystone Ave # 224
Reno, NV 89503-4304, USA

Diamont, Anita (Writer)
Charles Scribner's Sons
866 3rd Ave
New York, NY 10022-6221, USA

Diamont, Don (Actor)
Craig Mgmt
125 S Sycamore Ave
Los Angeles, CA 90036-2938, USA

Diana, Rich (Football Player)
Miami Dolphins
2 Munson Dr Unit 7
Wallingford, CT 06492-5366, USA

Dias, Ivan Cardinal (Religious Leader)
Archbishop's House
21 Nathalal Parekh Marg
Mumbai, MS 400001, INDIA

Dias Dos Santos, Fernando da Piedade (Prime Minister)
Prime Minister's Office
Council of Ministers
Luanda, ANGOLA

Diaw, Boris (Basketball Player)
Atlanta Hawks
190 Marietta St NW
Atlanta, GA 30303-2717, USA

Diaz, Alex (Journalist)
Associated Press
450 W 33rd St Fl 7
New York, NY 10001-2606, USA

Diaz, Arnold (Correspondent)
c/o Staff Member *20/20*
147 Columbus Ave
Abc
New York, NY 10023-6503, USA

Diaz, Cameron (Actor)
c/o Rick Yorn *The Firm*
9465 Wilshire Blvd Fl 6
Beverly Hills, CA 90212-2605, USA

Diaz, Carlos (Baseball Player)
Atlanta Braves
47-709 Waiohia St
Kaneohe, HI 96744-4938, USA

Diaz, Carlos (Baseball Player)
Toronto Blue Jays
3037 Homestead Oaks Dr
Clearwater, FL 33759-1626, USA

Diaz, Einar (Baseball Player)
Cleveland Indians
4315 70th Ave E
Ellenton, FL 34222-7329, USA

Diaz, Guillermo (Actor)
c/o Staff Member *Abrams Artists Agency (LA)*
9200 W Sunset Blvd Ph 11
Los Angeles, CA 90069-3601, USA

Diaz, Helga (Actor)
c/o Gabriel Blanco *Gabriel Blanco Iglesias (Mexico)*
Rio Balsas 35-32
Colonia Cuauhtemoc
DF 06500, MEXICO

Diaz, Jorge (Football Player)
Tampa Bay Buccaneers
230 W Henrietta Ave
Kingsville, TX 78363-4424, USA

Diaz, Laura (Golfer)
c/o Staff Member *Ladies Pro Golf Association (LPGA)*
100 International Golf Dr
Daytona Beach, FL 32124-1082, USA

Diaz, Manny (Politician)
Mayor's Office
3500 Pan American Dr
Miami, FL 33133-5504, USA

Diaz, Matt (Baseball Player)
Tampa Bay Devil Rays
1124 Afton St
Lakeland, FL 33803-3202, USA

Diaz, Mike (Baseball Player)
Chicago Cubs
416 Athenian Way
Pacifica, CA 94044-3901, USA

Diaz, Norberto (Actor)
c/o Staff Member *Telefe - Argentina*
Pavon 2444 (C1248AAT)
Buenos Aires, ARGENTINA

Diaz, Robison (Actor)
c/o Staff Member *TV Caracol*
Calle 76 #11 - 35
Piso 10AA
Bogota DC 26484, COLOMBIA

Diaz Balart, Jose (Actor)
c/o Staff Member *Telemundo*
2470 W 8th Ave
Hialeah, FL 33010-2000, USA

Diaz-Balart, Jose (Correspondent)
CBS-TV
51 W 52nd St
News Dept
New York, NY 10019-6119, USA

Diaz-Rahi, Yamila (Model)
Next Model Mgmt
23 Watts St
New York, NY 10013, USA

Dibble, Dorne (Football Player)
Detroit Lions
18601 Jamestown Cir
Northville, MI 48168-1834, USA

Dibble, Rob (Baseball Player, Television Host)
c/o Staff Member *Best Damned Sports Show Period, The*
10201 W Pico Blvd
Fox Sports Net
Los Angeles, CA 90064-2606, USA

Dibel, John C (Business Person)
Meade Instruments Corp
6001 Oak Cyn
Irvine, CA 92618-5200, USA

DiBeliglojoso, Lodovico B (Architect)
Studio Architetti BBPR
2 Via Dei Chiostri
Milan 20121, ITALY

Dibernardo, Rick (Football Player)
St Louis Cardinals
31942 Via Oso
Trabuco Canyon, CA 92679-3900, USA

DiBiaggio, John A (Educator)
Tufts University
President's Office
Medford, MA 02155, USA

DiBlasio, Raul (Musician)
Esterfan Enterprises
420 Jefferson Ave
Miami Beach, FL 33139-6503, USA

Diblassio, Raul (Musician)
c/o Staff Member *BMG*
1540 Broadway
New York, NY 10036-4074, USA

DiBona, Craig (Cinematographer)
333 E 66th St Apt 7O
New York, NY 10065-6274, USA

Dibos, Alicia (Golfer)
1465 E Putnam Ave Apt 112E
Old Greenwich, CT 06870-1330, USA

Dibra, Bash
c/o Daniel A (Dan) Strone *Trident Media Group LLC*
41 Madison Ave Fl 36
New York, NY 10010-2257, USA

Dicamillo, Gary T (Business Person)
1001 W Saint Georges Rd
Baltimore, MD 21210-1412, USA

DiCaprio, Leonardo (Actor)
c/o Staff Member *Appian Way*
9255 W Sunset Blvd Ste 615
West Hollywood, CA 90069-3303, USA

DiCenzo, George (Actor)
Michael Hartig Agency
156 5th Ave Ste 820
New York, NY 10010-7767, USA

Dichter, Misha (Musician)
Columbia Artists Mgmt Inc
1790 Broadway Fl 6
New York, NY 10019-1412, USA

Dicillo, Tom (Director)
William Morris Agency
151 El Camino Dr
Beverly Hills, CA 90212-2775, USA

Dick, Andy (Actor, Comedian)
c/o David (Dave) Becky *3 Arts Entertainment Inc*
9460 Wilshire Blvd Fl 7
Beverly Hills, CA 90212-2713, USA

Dick, Douglas (Actor)
604 S Gretna Green Way
Los Angeles, CA 90049-4035, USA

Dick, Ed (Baseball Player)
TCMA
16227 Lamey Bridge Rd
Biloxi, MS 39532-2861, USA

Dickau, Dan (Basketball Player)
Atlanta Hawks
190 Marietta St NW
Atlanta, GA 30303-2717, USA

Dickel, Dan (Football Player)
Baltimore Colts
3573 Maplewood Dr NE
Iowa City, IA 52240, USA

Dicken, Paul (Baseball Player)
Cleveland Indians
1901 NW 28th Ave
Ocala, FL 34475-4709, USA

Dickens, Jimmy (Musician)
5010 W Concord Rd
Brentwood, TN 37027-6520, USA

Dickens, Kim (Artist)
c/o Staff Member *Gersh Agency, The (LA)*
232 N Canon Dr
Beverly Hills, CA 90210-5302, USA

Dickenson, Gary (Bowler)
501 Wade Martin Rd
Edmond, OK 73034-6716, USA

Dickerson, Eric (Football Player, Sportscaster)
Los Angeles Rams
26815 Mulholland Hwy
Calabasas, CA 91302-1947, USA

Dickerson, Ernest R (Director)
c/o David Gersh *Gersh Agency, The (LA)*
232 N Canon Dr
Beverly Hills, CA 90210-5302, USA

Dickerson, Henry (Basketball Player)
Detroit Pistons
3204 Skybrook Ln
Durham, NC 27703-5983, USA

Dickerson, John (Baseball Player)
Homestead Grays
1702 26th St N
Columbus, MS 39701-2606, USA

Dickerson, Kenneth (Football Player)
Miami Dolphins
2811 Moton Cir
Tuskegee Institute, AL 36088-2875, USA

Dickerson, Sandra (Actor)
Howes & Prior
Berkeley House
Hay Hill
London W1X 7LH, UNITED KINGDOM (UK)

Dickey, Boh A (Business Person)
SAFECO Corp
Safeco Plaza
Seattle, WA 98185-0001, USA

Dickey, R A (Baseball Player)
Texas Rangers
701 Cantrell Ave
Nashville, TN 37215-1022, USA

Dickey, Richard (Basketball Player)
Boston Celtics
1109 Red Maple Dr
Plymouth, IN 46563-3697, USA

Dickinson, Angie (Actor)
c/o Merritt Blake *The Blake Agency*
1333 Ocean Ave
Santa Monica, CA 90401-1023, USA

Dickinson, Bruce (Musician)
c/o Staff Member *Agency Group Ltd, The (UK)*
361-373 City Road
London EC1V 1PQ, UNITED KINGDOM (UK)

Dickinson, David (Actor)
Bargain Hunt
PO Box 229
Bristol BS99 7JN, ENGLAND

Dickinson, Janice (Model, Reality TV Star)
c/o Itay Reiss *United Talent Agency (UTA)*
9560 Wilshire Blvd Ste 500
Beverly Hills, CA 90212-2401, USA

Dickinson, Judy (Golfer)
18277 SE Heritage Dr
Jupiter, FL 33469-1439, USA

Dickinson, Parnell (Football Player)
Tampa Bay Buccaneers
1646 Wallace Rd
Lutz, FL 33549-3933, USA

Dickinson, Richard (Football Player)
Dallas Texans
PO Box 166
New Augusta, MS 39462-0166, USA

Dickinson, Steve (Cartoonist)
King Features Syndicate
888 7th Ave Ste 201
New York, NY 10106-0201, USA

Dickman, James B (Journalist)
1471 Peach Creek Dr
Splendora, TX 77372, USA

Dickson, Clarence (Lawyer)
Police Department
1351 NW 12th St
Metro Justice
Miami, FL 33125-1644, USA

Dickson, Jason (Baseball Player)
California Angels
9022 E Helm Dr
Scottsdale, AZ 85260-2704, USA

Dickson, Jennifer (Artist, Photographer)
20 Osborne St
Ottawa, ON K1S 4Z9, CANADA

Dickson, Jim (Baseball Player)
Houston Colt.45's
90580 Sunset Lake Rd Apt 1
Warrenton, OR 97146-7285, USA

Dickson, John (Basketball Player)
New Orleans Buccaneers
4646 Wynmeade Park NE
Marietta, GA 30067-4098, USA

Dickson, Lance (Baseball Player)
Chicago Cubs
4615 N Placita Roca Blanca
Tucson, AZ 85718-7476, USA

Dickson, Neil (Actor)
International Creative Mgmt
76 Oxford St
London W1N 0AX, UNITED KINGDOM (UK)

Dickson, Ngila (Designer)
c/o Staff Member *Sandra Marsh Management*
9150 Wilshire Blvd Ste 220
Beverly Hills, CA 90212-3429, USA

Dickson, Paul (Football Player)
Los Angeles Rams
10340 Portland Ave S
Bloomington, MN 55420-5434, USA

Dicus, Charles (Chuck) (Football Player)
San Diego Chargers
1500 E Clark St
Fayetteville, AR 72701-3710, USA

Diddley, Bo (Musician)
c/o Margo Lewis *Talent Consultants International (TCI)*
105 Shad Row Ste B
Piermont, NY 10968-3001, USA

Didier, Bob (Baseball Player)
Atlanta Braves
544 SW 335th St
Federal Way, WA 98023-6189, USA

Didier, Clint (Football Player)
Washington Redskins
8770 N Glade Rd
Pasco, WA 99301-8720, USA

Didion, Joan (Writer)
Janklow & Nesbit
445 Park Ave # 1300
New York, NY 10022-2606, USA

Didion, John (Football Player)
Washington Redskins
48 Elk Ridge Ln
Naselle, WA 98638-8515, USA

Dido (Musician, Songwriter)
c/o Staff Member *Helter Skelter (UK)*
535 Kings Rd
The Plaza
London SW10 0SZ, UNITED KINGDOM (UK)

Diebold, John (Business Person)
Diebold Group
PO Box 515
Bedford Hills, NY 10507-0515, USA

Diehl, Digby (Journalist)
788 S Lake Ave
Pasadena, CA 91106-3948, USA

Diehl, John (Actor)
c/o Sandi Dudek *Paradigm (LA)*
360 N Crescent Dr
North Bldg
Beverly Hills, CA 90210-6820, USA

Diehl, John A (Football Player)
Baltimore Colts
900 S Henry St
Williamsburg, VA 23185-3989, USA

Dieken, Doug H (Football Player)
Cleveland Browns
209 Prospect Ave
Streator, IL 61364-1477, USA

Diemecke, Enrique Arturo (Conductor)
Herbert Barrett
266 W 37th St Fl 20
New York, NY 10018-6648, USA

Diener, Theodor O (Misc)
PO Box 272
11711 Battersea Dr
Beltsville, MD 20704-0272, USA

Dienhart, Mark (Football Player)
Buffalo Bills
1944 Bayard Ave
Saint Paul, MN 55116-1216, USA

Dierassi, Carl (Inventor)
2325 Bear Gulch Rd
Redwood City, CA 94062-4405, USA

Dierassi, Issac (Doctor)
2034 Delancey St
Philadelphia, PA 19103-6510, USA

Dierdorf, Dan (Football Player)
St Louis Cardinals
13302 Buckland Hall Rd
Saint Louis, MO 63131-1214, USA

Diering, Chuck (Baseball Player)
St Louis Cardinals
1 Nob Hill Dr
Saint Louis, MO 63138-1400, USA

Dierker, Lawrence E (Larry) (Baseball Player)
Houston Colt.45's
8318 N Tahoe Dr
Houston, TX 77040-1258, USA

Dierker, Robert R (General)
Deputy Commander Pacific Fleet
Camp H M Smith
Honolulu, HI 96861, USA

Dierking, Connie (Basketball Player)
Syracuse Nationals
5665 Kugler Mill Rd
Cincinnati, OH 45236-2163, USA

Dierking, Scott (Football Player)
New York Jets
1862 Wingate Ln
Wheaton, IL 60187-7881, USA

Diesel
26 Stokescroft #100
Bristol, ENGLAND BS1 3QD, UNITED KINGDOM (UK)

Diesel, Vin (Actor, Director, Producer, Writer)
c/o Staff Member *One Race Productions*
9100 Wilshire Blvd
East Tower #333
Beverly Hills, CA 90212-3401, USA

Dieterich, Chris (Football Player)
Detroit Lions
804 Edisto River Rd
Myrtle Beach, SC 29588-7439, USA

Dietrich, Dena (Actor)
Peter Strain
5455 Wilshire Blvd Ste 1812
Los Angeles, CA 90036-4268, USA

Dietrich, William A (Bill) (Journalist)
Seattle Times
1120 John St
Editorial Dept
Seattle, WA 98109-5321, USA

Dietrick, Coby (Basketball Player)
Memphis Pros
644 Patterson Ave
San Antonio, TX 78209-5655, USA

Dietz, Bob (Basketball Player)
Indianapolis Kautskys
12426 Medalist Pkwy
Carmel, IN 46033-8933, USA

Dietz, Eileen (Actor)
c/o Hazel Shallon *Shallon Star Management*
15030 Ventura Blvd Ste 911
Sherman Oaks, CA 91403-5470, USA

Dietzel, Roy (Baseball Player)
Washington Senators
8421 Coulwood Oak Ln
Charlotte, NC 28214-1165, USA

Difani, Jay (Baseball Player)
Washington Senators
1186 Weaver Rd
Festus, MO 63028-4242, USA

Difelice, Mike (Baseball Player)
St Louis Cardinals
9409 Trails End Rd
Knoxville, TN 37931-4218, USA

Diffie, Joe (Musician)
Buddy Lee Attractions
38 Music Sq E Ste 200
Nashville, TN 37203-4304, USA

Diffie, Whitfield (Inventor)
Sun Microsystems
901 San Antonio Rd
Ms Umtv29-116
Palo Alto, CA 94303-4900, USA

Diffrient, Niels (Designer)
General Delivery
Ridgefield, CT 06877-9999, USA

DiFranco, Ani (Musician, Songwriter, Writer)
c/o Staff Member *Primary Talent International (UK)*
2-12 Pentonville Rd Fl 5
London N1 9PL, UNITED KINGDOM (UK)

DiGenova, Joseph E (Lawyer)
DiGenova & Toensing
1776 K St NW Ste 700
Washington, DC 20006-2326, USA

Diggins, Ben (Baseball Player)
Milwaukee Brewers
PO Box 2887
Vero Beach, FL 32961-2887, USA

Diggs, Nail (Football Player)
Green Bay Packers
6915 Rea Croft Dr
Charlotte, NC 28226-3329, USA

Diggs, Shelton (Football Player)
New York Jets
261 Washington Ave Apt 3R
New Rochelle, NY 10801-5967, USA

Diggs, Taye (Actor)
c/o Greg Siegel *Endeavor Agency LLC (LA)*
9601 Wilshire Blvd Fl 3
Beverly Hills, CA 90210-5204, USA

Digiacomo, Curt (Football Player)
San Diego Chargers
830 Ida Ave
Solana Beach, CA 92075-2439, USA

Digible Planets (Music Group)
345 N Maple Dr Ste 123
Beverly Hills, CA 90210-6117, USA

DiGirolamo, Vincent A (Financier)
National City Corp
1900 E 9th St
National City Center
Cleveland, OH 44114-3484, USA

DiGregorio, Ernie (Basketball Player)
Buffalo Braves
60 Chestnut Ave
Narragansett, RI 02882-6113, USA

Dilauro, Jack (Baseball Player)
New York Mets
168 E Mohawk Dr
Malvern, OH 44644-9539, USA

Dilba (Musician)
United Stage Production
PO Box 11029
Stockholm 10061, SWEDEN

Dilfer, Trent F (Football Player)
Tampa Bay Buccaneers
15288 Quito Rd
Saratoga, CA 95070-6227, USA

Dilger, Ken (Football Player)
Indianapolis Colts
10403 Windemere
Carmel, IN 46032-8594, USA

Dilip (Actor)
74 Baskara Colony
Virugambakkam
Chennai, TN 600 092, INDIA

Dill, Craig (Basketball Player)
Pittsburgh Pipers
10200 Thomas Woods Rd
Saginaw, MI 48609-9512, USA

Dill, Laddie John (Artist)
1625 Electric Ave
Venice, CA 90291-4803, USA

Dill, Terry (Golfer)
9 Swiftwater Trl
The Hills, TX 78738-1417, USA

Dillahunt, Garret (Actor)
c/o Edith Rea *Allman/Rea Management*
141 S Barrington Ave Ste E
Los Angeles, CA 90049-3314, USA

Dillam, Bradford (Actor)
770 Hot Springs Rd
Santa Barbara, CA 93108-1107, USA

Dillane, Stephen (Actor)
Michelle Braidman
10/11 Lower John St
#300
London W1R 3PE, UNITED KINGDOM (UK)

Dillard, Alex (Business Person)
Dillard's Inc
1600 Cantrell Rd
Little Rock, AR 72201-1145, USA

Dillard, Don (Baseball Player)
Cleveland Indians
45 Bream Ln
Waterloo, SC 29384-4868, USA

Dillard, Doug (Actor, Musician)
Superior Communications Co Talent
340 S Columbus Blvd
C/O Randy Campbell
Tucson, AZ 85711-4138, USA

Dillard, Gordon (Baseball Player)
Baltimore Orioles
840 Via Manzana
Aromas, CA 95004-9026, USA

Dillard, Harrison
3449 Glencairn Rd
Shaker Heights, OH 44122-4801, USA

Dillard, Mickey (Basketball Player)
Cleveland Cavaliers
224 SW 11th Ave
Dania, FL 33004-3515, USA

Dillard, Rodney (Actor, Musician)
Superior Communications Co. Talent
340 S Columbus Blvd
C/O Randy Campbell
Tucson, AZ 85711-4138, USA

Dillard, Stacey (Football Player)
New York Giants
3188 County Road 4220
Annona, TX 75550-4037, USA

Dillard, Steve (Baseball Player)
Boston Red Sox
154 Drive 841
Saltillo, MS 38866-9362, USA

Dillard, W Harrison (Athlete, Track Athlete)
3449 Glencairn Rd
Shaker Heights, OH 44122-4801, USA

Dillard, William T Jr (Business Person)
Dillard's Inc
1600 Cantrell Rd
Little Rock, AR 72201-1145, USA

Dillehay, Thomas (Tom) (Misc)
University of Kentucky
Anthropology Dept
Lexington, KY 40506-0001, USA

Dilleita, Dilleita Mohamed (Prime Minister)
Prime Minister's Office
PO Box 2086
Djibouti, DJIBOUTI

Diller, Barry (Business Person)
IAC/InterActive Corp
555 W 18th St
New York, NY 10011-2822, USA

Diller, Phyllis (Actor, Comedian)
163 S Rockingham Ave
Los Angeles, CA 90049-2513, USA

Dillinger, Bob (Baseball Player)
St Louis Browns
15380 Rhododendron Dr
Canyon Country, CA 91387-1851, USA

Dillinger, Darlene
3104A Highland Ave
Manhattan Beach, CA 90266, USA

Dillion, Steve (Baseball Player)
New York Mets
110 Hyatt Ave
Yonkers, NY 10704-4315, USA

Dillman, Bill (Baseball Player)
Baltimore Orioles
PO Box 5167
Winter Park, FL 32793-5167, USA

Dillman, Bradford (Actor)
770 Hot Springs Rd
Santa Barbara, CA 93108-1107, USA

Dillman, Brooke (Actor)
c/o Staff Member *Sweet Mud Group*
648 Broadway # 1002
New York, NY 10012-2301, USA

Dillon, Bobby (Football Player)
Green Bay Packers
1289 Morgan Dr
Temple, TX 76502-4245, USA

Dillon, Corey (Football Player)
c/o Staff Member *New England Patriots*
60 Washington St
Gillette Stadium - RR 1
Foxboro, MA 02035-1388, USA

Dillon, David B (Business Person)
Kroger Co
1014 Vine St
Cincinnati, OH 45202-1100, USA

Dillon, Denny (Actor, Comedian)
International Creative Mgmt
8942 Wilshire Blvd # 219
Beverly Hills, CA 90211-1908, USA

Dillon, John T (Business Person)
International Paper Co
2 Manhattanville Rd
Purchase, NY 10577-2113, USA

Dillon, Kevin (Actor)
49 W 9th St Apt 5B
New York, NY 10011-9202, USA

Dillon, Marc (Musician)
c/o Staff Member *Pop Idol (Fremantle
Media)*
2700 Colorado Ave Ste 450
Santa Monica, CA 90404-3599, USA

Dillon, Matt (Actor, Director)
c/o Vic Ramos *Vic Ramos Management*
49 W 9th St Apt 5B
New York, NY 10011-9202, USA

Dillon, Melinda (Actor)
c/o Staff Member *Innovative Artists (LA)*
1505 10th St
Santa Monica, CA 90401-2805, USA

Dillon, Mike (Race Car Driver)
PO Box 30414
Winston Salem, NC 27130-0414, USA

Dilmancheff, Babe (Football Player)
Boston Yanks
3917 Edgehill Dr
Los Angeles, CA 90008-2617, USA

Dilone, Miguel (Baseball Player)
Pittsburgh Pirates
Calle El Sol #190
Santiago, DOMINICAN REPUBLIC

Dils, Steve (Football Player)
Minnesota Vikings
10285 Midway Ave
Alpharetta, GA 30022-6028, USA

Dilts, Douglas (Football Player)
Denver Broncos
1231 Defoor Ct NW
Atlanta, GA 30318-2973, USA

DiMaggio, John (Actor)
c/o Paul Rosicker *Gersh Agency, The (LA)*
232 N Canon Dr
Beverly Hills, CA 90210-5302, USA

DiMarco, Chris (Golfer)
1408 Langham Ter
Lake Mary, FL 32746-1965, USA

Dimas, Trent (Gymnast)
Gold Cup Gymnastics School
6009 Carmel Ave NE
Albuquerque, NM 87113-1741, USA

Dimbleby, David (Correspondent,
Journalist)
14 King St
Richmond
Surrey TW9 1NF, UNITED KINGDOM
(UK)

DiMeo, Paul (Actor, Reality TV Star)
c/o Staff Member *Extreme Makeover:
Home Edition*
9255 W Sunset Blvd Ste 1100
Endemol Entertainment USA
Los Angeles, CA 90069-3308, USA

DiMeola, Al (Musician)
Don't Worry
111 W 57th St Ste 1120
New York, NY 10019-2211, USA

Dimichele, Frank (Baseball Player)
California Angels
812 Tasker St
Philadelphia, PA 19148-1240, USA

Dimitriades, Alex (Actor)
c/o Staff Member *Shanahan Management*
PO Box 1509
Darlinghurst 1300, AUSTRALIA

Dimitrova, Ghena (Opera Singer)
I C M Artists
40 W 57th St
New York, NY 10019-4001, USA

Dimmel, Mike (Baseball Player)
Baltimore Orioles
526 Country Ln
Coppell, TX 75019-5129, USA

Dimmick, Thomas (Football Player)
Philadelphia Eagles
204 Broadmoor Blvd
Lafayette, LA 70503-5114, USA

Dimon, James (Jamie) (Business Person)
J P Morgan Chase
270 Park Ave Fl 12
New York, NY 10017-7924, USA

Dimple (Actor, Bollywood)
The Gallop Broad Acres Stud Farm
Avan Hali Estate
Bangalore, KA, INDIA

Dimry, Charles (Football Player)
Atlanta Falcons
611 S Myers St Apt 1
Oceanside, CA 92054-3904, USA

DiMucci, Dion
1650 Broadway Ste 503
New York, NY 10019-6833, USA

Dinapoli, Gennaro (Football Player)
Oakland Raiders
156 Taunton Hill Rd
Newtown, CT 06470-1723, USA

diNapoli, Marc
8 rue de Georges-de-Porto-Riche
Paris F-75014, FRANCE

DiNardo, Gerry (Coach, Football Coach)
Indiana University
Athletic Dept
Bloomington, IN 47405, USA

Dindal, Mark (Director)
c/o Peter Nichols *Lichter Grossman
Nichols Adler & Goodman*
9200 W Sunset Blvd Ste 1200
Los Angeles, CA 90069-3607, USA

Dine, James (Artist)
Pace Gallery
32 E 57th St
New York, NY 10022-2530, USA

Dineen, Gary (Hockey Player)
177 Sawmill Rd
West Springfield, MA 01089-1668, USA

Dineen, Kevin (Hockey Player)
30 Rivermead
Avon, CT 06001-2063, USA

Dineen, William P (Bill) (Coach)
Saint Louis Blues
1401 Clark Ave
Sawis Center
Saint Louis, MO 63103-2700, USA

Dinerstein, James (Artist)
Salander-O'Reilly Gallery
20 E 79th St
New York, NY 10075-0106, USA

Dingle, Mike (Football Player)
Cincinnati Bengals
512 Menlo Dr
Columbia, SC 29210-6537, USA

Dingman, Craig (Baseball Player)
New York Yankees
3573 Del Sienno St
Wichita, KS 67203-4349, USA

Dini, Paul (Actor, Producer, Writer)
c/o Staff Member *United Talent Agency
(UTA)*
9560 Wilshire Blvd Ste 500
Beverly Hills, CA 90212-2401, USA

Dinkel, Tom (Football Player)
Cincinnati Bengals
877 Squire Lake Ct
Villa Hills, KY 41017-1362, USA

Dinkeloo, John (Architect)
Roche & Dinkeloo
20 Davis St
Hamden, CT 06517-3501, USA

Dinklage, Peter (Actor)
c/o Charles Silver *SMS Talent Inc*
8730 W Sunset Blvd Ste 440
Los Angeles, CA 90069-2277, USA

Dinner, Michael (Director)
c/o Staff Member *Creative Artists Agency
LCC (CAA-LA)*
2000 Avenue Of The Stars
Los Angeles, CA 90067-4700, USA

Dinnigan, Collette (Designer, Fashion
Designer)
22-24 Hutchinson St
Surry Hills
Sydney, NSW 2010, AUSTRALIA

Dion (Musician)
Fox Entertainment
1650 Broadway Ste 503
New York, NY 10019-6833, USA

Dion, Celine (Musician)
c/o Alix Gucovsky *Special Artists Agency*
9465 Wilshire Blvd Ste 890
Beverly Hills, CA 90212-2607, USA

Dion, Colleen (Actor)
Abrams Artists
9200 W Sunset Blvd Ste 1125
Los Angeles, CA 90069-3610, USA

Dionisi, Stefano (Actor)
Carol Levi Co
Via Giuseppe Pisanelli
Rome 00196, ITALY

Dionne, Joseph L (Business Person,
Publisher)
McGraw-Hill Inc
1221 Avenue Of The Americas
New York, NY 10020-1095, USA

Dionne, Marcel E (Hockey Player)
Dionne Enterprises
9930 Keller Rd
Clarence Center, NY 14032-9774, USA

Diop, DeSagana (Basketball Player)
Cleveland Cavaliers
1 Center Ct
Gund Arena
Cleveland, OH 44115-4001, USA

Diop, Majhemout (President)
210 HCM Guediawaye
Dakar, SENEGAL

Dior, Christian (Designer, Fashion
Designer)
St-Anna-Platz 2
Munich 80538, GERMANY

Diorio, Nick (Soccer Player)
273 Clark St
Lemoyne, PA 17043-2010, USA

Diorio, Ron (Baseball Player)
Philadelphia Phillies
2 White Oak Ln
Waterbury, CT 06705-1835, USA

DiPasquale, James (Composer)
Gorfaine/Schwartz
4111 W Alameda Ave Ste 509
Burbank, CA 91505-4171, USA

Dipierro, Ramon (Football Player)
Green Bay Packers
1750 Brownstone Blvd Apt H
Toledo, OH 43614-1362, USA

Dipietro, Bob (Baseball Player)
Boston Red Sox
909 Carriage Hill Dr
Yakima, WA 98908-2414, USA

DiPietro, Rick (Hockey Player)
63 Loring Rd
Winthrop, MA 02152-2319, USA

Dipino, Frank (Baseball Player)
Milwaukee Brewers
5479 Pebble Beach Dr
Camillus, NY 13031-8651, USA

Dipoto, Jerry (Baseball Player)
15130 E Camelview Dr
Fountain Hills, AZ 85268-6405, USA

DiPreta, Tony (Cartoonist)
North American Syndicate
235 E 45th St
New York, NY 10017-3305, USA

DiPrete, Edward D (Governor)
555 Wilbur Ave
Cranston, RI 02921-1435, USA

Dirda, Michael (Journalist)
Washington Post
Editorial Dept
1150 15th St NW
Washington, DC 20071-0001, USA

Dirden, Johnnie (Football Player)
Houston Oilers
1403 S Ulster St
Denver, CO 80231-2744, USA

Director, Kim (Actor)
c/o Rachel Sheedy *Don Buchwald &
Associates Inc (LA)*
6500 Wilshire Blvd Ste 2200
Los Angeles, CA 90048-4942, USA

Direnzo, Daniel (Football Player)
Philadelphia Eagles
PO Box 958
Albrightsville, PA 18210-0958, USA

Direnzo, Fred (Football Player)
New York Giants
5 Togno St
Netcong, NJ 07857-1608, USA

Dirie, Waris (Activist, Model)
London Mgmt
2-4 Noel Street
London W1V 3RB, UNITED KINGDOM
(UK)

Dirnt, Mike (Musician)
c/o Staff Member *Creative Artists Agency
LCC (CAA-LA)*
2000 Avenue Of The Stars
Los Angeles, CA 90067-4700, USA

Dirt Band, The
PO Box 1915
Aspen, CO 81612-1915, USA

Dirty Pretty Things (Music Group)
c/o Staff Member *Paradigm (Monterey)*
509 Hartnell St
Monterey, CA 93940-2825, USA

Disarcina, Gary (Baseball Player)
California Angels
6 Patrick Ave
Billerica, MA 01821-5503, USA

Disch, Thomas M (Writer)
Karpfinger Agency
357 W 20th St
New York, NY 10011-3379, USA

Dischinger, Terry (Basketball Player)
1259 Lake Garden Ct
Lake Oswego, OR 97034-2832, USA

Disco, Shanthi (Actor, Bollywood)
19 Habibullah Road
T Nagar
Chennai, TN 600017, INDIA

Disco Biscuits, The (Music Group)
c/o Staff Member *Paradigm (Monterey)*
509 Hartnell St
Monterey, CA 93940-2825, USA

Disel, Vin (Actor, Director)
c/o Stacy Boniello *The Firm*
9465 Wilshire Blvd Fl 6
Beverly Hills, CA 90212-2605, USA

Dishman, Chris (Football Player)
c/o Staff Member *Saint Louis Rams*
1 Rams Way
Earth City, MO 63045-1525, USA

Dishman, Cris E (Football Player)
1561 Raymond Rd
Garland, NE 68360-9347, USA

Dishman, Glenn (Baseball Player)
San Diego Padres
5400 Fairway Dr
San Jose, CA 95127-1609, USA

Dishy, Bob (Actor)
20 E 9th St
New York, NY 10003-5944, USA

Disi, Ursula (Skier)
Krumme Gasse 10A
Ruhpolding 83324, GERMANY

Disi, Uschi (Misc)
Unterer Plattenberg 6
Flossenberg 92696, GERMANY

Disney, Anthea (Editor)
News Corporation
1211 Avenue Of The Americas Fl 8
New York, NY 10036-8706, USA

Disney, Roy (Business Person)
Walt Disney Company
500 S Buena Vista St
Burbank, CA 91521-0007, USA

Disney, William (Speed Skater)
1610 Kirk Dr
Lake Havasu City, AZ 86404-2449, USA

DiSpirito, Rocco (Actor, Reality TV Star)
c/o Staff Member *William Morris Agency (WMA-NY)*
1325 Avenue Of The Americas
New York, NY 10019-6026, USA

Distaso, Alec (Baseball Player)
Chicago Cubs
PO Box 721
Macomb, IL 61455-0721, USA

Distefano, Benny (Baseball Player)
Pittsburgh Pirates
9911 Murray Lndg
Missouri City, TX 77459-6417, USA

Distel, Sascha
20 rue de Fosses-Saint-Jacques
Paris F-75005, FRANCE

Distler, Natalie (Actor)
c/o Cynthia Booth *Agency Group Ltd, The (LA)*
1880 Century Park E Ste 711
Los Angeles, CA 90067-1618, USA

Disturbed (Music Group)
c/o Staff Member *Helter Skelter (UK)*
535 Kings Rd
The Plaza
London SW10 0SZ, UNITED KINGDOM (UK)

DiSuvero, Mark (Artist)
PO Box 2218
Astoria, NY 11102-0218, USA

Ditka, Mike (Coach, Football Coach, Football Player)
PPI Marketing
15601 Dallas Pkwy Ste 525
Addison, TX 75001-6055, USA

Ditmar, Arthur J (Art) (Baseball Player)
Philadelphia Athletics
6687 Wisteria Dr
Myrtle Beach, SC 29588-6481, USA

Dittmer, Andreas (Athlete)
Fischerbank 5
Neubrandenburg 17033, GERMANY

Dittmer, Edward C (Scientist)
702 Old Mescalero Rd
Tularosa, NM 88352-2525, USA

Dittmer, Jack (Baseball Player)
Boston Braves
200 N Main Street
Elkader, IA 52043, USA

Dityatin, Aleksandr N (Gymnast)
Nevski Prosp 18
#25
Saint Petersburg, RUSSIA

Ditz, Nancy (Athlete, Track Athlete)
524 Moore Rd
Woodside, CA 94062-1109, USA

Diulio, Albert J (Educator)
Marquette University
President's Office
Milwaukee, WI 53233, USA

Diva, Amanda (Television Host)
c/o Michael (Mike) Esterman *Esterman Entertainment*
214 Park Rd
Riva, MD 21140-1224, USA

Divac, Viade (Basketball Player)
c/o Staff Member *Sacramento Kings*
1 Sports Pkwy
Arco Arena
Sacramento, CA 95834-2301, USA

Divac, Vlade (Basketball Player)
c/o Team Member *Los Angeles Lakers (LA Lakers)*
1111 S Figueroa St
Staples Center
Los Angeles, CA 90015-1300, USA

Divina, Luz (DJ)
c/o Len Evans *Project Publicity*
312 W 53rd St
New York, NY 10019-5743, USA

Divine, Gary W (Misc)
National Federation of Federal Employees
1016 16th St
Washington, DC 20038, USA

Divine Comedy, The (Music Group)
c/o Staff Member *Paradigm (Monterey)*
509 Hartnell St
Monterey, CA 93940-2825, USA

Divins, Charles (Actor)
c/o Staff Member *Innovative Artists (LA)*
1505 10th St
Santa Monica, CA 90401-2805, USA

Diwakar, R R (Writer)
Sri Arvind Krupa
233 Sadashiv Nagar
Bangalore, Karnataka 560006, INDIA

Dix, Drew D (War Hero)
1829 S Pueblo Blvd
Pueblo, CO 81005-2105, USA

Dixie Chicks, The (Music Group)
c/o Staff Member *Creative Artists Agency LCC (CAA-LA)*
2000 Avenue Of The Stars
Los Angeles, CA 90067-4700, USA

Dixie Cups, The (Music Group)
2535 Noble St
North Las Vegas, NV 89030-3819, USA

Dixieland Rhythm Kings, The
PO Box 12403
Atlanta, GA 30355-2403, USA

Dixit, Madhuri (Actor, Bollywood)
Vijaydeep 3rd Floor Iris Park
Juhu
Mumbai, MS 400049, INDIA

Dixon, Al (Football Player)
New York Giants
120 W 7th St Ste 216
Plainfield, NJ 07060-1629, USA

Dixon, Alan J (Senator)
7606 Foley Dr
Belleville, IL 62223-2322, USA

Dixon, Becky (Sportscaster)
ABC-TV
77 W 66th St
Sports Dept
New York, NY 10023-6201, USA

Dixon, Cal (Football Player)
New York Jets
179 Las Palmas
Merritt Island, FL 32953-2902, USA

Dixon, Craig (Athlete, Track Athlete)
10630 Wellworth Ave
Los Angeles, CA 90024-5012, USA

Dixon, D Jeremy (Architect)
41 Shelton St
London WC2H 9HJ, UNITED KINGDOM (UK)

Dixon, Donna (Actor)
Edrick/Rich Mgmt
8955 Norma Pl
Los Angeles, CA 90069-4818, USA

Dixon, Dwayne (Football Player)
Tampa Bay Buccaneers
78 Westfield Pl
Athens, OH 45701-3857, USA

Dixon, Floyd (Musician)
Folklore Prod
1671 Appian Way
Santa Monica, CA 90401-3258, USA

Dixon, Frank J (Misc)
2355 Avenida De La Playa
La Jolla, CA 92037-3202, USA

Dixon, Gerald (Football Player)
Cleveland Browns
548 Jedburgh Way
Rock Hill, SC 29730-7475, USA

Dixon, Hanford (Football Player)
Cleveland Browns
1970 Bradley Rd
Westlake, OH 44145-6810, USA

Dixon, Ivan (Actor, Director)
11513 Black Maple Ave
Charlotte, NC 28269-5165, USA

Dixon, Juan (Basketball Player)
Washington Wizards
601 F St NW
Mcl Centre
Washington, DC 20004-1605, USA

Dixon, Ken (Baseball Player)
Baltimore Orioles
40 Clinton Hill Ct
Catonsville, MD 21228-3678, USA

Dixon, Leslie (Director, Producer, Writer)
c/o Todd Feldman *Creative Artists Agency LCC (CAA-LA)*
2000 Avenue Of The Stars
Los Angeles, CA 90067-4700, USA

Dixon, Mark (Football Player)
Miami Dolphins
4016 Ivy Ln
Kitty Hawk, NC 27949-4347, USA

Dixon, Randolph C (Randy) (Football Player)
Indianapolis Colts
9910 Summerlakes Dr
Carmel, IN 46032-9307, USA

Dixon, Robert J (General)
5100 John D Ryan Blvd Apt 2206
San Antonio, TX 78245-3513, USA

Dixon, Rodney (Rod) (Athlete, Track Athlete)
22 Entrican Ave
Remuera
Auckland 5, NEW ZEALAND

Dixon, Ronnie (Football Player)
New Orleans Saints
881 Holyoke Dr
Cincinnati, OH 45240-1840, USA

Dixon, Sonny (Baseball Player)
Washington Senators
2912 Iron Gate Ln
Charlotte, NC 28212-3646, USA

Dixon, Steve (Baseball Player)
St Louis Cardinals
6510 Hollow Tree Rd
Louisville, KY 40228-1336, USA

Dixon, Tamecka (Basketball Player)
Los Angeles Sparks
1111 S Figueroa St
Staples Center
Los Angeles, CA 90015-1300, USA

Dixon, Tom (Baseball Player)
Houston Astros
2945 Delaney St
Orlando, FL 32806-6256, USA

Dixon, Tony (Football Player)
Dallas Cowboys
440 Misty Ln
Lewisville, TX 75067-6251, USA

Dizon, Jesse
PO Box 572105
Tarzana, CA 91357-2105, USA

DJ, Premier (Artist)
William Morris Agency
151 El Camino Dr
Beverly Hills, CA 90212-2775, USA

DJ Jazzy Jeff (Actor, Musician)
c/o Staff Member *Coast to Coast Talent Group*
3350 Barham Blvd
Los Angeles, CA 90068-1404, USA

DJ Mendez (Musician)
c/o Leopoldo Mendez *Macabro Records*
Bolidenvagen 10
Johanneshov 121 63, SWEDEN

DJ Tiesto (Tiŏsto) (Actor, Musician)
c/o Staff Member *Primetime Magement*
P.O. Box 7042
Breda 4800 GA, THE NETHERLANDS

Djalili, Omid (Actor)
c/o Cara Stein *William Morris Agency (WMA-NY)*
1325 Avenue Of The Americas
New York, NY 10019-6026, USA

Djodjov Pejoski, Marjan (Designer, Fashion Designer)
c/o Staff Member *Marjan Djodjov Pejoski*
75 Garden Flat
Warwick Avenue
London, England W1Y 1DH, UNITED KINGDOM (UK)

Djoussouf, Abbass (Prime Minister)
Prime Minister's Office
Moroni, BP 421, COMOROS

Djukanovic, Milo (President)
Executive Council
Bul Lenjina 2
Novi Belgrad 11075, SERBIA-MONTENEGRO

D'Lyn, Shae (Actor)
c/o Miles Levy *James/Levy/Jacobson Management*
3500 W Olive Ave Ste 1470
Burbank, CA 91505-5514, USA

Dmitriev, Artur (Figure Skater)
Russian Skating Federation
Luchneksaia Nab 8
Moscow 119871, RUSSIA

DMX (Actor, Musician)
c/o Charles King *William Morris Agency (WMA-LA)*
1 William Morris Pl
Beverly Hills, CA 90212-4261, USA

Do Amaral, Diogo F (Government Official)
Ave Fontes Perelra de Melo 35 #13A
Lisbon 1050, PORTUGAL

Do Muoi (Politician)
Chairman's Office
Council of Ministers
Hanoi, VIETNAM

Do Nascimento, Alexandre Cardinal (Religious Leader)
Arcebispado
CP 87
Luanda 1230 C, ANGOLA

Doan, Charles A (Doctor)
4935 Oletangy Blvd
Columbus, OH 43214, USA

Doan, Shane (Hockey Player)
6751 N White Out Way # 200
Glendale, AZ 85305-3162, USA

Doar, John (Lawyer)
9 E 63rd St
New York, NY 10065-7236, USA

Dobbek, Dan (Baseball Player)
Washington Senators
4042 SE Yamhill St
Portland, OR 97214-4445, USA

Dobbin, Edmund J (Educator)
Villanova University
President's Office
Villanova, PA 19085, USA

Dobbins, Herb (Football Player)
Philadelphia Eagles
10 Keating Point
Saint Albert, AB T8N 5W8, CANADA

Dobbins, Oliver (Football Player)
Buffalo Bills
11126 Piscataway Rd
Clinton, MD 20735-9519, USA

Dobbs, Lou (Television Host)
Lou Dobbs Tonight
1 Time Warner Ctr Fl 4
Cnn
New York, NY 10019-8012, USA

Dobbs, Mattiwilda (Opera Singer)
1101 S Arlington Ridge Rd
Arlington, VA 22202-1951, USA

Dobek, Michelle (Golfer)
292 Chicopee St
Chicopee, MA 01013-1744, USA

Dobelstein, Bob (Football Player)
New York Giants
1473 SE Loquat Way
Lake City, FL 32025-6993, USA

Dobie, Alan
Pontus Molash
Kent CT4 8HW, ENGLAND

Dobkin, David (Director)
H S I Productions
3630 Eastham Dr
Culver City, CA 90232-2411, USA

Dobkin, Lawrence
1787 Old Ranch Rd
Los Angeles, CA 90049-2507, USA

Dobkins, Carl Jr (Musician)
7640 Cheviot Rd Apt 212
Cincinnati, OH 45247-4011, USA

Dobler, Conrad F (Football Player)
St Louis Cardinals
12600 Fairway Rd
Shawnee Mission, KS 66209-2453, USA

Dobler, David (Religious Leader)
Presbyterian Church USA
100 Witherspoon St
Louisville, KY 40202-6300, USA

Dobo, Kata (Actor)
Ramaker Management
400 N Gardner St
Los Angeles, CA 90036-5728, USA

Dobslow, Bill (Musician)
945 Handlebar Rd
Mishawaka, IN 46544-6647, USA

Dobson, Chuck (Baseball Player)
Kansas City A's
4208 Locust St
Kansas City, MO 64110-1017, USA

Dobson, Fefe (Musician)
c/o Staff Member *Island Records*
825 8th Ave
New York, NY 10019-7472, USA

Dobson, Helen (Golfer)
7638 Eagle Creek Dr
Sarasota, FL 34243-4613, USA

Dobson, James C (Religious Leader)
Focus on the Family
8605 Explorer Dr
Colorado Springs, CO 80920-1051, USA

Dobson, Kevin (Actor)
c/o Dede Binder-Goldsmith *Defining Artists*
10 Universal City Plz Ste 2000
Universal City, CA 91608-1074, USA

Dobson, Pat (Baseball Player)
Detroit Tigers
2565 Ingulf Pl
San Diego, CA 92110-2361, USA

Dobson, Peter (Actor)
1351 N Crescent Heights Blvd Apt 318
West Hollywood, CA 90046-4579, USA

Dockery, John (Football Player)
New York Jets
17 Garden Pl
Brooklyn, NY 11201-4501, USA

Dockson, Robert R (Financier)
1301 Collingwood Pl
Los Angeles, CA 90069-1219, USA

Dockstader, Frederick J (Misc)
165 W 66th St
New York, NY 10023-6508, USA

Doctorow, Edgar Lawrence (E L) (Writer)
c/o Ron Bernstein *International Creative Management (ICM-LA)*
10250 Constellation Blvd
Los Angeles, CA 90067-6200, USA

Doda, Carol (Actor, Dancer)
PO Box 387
Fremont, CA 94537-0387, USA

Dodd, Deryl (Musician, Songwriter, Writer)
823 Mgmt
PO Box 186
Waring, TX 78074-0186, USA

Dodd, Jamie (Actor)
c/o Staff Member *Nikki Bond Management*
Aspect Court
47 Park Square East
Leeds LS1 2NL, UNITED KINGDOM (UK)

Dodd, Maurice (Cartoonist)
Daily Mirror
Editorial Dept
1 Canada Square
London E14 5AP, UNITED KINGDOM (UK)

Dodd, Michael T (Mike) (Volleyball Player)
1017 Manhattan Ave
Manhattan Beach, CA 90266-5452, USA

Dodd, Patty D (Volleyball Player)
1017 Manhattan Ave
Manhattan Beach, CA 90266-5452, USA

Dodd, Robert (Baseball Player)
Philadelphia Phillies
500 New York Ave Apt 12
Dunedin, FL 34698-7858, USA

Dodd, Tom (Baseball Player)
Baltimore Orioles
3735 NE Shaver St
Portland, OR 97212-1871, USA

Dodds, Trevor (Golfer)
13103 Beaver Dam Rd
Saint Louis, MO 63131-2109, USA

Dodge, Brooks (Skier)
PO Box C
Jackson, NH 03846-0802, USA

Dodge, GeaHrey (Publisher)
Money Magazine
Time-Life Building
New York, NY 10020, USA

Dodge, Geoffrey (Publisher)
Money Magazine
Time-Life Building
New York, NY 10020, USA

Dodrill, Dale (Football Player)
Pittsburgh Steelers
2579 S Independence St
Lakewood, CO 80227-2847, USA

Dodson, Pat (Baseball Player)
Boston Red Sox
4104 Holly Hill Rd
Mebane, NC 27302-8232, USA

Dodson, Richard (Football Player)
Denver Broncos
PO Box 81302
Phoenix, AZ 85069-1302, USA

Doe, Cathy Jeneen (Actor)
c/o Michael Greene *Greene & Associates*
190 N Canon Dr Ste 200
Beverly Hills, CA 90210-5319, USA

Doelling, Fred (Football Player)
Dallas Texans
60 South St
Valparaiso, IN 46383-6445, USA

Doerger, Jerome (Football Player)
Chicago Bears
8309 Ridgevalley Ct
Cincinnati, OH 45247-3597, USA

Doering, Chris (Football Player)
Indianapolis Colts
1015 NW 21st Ave # 124
Gainesville, FL 32609-3448, USA

Doerr, Robert P (Bobby) (Baseball Player)
33705 Illamo-Agness Road
Agness, OR 97406, USA

Doerre-Heinig, Katrin (Athlete, Track Athlete)
Westring 53
Erbach 6471, GERMANY

Dog Star (Music Group)
1900 Avenue Of The Stars # 1040
Los Angeles, CA 90067-4301, USA

Dogg, Nate (Musician)
Elektra Records
75 Rockefeller Plz
New York, NY 10019-6908, USA

Dogins, Kevin (Football Player)
Tampa Bay Buccaneers
8861 Cameron Crest Dr
Tampa, FL 33626-4732, USA

Doherty, John (Baseball Player)
California Angels
109 Wakefield St
Reading, MA 01867-1854, USA

Doherty, John (Baseball Player)
Detroit Tigers
202 Alpine Pl
Tuckahoe, NY 10707-3086, USA

Doherty, Laura (Musician)
c/o Staff Member *Pop Idol (Fremantle Media)*
2700 Colorado Ave Ste 450
Santa Monica, CA 90404-3599, USA

Doherty, Peter C (Nobel Prize Laureate)
172 Kimbrough Pl Apt 506
Memphis, TN 38104-6724, USA

Doherty, Shannen (Actor)
c/o John Carrabino *John Carrabino Management*
5900 Wilshire Blvd Ste 406
Los Angeles, CA 90036-5015, USA

Dohm, Gaby (Actor)
Omnis Agentur
Wiedenmayerstr 11
Munich 80538, GERMANY

Dohring, Jason (Actor)
c/o Joel Stevens *Joel Stevens Entertainment*
206 S Brand Blvd
Glendale, CA 91204-1310, USA

Dohrmann, Angela (Actor)
Innovative Artists
1505 10th St
Santa Monica, CA 90401-2805, USA

Dohrmann, George (Journalist)
Saint Paul Pioneer Press
345 Cedar St
Editorial Dept
Saint Paul, MN 55101-1057, USA

Doi, Takako (Government Official)
Daini Giinkaikan
2-1-2 Nagatacho
Chiyodaku
Tokyo, JAPAN

Doi, Takao (Astronaut)
NASDA
Tsukuba Space Ctr
2-1-2 Sengern
Tukubashi, Ibaraki, JAPAN

Doig, Lex (Actor)
Andromeda Productions
8651 Eastlake Drive
Vancouver, BC V5A 4T7, CANADA

Doig, Lexa (Actor)
c/o Adam Levine *Anthem Entertainment*
6100 Wilshire Blvd Ste 1170
Los Angeles, CA 90048-5116, USA

Doig, Steve (Football Player)
Detroit Lions
PO Box 206
North Reading, MA 01864-0206, USA

Dokish, Wanita (Baseball Player)
403 Todd Farm Rd
Belle Vernon, PA 15012-3869, USA

Dokken, Don (Musician)
Agency for Performing Arts
405 S Beverly Dr Ste 500
Beverly Hills, CA 90212-4425, USA

Doktor, Martin (Athlete)
Canoe Prosport Sezemice
Slinecni 627
Sezemice 533 04, CZECH REPUBLIC

Dolan, Don (Actor)
14228 Emelita St
Van Nuys, CA 91401-4208, USA

Dolan, Ellen (Actor)
Don Buchwald
10 E 44th St
New York, NY 10017-3654, USA

Dolan, Louise A (Physicist)
University of North Carolina
Physics Dept
Chapel Hill, NC 27599, USA

Dolan, Michael P (Government Official)
Internal Revenue Service
1111 Constitution Ave NW
Washington, DC 20224-0002, USA

Dolan, Tom
1 Olympic Plz
Colorado Springs, CO 80909-5780, USA

Dolbin, Jack (Football Player)
Denver Broncos
1775 Howard Ave
Pottsville, PA 17901-3215, USA

Dolby, David C (War Hero)
PO Box 218
Pekiomen Ave
Oaks, PA 19456-0218, USA

Dolby, Raymond M (Ray) (Engineer, Inventor)
Dolby Laboratories
100 Potrero Ave
San Francisco, CA 94103-4813, USA

Dolby, Thomas (Musician, Songwriter, Writer)
Inteinational Talent Group
729 7th Ave Rm 1600
New York, NY 10019-6880, USA

Dolce (Musician)
c/o Staff Member *Diva Central Inc*
7510 W Sunset Blvd Ste 1445
Los Angeles, CA 90046-3408, USA

Dolce, Domenico (Designer, Fashion Designer)
Dolce & Gabbana
Via Santa Cecilia 7
Milan 20122, ITALY

Dolci, Danilo (Activist, Writer)
Centro Iniziative Studl
Largo Scalia 5
Partinico/Palermo
Sicily, ITALY

Dold, R Bruce (Journalist)
501 N Park Rd # Hse
La Grange Park, IL 60526-5516, USA

Dole, Elizabeth H (Politician, Secretary)
601 Pennsylvania Ave NW Fl 10
Washington, DC 20004-2601, USA

Dole, Robert J (Bob) (Senator)
601 Pennsylvania Ave NW Fl 10
Washington, DC 20004-2601, USA

Dole, Vincent P (Misc, Scientist)
Rockefeller University
1230 York Ave
New York, NY 10065-6399, USA

Doleac, Michael (Basketball Player)
7372 Comslock Circle
Salt Lake City, UT 84121, USA

Doleman, Christopher J (Chris) (Football Player)
Minnesota Vikings
1025 Leadenhall St
Alpharetta, GA 30022-8491, USA

Dolenz, Ami (Actor)
1860 Bel Air Rd
Los Angeles, CA 90077-2729, USA

Dolenz, Micky (Actor, Musician)
c/o Staff Member *Grant Management*
1158 26th St # 414
Santa Monica, CA 90403-4698, USA

Doll, Donald (Football Player)
Detroit Lions
32001 Via La Plata
San Juan Capistrano, CA 92675-3817, USA

Dollar, Aubrey (Actor)
c/o Rhonda Price *Gersh Agency, The (NY)*
41 Madison Ave Fl 33
New York, NY 10010-2202, USA

Dollar, Linda (Coach)
Southwest Missouri State University
Athletic Dept
Springfield, MO 65804, USA

Dollard, Christopher Edward (Actor)
Gold Marshak Liedtke
3500 W Olive Ave Ste 1400
Burbank, CA 91505-5512, USA

Dollens, Ronald (Business Person)
Guidant Corp
111 Monument Cir
Indianapolis, IN 46204-5129, USA

Dollfus, Audouin (Astronomer, Physicist)
77 Rue Albert Perdreaux
92370, Chaville 92370, FRANCE

Dolls, Goo Goo (Musician)
c/o David Levine *William Morris Agency (WMA-LA)*
1 William Morris Pl
Beverly Hills, CA 90212-4261, USA

Dolmayan, John (Musician)
Velvet Hammer
9911 W Pico Blvd # 350
Los Angeles, CA 90035-2703, USA

Dologuele, Anicet Georges (Prime Minister)
Prime Minister's Office
Bangui, CENTRAL AFRICAN REPUBLIC

Doman, Brandon (Football Player)
San Francisco 49ers
5260 Rogers Rd Apt E7
Hamburg, NY 14075-3587, USA

Doman, John (Actor)
c/o Staff Member *Peter Strain & Associates Inc (NY)*
1501 Broadway
New York, NY 10036-5601, USA

Domar, Evsey D (Economist)
264 Heaths Bridge Rd
Concord, MA 01742-4921, USA

Dombasle, Arielle (Actor)
Agence Intertalent
5 Rue Clemet Marot
Paris 75008, FRANCE

Dombroski, Paul (Football Player)
Kansas City Chiefs
19122 Beckett Dr
Odessa, FL 33556-2274, USA

Dombrowski, Dave (Baseball Player)
Detroit Tigers
345 Woodridge Rd
Bloomfield Hills, MI 48304-3468, USA

Dombrowski, James M (Jim) (Football Player)
New Orleans Saints
220 Evangeline Dr
Mandeville, LA 70471-1874, USA

Domi, Tie (Hockey Player)
c/o Staff Member *Professional Sports Source Inc*
PO Box 6800 #311
Toronto, ON M1S 3C6, CANADA

Domi, Tim (Hockey Player)
46 Florence St
Ottawa, ON K2P 0W7, CANADA

Dominczyk, Dagmara (Actor)
c/o Bill Butler *Gersh Agency, The (NY)*
41 Madison Ave Fl 33
New York, NY 10010-2202, USA

Dominczyk, Marika (Actor)
c/o Sally Ware *Gersh Agency, The (NY)*
41 Madison Ave Fl 33
New York, NY 10010-2202, USA

Domingo, Placido (Opera Singer)
Zaungergasse 1-3
Tur 16
Vienna 1030, AUSTRIA

Dominguez, Fernandez Adolfo (Designer, Fashion Designer)
Polingono Industrial Calle 4
San Ciprian de Vinas, Ourense 32901, SPAIN

Dominik, Andrew (Director, Writer)
c/o Spencer Baumgarten *Creative Artists Agency LCC (CAA-LA)*
2000 Avenue Of The Stars
Los Angeles, CA 90067-4700, USA

Dominis, John (Photographer)
16 Jackson St
East Hampton, NY 11937-2617, USA

Dominy, Charles E (Chuck) (General)
300 Fox Mill Road
Oakton, VA 22124, USA

Domnanovich, Joseph (Joe) (Football Player)
Boston Yanks
4949 Nottingham Ln
Birmingham, AL 35223-1667, USA

Domres, Martin F (Marty) (Football Player)
San Diego Chargers
24 Mansel Dr
Reisterstown, MD 21136-5662, USA

Donahue, Aichie G (War Hero)
2402 Lary Lake Dr
Harlingen, TX 78550, USA

Donahue, Archie G (War Hero)
2402 Lazy Lake Dr
Harlingen, TX 78550-8630, USA

Donahue, Deacon (Baseball Player)
Philadelphia Phillies
150 Weiland Rd # 120
Buffalo Grove, IL 60089-7047, USA

Donahue, Elinor (Actor)
78533 Sunrise Mountain Vw
Palm Desert, CA 92211-2403, USA

Donahue, Heather (Actor)
Rigberg Roberts Rugolo
1180 S Beverly Dr Ste 601
Los Angeles, CA 90035-1158, USA

Donahue, Kenneth (Misc)
245 S Westgate Ave
Los Angeles, CA 90049-4205, USA

Donahue, Mitch (Football Player)
San Francisco 49ers
2220 Beloit Dr
Billings, MT 59102-5706, USA

Donahue, Phil (Entertainer)
244 Madison Ave # 707
New York, NY 10016-2817, USA

Donahue, Terry (Baseball Player)
215 N 3rd Ave
Saint Charles, IL 60174-2005, USA

Donahue, Thomas R (Misc)
American Federation of Labor
815 L6TH St NW
Washington, DC 20006, USA

Donald, David Herbert (Writer)
41 Lincoln Rd
PO Box L58
Lincoln, MA 01773, USA

Donald, Kirkland H (Admiral)
7958 Blandy Rd
Commander Submarine Command
Atlantic
Norfolk, VA 23551-2492, USA

Donald, Mike (Golfer)
2400 NW 65th Way
Hollywood, FL 33024-4046, USA

Donaldson, Colby (Actor, Reality TV Star)
c/o Nicole David *William Morris Agency (WMA-LA)*
1 William Morris Pl
Beverly Hills, CA 90212-4261, USA

Donaldson, Eugene (Football Player)
Buffalo Bills
114 Maud St
Clarksburg, WV 26301-3036, USA

Donaldson, James (Basketball Player)
Seattle SuperSonics
2843 34th Ave W
Seattle, WA 98199-2602, USA

Donaldson, John (Football Player)
Chicago Hornets
3913 Yates Ct
Charlotte, NC 28215-3955, USA

Donaldson, Raymond C (Ray) (Football Player)
Baltimore Colts
10507 Bishop Cir
Carmel, IN 46032-8599, USA

Donaldson, Roger (Director)
Creative Artists Agency
9830 Wilshire Blvd
Beverly Hills, CA 90212-1804, USA

Donaldson, Samuel A (Sam) (Correspondent)
1125 Crest Ln
McLean, VA 22101-1805, USA

Donaldson, William H (Financier, Government Official)
Securities & Exchange Commision
450 5th St NW
Washington, DC 20549-0001, USA

Donan, Holland R (Football Player)
212 Valley Vw
Pompton Plains, NJ 07444-2166, USA

Donat, Peter (Actor)
PO Box 441
Wolfville, NS B0P 1X0, CANADA

Donatelli, Don (Football Player)
Houston Oilers
54846 Seneca Lake Rd
Quaker City, OH 43773-9659, USA

Donath, Helen (Opera Singer)
Bergstr 5
Wedemark 30900, GERMANY

Donckers, William (Football Player)
St Louis Cardinals
13708 SE 141st St
Renton, WA 98059-5416, USA

Done, Kenneth S (Ken) (Artist, Misc)
28 Hopetoun Ave
Mosman, NSW 2088, AUSTRALIA

Donegan, Dan (Music Group, Musician)
Mitch Schneider Organization
14724 Ventura Blvd Ste 710
Sherman Oaks, CA 91403-3520, USA

Donella, Chad E (Actor)
c/o Staff Member *TalentWorks (LA)*
3500 W Olive Ave Ste 1400
Burbank, CA 91505-5512, USA

Donelly, Tanya (Music Group, Songwriter, Writer)
Helter Skelter
Plaza 535 Kings Road
London SW10 0S, UNITED KINGDOM (UK)

Donen, Stanley (Director)
30 W 63rd St # 25
New York, NY 10023-7103, USA

Dong Ghua, Li
rue des O'Euches 10
Moutier 1 CP 359 274, SWITZERLAND

Doniger, Wendy (Historian, Misc)
1319 E 55th St
Chicago, IL 60615-5301, USA

Donlan, Yolande (Actor)
11 Mellina Place
London NW8, UNITED KINGDOM (UK)

Donleavy, James Patrick (J P) (Writer)
Levington Park Mullingar
County Westmeath, IRELAND

Donley, Doug (Football Player)
Dallas Cowboys
8005 Pullam Cir
Plano, TX 75024-6849, USA

Donlon, Roger H C (War Hero)
2101 Wilson Ave
Leavenworth, KS 66048-4634, USA

Donnahoo, Roger (Football Player)
New York Titans
20 Rock Brook Cv
Rossville, GA 30741-5355, USA

Donnalley, Kevin (Football Player)
Houston Oilers
8910 Dove Stand Ln
Charlotte, NC 28226-2671, USA

Donnan, Jim (Coach, Football Coach)
University of Georgia
Athletic Dept
Athens, GA 30602, USA

Donnas, The (Music Group)
c/o Molly Neuman *Lookout! Records*
PO Box 11374
Berkeley, CA 94712-2374, USA

Donnellan, Declan (Director)
Cheek by Jowl Theatre Co
Aveline St
London SW11 5DQ, UNITED KINGDOM (UK)

Donnelley, James R (Business Person)
R R Donnelley & Sons
77 W Wacker Dr
Chicago, IL 60601-1604, USA

Donnelley, Rick (Football Player)
Atlanta Falcons
10408 Buck Brush Rd
Cheyenne, WY 82009-8830, USA

Donnelly, Brendan (Baseball Player)
Anaheim Angels
4149 E Peach Tree Dr
Chandler, AZ 85249-7349, USA

Donnelly, Declan (Actor, Television Host)
c/o Staff Member *Rabbit Vocal Management*
18 Broad Wick St Fl 2
London W1F 8HS, UNITED KINGDOM (UK)

Donnelly, George (Football Player)
San Francisco 49ers
2S530 Beechwood Rd
Glen Ellyn, IL 60137-6955, USA

Donnelly, Rick (Football Player)
Atlanta Falcons
1796 Danforth Dr
Marietta, GA 30062-5544, USA

Donnelly, Russell J (Physicist)
2175 Olive St
Eugene, OR 97405-2837, USA

Donnels, Chris (Baseball Player)
New York Mets
21256 Oakridge Ln
Trabuco Canyon, CA 92679-3305, USA

Donner, Clive (Director)
20 Thames Reach
80 Rainville Road
London W6 9HS, UNITED KINGDOM (UK)

Donner, Jom J (Director)
Pohjoisranta 12
Helsinki 17 00170, FINLAND

Donner, Jorn
Pohjoisranta 12
Helsinki SF-00170, FINLAND

Donner, Lauren Shuler (Producer)
c/o Staff Member *Donners' Company, The*
9465 Wilshire Blvd Ste 420
Beverly Hills, CA 90212-2603, USA

Donner, Richard (Director)
c/o Staff Member *Donners' Company, The*
9465 Wilshire Blvd Ste 420
Beverly Hills, CA 90212-2603, USA

Donnovan, Elisa (Actor)
SMS Talent
8730 W Sunset Blvd Ste 440
Los Angeles, CA 90069-2277, USA

D'Onofrio, Mark (Football Player)
Green Bay Packers
295 Harmon Ave
Fort Lee, NJ 07024-4446, USA

D'Onofrio, Vincent (Actor, Producer)
c/o Ken Christmas *Ken Christmas Group, The*
1635 N Cahuenga Blvd Fl 4
Los Angeles, CA 90028-6201, USA

Donohoe, Amanda (Actor)
Markham & Froggatt
Julian House
4 Windmill Street
London W1P 1HF, UNITED KINGDOM (UK)

Donohoe, Michael (Football Player)
Atlanta Falcons
505 Juneberry Rd
Riverwoods, IL 60015-3715, USA

Donohoe, Peter (Music Group, Musician)
82 Hampton Lane Solihull
West Midlands B91 2RS, UNITED KINGDOM (UK)

Donohue, Jim (Baseball Player)
Detroit Tigers
16 Huntleigh Downs
Saint Louis, MO 63131-3416, USA

Donohue, Leon (Football Player)
San Francisco 49ers
1904 Bechelli Ln
Redding, CA 96002-0132, USA

Donohue, Terry
11918 Laurelwood Dr
Studio City, CA 91604-3749, USA

Donohue, Timothy (Business Person)
Nextel Communications
2001 Edmund Halley Dr
Reston, VA 20191-3436, USA

Donohue, Tom (Baseball Player)
California Angels
249 Liberty Ave
Westbury, NY 11590-2135, USA

Donoso, Jose (Writer)
Calceite
Province of Teruel, SPAIN

Donovan (Music Group, Songwriter, Writer)
P O Box 1119
London SW9 9JW, UNITED KINGDOM (UK)

Donovan, Alan B (Educator)
State University of New York College
President's Office
Oneonta, NY 13820, USA

Donovan, Anne (Basketball Player, Coach)
3638 Cordwood Ln
Indianapolis, IN 46214, USA

Donovan, Billy (Basketball Player)
New York Knicks
8515 SW 31st Ave
Gainesville, FL 32608-2725, USA

Donovan, Brian (Journalist)
Newsday
235 Pinelawn Rd
Editorial Dept
Melville, NY 11747-4250, USA

Donovan, Elisa (Actor)
c/o Staff Member *Seven Summits Pictures & Management*
8906 W Olympic Blvd Ground Floor
Beverly Hills, CA 90211, USA

Donovan, Francis R (Frank) (Admiral)
9216 Dellwood Dr
Vienna, VA 22180-6121, USA

Donovan, Harry (Basketball Player)
New York Knicks
836 Bay Quarter Dr
Heathsville, VA 22473-2117, USA

Donovan, Jason S (Actor, Music Group)
Richard East Productions
PO Box 342
South Yarra, VIC 3141, AUSTRALIA

Donovan, Jeffrey (Actor)
c/o Staff Member *Principal Entertainment (LA)*
1964 Westwood Blvd Ste 400
Los Angeles, CA 90025-4695, USA

Donovan, Landon (Soccer Player)
Los Angeles Galaxy
18400 Avalon Blvd Ste 200
Carson, CA 90746-2181, USA

Donovan, Martin (Actor)
Paradigm Agency
10100 Santa Monica Blvd Ste 2500
Los Angeles, CA 90067-4116, USA

Donovan, Pat (Football Player)
Dallas Cowboys
113 S Prairiesmoke Cir
Whitefish, MT 59937-8182, USA

Donovan, Raymond J (Misc, Secretary)
1600 Paterson Plank Rd
Secaucus, NJ 07094, USA

Donovan, Tate (Actor)
c/o Staff Member *Gersh Agency, The (LA)*
232 N Canon Dr
Beverly Hills, CA 90210-5302, USA

Donovan Jr, Arthur J (Art) (Athlete, Football Player)
Baltimore Colts
1512 Jeffers Rd
Valley Country Club
Baltimore, MD 21204-1931, USA

Donovan (Leich)
PO Box 106
Rochdale OL16 4HW, ENGLAND

Donowho, Ryan (Actor)
c/o Mara Glauberg *Cunningham Escott Slevin & Doherty (NY)*
257 Park Ave S Rm 950
New York, NY 10010-7304, USA

Doobie Brothers (Music Group)
c/o Staff Member *Paradigm (Monterey)*
509 Hartnell St
Monterey, CA 93940-2825, USA

Doody, Alison (Actor)
Julian Belfarge
46 Albermarle St
London W1X 4PP, UNITED KINGDOM (UK)

Doolan, Wendy (Golfer)
3353 Tumberry Dr
Lakeland, FL 33803, USA

Dooley, Jim (Football Player)
Chicago Bears
1350 N Western Ave Apt 212
Lake Forest, IL 60045-1264, USA

Dooley, Paul (Actor)
Innovative Artists
1505 10th St
Santa Monica, CA 90401-2805, USA

Dooley, Taylor (Actor)
c/o Meredith Wechter *International Creative Management (ICM-LA)*
10250 Constellation Blvd
Los Angeles, CA 90067-6200, USA

Dooley, Thomas (Soccer Player)
55 San Simeon
Laguna Niguel, CA 92677-7951, USA

Dooley, Vince
PO Box 1472
Athens, GA 30603-1472, USA

Dooling, Keyon (Basketball Player)
Los Angeles Clippers
1111 S Figueroa St
Staples Center
Los Angeles, CA 90015-1300, USA

Doolittle, Melinda (Musician, Reality TV Star)
c/o Staff Member *American Idol*
7800 Beverly Blvd # 251
Los Angeles, CA 90036-2112, USA

Doornink, Dan (Football Player)
New York Giants
402 S 12th Ave
Yakima, WA 98902-3115, USA

Dopazo, Cecilia (Actor)
c/o Staff Member *Telefe - Argentina*
Pavon 2444 (C1248AAT)
Buenos Aires, ARGENTINA

Dopson, John (Baseball Player)
Montreal Expos
3337 Old Gamber Rd
Finksburg, MD 21048-2223, USA

Doran, Bill (Baseball Player)
Houston Astros
5720 Grand Legacy Dr
Maineville, OH 45039-7757, USA

Doran, Walter F (Admiral)
Chairman Joint Chiefs Of Staff Pentagon
Washington, DC 20318-0001, USA

Dore, Andre (Hockey Player)
73 Betsys Lane
Kingston, ON K7M 7B6, CANADA

Dore, Jimmy (Comedian)
c/o Staff Member *OmniPop Inc (LA)*
4605 Lankershim Blvd Ste 201
North Hollywood, CA 91602-1874, USA

Dore, Patricia (Actor)
Cineart
36 Rue de Ponthieu
Paris 75008, FRANCE

Dore, Ronald Philip (Educator)
157 Surrenden Road Brighton
East Sussex BN1 6ZA, UNITED KINGDOM (UK)

Dorensky, Sergey L (Music Group, Musician)
Bryusov Per 8/10 #75
Moscow 103009, RUSSIA

Dorff, Stephen (Actor)
c/o David Unger *International Creative Management (ICM-LA)*
10250 Constellation Blvd
Los Angeles, CA 90067-6200, USA

Dorfman, Ariel (Writer)
Duke University
International Studies Center
2122 Campus Dr
Durham, NC 27706, USA

Dorfman, Dan (Correspondent, Misc)
CBS-TV
51 W 52nd St
News Dept
New York, NY 10019-6119, USA

Dorfman, David (Actor)
c/o Staff Member *Abrams Artists Agency (LA)*
9200 W Sunset Blvd Ph 11
Los Angeles, CA 90069-3601, USA

Dorfmeister, Michaela (Skier)
Quellensteig
Neusiedl 2763, AUSTRIA

Dorin, Francoise (Actor, Writer)
Artmedia
20 Ave Rapp
Paris 75007, FRANCE

Dorio, Gabriella (Athlete, Track Athlete)
Federation of Light Athletics
Viale Tialano 70
Rome 00196, ITALY

Dority, Douglas R (Misc)
United Food & Commercial Workers Union
1775 K St NW Bsmt
Washington, DC 20006-1521, USA

Dorman, David (Business Person)
American Telephone & Telegraph Corp
32 Avenue Of The Americas
New York, NY 10013-2473, USA

Dorman, Lee (Music Group, Musician)
Entertainment Services Int'l
6400 Pleasant Park Dr
Chanhassen, MN 55317-8804, USA

Dormann, Dana (Golfer)
4887 Ariene Pl
Pleasanton, CA 94566, USA

Dorn, Dolores (Dody) (Editor)
Skouras Agency
631 Wilshire Blvd
2nd Floor Suite C
Santa Monica, CA 90401-1510, USA

Dorn, Michael (Actor)
15030 Ventura Blvd # 710
Sherman Oaks, CA 91403-5470, USA

Dornbrook, Thom (Football Player)
Pittsburgh Steelers
5918 Emerald Lakes Dr
Medina, OH 44256-7464, USA

Dorney, Keith R (Football Player)
Detroit Lions
2450 Blucher Valley Rd
Sebastopol, CA 95472-5355, USA

Doro & Warlock
Postfach 87 21
Dusseldorf D-40086, GERMANY

Doronina, Tatyana (Actor)
Gorky Arts Theater
22 Tverskoi Blvd
Moscow 119146, RUSSIA

Dorough, Howie (Music Group)
Mitch Schneider Organization
14724 Ventura Blvd Ste 710
Sherman Oaks, CA 91403-3520, USA

Dorow, Al (Football Player)
Washington Redskins
4933 Loma Loop
Sierra Vista, AZ 85635-5753, USA

Dorrell, Karl (Coach, Football Coach)
University of California
Athletic Dept
Los Angeles, CA 90024, USA

Dorris, Andrew (Football Player)
St Louis Cardinals
RR 22 Box 549
Conroe, TX 77303, USA

Dorris, Derek (Football Player)
New York Giants
2610 E Williamsburg Mnr
Arlington, TX 76014-1221, USA

Dorroh, Jefferson D (War Hero)
24603 12th Ave S
Des Moines, WA 98198-3866, USA

D'Orsay, Brooke (Actor)
c/o Chris Fenton *H2F*
345 N Maple Dr Ste 200
Beverly Hills, CA 90210-3860, USA

Dorsen, Norman (Attorney, Attorney General, General)
New York University
40 Washington Sq S
Law School
New York, NY 10012-1005, USA

Dorsett, Anthony D (Tony) (Football Player)
Dallas Cowboys
5990 Haley Way
Frisco, TX 75034-4878, USA

Dorsett, Brian (Baseball Player)
Cleveland Indians
700 Dobbs Glen St
Terre Haute, IN 47803-2480, USA

Dorsey, Eric (Football Player)
New York Giants
5 London Ct
Teaneck, NJ 07666-6461, USA

Dorsey, Jacky (Basketball Player)
Denver Nuggets
1231 S Eak Estates Cir
Fresno, TX 77545, USA

Dorsey, Jim (Baseball Player)
California Angels
335 Elm St
Seekonk, MA 02771-1724, USA

Dorsey, John (Football Player)
Green Bay Packers
1644 Charles St
De Pere, WI 54115-3402, USA

Dorsey, Ken (Football Player)
San Francisco 49ers
4949 Centennial Blvd
Santa Clara, CA 95054-1229, USA

Dorsey, Nate (Football Player)
New England Patriots
6915 Silver Run Dr Apt 202
Tampa, FL 33617-9071, USA

Dorsey, Ron (Basketball Player)
Carolina Cougars
3925 Mallard Way
Cumming, GA 30028-4862, USA

Dorsey Brothers Orchestra (Music Group)
PO Box 643176
Vero Beach, FL 32964-3176, USA

Dos Santos, Alexandre J M Cardinal (Religious Leader)
Paco Arquiepiscopal
Avenida Eduardo Mondlane
CP Maputo 1448, MOZAMBIQUE

Doshi, Balkkrishna V (Architect)
Sangath Thaltej Road
Ahmedbad, GJ 380 054, INDIA

Doss, Desmond T (War Hero)
372 Valley Creek Rd
Piedmont, AL 36272-7969, USA

Doss, Murphy (Actor)
52 Hospital Road
Saidapet
Chennai, TN 600 015, INDIA

Doss, Noble (Football Player)
Philadelphia Eagles
4410 Balcones Dr
Austin, TX 78731-5710, USA

Doster, David (Baseball Player)
Philadelphia Phillies
9320 Old Grist Mill Pl
Fort Wayne, IN 46835-9301, USA

Dotrice, Roy (Actor)
Lord
6 Meadow Lane Leasingham
Sleaford
Lincolnshire NG34 8LL, UNITED KINGDOM (UK)

Dotson, Al (Football Player)
Kansas City Chiefs
Coyues 24 Las Playas
Acapulco 39390, MEXICO

Dotson, Dewayne (Football Player)
Miami Dolphins
1210 Williamsburg Dr
Hendersonville, TN 37075-5768, USA

Dotson, Earl (Football Player)
Green Bay Packers
1112 Azalea Dr
Longview, TX 75601-3214, USA

Dotson, Richard E (Rich) (Baseball Player)
Chicago White Sox
7 Colonel Watson Dr
New Richmond, OH 45157-9002, USA

Dotson, Santana (Football Player)
Tampa Bay Buccaneers
11002 Greenbay St
Houston, TX 77024-6829, USA

Dotter, Bobby (Race Car Driver)
MPH Racing
118 Stutts Rd
Mooresville, NC 28117, USA

Dotter, Gary (Baseball Player)
Minnesota Twins
17 Edgemere Dr
Roanoke, TX 76262-9736, USA

Dottley, John (Football Player)
Chicago Bears
1438 Wisteria Dr
Vicksburg, MS 39180-4757, USA

Douaihy, Saliba (Artist)
Vining Road
Windham, NY 12496, USA

Doubleday, Nelson (Baseball Player)
New York Mets
84 Gomez Rd
Hobe Sound, FL 33455-2330, USA

Doucet, Michael (Music Group, Musician)
Rosebud Agency
PO Box 170429
San Francisco, CA 94117-0429, USA

Doucett, Linda (Actor, Model)
Michael Slessinger
8730 W Sunset Blvd Ste 220W
Los Angeles, CA 90069-2275, USA

Doug, Doug E (Musician)
4024 Radford Ave # 3
Studio City, CA 91604-2101, USA

Dougan, Angel Serafin Seriche (Prime Minister)
Prime Minister's Office
Malabo, EQUATORIAL GUINEA

Doughboys (Musician)
Box 5559 Station B
Montreal, PQ H3P 4P1, CANADA

Dougherty, Dennis A (Misc)
1817 Bushnell Ave
South Pasadena, CA 91030-4905, USA

Dougherty, Ed (Golfer)
448 SW Fairway Vis
Port Saint Lucie, FL 34986-2131, USA

Dougherty, Jim (Baseball Player)
Houston Astros
PO Box 1737
Kitty Hawk, NC 27949-1737, USA

Dougherty, Joseph (Joe) (Director, Producer, Writer)
c/o Ken Freimann *William Morris Agency (WMA-LA)*
1 William Morris Pl
Beverly Hills, CA 90212-4261, USA

Dougherty, Robert W (Football Player)
Los Angeles Rams
864 Flint Rdg
Newport, KY 41076-7112, USA

Dougherty, William A Jr (Admiral)
1505 Colonial Ct
Arlington, VA 22209-1439, USA

Doughty, Glenn (Football Player)
Baltimore Colts
8808 Saint Charles Rock Rd
Saint Louis, MO 63114-4340, USA

Doughty, Kenny (Actor)
c/o Risa Shapiro *International Creative Management (ICM-LA)*
10250 Constellation Blvd
Los Angeles, CA 90067-6200, USA

Douglas, Anslem (Composer, Entertainer)
JW Records
2833 Church Ave
Brooklyn, NY 11226-4168, USA

Douglas, Barry (Music Group, Musician)
I C M Artists
40 W 57th St
New York, NY 10019-4001, USA

Douglas, Bobby (Coach, Wrestler)
Iowa State University
Athletic Dept
Ames, IA 50011-0001, USA

Douglas, Cameron (Actor)
c/o Edward G (Eddie) Horowitz *Creative Management Group (CMG)*
8522 National Blvd Ste 108
Culver City, CA 90232-2454, USA

Douglas, Carl
6611 Shenandoah Ave
Los Angeles, CA 90056-2115, USA

Douglas, Carol (Music Group)
Famous Artists Agency
250 W 57th St
New York, NY 10107-0001, USA

Douglas, Cathleen (Lawyer, Misc)
815 Connecticut Ave NW
Washington, DC 20006-4004, USA

Douglas, Charles (Baseball Player)
Pittsburgh Pirates
PO Box 231
Hubert, NC 28539-0231, USA

Douglas, David (Football Player)
Cincinnati Bengals
605 Snowshill Way
Maryville, TN 37803-6387, USA

Douglas, Denzil L (Prime Minister)
Premier's Office
Government Building
Basseterre, SAINT KITTS & NEVIS

Douglas, Diana (Actor)
c/o Staff Member *Bauman Redanty & Shaul Agency*
5757 Wilshire Blvd Ste 473
Los Angeles, CA 90036-3632, USA

Douglas, Donna (Actor)
c/o Staff Member *The Bazel Group Inc*
4636 Lebanon Pike # 308
Hermitage, TN 37076-1316, USA

Douglas, Hugh (Football Player)
Jacksonville Jaguars
1 Alltel Stadium Pl
Jacksonville, FL 32202-1917, USA

Douglas, Ileana (Actor)
c/o Staff Member *Baumgarten Merims Entertainment*
1640 S Sepulveda Blvd Ste 218
Los Angeles, CA 90025-7535, USA

Douglas, Illeana (Actor)
c/o Jason Weinberg *Untitled Entertainment (LA)*
331 N Maple Dr Fl 3
Beverly Hills, CA 90210-3827, USA

Douglas, James (Buster) (Athlete, Boxer)
PO Box 342
Johnstown, OH 43031-0342, USA

Douglas, Jay (Football Player)
San Diego Chargers
2909 Laurel Cherry Way
The Woodlands, TX 77380-4004, USA

Douglas, Jerry (Actor)
17336 Rancho St
Encino, CA 91316-3945, USA

Douglas, John (Football Player)
New Orleans Saints
3094 Phillip Dr
Hurst, TX 76054-2072, USA

Douglas, Katie (Basketball Player)
Connecticut Sun
Mohegan Sun Arena
Uncasville, CT 06382, USA

Douglas, Kirk (Actor)
805 N Rexford Dr
Beverly Hills, CA 90210-2908, USA

Douglas, Kyan (Television Host)
c/o Staff Member *Queer Eye for the Straight Guy*
119 Braintree St
Boston, MA 02134-1628, USA

Douglas, Leon (Basketball Player)
Detroit Pistons
6265 Sun Blvd Apt 402G
Saint Petersburg, FL 33715-1034, USA

Douglas, Leon (Basketball Player)
PO Box 58
Leighton, AL 35646-0058, USA

Douglas, Merrill (Football Player)
Chicago Bears
2185 E 3970 S
Salt Lake City, UT 84124-1754, USA

Douglas, Michael (Actor)
15030 Ventura Blvd # 710
Sherman Oaks, CA 91403-5470, USA

Douglas, Santiago (Actor)
c/o Charlton Blackburne *A Management*
9107 Wilshire Blvd Ste 650
Beverly Hills, CA 90210-5544, USA

Douglas, Sarah (Actor)
c/o Staff Member *Time Machine*
2109 S Wilbur Ave
Walla Walla, WA 99362-9048, USA

Douglas, Sherman (Basketball Player)
New Jarsey Nets
390 Murray Hill Pkwy
East Rutherford, NJ 07073-2109, USA

Douglass, Bobby (Football Player)
Chicago Bears
41 S June Ter
Lake Forest, IL 60045-3206, USA

Douglass, Dale (Golfer)
6601 E San Miguel Ave
Paradise Valley, AZ 85253-5983, USA

Douglass, Maurice (Football Player)
c/o Staff Member *Saint Louis Rams*
1 Rams Way
Earth City, MO 63045-1525, USA

Douglass, Michael R (Mike) (Football Player)
Green Bay Packers
1725 Porterfield Pl
El Cajon, CA 92019-4122, USA

Douglass, Robyn (Actor)
c/o Rick Halprin
407 S Dearborn St Ste 1675
Chicago, IL 60605-1144, USA

Douglass, Sean (Baseball Player)
Baltimore Orioles
44437 Benald St
Lancaster, CA 93535-3440, USA

Doumit, Sam (Actor)
c/o Staff Member *Handprint Entertainment*
1100 Glendon Ave Ste 1000
Los Angeles, CA 90024-3514, USA

Dourda, Abu Zaid Umar (Prime Minister)
Prime Minister's Office
Bab el Aziziya Barracks
Tripoli, LIBYA

Dourdan, Gary (Actor)
c/o Jai Khanna *Brillstein-Grey Entertainment*
9150 Wilshire Blvd Ste 350
Beverly Hills, CA 90212-3453, USA

Dourif, Brad (Actor)
c/o Steve LaManna *Innovative Artists (LA)*
1505 10th St
Santa Monica, CA 90401-2805, USA

Douse, Joseph (Baseball Player)
Kansas City Monarchs
16722 Fenmore St
Detroit, MI 48235-3423, USA

Douthitt, Earl (Football Player)
Chicago Bears
8100 Central Ave Apt 211
Cleveland, OH 44104-2173, USA

Dove, Eddie (Football Player)
San Francisco 49ers
1750 Poppy Ave
Menlo Park, CA 94025-5738, USA

Dove, Rita F (Writer)
1757 Lambs Rd
Charlottesville, VA 22901-8911, USA

Dove, Robert (Bob) (Football Player)
Chicago Rockets
6 Neff Dr
Canfield, OH 44406-1343, USA

Dove, Ronnie (Music Group)
c/o Staff Member *Time Machine*
2109 S Wilbur Ave
Walla Walla, WA 99362-9048, USA

Doves (Music Group)
c/o Staff Member *Paradigm (Monterey)*
509 Hartnell St
Monterey, CA 93940-2825, USA

Dow, Ellen Albertini (Actor)
c/o Staff Member *GVA Talent Agency Inc*
9229 W Sunset Blvd Ste 320
Los Angeles, CA 90069-3403, USA

Dow, Harley (Football Player)
San Francisco 49ers
13428 The Sq
Poway, CA 92064-1309, USA

Dow, Peggy (Actor)
2121 South Yorkstown Ave
Tulsa, OK 74114, USA

Dow, Tony (Actor)
Diamond Artists
9200 W Sunset Blvd Ste 701
West Hollywood, CA 90069-3602, USA

Dowd, Maureen (Editor)
New York Times
229 W 43rd St
Editorial Dept
New York, NY 10036-3959, USA

Dowdell, Marcus (Football Player)
New Orleans Saints
4117 Chateau Blvd Apt A
Kenner, LA 70065-5729, USA

Dowdy, Steven (Misc, Scientist)
Howard Hughes Medical Institute
Washington Univesity
Saint Louis, MO 63110, USA

Dowell, Anthony J (Ballerina)
Royal Ballet
Convent Garden Bow St
London WC2E 9DD, UNITED KINGDOM
(UK)

Dowell, Ken (Baseball Player)
Philadelphia Phillies
5640 33rd Ave
Sacramento, CA 95824-1704, USA

Dower, John W (Writer)
Massachusetts Institute of Technology
History Dept
Cambridge, MA 02139, USA

Dowle, David (Music Group, Musician)
Int'l Talent Booking
27A Floral St #300
London WC2E 9DQ, UNITED KINGDOM
(UK)

Dowler, Boyd H (Football Player)
Green Bay Packers
3013 Grove View Ct
Dacula, GA 30019-6896, USA

Dowling, Brian (Football Player)
New England Patriots
114 Arboretum Way
Burlington, MA 01803-3827, USA

Dowling, Dave (Baseball Player)
St Louis Cardinals
6131 W Rose Garden Ln
Glendale, AZ 85308-6270, USA

Dowling, Robert J (Editor, Publisher)
Hollywood Reporter
5055 Wilshire Blvd
Los Angeles, CA 90036-4396, USA

Dowling, Timothy (Actor)
c/o Staff Member *Endeavor Agency LLC
(LA)*
9601 Wilshire Blvd Fl 3
Beverly Hills, CA 90210-5204, USA

Dowling, Vincent (Director, Writer)
322 E River Rd
Huntington, MA 01050-9645, USA

Down, Lesley-Anne (Actor)
All-Media Public Relations
5664 Cahuenga Blvd # 231
North Hollywood, CA 91601-2103, USA

Down, Sarah (Cartoonist)
Playboy Magazine
680 N Lake Shore Dr
Reader Services
Chicago, IL 60611-4546, USA

Down, System of a (Music Group)
c/o Staff Member *Sony Records*
2100 Colorado Ave
Santa Monica, CA 90404-3504, USA

Downes, Edward (Opera Singer)
Royal Opera House
Covent Garden
London WC2E 9DD, UNITED KINGDOM
(UK)

Downes, Robin Atkin (Actor)
c/o Staff Member *Gordon Agency*
260 S Beverly Dr Ste 308
Beverly Hills, CA 90212-3814, USA

Downey, Bill (Basketball Player)
Providence Steamrollers
1035 S Moorings Dr
Arlington Heights, IL 60005-3217, USA

Downey, Jim (Writer)
c/o Staff Member *3 Arts Entertainment Inc*
9460 Wilshire Blvd Fl 7
Beverly Hills, CA 90212-2713, USA

Downey, Robert J (Director)
55 W 900 S
Salt Lake City, UT 84101-2931, USA

Downey, Roma (Actor)
c/o Ken Kaplan *Gersh Agency, The (LA)*
232 N Canon Dr
Beverly Hills, CA 90210-5302, USA

Downey Jr, Robert (Actor)
c/o Bryan Lourd *Creative Artists Agency
LCC (CAA-LA)*
2000 Avenue Of The Stars
Los Angeles, CA 90067-4700, USA

Downie, Leonard Jr (Editor)
Washington Post
Editorial Dept 1150 15th St NW
Washington, DC 20071-0001, USA

Downing, Alphonso E (Al) (Baseball
Player)
New York Yankees
752 Edgewood Ave
Trenton, NJ 08618-5404, USA

Downing, Brian J (Baseball Player)
8095 County Road 135
Celina, TX 75009-2539, USA

Downing, George (Misc, Yachtsman)
Get Wet!
3021 Waialae Ave
Honolulu, HI 96816-1505, USA

Downing, Kathryn (Publisher)
Mypotential.com
2821 Main St
Santa Monica, CA 90405-4009, USA

Downing, Sara (Actor)
c/o Staff Member *Lighthouse
Entertainment*
409 N Camden Dr Ste 202
Beverly Hills, CA 90210-4423, USA

Downing, Walt (Football Player)
San Francisco 49ers
1141 Durham Cir NW
Massillon, OH 44646-2121, USA

Downing, Wayne A (General)
4515 N Grandview Dr
Peoria Heights, IL 61616-6629, USA

Downs, Dave (Baseball Player)
Philadelphia Phillies
925 E 1050 N
Bountiful, UT 84010-2620, USA

Downs, Hugh H (Correspondent)
Arizona State University
Human Communications Department
Tempe, AZ 85287-0001, USA

Downs, Kelly (Baseball Player)
San Francisco Giants
244 W 1750 N
Centerville, UT 84014-3136, USA

Downs, Michael (Football Player)
Dallas Cowboys
5926 Stoneshire Ct
Dallas, TX 75252-5159, USA

Downs, Nicholas (Actor)
c/o Andrew Stawiarski *ADS Management*
269 S Beverly Dr # 441
Beverly Hills, CA 90212-3851, USA

Downs, Robert (Football Player)
San Francisco 49ers
28024 High Vista Dr
Escondido, CA 92026-7215, USA

Downs, Scott (Baseball Player)
Chicago Cubs
6814 Barbrook Rd
Louisville, KY 40258-2668, USA

Dowson, Philip M (Architect)
Royal Academy of the Arts
Piccadilly
London W1V 0DS, UNITED KINGDOM
(UK)

Doyle, Allen (Golfer)
512 Riverside Dr
Lagrange, GA 30240-9633, USA

Doyle, Brian (Baseball Player)
New York Yankees
PO Box 9156
Winter Haven, FL 33883-9156, USA

Doyle, Chris (Cinematographer)
10866 Wilshire Blvd # 1000
Los Angeles, CA 90024-4300, USA

Doyle, Christopher (Cinematographer)
c/o Staff Member *International Creative
Management (ICM-LA)*
10250 Constellation Blvd
Los Angeles, CA 90067-6200, USA

Doyle, Danny (Baseball Player)
Boston Red Sox
3805 Quail Creek Farms
Stillwater, OK 74074-2422, USA

Doyle, Denny (Baseball Player)
Philadelphia Phillies
PO Box 9156
Winter Haven, FL 33883-9156, USA

Doyle, James H Jr (Admiral)
5121 Baltan Rd
Bethesda, MD 20816-2309, USA

Doyle, Jeff (Baseball Player)
Philadelphia Phillies
830 SE Bayshore Cir
Corvallis, OR 97333-3206, USA

Doyle, Patrick (Composer)
Air-Edel
18 Rodmarton St
London W1H 3FW, UNITED KINGDOM
(UK)

Doyle, Paul (Baseball Player)
Atlanta Braves
5832 Woodboro Dr
Huntington Beach, CA 92649-4963, USA

Doyle, Roddy (Writer)
Secker & Warburg
38A West Road Bromsgrove
Worc B60 2NQ, UNITED KINGDOM
(UK)

Doyle, Ted (Football Player)
Pittsburgh Pirates
10521 S 176th St
Omaha, NE 68136-1949, USA

Doyle & Debbie Show, The (Music
Group)
c/o Staff Member *Paradigm (Monterey)*
509 Hartnell St
Monterey, CA 93940-2825, USA

Doyle-Childress, Cartha (Baseball Player)
1516 Carowinds Cir
Maryville, TN 37803-7704, USA

Doyle Kennedy, Maria (Actor)
c/o Ruth Young *Peters Fraser & Dunlop
(PFD - UK)*
Drury House
34-43 Russell St
London WC2B 5HA, UNITED KINGDOM
(UK)

Dozier, Buzz (Baseball Player)
Washington Senators
2909 Braemar St
Waco, TX 76710-2122, USA

Dozier, D J (Baseball Player, Football
Player)
Minnesota Vikings
5821 N Cherokee Cluster
Virginia Beach, VA 23462-3214, USA

Dozier, James L (General)
2150 Channel Way
North Fort Myers, FL 33917-2514, USA

Dozier, Tom (Baseball Player)
Oakland A's
1231 Willow Ave Apt D7
Hercules, CA 94547-1200, USA

Dr Demento (Entertainer)
6102 Pimenta Ave
Lakewood, CA 90712-1042, USA

Dr Dog (Musician)
c/o Staff Member *Paradigm (Monterey)*
509 Hartnell St
Monterey, CA 93940-2825, USA

Dr John (Music Group, Musician,
Songwriter, Writer)
Impact Artists
356 W 123rd St
New York, NY 10027-5123, USA

Drabble, Margaret (Writer)
P F D
Drury House 34-43 Russell St
London WC2B 5HA, UNITED KINGDOM
(UK)

Drabek, Douglas D (Doug) (Baseball
Player)
New York Yankees
15 Ivy Pond Pl
The Woodlands, TX 77381-6326, USA

Drabinsky, Garth H (Producer)
Livent Inc
165 Avenue Road #600
Toronto, ON M5R 3S4, CANADA

Drabowsky, Myron W (Moe) (Baseball
Player)
Chicago Cubs
4741 Oak Run Dr
Sarasota, FL 34243-4537, USA

Draffen, Willis (Music Group)
16103 Vista Del Mar Dr
Houston, TX 77083-2309, USA

Draft, Chris (Football Player)
Chicago Bears
970 E Oak St
Anaheim, CA 92805-4138, USA

Draglia, Stacy (Athlete, Track Athlete)
1112 E Monte Cristo Ave
Phoenix, AZ 85022-3150, USA

Drago, Billy (Actor)
3800 Barham Blvd Ste 303
Los Angeles, CA 90068-1042, USA

Drago, Richard A (Dick) (Baseball Player)
Kansas City Royals
12626 Castle Hill Dr
Tampa, FL 33624-4141, USA

Dragon
122 McEvoy Street
Alexandria, NSW 2015, AUSTRALIA

Dragon, Daryl (Musician)
Cheri Ingrams Enterprises
7500 W Lake Mead Blvd # 9492
Las Vegas, NV 89128-0297, USA

Dragoti, Stan (Director)
1800 Avenue Of The Stars Ste 430
Los Angeles, CA 90067-4206, USA

Dragpejvic, Srdjan (Director, Writer)
William Morris Agency
151 El Camino Dr
Beverly Hills, CA 90212-2775, USA

Drahman, Brian (Baseball Player)
Chicago White Sox
4050 NE 15th Ave
Oakland Park, FL 33334-4643, USA

Drahos, Nick (Football Player)
New York Americans
3158 State Route 90
Aurora, NY 13026-9741, USA

Drai, Victor (Producer)
10527 Bellagio Road
Beverly Hills, CA 90210, USA

Draiman, Dave (Music Group)
Mitch Schneider Organization
14724 Ventura Blvd Ste 710
Sherman Oaks, CA 91403-3520, USA

Drake, Bebe (Actor)
c/o Staff Member *Baron Entertainment*
5757 Wilshire Blvd Ste 659
Los Angeles, CA 90036-3682, USA

Drake, Betsy (Actor)
10850 Wilshire Blvd Ste 575
Los Angeles, CA 90024-4336, USA

Drake, Dallas (Hockey Player)
11472 E Cedar Bay Trl
Traverse City, MI 49684-6841, USA

Drake, Jerry (Football Player)
Arizona Cardinals
2857 Regal Cir Apt E
Birmingham, AL 35216-4632, USA

Drake, Joe (Football Player)
Philadelphia Eagles
873 University St
San Francisco, CA 94134-1843, USA

Drake, Judith (Actor)
20th Century Artists
4605 Lankershim Blvd Ste 305
North Hollywood, CA 91602-1875, USA

Drake, Juel D (Misc)
Iron Workers Union
1750 New York Ave NW Ste 400
Washington, DC 20006-5301, USA

Drake, Larry (Actor)
15260 Ventura Blvd Ste 2100
Sherman Oaks, CA 91403-5360, USA

Drake, Sammy (Baseball Player)
Chicago Cubs
4415 Springdale Dr
Los Angeles, CA 90043-2107, USA

Drake, Solly (Baseball Player)
Chicago Cubs
1732 S Corning St
Los Angeles, CA 90035-4302, USA

Drakeford, Tyronne (Football Player)
San Francisco 49ers
2311 Baron Dekalb Rd
Camden, SC 29020-8224, USA

Drane, Ashley (Actor)
c/o Kathy Carter *Axiom Management*
16302 Crowne Brook Cir
Franklin, TN 37067-1673, USA

Drane, Dwight (Football Player)
Buffalo Bills
200 NW 107th Ave
Plantation, FL 33324-1700, USA

Dransfeldt, Kelly (Baseball Player)
Texas Rangers
1810 Jana Ln
Morris, IL 60450-1162, USA

Draper, Courtnee
c/o Steve Simon *Landis-Simon
Productions Talent Management*
8899 Beverly Blvd Ste 815
West Hollywood, CA 90048-2452, USA

Draper, E Lynn Jr (Business Person)
American Electric Power
1 Riverside Plz
Columbus, OH 43215-2373, USA

Draper, Mike (Baseball Player)
New York Mets
18317 Manor Church Rd
Boonsboro, MD 21713-2502, USA

Draper, Polly (Actor)
c/o Staff Member *Innovative Artists (LA)*
1505 10th St
Santa Monica, CA 90401-2805, USA

Draper, William H III (Financier)
91 Tallwood Ct
Atherton, CA 94027-6431, USA

Drasner, Fred (Publisher)
New York Daily News
220 E 42nd St
New York, NY 10017-5806, USA

Dratch, Rachel (Actor, Comedian)
c/o Jim Hess *Paradigm (LA)*
360 N Crescent Dr
North Bldg
Beverly Hills, CA 90210-6820, USA

Dravecky, David F (Dave) (Baseball Player)
Outreach of Hope
13840 Gleneagle Dr
Colorado Springs, CO 80921-3214, USA

Draven, Jamie (Actor)
c/o Staff Member *International Creative Management (ICM-UK)*
Oxford House
76 Oxford St
London W1N OAX, UNITED KINGDOM (UK)

Draves, Victoria (Vickie) (Misc, Swimmer)
23842 Shady Tree Cir
Laguna Niguel, CA 92677-1704, USA

Drayton, Charlie (Music Group, Musician)
Direct Mangement Group
947 N La Cienega Blvd # 2
Los Angeles, CA 90069-4782, USA

Drayton, Troy (Football Player)
Los Angeles Rams
31 Oak St Ste 1
Eric Rothman
Patchogue, NY 11772-2841, USA

Dream (Music Group)
c/o Johnny Wright *Wright-Crear Management*
3815 Hughes Ave
Culver City, CA 90232-2715, USA

Dream So Real
PO Box 8061
Athens, GA 30603-8061, USA

Dream Warriors
1505 W 2nd Ave #200
Vancouver, BC V6H 3Y4, CANADA

Dreamstreet (Music Group)
c/o Staff Member *Adonis Productions*
175 Skillman St
Brooklyn, NY 11205-3901, USA

Drechsler, Dave (Football Player)
Green Bay Packers
1135 Arabian Farms Rd
Clover, SC 29710-8562, USA

Drechsler, Heike (Athlete, Track Athlete)
LAC Chemnitz
Reichenhainer Str 154
Chmnitz 09135, GERMANY

Drees, Tom (Baseball Player)
Chicago White Sox
14723 Boulder Pointe Rd
Eden Prairie, MN 55347, USA

Dreesen, Tom (Actor, Comedian)
14538 Benefit St Unit 301
Sherman Oaks, CA 91403-5507, USA

Dreifort, Darren (Baseball Player)
Los Angeles Dodgers
821 Alma Real Dr
Pacific Palisades, CA 90272-3705, USA

Dreifuss, Ruth (President)
Federal Chancellery
Bundeshaus-W
Bundesgasse
Beme 3033, SWITZERLAND

Drell, Persis (Physicist)
Stanford University
Linear Accelerator Center
Stanford, CA 94305, USA

Drell, Sidney D (Physicist)
620 Sand Hill Rd Apt 420D
Palo Alto, CA 94304-2075, USA

Drescher, Fran (Actor)
c/o Iris Grossman *International Creative Management (ICM-LA)*
10250 Constellation Blvd
Los Angeles, CA 90067-6200, USA

Dreschler, David (Football Player)
1135 Arablan Farms Road
Clover, SC 29710, USA

Drese, Ryan (Baseball Player)
Cleveland Indians
1030 Sunnyhills Rd
Oakland, CA 94610-2417, USA

Dressel, Chris (Football Player)
Houston Oilers
410 Whiskey Hill Rd
Woodside, CA 94062-2571, USA

Dresselhaus, Mildred S (Engineer, Physicist)
Energy Department
1000 Independence Ave SW
Washington, DC 20585-0001, USA

Dressendorfer, Kirk (Baseball Player)
Oakland A's
1004 Oaklands Dr
Round Rock, TX 78681-4033, USA

Dressler, Doug (Football Player)
Cincinnati Bengals
540A 9th Ave
Menlo Park, CA 94025-1866, USA

Dressler, Rob (Baseball Player)
San Francisco Giants
2037 17th Ave
Forest Grove, OR 97116-2709, USA

Drew, B Alvin (Astronaut)
2814 Lighthouse Dr
Houston, TX 77058-4320, USA

Drew, Cameron (Baseball Player)
Houston Astros
31 Highbridge Rd
Yardville, NJ 08620-9632, USA

Drew, David Jonathan (J D) (Baseball Player)
Saint Louis Cardinals
250 Stadium Plz
Busch Stadium
Saint Louis, MO 63102, USA

Drew, Dennis (Music Group, Musician)
Agency for Performing Arts
405 S Beverly Dr Ste 500
Beverly Hills, CA 90212-4425, USA

Drew, Elizabeth H (Publisher)
Avon/William Morrow
1350 Avenue Of The Americas
New York, NY 10019-4702, USA

Drew, Griffin (Actor, Model)
9066 Cambridge Cir
Vallejo, CA 94591-8593, USA

Drew, Heather (Golfer)
76160 Desert Mountain Cir
Indio, CA 92203, USA

Drew, J D (Baseball Player)
St Louis Cardinals
1204 Suncast Ln Ste 2
El Dorado Hills, CA 95762-9665, USA

Drew, Larry (Basketball Player)
Detroit Pistons
4942 Densmore Ave
Encino, CA 91436-1538, USA

Drew, Tim (Baseball Player)
Cleveland Indians
5006 Old US 41 N
Hahira, GA 31632-4405, USA

Drew, Urban (War Hero)
451 Neptune Ave
Encinitas, CA 92024-2016, USA

Drewrey, Willie (Football Player)
Houston Oilers
2714 Cheryl Ct
Missouri City, TX 77459-2930, USA

Drexler, Clyde (Basketball Player)
Portland Trail Blazers
5353 Westheimer Rd # 2607
Houston, TX 77056-5402, USA

Drexler, Clyde (Basketball Player, Coach)
Dade/Schultz
6442 Coldwater Canyon Ave Ste 206
North Hollywood, CA 91606-1137, USA

Dreyer, Steve (Baseball Player)
Texas Rangers
6018 Greywood Cir
Johnston, IA 50131-1687, USA

Dreyfus, George (Composer)
3 Grace St
Camberwell, VIC 3124, AUSTRALIA

Dreyfus, Lee S (Governor)
3159 Madison St
Waukesha, WI 53188-4409, USA

Dreyfuss, Richard S (Actor, Producer)
PO Box 10459
Burbank, CA 91510-0459, USA

Driedger, Florence G (Activist, Misc)
3833 Montaigne St
Regina, SK S4S 3J6, CANADA

Driessen, Dan (Baseball Player)
Cincinnati Reds
97 William Hilton Pkwy
Hilton Head Island, SC 29926-1205, USA

Driest, Burkhard
Alter Militarring 8
Koln 50933, GERMANY

Drinan, Robert F (Educator, Misc)
Georgetown University
1507 Isherwood St NE Apt 1
Washington, DC 20002-5564, USA

Drinkard, Bobby Jon (Reality TV Star)
c/o Staff Member *Mark Burnett Productions*
640 N Sepulveda Blvd
Los Angeles, CA 90049-2108, USA

Drinkwater-Simmons, Maxine (Baseball Player)
18 Belmont Ave
Camden, ME 04843-2028, USA

Driscoll, Jean (Athlete, Motivational Speaker, Olympic Athlete)
Pat Fettig
8142 Traverse Ct
Cincinnati, OH 45242-7224, USA

Driscoll, Jim (Baseball Player)
Oakland A's
4135 N 81st St
Scottsdale, AZ 85251-2670, USA

Driscoll, John (Actor)
c/o Staff Member *Talented Managers*
65 West 90th Stste 7D
Nyc, NY 10024, USA

Driscoll, Terry (Basketball Player)
Detroit Pistons
200 Vanrage Terrace
Duxbury, MA 02332, USA

Driskill, Travis (Baseball Player)
Baltimore Orioles
800 Blue Spring Cir
Round Rock, TX 78681-4047, USA

Driver, Bruce (Hockey Player)
21A Crest Ter
Montville, NJ 07045-9370, USA

Driver, Minnie (Actor)
c/o Jason Weinberg *Untitled Entertainment (LA)*
331 N Maple Dr Fl 3
Beverly Hills, CA 90210-3827, USA

Driver, William J (Government Official)
215 W Columbia St
Falls Church, VA 22046-3412, USA

D'Rivera, Paquito
Charismic Productions
2704 Mozart Place NW
Washington, DC 20009, USA

Drnovsek, Janez (Prime Minister)
Prime Minister's Office
Gregorcicova St 20
Ljubljana 61000, SLOVENIA

Dro, Bob (Basketball Player)
Indianapolis Kautskys
10708 Lakeview Dr
Carmel, IN 46033-3933, USA

Drobny, Jaroslav (Actor)
23 Kenilworth Court
Lower Richmond Road
London SW15 1EW, UNITED KINGDOM (UK)

Drollinger, Ralph (Basketball Player)
Dallas Mavericks
22831 Market St
Santa Clarita, CA 91321-3605, USA

Dropo, Walter (Walt) (Baseball Player)
Boston Red Sox
104 Brooksby Village Dr Unit 104
Peabody, MA 01960-1470, USA

Drosdick, John G (Business Person)
Sunoco Inc
10 Penn Center 1801 Market St
Philadelphia, PA 19103, USA

Drougas, Tom (Football Player)
Baltimore Colts
600 Northwood Way
Ketcham, ID 83340, USA

Droughns, Reuben (Football Player)
Detroit Lions
5200 S Ulster St Apt 1419S
Greenwood Village, CO 80111-2865, USA

Drowning Pool (Music Group)
c/o Staff Member *Wind-up Records*
72 Madison Ave Fl 8
New York, NY 10016-8731, USA

Drozdova, Margarita S (Ballerina)
Stanislavsky Musical Theater
Pushkinskaya Str 17
Moscow, RUSSIA

Dru Hill (Music Group)
c/o Staff Member *Endeavor Agency LLC (LA)*
9601 Wilshire Blvd Fl 3
Beverly Hills, CA 90210-5204, USA

Druck, Mirchea (Prime Minister)
Str 31 August 123 #7
Kishinev 277012, MOLDOVA

Druckenmiller, Jim (Football Player)
San Francisco 49ers
2351 E Aragon Blvd Unit 6
Sunrise, FL 33313-8045, USA

Drucker, Eugene (Music Group, Musician)
I M G Artists
3 Burlington Lane
Chiswick
London W4 2TH, UNITED KINGDOM (UK)

Drucker, Mort (Cartoonist)
Famous Artists Agency
250 W 57th St
New York, NY 10107-0001, USA

Drudge, Matt (Journalist)
1425 Brickell Ave Apt 47C
Miami, FL 33131-3402, USA

Druker, Brian J (Misc)
Oregon Health Science University
Cancer Research Center
Portland, OR 97201, USA

Drulis, Al (Football Player)
Chicago Cardinals
1114 Cooperskill Rd
Cherry Hill, NJ 08034-2835, USA

Drummond, Alice (Actor)
351 E 50th St
New York, NY 10022-7975, USA

Drummond, Jonathan (Jon) (Athlete, Track Athlete)
113 Cascade Lake St
Las Vegas, NV 89148-2792, USA

Drummond, Roscoe (Misc, Writer)
6637 Maclean Dr Olde Dominion Square
McLean, VA 22101, USA

Drummond, Ryan (Actor)
c/o Staff Member *Bobby Ball Talent Agency*
4605 Lankershim Blvd Ste 721
North Hollywood, CA 91602-1878, USA

Drummond, Tim (Baseball Player)
Pittsburgh Pirates
102 Haldane Ct
La Plata, MD 20646-4308, USA

Drumright, Keith (Baseball Player)
Houston Astros
1333 W Lindberg St
Springfield, MO 65807-2385, USA

Drury, Chris (Hockey Player)
57 E Oak Hills Dr
Castle Rock, CO 80108-9251, USA

Drury, James (Actor)
12126 Osage Park Dr
Houston, TX 77065-3812, USA

Drury, Ted (Hockey Player)
64 Glenwood Ave
Point Lookout, NY 11569, USA

Druschel, Rich (Football Player)
Pittsburgh Steelers
724 Cochran Dr
Greensburg, PA 15601-4610, USA

Drut, Guy J (Athlete, Track Athlete)
Maine
Coulommiers 77120, FRANCE

Druze, John (Football Player)
Brooklyn Dodgers
1051 S Rochester
Mesa, AZ 85206-2753, USA

Dryburgh, Stuart (Cinematographer)
Sandra Marsh Mgmt
9150 Wilshire Blvd Ste 220
Beverly Hills, CA 90212-3429, USA

Dryden, Ken (Athlete, Hockey Player)
58 Poplar Plains Road
Toronto, ON M5J 2M8, CANADA

Dryer, Fred (Football Player)
New York Giants
1700 W Burbank Blvd Ste 100
Burbank, CA 91506-1313, USA

Dryke, Matthew (Matt) (Misc)
4702 Davis Ave S Apt 2B102
Renton, WA 98055-6253, USA

Drynan, Jeanie (Actor)
c/o Staff Member *Essential Talent Management*
6399 Wilshire Blvd Ste 400
Los Angeles, CA 90048-5716, USA

Drysdale, Cliff (Sportscaster, Tennis Player)
Landfall
1801 Eastwood Rd # F
Wilmington, NC 28403, USA

Drzewiecki, Ron (Football Player)
Chicago Bears
5977 S 34th St
Milwaukee, WI 53221-4725, USA

D'Souza, Lawrence (Bollywood, Director, Filmmaker, Producer)
302B Red Rose New Link Road
Versova Andheri
Bombay, MS 400 058, INDIA

du Tertre, Celine (Actor)
c/o Mara Glauberg *Cunningham Escott Slevin & Doherty (LA)*
10635 Santa Monica Blvd Ste 130
Los Angeles, CA 90025-8306, USA

Du Toit, Elize (Actor)
c/o Vanessa Pereira *Artists Independent Management (LA)*
825 Nowita Pl
Venice, CA 90291-3836, USA

Duany, Andres (Architect)
Duany & Plater-Zaberk Architects
1023 SW 25th Ave
Miami, FL 33135-4824, USA

DuArt, Louise (Religious Leader, Television Host)
c/o Staff Member *Living the Life* Christian Broadcasting Network
977 Centerville Tpke
Virginia Beach, VA 23463-0001, USA

Dubbels, Britta (Model)
Ford Model Agency
142 Greene St # 400
New York, NY 10012-3236, USA

Dubble, Curtis (Religious Leader)
Church of Brethren
1451 Dundee Ave
Elgin, IL 60120-1694, USA

Dube, Joseph (Joe) (Misc, Wrestler)
8821 Eaton Ave
Jacksonville, FL 32211-0306, USA

Dube, Lucky (Musician)
Fast Lane Int'l
4856 Haygood Rd Ste 200
Virginia Beach, VA 23455-5349, USA

Dubenion, Elbert (Football Player)
Buffalo Bills
610 E Walnut St
Westerville, OH 43081-2423, USA

Dubia, John A (General)
10095 Cover Pl
Fairfax, VA 22030-2494, USA

Dubinbaum, Gail (Opera Singer)
Metropolitan Opera Assn
Lincoln Center Plaza
New York, NY 10023, USA

Dubinin, Yuri V (Government Official)
Gazprom RAO Nametkina Str 16
Moscow 117884, RUSSIA

Dublinski, James L (Football Player)
Washington Redskins
723 S 900 E
Salt Lake City, UT 84102-3605, USA

Dublinski, Tom (Football Player)
Detroit Lions
15918 E El Lago Blvd
Fountain Hills, AZ 85268-3935, USA

Dubois, Brian (Baseball Player)
Detroit Tigers
359 E Ridge St
Braidwood, IL 60408-2095, USA

Dubois, Janet (Actor)
c/o Staff Member *Cunningham Escott
Slevin & Doherty (LA)*
10635 Santa Monica Blvd Ste 130
Los Angeles, CA 90025-8306, USA

DuBois, Marta (Actor)
Three Moons Entertainment
5441 E Beverly Blvd Ste G
Los Angeles, CA 90022-2243, USA

Dubois, Phil (Football Player)
Washington Redskins
405 Speedway Ave
Missoula, MT 59802-5475, USA

Dubose, Brian (Baseball Player)
Ted Williams
15336 Oakfield St
Detroit, MI 48227-1532, USA

Dubose, Eric (Baseball Player)
Baltimore Orioles
326 County Road 8
Gilbertown, AL 36908-2211, USA

DuBose, G Thomas (Misc)
United Transportation Union
14600 Detroit Ave
Cleveland, OH 44107-4250, USA

Dubose, Jimmy (Football Player)
Tampa Bay Buccaneers
11420 Walker Rd
Thonotosassa, FL 33592-3616, USA

Dubzinski, Walt (Football Player)
New York Giants
158 Lovewell St
Gardner, MA 01440-3552, USA

Ducasse, Alain (Chef)
Louis XV Restaurant
Hotel de Paris
Monte Carlo, MONACO

Ducey, Rob (Baseball Player)
Toronto Blue Jays
699 Richmond Close
Tarpon Springs, FL 34688-8423, USA

Duchesnay, Isamelle (Dancer)
Im Steinach 30
Oberstdorf 87561, GERMANY

Duchesnay, Paul (Figure Skater)
Bundesleistungszentrum
Rossbichstr 2-6
Oberstdorf 87561, GERMANY

Duchin, Peter (Music Group, Musician)
Peter Duchin Orchestra
60 E 42nd St Ste 1625
New York, NY 10165-6210, USA

Duchovny, David (Actor)
c/o Melanie Greene *Melanie Greene
Management & Productions*
425 N Robertson Blvd
West Hollywood, CA 90048-1735, USA

Duchscherer, Justin (Baseball Player)
Texas Rangers
4700 Green Oaks Dr
Colleyville, TX 76034-4765, USA

DuCille, Michel (Journalist, Photographer)
9571 Pine Meadows Ln
Burke, VA 22015-1550, USA

Duckett, Mahlon (Baseball Player)
Philadelphia Stars
259 S 52nd St
Philadelphia, PA 19139-4148, USA

Duckett, Richard (Basketball Player)
Cincinnati Royals
22 Cedar St
Westborough, MA 01581-1606, USA

Ducksworth, Sheila (Producer)
c/o Staff Member *Creative Artists Agency
LCC (CAA-LA)*
2000 Avenue Of The Stars
Los Angeles, CA 90067-4700, USA

Duckworth, Brandon (Baseball Player)
Philadelphia Phillies
4460 W 6095 S
Kearns, UT 84118-5289, USA

Duckworth, Jim (Baseball Player)
Washington Senators
405 Esther Ct
Fort Mill, SC 29708-5707, USA

Duckworth, Joe (Football Player)
Washington Redskins
1817 Calash Way
Virginia Beach, VA 23454-6041, USA

Duckworth, Tyler (Reality TV Star)
c/o Len Evans *Project Publicity*
312 W 53rd St
New York, NY 10019-5743, USA

Ducsmal, Agnieszka
Polish Radio Orchestra
Al Marchinkowskiego 3
Pozna 61-745, POLAND

Duda, Mark (Football Player)
St Louis Cardinals
1707 Cherry St
Scranton, PA 18505-3972, USA

Dudek, Anne (Actor)
c/o Staff Member *Industry Entertainment*
955 Carrillo Dr Ste 300
Los Angeles, CA 90048-5400, USA

Dudek, Joseph A (Joe) (Football Player)
Denver Broncos
17 Adam Dr
Hudson, NH 03051-3235, USA

Dudek, Mitch (Football Player)
New York Jets
1241 Forest Ave
Wilmette, IL 60091-1656, USA

Duden, H Richard (Dick) Jr (Football Player)
New York Giants
11 Old Station Rd
Severna Park, MD 21146-4618, USA

Duderstadt, James J (Educator, Government Official)
National Science Foundation
1800 G St NW
Washington, DC 20006-4403, USA

Dudikoff, Michael (Actor)
c/o Sid Craig *Craig Management*
2240 Miramonte Cir E Unit C
Palm Springs, CA 92264-5734, USA

Dudley, Brian (Football Player)
Cleveland Browns
6319 London Ave
Alta Loma, CA 91737-3646, USA

Dudley, Charles (Basketball Player)
Seattle SuperSonics
4032 42nd Ave S
Seattle, WA 98118-1121, USA

Dudley, Chris (Athlete, Basketball Player)
Cleverland Cavaliers
1150 Fairway Rd
Lake Oswego, OR 97034-2818, USA

Dudley, D-Von (Wrestler)
c/o Staff Member *World Wrestling
Entertainment (WWE)*
1241 E Main St
Stamford, CT 06902-3520, USA

Dudley, Debra
PO Box 40
Bonnieville, KY 42713-0040, USA

Dudley, James (Baseball Player)
Baltimore Elite Giants
607 Delafield Pl NW
Washington, DC 20011-4054, USA

Dudley, Rick (Coach, Hockey Player, Misc)
5150 Oakhill Dr
Lewiston, NY 14092-1857, USA

Dudley, Rickey (Football Player)
Oakland Raiders
4529 Mahogany Ln
Lewisville, TX 75077-8546, USA

Dudley, William M (Bill) (Football Player)
Pittsburgh Steelers
303 Barkley Ct
Lynchburg, VA 24503-4222, USA

Duenkel Fuldner, Virginia (Swimmer)
2132 NE 17th Ter # 500
Wilton Manors, FL 33305-2414, USA

Duerod, Terry (Basketball Player)
Detroit Pistons
26606 Glendale
Redford, MI 48239-2721, USA

Duerson, David R (Dave) (Football Player)
Chicago Bears
19333 Collins Ave Apt 603
Sunny Isles Beach, FL 33160-2368, USA

Dues, Hal (Baseball Player)
Montreal Expos
PO Box R
Dickinson, TX 77539-2018, USA

Dueto Voces del Rancho (Musician)
c/o Staff Member *Sony Music Miami*
605 Lincoln Rd Fl 7
Miami Beach, FL 33139-2900, USA

Dufay, Rick (Music Group, Musician)
H K Mgmt
9200 W Sunset Blvd Ste 530
Los Angeles, CA 90069-3509, USA

Dufek, Don (Football Player)
Seattle Seahawks
570 S Maple Rd
Ann Arbor, MI 48103-3837, USA

Dufek, Joe (Football Player)
Buffalo Bills
17015 N 7th St Ste 1
Phoenix, AZ 85022-2404, USA

Duff, Haylie (Actor, Composer, Musician)
c/o Susan Curtis *Curtis Talent
Management*
9607 Arby Dr
Beverly Hills, CA 90210-1202, USA

Duff, Hilary (Actor, Model, Musician)
c/o Susan Curtis *Curtis Talent
Management*
9607 Arby Dr
Beverly Hills, CA 90210-1202, USA

Duff, Jamal (Football Player)
New York Giants
530 Ocean Blvd Apt 1911
Long Beach, CA 90802, USA

Duff, John (Football Player)
Oakland Raiders
PO Box 20058
Long Beach, CA 90801-3058, USA

Duff, John B (Educator)
Columbia College
President's Office
Chicago, IL 60605, USA

Duff, John E (Artist, Misc)
7 Doyers St
New York, NY 10013-5112, USA

Duff, Matt (Baseball Player)
St Louis Cardinals
1701 27th St E
Bradenton, FL 34208-7831, USA

Duff, T Richard (Dick) (Hockey Player)
4-7 Elmwood Ave S
Mississauga, ON L5G 3J6, CANADA

Duffalo, Jim (Baseball Player)
San Francisco Giants
PO Box 1082
Du Bois, PA 15801-1082, USA

Duffell, Peter
29 Roehampton Gate
London, ENGLAND SW15 5JR, UNITED KINGDOM (UK)

Duffie, John (Baseball Player)
Los Angeles Dodgers
177 Lakeside Cir
Douglas, GA 31535-6627, USA

Duffield, David (Business Person)
PeopleSoft Inc
4460 Hacienda Dr
Pleasanton, CA 94588-2761, USA

Duffner, Mark (Coach, Football Coach)
University of Maryland
Athletic Dept
College Park, MD 20740, USA

Duffy, Brian (Astronaut)
14805 Pristine Dr
Colorado Springs, CO 80921-3549, USA

Duffy, Brian (Cartoonist, Editor)
Des Moines Regester
PO Box 957
Editorial Dept
Des Moines, IA 50306-0957, USA

Duffy, Dorothy (Actor)
PFD
Drury House
34-43 Russell St
London WC2B 5HA, UNITED KINGDOM (UK)

Duffy, Frank (Baseball Player)
Cincinnati Reds
1740 E Silver St
Tucson, AZ 85719-3152, USA

Duffy, J C (Cartoonist)
Universal Press Syndicate
4520 Main St
Kansas City, MO 64111-1876, USA

Duffy, James (Business Person)
Saint Paul Companies
385 Washington St
Saint Paul, MN 55102-1396, USA

Duffy, John (Composer)
Meet the Composer
2112 Broadway
New York, NY 10023-2105, USA

Duffy, Julia (Actor)
Lacey
5699 Kanan Rd # 285
Agoura, CA 91301-3358, USA

Duffy, Karen (Actor, Model)
Ford Model Agency
142 Greene St # 400
New York, NY 10012-3236, USA

Duffy, Keith (Music Group)
Carol Assoc-War Mgmt
Bushy Park Road 57 Meadowgate
Dublin, IRELAND

Duffy, Matthew (DJ)
c/o Len Evans *Project Publicity*
312 W 53rd St
New York, NY 10019-5743, USA

Duffy, Patrick (Actor, Director, Producer)
c/o Craig Dorfman *Blueprint Management*
5670 Wilshire Blvd Ste 2525
Los Angeles, CA 90036-5647, USA

Duffy, Roger (Football Player)
New York Jets
6509 Lutz Ave NW
Massillon, OH 44646-9512, USA

Duffy, Troy (Actor, Director, Writer)
c/o Staff Member *William Morris Agency
(WMA-LA)*
1 William Morris Pl
Beverly Hills, CA 90212-4261, USA

Dufner, Jason (Golfer)
2002 Saint Patrick Ct
Auburn, AL 36830-6962, USA

Dugan, Dennis (Actor, Director)
15611 Royal Oak Rd
Encino, CA 91436-3905, USA

Dugan, Fred (Football Player)
San Francisco 49ers
1827 Tamiami Trl N
Nokomis, FL 34275-1456, USA

Dugan, Michael J (General, Misc)
National Multiple Sclerosis Society
733 3rd Ave
New York, NY 10017-3288, USA

Duggan, Jim (Football Player, Wrestler)
Atlanta Falcons
1328 Hornsby Cir
Lugoff, SC 29078-9722, USA

Dugger, John S (Artist)
410 Evelyn Ave Apt 201
Albany, CA 94706-1358, USA

Duguary, Ron (Actor, Hockey Player)
982 Porte Vedra Blvd
Porta Vedra Beach, FL 32082, USA

Duhamel, Josh (Actor)
c/o Rhonda Price *Gersh Agency, The (NY)*
41 Madison Ave Fl 33
New York, NY 10010-2202, USA

Duhart, Paul (Football Player)
Green Bay Packers
5 San Jose Dr
Palm Coast, FL 32137-2335, USA

Duhe, Adam J (A J) Jr (Football Player)
Miami Dolphins
379 Coconut Cir
Weston, FL 33326-3320, USA

Duhe, John M Jr (Judge)
US Court of Appeals
556 Jefferson St
Lafayette, LA 70501-6950, USA

Duhon, Robert (Football Player)
New York Giants
14204 S Hospital Dr
Abbeville, LA 70510-8819, USA

Duich, Steve (Football Player)
Atlanta Falcons
PO Box 2
Descanso, CA 91916-0002, USA

Dukakis, Kitty
85 Perry St
Brookline, MA 02446-6935, USA

Dukakis, Michael (Governor)
85 Perry St
Brookline, MA 02446-6935, USA

Dukakis, Olympia (Actor)
684 Broadway Apt 6E
New York, NY 10012-1123, USA

Duke, Bill (Director)
Duke Media
7510 W Sunset Blvd # 523
Los Angeles, CA 90046-3408, USA

Duke, Charles
PO Box 310345
New Braunfels, TX 78131-0345, USA

Duke, Charles M Jr (Astronaut, General)
280 Lakeview Blvd
New Braunfels, TX 78130-5200, USA

Duke, George (Music Group, Songwriter,
Writer)
Associated Booking Corp
PO Box 2055
New York, NY 10021-0051, USA

Duke, Ken (Golfer)
3612 SW Rivers End Way
Palm City, FL 34990-7606, USA

Duke, Norm (Bowler)
10836 County Rd 561A
Clermont, FL 34711-9400, USA

Duke, Patty (Actor)
c/o Mitchell Stubbs *Mitchell K Stubbs &
Assoc (MKS)*
8695 Washington Blvd Ste 204
Culver City, CA 90232-7419, USA

Duke, Paul (Football Player)
New York Yankees
3833 Randall Ridge Rd NW
Atlanta, GA 30327-3105, USA

Duke Special
c/o Staff Member *Paradigm (Monterey)*
509 Hartnell St
Monterey, CA 93940-2825, USA

Duke Spirit, The (Music Group)
c/o Staff Member *Paradigm (Monterey)*
509 Hartnell St
Monterey, CA 93940-2825, USA

Dukes, Jamie (Football Player)
Atlanta Falcons
2452 Stone Manor Dr
Buford, GA 30519-7686, USA

Dukes, Jan (Baseball Player)
Washington Senators
959 Helena Dr
Sunnyvale, CA 94087-4126, USA

Dukes, Michael (Football Player)
Houston Oilers
5810 Bret Ln
Beaumont, TX 77713-9228, USA

Dukes, The (Music Group)
11 Chartfield Square
London, England SW15, UNITED
KINGDOM (UK)

Dukes, Tom (Baseball Player)
Houston Astros
325 Monte Vista Rd
Arcadia, CA 91007-6147, USA

Dukes of Dixieland, The
PO Box 56757
New Orleans, LA 70156-6757, USA

Dukochitz, Jonathan (Actor, Musician)
c/o Staff Member *Innovative Artists (LA)*
1505 10th St
Santa Monica, CA 90401-2805, USA

Dulany, Caitlin (Actor)
Gersh Agency
232 N Canon Dr
Beverly Hills, CA 90210-5302, USA

Dulbecco, Renato (Nobel Prize Laureate)
7525 Hillside Dr
La Jolla, CA 92037-3941, USA

Duley, Ed (Football Player)
Houston Oilers
5219 N Casa Blanca Dr
Paradise Valley, AZ 85253-6201, USA

Dulgan, John (Director)
54A Tite St
London SW3 4JA, UNITED KINGDOM
(UK)

Dulhalde, Eduardo (President)
Casa de Gobiemo
Balcarce 50
Buenos Aires 1064, ARGENTINA

Duliba, Bob (Baseball Player)
St Louis Cardinals
327 Philadelphia Ave
West Pittston, PA 18643-2146, USA

Dullea, Keir (Actor)
310 W 72nd St # 9B
New York, NY 10023-2675, USA

Dulles, Avery R Cardinal (Misc)
Fordham University
Jesuit Community
Bronx, NY 10458, USA

Dulli, Greg (Music Group)
Real Time
48 Laight St
New York, NY 10013-2016, USA

Dumars, Joe III (Basketball Player)
Detroit Pistons
3499 Franklin Rd
Bloomfield Hills, MI 48302-0960, USA

Dumart, Woodrow W C (Woody)
(Hockey Player)
36 Old Farm Rd
Needham, MA 02492, USA

Dumas, Amy (Lita) (Wrestler)
c/o Staff Member *World Wrestling
Entertainment (WWE)*
1241 E Main St
Stamford, CT 06902-3520, USA

Dumas, Mike (Football Player)
Houston Oilers
6735 Alden Nash Ave SE
Alto, MI 49302-9682, USA

Dumas, Tony (Basketball Player)
Dallas Mavericks
7840 Tumbling Creek Dr
Millington, TN 38053-2216, USA

Dumbauld, Jonathan (Football Player)
New Orleans Saints
1530 E Sagebrush Ct
Gilbert, AZ 85296-2522, USA

Dumler, Doug (Football Player)
New England Patriots
1526 Peterson St
Fort Collins, CO 80524-4130, USA

Dummar, Melvin
Dummar's Restaurant
Gabbs, NV 89409, USA

Dummett, Michael A E (Misc)
54 Park Town
Oxford OX2 6SJ, UNITED KINGDOM
(UK)

Dumont, J P (Hockey Player)
Buffalo Sabres
1 Seymour St
Hsbc Arena
Buffalo, NY 14210, USA

Dumont, Sky (Actor)
ZBF Agentur
Leopoldstr 19
Munich 80802, GERMANY

Dumont, Tom (Music Group, Musician)
Rebel Waltz Inc
31652 2nd Ave
Laguna Beach, CA 92651-8244, USA

Dumoulin, Dan (Baseball Player)
Cincinnati Reds
202 Nancy Dr
Kokomo, IN 46901-5907, USA

Dunagin, Ralph (Cartoonist)
North American Syndicate
235 E 45th St
New York, NY 10017-3305, USA

Dunaway, Faye (Actor)
c/o David Herd *Innovative Artists (LA)*
1505 10th St
Santa Monica, CA 90401-2805, USA

Dunaway, James E (Football Player)
Buffalo Bills
169 Mount Carmel Church Rd
Sandy Hook, MS 39478-9365, USA

Dunbar, Bonnie J (Astronaut)
2200 Todville Rd
Seabrook, TX 77586-3005, USA

Dunbar, Huey (Musician)
c/o Staff Member *Sony Music Miami*
605 Lincoln Rd Fl 7
Miami Beach, FL 33139-2900, USA

Dunbar, Matt (Baseball Player)
Florida Marlins
6328 County Donegal Ct
Charlotte, NC 28277-9652, USA

Dunbar, Rockmond (Actor)
c/o Ryan Martin *Agency for the
Performing Arts (APA-LA)*
405 S Beverly Dr
Beverly Hills, CA 90212-4416, USA

Dunbar, Tommy (Baseball Player)
Texas Rangers
558 Palm Dr S
Aiken, SC 29803-5450, USA

Duncan, Andy (Basketball Player)
Rochester Royals
608 Berry Pi
Marion, VA 24354, USA

Duncan, Angus (Actor)
Thomas Jennings
28035 Dorothy Dr Ste 210A
Agoura, CA 91301-2685, USA

Duncan, Arthur (Dancer)
Greg Purcott Productions
PO Box 276005
Boca Raton, FL 33427-6005, USA

Duncan, Brian (Football Player)
Cleveland Browns
739 Elm St
Graham, TX 76450-3018, USA

Duncan, Charles K (Admiral)
813 1st St
Coronado, CA 92118-1301, USA

Duncan, Charles W Jr (Secretary)
9 Briarwood Ct
Houston, TX 77019-5801, USA

Duncan, Cleveland (Cleve) (Music Group)
David Harris Enterprises
24210 E East Fork Rd Spc 9
Azusa, CA 91702-6249, USA

Duncan, Courtney (Baseball Player)
Chicago Cubs
121 Adalene Ln
Madison, AL 35757-8423, USA

Duncan, Curtis (Football Player)
Houston Oilers
4915 Glen Hollow St
Sugar Land, TX 77479-3804, USA

Duncan, Dave (Baseball Player)
Kansas City A's
10166 N Valle Del Oro Dr
Tucson, AZ 85737-7620, USA

Duncan, David Douglas (Journalist, Photographer)
Castellaras Mouans-Sartoux 06370, FRANCE

Duncan, H Randolph (Randy) (Football Player)
907 Ashworth Rd Apt 106
West Des Moines, IA 50265-3659, USA

Duncan, Jeff (Baseball Player)
New York Mets
825 Lincoln Ln
Frankfort, IL 60423-1087, USA

Duncan, Ken (Football Player)
Green Bay Packers
661 Colina Vis
Ventura, CA 93003-1355, USA

Duncan, Lindsay (Actor)
Ken McReddie
91 Regent St
London W1R 7TB, UNITED KINGDOM (UK)

Duncan, Mariano (Baseball Player)
Los Angeles Dodgers
Ingenio Angelina #137
San Pedro de Macoris, DOMINICAN REPUBLIC

Duncan, Melvin (Baseball Player)
Kansas City Monarchs
731 Arbor Dr
Ypsilanti, MI 48197-5174, USA

Duncan, Michael Clarke (Actor)
Dolores Robinson
3815 Hughes Ave # 3
Culver City, CA 90232-2715, USA

Duncan, Patrick S (Director, Producer, Writer)
c/o David Kanter *Jeff Morrone Management*
9350 Wilshire Blvd Ste 224
Beverly Hills, CA 90212-3204, USA

Duncan, Robert (Astronomer, Misc, Physicist)
University of Texas
Astronomy Dept
Austin, TX 78712, USA

Duncan, Sandy (Actor)
Litke/Gale Madden
1640 S Sepulveda Blvd Ste 530
Los Angeles, CA 90025-7538, USA

Duncan, Speedy (Football Player)
San Diego Chargers
1607 Porter Way
Stockton, CA 95207-4126, USA

Duncan, Taylor (Baseball Player)
St Louis Cardinals
83 Hampton St
Asheville, NC 28803-1641, USA

Duncan, Tim (Basketball Player)
San Antonio Spurs
Attn: Alumni Association
Wake Forest University P O Box 7426
Winston Salem, NC 27109, USA

Duncan, Tim (Basketball Player)
San Antonio Spurs
Alamodome 1 Sbc Center
San Antonio, TX 78219, USA

Dundee, Angelo (Boxer)
5060 Pinnacle Dr
Oldsmar, FL 34677-1926, USA

Dunderstadt, James (Educator)
University of Michigan
President's Office
Ann Arbor, MI 48109, USA

Dunegan, Jim (Baseball Player)
Chicago Cubs
20246 180th St
New London, IA 52645-8555, USA

Dungey, Merrin (Actor)
c/o Daniel (Dan) Spilo *Artistry Management*
525 Westbourne Dr
West Hollywood, CA 90048-1913, USA

Dungy, Tony (Coach, Football Coach, Football Player)
c/o Staff Member *Indianapolis Colts*
7001 W 56th St
Indianapolis, IN 46254-9698, USA

Dunham, Archie W (Business Person)
ConocoPhilips Inc
600 N Dairy Ashford St
Houston, TX 77079-1175, USA

Dunham, Chip (Cartoonist)
Universal Press Syndicate
4520 Main St
Kansas City, MO 64111-1876, USA

Dunham, Duane R (Business Person)
Bethlehem Steel Corp
1 E Broad St Ste 210
Bethlehem, PA 18018-5951, USA

Dunham, Jeff (Comedian)
On A Stick Productions, Inc
13801 Ventura Blvd
Sherman Oaks, CA 91423-3603, USA

Dunham, John L (Business Person)
May Department Stores
611 Olive St
Saint Louis, MO 63101-1756, USA

Dunham, Michael (Mike) (Hockey Player)
277 Gloucester Ct
Matawan, NJ 07747-1878, USA

Dunham, Russell E (War Hero)
31405 Sunderland Rd
Jerseyville, IL 62052-6497, USA

Dunham, Stephen (Actor)
c/o Connie Tavel *Forward Entertainment*
9255 W Sunset Blvd Ste 805
Los Angeles, CA 90069-3305, USA

Dunitz, Jack D (Misc)
Obere Heslibachstr 77
Kusnacht 8700, SWITZERLAND

Dunkie, Nancy (Basketball Player)
University of California
Campus Police
Berkeley, CA 94720-0001, USA

Dunkle, Nancy (Basketball Player)
Olympics
University Of California Campus
Berkeley, CA 94720-0001, USA

Dunlap, Alexander W (Astronaut)
721 Parkside Dr
Woodstock, GA 30188-6057, USA

Dunlap, Carla (Gymnast, Misc)
Diamond
732 Irvington Ave
Maplewood, NJ 07040-1610, USA

Dunlap, Grant (Baseball Player)
St Louis Cardinals
1431 Alga Ct
Vista, CA 92081-5016, USA

Dunlap, Page (Golfer)
8728 Misty Creek Dr
Sarasota, FL 34241-9561, USA

Dunlap, Robert H (War Hero)
PO Box 584
Monmouth, IL 61462-0584, USA

Dunlap, Scott (Golfer)
104 Summerour Vale
Duluth, GA 30097-2464, USA

Dunleavy, Mary (Opera Singer)
Columbia Artists Mgmt
1790 Broadway Fl 6
New York, NY 10019-1412, USA

Dunleavy, Michael J (Mike) (Basketball Player, Coach)
Philadelphia 76ers
555 S Barrington Ave
Los Angeles, CA 90049-4344, USA

Dunleavy, Mike (Basketball Player)
Golden State Warriors
1001 Broadway
Oakland, CA 94607-4019, USA

Dunlop, Andy (Music Group, Musician)
Wildlife Entertainment
21 Heathmans Road
London SW6 4TJ, UNITED KINGDOM (UK)

Dunn, Adam (Baseball Player)
Cincinnati Reds
PO Box 105
Porter, TX 77365-0105, USA

Dunn, Andrew W (Cinematographer)
525 Broadway Ste 250
Santa Monica, CA 90401-2419, USA

Dunn, Gary (Football Player)
Pittsburgh Steelers
243 Navajo St
Tavernier, FL 33070-2119, USA

Dunn, Gertie (Baseball Player)
PO Box 88
Chadds Ford, PA 19317-0088, USA

Dunn, Gregory (Publisher)
Redbook Magazine
224 W 57th St
New York, NY 10019-3200, USA

Dunn, Holly (Actor, Musician)
Holly Dunn Enterprises
PO Box 2525
Hendersonville, TN 37077-2525, USA

Dunn, Keldrick (Football Player)
Tampa Bay Buccaneers
2264 Colleen Ct
Decatur, GA 30032-7153, USA

Dunn, Kevin (Actor)
c/o Staff Member *Lighthouse Entertainment*
409 N Camden Dr Ste 202
Beverly Hills, CA 90210-4423, USA

Dunn, Martin (Editor)
New York Daily News
220 E 42nd St
Editorial Dept
New York, NY 10017-5806, USA

Dunn, Mignon (Opera Singer)
Warden Assoc
5626 N Deer Run Rd
Doylestown, PA 18902-1912, USA

Dunn, Mike (Race Car Driver)
Circle A Racing
RR 24 Box 537A Keeney Lane
York, PA 17406, USA

Dunn, Moira (Golfer)
15803 Bridgewater Ln
Tampa, FL 33624-1044, USA

Dunn, Nora (Actor, Comedian)
c/o Steven Siebert *Lighthouse Entertainment*
409 N Camden Dr Ste 202
Beverly Hills, CA 90210-4423, USA

Dunn, Patricia (Tricia) (Hockey Player)
5 Twinbrook Dr
Derry, NH 03038-4358, USA

Dunn, Perry Lee (Football Player)
Dallas Cowboys
64 Glenway Pl
Brandon, MS 39042-2545, USA

Dunn, Ron (Baseball Player)
Chicago Cubs
1161 Husted Ave
San Jose, CA 95125-3633, USA

Dunn, Ronnie (Music Group, Songwriter, Writer)
Brooks & Dunn
PO Box 120669
Nashville, TN 37212-0669, USA

Dunn, Stephen (Writer)
Stockton State College
Humanities/Fine Arts Arts Dept
Pomona, NJ 08240, USA

Dunn, Stephen L (Religious Leader)
Churches of God General Conference
7176 Glenmeadow Ct
Frederick, MD 21703-1828, USA

Dunn, Steve (Baseball Player)
Minnesota Twins
484 Broadmoor Dr
Maryville, TN 37803-6575, USA

Dunn, Susan (Opera Singer)
1212 Lancaster Dr
Champaign, IL 61821-7002, USA

Dunn, T R (Basketball Player)
Portland Trail Blazers
1014 19th St SW
Birmingham, AL 35211-3623, USA

Dunn, Todd (Baseball Player)
Milwaukee Brewers
12030 London Lake Dr W
Jacksonville, FL 32258-3317, USA

Dunn, Warrick (Football Player)
Tampa Bay Buccaneers
305 Inner Harbour Cir
Tampa, FL 33602-5970, USA

Dunne, Dominick (Writer)
155 E 49th St
New York, NY 10017-1200, USA

Dunne, Griffin (Actor, Director)
c/o Geyer Kosinski *Media Talent Group*
9200 W Sunset Blvd Ste 810
W Hollywood, CA 90069-3603, USA

Dunne, Mike (Baseball Player)
Pittsburgh Pirates
5115 W Ancient Oak Dr
Peoria, IL 61615, USA

Dunne, Robin (Actor)
United Talent Agency
9560 Wilshire Blvd Ste 500
Beverly Hills, CA 90212-2401, USA

Dunne, Roisin (Music Group, Musician)
Rave Booking
PO Box 310780
Jamaica, NY 11431-0780, USA

Dunnigan, Frank J (Publisher)
1500 Palisade Ave
Fort Lee, NJ 07024-5337, USA

Dunnigan, T Kevin (Business Person)
Thomas & Betts Corp
8155 Thomas & Betts Blvd
Memphis, TN 38125, USA

Dunning, Debbe (Actor, Model)
1373 Crest Rd
Del Mar, CA 92014-2528, USA

Dunning, Steve (Baseball Player)
Cleveland Indians
609 Thackeray Ln
Fox River Grove, IL 60021-1839, USA

Dunphy, Jessica (Actor)
c/o Edie Robb *Creative Management Group*
3815 Hughes Ave Fl 3
Culver City, CA 90232-2715, USA

Dunphy, Marv (Coach, Volleyball Player)
33370 Decker School Rd
Malibu, CA 90265-2344, USA

Dunphy, T J Dermot (Business Person)
Sealed Air Corp
Park 80 Plaza E
Saddle Park, NJ 07663, USA

Dunsmore, Barrie (Correspondent)
ABC-TV
5010 Creston St
News Dept
Hyattsville, MD 20781-1216, USA

Dunst, Kirsten (Actor)
c/o Eric Kranzler *Management 360*
9111 Wilshire Blvd
Beverly Hills, CA 90210-5508, USA

Dunst, Kristen (Actor)
8916 Ashcroft Ave
West Hollywood, CA 90048-2404, USA

Dunstan, William (Football Player)
Philadelphia Eagles
PO Box 514
Rancho Mirage, CA 92270-0514, USA

Dunston, Shawon D (Baseball Player)
Chicago Cubs
957 Corte Del Sol
Fremont, CA 94539-4925, USA

Dunton, Gary C (Financier)
MBIA Inc
113 King St
Armonk, NY 10504-1610, USA

Dunwoody, Richard (Jockey, Race Car Driver)
14 Saint Maur Road Fulham
London SW6 4DP, UNITED KINGDOM (UK)

Dunwoody, Todd (Baseball Player)
Florida Marlins
1704 King Eider Dr
West Lafayette, IN 47906-6504, USA

Dunye, Cheryl (Actor, Director, Producer, Writer)
c/o Staff Member *Broder Webb Chervin Silbermann Agency, The (BWCS)*
10250 Constellation Blvd Ste P
Los Angeles, CA 90067-6213, USA

DuPlessis, Christian (Opera Singer)
Performing Arts
1 Hinde St
London W1M 5RH, UNITED KINGDOM (UK)

Dupont, Jacques (Misc, Politician)
Minister of State's Office
Boite Postale 522
Monaco-Cedex 98015, MONACO

DuPont, Margaret Osborne (Tennis Player)
415 Camino Real Ave
El Paso, TX 79922-2003, USA

DuPont, Pierre (Ex-Governor, Governor)
Richards Layton Finger
PO Box 551
1 Rodney Square
Wilmington, DE 19899-0551, USA

Dupont, Tiffany (Actor)
c/o Jeff Raymond *Nancy Iannios PR*
8687 Melrose Ave
West Hollywood, CA 90069-5701, USA

DuPree, Billy Joe (Football Player)
Dallas Cowboys
PO Box 720330
Dallas, TX 75372, USA

Dupree, Donald (Don) (Athlete)
3 Center St
Saranac Lake, NY 12983, USA

Dupree, Marcus (Football Player)
Los Angeles Rams
274 Davis St
Philadelphia, MS 39350-3431, USA

Dupree, Mike (Baseball Player)
San Diego Padres
2358 E Richmond Ave
Fresno, CA 93720-0438, USA

DuPrez, John (Composer)
Air-Edel
9255 W Sunset Blvd # 200
West Hollywood, CA 90069-3309, USA

Dupri, Jermaine (Musician)
c/o Staff Member *William Morris Agency (WMA-LA)*
1 William Morris Pl
Beverly Hills, CA 90212-4261, USA

Dupuis, Roy (Actor)
Agence Premier Role Inc
3451 Hotel de Ville
Montreal, PQ H2X 3B5, CANADA

Duque, Bernardo (Musician)
c/o Gabriel Blanco *Gabriel Blanco Iglesias (Mexico)*
Rio Balsas 35-32
Colonia Cuauhtemoc
DF 06500, MEXICO

Duque, Pedro (Astronaut)
1103 Virginia St
South Houston, TX 77587-3945, USA

Durack, David T (Physicist)
815 W Knox St
Durham, NC 27701-1645, USA

Duran, Clarence (Football Player)
St Louis Cardinals
13909 Alfeld Ave
Los Angeles, CA 90061-2123, USA

Duran, Dan (Baseball Player)
Texas Rangers
104 Brisbane Ter
Sunnyvale, CA 94086-5064, USA

Duran, Micki (Actor)
c/o Staff Member *DDO Artist Agency*
8322 Beverly Blvd Ste 301
Los Angeles, CA 90048-2665, USA

Duran, Roberto (Boxer)
Nuevo Reperto El Carmen
PANAMA

Duran Duran (Music Group)
c/o Staff Member *DD Productions*
93A Westbourne Park Villas
London W2 5ED, UNITED KINGDOM (UK)

Durance, Erica (Actor)
c/o Jeff Palffy *Ford Models (LA)*
8826 Burton Way
Beverly Hills, CA 90211-1715, USA

Durand, Kevin (Actor)
Stubbs Agency
1450 S Robertson Blvd
Los Angeles, CA 90035-3402, USA

Duranko, Peter (Football Player)
Denver Broncos
417 S Clearfield St
Johnstown, PA 15905-3327, USA

Durant, Graham J (Inventor)
Cambridge NeuroScience
333 Boston Providence Tumpike
Norwood, MA 02062, USA

Durant, Joe (Golfer)
8451 Sunshine Hill Rd
Molino, FL 32577-4168, USA

Durant, Mike (Baseball Player)
Minnesota Twins
7520 Marston Ln
Dublin, OH 43016-7029, USA

Durante, Viviana P (Ballerina)
20 Bristol Gardens Little Venice
London W9, UNITED KINGDOM (UK)

Durao Barroso, Jose Manuel (Prime Minister)
Prime Minister's Office
Rua do Imprensa a Estrela 8
Lisbon 1300, PORTUGAL

Durazo, Erubiel (Athlete, Baseball Player)
c/o Staff Member *Oakland Athletics*
7000 Coliseum Way
Oakland, CA 94621-1992, USA

Durbin, Chad (Baseball Player)
Kansas City Royals
15705 Malvem Hill Ave
Baton Rouge, LA 70817, USA

Durbin, Deanna (Actor, Music Group)
BP 3315
Paris Cedex 03 75123, FRANCE

Durbin, Mike (Bowler)
Professional Bowlers Assn
719 2nd Ave Ste 701
Seattle, WA 98104-1747, USA

Durcal, Rocio (Musician)
c/o Staff Member *BMG*
1540 Broadway
New York, NY 10036-4074, USA

Duren, John (Basketball Player)
Utah Jazz
1107 1st St NW
Washington, DC 20001-1304, USA

Duren, Rinold G (Ryne) (Baseball Player)
Baltimore Orioles
4068 Dunmore Dr
Lake Wales, FL 33859-5738, USA

Durham, Don (Baseball Player)
St Louis Cardinals
2627 Pennington Bend Rd
Nashville, TN 37214-1107, USA

Durham, Hugh (Basketball Player, Coach)
Jacksonville University
Athletic Dept
Jacksonville, FL 32211, USA

Durham, Jarrett (Basketball Player)
New Jersey Nets
18 McKelvey Ave
Pittsburgh, PA 15218-1454, USA

Durham, Joe (Baseball Player)
Chicago American Giants
9715 Mendoza Rd
Randallstown, MD 21133-2530, USA

Durham, Leon (Baseball Player)
St Louis Cardinals
1553 Williamson Dr
Cincinnati, OH 45240-1549, USA

Durham, Ray (Sugar Ray) (Baseball Player)
Chicago White Sox
721 Enterprise Dr Ste 201
Oak Brook, IL 60523-1994, USA

Duritz, Adam (Misc, Music Group, Songwriter, Writer)
Interscope Geffen A&M Records
2220 Colorado Ave
Santa Monica, CA 90404-3506, USA

Durkee, Charlie (Football Player)
New Orleans Saints
1210 Danbury Dr
Mansfield, TX 76063-3809, USA

Durkin, Clare (Model)
Ford Model Agency
142 Greene St # 400
New York, NY 10012-3236, USA

Durkin, John A (Senator)
60 Lenz St
Manchester, NH 03102-4918, USA

Durko, Sandy (Football Player)
Cincinnati Bengals
2020 Paseo Del Mar
Palos Verdes Estates, CA 90274-2659, USA

Durnbaugh, Bobby (Baseball Player)
Cincinnati Reds
1638 N Central Dr
Dayton, OH 45432-2118, USA

Durning, Charles (Actor)
10590 Wilshire Blvd Apt 506
Los Angeles, CA 90024-7333, USA

Durocher, Jayson (Baseball Player)
Milwaukee Brewers
34042 N 43rd St
Cave Creek, AZ 85331-4016, USA

Durr, Francoise
195 rue de Lourmel
Paris F-75015, FRANCE

Durr, Jason (Actor)
c/o Staff Member *Ken McReddie Ltd*
Paurelle House
91 Regent St
London W1R7TB, UNITED KINGDOM
(UK)

Durr Browning, Francoise (Tennis Player)
195 Rue de Lourmel
Paris, 75015, FRANCE

Durrance, Samuel T (Astronaut,
Astronomer)
770 Kerry Downs Cir
Melbourne, FL 32940-1774, USA

Durrant, Devin (Basketball Player)
Indiana Pacers
1716 W 1825 N
Provo, UT 84604-1115, USA

Durringer, Annemarie
Hawelgasse 17
Vienna 1180, AUSTRIA

Durrington, Trent (Baseball Player)
Anaheim Angels
499 N Canon Dr Apt 400
Beverly Hills, CA 90210-4842, USA

Durslag, Melvin
PO Box 559
Salisbury, NC 28145-0559, USA

Durst, Fred (Musician)
c/o Rick Yorn *The Firm*
9465 Wilshire Blvd Fl 6
Beverly Hills, CA 90212-2605, USA

Durst, Will (Actor, Comedian)
Entertainment Alliance
PO Box 1544
Mendocino, CA 95460-1544, USA

Dusay, Debra (Actor)
Susan Nathe
8281 Melrose Ave Ste 200
Los Angeles, CA 90046-6890, USA

Dusay, Mari (Actor)
320 W 66th St
New York, NY 10023-6304, USA

Dusay, Marj (Actor)
Susan Nathe
8281 Melrose Ave Ste 200
Los Angeles, CA 90046-6890, USA

Dusbabek, Mark (Football Player)
Minnesota Vikings
11452 Dona Dorotea Dr
Studio City, CA 91604-4246, USA

Dusek, Brad (Football Player)
Washington Redskins
The 4th Quarter Ranch 8311 Fm 2086
Temple, TX 76501, USA

Dusenberry, Ann (Actor)
1615 San Leandro Ln
Montecito, CA 93108, USA

Duser, Carl (Baseball Player)
Kansas City A's
3021 Cornwall Rd
Bethlehem, PA 18017-3313, USA

Dushku, Eliza (Actor)
c/o Jim Toth *Creative Artists Agency LCC
(CAA-LA)*
2000 Avenue Of The Stars
Los Angeles, CA 90067-4700, USA

Dushku, Nate (Actor)
c/o Matt Schwartz *Atlas Entertainment*
6100 Wilshire Blvd Ste 1170
Los Angeles, CA 90048-5116, USA

Dussault, Jean H (Misc)
Laval Medical Center
2705 Blvd Laurier
Sainte Foy, PQ G1V 4G2, CANADA

Dussault, Nancy (Actor, Music Group)
4406 Moorpark Way
Toluca Lake, CA 91602-2409, USA

Dust, Angel (Music Group)
Digger International
164 Division St Ste 408
Elgin, IL 60120-5530, USA

Dustrude-Roberson, Beverly (Baseball
Player)
2422 Lobelia Dr
Oxnard, CA 93036-6260, USA

Dutch, Deborah (Actor)
850 N Kings Rd # 100
West Hollywood, CA 90069-5442, USA

Dutilleux, Henri (Composer)
12 Rue Saint Louis-en-l'sle
Paris 75004, FRANCE

Dutoit, Charles E
Montreal Symphony
85 Sainte Catherine St W
Montreal, PQ H2X 3P4, CANADA

Dutt, Hank (Music Group, Musician)
Kronos Quartet
1235 9th Ave
San Francisco, CA 94122-2306, USA

Dutt, Sanjay (Actor, Bollywood)
58 Smt Nargis Dutt Road
Pali Hill Bandra(W)
Mumbai, MS 400050, INDIA

Dutta, Divya (Actor, Bollywood)
C-17 Nehru Nagar
Kishore Kumar Gangulay Marg Juhu Tara
Road
Mumbai, MS 400049, INDIA

Dutta, Lara (Beauty Pageant Winner)
c/o Staff Member *Miss Universe
Organization, The*
1370 Avenue Of The Americas Fl 16
New York, NY 10019-4602, USA

Dutton, Charles S (Actor)
10061 Riverside Dr # 821
Toluca Lake, CA 91602-2560, USA

Dutton, John O (Football Player)
Baltimore Colts
5706 Moss Creek Trl
Dallas, TX 75252-2380, USA

Dutton, Lawrence (Music Group,
Musician)
I M G Artists
3 Burlington Lane Chiswick
London W4 2TH, UNITED KINGDOM
(UK)

Dutton, Simon (Actor)
Marmont Management
Langham House 302/8 Regent St
London W1R 5AL, UNITED KINGDOM
(UK)

Duva, Lou (Boxer, Misc)
Main Events
811 Totowa Rd # 100
Totowa, NJ 07512-1207, USA

Duval, David (Golfer)
c/o Staff Member *Pro Golfers Assoc of
America (PGA)*
100 Avenue Of The Champions
Palm Beach Gardens, FL 33418-3653,
USA

Duval, Dennis (Basketball Player)
Washington Bullets
8105 Verbeck Dr
Manlius, NY 13104-9306, USA

Duval, Helen (Bowler)
1624 Posen Ave
Berkeley, CA 94707-2736, USA

Duval, James (Jimmy) (Actor)
c/o Ryan Revel *Imparato Fay Management*
1126 Roxbury Dr
Los Angeles, CA 90035-1031, USA

Duval, Juliette (Actor)
Cineart
36 Rue de Ponthieu
Paris 75008, FRANCE

Duval, Mike (Baseball Player)
Tampa Bay Devil Rays
2743 Nature Pointe Loop
Fort Myers, FL 33905-2468, USA

Duvall, Brad (Baseball Player)
Bowman
438 Sycamore Trl
Woodstock, GA 30189-7423, USA

Duvall, Carol (Television Host)
c/o Staff Member *HGTV/Home & Garden
Television*
9721 Sherrill Blvd
Knoxville, TN 37932-3330, USA

DuVall, Clea (Actor)
Innovative Artists
1505 10th St
Santa Monica, CA 90401-2805, USA

Duvall, Jed (Correspondent)
ABC-TV
5010 Creston St
News Dept
Hyattsville, MD 20781-1216, USA

Duvall, Robert (Actor)
c/o Staff Member *Butchers Run Films*
1041 N Formosa Ave
Santa Monica Bldg E #200
W Hollywood, CA 90046-6703, USA

Duvall, Sammy (Skier)
PO Box 871
Windermere, FL 34786-0871, USA

Duvall-Hero, Camille (Skier)
PO Box 871
Windermere, FL 34786-0871, USA

Duvignaud, Jean (Writer)
28 Rue Saint-Leonard
La Rochelle 1700, FRANCE

Duvillard, Henri (Skier)
Le Monte d'Arbois
Megere 74120, FRANCE

Duwelius, Rick (Volleyball Player)
345 W Juniper St Apt 5
San Diego, CA 92101-1347, USA

Duwez, Pol E (Physicist)
1535 Oakdale St
Pasadena, CA 91106-3552, USA

Dvorak, Richard (Football Player)
New York Giants
13587 SE 230 Rd
Spearville, KS 67876-7506, USA

Dvorovenko, Irina (Ballerina)
Amirican Ballet Theatre
890 Broadway
New York, NY 10003-1278, USA

Dvorsky, Peter (Opera Singer)
Bradianska Ulica 11
Bratislave SK-811 08, SLOVAKIA

Dwight, Edward Jr (Astronaut)
4022 Montview Blvd
Denver, CO 80207-3713, USA

Dwight, Tim (Football Player)
Atlanta Falcons
26164 Indigo Dr
Park Rapids, MN 56470-5189, USA

Dwork, Melvin (Designer)
Melvin Dwork Inc
196 Avenue Of The Americas
New York, NY 10013-1234, USA

Dworkins, Lenny (Len) (Cartoonist)
2906 Wilmette Ave
Wilmette, IL 60091-2136, USA

Dworsky, Daniel L (Dan) (Architect,
Football Player)
Los Angeles Dons
9225 Nightingale Dr
Los Angeles, CA 90069-1117, USA

Dwyer, Bil (Game Show Host)
c/o Staff Member *OmniPop Inc (LA)*
4605 Lankershim Blvd Ste 201
North Hollywood, CA 91602-1874, USA

Dwyer, Jim (Baseball Player)
St Louis Cardinals
7607 159th Pl
Tinley Park, IL 60477-1314, USA

Dwyer, Karyn (Actor)
Oscars Abrams Zimel
438 Queen St E
Toronto, ON M5A 1T4, CANADA

Dyal, Mike (Football Player)
Oakland Raiders
609 Rock Creek Loop
Kerrville, TX 78028-6506, USA

Dybdahl, Thomas (Musician)
c/o Staff Member *Paradigm (Monterey)*
509 Hartnell St
Monterey, CA 93940-2825, USA

Dybzinski, Jerry (Baseball Player)
Cleveland Indians
1626 Haywood Pl
Fort Collins, CO 80526-2289, USA

Dychtwald, Ken (Doctor, Misc)
Age Wave Inc
1900 Powell St
Emeryville, CA 94608-1811, USA

Dydek, Malforzata (Margo) (Basketball
Player)
San Antonio Silver Stars
1 Sbc Center Pkwy
San Antonio, TX 78219-3604, USA

Dye, Cameron (Actor)
13035 Woodbridge St
Studio City, CA 91604-1431, USA

Dye, Ernest (Football Player)
Phoenix Cardinals
114 Flatwood Rd
Hodges, SC 29653-9493, USA

Dye, Ian (Composer)
Gorfaine/Schwartz
4111 W Alameda Ave Ste 509
Burbank, CA 91505-4171, USA

Dye, Jermaine (Baseball Player)
Atlanta Braves
6855 N 66th Pl
Paradise Valley, AZ 85253, USA

Dye, John (Actor)
William Morris Agency
151 El Camino Dr
Beverly Hills, CA 90212-2775, USA

Dye, Lee (Architect, Golfer, Misc)
Dye Designs
5500 E Yale Ave
Denver, CO 80222-6925, USA

Dye, Melissa Dori (Musician)
c/o Staff Member *Dye Productions*
5403 Everhart Rd # 140
Corpus Christi, TX 78411-4805, USA

Dye, Nancy Schrom (Educator)
Oberlin College
President's Office
Oberlin, OH 44074, USA

Dye, Tyrone (Football Player)
Washington Redskins
410 E Washington St
City Of Iowa City Parking Dept Attn:
Enforcement Division
Iowa City, IA 52240-1825, USA

Dyer, Danny (Actor)
c/o Staff Member *International Creative
Management (ICM-LA)*
10250 Constellation Blvd
Los Angeles, CA 90067-6200, USA

Dyer, David W (Judge)
US Court of Appeals
300 NE 1st Ave Ste 115
Miami, FL 33132-2136, USA

Dyer, Duffy (Baseball Player)
New York Mets
742 W Las Palmaritas Dr
Phoenix, AZ 85021-5545, USA

Dyer, Hector (Athlete, Track Athlete)
1620 E Chapman Ave # 214
Fullerton, CA 92831-4016, USA

Dyer, Henry (Football Player)
Los Angeles Rams
23464 Reames Rd
Zachary, LA 70791-6603, USA

Dyer, Joseph W Jr (Admiral)
Commander Naval Air Systems Command
Patuxent River, MD 20670, USA

Dyer, Ken (Football Player)
San Diego Chargers
1151 S Sandstone Ct
Gilbert, AZ 85296-3743, USA

Dyer, Mike (Baseball Player)
Minnesota Twins
22392 Manacor
Mission Viejo, CA 92692-1188, USA

Dyer, Wayne W (Writer)
Hay House
PO Box 5100
Carlsbad, CA 92018-5100, USA

Dyk, Timothy B (Judge)
US Court of Appeals
717 Madison Pl NW
Washington, DC 20439-0001, USA

Dyke, Charles W (General, Misc)
International Technical/Trade Assoc
1330 Connecticut Ave NW
Washington, DC 20036-1704, USA

Dykema, Craig (Basketball Player)
Phoenix Suns
10525 Destino St
Bellflower, CA 90706-7125, USA

Dykes, Hart Lee (Football Player)
New England Patriots
30 Dorothea Ln
Sugar Land, TX 77479-2446, USA

Dykes Bower, John (Music Group,
Musician)
4Z Artillery Mansions Westminster
London SW1, UNITED KINGDOM (UK)

Dykhoff, Radhames (Baseball Player)
Baltimore Orioles
105 Angelfish Ln
Jupiter, FL 33477-7227, USA

Dykinga, Jack (Journalist, Photographer)
1519 E Tascal Loop
Tucson, AZ 85737-8570, USA

Dykstra, John (Animator, Artist,
Cinematographer)
15060 Encanto Dr
Sherman Oaks, CA 91403-4408, USA

Dykstra, Leonard K (Lenny) (Baseball
Player)
New York Mets
1072 Newbern Ct
Thousand Oaks, CA 91361-5346, USA

Dylan, Bob (Music Group, Songwriter,
Writer)
c/o Brian Greenbaum *Creative Artists
Agency LCC (CAA-LA)*
2000 Avenue Of The Stars
Los Angeles, CA 90067-4700, USA

Dylan, Jakob (Music Group)
H K Mgmt
9200 W Sunset Blvd Ste 530
Los Angeles, CA 90069-3509, USA

Dymally, Mervyn M (Misc)
Dymally International Group
9111 S La Cienega Blvd
Compton, CA 90220, USA

Dyrdek, Rob (Skateboarder)
c/o Staff Member *MTV Films*
5555 Melrose Ave
Modular Bldg #213
Los Angeles, CA 90038-3989, USA

Dysart, Richard (Actor)
654 Copeland Ct
Santa Monica, CA 90405-4416, USA

Dyson, Andre (Football Player)
Tennessee Titans
3367 N Shoreline Cir
Layton, UT 84040-7128, USA

Dyson, Esther (Business Person, Writer)
Edventure Holdings
104 5th Ave # 2000
New York, NY 10011-6901, USA

Dyson, Freeman J (Physicist, Writer)
105 Battle Road Cir
Princeton, NJ 08540-4904, USA

Dyson, Michael Eric (Writer)
DePaul University
English Dept
Chicago, IL 60604, USA

Dystel, Oscar (Publisher)
Springs Purchase Hills Dr
Purchase, NY 10577, USA

Dzau, Victor (Misc, Scientist)
Stanford University Hospital
Cardiovascular Medicine Div
Stanford, CA 94305, USA

Dzeliwe (Misc)
Royal Palace
Mbabane, SWAZILAND

Dzhanibekov, Vladimir A (Astronaut,
General, Misc)
Potchta Kosmonavtov
Moskovskoi Oblasti
Syvisdny Goroduk 141160, RUSSIA

Dzhanibelkov, Vladimir
Potchka Kosmon 141 160 Svyosdny
Gorodok
Moscow, RUSSIA

Dziena, Alexis (Actor)
c/o Paul Martino *International Creative
Management (ICM-NY)*
40 W 57th St
New York, NY 10019-4001, USA

Dziura, Jennifer (Comedian)
316 W 39th St Apt 3W
New York, NY 10018-1420, USA

Dzundza, George (Actor)
c/o Glen Robbins *Raw Talent
Management*
9615 Brighton Way Ste 300
Beverly Hills, CA 90210-5118, USA

Dzurlnda, Mikulas (Prime Minister)
Prime Minister's Office
Nam Slobody 1
Bratislava 1 81370, SLOVAKIA

E 40 (Music Group)
BME Recordings
2144 Hills Ave NW Ste D2
Atlanta, GA 30318-2805, USA

E-Type (Music Group)
c/o Staff Member *Agency Group Ltd, The
(Denmark)*
Slotsgade 2 Fl 2
Copenhagen 2200, DENMARK

Eackles, Ledell (Basketball Player)
Washington Bullets
9134 Elmgrove Garden Dr
Baton Rouge, LA 70807-4307, USA

Eaddy, Don (Baseball Player)
Chicago Cubs
5394 Effingham Dr SE
Grand Rapids, MI 49508-6308, USA

Eade, George J (General)
1131 Sunnyside Dr
Healdsburg, CA 95448-3536, USA

Eads, Ora W (Religious Leader)
Christian Congregation
804 W Hemlock St
La Follette, TN 37766, USA

Eads III, George Coleman (Actor)
c/o Alan Iezman *Shelter Entertainment*
9255 W Sunset Blvd Ste 1010
Los Angeles, CA 90069-3307, USA

Eagan, James (Writer)
c/o Greg Cavic *Creative Artists Agency
LCC (CAA-LA)*
2000 Avenue Of The Stars
Los Angeles, CA 90067-4700, USA

Eagle, Ian (Sportscaster)
CBS-TV
51 W 52nd St
Sports Dept
New York, NY 10019-6119, USA

Eagle-Eye Cherry (Music Group)
c/o Staff Member *Paradigm (Monterey)*
509 Hartnell St
Monterey, CA 93940-2825, USA

Eagleburger, Lawrence S (Secretary)
1450 Osensville Rd
Charlottesville, VA 22901, USA

Eaglen, Jane (Opera Singer)
Columbia Artists Mgmt Inc
1790 Broadway Fl 6
New York, NY 10019-1412, USA

Eagles, The (Musician)
c/o Staff Member *William Morris Agency
(WMA-LA)*
1 William Morris Pl
Beverly Hills, CA 90212-4261, USA

Eagleson, Alan (Hockey Player)
37 Maitland St
Toronto, ON M4Y 1C8, CANADA

Eagleton, Thomas (Ex-Senator, Senator)
1 Mercantile Center
St Louis, MO 63101, USA

Eagleton, Thomas F (Senator)
1 Firstar Center
Saint Louis, MO 63101, USA

Eagling, Wayne J (Choreographer,
Dancer)
Postbus 16486
1001 RN
Amsterdam, THE NETHERLANDS

Eakes, Bobbie (Actor)
c/o Staff Member *William Morris Agency
(WMA-LA)*
1 William Morris Pl
Beverly Hills, CA 90212-4261, USA

Eakin, Richard R (Educator)
East Carolina University
Chancellor's Office
Greenville, NC 27858, USA

Eakin, Thomas C (Business Person)
245 Sandover Dr
Shaker Heights
Aurora, OH 44202-8774, USA

Eakins, Gretchen (Actor)
Mattie Management
1438 N Gower St Ste 34 Ste 2
C/O Mattie Semradek
Los Angeles, CA 90028-8362, USA

Eakins, James(Jim) (Basketball Player)
2575 E 9600 S
Sandy, UT 84092-3469, USA

Eakins, Jim (Basketball Player)
Oakland Oaks
2575 Little Cottonwood Rd
Sandy, UT 84092-3469, USA

Eaks, R W (Golfer)
9129 E Daveport Dr
Scottsdale, AZ 85260, USA

Ealy, Michael (Actor)
c/o Darryl Taja *Epidemic Pictures and
Management*
1635 N Cahuenga Blvd Fl 5
Hollywood, CA 90028-6201, USA

Earl, Anthony S (Governor)
2810 Arbor Dr Unit B
Madison, WI 53711-1809, USA

Earl, Robin D (Football Player)
Chicago Bears
9 Middlebury Ln
Lincolnshire, IL 60069-4027, USA

Earl, Roger (Musician)
Lustig Talent
PO Box 770850
Orlando, FL 32877-0850, USA

Earl, Scott (Baseball Player)
Detroit Tigers
37 Henry St
North Vernon, IN 47265-1048, USA

Earle, Acie (Basketball Player)
Boston Celtics
2301 14th Ave
Moline, IL 61265-3203, USA

Earle, Ed (Basketball Player)
Syracuse Nationals
1940 Burton Ln
Park Ridge, IL 60068-1572, USA

Earle, Sylvia Alice (Oceanographer)
12812 Skyline Blvd
Oakland, CA 94619-3125, USA

Earley, Anthony F Jr (Business Person)
Detroit Edison
2000 2nd Ave
Detroit, MI 48226-1203, USA

Earley, Bill (Baseball Player)
St Louis Cardinals
112 Carruthers Pond Dr
Cincinnati, OH 45246-3854, USA

Earley, Liz (Golfer)
24 Morton Dr
Buffalo, NY 14226-3338, USA

Earley, Michael M (Business Person)
Triton Group
550 W C St
San Diego, CA 92101-3540, USA

Early, Gerald L (Writer)
Washington University
English Dept
Saint Louis, MO 63130, USA

Earnhardt, R Dale Jr (Race Car Driver)
1675 Coddle Creek Hwy
Mooresville, NC 28115, USA

Earon, Blaine (Football Player)
Detroit Lions
6640 Lake Run Dr
Flowery Branch, GA 30542-3895, USA

Earp, Mildred (Baseball Player)
217 Dolly
West Fork, AR 72774, USA

Earth Wind & Fire (Music Group)
c/o Jeff Frasco *Creative Artists Agency
LCC (CAA-LA)*
2000 Avenue Of The Stars
Los Angeles, CA 90067-4700, USA

Easler, Mike (Baseball Player)
Houston Astros
5650 Red Roof St
North Las Vegas, NV 89081-2439, USA

Easley, Bill (Musician)
Hot Jazz Mgmt
328 W 43rd St # 4fw
New York, NY 10036, USA

Easley, Damlon (Baseball Player)
California Angels
14125 N 65th Ave
Glendale, AZ 85306-3757, USA

Easley, Kenny (Football Player)
Seattle Seahawks
3906 Kegagie Dr
Norfolk, VA 23518-1500, USA

Eason, Eric (Actor)
c/o Staff Member *Creative Artists Agency
LCC (CAA-LA)*
2000 Avenue Of The Stars
Los Angeles, CA 90067-4700, USA

Eason, Tony (Football Player)
851 Cocos Dr
San Marcos, CA 92078-5058, USA

East, Jeff (Actor)
c/o Vaughn Hart *Vaughn Hart &
Associates*
8899 Beverly Blvd
Los Angeles, CA 90048-2412, USA

East, Ron (Football Player)
Dallas Cowboys
22125 NE 62nd Pl
Redmond, WA 98053-2306, USA

East 17
Box 153 Stanmore
Middlesex, ENGLAND HA7 2HF,
UNITED KINGDOM (UK)

Easterbrook, Frank (Judge)
US Court of Appeals
111 N Canal St Bldg 6
Chicago, IL 60606-7206, USA

Easterbrook, Leslie (Actor)
c/o Richard Kerner *KMA*
311 N Robertson Blvd # 288
Beverly Hills, CA 90211-1705, USA

Easterling, Ray (Football Player)
Atlanta Falcons
3420 Traylor Dr
Richmond, VA 23235-1750, USA

Easterly, David E (Business Person)
Cox Enterprises
1400 Lake Hearn Dr NE
Atlanta, GA 30319-1418, USA

Easterly, Jamie (Baseball Player)
Atlanta Braves
1306 Plantation Dr
Crockett, TX 75835-2314, USA

Easterly, Richard (Football Player)
San Francisco 49ers
206 S Gardenia Ave
Tampa, FL 33609-2506, USA

Eastern Conference Champions (Music
Group)
c/o Staff Member *Paradigm (Monterey)*
509 Hartnell St
Monterey, CA 93940-2825, USA

Eastham, Dean E (Physicist)
281 Bloomingbank Rd
Riverside, IL 60546-2246, USA

Eastin, Steve (Actor)
c/o Staff Member *Agency for the
Performing Arts (APA-LA)*
405 S Beverly Dr
Beverly Hills, CA 90212-4416, USA

Eastman, John (Attorney, Attorney
General, General)
Eastman & Eastman
39 W 54th St
New York, NY 10019-5404, USA

Eastman, Kevin (Cartoonist)
Teenage Mutant ninja Turtles
PO Box 417
Haydenville, MA 01039-0417, USA

Eastman, Madeline (Musician)
Prince/SF Productions
1450 Southgate Ave Apt 206
Daly City, CA 94015-4021, USA

Eastman, Marilyn (Actor)
Hardman-Eastman Studios
138 Hawthome St
Pittsburgh, PA 15218, USA

Eastman, Rodney (Actor)
c/o Staff Member *Leslie Allan-Rice
Management*
7524 Mulholland Dr
Los Angeles, CA 90046-1239, USA

Easton, Michael (Actor)
c/o Danielle Allman *Allman/Rea
Management*
141 S Barrington Ave Ste E
Los Angeles, CA 90049-3314, USA

Easton, Millard E (Bill) (Coach)
1704 NW Weatherstone Dr
Blue Springs, MO 64015-6317, USA

Easton, Robert
Paul Kohner
9300 Wilshire Blvd Ste 555
Beverly Hills, CA 90212-3211, USA

Easton, Sheena (Musician)
Emmis Mgmt
18136 Califa St
Tarzana, CA 91356-1718, USA

Eastwick, Rawly (Baseball Player)
Cincinnati Reds
10 River Meadow Dr
West Newbury, MA 01985-1400, USA

Eastwick-Field, Elizabeth (Architect)
Low Farm Low Road
Denham Eye
Suffolk IP21 5ET, UNITED KINGDOM
(UK)

Eastwood, Alison (Actor, Model)
c/o Bob McGowan *McGowan
Management*
8733 W Sunset Blvd Ste 103
W Hollywood, CA 90069-2241, USA

Eastwood, Bob (Golfer)
PO Box 14769
Haltom City, TX 76117-0769, USA

Eastwood, Clint (Actor, Producer)
c/o Staff Member *Malpaso Productions*
4000 Warner Bros Ste 101 Bldg 81
Burbank, CA 91522-0001, USA

Eastwood, Kyle
2049 Century Park E Ste 3500
Los Angeles, CA 90067-3217, USA

Easum, Donald B (Diplomat)
801 W End Ave Apt 3A
New York, NY 10025-5361, USA

Easy, Omar (Football Player)
Kansas City Chiefs
40 Willow Dr
Saint Augustine, FL 32080-5937, USA

Eathorne, A J (Golfer)
23023 N 25th Pl
Phoenix, AZ 85024-7567, USA

Eaton, Adam (Baseball Player)
401 N Angford Dr
Ellensburg, WA 98926-3276, USA

Eaton, Andrew (Producer)
c/o Staff Member *Revolution Films*
9A Dallington St
London EC1V 0BQ, UNITED KINGDOM
(UK)

Eaton, Brando (Actor)
c/o Staff Member *Art Work Entertainment*
5900 Wilshire Blvd Ste 2150
Los Angeles, CA 90036-5021, USA

Eaton, Craig (Baseball Player)
3307 Baltusrol Ln
Lake Worth, FL 33467-1301, USA

Eaton, Dan L (Doctor)
Genentech Inc
460 Point San Bruno Blvd
South San Francisco, CA 94080-4939,
USA

Eaton, Don (Babtunde) (Composer,
Musician)
Agency Group Ltd
370 City Road
London EC1V 2QA, UNITED KINGDOM
(UK)

Eaton, John C (Composer)
4585 N Hartstrait Rd
Bloomington, IN 47404-9318, USA

Eaton, Mark (Basketball Player)
Utah Jazz
2104 Dayton Ave NE
Renton, WA 98056-2719, USA

Eaton, Mark E (Basketball Player)
PO Box 982108
Park City, UT 84098-2108, USA

Eaton, Meredith (Actor)
Susan Smith
1344 N Wetherly Dr
Los Angeles, CA 90069-1817, USA

Eaton, Shirley (Actor)
Guild House
Upper Saint Martin's Lane
London WC2H PEG, UNITED KINGDOM
(UK)

Eaton, Tracey (Football Player)
Houston Oilers
PO Box 881
Preston, WA 98050-0881, USA

Eave, Gary (Baseball Player)
Atlanta Braves
1601 King Ave
Bastrop, LA 71220-4957, USA

Eaves, Jerry (Basketball Player)
Utah Jazz
10 Perch Pl
Greensboro, NC 27455-3437, USA

Ebadi, Shirin (Nobel Prize Laureate)
University of Tehran
Enghelab Ave & 16 Azar St
Tehran, IRAN

Ebanks, Selita (Actor)
c/o Staff Member *Blueprint Management*
5670 Wilshire Blvd Ste 2525
Los Angeles, CA 90036-5647, USA

Ebashi, Setsuro (Physicist)
17-503 Nahaizumi Myodaiji
Okazaki 444, JAPAN

Ebben, Bill (Basketball Player)
Detroit Pistons
12254 Colliers Reserve Dr
Naples, FL 34110-0910, USA

Ebel, David M (Judge)
US Court of Appeals
1929 Stout St
US Courthouse
Denver, CO 80294-0003, USA

The Celebrity Black Book 2008

Eben, Petr (Composer)
Hamsikova 19
Prague 150 00 Prague 5, CZECH
REPUBLIC

Ebensteiner, June
20100 Wells Dr
Woodland Hills, CA 91364-4728, USA

Eber, Richard (Football Player)
Atlanta Falcons
13 Stoney Pt
Laguna Niguel, CA 92677-1000, USA

Eberhard, Al (Basketball Player)
Detroit Pistons
203 W Parkway Dr
Columbia, MO 65203-3450, USA

Eberhart, Ralph E (Ed) (General)
Commander
US Northen Command
Peterson Air Force Base, CO 80914, USA

Eberharter, Stefan (Skier)
Dorfstr 21
6272 Stumm
AUSTRIA

Eberle, Markus (Skier)
Unterwestweg 27
Rieztem 87567, GERMANY

Eberle, William D (Business Person)
13 Garland Rd
Concord, MA 01742-2214, USA

Ebershoff, David (Writer)
Viking Press
375 Hudson St
New York, NY 10014-3658, USA

Ebersole, Dick (Business Person)
174 West St # 54
Litchfield, CT 06759-3434, USA

Ebersole, Drew (Actor)
c/o Staff Member *The House of
Representatives*
211 S Beverly Dr Ste 208
Beverly Hills, CA 90212-3879, USA

Ebersole, John (Football Player)
New York Jets
1470 Village Sq
Mount Pleasant, SC 29464-4626, USA

Ebert, Derrin (Baseball Player)
Atlanta Braves
6866 Svl Box
Victorville, CA 92395-5174, USA

Ebert, Peter (Musician)
Col di Mura
06010 Lippiano, ITALY

Ebert, Robert D (Physicist)
16 Brewster Rd
Wayland, MA 01778-3704, USA

Ebert, Roger (Actor, Critic, Writer)
Ephraim & Associates P.C.
108 W Grand Ave
Chicago, IL 60610-4206, USA

Eberts, Jake (Producer)
c/o Staff Member *National Geographic
Feature Films*
9100 Wilshire Blvd Ste 401E
Beverly Hills, CA 90212-3400, USA

Ebi, Ndudi (Basketball Player)
Minnesota Timberwolves
600 1st Ave N
Target Center
Minneapolis, MN 55403-1416, USA

Ebli, Ray (Football Player)
Chicago Cardinals
2091 Balsam Way
Green Bay, WI 54313-9344, USA

Ebrahim, Vincent (Actor)
c/o Staff Member *BBC Artist Mail*
PO Box 1116
Belfast BT2 7AJ, UNITED KINGDOM
(UK)

Ebron, Roy (Basketball Player)
Utah Stars
550 Ahoskie Cofield Rd
Ahoskie, NC 27910-8270, USA

Ebsen, Bonnie (Actor)
PO Box 356
Agoura, CA 91376-0356, USA

Eccleston, Christopher (Actor)
c/o Brian Swardstrom *Endeavor Agency
LLC (LA)*
9601 Wilshire Blvd Fl 3
Beverly Hills, CA 90210-5204, USA

Ecclestone, Bernie (Race Car Driver)
Formula One Ltd
6 Prince's Gate
London, England SW7 1QJ, UNITED
KINGDOM (UK)

Ecclestone, Timothy J (Tim) (Hockey
Player)
10095 Fairway Village Dr
Roswell, GA 30076-3718, USA

Ecevit, Bulent (Prime Minister)
Or-An Sehri 69/5
Ankara, TURKEY

Echevarria, Angel (Baseball Player)
Colorado Rockies
23830 231st Pl SE
Maple Valley, WA 98038-5257, USA

Echeverria Alvarez, Luis (President)
Magnolia 131
San Jeronimo Lidice
Magdalena Contreras, CP 10200,
MEXICO

Echikunwoke, Megalyn (Actor)
c/o Sandy Bresler *Bresler Kelly &
Associates*
11500 W Olympic Blvd Ste 352
Los Angeles, CA 90064-1525, USA

Eck, Keith (Football Player)
New York Giants
7426 Solano St
Carlsbad, CA 92009-7527, USA

Eckenstahler, Eric (Baseball Player)
Detroit Tigers
305 S Prospect Rd Apt 2
Bloomington, IL 61704-4553, USA

Eckersley, Dennis (Baseball Player)
6 Macy Ln
Ipswich, MA 01938-1185, USA

Eckert, Aaron (Actor)
Creative Artists Agency
9830 Wilshire Blvd
Beverly Hills, CA 90212-1804, USA

Eckert, Robert (Business Person)
Mattel Inc
333 Continental Blvd
El Segundo, CA 90245-5032, USA

Eckert, Shari (Actor)
PO Box 5761
Sherman Oaks, CA 91413-5761, USA

Eckhart, Aaron (Actor)
Creative Artists Agency
9830 Wilshire Blvd
Beverly Hills, CA 90212-1804, USA

Eckholdt, Steven (Actor)
137 N Larchmont Blvd # 138
Los Angeles, CA 90004-3704, USA

Eckhouse, James
4222 Murietta Ave
Sherman Oaks, CA 91423-4225, USA

Ecklund, Brad (Football Player)
New York Yankees
155 Huntington Dr
Southampton, NJ 08088-1255, USA

Ecko, Marc (Fashion Designer, Producer)
c/o David Schiff *Schiff Company*
9465 Wilshire Blvd Ste 480
Beverly Hills, CA 90212-2603, USA

Eckstein, David (Baseball Player)
Anaheim Angels
103 Aldean Dr
Sanford, FL 32771-3612, USA

Eckwood, Jerry (Football Player)
Tampa Bay Buccaneers
496 Pickett Rd
Memphis, TN 38109-7365, USA

Eco, Umberto (Tennis Player)
Piazza Castello 13
Milan 20121, ITALY

Econoline Crush
1505 N. 2nd Ave. #200
Vancouver, BC V6H 3Y4, CANADA

Edberg, Stefan (Tennis Player)
ProServe
1101 Woodrow Wilson Blvd #1800
Arlington, VA 22209, USA

Eddie, Patrick (Basketball Player)
New York Knicks
4424 N 76th St Apt 3
Milwaukee, WI 53218-5336, USA

Eddie X (DJ)
c/o Staff Member *Diva Central Inc*
7510 W Sunset Blvd Ste 1445
Los Angeles, CA 90046-3408, USA

Eddings, Floyd (Football Player)
New York Giants
825 Franklin Ave SW
Birmingham, AL 35211, USA

Eddy, Chris (Baseball Player)
Oakland A's
47 Winterbury Cir
Wilmington, DE 19808-1429, USA

Eddy, Don (Baseball Player)
Chicago White Sox
PO Box 537
Rockwell, IA 50469-0537, USA

Eddy, Nicholas M (nick) (Football Player)
Detroit Lions
2225 London Cir
Modesto, CA 95356-0731, USA

Eddy, Sonya (Actor)
c/o Staff Member *Marshak/Zachary
Company, The*
8840 Wilshire Blvd Fl 1
Beverly Hills, CA 90211-2606, USA

Eddy, Steve (Baseball Player)
California Angels
700 N Dobson Rd Unit 38
Chandler, AZ 85224-6940, USA

Edelen, Joe (Baseball Player)
St Louis Cardinals
PO Box 38
Washington, OK 73093-0038, USA

Edelin, Kent (Basketball Player)
Indiana Pacers
1200 Braddock Pi Apt 211
Alexandria, VA 22314, USA

Edell, Marc Z (Attorney, Attorney
General, General)
Budd Larner Gross
150 John F Kennedy Pkwy Ste 301
Short Hills, NJ 07078-2701, USA

Edelman, Brad M (Football Player)
New Orleans Saints
14813 Grantley Dr
Chesterfield, MO 63017-5566, USA

Edelman, Gerald M (Nobel Prize
Laureate)
Scripps Research Institute
Neurobiology Dept
La Jolla, CA 92037, USA

Edelman, Marian Wright (Business
Person)
Children's Defense Fund
25 E St NW
Washington, DC 20001-1591, USA

Edelman, Pawel (Cinematographer)
c/o Staff Member *International Creative
Management (ICM-LA)*
10250 Constellation Blvd
Los Angeles, CA 90067-6200, USA

Edelman, Randy (Composer)
Gorfaine/Schwartz
4111 W Alameda Ave Ste 509
Burbank, CA 91505-4171, USA

Edelstein, Jean (Artist)
48 Brooks Ave
Venice, CA 90291-3226, USA

Edelstein, Lisa (Actor)
I F A Talent Agency
8730 W Sunset Blvd Ste 490
Los Angeles, CA 90069-2248, USA

Edelstein, Lisa (Actor)
c/o Staff Member *Anthem Entertainment*
6100 Wilshire Blvd Ste 1170
Los Angeles, CA 90048-5116, USA

Edelstein, Michael (Producer)
c/o Staff Member *Industry Entertainment*
955 Carrillo Dr Ste 300
Los Angeles, CA 90048-5400, USA

Edelstein, Victor (Designer, Fashion
Designer)
3 Stanhope Mews West
London SW7 5RB, UNITED KINGDOM
(UK)

Eden, Barbara (Actor)
9816 Denbigh Dr
Beverly Hills, CA 90210-1014, USA

Eden, Mike (Baseball Player)
Atlanta Braves
11531 Forest Hills Dr
Tampa, FL 33612-5121, USA

Eden, Richard (Actor)
The Agency
1800 Avenue Of The Stars Ste 400
Los Angeles, CA 90067-4206, USA

Edenfield, Ken (Baseball Player)
California Angels
4407 Barbara Dr
Knoxville, TN 37918-4403, USA

Edens, Tom (Baseball Player)
New York Mets
2033 Quailridge Ct
Clarkston, WA 99403-1787, USA

Eder, Elfriede
Rain 12
Leogang 5771, AUSTRIA

Eder, Linda (Actor)
c/o Staff Member *Agency Group Ltd, The (LA)*
1880 Century Park E Ste 711
Los Angeles, CA 90067-1618, USA

Eder, Richard G (Journalist)
Los Angeles Times
202 W 1st St
Editorial Dept
Los Angeles, CA 90012-4105, USA

Edgar, David
917 NE 16th Ave Apt 13
Ft Lauderdale, FL 33304-4497, USA

Edgar, David (Dave) (Swimmer)
2633 Middle River Dr Apt 3
Fort Lauderdale, FL 33306-1437, USA

Edgar, Jim (Governor)
State House 207 E Capitol Ave
Springfield, IL 62706-0001, USA

Edgar, Robert W (Religious Leader)
National Council of Churches
475 Riverside Dr Ste 817
New York, NY 10115-0697, USA

Edge (Musician)
Regine Moylet
145A Ladbroke Grove
London W10 6HJ, UNITED KINGDOM (UK)

Edge, Butch (Baseball Player)
Toronto Blue Jays
2491 Michelle Dr
Sacramento, CA 95821-2342, USA

Edge, Graeme (Musician)
Insight Mgmt
1222 16th Ave S # 300
Nashville, TN 37212-2926, USA

Edge, Mitzi (Golfer)
118 Kings Chapel Rd
Augusta, GA 30907-4002, USA

Edgerson, Booker (Football Player)
Buffalo Bills
68 Union Cmn
Buffalo, NY 14221-7744, USA

Edgerton, Bill (Baseball Player)
Kansas City A's
1725 E Jefferson Blvd
Mishawaka, IN 46545-7233, USA

Edgerton, Joel (Actor)
c/o Ann Churchill-Brown *Shanahan Management*
PO Box 1509
Darlinghurst 1300, AUSTRALIA

Edgley, Gigi
Forster - Delaney Management
12533 Woodgreen St
Los Angeles, CA 90066-2723, USA

Edinger, Paul (Football Player)
Chicago Bears
2313 York Pl
Lakeland, FL 33810-4883, USA

Edlen, Bengt (Physicist)
University of Lund
Physics Dept
Lund, SWEDEN

Edler, Dave (Baseball Player)
Seattle Mariners
1504 S 34th Ave
Yakima, WA 98902-4808, USA

Edler, Inge G (Doctor)
University Hospital
Cadiology Dept
Lund, SWEDEN

Edler, Lee
1725 K St NW Ste 1202
Washington, DC 20006-1407, USA

Edlund, David J (Inventor)
Northwest Power Systems
PO Box 5339
Bend, OR 97708-5339, USA

Edlund, Richard P (Cinematographer)
2710 Wilshire Blvd
Santa Monica, CA 90403-4706, USA

Edmiston, Mark M (Publisher)
Jordan Edmiston Group
885 3rd Ave
New York, NY 10022-4834, USA

Edmonds, James P (Jim) (Baseball Player)
California Angels
114 Hunters Grove Dr
Saint Louis, MO 63141-7669, USA

Edmonds, Kenneth (Babyface) (Musician, Producer)
15030 Ventura Blvd # 710
Sherman Oaks, CA 91403-5470, USA

Edmonds, Louis
250 W 57th St Ste 2317
New York, NY 10107-2306, USA

Edmonds, Tracey E (Producer)
c/o Staff Member *Edmonds Entertainment*
1635 N Cahuenga Blvd Fl 5
Los Angeles, CA 90028-6201, USA

Edmondson, Brian (Baseball Player)
Atlanta Braves
304 Ridgeview Trce
Canton, GA 30114-7000, USA

Edmondson, James L (Judge)
US Court of Appeals
56 Forsyth St NW
Atlanta, GA 30303-2295, USA

Edmund-Davies, Herbert E (Judge)
5 Gray's Inn Square
London WC1R 5EU, UNITED KINGDOM (UK)

Edmunds, Dave (Musician, Songwriter, Writer)
Entertainment Services
Main Street Plaza 1000 #303
Voorhees, NJ 08043, USA

Edmunds, Ferrell (Football Player)
Miami Dolphins
272 Wilkerson Rd
Danville, VA 24540-0654, USA

Edmunds, Randall (Football Player)
Miami Dolphins
2307 Amity Woodlawn Rd
Lincolnton, GA 30817-1910, USA

Edna, Dame (Actor, Comedian)
c/o Staff Member *PBJ Management*
7 Soho Street
London W1D 3DQ, UNITED KINGDOM (UK)

Edner, Bobby (Actor)
c/o Mitchell Gossett *Cunningham Escott Slevin & Doherty (LA)*
10635 Santa Monica Blvd Ste 130
Los Angeles, CA 90025-8306, USA

Edney, Leon A (Bud) (Admiral)
1037 Encino Row
Coronado, CA 92118-2813, USA

Edney, Tyus (Basketball Player)
1800 S Floyd Ct
La Habra, CA 90631-2058, USA

Edson, Hilary (Actor)
400 S Beverly Dr Ste 216
Beverly Hills, CA 90212-4404, USA

Eduardo dos Santos, Jose (President)
President's Office
Palacio do Povo
Luanda, ANGOLA

Edward (Prince)
Bagshot
Bagshot Park
Surrey, ENGLAND GU19 5PN, UNITED KINGDOM (UK)

Edward, John (Psychic)
c/o Gina Rugolo-Judd *Rigberg-Rugolo Entertainment*
1180 S Beverly Dr Ste 601
Los Angeles, CA 90035-1158, USA

Edwards, Al (Football Player)
Buffalo Bills
1729 Laurel Ridge Ln
Lawrenceville, GA 30043-3008, USA

Edwards, Anthony (Actor, Producer)
c/o Steve Lovett *Lovett Management*
1327 Brinkley Ave
Los Angeles, CA 90049-3619, USA

Edwards, Antonio (Football Player)
Seattle Seahawks
716 2nd St NW
Moultrie, GA 31768-3330, USA

Edwards, Antuan (Football Player)
Green Bay Packers
149 Northside Dr
Starkville, MS 39759-2414, USA

Edwards, Barbara (Actor, Model)
Hansen
7767 Hollywood Blvd Apt 202
Los Angeles, CA 90046-2643, USA

Edwards, Bill
17 Bishop's Rd.
Tewin Wood Herts., ENGLAND, UNITED KINGDOM (UK)

Edwards, Blue (Basketball Player)
Miami Heat
601 Biscayne Blvd
American Airlines Arena
Miami, FL 33132-1801, USA

Edwards, Carl (Race Car Driver)
Roush Racing
122 Knob Hill Rd
Mooresville, NC 28117-6847, USA

Edwards, Charles C (Physicist)
10666 N Torrey Pines Rd
Keeney Park
La Jolla, CA 92037-1027, USA

Edwards, Cid (Football Player)
St Louis Cardinals
5343 Adobe Falls Rd
San Diego, CA 92120-4403, USA

Edwards, Dave (Baseball Player)
Minnesota Twins
5059 Quail Run Rd Apt 75
Riverside, CA 92507-6485, USA

Edwards, David (Golfer)
5 Champion Pl
Stillwater, OK 74074-1065, USA

Edwards, Dennis (Musician, Opera Singer, Songwriter, Writer)
Green Light Talent Agency
PO Box 3172
Beverly Hills, CA 90212-0172, USA

Edwards, Dixon III (Football Player)
Dallas Cowboys
8756 Lunski Ln
Eden Prairie, MN 55347-2440, USA

Edwards, Don (Hockey Player)
530 Saint Andrews Rd Unit 4
Saginaw, MI 48638-5943, USA

Edwards, Don (Music Group, Musician, Songwriter, Writer)
Scott O'Malley Assoc
433 S Cuchamas St
Colorado Springs, CO 80903, USA

Edwards, Earl (Football Player)
San Francisco 49ers
1534 W Saint Thomas Dr
Gilbert, AZ 85233-6534, USA

Edwards, Eddie (Football Player)
Cincinnati Bengals
9440 NW 13th St
Plantation, FL 33322-4202, USA

Edwards, Elizabeth (Politician)
One America Commitee
1001 G St NW Ste 400W
Washington, DC 20001-4581, USA

Edwards, Eric (Cinematographer)
3404 SW Water Ave
Portland, OR 97239-4636, USA

Edwards, Gail
651 N Kilkea Dr
Los Angeles, CA 90048-2213, USA

Edwards, Gareth (Soccer Player)
211 West Rd
Nottage
Porthcawl, Mid-Clamorgan
WALES CF363RT, UNITED KINGDOM (UK)

Edwards, Geoff
249 Main
Ilderton, ON N0M 2, CANADA

Edwards, Glen (Football Player)
Pittsburgh Steelers
1175 Pinellas Point Dr S Apt 281
St Petersburg, FL 33705-6065, USA

Edwards, Harry (Activist, Educator)
University of California
Sociology Dept
Berkeley, CA 94720-0001, USA

Edwards, Harry T (Judge)
US Court of Appeals
333 Constitution Ave NW
Washington, DC 20001-2866, USA

Edwards, Herm (Football Player)
Philadelphia Eagles
433 Ward Pkwy Apt 1N
Kansas City, MO 64112-2128, USA

Edwards, Herman L (Coach, Football Coach, Football Player)
1627 Highland St
Seaside, CA 93955-4511, USA

Edwards, Howard (Baseball Player)
Cleveland Indians
3706 Driftwood Dr
San Angelo, TX 76904-5972, USA

Edwards, James (Basketball Player)
3890 Lakeland Ln
Bloomfield Township, MI 48302-1327, USA

Edwards, James B (Governor, Secretary)
100 Venning St
Mount Pleasant, SC 29464-5323, USA

Edwards, Jay (Basketball Player)
121 N Washington St Apt 506
Marion, IN 46952-2865, USA

Edwards, Jennifer (Actor)
4123 Saint Clair Ave
Studio City, CA 91604-1608, USA

Edwards, Jesse E (Doctor)
211 2nd St NW Apt 1911
Rochester, MN 55901-3101, USA

Edwards, Joe F Jr (Astronaut)
Enron Broadband Services
PO Box 1188
Houston, TX 77251-1188, USA

Edwards, Joel (Golfer)
280 Benson Ln
Coppell, TX 75019-4548, USA

Edwards, John (Musician)
Buddy Allen Mgmt
3750 Hudson Manor Ter Apt 3ae
Bronx, NY 10463-1167, USA

Edwards, John (Politician)
One America Committee
1001 G St NW Ste 400W
Washington, DC 20001-4581, USA

Edwards, John (Psychic)
Get Psych'd Inc
PO Box 383
Huntington, NY 11743-0383, USA

Edwards, Jonathan (Athlete, Track Athlete)
MTC
10 Kendall Place
London, England W1H3AH, UNITED
KINGDOM (UK)

Edwards, Jonathan (Music Group,
Songwriter, Writer)
Northern Lights
437 Live Oak Loop NE
Albuquerque, NM 87122-1406, USA

Edwards, Kalimba (Athlete)
c/o Staff Member Detroit Lions
222 Republic Dr
Allen Park, MI 48101-3650, USA

Edwards, Kelvin (Football Player)
New Orleans Saints
1716 Brookarbor Ct
Arlington, TX 76018-2420, USA

Edwards, Lena F (Physicist)
821 Woodland Dr
Lakewood, NJ 08701-3038, USA

Edwards, Luke (Actor)
Ensemble Entertainment
10474 Santa Monica Blvd Ste 380
Los Angeles, CA 90025-6943, USA

Edwards, Marc (Football Player)
San Francisco 49ers
4304 Ashland Ave
Norwood, OH 45212-3211, USA

Edwards, Mario (Football Player)
c/o Staff Member Dallas Cowboys
1 Cowboys Pkwy
Irving, TX 75063-4999, USA

Edwards, Marshall (Baseball Player)
Milwaukee Brewers
8948 La Cintura Ct
San Diego, CA 92129-3316, USA

Edwards, Mike (Baseball Player)
Pittsburgh Pirates
11370 Moreno Beach Dr
Moreno Valley, CA 92555-5240, USA

Edwards, Mike (Baseball Player)
Oakland A's
502 Sharon Ave
Mechanicsburg, PA 17055-6630, USA

Edwards, Paddi
1800 Avenue Of The Stars Ste 400
Los Angeles, CA 90067-4206, USA

Edwards, R Lavell (Coach, Football
Coach, Football Player)
Brighan Young University
Athletic Dept
Provo, UT 84602, USA

Edwards, Randy (Football Player)
Seattle Seahawks
1369 Mountain Park Dr NW
Kennesaw, GA 30152-4780, USA

Edwards, Robert (Football Player)
New England Patriots
931 Knight Rd
Tennille, GA 31089-4210, USA

Edwards, Robert A (Bob) (Correspondent)
National Public Radio
635 Massachusetts Ave NW
News Dept
Washington, DC 20001-3753, USA

Edwards, Robert G (Physicist)
Duck End Farm
Dry Drayton
Cambridge, England CB38DB, UNITED
KINGDOM (UK)

Edwards, Robert J (Editor)
Williamscot House
near Banbury
England Oxon OX17 1AE, UNITED
KINGDOM (UK)

Edwards, Ronnie Claire (Actor)
c/o Staff Member The Artists Group Ltd
(LA)
1650 Broadway Ste 610
New York, NY 10019-6833, USA

Edwards, Sian (Conductor)
70 Twisden Road
London, England NW5 1DN, UNITED
KINGDOM (UK)

Edwards, Stacy (Actor)
Paradigm Agency
10 100 Santa Monica Blvd #2500
Los Angeles, CA 90067, USA

Edwards, Stephanie (Actor)
c/o Staff Member Tisherman Agency Inc
6767 Forest Lawn Dr Ste 101
Los Angeles, CA 90068-1050, USA

Edwards, Steve (Composer)
3980 Royal Oak Pl
Encino, CA 91436-3918, USA

Edwards, Teresa (Basketball Player)
291 Union Grove Church Rd SE
Calhoun, GA 30701-3737, USA

Edwards, Tommy Lee (Cartoonist)
DC Comics
1700 Broadway
New York, NY 10019-5914, USA

Edwards, Tonya (Basketball Player)
Phoenix Mercury
201 E Jefferson St
American West Arena
Phoenix, AZ 85004-2412, USA

Edwards, Troy (Football Player)
Pittsburgh Steelers
3559 Highland Glen Ct
Jacksonville, FL 32224-1612, USA

Edwards, W Blake (Actor, Director,
Producer, Writer)
c/o Caren Bohrman The Bohrman Agency
8899 Beverly Blvd Ste 811
Los Angeles, CA 90048-2452, USA

Edwards, Wayne (Baseball Player)
Chicago White Sox
9738 Aqueduct Ave
Sepulveda, CA 91343-2035, USA

Edwards Jr, Charles C (Publisher)
Des Moines Register & Tribune
715 Locust St
Des Moines, IA 50309-3703, USA

Eenhoorn, Robert (Baseball Player)
New York Yankees
Zermilieplaats 15 3068J
Rotterdam, THE NETHERLANDS

Efron, Zac (Actor)
c/o Jason Barrett Alchemy Entertainment
9229 W Sunset Blvd Ste 720
Los Angeles, CA 90069-3407, USA

Egan, Dick (Baseball Player)
Cincinnati Reds
1611 W Thurderhill Dr
Phoenix, AZ 85045, USA

Egan, Edward M Cardinal (Religious
Leader)
Archdiocese of New York
1011 1st Ave
New York, NY 10022-4112, USA

Egan, Jennifer (Writer)
Doubleday Press
1540 Broadway
New York, NY 10036-4039, USA

Egan, John (Johnny) (Basketball Player)
2124 Nantucket Dr # B
Houston, TX 77057-2906, USA

Egan, John L (Business Person)
130 Wilton Road
London, England SW1V 1LQ, UNITED
KINGDOM (UK)

Egan, Kian (Musician)
c/o Staff Member Solo Agency Ltd (UK)
55 Fulham High St
London SW6 3JJ, UNITED KINGDOM
(UK)

Egan, Peter (Actor)
James Sharkey
21 Golden Square
London, England W1R 3PA, UNITED
KINGDOM (UK)

Egan, Richard J (Business Person)
ECM Corp
35 Parkwood Dr
Hopkinton, MA 01748-1659, USA

Egan, Susan (Actor)
Himber Entertainment
15760 Ventura Blvd Ste 700
Encino, CA 91436-3016, USA

Egan, Tom (Baseball Player)
California Angels
184 E Myrna Ln
Tempe, AZ 85284-3118, USA

Egbert, Dave (Television Host)
The Coastal Gardener TV Show
PO Box 455
Big Sur, CA 93920-0455, USA

Egdahl, Richard H (Doctor)
505 Tremont St Unit 704
Boston, MA 02116-6353, USA

Ege, Julie (Actor)
Guild House
Upper Saint Martins
London, England WC2H 9EG, UNITED
KINGDOM (UK)

Eger, David (Golfer)
501 Marsh Cove Ln
Ponte Vedra Beach, FL 32082-1660, USA

Egerszegi, Kristina
Feszti A. u 4
Budapest 1032, HUNGARY

Egerszegi, Krisztina (Swimmer)
Budapest Spartacus
Koer Utca 1/A
1103 Budapest, HUNGARY

Eggar, Samantha (Actor)
c/o Staff Member Diverse Talent Group
1875 Century Park E Ste 2250
Los Angeles, CA 90067-2563, USA

Eggby, David (Cinematographer)
4344 Promenade Way Unit 209
Marina Del Rey, CA 90292-6291, USA

Eggeling, Dale (Golfer)
8918 Magnolia Chase Cir
Tampa, FL 33647-2219, USA

Eggers, Dave (Writer)
Simon & Schuster
1230 Avenue Of The Americas
New York, NY 10020-1586, USA

Eggers, Doug (Football Player)
Baltimore Colts
12803 Cedarbrook Ln
Laurel, MD 20708-2449, USA

Eggert, Nicole (Actor)
4510 Radford Ave
Valley Village, CA 91607-4137, USA

Eggert, Robert J (Economist)
Eggert Economics Enterprises
1195 S Bates Rd
Cottonwood, AZ 86326-5415, USA

Eggerth, Marta
Park Dr. No.
Rye, NY 10580, USA

Egglesfield, Colin (Actor)
c/o Colton Gramm Brillstein-Grey
Entertainment
9150 Wilshire Blvd Ste 350
Beverly Hills, CA 90212-3453, USA

Eggleston, William (Photographer)
Robert Miller Gallery
526 W 26th St Rm 10A
New York, NY 10001-5541, USA

Eggleton, Arthur C (Government Official)
National Defence Ministry
101 Colonel By Dr
Ottawa, ON K1A 0K2, CANADA

Egielski, Richard
525 B St Ste 1900
San Diego, CA 92101-4495, USA

Egloff, Bruce (Baseball Player)
Cleveland Indians
3136 S Emporia Ct
Denver, CO 80231-4739, USA

Egloff, Ron (Football Player)
Denver Broncos
975 Lincoln St
Denver, CO 80203-2725, USA

Egnew, Danielle (Musician)
Danielle Egnew Spiritual Advisory
15030 Ventura Blvd Ste 843
Sherman Oaks, CA 91403-5470, USA

Egoyan, Atom (Actor)
Ego Film Artiosts
80 Niagara St
Toronto, ON M5V 1C5, CANADA

Ehle, Jennifer (Actor)
c/o Staff Member *International Creative Management (ICM-LA)*
10250 Constellation Blvd
Los Angeles, CA 90067-6200, USA

Ehlers, Beth (Actor)
c/o Staff Member *Stone Manners Talent & Literary (LA)*
6500 Wilshire Blvd Ste 550
Los Angeles, CA 90048-4950, USA

Ehlers, Tom (Football Player)
Philadelphia Eagles
13898 Layton Rd
Mishawaka, IN 46544-9498, USA

Ehlers, Walter D (War Hero)
8382 Valley View St
Buena Park, CA 90620-2738, USA

Ehrlich, S Paul Jr (Physicist)
1132 Seaspray Ave
Delray Beach, FL 33483-7140, USA

Ehrman, Bart D (Writer)
The Department of Religious Studies
125 Saunders Hall, Cb# 3225
University Of North Carolina At Chapel Hill
Chapel Hill, NC 27599, USA

Ehrmann, Joe (Football Player)
Baltimore Colts
5 Elmhurst Rd
Baltimore, MD 21210-2216, USA

Eiber, Janet
9300 Wilshire Blvd # 410
Beverly Hills, CA 90212-3213, USA

Eichelberger, Charles B (General)
California Microwave
124 Sweetwater Oaks
Peachtree City, GA 30269-2110, USA

Eichelberger, Dave (Golfer)
PO Box 2303
Waco, TX 76703-2303, USA

Eichelberger, Juan (Baseball Player)
San Diego Padres
14674 Silverset St
Poway, CA 92064-6408, USA

Eichhorn, Lisa (Actor)
1919 W 44th St #1000
New York, NY 10036, USA

Eichhorn, Mark (Baseball Player)
Toronto Blue Jays
147 Norma Ct
Aptos, CA 95003-9789, USA

Eichorn, Lisa
1501 Broadway Ste 2600
New York, NY 10036-5600, USA

Eidson, Jim (Football Player)
Dallas Cowboys
3116 Purdue Ave
Dallas, TX 75225-7721, USA

Eifrid, Jim (Football Player)
Denver Broncos
2710 Tyler Ave
Fort Wayne, IN 46808-1944, USA

Eigeman, Chris (Actor)
c/o Thomas Cushing *Innovative Artists (LA)*
1505 10th St
Santa Monica, CA 90401-2805, USA

Eighth Wonder
50 Lisson St Unit 1B
London, ENGLAND NW1 5DF, UNITED KINGDOM (UK)

Eigsti, Roger H (Business Person)
SAFECO Corp
Safeco Plaza
Seattle, WA 98185-0001, USA

Eikenberry, Jill (Actor)
509 Pixie Trl
Mill Valley, CA 94941-3386, USA

Eikenes, Adele (Opera Singer)
Van Walsum Mgmt
4 Addison Bridge Place
London, England W14 8XP, UNITED KINGDOM (UK)

Eiland, Dave (Baseball Player)
New York Yankees
2824 Blue Springs Pl
Wesley Chapel, FL 33544-8746, USA

Eilbacher, Cynthia
PO Box 8920
Universal Cty, CA 91618-8920, USA

Eilbacher, Lisa (Actor)
4600 Petit Ave
Encino, CA 91436-3216, USA

Eilers, Dave (Baseball Player)
602 Perkins Ln
Brenham, TX 77833-4394, USA

Eilers, Pat (Football Player)
Minnesota Vikings
177 De Windt Rd
Winnetka, IL 60093-3708, USA

Eilts, Hermann F (Diplomat)
67 Cleveland Rd
Wellesley, MA 02481-2434, USA

Einertson, Darrell (Baseball Player)
New York Yankees
427 NW Skyline Dr
Ankeny, IA 50023-8701, USA

Einstein, Bob (Super Dave Osbourne) (Actor)
8383 Wilshire Blvd Ste 500
Beverly Hills, CA 90211-2404, USA

Einziger, Mike (Music Group)
Artist Direct
1601 Cloverfield Blvd # 400
Santa Monica, CA 90404-4082, USA

Eischeid, Mike (Football Player)
Oakland Raiders
306 Auburn St
West Union, IA 52175-1067, USA

Eischen, Joey (Baseball Player)
Montreal Expos
1428 E Herring Ave
West Covina, CA 91791-3111, USA

Eisen, Herman N (Doctor)
9 Homestead St
Waban, MA 02468-2008, USA

Eisen, Thelma (Baseball Player)
396 Pintoresca Dr
Pacific Palisades, CA 90272-3318, USA

Eisen, Tripp (Music Group)
Andy Gould Mgmt
9100 Wilshire Blvd Ste 400W
Beverly Hills, CA 90212-3464, USA

Eisenberg, Hallie Kate (Actor)
c/o Staff Member *Endeavor Agency LLC (LA)*
9601 Wilshire Blvd Fl 3
Beverly Hills, CA 90210-5204, USA

Eisenberg, Jesse (Actor)
c/o Staff Member *William Morris Agency (WMA-LA)*
1 William Morris Pl
Beverly Hills, CA 90212-4261, USA

Eisenberg, Lee B (Editor)
Edison Project
3286 N Park Blvd
Alcoa, TN 37701-3274, USA

Eisenberg, Leon (Doctor)
130 Mount Auburn St Apt 310
Cambridge, MA 02138-5779, USA

Eisenberg, Melvin A (Attorney, Attorney General, Educator, General)
1197 Keeler Ave
Berkeley, CA 94708-1753, USA

Eisenberg, Warren (Business Person)
Bed Bath & Beyond
650 Liberty Ave
Union, NJ 07083-8135, USA

Eisenhauer, Lawrence (Football Player)
Boston Patriots
2 Winter St
Pro Action
Waltham, MA 02451-0944, USA

Eisenhauer, Peggy (Designer, Special Effects Designer)
International Creative Mgmt
40 W 57th St Ste 1800
New York, NY 10019-4001, USA

Eisenhauer, Stephen S (Steve) (Football Player)
105 Abbey Rd
Winchester, VA 22602-7402, USA

Eisenhooth, John (Football Player)
Seattle Seahawks
546 Walnut St
Howard, PA 16841, USA

Eisenhower, David
Foxall Lane
Berwyn, PA 19312, USA

Eisenhower, John
27318 Morris Rd
Trappe, MD 21673-1915, USA

Eisenhower, Julie Nixon
Foxall Lane
Berwyn, PA 19312, USA

Eisenhower, Susan
1050 17th St NW Ste 600
Washington, DC 20036-5517, USA

Eisenman, Peter D (Architect)
Eisenman Architects
40 W 25th St
New York, NY 10010-2707, USA

Eisenmann, Ike
6556 Blucher Ave
Van Nuys, CA 91406-6207, USA

Eisenreich, James M (Jim) (Baseball Player)
Minnesota Twins
21300 E 34th St S
Independence, MO 64057-3410, USA

Eisenstein, Michael (Music Group)
Little Big Man
155 Avenue Of The Americas Rm 700
New York, NY 10013-1507, USA

Eisler, Lloyd
211-800 Montarville
Boucherville, PQ JYB 125, CANADA

Eisley, Howard (Athlete, Basketball Player)
20250 Rodeo Ct
Southfield, MI 48075-1285, USA

Eisman, Hy (Cartoonist)
99 Boulevard
Glen Rock, NJ 07452-2003, USA

Eisner, Michael (Business Person)
The Tornante Company
9401 Wilshire Blvd Ste 760
Beverly Hills, CA 90212-2919, USA

Eitan, Raphael (Admiral, General)
Tsomet Party
Knesset, Tel-Aviv, ISRAEL

Eitzel, Mark (Music Group, Songwriter, Writer)
Legends of 21st Century
7 Trinity Row
Florence, MA 01062-1931, USA

Eizenstat, Stuart E (Diplomat, Government Official)
9107 Briety Road
Chevy Chase, MD 20815, USA

Ejiofor, Chiwetel (Actor)
c/o John Burnham *International Creative Management (ICM-LA)*
10250 Constellation Blvd
Los Angeles, CA 90067-6200, USA

Ejogo, Carmen (Actor)
P F D
Drug House
34-43 Russell St
London WC2B, UNITED KINGDOM (UK)

Ekberg, Ulf (Musician)
Basic Music Mgmt
Norrtullsgatan 52
Stockholm 113 45, SWEDEN

Ekberg Anita
Via Aspro N(2 Genzano Di
Roma 00045, ITALY

Ekland, Britt (Actor)
1888 N Crescent Heights Blvd
Los Angeles, CA 90069-1647, USA

Eklund, A Sigvard (Physicist)
Krapfenwaldgasse 48
Vienna 1190, AUSTRIA

Eklund, Greg (Music Group)
Pinnacle Entertainment
30 Glenn St
White Plains, NY 10603-3254, USA

Ektaa (Actor, Bollywood)
Sagar Sangeet
Opp. Colaba Post Office
Mumbai, MS 400005, INDIA

El, Antwaan Randle (Football Player)
c/o Staff Member *Pittsburgh Steelers*
3400 S Water St
Pittsburgh, PA 15203-2349, USA

El Fadil, Siddig (Actor)
Paramount
5555 Melose Ave
Los Angeles, CA 90038, USA

El Sitio (Moris y Santiago) (Musician)
c/o Gabriel Blanco *Gabriel Blanco Iglesias (Mexico)*
Rio Balsas 35-32
Colonia Cuauhtemoc
DF 06500, MEXICO

Elam, Jason (Football Player)
c/o Staff Member *Denver Broncos*
13655 Broncos Pkwy
Englewood, CO 80112-4150, USA

Elam, Merrill (Architect)
Scogin Elam Bray
1819 Peachtree Rd NE Ste 700
Atlanta, GA 30309-1849, USA

Elarton, Scott (Baseball Player)
Houston Astros
13501 County Road 33
Karval, CO 80823-9305, USA

Elavarasan (Actor)
7 Mahalinga Road
Chennai, TN 600 034, INDIA

Elba, Idris (Actor)
c/o Sara Ramaker *Paradigm (LA)*
360 N Crescent Dr
North Bldg
Beverly Hills, CA 90210-6820, USA

Elbaradel, Mohamed (Government Official)
International Atomic Energy Agency
Wagramserstr
Vienna 1400, AUSTRIA

Eldard, Ron (Actor)
c/o William Choi *Management 360*
9111 Wilshire Blvd
Beverly Hills, CA 90210-5508, USA

Elder, Dave (Baseball Player)
2642 High St SW
Conyers, GA 30094-6843, USA

Elder, George (Baseball Player)
St Louis Browns
423 Amethyst Dr
Fruita, CO 81521-8813, USA

Elder, Larry (Actor)
c/o Ariel (Ari) Emanuel *Endeavor Agency LLC (LA)*
9601 Wilshire Blvd Fl 3
Beverly Hills, CA 90210-5204, USA

Elder, Lee E (Golfer)
1440 S Ocean Blvd Apt 3C
Pompano Beach, FL 33062-7368, USA

Elder, Mark P
Natinal Opera
London Coliseum
London WC2N 4ES, UNITED KINGDOM (UK)

Elder, Will (Cartoonist)
311 Jutland Dr #A
Monroe Township, NJ 08831, USA

Elders, M Jocelyn (Doctor, Government Official)
University of Arkansas Medical School
Pediatrics Dept
Little Rock, AR 72205, USA

Eldred, Cal (Baseball Player)
Milwaukee Brewers
1893 Horn Rd
Mount Vernon, IA 52314-9517, USA

Eldredge, Allison (Music Group)
C M Artists
40 W 25th St
New York, NY 10010-2707, USA

Elegant, Robert S (Writer)
Manor House
Middle Green near Langley
Bucks SL3 6BS, UNITED KINGDOM (UK)

Eleniak, Erika (Actor, Model)
c/o Staff Member *Melissa Prophet Management*
4321 Matilija Ave Apt 21
Sherman Oaks, CA 91423-3672, USA

Elfman, Bodhi (Actor)
c/o Staff Member *Stone Manners Talent & Literary (LA)*
6500 Wilshire Blvd Ste 550
Los Angeles, CA 90048-4950, USA

Elfman, Danny (Composer, Director, Music Group, Musical Director, Musician)
c/o Staff Member *Kraft-Engel Management*
15233 Ventura Blvd Ste 200
Sherman Oaks, CA 91403-2244, USA

Elfman, Jenna (Actor, Model)
c/o Kevin Huvane *Creative Artists Agency LCC (CAA-LA)*
2000 Avenue Of The Stars
Los Angeles, CA 90067-4700, USA

Elgart, Larry
2065 Gulf Of Mexico Dr
Longboat Key, FL 34228-3202, USA

Elgen, Manfred (Nobel Prize Laureate)
Georg-Dehio-Weg 4
37075 Gottingen, GERMANY

Eli Young Band (Music Group)
c/o Staff Member *Paradigm (Monterey)*
509 Hartnell St
Monterey, CA 93940-2825, USA

Elia, Bruce (Football Player)
Miami Dolphins
1409 John St
Fort Lee, NJ 07024-2565, USA

Elia, Lee (Baseball Player)
Chicago White Sox
11613 Innfields Dr
Odessa, FL 33556-5407, USA

Elias, Eliane (Composer, Director, Music Group, Musical Director, Musician)
Bennett Morgan
RR 376 Box 1282
Wappingers Falls, NY 12590, USA

Elias, Hector (Actor)
28 N Mansfield Ave
Los Angeles, CA 90038, USA

Elias, Homer (Football Player)
Detroit Lions
2049 E 128th St
Grant, MI 49327-9321, USA

Elias, Jonathan (Composer)
Gorfaine/Schwartz
4111 W Alameda Ave Ste 509
Burbank, CA 91505-4171, USA

Elias, Keith (Football Player)
New York Giants
512 Maplewood Dr
Lanoka Harbor, NJ 08734-2835, USA

Elias, Patrick (Composer)
1005 Smith Manor Blvd # 98
West Orange, NJ 07052-4227, USA

Elias, Rosalind (Opera Singer)
Rober Lombardo
61 W 62nd St Apt 6F
Harkness Plaza
New York, NY 10023-7017, USA

Eliason, Donald (Basketball Player, Football Player)
Brooklyn Dodgers
5690 Fisher St
Saint Paul, MN 55110-2264, USA

Eliel, Ernest L (Misc)
345 Carolina Meadows Villa
Chapel Hill, NC 27517-7519, USA

Eliff, Tom (Religious Leader)
Southern Baptist Convention
901 Commerce St Ste 750
Nashville, TN 37203-3600, USA

Elinson, Jack (Scientist)
655 Pomander Walk Apt 355
Teaneck, NJ 07666-1673, USA

Eliopulos, Jim (Football Player)
St Louis Cardinals
2500 Macero St
Roseville, CA 95747-5000, USA

Eliot, Alison
2 Ironsides St # 18
Marina Del Rey, CA 90292, USA

Eliot, Jan (Cartoonist)
PO Box 50032
Eugene, OR 97405-0967, USA

Elise, Christine (Actor)
c/o Will Ward *ROAR LLC*
9701 Wilshire Blvd Ste 850
Beverly Hills, CA 90212-2032, USA

Elise, Kimberly (Actor)
c/o Evan Hainey *Untitled Entertainment (LA)*
331 N Maple Dr Fl 3
Beverly Hills, CA 90210-3827, USA

Elisha, Walter Y (Business Person)
Springs Industries
205 N White St
Fort Mill, SC 29715-1654, USA

Elizabeth, Princess
1526 N Beverly Dr
Beverly Hills, CA 90210-2314, USA

Elizabeth, Shannon (Actor)
c/o Steven Fenton *Fenton-Kritzer Entertainment*
8840 Wilshire Blvd Fl 3
Beverly Hills, CA 90211-2606, USA

Elizondo, Hector (Actor)
15030 Ventura Blvd # 710
Sherman Oaks, CA 91403-5470, USA

Elk, Jim (Actor)
Dade/Schultz
6442 Coldwater Canyon Ave Ste 206
North Hollywood, CA 91606-1137, USA

Elkes, Joel (Doctor, Psychic)
University of Louisville
Psychiatry/Behavioral Sci Dept
Louisville, KY 40292-0001, USA

Elkind, Mortimer M (Physicist)
16925 Hierba Dr
San Diego, CA 92128-2688, USA

Elkington, Steve (Golfer)
7010 Kelsey Rae Ct
Houston, TX 77069-1102, USA

Elkins, Hillard (Producer)
1335 N Doheny Dr
Los Angeles, CA 90069-1760, USA

Elkins, Larry
111 S Saint Joseph St
South Bend, IN 46601-1901, USA

Elkins, Larry (Football Player)
Houston Oilers
4407 McArthur Cir
Brownwood, TX 76801-7334, USA

Elkins, Lawrence C (Larry) (Football Player)
Saline Water Corp
PO Box 60889
Al Riyadh 11555, SAUDI ARABIA

Ellard, Henry A (Football Player)
Los Angeles Rams
4631 E Byrd Ave
Fresno, CA 93725-1640, USA

Ellena, Jack (Football Player)
Los Angeles Rams
PO Box 610
Mountain Meadow Ranch
Susanville, CA 96130-0610, USA

Ellenbogen, Bill (Football Player)
New York Giants
777 Pelham Rd # 12-G
New Rochelle, NY 10805-1158, USA

Ellenstein, Robert (Actor)
5212 Sepulveda Blvd # 23F
Culver City, CA 90230, USA

Ellenthal, Ira (Publisher)
New York Daily News
220 E 42nd St
New York, NY 10017-5806, USA

Eller, Carl (Football Player, Misc)
Minnesota Vikings
1035 Washburn Ave N
Minneapolis, MN 55411-3557, USA

Ellerbee, Linda (Correspondent)
c/o Staff Member *Lucky Duck Productions*
96 Morton St Fl 4
New York, NY 10014-3375, USA

Ellerson, Gary (Football Player)
Green Bay Packers
S86W18643 Sue Marie Ln
Muskego, WI 53150-8718, USA

Elliman, Donald M Jr (Publisher)
Sports Illustrated Magazine
Rockefeller Center
New York, NY 10020, USA

Elliman, Yvonne (Music Group)
Talent Consultants International
105 Shad Row Ste B
Piermont, NY 10968-3001, USA

Ellin, Doug (Director)
Creative Artists Agency
9830 Wilshire Blvd
Beverly Hills, CA 90212-1804, USA

Elling, Kurt (Music Group)
Open Door Mgmt
15327 W Sunset Blvd # 365
Pacific Palisades, CA 90272-3614, USA

Ellingsen, Bruce (Baseball Player)
Cleveland Indians
5873 Daneland St
Lakewood, CA 90713-1830, USA

Ellingson, Evan (Actor)
c/o Staff Member *Ann Waugh Talent Agency*
4741 Laurel Canyon Blvd Ste 200
North Hollywood, CA 91607-5910, USA

Elliot, Carlton (Football Player)
Green Bay Packers
5109 Presidio Dr
Garland, TX 75043-3108, USA

Elliot, Larry (Baseball Player)
Pittsburgh Pirates
13010 Caminito Bracho
San Diego, CA 92128-1808, USA

Elliot, Lenvil (Football Player)
Cincinnati Bengals
101 Woodson Ave
Richmond, MO 64085-1444, USA

Elliot, Lin (Football Player)
Dallas Cowboys
5409 Links Dr
Waco, TX 76708-5714, USA

Elliot, Ross
5702 Graves Ave
Encino, CA 91316-1441, USA

Elliot, Stephan
Box 452
Paddington NSW 2021, AUSTRALIA

Elliot, Tony (Football Player)
Green Bay Packers
45907 Riverwoods Dr
Macomb, MI 48044-5788, USA

Elliott, Alecia (Actor, Music Group)
PO Box 3075
Muscle Shoals, AL 35662-3075, USA

Elliott, Alison (Actor)
2 Ironsides St # 18
Marina Del Rey, CA 90292, USA

Elliott, Allison
1505 10th St
Santa Monica, CA 90401-2805, USA

Elliott, Bill
3323 Dillard Rd W
Blairsville, GA 30512-5116, USA

Elliott, Brennan (Actor)
c/o Christopher (Chris) Wright *Christopher Wright Management*
3207 Winnie Dr
Los Angeles, CA 90068-1439, USA

Elliott, Chalmers (Bump) (Coach, Football Coach, Football Player)
University of Iowa
Athletic Dept
Iowa City, IA 52242, USA

Elliott, Chris (Actor, Comedian)
c/o Judy Hofflund *Hofflund/Polone*
9465 Wilshire Blvd Ste 890
Beverly Hills, CA 90212-2607, USA

Elliott, David James (Actor)
c/o Bob McGowan *McGowan Management*
8733 W Sunset Blvd Ste 103
W Hollywood, CA 90069-2241, USA

Elliott, Dennis (Music Group)
Hard to Handle Mgmt
16501 Ventura Blvd Ste 602
Encino, CA 91436-2072, USA

Elliott, Donnie (Baseball Player)
San Diego Padres
1206 Bayou Vista Dr
Deer Park, TX 77536-6902, USA

Elliott, Gordon (Chef)
Food Network
1180 Avenue Of The Americas Ste 1200
New York, NY 10036-8401, USA

Elliott, Harry (Baseball Player)
St Louis Cardinals
1154 Random Rd
El Cajon, CA 92020-7743, USA

Elliott, Herbert (Herb) (Athlete, Track Athlete)
Athletics Australia
431 St Kilda Rd
#22
Melbourne, VIC 3004, AUSTRALIA

Elliott, Joe (Music Group)
Q Prime Inc
729 7th Ave Rm 1400
New York, NY 10019-6889, USA

Elliott, John (Football Player)
PO Box 340
Warren, TX 77664-0340, USA

Elliott, Michael (Misc)
45 Larkfield
Ewhurst Cranleigh
Surrey GU6 7QU, UNITED KINGDOM (UK)

Elliott, Missy (Misdemeanor) (Actor, Musician, Producer)
c/o Seth Rodsky *Creative Artists Agency LCC (CAA-LA)*
2000 Avenue Of The Stars
Los Angeles, CA 90067-4700, USA

Elliott, Osborn (Journalist)
31 E 72nd St # 6B
New York, NY 10021-4131, USA

Elliott, Paul H (Cinematographer)
Sandra Marsh Mgmt
9150 Wilshire Blvd Ste 220
Beverly Hills, CA 90212-3429, USA

Elliott, Peggy Gordon (Educator)
929 Harvey Dunn St
Brookings, SD 57006-1347, USA

Elliott, Pete3
003 Dunbarton Ave. NW
Canton, OH 44708, USA

Elliott, Peter R (Pete) (Coach, Football Coach, Football Player)
3003 Dunbarton Ave NW
Canton, OH 44708-1818, USA

Elliott, R Keith (Business Person)
Hercules Inc
Hercules Plaza 1313 N Market St
Wilmington, DE 19894-0001, USA

Elliott, Ralph E (War Hero)
5150 Damascus Rd S
Jacksonville, FL 32207-5772, USA

Elliott, Randy (Baseball Player)
San Diego Padres
PO Box 834
Somis, CA 93066-0834, USA

Elliott, Sam (Actor)
33050 Pacific Coast Hwy
Malibu, CA 90265-2300, USA

Elliott, Sean M (Basketball Player)
San Antonio Spurs
Alamodome 1 Sbc Center
San Antonio, TX 78219, USA

Elliott, Ted (Writer)
c/o Staff Member *Creative Artists Agency LCC (CAA-LA)*
2000 Avenue Of The Stars
Los Angeles, CA 90067-4700, USA

Ellis, Albert (Doctor)
Institute of Rational-Emotional Therapy
75 W End Ave Apt C14J
New York, NY 10023-7862, USA

Ellis, Allan (Football Player)
Chicago Bears
4318 Mayfair Ct
Country Club Hills, IL 60478-5132, USA

Ellis, Alton (Musician)
27 McConnell House
Deeley Road
London SW8, UNITED KINGDOM (UK)

Ellis, Anita
130 E End Ave
New York, NY 10028-7553, USA

Ellis, Aunjanue (Actor)
c/o Howard Axel *TMT Entertainment Group*
648 Broadway # 1002
New York, NY 10012-2301, USA

Ellis, Bret Easton (Writer)
International Creative Mgmt
40 W 57th St Ste 1800
New York, NY 10019-4001, USA

Ellis, Caroline (Actor)
8060 Saint Clair Ave
North Hollywood, CA 91605-1321, USA

Ellis, Chris
c/o Staff Member *Bauman Redanty & Shaul Agency*
5757 Wilshire Blvd Ste 473
Los Angeles, CA 90036-3632, USA

Ellis, Clarence J Jr (Football Player)
Atlanta Falcons
120 Hights Holw
Fayetteville, GA 30215-5139, USA

Ellis, Cliff (Basketball Player, Coach)
Auburn University
Athletic Dept
Auburn, AL 36831, USA

Ellis, Danny (Golfer)
1543 Cherry Lake Way
Lake Mary, FL 32746-1906, USA

Ellis, Dock P (Baseball Player)
Pittsburgh Pirates
13274 Desert Vista Dr
Victorville, CA 92392-6801, USA

Ellis, Don (Bowler)
34 Crestwood Cir
Sugar Land, TX 77478-3914, USA

Ellis, Elmer (Historian)
3300 New Haven Ave # 223
Columbia, MO 65201-5423, USA

Ellis, Gerry (Football Player)
Green Bay Packers
250 Cavil Way
De Pere, WI 54115-3772, USA

Ellis, Gregory (Football Player)
Dallas Cowboys
1207 Club House Ct
Southlake, TX 76092-9636, USA

Ellis, Hunter (Actor, Reality TV Star)
c/o Lauren Feeney *Ideal Management*
5780 Cencinela Av Suite 313
Los Angele, CA 90045, USA

Ellis, James R (General)
4213 W Swann Ave
Tampa, FL 33609-4330, USA

Ellis, Janet (Actor)
Arlington Entertainments
1/3 Charlotte St
London W1P 1HD, UNITED KINGDOM (UK)

Ellis, Jim (Baseball Player)
Chicago Cubs
13608 Avenue 224
Tulare, CA 93274-9304, USA

Ellis, Jimmy (Boxer)
5218 Saint Gabriel Ln
Louisville, KY 40291-1610, USA

Ellis, Joseph J (Writer)
Mount Holyoke College
History Dept
South Hadley, MA 01075, USA

Ellis, Kathleen (Kathy) (Swimmer)
3024 Woodshore Ct
Carmel, IN 46033-3643, USA

Ellis, Kenneth (Football Player)
Green Bay Packers
13826 Brantley Dr
Baker, LA 70714-4634, USA

Ellis, LaPhonso (Basketball Player)
7041 Old Cutler Rd
Coral Gables, FL 33143-6368, USA

Ellis, Larry R (General)
Deputy Chief Of Staff Operations/Plans
Hqusa Pentagon
Washington, DC 20310-0001, USA

Ellis, Luther (Football Player)
527 Riverside Ave
Mancos, CO 81328, USA

Ellis, M Herbert (Herb) (Music Group)
Producers Inc
11806 N 56th St
Tampa, FL 33617-1652, USA

Ellis, Mark (Baseball Player)
Oakland A's
318 Kinney Ave
Rapid City, SD 57702-2332, USA

Ellis, Mary
54 Eaton Square
London, ENGLAND SW1 W9BE, UNITED KINGDOM (UK)

Ellis, Maurice (Bo) (Basketball Player)
516 N 14th St
Milwaukee, WI 53233, USA

Ellis, Osian G (Misc)
90 Chandos Ave
London N20 9DZ, UNITED KINGDOM (UK)

Ellis, Patrick (H J) (Educator)
Catholic University
President's Office
Washington, DC 20064-0001, USA

Ellis, Ray (Football Player)
Philadelphia Eagles
449 N Citrus Ln
Gilbert, AZ 85234-7834, USA

Ellis, Rob (Baseball Player)
Milwaukee Brewers
2020 Krislin Dr NE
Grand Rapids, MI 49505-7160, USA

Ellis, Robert (Baseball Player)
California Angels
2066 75th Ave
Baton Rouge, LA 70807-5836, USA

Ellis, Roger (Football Player)
New York Titans
PO Box 575
Holden, ME 04429-0575, USA

Ellis, Romallis (Boxer)
2062 San Marco Dr
Ellenwood, GA 30294-1009, USA

Ellis, Ronald J E (Ron) (Hockey Player)
B C E Place
30 Yonge St
Toronto, ON M5E 1X8, CANADA

Ellis, Sammy (Baseball Player)
Cincinnati Reds
12511 Forest Highlands Dr
Dade City, FL 33525-8273, USA

Ellis, Scott (Director)
420 Central Park W Apt 5B
New York, NY 10025-4315, USA

Ellis, Shuan (Football Player)
New York Jets
1000 Fulton Ave
Hempstead, NY 11550-1030, USA

Ellis, Terry (Music Group)
East West Records
75 Rockefeller Plz # 1200
New York, NY 10019-6908, USA

Ellis-Bextor, Sophie (Actor, Musician)
c/o Staff Member *Universal Music Ltd (UK)*
22 St Peters Square
London W6 9NW, UNITED KINGDOM (UK)

Ellis Brothers
PO Box 50221
Nashville, TN 37205-0221, USA

Ellison, David (Actor)
c/o Eddie Michaels *Insignia Public Relations*
9255 W Sunset Blvd Ste 920
Los Angeles, CA 90069-3306, USA

Ellison, Harlan
PO Box 55548
Sherman Oaks, CA 91413-0548, USA

Ellison, Jennifer (Actor)
c/o Colette Fenlon *Colette Fenlon Management*
2A Eaton Rd
West Derby
Liverpool L2 7JJ, UNITED KINGDOM (UK)

Ellison, Larry (Business Person)
Oracle Corporation
500 Oracle Pkwy
Redwood City, CA 94065-1675, USA

Ellison, Pervis (Basketball Player)
36 Bishop Ter
Waltham, MA 02452, USA

Ellison, Riki (Football Player)
San Francisco 49ers
1505 Crystal Dr # 1124
Arlington, VA 22202-4115, USA

Ellison, William H (Willie) (Football Player)
Los Angeles Rams
3503 Mosley Ct
Houston, TX 77004-4114, USA

Elliss, Luther (Football Player)
Detroit Lions
2521 Plum Creek Ct
Oakland, MI 48363-2153, USA

Ellroy, James (Writer)
Sobel Weber Assoc
146 E 19th St
New York, NY 10003-2404, USA

Ellsberg, Daniel (Politician)
90 Norwood Ave
Kensington, CA 94707-1150, USA

Ellsworth, Frank L (Educator)
465 W 23rd St Apt 15I
New York, NY 10011-2118, USA

Ellsworth, Kiko (Actor)
c/o Kathy Carter *Axiom Management*
16302 Crowne Brook Cir
Franklin, TN 37067-1673, USA

Ellsworth, Percy (Football Player)
New York Giants
11261 Fortsville Road
Drewryville, VA 23844, USA

Ellsworth, Richard C (Dick) (Baseball Player)
Chicago Cubs
1099 W Morris Ave
Fresno, CA 93711-2432, USA

Ellsworth, Steve (Baseball Player)
Boston Red Sox
546 W Enterprise Ave
Clovis, CA 93619-8356, USA

Ellwood, Paul M Jr (Physicist)
Jackson Hole Group
PO Box 270
Bondurant, WY 82922-0270, USA

Ellzey, Charley (Football Player)
St Louis Cardinals
116 Roosevelt St
Quitman, MS 39355-2018, USA

Elman, Jamie (Actor)
c/o Staff Member *Kohner Agency, The*
9300 Wilshire Blvd Ste 555
Beverly Hills, CA 90212-3211, USA

Elmendorf, Dave (Football Player)
Los Angeles Rams
17990 Fm 1452 W
Normangee, TX 77871-4174, USA

Elmes, Fredrick (Cinematographer)
Mirisch Agency
1801 Century Park E Ste 1801
Los Angeles, CA 90067-2320, USA

Elmore, Henry (Baseball Player)
Birmingham Black Barons
4311 43rd Pl N
Birmingham, AL 35217-3925, USA

Elmore, Len (Basketball Player)
7118 Deer Valley Rd
Highland, MD 20777-9512, USA

Elrod, Jack (Cartoonist)
7240 Hunters Branch Dr NE
Atlanta, GA 30328-1719, USA

Elrod, James (Football Player)
Kansas City Chiefs
10124 S Maplewood Ave
Tulsa, OK 74137-7085, USA

Elrod, Scott (Actor)
c/o Steven Jensen *The Independent Group LLC*
8721 W Sunset Blvd Ste 105
Los Angeles, CA 90069-2271, USA

Els, Ernie (Golfer)
Legends Inc
PO Box 2255
Parklands 2121, SOUTH AFRICA

Elsna, Hebe (Writer)
Curtis Brown
162/168 Regent St
London W1R 5TB, UNITED KINGDOM (UK)

Elsner, Hannelore
ZBF Leopoldstr. 19
Munich D-80802, GERMANY

Elson, Karen (Model)
Ford Models Agence
9 Rue Scribe
Paris 75009, FRANCE

Elster, Kevin D (Baseball Player)
New York Mets
5801 Marshall Dr
Huntington Beach, CA 92649-2727, USA

Elsworth, Michael (Actor)
Sharon Power
PO Box 1243
Wellington, NEW ZEALAND

Elswrit, Richard (Rik) (Music Group)
Artists Int'l Mgmt
9850 Sandalwood Blvd #458
Boca Raton, FL 33428, USA

Elter, Leo (Football Player)
Pittsburgh Steelers
13 Emma Dr
Pittsburgh, PA 15223-1201, USA

Elton, Ben (Actor, Comedian)
Phil McIntyre Mgmt
35 Soho Square
London W1V 5DG, UNITED KINGDOM (UK)

Elvin, Violetta (Ballerina)
Marina di Equa
80066 Seiano
Bay of Naples, ITALY

Elvira, (Cassandra Peterson) (Actor)
Queen B Productions
PO Box 38246
Los Angeles, CA 90038-0246, USA

Elway, John A (Football Player)
c/o Staff Member *Denver Broncos*
13655 Broncos Pkwy
Englewood, CO 80112-4150, USA

Elwes, Cary (Actor)
15030 Ventura Blvd # 710
Sherman Oaks, CA 91403-5470, USA

Ely, Alexandre (Soccer Player)
5526 N 2nd St
Philadelphia, PA 19120-2904, USA

Ely, Jack (Music Group)
Jeff Hubbard Productions
PO Box 53664
Indianapolis, IN 46253-0664, USA

Ely, Joe (Music Group, Songwriter, Writer)
Fitzgerald-Hartley
34 N Palm St # 100
Ventura, CA 93001-2635, USA

Ely, Larry (Football Player)
Cincinnati Bengals
12190 Waters Edge Ct
Loveland, OH 45140-4828, USA

Ely, Melvin (Basketball Player)
Los Angeles Clippers
1111 S Figueroa St
Staples Center
Los Angeles, CA 90015-1300, USA

Eman, J H A (Henny) (Prime Minister)
Prime Minister's Office
Oranjestad, ARUBA

Emanuel, Alphonsia (Actor)
Marina Martin
12/13 Poland St
London W1V 2DE, UNITED KINGDOM (UK)

Emanuel, Bert (Football Player)
Atlanta Falcons
15 Bees Creek Ct
Missouri City, TX 77459-6734, USA

Emanuel, Elizabeth F (Designer, Fashion Designer)
42A Warrington Crescent
Maida Vale
London W9 1EP, UNITED KINGDOM (UK)

Emanuel, Frank (Football Player)
Miami Dolphins
16614 E Course Dr
Tampa, FL 33624-6705, USA

Emanuel, Rahm (Government Official, Journalist)
Whit House
1600 Pennsylvania Ave NW
Washington, DC 20500-0004, USA

Embach, Carsten (Athlete)
BSR Rennsteig e V
Grafenrodaer Str 2
Oberhof 98559, GERMANY

Emberg, Kelly (Actor, Model)
2835 McConnell Dr
Los Angeles, CA 90064-4635, USA

Embery, Joan
San Diego Zoo
2920 Zoo Dr
Park Blvd
San Diego, CA 92101-1693, USA

Embrace (Music Group)
c/o Staff Member *Paradigm (Monterey)*
509 Hartnell St
Monterey, CA 93940-2825, USA

Embree, Alan (Baseball Player)
Cleveland Indians
29400 NE 70th Cir
Camas, WA 98607-7049, USA

Embree, John (Football Player)
Denver Broncos
431 E Moorehaven Dr
Carson, CA 90746-1150, USA

Embree, Jon (Football Player)
Los Angeles Rams
14417 Reeds St
Overland Park, KS 66223-1229, USA

Embry, Ethan (Actor)
c/o Staff Member *William Morris Agency (WMA-LA)*
1 William Morris Pl
Beverly Hills, CA 90212-4261, USA

Embry, Wayne (Basketball Player, Misc)
130 W Juniper Ln
Moreland Hills, OH 44022-1382, USA

Emburey, John E (Cricketer)
Northantshire Cricket Club
Wantage Road
Northampton NN1 4TJ, UNITED KINGDOM (UK)

Emerick, Bob (Football Player)
Detroit Lions
5700 Old Providence Rd
Charlotte, NC 28226, USA

Emerick, Kate (Actor)
c/o Matt Sherman *Matt Sherman Management*
7510 W Sunset Blvd # 1413
Los Angeles, CA 90046-3408, USA

Emerson, Alice F (Educator)
Andrew Mellon Fondation
140 E 62nd St
New York, NY 10065-8124, USA

Emerson, David F (Admiral)
PO Box 90892
Brooklyn, NY 11209-0892, USA

Emerson, Douglas (Actor)
1450 Belfast Dr
Los Angeles, CA 90069-1327, USA

Emerson, George H (Educator)
Utah State University
President's Office
Logan, UT 84322-0001, USA

Emerson, J Martin (Misc)
American Federation of Musicians
1501 Broadway
New York, NY 10036-5601, USA

Emerson, Keith (Musician)
Columbia Artists Mgmt Inc
1790 Broadway Fl 6
New York, NY 10019-1412, USA

Emerson, Roy
2221 Alta Vista Dr
Newport Beach, CA 92660-4128, USA

Emerson Drive (Music Group)
c/o Staff Member *Creative Artists Agency (CAA-Nashville)*
3310 W End Ave Fl 5
Nashville, TN 37203-1028, USA

Emery, Cal (Baseball Player)
Philadelphia Phillies
4817 S 195th East Ave
Broken Arrow, OK 74014-8068, USA

Emery, John (Athlete)
2001 Union St
San Francisco, CA 94123-4114, USA

Emery, Julie Ann (Actor)
c/o Stacey Bock-McLaughlin *Principal Entertainment (LA)*
1964 Westwood Blvd Ste 400
Los Angeles, CA 90025-4695, USA

Emery, Kenneth O (Oceanographer)
35 Horseshoe Ln
North Falmouth, MA 02556-3021, USA

Emery, Lin (Artist, Misc)
7820 Dominican St
New Orleans, LA 70118-3744, USA

Emery, Oren D (Religious Leader)
Wesleyan International
6060 Castlway W Dr
Indianapolis, IN 46250-1930, USA

Emery, Ralph (Entertainer)
PO Box 23470
Nashville, TN 37202-3470, USA

Emery, Victor (Athlete)
61 Walton St
London SW 3J, UNITED KINGDOM (UK)

Emick, Jarrod (Actor)
Gersh Agency
232 N Canon Dr
Beverly Hills, CA 90210-5302, USA

Emilio (Music Group)
Refugee Mgmt
209 10th Ave S Ste 347
Nashville, TN 37203-0762, USA

Emir of Bahrain
721 5th Ave Fl 60
New York, NY 10022-2523, USA

Emir of Kuwait
Banyan Palace
Kuwait City, KUWAIT

Emmanuel (Musician)
Sendyk Leonard
532 Colorado Ave
Santa Monica, CA 90401-2408, USA

Emmanuel, Tommy (Musician)
c/o Staff Member *Paradigm (Monterey)*
509 Hartnell St
Monterey, CA 93940-2825, USA

Emme (Model)
Ford Model Agency
142 Greene St # 400
New York, NY 10012-3236, USA

Emmerich, Noah (Actor)
William Morris Agency
151 El Camino Dr
Beverly Hills, CA 90212-2775, USA

Emmerich, Roland (Director, Producer)
c/o Staff Member *Centropolis Entertainment*
1445 N Stanley Ave Fl 3
Los Angeles, CA 90046-4015, USA

Emmerson, Roy
Private Bag 6060
Richmond South Vic. 3121, AUSTRALIA

Emmet, Mark (Educator)
Louisiana State University
President's Office
Baton Rouge, LA 70803-0001, USA

Emmerton, Bill (Athlete, Track Athlete)
615 Ocean Ave
Santa Monica, CA 90402-2611, USA

Emmett, John C (Inventor)
Oak House Hatfield Broad Oak
Bishop's Stortford
Herts CM22 7HG, UNITED KINGDOM (UK)

Emmons, Frank (Football Player)
Philadelphia Eagles
4207 Phinney Ave N Apt 105
Seattle, WA 98103-7132, USA

Emmott, Bill (Editor)
Economist Magazine
25 Saint James's St
London SW1A 1HG, UNITED KINGDOM (UK)

Emory, Sonny (Misc, Music Group)
Great Scott Productions
4750 Lincoln Blvd Apt 229
Marina Del Rey, CA 90292-6991, USA

Emotions (Music Group)
c/o Staff Member *Diva Central Inc*
7510 W Sunset Blvd Ste 1445
Los Angeles, CA 90046-3408, USA

Emtman, Steven C (Steve) (Football Player)
Indianapolis Colts
19601 S Cheney Spangle Rd
Cheney, WA 99004-9040, USA

En Blanco Y Negro (Music Group)
c/o Staff Member *Sony Music Miami*
605 Lincoln Rd Fl 7
Miami Beach, FL 33139-2900, USA

En Vogue (Music Group)
c/o Phil Casey *International Creative Management (ICM-LA)*
10250 Constellation Blvd
Los Angeles, CA 90067-6200, USA

Enan, Susan (Musician)
c/o Staff Member *Paradigm (Monterey)*
509 Hartnell St
Monterey, CA 93940-2825, USA

Enberg, Alexander (Actor)
c/o Staff Member *TalentWorks (LA)*
3500 W Olive Ave Ste 1400
Burbank, CA 91505-5512, USA

Enberg, Dick (Sportscaster)
1275 Virginia Way
La Jolla, CA 92037-5231, USA

Enbom, John (Writer)
c/o Staff Member *Creative Artists Agency LCC (CAA-LA)*
2000 Avenue Of The Stars
Los Angeles, CA 90067-4700, USA

End of Fashion (Music Group)
c/o Staff Member *Paradigm (Monterey)*
509 Hartnell St
Monterey, CA 93940-2825, USA

Endelman, Stephen (Composer)
Gorfaine/Schwartz
4111 W Alameda Ave Ste 509
Burbank, CA 91505-4171, USA

Ender, Grummt Kornelia (Swimmer)
DSV
Postfach 420140
Kassel 34070, GERMANY

Enderle, Richard (Football Player)
Atlanta Falcons
146 E 49th St Apt 6A
New York, NY 10017-1248, USA

Enders, Erica (Race Car Driver)
c/o Staff Member *Big Machine Media*
404 E 76th St Apt 5K
New York, NY 10021-1411, USA

Enders, Trevor (Baseball Player)
Tampa Bay Devil Rays
930 1/2 32nd Ave N
Saint Petersburg, FL 33704-2047, USA

Endicott, Bill (Baseball Player)
St Louis Cardinals
14219 Oak Knoll Rd
Sonora, CA 95370-8822, USA

Endress, Albert (Football Player)
San Francisco 49ers
4917 Ravenswood Dr Apt 1765
San Antonio, TX 78227-4359, USA

Enevoldsen, Einar (Astronaut, Misc)
9651 Lewis Ave
California City, CA 93505-6203, USA

Engel, Albert E (Geophysicist, Physicist)
University of California
Scripps Institute Geology Dept
La Jolla, CA 92093, USA

Engel, Albert J (Judge)
US Court of Appeals
110 Michigan St NW
Grand Rapids, MI 49503-2300, USA

Engel, Georgia (Actor)
10820 Camanlio St #3
Nort Hollywood, CA 91602, USA

Engel, Steve (Baseball Player)
6212 Old Stone Ct
Hamilton, OH 45011-0003, USA

Engel, Susan
43A Princess Rd. Regents Park
London, ENGLAND NW1 8JS, UNITED KINGDOM (UK)

Engelbart, Douglas C (Scientist)
89 Catalpa Dr
Menlo Park, CA 94027-2167, USA

Engelbrecht, Constanze
17 pass. du Montenegro
Paris F-75019, FRANCE

Engelhard, David H (Religious Leader)
Cristian Reformed Church
2850 Kalamazoo Ave SE
Grand Rapids, MI 49560-0001, USA

Engelhardt, Thomas A (Tom) (Cartoonist, Editor)
Saint Louis Post-Dispatch
900 N Tucker Blvd
Editorial Dept
Saint Louis, MO 63101-1099, USA

Engen, D Travis (Business Person)
ITT Industries
4 W Red Oak Ln
White Plains, NY 10604-3617, USA

Engerman, Stanley L (Economist, Historian)
181 Warrington Dr
Rochester, NY 14618-1122, USA

Engholm, Bjorn (Government Official)
Jurgen-Wallenwever-Str 9
Lubeck, GERMANY

Engibous, Thomas J (Business Person)
Texas Instruments
PO Box 660199
8505 Forest Lane
Dallas, TX 75266-0199, USA

England, Anthony (Astronaut, Geophysicist, Physicist)
7949 Ridgeway Ct
Dexter, MI 48130-9700, USA

England, Audie
6100 Wilshire Blvd Ste 1170
Los Angeles, CA 90048-5116, USA

England, Dan
PO Box 220082
Great Neck, NY 11022-0082, USA

England, Gordon R (Secretary)
Homeland Security Department
Washington, DC 20528-0001, USA

England, Richard (Architect)
26/1 Merchants St
Valletta, MALTA

England, Ty
3322 W End Ave # 520
Nashville, TN 37203-1031, USA

England, Tyler (Music Group)
Buddy Lee
38 Music Sq E Ste 200
Nashville, TN 37203-4304, USA

Englander, Herold R (Doctor, Scientist)
11502 Whisper Bluff St
San Antonio, TX 78230-3704, USA

Engle, Dave (Baseball Player)
Minnesota Twins
5343 Castle Hills Dr
San Diego, CA 92109-1926, USA

Engle, Doug (Baseball Player)
Montreal Expos
17282 Helser Rd
Berlin Center, OH 44401, USA

Engle, Eleanor (Baseball Player)
Archives
319 W Main St
Camp Hill, PA 17011-6333, USA

Engle, Joe (Astronaut, General)
3280 Cedar Heights Dr
Colorado Springs, CO 80904-4728, USA

Engle, Robert F (Nobel Prize Laureate)
New York University
Stem Business School
New York, NY 10012, USA

Englehart, Robert W (Bob) Jr (Cartoonist, Editor)
Hartford Courant
280 Broad St
Editorial Dept
Hartford, CT 06105, USA

Engler, John M (Governor)
PO Box 30013
Lansing, MI 48909-7513, USA

Engles, Rick (Football Player)
Seattle Seahawks
11307 S Vine St
Jenks, OK 74037-2466, USA

English, Alexander (Alex) (Basketball Player)
596 Rimer Pond Rd
Blythewood, SC 29016-9448, USA

English, Corri (Actor)
c/o Staff Member *SMS Talent Inc*
8730 W Sunset Blvd Ste 440
Los Angeles, CA 90069-2277, USA

English, Diane (Writer)
c/o Staff Member *Shukovsky/English Entertainment*
4605 Lankershim Blvd Ste 510
North Hollywood, CA 91602-1877, USA

English, Edmond J (Business Person)
TJX Companies
770 Cochituate Rd
Framingham, MA 01701-4666, USA

English, Floyd L (Business Person)
Andrew Corp
10500 W 153rd St
Orland Park, IL 60462-3467, USA

English, James F Jr (Educator)
31 Potter St
Groton, CT 06340-5734, USA

English, Joseph T (Doctor)
Saint Vincent's Hospital
203 W 12th St
New York, NY 10011-7762, USA

English, Kim (Musician)
c/o Staff Member *Diva Central Inc*
7510 W Sunset Blvd Ste 1445
Los Angeles, CA 90046-3408, USA

English, L Douglas (Doug) (Football Player)
Detroit Lions
4306 Bennedict Ln
Austin, TX 78746-1940, USA

English, Madeline (Baseball Player)
55 Clinton St
Everett, MA 02149-4640, USA

English, Michael (Music Group)
Trifecta Entertainment
209 10th Ave S Ste 302
Nashville, TN 37203-0730, USA

English, Paul (Actor)
Wurzel Talent Mgmt
19528 Ventura Blvd # 501
Tarzana, CA 91356-2917, USA

Engluand, Robert (Actor)
1616 Santa Cruz St
Laguna Beach, CA 92651-3350, USA

Englund, Robert (Actor)
1278 Glenneyre St Pmb 73
Laguna Beach, CA 92651-3103, USA

Engstrom, Ted W (Misc)
World Vision
919 W Huntington Dr
Arcadia, CA 91007-8811, USA

Engvall, Bill (Actor, Comedian)
c/o John MacDonald *Parallel Entertainment*
9229 W Sunset Blvd Ste 311
West Hollywood, CA 90069-3403, USA

Enich, Steve (Football Player)
Chicago Cardinals
8621 W Beloit Rd Apt 119
Milwaukee, WI 53227-3759, USA

Enigma (Music Group)
c/o Staff Member *Virgin Records (NY)*
304 Park Ave S Fl 5
New York, NY 10010-4316, USA

Enis, Curtis (Football Player)
Chicago Bears
10972 Comanche Dr
Sidney, OH 45365-9586, USA

Enis, Hunter (Football Player)
Dallas Texans
RR 3
Jacksboro, TX 76458, USA

Enke, Fred (Football Player)
Detroit Lions
206 E McMurray Blvd
Casa Grande, AZ 85222-3415, USA

Enke, Werner
Moltkestr. 6
Munich D-80803, GERMANY

Enke-Kania, Karin (Skier)
Tolstoistr 3
Dresden 01326, GERMANY

Enkhbayar, Nambaryn (Prime Minister)
Prime Minister's Office
Great Hural
Ulan Bator 12, MONGOLIA

Enn, Hans (Skier)
Hinterglemm 400
Saalbach 5754, AUSTRIA

Ennis, Ralph (Musician)
2 Kirklake Bank
Formby
Liverpool L37 2Y5, UNITED KINGDOM (UK)

Ennis, Ray (Musician)
2 Kirklake Bank
Formby
Liverpool L37 2Y5, UNITED KINGDOM (UK)

Ennis Sisters, The (Music Group)
c/o Staff Member *Paradigm (Monterey)*
509 Hartnell St
Monterey, CA 93940-2825, USA

Eno, Brian (Actor)
c/o Brian Loucks *Creative Artists Agency LCC (CAA-LA)*
2000 Avenue Of The Stars
Los Angeles, CA 90067-4700, USA

Eno, Brian (Composer, Musician)
Opal Music
3 Pembridge Mews
London W11 3Eq, UNITED KINGDOM (UK)

Enoch, Russell
43A Princess Rd. Regents Park
London, ENGLAND NW1 8JS, UNITED KINGDOM (UK)

Enos, John (Actor)
c/o Lara Rosenstock *Lara Rosenstock Management*
8371 Blackburn Ave Apt 1
Los Angeles, CA 90048-4245, USA

Enrico, Roger A (Business Person)
Pepsi Co Inc
700 Anderson Hill Rd
Purchase, NY 10577-1444, USA

Enright, George (Baseball Player)
Montreal Expos
3075 Strawflower Way
Lake Worth, FL 33467-1465, USA

Enrique, Luis (Musician)
c/o Staff Member *Verve Music Group*
1755 Broadway Frnt 3
New York, NY 10019-3743, USA

Enriquez, Jocelyn
1135 Francisco St Apt 7
San Francisco, CA 94109-1075, USA

Enriquez, Joy (Musician)
c/o Staff Member *William Morris Agency (WMA-LA)*
1 William Morris Pl
Beverly Hills, CA 90212-4261, USA

Ensberg, Morgan (Baseball Player)
Houston Astros
1132 3rd St
Hermosa Beach, CA 90254-4901, USA

Ensher, Jason R (Physicist)
University of Colorado
Physics Dept
Boulder, CO 80309-0001, USA

Ensign, Michael (Actor)
Abrams Artists
9200 W Sunset Blvd Ste 1125
Los Angeles, CA 90069-3610, USA

Ensler, Eve (Actor, Producer, Writer)
c/o Staff Member *William Morris Agency (WMA-LA)*
1 William Morris Pl
Beverly Hills, CA 90212-4261, USA

Ensley, Frank (Baseball Player)
Kansas City Monarchs
601 Monday Road
Grambling, LA 71245, USA

Entner, Warren (Music Group)
Thomas Cassidy
11761 E Speedway Blvd
Tucson, AZ 85748-2017, USA

Entremont, Philippe
Schwarzenbergplatz 10/7
Vienna A-1040, AUSTRIA

Entremont, Philippe (Musician)
10 Rue de Castuglione
Paris 75001, FRANCE

Entwhistle, John
PO Box 241
Lake Peekskill, NY 10537-0241, USA

Enya (Composer, Musician)
c/o Staff Member *Shore Fire Media*
32 Court St Ste 1600
Brooklyn, NY 11201-4441, USA

Enyart, Terry (Baseball Player)
Montreal Expos
3444 Foxwood Blvd
Zephyrhills, FL 33543-5155, USA

Enzensberger, Hans M (Writer)
Lindenstr 29
Frankfurt am Maim 60325, GERMANY

Eotvos, Peter (Composer)
Naardeweg 56
Blaircum 1261 BV, THE NETHERLANDS

Ephriam, Mablean (Judge)
c/o Sean Perry *Endeavor Agency LLC (LA)*
9601 Wilshire Blvd Fl 3
Beverly Hills, CA 90210-5204, USA

Ephron, Nora (Director, Producer, Writer)
c/o Staff Member *William Morris Agency (WMA-LA)*
1 William Morris Pl
Beverly Hills, CA 90212-4261, USA

Epic (Artist, Musician)
Wyze Mgmt
34 Maple St
London W1 5GD, UNITED KINGDOM (UK)

Eppard, Jim (Baseball Player)
California Angels
23115 153rd Ave
Rapid City, SD 57703-9041, USA

Epperson-Doumani, Brenda (Actor)
kazarian/Spencer
11365 Ventura Blvd Ste 100
Studio City, CA 91604-3148, USA

Eppinger, Dale L (War Hero)
101 Windy Hollow St
Victoria, TX 77904-3405, USA

Epple, Maria (Skier)
Gunzesried 3
Blaicach 87544, GERMANY

Epple-Beck, Irene (Skier)
Autmberg 235
Seeg 87637, GERMANY

Eppler, Dieter
Franziskaweg 17
Stuttgart D-70599, GERMANY

Epps, Bobby (Football Player)
New York Giants
934 Illinois Ave
Pittsburgh, PA 15221-4718, USA

Epps, Hal (Baseball Player)
St Louis Cardinals
11900 Barryknoll Ln Apt 2112
Houston, TX 77024-4322, USA

Epps, Mike (Actor)
c/o Chris Smith *International Creative Management (ICM-LA)*
10250 Constellation Blvd
Los Angeles, CA 90067-6200, USA

Epps, Omar (Actor)
c/o Raelle Koota *Anonymous Content (NY)*
8522 National Blvd Ste 101
Culver City, CA 90232-2454, USA

Epps, Phil (Football Player)
Green Bay Packers
212 Boulder Creek Dr
Desoto, TX 75115-5324, USA

Epstein, Daniel M (Writer)
843 W University Pkwy
Baltimore, MD 21210-2911, USA

Epstein, Gabriel (Architect)
3 Rue Mazet
Paris 75006, FRANCE

Epstein, Jake (Actor)
AMI Artist Management Inc
550 Queen Street East
Suite 315
Toronto, ON M5A 1V2, CANADA

Epstein, Jason (Editor)
Random House
1745 Broadway # B1
New York, NY 10019-4305, USA

Epstein, Joseph (Educator, Writer)
522 Church St Apt 6B
Evanston, IL 60201-4559, USA

Epstein, Mike (Baseball Player)
Baltimore Orioles
6384 S Blackhawk Way
Aurora, CO 80016-3112, USA

Erardi, Greg (Baseball Player)
Seattle Mariners
42 Westgate Rd
Massapequa Park, NY 11762-1953, USA

Erasure (Music Group)
c/o Jonny (Jon) Podell *Podell Talent Agency LLC*
22 W 21st St Fl 9
New York, NY 10010-7095, USA

Erautt, Eddie (Baseball Player)
Cincinnati Reds
7252 Walte Dr
La Mesa, CA 91941, USA

Erb, Christy (Golfer)
4043 Country Trl
Bonita, CA 91902-3025, USA

Erb, Donald J (Composer)
2073 Bluestone Road
Cleveland, OH 44121, USA

Erb, Richard D (Government Official)
International Monetary Fund
700 19th St NW
Washington, DC 20431-0002, USA

Erbakan, Necmettin (Prime Minister)
National Salvation Party
Balgat
Ankara, TURKEY

Erbe, Kathryn (Actor)
LMR
1964 Westwood Blvd Ste 400
Los Angeles, CA 90025-4695, USA

Erburu, Robert F (Business Person, Publisher)
1518 Blue Jay Way
Los Angeles, CA 90069-1215, USA

Erdlitz, Dick (Football Player)
Philadelphia Eagles
134 US Highway 64W
Cashiers, NC 28717, USA

Erdman, Dennis (Actor, Director, Producer)
c/o Staff Member *International Creative Management (ICM-LA)*
10250 Constellation Blvd
Los Angeles, CA 90067-6200, USA

Erdman, Paul E (Writer)
1817 Lytton Springs Rd
Healdsburg, CA 95448-9145, USA

Erdman, Richard (Actor)
5655 Greenbush Ave
Van Nuys, CA 91401-4513, USA

Erdmann, Susi-Lisa (Athlete)
Karwendelstr 8A
Munich 81369, GERMANY

Erdo, Peter Cardinal (Religious Leader)
Mindszenty Hercegprimas Ter 2
Esztergom Magyarirszay 2501,
HUNGARY

Erdogan, Recep Tayyip (Prime Minister)
Premier's Office
Eski Basbakanlik
Bakanliklar
Ankara, TURKEY

Erdos, Todd (Baseball Player)
San Diego Padres
118 Windsor Ct
Cranberry Twp, PA 16066-3216, USA

Erenberg, Richard (Football Player)
Pittsburgh Steelers
318 Snowberry Cir
Venetia, PA 15367-1043, USA

Ergen, Charles W (Business Person)
EchoStar Communications Corp
5701 S Santa Fe Dr
Littleton, CO 80120-1813, USA

Erhardt, Warren R (Publisher)
455 Wakefield Dr
Metuchen, NJ 08840-1626, USA

Erhuero, Oris (Actor)
c/o Staff Member *Midwest Talent Management Inc*
4821 Lankershim Blvd Ste F
Pmb 149
N Hollywood, CA 91601-4572, USA

Eric, B (Music Group, Musician)
Rush Artists
1600 Varick St
New York, NY 10013, USA

Eric Kaplan, Bruce (Producer)
c/o Staff Member *William Morris Agency (WMA-LA)*
1 William Morris Pl
Beverly Hills, CA 90212-4261, USA

Ericks, John (Baseball Player)
Philadelphia Phillies
17000 Oketo Ave
Tinley Park, IL 60477-2630, USA

Erickson, Arthur C (Architect)
Arthur Erickson Architects
1672 W 1st Ave
Vancouver, BC V6J 1G1, CANADA

Erickson, Bud (Football Player)
Washington Redskins
14523 165th Pl NE
Woodinville, WA 98072-9037, USA

Erickson, Craig (Football Player)
Tampa Bay Buccaneers
420 N Country Club Dr
Lake Worth, FL 33462-1004, USA

Erickson, Dennis (Coach, Football Coach)
San Francisco 49ers
4949 Centennial Blvd
Santa Clara, CA 95054-1229, USA

Erickson, Don (Baseball Player)
Philadelphia Phillies
1929 Montana Dr
Springfield, IL 62704-4150, USA

Erickson, Ethan (Actor)
c/o Staff Member *Diverse Talent Group*
1875 Century Park E Ste 2250
Los Angeles, CA 90067-2563, USA

Erickson, Hal (Baseball Player)
Detroit Tigers
4000 Brinker Ave Apt 10
Ogden, UT 84403-2452, USA

Erickson, keith (Basketball Player, Volleyball Player)
333 23rd St
Santa Monica, CA 90402-2513, USA

Erickson, Robert (Composer)
University of California
Music Dept
La Jolla, CA 92093, USA

Erickson, Roger (Baseball Player)
Minnesota Twins
2647 Delaware Dr
Springfield, IL 62702-1213, USA

Erickson, Scott (Actor)
501 Chicago Ave
Minneapolis, MN 55415-1517, USA

Erickson, Scott G (Baseball Player)
Minnesota Twins
PO Box 2790
Stateline, NV 89449-2790, USA

Erickson, Steve (Writer)
Poseidon Press
1230 Avenue Of The Americas
New York, NY 10020-1513, USA

Erickson-Sauer, Louise (Baseball Player)
917 Pleasant Ave
Arcadia, WI 54612-1859, USA

Ericson, John (Actor)
7 Avenida Vista Grande # 310
Santa Fe, NM 87508-9198, USA

Eriksen, Stein (Skier)
7700 Stein Way
Park City, UT 84060-5132, USA

Erikson, Duke (Misc)
Borman Entertainment
1250 6th St Ste 401
Santa Monica, CA 90401-1638, USA

Erikson, Raymond L (Doctor)
Harvard University
25 Shattuck St
Medical School
Boston, MA 02115-6027, USA

Erixon, Jan (Hockey Player)
PO Box 90111
Arlington, TX 76004-3111, USA

Erlandson, Eric (Songwriter, Writer)
Artist Group International
9560 Wilshire Blvd Ste 400
Beverly Hills, CA 90212-2416, USA

Erlandson, Tom Sr (Football Player)
Denver Broncos
1045 E Possee Rd
Castle Rock, CO 80108-9312, USA

Erman, John (Director)
c/o Johnnie Planco *Untitled Entertainment (NY)*
322 8th Ave Ste 601
New York, NY 10001-6715, USA

Ermer, Cal (Baseball Player)
Washington Senators
120 Ashton Park
Peachtree City, GA 30269-3663, USA

Ermy, R Lee
4348 W Avenue N3
Palmdale, CA 93551-1823, USA

Erna, Sully (Actor, Music Group)
c/o Staff Member *William Morris Agency (WMA-LA)*
1 William Morris Pl
Beverly Hills, CA 90212-4261, USA

Ernaga, Frank (Baseball Player)
Chicago Cubs
50 N Roop St
Susanville, CA 96130-3926, USA

Erni, Hans (Artist)
6045 Meggen
Lucerne, SWITZERLAND

Ernst, Bret (Actor, Comedian)
c/o Joan Green *Joan Green Management*
1836 Courtney Ter
Los Angeles, CA 90046-2106, USA

Ernst, Richard R (Nobel Prize Laureate)
Kurlistr 24
Winterthur, SWITZERLAND

Eroy, Iran (Actor)
c/o Staff Member *Televisa*
Blvd Adolfo Lopez Mateos 232
Colonia San Angel INN
DF CP 01060, MEXICO

Errazuriz Ossa, Francisco J Cardinal
(Religious Leader)
Casilla 30D
Erasmo Escala 1894
Santiago, CHILE

Errico, Melissa (Actor)
c/o Staff Member *International Creative Managemnet*
8942 Wilshire Blvd
Beverly Hills, CA 90211-1908, USA

Erskine, Carl D (Baseball Player)
Brooklyn Dodgera
4031 Fallbrook Ln
Anderson, IN 46011-1609, USA

Erskine, Peter (Musician)
1727 Hill St
Santa Monica, CA 90405-4843, USA

Erskine, Ralph (Architect)
Box 156
Gustav III's Vag
Drottningholm 170 11, SWEDEN

Erstad, Darin C (Baseball Player)
California Angels
3224 35 1/2 Court Ave S
Fargo, ND 58104-8879, USA

Ertl, Martina (Skier)
Erthofe 17
Lenggries 83661, GERMANY

Ertl, Sue (Golfer)
314 N 6th St
Quincy, IL 62301-2702, USA

Eruzione, Michael (Mike) (Hockey Player)
% Boston University
599 Commonwealth Ave
Athletic Dept
Boston, MA 02215, USA

Erving, Julius
PO Box 914100
Longwood, FL 32791-4100, USA

Erving, Jullus W (Dr J) (Basketball Player)
400 E Colonial Dr Apt 1607
Orlando, FL 32803-4522, USA

Ervolino, Frank (Politician)
Laundry & Dry Cleaning Union
107 Delaware Ave
Buffalo, NY 14202-2810, USA

Erwin, Bill (Actor)
12324 Moorpark St
Studio City, CA 91604-1233, USA

Erwin, Hank
4213rd St. NE
Leeds, AL 35094, USA

Erwin, Mike (Actor)
c/o Loch Powell *Leverage Management*
1610 Broadway
Santa Monica, CA 90404-2792, USA

Erwitt, Elliott R (Photographer)
88 Central Park W
New York, NY 10023-5209, USA

Erxleban, Russell A (Football Player)
144 World Of Tennis Sq
Lakeway, TX 78738-1104, USA

Erxleben, Russell (Football Player)
New Orleans Saints
306 Saddlehorn Dr
Dripping Springs, TX 78620-2740, USA

Esaki, Leo (Nobel Prize Laureate)
2484 Uenomuro
Tsukuba Ibaraki 305, JAPAN

Esasky, Nick (Baseball Player)
Cincinnati Reds
1779 Starlight Dr
Marietta, GA 30062-1942, USA

Escalante, Jaime A (Educator)
Hiram Johnson High School
6879 14th Ave
Sacramento, CA 95820-3499, USA

Escape (DJ)
c/o Len Evans *Project Publicity*
312 W 53rd St
New York, NY 10019-5743, USA

Escarpeta, Arlen (Actor)
c/o Jerry Shandrew *Shandrew Public Relations*
1050 S Stanley Ave
Los Angeles, CA 90019-6634, USA

Eschbach, Jesse E (Judge)
US Court of Appeals
701 Clematis St
US Courthouse
West Palm Beach, FL 33401-5101, USA

Eschelman, Vaughn (Baseball Player)
Boston Red Sox
30106 Falher Dr
Spring, TX 77386-1683, USA

Eschen, Larry (Baseball Player)
Philadelphia Athletics
3649 Garden Blvd
Gainesville, GA 30506-1552, USA

Eschenbach, Christoph
2 Ave. d'Alena
Paris 75016, FRANCE

Eschenbach, Christoph (Musician)
Maspalomas
Monte Leon 760625
Gran Canaria, SPAIN

Eschenmoser, Albert J (Misc)
Bergstra 9
Kusnacht, ZH 8700, SWITZERLAND

Eschert, Jurgen (Athlete)
Tornowstr 8
Potsdam 1447, GERMANY

Escovedo, Pete (Musician)
PO Box 1741
C/O Victor Pamiroyan
Alameda, CA 94501-0199, USA

Esiason, Norman J (Boomer) (Football Player)
Cincinnati Bengals
25 Heights Rd
Plandome, NY 11030-1412, USA

Eskell, Diana
41 Bushgrove Stanmore
Middlesex, ENGLAND HA7 2DY,
UNITED KINGDOM (UK)

Esler-Smith, Frank (Misc)
Agency for Peroforming Arts
405 S Beverly Dr Ste 500
Beverly Hills, CA 90212-4425, USA

Esparza, Moctesuma (Producer)
c/o Staff Member *International Creative Management (ICM-LA)*
10250 Constellation Blvd
Los Angeles, CA 90067-6200, USA

Esperon, Natalia (Actor)
c/o Staff Member *Televisa*
Blvd Adolfo Lopez Mateos 232
Colonia San Angel INN
DF CP 01060, MEXICO

Espino, Gaby (Actor)
c/o Gabriel Blanco *Gabriel Blanco Iglesias (Mexico)*
Rio Balsas 35-32
Colonia Cuauhtemoc
DF 06500, MEXICO

Espinoza, Alvaro (Baseball Player)
Minnesota Twins
707 SW Lake Charles Cir
Port Saint Lucie, FL 34986-3447, USA

Espinoza, Mark (Actor)
c/o Staff Member *Howard Entertainment*
10850 Wilshire Blvd Ste 1260
Los Angeles, CA 90024-4337, USA

Esposito, Frank (Bowler)
200 N State Rt 17
Paramus, NJ 07652-2902, USA

Esposito, Giancarlo (Actor)
c/o Staff Member *Untitled Entertainment (LA)*
331 N Maple Dr Fl 3
Beverly Hills, CA 90210-3827, USA

Esposito, Jennifer (Actor)
648 Broadway # 912
New York, NY 10012-2301, USA

Esposito, Laura (Actor)
Gersh Agency
232 N Canon Dr
Beverly Hills, CA 90210-5302, USA

Esposito, Mike (Football Player)
Atlanta Falcons
8 Hovey Meadow Rd
Atkinson, NH 03811, USA

Esposito, Phil (Hockey Player)
4807 Tea Rose Ct
Lutz, FL 33558-9004, USA

Esposito, Sammy (Baseball Player)
Chicago White Sox
8303 Amber Leaf Ct
Raleigh, NC 27612-7388, USA

Esposito, Tony
418 55th Ave
St Pete Beach, FL 33706-2311, USA

Espy, A Michael (Mike) (Secretary)
154 Deertrail Ln
Madison, MS 39110-9309, USA

Espy, Cecil (Baseball Player)
Los Angeles Dodgers
5480 Encina Dr
San Diego, CA 92114-6307, USA

Esquivel, Laura (Writer)
Creative Artists Agency
9830 Wilshire Blvd
Beverly Hills, CA 90212-1804, USA

Esquivel, Manuel (Prime Minister)
United Democratic Party
19 King St
PO Box 1143
Belize City, BELIZE

Essany, Michael (Actor, Talk Show Host)
Michael Essany Show
139 Concord Cir
C/O Mike Randazzo
Valparaiso, IN 46385-8070, USA

Essegian, Chuck (Baseball Player)
Philadelphia Phillies
15639 Bronco Dr
Canyon Country, CA 91387-4717, USA

Essensa, Bob (Hockey Player)
Boston Bruins
1 Fleetcenter Pl Ste 250
Boston, MA 02114-1390, USA

Esser, Clarence (Football Player)
Chicago Cardinals
10 S Brown Ave
Orlando, FL 32801, USA

Esser, Mark (Baseball Player)
Chicago White Sox
208 Ridge Rd
Jupiter, FL 33477-9652, USA

Essex, David
5 Stratford Saye 20-22 Wellington
Bournemouth Dorset, ENGLAND BG8
8JN, UNITED KINGDOM (UK)

Essian, James (Jim) (Baseball Player)
Philadelphia Phillies
134 Eckford Dr
Troy, MI 48085-4745, USA

Essink, Ron (Football Player)
Seattle Seahawks
PO Box 265
Hamilton, MI 49419-0265, USA

Esslinger, Hartmut (Designer)
FrogDesign
3460 Hillview Ave
Palo Alto, CA 94304-1338, USA

Essman, Susie (Comedian)
c/o Staff Member *William Morris Agency (WMA-LA)*
1 William Morris Pl
Beverly Hills, CA 90212-4261, USA

Esswood, Paul L V (Opera Singer)
Jasmine Cottage
42 Ferring Lane
West Sussex BN12 6QT, UNITED
KINGDOM (UK)

Estacea, Elizabeth (Musician)
PO Box 691481
Charlotte, NC 28227-7025, USA

Estalelia, Bobby (Baseball Player)
Philadelphia Phillies
1850 NW 139th Ave
Pembroke Pines, FL 33028-2839, USA

Esteban, Samantha (Actor)
c/o Staff Member *James/Levy/Jacobson Management*
3500 W Olive Ave Ste 1470
Burbank, CA 91505-5514, USA

Estefan, Emilio (Musician)
Estefan Enterprises
420 Jefferson Ave
Miami Beach, FL 33139-6503, USA

Estefan, Gloria (Musician)
c/o Emanuel Nunez *Creative Artists Agency LCC (CAA-LA)*
2000 Avenue Of The Stars
Los Angeles, CA 90067-4700, USA

Estefan, Lili (Actor)
c/o Staff Member *Univision*
605 3rd Ave Fl 12
New York, NY 10158-1299, USA

Estefan, Manuel A (Educator)
California State University
President's Office
Chico, CA 95929-0001, USA

Estelle, Dick (Baseball Player)
San Francisco Giants
2221 Taylor St
Point Pleasant Boro, NJ 08742-3839, USA

Esten, Charles (Actor)
c/o Staff Member *Stone Manners Talent & Literary (LA)*
6500 Wilshire Blvd Ste 550
Los Angeles, CA 90048-4950, USA

Estern, Neil (Misc)
432 Cream Hill Rd
West Cornwall, CT 06796-1210, USA

Estes, A Shawn (Baseball Player)
c/o Staff Member *Arizona Diamondbacks*
401 E Jefferson St
Bank One Ballpark
Phoenix, AZ 85004-2438, USA

Estes, Billy Sol
1004 S College St
Brady, TX 76825-5528, USA

Estes, Bob (Golfer)
4408 Long Champ Dr Apt 21
Austin, TX 78746-1186, USA

Estes, Ellen (Misc)
Stanford University
Athletic Dept
Stanford, CA 94305, USA

Estes, Howell M Jr (Business Person, General)
7603 Shadywood Rd
Bethesda, MD 20817-2066, USA

Estes, James (Cartoonist)
1103 Callahan St
Amarillo, TX 79106-4201, USA

Estes, Larry (Football Player)
New Orleans Saints
629 Day St
Louisville, MS 39339-8517, USA

Estes, Rob (Actor)
c/o Elizabeth Much *Much and House Public Relations*
8075 W 3rd St Ste 500
Los Angeles, CA 90048-4325, USA

Estes, Robert (Actor)
910 Idaho Ave
Santa Monica, CA 90403-2904, USA

Estes, Simon L (Opera Singer)
Hochstr 43
Feldmeilen 8706, SWITZERLAND

Estes, Will (Actor)
c/o Liza Anderson *Warren Cowan & Associates PR*
8899 Beverly Blvd Ste 919
Los Angeles, CA 90048-2436, USA

Estes, William K (Physicist)
1145 Linden Dr
Bloomington, IN 47408-1277, USA

Esteve-Coll, Elizabeth (Misc)
27 Ursulu St
London SW11 3DW, UNITED KINGDOM (UK)

Estevez, Emilio (Actor, Director)
c/o Matt Kuiper *900 Frames*
12910 Culver Blvd Ste G
Los Angeles, CA 90066-6710, USA

Estevez, Luis (Designer, Fashion Designer)
122 E 7th St
Los Angeles, CA 90014-2014, USA

Estevez, Ramon (Actor)
837 Ocean Ave # 101
Santa Monica, CA 90403, USA

Estevez, Renee (Actor)
Michael Mann Talent
977 Lake St
Venice, CA 90291-2853, USA

Esthero (Musician)
c/o Staff Member *ArtistDirect*
1601 Cloverfield Blvd # 400
Santa Monica, CA 90404-4082, USA

Estill, Michelle (Golfer)
642 Yacavona St
Kent, OH 44240-3318, USA

Estleman, Loren Daniel (Writer)
5552 Walsh Rd
Whitmore Lake, MI 48189-9673, USA

Estock, George (Baseball Player)
595 Ray St
Sebastian, FL 32958-4245, USA

Estrada, Charle L (Chuck) (Baseball Player)
Baltimore Orioles
1289 Manzanita Way
San Luis Obispo, CA 93401-7838, USA

Estrada, Erik (Actor)
c/o Konrad Leh *Sterling/Winters Company, The*
10900 Wilshire Blvd Ste 1550
Los Angeles, CA 90024-6525, USA

Estrada, Erik-Michael (Musician)
c/o PJ Shapiro *Ziffren Brittenham Branca Fischer Gilbert-Lurie, Stiffman & Cook*
1801 Century Park W
Los Angeles, CA 90067-6409, USA

Estrella, Alberto (Actor)
c/o Staff Member *Televisa*
Blvd Adolfo Lopez Mateos 232
Colonia San Angel INN
DF CP 01060, MEXICO

Estrella, Leo (Baseball Player)
Toronto Blue Jays
5462 NW Boydga Ave
Port St Lucie, FL 34986-4038, USA

Estrich, Susan (Attorney, Attorney General, General)
9255 Doheny Rd Apt 802
West Hollywood, CA 90069-3206, USA

Estrin, Zack (Writer)
c/o Staff Member *Endeavor Agency LLC (LA)*
9601 Wilshire Blvd Fl 3
Beverly Hills, CA 90210-5204, USA

Eszterhas, Joe
8942 Wilshire Blvd
Beverly Hills, CA 90211-1908, USA

Eszterhas, Joseph A (Writer)
Rogers & Cowan
8687 Melrose Ave
West Hollywood, CA 90069-5701, USA

Etaix, Pierre (Actor, Director)
Cirque Fratellini
2 Rue de la Cloture
Paris 75019, FRANCE

Etchebarren, Andy (Baseball Player)
Baltimore Orioles
1488 Vermeer Dr
Nokomis, FL 34275-4470, USA

Etchegaray, Roger Cardinal (Religious Leader)
Piazza San Calisto
Vatican City 00120, VATICAN CITY

Etcheverry, Marco (Soccer Player)
DC United
14120 Newbrook Dr
Chantilly, VA 20151-2273, USA

Etcheverry, Michel (Actor)
47 Rue du Borrego
Paris 75020, FRANCE

Etebari, Eric (Actor)
c/o Staff Member *Agency for the Performing Arts (APA-LA)*
405 S Beverly Dr
Beverly Hills, CA 90212-4416, USA

Etharton, Seth (Baseball Player)
Anaheim Angels
16 Saint John
Dana Point, CA 92629-4127, USA

Etheredge, Carlos (Football Player)
Indianapolis Colts
1231 Tuscumbia Rd
Collierville, TN 38017-3418, USA

Etheridge, Bobby (Baseball Player)
San Francisco Giants
118 Portland Rd
Eudora, AR 71640-2174, USA

Etheridge, Joe (Football Player)
Green Bay Packers
900 E Bryan St
Kermit, TX 79745-3623, USA

Etheridge, Melissa (Musician, Songwriter, Writer)
c/o Marcel Pariseau *True Public Relations*
6725 W Sunset Blvd Ste 570
Los Angeles, CA 90028-7180, USA

Ethridge, Mark F III (Editor)
5516 Gorham Dr
Charlotte, NC 28226-6414, USA

Etienne-Martin (Artist)
7 Rue du Pot de Fer
Paris 75005, FRANCE

Etrog, Sorel (Artist)
PO Box 67034
23 Yonge St
Toronto, ON M4P 1E0, CANADA

Etsel, Edward (Ed) (Misc)
University of Virginia
Athletic Dept
Charlottesville, VA 22906, USA

Etsou-Nzabi-Bamungwabi, Frederic (Religious Leader)
Archdiocese of Kinshasa
BP 8431
Kinshasa 1, CONGO DEMOCRATIC REPUBLIC

Etter, Bob (Football Player)
Atlanta Falcons
8609 La Riviera Dr Apt F
Sacramento, CA 95826-1775, USA

Ettinger, Cynthia (Actor)
c/o Dan Barnhardt *Thruline Entertainment*
9250 Wilshire Blvd Ground Fl
Beverly Hills, CA 90210, USA

Ettles, Mark (Baseball Player)
San Diego Padres
3-10 Rose Avenue
South Perth 6151, AUSTRALIA

Etzel, Gregory A M (War Hero)
7822 Wonder St
Citrus Heights, CA 95610-2422, USA

Etzioni, Amitai W (Activist)
7110 Arran Pl
Bethesda, MD 20817-4771, USA

Etzwiler, Donnell D (Doctor)
7611 Bush Lake Dr
Minneapolis, MN 55438-1695, USA

Eubank, Chris (Boxer)
9 Upper Dr
Hove, East Sussex BN3 6GR, UNITED KINGDOM (UK)

Eubanks, Bob (Television Host)
PO Box 1634
Santa Ynez, CA 93460-1634, USA

Eubanks, Kevin (Musician)
Ted Kurland
173 Brighton Ave
Boston, MA 02134-2003, USA

Eufernia, Frank (Baseball Player)
Minnesota Twins
10 Mariners Rd
Seaside Heights, NJ 08751-1335, USA

Eure, Wesley (Actor)
Irv Schechter
9300 Wilshire Blvd # 410
Beverly Hills, CA 90212-3213, USA

Europe
Box 22036
Stockholm S-10422, SWEDEN

Eurythmics (Music Group)
c/o Staff Member *William Morris Agency (WMA-LA)*
1 William Morris Pl
Beverly Hills, CA 90212-4261, USA

Eusebio, Tony (Baseball Player)
Houston Astros
2078 Shannon Lakes Blvd
Kissimmee, FL 34743-3648, USA

Evan & Jaron (Music Group)
c/o Billy Lazarus *United Talent Agency (UTA)*
9560 Wilshire Blvd Ste 500
Beverly Hills, CA 90212-2401, USA

Evanescence (Music Group)
c/o Dennis Rider *Dennis Rider Management*
931 Hilldale Ave
West Hollywood, CA 90069-4404, USA

Evangelista, Daniella (Actor)
c/o Steve Chasman *Ace Media*
1411 5th St Ste 405
Santa Monica, CA 90401-2417, USA

Evangelista, Linda (Actor, Model)
c/o Didier Fernandez *DNA Model Management*
520 Broadway Fl 11
New York, NY 10012-4436, USA

Evanovich, Janet (Writer)
PO Box 5487
Hanover, NH 03755-5487, USA

Evans, Alice (Actor)
c/o Joe Vance *Domain*
9229 W Sunset Blvd Ste 415
West Hollywood, CA 90069-3404, USA

Evans, Andrea (Actor)
ARL
8075 W 3rd St # 303
Los Angeles, CA 90048-4318, USA

Evans, Anthony H (Educator)
California State University
President's Office
San Bermardino, CA 92407, USA

Evans, Barry (Baseball Player)
San Diego Padres
8303 Seven Oaks Dr
Jonesboro, GA 30236-4025, USA

Evans, Bart (Baseball Player)
Kansas City Royals
332 S Woodstock Avenue
Springfield, MO 65809, USA

Evans, Bill (Misc)
Dept of Field Mgmt
1501 Broadway Ste 1304
New York, NY 10036-5505, USA

Evans, Byron (Football Player)
Philadelphia Eagles
1763 E Carter Rd
Phoenix, AZ 85042-5754, USA

Evans, Charlie (Football Player)
New York Giants
12513 Marradi Ave
Bakersfield, CA 93312-6419, USA

Evans, Chris (Actor)
c/o Brad Stokes *Kass & Stokes Management*
9229 W Sunset Blvd Ste 504
Los Angeles, CA 90069-3405, USA

Evans, Daniel J (Educator, Governor, Senator)
Daniel J Evans Assoc
4000D NE 41st St
Seattle, WA 98105, USA

Evans, David Mickey (Director)
c/o Gleb Klioner *Schachter Entertainment*
1157 S Beverly Dr Fl 2
Los Angeles, CA 90035-1119, USA

Evans, Dick (Football Player)
Green Bay Packers
4540 Bee Ridge Rd Apt 328
Sarasota, FL 34233-2501, USA

Evans, Dick (Writer)
121 Morning Dove Ct
Daytona Beach, FL 32119-8739, USA

Evans, Donald (Football Player)
Los Angeles Rams
1009 Dickinson Cir
Raleigh, NC 27614-8445, USA

Evans, Donald L (Secretary)
Commerce Department
14th St & Constitution Ave NW
Washington, DC 20230-0001, USA

Evans, Donna (Actor)
c/o Staff Member *United Stuntwomen's Association*
3518 Cahuenga Blvd W # 206B
Hollywood, CA 90068, USA

Evans, Doug (Football Player)
Green Bay Packers
8099 Highway 534
Haynesville, LA 71038-5030, USA

Evans, Dwayne (Athlete)
PO Box 91219
Phoenix, AZ 85066-1219, USA

Evans, Dwight (Baseball Player)
Atlanta Braves
3 Jordan Rd
Lynnfield, MA 01940-1220, USA

Evans, Edward P (Publisher)
712 5th Ave Ste 4900
New York, NY 10019-4108, USA

Evans, Evans (Actor)
3114 Abington Dr
Beverly Hills, CA 90210-1101, USA

Evans, Faith (Musician)
J L entertainment
18653 Ventura Blvd # 340
Tarzana, CA 91356-4103, USA

Evans, Frank (Baseball Player)
Cleveland Buckeyes
PO Box 153
Loachapoka, AL 36865-0153, USA

Evans, Fred (Football Player)
Cleveland Rams
3422 W 148th St
Cleveland, OH 44111-2118, USA

Evans, George (Cartoonist)
King Features Syndicate
888 7th Ave Ste 201
New York, NY 10106-0201, USA

Evans, Greg (Cartoonist)
216 Country Garden Ln
San Marcos, CA 92069-9759, USA

Evans, Harold J (Physicist)
17360 Holy Names Dr Unit 2037
Lake Oswego, OR 97034-5186, USA

Evans, Harold M (Editor)
Random House
1745 Broadway # B1
New York, NY 10019-4305, USA

Evans, J Handel (Educator)
San Jose State University
President's Office
San Jose, CA 95192-0001, USA

Evans, J Thomas (Wrestler)
607 S Fir Ct
Broken Arrow, OK 74012-3435, USA

Evans, James B (Jim) (Baseball Player)
1801 Rogge Ln
Austin, TX 78723-3416, USA

Evans, Janet (Swimmer)
c/o Evan Morgenstein *PMG Sports*
700 Evanvale Ct
Cary, NC 27518-2806, USA

Evans, Jay (Football Player)
Denver Broncos
8878 N Highway 5
Camdenton, MO 65020, USA

Evans, Jerry (Football Player)
Denver Broncos
4139 Ivanhoe Dr
Lorain, OH 44053-1560, USA

Evans, John (Business Person)
Alcan Aluminium
1188 Sherbrooke St W
Montreal, PC H3A 3G2, CANADA

Evans, John A (Football Player)
Cleveland Browns
North Carolina State University Attn:
Alumni Association
PO Box 8501
Raleigh, NC 27695-0001, USA

Evans, John E (Business Person)
Allied Group
701 5th Ave
Des Moines, IA 50391-1007, USA

Evans, John R (Misc)
Rockefeller Foundation
113 Avenue Of The Americas
New York, NY 10013, USA

Evans, John V (Governor)
D L Evans Bank
397 N Overland Ave
Burley, ID 83318-3432, USA

Evans, Josh (Football Player)
Houston Oilers
PO Box 273309
Boca Raton, FL 33427-3309, USA

Evans, Karin
Laubenheimer Str. I
Berlin D-14197, GERMANY

Evans, Larry (Football Player)
Denver Broncos
5316 S Broadway Cir Apt 208
Englewood, CO 80113-6735, USA

Evans, Lee (Actor, Comedian, Writer)
c/o Staff Member *William Morris Agency
(WMA-LA)*
1 William Morris Pl
Beverly Hills, CA 90212-4261, USA

Evans, Lee E (Actor, Athlete, Track
Athlete)
2650 College Pl
Fullerton, CA 92831-3709, USA

Evans, Linda (Actor)
c/o Staff Member *TalentWorks (LA)*
3500 W Olive Ave Ste 1400
Burbank, CA 91505-5512, USA

Evans, Lynn (Musician)
Richard Paul Assoc
16207 Mott Dr
Macomb, MI 48044-5650, USA

Evans, Marc (Director)
c/o Jane Villiers *Tessa Sayle Agency*
11 Jubilee Pl
London SW3 3TE, UNITED KINGDOM
(UK)

Evans, Marsha Johnson (Admiral)
American Red Cross
431 18th St NW
Washington, DC 20006-5304, USA

Evans, Martin J (Misc, Scientist)
Castle Rise 41
Rumney
Cardiff, WALES CF3 9BB, UNITED
KINGDOM (UK)

Evans, Mary Beth (Actor, Director)
c/o Michael Bruno *The Michael Bruno
Group*
13576 Cheltenham Dr
Sherman Oaks, CA 91423-4818, USA

Evans, Mike (Football Player)
Kansas City Chiefs
18717 Pinehurst St
Detroit, MI 48221-1958, USA

Evans, Murray (Football Player)
Detroit Lions
46 Courtside Cir
San Antonio, TX 78216-7843, USA

Evans, Nicholas (Nick) (Writer)
Delacorte Press
1540 Broadway
New York, NY 10036-4039, USA

Evans, Norm (Football Player)
Houston Oilers
360 NW Boulder Pl
Issaquah, WA 98027-5645, USA

Evans, Norm E (Football Player)
4143 Via Marina
Marina Del Rey, CA 90292-5303, USA

Evans, Raymond R (Ray) (Basketball
Player, Football Player)
8449 Somerset Dr
Prairie Village, KS 66207-1845, USA

Evans, Reggie (Football Player)
Washington Redskins
2813 Juniper Street
Merrifield, VA 22116, USA

Evans, Richard (Misc, Sportscaster)
Madison Square Garden
4 Pennsylvania Plaza
New York, NY 10001, USA

Evans, Richard Paul (Writer)
Simon & Schuster
1230 Avenue Of The Americas
New York, NY 10020-1586, USA

Evans, Rob (Coach)
Arizona State University
Athletic Dept
Tempe, AZ 85287-0001, USA

Evans, Robert (Bob/ Bobby) (Actor,
Producer, Writer)
c/o Staff Member *Robert Evans Company,
The*
5555 Melrose Ave
Lubitsch Bldg 117
Los Angeles, CA 90038-3989, USA

Evans, Robert C (Mountaineer)
Ardincaple
Capel Curig
Betws-y-Coed, Northern Wales, UNITED
KINGDOM (UK)

Evans, Robert S (Business Person)
Crane Co
100 Stamford Pl
Stamford, CT 06902-6784, USA

Evans, Ronald E
6134 E Mescal St
Scottsdale, AZ 85254-5419, USA

Evans, Ronald M (Doctor)
Salk Institute
10100 N Torrey Pines Rd
La Jolla, CA 92037, USA

Evans, Sara (Musician)
c/o Keith Miller *William Morris Agency
(WMA-TN)*
1600 Division St Ste 300
Nashville, TN 37203-2755, USA

Evans, Shaun (Actor)
c/o Stacey Boniello *The Firm*
9465 Wilshire Blvd Fl 6
Beverly Hills, CA 90212-2605, USA

Evans, Thomas (Business Person)
Collins & Aikman Corporation
PO Box 5145
Southfield, MI 48086-5145, USA

Evans, Troy (Actor)
PO Box 834
Lakeside, MT 59922-0834, USA

Evans, Walker (Race Car Driver)
Walker Evans Racing
PO Box 2469
Riverside, CA 92516-2469, USA

Evansen, Paul (Football Player)
San Francisco 49ers
1300 Eureka Cir
Medford, OR 97504-7456, USA

Evashevski, Forest (Coach, Football
Coach)
5820 Clubhouse Dr
Vero Beach, FL 32967-7552, USA

Evdokimova, Eva (Ballerina)
Gregori Productions
PO Box 1586
New York, NY 10150-1586, USA

Eve (Actor)
c/o Staff Member *United Talent Agency
(UTA)*
9560 Wilshire Blvd Ste 500
Beverly Hills, CA 90212-2401, USA

Eve (Actor, Musician)
c/o Staff Member *William Morris Agency
(WMA-LA)*
1 William Morris Pl
Beverly Hills, CA 90212-4261, USA

Eve, Trevor
76 Oxford St.
London, ENGLAND W1N 0AX, UNITED
KINGDOM (UK)

Evelyn, Lionel (Baseball Player)
New York Cubans
2508 Edgemere Ave
Far Rockaway, NY 11691-2716, USA

Everclear (Music Group)
c/o Staff Member *Manatt Phelps & Phillips
LLP*
11355 W Olympic Blvd
Los Angeles, CA 90064-1631, USA

Everett, Adam (Baseball Player)
Boston Red Sox
70 Colonial Way
Dallas, GA 30157-1084, USA

Everett, Carl E (Baseball Player)
Florida Marlins
19108 Harborbridge Ln
Lutz, FL 33558-9717, USA

Everett, Chad (Actor)
5472 Island Forest Pl
Westlake Village, CA 91362-5406, USA

Everett, Danny (Athlete)
Santa Monica Track Club
1801 Ocean Park Blvd Apt 112
Santa Monica, CA 90405-4925, USA

Everett, James S (Jim) (Football Player)
Los Angeles Rams
30342 Esperanza
Rancho Santa Margarita, CA 92688-2118,
USA

Everett, Major (Football Player)
Philadelphia Eagles
PO Box 1441
Pine Lake, GA 30072-1441, USA

Everett, Rupert (Actor)
c/o Annett Wolf *Wolf Kasteler Van Iden &
Associates (LA)*
335 N Maple Dr Ste 351
Beverly Hills, CA 90210-3860, USA

Everett, Thomas G (Football Player)
Pittsburgh Steelers
PO Box 795337
Dallas, TX 75379-5337, USA

Everhard, Nancy (Actor)
Kazarian /Spencer
11365 Ventura Blvd Ste 100
Studio City, CA 91604-3148, USA

Everhart, Angie (Actor, Producer)
c/o Staff Member *PTI Talent Agency*
14724 Ventura Blvd Ph
Sherman Oaks, CA 91403-3513, USA

Everhart, Arigie (Actor, Model)
Karin
524 Broadway Rm 404
New York, NY 10012-4408, USA

Everitt, Leon (Baseball Player)
San Diego Padres
367 Henry Everitt Rd
Marshall, TX 75672-3919, USA

Everitt, Mike (Baseball Player)
12381 Walnut Ridge Ct
Clive, IA 50325-8127, USA

Everitt, Steve (Football Player)
Cleveland Browns
17252 Snapper Ln
Summerland Key, FL 33042-3669, USA

Everly Brothers (Musician)
Beehive
PO Box 3933
Seattle, WA 98124-3933, USA

Evermore (Music Group)
c/o Staff Member *Paradigm (Monterey)*
509 Hartnell St
Monterey, CA 93940-2825, USA

Evers, Bill (Athlete)
PO Box 507
Durham, NC 27702-0507, USA

Evers, Charles (Civil Rights Activist)
1018 Pecan Park Cir
Jackson, MS 39209-6913, USA

Evers, Jackson (Actor)
232 N Crescent Dr Apt 101
Beverly Hills, CA 90210-4827, USA

Evers, John (Comedian)
PO Box 169
Mount Airy, NC 27030-0169, USA

Evers-Williams, Myrlie (Misc)
15 SW Colorado Ave Ste 310
Bend, OR 97702-1149, USA

Eversgerd, Bryan (Baseball Player)
St Louis Cardinals
634 Quali Run
O Fallon, IL 62269, USA

Eversley, Frederick J (Artist)
1110 W Albert Kinney Blvd
Venice, CA 90219, USA

Everson, Corinna (Cory) (Misc)
23705 Vanowen St
West Hills, CA 91307-3030, USA

Everson, Cory (Athlete)
23705 Vanowen St # 209
West Hills, CA 91307-3030, USA

Everson, Mark (Government Official)
Internal Revenue Service
111 Constitution Ave NW
Washington, DC 20224-0001, USA

Evert, Christine M (Chris) (Tennis Player)
8563 Horseshoe Ln
Boca Raton, FL 33496-1231, USA

Every Move A Picture (Music Group)
c/o Staff Member *Paradigm (Monterey)*
509 Hartnell St
Monterey, CA 93940-2825, USA

Evetts, Hayley (Musician)
c/o Staff Member *Pop Idol (Fremantle Media)*
2700 Colorado Ave Ste 450
Santa Monica, CA 90404-3599, USA

Evey, Dick (Football Player)
Chicago Bears
335 S Springview Rd
Maryville, TN 37801-0977, USA

Evigan, Greg (Actor)
c/o Daniel (Dan) Spilo *Artistry Management*
525 Westbourne Dr
West Hollywood, CA 90048-1913, USA

Evora, Cesar (Actor)
c/o Staff Member *Televisa*
Blvd Adolfo Lopez Mateos 232
Colonia San Angel INN
DF CP 01060, MEXICO

Evora, Cesaria (Musician)
Monterey International
200 W Superior St Ste 202
Chicago, IL 60610-3554, USA

Evren, Kenan (General, President)
Beyaz Ev Sokak 21
Armutalan, Marmaris, TURKEY

Evron, Ephraim (Government Official)
Ministry of Foreign Affairs
Tel-Aviv, ISRAEL

Ewald, Elwyn (Religious Leader)
Free Lutheran Congregations
12015 Manchester Rd
Saint Louis, MO 63131-4423, USA

Ewald, Esther (Baseball Player)
8455 N Ozanam Ave
Niles, IL 60714-1935, USA

Ewald, Reinhold (Cosmonaut)
DLR Astronauterburo WT/AN
Linder Hohe
Cologne 51140, GERMANY

Ewell, Dwight (Actor)
c/o Margrit Polak *Margrit Polak Management*
8170 Beverly Blvd Ste 102
Los Angeles, CA 90048-4533, USA

Ewell, Kayla (Actor)
c/o Brad Warshaw *Sneak Preview Entertainment*
PO Box 3238
Hollywood, CA 90078-3238, USA

Ewing, Barbara (Actor)
Flat 4
1 Candover St
York House, London W1W 7DG,
UNITED KINGDOM (UK)

Ewing, Maria L (Opera Singer)
33 Bramerton St
London SW3, UNITED KINGDOM (UK)

Ewing, Patrick (Basketball Player)
37 Summit St
Englewood Cliffs, NJ 07632-1525, USA

Ewing, Sam (Baseball Player)
Chicago White Sox
1048 Cedarview Ln
Franklin, TN 37067-4068, USA

Exile
PO Box 1547
Goodlettsville, TN 37070-1547, USA

Expose (Music Group)
c/o Staff Member *Richard Walters Entertainment, Inc*
1800 Argyle Ave Ste 408
Los Angeles, CA 90028-5253, USA

Extreme
189 Carlton St.
Toronto, ON M5A 2, CANADA

Eyes, Raymond (Publisher)
McCall's Magazine
375 Lexington Ave
New York, NY 10017-5644, USA

Eyharts, Leopold
49 Rue Desnouttes
Paris 75015, FRANCE

Eyre, Richard (Director)
Judy Daish
2 Saint Charles Place
London W10 6EG, UNITED KINGDOM
(UK)

Eyre, Scott (Baseball Player)
Chicago White Sox
7010 190th St E
Bradenton, FL 34211-7242, USA

Eyrich, George (Baseball Player)
Chicago White Sox
46 N 2nd St
Womelsdorf, PA 19567-1212, USA

Eysenck, Hans J (Misc)
10 Dorchester Dr
London SE24, UNITED KINGDOM (UK)

Eyskens, Mark (Government Official)
Graaf de Grunnelaan
Heverlee 3001, BELGIUM

Eytchison, Ronald M (Admiral)
11 Prentice Ln
Signal Mountain, TN 37377-2081, USA

Ezor, Blake (Football Player)
Denver Broncos
10622 Salmon Leap St
Las Vegas, NV 89183-4917, USA

Ezra, Derek (Government Official)
2 Salisbury Road
Wimbledon
London SW19 4EZ, UNITED KINGDOM
(UK)

Fabac-Bretting, Elizabeth (Baseball Player)
1455 Mesa St
Redding, CA 96001-2310, USA

Fabares, Shelley (Actor)
PO Box 6010-909
Sherman Oaks, CA 91413, USA

Fabbricini, Tiziana (Opera Singer)
Gianni Testa
Via Wrenteggio 31/6
Milan 20146, ITALY

Fabel, Brad (Golfer)
247 Windsor Terrace Dr
Nashville, TN 37221-2279, USA

Fabi, Ted
9350 Castlegate Dr
Indianapolis, IN 46256-1001, USA

Fabian, Ava (Actor)
c/o Staff Member *Commercial Talent Agency*
9255 W Sunset Blvd Ste 505
West Hollywood, CA 90069-3301, USA

Fabian, John M (Astronaut)
100 Shine Rd
Port Ludlow, WA 98365-9274, USA

Fabian, Lara
BP 37
Boussu-1 7301, BELGIUM

Fabian, Lara (Actor)
c/o Staff Member *Creative Artists Agency LCC (CAA-LA)*
2000 Avenue Of The Stars
Los Angeles, CA 90067-4700, USA

Fabian, Lara (Musician, Songwriter, Writer)
Alian Productions
1 Place du Commerce
Nun's Island, PQ H3E 1A2, CANADA

Fabian, Patrick (Actor)
Writers & Artists
360 N Crescent Dr Bldg North
Beverly Hills, CA 90210-6818, USA

Fabiani, Joe (Reality TV Star)
c/o Staff Member *NBC Television (LA)*
3000 W Alameda Ave # 5366
Burbank, CA 91523-0001, USA

Fabini, Jason (Football Player)
New York Jets
17 Tappanwood Rd
Locust Valley, NY 11560-1321, USA

Fabio (Actor, Model)
c/o Eric Ashenberg *Thor Four LLC*
3000 Olympic Blvd
Santa Monica, CA 90404-5073, USA

Fabiola Moray Aragon, Dona (Royalty)
Royal Palace of Laeken
Laeken-Brussels, BELGIUM

Fabius, Laurent (Misc)
Mairie
Le Grand-Quevilly 76120, FRANCE

Fabolous (Musician)
c/o Staff Member *American Talent Agency*
173 Main St
Ossining, NY 10562-4704, USA

Fabray, Nanette (Actor, Musician)
Webb
13834 Magnolia Blvd
Sherman Oaks, CA 91423-1202, USA

Fabregas, Francesc (Soccer Player)
Arsenal Football Club
Highbury House
75 Drayton Park
London N5 1BU, UNITED KINGDOM
(UK)

Fabregas, Jorge (Baseball Player)
California Angels
9504 SW 125th Ter
Miami, FL 33176-5050, USA

Fabulous, Moolah (Wrestler)
101 Moolah Dr
Columbia, SC 29223-3931, USA

Face, Elroy L (Roy) (Baseball Player)
608 Della Dr Apt 5F
North Versailles, PA 15137-1518, USA

Facinelli, Peter (Actor)
c/o Judy Hofflund *Hofflund/Polone*
9465 Wilshire Blvd Ste 890
Beverly Hills, CA 90212-2607, USA

Faddis, Jonathan (Jon) (Misc)
Carolyn McClair
PO Box 55
Radio Station
New York, NY 10101-0055, USA

Fadeyechev, Aleksei (Dancer)
Bolshoi Theater
Teatralnaya Pl 1
Moscow 103009, RUSSIA

Fadeyechev, Nicolai B (Dancer)
Bolshoi Theater
Teatralnaya Pl 1
Moscow 103009, RUSSIA

Fadul, Francisco Jose (Prime Minister)
Prime Minister's Office
Bissau, GUINEA-BISSAU

Faedo, Len (Baseball Player)
Minnesota Twins
2920 W Collins St
Tampa, FL 33607-6702, USA

Fagan, Garth (Choreographer)
Garth Fagan Dance
50 Chestnut St Ste 1
Rochester, NY 14604-2318, USA

Fagan, John J (Misc)
International teamsters Brotherhood
25 Louisiana Ave NW
Washington, DC 20001-2130, USA

Fagan, Julian (Football Player)
New Orleans Saints
208 Mallory Ct
Madison, MS 39110-9038, USA

Fagan, kevin (Cartoonist)
26771 Ashford
Mission Viejo, CA 92692-4106, USA

Fagan, Kevin (Football Player)
San Francisco 49ers
11441 Camp Dr
Dunnellon, FL 34432-8321, USA

Fagen, Clifford B (Basketball Player)
1021 Royal Saint George Dr
Naperville, IL 60563-2322, USA

Fagen, Donald (Musician, Songwriter, Writer)
Howard Rose
9460 Wilshire Blvd Ste 310
Beverly Hills, CA 90212-2710, USA

Fagerbakke, Bill (Actor)
1500 Will Geer Rd
Topanga, CA 90290-4238, USA

Fagg, George G (Judge)
US Court of Appeals
US Courthouse
East 1st & Walnut
Des Moines, IA 50309, USA

Faggs, Starr H Mae (Athlete, Track Athlete)
10152 Shady Ln
Cincinnati, OH 45215-1322, USA

Fahd bin Ibn, Abdul al-Aziz al Saud (King)
Royal Palace
Royal Court
Riyadh, SAUDI ARABIA

Fahey, Bill (Baseball Player)
Washington Senators
5740 Mona Ln
Dallas, TX 75236-1722, USA

Fahey, Damien (Television Host)
c/o Michael (Mike) Esterman *Esterman Entertainment*
214 Park Rd
Riva, MD 21140-1224, USA

Fahey, Jeff (Actor)
c/o Hillard Elkins *Elkins Entertainment*
8306 Wilshire Blvd
Beverly Hills, CA 90211-2304, USA

Fahnhorst, James (Football Player)
San Francisco 49ers
2365 Brockton Ln N
Plymouth, MN 55447-2043, USA

Fahnhorst, Keith (Football Player)
San Francisco 49ers
12216 Chadwick Ln
Eden Prairie, MN 55344-3292, USA

Fahr, Alicia (Actor)
c/o Staff Member *Televisa*
Blvd Adolfo Lopez Mateos 232
Colonia San Angel INN
DF CP 01060, MEXICO

Fahr, Red (Baseball Player)
Cleveland Indians
7749 Highway 49 N
Marmaduke, AR 72443, USA

Faia, Renee (Actor)
c/o Staff Member *Abrams Artists Agency (LA)*
9200 W Sunset Blvd Ph 11
Los Angeles, CA 90069-3601, USA

Fain, Farris
PO Box 1357
Georgetown, CA 95634-1357, USA

Fain, Richard (Football Player)
Cincinnati Bengals
1539 SW 49th Ter
Cape Coral, FL 33914-6976, USA

Faine, Jeff (Football Player)
Cleveland Browns
76 Lou Groza Blvd
Berea, OH 44017-1269, USA

Fainsilber, Adrien (Architect)
7 Rue Salvador Allende
Nanterre 92000, FRANCE

Fair, Terry (Football Player)
Detroit Lions
12910 W Monte Vista Rd
Avondale, AZ 85392-7140, USA

Fairbairn, Bruce (Actor)
Century Artists
PO Box 59747
Santa Barbara, CA 93150, USA

Fairbank, Richard W (Financier)
Capital One Financial
1680 Capital One Dr # 1
Mc Lean, VA 22102-3407, USA

Fairchild, Barbara (Musician, Songwriter, Writer)
Blackwood Mgmt
PO Box 5331
Sevierville, TN 37864-5331, USA

Fairchild, John B (Publisher)
CHalet Bianchina
Talstr GR
Klosters 7250, SWITZERLAND

Fairchild, Morgan (Actor)
c/o Staff Member *Bauman Redanty & Shaul Agency*
5757 Wilshire Blvd Ste 473
Los Angeles, CA 90036-3632, USA

Fairchild, Paul (Football Player)
New England Patriots
22249 W 183rd St
Olathe, KS 66062-9284, USA

Fairchild, Thomas E (Judge)
US Court of Appeals
111 N Cancal St Building 6
Chicago, IL 60606, USA

Faircloth, Arthur (Football Player)
New York Giants
10010 Sandwedge Ct
Fredericksburg, VA 22408-9546, USA

Faircloth, D McLauchlin (Lauch) (Senator)
813 Beaman St
Clinton, NC 28328, USA

Faircloth, Michael (Designer, Fashion Designer)
Lilly Dodson
4227 Lomo Alto Ct
Dallas, TX 75219-1508, USA

Fairey, Jim (Baseball Player)
Los Angeles Dodgers
218 Strawberry Ln
Clemson, SC 29631-1363, USA

Fairly, Ronald R (Ron) (Baseball Player)
Los Angeles Dodgers
75369 Spyglass Dr
Indian Wells, CA 92210-7650, USA

Fairs, Eric (Football Player)
Houston Oilers
32707 Wales Cir
Fulshear, TX 77441-4250, USA

Faison, Donald (Actor)
c/o Glenn Rigberg *Rigberg-Rugolo Entertainment*
1180 S Beverly Dr Ste 601
Los Angeles, CA 90035-1158, USA

Faison, Matthew (Actor)
13701 Kagel Canyon Rd
Sylmar, CA 91342, USA

Faison, Tiffani (Chef)
c/o Staff Member *Magical Elves Inc*
453 S Spring St
Los Angeles, CA 90013-2013, USA

Faison, William E (Earl) (Football Player)
San Diego Chargers
1452 Kwana Ct
Prescott, AZ 86301-4447, USA

Faith No More
5550 Wilshire Blvd Ste 202
Los Angeles, CA 90036-3888, USA

Faithfull, Marianne (Actor, Songwriter)
Susan Dewsap
235 Gootscray Rd
New Eltham
London SE9 2EL, UNITED KINGDOM (UK)

Faithless (Music Group)
c/o Staff Member *Paradigm (Monterey)*
509 Hartnell St
Monterey, CA 93940-2825, USA

Fakir, Abdul (Duke) (Music Group)
William Morris Agency
151 El Camino Dr
Beverly Hills, CA 90212-2775, USA

Falana, Lola (Dancer, Music Group)
Capital Entertainment
217 Seaton Pl NE
Washington, DC 20002-1528, USA

Falcam, Leo A (President)
President's Office
Palikjr
Kolonia
Pohnpei, FM 96941, MICRONESIA

Falcao, Jose Freire Cardinal (Religious Leader)
QL 12-CJ12
Lote 1
Lago Sul, Brasilia DF 71630-325, BRAZIL

Falcao, Jose Friere Cardinal (Religious Leader)
QL 12-CJ 12 Lote 1 Lago Sul
Brasilia DF 71630-325, BRAZIL

Falco, Edie (Actor)
c/o Staff Member *Innovative Artists (NY)*
235 Park Ave S Fl 7
New York, NY 10003-1405, USA

Falcone, Ben (Actor)
c/o Staff Member *Osbrink Talent Agency*
4343 Lankershim Blvd # 100
North Hollywood, CA 91602-2705, USA

Falcone, Pete (Baseball Player)
Los Angeles Dodgers
2232 Thomton Ct
Indian Wells, CA 92210, USA

Faldo, Nick (Golfer)
9108 Sloane St
Orlando, FL 32827-7024, USA

Falik, Yuri (Composer, Conductor)
Fihlyandsky Prospekt 1 #54
Saint Petersburg 194044, RUSSIA

Falk, David (Lawyer)
Falk Assoc
5335 Wiconsin Ave NW #850
Washington, DC 20015, USA

Falk, David B (Attorney, Attorney General, General, Misc)
Falk Assoc
5335 Wisconsin Ave NW Ste 850
Washington, DC 20015-2052, USA

Falk, Lisanne
9255 W Sunset Blvd Ste 515
Los Angeles, CA 90069-3301, USA

Falk, Paul (Figure Skater)
Sybelstr 21
Dusseldorf 40239, GERMANY

Falk, Peter (Actor)
c/o Norman Aladjem *Paradigm (LA)*
360 N Crescent Dr
North Bldg
Beverly Hills, CA 90210-6820, USA

Falk, Quentin
Old Barn Cottage Little Marlow
Bucks., ENGLAND, UNITED KINGDOM (UK)

Falk, Randall M (Religious Leader)
Temple
5015 Harding Rd
Nashville, TN 37205-2890, USA

Falkenburg, Bob
259 St Pierre Rd
Los Angeles, CA 90077-3430, USA

Falkenstein, Claire (Artist)
719 Ocean Front Walk
Venice, CA 90291-3212, USA

Falkner, Keith (Musician)
Low Cottages Ilketshall Saint Margaraet
Bungay
Suffolk, UNITED KINGDOM (UK)

Fall, Jim (Actor)
c/o Staff Member *United Talent Agency (UTA)*
9560 Wilshire Blvd Ste 500
Beverly Hills, CA 90212-2401, USA

Fall, Timothy (Actor)
Gersh Agency
232 N Canon Dr
Beverly Hills, CA 90210-5302, USA

Falldin, N O Thorbjom (Prime Minister)
As
Ramvik 870 16, SWEDEN

Fallon, Bob (Baseball Player)
Chicago White Sox
801 Somerset Cir
Hanover Park, IL 60133-2722, USA

Fallon, Jimmy (Actor, Comedian)
c/o Jason Heyman *Creative Artists Agency LCC (CAA-LA)*
2000 Avenue Of The Stars
Los Angeles, CA 90067-4700, USA

Falloon, Pat (Hockey Player)
Pittsburgh Penguins
66 Mario Lemieux Pl
Mellon Arena
Pittsburgh, PA 15219-3504, USA

Fallout Boy (Music Group)
c/o Staff Member *Island Records*
825 8th Ave
New York, NY 10019-7472, USA

Falls, Mike (Football Player)
Dallas Cowboys
5831 Secrest Dr
Austin, TX 78759-2416, USA

Faloona, Christopher J (Cinematographer)
138 Via La Soledad
Redondo Beach, CA 90277-6624, USA

Falossi, David (Artist)
Adrienne Editions
377 Geary St
San Francisco, CA 94102-1801, USA

Falteisek, Steve (Baseball Player)
Montreal Expos
12 Verbena Ave
Floral Park, NY 11001-2712, USA

Faltermayer, Harold (Composer)
Creative Artists Agency
9830 Wilshire Blvd
Beverly Hills, CA 90212-1804, USA

Faltskog, Agnetha (Musician)
Agnetha Faltskog Productions
SYdra Brob`nken 41A
Stockholm 111 49, SWEDEN

Faludi, Susan C (Journalist)
1032 Irving St # 204
San Francisco, CA 94122-2216, USA

Falvey, Justin (Producer)
c/o Staff Member *Dreamworks Television*
100 Universal Plaza Bldg 10
Universal City, CA 91608, USA

Fambrough, Charles (Musician)
Zane Mgmt
Bellvue
Broad & Walnut Sts
Philadelphia, PA 19102, USA

Fambrough, Henry (Music Group)
Buddy Allen Management
3750 Hudson Manor Ter # 3ag
Bronx, NY 10463-1126, USA

Famiglietti, Mark (Actor)
c/o Robert Stein *Robert Stein Management*
345 N Maple Dr Ste 317
Beverly Hills, CA 90210-3856, USA

Famuyiwa, Rick (Director, Writer)
c/o Philip Raskind *Endeavor Agency LLC (LA)*
9601 Wilshire Blvd Fl 3
Beverly Hills, CA 90210-5204, USA

Fancher, Hampton (Director)
262 Old Topanga Canyon Rd
Topanga, CA 90290-3810, USA

Fanchetti, Peter
151 El Camino Dr
Beverly Hills, CA 90212-2704, USA

Fancy, Richard (Actor)
c/o Paul Kohner *Kohner Agency, The*
9300 Wilshire Blvd Ste 555
Beverly Hills, CA 90212-3211, USA

Faneca, Alan (Football Player)
Pittsburgh Steelers
201 Whetherburn Dr
Wexford, PA 15090-8869, USA

Faneyte, Rikkert (Baseball Player)
San Francisco Giants
7408 E Osborn Rd
Scottsdale, AZ 85251-6424, USA

Fang, Lizhi (Activist, Misc, Physicist, Politician)
University of Arizona
Physics Dept
Tucson, AZ 85721-0001, USA

Fangio, Juan Manuel II (Race Car Driver)
All-American Racers
2334 S Broadway
Santa Ana, CA 92707-3250, USA

Fankhauser, Merrell (Composer, Musician)
PO Box 1504
Arroyo Grande, CA 93421-1504, USA

Fann, Al (Actor)
6051 Hollywood Blvd Ste 207
Hollywood, CA 90028-5496, USA

Fanning, Dakota (Actor)
c/o Cindy Osbrink *Osbrink Talent Agency*
4343 Lankershim Blvd # 100
North Hollywood, CA 91602-2705, USA

Fanning, Elle (Actor)
c/o Cindy Osbrink *Osbrink Talent Agency*
4343 Lankershim Blvd # 100
North Hollywood, CA 91602-2705, USA

Fanning, Jim (Baseball Player)
Chicago Cubs
154 Tiner Avenue
Dorchester, ON N0L 1G2, CANADA

Fanning, Michael L (Mike) (Football Player)
Los Angeles Rams
28808 S 4190 Rd
Inola, OK 74036-5276, USA

Fanning, Shawn (Business Person)
c/o Staff Member *Roxio Inc*
455 El Camino Real
Santa Clara, CA 95050-4377, USA

Fannypack (Music Group)
Famous Celebrity Sound
29 John St Ste 230
New York, NY 10038-4005, USA

Fano, Robert M (Engineer, Scientist)
51 Woodland Way
North Chatham, MA 02650-1019, USA

Fanok, Harry (Baseball Player)
St Louis Cardinals
12373 Old State Rd
Chardon, OH 44024-9560, USA

Fanovich, Frank (Baseball Player)
Cincinnati Reds
3 Fairgreen Ave
New Smyrna Beach, FL 32168-6112, USA

Fante, Ricky (Musician)
c/o Staff Member *Virgin Records (NY)*
304 Park Ave S Fl 5
New York, NY 10010-4316, USA

Fantetti, Ken (Football Player)
Detroit Lions
1211 SE 175th Pl
Portland, OR 97233-4631, USA

Fantoni, Sergio
Via del Cappellari 35
Rome 00186, ITALY

Faracy, Stephanie (Actor)
8765 Lookout Mountain Ave
Los Angeles, CA 90046-1861, USA

Faralla, Lillian (Baseball Player)
102 Antigua Ct
Coronado, CA 92118-3315, USA

Farar, Hassan Abshir (Prime Minister)
Prime Minister's Office
People's Palace
Mogadishy, SOMALIA

Farasopoulos, Chris (Football Player)
New York Jets
195 Migues Mountain Ln
Aptos, CA 95003-9628, USA

Farber, Barry
2211 Broadway # 3A
New York, NY 10024-6264, USA

Farber, Hap (Football Player)
Minnesota Vikings
200 Dominican Dr
Madison, MS 39110-8630, USA

Farber, Stacey (Actor)
c/o Yanick Landry *Newton-Landry Management*
19 Isabella Street
Toronto, ON M4Y 1M7, CANADA

Faregalli, Lindy (Bowler)
113 N 5th Ave
Manville, NJ 08835-1201, USA

Farenthold, Frances T (Activist, Educator)
2929 Buffalo Speedway # 18B
Houston, TX 77098-1720, USA

Farentino, Debrah
1505 10th St
Santa Monica, CA 90401-2805, USA

Farentino, James (Actor)
1340 Londonderry Pl
Los Angeles, CA 90069-1335, USA

Fares, Muhammad Ahmed Al (Cosmonaut)
PO Box 1272
Aleppo, SYRIA

Fargas, Antonio (Actor)
H David Moss
733 Seward St Ph
Los Angeles, CA 90038-3503, USA

Fargis, Joe (Horse Racer)
PO Box 2168
Middleburg, VA 20118-2168, USA

Fargo, Donna (Music Group)
PO Box 210877
Nashville, TN 37221-0877, USA

Fargo, Thomas B (Admiral)
Commander Pacific Fleet
Camp H M Smith
Honolulu, HI 96861, USA

Farha (Actor, Bollywood)
308 Dara Villa A B Nair Road
Juhu
Mumbai, MS 400049, INDIA

Farina, Battista (Pinin) (Designer)
Pinitarina SpA
Via Lesna 78
Turin
Grugliasco 10095, ITALY

Farina, David (Religious Leader)
Chrishtian Church of North America
41 Sherbrooke Rd
Trenton, NJ 08638-2416, USA

Farina, Dennis (Actor)
c/o Amy Guenther *Gateway Management Partners*
5225 Wilshire Blvd Ste 702
Los Angeles, CA 90036-4351, USA

Farina, Johnny (Music Group)
Bellrose Music
308 E 6th St Apt 13
New York, NY 10003-8760, USA

Faris, Anna (Actor)
Row Talent
9615 Brighton Way Ste 300
Beverly Hills, CA 90210-5118, USA

Faris, Sean (Actor)
c/o Dino May *Dino May Management*
11262 Ventura Blvd Ph
Studio City, CA 91604-3135, USA

Faris, Valerie (Director, Producer)
Bob Industries
1313 5th St
Santa Monica, CA 90401-1414, USA

Farish, William S (Diplomat)
US Embassy
Grosvenor Square 55 Upper Brook St
London W1A 2LQ, UNITED KINGDOM (UK)

Farkas, Bertalan (Astronaut, Misc)
A Magyar Koztarsasag Kutato Urhajosa
Pf 25
Budapest 1885, HUNGARY

Farkas, Ferenc (Composer)
Nagyatai Utca 12
Budapest 1026, HUNGARY

Farley, Carole (Music Group, Opera Singer)
270 Riverside Dr
New York, NY 10025-5209, USA

Farley, Dale (Football Player)
Miami Dolphins
RR 8 Box 472
Sparta, TN 38583, USA

Farley, David (Writer)
c/o Staff Member *MBST Entertainment*
345 N Maple Dr Ste 200
Beverly Hills, CA 90210-3860, USA

Farley, Lillian
84 Kenneth Ave
Huntington, NY 11743-4929, USA

Farmer, Art
49 E 96th St
New York, NY 10128-0782, USA

Farmer, Billy (Baseball Player)
18987 E Wilshire Blvd
Jones, OK 73049-5917, USA

Farmer, Danny (Football Player)
Cincinnati Bengals
332 Lorraine Blvd
Los Angeles, CA 90020-4728, USA

Farmer, Dave (Football Player)
Tampa Bay Buccaneers
141 Via Medici
Aptos, CA 95003-5838, USA

Farmer, Ed (Athlete)
333 W 35th St
Chicago, IL 60616-3651, USA

Farmer, Evan (Actor, Television Host)
c/o Robert Attermann *Abrams Artists Agency (LA)*
9200 W Sunset Blvd Ph 11
Los Angeles, CA 90069-3601, USA

Farmer, George (Football Player)
Chicago Bears
332 Lorraine Blvd
Los Angeles, CA 90020-4728, USA

Farmer, George III (Football Player)
Los Angeles Rams
12422 S Denker Ave
Los Angeles, CA 90047-5339, USA

Farmer, John Jr (Governor)
Attorney General's Office
Hughes Justice Complex
Trenton, NJ 08625, USA

Farmer, Mike (Basketball Player, Coach)
308 W Macdonald Ave
Richmond, CA 94801-2942, USA

Farmer, Mimsy (Actor)
Cineart
36 Rue de Ponthieu
Paris 75008, FRANCE

Farmer, Phillip W (Business Person)
Harris Corp
1025 W Nasa Blvd
Melbourne, FL 32919-0001, USA

Farmer, Richard G (Doctor)
9126 Town Gate Ln
Bethesda, MD 20817-4111, USA

Farmiga, Vera (Actor)
Innovative Artists
1505 10th St
Santa Monica, CA 90401-2805, USA

Farner, Mark (Music Group, Musician)
Bobby Roberts
PO Box 1547
Goodlettsville, TN 37070-1547, USA

Farnham, John
Box 6500 St. Kilda Rd.
Central Melbourne 3004, AUSTRALIA

Farnham, John P (Music Group)
TalentWorks
663 Victoria St
Abbottsford, VIC 3067, AUSTRALIA

Farnon, Shannon
12743 Milbank St
Studio City, CA 91604-1310, USA

Farnsworth, Kyle (Baseball Player)
c/o Staff Member *Chicago Cubs*
1060 W Addison St
Wrigley Field
Chicago, IL 60613-4397, USA

Farquhar, John W (Doctor)
Stanford University
Med School
Disease Prevention Center
Stanford, CA 94305, USA

Farquhar, Robert W (Scientist)
Johns Hopkins University
Applied Physics Laboratory
Laurel, MD 20723, USA

Farr, Bruce (Architect)
Bruce Farr Assoc
613 Third St Ste 20
Annapolis, MD 21403-3248, USA

Farr, Diane (Actor)
c/o Steven Fenton *Fenton-Kritzer Entertainment*
8840 Wilshire Blvd Fl 3
Beverly Hills, CA 90211-2606, USA

Farr, Felicia (Actor)
1143 Tower Rd
Beverly Hills, CA 90210-2130, USA

Farr, Jaime (Actor)
51 Ranchero Rd
Bell Canyon, CA 91307, USA

Farr, Kimberly (Actor)
Tisherman Agency
6767 Forest Lawn Dr Ste 101
Los Angeles, CA 90068-1050, USA

Farr, Mel Jr (Football Player)
Los Angeles Rams
4525 Lakeview Ct
Bloomfield Hills, MI 48301-1412, USA

Farr, Melvin (Mel) Sr (Football Player)
Detroit Lions
10550 W 8 Mile Rd
Ferndale, MI 48220-2152, USA

Farr, Michael (Football Player)
Detroit Lions
3950 Paran Rdg NW
Atlanta, GA 30327-3030, USA

Farr, Miller (Football Player)
Denver Broncos
27085 Greenwich Cir
Farmington Hills, MI 48331-3673, USA

Farragut, Ken (Football Player)
Philadelphia Eagles
605 Creek Ln
Flourtown, PA 19031-1114, USA

Farrakhan, Louis (Religious Leader)
Nation of Islam
734 W 79th St
Chicago, IL 60620-2424, USA

Farrar, Frank L (Governor)
203 9th Ave
Britton, SD 57430, USA

Farrel, Franklin (Hockey Player)
89 Notch Hill Rd # 223
North Branford, CT 06471, USA

Farreley, Alexander (Governor)
Governor's Office
Government Offices
Charlotte Amalie, VI 00801, USA

Farrell, Christopher (Musician)
c/o Mike Rosen *Working Artists Agency*
13525 Ventura Blvd
Sherman Oaks, CA 91423-3801, USA

Farrell, Colin (Actor)
c/o Josh Lieberman *Creative Artists Agency LCC (CAA-LA)*
2000 Avenue Of The Stars
Los Angeles, CA 90067-4700, USA

Farrell, Jon (Baseball Player)
1331 N Kyle Way
Saint Johns, FL 32259-1927, USA

Farrell, Mike (Actor)
14011 Ventura Blvd
Sherman Oaks, CA 91423-3533, USA

Farrell, Paul (Football Player)
Cleveland Browns
PO Box 804
Dennis Port, MA 02639-0804, USA

Farrell, Perry (Music Group)
H K Mgmt
9200 W Sunset Blvd Ste 530
Los Angeles, CA 90069-3509, USA

Farrell, Sean (Football Player)
Tampa Bay Buccaneers
17754 Esprit Dr
Tampa, FL 33647-2508, USA

Farrell, Sharon (Actor)
360 S Doheny Dr
Beverly Hills, CA 90211-3581, USA

Farrell, Shea (Actor)
Artists Agency
1180 S Beverly Dr Ste 301
Los Angeles, CA 90035-1154, USA

Farrell, Suzanne (Ballerina)
Kennedy Center for Performing Arts
Education Dept
Washington, DC 20566-0001, USA

Farrell, Terence (Terry) (Architect)
17 Hatton St
London NW8 8PL, UNITED KINGDOM (UK)

Farrell, Terry (Actor)
Don Buchwald
6500 Wilshire Blvd Ste 2200
Los Angeles, CA 90048-4942, USA

Farrelly, Bobby (Director)
Creative Artists Agency
9830 Wilshire Blvd
Beverly Hills, CA 90212-1804, USA

Farrelly, Peter (Director)
9830 Wilshire Blvd
Beverly Hills, CA 90212-1804, USA

Farrimond, Richard A (Astronaut)
Metra Marconi Center
Gunnels Wood Rd Stevenage
Herts SG1 2AS, UNITED KINGDOM (UK)

Farrington, Amy
c/o Megan Schumacher *Himber Entertainment Inc*
15760 Ventura Blvd Ste 700
Encino, CA 91436-3016, USA

Farrington, Robert G (Bob) (Race Car Driver)
201 Lake Hinsdale Dr Apt 211
Willowbrook, IL 60527-2688, USA

Farrior, James (Football Player)
New York Jets
300 S Pointe Dr Apt 1005
Miami Beach, FL 33139-7353, USA

Farris, Dionne (Music Group)
Creative Artists Agency
9830 Wilshire Blvd
Beverly Hills, CA 90212-1804, USA

Farris, Jerome
US Court of Appeals
1010 5th Ave
US Courthouse
Seattle, WA 98104-1195, USA

Farris, Joseph (Cartoonist)
68 Sunburst Cir
Fairport, NY 14450-9019, USA

Farris, Rachel (Musician)
c/o Staff Member *Logic House Media*
3013 Brightwood Ave
Nashville, TN 37212-6019, USA

Farris, Tom (Football Player)
Chicago Bears
7039 La Costa Ln
Citrus Heights, CA 95621-4205, USA

Farriss, Andrew (Music Group)
8 Hayes St #1
Neutral Bay, NSW 20891, AUSTRALIA

Farriss, Jon (Music Group, Musician)
8 Hayes St #1
Neutral Bay, NSW 20891, AUSTRALIA

Farriss, Tim (Music Group, Musician)
8 Hayes St #1
Neutral Bay, NSW 20891, AUSTRALIA

Farrow, Mallory (Actor)
Hervey/Grimes
PO Box 64249
Los Angeles, CA 90064-0249, USA

Farrow, Mia (Actor)
124 Henry Sanford Rd
Bridgewater, CT 06752-1213, USA

Farrow, Yvonne (Actor)
Geddes Agency
8430 Santa Monica Blvd Ste 200
West Hollywood, CA 90069-4253, USA

Farrow-Rapp, Elizabeth (Baseball Player)
401 Quail Run
Metamora, IL 61548-8360, USA

Farulli, Piero (Musician)
Via G D'Annunzio 153
Florence, ITALY

Farwig, Stephanie (Golfer)
2308 E Taro Ln
Phoenix, AZ 85024-2416, USA

Faryniarz, Brett (Football Player)
Los Angeles Rams
1185 S Summer Breeze Ln
Anaheim, CA 92808-2529, USA

Fasano, John (Actor, Director, Producer, Writer)
c/o Craig Baumgarten *Baumgarten Merims Entertainment*
1640 S Sepulveda Blvd Ste 216
Los Angeles, CA 90025-7535, USA

Fass, Horst (Journalist, Photographer)
12 Norwich St
London EC4A, UNITED KINGDOM (UK)

Fassbaender, Brigitte (Opera Singer)
Am Theater
Braunschweig 38100, GERMANY

Fassbender, Michael (Actor)
Troika
74 Clerkenwell Rd 3rd Fl
London EC1M 5QA, UNITED KINGDOM (UK)

Fassell, Jim (Coach, Football Coach)
Baltimore Ravens
Ravens Stadium
11001 Russell St
Baltimore, MD 21230, USA

Fast, Darrell (Religious Leader)
Mennonite Church General Conference
PO Box 347
Newton, KS 67114-0347, USA

Fast, Larry (Composer, Musician)
Polydor Records
70 Universal City Plz
Universal City, CA 91608-1011, USA

Fatboy Slim
c/o Sam Kirby *William Morris Agency (WMA-NY)*
1325 Avenue Of The Americas
New York, NY 10019-6026, USA

Fatel, Mitch (Musician)
c/o Staff Member *Paradigm (Monterey)*
509 Hartnell St
Monterey, CA 93940-2825, USA

Fath, Farah (Actor)
c/o Kurt Patino *LINK Talent Group*
4741 Laurel Canyon Blvd Ste 106
Valley Village, CA 91607-5907, USA

Fatone, Joey Jr (Dancer, Musician)
c/o Kenny Goodman *William Morris Agency (WMA-LA)*
1 William Morris Pl
Beverly Hills, CA 90212-4261, USA

Fauci, Anthony S (Doctor)
3012 43rd St NW
Washington, DC 20016-3547, USA

Faucon, Bernard (Photographer)
6 Rue Barbanegre
Paris 75019, FRANCE

Faulk, Marshall (Football Player)
Indianapolis Colts
6430 Clayton Rd # 305
Saint Louis, MO 63117, USA

Faulkner, Eric (Music Group, Musician)
27 Preston Grange
Preston Pans E
Lothian, SCOTLAND

Faulkner, John (Scientist)
Scripps Institution of Oceanography
La Jolla, CA 92093, USA

Faumui, Taase (Football Player)
Pittsburgh Steelers
94-249 Waikele Rd Apt A104
Waipahu, HI 96797-2627, USA

Faure, Maurice H (Government Official)
28 Blvd Raspail
Paris 75007, FRANCE

Fauria, Christian (Football Player)
Seattle Seahawks
11237 NE 58th Pl
Kirkland, WA 98033-7518, USA

Fauser, Mark (Writer)
c/o Staff Member *United Talent Agency (UTA)*
9560 Wilshire Blvd Ste 500
Beverly Hills, CA 90212-2401, USA

Faust, Chad (Actor)
c/o Mimi DiTrani *Untitled Entertainment (LA)*
331 N Maple Dr Fl 3
Beverly Hills, CA 90210-3827, USA

Faust, Paul (Football Player)
Minnesota Vikings
5522 Highwood Dr W
Minneapolis, MN 55436-1227, USA

Faustino, David (Actor)
c/o David Rose *Innovative Artists (LA)*
1505 10th St
Santa Monica, CA 90401-2805, USA

Faut-Eastman, Jean (Baseball Player)
406 Warrington Pl
Rock Hill, SC 29732-7408, USA

Fauts, Dan
4020 Murphy Canyon Rd
San Diego, CA 92123-4407, USA

Fauza, Dario (Doctor, Misc)
Harvard Medical School
25 Shattuck St
Boston, MA 02115-6092, USA

Faverty, Hal (Football Player)
Green Bay Packers
18 Blenheim Pl
Port Townsend, WA 98368-9515, USA

Favier, Jean-Jacques (Misc)
Technologies Avances
17 Ave des Martys
Grenoble Cedex 38054, FRANCE

Favor-Hamilton, Suzy
PO Box 120
Indianapolis, IN 46206, USA

Favors, Gregory (Football Player)
Kansas City Chiefs
3182 Holly Mill Run
Marietta, GA 30062-5474, USA

Favre, Brett L (Football Player)
c/o Staff Member *Green Bay Packers*
PO Box 10628
Green Bay, WI 54307-0628, USA

Favreau, Jon (Actor, Writer)
c/o Spencer Baumgarten *Creative Artists Agency LCC (CAA-LA)*
2000 Avenue Of The Stars
Los Angeles, CA 90067-4700, USA

Fawcett, Don W (Doctor, Misc)
3710 American Way Apt 325
Missoula, MT 59808-1927, USA

Fawcett, Farrah (Actor, Model)
10580 Wilshire Blvd # 14ne
Los Angeles, CA 90024-4500, USA

Fawcett, John (Director)
c/o Scott Yoselow *Gersh Agency, The (NY)*
41 Madison Ave Fl 33
New York, NY 10010-2202, USA

Fawcett, Sherwood L (Physicist, Scientist)
1800 Riverside Dr Apt 2314
Columbus, OH 43212-1823, USA

Faxon Jr, Brad (Golfer)
85 Navatt Rd
Barrington, RI 02805, USA

Fay, David B (Golfer)
US Golf Assn
Liberty Corner Road
Golf House
Far Hills, NJ 07931, USA

Fay, Martin (Music Group, Musician)
Macklam Feldman Mgmt
1505 W 2nd Ave #200
Vancouver, BC V6H 3Y4, CANADA

Fay, Meagan (Actor)
c/o Staff Member *Paradigm (LA)*
360 N Crescent Dr
North Bldg
Beverly Hills, CA 90210-6820, USA

Fay, Meagen (Actor)
c/o Staff Member *Main Title Entertainment*
5225 Wilshire Blvd Ste 500
Los Angeles, CA 90036-4349, USA

Fay, Peter T (Judge)
US Court of Appeals
99 NE 4th St Rm 1212
Miami, FL 33132-2140, USA

Faydoedeelay (Music Group, Musician)
Q Prime
729 7th Ave Rm 1600
New York, NY 10019-6880, USA

Fayed, Mohamed al- (Business Person)
Craven Cottage Stevenage Road
Fulham
London SW6 6HH, UNITED KINGDOM (UK)

Fazio, Ernie
2310 Royal Oaks Dr
Alamo, CA 94507-2223, USA

Fazio, Tom (Architect, Golfer)
Fazio Golf Course Designers
401 N Main St Ste 400
Hendersonville, NC 28792-4915, USA

Fazzini, Enrico (Doctor)
New York University
550 1st Ave
Medical Center
New York, NY 10016-6402, USA

Feagles, Jeff (Football Player)
New England Patriots
326 W End Ave
Ridgewood, NJ 07450-4940, USA

Feamster, Tom (Football Player)
Baltimore Colts
RR 1
Elk Creek, VA 24326, USA

Fearnley-Whittingstall, Hugh (Chef)
c/o Staff Member *BBC Artist Mail*
PO Box 1116
Belfast BT2 7AJ, UNITED KINGDOM (UK)

Fearon, Douglas T (Doctor, Misc)
Wellcome Trust Immunology Unit
Hills Road
Cambridge CB2 2SP, UNITED KINGDOM (UK)

Feaster, Allison (Basketball Player)
Charlotte Sting
333 E Trade St
Charlotte, NC 28202-2331, USA

Feck, Luke M (Editor)
6880 Worthington Rd
Westerville, OH 43082-9491, USA

Federer, Roger (Tennis Player)
Int'l Mgmt Group
1 Erieview Plz
1360 E 9th St #1300
Cleveland, OH 44114-1738, USA

Federico, Anthony (Football Player)
Boston Patriots
12306 Van Nuys Blvd
Sylmar, CA 91342-6049, USA

Federko, Bernie (Hockey Player)
2219 Devonsbrook Dr
Chesterfield, MO 63005-4519, USA

Federline, Kevin (Actor, Choreographer, Musician)
c/o Nina Nisenholtz *N2N Entertainment*
1230 Montana Ave Apt 203
Santa Monica, CA 90403-5987, USA

Federov, Sergei (Hockey Player)
1966 Tiverton Rd
Bloomfield Hills, MI 48304-2347, USA

Federspiel, Joe (Football Player)
New Orleans Saints
2016 Lakeside Dr
Lexington, KY 40502-3017, USA

Fedewa, Tim (Race Car Driver)
1737 Onondaga Rd
Holt, MI 48842-8600, USA

Fedoseyev, Vladimir I
Moscow House of Recording
Kachalova 24
Moscow 121069, RUSSIA

Fedotov, Maxim V (Musician)
Tolbukhin Str 8 #6
Moscow 121596, RUSSIA

Fee, Melinda (Actor)
145 S Fairfax Ave Ste 310
Los Angeles, CA 90036-2176, USA

Feeder (Music Group)
Feeder Central
PO Box 2539
London W1A 3HZ, UNITED KINGDOM (UK)

Feehery, Gerry (Football Player)
Philadelphia Eagles
5 Sharpless Ln
Media, PA 19063-3931, USA

Feehily, Mark (Musician)
c/o Staff Member *Solo Agency Ltd (UK)*
55 Fulham High St
London SW6 3JJ, UNITED KINGDOM (UK)

Feeley, A J (Football Player)
Philadelphia Eagles
1112 SW 9th Ave
Ontario, OR 97914-3322, USA

Feeney, Joe
32630 Concord Dr
Madison Heights, MI 48071-1110, USA

Fegley, Richard (Photographer)
Playboy Magazine
680 N Lake Shore Dr
Reader Services
Chicago, IL 60611-4546, USA

Feher, George (Physicist)
University of California
9500 Gilman Dr
Physics Dept
La Jolla, CA 92093-5004, USA

Feherty, David (Golfer)
6422 Prestonshire Ln
Dallas, TX 75225-2309, USA

Fehr, Brendan (Actor)
c/o Jim Sheasgreen *Look Management*
1529 W 6th Ave #110
Vancouver, BC V6J 1R, CANADA

Fehr, Oded (Actor)
c/o Wendy Murphey *IFA Talent Agency*
8730 W Sunset Blvd Ste 490
Los Angeles, CA 90069-2248, USA

Fehr, Rick (Golfer)
c/o Staff Member *Pro Golfers Association (PGA) Tour*
112 Tpc Blvd
Ponte Vedra Beach, FL 32082, USA

Fehr, Steve (Bowler)
1329 Castlebridge Ct
Cincinnati, OH 45233-5214, USA

Feiffer, Jules (Cartoonist)
325 W End Ave Apt 12A
New York, NY 10023-8144, USA

Feigenbaum, Armand V (Business Person, Engineer)
General Systems
23 South St # 250
Pittsfield, MA 01201, USA

Feigenbaum, Edward A (Scientist)
1017 Cathcart Way
Stanford, CA 94305-1048, USA

Feilden, Bernard M (Architect)
Stiffkey Old Hall
Wells-next-to-the-Sea
Norfolk NR23 1QJ, UNITED KINGDOM (UK)

Feinberg, Alan (Musician)
Cramer/Marder Artists
3436 Springhill Rd
Lafayette, CA 94549-2535, USA

Feinberg, Wilfred (Judge)
US Court of Appeals
US Courthouse Foley Square
New York, NY 10007, USA

Feingold, Russell (Senator)
7114 Donna Dr
Middleton, WI 53562-1709, USA

Feinstein, A Richard (Doctor, Physicist)
1760 2nd Ave Apt 32C
New York, NY 10128-5397, USA

Feinstein, Alan (Actor)
Badgley Connor Talent
1680 Vine St Ste 1016
Los Angeles, CA 90028-8800, USA

Feinstein, Dianne (Politician)
c/o Staff Member *United States Senate*
(Hart Office)
316 Hart Senate Office Building
Washington, DC 20510-0001, USA

Feinstein, Michael (Music Group, Musician)
4647 Kingswell Ave # 110
Los Angeles, CA 90027-4301, USA

Feist, Raymond E(lias) (Writer)
c/o Staff Member *Doubleday*
1540 Broadway
New York, NY 10036-4039, USA

Fekete, Gene (Football Player)
Cleveland Rams
963 Norway Dr
Columbus, OH 43221-1655, USA

Felashia
PO Box 31734
Tucson, AZ 85751-1734, USA

Felber, Dean (Music Group, Musician)
FishCo Mgmt
PO Box 5456
Columbia, SC 29250, USA

Felch, William C (Doctor, Physicist)
8545 Carmel Valley Rd
Carmel, CA 93923-9556, USA

Feld, Eliot (Choreographer, Dancer)
Feld Ballet
890 Broadway # 800
New York, NY 10003-1211, USA

Feldenkrais, Moshe (Doctor, Misc)
University of Tel-Aviv
Psychology Dept
Tel-Aviv, ISRAEL

Felder, Benny (Baseball Player)
Newark Eagles
5012 N 39th St
Tampa, FL 33610-6628, USA

Felder, Don (Musician)
PO Box 6051
Malibu, CA 90264-6051, USA

Felder, Kenny (Baseball Player)
2902 W Amberwood Dr
Phoenix, AZ 85045-2289, USA

Felder, Raoul Lionel (Attorney, Attorney General, General)
437 Madison Ave
New York, NY 10022-7001, USA

Feldhausen, Paul (Football Player)
Boston Patriots
W137S6949 Clarendon Pl
Muskego, WI 53150-3207, USA

Feldman, Bella (Artist)
12 Summit Ln
Berkeley, CA 94708-2213, USA

Feldman, Corey (Actor)
c/o Liza Anderson *Warren Cowan & Associates PR*
8899 Beverly Blvd Ste 919
Los Angeles, CA 90048-2436, USA

Feldman, Ed
7700 Wisconsin Ave
Bethesda, MD 20814-3578, USA

Feldman, Jerome M (Doctor, Physicist)
2744 Sevier St
Durham, NC 27705-5745, USA

Feldman, Michelle (Bowler)
Gary Feldman
PO Box 713
Skaneateles, NY 13152-0713, USA

Feldman, Myer (Government Official)
Ginsberg Feldman Bress
1250 Connecticut Ave NW
Washington, DC 20036-2603, USA

Feldman, Sandra (Misc)
American Federation of Teachers
555 New Jersey Ave NW
Washington, DC 20001-2079, USA

Feldman, Tamara (Actor)
c/o Staff Member *United Talent Agency (UTA)*
9560 Wilshire Blvd Ste 500
Beverly Hills, CA 90212-2401, USA

Feldmann, Marc (Doctor, Misc)
Charing Cross Hospital
Saint Dunstan's Road
London W6 8RP, UNITED KINGDOM (UK)

Feldon, Barbara (Actor, Model)
14 E 74th St
New York, NY 10021-2628, USA

Feldott, Jennifer (Golfer)
PO Box 2995
Lake Arrowhead, CA 92352-2995, USA

Feldshuh, Tovah S (Actor)
322 Central Park W # 11B
New York, NY 10025-7629, USA

Feldstein, Martin (Economist, Government Official)
147 Clifton St
Belmont, MA 02478-2603, USA

Felici, Angelo Cardinal (Religious Leader)
Piazza della Citta Leonina 9
Rome 00193, ITALY

Feliciano, Jose (Music Group, Musician)
World Entertainment Assoc
297101 Kinderkamack Road #128
Oradell, NJ 07649, USA

Felipe (Prince)
Palacio de la Zarzuela
Madrid 28080, SPAIN

Felix the Cat
12020 Chandler Blvd Ste 200
N Hollywood, CA 91607-4617, USA

Felke, Petra (Athlete, Track Athlete)
SC Motor Jena
Wollnitzevstr 42
Jena 07749, GERMANY

Felker, Clay (Editor)
322 E 57th St
New York, NY 10022-2949, USA

Fell, Ray
1555 E Flamingo Rd Ste 252
Las Vegas, NV 89119-5283, USA

Feller, Robert W A (Bob) (Baseball Player)
PO Box 157
Gates Mills, OH 44040-0157, USA

Fellowes, Julian (Actor)
International Creative Mgmt
76 Oxford St
London W1N 0AX, UNITED KINGDOM (UK)

Fellows, Edith (Actor)
2016 1/2 Vista Del Mar St
Los Angeles, CA 90068-4065, USA

Fellows, Mark (Football Player)
San Diego Chargers
PO Box 517
Choteau, MT 59422-0517, USA

Fellows, Ron (Football Player)
Dallas Cowboys
Sawmill Road
Dayton, TX 77535, USA

Felmy, Hansjorg
Berghofen
Eching D-84174, GERMANY

Felsenstein, Lee (Inventor)
1479 Regent St
Redwood City, CA 94061-2821, USA

Felt, Richard (Football Player)
New York Titans
3993 N 750 E
Provo, UT 84604-4773, USA

Felton, Dennis (Basketball Player)
University of Georgia
Athletic Dept
Athens, GA 30602, USA

Felton, Eric (Football Player)
New Orleans Saints
PO Box 1355
Coppell, TX 75019-1355, USA

Felton, John (Musician)
GMS
PO Box 1031
Montrose, CA 91021-1031, USA

Felton, Ralph (Football Player)
Washington Redskins
PO Box 277
1207 2nd St
Midway, PA 15060-0277, USA

Felton, Tom (Actor)
c/o Staff Member *Harry Potter Production*
Leavesden Studios
PO Box 3000
Leavesden, Hertfordshire WD2 7LT,
UNITED KINGDOM (UK)

Felts, Narvel (Musician, Songwriter, Writer)
2005 Narvel Felts Dr
Malden, MO 63863-1243, USA

Feltsman, Vladimir (Musician)
Columbia Artists Mgmt Inc
1790 Broadway Fl 6
New York, NY 10019-1412, USA

Feltus, Alan E (Artist)
Porziano 68
Assisi PG 06081, ITALY

Feltz, Vanessa (Actor)
c/o Staff Member *XS Promotions*
57 Fonthill Rd
Aberdeen AB11 6UQ, UNITED
KINGDOM (UK)

Fem 2 Fem
1122 B St Ste 308
Hayward, CA 94541-4274, USA

Femia, John
1650 Broadway Ste 714
New York, NY 10019-6833, USA

Fencik, J Gary (Football Player)
Chicago Bears
1134 W Schubert Ave
Chicago, IL 60614-1309, USA

Fenech, Edwige (Actor)
Carol Levi Co
Via Giuseppe Pisanelli
Rome 00196, ITALY

Fenech, Jeff (Boxer)
PO Box 21
Hardys Bay, NSW 2257, AUSTRALIA

Fenech-Adami, Edward (Prime Minister)
176 Main St
Birkikara, MALTA

Fenenbock, Charles (Football Player)
Detroit Lions
6000 S Land Park Dr Apt 105
Sacramento, CA 95822-3362, USA

Fenerty, Gill (Football Player)
New Orleans Saints
618 Honore Dr
New Orleans, LA 70121-1607, USA

Feng, Ying (Ballerina)
Central Ballet of China
3 Taiping St
Beijing 100050, CHINA

Fenimore, Robert D (Bob) (Football Player)
Chicago Bears
1214 S Fairway Dr
Stillwater, OK 74074-1316, USA

Fenley, Molissa (Choreographer, Dancer)
59 Walder St #4
New York, NY 10013, USA

Fenn, John B (Nobel Prize Laureate)
4909 Cary Street Rd
Richmond, VA 23226-1619, USA

Fenn, Sherilyn (Actor)
c/o Todd Eisner *Agency for the Performing Arts (APA-LA)*
405 S Beverly Dr
Beverly Hills, CA 90212-4416, USA

Fennema, Carl (Football Player)
New York Giants
2470 Dexter Ave N Apt 402
Seattle, WA 98109-2248, USA

Fenner, Derrick (Football Player)
Seattle Seahawks
7533 33rd Ave NW
Seattle, WA 98117-4712, USA

Fenner, Lane (Football Player)
San Diego Chargers
412 Labarre Ct
Saint Johns, FL 32259-4024, USA

Fenney, Rick (Football Player)
Minnesota Vikings
772 E Willetta St
Mesa, AZ 85207, USA

Fenske, Chuck
3 Tattnall Pl
Hilton Head, SC 29928-3908, USA

Fenton, James (Writer)
P F D Drury House
34-43 Russell St
London WC2B 5HA, UNITED KINGDOM (UK)

Fenton, Paul (Hockey Player)
524 Laurel St
Longmeadow, MA 01106-1914, USA

Fenton, Peggy (Baseball Player)
11131 Cottonwood Dr
Palos Hills, IL 60465-2528, USA

Fenty, Rihanna 'Rihanna' (Musician)
c/o Staff Member *Island Def Jam Music Group*
825 8th Ave Fl 28
New York, NY 10019-7416, USA

Feoktistov, Konstantin P (Cosmonaut)
Potcha Kosmonavtov
Moskovskoi Oblasti
Syvisdny Goroduk 141160, RUSSIA

Feore, Colm (Actor)
c/o Staff Member *Endeavor Agency LLC (LA)*
9601 Wilshire Blvd Fl 3
Beverly Hills, CA 90210-5204, USA

Ferarone, Jessica (Actor)
c/o Tiffany Kuzon *Evolution Entertainment (LA)*
901 N Highland Ave
Los Angeles, CA 90038-2412, USA

Feraud, Gianfranco (Designer, Fashion Designer)
25 Rue Saint Honore
Paris 75001, FRANCE

Ferdin, Pamela (Actor)
171 Pier Ave # 453
Santa Monica, CA 90405-5311, USA

Ferdinand, Franz (Musician)
c/o Staff Member *Paradigm (Monterey)*
509 Hartnell St
Monterey, CA 93940-2825, USA

Ferdinand, Marie (Basketball Player)
San Antonio Silver Stars
1 Sbc Center Pkwy
San Antonio, TX 78219-3604, USA

Ferdinand, Rio (Soccer Player)
c/o Staff Member *Manchester United PLC*
Sir Matt Busby Way
Old Trafford
Manchester M160RA, UNITED KINGDOM (UK)

Ferdinand, Ron
PO Box 1997
Monterey, CA 93942-1997, USA

Ferentz, Kirk (Coach, Football Coach)
University of Iowa
Athletic Dept
Iowa City, IA 52242, USA

Fergason, James L (Jim) (Inventor)
145 Gartland Dr
Menlo Park, CA 94025, USA

Fergon, Vicki (Golfer)
41094 Laguna Seca Ct
Bermuda Dunes, CA 92203-1183, USA

Fergus, Keith (Golfer)
11515 Noblewood Crest Ln
Houston, TX 77082-6814, USA

Fergus-Thompson, Gordo (Musician)
150 Audley Road
Hendon
London NW4 3EG, UNITED KINGDOM (UK)

Ferguson, Alexander C (Alex) (Soccer Player)
Manchester United FC
Old Trafford
Manchester M16 0RA, UNITED KINGDOM (UK)

Ferguson, Bob (Football Player)
Pittsburgh Steelers
1380 E 22nd Ave
Columbus, OH 43211-2526, USA

Ferguson, Charles A (Editor)
1448 Joseph St
New Orleans, LA 70115-4263, USA

Ferguson, Charley (Football Player)
Cleveland Browns
81 Stonecroft Ln
Eggertsville, NY 14226-4129, USA

Ferguson, Christopher J (Astronaut)
16111 Park Center Way
Houston, TX 77059-4083, USA

Ferguson, Clarence C Jr (Attorney, Attorney General, Diplomat, General)
Harvard University
Law School
Cambridge, MA 02138, USA

Ferguson, Colin (Actor)
c/o Perry Zimel *Oscars Abrams Zimel & Associates*
438 Queen St E
Toronto, ON M5A 1T4, CANADA

Ferguson, Craig (Actor, Comedian, Television Host)
Late Late Show with Craig Ferguson
7800 Beverly Blvd # 244
Los Angeles, CA 90036-2112, USA

Ferguson, Cullum Cathy (Swimmer)
515 Amanda Dr
Bear, DE 19701-1961, USA

Ferguson, Frederick E (War Hero)
106 S Stellar Pkwy
Chandler, AZ 85226-3725, USA

Ferguson, Howard (Football Player)
Green Bay Packers
1000 Darby Ln Apt 207
New Iberia, LA 70560-1471, USA

Ferguson, James (Jim) (Misc)
26931 Whitehouse Road
Santa Clarita, CA 91351, USA

Ferguson, James L (Business Person)
General Foods Corp
800 Westchester Ave
Rye Brook, NY 10573-1354, USA

Ferguson, Jay (Actor)
c/o Robert Marsala *Bauer Company, The*
9300 Wilshire Blvd Ph
Beverly Hills, CA 90212-3213, USA

Ferguson, Keith (Football Player)
San Diego Chargers
2631 Preakness Way
Fresno, TX 77545, USA

Ferguson, Lynda (Actor)
606 N Larchmont Blvd Ste 309
Los Angeles, CA 90004-1309, USA

Ferguson, Roger W Jr (Economist, Government Official)
Federal Reserve Board
20th & Constitution Ave NW
Washington, DC 20551-0001, USA

Ferguson, Sarah (Royalty)
c/o Hartmoor, LLC
590 Madison Ave Rm 2602
New York, NY 10022-8540, USA

Ferguson, Stacy (Fergie) (Actor, Musician)
c/o Sara Ramaker *Paradigm (LA)*
360 N Crescent Dr
North Bldg
Beverly Hills, CA 90210-6820, USA

Ferguson, Thomas A Jr (Business Person)
Newell Rubbermaid Inc
29 E Stephenson St
Newell Center
Freeport, IL 61032-0943, USA

Ferguson, Vasquero D (Vagas) (Football Player)
New England Patriots
380 Hub Etchison Pkwy
Richmond High School Attn: Assistant Principal
Richmond, IN 47374-5339, USA

Ferguson, Warren J (Judge)
US Courts of Appeals
34 Civic Center Plz
Santa Ana, CA 92701-4025, USA

Ferguson, William (Football Player)
New York Jets
9507 N Division St Ste J
Spokane, WA 99218-1553, USA

Ferguson-Winn, Mabel (Athlete, Track Athlete)
2575 Steele Rd Apt 206
San Bernardino, CA 92408-3979, USA

Fergusson, Frances D (Educator)
Vassar College
President's Office
Poughkeepsie, NY 12603, USA

Ferigno, Lou (Actor)
Lou Ferrigno Enterprises Inc
PO Box 1671
Santa Monica, CA 90406-1671, USA

Ferland, E James (Business Person)
Public Service Enterprise
80 Park Plz
PO Box 1171
Newark, NJ 07102-4194, USA

Ferland, Jodelle (Actor)
c/o Staff Member *Pacific Artists Management*
1404-510 W Hastings St
Vancouver, BC V6B 1L8, CANADA

Ferlinghetti, Lawrence (Publisher, Writer)
City Lights Booksellers
261 Columbus Ave
San Francisco, CA 94133-4586, USA

Ferlito, Vanessa (Actor)
c/o Jeff Golenberg *The Collective*
9100 Wilshire Blvd # 700 W
Beverly Hills, CA 90212-3401, USA

Fernandez, Adrian (Race Car Driver)
7140 E Bronco Dr
Paradise Valley, AZ 85253-3186, USA

Fernandez, Alejandro (Musician)
Hauser Entertainment
11003 Rocks Road
Whittier, CA 90601, USA

Fernandez, Bernardo (Baseball Player)
Atlanta Black Crackers
2547 Ellsworth St
Philadelphia, PA 19146-3926, USA

Fernandez, C Sidney (Sid) (Baseball Player)
543 Punaa St
Kailua, HI 96734-2262, USA

Fernandez, Chico
3322 24th St
Detroit, MI 48208-2412, USA

Fernandez, Craig (Director, Writer)
c/o Staff Member *The Gotham Group Inc*
9255 W Sunset Blvd Ste 515
Los Angeles, CA 90069-3301, USA

Fernandez, Ester
Mitla 112 esq. Xola Colonia Narvarte
Mexico DF, MEXICO

Fernandez, Evalina
5911 Allison St.
Los Angeles, CA 90022, USA

Fernandez, Ferdinand F (Judge)
US Courts of Appeals
125 S Grand Ave
Pasadena, CA 91105-1652, USA

Fernandez, Gigi (Tennis Player)
Gigi Tennis Camp
4202 E Fowler Ave # 214
Tampa, FL 33620-9951, USA

Fernandez, Giselle (Television Host)
NHD International Service
PO Box 498
Quakertown, PA 18951-0498, USA

Fernandez, Juan (Actor)
Don Buchwald
6500 Wilshire Blvd Ste 2200
Los Angeles, CA 90048-4942, USA

Fernandez, Lisa (Misc)
1460 Homewood Rd Apt 95B
Seal Beach, CA 90740-4627, USA

Fernandez, Lujan (Actor)
c/o Staff Member *Innovative Artists (LA)*
1505 10th St
Santa Monica, CA 90401-2805, USA

Fernandez, Manny (Football Player)
Miami Dolphins
5805 SW 120th Ave
Cooper City, FL 33330-3328, USA

Fernandez, Mary Jo
133 1st St NE
St Petersburg, FL 33701-3307, USA

Fernandez, Mary Joe (Tennis Player)
6040 SW 104th St
Miami, FL 33156-1902, USA

Fernandez, Mervyn (Football Player)
Los Angeles Raiders
1546 Morning Star Dr
Morgan Hill, CA 95037-9033, USA

Fernandez, O Antonio (Tony) (Baseball Player)
950 Peninsula Corporate Cir Ste 2000
Boca Raton, FL 33487-1386, USA

Fernandez, Pedro (Musician, Songwriter, Writer)
Exclusive Artists Productions
PO Box 65948
Los Angeles, CA 90065-0948, USA

Fernandez, Vicente (Musician)
Hauser Entertainment
11003 Rocks Road
Whittier, CA 90601, USA

Ferneyhough, Brian J P (Composer)
848 Allardice Way
Stanford, CA 94305-1056, USA

Ferragamo, Vince (Football Player)
Los Angeles Rams
6200 E Canyon Rim Rd
Touchdown Real Estate
Anaheim, CA 92807-4317, USA

Ferrante, Art (Musician)
Scott Smith
12224 Avila Dr
Kansas City, MO 64145-1750, USA

Ferrante, Orlando (Football Player)
Los Angeles Chargers
1223 Adair St
San Marino, CA 91108-1806, USA

Ferrara, Abel (Director)
International Creative Mgmt
8942 Wilshire Blvd # 219
Beverly Hills, CA 90211-1908, USA

Ferrara, Adam (Actor)
Conversation Co
697 Middle Neck Rd
Great Neck, NY 11023-1216, USA

Ferrara, Jerry (Actor)
c/o Stephen (Steve) Levinson *Leverage Management*
3030 Pennsylvania Ave
Santa Monica, CA 90404-4112, USA

Ferrare, Cristina (Entertainer, Model)
10727 Wilshire Blvd Apt 1602
Los Angeles, CA 90024-7334, USA

Ferrari, Michael R Jr (Educator)
570 Greenway Dr
Lake Forest, IL 60045-4801, USA

Ferrari, Tina (Dancer, Wrestler)
2901 Las Vegas Blvd S
Las Vegas, NV 89109-1933, USA

Ferrario, Bill (Football Player)
Green Bay Packers
116 Hensy Court
Scranton, PA 18504, USA

Ferraro, Dave (Bowler)
672 E Chester St
Kingston, NY 12401-1742, USA

Ferraro, Geraldine (Politician, Writer)
575 Park Ave
New York, NY 10065-7332, USA

Ferratti, Rebecca (Actor, Model)
10061 Riverside Dr # 721
Toluca Lake, CA 91602-2560, USA

Ferrazzi, Ferruccio (Artist)
Piazza delle Muse
Via G G Porro 27
Rome 00197, ITALY

Ferrazzi, Pierpaolo (Athlete)
EuroGrafica
Via del Progresso
Marano Vicenza 36035, ITALY

Ferre, Gianfranco (Designer, Fashion Designer)
Villa Della Spiga 19/A
Milan 20121, ITALY

Ferree, Jim (Golfer)
12 Kings Tree Rd
Hilton Head Island, SC 29928-6101, USA

Ferreira, Wayne (Tennis Player)
Int'l Mgmt Group
1 Erieview Plz
1360 E 9th St #1300
Cleveland, OH 44114-1738, USA

Ferrell, Bob (Football Player)
San Francisco 49ers
88 Emory Ave
Beaumont, CA 92223-3117, USA

Ferrell, Conchata (Actor)
1335 Seward St
Los Angeles, CA 90028-7816, USA

Ferrell, Earl (Football Player)
St Louis Cardinals
107 E Forest Trl
South Boston, VA 24592-4366, USA

Ferrell, Rachel (Musician)
Vida Music Group
19800 Cornerstone Sq Apt 415
Ashburn, VA 20147-4250, USA

Ferrell, Tyra (Actor)
c/o Staff Member *Gersh Agency, The (LA)*
232 N Canon Dr
Beverly Hills, CA 90210-5302, USA

Ferrell, Will (Actor, Comedian)
c/o Jimmy Miller *Mosaic Media Group*
24 Music Sq W Fl 1
Nashville, TN 37203-6661, USA

Ferrell Edmonson, Barbara A (Athlete, Track Athlete)
University of Newada
Athletic Dept
Las Vegas, NV 89154, USA

Ferreol, Andrea
10 Ave. George V
Paris F-75008, FRANCE

Ferrer, Danay (Musician)
Evolution Talent
1776 Broadway Ste 1500
New York, NY 10019-2002, USA

Ferrer, Lupita
861 Stone Canyon Rd
Los Angeles, CA 90077-2911, USA

Ferrer, Mel (Actor)
6590 Camino Carreta
Carpinteria, CA 93013-3102, USA

Ferrer, Miguel (Actor)
1007 Maybrook Dr
Beverly Hills, CA 90210-2715, USA

Ferrera, America (Actor)
c/o Jon Rubinstein *Jon Rubinstein Ltd*
740 Broadway Ste 201
New York, NY 10003-9518, USA

Ferreras, Francisco (Pipin) (Misc)
7548 W Treasure Dr
North Bay Village, FL 33141-4118, USA

Ferrero, Louis P (Business Person)
PO Box 675744
Rancho Santa Fe, CA 92067-5744, USA

Ferrin, Arnie (Basketball Player)
910 Donner Way Apt 301
Salt Lake City, UT 84108-4119, USA

Ferrin, Jennifer (Actor)
c/o Staff Member *As The World Turns*
1268 E 14th St
Jc Studios
Brooklyn, NY 11230-5241, USA

Ferris, John (Swimmer)
1961 Klamath River Dr
Rancho Cordova, CA 95670-2910, USA

Ferris, Michael (Mike) (Producer, Writer)
c/o Staff Member *Broder Webb Chervin Silbermann Agency, The (BWCS)*
10250 Constellation Blvd Ste P
Los Angeles, CA 90067-6213, USA

Ferris, Pamela
16601 Marquez Ave Unit 405
Pacific Palisades, CA 90272-3263, USA

Ferriss, David M (Boo) (Baseball Player)
510 Robinson Dr
Cleveland, MS 38732-2214, USA

Ferritor, Daniel E (Educator)
University of Arkansas
Chancellor's Office
Fayetteville, AR 72701, USA

Ferron (Musician, Songwriter, Writer)
JR Productions
4930 Paradise Dr
Tiburon, CA 94920-1060, USA

Ferry, Bryan (Musician, Songwriter, Writer)
IE Mgmt
59-A Chesson Rd
London W14 9QS, UNITED KINGDOM (UK)

Ferry, Daniel J W (Danny) (Basketball Player)
San Antonio Spurs
1 Sbc Center Pkwy
Alamodome
San Antonio, TX 78219-3604, USA

Ferry, David R (Writer)
Wellesley College
English Dept
Wellesley, MA 02181, USA

Ferry, John D (Misc)
6175 Mineral Point Rd
Madison, WI 53705-4457, USA

Ferry, Lou (Football Player)
Green Bay Packers
800 E Lancaster Ave
Villanova University Attn Football Program
Villanova, PA 19085-1603, USA

Ferry, Robert (Bob) (Basketball Player)
2129 Beach Haven Rd
Annapolis, MD 21409-5744, USA

Fersen, Paul (Football Player)
New Orleans Saints
990 Danby Mt Rd
Dorset, VT 05251-9715, USA

Fersht, Alan R (Misc)
2 Barrow Close
Cambridge CB2 2AT, UNITED KINGDOM (UK)

Fesperman, John E (Business Person)
J C Penney Co
6501 Legacy Dr
Plano, TX 75024-3698, USA

Fest, Howard (Football Player)
Cincinnati Bengals
20 River Ranch Dr
Bandera, TX 78003, USA

Festinger, Leon (Misc)
37 W 12th St
New York, NY 10011-8502, USA

Fetchick, Mike (Golfer)
4 White Birch Dr
Dix Hills, NY 11746-7720, USA

Fetisov, Viachesiav (Slava) (Hockey Player)
65 Avon Dr
Essex Fells, NJ 07021-1717, USA

Fetter, Trevor (Business Person)
Tenet Healthcare Corp
13737 Noel Rd Ste 100
Dallas, TX 75240-2017, USA

Fetterhoff, Robert (Religious Leader)
Fellowship of Grace Brethem
PO Box 386
Winona Lake, IN 46590-0386, USA

Fettig, Jeff M (Business Person)
Whirlpool Corp
2000 N State St
RR 63
Benton Harbor, MI 49022, USA

Fetting, Katie (Actor)
c/o Staff Member *Niad Management*
15030 Ventura Blvd Ste 19 Ste 860
Sherman Oaks, CA 91403-2444, USA

Fetting, Ralner (Artist)
Hasenhelde 61
Berlin 61, GERMANY

Fettman, Martin J (Astronaut)
1572 N Saguaro Cliffs Ct
Tucson, AZ 85745-8839, USA

Feuer, Debra
9560 Wilshire Blvd Ste 500
Beverly Hills, CA 90212-2401, USA

Feuerstein, Mark (Actor)
c/o Steven Levy *Framework Entertainment (LA)*
9057 Nemo St # C
W Hollywood, CA 90069-5511, USA

Feulner, Edvin J Jr (Misc)
Heritage Foundation
214 Massachusetts Ave NE
Washington, DC 20002-4999, USA

Feustel, Andrew J (Astronaut)
4003 Elm Crest Trl
Houston, TX 77059-3281, USA

Fewx, Gene (Misc)
666 15th St NE
Salem, OR 97301-2616, USA

Fey (Musician)
RAC Paseo Palmas 1005
#1
Chapultapec Lomas
Mexico City 11000, MEXICO

Fey, Michael (Cartoonist)
United Feature Syndicate
200 Madison Ave
New York, NY 10016-3911, USA

Fey, Tina (Actor, Comedian)
c/o David Miner *3 Arts Entertainment Inc*
9460 Wilshire Blvd Fl 7
Beverly Hills, CA 90212-2713, USA

Fezler, Forrest (Golfer)
6270 Old Water Oak Rd
Tallahassee, FL 32312-3861, USA

Fiala, John (Football Player)
Pittsburgh Steelers
12113 268th Dr NE
Duvall, WA 98019-9610, USA

Fialkowska, Janina (Musician)
ICM Artists
40 W 57th St
New York, NY 10019-4001, USA

Fiasco, Lupe (Musician)
c/o Staff Member *Atlantic Records (NY)*
1290 Avenue Of The Americas
New York, NY 10104-0184, USA

Ficca, Dan (Football Player)
Oakland Raiders
1508 Kansas Ln
Kulpmont, PA 17834-1938, USA

Fichtel, Anja
Stauferring 104
Tauberbischofsheim D-97941, GERMANY

Fichter, Rick T (Cinematographer)
7 Kramer Pl
San Francisco, CA 94133-2903, USA

Fichtner, Hans J (Scientist)
612 Cleemont Dr SE
Huntsville, AL 35801, USA

Fichtner, Ross (Football Player)
Cleveland Browns
46833 Danbridge St
Plymouth, MI 48170-3079, USA

Fichtner, William (Actor)
c/o Andrea Pett-Joseph *Brillstein-Grey Entertainment*
9150 Wilshire Blvd Ste 350
Beverly Hills, CA 90212-3453, USA

Fidrych, Mark (Baseball Player)
260 West St
Northborough, MA 01532-1223, USA

Fiedel, Brad (Composer)
Gortaine/Schwartz
13245 Riverside Dr # 430
Sherman Oaks, CA 91423-5625, USA

Fiedler, Jay (Football Player)
Minnesota Vikings
2266 SW 105th Ter
Davie, FL 33324, USA

Fiedler, Jens
Bruno-Granz-Str. 48
Chemnitz D-09122, GERMANY

Fieger, Geoffrey (Attorney, Attorney General, General)
Fieger Fieger Schwartz
19390 W 10 Mile Rd
Southfield, MI 48075-2458, USA

Field, Arabella (Actor)
S M S Talent
8730 W Sunset Blvd Ste 440
Los Angeles, CA 90069-2277, USA

Field, Ayda (Actor)
c/o Staff Member *Brillstein-Grey Entertainment*
9150 Wilshire Blvd Ste 350
Beverly Hills, CA 90212-3453, USA

Field, Chelsea (Actor)
Troxell
15263 Mulholland Dr
Los Angeles, CA 90077-1620, USA

Field, Helen (Opera Singer)
Athole Still
Foresters Hall
25-27 Westow St
London SE19 3RY, UNITED KINGDOM
(UK)

Field, Sally (Actor)
c/o Judy Hofflund *Hofflund/Polone*
9465 Wilshire Blvd Ste 890
Beverly Hills, CA 90212-2607, USA

Field, Shirley Ann
2-4 Noel St.
London, ENGLAND W1V 2RB, UNITED
KINGDOM (UK)

Field, Todd (Actor)
Three Arts Entertainment
9460 Wilshire Blvd Ste 700
Beverly Hills, CA 90212-2713, USA

Fielding, Fred F (Attorney, Attorney General, General, Government Official)
Wiley Rein Fielding
7925 Jones Branch Dr # 6200
McLean, VA 22102-3321, USA

Fielding, Helen (Writer)
c/o Elizabeth (Beth) Swofford *Creative Artists Agency LCC (CAA-LA)*
2000 Avenue Of The Stars
Los Angeles, CA 90067-4700, USA

Fielding, Joy (Writer)
Atria Books
1230 Avenue Of The Americas
New York, NY 10020-1513, USA

Fielding, Yvette (Actor, Misc)
Antix Productions
128 Grove Ln
Cheadle Hulme
Cheshire SK8 7ND, UNITED KINGDOM
(UK)

Fields, Edgar (Football Player)
Atlanta Falcons
435 Musket Entry
Roswell, GA 30076-3411, USA

Fields, Freddie
8899 Beverly Blvd Ste 918
Los Angeles, CA 90048-2427, USA

Fields, Harold T Jr (General)
126 Deer Run Strut
Enterprise, AL 36330-7812, USA

Fields, Holly (Actor)
Don Buchwald
6500 Wilshire Blvd Ste 2200
Los Angeles, CA 90048-4942, USA

Fields, Jitter (Football Player)
New Orleans Saints
5776 Kensington Ave
Detroit, MI 48224-2071, USA

Fields, Joseph C (Joe) Jr (Football Player)
1 University Pl
Widener University Alumni Association
Chester, PA 19013-5700, USA

Fields, Kim (Actor)
c/o Staff Member *Shapiro-Lichtman Talent Agency*
1333 Beverly Green Dr
Los Angeles, CA 90035-1018, USA

Fields, Scott (Football Player)
Atlanta Falcons
7513 Santa Lucia St
Fontana, CA 92336-3603, USA

Fields, Stephen (Baseball Player)
8306 Wickham Rd
Springfield, VA 22152-1708, USA

Fields, Valerie
PO Box 4025
Niagara Falls, NY 14304-8025, USA

Fieldstad, Oivin
Damfaret 59
Bryn-Oslo 6, NORWAY

Fiennes, Joseph (Actor)
c/o Gene Parseghian *Untitled Entertainment (NY)*
322 8th Ave Ste 601
New York, NY 10001-6715, USA

Fiennes, Ralph (Actor)
15030 Ventura Blvd # 710
Sherman Oaks, CA 91403-5470, USA

Fierek, Wolfgang
Ottobrunner Str. 15
Brunnthal D-85649, GERMANY

Fierstein, Harvey (Actor, Musician, Writer)
1419 Peerless Pl Apt 119
Los Angeles, CA 90035-2865, USA

Fieser, Louis (Inventor)
58 Medford St
Arlington, MA 02474-3124, USA

Fife, Dan (Baseball Player)
Minnesota Twins
5854 Misty Hill Dr
Clarkston, MI 48346-3033, USA

Figaro, Cedric (Football Player)
San Diego Chargers
205 Staten St
Lafayette, LA 70501-1745, USA

Figg-Currier, Cindy (Golfer)
109 Blue Jay Dr
Lakeway, TX 78734-5101, USA

Figga, Mike (Baseball Player)
New York Yankees
16434 Turnbury Oak Dr
Odessa, FL 33556-2896, USA

Figgins, Chone (Baseball Player)
Anaheim Angels
208 Ravenway Dr
Seffner, FL 33584-5756, USA

Figgis, Michael (Mike) (Director)
Steven R Pines
2001 Wilshire Blvd Ste 250
Santa Monica, CA 90403-5681, USA

Figgis, Mike (Director)
520 Broadway Ste 600
Santa Monica, CA 90401-2463, USA

Figini, Luigi (Architect)
Via Perone di S Martino 8
Milan, ITALY

Figini, Michela (Skier)
Ariolo
Prato Lavenina 6799, SWITZERLAND

Figlo-Gill, Josephine (Baseball Player)
99 Washington Rd
Sayreville, NJ 08872-1732, USA

Figo, Luis (Soccer Player)
Real Madrid FC
Avda Cincha Espina 1
Madrid 28036, SPAIN

Figueras-Dotti, Marta (Golfer)
6174 Palomino Cir
Bradenton, FL 34201-2384, USA

Figueroa, Blen (Baseball Player)
St Louis Cardinals
3909 Reserve Dr Apt 1522
Tallahassee, FL 32311-1283, USA

Figueroa, Ed (Baseball Player)
California Angels
Calle 41 A-N15
Santa Juanita, PR 00619, USA

Figueroa, Efrain (Actor)
c/o Staff Member *Mitchell K Stubbs & Assoc (MKS)*
8695 Washington Blvd Ste 204
Culver City, CA 90232-7419, USA

Figueroa, Nelson (Baseball Player)
Arizona Diamondbacks
14 Clover Ln
Quakertown, PA 18951-3920, USA

Figura, Maria Louisa (Actor)
c/o Staff Member *Select Artists Ltd (CA-Westside Office)*
1138 12th St Apt 1
Santa Monica, CA 90403-5459, USA

Figures, Deon (Football Player)
Pittsburgh Steelers
1520 S Visalia Ave
Compton, CA 90220-3947, USA

Fikac, Jeremy (Baseball Player)
Sad Diego Padres
1709 Cody Dr
Shiner, TX 77984-8302, USA

Fike, Dan (Football Player)
Cleveland Browns
23479 Wingedfoot Dr
Westlake, OH 44145-4371, USA

Fikrig, Erol (Doctor)
Yale University
Medical Center
Infectious Disease Dept
New Haven, CT 06510, USA

Filan, Shane (Musician)
c/o Staff Member *Solo Agency Ltd (UK)*
55 Fulham High St
London SW6 3JJ, UNITED KINGDOM
(UK)

Filardi, Peter (Director, Producer, Writer)
c/o Robert Marsala *Bauer Company, The*
9300 Wilshire Blvd Ph
Beverly Hills, CA 90212-3213, USA

Filarski-Steffes, Helen (Baseball Player)
19623 Damman St
Harper Woods, MI 48225-1753, USA

Filatova, Ludmila P (Opera Singer)
Ryleyevastr 6
#13
Saint Petersburg, RUSSIA

File, Bob (Baseball Player)
Toronto Blue Jays
509 Larkspur St
Philadelphia, PA 19116-2803, USA

File, Sam (Baseball Player)
Philadelphia Phillies
264 Windjammer Rd
Berlin, MD 21811-1831, USA

Filer, Sam (Baseball Player)
Chicago Cubs
425 Fox Hollow Dr
Langhorne, PA 19053-2495, USA

Files, Jim (Football Player)
New York Giants
633 Fallstone Rd
Fort Smith, AR 72916, USA

Filicia, Thom (Television Host)
c/o Staff Member *Queer Eye for the Straight Guy*
119 Braintree St
Boston, MA 02134-1628, USA

Filiol, Jalme (Tennis Player)
Advantage International
1025 Thomas Jefferson St NW # 430
Washington, DC 20007-5201, USA

Filion, Herve (Race Car Driver)
18 Evans Ave
Albertson, NY 11507-1902, USA

Filipacchi, Daniel (Publisher)
Hachette Filipacchi
149-51 Rue Anatole-France
Levallois 92534, FRANCE

Filipchenko, Anatoli N (Cosmonaut, General)
Potcha Kosmonavtov Moskovskoi Oblasti
Syvisdny Goroduk 141160, RUSSIA

Filippo, Lou
7826 Botany St
Downey, CA 90240-2624, USA

Filippo (Fillipo/Filippo), Fabrizio (Fab) (Actor)
c/o David Lillard *IFA Talent Agency*
8730 W Sunset Blvd Ste 490
Los Angeles, CA 90069-2248, USA

Filipski, Gene (Football Player)
1285 Caribou Ln
Hoffman Estates, IL 60192-4601, USA

Fill, Shannon (Actor)
260 S Beverly Dr Ste 200
Beverly Hills, CA 90212-3812, USA

Fillion, Nathan (Actor)
c/o Staff Member *3 Arts Entertainment Inc*
9460 Wilshire Blvd Fl 7
Beverly Hills, CA 90212-2713, USA

Filson, Pete (Baseball Player)
Minnesota Twins
1034 10th Ave
Folsom, PA 19033-1112, USA

Filter (Music Group)
c/o Staff Member *Warner Bros Records (NY)*
75 Rockefeller Plz
New York, NY 10019-6908, USA

Fimmel, Travis (Actor, Model)
c/o David Seltzer *Management 360*
9111 Wilshire Blvd
Beverly Hills, CA 90210-5508, USA

Fimple, Dennis
3518 Cahuenga Blvd W # 306
Los Angeles, CA 90068, USA

Fimple, Jack (Baseball Player)
Los Angeles Dodgers
8012 Cliffrose St
Windsor, CA 95492-9537, USA

Fina, John (Football Player)
Buffalo Bills
5180 E Fort Lowell Rd
Tucson, AZ 85712-1309, USA

Finch, Jennie (Athlete, Olympic Athlete)
Finch Windmill
PO Box 97
La Mirada, CA 90637-0097, USA

Finch, Joel (Baseball Player)
Boston Red Sox
68571 Oak Spring Rd
Edwardsburg, MI 49112-9502, USA

Finch, Jon (Actor)
London Mgmt
2-4 Noel St
London W1V 3RB, UNITED KINGDOM (UK)

Finch, Karl (Football Player)
Los Angeles Chargers
4408 Copper Crest Ln
Modesto, CA 95355-8970, USA

Finch, Larry (Basketball Player, Coach)
5962 Lake Tide Cv
Memphis, TN 38120-4121, USA

Finch, Linda (Misc)
World Flight
211 Switch Oak
Shavano Park, TX 78230-5621, USA

Finch, Tyrone (Comedian)
c/o Staff Member *United Talent Agency (UTA)*
9560 Wilshire Blvd Ste 500
Beverly Hills, CA 90212-2401, USA

Finchem, Timothy W (Golfer)
Professional Golfer's Assn
Sawgrass
Ponte Vedra Beach, FL 32082, USA

Fincher, David (Director)
c/o Matthew (Matt) Del Piano *Creative Artists Agency LCC (CAA-LA)*
2000 Avenue Of The Stars
Los Angeles, CA 90067-4700, USA

Finck, George C (War Hero)
143 Beaver Ln
Benton, LA 71006-9332, USA

Fincke, E Michael (Mike) (Astronaut)
15819 El Dorado Oaks Dr
Houston, TX 77059-4045, USA

Finckel, David (Musician)
I M G Artists
3 Burlington Lane
London W4 2TH, UNITED KINGDOM (UK)

Findlay, Conn F (Athlete, Yachtsman)
1920 Oak Knoll Dr
Belmont, CA 94002-1755, USA

Fine, David (Writer)
c/o Staff Member *Endeavor Agency LLC (LA)*
9601 Wilshire Blvd Fl 3
Beverly Hills, CA 90210-5204, USA

Fine, Jeanna
19 Hanover Pl Pmb 313
Hicksville, NY 11801, USA

Fine, Tom (Baseball Player)
Boston Red Sox
2605 Cascade Cove Dr
Little Elm, TX 75068-7603, USA

Fine, Travis (Actor)
Vaughn D Hart
200 N Robertson Blvd # 219
Beverly Hills, CA 90211-1769, USA

Finfera, Joe (Actor)
c/o Staff Member *Select Artists Ltd (CA-Westside Office)*
1138 12th St Apt 1
Santa Monica, CA 90403-5459, USA

Finger Eleven (Music Group)
c/o Staff Member *Wind-up Records*
72 Madison Ave Fl 8
New York, NY 10016-8731, USA

Fingers, Rollie (Baseball Player)
10675 Fairfield Ave
Las Vegas, NV 89183-4635, USA

Fink, Gerald R (Doctor, Scientist)
40 Allston St
West Newton, MA 02465, USA

Fink, John
1680 Vine St Ste 614
Hollywood, CA 90028-8833, USA

Fink, Mitchell
1835 E Michelle St
West Covina, CA 91791-3942, USA

Fink, Natascha (Golfer)
Golfclub Murhof Adriach 54
Frohnleiten A-8130, AUSTRIA

Finkel, Fyvush (Actor)
155 E 50th St # 6E
New York, NY 10022-9503, USA

Finkel, Henry (Hank) (Basketball Player)
2 Pocahontas Way
Lynnfield, MA 01940-1042, USA

Finkel, Shelly
310 Madison Ave # 804
New York, NY 10017, USA

Finlay, Frank (Actor)
Ken McReddie
91 Regent St
London W1R 7TB, UNITED KINGDOM (UK)

Finley, Charles E (Chuck) (Baseball Player)
California Angels
117 Old Course Dr
Newport Beach, CA 92660-4289, USA

Finley, David (Opera Singer)
1642 Milvia St Apt 3S
Berkeley, CA 94709-2001, USA

Finley, Gerald H (Opera Singer)
I M G Artists
3 Burlington Lane
Chiswick
London W4 2TH, UNITED KINGDOM (UK)

Finley, John L (Astronaut)
700 Colonial Rd Ste 120
Memphis, TN 38117-5191, USA

Finley, Karen (Artist)
Creative Time
59 E 4th St Ste 6E
New York, NY 10003-8991, USA

Finley, Margot (Actor)
c/o Staff Member *Pacific Artists Management*
1404-510 W Hastings St
Vancouver, BC V6B 1L8, CANADA

Finley, Michael (Basketball Player)
Dallas Mavericks
2909 Taylor St
Dallas, TX 75226-1909, USA

Finley, Steven A (Steve) (Baseball Player)
Baltimore Orioles
PO Box 2101
Rancho Santa Fe, CA 92067-2101, USA

Finn, Jim (Football Player)
Indianapolis Colts
398 Kingston Ct
West New York, NJ 07093-8335, USA

Finn, John (Actor)
c/o Gabrielle Krengel *Domain*
4526 Wilshire Blvd
Los Angeles, CA 90010-3801, USA

Finn, John W (War Hero)
36585 Old Highway 80
Pine Valley, CA 91962, USA

Finn, Neil (Musician, Songwriter, Writer)
c/o Staff Member *William Morris Agency (WMA-LA)*
1 William Morris Pl
Beverly Hills, CA 90212-4261, USA

Finn, Patrick (Actor)
c/o Staff Member *Brillstein-Grey Entertainment*
9150 Wilshire Blvd Ste 350
Beverly Hills, CA 90212-3453, USA

Finn, Tim (Musician)
Grant Thomas Mgmt
98 Surrey St
Darlinghurst, NSW 2010, AUSTRALIA

Finn, Veronica (Musician)
Evolution Talent
1776 Broadway Ste 1500
New York, NY 10019-2002, USA

Finn, William (Composer, Songwriter, Writer)
New York University
Music Dept
New York, NY 10012, USA

Finneran, Gary (Football Player)
Los Angeles Chargers
17021 Paulette Pl
Granada Hills, CA 91344-1651, USA

Finneran, John G (Admiral)
2904 N Leisure World Blvd Apt 404
Silver Spring, MD 20906-1394, USA

Finneran, Rittenhouse Sharon (Swimmer)
212 Harbor Dr
Santa Cruz, CA 95062-3442, USA

Finnerty, Dan (Actor, Musician)
c/o Staff Member *William Morris Agency (WMA-LA)*
1 William Morris Pl
Beverly Hills, CA 90212-4261, USA

Finnessey, Shandi (Beauty Pageant Winner)
c/o Staff Member *Miss Universe Organization, The*
1370 Avenue Of The Americas Fl 16
New York, NY 10019-4602, USA

Finney, Albert (Actor)
Michael Simkins
45/51 Whitfield St
London W1P 6AA, UNITED KINGDOM (UK)

Finney, Allison (Golfer)
78160 Desert Mountain Cir
Bermuda Dunes, CA 92203-8151, USA

Finney, Tom (Soccer Player)
Preston North End FC
Deepdale
Sir Finney Way
Preston PR1 6RU, UNITED KINGDOM (UK)

Finnie, Linda A (Musician)
16 Golf Course Girvan
Ayrshire KA26 9HW, UNITED KINGDOM (UK)

Finnie, Roger (Football Player)
New York Jets
2307 NW 56th St
Miami, FL 33142-2927, USA

Finnigan, Jennifer (Actor)
c/o John Carrabino *John Carrabino Management*
5900 Wilshire Blvd Ste 406
Los Angeles, CA 90036-5015, USA

Finnvold, Gar (Baseball Player)
Boston Red Sox
1204 NE 4th Ave
Boca Raton, FL 33432-2808, USA

Finsterwald, Dow (Golfer)
6330 Masters Blvd
Orlando, FL 32819-4869, USA

Finzer, Dave (Football Player)
Chicago Bears
1435 Kaywood Ln
Glenview, IL 60025-2341, USA

Fiore, Dave (Football Player)
San Francisco 49ers
5177 Englewood Dr
San Jose, CA 95129-4235, USA

Fiore, Kathryn (Actor)
c/o Michael P Levine *Levine Management*
9028 W Sunset Blvd # Ph1
Los Angeles, CA 90069-1846, USA

Fiore, Mike (Baseball Player)
US Olympic Team
3032 Zimmerman Pl
Tustin, CA 92782-0938, USA

Fiore, Tony (Baseball Player)
Minnesota Twins
19021 Fishermans Bend Dr
Lutz, FL 33558-9754, USA

Fiorentino, Linda (Actor)
c/o Robert Stein *Paradigm (LA)*
360 N Crescent Dr
North Bldg
Beverly Hills, CA 90210-6820, USA

Fiori, Ed (Golfer)
50 Burwick St
Sugar Land, TX 77479-2997, USA

Fiori, Fernando (Actor)
c/o Staff Member *Latin World
Entertainment Agency (WEA)*
2601 S Bayshore Dr Ste 235
Miami, FL 33133-5432, USA

Fiorillo, Elisbatta (Opera Singer)
Columbia Artists Mgmt Inc
1790 Broadway Fl 6
New York, NY 10019-1412, USA

Fiorito, Jaelle (Actor, Television Host)
c/o Staff Member *Rebel Entertainment
Partners Inc*
5700 Wilshire Blvd Ste 456
Los Angeles, CA 90036-3648, USA

Firbank, Ann
76 Oxford St.
London, ENGLAND W1N OAX, UNITED
KINGDOM (UK)

Firefall
6400 Pleasant Park Dr
Chanhassen, MN 55317-8804, USA

Fireman, Paul B (Business Person)
Reebok International
1895 J W Foster Blvd
Canton, MA 02021-1099, USA

Fireovid, Steve (Baseball Player)
San Diego Padres
1408 Woodstream Dr
Bryan, OH 43506-9049, USA

Fires, Earlie S (Jockey)
16337 Rivervale Lane
Rivervale, AR 72377, USA

Firestone, Andrew (Actor, Reality TV Star)
c/o Staff Member *Paradigm (LA)*
360 N Crescent Dr
North Bldg
Beverly Hills, CA 90210-6820, USA

Firestone, Eddie
303 S Crescent Heights Blvd
Los Angeles, CA 90048-4403, USA

Firestone, Roy (Sportscaster)
Seizen/Wallach Productions
257 S Rodeo Dr
Beverly Hills, CA 90212-3803, USA

Firm, The
57A Great Titchfield St.
London, ENGLAND W1P 7FL, UNITED
KINGDOM (UK)

Firova, Dan (Baseball Player)
Seattle Mariners
5115 Coos Bay
Laredo, TX 78041-1963, USA

First, Neal L (Misc)
9437 W Garnette Dr
Sun City, AZ 85373-1732, USA

Firth, Colin (Actor)
c/o Chris Andrews *Creative Artists Agency
LCC (CAA-LA)*
2000 Avenue Of The Stars
Los Angeles, CA 90067-4700, USA

Firth, Peter (Actor)
Markham & Froggatt
Julian House
4 Windmill St
London W1P 1HF, UNITED KINGDOM
(UK)

Fischbach, Ephraim (Physicist)
5821 Farm Ridge Rd
West Lafayette, IN 47906-9492, USA

Fischer, Adam
Askonas Holt Ltd
27 Chancery Lane
London WC2A 1PF, UNITED KINGDOM
(UK)

Fischer, Bernard
208 W King Rd
Kuna, ID 83634, USA

Fischer, Bill (Baseball Player)
Chicago White Sox
139 Upland Dr
Council Bluffs, IA 51503-4823, USA

Fischer, Bill (Football Player)
Chicago Cardinals
23191 Shady Oak Ln
Estero, FL 33928-4383, USA

Fischer, Bobby
186 Rt. 9W
New Windsor, NY 12550, USA

Fischer, Edmond H (Nobel Prize Laureate)
5540 NE Windermere Rd
Seattle, WA 98105-2849, USA

Fischer, Ernst Otto (Nobel Prize Laureate)
Sohnckestr 16
Munich 81479, GERMANY

Fischer, Hank (Baseball Player)
Montreal Expos
215 Worth Ct N
West Palm Beach, FL 33405-2751, USA

Fischer, Heinz (President)
Prasidentschaftskanzlei
Hofburg
Alderstiege
Vienna 1010, AUSTRIA

Fischer, Helmut
Kaiserplatz 5
Munich D-80803, GERMANY

Fischer, Ivan
1 Andrassy Utca 27
Budapest 1061, HUNGARY

Fischer, Jenna (Actor)
c/o Naomi Odenkirk *Odenkirk Talent
Management*
650 N Bronson Ave Bldg B145
Raleigh Studios
Los Angeles, CA 90004-1404, USA

Fischer, Kate (Actor)
c/o Staff Member *Current Entertainment*
9200 W Sunset Blvd
West Hollywood, CA 90069-3502, USA

Fischer, Lisa (Musician)
Alive Enterprices
3264 S Kihei Rd
Kihei, HI 96753-9605, USA

Fischer, Michael L (Misc)
California Coastal Conservancy
1330 Broadway Ste 1300
Oakland, CA 94612-2530, USA

Fischer, Patrick (Pat) (Football Player)
St Louis Cardinals
PO Box 4289
Leesburg, VA 20177-8401, USA

Fischer, Schmidt Birgit (Athlete)
Kuckuckswald 11
Kleinmachnow 14532, GERMANY

Fischer, Stanley (Economist)
399 Park Ave Frnt 2
New York, NY 10022-4661, USA

Fischer, Sven (Athlete)
Schillerhoehe 7
Schmalkalden 98574, GERMANY

Fischer, Todd (Baseball Player)
California Angels
12734 Newtown Rd
Unionville, TN 37180-5004, USA

Fischer, Todd (Golfer)
7347 Linwood Ct
Pleasanton, CA 94588-4877, USA

Fischer, Van (Director)
Gersh Agency
232 N Canon Dr
Beverly Hills, CA 90210-5302, USA

Fischer, Veronika
Glockengiesserwall 3
Hamburg D-20095, GERMANY

Fischer-Diskau, Dietrich
Lindenallee 22
Berlin D-14050, GERMANY

Fischerspooner (Music Group)
c/o Staff Member *Paradigm (Monterey)*
509 Hartnell St
Monterey, CA 93940-2825, USA

Fischetti, Brad (Musician)
Evolution Talent Agency
1776 Broadway Fl 15
New York, NY 10019-2002, USA

Fischler, Patrick (Actor)
c/o Staff Member *Peter Strain &
Associates Inc (LA)*
5455 Wilshire Blvd Ste 1812
Los Angeles, CA 90036-4268, USA

Fischlin, Mike (Baseball Player)
Houston Astros
1010 Curtright Pl
Greensboro, GA 30642-7432, USA

Fish, Ginger (Musician)
c/o Staff Member *Interscope Records (LA)
- Main*
2220 Colorado Ave
Santa Monica, CA 90404-3506, USA

Fish, Howard M (General)
1223 Capilano Dr
Shreveport, LA 71106-8286, USA

Fishbacher, Siegfried (Magician)
Mirage Hotel & Casino
3400 Las Vegas Blvd S
Las Vegas, NV 89109-8907, USA

Fishback, Joe (Football Player)
Atlanta Falcons
1402 Battlecreek Village Dr
Jonesboro, GA 30236-8532, USA

Fishbone
PO Box 4450
New York, NY 10163-4450, USA

Fishburne, Laurence (Actor)
c/o Staff Member *Cinema Gypsy*
4116 W Magnolia Blvd Ste 101
Burbank, CA 91505-2700, USA

Fishel, Danielle (Actor)
c/o Staff Member *Innovative Artists (LA)*
1505 10th St
Santa Monica, CA 90401-2805, USA

Fishel, John (Baseball Player)
Houston Astros
329 Marjoram Dr
Gahanna, OH 43230-7027, USA

Fisher, Anna L (Astronaut)
1912 Elmen St
Houston, TX 77019-6144, USA

Fisher, Bernard (Doctor)
5636 Aylesboro Ave
Pittsburgh, PA 15217-1402, USA

Fisher, Bernard F (War Hero)
4200 W King Rd
Kuna, ID 83634-1610, USA

Fisher, Brian (Baseball Player)
New York Yankees
3660 S Uravan St
Aurora, CO 80013-3458, USA

Fisher, Bryan (Actor)
c/o Jamie Freed *The Collective*
8530 Wilshire Blvd Fl 5
Beverly Hills, CA 90211-3102, USA

Fisher, Carrie (Actor)
c/o Carin Sage *Creative Artists Agency
LCC (CAA-LA)*
2000 Avenue Of The Stars
Los Angeles, CA 90067-4700, USA

Fisher, Charles (Football Player)
Cincinnati Bengals
1040 Knoll St
Aliquippa, PA 15001-3912, USA

Fisher, Climie
30 Bridstow Pl.
London, ENGLAND W2 5AE, UNITED
KINGDOM (UK)

Fisher, Derek (Basketball Player)
Los Angeles Lakers
1111 S Figueroa St
Staples Center
Los Angeles, CA 90015-1300, USA

Fisher, Ed (Football Player)
Houston Oilers
4734 E Redfield Rd
Phoenix, AZ 85032-5520, USA

Fisher, Eddie (Actor, Musician)
1177 California St Apt 931
San Francisco, CA 94108-2222, USA

Fisher, Eddie G (Baseball Player)
San Francisco Giants
408 Cardinal Cir S
Altus, OK 73521-1714, USA

Fisher, Elder A (Bud) (Bowler)
7551 Brackenwood Cir N
Indianapolis, IN 46260-5439, USA

Fisher, Evan (Musician)
GEMS
PO Box 1031
Montrose, CA 91021-1031, USA

Fisher, Frances (Actor)
c/o Tammy Rosen *Melanie Greene
Management & Productions*
425 N Robertson Blvd
West Hollywood, CA 90048-1735, USA

Fisher, Fritz (Baseball Player)
Detroit Tigers
3703 Barcelona Dr
Toledo, OH 43615-1203, USA

Fisher, Gerry
River Bank Hartsfield Rd.
W. Molesey Surrey, ENGLAND, UNITED
KINGDOM (UK)

Fisher, Isla (Actor)
c/o David (Dave) Fleming *Mosaic Media Group*
24 Music Sq W Fl 1
Nashville, TN 37203-6661, USA

Fisher, Jeff (Coach, Football Coach)
Tennessee Titans
460 Great Circle Rd
Nashville, TN 37228-1404, USA

Fisher, Jeff (Football Player)
Chicago Bears
385 Lake Valley Dr
Franklin, TN 37069-4652, USA

Fisher, Joel (Artist)
PO Box 65
Palisades, NY 10964-0065, USA

Fisher, Joely (Actor)
c/o John Carrabino *John Carrabino Management*
5900 Wilshire Blvd Ste 406
Los Angeles, CA 90036-5015, USA

Fisher, Jules E (Designer)
Jules Fisher Enterprises
126 5th Ave
New York, NY 10011-5606, USA

Fisher, Kimberly (Model)
PO Box 69330
703
West Hollywood, CA 90069-0330, USA

Fisher, Mary (Misc)
Charles Scribner's Sons
866 3rd Ave
New York, NY 10022-6221, USA

Fisher, Matthew (Misc)
39 Croham Road
South Croydon CR2 7HD, UNITED KINGDOM (UK)

Fisher, Maury (Baseball Player)
Cincinnati Reds
15920 Lucerne Rd
Fredericktown, OH 43019-9531, USA

Fisher, Raymond C (Judge)
US Courts of Appeals
125 S Grand Ave
Pasadena, CA 91105-1652, USA

Fisher, Red (Writer)
Montreal Gazette
250 Saint Antoine W
Montreal, PQ H2Y 3R7, CANADA

Fisher, Rob
45 Montague Rd.
Richmond Surrey, ENGLAND, UNITED KINGDOM (UK)

Fisher, Robert (Business Person)
Gap Inc
2 Folsom St
San Francisco, CA 94105-1205, USA

Fisher, Roger (Musician)
Borman Entertainment
1250 6th St Ste 401
Santa Monica, CA 90401-1638, USA

Fisher, Steve (Coach)
San Diego State University
Athletic Dept
San Diego, CA 92182, USA

Fisher, Terry Louise
5314 Pacific Ave
Marina Del Rey, CA 90292-7118, USA

Fisher, Thomas L
Nicor Inc
1844 W Ferry Rd
Naperville, IL 60563-9600, USA

Fisher, Tom (Baseball Player)
Baltimore Orioles
8515 Lake Suzzanne Cir
Panama City, FL 32404, USA

Fisher, Trisha Leigh
243 Delfern Dr
Los Angeles, CA 90077-3544, USA

Fisher, William F (Astronaut)
1119 Woodland Dr
Seabrook, TX 77586-6044, USA

Fisher-Stevens, Lorraine (Baseball Player)
120 Birdsell St
Jackson, MI 49203-4670, USA

Fishman, Jerald G (Business Person)
Analog Devices Inc
1 Technology Way
Norwood, MA 02062-2666, USA

Fishman, Jon (Musician)
Dionyslan Productions
431 Pine St
Burlington, VT 05401-4726, USA

Fisk, Carlton E (Baseball Player)
PO Box 1317
New Lenox, IL 60451-6317, USA

Fisk, Pliny III (Architect)
Maximum Potential Building Systems Center
8604 Fm 969
Austin, TX 78724-6200, USA

Fisk, Schuyler (Actor)
c/o Staff Member *Creative Artists Agency LCC (CAA-LA)*
2000 Avenue Of The Stars
Los Angeles, CA 90067-4700, USA

Fisk, William (Football Player)
Detroit Lions
3809 Sandune Ln
Corona Del Mar, CA 92625-1623, USA

Fiske, Robert B Jr (Attorney, Attorney General, General)
19 Juniper Rd
Darien, CT 06820-5707, USA

Fisker, Bruce L (General)
9001 Jimson Weed Way
Highlands Ranch, CO 80126-2642, USA

Fiss, Galen (Football Player)
Cleveland Browns
4609 W 125th St
Shawnee Mission, KS 66209-3145, USA

Fitch, Val L (Nobel Prize Laureate)
292 Hartley Ave
Princeton, NJ 08540-5656, USA

Fites, Donald V (Business Person)
Caterpillar Inc
100 NE Adams St
Peoria, IL 61629-0002, USA

Fitt of Bell's Hill, Gerald (Government Official)
irish Club
82 Eaton Square
London SW1, UNITED KINGDOM (UK)

Fittipaldi, Christian (Race Car Driver)
282 Alphaville Barueri
Sao Paulo 064500, BRAZIL

Fittipaldi, Emerson (Race Car Driver)
735 Crandon Blvd Apt 503
Miami, FL 33149-2526, USA

Fitts, Rick
1903 Dracena Dr
Los Angeles, CA 90027-3106, USA

Fitz, Raymond L (Educator)
University of Dayton
President's Office
Dayton, OH 45414, USA

Fitzgerald, A Ernest (Government Official, Lawyer)
Air Force Management Systems
Pentagon
Washington, DC 20330-0001, USA

Fitzgerald, Brian (Baseball Player)
Seattle Mariners
7226 John Taylor Mews
Ruther Glen, VA 22546-4816, USA

Fitzgerald, Ed (Baseball Player)
Pittsburgh Pirates
431 Christopher St
Folsom, CA 95630-1706, USA

Fitzgerald, Fern (Actor)
Boutique
10 Universal City Plz Ste 2000
Universal City, CA 91608-1074, USA

FitzGerald, Frances (Writer)
Simon & Schuster
1230 Avenue Of The Americas
New York, NY 10020-1586, USA

FitzGerald, Garret (Prime Minister)
30 Palmerston Road
Dublin 6, IRELAND

Fitzgerald, Glenn (Actor)
c/o Bonnie Bernstein *Endeavor Agency LLC (NY)*
23 Watts St Fl 6
New York, NY 10013, USA

FitzGerald, Helen (Actor)
Paul Lohner
9300 Wilshire Blvd Ste 555
Beverly Hills, CA 90212-3211, USA

Fitzgerald, Jack (Actor)
William Kerwin Agency
1605 N Cahuenga Blvd Ste 202
Los Angeles, CA 90028-6288, USA

Fitzgerald, James F (Misc)
Golden State Warriors
1001 Broadway
Oakland, CA 94607-4019, USA

Fitzgerald, John (Baseball Player)
San Francisco Giants
1913 Greve Ave Apt I
Spring Lake, NJ 07762-2354, USA

Fitzgerald, John (Football Player)
Dallas Cowboys
408 Arborcrest Dr
Richardson, TX 75080-2606, USA

Fitzgerald, Larry (Football Player)
Arizona Cardinals
PO Box 888
Phoenix, AZ 85001-0888, USA

Fitzgerald, Melissa (Actor)
c/o Staff Member *Geddes Agency, The*
8430 Santa Monica Blvd Ste 200
Los Angeles, CA 90069-4253, USA

Fitzgerald, Mike (Baseball Player)
St Louis Cardinals
1607 E 37th St
Savannah, GA 31404-3535, USA

Fitzgerald, Mike (Baseball Player)
New York Mets
502 Flint Ave
Long Beach, CA 90814-2039, USA

Fitzgerald, Mosley Benita (Athlete)
Women in Cable/Telecommunications
14555 Avion Pkwy Ste 250
Chantilly, VA 20151-1117, USA

FitzGerald, Niali W A (Business Person)
Unilever NV
Weena 455
Rotterdam, DK 3000, THE NETHERLANDS

Fitzgerald, Tac (Actor)
c/o Staff Member *Iris Burton Agency*
8916 Ashcroft Ave
West Hollywood, CA 90048-2404, USA

Fitzgerald, Tara (Actor)
Caroline Dawson
125 Gloucester Road
London SW7 4IE, UNITED KINGDOM (UK)

Fitzgerald-Leclair, Meryle (Baseball Player)
909 E Hanson Ave
Mitchell, SD 57301-3635, USA

Fitzkee, Scott (Football Player)
Philadelphia Eagles
1611 Grafton Shop Rd
Forest Hill, MD 21050-2535, USA

Fitzmaurice, David J (Misc)
Electrical Radio & Machinists Union
11256 156th St NW
Washington, DC 20005, USA

Fitzmaurice, Michael J (War Hero)
PO Box 178
Hartford, SD 57033-0178, USA

Fitzmaurice, Shaun (Baseball Player)
New York Mets
1911 Normanstone Dr
Midlothian, VA 23113, USA

Fitzmorris, Al (Baseball Player)
Kansas City Royals
17512 W 159th Ter
Olathe, KS 66062-4017, USA

Fitzpatrick, Leo (Actor)
9350 Wilshire Blvd Ste 328
Beverly Hills, CA 90212-3206, USA

Fitzpatrick, Michael (Baseball Player)
262 Lodge Ln
Kalamazoo, MI 49009-9161, USA

Fitzpatrick, Sonya (Psychic, Writer)
Animals Are Forever LLC
12121 Wilshire Blvd Ste 301
Los Angeles, CA 90025-1166, USA

Fitzsimonds, Roger L (Financier)
Firstar Corp
777 E Wisconsin Ave
Milwaukee, WI 53202-5342, USA

Fitzwater, Marlin (Government Official)
851 Cedar Dr
Deale, MD 20751-9613, USA

Five for Fighting (Music Group)
c/o Staff Member *Paradigm (NY)*
360 Park Ave S Fl 16
New York, NY 10010-1716, USA

Fix, Oliver (Athlete)
Ringstr 6
Stadtbergen, GERMANY

Fixman, Marshall (Misc)
Colorado State University
Chemistry Dept
Fort Collins, CO 80523-0001, USA

Fizer, Marcus (Basketball Player)
Charlotte Bobcats
333 E Trade St
Charlotte, NC 28202-2331, USA

Flach, Ken (Coach, Tennis Player)
Vanderbilt University
Athletic Dept
Nashville, TN 37240-0001, USA

Flack, Enya (Actor)
c/o Staff Member *The House of
Representatives*
211 S Beverly Dr Ste 208
Beverly Hills, CA 90212-3879, USA

Flade, H Kiaus-Dietrich (Cosmonaut)
Airbus Industries
1 Rond Point M Bellonte
Blagnac Cedex 31707, FRANCE

Flagg, Fannie (Actor, Comedian)
c/o Sally Wilcox *Creative Artists Agency
LCC (CAA-LA)*
2000 Avenue Of The Stars
Los Angeles, CA 90067-4700, USA

Flaherty, Harry (Football Player)
Dallas Cowboys
23 Elizabeth Dr
Oceanport, NJ 07757-1050, USA

Flaherty, Joe
c/o Staff Member *Silver Massetti &
Szatmary (SMS-NY)*
145 W 45th St # 1204
New York, NY 10036-4008, USA

Flaherty, John (Baseball Player)
Boston Red Sox
17 Joseph Bow Ct
Pearl River, NY 10965-2868, USA

Flaherty, Maureen
PO Box 15967
Long Beach, CA 90815-0967, USA

Flaherty, Stephen (Composer)
William Morris Agency
151 El Camino Dr
Beverly Hills, CA 90212-2775, USA

Flaman, Ferdinand C (Fernle) (Hockey
Player)
29 Church St
Westwood, MA 02090-3511, USA

Flamingos, The
2375 E Tropicana Ave Ste 304
Las Vegas, NV 89119-9808, USA

Flanagan, Barry (Artist)
5E Fawe St
London E14 6PD, UNITED KINGDOM
(UK)

Flanagan, Crista (Actor)
c/o Kay Liberman *Liberman/Zerman
Management*
252 N Larchmont Blvd Ste 200
Los Angeles, CA 90004-3754, USA

Flanagan, Ed (Football Player)
Detroit Lions
10981 Clayton St
Northglenn, CO 80233-4671, USA

Flanagan, Edward M Jr (General)
12 Oyster Catcher Rd
Parade Rest
Beaufort, SC 29907-1221, USA

Flanagan, Fionnula (Actor)
c/o Dick Guttman *Guttman Associates*
118 S Beverly Dr Ste 201
Beverly Hills, CA 90212-3016, USA

Flanagan, Michael K (Mike) (Baseball
Player)
Baltimore Orioles
15010 York Rd
Sparks, MD 21152-9669, USA

Flanagan, Mike (Football Player)
Green Bay Packers
4127 Hollister Ave
Carmichael, CA 95608-2512, USA

Flanagan, Tommy (Actor)
P F D
Drury House
34-43 Russell St
London WC2B 5HA, UNITED KINGDOM
(UK)

Flanery, Bridget
8428 Melrose Pl Ste C
Los Angeles, CA 90069-5300, USA

Flanery, Sean Patrick (Actor)
6351 Bryn Mawr Dr
Los Angeles, CA 90068-2808, USA

Flanigan, Jim (Football Player)
Green Bay Packers
3820 Sand Bay Point Rd
Sturgeon Bay, WI 54235-8418, USA

Flanigan, Jim (Football Player)
Chicago Bears
4511 Wyandot Trl
Green Bay, WI 54313-6789, USA

Flanigan, Joe (Actor)
c/o John Carrabino *John Carrabino
Management*
5900 Wilshire Blvd Ste 406
Los Angeles, CA 90036-5015, USA

Flanigan, Lauren (Opera Singer)
Robert Lombardo
61 W 62nd St Apt 6F
Harkness Plaza
New York, NY 10023-7017, USA

Flanigan, Tom (Baseball Player)
Chicago White Sox
114 E 40th St
Covington, KY 41015-1802, USA

Flannery, John (Baseball Player)
Chicago White Sox
9002 Scottish Pastures Dr
Austin, TX 78750-3582, USA

Flannery, Susan (Actor)
Flannery-Daedy-Leona
6977 Shepard Mesa Rd
Carpinteria, CA 93013-3134, USA

Flannery, Thomas (Cartoonist, Editor)
911 Dartmouth Gien Way
Baltimore, MD 21212, USA

Flannery, Tim (Baseball Player)
San Diego Padres
715 Hymettus Ave
Encinitas, CA 92024-2148, USA

Flannigan, Maureen (Actor)
Gold Marshak Liedtke
3500 W Olive Ave Ste 1400
Burbank, CA 91505-5512, USA

Flatley, Michael (Actor, Dancer)
c/o Staff Member *Creative Artists Agency
LCC (CAA-LA)*
2000 Avenue Of The Stars
Los Angeles, CA 90067-4700, USA

Flatley, Patrick (Pat) (Hockey Player)
69 Cherrylawn Ave
North York, ON M9L 2B3, CANADA

Flatley, Paul R (Football Player)
Minnesota Vikings
795 Woods Rd
Richmond, IN 47374-9409, USA

Flatt, Lester
PO Box 647
Hendersonville, TN 37077-0647, USA

Flaum, Joel M (Judge)
US District Court
219 S Dearborn St
Chicago, IL 60604-1800, USA

Flavell, Richard A (Misc)
Yale University
Medical Center
Immunology Dept
New Haven, CT 06520, USA

Flavin, Jennifer (Model)
30 Beverly Park
Beverly Hills, CA 90210-1546, USA

Flavin, John (Baseball Player)
Chicago Cubs
23060 16th St
Newhall, CA 91321-1054, USA

Flavio, Alfaro (Baseball Player)
US Olympic Team
3240 N Bass Island Rd
West Sacramento, CA 95691-5848, USA

Flavor, Flav (Actor, Artist, Comedian)
William Morris Agency
151 El Camino Dr
Beverly Hills, CA 90212-2775, USA

Flay, Bobby (Chef, Television Host)
c/o Staff Member *Food Network, The*
75 9th Ave
New York, NY 10011-7006, USA

Flchter, Michael (Baseball Player)
8821 Jackson Ct
Munster, IN 46321-2410, USA

Flea (Musician)
Q Prime
729 7th Ave Rm 1600
New York, NY 10019-6880, USA

Fleck, Bela (Composer, Musician)
Agency for Performing Arts
405 S Beverly Dr Ste 500
Beverly Hills, CA 90212-4425, USA

Fleck, Jack (Golfer)
12006 Edgewater Rd
Fort Smith, AR 72903-5889, USA

Fleckman, Marty (Golfer)
26411 Ridgestone Park Ln
Cypress, TX 77433-1279, USA

Fleder, Gary R (Director)
ACTW Filmworks
624 Sunset Ave
Venice, CA 90291-2733, USA

Fleeshman, Richard (Actor)
Pemberton Associates
193 Wardour Street
London W1V 3FA, UNITED KINGDOM
(UK)

Fleetwood, Ken (Designer, Fashion
Designer)
14 Savile Row
London SW1, UNITED KINGDOM (UK)

Fleetwood, Mick (Musician)
Courage Mgmt
2899 Agoura Rd # 582
Westlake Village, CA 91361-3218, USA

Fleischer, Arthur Jr (Attorney, Attorney
General, General)
Fried Frank Harris Shriver Jacobson
1 New York Plz
New York, NY 10004-1980, USA

Fleischer, Charles
749 N Crescent Heights Blvd
Los Angeles, CA 90046-7001, USA

Fleischer, Daniel (Religious Leader)
201 Princess Dr
Corpus Christi, TX 78410-1615, USA

Fleischman, Paul (Writer)
PO Box 646
Aromas, CA 95004-0646, USA

Fleischmann, Peter (Director, Producer)
Filmzentrum Babelsberg
August-Bebel-Str 26-53
Potsdam 14482, GERMANY

Fleisher, Bruce (Golfer)
11722 Cardena Ct
Palm Beach Gardens, FL 33418-1564,
USA

Fleisher, Leon (Musician)
20 Merrymount Rd
Baltimore, MD 21210-1909, USA

Fleiss, Heidi (Business Person)
One Hour Entertainment
PO Box 291831
C/O Development Dept
Los Angeles, CA 90029-8831, USA

Fleiss, Michael (Mike) (Director,
Producer, Writer)
c/o Staff Member *Next Entertainment*
3300 W Olive Ave Unit 500
Burbank, CA 91505-4665, USA

Fleiss, Noah (Actor)
c/o Nick Frenkel *3 Arts Entertainment
(NY)*
9460 Wilshire Blvd Ste 700
Beverly Hills, CA 90212-2713, USA

Fleitas, Angel (Baseball Player)
Washington Senators
8540 SW 133rd Avenue Rd Apt 107
Miami, FL 33183-4508, USA

Fleming, Bill (Baseball Player)
Boston Red Sox
6150 Windflower Dr
Powder Springs, GA 30127-8321, USA

Fleming, Cory (Football Player)
Dallas Cowboys
1404 Madison Dr
La Vergne, TN 37086-3996, USA

Fleming, David (Baseball Player)
Seattle Mariners
37 Laurelwood Ln
Southbury, CT 06488-4657, USA

Fleming, Ed
RR 3 Box 261K
Greensburg, PA 15601-9426, USA

Fleming, James P (War Hero)
PO Box 487
Manvel, TX 77578-0487, USA

Fleming, Mac A (Misc)
Maintenance of Ways Brotherhood
26555 Evergreen Rd
Southfield, MI 48076-4206, USA

Fleming, Marvin (Marv) (Football Player)
Green Bay Packers
909 Howard St
Marina Del Rey, CA 90292-5518, USA

Fleming, Peggy (Figure Skater)
16387 Aztec Ridge Dr
Los Gatos, CA 95030-7503, USA

Fleming, Peter E Jr (Attorney, Attorney
General, General)
Curtis Mallet-Prevost Colt Mosle
101 Park Ave Fl 34
New York, NY 10178-3499, USA

Fleming, Reginald S (Reggie) (Hockey
Player)
1605 E Central Rd Unit 406A
Arlington Heights, IL 60005-3342, USA

Fleming, Renee (Opera Singer)
M L Falcone
155 W 68th St Apt 1104
New York, NY 10023-5816, USA

Fleming, Rhonda (Actor)
10281 Century Woods Dr
Los Angeles, CA 90067-6312, USA

Fleming, Scott (Government Official)
2750 Shasta Rd
Berkeley, CA 94708-1924, USA

Fleming, Vern (Basketball Player)
10713 Brixton Ln
Fishers, IN 46037-8707, USA

Flemming, Catherine
Goethestr. 17
Munich D-80336, GERMANY

Flemming, John (Artist)
1409 Cambronne St
New Orleans, LA 70118-1301, USA

Flemming, William N (Bill) (Sportscaster)
ABC-TV Sports Dept
77 W 66th St
New York, NY 10023-6201, USA

Flemyng, Gordon (Director)
1 Albert Road
Wilmslow
Cheshire SK9 5HT, UNITED KINGDOM
(UK)

Flemyng, Jason (Actor)
Conway Van Gelder Robinson
18-21 Jermyn St
London SW1Y 6NB, UNITED KINGDOM
(UK)

Flemyng, Robert (Actor)
4 Netherbourne Road
London SW4, UNITED KINGDOM (UK)

Flener, Huck (Baseball Player)
Toronto Blue Jays
2012 Blackridge Ave
Sacramento, CA 95835-1248, USA

Flennes, Ranulph T-W (Misc)
Greenlands Extord
Minehead
West Sussex, UNITED KINGDOM (UK)

Flerstein, Harvey F (Actor, Musician,
Writer)
1479 Carla Rdg
Beverly Hills, CA 90210-2510, USA

Flesch, Steve (Golfer)
10710 Meadow Stable Ln
Union, KY 41091-7986, USA

Flessel, Craig (Cartoonist)
40 Camino Alto Apt 2306
Mill Valley, CA 94941-2976, USA

Fletcher, Andrew (Baseball Player)
3282 Kinderhill Ln
Germantown, TN 38138-8210, USA

Fletcher, Andy (Musician)
Reach Media
295 Greenwich St # 109
New York, NY 10007-1049, USA

Fletcher, Betty Binns (Judge)
US Court of Appeals
1010 5th Ave
US Courthouse
Seattle, WA 98104-1195, USA

Fletcher, Brendan (Actor)
Seven Summits Mgmt
8447 Wilshire Blvd Ste 200
Beverly Hills, CA 90211-3207, USA

Fletcher, Charles M (Physicist, Scientist)
2 Coastguard Cottages
Newtown PO30 4PA, UNITED
KINGDOM (UK)

Fletcher, Chris (Football Player)
San Diego Chargers
12868 Isleworth Dr
Jacksonville, FL 32225-4752, USA

Fletcher, Darrin (Baseball Player)
Los Angeles Dodgers
9146 E 2100 North Rd
Oakwood, IL 61858-6285, USA

Fletcher, Derrick (Football Player)
New England Patriots
2100 S 8th St Apt 2106
Waco, TX 76706-3192, USA

Fletcher, Dexter
1 Kingsway House Albion Rd.
London, ENGLAND N16, UNITED
KINGDOM (UK)

Fletcher, Diane (Actor)
Ken McReddie
91 regent St
London W1R 7TB, UNITED KINGDOM
(UK)

Fletcher, Guy (Musician)
Damage Mgmt
16 Lambton Place
London W11 2SH, UNITED KINGDOM
(UK)

Fletcher, Louise (Actor)
1520 Camden Ave Apt 105
Los Angeles, CA 90025-3443, USA

Fletcher, Martin (Correspondent)
NBC-TV
4001 Nebraska Ave NW
News Dept
Washington, DC 20016-2733, USA

Fletcher, Paul (Baseball Player)
Philadelphia Phillies
548 Mockingbird Way
Warrington, PA 18976-3017, USA

Fletcher, Scott B (Baseball Player)
Chicago Cubs
300 Birkdale Dr
Fayetteville, GA 30215-2720, USA

Fletcher, Simon (Football Player)
Denver Broncos
2225 S Ensenada St
Aurora, CO 80013-6230, USA

Fletcher, Terrell (Football Player)
San Diego Chargers
PO Box 711960
San Diego, CA 92171-1960, USA

Fletcher, Tom (Baseball Player)
Detroit Tigers
9287 E 2085 North Rd
Oakwood, IL 61858-6252, USA

Fletcher, Van (Baseball Player)
Detroit Tigers
2404 Whitaker Rd
Boonville, NC 27011-9204, USA

Fletcher, William A (Judge)
US Court of Appeals
95 7th St
Courts Building
San Francisco, CA 94103-1518, USA

Fleury, Theoren (Hockey Player)
Chicago Blackhawks
1901 W Madison St
United Center
Chicago, IL 60612-2459, USA

Flick, Bob (Misc)
Bob Flick Productions
300 Vine St Ste 14
Seattle, WA 98121-1465, USA

Flick, Mick
Sherry Netherlands 5th & 59th
New York, NY 10003, USA

Flick, Tom (Football Player)
Washington Redskins
9718 208th Ave NE
Redmond, WA 98053-5216, USA

Flicker, John (Misc)
National Audubon Society
700 Broadway
President's Office
New York, NY 10003-9536, USA

Flinelt, Flemming O (Choreographer,
Dancer)
Christiansholms Parkv 24
Klampenborg 2930, DENMARK

Flinn, John (Baseball Player)
Baltimore Orioles
6221 Lake Providence Ln
Charlotte, NC 28277-0565, USA

Flint, George (Football Player)
Buffalo Bills
PO Box 2486
Prescott, AZ 86302-2486, USA

Flint, Judson (Football Player)
Cleveland Browns
306 Federal St
Farrell, PA 16121-1925, USA

Flint, Keith (Dancer, Musician)
c/o Staff Member *Maverick Recording Co
(LA)*
3300 Warner Blvd
Burbank, CA 91505-4632, USA

Flippin, Lucy Lee
1753 S Canfield Ave
Los Angeles, CA 90035-4216, USA

Flitcroft, Garry (Soccer Player)
c/o Staff Member *Blackburn Rovers
Football Club*
Ewood Park
Blackburn
Lancashire BB2 4JF, UNITED KINGDOM
(UK)

Flock of Seagulls
526 Nicolett Mall
Minneapolis, MN 55402, USA

Flockhart, Calista (Actor)
c/o Barry Tyerman *Jackoway Tyerman
Wertheimer Austen Mandelbaum &
Morris*
1888 Century Park E Fl 18
Los Angeles, CA 90067-1702, USA

Floethe, Chris (Baseball Player)
5634 Mount Hood Ct
Martinez, CA 94553-5837, USA

Floetry (Music Group)
c/o Cara Lewis *William Morris Agency
(WMA-NY)*
1325 Avenue Of The Americas
New York, NY 10019-6026, USA

Flom, Joseph H (Attorney, Attorney
General, General)
Skadden Arps State Meagher Flom
4 Times Sq
New York, NY 10036-6518, USA

Flood, Ann (Actor)
15 E 91st St
New York, NY 10128-0648, USA

Flood, Staci (Model, Musician)
Clear Talent Group
10950 Ventura Blvd
Studio City, CA 91604-3340, USA

Flor, Claus Peter (Conductor)
Intermusica Artists
16 Duncan Terrace
London N1 8BZ, UNITED KINGDOM
(UK)

Flora, Kevin (Baseball Player)
California Angels
3854 Lealma Ave
Claremont, CA 91711-3023, USA

Florance, Sheila (Actor)
Melbourne Artists
643 Saint Kikla Road
Melbourne, VIC 3004, AUSTRALIA

Florek, Dann (Actor)
145 W 45th St # 1204
New York, NY 10036-4008, USA

Florence, Don (Baseball Player)
New York Mets
144 Bedford Rd
New Boston, NH 03070-4301, USA

Florence, Tyler (Chef, Television Host)
c/o Staff Member *Food Network, The*
75 9th Ave
New York, NY 10011-7006, USA

Flores, Facusse Carlos (President)
Casa Presidencial
Blvd Juan Pablo II
Tegucigalpa, HONDURAS

Flores, Francisco (President)
President's Office
Casa Presidencial
San Salvador, EL SALVADOR

Flores, Nikki (Musician)
c/o Staff Member *Sony Music
International*
550 Madison Ave Fl 6
New York, NY 10022-3211, USA

Flores, Patrick F (Religious Leader)
Archbishop's Residence
2600 W Woodlawn Ave
San Antonio, TX 78228-5122, USA

Flores, Randy (Baseball Player)
Texas Rangers
7313 Moonlight View Ct
Las Vegas, NV 89129-5945, USA

Flores, Thomas R (Tom) (Coach, Football
Coach, Football Executive, Football
Player)
Oakland Raiders
77741 Cove Pointe Cir
Indian Wells, CA 92210-6101, USA

Flores, Tom
11220 NE 53rd St
Kirkland, WA 98033-7505, USA

Floria, Holly (Actor)
Epstein-Wyckoff
280 S Beverly Dr Ste 400
Beverly Hills, CA 90212-3904, USA

Floria, James J (Jim) (Governor)
Mudge Rose Guthrie
1673 E 16th St # 16
Coporate Center 2
Brooklyn, NY 11229-2901, USA

Florie, Bryce (Baseball Player)
San Diego Padres
PO Box 1744
Goose Creek, SC 29445-1744, USA

Florin, Susan (Golfer)
c/o Staff Member *Ladies Pro Golf Association (LPGA)*
100 International Golf Dr
Daytona Beach, FL 32124-1082, USA

Florio, Steven T (Publisher)
Conde Nast Publications
4 Times Sq
Publisher's Office
New York, NY 10036-6561, USA

Florio, Thomas A (Actor)
New Yorker Magazine
4 Times Sq
Publisher's Office
New York, NY 10036-6592, USA

Flory, Med (Actor)
6044 Ensign Ave
North Hollywood, CA 91606-4905, USA

Flournoy, Craig (Journalist)
Dallas News
Communications Center
Editorial Dept
Dallas, TX 75211, USA

Flower, Joseph R (Religious Leader)
Assemblies of God
1445 N Boonville Ave
Springfield, MO 65802-1894, USA

Flowers, Ben (Baseball Player)
Boston Red Sox
901 Treemont Rd NW
Wilson, NC 27896-2050, USA

Flowers, Bernard (Football Player)
Baltimore Colts
3819 Old Farm Rd
Lafayette, IN 47909-3521, USA

Flowers, Charles (Charlie) (Football Player)
Los Angeles Chargers
6170 Mount Brook Way NW
Atlanta, GA 30342, USA

Flowers, Frank E (Director, Writer)
c/o Aleen Keshishian *Brillstein-Grey Entertainment*
9150 Wilshire Blvd Ste 350
Beverly Hills, CA 90212-3453, USA

Flowers, Gennifer
4859 Cedar Springs Rd Apt 241
Dallas, TX 75219-1215, USA

Flowers, Richmond (Football Player)
Dallas Cowboys
3434 Indian Lake Dr
Pelham, AL 35124-2713, USA

Flowers of Queen's Gate, Brian H
(Physicist)
53 Athenaeum Road
London N2O 9AL, UNITED KINGDOM (UK)

Floyd, Bobby (Baseball Player)
Baltimore Orioles
1757 SE Dominic Ave
Port Saint Lucie, FL 34952-5815, USA

Floyd, Bobby Jack (Football Player)
Green Bay Packers
3428 Kensington Ct
Rocklin, CA 95765-5626, USA

Floyd, C Clifford (Cliff) (Baseball Player)
Montreal Expos
10863 Blackhawk St
Plantation, FL 33324-2180, USA

Floyd, Carlisie (Composer)
4491 Yoakum Blvd
Houston, TX 77006-5819, USA

Floyd, Eddie (Musician, Songwriter, Writer)
Jason West
Gables House
Saddlebow Kings Lynn PE34 3AR, UNITED KINGDOM (UK)

Floyd, Eric (Sleepy) (Basketball Player)
22136 Westheimer Pkwy # 201
Katy, TX 77450-8296, USA

Floyd, George (Football Player)
New York Jets
7085 Burlington Pike
Boone County High School Attn: Faculty Staff
Florence, KY 41042, USA

Floyd, Heather (Musician)
TBA Artists Mgmt
300 10th Ave S
Nashville, TN 37203-4125, USA

Floyd, Leslie (Baseball Player)
Detroit Tigers
PO Box 7619
Texarkana, TX 75505-7619, USA

Floyd, Marlene (Golfer)
Marlene Floyd Golf School
5370 Clubhouse Ln
Hope Mills, NC 28348-9794, USA

Floyd, Pink
370 City Rd. Islington
London, ENGLAND EC1V 2QA, UNITED KINGDOM (UK)

Floyd, Ray
PO Box 545957
Surfside, FL 33154-5957, USA

Floyd, Susan
PO Box 5617
Beverly Hills, CA 90209-5617, USA

Floyd, Tim (Coach)
New Orleans Hornets
1250 Poydras St # 19
New Orleans Arena
New Orleans, LA 70113-1804, USA

Fluckey, Eugene B (Admiral, War Hero)
1016 Sandpiper Ln
Annapolis, MD 21403-4633, USA

Fluegel, Darlanne (Actor)
Shelter Entertainment
9255 W Sunset Blvd Ste 1010
Los Angeles, CA 90069-3307, USA

Flueger, Patrick (Actor)
c/o Theresa Peters *William Morris Agency (WMA-LA)*
1 William Morris Pl
Beverly Hills, CA 90212-4261, USA

Fluno, Jere D (Business Person)
W W Grainger Inc
5500 Howard St
Skokie, IL 60077-2620, USA

Flutie, Darren (Football Player)
San Diego Chargers
430 Franklin Village Dr # 246
Franklin, MA 02038-4007, USA

Flutie, Doug (Football Player)
Chicago Bears
22 Chieftain Ln
Natick, MA 01760-6083, USA

Flyleaf (Music Group)
Octone Records
560 Broadway Rm 500
New York, NY 10012-3946, USA

Flynn, Barbara (Actor)
Markham & Froggatt
Julian House
4 Windmill St
London W1P 1HF, UNITED KINGDOM (UK)

Flynn, Colleen (Actor)
LGM
10390 Santa Monica Blvd Ste 300
Los Angeles, CA 90025-5091, USA

Flynn, Don (Football Player)
Dallas Texans
6511 S Indianapolis Ave
Tulsa, OK 74136-1416, USA

Flynn, Doug (Baseball Player)
Detroit Tigers
2465 Vale Dr
Lexington, KY 40514-1421, USA

Flynn, George W (Misc)
382 Summit Ave
Leonia, NJ 07605-1337, USA

Flynn, Jackie (Comedian)
c/o Staff Member *Don Buchwald & Associates Inc (LA)*
6500 Wilshire Blvd Ste 2200
Los Angeles, CA 90048-4942, USA

Flynn, Luke (Actor, Producer, Writer)
c/o Kay Liberman *Liberman/Zerman Management*
252 N Larchmont Blvd Ste 200
Los Angeles, CA 90004-3754, USA

Flynn, Neil (Actor)
c/o Christopher (Chris) Wright *Christopher Wright Management*
3207 Winnie Dr
Los Angeles, CA 90068-1439, USA

Flynn, Raymond L (Diplomat, Politician)
Catholic Alliance
PO Box 1872
Via Cathollcity
Chesapeake, VA 23327-1872, USA

Flynn, Sean (Actor)
c/o Meredith Fine *Coast to Coast Talent Group*
3350 Barham Blvd
Los Angeles, CA 90068-1404, USA

Flynn, Tom (Football Player)
Green Bay Packers
4008 Holiday Park Dr
Murrysville, PA 15668-8529, USA

Flynn, Vince (Writer)
Cloak & Dagger Press
2316 Delaware Ave Ste 266
Buffalo, NY 14216-2607, USA

Flynt, Larry (Publisher)
LFP Inc
8484 Wilshire Blvd Ste 900
Beverly Hills, CA 90211-3218, USA

Flynville Train (Music Group)
c/o Staff Member *Paradigm (Monterey)*
509 Hartnell St
Monterey, CA 93940-2825, USA

Flythe, Mark (Football Player)
New York Giants
205 Montrose Ave Apt 7
Brooklyn, NY 11206-2738, USA

Fo, Dario (Nobel Prize Laureate)
Pietro Sclotta
Via Alessandria 4
Milan 20144, ITALY

Foale, C Michael (Mike) (Astronaut)
2101 Todville Rd # 11
Seabrook, TX 77586, USA

Fobbs, Brandon
c/o Todd Justice *Venture IAB*
2509 Wilshire Blvd
Los Angeles, CA 90057-4302, USA

Foch, Nina (Actor)
PO Box 1884
Beverly Hills, CA 90213-1884, USA

Fodge, Gene (Baseball Player)
Chicago Cubs
1505 N Chicago St
South Bend, IN 46628-1421, USA

Fodor, Eugene (Musician)
22314 N Turkey Creek Rd
Morrison, CO 80465-9028, USA

Foege, William H (Misc)
10610 SW Cowan Rd
Vashon, WA 98070-3054, USA

Foeger, Luggi (Skier)
Christopher Foeger
230 S Balsamina Way
Portola Valley, CA 94028-7503, USA

Fogdoe, Tomas (Skier)
Skogsvagen 18
Gallvare 970 02, SWEDEN

Fogel, Robert W (Nobel Prize Laureate)
5321 S University Ave
Chicago, IL 60615-5105, USA

Fogelberg, Dan (Musician, Songwriter, Writer)
H K Mgmt
9200 W Sunset Blvd Ste 530
Los Angeles, CA 90069-3509, USA

Fogerty, John (Musician, Songwriter, Writer)
4570 Van Nuys Blvd # 3517
Sherman Oaks, CA 91403-2913, USA

Fogg, Josh (Baseball Player)
Chicago White Sox
593 NW 70th Way
Margate, FL 33063-4314, USA

Fogg, Kirk (Actor)
c/o Staff Member *Brady Brannon & Rich*
5670 Wilshire Blvd Ste 820
Los Angeles, CA 90036-5613, USA

Foggie, Fred (Football Player)
Cleveland Browns
337 N Emerald Rd Apt Dd6
Greenwood, SC 29646-3049, USA

Foggs, Edward L (Religious Leader)
Church of God
PO Box 2420
Anderson, IN 46018-2420, USA

Fogleman, Ronald R (Ron) (General)
406 Snowshoe Ln
Durango, CO 81301, USA

Fogler, Eddie (Basketball Player)
University of South Carolina
Athletic Dept
Columbia, SC 53233, USA

Foglesong, Robert H (Doc) (General)
Vice Chief Of Staff
Hqusaf Pentagon
Washington, DC 20330-0001, USA

Foiles, Hank (Baseball Player)
Cincinnati Reds
4333 Silverleaf Ct
Virginia Beach, VA 23462-5738, USA

Foiles, Lisa (Actor)
Boutique Talent Agency
10 Universal City Plz Ste 2000
C/O Nancy Schmidt Sanford
Universal City, CA 91608-1074, USA

Fokin, Vitold P (Prime Minister)
Cabinet of Ministers
Government Building
Klev, UKRAINE

Folau, Spencer (Football Player)
Baltimore Ravens
14003 Woodens Ln
Reisterstown, MD 21136-4536, USA

Foldberg, Henry C (Hank) (Football Player)
1204 S 12th St
Rogers, AR 72756-5110, USA

Folder-Powell, Rose (Baseball Player)
PO Box 415
Carnation, WA 98014-0415, USA

Folds, Ben (Musician, Songwriter, Writer)
CEC
1123 Broadway Ste 317
New York, NY 10010-2093, USA

Foley, Dave (Comedian)
Baker/Winokur/Ryder
9100 Wilshire Blvd # 600
Beverly Hills, CA 90212-3401, USA

Foley, Dave (Football Player)
New York Jets
4500 Redmond Rd
Springfield, OH 45505-1722, USA

Foley, ex-Speaker Tom
601 W 1st Ave # 2W
Spokane, WA 99201-3825, USA

Foley, Jeremy (Actor)
Academy Kids Mgmt
4942 Vineland Ave Ste 103
North Hollywood, CA 91601-5639, USA

Foley, Linda (Misc)
Newspaper Guild
8611 2nd Ave
Silver Spring, MD 20910-3372, USA

Foley, Marv (Baseball Player)
Chicago White Sox
4970 Country Meadows Blvd
Sarasota, FL 34235-8219, USA

Foley, Maurice B (Judge)
US Tax Court
400 2nd St NW
Washington, DC 20217-0002, USA

Foley, Mick (Wrestler)
c/o Staff Member *World Wrestling
Entertainment (WWE)*
1241 E Main St
Stamford, CT 06902-3520, USA

Foley, Scott (Actor)
c/o David Guillod *United Talent Agency
(UTA)*
9560 Wilshire Blvd Ste 500
Beverly Hills, CA 90212-2401, USA

Foley, Steve
8942 Wilshire Blvd
Beverly Hills, CA 90211-1908, USA

Foley, Steve (Football Player)
Denver Broncos
6321 S Newport Ct
Centennial, CO 80111-4630, USA

Foley, Sylvester R Jr (Admiral)
50 Apple Hill Dr
Tewksbury, MA 01876-1140, USA

Foley, Thomas S (Diplomat)
PO Box 1047
Medical Lake, WA 99022-1047, USA

Foley, Tim (Football Player)
Miami Dolphins
11541 Lane Park Rd
Tavares, FL 32778-9674, USA

Foley, Tim J (Football Player)
Baltimore Colts
2851 Old Clifton Rd
Springfield, OH 45502-9455, USA

Foley, Tom (Baseball Player)
Cincinnati Reds
5237 Karlsburg Pl
Palm Harbor, FL 34685-3696, USA

Folger, Franklin (Cartoonist)
King Features Syndicate
888 7th Ave Ste 201
New York, NY 10106-0201, USA

Foli, Tim (Baseball Player)
525 Timberline Dr
Lenoir City, TN 37772-6934, USA

Foligno, Mike (Hockey Player)
1179 Jill Dr
Hummelstown, PA 17036-9004, USA

Folkenberg, Robert S (Religious Leader)
Seventh-Day Adventists
12501 Old Columbia Pike
Silver Spring, MD 20904-6600, USA

Folkers, Rich (Baseball Player)
New York Mets
7100 3rd Ave N
Saint Petersburg, FL 33710-7502, USA

Folkins, Lee (Football Player)
Dallas Cowboys
14439 Fawnhaven Ct
Orlando, FL 32828-7843, USA

Folkman, M Judah (Doctor)
18 Chatham Cir
Brookline, MA 02446-5454, USA

Foll, Tim (Baseball Player)
New York Mets
1003 Hilltop Ln
Kodak, TN 37764-1838, USA

Follesdal, Dagfinn K (Misc)
Staverhagen 7
Slepemdem 1312, NORWAY

Follett, Ken (Writer)
Box 4
Knebworth SG3 6UT, UNITED
KINGDOM (UK)

Follows, Megan (Actor)
Susan Smith
1344 N Wetherly Dr
Los Angeles, CA 90069-1817, USA

Folon, Jean-Michel (Artist)
Burcy
Beaumont-du-Gatinais 77890, FRANCE

Folsom, Allan R (Writer)
Little Brown
3 Center Plz
Boston, MA 02108-2084, USA

Folsom, James E (Jim) Jr (Governor)
1482 Orchard Dr NE
Cullman, AL 35055-2145, USA

Foltz, Vern (Football Player)
Washington Redskins
327 Ballard Ave
Baltimore, MD 21220-3605, USA

Fonda, Bridget (Actor)
c/o Staff Member *IFA Talent Agency*
8730 W Sunset Blvd Ste 490
Los Angeles, CA 90069-2248, USA

Fonda, Jane (Actor)
Fonda Inc
PO Box 5840
Atlanta, GA 31107-0840, USA

Fonda, Peter (Actor)
21 Foothills Dr
Bozeman, MT 59718-8352, USA

Fondren, Debra Jo (Actor, Model)
PO Box 4351-856
Los Angeles, CA 90078, USA

Foner, Eric (Historian)
606 W 116th St
New York, NY 10027-7011, USA

Fong, Darryl
247 S Beverly Dr # 102
Beverly Hills, CA 90212-3830, USA

Fonseca, Adriana (Actor)
c/o Staff Member *Televisa*
Blvd Adolfo Lopez Mateos 232
Colonia San Angel INN
DF CP 01060, MEXICO

Fonseca, Chris (Actor)
Strauss-McGarr Entertainment
1199 Boise Way
Costa Mesa, CA 92626-2704, USA

Fonseca, Lyndsy (Actor)
c/o Felicia Sager *Art Work Entertainment*
5900 Wilshire Blvd Ste 2150
Los Angeles, CA 90036-5021, USA

Fontaine, Joan (Actor)
c/o Staff Member *Gage Group, The (LA)*
14724 Ventura Blvd Ste 505
Sherman Oaks, CA 91403-3505, USA

Fontaine, Maurice A (Misc)
25 Rue Pierre Nicole
Paris 75005, FRANCE

Fontana, D J
PO Box 262
Carteret, NJ 07008-0262, USA

Fontana, Isabeli (Model)
Women Model Mgmt
107 Greene St # 200
New York, NY 10012-3803, USA

Fontana, Wayne (Musician)
Brian Gannon Mgmt
PO Box 106
Rochdale OL16 4HW, UNITED
KINGDOM (UK)

Fontenot, Albert (Football Player)
Chicago Bears
4919 Gammage St
Houston, TX 77021-3205, USA

Fontenot, Jerry (Football Player)
Chicago Bears
938 Bristol Dr
Deerfield, IL 60015-4843, USA

Fontenot, Joe (Baseball Player)
Florida Marlins
115 Logan St
Lafayette, LA 70506-9533, USA

Fontenot, Ray (Baseball Player)
New York Yankees
1674 S Crestview Dr
Lake Charles, LA 70605, USA

Fontes, Wayne H (Coach, Football Coach,
Football Player)
New York Titans
2043 Harbour Watch Cir
Tarpon Springs, FL 34689-2055, USA

Fonville, Chad (Baseball Player)
Montreal Expos
131 Old Rocky Run Rd
Midway Park, NC 28544-1240, USA

Fonville, Charles (Athlete, Track Athlete)
1845 Wintergreen Ct
Ann Arbor, MI 48103-9727, USA

Foo Fighters (Music Group)
c/o Staff Member *Creative Artists Agency
LCC (CAA-LA)*
2000 Avenue Of The Stars
Los Angeles, CA 90067-4700, USA

Foor, Jim (Baseball Player)
Detroit Tigers
2018 Bolsover St
Houston, TX 77005-1616, USA

Foose, Chip (Actor)
Foose Design Inc
17811 Sampson Ln
Huntington Beach, CA 92647-7199, USA

Foot, Michael M (Government Official)
308 Gray's Inn Road
London WC1X 8DY, UNITED KINGDOM
(UK)

Foote, Adam (Hockey Player)
11 Mountain Laurel Dr
Littleton, CO 80127, USA

Foote, Barry (Baseball Player)
Montreal Expos
2705 Middle Sound Loop Rd
Wilmington, NC 28411-7835, USA

Foote, Dan (Cartoonist, Editor)
Dallas Times Herald
Herald Square
Editorial Dept
Dallas, TX 75215, USA

Foote, Horton (Writer)
PO Box 1109
Wharton, TX 77488-1109, USA

Foote II, Edward T (Educator)
University of Miami
President's Office
Coral Gables, FL 33124, USA

Footman, Dan (Football Player)
Cleveland Browns
1311 Windsor Pl
Jacksonville, FL 32205-7962, USA

Foray, June (Actor)
22745 Erwin St
Woodland Hills, CA 91367-3212, USA

Forbert, Steve (Musician, Songwriter, Writer)
Mongrel Music
743 Center Blvd
Fairfax, CA 94930-1764, USA

Forbes, Brian
Seven Pines Wentworth
Surrey, ENGLAND, UNITED KINGDOM (UK)

Forbes, Bryan (Director, Writer)
Bookshop
Virginia Water, Surrey, UNITED KINGDOM (UK)

Forbes, Kristin (Economist, Government Official)
Council of Economic Advisers
Old Executive Office Bldg
Washington, DC 20500, USA

Forbes, Malcolm S (Steve) Jr (Editor)
Forbes Magazine
60 5th Ave
Editorial Dept
New York, NY 10011-8868, USA

Forbes, Michelle (Actor)
c/o Joe Vance *Domain*
9229 W Sunset Blvd Ste 415
West Hollywood, CA 90069-3404, USA

Forbes, P J (Baseball Player)
Baltimore Orioles
503 W 5th St
Pittsburg, KS 66762-3704, USA

Forbes, West (Musician)
Paramount Entertainment
PO Box 12
Far Hills, NJ 07931-0012, USA

Force, John (Race Car Driver)
John Force Racing
22722 Old Canal Rd
Yorba Linda, CA 92887-4602, USA

Ford, Bette
1801 Avenue Of The Stars Ste 902
Los Angeles, CA 90067-5981, USA

Ford, Brian (Football Player)
New Orleans Saints
20225 Bothell Everett Hwy Apt 1131
Bothell, WA 98012-8186, USA

Ford, Charlie (Football Player)
Chicago Bears
15207 Carol Chase Cir
Missouri City, TX 77489-2316, USA

Ford, Charlotte
25 Sutton Pl
New York, NY 10022-2453, USA

Ford, Cheryl (Basketball Player)
Detroit Shock Palace
2 Championship Dr
Auburn Hills, MI 48326-1753, USA

Ford, Chris (Basketball Player, Coach)
424 N Vendome Ave
Margate City, NJ 08402-1265, USA

Ford, Colton (Musician)
c/o Staff Member *Diva Central Inc*
7510 W Sunset Blvd Ste 1445
Los Angeles, CA 90046-3408, USA

Ford, Curt (Baseball Player)
St Louis Cardinals
1420 Heritage Lndg Apt 307
Saint Charles, MO 63303-6194, USA

Ford, Dale (Baseball Player)
678 Brethern Church Rd
Jonesborough, TN 37659-3923, USA

Ford, Danny (Baseball Player)
Minnesota Twins
8807 Digger Pine Dr
Riverside, CA 92508-3037, USA

Ford, Dave (Baseball Player)
Baltimore Orioles
19523 N Sagamore Rd
Cleveland, OH 44126-1662, USA

Ford, David (Musician)
c/o Staff Member *Paradigm (Monterey)*
509 Hartnell St
Monterey, CA 93940-2825, USA

Ford, Diane
201 San Vicente Blvd Apt 6
Santa Monica, CA 90402-1579, USA

Ford, Doug (Golfer)
4070 Chestnut Ave
Palm Beach Gardens, FL 33410-2146, USA

Ford, Edward C (Whitey) (Baseball Player)
3750 Galt Ocean Dr Apt 1411
Fort Lauderdale, FL 33308-7623, USA

Ford, Eileen
344 E 59th St
New York, NY 10022-1593, USA

Ford, Elizabeth B (Betty) (Ex-First Lady, First Lady)
40365 Sand Dune Rd
Rancho Mirage, CA 92270-3551, USA

Ford, Elleen O (Misc)
Ford Model Agency
142 Greene St # 400
New York, NY 10012-3236, USA

Ford, Ervin (Baseball Player)
Indianapolis Clowns
429 Banks St
Greensboro, NC 27401-3105, USA

Ford, Faith (Actor)
c/o Rebecca (Becca) Kovacik *Hofflund/Polone*
9465 Wilshire Blvd Ste 890
Beverly Hills, CA 90212-2607, USA

Ford, Frankie (Musician, Songwriter, Writer)
Ken Keane Artists
PO Box 1875
Gretna, LA 70054-1875, USA

Ford, Frederick (Adult Film Star)
c/o Staff Member *Diva Central Inc*
7510 W Sunset Blvd Ste 1445
Los Angeles, CA 90046-3408, USA

Ford, Gerald W (Misc)
Ford Model Agency
142 Greene St # 400
New York, NY 10012-3236, USA

Ford, Gilbert (Gib) (Basketball Player, Coach)
264 Edgemere Way E
Naples, FL 34105-7150, USA

Ford, Harrison (Actor)
c/o Jim Berkus *United Talent Agency (UTA)*
9560 Wilshire Blvd Ste 500
Beverly Hills, CA 90212-2401, USA

Ford, Henry (Football Player)
Cleveland Browns
PO Box 46403
Monroeville, PA 15146-8843, USA

Ford, Henry (Football Player)
Houston Oilers
809 Glendevon Dr
McKinney, TX 75071-6543, USA

Ford, Henry (Football Player)
3729 Brett Dr
Fort Worth, TX 76123-1333, USA

Ford, Jack (Correspondent)
CBS-TV
51 W 52nd St
News Dept
New York, NY 10019-6119, USA

Ford, James L (Football Player)
New Orleans Saints
2168 College Cir N
Jacksonville, FL 32209-5980, USA

Ford, Katie (Misc)
Ford Model Agency
142 Greene St # 400
New York, NY 10012-3236, USA

Ford, Kevin A (Astronaut)
3526 E 200 N
Hartford City, IN 47348-9243, USA

Ford, Lew (Baseball Player)
Minnesota Twins
1703 Mountain Lake Rd
Dallas, TX 75224-1639, USA

Ford, Lita (Musician)
RCA Records
1540 Broadway # 3500
New York, NY 10036-4039, USA

Ford, Matt (Baseball Player)
Milwaukee Brewers
6106 Nantucket Ln
Spring Hill, FL 34608-1151, USA

Ford, Melyssa (Model)
c/o Michael (Mike) Esterman *Esterman Entertainment*
214 Park Rd
Riva, MD 21140-1224, USA

Ford, Mick
47 Courtfield Rd. #9
London, ENGLAND SW7 4DB, UNITED KINGDOM (UK)

Ford, Mike (Football Player)
Tampa Bay Buccaneers
9798 Fm 1565
Terrell, TX 75160-8516, USA

Ford, Richard (Writer)
International Creative Mgmt
40 W 57th St Ste 1800
New York, NY 10019-4001, USA

Ford, Ruth (Actor)
Dakota Hotel
1 W 72nd St
New York, NY 10023-3486, USA

Ford, Scott (Business Person)
Alltel Corp
PO Box 94255
Palatine, IL 60094-4255, USA

Ford, T J (Basketball Player)
Milwaukee Bucks
1001 N 4th St
Bradley Center
Milwaukee, WI 53203-1312, USA

Ford, Ted (Baseball Player)
Cleveland Indians
6220 N 11th St Apt 19
McAllen, TX 78504-3275, USA

Ford, Thomas Mikal (Actor)
c/o Staff Member *TalentWorks (LA)*
3500 W Olive Ave Ste 1400
Burbank, CA 91505-5512, USA

Ford, Tom (Designer, Fashion Designer)
c/o Staff Member *Estee Lauder Inc*
767 5th Ave
Corporate Headquarters
New York, NY 10153-0003, USA

Ford, Trent (Actor)
c/o Staff Member *Paradigm (LA)*
360 N Crescent Dr
North Bldg
Beverly Hills, CA 90210-6820, USA

Ford, Wendell H (Governor, Senator)
423 Frederica St # 314
Owensboro, KY 42301-3013, USA

Ford, Willa (Musician)
c/o Michael (Mike) Esterman *Esterman Entertainment*
214 Park Rd
Riva, MD 21140-1224, USA

Ford, William C Jr (Business Person)
Ford Motor Co
American Road
Dearborn, MI 48126, USA

Ford Jr, Gerald R (Ex-President, Politician, President)
40365 Sand Dune Rd
Rancho Mirage, CA 92270-3551, USA

Fordham, Julia (Musician, Songwriter, Writer)
Vanguard Records
2700 Pennsylvania Ave
Santa Monica, CA 90404-4066, USA

Fordham, Tom (Baseball Player)
Chicago White Sox
14559 Miguel Ln
El Cajon, CA 92021-2843, USA

Fordham, Willie (Baseball Player)
Negro Baseball Leagues
3608 Tudor Dr
Harrisburg, PA 17109-1235, USA

Fordyce, Brook (Baseball Player)
New York Mets
5 River Crest Ct
Stuart, FL 34996-6515, USA

Foreigner (Music Group)
c/o Staff Member *Creative Artists Agency LCC (CAA-LA)*
2000 Avenue Of The Stars
Los Angeles, CA 90067-4700, USA

Foreman, Amanda (Actor)
c/o Lauren Lloyd *Lloyd and Kass Entertainment*
10202 Washington Blvd Bldg Astaire 2210
Culver City, CA 90232-3119, USA

Foreman, Carol L T (Government Official)
5600 Wisconsin Ave Apt 502
Chevy Chase, MD 20815-4410, USA

Foreman, Chuck
574 Prairie Center Dr # 156
Eden Prairie, MN 55344-7930, USA

Foreman, Deborah
9014 Melrose Ave
W Hollywood, CA 90069-5610, USA

Foreman, George (Boxer)
c/o Mirium Altshuler *Miriam Altshuler Literary Agency*
53 Old Post Rd N
Red Hook, NY 12571-2262, USA

Foreman, Walter E (Chuck) (Football Player)
Minnesota Vikings
9716 Mill Creek Dr
Eden Prairie, MN 55347-4307, USA

Forest, Michael
PO Box 69590
Los Angeles, CA 90069-0590, USA

Forester, Bill (Football Player)
Green Bay Packers
10448 Stone Canyon Rd Apt 204
Dallas, TX 75230-4879, USA

Forester, Herschel (Football Player)
Cleveland Browns
8502 Edgemere Rd Apt 226
Dallas, TX 75225-3553, USA

Forester, Nicole (Actor)
Gage Group
14724 Ventura Blvd Ste 505
Sherman Oaks, CA 91403-3505, USA

Forester Sisters
3322 W End Ave
Nashville, TN 37203-1031, USA

Foret, Sarah (Actor)
c/o Todd Neville *Agency for the Performing Arts (APA-LA)*
405 S Beverly Dr
Beverly Hills, CA 90212-4416, USA

Forget, Guy (Tennis Player)
Rue des Pacs 2
Neuchatel 2000, SWITZERLAND

Forkovitch, Nick (Football Player)
Brooklyn Dodgers
305 Fairway Dr
Harrisonburg, VA 22802-8704, USA

Forlani, Arnaldo (Prime Minister)
Piazzale Schumann 15
Rome, ITALY

Forlani, Claire (Actor)
c/o Marsha McManus *Principal Entertainment (LA)*
1964 Westwood Blvd Ste 400
Los Angeles, CA 90025-4695, USA

Forman, Al (Baseball Player)
219 W Tateway Rd Apt B
Kitty Hawk, NC 27949-4377, USA

Forman, Milos (Director)
Lantz
200 W 57th St Ste 503
New York, NY 10019-3211, USA

Forman, Stanley (Journalist, Photographer)
17 Cherry Rd
Beverly, MA 01915-1511, USA

Forman, Tom (Cartoonist)
10544 James Rd
Celina, TX 75009-3744, USA

Formesa, Fern
5018 N 61st Ave
Glendale, AZ 85301-7310, USA

Formia, Osvaldo (Horse Racer)
6501 Winfield Blvd # A10
Margate, FL 33063-7168, USA

Forney, Carl (Baseball Player)
Indianapolis Clowns
476 S Weldon St Apt E
Gastonia, NC 28052-2900, USA

Forney, G David Jr (Scientist)
6 Coolidge Hill Rd
Cambridge, MA 02138-5510, USA

Foronly, Richard (Actor)
House of Representatives
211 S Beverly Dr Ste 208
Beverly Hills, CA 90212-3879, USA

Forrest, Frederic (Actor)
11300 W Olympic Blvd Ste 610
Los Angeles, CA 90064-1643, USA

Forrest, Katherine Virginia (Writer)
PO Box 31613
San Francisco, CA 94131-0613, USA

Forrest, Mark
13266 Bracken St
Arleta, CA 91331-5703, USA

Forrest, Sally (Actor)
1125 Angelo Dr
Beverly Hills, CA 90210-2703, USA

Forrest, Steve (Actor)
1605 Michael Ln
Pacific Palisades, CA 90272-2029, USA

Forrestal, Robert P (Financier, Government Official)
3949 Vermont Rd NE
Atlanta, GA 30319-1212, USA

Forrester, James (Scientist)
Cedars-Sinai Medical Center
8700 Beverly Blvd
West Hollywood, CA 90048-1865, USA

Forrester, Jay W (Inventor)
Massachusetts Institute of Technology Management School
Cambridge, MA 02139, USA

Forrester, Patrick G (Astronaut)
3923 Park Circle Way
Houston, TX 77059-3019, USA

Forrester Sisters (Music Group)
c/o Staff Member *Warner Bros Music*
4000 Warner Blvd
Burbank, CA 91522-0001, USA

Forsberg, Fred (Football Player)
Denver Broncos
PO Box 771
Nhc Corporation
Issaquah, WA 98027-0028, USA

Forsberg, Peter (Hockey Player)
c/o Staff Member *Philadelphia Flyers*
3601 S Broad St
First Union Spectrum
Philadelphia, PA 19148-5297, USA

Forsch, Kenneth R (Ken) (Baseball Player)
Houston Astros
881 S Country Glen Way
Anaheim, CA 92808-2635, USA

Forsch, Robert H (Bob) (Baseball Player)
St Louis Cardinals
9 Westmeade Ct
Chesterfield, MO 63005-4619, USA

Forslund, Constance (Actor)
165 W 46th St Ste 1109
New York, NY 10036-2516, USA

Forsman, Dan (Golfer)
88 W 4500 N
Provo, UT 84604-5517, USA

Forst, Bill (Cartoonist)
2320 Byer Rd
Santa Cruz, CA 95062-1949, USA

Forster, Brian
16172 Flamstead Dr
Hacienda Heights, CA 91745-3644, USA

Forster, Marc (Director, Producer)
c/o Todd Feldman *Creative Artists Agency LCC (CAA-LA)*
2000 Avenue Of The Stars
Los Angeles, CA 90067-4700, USA

Forster, Robert (Actor)
c/o Eli Selden *The Firm*
9465 Wilshire Blvd Fl 6
Beverly Hills, CA 90212-2605, USA

Forster, Scott (Baseball Player)
Montreal Expos
17 Rose Ln
Flourtown, PA 19031-1909, USA

Forster, Terry (Baseball Player)
Chicago White Sox
PO Box 711658
Santee, CA 92072-1658, USA

Forster, William H (General)
10245 Fairfax Dr
Fort Belvoir, VA 22060-2123, USA

Forsyth, Bill (Director)
P F D
Drury House
34-43 Russell St
London WC2B 5HA, UNITED KINGDOM (UK)

Forsyth, Bruce (Actor, Comedian)
Kent House
Upper Ground
London SE1, UNITED KINGDOM (UK)

Forsyth, Frederick (Writer)
Trans World Publishers
61-63 Oxbridge Rd
Ealing
London W5 5SA, UNITED KINGDOM (UK)

Forsythe, Bill
20 Winton Dr.
Glasgow G12 0QA, SCOTLAND

Forsythe, Gerald (Gary) (Motorcycle Race, Motorcycle Racer)
Forsythe Racing
7231 Georgetown Rd
Indianapolis, IN 46268-4126, USA

Forsythe, Gerry
9350 Castlegate Dr
Indianapolis, IN 46256-1001, USA

Forsythe, John (Actor)
3849 Roblar Ave
Santa Ynez, CA 93460-9580, USA

Forsythe, Rosemary (Actor)
1591 Benedict Canyon Dr
Beverly Hills, CA 90210-2023, USA

Forsythe, William (Actor)
7532 Melba Ave
Canoga Park, CA 91304-5361, USA

Forsythe, William (Choreographer)
Frankfurt Ballet
Untermainanlage 11
Frankfurt 60311, GERMANY

Fort, Edward B (Educator)
North Carolina A&T State University
Chancellor's Office
Greensboro, NC 27411-0001, USA

Fort-Brescia, Bernardo (Architect)
Arquitectonica International
550 Brickell Ave # 200
Miami, FL 33131, USA

Forte, Aldo (Football Player)
Chicago Bears
10980 Willow Ridge Loop
Orlando, FL 32825-4408, USA

Forte, Fabian
6671 W Sunset Blvd Ste 1502
Los Angeles, CA 90028-7235, USA

Forte, Ike (Football Player)
New England Patriots
5811 Winchester Dr
Texarkana, TX 75503-4602, USA

Forte, Joseph (Basketball Player)
355 Elmcroft Blvd # 621
Rockville, MD 20850-5662, USA

Forte, Will (Actor)
c/o Jason Heyman *Creative Artists Agency LCC (CAA-LA)*
2000 Avenue Of The Stars
Los Angeles, CA 90067-4700, USA

Fortier, Claude (Misc)
1014 De Grenoble
Sainte-Foy
Quebec, PQ G1V 2Z9, CANADA

Fortier, Laurie (Actor)
Kritzer Entertainment
12200 W Olympic Blvd Ste 400
Los Angeles, CA 90064-1047, USA

Fortin, Roman (Football Player)
Detroit Lions
10741 Bell Rd
Duluth, GA 30097-1801, USA

Fortner, Nell (Coach)
Auburn University
Athletic Dept
Auburn, AL 36849, USA

Fortugno, Tim (Baseball Player)
California Angels
3604 Babson Dr
Elk Grove, CA 95758-4576, USA

Fortunato, Don (Football Player)
Chicago Cardinals
222 Regent Wood Rd
Northfield, IL 60093-2767, USA

Fortunato, Joseph F (Joe) (Football Player)
Chicago Bears
PO Box 934
Natchez, MS 39121-0934, USA

Fortune, Jimmy (Musician)
American Major Talent
8747 Highway 304
Hernando, MS 38632-8445, USA

Foruria, John (Football Player)
Pittsburgh Steelers
5603 Edson St
Boise, ID 83705-1852, USA

Fosbury, Dick
709 Canyon Run Box 1791
Ketchum, ID 83340, USA

Fosnow, Jerry (Baseball Player)
Minnesota Twins
369 Caddie Dr
Debary, FL 32713-4512, USA

Foss, Anita (Baseball Player)
2107 Ashland Ave
Santa Monica, CA 90405-6025, USA

Foss, John W II (General)
16 Hampton Key
Williamsburg, VA 23185-5538, USA

Foss, Larry (Baseball Player)
Pittsburgh Pirates
4303 E English St
Wichita, KS 67218-1320, USA

Foss, Lukas (Composer, Musician)
1140 5th Ave # 4B
New York, NY 10128-0806, USA

Fossas, Tony (Baseball Player)
Texas Rangers
11302 NW 9th St
Plantation, FL 33325-1501, USA

Fosse, Ray (Baseball Player)
Cleveland Indians
6847 E Amber Sun Dr
Scottsdale, AZ 85266-7034, USA

Fossey, Brigitte (Actor)
18 Rue Troyon
Paris 75017, FRANCE

Fossum, Casey (Baseball Player)
Boston Red Sox
209 10th Ave S Ste 405
Nashville, TN 37203-0764, USA

Fossum, Michael E (Astronaut)
822 Rolling Run Ct
Houston, TX 77062-2100, USA

Foster, Barry (Football Player)
Pittsburgh Steelers
1905 Ashton Ct
Colleyville, TX 76034-4401, USA

Foster, Ben (Actor)
c/o Ken Jacobson *James/Levy/Jacobson Management*
3500 W Olive Ave Ste 1470
Burbank, CA 91505-5514, USA

Foster, Bill (Basketball Player)
Virginia Polytechnic Institute
Athletic Dept
Blacksburg, VA 24061-0001, USA

Foster, Brendan (Athlete, Track Athlete)
Whitegates
31 Meadowfield Road
Stocksfield, Northumberland, UNITED KINGDOM (UK)

Foster, Coy (Misc)
5486 Glen Lakes Dr
Dallas, TX 75231-4308, USA

Foster, David (Musician, Songwriter, Writer)
3469 Cross Creek Rd
Malibu, CA 90265-4966, USA

Foster, Frank B III (Composer, Musician)
Joel Chriss
300 Mercer St Apt 3J
New York, NY 10003-6732, USA

Foster, George (Baseball Player)
San Francisco Giants
15 E Putnam Ave # 320
Greenwich, CT 06830-5424, USA

Foster, Jerome (Football Player)
Houston Oilers
18900 Goldwin St
Southfield, MI 48075-7218, USA

Foster, Jodie (Actor, Director)
c/o Pat Kingsley *PMK/HBH Public Relations (PMK-LA)*
700 N San Vicente Blvd Ste G910
West Hollywood, CA 90069-5061, USA

Foster, John (Actor)
c/o Staff Member *Windfall*
3000 W Alameda Ave
Burbank, CA 91523-0001, USA

Foster, John (Baseball Player)
Atlanta Braves
519 Airway Ave
Lewiston, ID 83501-4503, USA

Foster, Jon (Actor)
c/o Ken Jacobson *James/Levy/Jacobson Management*
3500 W Olive Ave Ste 1470
Burbank, CA 91505-5514, USA

Foster, Kevin (Baseball Player)
Philadelphia Phillies
1374 S Park Grove Ct
Gilbert, AZ 85296-4168, USA

Foster, Kris (Baseball Player)
Baltimore Orioles
116 Johns Ave
Lehigh Acres, FL 33936-2135, USA

Foster, Larry (Baseball Player)
Detroit Tigers
205 W Obell St
Whitehall, MI 49461-1742, USA

Foster, Lawrence T (Conductor)
International Creative Mgmt
40 W 57th St Ste 1800
New York, NY 10019-4001, USA

Foster, Leo (Baseball Player)
Atlanta Braves
699 Glensprings Dr
Cincinnati, OH 45246-2129, USA

Foster, Marty (Baseball Player)
319 W 5th Ave
Denver, CO 80204-5118, USA

Foster, Meg (Actor)
Judy Schoen
606 N Larchmont Blvd Ste 309
Los Angeles, CA 90004-1309, USA

Foster, Norman R (Architect)
Foster Assoc
Riverside 3
22 Hester Road
London SW11 4AN, UNITED KINGDOM (UK)

Foster, Radney (Musician, Songwriter, Writer)
PO Box 121452
Nashville, TN 37212-1452, USA

Foster, Robert W (Bob) (Boxer)
913 Valencia Dr NE
Albuquerque, NM 87108-1753, USA

Foster, Ron (Football Player)
Los Angeles Raiders
17819 Merridy St Apt 117
Northridge, CA 91325-4604, USA

Foster, Roy (Baseball Player)
Cleveland Indians
650 E 27th Pl N
Tulsa, OK 74106-2409, USA

Foster, Roy A (Football Player)
Miami Dolphins
11522 W State Road 84 # 267
Davie, FL 33325-4022, USA

Foster, Sara (Actor)
c/o Geyer Kosinski *Media Talent Group*
9200 W Sunset Blvd Ste 810
W Hollywood, CA 90069-3603, USA

Foster, Scott M (Actor)
c/o John Tae Lee *Shapiro/West & Associates*
141 El Camino Dr Ste 205
Beverly Hills, CA 90212-2718, USA

Foster, Steven (Baseball Player)
Cincinnati Reds
1201 Hillview Dr
Waxahachie, TX 75165-6032, USA

Foster, Susanna
155 W Hudson Ave
Englewood, NJ 07631-1609, USA

Foster, Susannah (Actor, Musician)
11255 Morrison St Apt F
North Hollywood, CA 91601-4423, USA

Foster, Todd (Boxer)
249 21st Ave NW
Great Falls, MT 59404-1425, USA

Foster, William E (Bill) (Coach)
152 Hollywood Dr
Coppell, TX 75019-7302, USA

Foster Jr, John S (Physicist)
TRW Inc
1 Space Park Blvd
Redondo Beach, CA 90278-1001, USA

Fou, Ts'ong (Musician)
62 Aberdeen Park
London N5 2BL, UNITED KINGDOM (UK)

Foucault, Steve (Baseball Player)
Texas Rangers
109 Tropic Pl
Rockledge, FL 32955-5608, USA

Foudy, Judy (Julie) (Model, Soccer Player)
US Soccer Federation
1801 S Prairie Ave
Chicago, IL 60616-1319, USA

Foudy, Julie
1801 S Prairie Ave
Chicago, IL 60616-1319, USA

Fought, John (Golfer)
16 Laurel Valley Dr
Brownsburg, IN 46112-8351, USA

Foulke, Keith C (Baseball Player)
c/o Staff Member *Boston Red Sox*
Fenway Park
4 Yawkey Way
Boston, MA 02215-3496, USA

Foulkes, Llyn (Artist)
6010 Eucalyptus Ln
Los Angeles, CA 90042-1244, USA

Fountain, Pete
237 N Peters St # 400
New Orleans, LA 70130-1019, USA

Fountain, Peter D (Pete) Jr (Musician)
Paradise Artists
108 E Matilija St
Ojai, CA 93023-2639, USA

Fountain, Rex
10475 Bellagio Rd
Los Angeles, CA 90077-3818, USA

Fountaine, Jamal (Football Player)
San Francisco 49ers
245 SW Lincoln Apt 122
Portland, OR 97201-5083, USA

Fountains of Wayne (Music Group)
c/o Staff Member *Big Hassle*
157 Chambers St Fl 12
New York, NY 10007-1015, USA

Four Aces, The
11761 E Speedway Blvd
Tucson, AZ 85748-2017, USA

Four Freshman, The
PO Box 93534
Las Vegas, NV 89193-3534, USA

Four Non Blondes
PO Box 170545
San Francisco, CA 94117-0545, USA

Four Tops (Music Group)
c/o Staff Member *Famous Artists Agency*
250 W 57th St # 821
New York, NY 10107-0001, USA

Fourcade, John (Football Player)
New Orleans Saints
2749 Long Branch Dr
Marrero, LA 70072-5856, USA

Fournier, Brigitte (Opera Singer)
EMI America Records
1370 Avenue Of The Americas
New York, NY 10019-4602, USA

Foust, Nina (Golfer)
901 East Dr
Morehead City, NC 28557-3009, USA

Fouts, Dan (Football Player)
San Diego Chargers
16820 Varco Rd
Bend, OR 97701-9135, USA

Fouts, Daniel F (Dan) (Football Player, Sportscaster)
ABC-TV
77 W 66th St
Sports Dept
New York, NY 10023-6201, USA

Fowler, Bobby (Football Player)
New Orleans Saints
808 Chateau Pl
Richmond, TX 77469-5106, USA

Fowler, Chris (Sportscaster)
c/o Staff Member *ESPN (Main)*
935 Middle St
Espn Plaza
Bristol, CT 06010-1000, USA

Fowler, E Michael C (Architect)
Branches Giffords Road
Bienheim RD 3, NEW ZEALAND

Fowler, J Arthur (Art) (Baseball Player)
Cincinnati Reds
3046 E Main Street Ext
Spartanburg, SC 29307-1225, USA

Fowler, Jaimie (Race Car Driver)
c/o Staff Member *Agency for the Performing Arts (APA-LA)*
405 S Beverly Dr
Beverly Hills, CA 90212-4416, USA

Fowler, Jim (Actor)
Wild Kingdom
Mutual Of Omaha
Mutual Of Omaha Plaza
Omaha, NE 68175-0001, USA

Fowler, Kevin (Musician)
c/o Staff Member *Paradigm (Monterey)*
509 Hartnell St
Monterey, CA 93940-2825, USA

Fowler, Peggy Y (Business Person)
Portland General Electric
121 SW Salmon St
Portland, OR 97204-2977, USA

Fowler, Todd (Football Player)
Dallas Cowboys
10024 Fm 3053 N
Kilgore, TX 75662-4721, USA

Fowler, W Wyche Jr (Diplomat, Senator)
701 A St NE
Washington, DC 20002-6031, USA

Fowler, Willmer (Football Player)
Buffalo Bills
517 Lily St
Mansfield, OH 44903-1314, USA

Fowlkes, Alan (Baseball Player)
San Francisco Giants
405 Emerald Lake Dr
Lumberton, NC 28358-8022, USA

Fox, Allen (Coach, Tennis Player)
Pepperdine University
Athletic Dept
Malibu, CA 90265, USA

Fox, Andy (Baseball Player)
New York Yankees
8008 Sacramento St
Fair Oaks, CA 95628-7527, USA

Fox, Bernard (Actor)
6601 Burnet Ave
Van Nuys, CA 91405-4515, USA

Fox, Chad (Baseball Player)
Atlanta Braves
6007 Windrose Hollow Ln
Spring, TX 77379-8904, USA

Fox, Charles I (Composer, Conductor)
American Int'l Artists
356 Pine Valley Rd
Hoosick Falls, NY 12090-3859, USA

Fox, Charlie (Baseball Player)
New York Yankees
55 W 5th Ave Apt 10A
San Mateo, CA 94402-2052, USA

Fox, Crystal (Actor)
Writers & Artists
360 N Crescent Dr Bldg North
Beverly Hills, CA 90210-6818, USA

Fox, Edward (Actor)
25 Maida Ave
London W2, UNITED KINGDOM (UK)

Fox, Emilia
125 Glouster Rd.
London, ENGLAND SW7 4TE, UNITED
KINGDOM (UK)

Fox, Eric (Baseball Player)
Oakland A's
PO Box 577198
Modesto, CA 95357-7198, USA

Fox, Everett (Misc)
Clark University
Jewish Studies Program
Worcester, MA 01610, USA

Fox, George
4950 Yonge St. #2400
Toronto, ON M2N 6K, CANADA

Fox, Jackie
23368 Ostronic Dr
Woodland Hills, CA 91367-6045, USA

Fox, James (Actor)
International Creative Mgmt
76 Oxford St
London W1N 0AX, UNITED KINGDOM
(UK)

Fox, Jessica (Actor)
Associated International Management
Nederlander House 7 Great Russell Street
London
WC1B 3NH UK, UNITED KINGDOM
(UK)

Fox, John (Coach, Football Coach)
Carolina Panthers
800 S Mint St
Ericsson Stadium
Charlotte, NC 28202-1640, USA

Fox, Jorja (Actor)
Flick East-West
9057 Nemo St # A
West Hollywood, CA 90069-5511, USA

Fox, Marye Anne (Misc)
1530 Soledad Ave
La Jolla, CA 92037-3815, USA

Fox, Matthew (Actor, Director)
c/o William Choi *Management 360*
9111 Wilshire Blvd
Beverly Hills, CA 90210-5508, USA

Fox, Matthew (Religious Leader)
Grace Episcopal Cathedral
1 Nob Hill Cir
San Francisco, CA 94108-2232, USA

Fox, Megan (Actor)
c/o Staff Member *Stone Manners Talent &
Literary (LA)*
6500 Wilshire Blvd Ste 550
Los Angeles, CA 90048-4950, USA

Fox, Michael J (Actor)
c/o Staff Member *Lottery Hill
Entertainment*
Pier 62 Ste 303
New York, NY 10011, USA

Fox, Neil (Actor)
c/o Staff Member *MPC Entertainment*
MPC House
15-16 Maple Mews
London NW6 5UZ, UNITED KINGDOM
(UK)

Fox, Rick (Actor, Basketball Player)
c/o Staff Member *William Morris Agency
(WMA-LA)*
1 William Morris Pl
Beverly Hills, CA 90212-4261, USA

Fox, Samantha (Model, Musician)
Fox 2000
PO Box 7834
London NW3 3ZT, UNITED KINGDOM
(UK)

Fox, Shayna
6212 Banner Ave
Los Angeles, CA 90038-2802, USA

Fox, Sheldon (Architect)
Kohn Pederson Fox Assoc
111 W 57th St
New York, NY 10019-2272, USA

Fox, Terry (Baseball Player)
Milwaukee Braves
2317 Sugar Mill Rd
New Iberia, LA 70563-8648, USA

Fox, Tim (Football Player)
New England Patriots
11 Glover Ave
Hull, MA 02045-1464, USA

Fox, Vernon (Football Player)
San Diego Chargers
6704 Willow River Ct
Las Vegas, NV 89108-5033, USA

Fox, Vicente (Politician, President)
Patacio Nacional
Patio de Honor
2 Piso
Mexico City DF 06067, MEXICO

Fox, Vivica A (Actor)
c/o Lita Richardson *Lita Richardson
Entertainment*
13400 Chandler Blvd
Sherman Oaks, CA 91401-5326, USA

Fox, Wesley L (War Hero)
855 Deercroft Dr
Blacksburg, VA 24060-0272, USA

Fox Brothers
Rt. 6 Bending Chestnut
Franklin, TN 37064, USA

Foxworth, Robert (Actor)
c/o Chris Schmidt *Paradigm (LA)*
360 N Crescent Dr
North Bldg
Beverly Hills, CA 90210-6820, USA

Foxworthy, Jeff (Actor, Comedian)
c/o John Ferriter *William Morris Agency
(WMA-LA)*
1 William Morris Pl
Beverly Hills, CA 90212-4261, USA

Foxx, Jamie (Actor, Comedian)
c/o Jamie King *King Management*
9229 W Sunset Blvd Ste 830
Los Angeles, CA 90069-3400, USA

Foxx, Shyla (Adult Film Star)
c/o Staff Member *Atlas Multimedia Inc*
9035 Independence Ave
Canoga Park, CA 91304-1743, USA

Foxx, Tanya
901 W Victoria St Ste G
Compton, CA 90220-5819, USA

Foy, Eddie III (Actor)
3003 W Olive Ave
Burbank, CA 91505-4538, USA

Foytack, Paul (Baseball Player)
Detroit Tigers
1910 Portview Dr
Spring Hill, TN 37174-8249, USA

Frabotta, Don
PO Box 962
Douglas, MA 01516-0962, USA

Fradkov, Mikhail (Prime Minister)
Prime Minister's Office
Kremlin
Staraya Pl 4
Moscow 103132, RUSSIA

Fradon, Dana (Cartoonist)
2 Brushy Hill Rd
Newtown, CT 06470, USA

Fradon, Ramona (Cartoonist)
Tribune Media Services
435 N Michigan Ave Ste 1500
Chicago, IL 60611-4012, USA

Frailing, Ken (Baseball Player)
Chicago White Sox
2150 Shadow Oaks Rd
Sarasota, FL 34240-9324, USA

Frain, James (Actor)
PFD
Drury House
34-43 Russell St
London WC2B 5HA, UNITED KINGDOM
(UK)

Fraiture, Nikolai (Musician)
MVO Ltd
370 7th Ave # 807
New York, NY 10001-3912, USA

Fraker, William A (Cinematographer)
337 Lorraine Blvd
Los Angeles, CA 90020-4727, USA

Frakes, Jonathan (Actor, Director)
10990 Wilshire Blvd Ste 1600
Los Angeles, CA 90024-3925, USA

Fralic, William (Bill) (Football Player)
Atlanta Falcons
280 Galsworthy Ct
Roswell, GA 30075-6354, USA

Frampton, Peter (Musician, Songwriter,
Writer)
c/o Staff Member *Cunningham Escott
Slevin & Doherty (LA)*
10635 Santa Monica Blvd Ste 130
Los Angeles, CA 90025-8306, USA

Franca, Celia (Ballerina, Choreographer)
157 King St E
Toronto, ON M5C 1G9, CANADA

France, Brian (Misc)
National Assn of Stock Car Racing
1801 Speedway Blvd
Daytona Beach, FL 32114-1215, USA

Franchione, Dennis (Coach, Football
Coach)
Texas A&M University
Athletic Dept
College Station, TX 77843-0001, USA

Franchitti, Dario (Race Car Driver)
7615 Zionsville Rd
Indianapolis, IN 46268-2174, USA

Francis, Anne (Actor)
PO Box 5608
Santa Barbara, CA 93150-5608, USA

Francis, Betty (Baseball Player)
11750 S Homan Ave Trlr 19A
Merrionette Park, IL 60803-4513, USA

Francis, Bob (Coach, Hockey Player)
7510 E Monterra Way
Scottsdale, AZ 85266, USA

Francis, Clarence (Bevo) (Basketball
Player)
18340 Steubenyille Pike Road
Salineville, OH 43945, USA

Francis, Connie (Actor, Musician)
6413 NW 102nd Ter
Parkland, FL 33076-2357, USA

Francis, Dick (Writer)
John Johnson Ltd
45/47 Clerkenwell Green
London EC1R 0HT, UNITED KINGDOM
(UK)

Francis, Don (Scientist)
Genentech Inc
460 Point San Bruno Blvd
South San Francisco, CA 94080-4939,
USA

Francis, Emile P (Coach)
7220 Crystal Lake Dr
West Palm Beach, FL 33411-5713, USA

Francis, Fred (Correspondent)
NBC-TV
4001 Nebraska Ave NW
News Dept
Washington, DC 20016-2733, USA

Francis, Genie (Actor)
10990 Wilshire Blvd Ste 1600
Los Angeles, CA 90024-3925, USA

Francis, Harrison (Football Player)
Chicago Bears
207 S Susan Ave
Wagoner, OK 74467-4843, USA

Francis, James (Football Player)
Cincinnati Bengals
2903 Main St
La Marque, TX 77568-5110, USA

Francis, Joe (Football Player)
Green Bay Packers
45-570 Kaaluna Pl
Kaneohe, HI 96744-3410, USA

Francis, Joe (Producer)
c/o Staff Member *Mantra Films*
PO Box 150
Hollywood, CA 90078-0150, USA

Francis, Paul (Actor)
c/o Staff Member *Gilbertson-Kincaid Management*
1334 3rd Street Promenade Ste 201
Santa Monica, CA 90401-1320, USA

Francis, Richard S (Dick) (Writer)
PO Box 30866
Seven Mile Beach
Grand Cayman, WEST INDIES

Francis, Ron (Football Player)
Dallas Cowboys
2903 Main St
La Marque, TX 77568-5110, USA

Francis, Ron (Hockey Player)
12312 Birchfalls Dr
Raleigh, NC 27614-7900, USA

Francis, Russ (Football Player)
New England Patriots
692 Kuliouou Rd
Honolulu, HI 96821-2429, USA

Francis, Steve (Basketball Player)
Houston Rockets
2 Greenway Plz
Toyota Center
Houston, TX 77046-0297, USA

Francis, Wally (Football Player)
Buffalo Bills
1307 Walton Ln SE
Smyrna, GA 30082-3875, USA

Francis, William (Bill) (Musician)
Artists International
9850 Sandalwood Blvd #458
Boca Raton, FL 33428, USA

Francisco, Don (Television Host)
c/o Staff Member *Univision*
605 3rd Ave Fl 12
New York, NY 10158-1299, USA

Francisco, George J (Misc)
Fireman & Oilers Union
1100 Cir 75 Pkwy
Atlanta, GA 30339-3064, USA

Franck, George H (Sonny) (Football Player)
New York Giants
2714 29th Ave
Rock Island, IL 61201-5447, USA

Franckowiak, Mike (Football Player)
Denver Broncos
73 Fitch Way
Princeton, NJ 08540-7609, USA

Francks, Rainbow Sun (Actor)
c/o Staff Member *Sci-FI Channel, The*
100 Universal Plaza Bldg 1280/12
Universal City, CA 91608, USA

Franco, Carlos (Golfer)
10561 NW 51st St
Doral, FL 33178-3209, USA

Franco, James (Actor)
c/o Miles Levy *James/Levy/Jacobson Management*
3500 W Olive Ave Ste 1470
Burbank, CA 91505-5514, USA

Franco, John A (Baseball Player)
Cincinnati Reds
111 Helena Rd
Staten Island, NY 10304-1353, USA

Franco, Julio C (Baseball Player)
651 NE 23rd Ct
Pompano Beach, FL 33064-5504, USA

Franco, Liliana (Actor)
c/o Staff Member *Eileen O'farrell Personal Management*
11653 Blix St Apt 5
Studio City, CA 91602-1051, USA

Franco, Matt (Baseball Player)
New York Mets
1008 Clear Sky Pl
Simi Valley, CA 93065-8331, USA

Francois-Poncet, Jean A (Financier, Government Official)
6 Blvd Suchet
Paris 75116, FRANCE

Francona, John P (Tito) (Baseball Player)
Baltimore Orioles
1109 Penn Ave
New Brighton, PA 15066-1632, USA

Francona, Terry J (Baseball Player)
Montreal Expos
750 Newton St
Chestnut Hill, MA 02467-2606, USA

Frangione, Nancy
280 S Beverly Dr Ste 400
Beverly Hills, CA 90212-3904, USA

Frangoulis, Mario (Musician)
c/o Staff Member *Sony Music International*
550 Madison Ave Fl 6
New York, NY 10022-3211, USA

Frank, Anthony M (Financier, Government Official)
Independent Bancorp
3800 N Central Ave
Phoenix, AZ 85012-1992, USA

Frank, Barney (Politician)
Congressman Barney Frank
2252 Rayburn Hob
Washington, DC 20515-2104, USA

Frank, Brian (Basketball Player)
Anderson Duffy Packers
19231 N Shore Ct
Baton Rouge, LA 70817-3981, USA

Frank, Charles (Actor)
S D B Partners
1801 Avenue Of Stars Ste 902
Los Angeles, CA 90067-5981, USA

Frank, Claude (Musician)
Columbia Artists Mgmt Inc
1790 Broadway Fl 6
New York, NY 10019-1412, USA

Frank, Darryl (Producer)
c/o Staff Member *Dreamworks Television*
100 Universal Plaza Bldg 10
Universal City, CA 91608, USA

Frank, Diana (Actor)
The Agency
1800 Avenue Of Stars Ste 400
Los Angeles, CA 90067-4206, USA

Frank, Donald (Football Player)
San Diego Chargers
1000 Elm St
Tarboro, NC 27886-3126, USA

Frank, Gary (Actor)
1401 S Bentley Ave Apt 202
Los Angeles, CA 90025-8031, USA

Frank, Howard (Business Person)
Carnival Corp
3655 NW 87th Ave
Doral, FL 33178-2428, USA

Frank, Jason David (Actor, Comedian)
Richard Stone
2 Henrietta St
London WC2E 8PS, UNITED KINGDOM (UK)

Frank, Jerome D (Educator)
818 W 40th St # K
Baltimore, MD 21211-2101, USA

Frank, Joanna (Actor)
1274 Capri Dr
Pacific Palisades, CA 90272-4001, USA

Frank, Joe (Entertainer)
KCRW-FM
1900 Pico Blvd
Santa Monica, CA 90405-1628, USA

Frank, Larry (Race Car Driver)
Larry Frank Auto Body Works
832 Fork Shoals Rd
Greenville, SC 29605-5832, USA

Frank, Mike (Baseball Player)
Cincinnati Reds
1343 W 19th St
Upland, CA 91784-7433, USA

Frank, Neil L (Misc)
National Hurricane Center
1320 S Dixie Hwy
Coral Gables, FL 33146-2926, USA

Frank, Phil (Cartoonist)
500 Turley St
Sausalito, CA 94965, USA

Frank-Dummerth, Edna (Baseball Player)
5044 Tealby Ln
Saint Louis, MO 63128-2952, USA

Frankel, Felice (Artist, Photographer)
Massachusetts Institute of Technology
Edgerton Center
Cambridge, MA 02139, USA

Frankel, Max (Editor)
New York Times
229 W 43rd St
Editorial Dept
New York, NY 10036-3959, USA

Franken, Al (Actor, Comedian, Writer)
c/o John Mass *William Morris Agency (WMA-LA)*
1 William Morris Pl
Beverly Hills, CA 90212-4261, USA

Franken, Steve (Actor)
Acme Talent
4727 Wilshire Blvd Ste 333
Los Angeles, CA 90010-3874, USA

Frankenthaler, Helen (Artist)
19 Contentment Island Rd
Darien, CT 06820-6208, USA

Frankl, Peter (Musician)
5 Gresham Gardens
London NW11 8NX, UNITED KINGDOM (UK)

Franklin, Allen (Business Person)
Southern Co
270 Peachtree St NW
Atlanta, GA 30303-1283, USA

Franklin, Andra (Football Player)
Miami Dolphins
5236 Myrtle St
Lincoln, NE 68506-2644, USA

Franklin, Anthony R (Tony) (Football Player)
Philadelphia Eagles
117 Shady Trail St
San Antonio, TX 78232-1313, USA

Franklin, Aretha (Musician)
8450 Linwood St
Detroit, MI 48206, USA

Franklin, Barbara Hackman (Secretary)
1875 Perkins St
Bristol, CT 06010-8910, USA

Franklin, Bobby (Football Player)
Cleveland Browns
510 N Panola St Athletic Dept
Northwest Mississippi College
Senetobia, MS 38668, USA

Franklin, Bonnie (Actor)
c/o Staff Member *Cunningham Escott Slevin & Doherty (LA)*
10635 Santa Monica Blvd Ste 130
Los Angeles, CA 90025-8306, USA

Franklin, Byron (Football Player)
Buffalo Bills
2613 Singapore Dr
Birmingham, AL 35211-6924, USA

Franklin, Carl M (Director)
Broder Kurland Webb Uffner
10250 Constellation Blvd
Los Angeles, CA 90067-6200, USA

Franklin, Diane (Actor)
Third Hill Entertainment
195 S Beverly Dr Ste 400
Beverly Hills, CA 90212-3044, USA

Franklin, Don
10101 Santa Monica Blvd # 2500
Los Angeles, CA 90067, USA

Franklin, Don (Actor)
Paradigm Agency
10100 Santa Monica Blvd Ste 2500
Los Angeles, CA 90067-4116, USA

Franklin, Farrah (Musician)
c/o Staff Member *Supreme Entertainment*
262 Chestnut Hill Ave
Boston, MA 02135-5902, USA

Franklin, Gary
7610 Beverly Blvd # 480820
Los Angeles, CA 90048-9996, USA

Franklin, Howard (Director, Writer)
Creative Artists Agency
9830 Wilshire Blvd
Beverly Hills, CA 90212-1804, USA

Franklin, Jay (Baseball Player)
San Diego Padres
2450 Massanutten Ter
Winchester, VA 22601-2774, USA

Franklin, Joe
PO Box 1
Lynbrook, NY 11563-0001, USA

Franklin, John (Actor)
Gilla Roos
9744 Wilshire Blvd Ste 203
Beverly Hills, CA 90212-1812, USA

Franklin, John Hope (Historian, Judge)
208 Pineview Rd
Durham, NC 27707-2846, USA

Franklin, Jon D (Journalist)
9650 Strickland Rd
Raleigh, NC 27615-1902, USA

Franklin, Kirk (Musician)
c/o Staff Member *Paradigm (Monterey)*
509 Hartnell St
Monterey, CA 93940-2825, USA

Franklin, Larry (Football Player)
Tampa Bay Buccaneers
9390 Afton Grove Rd
Cordova, TN 38018-7519, USA

Franklin, Melissa (Physicist)
Harvard University
Physics Dept
Cambridge, MA 02138, USA

Franklin, Micah (Baseball Player)
St Louis Cardinals
48 Hope Dr
Plainview, NY 11803-5600, USA

Franklin, Richard
8383 Wilshire Blvd Ste 550
Beverly Hills, CA 90211-2417, USA

Franklin, Robert (Business Person)
Placer Dome Inc
1600-1055 Dunsmuir St
Vancouver, BC V7X 1P1, CANADA

Franklin, Roshawn (Actor)
c/o Andrew Stawiarski *Braverman/Bloom Company*
6399 Wilshire Blvd Ste 901
Los Angeles, CA 90048-5712, USA

Franklin, Ryan (Baseball Player)
Seattle Mariners
PO Box 321
Shawnee, OK 74802-0321, USA

Franklin, Shirley (Politician)
Mayor's Office
55 Trinity Ave SW
City Hall
Atlanta, GA 30303-3539, USA

Franklin, Wayne (Baseball Player)
Houston Astros
3800 Grandlake Blvd Apt 103
Kenner, LA 70065-6510, USA

Franklin, William (Boxer, Misc)
920 La Sombra Dr
San Marcos, CA 92078-1320, USA

Franklyn, Sabina (Actor)
CCA Mgmt
4 Court Lodge
48 Sloane Square
London SW1W 8AT, UNITED KINGDOM (UK)

Franks, Daniel (Football Player)
Green Bay Packers
1019 Stadium Ave
Big Spring, TX 79720-3129, USA

Franks, Dennis (Football Player)
Philadelphia Eagles
4 Westmount Ct
Greensboro, NC 27410-2183, USA

Franks, Elvis (Football Player)
Cleveland Browns
2200 Avenue A
Beaumont, TX 77701-6910, USA

Franks, Frederick M Jr (General)
6364 Brampton Ct
Alexandria, VA 22304-3509, USA

Franks, Gerold
1745 Camino Palmero St
Los Angeles, CA 90046-2945, USA

Franks, Herman (Baseball Player)
St Louis Cardinals
2745 Comanche Dr
Salt Lake City, UT 84108-2810, USA

Franks, Hermine (Baseball Player)
422 Pecor St
Oconto, WI 54153-1800, USA

Franks, Michael (Musician, Songwriter, Writer)
Agency of Performing Arts
405 S Beverly Dr Ste 500
Beverly Hills, CA 90212-4425, USA

Frankston, Robert M (Bob) (Designer)
State Corp
15035 N 73rd St
Scottsdale, AZ 85260-2468, USA

Fransioli, Thomas A (Artist)
55 Dodges Row
Wenham, MA 01984-1627, USA

Franti, Michael (Musician)
William Morris Agency
151 El Camino Dr
Beverly Hills, CA 90212-2775, USA

Frantz, Adrienne (Actor)
c/o Marnie Sparer *Innovative Artists (LA)*
1505 10th St
Santa Monica, CA 90401-2805, USA

Frantz, Art (Baseball Player)
9128 W Terrace Dr Apt 1 E
Niles, IL 60714-5854, USA

Frantz, Chris (Musician)
Premier Talent
3 E 54th St # 1100
New York, NY 10022-3108, USA

Franz, Arthur (Actor)
PO Box 974
El Prado, NM 87529-0974, USA

Franz, Dennis (Actor)
c/o Alisa Adler *Paradigm (LA)*
360 N Crescent Dr
North Bldg
Beverly Hills, CA 90210-6820, USA

Franz, Frederick W (Religious Leader)
Jehovah's Witnesses
25 Columbia Hts
Brooklyn, NY 11201-1300, USA

Franz, Judy R (Physicist)
American Physical Society
1 Physics Eclipse
College Park, MD 20740, USA

Franz, Nolan (Football Player)
Green Bay Packers
327 31st St
Gulfport, MS 39507-2341, USA

Franz, Rodney T (Rod) (Football Player)
1448 Engberg Ct
Carmichael, CA 95608-5812, USA

Franzen, Jonathan (Writer)
Farrar Straus Giroux
19 Union Sq W Fl 11
New York, NY 10003-3304, USA

Franzen, Ulrich J (Architect)
975 Park Ave
New York, NY 10028-0323, USA

Frasca, Robert J (Architect)
Zimmer Gunsul Frasca
320 SW Oak St Ste 500
Portland, OR 97204-2737, USA

Frascatore, John (Baseball Player)
St Louis Cardinals
PO Box 1411
Brooksville, FL 34605-1411, USA

Frasconi, Antonio (Artist)
26 Dock Rd
Norwalk, CT 06854-4717, USA

Frase, Paul (Football Player)
New York Jets
5150 Palm Valley Rd Ste 210
Ponte Vedra Beach, FL 32082-4631, USA

Fraser, Antonia (Writer)
Curtis Brown
Haymarket House
28/29 Haymarket
London SW1Y 4SP, UNITED KINGDOM (UK)

Fraser, Brad (Writer)
Great North Artists Mgmt
350 Dupont Ave
Toronto, ON M5R 1V9, CANADA

Fraser, Brendan (Actor)
2118 Wilshire Blvd # 513
Santa Monica, CA 90403-5784, USA

Fraser, Brooke (Musician)
c/o Staff Member *Paradigm (Monterey)*
509 Hartnell St
Monterey, CA 93940-2825, USA

Fraser, Dawn (Athlete, Swimmer)
87 Birchgrove Road
Balmain NSW, AUSTRALIA

Fraser, Douglas (Misc)
United Auto Workers
8000 E Jefferson Ave
Detroit, MI 48214-3963, USA

Fraser, George MacDonald (Writer)
Curtis Brown
28/29 Haymarket
London SW1Y 4SP, UNITED KINGDOM (UK)

Fraser, Gretchen
5023 236th Pl SE
Woodinville, WA 98072-8610, USA

Fraser, Hon
MalcolmThurulgoona
Redhill Vic. 3937, AUSTRALIA

Fraser, Honor (Model)
c/o Staff Member *Fam*
boul. Vital Bouhot 30
Neuilly-sur-Seine,Paris 75008, FRANCE

Fraser, Hugh (Actor)
Jonathan Altaras
13 Shorts Gardens
London WC2H 9AT, UNITED KINGDOM (UK)

Fraser, Ian E (War Hero)
Innisfallen
47 Warren Dr
Wallasey, Merseyside, UNITED KINGDOM (UK)

Fraser, Laura (Actor)
c/o Tammy Rosen *Melanie Greene Management & Productions*
425 N Robertson Blvd
West Hollywood, CA 90048-1735, USA

Fraser, Malcolm (Prime Minister)
Thurulgoona
Redhill, VIC 3937, AUSTRALIA

Fraser, Neale (Tennis Player)
21 Bolton Ave
Hampton, VIC 3188, AUSTRALIA

Fraser, Ware Dawn (Swimmer)
403 Darling St
Balmain, NSW 2041, AUSTRALIA

Fraser, Willie (Baseball Player)
California Angels
3908 Plantation Blvd
Leesburg, FL 34748-7431, USA

Frashilla, Fran (Coach)
New Mexico University
Athletic Dept
Albuquerque, NM 87131-0001, USA

Fratangelo, Dawn (Journalist)
c/o Staff Member *William Morris Agency (WMA-LA)*
1 William Morris Pl
Beverly Hills, CA 90212-4261, USA

Fratello, Michael R (Mike) (Coach, Sportscaster)
c/o Staff Member *Memphis Grizzlies*
191 Beale St
Memphis, TN 38103-3715, USA

Fratianne, Linda S (Figure Skater)
15691 Borgas Court
Moorpark, CA 93021, USA

Frattare, Lanny (Baseball Player, Sportscaster)
Pittsburgh Pirates
1009 Perry Hwy
Pittsburgh, PA 15237-2108, USA

Fraumeni, Joseph F Jr (Inventor)
National Cancer Institute
Cancer Etiology Division
Bethesda, MD 20892-0001, USA

Frayn, Michael (Writer)
Greene & Heaton
37A Goldhawk Road
London W12 8QQ, UNITED KINGDOM (UK)

Frazar, Harrison (Golfer)
3208 Villanova St
Dallas, TX 75225-4839, USA

Frazer, Liz (Actor)
Peter Charlesworth
68 Old Brompton Road
#200
London SW7 3LQ, UNITED KINGDOM (UK)

Frazetta, Frank (Artist)
Frazetta Art Museum
82 S Courtland St
East Stroudsburg, PA 18301, USA

Frazier, Albert (Baseball Player)
Jacksonville Red Caps
5749 Copper Hill Ln E
Jacksonville, FL 32218-7311, USA

Frazier, Charley (Football Player)
Houston Oilers
4018 Brookston St
Houston, TX 77045-3412, USA

Frazier, Dallas (Musician, Songwriter, Writer)
RR 5 Box 133
Longhollow Pike
Gallatin, TN 37066, USA

Frazier, George (Baseball Player)
St Louis Cardinals
2001 Blake St
Denver, CO 80205-2008, USA

Frazier, Herman (Athlete, Track Athlete)
1777 Ala Moana Blvd
Honolulu, HI 96815-1603, USA

Frazier, Ian (Writer)
Farrar Straus Giroux
19 Union Sq W Fl 11
New York, NY 10003-3304, USA

Frazier, Joe (Baseball Player)
Cleveland Indians
519 Fairway Dr
Broken Arrow, OK 74011-8407, USA

Frazier, Joe (Smokin' Joe) (Boxer)
2917 N Broad St
Philadelphia, PA 19132-2402, USA

Frazier, Kevin (Actor, Television Host)
c/o Staff Member *Entertainment Tonight (ET)*
5555 Melrose Ave
Mae West Bldg Fl 2
Los Angeles, CA 90038-3989, USA

Frazier, Leslie (Football Player)
Chicago Bears
13560 Technology Dr Apt 1210
Eden Prairie, MN 55344-2262, USA

Frazier, Lisa (Musician)
c/o Staff Member *Diva Central Inc*
7510 W Sunset Blvd Ste 1445
Los Angeles, CA 90046-3408, USA

Frazier, Lou (Baseball Player)
Montreal Expos
1371 N Concord Ave
Chandler, AZ 85225-8624, USA

Frazier, Mavis (Boxer)
2917 N Broad St
Philadelphia, PA 19132-2402, USA

Frazier, Owsley B (Business Person)
Brown-Forman Corp
850 Dixie Hwy
Louisville, KY 40210-1038, USA

Frazier, Sheila (Actor)
c/o Daniel Hoff *Daniel Hoff Agency*
5455 Wilshire Blvd Ste 1100
Los Angeles, CA 90036-4277, USA

Frazier, Walt
675 Flamingo Dr SW
Atlanta, GA 30311-2403, USA

Frazier, Walter (Clyde) II (Basketball Player)
WFAN-AM
3412 36th St
Long Island City, NY 11106-1214, USA

Frazier, Wayne (Football Player)
San Diego Chargers
PO Box 413
Brewton, AL 36427-0413, USA

Frazier, Willie (Football Player)
Houston Oilers
6203 Bankside Dr
Houston, TX 77096-5608, USA

Frears, Stephen A (Director)
93 Talbot Road
London W2, UNITED KINGDOM (UK)

Freberg, Stanley V (Stan) (Actor, Comedian)
Radio Spirits
PO Box 3107
Wallingford, CT 06492-1591, USA

Frechette, Peter (Actor)
c/o Staff Member *Don Buchwald & Associates Inc (LA)*
6500 Wilshire Blvd Ste 2200
Los Angeles, CA 90048-4942, USA

Freddie & The Dreamers
9 Ridge Rd
Emerson, NJ 07630-1329, USA

Frederick, Andrew B (Football Player)
Dallas Cowboys
7247 Alexander Dr
Dallas, TX 75214-3216, USA

Frederick, Kevin (Baseball Player)
Minnesota Twins
20512 N Clarice Ave
Lincolnshire, IL 60069-9618, USA

Fredericks, Frank (Frankie) (Athlete, Track Athlete)
4497 Wimbledon Dr
Provo, UT 84604-5394, USA

Fredericks, Fred (Cartoonist)
PO Box 475
Eastham, MA 02642-0475, USA

Frederickson, Ivan C (Tucker) (Football Player)
New York Giants
12414 Indian Rd
North Palm Beach, FL 33408-2539, USA

Frederickson, Rob (Football Player)
Los Angeles Raiders
5942 E Caballo Ln
Paradise Valley, AZ 85253-2216, USA

Frederickson, Scott (Baseball Player)
Colorado Rockies
12637 King Oaks Dr
Live Oak, TX 78233-2408, USA

Fredrickson, George M (Historian)
741 Esplanada Way
Palo Alto, CA 94305-1013, USA

Fredriksson, Gert (Athlete)
Bruunsgat 13
Nykoping 61122, SWEDEN

Fredriksson, Marie (Musician, Songwriter, Writer)
D &D Mgmt
Lilla Nygatan 19
Stockholm 11128, SWEDEN

Free (Actor, Musician)
c/o Damu Bobb *Identity Talent Agency (ID)*
9107 Wilshire Blvd Ste 450
Beverly Hills, CA 90210-5535, USA

Free, Helen M (Inventor)
3752 E Jackson Blvd
Elkhart, IN 46516-5205, USA

Free, World B (Baseball Player, Coach)
Philadelphia 76ers
3601 S Broad St
1st Union Center
Philadelphia, PA 19148-5287, USA

Freebo
740 N Hayworth Ave
Los Angeles, CA 90046-7142, USA

Freed, Audley (Musician)
Mitch Schneider Organization
14724 Ventura Blvd Ste 710
Sherman Oaks, CA 91403-3520, USA

Freed, Jack H (Misc)
108 Homestead Cir
Ithaca, NY 14850-6214, USA

Freedman, Alix M (Journalist)
Wall Street Journal
200 Liberty St
Editorial Dept
New York, NY 10281-0084, USA

Freedman, Eric (Journalist)
Detroit News
615 W Lafayette Blvd
Editorial Dept
Detroit, MI 48226-3142, USA

Freedman, Gerald A (Director, Opera Singer)
Theatre Julliard School
Lincoln Center Plaza
New York, NY 10023, USA

Freedman, James O (Educator)
Dartmouth College
President's Office
Hanover, NH 03755, USA

Freedman, Ronald (Activist)
1200 Earhart Rd # 228
Ann Arbor, MI 48105-2768, USA

Freeh, Louis FBI
9th & Pennsylvania Ave. NW
Washington, DC 20035, USA

Freehan, William A (Bill) (Baseball Player)
Detroit Tigers
6999 Indian Garden Rd
Petoskey, MI 49770-8708, USA

Freel, Ryan (Baseball Player)
Toronto Blue Jays
4409 Stone Meadow Dr
Orlando, FL 32826-4263, USA

Freelon, Nnenna (Musician)
Ted Kurland
173 Brighton Ave
Boston, MA 02134-2003, USA

Freelon, Solomon (Football Player)
Houston Oilers
7214 Towerview Ln
Missouri City, TX 77489-2434, USA

Freeman, Arturo (Football Player)
Miami Dolphins
PO Box 291386
Fort Lauderdale, FL 33329-1386, USA

Freeman, Bob (Football Player)
Cleveland Browns
PO Box 1910
Auburn, AL 36831-1910, USA

Freeman, Bobby (Musician)
Lustig Talent
PO Box 770850
Orlando, FL 32877-0850, USA

Freeman, Cathy (Athlete, Track Athlete)
PO Box 700
South Melbourne, VIC 3205, AUSTRALIA

Freeman, Charles W Jr (Diplomat)
Project International
1800 K St NW Ste 1010
Washington, DC 20006-2234, USA

Freeman, Crispin (Actor, Writer)
c/o Staff Member *Arlene Thornton & Associates*
12711 Ventura Blvd Ste 490
Studio City, CA 91604-2477, USA

Freeman, Hersh (Baseball Player)
Toronto Blue Jays
4409 Stone Meadow Dr
Orlando, FL 32826-4263, USA

Freeman, Isaac (Musician)
Keith Case Assoc
1025 17th Ave S Fl 2
Nashville, TN 37212-2211, USA

Freeman, J E (Actor)
Gersh Agency
232 N Canon Dr
Beverly Hills, CA 90210-5302, USA

Freeman, Jennifer Nicole (Actor)
c/o Nils Larsen *Elements Entertainment*
1635 N Cahuenga Blvd Fl 5
Los Angeles, CA 90028-6201, USA

Freeman, Jimmy (Baseball Player)
Atlanta Braves
4716 E 106th St
Tulsa, OK 74137-6805, USA

Freeman, K Todd (Actor)
c/o Staff Member *Steppenwolf Theatre Co*
758 W North Ave Fl 4
Chicago, IL 60610-1047, USA

Freeman, Lavel (Baseball Player)
Milwaukee Brewers
2501 Gardendale Rd
Sacramento, CA 95822-5448, USA

Freeman, Mark (Baseball Player)
New York Yankees
40270 Paseo Del Rey
Rancho Mirage, CA 92270-3322, USA

Freeman, Marvin (Baseball Player)
Philadelphia Phillies
20135 Mohawk Trl
Olympia Fields, IL 60461-1135, USA

Freeman, Mona (Actor)
608 N Alpine Dr
Beverly Hills, CA 90210-3304, USA

Freeman, Morgan (Actor)
c/o Staff Member *Revelations Entertainment*
1221 2nd St Fl 4
Santa Monica, CA 90401-1150, USA

Freeman, Orville (Ex-Governor, Governor)
3701 Bryant Ave S Apt 802
Minneapolis, MN 55409-1091, USA

Freeman, Phil (Football Player)
Tampa Bay Buccaneers
1222 S Stanley Ave
Los Angeles, CA 90019-6617, USA

Freeman, Reggie (Football Player)
New Orleans Saints
PO Box 1694
Clewiston, FL 33440-1694, USA

Freeman, Robin (Golfer)
115 Chelsea Cir
Palm Desert, CA 92260-4688, USA

Freeman, Russ (Football Player)
Denver Broncos
4090 Summit Crossing Dr
Decatur, GA 30034-3542, USA

Freeman, Russell (Writer)
280 Riverside Dr
New York, NY 10025-9010, USA

Freeman, Sandi (Correspondent)
Cable News Network
820 1st St NE
News Dept
Washington, DC 20002-4243, USA

Freeman, Steve (Football Player)
Buffalo Bills
PO Box 5308
Mississippi State University Attn: Alumni Association
Mississippi State, MS 39762-5308, USA

Freeman, Yvette (Actor, Musician)
Stone Manners
6500 Wilshire Blvd Ste 550
Los Angeles, CA 90048-4950, USA

Freeman Jr, Al (Actor)
Artists Agency
1180 S Beverly Dr Ste 301
Los Angeles, CA 90035-1154, USA

Freeney, Dwight (Football Player)
Indianapolis Colts
7001 W 56th St
Indianapolis, IN 46254-9698, USA

Freese, Gene (Baseball Player)
Pittsburgh Pirates
6504 Glendale St
Metairie, LA 70003-3011, USA

Freese, George (Baseball Player)
Detroit Tigers
3341 SW Marigold St
Portland, OR 97219-5309, USA

Fregosi, James L (Jim) (Baseball Player)
1092 Copeland Ct
Tarpon Springs, FL 34688-7622, USA

Fregoso, Ramon (Actor)
c/o Staff Member *TV Azteca*
Periferico Sur 4121
Colonia Fuentes del Pedregal
DF CP 14141, MEXICO

Frehley, Ace (Musician)
McGhee Entertainment
8730 W Sunset Blvd Ste 200
West Hollywood, CA 90069-2275, USA

Frei, Emil III (Misc)
Dana-Farber Cancer Institute
44 Binney St
Boston, MA 02115-6084, USA

Frei Ruiz-Tagle, Eduardo (President)
President's Office
Palacio de la Monedo
Santiago, CHILE

Freiberger, Marcus (Basketball Player)
14100 Hickory Marsh Ln Apt 95
Fort Myers, FL 33912-7873, USA

Freidheim, Cyrus (Business Person)
Chiquita Brands International
250 E 5th St
Cincinnati, OH 45202-5190, USA

Freigang, Stephan
Strasse der Jugend 58
Cottbus D-03050, GERMANY

Freilicher, Jane (Artist)
Fishbach Gallery
210 11th Ave Rm 801
New York, NY 10001-1224, USA

Freire, Nelson (Musician)
Columbia Artists Mgmt Inc
1790 Broadway Fl 6
New York, NY 10019-1412, USA

Freireich, Emil J (Doctor)
M D Anderson Medical Center
1515 Holcombe Blvd
Houston, TX 77030-4000, USA

Freis, Edward DJ (Doctor)
4515 Willard Ave
Chevy Chase, MD 20815-3622, USA

Freisleben, Dave (Baseball Player)
San Diego Padres
1326 Diamante Dr
Pasadena, TX 77504-1479, USA

Freitas, Jesse (Football Player)
San Diego Chargers
1863 Heather Ln
Petaluma, CA 94954-8592, USA

Freitas, Rockne (Football Player)
Detroit Lions
2667 East Manoa Rd
Honolulu, HI 96822-1817, USA

Frelich, Phyllis (Actor)
Artists Group
1650 Broadway Ste 610
New York, NY 10019-6833, USA

French, Dawn (Actor, Comedian)
P F D Drury House
34-43 Russell St
London WC2B 5HA, UNITED KINGDOM
(UK)

French, Heather
567 Circle Dr
Maysville, KY 41056-9124, USA

French, Jim (Baseball Player)
Washington Senators
PO Box 6
Mesa, CO 81643-0006, USA

French, Leigh (Actor)
1850 N Vista St
Los Angeles, CA 90046-2237, USA

French, Marilyn (Writer)
Charlotte Sheedy Agency
65 Bleecker St # 1200
New York, NY 10012-2420, USA

French, Niki (Musician)
Mega Artists Mgmt
PO Box 89
Edam, ZJ 1135, THE NETHERLANDS

French, Paige (Actor)
Gersh Agency
232 N Canon Dr
Beverly Hills, CA 90210-5302, USA

French, Rufus (Football Player)
Green Bay Packers
PO Box 10628
Green Bay, WI 54307-0628, USA

French, Susan
110 E 9th St Ste C1005
Los Angeles, CA 90079-6005, USA

Freni, Mirelia (Opera Singer)
John Coast Mgmt
31 Sinclair Road
London W14 0NS, UNITED KINGDOM
(UK)

Freni, Mirella (Opera Singer)
Decca/Universal Classics Records
825 8th Ave
New York, NY 10019-7416, USA

Frenkiel, Richard H (Engineer, Inventor)
Rutgers University
PO Box 909
Winlab
Piscataway, NJ 08855, USA

Frentzen, Heinz-Harald (Race Car Driver)
Formula One Ltd
Silverstone Circuit
Northamptonshire NN12 8TN, UNITED
KINGDOM (UK)

Freotte, Gus (Football Player)
Washington Redskins
1360 Herschel Ave
Cincinnati, OH 45208-2511, USA

Freotte, Mitch (Football Player)
Buffalo Bills
445 Reynolds Ave
Kittanning, PA 16201-2713, USA

Frerotte, Gus (Football Player)
10040 Litzsinger Rd
Saint Louis, MO 63124-1132, USA

Fresco, Paolo (Business Person)
Fiat SpA
Corso Marconi 10/20
Turin 10125, ITALY

Fresh, Doug E (Musician)
Agency Group Ltd
1775 Broadway Ste 515
New York, NY 10019-1903, USA

Fresh, Mannie (Musician, Producer)
c/o Staff Member *Universal Music Group*
(UMG - LA)
2220 Colorado Ave
Santa Monica, CA 90404-3506, USA

Freston, Tom (Business Person)
Viacom
1515 Broadway
New York, NY 10036-8901, USA

Freud, Bella (Designer, Fashion Designer)
48 Rawstorne St
London EC1V 7ND, UNITED KINGDOM
(UK)

Freud, Lucian (Artist)
Rawstron-Derrick
90 Fetter Lane
London EC4A 1EQ, UNITED KINGDOM
(UK)

Freundlich, Bart (Director, Producer,
Writer)
c/o Glenn Bickel *Creative Artists Agency
LCC (CAA-LA)*
2000 Avenue Of The Stars
Los Angeles, CA 90067-4700, USA

Frewer, Matt (Actor)
c/o Carol Gettko *Warren Cowan &
Associates PR*
8899 Beverly Blvd Ste 919
Los Angeles, CA 90048-2436, USA

Frey, Christopher
The Toft E. Dean nr. Chichester
Sussex, ENGLAND, UNITED KINGDOM
(UK)

Frey, Donald N (Business Person,
Engineer)
2758 Sheridan Rd
Evanston, IL 60201-1728, USA

Frey, Glenn (Actor, Musician, Songwriter,
Writer)
5020 Brent Knoll Ln
Suwanee, GA 30024-1376, USA

Frey, James G (Jim) (Baseball Player)
12101 Tullamore Ct Unit 406
Timonium, MD 21093-8148, USA

Frey, Lonnie (Baseball Player)
Brooklyn Dodgers
995 W Woodlawn Dr
Hayden, ID 83835-8810, USA

Frey, Richard (Football Player)
Kansas City Chiefs
PO Box 1967
Tomball, TX 77377-1967, USA

Frey, Sami
21 Place des Vosges
Paris F-75003, FRANCE

Frey, Steve (Baseball Player)
Montreal Expos
1414 2nd Street Pike
Southampton, PA 18966-3931, USA

Freyndlikh, Alisa B (Actor)
Rubinstein Str 11
#7
Saint Petersburg 191002, RUSSIA

Freytag, Arny (Photographer)
22735 Macfarlane Dr
Woodland Hills, CA 91364-1322, USA

Frick, Gottlob (Opera Singer)
Eichelberg-Haus Waldfrieden
Olbronn-Durrn 75248, GERMANY

Frick, Ray (Football Player)
Brooklyn Dodgers
623 County Road 513
Pittstown, NJ 08867-5162, USA

Frick, Stephen N (Astronaut)
4322 Towering Oak Ct
Houston, TX 77059-3146, USA

Fricke, Janie (Musician)
Janie Fricke Concerts
PO Box 798
Lancaster, TX 75146-0798, USA

Fricker, Brenda (Actor)
Meyer & Eden
34 Kingly Court
London W1R 5LE, UNITED KINGDOM
(UK)

Frickle, Ben (Football Player)
Dallas Cowboys
1323 Alta Vista Ave
Austin, TX 78704-2514, USA

Frickman, Andy (Director)
c/o Staff Member *Endeavor Agency LLC
(LA)*
9601 Wilshire Blvd Fl 3
Beverly Hills, CA 90210-5204, USA

Friday Jr, Elbert W (Government Official)
US National Weather Service
1125 E West Hwy
Silver Spring, MD 20910, USA

Fridell, Squire
13563 Ventura Blvd # 200
Sherman Oaks, CA 91423-6100, USA

Fridovich, Irwin (Misc)
3517 Courtland Dr
Durham, NC 27707-5134, USA

Fridriksson, Fridrik T (Director)
Bjarkgata 8
Reykjavik 101, ICELAND

Friebe, Anika
111 E 22nd St Rm 200
New York, NY 10010-5414, USA

Fried, Charles (Educator, Government
Official)
Harvard University
Law School
Cambridge, MA 02138, USA

Friede, Mike (Football Player)
Detroit Lions
7727 Park Ridge Cir
Fort Collins, CO 80528-8909, USA

Friedel, Jacques (Physicist)
2 Rue Jean-Francois Gerbillon
Paris 75006, FRANCE

Friedgen, Ralph (Coach, Football Coach)
University of Maryland
Athletic Dept
College Park, MD 20742-0001, USA

Friedkin, William (Director)
10741 Levico Way
Los Angeles, CA 90077-1918, USA

Friedlander, Lee (Artist, Photographer)
44 S Mountain Rd
New City, NY 10956-2315, USA

Friedle, Will (Actor)
c/o Steven Muller *Innovative Artists (LA)*
1505 10th St
Santa Monica, CA 90401-2805, USA

Friedman, Daniel M (Judge)
US Court of Appeals
717 Madison Pl NW
Washington, DC 20439-0001, USA

Friedman, Emanuel A (Educator)
Beth-Israel Hospital
330 Brookline Ave
Boston, MA 02215-5491, USA

Friedman, Jeffrey (Misc)
Rockefeller University
Hughes Medical Institute
New York, NY 10021, USA

Friedman, Jerome I (Nobel Prize Laureate)
75 Greenough St
Brookline, MA 02445-6152, USA

Friedman, Kinky (Politician)
906 1/2 Congress
Austin, TX 78701-2422, USA

Friedman, Lawrence M (Educator, Lawyer)
724 Frenchmans Rd
Palo Alto, CA 94305-1005, USA

Friedman, Peter (Actor, Musician)
J Michael Bloom
233 Park Ave S # 1000
New York, NY 10003-1606, USA

Friedman, Philip (Writer)
Ivy Books/Random House Inc
1745 Broadway # B1
New York, NY 10019-4305, USA

Friedman, Sonya
208 Harristown Rd
Glen Rock, NJ 07452-3308, USA

Friedman, Stephen (Financier, Government Official)
White House
1600 Pennsylvania Ave NW
Washington, DC 20500-0004, USA

Friedman, Thomas L (Journalist, Writer)
New York Times
229 W 43rd St
Editorial Dept
New York, NY 10036-3959, USA

Friedman, Tom (Artist)
Artists on the Corner
802 De Mun Ave
Clayton, MO 63105-3197, USA

Friedman, Yona (Architect)
33 Blvd Garibaldi
Paris 75015, FRANCE

Friedmann, Phil (Musician)
Overland Productions
156 W 56th St # 500
New York, NY 10019-3800, USA

Friel, Anna (Actor)
Conway Van Gelder Robinson
18-21 Jermyn St
London, CA SW1Y 6NB, UNITED KINGDOM (UK)

Friel, Brian (Writer)
Drumaweir House
Greencastle, County Donegal, IRELAND

Friels, Colin (Actor)
129 Brooke St
Woollomooloo
Sydney, NSW 2011, AUSTRALIA

Friend, Lionel (Conductor)
136 Rosendale Road
London SE21 8LG, UNITED KINGDOM (UK)

Friend, Owen (Baseball Player)
St Louis Cardinals
2055 Porter St Spt 103
Wichita, KS 67203, USA

Friend, Patricia A (Misc)
1275 K St NW # 5
Washington, DC 20005-4083, USA

Friend, Richard H (Misc)
Cavendish Laboratory
Chemistry Dept
Cambridge, UNITED KINGDOM (UK)

Friend, Robert B (Bob) (Baseball Player)
Pittsburgh Pirates
4 Salem Cir
Pittsburgh, PA 15238-2525, USA

Frier, Mike (Football Player)
Cincinnati Bengals
3021 N Tower Way NE
Conyers, GA 30012-2653, USA

Fries, Chuck
6922 Hollywood Blvd
Los Angeles, CA 90028-6117, USA

Fries, Donald B (Publisher)
Life Magazine
Time-Life Building
New York, NY 10020, USA

Friesen, David (Musician)
Thomas Cassidy
11761 E Speedway Blvd
Tucson, AZ 85748-2017, USA

Friesen, Don (Musician)
c/o Staff Member *Paradigm (Monterey)*
509 Hartnell St
Monterey, CA 93940-2825, USA

Friesen, Gil
770 N Bonhill Rd
Los Angeles, CA 90049-2304, USA

Friesinger, Anni (Speed Skater)
WIGE Media AG
Geilbelweg 24
Fellbach 70736, GERMANY

Friesz, John (Football Player)
San Diego Chargers
624 Arboretum Way
Canton, MA 02021-2732, USA

Frigid Pink
32885 Northampton Dr
Warren, MI 48093-6164, USA

Frimout, Dirk D (Astronaut)
c/o Staff Member *NASA*
2101 Nasa Pkwy
Johnson Space Center
Houston, TX 77058-3691, USA

Frisbee, Rob (Athlete)
c/o Jerry Shandrew *Shandrew Public Relations*
1050 S Stanley Ave
Los Angeles, CA 90019-6634, USA

Frischman, Daniel
145 S Fairfax Ave Ste 310
Los Angeles, CA 90036-2176, USA

Frischmann, Justine (Musician)
CMO Mgmt
Ransomes Dock
357-37 Parkgate Road
London SW11 4NP, UNITED KINGDOM (UK)

Frisell, William R (Bill) (Musician)
Nonesuch Records
75 Rockefeller Plz
New York, NY 10019-6908, USA

Frishberg, David L (Composer, Musician)
Irvin Arthur Assoc
1441 3rd Ave Apt 12C
New York, NY 10028-1976, USA

Frist, Bill Frist (Senator)
VOLPAC
PO Box 158552
Nashville, TN 37215-8552, USA

Fritsch, Ted Jr (Football Player)
Atlanta Falcons
5014 Odins Way
Marietta, GA 30068-1660, USA

Fritsch, Toni (Football Player)
Dallas Cowboys
6 Heather Wisp Ct
Spring, TX 77381-6406, USA

Fritz, Harold A (War Hero)
1017 W Scottwood Dr
Peoria, IL 61615-1056, USA

Fritz, Larry (Baseball Player)
Philadelphia Phillies
2632 Schrage Ave
Whiting, IN 46394-2117, USA

Fritz, Nikki (Actor)
PO Box 57764
Sherman Oaks, CA 91413-2764, USA

Frizzell, David (Musician)
4694 E Robertson Rd
Cross Plains, TN 37049-4827, USA

Frizzell, John (Composer)
B M I
8730 W Sunset Blvd Ste 300
Los Angeles, CA 90069-2276, USA

Frizzelle, William J (Football Player)
Detroit Lions
8001 Tylerton Dr
Raleigh, NC 27613-1557, USA

Frobel, Doug (Baseball Player)
Pittsburgh Pirates
37 Willow Crossing Rd
Greensburg, PA 15601-9125, USA

Froboess, Cornelia
Rinklhof Kleinholzhausen
Raubling D-83064, GERMANY

Froemming, Bruce N (Baseball Player)
702 W Haddonstone Pl
Thiensville, WI 53092-5966, USA

Froese, Bob (Hockey Player)
5140 Stricker Road
Clarence, NY 14031, USA

Frohnmayer, David B (Dave) (Educator)
University of Oregon
President's Office
Eugene, OR 97401, USA

Frohnmayer, John E (Government Official)
1335 SW Timian St
Corvallis, OR 97333-3932, USA

Frohwirth, Todd (Baseball Player)
Philadelphia Phillies
6608 W Chambers St
Milwaukee, WI 53210-1329, USA

Froines, John (Activist, Educator)
University of California
Public Health School
Los Angeles, CA 90024, USA

Frolov, Diane (Actor)
c/o Richard Weitz *Endeavor Agency LLC (LA)*
9601 Wilshire Blvd Fl 3
Beverly Hills, CA 90210-5204, USA

Fromherz, Peter (Physicist)
Max Pianck Biochemistry Institute
Biophysics Dept
Martinsried, GERMANY

Fromm, Fritz (Misc)
An der Bismarckschule 64
Hannover 30173, GERMANY

Frommelt, Paul (Skier)
Liechtenstein Ski Federation
Vaduz, LIECHTENSTEIN

Fron, Kenneth (Designer)
Kenneth Fron Designs
333 W North Ave # 133
Chicago, IL 60610-1293, USA

Frongillo, John (Football Player)
Houston Oilers
10230 Elmhurst Dr NW
Albuquerque, NM 87114-4617, USA

Froning-O'Meara, Mary (Baseball Player)
417 Bay Hill Dr
Madison, WI 53717-2650, USA

Fronius, Hans (Artist)
Guggenberggasse 18
Perchtoldadorf bel Vienna 2380, AUSTRIA

Frontiere, Dominic
280 S Beverly Dr Ste 411
Beverly Hills, CA 90212-3904, USA

Frontiere, Georgia (Misc)
Saint Louis Rams
901 N Broadway
Saint Louis, MO 63101-2800, USA

Froom, Mitchell (Misc)
Gary Stamler Mgmt
3055 Overland Ave Ste 200
Los Angeles, CA 90034-3431, USA

Frosch, Robert A (Government Official)
1 Heritage Hills Dr
#42 A
Somers, NY 10589-1516, USA

Frost, Craig (Misc)
Lustig Talent
PO Box 770850
Orlando, FL 32877-0850, USA

Frost, Dave (Baseball Player)
Chicago White Sox
2206 Ocana Ave
Long Beach, CA 90815-2125, USA

Frost, David (Golfer)
Professional Golfer's Association
PO Box 109601
Palm Beach Gardens, FL 33410-9601, USA

Frost, David P (Entertainer)
4245 N Central Expy Ste 350
Dallas, TX 75205-4570, USA

Frost, Jo (Actor, Reality TV Star)
c/o Staff Member *Supernanny (USA)*
2300 W Riverside Dr
Abc Television
Burbank, CA 91506-2976, USA

Frost, Ken (Football Player)
Dallas Cowboys
103 Silver Birch Ln
La Vergne, TN 37086-4162, USA

Frost, Lindsay (Actor)
William Morris Agency
151 El Camino Dr
Beverly Hills, CA 90212-2775, USA

Frost, Mark (Writer)
Mark Frost Productions
PO Box 1723
North Hollywood, CA 91614-0723, USA

Frost, Sadie (Actor)
Julian Belfarge
46 Albermarle St
London W1X 4PP, UNITED KINGDOM (UK)

Frost, Scott (Football Player)
New York Jets
3944 S Lake Creek Drive
Jackson, WY 83001, USA

Frost, Sir David
BBC Centre Wood Lane
London, ENGLAND W12 7RJ, UNITED
KINGDOM (UK)

Fruedek, Jacques (Physicist)
2 Rue Jean-Francois Gerbillon
Paris 70006, FRANCE

Fruh, Eugen (Artist)
Romergasse 9
Zurich 8001, SWITZERLAND

Fruhbeck de Burgos, Rafael (Conductor)
Avenida dek Mediterraneo 21
Madrid 28007, SPAIN

Frusciante, John (Musician)
Boeing
8942 Wilshire Blvd
Everett, WA 98208, USA

Frutig, Ed (Football Player)
Green Bay Packers
8343 Sego Ln
Vero Beach, FL 32963-4200, USA

Fruton, Joseph S (Misc)
123 York St
New Haven, CT 06511-5614, USA

Fruwirth, Amy (Golfer)
26431 N 44th Way
Phoenix, AZ 85050-8579, USA

Fry, Arthur L (Inventor)
Minnesota Mining & Manufacturing
3M Center Bldg 230-2S
Saint Paul, MN 55144-1001, USA

Fry, Jay (Football Player)
New York Giants
PO Box 53
College Corner, OH 45003, USA

Fry, Jerry (Baseball Player)
Montreal Expos
3300 Stanton St
Springfield, IL 62703-4830, USA

Fry, Jordan (Actor)
c/o Carlyne Grager *Dramatic Artists Agency*
50 16th Ave
Kirkland, WA 98033-4909, USA

Fry, Robert (Football Player)
Los Angeles Rams
1604 Bexley Dr
Wilmington, NC 28412-2049, USA

Fry, Scott A (Admiral)
Director Joint Staff Operations
Pentagon
Washington, DC 20318-0001, USA

Fry, Stephen (Actor)
c/o Staff Member *William Morris Agency (WMA-LA)*
1 William Morris Pl
Beverly Hills, CA 90212-4261, USA

Fry, Stephen J (Actor, Comedian, Writer)
Lorraine Hamilton Asper
76 Oxford St
London W1N 0AT, UNITED KINGDOM (UK)

Fry-Irvin, Shirley (Tennis Player)
1970 Asylum Ave
West Hartford, CT 06117-3007, USA

Fryar, Irving D (Football Player, Sportscaster)
New England Patriots
51 Applegate Rd
Jobstown, NJ 08041-2202, USA

Fryce, Trevor (Football Player)
Denver Broncos
20293 E Lake Cir
Centennial, CO 80016-1282, USA

Frye, Jeff (Baseball Player)
Texas Rangers
6833 Lahontan Dr
Fort Worth, TX 76132-5457, USA

Frye, Meno
2713 N Keystone St
Burbank, CA 91504-1602, USA

Frye, Shawn
2713 N Keystone St
Burbank, CA 91504-1602, USA

Frye, Soleil Moon (Actor)
PO Box 3743
Glendale, CA 91221-0743, USA

Fryling, Victor J (Business Person)
CMS Energy Fairlane Plaza South
330 Town Center Dr
Dearborn, MI 48126-2738, USA

Fryman, D Travis (Baseball Player)
Detroit Tigers
2600 Highway 196
Molino, FL 32577-9502, USA

Fryman, Woodrow T (Woodie) (Baseball Player)
Pittsburgh Pirates
RR 1 Box 21
Ewing, KY 41039, USA

Ftorek, Robert B (Robbie) (Coach, Hockey Player)
79 Sunset Point Rd
Wolfeboro, NH 03894-4907, USA

Fu, Mingxia (Swimmer)
General Physical Culture Bureau
9 Tiyuguan Road
Bejing, CHINA

Fuchs, Ann Sutherland (Publisher)
Vogue Magazine
350 Madison Ave
New York, NY 10017-3700, USA

Fuchs, Joseph L (Publisher)
Mademoiselle Magazine
350 Madison Ave
New York, NY 10017-3700, USA

Fuchs, Leo
609 N Kilkea Dr
Los Angeles, CA 90048-2213, USA

Fuchs, Michael J (Television Host)
Home Box Office
1100 Avenue Of The Americas
New York, NY 10036-6712, USA

Fuchs, Victor R (Economist)
796 Cedro Way
Stanford, CA 94305-1032, USA

Fuchsberger, Joachin
Hubertusstr. 62
Grunwald D-82031, GERMANY

Fudge, Alan (Actor)
11835 Juniette St
Culver City, CA 90230-6227, USA

Fuel (Music Group)
c/o Staff Member *Paradigm (Monterey)*
509 Hartnell St
Monterey, CA 93940-2825, USA

Fuente, David I (Business Person)
Office Depot Inc
2200 Old Germantown Rd
Delray Beach, FL 33445-8299, USA

Fuente, Luis (Dancer)
98 Rue Lepic
Paris 75018, FRANCE

Fuentealba, Victor W (Misc)
4501 Arabia Ave
Baltimore, MD 21214-3306, USA

Fuentes, Brian (Baseball Player)
Seattle Mariners
3220 Santa Fe St
Riverbank, CA 95367-2315, USA

Fuentes, Carlos (Writer)
Harvard University
Latin American Studies Dept
Cambridge, MA 02138, USA

Fuentes, Daisy (Entertainer, Model)
c/o Marleah Leslie *Marleah Leslie & Associates PR*
8370 Wilshire Blvd Ste 210
Beverly Hills, CA 90211-2335, USA

Fuentes, Julio M (Judge)
US Court of Appeals
50 Walnut St Rm 5040
US Courthouse
Newark, NJ 07102-3571, USA

Fuentes, Mike (Baseball Player)
Montreal Expos
9626 Sycamore Ct
Davie, FL 33328-6768, USA

Fuentes, Rigoberto (Baseball Player)
San Francisco Giants
61 S Maddux Dr
Reno, NV 89512-1832, USA

Fuentes, Tito
61 S Maddux Dr
Reno, NV 89512-1832, USA

Fugard, Athol H (Writer)
PO Box 5090
Walmer
Port Elizabeth 6065, SOUTH AFRICA

Fugate, Judith (Ballerina)
New York City Ballet
Lincoln Center Plaza
New York, NY 10023, USA

Fugees, The
83 Riverside Dr
New York, NY 10024-5713, USA

Fugelsang, John (Actor, Comedian)
William Morris Agency
151 El Camino Dr
Beverly Hills, CA 90212-2775, USA

Fugere, Joe (Baseball Player)
1150 Hillsboro Mile Apt 404
Hillsboro Beach, FL 33062-1737, USA

Fugett, Jean (Football Player)
Dallas Cowboys
4801 Westparkway
Baltimore, MD 21229-1336, USA

Fugit, David (Actor)
c/o Alex Yarosh *Gersh Agency, The (LA)*
232 N Canon Dr
Beverly Hills, CA 90210-5302, USA

Fugit, Patrick (Actor)
Gersh Agency
232 N Canon Dr
Beverly Hills, CA 90210-5302, USA

Fuglesang, Christer (Astronaut)
108 Englewood St
Bellaire, TX 77401-5340, USA

Fuhrman, Mark
PO Box 333
Sagle, ID 83860-0333, USA

Fujisaki, Judge Hiroshi
1705 Main St # Q
Santa Monica, CA 90401, USA

Fukuto, Maru (Director)
Jim Preminger Agency
10866 Wilshire Blvd Fl 10
Los Angeles, CA 90024-4350, USA

Fukuyarna, Francis (Activist)
George Mason University
Public Policy Dept
Fairfax, VA 22030, USA

Fulcher, Bill (Football Player)
Los Angeles Rams
127 Erwin Dr
Mayfield, KY 42066-1908, USA

Fulcher, David (Football Player)
Cincinnati Bengals
PO Box 378
Mason, OH 45040-0378, USA

Fulcher, Modriel (Football Player)
Oakland Raiders
3724 Oak Ridge Ln
Weston, FL 33331-3700, USA

Fuld, Richard S Jr (Financier)
Lehman Bros
745 7th Ave
New York, NY 10019-6801, USA

Fulford, Cariton W Jr (General)
Deputy Cinc
US European Command Stuttgart-Vaihingen Germany
APO, AE 09128, USA

Fulgham, John (Baseball Player)
St Louis Cardinals
769 Cricklewood Ter
Lake Mary, FL 32746-5310, USA

Fulgham, Robert (Writer)
Random House
299 Park Ave
New York, NY 10171-0002, USA

Fulghum, Robert (Writer)
Random House
1745 Broadway # B1
New York, NY 10019-4305, USA

Fulhage, Scott (Football Player)
Cincinnati Bengals
2430 N Rd
Beloit, KS 67420-3064, USA

Fulks, Robbie (Musician, Songwriter, Writer)
Mongrel Music
743 Center Blvd
Fairfax, CA 94930-1764, USA

Fuller, Amanda (Actor)
c/o Amy Abell *Innovative Artists (LA)*
1505 10th St
Santa Monica, CA 90401-2805, USA

Fuller, Bob B (Writer)
37 Langton Way
London 5E3, UNITED KINGDOM (UK)

Fuller, Curtis D (Musician)
Denon Records
135 W 50th St # 1915
New York, NY 10020-1201, USA

Fuller, Deiores (Actor, Songwriter, Writer)
3628 Ottawa Cir
Las Vegas, NV 89169-3301, USA

Fuller, Dolores
3628 Ottawa Cir
Las Vegas, NV 89169-3301, USA

Fuller, Drew (Actor)
c/o Stephanie Simon *Untitled Entertainment (LA)*
331 N Maple Dr Fl 3
Beverly Hills, CA 90210-3827, USA

Fuller, Jack W (Editor, Publisher)
Chicago Tribune
435 N Michigan Ave
Editorial Dept
Chicago, IL 60611-4024, USA

Fuller, Jeff (Race Car Driver)
S-T Motorsports
103 Commercial Park Dr
Concord, NC 28027-9014, USA

Fuller, Jim (Baseball Player)
Baltimore Orioles
4215 Haiti Ln
Pasadena, TX 77505-4028, USA

Fuller, Joe (Football Player)
San Diego Chargers
8906 Farnsworth Ave N
Brooklyn Park, MN 55443-1752, USA

Fuller, John (Baseball Player)
Atlanta Braves
31912 Paseo Terraza
San Juan Capistrano, CA 92675-3060, USA

Fuller, Johnny (Football Player)
San Francisco 49ers
1925 Highland Dr
Salado, TX 76571-5792, USA

Fuller, Kathryn S (Misc)
World Wildlift Fund
1250 24th St NW
Washington, DC 20037-1193, USA

Fuller, Kurt (Actor)
c/o Staff Member *Brady Brannon & Rich*
5670 Wilshire Blvd Ste 820
Los Angeles, CA 90036-5613, USA

Fuller, Lance
1900 S Longwood Ave
Los Angeles, CA 90016-1408, USA

Fuller, Linda (Activist)
Habitat for Humanity
121 Habitat St
Americus, GA 31709-3498, USA

Fuller, Mark (Artist)
Wet Design
90 Universal City Plz
Universal City, CA 91608-1002, USA

Fuller, Marvin D (General)
6799 Patton Dr
Fort Hood, TX 76544-1343, USA

Fuller, Mike (Football Player)
San Diego Chargers
4241 Abingdon Trl
Birmingham, AL 35243-1737, USA

Fuller, Millard (Activist)
Habitat for Humanity
121 Habitat St
Americus, GA 31709-3498, USA

Fuller, Penny (Actor)
12428 Hesby St
North Hollywood, CA 91607-3020, USA

Fuller, Randy (Football Player)
Denver Broncos
2257 Patsy Ln
Columbus, GA 31903-3436, USA

Fuller, Robert (Bob) (Actor)
5012 Auckland Ave
North Hollywood, CA 91601-4102, USA

Fuller, Simon (Producer, Writer)
c/o Staff Member *19 Management Ltd*
33 Ransomes Dock
35-37 Parkgate Rd
London SW11 4NP, UNITED KINGDOM (UK)

Fuller, Steve (Football Player)
Kansas City Chiefs
81 Oak Tree Rd
Bluffton, SC 29910-4960, USA

Fuller, Vem (Baseball Player)
Cleveland Indians
155 Ironwood Cir
Aurora, OH 44202-9156, USA

Fuller, William H Jr (Football Player)
Houston Oilers
1424 Blue Heron Rd
Virginia Beach, VA 23454-1700, USA

Fullerton, C Gordon (Astronaut)
44046 28th St W Bldg 4800D
Lancaster, CA 93536-6026, USA

Fullerton, Ed (Football Player)
Pittsburgh Steelers
135 Point Vue Dr
Pittsburgh, PA 15237-1883, USA

Fullerton, Fiona (Actor)
London Mgmt
2-4 Noel St
London W1V 3RB, UNITED KINGDOM (UK)

Fullerton, Larry (Inventor)
Time Domain
6700 Odyssey Dr NW
Huntsville, AL 35806-3303, USA

Fullington, Darrell (Football Player)
Minnesota Vikings
1023 W Patrick Cir
Daytona Beach, FL 32117-4565, USA

Fullmer, Brad (Baseball Player)
Montreal Expos
2826 Bellini Dr
Henderson, NV 89052-3119, USA

Fullmer, Gene (Boxer)
9250 S 2200 W
West Jordan, UT 84088-6405, USA

Fullwood, Brent (Football Player)
Green Bay Packers
4002 Maybreeze Rd
Marietta, GA 30066-2734, USA

Fulmer, Phillip (Coach, Football Coach)
University of Tennessee
Athletic Dept
Knoxville, TN 37996-0001, USA

Fulton, Bill (Baseball Player)
New York Yankees
3001 Lexington Ct
Export, PA 15632-9061, USA

Fulton, Eileen (Actor, Musician)
As the World Turns Show' CBS-TV
524 W 57th St
New York, NY 10019-2930, USA

Fulton, Fitz
1023 E Avenue J5
Lancaster, CA 93535-4239, USA

Fulton, Fitzhugh Jr (Misc)
1023 E Avenue J # 5
Lancaster, CA 93535-3839, USA

Fulton, Soren (Actor)
c/o Staff Member *Savage Agency*
6212 Banner Ave
Los Angeles, CA 90038-2802, USA

Fultz, Mike (Football Player)
New Orleans Saints
1900 W Foothills Rd
Lincoln, NE 68523-9389, USA

Fumero, David (Actor)
c/o Staff Member *Latin World Entertainment Agency (WEA)*
2601 S Bayshore Dr Ste 235
Miami, FL 33133-5432, USA

Fumusa, Dominic (Actor)
c/o Staff Member *Don Buchwald & Associates Inc (LA)*
6500 Wilshire Blvd Ste 2200
Los Angeles, CA 90048-4942, USA

Fun Affairs
Flossergasse 7
Munich D-81369, GERMANY

Funaki, Kazuyoshi (Skier)
Japanese Olympic Committee
1-1-1 Jinan Shilbuya-Ku
Tokyo 150, JAPAN

Func, Eric (Composer)
PO Box 1073
Helena, MT 59624-1073, USA

Func, Fred (Golfer)
24711 Harbour View Dr
Ponte Vedra, FL 32082-1508, USA

Funchess, Tom (Football Player)
Boston Patriots
1015 Funchess St
Crystal Springs, MS 39059-3017, USA

Funderburk, Leonard J (War Hero)
2311 Lathan Rd
Monroe, NC 28112-8023, USA

Funderburk, Mark (Baseball Player)
Minnesota Twins
6924 Old Providence Rd
Charlotte, NC 28226-7740, USA

Funicello, Annette (Actor, Musician)
c/o Joe Funicello *International Creative Management (ICM-LA)*
10250 Constellation Blvd
Los Angeles, CA 90067-6200, USA

Funk, Caribbean (Music Group)
c/o Staff Member *Sony Music Miami*
605 Lincoln Rd Fl 7
Miami Beach, FL 33139-2900, USA

Funk, Frank (Baseball Player)
Cleveland Indians
4022 S Alamandas Way
Gold Canyon, AZ 85218-1899, USA

Funk, Fred (Golfer)
24729 Harbour View Dr
Ponte Vedra Beach, FL 32082-1509, USA

Funk, Tom (Baseball Player)
Houston Astros
6952 N Olive St
Kansas City, MO 64118-2876, USA

Funke, Alex (Cinematographer)
1176 Fiske St
Pacific Palisades, CA 90272-3845, USA

Funkmaster Flex (DJ)
c/o Staff Member *Coast II Coast Entertainment (LA)*
3350 Wilshire Blvd Ste 1200
Los Angeles, CA 90010-1836, USA

Funt, Peter
PO Box 827
Monterey, CA 93942-0827, USA

Fuqua, Antoine (Director)
c/o Scott Greenberg *Creative Artists Agency LCC (CAA-LA)*
2000 Avenue Of The Stars
Los Angeles, CA 90067-4700, USA

Fuqua, John (Football Player)
New York Giants
13983 Glastonbury Ave
Detroit, MI 48223-2921, USA

Furay, Richie (Musician)
c/o Staff Member *Agency Group Ltd, The (NY)*
1775 Broadway Ste 515
New York, NY 10019-1903, USA

Furcal, Rafael (Athlete, Baseball Player)
c/o Staff Member *Atlanta Braves*
PO Box 4064
Turner Field
Atlanta, GA 30302-4064, USA

Furchgott, Robert F (Nobel Prize Laureate)
State University of New York
Health Science Center
Brooklyn, NY 11203, USA

Furey, John (Actor)
House of Representatives
211 S Beverly Dr Ste 208
Beverly Hills, CA 90212-3879, USA

Furgler, Kurt (President)
Dufourstr 34
Saint-Gail 9000, SWITZERLAND

Furian, Mira (Actor)
6410 Blarney Stone Ct
Springfield, VA 22152-2129, USA

Furianetto, Ferruccio (Opera Singer)
Metropolitan Opera Assn
Lincoln Center Plaza
New York, NY 10023, USA

Furie, Sidney (Director, Producer, Writer)
c/o Jack Gilardi *International Creative Management (ICM-LA)*
10250 Constellation Blvd
Los Angeles, CA 90067-6200, USA

Furjanic, Anthony (Football Player)
Buffalo Bills
15220 Cottonwood Ct
Orland Park, IL 60467-7346, USA

Furlan, Mira
247 S Beverly Dr # 102
Beverly Hills, CA 90212-3830, USA

Furlong, Edward (Actor)
c/o Mark Rousso *New Wave Entertainment (LA)*
2660 W Olive Ave
Burbank, CA 91505-4525, USA

Furlong, Shirley (Golfer)
16412 S 18th Dr
Phoenix, AZ 85045-1628, USA

Furmann, Benno (Actor)
c/o Staff Member *Artists Independent Management (UK)*
32 Tavistock St
London WC2E 7PB, UNITED KINGDOM (UK)

Furniss, Bruce (Swimmer)
655 S Westford St
Anaheim, CA 92807-3643, USA

Furno, Carlo Cardinal (Religious Leader)
Piazza Della Citta Leonina
Rome 92807, ITALY

Furst, Anthony (Football Player)
Detroit Lions
3001 Big Hill Rd
Dayton, OH 45419-1303, USA

Furst, Janos K (Conductor)
I M G Artists
3 Burlington Lane
Chiswick
London W4 2TH, UNITED KINGDOM
(UK)

Furst, Nathan (Musician)
c/o Mike Rosen *Working Artists Agency*
13525 Ventura Blvd
Sherman Oaks, CA 91423-3801, USA

Furst, Stephen (Actor, Comedian)
Gold Marshak Liedtke
3500 W Olive Ave Ste 1400
Burbank, CA 91505-5512, USA

Furstenfeld, Jeremy (Musician)
Ashley Talent
2002 Hogback Rd Ste 20
Ann Arbor, MI 48105-9736, USA

Furstenfeld, Justin (Musician)
Ashley Talent
2002 Hogback Rd Ste 20
Ann Arbor, MI 48105-9736, USA

Furtado, Nelly (Musician, Songwriter,
Writer)
c/o Staff Member *Chris Smith
Management Inc*
21 Camden St Fl 5
Toronto, ON M5V 1V2, CANADA

Furth, George (Actor, Writer)
Bresler Kelly Assoc
11500 W Olympic Blvd Ste 510
Los Angeles, CA 90064-1527, USA

Furuhashi, Hironshin (Swimmer)
3-9-11 Nozawa
Setagayaku
Tokyo, JAPAN

Furukawa, Masaru (Swimmer)
5-5-12 Shinohara Honmachi
Nadaku
Kobe, JAPAN

Furukawa, Satoshi (Astronaut)
NASDA
Tsukuba Space Center
2-1-1 Sengen
Tukuhashi, Ibaraka 305, JAPAN

Furuseth, Ole Christian (Skier)
John Colletts Alle 74
Oslo 0854, NORWAY

Fury, Ed
6729 Babcock Ave
North Hollywood, CA 91606-1310, USA

Furyk, Jim (Golfer)
240 Deer Haven Dr
Ponte Vedra Beach, FL 32082-2107, USA

Fusina, Chuck A (Football Player)
Tampa Bay Buccaneers
1548 King James Dr
Pittsburgh, PA 15237-1588, USA

Fussell, Chris (Baseball Player)
Baltimore Orioles
644 Ansonia St
Oregon, OH 43616-2706, USA

Futey, Bohdan A (Judge)
US Claims Court
717 Madison Pl NW
Washington, DC 20439-0001, USA

Futral, Elizabeth (Opera Singer)
Neil Funkhouser Mgmt
105 Arden St Apt 5G
New York, NY 10040-1119, USA

Futrell, Mary H (Misc)
George Washington University
Education School
Washington, DC 20052-0001, USA

Futter, Ellen V (Educator)
American Natural History Museum
Park Ave West & 79th St
New York, NY 10034, USA

Futterman, Dan (Actor)
Gersh Agency
232 N Canon Dr
Beverly Hills, CA 90210-5302, USA

Futureheads, The (Music Group)
c/o Staff Member *Paradigm (Monterey)*
509 Hartnell St
Monterey, CA 93940-2825, USA

Fuzz (Musician)
Mitch Schneider Organization
14724 Ventura Blvd Ste 710
Sherman Oaks, CA 91403-3520, USA

Fyhrie, Mike (Baseball Player)
New York Mets
4 Wellesley Ct
Coto De Caza, CA 92679-4725, USA

G, Franky (Actor)
c/o Jimmy Darmody *Creative Artists
Agency LCC (CAA-LA)*
2000 Avenue Of The Stars
Los Angeles, CA 90067-4700, USA

G, Kenny (Musician)
c/o Staff Member *William Morris Agency
(WMA-LA)*
1 William Morris Pl
Beverly Hills, CA 90212-4261, USA

G K (Actor)
11 Shyamala Vadana Street
Koyathoppu
Chennai, TN 600 024, INDIA

G Love & Special Sauce (Music Group)
c/o Staff Member *Paradigm (Monterey)*
509 Hartnell St
Monterey, CA 93940-2825, USA

G Ponnambalam (Actor)
10 Dr Subbarray Nagar
II Street Kodambakkam
Chennai, TN 600 024, INDIA

G Unit (Music Group)
c/o Staff Member *Interscope Records (NY)*
1790 Broadway
New York, NY 10019-1412, USA

Gaarder, Jostein (Misc)
Gullkroken 22A
Oslo 0377, NORWAY

Gabaldon, Diana (Writer)
Delacorte Press
1540 Broadway
New York, NY 10036-4039, USA

Gabbaja, Stefano
via Santa Cecilia 7
Milan 20122, ITALY

Gable, Brian (Cartoonist)
67 Riverside Dr Apt 1D
New York, NY 10024-6155, USA

Gable, Daniel M (Danny) (Coach,
Wrestler)
RR 2 Box 55
Iowa City, IA 52240, USA

Gable, John Clark
Jack Scagnetti Talent Agency
5118 Vineland Ave Ste 102
North Hollywood, CA 91601-3814, USA

Gabler, Bill (Baseball Player)
Chicago Cubs
4443 Mattis Rd
Saint Louis, MO 63128-3136, USA

Gabler, John (Baseball Player)
New York Yankees
8606 W 81st St
Overland Park, KS 66204-3444, USA

Gabor, Zsa Zsa (Actor)
1001 Bel Air Rd
Los Angeles, CA 90077-3011, USA

Gaborik, Marian (Hockey Player)
Minnesota Wild
175 Kellogg Blvd W
Xcel Energy Arena
Saint Paul, MN 55102-1206, USA

Gabriel, Ana (Musician)
AG Ediciones Musicales
Peten 117 Col Narvarte
Mexico City 03020, MEXICO

Gabriel, Charles A (General)
Flight International
International Airport
Newport News, VA 23602, USA

Gabriel, Gunter
Vorhelmer Str. 63
Ennigerloh-Enniger D-59320, GERMANY

Gabriel, John (Actor)
130 W 42nd St Ste 1804
New York, NY 10036-7902, USA

Gabriel, Juan (Musician, Songwriter,
Writer)
Hauser Entertainment
11003 Rooks Rd
Whittier, CA 90601-1624, USA

Gabriel, Michael (Artist)
Dlouha 32
Prague 1 110 00, CZECH REPUBLIC

Gabriel, Peter (Musician, Songwriter,
Writer)
c/o Staff Member *Real World Records*
Box Mill
Box Corsham
Wiltshire SN1 38PN, UNITED KINGDOM
(UK)

Gabriel, Roman
16817 McKee Rd
Charlotte, NC 28278-8406, USA

Gabriel, Roman I Jr (Football Player)
Los Angeles Rams
PO Box 1676
Little River, SC 29566-1676, USA

Gabrielle, Josefina (Actor)
c/o Staff Member *Stone Manners Talent &
Literary (LA)*
6500 Wilshire Blvd Ste 550
Los Angeles, CA 90048-4950, USA

Gabrielle, Monique (Actor, Model)
Purrfect Productions
PO Box 1771
Pompano Beach, FL 33061-1771, USA

Gabrielson, Len (Baseball Player)
Milwaukee Braves
24230 Hillview Rd
Los Altos, CA 94024-5221, USA

Gacioch, Rose (Baseball Player)
17001 17 Mile Rd
Clinton Township, MI 48038-2801, USA

Gacki, Sebastian (Actor)
c/o Staff Member *Lizbell Agency*
216-309 W Cordova St
Vancouver, BC V6B 1E5, CANADA

Gacy, Madonna Wayne (Musician)
Artists & Audience Entertainment
PO Box 35
Pawling, NY 12564-0035, USA

Gaddafi, Muammar Muhammad al
(President)
President's Office
Bab el Aziziya Barracks
Tripoli, LIBYA

Gaddis, John L (Historian)
Ohio University
Contemporary History Institute
Brown House
Athens, OH 45701, USA

Gaddis, Robert (Football Player)
Buffalo Bills
1022 Gaddis Rd
Edwards, MS 39066-8007, USA

Gade, Ariel (Actor)
c/o Jennifer Millar *Abrams Artists Agency
(LA)*
9200 W Sunset Blvd Ph 11
Los Angeles, CA 90069-3601, USA

Gadinsky, Brian (Producer)
c/o Staff Member *William Morris Agency
(WMA-LA)*
1 William Morris Pl
Beverly Hills, CA 90212-4261, USA

Gadsby, William A (Bill) (Hockey Player)
28765 E Kalong Cir
Southfield, MI 48034-5650, USA

Gadsden, Oronde (Football Player)
Miami Dolphins
11241 NW 15th St
Plantation, FL 33323-2433, USA

Gadzhiev, Raul S O (Composer)
Azerbaijan State Popular Orchestra
Baku, AZERBAIJAN

Gaechter, Mike (Football Player)
Dallas Texans
13 Horizon Pt
Frisco, TX 75034-6840, USA

Gaeta, John (Designer, Special Effects
Designer)
c/o Staff Member *International Creative
Management (ICM-LA)*
10250 Constellation Blvd
Los Angeles, CA 90067-6200, USA

Gaetti, Gary (Baseball Player)
Minnesota Twins
78255 Highway 1082
Covington, LA 70435-4656, USA

Gaff, Brent (Baseball Player)
New York Mets
5925 S State Road 9
Albion, IN 46701-9623, USA

Gaffigan, Jim (Actor, Comedian)
c/o Estelle Lasher *Principal Entertainment
(LA)*
1964 Westwood Blvd Ste 400
Los Angeles, CA 90025-4695, USA

Gaffney, Derrick T (Football Player)
New York Jets
11750 Cherry Bark Dr E
Jacksonville, FL 32218-7674, USA

Gaffney, F Andrew (Drew) (Astronaut)
6613 Chatsworth Pl
Nashville, TN 37205-3955, USA

Gaffney, Mo (Actor)
Stone Manners
8436 W 3rd St Ste 740
Los Angeles, CA 90048-4130, USA

Gaffney, Paul F (Admiral)
President National Defense University
Fort Lesley McNair
Washington, DC 20319-0001, USA

Gage, Bob (Football Player)
Pittsburgh Steelers
520 Chick Springs Rd
Greenville, SC 29609-4828, USA

Gage, Fred H (Misc)
Salk Biological Study Institute
10110 N Torrey Pines Rd
La Jolla, CA 92037, USA

Gage, Nathaniel L (Educator)
85 Peter Courts Circle
Palo Alto, CA 94305, USA

Gage, Nicholas (Journalist)
37 Nelson St
North Grafton, MA 01536-1424, USA

Gage, Paul (Inventor)
Craig Research
Highway 178 N
Chippewa Falls, WI 55402, USA

Gagliano, Phil (Baseball Player)
St Louis Cardinals
1095 Crescent Dr
Hollister, MO 65672-4884, USA

Gagliano, Ralph (Baseball Player)
Cleveland Indians
1756 Overton Park Ave
Memphis, TN 38112-5344, USA

Gagliano, Robert F (Bob) (Football Player)
Kansas City Chiefs
1560 Newbury Rd
Newbury Park, CA 91320-3452, USA

Gagliardi, John (Coach, Football Coach)
Saint John's University
Athletic Dept
Collegeville, MN 56321, USA

Gagne, Eric S (Baseball Player)
Los Angeles Dodgers
1000 Elysian Park Ave
Stadium
Los Angeles, CA 90012-1199, USA

Gagne, Greg (Baseball Player)
Minnesota Twins
746 Whetstone Hill Rd
Somerset, MA 02726-3702, USA

Gagne, Simon (Hockey Player)
Philadelphia Flyers
3601 S Broad St
1st Union Center
Philadelphia, PA 19148-5297, USA

Gagner, Dave (Hockey Player)
Custon Ice
404179 Harvester Road
Burlington, ON L7L 5M4, CANADA

Gagner, Larry (Football Player)
Pittsburgh Steelers
205 W Curtis St
Tampa, FL 33603-3649, USA

Gagnier, Holly (Actor)
Stone Manners
6500 Wilshire Blvd Ste 550
Los Angeles, CA 90048-4950, USA

Gagnon, Andre Philippe
89 Rue Alexandra
Granby, PQ J2C 2P4, CANADA

Gagnon, Edouard Cardinal (Religious Leader)
Pontifical Family Council
Palazzo S Calisto
00120, VATICAN CITY

Gago, Jenny (Actor)
Metropolitan Talent Agency
4500 Wilshire Blvd Fl 2
Los Angeles, CA 90010-3858, USA

Gagosian, Larry (Business Person)
Gagosian Gallery
980 Madison Ave Ph
New York, NY 10075-1848, USA

Gahan, David (Musician)
Reach Media
295 Greenwich St # 109
New York, NY 10007-1049, USA

Gahan, David (Dave) (Musician)
c/o Carole Kinzel *Creative Artists Agency LCC (CAA-LA)*
2000 Avenue Of The Stars
Los Angeles, CA 90067-4700, USA

Gaidar, Yegor T (Prime Minister)
Gazetny Per 5
Moscow 111024, RUSSIA

Gail, David
c/o Staff Member *Henze Management*
1925 Century Park E Ste 2320
Los Angeles, CA 90067-2724, USA

Gaile, Jeri
880 Hilldale Ave Apt 3
Los Angeles, CA 90069-4921, USA

Gailey, T Chandler (Chan) (Coach, Football Coach, Football Player)
3497 Paces Valley Rd NW
Atlanta, GA 30327-3201, USA

Gaillard, Bob (Coach)
50 Bonnie Brae Dr
Novato, CA 94949-5851, USA

Gaillard, Eddie (Baseball Player)
Detroit Tigers
834 Peppertree Ct
Wellington, FL 33414-4925, USA

Gaillard, Mary Katharine (Physicist)
University of California
Physics Dept
Berkeley, CA 94720-0001, USA

Gaiman, Neil (Writer)
c/o Jon Levin *Creative Artists Agency LCC (CAA-LA)*
2000 Avenue Of The Stars
Los Angeles, CA 90067-4700, USA

Gain, Robert (Bob) (Football Player)
Cleveland Browns
11 Nokomis Dr
Eastlake, OH 44095-1943, USA

Gainer, Derrick (Football Player)
Cleveland Browns
711 E McDonald Rd
Plant City, FL 33567, USA

Gainer, Jay (Baseball Player)
Colorado Rockies
1035 E 8th St
Panama City, FL 32401-3594, USA

Gaines, Ambrose (Rowdy) IV (Swimmer)
6800 Hawaii Kai Dr
Honolulu, HI 96825-1505, USA

Gaines, Boyd (Actor, Musician)
Duva/Flack
200 W 57th St Ste 1407
New York, NY 10019-3211, USA

Gaines, Clark (Football Player)
New York Jets
6 Farnham Pl
Metairie, LA 70005-4008, USA

Gaines, Davis
315 W 57th St Frnt 4H
New York, NY 10019-3158, USA

Gaines, Ernest J (Writer)
PO Box 81
Oscar, LA 70762-0081, USA

Gaines, Joe (Baseball Player)
Cincinnati Reds
77 Anair Way
Oakland, CA 94605-4874, USA

Gaines, Lawrence (Football Player)
Detroit Lions
4963 Cherry Blossom Cir
West Bloomfield, MI 48324-1297, USA

Gaines, Reese (Baseball Player)
Houston Rockets
2 Greenway Plz
Toyota Center
Houston, TX 77046-0297, USA

Gaines, Rowdy
6800 Hawaii Kai Dr
Honolulu, HI 96825-1505, USA

Gaines, William C (Journalist)
Chicago Tribune
435 N Michigan Ave
Editorial Dept
Chicago, IL 60611-4024, USA

Gainey, Robert M (Bob) (Coach, Hockey Player)
PO Box 829
Coppell, TX 75019-0829, USA

Gainey, Ty (Baseball Player)
Houston Astros
3040 W Market Street Ext
Cheraw, SC 29520-5587, USA

Gainsbourg, Charlotte (Actor)
c/o Dominique Besnehard *ArtMedia*
20 av Rapp
Paris 75007, FRANCE

Gaiser, George (Football Player)
Denver Broncos
8637 Fair Oaks Pkwy
Boerne, TX 78015-4604, USA

Gaison, Blane (Football Player)
Atlanta Falcons
45-444 Koa Kahiko St
Kaneohe, HI 96744-2008, USA

Gaiter, Tony (Football Player)
New England Patriots
9235 NW 35th Ct
Miami, FL 33147-2829, USA

Gaither, Bill (Musician, Songwriter, Writer)
Gaither Music Co
PO Box 737
Alexandria, IN 46001-0737, USA

Gajan, Hokie (Football Player)
New Orleans Saints
213 Cottonwood Ln
Mandeville, LA 70471-2552, USA

Gajarsa, Arthur J (Judge)
Us Court of Appeals
717 Madison Pl NW
Washington, DC 20439-0001, USA

Gajdusek, D Carieton (Nobel Prize Laureate)
Human Virology Institute
725 W Lombard St # N460
Baltimore, MD 21201-1009, USA

Gajkowski, Steve (Baseball Player)
Seattle Mariners
416 Turner St NE
Olympia, WA 98506-4663, USA

Gakeler, Dan (Baseball Player)
Detroit Tigers
3501 Terrault Dr
Greensboro, NC 27410-8240, USA

Galabru, Michael
11 rue Boissiere
Paris F-75116, FRANCE

Galambos, Robert (Misc)
8826 La Jolla Scenic Dr N
La Jolla, CA 92037-1608, USA

Galanos, James (Designer, Fashion Designer)
1316 Sunset Plaza Dr
Los Angeles, CA 90069-1235, USA

Galanos, Mike (Television Host)
Prime News Tonight
1 Time Warner Ctr
Cnn
New York, NY 10019-6038, USA

Galarraga, Andres (Baseball Player)
c/o Staff Member *New York Mets*
12301 Roosevelt Ave
Shea Stadium
Flushing, NY 11368-1699, USA

Galarrage, Andres J P (Baseball Player)
Barrio Nuevo Chapellin
Clejon Soledad #5
Caracas, VENEZUELA

Galasso, Bob (Baseball Player)
Seattle Mariners
1449 Minstrel Dr Apt 2
Dayton, OH 45449-5363, USA

Galati, Frank J (Director)
2990 Emathla St
Miami, FL 33133-3223, USA

Galbraith, Clint (Race Car Driver)
PO Box 902
Edwardsville, IL 62025-0902, USA

Galbraith, Evan G (Diplomat, Financier)
133 E 64th St
New York, NY 10065-7045, USA

Galbraith, Scott (Football Player)
Cleveland Browns
3649 Plymouth Dr
North Highlands, CA 95660-3309, USA

Galbreath, Harry (Football Player)
Miami Dolphins
728 McGraw St
Clarksville, TN 37040-4220, USA

Galbreath, Tony (Football Player)
New Orleans Saints
411 W 9th St
Fulton, MO 65251-1178, USA

Galdikas, Birute M F (Misc)
Orangutan Foundation International
822 Wellesley Ave
Los Angeles, CA 90049-5213, USA

Galdonik, Barbara (Baseball Player)
4016 7th Ave
Kenosha, WI 53140-5532, USA

Gale, Ed (Actor)
c/o Cindy Osbrink *Osbrink Talent Agency*
4343 Lankershim Blvd # 100
North Hollywood, CA 91602-2705, USA

Gale, Joseph H (Judge)
US Tax Court
400 2nd St NW
Washington, DC 20217-0002, USA

Gale, Rich (Baseball Player)
Kansas City Royals
869 Center Park St
Daniel Island, SC 29492-7569, USA

Gale, Robert P (Inventor)
980 Bluegrass Ln
Los Angeles, CA 90049-1433, USA

Galecki, Johnny (Actor)
c/o Staff Member *Handprint Entertainment*
1100 Glendon Ave Ste 1000
Los Angeles, CA 90024-3514, USA

Galella, Ronald E (Ron) (Photographer)
Ron Galella Ltd
12 Nelson Ln
Montville, NJ 07045-9306, USA

Galer, Robert E (General)
3525 Turtle Creek Blvd Apt 6D
Dallas, TX 75219-5515, USA

Galiena, Anna (Actor)
c/o Dominique Besnehard *ArtMedia*
20 av Rapp
Paris 75007, FRANCE

Galifinakis, Zach (Comedian)
c/o Staff Member *William Morris Agency (WMA-LA)*
1 William Morris Pl
Beverly Hills, CA 90212-4261, USA

Galigher, Ed (Football Player)
New York Jets
1465 Paint Mountain Rd
Escondido, CA 92029-5926, USA

Galik, Denise (Actor)
Badgley Connor Talent
1680 Vine St Ste 1016
Los Angeles, CA 90028-8800, USA

Galina, Stacy (Actor)
c/o Staff Member *Alan Siegel Entertainment*
345 N Maple Dr Ste 375
Beverly Hills, CA 90210-5942, USA

Galindo, Rudy (Figure Skater)
c/o Staff Member *Champions on Ice*
3500 W 80th St
Tom Collins Enterprises Inc
Minneapolis, MN 55431-1068, USA

Gall, Hugues (Opera Singer)
Grand Theatre de Geneva
11 Blvd du Theatre
Geneva 1211, SWITZERLAND

Gallacher, Kevin (Soccer Player)
Blackbum Rovers
Ewood Park
Blackbum
Lancashire BB2 4JF, UNITED KINGDOM
(UK)

Gallagher (Misc)
14984 Roan Ct
Wellington, FL 33414-1015, USA

Gallagher, Al (Baseball Player)
San Francisco Giants
2920 N Sherman Ave
Madison, WI 53704-3000, USA

Gallagher, Bob (Baseball Player)
Boston Red Sox
315 Fair Ave
Santa Cruz, CA 95060-6343, USA

Gallagher, Brian (Misc)
United Way of America
701 N Fairfax Ave
Alexandria, VA 22314-2062, USA

Gallagher, Bronagh (Actor)
Marmont Mgmt
Langham House
302/8 Regent St
London W1R 5AL, UNITED KINGDOM
(UK)

Gallagher, Dave (Baseball Player)
Cleveland Indians
Stridell 177 Applegate Dr
Trenton, NJ 08690, USA

Gallagher, Dave (Football Player)
Chicago Bears
2740 California Ct
Columbus, IN 47201-2924, USA

Gallagher, David (Actor)
c/o Abby Bluestone *Innovative Artists (LA)*
1505 10th St
Santa Monica, CA 90401-2805, USA

Gallagher, Delia (Anchor)
c/o Staff Member *CNN (LA)*
6430 W Sunset Blvd Ste 300
Hollywood, CA 90028-7906, USA

Gallagher, Doug (Baseball Player)
Detroit Tigers
1690 Maple Ln
Fremont, OH 43420-3612, USA

Gallagher, Frank (Football Player)
Detroit Lions
6572 Enclave Dr
Clarkston, MI 48348-4859, USA

Gallagher, Helen (Actor, Musician)
260 W End Ave
New York, NY 10023-3614, USA

Gallagher, John (Religious Leader)
Advent Christian Church
PO Box 551
Presque Isle, ME 04769-0551, USA

Gallagher, Liam (Musician)
Ignition Mgmt
54 Linhope St
London NW1 6HL, UNITED KINGDOM
(UK)

Gallagher, Mary (Actor)
c/o Jason M Solomon *Full Circle Management*
8961 W Sunset Blvd
Los Angeles, CA 90069-1807, USA

Gallagher, Megan (Actor)
Don Buchwald
6500 Wilshire Blvd Ste 2200
Los Angeles, CA 90048-4942, USA

Gallagher, Mike (Radio Personality)
Gallagher Networks
350 5th Ave Ste 1818
New York, NY 10118-1818, USA

Gallagher, Noel (Musician, Songwriter, Writer)
c/o Staff Member *Ignition Management*
54 Linhope St
London NW1 6HL, UNITED KINGDOM
(UK)

Gallagher, Peter (Actor)
c/o Raelle Koota *Anonymous Content (NY)*
8522 National Blvd Ste 101
Culver City, CA 90232-2454, USA

Gallagher Jr, Jim (Golfer)
PO Box 507
Greenwood, MS 38935-0507, USA

Gallagher-Smith, Jackie (Golfer)
193 Paradise Cir
Jupiter, FL 33458-2853, USA

Gallant, Matt (Actor, Television Host)
608 Idaho Ave Unit 8
Santa Monica, CA 90403-2712, USA

Gallant, Mavis (Writer)
14 Rue Jean Ferrandi
Paris 75006, FRANCE

Gallardo, Camilo
1505 10th St
Santa Monica, CA 90401-2805, USA

Gallardo, Silvana
10637 Burbank Blvd
N Hollywood, CA 91601-2512, USA

Gallatin, Harry J (Basketball Player, Coach)
2010 Madison Ave
Edwardsville, IL 62025-2623, USA

Galle, Stan (Baseball Player)
Washington Senators
7 N Reed Ave
Mobile, AL 36604-1325, USA

Gallego, Gina (Actor)
The Agency
1800 Avenue Of Stars Ste 400
Los Angeles, CA 90067-4206, USA

Gallegos, Gilbert G (Misc)
Fraternal Order of Police
1410 Donaldson Pike
Nashville, TN 37217, USA

Gallery, Robert (Football Player)
Oakland Raiders
1220 Harbor Bay Pkwy
Alameda, CA 94502-6570, USA

Galles, John (Misc)
National Small Business United
1156 15th St NW Ste 1100
Washington, DC 20005-1755, USA

Galliano, John C (Designer, Fashion Designer)
House of Dior
60 Rue D'Avron
Paris 75020, FRANCE

Gallico, Gregory III (Doctor, Inventor)
Massachusetts General Hospital
275 Cambridge St
Boston, MA 02114-3130, USA

Galligan, Zach
151 El Camino Dr
Beverly Hills, CA 90212-2704, USA

Gallison, Joe (Actor)
PO Box 10187
Wilmington, NC 28404-0187, USA

Gallner, Kyle (Actor)
c/o Sarah Shyn *Gersh Agency, The (LA)*
232 N Canon Dr
Beverly Hills, CA 90210-5302, USA

Gallo, Carla (Actor)
c/o April Lim *Global Artists Agency*
1648 Wilcox Ave Ste 3
Los Angeles, CA 90028-6898, USA

Gallo, Ernest (Business Person)
E & J Gallo Winery
600 Yosernite Blvd
Modesto, CA 95354, USA

Gallo, Frank (Artist)
University of Illinios
Art Dept
Urbana, IL 61801, USA

Gallo, Robert C (Scientist)
University of Maryland
Study Of Viruses Institute
Baltimore, MD 21228, USA

Gallo, Vincent (Actor, Director)
432 La Guardia Pl #600
New York, NY 10012, USA

Gallo, William V (Bill) (Boxer, Cartoonist)
1 Mayflower Dr
Yonkers, NY 10710-3801, USA

Gallop, Tom (Actor)
c/o Dan Baron *Agency for the Performing Arts (APA-LA)*
405 S Beverly Dr
Beverly Hills, CA 90212-4416, USA

Galloway, David (Football Player)
St Louis Cardinals
19018 NW 52nd Pl
Miami Gardens, FL 33055-2389, USA

Galloway, Don (Actor)
2501 Colorado Ave Ste 350
Santa Monica, CA 90404-3583, USA

Galloway, Jean (Religious Leader)
Volunteers of America
1660 Duke St
Alexandria, VA 22314-3473, USA

Galloway, Joey (Football Player)
Seattle Seahawks
14732 Waterchase Blvd
Tampa, FL 33626-3317, USA

Galotti, Donna (Publisher)
Ladies Home Journal
100 Park Ave
New York, NY 10017-5516, USA

Galotti, Ronald A (Publisher)
Conde Nast Publications
4 Times Sq
Publisher's Office
New York, NY 10036-6561, USA

Galvin, James (Writer)
University of Iowa
Writer's Workshop
Iowa City, IA 52242, USA

Galvin, John (Football Player)
New York Jets
136 Parkview Ave
Lowell, MA 01852-3811, USA

Galvin, John R (General)
2714 Jodeco Cir
Jonesboro, GA 30236-5329, USA

Galvin, Robert W (Business Person)
Motorola Corporate Office
1303 E Algonquin Rd
Schaumburg, IL 60196-4041, USA

Galway, James (Musician)
Benzeholzstr 11
Meggen 6045, SWITZERLAND

Galyon, Gregory (Football Player)
New York Giants
2352 Monticello Dr
Maryville, TN 37803-7528, USA

Gam, Rita (Actor)
180 W 58th St # 8B
New York, NY 10019-2145, USA

Gamar, Charles D
7660 N 159th Street Ct E
Benton, KS 67017-8926, USA

Gambee, Dave (Basketball Player)
PO Box 3070
Portland, OR 97208-3070, USA

Gamble, Ed (Cartoonist)
Florida Times-Union
1 Riverside Ave
Editorial Dept
Jacksonville, FL 32202-4904, USA

Gamble, John (Baseball Player)
Detroit Tigers
369 Caliente St
Reno, NV 89509-2729, USA

Gamble, Kenny (Ken) (Football Player)
Kansas City Chiefs
4 Algonquin Dr
Wilbraham, MA 01095-2373, USA

Gamble, Kevin (Basketball Player)
41 Forest Rdg
Springfield, IL 62712-8910, USA

Gamble, Mason (Actor)
United Talent Agency
9560 Wilshire Blvd Ste 500
Beverly Hills, CA 90212-2401, USA

Gamble, Oscar (Baseball Player)
Chicago Cubs
9705 Bent Brook Dr
Montgomery, AL 36117-7445, USA

Gamboa, Juan Pablo (Actor)
c/o Staff Member *Televisa*
Blvd Adolfo Lopez Mateos 232
Colonia San Angel INN
DF CP 01060, MEXICO

Gambol, Chris (Football Player)
Indianapolis Colts
6450 Double Eagle Dr Apt 416
Woodridge, IL 60517-1594, USA

Gambon, Michael (Actor)
c/o Staff Member *Paradigm (LA)*
360 N Crescent Dr
North Bldg
Beverly Hills, CA 90210-6820, USA

Gambon, Michael J (Actor)
International Creative Mgmt
40 W 57th St Ste 1800
New York, NY 10019-4001, USA

Gambon, Sir Michael (Actor)
c/o Staff Member *International Creative Management (ICM-LA)*
10250 Constellation Blvd
Los Angeles, CA 90067-6200, USA

Gambrell, Bill (Football Player)
St Louis Cardinals
341 Osceola Ave
Bogart, GA 30622-1511, USA

Gambrell, David H (Senator)
3205 Arden Rd NW
Atlanta, GA 30305-1918, USA

Gambril, Don (Coach)
4409 Spring Row
Northport, AL 35473-5231, USA

Gambucci, Andre (Coach, Hockey Player)
660 Southpointe Ct
Colorado Springs, CO 80906-3804, USA

Gammon, James (Actor)
414 N Sycamore Ave Apt 3
Los Angeles, CA 90036-2654, USA

Gammon, Kendall (Football Player)
Pittsburgh Steelers
14429 Maple St
Overland Park, KS 66223-1256, USA

Gammons, Peter (Baseball Player, Writer)
Boston Globe
Editorial Dept
PO Box 2378
Boston, MA 02107, USA

Ganassi, Sonia (Opera Singer)
Columbia Artists Mgmt Inc
1790 Broadway Fl 6
New York, NY 10019-1412, USA

Ganatra, Nisha (Director)
c/o Roger E Kass *Cowan, DeBaets, Abrahams & Sheppard LLP*
40 W 57th St Ste 2104
New York, NY 10019-4001, USA

Gand, Gale (Chef, Television Host)
c/o Staff Member *Food Network, The*
75 9th Ave
New York, NY 10011-7006, USA

Gandarillas, Gus (Baseball Player)
Milwaukee Brewers
6320 NW 114th St
Hialeah, FL 33012-2334, USA

Gandee, Sherwin (Football Player)
Detroit Lions
148 Viking Way
Naples, FL 34110-1136, USA

Gandhi, Sonia (Government Official, Politician)
All India Congress Party
24 Akbar Road
New Delhi, New Delhi 110011, INDIA

Gandhimathi (Actor, Bollywood)
59 Saidapet Road
Chennai, TN 600026, INDIA

Gandler, Markus (Skier)
Sinwell 22
Kitzbuhel 6370, AUSTRIA

Gandolfi, Michael (Model)
c/o Staff Member *Ford Models (NY)*
111 5th Ave Fl 9
New York, NY 10003-1005, USA

Gandolfini, James (Actor)
c/o Nina Nisenholtz *N2N Entertainment*
1230 Montana Ave Apt 203
Santa Monica, CA 90403-5987, USA

Gandy, Wayne L (Football Player)
Los Angeles Rams
130 Sand Pine Ln
Davenport, FL 33837-5510, USA

Ganellin, C Robin (Inventor)
University College
Chemistry Dept
20 Gordon
London WC1H OAJ, UNITED KINGDOM (UK)

Ganesh, Gemini (Actor)
6 Nungambakkam High Road
Chennai, TN 600 034, INDIA

Ganev, Tzetzi
1751 N Berendo St # 21
Los Angeles, CA 90027, USA

Gang of Four (Music Group)
c/o Staff Member *Paradigm (Monterey)*
509 Hartnell St
Monterey, CA 93940-2825, USA

Ganga (Actor)
6 South Mada Street
Mylapore
Chennai, TN 600 004, INDIA

Gangel, Jamie (Correspondent)
NBC-TV News Dept
30 Rockefeller Plz Ste 270E
New York, NY 10112-0299, USA

Gannascoli, Joseph (Joe) (Actor)
c/o Greg Meyer *Acme Talent & Literary (LA)*
4727 Wilshire Blvd Ste 333
Los Angeles, CA 90010-3874, USA

Gannon, Richard J (Rich) (Football Player)
Oakland Raiders
1220 Harbor Bay Pkwy
Alameda, CA 94502-6570, USA

Ganote-Weise, Gertrude (Baseball Player)
1630 Berry Blvd
Louisville, KY 40215-1902, USA

Gans, Danny (Entertainer)
D G Entertainment Inc
3400 Las Vegas Blvd S
C/O The Mirage Hotel
Las Vegas, NV 89109-8923, USA

Gansler, Bob (Coach, Soccer Player)
Kansas City Wizards
8900 State Line Rd
Leawood, KS 66206-1941, USA

Ganson, Arthur (Artist)
Massachusetts Institute of Technology
Compton Gallery
Cambridge, MA 02139, USA

Gant, Harry (Race Car Driver)
RR 3 Box 587
Taylorsville, NC 28681, USA

Gant, Kenny (Football Player)
Dallas Cowboys
8639 N Himes Ave Apt 2301
Tampa, FL 33614-1623, USA

Gant, Reuben (Football Player)
Buffalo Bills
PO Box 3051
Tulsa, OK 74101-3051, USA

Gant, Robert (Actor)
c/o Staff Member *Mythgarden*
11026 Ventura Blvd Ste 8
Studio City, CA 91604-3570, USA

Gant, Ronald E (Ron) (Baseball Player)
Atlanta Braves
1090 Olde Towne Ln
Woodstock, GA 30189-8187, USA

Gantin, Bernardin Cardinal (Religious Leader)
Congregation for Bishops
Plazza Pio XII 10
Rome 00193, ITALY

Gantner, Jim (Baseball Player)
Milwaukee Brewers
PO Box 156
Eden, WI 53019-0156, USA

Gantos, Jack (Writer)
Farrar Straus Giroux
19 Union Sq W Fl 11
New York, NY 10003-3304, USA

Gantt, Greg (Football Player)
New York Jets
6400 Glenview Cir
Gardendale, AL 35071-2102, USA

Gantt, Harvey
RR 1 Box 587
Taylorsville, NC 28681, USA

Gantt, Jerry (Football Player)
Buffalo Bills
1511 Atwick Dr
Fayetteville, NC 28304-3901, USA

Ganz, Bruno (Actor)
Mgmt Ema Baumbauer
Keplerstrasse 2
Munich 81679, GERMANY

Ganzel, Teresa (Actor)
Irv Schechter
9300 Wilshire Blvd # 410
Beverly Hills, CA 90212-3213, USA

Gao, Xiang (Musician)
Columbia Artists Mgmt Inc
1790 Broadway Fl 6
New York, NY 10019-1412, USA

Gao, Xingjian (Nobel Prize Laureate)
Chinese University of Hong Kong Press
Shatin
Hong Kong, CHINA

Gaona, Jessica (Actor)
c/o Staff Member *Abrams Artists Agency (LA)*
9200 W Sunset Blvd Ph 11
Los Angeles, CA 90069-3601, USA

Gap Band, The
89 5th Ave Ste 700
New York, NY 10003-3020, USA

Garabaldi, Bob
2143 Oregon Ave
Stockton, CA 95204-4617, USA

Garagiola, Joe (Baseball Player)
Milwaukee Brewers
7433 E Tuckey Ln
Scottsdale, AZ 85250-4640, USA

Garagozzo, Keith (Baseball Player)
Cincinnati Reds
16 Foxcroft Way
Mount Laurel, NJ 08054-5732, USA

Garai, Romola (Actor)
c/o Staff Member *Creative Artists Agency LCC (CAA-LA)*
2000 Avenue Of The Stars
Los Angeles, CA 90067-4700, USA

Garalczyk, Mark (Football Player)
St Louis Cardinals
8096 N 85th Way Ste 101
Scottsdale, AZ 85258-4322, USA

Garan, Ronald J Jr (Astronaut)
2002 Sea Cove Ct
Houston, TX 77058-4228, USA

Garant, Robert Ben (Actor, Director, Producer, Writer)
c/o Joseph Cohen *Creative Artists Agency LCC (CAA-LA)*
2000 Avenue Of The Stars
Los Angeles, CA 90067-4700, USA

Garas, Kaz (Actor)
10145 N Buchanan Ave
Portland, OR 97203, USA

Garavito, R Michael (Misc)
Michigan State University
Biochemistry Dept
East Lansing, MI 48824, USA

Garbage (Music Group)
c/o Staff Member *Creative Artists Agency LCC (CAA-LA)*
2000 Avenue Of The Stars
Los Angeles, CA 90067-4700, USA

Garbarek, Jan (Musician)
Niels Juels Gate 42
Oslo 0257, NORWAY

Garber, H Eugene (Gene) (Baseball Player)
Pittsburgh Pirates
771 Stonemill Dr
Elizabethtown, PA 17022-9717, USA

Garber, Terri (Actor)
Metropolitan Talent Agency
4500 Wilshire Blvd Fl 2
Los Angeles, CA 90010-3858, USA

Garber, Victor (Actor)
c/o Bill Butler *Gersh Agency, The (NY)*
41 Madison Ave Fl 33
New York, NY 10010-2202, USA

Garbowski, Alex (Baseball Player)
Detroit Tigers
100 Oak Ridge Dr
Putnam Valley, NY 10579-1325, USA

Garces, Paula (Actor)
c/o Staff Member *Untitled Entertainment (NY)*
322 8th Ave Ste 601
New York, NY 10001-6715, USA

Garces, Rich (Baseball Player)
Minnesota Twins
605 Swigert St
Kerrville, TX 78028-3140, USA

Garcetti, Gil
139 N Cliffwood Ave
Los Angeles, CA 90049-2613, USA

Garci, Jose Luis (Director)
Direccion General del Libro
Paseo de la Castellana 109
Madrid 16, SPAIN

Garcia, Adam (Actor)
c/o Peter Safran *The Safran Company*
9150 Wilshire Blvd Ste 350
Beverly Hills, CA 90212-3453, USA

Garcia, Aimee (Actor)
c/o Staff Member *Essential Talent Management*
6399 Wilshire Blvd Ste 400
Los Angeles, CA 90048-5716, USA

Garcia, Andy (Actor, Musician)
c/o Staff Member *CineSon Productions Inc*
4519 Varna Ave
Sherman Oaks, CA 91423-3127, USA

Garcia, Armand (Actor)
c/o Rob D'Avola *Identity Talent Agency (ID)*
9107 Wilshire Blvd Ste 450
Beverly Hills, CA 90210-5535, USA

Garcia, Danna (Actor)
c/o Staff Member *Telemundo*
2470 W 8th Ave
Hialeah, FL 33010-2000, USA

Garcia, Danny (Baseball Player)
Kansas City Royals
274 Fairhaven Mall Apt A8
Jericho, NY 11753-2446, USA

Garcia, David (Dave) (Baseball Player)
15420 Olde Highway 80 Spc 19
El Cajon, CA 92021-2412, USA

Garcia, Eddie (Football Player)
Green Bay Packers
4914 Oreilly Rd
Omro, WI 54963, USA

Garcia, Freddy A (Baseball Player)
Quisquella Qta
Etapa M22 #52
La Romana, DOMINICAN REPUBLIC

Garcia, James (Football Player)
Cleveland Browns
999 E Basse Rd Ste 180
San Antonio, TX 78209-1807, USA

Garcia, Jeff (Football Player)
c/o Team Member *Cleveland Browns*
76 Lou Groza Blvd
Berea, OH 44017-1269, USA

Garcia, Jesus (Actor)
c/o Staff Member *Columbia Artists Mgmt Inc*
1790 Broadway Fl 6
New York, NY 10019-1412, USA

Garcia, JoAnna (Actor)
c/o Staff Member *Lovett Management*
1327 Brinkley Ave
Los Angeles, CA 90049-3619, USA

Garcia, Jorge (Actor)
c/o Erik Kritzer *Fenton-Kritzer Entertainment*
8840 Wilshire Blvd Fl 3
Beverly Hills, CA 90211-2606, USA

Garcia, Jsu (Actor)
c/o Devin Klein *Carlyle Productions & Management*
2050 Laurel Canyon Blvd
Los Angeles, CA 90046-2065, USA

Garcia, Juan Carlos (Actor)
c/o Gabriel Blanco *Gabriel Blanco Iglesias (Mexico)*
Rio Balsas 35-32
Colonia Cuauhtemoc
DF 06500, MEXICO

Garcia, Karim (Athlete, Baseball Player)
c/o Staff Member *Cleveland Indians*
2401 Ontario St
Jacobs Field
Cleveland, OH 44115-4003, USA

Garcia, Kiko (Baseball Player)
Baltimore Orioles
526 Trailview Cir
Martinez, CA 94553-3563, USA

Garcia, Leonardo (Actor)
c/o Staff Member *TV Azteca*
Periferico Sur 4121
Colonia Fuentes del Pedregal
DF CP 14141, MEXICO

Garcia, Lilian
1100 Valley Brook Ave
Lyndhurst, NJ 07071-3620, USA

Garcia, Nina (Business Person, Designer)
Elle Magazine
1633 Broadway Fl 44
New York, NY 10019-6708, USA

Garcia, Odalys (Actor)
c/o Staff Member *Univision*
605 3rd Ave Fl 12
New York, NY 10158-1299, USA

Garcia, Pedro (Baseball Player)
L4 Parq Del Condado
Caguas, PR 00727-1224, USA

Garcia, Ralph (Baseball Player)
San Diego Padres
7441 Brian Ln
La Palma, CA 90623-1312, USA

Garcia, Ramon (Baseball Player)
Washington Senators
Hatuey 259 E Oriente Camaguey Arroyo
Havana, CUBA

Garcia, Rich (Baseball Player)
PO Box 3276
Clearwater Beach, FL 33767-8276, USA

Garcia, Rodrigo (Director)
c/o Adriana Alberghetti *Endeavor Agency LLC (LA)*
9601 Wilshire Blvd Fl 3
Beverly Hills, CA 90210-5204, USA

Garcia, Russ
7920 W Sunset Blvd Ste 300
Los Angeles, CA 90046-3300, USA

Garcia Marquez, Gabriel (Nobel Prize Laureate)
Fuego 144
Pedregal de San Angel
Mexico City, DF, MEXICO

Garcia Posey, Tyler (Actor)
c/o Staff Member *SDB Partners Inc*
1801 Avenue Of The Stars Ste 902
Los Angeles, CA 90067-5981, USA

Garciaparra, Nomar (Baseball Player)
Boston Red Sox
120 16th St
Manhattan Beach, CA 90266-4617, USA

Gardeazabal, Marcela (Actor)
c/o Staff Member *TV Caracol*
Calle 76 #11 - 35
Piso 10AA
Bogota DC 26484, COLOMBIA

Gardell, Billy (Actor)
c/o Paul Santana *Agency for the Performing Arts (APA-LA)*
405 S Beverly Dr
Beverly Hills, CA 90212-4416, USA

Gardella, Al (Baseball Player)
4367 SW 10th Pl Apt 106
Deerfield Beach, FL 33442-8330, USA

Gardener, Daryl (Football Player)
Miami Dolphins
9045 Willow Springs Ln
Conroe, TX 77302-3453, USA

Gardenhire, Ronald C (Ron) (Baseball Player)
New York Mets
668 County Road B2 E
Little Canada, MN 55117-1611, USA

Gardin, Ron (Football Player)
Baltimore Colts
PO Box 66051
Tucson, AZ 85728-6051, USA

Gardiner, John Eliot (Conductor)
Gore Farm
Ashmore
Salisbury, Wilts SP5 5AR, UNITED KINGDOM (UK)

Gardiner, Mike (Baseball Player)
Seattle Mariners
26 Read Dr
Hanover, MA 02339-2632, USA

Gardiner, Robert K A (Misc)
PO Box 9274
The Airport
Accra, GHANA

Gardner, Art (Baseball Player)
Houston Astros
RR 2 Box 41
Walnut Grove, MS 39189, USA

Gardner, Ashley (Actor)
S M S Talent
8730 W Sunset Blvd Ste 440
Los Angeles, CA 90069-2277, USA

Gardner, Barry (Football Player)
Philadelphia Eagles
15415 Ashland Ave
Harvey, IL 60426-3620, USA

Gardner, Calvin P (Cal) (Hockey Player)
1979 Remo Dr
Brights Grove, ON N0N 1C0, CANADA

Gardner, Carl (Musician)
Veta Gardner
1661 SE Goucho Ave
Port Saint Lucie, FL 34952-4943, USA

Gardner, Carwell (Football Player)
Buffalo Bills
9603 Galene Dr
Louisville, KY 40299-3231, USA

Gardner, Chris (Baseball Player)
Houston Astros
2304 SW Abalon Cir
Port Saint Lucie, FL 34953-5718, USA

Gardner, Christopher (Writer)
Rubenstein Communications
1345 Avenue Of The Americas Fl 30
C/O Rachel Nagler
New York, NY 10105-0109, USA

Gardner, Dale (Astronaut)
c/o Staff Member *NASA*
2101 Nasa Pkwy
Johnson Space Center
Houston, TX 77058-3691, USA

Gardner, David P (Educator)
Hewlett Foundation
2121 Sand Hill Rd
Menlo Park, CA 94025-6909, USA

Gardner, Guy S (Astronaut)
PO Box 2730
Gainesville, GA 30503-2730, USA

Gardner, Howard E (Physicist)
Harvard University
Graduate Education School
Cambridge, MA 02138, USA

Gardner, James H (Basketball Player, Coach)
5465 Bromely Dr
Oak Park, CA 91377-4750, USA

Gardner, Jeff (Baseball Player)
New York Mets
1906 Port Weybridge Pl
Newport Beach, CA 92660-5431, USA

Gardner, John (Dancer)
American Ballet Theatre
890 Broadway
New York, NY 10003-1278, USA

Gardner, Lee (Baseball Player)
Tampa Bay Devil Rays
2215 Fenton Rd
Hartland, MI 48353-3105, USA

Gardner, Mark (Baseball Player)
Montreal Expos
489 Burgan Ave
Clovis, CA 93611-0610, USA

Gardner, Moe (Football Player)
Atlanta Falcons
240 May Apple Ln
Alpharetta, GA 30005-6903, USA

Gardner, Randy (Figure Skater)
4640 Glencove Ave #6
Marina Del Rey, CA 90291, USA

Gardner, Rob (Baseball Player)
New York Mets
727 Via Tripoli Apt 123
Punta Gorda, FL 33950-6794, USA

Gardner, Rod (Football Player)
Washington Redskins
5720 Perry St
Jacksonville, FL 32208-5136, USA

Gardner, Rulon (Wrestler)
6791 Brook Forest Dr
Evergreen, CO 80439-6827, USA

Gardner, W Booth (Governor)
801 2nd Ave Ste 1300
Norton Building
Seattle, WA 98104-1517, USA

Gardner, Wee Willie
400 E Van Buren St Ste 300
Phoenix, AZ 85004-2257, USA

Gardner, Wes (Baseball Player)
New York Mets
2 River Crest Cir
Benton, AR 72019-2175, USA

Gardner, Wilford R (Physicist)
University of California
Natural Resources College
Berkeley, CA 94720-0001, USA

Gardner, William F (Billy) (Baseball Player)
New York Giants
35 Dayton Rd
Waterford, CT 06385-4205, USA

Gardocki, Christopher A (Chris) (Football Player)
Pittsburgh Steelers
3400 S Water St
Pittsburgh, PA 15203-2349, USA

Gare, Danny (Hockey Player)
60 E Spring St Apt 312
Columbus, OH 43215-7523, USA

Garelick, Jeremy (Producer)
c/o Staff Member *Principato/Young Management*
9665 Wilshire Blvd Ste 500
Beverly Hills, CA 90212-2312, USA

Garewal, Simi (Actor, Bollywood)
Paviova 6th Floor Little Gibb's Road
Malabar Hill
Bombay, MS 400 006, INDIA

Garfat, Jance (Musician)
Artists Int'l Mgmt
9850 Sandalwood Blvd #458
Boca Raton, FL 33428, USA

Garfield, Allen
8271 Melrose Ave Ste 202
Los Angeles, CA 90046-6826, USA

Garfinkle, David (Producer)
c/o Staff Member *Renegade 83 Entertainment*
5700 Wilshire Blvd
6th Floor
Los Angeles, CA 90036-3659, USA

Garfunkel, Art (Actor, Musician)
c/o Staff Member *William Morris Agency (WMA-LA)*
1 William Morris Pl
Beverly Hills, CA 90212-4261, USA

Garity, Troy (Actor)
c/o William Choi *Management 360*
9111 Wilshire Blvd
Beverly Hills, CA 90210-5508, USA

Garland, Beverly (Actor)
8014 Briar Summit Dr
Los Angeles, CA 90046-1127, USA

Garland, Carrington
8014 Briar Summit Dr
Los Angeles, CA 90046-1127, USA

Garland, George D (Physicist)
5 Mawhiney Court
Huntsville, ON P0A 1K0, CANADA

Garland, Jon (Baseball Player)
Chicago White Sox
16833 Armstead St
Granada Hills, CA 91344-2704, USA

Garland, Merrick B (Judge)
US Court of Appeals
333 Constitution Ave NW
Washington, DC 20001-2866, USA

Garland, Wayne (Baseball Player)
Baltimore Orioles
1026 Ridgegreen Loop N
Lakeland, FL 33809-0866, USA

Garlick, Jessica (Musician)
c/o Staff Member *Pop Idol (Fremantle Media)*
2700 Colorado Ave Ste 450
Santa Monica, CA 90404-3599, USA

Garlick, Scott (Soccer Player)
Colorado Rapids
1000 Chopper Cir
Denver, CO 80204-5805, USA

Garlin, Jeff (Actor, Producer)
c/o Staff Member *3 Arts Entertainment Inc*
9460 Wilshire Blvd Fl 7
Beverly Hills, CA 90212-2713, USA

Garlits, Donald G (Big Daddy) (Race Car Driver)
Garlits Racing Museum
13700 SW 16th Ave
Ocala, FL 34473-3970, USA

Garmaker, Dick (Basketball Player)
5824 E 11th St
Tulsa, OK 74137, USA

Garman, Mike (Baseball Player)
Boston Red Sox
15144 Kings Row Rd
Caldwell, ID 83607-8371, USA

Garman-Hosted, Ann (Baseball Player)
6582 N 100 E
Wawaka, IN 46794-9724, USA

Garmann, Greg (Actor)
8383 Wilshire Blvd Ste 550
Beverly Hills, CA 90211-2417, USA

Garn, E Jacob (Jake) (Astronaut, Senator)
1626 Yale Ave
Salt Lake City, UT 84105-1720, USA

Garn, Jake (Ex-Senator, Senator)
500 Huntsman Way
Salt Lake City, UT 84108-1235, USA

Garn, Stanley M (Misc)
1200 Earhart Rd # 223
Ann Arbor, MI 48105-2768, USA

Garneau, Marc (Astronaut)
Space Agency
6767 Route de Aeroport
Sainte-Hubert, PQ J3Y 8Y9, CANADA

Garner, Charlie (Football Player)
Philadelphia Eagles
12944 Royal George Ave
Odessa, FL 33556-5709, USA

Garner, James (Actor)
c/o Bill Robinson *Bill Robinson Management*
PO Box 6284
Malibu, CA 90264-6284, USA

Garner, Jennifer (Actor)
c/o Nicole King *Management 360*
9111 Wilshire Blvd
Beverly Hills, CA 90210-5508, USA

Garner, Kelli (Actor)
c/o Alissa Vradenburg *Untitled Entertainment (LA)*
331 N Maple Dr Fl 3
Beverly Hills, CA 90210-3827, USA

Garner, Philip M (Phil) (Baseball Player)
c/o Staff Member *Houston Astros*
501 Crawford St
Astros Field
Houston, TX 77002-2113, USA

Garner, Wendell R (Physicist)
PO Box 650
Branford, CT 06405-0650, USA

Garner, William S (Cartoonist)
Memphis Commercial Appeal
495 Union Ave
Editorial Dept
Memphis, TN 38103-3217, USA

Garnes, Sam (Football Player)
New York Giants
101 Hearthstone Dr
West Milford, NJ 07480-3751, USA

Garnett, Dave (Football Player)
Minnesota Vikings
4527 Tyrone Ave
Sherman Oaks, CA 91423-2628, USA

Garnett, Kevin (Basketball Player)
Minnesota Timberwolves
600 1st Ave N
Target Center
Minneapolis, MN 55403-1416, USA

Garnett, Winfield (Football Player)
Minnesota Vikings
2029 S 16th Ave
Broadview, IL 60155-3015, USA

Garofalo, Janeane (Actor)
c/o Dave Rath *Generate Management*
1545 26th St # 200
Santa Monica, CA 90404-5557, USA

Garouste, Gerard (Artist)
La Mesangere
Marcilly-sur-Eure 27810, FRANCE

Garr, Ralph A (Baseball Player)
Atlanta Braves
22314 Auburn Canyon Ln
Richmond, TX 77469-5639, USA

Garr, Teri (Terri/Terry) (Actor)
c/o Chris Schmidt *Paradigm (LA)*
360 N Crescent Dr
North Bldg
Beverly Hills, CA 90210-6820, USA

Garrahy, J Joseph (Governor)
250 Centerville Rd Bldg B
Warwick, RI 02886-4353, USA

Garrard, Rose (Artist)
105 Carpenters Road
#21
London E18, UNITED KINGDOM (UK)

Garreis, Robert M (Geophysicist, Physicist)
South Florida University
Marine Science Dept
Saint Petersburg, FL 33701, USA

Garrelts, Scott (Baseball Player)
San Francisco Giants
11070 Ashland Way
Shreveport, LA 71106-9348, USA

Garret, Peter (Musician)
PO Box 249
Maroubra, NSW 2035, AUSTRALIA

Garrett, Adrian (Baseball Player)
Atlanta Braves
PO Box 201
Manchaca, TX 78652-0201, USA

Garrett, Alvin (Football Player)
New York Giants
2600 Napoleon Ct
Birmingham, AL 35243-5452, USA

Garrett, Beau (Actor)
c/o Sean Fay *Imparato Fay Management*
1126 Roxbury Dr
Los Angeles, CA 90035-1031, USA

Garrett, Betty (Actor, Musician)
3231 Oakdell Rd
Studio City, CA 91604-4222, USA

Garrett, Brad (Actor, Comedian)
c/o Glen Robbins *Raw Talent Management*
9615 Brighton Way Ste 300
Beverly Hills, CA 90210-5118, USA

Garrett, Carl (Football Player)
Boston Patriots
314 Teal St
Pittsburg, TX 75686-1530, USA

Garrett, Clifton (Baseball Player)
Bowman
7504 Kennicott Ln
Plainfield, IL 60586-4173, USA

Garrett, George P Jr (Writer)
1845 Wayside Pl
Charlottesville, VA 22903-1630, USA

Garrett, Jason (Football Player)
Dallas Cowboys
3512 Lindenwood Ave
Dallas, TX 75205-3230, USA

Garrett, Jeremy (Actor)
c/o Staff Member *Paradigm (LA)*
360 N Crescent Dr
North Bldg
Beverly Hills, CA 90210-6820, USA

Garrett, John (Football Player)
University of Virginia Football
PO Box 400837
McCue Center
Charlottesville, VA 22904-4837, USA

Garrett, Judd (Football Player)
Dallas Cowboys
18 Spring Mill Woods Ct
Saint Charles, MO 63303-1343, USA

Garrett, Kathleen (Actor)
The Agency
1800 Avenue Of Stars Ste 400
Los Angeles, CA 90067-4206, USA

Garrett, Kenneth (Photographer)
National Geographic Magazine
1145 17th St NW
Washington, DC 20036-4688, USA

Garrett, Kenny (Musician)
Von Productions
1915 Cullen Ave
Austin, TX 78757-2435, USA

Garrett, Leif (Actor, Musician)
Barbara Papageorge
790 Amsterdam Ave Apt 4E
New York, NY 10025-5710, USA

Garrett, Len (Football Player)
Green Bay Packers
9413 W Tampa Dr
Baton Rouge, LA 70815-8951, USA

Garrett, Lesley (Opera Singer)
PV Productions
Park Offices
121 Dora Road
London SW19 7JT, UNITED KINGDOM
(UK)

Garrett, Lila (Director)
1245 Laurel Way
Beverly Hills, CA 90210, USA

Garrett, Michael L (Mike) (Football
Player)
Kansas City Chiefs
University Of Southern California Athletic
Dept
Los Angeles, CA 90089-0001, USA

Garrett, Mike S (Football Player)
Baltimore Colts
1040 Dogwood Dr
Greensboro, GA 30642-4827, USA

Garrett, MJ (Reality TV Star)
c/o Michael (Mike) Esterman *Esterman
Entertainment*
214 Park Rd
Riva, MD 21140-1224, USA

Garrett, Pat (Musician, Songwriter,
Writer)
Patrick Sickafus
PO Box 84
Strausstown, PA 19559-0084, USA

Garrett, Reggie (Football Player)
Pittsburgh Steelers
3 Martino Way
Somerset, NJ 08873-4952, USA

Garrett, Wayne (Baseball Player)
New York Mets
4331 Linwood St
Sarasota, FL 34232-3905, USA

Garrett, Wilbur E (Editor)
National Geographic Magazine
17th & M Sts
Washington, DC 20036, USA

Garrett, William E (Photographer)
209 Seneca Rd
Great Falls, VA 22066-1108, USA

Garrett III, H Lawrence (Government
Official)
RR 1 Box 136-18
Boyce, VA 22620, USA

Garrido, Gil (Baseball Player)
San Francisco Giants
PO Box 527948
Miami, FL 33152-7948, USA

Garrido, Norberto (Football Player)
Carolina Panthers
15633 Briarbank St
La Puente, CA 91744-1106, USA

Garriott, Owen K (Astronaut)
111 Lost Tree Dr SW
Huntsville, AL 35824-1313, USA

Garrison, David (Actor)
630 Estrada Redonda
Santa Fe, NM 87506, USA

Garrison, Gary (Football Player)
San Diego Chargers
25 Aliso Rd
Carmel Valley, CA 93924-9442, USA

Garrison, John (Hockey Player)
Old Concord Road
Lincoln, MA 01773, USA

Garrison, Lane (Actor)
c/o Dannielle Thomas *Untitled
Entertainment (LA)*
331 N Maple Dr Fl 3
Beverly Hills, CA 90210-3827, USA

Garrison, Walt (Football Player)
San Diego Chargers
187 E Hickory Hill Rd
Argyle, TX 76226, USA

Garrison, Webster (Baseball Player)
Oakland A's
2038 Rue Racine
Marrero, LA 70072-4729, USA

Garrison-Jackson, Zina (Tennis Player)
1701 Hermann Dr Unit 705
Houston, TX 77004-7348, USA

Garrity, Gregg (Football Player)
Pittsburgh Steelers
86 Seldom Seen Rd
Bradfordwoods, PA 15015-1320, USA

Garron, Larry (Football Player)
Boston Patriots
987 Pleasant St
Framingham, MA 01701-8853, USA

Garron, Leon (Football Player)
Buffalo Bills
2051 S Woodlawn Dr # A
Mobile, AL 36605-2385, USA

Garrum, Larry (Hockey Player)
987 Pleasant St
Framingham, MA 01701-8853, USA

Garson, Willie (Actor)
Writers & Artists
360 N Crescent Dr Bldg North
Beverly Hills, CA 90210-6818, USA

Garten, Ina (Writer)
Clarkson Potter
1745 Broadway
Author Mail
New York, NY 10019-4305, USA

Garth, Jennie (Actor)
c/o Randy James *James/Levy/Jacobson
Management*
3500 W Olive Ave Ste 1470
Burbank, CA 91505-5514, USA

Garth, Leonard I (Judge)
US Court of Appeals
50 Walnut St Rm 5040
US Courthouse
Newark, NJ 07102-3571, USA

Gartner, Claus-Theo
Postfach 230313
Essen 45071, GERMANY

Gartner, Mike (Hockey Player)
NHL Players Association
2400-777 Bay St
Toronto, ON M5G 2C8, CANADA

Garver, Cathy (Actor)
550 Mountain Home Rd
Woodside, CA 94062-2515, USA

Garver, Kathy (Actor)
c/o Staff Member *The Morgan Agency*
1200 N Doheny Dr
Los Angeles, CA 90069-1723, USA

Garver, Ned F (Baseball Player)
St Louis Cardinals
1121 Town Line Rd Unit 164
Bryan, OH 43506-8732, USA

Garvey, Steve (Baseball Player)
1806 Watermere Ln
Windermere, FL 34786-6121, USA

Garvey-Truhan, Cyndy
13924 Panay Way Apt 309
Marina Del Rey, CA 90292-6196, USA

Garvin, Jerry (Baseball Player)
Toronto Blue Jays
1082 Perazzo Cir
Folsom, CA 95630-7667, USA

Garwin, Richard L (Physicist)
16 Ridgecrest E
Scarsdale, NY 10583-2012, USA

Garwood, William L (Will) (Judge)
US Court of Appeals
903 San Jacinto Blvd
Austin, TX 78701-2449, USA

Gary, Cleveland (Football Player)
Los Angeles Rams
720 SE Martin Luther King Jr Blvd
Stuart, FL 34994-2310, USA

Gary, Cleveland E (Football Player)
1446 SW 169th Ave
Indiantown, FL 37956, USA

Gary, Keith (Football Player)
Pittsburgh Steelers
450 Massachusetts Ave NW Apt 903
Washington, DC 20001-6220, USA

Gary, Lorraine (Actor)
1158 Tower Rd
Beverly Hills, CA 90210-2131, USA

Garza, David (Musician)
Partisan Arts
PO Box 5085
Larkspur, CA 94977-5085, USA

Garza, Emilio M (Judge)
US Court of Appeals
US Courthouse
8200 1-10 W
San Antonio, TX 78230, USA

Garza, Nicole (Actor)
c/o Todd Neville *Agency for the
Performing Arts (APA-LA)*
405 S Beverly Dr
Beverly Hills, CA 90212-4416, USA

Gascoigne, Paul J (Soccer Player)
Arran Gardner
Holborn Hall
10 Grays Inn Road
London WC1X 8BY, UNITED KINGDOM
(UK)

Gascoine, Jill (Actor)
Marina Martin
12/13 Poland St
London W1V 3DE, UNITED KINGDOM
(UK)

Gascolgne, Sheryl
Stanstead Abbots
Hertfordshire, ENGLAND, UNITED
KINGDOM (UK)

Gascon, Elleen (Baseball Player)
249 Trowbridge Rd
Elk Grove Village, IL 60007-3820, USA

Gash, Samuel L (Sam) (Football Player)
New England Patriots
721 Prince Dr
Hendersonville, NC 28791, USA

Gash, Thane (Football Player)
Cleveland Browns
201 Whispering Hills Dr
Hendersonville, NC 28792-1213, USA

Gaskill, Brian (Actor)
c/o Todd Neville *Agency for the
Performing Arts (APA-LA)*
405 S Beverly Dr
Beverly Hills, CA 90212-4416, USA

Gasol, Pau (Basketball Player)
Memphis Grizzlies
191 Beale St
Memphis, TN 38103-3715, USA

Gaspar, Rod (Baseball Player)
New York Mets
28771 Peach Blossom
Mission Viejo, CA 92692-1072, USA

Gaspari, Rich (Misc)
PO Box 29
Milltown, NJ 08850-0029, USA

Gass, William H (Writer)
6304 Westminster Pl
Saint Louis, MO 63130-4727, USA

Gassert, Ron (Football Player)
Green Bay Packers
11 Sheffield Pl
Southampton, NJ 08088-1306, USA

Gasslyev, Nikolal T (Opera Singer)
Mariinsky Theater
Teartainaya Pl 1
Saint Petersburg, RUSSIA

Gassman, Alessandro (Actor)
Christian Cucchini Mgmt
Lungotevere del Mellini 10
Rome 00193, ITALY

Gast, Leon (Director)
William Morris Agency
151 El Camino Dr
Beverly Hills, CA 90212-2775, USA

Gasteyer, Ana (Actor, Comedian)
c/o Jennifer Craig *Gersh Agency, The (LA)*
232 N Canon Dr
Beverly Hills, CA 90210-5302, USA

Gastineau, Brittny (Actor, Reality TV Star)
c/o Staff Member *True Entertainment*
435 W 19th St
New York, NY 10011-3803, USA

Gastineau, Lisa (Actor, Reality TV Star)
c/o Staff Member *True Entertainment*
435 W 19th St
New York, NY 10011-3803, USA

Gastineau, Marcus D (Mark) (Football
Player)
National Athelets Organization
1806 Watermere Ln
Windermere, FL 34786-6121, USA

Gaston, Clarence E (Cito) (Baseball
Player)
Atlanta Braves
2 Blyth Dale Rd
Toronto, ON M4N 3M2, CANADA

Gaston, Hiram (Baseball Player)
Birmingham Black Barons
18 Burntwood Cres
Winnipeg, AB R2J 3A1, CANADA

Gately, Stephen (Musician)
Carol Assoc-War Mgmt
Bushy Park Road
57 Meadowbanl
Dublin, IRELAND

Gates, Bill (Business Person)
c/o Staff Member *Microsoft Corporation*
1 Microsoft Way
Redmond, WA 98052-8300, USA

Gates, Brent (Baseball Player)
Oakland A's
234 Grayfield Ct SE
Ada, MI 49301-9162, USA

Gates, Daryl
24876 Sunstar Ln
Dana Point, CA 92629-1930, USA

Gates, David (Musician, Songwriter, Writer)
Paradise Artists
108 E Matilija St
Ojai, CA 93023-2639, USA

Gates, Gareth (Musician)
c/o Staff Member *Pop Idol (Fremantle Media)*
2700 Colorado Ave Ste 450
Santa Monica, CA 90404-3599, USA

Gates, Henry Lewis Jr (Educator)
Harvard University
Afro-American Studies Dept
Cambridge, MA 02138, USA

Gates, Joe (Baseball Player)
Chicago White Sox
1517 E 19th Ave
Gary, IN 46407-1607, USA

Gates, Mike (Baseball Player)
Montreal Expos
131 Edgewater Rd
Kooskia, ID 83539-5024, USA

Gates, Robert M (Educator, Government Official)
Texas A&M University
President's Office
College Station, TX 77843-0001, USA

Gatewood, Aubrey (Baseball Player)
Los Angeles Dodgers
5 Pine Tree Loop
North Little Rock, AR 72116-8313, USA

Gatewood, Les (Football Player)
Green Bay Packers
PO Box 414
Kirbyville, TX 75956-0414, USA

Gatewood, Tom (Football Player)
New York Giants
1040 1st Ave Apt 333
New York, NY 10022-2991, USA

Gatlin, Justin (Athlete, Track Athlete)
c/o Staff Member *USA Track & Field*
1 Rca Dome Ste 140
Indianapolis, IN 46225-1023, USA

Gatlin, Larry
5100 Harris Ave
Kansas City, MO 64133-2331, USA

Gatlin, Larry W (Musician, Songwriter, Writer)
McLachlan-Scruggs
2821 Bransford Ave
Nashville, TN 37204-3101, USA

Gatti, Arturo (Boxer)
3208 Bergenline Ave
Union City, NJ 07087-3929, USA

Gatti, Jennifer (Actor)
S D B Partners
1801 Avenue Of Stars Ste 902
Los Angeles, CA 90067-5981, USA

Gatting, Michael W (Cricketer)
Middlesex Cricket Club
Saint John's Wood Road
London NW8 8QN, UNITED KINGDOM
(UK)

Gattorno, Francisco (Actor)
c/o Gabriel Blanco *Gabriel Blanco Iglesias (Mexico)*
Rio Balsas 35-32
Colonia Cuauhtemoc
DF 06500, MEXICO

Gaubatz, Dennis (Football Player)
Detroit Lions
1250 County Road 943
West Columbia, TX 77486-9454, USA

Gaucho, Ronaldinho (Soccer Player)
Futbol Club Barcelona
Avenida Aristides Mailol
Barcelona 08028, SPAIN

Gauci, Miriam (Opera Singer)
Kunstleragentur Raab & Bohm
Plankengasse 7
Vienna 1010, AUSTRIA

Gaudet, Jim (Baseball Player)
Kansas City Royals
3336 Vineville Ave
Macon, GA 31204-2328, USA

Gaudiani, Claire L (Educator)
53 Neptune Dr
Groton, CT 06340-5421, USA

Gaudin, Chad (Baseball Player)
c/o Staff Member *Oakland Athletics*
7000 Coliseum Way
Oakland, CA 94621-1992, USA

Gaudio, Robert (Football Player)
Cleveland Browns
8090 SW 143rd St
Palmetto Bay, FL 33158-1567, USA

Gaul, Frank (Football Player)
New York Bulldogs
3420 Balsam Dr
Westlake, OH 44145-4407, USA

Gaul, Gilbert M (Journalist)
Philadelphia Inquirer
400 N Broad St
Editorial Dept
Philadelphia, PA 19130-4099, USA

Gault, William Campbell (Writer)
481 Mountain Dr
Santa Barbara, CA 93103-1700, USA

Gault, Willie J (Football Player)
Chicago Bears
PO Box 10759
Marina Del Rey, CA 90295-6759, USA

Gaurav, Kumar (Actor)
Dimple 7 Pali Hill
Bandra
Bombay, MS 400 050, INDIA

Gauthreaux, Joe (DJ)
c/o Staff Member *Diva Central Inc*
7510 W Sunset Blvd Ste 1445
Los Angeles, CA 90046-3408, USA

Gautier, Dick (Actor)
11333 Moor Park St # 59
N Hollywood, CA 91602-2618, USA

Gava, Cassandra (Actor)
1745 Camino Palmero St Apt 210
Los Angeles, CA 90046-2918, USA

Gavaskar, Sunil M (Cricketer)
40 Bhalchandra Road #A Dadar
Bombay, MS 400014, INDIA

Gavilan, Kid
1 Hall Of Fame Dr
Canastota, NY 13032-1175, USA

Gavin, Charles E (Football Player)
Denver Broncos
1800 Grape St
Denver, CO 80220, USA

Gavin, Diarmuid (Actor)
c/o Staff Member *John Noel Management*
10A Belmont St
Floor 2
London NW1 8HH, UNITED KINGDOM
(UK)

Gavin, John (Actor, Diplomat)
2100 Century Park W # 10263
Los Angeles, CA 90067-6900, USA

Gaviria, Trujillo Cesar (President)
Organization of American States
17th & Constitution NW
Washington, DC 20006, USA

Gavitt, Dave (Basketball Player, Misc)
Boston Celtics
151 Merrimac St # 1
Boston, MA 02114-4714, USA

Gavrilov, Andrei V (Music Group, Musician)
Konzertdirektion Schlote
Danreitergasse 4
Salzburg 5020, GERMANY

Gay, Don
1818 Rodeo Dr
Mesquite, TX 75149-3800, USA

Gay, Everett (Football Player)
Dallas Cowboys
700 E Johnson St
Waco, TX 76705-3816, USA

Gay, George
588 Charlton Ct NW
Marietta, GA 30064-1451, USA

Gay, Gerald H (Jerry) (Journalist, Photographer)
PO Box 33848
Seattle, WA 98133-0848, USA

Gay, Peter J (Historian)
270 Riverside Dr Apt 8C
New York, NY 10025-5211, USA

Gay, William T (Football Player)
Chicago Cardinals
824 Lisdowney Dr
Lockport, IL 60441-2794, USA

Gaydos, Joey (Actor)
c/o Staff Member *Cunningham Escott Slevin & Doherty (LA)*
10635 Santa Monica Blvd Ste 130
Los Angeles, CA 90025-8306, USA

Gaydos, Kent (Football Player)
Green Bay Packers
1117 Saint Andrews Dr
Mansfield, TX 76063-2691, USA

Gaydukov, Sergei N (Astronaut, Misc)
Potchta Kosmonavtov
Moskovskoi Oblasti
Syvisdny Goroduk 141160, RUSSIA

Gayheart, Rebecca (Actor, Model)
c/o Jennifer Craig *Gersh Agency, The (LA)*
232 N Canon Dr
Beverly Hills, CA 90210-5302, USA

Gayle, Crystal (Music Group, Musician)
51 Music Sq E
Nashville, TN 37203-4324, USA

Gayle, Shaun (Football Player)
Chicago Bears
1530 N Elk Grove Ave Apt I
Chicago, IL 60622-2059, USA

Gaylor, Noel (Admiral)
2111 Mason Hill Dr
Alexandria, VA 22306-2416, USA

Gaylord, Scott
1451 Depen
Lakewood, CO 80214, USA

Gaylords, The
32630 Concord Dr
Madison Heights, MI 48071-1110, USA

Gaynes, George (Actor)
3344 Campanil Dr
Santa Barbara, CA 93109-1017, USA

Gaynor, Gloria (Music Group, Musician)
c/o Staff Member *Richard De La Font Agency*
4845 S Sheridan Rd Ste 505
Tulsa, OK 74145-5719, USA

Gaynor, Mitzi (Actor, Dancer, Music Group, Musician)
610 N Arden Dr
Beverly Hills, CA 90210-3510, USA

Gayoom, Maumoon Abdul (President)
Presidential Palace
Orchid Magu
Male 20-05, MALDIVES

Gayson, Eunice (Actor)
Spotlight
7 Leicester Place
London WC2H 7BP, UNITED KINGDOM
(UK)

Gayton, Joe (Writer)
c/o David Saunders *Agency for the Performing Arts (APA-LA)*
405 S Beverly Dr
Beverly Hills, CA 90212-4416, USA

Gayton, Tony (Writer)
c/o Matt Ochacher *Agency for the Performing Arts (APA-LA)*
405 S Beverly Dr
Beverly Hills, CA 90212-4416, USA

Gaziano, Frank (Football Player)
Boston Yanks
29 Pilot Point Rd
Cape Elizabeth, ME 04107-2808, USA

Gazit, Doron (Artist)
Air Dimensional Inc
14141 Covello St Bldg 1
Van Nuys, CA 91405-1491, USA

Gazzara, Ben (Actor)
c/o Tim Stone *Stone Manners Talent & Literary (LA)*
6500 Wilshire Blvd Ste 550
Los Angeles, CA 90048-4950, USA

Gbagbo, Laurent (President)
President's Office
Boulevard Clozel
Abidjan, IVORY COAST

Gearan, Mark (Educator, Government Official)
Hobart & William Smith College
President's Office
Geneva, NY 14456, USA

Geary, Cynthia (Actor)
Baumgarten/Prophet
1041 N Formosa Ave # 200
West Hollywood, CA 90046-6703, USA

Geary, Geoff (Baseball Player)
Philadelphia Phillies
1060 Rippey St
El Cajon, CA 92020-1738, USA

Geary, Tony
7010 Pacific View Dr
Los Angeles, CA 90068-2038, USA

Geathers, James (Football Player)
New Orleans Saints
200 Tony Dr
Georgetown, SC 29440-2059, USA

Gebhard, Bob (Baseball Player)
Minnesota Twins
5242 E Otero Pl
Centennial, CO 80122-3889, USA

Gebo, Daniel (Scientist)
Northern Illinois University
Paleontology Dept
De Kalb, IL 60115, USA

Gebrian, Pete (Baseball Player)
Chicago White Sox
811 SW South River Dr Apt 207
Stuart, FL 34997-3271, USA

Gebrselassie, Haile (Athlete, Track Athlete)
Ethiopian Athletic Federation
P O Box 3241
Addis Ababa, ETHIOPIA

Gedda, Nicolai (Opera Singer)
Valhallavagen 128
Stockholm 11441, SWEDEN

Geddes, Anne (Photographer)
Kel Geddes Management
2 York Street
Parnell
Auckland 1001, NEW ZEALAND

Geddes, Bob (Football Player)
Denver Broncos
1115 Ferrelo Rd
Santa Barbara, CA 93103-2118, USA

Geddes, Jane (Golfer)
3396 Sterling Ridge Ct
Longwood, FL 32779-3182, USA

Geddes, Jim (Baseball Player)
Chicago White Sox
6738 Harrisburg London Rd
Orient, OH 43146-9454, USA

Geddes, Ken (Football Player)
Los Angeles Rams
7702 147th Ave NE
Redmond, WA 98052-4168, USA

Gedman, Rich (Baseball Player)
Boston Red Sox
10 Parmenter Rd
Framingham, MA 01701-3019, USA

Gedney, Chris (Football Player)
Chicago Bears
4981 Boneta Rd
Medina, OH 44256-8141, USA

Gedrick, Jason (Actor)
I F A Talent Agency
8730 W Sunset Blvd Ste 490
Los Angeles, CA 90069-2248, USA

Gee, E Gordon (Educator)
Vanderbilt University
Chancellor's Office
Nashville, TN 37240-0001, USA

Gee, James D (Religious Leader)
Penecostal Church of God
4901 Pennsylvania Ave
Joplin, MO 64804-4947, USA

Gee, Kim (Musician)
c/o Staff Member *Pop Idol (Fremantle Media)*
2700 Colorado Ave Ste 450
Santa Monica, CA 90404-3599, USA

Gee, Prunella (Actor)
Michael Ladkin Mgmt
1Duchess St #1
London W1N 3DE, UNITED KINGDOM (UK)

Geer, Dennis (Financier)
Federal Deposit Insurance
550 17th St NW
Washington, DC 20429-0002, USA

Geer, Ellen (Actor)
21418 Entrada Rd
Topanga, CA 90290-3539, USA

Geertz, Clifford J (Misc)
Institute for Advanced Study
Social Science Dept
Princeton, NJ 08540, USA

Gees, Bee, The (Musician)
c/o Staff Member *William Morris Agency (WMA-LA)*
1 William Morris Pl
Beverly Hills, CA 90212-4261, USA

Geeson, Judy (Actor)
Media Artists Group
6300 Wilshire Blvd Ste 1470
Los Angeles, CA 90048-5200, USA

Geffen, Aviv
Bugroashov 26
Tel Aviv 63342, ISRAEL

Geffen, David (Business Person, Producer)
c/o Staff Member *DreamWorks SKG*
100 Universal City Plz
Universal City, CA 91608-1002, USA

Gegenhuber, John
9171 Wilshire Blvd Ste 441
Beverly Hills, CA 90210-5516, USA

Gehman, Martha
2488 Cheremoya Ave
Los Angeles, CA 90068-3070, USA

Gehring, Walter J (Doctor, Misc, Scientist)
Hochfeldstr 32
Therwill 4106, SWITZERLAND

Gehringer, Rick (Musician)
c/o Staff Member *Brothers Management Associates Inc*
141 Dunbar Ave
Fords, NJ 08863-1551, USA

Gehrke, Jack (Football Player)
Kansas City Chiefs
1253 Keystone Ranch Rd
Keystone, CO 80435, USA

Gehry, Franko O (Architect)
Gehry Partners
12541 Beatrice St
Los Angeles, CA 90066-7001, USA

Geiberger, Al (Golfer)
Professional Golfer's Assn
PO Box 109601
Palm Beach Gardens, FL 33410-9601, USA

Geiberger, Brent (Golfer)
Cross Consulting
5 Cathy Pl
Menlo Park, CA 94025-5602, USA

Geier, Philip H Jr (Business Person)
Interpublic Group
1271 Avenue Of The Americas
New York, NY 10020-1300, USA

Geiger, Ken (Journalist, Photographer)
Dallas Mornig News
Communications Center
Dallas, TX 75211, USA

Geiger, Matt (Basketball Player)
1561 Hillside Landing Dr
Tarpon Springs, FL 34688-5301, USA

Geiger, Teddy (Musician)
c/o John Geiger
11 Tamarron Way
Pittsford, NY 14534-3347, USA

Geimer, Samantha
4245 Waipua St
Kilauea, HI 96754, USA

Geingob, Hage G (Prime Minister)
Prime Minister's Office
Private Bag 13338
Windhoek 9000, NAMIBIA

Geisel, Dave (Baseball Player)
Chicago Cubs
4 Blacksmith Ln
Media, PA 19063-4411, USA

Geishert, Vern (Baseball Player)
California Angels
984 N Park St
Richland Center, WI 53581-1428, USA

Geismar, Thomas H (Architect)
Cambridge Seven Assoc
1050 Massachusetts Ave
Cambridge, MA 02138-5359, USA

Geiss, Johannes (Physicist)
University of Beme
Physics Instit Sidlerstr 5
Beme 3012, SWITZERLAND

Geissendorfer, Hans
An den Herrenbergen 21a
Neustadt/Aisch D-91413, GERMANY

Geissinger-Harding, Jean (Baseball Player)
539 Hodunk Rd
Coldwater, MI 49036-9273, USA

Geithner, Timothy (Financier)
Federal Reserve Bank
33 Liberty St
New York, NY 10045-0001, USA

Gelb, Leslie H (Educator)
Council of Foreign Relations
58 E 68th St
New York, NY 10065-5953, USA

Gelbart, Larry (Producer, Writer)
807 N Alpine Dr
Beverly Hills, CA 90210-2901, USA

Geldof, Bob (Actor, Musician)
Ten Alps Broadcasting
6 Anglers Lane
Kentish Town, London NW5 3DG, UNITED KINGDOM (UK)

Gelfant, Alan (Actor)
Peter Strain
5455 Wilshire Blvd Ste 1812
Los Angeles, CA 90036-4268, USA

Gelinas, Gratien (Actor, Writer)
316 Girouard St #207
Oka, PQ J0N 1E0, CANADA

Gell-Mann, Murray (Nobel Prize Laureate)
Santa Fe Institute
1399 Hyde Park Rd
Santa Fe, NM 87501-8943, USA

Gellar, Sarah Michelle (Actor)
c/o JoAnne Colonna *Brillstein-Grey Entertainment*
9150 Wilshire Blvd Ste 350
Beverly Hills, CA 90212-3453, USA

Geller, Uri (Actor)
c/o Staff Member *Celeb Agents*
77 Oxford St
London ON W1D 2ES, UNITED KINGDOM (UK)

Gelman, Larry (Actor)
5121 Greenbush Ave
Sherman Oaks, CA 91423-1507, USA

Gelman, Michael
7 Lincoln Sq
New York, NY 10023-6201, USA

Gelnar, John (Baseball Player)
Pittsburgh Pirates
36186 E County Road 1380
Granite, OK 73547-5120, USA

Gemma, Giuliano
Via dei Riari 66
Rome 00165, ITALY

Gems, Pam (Writer)
Cassarotto
60/66 Wardour St
London W1V 4ND, UNITED KINGDOM (UK)

Genaux, Vivica (Opera Singer)
Robert Lombardo
61 W 62nd St Apt 6F
Harkness Plaza
New York, NY 10023-7017, USA

Gendron, George (Editor)
Inc Magazine
77 N Washington St
Editorial Dept
Boston, MA 02114-1908, USA

Generation, The X
184 Glochester Pl.
London, ENGLAND NW1, UNITED KINGDOM (UK)

Genesis (Music Group)
c/o Staff Member *Hit and Run Music Ltd*
25 Ives Street
South Kensington
London SW3 2ND, UNITED KINGDOM (UK)

Genet, Sabryn
7800 Beverly Blvd # 3305
Los Angeles, CA 90036-2112, USA

Genitallica (Music Group)
c/o Staff Member *Sony Music Miami*
605 Lincoln Rd Fl 7
Miami Beach, FL 33139-2900, USA

Genovese, Eugene D (Historian)
1487 Sheridan Walk NE
Atlanta, GA 30324-3253, USA

Genovese, George (Baseball Player)
Washington Senators
11474 Erwin St
North Hollywood, CA 91606-4126, USA

Genscher, Hans-Dietrich
Am Kottenforst 16
Wachtberg 3 5307, GERMANY

Gensler, M Arthur Jr (Architect)
Gensler & Assoc Architects
550 Kearny St
San Francisco, CA 94108, USA

Gent, Peter (Football Player)
Dallas Cowboys
208 Center St
South Haven, MI 49090, USA

Gentile, Jim (Baseball Player)
Brooklyn Dodgers
1016 S Neptune Rd
Edmond, OK 73003-6071, USA

Gentry, Alvin (Basketball Player, Coach, Misc)
New Orleans Hornets
1501 Girod St
New Orleans Arena
New Orleans, LA 70113-3124, USA

Gentry, Bobbie (Music Group)
269 S Beverly Dr # 368
Beverly Hills, CA 90212-3851, USA

Gentry, Curtis (Football Player)
Chicago Bears
387 Meadow Green Ln
Round Lake Beach, IL 60073-1326, USA

Gentry, Gary (Baseball Player)
New York Mets
PO Box 44945
Phoenix, AZ 85064-4945, USA

Gentry, Harvey (Baseball Player)
New York Giants
109 Eaton Ln
Bristol, TN 37620-2820, USA

Gentry, Montgomery (Musician)
c/o Staff Member *Paradigm (Nashville)*
124 12th Ave S Ste 410
Nashville, TN 37203-3170, USA

Gentry, Race
2379 Mountain View Dr
Escondido, CA 92027-4951, USA

Gentry, Teddy W (Music Group, Musician)
PO Box 529
Fort Payne, AL 35968, USA

Gentry, Troy (Music Group)
Hallmark Direction
713 18th Ave S
Nashville, TN 37203-3214, USA

Genzel, Carrie (Actor)
Pakula/King
9229 W Sunset Blvd Ste 315
Los Angeles, CA 90069-3403, USA

Genzmer, Harald (Composer)
Eisensteinstr 10
Munich 81679, GERMANY

Geoffrin, Bernard (Boom Boom) (Hockey Player)
4431 Dobbs Ferry Crossing Dr
Marietta, GA 30068, USA

Geoffripn, Scott (Race Car Driver)
592 Explorer St Ste B
Brea, CA 92821-3137, USA

George, Alex (Baseball Player)
Kansas City A's
8432 Linden Ln
Prairie Village, KS 66207-1834, USA

George, Boy (Music Group)
McKorkindale & Holton
1-2 Langham Place
London W1A 3DD, UNITED KINGDOM (UK)

George, Chris (Baseball Player)
Milwaukee Brewers
428 Kathy Lynn Dr
Pittsburgh, PA 15239-1708, USA

George, Chris (Baseball Player)
Kansas City Royals
7520 Boudreaux Rd
Spring, TX 77379-2407, USA

George, Christopher S (Chris) (Baseball Player)
121 E Maranta Rd
Mooresville, NC 28117-6335, USA

George, Ed (Football Player)
Baltimore Colts
1460 Golden Gate Pkwy Ste 103
Naples, FL 34105-3128, USA

George, Eddie (Actor)
c/o Al Hassas *United Talent Agency (UTA)*
9560 Wilshire Blvd Ste 500
Beverly Hills, CA 90212-2401, USA

George, Eddie (Football Player)
Houston Oilers
9538 Sanctuary Pl
Brentwood, TN 37027, USA

George, Edward A J (Financier)
Bank of England
Threadneedle St
London EC2R 8AH, UNITED KINGDOM (UK)

George, Elizabeth (Writer)
William Morris Agency
151 El Camino Dr
Beverly Hills, CA 90212-2775, USA

George, Eric (Actor)
Lasher McManus Robinson
1964 Westwood Blvd Ste 400
Los Angeles, CA 90025-4695, USA

George, Francis E Cardinal (Religious Leader)
Chicago Archidiocese
1555 N State Pkwy
Chicago, IL 60610-1613, USA

George, Gotz
Terrassenstr. 32
Berlin D-14129, GERMANY

George, Jason (Actor)
c/o Staff Member *The Artists Group Ltd (LA)*
1650 Broadway Ste 610
New York, NY 10019-6833, USA

George, Jeffrey S (Jeff) (Football Player)
Indianapolis Colts
1980 Schwier Ct
Indianapolis, IN 46229, USA

George, Lynda Day
10310 Riverside Dr Apt 104
Toluca Lake, CA 91602-2457, USA

George, Matt (Football Player)
Pittsburgh Steelers
26514 Big Horn Way
Valencia, CA 91354-2523, USA

George, Melissa (Actor)
c/o Pam Kohl *3 Arts Entertainment Inc*
9460 Wilshire Blvd Fl 7
Beverly Hills, CA 90212-2713, USA

George, Phyllis (Beauty Pageant Winner, Misc, Television Host)
Miss America Organization
2 Miss America Way Ste 1000
Atlantic City, NJ 08401-4142, USA

George, Steve (Football Player)
St Louis Cardinals
5922 W Airport Blvd
Houston, TX 77035-5302, USA

George, Susan (Actor)
McKorkindale & Holton
1-2 Langham Place
London W1A 3DD, UNITED KINGDOM (UK)

George, Terry (Writer)
c/o Ariel (Ari) Emanuel *Endeavor Agency LLC (LA)*
9601 Wilshire Blvd Fl 3
Beverly Hills, CA 90210-5204, USA

George, Tim (Football Player)
Cincinnati Bengals
77 Saddle Ln
Easton, PA 18045-3115, USA

George, Tony (Race Car Driver)
Indianapolis Motor Speedway
4790 W 16th St
Indianapolis, IN 46222-2573, USA

George, William W (Business Person)
Medtronic Inc
7000 Central Ave NE
Minneapolis, MN 55432-3576, USA

George-McFaul, Jean (Baseball Player)
2432 Kilkeer Ste 9
N Battleford, SK S9I 3Y5, CANADA

Georgel, Pierre (Misc)
24 Rue Richer
Paris 76009, FRANCE

Georges, Anne (Baseball Player)
407 Oak St
Des Plaines, IL 60016-4429, USA

Georgi, Howard (Physicist)
Harvard University
Physics Dept Lyman Laboratory
Cambridge, MA 02138, USA

Georgian, Theodore J (Religious Leader)
Orthodox Presbyterian Church
PO Box P
Willow Grove, PA 19090, USA

Georgievski, Ljubisa (Ljupco) (Prime Minister)
Prime Minister's Office
Dame Grueva 6
Skopje 91000, MACEDONIA

Georgije, Bishop (Religious Leader)
Serbian Orthodox Church
PO Box 519
Sava Monastery
Libertyville, IL 60048-0519, USA

Gephardt, Richard (Congressman, Politician)
Office of Congressman Richard Gehhardt
1236 Longworth House Office Building
Washington, DC 20515-0001, USA

Geraci, Sonny (Music Group)
Mars Talent
27 L Ambiance Ct
Bardonia, NY 10954-1421, USA

Geraghty, Brian (Actor)
c/o Lena Roklin *Roklin Management*
8530 Wilshire Blvd Ste 550
Beverly Hills, CA 90211-3133, USA

Gerard, Dave (Baseball Player)
Chicago Cubs
318 Doone Pl
Fairless Hills, PA 19030-2225, USA

Gerard, Gil (Actor)
23679 Calabasas Rd # 325
Calabasas, CA 91302-1502, USA

Gerard, Jean Shevlin (Diplomat)
American Embassy
22 Blvd Emannanuel Servais
2535, LUXEMBOURG

Gerard, Tara (Reality TV Star)
c/o Michael (Mike) Esterman *Esterman Entertainment*
214 Park Rd
Riva, MD 21140-1224, USA

Gerardo (Mejia) (Artist, Music Group)
Tapestry Artists
17337 Ventura Blvd Ste 208
Encino, CA 91316-3992, USA

Gerber, Craig (Baseball Player)
California Angels
4297 N Pershing Ave
San Bernardino, CA 92407-3737, USA

Gerber, David
10800 Chalon Rd
Los Angeles, CA 90077-3220, USA

Gerber, H Joseph (Business Person)
Gerber Scientific Inc
83 Gerber Rd W
South Windsor, CT 06074-3230, USA

Gerber, Joel (Judge)
US Tax Court
400 2nd St NW
Washington, DC 20217-0002, USA

Gerberding, Julie (Doctor, Government Official, Physicist)
Centers for Disease Control
1600 Clifton Rd NE
Atlanta, GA 30329-4018, USA

Gerberman, George (Baseball Player)
Chicago Cubs
1501 Michael St
El Campo, TX 77437-9345, USA

Gere, Richard (Actor)
15030 Ventura Blvd # 710
Sherman Oaks, CA 91403-5470, USA

Geredine, Tom (Football Player)
Atlanta Falcons
1155 Woodlands Dr
Kyle, TX 78640-5530, USA

Gerela, Roy (Football Player)
Houston Oilers
3933 Ramrod Frg
Las Cruces, NM 88012-6008, USA

Geren, Bob (Baseball Player)
New York Yankees
2710 Bay Canyon Ct
San Diego, CA 92117-6704, USA

Gerety, Tom Jr (Educator)
Amherst College
President's Office
Amherst, MA 01003, USA

Gerg, Hilde (Skier)
Brauneck Tolzer Hutte
Lenggries 83661, GERMANY

Gerg-Leitner, Michaela (Skier)
Jachenauer Str 26
Lenggries 83661, GERMANY

Gergen, David R (Editor)
31 Ash St
Cambridge, MA 02138-4840, USA

Gergiev, Valery A
Kunstleragentur Raab & Bohm
Plankengasse 7
Vienna 1010, AUSTRIA

Gerhardt, Alben (Musician)
Columbia Artists Mgmt Inc
1790 Broadway Fl 6
New York, NY 10019-1412, USA

Gerhardt, Rusty (Baseball Player)
San Diego Padres
PO Box 426
New London, TX 75682-0426, USA

Gerhart, Ken (Baseball Player)
Baltimore Orioles
1603 Ashford Ct
Murfreesboro, TN 37129-5888, USA

Gering, Galen (Actor)
c/o Staff Member *Passions*
4024 Radford Ave
Studio City, CA 91604-2101, USA

Gering, Jenna (Actor)
c/o Jonathan Bluman *Paradigm (LA)*
360 N Crescent Dr
North Bldg
Beverly Hills, CA 90210-6820, USA

Gerlach, Gary (Publisher)
Des Moines Register & Tribune
715 Locust St
Des Moines, IA 50309-3703, USA

Germain, Stephanie (Producer)
c/o Staff Member *Creative Artists Agency
LCC (CAA-LA)*
2000 Avenue Of The Stars
Los Angeles, CA 90067-4700, USA

German, Aleksei G (Director)
Marsovo Pole 7 #37
Saint Petersburg 191041, RUSSIA

German, Jammi (Football Player)
Atlanta Falcons
3215 Stella St
Fort Myers, FL 33916-5725, USA

German, Lauren (Actor)
c/o Doug Wald *Raw Talent Management*
9615 Brighton Way Ste 300
Beverly Hills, CA 90210-5118, USA

German, William (Editor)
San Francisco Chronicle
Editorial Dept 901 Mission
San Francisco, CA 94103, USA

Germani, Fernando (Music Group,
Musician)
Via Delle Terme Decians 11
Rome, ITALY

Germann, Greg (Actor, Director)
c/o Jeff Golenberg *The Collective*
9100 Wilshire Blvd # 700 W
Beverly Hills, CA 90212-3401, USA

Germano, Lisa (Music Group, Musician)
Artists & Audience Entertainment
PO Box 35
Pawling, NY 12564-0035, USA

Germany, Reggie (Football Player)
Buffalo Bills
5565 Mallards Marsh
Columbus, OH 43229-9316, USA

Germany, Willie (Football Player)
Atlanta Falcons
4401 Pratt St
Omaha, NE 68111-2533, USA

Germar, Manfred (Athlete, Track Athlete)
DLV
Alsfelder Str 27
Darmstadt 642889, GERMANY

Germeshausen, Bernhard (Athlete)
Hinter Dem Salon 39
Schwansee 99195, GERMANY

Germond, Jack
1627 K St NW Ste 1100
Washington, DC 20006-1710, USA

Gernander, Ken (Hockey Player)
311 Lakeview Dr
Grand Rapids, MN 55744, USA

Gerner, Robert (Doctor, Misc)
University of California
Neuropsychiatric Institute
Los Angeles, CA 90024, USA

Gernert, Dick (Baseball Player)
Boston Red Sox
1420 Rose Virginia Rd
Reading, PA 19611-1738, USA

Gernhardt, Michael L (Astronaut)
3005 S Island Dr
Seabrook, TX 77586-1649, USA

Gero, Gary D (Cinematographer)
2 McLaren Ste A
Irvine, CA 92618-2815, USA

Geronimo, Cesar F (Baseball Player)
Tefeda Flo #46
Santo Domingo, DOMINICAN REPUBLIC

Gerrard, Steven (Soccer Player)
Liverpool FC
Anfield Road
Liverpool
Merseyside L4 OTH, UNITED KINGDOM
(UK)

Gerring, Cathy (Golfer)
Tarrant Springs Trail
Fort Wayne, IN 46804, USA

Gersbach, Carl (Football Player)
Philadelphia Eagles
PO Box 433
Devon, PA 19333-0433, USA

Gershon, Gina (Actor)
200 Park Ave S # 800
New York, NY 10003-1503, USA

Gerson, Mark (Photographer)
3 Regal Lane Regent's Park
London NW1 7TH, UNITED KINGDOM
(UK)

Gerstell, A Frederick (Business Person)
CalMat Co
3200 N San Fernando Rd
Los Angeles, CA 90065-1415, USA

Gerstner V, Jr, Louis (Business Person)
IBM Corp
1 N Castle Dr
Armonk, NY 10504-1784, USA

Gerth, Jeff (Journalist)
New York Times
229 W 43rd St
Editorial Dept
New York, NY 10036-3959, USA

Gertz, Jami (Actor)
15030 Ventura Blvd # 710
Sherman Oaks, CA 91403-5470, USA

Gerut, Jody (Baseball Player)
Cleveland Indians
623 Rochdale Cir
Lombard, IL 60148-4730, USA

Gervais, Ricky (Actor, Director, Producer,
Writer)
c/o Duncan Hayes *Peters Fraser &
Dunlop (PFD - UK)*
Drury House
34-43 Russell St
London WC2B 5HA, UNITED KINGDOM
(UK)

Gervin, George (Basketball Player, Coach)
San Antonio Spurs
Alamodome 1SBC Center
San Antonio, TX 78219, USA

Gerwick, Ben C Jr (Architect, Engineer)
5727 Country Club Dr
Oakland, CA 94618-1717, USA

Geschke, Charles (Business Person)
Adobe Systems
345 Park Ave
San Jose, CA 95110-2704, USA

Gesek, John (Football Player)
Oakland Raiders
105 Sand Point Ct
Coppell, TX 75019-5359, USA

Gesinger, Michael (Photographer)
1136 Umatilla Ave
Port Townsend, WA 98368-4809, USA

Gessendorf, Mechthild (Opera Singer)
Columbia Artists Mgmt Inc
1790 Broadway Fl 6
New York, NY 10019-1412, USA

Gessle, Per (Music Group, Musician)
D&D Mgmt
Lilla Nygatan 19
Stockholm 111 28, SWEDEN

Gest, David (Actor, Producer)
c/o Monique Moss *Warren Cowan &
Associates PR*
8899 Beverly Blvd Ste 919
Los Angeles, CA 90048-2436, USA

Get Up Kids (Music Group)
c/o Staff Member *Creative Artists Agency
LCC (CAA-LA)*
2000 Avenue Of The Stars
Los Angeles, CA 90067-4700, USA

Getherall, Joey (Football Player)
Miami Dolphins
2440 Amelgado Dr
Hacienda Heights, CA 91745-4801, USA

Gethers, Peter (Writer)
c/o Catherine Brackey *International
Creative Management (ICM-LA)*
10250 Constellation Blvd
Los Angeles, CA 90067-6200, USA

Gets, Malcolm (Actor)
c/o Lisa Kussell *BWR (BWR-NY)*
909 3rd Ave Fl 10
New York, NY 10022-4731, USA

Gettel, Al (Baseball Player)
New York Yankees
5620 Parliament Dr
Virginia Beach, VA 23462-3319, USA

Gettelfinger, Ron (Misc)
United Auto Workers
800 E Jefferson Ave
Detroit, MI 48214, USA

Getty, Andrew
2936 Montcalm Ave
W Hollywood, CA 90046-1304, USA

Getty, Balthazar (Actor)
Three Arts Entertainment
9460 Wilshire Blvd Ste 700
Beverly Hills, CA 90212-2713, USA

Getty, Balthazar (Actor)
c/o Staff Member *Gersh Agency, The (LA)*
232 N Canon Dr
Beverly Hills, CA 90210-5302, USA

Getty, Charlie (Football Player)
Kansas City Chiefs
3736 W Morningside St
Springfield, MO 65807-5581, USA

Getty, Estelle (Actor)
c/o Staff Member *Innovative Artists (LA)*
1505 10th St
Santa Monica, CA 90401-2805, USA

Getty, Gordon
2880 Broadway St
San Francisco, CA 94115-1061, USA

Getz, John (Actor)
4124 Wade St
Los Angeles, CA 90066-5732, USA

Getzlaff, James (Actor)
c/o Staff Member *Douglas Gorman
Rothacker & Wilhelm Inc*
1501 Broadway Ste 703
New York, NY 10036-5505, USA

Geyer, Georgie Anne (Editor, Misc)
Plaza
800 25th St NW
Washington, DC 20037-2208, USA

Geyer, Hugh (Music Group)
2218 Ridge Rd
McKeesport, PA 15135-3037, USA

Geyer, William (Football Player)
Chicago Bears
39 Afterglow Way
Verona, NJ 07044-5103, USA

Ghadie, Samia (Actor)
c/o *Granada TV*
Quay Street
Manchester M60 9EA, UNITED
KINGDOM (UK)

Ghai, Subhash (Bollywood, Director,
Filmmaker, Producer)
12 Cliff Tower
Mount Mary Church Road Bandra (W)
Mumbai, MS 400050, INDIA

Ghannouchi, Mohamed (Prime Minister)
Prime Minister's Office
Place du Gouvernement
Tunis, TUNISIA

Ghattas, Stephenos II Cardinal (Religious
Leader)
Patriarcat Copte Catholique
BP 69 Rue Ibn Sandar
Cairo 11712, EGYPT

Ghauri, Yasmine (Model)
Next Model Mgmt
23 Watts St
New York, NY 10013, USA

Ghelfi, Tony (Baseball Player)
Philadelphia Phillies
3414 Geneva Ln
La Crosse, WI 54601-8302, USA

Gheorghiu, Angela (Opera Singer)
Levon Sayan
2 Rue du Prieure
Nyon 1260, SWITZERLAND

Gheorghiu, Ion A (Artist)
27-29 Emil Pangratti St
Bucharest, ROMANIA

Ghesquiere, Nicolas (Fashion Designer)
11 Avenue dlena
Balenciaga, Paris 75016, FRANCE

Ghiardi, John F L (Economist, Government Official)
12 Park Overlook Ct
Bethesda, MD 20817-2720, USA

Ghiglia, Oscar A (Music Group, Musician)
Helfembergstr 14
Basel 4059, SWITZERLAND

Ghigliotti, Marilyn (Actor)
Redrock Entertainment Development
118 S Cordova St
3rd Fl
Burbank, CA 91505-4610, USA

Ghiorso, Albert (Misc, Scientist)
Lawrence Berkeley Laboratory
1 Cyclotron Rd
Berkeley, CA 94720-8099, USA

Ghiuselev, Nicola (Opera Singer)
Villa della Pisana 370/B-2
Rome 00163, ITALY

Ghizikis, Phaidon (General, President)
25 Kountouriotou
Pefki 151 21, GREECE

Ghosh, Gautam (Director)
28/1-A Gariahat Road Block 5 #50
Calcutta, WB 700029, INDIA

Ghosh, Partho (Bollywood, Director, Filmmaker, Producer)
D1 Hawa Apartments Opp Holy Spirit Hospital
Mahakali Caves Road Andheri (E)
Bombay, MS 400 093, INDIA

Ghost, Amanda (Musician)
c/o Staff Member *Basina Recording Company*
PO Box 8121
Pittsburgh, PA 15217-0121, USA

Ghostface, Killa (Music Group, Musician)
Famous Artists Agency
250 W 57th St
New York, NY 10107-0001, USA

Ghostland Observatory (Music Group)
c/o Staff Member *Paradigm (Monterey)*
509 Hartnell St
Monterey, CA 93940-2825, USA

Ghuman Jr, JB (Actor)
c/o Steven Levy *The Firm*
9465 Wilshire Blvd Fl 6
Beverly Hills, CA 90212-2605, USA

Giacconi, Riccardo (Nobel Prize Laureate)
Associated Universities Inc
1440 16th St NW # 730
Washington, DC 20036, USA

Giacomarro, Ralph (Football Player)
Atlanta Falcons
3945 Mantle Ridge Dr
Cumming, GA 30041-5620, USA

Giacomin, Eddie (Hockey Player)
6575 Red Maple Ln
Bloomfield Hills, MI 48301-3225, USA

Giacomin, Edward (Ed) (Hockey Player)
6575 Red Maple Ln
Bloomfield Hills, MI 48301-3225, USA

Giaever, Ivar (Nobel Prize Laureate)
2080 Van Antwerp Rd
Schenectady, NY 12309-1124, USA

Giallombardo, Bob (Baseball Player)
Los Angeles Dodgers
7903 Antique Cir
Waxhaw, NC 28173-7858, USA

Giamatti, Marcus
c/o Mitchell Stubbs *Mitchell K Stubbs & Assoc (MKS)*
8695 Washington Blvd Ste 204
Culver City, CA 90232-7419, USA

Giamatti, Paul (Actor)
c/o Perri Kipperman *Kipperman Management*
130 W 42nd St
New York, NY 10036-7902, USA

Giambalvo, Louis (Actor)
c/o Staff Member *Judy Schoen & Associates*
606 N Larchmont Blvd Ste 309
Los Angeles, CA 90004-1309, USA

Giambastiani, Edmund P Jr (Admiral)
Deputy Cno For Resources/Warfare Requirements
Hqusn
Washington, DC 20350-0001, USA

Giambi, Jason G (Baseball Player)
Oakland A's
1034 E Belmont Abbey Ln
Claremont, CA 91711-1463, USA

Giambi, Jeremy (Baseball Player)
Kansas City Royals
1034 E Belmont Abbey Ln
Claremont, CA 91711-1463, USA

Giambra, Joey (Boxer)
7950 W Flamingo Rd Unit 1188
Las Vegas, NV 89147-4234, USA

Giammona, Louie (Football Player)
New York Jets
525 Parrish St
Philadelphia, PA 19123-2111, USA

Gian, Joey (Musician)
Joey Gian Entertainment
13351D Riverside Dr # 294
Sherman Oaks, CA 91423-2508, USA

Gian, Joseph
8271 Melrose Ave Ste 110
Los Angeles, CA 90046-6800, USA

Giancanelli, Hal (Football Player)
Philadelphia Eagles
2227 Portola Ln
Westlake Village, CA 91361-1748, USA

Gianelli, John (Basketball Player)
PO Box 1097
Pinecrest, CA 95364-0097, USA

Gianelli, Ray (Baseball Player)
Toronto Blue Jays
56 E Saltaire Rd
Lindenhurst, NY 11757-6829, USA

Giannini, Andriano (Actor)
c/o Lindy King *Peters Fraser & Dunlop (PFD - UK)*
Drury House
34-43 Russell St
London WC2B 5HA, UNITED KINGDOM (UK)

Giannini, Giancario (Actor)
Via Salaria 292
Rome 00199, ITALY

Giannini, Giancarlo (Actor)
Via della Giuliana 101
Rome I-00195, ITALY

Giannulli, Mossimo (Designer, Fashion Designer)
Mossimo Supply
2450 White Rd # 200
Irvine, CA 92614-6250, USA

Gianopoulos, David (Actor)
c/o Staff Member *GVA Talent Agency Inc*
9229 W Sunset Blvd Ste 320
Los Angeles, CA 90069-3403, USA

Gianulias, Nicole (Nikki) (Bowler)
Ladies Professional Bowling Tour
7200 Harrison Ave # 7171
Rockford, IL 61112-1017, USA

Giaquinto, Nick (Football Player)
Miami Dolphins
316 3rd Ave
Stratford, CT 06615-7736, USA

Giardello, Joey (Boxer)
1214 Severn Ave
Cherry Hill, NJ 08002-3243, USA

Giarraputo, Jack (Producer, Writer)
c/o Staff Member *Happy Madison Productions*
10202 Washington Blvd
Judy Garland Bldg
Culver City, CA 90232-3119, USA

Gibara, Samir (Business Person)
Goodyear Tire & Rubber
1144 W Market St
Akron, OH 44316, USA

Gibb, Barry (Music Group, Musician, Songwriter, Writer)
c/o Staff Member *United Talent Agency (UTA)*
9560 Wilshire Blvd Ste 500
Beverly Hills, CA 90212-2401, USA

Gibb, Cynthia (Actor)
1139 S Hill St # 177
Los Angeles, CA 90015-2207, USA

Gibb, Donald (Actor)
Ashby/Rojo Entertainment
1485 S Beverly Dr
Los Angeles, CA 90035-3021, USA

Gibb, Robin (Music Group, Musician, Songwriter, Writer)
Middle Ear
5820 N Bay Rd
Miami Beach, FL 33140-2043, USA

Gibberd, Frederick (Architect)
House Marsh Lane Old Harlow
Essex CM17 0NA, UNITED KINGDOM (UK)

Gibbon, Joe (Baseball Player)
Pittsburgh Pirates
26 County Road 24142
Newton, MS 39345-8946, USA

Gibbons, Beth (Music Group, Songwriter, Writer)
Fruit
Saga Center 326 Kensal Road
London W10 5BZ, UNITED KINGDOM (UK)

Gibbons, Billy (Music Group, Musician)
Lone Wolf Mgmt
PO Box 16390
Austin, TX 78761, USA

Gibbons, Brian (Baseball Player)
51788 Whitestable Ln
South Bend, IN 46637-1370, USA

Gibbons, Jim (Football Player)
Detroit Lions
9 Sagewood Ct
Basalt, CO 81621-8314, USA

Gibbons, John (Baseball Player)
New York Mets
3602 Hunters Quail
San Antonio, TX 78230-2052, USA

Gibbons, John D (Prime Minister)
Leeward 5 Leeside Dr
Pembroke HM 05, BERMUDA

Gibbons, Kaye (Writer)
c/o Lynn Pleshette *Lynn Pleshette Literary Agency*
2700 N Beachwood Dr
Los Angeles, CA 90068-1922, USA

Gibbons, Leeza (Entertainer)
c/o Staff Member *Leeza Gibbons Enterprises (LGE)*
20700 Ventura Blvd Ste 328
Woodland Hills, CA 91364-6282, USA

Gibbons, Mike (Football Player)
New York Giants
1315 Moorwick Ln
Houston, TX 77043-4540, USA

Gibbons, Tim (Producer)
c/o Staff Member *International Creative Management (ICM-LA)*
10250 Constellation Blvd
Los Angeles, CA 90067-6200, USA

Gibbons, Walter (Baseball Player)
Indianapolis Clowns
103 E North St
Tampa, FL 33604-6156, USA

Gibbs, H Jarrell (Business Person)
Texas Utilities Co
1601 Bryan St
Energy Plaza
Dallas, TX 75201-3430, USA

Gibbs, Jerry D (Jake) (Baseball Player)
New York Yankees
223 Saint Andrews Cir
Oxford, MS 38655-2518, USA

Gibbs, Joe (Race Car Driver)
Joe Gibbs Racing
13415 Reese Blvd W
Huntersville, NC 28078-7933, USA

Gibbs, L Richard (Cricketer)
276 Republic Park
Peter's Hall EBD, GUYANA

Gibbs, Lawrence B (Government Official)
Miller & Chevalier
655 15th St NW Ste 900
Washington, DC 20005-5799, USA

Gibbs, Marla (Actor, Music Group)
3500 W Manchester Blvd Unit 267
Inglewood, CA 90305-4267, USA

Gibbs, Pat (Football Player)
Philadelphia Eagles
4835 Corley St
Beaumont, TX 77707-4224, USA

Gibbs, Patt (Misc)
Flght Attendants Assn
1275 K St NW Ste 500
Washington, DC 20005-4040, USA

Gibbs, Terri (Music Group, Songwriter, Writer)
1439 Clary Cut Rd
Appling, GA 30802-2109, USA

Gibbs, Terry (Music Group, Musician)
Thomas Cassidy
11761 E Speedway Blvd
Tucson, AZ 85748-2017, USA

Gibbs, Timothy (Actor)
c/o Julia Buchwald *Don Buchwald & Associates Inc (LA)*
6500 Wilshire Blvd Ste 2200
Los Angeles, CA 90048-4942, USA

Gibgot, Adam (Writer)
c/o Adriana Alberghetti *Endeavor Agency LLC (LA)*
9601 Wilshire Blvd Fl 3
Beverly Hills, CA 90210-5204, USA

Giblett, Eloise R (Doctor, Misc)
6533 53rd Ave NE
Seattle, WA 98115-7748, USA

Giblin, Robert (Football Player)
New York Giants
2818 Reynolds Ln
Port Neches, TX 77651-5410, USA

Gibney, Rebecca
128 Rupert St.
Collingwood Vic. 3066, AUSTRALIA

Gibney, Susan (Actor)
c/o Matthew Lesher *Lesher Entertainment Inc*
1134 S Cloverdale Ave
Los Angeles, CA 90019-6737, USA

Gibraltor, Steve (Baseball Player)
Cincinnati Reds
3510 Turtle Creek Blvd Apt 5B
Dallas, TX 75219-5543, USA

Gibran, Kahill (Artist, Misc)
160 W Canton St
Boston, MA 02118-1216, USA

Gibson, Aaron (Football Player)
Detroit Lions
PO Box 637
Roanoke, IN 46783-0637, USA

Gibson, Antonio (Football Player)
New Orleans Saints
1013 Sun Meadow Ct
College Station, TX 77845-7291, USA

Gibson, Bob (Baseball Player)
215 Bellevue Blvd S
Bellevue, NE 68005-2442, USA

Gibson, Bob (Baseball Player)
Milwaukee Brewers
751 W Rolling Rd
Springfield, PA 19064-1131, USA

Gibson, Charles (Television Host)
c/o Staff Member *Good Morning America (NY)*
147 Columbus Ave Fl 6
Abc
New York, NY 10023-6503, USA

Gibson, Claude (Football Player)
San Diego Chargers
47 Gladstone Rd
Asheville, NC 28805-2454, USA

Gibson, Damon (Football Player)
Cincinnati Bengals
4332 Dell Rd Apt J
Lansing, MI 48911-8126, USA

Gibson, Deborah (Actor, Musician)
GMI Entertainment
656 5th Ave # 302
New York, NY 10103, USA

Gibson, Dennis (Football Player)
Detroit Lions
PO Box 442
Ankeny, IA 50021-0442, USA

Gibson, Derrick (Baseball Player)
Colorado Rockies
138 Buckeye Loop Rd
Winter Haven, FL 33881-2703, USA

Gibson, Derrick (Football Player)
Oakland Raiders
1220 Harbor Bay Pkwy
Alameda, CA 94502-6570, USA

Gibson, Ernest (Football Player)
New England Patriots
1749 Kinsmon Cv
Marietta, GA 30062-8173, USA

Gibson, Everett K Jr (Geophysicist, Misc, Physicist)
1015 Trowbridge Dr
Houston, TX 77062-2726, USA

Gibson, George (Football Player)
Frankford Yellow Jackets
1419 Ainslee St
Midland, TX 79701-3920, USA

Gibson, Greg (Baseball Player)
20305 Country Club Dr
Catlettsburg, KY 41129-8602, USA

Gibson, Henry (Actor)
26740 Latigo Shore Dr
Malibu, CA 90265-4510, USA

Gibson, Joe (Football Player)
Cleveland Rams
5535 Clarendon Way
Carmichael, CA 95608-5506, USA

Gibson, Mel (Actor, Director, Producer)
c/o Staff Member *ICON Productions Inc*
808 Wilshire Blvd Fl 4
Santa Monica, CA 90401-1889, USA

Gibson, Oliver (Football Player)
Pittsburgh Steelers
2112 Cranberry Ct
Naperville, IL 60565-2849, USA

Gibson, Paul (Baseball Player)
Detroit Tigers
PO Box 354
Center Moriches, NY 11934-0354, USA

Gibson, Ralph H (Photographer)
331 W Broadway
New York, NY 10013-2265, USA

Gibson, Reginald W (Judge)
US Claims Court
717 Madison Pl NW
Washington, DC 20439-0001, USA

Gibson, Robert L
1709 Shagbark Trl
Murfreesboro, TN 37130-1136, USA

Gibson, Russ (Baseball Player)
Boston Red Sox
495 Gardners Neck Rd
Swansea, MA 02777-3131, USA

Gibson, Thomas (Actor)
c/o Craig Dorfman *Blueprint Management*
5670 Wilshire Blvd Ste 2525
Los Angeles, CA 90036-5647, USA

Gibson, Tom (Football Player)
Cleveland Browns
6719 E Paradise Ln
Scottsdale, AZ 85254-5604, USA

Gibson, Tyrese (Actor, Musician, Producer, Writer)
c/o Staff Member *HQ Pictures*
1635 N Cahuenga Blvd Fl 2
Los Angeles, CA 90028-6201, USA

Gick, George (Baseball Player)
Chicago White Sox
3 Brady Lane Ct
Lafayette, IN 47909-3801, USA

Gidada, Negasso (President)
President's Office
P O Box 5707
Addis Ababa, ETHIOPIA

Giddens, Frank (Football Player)
Philadelphia Eagles
2602 Carver St
Carlsbad, NM 88220-4711, USA

Gideon, Brett (Baseball Player)
Pittsburgh Pirates
PO Box 822
Georgetown, TX 78627-0822, USA

Gideon, Jim (Baseball Player)
Texas Rangers
104 Plum Tree Ter Apt 120
Houston, TX 77077-5375, USA

Gideon, Raynold (Actor, Writer)
3524 Multiview Dr
Los Angeles, CA 90068-1222, USA

Gidley, Pamela (Actor)
c/o Tom Harrison *Diverse Talent Group*
1875 Century Park E Ste 2250
Los Angeles, CA 90067-2563, USA

Gidzenko, Yuri P (Astronaut, Misc)
Potchta Kosmonavtov
Moskovskoi Oblasti
Syvisdny Goroduk 141160, RUSSIA

Giebell, Floyd (Baseball Player)
Detroit Tigers
607 Laurelwood Dr
Wilkesboro, NC 28697-8118, USA

Gielen, Michael A (Composer, Conductor)
Hans Ulrich Schmid
Postfach 1617
Hanover 30016, GERMANY

Giella, Joseph (Cartoonist)
191 Morris Dr
East Meadow, NY 11554-1317, USA

Gien, Pamela (Actor, Writer)
c/o Heather Schroder *International Creative Management (ICM-NY)*
40 W 57th St
New York, NY 10019-4001, USA

Gienger, Eberhard
Friedrich-Schaal-Str. 53
Tubingen D-72074, GERMANY

Gierasch, Stefan (Actor)
c/o Staff Member *Brandon's Commercials Unlimited*
190 N Canon Dr Ste 302
Beverly Hills, CA 90210-5314, USA

Gierer, Vincent A Jr (Business Person)
UST Inc
100 W Putnam Ave
Greenwich, CT 06830-5316, USA

Gierowski, Stefen (Artist)
Ul Gagarina 15 m 97
Warsaw 00-753, POLAND

Giesler, Jon (Football Player)
Miami Dolphins
141 Via Isabela
Jupiter, FL 33458-6925, USA

Giessinger, Andrew (Football Player)
San Diego Chargers
1667 Union Ave
Barberton, OH 44203-7644, USA

Gifford, Frank N (Football Player, Sportscaster)
New York Giants
108 Cedar Cliff Rd
Riverside, CT 06878-2606, USA

Gifford, Gloria (Actor)
Schiowitz/Clay/Rose
1680 Vine St Ste 1016
Los Angeles, CA 90028-8800, USA

Gifford, Kathie Lee (Correspondent, Entertainer)
c/o Sam Haskell *William Morris Agency (WMA-LA)*
1 William Morris Pl
Beverly Hills, CA 90212-4261, USA

Gift, Roland (Actor, Music Group)
Primary Talent Int'l
1-12 Petonville Road
London N1 9PL, UNITED KINGDOM (UK)

Giggle, Bob (Baseball Player)
Milwaukee Braves
89 McAndrew Rd
Braintree, MA 02184-8245, USA

Gigli, Romeo (Designer, Fashion Designer)
37 W 57th St Ste 900
New York, NY 10019-3411, USA

Gigon, Norm (Baseball Player)
Chicago Cubs
205 Paxinosa Rd E
Easton, PA 18040-1334, USA

Gigot, Paul (Journalist)
Wall Street Journal
200 Liberty St
Editorial Dept
New York, NY 10281-0084, USA

Giguere, Russ (Music Group, Musician)
Variety Artists
793 Higuera St Ste 6
San Luis Obispo, CA 93401-0500, USA

Giheno, John (President)
Prime Minister's Office
Marera Hau
Port Moresby, PAPUA NEW GUINEA

Gil, Ariadna (Actor)
Cineart
36 Rue de Ponthieu
Paris 75008, FRANCE

Gil, Geronimo (Athlete, Baseball Player)
c/o Staff Member *Baltimore Orioles*
333 W Camden St
Oriole Park
Baltimore, MD 21201-2435, USA

Gil, Gilberto (Music Group, Songwriter, Writer)
BPR
36 Como St Ramford
Essex RM 7 7DR, UNITED KINGDOM (UK)

Gil, Gus (Baseball Player)
Cleveland Indians
6494 King Louis Dr Apt 303
Alexandria, VA 22312-1662, USA

Gil, R Benjamin (Benji) (Baseball Player)
Texas Rangers
504 Unbridled Ln
Keller, TX 76248-8724, USA

Gilbert, Brad
888 17th St NW Ste 1200
Washington, DC 20006-3320, USA

Gilbert, Bradley (Brad) (Tennis Player)
ProServe
1101 Woodrow Wilson Blvd #1800
Arlington, VA 22209, USA

Gilbert, Brantley (Musician)
c/o Staff Member *Paradigm (Monterey)*
509 Hartnell St
Monterey, CA 93940-2825, USA

Gilbert, Buddy (Baseball Player)
Cincinnati Reds
1913 Belcaro Dr
Knoxville, TN 37918-3709, USA

Gilbert, Chris (Football Player)
Greenbriar Mgmt
4422 Fm 1960 Rd W
Houston, TX 77068-3419, USA

Gilbert, Daren (Football Player)
New Orleans Saints
13926 Villanova Ave
Chino, CA 91710-7116, USA

Gilbert, David (Cartoonist)
King Features Syndicate
888 7th Ave Ste 201
New York, NY 10106-0201, USA

Gilbert, Elsie
1016 N Orange Grove Ave Apt 4
West Hollywood, CA 90046-6127, USA

Gilbert, Felix (Historian)
918 Bluffwood Dr
Iowa City, IA 52245-3516, USA

Gilbert, Greg (Coach, Hockey Player)
303 Main St
Worcester, MA 01608-1511, USA

Gilbert, J Freeman (Geophysicist, Physicist)
780 Kalamath Dr
Del Mar, CA 92014-2630, USA

Gilbert, Joe (Baseball Player)
Montreal Expos
1952 N Bowie St
Jasper, TX 75951, USA

Gilbert, Kenneth A (Music Group, Musician)
23 Cloitre Notre-Dame
Chartres 28000, FRANCE

Gilbert, Lewis (Director, Producer)
19 Blvd de Suisse
Monte Carlo, MONACO

Gilbert, Mark (Baseball Player)
Chicago White Sox
2340 NW 45th St
Boca Raton, FL 33431-8437, USA

Gilbert, Martin J (Historian)
Merton College
Oxford OX1 4JD, UNITED KINGDOM
(UK)

Gilbert, Melissa (Actor)
c/o Erwin Moore *William Morris Agency (WMA-LA)*
1 William Morris Pl
Beverly Hills, CA 90212-4261, USA

Gilbert, O'Neill (Coach, Football Coach, Football Player)
San Francisco 49ers
Tennessee Titans 460 Great Circle Rd
Attn Coaching Staff
Nashville, TN 37228, USA

Gilbert, Peter (Director)
Innovative Artists
1505 10th St
Santa Monica, CA 90401-2805, USA

Gilbert, Richard W (Publisher)
Des Moines Register & Tribune
715 Locust St
Des Moines, IA 50309-3703, USA

Gilbert, Rodrique G (Rod) (Hockey Player)
344 Pacific Ave
Cedarhurst, NY 11516-1814, USA

Gilbert, Ronnie (Music Group)
Donna Korones Mgmt
PO Box 8388
Berkeley, CA 94707-8388, USA

Gilbert, S J Sr (Religious Leader)
Baptist Convention of America
6717 Centennial Blvd
Nashville, TN 37209-1017, USA

Gilbert, Sara (Actor)
c/o Steven Levy *Framework Entertainment (LA)*
9057 Nemo St # C
W Hollywood, CA 90069-5511, USA

Gilbert, Sean (Football Player)
Los Angeles Rams
7912 Baltusrol Ln
Charlotte, NC 28210-4933, USA

Gilbert, Shawn (Baseball Player)
New York Mets
1644 W Wrenwood Ave
Fresno, CA 93711-2938, USA

Gilbert, Simon (Music Group, Musician)
Interceptor Enterprises
98 White Lion St
London N1 9PF, UNITED KINGDOM
(UK)

Gilbert, Walter (Nobel Prize Laureate)
15 Gray Gdns W
Cambridge, MA 02138-2311, USA

Gilberto, Astrud (Music Group)
Absolute Artists
530 Howard St Ste 200
San Francisco, CA 94105-3018, USA

Gilberto, Bebel (Music Group)
Miracle Prestige
1 Water Lane Camden Town
London NW1 8NZ, UNITED KINGDOM
(UK)

Gilbertson, Keith (Coach, Football Coach)
University of Washington
Athletic Dept
Seattle, WA 98195-0001, USA

Gilbreth, Bill (Baseball Player)
Detroit Tigers
709 Gary Ln
Abilene, TX 79601-5537, USA

Gilbreth, David (Writer)
c/o Ryan Saul *Jim Preminger Agency*
10866 Wilshire Blvd Fl 10
Los Angeles, CA 90024-4350, USA

Gilbride, Kevin (Coach, Football Player)
Pittsburgh Steelers
3400 S Water St
Pittsburgh, PA 15203-2349, USA

Gilburg, Tom (Football Player)
Baltimore Colts
64 Blachley Rd # B
Stamford, CT 06902-4320, USA

Gilchrist, Carlton (Football Player)
Buffalo Bills
2017 W Girard Ave
Philadelphia, PA 19130-1420, USA

Gilchrist, Jeanne (Baseball Player)
218-67 Miner Street
New Westminster, BC V3L 5N5,
CANADA

Gilchrist, Pual R (Religious Leader)
Presbyterian Church in America
1862 Century Pl NE
Atlanta, GA 30345, USA

Gilder, Bob (Golfer)
1977 NW Bonney Dr
Corvallis, OR 97330-9161, USA

Gilder, George F (Economist, Writer)
Main Road
Tyringham, MA 01264, USA

Gildon, Jason (Football Player)
Pittsburgh Steelers
1562 Barrington Dr
Wexford, PA 15090-9377, USA

Gile, Don (Baseball Player)
Boston Red Sox
570 Seahorse Ln
Redwood City, CA 94065-1223, USA

Giles, Bill (Baseball Player)
Philadelphia Phillies
1755 Cedar Ln
Villanova, PA 19085-2018, USA

Giles, Brian (Baseball Player)
c/o Staff Member *San Diego Padres*
100 Park Blvd
San Diego, CA 92101-7405, USA

Giles, Jimmie (Football Player)
Houston Oilers
10429 Greenmont Dr
Tampa, FL 33626-5306, USA

Giles, Marcus (Athlete, Baseball Player)
c/o Staff Member *Atlanta Braves*
PO Box 4064
Turner Field
Atlanta, GA 30302-4064, USA

Giles, Nancy (Actor)
12047 178th St
Jamaica, NY 11434-2719, USA

Giles, Sandra
350 N Crescent Dr
Beverly Hills, CA 90210-4847, USA

Giletti, Alain (Figure Skater)
103 Place de L'Eglise
Chamonix 74400, FRANCE

Gilfillan, Jason (Baseball Player)
Kansas City Royals
153 Gilfillan Rd
Blacksburg, SC 29702-8521, USA

Gilfry, Rodney (Opera Singer)
Columbia Artists Mgmt Inc
1790 Broadway Fl 6
New York, NY 10019-1412, USA

Gilgorov, Kiro (President)
President's Office
Skopje, MACEDONIA

Gilkey, Bernard (Baseball Player)
St Louis Cardinals
7895 Trenton Ave
University City, MO 63130-1227, USA

Gill, AJ (Musician)
c/o Staff Member *Fox Television Studios*
10201 W Pico Blvd Bldg 41
Los Angeles, CA 90064-2606, USA

Gill, George N (Publisher)
Louisville Courier-Journal & Times
525 W Broadway
Louisville, KY 40202-2206, USA

Gill, Janis (Music Group)
Monty Hitchcock Mgmt
5101 Overton Rd
Nashville, TN 37220-1920, USA

Gill, Johnny (Music Group, Musician, Songwriter, Writer)
4924 Balboa Blvd # 366
Encino, CA 91316-3402, USA

Gill, Kendall (Basketball Player)
c/o Staff Member *Milwaukee Bucks*
1001 N 4th St
Bradley Center
Milwaukee, WI 53203-1312, USA

Gill, Priya (Actor, Bollywood)
606 Nestle - B 4th Cross Road
Lokhandwala Complex Andheri (W)
Mumbai, MS 400058, INDIA

Gill, Tim (Designer, Engineer, Misc)
Gill Foundation
2215 Market St
Denver, CO 80205-2026, USA

Gill, Vince (Music Group, Musician, Songwriter, Writer)
c/o Rick Shipp *William Morris Agency (WMA-TN)*
1600 Division St Ste 300
Nashville, TN 37203-2755, USA

Gill, William A Jr (Government Official, Misc)
15975 Cove Ln
Dumfries, VA 22025-1412, USA

Gillan, Ian (Musician)
Miracle Prestige
1 Water Lane
Camden Town
London NW1 8N2, UNITED KINGDOM
(UK)

Gillbreath, Rod (Baseball Player)
Atlanta Braves
1438 Ridgeland Way SW
Lilburn, GA 30047-4352, USA

Gillen, Aidan (Actor)
c/o Sally Long-Innes *International Creative Management (ICM-UK)*
Oxford House
76 Oxford St
London W1N OAX, UNITED KINGDOM
(UK)

Giller, Walter
Via Tamporiva 26
Castagnola CH-6976, SWITZERLAND

Gilles, Daniel (Writer)
161 Ave Churchill
Brussels 1180, BELGIUM

Gilles, Tom (Baseball Player)
Toronto Blue Jays
3116 N Emery Ave
Peoria, IL 61604-1444, USA

Gillespie, Ann (Actor)
Greene Assoc
7080 Hollywood Blvd Ste 1017
Los Angeles, CA 90028-6937, USA

Gillespie, Charles A Jr (Diplomat)
Scowcroft Group
900 17th St NW Ste 500
Washington, DC 20006-2507, USA

Gillespie, Rhondda (Music Group, Musician)
2 Princess Road
Saint Leonards-on-Sea
East Sussex TN37 6EL, UNITED
KINGDOM (UK)

Gillespie, Robert (Financier)
KeyCorp
127 Public Sq
Cleveland, OH 44114-1306, USA

Gillespie, Ronald J (Doctor, Misc)
McMaster University
Chemistry Dept
Hamilton, ON L8S 4M1, CANADA

Gillette (Musician)
c/o Staff Member *Diva Central Inc*
7510 W Sunset Blvd Ste 1445
Los Angeles, CA 90046-3408, USA

Gillette, Anita (Actor)
501 S Beverly Dr Fl 3
Beverly Hills, CA 90212-4520, USA

Gillette, Walker (Football Player)
San Diego Chargers
401 N College Dr
Franklin, VA 23851-2401, USA

Gilley, J Wade (Educator)
University of Tennessee
President's Office
Knoxville, TN 37996-0001, USA

Gilley, Mickey (Music Group, Songwriter, Writer)
Gilley's Interests
PO Box 1242
Pasadena, TX 77501-1242, USA

Gilliam, Armon (Basketball Player)
Pennsylvania State University
Athletic Dept
M Keesport, PA 15131, USA

Gilliam, Burton
1427 Tascosa Ct
Allen, TX 75013-1111, USA

Gilliam, Elijah (Baseball Player)
Birmingham Black Barons
1617 5th Ave N
Birmingham, AL 35203-1953, USA

Gilliam, Herm (Basketball Player)
2701 Bon Air Ave
Winston Salem, NC 27105-4306, USA

Gilliam, John (Football Player)
New Orleans Saints
1181 Braemar Ave SW
Atlanta, GA 30311-3017, USA

Gilliam, Jon (Football Player)
Dallas Texans
208 Buffalo Creek Dr
Waxahachie, TX 75165-1539, USA

Gilliam, Seth (Actor)
c/o Jason Gutman *Gersh Agency, The (NY)*
41 Madison Ave Fl 33
New York, NY 10010-2202, USA

Gilliam, Terry (Actor, Animator, Writer)
Old Hall South Grove
Highgate
London N6 6BP, UNITED KINGDOM (UK)

Gilliand, Herman (Baseball Player)
Chicago Cubs
1833 Kern Mountain Way
Antioch, CA 94531-7497, USA

Gilliangham, Gale (Football Player)
Green Bay Packers
1605 W River Rd
Little Falls, MN 56345-4155, USA

Gilliatt, Penelope
31 Chester Sq.
London, ENGLAND SW1W 9HT, UNITED KINGDOM (UK)

Gillie, Nick (Producer)
c/o Staff Member *Metropolitan*
4500 Wilshire Blvd Fl 2
Los Angeles, CA 90010-3858, USA

Gillies, Ben (Music Group, Musician)
John Watson Mgmt
P O Box 281
Sunny Hills, NSW 2010, AUSTRALIA

Gillies, Clark (Hockey Player)
225 Old Country Rd
Melville, NY 11747-2719, USA

Gillies, Daniel (Actor)
c/o Ben Levine *Evolution Entertainment (LA)*
10585 Santa Monica Blvd Ste 120
Los Angeles, CA 90025-4984, USA

Gilliford, Paul (Baseball Player)
Baltimore Orioles
7 Woodland Dr
Malvern, PA 19355-3308, USA

Gilligan, Carol (Educator)
Harvard University
Gender Studies Dept
Cambridge, MA 02138, USA

Gillilan, William J III (Business Person)
Centex Corp
PO Box 199000
Dallas, TX 75219-9000, USA

Gilliland, Richard (Actor)
Metropolitan Talent Agency
4500 Wilshire Blvd Fl 2
Los Angeles, CA 90010-3858, USA

Gilliland, Robert J (Misc)
PO Box 6367
Burbank, CA 91510-6367, USA

Gillingwater, Leah (Reality TV Star)
c/o Staff Member *Real World, The*
6007 Sepulveda Blvd
Van Nuys, CA 91411-2502, USA

Gillins, Don (Football Player)
Chicago Cardinals
4658 Oso Pkwy
Corpus Christi, TX 78413-5269, USA

Gillis, Louis (Baseball Player)
Birmingham Black Barons
2920 33rd Way N
Birmingham, AL 35207-3720, USA

Gillis, Malcolm (Educator)
Rice University
President's Office
Houston, TX 77047, USA

Gillman, Sid
2968 Playa Rd.
Carlsbad, CA 92009, USA

Gillom, Jennifer (Basketball Player)
c/o Staff Member *LA Sparks*
555 N Nash St
El Segundo, CA 90245-2818, USA

Gillooly (Stone), Jeff
10408 SE 82nd Ave
Happy Valley, OR 97086-2312, USA

Gilman, Alfred G (Nobel Prize Laureate)
10996 Crooked Creek Dr
Dallas, TX 75229-4304, USA

Gilman, Billy (Music Group)
c/o Rodney (Rod) Essig *Creative Artists Agency (CAA-Nashville)*
3310 W End Ave Fl 5
Nashville, TN 37203-1028, USA

Gilman, Dorothy (Writer)
321 N Highland Ave
Ossining, NY 10562-2331, USA

Gilman, Kenneth B (Business Person)
Limited Inc
3 Limited Pkwy
P O Box 1600
Columbus, OH 43230-1467, USA

Gilman, Richard H (Publisher)
Boston Globe
Publisher's Office
135 W T Morrissey Blvd
Dorchester, MA 02125, USA

Gilman, Sid (Doctor, Misc)
3441 Geddes Rd
Ann Arbor, MI 48105, USA

Gilmartin, Paul (Comedian)
c/o Staff Member *Agency for the Performing Arts (APA-LA)*
405 S Beverly Dr
Beverly Hills, CA 90212-4416, USA

Gilmartin, Raymond V (Business Person)
Merck Co
PO Box 100
1 Merck Dr
Whitehouse Station, NJ 08889-0100, USA

Gilmer, Harry V (Football Player)
Washington Redskins
7467 Highway N
O Fallon, MO 63368-7014, USA

Gilmore, Artis (Basketball Player)
11043 Turnbridge Dr
Jacksonville, FL 32256-2329, USA

Gilmore, Clarence P (Editor)
1629 Boston Post Rd
Westbrook, CT 06498-2047, USA

Gilmore, Jimmie Dale (Music Group, Songwriter, Writer)
Crowley Artists Mgmt
602 Wayside Dr
Wimberley, TX 78676-5151, USA

Gilmore, Kenneth O (Editor)
Charles Road
Mount Kisco, NY 10549, USA

Gilmore, Len (Baseball Player)
Pittsburgh Pirates
RR 2 Box 213C
Jones, OK 73049, USA

Gilmour, Buddy (Race Car Driver)
PO Box 812
Bellmore, NY 11710-0812, USA

Gilmour, David (Music Group, Musician)
P O Box 62 Heathfield
East Sussex TN21 8ZE, UNITED KINGDOM (UK)

Gilmour, Doug (Hockey Player)
Octagon
1751 Pinnacle Dr Ste 1500
McLean, VA 22102-3833, USA

Gilmour of Craigmillar, Ian (Government Official)
Ferry House Old Isleworth
Middx, UNITED KINGDOM (UK)

Gilpin, Peri (Actor)
William Morris Agency
151 El Camino Dr
Beverly Hills, CA 90212-2775, USA

Gilroy, Frank D (Writer)
6 Magnin Rd
Monroe, NY 10950, USA

Gilroy, Tom (Actor, Director, Producer, Writer)
c/o Staff Member *William Morris Agency (WMA-LA)*
1 William Morris Pl
Beverly Hills, CA 90212-4261, USA

Gilsig, Jessalyn (Actor)
c/o Staff Member *Innovative Artists (LA)*
1505 10th St
Santa Monica, CA 90401-2805, USA

Gilson, Hal (Baseball Player)
St Louis Cardinals
2778 S Lansing Way
Aurora, CO 80014-3062, USA

Gilyard Jr, Clarence (Actor)
24040 Camino Del Avion # A239
Monarch Bay, CA 92629-4005, USA

Gimbel, Norman (Songwriter, Writer)
PO Box 50013
Santa Barbara, CA 93150-0013, USA

Gimbrone, Michael A Jr (Doctor, Misc)
Brigham & Women's Hospital
Vascular Pathlogy Dept
Boston, MA 02115, USA

Gimeno, Andres (Tennis Player)
Paseo de la Bnanova 38
Barcelona 6, SPAIN

Gimpel, Erica
c/o Staff Member *Innovative Artists (LA)*
1505 10th St
Santa Monica, CA 90401-2805, USA

Gin Blossoms
PO Box 429094
San Francisco, CA 94142-9094, USA

Gina G (Music Group)
What Mgmt
PO Box 1463
Culver City, CA 90232-1463, USA

Ging, Jack (Actor)
48701 San Pedro St
La Quinta, CA 92253-6229, USA

Gingerich, Philip D (Misc, Scientist)
University of Michigan
Paleontology Dept
Ann Arbor, MI 48109, USA

Gingrich, Newton L (Newt) (Politician)
1301 K St NW Ste 800W
Washington, DC 20005-3317, USA

Ginibre, Jean-Louis (Editor)
Hachett Filipacchi
1633 Broadway
New York, NY 10019-6741, USA

Ginn, Hubert (Football Player)
Miami Dolphins
16 Egrets Nest Dr
Savannah, GA 31406-4258, USA

Ginn, William H Jr (General)
1002 Priscilla Ln
Alexandria, VA 22308-2645, USA

Ginobili, Emanuel (Basketball Player)
c/o Staff Member *San Antonio Spurs*
100 Montana St
Alamodome
San Antonio, TX 78203-1031, USA

Ginsberg, Joe (Baseball Player)
Detroit Tigers
12635 SW Kingsway Cir # D1
Lake Suzy, FL 34269-4585, USA

Ginsberg, Justice Ruth Bader
700 New Hampshire Ave NW
Washington, DC 20037-2407, USA

Ginsburg, Art (Television Host)
Mr. Food
1770 NW 64th St Ste 500
King World Productions
Ft Lauderdale, FL 33309-1853, USA

Ginsburg, Douglas H (Judge)
US Court of Appeals
333 Constitution Ave NW
Washington, DC 20001-2866, USA

Ginsburg, Ruth Bader (Judge, Lawyer, Misc)
US Supreme Court
1 1st St NE
Washington, DC 20543-0002, USA

Ginsburg, William
10100 Santa Monica Blvd Ste 800
Los Angeles, CA 90067-4105, USA

Ginter, Keith (Baseball Player)
Houston Astros
2907 Maple Ave
Fullerton, CA 92835-2126, USA

Ginter, Matt (Baseball Player)
Chicago White Sox
3320 Boonesboro Rd
Winchester, KY 40391-9292, USA

Ginty, Robert (Actor)
Introvision
1011 N Fuller Ave
West Hollywood, CA 90046-6651, USA

Ginuwine (Music Group)
International Creative Mgmt
8942 Wilshire Blvd # 219
Beverly Hills, CA 90211-1908, USA

Ginzburg, Vitaly L (Nobel Prize Laureate)
Lebedev Physical Institute
Leninsky Prospect 53
Moscow 117924, RUSSIA

Ginzton, Edward L (Business Person, Engineer)
Varian Assoc
3100 Hansen Way
Palo Alto, CA 94304-1038, USA

Giofriddo, Al
64 Bristol Pl
Goleta, CA 93117-1949, USA

Gioia (Musician)
c/o Staff Member *Diva Central Inc*
7510 W Sunset Blvd Ste 1445
Los Angeles, CA 90046-3408, USA

Giola, Dana (Government Official, Writer)
National Endowment for Arts
1100 Pennsylvania Ave NW
Washington, DC 20506-0001, USA

Giordano, Michele Cardinal (Religious Leader)
Arcivescovado di Napoli
Largo Donnaregina 22
Naples 80138, ITALY

Giordano, Tommy (Baseball Player)
Philadelphia Athletics
176 Riverside Ave
Amityville, NY 11701-3738, USA

Giovanni, Joseph (Architect)
Giovanni Assoc
140 E 40th St
New York, NY 10016-1701, USA

Giovanni, Nikki E (Writer)
Virginia Polytechnic Institute
English Dept
Blacksburg, VA 24061-0001, USA

Giovanola, Ed (Baseball Player)
Atlanta Braves
1741 Nomark Ct
San Jose, CA 95125-3948, USA

Giovinazzo, Carmine (Actor)
c/o Craig Shapiro *Innovative Artists (LA)*
1505 10th St
Santa Monica, CA 90401-2805, USA

Gipson, Charles (Baseball Player)
Seattle Mariners
632 S Earlham St
Orange, CA 92869-5406, USA

Gipsy Kings (Music Group)
350 Lincoln Rd Ste 415
Miami Beach, FL 33139-3155, USA

Giradeau, Bernard
37 rue Froidevaux
Paris 75014, FRANCE

GiradelII, Marc (Skier)
9413 Oberegg-Sulzbach
SWITZERLAND

Giradelli, Marc
Obererg-
Sulzbach CH-9413, SWITZERLAND

Giraldi, Robert N (Bob) (Director)
Giraldi Saurez
581 Avenue Of The Americas
New York, NY 10011-2021, USA

Giraldo, Greg (Actor, Comedian)
c/o Staff Member *William Morris Agency (WMA-LA)*
1 William Morris Pl
Beverly Hills, CA 90212-4261, USA

Giraldo, Neil (Musician, Producer)
c/o Staff Member *William Morris Agency (WMA-LA)*
1 William Morris Pl
Beverly Hills, CA 90212-4261, USA

Girardi, Joseph E (Joe) (Baseball Player)
1845 S James Ct N
Lake Forest, IL 60045-4624, USA

Girardot, Annie (Actor)
c/o Josette Arrigoni *ArtMedia*
20 av Rapp
Paris 75007, FRANCE

Giraudeau, Bernard (Actor)
Cineart
36 Rue de Ponthieu
Paris 75008, FRANCE

Giri, Tulsi (Prime Minister)
Jawakpurdham
District Dhanuka, NEPAL

Girls Aloud
c/o Staff Member *Concorde Intl Artists Ltd*
101 Shepherds Bush Rd
London W6 7LP, UNITED KINGDOM (UK)

Girls Aloud (Music Group)
Polydor
72 Black Lion Ln
London W6 9BE, UNITED KINGDOM (UK)

Girone, Remo (Actor)
Cineart
36 Rue de Ponthieu
Paris 75008, FRANCE

Giroux, Bonny (Actor)
c/o Staff Member *Deborah Harry Talent*
408-1917 W 4th Ave
Vancouver, BC V6J 1M7, CANADA

Giroux, Robert (Publisher)
Farrar Straus Giroux
19 Union Sq W Fl 11
New York, NY 10003-3304, USA

Giscard, d'Estaing Valery (President)
199 Blvd Saint-Germain
Paris 75007, FRANCE

Gish, Annabeth (Actor)
2104 E Main St # 841
Ventura, CA 93001-3504, USA

Gisler, Mike (Football Player)
New England Patriots
407 Tampa Dr
Victoria, TX 77904-1649, USA

Gismonti, Egberto (Music Group, Musician)
International Music Network
278 S Main St #400
Gloucester, MA 01930, USA

Gitlin, Todd (Historian)
New York University
Culture & Communications Dept
New York, NY 10012, USA

Gitomer, Jeffrey (Business Person)
BuyGitomer Inc
310 Arlington Ave Unit 329
Charlotte, NC 28203-4296, USA

Giuffre, Carlo
Via Massimi 45
Rome I-00136, ITALY

Giuffre, James P (Jimmy) (Music Group, Musician)
Legacy Records
550 Madison Ave # 1700
New York, NY 10022-3211, USA

Giuliani, Tony (Baseball Player)
St Louis Cardinals
1985 Norfolk Ave
Saint Paul, MN 55116-2631, USA

Giuliano, Louis J (Business Person)
ITT Industries
4 W Red Oak Ln
White Plains, NY 10604-3617, USA

Giuliano, Tom (Music Group)
6929 N Hayden Rd
Scottsdale, AZ 85250-7978, USA

Giullani, Rudolph W (Misc, Politician)
Guiliani Partners
5 Times Sq Fl 6
New York, NY 10036-6528, USA

Giuranna, Bruno (Music Group, Musician)
Via Bembo 96
Asolo TV 31011, ITALY

Giusti, David J (Dave) (Baseball Player)
Houston Colt .45's
524 Clair Dr
Pittsburgh, PA 15241-2013, USA

Givenchy, Hubert
3 Ave. George V
Paris 75008, FRANCE

Givens, Adele
c/o Staff Member *William Morris Agency (WMA-LA)*
1 William Morris Pl
Beverly Hills, CA 90212-4261, USA

Givens, Jack (Basketball Player, Misc)
1536 Frazier Ave
Orlando, FL 32811-3920, USA

Givens, Robin (Actor)
c/o Alan Iezman *Shelter Entertainment*
9255 W Sunset Blvd Ste 1010
Los Angeles, CA 90069-3307, USA

Givins, Brian (Baseball Player)
Milwaukee Brewers
719 Stonemont Ct
Castle Rock, CO 80108-8238, USA

Givins, Ernest (Football Player)
Houston Oilers
2701 Union St S
Saint Petersburg, FL 33712-3836, USA

Gizzi, Claudio (Composer)
SIAE
Viaile dell Letteratura 30
Rome 00100, ITALY

Gladden, Danny (Dan) (Baseball Player)
San Francisco Giants
888 Brookgrove Ln
Cupertino, CA 95014-4634, USA

Gladding, Fred (Baseball Player)
Detroit Tigers
4721 Macmont Cir
Powell, TN 37849-4520, USA

Gladieux, Robert (Football Player)
Boston Patriots
802 Arch Ave
South Bend, IN 46601-3204, USA

Gladwell, Malcolm (Business Person, Writer)
410 W 24th St Apt 19A
New York, NY 10011-1309, USA

Glamack, George (Basketball Player)
50 Pleasant Way
Rochester, NY 14622-1227, USA

Glance, Harvey (Athlete, Track Athlete)
2408 Old Creek Rd
Montgomery, AL 36117-2420, USA

Glanville, Doug (Baseball Player)
Chicago Cubs
2043 W McLean Ave
Chicago, IL 60647-4532, USA

Glanville, Jerry (Coach, Football Coach, Sportscaster)
CBS-TV
51 W 52nd St
Sports Dept
New York, NY 10019-6119, USA

Glasbergen, Randy (Cartoonist)
King Features Syndicate
888 7th Ave Ste 201
New York, NY 10106-0201, USA

Glaser, Donald A (Nobel Prize Laureate)
University of California
Molecular Biology Laboratory
Berkeley, CA 94720-0001, USA

Glaser, Gabrielle (Gabby) (Music Group, Musician)
Metropolitan Entertainment
2 Penn Plz # 2600
New York, NY 10121-0101, USA

Glaser, Jim (Music Group)
Joe Taylor Artist Agency
2802 Columbine Pl
Nashville, TN 37204-3104, USA

Glaser, Jon (Actor, Writer)
c/o Staff Member *3 Arts Entertainment Inc*
9460 Wilshire Blvd Fl 7
Beverly Hills, CA 90212-2713, USA

Glaser, Milton (Artist, Misc)
Milton Glaser Assoc
207 E 32nd St
New York, NY 10016-6305, USA

Glaser, Paul Michael (Actor, Director)
c/o Mark Teitelbaum *Teitelbaum Artists Group*
8840 Wilshire Blvd # 200
Beverly Hills, CA 90211-2606, USA

Glaser, Robert (Doctor, Misc)
University of Pittsburgh
Psychology Dept
Pittsburgh, PA 15260, USA

Glaser, Robert J (Misc)
555 Byron St Apt 305
Palo Alto, CA 94301-2038, USA

Glaser, Rose Mary (Baseball Player)
2188 South Rd
Cincinnati, OH 45233-4266, USA

Glaser Brothers
91619th Ave
Nashville, TN 37212, USA

Glasgow, Brian (Football Player)
Chicago Bears
5 Sage Ct
Bolingbrook, IL 60490-3220, USA

Glasgow, Nesby (Football Player)
Baltimore Colts
8221 NE 115th Way
Kirkland, WA 98034-3506, USA

Glasgow, W Victor (Vic) (Basketball
Player)
6312 King Dr
Bartlesville, OK 74006-8949, USA

Glashow, Sheldon Lee (Nobel Prize
Laureate)
30 Prescott St
Brookline, MA 02446-4038, USA

Glaspie, April (Diplomat)
State Department
2201 C St NW
Washington, DC 20520-0099, USA

Glass, David (Baseball Player)
Kansas City Royals
17 Glenbrook
Bentonville, AR 72712-3840, USA

Glass, Glenn (Football Player)
Pittsburgh Steelers
301 Portsmouth Blvd
Knoxville, TN 37909-3020, USA

Glass, Leland (Football Player)
Green Bay Packers
1800 Hunters Run
Tuscaloosa, AL 35405-6743, USA

Glass, Nancy (Journalist)
Glass DiFede Productions
211 Rock Hill Rd Ste 100
Bala Cynwyd, PA 19004-2052, USA

Glass, Philip (Composer)
c/o Staff Member *Kraft-Engel Management*
15233 Ventura Blvd Ste 200
Sherman Oaks, CA 91403-2244, USA

Glass, Ron (Actor)
c/o Mitchell Stubbs *Mitchell K Stubbs &
Assoc (MKS)*
8695 Washington Blvd Ste 204
Culver City, CA 90232-7419, USA

Glass, Todd (Actor)
c/o Alex Murray *Nine Yards Entertainment*
8530 Wilshire Blvd Fl 5
Beverly Hills, CA 90211-3102, USA

Glass, William S (Bill) (Football Player)
Detroit Lions
PO Box 761101
Bill Glass Ministries
Dallas, TX 75376-1101, USA

Glass Tiger
238 Davenport #126
Toronto, ON M5R 1J, CANADA

Glasser, Erika (Actor)
c/o Gabriel Blanco *Gabriel Blanco
Iglesias (Mexico)*
Rio Balsas 35-32
Colonia Cuauhtemoc
DF 06500, MEXICO

Glasser, Ira S (Activist, Attorney, Attorney
General, General, Lawyer, Misc)
American Civil Liberties Union
132 W 43rd St
New York, NY 10036, USA

Glasser, Isabel (Actor)
c/o Kyle Luker *LaSalle Holland*
141 W 28th St Rm 300
New York, NY 10001-6187, USA

Glasser, William (Doctor, Misc)
11633 San Vincente Blvd
Los Angeles, CA 90049, USA

Glatter, Lesli L (Director)
United Talent Agency
9560 Wilshire Blvd Ste 500
Beverly Hills, CA 90212-2401, USA

Glattes, Wolfgang (Producer)
c/o Staff Member *Mirisch Agency*
1801 Century Park E Ste 1801
Los Angeles, CA 90067-2320, USA

Glatzeder, Winfried
Gosslerstrasse 24
Berlin D-12161, GERMANY

Glau, Summer (Actor)
c/o Amanda Glazer *Kohner Agency, The*
9300 Wilshire Blvd Ste 555
Beverly Hills, CA 90212-3211, USA

Glaudini, Lola (Actor)
c/o Staff Member *Innovative Artists (LA)*
1505 10th St
Santa Monica, CA 90401-2805, USA

Glaus, Troy (Baseball Player)
Anaheim Angels
4300 Bibleway Ct
Holly Springs, NC 27540-3305, USA

Glave, Matthew (Actor)
c/o Staff Member *Innovative Artists (LA)*
1505 10th St
Santa Monica, CA 90401-2805, USA

Glaviano, Tommy (Baseball Player)
St Louis Cardinals
5413 Marconi Ave Apt 11
Carmichael, CA 95608-4479, USA

Glavin, Denis Joseph (Misc)
*Electrical Radio & Machine Worders
Union*
11 E 1st St
New York, NY 10003-8996, USA

Glavine, Tom (Athlete)
8925 Old Southwick Pass
Alpharetta, GA 30022-7140, USA

Glazer, Jay (Sportscaster)
CBS-TV
51 W 52nd St
Sports Dept
New York, NY 10019-6119, USA

Glazer, Jonathan (Director, Writer)
c/o David Naylor *David Naylor &
Associates*
6535 Santa Monica Blvd
Los Angeles, CA 90038-1407, USA

Glazer, Mitch (Producer)
c/o Staff Member *Creative Artists Agency
LCC (CAA-LA)*
2000 Avenue Of The Stars
Los Angeles, CA 90067-4700, USA

Glazer, Nathan (Activist, Misc)
12 Scott St
Cambridge, MA 02138-2016, USA

Glazier, Nancy (Artist)
Somerset House Publishing
PO Box 869
Fulshear, TX 77441-0869, USA

Glazkov, Yuri N (Astronaut, General,
Misc)
Potchta Kosmonavtov
Moskovskoi Oblasti
Syvisdny Goroduk 141160, RUSSIA

Glazunov, Ilya S (Artist)
Razhviz Academy
Kamergersky Per 2
Moscow 103009, RUSSIA

Gleason, Joanna (Actor)
c/o Leslie Maskin *United Talent Agency
(UTA)*
9560 Wilshire Blvd Ste 500
Beverly Hills, CA 90212-2401, USA

Gleason, Mary Pat (Actor, Writer)
c/o Holly Shelton *Stone Manners Talent &
Literary (LA)*
6500 Wilshire Blvd Ste 550
Los Angeles, CA 90048-4950, USA

Gleason, Roy (Baseball Player)
Los Angeles Dodgers
41770 Margarita Rd Apt 1043
Temecula, CA 92591-1945, USA

Gleaton, Jerry Don (Baseball Player)
Texas Rangers
3008 Avenue K
Brownwood, TX 76801-6016, USA

Gleeson, Brendan (Actor)
c/o Joan Scott *Keylight Entertainment
(Joan Scott Management)*
888 7th Ave
35th Floor
New York, NY 10106-0001, USA

Glemp, Jozef Cardinal (Religious Leader)
Sekretariat Prymasa Kolski
Ul Miodowa 17
Warsaw 00 246, POLAND

Glen, John (Director)
Spyros Skouras
1015 Gayley Ave # 300
Los Angeles, CA 90024-3413, USA

Glenn, Aaron (Football Player)
New York Jets
30 Commanders Cv
Missouri City, TX 77459-6518, USA

Glenn, Bill (Football Player)
Chicago Bears
39 Lovell Valley Dr
Springfield, IL 62702-1672, USA

Glenn, Hubert (Baseball Player)
Philadelphia Stars
248 9th Avenue Dr NE
Hickory, NC 28601-3828, USA

Glenn, Jason (Football Player)
New York Jets
15530 Ella Blvd Apt 501
Houston, TX 77090-5309, USA

Glenn, John (Baseball Player)
St Louis Cardinals
1317 Perry Ave
Augusta, GA 30901-3251, USA

Glenn, Scott (Actor)
c/o Johnnie Planco *Untitled Entertainment
(NY)*
322 8th Ave Ste 601
New York, NY 10001-6715, USA

Glenn, Stanley (Baseball Player)
Philadelphia Stars
9 Baily Rd
Yeadon, PA 19050-2817, USA

Glenn, Tarik (Football Player)
Indianapolis Colts
10481 Titan Run
Carmel, IN 46032-8232, USA

Glenn, Terry (Football Player)
Dallas Cowboys
1 Cowboys Pkwy
Irving, TX 75063-4999, USA

Glenn, Vencie (Football Player)
New England Patriots
13833 Tummore Rd
Silver Spring, MD 20906, USA

Glenn, Wayne E (Misc)
United Paperworkers Int'l Union
3340 Perimeter Hill Dr
Nashville, TN 37211-4123, USA

Glenn Jr, John H (Astronaut, Senator)
Ohio State University
1947 N College Rd
Stillman Hall
Columbus, OH 43210-1181, USA

Glennan, Robert E Jr (Educator)
Emporia State University
President's Office
Emporia, KS 66801, USA

Glennie, Brian (Hockey Player)
Mortimer's Point Road
Port Carling, ON P0B 1J0, CANADA

Glennie, Evelyn E A (Music Group,
Musician)
P O Box 6 Sawtry Huntingdon
Cambs PE17 5WE, UNITED KINGDOM
(UK)

Glennie-Smith, Nick (Composer)
Vangelos Mgmt
15233 Ventura Blvd Ste 200
Sherman Oaks, CA 91403-2244, USA

Gless, Sharon (Actor)
Rosenzweig Productions
PO Box 48005
Los Angeles, CA 90048-0005, USA

Glick, Frederick (Freddie) (Football
Player)
Chicago Cardinals
4226 Antlers Ct
Fort Collins, CO 80526-6411, USA

Glick, Gary (Football Player)
Pittsburgh Steelers
2801 Middlesborough Ct
Fort Collins, CO 80525-2331, USA

Glickman, Daniel R (Misc, Secretary)
Harvard University
Kennedy Government School
Cambridge, MA 02138, USA

Glidden, Bob (Race Car Driver)
PO Box 173
Whiteland, IN 46184-0173, USA

Glidden, Robert (Educator)
Ohio University
President's Office
Athens, OH 45701, USA

Glidewell, Iain (Judge)
Rough Heys Farm Macclesfield
Cheshire SK11 9PF, UNITED KINGDOM
(UK)

Glimcher, Arnold O (Arne) (Artist, Misc)
Pace Gallery
32 E 57th St
New York, NY 10022-2530, USA

Glinatsis, George (Baseball Player)
Seattle Mariners
13742 W 59th Ave
Arvada, CO 80004-3740, USA

Glitman, Maynard W (Diplomat)
PO Box 438
Jeffersonville, VT 05464-0438, USA

Glitter, Gary (Music Group, Songwriter, Writer)
Jef Hanlon Mgmt
1 York St
London W1H 1PZ, UNITED KINGDOM
(UK)

Glmble, Johnny (Misc)
Nancy Fly Agency
6618 Wolfcreek Pall
Austin, TX 78749, USA

Gload, Ross (Baseball Player)
Chicago Cubs
23 Harrison Ave
East Hampton, NY 11937-2051, USA

Globus, Yoram (Producer)
Pathe International
8670 Wilshire Blvd
Beverly Hills, CA 90211-2924, USA

Glockner, Michael
Kaiserslautener Str. 54
Saarbrucken D-66123, GERMANY

Gloden, Fred (Football Player)
Philadelphia Eagles
3821 Andrea Rd
Philadelphia, PA 19154-4211, USA

Glory, New Found (Music Group)
c/o Staff Member *Ellis Industries Inc*
234 Shoreward Dr
Great Neck, NY 11021-2734, USA

Glosson, Clyde (Football Player)
Buffalo Bills
5803 Lake Falls Dr
San Antonio, TX 78222-2405, USA

Glossop, Peter (Opera Singer)
End Cottage 7 Gate Close
Hawkchurch near Axminster
Devon, UNITED KINGDOM (UK)

Glouberman, Michael (Producer)
c/o Staff Member *United Talent Agency (UTA)*
9560 Wilshire Blvd Ste 500
Beverly Hills, CA 90212-2401, USA

Glover, Andrew (Football Player)
Oakland Raiders
23106 Dew Wood Ln
Spring, TX 77373-6905, USA

Glover, Bloc (Motorcycle Race, Motorcycle Racer)
American Motorcycle Assn
13515 Yarmouth Dr
Pickerington, OH 43147-8273, USA

Glover, Brian (Actor)
DeWolfe
Manfield House
376/378 Strand
London WC2R OLR, UNITED KINGDOM
(UK)

Glover, Bruce (Actor)
11449 Woodbine St
Los Angeles, CA 90066-1229, USA

Glover, Chris (Musician)
c/o Staff Member *Paradigm (Monterey)*
509 Hartnell St
Monterey, CA 93940-2825, USA

Glover, Crispin (Actor)
3573 Carnation Ave
Los Angeles, CA 90026-1103, USA

Glover, Danny (Actor)
PO Box 170069
San Francisco, CA 94117-0069, USA

Glover, Gary (Baseball Player)
Toronto Blue Jays
2135 Penn Dr
Deland, FL 32724-8356, USA

Glover, Jane A
Kaylor Mgmt
130 W 57th St Apt 8G
New York, NY 10019-3311, USA

Glover, John (Actor)
130 W 42nd St # 2400
New York, NY 10036-7902, USA

Glover, Julian (Actor)
200 Fulham Road
London SW10 9PN, UNITED KINGDOM
(UK)

Glover, Kevin B (Football Player)
Detroit Lions
11553 Manorstone Ln
Columbia, MD 21044-5413, USA

Glover, La'Roi (Football Player)
Oakland Raiders
841 49th St
San Diego, CA 92102-3711, USA

Glover, Richard E (Rich) (Football Player)
New York Giants
215 Claremont Ave
Jersey City, NJ 07305-3623, USA

Glover, Stephen (Steve-O) (Actor, Writer)
c/o Cal Boyington *Paradigm (LA)*
360 N Crescent Dr
North Bldg
Beverly Hills, CA 90210-6820, USA

Glowacki, Janusz (Writer)
845 W End Ave Apt 4B
New York, NY 10025-8436, USA

Gluck, Carol (Historian)
440 Riverside Dr
New York, NY 10027-6828, USA

Gluck, Louise E (Writer)
Williams College
English Dept
Williamstown, MA 02167, USA

Glueck, Larry (Football Player)
Chicago Bears
104B Heritage Hls
Somers, NY 10589-1316, USA

Glushchenko, Fedor I
1st Prydilnaya Str 11 #5
Moscow 105037, RUSSIA

Glynn, Bill (Baseball Player)
Philadelphia Phillies
6916 51st St
San Diego, CA 92120-1212, USA

Glynn, Carlin (Actor)
1165 5th Ave
New York, NY 10029-6931, USA

Glynn, Ed (Baseball Player)
Detroit Tigers
157 San Carlos St
Toms River, NJ 08757-6222, USA

Glynn, Ian M (Misc, Physicist)
Daylesford Conduit Head Road
Cambridge CB3 0EY, UNITED KINGDOM
(UK)

Glynn, Robert D Jr (Business Person)
PG&E Corp
1 Market St
Spear Tower
San Francisco, CA 94105-1420, USA

Glynn, Ryan (Baseball Player)
Texas Rangers
3648 Kings Rd # 5-102
Palm Harbor, FL 34685-4195, USA

Gminski, Mike (Basketball Player, Sportscaster)
1309 Canterbury Hill Cir
Charlotte, NC 28211-1454, USA

Gnarls Barkley (Music Group)
Downtown Records
73 Spring St Rm 504
New York, NY 10012-5802, USA

Gnedovsky, Yuri P (Architect)
Union of Architects
Granatny Per 22
Moscow 103001, RUSSIA

Go-Go's, The (Musician)
c/o Bradford Cobb *Direct Management Group*
947 N La Cienega Blvd Ste G
Los Angeles, CA 90069-4700, USA

Goad, Tim (Football Player)
New England Patriots
138 Birchwood Dr
Pittsboro, NC 27312-8737, USA

Gob, Art (Football Player)
Washington Redskins
123 Hiscott Dr
Pittsburgh, PA 15241-1105, USA

Gobble, Jimmy (Baseball Player)
Kansas City Royals
18668 Benhams Rd
Bristol, VA 24202-0460, USA

Goble, Les (Football Player)
Chicago Cardinals
21 Dodge Ave
Waverly, NY 14892-9568, USA

Gocke, Justin
6763 Pistachio Pl
Palmdale, CA 93551-1930, USA

Godard, Jean-Luc (Director)
15 Rue du Nord
Roulle 1180, SWITZERLAND

Godbold, John C (Judge)
US Court of Appeals
PO Box 3038
Montgomery, AL 36109-0038, USA

Godboldo, Dale (Actor)
c/o Staff Member *Burstein Company, The*
15304 W Sunset Blvd Ste 208
Pacific Palisades, CA 90272-3656, USA

Godby, Danny (Baseball Player)
St Louis Cardinals
RR 2 Box 17A
Chapmanville, WV 25508-9773, USA

Godchaux, Stephen (Producer)
c/o Staff Member *William Morris Agency (WMA-LA)*
1 William Morris Pl
Beverly Hills, CA 90212-4261, USA

Goddard, Anna-Marie (Model)
PO Box 7624
Capistrano Beach, CA 92624-7624, USA

Goddard, Daniel (Actor)
c/o Paul Nelson *Mosaic Media Group*
24 Music Sq W Fl 1
Nashville, TN 37203-6661, USA

Goddard, Joe (Baseball Player)
San Diego Padres
304 Ridgepark Dr
Beckley, WV 25801-9593, USA

Goddard, John (Misc, Scientist)
4224 Beulah Dr
La Canada, CA 91011-3826, USA

Goddard, Mark (Actor)
PO Box 778
Middleboro, MA 02346-0778, USA

Goddard, Samuel P (Sam) Jr (Governor)
4724 E Camelback Canyon Dr
Phoenix, AZ 85018, USA

Godecki, Marzena (Actor)
Jonathan M. Shiff Productions
373 Bay Street
Port Melbourne
Victoria 3207, AUSTRALIA

Godfrey, Paul V (Publisher)
Toronto Sun
333 King St E
Toronto, ON M5A 3X5, CANADA

Godfrey, Randall (Football Player)
Dallas Cowboys
PO Box 9511
Rancho Santa Fe, CA 92067-4511, USA

Godin, Seth (Business Person, Writer)
c/o Staff Member *Greater Talent Network Inc*
437 5th Ave Fl 7
New York, NY 10016-2205, USA

Godina, John
PO Box 120
Indianapolis, IN 46204, USA

Godley, Georgina (Designer, Fashion Designer)
42 Bassett Road
London W10 6UL, UNITED KINGDOM
(UK)

Godley, Kevin (Music Group, Musician)
Heronden Hall Tenterden
Kent, UNITED KINGDOM (UK)

Godmanis, Ivars (Misc, Politician)
Palasta St 1
Riga 1954, LATVIA

Godreche, Judith (Actor)
William Morris Agency
151 El Camino Dr
Beverly Hills, CA 90212-2775, USA

Godwin, Fay S (Photographer)
Fay Godwin Network
3-4 Kerby St
London E4N 8TS, UNITED KINGDOM
(UK)

Godwin, Gail K (Writer)
PO Box 946
Woodstock, NY 12498-0946, USA

Godwin, Linda M (Astronaut, Physicist)
16923 Cottonwood Way
Houston, TX 77059-3102, USA

Godynyuk, Alexander (Hockey Player)
VIP Sports International
110 E 59th St
New York, NY 10022-1304, USA

Goeas, Leo (Football Player)
San Diego Chargers
18083 Chieftain Ct
San Diego, CA 92127-3118, USA

Goebel, Timothy (Figure Skater)
c/o Staff Member *Champions on Ice*
3500 W 80th St
Tom Collins Enterprises Inc
Minneapolis, MN 55431-1068, USA

Goeddeke, George (Football Player)
Denver Broncos
1227 Pinecrest Dr
White Lake, MI 48386-3655, USA

Goehr, Alexander
11 West Rd.
Cambridge, ENGLAND, UNITED
KINGDOM (UK)

Goehr, P Alexander (Composer)
University of Cambridge
Music Faculty 11 West Road
Cambridge, UNITED KINGDOM (UK)

Goel, Jyotin (Actor, Bollywood)
258 Famous Cine Building
Mahalaxmi
Bombay, MS 400 011, INDIA

Goellner, Marc-Kevin (Athlete, Tennis
Player)
Blau-Weiss Neuss
Tennishall Jahnstrasse
Neuss 41464, GERMANY

Goelz, Dave (Gonzo) (Artist, Misc)
Jim Henson Productions
117 E 69th St
New York, NY 10021-5004, USA

Goen, Bob (Entertainer)
21767 Planewood Dr
Woodland Hills, CA 91364-5216, USA

Goerke, Glenn A (Educator)
University of Houston
President's Office
Houston, TX 77204-0001, USA

Goestenkors, Gail (Basketball Player,
Coach)
Duke University
Athletic Dept
Durham, NC 27708-0001, USA

Goestschi, Renate (Skier)
Schwarzenbach 3
Obdach 8742, AUSTRIA

Goettmann, Georgia
344 E 59th St
New York, NY 10022-1593, USA

Goetz, Bernhard
55 W 14th St
New York, NY 10011-7407, USA

Goetz, Eric (Misc, Yachtsman)
Eric Goetz Marine & Technology
15 Broad Common Rd
Bristol, RI 02809-2721, USA

Goetz, John (Baseball Player)
Chicago Cubs
3253 Myddleton Dr
Troy, MI 48084-1274, USA

Goetz, Peter Michael (Actor)
c/o Staff Member *SMS Talent Inc*
8730 W Sunset Blvd Ste 440
Los Angeles, CA 90069-2277, USA

Goetz, Russ (Baseball Player)
937 Fawcett Ave
McKeesport, PA 15132-1409, USA

Goetzman, Gary (Producer)
c/o Staff Member *Creative Artists Agency
LCC (CAA-LA)*
2000 Avenue Of The Stars
Los Angeles, CA 90067-4700, USA

Goff, Jerry (Baseball Player)
Montreal Expos
3 Oak Valley Dr
Novato, CA 94947-1964, USA

Goff, Mike (Football Player)
Cincinnati Bengals
2225 5th St
Peru, IL 61354-2506, USA

Goff, Willard (Football Player)
Atlanta Falcons
441 E 10th Ave
Springfield, CO 81073, USA

Goffin, David (Producer)
c/o Staff Member *International Creative
Management (ICM-LA)*
10250 Constellation Blvd
Los Angeles, CA 90067-6200, USA

Goffin, Gerry (Misc, Songwriter, Writer)
9171 Hazen Dr
Beverly Hills, CA 90210-1825, USA

Gofourth, Derrel (Football Player)
Green Bay Packers
1119 S Woodcrest Dr
Stillwater, OK 74074-1433, USA

Goganious, Keith (Football Player)
Buffalo Bills
4173 Cheswick Ln
Virginia Beach, VA 23455-6560, USA

Goggin, Chuck (Baseball Player)
Pittsburgh Pirates
4311 Crystal Lake Dr Apt 211
Pompano Beach, FL 33064-1244, USA

Goggins, Walton (Actor)
c/o Staff Member *Abrams Artists Agency
(LA)*
9200 W Sunset Blvd Ph 11
Los Angeles, CA 90069-3601, USA

Gogolak, Charlie (Football Player)
Washington Redskins
47 Village Ave Unit 211
Dedham, MA 02026-4233, USA

Gogolak, Peter (Pete) (Football Player)
Buffalo Bills
24 Arrowhead Way
Darien, CT 06820-5505, USA

Gogolewski, Bill (Baseball Player)
Washington Senators
1522 Graham Ave
Oshkosh, WI 54902-2623, USA

Goh, Kun (Prime Minister)
Prime Minister's Office
77 Sejonh-no
Chongnoku
Seoul, SOUTH KOREA

Goh, Michelle (Actor)
c/o Leonard Bonnell *Characters Talent
Agency, The (Vancouver)*
1505 W 2nd Ave #200
Vancouver, BC V6H 3Y4, CANADA

Goh, Rex (Music Group, Musician)
Agency for Performing Arts
405 S Beverly Dr Ste 500
Beverly Hills, CA 90212-4425, USA

Goh Chok Tong (Prime Minister)
Prime Minister's Office
Istana Annexe
Singapore 0923, SINGAPORE

Goheen, Robert F (Diplomat, Educator)
1 Orchard Cir
Princeton, NJ 08540-3025, USA

Gohr, Greg (Baseball Player)
Detroit Tigers
77 Scotland Rd
Reading, MA 01867-3323, USA

Goich, Dan (Football Player)
Detroit Lions
PO Box 19068
Las Vegas, NV 89132-0068, USA

Going, Joanna (Actor)
c/o Staff Member *Cunningham Escott
Slevin & Doherty (LA)*
10635 Santa Monica Blvd Ste 130
Los Angeles, CA 90025-8306, USA

Goings, E V (Business Person)
Tupperware Corp
PO Box 2353
Orlando, FL 32802-2353, USA

Goings, Nick (Athlete)
c/o Staff Member *Carolina Panthers*
800 S Mint St
Ericsson Stadium
Charlotte, NC 28202-1640, USA

Goitschel-Beranger, Marielle (Skier)
Val Thorens
Saint-Martin de Belleville 73440, FRANCE

Gola, Tom
15 Kings Oak Ln
Philadelphia, PA 19115-4008, USA

Gold, Andrew (Music Group, Songwriter,
Writer)
Store
5317 Felice Pl
Woodland Hills, CA 91364-3525, USA

Gold, Brandy (Actor)
Gold Marshak Liedtke
3500 W Olive Ave Ste 1400
Burbank, CA 91505-5512, USA

Gold, Elon (Actor, Comedian)
United Talent Agency
9560 Wilshire Blvd Ste 500
Beverly Hills, CA 90212-2401, USA

Gold, Herbert (Writer)
1051 Broadway # A
San Francisco, CA 94133-4205, USA

Gold, Ian (Football Player)
Denver Broncos
10275 Tradition Pl
Lone Tree, CO 80124-8505, USA

Gold, Jack (Director)
24 Wood Vale
London N10 3DP, UNITED KINGDOM
(UK)

Gold, Jaime (Misc)
Buzznation LLC
11601 Wilshire Blvd Ste 22
Los Angeles, CA 90025-0509, USA

Gold, Jimmy
11990 San Vicente Blvd Ste 340
Los Angeles, CA 90049-6608, USA

Gold, Judy (Comedian)
c/o Ross Mark *ReBar Management*
10061 Riverside Dr # 722
Toluca Lake, CA 91602-2560, USA

Gold, Missy
3500 W Olive Ave Ste 1400
Burbank, CA 91505-5512, USA

Gold, Murray (Musician)
Manners McDade Artist Management
c/o Catherine Manners
18 Broadwick St 4th Fl
London W1F 8HS, UNITED KINGDOM
(UK)

Gold, Seth (DJ)
c/o Len Evans *Project Publicity*
312 W 53rd St
New York, NY 10019-5743, USA

Gold, Todd
c/o Daniel A (Dan) Strone *Trident Media
Group LLC*
41 Madison Ave Fl 36
New York, NY 10010-2257, USA

Gold, Tracey (Actor)
c/o Harry Gold *TalentWorks (LA)*
3500 W Olive Ave Ste 1400
Burbank, CA 91505-5512, USA

Goldberg, Adam (Actor)
Innovative Artists
1505 10th St
Santa Monica, CA 90401-2805, USA

Goldberg, Bill (Football Player)
c/o Barry McPherson *Agency for the
Performing Arts (APA-LA)*
405 S Beverly Dr
Beverly Hills, CA 90212-4416, USA

Goldberg, Edward D (Geophysicist, Misc,
Physicist)
750 Val Sereno Dr
Encinitas, CA 92024-6919, USA

Goldberg, Eric (Animator)
c/o Ellen Goldsmith-Vein *The Gotham
Group Inc*
9255 W Sunset Blvd Ste 515
Los Angeles, CA 90069-3301, USA

Goldberg, Gary David (Actor, Director,
Producer, Writer)
c/o Staff Member *UBU Productions*
4024 Radford Ave
Bungalow 14
Studio City, CA 91604-2101, USA

Goldberg, Leonard (Producer)
Spectradyne Inc
1198 Commerce Dr
Richardson, TX 75081-2307, USA

Goldberg, Lucianne
255 W 84th St Apt 6A
New York, NY 10024-4323, USA

Goldberg, Luella G (Educator)
7019 Tupa Dr
Minneapolis, MN 55439-1643, USA

Goldberg, Marshall (Football Player)
Chicago Cardinals
180 E Pearson St Apt 4202
Chicago, IL 60611-2110, USA

Goldberg, Marshall (Biggie) (Artist)
222 Bowery
New York, NY 10012-4216, USA

Goldberg, Richard W (Judge)
US International Trade Court
1 Federal Plz
New York, NY 10278-0001, USA

Goldberg, Stan (Cartoonist)
8 White Birch Ln
Scarsdale, NY 10583-7635, USA

Goldberg, Whoopi (Actor, Comedian)
c/o Brad Cafarelli *Bragman/Nyman/
Cafarelli (BNC)*
8687 Melrose Ave Fl 8
Pacific Design Center
Los Angeles, CA 90069-5701, USA

Goldberger, Andi
Bleckenwegen 4
Waldzell 4924, AUSTRIA

Goldberger, Andreas (Skier)
Bleckenwegen 4
Waldzell 4924, AUSTRIA

Goldberger, Marvin L (Educator,
Physicist)
621 Mira Monte
La Jolla, CA 92037-6728, USA

Goldberger, Paul J (Critic, Journalist)
New York Times
229 W 43rd St
Editorial Dept
New York, NY 10036-3959, USA

Goldblatt, Stephen L (Cinematographer)
Spyros Skouras
631 Wilshire Blvd # 2C
Santa Monica, CA 90401-1510, USA

Goldblum, Jeff (Actor)
15030 Ventura Blvd # 710
Sherman Oaks, CA 91403-5470, USA

Golden, Arthur (Writer)
c/o Lynn Pleshette *Lynn Pleshette Literary
Agency*
2700 N Beachwood Dr
Los Angeles, CA 90068-1922, USA

Golden, Harry (Bowler, Misc)
Professional Bowlers Assn
719 2nd Ave Ste 701
Seattle, WA 98104-1747, USA

Golden, Jim (Baseball Player)
Los Angeles Dodgers
8630 SW 10th Ave
Topeka, KS 66615-9688, USA

Golden, Kit (Producer)
c/o Staff Member *Manhattan Project*
1775 Broadway Ste 410
New York, NY 10019-1903, USA

Golden, Michael (Business Person)
New York Times Co
229 W 43rd St
New York, NY 10036-3959, USA

Golden, William Lee (Music Group,
Songwriter, Writer)
PO Box 1795
Hendersonville, TN 37077-1795, USA

Goldens, The
PO Box 1795
Hendersonville, TN 37077-1795, USA

Goldenthal, Elliot (Composer)
Gorfaine/Schwartz
4111 W Alameda Ave Ste 509
Burbank, CA 91505-4171, USA

Goldfinger, Sarah (Actor)
c/o Staff Member *Creative Artists Agency
LCC (CAA-LA)*
2000 Avenue Of The Stars
Los Angeles, CA 90067-4700, USA

Goldhaber, Maurice (Physicist)
91 S Gillette Ave
Bayport, NY 11705-2226, USA

Goldin, Claudia D (Economist)
Harvard University
Economics Dept
Cambridge, MA 02138, USA

Goldin, Judah (Educator)
3300 Darby Rd
Haverford, PA 19041-1061, USA

Goldin, Nan (Photographer)
334 Bowery
New York, NY 10012-2430, USA

Goldin, Ricky Paull (Actor)
Metropolitan Talent Agency
4500 Wilshire Blvd Fl 2
Los Angeles, CA 90010-3858, USA

Goldin, Ricky Paull (Actor)
365 W 52nd St # Le
New York, NY 10019-6250, USA

Golding, Meta (Actor)
c/o Charlton Blackburne *A Management*
9107 Wilshire Blvd Ste 650
Beverly Hills, CA 90210-5544, USA

Goldman, Bo (Writer)
Creative Artists Agency
9830 Wilshire Blvd
Beverly Hills, CA 90212-1804, USA

Goldman, Les (Football Player)
Green Bay Packers
800 E Cypress Creek Rd Ste 203
Fort Lauderdale, FL 33334-3522, USA

Goldman, William (Writer)
Janklow & Nesbit
445 Park Ave # 1300
New York, NY 10022-2606, USA

Goldoni, Lelia
15459 Wyandotte St
Van Nuys, CA 91406-3334, USA

Goldrup, Ray
2383 Broderick Dr
West Jordan, UT 84084-5703, USA

Goldsboro, Bobby (Music Group,
Songwriter, Writer)
La Rana Productions
PO Box 4979
Ocala, FL 34478-4979, USA

Goldschmidt, Neil E (Governor, Misc,
Secretary)
222 SW Columbia St
Portland, OR 97201-6600, USA

Goldsman, Akiva (Director)
c/o Risa Gertner *Creative Artists Agency
LCC (CAA-LA)*
2000 Avenue Of The Stars
Los Angeles, CA 90067-4700, USA

Goldsmith, Barbara (Writer)
Janklow Nesbit Assocs
445 Park Ave # 1300
New York, NY 10022-2606, USA

Goldsmith, Bethany (Baseball Player)
1000 E Michigan St Apt A
Orlando, FL 32806-4736, USA

Goldsmith, Judy (Activist)
National Organization for Women
425 13th St NE
Washington, DC 20002-6327, USA

Goldsmith, Kelly (Actor)
c/o Dede Binder-Goldsmith *Defining
Artists*
10 Universal City Plz Ste 2000
Universal City, CA 91608-1074, USA

Goldsmith, Paul
1148 Vivian Ln
Munster, IN 46321-2537, USA

Goldsmith, Stephen (Misc, Politician)
Governor's Office
State House
Indianapolis, IN 46204-2728, USA

Goldsmith-Thomas, Elaine (Producer)
c/o Staff Member *Red Om Films Inc*
16 W 19th St Fl 12
New York, NY 10011-4205, USA

Goldstein, Avram (Misc)
620 Sand Hill Rd Apt 120D
Palo Alto, CA 94304-2095, USA

Goldstein, Jenette
3932 Marathon St
Los Angeles, CA 90029-3602, USA

Goldstein, Joseph L (Nobel Prize
Laureate)
3831 Turtle Creek Blvd Apt 22B
Dallas, TX 75219-4538, USA

Goldstein, Lonnie (Baseball Player)
Cincinnati Reds
3401 Premier Dr Apt 213
Plano, TX 75023-7093, USA

Goldstein, Murray (Misc, Physicist)
United Cerebral Palsey Foundation
1025 Connecticut Ave NW Ste 701
Washington, DC 20036-5447, USA

Goldstone, Jeffrey (Physicist)
77 Massachusetts Ave # 6-313
Cambridge, MA 02139-4301, USA

Goldstone, Ralph (Football Player)
Philadelphia Eagles
4813 Westchester Dr Apt 119
Youngstown, OH 44515-2511, USA

Goldstone, Richard J (Judge)
Constitutional Court Private Bag X32
Braamfontein 2017, SOUTH AFRICA

Goldsworthy, Andrew C (Andy) (Artist,
Photographer)
Hue-Williams Fine Art
21 Cork St
London W1X 1HB, UNITED KINGDOM
(UK)

Goldthwait, Bob (Bobcat) (Actor,
Comedian)
c/o Rick Greenstein *Gersh Agency, The
(LA)*
232 N Canon Dr
Beverly Hills, CA 90210-5302, USA

Goldwater Jr, Barry
4401 Connecticut Ave NW Pmb 850
Washington, DC 20077-0001, USA

Goldwyn, Tony (Actor, Director)
Creative Artists Agency
9830 Wilshire Blvd
Beverly Hills, CA 90212-1804, USA

Goldwyn Jr, Samuel (Producer)
c/o Staff Member *Samuel Goldwyn
Company*
9570 W Pico Blvd Ste 400
Los Angeles, CA 90035-1216, USA

Goldy, Purnal (Baseball Player)
Detroit Tigers
1318 Cherryville Rd
Greenwood Village, CO 80121-1222,
USA

Golembiewski, Billy (Bowler)
4966 N Wise Rd
Coleman, MI 48618-9658, USA

Golenbock, Peter (Baseball Player, Writer)
849 Jennings Ave N
Saint Petersburg, FL 33704-1142, USA

Golic, Mike (Football Player)
Houston Oilers
108 Westland Rd
Avon, CT 06001-2349, USA

Golic, Robert P (Bob) (Football Player,
Sportscaster)
New England Patriots
6130 Loch Lomond Ct
Solon, OH 44139-5945, USA

Golina, Stacy
325 S Swall Dr Apt 502
Los Angeles, CA 90048-3078, USA

Golino, Valeria (Actor)
Creative Artists Agency
9830 Wilshire Blvd
Beverly Hills, CA 90212-1804, USA

Golisano, B Thomas (Business Person)
Paychex Inc
911 Panorama Trl S
Rochester, NY 14625-2396, USA

Gollat, Mike (Baseball Player)
Philadelphia Phillies
2650 Greenlawn Dr
Seven Hills, OH 44131-3623, USA

Golodryga, Bianna (Actor, Anchor)
c/o Staff Member *CNBC*
900 Sylvan Ave
Englewood Cliffs, NJ 07632-3312, USA

Golonka, Arlene (Actor)
Silver/Kass/Massetti
8730 W Sunset Blvd Ste 480
Los Angeles, CA 90069-2277, USA

Golson, Benny (Composer, Music Group,
Musician)
Abby Hoffer
223 1/2 E 48th St
New York, NY 10017, USA

Golsteyn, Jerry (Football Player)
New York Giants
243 Tadcaster Ct
Raeford, NC 28376-6623, USA

Goltz, Dave (Baseball Player)
Minnesota Twins
1009 Stony Brook Mnr
Fergus Falls, MN 56537-4413, USA

Golub, Richard
42 E 64th St
New York, NY 10065-7306, USA

Gomes, Wayne (Baseball Player)
Philadelphia Phillies
4 Boykin Ln
Hampton, VA 23663-1009, USA

Gomez (Music Group)
c/o Staff Member *Paradigm (Monterey)*
509 Hartnell St
Monterey, CA 93940-2825, USA

Gomez, Andres (Tennis Player)
ProServe
1101 Woodrow Wilson Blvd #1800
Arlington, VA 22209, USA

Gomez, Chris (Baseball Player)
Detroit Tigers
8 Vernal Spg
Irvine, CA 92603-0405, USA

Gomez, Hector (Actor)
c/o Staff Member *Televisa*
Blvd Adolfo Lopez Mateos 232
Colonia San Angel INN
DF CP 01060, MEXICO

Gomez, Ian (Actor)
c/o Gabrielle Krengel *Domain*
4526 Wilshire Blvd
Los Angeles, CA 90010-3801, USA

Gomez, Javier (Actor)
c/o Gabriel Blanco *Gabriel Blanco Iglesias (Mexico)*
Rio Balsas 35-32
Colonia Cuauhtemoc
DF 06500, MEXICO

Gomez, Jill (Opera Singer)
16 Milton Park
London N6 5QA, UNITED KINGDOM
(UK)

Gomez, Leo (Baseball Player)
Baltimore Orioles
11760 Frederick Rd
Ellicott City, MD 21042-1032, USA

Gomez, Luis (Baseball Player)
Minnesota Twins
676 Chesterfield Dr
Lawrenceville, GA 30044-5624, USA

Gomez, Panchito
PO Box 7016
Burbank, CA 91510-7016, USA

Gomez, Pat (Baseball Player)
San Diego Padres
7217 Oakberry Way
Citrus Heights, CA 95621-1230, USA

Gomez, Preston (Baseball Player)
Washington Senators
15765 Sleepy Oak Rd
Chino Hills, CA 91709-3845, USA

Gomez, Rick (Actor)
c/o Sam Maydew *The Collective*
9615 Brighton Way Ste 426
Beverly Hills, CA 90210-5118, USA

Gomez, Scott (Hockey Player)
1812 Toklat St
Anchorage, AK 99508-3253, USA

Gomez-Preston, Reagan (Actor)
c/o Mara Santino *Kazarian/Spencer & Assoc (LA)*
11969 Ventura Blvd
Box 7409 Fl 3
Studio City, CA 91604-2630, USA

Gomez-Preston, Reagen (Actor)
c/o Staff Member *Jeff Morrone Management*
9350 Wilshire Blvd Ste 224
Beverly Hills, CA 90212-3204, USA

Gompers, Bill (Football Player)
Buffalo Bills
181 Roscommon Pl
Mc Murray, PA 15317-2445, USA

Gompf, Thomas (Tom) (Misc, Swimmer)
2716 Barrel Ave
Plant City, FL 33566, USA

Goncalves, Vascos dos Santos (General, Prime Minister)
Ave Estados Unidos da America 86
5 Esq
Lisbon 1700, PORTUGAL

Gonchar, Sergei (Hockey Player)
Int'l Management Group
801 6th St SW #235
Calgary, AB T2P 3V8, CANADA

Gonda, George (Football Player)
Pittsburgh Steelers
2919 Grayland Ave
Richmond, VA 23221-3523, USA

Gonder, Jesse (Baseball Player)
New York Yankees
604 56th St
Oakland, CA 94609-1606, USA

Gondry, Michel (Director, Writer)
c/o Dan Aloni *Creative Artists Agency LCC (CAA-LA)*
2000 Avenue Of The Stars
Los Angeles, CA 90067-4700, USA

Gonick, Larry (Cartoonist)
247 Missouri St
San Francisco, CA 94107-2404, USA

Gonnenwein, Wolfgang
Opera et Concert
Maximilianstr 22
Munich 80539, GERMANY

Gonshaw, Francesca (Actor)
Greg Mellard
12 D'Arblay St #200
London W1V 3FP, UNITED KINGDOM
(UK)

Gonsoulin, Austin (Goose) (Football Player)
Denver Broncos
5966 Reeves Dr
Silsbee, TX 77656-8987, USA

Gonzaga, John (Football Player)
San Francisco 49ers
5812 Glen Eagles Dr
West Bloomfield, MI 48323-2205, USA

Gonzales, Alberto (Government Official, Judge)
White House
1600 Pennsylvania Ave NW
Washington, DC 20500-0004, USA

Gonzales, Carlos (Cinematographer)
1549 1/2 N Commonwealth Ave
Los Angeles, CA 90027-5513, USA

Gonzales, Dan (Baseball Player)
Detroit Tigers
429 W Silvertip Rd
Tucson, AZ 85737-3704, USA

Gonzales, Raul (Soccer Player)
Sergio Cerro Luengas
Alcala 694 1
Madrid 28019, SPAIN

Gonzales, Rene (Baseball Player)
Montreal Expos
755 E Orangewood Dr
Covina, CA 91723-3620, USA

Gonzalez, Alexander S (Alex) (Baseball Player)
8620 SW 102nd Ave
Miami, FL 33173-3943, USA

Gonzalez, Araceli (Actor)
c/o Staff Member *Telefe - Argentina*
Pavon 2444 (C1248AAT)
Buenos Aires, ARGENTINA

Gonzalez, Arthur (Judge)
US Bankruptcy Court
1 Bowling Grn
New York, NY 10004-1400, USA

Gonzalez, Clifton
955 Carrillo Dr Ste 300
Los Angeles, CA 90048-5400, USA

Gonzalez, Edith (Actor)
c/o Staff Member *Televisa*
Blvd Adolfo Lopez Mateos 232
Colonia San Angel INN
DF CP 01060, MEXICO

Gonzalez, Gabe (Baseball Player)
Florida Marlins
920 Cerritos Ave
Long Beach, CA 90813-4812, USA

Gonzalez, Hector (Religious Leader)
Baptist Churches USA
PO Box 851
Valley Forge, PA 19482-0851, USA

Gonzalez, Juan (Athlete, Baseball Player)
c/o Staff Member *Texas Rangers*
1000 Ballpark Way Ste 306
Arlington, TX 76011-5169, USA

Gonzalez, Juan A (Baseball Player)
Ext Catoni A9
Vega Baja, PR 00693, USA

Gonzalez, Juan Miguel & Elian
Marcelo Salado
Cardenas, CUBA

Gonzalez, Julio (Baseball Player)
Houston Astros
PO Box 75755
Caguas, PR 00725, USA

Gonzalez, Lazaro & Marisleysis
2319 NW 2nd St
Miami, FL 33125-5207, USA

Gonzalez, Leon (Football Player)
Dallas Cowboys
4025 Leonnie Rd
Jacksonville, FL 32208-2947, USA

Gonzalez, Luis E (Baseball Player)
Houston Astros
6026 E Jenan Dr
Scottsdale, AZ 85254-4907, USA

Gonzalez, Macchi Luis (President)
Palacio de Gobierno
Ave Marisol Lopez
Asuncion, PARAGUAY

Gonzalez, Marquez Felipe (Prime Minister)
Foudacion Socialismo XXI
Gobefas 31
Madrid 28023, SPAIN

Gonzalez, Mike (Baseball Player)
Pittsburgh Pirates
2414 Pine Brook Ct
Deer Park, TX 77536-1518, USA

Gonzalez, Miriam (Actor, Model)
c/o Staff Member *Playboy Entertainment Group Inc*
2112 Broadway
Santa Monica, CA 90404-2912, USA

Gonzalez, Nicholas (Actor)
c/o Chuck James *Gersh Agency, The (LA)*
232 N Canon Dr
Beverly Hills, CA 90210-5302, USA

Gonzalez, Orlando (Baseball Player)
Cleveland Indians
PO Box 441514
Miami, FL 33144-1514, USA

Gonzalez, Pedro (Baseball Player)
New York Yankees
San Pedro de Macoris
Dominican Republic, DOMINICAN REPUBLIC

Gonzalez, Phoenix (Actor)
c/o Staff Member *Select Artists Ltd (CA-Westside Office)*
1138 12th St Apt 1
Santa Monica, CA 90403-5459, USA

Gonzalez, Raul (Soccer Player)
Real Madrid FC
Avda Concha Espina 1
Madrid 28036, SPAIN

Gonzalez, Rick (Actor)
c/o Staff Member *Paradigm (LA)*
360 N Crescent Dr
North Bldg
Beverly Hills, CA 90210-6820, USA

Gonzalez, Susana (Actor)
c/o Staff Member *Televisa*
Blvd Adolfo Lopez Mateos 232
Colonia San Angel INN
DF CP 01060, MEXICO

Gonzalez, Tony (Athlete, Football Player)
c/o Staff Member *Kansas City Chiefs*
1 Arrowhead Dr
Kansas City, MO 64129-1651, USA

Gonzalez, Victor (Actor)
c/o Gabriel Blanco *Gabriel Blanco Iglesias (Mexico)*
Rio Balsas 35-32
Colonia Cuauhtemoc
DF 06500, MEXICO

Gonzalez Zumarraga, Antonio J Cardinal (Religious Leader)
Arzobispado
Apartado 17-01-00106
Called Chile
Quito 1140, ECUADOR

Gonzalo, Julie (Actor)
c/o Sharon Lane *Lane Management Group*
13017 Woodbridge St
Studio City, CA 91604-1431, USA

Gooch, Jeff (Football Player)
Tampa Bay Buccaneers
8514 Fawn Creek Dr
Tampa, FL 33626-2323, USA

Good, Hugh W (Religious Leader)
Primitive Advent Christian Church
273 Frame Rd
Elkview, WV 25071-9626, USA

Good, Meagan (Actor)
c/o Evan Hainey *Untitled Entertainment (LA)*
331 N Maple Dr Fl 3
Beverly Hills, CA 90210-3827, USA

Good, Melanie (Actor)
11288 Ventura Blvd # 175
Studio City, CA 91604-3187, USA

Good, Michael T (Astronaut)
2617 Broussard Ct
Seabrook, TX 77586-3361, USA

Good Charlotte (Music Group)
81 Pondfield Rd # 358
Bronxville, NY 10708-3818, USA

Goodacre, Connick Jill (Model)
Harry Connick
Wilkins Mgmt 323 Broadway
Cambridge, MA 02139, USA

Goodacre, Glenna (Artist, Misc)
National Academy Museum
1083 5th Ave
New York, NY 10126-0001, USA

Goodall, Caroline (Actor)
P F D Drury House
34-43 Russell St
London WC2B 5HA, UNITED KINGDOM
(UK)

Goodburn, Kelly (Football Player)
Kansas City Chiefs
3710 W 52nd Pl
Shawnee Mission, KS 66205-2766, USA

Goode, Chris (Football Player)
Indianapolis Colts
PO Box 19126
Birmingham, AL 35219-9126, USA

Goode, David R (Business Person)
Norfolk Southern Corp
3 Commercial Pl
Norfolk, VA 23510-2108, USA

Goode, Don (Football Player)
San Diego Chargers
4935 Dafter Pl
San Diego, CA 92102-1309, USA

Goode, Irvin (Football Player)
St Louis Cardinals
951 Shulte Rd
Saint Louis, MO 63146, USA

Goode, Joe (Artist)
1645 Electric Ave
Venice, CA 90291-4803, USA

Goode, Kerry (Football Player)
Tampa Bay Buccaneers
639 Herron Ct
Fairburn, GA 30213-2398, USA

Goode, Matthew (Actor)
c/o Simon Beresford *Dalzell & Beresford Ltd*
26 Astwood Mews
London SW7 4DE, UNITED KINGDOM (UK)

Goode, Richard S (Music Group, Musician)
Frank Salonon
201 W 54th St Apt 1C
New York, NY 10019-5520, USA

Goode, Rob (Football Player)
Washington Redskins
1902 Oakridge Trl
Bridgeport, TX 76426-2620, USA

Goode, Tom (Football Player)
Houston Oilers
9190 Tom Goode Rd
West Point, MS 39773-4487, USA

Goodell, Brian S (Swimmer)
27040 S Ridge Dr
Mission Viejo, CA 92692-5015, USA

Gooden, Drew (Basketball Player)
Orlando Magic
8701 Maitland Summit Blvd
Waterhouse Center
Orlando, FL 32810-5915, USA

Gooden, Dwight (Baseball Player)
New York Mets
8349 Golden Prairie Dr
Tampa, FL 33647-3242, USA

Goodenough, Ward H (Misc)
3300 Darby Rd Apt 5306
Haverford, PA 19041-7707, USA

Goodeve, Charles P (Misc)
38 Middleway
London NW11, UNITED KINGDOM (UK)

Goodeve, Grant (Actor)
21416 NE 68th Ct
Redmond, WA 98053-2393, USA

Goodfellow, Peter N (Misc, Scientist)
Cancer Research Fund
Lincoln Inn Fields
London WC2A 3PX, UNITED KINGDOM (UK)

Goodfriend, Linda
338 S Beachwood Dr
Burbank, CA 91506-2713, USA

Gooding, Cuba Jr (Actor)
c/o Michael Rotenberg *3 Arts Entertainment Inc*
9460 Wilshire Blvd Fl 7
Beverly Hills, CA 90212-2713, USA

Gooding, Omar
3500 W Olive Ave Ste 1400
Burbank, CA 91505-5512, USA

Goodlin, Chalmers (Misc)
7620 Red River Rd
West Palm Beach, FL 33411-5812, USA

Goodman, Alfred (Composer)
Bodenstedtstr 31
Munich 81241, GERMANY

Goodman, Allegra (Writer)
Dial Press
375 Hudson St
New York, NY 10014-3658, USA

Goodman, Brian (Actor)
c/o Paul Santana *Agency for the Performing Arts (APA-LA)*
405 S Beverly Dr
Beverly Hills, CA 90212-4416, USA

Goodman, Dody
Scott Stander
13701 Riverside Dr Ste 201
Sherman Oaks, CA 91423-2447, USA

Goodman, Ellen H (Editor, Misc)
Boston Globe
Editorial Dept
135 W T Morrissey Blvd
Dorchester, MA 02125, USA

Goodman, Henry (Football Player)
Detroit Lions
2015 Broad St Apt 108
Cranston, RI 02905-3346, USA

Goodman, John (Actor, Musician, Producer)
c/o Bob Gersh *Gersh Agency, The (LA)*
232 N Canon Dr
Beverly Hills, CA 90210-5302, USA

Goodman, John (Football Player)
Pittsburgh Steelers
800 E 9th St
Edmond, OK 73034-5407, USA

Goodman, Oscar (Attorney, Attorney General, General)
520 S 4th St
Las Vegas, NV 89101-6520, USA

Goodman, Richard (Producer)
c/o Staff Member *Endeavor Agency LLC (LA)*
9601 Wilshire Blvd Fl 3
Beverly Hills, CA 90210-5204, USA

Goodnoff, Irvin (Cinematographer)
29997 Mulholland Hwy
Agoura Hills, CA 91301-3009, USA

Goodreault, Gene J (Football Player)
7 Via Corte
Orinda, CA 94563-2238, USA

Goodrem, Delta (Musician)
c/o Staff Member *Sony Music Entertainment (Australia)*
11-19 Hargrave St
E Sydney
NSW 2010, AUSTRALIA

Goodrich, Gail
PO Box 4969
Greenwich, CT 06831-0419, USA

Goodrich, Gail C Jr (Basketball Player)
270 Oceano Dr
Los Angeles, CA 90049-4124, USA

Goodrich, Jon (Baseball Player)
123 W Agua Caliente Rd
Sonoma, CA 95476-3340, USA

Goodrum, Charles (Football Player)
Minnesota Vikings
Boat Ramp Road
East Palatka, FL 32131, USA

Goodson, Ed (Baseball Player)
San Francisco Giants
23330 Cold Springs Ln
Galax, VA 24333, USA

Goodson, James A (War Hero)
37 Carolina Trl
Marshfield, MA 02050-6373, USA

Goodwill, Oliver (Actor)
Asylum Entertainment
7920 W Sunset Blvd Fl 2
C/O Marcello Robinson
Los Angeles, CA 90046-3300, USA

Goodwin, Curtis (Baseball Player)
Baltimore Orioles
14939 Western Ave
San Leandro, CA 94578-3627, USA

Goodwin, Danny (Baseball Player)
California Angels
3628 Meadowglenn Village Ln Apt G
Atlanta, GA 30340-5626, USA

Goodwin, Doris Kearns (Historian)
General Delivery
1649 Monument St
Concord, MA 01742, USA

Goodwin, Doug (Football Player)
Buffalo Bills
70 N Grove St Apt 2H
Freeport, NY 11520-3018, USA

Goodwin, Ginnifer (Actor)
c/o Esther Chang *William Morris Agency (WMA-LA)*
1 William Morris Pl
Beverly Hills, CA 90212-4261, USA

Goodwin, Hunter (Football Player)
Minnesota Vikings
PO Box 725
Bellville, TX 77418-0725, USA

Goodwin, Jim (Baseball Player)
Chicago White Sox
11533 Francetta Ln
Saint Louis, MO 63138-1718, USA

Goodwin, Michael (Actor)
8271 Melrose Ave Ste 110
Los Angeles, CA 90046-6800, USA

Goodwin, Ron
Black Nest Cottage Hackford Lane
Brimpton Common, ENGLAND RG7 4RP,
UNITED KINGDOM (UK)

Goodwin, Ron (Football Player)
Philadelphia Eagles
3702 Sul Ross St
San Angelo, TX 76904-6229, USA

Goodwin, Tom (Baseball Player)
Los Angeles Dodgers
6480 Pool Rd
Grapevine, TX 76051-6877, USA

Goodwin, Trudie (Actor)
Bosun House
1 Deer Park Rd
Merton
London SW19 3TL, ENGLAND

Goody, Joan E (Architect)
Goody Clancy Assoc
334 Boylston St
Boston, MA 02116-3899, USA

Goodyear, Scott (Race Car Driver)
Scott Goodyear Racing
PO Box 589
Carmel, IN 46082-0589, USA

Goolagong Cawley, Evonne F (Tennis Player)
Private Bag 6060
Richmond, SV 3121, AUSTRALIA

Goorjian, Michael (Actor)
Evolution Entertainment
901 N Highland Ave
Los Angeles, CA 90038-2412, USA

Goosen, Don (Boxer, Misc)
6320 Van Nuys Blvd
Van Nuys, CA 91401-2617, USA

Goosen, Retief (Golfer)
c/o Staff Member *Pro Golfers Assoc of America (PGA)*
100 Avenue Of The Champions
Palm Beach Gardens, FL 33418-3653,
USA

Goossen, Greg (Baseball Player)
New York Mets
4555 Fulton Ave Apt 204
Sherman Oaks, CA 91423-3201, USA

Gopi (Actor)
M3/F Anugraha Colony 3rd Avenue
Ashok Nagar
c, TN 600 083, INDIA

Gopi Krishna, B M (Actor)
14 Soundara Rajan Street
T Nagar
Chennai, TN 600 017, INDIA

Goranson, Alicia (Actor)
c/o Staff Member *Paradigm (LA)*
360 N Crescent Dr
North Bldg
Beverly Hills, CA 90210-6820, USA

Gorbachev, Mikhail S (General, Nobel Prize Laureate, Politician, Secretary)
Leningradsky Prospekt 49
Moscow 125468, RUSSIA

Gorbachev, Yuri (Artist)
Adrienne Editions
377 Geary St
San Francisco, CA 94102-1801, USA

Gorbatko, Viktor V (Astronaut, General, Misc)
Potchta Kosmonavtov
Moskovskoi Oblasti
Svyisdny Goroduk 141160, RUSSIA

Gorchakova, Galina (Opera Singer)
Askonas Holt Ltd
27 Chancery Lane
London WC2A 1PF, UNITED KINGDOM
(UK)

Gordeeva, Ekaterina (Figure Skater)
International Skating Center
152 W 57th St
New York, NY 10019-3386, USA

Gordeyev, Vyacheslav M (Ballerina, Choreographer, Dancer)
Tverskaya Str 9 #78
Moscow 103009, RUSSIA

Gordimer, Nadine (Nobel Prize Laureate)
7 Frere Road Parktown
Johannesburg 2193, SOUTH AFRICA

Gordin, Charles (Actor)
187 Chestnut Hill Rd
Wilton, CT 06897-4108, USA

Gordon, Barry (Actor, Music Group)
1912 Kaweah Dr
Pasadena, CA 91105-3604, USA

Gordon, Bert I (Director)
9640 Arby Dr
Beverly Hills, CA 90210-1202, USA

Gordon, Bridgette (Basketball Player)
421 E Chelsea St
Deland, FL 32724-6900, USA

Gordon, Bruce (Actor)
231 Tano Rd # C
Santa Fe, NM 87506-7030, USA

Gordon, Carl
8661 Pine Tree Pl
Los Angeles, CA 90069-1201, USA

Gordon, Cornell (Football Player)
New York Jets
4029 Spring Meadow Cres
Chesapeake, VA 23321-3117, USA

Gordon, Danso (Actor)
c/o Paul Nicholls *Artistry Management*
525 Westbourne Dr
West Hollywood, CA 90048-1913, USA

Gordon, Darrien (Football Player)
San Diego Chargers
1800 Leeds Dr
Southlake, TX 76092-3576, USA

Gordon, David (Choreographer)
47 Great Jones St # 2
New York, NY 10012-1118, USA

Gordon, Dick (Football Player)
Chicago Bears
7119 Sandy Springs Rd
Maumee, OH 43537-9774, USA

Gordon, Don
6853 Pacific View Dr
Los Angeles, CA 90068-1831, USA

Gordon, Don (Actor)
Acme Talent
4727 Wilshire Blvd Ste 333
Los Angeles, CA 90010-3874, USA

Gordon, Don (Baseball Player)
Toronto Blue Jays
711 Sunset Mountain Dr
Chattanooga, TN 37421-2076, USA

Gordon, Ed (Correspondent)
NBC-TV
30 Rockefeller Plz
News Dept
New York, NY 10112-0015, USA

Gordon, Eve
10100 Santa Monica Blvd Ste 2500
Los Angeles, CA 90067-4116, USA

Gordon, Hannah Taylor (Actor)
Hutton Mgmt
4 Old Manor Close Askett
Buckinghamshire HP27 9NA, UNITED
KINGDOM (UK)

Gordon, Harold P (Business Person)
Hasbro Inc
1027 Newport Ave
Pawtucket, RI 02861-2500, USA

Gordon, Herold (Baseball Player)
Chicago American Giants
8798 Traverse St
Detroit, MI 48213-1158, USA

Gordon, Howard (Producer, Writer)
c/o Rick Rosen *Endeavor Agency LLC (LA)*
9601 Wilshire Blvd Fl 3
Beverly Hills, CA 90210-5204, USA

Gordon, Ira (Football Player)
San Diego Chargers
PO Box 3222
Kent, WA 98089-0204, USA

Gordon, Jeff (Race Car Driver)
The Jeff Gordon Network
4345 Papa Joe Hendrick Blvd
Charlotte, NC 28262-5701, USA

Gordon, John (Football Player)
40 Calle Fresno
San Clemente, CA 92672-9421, USA

Gordon, Keith (Actor, Director, Writer)
c/o Dan Aloni *Creative Artists Agency
LCC (CAA-LA)*
2000 Avenue Of The Stars
Los Angeles, CA 90067-4700, USA

Gordon, Keith (Baseball Player)
Cincinnati Reds
4601 Thornhurst Dr
Olney, MD 20832-1826, USA

Gordon, Lawrence (Business Person)
Largo Entertainment
20th Century Fox 10201 W Pico Blvd
Los Angeles, CA 90064, USA

Gordon, Leo
9977 Wornom Ave
Sunland, CA 91040-1549, USA

Gordon, Lincoln (Diplomat, Economist)
10450 Lottsford Rd Apt 253
Bowie, MD 20721-3303, USA

Gordon, Mark (Actor)
Fifi Oscard Agency
24 W 40th St # 1700
New York, NY 10018-3904, USA

Gordon, Mikalah (Musician)
c/o Staff Member *American Idol*
7800 Beverly Blvd # 251
Los Angeles, CA 90036-2112, USA

Gordon, Mike (Baseball Player)
Chicago Cubs
35 Longview Rd
Brockton, MA 02301-5637, USA

Gordon, Mike (Musician)
c/o Staff Member *Paradigm (Monterey)*
509 Hartnell St
Monterey, CA 93940-2825, USA

Gordon, Milton A (Educator)
California State University
President's Office
Fullerton, CA 99264, USA

Gordon, Mita (Governor)
Belize House
Belnopan, BELIZE

Gordon, Nathan G (War Hero)
606 Green St
Morrilton, AR 72110-3530, USA

Gordon, Nina (Musician)
c/o Staff Member *Paradigm (Monterey)*
509 Hartnell St
Monterey, CA 93940-2825, USA

Gordon, Pamela (Prime Minister)
United Bermuda Party
Burrows Bldg
Hamilton HM, CX, BERMUDA

Gordon, Phil (Misc)
Much and House Public Relations
8075 W 3rd St Ste 500
Los Angeles, CA 90048-4325, USA

Gordon, Richard
1 Craven Hill
London, ENGLAND W2 3EN, UNITED
KINGDOM (UK)

Gordon, Richard F Jr (Astronaut)
65 Woodside Dr
Prescott, AZ 86305-5092, USA

Gordon, Robby (Race Car Driver)
Robby Gordon Motorsports
10615 Twin Lakes Pkwy
Charlotte, NC 28269-7659, USA

Gordon, Sean (Model)
c/o Staff Member *IMG Models*
304 Park Ave S Fl 12
New York, NY 10010-4301, USA

Gordon, Tom (Baseball Player)
Kansas City Royals
115 E State St
Avon Park, FL 33825-4143, USA

Gordon, William E (Physicist)
Rice University
PO Box 1892
Space Physics Dept
Houston, TX 77251-1892, USA

Gordon-Levitt, Joey
4024 Radford Ave Bldg 3
Studio City, CA 91604-2101, USA

Gordon-Levitt, Joseph (Actor)
Gersh Agency
232 N Canon Dr
Beverly Hills, CA 90210-5302, USA

Gordy, Berry
878 Stradella Rd
Los Angeles, CA 90077-3310, USA

Gordy, John (Football Player)
Detroit Lions
40 Calle Fresno
San Clemente, CA 92672-9421, USA

Gordy, Walter (Physicist)
2521 Perkins Rd
Durham, NC 27705-1018, USA

Gore, Al (Politician)
312 Lynnwood Blvd
Nashville, TN 37205-2927, USA

Gore, Lesley (Musician, Songwriter,
Writer)
World Entertainment Assoc
297101 Kinderkamack Road #128
Oradell, NJ 07649, USA

Gore, Martin (Musician)
c/o Carole Kinzel *Creative Artists Agency
LCC (CAA-LA)*
2000 Avenue Of The Stars
Los Angeles, CA 90067-4700, USA

Gore, Michael
15622 Royal Oak Rd
Encino, CA 91436-3906, USA

Gore, Tipper (Politician)
1201 26th St S
Arlington, VA 22202-2202, USA

Gorecki, Henryk M (Composer)
Ul HA Gornika 4 m 1
Katowice 40-133, POLAND

Gorecki, Rick (Baseball Player)
Los Angeles Dodgers
9630 County Line Rd
Crown Point, IN 46307-9163, USA

Goren, Shlomo (General, Religious
Leader)
Chief Rabbinate
Hechal Shlomo
Jerusalem, ISRAEL

Gorenstein, Mark B (Conductor)
Rublevskoye Shosses 28
#25
Moscow 121609, RUSSIA

Goretta, Claude (Director)
10 Tour de Boel
Geneva 1204, SWITZERLAND

Gorgal, Ken (Football Player)
Cleveland Browns
4 The Court Of Harborside
Northbrook, IL 60062-3207, USA

Gorham, Christopher (Actor)
c/o Glenn Rigberg *Rigberg-Rugolo
Entertainment*
1180 S Beverly Dr Ste 601
Los Angeles, CA 90035-1158, USA

Gorham, Eville (Misc)
1933 E River Ter
Minneapolis, MN 55414-3673, USA

Gorie, Dominic L (Astronaut)
16522 Craighurst Dr
Houston, TX 77059-6518, USA

Gorillaz (Musician)
Virgin Records
1750 Vine St
Los Angeles, CA 90028-5209, USA

Gorin, Brandon (Football Player)
San Diego Chargers
3401 E Miami Trl
Muncie, IN 47302-8663, USA

Gorin, Charles
2617 S 1st St
Austin, TX 78704-5451, USA

Gorin, Charlie (Baseball Player)
Milwaukee Braves
2617 Fiset Dr
Austin, TX 78731-5613, USA

Goring, Robert T (Butch) (Hockey Player)
245 W 5th Ave Ste 108
Anchorage, AK 99501-2300, USA

Gorinski, Bob (Baseball Player)
Minnesota Twins
PO Box 133
Calumet, PA 15621-0133, USA

Goris, Eva (Actor)
International Creative Mgmt
8942 Wilshire Blvd # 219
Beverly Hills, CA 90211-1908, USA

Gorlin, Alexander (Architect)
Alexander Gorlin Architect
137 Varick St
New York, NY 10013-1105, USA

Gorman, Brian (Baseball Player)
PO Box 1208
Somis, CA 93066-1208, USA

Gorman, Burn
c/o Staff Member *Conway Van Gelder Ltd*
18-21 Jermyn St Fl 3
London SW1Y 6HP, UNITED KINGDOM
(UK)

Gorman, Cliff
333 W 57th St
New York, NY 10019-3159, USA

Gorman, Joseph T (Business Person)
TRW Inc
1900 Richmond Rd
Cleveland, OH 44124, USA

Gorman, Paul F Jr (General)
9175 Batesville Rd
Afton, VA 22920-2620, USA

Gorman, R C (Artist)
PO Box 1258
El Prado, NM 87529-1258, USA

Gorman, Steve (Musician)
Mitch Schneider Organization
14724 Ventura Blvd Ste 710
Sherman Oaks, CA 91403-3520, USA

Gorman, Tom (Baseball Player)
Montreal Expos
1615 SW 5th Ave
Portland, OR 97201-5403, USA

Gorman, Tom (Tennis Player)
ProServe
1101 Woodrow Wilson Blvd #1800
Arlington, VA 22209, USA

Gorman-Cahill, Margaret
4216 38th St NW
Washington, DC 20016-2258, USA

Gorme, Eydie (Musician)
944 Pinehurst Dr
Las Vegas, NV 89109-1569, USA

Gormley, Antony (Artist)
13 South Villas
London NW1 9BS, UNITED KINGDOM
(UK)

Gorney, Karen Lynn (Actor)
Karen Company
PO Box 231060
New York, NY 10023-0018, USA

Gorouuch, Edward Lee (Educator)
University of Alaska
President's Office
Anchorage, AK 99508, USA

Gorrell, Bob (Cartoonist)
Creators Syndicate
5777 W Century Blvd Ste 700
Los Angeles, CA 90045-9023, USA

Gorrell, Fred (Misc)
501 E Port Au Prince Ln
Phoenix, AZ 85022-3670, USA

Gorris, Marleen (Director, Writer)
c/o Howard Cohen *United Talent Agency*
(UTA)
9560 Wilshire Blvd Ste 500
Beverly Hills, CA 90212-2401, USA

Gorski, Tamara (Actor)
Steve Young & Associates
18 Gloucester Lane #200
Toronto, ON M4Y 1L5, CANADA

Gorter, Cornelis J (Physicist)
Klobeniersburgwal 29
Amsterdam, THE NETHERLANDS

Gortman, Shaunzinski (Basketball Player)
Charlotte Sting
333 E Trade St
Charlotte, NC 28202-2331, USA

Goryl, John (Baseball Player)
Chicago Cubs
1888 Cranberry Isles Way
Apopka, FL 32712-2138, USA

Gosger, Jim (Baseball Player)
Boston Red Sox
1823 7th St
Port Huron, MI 48060-6301, USA

Goslin, Thomas B Jr (General)
US Strategic Command
Deputy Cinc
Offutt Air Force Base, NE 68113, USA

Gosling, James (Designer)
Sun Microsystems
2550 Garcia Ave
Mountain View, CA 94043-1109, USA

Gosling, Ryan (Actor)
c/o Carolyn Govers *Artist Management*
1118 15th St Apt 1
Santa Monica, CA 90403-5580, USA

Gosnell, Raja (Director)
c/o Dan Aloni *Creative Artists Agency*
LCC (CAA-LA)
2000 Avenue Of The Stars
Los Angeles, CA 90067-4700, USA

Goss, Luke (Actor)
Insomnia Media Group
C/O Jeff Bowler
100 Universal Dr Bungalow 7151
Universal City, CA 91608, USA

Goss, Matt (Actor)
Classic Management
5 Jubilee Pl
London SW3 3TD, UNITED KINGDOM
(UK)

Goss, Porter (Misc)
Central Intelligence Agency
Office Of Public Affairs
Washington, DC 20505-0001, USA

Goss, Robert F (Misc)
Oil Chemical & Atomic International
1636 Champa St
Denver, CO 80202-2703, USA

Gossage, Gene (Football Player)
Philadelphia Eagles
793 Toby Hill Rd
Westbrook, CT 06498-3502, USA

Gossage, Goose
35 Marland Rd
Colorado Springs, CO 80906-4328, USA

Gossage, Rich (Baseball Player)
Chicago White Sox
35 Marland Rd
Colorado Springs, CO 80906-4328, USA

Gossard, Stone (Musician)
Annie Ohayon Media Relations
525 Broadway # 600
New York, NY 10012-4411, USA

Gosselaar, Mark-Paul (Actor)
c/o Miles Levy *James/Levy/Jacobson*
Management
3500 W Olive Ave Ste 1470
Burbank, CA 91505-5514, USA

Gosselin, Mario (Hockey Player)
3225 NE 16th St
Pompano Beach, FL 33062-3303, USA

Gossett, D Bruce (Football Player)
Los Angeles Rams
6109 Puerto Dr
Rancho Murieta, CA 95683-9320, USA

Gossett, Robert (Actor)
c/o Staff Member *Leavitt Talent Group*
6404 Wilshire Blvd Ste 950
Los Angeles, CA 90048-5529, USA

Gossett Jr, Louis (Actor)
c/o Norman Aladjem *Paradigm (LA)*
360 N Crescent Dr
North Bldg
Beverly Hills, CA 90210-6820, USA

Gossick Crockatt, Sue (Swimmer)
13768 Christian Barrett Dr
Moorpark, CA 93021-2802, USA

Goswami, Kunal (Director)
47 Jaihind Society 11th N S Road
JVPD Scheme
Bombay, MS 400 049, INDIA

Gotch, Karl
18530 Wayne Rd
Odessa, FL 33556-4739, USA

Gothard, Michael
18 Shirlock Rd.
London, ENGLAND NW3 2HS, UNITED
KINGDOM (UK)

Gothard, Preston (Football Player)
Pittsburgh Steelers
13654 Vaughn Rd
Pike Road, AL 36064-2332, USA

Gotshalk, Leonard (Football Player)
Atlanta Falcons
1200 Butler Creek Rd
Ashland, OR 97520-9370, USA

Gott, Jim (Baseball Player)
Toronto Blue Jays
1739 Windsor Rd
San Marino, CA 91108-2527, USA

Gott, Karel (Musician)
Nad Bertramkou 18
Prague 160 00, CZECH REPUBLIC

Gottfried, Brian (Tennis Player)
129 Teal Pointe Ln
Ponte Vedra Beach, FL 32082-1937, USA

Gottfried, Gilbert (Actor, Comedian)
c/o Staff Member *William Morris Agency*
(WMA-LA)
1 William Morris Pl
Beverly Hills, CA 90212-4261, USA

Gotti, Carmine (Reality TV Star)
c/o Staff Member *Growing Up Gotti*
13400 Riverside Dr Ste 300
Sherman Oaks, CA 91423-2546, USA

Gotti, John, Jr (Reality TV Star)
c/o Staff Member *Growing Up Gotti*
13400 Riverside Dr Ste 300
Sherman Oaks, CA 91423-2546, USA

Gotti, Victoria (Actor, Producer, Reality
TV Star)
c/o Staff Member *Growing Up Gotti*
13400 Riverside Dr Ste 300
Sherman Oaks, CA 91423-2546, USA

Gottlieb, Michael (Director)
2436 Washington Ave
Santa Monica, CA 90403-2128, USA

Gottlieb, Robert A (Editor, Publisher)
237 E 48th St
New York, NY 10017-1538, USA

Gougeon, Donni (Misc)
Variety Artists
793 Higuera St Ste 6
San Luis Obispo, CA 93401-0500, USA

Gough, Alfred (Writer)
c/o Renee Kurtz *William Morris Agency*
(WMA-LA)
1 William Morris Pl
Beverly Hills, CA 90212-4261, USA

Gough, Michael (Actor)
Torleigh Green Lane
Ashmore
Salisbury, Wills SP5 5AO, UNITED
KINGDOM (UK)

Gough, Tommy (Musician)
Brothers Mgmt
141 Dunbar Ave
Fords, NJ 08863-1551, USA

Gould, Alexander (Actor)
c/o TJ Stein *Stein Entertainment Group*
11271 Ventura Blvd # 477
Studio City, CA 91604-3136, USA

Gould, Dana (Actor, Producer, Writer)
c/o Blair Belcher *United Talent Agency*
(UTA)
9560 Wilshire Blvd Ste 500
Beverly Hills, CA 90212-2401, USA

Gould, Elizabeth (Doctor)
Princeton University
Medical Center
Neurosciences Dept
Princeton, NJ 08544-0001, USA

Gould, Elliott (Actor)
c/o Steve Kenis *Steve Kenis & Company*
72 Dean St
London W1D 3SG, UNITED KINGDOM
(UK)

Gould, Hal (Baseball Player)
Philadelphia Stars
126 Rogers Ave
Millville, NJ 08332-9723, USA

Gould, Harold (Actor)
c/o Alan Siegel *Alan Siegel Entertainment*
345 N Maple Dr Ste 375
Beverly Hills, CA 90210-5942, USA

Gould, Lawrence M (Misc)
201 E Rudasill Rd
Tucson, AZ 85704-6024, USA

Gould, Matt Kennedy (Reality TV Star)
c/o Staff Member *William Morris Agency*
(WMA-LA)
1 William Morris Pl
Beverly Hills, CA 90212-4261, USA

Gould, Ronald M (Judge)
US Court of Appeals
1010 5th Ave
US Courthouse
Seattle, WA 98104-1195, USA

Gould, Shane
207 Kent St.Level 18
Sydney NSW 2000, AUSTRALIA

Gould, Terry (Producer)
c/o Staff Member *Lenhoff & Lenhoff*
830 Palm Ave
West Hollywood, CA 90069-4009, USA

Gould Innes, Shane (Swimmer)
207 Kent St
Level 18
Sydney, NSW 2000, AUSTRALIA

Goulet, Michael (Hockey Player)
1283 Buffalo Ridge Rd
Castle Rock, CO 80108-8192, USA

Goundamani (Actor)
7 Cenatop Ist Cross Street
Teynampet
Chennai, TN 600 018, INDIA

Gourley, Roark (Artist)
Roark Gourley Art Gallery
33151 Paso Dr
South Laguna Beach, CA 92677, USA

Gove, Jeff (Golfer)
21323 31st Ave SE
Bothell, WA 98021-7871, USA

Govich, Milena (Actor)
c/o Rhonda Price *Gersh Agency, The (NY)*
41 Madison Ave Fl 33
New York, NY 10010-2202, USA

Govinda (Actor, Bollywood)
105 Jal Darshan
A' Wing Ruia Park Juhu
Mumbai, MS 400049, INDIA

Gov't Mule (Music Group)
c/o Staff Member *Paradigm (Monterey)*
509 Hartnell St
Monterey, CA 93940-2825, USA

Gowan, Caroline (Golfer)
209 Crescent Ave
Greenville, SC 29605-2814, USA

Gowan, James (Architect)
2 Linden Gardens
London W2 4ES, UNITED KINGDOM
(UK)

Gowan, Lawrence (Musician)
c/o Sterling Bacon *TBA Artist
Management (Atlanta)*
1111 Alderman Dr Ste 285
Alpharetta, GA 30005-5433, USA

Gowdy, Cornell (Football Player)
Dallas Cowboys
4611 John St
Suitland, MD 20746-3772, USA

Gowell, Larry (Baseball Player)
Toronto Blue Jays
4 Carson St
Auburn, ME 04210-3706, USA

Gower, David I (Cricketer)
David Gower Promotions
6 George St
Nottingham NG1 3BE, UNITED
KINGDOM (UK)

Gower, Jessica (Actor)
c/o Jason Newman *Untitled Entertainment
(LA)*
331 N Maple Dr Fl 3
Beverly Hills, CA 90210-3827, USA

Gowon, Yakub (General, President)
National Oil/Chemical Marketing Co
38-39 Marina
Lagos 2052, NIGERIA

Gowrie, Earl of (Government Official)
Government Securities
Stag Place
London SW1E 5DS, UNITED KINGDOM
(UK)

Gowtham (Actor)
9 Pooram prakash Rao Road
Balaji Nagar
Chennai, TN 600 014, INDIA

Gowthami (Actor, Bollywood)
2-B, Syamvilla 2nd Main Road
C.I.T.Colony Mylapore
Chennai, TN 600004, INDIA

Goycoechea, Sergio (Soccer Player)
Argentine Football Assn
Via Monte 1366-76
Buenos Aires 1053, ARGENTINA

Goydos, Paul (Golfer)
c/o Staff Member *Pro Golfers Association
(PGA) Tour*
112 Tpc Blvd
Ponte Vedra Beach, FL 32082, USA

Goyer, David S (Director, Producer,
Writer)
Phantom Four
4000 Warner Blvd Bldg 81 # 207A
Burbank, CA 91522-0001, USA

Goyette, J G Philippe (Phil) (Hockey
Player)
815 38-E Ave
Lachine, PQ H8T 2C4, CANADA

Goyri, Sergio (Actor)
c/o Staff Member *Televisa*
Blvd Adolfo Lopez Mateos 232
Colonia San Angel INN
DF CP 01060, MEXICO

Gozzo, Mauro (Baseball Player)
New York Yankees
956 Cold Creek Cv
Collierville, TN 38017-4972, USA

GQ
1560 Broadway # 1308
New York, NY 10036-1518, USA

Grabarkewitz, Billy (Baseball Player)
Los Angeles Dodgers
PO Box 92307
Southlake, TX 76092-0103, USA

Grabe, Ronald J (Astronaut)
2652 E Scorpio Pl
Chandler, AZ 85249-5253, USA

Grabeel, Lucas (Actor)
3800 W Alameda Ave
Burbank, CA 91505-4300, USA

Graber, Bill (Athlete, Track Athlete)
PO Box 5019
Upland, CA 91785-5019, USA

Graber, Rod (Baseball Player)
Cleveland Indians
4674 Mount Armet Dr
San Diego, CA 92117-4719, USA

Graber, Susan P (Judge)
US Courts of Appeals
700 SW 6th Ave Ste 211
Pioneer Courthouse
Portland, OR 97204-1434, USA

Grabois, Neil R (Educator)
Colgate University
President's Office
Hamilton, NY 13346, USA

Grabow, John (Baseball Player)
Pittsburgh Pirates
114 Franklin Ave
San Gabriel, CA 91775-2842, USA

Grabowski, James S (Jim) (Football
Player)
Green Bay Packers
1523 W Withom Lane
Palatine, IL 60067, USA

Grabowski, Jason (Baseball Player)
Oakland A's
131 Beach Park Rd
Clinton, CT 06413-2335, USA

Grace, April (Actor)
c/o Lenore Zerman *Liberman/Zerman
Management*
252 N Larchmont Blvd Ste 200
Los Angeles, CA 90004-3754, USA

Grace, Bud (Cartoonist)
PO Box 66
Oakton, VA 22124-0066, USA

Grace, Maggie (Actor)
c/o Staff Member *Lost/Touchstone
Television*
Production Bldg #343
500 South Buena Vista
Burbank, CA 91521-0001, USA

Grace, Mark (Baseball Player)
Chicago Cubs
5624 E Via Buena Vis
Paradise Valley, AZ 85253-8129, USA

Grace, Mike (Baseball Player)
Philadelphia Phillies
1156 Buell Ave
Joliet, IL 60435-6809, USA

Grace, Mike (Baseball Player)
Cincinnati Reds
12791 Big Lake Rd
Davisburg, MI 48350-3419, USA

Grace, Nancy (Lawyer, Television Host)
The Nancy Grace Show
1 Time Warner Ctr
Cnn
New York, NY 10019-6038, USA

Grace, Topher (Actor)
c/o John Fogelman *William Morris
Agency (WMA-LA)*
1 William Morris Pl
Beverly Hills, CA 90212-4261, USA

Grace, Willie (Baseball Player)
Cincinnati Buckeyes
3550 Imperial Dr
Erie, PA 16506-1964, USA

Graceland
3765 Elvis Presley Blvd
Memphis, TN 38116-4105, USA

Gracen, Elizabeth (Actor, Beauty Pageant
Winner)
Metropolitan Talent Agency
4500 Wilshire Blvd Fl 2
Los Angeles, CA 90010-3858, USA

Gracey, James S (Admiral, Business
Person)
2445 M St NW # 260
1 Westin Center
Washington, DC 20037-1435, USA

Grach, Eduard D (Musician)
1st Smolensky Per 9
#98
Moscow 113324, RUSSIA

Grachev, Pavel S (General)
Ovchinnikovskaya Nab 18/1
Moscow 113324, RUSSIA

Gracheva, Nadezhda A (Ballerina)
1st Truzhennikov Per 17
#49
Moscow 119121, RUSSIA

Grachvogel, Maria (Designer, Fashion
Designer)
c/o Staff Member *Maria Grachvogel*
5 South Molton Street
London, England W11 1LT, UNITED
KINGDOM (UK)

Gracie, Charlie (Musician)
Jeff Hubbard Productions
PO Box 53664
Indianapolis, IN 46253-0664, USA

Gracie, Royce (Athlete, Wrestler)
KhonKhor Enterprises, Inc
PO Box 10346
Torrance, CA 90505-1246, USA

Gracin, Joshua (Musician)
c/o Staff Member *William Morris Agency
(WMA-TN)*
1600 Division St Ste 300
Nashville, TN 37203-2755, USA

Gradishar, Randy C (Football Player)
Denver Broncos
7628 Pineridge Ter
Castle Rock, CO 80108-8260, USA

Grady, Ellen
150 E Olive Ave Ste 111
Burbank, CA 91502-1849, USA

Grady, James T (Politician)
International Teamsters Brotherhood
25 Louisiana Ave NW
Washington, DC 20001-2130, USA

Grady, Wayne (Golfer)
PO Box 78
Coolum Beach, QLD 4573, AUSTRALIA

Graeber, Clark (Tennis Player)
411 Harbor Road
Fairfield, CT 06431, USA

Graelis, Francisco (Pancho) (Cartoonist,
Editor)
Le Monde
Editorial Dept
21 Bis Rue Claude Bernard
Paris 75005, FRANCE

Graf, Bianca
Oppenheimstr. 6b
Wolfen D-06766, GERMANY

Graf, Dave (Football Player)
Cleveland Browns
1825 SE 21st Ave
Pompano Beach, FL 33062-7642, USA

Graf, Hans
Houston Symphony
615 Louisiana St Ste 102
Jesse Jones Hall
Houston, TX 77002-2715, USA

Graf, Richard (Football Player)
Miami Dolphins
11108 Bluestem Ln
Eden Prairie, MN 55347-4731, USA

Graf, Stefanie M (Steffi) (Tennis Player)
8921 Andre Dr
Las Vegas, NV 89148-1405, USA

Graff, Ilene
11455 Sunshine Ter
Studio City, CA 91604-3129, USA

Graff, Milt (Baseball Player)
Kanas City A's
1112 Austin Ave
College Station, TX 77845-5136, USA

Graff, Neil (Football Player)
New England Patriots
PO Box 2696
Graff Capital Management
Sioux Falls, SD 57101-2696, USA

Graff, Randy (Actor)
Peter Strawn Assoc
1501 Broadway Ste 2900
New York, NY 10036-5600, USA

Graff, Todd
547 Hudson St
New York, NY 10014-3290, USA

Graffanino, Tony (Baseball Player)
Atlanta Braves
16 Amberfield Ln
Hockessin, DE 19707-2089, USA

Graffin, Guillaume (Ballerina)
American Ballet Theatre
890 Broadway
New York, NY 10003-1278, USA

Graffman, Gary (Musician)
Curtis Institute of Music
1726 Locust St
Philadelphia, PA 19103-6187, USA

Grafstein, Bernice (Physicist, Scientist)
Weill Medical College
1300 York Ave
Physiology Dept
New York, NY 10065-4805, USA

Grafton, Sue (Writer)
PO Box 41446
Santa Barbara, CA 93140-1446, USA

Graham, Alex (Cartoonist)
Tribune Media Services
435 N Michigan Ave Ste 1500
Chicago, IL 60611-4012, USA

Graham, Art (Football Player)
Boston Patriots
PO Box 785
South Orleans, MA 02662-0785, USA

Graham, Aubrey (Actor)
c/o Staff Member *Noble Kaplan Agency*
1260 Yonge St Fl 2
Toronto, ON M4T 1W6, CANADA

Graham, Bill (Baseball Player)
Detroit Tigers
RR 2 Box 275
Flemingsburg, KY 41041, USA

Graham, Bill (Football Player)
Detroit Lions
11013 Sierra Verde Trl
Austin, TX 78759-5129, USA

Graham, Bob (Senator)
14814 Breckness Pl
Miami Lakes, FL 33016-1458, USA

Graham, Charles P (General)
134 Wabler Way
Georgetown, TX 78628, USA

Graham, Currie
c/o Vera Mihailovich *Forward Entertainment*
9171 Wilshire Blvd Ste 406
Beverly Hills, CA 90210-5516, USA

Graham, Dan (Baseball Player)
Minnesota Twins
225 N Standage Unit 33
Mesa, AZ 85201-6243, USA

Graham, Daniel (Football Player)
New England Patriots
60 Washington St
Gillete Stadium RR 1
Foxboro, MA 02035-1388, USA

Graham, David (Golfer)
PO Box 4997
Whitefish, MT 59937-4997, USA

Graham, Derrick (Football Player)
Kansas City Chiefs
770 Blue St
Groveland, FL 34736, USA

Graham, Dirk (Coach, Hockey Player)
45 Christine Dr
West Springfield, MA 01089-2220, USA

Graham, Donald E (Publisher)
Washington Post Co
1150 15th St NW
Washington, DC 20071-0002, USA

Graham, Ed (Musician)
c/o Sue Whitehouse *Whitehouse Management*
PO Box 43829
London NW6 3PJ, UNITED KINGDOM (UK)

Graham, Franklin (Religious Leader)
Samantan's Purse
PO Box 3000
Boone, NC 28607-3000, USA

Graham, Gail (Golfer)
Landmark Sport Group 277 Richmond St NW
Toronto, ON M5V 1X1, CANADA

Graham, Gerrit (Actor)
S M S Talent
8730 W Sunset Blvd Ste 440
Los Angeles, CA 90069-2277, USA

Graham, Glen (Musician)
Shapiro Co
9229 W Sunset Blvd Ste 607
Los Angeles, CA 90069-3406, USA

Graham, Heather (Actor, Producer)
c/o Mary Putnam Greene *Brillstein-Grey Entertainment*
9150 Wilshire Blvd Ste 350
Beverly Hills, CA 90212-3453, USA

Graham, Jeff (Football Player)
Pittsburgh Steelers
4027 Fairbanks Ave
Dayton, OH 45402-5226, USA

Graham, John R (Writer)
University of California
Astronomy Dept
Berkeley, CA 94720-0001, USA

Graham, Jorie (Writer)
General Delivery
West Tisbury, MA 02575-9999, USA

Graham, Katherine
2920 R St NW
Washington, DC 20007-2920, USA

Graham, Kent (Football Player)
New York Giants
1001 N Washington St
Wheaton, IL 60187-3857, USA

Graham, Larry (Musician)
Groove Entertainment
1005 N Alfred St Apt 2
West Hollywood, CA 90069-4757, USA

Graham, Lauren (Actor)
c/o John Carrabino *John Carrabino Management*
5900 Wilshire Blvd Ste 406
Los Angeles, CA 90036-5015, USA

Graham, Lee (Baseball Player)
Boston Red Sox
481 Richmond Rd
Cleveland, OH 44143-2745, USA

Graham, Linda (Bowler)
4147 E Seneca Ave
Des Moines, IA 50317-8123, USA

Graham, Loren R (Historian)
7 Francis Ave
Cambridge, MA 02138-2009, USA

Graham, Lou (Golfer)
85 Concord Park W
Nashville, TN 37205-4707, USA

Graham, Mikey (Musician)
JC Music
84A Strand on the Green
London W43 PU, UNITED KINGDOM (UK)

Graham, Parker (Musician)
Performers of the World
8901 Melrose Ave # 200
West Hollywood, CA 90069-5605, USA

Graham, R A (Football Player)
Rochester Jeffersons
5 River Ln
Westport, CT 06880-1926, USA

Graham, Samaria
c/o Steven Jensen *The Independent Group LLC*
947 N La Cienega Blvd Ste G
Los Angeles, CA 90069-4700, USA

Graham, Susan (Opera Singer)
Columbia Artists Mgmt Inc
1790 Broadway Fl 6
New York, NY 10019-1412, USA

Graham, Tommy (Football Player)
Denver Broncos
4084 S Wisteria Way
Denver, CO 80237-1714, USA

Graham, Wayne (Baseball Player)
Philadelphia Phillies
2017 Dryden Rd
Houston, TX 77030-1205, USA

Graham, William B (Business Person)
40 Devonshire Ln
Kenilworth, IL 60043-1205, USA

Graham, William F (Billy) (Misc)
Billy Graham Evangelistic Assoc
1 Billy Graham Pkwy
Charlotte, NC 28201, USA

Graham, William R (Government Official)
Xsirius Inc
1110 N Glebe Rd # 620
Arlington, VA 22201-4795, USA

Graham-Douglas, Mary Lou (Baseball Player)
9990 N Hillview Dr
Tucson, AZ 85737-7940, USA

Grahe, Joe (Baseball Player)
California Angels
2317 N Wallen Dr
West Palm Beach, FL 33410-2558, USA

Grahn, Nancy
4910 Agnes Ave
N Hollywood, CA 91607-3705, USA

Grahn, Nancy Lee (Actor)
c/o Staff Member *Innovative Artists (LA)*
1505 10th St
Santa Monica, CA 90401-2805, USA

Grainger, David W (Business Person)
WW Grainger Inc
100 Grainger Pkwy
Lake Forest, IL 60045-5201, USA

Gralish, Tom (Journalist, Photographer)
203 E Cottage Ave
Haddonfield, NJ 08033-1824, USA

Gralla, Lawrence (Publisher)
Gralla Publications
1515 Broadway
New York, NY 10036-8901, USA

Gralla, Milton (Publisher)
Gralla Publications
1515 Broadway
New York, NY 10036-8901, USA

Gramanis, Paul (Football Player)
Chicago Bears
989 Parkview Dr
Tallahassee, FL 32311-1245, USA

Gramatica, Bill (Football Player)
Arizona Cardinals
1170 N Judd Pl
Chandler, AZ 85226-8703, USA

Gramatica, Martin (Football Player)
Tampa Bay Buccaneers
3912 Northampton Way
Tampa, FL 33618-8443, USA

Gramlich, Edward M (Economist, Government Official)
Federal Reserve Board
20th & Constitution Aves NW
Washington, DC 20551-0001, USA

Gramly, Tommy (Baseball Player)
Cleveland Indians
16485 Red Wood Cir W RR 1
Mc Kinney, TX 75071-6198, USA

Gramm, Lou (Musician)
c/o Staff Member *Creative Artists Agency LCC (CAA-LA)*
2000 Avenue Of The Stars
Los Angeles, CA 90067-4700, USA

Gramm, W Philip (Phil) (Senator)
UBS Warburg
299 Park Ave Fl 8
New York, NY 10171-3799, USA

Gramm, Wendy L (Government Official)
Commodity Futures Trading Commission
2033 K St NW
Washington, DC 20006-1002, USA

Grammas, Alex (Baseball Player)
St Louis Cardinals
3432 Oakdale Dr
Birmingham, AL 35223-2210, USA

Grammer, Kathy (Actor)
Artists Agency
1180 S Beverly Dr Ste 301
Los Angeles, CA 90035-1154, USA

Grammer, Kelsey (Actor)
c/o Staff Member *Grammnet Productions*
5555 Melrose Ave
Lucy Bungalow 206 (Tv)
Los Angeles, CA 90038-3989, USA

Gran, Phyllis
Penguin/Pitnam Publishing
200 Madison Ave
New York, NY 10016-3903, USA

Granatelli, Andy (Misc)
1469 Edgecliff Ln
Montecito, CA 93108-2810, USA

Granato, Catherine (Cammi) (Hockey Player)
13454 Wood Duck Dr
Plainfield, IL 60585-7766, USA

Granato, Tony (Coach, Hockey Player)
11657 E Berry Dr
Englewood, CO 80111-4154, USA

Grand Funk Railroad (Musician)
c/o Staff Member *Paradigm (Monterey)*
509 Hartnell St
Monterey, CA 93940-2825, USA

Grand Ole Opry
2804 Opryland Dr
Nashville, TN 37214-1209, USA

Grandberry, Ken (Football Player)
Chicago Bears
108 E Mark Rd
Harker Heights, TX 76548-1224, USA

Grandberry, Omari (Omarion) (Actor)
c/o Chris Stokes *Ultimate Group, The*
848 N La Cienega Blvd Ste 201
West Hollywood, CA 90069-6600, USA

Grandelius, Everett (Football Player)
New York Giants
31531 Robinhood Dr
Beverly Hills, MI 48025-3532, USA

Granderson, Rufus (Football Player)
Dallas Texans
3080 Creek Dr SE
Grand Rapids, MI 49512-8167, USA

Grandin, Temple (Scientist)
2918 Silverplume Dr Apt C3
Fort Collins, CO 80526-2402, USA

Grandmaster, Mele-Mel (Musician)
Groove Entertainment
1005 N Alfred St Apt 2
West Hollywood, CA 90069-4757, USA

Grandmont, Jean-Michel (Economist)
55 Blvd de Charonne
Les Doukas 23
Paris 75011, FRANCE

Grandpre, Mary (Designer)
Scholastic Press
555 Broadway
New York, NY 10012-3919, USA

Grandy, Fred (Actor)
9417 Spruce Tree Cir
Bethesda, MD 20814-1654, USA

Granger, Charley (Football Player)
Dallas Cowboys
621 Burbridge St
Port Allen, LA 70767-2128, USA

Granger, Clive W J (Nobel Prize Laureate)
University of California
9500 Gilman Dr
Economics Dept
La Jolla, CA 92093-5004, USA

Granger, David (Athlete)
Ingalls & Snyder
61 Broadway Fl 31
New York, NY 10006-2872, USA

Granger, Hoyle (Football Player)
Houston Oilers
10611 Cranbrook Rd
Houston, TX 77042-1436, USA

Granger, Jeff (Baseball Player)
Kansas City Royals
2905 Glasgow Dr
Arlington, TX 76015-2226, USA

Granger, Wayne (Baseball Player)
St Louis Cardinals
PO Box 134
Huntington, MA 01050-0134, USA

Grannis, Paul D (Physicist)
Fermi Nat Accelerator Lab
PO Box 500
Cdf Collaboration
Batavia, IL 60510-5011, USA

Grant, Alan (Football Player)
Indianapolis Colts
2474 40th Ave
San Francisco, CA 94116-2115, USA

Grant, Amy (Musician, Songwriter, Writer)
c/o John Huie *Creative Artists Agency (CAA-Nashville)*
3310 W End Ave Fl 5
Nashville, TN 37203-1028, USA

Grant, Beth
2852 Hollyridge Dr
Los Angeles, CA 90068-2321, USA

Grant, Boyd (Coach)
Colorado State University
Athletic Dept
Fort Collins, CO 80523-0001, USA

Grant, Brian (Basketball Player)
13621 Deering Bay Dr Apt 404
Coral Gables, FL 33158-2846, USA

Grant, Bud (Football Player)
Philadelphia Eagles
8134 Oakmere Rd
Bloomington, MN 55438-1333, USA

Grant, Charles (Actor)
Media Artists Group
6300 Wilshire Blvd Ste 1470
Los Angeles, CA 90048-5200, USA

Grant, Darryl (Football Player)
Washington Redskins
6931 Compton Ln
Centreville, VA 20121-5009, USA

Grant, David Marshall (Actor)
c/o Michael Katcher *Creative Artists Agency LCC (CAA-LA)*
2000 Avenue Of The Stars
Los Angeles, CA 90067-4700, USA

Grant, Deborah (Actor)
Larry Datzall
17 Broad Ct #12
London WC2B 5QN, UNITED KINGDOM (UK)

Grant, Edmond (Eddy) (Musician, Songwriter, Writer)
Consolidated Ale
PO Box 87
Tarporley CW6 9FN, UNITED KINGDOM (UK)

Grant, Faye (Actor)
B & B Entertainment
1640 S Sepulveda Blvd Ste 530
Los Angeles, CA 90025-7538, USA

Grant, Frank (Football Player)
Washington Redskins
2126 Glencourse Ln
Reston, VA 20191-1315, USA

Grant, Gil (Producer)
c/o Staff Member *Principal Entertainment (LA)*
1964 Westwood Blvd Ste 400
Los Angeles, CA 90025-4695, USA

Grant, Gogi (Musician)
10323 Alamo Ave #202
Los Angeles, CA 90064, USA

Grant, Horace (Basketball Player)
719 N Eucalyptus Ave Apt 25B
Inglewood, CA 90302-2254, USA

Grant, Hugh (Actor)
c/o Robert Garlock *42West*
220 W 42nd St Fl 12
New York, NY 10036-7200, USA

Grant, James T (Mudcat) (Baseball Player)
1020 S Dunsmuir Ave
Los Angeles, CA 90019-6754, USA

Grant, John (Football Player)
Denver Broncos
PO Box 8506
Denver, CO 80201-8506, USA

Grant, Johnny
7000 Hollywood Blvd Ph
Hollywood, CA 90028-6003, USA

Grant, Lee (Actor, Director)
c/o Joel Dean *TalentWorks (LA)*
3500 W Olive Ave Ste 1400
Burbank, CA 91505-5512, USA

Grant, Mark (Baseball Player)
San Francisco Giants
123 Fairlane Dr
Joliet, IL 60435-5213, USA

Grant, Mickie (Actor)
250 W 94th St # 6G
New York, NY 10025-6954, USA

Grant, Paul (Basketball Player)
Milwaukee Bucks
1001 N 4th St
Bradley Center
Milwaukee, WI 53203-1312, USA

Grant, Rachel (Actor)
Bloomfields Management
34 South Molton Street
London W1K 5BP, UNITED KINGDOM (UK)

Grant, Reginald (Football Player)
New York Jets
PO Box 15602
Los Angeles, CA 90015-0602, USA

Grant, Richard E (Actor)
International Creative Mgmt
76 Oxford St
London W1N 0AX, UNITED KINGDOM (UK)

Grant, Robert M (Educator)
RR 1 Box 1423
Berlin, NH 03570, USA

Grant, Rodney A. (Actor)
c/o Ann Geddes *Geddes Agency, The*
8430 Santa Monica Blvd Ste 200
Los Angeles, CA 90069-4253, USA

Grant, Susannah (Director, Writer)
c/o Risa Gertner *Creative Artists Agency LCC (CAA-LA)*
2000 Avenue Of The Stars
Los Angeles, CA 90067-4700, USA

Grant, Tom (Baseball Player)
Chicago Cubs
36 Millville Rd
Mendon, MA 01756-1231, USA

Grant, Tom (Musician)
Brad Simon Organization
122 E 57th St # 300
New York, NY 10022-2623, USA

Grant, Toni (Misc)
610 S Ardmore Ave
Los Angeles, CA 90005-2322, USA

Grant, Wesley (Football Player)
Buffalo Bills
3870 Crenshaw Blvd # 926
Los Angeles, CA 90008-1837, USA

Grantham, Larry (Football Player)
New York Titans
1971 Tissington Dr
Horn Lake, MS 38637-3752, USA

Grapenthin, Dick (Baseball Player)
Montreal Expos
500 Argylls Crst
Alpharetta, GA 30022-6118, USA

Grasmick, Lou (Baseball Player)
Philadelphia Phillies
6715 Quad Ave
Baltimore, MD 21237-2406, USA

Grass, Darren (Baseball Player)
US Olympic Team
1086 174th St
Hammond, WI 54015-4831, USA

Grass, Gunter (Nobel Prize Laureate)
Sekfretariat Glockengiesserstr 21
Lubeck 23552, GERMANY

Grass, Gunther
Glockengiesserstr. 21
Lubeck D-23552, GERMANY

Grassie, Karen (Actor)
PO Box 913
Pacific Palisades, CA 90272-0913, USA

Grassle, Karen
2646 Francisco Way
El Cerrito, CA 94530-1531, USA

Grasso, Richard A (Financier)
New York Stock Exchange
11 Wall St
New York, NY 10005-1974, USA

Grassroots, The
108 E Matilija St
Ojai, CA 93023-2639, USA

Grata, Enrique (Actor)
c/o Staff Member *Univision*
605 3rd Ave Fl 12
New York, NY 10158-1299, USA

Grate, Carl (Football Player)
New York Giants
205 Wind Ship Ln
Woodstock, GA 30189-5286, USA

Grate, Don (Baseball Player)
Philadelphia Phillies
1245 NW 203rd St
Miami, FL 33169-2312, USA

Grateful Dead
PO Box 1073-C
San Rafael, CA 94915, USA

Grater, Mark (Baseball Player)
St Louis Cardinals
1136 Indiana Ave
Monaca, PA 15061-2025, USA

Grau, Shirley Ann (Writer)
12 Nassau Dr
Metairie, LA 70005-4434, USA

Grausman, Philip (Artist)
21 Barnes Rd
Washington, CT 06793, USA

Gravel, Maurice R (Mike) (Senator)
1600 N Oak St Apt 1412
Arlington, VA 22209-2757, USA

Graveline, Duane E (Astronaut)
494 Pleasant St
Island Pond, VT 05846-9738, USA

Gravelle, Gordon (Football Player)
Pittsburgh Steelers
2208 Cordoba Ct
Antioch, CA 94509-5861, USA

Graves, Adam (Hockey Player)
574 Lis Crescent
Windsor, ON N9G 2M5, CANADA

Graves, Alex (Producer)
c/o Staff Member *International Creative Management (ICM-LA)*
10250 Constellation Blvd
Los Angeles, CA 90067-6200, USA

Graves, Danny (Baseball Player)
Cleveland Indians
24120 Weldon Dr
Eustis, FL 32736-7926, USA

Graves, Denyce (Actor)
c/o Staff Member *Don Buchwald & Associates Inc (LA)*
6500 Wilshire Blvd Ste 2200
Los Angeles, CA 90048-4942, USA

Graves, Denyce (Opera Singer)
Columbia Artists Mgmt Inc
1790 Broadway Fl 6
New York, NY 10019-1412, USA

Graves, Earl G (Publisher)
Black Enterprise Magazine
130 5th Ave
New York, NY 10011-4306, USA

Graves, Ernest Jr (General)
2328 S Nash St
Arlington, VA 22202-1548, USA

Graves, Harold N Jr (Government
Official, Journalist)
4816 Grantham Ave
Chevy Chase, MD 20815-5538, USA

Graves, Michael (Architect)
341 Nassau St
Princeton, NJ 08540-4602, USA

Graves, Peter (Actor)
c/o Cary Berman *William Morris Agency
(WMA-LA)*
1 William Morris Pl
Beverly Hills, CA 90212-4261, USA

Graves, Ray (Coach, Football Coach,
Football Player)
Philadelphia Eagles
4230 Hartwood Ln
Tampa, FL 33618-7536, USA

Graves, Richard G (General)
12069 Sage Hollow Cir
Kamas, UT 84036-9348, USA

Graves, Rory (Football Player)
Los Angeles Raiders
PO Box 2460
Jonesboro, GA 30237-2460, USA

Graves, Rupert (Actor)
P F D
Drury House
34-43 Russell St
London WC2B 5HA, UNITED KINGDOM
(UK)

Graves, Tom (Football Player)
Pittsburgh Steelers
1902 Montclair Ave
Norfolk, VA 23523-2322, USA

Graves, White (Football Player)
Boston Patriots
2610 Birchwood Dr
Monroe, LA 71201-2337, USA

Gravitte, Beau (Actor)
Paradigm Agency
10100 Santa Monica Blvd Ste 2500
Los Angeles, CA 90067-4116, USA

Gray, Alasdair J (Writer)
McAlpine
2 Marchmont Terrace
Glasgow G12 9LT, SCOTLAND

Gray, Alfred M Jr (General)
6317 Chaucer View Cir
Alexandria, VA 22304-3548, USA

Gray, Billy (Actor)
19612 Grand View Dr
Topanga, CA 90290-3353, USA

Gray, C Boyden (Government Official)
Wilmer Cutler Pickering
2445 M St NW Ste 500
Washington, DC 20037-1448, USA

Gray, Colleen
2337 Roscomare Rd # 2-112
Los Angeles, CA 90077-1854, USA

Gray, Dave (Baseball Player)
Boston Red Sox
PO Box 12524
Ogden, UT 84412-2524, USA

Gray, David (Musician, Songwriter)
c/o Rob Holden *Mondo Management*
26-32 Voltaire Rd #2D
London SW6 6DH, UNITED KINGDOM
(UK)

Gray, Dick (Baseball Player)
Los Angeles Dodgers
503 S Hampton St
Anaheim, CA 92804-2233, USA

Gray, Dobie (Musician)
2211 Elliott Ave
Nashville, TN 37204-2109, USA

Gray, Doug (Musician)
Ron Rainey Mgmt
315 S Beverly Dr Ste 407
Beverly Hills, CA 90212-4301, USA

Gray, Duicie (Actor)
Barry Burnett
31 Coventry St
London W1V 8AS, UNITED KINGDOM
(UK)

Gray, Dulcie
44 Brunswick Gardens #2
London W8 4AN, ENGLAND

Gray, D'Wayne (General)
3423 Barger Dr
Falls Church, VA 22044-1202, USA

Gray, Earnest (Football Player)
New York Giants
6746 Kirby Oaks Ln
Memphis, TN 38119-8328, USA

Gray, Ed (Basketball Player)
Houston Rockets
2 Greenway Plz
Toyota Center
Houston, TX 77046-0297, USA

Gray, Erin (Actor, Model)
10921 Alta View Dr
Studio City, CA 91604-3904, USA

Gray, F Gary (Director)
H S I Productions
3630 Eastham Dr
Culver City, CA 90232-2411, USA

Gray, Fred Sr (Attorney, Attorney
General, General)
1005 E Lakeshore Dr
Tuskegee, AL 36083-1935, USA

Gray, Gary (Baseball Player)
Texas Rangers
PO Box 98
La Place, LA 70069-0098, USA

Gray, George W (Misc)
Juniper House
Furzehill
Wimborne, Dorset BH21 4HD, UNITED
KINGDOM (UK)

Gray, Harry B (Misc)
1415 E California Blvd
Pasadena, CA 91106-4101, USA

Gray, Hector (Football Player)
Detroit Lions
751 Dove Ave
Miami Springs High School
Miami Springs, FL 33166-3203, USA

Gray, James (Director, Writer)
United Talent Agency
9560 Wilshire Blvd Ste 500
Beverly Hills, CA 90212-2401, USA

Gray, Jeff (Baseball Player)
Cincinnati Reds
17634 Esprit Dr
Tampa, FL 33647-2505, USA

Gray, Jerry (Football Player)
Los Angeles Rams
27 Birdsong Pkwy
Orchard Park, NY 14127-3046, USA

Gray, Jim (Actor)
3325 Blair Dr
Los Angeles, CA 90068-1409, USA

Gray, John (Baseball Player)
Philadelphia Athletics
10645 Greenbriar Ct
Boca Raton, FL 33498-1644, USA

Gray, John (Writer)
John Gray Inc
20 Sunnyside Ave # A130
Mill Valley, CA 94941-1933, USA

Gray, Johnnie (Football Player)
Green Bay Packers
229 Crestview Ln
De Pere, WI 54115-3452, USA

Gray, Ken (Football Player)
Chicago Cardinals
356 Camoa Pajama Lane
Kingsland, TX 78639, USA

Gray, Linda (Actor)
PO Box 5064
Sherman Oaks, CA 91413-5064, USA

Gray, Lorenzo (Baseball Player)
Chicago White Sox
301 Trotters Ct
Jefferson, GA 30549-4308, USA

Gray, Macy (Musician, Songwriter,
Writer)
c/o Staff Member *Creative Artists Agency
LCC (CAA-LA)*
2000 Avenue Of The Stars
Los Angeles, CA 90067-4700, USA

Gray, Michael
9294 Civic Center Dr
Beverly Hills, CA 90210-3714, USA

Gray, Moses (Football Player)
New York Titans
1313 Aggie Ln
Indianapolis, IN 46260-4096, USA

Gray, Natalie (Actor, Writer)
c/o Monique Moss *Warren Cowan &
Associates PR*
8899 Beverly Blvd Ste 919
Los Angeles, CA 90048-2436, USA

Gray, Simon J H (Writer)
Judy Daish
2 Saint Charles Place
London W10 6EG, UNITED KINGDOM
(UK)

Gray, Spaiding (Artist, Writer)
22 Wooster St
New York, NY 10013-2300, USA

Gray, Tamyra (Musician)
c/o Jeff Frasco *Creative Artists Agency
LCC (CAA-LA)*
2000 Avenue Of The Stars
Los Angeles, CA 90067-4700, USA

Gray, Theordore G (Ted) (Baseball
Player)
Detroit Tigers
2917 S Ocean Blvd Apt 1005
Highland Beach, FL 33487-1882, USA

Gray, Torrian (Football Player)
Minnesota Vikings
1045 Roselle Ave
Lakeland, FL 33805-4146, USA

Gray, William H III (Misc)
United Negro College Fund
500 E 62nd St
New York, NY 10065-8314, USA

Gray Cabey, Noah (Actor)
c/o Cindy Osbrink *Osbrink Talent Agency*
4343 Lankershim Blvd # 100
North Hollywood, CA 91602-2705, USA

Gray-Stanford, Jason (Actor)
c/o Scott Zimmerman *Untitled
Entertainment (LA)*
331 N Maple Dr Fl 3
Beverly Hills, CA 90210-3827, USA

Graybeal, Mike (Actor)
c/o TJ Stein *Stein Entertainment Group*
11271 Ventura Blvd # 477
Studio City, CA 91604-3136, USA

Graybiel, Ann M (Scientist)
Massachusetts Institute of Technology
Cognitive Sci Dept
Cambridge, MA 02139, USA

Grayden, Sprague (Actor)
c/o Staff Member *Abrams Artists Agency
(LA)*
9200 W Sunset Blvd Ph 11
Los Angeles, CA 90069-3601, USA

Graydon, Joe
1870 Caminito Del Cielo
Glendale, CA 91208-3049, USA

Grayhm, Steven (Actor)
c/o Ben Levine *Evolution Entertainment
(LA)*
10585 Santa Monica Blvd Ste 120
Los Angeles, CA 90025-4984, USA

Graysmith, Robert (Cartoonist, Editor)
San Francisco Chronicle
901 Mission St
San Francisco, CA 94103-2934, USA

Grayson, C Jackson Jr (Educator,
Government Official)
123 N Post Oak Ln
Houston, TX 77024-7715, USA

Grayson, David Lee (Football Player)
Cleveland Browns
860 Turquoise St Unit 332
San Diego, CA 92109-1143, USA

Grayson, Kathryn (Actor, Musician)
c/o Sally Sherman
2009 La Mesa Dr
Santa Monica, CA 90402-2324, USA

Grayson Sr, Dave (Football Player)
Dallas Texans
PO Box 601292
San Diego, CA 92160-1292, USA

Grazer, Brian (Producer)
c/o Staff Member *Imagine Entertainment*
9465 Wilshire Blvd Fl 7
Beverly Hills, CA 90212-2606, USA

Grazia, Eugene (Hockey Player)
2421 NE 49th St
Fort Lauderdale, FL 33308-4788, USA

Graziadei, Michael (Actor)
c/o Amy Abell *Innovative Artists (LA)*
1505 10th St
Santa Monica, CA 90401-2805, USA

Graziani, Ariel (Soccer Player)
San Jose Earthquakes
100 N Almaden Ave
San Jose, CA 95110-2437, USA

Grazioso, Claudia (Producer, Writer)
c/o Nicole Clemens *International Creative
Management (ICM-LA)*
10250 Constellation Blvd
Los Angeles, CA 90067-6200, USA

Grazzola, Kenneth E (Publisher)
Aviation Week Magazine
1221 Avenue Of The Americas
New York, NY 10020-1014, USA

Grba, Eli (Baseball Player)
New York Yankees
106 Fox Run
Florence, AL 35633-1465, USA

Grbac, Elvis (Football Player)
San Francisco 49ers
17361 Coldwater Trl
Chagrin Falls, OH 44023-1413, USA

Greason, Bill (Baseball Player)
St Louis Cardinals
4536 Hillman Dr SW
Birmingham, AL 35221-1816, USA

Greason, Staci
8831 W Sunset Blvd # 304
Los Angeles, CA 90069, USA

Great Big Sea (Musician)
Fleming & Associates
733 N Main St # 735
Ann Arbor, MI 48104-1030, USA

Greatbatch, Wilson (Inventor)
10000 Wehrie Dr
Clarence, NY 14031, USA

Greaves, Gary (Football Player)
Houston Oilers
8221 SW 176th St
Palmetto Bay, FL 33157-6147, USA

Grebeck, Craig (Baseball Player)
Chicago White Sox
27856 Homestead Rd
Laguna Niguel, CA 92677-3763, USA

Grebenshchikov, Boris (Musician)
2 Marata St
#3
Saint Petersburg, RUSSIA

Grechko, Georgi M (Cosmonaut)
Potcha Kosmonavtov
Moskovskoi Oblasti
Syvisdny Goroduk 141160, RUSSIA

Greco, Buddy (Musician)
Zane Mgmt
1301 Yarmouth Rd
Wynnewood, PA 19096-3642, USA

Greco, Emilio (Artist)
Viale Cortina d'Ampezzo 132
Rome 00135, ITALY

Greco, Juliette (Actor, Musician)
Maurice Maraouani
37 Rue Marbeuf
Paris 75008, FRANCE

Greco, Michael (Actor)
EastEnders
BBC Elstree Centre
Clarendon Road
Borehamwood, Herts WD6 1JF, UNITED
KINGDOM (UK)

Greczyn, Alice
c/o Joseph Le *Amatruda Benson &
Associates (ABA)*
9107 Wilshire Blvd Ste 500
Beverly Hills, CA 90210-5526, USA

Greeley, Andrew
6030 S Ellis Ave
Chicago, IL 60637-2608, USA

Green, A C (Basketball Player)
201 E Jefferson St
Phoenix, AZ 85004-2412, USA

Green, Adolph
211 Central Park W # 19E
New York, NY 10024-6020, USA

Green, Ahman (Football Player)
c/o Staff Member *Green Bay Packers*
PO Box 10628
Green Bay, WI 54307-0628, USA

Green, Al (Musician)
c/o Staff Member *William Morris Agency
(WMA-NY)*
1325 Avenue Of The Americas
New York, NY 10019-6026, USA

Green, Al (Musician, Songwriter, Writer)
PO Box 456
Millington, TN 38083-0456, USA

Green, B Eric (Football Player)
Pittsburgh Steelers
13131 Luntz Point Ln
Windermere, FL 34786-5802, USA

Green, Barrett (Football Player)
Detroit Lions
808 Brickell Key Dr Apt 802
Miami, FL 33131-2685, USA

Green, Barry (Misc)
Team Green
7615 Zionsville Rd
Indianapolis, IN 46268-2174, USA

Green, Benny (Musician)
Jazz Tree
211 Thompson St Apt 1D
New York, NY 10012-1366, USA

Green, Boyce (Football Player)
Cleveland Browns
4156 1st Street Pl NW
Hickory, NC 28601-8075, USA

Green, Brian Austin (Actor)
c/o Tracy Samuels *Interlink Management*
19366 Rosita St
Tarzana, CA 91356-5055, USA

Green, Charlie (Football Player)
Oakland Raiders
735 S Alton Way
Denver, CO 80247-1864, USA

Green, Chris (Baseball Player)
Pittsburgh Pirates
1423 W 85th St
Los Angeles, CA 90047-5412, USA

Green, Chris (Football Player)
Miami Dolphins
331 Patio Village Ter
Weston, FL 33326-1622, USA

Green, Cleveland (Football Player)
Miami Dolphins
12340 I 20
Edwards, MS 39066-9081, USA

Green, Cornell (Football Player)
Dallas Cowboys
2106 Trinidad Dr
Dallas, TX 75232-2750, USA

Green, Dallas (Baseball Player)
Philadelphia Phillies
846 Conowingo Rd
Conowingo, MD 21918-1307, USA

Green, Darrell (Football Player)
Washington Redskins
20998 Rostormel Ct
Ashburn, VA 20147-4780, USA

Green, David (Baseball Player)
St Louis Cardinals
1440 Cove Ln
Saint Louis, MO 63138-2408, USA

Green, David (Director)
International Creative Mgmt
76 Oxford St
London W1N 0AX, UNITED KINGDOM
(UK)

Green, David E (Football Player)
Houston Oilers
8311 Pat Blvd
Tampa, FL 33615-1810, USA

Green, David E (Misc)
5339 Brody Dr
Madison, WI 53705-5425, USA

Green, David Gordon (Director,
Producer, Writer)
c/o Craig Gering *Creative Artists Agency
LCC (CAA-LA)*
2000 Avenue Of The Stars
Los Angeles, CA 90067-4700, USA

Green, David T (Inventor)
US Surgical Corp
150 Glover Ave
Norwalk, CT 06850-1346, USA

Green, Debbie (Volleyball Player)
239 5th St
Seal Beach, CA 90740-6116, USA

Green, Dennis (Coach, Football Coach)
FLW Outdoors
Pax-Tv
601 Cleanwater Park Road
West Palm Beach, FL 33401, USA

Green, Dick (Baseball Player)
Kansas City A's
3924 Ridgemoor Dr
Rapid City, SD 57702-5328, USA

Green, Donnie (Football Player)
Buffalo Bills
29 W Washington St Apt 210
Annapolis, MD 21401-1946, USA

Green, Ernie (Football Player)
Cleveland Browns
424 Rue Marseille
Dayton, OH 45429-1878, USA

Green, Eva (Actor)
c/o Michelle Bohan *Endeavor Agency LLC
(LA)*
9601 Wilshire Blvd Fl 3
Beverly Hills, CA 90210-5204, USA

Green, Gary (Baseball Player)
San Diego Padres
939 Kennebec St
Pittsburgh, PA 15217-2604, USA

Green, Gary F (Football Player)
Kansas City Chiefs
16330 Walnut Creek Dr
San Antonio, TX 78247-5636, USA

Green, Gerald (Writer)
88 Arrowhead Trl
New Canaan, CT 06840-3441, USA

Green, Hamilton (Prime Minister)
Plot D Lodge
Georgetown, GUYANA

Green, Harold (Football Player)
Cincinnati Bengals
212 Holly Ridge Ln
Columbia, SC 29229-9406, USA

Green, Howard (Physicist)
Harvard Medical School
Physiology & Biophysics Dept
Boston, MA 02115, USA

Green, Hugh (Football Player)
Tampa Bay Buccaneers
4758 Highway 61
Fayette, MS 39069-5422, USA

Green, Jacob (Football Player)
Seattle Seahawks
4921 Whistling Straits Loop
College Station, TX 77845-3866, USA

Green, Janine (Actor)
c/o David Sweeney *Sweeney
Management*
8755 Lookout Mountain Ave
Los Angeles, CA 90046-1861, USA

Green, Jeff (Race Car Driver)
Continental
5909 Peachtree Dunwoody Rd NE
Atlanta, GA 30328-8102, USA

Green, Jessie (Football Player)
Green Bay Packers
314 Lakeside Hills
Granbury, TX 76408, USA

Green, John (Football Player)
Buffalo Bills
7417 Jester Ct
Ooltewah, TN 37363-7150, USA

Green, John M (Johnny) (Basketball
Player)
9 Susan Ln
Dix Hills, NY 11746-5140, USA

Green, John N (Jack) Jr
(Cinematographer)
516 Esplanade Apt E
Redondo Beach, CA 90277-4077, USA

Green, Kate (Writer)
Bantam/Delacorte/Dell/Doubleday Press
1540 Broadway
New York, NY 10036-4039, USA

Green, Ken (Golfer)
4520 Feivel Rd Apt 56
West Palm Beach, FL 33417-8078, USA

Green, Lenny (Baseball Player)
Baltimore Orioles
18693 Sunset St
Detroit, MI 48234-2043, USA

Green, Leonard I (Business Person)
Rite Aid Corp
30 Hunter Ln
Camp Hill, PA 17011-2410, USA

Green, Lucinda (Misc)
Appleshaw House
Andover
Hants, UNITED KINGDOM (UK)

Green, Mark (Race Car Driver)
Trackside Marketing Group
345 Marblerock Way
Lexington, KY 40503-6321, USA

Green, Mark A (Football Player)
Chicago Bears
1087 Creek Bend Dr
Vernon Hills, IL 60061-3307, USA

Green, Mark J (Activist, Attorney, Attorney General, General, Writer)
Democracy Project
43 E 19th St Fl 3
New York, NY 10003-1304, USA

Green, Maurice Spurgeon (Editor)
Hermitage
Twyford House
Hants, UNITED KINGDOM (UK)

Green, Michael (Cinematographer)
11 Stevenson Ln
Upper Saddle River, NJ 07458-2136, USA

Green, Mike (Football Player)
San Diego Chargers
15271 Peach St
Chino Hills, CA 91709-2565, USA

Green, Pat (Musician, Songwriter, Writer)
William Morris Agency
1600 Division St Ste 300
Nashville, TN 37203-2755, USA

Green, Patricia (Producer, Writer)
c/o David Greenblatt *Key Creatives*
9595 Wilshire Blvd Ste 800
Beverly Hills, CA 90212-2508, USA

Green, Paul (Football Player)
Seattle Seahawks
8790 Lookout Mountain Ave
Los Angeles, CA 90046-1859, USA

Green, Pumpsie (Baseball Player)
Boston Red Sox
2105 Harper St
El Cerrito, CA 94530-1724, USA

Green, Ray (Football Player)
Carolina Panthers
180 Dunnemann Ave
Charleston, SC 29403-3510, USA

Green, Rick (Hockey Player)
RR 1
Peterborough, ON K9J 6X2, CANADA

Green, Robin (Writer)
c/o Staff Member *Broder Webb Chervin Silbermann Agency, The (BWCS)*
10250 Constellation Blvd Ste P
Los Angeles, CA 90067-6213, USA

Green, Robson (Actor)
c/o Staff Member *Coastal Productions*
25B Broadchare
The Quayside
Newcastle-Upon-Tyne NE1 3DQ,
UNITED KINGDOM (UK)

Green, Sarah (Producer)
c/o Staff Member *International Creative Management (ICM-LA)*
10250 Constellation Blvd
Los Angeles, CA 90067-6200, USA

Green, Seth (Actor, Comedian, Producer, Writer)
c/o Trice Koopman *Koopman Management*
PO Box 1317
Pacific Palisades, CA 90272-1317, USA

Green, Sidney (Basketball Player, Coach)
Florida Atlantic University
Athletic Dept
Boca Raton, FL 33431, USA

Green, Suzy (Golfer)
891 Westhills Dr Apt 1
South Lyon, MI 48178-2533, USA

Green, Tammie (Golfer)
4990 Township Road 147 NE
Somerset, OH 43783-9753, USA

Green, Timothy J (Tim) (Football Player, Sportscaster)
Atlanta Falcons
1194 Breenfield Lane
Skaneateles, NY 13152, USA

Green, Tom (Actor, Comedian)
William Morris Agency
151 El Camino Dr
Beverly Hills, CA 90212-2775, USA

Green, Travis (Hockey Player)
4-810 Marine Dr
Gibsons, BC V0N 1V0, CANADA

Green, Trent (Football Player)
Kansas City Chiefs
1 Arrowhead Dr
Kansas City, MO 64129-1651, USA

Green, Tyler (Baseball Player)
Philadelphia Phillies
5892 S Havana Ct
Englewood, CO 80111, USA

Green, Van (Football Player)
Cleveland Browns
311 Leta St
Auburndale, FL 33823-4313, USA

Green, Victor (Football Player)
New York Jets
3904 Merriweather Woods
Alpharetta, GA 30022-7150, USA

Green, Vivian (Actor)
c/o Staff Member *Endeavor Agency LLC (LA)*
9601 Wilshire Blvd Fl 3
Beverly Hills, CA 90210-5204, USA

Green, Willie (Football Player)
Detroit Lions
152 Farmington Rd
Shelby, NC 28150-8698, USA

Green, Woody (Football Player)
Kansas City Chiefs
3819 NE Garfield Ave
Portland, OR 97212-1022, USA

Green, Yatil (Football Player)
Miami Dolphins
2000 Island Blvd Apt 3002
Aventura, FL 33160-4966, USA

Green Day (Music Group)
c/o Staff Member *Creative Artists Agency LCC (CAA-LA)*
2000 Avenue Of The Stars
Los Angeles, CA 90067-4700, USA

Greenaway, Peter (Director)
Allarts Ltd
387B King St
London W6 9NH, UNITED KINGDOM (UK)

Greenberg, Adam (Cinematographer)
Gersh Agency
232 N Canon Dr
Beverly Hills, CA 90210-5302, USA

Greenberg, Alan C (Financier)
Bear Steams Co
383 Madison Ave
New York, NY 10017, USA

Greenberg, Carl (Journalist)
6001 Canterbury Dr
Culver City, CA 90230-6876, USA

Greenberg, Evan (Business Person)
American International Group
70 Pine St
New York, NY 10270-0094, USA

Greenberg, Jack (Attorney, Attorney General, Educator, General)
118 Riverside Dr
New York, NY 10024-3708, USA

Greenberg, Maurice R (Business Person)
American International Group
70 Pine St
New York, NY 10270-0094, USA

Greenberg, Morton I (Judge)
US Court of Appeals
402 E State St
Judicial Complex
Trenton, NJ 08608-1507, USA

Greenberg, Peter (Television Host)
c/o Staff Member *Today Show, The*
30 Rockefeller Plz # 374E
New York, NY 10112-0015, USA

Greenberg, Robbie S (Cinematographer)
11 Reef St
Marina Del Rey, CA 90292-6725, USA

Greenblatt, Stephen J (Writer)
Harvard University
English Dept
Cambridge, MA 02138, USA

Greenblatt, William
30710 Monte Lado Dr
Malibu, CA 90265-3128, USA

Greenburg, Dan (Writer)
323 E 50th St
New York, NY 10022-7901, USA

Greenburg, Paul (Journalist)
5900 Scenic Dr
Little Rock, AR 72207-2833, USA

Greenbush, Rachel Lindsay (Actor)
Gold Marshak Liedtke
3500 W Olive Ave Ste 1400
Burbank, CA 91505-5512, USA

Greenbush, Sidney Robin (Actor)
Gold Marshak Liedtke
3500 W Olive Ave Ste 1400
Burbank, CA 91505-5512, USA

Greene, Al (Baseball Player)
Detroit Tigers
18294 Marlowe St
Detroit, MI 48235-2762, USA

Greene, Charles E (Charlie) (Athlete, Track Athlete)
PO Box 6938
Lincoln, NE 68506-0938, USA

Greene, Charlie (Baseball Player)
New York Mets
1449 Oldfield Dr
Tallahassee, FL 32308-0534, USA

Greene, David (Actor)
c/o Lenore Zerman *Liberman/Zerman Management*
252 N Larchmont Blvd Ste 200
Los Angeles, CA 90004-3754, USA

Greene, Ellen (Musician)
Innovative Artists
1505 10th St
Santa Monica, CA 90401-2805, USA

Greene, Graham (Actor)
Susan Smith
1344 N Wetherly Dr
Los Angeles, CA 90069-1817, USA

Greene, Jack (Musician)
Ace Productions
PO Box 428
Portland, TN 37148-0428, USA

Greene, Jack P (Historian)
1974 Division Rd
East Greenwich, RI 02818-1211, USA

Greene, James
60 Pope's Grove Twickenham
Middlesex, ENGLAND, UNITED KINGDOM (UK)

Greene, John (Football Player)
Detroit Lions
39400 Woodward Ave Ste 255
Bloomfield Hills, MI 48304-5155, USA

Greene, Kenneth E (Football Player)
St Louis Cardinals
1620 E Bulldog Ln
Fresno, CA 93740-0001, USA

Greene, Kevin (Football Player)
Los Angeles Rams
928 Bambi Dr
Destin, FL 32541-1833, USA

Greene, Leonard M (Inventor)
1010 Greacen Point Rd
Mamaroneck, NY 10543-4609, USA

Greene, Maurice (Athlete, Track Athlete)
HSI Sports Mgmt
2600 Michelson Dr Ste 680
Irvine, CA 92612-6526, USA

Greene, Michelle
PO Box 29117
Los Angeles, CA 90029-0117, USA

Greene, Pat (Actor)
c/o Staff Member *GVA Talent Agency Inc*
9229 W Sunset Blvd Ste 320
Los Angeles, CA 90069-3403, USA

Greene, Robert B (Bob) Jr (Writer)
Chicago Tribune
435 N Michigan Ave
Editorial Dept
Chicago, IL 60611-4024, USA

Greene, Shecky (Actor, Comedian)
1642 S La Verne Way
Palm Springs, CA 92264-9296, USA

Greene, Todd (Baseball Player)
California Angels
725 Pine Leaf Ct
Alpharetta, GA 30022-1026, USA

Greene, Tommy (Baseball Player)
Atlanta Braves
6001 Dalecross Way
Glen Allen, VA 23059-6962, USA

Greene, Tony (Football Player)
Buffalo Bills
9001 Brookville Rd
Southeast Recycling
Silver Spring, MD 20910-1819, USA

Greene, Tony (Football Player)
Southeast Recycling
9001 Brookville Rd
Silver Spring, MD 20910-1819, USA

Greene, Willie (Baseball Player)
Cincinnati Reds
143 Greenview Ter
Macon, GA 31220-8750, USA

Greenfield, James L (Journalist)
470 Park Ave # 9A
New York, NY 10022-1990, USA

Greenfield, Jeff (Correspondent)
Cable News Network
820 1st St NE
News Dept
Washington, DC 20002-4243, USA

Greenfield, Lauren (Director, Photographer, Producer)
Lauren Greenfield Photography
2417 McKinley Ave
Venice, CA 90291-4625, USA

Greenfield, Max (Actor, Producer)
c/o Loch Powell *Leverage Management*
3030 Pennsylvania Ave
Santa Monica, CA 90404-4112, USA

Greenfield, Tom (Football Player)
Green Bay Packers
6115 E San Cristobal St
Tucson, AZ 85715-3013, USA

Greengard, Paul (Nobel Prize Laureate)
362 E 69th St
New York, NY 10021-5706, USA

Greengrass, Jim (Baseball Player)
Cincinnati Reds
232 Talking Rock Creek Pro Rd
Chatsworth, GA 30705-6895, USA

Greenhouse, Linda (Journalist)
New York Times
229 W 43rd St
Editorial Dept
New York, NY 10036-3959, USA

Greenlee, David (Actor)
1811 Whitley Ave Apt 800
Los Angeles, CA 90028-4960, USA

Greenspan, Alan (Business Person)
c/o Staff Member *International Arts Entertainment*
8899 Beverly Blvd Ste 800
Los Angeles, CA 90048-2451, USA

Greenspan, Alan (Financier, Government Official)
Federal Reserve Board
20th St & Constitution Ave NW
Washington, DC 20551-0001, USA

Greenspan, Bud (Director, Producer)
118 E 57th St
New York, NY 10022-2601, USA

Greenspan, Melissa (Actor)
c/o Staff Member *International Creative Management (ICM-LA)*
10250 Constellation Blvd
Los Angeles, CA 90067-6200, USA

Greenspoon, Jimmy (Musician)
McKenzie Accountancy
5171 Caliente St Unit 134
Las Vegas, NV 89119-2198, USA

Greenstein, Jeff (Producer)
c/o Staff Member *Broder Webb Chervin Silbermann Agency, The (BWCS)*
10250 Constellation Blvd Ste P
Los Angeles, CA 90067-6213, USA

Greenville, Georgina (Model)
Next Model Mgmt
188 Rue de Rivoli
Paris 75001, FRANCE

Greenwald, Milton (Misc)
University of California
Museum Of Paleontology
Berkeley, CA 94720-0001, USA

Greenwalt, T Jack (Misc)
2444 Madison Rd Unit 1501
Cincinnati, OH 45208-1228, USA

Greenwell, Michael L (Mike) (Baseball Player)
Boston Red Sox
35 NE Pine Island Rd
Greenwell's Family Fun Park
Cape Coral, FL 33909-2559, USA

Greenwich, Ellie (Musician)
203 SW 3rd Ave
Gainesville, FL 32601-6519, USA

Greenwood, Bruce (Actor)
1465 Lindacrest Dr
Beverly Hills, CA 90210-2519, USA

Greenwood, Colin (Musician)
Nasty Little Man
72 Spring St # 1100
New York, NY 10012-4019, USA

Greenwood, Jonny (Musician)
Nasty Little Man
72 Spring St # 1100
New York, NY 10012-4019, USA

Greenwood, L C (Football Player)
Pittsburgh Steelers
PO Box 614
Pro Athlete Marketing
Beaver Falls, PA 15010-0614, USA

Greenwood, L C H (L C) (Football Player)
329 S Dallas Ave
Pittsburgh, PA 15208-2627, USA

Greenwood, Lee (Musician, Songwriter, Writer)
c/o Staff Member *William Morris Agency (WMA-LA)*
1 William Morris Pl
Beverly Hills, CA 90212-4261, USA

Greenwood, Michael
Princes Gate1 4 Kingston House E
London, ENGLAND SW7, UNITED KINGDOM (UK)

Greenwood, Morlon (Football Player)
Miami Dolphins
18117 SW 24th St
Miramar, FL 33029-5118, USA

Greenwood, Norman (Misc)
University of Leeds
Chemistry Dept
Leeds LS2 9JT, UNITED KINGDOM (UK)

Greer, Brian (Baseball Player)
San Diego Padres
307 Bagnall Ave
Placentia, CA 92870-1904, USA

Greer, Brodie
300 S Raymond Ave # II
Pasadena, CA 91105-2620, USA

Greer, David S (Misc)
Brown University
PO Box G
Providence, RI 02912-0001, USA

Greer, Donovan (Football Player)
Atlanta Falcons
12023 Bissonnet St Apt 1511
Houston, TX 77099-1451, USA

Greer, Germaine (Writer)
Atkin & Stone
29 Fernshaw Road
London SW10 0TG, UNITED KINGDOM (UK)

Greer, Gordon G (Editor)
Better Homes & Gardens Magazine
1716 Locust St
Des Moines, IA 50309-3038, USA

Greer, Harold E (Hal) (Basketball Player)
7900 E Princess Dr Apt 1021
Scottsdale, AZ 85255-5824, USA

Greer, Howard (Admiral)
8539 Prestwick Dr
La Jolla, CA 92037-2025, USA

Greer, Judy (Actor)
Creative Artists Agency
9830 Wilshire Blvd
Beverly Hills, CA 90212-1804, USA

Greer, Kenny (Baseball Player)
New York Mets
17 Hill St
Cohasset, MA 02025-2218, USA

Greer, Rusty (Baseball Player)
Texas Rangers
3930 Glade Rd Ste 108
Colleyville, TX 76034-5930, USA

Greevy, Bernadette (Musician)
Melrose
672 Howth Road
Dublin 5, IRELAND

Greezyn, Alice (Actor)
c/o Staff Member *Windfall*
3000 W Alameda Ave
Burbank, CA 91523-0001, USA

Gregg, A Forrest (Coach, Football Coach, Football Executive, Football Player)
Green Bay Packers
2985 Plaza Azul
Santa Fe, NM 87507-5337, USA

Gregg, Clark (Actor)
United Talent Agency
9560 Wilshire Blvd Ste 500
Beverly Hills, CA 90212-2401, USA

Gregg, John
1/1 Punch St.
Mosman NSW 2088, AUSTRALIA

Gregg, Kevin (Baseball Player)
Anaheim Angels
6 NW Edgewood Dr
Corvallis, OR 97330-2302, USA

Gregg, Ricky Lynn (Musician)
ER Rimes Mgmt
1103 Bell Grimes Ln
Nashville, TN 37207-1605, USA

Gregg, Stephen (Writer)
c/o Staff Member *Creative Artists Agency LCC (CAA-LA)*
2000 Avenue Of The Stars
Los Angeles, CA 90067-4700, USA

Gregg, Stephen R (War Hero)
280 Main St Apt 310
Little Falls, NJ 07424-1375, USA

Gregg, Tommy (Baseball Player)
Pittsburgh Pirates
300 Winding Forest Dr
Winston Salem, NC 27104-3643, USA

Gregorian, Vartan (Educator)
Carnegie Corp
437 Madison Ave
President's Office
New York, NY 10022-7034, USA

Gregorio, Rose (Actor)
Don Buchwald
6500 Wilshire Blvd Ste 2200
Los Angeles, CA 90048-4942, USA

Gregorio, Tom (Baseball Player)
Anaheim Angels
66 McArthur Ave
Staten Island, NY 10312-1925, USA

Gregorios, Metropolitan Paulos M (Religious Leader)
Orthodox Seminary
PO Box 98
Kottayam, Kerala 686001, INDIA

Gregory, Adam (Musician)
c/o Staff Member *SL Feldman & Associates*
1505 W 2nd Ave #200
Vancouver, BC V6H 3Y4, CANADA

Gregory, Andre (Actor)
c/o Jeff Hunter *William Morris Agency (WMA-NY)*
1325 Avenue Of The Americas
New York, NY 10019-6026, USA

Gregory, Bettina L (Correspondent)
ABC-TV
5010 Creston St
News Dept
Hyattsville, MD 20781-1216, USA

Gregory, Cynthia (Ballerina)
American Ballet Theatre
890 Broadway
New York, NY 10003-1278, USA

Gregory, David
2200 Fletcher Ave
Fort Lee, NJ 07024-5005, USA

Gregory, Dick (Activist, Actor, Comedian)
Dick Gregory Health Enterprise
PO Box 3270
Plymouth, MA 02361-3270, USA

Gregory, Dorian (Actor, Television Host)
c/o Deborah Miller *Compass Entertainment Group*
9255 W Sunset Blvd Ste 727
Los Angeles, CA 90069-3304, USA

Gregory, Frederick D (Astronaut)
506 Tulip Rd
Annapolis, MD 21403-1326, USA

Gregory, Garland (Football Player)
San Francisco 49ers
1201 Lakeview Dr
Ruston, LA 71270-5237, USA

Gregory, Glynn (Football Player)
Dallas Cowboys
7007 Joyce Way
Dallas, TX 75225-1728, USA

Gregory, Jack (Football Player)
Cleveland Browns
108 Robertson St
Okolona, MS 38860-1619, USA

Gregory, Kathy (Cartoonist)
Playboy Magazine
680 N Lake Shore Dr
Reader Services
Chicago, IL 60611-4546, USA

Gregory, Lee (Baseball Player)
Chicago Cubs
6456 N Teilman Ave
Fresno, CA 93711-1315, USA

Gregory, Nick (Actor)
Writers & Artists
360 N Crescent Dr Bldg North
Beverly Hills, CA 90210-6818, USA

Gregory, Paul
PO Box 415
Desert Hot Springs, CA 92240-0415, USA

Gregory, Richard (Religious Leader)
Independent Fundamental Churches
2684 Meadowridge Dr SW
Byron Center, MI 49315-9242, USA

Gregory, Roberta (Artist)
c/o Staff Member *Fantagraphics Books*
7563 Lake City Way NE
Seattle, WA 98115-4218, USA

Gregory, Stephen (Actor)
Carey
64 Thornton Ave
London W4 1QQ, UNITED KINGDOM
(UK)

Gregory, William G (Astronaut)
2027 E Freeport Ln
Gilbert, AZ 85234-2829, USA

Gregory, William H (Editor)
Aviation Week Magazine
1221 Avenue Of The Americas
New York, NY 10020-1014, USA

Gregory, William Jr (Football Player)
Dallas Cowboys
4317 Cityview Dr
Plano, TX 75093-3236, USA

Gregory, Wilton D (Religious Leader)
Illinois Diocese
222 S 3rd St
Chancery Office
Belleville, IL 62220-1916, USA

Gregory Moss, Shad (Lil Bow Wow)
(Actor, Musician)
c/o Jeff Frasco *Creative Artists Agency
LCC (CAA-LA)*
2000 Avenue Of The Stars
Los Angeles, CA 90067-4700, USA

Gregory-Paul, Zoe (Actor)
c/o Staff Member *Gordon Rael Agency
LLC (GRA)*
9229 Sunset Blvd #310
Beverly Hills, CA 90069, USA

Gregson, Wallace C (General)
Commanding General
Marine Forces Pacific
Camp Hm Smith, HI 96861, USA

Gregson-Williams, Harry (Composer)
Gorfaine/Schwartz
4111 W Alameda Ave Ste 509
Burbank, CA 91505-4171, USA

Grehl, Michael (Editor)
Memphis Commercial Appeal
495 Union Ave
Editorial Dept
Memphis, TN 38103-3217, USA

Greif, Bill (Baseball Player)
Houston Astros
807 E 31st St
Austin, TX 78705-3205, USA

Greiner, William R (Educator)
State University of New York
President's Office
Buffalo, NY 14221, USA

Greiner-Petter-Memm, Simone (Athlete)
Am Sportplatz 14
Waldau 98667, GERMANY

Greise, Bob (Athlete)
3195 Ponce De Leon Blvd # 412
Coral Gables, FL 33134-6801, USA

Greisen, Chris (Football Player)
Arizona Cardinals
1710 Arabian Dr
Green Bay, WI 54313-4388, USA

Greisen, Nick (Football Player)
New York Giants
1028 S 19th Pl
Sturgeon Bay, WI 54235-1091, USA

Greisinger, Seth (Baseball Player)
Detroit Tigers
6460 Overbrook St
Falls Church, VA 22043-1914, USA

Greist, Kim (Actor)
Innovative Artists
1505 10th St
Santa Monica, CA 90401-2805, USA

Grelf, Michael (Director)
La Jolla Playhouse
PO Box 12039
La Jolla, CA 92039-2039, USA

Grenier, Adrian (Actor)
1610 Broadway
Santa Monica, CA 90404-2792, USA

Grenier, Sylvain (Wrestler)
c/o Staff Member *World Wrestling
Entertainment (WWE)*
1241 E Main St
Stamford, CT 06902-3520, USA

Grenier, Zach (Actor)
c/o Don Spradlin *Essential Talent
Management*
6399 Wilshire Blvd Ste 400
Los Angeles, CA 90048-5716, USA

Grentz, Theresa Shank (Coach)
University of Illinois
Athletic Dept
Champaign, IL 61820, USA

Gretch, Joel (Actor)
c/o Molly Madden *3 Arts Entertainment
Inc*
9460 Wilshire Blvd Fl 7
Beverly Hills, CA 90212-2713, USA

Gretzky, Wayne (Hockey Player)
Goldman Grant Tani
9100 Wilshire Blvd Ste 1000W
Beverly Hills, CA 90212-3463, USA

Grevey, Kevin (Basketball Player)
528 River Bend Rd
Great Falls, VA 22066-2716, USA

Grey, Beryl E (Ballerina)
Fernhill Priory Road
Forest Row
East Sussex RH18 5JE, UNITED
KINGDOM (UK)

Grey, Jennifer (Actor)
c/o Constance Freiberg *Envision
Entertainment*
9255 W Sunset Blvd Ste 500
West Hollywood, CA 90069-3301, USA

Grey, Joel (Actor)
c/o Nevin Dolcefino *Innovative Artists
(LA)*
1505 10th St
Santa Monica, CA 90401-2805, USA

Greyeyes, Michael
3500 W Olive Ave Ste 1400
Burbank, CA 91505-5512, USA

Grgich, Visco (Football Player)
San Francisco 49ers
4205 Belvedere Ct
Modesto, CA 95357-0839, USA

Gribbon, Melissa (Actor)
c/o Dianne Hooper *Starcraft Talent
Agency*
1516 N Formosa Ave
Los Angeles, CA 90046, USA

Gribow, Patti
3303 Clerendon Rd
Beverly Hills, CA 90210-1061, USA

Grich, Robert A (Bobby) (Baseball Player)
Baltimore Orioles
31 Madison Ln
Coto De Caza, CA 92679-5012, USA

Grieco, Richard (Actor)
CR&G Enterprises
95 Public Sq Ste 304
Watertown, NY 13601-2642, USA

Grieder, William (Journalist)
Simon & Schuster
1230 Avenue Of The Americas
New York, NY 10020-1586, USA

Griem, Helmut (Actor)
Mgmt Erna Baumbauer
Keplerstr 2
Munich 81679, GERMANY

Grier, David Alan (Actor, Comedian)
c/o Sean Elliott *Endeavor Agency LLC (LA)*
9601 Wilshire Blvd Fl 3
Beverly Hills, CA 90210-5204, USA

Grier, Pam (Actor)
c/o Stephen LaManna *Innovative Artists
(LA)*
1505 10th St
Santa Monica, CA 90401-2805, USA

Grier, Roosevelt (Rosey) (Actor, Football
Player)
1250 4th St # 600
Santa Monica, CA 90401-1366, USA

Gries, Jonathan (Jon) (Actor, Director,
Producer)
c/o Cynthia Booth *Agency Group Ltd, The
(LA)*
1880 Century Park E Ste 711
Los Angeles, CA 90067-1618, USA

Griese, Brian (Football Player)
Denver Broncos
210 Hazel Ave
Glencoe, IL 60022-1735, USA

Griesemer, John N (Government Official)
RR 2 Box 204B
Springfield, MO 65802, USA

Grieve, Ben (Baseball Player)
Oakland A's
3620 Hanover St
Dallas, TX 75225-7210, USA

Grieve, Pierson M (Business Person)
Ecolab Inc
370 Wabasha St N
Ecolab Center
Saint Paul, MN 55102-1349, USA

Grieve, Tom (Baseball Player)
Washington Senators
4107 Carnation Dr
Arlington, TX 76016-3922, USA

Griffeth, Lee (Baseball Player)
Philadelphia Athletics
PO Box 51641
Durham, NC 27717-1641, USA

Griffey, Ken Jr (Baseball Player)
c/o Staff Member *Cincinnati Reds*
100 Cinergy Fld
Cinergy Field
Cincinnati, OH 45202, USA

Griffey, Ken Sr (Baseball Player)
Cincinnati Reds
8216 Princeton Glendale Rd # 103
West Chester, OH 45069-1675, USA

Griffin, Adrian (Basketball Player)
Dallas Marvericks
2909 Taylor St
Dallas, TX 75226-1909, USA

Griffin, Alfredo (Baseball Player)
Cleveland Indians
9731 NW 41st St
Doral, FL 33178-2944, USA

Griffin, Archie
4965 Saint Andrews Dr
Westerville, OH 43082, USA

Griffin, Archie M (Football Player)
Cincinnati Bengals
6845 Temperance Point Pl
Westerville, OH 43082-8704, USA

Griffin, Bo (Correspondent, Television
Host)
c/o Staff Member *Good Day Live*
20th Century Fox Television
10201 W Pico Blvd Blg 88 Rm 29
Los Angeles, CA 90035, USA

Griffin, Cornelius (Football Player)
New York Giants
1207 Forestburg Dr
Houston, TX 77038-2122, USA

Griffin, Courtney (Football Player)
Los Angeles Rams
6302 N Selland Ave
Fresno, CA 93711-0872, USA

Griffin, David
13 Spencer Gardens
London, ENGLAND SW14 7AH, UNITED
KINGDOM (UK)

Griffin, Don (Football Player)
Chicago Rockets
2475 Tracy Ln
Aurora, IL 60506-4229, USA

Griffin, Doug (Baseball Player)
California Angels
43 Highland Vw
Irvine, CA 92603-3704, USA

Griffin, Eddie (Actor, Comedian,
Producer, Writer)
c/o Daniel (Dan) Spilo *Artistry
Management*
525 Westbourne Dr
West Hollywood, CA 90048-1913, USA

Griffin, Eddie (Basketball Player)
c/o Staff Member *Minnesota
Timberwolves*
600 1st Ave N
Target Center
Minneapolis, MN 55403-1416, USA

Griffin, Eric (Boxer)
PO Box 964
Jasper, TN 37347-0964, USA

Griffin, Forrest (Athlete, Wrestler)
c/o Jervis L Cole
5 E River Park Pl W Ste 203
Fresno, CA 93720-1557, USA

Griffin, James
25 Paulson Dr
Burlington, MA 01803-2819, USA

Griffin, James Bennett (Misc)
5023 Wyandot Ct
Bethesda, MD 20816-2205, USA

Griffin, John W (Football Player)
Los Angeles Rams
10315 Herons Ridge Rd
Lakeland, TN 38002-8292, USA

Griffin, Kathy (Actor)
c/o Suzy Unger *William Morris Agency
(WMA-LA)*
1 William Morris Pl
Beverly Hills, CA 90212-4261, USA

Griffin, Keith (Football Player)
Washington Redskins
4330 Canada Hills Ct
Waldorf, MD 20602-3106, USA

Griffin, Larry (Football Player)
Houston Oilers
5617 Silchester Ln
Charlotte, NC 28215-5327, USA

Griffin, Leonard (Football Player)
Kansas City Chiefs
PO Box 480
Calhoun, LA 71225-0480, USA

Griffin, Mike (Baseball Player)
New York Yankees
1620 Grove Ave
Woodland, CA 95695-5149, USA

Griffin, Nikki (Actor)
c/o Staff Member *Agency for the Performing Arts (APA-LA)*
405 S Beverly Dr
Beverly Hills, CA 90212-4416, USA

Griffin, Patty (Musician, Songwriter, Writer)
Monterey Peninsula Artists
509 Hartnell St
Monterey, CA 93940-2825, USA

Griffin, Robert P (Judge, Senator)
Michigan Supreme Court
PO Box 30052
Lansing, MI 48909-7552, USA

Griffin, Rod L (Writer)
c/o Staff Member *$olvency International Inc*
PO Box 17802
Clearwater, FL 33762-0802, USA

Griffin, Thomas N Jr (General)
9749 South Park Cir
Fairfax Station, VA 22039-2943, USA

Griffin, Tom (Baseball Player)
Houston Astros
13147 Avenida La Valencia
Poway, CA 92064-1905, USA

Griffin, Tony (Actor, Director, Writer)
c/o Staff Member *Merv Griffin Entertainment*
130 El Camino Dr
Beverly Hills, CA 90212-2705, USA

Griffin, Warren (Warren G) (Actor, Musician)
c/o Staff Member *Warning Management*
9440 Santa Monica Blvd
Beverly Hills, CA 90210-4610, USA

Griffing, Glynn (Football Player)
New York Giants
2318 Irving Pl
Jackson, MS 39211-6133, USA

Griffith, Alan R (Financier)
Bank of New York
1 Wall St
New York, NY 10286-0001, USA

Griffith, Andy (Actor, Musician, Producer, Writer)
c/o Jeff Kolodny *William Morris Agency (WMA-LA)*
1 William Morris Pl
Beverly Hills, CA 90212-4261, USA

Griffith, Bill (Cartoonist)
Pinhead Productions
PO Box 88
Hadlyme, CT 06439-0088, USA

Griffith, Calvin (Baseball Player)
Minnesota Twins
501 Chicago Ave
Minneapolis, MN 55415-1596, USA

Griffith, Darrell (Basketball Player)
3021 Falmouth Dr
Louisville, KY 40205-2876, USA

Griffith, Emile A (Boxer)
150 Washington St Apt 6J
Hempstead, NY 11550-3133, USA

Griffith, Howard (Football Player)
Los Angeles Rams
9152 S Clyde Ave
Chicago, IL 60617-3740, USA

Griffith, James (Business Person)
Timken Co
1835 Dueber Ave SW
Canton, OH 44706-2798, USA

Griffith, Melanie (Actor, Producer)
c/o Nicole David *William Morris Agency (WMA-LA)*
1 William Morris Pl
Beverly Hills, CA 90212-4261, USA

Griffith, Robert (Football Player)
Cleveland Browns
76 Lou Groza Blvd
Berea, OH 44017-1269, USA

Griffith, Thomas Ian (Actor)
c/o Lou Pitt *Pitt Group, The*
9465 Wilshire Blvd Ste 480
Beverly Hills, CA 90212-2603, USA

Griffith, Thomas Ian (Actor)
Endeavor Talent Agency
9701 Wilshire Blvd Ste 1000
Beverly Hills, CA 90212-2010, USA

Griffith, Tom W (Misc)
Rural Letter Carriers Assn
1448 Duke St # 100
Alexandria, VA 22314-3403, USA

Griffith, Wendy (Religious Leader, Television Host)
c/o Staff Member *CBN News*
977 Centerville Turnpike
Christian Broadcasting Network
Virginia Beach, VA 23464, USA

Griffith, Yolanda (Basketball Player)
Sacramento Monarchs
1 Sports Pkwy
Arco Arena
Sacramento, CA 95834-2300, USA

Griffiths, Brian (Baseball Player)
16022 SE Goosehollow Dr
Damascus, OR 97089-7859, USA

Griffiths, Derrell (Baseball Player)
Los Angeles Dodgers
201 E Central Blvd
Anadarko, OK 73005-3431, USA

Griffiths, Jeremy (Baseball Player)
New York Mets
120 Beachdale Dr
Avon Lake, OH 44012-1611, USA

Griffiths, Rachel (Actor)
c/o Michael D Aglion *Michael Aglion Management*
205 S Beverly Dr Ste 208
Beverly Hills, CA 90212-3867, USA

Griffiths, Richard (Actor)
c/o Staff Member *BBC Television Centre*
Incoming Mail
Wood Lane
London W12 7RJ, UNITED KINGDOM (UK)

Griffiths, Susan
9300 Wilshire Blvd # 410
Beverly Hills, CA 90212-3213, USA

Griggs, Acle (Baseball Player)
Birmingham Black Barons
820 Newwau Ave SW
Birmingham, AL 35221, USA

Griggs, Andy (Musician)
PO Box 120835
Nashville, TN 37212-0835, USA

Griggs, Hal (Baseball Player)
Washington Senators
2530 W Tenbrook Way
Tucson, AZ 85741-3782, USA

Griggs, William E (Football Player)
New York Jets
18 Summerhill Ln
Medford, NJ 08055-2365, USA

Grigonis, Frank (Football Player)
Detroit Lions
4585 Wieuca Rd NE
Atlanta, GA 30342-3355, USA

Grigorian, Irina (Figure Skater)
c/o Staff Member *Champions on Ice*
3500 W 80th St
Tom Collins Enterprises Inc
Minneapolis, MN 55431-1068, USA

Grigsby, Benji (Baseball Player)
118 Teakwood Dr SW
Huntsville, AL 35801-3453, USA

Grijalva, Lucy (Writer)
PO Box 1634
Benicia, CA 94510-4634, USA

Grijalva, Victor E (Business Person)
Schlumberger Ltd
277 Park Ave
New York, NY 10172-0003, USA

Grill, Rob (Musician)
Paradise Artists
108 E Matilija St
Ojai, CA 93023-2639, USA

Grilli, Guido (Baseball Player)
Boston Red Sox
250 Sloan Ln
Locust Grove, AR 72550-9000, USA

Grilli, Jason (Baseball Player)
Florida Marlins
9037 Point Cypress Dr
Orlando, FL 32836-5475, USA

Grilli, Steve (Baseball Player)
Detroit Tigers
8637 Briar Patch
Baldwinsville, NY 13027-8914, USA

Grillo, Frank
c/o Steven Muller *Innovative Artists (LA)*
1505 10th St
Santa Monica, CA 90401-2805, USA

Grim, Robert (Bob) (Football Player)
Minnesota Vikings
18 NW Saginaw Ave
Bend, OR 97701-1221, USA

Grimaldi, Dan (Actor)
c/o Staff Member *Sopranos, The*
9150 Wilshire Blvd Ste 350
Brad Grey Television
Beverly Hills, CA 90212-3453, USA

Grimaud, Helene (Musician)
I C M Artists
40 W 57th St
New York, NY 10019-4001, USA

Grimes, Billy Joe (Football Player)
Green Bay Packers
3140 NW 24th St
Oklahoma City, OK 73107-1906, USA

Grimes, Gary
4578 W 165th St
Lawndale, CA 90260-2805, USA

Grimes, Karolyn
PO Box 145
Carnation, WA 98014-0145, USA

Grimes, Martha (Writer)
115 D St SE Apt G6
Washington, DC 20003-1822, USA

Grimes, Randy (Football Player)
Tampa Bay Buccaneers
350 Kingscourt Dr
Houston, TX 77015-2321, USA

Grimes, Scott (Actor)
c/o Adam Levine *Anthem Entertainment*
6100 Wilshire Blvd Ste 1170
Los Angeles, CA 90048-5116, USA

Grimes, Tammy (Actor, Musician)
Don Buchwald
10 E 44th St
New York, NY 10017-3654, USA

Grimes, Tinsley (Actor)
c/o Staff Member *Innovative Artists (LA)*
1505 10th St
Santa Monica, CA 90401-2805, USA

Griminelli, Andrea (Musician)
Columbia Artists Mgmt Inc
1790 Broadway Fl 6
New York, NY 10019-1412, USA

Grimm, Dan (Football Player)
Green Bay Packers
2514 Smith Harbour Dr
Denver, NC 28037-8093, USA

Grimm, Russ (Coach, Football Coach, Football Player)
Washington Redskins
12177 Hickory Knoll Pl
Fairfax, VA 22033-1823, USA

Grimm, Tim (Actor)
Abrams Artists
9200 W Sunset Blvd Ste 1125
Los Angeles, CA 90069-3610, USA

Grimshaw, Nicholas T (Architect)
1 Conway St
Fitzroy Square
London W1P 5HA, UNITED KINGDOM (UK)

Grimsley, Jason (Baseball Player)
Philadelphia Phillies
PO Box 24085
Overland Park, KS 66283-4085, USA

Grimsley, John (Football Player)
Houston Oilers
3615 Robinson Rd
Missouri City, TX 77459-4313, USA

Grimsley, Ross A (Baseball Player)
Cincinnati Reds
92 Conewago Ct
Owings Mills, MD 21117-5049, USA

Grimsson, Olafur Ragnar (President)
President's Office
Sto'marradshusini v/Lackjartog
Reykjavik, ICELAND

Grinberg, Anouk (Actor)
Artmedia
20 Ave Rapp
Paris 75007, FRANCE

Grindenko, Tatyana T (Musician)
Moscow State Philharmonic
Tverskaya Str 31
Moscow 103050, RUSSIA

Grinder, Scott (Baseball Player)
1323 14th Ave N
Birmingham, AL 35204, USA

Grindlay, Annie (Actor)
Lichtman/Salners
15865 Royal Haven Pl
Sherman Oaks, CA 91403-4724, USA

Griner, Paul (Writer)
Random House
1745 Broadway # B1
New York, NY 10019-4305, USA

Grinham, Rawley Judy (Swimmer)
103 Green Lane Northwood
Middx HA6 1AP, UNITED KINGDOM
(UK)

Grinnell, Alan D (Physicist)
University of California
Lewis Center
Medical School
Los Angeles, CA 90024, USA

grinnell, todd (Actor)
c/o DEBRA MANNERS *Daniel Hoff
Agency*
5455 Wilshire Blvd Ste 1100
Los Angeles, CA 90036-4277, USA

Grinstead, Irish (Musician)
Creative Artists Agency
9830 Wilshire Blvd
Beverly Hills, CA 90212-1804, USA

Grinstead, LeMisha (Musician)
Creative Artists Agency
9830 Wilshire Blvd
Beverly Hills, CA 90212-1804, USA

Grinstein, Gerald (Business Person)
Delta Airlines
Hartsfield International Airport
Atlanta, GA 30320, USA

Grint, Rupert (Actor)
c/o Chris Harris *Actual Management
Company*
7 Great Russell Street
London WC1B 3NH, UNITED KINGDOM
(UK)

Grinville, Patrick (Writer)
Academie Goncourt
38 Rue du Faubourg Saint Jacques
Paris 75014, FRANCE

Grisanti, Eugene P (Business Person)
International Flavors
521 W 57th St
New York, NY 10019-2929, USA

Grisez, Germain (Misc)
Mount Saint Mary's College
Christain Ethics Dept
Emmitsburg, MD 21727, USA

Grisham, John (Writer)
c/o David Gernert *Gernert Company*
136 E 57th St
New York, NY 10022-2707, USA

Grishin, Evgenil (Speed Skater)
Committee of Physical Culture
Skatertny Pl 4
Moscow, RUSSIA

Grishuk, Okasana (Pasha) (Dancer)
Int'l Mgmt Group
22 E 71st St
New York, NY 10021-4975, USA

Grishuk, Pasha
Luzhnetskaia nab. 8
Moscow 119871, RUSSIA

Grisman, David (Composer, Musician)
CM Mgmt
5749 Larryan Dr
Woodland Hills, CA 91367-4041, USA

Grissom, Marguis D (Baseball Player)
PO Box 741810
Riverdale, GA 30274-1333, USA

Grissom, Marv (Baseball Player)
New York Giants
13975 Noble Way
Red Bluff, CA 96080-9332, USA

Grissom, Steve (Race Car Driver)
Source International
3475 Myer Lee Dr
Winston Salem, NC 27101-6209, USA

Grist, Reri (Opera Singer)
Columbia Artists Mgmt Inc
1790 Broadway Fl 6
New York, NY 10019-1412, USA

Grizzard, George (Actor)
400 E 54th St
New York, NY 10022-5164, USA

Grizzard, George (Baseball Player,
Basketball Player)
Champion Lakes
PO Box 288
Bolivar, PA 15923-0288, USA

Groat, Dick (Baseball Player)
Pittsburgh Pirates
PO Box 288
Champion Lakes Country Club
Bolivar, PA 15923-0288, USA

Grob, Mike (Golfer)
3611 Quimet Cir
Billings, MT 59106-1009, USA

Groban, Josh (Musician, Songwriter,
Writer)
c/o Staff Member *Special Artists Agency*
9465 Wilshire Blvd Ste 890
Beverly Hills, CA 90212-2607, USA

Grobell, Werner (Mr Frick) (Misc)
PO Box 7886
Incline Village, NV 89452-7886, USA

Groce, Clifton (Football Player)
Indianapolis Colts
1632A Park Pl
College Station, TX 77840-3123, USA

Grocholewski, Zenon Cardinal (Religious
Leader)
Palazzo della Congregazioni
Piazzo Pio XII #3
Rome 00193, ITALY

Grodin, Charles
c/o Tim Curtis *William Morris Agency
(WMA-LA)*
1 William Morris Pl
Beverly Hills, CA 90212-4261, USA

Groener, Harry (Actor)
Susan Smith
1344 N Wetherly Dr
Los Angeles, CA 90069-1817, USA

Groening, Matthew (Matt) (Cartoonist)
c/o Michael A Neidorf *Caplan-Groening
Family Foundation*
9720 Wilshire Blvd Fl 3
Beverly Hills, CA 90212-2015, USA

Groetzinger Jr, Jon (Business Person)
American Greetings Corp
1 American Rd
Cleveland, OH 44144-2398, USA

Grofe Jr, Ferde
18139 Coastline Dr
Malibu, CA 90265-5738, USA

Grogan, John (Writer)
HarperCollins Publishers L.L.C.
1000 Keystone Industrial Park
Dunmore, PA 18512-4621, USA

Grogan, Steven J (Steve) (Football Player)
New England Patriots
6 Country Club Ln
Foxboro, MA 02035-2756, USA

Groh, Al (Coach, Football Coach)
University of Virginia
Athletic Dept
Charlottesburg, VA 22903, USA

Groh, David (Actor)
c/o Alexandra Karrys *Divine Management*
117 N Orlando Ave
Los Angeles, CA 90048-3403, USA

Groh, Gary (Golfer)
331 Signe Ct
Lake Bluff, IL 60044-1219, USA

Grohl, Dave (Musician)
c/o Erin Culley-LaChapelle *Creative Artists
Agency LCC (CAA-LA)*
2000 Avenue Of The Stars
Los Angeles, CA 90067-4700, USA

Groman, William (Football Player)
Houston Oilers
7906 Scherzo Ln
Houston, TX 77040-2529, USA

Gronemeyer, Herbert
Leopoldstr. 19
Munich D-80802, GERMANY

Gronk (Artist)
Saxon-Lee Gallery
7525 Beverly Blvd
Los Angeles, CA 90036-2722, USA

Gronman, Tuomas (Hockey Player)
Pittsburgh Penguins
66 Mario Lemieux Pl
Mellon Arena
Pittsburgh, PA 15219-3504, USA

Groom, Buddy (Baseball Player)
Detroit Tigers
216 Pierce Rd
Red Oak, TX 75154, USA

Groom, Jerome P (Jerry) (Football Player)
Chicago Cardinals
625 Beach Rd # 201
Sarasota, FL 34242-1948, USA

Groom, Sam (Actor)
8730 W Sunset Blvd Ste 440
Los Angeles, CA 90069-2277, USA

Gropp, Louis Oliver (Editor)
140 Riverside Dr # 6G
New York, NY 10024-2605, USA

Gros, Earl (Football Player)
Green Bay Packers
17424 Airline Hwy Ste 12
Prairieville, LA 70769-3352, USA

Gros, Francois (Misc)
102 Rue de la Tour
Paris 75116, FRANCE

Gros Louis, Kenneth R R (Educator)
Indiana University
President's Office
Bloomington, IN 47405, USA

Grosbard, Ulu (Director)
29 W 10th St
New York, NY 10011-8739, USA

Gross, Alfred E (Football Player)
Cleveland Browns
8227 Grandstaff Dr
Sacramento, CA 95823-5970, USA

Gross, Arye
c/o Paul Greenstone *Paul Greenstone
Entertainment*
1227 Union St
San Francisco, CA 94109-1922, USA

Gross, Charles G (Psychic)
45 Woodside Ln
Princeton, NJ 08540-5417, USA

Gross, David (Comedian)
c/o Staff Member *United Talent Agency
(UTA)*
9560 Wilshire Blvd Ste 500
Beverly Hills, CA 90212-2401, USA

Gross, Don (Baseball Player)
Cincinnati Reds
1299 E Farrand Rd
Clio, MI 48420-9137, USA

Gross, George (Football Player)
San Diego Chargers
8 Troyer Ct
Fairhope, AL 36532-3611, USA

Gross, Greg (Baseball Player)
Houston Astros
802 Hallowell Dr
West Chester, PA 19382-5243, USA

Gross, Henry (Musician)
Zelda Mgmt
PO Box 150163
Nashville, TN 37215-0163, USA

Gross, Jordan (Football Player)
Carolina Panthers
800 S Mint St
Ericsson Stadium
Charlotte, NC 28202-1640, USA

Gross, Kevin (Baseball Player)
Philadelphia Phillies
PO Box 144
Claremont, CA 91711-0144, USA

Gross, Kip (Baseball Player)
Cincinnati Reds
2015 Ridgeview Ct
Redlands, CA 92373-6979, USA

Gross, Lee (Football Player)
New Orleans Saints
871 Holland Rd
Newton, AL 36352-8035, USA

Gross, Mary (Actor, Comedian)
9100 W Sunset Blvd # 300
Los Angeles, CA 90069-3110, USA

Gross, Michael (Actor)
c/o Staff Member *Silver Massetti &
Szatmary (SMS-NY)*
145 W 45th St # 1204
New York, NY 10036-4008, USA

Gross, Michael (Swimmer)
Paul-Ehrlich-Str 6
Frankfurt/Main 60596, GERMANY

Gross, Paul (Actor)
c/o Staff Member *Alliance
Communications*
121 Floor E #1400
Toronto, ON M4M 3M5, CANADA

Gross, Ricco (Athlete)
Waldbahnstr 34A
Ruhpolding 83324, GERMANY

Gross, Robert A (Physicist)
14 Sunnyside Way
New Rochelle, NY 10804-2109, USA

Gross, Robert (Bob) (Basketball Player)
13466 SE Red Rose Ln
Happy Valley, OR 97086-9752, USA

Gross, Terry R (Correspondent)
WHYY-Radio
Independence Mall W
News Dept
Philadelphia, PA 19106, USA

Gross, Wayne (Baseball Player)
Oakland A's
45 Leonard Ct
Danville, CA 94526-1911, USA

Grosscup, Lee (Football Player)
New York Giants
703 Atlantic Ave Apt 110
Alameda, CA 94501-2177, USA

Grossfeld, Stanley (Journalist)
Boston Globe
Editorial Dept
135 W T Morrissey Blvd
Dorchester, MA 02125, USA

Grosskios, Howdie (Baseball Player)
Pittsburgh Pirates
310 Llwyds Ln
Vero Beach, FL 32963-3253, USA

Grossman, Allen R (Writer)
4 Jeffrey Ter
Lexington, MA 02420-1324, USA

Grossman, Harley (Baseball Player)
Washington Senators
5605 Harmony Woods Ln
Evansville, IN 47720-2479, USA

Grossman, Judith (Football Player)
Chicago Bears
1000 Football Dr
Lake Forest, IL 60045-4829, USA

Grossman, Judith (Writer)
Warren Wilson College
English Dept
Swannanoa, NC 28778, USA

Grossman, Leslie (Actor)
c/o Staff Member *Metropolitan*
4500 Wilshire Blvd Fl 2
Los Angeles, CA 90010-3858, USA

Grossman, Randy (Football Player)
Pittsburgh Steelers
204 Ridge Rd
Pittsburgh, PA 15238-1522, USA

Grossman, Rex (Football Player)
c/o Staff Member *Chicago Bears*
1000 Football Dr
Lake Forest, IL 60045-4829, USA

Grossman, Robert (Misc)
19 Crosby St
New York, NY 10013-3102, USA

Grosvenor, Gilbert M (Publisher)
National Geographic Society
17th & M NW
Washington, DC 20036, USA

Grote, Jerry (Baseball Player)
Houston Colt .45's
5807 Babcock Rd # 215
San Antonio, TX 78240-2196, USA

Grotenfelt, Georg E J (Architect)
Kapteeninkatu 20D
Helsinki 00140, FINLAND

Grotewold, Jeff (Baseball Player)
Philadelphia Phillies
103 E 48th St
San Bernardino, CA 92404-1211, USA

Groth, Ernie (Baseball Player)
Cleveland Indians
Blackhawk-Negly Road
Beaver Falls, PA 15010, USA

Groth, Jeff (Football Player)
Miami Dolphins
13824 Driftwood Dr
Carmel, IN 46033-8510, USA

Groth, Johnny (Baseball Player)
Detroit Tigers
170 N Ocean Blvd Apt 307
Palm Beach, FL 33480-3931, USA

Grott, Matt (Baseball Player)
Cincinnati Reds
4714 Rolling Green Dr
Ooltewah, TN 37363-9073, USA

Grottkau, Robert (Football Player)
Detroit Lions
5105 S Muirfield Ln
Spokane, WA 99223-6362, USA

Grouch, Roger K (Astronaut)
Life/Microgravity Sciences Office
Nasa Headquarters
Washington, DC 20546-0001, USA

Grove, Andrew S (Business Person)
Intel Corp
2200 Mission College Blvd
Santa Clara, CA 95054-1549, USA

Grover, Gushan (Actor)
501/601 Woodstock J P Road
7 Bangalows Versova Andheri (W)
Bombay, MS 400 061, INDIA

Groves, George (Football Player)
Buffalo Bisons
3150 Frembes Rd
Waterford, MI 48329-4014, USA

Groves, Napiera Danielle (Actor)
c/o Christine Thomas *Sweet Mud Group*
648 Broadway # 1002
New York, NY 10012-2301, USA

Groves, Richard H (General)
400 Madison St Apt 1302
Alexandria, VA 22314-1722, USA

Grow, Carol (Actor, Model)
Xposure Public Relations
8271 Melrose Ave Ste 110
C/O Jon Orlando
Los Angeles, CA 90046-6800, USA

Growney, Robert L (Business Person)
Motorola Inc
1303 E
Schaumburg, IL 60196-0001, USA

Grroms, Charles R (Red) (Artist)
85 Walker St
New York, NY 10013-3523, USA

Grubb, John (Baseball Player)
San Diego Padres
6618 Bel Lac Dr
Chester, VA 23831-1431, USA

Grubb, Kevin (Race Car Driver)
c/o Grubb Motorsports
5120 Jefferson Davis Hwy
Richmond, VA 23234-2252, USA

Grubb, Robert
129 Bourke St.
Woolloomooloo NSW 2011, AUSTRALIA

Grubbs, Gary (Actor)
Parasigm Agency
10100 Santa Monica Blvd Ste 2500
Los Angeles, CA 90067-4116, USA

Grubbs, Robert H (Misc)
California Institute of Technology
Chemistry Dept
Pasadena, CA 91125-0001, USA

Gruber, Kelly W (Baseball Player)
Toronto Blue Jays
3300 Bee Cave Rd # 650-227
West Lake Hills, TX 78746-6600, USA

Gruber, Paul (Football Player)
Tampa Bay Buccaneers
PO Box 4239
Edwards, CO 81632-4201, USA

Gruberova, Edita (Opera Singer)
Opera et Concert
Maximillianstr 22
Munich 80539, GERMANY

Grubman, Allen J (Lawyer)
Grubman Indursky Schindler Goldstein
152 W 57th St
New York, NY 10019-3386, USA

Gruden, Jon (Coach)
Tampa Bay Buccaneers
1 W Buccaneer Place
Tampa, FL 33607, USA

Grudens, Richard
Box 344 Main St.
Stony Brook, NY 11790, USA

Grudzielanek, Mark (Baseball Player)
Montreal Expos
PO Box 1581
Rancho Santa Fe, CA 92067-1581, USA

Grudzlelanek, Mark J (Baseball Player)
Tom Grudzielanek
550 E Mona Dr
Oak Creek, WI 53154-3095, USA

Gruenberg, Erich (Musician)
80 Northway
Hampstead Garden Suburb
London NW11 6PA, UNITED KINGDOM
(UK)

Gruffudd, Ioan (Actor)
Hamilton Hodell
24 Hanway St
London W1T 1UH, UNITED KINGDOM
(UK)

Grum, Clifford J (Business Person)
Temple-Inland Inc
303 S Temple Dr
Diboll, TX 75941-2419, USA

Grumman, Cornelia (Journalist)
Chicago Tribune
435 N Michigan Ave
Editorial Dept
Chicago, IL 60611-4024, USA

Grummer, Elisabeth (Opera Singer)
Am Schlachtensee 104
Berlin 14163, GERMANY

Grunberg, Greg (Actor)
Greene Assoc
7080 Hollywood Blvd Ste 1017
Los Angeles, CA 90028-6937, USA

Grunberg-Manago, Marianne (Misc)
80 Boulevard Pasteur
Paris 75015, FRANCE

Grundfest, Joseph A (Government
Official)
Stanford University
Law School
Stanford, CA 94305, USA

Grundhofer, Jerry A (Financier)
Firstar Corp
777 E Wisconsin Ave
Milwaukee, WI 53202-5342, USA

Grundhofer, John F (Financier)
US Bancorp
601 2nd Ave S
US Bank Place
Minneapolis, MN 55402-1902, USA

Grundman, Bernie (Musician)
Bernie Grundman Mastering
1640 N Gower St
Hollywood, CA 90028-6518, USA

Grundt, Ken (Baseball Player)
Boston Red Sox
4814 W Parker Ave
Chicago, IL 60639-1712, USA

Grundy, Hugh (Musician)
Lustig Talent
PO Box 770850
Orlando, FL 32877-0850, USA

Grune, George V (Publisher)
PO Box 2348
Ponte Vedra Beach, FL 32004-2348, USA

Gruneisen, Sam (Football Player)
San Diego Chargers
569 Finsbay Ct
Ocoee, FL 34761-5658, USA

Grunfeld, Ernie (Basketball Player)
10121 Counselman Rd
Potomac, MD 20854-5021, USA

Grunhard, Tim (Football Player)
Kansas City Chiefs
6975 S Atlantic Ave
New Smyrna Beach, FL 32169-5007, USA

Grunsfeld, John M (Astronaut)
4202 Lake Grove Dr
Seabrook, TX 77586-4113, USA

Grunwald, Al (Baseball Player)
Pittsburgh Pirates
21001 Plummer St Spc 11
Chatsworth, CA 91311-0511, USA

Grunwald, Ernie (Actor)
c/o Suzanne (Sue) Wohl *TalentWorks (LA)*
3500 W Olive Ave Ste 1400
Burbank, CA 91505-5512, USA

Grunwald, Henry A (Diplomat, Editor)
62A Barkers Point Rd
Port Washington, NY 11050-1323, USA

Grunwald, Norten
Nyborggade Strandboulevarden 160-162
DK-2100
Copenhagen, DENMARK

Grupo Mania (Music Group)
c/o Staff Member *Sony Music Miami*
605 Lincoln Rd Fl 7
Miami Beach, FL 33139-2900, USA

Grupp, Robert (Football Player)
Kansas City Chiefs
305 Hill Ave
Langhorne, PA 19047-2819, USA

Grushin, Dave
200 W Superior St Ste 202
Chicago, IL 60610-3554, USA

Grutman, N Roy (Lawyer)
Grutman Miller Greenspoon Hendler
505 Park Ave
New York, NY 10022-1106, USA

Gruttadauria, Mike (Football Player)
St Louis Rams
1715 South Dr
Sarasota, FL 34239-5040, USA

Gryboski, Kevin (Baseball Player)
Atlanta Braves
130 Maffett St
Wilkes Barre, PA 18705-1003, USA

Grygiel, George (Baseball Player)
451 W Bazille Way
Green Valley, AZ 85614-5270, USA

Grymes, Darrell (Football Player)
Detroit Lions
915 McCleary Ave Apt C
Dayton, OH 45406-2829, USA

Grzanich, Mike (Baseball Player)
Houston Astros
170 Highland Cv
Jackson, MS 39272-8958, USA

Grzenda, Joe (Baseball Player)
Detroit Tigers
202 Hillcrest Dr
Gouldsboro, PA 18424-9475, USA

Guadagnino, Kathy Baker (Golfer)
1535 SW 4th Cir
Boca Raton, FL 33486-4414, USA

Guard, Christopher
76 Oxford St.
London, ENGLAND W1N OAX, UNITED
KINGDOM (UK)

Guardado, Edward A (Eddie) (Baseball
Player)
Detroit Tigers
11268 Overlook Pt
Tustin, CA 92782-4314, USA

Guardino, Harry (Actor)
2949 E Via Vaquero Rd
Palm Springs, CA 92262-7941, USA

Guarini, Justin (Musician)
c/o Benny Medina *Handprint
Entertainment*
1100 Glendon Ave Ste 1000
Los Angeles, CA 90024-3514, USA

Guarrera, Frank (Opera Singer)
4514 Latona Ave NE
Seattle, WA 98105-4848, USA

Guaty, Camille (Actor)
c/o Staff Member *Innovative Artists (LA)*
1505 10th St
Santa Monica, CA 90401-2805, USA

Gubaidulina, Sofia A (Composer)
2D Pugachevskaya 8
Korp 5 #130
Moscow 107061, RUSSIA

Gubanich, Creighton (Baseball Player)
Boston Red Sox
10 Galicia Dr
Phoenixville, PA 19460-2010, USA

Gubarev, Aleksei A (Cosmonaut, General)
Potchta Kosmonavtov
Moskovskoi Oblasti
Syvisdny Goroduk 141160, RUSSIA

Guber, Peter (Producer)
Mandaly Entertainment
10202 Washington Blvd # 1070
Culver City, CA 90232-3119, USA

Gubert, Walter A (Financier)
J P Morgan Chase
270 Park Ave Fl 12
New York, NY 10017-7924, USA

Gubicza, Mark (Baseball Player)
Kansas City Royals
11808 Macoda Ln
Chatsworth, CA 91311-1271, USA

Guccione, Bob
11 Penn Plz Fl 12
New York, NY 10001-2006, USA

Guccione, Christopher (Baseball Player)
88 Paloma Ave
Brighton, CO 80601-8791, USA

Gucclardo, Pat (Football Player)
New York Jets
5038 Olde Mill Ct
Sylvania, OH 43560-1800, USA

Guckert, Elmer (Baseball Player)
1212 Balmoral Dr
Pittsburgh, PA 15237-6222, USA

Gudauskas, Pete (Football Player)
Cleveland Rams
2780 Highcrest Ct
Cincinnati, OH 45251-4216, USA

Gudmundson, Scott (Football Player)
Boston Yankees
11 Guindola Way # 268
Hot Springs Village, AR 71909-7128, USA

Guelleh, Ismail Omar (President)
President's Office
8-10 Ahmed Nessim St
Djibouti, DJIBOUTI

Guennel, Joe (Soccer Player)
835 Front Range Rd
Littleton, CO 80120-4005, USA

Gueno, James (Football Player)
Green Bay Packers
6939 General Haig St
New Orleans, LA 70124-4030, USA

Guenther, Johnny (Bowler)
23826 115th Pl W
Woodway, WA 98020-5212, USA

Guerard, Michael E (Chef)
Les Pres d'Eugenie
Eugenie les Bains 40320, FRANCE

Guerin, Bill (Hockey Player)
11 Wagon Dr
Wilbraham, MA 01095-1680, USA

Guerin, Richie (Basketball Player)
1355 Bear Island Dr
West Palm Beach, FL 33409-2042, USA

Guerra, Blanca (Actor)
c/o Staff Member *Televisa*
Blvd Adolfo Lopez Mateos 232
Colonia San Angel INN
DF CP 01060, MEXICO

Guerra, Eddie (Actor)
c/o Peter Micelli *Creative Artists Agency
LCC (CAA-LA)*
2000 Avenue Of The Stars
Los Angeles, CA 90067-4700, USA

Guerra, Jackie (Comedian)
c/o Staff Member *Brillstein-Grey
Entertainment*
9150 Wilshire Blvd Ste 350
Beverly Hills, CA 90212-3453, USA

GUERRA, Juan Luis (Musician)
Integrity Music
1000 Cody Rd S
Mobile, AL 36695-3499, USA

Guerra, Saverio (Actor)
Writers & Artists
360 N Crescent Dr Bldg North
Beverly Hills, CA 90210-6818, USA

Guerra, Vida (Actor, Model)
c/o Juliette Harris *It Girl Public Relations*
3763 Eddingham Ave
Calabasas, CA 91302-5835, USA

Guerrero, Julen (Soccer Player)
AC Bilbao
Alameda Mazarredo 23
Bilbao 48009, SPAIN

Guerrero, Mario (Baseball Player)
Boston Red Sox
Calle Duarte
#450
Santa Domingo, DOMINICAN REPUBLIC

Guerrero, Roberto (Race Car Driver)
31642 Via Cervantes
San Juan Capistrano, CA 92675-3390,
USA

Guerrero, Viadmir (Baseball Player)
Montreal Expos
Plympic Stadium
Montreal, PQ H1V 3N7, CANADA

Guerrero, Vladimir (Baseball Player)
c/o Staff Member *Anaheim Angels*
2000 E Gene Autry Way
Edison Field
Anaheim, CA 92806-6143, USA

Guerrero Coles, Lisa (Actor, Sportscaster)
ABC-TV
77 W 66th St
Sports Dept
New York, NY 10023-6201, USA

Guers, Paul
40 rue de Buci
Paris 75006, FRANCE

Guess Who
31 Hemlock Pl.
Winnepeg, MB R2H 1L8, CANADA

Guest, Christopher H (Actor, Director)
c/o Sharon Sheinwold *United Talent
Agency (UTA)*
9560 Wilshire Blvd Ste 500
Beverly Hills, CA 90212-2401, USA

Guest, Cornelia (Model)
1419 Donhill Dr
Beverly Hills, CA 90210-2216, USA

Guest, Douglas (Misc)
Gables
Minchinhampton
Gloscester GL6 9JE, UNITED KINGDOM
(UK)

Guest, Lance
2269 La Granada Dr
Los Angeles, CA 90068-2723, USA

Guetary, Francois (Actor)
Cineart
36 Rue de Ponthieu
Paris 75008, FRANCE

Guetterman, Lee (Baseball Player)
Seattle Mariners
108 1/2 E Broadway St
Lenoir City, TN 37771-2908, USA

Guffey Jr, John W (Business Person)
Coltec Industries
2550 W Tyvola Rd
Charlotte, NC 28217-4574, USA

Gugelmin, Mauricio (Race Car Driver)
PacWest Reacing Group
PO Box 1607
Bellevue, WA 98009-1607, USA

Guggemos, Neal (Football Player)
Minnesota Vikings
8173 Drexel Ct
Eden Prairie, MN 55347-2189, USA

Guggenheim, Alan (Inventor)
Northwest Power Systems
PO Box 5339
Bend, OR 97708-5339, USA

Guggenheim, Marc (Actor)
c/o Staff Member *United Talent Agency
(UTA)*
9560 Wilshire Blvd Ste 500
Beverly Hills, CA 90212-2401, USA

Gugino, Carla (Actor)
c/o Michael Katcher *Creative Artists
Agency LCC (CAA-LA)*
2000 Avenue Of The Stars
Los Angeles, CA 90067-4700, USA

Guglielmi, Ralph (Football Player)
Washington Redskins
159 Red Berry Dr
Wallace, NC 28466-2377, USA

Gugloitta, Tom (Basketball Player)
1267 Francis St NW
Atlanta, GA 30318-5323, USA

Guice, Jackson (Cartoonist)
DC Comics
1700 Broadway
New York, NY 10019-5914, USA

Guida, Gloria
Via Francesco Denza 48
Rome I-00197, ITALY

Guida, Lou (Misc)
4800 Highway A1A Apt 505
Vero Beach, FL 32963-1224, USA

Guidi, Osvaldo (Actor)
c/o Staff Member *Telefe - Argentina*
Pavon 2444 (C1248AAT)
Buenos Aires, ARGENTINA

Guidoni, Umberto (Astronaut)
15010 Cobre Valley Dr
Houston, TX 77062-2810, USA

Guidry, Kevin (Football Player)
Denver Broncos
4045 W Briarfield St
Lake Charles, LA 70607-3658, USA

Guidry, Mark
1264 Camelot Ln
Lemont, IL 60439-8505, USA

Guidry, Paul (Football Player)
Buffalo Bills
880 Noel Dr
Mount Juliet, TN 37122-1352, USA

Guidry, Ronald A (Ron) (Baseball Player)
PO Box 278
Scott, LA 70583-0278, USA

Guilland, Richard
4526 Wilshire Blvd
Los Angeles, CA 90010-3801, USA

Guilbaut, Jeremy (Actor)
c/o Russ Mortensen *Pacific Artists
Management*
1404-510 W Hastings St
Vancouver, BC V6B 1L8, CANADA

Guilbe, Felix (Baseball Player)
Baltimore Elite Giants
Los Cabos Calle Carambala
Ponce, PR 00716, USA

Guilbert, Ann (Actor)
550 Erskine Dr
Pacific Palisades, CA 90272-4247, USA

Guilford, Eric (Football Player)
Minnesota Vikings
8111 W Wacker Rd Unit 51
Peoria, AZ 85381-4943, USA

Guilfoyle, Paul (Actor)
c/o Donna Massetti *SMS Talent Inc*
8730 W Sunset Blvd Ste 440
Los Angeles, CA 90069-2277, USA

Guillaume, Robert (Actor)
c/o Alan David *Alan David Management*
8840 Wilshire Blvd
Beverly Hills, CA 90211-2606, USA

Guillem, Sylvie (Ballerina)
Royal Ballet
Convent Garden
Bow St
London WC2E 9DD, UNITED KINGDOM
(UK)

Guillemin, Roger C L (Nobel Prize
Laureate)
7316 Encelia Dr
La Jolla, CA 92037-5728, USA

Guillen, Francesca (Actor)
c/o Staff Member *Televisa*
Blvd Adolfo Lopez Mateos 232
Colonia San Angel INN
DF CP 01060, MEXICO

Guillen, Michael (Correspondent, Doctor)
c/o Staff Member *20/20*
147 Columbus Ave
Abc
New York, NY 10023-6503, USA

Guillen, Oswaldo J (Ozzie) (Baseball
Player)
Chicago White Sox
19462 38th Ct
Golden Beach, FL 33160-2298, USA

Guillermin, John
309 S Rockingham Ave
Los Angeles, CA 90049-3637, USA

Guillo, Dominque (Actor)
Cineart
36 Rue de Ponthieu
Paris 75008, FRANCE

Guillory, Bennet
1519 Galaxy Ct
Rohnert Park, CA 94928-5611, USA

Guillory, Sienna (Actor)
c/o David Adamson *William Morris
Agency (WMA-LA)*
1 William Morris Pl
Beverly Hills, CA 90212-4261, USA

Guinan, Francis
606 N Larchmont Blvd # 309la
Los Angeles, CA 90004-1321, USA

Guindon, Bob (Baseball Player)
Boston Red Sox
55 General Edwards Highway
East Walpole, MA 02032, USA

Guindon, Richard G (Cartoonist)
321 W Lafayette Blvd
Detroit, MI 48226-2703, USA

Guinee, Tim (Actor)
c/o Jonathan Howard *Innovative Artists
(LA)*
1505 10th St
Santa Monica, CA 90401-2805, USA

Guinier, Lani (Educator, Lawyer)
University of Pennsylvania
3400 Chestnut St Ste 1
Law School
Philadelphia, PA 19104-6204, USA

Guinn, Skip (Baseball Player)
Atlanta Braves
RR 3 Box 790
Stilwell, OK 74960-9511, USA

Guinney, Bob (Reality TV Star)
c/o Staff Member *Bachelor, The*
15301 Ventura Blvd Bldg E
Sherman Oaks, CA 91403-5885, USA

Guirgis, Stephen Adly (Comedian)
c/o Staff Member *Gersh Agency, The (LA)*
232 N Canon Dr
Beverly Hills, CA 90210-5302, USA

Guiry, Thomas (Actor)
c/o Rhonda Price *Gersh Agency, The (NY)*
41 Madison Ave Fl 33
New York, NY 10010-2202, USA

Guisewite, Cathy L (Cartoonist)
4039 Camellia Ave
Studio City, CA 91604-3007, USA

Gujral, Inder Kumar (Prime Minister)
5 Janpath
New Delhi, Delhi 110011, INDIA

Gulager, Clu (Actor)
Clu Gulager Acting
320 Wilshire Blvd
Santa Monica, CA 90401-1315, USA

Gulan, Mike (Baseball Player)
St Louis Cardinals
151 Hollywood Blvd
Steubenville, OH 43952-1244, USA

Gulbinowicx, Henryk Roman Cardinal
(Religious Leader)
Metropolita Wroclawski
UL Katedraina 11
Wroclaw 50-328, POLAND

Gulbis, Natalie (Golfer)
Octagon
7100 Forest Ave Ste 201
C/O Giff Breed
Richmond, VA 23226-3742, USA

Guldelli, Giovanni (Actor)
Carol Levi Co
Via Giuseppe Pisanelli
Rome 00196, ITALY

Gulden, Brad (Baseball Player)
Los Angeles Dodgers
15820 Lundstead Rd
Carver, MN 55315-9702, USA

Guleghina, Maria (Opera Singer)
Askonas Holt Ltd
27 Chancery Lane
London WC2A 1PF, UNITED KINGDOM
(UK)

Gullett, Donald E (Don) (Baseball Player)
Cincinnati Reds
194 Kingsway Dr
South Shore, KY 41175-7934, USA

Gulli, Franco (Musician)
Columbia Artists Mgmt Inc
1790 Broadway Fl 6
New York, NY 10019-1412, USA

Gullickson, William L (Bill) (Baseball
Player)
Montreal Expos
3 Banchory Ct
Palm Beach Gardens, FL 33418-6811,
USA

Gullikson, Tom (Athlete)
Tim & Tom Gullikson Foundation
233 S Wacker Dr Ste 8000
Chicago, IL 60606-6448, USA

Gullit, Ruud (Soccer Player)
FC Chelsea
Stamford Bridge
Fulham Road
London SW6 1HS, UNITED KINGDOM
(UK)

Gulliver, Dorothy
28792 Lajos Ln
Valley Center, CA 92082-6107, USA

Gulliver, Glenn (Baseball Player)
Baltimore Orioles
8123 Cortland Ave
Allen Park, MI 48101-2215, USA

Gulliver, Harold (Editor)
Atlanta Constitution
72 Marietta St NW
Editorial Dept
Atlanta, GA 30303-2899, USA

Gulman, Gary (Musician)
c/o Staff Member *Paradigm (Monterey)*
509 Hartnell St
Monterey, CA 93940-2825, USA

Gulyas, Denes (Opera Singer)
Hungarian State Opera
Andrassy Utca 22
Budapest 1062, HUNGARY

Gulzar (Bollywood, Songwriter, Writer)
Boskiyana Pali Hill
Bandra (W)
Mumbai, MS 400050, INDIA

Guman, Michael D (Mike) (Football
Player)
Los Angeles Rams
3913 Pleasant Ave
Allentown, PA 18103-9773, USA

Gumbel, Bryant C (Correspondent,
Television Host)
Real Sports with BRyant Gumbel
1100 Avenue Of The Americas
New York, NY 10036-6712, USA

Gumbel, Greg (Sportscaster, Television
Host)
c/o Staff Member *CBS Television*
51 W 52nd St
New York, NY 10019-6119, USA

Gummersall, Devon (Actor)
c/o Peg Donegan *Framework
Entertainment (LA)*
9057 Nemo St # C
W Hollywood, CA 90069-5511, USA

Gump, Scott (Golfer)
11225 Willow Gardens Dr
Windermere, FL 34786-6020, USA

Gumpert, Dave (Baseball Player)
Detroit Tigers
68371 Fleetwood Dr
South Haven, MI 49090-8357, USA

Gumpert, Randy (Baseball Player)
Philadelphia Athletics
49 School St
Douglassville, PA 19518-9777, USA

Gun, Jang Dong (Actor)
152-4-4 bukit gembira condo
off jalan kuchai lama
kuala lumpur, wilayah
persekutuan 58200, MALAYSIA

Gund, Agnes (Misc)
Museum of Modern Art
11 W 53rd St
New York, NY 10019-5497, USA

Gunderman, Robert (Football Player)
Pittsburgh Steelers
11 Post Brook Rd S
West Milford, NJ 07480-4518, USA

Gunderson, Eric (Baseball Player)
San Francisco Giants
712 SE 97th Ave
Camas, WA 98607, USA

Gundi (Actor)
RR1
Roseneath, ON K0K 2X0, CANADA

Gundlach, Herman (Football Player)
Boston Redskins
RR 1
Houghton, MI 49931, USA

Gundu, Kalyanam (Actor)
D-1 Block Lloyds Colony
Royapettah
Chennai, TN 600 014, INDIA

Gunn, Anna
10100 Santa Monica Blvd Ste 2500
Los Angeles, CA 90067-4116, USA

Gunn, Lance (Football Player)
Cincinnati Bengals
19114 Milloak Dr
Humble, TX 77346-4004, USA

Gunn, Nathan (Opera Singer)
ICM Artists
40 W 57th St
New York, NY 10019-4001, USA

Gunn, Richard
12216 Moorpark St
Studio City, CA 91604-5228, USA

Gunn, Sean (Actor)
1421 S Shenandoah St Apt 1
Los Angeles, CA 90035-3523, USA

Gunn, Tim (Fashion Designer, Reality TV
Star)
c/o Staff Member *Project Runway*
915 Broadway Fl 20
New York, NY 10010-7130, USA

Gunnell, Sally (Athlete, Track Athlete)
18 Shepherd's Croft
Brighton
East Sussex, UNITED KINGDOM (UK)

Gunnels, Riley (Football Player)
Philadelphia Eagles
606 Wesley Ave
Ocean City, NJ 08226-3856, USA

Gunner, Harry (Football Player)
Cincinnati Bengals
248 Emory Ln
Port Arthur, TX 77642-4769, USA

Guns N' Roses (Music Group)
c/o Doug Goldstein *Sanctuary Music
Management (LA)*
301 Arizona Ave Ste 200
Santa Monica, CA 90401-1364, USA

Gunter, Dan (Actor)
Century Artists
PO Box 59747
Santa Barbara, CA 93150, USA

Guokas Jr, Matt (Basketball Player,
Coach)
458 Devon Pl
Heathrow, FL 32746-5002, USA

Gupta, Neena (Actor)
129 Aram Nagar II Versova Road
Andheri
Bombay, MS 400 061, INDIA

Gupta, Raj (Business Person)
Rohm & Haas Co
100 S Independence Mall W Ste 1A
Philadelphia, PA 19106-2399, USA

Gupta, Sudhir (Misc)
University of California
Medicine Dept
Irvine, CA 92717, USA

Gur, Mordechai (General)
25 Mishmeret St
Afeka
Tel-Aviv 69694, ISRAEL

Gura, Larry C (Baseball Player)
Chicago Cubs
PO Box 94
Litchfield Park, AZ 85340-0094, USA

Gurchenko, Ludmilla M (Actor)
Trekjprudny Per 5/15
#22
Moscow 103001, RUSSIA

Gurdon, John B (Misc)
Magdalene College
Master's Cottage
Cambridge CB3 0AG, UNITED
KINGDOM (UK)

Guren, Peter (Cartoonist)
Creators Syndicate
5777 W Century Blvd Ste 700
Los Angeles, CA 90045-9023, USA

Gurewitz, Brett (Musician)
William Morris Agency
151 El Camino Dr
Beverly Hills, CA 90212-2775, USA

Gurganus, Alan (Writer)
Vintage/Anchor Publicity
1745 Broadway Fl 20
New York, NY 10019-4305, USA

Gurian, Michael (Writer)
417 W 32nd Ave
Spokane, WA 99203-1777, USA

Gurney, Dan
2334 S Broadway
Santa Ana, CA 92707-3250, USA

Gurney, Hilda (Horse Racer)
8430 Waters Rd
Moorpark, CA 93021-8715, USA

Gurney, Scott (Actor)
c/o Staff Member Guttman Associates
118 S Beverly Dr Ste 201
Beverly Hills, CA 90212-3016, USA

Gurney Jr, Albert R (A R) (Writer)
40 Wellers Bridge Rd
Roxbury, CT 06783, USA

Gurraggchaa, Jugderdemidijn
(Cosmonaut, General)
Lyotchik Kosmonavt
MNR Central Post Office Box 378
Ulan Bator, MONGOLIA

Gurry, Kick (Actor)
c/o Steve Himber Himber Entertainment Inc
15760 Ventura Blvd Ste 700
Encino, CA 91436-3016, USA

Gursky, Al (Football Player)
New York Giants
54 Securda Rd
Reading, PA 19607-2521, USA

Guru (Musician)
William Morris Agency
151 El Camino Dr
Beverly Hills, CA 90212-2775, USA

Gurwitch, Annabelle (Actor)
Don Buchwald
6500 Wilshire Blvd Ste 2200
Los Angeles, CA 90048-4942, USA

Gus Gus
PO Box 1141 121 Reykjavik
ICELAND

Gusarov, Alexei (Hockey Player)
Saint Louis Blues
1401 Clark Ave
Sawis Center
Saint Louis, MO 63103-2700, USA

Gusella, James (Inventor)
Harvard Medical School
25 Shattuck St
Boston, MA 02115-6092, USA

Gushiken, Koji (Gymnast)
Nippon Physical Education College
Judo School
Tokyo, JAPAN

Gusmao, Jose Alexandre (Xanana)
(President)
President's Office
Dili, EAST TIMOR

Guss, Louis (Actor)
Amset Eisenstadt Frazier
5055 Wilshire Blvd Ste 860
Los Angeles, CA 90036-6108, USA

Gustafson, Ed (Football Player)
Brooklyn Dodgers
6209 Mineral Point Rd Apt 1007
Madison, WI 53705-4555, USA

Gustafson, Kathryn (Architect)
Gustafson Guthrie Nichol
31101 Alaskan Way Pier 55
Seattle, WA 98101, USA

Gustafson, Steven (Musician)
Agency for Performing Arts
405 S Beverly Dr Ste 500
Beverly Hills, CA 90212-4425, USA

Gustav, King Carl XVI HM
Kungliga Slottet
Stockholm 11130, SWEDEN

Guster (Music Group)
c/o Staff Member Nettwerk Management (NY)
345 7th Ave Fl 24
New York, NY 10001-5030, USA

Gutensohn-Knopf, Katrin (Skier)
Oberfeldweg 12
Oberaudorf 83080, GERMANY

Guterman, Lawrence M (Director)
c/o Staff Member Endeavor Agency LLC (LA)
9601 Wilshire Blvd Fl 3
Beverly Hills, CA 90210-5204, USA

Guth, Alan H (Physicist)
Massachusetts Institute of Technology
Physics Dept
Cambridge, MA 02139, USA

Guth, Bucky (Baseball Player)
Minnesota Twins
202 Morris Dr
Salisbury, MD 21804-7229, USA

Guthe, Manfred (Cinematographer)
122 Collier St
Toronto, ON M4W 1M3, CANADA

Guthman, Edwin O (Editor)
Philadelphia Inquirer
400 N Broad St
Editorial Dept
Philadelphia, PA 19130-4099, USA

Guthrie, Arlo (Music Group, Songwriter, Writer)
The Farm
Washington, MA 01223, USA

Guthrie, Janet (Race Car Driver)
PO Box 505
Aspen, CO 81612-0505, USA

Guthrie, Jennifer (Actor)
Don Buchwald
6500 Wilshire Blvd Ste 2200
Los Angeles, CA 90048-4942, USA

Guthrie, Mark (Baseball Player)
Minnesota Twins
4502 N Tamiami Trl
Sarasota, FL 34234-3866, USA

Gutierrez, Carlos M (Business Person)
Kellogg Co
1 Kellogg Sq
PO Box 3599
Battle Creek, MI 49017-3517, USA

Gutierrez, Diego (Actor)
c/o Staff Member Creative Artists Agency LCC (CAA-LA)
2000 Avenue Of The Stars
Los Angeles, CA 90067-4700, USA

Gutierrez, Gustavo (Misc)
Instituto Bartolome Las Casas-Rimac
Apartado 3090
Lima 100, PERU

Gutierrez, Horacio (Music Group, Musician)
I C M Artists
40 W 57th St
New York, NY 10019-4001, USA

Gutierrez, Jackie (Baseball Player)
Boston Red Sox
10631 SW 126th Ave
Miami, FL 33186-3744, USA

Gutierrez, Luclo (President)
Palacio de Gobiemo
Garcia Moreno
Quito 1043, ECUADOR

Gutierrez, Ricky (Baseball Player)
San Diego Padres
13754 NW 18th Ct
Pembroke Pines, FL 33028-2603, USA

Gutierrez, Sidney M (Astronaut)
324 Sarah Ln NW
Albuquerque, NM 87114-1026, USA

Gutman, Natalia G (Music Group, Musician)
Askonas Holt Ltd
27 Chancery Lane
London WC2A 1PF, UNITED KINGDOM (UK)

Gutman, Roy W (Journalist)
1349 Windy Hill Rd
Mc Lean, VA 22102-2803, USA

Gutmann, Amy (Educator)
Princeton University
President's Office
Princeton, NJ 08544-0001, USA

Gutsche, TorstenHans- (Athlete)
Hans-Marchwitza-Ring 51
Potsdam 14473, GERMANY

Guttenberg, Steve (Actor)
15030 Ventura Blvd # 710
Sherman Oaks, CA 91403-5470, USA

Gutteridge, Don (Baseball Player)
St Louis Cardinals
804 Lakeview Dr
Pittsburg, KS 66762-6150, USA

Gutteridge, Lucy
76 Oxford St.
London, ENGLAND W1N 0AX, UNITED KINGDOM (UK)

Gutz, Julie (Baseball Player)
9940 Gappa Rd
Kabetogama, MN 56669, USA

Guy, Buddy (Music Group, Musician)
Monterey International
200 W Superior St Ste 202
Chicago, IL 60610-3554, USA

Guy, Fabrice
50 rue de Marquisats F-74011
Annecy Cedex, FRANCE

Guy, Francois-Frederic (Music Group, Musician)
Van Walsum Mgmt
4 Addison Bridge Place
London W14 8XP, UNITED KINGDOM (UK)

Guy, Jasmine (Actor)
c/o Staff Member Stone Manners Talent & Literary (LA)
6500 Wilshire Blvd Ste 550
Los Angeles, CA 90048-4950, USA

Guy, Louis (Football Player)
New York Giants
2127 Sheffield Dr
Jackson, MS 39211-5851, USA

Guy, Melwood (Football Player)
New York Giants
345 Castle St
Lowell, IN 46356-1810, USA

Guy, Ray (Football Player)
Oakland Raiders
1389 Wrightsboro Rd
Thomson, GA 30824-7529, USA

Guy, Sebastien (Actor)
c/o Staff Member Acme Talent & Literary (LA)
4727 Wilshire Blvd Ste 333
Los Angeles, CA 90010-3874, USA

Guy, William L (Governor)
5210 12th St S Apt 105
Fargo, ND 58104-6440, USA

Guyer, Cindy
2 Lincoln Sq
New York, NY 10023-6229, USA

Guyer, David B (Misc)
Save the Children Foundation
514 2nd St
Owyhee, NV 89832, USA

Guynn, Jack (Financier, Government Official)
Federal Reserve Bank
1000 Peachtree St NE
Atlanta, GA 30309-4470, USA

Guyon, John C (Educator)
Southern Illinois Univesity
President's Office
Carbondale, IL 62901, USA

Guyot, Paul (Actor, Producer, Writer)
c/o Kathy White Creative Artists Agency LCC (CAA-LA)
2000 Avenue Of The Stars
Los Angeles, CA 90067-4700, USA

Guyton, Myron (Football Player)
New York Giants
302 Shadow Gln
McDonough, GA 30253-4294, USA

Guzik, John (Football Player)
Los Angeles Rams
905 Rider Ave
Salinas, CA 93905-1090, USA

Guzman, Alejandra (Musician)
c/o Staff Member *BMG*
1540 Broadway
New York, NY 10036-4074, USA

Guzman, Andrea (Actor)
c/o Staff Member *TV Caracol*
Calle 76 #11 - 35
Piso 10AA
Bogota DC 26484, COLOMBIA

Guzman, Cristian (Baseball Player)
c/o Staff Member *Washington Nationals*
2400 East Capitol Street SE
Rfk Stadium
Washington, DC 20003, USA

Guzman, Jose (Baseball Player)
Texas Rangers
1104 Somerset Blvd
Colleyville, TX 76034-4276, USA

Guzman, Juan (Baseball Player)
Toronto Blue Jays
176 Dockside Cir
Weston, FL 33327-1100, USA

Guzman, Luis (Actor)
Gersh Agency
232 N Canon Dr
Beverly Hills, CA 90210-5302, USA

Guzman, Santiago (Baseball Player)
St Louis Cardinals
1712 N Douty St
Hanford, CA 93230-2155, USA

Guzy, Carol (Journalist, Photographer)
2145 Fort Scott Dr
Arlington, VA 22202, USA

Gwathmey, Charles (Architect)
Gwathmey Siegel Architects
475 10th Ave Fl 3
New York, NY 10018-9724, USA

Gwinn, Mary Ann (Journalist)
Seattle Times
1120 John St
Editorial Dept
Seattle, WA 98109-5321, USA

Gwinn, Ross (Football Player)
New Orleans Saints
1736 Washington St
Natchitoches, LA 71457-4926, USA

Gwosdz, Doug (Baseball Player)
San Diego Padres
2108 Rose Rd
Pearland, TX 77581-3844, USA

Gwynn, Chris (Baseball Player)
Los Angeles Dodgers
10975 Hillside Rd
Alta Loma, CA 91737-2458, USA

Gwynn, Darrell (Race Car Driver)
4850 SW 52nd St
Davie, FL 33314-5526, USA

Gwynn, Tony
15643 Boulder Ridge Ln
Poway, CA 92064-2172, USA

Gwynne, A Patrick (Architect)
Homewood Esher
Surrey KT10 9JL, UNITED KINGDOM
(UK)

Gyanendra (King)
Royal Palace
Narayanhiti Durbag Marg
Kathmandu, NEPAL

Gyll, J Soren (Business Person)
Volvo AB
Goteborg 405 08, SWEDEN

Gyllenhaal, Jake (Actor)
c/o Evelyn O'Neill *Management 360*
9111 Wilshire Blvd
Beverly Hills, CA 90210-5508, USA

Gyllenhaal, Maggie (Actor)
c/o Courtney Kivowitz *Benderspink*
110 S Fairfax Ave Ste 350
Los Angeles, CA 90036-2179, USA

Gyllenhaal, Stephen G (Director,
Producer, Writer)
c/o Staff Member *William Morris Agency
(WMA-LA)*
1 William Morris Pl
Beverly Hills, CA 90212-4261, USA

Gyllenhammer, Pehr G (Business Person)
CHU PLC Saint Helen's 1 Undershaft
London EC3P 3DQ, UNITED KINGDOM
(UK)

Gypsy Kings, The (Music Group)
c/o Jonny (Jon) Podell *Podell Talent
Agency LLC*
22 W 21st St Fl 9
New York, NY 10010-7095, USA

GZA (Music Group, Musician)
Agency Group Ltd
1775 Broadway Ste 515
New York, NY 10019-1903, USA

Ha Jin (Writer)
Emory University
English Dept
Atlanta, GA 30332-0001, USA

Haag, Rudolf (Physicist)
Waldschmidt Str 4B
Schliersee-Neuhaus 83727, GERMANY

Haake, James
1256 N Flores St # L
Los Angeles, CA 90069-2963, USA

Haakon (Prince)
Det Kongeligel Slottet
Drammensveien 1
Oslo 0010, NORWAY

Haas, Andrew T (Misc)
Auto Aero & Agricultural Union
1300 Connecticut Ave NW
Washington, DC 20036-1703, USA

Haas, Carl
500 Tower Pkwy
Lincolnshire, IL 60069-3600, USA

Haas, Dave (Baseball Player)
Detroit Tigers
160 E 6th Pl
Mesa, AZ 85201-5068, USA

Haas, Eddie (Baseball Player)
Chicago Cubs
8314 Alpena Way
Louisville, KY 40242-2502, USA

Haas, Ernest (Photographer)
853 7th Ave
New York, NY 10019-5215, USA

Haas, Hunter (Golfer)
4078 Lively Ln
Dallas, TX 75220-1825, USA

Haas, Jay (Golfer)
4 Tuscany Ct
Greer, SC 29650-4021, USA

Haas, Lucas (Actor)
Lighthouse
409 N Camden Dr Ste 202
Beverly Hills, CA 90210-4423, USA

Haas, Lukas (Actor)
c/o Jason Weinberg *Untitled
Entertainment (LA)*
331 N Maple Dr Fl 3
Beverly Hills, CA 90210-3827, USA

Haas, Moose (Baseball Player)
Milwaukee Brewers
4351 E Lariat Ln
Phoenix, AZ 85050-8905, USA

Haas, Philip (Actor)
c/o Staff Member *Gersh Agency, The (LA)*
232 N Canon Dr
Beverly Hills, CA 90210-5302, USA

Haas, Richard J (Artist)
29 Overcliff St
Yonkers, NY 10705-1418, USA

Haas, Robert D (Business Person)
Levi Strauss Assoc
1155 Battery St
San Francisco, CA 94111-1264, USA

Haas, Thomas (Tommy) (Tennis Player)
TC Weiden am Postkeller
Schmiritzer Weg
Weiden 92637, GERMANY

Haas, Waltraud
Kuniglberggasse 45
Vienna A-1130, AUSTRIA

Haase, Andy (Football Player)
New York Giants
1508 Bon Homme Richard Dr
Fort Collins, CO 80526-9695, USA

Habash, George (Politician)
Popular Front for Palestine Liberation
PO Box 12144
Damascus, SYRIA

Habel, Karl (Misc, Scientist)
Reading Institute of Rehabilitation
RR 1 Box 252
Reading, PA 19607, USA

Haber, Norman (Inventor)
Haber Inc
470 Main Rd
Towaco, NJ 07082-1248, USA

Habermann, Eva
Kuckuchsberg 9
Lutiansee D-22952, GERMANY

Habermas, Jurgen (Misc)
Ringstr 8B
Stamberg 82319, GERMANY

Habib, Brian (Football Player)
Minnesota Vikings
17235 Sangallo Ln
San Diego, CA 92127-2807, USA

Habib, Munir (Astronaut, Misc)
Potchta Kosmonavtov
Moskovskoi Oblasti
Syvisdny Goroduk 141160, RUSSIA

Habibie, Baharuddin Jusuf (President)
President's Office
15 Jalan Merdeka Utara
Jakarta, INDONESIA

Habiger, Eugene E (Gene) (General)
Energy Department
Security Ops 1000 Independence NW
Independence
Washington, DC 20585-0001, USA

Habraken, Nicolaas J (Architect)
63 Wildemislaan
Apeldoom 7313 BD, THE NETHERLANDS

Habyan, John (Baseball Player)
Baltimore Orioles
4 Dorfer Ln
Nesconset, NY 11767-1067, USA

Hachette, Jean-Louis (Publisher)
Hachette Livre
83 Ave Marceau
Paris 75116, FRANCE

Hachten, William (Football Player)
New York Giants
6205 Mineral Point Rd Apt 210
Madison, WI 53705-4577, USA

Hack, Olivia (Actor)
c/o Staff Member *Gilbertson-Kincaid
Management*
1334 3rd Street Promenade Ste 201
Santa Monica, CA 90401-1320, USA

Hack, Shelley (Actor, Model)
1208 Georgina Ave
Santa Monica, CA 90402-2120, USA

Hackbart, Dale (Football Player)
Green Bay Packers
2541 Cowley Dr
Lafayette, CO 80026-9175, USA

Hacker, Rich (Baseball Player)
Montreal Expos
2900 18th Fairway Dr
Belleville, IL 62220-4840, USA

Hackerman, Norman (Misc)
5842 Westslope Dr
Austin, TX 78731-3633, USA

Hackett, Dino (Football Player)
Kansas City Chiefs
1152 Kearns Hackett Rd
Pleasant Garden, NC 27313-8218, USA

Hackett, Grant (Swimmer)
PO Box 940
Dickson, ACT 2602, AUSTRALIA

Hackett, Joey (Football Player)
Denver Broncos
1147 Kearns Hackett Rd
Pleasant Garden, NC 27313-8218, USA

Hackett, Martha (Actor)
Vaughn D Hart
12304 Santa Monica Blvd Ste 111
Los Angeles, CA 90025-2586, USA

Hackett, Paul (Politician)
Hackett for US Senate
1014 Vine St Ste 1690
Cincinnati, OH 45202-1121, USA

Hackford, Taylor (Director, Producer)
c/o David Styne *Creative Artists Agency
LCC (CAA-LA)*
2000 Avenue Of The Stars
Los Angeles, CA 90067-4700, USA

Hackl, Georg (Athlete)
Caftehaus Soamatl Ramsauerstr 100
Berchtesgaden-Engedey 83471,
GERMANY

Hackman, Gene (Actor)
c/o Fred Specktor *Creative Artists Agency
LCC (CAA-LA)*
2000 Avenue Of The Stars
Los Angeles, CA 90067-4700, USA

Hackman, Luther (Baseball Player)
Colorado Rockies
338 Concourse Rd
Columbus, MS 39702-8501, USA

Hackney, Lisa (Golfer)
Signature Sports Group
4150 Olson Memorial Hwy Ste 110
Minneapolis, MN 55422-4804, USA

Hackney, Roderick P (Architect)
Saint Peter's House
Windmill St Macclesfield
Cheshire SK11 7HS, UNITED KINGDOM
(UK)

Hackwith, Scott (Music Group, Musician, Songwriter, Writer)
Overland Productions
156 W 56th St # 500
New York, NY 10019-3800, USA

Hadas, Rachel C (Educator, Writer)
838 W End Ave Apt 3A
New York, NY 10025-5365, USA

Haddad, Drew (Football Player)
Indianapolis Colts
28532 E Brockway Dr
Westlake, OH 44145-5246, USA

Haddix, Michael (Football Player)
Philadelphia Eagles
1825 Arrowhead Trl
Vineland, NJ 08361-6403, USA

Haddix, Wayne (Football Player)
New York Giants
1213 Vinetree Dr
Brandon, FL 33510-2089, USA

Haddon, Dayle (Actor, Model)
Hyperion Books
114 5th Ave
New York, NY 10011-5690, USA

Haddon, Lawrence (Actor)
14950 Sutton St
Sherman Oaks, CA 91403-4018, USA

Haden, Charles E (Charlie) (Composer, Music Group, Musician)
Merlin Co
17609 Ventura Blvd Ste 212
Encino, CA 91316-5125, USA

Haden, Nate (Actor)
c/o Staff Member *Diverse Talent Group*
1875 Century Park E Ste 2250
Los Angeles, CA 90067-2563, USA

Haden, Nick (Football Player)
Oakland Raiders
329 Sarah St
West Mifflin, PA 15122, USA

Haden, Patrick C (Pat) (Football Player, Sportscaster)
Los Angeles Rams
1525 Wilson Ave
San Marino, CA 91108-2364, USA

Hadfield, Chris A (Astronaut)
638 Shorewood Dr
Kemah, TX 77565, USA

Hadid, Zaha (Architect)
Studio 9
10 Bowling Green Lane
London WC1R 0BD, UNITED KINGDOM
(UK)

Hadl, John W (Football Player)
San Diego Chargers
3700 Quail Creek Ct
Lawrence, KS 66047-2135, USA

Hadlee, Richard J (Cricketer)
PO Box 29186
Christchurch, NEW ZEALAND

Hadley, Brett (Actor)
5070 Woodley Ave
Encino, CA 91436-1411, USA

Hadley, Kent (Baseball Player)
Kansas City A's
1630 Huntington Dr
Pocatello, ID 83204-4679, USA

Hadley, Ron (Football Player)
San Francisco 49ers
4533 131st Pl SW
Mukilteo, WA 98275-5826, USA

Hadley, Tony (Music Group)
Mission Control
Business Center Lower Road
London SE16 2XB, UNITED KINGDOM
(UK)

Haebler, Ingrid (Music Group, Musician)
Ibbs & Tillett
420-452 Edgware Road
London W2 1EG, UNITED KINGDOM
(UK)

Haechen, Hartmut (Conductor)
Organisation Int'l Artistique
16 Ave F D Roosevelt
Paris 75008, FRANCE

Haefner, Ruby (Baseball Player)
1436 Union Rd Apt 329
Gastonia, NC 28054-2310, USA

Haegele, Patricia (Publisher)
Good Housekeeping Magazine
959 8th Ave
New York, NY 10019-3737, USA

Haegg, Gunder (Athlete, Track Athlete)
Swedish Olympic Committee
Idrottens Hus
Farsta 12387, SWEDEN

Haendel, Ida (Music Group, Musician)
Harlod Holt
31 Sinclair Road
London W14 0NS, UNITED KINGDOM
(UK)

Haenicke, Diether H (Educator)
Western Michigan University
President's Office
Kalamazoo, MI 49008, USA

Hafen, Barney (Football Player)
Detroit Lions
1125 Goldenrod Cir
Saint George, UT 84790-7512, USA

Hafer, Fred D (Business Person)
GPU Inc
300 Madison Ave
Morristown, NJ 07960-6118, USA

Hafner, Dudley H (Misc)
140 Estrada Maya
Santa Fe, NM 87506-8560, USA

Hafner, Travis (Baseball Player)
Texas Rangers
5133 Highway 200
Sykeston, ND 58486-9577, USA

Hafstein, Johann (Prime Minister)
Sjalfstaedisflokkurinn Laufasvegi 46
Reykjavik, ICELAND

Hag, Sid (Actor)
Kathleen Schultz Associates Talent Agency
6442 Coldwater Canyon Ave Ste 206
North Hollywood, CA 91606-1137, USA

Hagan, Cliff O (Basketball Player)
3637 Castlegate West Wynd
Lexington, KY 40502, USA

Hagan, Molly (Actor)
c/o Staff Member *Kohner Agency, The*
9300 Wilshire Blvd Ste 555
Beverly Hills, CA 90212-3211, USA

Hagan, Sarah (Actor)
c/o Staff Member *Mark Robert Management*
14014 Moorpark St Apt 316
Sherman Oaks, CA 91423-3494, USA

Hagar, Sammy (Music Group, Musician, Songwriter, Writer)
c/o Staff Member *Azoffmusic Management*
1100 Glendon Ave Ste 2000
Los Angeles, CA 90024-3524, USA

Hagee, Michael W (General)
Commandant Hqusmc
2 Navy Annex
Washington, DC 20380-0001, USA

Hagegard, Hakan (Opera Singer)
Gunnarsbyn
Edane 670 30, SWEDEN

Hageman, Fred (Football Player)
Washington Redskins
4608 Merion Ct
Lawrence, KS 66047-1811, USA

Hagemeister, Charles C (War Hero)
1908 Canterbury Ct
Leavenworth, KS 66048-6525, USA

Hagen, Alexander
Mittelweg 58
Hamburg D-20149, GERMANY

Hagen, Halvor (Football Player)
Dallas Cowboys
32 Algonquin Rd
Canton, MA 02021-1202, USA

Hagen, Kevin (Baseball Player)
St Louis Cardinals
24826 164th Ave SE
Covington, WA 98042-5232, USA

Hagen, Bob
4001 Nebraska Ave NW
Washington, DC 20016-2733, USA

Hager, Kristen (Actor)
c/o Staff Member *Magnolia Entertainment*
9595 Wilshire Blvd Ste 601
Beverly Hills, CA 90212-2506, USA

Hager, Robert (Correspondent)
NBC-TV
4001 Nebraska Ave NW
News Dept
Washington, DC 20016-2733, USA

Hager Twins
PO Box 1516
Champaign, IL 61824-1516, USA

Hagerty, Julie (Actor)
c/o Steven Levy *The Firm*
9465 Wilshire Blvd Fl 6
Beverly Hills, CA 90212-2605, USA

Hagerty, Michael (Actor)
c/o Michael Greene *Greene & Associates*
190 N Canon Dr Ste 200
Beverly Hills, CA 90210-5319, USA

Haggard, Merle (Music Group, Songwriter, Writer)
235 Murrell Meadows Dr # 72
Sevierville, TN 37876-2087, USA

Hagge, Mariene (Golfer)
PO Box 2212
Palm Desert, CA 92261-2212, USA

Haggerty, Dan (Actor)
C/O Doc Cleland
2134 62nd Pl SE
Auburn, WA 98092-8027, USA

Haggerty, Julie (Actor)
c/o Staff Member *Framework Entertainment (LA)*
9057 Nemo St # C
W Hollywood, CA 90069-5511, USA

Haggerty, Mike (Football Player)
Pittsburgh Steelers
511 Potomac Ct
Gibsonia, PA 15044-8028, USA

Haggerty, Steve (Football Player)
Denver Broncos
3313 E Costilla Ave
Centennial, CO 80122-1849, USA

Haggerty, Tim (Cartoonist)
United Feature Syndicate
200 Madison Ave
New York, NY 10016-3911, USA

Haggins, Raymond (Baseball Player)
Birmingham Black Barons
PO Box 462
Montevallo, AL 35115-0462, USA

Haggis, Paul (Director, Producer, Writer)
c/o Larry Becsey *Becsey/Wisdom/Kalajian*
849 S Wooster St Apt 7
Los Angeles, CA 90035-1792, USA

Hagins, Ike (Football Player)
Tampa Bay Buccaneers
1723 Madison Ave
Shreveport, LA 71103-2431, USA

Hagler, Marvin (Boxer)
c/o Valerie Swett *Deutsch Williams*
99 Summer St
Boston, MA 02110-1235, USA

Hagman, Larry (Actor)
9950 Sulphur Mountain Rd
Ojai, CA 93023-9374, USA

Hagn, Johanna (Athlete)
ASG Elsdorf
Behrgasse 6
Elsdorf 50198, GERMANY

Hague, William MP (Government Official)
House of Commons
Westminster
London SW1A 0AA, UNITED KINGDOM
(UK)

Hahn, Don (Baseball Player)
Montreal Expos
1046 Boise Dr
Campbell, CA 95008-0306, USA

Hahn, Erwin L (Physicist)
69 Stevenson Ave
Berkeley, CA 94708-1732, USA

Hahn, Frank H (Economist)
61 Adams Road
Cambridge CB3 9AD, UNITED KINGDOM (UK)

Hahn, Hilary (Music Group, Musician)
Hans Ulrich Schmid
Postfach 1617
Hanover 30016, GERMANY

Hahn, James (Politician)
Mayor's Office
200 N Spring St
City Hall
Los Angeles, CA 90012-4801, USA

Hahn, Jessica (Actor, Model)
6345 Balboa Blvd Ste 375
Encino, CA 91316-5238, USA

Hahn, Joseph (Music Group)
Artist Group International
9560 Wilshire Blvd Ste 400
Beverly Hills, CA 90212-2416, USA

Hahn, Kathryn (Actor)
c/o Lindsey Porter *Gersh Agency, The (NY)*
41 Madison Ave Fl 33
New York, NY 10010-2202, USA

Hai, Do Thi (Actor)
c/o Barry McPherson *Agency for the Performing Arts (APA-LA)*
405 S Beverly Dr
Beverly Hills, CA 90212-4416, USA

Haid, Charles (Actor)
4376 Forman Ave
Toluca Lake, CA 91602-2944, USA

Haider, Jorg (Government Official)
Freedom Party
Kamtnerstr 28
Vienna 1010, AUSTRIA

Haig, Alexander M Jr (General, Secretary)
622 N Flagler Dr Apt 801
West Palm Beach, FL 33401-4031, USA

Haig, Sid (Actor)
c/o Staff Member *Kathleen Schultz Associates Talent Agency*
6442 Coldwater Canyon Ave Ste 206
North Hollywood, CA 91606-1137, USA

Haight, Mike (Football Player)
New York Jets
2960 N Liberty Rd NE
Iowa City, IA 52240-7909, USA

Haignere, Jean-Pierre (Misc)
CNES
2Place Maurice Quentin
Paris Cedeux 75039, FRANCE

Haik, Mac (Football Player)
Houston Oilers
11738 Wood Ln
Houston, TX 77024-5129, USA

Hailey, Joel (Actor, Musician)
c/o Dennis Ashley *Creative Artists Agency LCC (CAA-LA)*
2000 Avenue Of The Stars
Los Angeles, CA 90067-4700, USA

Hailey, Leisha (Music Group, Songwriter, Writer)
c/o Staff Member *LW1/Light Wilhelmina*
7257 Beverly Blvd Fl 2
Los Angeles, CA 90036-2503, USA

Hailey, Oliver
11747 Canton Pl
Studio City, CA 91604-4166, USA

Haill, Gary H (Football Player)
Minnesota Vikings
6207 Surflanding Ln
Huntington Beach, CA 92648-7507, USA

Hailston, Earl B (General)
Commanding General
Marine Corps Forces Pacific
Camp H M Smith, HI 96861, USA

Haim, Corey (Actor)
Scott Carlson Entertainment
5627 Sepulveda Blvd Ste 230
C/O Scott Carlson
Van Nuys, CA 91411-2944, USA

Haimovitz, Jules (Business Person)
King Worls Productions
12400 Wilshire Blvd
Los Angeles, CA 90025-1019, USA

Haimovitz, Matt (Music Group, Musician)
Columbia Artists Mgmt Inc
1790 Broadway Fl 6
New York, NY 10019-1412, USA

Haine-Daniels, Audrey (Baseball Player)
618 Revere Dr
Bay Village, OH 44140-1971, USA

Haines, Byron (Football Player)
Pittsburgh Steelers
16625 1st Ave S Apt 202
Burien, WA 98148-1472, USA

Haines, Connie (Music Group)
880 Mandalay Ave # 3-109
Clearwater, FL 33767-1242, USA

Haines, Emily (Musician)
c/o Staff Member *Paradigm (Monterey)*
509 Hartnell St
Monterey, CA 93940-2825, USA

Haines, John (Football Player)
Minnesota Vikings
4000 Chamisa Dr
Austin, TX 78730-3301, USA

Haines, Kris (Football Player)
Washington Redskins
1610 N La Salle Dr
Chicago, IL 60614, USA

Haines, Lee M (Religious Leader)
Wesleyan Church
PO Box 50434
Indianapolis, IN 46250-0434, USA

Haines, Martha (Baseball Player)
144 Langshire Ct
Florence, KY 41042-3542, USA

Haines, Randa (Director)
1429 Avon Park Ter
Los Angeles, CA 90026-2007, USA

Hair, Harlod (Baseball Player)
Birmingham Black Barons
1645 W 20th St
Jacksonville, FL 32209-4817, USA

Haire, John E (Publisher)
Time Magazine
Rockefeller Center
New York, NY 10020, USA

Hairi, Gisue (Architect)
Hairi & Hairi
18 E 12th St
New York, NY 10003-4458, USA

Hairi, Moigan (Architect)
Hairi & Hairi
18 E 12th St
New York, NY 10003-4458, USA

Hairston, Carl (Football Player)
Philadelphia Eagles
3514 Spyglass Hill Dr
Green Bay, WI 54311-6122, USA

Hairston, Harold (Baseball Player)
Homestead Grays
542 E 107th St
Cleveland, OH 44108-1432, USA

Hairston, Jerry (Baseball Player)
Chicago White Sox
7831 W Peace Pipe Rd
Tucson, AZ 85743-5207, USA

Hairston, Jerry Jr (Baseball Player)
Baltimore Orioles
6 Austringer Ct
Pikesville, MD 21208-2153, USA

Hairston, John (Baseball Player)
Chicago Cubs
4226 NE 22nd Ave
Portland, OR 97211-5757, USA

Hairston, Stacey (Football Player)
Cleveland Browns
957 Kingswood Dr
Lima, OH 45804-3367, USA

Haise, Fred W
14316 Fm 2354 Rd
Baytown, TX 77520-9869, USA

Haise, Fred W Jr (Astronaut, Misc)
PO Box 5765
Pasadena, TX 77508-5765, USA

Haise, Jim (Baseball Player)
Washington Senators
2425 Albion Ave
Orlando, FL 32833-3981, USA

Haislip, Marcus (Basketball Player)
Milwaukee Bucks
1001 N 4th St
Bradley Center
Milwaukee, WI 53203-1312, USA

Haitink, Bernard J H (Conductor)
Harold Holt
31 Sinclair Road
London W14 0NS, UNITED KINGDOM (UK)

Hajak, Ron
17420 Ventura Blvd # 4
Encino, CA 91316-3846, USA

Hajduk, Chet (Baseball Player)
Chicago White Sox
6838 N Concord Ln
Niles, IL 60714-4432, USA

Hajek, Andreas (Athlete)
Weissbundenweg 18
Halle/Saale 06128, GERMANY

Hajek, Dave (Baseball Player)
Houston Astros
5190 Bitterweed Ln
Colorado Springs, CO 80917-1302, USA

Haji-Sheikh, Ali (Football Player)
New York Giants
550 S Spinningwheel Ln
Bloomfield Township, MI 48304-1318, USA

Hajiro, Barney (War Hero)
94-535 Awamoi St
Waipahu, HI 96797-1612, USA

Hakim, Az-Zahir (Football Player)
St Louis Rams
210 Canaan Glen Way SW
Atlanta, GA 30331-8055, USA

Hakkinen, Mikka (Race Car Driver)
McLaren International
Albert Dr
Woking
Surrey GU21 5JY, UNITED KINGDOM (UK)

Halama, John (Baseball Player)
Houston Astros
7615 Fort Hamilton Pkwy
Brooklyn, NY 11228-2325, USA

Haland, Bjoro
Sor-Audnedal N-4520, NORWAY

Halas, John (Animator)
Educational Film Center
5-7 Kean St
London WC2B 4AT, UNITED KINGDOM (UK)

Halbert, David (Business Person)
Advance PCS
750 W John Carpenter Fwy Ste 1200
Irving, TX 75039-2507, USA

Halbreich, Kathy (Director, Misc)
Walker Art Center
725 Vineland Pl
Minneapolis, MN 55403-1195, USA

Haldeman, Charles (Ed) (Financier)
Putnam Investments
1 Post Office Sq Ste 500
Boston, MA 02109-2199, USA

Haldorson, Burdette (Burdie) (Basketball Player)
2422 Zane Pl
Colorado Springs, CO 80909-1725, USA

Hale, Alan Spencer
5476 St. Paul Rd
Morristown, NJ 07813, USA

Hale, Barbara (Actor)
PO Box 6061-261
Sherman Oaks, CA 91413, USA

Hale, Bob (Baseball Player)
Baltimore Orioles
616 Overhill Ave
Park Ridge, IL 60068-3455, USA

Hale, Chip (Baseball Player)
Minnesota Twins
190 Driftwood Ct
Aptos, CA 95003-5769, USA

Hale, Dave (Football Player)
Chicago Bears
1420 Pioneer Rd
McPherson, KS 67460-8042, USA

Hale, Georgina (Actor)
74A St John's Wood High St
London NW8, UNITED KINGDOM (UK)

Hale, John (Baseball Player)
Los Angeles Dodgers
2200 Pine St
Bakersfield, CA 93301-3429, USA

Hale, Monte (Actor, Music Group)
11732 Moorpark St Apt B
Studio City, CA 91604-2115, USA

Haley, Charles J (Football Player)
San Francisco 49ers
3787 Royal Cove Dr
Dallas, TX 75229-5237, USA

Haley, Jackie Earle (Actor)
c/o Warren Zavala *Gersh Agency, The (LA)*
232 N Canon Dr
Beverly Hills, CA 90210-5302, USA

Haley, Maria (Financier)
Export-Import Bank
811 Vermont Ave NW
Washington, DC 20571-0002, USA

Halffter, Cristobal J (Composer, Conductor)
Jurgen Erlebach
Grillparsestr 24
Hamburg 22085, GERMANY

Halford, Rob (Music Group)
International Creative Mgmt
40 W 57th St Ste 1800
New York, NY 10019-4001, USA

Halfpenny, Jill (Actor)
c/o Staff Member *Talking Heads*
2-4 Noel St
London W1F 8GB, UNITED KINGDOM (UK)

Halfvarson, Eric (Opera Singer)
Munro Artist Mgmt
786 Dartmouth St
South Dartmouth, MA 02748-3247, USA

Haliburton, Ronnie (Football Player)
Denver Broncos
PO Box 1283
Port Arthur, TX 77641-1283, USA

Halicki, Ed (Baseball Player)
San Francisco Giants
19605 Paddlewheel Ln
Reno, NV 89521-7850, USA

Hall, Alaina Reed (Actor)
10636 Rathburn Ave
Northridge, CA 91326-3127, USA

Hall, Albert (Baseball Player)
Atlanta Braves
1628 Spaulding Ishkooda Rd
Birmingham, AL 35211-5520, USA

Hall, Anthony Michael (Actor)
c/o Jonathan Brandstein *MBST Entertainment*
345 N Maple Dr Ste 200
Beverly Hills, CA 90210-3860, USA

Hall, Arsenio (Actor, Entertainer, Musician, Writer)
c/o Erik Kritzer *Fenton-Kritzer Entertainment*
8840 Wilshire Blvd Fl 3
Beverly Hills, CA 90211-2606, USA

Hall, Art (Football Player)
Boston Patriots
Cardinal Gibbons High School 4601 Bayview Dr
Fort Lauderdale, FL 33308, USA

Hall, Barbara (Producer, Writer)
c/o Chris Harbert *Creative Artists Agency LCC (CAA-LA)*
2000 Avenue Of The Stars
Los Angeles, CA 90067-4700, USA

Hall, Bill (Baseball Player)
Milwaukee Brewers
New Chapel Road
Nettleton, MS 38858, USA

Hall, Bobby
20122 Hall Dr
Brooksville, FL 34601, USA

Hall, Bridget (Model)
I M G Models
304 Park Ave S # 1200
New York, NY 10010-4301, USA

Hall, Bruce Michael (Actor)
c/o Jerry Shandrew *Shandrew Public Relations*
1050 S Stanley Ave
Los Angeles, CA 90019-6634, USA

Hall, Bug (Actor)
c/o Laina Cohn *Relativity Management*
8899 Beverly Blvd Ste 510
Los Angeles, CA 90048-2449, USA

Hall, Charles (Inventor)
Basic Designs
5815 Bennett Valley Rd
Santa Rosa, CA 95404-8565, USA

Hall, Charlie (Football Player)
Cleveland Browns
602 Lavaca St
Yoakum, TX 77995-4136, USA

Hall, Cory (Football Player)
Cincinnati Bengals
1013 Port West Dr
Auburn, GA 30011-4605, USA

Hall, Courtney (Football Player)
San Diego Chargers
19912 Enslow Dr
Carson, CA 90746-3028, USA

Hall, Cynthia Holcomb (Judge)
US Court of Appeals
125 S Grand Ave
Pasadena, CA 91105-1652, USA

Hall, Dana (Football Player)
San Francisco 49ers
6 W Raymond Ave
Danville, IL 61832-1720, USA

Hall, Dante (Athlete)
c/o Staff Member *Kansas City Chiefs*
1 Arrowhead Dr
Kansas City, MO 64129-1651, USA

Hall, Darren (Baseball Player)
Toronto Blue Jays
3028 Monet Ct
Flower Mound, TX 75022-5561, USA

Hall, Daryl (Music Group, Songwriter, Writer)
Creative Artists Agency
9830 Wilshire Blvd
Beverly Hills, CA 90212-1804, USA

Hall, Deidre (Actor)
c/o Staff Member *David Shapira & Associates*
193 N Robertson Blvd
Beverly Hills, CA 90211-2103, USA

Hall, Delores (Actor, Music Group)
Agency for Performing Arts
485 Madison Ave
New York, NY 10022-5803, USA

Hall, Delton (Football Player)
Pittsburgh Steelers
3810 California Ave
Pittsburgh, PA 15212-1634, USA

Hall, Dick (Baseball Player)
Pittsburgh Pirates
405 Plumbridge Ct Unit 403
Lutherville Timonium, MD 21093-8136, USA

Hall, Donald (Writer)
Eagle Point Farm
Wilmot, NH 03287, USA

Hall, Donald J (Business Person)
Hallmark Cards
2501 McGee St
Kansas City, MO 64108-2600, USA

Hall, Donald R (Football Player)
Cleveland Browns
355 Chestnut Neck Rd
Port Republic, NJ 08241-9703, USA

Hall, Drew (Baseball Player)
Chicago Cubs
177 Fighting Frk
Grayson, KY 41143-8898, USA

Hall, Edward T (Doctor, Writer)
8 Calle Jacinta
Santa Fe, NM 87508-9561, USA

Hall, Ervin (Erv) (Athlete, Track Athlete)
Citicorp Mortgage
670 Mason Ridge Center Dr
Saint Louis, MO 63141-8573, USA

Hall, Fawn -
1568 Viewsite Dr
Los Angeles, CA 90069, USA

Hall, Galen (Coach, Football Coach, Football Player)
Pennsylvania State University
Greenberg Complex
University Park, PA 16802, USA

Hall, Glenn H (Hockey Player)
CSAS
PO Box 60036
RPO Glen Abbey
Oakville, ON L6M 3H2, CANADA

Hall, Greff Kaye (Swimmer)
906 3rd St
Mukilteo, WA 98275-1634, USA

Hall, Irv (Baseball Player)
Philadelphia Athletics
1153 Deanwood Rd
Baltimore, MD 21234-6618, USA

Hall, James E (Jim) (Misc, Race Car Driver)
RR 7 Box 640
Midland, TX 79706, USA

Hall, James S (Jim) (Music Group, Musician)
Jazz Tree
211 Thompson St Apt Ld
New York, NY 10012-1366, USA

Hall, Jeff (Football Player)
Washington Redskins
2201 Lake Ave Apt 205
Knoxville, TN 37916-2814, USA

Hall, Jerry (Actor, Model)
c/o Staff Member *Ford Models (LA)*
8826 Burton Way
Beverly Hills, CA 90211-1715, USA

Hall, Jerry (Doctor, Misc)
George Washington University
Med Center
2300 St NW
Washington, DC 20037, USA

Hall, Jimmie (Baseball Player)
Minnesota Twins
8622 Carter Grove Dr
Elm City, NC 27822-7926, USA

Hall, Joe (Baseball Player)
Chicago White Sox
1034 Dundale Rd
Paducah, KY 42003-5016, USA

Hall, Joe B (Basketball Player, Coach)
Central Bank & Trust Co
300 W Vine St
Lexington, KY 40507-1666, USA

Hall, Josh (Baseball Player)
Cincinnati Reds
3512 Hawkins Mill Rd
Lynchburg, VA 24503-4923, USA

Hall, Karen (Writer)
9242 Beverly Blvd Ste 200
Beverly Hills, CA 90210-3731, USA

Hall, Kevan (Designer, Fashion Designer)
Kevan Hall Studio
756 S Spring St Ste 11E
Los Angeles, CA 90014-2953, USA

Hall, Kristen (Musician)
c/o Staff Member *Gail Gellman Management*
23852 Pch #920
Malibu, CA 90265, USA

Hall, L Parker (Football Player)
4712 Cole Rd
Memphis, TN 38117-4013, USA

Hall, Lani (Music Group)
31930 Pacific Coast Hwy
Malibu, CA 90265-2524, USA

Hall, Lanny (Educator)
Hardin-Simmons University
President's Office
Abilene, TX 79698-0001, USA

Hall, Lemanski (Football Player)
Houston Oilers
2336 Wimbledon Cir
Franklin, TN 37069-1862, USA

Hall, Lloyd M Jr (Religious Leader)
Congregation Christian Church Assn
PO Box 1620
Oak Creek, MI 53154, USA

Hall, Michael C (Actor)
Jon Rubinstein Ltd
740 Broadway Ste 201
C/O Jon Rubinstein
New York, NY 10003-9518, USA

Hall, Monty
519 N Arden Dr
Beverly Hills, CA 90210-3507, USA

Hall, Nigel J (Artist)
11 Kensington Park Gardens
London W11 3HD, UNITED KINGDOM (UK)

Hall, Parker (Football Player)
Cleveland Rams
940 Warrenton Rd
Vicksburg, MS 39180-5924, USA

Hall, Peter R F (Director)
Peter Hall Co
18 Exeter St
London WC2E 7DU, UNITED KINGDOM (UK)

Hall, Philip Baker (Actor)
c/o Chris Schmidt *Paradigm (LA)*
360 N Crescent Dr
North Bldg
Beverly Hills, CA 90210-6820, USA

Hall, Pooch (Actor)
c/o Mark Turner *Abrams Artists Agency (LA)*
9200 W Sunset Blvd Ph 11
Los Angeles, CA 90069-3601, USA

Hall, Randy (Football Player)
Baltimore Colts
PO Box 447
Genesee, ID 83832-0447, USA

Hall, Reamy (Actor)
c/o Staff Member *Irv Schechter Company*
9460 Wilshire Blvd Ste 300
Beverly Hills, CA 90212-2710, USA

Hall, Regina (Actor)
c/o Nancy Sanders *Sanders/Armstrong Management*
2120 Colorado Ave Ste 120
Santa Monica, CA 90404-3561, USA

Hall, Robert David (Actor)
c/o Staff Member *CSI*
7800 Beverly Blvd
Los Angeles, CA 90036-2112, USA

Hall, Robert N (Inventor)
2315 Gurenson Ln
Niskayuna, NY 12309-5908, USA

Hall, Ron (Football Player)
Pittsburgh Steelers
14008 NE 162nd St
Kearney, MO 64060-8107, USA

Hall, Samuel (Sam) (Misc, Swimmer)
5759 Wilcke Way
Dayton, OH 45459-1637, USA

Hall, Sonny (Misc)
Transport Workers Union
80 W End Ave
New York, NY 10023-6399, USA

Hall, Toby (Baseball Player)
Tampa Bay Devil Rays
17209 Journeys End Dr
Odessa, FL 33556-2444, USA

Hall, Tom (Baseball Player)
Minnesota Twins
3592 Lillian St
Riverside, CA 92504-3609, USA

Hall, Tom (Football Player)
Detroit Lions
PO Box 60441
Longmeadow, MA 01116-0441, USA

Hall, Tom T (Music Group, Songwriter, Writer)
Tom T Hall Enterprises
PO Box 1246
Franklin, TN 37065-1246, USA

Hall, Walter (Golfer)
271 Orchard Park Dr
Advance, NC 27006-7481, USA

Hall, Windlan (Football Player)
San Francisco 49ers
13609 Pleasant Ln
Burnsville, MN 55337-4547, USA

Hall & Oates (Music Group)
c/o Brian Doyle *Doyle-Kos Entertainment*
1 Penn Plz Ste 2107
New York, NY 10119-2107, USA

Hall-Garmes, Ruth (Actor)
432 Alandele Ave
Los Angeles, CA 90036-3153, USA

Hall Jr, Gary (Swimmer)
2409 E Luke Ave
Phoenix, AZ 85016-2808, USA

Halla, Brian L (Business Person)
National Semiconductor
2900 Semiconductor Dr
Santa Clara, CA 95051-0695, USA

Halladay, H Leroy (Roy) (Baseball Player)
Toronto Blue Jays
18509 Council Crest Dr
Odessa, FL 33556-5039, USA

Hallam, John
51 Lansdowne Gardens
London, ENGLAND SW8 2EL, UNITED KINGDOM (UK)

Hallberg, Gary (Golfer)
12516 Ventana Mesa Cir
Castle Rock, CO 80108-9147, USA

Halldorson, Dan (Golfer)
209 South Rd
Cambridge, IL 61238-1429, USA

Hallen, Bob (Football Player)
Atlanta Falcons
7052 Rushmore Way
Painesville, OH 44077-2301, USA

Haller, Alan (Football Player)
Pittsburgh Steelers
12800 Chartreuse Dr
Dewitt, MI 48820-7868, USA

Haller, Bill (Baseball Player)
RR 2 Box 82C
Brownstown, IL 62418-9630, USA

Haller, Gordon (Athlete)
20514 E Caley Dr
Centennial, CO 80016-3800, USA

Haller, Kevin (Hockey Player)
113-276 Midpark Way SE
Calgary, AB T2X 1J6, CANADA

Hallervorden, Dieter
Nurnberger Str. 33
Berlin D-10777, GERMANY

Hallett, Andy (Actor)
c/o Pat Brady *Cunningham Escott Slevin & Doherty (LA)*
10635 Santa Monica Blvd Ste 130
Los Angeles, CA 90025-8306, USA

Hallick, Tom
13900 Tahiti Way Apt 108
Marina Del Rey, CA 90292-6568, USA

Halliday, Nathan (Actor)
c/o Sharon Lane *Lane Management Group*
13017 Woodbridge St
Studio City, CA 91604-1431, USA

Hallier, Lori (Actor)
c/o Richard Lucas *Lucas Talent Inc*
Sun Tower Floor 7
100 W Pender St
Vancouver, BC V6B 1R8, CANADA

Hallinan, Joseph T (Journalist)
Random House
1745 Broadway # B1
New York, NY 10019-4305, USA

Hallion, Tom (Baseball Player)
4040 Ormond Rd
Louisville, KY 40207-2036, USA

Hallisay, Brian (Actor)
c/o Melisa Spamer *Domain*
9229 W Sunset Blvd Ste 415
West Hollywood, CA 90069-3404, USA

Halliwell, Geri (Music Group)
c/o Jenny Frankfurt *Handprint Entertainment*
1100 Glendon Ave Ste 1000
Los Angeles, CA 90024-3514, USA

Hallman, Tom Jr (Journalist)
Portland Oregonian
1320 SW Broadway
Editorial Dept
Portland, OR 97201-3411, USA

Hallock, Ty (Football Player)
Detroit Lions
3676 Hunters Way Dr SE
Ada, MI 49301-8351, USA

Hallstrom, Holly (Entertainer, Model)
5757 Wilshire Blvd Ste 206
Los Angeles, CA 90036-3682, USA

Hallstrom, Lasse (Director)
United Talent Agency
9560 Wilshire Blvd Ste 500
Beverly Hills, CA 90212-2401, USA

Hallstrom, Ron (Football Player)
Green Bay Packers
PO Box 379
Hallstroms Marina
Woodruff, WI 54568-0379, USA

Hallwachs, Hans-Peter
Lindenstr. 9a
Grunwald 83021, GERMANY

Hallyday, Johnny (Actor, Music Group)
CC Productions
6 Rue Daubigny
Paris 75017, FRANCE

Halonen Tarja, Kaarina (President)
Presidential Palace
Pohjoisesplandi 1
Helsinki 17 00170, FINLAND

Halperin, Bertrand I (Physicist)
Harvard University
Physics Dept
Cambridge, MA 02138, USA

Halpern, Daniel (Writer)
9 Mercer St
Princeton, NJ 08540-6807, USA

Halpern, Jack (Misc)
5801 S Dorchester Ave Apt 4A
Chicago, IL 60637-1757, USA

Halpern, James S (Judge)
US Tax Court
400 2nd St NW
Washington, DC 20217-0002, USA

Halpin, Brandan Dean (Actor)
c/o Dino May *Dino May Management*
11262 Ventura Blvd Ph
Studio City, CA 91604-3135, USA

Halprin, Lawrence (Architect, Misc)
125 E Sir Francis Drake Blvd
Larkspur, CA 94939-1860, USA

Halsell, James D Jr (Astronaut)
257 River Cove Rd
Huntsville, AL 35811-8010, USA

Halter, Shane (Baseball Player)
Kansas City Royals
2701 W 140th St
Overland Park, KS 66224-3940, USA

Haluska, Jim (Football Player)
Chicago Bears
4325 W Cleveland Ave
Milwaukee, WI 53219-3209, USA

Halverson, Dean (Football Player)
Los Angeles Rams
3708B Wesley Loop NW
Olympia, WA 98502-3748, USA

Ham, Jack R (Football Player)
Pittsburgh Steelers
540 Lindergh Dr
Moon Township, PA 15108, USA

Ham, Kenneth T (Astronaut)
1315 Falling Leaf Dr
Friendswood, TX 77546-4615, USA

Hamao, Stephen Fumio Cardinal (Religious Leader)
Pastoral Care of Migrants
Piazza S Calisto 16
00120, VATICAN CITY

Hamari, Julia (Opera Singer)
Max Brod-Weg 14
Stuttgart 70437, GERMANY

Hambling, Maggi (Artist)
Morley College
Westminster Bridge Road
London SE1 7HT, UNITED KINGDOM (UK)

Hambright, Roger (Baseball Player)
New York Yankees
8709 NE 37th Ave
Vancouver, WA 98665-1065, USA

Hamburger, Michael P L (Writer)
John Johnson
45/47 Clerkenwell Green
London EC1R 0HT, UNITED KINGDOM (UK)

Hamed, Nihad (Religious Leader)
Islamic Assn in US/Canada
25351 5 Mile Rd
Redford, MI 48239-3703, USA

Hamed, Prince Naseem (Athlete, Boxer)
Mowbray House
Mowbray Street
Stockport, Cheshire SK1 3EJ, UNITED KINGDOM (UK)

Hamel, Alan
PO Box 827
Monterey, CA 93942-0827, USA

Hamel, Dean (Football Player)
Washington Redskins
902 Hemlock Dr NE
Lenoir, NC 28645-3850, USA

Hamel, Michael A (Astronaut)
150 Vandenberg St Ste 1105
Hq Afspc/Dr
Colorado Springs, CO 80914-4184, USA

Hamel, Veronica (Actor, Model)
c/o Staff Member *Cunningham Escott Slevin & Doherty (LA)*
10635 Santa Monica Blvd Ste 130
Los Angeles, CA 90025-8306, USA

Hamel, William (Religious Leader)
Evangelical Free Church
901 E 78th St
Minneapolis, MN 55420-1300, USA

Hamelin, Bob (Baseball Player)
Kansas City Royals
51 Patton Ct SE
Concord, NC 28025-3742, USA

Hamill, Dorothy (Figure Skater)
c/o Staff Member *William Morris Agency (WMA-LA)*
1 William Morris Pl
Beverly Hills, CA 90212-4261, USA

Hamill, Mark (Actor)
PO Box 287
Grand Blanc, MI 48480-0287, USA

Hamill, W Pete (Editor, Writer)
8 Whiskey Hill Rd
Wallkill, NY 12589-3421, USA

Hamilton, Allan G (Al) (Hockey Player)
2452 11th St
Edmonton, AB T6J 3S1, CANADA

Hamilton, Anthony (Musician)
c/o Nancy Josephson *Endeavor Agency LLC (LA)*
8942 Wilshire Blvd
Beverly Hills, CA 90211-1908, USA

Hamilton, Arthur Lee (Baseball Player)
Indianapolis Clowns
2243 College Cir N
Jacksonville, FL 32209-5916, USA

Hamilton, Ashley (Actor)
9255 Doheny Rd Apt 2302
Los Angeles, CA 90069-3228, USA

Hamilton, Ben (Football Player)
Denver Broncos
23976 E Willowbrook Ave
Parker, CO 80138-5721, USA

Hamilton, Bobby Jr (Race Car Driver)
Motorsports Decisions
1435 W Morehead St Ste 190
Charlotte, NC 28208-5291, USA

Hamilton, Darryl (Baseball Player)
Milwaukee Brewers
4721 Southwind Dr
Baton Rouge, LA 70816-4738, USA

Hamilton, Dave (Baseball Player)
Oakland A's
9464 Cherry Hills Ln
San Ramon, CA 94583-3935, USA

Hamilton, David (Photographer)
41 Blvd du Montpamasse
Paris 75006, FRANCE

Hamilton, Derek (Actor)
c/o PJ Shapiro Ziffren Brittenham Branca
Fischer Gilbert-Lurie, Stiffman & Cook
1801 Century Park W
Los Angeles, CA 90067-6409, USA

Hamilton, Forestom (Chico) (Music
Group, Musician)
Chico Hamilton Productions
321 E 45th St Ph
New York, NY 10017-3427, USA

Hamilton, George (Actor)
c/o Joan Vento-Hall Law Offices of Joan
Vento-Hall, The
10250 Constellation Blvd Fl 19
Los Angeles, CA 90067-6219, USA

Hamilton, George IV (Music Group,
Musician, Songwriter, Writer)
Blade Agency
203 SW 3rd Ave
Gainesville, FL 32601-6519, USA

Hamilton, Guy (Director)
Puerto de Andraitz
Apartado III
Palma de Mallorca, SPAIN

Hamilton, Harry (Football Player)
New York Jets
PO Box 986
Lemont, PA 16851-0986, USA

Hamilton, Jack (Baseball Player)
Philadelphia Phillies
109 Rocky Rd
Ridgedale, MO 65739-9746, USA

Hamilton, James (Football Player)
Jacksonville Jaguars
242 McGirt Rd
Hamlet, NC 28345-9124, USA

Hamilton, Jeff (Baseball Player)
Los Angeles Dodgers
2485 Golfview Cir
Fenton, MI 48430-9633, USA

Hamilton, Joe Frank & Reynolds
1629 E Sahara Ave
Las Vegas, NV 89104-3475, USA

Hamilton, Joey (Baseball Player)
Los Angeles Dodgers
234 Allenwood Dr
Statesboro, GA 30458-4477, USA

Hamilton, Josh (Baseball Player)
314 Bluff Ridge Ln
Angier, NC 27501-5840, USA

Hamilton, Keith (Football Player)
New York Giants
6 Bonnieview Ln
Towaco, NJ 07082-1289, USA

Hamilton, Laird (Athlete)
5111 Ocean Front Walk Apt 4
Marina Del Rey, CA 90292-7143, USA

Hamilton, Lee H (Misc, Politician)
Wilson Int'l Schorlars Center
1300 Pennsylvania Ave NW
Washington, DC 20004-3002, USA

Hamilton, Leonard (Basketball Player,
Coach)
Florida State University
Athletic Dept
Tallahassee, FL 32306, USA

Hamilton, Linda (Actor)
c/o Sarah Clossey Paradigm (LA)
360 N Crescent Dr
North Bldg
Beverly Hills, CA 90210-6820, USA

Hamilton, Lisa Gay (Actor)
Writers & Artists
360 N Crescent Dr Bldg North
Beverly Hills, CA 90210-6818, USA

Hamilton, Lynn
1042 S Burnside Ave
Los Angeles, CA 90019-6718, USA

Hamilton, Marcus
12225 Ranburne Rd
Charlotte, NC 28227-5623, USA

Hamilton, Michael (Artist)
2012 N 19th St
Boise, ID 83702-0821, USA

Hamilton, Michael (Football Player)
San Diego Chargers
6755 Mira Mesa Blvd # 123-227
San Diego, CA 92121-4392, USA

Hamilton, Milo (Baseball Player,
Sportscaster)
Houston Astros
2001 Holcombe Blvd Unit 901
Houston, TX 77030-4214, USA

Hamilton, Natasha (Musician)
c/o Staff Member Concorde Intl Artists Ltd
101 Shepherds Bush Rd
London W6 7LP, UNITED KINGDOM
(UK)

Hamilton, Paula (Actor)
PFD Drury House
34-43 Russell St
London WC2B 5HA, UNITED KINGDOM
(UK)

Hamilton, Ray (Football Player)
New England Patriots
PO Box 363
Sharon, MA 02067-0363, USA

Hamilton, Richard (Artist)
Northend Form
Northend
Oxon RG9 6LQ, UNITED KINGDOM
(UK)

Hamilton, Richard (Athlete, Basketball
Player)
c/o Staff Member Detroit Pistons
2 Championship Dr
Palace
Auburn Hills, MI 48326-1753, USA

Hamilton, Ruffin (Football Player)
Green Bay Packers
400 Norton Xing
Woodstock, GA 30188-7821, USA

Hamilton, Scott S (Figure Skater)
13921 Valley Vista Blvd
Sherman Oaks, CA 91423-4652, USA

Hamilton, Suzanna (Actor)
Julian Belfarge
46 Albermarie St
London W1X 4PP, UNITED KINGDOM
(UK)

Hamilton, Suzy
4121 Nakoma Rd
Madison, WI 53711-3018, USA

Hamilton, Todd (Golfer)
2004 Rock Dove Ct
Westlake, TX 76262-9076, USA

Hamilton, Victoria (Actor)
c/o Michael Lazo Paradigm (LA)
360 N Crescent Dr
North Bldg
Beverly Hills, CA 90210-6820, USA

Hamilton-Klemperer, Kim
44 W 62nd St Fl 10
New York, NY 10023-7008, USA

Hamiter, Uhuru (Football Player)
New Orleans Saints
5737 Hazel Ave
Philadelphia, PA 19143-1910, USA

Hamlin, Brooke (Actor)
c/o Staff Member Coast to Coast Talent
Group
3350 Barham Blvd
Los Angeles, CA 90068-1404, USA

Hamlin, Eugene (Football Player)
Washington Redskins
26411 24 Mile Rd
Chesterfield, MI 48051-1514, USA

Hamlin, Harry (Actor)
c/o Cynthia Campos-Greenberg Anthem
Entertainment
6100 Wilshire Blvd Ste 1170
Los Angeles, CA 90048-5116, USA

Hamlin, Ken (Baseball Player)
Pittsburgh Pirates
5242 County Road 413
Mc Millan, MI 49853-9266, USA

Hamlin, Shelley (Golfer)
4311 W Ardmore Rd
Laveen, AZ 85339-2112, USA

Hamlisch, Marvin (Composer, Conductor)
970 Park Ave # 501
New York, NY 10028-0324, USA

Hamm, Jon (Actor)
c/o Toni Howard International Creative
Management (ICM-LA)
10250 Constellation Blvd
Los Angeles, CA 90067-6200, USA

Hamm, Mia (Model, Soccer Player)
Mia Hamm Foundation
PO Box 56
Chapel Hill, NC 27514-0056, USA

Hamm, Morgan (Olympic Athlete)
C/O Ohio State University
1160 Steelwood Rd
Steelwood Training Facility
Columbus, OH 43212-1356, USA

Hamm, Nick (Director)
International Creative Mgmt
8942 Wilshire Blvd # 219
Beverly Hills, CA 90211-1908, USA

Hamm, Paul (Olympic Athlete)
C/O Ohio State University
1160 Steelwood Rd
Steelwood Training Facility
Columbus, OH 43212-1356, USA

Hamm, Pete (Baseball Player)
Minnesota Twins
525 Lockhart Gulch Rd
Santa Cruz, CA 95066-3034, USA

Hamm, Richard L (Religious Leader)
Christian Church Disciples of Christ
PO Box 1986
Indianapolis, IN 46206-1986, USA

Hammack, Mal (Football Player)
Chicago Cardinals
936 Big Bend Station Dr
Valley Park, MO 63088-1428, USA

Hammad al-Bassam, Abd al-Mohsin
(Cosmonaut)
Royal Embassy of Saudi Arabia
22 Holland Park
London W11, UNITED KINGDOM (UK)

Hammaker, Atlee (Baseball Player)
Kansas City Royals
2739 Stubbs Bluff Rd
Knoxville, TN 37932-1728, USA

Hammel, Eugene A (Misc)
2332 Piedmont Ave
Berkeley, CA 94720-0001, USA

Hammel, Penny (Golfer)
4786 Orchard Ln
Delray Beach, FL 33445-5306, USA

Hammer (Music Group, Musician)
Terrie Williams Agency
1500 Broadway Fl 7
New York, NY 10036-4055, USA

Hammer, AJ (Television Host)
Showbiz Tonight
1 Time Warner Ctr
Cnn
New York, NY 10019-6038, USA

Hammer, MC (Actor, Musician,
Songwriter, Writer)
c/o Staff Member Richard De La Font
Agency
4845 S Sheridan Rd Ste 505
Tulsa, OK 74145-5719, USA

Hammer, Victor S (Cinematographer)
PO Box 10788
Marina Del Rey, CA 90295-6788, USA

Hammer Jr, Jan (Composer, Musician)
2 W 45th St Ste 1102
New York, NY 10036-4249, USA

Hammergren, John H (Business Person)
McKesson HBOC Inc
1 Post St
San Francisco, CA 94104-5277, USA

Hammerman, Stephen (Financier)
Merrill Lynch Co
2 Vesey St
World Financial Center
New York, NY 10007, USA

Hammes, Gordon G (Misc)
11 Staley Pl
Durham, NC 27705-2421, USA

Hammett, Kirk (Music Group, Musician)
2505 Divisadero St
San Francisco, CA 94115-1119, USA

Hammock, Robby (Baseball Player)
Arizona Diamondbacks
4200 Chatham View Dr
Buford, GA 30518-4913, USA

Hammon, Becky (Basketball Player)
New York Liberty
2 Penn Plz
Madison Square Garden
New York, NY 10121-1703, USA

Hammon, Jennifer
270 N Canon Dr # 1064
Beverly Hills, CA 90210-5323, USA

Hammond, Albert Jr (Music Group,
Musician)
MVO Ltd
370 7th Ave # 807
New York, NY 10001-3912, USA

Hammond, Bobby (Football Player)
New York Giants
2535 Butler St
East Elmhurst, NY 11369-1628, USA

Hammond, Caleb D Jr (Misc, Publisher)
PO Box 194
Mendham, NJ 07945-0194, USA

Hammond, Chris (Baseball Player)
Cincinnati Reds
908 Old Highway 431
Wedowee, AL 36278-4612, USA

Hammond, Darrell (Actor, Comedian)
c/o Geoff Cheddy *Brillstein-Grey
Entertainment*
9150 Wilshire Blvd Ste 350
Beverly Hills, CA 90212-3453, USA

Hammond, Donnie (Golfer)
1642 Bridgewater Dr
Lake Mary, FL 32746-4103, USA

Hammond, Fred (Music Group)
Face to Face
21421 Hilltop St Ste 20
Southfield, MI 48033-4002, USA

Hammond, Gary (Football Player)
St Louis Cardinals
5321 Seascape Ln
Plano, TX 75093-4121, USA

Hammond, Henry (Football Player)
Chicago Bears
222 Polk Ave Apt 601
Nashville, TN 37203-3592, USA

Hammond, James T (Religious Leader)
Pentecostal Free Will Baptist Church
PO Box 1568
Dunn, NC 28335-1568, USA

Hammond, Joan H (Opera Singer)
Private Bag 101
Geelong Mail Center, VIC 3221,
AUSTRALIA

Hammond, John (Music Group, Musician)
c/o Staff Member *Shore Fire Media*
32 Court St Ste 1600
Brooklyn, NY 11201-4441, USA

Hammond, Kim (Football Player)
Miami Dolphins
9 Creek Bluff Run
Flagler Beach, FL 32136-5106, USA

Hammond, L Blaine Jr (Astronaut)
Gulfstream Aircraft
4150 E Donald Douglas Dr # 926
Long Beach, CA 90808-1725, USA

Hammond, Robert D (General)
PO Box 222032
Carmel, CA 93922-2032, USA

Hammond, Steve (Baseball Player)
Kansas City Royals
11104 Lake Butler Blvd
Windermere, FL 34786-7808, USA

Hammond, Tom (Sportscaster)
NBC-TV
30 Rockefeller Plz
Sprots Dept
New York, NY 10112-0015, USA

Hammonds, Jeff (Baseball Player)
Baltimore Orioles
2950 Meadow Ln
Weston, FL 33331-3018, USA

Hammons, David (Artist)
Studio Museum in Harlem
144 W 125th St
New York, NY 10027-4498, USA

Hammons, Roger (Religious Leader)
Primitive Advent Christian Church
273 Frame Rd
Elkview, WV 25071-9626, USA

Hamner, Earl
11575 Amanda Dr
Studio City, CA 91604-4144, USA

Hamner, Garvin (Baseball Player)
Philadelphia Phillies
6399 Studley Rd
Mechanicsville, VA 23116-4751, USA

Hamnett, Katharine (Designer, Fashion
Designer)
Katharine Hamnett Ltd
202 New North Road
London N1, UNITED KINGDOM (UK)

Hampel, Olaf (Athlete)
Pommenweg 2
Bielefeld 33689, GERMANY

Hampshire, Susan (Actor)
Chatto & Linnit
Prince of Wales Coventry St
London W1V 7FE, UNITED KINGDOM
(UK)

Hampson, Blake (Actor)
c/o Staff Member *Nickelodeon UK*
PO Box 6425
LONDON W1A 6UR, UNITED
KINGDOM (UK)

Hampson, Thomas (Opera Singer)
Starkriedgasse 53
Vienna 1180, AUSTRIA

Hampton, Brenda (Producer)
c/o Cliff Gilbert-Lurie *Ziffren Brittenham
Branca Fischer Gilbert-Lurie, Stiffman &
Cook*
1801 Century Park W
Los Angeles, CA 90067-6409, USA

Hampton, Casey (Football Player)
Pittsburgh Steelers
105 Conover Rd
Pittsburgh, PA 15208-2601, USA

Hampton, Christopher J (Writer)
2 Kensington Park Gardens
London W11, UNITED KINGDOM (UK)

Hampton, Daniel O (Dan) (Football
Player)
Chicago Bears
9191 Falling Waters Dr E
Burr Ridge, IL 60527-0716, USA

Hampton, Ike (Baseball Player)
New York Mets
2 Walden St
Ladera Ranch, CA 92694-0212, USA

Hampton, James (Actor)
102 Forest Hill Dr
Roanoke, TX 76262-5522, USA

Hampton, Locksley (Slide) (Music Group,
Musician)
Charismic Productions
2604 Mozart Pl NW
Washington, DC 20009-3601, USA

Hampton, Lorenzo (Football Player)
Miami Dolphins
1251 Nottoway Trl
Marietta, GA 30066-7811, USA

Hampton, Michael W (Mike) (Baseball
Player)
c/o Staff Member *Atlanta Braves*
PO Box 4064
Turner Field
Atlanta, GA 30302-4064, USA

Hampton, Millard (Athlete, Track Athlete)
201 W Mission St
San Jose, CA 95110-1701, USA

Hampton, Ralph C Jr (Religious Leader)
Free Will Baptist Bible College
3606 W End Ave
Nashville, TN 37205-2498, USA

Hampton, Rodney (Football Player)
New York Giants
5603 Grand Floral Blvd
Houston, TX 77041-5563, USA

Hamrick, Ray (Baseball Player)
Philadelphia Phillies
349 Saint Andrews Dr
Franklin, TN 37069-7078, USA

Hamrlik, Roman (Hockey Player)
New York Islanders
Hempstead Turnpike
Nassau Coliseum
Uniondale, NY 11553, USA

Hamzah (Prince)
Crown Prince's Office
Royal Palace
Amman, JORDAN

Han, Suyin (Writer)
37 Montoie
Lausanne 1007, SWITZERLAND

Hanauer, Terri
8271 Melrose Ave Ste 110
Los Angeles, CA 90046-6800, USA

Hanburger, Christian (Chris) Jr (Football
Player)
Washington Redskins
708 Winter Hill Dr
Apex, NC 27502-1376, USA

Hanbury-Tension, Robin (Scientist)
Maidenwell
Cardinham Bodmin
Comwall PL3O 4DW, UNITED
KINGDOM (UK)

Hance Jr, James H (Financier)
Bank of America Corp
100 N Tyron St
Charlotte, NC 28255-0001, USA

Hancken, Buddy (Baseball Player)
Philadelphia Athletics
850 Cactus St
Bridge City, TX 77611-3308, USA

Hancock, Anthony (Football Player)
Kansas City Chiefs
8233 Corteland Dr
Knoxville, TN 37909-2116, USA

Hancock, Eddie (Baseball Player)
Memphis Red Sox
2104 W 15th St
Pueblo, CO 81003-1126, USA

Hancock, Garry (Baseball Player)
Boston Red Sox
2217 Greenhills Dr
Valrico, FL 33596-5215, USA

Hancock, Herbert J (Herbie) (Composer,
Musician)
DL Media
PO Box 2728
Bala Cynwyd, PA 19004-6728, USA

Hancock, John D (Director)
7355 N Fail Rd
La Porte, IN 46350-7108, USA

Hancock, John Lee (Director, Producer,
Writer)
c/o David O'Connor *Creative Artists
Agency LCC (CAA-LA)*
2000 Avenue Of The Stars
Los Angeles, CA 90067-4700, USA

Hancock, Josh (Baseball Player)
Boston Red Sox
2201 Edison Ave
Fort Myers, FL 33901-3869, USA

Hancock, Lee (Baseball Player)
Pittsburgh Pirates
2580 Caddle Ct
Brentwood, CA 94513, USA

Hancock, Leroy (Baseball Player)
New Orleans Eagles
2010 Haywood Ave
Forrest City, AR 72335-4518, USA

Hancock, Phillip (Golfer)
3215 W Swann Ave Apt 30
Tampa, FL 33609-4663, USA

Hancock, Ryan (Baseball Player)
California Angels
1493 Green Apple St
South Jordan, UT 84095-4637, USA

Hand, Jon T (Football Player)
Indianapolis Colts
13013 Broad St
Carmel, IN 46032-7226, USA

Hand, Larry (Football Player)
Detroit Lions
4414 Robinhood Rd
Winston Salem, NC 27106-4236, USA

Hand, Rich (Baseball Player)
Cleveland Indians
3824 Bay Ct
Fort Worth, TX 76179-3831, USA

Handelsman, J B (Cartoonist)
New Yorker Magazine
4 Times Sq
Editorial Dept
New York, NY 10036-6592, USA

Handelsman, Walt (Cartoonist, Editor)
Newsday
235 Pinelawn Rd
Editorial Dept
Melville, NY 11747-4250, USA

Handford, Martin (Cartoonist)
Walker Books
87 Vauxhall Walk
London SE11 5HU, UNITED KINGDOM
(UK)

Handler, Chelsea (Actor, Writer)
c/o Mark Schulman *3 Arts Entertainment
Inc*
9460 Wilshire Blvd Fl 7
Beverly Hills, CA 90212-2713, USA

Handler, Daniel (Actor, Writer)
c/o Esther Newberg *International Creative
Management (ICM-NY)*
40 W 57th St
New York, NY 10019-4001, USA

Handler, Evan (Actor)
c/o Lenore Zerman *Liberman/Zerman
Management*
252 N Larchmont Blvd Ste 200
Los Angeles, CA 90004-3754, USA

Handley, Gene (Baseball Player)
Philadelphia Athletics
393 Hospital Rd # 16
Newport Beach, CA 92663-3501, USA

Handley, Taylor (Actor)
c/o Booh Schut *Booh Schut Company*
11365 Sunshine Ter
Studio City, CA 91604-3141, USA

Handley, Vernon G (Conductor)
Cwm Cottage
Bettws Abergavenny
Monmouhshire, WALES NP7 7LG,
UNITED KINGDOM (UK)

Handlin, Oscar (Historian)
18 Agassiz St
Cambridge, MA 02140-2802, USA

Handrahan, Vern (Baseball Player)
Kansas City A's
36 Newland Cres
Charlottetown, PE C1A 4H5, CANADA

Hands, Terence (Director)
Clwyd Theater Cymru
Mold
Flintshire, NORTH WALES

Hands, William A (Bill) (Baseball Player)
San Francisco Giants
PO Box 334
Orient, NY 11957-0334, USA

Handsome
9255 W Sunset Blvd # 200
Los Angeles, CA 90069-3309, USA

Handy, John W (General)
Commander-In-Chief
Transportation Command
Scott Air Force Base, IL 62225, USA

Hanes, Ken
8281 Melrose Ave Ste 200
Los Angeles, CA 90046-6890, USA

Haney, Chris (Baseball Player)
Montreal Expos
PO Box 97
Barboursville, VA 22923-0097, USA

Haney, Hank (Golfer)
Hank Haney Golf Ranch
2791 S Stemmons Fwy
Lewisville, TX 75067-4138, USA

Haney, Larry (Baseball Player)
Baltimore Orioles
PO Box 157
Barboursville, VA 22923-0157, USA

Haney, Lee (Writer)
Lee Haney Enterprises
105 Trail Point Cir
Fairburn, GA 30213-3433, USA

Haney, Todd (Baseball Player)
Montreal Expos
5404 Pointwood Cir
Waco, TX 76710-1265, USA

Hanfmann, George M A (Archaeologist)
Harvard University
32 Quincy St
Fogg Art Museum
Cambridge, MA 02138-3845, USA

Hanft, Ruth S (Scientist)
3340 Brookside Dr
Charlottesville, VA 22901-9566, USA

Hanin, Roger (Actor)
9 rue du Boccador
Paris 75008, FRANCE

Hankins, Jay (Baseball Player)
Kansas City A's
26509 East 150 Highway
Greenwood, MO 64034, USA

Hankinson, Tim (Coach, Soccer Player)
Columbus Crew
2121 Velman Ave
Columbus, OH 43211, USA

Hanks, Colin (Actor)
Creative Artists Agency
9830 Wilshire Blvd
Beverly Hills, CA 90212-1804, USA

Hanks, Merton (Football Player)
c/o Staff Member *National Football League (NFL)*
280 Park Ave Fl 12W
New York, NY 10017-1206, USA

Hanks, Tom (Actor, Producer)
c/o Staff Member *Playtone Productions*
PO Box 7340
Santa Monica, CA 90406-7340, USA

Hankton, Karl (Football Player)
Philadelphia Eagles
11448 Mangla Dr
Charlotte, NC 28214-8885, USA

Hanley, Bridget
12021 Hesby St
Valley Village, CA 91607-3115, USA

Hanley, Charles (Journalist)
Associated Press
450 W 33rd St Fl 7
New York, NY 10001-2606, USA

Hanley, Frank (Misc)
Int'l Union of Operating Engineers
1125 17th St NW
Washington, DC 20036-4707, USA

Hanley, Jenny (Actor)
MGA
Southbank House
Black Prince Road
London SE1 7SJ, UNITED KINGDOM (UK)

Hanley, Kay (Music Group)
c/o Staff Member *Paradigm (Monterey)*
509 Hartnell St
Monterey, CA 93940-2825, USA

Hanley, Richard (Swimmer)
E266 Lake Rd
Ironwood, MI 49938-9736, USA

Hanlon, Edward Jr (General)
Commanding General
Marine Combat Development Command
Quantico, VA 22134, USA

Hanlon, Glen (Hockey Player)
8781 Piney Orchard Pkwy
Odenton, MD 21113-2244, USA

Hann, Judith
56 Wood Lane
London, ENGLAND W12 7RJ, UNITED KINGDOM (UK)

Hanna, Jack
PO Box 400
Powell, OH 43065-0400, USA

Hanna, Jerome (Music Group)
Paramount Entertainment
PO Box 12
Far Hills, NJ 07931-0012, USA

Hanna, Preston (Baseball Player)
Atlanta Braves
5552 Mayfair Dr
Pensacola, FL 32506-5392, USA

Hannah, Bob (Baseball Player, Coach)
University of Delaware
Athletic Dept
Newark, DE 19716, USA

Hannah, Bob (Motorcycle Race, Motorcycle Racer)
American Motorcycle Assn
13515 Yarmouth Dr
Pickerington, OH 43147-8273, USA

Hannah, Charles A (Charley) (Football Player)
Tampa Bay Buccaneers
PO Box 2671
Lutz, FL 33548-2671, USA

Hannah, Daryl (Actor)
c/o Chuck Binder *Binder & Associates*
1465 Lindacrest Dr
Beverly Hills, CA 90210-2519, USA

Hannah, Herb (Football Player)
New York Giants
199 Hannah Dr
Albertville, AL 35951-4331, USA

Hannah, John (Actor)
William Morris Agency
52/53 Poland Place
London W1F 7LX, UNITED KINGDOM (UK)

Hannah, John (Football Player)
2407 Hideaway Pl SE
Decatur, AL 35603-5602, USA

Hannah, Travis (Football Player)
Houston Oilers
6123 Heatherbloom Dr
Houston, TX 77085-3205, USA

Hannah, Wayne (Religious Leader)
Fellowship of Grace Brethren Churches
PO Box 386
Winona Lake, IN 46590-0386, USA

Hannahs, Gerald (Baseball Player)
Montreal Expos
1411 Andover Rdg
Little Rock, AR 72227-3971, USA

Hannan, Jim (Baseball Player)
Washington Senators
3907 Cherry Hill Way
Annandale, VA 22003-2220, USA

Hannawald, Sven (Skier)
WH Sport Int'l GmbH
Im Sabel 4
Trier 54294, GERMANY

Hanneman, Steve (Actor)
c/o Staff Member *Abrams Artists Agency (LA)*
9200 W Sunset Blvd Ph 11
Los Angeles, CA 90069-3601, USA

Hanner, Dave (Football Player)
Green Bay Packers
General Delivery
Florence, WI 54121-9999, USA

Hannigan, Alyson (Actor)
c/o Adena Chawke *Greenlight Management*
315 S Beverly Dr Ste 300
Beverly Hills, CA 90212-4309, USA

Hannigan, Mackenzie (Actor)
c/o Staff Member *Martin Weiss Management*
PO Box 5656
Santa Monica, CA 90409-5656, USA

Hannity, Sean (Correspondent)
c/o Staff Member *Hannity & Colmes*
1211 Avenue Of The Americas
New York, NY 10036-8701, USA

Hannity, Shawn (Talk Show Host)
ABC Radio Networks
125 W End Ave Fl 6
New York, NY 10023-6387, USA

Hannon, Tom (Football Player)
Minnesota Vikings
17398 Roxbury Ave
Southfield, MI 48075-7609, USA

Hannuia, Dick (Coach, Swimmer)
1021 S Westley Dr
Tacoma, WA 98465-1426, USA

Hanratty, Terrance R (Terry) (Football Player)
Pittsburgh Steelers
22 Hunters Creek Ln
New Canaan, CT 06840-2002, USA

Hans-Adam II (Prince)
Schloss Vaduz
9490 Vaduz
LIECHTENSTEIN

Hansell, Greg (Baseball Player)
Los Angeles Dodgers
1791 W Prescott Dr
Chandler, AZ 85248-4845, USA

Hansen, Alfred G (Business Person, General)
Lockheed Aero Systems
86 S Cobb Dr
Marietta, GA 30063-0001, USA

Hansen, Beck (Beck) (Musician, Songwriter, Writer)
c/o Staff Member *Nasty Little Man*
110 Greene St Ste 605
New York, NY 10012-3838, USA

Hansen, Bob (Baseball Player)
Milwaukee Brewers
19 N Kelsey Ave
Evansville, IN 47711-6051, USA

Hansen, Bruce (Football Player)
New England Patriots
480 N 1100 E
American Fork, UT 84003-1992, USA

Hansen, Chris (Correspondent, Television Host)
c/o Staff Member *Dateline NBC*
30 Rockefeller Plz Ste 270E
Nbc News
New York, NY 10112-0299, USA

Hansen, Cliff (Football Player)
Chicago Cardinals
3008 Southbrook Dr
Minneapolis, MN 55431-2449, USA

Hansen, Clifford P (Governor, Senator)
PO Box 448
Jackson, WY 83001-0448, USA

Hansen, Courtney (Actor)
c/o Staff Member *Don Buchwald & Associates Inc (LA)*
6500 Wilshire Blvd Ste 2200
Los Angeles, CA 90048-4942, USA

Hansen, David (Baseball Player)
Los Angeles Dodgers
9852 Orchard Ln
Villa Park, CA 92861-3105, USA

Hansen, Don (Football Player)
Minnesota Vikings
919 Lakeview Rd
Grayson, GA 30017-1146, USA

Hansen, Frederick M (Fred) (Athlete, Track Athlete)
201 Vanderpool Ln Apt 12
Houston, TX 77024-6151, USA

Hansen, Gale (Actor)
721 SE 29th Ave
Portland, OR 97214-3027, USA

Hansen, Gunnar (Actor)
PO Box 368
Northeast Harbor, ME 04662-0368, USA

Hansen, Jacqueline (Athlete, Track Athlete)
1133 9th St
Santa Monica, CA 90403-5247, USA

Hansen, James E (Physicist, Scientist)
Goddard Institute for Space Studies
2880 Broadway
New York, NY 10025-7886, USA

Hansen, Jed (Baseball Player)
Kansas City Royals
1534 12th Lane Fi
Fox Island, WA 98333-9664, USA

Hansen, Mark Victor (Business Person)
M.V. Hansen & Associates
PO Box 7665
Newport Beach, CA 92658-7665, USA

Hansen, Patti (Model)
Redlands W Wittering
Chichester
Sussex, UNITED KINGDOM (UK)

Hansen, Peter (Actor)
Stone Manners
6500 Wilshire Blvd Ste 550
Los Angeles, CA 90048-4950, USA

Hansen, Phil (Football Player)
Buffalo Bills
24921 N Melissa Dr
Detroit Lakes, MN 56501-7266, USA

Hansen, Rick (Athlete)
Rick Hansen Man In Motion Foundation
520 West 6th Ave 5th Fl
Vancouver, BC V5Z 1A1, CANADA

Hansen, Ron (Baseball Player)
Baltimore Orioles
13602 Alliston Dr
Baldwin, MD 21013-9748, USA

Hansen, Roscoe (Football Player)
Philadelphia Eagles
638 Sooy Ln
Absecon, NJ 08201-1325, USA

Hanson (Music Group)
1045 N 78th East Ave
Tulsa, OK 74115-6909, USA

Hanson, Carl T (Admiral)
900 Birdseye Road
Orient, NY 11967, USA

Hanson, Curtis (Director, Writer)
c/o Staff Member *Deuce Three Productions*
1041 N Formosa Ave
Santa Monica Bldg #E
West Hollywood, CA 90046-6703, USA

Hanson, Erik (Baseball Player)
Seattle Mariners
20333 N 83rd Pl
Scottsdale, AZ 85255-3931, USA

Hanson, Jason D (Football Player)
Detroit Lions
3165 Midvale Dr
Rochester Hills, MI 48309-4124, USA

Hanson, Jennifer (Musician)
c/o Staff Member *Creative Artists Agency (CAA-Nashville)*
3310 W End Ave Fl 5
Nashville, TN 37203-1028, USA

Hanson, Stan
PO Box 970
Hotchkiss, CO 81419-0970, USA

Hanson, Taylor (Music Group, Musician, Songwriter, Writer)
Tenth Street Entertainment
568 Broadway Rm 608
C/O Allen Kovac
New York, NY 10012-3260, USA

Hanson, Tracy (Golfer)
451 Pine Wood Ct
Holland, MI 49424-6625, USA

Hanson, William R (Artist)
78 W Notre Dame St
Glens Falls, NY 12801-2721, USA

Hanson, Zachary (Music Group, Musician, Songwriter, Writer)
1045 N 78th East Ave
Tulsa, OK 74115-6909, USA

Hansraj, Jugal (Actor, Bollywood)
14-A Queens Apt
Pali Hill Bandra (W)
Mumbai, MS 400050, INDIA

Hanss, Ted (Scientist)
Information Technology Intergration Center
3025 Boardwalk St
Ann Arbor, MI 48108-3230, USA

Hantla, Robert (Football Player)
San Francisco 49ers
7815 E Monte Vista Rd
Scottsdale, AZ 85257-2209, USA

Hantuchova, Daniela (Tennis Player)
c/o Staff Member *Women's Tennis Association (WTA (US))*
1 Progress Plz Ste 1500
St Petersburg, FL 33701-4335, USA

Hanuja (Actor, Bollywood)
No 20 Periyar Street
Gandhi Nagar
Chennai, TN, INDIA

Hanulak, Chet (Football Player)
Cleveland Browns
225 Canal Park Dr Apt 6
Salisbury, MD 21804-7266, USA

Hanzlik, Bill (Basketball Player, Coach)
5701 Green Oaks Dr
Greenwood Village, CO 80121-1336, USA

Hape, Patrick (Football Player)
Tampa Bay Buccaneers
105 Sutton Cir
Birmingham, AL 35242-7075, USA

Hapke, Bruce (Misc)
1702 Georgetown Pl
Pittsburgh, PA 15235-4916, USA

Harada, Masahiko (Fighting) (Boxer)
2-21-5 Azabu-Juban
Minatoku
Tokyo 106, JAPAN

Harald V (King)
Det Kongelige Slott
Drammensvelen 1
Oslo 0010, NORWAY

Harang, Aaron (Baseball Player)
Oakland A's
6411 Glenroy St
San Diego, CA 92120-2713, USA

Harbach, Otto
3455 Congress St
Fairfield, CT 06824-2036, USA

Harbaugh, Gregory J (Astronaut)
1936 Thornwood Ave
Wilmette, IL 60091-1403, USA

Harbaugh, James J (Jim) (Football Player)
Chicago Bears
5998 Alcala Park
San Diego, CA 92110-8001, USA

Harbaugh, Robert E (Doctor)
Dartmouth-Hitchcock Medical Center
Surgery Dept
Hanover, NH 03756, USA

Harbison, John H (Composer)
479 Franklin St
Cambridge, MA 02139-3115, USA

Harcourt, Ed (Musician)
c/o Staff Member *Paradigm (Monterey)*
509 Hartnell St
Monterey, CA 93940-2825, USA

Hard, Darlene R (Tennis Player)
22924 Erwin St
Woodland Hills, CA 91367-3215, USA

Hardaway, Anfemee (Penny) (Basketball Player)
PO Box 2132
Farmington Hills, MI 48333-2132, USA

Hardaway, Anfernee (Basketball Player)
c/o Team Member *Orlando Magic*
8701 Maitland Summit Blvd
Orlando, FL 32810-5915, USA

Hardaway, Timothy D (Tim) (Basketball Player)
10050 SW 62nd Ave
Miami, FL 33156-3378, USA

Hardeman, Buddy (Football Player)
Washington Redskins
5711 Heming Ave
Springfield, VA 22151-2714, USA

Hardeman, Don (Football Player)
Houston Oilers
6100 E Rancier Ave Lot 264
Killeen, TX 76543-8610, USA

Harden, Bobby (Football Player)
Miami Dolphins
1750 NW 36th Ter
Fort Lauderdale, FL 33311-4128, USA

Harden, Marcia Gay (Actor)
c/o Maryellen Mulcahy *Framework Entertainment (LA)*
9057 Nemo St # C
W Hollywood, CA 90069-5511, USA

Harden, Michael (Football Player)
Denver Broncos
7150 Leetsdale Dr # 315
Denver, CO 80224-3529, USA

Hardenberger, Hahan (Music Group, Musician)
Columbia Artists Mgmt Inc
1790 Broadway Fl 6
New York, NY 10019-1412, USA

Hardesty Jr, David C (Educator)
West Virginia University
President's Office
Morgantown, WV 26506, USA

Hardie, Kate (Actor)
Jonathan Altaras
13 Shorts Gardens
London WC2H 9AT, UNITED KINGDOM (UK)

Hardin, Clifford M (Secretary)
10 Road Lane
Saint Louis, MO 63124, USA

Hardin, Jerry
3033 Vista Crest Dr
Los Angeles, CA 90068-1824, USA

Hardin, Melora (Actor)
c/o Staff Member *Kohner Agency, The*
9300 Wilshire Blvd Ste 555
Beverly Hills, CA 90212-3211, USA

Hardin, Paul III (Educator)
University of North Carolina
Chancellor's Office
Chapel Hill, NC 27599, USA

Hardin, Ty (Actor)
2210 87th Street Ct NW
Gig Harbor, WA 98332-7550, USA

Harding, Daniel (Musician)
c/o Staff Member *International Creative Management (ICM-LA)*
10250 Constellation Blvd
Los Angeles, CA 90067-6200, USA

Harding, John Wesley (Music Group, Songwriter, Writer)
Sincere Mgmt
6 Bravington Road #6
London W9 3AH, UNITED KINGDOM (UK)

Harding, Roger (Football Player)
Cleveland Rams
1911 Kalakaua Ave Apt 601
Honolulu, HI 96815-1809, USA

Harding, Tonya M (Actor, Figure Skater)
11805 Bastrop St
Manor, TX 78653-4928, USA

Hardis, Stephen R (Business Person)
Eaton Corp
1111 Superior Ave E
Eaton Center
Cleveland, OH 44114-2535, USA

Hardison, Dee (Football Player)
Buffalo Bills
135 Reuben Dr
Statesville, NC 28677-1726, USA

Hardison, Kadeem (Actor)
19743 Valley View Dr
Topanga, CA 90290-3257, USA

Hardisty, Huntington (Admiral)
Lexington Institute
1600 Wilson Blvd Ste 900
Arlington, VA 22209-2510, USA

Hardman, Cedrick (Football Player)
San Francisco 49ers
364 Myrtle St
Laguna Beach, CA 92651-1533, USA

Hardman, Earl
1400 E Carson St
Pittsburgh, PA 15203-1556, USA

Hardnett, Charles (Charlie) (Basketball Player, Coach)
1906 Swainsboro Dr
Louisville, KY 40218-2417, USA

Hardt, Eloise (Actor)
Daje Garrick
8831 W Sunset Blvd # 402
Los Angeles, CA 90069, USA

Hardt, Michael (Educator)
Duke Univesity
English Dept
Durham, NC 27708-0001, USA

Hardtke, Jason (Baseball Player)
New York Mets
52 Marwood Rd N
Port Washington, NY 11050-1441, USA

Hardwick, Billy
1576 S White Station Rd
Memphis, TN 38117-7220, USA

Hardwick, Catherine (Director)
c/o Staff Member *International Creative Management (ICM-LA)*
10250 Constellation Blvd
Los Angeles, CA 90067-6200, USA

Hardwick, Chris (Actor)
c/o Staff Member *Agency for the Performing Arts (APA-LA)*
405 S Beverly Dr
Beverly Hills, CA 90212-4416, USA

Hardwick, Elizabeth (Writer)
15 W 67th St
New York, NY 10023-6226, USA

Hardwick, Gary C (Director, Producer, Writer)
c/o Bruce Kaufman *Broder Webb Chervin Silbermann Agency, The (BWCS)*
10250 Constellation Blvd Ste P
Los Angeles, CA 90067-6213, USA

Hardwick, Johnny (Artist, Voice Over Artist, Writer)
c/o Staff Member *Creative Artists Agency LCC (CAA-LA)*
2000 Avenue Of The Stars
Los Angeles, CA 90067-4700, USA

Hardwicke, Edward (Actor)
c/o Staff Member *International Creative Management (ICM-LA)*
10250 Constellation Blvd
Los Angeles, CA 90067-6200, USA

Hardy, Adrian (Football Player)
San Francisco 49ers
7530 Kingsport Blvd
New Orleans, LA 70128-2114, USA

Hardy, Bruce A (Football Player)
Miami Dolphins
3310 Pinewalk Dr N Apt 1826
Margate, FL 33063-9341, USA

Hardy, Carroll (Baseball Player, Football Player)
Cleveland Indians
27875 Whitewood Dr E
Steamboat Springs, CO 80487, USA

Hardy, David (Football Player)
Los Angeles Raiders
PO Box 1270
New Waverly, TX 77358-1270, USA

Hardy, Hagood (Composer, Musician)
SOCAN
41 Valleybrook Dr
Don Mills, ON M3B 2S6, CANADA

Hardy, Hugh (Architect)
Hardy Holzman Pfeiffer
902 Broadway
New York, NY 10010-6082, USA

Hardy, Jeff (Wrestler)
c/o Staff Member *HarperCollins Publishers*
10 E 53rd St Fl 17
New York, NY 10022-5244, USA

Hardy, Jim (Football Player)
Los Angeles Rams
48490 San Vicente St
La Quinta, CA 92253-6253, USA

Hardy, John (Baseball Player)
Chicago White Sox
1260 NW 192nd Ln
Pembroke Pines, FL 33029-4520, USA

Hardy, Kevin (Football Player)
Jacksonville Jaguars
1228 Windsor Harbor Dr
Jacksonville, FL 32225-2651, USA

Hardy, Kevin (Football Player)
San Francisco 49ers
298 Paraiso Dr
Danville, CA 94526-4950, USA

Hardy, Larry (Baseball Player)
San Diego Padres
7 Jennifer Ct
Trophy Club, TX 76262-5402, USA

Hardy, Larry (Football Player)
New Orleans Saints
1711 Fairwood Dr
Jackson, MS 39213-7918, USA

Hardy, Mark (Hockey Player)
33 W Ontario St Apt 50B
Chicago, IL 60610-7774, USA

Hardy, Matt (Wrestler)
c/o Staff Member *World Wrestling Entertainment (WWE)*
1241 E Main St
Stamford, CT 06902-3520, USA

Hardy, Robert (Actor)
Chatto & Linnit
Prince of Wales
Coventry St
London W1V 7FE, UNITED KINGDOM (UK)

Hardy, Sophie (Doctor)
332 Ave du Marechal Juin
Boulogne 92100, FRANCE

Hardy, Terry (Football Player)
Arizona Cardinals
3109 S Rick Dr
Montgomery, AL 36108-3821, USA

Hare, David (Writer)
95 Linden Gardens
London WC2, UNITED KINGDOM (UK)

Hare, Eddie (Football Player)
New England Patriots
802 Walker School Rd
Sugar Land, TX 77479-5807, USA

Hare, Shawn (Baseball Player)
Detroit Tigers
1975 Deer Path Trl
Oxford, MI 48371-6062, USA

Harelik, Mark (Actor)
c/o Staff Member *Gersh Agency, The (LA)*
232 N Canon Dr
Beverly Hills, CA 90210-5302, USA

Harewood, Dorien
2 Bearwood Dr
Toronto, ON M9A 4, CANADA

Harewood, Nancy (Actor)
Metropolitan Talent Agency
4500 Wilshire Blvd Fl 2
Los Angeles, CA 90010-3858, USA

Hargain, Tony (Football Player)
Kansas City Chiefs
6440 Shady Springs Way
Citrus Heights, CA 95621-3514, USA

Hargan, Steve (Baseball Player)
Cleveland Indians
2502 E Morongo Trl
Palm Springs, CA 92264-4839, USA

Hargesheimer, Alan (Baseball Player)
San Francisco Giants
107 N Evanston Ave
Arlington Heights, IL 60004-6617, USA

Hargett, Edd (Football Player)
New Orleans Saints
379 County Road 222
Nacogdoches, TX 75965-4806, USA

Hargis, Gary (Baseball Player)
Pittsburgh Pirates
157 Gemini St
Lompoc, CA 93436-1244, USA

Hargitay, Mariska (Actor)
c/o Staff Member *Law & Order: SVU*
100 Universal City Plz Bldg 2252
Universal City, CA 91608-1002, USA

Hargrove, D Michael (Mike) (Baseball Player)
Texas Rangers
3925 Ramblewood Dr
Richfield, OH 44286-9642, USA

Hargrove, Linda (Coach)
Washington Mystics
601 E St NW
Mci Center
Washington, DC 20004, USA

Hargrove, Marion
401 Montana Ave # 6
Santa Monica, CA 90403-1303, USA

Harikkala, Tim (Baseball Player)
Seattle Mariners
1721 Crestwood Blvd
Lake Worth, FL 33460-1756, USA

Haris, Niki (Musician)
c/o Staff Member *Diva Central Inc*
7510 W Sunset Blvd Ste 1445
Los Angeles, CA 90046-3408, USA

Harker, Al (Soccer Player)
409 2nd St
Lafayette Hill, PA 19444-1403, USA

Harker, Susannah
55 Ashburnham Grove Greenwich
London, ENGLAND SW10 8UJ, UNITED KINGDOM (UK)

Harket, Morten (Music Group)
Bandana Mgmt
11 Elvaston Place #300
London SW7 5QC, UNITED KINGDOM (UK)

Harkey, Lem (Football Player)
San Francisco 49ers
2402 SW 14th St
Lawton, OK 73501-8060, USA

Harkey, Mike (Baseball Player)
Chicago Cubs
23930 Strange Creek Dr
Diamond Bar, CA 91765-1144, USA

Harkey, Steve (Football Player)
New York Jets
6582 Cherry Tree Ln NE
Sandy Springs, GA 30328-3319, USA

Harkin, Tom (Senator)
880 Locust St Ste 125
Dubuque, IA 52001-6700, USA

Harkleroad, Ashley (Tennis Player)
c/o Jill Smoller *William Morris Agency (WMA-LA)*
1 William Morris Pl
Beverly Hills, CA 90212-4261, USA

Harkless, Burkley (Football Player)
Baltimore Colts
2308 E Windsor Dr
Denton, TX 76209-1447, USA

Harkness, Ned (Coach, Hockey Player)
12 Flower Ave
Glens Falls, NY 12801, USA

Harkness, Tim (Baseball Player)
Los Angeles Dodgers
70 Homefield Sq
Courtice, ON L1E 1L3, CANADA

Harlan, Jack R (Scientist)
University of Illinois
Agronomy Dept
Urbana, IL 61801, USA

Harlan, Kevin (Sportscaster)
CBS-TV
51 W 52nd St
Sprots Dept
New York, NY 10019-6119, USA

Harlem Globetrotters
400 E Van Buren St Ste 300
Phoenix, AZ 85004-2257, USA

Harley, Steve (Music Group)
Work Hard
19D Pinfold Road
London SW16 2SL, UNITED KINGDOM (UK)

Harlin, Renny (Director, Producer)
Midnight Sun Pictures
8800 W Sunset Blvd # 400
Los Angeles, CA 90069-2105, USA

Harlow, Shalom (Model)
38 Stephen Ave
Courtice, ON L1E 1Z1, CANADA

Harlow, Terry (Baseball Player)
Baltimore Orioles
26348 W Burnett Rd
Buckeye, AZ 85396-9239, USA

Harman, Bill (Baseball Player)
Philadelphia Phillies
9 Guyenne Rd
Wilmington, DE 19807-1413, USA

Harman, Katie (Beauty Pageant Winner)
c/o Staff Member *The Miss America Organization*
2 Miss America Way Ste 1000
Atlantic City, NJ 08401-4142, USA

Harmon, Andrew P (Football Player)
Philadelphia Eagles
1258 Waters Edge Dr
Dayton, OH 45458-3937, USA

Harmon, Chuck (Baseball Player)
Indianapolis Clowns
6035 Ridgeacres Dr Unit A
Cincinnati, OH 45237-4733, USA

Harmon, Clarence (Football Player)
Washington Redskins
PO Box 571
Verona, MS 38879-0571, USA

Harmon, Debbie
47385 Via Florence
La Quinta, CA 92253-2126, USA

Harmon, Joy (Actor)
9901 Poole Ave
Sunland, CA 91040-1335, USA

Harmon, Kelly (Actor, Model)
13224 Old Oak Ln
Los Angeles, CA 90049-2502, USA

Harmon, Larry
10590 Wilshire Blvd Apt 1604
Los Angeles, CA 90024-4563, USA

Harmon, Manny -
8350 Santa Monica Blvd
Los Angeles, CA 90069-4393, USA

Harmon, Mark (Actor)
c/o Staff Member *Wings Productions Inc*
2236 Encinitas Blvd Ste A
Encinitas, CA 92024-4353, USA

Harmon, Merle (Sportscaster)
424 E Lamar Blvd Ste 210
Arlington, TX 76011-3606, USA

Harmon, Nigel (Astronaut)
Church Crookham
Aldershot, UNITED KINGDOM (UK)

Harmon, Robert (Director)
c/o Andrew Ruf *Paradigm (LA)*
360 N Crescent Dr
North Bldg
Beverly Hills, CA 90210-6820, USA

Harmon, Ronnie K (Football Player)
Buffalo Bills
13022 218th St
Laurelton, NY 11413-1231, USA

Harmon, Terry (Baseball Player)
Philadelphia Phillies
62 Oakwood Dr
Medford, NJ 08055-8824, USA

Harmon, Winsor
c/o Jerry Shandrew *Shandrew Public Relations*
1050 S Stanley Ave
Los Angeles, CA 90019-6634, USA

Harmon-Sehorn, Angie (Actor)
c/o John Carrabino *John Carrabino Management*
5900 Wilshire Blvd Ste 406
Los Angeles, CA 90036-5015, USA

Harmonica Rascals, The
4585 N River Rd
Zanesville, OH 43701-7768, USA

Harms, Alfred G Jr (Admiral)
Chief Education/Training
Naval Air Station
Pensacola, FL 32508, USA

Harms, Kristin (Producer)
c/o Staff Member *West Wing, The*
4000 Warner Blvd Trlr 8
Burbank, CA 91522-0001, USA

Harnden, Arthur (Art) (Athlete, Track Athlete)
7218 Pepper Ridge Rd
Corpus Christi, TX 78413-5005, USA

Harnes, Robert (Baseball Player)
Chicago Giants
833 E Drexel Sq
Chicago, IL 60615-3705, USA

Harness, William E (Opera Singer)
PO Box 328
Washougal, WA 98671-0328, USA

Harney, Paul (Golfer)
72 Club Valley Dr
East Falmouth, MA 02536, USA

Harnisch, Peter T (Pete) (Baseball Player)
Baltimore Orioles
2 Cornfield Ln
Commack, NY 11725-2702, USA

Harnois, Elisabeth (Actor)
c/o Ted Schachter *Schachter Entertainment*
1157 S Beverly Dr Fl 2
Los Angeles, CA 90035-1119, USA

Harnoncourt, Nikolaus
38 Piaristangasse
Vienna 1080, AUSTRIA

Harnos, Christine (Actor)
Gersh Agency
232 N Canon Dr
Beverly Hills, CA 90210-5302, USA

Harnoy, Ofra (Musician)
437 Spadina Road
PO Box 23046
Toronto, ON M5P 2W0, CANADA

Harold, Erika (Beauty Pageant Winner)
c/o Staff Member *The Miss America Organization*
2 Miss America Way Ste 1000
Atlantic City, NJ 08401-4142, USA

Harold, Gale (Actor)
c/o Suzanne DeWalt *Dewalt & Musik Management*
623 N Parish Pl
Burbank, CA 91506-1701, USA

Harout, Magda (Actor)
13452 Vose St
Van Nuys, CA 91405-3416, USA

Harper, Alvin C (Football Player)
Dallas Cowboys
8 Barberry Ct
Upper Marlboro, MD 20774-1657, USA

Harper, Ben (Music Group, Musician, Songwriter, Writer)
c/o Staff Member *Virgin Records (NY)*
304 Park Ave S Fl 5
New York, NY 10010-4316, USA

Harper, Brian (Baseball Player)
California Angels
8319 E Shetland Trl
Scottsdale, AZ 85258-1343, USA

Harper, Charles M (Business Person)
6625 State St
Omaha, NE 68152-1633, USA

Harper, Dave (Football Player)
Dallas Cowboys
4494 Cedar St
Eureka, CA 95503-8901, USA

Harper, Derek (Basketball Player)
2215 High Point Cir
Carrollton, TX 75007, USA

Harper, Donald D W (Don) (Swimmer)
1765 Lynnhaven Dr
Columbus, OH 43221-1409, USA

Harper, Dwayne (Football Player)
Seattle Seahawks
104 Cue St
Orangeburg, SC 29115-7593, USA

Harper, Edward J (Composer)
7 Morningside Park
Edinburgh EH10 5HD, SCOTLAND

Harper, Heather M (Opera Singer)
20 Milverton Road
London NW6 7AS, UNITED KINGDOM (UK)

Harper, Heck
13647 Gaffney Ln Apt 17
Oregon City, OR 97045-8970, USA

Harper, Herschel (Baseball Player)
Negro Baseball Leagues
3302 Hazelwood Dr SW
Atlanta, GA 30311-3038, USA

Harper, Hill (Actor)
c/o Lorrie Bartlett *Gersh Agency, The (LA)*
232 N Canon Dr
Beverly Hills, CA 90210-5302, USA

Harper, Jessica (Actor, Music Group)
15430 Brownwood Pl
Los Angeles, CA 90077-1609, USA

Harper, John
9700 Kessler Ave
Chatsworth, CA 91311-5503, USA

Harper, Mark (Football Player)
Cleveland Browns
2162 Albany Ave
Memphis, TN 38108-3011, USA

Harper, Robert (Actor)
Karg/Weissenbach
329 N Wetherly Dr Ste 101
Beverly Hills, CA 90211-1674, USA

Harper, Roger (Football Player)
Atlanta Falcons
1921 Holburn Ave
Columbus, OH 43207-1683, USA

Harper, Roland (Football Player)
Chicago Bears
1391 Westbourne Pkwy
Algonquin, IL 60102-6052, USA

Harper, Ron (Actor)
c/o Staff Member *Tisherman Agency Inc*
6767 Forest Lawn Dr Ste 101
Los Angeles, CA 90068-1050, USA

Harper, Ron (Basketball Player)
8934 Brecksville Rd # 417
Cleveland, OH 44141-2318, USA

Harper, Terry (Baseball Player)
Atlanta Braves
4225 Jailette Rd
Atlanta, GA 30349-1848, USA

Harper, Tess (Actor)
6249 Ventura Canyon Ave
Van Nuys, CA 91401-2433, USA

Harper, Tommy (Baseball Player)
Cincinnati Reds
5 Cow Hill Rd
Sharon, MA 02067-2987, USA

Harper, Travis (Baseball Player)
Tampa Bay Devil Rays
HC 77 Box 13
Riverton, WV 26814-9503, USA

Harper, Valarie (Actor)
David Shapira
193 N Robertson Blvd
Beverly Hills, CA 90211-2103, USA

Harper, Valerie
PO Box 7187
Beverly Hills, CA 90212-7187, USA

Harper, Willie M (Football Player)
San Francisco 49ers
2525 Berryessa Ct
Tracy, CA 95304-5825, USA

Harpring, Matt (Basketball Player)
c/o Staff Member *Utah Jazz*
301 W South Temple
Delta Center
Salt Lake City, UT 84101-1216, USA

Harptones, The
55 W 119th St
New York, NY 10026-1454, USA

Harrah, Colbert D (Toby) (Baseball Player)
Washington Senators
316 Leewood Cir
Azle, TX 76020, USA

Harrah, Dennis W (Football Player)
Los Angeles Rams
38777 Via De Oro
Temecula, CA 92592-8884, USA

Harrar, J George (Misc)
125 Puritan Dr
Scarsdale, NY 10583-6734, USA

Harraway, Charlie (Football Player)
Cleveland Browns
7961 Megan Hammock Way
Sarasota, FL 34240-8244, USA

Harrell, Anthony (Actor)
c/o Michael Greene *Greene & Associates*
190 N Canon Dr Ste 200
Beverly Hills, CA 90210-5319, USA

Harrell, Billy (Baseball Player)
Birmingham Black Barons
253 Mount Hope Dr
Albany, NY 12202-1017, USA

Harrell, James A (Geophysicist, Physicist)
University of Toledo
Geology Dept
Toledo, OH 43606, USA

Harrell, John (Baseball Player)
San Francisco Giants
756 Erie Cir
Milpitas, CA 95035-3551, USA

Harrell, Lynn M (Musician)
I M G Artists
420 W 45th St
New York, NY 10036-3503, USA

Harrell, Tom (Music Group, Musician)
Joel Chriss
300 Mercer St Apt 3J
New York, NY 10003-6732, USA

Harrell, Willard (Football Player)
Green Bay Packers
8 Scarlet Oak Ct
Lake Saint Louis, MO 63367-2143, USA

Harrell-Doyle, Dorothy (Baseball Player)
68670 Raposa Rd
Cathedral City, CA 92234-8148, USA

Harrelson, Bill (Baseball Player)
California Angels
6900 Kimberly Ave
Bakersfield, CA 93308-3923, USA

Harrelson, Brett (Actor)
Agency for Performing Arts
405 S Beverly Dr Ste 500
Beverly Hills, CA 90212-4425, USA

Harrelson, Derrell M (Bud) (Baseball Player)
New York Mets
357 Ridgefield Rd
Hauppauge, NY 11788-2314, USA

Harrelson, Kenneth S (Ken) (Baseball Player)
Kansas City A's
90006 Shawn Park Pl
Orlando, FL 32819, USA

Harrelson, Woody (Actor)
c/o Jeremy Plager *Creative Artists Agency LCC (CAA-LA)*
2000 Avenue Of The Stars
Los Angeles, CA 90067-4700, USA

Harrick, Jim (Basketball Player, Coach)
Denver Nuggets
1000 Chopper Cir
Pepsi Center
Denver, CO 80204-5805, USA

Harriger, Denny (Baseball Player)
Detroit Tigers
RR 1
Rimersburg, PA 16248, USA

Harring, Laura Elena (Actor, Beauty Pageant Winner)
12335 Santa Monica Blvd # 302
Los Angeles, CA 90025-2519, USA

Harrington, Bill (Baseball Player)
Philadelphia Athletics
7219 Cleveland School Rd
Garner, NC 27529-8928, USA

Harrington, David (Music Group, Musician)
Kronos Quartet
1235 9th Ave
San Francisco, CA 94122-2306, USA

Harrington, Desmond (Actor)
c/o Stephanie Simon *Untitled Entertainment (LA)*
331 N Maple Dr Fl 3
Beverly Hills, CA 90210-3827, USA

Harrington, Donald J (Educator)
Saint John's Univesity
President's Office
Jamaica, NY 11439-0001, USA

Harrington, Jay (Actor)
c/o Abe Hoch *Magus Entertainment*
9107 Wilshire Blvd Ste 650
Beverly Hills, CA 90210-5544, USA

Harrington, Joey (Football Player)
Detroit Lions
222 Republic Dr
Allen Park, MI 48101-3650, USA

Harrington, John (Coach, Hockey Player)
Saint John's Univesity
PO Box 7277
Athletic Dept
Collegeville, MN 56321-7277, USA

Harrington, Mike (Baseball Player)
Philadelphia Phillies
135 Scenic Dr
Hattiesburg, MS 39401-8403, USA

Harrington, Pat
730 Marzella Ave
Los Angeles, CA 90049-2043, USA

Harrington, Perry (Football Player)
Philadelphia Eagles
1302 Roxbury Ct
Jackson, MS 39211-6367, USA

Harrington, Robert (Race Car Driver)
2609 Woodshade Ave
Kannapolis, NC 28127, USA

Harriott, Ainsley
12 Ogle St.
London, ENGLAND W1P 7LG, UNITED KINGDOM (UK)

Harris, A E (Football Player)
Brooklyn Dodgers
1090 Magnolia Dr
Highland Home, AL 36041-3412, USA

Harris, Al (Football Player)
Chicago Bears
12 Stone Ridge Dr
South Barrington, IL 60010-9593, USA

Harris, Alonzo (Baseball Player)
Houston Astros
7378 Tyler Ln
Fontana, CA 92336-5408, USA

Harris, Barbara
159 W 53rd St # 12-D
New York, NY 10019-6005, USA

Harris, Barbara C (Activist, Religious Leader)
Episcopal Diocese of Massachusetts
138 Tremont St
Boston, MA 02111-1356, USA

Harris, Barry (DJ, Music Group, Musician)
Brad Simon Organization
122 E 57th St # 300
New York, NY 10022-2623, USA

Harris, Bernard A Jr (Astronaut)
3411 Erin Knoll Ct
Houston, TX 77059-3716, USA

Harris, Bill (Baseball Player)
Brooklyn Dodgers
322 S Reed St
Kennewick, WA 99336-4264, USA

Harris, Bill (Critic)
12747 Riverside Dr Apt 208
Valley Village, CA 91607-3303, USA

Harris, Billy (Baseball Player)
Cleveland Indians
114 W Brandywine Cir
Wilmington, NC 28411-9703, USA

Harris, Bishop Barbara
138 Tremont St
Boston, MA 02111-1318, USA

Harris, Bo (Football Player)
Cincinnati Bengals
231 Highland Villa Cir
Nashville, TN 37211-7320, USA

Harris, Buddy (Baseball Player)
Houston Astros
2305 Carol Ln
Norristown, PA 19401-2046, USA

Harris, Charles (Baseball Player)
Philadelphia Athletics
PO Box 159
Nobleton, FL 34661-0159, USA

Harris, Cliff (Football Player)
Dallas Cowboys
722 Kentwood Dr
Rockwall, TX 75032-7506, USA

Harris, Corey (Football Player)
Houston Oilers
933 N Tremont St
Indianapolis, IN 46222-3738, USA

Harris, Cristi Ellen
c/o Staff Member *The House of Representatives*
211 S Beverly Dr Ste 208
Beverly Hills, CA 90212-3879, USA

Harris, Damian (Director)
International Creative Mgmt
8942 Wilshire Blvd # 219
Beverly Hills, CA 90211-1908, USA

Harris, Danielle (Actor)
c/o Staff Member *Metropolitan*
4500 Wilshire Blvd Fl 2
Los Angeles, CA 90010-3858, USA

Harris, Danneel (Actor)
c/o Rob D'Avola *Identity Talent Agency (ID)*
9107 Wilshire Blvd Ste 450
Beverly Hills, CA 90210-5535, USA

Harris, Donald (Baseball Player)
Texas Rangers
916 Hubert St
Waco, TX 76704-1936, USA

Harris, Ed (Actor)
Creative Artists Agency
9830 Wilshire Blvd
Beverly Hills, CA 90212-1804, USA

Harris, Emmylou (Music Group, Songwriter, Writer)
c/o Staff Member *Vector Management*
1607 17th Ave S
Nashville, TN 37212-2812, USA

Harris, Ernest (Baseball Player)
Birmingham Black Barons
1007 46th St W
Birmingham, AL 35208-1434, USA

Harris, Estelle (Actor)
Agy for Performing Arts
405 S Beverly Dr Ste 500
Beverly Hills, CA 90212-4425, USA

Harris, Franco (Football Player)
Pittsburgh Steelers
200 Chaucer Ct S
Sewickley, PA 15143-8726, USA

Harris, Gail (Baseball Player)
New York Giants
9008 Weir St
Manassas, VA 20110-4913, USA

Harris, Gail Robyn (Actor)
Don Gerler
3349 Cahuenga Blvd W Ste 1
Los Angeles, CA 90068-1379, USA

Harris, Gene (Baseball Player)
Montreal Expos
1267 NE 16th Ave
Okeechobee, FL 34972-3066, USA

Harris, Greg (Baseball Player)
San Diego Padres
12613 Richmond Run Ct
Raleigh, NC 27614, USA

Harris, Greg (Baseball Player)
San Diego Padres
11248 Barbi Ln
Los Alamitos, CA 90720-3931, USA

Harris, Hernando (Baseball Player)
California Angels
995 Ten Oaks Dr
Lancaster, SC 29720-9039, USA

Harris, James L (Football Player)
Buffalo Bills
9722 Groffs Mill Dr # 106
Owings Mills, MD 21117-6341, USA

Harris, Jay (Cartoonist)
King Features Syndicate
888 7th Ave Ste 201
New York, NY 10106-0201, USA

Harris, Jim B (Football Player)
Philadelphia Eagles
3455 Calumet Dr
Shreveport, LA 71107-7407, USA

Harris, Joe Frank (Governor)
712 West Ave
Cartersville, GA 30120-3441, USA

Harris, John (Football Player)
Seattle Seahawks
270 NW 120th St
Miami, FL 33168-3525, USA

Harris, John (Golfer)
4316 Fremont Ave S
Minneapolis, MN 55409-1721, USA

Harris, John R (Architect)
24 Devonshire Place
London W1N 2BX, UNITED KINGDOM (UK)

Harris, Jon (Football Player)
Philadelphia Eagles
930 Coral Ridge Dr Apt 204
Coral Springs, FL 33071-4144, USA

Harris, Joshua (Actor)
1800 Vine St Ste 305
Los Angeles, CA 90028-5237, USA

Harris, Julie (Actor)
132 Barn Hill Road #1267
West Chatham, MA 02669, USA

Harris, Katherine
c/o Daniel A (Dan) Strone *Trident Media Group LLC*
41 Madison Ave Fl 36
New York, NY 10010-2257, USA

Harris, Kwame (Football Player)
San Francisco 49ers
4949 Centennial Blvd
Santa Clara, CA 95054-1229, USA

Harris, Lara
400 S Beverly Dr Ste 101
Beverly Hills, CA 90212-4403, USA

Harris, Larry (Football Player)
Houston Oilers
340 E Mosholu Pkwy S Apt 6F
Bronx, NY 10458-1768, USA

Harris, Lenny (Baseball Player)
Cincinnati Reds
7435 N Augusta Dr
Hialeah, FL 33015-2050, USA

Harris, Leon (Correspondent)
Cable News Network
1050 Techwood Dr NW
News Dept
Atlanta, GA 30318-5604, USA

Harris, Leonard (Football Player)
Tampa Bay Buccaneers
1817 Trilogy Park Dr
Hoschton, GA 30548-6237, USA

Harris, Leroy (Football Player)
Miami Dolphins
1919 Live Oak St
Savannah, GA 31404-3336, USA

Harris, M L (Football Player)
Cincinnati Bengals
4323 Eastpoint Dr
Columbus, OH 43232-4202, USA

Harris, Marilyn
217 N San Marino Ave
San Gabriel, CA 91775-2909, USA

Harris, Mel (Actor)
VOX
5670 Wilshire Blvd Ste 820
Los Angeles, CA 90036-5613, USA

Harris, Moira (Actor)
Writers & Artists
360 N Crescent Dr Bldg North
Beverly Hills, CA 90210-6818, USA

Harris, Naomie (Actor)
c/o Staff Member *Artists Rights Group (ARG London)*
4 Great Portland St
London W1W 8PA, UNITED KINGDOM (UK)

Harris, Neil (Historian)
5555 S Everett Ave
Chicago, IL 60637-1968, USA

Harris, Neil Patrick (Actor)
c/o Chris Schmidt *Paradigm (LA)*
360 N Crescent Dr
North Bldg
Beverly Hills, CA 90210-6820, USA

Harris, Odie L Jr (Football Player)
Tampa Bay Buccaneers
1404 Knob Hill Dr
Desoto, TX 75115-5336, USA

Harris, Rachael (Comedian)
c/o Staff Member *Principato/Young Management*
9665 Wilshire Blvd Ste 500
Beverly Hills, CA 90212-2312, USA

Harris, Raymont (Football Player)
Chicago Bears
1144 Aroya Ct
New Albany, OH 43054-9205, USA

Harris, Reggie (Baseball Player)
Cincinnati Reds
55 Ashleigh Dr # 8
Waynesboro, VA 22980, USA

Harris, Rene (President)
President's Office
Government Offices
Yaren, NAURU

Harris, Richard (Football Player)
Philadelphia Eagles
9202 NE 132nd Pl
Kirkland, WA 98034-2634, USA

Harris, Richard (Music Group)
Paramount Entertainment
PO Box 12
Far Hills, NJ 07931-0012, USA

Harris, Rickie (Football Player)
Washington Redskins
613 Q St NW
Washington, DC 20001-3404, USA

Harris, Robert (Football Player)
Minnesota Vikings
2711 13th St SW
Lehigh Acres, FL 33976-3114, USA

Harris, Rolf (Entertainer)
Billy Marsh Assoc
174-178 N Gower St
London NW1 2NB, UNITED KINGDOM
(UK)

Harris, Ronald W (Ronnie) (Boxer)
1365 Glennview St NE
Canton, OH 44721-1916, USA

Harris, Rosemary (Actor)
International Creative Mgmt
76 Oxford St
London W1N 0AX, UNITED KINGDOM
(UK)

Harris, Ross
6542 Fulcher Ave
N Hollywood, CA 91606-2717, USA

Harris, Sam (Music Group)
Scott Stander
13701 Riverside Dr Ste 201
Sherman Oaks, CA 91423-2447, USA

Harris, Samantha (Actor)
c/o Staff Member *Visionary Entertainment*
1558 N Stanley Ave
West Hollywood, CA 90046-2711, USA

Harris, Sidney (Cartoonist)
302 W 86th St Apt 9A
New York, NY 10024-3154, USA

Harris, Stefon (Misc)
Joel Chriss
300 Mercer St Apt 3J
New York, NY 10003-6732, USA

Harris, Steve (Actor)
c/o Colton Gramm *Brillstein-Grey
Entertainment*
9150 Wilshire Blvd Ste 350
Beverly Hills, CA 90212-3453, USA

Harris, Steve (Musician)
Sanctuary Music Mgmt
82 Bishop's Bridge Road
London W2 6BB, UNITED KINGDOM
(UK)

Harris, Susan (Producer)
11828 La Grange Ave # 200
Los Angeles, CA 90025-5212, USA

Harris, Thomas (Director, Writer)
c/o Robert (Bob) Bookman *Creative Artists
Agency LCC (CAA-LA)*
2000 Avenue Of The Stars
Los Angeles, CA 90067-4700, USA

Harris, Tim (Football Player)
Pittsburgh Steelers
11644 Acacia Ave Apt 17
Hawthorne, CA 90250-2348, USA

Harris, Tim (Football Player)
Green Bay Packers
1004 Parkwood Cir
Birmingham, AL 35215-4372, USA

Harris, Timothy D (Tim) (Football Player)
San Francisco 49ers
4949 Centennial Blvd
Santa Clara, CA 95054-1229, USA

Harris, Tommie (Football Player)
Chicago Bears
1000 Football Dr
Lake Forest, IL 60045-4829, USA

Harris, Vic (Baseball Player)
Texas Rangers
5420 S Garth Ave
Los Angeles, CA 90056-1116, USA

Harris, Walt (Football Player)
Chicago Bears
4103 Shinault Ln
Olive Branch, MS 38654-8039, USA

Harris, Wendell (Football Player)
Baltimore Colts
2368 Wisteria St # 368
Baton Rouge, LA 70806-5352, USA

Harris, William M (Football Player)
St Louis Cardinals
2118 Laurel Forest Way
Houston, TX 77014-2452, USA

Harris, Willie (Baseball Player)
Philadelphia Stars
108 Page Ave
Birmingham, AL 35214-5129, USA

Harris, Wilmer (Baseball Player)
Philadelphia Stars
441 Tomlinson Rd Apt F3
Philadelphia, PA 19116-3227, USA

Harris, Wood (Actor)
Gersh Agency
232 N Canon Dr
Beverly Hills, CA 90210-5302, USA

Harris Jr, Clifford (TI) (Musician)
c/o Staff Member *International Creative
Management (ICM-LA)*
10250 Constellation Blvd
Los Angeles, CA 90067-6200, USA

Harris-Stewart, Lusia M (Lucy) (Basketball
Player)
1002 Cherry St
Greenwood, MS 38930-6506, USA

Harrison, Alvin (Athlete, Track Athlete)
Octagon
1751 Pinnacle Dr Ste 1500
McLean, VA 22102-3833, USA

Harrison, Bertram C (General)
PO Box 209
Leesburg, VA 20178-0209, USA

Harrison, Bob (Baseball Player)
Baltimore Orioles
16777 Loch Cir
Noblesville, IN 46060-4482, USA

Harrison, Bob (Football Player)
San Francisco 49ers
3 Westwind Cir
Stamford, TX 79553-6117, USA

Harrison, Bret (Actor)
c/o Staff Member *United Talent Agency
(UTA)*
9560 Wilshire Blvd Ste 500
Beverly Hills, CA 90212-2401, USA

Harrison, C Richard (Business Person)
Parametric Technology
140 Kendrick St
Needham Heights, MA 02494-2739, USA

Harrison, Chris (Actor, Reality TV Star)
c/o Staff Member *Bachelor, The*
15301 Ventura Blvd Bldg E
Sherman Oaks, CA 91403-5885, USA

Harrison, Chuck (Baseball Player)
Houston Astros
222 Buckskin Rd
Abilene, TX 79602-4508, USA

Harrison, Dennis (Football Player)
Philadelphia Eagles
1048 Hickory Hollow Rd
Nashville, TN 37221-1139, USA

Harrison, Dwight (Football Player)
Denver Broncos
2265 Buchanan St
Beaumont, TX 77703-2255, USA

Harrison, Glynn (Football Player)
Kansas City Chiefs
485 Huntington Rd Ste 203
Athens, GA 30606-1845, USA

Harrison, Granville (Football Player)
200 S High St
Franklin, VA 23851-1631, USA

Harrison, Gregory (Actor)
c/o Staff Member *Stone Manners Talent &
Literary (LA)*
6500 Wilshire Blvd Ste 550
Los Angeles, CA 90048-4950, USA

Harrison, Jenilee (Actor)
JLeeCorp
19528 Ventura Blvd # 365
Tarzana, CA 91356-2917, USA

Harrison, Jerry (Musician)
Sire/Warner Bros Records
3300 Warner Blvd
Burbank, CA 91505-4694, USA

Harrison, Jim (Football Player)
Chicago Bears
4916 Hemphill Dr
San Antonio, TX 78228-3724, USA

Harrison, Jim (Writer)
Longstreet Press
325 N Milledge Ave
Athens, GA 30601-3805, USA

Harrison, Kathryn (Writer)
Random House
1745 Broadway # B1
New York, NY 10019-4305, USA

Harrison, Linda (Actor)
9846 Portola Dr
Beverly Hills, CA 90210-1421, USA

Harrison, Mark (Editor)
The Gazette
250 Saint Antoine St W
Montreal, PQ H2Y 2R7, CANADA

Harrison, Martin (Football Player)
San Francisco 49ers
10624 S Eastern Ave # A-251
Henderson, NV 89052-2982, USA

Harrison, Marvin (Athlete, Football
Player)
c/o Staff Member *Indianapolis Colts*
7001 W 56th St
Indianapolis, IN 46254-9698, USA

Harrison, Matthew (Director)
Rigberg Roberts Rugolo
1180 S Beverly Dr Ste 601
Los Angeles, CA 90035-1158, USA

Harrison, Michael Allen (Composer,
Musician)
MAH Records
828 NE Prescott St
Portland, OR 97211-4544, USA

Harrison, Nolan (Football Player)
Oakland Raiders
4605 Blarney Dr
Matteson, IL 60443-1886, USA

Harrison, Olivia (Actor, Producer)
c/o Craig Fruin *H.K. Management*
1100 Glendon Ave Ste 1100
Los Angeles, CA 90024-3515, USA

Harrison, Randy (Actor)
c/o Jason Weinberg *Untitled
Entertainment (LA)*
331 N Maple Dr Fl 3
Beverly Hills, CA 90210-3827, USA

Harrison, Reggie (Football Player)
St Louis Cardinals
1912 Halifax Rd
Woodbridge, VA 22191-2407, USA

Harrison, Roric (Baseball Player)
Baltimore Orioles
2301 Dupont Dr Ste 300
Irvine, CA 92612-7531, USA

Harrison, Schae
7800 Beverly Blvd # 3371
Los Angeles, CA 90036-2112, USA

Harrison, Tom (Baseball Player)
Kansas City A's
2932 Channing Way
Los Alamitos, CA 90720-4049, USA

Harrison, Tony (Writer)
Gordon Dickinson
2 Crescent Grove
London SW4 7AH, UNITED KINGDOM
(UK)

Harrison, William B Jr (Financier)
JP Morgan Chase Corp
270 Park Ave Fl 12
New York, NY 10017-7924, USA

Harrison, William H (General)
7302 Amber Ln SW
Tacoma, WA 98498-5045, USA

Harrison Breetzke, Joan (Swimmer)
16 Clevedon Road
East London 5201, SOUTH AFRICA

Harrold, Kathryn (Actor)
9255 W Sunset Blvd Ste 901
Los Angeles, CA 90069-3306, USA

Harron, Mary (Director)
William Morris Agency
151 El Camino Dr
Beverly Hills, CA 90212-2775, USA

Harrow, Lisa
46 Albermarle St
London, ENGLAND W1X 4PP, UNITED
KINGDOM (UK)

Harry (Prince)
Clarence House
Stable Yard Gate
London SW1, UNITED KINGDOM (UK)

Harry, Deborah (Actor)
c/o Staff Member *Untitled Entertainment (LA)*
331 N Maple Dr Fl 3
Beverly Hills, CA 90210-3827, USA

Harry, Deborah A (Debbie) (Actor, Musician, Songwriter)
c/o Staff Member *Paradigm (NY)*
360 Park Ave S Fl 16
New York, NY 10010-1716, USA

Harry, Emile (Football Player)
Kansas City Chiefs
Cl-14 Box 2
South Padre Island, TX 78597, USA

Harry, HRH Prince (Prince)
Highgrove House
Gloucestershire, UNITED KINGDOM (UK)

Harry, Jackee (Actor, Director)
c/o Christopher Barrett *Metropolitan*
4500 Wilshire Blvd Fl 2
Los Angeles, CA 90010-3858, USA

Harryhausen, Ray
2 Ilchester Pl
London, ENGLAND W14 8AA, UNITED KINGDOM (UK)

Harsch, Eddie (Music Group, Musician)
Mitch Schneider Organization
14724 Ventura Blvd Ste 710
Sherman Oaks, CA 91403-3520, USA

Harshman, Margo (Actor)
c/o Elain Lively *LA Entertainment*
1317 N San Fernando Blvd # 155
Burbank, CA 91504-4236, USA

Harshman, Marvel K (Marv) (Basketball Player, Coach)
19221 90th Pl NE
Bothell, WA 98011-2253, USA

Hart, Bob (Bowler)
5740 Laurel Oak Dr
Suwanee, GA 30024-3370, USA

Hart, Bret
435 Patina Place SE
Calgary, AB T3H 2P, CANADA

Hart, Christopher
1423 N Martel Ave Apt 4
Los Angeles, CA 90046-4204, USA

Hart, Corey
1445 Lambert Close #300
Montreal, PQ H3H 1Z5, CANADA

Hart, Dolores (Mother Dolores) (Actor)
Regina Laudis Abbey
275 Flanders Rd
Bethlehem, CT 06751, USA

Hart, Doris (Tennis Player)
600 Biltmore Way Apt 306
Coral Gables, FL 33134-7528, USA

Hart, Dorothy
43 Martindale Rd
Asheville, NC 28804-1427, USA

Hart, Doug (Football Player)
Green Bay Packers
19047 Evergreen Rd
Fort Myers, FL 33967-3654, USA

Hart, Dudley (Golfer)
5130 Rockledge Dr
Clarence, NY 14031-2442, USA

Hart, Freddie (Music Group, Musician, Songwriter, Writer)
317 N Kenwood St
Burbank, CA 91505-3446, USA

Hart, Gary (Ex-Senator, Senator)
950 17th St Ste 2050
Denver, CO 80202-2825, USA

Hart, Gary W (Senator)
730 17th St Ste 300
Denver, CO 80202-3513, USA

Hart, Harold J (Football Player)
Oakland Raiders
2004 E Caracas St
Tampa, FL 33610-5025, USA

Hart, Herbert L A (Lawyer, Misc)
11 Manor Place
Oxford, UNITED KINGDOM (UK)

Hart, Ian (Actor)
P F D
Drury House 34-43 Russell St
London WC2B 5HA, UNITED KINGDOM (UK)

Hart, James V (Director, Producer, Writer)
c/o Jon Levin *Creative Artists Agency LCC (CAA-LA)*
2000 Avenue Of The Stars
Los Angeles, CA 90067-4700, USA

Hart, Jason (Baseball Player)
Texas Rangers
1225 W Berkeley St
Springfield, MO 65807-7201, USA

Hart, Jeff (Golfer)
105 Guanajuato Ct
Solana Beach, CA 92075-2510, USA

Hart, Jim (Football Player)
St Louis Cardinals
3141 Dominica Way
Naples, FL 34119-1606, USA

Hart, Jim Ray (Baseball Player)
Manteca, CA 95336, USA

Hart, Jim Ray (Baseball Player)
San Francisco Giants
17074 Templeton Ln
Lathrop, CA 95330-8634, USA

Hart, John (Actor)
35109 Highway 79 Spc 134
Warner Springs, CA 92086-9704, USA

Hart, John R (Correspondent)
International Creative Mgmt
40 W 57th St Ste 1800
New York, NY 10019-4001, USA

Hart, Kevin (Actor, Comedian)
c/o David (Dave) Becky *3 Arts Entertainment Inc*
9460 Wilshire Blvd Fl 7
Beverly Hills, CA 90212-2713, USA

Hart, Leon
3904 Cottontail Ln
Bloomfield, MI 48301-1908, USA

Hart, Leslie (Football Player)
Staten Island Stapletons
601 Bank Ave
Riverton, NJ 08077-1144, USA

Hart, Linda (Actor)
c/o Staff Member *Gage Group, The (LA)*
14724 Ventura Blvd Ste 505
Sherman Oaks, CA 91403-3505, USA

Hart, Margie
228 S Hudson Ave
Los Angeles, CA 90004-1036, USA

Hart, Mary (Television Host)
c/o Staff Member *Entertainment Tonight (ET)*
5555 Melrose Ave
Mae West Bldg Fl 2
Los Angeles, CA 90038-3989, USA

Hart, Melissa Joan (Actor)
c/o Staff Member *Artistry Management*
525 Westbourne St
West Hollywood, CA 90048-1913, USA

Hart, Mickey (Music Group, Musician)
c/o Staff Member *360° Productions, Inc.*
PO Box 1636
Sebastopol, CA 95473-1636, USA

Hart, Mike (Baseball Player)
Texas Rangers
409 Larkspur Ave
Portage, MI 49002-6243, USA

Hart, Mike (Baseball Player)
Minnesota Twins
16552 W Crescent Dr
New Berlin, WI 53151-6514, USA

Hart, Parker T (Diplomat)
4705 Berkeley Ter NW
Washington, DC 20007-1508, USA

Hart, Richard (Football Player)
Philadelphia Eagles
273 Oarlock Cir
East Syracuse, NY 13057-3123, USA

Hart, Roxanne
Agency for Performing Arts
405 S Beverly Dr Ste 500
Beverly Hills, CA 90212-4425, USA

Hart, Stanley R (Geophysicist, Physicist)
53 Quonset Rd
Falmouth, MA 02540-1656, USA

Hart, Terry J (Astronaut)
PO Box V
Hellertown, PA 18055-0218, USA

Hart, Tommy (Football Player)
San Francisco 49ers
3503 Highland Ave
Redwood City, CA 94062-3109, USA

Hartack, Bill
PO Box 250
Lexington, KY 40588-0250, USA

Hartack, William J (Bill) (Jockey)
Jockey's Guild
PO Box 150
Monrovia, CA 91017-0150, USA

Harte, Houston H (Publisher)
Harte-Hanks Communications
200 Concord Plaza Dr
San Antonio, TX 78216-6900, USA

Hartenstein, Chuck (Baseball Player)
Chicago Cubs
10735 Cassia Dr
Austin, TX 78759-6452, USA

Hartenstine, Michael A (Mike) (Football Player)
Chicago Bears
322 Winchester Ct
Lake Bluff, IL 60044-1930, USA

Harter, Dick (Basketball Player, Coach)
Philadelphia 76ers
3601 S Broad St
1st Union Center
Philadelphia, PA 19148-5287, USA

Hartgraves, Dean (Baseball Player)
Houston Astros
515 Kings Ct
Central Point, OR 97502-2120, USA

Harth, Sidney (Musician)
135 Westland Dr
Pittsburgh, PA 15217-2538, USA

Hartigan, Grace (Artist)
1701 1/2 Eastern Ave
Baltimore, MD 21231, USA

Hartings, Jeff (Football Player)
Detroit Lions
104 Player Ln
Sewickley, PA 15143-7501, USA

Hartley, Bob (Coach, Hockey Player)
Atlanta Thrashers
13 South Ave SE
Philips Arena
Atlanta, GA 30315, USA

Hartley, Hal (Director)
True Fiction Pictures
39 W 14th St Ste 406
New York, NY 10011-7404, USA

Hartley, Harry J (Educator)
University of Connecticut
President's Office
Storrs Mansfield, CT 06269-0001, USA

Hartley, Howard (Football Player)
Washington Redskins
226 Glenbrooke Way
Greenville, SC 29615-1299, USA

Hartley, Justin (Actor)
c/o Theodore B Gekis *Gekis Management*
4217 Verdugo View Dr
Los Angeles, CA 90065-4317, USA

Hartley, Mariette (Actor)
Dayton Milrad Cho Management
8306 Wilshire Blvd # 56
C/O Judy Milrad
Beverly Hills, CA 90211-2304, USA

Hartley, Mike (Baseball Player)
Mesa Miners Pro Baseball
123 N Centennial Way Ste 150
Mesa, AZ 85201-6689, USA

Hartley, Ted
524 N Rockingham Ave
Los Angeles, CA 90049-2640, USA

Hartline, Mary (Actor)
c/o Staff Member *Pierce & Shelly*
13775A Mono Way # 220
Sonora, CA 95370-8813, USA

Hartman, Arthur A (Diplomat)
APCO Consulting Group
1615 L St NW
Washington, DC 20036-5610, USA

Hartman, Bob (Baseball Player)
Milwaukee Braves
2580 18th St Apt 1
Kenosha, WI 53140-4674, USA

Hartman, David
16-00 Rt. 208 Box 770
Fair Lawn, NJ 07410, USA

Hartman, George E (Architect)
107 Hesketh St
Chevy Chase, MD 20815-4222, USA

Hartman, J C (Baseball Player)
Kansas City Monarchs
3425 Rosedale St
Houston, TX 77004-6312, USA

Hartman, Kevin (Soccer Player)
Los Angeles Galaxy
1010 Rose Bowl Dr
Pasadena, CA 91103, USA

Hartman, William C (Bill) Jr (Football Player)
Washington Redskins
999 Hood Rd NE Apt 282
Marietta, GA 30068-2273, USA

Hartman, William K (Bill) (Misc)
Planetary Science Institute
1700 E Fort Lowell Rd Ste 106
Tucson, AZ 85719-2395, USA

Hartmann, Frederick W (Editor)
Florida Times-Union
1 Riverside Ave
Editorial Dept
Jacksonville, FL 32202-4904, USA

Hartmann, Robert T (Government Official)
4129 Estate La Grande Princess # C
Christiansted, VI 00820-4280, USA

Hartnett, Josh (Actor)
c/o Kevin Huvane *Creative Artists Agency LCC (CAA-LA)*
2000 Avenue Of The Stars
Los Angeles, CA 90067-4700, USA

Hartog, Jan de (Writer)
Andrew Nurnberg Assoc
45/47 Clerkenwell Green
London EC1R 0HT, UNITED KINGDOM (UK)

Harts, Greg (Baseball Player)
New York Mets
829 Humphries St SW
Atlanta, GA 30310-2165, USA

Hartsfield, Henry W
422 Willow Vista Dr
Seabrook, TX 77586-6020, USA

Hartsfield, Roy (Baseball Player)
Boston Red Sox
PO Box 236
East Ellijay, GA 30539-0004, USA

Hartshorn, Lawrence (Football Player)
Chicago Cardinals
PO Box 1542
Cedar Ridge, CA 95924-1542, USA

Hartsock, Jeffrey (Baseball Player)
Chicago Cubs
1720 Swannnoa Dr
Greensboro, NC 27410, USA

Hartung, Clint (Baseball Player)
New York Giants
1018 E Fulton St
Sinton, TX 78387-2715, USA

Hartung, James (Gymnast)
3621 Portia St
Lincoln, NE 68521-1782, USA

Hartwell, Edgerton (Football Player)
Baltimore Ravens
2723 Carla Ave
North Las Vegas, NV 89030-4621, USA

Hartwell, Leland H (Lee) (Nobel Prize Laureate)
Hutchinson Cancer Research Center
PO Box 19024
Seattle, WA 98109-1024, USA

Hartzell, Paul (Baseball Player)
California Angels
PO Box 2860
Hailey, ID 83333-2860, USA

Hartzog, George B Jr (Government Official)
1643 Chain Bridge Rd
McLean, VA 22101-4329, USA

Haruf, Kent (Writer)
Southern Illinois University
English Dept
Carbondale, IL 62901, USA

Harvey, Anthony (Director)
Arthur Greene
101 Park Ave Rm 2607
New York, NY 10178-2602, USA

Harvey, Bryan (Baseball Player)
California Angels
1224 Astoria Pkwy
Catawba, NC 28609-8885, USA

Harvey, Claude (Football Player)
Houston Oilers
2918 Dragonwick Dr
Houston, TX 77045-4708, USA

Harvey, Cynthia T (Ballerina)
American Ballet Theater
890 Broadway
New York, NY 10003-1278, USA

Harvey, David R (Business Person)
Sigme-Aldrich Corp
3050 Spruce St
Saint Louis, MO 63103-2530, USA

Harvey, Don
6310 San Vicente Blvd Ste 520
Los Angeles, CA 90048-5421, USA

Harvey, Donnell (Basketball Player)
Orlando Magic
8701 Maitland Summit Blvd
Waterhouse Center
Orlando, FL 32810-5915, USA

Harvey, Fred
397 Parkhurst Dr
Fredericton, NB E3B 2K2, CANADA

Harvey, H Douglas (Doug) (Baseball Player)
32398 River Island Dr
Springville, CA 93265-9632, USA

Harvey, Harry (Educator, Horse Racer)
34 Deep Hollow Ln N
Columbus, NJ 08022-1018, USA

Harvey, James B (Football Player)
Oakland Raiders
3685 Clairice Cv
Memphis, TN 38133-0979, USA

Harvey, Jan
169 Queensgate #8A
London, ENGLAND SW7 5EH, UNITED KINGDOM (UK)

Harvey, Jonathan D (Composer)
Faber Music
3 Queen Square
London WC1N 3AU, UNITED KINGDOM (UK)

Harvey, Ken (Football Player)
Phoenix Cardinals
11600 Great Falls Way
Great Falls, VA 22066-1150, USA

Harvey, Nancy (Golfer)
7006 E Jensen St Unit 62
Mesa, AZ 85207-2833, USA

Harvey, Paul (Correspondent)
Paulyanne
1035 Park Ave
River Forest, IL 60305-1307, USA

Harvey, PJ (Musician)
c/o Staff Member *Creative Artists Agency LCC (CAA-LA)*
2000 Avenue Of The Stars
Los Angeles, CA 90067-4700, USA

Harvey, Polly Jean (P J) (Music Group, Musician, Songwriter, Writer)
Helter Skelter
Plaza 535 Kings Road
London SW10 0S, UNITED KINGDOM (UK)

Harvey, Steve (Actor, Comedian)
c/o Sean Perry *Endeavor Agency LLC (LA)*
9601 Wilshire Blvd Fl 3
Beverly Hills, CA 90210-5204, USA

Harvey, Terry (Baseball Player)
US Olympic Team
215 Annandale Dr
Cary, NC 27511-6503, USA

Harvick, Kevin (Race Car Driver)
Richard Childress Racing
PO Box 1189
Industrial Dr
Welcome, NC 27374-1189, USA

Harville, Chad (Baseball Player)
Oakland A's
261 Farmington Rd
Savannah, TN 38372-5635, USA

Harwell, Ernie (Baseball Player, Sportscaster)
Detroit Tigers
41110 Fox Run Apt 211
Novi, MI 48377-4880, USA

Harwell, Steve (Music Group)
Creative Artists Agency
9830 Wilshire Blvd
Beverly Hills, CA 90212-1804, USA

Hary, Armin (Athlete, Track Athlete)
Schloss
Diessen/Ammersee 86911, GERMANY

Hase, Dagmar (Swimmer)
Niederndodeleber Str 14
Magdeburg 29110, GERMANY

Hasegawa, Shigetoshi (Baseball Player)
Anaheim Angels
110 Newport Center Dr Ste 200
Newport Beach, CA 92660-6973, USA

Hasek, Dominik (Hockey Player)
Ottawa Senators
1000 Palladium Dr
Kanata, ON K2V 1A4, CANADA

Haselkorn, Robert (Scientist)
5834 S Stony Island Ave
Chicago, IL 60637-2060, USA

Haselman, Bill (Baseball Player)
Texas Rangers
14501 SE 85th St
Newcastle, WA 98059-9218, USA

Haselrig, Carlton (Football Player)
Pittsburgh Steelers
386 William Penn Ave
Johnstown, PA 15901-1253, USA

Haseltine, Dan (Music Group)
Flood Bumstead McCarthy
1700 Hayes St Ste 304
Nashville, TN 37203-3014, USA

Hasen, Irvin H (Cartoonist)
68 E 79th St
New York, NY 10075-0224, USA

Hasenmayer, Don (Baseball Player)
Philadelphia Phillies
721 Golf Dr
Warrington, PA 18976-2053, USA

Hasenohrl, George (Football Player)
New York Giants
14836 Corridon Ave
Maple Heights, OH 44137-3241, USA

Hash, Herb (Baseball Player)
Boston Red Sox
PO Box 191
Culpeper, VA 22701-0191, USA

Hasham, Josephine (Baseball Player)
575 SW 11th St
Miami, FL 33129-1034, USA

Haskell, Colleen Marie (Actor)
c/o Andy Cohen *International Creative Management (ICM-LA)*
10250 Constellation Blvd
Los Angeles, CA 90067-6200, USA

Haskell, Jimmie
11800 Laughton Way
Northridge, CA 91326-1313, USA

Haskell, Peter (Actor)
19924 Acre St
Northridge, CA 91324-3201, USA

Haskins, Clem (Basketball Player, Coach)
2632 Roberts Rd
Campbellsville, KY 42718, USA

Haskins, Dennis (Actor)
c/o Staff Member *Tisherman Agency Inc*
6767 Forest Lawn Dr Ste 101
Los Angeles, CA 90068-1050, USA

Haskins, Don (Basketball Player)
Chicago Bulls
1901 W Madison St
United Center
Chicago, IL 60612-2459, USA

Haskins, Jon (Football Player)
San Diego Chargers
4055 Higel Ave
Sarasota, FL 34242-1138, USA

Haskins, Michael D (Admiral)
Inspector General Hqusn
Pentagon
Washington, DC 20350-0001, USA

Haskins, Samuel J (Sam) (Photographer)
PO Box 59
Wimbledon
London SW19, UNITED KINGDOM (UK)

Hasler, Otmar (Prime Minister)
Primier's Office
Regierungsgebaude
Vaduz 9490, LIECHTENSTEIN

Haslett, James D (Jim) (Coach, Football Player)
Buffalo Bills
118 Crandon Dr
Saint Louis, MO 63105-3606, USA

Hasluck, Paul M C (Government Official)
2 Adams Road
Dalkeith, WA 6009, AUSTRALIA

Hass, Robert (Writer)
University of California
English Dept
Berkeley, CA 94720-0001, USA

Hassan, Fred (Business Person)
Schering-Plough Corp
2000 Galloping Hill Rd
Kenilworth, NJ 07033-1328, USA

Hassan, Kamal (Actor, Director, Filmmaker, Producer)
63 Luz Church Road
Chennai, TN 600 004, INDIA

Hassan Ibn Talal (Prince)
Deputy King's Office
Royal Palace
Amman, JORDAN

Hassel, Gerald L (Financier)
Bank of New York
1 Wall St
New York, NY 10286-0001, USA

Hasselbeck, Donald W (Don) (Football Player)
New England Patriots
38 Noon Hill Ave
Norfolk, MA 02056-1145, USA

Hasselbeck, Elisabeth (Reality TV Star, Television Host)
c/o Staff Member *View, The*
320 W 66th St
New York, NY 10023-6304, USA

Hasselbeck, Matt (Football Player)
c/o Staff Member *Seattle Seahawks*
11220 NE 53rd St
Kirkland, WA 98033-7595, USA

Hasselhoff, David (Actor, Music Group)
c/o Joel Dean *TalentWorks (LA)*
3500 W Olive Ave Ste 1400
Burbank, CA 91505-5512, USA

Hasselmo, Nils (Educator)
Assn of American Universities
1200 New York Ave NW Ste 550
Washington, DC 20005-6122, USA

Hassenfeld, Alan G (Business Person)
Hasbro Inc
1027 Newport Ave
Pawtucket, RI 02861-2500, USA

Hassett, Marilyn (Actor)
8905 Rosewood Ave
West Hollywood, CA 90048-2409, USA

Hassey, Ron (Baseball Player)
Cleveland Indians
6330 N Calle Tregua Serena
Tucson, AZ 85750-0951, USA

Hassler, Andy (Baseball Player)
California Angels
PO Box 15932
Phoenix, AZ 85060-5932, USA

Hasson, Gene (Baseball Player)
Philadelphia Athletics
535 E Bonita Ave
San Dimas, CA 91773-3124, USA

Hasson, Maurice (Musician)
18 West Heath Court
North End Road
London NW11, UNITED KINGDOM (UK)

Hast, Adele (Editor)
Newberry Library
2905 N Harding Ave
Chicago, IL 60618-7215, USA

Hastert, Speaker Dennis
2438 Rayburn Hob
Washington, DC 20515-3518, USA

Hastings, Andre (Football Player)
Pittsburgh Steelers
700 N Dobson Rd Unit 37
Chandler, AZ 85224-6940, USA

Hastings, Barry G (Financier)
Northern Trust Corp
50 S La Salle St
Chicago, IL 60603-1003, USA

Hastings, Bob
620 S Sparks St
Burbank, CA 91506-3034, USA

Hastings, Don (Actor)
524 W 57th St # 5330
New York, NY 10019-2930, USA

Haston, Kirk (Basketball Player)
PO Box 186
Linden, TN 37096-0186, USA

Hasty, James (Football Player)
New York Jets
8212 127th Ave SE
Newcastle, WA 98056-9146, USA

Hatalsky, Morris (Golfer)
201 S Ocean Grande Dr # Ph5
Ponte Vedra, FL 32082-6515, USA

Hatch, Harold A (General)
8655 White Beech Way
Vienna, VA 22182-5056, USA

Hatch, Henry J (General)
2715 Silkwood Ct
Oakton, VA 22124-1455, USA

Hatch, Monroe W Jr (General)
8210 Thomas Ashleigh Ln
Clifton, VA 20124-2245, USA

Hatch, Orrin (Senator)
2127 Galloping Way
Vienna, VA 22181-2934, USA

Hatch, Richard (Actor)
MerlinQuest Entertainment
PO Box 461519
Los Angeles, CA 90046-9519, USA

Hatch, Richard (Actor, Reality TV Star)
c/o Alan David *Alan David Management*
8840 Wilshire Blvd
Beverly Hills, CA 90211-2606, USA

Hatchell, Sylvia (Basketball Player)
University of North Carolina
Athletic Dept
Chapell Hill, NC 27515, USA

Hatcher, Billy (Baseball Player)
Chicago Cubs
5096 Rollman Estates Dr
Cincinnati, OH 45236-1448, USA

Hatcher, Chris (Baseball Player)
Kansas City Royals
1406 250th St
Audubon, IA 50025-7356, USA

Hatcher, Kevin (Hockey Player)
1225 S Water St
Marine City, MI 48039-3600, USA

Hatcher, Mickey (Baseball Player)
Los Angeles Dodgers
726 E Appaloosa Rd
Gilbert, AZ 85296-2906, USA

Hatcher, R Dale (Football Player)
Los Angeles Rams
906 White Plains Rd
Gaffney, SC 29340-5473, USA

Hatcher, Teri (Actor)
c/o Staff Member *Desperate Housewives*
2300 W Riverside Dr
Abc Television
Burbank, CA 91506-2976, USA

Hatchett, Derrick (Football Player)
Baltimore Colts
504 W 24th St # 84
Austin, TX 78705-5234, USA

Hatchett, Joseph W (Judge)
US Court of Appeals
810 Lewis State Bank Building
Tallahassee, FL 32302, USA

Hatfield, Juliana (Music Group, Songwriter, Writer)
Fort Apache Mgmt
1 Camp St
Cambridge, MA 02140-1103, USA

Hatfield, Mark (Ex-Governor, Ex-Senator, Governor, Philanthropist, Politician, Senator)
Natl Institute of Health
6100 Executive Blvd #3C01
Msc 7511
Bethesda, MD 20892-0001, USA

Hatfield, Mark O (Governor, Senator)
17400 Holy Names Dr # E306
Lake Oswego, OR 97034-5187, USA

Hathaway, Amy
4526 Wilshire Blvd
Los Angeles, CA 90010-3801, USA

Hathaway, Anne (Actor)
c/o Suzan Bymel *Management 360*
9111 Wilshire Blvd
Beverly Hills, CA 90210-5508, USA

Hathaway, Hilly (Baseball Player)
California Angels
3140 Southern Hills Cir W
Jacksonville, FL 32225-5762, USA

Hathaway, Noah (Actor)
5150 Choppers & Hot Rods
228 Grand Ave
Perryville, MO 63775-1806, USA

Hathaway, Ray (Baseball Player)
Brooklyn Dodgers
25 Leisure Mountain Rd
Asheville, NC 28804-1147, USA

Hathaway, William D (Senator)
Federal Maritime Commission
800 N Capitol St NW
Washington, DC 20002-4244, USA

Hathcock, Dave (Football Player)
Green Bay Packers
417 Rolling Mill Rd
Old Hickory, TN 37138-2137, USA

Hatori, Miho (Music Group)
Billions Corp
833 W Chicago Ave Ste 101
Chicago, IL 60622-8408, USA

Hatosy, Shawn (Actor)
853 7th Ave Apt 9A
New York, NY 10019-5222, USA

Hatsopoulos, George N (Business Person, Engineer)
Thermo Electron Corp
81 Wyman St
PO Box 9046
Waltham, MA 02451-1271, USA

Hatteberg, Scott (Baseball Player)
Boston Red Sox
802 Berg Ct NW
Gig Harbor, WA 98335-7709, USA

Hatten, Tom (Actor)
1759 Sunset Plaza Dr
Los Angeles, CA 90069-1311, USA

Hattersley, Roy S G (Government Official)
House of Lords
Westminster
London SW1A 0PW, UNITED KINGDOM (UK)

Hattestad, Stine Lise (Skier)
Sundlia 1B
Nesoya 1315, NORWAY

Hatton, Grady (Baseball Player)
Cincinnati Reds
PO Box 97
Warren, TX 77664-0097, USA

Hatton, Vernon (Basketball Player)
PO Box 8405
Lexington, KY 40533-8405, USA

Hatzell-Volkert, Beverly (Baseball Player)
410 W High St
Hicksville, OH 43526-1036, USA

Hau, Lene Vestergaard (Physicist)
Harvard University
Applied Physics Dept
Cambridge, MA 01238, USA

Hauck, Frederick H (Rick) (Astronaut)
2 Redwood Ln
Falmouth, ME 04105-1368, USA

Hauck, Silke 16
Mt. Bundt Verlag K2
Mannheim 69159, GERMANY

Hauck, Tim (Football Player)
New England Patriots
PO Box 984
Marion, MT 59925-0984, USA

Hauer, Rutger (Actor)
1601 Cloverfield Blvd Ste 5000N
Santa Monica, CA 90404-4085, USA

Hauerwas, Stanley (Misc, Religious Leader)
Duke University
Divinity School
Durham, NC 27706, USA

Haughey, Chris (Baseball Player)
Brooklyn Dodgers
4141 Stevenson Blvd Apt 202
Fremont, CA 94538-2717, USA

Haught, Gary (Baseball Player)
Oakland A's
16445 Lynn St
Choctaw, OK 73020-7926, USA

Hauk, A Andrew (Judge, Skier)
US Court House
312 N Spring St Ste G33
Los Angeles, CA 90012-4711, USA

Haun, Darla
300 S Raymond Ave Ste 11
Pasadena, CA 91105-2639, USA

Haun, Lindsey (Actor)
c/o Staff Member *Kazarian/Spencer & Assoc (LA)*
11969 Ventura Blvd
Box 7409 Fl 3
Studio City, CA 91604-2630, USA

Hauptman, Herbert A (Nobel Prize Laureate)
121 Woodbury Dr
Buffalo, NY 14226-3536, USA

Haus, Herman A (Engineer, Scientist)
38 Jeffrey Ter
Lexington, MA 02420, USA

Hauser, Art (Football Player)
Los Angeles Rams
2816 Walsh Rd
Cincinnati, OH 45208-3426, USA

Hauser, Cole (Actor)
c/o David Guillod *United Talent Agency (UTA)*
9560 Wilshire Blvd Ste 500
Beverly Hills, CA 90212-2401, USA

Hauser, Erich (Artist)
Saline 36
Rottweil 78628, GERMANY

Hauser, Tim (Music Group)
c/o Staff Member *The Merlin Company*
16574 Bosque Dr
Encino, CA 91436-3747, USA

Hauser, Wings (Actor)
9450 Chivers Ave
Sun Valley, CA 91352-2654, USA

Hausman, Jerry A (Economist)
Massachussetts Institute of Technology
Economics Dept
Cambridge, MA 02139, USA

Hausman, Tom (Baseball Player)
Milwaukee Brewers
3165 Westfield Cir
Las Vegas, NV 89121-3332, USA

Hausmann, George (Baseball Player)
New York Giants
339 Fm 474
Boerne, TX 78006-7809, USA

Hauss, Lenard M (Len) (Football Player)
Washington Redskins
181 E Brazell St
Reidsville, GA 30453, USA

Havel, Vaclav (President, Writer)
Kancelar Prezidenta Republiky
Hradecek
Prague 119 08, CZECH REPUBLIC

Havelange, Jean M F G (Joao) (Soccer Player)
Ave Rio Branco 89B
Conj 602 Centro
Rio de Janiero 20040-004, BRAZIL

Havelange, JoaoRua
Prudente de Marosa 1700 Apto. 1001
Rio de Janeiro BR 20420-0, BRAZIL

Havelid, Niclas (Hockey Player)
Anaheim Mighty Ducks
2000 E Gene Autry Way
Anaheim, CA 92806-6143, USA

Haven, Annette
PO Box 1244
Sausalito, CA 94966-1244, USA

Haven, James (Actor)
c/o Staff Member *Saffron Management*
9171 Wilshire Blvd Ste 441
Beverly Hills, CA 90210-5516, USA

Havens, Brad (Baseball Player)
Minnesota Twins
3227 Eden Trl
Brighton, MI 48114-9185, USA

Havens, Frank B (Athlete)
PO Box 55
Harborton, VA 23389-0055, USA

Havens, Richie (Music Group, Musician, Songwriter, Writer)
177 Woodland Ave
Westwood, NJ 07675-3218, USA

Haverdink, Kevin (Football Player)
New Orleans Saints
15844 Prairie Ronde Rd
Schoolcraft, MI 49087-9124, USA

Havers, Nigel (Actor)
Michael Whitehall
125 Gloucester Road
London SW7 4TE, UNITED KINGDOM
(UK)

Havig, Dennis (Football Player)
Atlanta Falcons
5964 Old Stilesboro Rd NW
Acworth, GA 30101-4304, USA

Havin, Alexa (Actor)
c/o Staff Member *Mattie Management*
1438 N Gower St Ste 57
Los Angeles, CA 90028-8358, USA

Havins, Alexa (Actor)
c/o Noreen Konkle *AKA Talent Agency*
6310 San Vicente Blvd Ste 200
Los Angeles, CA 90048-5488, USA

Havlat, Martin (Hockey Player)
Ottawa Senators
1000 Palladium Dr
Kanata, ON K2V 1A4, CANADA

Havlish, Jean (Baseball Player)
PO Box 122
Rockville, MN 56369-0122, USA

Havoc, June (Actor)
405 Old Long Ridge Rd
Stamford, CT 06903-1133, USA

Havrilak, Sam (Football Player)
Baltimore Colts
1 Trojan Horse Dr
Phoenix, MD 21131-1345, USA

Havrilla, Jo Ann
9751 Old Route 99
Mc Kean, PA 16426, USA

Hawass, Zahi (Writer)
Supreme Council of Antiquities
3 Al-Adel Bakr St
Zamalek, Cairo, EGYPT

Hawblitzel, Ryan (Baseball Player)
Colorado Rockies
7972 S Four Oaks Pt
Floral City, FL 34436-2623, USA

Hawerchuck, Dale (Hockey Player)
Grand Farms
95404 7th Line EHS
RR 5
Orangeville, ON L9W 2Z2, CANADA

Hawes, Roy (Baseball Player)
Washington Senators
PO Box 854
Ringgold, GA 30736-0854, USA

Hawk, John D (War Hero)
3243 Solie Ave
Bremerton, WA 98310-2821, USA

Hawk, Tony (Actor, Athlete, Skateboarder)
c/o Staff Member *900 Films*
1611A S Melrose Dr # 362
Vista, CA 92081-5471, USA

Hawke, Bob
GPO Box 36
Sydney NSW 2001, AUSTRALIA

Hawke, Ethan (Actor)
c/o Erwin Stoff *3 Arts Entertainment Inc*
9460 Wilshire Blvd Fl 7
Beverly Hills, CA 90212-2713, USA

Hawke, Jason (Adult Film Star)
c/o Staff Member *Diva Central Inc*
7510 W Sunset Blvd Ste 1445
Los Angeles, CA 90046-3408, USA

Hawkes, Christopher (Archaeologist)
19 Walton St
Oxford OX1 2HQ, UNITED KINGDOM
(UK)

Hawkes, John (Artist)
c/o Staff Member *Rigberg-Rugolo Entertainment*
1180 S Beverly Dr Ste 601
Los Angeles, CA 90035-1158, USA

Hawking, Stephen (Physicist)
University of Cambridge
Applied Math Dept
Cambridge CB3 9EW, UNITED
KINGDOM (UK)

Hawkins, Alex (Football Player)
Baltimore Colts
215 Bonanza Rd
Denmark, SC 29042-9311, USA

Hawkins, Andy (Baseball Player)
San Diego Padres
PO Box 3783 Attn Coaching Staff
Sawannah Sand Gnats
Savannah, GA 31414-3783, USA

Hawkins, Artrell (Football Player)
Cincinnati Bengals
12166 Peak Dr
Cincinnati, OH 45246-1400, USA

Hawkins, Barbara (Music Group)
Superstars Unlimited
PO Box 371371
Las Vegas, NV 89137-1371, USA

Hawkins, Benjamin C (Ben) (Football Player)
Philadelphia Eagles
104 Deforest St
Roslindale, MA 02131-4920, USA

Hawkins, Bill (Football Player)
Los Angeles Rams
19183 SE Jupiter River Dr
Jupiter, FL 33458-1023, USA

Hawkins, Brad
47 Music Sq E
Nashville, TN 37203-4324, USA

Hawkins, Cornelius (Connie) (Basketball Player)
Phoenix Suns
201 E Jefferson St
Phoenix, AZ 85004-2412, USA

Hawkins, Courtney (Football Player)
Tampa Bay Buccaneers
8305 Gale Rd
Goodrich, MI 48438-9436, USA

Hawkins, Dale (Music Group, Musician, Songwriter, Writer)
4618 John F Kennedy Blvd # 107
North Little Rock, AR 72116-7311, USA

Hawkins, Dan (Musician)
c/o Sue Whitehouse *Whitehouse Management*
PO Box 43829
London NW6 3PJ, UNITED KINGDOM
(UK)

Hawkins, Edwin (Music Group)
PAZ Entertainment
2041 Locust St
Philadelphia, PA 19103-5629, USA

Hawkins, Frank (Football Player)
Oakland Raiders
2300 Alta Dr
Las Vegas, NV 89107-4616, USA

Hawkins, Hersey R Jr (Basketball Player)
New Orleans Hornets
1250 Poydras St # 19
New Orleans Arena
New Orleans, LA 70113-1804, USA

Hawkins, Jennifer (Actor, Beauty Pageant Winner)
c/o Staff Member *Miss Universe Organization, The*
1370 Avenue Of The Americas Fl 16
New York, NY 10019-4602, USA

Hawkins, Justin (Musician)
c/o Sue Whitehouse *Whitehouse Management*
PO Box 43829
London NW6 3PJ, UNITED KINGDOM
(UK)

Hawkins, Latroy (Baseball Player)
Minnesota Twins
9802 Honeysuckie Dr
Frisco, TX 75035, USA

Hawkins, Michael Daly (Judge)
US Court of Appeals
230 N 1st
Phoenix, AZ 85025, USA

Hawkins, Mike (Football Player)
New England Patriots
2320 Bordeaux Dr
Bay City, TX 77414-8512, USA

Hawkins, Paula (Senator)
1214 Park Ave N
Winter Park, FL 32789-2542, USA

Hawkins, Rip (Football Player)
Minnesota Vikings
100 Tower Carlile Rd
Devils Tower, WY 82714-8702, USA

Hawkins, Ronnie (Music Group)
Agency Group Ltd
59 Berkeley St
Toronto, ON M5A 2W5, CANADA

Hawkins, Rosa (Music Group)
Superstars Unlimited
PO Box 371371
Las Vegas, NV 89137-1371, USA

Hawkins, Rowena
PO Box 15277
Chattanooga, TN 37415-0277, USA

Hawkins, Sally (Actor)
c/o John Grant *Conway Van Gelder Ltd*
18-21 Jermyn St Fl 3
London SW1Y 6HP, UNITED KINGDOM
(UK)

Hawkins, Sophie B (Music Group, Musician, Songwriter, Writer)
Trumpet Swan Productions
520 Washington Blvd # 337
Marina Del Rey, CA 90292, USA

Hawkins, Tommy (Basketball Player)
1745 Manzanita Park Ave
Malibu, CA 90265-3013, USA

Hawkins, Wynn (Baseball Player)
Cleveland Indians
5326 Cottage Dr
Cortland, OH 44410-9521, USA

Hawkinson, Tim (Artist)
Ace Gallery
5514 Wilshire Blvd Ste 200
Los Angeles, CA 90036-3877, USA

Hawks, Steve (Artist)
Hadley House
1101 Hampshire Road S
Bloomington, MN 55438, USA

Hawksworth, John
24 Cottesmore Gardens #2
London, ENGLAND W8 5PR, UNITED
KINGDOM (UK)

Hawlata, Franz (Opera Singer)
I M G Artists
3 Burlington Lane
Chiswick
London W4 2TH, UNITED KINGDOM
(UK)

Hawley, Frank (Race Car Driver)
Frank Hawley Drag Racing School
County Road 225
Gainesville, FL 32609, USA

Hawley, Sandy (Jockey)
9625 Merrill Rd
Silverwood, MI 48760-9532, USA

Hawley, Steven A (Astronaut)
3929 Walnut Pond Dr
Houston, TX 77059-4014, USA

Hawn, Goldie (Actor)
c/o Alan Nevins *The Firm*
9465 Wilshire Blvd Fl 6
Beverly Hills, CA 90212-2605, USA

Haworth, Jill (Actor)
300 E 51st St
New York, NY 10022-7806, USA

Hawpe, David V (Editor)
Louisville Courier-Jounal
525 Broadway
Editorial Dept
Louisville, KY 40202, USA

Hawthorne, Greg (Football Player)
Pittsburgh Steelers
1428 E Jefferson Ave
Fort Worth, TX 76104-5714, USA

Hawthorne, Sir Nigel
Febdens Park Cold Christmas Lane
Thundridge Herts, ENGLAND SG12 QUE,
UNITED KINGDOM (UK)

Hax, Carolyn (Writer)
Washington Post
Editorial Dept
1150 15th St NW
Washington, DC 20071-0001, USA

Hay, Colin (Music Group)
TPA
PO Box 125
Round Corner, NSW 2158, AUSTRALIA

Hay, Louise L (Writer)
Hay House
PO Box 5100
Carlsbad, CA 92018-5100, USA

Hayareet, Haya
Herons Flight Marlow
Buckinghamshire, ENGLAND, UNITED
KINGDOM (UK)

Hayashi, Henry
5127 Klump Ave
N Hollywood, CA 91601-3775, USA

Hayashi, Shizuya (War Hero)
1331 Hoohui St
Pearl City, HI 96782, USA

Haydee, Marcia (Ballerina)
Stuttgart Ballet
Oberer Schlossgarten 6
Stuttgart 70173, GERMANY

Haydel, Hal (Baseball Player)
Minnesota Twins
304 Lynwood Dr
Houma, LA 70360-6228, USA

Hayden
431-67 Mowat Ave
Toronto, ON M6K 3, CANADA

Hayden, Aaron (Football Player)
San Diego Chargers
504 Stone Oaks Cv
Collierville, TN 38017-9124, USA

Hayden, Gene (Baseball Player)
Cincinnati Reds
424 W Locust St
Lodi, CA 95240-2018, USA

Hayden, J Michael (Mike) (Governor)
5809 Sagamore Ct
Lawrence, KS 66047-2071, USA

Hayden, Jim (Publisher)
Philadelphia Inquirer
400 N Broad St
Philadelphia, PA 19130-4099, USA

Hayden, Leo (Football Player)
Minnesota Vikings
7664 Hidden Hollow Dr
Columbus, OH 43235-1765, USA

Hayden, Linda (Actor)
Michael Ladkin Mgmt
1 Duchess St #1
London W1N 3DE, UNITED KINGDOM
(UK)

Hayden, Michael (Actor)
H W A Talent
3500 W Olive Ave Ste 1400
Burbank, CA 91505-5512, USA

Hayden, Michael V (General)
Director National Security Agency
Fort George C Meade, MD 20755, USA

Hayden, Neil Steven (Publisher)
1755 York Ave Apt 19A
New York, NY 10128-6870, USA

Hayden, Nicky (Motorcycle Racer)
Nicky Hayden Inc
419 Medina Rd
Medina, OH 44256-9619, USA

Hayden, Tom (Politician)
152 Wadsworth Ave
Santa Monica, CA 90405-3510, USA

Hayden, William G (General, Governor)
GPO Box 7829
Waterfront Place
Brisbane, QLD 4001, AUSTRALIA

Haydon, Jones Ann (Tennis Player)
85 Westerfield Road
Edglaoston
Birmingham 15, UNITED KINGDOM
(UK)

Haydon, Nicky (Motorcycle Racer)
c/o Steve Dicterow *International Racers,
Inc*
8001 Irvine Center Dr Ste 820
Irvine, CA 92618-2965, USA

Hayek, Julie
5645 Burning Tree Dr
La Canada, CA 91011-2861, USA

Hayek, Nicolas G (Designer)
SMH
Seevorstadt 6
Biel 2502, SWITZERLAND

Hayek, Salma (Actor, Model)
c/o Evelyn O'Neill *Management 360*
9111 Wilshire Blvd
Beverly Hills, CA 90210-5508, USA

Hayers, Sidney A (Director)
John Redway
5 Denmark St
London WC2H 8LP, UNITED KINGDOM
(UK)

Hayes, Amy (Model, Sportscaster)
641 N Hardin Hts
Harrodsburg, KY 40330-9234, USA

Hayes, Ben (Baseball Player)
Cincinnati Reds
3501 10th St NE
Saint Petersburg, FL 33704-1605, USA

Hayes, Bill (Actor, Music Group)
4528 Beck Ave
North Hollywood, CA 91602-1904, USA

Hayes, Bill (Baseball Player)
Chicago Cubs
4602 E Earll Dr
Phoenix, AZ 85018-6531, USA

Hayes, Billie (Football Player)
New Orleans Saints
2876 Avalon St
Riverside, CA 92509-2013, USA

Hayes, Bob
2717 King Cole Dr
Dallas, TX 75216-3430, USA

Hayes, Brian
60 Charlotte St.
London, ENGLAND W1P 1LS, UNITED
KINGDOM (UK)

Hayes, Charlie (Baseball Player)
San Francisco Giants
22503 Holly Creek Trl
Tomball, TX 77377-3656, USA

Hayes, Dade
c/o Daniel A (Dan) Strone *Trident Media
Group LLC*
41 Madison Ave Fl 36
New York, NY 10010-2257, USA

Hayes, Denis A (Geophysicist, Misc,
Physicist)
Green Seal
PO Box 18237
Washington, DC 20036-8237, USA

Hayes, Dennis C (Engineer, Inventor)
Hayes Microcomputer Products
945 E Paces Ferry Rd NE
Atlanta, GA 30326-1160, USA

Hayes, Elvin E (Basketball Player)
252 Piney Point Rd
Houston, TX 77024-7325, USA

Hayes, Erinn (Actor)
c/o David Sweeney *Sweeney
Management*
8755 Lookout Mountain Ave
Los Angeles, CA 90046-1861, USA

Hayes, Gemma (Musician)
c/o Staff Member *Paradigm (Monterey)*
509 Hartnell St
Monterey, CA 93940-2825, USA

Hayes, Isaac (Actor)
c/o Alan Saffron *Saffron Management*
9171 Wilshire Blvd Ste 441
Beverly Hills, CA 90210-5516, USA

Hayes, J P (Golfer)
740 Camino Real Ave
El Paso, TX 79922-2010, USA

Hayes, Jarvis (Basketball Player)
Washington Wizards
601 F St NW
Mcl Center
Washington, DC 20004-1605, USA

Hayes, Jonathan (Football Player)
Kansas City Chiefs
1231 Obannon Creek Ln
Loveland, OH 45140-6027, USA

Hayes, Louis S (Music Group, Musician)
Abby Hoffer
223 1/2 E 48th St
New York, NY 10017, USA

Hayes, Mark (Golfer)
1014 Saint Andrews Dr
Edmond, OK 73025-2645, USA

Hayes, Mercury (Football Player)
New Orleans Saints
138 W Whitney St
Houston, TX 77018-4515, USA

Hayes, Ray (Football Player)
New York Jets
5000 Laur Rd
North Branch, MI 48461-9782, USA

Hayes, Reggie (Actor)
c/o Staff Member *TalentWorks (LA)*
3500 W Olive Ave Ste 1400
Burbank, CA 91505-5512, USA

Hayes, Robert M (Activist)
National Coalition for the Homeless
105 E 22nd St
New York, NY 10010-5413, USA

Hayes, Sean (Actor)
c/o Staff Member *Hazy Mills Productions*
1258 N Highland Ave Ste 301
Los Angeles, CA 90038-1227, USA

Hayes, Susan Seaforth
4528 Beck Ave
N Hollywood, CA 91602-1904, USA

Hayes, Wade (Music Group)
Trey Turner Assoc
40 Music Sq W
Nashville, TN 37203-3206, USA

Hayes, Wendell (Football Player)
Dallas Cowboys
1935 E 30th St Apt 23
Oakland, CA 94606-3486, USA

Hayhoe, Bill (Football Player)
Green Bay Packers
5146 Santa Anita Dr
Sparks, NV 89436-0801, USA

Haylett, Alice (Baseball Player)
243 Pearl Ave
Lakeland, FL 33815-3737, USA

Hayman, David T (Actor, Director)
c/o Staff Member *International Creative
Management (ICM-UK)*
Oxford House
76 Oxford St
London W1N OAX, UNITED KINGDOM
(UK)

Hayman, Fred (Designer, Fashion
Designer)
6946 Wildlife Rd
Malibu, CA 90265-4309, USA

Hayman, Gorgon I (Cinematographer)
54 Lakes Lane
Beaconsfield
London HP9 2LB, UNITED KINGDOM
(UK)

Hayman, James (Director)
c/o Staff Member *Creative Artists Agency
LCC (CAA-LA)*
2000 Avenue Of The Stars
Los Angeles, CA 90067-4700, USA

Haymond, Alvin (Football Player)
Baltimore Colts
2857 Mantis Dr
San Jose, CA 95148-2136, USA

Haynes, Abner (Football Player)
Dallas Texans
2434 South Blvd
Dallas, TX 75215-2332, USA

Haynes, Al (Misc)
4410 S 182nd St
Seatac, WA 98188-4560, USA

Haynes, Betsy (Writer)
5973 Sandhill Cir
The Colony, TX 75056-3678, USA

Haynes, Haynes
7200 Sandering Ct.
Carlsbad, CA 92009, USA

Haynes, Heath (Baseball Player)
Montreal Expos
245 Springdale Ave
Wheeling, WV 26003, USA

Haynes, Jimmy (Baseball Player)
Baltimore Orioles
160 Pine Cir
Lagrange, GA 30241-2532, USA

Haynes, Louis (Football Player)
Kansas City Chiefs
PO Box 482
Desoto, TX 75123-0482, USA

Haynes, Mark (Football Player)
New York Giants
8101 E Dartmouth Ave Unit 11
Shaka Franklin Foundation
Denver, CO 80231-4258, USA

Haynes, Marques O (Basketball Player, Coach)
PO Box 191
Dallas, TX 75221, USA

Haynes, Michael (Football Player)
Atlanta Falcons
1580 Arbour Glenn Dr
Lawrenceville, GA 30043-7154, USA

Haynes, Michael (Football Player)
Chicago Bears
1000 Football Dr
Lake Forest, IL 60045-4829, USA

Haynes, Reggie (Football Player)
Washington Redskins
2324 Antiqua Ct
Reston, VA 20191-1706, USA

Haynes, Richard (Attorney, Attorney General, General)
2701 Fannin St
Houston, TX 77002-9217, USA

Haynes, Roy O (Musician)
Ted Kurland
173 Brighton Ave
Boston, MA 02134-2003, USA

Haynes, Todd (Director)
c/o Staff Member *Creative Artists Agency LCC (CAA-LA)*
2000 Avenue Of The Stars
Los Angeles, CA 90067-4700, USA

Haynes, Warren (Musician)
c/o Staff Member *Paradigm (Monterey)*
509 Hartnell St
Monterey, CA 93940-2825, USA

Haynes Jr, Cornell (Nelly) (Musician)
c/o Scott Vener *Schiff Company*
9465 Wilshire Blvd Ste 480
Beverly Hills, CA 90212-2603, USA

Haynesworth, Albert (Football Player)
Tennessee Titans
460 Great Circle Rd
Nashville, TN 37228-1404, USA

Haynie, Jim
10100 Santa Monica Blvd Ste 2500
Los Angeles, CA 90067-4116, USA

Hays, Harold (Football Player)
Dallas Cowboys
10410 Ravenswood Rd
Granbury, TX 76049-4543, USA

Hays, Robert (Actor)
919 Victoria Ave
Venice, CA 90291-3933, USA

Hays, Ronald J (Admiral)
869 Kamoi Pl
Honolulu, HI 96825-1318, USA

Hays, Thomas C (Business Person)
Fortune Brands Inc
300 Tower Pkwy
Lincolnshire, IL 60069-3665, USA

Haysbert, Dennis (Actor)
c/o Michael P Levine *Levine Management*
9028 W Sunset Blvd # Ph1
Los Angeles, CA 90069-1846, USA

Hayter, David (Writer)
c/o Staff Member *Kaplan/Perrone Entertainment*
10202 Washington Blvd
Astaire Bldg, Suite #3003
Culver City, CA 90232-3119, USA

Hayward, Brooke
305 Madison Ave # 956
New York, NY 10165-6201, USA

Hayward, Charles E (Publisher)
Little Brown Co
Rockefeller Center
Time-Life Building
New York, NY 10020, USA

Hayward, Justin (Musician)
The Threshold Record Co Ltd
53 High St
Cobham, Surrey KT11 3DP, UNITED KINGDOM (UK)

Hayward, Ray (Baseball Player)
San Diego Padres
5113 Deerhurst Dr
Norman, OK 73072-3882, USA

Hayward, Thomas B (Admiral)
2200 Ross Ave Ste 3800
Dallas, TX 75201-7967, USA

Haywood, Bill (Baseball Player)
Washington Senators
867 Villa Dr
North Myrtle Beach, SC 29582-2575, USA

Haywood, Spencer (Basketball Player)
46866 Mornington Rd
Canton, MI 48188-3016, USA

Hayworth, Red (Baseball Player)
St Louis Browns
1765 Westchester Dr Apt 128
High Point, NC 27262-7241, USA

Hayworth, Tracy (Football Player)
Detroit Lions
528 Knights Church Rd
Decherd, TN 37324, USA

Hazard, Geoffrey C Jr (Attorney, Attorney General, Educator, General)
200 W Willow Grove Ave
Philadelphia, PA 19118-3919, USA

Haze, Jonathan
3636 Woodhill Canyon Rd
Studio City, CA 91604-3658, USA

Hazelton, Major (Football Player)
Chicago Bears
6803 S Crandon Ave
Chicago, IL 60649-1210, USA

Hazen, Maya (Actor)
c/o Adam Griffin *The Collective*
9100 Wilshire Blvd # 700 W
Beverly Hills, CA 90212-3401, USA

Hazewood, Drungo (Baseball Player)
Baltimore Orioles
7991 Westboro Way
Sacramento, CA 95823-4934, USA

Haziza, Shlomi (Artist)
H Studio
8640 Tamarack Ave
Sun Valley, CA 91352-2504, USA

Hazzard, Johnny (Adult Film Star)
c/o Staff Member *Diva Central Inc*
7510 W Sunset Blvd Ste 1445
Los Angeles, CA 90046-3408, USA

Hazzard, Shirley (Writer)
200 E 66th St
New York, NY 10065-9175, USA

Head, Anthony (Actor)
Gordon & French
12-13 Poland St
London W1F 8QB, ENGLAND

Head, Anthony Stewart (Actor)
c/o Staff Member *Innovative Artists (LA)*
1505 10th St
Santa Monica, CA 90401-2805, USA

Head, James W (Scientist)
Brown University
Geological Sciences Dept
Providence, RI 02912-0001, USA

Head, John (Baseball Player)
Kansas City Monarchs
12677 Tremblewood Dr
Florissant, MO 63033-4729, USA

Head, Roy (Musician)
Texas Sounds Entertainment
PO Box 1644
Dickinson, TX 77539-1644, USA

Headden, Susan M (Journalist)
Indianapolis Star
307 N Pennsylvania St
Editorial Dept
Indianapolis, IN 46204-1899, USA

Headen, Andy (Football Player)
New York Giants
PO Box 821
Liberty, NC 27298-0821, USA

Headey, Lena (Actor)
c/o Jimmy Darmody *Creative Artists Agency LCC (CAA-LA)*
2000 Avenue Of The Stars
Los Angeles, CA 90067-4700, USA

Headley, Glenne
8942 Wilshire Blvd
Beverly Hills, CA 90211-1908, USA

Headley, Heather (Actor, Musician)
40 W 56th St Apt 5F
New York, NY 10019-3813, USA

Headley, Shari
11226 178th St
Jamaica, NY 11433-4118, USA

Headly, Glenne (Actor)
c/o Brian Mann *International Creative Management (ICM-LA)*
10250 Constellation Blvd
Los Angeles, CA 90067-6200, USA

Headrick, Sherrill (Football Player)
Dallas Texans
5621 S Schilder Dr
River Oaks, TX 76114-3216, USA

Heafner, Vance (Golfer)
6212 Godfrey Dr
Raleigh, NC 27612-6717, USA

Heald, Anthony (Actor)
Endeavor Talent Agency
9701 Wilshire Blvd Ste 1000
Beverly Hills, CA 90212-2010, USA

Healey, Danis W (Government Official)
Pingles Place
Alfriston
East Sussex BN26 5TT, UNITED KINGDOM (UK)

Healey, Derek E (Composer)
29 Stafford Road
Ruislip Gardens
Middx H4A 6PB, UNITED KINGDOM (UK)

Healey, James
415 S Spalding Dr Unit 306
Beverly Hills, CA 90212-4160, USA

Healey, John G (Misc)
Amnesty International USA
322 8th Ave
New York, NY 10001-8001, USA

Healy, Bernadine (Doctor)
430 17th St NW
Washington, DC 20006-5307, USA

Healy, Cornelius T (Misc)
Plate Die Engravers Union
228 S Swarthmore Ave
Ridley Park, PA 19078-1214, USA

Healy, Don (Football Player)
Chicago Bears
3427 Boca Ciega Dr
Naples, FL 34112-6809, USA

Healy, Fran (Baseball Player)
Kansas City Royals
1 Primrose Ln
Holyoke, MA 01040-1523, USA

Healy, Fran (Music Group)
Wildlife Entertainment
21 Heathmans Road
London SW6 4TJ, UNITED KINGDOM (UK)

Healy, Jane E (Journalist)
Orlando Sentinel
633 N Orange Ave
Editrial Dept
Orlando, FL 32801-1349, USA

Healy, Jeremiah (Writer)
PO Box 442
Kents Hill, ME 04349-0442, USA

Healy, Mary (Actor)
8641 Robinson Ridge Dr
Las Vegas, NV 89117-5807, USA

Healy, Patricia (Actor)
Shelter Entertainment
9255 W Sunset Blvd Ste 1010
Los Angeles, CA 90069-3307, USA

Heames, Darin (Actor)
c/o Andrew Stawiarski *ADS Management*
269 S Beverly Dr # 441
Beverly Hills, CA 90212-3851, USA

Heaney, Gerald W (Judge)
US Court of Appeals
Federal Building
Duluth, MN 55802, USA

Heaney, Seamus
3 Queens Sq.
London, ENGLAND WC1N 3AU, UNITED KINGDOM (UK)

Heaney, Seamus J (Nobel Prize Laureate)
191 Strand Road
Dublin 4, IRELAND

Heap, Joseph (Football Player)
New York Giants
410 Laurelleaf Ln
Covington, LA 70433-7203, USA

Heap, Todd (Football Player)
Baltimore Ravens
10 Falling Waters Ct
Reisterstown, MD 21136-5659, USA

Heard, G Alexander (Educator, Politician, Scientist)
2100 Golf Club Ln
Nashville, TN 37215-1224, USA

Heard, Herman Jr (Football Player)
Kansas City Chiefs
5251 Grey Swallow St
Brighton, CO 80601-8748, USA

Heard, Jerry (Golfer)
293 Talawah Rd
Purvis, MS 39475-5047, USA

Heard, John (Actor)
853 7th Ave Apt 9A
New York, NY 10019-5222, USA

Hearn, Chick
4362 Avocado Ave
Yorba Linda, CA 92886-2506, USA

Hearn, Ed (Baseball Player)
New York Mets
5737 Theden St
Shawnee, KS 66218-9199, USA

Hearn, George (Actor, Music Group)
211 S Beverly Dr Ste 211
Beverly Hills, CA 90212-3866, USA

Hearn, J Woodrow (Religious Leader)
United Methodist Church
PO Box 320
Nashville, TN 37202-0320, USA

Hearn, Kevin (Musician)
Nettwerk Mgmt
8730 Wilshire Blvd # 304
Beverly Hills, CA 90211-2716, USA

Hearn, Thomas K Jr (Educator)
Wake Forest University
President's Office
Winston Salem, NC 27109, USA

Hearn, Tom (Golfer)
Links Mmg
5068 W Plano Pkwy Ste 256
Plano, TX 75093-4441, USA

Hearne, Bill (Music Group, Musician)
Class Act Entertainment
PO Box 160236
Nashville, TN 37216-0236, USA

Hearnes, Warren E (Governor)
118 N Main St
Charleston, MO 63834, USA

Hearns, Tommy (Boxer)
c/o Staff Member *The National Organization of Professional Athletes*
1806 Watermere Ln
Windermere, FL 34786-6121, USA

Hearron, Jeff (Baseball Player)
Toronto Blue Jays
322 Ivy Manor Dr NW
Marietta, GA 30064-5117, USA

Hearst, G Garrison (Football Player)
Phoenix Cardinals
3753 Augusta Hwy
Lincolnton, GA 30817-4402, USA

Hearst, Rick (Actor)
Stone Manners
6500 Wilshire Blvd Ste 550
Los Angeles, CA 90048-4950, USA

Hearst, Victoria
865 Comstock Ave
Los Angeles, CA 90024-2572, USA

Hearst Shaw, Patricia C (Patty) (Actor)
110 5th St
San Francisco, CA 94103-2918, USA

Heart (Musician)
c/o Jeff Frasco *Creative Artists Agency LCC (CAA-LA)*
2000 Avenue Of The Stars
Los Angeles, CA 90067-4700, USA

Heaslip, Mark (Hockey Player)
11 Leland Ct
Chevy Chase, MD 20815-4906, USA

Heat, Mike (Baseball Player)
New York Yankees
1107 Sweet Breeze Dr
Valrico, FL 33594-4085, USA

Heater, Don (Football Player)
St Louis Cardinals
8704 Manchester Ave
Kansas City, MO 64138-4167, USA

Heath, Albert (Tootie) (Music Group, Musician)
Ted Kurland
173 Brighton Ave
Boston, MA 02134-2003, USA

Heath, Bill (Baseball Player)
Chicago White Sox
1626 Lake Charlotte Ln
Richmond, TX 77469-7016, USA

Heath, James E (Jimmy) (Composer, Music Group, Musician)
Ted Kurland
173 Brighton Ave
Boston, MA 02134-2003, USA

Heath, Kelly (Baseball Player)
Kansas City Royals
2249 Portofino Pl Apt 2222
Palm Harbor, FL 34683-7740, USA

Heath, Leon (Football Player)
Washington Redskins
1319 Arizona Ave
Chickasha, OK 73018-6606, USA

Heath-Stubbs, John F A (Writer)
22 Artesian Road
London W2 5AR, UNITED KINGDOM (UK)

Heathcock, Clayton H (Misc)
5235 Alhambra Valley Rd
Martinez, CA 94553-9765, USA

Heathcock, Jeff (Baseball Player)
Houston Astros
24962 Calle Vecindad
Lake Forest, CA 92630-2105, USA

Heathcote, Jud (Basketball Player, Coach)
5418 S Quail Ridge Cir
Spokane, WA 99223-6391, USA

Heathcott, Mike (Baseball Player)
Chicago White Sox
711 E Thomas St
Arlington Heights, IL 60004-4921, USA

Heatherly, Eric (Actor)
c/o Staff Member *The Bobby Roberts Company Inc*
PO Box 1547
Goodlettsville, TN 37070-1547, USA

Heaton, Neal (Baseball Player)
Cleveland Indians
3 Nursery Ct
East Patchogue, NY 11772-6152, USA

Heaton, Patricia (Actor)
c/o Staff Member *FourBoys Films*
1037 N Laurel Ave # 19C
West Hollywood, CA 90046-6097, USA

Heatwave
6464 W Sunset Blvd Ste 1010
Hollywood, CA 90028-8012, USA

Heaverio, Dave (Baseball Player)
San Francisco Giants
3720 W Lakeshore Dr
Moses Lake, WA 98837-3003, USA

Heavy D (Artist, Music Group)
Soul On Soul
PO Box 1009
Pelham, NY 10803-8009, USA

Hebert, Bobby (Football Player)
New Orleans Saints
530 Avala Ct
Alpharetta, GA 30022-5576, USA

Hebert, Bud (Football Player)
New York Giants
PO Box 250342
Plano, TX 75025-0342, USA

Hebert, Johnny (Race Car Driver)
Team Lotus
Kettering Hamm Hall
Wymondham
Norfolk NR18 7HW, UNITED KINGDOM (UK)

Hebner, Rich (Baseball Player)
Pittsburgh Pirates
6 Tetreault Dr
Walpole, MA 02081-2224, USA

Hebron, Vaughn (Football Player)
Philadelphia Eagles
313 Melvin Ave
Baltimore, MD 21228-3109, USA

Hebson, Bryan (Baseball Player)
Montreal Expos
1151 Fairmont Ln
Auburn, AL 36830-2105, USA

Heche, Anne (Actor)
c/o Jason Weinberg *Untitled Entertainment (LA)*
331 N Maple Dr Fl 3
Beverly Hills, CA 90210-3827, USA

Hecht, Albie (Producer, Writer)
c/o Staff Member *Spike TV*
1515 Broadway
New York, NY 10036-8901, USA

Hecht, Duvall (Misc)
2910 W Garry Ave
Santa Ana, CA 92704-6510, USA

Hecht, Jessica (Actor)
c/o Staff Member *Innovative Artists (LA)*
1505 10th St
Santa Monica, CA 90401-2805, USA

Hecht-Herskowitz, Gina (Actor)
5930 Foothill Dr
Los Angeles, CA 90068-3524, USA

Hechter, Daniel (Designer, Fashion Designer)
4 Ave Ter Hoche
Paris 75008, FRANCE

Heck, Andy (Football Player)
Seattle Seahawks
1 Bullrush Ct
Stafford, VA 22554-8501, USA

Heck, Ralph (Football Player)
Philadelphia Eagles
5575 Howland Ct
Atlanta, GA 30338-2913, USA

Heck, Robert (Football Player)
Chicago Hornets
1939 Tarpon Rd
Naples, FL 34102-1565, USA

Hecker, Zvi (Architect)
19 Elzar St
Tel Aviv 65157, ISRAEL

Heckerling, Amy (Director, Producer)
1330 Schuyler Rd
Beverly Hills, CA 90210-2539, USA

Heckler, Margaret M (Secretary)
1401 N Oak St
Arlington, VA 22209-3699, USA

Heckman, James J (Nobel Prize Laureate)
4807 S Greenwood Ave
Chicago, IL 60615-1913, USA

Heckscher, August (Writer)
333 E 68th St
New York, NY 10065-5693, USA

Hector, Johnny (Football Player)
New York Jets
525 Caroline St
New Iberia, LA 70560-4913, USA

Hedaya, Dan (Actor)
Gersh Agency
232 N Canon Dr
Beverly Hills, CA 90210-5302, USA

Hedeman, Richard (Tuff) (Misc)
PO Box 224
Morgan Mill, TX 76465-0224, USA

Heder, Jon (Actor)
c/o Judy Wixon-Darmody *Mosaic Media Group*
24 Music Sq W Fl 1
Nashville, TN 37203-6661, USA

Hedford, Eric (Music Group, Musician)
Monqui Mgmt
PO Box 5908
Portland, OR 97228-5908, USA

Hedges, Clifton
10475 Crosspoint Blvd
Indianapolis, IN 46256-3386, USA

Hedges, Peter (Director, Writer)
c/o Michael Peretzian *Creative Artists Agency LCC (CAA-LA)*
2000 Avenue Of The Stars
Los Angeles, CA 90067-4700, USA

Hedican, Bret (Hockey Player)
2500 E Las Olas Blvd Apt 502
Fort Lauderdale, FL 33301-1585, USA

Hedison, Alexandra (Actor)
c/o Harley Neuman *Neuman & Associates CPA*
16255 Ventura Blvd Ste 920
Encino, CA 91436-2317, USA

Hedison, David (Actor)
c/o Staff Member *Young and the Restless, The*
7800 Beverly Blvd Ste 3305
Los Angeles, CA 90036-2112, USA

Hedlund, Garrett (Actor)
c/o Cynthia Pett-Dante *Brillstein-Grey Entertainment*
9150 Wilshire Blvd Ste 350
Beverly Hills, CA 90212-3453, USA

Hedlund, Mike (Baseball Player)
Cleveland Indians
2412 Klinger Rd
Arlington, TX 76016-1143, USA

Hedquist, Julien
c/o Staff Member *IMG Models*
304 Park Ave S Fl 12
New York, NY 10010-4301, USA

Hedren, Tippi (Actor)
6867 Soledad Canyon Rd
Acton, CA 93510-2221, USA

Hedrick, Jerry L (Misc)
25280 Cartsbad Ave
Davis, CA 95616, USA

Hedrick, Joan D (Writer)
Trinity College
300 Summit St
Women's Studies Program
Hartford, CT 06106-3186, USA

Hedrick, Larry
PO Box 749
Statesville, NC 28687-0749, USA

Heeger, Alan J (Nobel Prize Laureate)
1042 Las Alturas Rd
Santa Barbara, CA 93103-1608, USA

Heenan, Pat (Football Player)
Washington Redskins
10007 Raynor Rd
Silver Spring, MD 20901-2124, USA

Heep, Danny (Baseball Player)
Houston Astros
327 Teakwood Ln
San Antonio, TX 78216-6825, USA

Heera (Actor, Bollywood)
Nungambakkam
Chennai, TN 600034, INDIA

Heesters, Johannes
Heimgartenstr. 21
Starnberg D-82319, GERMANY

Heeter, Carrie (Inventor)
Michigan State Univesity
Communication Technology Lab
East Lansing, MI 48824, USA

Heffeman, Bert (Baseball Player)
Seattle Mariners
228 Brookville Ave
Islip, NY 11751-1710, USA

Heffernan, Dave (Football Player)
Tampa Bay Buccaneers
8101 SW 79th Ter
Miami, FL 33143, USA

Heffernan, Kevin (Comedian)
c/o Staff Member *United Talent Agency
(UTA)*
9560 Wilshire Blvd Ste 500
Beverly Hills, CA 90212-2401, USA

Heffner, Bob (Baseball Player)
Boston Red Sox
910 N 12th St
Allentown, PA 18102-1102, USA

Heffner, Kyle (Actor)
c/o Melanie Sharp-Snyder *Sharp Talent*
117 N Orlando Ave
Los Angeles, CA 90048-3403, USA

Heffron, John (Actor, Comedian)
c/o Peter Rosegarten *Conversation
Company*
1044 Northern Blvd Ste 304
Roslyn, NY 11576-1589, USA

Heffron, Richard T (Director)
c/o Staff Member *Shapiro-Lichtman Talent
Agency*
1333 Beverly Green Dr
Los Angeles, CA 90035-1018, USA

Heflin, Bronson (Baseball Player)
Philadelphia Phillies
108 Rivers Edge Ct
Nashville, TN 37214-2375, USA

Heflin, Vince (Football Player)
Miami Dolphins
5603 Regency Park Ct Apt 3
Suitland, MD 20746-3328, USA

Hefner, Christie (Publisher)
Playboy Enterprises
680 N Lake Shore Dr Ste 1500
Chicago, IL 60611-4455, USA

Hefner, Hugh (Producer, Publisher)
Playboy Mansion
10236 Charing Cross Rd
Los Angeles, CA 90024-1815, USA

Hefner, Larry (Football Player)
Green Bay Packers
1208 Arboretum Dr
Lewisville, NC 27023-8658, USA

Hefner, Lene
15127 Califa St
Van Nuys, CA 91411-3021, USA

Heft, Bob
4098 Green St
Saginaw, MI 48638-6618, USA

Heft, Robert (Bob) (Designer)
PO Box 20404
Saginaw, MI 48602-0404, USA

Hefti, Neal (Composer)
Encino Music
9454 Wilshire Blvd Ste 405
Beverly Hills, CA 90212-2907, USA

Hegan, Mike (Baseball Player)
New York Yankees
7 Wild Turkey Run
Hilton Head Island, SC 29926-1901, USA

Heger, Rene (Actor)
c/o Jerry Shandrew *Shandrew Public
Relations*
1050 S Stanley Ave
Los Angeles, CA 90019-6634, USA

Hegerland, Anita
1315 Nesoya
NORWAY

Heggtveit, Ann Hamilton (Skier)
General Delivery
Grand Isle, VT 05458-9999, USA

Hegman, Bob (Baseball Player)
Kansas City Royals
3529 NW Winding Woods Dr
Lees Summit, MO 64064-1879, USA

Hegman, Mike (Football Player)
Dallas Cowboys
2958 Suesand Dr
Memphis, TN 38128-5941, USA

Hegyes, Robert (Actor)
PO Box 1774
Venice, CA 90294-1774, USA

Hehn, Sascha
Postfach 100823
Munich D-80082, GERMANY

Heidei, James (Football Player)
St Louis Cardinals
1425 Wisteria Dr
Vicksburg, MS 39180-4756, USA

Heidelberger, Charles (Misc)
1495 Poppy Peak Dr
Pasadena, CA 91105-2705, USA

Heidemann, Jack (Baseball Player)
Cleveland Indians
1816 S Salida Del Sol Cir
Mesa, AZ 85202-5529, USA

Heiden, Beth
PO Box 110
Dollar Bay, MI 49922-0110, USA

Heiden, Eric (Misc, Speed Skater)
1219 Cottonwood Ln
Park City, UT 84098-7602, USA

Heiden, Steve (Football Player)
San Diego Chargers
30119 Aspen Rd
Rushford, MN 55971-5043, USA

Heidmann, Manfred
Borbecker Str. 237
Essen D-45355, GERMANY

Heidt Jr, Horace
4151 Witzel Dr
Sherman Oaks, CA 91423-4613, USA

Height, Dorothy I (Activist)
Duane Morris Heckscher
1667 K St NW
Washington, DC 20006-1608, USA

Heigl, Jennifer (Actor)
Writers & Artists
360 N Crescent Dr Bldg North
Beverly Hills, CA 90210-6818, USA

Heigl, Katherine (Actor, Model)
c/o Staff Member *Grey's Anatomy*
500 S Buena Vista St
Burbank, CA 91521-0001, USA

Heilbron, Lorna (Actor)
Brunskill
169 Queen's Gate
London SW7 5HE, UNITED KINGDOM
(UK)

Heilbroner, Robert L (Economist)
412 W End Ave Apt 3E
New York, NY 10024-5775, USA

Heilman, Aaron (Baseball Player)
New York Mets
702 Harbor Walk Dr
Fort Wayne, IN 46819-2623, USA

Heilmeier, George H (Inventor)
Telecordia Technologies
1 Telcordia Dr
Piscataway, NJ 08854-4151, USA

Heim-McDaniel, Kay (Baseball Player)
3390 143rd St W
Rosemount, MN 55068-4057, USA

Heimbold, Charles A Jr (Business Person)
Bristol-Myers Squibb
345 Park Ave Bsmt Lc3
New York, NY 10154-0019, USA

Heimburger, Craig (Football Player)
Green Bay Packers
311 Flagstone Dr
Belleville, IL 62221-5821, USA

Heimel, Cynthia (Writer)
Simon & Schuster
1230 Avenue Of The Americas
New York, NY 10020-1586, USA

Heimlich, Henry J (Doctor, Physicist)
2347 Bedford Ave # 1D
Cincinnati, OH 45208-2656, USA

Heimueller, Gorman (Baseball Player)
Oakland A's
2148 Glen Ave
Riverton, UT 84065-7079, USA

Heimuli, Lakei (Football Player)
Chicago Bears
1563 N 400 W
Bountiful, UT 84010-6727, USA

Heine, Jutta (Athlete, Track Athlete)
Blaue Muhle
Burglahr 57614, GERMANY

Heineman, Ken (Football Player)
Cleveland Browns
13012 Fairfield Oaks Rd
Saint Louis, MO 63141-8551, USA

Heinen, Mike (Golfer)
4518 E Meadow Ln
Lake Charles, LA 70605-5318, USA

Heinkel, Don (Baseball Player)
Detroit Tigers
22207 Nick Davis Rd
Athens, AL 35613-5806, USA

Heinle, Amelia (Actor)
c/o John Carrabino *John Carrabino
Management*
5900 Wilshire Blvd Ste 406
Los Angeles, CA 90036-5015, USA

Heinsohn, Thomas W (Tom) (Basketball
Player, Coach)
PO Box 422
Newton Upper Falls, MA 02464-0002,
USA

Heintzelman, Tom (Baseball Player)
St Louis Cardinals
602 E Wethersfield Rd
Scottsdale, AZ 85254, USA

Heinz, Bob (Football Player)
Miami Dolphins
1350 Delfino Way
Menlo Park, CA 94025-6024, USA

Heinz, W C (Sportscaster, Writer)
1150 Nichols Hill Rd
Dorset, VT 05251-9536, USA

Heinzer, Franz (Skier)
Lauenen
Rickenbach/Schwyz 6432,
SWITZERLAND

Heise, Bob (Baseball Player)
New York Mets
537 Live Oak Rd
Angels Camp, CA 95222, USA

Heiser, Roy (Baseball Player)
Washington Senators
1038 Grovehill Rd
Baltimore, MD 21227-3802, USA

Heiserman, Rick (Baseball Player)
St Louis Cardinals
17252 Adams St
Omaha, NE 68135-3078, USA

Heiss Jenkins, Carol (Figure Skater)
3183 Regency Pl
Westlake, OH 44145-6735, USA

Heist, Al (Baseball Player)
Chicago Cubs
PO Box 70
Cookson, OK 74427-0070, USA

Heitmeyer, Jayne
4450 W Lakeside Dr Ste 350
Burbank, CA 91505-4064, USA

Hejduk, Milan (Hockey Player)
8651 Sawgrass Dr
Lone Tree, CO 80124-8504, USA

Hekkers, George (Football Player)
Detroit Lions
431 W Main St
Waukesha, WI 53186-4612, USA

Held, Archie (Artist, Misc)
A New Leaf Garden
1286 Gilman St
Berkeley, CA 94706-2353, USA

Held, Carl
1817 Hillcrest Rd Apt 51
Los Angeles, CA 90068-3150, USA

Held, Franklin (Bud) (Athlete, Track Athlete)
13367 Caminito Mar Villa
Del Mar, CA 92014-3613, USA

Held, Mel (Baseball Player)
Baltimore Orioles
103 Hogan Ln
Bryan, OH 43506-9161, USA

Held, Paul (Football Player)
Pittsburgh Steelers
29055 Blue Moon Dr
Menifee, CA 92584-7302, USA

Held, Richard M (Doctor)
Massachusetts Institute of Technology
Psychology Dept
Cambridge, MA 02139, USA

Held, Woodie (Baseball Player)
New York Yankees
Big Diamond Ranch
Dubois, WY 82513, USA

Helde, Annette
8430 Santa Monica Blvd Ste 200
Los Angeles, CA 90069-4253, USA

Heldt, Mike (Football Player)
Indianapolis Colts
7908 Riverwood Blvd
Tampa, FL 33615-2033, USA

Helfand, Eric (Baseball Player)
Oakland A's
8679 Circle R Valley Ln
Escondido, CA 92026-5909, USA

Helfer, Ricki Tigert (Financier)
Federal Deposit Insurance
550 17th St NW
Washington, DC 20429-0002, USA

Helfer, Tricia (Actor)
c/o Steven Muller *Innovative Artists (LA)*
1505 10th St
Santa Monica, CA 90401-2805, USA

Helford, Bruce (Producer, Writer)
c/o Staff Member *United Talent Agency (UTA)*
9560 Wilshire Blvd Ste 500
Beverly Hills, CA 90212-2401, USA

Helgeland, Brian (Director)
c/o Robert Newman *International Creative Management (ICM-LA)*
10250 Constellation Blvd
Los Angeles, CA 90067-6200, USA

Helgenberger, Marg (Actor)
c/o Nancy Sanders *Sanders/Armstrong Management*
2120 Colorado Ave Ste 120
Santa Monica, CA 90404-3561, USA

Helix
1505 W. 2nd Ave. #200
Vancouver, BC V6H 3Y4, CANADA

Hellawell, Keith (Government Official, Lawyer)
Government Offices
Great George St
London SW1A 2AL, UNITED KINGDOM (UK)

Heller, Andre
Singerstr. 8
Vienna A-1010, AUSTRIA

Heller, Daniel M (Attorney, Attorney General, General)
14 NE 1st Ave
Israel Discount Bank Building
Miami, FL 33132-2431, USA

Heller, Jane (Writer)
1014 Ladera Ln
Santa Barbara, CA 93108-1630, USA

Heller, Jeffrey M (Business Person)
Electronic Data Systems
5400 Legacy Dr
Plano, TX 75024-3199, USA

Heller, John H (Scientist)
74 Horseshoe Rd
Wilton, CT 06897-3400, USA

Heller, Ron (Football Player)
San Francisco 49ers
3894 Nathan Rd
Santa Barbara, CA 93110-1579, USA

Hellerman, Fred (Music Group, Songwriter, Writer)
83 Good Hill Rd
Weston, CT 06883-2802, USA

Hellestrae, Dale (Football Player)
Buffalo Bills
11705 E Charter Oak Dr
Scottsdale, AZ 85259-2743, USA

Hellickson, Russell (Russ) (Wrestler)
6893 Lauren Pl
Columbus, OH 43235-2188, USA

Helling, Ricky A (Rick) (Baseball Player)
Texas Rangers
3672 Landings Dr
Excelsior, MN 55331-9709, USA

Hellion
18653 Ventura Blvd # 307
Tarzana, CA 91356-4103, USA

Helliwell, Robert A (Scientist)
2240 Page Mill Road
Palo Alto, CA 94304, USA

Hellman, Bonnie
1680 Vine St Ste 614
Hollywood, CA 90028-8833, USA

Hellman, Martin E (Inventor)
855 Serra St
Stanford, CA 94305, USA

Hellman, Monte (Director)
8588 Appian Way
Los Angeles, CA 90046-7729, USA

Hellmann, Martina (Athlete, Track Athlete)
Neue Leipziger Str 14
Leipzig 04205, GERMANY

Hellmuth, George F (Architect)
10111 Ingleside Dr
Saint Louis, MO 63124-1246, USA

Helluin, Francis (Football Player)
Cleveland Browns
3930 Southdown Mandalay Rd
Houma, LA 70360-3001, USA

Hellyer, Paul T (Government Official)
65 Harbour Square #506
Toronto, ON M5J 2L4, CANADA

Helm, Levon (Actor, Music Group, Musician)
160 Plochmann Ln
Woodstock, NY 12498-2007, USA

Helm, Peter
1480 S Wild Oaks Dr
Nixa, MO 65714-8269, USA

Helm, Val (Baseball Player)
Chicago White Sox
PO Box 423
Superior, NE 68978-0423, USA

Helmberger, Don V (Misc)
California Institute of Technology
Seismology Dept
Pasadena, CA 91125-0001, USA

Helmerich, Hans C (Business Person)
Helmerich & Payne Inc
Utica & 21st St
Tulsa, OK 74114, USA

Helmerich, Walter H III (Business Person)
Helmerich & Payne Inc
Utica & 21st St
Tulsa, OK 74114, USA

Helmerson, Frans (Music Group, Musician)
Columbia Artists Mgmt Inc
1790 Broadway Fl 6
New York, NY 10019-1412, USA

Helmly, James R (General)
Commander
US Army Reserves
Hqusa Pentagon
Washington, DC 20310-0001, USA

Helmond, Katherine (Actor)
c/o Jeff Witjas *Agency for the Performing Arts (APA-NY)*
888 7th Ave
New York, NY 10106-0001, USA

Helmreich, Ernst J M (Misc)
University of Wurzburg Biozentrum
Am Hubland
Wurzburg 97074, GERMANY

Helms, Edward (Ed) (Actor, Comedian)
c/o Peter Principato *Principato/Young Management*
9665 Wilshire Blvd Ste 500
Beverly Hills, CA 90212-2312, USA

Helms, Jesse (Senator)
403 Dirksen Bldg
Washington, DC 20510-0001, USA

Helms, L S (Financier)
KeyCorp
127 Public Sq
Cleveland, OH 44114-1306, USA

Helms, Susan J (Astronaut)
NASA
2101 Nasa Pkwy
Johnson Space Center
Houston, TX 77058-3691, USA

Helms, Tommy (Baseball Player)
Cincinnati Reds
5427 Bluesky Dr
Cincinnati, OH 45247-7865, USA

Helms, Wes (Baseball Player)
Atlanta Braves
2205 Pamela St
Gastonia, NC 28054-1907, USA

Helms, Wes (Baseball Player)
Cleveland Indians
5555 Canyon Crest Dr Apt 3D
Riverside, CA 92507-6453, USA

Helmsley, Leona M (Business Person)
36 Central Park S
New York, NY 10019-1600, USA

Helmstetter, Shad (Motivational Speaker, Writer)
Goals-On-Line.com Corporate Offices
362 Gulf Breeze Pkwy Ste 104
Gulf Breeze, FL 32561-4492, USA

Helmut
1775 Broadway Ste 433
New York, NY 10019-1903, USA

Helmuth, Phil (Misc)
1101 University Ave
Palo Alto, CA 94301-2239, USA

Helnwein, Gottfried (Artist)
Aul der Burg 2
Burgbrol 56659, GERMANY

Heloise
PO Box 795000
San Antonio, TX 78279-5000, USA

Helpern, Joan G (Designer, Fashion Designer)
Joan & David Helpern Inc
46 W 56th St # 200
New York, NY 10019-3801, USA

Heltau, Michael (Actor, Music Group)
Sulzweg 11
Vienna 1190, AUSTRIA

Helton, Bill D (Business Person)
New Century Energies
1225 17th St Ste 100
Denver, CO 80202-5518, USA

Helton, Darius (Football Player)
Kansas City Chiefs
5816 Amity Springs Dr
Charlotte, NC 28212-2604, USA

Helton, RJ (Musician)
PO Box 246
1400 Market Place Blvd
Cumming, GA 30028-0246, USA

Helton, Todd L (Baseball Player)
Colorado Rockies
8720 E 127th Ct
Brighton, CO 80602-8111, USA

Helvin, Marie (Model)
IMG Models
23 Eyot Gardens
London W6 9TN, UNITED KINGDOM (UK)

Hely, Steve (Actor)
c/o Staff Member *William Morris Agency (WMA-LA)*
1 William Morris Pl
Beverly Hills, CA 90212-4261, USA

Hemandez, Angel (Baseball Player)
500 Cypress Xing
Wellington, FL 33414-6368, USA

Hemenway, Robert E (Educator)
University of Kansas
President's Office
Lawrence, KS 66045-0001, USA

Hemingway, Gerardine (Designer, Fashion Designer)
Red or Dead Ltd
Courtney Road Bldg 201
Wembley
Middx HA9 7PP, UNITED KINGDOM (UK)

Hemingway, Mariel (Actor, Model)
PO Box 2249
Ketchum, ID 83340-2249, USA

Hemingway, Wayne (Designer, Fashion Designer)
Red or Dead Ltd
Courtney Road Bldg 201
Wembley
Middx HA9 7PP, UNITED KINGDOM (UK)

Hemme, Christy (Actor)
c/o Liza Anderson *Warren Cowan & Associates PR*
8899 Beverly Blvd Ste 919
Los Angeles, CA 90048-2436, USA

Hemmer, Bill (Correspondent)
c/o Staff Member *Fox News Channel (NY)*
1211 Avenue Of The Americas
Level C1
New York, NY 10036-8701, USA

Hemmi, Heini (Skier)
Chalet Bel-Lia
Valbella 7077, SWITZERLAND

Hemming, Lindy (Designer, Stylist)
c/o Robert Arakelian *United Talent Agency (UTA)*
9560 Wilshire Blvd Ste 500
Beverly Hills, CA 90212-2401, USA

Hemmis, Paige (Actor, Reality TV Star)
c/o Staff Member *Extreme Makeover: Home Edition*
9255 W Sunset Blvd Ste 1100
Endemol Entertainment USA
Los Angeles, CA 90069-3308, USA

Hemond, Scott (Baseball Player)
Oakland A's
263 Florida Ave
Dunedin, FL 34698-7530, USA

Hemphill, Bret (Baseball Player)
Anaheim Angels
1273 Trehowell Dr
Roseville, CA 95678-6110, USA

Hemphill, Joel (Music Group)
Harper Agency
PO Box 144
Goodlettsville, TN 37070-0144, USA

Hemphill, Labreeska (Music Group)
Harper Agency
PO Box 144
Goodlettsville, TN 37070-0144, USA

Hemphill, Richard (Baseball Player)
Kansas City Monarchs
422 Barnes St
Rock Hill, SC 29730-5044, USA

Hempstead, Hessley (Football Player)
Detroit Lions
52900 Winsome Ln
Chesterfield, MI 48051-3723, USA

Hempstone, Smith Jr (Diplomat, Writer)
7611 Fairfax Rd
Bethesda, MD 20814-1313, USA

Hemsley, Nate (Football Player)
Dallas Cowboys
26 Roberts Pl
Willingboro, NJ 08046-2514, USA

Hemsley, Stephen J (Business Person)
United HealthCare Corp
9900 Bren Rd E
Opus Center
Minnetonka, MN 55343-4402, USA

Hemus, Solly (Baseball Player)
St Louis Cardinals
6565 West Loop S Ste 555
Bellaire, TX 77401-3597, USA

Hencken, John F (Swimmer)
PO Box 2540
Weaverville, NC 28787-2540, USA

Hendershot, Larry (Football Player)
Washington Redskins
1721 W 6th St
Muncie, IN 47302-2108, USA

Henderson, Alan (Basketball Player)
Atlanta Hawks
190 Marietta St NW
Atlanta, GA 30303-2717, USA

Henderson, Chris (Soccer Player)
Columbus Crew
2121 Velman Ave
Columbus, OH 43211, USA

Henderson, David L (Dave) (Baseball Player)
6004 142nd Ct SE
Bellevue, WA 98006-4901, USA

Henderson, Donald A (Educator, Misc)
3802 Greenway
Baltimore, MD 21218-1825, USA

Henderson, Felicia (Writer)
c/o Scott Schwartz *Vision Art Management*
9200 W Sunset Blvd Ph 1
Los Angeles, CA 90069-3601, USA

Henderson, Florence (Actor, Music Group)
Cliff Ayers Enterprises
PO Box 17059
Nashville, TN 37217-0059, USA

Henderson, Gordon (Designer, Fashion Designer)
World Hong Kong
80 W 40th St
New York, NY 10018-2682, USA

Henderson, James A (Business Person)
Cummins Engine Co
PO Box 3005
500 Jackson St
Columbus, IN 47202-3005, USA

Henderson, Joe (Baseball Player)
Chicago White Sox
6026 Casa Nicole Way
Sacramento, CA 95824-1565, USA

Henderson, John (Football Player)
Jacksonville Jaguars
1 Alltel Stadium Pl
Jacksonville, FL 32202-1917, USA

Henderson, John (Football Player)
Detroit Lions
18130 19th Ave N
Plymouth, MN 55447-2634, USA

Henderson, Josh (Actor)
c/o Michael Baum *Handprint Entertainment*
1100 Glendon Ave Ste 1000
Los Angeles, CA 90024-3514, USA

Henderson, Karen LeCraft (Judge)
US Court of Appeals
333 Constitution Ave NW
Washington, DC 20001-2866, USA

Henderson, Keith (Football Player)
San Francisco 49ers
PO Box 3231
Cartersville, GA 30120-1704, USA

Henderson, Ken (Baseball Player)
San Francisco Giants
182 La Montagne Ct
Los Gatos, CA 95032-1703, USA

Henderson, Martin (Actor)
c/o Peter Kiernan *Management 360*
9111 Wilshire Blvd
Beverly Hills, CA 90210-5508, USA

Henderson, Neale (Baseball Player)
Kansas City Monarchs
341 Los Soneto Dr
San Diego, CA 92114-5922, USA

Henderson, Paul III (Journalist)
Seattle Times
1120 John St
Editorial Dept
Seattle, WA 98109-5321, USA

Henderson, Reuben (Football Player)
Chicago Bears
3918 Hunters Ridge Dr Apt 4
Lansing, MI 48911-1106, USA

Henderson, Rickey (Baseball Player)
Oakland A's
10561 Englewood Dr
Oakland, CA 94605-5013, USA

Henderson, Rod (Baseball Player)
Montreal Expos
3641 Fair Ridge Dr
Lexington, KY 40509-1856, USA

Henderson, Shirley (Actor)
Hamilton Hodell
24 Hanway St
London W1T 1UH, UNITED KINGDOM (UK)

Henderson, Steve (Baseball Player)
New York Mets
3010 W Saint Conrad St
Tampa, FL 33607-2955, USA

Henderson, Tareva
PO Box 82911
Baton Rouge, LA 70884-2911, USA

Henderson, Thomas
7 Seafield Ln
Westhampton Beach, NY 11978-2714, USA

Henderson, Thomas (Football Player)
Dallas Cowboys
8403 Mesa Dr
Anderson High School Attn: Athletic Dept
Austin, TX 78759-8117, USA

Henderson, Thomas (Tom) (Basketball Player)
14003 Piney Run Ct
Houston, TX 77066-5519, USA

Henderson, Zachary (Football Player)
Philadelphia Eagles
1224 Brentwood Pt
Brentwood, TN 37027-2943, USA

Hendler, Lauri
4034 Stone Canyon Ave
Sherman Oaks, CA 91403-4541, USA

Hendley, Bob (Baseball Player)
Milwaukee Braves
645 Wimbish Rd
Macon, GA 31210-4328, USA

Hendley, Dick (Football Player)
Pittsburgh Steelers
6 Sun Flare Ct
Greer, SC 29650-4419, USA

Hendrick, George (Baseball Player)
Oakland A's
10672 Blue Nile Ct
Las Vegas, NV 89144-4115, USA

Hendricks, Barbara (Opera Singer)
I M G Artists
420 W 45th St
New York, NY 10036-3503, USA

Hendricks, Christina (Actor)
c/o Ben Levine *Evolution Entertainment (LA)*
10585 Santa Monica Blvd Ste 120
Los Angeles, CA 90025-4984, USA

Hendricks, Elrod (Baseball Player)
Baltimore Orioles
4113 Holbrook Rd
Randallstown, MD 21133-1116, USA

Hendricks, Jon (Music Group)
Virginia Wicks
2737 Edwin Pl
Los Angeles, CA 90046-1031, USA

Hendricks, L H (Baseball Player)
Negro Baseball Leagues
12 Sunset Blvd
Beaufort, SC 29907, USA

Hendricks, Susan (Anchor)
c/o Staff Member *CNN (Atlanta)*
1 Cnn Ctr NW
PO Box 105366
Atlanta, GA 30303-2762, USA

Hendricks, Theodore P (Ted) (Football Player)
Baltimore Colts
165 Sunset Way
Miami Springs, FL 33166-5153, USA

Hendrickson, Mark (Baseball Player)
Toronto Blue Jays
17289 Dunbar Rd
Mount Vernon, WA 98273-8761, USA

Hendrickson, Steve (Football Player)
Dallas Cowboys
2558 Miller Ave
Escondido, CA 92029-5704, USA

Hendrix, Elaine (Actor)
Rigberg Roberts Rugolo
1180 S Beverly Dr Ste 601
Los Angeles, CA 90035-1158, USA

Hendrix, John W (General)
Commanding General
Army Forces Command
Atlanta, GA 30330-0001, USA

Hendrix, Terri (Musician)
Wilory Records
PO Box 2340
San Marcos, TX 78667-2340, USA

Hendrix, Tim (Football Player)
Dallas Cowboys
7251 Hamilton Dr
Midlothian, TX 76065-6974, USA

Hendry, Gloria (Actor)
H David Moss
733 Seward St Ph
Los Angeles, CA 90038-3503, USA

Hendry, Ted (Baseball Player)
14740 N 90th Pl
Scottsdale, AZ 85260-2700, USA

Hendryx, Nona (Musician)
Black Rock
6201 W Sunset Blvd # 329
Hollywood, CA 90028, USA

Hendy, John (Football Player)
San Diego Chargers
2120 Brown Ave
Santa Clara, CA 95051-1722, USA

Henenlotter, Frank (Director)
81 Bedford St Apt 6E
New York, NY 10014-5749, USA

Hengel, Dave (Baseball Player)
Seattle Mariners
2642 Kingfisher Ln
Lincoln, CA 95648-8753, USA

Henin-Hardenne, Justine (Tennis Player)
Octagon
1751 Pinnacle Dr Ste 1500
McLean, VA 22102-3833, USA

Henke, Brad (Actor)
c/o Matt Schwartz *Atlas Entertainment*
6100 Wilshire Blvd Ste 1170
Los Angeles, CA 90048-5116, USA

Henke, Edgar (Football Player)
San Francisco 49ers
769 Lisa Ln
Ashland, OR 97520-3156, USA

Henke, Karl (Football Player)
New York Jets
1180 Bogota Ct
Oxnard, CA 93035-2608, USA

Henke, Nolan (Golfer)
1323 Florida Ave
Fort Myers, FL 33901-7707, USA

Henke, Tom (Baseball Player)
Texas Rangers
RR 6
Jefferson City, MO 65101, USA

Henkel, Andrea (Athlete)
TKW Sport-Promotion
Lerchenstr 39
Memmingen 87700, GERMANY

Henkel, Heike (Athlete, Track Athlete)
Tannenbergstr 57
Leverkusen 51373, GERMANY

Henkel, Herbert L (Business Person)
Ingersoll-Rand Co
155 Chestnut Ridge Rd
Montvale, NJ 07645-1115, USA

Henkin, Louis (Attorney, Attorney General, Educator, General)
460 Riverside Dr
New York, NY 10027-6821, USA

Henle, Gertrude (Scientist)
533 Ott Rd
Bala Cynwyd, PA 19004-2509, USA

Henley, Carey (Football Player)
Buffalo Bills
1611 S Clayton Ave
Chattanooga, TN 37412-1107, USA

Henley, Darryl (Football Player)
Los Angeles Rams
10178 Woodridge Dr
Rancho Cucamonga, CA 91737-6834, USA

Henley, Don (Music Group, Songwriter, Writer)
c/o Staff Member *Azoffmusic Management*
1100 Glendon Ave Ste 2000
Los Angeles, CA 90024-3524, USA

Henley, Edward T (Misc)
Hotel & Restaurant Employees Union
1219 28th St NW
Washington, DC 20007-3362, USA

Henley, Gail (Baseball Player)
Pittsburgh Pirates
7338 Alta Vis
La Verne, CA 91750-1115, USA

Henley, Georgie (Actor)
c/o Christian Hodell *Hamilton Hodell Ltd*
66 - 68 Margaret St 5th Fl
London W1W 8SR, UNITED KINGDOM (UK)

Henley, J Smith (Judge)
US Court of Appeals
200 Federal Building
Harrison, AR 72601, USA

Henley, Larry (Composer)
Creative Directions
PO Box 335
Brentwood, TN 37024-0335, USA

Henley, Patricia
PO Box 259
Battle Ground, IN 47920-0259, USA

Henley, Robert (Ballerina)
Montreal Expos
11050 Moreland Dr E
Grand Bay, AL 36541-6626, USA

Henman, Graham (Director)
Agency for Performing Arts
405 S Beverly Dr Ste 500
Beverly Hills, CA 90212-4425, USA

Henman, Tim (Tennis Player)
14497 N Dale Mabry Hwy Ste 205
Tampa, FL 33618-2047, USA

Henn, Mark (Animator)
Walt Disney Animation
PO Box 10200
Lake Buena Vista, FL 32830-0200, USA

Henn, Walter (Architect)
Ramsachleite 13
Mumau 82418, GERMANY

Henneman, Brian (Music Group)
Hard Head Productions
180 Varick St Rm 810
New York, NY 10014-5416, USA

Henneman, Mike (Baseball Player)
Detroit Tigers
806 Lake Creek Dr
McKinney, TX 75070-5590, USA

Hennen, Thomas J (Astronaut)
522 Villa Dr
Seabrook, TX 77586-3034, USA

Henner, Marilu (Actor)
c/o Dick Guttman *Guttman Associates*
118 S Beverly Dr Ste 201
Beverly Hills, CA 90212-3016, USA

Hennessey, Tom (Bowler)
157 Forest Brook Ln
Saint Louis, MO 63146-5601, USA

Hennessy, Jill (Actor)
c/o Scott Lambert *William Morris Agency (WMA-LA)*
1 William Morris Pl
Beverly Hills, CA 90212-4261, USA

Hennessy, John (Educator)
Stanford University
President's Office
Stanford, CA 94305, USA

Hennessy, John B (Archaeologist)
497 Old Windsor Road
Kellyville, NSW 2153, AUSTRALIA

Henney, Jane (Government Official)
Food & Drug Administration
5600 Fishers Ln
Rockville, MD 20852-1750, USA

Hennigan, Charley (Football Player)
Houston Oilers
157 Rocking G Farms Rd
Livingston, TX 77351-1226, USA

Hennigan, Mike (Football Player)
Detroit Lions
943 Robin Ln
Cookeville, TN 38501-2911, USA

Hennigan, Phil (Baseball Player)
Cleveland Indians
PO Box 1212
Center, TX 75935-1212, USA

Henning, Dan (Football Player)
San Diego Chargers
11205 NW 15th Pl
Pembroke Pines, FL 33026-2601, USA

Henning, John F Jr (Publisher)
Sunset Magazine
80 Willow Rd
Menlo Park, CA 94025-3691, USA

Henning, Larry
7426 43rd Ave SE
Saint Cloud, MN 56304-9579, USA

Henning, Linda (Actor)
10765 Wrightwood Ln
Studio City, CA 91604-3951, USA

Henning, Lorne E (Coach, Hockey Player)
18 Coldbrook
Irvine, CA 92604-4649, USA

Henning-Walker, Anne (Speed Skater)
5001 W Portland Dr
Littleton, CO 80128-6409, USA

Henninger, Rick (Baseball Player)
Texas Rangers
373 Maple Dr
Pottsboro, TX 75076-5344, USA

Hennings, Chad W (Football Player)
Dallas Cowboys
6101 Bay Valley Ct
Flower Mound, TX 75022-5575, USA

Hennis, Randy (Baseball Player)
Houston Astros
1747 Sienna Dr
Melbourne, FL 32934-9030, USA

Henrich, Bobby (Baseball Player)
Cincinnati Reds
1531 Via Los Coyotes
La Habra, CA 90631-7655, USA

Henrich, Dieter (Misc)
Gerlichstr 7A
Munich 81245, GERMANY

Henrich, Thomas D (Tommy) (Baseball Player)
New York Yankees
13801 Woodbine Ave
Dayton, OH 45420, USA

Henrich, Tom
1547 Albino Trail
Dewey, AZ 86327, USA

Henrichsen, Brett (DJ)
c/o Len Evans *Project Publicity*
312 W 53rd St
New York, NY 10019-5743, USA

Henricks, Jon N (Swimmer)
254 Laurel Ave
Des Plaines, IL 60016-4321, USA

Henricks, Terence T (Tom) (Astronaut)
Timken Aerospace
PO Box 547
Keene, NH 03431-0547, USA

Henrie, David (Actor)
Noble Media Group Inc
53 Sunrise Creek Rd
Superior, MT 59872-9746, USA

Henrik (Prince)
Amalienborg Palace
Copenhagen K 1257, DENMARK

Henriksen, Lance (Actor)
Innovative Artists
1505 10th St
Santa Monica, CA 90401-2805, USA

Henriquez, Ron (Actor)
PO Box 38027
Los Angeles, CA 90038-0027, USA

Henry, Bill (Baseball Player)
New York Yankees
26 Stoney Creek Rd
Hilton Head Island, SC 29928-2909, USA

Henry, Bill (Baseball Player)
Boston Red Sox
2313 Kilkenny Ln
Deer Park, TX 77536-3955, USA

Henry, Buck (Actor, Writer)
117 E 57th St
New York, NY 10022-2002, USA

Henry, Butch (Baseball Player)
Houston Astros
12072 Paseo De Amor Ln
El Paso, TX 79936-4499, USA

Henry, Clarence (Forgman) (Music Group, Songwriter, Writer)
3309 Lawrence St
New Orleans, LA 70114-3230, USA

Henry, David (Actor)
c/o Dallas Smith *Peters Fraser & Dunlop (PFD - UK)*
Drury House
34-43 Russell St
London WC2B 5HA, UNITED KINGDOM (UK)

Henry, Doug (Baseball Player)
Milwaukee Brewers
2804 Burries Rd
Hartland, WI 53029-8823, USA

Henry, Dwayne (Baseball Player)
Texas Rangers
502 E Hampstead Ct
Middletown, DE 19709-1209, USA

Henry, Geoffrey A (Prime Minister)
PO Box 281
Rarotonga, COOK ISLANDS

Henry, Gloria (Actor)
849 N Harper Ave
Los Angeles, CA 90046-6803, USA

Henry, Gregg (Actor)
8956 Appian Way
Los Angeles, CA 90046-7737, USA

Henry, J J (Golfer)
6720 Medinah Dr
Fort Worth, TX 76132-4574, USA

Henry, Joe (Baseball Player)
Memphis Red Sox
220 N 7th Street
Lovejoy, IL 62059, USA

The Celebrity Black Book 2008

Henry, Joe (Music Group, Songwriter, Writer)
Monterey Peninsula Artists
509 Hartnell St
Monterey, CA 93940-2825, USA

Henry, John (Baseball Player)
Florida Marlins
4698 Sanctuary Ln
Boca Raton, FL 33431-5206, USA

Henry, Joseph L (Doctor)
60 Marinita Ave
San Rafael, CA 94901-3431, USA

Henry, Justin (Actor)
c/o Staff Member *Slamdunk Films*
202 Main St Ste 14
Venice, CA 90291-5211, USA

Henry, Lenny (Actor)
c/o Staff Member *William Morris Agency (WMA-LA)*
1 William Morris Pl
Beverly Hills, CA 90212-4261, USA

Henry, Mike (Actor)
Pittsburgh Steelers
10803 Blix St Unit 3
North Hollywood, CA 91602-3822, USA

Henry, Pierre (Composer)
32 Rue Toul
Paris 75012, FRANCE

Henry, Piper
1680 Vine St Ste 614
Hollywood, CA 90028-8833, USA

Henry, Robert H (Judge)
US Court of Appeals
PO Box 1767
Oklahoma City, OK 73101-1767, USA

Henry, Thierry (Titi) (Soccer Player)
Arsenal FC
Arsenal Stadium
Avenell Rd Highbury
London N5 1BU, UNITED KINGDOM (UK)

Henry, William H Jr (Producer)
Time-Life Books
Rockefeller Center
New York, NY 10020, USA

Hensby, Mark (Golfer)
8121 E Echo Canyon St
Mesa, AZ 85207-7186, USA

Hensel, Bruce (Doctor)
17526 Tramonto Dr
Pacific Palisades, CA 90272-3127, USA

Hensel, Robert M (World Record Holder)
wheelierecord@yahoo.com
138 E 3rd St # A
Oswego, NY 13126-2607, USA

Hensel, Witold (Archaeologist)
Ul Marszalkowska 84/92M
Warsaw 109 00-514, POLAND

Hensilwood, Christopher (Misc, Scientist)
Iziko Museum
25 Queen Victoria St
Cape Town, SOUTH AFRICA

Hensley, Chuck (Baseball Player)
San Francisco Giants
259 Bonanza Dr
Erie, CO 80516-8451, USA

Hensley, Jimmy (Race Car Driver)
152 S Iredell Industrial Park Rd
Mooresville, NC 28115-7128, USA

Hensley, John (Actor)
c/o Staff Member *Innovative Artists (LA)*
1505 10th St
Santa Monica, CA 90401-2805, USA

Hensley, Kirby J (Religious Leader)
Universal Life Church
601 3rd St
Modesto, CA 95351-3395, USA

Hensley, Pamela (Actor)
9526 Dalegrove Dr
Beverly Hills, CA 90210-1711, USA

Henson, Champ (Football Player)
Cincinnati Bengals
PO Box 3
Ashville, OH 43103-0003, USA

Henson, Darrin (Actor)
c/o Staff Member *Don Buchwald & Associates Inc (LA)*
6500 Wilshire Blvd Ste 2200
Los Angeles, CA 90048-4942, USA

Henson, Darrin Dewitt (Actor)
c/o Steven Muller *Innovative Artists (LA)*
1505 10th St
Santa Monica, CA 90401-2805, USA

Henson, Drew (Baseball Player)
New York Yankees
2931 Magnolia Hill Ct
Dallas, TX 75201-1680, USA

Henson, Elden (Actor)
c/o Chuck Binder *Binder & Associates*
1465 Lindacrest Dr
Beverly Hills, CA 90210-2519, USA

Henson, John (Actor, Comedian)
Conversation Co
1044 Northern Blvd Ste 304
Roslyn, NY 11576-1589, USA

Henson, Lisa (Producer)
Columbia Pictures
2400 Riverside Dr
Burbank, CA 91505, USA

Henson, Lou (Basketball Player, Coach)
New Mexico State University
Athletic Dept
Las Cruces, NM 88033, USA

Henson, Luther (Football Player)
New England Patriots
5395 Maple Grove Ave
Blanchester, OH 45107-1533, USA

Henson, Taraji P (Actor)
c/o Vincent Cirrincione *Vincent Cirrincione Associates*
1516 N Fairfax Ave
Los Angeles, CA 90046-2608, USA

Henstridge, Natasha (Actor, Model)
345 N Maple Dr Ste 397
Beverly Hills, CA 90210-3856, USA

Hentoff, Nathan I (Nat) (Critic, Musician)
Village Voice
36 Cooper Sq
Editorial Dept
New York, NY 10003-7149, USA

Henton, John (Actor)
c/o Staff Member *Gersh Agency, The (LA)*
232 N Canon Dr
Beverly Hills, CA 90210-5302, USA

Hentrich, Craig (Football Player)
Green Bay Packers
604 Canters Ct
Franklin, TN 37067-5047, USA

Hentrich, Helmut (Architect)
Dusseldorfer Str 67
Dusseldorf-Oberkassel 40545, GERMANY

Henze, Hans Werner (Composer, Conductor)
Weihergarten 1-5
Mainz 55116, GERMANY

Hepburn, Cassandra (Actor)
c/o Glenn Hughes III *Gem Entertainment Group*
2530 Wilshire Blvd Fl 3
Santa Monica, CA 90403-4643, USA

Hepler, Bill (Baseball Player)
New York Mets
12518 Fort King Rd
Dade City, FL 33525-5609, USA

Heppner, Ben (Opera Singer)
Columbia Artists Mgmt Inc
1790 Broadway Fl 6
New York, NY 10019-1412, USA

Her Majesty The Queen, Elizabeth II (Royalty)
Buckingham Palace
London SW1A 1AA, UNITED KINGDOM (UK)

Herb, Marvin (Business Person)
Coca-Cola Bottling Company of Chicago
7400 N Oak Park Ave
Niles, IL 60714-3818, USA

Herbert, Bob (Writer)
New York Times
229 W 43rd St
Editorial Dept
New York, NY 10036-3959, USA

Herbert, Holly (Journalist)
Celebrity Justice c/o Warner Bros
4000 Warner Blvd
Burbank, CA 91522-0001, USA

Herbert, James (Writer)
David Higham Associates
5-8 Lower John St
London W1R 4HA, UNITED KINGDOM (UK)

Herbert, Johnny (Race Car Driver)
PP Sayber AG
Wildbachstr 9
Hinwil 8340, SWITZERLAND

Herbert, Michael K (Editor)
990 Grove St
Evanston, IL 60201-6510, USA

Herbert, Ray (Baseball Player)
Detroit Tigers
9360 Taylors Turn
Stanwood, MI 49346-9686, USA

Herbert, Raymond E (Ray) (Baseball Player)
Detroit Tigers
9360 Taylors Turn
Stanwood, AL 35901, USA

Herbert, Walter W (Wally) (Scientist)
Rowan Cottage
Catlodge
Laggan
Inverness-shire PH20 1AH, UNITED KINGDOM (UK)

Herbert of Hemingford, D Nicholas (Publisher)
Old Rectory
Hemingford Abbots
Huntington Cambs PE18 9AN, UNITED KINGDOM (UK)

Herbig, Gunther
Toronto Symphony
60 Simcoe St #C116
Toronto, ON MJ5 2H5, CANADA

Herbst, Rebecca (Actor)
c/o Staff Member *General Hospital*
500 S Buena Vista St
Burbank, CA 91521-0001, USA

Herchman, Bill (Football Player)
San Francisco 49ers
114 Willowbrook Dr
Duncanville, TX 75116-4508, USA

Herczegh, Gezar G (Judge)
Int'l Court of Justice
Camegieplein 2
KJ Hague 2517, THE NETHERLANDS

Herd, Carla
8281 Melrose Ave Ste 200
Los Angeles, CA 90046-6890, USA

Herd, Richard (Actor)
PO Box 56297
Sherman Oaks, CA 91413-1297, USA

Herda, Frank A (War Hero)
PO Box 34239
Cleveland, OH 44134-0939, USA

Heredia, Felix (Baseball Player)
Florida Marlins
2655 S Le Jeune Rd
Miami, FL 33134-5832, USA

Heredia, Gil (Baseball Player)
San Francisco Giants
4710 W Calle Don Manuel
Tucson, AZ 85757-9227, USA

Heredia, Wilson (Actor)
c/o Sarah Fargo *Paradigm (NY)*
360 Park Ave S Fl 16
New York, NY 10010-1716, USA

Heredia, Wilson Jermaine (Actor)
c/o Leanne Coronel *Endeavor Agency LLC (LA)*
9601 Wilshire Blvd Fl 3
Beverly Hills, CA 90210-5204, USA

Herek, Stephen R (Director)
Endeavor Talent Agency
9701 Wilshire Blvd Ste 1000
Beverly Hills, CA 90212-2010, USA

Herera, Sue (Correspondent, Television Host)
c/o Staff Member *CNBC*
900 Sylvan Ave
Englewood Cliffs, NJ 07632-3312, USA

Hergert, Joe (Football Player)
Buffalo Bills
875 Tater Rd
New Smyrna Beach, FL 32168-9140, USA

Herges, Matt (Baseball Player)
Los Angeles Dodgers
2406 Prairieridge Pl
Champaign, IL 61822-9330, USA

Herincx, Raimund (Opera Singer)
Monk's Vineyard
Larkbarrow
Shepton Mallet
Somerset BA4 4NR, UNITED KINGDOM (UK)

Herkenhoff, Matt (Football Player)
Kansas City Chiefs
16000 Baywood Ln
Eden Prairie, MN 55346-2409, USA

Herles, Kathleen (Actor)
Shirley Grant Management
PO Box 866
Teaneck, NJ 07666-0866, USA

Herline, Alan (Football Player)
New England Patriots
610 Post Oak Cir
Brentwood, TN 37027-5189, USA

Herman, Axel (Model)
c/o Celebrity Stylist *Ford Models (NY)*
111 5th Ave Fl 9
New York, NY 10003-1005, USA

Herman, Dave (Football Player)
New York Jets
19 Stephens Ln
Valhalla, NY 10595-1601, USA

Herman, David J (Business Person)
Adam Opel AG
Bahnhofplatz 1
Russelsheim 65429, GERMANY

Herman, Pee Wee
PO Box 29373
Los Angeles, CA 90029-0373, USA

Hermann, Allen M (Physicist)
2704 Lookout View Dr
Golden, CO 80401-2520, USA

Hermann, Mark (Football Player)
Denver Broncos
8525 Tidewater Dr
Indianapolis, IN 46236-8917, USA

Hermannson, Dustin M (Baseball Player)
9002 E Rimrock Dr
Scottsdale, AZ 85255-9133, USA

Hermannsson, Steingrimur (Prime Minister)
Mavanes 19
Gardaba 210, ICELAND

Hermansen, Chad (Baseball Player)
Pittsburgh Pirates
678 Cervantes Dr
Henderson, NV 89014-4067, USA

Hermanski, Gene (Baseball Player)
Brooklyn Dodgers
1 Fairwoods Ct
Homosassa, FL 34446-8239, USA

Hermaszewski, Miroslav (Astronaut, General)
Ul Czeczota 25
Warsaw 02-650, POLAND

Hermeling, Terry (Football Player)
Washington Redskins
4409 Jim Mitchell Trl E
Colleyville, TX 76034-4581, USA

Hermits s/ Peter Noone, Herman's (Musician)
c/o Staff Member *Paradise Artists*
108 E Matilija St
Ojai, CA 93023-2639, USA

Hermlin, Stephan (Writer)
Hermann-Hesse-Str 39
Berlin 13156, GERMANY

Hermon, John C (Government Official, Lawyer)
Warren Road
Donaghadee
County Down, NORTHERN IRELAND

Herms, George (Artist)
Jack Rutberg Fine Arts
357 N La Brea Ave
Los Angeles, CA 90036-2517, USA

Hernandez, Evelio (Baseball Player)
Washington Senators
3004 SW 113th Ave
Miami, FL 33165-2228, USA

Hernandez, Genaro (Boxer)
24442 Ferrocarril
Mission Viejo, CA 92691-4027, USA

Hernandez, Guillermo (Willie) (Baseball Player)
PO Box 125 Bo Espina
Calle C Buzon
Aguada, PR 00602-0125, USA

Hernandez, Jackie (Baseball Player)
California Angels
13390 NE 7th Ave Apt 103
North Miami, FL 33161-7509, USA

Hernandez, Jay (Actor)
United Talent Agency
9560 Wilshire Blvd Ste 500
Beverly Hills, CA 90212-2401, USA

Hernandez, Jeremy (Baseball Player)
San Diego Padres
13611 Branford St
Arleta, CA 91331-6210, USA

Hernandez, Keith (Baseball Player)
255 E 49th St Apt 28D
New York, NY 10017-1544, USA

Hernandez, Los Bros (Artist)
c/o Staff Member *Fantagraphics Books*
7563 Lake City Way NE
Seattle, WA 98115-4218, USA

Hernandez, Matt (Football Player)
Seattle Seahawks
PO Box 682
Eastpointe, MI 48021-0682, USA

Hernandez, Orlando (Athlete, Baseball Player)
c/o Staff Member *Montreal Expos*
4549 Avenue Pierre de Coubertin
Montreal, PQ H1V 3N7, CANADA

Hernandez, Robert J (Business Person)
USX Corp
600 Grant St
Pittsburgh, PA 15219-2800, USA

Hernandez, Rodolfo P (War Hero)
5328 Bluewater Pl
College Lakes
Fayetteville, NC 28311-1224, USA

Hernandez Colon, Rafael (Governor)
Puerta De Tierra
PO Box 5788
San Juan, PR 00901, USA

Herndon, Kelly (Football Player)
Denver Broncos
1968 Cambridge St
Twinsburg, OH 44087-2008, USA

Herndon, Mark J (Music Group, Musician)
RR 1 Box 239A
Mentone, AL 35984, USA

Herndon, Ty (Music Group)
PO Box 121858
Nashville, TN 37212-1858, USA

Heron, Fred (Football Player)
St Louis Cardinals
3908 Brook Valley Cir
Stockton, CA 95219, USA

Herr, John C (Scientist)
University of Virginia
Med Center
Immunology Dept
Charlottesville, VA 22903, USA

Herr, Thomas M (Tommy) (Baseball Player)
1077 Olde Forge Xing
Lancaster, PA 17601-1738, USA

Herranz Casado, Julian Cardinal (Religious Leader)
Legislative Texts Curia
Piazza Pio XII #10
Rome 00193, ITALY

Herren, James (Football Player)
New York Jets
224 Monongahela Ave
Glassport, PA 15045-1319, USA

Herrera, Carolina (Designer, Fashion Designer)
Carolina Herrera Ltd
501 Fashion Ave Fl 17
New York, NY 10018-5911, USA

Herrera, Caroline (Designer, Fashion Designer)
501 7th Ave Fl 17
New York, NY 10018-5911, USA

Herrera, Efren (Football Player)
Dallas Cowboys
861 Atlanta Ct
Claremont, CA 91711-2515, USA

Herrera, Kristin (Actor)
c/o David Eisenberg *Protege Entertainment*
710 E Angeleno Ave
Burbank, CA 91501-2213, USA

Herrera, Pamela (Ballerina)
American Ballet Theatre
890 Broadway
New York, NY 10003-1278, USA

Herrera, Pancho (Baseball Player)
Kansas City Monarchs
18700 NW 78th Ave
Hialeah, FL 33015-5244, USA

Herrera, Silvestre S (War Hero)
7222 W Windsor Blvd
Glendale, AZ 85303-6130, USA

Herres, Robert T (Business Person, General)
United Services Automobile Assn
Usaa Building
San Antonio, TX 78288-0001, USA

Herring, Harold (Football Player)
Cleveland Browns
8673 Laurel Dr
Pinellas Park, FL 33782-4304, USA

Herring, Laura
4702 N 36th St
Phoenix, AZ 85018-3423, USA

Herring, Lynn (Actor)
37900 Road 800
Raymond, CA 93653-9714, USA

Herring, Vincent (Composer, Musician)
Fat City Artists
1906 Chet Atkins Blvd Apt 502
Nashville, TN 37212-2122, USA

Herring-James, Katie (Baseball Player)
143 Grouse Ridge Rd
Tamaqua, PA 18252-5442, USA

Herrington, John B (Astronaut)
4367 Bays Water Dr
Colorado Springs, CO 80920-7636, USA

Herrington, John S (Business Person, Secretary)
Harcourt Brace
525 B St
San Diego, CA 92101-4401, USA

Herrmann, Don (Football Player)
New York Giants
PO Box 318
Brookside, NJ 07926-0318, USA

Herrmann, Edward (Ed) (Actor)
220 E 23rd St Ste 400
New York, NY 10010-4669, USA

Herrod, Jeff (Football Player)
Indianapolis Colts
7645 Ballinshire N
Indianapolis, IN 46254-9647, USA

Herron, Bruce (Football Player)
Chicago Bears
8504 S Calumet Ave
Chicago, IL 60619-6026, USA

Herron, Cindy (Music Group)
East West Records
75 Rockefeller Plz # 1200
New York, NY 10019-6908, USA

Herron, Denis (Hockey Player)
12841 Marsh Pointe Way
West Palm Beach, FL 33418-6973, USA

Herron, Robert J (Architect)
Herron Assoc
28-30 Rivington St
London EC2A 3DU, UNITED KINGDOM (UK)

Herron, Tim (Golfer)
50 Kimberly Ln N
Minneapolis, MN 55447-4106, USA

Hersch, Fred (Music Group, Musician)
SRO Artists
PO Box 9532
Madison, WI 53715, USA

Hersch, Michael (Composer)
21C Music Publishing
30 W 63rd St Apt 15S
New York, NY 10023-7115, USA

Herschler, E David (Artist)
PO Box 5859
Santa Barbara, CA 93150-5859, USA

Hersh, Kristin (Music Group, Songwriter, Writer)
c/o Staff Member *Concerted Efforts*
59 Parsons St
West Newton, MA 02465-2137, USA

Hersh, Seymour (Journalist, Writer)
1211 Connecticut Ave NW
Washington, DC 20036-2701, USA

Hershey, Barbara (Actor)
c/o Jill Littman *Handprint Entertainment*
1100 Glendon Ave Ste 1000
Los Angeles, CA 90024-3514, USA

Hershey, Erin (Actor)
PO Box 16212
Irvine, CA 92623-6212, USA

Hershey, Maralyn
37337 Green Level Rd
Wakefield, VA 23888-2525, USA

Hershey-Reeser, Esther Anne (Baseball Player)
3450 Compass Rd
Gap, PA 17527-9006, USA

Hershiser, Orel (Athlete, Baseball Player, Sportscaster)
5277 Isleworth Country Club Dr
Windermere, FL 34786-8964, USA

Hershiser, Orel L Q (Baseball Player, Sportscaster)
7163 Helsem Bnd
Dallas, TX 75230-1946, USA

Herta, Bryan (Race Car Driver)
Bryan Herta Racing, Inc
3331 Shellbrook Ct
C/O Gary Herta
Arlington, TX 76016-2064, USA

Hertel, Rob (Football Player)
Cincinnati Bengals
1707 Camden Pkwy
South Pasadena, CA 91030-4913, USA

Hertwig, Craig (Football Player)
Detroit Lions
249 Bloomfield St
Athens, GA 30605-1203, USA

Hertz, C Hellmuth (Physicist)
Lund INstitute of Technology
Physics School
Lund, SWEDEN

Hertz, Steve (Baseball Player)
Houston Colt .45's
10211 SW 96th Ter
Miami, FL 33176-2704, USA

Hertzberg, Daniel (Journalist)
Wall Street Journal
200 Liberty St
Editorial Dept
New York, NY 10281-0084, USA

Hertzberger, Herman (Architect)
Architectourstudio
Box 74665
Amsterdam, BR 1070, THE
NETHERLANDS

Hervey, Jason (Actor)
2049 Century Park E Ste 2500
Los Angeles, CA 90067-3127, USA

Herzenberg, Caroline Littlejohn
(Physicist)
1700 E 56th St Apt 2707
Chicago, IL 60637-5092, USA

Herzfeld, John (Director)
c/o Staff Member *Endeavor Agency LLC*
(LA)
9601 Wilshire Blvd Fl 3
Beverly Hills, CA 90210-5204, USA

Herzfeld, John M (Director)
Industry Entertainment
955 Carrillo Dr Ste 300
Los Angeles, CA 90048-5400, USA

Herzigova, Eva (Model)
Men/Women Model Inc
199 Lafayette St # 700
New York, NY 10012-4003, USA

Herzog, Arthur III (Writer)
4 E 81st St
New York, NY 10028-0235, USA

Herzog, Jacques (Architect, Misc)
Herzog & De Meuron Architekten
Rheinschanze 6
Basel 4056, SWITZERLAND

Herzog, Maurice (Mountaineer)
84 Chemin De La Tournette
Chamoinix-Mont-Blanc 74400, FRANCE

Herzog, Roman (Ex-President, Politician,
President)
Schloss Bellevue
Spreeweg 1
Berlin 10557, GERMANY

Herzog, Werner (Director)
Herzog Film Productions
Turkenstr 91
Munich 80799, GERMANY

Herzog, Whitey
9426 Sappington Estates Dr
Saint Louis, MO 63127-1664, USA

Hesburgh, Father Theodore
1320 Hesburgh Library
South Bend, IN 46566, USA

Hesburgh, Theodore M (Educator)
University of Natre Dame
1301 Hesburgh Library
Notre Dame, IN 46556-5629, USA

Heseltine, Michael R D (Government
Official)
Thenford House near Banbury
Oxon OX17 2BX, UNITED KINGDOM
(UK)

Heskin, Kam (Actor)
c/o Susan Calogerakis *Thruline
Entertainment*
9250 Wilshire Blvd Ground Fl
Beverly Hills, CA 90210, USA

Heslov, Grant (Actor)
c/o Rick Ax *Gold Coast Management*
1023 1/2 Abbot Kinney Blvd
Venice, CA 90291-5536, USA

Hess, Erika (Skier)
Aeschi
Gratenort 6388, SWITZERLAND

Hess, Ilse
Gailenberg 22
Hindelang/Allgau D-87541, GERMANY

Hess, Jared (Director, Writer)
c/o Jim Berkus *United Talent Agency
(UTA)*
9560 Wilshire Blvd Ste 500
Beverly Hills, CA 90212-2401, USA

Hess, John B (Business Person)
Amerada Hess Corp
1185 Avenue Of The Americas
New York, NY 10036-2665, USA

Hesseman, Howard (Actor)
Innovative Artists
1505 10th St
Santa Monica, CA 90401-2805, USA

Hessenland, Dagmar
Amsterdamer Str. 3
Munich D-80805, GERMANY

Hessler, Curtis A (Publisher)
Times-Mirror Co
Times-Mirror Square
Los Angeles, CA 90053, USA

Hessler, Gordon (Director)
8910 Holly Pl
Los Angeles, CA 90046-1836, USA

Hessler, Robert R (Oceanographer)
Scripps Institute of Oceanography
Biodiversity Dept
La Jolla, CA 92037, USA

Hest, Ari (Musician)
c/o Staff Member *Paradigm (Monterey)*
509 Hartnell St
Monterey, CA 93940-2825, USA

Hester, Jesse (Football Player)
Oakland Raiders
12813 Pineacre Ct
Wellington, FL 33414-4140, USA

Hester, Paul V (General)
Commander
Special Operations Command
Hurlburt Field, FL 32544, USA

Heston, Charlton (Actor)
c/o Staff Member *Agamemnon Films*
650 N Bronson Ave # B-225
Los Angeles, CA 90004-1404, USA

Hetfield, James (Music Group, Musician)
2020 Union St
San Francisco, CA 94123-4103, USA

Hetherington, Eileen M (Doctor)
University of Virginia
Gilmer Hall
Psychology Dept
Charlottesville, VA 22903, USA

Hetki, Johnny (Baseball Player)
Cincinnati Reds
4004 Stary Dr
Parma, OH 44134-5823, USA

Hetrick, Jennifer (Actor)
c/o Staff Member *AKA Talent Agency*
6310 San Vicente Blvd Ste 200
Los Angeles, CA 90048-5488, USA

Hettema, Dave (Football Player)
San Francisco 49ers
31 Desert Sky Rd SE
Albuquerque, NM 87123-3983, USA

Hettich, Arthur M (Editor)
606 Shore Acres Dr
Mamaroneck, NY 10543-4011, USA

Hetzel, Eric (Baseball Player)
Boston Red Sox
2271 Hetzei Rd
Crowley, LA 70526, USA

Hetzel, Fred (Basketball Player)
218 Corwall St NW
Leesburg, VA 20176, USA

Heuga, Jimmie (Skier)
PO Box 686
111 Rawhide
Avon, CO 81620-0686, USA

Heuring, Lori (Actor)
c/o David (Dave) Fleming *Mosaic Media
Group*
24 Music Sq W Fl 1
Nashville, TN 37203-6661, USA

Heverly-Williams, Ruth (Baseball Player)
520 Tennis Ave
Ambler, PA 19002-6015, USA

Hewett, Christopher
1422 N Sweetzer Ave Apt 110
Los Angeles, CA 90069-1527, USA

Hewett, Howard (Music Group)
GHR Entertainment
6014 N Pointe Pl
Woodland Hills, CA 91367-5500, USA

Hewgley, Claude (Football Player)
New York Jets
55 Silvermont Dr
Spring, TX 77382-2007, USA

Hewish, Anthony (Nobel Prize Laureate)
Pryor's Cottage
Kingston
Cambridge CB3 7NQ, UNITED
KINGDOM (UK)

Hewitt, Angela (Musician)
Cramer/Marder Artists
3436 Springhill Rd
Lafayette, CA 94549-2535, USA

Hewitt, Bob (Tennis Player)
822 Boylston St Ste 203
Chestnut Hill, MA 02467-2504, USA

Hewitt, Christopher (Actor)
154 E 66th St
New York, NY 10065-6643, USA

Hewitt, Don (Producer)
CBS-TV
51 W 52nd St
News Dept
New York, NY 10019-6119, USA

Hewitt, Heather
6324 Tahoe Dr
Los Angeles, CA 90068-1654, USA

Hewitt, Jennifer Love (Actor, Music
Group)
c/o Danielle Thomas *Untitled
Entertainment (LA)*
331 N Maple Dr Fl 3
Beverly Hills, CA 90210-3827, USA

Hewitt, Martin (Actor)
1147 Horn Ave Apt 3
Los Angeles, CA 90069-2113, USA

Hewitt, Paul (Basketball Player, Coach)
Georgia Institute of Technology
Athletic Dept
Atlanta, GA 30332-0001, USA

Hewitt, Peter (Director)
Creative Artists Agency
9830 Wilshire Blvd
Beverly Hills, CA 90212-1804, USA

Hewko, Robert (Football Player)
Tampa Bay Buccaneers
100 Lincoln Rd Apt 634
Miami, FL 33139-2013, USA

Hewlett, David (Actor)
c/o Shelly Browning *Magnolia
Entertainment*
9595 Wilshire Blvd Ste 601
Beverly Hills, CA 90212-2506, USA

Hewlett, Donald
King's Head House Island Wall
Whitstable
Kent, ENGLAND CT5 1EP, UNITED
KINGDOM (UK)

Hewlett, Howard (Music Group)
Green Light Talent Agency
PO Box 3172
Beverly Hills, CA 90212-0172, USA

Hewlett, Mark (Reality TV Star)
c/o Jerry Shandrew *Shandrew Public
Relations*
1050 S Stanley Ave
Los Angeles, CA 90019-6634, USA

Hewson, John (Government Official)
ABN Amro Australia
10 Spring St #14
Sydney, NSW 2000, AUSTRALIA

Hextall, Dennis H (Hockey Player)
2631 Harvest Hill Dr
Brighton, MI 48114-8299, USA

Hextall, Ronald (Ron) (Hockey Player)
Philadelphia Flyers
3601 S Broad St
1st Union Center
Philadelphia, PA 19148-5297, USA

Hey, John D (Economist, Mathematician)
University of York
Economics Dept
Heslington
York YO1 5DD, UNITED KINGDOM
(UK)

Hey, Virginia (Actor)
Anthony Williams Mgmt
50 Oxford St
Paddington, NSW 2021, AUSTRALIA

Heyderman, Greg (Baseball Player)
Los Angeles Dodgers
702 Ramona Ave
Monterey, CA 93940-5430, USA

Heyland, Rob
The Manor Middle Lyttleton
Worcestershire, ENGLAND, UNITED
KINGDOM (UK)

Heyliger, Vic (Coach, Hockey Player)
2122 Hercules Dr
Colorado Springs, CO 80906-1136, USA

Heyman, Arthur B (Art) (Basketball
Player)
321 Lincoln Ave
Rockville Centre, NY 11570-6018, USA

Heywood, Anne (Actor)
9966 Liebe Dr
Beverly Hills, CA 90210-1037, USA

Heywood, Joanne
122 Wardour St.
London, ENGLAND W1V 3LA, UNITED
KINGDOM (UK)

Heywood, Ralph (Football Player)
Detroit Lions
2914 State Highway 173 S
Bandera, TX 78003-4602, USA

Hi-Five
PO Box 313030
Jamaica, NY 11431-3030, USA

Hiatt, Jack (Baseball Player)
Los Angeles Angels
715 E 1st St
Coquille, OR 97423-1904, USA

Hiatt, John (Music Group, Musician,
Songwriter, Writer)
c/o Staff Member *United Talent Agency
(UTA)*
9560 Wilshire Blvd Ste 500
Beverly Hills, CA 90212-2401, USA

Hiatt, Phil (Baseball Player)
Kansas City Royals
563 S 72nd Ave Apt 1
Pensacola, FL 32506-7621, USA

Hiatt, Shana (Actor, Model)
c/o Jerry Shandrew *Shandrew Public
Relations*
1050 S Stanley Ave
Los Angeles, CA 90019-6634, USA

Hibbard, Greg (Baseball Player)
Chicago White Sox
1957 Arden Landing Cv S
Germantown, TN 38139-5704, USA

Hibbert, Edward (Actor)
Gage Group
14724 Ventura Blvd Ste 505
Sherman Oaks, CA 91403-3505, USA

Hibbs, Jim (Baseball Player)
California Angels
4659 Foothill Rd
Ventura, CA 93003-1903, USA

Hick, Graeme A (Cricketer)
Worcestershire County Cricket Club
New Road
Worcester, UNITED KINGDOM (UK)

Hick, John H (Religious Leader)
144 Oak Tree Lane
Selly Oak
Birmingham B29 6HU, UNITED
KINGDOM (UK)

Hickam, Homer H Jr (Writer)
9532 Hemlok Dr SE
Huntsville, AL 35803, USA

Hickcox, Charles B (Charlie) (Swimmer)
8315 E Redfield Rd
Scottsdale, AZ 85260-3535, USA

Hicke, William A (Bill) (Hockey Player)
61 Dogwood Place
Regina, SK S4S 5A1, CANADA

Hickel, Walter J (Governor, Secretary)
1905 Loussac Dr
Anchorage, AK 99517-1225, USA

Hickenbottom, Michael (Wrestler)
c/o Staff Member *World Wrestling
Entertainment (WWE)*
1241 E Main St
Stamford, CT 06902-3520, USA

Hickerson, Bryan (Baseball Player)
San Francisco Giants
275 S Hunters Rdg
Warsaw, IN 46582-5645, USA

Hickerson, R Gene (Football Player)
Cleveland Browns
4471 Nagel Rd
Avon, OH 44011-2735, USA

Hickey, Bo (Football Player)
Denver Broncos
PO Box 1143
New Canaan, CT 06840-1143, USA

Hickey, John Benjamin (Actor)
c/o Staff Member *Paradigm (LA)*
360 N Crescent Dr
North Bldg
Beverly Hills, CA 90210-6820, USA

Hickey, Kevin (Baseball Player)
Chicago White Sox
5715 S Mason Ave
Chicago, IL 60638-3606, USA

Hickey, Maurice (Publisher)
Denver Post
65015th St
Denver, CO 80202, USA

Hickey, Red (Football Player)
Pittsburgh Steelers
3400 Paul Sweet Rd Unit D114
Santa Cruz, CA 95065-1542, USA

Hickey, Thomas J (General)
2127 Bobbyber Dr
Vienna, VA 22182-4026, USA

Hickey, William V (Business Person)
Sealed Air Corp
Park 80 E
Saddle Brook, NJ 07663, USA

Hickland, Catherine (Actor)
255 W 84th St Apt 2A
New York, NY 10024-4322, USA

Hickman, Dallas (Football Player)
Washington Redskins
6521 E Dreyfus Ave
Scottsdale, AZ 85254-3915, USA

Hickman, Darryl (Actor)
171 Hermosillo Rd
Santa Barbara, CA 93108-2414, USA

Hickman, Dwayne (Actor)
PO Box 17226
Encino, CA 91416-7226, USA

Hickman, Fred (Sportscaster)
Cable News Network
1050 Techwood Dr NW
Sports Dept
Atlanta, GA 30318-5604, USA

Hickman, Jess (Baseball Player)
Kansas City A's
1801 Jewel St
Pineville, LA 71360-5156, USA

Hickman, Jim (Baseball Player)
New York Mets
PO Box 455
Henning, TN 38041-0455, USA

Hickman, Larry (Football Player)
Chicago Cardinals
5519 Westchester Dr
Tyler, TX 75703-6009, USA

Hickox, Edwin (Baseball Player)
1721 Baron Ct
Port Orange, FL 32128-6789, USA

Hickox, Marc
10 St. Mary St. #308
Toronto, ON M4Y 1, CANADA

Hickox, Richard S (Conductor)
35 Ellington St
London N7 8PN, UNITED KINGDOM
(UK)

Hicks, Buddy (Baseball Player)
Detroit Tigers
1526 N Dixie Downs Rd Unit 26
Saint George, UT 84770-4105, USA

Hicks, Dan (Music Group)
Leslie Wiener
PO Box 245
Sausalito, CA 94966-0245, USA

Hicks, Dan (Sportscaster)
NBC-TV
30 Rockefeller Plz Ste 270E
Sports Dept
New York, NY 10112-0299, USA

Hicks, Eric (Football Player)
Washington Redskins
5761 Carriage Hill Dr
Erie, PA 16509-3161, USA

Hicks, Jim (Baseball Player)
Chicago White Sox
9331 Portal Dr
Houston, TX 77031-2210, USA

Hicks, Joe (Baseball Player)
Chicago White Sox
2707 Brookmere Rd
Charlottesville, VA 22901-1106, USA

Hicks, John C Jr (Football Player)
New York Giants
3287 Green Cook Rd
Johnstown, OH 43031-9208, USA

Hicks, Michael (Actor)
c/o Louise Spinner Ward *William Morris
Agency (WMA-LA)*
1505 10th St
Santa Monica, CA 90401-2805, USA

Hicks, Michael (Basketball Player)
c/o Staff Member *New York Knicks*
4 Penn Plz
Madison Square Garden
New York, NY 10121-0004, USA

Hicks, Michele (Actor)
c/o Eric Black *Anonymous Content (CA)*
3532 Hayden Ave
Culver City, CA 90232-2413, USA

Hicks, Michelle (Actor)
c/o Staff Member *Innovative Artists (LA)*
1505 10th St
Santa Monica, CA 90401-2805, USA

Hicks, Robert (Football Player)
Buffalo Bills
2544 Hightower Ct NW
Atlanta, GA 30318-7412, USA

Hicks, Scott (Director)
PO Box 824
Kent Town 5071, SOUTH AFRICA

Hicks, Sylvester (Football Player)
Kansas City Chiefs
144 Sweetbay Dr
Jackson, TN 38301-3569, USA

Hicks, Taylor (Musician, Reality TV Star)
c/o Jon Leshay *The Firm*
9465 Wilshire Blvd Fl 6
Beverly Hills, CA 90212-2605, USA

Hicks, Thomas O (Baseball Player)
Texas Rangers
5511 Walnut Hill Ln
Dallas, TX 75229, USA

Hicks, Tom (Football Player)
Chicago Bears
207 Rivershire Ln Apt 106
Lincolnshire, IL 60069-3808, USA

Hicks, W K (Football Player)
Houston Oilers
15207 Tayport Ln
Channelview, TX 77530-4727, USA

Hidalgo, John (Government Official)
May's Valentine Davenport Moore
1899 L St NW
Washington, DC 20036-3804, USA

Hide, Chris (Musician)
c/o Staff Member *Pop Idol (Fremantle
Media)*
2700 Colorado Ave Ste 450
Santa Monica, CA 90404-3599, USA

Hide, Herbie (Boxer)
Matchroom
10 Western Road
Romford
Essex RM1 3JT, UNITED KINGDOM (UK)

Hide, Raymond (Geophysicist, Physicist)
University of Oxford
Jesus College
Oxford OX1 3DW, UNITED KINGDOM
(UK)

Hieb, Richard J (Astronaut)
Allied Signal Tech Services
7515 Mission Dr Lbby
Lanham Seabrook, MD 20706-2212, USA

Hiebert, Erwin N (Historian)
40 Payson Rd
Belmont, MA 02478-2718, USA

Hiemstra, Ed (Football Player)
New York Giants
40 Canyon Road # B
Heppner, OR 97836, USA

Hier, Marvin (Activist, Religious Leader)
Simon Wiesenthal Holocaust Center
9766 W Pico Blvd
Los Angeles, CA 90035, USA

Hieronymus, Clara W (Journalist)
50 Spring St
Savannah, TN 38372-1454, USA

Higashi, Satoshi (Golfer)
Bridgestone Sports
45 Higashi-Matsushita-Cho Kanda
Chiyoda-ku
Tokyo 101, JAPAN

Higdon, Bruce (Cartoonist)
210 Canvasback Ct
Murfreesboro, TN 37130-8855, USA

Higginbotham, Joan E (Astronaut)
1409 Mija Ln
Seabrook, TX 77586-2406, USA

Higginbotham, Patrick E (Judge)
US Court of Appeals
1100 Commerce St
US Courthouse
Dallas, TX 75242-1027, USA

Higgins, Al (Producer)
c/o Staff Member *Creative Artists Agency LCC (CAA-LA)*
2000 Avenue Of The Stars
Los Angeles, CA 90067-4700, USA

Higgins, Chester Jr (Photographer)
New York Times
229 W 43rd St
Editorial Dept
New York, NY 10036-3959, USA

Higgins, Dennis (Baseball Player)
Chicago White Sox
1123 Boonville Rd
Jefferson City, MO 65109-0621, USA

Higgins, J Kenneth (Misc)
Boeing Commercial Airplane Group
PO Box 3707
Seattle, WA 98124-2207, USA

Higgins, Jack (Cartoonist, Editor)
59 Waverly Ave
Clarendon Hills, IL 60514-1236, USA

Higgins, Jack (Writer)
September Tide
Mont de la Rocque Jersey
Channel Island, UNITED KINGDOM (UK)

Higgins, John (Coach, Swimmer)
40 Williams Dr
Annapolis, MD 21401-2265, USA

Higgins, John Michael (Actor)
c/o Dan Baron *Agency for the Performing Arts (APA-LA)*
405 S Beverly Dr
Beverly Hills, CA 90212-4416, USA

Higgins, Kevin (Baseball Player)
San Diego Padres
10551 Haywood Dr
Las Vegas, NV 89135-2851, USA

Higgins, Mark (Baseball Player)
Cleveland Indians
2999 Abbotts Oak Way
Duluth, GA 30097-2193, USA

Higgins, Michael (Actor)
Michael Hartig Agency
156 5th Ave Ste 820
New York, NY 10010-7767, USA

Higgins, Robert (Business Person)
Fleet Boston Corp
1 Federal St
Boston, MA 02110-2012, USA

Higgins, Rosalyn (Judge)
International Court of Justice
Peace Palace
Hague, KJ 2517, THE NETHERLANDS

Higgins, Scott (Baseball Player)
3591 Indian Clover St
Plumas Lake, CA 95961-8740, USA

Higgins, Tom (Football Player)
Buffalo Bills
127 Hillgrove Cres SW
Calgary, AB T2V 3K9, CANADA

Higginson, Bobby (Baseball Player)
Detroit Tigers
2039 Indian Sky Cir
Lakeland, FL 33813-4859, USA

Higginson, John (Doctor)
16 Sundew Rd
Savannah, GA 31411-2955, USA

Higginson, Torri (Actor)
c/o Staff Member *Sci-Fi Channel, The*
100 Universal Plaza Bldg 1280/12
Universal City, CA 91608, USA

Higgs, Mark (Football Player)
Dallas Cowboys
45 NW 156th Ln
Pembroke Pines, FL 33028-1500, USA

High Speed Scene, The (Music Group)
c/o Staff Member *Paradigm (Monterey)*
509 Hartnell St
Monterey, CA 93940-2825, USA

Higham, Scott (Journalist)
Washington Post
Editorial Dept
1150 15th St NW
Washington, DC 20071-0001, USA

Highman, Charles
4027 Farmouth Dr
Los Angeles, CA 90027-1314, USA

Highmore, Freddie (Actor)
c/o Sue Latimer *Artists Rights Group (ARG London)*
4 Great Portland St
London W1W 8PA, UNITED KINGDOM (UK)

Highsmith, Don (Football Player)
Oakland Raiders
221 S 9th Ave
Highland Park, NJ 08904-3145, USA

Hightower, John B (Director)
394 Emily Dickinson N
Newport News, VA 23606-1486, USA

Hightower, Rosella (Ballerina, Choreographer, Dancer)
Villa Piege Luiere
Parc Florentina Ave Vallauris
Cannes 06400, FRANCE

Highway 101
PO Box 1547
Goodlettsville, TN 37070-1547, USA

Hijuelos, Oscar (Writer)
Hofstra University
English Dept
10000 Fulton Ave
Hempstead, NY 11550, USA

Hikaru, Utada (Musician)
c/o Staff Member *Island Records*
825 8th Ave
New York, NY 10019-7472, USA

Hiken, Gerald
910 Moreno Ave
Palo Alto, CA 94303-3731, USA

Hil St Soul (Music Group)
c/o Staff Member *Paradigm (Monterey)*
509 Hartnell St
Monterey, CA 93940-2825, USA

Hilario, Maybyner (Nene) (Basketball Player)
Denver Nuggets
1000 Chopper Cir
Pepsi Center
Denver, CO 80204-5805, USA

Hilario, Nene (Basketball Player)
c/o Staff Member *Denver Nuggets*
1000 Chopper Cir
Pepsi Center
Denver, CO 80204-5805, USA

Hilbe, Alfred J (Government Official)
9494 Schaan
Garsill 11, LIECHTENSTEIN

Hildebrandt, Dieter
Rollenhagenstr. 3a
Munich D-81739, GERMANY

Hildebrandt, Greg (Cartoonist)
Dark Horse
10956 SE Main St
Milwaukie, OR 97222-7644, USA

Hildreth, Eugene A (Doctor)
2000 Cambridge Ave Apt 129
Reading, PA 19610-2741, USA

Hilfiger, Ally (Heir/Heiress, Reality TV Star)
c/o Staff Member *Tommy Hilfiger*
601 W 26th St Rm 500
New York, NY 10001-1142, USA

Hilfiger, Tommy (Designer, Fashion Designer)
Tommy Hilfiger Corporate Foundation
601 W 26th St Rm 500
New York, NY 10001-1142, USA

Hilgenberg, Jay W (Football Player)
Chicago Bears
1296 Kimmer Ct
Lake Forest, IL 60045-3669, USA

Hilgenberg, Joel (Football Player)
New Orleans Saints
2027 Ridgeway Dr
Iowa City, IA 52245-3239, USA

Hilgenberg, Wally (Football Player)
Detroit Lions
18526 Judicial Rd
Prior Lake, MN 55372-9165, USA

Hilgendorf, Tom (Baseball Player)
St Louis Cardinals
PO Box 124
Camanche, IA 52730-0124, USA

Hilger, Rusty (Football Player)
Oakland Raiders
1145 SW 78th Ter
Oklahoma City, OK 73139-2417, USA

Hiljus, Erik (Baseball Player)
Detroit Tigers
16944 Tupper St
Northridge, CA 91343-3535, USA

Hill, A Derek (Artist)
National Art Collections Fund
20 John Islip St
London SW1, UNITED KINGDOM (UK)

Hill, Andrew (Drew) (Football Player)
Los Angeles Rams
PO Box 741143
Riverdale, GA 30274-1301, USA

Hill, Anita (Educator)
600 3rd Ave # 200
New York, NY 10016-1901, USA

Hill, Bernard (Actor)
Julian Belfarge
46 Albermarle St
London W1X 4PP, UNITED KINGDOM (UK)

Hill, Bobby (Baseball Player)
Chicago Cubs
113 Constellation Cir
Jackson, TN 38305-6669, USA

Hill, Brendan (Music Group, Musician)
ArtistDirect
1601 Cloverfield Blvd # 400
Santa Monica, CA 90404-4082, USA

Hill, Bruce (Football Player)
Tampa Bay Buccaneers
1919 E Citation Ln
Tempe, AZ 85284-4704, USA

Hill, Calvin (Football Player)
Dallas Cowboys
10300 Walker Lake Dr
Great Falls, VA 22066-3557, USA

Hill, Carolyn (Golfer)
5906 Skimmer Point Blvd S
Gulfport, FL 33707-3938, USA

Hill, Damon G D (Race Car Driver)
PO Box 100
Nelson
Lanscashire BB9 8AQ, UNITED KINGDOM (UK)

Hill, Dan
1407 Mt. Pleasant Rd.
Toronto, ON M4N 2, CANADA

Hill, Dan (Music Group, Songwriter, Writer)
Paquin Entertainment
1067 Sherwin Road
Winnipeg, MB R3H 0TB, CANADA

Hill, Daniel W (Dan) (Football Player)
171 Montrose Dr
Dunbarton
Durham, NC 27707-3929, USA

Hill, Dave (Baseball Player)
Kansas City A's
125 Jenny Lind Dr
Hendersonville, NC 28791-1321, USA

Hill, Dave (Golfer)
Eddie Elias Enterprises
3641 Bay Hill Dr
Akron, OH 44333-9227, USA

Hill, David H (Football Player)
Kansas City Chiefs
921 Clements Cir
Moody, AL 35004-2512, USA

Hill, David L (Tex) (War Hero)
317 Elizabeth Rd
San Antonio, TX 78209-5932, USA

Hill, Derek (Football Player)
Pittsburgh Steelers
8939 Gallatin Rd
Pico Rivera, CA 90660-1693, USA

Hill, Donnie (Baseball Player)
Oakland A's
26161 Paseo Marbella
San Juan Capistrano, CA 92675-4454, USA

Hill, Draper (Cartoonist, Editor)
368 Washington Rd
Grosse Pointe Woods, MI 48230-1616, USA

Hill, Dule (Actor)
c/o Katherine Atkinson *Washington Square Arts (LA)*
1041 N Formosa Ave
Writers Bldg #305
West Hollywood, CA 90046-6703, USA

Hill, Dusty (Music Group, Musician)
Lone Wolf Mgmt
PO Box 163690
Austin, TX 78716-3690, USA

Hill, Eric (Football Player)
Phoenix Cardinals
5500 Palm Cir
Galveston, TX 77551-5566, USA

Hill, Erica (Television Host)
Prime News Tonight
1 Time Warner Ctr
Cnn
New York, NY 10019-6038, USA

Hill, Faith (Music Group, Musician)
c/o John Huie *Creative Artists Agency LCC (CAA-LA)*
2000 Avenue Of The Stars
Los Angeles, CA 90067-4700, USA

Hill, Fred (Football Player)
Philadelphia Eagles
31441 Paseo Riobo
San Juan Capistrano, CA 92675-5524, USA

Hill, Garry (Baseball Player)
Atlanta Braves
PO Box 8
Newell, NC 28126-0008, USA

Hill, Gary (Artist)
Comish College of the Arts Galleries
1000 Lenora St
Seattle, WA 98121-2707, USA

Hill, Geoffrey W (Writer)
Boston University
745 Commonwealth Ave
University Professors
Boston, MA 02215-1401, USA

Hill, George Roy
425 Madison Ave
New York, NY 10017-1110, USA

Hill, Glenallen (Baseball Player)
Toronto Blue Jays
108 Calvin Pl
Santa Cruz, CA 95060-3124, USA

Hill, Grant (Basketball Player)
c/o Team Member *Orlando Magic*
8701 Maitland Summit Blvd
Orlando, FL 32810-5915, USA

Hill, Greg (Football Player)
Houston Oilers
8014 Dowington Ct
Spring, TX 77379, USA

Hill, Greg (Football Player)
Kansas City Chiefs
PO Box 43210
Port Hueneme, CA 93044-3210, USA

Hill, Gregory (Director)
c/o Staff Member *Paul Lane Entertainment*
468 N Camden Dr
Beverly Hills, CA 90210-4507, USA

Hill, Harlon (Football Player)
Chicago Bears
RR 2 Box 276
Killen, AL 35645, USA

Hill, Henry (Writer)
Plesco Publishing
PO Box 88333
Seattle, WA 98138-2333, USA

Hill, Ike (Football Player)
Buffalo Bills
412 Randolph St
Oak Park, IL 60302-3260, USA

Hill, J D (Football Player)
Buffalo Bills
1550 S Yucca St
Chandler, AZ 85286-6859, USA

Hill, Jack (Director, Producer)
1445 N Fairfax Ave Apt 205
West Hollywood, CA 90046-3927, USA

Hill, James C (Judge)
US Court of Appeals
56 Forsyth St NW
Atlanta, GA 30303-2295, USA

Hill, James T (General)
Commanding General
Army Forces Command
Atlanta, GA 30330-0001, USA

Hill, Jeremy (Baseball Player)
Kansas City Royals
10050 Goodling Dr
Dallas, TX 75229, USA

Hill, Jessie (Music Group, Musician)
1210 Caffin Ave
New Orleans, LA 70117-2438, USA

Hill, Jim (Football Player)
San Diego Chargers
4120 Parva Ave
Los Angeles, CA 90027-1365, USA

Hill, Jim (Sportscaster)
ABC-TV
77 W 66th St
Sprots Dept
New York, NY 10023-6201, USA

Hill, John S (Football Player)
New York Giants
2005 Boyce Bridge Rd
Creedmoor, NC 27522-8023, USA

Hill, Jonah (Actor)
c/o Peter Principato *Principato/Young Management*
9665 Wilshire Blvd Ste 500
Beverly Hills, CA 90212-2312, USA

Hill, Julia Butterfly (Misc)
Circle of Life Foundation
PO Box 3764
Oakland, CA 94609-0764, USA

Hill, Ken (Baseball Player)
St Louis Cardinals
1360 Shady Oaks Dr
Southlake, TX 76092-4208, USA

Hill, Kenneth (Football Player)
Oakland Raiders
121 Hawkins Pl
Boonton, NJ 07005-1127, USA

Hill, Kent (Football Player)
Los Angeles Rams
630 Hawthorne Pl
Fayetteville, GA 30214-1218, USA

Hill, Kim (Music Group)
Ambassador Artist Agency
PO Box 50358
Nashville, TN 37205-0358, USA

Hill, King (Football Player)
St Louis Cardinals
7611 Sands Terrace Ln
Spring, TX 77389-2131, USA

Hill, Koyle (Baseball Player)
Los Angeles Dodgers
2819 Oriole Dr
Wichita, KS 67204-5342, USA

Hill, Lauryn (Actor, Musician, Producer)
c/o Nicole David *William Morris Agency (WMA-LA)*
1 William Morris Pl
Beverly Hills, CA 90212-4261, USA

Hill, Madre (Football Player)
Cleveland Browns
18 Charleston Ct
Elgin, SC 29045-8521, USA

Hill, Marc (Baseball Player)
St Louis Cardinals
203 Maple St
Elsberry, MO 63343-1604, USA

Hill, Mike (Golfer)
6750 Jefferson Rd
Brooklyn, MI 49230-9717, USA

Hill, Milt (Baseball Player)
Cincinnati Reds
1618 Middleton Way
West Palm Beach, FL 33409, USA

Hill, Pat (Football Player)
California State University
Athletic Dept
Fresno, CA 93740-0001, USA

Hill, Phil (Race Car Driver)
PO Box 3008
Santa Monica, CA 90408-3008, USA

Hill, Randal (Football Player)
Miami Dolphins
5360 SW 130th Ter
Miramar, FL 33027-5411, USA

Hill, Ron (Athlete, Track Athlete)
PO Box 11
Hyde
Cheshire SK14 1RD, UNITED KINGDOM (UK)

Hill, Sean (Hockey Player)
12441 Bagleaf Church Road
Raleigh, NC 27614, USA

Hill, Steven (Actor)
18 Jill Ln
Monsey, NY 10952-2619, USA

Hill, Susan E (Writer)
Longmoor Farmhouse Ebrington
Chipping Campden
Glos GL55 6NW, UNITED KINGDOM (UK)

Hill, Terence (Actor)
3 Los Pinos Rd
Santa Fe, NM 87507-4300, USA

Hill, Thomas (Tom) (Athlete, Track Athlete)
428 Elmcrest Dr
Norman, OK 73071-7053, USA

Hill, Tony (Football Player)
Dallas Cowboys
729 Forest Bend Dr
Plano, TX 75025-3205, USA

Hill, Tyrone (Baseball Player)
Pinnacle
5594 Electric Ave
San Bernardino, CA 92407-2713, USA

Hill, Virgil (Boxer)
1618 Santa Gertrudis Loop
Bismarck, ND 58503-0866, USA

Hill, Virgil L Jr (Admiral)
1000 Glendon Court
Ambler, PA 19002, USA

Hill, Walter (Director)
836 Greenway Dr
Beverly Hills, CA 90210-3006, USA

Hill, Winston (Football Player)
New York Jets
101 Lane Dr
Gladewater, TX 75647-5369, USA

Hill Hearth, Amy
c/o Daniel A (Dan) Strone *Trident Media Group LLC*
41 Madison Ave Fl 36
New York, NY 10010-2257, USA

Hill Smith, Marilyn (Opera Singer)
Music International
13 Ardilaun Road
Highbury
London N5 2QR, UNITED KINGDOM (UK)

Hill-Westerman, Joyce (Baseball Player)
1565 47th Ave
Kenosha, WI 53144-1289, USA

Hillaby, John (Writer)
Constable Co
Lanchesters
102 Fulham Palace Road
London W6 9ER, UNITED KINGDOM (UK)

Hillan, Patrick (Actor)
11005 Morrison St Apt 206
N Hollywood, CA 91601-3899, USA

Hillary, Edmund P (Mountaineer, Scientist)
278A Remuera Road
Auckland SE2, NEW ZEALAND

Hillary, Sir Edmund
278A Remuera Rd.
Auckland SE 2, NEW ZEALAND

Hille, Bertil (Doctor)
10630 Lakeside Ave NE
Seattle, WA 98125-6934, USA

Hillebrand, Gerald (Football Player)
New York Giants
23 Madison Cir
Davenport, IA 52806-2812, USA

Hillebrecht, Rudolf F H (Architect)
Gneiststr 7
Hanover 30169, GERMANY

Hillegas, Shawn (Baseball Player)
Los Angeles Dodgers
870 Rockville Rd
South Fork, PA 15956-3503, USA

Hillel, Shlomo (Government Official)
14 Gelber St
Jerusalem 96755, ISRAEL

Hillen, Bobby (Race Car Driver)
Donlavey Racing
5011 Midlothian Turnpike
Richmond, VA 23225, USA

Hillenbrand, Daniel A (Business Person)
Hillenbrand Industries
700 State RR 46 E
Batesville, IN 47006, USA

Hillenbrand, Laura (Writer)
Random House
1745 Broadway # B1
New York, NY 10019-4305, USA

The Celebrity Black Book 2008

Hillenbrand, Martin J (Diplomat)
University of Georgia
International Trade/Security Center
Athens, GA 30602, USA

Hillenbrand, Shea (Baseball Player)
Boston Red Sox
2614 E Via De Palmas
Gilbert, AZ 85298-2068, USA

Hillenburg, Stephen (Producer, Writer)
c/o Staff Member *Spongebob Squarepants*
231 W Olive Ave
Burbank, CA 91502-1825, USA

Hiller, Arthur (Director)
1218 Benedict Canyon Dr
Beverly Hills, CA 90210-2728, USA

Hiller, John (Baseball Player)
Detroit Tigers
W8085 Becker Dr
Iron Mountain, MI 49801-9385, USA

Hiller, Susan (Artist)
83 Loudoun Road
London NW8 0DL, UNITED KINGDOM
(UK)

Hillerman, John (Actor)
1110 Bade St
Houston, TX 77055-7404, USA

Hillerman, Tony (Writer)
1632 Francisca Rd NW
Albuquerque, NM 87107-7118, USA

Hillery, Patrick J (President)
Grasmere Greenfield Road
Sutton
Dublin 13, IRELAND

Hilliard, Dalton (Football Player)
New Orleans Saints
23 Hermitage Dr
Destrehan, LA 70047-3701, USA

Hilliard, Ike (Football Player)
New York Giants
Giants Stadium
East Rutherford, NJ 07073, USA

Hilliard, Issac (Football Player)
New York Giants
8240 SW 164th Ter
Palmetto Bay, FL 33157-3653, USA

Hillier, James (Inventor)
22 Arreton Rd # Cr31
Princeton, NJ 08540-1402, USA

Hillier, Steve (Music Group, Musician)
Primary Talent Int'l
2-12 Petonville Road
London N1 9PL, UNITED KINGDOM
(UK)

Hillis, Ali (Actor)
4460 Stern Ave
Back Guest House
Sherman Oaks, CA 91423-3521, USA

Hillis, W Daniel (Danny) (Scientist)
Applied Minds
1209 Grand Central Ave
Glendale, CA 91201-2425, USA

Hillman, Chris (Music Group, Musician,
Songwriter, Writer)
McMullen Co
433 N Camden Dr Ste 400
Beverly Hills, CA 90210-4408, USA

Hillman, Dave (Baseball Player)
Chicago Cubs
849 Mimosa Dr
Kingsport, TN 37660-2563, USA

Hillman, Eric (Baseball Player)
New York Mets
157 Bellaire St
Denver, CO 80220-5632, USA

Hills, Carla (Secretary)
3125 Chain Bridge Rd NW
Washington, DC 20016-3411, USA

Hills, Roderick M (Business Person,
Government Official)
Mudge Rose Guthrie Alexander Ferdon
1200 19th St NW
Washington, DC 20036-2412, USA

Hillton, Dave (Baseball Player)
San Diego Padres
4910 E Sunnyside Dr
Scottsdale, AZ 85254-4671, USA

Hilmers, David C (Astronaut)
2846 Bellefontaine St
Houston, TX 77025-1610, USA

Hilmes, Jerome B (General)
4900 Windsor Park
Sarasota, FL 34235-2609, USA

Hilton, Barron (Business Person)
Hilton Hotels Corp
9336 Civic Center Dr
Beverly Hills, CA 90210-3698, USA

Hilton, Howard (Baseball Player)
St Louis Cardinals
1453 Zion Way
Ventura, CA 93003-7339, USA

Hilton, Janet (Music Group, Musician)
Holly House E Downs Road
Bowdon Altrincham
Cheshire WA14 2LH, UNITED
KINGDOM (UK)

Hilton, John J (Football Player)
Pittsburgh Steelers
3911 S Fairway Dr
Powhatan, VA 23139-7022, USA

Hilton, Nicky (Heir/Heiress)
Venture IAB
2509 Wilshire Blvd
Los Angeles, CA 90057-4302, USA

Hilton, Paris (Heir/Heiress, Reality TV
Star)
c/o Jason Moore *Paris Hilton
Entertainment*
250 N Canon Dr Fl 2
Beverly Hills, CA 90210-5306, USA

Hilton, Roy (Football Player)
Baltimore Colts
8332 Merrymount Dr
Baltimore, MD 21244-2242, USA

Hilton, Tyler (Actor)
c/o Victoria Blake *Victoria Blake
Management*
23801 Calabasas Rd Ste 2023
Calabasas, CA 91302-1558, USA

Hilton (Lavandeira), Perez (Mario)
(Writer)
8174 W Sunset Blvd # 993
West Hollywood, CA 90046-2426, USA

Hiltz, Nichole (Actor)
c/o Steve Caserta *Sanders/Armstrong
Management*
2120 Colorado Ave Ste 120
Santa Monica, CA 90404-3561, USA

Hiltzik, Michael A (Journalist)
Los Angeles Times
202 W 1st St
Editorial Dept
Los Angeles, CA 90012-4105, USA

H.I.M. (Music Group)
Oy Heartagram Ltd
PL 194
Helsinki fin-00121, FINLAND

HIM (Music Group)
Oy Heartagram Ltd
PL 194
Helsinki fin-00121, FINLAND

Himelstein, Aaron (Actor)
c/o Staff Member *Stewart Talent*
58 W Huron St
Chicago, IL 60610-3806, USA

Himes, Dick (Football Player)
Green Bay Packers
431 Prairie Ln
Luxemburg, WI 54217-1054, USA

Himmelfarb, Gertrude (Historian)
2510 Virginia Ave NW
Washington, DC 20037-1902, USA

Hinault, Bernard
7 rue de la Sauvaie 21 Sud-Est.
Rennes F-35000, FRANCE

Hinch, A J (Baseball Player)
Oakland A's
16406 N 106th Way
Scottsdale, AZ 85255-9014, USA

Hinckley, Gordon B (Religious Leader)
Church of Latter Day Saints
50 E North Temple
Salt Lake City, UT 84150-0002, USA

Hinckley Jr, John
2700 Martin Luther King Jr Ave SE
Washington, DC 20032-2601, USA

Hinder (Music Group)
Universal Motown Records
1755 Broadway Fl 6
New York, NY 10019-3743, USA

Hindle, Art (Actor)
Buzz Halliday & Assoc
PO Box 481275
Los Angeles, CA 90048-9766, USA

Hindman, Stan (Football Player)
San Francisco 49ers
824 Creed Rd
Oakland, CA 94610-1827, USA

Hinds, Aisha (Actor)
c/o Michael Greene *Greene & Associates*
190 N Canon Dr Ste 200
Beverly Hills, CA 90210-5319, USA

Hinds, Ciaran (Actor)
c/o Larry Dalzell *Dalzell & Beresford Ltd*
26 Astwood Mews
London SW7 4DE, UNITED KINGDOM
(UK)

Hinds, Cirian (Actor)
c/o Staff Member *Endeavor Agency LLC
(LA)*
9601 Wilshire Blvd Fl 3
Beverly Hills, CA 90210-5204, USA

Hinds, Samuel A A (Prime Minister)
Prime Minister's Office
Public Buildings
Georgetown, GUYANA

Hinds, William E (Cartoonist)
1301 Spring Oaks Cir
Houston, TX 77055-4703, USA

Hine, Maynard K (Doctor)
1121 W Michigan St
Indianapolis, IN 46202-5211, USA

Hine, Patrick (Misc)
Lloyd's Bank
Cox's & Kings
7 Pall Mall
London SW1 5NA, UNITED KINGDOM
(UK)

Hiner, Glen H (Business Person)
Owens-Coming
1 Owens Coming Parkway
Toledo, OH 43659-0001, USA

Hines, Andre (Football Player)
Seattle Seahawks
1906 N 44th St
Kansas City, KS 66102-1814, USA

Hines, Cheryl (Actor)
c/o Peter Principato *Principato/Young
Management*
9665 Wilshire Blvd Ste 500
Beverly Hills, CA 90212-2312, USA

Hines, Deni (Music Group)
Peter Rix Mgmt
49 Hume St #200
Crows Nest, NSW 2065, AUSTRALIA

Hines, Glen Ray (Football Player)
Houston Oilers
861 N Queen Annes Lace Dr
Fayetteville, AR 72704-5106, USA

Hines, Mimi
1605 S 11th St
Las Vegas, NV 89104-1614, USA

Hingis, Martina (Tennis Player)
30165 Fairway Dr
Wesley Chapel, FL 33543-4400, USA

Hingle, Pat (Actor)
PO Box 2228
Carolina Beach, NC 28428-2228, USA

Hings, Donald L (Inventor)
281 Howard Ave
North Burnaby, BC V5B 4Y7, CANADA

Hingsen, Jurgen (Athlete, Track Athlete)
655 Circle Dr
Santa Barbara, CA 93108-1001, USA

Hinkle, George (Football Player)
San Diego Chargers
4998 Willowford Rd
Robertsville, MO 63072-1618, USA

Hinkle, Jack (Football Player)
New York Giants
2114 Weber Ln
Norristown, PA 19403-3014, USA

Hinkle, Lon (Golfer)
PO Box 1347
Bigfork, MT 59911-1347, USA

Hinkle, Marin (Actor)
c/o Staff Member *Innovative Artists (LA)*
1505 10th St
Santa Monica, CA 90401-2805, USA

Hinkle, Robert
5225 Agnes Ave Apt 102
N Hollywood, CA 91607-2749, USA

Hinkley, Brent (Actor)
c/o Staff Member *Gage Group, The (LA)*
14724 Ventura Blvd Ste 505
Sherman Oaks, CA 91403-3505, USA

Hinman, Dayle (Misc)
c/o Staff Member *Story House
Productions, Inc*
2233 Wisconsin Ave NW Ste 420
Washington, DC 20007-4122, USA

Hinn, Benny (Religious Leader)
PO Box 162000
Irving, TX 75016-2000, USA

Hinnant, Michael (Football Player)
Pittsburgh Steelers
43 Ashford Way
Schwenksville, PA 19473-1693, USA

Hinners, Noel (Government Official)
7 Greyswood Ct
Rockville, MD 20854-6149, USA

Hino, Kazuyoshi (Designer, Fashion Designer)
Hino & Malee Inc
3701 N Ravenswood Ave
Chicago, IL 60613-3553, USA

Hinojosa, Ricardo H (Judge)
US District Court
PO Box 5007
McAllen, TX 78502-5007, USA

Hinojosa, Tish (Music Group, Songwriter, Writer)
PO Box 3304
Austin, TX 78764-3304, USA

Hinrich, Kirk (Basketball Player)
c/o Staff Member *Chicago Bulls*
1901 W Madison St
United Center
Chicago, IL 60612-2459, USA

Hinrichs, Paul (Baseball Player)
Boston Red Sox
1982 Brett Dr
Madisonville, KY 42431-9115, USA

Hinsche, Billy
2588 El Camino Real Ste F Pmb 101
Carlsbad, CA 92008-1212, USA

Hinshaw, George (Baseball Player)
San Diego Padres
1240 E Ontario Ave # 123
Corona, CA 92881-8671, USA

Hinske, Eric (Baseball Player)
Toronto Blue Jays
631 8th St
Menasha, WI 54952-2374, USA

Hinsley, Jerry (Baseball Player)
New York Mets
4255 Holliday Ln
Las Cruces, NM 88007-5760, USA

Hinson, Jordan (Actor)
c/o Bonnie Liedtke *William Morris Agency (WMA-LA)*
1 William Morris Pl
Beverly Hills, CA 90212-4261, USA

Hinson, Larry (Golfer)
RR 4 Box 397
Douglas, GA 31533, USA

Hinson, Roy (Basketball Player)
4272 State Highway 27
Monmouth Junction, NJ 08852, USA

Hinterseer, Ernst (Skier)
Hahnenkammstr
Kitzbuhel 6370, AUSTRIA

Hintikka, Jaakko J (Misc)
University of Helsinki
PO Box 24
Helsinki 00014, FINLAND

Hinton, Charles R (Football Player)
New York Giants
124 Tanglewood Rd
Natchez, MS 39120-4526, USA

Hinton, Chris (Football Player)
Baltimore Colts
650 Galway Dr
Roswell, GA 30076-5132, USA

Hinton, Christopher J (Chris) (Football Player)
5136 Falcon Chase Ln NE
Atlanta, GA 30342, USA

Hinton, Chuck (Baseball Player)
Washington Senators
6330 16th St NW
Washington, DC 20011-8010, USA

Hinton, Darby (Actor)
1267 Bel Air Rd
Los Angeles, CA 90077, USA

Hinton, Eddie (Football Player)
Baltimore Colts
34 Auburn Rdg
Spring Branch, TX 78070-6014, USA

Hinton, James David
2806 Oak Point Dr
Los Angeles, CA 90068, USA

Hinton, Rich (Baseball Player)
Chicago White Sox
7447 Hawkins Rd
Sarasota, FL 34241-9376, USA

Hinton, S E
8955 Beverly Blvd
West Hollywood, CA 90048-2423, USA

Hinton, Sam (Music Group, Songwriter, Writer)
1719 Addison St
Berkeley, CA 94703-1501, USA

Hinton of Bankside, Christopher (Engineer, Government Official)
Tiverton Lodge
Dulwich Common
London SG2 7EW, UNITED KINGDOM (UK)

Hintz, Donald C (Business Person)
Entergy Corp
10055 Grogans Mill Rd # 5A
The Woodlands, TX 77380-1059, USA

Hinzo, Tommy (Baseball Player)
Cleveland Indians
242 I St
Chula Vista, CA 91910-5603, USA

Hiort, Esbjonm (Architect)
Bel Colles Farm
Parkvej 6
Rungsted Kyst 2960, DENMARK

Hipp, I M (Football Player)
Oakland Raiders
27 Underwood Pl
Alexandria, VA 22304-4941, USA

Hipp, Paul
8383 Wilshire Blvd Ste 550
Beverly Hills, CA 90211-2417, USA

Hipple, Eric (Football Player)
Detroit Lions
7155 Driftwood Dr
Fenton, MI 48430-4304, USA

Hipps, Claude (Football Player)
Pittsburgh Steelers
1535 Dartmouth Rd
Columbus, GA 31904-1903, USA

Hipwell, Elizabeth
18 Gramercy Park S
New York, NY 10003-1724, USA

Hirase, Mayumi (Golfer)
I M G
1360 E 9th St Ste 100
Cleveland, OH 44114-1730, USA

Hird, Thora
21 Leinster Mews
London, ENGLAND W2 3EY, UNITED KINGDOM (UK)

Hire, Kathryn P (Kay) (Astronaut)
PO Box 580146
Houston, TX 77258-0146, USA

Hiroshima
1460 4th St Ste 205
Santa Monica, CA 90401-3414, USA

Hirosue, Ryoyo (Actor)
c/o Omiotek Maciej *OmniotComp*
Sowinskiego 27A
Grodzisk
Mazowiecki, POLAND

Hirsch, David
6255 W Sunset Blvd # 627
Los Angeles, CA 90028-7403, USA

Hirsch, E D Jr (Educator)
University of Virginia
Education Dept
Charlottesville, VA 22906, USA

Hirsch, Emile (Actor)
c/o Sam Maydew *The Collective*
9100 Wilshire Blvd # 700 W
Beverly Hills, CA 90212-3401, USA

Hirsch, Hallee (Actor, Musician)
c/o Amy Abell *Innovative Artists (LA)*
1505 10th St
Santa Monica, CA 90401-2805, USA

Hirsch, Judd (Actor)
c/o Joel Rudnick *Paradigm (LA)*
360 N Crescent Dr
North Bldg
Beverly Hills, CA 90210-6820, USA

Hirsch, Laurence E (Business Person)
Centex Corp
2728 N Harwood St
Dallas, TX 75201-1591, USA

Hirsch, Leon C (Inventor)
150 Glover Ave
Norwalk, CT 06850-1308, USA

Hirsch, Robert P (Actor)
1 Pl du Palais Bourbon
Paris 75007, FRANCE

Hirsch, Stan
16027 Ventura Blvd Ste 206
Encino, CA 91436-2774, USA

Hirschbeck, John (Baseball Player)
8730 Raintree Run
Youngstown, OH 44514-2987, USA

Hirschbeck, Mark (Baseball Player)
15 Blackberry Ln
Shelton, CT 06484-3774, USA

Hirschbiegel, Oliver (Director)
c/o Tobin Babst *United Talent Agency (UTA)*
9560 Wilshire Blvd Ste 500
Beverly Hills, CA 90212-2401, USA

Hirschfelder, David (Composer)
APRA
PO Box 567
Crows Nest, NSW 2065, AUSTRALIA

Hirschfielder, Gerald J (Cinematographer)
425 Ashland St
Ashland, OR 97520-3104, USA

Hirschman, Albert O (Economist)
16 Newlin Rd
Princeton, NJ 08540-4916, USA

Hirschmann, Ralph F (Misc)
711 Radcliff Ct
Lansdale, PA 19446-5895, USA

Hirson, Alice (Actor)
Halpem Assoc
PO Box 5597
Santa Monica, CA 90409-5597, USA

Hirst, Damien (Artist)
White Cube Gallery
Saint James's
44 Duke St
London SW1Y 6DD, UNITED KINGDOM (UK)

Hirtz, Dagmar
Jollystr. 14
Munich D-81545, GERMANY

Hiser, Gene (Baseball Player)
Chicago Cubs
1450 Caldwell Ln
Hoffman Estates, IL 60169-1202, USA

Hiskey, Babe (Golfer)
1706 12th St
Galena Park, TX 77547-2302, USA

Hisle, Larry E (Baseball Player)
Philadelphia Phillies
312 W Saddleworth Ct
Mequon, WI 53092-3564, USA

Hislop, Ian (Actor)
c/o Jenne Casarotto *Casarotto Ramsay & Associates Ltd (UK)*
National House
60-66 Wardour Street
London W1V 4ND, UNITED KINGDOM (UK)

Hisner, Harley (Baseball Player)
Boston Red Sox
14322 Monroeville Rd
Monroeville, IN 46773-9555, USA

Hitchcock, Billy (Baseball Player)
Detroit Tigers
1117 W Collinwood Cir
Opelika, AL 36801-2705, USA

Hitchcock, Ken (Hockey Player)
4531 Rheims Pl
Dallas, TX 75205-3628, USA

Hitchcock, Ray (Football Player)
Washington Redskins
2190 Arcade St
Saint Paul, MN 55109-2572, USA

Hitchcock, Robyn (Music Group, Songwriter, Writer)
Agency Group Ltd
1775 Broadway Ste 515
New York, NY 10019-1903, USA

Hitchcock, Russell (Musician)
Agency for Performing Arts
405 S Beverly Dr Ste 500
Beverly Hills, CA 90212-4425, USA

Hitchcock, Sterling (Baseball Player)
New York Yankees
255 Yucca Rd
Naples, FL 34102-5318, USA

Hitchins, Christopher
2022 Columbia Rd NW
Washington, DC 20009-1352, USA

Hite, Shere
PO Box 1037
New York, NY 10028-0007, USA

Hitt, Joel (Football Player)
Cleveland Rams
800 Founders Pointe Blvd
Franklin, TN 37064-0752, USA

Hitt, John C (Educator)
1000 Central Florida Blvd
Orlando, FL 32826-2404, USA

Hitt, Lee (Football Player)
Green Bay Packers
612 Crown Colony Dr
Arlington, TX 76006-3600, USA

Hittle, Lloyd (Baseball Player)
Washington Senators
2031 W Elm St
Lodi, CA 95242-2820, USA

Hix, William (Football Player)
Philadelphia Eagles
5070 White Dr
Batesville, AR 72501-9138, USA

Hjejle, Iben (Actor)
William Morris Agency
151 El Camino Dr
Beverly Hills, CA 90212-2775, USA

Hlinka, Nichol (Ballerina)
New York City Ballet
Lincoln Center Plaza
New York, NY 10023, USA

Hnatiuk, Glen (Golfer)
8746 Mississippi Run
Weeki Wachee, FL 34613-4046, USA

Hnilicka, Milan (Hockey Player)
Los Angeles Kings
1111 S Figueroa St
Staples Center
Los Angeles, CA 90015-1300, USA

Ho, David (Scientist)
Aaron Diamond AIDS Research Center
455 1st Ave
New York, NY 10016-9121, USA

Ho, Don
PO Box 90039
Honolulu, HI 96835-0039, USA

Ho, Donald T (Don) (Music Group)
277 Lewers St
Honolulu, HI 96815, USA

Ho, Tao (Architect)
Upper Deck North Point West
Passenger Ferry Pier
North Point, HONG KONG

Hoag, Charles (Basketball Player)
2927 SW Foxcroft Court #2
Topeka, KS 66614, USA

Hoag, Jan
855 N Martel Ave
Los Angeles, CA 90046-7561, USA

Hoag, Judith W (Actor)
HWA Talent
3500 W Olive Ave Ste 1400
Burbank, CA 91505-5512, USA

Hoag, Peter C (Misc)
3566 Little Rock Dr
Provo, UT 84604, USA

Hoag, Tami (Writer)
Delacorte Press
1540 Broadway
New York, NY 10036-4039, USA

Hoage, Terrell L (Terry) (Football Player)
New Orleans Saints
870 Arbor Rd
Paso Robles, CA 93446-8609, USA

Hoagland, Edward (Writer)
PO Box 51
Barton, VT 05822-0051, USA

Hoagland, Jaheim (Musician)
c/o Staff Member *JL Entertainment Inc*
18653 Ventura Blvd # 340
Tarzana, CA 91356-4103, USA

Hoagland, Jimmie L (Jim) (Journalist)
Washington Post
Editorial Dept
1150 15th St NW
Washington, DC 20071-0001, USA

Hoaglin, Fred (Coach, Football Coach, Football Player)
Cleveland Browns
7 Governors Rd
Hilton Head, SC 29928-3018, USA

Hoak, Dick (Football Player)
Pittsburgh Steelers
162 Crest View Dr
Greensburg, PA 15601-1414, USA

Hoar, Joseph P (General)
386 13th St
Del Mar, CA 92014-2555, USA

Hoard, Leroy (Football Player)
Cleveland Browns
4301 NE 15th Ave
Oakland Park, FL 33334-4712, USA

Hoare, Tony
430 Edgware Rd
London, ENGLAND W2 1EG, UNITED KINGDOM (UK)

Hoban, Mike (Football Player)
Chicago Bears
1917 Holly Ave
Darien, IL 60561-3518, USA

Hoban, Russell C (Writer)
6 Musgrave Crescent
London SW6 4PT, UNITED KINGDOM (UK)

Hobart, Nick (Cartoonist)
5632 Indiana Ave
New Port Richey, FL 34652-2333, USA

Hobaugh, Charles O (Astronaut)
NASA
2101 Nasa Pkwy
Johnson Space Center
Houston, TX 77058-3691, USA

Hobault, John (Scientist)
51 Winster Fax
Williamsburg, VA 23185-5543, USA

Hobbs, Becky (Musician)
Entertainment Artists
2409 21st Ave S Ste 100
Nashville, TN 37212-5317, USA

Hobbs, Chelsea (Actor)
c/o Jennifer Millar *Abrams Artists Agency (LA)*
9200 W Sunset Blvd Ph 11
Los Angeles, CA 90069-3601, USA

Hobbs, Franklin (Fritz) (Misc)
151 E 79th St
New York, NY 10075-0417, USA

Hobbs, Rebecca (Actor)
c/o Kathryn Rawlings *Kathryn Rawlings Actors Agency*
PO Box 105
Auckland Central 657, NEW ZEALAND

Hobby, Marion (Football Player)
New England Patriots
708 Nytol Cir
Birmingham, AL 35210-2919, USA

Hoblit, Gregory (Director)
c/o David Wirtschafter *William Morris Agency (WMA-LA)*
1 William Morris Pl
Beverly Hills, CA 90212-4261, USA

Hobson, Clell L (Butch) (Baseball Player)
3705 Dearing Downs Dr
Tuscaloosa, AL 35405-4653, USA

Hobson, J Allan (Scientist)
Harvard University
Sleep Laboratory
Cambridge, MA 02138, USA

Hobson, Jeff (Misc)
Jack Grenier Productions
32630 Concord Dr
Madison Heights, MI 48071-1110, USA

Hoch, Carin (Golfer)
I M G
1360 E 9th St Ste 100
Cleveland, OH 44114-1730, USA

Hoch, Danny (Artist)
Columbia Artists Mgmt Inc
1790 Broadway Fl 6
New York, NY 10019-1412, USA

Hoch, Scott (Golfer)
8800 Lake Sheen Ct
Orlando, FL 32836-5482, USA

Hochhuth, Rolf (Writer)
PO Box 661
Basel 4002, SWITZERLAND

Hochstrasser, Robin M (Misc)
University of Pennsylvania
Chemistry Dept
Philadelphia, PA 19104, USA

Hochwald, Bari (Actor)
Herb Tannen
10801 National Blvd Ste 101
Los Angeles, CA 90064-4140, USA

Hock, Dee Ward (Business Person)
Visa International
900 Metro Center Blvd
Foster City, CA 94404-2172, USA

Hocke, Stefan (Skier)
Sportgymnasium
Am Harzwald 3
Oberhof 98558, GERMANY

Hockenberry, John (Actor, Correspondent, Writer)
c/o Sally Wilcox *Creative Artists Agency LCC (CAA-LA)*
2000 Avenue Of The Stars
Los Angeles, CA 90067-4700, USA

Hockney, David (Artist)
7508 Santa Monica Blvd
West Hollywood, CA 90046-6407, USA

Hodder, Kane (Actor)
3701 Senda Calma
Calabasas, CA 91302-3066, USA

Hodder, Kenneth (Religious Leader)
Salvation Army
615 Slaters Ln
Alexandria, VA 22314-1112, USA

Hoddinott, Alun (Composer)
64 Gowerton Road
Three Crosses
Swansea, WALES SA4 3PX, UNITED KINGDOM (UK)

Hoddle, Glenn (Soccer Player)
Football Assn
16 Lancaster Gate
London W2 3LW, UNITED KINGDOM (UK)

Hodel, Donald P (Secretary)
1801 Sara Dr Ste L
Chesapeake, VA 23320-2647, USA

Hodge, Aldis (Actor)
c/o Andrew Rogers *Paradigm (LA)*
360 N Crescent Dr
North Bldg
Beverly Hills, CA 90210-6820, USA

Hodge, Charles E (Charlie) (Hockey Player)
21356 86A Crescent
Langley, BC V1M 2A2, CANADA

Hodge, Daniel A (Dan) (Wrestler)
General Delivery
Perry, OK 73077-9999, USA

Hodge, Douglas (Actor)
c/o Lindy King *Peters Fraser & Dunlop (PFD - UK)*
Drury House
34-43 Russell St
London WC2B 5HA, UNITED KINGDOM (UK)

Hodge, Kenneth R (Ken) Sr (Hockey Player)
1115 Main St
Lynnfield, MA 01940-1030, USA

Hodge, Patricia (Actor)
International Creative Mgmt
76 Oxford St
London W1N 0AX, UNITED KINGDOM (UK)

Hodge, Sedrick (Football Player)
New Orleans Saints
120 Victoria Pl
Fayetteville, GA 30214-1176, USA

Hodge, Stephanie (Actor)
Gersh Agency
232 N Canon Dr
Beverly Hills, CA 90210-5302, USA

Hodge, Sue
82 Constance Rd. Twickenham
Middlesex A, ENGLAND TW2 7J,
UNITED KINGDOM (UK)

Hodges, Bill (Basketball Player, Coach)
Georgia College
Athletic Dept
Milledgeville, GA 31061, USA

Hodges, Eric (Actor)
3800 W Alameda Ave
Burbank, CA 91505-4300, USA

Hodges, Louise
31A St. George's Rd Leyton
London, ENGLAND E10 5RH, UNITED KINGDOM (UK)

Hodges, Mike (Director)
Wesley Farm Durweston
Blanford Forum
Dorset DT11 0QG, UNITED KINGDOM (UK)

Hodges, Morris (Baseball Player)
1520 River Haven Ln
Birmingham, AL 35244-1259, USA

Hodges, Pat (Actor, Musician)
c/o Staff Member *Diva Central Inc*
7510 W Sunset Blvd Ste 1445
Los Angeles, CA 90046-3408, USA

Hodges, Trey (Athlete, Baseball Player)
c/o Staff Member *Atlanta Braves*
PO Box 4064
Turner Field
Atlanta, GA 30302-4064, USA

Hodgkin, Howard (Artist)
Anthony D'Offay Gallery
9/24 Dering St
London W1R 9AA, UNITED KINGDOM
(UK)

Hodgson, James D (Secretary)
10132 Hillgrove Dr
Beverly Hills, CA 90210-2733, USA

Hodgson, Pat (Football Player)
Washington Redskins
5 Wagon Trl
Mahwah, NJ 07430-3510, USA

Hodo, David (Music Group)
8255 W Sunset Blvd
West Hollywood, CA 90046-2417, USA

Hodson, Tom (Football Player)
New England Patriots
17938 Crossing Blvd
Baton Rouge, LA 70810-3840, USA

Hoechlin, Tyler (Actor)
c/o Brian Gersh *Blue Train Entertainment*
798 Brooktree Rd
Pacific Palisades, CA 90272-3901, USA

Hoeft, William F (Billy) (Baseball Player)
Canadian Lakes
9965 Lost Canyon Dr
Stanwood, MI 49346-9404, USA

Hoelscher, Joel (Football Player)
Washington Redskins
8931 N Star Fort Loramie Rd
Yorkshire, OH 45388-9750, USA

Hoenig, Michael (Composer)
Gorfaine/Schwartz
4111 W Alameda Ave Ste 509
Burbank, CA 91505-4171, USA

Hoenig, Thomas M (Financier,
Government Official)
615 W Meyer Blvd
Kansas City, MO 64113-1543, USA

Hoerner, Dick (Football Player)
Los Angeles Rams
15925 Alta Vista Dr Unit A
La Mirada, CA 90638-3265, USA

Hoest, Bunny (Cartoonist)
William Hoest Enterprises
27 Watch Way
Lloyd Neck
Lloyd Harbor, NY 11743-9707, USA

Hoey, George (Football Player)
St Louis Cardinals
530 Walden Way
Fort Collins, CO 80526-3235, USA

Hofer, Paul (Football Player)
San Francisco 49ers
1747 Overton Park Ave
Memphis, TN 38112-5343, USA

Hoff, Marcian E (Ted) Jr (Inventor)
12226 Colina Dr
Los Altos Hills, CA 94024-5299, USA

Hoff, Philip H (Governor)
Hoff Wilson Powell Lang
PO Box 567
Burlington, VT 05402-0567, USA

Hoffa, James P (Misc)
2593 Hounds Chase Dr
Troy, MI 48098-2338, USA

Hoffman, Alice (Writer)
3 Hurlbut St
Cambridge, MA 02138-1603, USA

Hoffman, Barbara (Baseball Player)
318 E Mill St
Millstadt, IL 62260-1218, USA

Hoffman, Basil (Actor)
26 Aller Ct
Glendale, CA 91206-1701, USA

Hoffman, Bill (Baseball Player)
Philadelphia Phillies
2 Robin Ln
Lafayette Hill, PA 19444-1402, USA

Hoffman, Bob (Football Player)
Washington Redskins
606 Washington Ave
Taft, CA 93268-4444, USA

Hoffman, Darleane C (Physicist)
Lawrence Berkeley Laboratory
1 Cyctotron Road
Berkeley, CA 94720-0001, USA

Hoffman, Dustin (Actor, Director,
Producer)
c/o Staff Member *Punch Productions*
11661 San Vicente Blvd Ste 222
Los Angeles, CA 90049-5110, USA

Hoffman, Elizabeth (Actor)
Bauman Assoc
5750 Wilshire Blvd # 473
Los Angeles, CA 90036-3697, USA

Hoffman, Elizabeth (Educator)
University of Colorado
President's Office
Boulder, CO 80309-0001, USA

Hoffman, Glenn E (Baseball Player)
Boston Red Sox
201 S Old Bridge Rd
Anaheim, CA 92808-1326, USA

Hoffman, Guy (Baseball Player)
Chicago White Sox
1016 Crooked Stick Ln
Normal, IL 61761-4897, USA

Hoffman, Jeffrey A (Astronaut)
US Embassy
2 Ave Gabriel
PSC 116/NASA
Paris Cedex 75382, FRANCE

Hoffman, John Robert (Writer)
c/o Rosalie Swedlin *Industry
Entertainment*
955 Carrillo Dr Ste 300
Los Angeles, CA 90048-5400, USA

Hoffman, Jorg (Swimmer)
Saarmunder Str 74
Potsdam 14478, GERMANY

Hoffman, Matt (Actor)
c/o Staff Member *DDK Talent*
3800 Barham Blvd Ste 303
Los Angeles, CA 90068-1042, USA

Hoffman, Michael (Director)
c/o Doug MacLaren *International Creative
Management (ICM-LA)*
10250 Constellation Blvd
Los Angeles, CA 90067-6200, USA

Hoffman, Paul Felix (Geophysicist,
Physicist)
162 Cypress St
Brookline, MA 02445-6767, USA

Hoffman, Philip Seymour (Actor,
Producer)
c/o Staff Member *Cooper's Town
Productions*
302A W 12th St # 214
New York, NY 10014-1947, USA

Hoffman, Ray (Baseball Player)
Washington Senators
14475 Thompson Rd
Alpharetta, GA 30004-6912, USA

Hoffman, Rick (Actor)
c/o Staff Member *Jeff Morrone
Management*
9350 Wilshire Blvd Ste 224
Beverly Hills, CA 90212-3204, USA

Hoffman, Robert (Actor, Dancer)
c/o Staff Member *Pakula/King &
Associates*
9229 W Sunset Blvd Ste 315
Los Angeles, CA 90069-3403, USA

Hoffman, Ted Jr (Bowler)
1568 Partarian Way
San Jose, CA 95129, USA

Hoffman, Toby (Music Group, Musician)
Columbia Artists Mgmt Inc
1790 Broadway Fl 6
New York, NY 10019-1412, USA

Hoffman, Trevor (Baseball Player)
Florida Marlins
2220 Ocean Front
Del Mar, CA 92014-2134, USA

Hoffman, William M (Songwriter, Writer)
190 Prince St
New York, NY 10012-2906, USA

Hoffmann, Christian (Skier)
Frunwald 7
Aigen 4160, AUSTRIA

Hoffmann, Frank N (Nordy) (Football
Player)
400 N Capitol St NW # 327
Washington, DC 20001-1511, USA

Hoffmann, Gaby
8942 Wilshire Blvd
Beverly Hills, CA 90211-1908, USA

Hoffmann, Isabella
6500 Wilshire Blvd Ste 2200
Los Angeles, CA 90048-4942, USA

Hoffmann, Roald (Nobel Prize Laureate)
4 Sugarbush Ln
Ithaca, NY 14850-6326, USA

Hoffs, Susanna (Musician)
Bangles Mall
PO Box 180
1341W Fullerton Ave
Chicago, IL 60690-0180, USA

Hofheimer, Charlie (Actor)
c/o Abby Bluestone *Innovative Artists (LA)*
1505 10th St
Santa Monica, CA 90401-2805, USA

Hofmann, Al (Race Car Driver)
PO Box 346
Umatilla, FL 32784-0346, USA

Hofmann, Detlef (Athlete)
Saarlandstr 164
Karlsruhe 76187, GERMANY

Hofmann, Douglas (Artist)
8602 Saxon Cir
Baltimore, MD 21236-2559, USA

Hofmann, Kenneth (Baseball Player)
Oakland A's
1380 Galaxy Way
Concord, CA 94520-4912, USA

Hofmann, Peter (Opera Singer)
Postfach 127
Kemnath 95474, GERMANY

Hofschneider, Marco (Actor)
Progressive Artists Agency
400 S Beverly Dr Ste 216
Beverly Hills, CA 90212-4404, USA

Hofstatter, Peter R (Doctor, Psychic)
Lehmkuhleweg 16
Buxtehude 21614, GERMANY

Hogan, Brooke (Musician, Reality TV Star)
Brookestar
130 Willadel Dr
Belleair, FL 33756-1942, USA

Hogan, Chris (Actor)
c/o Staff Member *Rigberg-Rugolo
Entertainment*
1180 S Beverly Dr Ste 601
Los Angeles, CA 90035-1158, USA

Hogan, Darrell (Football Player)
Pittsburgh Steelers
14988 Scenic Loop Rd
Helotes, TX 78023-3701, USA

Hogan, Hulk (Actor, Wrestler)
c/o Staff Member *Pink Sneakers
Productions*
1000 Colour Pl
Apopka, FL 32703-7753, USA

Hogan, Linda (Writer)
University of Colorado
English Dept
Boulder, CO 80309-0001, USA

Hogan, Marc (Football Player)
New York Jets
3761 Colby St
Pittsburgh, PA 15214-2134, USA

Hogan, Mike (Football Player)
Philadelphia Eagles
11 Walton Creek Dr SW
Rome, GA 30165-7228, USA

Hogan, Paul (Actor)
18 Marshall Crescent
Beacon Hill, NSW 2060, AUSTRALIA

Hogan, Paul (Actor)
c/o Staff Member *Silver Lion Films*
701 Santa Monica Blvd Ste 240
Santa Monica, CA 90401-2625, USA

Hogan, Paul (Reality TV Star)
c/o Staff Member *Acme Talent & Literary
(LA)*
4727 Wilshire Blvd Ste 333
Los Angeles, CA 90010-3874, USA

Hogan, Paul (PJ) (Director, Producer,
Writer)
c/o Richard Lovett *Creative Artists Agency
LCC (CAA-LA)*
2000 Avenue Of The Stars
Los Angeles, CA 90067-4700, USA

Hogan, Robert (Actor)
344 W 89th St Apt 1B
New York, NY 10024-2176, USA

Hogan, Terry
130 Willadel Dr
Belleair, FL 33756-1942, USA

Hogarth, Freddie
69 St. Quentin Ave. #1
London, ENGLAND W10 6PA, UNITED
KINGDOM (UK)

Hoge, Merril (Football Player)
Pittsburgh Steelers
105 Stanbery Rdg
Fort Thomas, KY 41075-1068, USA

Hogeboom, Gary (Football Player)
Dallas Cowboys
13635 Hofma Ct
Grand Haven, MI 49417-9669, USA

Hogestyn, Drake (Actor)
c/o Staff Member *Hines and Hunt Entertainment*
1213 W Magnolia Blvd
Burbank, CA 91506-1829, USA

Hogg, Christopher A (Business Person)
Courtaulds
18 Hanover Square
London W1A 2BB, UNITED KINGDOM (UK)

Hogg, James R (Admiral)
2556 W Main Rd
Prescott Farm
Portsmouth, RI 02871-1022, USA

Hoggard, Jay (Music Group, Musician)
Creative Music Consultants
181 Chrystie St # 300
New York, NY 10002-1275, USA

Hogland, Doug (Football Player)
San Francisco 49ers
1514 4th St
Tillamook, OR 97141-3426, USA

Hogue, Cal (Baseball Player)
Pittsburgh Pirates
1765 Piper Ln Apt 103
Dayton, OH 45440-5091, USA

Hogue, Stacey
10474 Santa Monica Blvd Ste 380
Los Angeles, CA 90025-6943, USA

Hogwood, Christopher J H (Conductor, Musician)
10 Brookside
Cambridge CB2 1JE, UNITED KINGDOM (UK)

Hohlmayer, Alice (Baseball Player)
5155 Cedarwood Rd Apt 47
Bonita, CA 91902-1946, USA

Hohmann, John (Misc)
Louis Berger Assoc
1110 E Missouri Ave Ste 200
Phoenix, AZ 85014-2754, USA

Hohn, Robert (Football Player)
Pittsburgh Steelers
2624 N 78th St
Lincoln, NE 68507-2965, USA

Hohne, Claus
An der Kiesgrube 3
Holzkirchen D-83607, GERMANY

Hoiby, Lee (Composer, Musician)
9807 County Hwy 28
Long Eddy, NY 12760-4204, USA

Hoiles, Chris (Baseball Player)
Baltimore Orioles
8688 Jerry City Rd
Wayne, OH 43466-9837, USA

Hoisington, Allan (Football Player)
Oakland Raiders
71371 Biskra Rd
Rancho Mirage, CA 92270-4251, USA

Hoke, Jon (Football Player)
Chicago Bears
2665 Corlington Dr
Dayton, OH 45440-1406, USA

Hoku (Musician)
c/o Staff Member *United Talent Agency (UTA)*
9560 Wilshire Blvd Ste 500
Beverly Hills, CA 90212-2401, USA

Holahan, Dennis
9250 Wilshire Blvd Ste 208
Beverly Hills, CA 90212-3344, USA

Holbert, Aaron (Baseball Player)
St Louis Cardinals
32015 Teague Way
Zephyrhills, FL 33545-1612, USA

Holbert, Jerry (Cartoonist, Editor)
Boston Herald
1 Herald St
Editorial Dept
Roxbury, MA 02118, USA

Holbert, Ray (Baseball Player)
San Diego Padres
20450 N 40th Dr
Glendale, AZ 85308-4737, USA

Holbrook, Bill (Cartoonist)
King Features Syndicate
888 7th Ave Ste 201
New York, NY 10106-0201, USA

Holbrook, Hal (Actor)
c/o Mark Turner *Abrams Artists Agency (LA)*
9200 W Sunset Blvd Ph 11
Los Angeles, CA 90069-3601, USA

Holbrook, Karen (Educator)
Presidint's Office
Ohio State University
Columbus, OH 43210, USA

Holbrook, Sam (Baseball Player)
2620 Sungale Ct
Lexington, KY 40513-1463, USA

Holbrook, Terry (Hockey Player)
8415 Hendricks Rd
Mentor, OH 44060-2259, USA

Holcomb, Corey (Comedian)
c/o Staff Member *William Morris Agency (WMA-LA)*
1 William Morris Pl
Beverly Hills, CA 90212-4261, USA

Holcombe, Ken (Baseball Player)
New York Yankees
32 Botany Dr
Asheville, NC 28805-1633, USA

Holden, Alexandra (Actor)
c/o Pamela Cole *United Talent Agency (UTA)*
9560 Wilshire Blvd Ste 500
Beverly Hills, CA 90212-2401, USA

Holden, Amanda (Actor)
c/o Melanie Greene *Melanie Greene Management & Productions*
425 N Robertson Blvd
West Hollywood, CA 90048-1735, USA

Holden, Gina (Actor)
Kirk Talent Agencies Inc
1006 Beach Avenue 8th Fl
Vancouver, BC V6E 1T7, CANADA

Holden, Henry (Misc)
1140 Bloomfield Ave Ste 220
West Caldwell, NJ 07006-7126, USA

Holden, Jennifer
115 S Topanga Canyon Blvd # 153
Topanga, CA 90290-3160, USA

Holden, Joyce
444 N El Camino Real Spc 89
Encinitas, CA 92024-1313, USA

Holden, Laurie (Actor)
c/o Jason Newman *Untitled Entertainment (LA)*
331 N Maple Dr Fl 3
Beverly Hills, CA 90210-3827, USA

Holden, Mariean (Actor)
L A Talent
8335 W Sunset Blvd Ste 200
Los Angeles, CA 90069-1534, USA

Holden, Steve (Football Player)
Cleveland Browns
1202 N Nevada Way
Mesa, AZ 85203-4323, USA

Holden, William Wildlife Foundation
PO Box 67981
Los Angeles, CA 90067, USA

Holden-Reid, Kristen (Actor)
c/o Staff Member *Paradigm (LA)*
360 N Crescent Dr
North Bldg
Beverly Hills, CA 90210-6820, USA

Holder, Christopher (Actor)
H David Moss
733 Seward St Ph
Los Angeles, CA 90038-3503, USA

Holder, Geoffrey (Actor, Dancer)
565 Broadway
New York, NY 10012-3925, USA

Holderness, Joan (Baseball Player)
1037 Summerwind Dr
Crossville, TN 38571-3691, USA

Holderness, Sue
10 Rectory Close Windsor
Berks., ENGLAND SL4 5ER, UNITED KINGDOM (UK)

Holding, John Simon
15060 Ventura Blvd Ste 360
Sherman Oaks, CA 91403-2483, USA

Holdman, Warrick (Football Player)
c/o Staff Member *Washington Redskins*
21300 Redskin Park Dr
Ashburn, VA 20147-6100, USA

Holdorf, Willi (Athlete, Track Athlete)
Adidas KG
Herzogenaurach 91074, GERMANY

Holdridge, David (Baseball Player)
Seattle Mariners
220 W San Angelo St Apt 1080
Gilbert, NC 28805, USA

Holdsclaw, Chamique (Basketball Player)
Washington Mystics
601 F St NW
Mci Center
Washington, DC 20004-1605, USA

Holdsworth, Fred (Baseball Player)
Detroit Tigers
1900 W Olney Ave
Attn: Baseball Program
Philadelphia, PA 19141-1108, USA

Hole
150 E 58th St Ste 1900
New York, NY 10155-1901, USA

Holecek, John (Football Player)
Buffalo Bills
1876 N Wilmot Ave
Chicago, IL 60647-4417, USA

Holgren, Paul H
724 Southwick Cir
Somerdale, NJ 08083-2312, USA

Holiday, Corey (Football Player)
Pittsburgh Steelers
315 Columbia Pi E
Chapel Hill, NC 27516, USA

Holiday, Debby (Musician)
c/o Staff Member *Diva Central Inc*
7510 W Sunset Blvd Ste 1445
Los Angeles, CA 90046-3408, USA

Holiday, Ron (Football Player)
San Diego Chargers
229 Balance Meeting Rd
Peach Bottom, PA 17563-9772, USA

Holik, Bobby (Hockey Player)
c/o Staff Member *Atlanta Thrashers*
101 Marietta St NW Ste 1900
Centennial Tower
Atlanta, GA 30303-2771, USA

Holl, Steven M (Architect)
Steven Holl Architects
435 Hudson St Rm 400
New York, NY 10014-3948, USA

Holladay, Robert (Football Player)
Los Angeles Rams
2369 Timberland Dr NE
Conyers, GA 30207, USA

Holladay, Wilhelmina Cole (Misc)
National Museum of Women in Arts
1250 New York Ave NW
Washington, DC 20005-3970, USA

Holland, Agnieszka (Director, Writer)
Agence Nicole Cann
1 Rue Alfred de Vigny
Paris 75008, FRANCE

Holland, Al (Baseball Player)
Pittsburgh Pirates
443 Lewiston St NW
Roanoke, VA 24017, USA

Holland, Dexter (Musician)
Rebel Waltz
31652 2nd Ave
Laguna Beach, CA 92651-8244, USA

Holland, Heinrich D (Geophysicist, Physicist)
1222 W Wynnewood Rd
Wynnewood, PA 19096-2457, USA

Holland, Jamie L (Football Player)
San Diego Chargers
410 Woody Hayes Dr
Ohio State University Attn Alumni Association
Columbus, OH 43210-1104, USA

Holland, John (Football Player)
Minnesota Vikings
3117 Flagstone Dr
Garland, TX 75044-5882, USA

Holland, John R (Religious Leader)
Foursquare Gospel Int'l Church
1910 W Sunset Blvd
Los Angeles, CA 90026-3275, USA

Holland, Johnny (Football Player)
Green Bay Packers
3303 Prestwick Sq
Missouri City, TX 77459-2888, USA

Holland, Jools (Music Group)
c/o Staff Member *Miracle Artists*
1 York Street
London
England W1U 6PA, UNITED KINGDOM (UK)

Holland, Josh
4533 Willis Ave
Sherman Oaks, CA 91403-2710, USA

Holland, Juliam M (Jools) (Musician)
One Fifteen
Gallery 28 Wood Wharf
Horseferry
London SE10 9BT, UNITED KINGDOM
(UK)

Holland, Paul (Musician)
Variety Artists
793 Higuera St Ste 6
San Luis Obispo, CA 93401-0500, USA

Holland, Richard
9019 Wonderland Park Ave
Los Angeles, CA 90046-1431, USA

Holland, Todd (Director)
c/o David Lonner *William Morris Agency
(WMA-LA)*
1 William Morris Pl
Beverly Hills, CA 90212-4261, USA

Holland, Willa (Actor)
c/o Brett Norensberg *Gersh Agency, The
(LA)*
232 N Canon Dr
Beverly Hills, CA 90210-5302, USA

Holland, Willard R Jr (Business Person)
FirstEnergy Corp
76 S Main St
Akron, OH 44308-1812, USA

Hollander, Dan (Figure Skater)
c/o Staff Member *Champions on Ice*
3500 W 80th St
Tom Collins Enterprises Inc
Minneapolis, MN 55431-1068, USA

Hollander, John (Writer)
Yale University
English Dept
New Haven, CT 06520, USA

Hollander, Lorin (Musician)
I C M Artists
40 W 57th St
New York, NY 10019-4001, USA

Hollander, Nicole (Cartoonist)
Sylvia Syndicate
1440 N Dayton St
Chicago, IL 60622-2644, USA

Hollander, Xaviera
Stadionweg 17
Amsterdam 1077 RU, THE
NETHERLANDS

Hollander, Zander (Writer)
3805 Yuma St NW
Washington, DC 20016-2213, USA

Hollandsworth, Todd M (Baseball Player)
Los Angeles Dodgers
1310 Macalpin Dr
Inverness, IL 60010-6424, USA

Hollas, Donald (Football Player)
Cincinnati Bengals
1811 Mayweather Ln
Richmond, TX 77469-1337, USA

Holle, Eric (Football Player)
Kansas City Chiefs
6646 Whitemarsh Valley Walk
Austin, TX 78746-6363, USA

Holle, Gary (Baseball Player)
Texas Rangers
820 5th Ave
Watervliet, NY 12189-3612, USA

Holle, Mabel (Baseball Player)
914 Valley Rd
Lake Forest, IL 60045-2919, USA

Hollein, Hans (Architect, Misc)
Eiskellerstr 1
Dusseldorf 40213, GERMANY

Holler, Ed (Football Player)
Green Bay Packers
4500 Ivy Hall Dr
Columbia, SC 29206-1229, USA

Holleran, Leslie (Producer)
c/o Staff Member *Laha Films*
115 E 92nd St
7C
New York, NY 10128-1688, USA

Hollerer, Walter F (Writer)
Heerstr 99
Berlin 14055, GERMANY

Holliday, Charles O (Business Person)
E I DuPont de Nemours
1007 N Market St
Wilmington, DE 19801-1227, USA

Holliday, Cheryl (Writer)
c/o Staff Member *United Talent Agency
(UTA)*
9560 Wilshire Blvd Ste 500
Beverly Hills, CA 90212-2401, USA

Holliday, Fred (Actor)
4610 Forman Ave
Toluca Lake, CA 91602-1617, USA

Holliday, Jennifer (Actor, Music Group)
Universal Attractions
W 57th St Ste 1500W
New York, NY 10019, USA

Holliday, Kathy
345 N Maple Dr Ste 397
Beverly Hills, CA 90210-3856, USA

Holliday, Kene
9300 Wilshire Blvd Ste 400
Beverly Hills, CA 90212-3210, USA

Holliday, Polly D (Actor, Music Group)
201 E 17th St Apt 23H
New York, NY 10003-3680, USA

Hollie, Doug (Football Player)
Seattle Seahawks
3917 Midvale Ave
Oakland, CA 94602-3940, USA

Hollier, Dwight (Football Player)
Miami Dolphins
5012 Woodview Ln
Matthews, NC 28104-8057, USA

Hollies, The
Hill Farm Hackleton
Northants., ENGLAND NN7 2DH,
UNITED KINGDOM (UK)

Holliger, Heinz (Composer, Musician)
Konzertgellschaft
Hochstr 51
Basel 4002, SWITZERLAND

Holliman, Earl (Actor)
PO Box 1969
Studio City, CA 91614-0969, USA

Hollimon, Ulysses (Baseball Player)
Birmingham Black Barons
3726 Benton Blvd
Kansas City, MO 64128-2515, USA

Hollings, Ernest (Senator)
261 Calhoun St Rm 304
Charleston, SC 29401-1378, USA

Hollings, Michael R (Religious Leader)
Saint Mary of Angels
Moorhouse Road Bayswater
London W2 5DJ, UNITED KINGDOM
(UK)

Hollingsworth, Shawn (Football Player)
Denver Broncos
6 Broyhill Ct
Stafford, VA 22554-7757, USA

Hollinquest, Lamont (Football Player)
Washington Redskins
13709 S San Pedro St
Los Angeles, CA 90061-2619, USA

Hollins, Damon (Baseball Player)
Atlanta Braves
112 El Campo Ct
Vallejo, CA 94589-2220, USA

Hollins, Dave (Baseball Player)
Philadelphia Phillies
20 Lakeridge Dr S
Orchard Park, NY 14127-3370, USA

Hollins, Jessie (Baseball Player)
Chicago Cubs
RR 1 Box 159A
Apple Springs, TX 75926, USA

Hollins, Lionel (Basketball Player, Coach)
7594 Tagg Dr
Germantown, TN 38138-5827, USA

Hollis, James (Writer)
5200 Montrose Blvd
Houston, TX 77006-6547, USA

Hollis, Michael (Football Player)
Jacksonville Jaguars
124 Sawbill Palm Dr
Ponte Vedra Beach, FL 32082-3840, USA

Hollister, Dave (Music Group)
Creative Artists Agency
9830 Wilshire Blvd
Beverly Hills, CA 90212-1804, USA

Hollister, Ken (Football Player)
New York Jets
8772 Linksway Dr
Powell, OH 43065-8299, USA

Hollit, Raye (Zapp)
2554 Lincoln Blvd # 638
Venice, CA 90291-5082, USA

Holloman, Laurel (Actor)
c/o Lindsey Porter *Gersh Agency, The
(NY)*
41 Madison Ave Fl 33
New York, NY 10010-2202, USA

Hollomon, Gus (Football Player)
Denver Broncos
2489 County Road 139
Cameron, TX 76520-3614, USA

Holloway, Brenda (Musician)
Universal Attractions
145 W 57th St # 1500
New York, NY 10019-2220, USA

Holloway, Brian (Football Player)
New England Patriots
742 State Route 43
Stephentown, NY 12169-1914, USA

Holloway, James L III (Admiral)
4800 Fillmore Ave Apt 1058
Alexandria, VA 22311-5076, USA

Holloway, Johnny (Football Player)
Dallas Cowboys
1500 W 9th St Apt 5
Lawrence, KS 66044-2462, USA

Holloway, Josh (Actor)
c/o Staff Member *Rough Diamond
Management*
1424 N Kings Rd
West Hollywood, CA 90069-1908, USA

Holloway, Ken (Music Group)
World Class/Berry Mgmt
1848 Tyne Blvd
Nashville, TN 37215-4702, USA

Holloway, Loleatta (Music Group)
c/o Staff Member *Diva Central Inc*
7510 W Sunset Blvd Ste 1445
Los Angeles, CA 90046-3408, USA

Holloway, Matt (Writer)
c/o Staff Member *Nine Yards
Entertainment*
8530 Wilshire Blvd Fl 5
Beverly Hills, CA 90211-3102, USA

Holloway, Robin G (Composer)
Gonville & Caius College
Music Dept
Cambridge CB2 1TA, UNITED
KINGDOM (UK)

Holloway, William J Jr (Judge)
US Court of Appeals
PO Box 1767
Oklahoma City, OK 73101-1767, USA

Hollowell, Matt (Baseball Player)
8 Oldwick Rd
Whitehouse Station, NJ 08889-3719, USA

Holly, Buddy Memorial Society
PO Box 6123
Lubbock, TX 79493-6123, USA

Holly, Jeff (Baseball Player)
Minnesota Twins
502 Village Rd
Port Hueneme, CA 93041-3035, USA

Holly, Lauren (Actor)
c/o Aaron Ray *Nine Yards Entertainment*
8530 Wilshire Blvd Fl 5
Beverly Hills, CA 90211-3102, USA

Holly, Molly (Wrestler)
c/o Staff Member *World Wrestling
Entertainment (WWE)*
1241 E Main St
Stamford, CT 06902-3520, USA

Hollyday, Christopher (Musician)
Ted Kurland
173 Brighton Ave
Boston, MA 02134-2003, USA

Holm, Celeste (Actor)
88 Central Park W
New York, NY 10023-5209, USA

Holm, Ian (Actor)
Markham & Froggatt
Julian House
4 Windmill St
London W1P 1HF, UNITED KINGDOM
(UK)

Holm, Jeanne M (General)
2707 Thyme Dr
Edgewater, MD 21037-1120, USA

Holm, Joan (Bowler)
5829 N Magnolia Ave
Chicago, IL 60660-3415, USA

Holm, Peter
1 rue de Fer Achevel Port Grimaud
Cogolin F- 83310, FRANCE

Holm, Richard H (Misc)
483 Pleasant St Apt 10
Belmont, MA 02478-3266, USA

Holm, Sir Ian
46 Albermarle St.
London, ENGLAND W1X 4PP, UNITED
KINGDOM (UK)

Holman, Brad (Baseball Player)
Seattle Mariners
4720 N Ridge Rd
Wichita, KS 67205-8837, USA

Holman, Brian (Baseball Player)
Montreal Expos
22232 17th Ave SE Ste 312
Ronald Blue And Company
Bothell, WA 98021-7425, USA

Holman, C Ray (Business Person)
Mallinckrodt Inc
675 McDonell Blvd
Saint Louis, MO 63134, USA

Holman, Gary (Baseball Player)
Washington Senators
PO Box 923
Aguanga, CA 92536-0923, USA

Holman, Marshall (Bowler)
288 Island Pointe Dr
Medford, OR 97504-9453, USA

Holman, Rodney (Football Player)
Cincinnati Bengals
41460 Herwig Bluff Rd
Slidell, LA 70461-5040, USA

Holman, Scott (Baseball Player)
New York Mets
215 Dublin Ct
Brandon, MS 39047-8035, USA

Holman, Scott (Football Player)
St Louis Cardinals
4 Comiso
Irvine, CA 92614-0224, USA

Holman, Shawn (Baseball Player)
Detroit Tigers
RR 3
Sewickley, PA 15143, USA

Holmberg, Mark (Musician)
MOB Agency
6404 Wilshire Blvd Ste 505
Los Angeles, CA 90048-5507, USA

Holmberg, Rob (Football Player)
Los Angeles Raiders
316 Coppersmith Ln
Strasburg, PA 17579-1021, USA

Holmes, A M (Writer)
Columbia Univesity
English Dept
New York, NY 10027, USA

Holmes, Ashton (Actor)
c/o Christopher Lockhart *International
Creative Management (ICM-LA)*
10250 Constellation Blvd
Los Angeles, CA 90067-6200, USA

Holmes, Clayton (Football Player)
Dallas Cowboys
1142 Hollings Ave
Florence, SC 29506-6725, USA

Holmes, Clint (Music Group)
Conversation Co
697 Middle Neck Rd
Great Neck, NY 11023-1216, USA

Holmes, D Brainerd (Business Person,
Engineer)
Bay Colony Corp Center
950 Winter St # 4350
Waltham, MA 02451-1424, USA

Holmes, Dame Kelly (Athlete)
*International Association of Athletics
Federations*
17 rue Princesse Florestine
BP 359
MC98007, MONACO

Holmes, Earl (Football Player)
Pittsburgh Steelers
2978 Stonybrook Ct
Tallahassee, FL 32309-2167, USA

Holmes, Ernie (Football Player)
Pittsburgh Steelers
PO Box 299
Wiergate, TX 75977-0299, USA

Holmes, Jennifer (Actor)
PO Box 6303
Carmel, CA 93921-6303, USA

Holmes, Jerry (Football Player)
New York Jets
107 Chatham Ter
Hampton, VA 23666-4105, USA

Holmes, Katie (Actor)
c/o John Carrabino *John Carrabino
Management*
5900 Wilshire Blvd Ste 406
Los Angeles, CA 90036-5015, USA

Holmes, Kenneth (Football Player)
Tennessee Titans
PO Box 273309
Boca Raton, FL 33427-3309, USA

Holmes, Larry (Boxer)
91 Larry Holmes Dr Ste 200
Easton, PA 18042-7745, USA

Holmes, Pat (Football Player)
Houston Oilers
221 Mack Hollimon Dr
Kerrville, TX 78028-6628, USA

Holmes, Priest (Football Player)
Kansas City Chiefs
1 Arrowhead Dr
Kansas City, KS, USA

Holmes, Rudell (Football Player)
Atlanta Falcons
1713 Lisa Ave
Vista, CA 92084-3057, USA

Holmes, Rupert (Music Group,
Songwriter, Writer)
Mars Talent
27 L Ambiance Ct
Bardonia, NY 10954-1421, USA

Holmes, Sherlock Society
221B Baker St.
London, ENGLAND W1, UNITED
KINGDOM (UK)

Holmes, Susan (Actor, Model)
c/o Jerry Shandrew *Shandrew Public
Relations*
1050 S Stanley Ave
Los Angeles, CA 90019-6634, USA

Holmes, Thomas F (Tommy) (Baseball
Player)
Boston Red Sox
42 Whooping Hollow Rd
East Hampton, NY 11937-2522, USA

Holmes, Tina (Actor)
c/o Brian Alexander *Essential Talent
Management*
6399 Wilshire Blvd Ste 400
Los Angeles, CA 90048-5716, USA

Holmgren, Janet L (Educator)
Mills College
President's Office
Oakland, CA 94613, USA

Holmgren, Michael G (Mike) (Coach,
Football Coach)
Seattle Seahawks
11220 NE 53rd St
Kirkland, WA 98033-7595, USA

Holmoe, Tom (Football Player)
San Francisco 49ers
1674 N 1670 W
Provo, UT 84604-7210, USA

Holmquest, Donald L (Astronaut)
205 Princeton Rd
Menlo Park, CA 94025-5217, USA

Holmstrom, Carl (Skier)
1703 E 3rd St Apt 101
Duluth, MN 55812-1743, USA

Holmstrom, Peter (Musician)
Monqui Mgmt
PO Box 5908
Portland, OR 97228-5908, USA

Holohan, Pete (Football Player)
San Diego Chargers
5131 Bothe Ave
San Diego, CA 92122-4016, USA

Holovak, Michael J (Mike) (Coach,
Football Player)
Chicago Bears
5051 Sandy Brook Cir
Wimauma, FL 33598-4023, USA

Holroyd, Michael (Writer)
85 Saint Marks Road
London W10 6JS, UNITED KINGDOM
(UK)

Holroyd, Scott (Actor)
c/o Staff Member *Stone Manners Talent &
Literary (NY)*
900 Broadway Ste 803
New York, NY 10003-1229, USA

Holst, Per (Producer)
Per Holst Film A/S
Rentemestervej 69A
Copenhagen, NV 2400, DENMARK

Holt, Chris (Baseball Player)
Houston Astros
739 Madison St
Coppell, TX 75019-2096, USA

Holt, David Lee (Musician)
AristoMedia
1620 16th Ave S
Nashville, TN 37212-2908, USA

Holt, Glenn L (Football Player)
Miami Dolphins
North Miami High School 800 NE 137th
St
North Miami, FL 33161, USA

Holt, Issiac (Football Player)
Minnesota Vikings
4028 Fairmont Pl
Birmingham, AL 35207-2732, USA

Holt, Jim (Baseball Player)
Minnesota Twins
2345 Walter Andrews Rd
Graham, NC 27253-5018, USA

Holt, Lester (Correspondent)
NBC-TV
30 Rockefeller Plz Ste 270E
News Dept
New York, NY 10112-0299, USA

Holt, Pierce (Football Player)
San Francisco 49ers
5408 County Road 339
Christoval, TX 76935-3003, USA

Holt, Robert J (Football Player)
Buffalo Bills
1332 Williams Ave
Desoto, TX 75115-3182, USA

Holt, Roger (Baseball Player)
New York Yankees
804 Hilltop St
Fruitland Park, FL 34731-2061, USA

Holt, Sandrine (Actor)
Somers Teitelbaum David
8840 Wilshire Blvd # 200
Beverly Hills, CA 90211-2606, USA

Holt, Torry (Football Player)
c/o Staff Member *Saint Louis Rams*
1 Rams Way
Earth City, MO 63045-1525, USA

Holt Jr, Jack
504 Temple Dr
Harrah, OK 73045, USA

Holt-Kramer, Toni
1229 Santa Monica Blvd
Santa Monica, CA 90404-1705, USA

Holtermann, E Louis Jr (Publisher)
Glamour Magazine
350 Madison Ave
New York, NY 10017-3700, USA

Holtgrave, Vern (Baseball Player)
Detroit Tigers
389 N 8th St
Breese, IL 62230-1107, USA

Holton, A Linwood Jr (Physicist)
64 Francis Ave
Cambridge, MA 02138-1912, USA

Holton, Brian (Baseball Player)
Los Angeles Dodgers
831 Stanislaus Cir
Claremont, CA 91711-2967, USA

Holton, Michael (Basketball Player,
Coach)
5822 NW Redfox Dr
Portland, OR 97229-2657, USA

Holtz, Louis L (Lou) (Coach, Football
Coach)
1300 Rosewood Dr
Columbia, SC 29208-0001, USA

Holtz, Mike (Baseball Player)
California Angels
RR 4
Ebensburg, PA 15931, USA

Holtzman, Elizabeth (Liz) (Misc)
2 Park Ave Rm 2100
New York, NY 10016-9301, USA

Holtzman, Jerome (Baseball Player,
Writer)
1225 Forest Ave
Evanston, IL 60202-1409, USA

Holtzman, Kenneth D (Ken) (Baseball
Player)
Chicago Cubs
256 Waterside Dr
Grover, MO 63040-1632, USA

Holtzman, Wayne H (Doctor)
3300 Foothill Dr
Austin, TX 78731-5823, USA

Holub, E J (Football Player)
Dallas Texans
2311 S County Road 1120
Midland, TX 79706-4942, USA

Holum, Dianne (Speed Skater)
1344 McIntosh Ave
Broomfield, CO 80020-2480, USA

Holum, Kristin (Speed Skater)
10596 Steele St
Northglenn, CO 80233-6117, USA

Holway, Jerome F (Cinematographer)
448 Spruce Dr
Exton, PA 19341-2020, USA

Holy, Steve (Musician)
c/o Staff Member *Paradigm (Nashville)*
124 12th Ave S Ste 410
Nashville, TN 37203-3170, USA

Holyfield, Evander (Boxer)
794 Evander Holyfield Hwy
Fairburn, GA 30213-3496, USA

Holz, Gordon (Football Player)
Denver Broncos
730 S Plaza Dr Apt 222
Saint Paul, MN 55120-1575, USA

Holzemer, Mark (Baseball Player)
California Angels
10044 Macalister Trl
Highlands Ranch, CO 80129, USA

Holzer, Helmut (Scientist)
2103 Greenwood Pl SW
Huntsville, AL 35802-4462, USA

Holzer, Jenny (Artist)
80 Hewitts Rd
Hoosick Falls, NY 12090, USA

Holzier, James (Actor)
c/o Danny Robinson *Agency for the Performing Arts (APA-LA)*
405 S Beverly Dr
Beverly Hills, CA 90212-4416, USA

Holzman, Malcolm (Architect)
Hardy Holzman Pfeiffer
902 Broadway
New York, NY 10010-6082, USA

Homan, Dennis (Football Player)
Dallas Cowboys
1950 Charlotte Ct
Florence, AL 35630-6768, USA

Homeier, Skip
247 Castellana N
Palm Desert, CA 92260-2118, USA

Homfeld, Conrad (Horse Racer)
Sandron
11744 Marblestone Ct
Wellington, FL 33414-6041, USA

Honda, Yuka (Music Group)
Billions Corp
833 W Chicago Ave Ste 101
Chicago, IL 60622-8408, USA

Honderich, Beland H (Publisher)
Toronto Star
1 Yonge St
Toronto, ON M5E 1E6, CANADA

Honderich, John H (Editor)
Toronto Star
Editorial Dept
1 Yonge St
Toronto, ON M5E 1E6, CANADA

Honegger, Fritz (President)
Schloss-Str 29
Ruschlidon 8803, SWITZERLAND

Honeycutt, Rick
207 Forrest Rd
Fort Oglethorpe, GA 30742-3706, USA

Honeycutt, Van B (Business Person)
Computer Sciences Corp
2100 E Grand Ave
El Segundo, CA 90245-5098, USA

Honeycyt (Music Group)
c/o Staff Member *Paradigm (Monterey)*
509 Hartnell St
Monterey, CA 93940-2825, USA

Honeyghan, Lloyd (Boxer)
50 Barnfield Wood Road
Park Langley
Beckenham
Kent, UNITED KINGDOM (UK)

Honeymoon Suite
1505 W. 2nd Ave. #200
Vancouver, BC V6H 3Y4, CANADA

Hong, James (Actor)
8235 W Sunset Blvd # 202
West Hollywood, CA 90046, USA

Hong Song Nam (Prime Minister)
Premier's Office
Pyongyong, NORTH KOREA

Honig, Edwin (Writer)
229 Medway St Apt 305
Providence, RI 02906-5300, USA

Honore, Jean Cardinal (Religious Leader)
Archeveche
BP 1117
27 Rue Jules-Simon
Tours Cedex 37011, FRANCE

Hoobastank (Music Group)
c/o Jenna Adler *Creative Artists Agency LCC (CAA-LA)*
2000 Avenue Of The Stars
Los Angeles, CA 90067-4700, USA

Hood, Don (Baseball Player)
Baltimore Orioles
708 Firestone Dr
Florence, SC 29501-8825, USA

Hood, Estus (Football Player)
Green Bay Packers
2105 W Grace St
Kankakee, IL 60901-4590, USA

Hood, Kenneth (Religious Leader)
5799 Bloomfield Ave
Verona, NJ 07044, USA

Hood, Leroy E (Inventor, Scientist)
1441 N 34th St
Seattle, WA 98103-8904, USA

Hood, Robert
Boys Life Magazine
1325 W Walnut Hill Ln
Editorial Dept
Irving, TX 75038-3008, USA

Hood, Robin (Golfer)
6705 Shoal Creek Dr
Arlington, TX 76001-8310, USA

Hoogstratten, Louise
12451 Mulholland Dr
Beverly Hills, CA 90210-1336, USA

Hook, Chris (Baseball Player)
San Francisco Giants
30 Northfield Dr
Florence, KY 41042-8924, USA

Hook, Jay (Baseball Player)
Cincinnati Reds
PO Box 90
Maple City, MI 49664-0090, USA

Hooker, Charles R (Artist)
28 Whippingham Road
Brighton
Sussex BN2 3PG, UNITED KINGDOM (UK)

Hooker, Fair (Football Player)
Cleveland Browns
3728 Rutherford Ct
Inglewood, CA 90305-2244, USA

Hooks, Benjamin L (Activist)
200 Wagner Pl # 407-8
Memphis, TN 38103-3617, USA

Hooks, Jan (Actor)
c/o Staff Member *Innovative Artists (LA)*
1505 10th St
Santa Monica, CA 90401-2805, USA

Hooks, Kevin (Director)
International Creative Mgmt
8942 Wilshire Blvd # 219
Beverly Hills, CA 90211-1908, USA

Hooks, Robert (Actor)
145 N Valley St
Burbank, CA 91505-4036, USA

Hooks, Roland (Football Player)
Buffalo Bills
3724 Calgary Dr
Reno, NV 89511-6096, USA

Hookstratten, Edward G (Attorney, Attorney General, General)
Ed Hookstratten Mgmt
9536 Wilshire Blvd Ste 500
Beverly Hills, CA 90212-2435, USA

Hoop, Jesca (Musician)
c/o Staff Member *Paradigm (Monterey)*
509 Hartnell St
Monterey, CA 93940-2825, USA

Hooper, Brandon
3003 3rd St Unit 4
Santa Monica, CA 90405-5488, USA

Hooper, C Darrow (Athlete, Track Athlete)
6 Braemore Pl
Dallas, TX 75230-1958, USA

Hooper, Tobe
PO Box 5617
Beverly Hills, CA 90209-5617, USA

Hoopes, Mitch (Football Player)
Dallas Cowboys
5000 Murray Blvd Apt F1
Salt Lake City, UT 84123-2674, USA

Hooten, Burt
3619 Grandby Ct.
San Antonio, TX 78217, USA

Hooten, Leon (Baseball Player)
Oakland A's
461 N 11th St
Coos Bay, OR 97420-1851, USA

Hootie & The Blowfish (Music Group)
c/o Staff Member *Paradigm (Monterey)*
509 Hartnell St
Monterey, CA 93940-2825, USA

Hoover, Alice (Baseball Player)
520 W Bellevue Ave
Reading, PA 19605-2100, USA

Hoover, Brad (Football Player)
Carolina Panthers
2130 Climbing Rose Ln
Matthews, NC 28104-6232, USA

Hoover, Dick (Bowler)
112 Melody Dr
Copley, OH 44321-1154, USA

Hoover, Herbert III
200 S Los Robles Ave # 520
Pasadena, CA 91101-2479, USA

Hoover, Houston (Football Player)
Atlanta Falcons
1216 Mareed Ave
Yazoo City, MS 39194-2831, USA

Hoover, John (Baseball Player)
Texas Rangers
1615 W Fountain Way
Fresno, CA 93705-3331, USA

Hoover, Paul (Baseball Player)
Tampa Bay Devil Rays
210 10th St SE
Washington, DC 20003-2117, USA

Hoover, Robert A (Bob) (Misc)
Bob Hoover Airshows
1100 E Imperial Ave
El Segundo, CA 90245-2608, USA

Hoovler, Skip (Football Player)
New York Jets
8249 Broad St SW
Pataskala, OH 43062-7831, USA

Hope, Alec D (Writer)
PO Box 7949
Alice Springs, NT 0871, AUSTRALIA

Hope, Jim (Producer)
c/o Staff Member *Endeavor Agency LLC (LA)*
9601 Wilshire Blvd Fl 3
Beverly Hills, CA 90210-5204, USA

Hope, John (Baseball Player)
Pittsburgh Pirates
835 SW 13th St
Fort Lauderdale, FL 33315-1448, USA

Hope, Leslie (Actor)
Kritzer
12200 W Olympic Blvd Ste 400
Los Angeles, CA 90064-1047, USA

Hope, Maurice (Boxer)
582 Kingsland Road
London E8, UNITED KINGDOM (UK)

Hope, Tamara (Actor)
c/o Matt Schwartz *Atlas Entertainment*
6100 Wilshire Blvd Ste 1170
Los Angeles, CA 90048-5116, USA

Hopkins, Anthony (Actor)
c/o Rick Nicita *Creative Artists Agency LCC (CAA-LA)*
2000 Avenue Of The Stars
Los Angeles, CA 90067-4700, USA

Hopkins, Antony (Composer, Writer)
Woodyard Cottage Ashridge
Berkhamsted
Herts HP4 1PS, UNITED KINGDOM (UK)

Hopkins, Bo (Actor)
6628 Ethel Ave
North Hollywood, CA 91606-1018, USA

Hopkins, Don (Baseball Player)
Oakland A's
6380 Commanche Dr
West Chester, OH 45069-1351, USA

Hopkins, Gail (Baseball Player)
Chicago White Sox
120 Canterbury Dr
Parkersburg, WV 26104-8048, USA

Hopkins, Gareth (Business Person)
c/o Staff Member *EMI Recorded Music (UK)*
4 Tenterden St
Hanover Square
London W1A 2AY, UNITED KINGDOM (UK)

Hopkins, Godfrey T (Photographer)
Wilmington Cottage Wilmington Road
Seaford
E Sussex BN25 2EH, UNITED KINGDOM (UK)

Hopkins, Jan (Correspondent)
Cable News Network
1050 Techwood Dr NW
News Dept
Atlanta, GA 30318-5604, USA

Hopkins, Jerry (Football Player)
Denver Broncos
6688 E Highway 6
Waco, TX 76705-5385, USA

Hopkins, Josh (Actor)
Gersh Agency
232 N Canon Dr
Beverly Hills, CA 90210-5302, USA

Hopkins, Kaitlin (Actor)
19528 Ventura Blvd # 559
Tarzana, CA 91356-2917, USA

Hopkins, Katherine
215 S La Cienega Blvd Ph
Beverly Hills, CA 90211-3322, USA

Hopkins, Linda (Music Group)
2055 Ivar Ave Ph
Los Angeles, CA 90068-3918, USA

Hopkins, Michael J (Architect)
27 Broadley Terrace
London NW1 6LG, UNITED KINGDOM
(UK)

Hopkins, Paul (Baseball Player)
Washington Senators
60 Boston Post Rd
Old Saybrook, CT 06475-1503, USA

Hopkins, Stephen
8942 Wilshire Blvd
Beverly Hills, CA 90211-1908, USA

Hopkins, Sy (Music Group)
Paramount Entertainment
PO Box 12
Far Hills, NJ 07931-0012, USA

Hopkins, Tamburo (Football Player)
New York Giants
2740 Maitland Crossing Way Apt 2208
Orlando, FL 32810-7130, USA

Hopkins, Telma (Actor, Music Group)
c/o Staff Member *Innovative Artists (LA)*
1505 10th St
Santa Monica, CA 90401-2805, USA

Hopkins, Wesley (Football Player)
Philadelphia Eagles
7412 White Oak Rd
Fairfield, AL 35064-2454, USA

Hoppe, Fred (Artist)
7401nw 105th St
Malcolm, NE 68402, USA

Hoppe, Wolfgang (Athlete)
Dieterstedter Str 11
Apolda 99510, GERMANY

Hopper, Dennis (Actor, Director, Writer)
c/o Jeff Golenberg *The Collective*
9100 Wilshire Blvd # 700 W
Beverly Hills, CA 90212-3401, USA

Hopper, Heather (Actor)
c/o Staff Member *Baron Entertainment*
5757 Wilshire Blvd Ste 659
Los Angeles, CA 90036-3682, USA

Hopper, John D Jr (General)
Commander
Air Education/Training Command
Randolph Air Force Base, TX 78155, USA

Hoppock, Doug (Football Player)
Kansas City Chiefs
13212 W 115th St
Shawnee Mission, KS 66210-3540, USA

Hoppus, Mark (Musician)
Creative Artists Agency
9830 Wilshire Blvd
Beverly Hills, CA 90212-1804, USA

Hopson, Dennis (Basketball Player)
5608 Brickstone Pl
Hilliard, OH 43026-3886, USA

Horan, Machael W (Mike) (Football Player)
Philadelphia Eagles
1232 Edgeview Dr
Santa Ana, CA 92705-2339, USA

Horbiger, Christiane
Frankengasse 28
Zurich CH-8001, SWITZERLAND

Horgan, Patrick (Actor)
201 E 89th St
New York, NY 10128-3421, USA

Horien, Joel (Baseball Player)
Chicago White Sox
3718 Chartwell Dr
San Antonio, TX 78230-3202, USA

Horinek, Ramon A (War Hero)
181 National Blvd
Universal City, TX 78148-4444, USA

Horlock, John H (Educator, Engineer)
2 The Avenue
Ampthill
Bedford MK45 2NR, UNITED KINGDOM
(UK)

Horn, Don (Football Player)
Green Bay Packers
2229 Wynterbrook Dr
Highlands Ranch, CO 80126-4210, USA

Horn, Gyula (Prime Minister)
Parliament
Kossuth Lajor Ter 1/3
Budapest 1055, HUNGARY

Horn, Herman (Baseball Player)
Kansas City Monarchs
2635 Benton Blvd
Kansas City, MO 64127-4151, USA

Horn, Joe (Football Player)
c/o Staff Member *New Orleans Saints*
5800 Airline Dr
Metairie, LA 70003-3876, USA

Horn, Marian Blank (Judge)
US Claims Court
717 Madison Pl NW
Washington, DC 20439-0001, USA

Horn, Paul J (Musician)
4601 Leyns Road
Victoria, BC V8N 3A1, CANADA

Horn, Roy (Magician)
Mirage Hotel & Casino
3400 Las Vegas Blvd S
Las Vegas, NV 89109-8907, USA

Horn, Sam (Baseball Player)
Boston Red Sox
PO Box 63
Birmingham, AL 35201-0063, USA

Horn, Shriley (Music Group)
1007 Towne Ln
Charlottesville, VA 22901-3173, USA

Hornaday, Ron (Race Car Driver)
PO Box 229
Mooresville, NC 28115, USA

Hornburg, Hal M (General)
Commander
Air Combat Command
Langley Air Force Base, VA 23665, USA

Hornby, Nick (Writer)
Cassarotto
60/66 Wardour St
London W1V 4ND, UNITED KINGDOM
(UK)

Horne, Donald R (Writer)
53 Grosvenor St
Woollahra
Sydney, NSW 2025, AUSTRALIA

Horne, Jimmy Bo (Dancer, Music Group, Musician)
Talent Consultants International
105 Shad Row Ste B
Piermont, NY 10968-3001, USA

Horne, John R (Business Person)
Navistar International
PO Box 1488
Warrenville, IL 60555-7488, USA

Horne, Lena (Actor, Musician)
c/o Staff Member *Casterbridge Ltd*
23 E 74th St
New York, NY 10021-2617, USA

Horne, Marilyn (Opera Singer)
The Marilyn Horne Foundation
250 W 57th St Ste 603
New York, NY 10107-0607, USA

Horne, Steve (Race Car Driver)
Tasman Motor Sports Group
4192 Weaver Ct S
Hilliard, OH 43026, USA

Horneber, Petra (Misc)
Ringstr 77
Kranzberg 85402, GERMANY

Horneff, Wil (Actor)
c/o Staff Member *Creative Artists Agency LCC (CAA-LA)*
2000 Avenue Of The Stars
Los Angeles, CA 90067-4700, USA

Horner, Bob (Baseball Player)
Atlanta Braves
209 Steeplechase Dr
Irving, TX 75062-3823, USA

Horner, Charles A (General)
2824 Jack Nicklaus Way
Shalimar, FL 32579-2226, USA

Horner, Freeman V (War Hero)
1501 Doubletree Dr
Columbus, GA 31904-2659, USA

Horner, James (Composer)
13245 Riverside Dr Ste 450
Sherman Oaks, CA 91423-2172, USA

Horner, John R (Jack) (Scientist)
70 Cougar Dr
Bozeman, MT 59718-8346, USA

Horner, Martina S (Business Person, Educator)
TIAA-CREF
730 3rd Ave
New York, NY 10017-3207, USA

Hornig, Donald F (Misc)
1 Little Pond Cove Rd
Little Compton, RI 02837-1422, USA

Hornsby, Bruce (Musician)
PO Box 3545
Williamsburg, VA 23187-3545, USA

Hornsby, Ron (Football Player)
New York Giants
2028 Washington St
Franklinton, LA 70438-2533, USA

Hornung, Paul V (Actor)
325 W Main St
Waterfront Plaza #1116
Louisville, KY 40202-4254, USA

Horovitz, Adam (King Ad-Rock) (Artist, Music Group, Musician)
c/o Staff Member *Endeavor Agency LLC (LA)*
9601 Wilshire Blvd Fl 3
Beverly Hills, CA 90210-5204, USA

Horovitz, Israel A (Writer)
146 W 11th St
New York, NY 10011-8306, USA

Horovitz, Joseph (Composer)
Royal College of Music
Prince Consort Road
London SW7 2BS, UNITED KINGDOM
(UK)

Horowitz, Jerome P (Scientist)
Michigan Cancer Foundation
110 E Warren Ave
Detroit, MI 48201-1380, USA

Horowitz, Paul (Doctor, Physicist)
111 Chilton St
Cambridge, MA 02138-6844, USA

Horowitz, Sari (Journalist)
Washington Post
Editorial Dept
1150 15th St NW
Washington, DC 20071-0001, USA

Horowitz, Scott J (Astronaut)
5491 Freestyle Way
Park City, UT 84098-7621, USA

Horrocks, Jane (Actor, Music Group)
P F D
Drury House
34-43 Russell St
London WC2B 5HA, UNITED KINGDOM
(UK)

Horry, Robert (Basketball Player)
9 E Rivercrest Dr
Houston, TX 77042-2513, USA

Horsey, David (Cartoonist, Editor)
Kings Features Syndicate
300 W 57th St Fl 15
New York, NY 10019-3741, USA

Horsford, Anna Maria (Actor)
PO Box 48082
Los Angeles, CA 90048-0082, USA

Horsley, Lee A (Actor)
c/o Laura Walsh *Central Artists*
3310 W Burbank Blvd # A
Burbank, CA 91505-2230, USA

Horsley, Richard D (Financier)
Regions Financial Corp
417 20th St N
Birmingham, AL 35203-3203, USA

Horsman, Vince (Baseball Player)
Toronto Blue Jays
1941 Pinehurst Dr
Clearwater, FL 33763-2228, USA

Horst, Lisa Ann
PO Box 8633
Lancaster, PA 17604-8633, USA

Horstman, Catherine (Baseball Player)
39018 Desert Greens Dr E
Palm Desert, CA 92260-1403, USA

Horton, Ethan S (Football Player)
Kansas City Chiefs
PO Box 30247
Wfnz-Radio
Charlotte, NC 28230-0247, USA

Horton, Frank E (Educator)
288 River Ranch Cir
Bayfield, CO 81122-8774, USA

Horton, Greg (Football Player)
Los Angeles Rams
1053 Lytle St
Redlands, CA 92374-6240, USA

Horton, Lawrence (Football Player)
Chicago Bears
1442 S 13th St
Harrisburg, PA 17104-3107, USA

Horton, Michael (Editor)
c/o Staff Member *Mirisch Agency*
1801 Century Park E Ste 1801
Los Angeles, CA 90067-2320, USA

Horton, Peter (Actor)
409 Santa Monica Blvd Ph
Santa Monica, CA 90401-2232, USA

Horton, Ray (Football Player)
Cincinnati Bengals
8014 Falcon Ct
Gibsonia, PA 15044-6057, USA

Horton, Robert (Actor)
5317 Andasol Ave
Encino, CA 91316-2504, USA

Horton, Willie(baseball)
15124 Warwick St
Detroit, MI 48223-2293, USA

Horvath, Bronco J (Hockey Player)
27 Oliver St
South Yarmouth, MA 02664-2901, USA

Horvitz, H Robert (Nobel Prize Laureate)
Massachusetts Institute of Technology
Biology Dept
Cambridge, MA 02139, USA

Horvitz, Louis J (Director)
c/o Staff Member *Gersh Agency, The (LA)*
232 N Canon Dr
Beverly Hills, CA 90210-5302, USA

Horwitz, Tony (Journalist)
Wall Street Journal
200 Liberty St
Editorial Dept
New York, NY 10281-0084, USA

Hosbein, Marion (Baseball Player)
1347 Cliff Barnes Dr
Kalamazoo, MI 49009-8329, USA

Hosea, Bobby
4526 Wilshire Blvd
Los Angeles, CA 90010-3801, USA

Hosey, Dwayne (Baseball Player)
Boston Red Sox
7868 Milliken Ave Apt 411
Rancho Cucamonga, CA 91730-8387, USA

Hosey, Steve (Baseball Player)
San Francisco Giants
6445 N Lead Ave
Fresno, CA 93711-1028, USA

Hosket, William (Bill) (Basketball Player)
7461 Worthington Galena Rd
Worthington, OH 43085-6715, USA

Hoskins, Bob (Actor)
Cassarotto
60/66 Wardour St
London W1V 4ND, UNITED KINGDOM (UK)

Hoskins, Derrick (Football Player)
Oakland Raiders
10491 Road 842
Philadelphia, MS 39350-8204, USA

Hosley, Tim (Baseball Player)
Detroit Tigers
112 Elena Dr
Moore, SC 29369-9657, USA

Hosmer, Bradley C (Brad) (General)
PO Box 1128
Cedar Crest, NM 87008-1128, USA

Hoss, Clark (Football Player)
Philadelphia Eagles
3140 Sabo Ln
West Linn, OR 97068-5618, USA

Hossein, Robert (Actor, Director)
Ghislaine de Wing
10 Rue du Docteur Roux
Paris 75015, FRANCE

Hostak, Al (Boxer)
11501 161st Ave SE
Renton, WA 98059-6145, USA

Hostetler, Dave (Baseball Player)
Montreal Expos
3404 Steeplechase Trl
Arlington, TX 76016-2325, USA

Hostetler, David L (Artist)
PO Box 989
Athens, OH 45701-0989, USA

Hostetler, Jeff (Football Player)
New York Giants
2032 Magnolia Dr
Morgantown, WV 26508-4467, USA

Hostetter, G Richard (Religious Leader)
Presbyterian Church in America
1852 Century Plaza
Atlanta, GA 30345, USA

Hoston, Ricky (Baseball Player)
St Louis Cardinals
16026 Aston Ct
Chesterfield, MO 63005-4575, USA

Hoston, Tony (Baseball Player)
Boston Red Sox
17001 Livorno Dr
Pacific Palisades, CA 90272-3232, USA

Hotchkiss, Rob (Musician)
Jon Landau
158 Rowayton Ave
Norwalk, CT 06853-1442, USA

Hotchkiss, Rollin D (Doctor, Scientist)
2-4 Rolling Hls
Lenox, MA 01240-2127, USA

Hotchner, Aaron
14 Hillandale Rd
Westport, CT 06880-5225, USA

Hottelet, Richard C (Correspondent)
120 Chestnut Hill Rd
Wilton, CT 06897-4608, USA

Hottman, Ken (Baseball Player)
Chicago White Sox
9537 2nd Ave
Elk Grove, CA 95624-1936, USA

Hoty, Dee
333 W 56th St
New York, NY 10019-3764, USA

Houbregs, Robert J (Bob) (Basketball Player)
1949 Arena Ct SE
Olympia, WA 98501-6874, USA

Houcke, Sara (Misc)
Feld Enterprises
1313 17th St E
Palmetto, FL 34221-2850, USA

Hough, Charlie (Athlete)
2266 Shadetree Cir
Brea, CA 92821-4423, USA

Hough, Jim (Football Player)
Minnesota Vikings
2440 Christian Dr
Chaska, MN 55318-1993, USA

Hough, John (Director)
Associated International Mgmt
5 Denmark St
London WC2H 8LP, UNITED KINGDOM (UK)

Hough, Joseph C Jr (Educator)
Union Theological Seminary
President's Office
New York, NY 10027, USA

Hough, Michael A (General)
Deputy Cofs Aviation
Hqusmc 2 Navy St
Washington, DC 20380-0001, USA

Hough, Stephen A G (Musician)
Harrison/Parrott
12 Penzance Place
London W11 4PA, UNITED KINGDOM (UK)

Houghton, Charles N (Director)
11 E 9th St
New York, NY 10003-5946, USA

Houghton, James (Business Person)
Field 36 Spencer Hill Road
Corning, NY 14830, USA

Houghton, John (Physicist)
Rutherford Appleton Laboratory
Chilton
Didcot Oxon OX11 0QX, UNITED KINGDOM (UK)

Houghton, Katherine (Actor)
Ambrosio/Mortimer
165 W 46th St
New York, NY 10036-2501, USA

Houghton of Sowerby, Douglas (Government Official)
110 Marsham Court
London SW1, UNITED KINGDOM (UK)

Hougland, William (Bill) (Basketball Player)
PO Box 2629
Edwards, CO 81632-2629, USA

Houk, Ralph (Baseball Player)
New York Yankees
3000 Plantation Rd
Winter Haven, FL 33884-1236, USA

Houle, Rejean (Hockey Player)
7941 Boul Lasalle
Lasalle, PQ H8P 3R1, CANADA

Hounsfield, Godfrey N (Nobel Prize Laureate)
15 Crane Park Road
Whitton Twickenham
Middx TW2 6DF, UNITED KINGDOM (UK)

Hounsou, Djimon (Actor, Model)
c/o Lorrie Bartlett *Gersh Agency, The (LA)*
232 N Canon Dr
Beverly Hills, CA 90210-5302, USA

House, Craig (Baseball Player)
Colorado Rockies
8845 Patricia Ellen Cv
Memphis, TN 38133-3807, USA

House, David (Dave) (Business Person)
Nortel Networks Corp
8200 Dixie Road
Brampton, ON L6T 5P6, CANADA

House, James
1313 16th Ave S
Nashville, TN 37212-2903, USA

House, Karen Ellot (Journalist)
58 Cleveland Ln
Princeton, NJ 08540-3077, USA

House, Kevin (Football Player)
Tampa Bay Buccaneers
9724 Mary Robin Dr
Riverview, FL 33569-5572, USA

House, Pat (Baseball Player)
Houston Astros
2554 W Penick Pointe Ct
Meridian, ID 83646-5182, USA

House, Stormy
12334 Gorham Ave
Los Angeles, CA 90049-5206, USA

House, Tom (Baseball Player)
Atlanta Braves
12794 Via Felino
Del Mar, CA 92014-3806, USA

House, Yoanna (Model, Television Host)
c/o Staff Member *Style Network*
5750 Wilshire Blvd
Los Angeles, CA 90036-3697, USA

House of Pain (Music Group)
c/o Staff Member *William Morris Agency (WMA-LA)*
1 William Morris Pl
Beverly Hills, CA 90212-4261, USA

Householder, Paul (Baseball Player)
Cincinnati Reds
521 N Swinton Ave
Delray Beach, FL 33444-3969, USA

Houseley, Phil (Hockey Player)
Chicago Blackhawks
1901 W Madison St
United Center
Chicago, IL 60612-2459, USA

Houser, Huell
450 N Rossmore Ave # 602
Los Angeles, CA 90004-2406, USA

Houser, Jerry (Actor)
8325 Skyline Dr
Los Angeles, CA 90046-1038, USA

Houser, Kevin (Football Player)
New Orleans Saints
941 Montclair Cir
Westlake, OH 44145-1445, USA

Housner, George W (Engineer, Misc)
California Institute of Technology
Engineering Dept
Pasadena, CA 91125-0001, USA

Houston (Adult Film Star)
c/o Staff Member *Atlas Multimedia Inc*
9035 Independence Ave
Canoga Park, CA 91304-1743, USA

Houston, Allan (Basketball Player)
New York Knicks
2 Penn Plz
Madison Square Garden
New York, NY 10121-1703, USA

Houston, Andy (Race Car Driver)
835F Williamson Rd # 36
C/O Global Performance Co
Mooresville, NC 28117-8597, USA

Houston, Byron (Basketball Player)
1732 Lionsgate Cir
Bethany, OK 73008-6167, USA

Houston, Cissy (Music Group, Musician)
2160 N Central Rd
Fort Lee, NJ 07024-7547, USA

Houston, Edwin A (Business Person)
Ryder System Inc
11690 NW 105th St
Medley, FL 33178-1103, USA

Houston, Ken (Football Player)
Houston Oilers
3603 Forest Village Dr
Humble, TX 77339-1819, USA

Houston, Marques (Batman) (Actor, Musician)
c/o Tyler Grasham *Agency for the Performing Arts (APA-LA)*
405 S Beverly Dr
Beverly Hills, CA 90212-4416, USA

Houston, Marquis (Actor, Musician)
c/o Chris Stokes *Ultimate Group, The*
848 N La Cienega Blvd Ste 201
West Hollywood, CA 90069-6600, USA

Houston, Penelope (Music Group)
Absolute Artists
8490 W Sunset Blvd Ste 403
West Hollywood, CA 90069-1926, USA

Houston, Russell (Artist)
General Delivery
Eagar, AZ 85925-9999, USA

Houston, Thelma (Musician)
J Cast Productions
2550 Greenvalley Rd
Los Angeles, CA 90046-1438, USA

Houston, Tyler (Baseball Player)
Atlanta Braves
325 Pleasant Summit Dr
Henderson, NV 89012-3486, USA

Houston, Wade (Basketball Player, Coach)
University of Tennessee
Athletic Dept
Knoxville, TN 37901, USA

Houston, Whitney (Musician)
c/o Nicole David *William Morris Agency (WMA-LA)*
1 William Morris Pl
Beverly Hills, CA 90212-4261, USA

Houston Calls (Music Group)
Drive Thru Records
3019 Olympic Blvd
Santa Monica, CA 90404-5001, USA

Houthakker, Hendrik S (Economist)
1 Ivy Pointe Way
Hanover, NH 03755-1407, USA

Hovan, Chris (Football Player)
Minnesota Vikings
9520 Viking Dr
Eden Prairie, MN 55344-3898, USA

Hove, Andrew C Jr (Financier)
Federal Deposit Insurance
550 17th St NW
Washington, DC 20429-0002, USA

Hovind, David J (Business Person)
PACCAR Inc
777 106th Ave NE
Bellevue, WA 98004-5027, USA

Hoving, Thomas (Director, Editor)
Hoving Assoc
150 E 73rd St
New York, NY 10021-4362, USA

Hovland, Tim (Volleyball Player)
Assn of Volleyball Pros
330 Washington Blvd # 400
Marina Del Rey, CA 90292-5141, USA

Hovley, Steve (Baseball Player)
Seattle Mariners
PO Box 655
Oak View, CA 93022-0655, USA

Hovsepian, Vatche (Religious Leader)
Armenian Church of America West
1201 N Vine St
Los Angeles, CA 90038-1611, USA

Howard, Adina (Musician)
International Creative Mgmt
40 W 57th St Ste 1800
New York, NY 10019-4001, USA

Howard, Adina (Musician)
c/o Staff Member *Diva Central Inc*
7510 W Sunset Blvd Ste 1445
Los Angeles, CA 90046-3408, USA

Howard, Alan (Actor)
Julian Belfrage
46 Albermarle St
London W1X 4PP, UNITED KINGDOM (UK)

Howard, Ann (Opera Singer)
Stafford Law Assoc
6 Barham Close
Weybridge
Surrey KT13 9PR, UNITED KINGDOM (UK)

Howard, Arliss (Actor, Director)
William Morris Agency
151 El Camino Dr
Beverly Hills, CA 90212-2775, USA

Howard, Barbara (Actor)
Artists Group
1650 Broadway Ste 610
New York, NY 10019-6833, USA

Howard, Bob (Football Player)
San Diego Chargers
2444 56th St
San Diego, CA 92105-5012, USA

Howard, Bobby (Football Player)
Tampa Bay Buccaneers
6192 Remington Park
Lithonia, GA 30058-6451, USA

Howard, Bruce (Baseball Player)
Chicago White Sox
8705 Misty Creek Dr
Sarasota, FL 34241-9562, USA

Howard, Bryce Dallas (Actor)
c/o Peter Kiernan *Management 360*
9111 Wilshire Blvd
Beverly Hills, CA 90210-5508, USA

Howard, Chris (Baseball Player)
Chicago White Sox
17 Sea View Ave
Nahant, MA 01908-1548, USA

Howard, Chris (Baseball Player)
Seattle Mariners
8655 Jones Rd Apt 301
Houston, TX 77065-5104, USA

Howard, Clint (Actor)
4286 N Clybourn Ave
Burbank, CA 91505-4002, USA

Howard, David (Baseball Player)
Kansas City Royals
6416 Beaver Way
Tampa, FL 33625-1633, USA

Howard, David (Football Player)
Minnesota Vikings
5516 E Rosedale St
Fort Worth, TX 76112-6859, USA

Howard, Desmond (Football Player)
Washington Redskins
7459 Winding Way
Brecksville, OH 44141-1923, USA

Howard, Doug (Baseball Player)
California Angels
8038 Deer Creek Rd
Salt Lake City, UT 84121-5762, USA

Howard, Dwight (Basketball Player)
Orlando Magic
8701 Maitland Summit Blvd
Waterhouse Center
Orlando, FL 32810-5915, USA

Howard, Eddie (Football Player)
San Francisco 49ers
1130 E Workman Ave
West Covina, CA 91790-2357, USA

Howard, Frank (Baseball Player)
Los Angeles Dodgers
24178 Lenah Woods Pl
Aldie, VA 20105-2369, USA

Howard, Fred (Baseball Player)
Chicago White Sox
250 Lake Lulu Dr
Winter Haven, FL 33880-4461, USA

Howard, Gene (Football Player)
New Orleans Saints
11051 Lavender Ave
Fountain Valley, CA 92708-2457, USA

Howard, George (Bowler)
8415 Brookwood Dr
Portage, MI 49024-5209, USA

Howard, George (Musician)
David Rubinson
PO Box 411197
San Francisco, CA 94141-1197, USA

Howard, Greg (Cartoonist)
3403 W 28th St
Minneapolis, MN 55416-4302, USA

Howard, Harry N (Historian)
6508 Greentree Rd
Bradley Hills Grove
Bethesda, MD 20817-3326, USA

Howard, James J III (Business Person)
Northern States Power
414 Nicollet Mall
Minneapolis, MN 55401-1927, USA

Howard, James Newton (Composer)
Gorfaine/Schwartz
4111 W Alameda Ave Ste 509
Burbank, CA 91505-4171, USA

Howard, Jan (Music Group)
c/o Staff Member *Tessier-Marsh Talent*
505 Canton Pass
Madison, TN 37115-5449, USA

Howard, Jeffrey R (Judge)
US Court of Appeals
55 Pleasant St
US Courthouse
Concord, NH 03301-3954, USA

Howard, Joe (Football Player)
Buffalo Bills
2501 Joseph Dr
Clinton, MD 20735-4540, USA

Howard, John W (Prime Minister)
Prime Minister's Office
Parliament House
Canbera, ACT 2600, AUSTRALIA

Howard, Josh (Basketball Player)
Dallas Mavericks
2909 Taylor St
Dallas, TX 75226-1909, USA

Howard, Joyce
147 Ocean Avenue Ext
Santa Monica, CA 90402-1211, USA

Howard, Juwan (Basketball Player)
c/o Staff Member *Houston Rockets*
1510 Polk St
Houston, TX 77002-1099, USA

Howard, Ken (Actor, Producer, Writer)
c/o Ross Fineman *Fineman Entertainment*
9437 Santa Monica Blvd Ste 206
Beverly Hills, CA 90210-4612, USA

Howard, Kyle (Actor)
c/o Steve Himber *Himber Entertainment Inc*
15760 Ventura Blvd Ste 700
Encino, CA 91436-3016, USA

Howard, Larry (Baseball Player)
Houston Astros
207 Innwood Dr
Georgetown, TX 78628-8311, USA

Howard, Lee (Baseball Player)
Pittsburgh Pirates
4650 Dulin Rd Spc 203
Fallbrook, CA 92028-8766, USA

Howard, Lisa
247 S Beverly Dr # 102
Beverly Hills, CA 90212-3830, USA

Howard, Matt (Baseball Player)
New York Yankees
37168 Delgado Way
Temecula, CA 92592-8896, USA

Howard, Michael (Government Official)
House of Commons
Westminster
London SW1A 0AA, UNITED KINGDOM (UK)

Howard, Mike (Baseball Player)
New York Mets
101 Kenbridge Ln
Madison, MS 39110-9773, USA

Howard, Miki (Musician)
c/o Mike Gardner *Gardener Entertainment*
5683 Hazelcrest Cir
Westlake Village, CA 91362-5426, USA

Howard, ohn
GPO Box 59
Sydney NSW 2001, AUSTRALIA

Howard, Rance (Actor)
4286 N Clybourn Ave
Burbank, CA 91505-4002, USA

Howard, Rebecca Lynn (Musician)
c/o Staff Member *Paradigm (Monterey)*
509 Hartnell St
Monterey, CA 93940-2825, USA

Howard, Reggie (Baseball Player)
Indianapolis Clowns
4332 Crimson Leaf Cv
Memphis, TN 38125-2905, USA

Howard, Richard (Writer)
23 Waverly Pl Apt 5X
New York, NY 10003-6717, USA

Howard, Robert (Hardcore Holly) (Wrestler)
c/o Staff Member *World Wrestling Entertainment (WWE)*
1241 E Main St
Stamford, CT 06902-3520, USA

Howard, Ron (Actor, Director, Producer, Writer)
c/o Staff Member *Imagine Entertainment*
9465 Wilshire Blvd Fl 7
Beverly Hills, CA 90212-2606, USA

Howard, Ron (Football Player)
Dallas Cowboys
14701 NE 61st Ct
Redmond, WA 98052-4751, USA

Howard, Ryan (Athlete, Baseball Player)
c/o Staff Member *Philadelphia Phillies*
3501 S Broad St
Veterans Stadium
Philadelphia, PA 19148, USA

Howard, Sherman (Football Player)
New York Yankees
5125 Thomas Dr
Richton Park, IL 60471-1639, USA

Howard, Sherri (Athlete, Track Athlete)
14059 Bridle Ridge Rd
Sylmar, CA 91342-1060, USA

Howard, Sherry
14059 Bridle Ridge Rd
Sylmar, CA 91342-1060, USA

Howard, Steven (Baseball Player)
Oakland A's
4712 Shetland Ave
Oakland, CA 94605-5629, USA

Howard, Susan (Actor)
PO Box 1456
Boerne, TX 78006-1456, USA

Howard, Terrence Dashon (Actor)
c/o Shakim Compere *Flavor Unit Entertainment*
155 Morgan St
Jersey City, NJ 07302-2932, USA

Howard, Thomas (Baseball Player)
San Diego Padres
822 8th Ave
Middletown, OH 45044-5519, USA

Howard, Tim (Soccer Player)
Manchester United FC
Sir Matt Busby Way
Old Trafford
Manchester M16 0RA, ENGLAND

Howard, Todd (Football Player)
Kansas City Chiefs
1300 Bienville Ave
Ruston, LA 71270-5204, USA

Howard, Traylor (Actor)
c/o John Carrabino *John Carrabino Management*
5900 Wilshire Blvd Ste 406
Los Angeles, CA 90036-5015, USA

Howard, Wilbur (Baseball Player)
Milwaukee Brewers
643 Walston Ln
Houston, TX 77060-5846, USA

Howard, William W Jr (Misc)
National Wildlife Federation
11100 Wildlife Center Dr
Reston, VA 20190-5362, USA

Howarth, Elgar (Composer)
27 Cromwell Ave
London N6 5HN, UNITED KINGDOM (UK)

Howarth, Jim (Baseball Player)
San Francisco Giants
275 Santini St
Biloxi, MS 39530-2958, USA

Howarth, Judith (Opera Singer)
Lies Askonas
6 Henrietta St
London WC2E 8LA, UNITED KINGDOM (UK)

Howarth, Roger (Actor)
K&H
1212 Avenue Of The Americas # 3
New York, NY 10036-1602, USA

Howarth, Thomas (Architect)
University of Toronto
230 College St
Toronto, ON M5S 1R1, CANADA

Howatch, Susan (Writer)
Atiken & Stone
29 Femshaw Road
London SW10 0TG, UNITED KINGDOM (UK)

Howe, Arthur (Journalist)
Philadelphia Inquirer
400 N Broad St
Editorial Dept
Philadelphia, PA 19130-4099, USA

Howe, Arthur H (Art) Jr (Baseball Player)
Pittsburgh Pirates
17214 Calico Peak Way
Cypress, TX 77433-2113, USA

Howe, Brian (Music Group, Musician)
Union Entertainment
1323 Newbury Rd Ste 104
Newbury Park, CA 91320-3679, USA

Howe, Cal (Baseball Player)
Chicago Cubs
7450 Boulder Bluff Dr Apt 51
Jenison, MI 49428-8941, USA

Howe, Delles (Football Player)
New Orleans Saints
1907 Crescent Dr
Monroe, LA 71202-3023, USA

Howe, G Woodson (Editor)
Omaha World-Herald
World-Herald Square
Editorial Dept
Omaha, NE 68102, USA

Howe, Garry (Football Player)
Pittsburgh Steelers
1159 McCartney St
Pittsburgh, PA 15220-4625, USA

Howe, Jonathan T (Admiral)
Arthur Vining Davis Foundation
225 Water St Ste 1510
Jacksonville, FL 32202-5175, USA

Howe, Mark S (Hockey Player)
9 Inverness Ln
Jackson, NJ 08527-4046, USA

Howe, Oscar (Artist)
5900 S Prairie View Ct
Sioux Falls, SD 57108-2003, USA

Howe, Steven R (Steve) (Baseball Player)
PO Box 1355
Warsaw, IN 46581-1355, USA

Howe, Tina (Writer)
333 W End Ave
New York, NY 10023-8128, USA

Howe of Aberavon, R E Geoffrey (Government Official)
Barclays Bank
Cavendish Square Branch
4 Vere St
London W1, UNITED KINGDOM (UK)

Howell, Alex (Cartoonist)
King Features Syndicate
888 7th Ave Ste 201
New York, NY 10106-0201, USA

Howell, Bailey (Basketball Player)
1989 S Montgomery St
Starkville, MS 39759-9610, USA

Howell, Brad
Gunterring 21
Hattersheim D-65795, GERMANY

Howell, C Thomas (Actor, Director, Producer, Writer)
c/o Jean-Pierre (JP) Henraux *Shelter Entertainment*
1041 N Formosa Ave
Santa Monica Bldg W #17
W Hollywood, CA 90046-6703, USA

Howell, David (Golfer)
c/o Staff Member *International Sports Management Ltd (ISM UK)*
Cherry Tree Farm
Cherry Tree Lane
Rostherne, Cheshire WA14 3RZ, UNITED KINGDOM (UK)

Howell, Francis C (Misc)
1994 San Antonio Ave
Berkeley, CA 94707-1620, USA

Howell, Henry V (Harry) (Hockey Player)
21 Bruce St
Hamilton, ON L8P 3M5, CANADA

Howell, Jack (Baseball Player)
California Angels
822 S Lehigh Dr
Tucson, AZ 85710-4741, USA

Howell, Jay (Baseball Player)
Cincinnati Reds
4920 Highway 9 N # 329
Alpharetta, GA 30004-2921, USA

Howell, Ken (Baseball Player)
Los Angeles Dodgers
22090 Buckingham Dr
Farmington Hills, MI 48335-5423, USA

Howell, Margaret (Actor)
Chateau/Billings Agency
8489 W 3rd St
Los Angeles, CA 90048-4124, USA

Howell, Margaret (Designer, Fashion Designer)
5 Garden House
8 Battersea Park Road
London SW8, UNITED KINGDOM (UK)

Howell, Mike (Football Player)
Cleveland Browns
200 Charlotte St
Monroe, LA 71202-3906, USA

Howell, Pat (Football Player)
Atlanta Falcons
7692 N Kincaid Ave
Fresno, CA 93711-0363, USA

Howell, Patrick (Baseball Player)
New York Mets
5228 Wilhelm Dr
Mobile, AL 36618-2437, USA

Howell, Roy (Baseball Player)
Texas Rangers
1201 E Cypress Ave
Lompoc, CA 93436-7039, USA

Howell, William R (Business Person)
JC Penney Co
PO Box 10001
Dallas, TX 75301-0001, USA

Howells, Anne (Opera Singer)
Milestone Broom Close
Esher Surrey, UNITED KINGDOM (UK)

Howells, William W (Misc)
11 Lawrence Ln
Kittery Point, ME 03905-5104, USA

Howes, Sally Ann (Actor, Music Group, Musician)
Saraband
265 Liverpool Road
London N1 1LX, UNITED KINGDOM (UK)

Howey, Steve (Actor)
c/o Brian Swardstrom *Endeavor Agency LLC (LA)*
9601 Wilshire Blvd Fl 3
Beverly Hills, CA 90210-5204, USA

Howfield, Bobby (Football Player)
Denver Broncos
5529 S Lowell Blvd
Littleton, CO 80123-2840, USA

Howfield, Ian (Football Player)
Houston Oilers
2851 Elk Canyon Ct
Las Vegas, NV 89117-2983, USA

Howitt, Dann (Baseball Player)
Oakland A's
63 Allison Dr
Battle Creek, MI 49037-1827, USA

Howitt, Peter (Director)
Industry Entertainment
955 Carrillo Dr Ste 300
Los Angeles, CA 90048-5400, USA

Howland, Ben (Basketball Player, Coach)
University of California
Athletic Dept
Los Angeles, CA 90024, USA

Howland, Beth (Actor)
255 Amalfi Dr
Santa Monica, CA 90402-1125, USA

Howland, Chris
Vordersten Buchel 11
Rosrath D-51503, GERMANY

Howle, Paul (Cartoonist)
United Feature Syndicate
200 Madison Ave
New York, NY 10016-3911, USA

Howlett, Liam (Composer, Musician)
Midi Mgmt
Jenkins Lane
Great Hallinsbury
Essex CM22 7QL, UNITED KINGDOM (UK)

Howley, Chuck (Football Player)
Chicago Bears
5234 Ravine Dr
Dallas, TX 75220-2260, USA

Howry, Bobby (Baseball Player)
Chicago White Sox
5440 W Park View Ln
Glendale, AZ 85310-2947, USA

Howton, Bill (Football Player)
Green Bay Packers
1796 County Road 10
Plainview, TX 79072-0929, USA

Howze, Leonard Earl (Actor)
c/o Siri Garber *Platform Public Relations*
2133 Holly Dr
Los Angeles, CA 90068-2851, USA

Hoy, Peter (Baseball Player)
Boston Red Sox
770 Lambert Street
Cardinal, ON K0E 1E0, CANADA

Hoyem, Steve (Football Player)
Buffalo Bills
28 Twilight Blf
Newport Coast, CA 92657-2126, USA

Hoying, Bobby (Football Player)
Philadelphia Eagles
60 Dogwood Dr
Fort Loramie, OH 45845, USA

Hoyland, John (Artist)
41 Charterhouse Square
London EC1M 6EA, UNITED KINGDOM
(UK)

Hoyos, Luis Fernando (Actor)
c/o Gabriel Blanco *Gabriel Blanco
Iglesias (Mexico)*
Rio Balsas 35-32
Colonia Cuauhtemoc
DF 06500, MEXICO

Hoyt, D LaMarr (Baseball Player)
Chicago White Sox
1594 Lost Creek Dr
Columbia, SC 29212-2859, USA

Hrabetin, Frank (Football Player)
Philadelphia Eagles
47 Casa Arroyo Lane
Sonoita, AZ 85637, USA

Hrabosky, Alan T (Al) (Baseball Player,
Sportscaster)
9 Frontenac Estates Dr
Saint Louis, MO 63131-2613, USA

Hrbek, Kent A (Baseball Player)
Atlanta Braves
2611 W 112th St
Bloomington, MN 55431-3965, USA

Hrdy, Sarah Blaffer (Misc)
University of California
Anthropology Dept
Davis, CA 95616, USA

Hriniak, Walt (Baseball Player)
Atlanta Braves
18 Stacy Dr
North Andover, MA 01845-1832, USA

Hrivnak, Gary (Football Player)
Chicago Bears
1508 W Plymouth Dr
Arlington Heights, IL 60004-2847, USA

Hrkac, Tony (Hockey Player)
9 Dunleith Dr
Saint Louis, MO 63124-1895, USA

Hrudey, Kelly (Hockey Player)
Hockey Night
PO Box 500 Station A
Toronto, ON M5W 1E6, CANADA

Hu, Jintao (President)
Communist Party Central Committee
1 Zhong Nan Hai
Beijing, CHINA

Hu, Kelly (Actor)
c/o Craig Shapiro *Innovative Artists (LA)*
1505 10th St
Santa Monica, CA 90401-2805, USA

Hu, Qili (Government Official)
Consultative Conference
23 Taipingqiao St
Beijing 100283, CHINA

Huang, Helen (Musician)
I C M Artists
40 W 57th St
New York, NY 10019-4001, USA

Huang, James (Actor)
c/o Staff Member *Cunningham Escott
Slevin & Doherty (LA)*
10635 Santa Monica Blvd Ste 130
Los Angeles, CA 90025-8306, USA

Huang, Nina
8007 Highland Trl
Los Angeles, CA 90046-2022, USA

Huang, Ying (Musician)
c/o Staff Member *Sony Records*
2100 Colorado Ave
Santa Monica, CA 90404-3504, USA

Huard, Damon (Football Player)
Miami Dolphins
12413 Delmar St
Leawood, KS 66209-2242, USA

Huard, John (Football Player)
Denver Broncos
40 Vista Dr
S Portland, ME 04106-6894, USA

Huarte, John (Football Player)
Boston Patriots
14959 La Cumbre Dr
Pacific Palisades, CA 90272-4457, USA

Huarte, John G (Football Player)
Arizona Tile Supply
8829 S Priest Dr
Tempe, AZ 85284-1905, USA

Hub (Musician)
William Morris Agency
1325 Avenue Of The Americas
New York, NY 10019-6091, USA

Hubbard, Elizabeth
1505 10th St
Santa Monica, CA 90401-2805, USA

Hubbard, Erica (Actor)
c/o Jenny Delaney *Forster-Delaney
Entertainment*
12533 Woodgreen St
Los Angeles, CA 90066-2723, USA

Hubbard, Frederick D (Freddie)
(Composer, Musician)
Thomas Cassidy
11761 E Speedway Blvd
Tucson, AZ 85748-2017, USA

Hubbard, Glenn (Baseball Player)
Atlanta Braves
1515 Kings Xing
Stone Mountain, GA 30087-1914, USA

Hubbard, Gregg (Hobbie) (Music Group,
Musician)
Sawyer Brown Inc
5200 Old Harding Rd
Franklin, TN 37064-9406, USA

Hubbard, John (Artist)
Chilcombe House
Chilcombe near Bridport
Dorset, UNITED KINGDOM (UK)

Hubbard, Marvin R (Marv) (Football
Player)
Oakland Raiders
5804 Dawn View Ct
Castro Valley, CA 94552-1803, USA

Hubbard, Mike (Baseball Player)
Chicago Cubs
2552 Brookstone Ln
Richmond, VA 23233-6914, USA

Hubbard, Philip (Phil) (Basketball Player,
Coach)
Washington Wizards
601 F St NW
Mci Center
Washington, DC 20004-1605, USA

Hubbard, Trent (Baseball Player)
Colorado Rockies
2654 E 77th St
Chicago, IL 60649-4725, USA

Hubbauer, Matt (Hockey Player)
c/o Staff Member *Toronto Maple Leafs*
Air Canada Centre
40 Bay St #400
Toronto, ON M5J 2X2, CANADA

Hubbell, Frank (Football Player)
Los Angeles Rams
PO Box 11729
Knoxville, TN 37939-1729, USA

Hubbert, Brad (Football Player)
San Diego Chargers
PO Box 360990
Decatur, GA 30036-0990, USA

Hubcaps
PO Box 1388
Dover, DE 19903-1388, USA

Hubel, David H (Nobel Prize Laureate)
98 Collins Rd
Waban, MA 02468-2235, USA

Hubenthal, Karl (Cartoonist, Editor)
3901 E Coast Hwy Apt 15
Corona Del Mar, CA 92625-5505, USA

Huber, Anke (Tennis Player)
Dieselstr 10
Karlsdorf-Neuthard 76689, GERMANY

Huber, Robert (Nobel Prize Laureate)
Planck Biochemie Instiut
Am Kiopferspitz
Manrinsried 82152, GERMANY

Hubert-Whitten, Janet
10061 Riverside Dr # 204
Toluca Lake, CA 91602-2560, USA

Hubka, Gene (Football Player)
Pittsburgh Steelers
1065 Marshall St
Milton, PA 17847-7647, USA

Hubley, Season (Actor)
31 Mansfield Ave
Essex Junction, VT 05452-3732, USA

Huckabee, Cooper (Actor)
1800 N El Cerrito Pl Apt 34
Los Angeles, CA 90068-3743, USA

Huckaby, Ken (Baseball Player)
Arizona Diamondbacks
4490 S Rio Dr
Chandler, AZ 85249-3382, USA

Huckleby, Harlan (Football Player)
Green Bay Packers
7473 Franklin Ridge Way
West Bloomfield, MI 48322-4128, USA

Hucknall, Mick (Musician)
Simply Red
PO Box 20197
London W10 6YQ, UNITED KINGDOM
(UK)

Huckstep, Ronald L (Doctor)
108 Sugarloaf Crescent
Castlecrag
Syndey, NSW 2068, AUSTRALIA

Hudd, Roy
652 Finchley Rd.
London, ENGLAND NW11 7NT, UNITED
KINGDOM (UK)

Huddleston, David (Actor)
9200 W Sunset Blvd Ste 612
Los Angeles, CA 90069-3609, USA

Hudecek, Vaclav (Musician)
Londynska 25
Prague 2 120 00, CZECH REPUBLIC

Hudgens, Dave (Baseball Player)
Oakland A's
2765 N Scottsdale Rd Ste 104
Scottsdale, AZ 85257-1371, USA

Hudgens, Vanessa Anne (Actor)
c/o Stephanie Simon *Untitled
Entertainment (LA)*
331 N Maple Dr Fl 3
Beverly Hills, CA 90210-3827, USA

Hudler, Rex (Baseball Player)
New York Yankees
1857 Oxford Ave
Cambria, CA 93428-5519, USA

Hudlin, Reginald (Actor, Director,
Producer, Writer)
c/o Norman Aladjem *Paradigm (LA)*
360 N Crescent Dr
North Bldg
Beverly Hills, CA 90210-6820, USA

Hudner, Thomas J Jr (War Hero)
31 Allen Farm Ln
Concord, MA 01742-2202, USA

Hudson, Bill
7023 Birdview Ave
Malibu, CA 90265-4106, USA

Hudson, Brett
151 El Camino Dr
Beverly Hills, CA 90212-2704, USA

Hudson, C B Jr (Business Person)
Torchmark Corp
2001 3rd Ave S
Birmingham, AL 35233-2115, USA

Hudson, Charles (Baseball Player)
Philadelphia Phillies
PO Box 56
Oakwood, TX 75855-0056, USA

Hudson, Charles (Baseball Player)
St Louis Cardinals
32 W Hooker Ave
Coalgate, OK 74538, USA

Hudson, Clifford G (Financier)
Securities Investor Protection
805 15th St NW
Washington, DC 20005-2215, USA

Hudson, Emie (Actor)
5711 Hoback Glen Rd
Hidden Hills, CA 91302-1229, USA

Hudson, Ernie (Actor, Producer)
c/o Darryl Marshak *Marshak/Zachary
Company, The*
8840 Wilshire Blvd Fl 1
Beverly Hills, CA 90211-2606, USA

Hudson, Garth (Music Group, Musician)
Skyline Music
32 Clayton St
Portland, ME 04103-2250, USA

Hudson, Gary (Actor)
c/o Staff Member *Origin Talent Agency*
4705 Laurel Canyon Blvd Ste 306
Studio City, CA 91607-5940, USA

Hudson, Hal (Baseball Player)
New York Mets
422 Sandpiper Dr Apt C
Fort Pierce, FL 34982-5112, USA

Hudson, Haley (Actor)
c/o Staff Member *Weeds*
10880 Wilshire Blvd Ste 1600
Showtime Newtworks (La)
Los Angeles, CA 90024-4117, USA

Hudson, Hugh (Director)
c/o Staff Member *International Creative
Management (ICM-LA)*
10250 Constellation Blvd
Los Angeles, CA 90067-6200, USA

Hudson, James (Doctor)
Harvard Medical School
25 Shattuck St
Psychiatry Dept
Boston, MA 02115-6092, USA

Hudson, Jennifer (Musician, Reality TV
Star)
c/o Gabrielle (Gaby) Morgerman *William
Morris Agency (WMA-LA)*
1 William Morris Pl
Beverly Hills, CA 90212-4261, USA

Hudson, Jesse (Baseball Player)
New York Mets
PO Box 1052
Mansfield, LA 71052-1052, USA

Hudson, Jim (Football Player)
New York Jets
3635 Perefrine Falcon Dr
Austin, TX 78746, USA

Hudson, Joe (Baseball Player)
Boston Red Sox
123 Queen Anne Ct
Dover, DE 19901-1511, USA

Hudson, John (Football Player)
Philadelphia Eagles
3320 Highway 77
Paris, TN 38242-5495, USA

Hudson, Kate (Actor)
c/o Patrick Whitesell *Endeavor Agency
LLC (LA)*
9601 Wilshire Blvd Fl 3
Beverly Hills, CA 90210-5204, USA

Hudson, Lou (Basketball Player)
2002 Lakeview Dr
Park City, UT 84060-7049, USA

Hudson, Lucy-Jo (Actor)
Granada Television
Quay St
Manchester M60 9EA, ENGLAND

Hudson, Luke (Baseball Player)
Cincinnati Reds
9912 Aster Cir
Fountain Valley, CA 92708-2309, USA

Hudson, Marvin (Baseball Player)
542 Metasville Rd
Washington, GA 30673-2604, USA

Hudson, Oliver (Actor, Producer)
c/o Staff Member *Workshed Entertaiment*
9255 W Sunset Blvd Ste 1010
West Hollywood, CA 90069-3307, USA

Hudson, Ray (Coach, Soccer Player)
DC United
14120 Newbrook Dr
Chantilly, VA 20151-2273, USA

Hudson, Rex (Baseball Player)
Los Angeles Dodgers
4704 Spring Meadow Ln
Midland, TX 79705-2966, USA

Hudson, Richard S (Football Player)
San Diego Chargers
315 S Wilson St
Henry County High School Attn: Assistant
Principal
Paris, TN 38242-5053, USA

Hudson, Robert W (Football Player)
New York Giants
3408 Dalrock Rd
Rowlett, TX 75088-5538, USA

Hudson, Sally (Skier)
PO Box 2343
Olympic Valley, CA 96146-2343, USA

Hudson, Sid (Baseball Player)
Washington Senators
PO Box 8637
Waco, TX 76714-8637, USA

Hudson, Timothy A (Tim) (Baseball
Player)
Oakland A's
600 Graystone Ct
Peachtree City, GA 30269-3379, USA

Hudson Brothers
151 El Camino Dr
Beverly Hills, CA 90212-2704, USA

Huerta, Carlos (Football Player)
Chicago Bears
3980 Howard Hughes Pkwy Ste 550
Las Vegas, NV 89169-5905, USA

Huertas, Jon (Actor)
Cirrincione Assoc
300 W 5th St
New York, NY 10019, USA

Hues, Frankie
2640 NE 135th St Apt 302
North Miami, FL 33181-3540, USA

Hues, Matthias (Actor)
Lou Records
32 rue des Ježneurs
Paris 75002, FRANCE

Hues Corporation
1560 Broadway # 1308
New York, NY 10036-1518, USA

Huff, Aubrey (Baseball Player)
Tampa Bay Devil Rays
11831 94th St
Largo, FL 33773-4302, USA

Huff, Brent (Actor)
Artists Group
1650 Broadway Ste 610
New York, NY 10019-6833, USA

Huff, Gary E (Football Player)
Chicago Bears
3175 Hawks Landing Dr
Tallahassee, FL 32309-7227, USA

Huff, Kenneth W (Ken) (Football Player)
Baltimore Colts
105 Blackford Ct
Durham, NC 27712-9497, USA

Huff, Mike (Baseball Player)
Los Angeles Dodgers
11 Avery Cir
Jackson, MS 39211-2403, USA

Huff, Robert L (Sam) (Football Player)
New York Giants
Middleburg Broadcasting Network
8 N Jay St
Middleburg, VA 20118, USA

Huff, Shawn
1505 10th St
Santa Monica, CA 90401-2805, USA

Huffington, Arianna (Actor, Writer)
Inkwell Management
521 5th Ave
New York, NY 10175-0003, USA

Huffington, Michael (Congressman, Ex-
Congressman, Politician)
3005 45th St NW
Washington, DC 20016-3528, USA

Huffman, Ben (Baseball Player)
St Louis Browns
122 N Hawksbill St
Luray, VA 22835-1126, USA

Huffman, Felicity (Actor)
c/o Staff Member *Desperate Housewives*
2300 W Riverside Dr
Abc Television
Burbank, CA 91506-2976, USA

Huffman, Phil (Baseball Player)
Toronto Blue Jays
194 Paxton Rd
Rochester, NY 14617-4657, USA

Huffman, Tim (Football Player)
Green Bay Packers
3365 Jubilee Trl
Dallas, TX 75229-3810, USA

Hufnagel, John (Football Player)
Denver Broncos
12859 Biggin Church Rd S
Jacksonville, FL 32224-7928, USA

Hufsey, Billy (Actor)
15415 Muskingum Blvd
Brook Park, OH 44142-2327, USA

Hufstedler, Shirley M (Educator,
Secretary)
720 Iverness Dr
La Canada-Flintridge, CA 91011, USA

Hug, Procter R Jr (Judge)
US Court of Appeals
400 S Virginia St
Reno, NV 89501-2116, USA

Huggins, Bob (Basketball Player, Coach)
207 Beecher Hall
Cincinnati, OH 45221-0001, USA

Hughes, Albert (Director)
Creative Artists Agency
9830 Wilshire Blvd
Beverly Hills, CA 90212-1804, USA

Hughes, Allen (Director)
Creative Artists Agency
9830 Wilshire Blvd
Beverly Hills, CA 90212-1804, USA

Hughes, Bobby (Baseball Player)
Milwaukee Brewers
14254 N 46th Pl
Phoenix, AZ 85032-5561, USA

Hughes, Carolyn (Actor, Sportscaster,
Television Host)
c/o Staff Member *Fox Sports Television
Group*
10201 W Pico Blvd Bldg 101
Los Angeles, CA 90064-2606, USA

Hughes, Danan (Football Player)
Kansas City Chiefs
49 W 19th St
Bayonne, NJ 07002-3609, USA

Hughes, David (Football Player)
Seattle Seahawks
5307 240th Ave NE
Redmond, WA 98053-2543, USA

Hughes, Dennis (Football Player)
Pittsburgh Steelers
360 Beechwood Dr
Athens, GA 30606-4010, USA

Hughes, Edward Z (Publisher)
American Heritage Magazine
60 5th Ave
Forbes Building
New York, NY 10011-8868, USA

Hughes, Ernie (Football Player)
San Francisco 49ers
2116 Camino Brazos
Pleasanton, CA 94566-5811, USA

Hughes, Finola (Actor)
c/o *Iannucci Management*
300 S Rexford Dr Apt 106
Beverly Hills, CA 90212-4635, USA

Hughes, Frank John (Actor)
c/o Nicole Nassar *Nicole Nassar PR*
1111 10th St Unit 104
Santa Monica, CA 90403-5363, USA

Hughes, George (Football Player)
Pittsburgh Steelers
1870 E Ocean View Ave
Norfolk, VA 23503-2502, USA

Hughes, H Richard (Architect)
47 Chiswick Quay
London W4 3UR, UNITED KINGDOM
(UK)

Hughes, Harold R (Harry) (Governor)
Patton Boggs Blow
2550 M St NW Ste 500
Washington, DC 20037-1350, USA

Hughes, Irene
500 N Michigan Ave Ste 1039
Chicago, IL 60611-3984, USA

Hughes, Jim (Baseball Player)
Minnesota Twins
7526 El Manor Ave
Los Angeles, CA 90045-1351, USA

Hughes, John (Director)
c/o Jake Bloom *Bloom Hergott Deimer
Rosenthall La Violette*
150 S Rodeo Dr Fl 3
Beverly Hills, CA 90212-2410, USA

Hughes, John (Hockey Player)
317 Laudholm Farm Rd
Wells, ME 04090-4707, USA

Hughes, John W (Director, Writer)
Hughes Entertainment
1 Westminster Pl
Lake Forest, IL 60045-5511, USA

Hughes, Karen (Government Official)
US Department of State
2201 C St NW
Washington, DC 20520-0099, USA

Hughes, Kathleen (Actor)
8818 Rising Glen Pl
Los Angeles, CA 90069-1222, USA

Hughes, Keith (Baseball Player)
New York Yankees
176 Sycamore Rd
Havertown, PA 19083-3508, USA

Hughes, Keith W (Financier)
Associates First Capital
250 E John Carpenter Fwy
Irving, TX 75062-2710, USA

Hughes, Larry (Basketball Player)
Washington Wizards
601 F St NW
Mci Centre
Washington, DC 20004-1605, USA

Hughes, Mark (Coach)
c/o Staff Member *Blackburn Rovers Football Club*
Ewood Park
Blackburn
Lancashire BB2 4JF, UNITED KINGDOM
(UK)

Hughes, Mervyn G (Cricketer)
Australian Cricket Board
90 Jollimant St
Melbourne, VIC 3002, AUSTRALIA

Hughes, Miko (Actor)
Jamieson Assoc
53 Sunrise Road
Superior, MT 59872, USA

Hughes, Pat (Football Player)
New York Giants
4 Woodside Dr
Stratham, NH 03885-6549, USA

Hughes, Randy (Football Player)
Dallas Cowboys
17608 Cedar Creek Canyon Dr
Dallas, TX 75252-4966, USA

Hughes, Richard H (Dick) (Baseball Player)
St Louis Cardinals
PO Box 598
Stephens, AR 71764-0598, USA

Hughes, Robert S F (Critic)
143 Prince St
New York, NY 10012-3113, USA

Hughes, Sarah (Figure Skater)
John Hughes
12 Channel Dr
Great Neck, NY 11024-1212, USA

Hughes, Shannon (Model, Reality TV Star)
c/o Staff Member *The Sports Illustrated Fresh Faces Competition*
Nbc Entertainment
3000 W Alameda Ave #5366
Burbank, CA 91523-0001, USA

Hughes, Suzan (Actor)
c/o Staff Member *International Creative Management (ICM-LA)*
10250 Constellation Blvd
Los Angeles, CA 90067-6200, USA

Hughes, Terry (Baseball Player)
Chicago Cubs
532 Pierpont Avenue Ext
Spartanburg, SC 29303-4100, USA

Hughes, Thomas J Jr (Admiral)
400 Mar Vista Dr Apt 4
Monterey, CA 93940-4359, USA

Hughes, Tom (Baseball Player)
St Louis Cardinals
610 Kimswick Ct
Deer Park, TX 77536-6139, USA

Hughes, Tyrone C (Football Player)
New Orleans Saints
4758 Eunice St
New Orleans, LA 70127-3420, USA

Hughes, Wendy (Actor)
129 Bourke St Woolloomooloo
Sydney, NSW 2011, AUSTRALIA

Hughes-Fulford, Millie (Astronaut)
Veterans Affairs Dept
4150 Clement St
Medical Center
San Francisco, CA 94121-1545, USA

Hughley, D L (Actor, Comedian)
c/o Staff Member *3 Arts Entertainment Inc*
9460 Wilshire Blvd Fl 7
Beverly Hills, CA 90212-2713, USA

Hugo, Chad (Musician)
c/o Scott Vener *Schiff Company*
9465 Wilshire Blvd Ste 480
Beverly Hills, CA 90212-2603, USA

Hugstedt, Petter (Skier)
Kongsberg 3600, NORWAY

Huguenin, G Richard (Inventor)
Millitech Corp
South Deerfield, MA 01373, USA

Huisgen, Rolf (Misc)
Kaulbachstr 10
Munich 80539, GERMANY

Huisman, Mark (Baseball Player)
Kansas City Royals
705 NE Lake Pointe Dr
Lees Summit, MO 64064-2135, USA

Huisman, Rick (Baseball Player)
Kansas City Royals
17W025 Oak Ln
Bensenville, IL 60106-2860, USA

Huizenga, John R (Scientist)
43 McMichael Dr
Pinehurst, NC 28374-6702, USA

Huizenga, Wayne (Baseball Player, Business Person)
Huizenga Holdings
200 S Andrews Ave
Fort Lauderdale, FL 33301-1864, USA

Hulce, Tom (Actor)
2305 Stanley Hills Dr
Los Angeles, CA 90046-1533, USA

Hulcher, Janet
Arnold Palmer Enterprises
9000 Bay Hill Blvd
Orlando, FL 32819-4880, USA

Hulett, Tim (Baseball Player)
Chicago White Sox
6154 Buncombe Rd
Shreveport, LA 71129-4125, USA

Hull, Brett A (Hockey Player)
3520 Eben Way
Stillwater, MN 55082-8102, USA

Hull, Dennis
115 E Maple St
Hinsdale, IL 60521-3730, USA

Hull, Dennis W (Hockey Player)
Rose City Dodge
435 West Side
Welland, ON L3B 5X1, CANADA

Hull, Don (Misc)
US Olympic Committe
1 Olympic Plz
Colorado Springs, CO 80909-5760, USA

Hull, J Kent (Football Player)
Buffalo Bills
RR 1 Box 5748
Greenwood, MS 38930, USA

Hull, James D (Admiral)
Commander US Coast Guard Atlantic
4131 Crawford St
Portsmouth, VA 23704, USA

Hull, Mike (Football Player)
Chicago Bears
3809 Vista Azul
San Clemente, CA 92672-4543, USA

Hull, Roger H (Educator)
Union College
Chancellor's Office
Schenectady, NY 12308, USA

Hullar, Theodore L (Educator)
3 Lowell Pl
Ithaca, NY 14850-2553, USA

Hulme, Denis (Race Car Driver)
CI-6
RDTE Puke
Bay of Plenny, NEW ZEALAND

Hulme, Etta (Cartoonist, Editor)
Fort Worth Star-Telegram
400 W 7th St
Editorial Dept
Fort Worth, TX 76102-4793, USA

Hulme, Keri (Writer)
Hodder & Stoughton
338 Euston Road
London NW1 3BH, UNITED KINGDOM
(UK)

Hulse, David (Baseball Player)
Texas Rangers
1301 Kenwood Dr
San Angelo, TX 76903-7261, USA

Hulse, Russell A (Nobel Prize Laureate)
PO Box 451
Princeton, NJ 08543-0451, USA

Hultz, Don (Football Player)
Minnesota Vikings
5078 Pleasant Ridge Rd
Millington, TN 38053-7752, USA

Huly, Jan C (General)
Deputy Cofs Plans Policies & Ops And Ops And Ops And Ops
Hqusmc 2 Navy St
Washington, DC 20380-0001, USA

Human League (Music Group)
c/o Staff Member *Performers Of the World/ Management Interests Associates (POW/MIA)*
8901 Melrose Ave
2nd Floor
West Hollywood, CA 90069-5605, USA

Humann, L Philip (Financier)
Sun Trust Banks
303 Peachtree St NE
Atlanta, GA 30308-3201, USA

Humayan, Mark S (Doctor)
Johns Hopkins University
Wilmer Ophthalmology Institute
Baltimore, MD 21218, USA

Humbert, John O (Religious Leader)
Christian Church Disciples of Christ
130 E Washington St Ste 130A
Indianapolis, IN 46204-4604, USA

Humbert, Richard (Football Player)
Philadelphia Eagles
12112 Ashton Park Dr
Glen Allen, VA 23059-7129, USA

Hume, A Britton (Brit) (Correspondent)
3100 N St NW Apt 9
Washington, DC 20007-3427, USA

Hume, Alan
Deanrise Deanwood Rd.
Jordans Bucks., ENGLAND, UNITED
KINGDOM (UK)

Hume, Brit (Television Host)
c/o Staff Member *Fox News Channel (DC)*
400 N Capitol St NW Ste 550
Washington, DC 20001-1502, USA

Hume, John (Nobel Prize Laureate)
5 Bayview Terrace
Derry BT48 7EE, NORTHERN IRELAND

Hume, Kirsty (Model)
Elite Model Mgmt
111 E 22nd St Rm 200
New York, NY 10010-5414, USA

Hume, Roger
9 Blenheim St.
London, ENGLAND W1Y 9LE, UNITED
KINGDOM (UK)

Hume, Stephen (Editor)
Vancouver Sun
2250 Granville St
Vancouver, BC V6H 3G2, CANADA

Hume, Tom (Baseball Player)
Cincinnati Reds
3810 Redfish Ct
Palmetto, FL 34221-5636, USA

Humes, Edward (Journalist)
Simon & Schuster
1230 Avenue Of The Americas
New York, NY 10020-1586, USA

Humes, John P (Diplomat)
Forest Mill Road
Mill Neck, NY 11765, USA

Humes, Mary Margaret
PO Box 1168-714
Studio City, CA 91604, USA

Humes, Mary-Margaret (Actor, Model)
Stone Manners
6500 Wilshire Blvd Ste 550
Los Angeles, CA 90048-4950, USA

Humiston, Mike (Football Player)
Buffalo Bills
311 N Richhill St
Waynesburg, PA 15370-1224, USA

Humm, David (Football Player)
Oakland Raiders
1701 Fairfield Ave
Las Vegas, NV 89102-2878, USA

Hummes, Claudio Hummes Cardinal (Religious Leader)
Avenida Higienopolis 890
CP 1670
Sao Paulo 01238-908, BRAZIL

Humperdinck, Engelbert (Musician)
c/o Staff Member *International Creative Management (ICM-LA)*
10250 Constellation Blvd
Los Angeles, CA 90067-6200, USA

Humphrey, Claude (Football Player)
Atlanta Falcons
3399 Lord Dunmore Cv
Bartlett, TN 38134-3089, USA

Humphrey, Gordon J (Senator)
78 Garvin Hill Rd
Chichester, NH 03258-6102, USA

Humphrey, Jay (Football Player)
Minnesota Vikings
14109 Brookridge Cir
Dallas, TX 75254-2709, USA

Humphrey, Paul (Football Player)
Brooklyn Dodgers
1120 E Davis Dr Apt 515
Terre Haute, IN 47802-4068, USA

Humphrey, Renee
9300 Wilshire Blvd Ste 555
Beverly Hills, CA 90212-3211, USA

Humphrey, Richard (Baseball Player)
21 Midland Dr
Morristown, NJ 07960-5064, USA

Humphrey, Ryan (Basketball Player)
Memphis Grizzlies
191 Beale St
Memphis, TN 38103-3715, USA

Humphrey, Terry (Baseball Player)
Montreal Expos
7 Oakmont
Trabuco Canyon, CA 92679-4728, USA

Humphreys, Bob (Baseball Player)
New York Yankees
1803 Oakwood St
Bedford, VA 24523-1217, USA

Humphreys, Mike (Baseball Player)
New York Yankees
1402 Lost Creek Dr
Desoto, TX 75115-3662, USA

Humphries, Barry (Actor)
5 Soho Square
London W1V 5DE, UNITED KINGDOM
(UK)

Humphries, Jay (Basketball Player)
PO Box 1810
Parker, CO 80134-1407, USA

Humphries, Stan (Football Player)
Washington Redskins
212 E Frenchmans Bend Rd
Monroe, LA 71203-8702, USA

Humphries, Stefan (Football Player)
Chicago Bears
8708 E Redwood Ln
Spokane, WA 99217-9757, USA

Humphry, Derek (Activist)
ERGO
24828 Norris Ln
Junction City, OR 97448, USA

Hun, Sen (Prime Minister)
Prime Minister's Office
Supreme National Council
Phnom Penh, CAMBODIA

Hundertwasser, FriedensreichMu
hle Odissenbach
Rapottenstein 3911, AUSTRIA

Hundley, Randy (Baseball Player)
San Francisco Giants
122 E Forest Ln
Palatine, IL 60067-7443, USA

Hundley, Rod (Hot Rod) (Basketball
Player, Sportscaster)
1860 Siggard Dr
Salt Lake City, UT 84106-3870, USA

Hundley, Todd (Baseball Player)
New York Mets
830 Raleigh Rd
Glenview, IL 60025-4328, USA

Hundt, Reed E (Government Official)
6416 Brookside Dr
Bethesda, MD 20815-6649, USA

Hung, Sammo (Actor)
c/o Staff Member *Innovative Artists (LA)*
1505 10th St
Santa Monica, CA 90401-2805, USA

Hung, William (Musician, Reality TV Star)
c/o Michael (Mike) Esterman *Esterman
Entertainment*
214 Park Rd
Riva, MD 21140-1224, USA

Hunger, Daniela (Swimmer)
SV Preussen
Hansastr 190
Berlin 13088, GERMANY

Huniford, James (Architect, Designer)
Sills Hunifor Assoc
30 E 67th St
New York, NY 10065-6120, USA

Hunley, Ricky C (Football Player)
Denver Broncos
9617 Stonemasters Dr
Loveland, OH 45140-6210, USA

Hunnam, Charlie (Actor)
c/o Joe Libonati *I/D PR (LA)*
8409 Santa Monica Blvd
West Hollywood, CA 90069-4209, USA

Hunnan, Charlie (Actor)
c/o Cynthia Pett-Dante *Brillstein-Grey
Entertainment*
9150 Wilshire Blvd Ste 350
Beverly Hills, CA 90212-3453, USA

Hunnicutt, Gayle (Actor)
174 Regents Park Road
London NW1, UNITED KINGDOM (UK)

Hunphrey, Bobby (Football Player)
Denver Broncos
4209 Woodbine Ln
Hoover, AL 35226-4122, USA

Hunt, Bobby (Football Player)
Dallas Texans
5928 Bentway Dr
Charlotte, NC 28226-8053, USA

Hunt, Bonnie (Actor, Director)
c/o Staff Member *Bob & Alice
Productions*
11693 San Vicente Blvd # 813
Los Angeles, CA 90049-5105, USA

Hunt, Bryan (Artist)
31 Great Jones St
New York, NY 10012-1178, USA

Hunt, Byron (Football Player)
New York Giants
PO Box 281
Rutherford, NJ 07070-0281, USA

Hunt, Cletidus (Football Player)
Green Bay Packers
7246 Creek Bend Dr
Memphis, TN 38125-3018, USA

Hunt, George (Football Player)
Baltimore Colts
40 N Pine Cir
Belleair, FL 33756-1640, USA

Hunt, Helen (Actor)
c/o Bryan Lourd *Creative Artists Agency
LCC (CAA-LA)*
2000 Avenue Of The Stars
Los Angeles, CA 90067-4700, USA

Hunt, Jimmy (Actor)
2279 Lansdale Ct
Simi Valley, CA 93065-2530, USA

Hunt, John (Football Player)
Dallas Cowboys
8 Ulverston Way
Blythewood, SC 29016-8941, USA

Hunt, John R (Religious Leader)
Evangelical Covenant Church
5101 N Francisco Ave
Chicago, IL 60625-3699, USA

Hunt, Ken (Baseball Player)
Cincinnati Reds
268 E 300 N
Morgan, UT 84050-9520, USA

Hunt, Kevin (Football Player)
Green Bay Packers
PO Box 612
Londonderry, NH 03053-0612, USA

Hunt, Lamar (Football Executive, Soccer
Player, Tennis Player)
1601 Elm St # 2800
Thanksgiving Tower
Dallas, TX 75201-4701, USA

Hunt, Linda (Actor)
1414 N Orange Grove Ave
West Hollywood, CA 90046-3902, USA

Hunt, Marsha (Actor)
13131 Magnolia Blvd
Van Nuys, CA 91423-1528, USA

Hunt, Nelson Bunker (Business Person)
Hunt Resources Investment Group
Fountain Place
1445 Ross At Field
Dallas, TX 75224, USA

Hunt, Peter
2337 Roscomare Rd Ste 2
Los Angeles, CA 90077-1833, USA

Hunt, R Timothy (Nobel Prize Laureate)
Imperial Cancer Research Fund
PO Box 123
London WC2A 3PX, UNITED KINGDOM
(UK)

Hunt, Randy (Baseball Player)
St Louis Cardinals
324 Holly Ridge Dr
Montgomery, AL 36109-3904, USA

Hunt, Ray
1401 Elm St
Dallas, TX 75202-2910, USA

Hunt, Richard
1017 W Lill Ave
Chicago, IL 60614-2205, USA

Hunt, Robert M (Publisher)
New York Daily News
220 E 42nd St
New York, NY 10017-5806, USA

Hunt, Ronald K (Ron) (Baseball Player)
2806 Jackson Rd
Wentzville, MO 63385-4205, USA

Hunt, Sam (Football Player)
New England Patriots
1708 Eliza St
Nacogdoches, TX 75961-5700, USA

Hunt, Van (Musician)
c/o Staff Member *Creative Artists Agency
LCC (CAA-LA)*
2000 Avenue Of The Stars
Los Angeles, CA 90067-4700, USA

Hunt, Wendy (DJ)
c/o Staff Member *Diva Central Inc*
7510 W Sunset Blvd Ste 1445
Los Angeles, CA 90046-3408, USA

Hunter, Anthony (Football Player)
Buffalo Bills
3553 Edgeview Dr
Cincinnati, OH 45213-2024, USA

Hunter, Arthur (Art) (Football Player)
Green Bay Packers
12521 Wedgewood Circle
Tustin, CA 92780, USA

Hunter, Bill
Box 478
King's Cross NSW 1340, AUSTRALIA

Hunter, Billy (Baseball Player)
St Louis Browns
104 E Seminary Ave
Lutherville, MD 21093-6127, USA

Hunter, Brian (Baseball Player)
Houston Astros
31203 NE 49th St
Camas, WA 98607-9671, USA

Hunter, Brian (Baseball Player)
Atlanta Braves
47 Vista Toscana
Lake Elsinore, CA 92532-0215, USA

Hunter, Buddy
Boston Red Sox
14616 Fir Cir
Plattsmouth, NE 68048-5112, USA

Hunter, Charlie (Music Group, Musician)
Figurehead Mgmt
3470 19th St
San Francisco, CA 94110-1740, USA

Hunter, Dorothy (Baseball Player)
2607 Miller Ave NW
Grand Rapids, MI 49544-1948, USA

Hunter, Holly (Actor)
c/o Eric Kranzler *Management 360*
9111 Wilshire Blvd
Beverly Hills, CA 90210-5508, USA

Hunter, Ian (Music Group, Musician,
Songwriter, Writer)
Helter Skelter
Plaza
535 Kings Road
London SW10 0S, UNITED KINGDOM
(UK)

Hunter, Jack D
22 Hypolita St
St Augustine, FL 32084-3606, USA

Hunter, James E (Football Player)
Detroit Lions
5846 Prado Ct
Orchard Lake, MI 48324-2945, USA

Hunter, Jeff (Football Player)
Buffalo Bills
3492 Monte Carlo Dr
Augusta, GA 30906-5717, USA

Hunter, Jesse (Music Group, Musician)
Friedman & LaRosa
1334 Lexington Ave
New York, NY 10128, USA

Hunter, Jim (Baseball Player)
Milwaukee Brewers
12939 Penshurst Ln
Windermere, FL 34786-6672, USA

Hunter, Jim (Skier)
Jungle Jim Hunter Mgmt
864 Woodpark Way SW
Calgary, AB T2W 2V8, CANADA

Hunter, Les (Basketball Player)
8712 W 92nd St
Overland Park, KS 66212-3817, USA

Hunter, Mellisa (Reality TV Star)
c/o Michael (Mike) Esterman *Esterman
Entertainment*
214 Park Rd
Riva, MD 21140-1224, USA

Hunter, Montgomery (Football Player)
Dallas Cowboys
175 S McKinley Ave
Dover, OH 44622-2020, USA

Hunter, Patrick (Football Player)
Seattle Seahawks
880 N David Ct
Chandler, AZ 85226-1659, USA

Hunter, Paul (Director, Editor, Writer)
c/o Rob Carlson *William Morris Agency (WMA-LA)*
1 William Morris Pl
Beverly Hills, CA 90212-4261, USA

Hunter, Rachel (Actor, Model)
c/o Staff Member *Celebrity Consultants LLC*
3340 Ocean Park Blvd Ste 3030
Santa Monica, CA 90405-3217, USA

Hunter, Rich (Baseball Player)
Philadelphia Phillies
26090 Madison Ave
Murrieta, CA 92562-6909, USA

Hunter, Ronald
8730 W Sunset Blvd Ste 480
Los Angeles, CA 90069-2277, USA

Hunter, Scott (Football Player)
Green Bay Packers
6386 Dolive Ct
Daphne, AL 36526-7159, USA

Hunter, Stephen (Writer)
Washington Post
Editorial Dept
1150 15th St NW
Washington, DC 20071-0001, USA

Hunter, Steven (Basketball Player)
Orlando Magic
8701 Maitland Summit Blvd
Waterhouse Center
Orlando, FL 32810-5915, USA

Hunter, Tab (Actor, Writer)
PO Box 50308
Santa Barbara, CA 93150-0308, USA

Hunter, Tim (Director)
c/o Staff Member *Gersh Agency, The (LA)*
232 N Canon Dr
Beverly Hills, CA 90210-5302, USA

Hunter, Torii K (Baseball Player)
2408 Belmoor Dr
Pine Bluff, AR 71601-5463, USA

Hunter, Torll (Baseball Player)
Minnesota Twins
PO Box 1357
Prosper, TX 75078-1357, USA

Hunter, Willard (Baseball Player)
Los Angeles Dodgers
2562 Poppleton Ave
Omaha, NE 68105-2303, USA

Hunter-Gault, Charlayne (Correspondent)
News Hour Show
2700 S Quincy St Ste 250
Arlington, VA 22206-2222, USA

Hunter Tommy
2806 Opryland Dr
Nashville, TN 37214-1209, USA

Hunthausen, Raymond G (Religious Leader)
Catholic Archdiocese of Seattle
710 9th Ave
Seattle, WA 98104-2017, USA

Huntington, Sam (Actor)
c/o Walter Hamada *H2F*
9000 W Sunset Blvd Ste 710
West Hollywood, CA 90069-5807, USA

Huntington, Samuel P (Politician)
Harvard University
Olin Institute
Political Science Dept
Cambridge, MA 02138, USA

Huntley, Noah (Actor)
c/o Lindy King *Peters Fraser & Dunlop (PFD - UK)*
Drury House
34-43 Russell St
London WC2B 5HA, UNITED KINGDOM (UK)

Huntley, Richard (Football Player)
Atlanta Falcons
6005 Williams Rd Apt A
Charlotte, NC 28215-3606, USA

Huntsman, Stanley H (Coach)
5532 Timbercrest Trl
Knoxville, TN 37909-1837, USA

Huntz, Steve (Baseball Player)
St Louis Cardinals
2788 Wooster Rd
Rocky River, OH 44116-2918, USA

Hunyadfi, Steven (Coach, Swimmer)
838 Ridgewood Dr Apt 12
Fort Wayne, IN 46805-5712, USA

Hunyady, Emese (Speed Skater)
Beim Spitzriegel 1/2/9
Baden 2500, AUSTRIA

Hunziker, Terry (Designer)
208 3rd Ave S
Seattle, WA 98104-2608, USA

Huo, Yaobang (General, Secretary)
Communist Party Central Committee
Zhongguo Gongchan Dang
Beijing, CHINA

Huot, Raymond P (General)
Inspector General Hqusaf
Pentagon
Washington, DC 20330-0001, USA

Hupp, Jana Marie (Actor)
Metropolitan Talent Agency
4500 Wilshire Blvd Fl 2
Los Angeles, CA 90010-3858, USA

Huppert, Dave (Baseball Player)
Baltimore Orioles
6732 Stephens Path
Zephyrhills, FL 33542-0652, USA

Huppert, Isabelle (Actor)
VMA
20 Ave Rapp
Paris 75007, FRANCE

Hurd, Douglas R (Government Official)
Hawkpoint
Crosby Court
4 Great Saint Helens
London EC3A 6HA, UNITED KINGDOM (UK)

Hurd, Gale Anne (Producer)
c/o Staff Member *Valhalla Motion Pictures*
8530 Wilshire Blvd Fl 4
Beverly Hills, CA 90211-3102, USA

Hurd, Michelle (Actor)
c/o Tina Thor *TMT Entertainment Group*
648 Broadway # 1002
New York, NY 10012-2301, USA

Hurdle, Clinton M (Clint) (Baseball Player)
Kansas City Royals
9068 Sturbridge Pl
Littleton, CO 80129-2236, USA

Hurford, Peter J (Musician)
Broom House Saint Bernard's Road
Saint Albans
Herts AL3 5RA, UNITED KINGDOM (UK)

Hurley, Alfred F (Historian)
University of North Texas
President's Office
Denton, TX 76203, USA

Hurley, Craig
9255 W Sunset Blvd Ste 515
Los Angeles, CA 90069-3301, USA

Hurley, Douglas G (Astronaut)
700 Thomwood Dr
Friendswood, TX 77546, USA

Hurley, Elizabeth (Actor, Model)
c/o Lucy George
Unit 3b 101 Farm Ln
London SW6 1QJ, UNITED KINGDOM (UK)

Hurn, David (Photographer)
Prospect Cottage
Tintem
Gwent, WALES, UNITED KINGDOM (UK)

Hurnick, Ilja (Composer, Musician)
Narodni Trida 35
Prague 1 11000, CZECH REPUBLIC

Hurst, Bill (Baseball Player)
Florida Marlins
9331 SW 192nd Dr
Cutler Bay, FL 33157-7973, USA

Hurst, Bruce (Baseball Player)
Boston Red Sox
1080 N Riata St
Gilbert, AZ 85234-3466, USA

Hurst, James (Baseball Player)
Texas Rangers
1413 Van Pelt Rd
Sebring, FL 33870, USA

Hurst, Jimmy (Baseball Player)
Detroit Tigers
1310 37th St E
Tuscaloosa, AL 35405-2544, USA

Hurst, Jonathan (Baseball Player)
Montreal Expos
308 Woodbum Creek Rd
Spartanburg, SC 29302, USA

Hurst, Maurice (Football Player)
New England Patriots
PO Box 431068
Dallas, TX 75343, USA

Hurst, Michael (Actor)
Bruce Ugly Agency
218 Richmond Road
Grey Lynn
Auckland 2, NEW ZEALAND

Hurst, Pat (Golfer)
c/o Staff Member *Ladies Pro Golf Association (LPGA)*
100 International Golf Dr
Daytona Beach, FL 32124-1082, USA

Hurst, Rick (Actor)
c/o Staff Member *Badgley-Connor Agency*
1680 Vine St Ste 1016
Los Angeles, CA 90028-8800, USA

Hurst, Ryan (Actor)
c/o Brian Swardstrom *Endeavor Agency LLC (LA)*
9601 Wilshire Blvd Fl 3
Beverly Hills, CA 90210-5204, USA

Hurston, Chuck (Football Player)
Kansas City Chiefs
9360 Prestwick Club Dr
Duluth, GA 30097-2400, USA

Hurt, Frank (Misc)
Bakery Confectionery Tobacco Union
10401 Connecticut Ave
Kensington, MD 20895-3961, USA

Hurt, John (Actor)
Julian Belfarge
46 Albermarle St
London W1X 4PP, UNITED KINGDOM (UK)

Hurt, Mary Beth (Actor)
1619 Broadway # 900
New York, NY 10019-7412, USA

Hurt, William (Actor)
c/o Hylda Queally *Creative Artists Agency LCC (CAA-LA)*
2000 Avenue Of The Stars
Los Angeles, CA 90067-4700, USA

Hurtado, Edwin (Baseball Player)
Toronto Blue Jays
1202 15th Ave N
Lake Worth, FL 33460-1725, USA

Hurtado Larrea, Oswaldo (President)
Suecia 277 y Av Los Shyris
Quito, ECUADOR

Hurwich, Leo M (Doctor)
University of Pennsylvania
Psychology Dept
Philadelphia, PA 19104, USA

Hurwicz, Leonid (Economist)
5015 35th Ave S Apt 605
Minneapolis, MN 55417-1566, USA

Hurwit, Bruce (Director)
c/o Staff Member *MBST Entertainment*
345 N Maple Dr Ste 200
Beverly Hills, CA 90210-3860, USA

Hurwitz, Emanuel H (Musician)
25 Dollis Ave
London N3 1DA, UNITED KINGDOM (UK)

Hurwitz, Mitchell
c/o Adam Berkowitz *Creative Artists Agency LCC (CAA-LA)*
2000 Avenue Of The Stars
Los Angeles, CA 90067-4700, USA

Husa, Karel J (Composer)
1 Bellwood Ln
Ithaca, NY 14850-5029, USA

Husain, Mishal (Journalist)
c/o Staff Member *BBC Artist Mail*
PO Box 1116
Belfast BT2 7AJ, UNITED KINGDOM (UK)

Husaini (Actor)
T 16/2 Kalasethra Colony
Besant Nagar
Chennai, TN 600 090, INDIA

Husak, Todd (Football Player)
Washington Redskins
1344 Braewood Ave
Littleton, CO 80129-5621, USA

Husar, Lubomyr Cardinal (Religious Leader)
Ploscha Sviatoho Jura 5
Lviv 290000, UKRAINE

Husbands, Clifford (General, Governor)
Governor General's Office
Bay St
Saint Michael
Bridgetown, BARBADOS

Huselius, Kristian (Hockey Player)
Florida Panthers
1 Panther Pkwy
Sunrise, FL 33323-5315, USA

Husen, Torsten (Educator)
Int'l Educational Institute
Armfeltsgatan 10
Stockholm 115 34, SWEDEN

Husenov, Surat (Prime Minister)
Prime Minister's Office
Baku, AZERBAIJAN

Hush, Lizabeth
4512 Gentry Ave
N Hollywood, CA 91607-4117, USA

Huskey, Robert L (Baseball Player)
New York Mets
PO Box 996
Apache, OK 73006-0996, USA

Husky, Rick
13565 Lucca Dr
Pacific Palisades, CA 90272-2722, USA

Husmann, Ed (Football Player)
Chicago Cardinals
27266 Orth Ln
Conroe, TX 77385-9087, USA

Hussain, Nasir (Director, Filmmaker, Producer)
24 Pali Hill
Bandra
Bombay, MS 400 050, INDIA

Hussey, Olivia (Actor)
c/o Staff Member *Richard Schwartz Management*
2934 1/2 N Beverly Glen Cir # 107
Los Angeles, CA 90077-1724, USA

Husted, Dave (Bowler)
16231 SE Norma Rd
Portland, OR 97267-5193, USA

Husted, Wayne D (Artist)
Keep Homestead Museum
Ely Road
Monson, MA 01057, USA

Huston, Anjelica (Actor, Director)
c/o Staff Member *Gray Angel Productions*
74 Market St
Venice, CA 90291-3603, USA

Huston, Carol
10100 Santa Monica Blvd Ste 2500
Los Angeles, CA 90067-4116, USA

Huston, Daniel (Danny) (Director)
William Morris Agency
151 El Camino Dr
Beverly Hills, CA 90212-2775, USA

Huston, Jack (Actor)
c/o Vanessa Pereira *Artists Independent Management (LA)*
825 Nowita Pl
Venice, CA 90291-3836, USA

Huston, John (Golfer)
307 Lakeview Dr
Tarpon Springs, FL 34689-5329, USA

Hutch, Jesse (Actor)
c/o Staff Member *Pacific Artists Management*
1404-510 W Hastings St
Vancouver, BC V6B 1L8, CANADA

Hutcherson, Josh (Actor)
c/o Ric Beddingfield *Beddingfield Company, The*
9255 W Sunset Blvd Ste 920
Los Angeles, CA 90069-3306, USA

Hutcherson, Robert (Bobby) (Musician)
Abby Hoffer
223 1/2 E 48th St
New York, NY 10017, USA

Hutchins, Jason (Baseball Player)
1417 Salem Ct
College Station, TX 77845-9497, USA

Hutchins, Mel (Basketball Player)
160 Sherri Ln
Oceanside, CA 92054-5327, USA

Hutchins, Paul (Football Player)
Green Bay Packers
8818 S Jeffery Blvd
Chicago, IL 60617-2909, USA

Hutchins, Will (Actor)
PO Box 371
Glen Head, NY 11545-0371, USA

Hutchinson, Anthony (Football Player)
Chicago Bears
124 Bellaire Ct
Bellaire, TX 77401-4219, USA

Hutchinson, Asa (Politician)
1501 N Pierce St Ste 102
1501 N Pierce #102
Little Rock, AR 72207-5222, USA

Hutchinson, Barbara (Misc)
American Federation of Labor
815 15th St NW
Washington, DC 20005, USA

Hutchinson, Chad (Baseball Player)
c/o Staff Member *Chicago Bears*
1000 Football Dr
Lake Forest, IL 60045-4829, USA

Hutchinson, Clyde A Jr (Misc)
University of Chicago
Searle Laboratory
Chimestry Dept
Chicago, IL 60637, USA

Hutchinson, Doug (Actor)
United Talent Agency
9560 Wilshire Blvd Ste 500
Beverly Hills, CA 90212-2401, USA

Hutchinson, Doug (Actor)
c/o Ryan Martin *Agency for the Performing Arts (APA-LA)*
405 S Beverly Dr
Beverly Hills, CA 90212-4416, USA

Hutchinson, Frederick E (Educator)
University of Maine
President's Office
Orono, ME 04469-0001, USA

Hutchinson, J Maxwell (Architect)
Cavendish Mansions
#61 Clerkenwell Road
London EC1R 5DH, UNITED KINGDOM (UK)

Hutchinson, Kay Bailey (Senator)
703 Hart Bldg
Washington, DC 20510-0001, USA

Hutchinson, Kieran (Actor)
c/o Adam Levine *Anthem Entertainment*
6100 Wilshire Blvd Ste 1170
Los Angeles, CA 90048-5116, USA

Hutchinson, Scott (Football Player)
Buffalo Bills
726 Forest Glen Ct
Maitland, FL 32751-5109, USA

Hutchinson, Steven (Football Player)
Seattle Seahawks
350 Calamus Cir
Hamel, MN 55340-9228, USA

Huth, Edward J (Doctor, Editor)
1124 Morris Ave
Bryn Mawr, PA 19010-1712, USA

Huth, Gerald (Football Player)
New York Giants
5009 Elm Grove Dr
Las Vegas, NV 89130-3639, USA

Huther, Bruce (Football Player)
Dallas Cowboys
1156 N Bonnie Brae St
Denton, TX 76201-2421, USA

Hutson, Brian (Football Player)
New England Patriots
6077 Arboretum Dr
Frisco, TX 75034-7270, USA

Hutson, Candace
3500 W Olive Ave Ste 920
Burbank, CA 91505-5514, USA

Hutson, Herb (Baseball Player)
Chicago Cubs
7203 W Suger Tree Ct
Savannah, GA 31410, USA

Hutson, Tracy (Actor, Reality TV Star)
c/o Staff Member *Extreme Makeover: Home Edition*
9255 W Sunset Blvd Ste 1100
Endemol Entertainment USA
Los Angeles, CA 90069-3308, USA

Hutt, Peter B (Attorney, Attorney General, General)
Covington & Berlin
1201 Pennsylvania Ave NW
Washington, DC 20004-2494, USA

Hutto, Jim (Baseball Player)
Philadelphia Phillies
1317 John Carroll Dr
Pensacola, FL 32504-7114, USA

Hutton, Anthony (Reality TV Star)
c/o Staff Member *Big Brother (UK)*
Channel 4 Television
124 Horseferry Rd
London SW1P 2TX, UNITED KINGDOM (UK)

Hutton, Danny (Music Group, Musician)
2437 Horse Shoe Canyon Rd
Los Angeles, CA 90046-1539, USA

Hutton, Lauren (Actor, Model, Producer, Writer)
c/o Staff Member *N2N Entertainment*
1230 Montana Ave Apt 203
Santa Monica, CA 90403-5987, USA

Hutton, Mark (Baseball Player)
New York Yankees
6 Corfu Court
Westlakes Adelaide 5021, AUSTRALIA

Hutton, Ralph (Swimmer)
Vancouver Police Department
312 Main St
Vancouver, BC, CANADA

Hutton, Rif
10100 Santa Monica Blvd Ste 2490
Los Angeles, CA 90067-4144, USA

Hutton, Timothy (Actor)
Creative Artists Agency
9830 Wilshire Blvd
Beverly Hills, CA 90212-1804, USA

Hutton, Tommy
Los Angeles Dodgers
18 Huntly Dr
Palm Beach Gardens, FL 33418-6812, USA

Hutzler, Brody (Actor)
c/o Staff Member *Pakula/King & Associates*
9229 W Sunset Blvd Ste 315
Los Angeles, CA 90069-3403, USA

Huxhold, Ken (Football Player)
Philadelphia Eagles
8524 Stone Harbor Ave
Las Vegas, NV 89145-5704, USA

Huxley, Andrew F (Nobel Prize Laureate)
Manor Field
1 Vicarage Dr Grantchester
Cambridge CB3 9NG, UNITED KINGDOM (UK)

Huxley, Laura (Doctor, Writer)
6233 Mulholland Hwy
Los Angeles, CA 90068-1645, USA

Huxtable, Ada Louise (Critic)
969 Park Ave
New York, NY 10028-0322, USA

Huyck, Willard (Director)
39 Oakmont Dr
Los Angeles, CA 90049-1901, USA

Hvorostovsky, Dmitri (Opera Singer)
Lies Askonas
6 Henrietta St
London WC2E 8LA, UNITED KINGDOM (UK)

Hyams, Joe
10375 Wilshire Blvd Apt 4D
Los Angeles, CA 90024-4729, USA

Hyams, Peter (Director)
PO Box 10
Basking Ridge, NJ 07920-0010, USA

Hyatt, Fred (Football Player)
St Louis Cardinals
19350 SE 52nd Pl
Morriston, FL 32668-3968, USA

Hybl, William J (Misc)
US Olympic Committee
1 Olympic Plz
Colorado Springs, CO 80909-5760, USA

Hyche, Heath (Comedian)
c/o Staff Member *Brillstein-Grey Entertainment*
9150 Wilshire Blvd Ste 350
Beverly Hills, CA 90212-3453, USA

Hyche, Steve (Football Player)
Chicago Bears
2801 Five Oaks Ln
Birmingham, AL 35243-2621, USA

Hyde, Dick (Baseball Player)
Washington Senators
1506 Cambridge Dr
Champaign, IL 61821-4957, USA

Hyde, Harry
PO Box 291
Harrisburg, NC 28075-0291, USA

Hyde, Jonathan (Actor)
William Morris Agency
52/53 Poland Place
London W1F 7LX, UNITED KINGDOM (UK)

Hyde-White, Alex (Actor)
Borinstein Oreck Bogart
3172 Dona Susana Dr
Studio City, CA 91604-4356, USA

Hyers, Tim (Baseball Player)
San Diego Padres
241 Ridge Rd
Covington, GA 30016-5138, USA

Hyland, Brian (Musician)
Stone Buffalo
PO Box 101
Helendale, CA 92342-0101, USA

Hyland, Robert (Football Player)
Green Bay Packers
30 Colonial Rd
White Plains, NY 10605-2212, USA

Hylton, Thomas J (Journalist)
Pottstown Mercury
Editorial Dept
Hanover & Kings Sts
Pottstown, PA 19464, USA

Hyman, B D
PO Box 7107
Charlottesville, VA 22906-7107, USA

Hyman, Dick
223 1/2 E 48th St
New York, NY 10017, USA

Hyman, Dorothy
7 Norman Close Barnsley
So. Yorks, ENGLAND S71 244, UNITED
KINGDOM (UK)

Hyman, Earle (Actor)
Manhattan Towers
484 W 43rd St Apt 33E
New York, NY 10036-6331, USA

Hyman, Fracaswell (Producer)
c/o Staff Member *William Morris Agency
(WMA-LA)*
1 William Morris Pl
Beverly Hills, CA 90212-4261, USA

Hyman, Kenneth
Sherwood House Tilehouse Lane Denham
Bucks, ENGLAND., UNITED KINGDOM
(UK)

Hyman, Misty (Swimmer)
3826 E Lupine Ave
Phoenix, AZ 85028-2125, USA

Hymowitz, Kay S. (Writer)
Manhattan Institute For Policy Research
52 Vanderbilt Ave Fl 2
New York, NY 10017-3808, USA

Hynd, Noel
c/o Susan Simons *Broder Webb Chervin
Silbermann Agency, The (BWCS)*
10250 Constellation Blvd Ste P
Los Angeles, CA 90067-6213, USA

Hynd, Ronald (Ballerina, Choreographer)
Fern Cottage Up Somerton
Bury Saint Edmonds
Suffolk IP29 4ND, UNITED KINGDOM
(UK)

Hynde, Chrissie (Actor, Musician)
c/o Barbara Skydell *William Morris
Agency (WMA-NY)*
1325 Avenue Of The Americas
New York, NY 10019-6026, USA

Hynes, Garry (Director)
Druid Theater Co
Chapel Lane
Galway, IRELAND

Hynes, Samuel (Writer)
130 Moore St
Princeton, NJ 08540-3359, USA

Hynes, Tyler (Actor)
201 Laurier Ave E #202
Ottawa, ON K1N 6P1, CANADA

Hynoski, Henry (Football Player)
Cleveland Browns
PO Box 257
Elysburg, PA 17824-0257, USA

Hyser, Joyce (Actor)
Artists Agency
1180 S Beverly Dr Ste 301
Los Angeles, CA 90035-1154, USA

Hysong, Nick (Athlete, Track Athlete)
2822 E Cholla St
Phoenix, AZ 85028-1935, USA

Hytner, Nicholas R (Director)
National Theatre
South Bank
London SE1 9PX, UNITED KINGDOM
(UK)

Hyzdu, Adam (Baseball Player)
Pittsburgh Pirates
7823 E Red Hawk Cir
Mesa, AZ 85207-1167, USA

Iacavazzi, Cosmo (Football Player)
New York Jets
90 Vine St
Taylor, PA 18517-1225, USA

Iaconio, Frank (Race Car Driver)
250 US Highway 206
Flanders, NJ 07836-9071, USA

Iafrate, Al A (Hockey Player)
27480 5 Mile Rd
Livonia, MI 48154, USA

Iakovas, Primate Archbishop (Religious
Leader)
31 Park Dr
South Rye, NY 10021, USA

Iaquaniello, Mike (Football Player)
Miami Dolphins
49105 Plum Tree Dr
Plymouth, MI 48170-3263, USA

Iassonga, Daniel (Baseball Player)
5950 N 78th St Unit 159
Scottsdale, AZ 85250-6183, USA

Ibanez, Raul (Baseball Player)
Seattle Mariners
7497 SW 109th Pl
Miami, FL 33173-2744, USA

Ibbetson, Arthur (Cinematographer)
Tanglewood Chalfont Lane
Chorley Wood
Herts, UNITED KINGDOM (UK)

Ibers, James A (Misc)
990 N Lake Shore Dr Apt 17C
Chicago, IL 60611-1376, USA

Ibiam, Francis A (Religious Leader)
Ganymede Unwana
PO Box 240 Afikpo
Imo State, NIGERIA

Ibn Salman Ibn ' Abd Al-' Aziz Al-Saud
(Astronaut, Misc)
PO Box 18368
Riyadh 11415, SAUDI ARABIA

Ibrahim, Abdullah (Dollar Brand)
(Composer, Musician)
Brad Simon Organization
122 E 57th St # 300
New York, NY 10022-2623, USA

Ibrahim, Barre Mainassara (Misc)
Head of State's Office
Presidential Palace
Niamey, NIGER

Ibuka, Yaeko (Activist)
Fukusei Byoin
Leprosarium
Mount Fuji, JAPAN

Icahn, Carl C (Business Person)
Ichan Co
100 S Bedford Rd
Mount Kisco, NY 10549-3425, USA

Ice
11500 W Olympic Blvd Ste 655
Los Angeles, CA 90064-1530, USA

Ice T (Actor, Artist)
Coast II Coast
3350 Wilshire Blvd Ste 1200
Los Angeles, CA 90010-1836, USA

Ice-T (Actor, Musician)
c/o Jorge Hinojosa *Caliente Entertainment*
6606 Maryland Dr
Los Angeles, CA 90048-4614, USA

Icehouse
Box KX-300 Kings Cross
Sydney 2011, AUSTRALIA

Ichaco, Leon (Director)
Creative Artists Agency
9830 Wilshire Blvd
Beverly Hills, CA 90212-1804, USA

Ichaso, Leon (Director)
c/o Staff Member *Innovative Artists (LA)*
1505 10th St
Santa Monica, CA 90401-2805, USA

Ickx, Jacky (Race Car Driver)
171 Chaussee de la Hulpe
Brussels 1170, BELGIUM

Idelson, Bill (Actor, Comedian)
710 Brooktree Rd
Pacific Palisades, CA 90272-3901, USA

Idle, Eric (Actor, Comedian)
Mayday Mgmt
68A Delancey St
Camden Town
London NW1 7RY, UNITED KINGDOM
(UK)

Idol, Billy (Musician, Songwriter, Writer)
c/o John Marx *William Morris Agency
(WMA-LA)*
1 William Morris Pl
Beverly Hills, CA 90212-4261, USA

Iduarte Foucher, Andres (Writer)
Calle Edimburgo 3
Colonia del Valle
Mexico City, DF 12, MEXICO

Idzlak, Slawomir (Cinematographer)
Ul Wazow 1-Z
Warsaw 01-986, POLAND

Ifans, Rhys (Actor)
Endeavor Talent Agency
9701 Wilshire Blve #1000
Beverly Hills, CA 90212, USA

Ifeanyi, Israel (Football Player)
San Francisco 49ers
3380 Kates Way
Duluth, GA 30097-5164, USA

Iger, Robert A (Business Person)
Walt Disney Co
500 S Buena Vista St
Burbank, CA 91521-0007, USA

Iginla, Jarome (Hockey Player)
Newport Mgmt
601-201 City Centre Dr
Mississauga, ON L58 2T4, CANADA

Iglesias, Enrique (Musician)
c/o Fernando Giaccardi *The Firm*
9465 Wilshire Blvd Fl 6
Beverly Hills, CA 90212-2605, USA

Iglesias, Julio (Musician)
c/o Robert Norman *Creative Artists
Agency LCC (CAA-LA)*
2000 Avenue Of The Stars
Los Angeles, CA 90067-4700, USA

Iglesias, Julio Jr (Music Group, Musician,
Songwriter, Writer)
c/o Doc McGhee *McGhee Entertainment*
8730 W Sunset Blvd Ste 175
Los Angeles, CA 90069-2246, USA

Ignarro, Louis J (Nobel Prize Laureate)
University of California
Medical School
10833 Leconte
Los Angeles, CA 90095-0001, USA

Ignasiak, Gary (Baseball Player)
Detroit Tigers
3084 Angelus Dr
Waterford, MI 48329-2506, USA

Ignasiak, Mike (Baseball Player)
Milwaukee Brewers
5821 Saline Ann Arbor Rd
Saline, MI 48176-9566, USA

Ignatius, Paul R (Government Official)
3650 Fordham Rd NW
Washington, DC 20016-1906, USA

Ignatius Zakka I Iwas, Patriarch
(Religious Leader)
Syrian Orthodox Patriarchate
Bab Toma
PB 22260
Damascus, SYRIA

Ignizo, Mildred (Bowler)
241 Shore Acres Dr
Rochester, NY 14612-5807, USA

Igwebuike, Donald (Football Player)
Tampa Bay Buccaneers
14231 Angelton Ter
Burtonsville, MD 20866-2077, USA

Iha, James (Music Group, Musician)
1245 W Glenlake Ave
Chicago, IL 60660-2503, USA

Ihara, Michio (Artist)
63 Wood St
Concord, MA 01742-2225, USA

Ihnatowicz, Zbigniew (Architect)
Ul Mokotowska 31 M 15
Warsaw 00-560, POLAND

Ilkin, Tunch (Football Player)
Pittsburgh Steelers
2610 Cedarvue Dr
Pittsburgh, PA 15241-2912, USA

Ike, Reverend (Religious Leader)
4140 Broadway
New York, NY 10033-3701, USA

Ikeda, Daisaku (Misc, Religious Leader)
Soka Gokkai
32 Shinanomachi
Shinjuku
Tokyo 160-8583, JAPAN

Iken, Monica
c/o Staff Member *William Morris Agency (WMA-LA)*
1 William Morris Pl
Beverly Hills, CA 90212-4261, USA

Ikenberry, Stanley O (Educator)
American Council on Education
1 Dupont Cir NW
Washington, DC 20036-1193, USA

Ikle, Fred C (Scientist)
7010 Glenbrook Road
Washington, DC 20014, USA

Ikola, Willard (Coach, Hockey Player)
5697 Green Circle Dr Apt 316
Minnetonka, MN 55343-9650, USA

Il Divo (Music Group)
c/o Staff Member *Sony Music Entertainment*
555 Madison Ave
New York, NY 10022-3301, USA

Ilavarasi (Actor, Bollywood)
69 Vedawali Street
Kannbiran Colony
Chennai, TN 600093, INDIA

Iler, Robert (Actor)
c/o Staff Member *Innovative Artists (LA)*
1505 10th St
Santa Monica, CA 90401-2805, USA

Iley, Barbara (Actor)
Paradigm Agency
10100 Santa Monica Blvd Ste 2500
Los Angeles, CA 90067-4116, USA

Ilg, Ray (Football Player)
Boston Patriots
252 Shindagan Rd
Wilmot, NH 03287-4621, USA

Ilg, Raymond P (Admiral)
1830 Fountain Dr Unit 1505
Reston, VA 20190-4475, USA

Ilgauskas, Zydrunas (Basketball Player)
Cleveland Cavaliers
1 Center Ct
Gund Arena
Cleveland, OH 44115-4001, USA

Ilgenfritz, Mark (Football Player)
Cleveland Browns
742 Sharp Mountain Crk SE
Marietta, GA 30067-5168, USA

Iliescu, Ion (President)
President's Office
Calea Victoriei 59-53
Bucharest, ROMANIA

Ilitch, Michael (Baseball Player, Hockey Player)
Detroit Tigers
769 Sebago Ln
Bloomfield Hills, MI 48304-3361, USA

Illmann, Margaret (Ballerina)
National Ballet of Canada
157 E King St
Toronto, ON M5C 1G9, CANADA

Illsley, John (Musician)
Damage Mgmt
16 Lambton Place
London W11 2SH, UNITED KINGDOM
(UK)

Iloilo, Ratu Josefa (President)
President's Office
PO Box 2513
Suva
Viti Levu, FIJI

Ilsley, Blaise (Baseball Player)
Chicago Cubs
127 E Lincoln St
Alpena, MI 49707-3710, USA

Ilyenko, Yuriy G (Cinematographer)
9 Michail Koyzybinksy Str #22
Kiev 252030, UKRAINE

Imai, Kenji (Architect)
4-12-28 Kitazawa
Setagayaku
Tokyo, JAPAN

Imai, Nobuko (Musician)
Irene Witmer Mgmt
Kerkstrat 97
Amsterdam, GD 1017, THE NETHERLANDS

Iman (Actor, Model)
c/o Cary Berman *William Morris Agency (WMA-LA)*
1 William Morris Pl
Beverly Hills, CA 90212-4261, USA

Iman, Ken (Football Player)
Green Bay Packers
2 W Thompson Ave
Springfield, PA 19064-2109, USA

Imbert, Bertrand S M (Engineer, Scientist)
50 Rue de Turenne
Paris 75003, FRANCE

Imbert, Peter M (Lawyer)
Lieutenancy Office
City Hall
Victoria St
London S1E 6QP, UNITED KINGDOM
(UK)

Imbrie, Andrew W (Composer)
2625 Rose St
Berkeley, CA 94708-1920, USA

Imbruglia, Natalie (Actor, Musician)
Russells
Regency House
1-4 Warwick St
London W1R 6LJ, UNITED KINGDOM
(UK)

Imes Jackson, Monique (Mo'Nique)
(Actor, Comedian, Television Host)
c/o Jeff Golenberg *The Collective*
9100 Wilshire Blvd # 700 W
Beverly Hills, CA 90212-3401, USA

Imhoff, Darrell (Athlete)
3637 Sterling Woods Dr
Eugene, OR 97408-7201, USA

Imhoff, Gary (Actor)
Samantha Group
300 S Raymond Ave
Pasadena, CA 91105-2620, USA

Imhoff, Martin (Football Player)
St Louis Cardinals
11224 Corte Playa Azteca
San Diego, CA 92124-4135, USA

Imle, John F Jr (Business Person)
Unocal Corp
2141 Rosecrans Ave
El Segundo, CA 90245-4747, USA

Immelt, Jeffrey (Jeff) (Business Person)
General Electric Co
3135 Easton Tpke
Fairfield, CT 06828-0001, USA

Immerfall, Daniel (Dan) (Speed Skater)
5421 Trempeleau Trl
Madison, WI 53705-4662, USA

Imperato, Carlo
6120 Cartwright Ave
N Hollywood, CA 91606-5005, USA

Imperioli, Michael (Actor)
c/o Tina Thor *TMT Entertainment Group*
648 Broadway # 1002
New York, NY 10012-2301, USA

Imus, Don (Radio Personality)
Imus in the Morning
3412 36th St
Astoria, NY 11106-1214, USA

IMX (Music Group)
c/o Staff Member *Pyramid Entertainment Group*
377 Rector Pl Apt 21A
New York, NY 10280-1439, USA

Inamori, Kazuo (Business Person)
KDDI Corp
3-22 Nishi-Shinjuku
Shinjuku
Tokyo 163-8003, JAPAN

Inarritu, Alejandro (Actor)
c/o John Lesher *Endeavor Agency LLC (LA)*
9601 Wilshire Blvd Fl 3
Beverly Hills, CA 90210-5204, USA

Inbal, Eliahu (Conductor)
Heissischer Rundfunk
Bertramstr 8
Frankfurt/Main 60320, GERMANY

Incandella, Sal (Race Car Driver)
Indy Racing Regency
5811 W 73rd St
Indianapolis, IN 46278-1743, USA

Incavglia, Peter J (Pete) (Baseball Player)
PO Box 526
Pebble Beach, CA 93953-0526, USA

Inclan, Rafael (Actor)
c/o Staff Member *Televisa*
Blvd Adolfo Lopez Mateos 232
Colonia San Angel INN
DF CP 01060, MEXICO

Incubus (Music Group)
c/o Marlene Tsuchii *Creative Artists Agency LCC (CAA-LA)*
2000 Avenue Of The Stars
Los Angeles, CA 90067-4700, USA

Indelicato, Mark (Actor)
c/o Staff Member *Station3*
8522 National Blvd Ste 108
Culver City, CA 90232-2454, USA

Indhu (Actor, Bollywood)
D/o G.K.Ram Kumar
2 Circular Road United India Colony
Chennai, TN 600024, INDIA

Indiana, Robert (Artist)
Press Box 464
Vinalhaven, ME 04863, USA

Indigo Girls (Music Group)
c/o Staff Member *Russell Carter Artist Management*
567 Ralph McGill Blvd NE
Atlanta, GA 30312-1110, USA

Indraja (Actor, Bollywood)
89 Krishna Nagar
Virugambakkam
Chennai, TN 600092, INDIA

Indurain, Miguel
Avendia Villava
Pamplona (Navarra) E-31013, SPAIN

Infante, Lindy (Coach, Football Coach)
6870 A1A S
Saint Augustine, FL 32080, USA

Infante, Tobo (Actor)
c/o Staff Member *Televisa*
Blvd Adolfo Lopez Mateos 232
Colonia San Angel INN
DF CP 01060, MEXICO

Infill, O Urcille Jr (Religious Leader)
African Methodist Church
PO Box 19039
Philadelphia, PA 19138-0039, USA

Ing, Hout (Government Official)
Foreign Affairs Ministry
Phnom Penh, CAMBODIA

Inge, Peter A (Misc)
House of Lords
Westminster
London SW1A 0PW, UNITED KINGDOM
(UK)

Ingels, Marty (Actor, Comedian)
c/o Deborah Zucker *Ingels Entertainment*
Suite One Productions
16400 Ventura Blvd Ste 335
Encino, CA 91436-2196, USA

Ingersoll, Ralph II (Publisher)
Ingersoll Publications
PO Box 1869
Lakeville, CT 06039-1869, USA

Inghram, Mark G (Physicist)
3077 Lakeshore Dr N
Holland, MI 49424-6022, USA

Ingle, Doug (Music Group, Musician)
Entertainment Services Int'l
6400 Pleasant Park Dr
Chanhassen, MN 55317-8804, USA

Ingle, John (Actor)
Artists Group
1650 Broadway Ste 610
New York, NY 10019-6833, USA

Ingle, Robert D (Editor)
San Jose Mercury News
750 Ridder Park Dr
Editorial Dept
San Jose, CA 95131-2432, USA

Inglis, Tim (Football Player)
Cincinnati Bengals
22 Hidden Meadow Dr
Holland, OH 43528-8276, USA

Ingman, Elnar H Jr (War Hero)
W4053 W Silver Lake Rd
Irma, WI 54442-9726, USA

Ingraham, Hubert A (Prime Minister)
Prime Minister's Office
Whitfield Center
Box CB10980
Nassau, BAHAMAS

Ingraham, Laura (Radio Personality)
c/o Staff Member *XM Satellite Radio Studios*
1500 Eckington Pl NE
Washington, DC 20002-2128, USA

Ingram, A John (Doctor)
4940 Sullivan Woods Cv
Memphis, TN 38117-2011, USA

Ingram, Brian (Football Player)
New England Patriots
2461 Winshire Dr
Decatur, GA 30035-4227, USA

Ingram, Garey (Baseball Player)
Los Angeles Dodgers
2901 Gatewood Dr
Phenix City, AL 36870-2335, USA

Ingram, Jack (Musician)
c/o Staff Member *Paradigm (Monterey)*
509 Hartnell St
Monterey, CA 93940-2825, USA

Ingram, James (Music Group, Musician,
Songwriter, Writer)
867 S Muirfield Rd
Los Angeles, CA 90005-3836, USA

Ingram, Preston (Baseball Player)
Negro Baseball Leagues
174 Douglas St SE
Atlanta, GA 30317-2626, USA

Ingram, Riccardo (Baseball Player)
Detroit Tigers
1571 Twin Oaks Dr
Toledo, OH 43615-4036, USA

Ingrao, Pietro (Government Official)
Centro Studie Iniziative Per La Reforma
Via Della Vite 13
Rome, ITALY

Ingrassia, Paul J (Journalist)
111 Division Ave
New Providence, NJ 07974, USA

Ink Spots, The
5100 Dupont Blvd Apt 10A
Ft Lauderdale, FL 33308-4301, USA

Inkeles, Alex (Activist)
1001 Hamilton Ave
Palo Alto, CA 94301-2215, USA

Inkster, Jull Simpson (Golfer)
23140 Mora Glen Dr
Los Altos Hills, CA 94024-6620, USA

Inman, Bobby Ray (Admiral, Government
Official)
701 Brazos St Ste 500
Austin, TX 78701-3232, USA

Inman, Jerry (Football Player)
Denver Broncos
PO Box 1113
Battle Ground, WA 98604-1113, USA

Inman, John (Actor)
AMG Ltd
8 King St
London WC2E 8HN, UNITED KINGDOM
(UK)

Inman, John (Golfer)
2210 Chase St
Durham, NC 27707-2228, USA

Inmon, Earl (Football Player)
Tampa Bay Buccaneers
38429 Jamestown St
Umatilla, FL 32784-9519, USA

Innauer, Anton (Toni) (Coach, Skier)
Steinbruckstr 8/11
Innsbruck 6024, AUSTRIA

Innes, Laura (Actor)
c/o Staff Member *Creative Artists Agency
LCC (CAA-LA)*
2000 Avenue Of The Stars
Los Angeles, CA 90067-4700, USA

Innis (Musician)
c/o Staff Member *Paradigm (LA)*
360 N Crescent Dr
North Bldg
Beverly Hills, CA 90210-6820, USA

Innis, Jeff (Baseball Player)
New York Mets
4920 Woodlong Ln
Cumming, GA 30040-5275, USA

Innis, Roy
800 Riverside Dr Apt 6E
New York, NY 10032-7407, USA

Innis, Roy E A (Activist)
817 Broadway
New York, NY 10003-4709, USA

Innocenti, Antonio Cardinal (Religious
Leader)
Piazza della Citta Lemonia 9
Rome 00193, ITALY

Inogradov, Pavel (Astronaut, Misc)
Potchta Kosmonavtov
Moskovskol Oblasti
Syvisdny Goroduk 141160, RUSSIA

Inoue, Yuichi (Artist)
Ohkamiyashiki 2475-2 Kurami
Samakawamachi 253-01 Kozagun
Kam, JAPAN

Inouye, Daniel K (Senator, War Hero)
300 Ala Moana Blvd Rm 7212
Honolulu, HI 96850-7212, USA

Inouye, Lisa (Actor)
Media Artists Group
6300 Wilshire Blvd Ste 1470
Los Angeles, CA 90048-5200, USA

Insane Clown Posse (Music Group)
c/o Staff Member *William Morris Agency
(WMA-LA)*
1 William Morris Pl
Beverly Hills, CA 90212-4261, USA

Insko, Delmer M (Del) (Horse Racer)
2360 Fischer Road
South Beloit, IL 61080, USA

Insley, Will (Artist)
231 Bowery
New York, NY 10002-1237, USA

Insolla, Anthony (Editor)
Newsday
235 Pinelawn Rd
Editorial Dept
Melville, NY 11747-4250, USA

Inspectah, Deck (Artist)
Famous Artists Agency
250 W 57th St
New York, NY 10107-0001, USA

INXS
c/o Michael Moses *Epic Records Group*
550 Madison Ave
New York, NY 10022-3211, USA

Inzaghi, Filippo (Soccer Player)
c/o Team Member *AC Milan*
Via Turati 3
Milan 20221, ITALY

Ionatana, Ionatana (Prime Minister)
Prime Minister's Office
Vaiaku
Funafuti, TUVALU

Iorg, Dane (Baseball Player)
Philadelphia Phillies
928 Sage Dr
Pleasant Grove, UT 84062-2021, USA

Iorg, Garth (Baseball Player)
Knoxville Yard Dogs
1216 Gettysvue Way
C/O Ken Denton
Knoxville, TN 37922-5978, USA

Ioss, Walter (Photographer)
152 Deforest Rd
Montauk, NY 11954-9619, USA

Iqbal Rashid, Ian (Director)
c/o Staff Member *United Talent Agency
(UTA)*
9560 Wilshire Blvd Ste 500
Beverly Hills, CA 90212-2401, USA

Irabu, Hideki (Baseball Player)
New York Yankees
2212 Via Velardo
Rancho Palos Verdes, CA 90275-6563,
USA

Irani, Aruna (Actor, Bollywood)
603 B Gazdar Apartments
Near Juhu Hotel Juhu
Mumbai, MS 400049, INDIA

Irani, Ray R (Business Person)
Occidental Petroleum
10889 Wilshire Blvd
Los Angeles, CA 90024-4201, USA

Irbe, Arturs (Hockey Player)
10733 Trego Trl
Raleigh, NC 27614-9660, USA

Iredale, Randle W (Architect)
1151 W 8th Ave
Vancouver, BC V6H 1C5, CANADA

Ireland, Dan (Director, Producer, Writer)
c/o Staff Member *Gersh Agency, The (LA)*
232 N Canon Dr
Beverly Hills, CA 90210-5302, USA

Ireland, Kathy (Actor, Model)
c/o Beverly Magid *Guttman Associates*
118 S Beverly Dr Ste 201
Beverly Hills, CA 90212-3016, USA

Ireland, Patricia (Misc)
Katz Kutler Haigler Assoc
801 Pennsylvania Ave NW Ste 750
Washington, DC 20004-2670, USA

Ireland, Rich (Baseball Player)
181 Glen Dr
Grants Pass, OR 97526-9018, USA

Ireland, Tim (Baseball Player)
Kansas City Royals
20932 Times Ave
Hayward, CA 94541-3754, USA

Iris, Donnie (Music Group, Musician,
Songwriter, Writer)
807 Darlington Rd
Beaver Falls, PA 15010-2817, USA

Irish Rovers, The
1505 W. 2nd Ave. #200
Vancouver, BC V6H 3Y4, CANADA

Irizarry, Vincent (Actor)
David Shapira
193 N Robertson Blvd
Beverly Hills, CA 90211-2103, USA

Irobe, Yoshiaki (Financier)
26-6-6 Saginomiya
Nakanoku
Tokyo, JAPAN

Iron Butterfly
PO Box 770850
Orlando, FL 32877-0850, USA

Iron Maiden (Music Group)
c/o Rick Roskin *Creative Artists Agency
LCC (CAA-LA)*
2000 Avenue Of The Stars
Los Angeles, CA 90067-4700, USA

Irons, Gerald (Football Player)
Oakland Raiders
30010 E Legends Trail Ct
Spring, TX 77386-2998, USA

Irons, Jeremy (Actor)
Hutton Mgmt
4 Old Manor Close
Askett
Buckinghamshire HP27 9NA, UNITED
KINGDOM (UK)

Irons, Nicholas (Actor)
Emptage Hallett
c/o Michael Emptage
24 Poland St
London W1F 8QL, UNITED KINGDOM
(UK)

Ironside, Michael (Actor, Producer,
Writer)
c/o Staff Member *Cunningham Escott
Slevin & Doherty (LA)*
10635 Santa Monica Blvd Ste 130
Los Angeles, CA 90025-8306, USA

Irrera, Dom (Actor, Comedian)
Irvin Arthur Assoc
1441 3rd Ave Apt 12C
New York, NY 10028-1976, USA

Irvan, Ernie (Race Car Driver)
629 El Cardenal Farm Ln
Mooresville, NC 28115, USA

Irvin, Anthony
1 Olympic Plz
Colorado Springs, CO 80909-5780, USA

Irvin, Cal (Baseball Player)
Newark Eagles
1311 Julian St
Greensboro, NC 27406-2158, USA

Irvin, Daryl (Baseball Player)
Boston Red Sox
2704 Hopkins Dr
McGaheysville, VA 22840-2150, USA

Irvin, John (Director)
c/o Jack Gilardi *International Creative
Management (ICM-LA)*
10250 Constellation Blvd
Los Angeles, CA 90067-6200, USA

Irvin, Ken (Football Player)
Buffalo Bills
8151 Nesbit Ferry Rd
Atlanta, GA 30350-1009, USA

Irvin, LeRoy Jr (Football Player)
Los Angeles Rams
2905 Ruby Dr Apt C
Fullerton, CA 92831-3249, USA

Irvin, Michael
1280 S Main St Ste 103
Grapevine, TX 76051-7509, USA

Irvin, Michael J (Football Player)
Dallas Cowboys
2339 Aberdeen Bnd
Carrollton, TX 75007-2040, USA

Irvin, Monte (Baseball Player)
Newark Eagles
1815 Enclave Pkwy Apt 6111
Houston, TX 77077-3668, USA

Irvine, Eddie (Race Car Driver)
Ferrari SpA
Casella Postale 589
Modena 41100, ITALY

Irvine, Paula
23852 Pacific Coast Hwy Pmb 195
Malibu, CA 90265-4876, USA

Irving, Amy (Actor)
Rigberg Roberts Rugolo
1180 S Beverly Dr Ste 601
Los Angeles, CA 90035-1158, USA

Irving, John (Writer)
c/o Robert (Bob) Bookman *Creative Artists Agency LCC (CAA-LA)*
2000 Avenue Of The Stars
Los Angeles, CA 90067-4700, USA

Irving, John W (Writer)
Turnbull Agency
PO Box 757
Dorset, VT 05251-0757, USA

Irving, Paul H (Attorney, Attorney General, General)
Manatt Phelps Phillips
11355 W Olympic Blvd
Los Angeles, CA 90064-1631, USA

Irving, Stu (Hockey Player)
93 Hart St
Beverly, MA 01915-2162, USA

Irving, Terry (Football Player)
Phoenix Cardinals
3205 Avenue R 1/2 Apt 2
Galveston, TX 77550-9651, USA

Irwin, Bill (Entertainer)
20 1st Ave
Nyack, NY 10960-2114, USA

Irwin, Bindi (Misc)
Australia Zoo
Glass House Mountains Tourist Route
Beerwah, Queensland 4519, AUSTRALIA

Irwin, Heath (Football Player)
New England Patriots
5530 N 115th St
Longmont, CO 80504-8434, USA

Irwin, Jennifer (Actor)
c/o Maureen Taran *New Wave Entertainment (LA)*
2660 W Olive Ave
Burbank, CA 91505-4525, USA

Irwin, Mark (Cinematographer)
1522 Olive St
Santa Barbara, CA 93101-1160, USA

Irwin, Paul G (Misc)
Humane Society of the United States
2100 L St NW Ste 500
Washington, DC 20037-1560, USA

Irwin, Robert W (Artist)
Pace Gallery
32 E 57th St
New York, NY 10022-2530, USA

Irwin, Tim (Football Player)
Minnesota Vikings
PO Box 2186
Law Office Of Tim Irwin
Knoxville, TN 37901-2186, USA

Irwin, Tom
PO Box 5617
Beverly Hills, CA 90209-5617, USA

Irwin-Mellencamp, Elaine (Model)
John Caugar Mellencamp
5072 Stevens Rd
Nashville, IN 47448-9484, USA

Isaac, Victor (Actor)
c/o Staff Member *Epstein Wyckoff & Assoc (LA)*
280 S Beverly Dr Ste 400
Beverly Hills, CA 90212-3904, USA

Isaacks, Levie C (Cinematographer)
6634 Sunnyslope Ave
Van Nuys, CA 91401-1213, USA

Isaacksen, Peter
4635 Placidia Ave
Toluca Lake, CA 91602-1541, USA

Isaacs, Jason (Actor)
c/o Jeff Golenberg *The Collective*
9100 Wilshire Blvd # 700 W
Beverly Hills, CA 90212-3401, USA

Isaacs, Jeremy I (Director)
Royal Opera House
Covent Garden Bow St
London WC1 7Q4, UNITED KINGDOM (UK)

Isaacs, John (Speed) (Basketball Player)
1412 Crotona Ave
Bronx, NY 10456-2217, USA

Isaacs, Susan (Writer)
Harper Collins Publishers
10 E 53rd St Fl Cellar2
New York, NY 10022-5076, USA

Isaacson, Julius (Misc)
Novelty & Production Workers Union
1815 Franklin Ave
Valley Stream, NY 11581, USA

Isaacson, Walter S (Journalist)
Simon & Schuster
1230 Avenue Of The Americas
New York, NY 10020-1586, USA

Isaak, Chris (Actor, Musician, Songwriter)
c/o Ilene Feldman *IFA Talent Agency*
8730 W Sunset Blvd Ste 490
Los Angeles, CA 90069-2248, USA

Isaak, Russell (Business Person)
CPI Corp
1706 Washington Ave
Saint Louis, MO 63103-1717, USA

Isabel, Margarita (Actor)
c/o Staff Member *TV Azteca*
Periferico Sur 4121
Colonia Fuentes del Pedregal
DF CP 14141, MEXICO

Isabelle, Katharine (Actor)
c/o Staff Member *IFA Talent Agency*
8730 W Sunset Blvd Ste 490
Los Angeles, CA 90069-2248, USA

Isacksen, Peter (Actor)
4214 W Kling St
Burbank, CA 91505-3702, USA

Isaksson, Irma Sara (Musician, Songwriter, Writer)
United Stage Artists
PO Box 11026
Stockholm 100 61, SWEDEN

Isales, Orlando (Baseball Player)
Philadelphia Phillies
14710 SW 106th Ave
Miami, FL 33176-7791, USA

Isard, Walter (Economist)
3218 Garrett Rd
Drexel Hill, PA 19026-2912, USA

Isbell, Joe Bob (Football Player)
Dallas Cowboys
1606 Nest Pl
Plano, TX 75093-6030, USA

Isbin, Sharon (Musician)
Columbia Artists Mgmt Inc
1790 Broadway Fl 6
New York, NY 10019-1412, USA

Iscove, Robert (Rob) (Director)
16045 Royal Oak Rd
Encino, CA 91436-3913, USA

Isdell, E Neville (Business Person)
Coca-Cola Co
310 North Ave NW
1 Coca-Cola Plaza
Atlanta, GA 30313-2499, USA

Isenbarger, John (Football Player)
San Francisco 49ers
6381 Franklin Ct
Fishers, IN 46038-4704, USA

Isham, Mark (Composer)
Ron Moss Mgmt
2635 Griffith Park Blvd
Los Angeles, CA 90039-2519, USA

Ishara, B R (Actor, Bollywood)
C36 North Bombay Housing Society
Juhu Tara Road
Mumbai, MS 400049, INDIA

Ishibashi, Kanichiro (Business Person)
1 Nagasakacho Azabu
Minatoku
Tokyo, JAPAN

Ishida, Jim (Actor)
871 N Vail Ave
Montebello, CA 90640-2432, USA

Ishiguro, Kazuo (Writer)
Rogers Coleridge White
20 Powis Mews
London W11 1JN, UNITED KINGDOM (UK)

Ishihara, Shintaro (Government Official)
Sanno Grand Building
#606 2-14-2 Nagatocho Chiyodaku
Tokyo, JAPAN

Ishii, Kazuhiro (Architect)
4-14-27 Akasaka
Minatoku
Tokyo 107, JAPAN

Ishikawa, Sigeru (Economist)
19-8-4 Chome Kugayama
Suginamiku
Tokyo 168-0082, JAPAN

Ishizaka, Kimishiga (Doctor)
Allergy/Immunology Institute
11149 N Torrey Pines Rd
La Jolla, CA 92037-1031, USA

Ishizaka, Teruko (Doctor)
Good Samaritan Hospital
5601 Loch Raven Blvd
Baltimore, MD 21239-2991, USA

Iskarder, Fazil A (Writer)
Krasnoarmeiskaya Str 23 #104
Moscow 125319, RUSSIA

Islas, Claudia (Actor)
c/o Staff Member *TV Azteca*
Periferico Sur 4121
Colonia Fuentes del Pedregal
DF CP 14141, MEXICO

Islas, Mauricio (Actor)
c/o Staff Member *Televisa*
Blvd Adolfo Lopez Mateos 232
Colonia San Angel INN
DF CP 01060, MEXICO

Isley, Ronald (Ron) (Musician)
Ron Weisner Mgmt
PO Box 261640
Encino, CA 91426-1640, USA

Isley Brothers (Music Group)
c/o Carleen Donovan *Keith Sherman & Associates*
234 W 44th St Ste 1004
New York, NY 10036-3909, USA

Ismail, Qadry (Football Player)
Minnesota Vikings
1506 Sunningdale Way
Bel Air, MD 21015-2101, USA

Ismail, Raghib R (Rocket) (Football Player)
Oakland Raiders
7423 Marigold Dr
Irving, TX 75063-5505, USA

Ison, Christopher J (Journalist)
Minneapolis-Saint Paul Star Tribune
425 Portland Ave
Minneapolis, MN 55488-1511, USA

Isozaki, Arata (Architect)
Arata Assoc
6-17-9 Adasaka
Minatoku
Tokyo 107, JAPAN

Israel, Werner (Physicist)
5189 Polson Terrace
Victoria, BC V8Y 2C5, CANADA

Isringhausen, Jason (Baseball Player)
New York Mets
550 E Lake Dr
Tarpon Springs, FL 34688, USA

Issel, Daniel P (Dan) (Basketball Player, Coach)
10163 E Fair Cir
Englewood, CO 80111-5448, USA

Isselbacher, Kurt J (Doctor)
20 Nobscot Rd
Newton Center, MA 02459-1323, USA

Isserlis, Steven (Musician)
Harrison/Parrott
12 Penzance Place
London W11 4PA, UNITED KINGDOM (UK)

Ito, Lance (Judge)
Los Angeles Superior Court
210 W Temple St
Los Angeles, CA 90012-3210, USA

Ito, Masayoshi (Government Official)
1-28-3 Chitose-Dai
Setagayaku
Tokyo 157, JAPAN

Ito, Midori (Figure Skater)
Skating Federation
Kryshi Taaikukan 1-1-1
Shibuyaku
Tokyo 10, JAPAN

Ito, Robert (Actor)
843 N Sycamore Ave
Los Angeles, CA 90038-3316, USA

Itzin, Gregory (Actor)
Borinstein Oreck Bogart
3172 Dona Susana Dr
Studio City, CA 91604-4356, USA

Ivanchenkov, Aleksandr S (Astronaut, Misc)
Potchta Kosmonavtov
Moskovskoi Oblasti
Syvisdny Goroduk 141160, RUSSIA

Ivanchenkov, Alexander
141 160 Zvezdny Gorodok
Moscow Obl., RUSSIA

Ivanek, Zeljko
145 W 45th St # 1204
New York, NY 10036-4008, USA

Ivanisevic, Goran (Tennis Player)
Alijnoviceva 28
Split 58000, SERBIA-MONTENEGRO

Ivanov, Igor S (Government Official)
Foreign Affairs Ministry
Smolenskaya-Sennaya 32/34
Moscow, RUSSIA

Ivanov, Kalina (Actor, Designer)
c/o Sandra Marsh *Sandra Marsh Management*
9150 Wilshire Blvd Ste 220
Beverly Hills, CA 90212-3429, USA

Ivens, Terri (Actor)
c/o Staff Member *Kohner Agency, The*
9300 Wilshire Blvd Ste 555
Beverly Hills, CA 90212-3211, USA

Ivers, Eileen (Athlete, Misc)
Sony Records
2100 Colorado Ave
Santa Monica, CA 90404-3504, USA

Iverson, Allen (Athlete, Basketball Player)
c/o Staff Member *Philadelphia 76ers*
3601 S Broad St
1st Union Center
Philadelphia, PA 19148-5287, USA

Iverson, Duke (Football Player)
New York Giants
616 Elm Dr
Petaluma, CA 94952-1838, USA

Iverson, Portia (Religious Leader)
11312 Highway 75
Plattsmouth, NE 68048-8268, USA

Ivery, Eddie Lee (Football Player)
Green Bay Packers
1080 Wrightsboro Rd
Thomson, GA 30824-7500, USA

Ives, J Atwood (Business Person)
Eastern Enterprises
201 Rivermoor St
West Roxbury, MA 02132-4905, USA

Ivey, Dana (Actor)
Paradigm Agency
10100 Santa Monica Blvd Ste 2500
Los Angeles, CA 90067-4116, USA

Ivey, James
5856 Dahlia Dr Apt 7
Orlando, FL 32807-3261, USA

Ivey, James B (Jim) (Cartoonist, Editor)
5840 Dahlia Dr Apt 7
Orlando, FL 32807-3251, USA

Ivey, Judith (Actor)
53 W 87th St # 2
New York, NY 10024-3057, USA

Ivey, Phil (Misc)
c/o Staff Member *Kolyma Corporation*
Full Tilt Poker
62 Lloyd G Smith Blvd
Oranjestad, AW, ARUBA

Ivie, Mike (Baseball Player)
San Diego Padres
894 Rocker Rd
Crawfordville, GA 30631-1339, USA

Ivins, Marsha S (Astronaut)
2811 Timber Briar Cir
Houston, TX 77059-2904, USA

Ivlow, John (Football Player)
Chicago Bears
15238 S Poppy Ln
Plainfield, IL 60544-9201, USA

Ivo, Tommy
247 S Orchard Dr
Burbank, CA 91506-2441, USA

Ivory, Horace O (Football Player)
New England Patriots
5321 Diaz Ave
Fort Worth, TX 76107-5903, USA

Ivory, James (Baseball Player)
Detroit Stars
3026 Wenonah Park Rd SW
Birmingham, AL 35211-5846, USA

Ivory, James F (Director, Filmmaker, Producer)
18 Patroon St
Claverack, NY 12513, USA

Ivosev, Aleksandra (Misc)
Sluzbeni put Zavoda 5
Careva Cuprija
Belgrad 11030, SERBIA-MONTENEGRO

Iwago, Mitsuaki (Photographer)
Edelhof Daichi Building #2F
8 Honsio-cho Shinjukuku
Tokyo 160, JAPAN

Iwanowski, Mark (Football Player)
New York Jets
523 N 12th St
Reading, PA 19604-2718, USA

Iwerks, Donald W (Business Person)
Iwerks Entertainment
4520 W Valerio St
Burbank, CA 91505-1046, USA

Iyer, Kalpana (Actor, Dancer)
E 43 Geeta Kiran Society J P Road Four Bangalows
Andheri
Bombay, MS 400 058, INDIA

Izibor, Laura (Musician)
c/o Staff Member *Paradigm (Monterey)*
509 Hartnell St
Monterey, CA 93940-2825, USA

Izo, George (Football Player)
Washington Redskins
313 Comstock Dr
Colonial Heights, VA 23834-2119, USA

Izquierdo, Hank (Baseball Player)
Minnesota Twins
12458 71st Pl N
West Palm Beach, FL 33412-1438, USA

Izturis, Cesar (Athlete, Baseball Player)
Toronto Blue Jays
375 Douglas Avenue
Clearwater, FL 33755, USA

Izzard, Eddie (Actor, Comedian)
c/o Tresa Redburn *Dept 56*
22410 Collins St
Woodland Hills, CA 91367-4430, USA

Izzo, Larry (Football Player)
Miami Dolphins
47 Chancery Pl
The Woodlands, TX 77381-6438, USA

Izzo, Tom (Basketball Player, Coach)
Michigan State University
Athletic Dept
East Lansing, MI 48824, USA

J-Bolt (Producer)
Lightning Bolt Entertainment
3342 S Sandhill Rd Ste 9-424
Las Vegas, NV 89121-3455, USA

Jablonski, Henryk (President)
Ul Filtrowa 61 m 4
Warsaw 02-056, POLAND

Jabs, Matthias (Musician)
c/o Staff Member *Agency Group Ltd, The (NY)*
1775 Broadway Ste 515
New York, NY 10019-1903, USA

Jace, Michael (Actor)
c/o Craig Dorfman *Blueprint Management*
5670 Wilshire Blvd Ste 2525
Los Angeles, CA 90036-5647, USA

Jack, Beau
1 Hall Of Fame Dr
Canastota, NY 13032-1175, USA

Jack, Eric (Football Player)
Atlanta Falcons
4206 W Ross Ave
Glendale, AZ 85308-4701, USA

Jack, Lind (Baseball Player)
Milwaukee Brewers
6132 E Redmont Dr
Mesa, AZ 85215-0878, USA

Jacke, Chris (Football Player)
Green Bay Packers
2120 S Ridge Rd
Green Bay, WI 54304-4327, USA

Jacke, Christoper L (Chris) (Football Player)
Arizona Cardinals
PO Box 888
Phoenix, AZ 85001-0888, USA

Jackee (Actor)
7250 Franklin Ave Apt 814
Los Angeles, CA 90046-3043, USA

Jacklin, Tony (Golfer, Sportscaster)
1175 51st St W
Bradenton, FL 34209-4259, USA

Jackman, Hugh (Actor)
c/o Staff Member *Seed Productions*
10201 W Pico Blvd Bldg 52 # 105
Los Angeles, CA 90064-2606, USA

Jacks Mannequin (Musician)
c/o Staff Member *Maverick Recording Co (LA)*
3300 Warner Blvd
Burbank, CA 91505-4632, USA

Jackson, Al (Baseball Player)
Pittsburgh Pirates
3321 SE Morningside Blvd
Port Saint Lucie, FL 34952, USA

Jackson, Alan (Musician, Songwriter, Writer)
c/o Jeff Hill *Creative Artists Agency (CAA-Nashville)*
3310 W End Ave Fl 5
Nashville, TN 37203-1028, USA

Jackson, Alfonza (Football Player)
Philadelphia Eagles
2701 Godwin Ln
Pensacola, FL 32526-9047, USA

Jackson, Alfred (Football Player)
Atlanta Falcons
1811 Kirby Dr
Houston, TX 77019-3415, USA

Jackson, Alphonso (Secretary)
Housing & Urban Development Department
451 7th St SW
Washington, DC 20410-0001, USA

Jackson, Anne (Actor)
90 Riverside Dr
New York, NY 10024-5306, USA

Jackson, Arthur J (War Hero)
1290 E Spring Ct
Boise, ID 83712-8313, USA

Jackson, Barry
29 Rathcoole Ave.
London, ENGLAND N8 9LY, UNITED KINGDOM (UK)

Jackson, Betty (Designer, Fashion Designer)
Betty Jackson Ltd
1 Netherwood Place
London W14 0BW, UNITED KINGDOM (UK)

Jackson, Bo (Baseball Player)
N'Genuity
9237 E Via De Ventura Ste 115
Scottsdale, AZ 85258-3329, USA

Jackson, Bo (Football Player)
Los Angeles Raiders
PO Box 158
Mobile, AL 36601-0158, USA

Jackson, Bobby (Basketball Player)
Sacramento Kings
1 Sports Pkwy
Arco Arena
Sacramento, CA 95834-2301, USA

Jackson, Bobby (Football Player)
Philadelphia Eagles
4009 Old Shell Rd Apt E9
Mobile, AL 36608-1385, USA

Jackson, Bobby (Football Player)
New York Jets
47 Tippin Dr
Huntington Station, NY 11746-2130, USA

Jackson, Calvin (Football Player)
Miami Dolphins
250 SW 28th Ter
Fort Lauderdale, FL 33312-1285, USA

Jackson, Charles (Football Player)
Kansas City Chiefs
PO Box 888285
Atlanta, GA 30356-0285, USA

Jackson, Chuck (Baseball Player)
Houston Astros
15821 SE 175th Pl
Renton, WA 98058-9122, USA

Jackson, Chuck (Musician)
Universal Attractions
225 W 57th St Ste 500
New York, NY 10019-2136, USA

Jackson, Clarence (Football Player)
New York Jets
5251 Appleleaf Ct
Richmond, VA 23234-2801, USA

Jackson, Curtis (50 Cent) (Actor, Musician)
c/o Cara Lewis *William Morris Agency (WMA-NY)*
1325 Avenue Of The Americas
New York, NY 10019-6026, USA

Jackson, Dallas (Producer, Writer)
c/o Holly Davis-Carter *Releve*
6255 W Sunset Blvd Ste 908
Hollywood, CA 90028-7410, USA

Jackson, Damian (Baseball Player)
Cleveland Indians
2038 Amparo Ct
Escondido, CA 92025-6662, USA

Jackson, Danny (Baseball Player)
Philadelphia Phillies
16200 S Switzer St
Olathe, KS 66062-9021, USA

Jackson, Darrell (Baseball Player)
Minnesota Twins
PO Box 4424
Downey, CA 90241-1424, USA

Jackson, Darrin (Baseball Player)
Chicago Cubs
432 E Mead Dr
Chandler, AZ 85249-5330, USA

Jackson, Daryl S (Architect)
161 Hotham St
East Melbourne, VIC 3002, AUSTRALIA

Jackson, Deanna (Basketball Player)
Indiana Fever
125 S Pennsylvania St
Conseco Fieldhouse
Indianapolis, IN 46204-3610, USA

Jackson, Donald
1080 Brocks
South Pickering, ON, CANADA

Jackson, Doris (Musician)
Nationwide Entertainment
2756 N Green Valley Pkwy
Henderson, NV 89014-2120, USA

Jackson, Earnest (Football Player)
San Diego Chargers
PO Box 585
Coraopolis, PA 15108-0585, USA

Jackson, Eddie (Bowler)
3961 Glenmore Ave
Cincinnati, OH 45211-3509, USA

Jackson, Ernie (Football Player)
New Orleans Saints
5124 36th St W
Bradenton, FL 34210-3268, USA

Jackson, Francis A (Composer, Musician)
Nether Garth
East Acklam
Malton North Yorkshire YO17 9RG,
UNITED KINGDOM (UK)

Jackson, Frank (Football Player)
Dallas Texans
5904 Gregory Ln
Allen, TX 75002-6710, USA

Jackson, Gildart (Actor)
c/o Chuck Binder *Binder & Associates*
1465 Lindacrest Dr
Beverly Hills, CA 90210-2519, USA

Jackson, Glenda (Actor)
Crouch Assoc
9-15 Neal St
London WC2H 9PF, UNITED KINGDOM
(UK)

Jackson, Grant (Baseball Player)
Philadelphia Phillies
212 Mesa Cir
Pittsburgh, PA 15241-1721, USA

Jackson, Harold (Coach, Football Player)
Los Angeles Rams
6144 Flight Ave
Los Angeles, CA 90056-1510, USA

Jackson, Harold (Journalist)
Birmingham News
2201 4th Ave N
Editorial Dept
Birmingham, AL 35203-3863, USA

Jackson, Harry A (Artist)
PO Box 2836
Cody, WY 82414-2836, USA

Jackson, Honor (Football Player)
New England Patriots
6091 Dinah Ct
Rohnert Park, CA 94928-2285, USA

Jackson, Huson (Architect)
Sert Jackson Assoc
442 Marrett Rd Ste 10
Lexington, MA 02421-7749, USA

Jackson, James A (Jim) (Basketball Player)
17827 Windflower Way
Dallas, TX 75252-5216, USA

Jackson, Janet (Actor, Dancer, Musician)
c/o Eric Kranzler *Management 360*
9111 Wilshire Blvd
Beverly Hills, CA 90210-5508, USA

Jackson, Jarious (Football Player)
Denver Broncos
2711 Driftwood Dr
Manvel, TX 77578-3240, USA

Jackson, Jeff (Baseball Player)
853 S Kingsley Dr Apt D
Los Angeles, CA 90005-4367, USA

Jackson, Jeff (Football Player)
Atlanta Falcons
5801 Castlebrook Dr
Douglasville, GA 30134-3607, USA

Jackson, Jermaine (Basketball Player)
Atlanta Hawks
190 Marietta St NW
Atlanta, GA 30303-2717, USA

Jackson, Jermaine (Music Group,
Musician, Songwriter, Writer)
c/o Vicki Roberts *Vicki M Roberts*
PO Box 642326
Los Angeles, CA 90064-7169, USA

Jackson, Jesse L (Activist, Politician,
Religious Leader)
400 T St NW
Washington, DC 20001-1809, USA

Jackson, Joe (Football Player)
Seattle Seahawks
3935 E Greenway Rd Apt 122
Phoenix, AZ 85032-4669, USA

Jackson, Joe (Musician, Songwriter)
c/o Staff Member *Paradigm (Monterey)*
509 Hartnell St
Monterey, CA 93940-2825, USA

Jackson, Joe M (War Hero)
25320 38th Ave S
Kent, WA 98032-5679, USA

Jackson, John (Baseball Player)
Houston Eagles
PO Box 898
Hodge, LA 71247-0898, USA

Jackson, John (Football Player)
Pittsburgh Steelers
5128 Karrington Dr
Gibsonia, PA 15044-6005, USA

Jackson, John David (Boxer)
1022 S State St
Tacoma, WA 98405-3042, USA

Jackson, John M (Actor)
JAG
5555 Melrose Ave
Clara Bow #204
Los Angeles, CA 90038-3989, USA

Jackson, Jonathan (Actor)
c/o David Guillod *United Talent Agency
(UTA)*
9560 Wilshire Blvd Ste 500
Beverly Hills, CA 90212-2401, USA

Jackson, Joshua (Actor)
c/o Michael Bircumshaw *Water Street
Management*
5225 Wilshire Blvd Ste 615
Los Angeles, CA 90036-4350, USA

Jackson, Kate (Actor)
c/o Staff Member *David Shapira &
Associates*
193 N Robertson Blvd
Beverly Hills, CA 90211-2103, USA

Jackson, Keith (Football Player)
Philadelphia Eagles
PO Box 241695
Little Rock, AR 72223-0012, USA

Jackson, Keith M (Sportscaster)
ABC-TV
77 W 66th St
Sports Dept
New York, NY 10023-6201, USA

Jackson, Ken (Baseball Player)
Philadelphia Phillies
PO Box 613
Waskom, TX 75692-0613, USA

Jackson, Ken (Football Player)
Philadelphia Eagles
Penn State University Athletic Dept
Attn: Football Coaching Staff
University Park, PA 16802, USA

Jackson, Kevin (Wrestler)
7215 Montarbor Dr
Colorado Springs, CO 80918-4757, USA

Jackson, Kirby (Football Player)
Los Angeles Rams
373 Vista Lake Ter
Suwanee, GA 30024-7418, USA

Jackson, Kwame (Business Person, Reality
TV Star)
c/o Staff Member *Mark Burnett
Productions*
640 N Sepulveda Blvd
Los Angeles, CA 90049-2108, USA

Jackson, Larron (Football Player)
Denver Broncos
1750 Saint Charles Ave Apt 229
New Orleans, LA 70130-6740, USA

Jackson, Larry R (Misc)
Grain Millers Federation
4949 Oslon Memorial Parkway
Minneapolis, MN 55422, USA

Jackson, LaToya (Model, Musician)
14126 Rosecrans Ave
Santa Fe Springs, CA 90670-5214, USA

Jackson, Lauren (Basketball Player)
Seattle Storm
351 Elliott Ave W Ste 500
Seattle, WA 98119-4153, USA

Jackson, Leshon (Football Player)
New York Jets
PO Box 957
Haskell, OK 74436-0957, USA

Jackson, Lillian (Baseball Player)
1050 W Camino Velasquez
Green Valley, AZ 85614-4527, USA

Jackson, Lucious (Luke) (Basketball
Player)
Cleveland Cavaliers
1 Center Ct
Gund Arena
Cleveland, OH 44115-4001, USA

Jackson, Mark A (Basketball Player)
628 Main St
Windsor, CO 80550-5133, USA

Jackson, Mark A (Football Player)
Denver Broncos
620 Mathews St Apt 202
Fort Collins, CO 80524-3037, USA

Jackson, Marlon
4641 Hayvenhurst Ave
Encino, CA 91436-3251, USA

Jackson, Mayor Maynard
68 Mitchell
Atlanta, GA 30303, USA

Jackson, Mel (Actor)
c/o Staff Member *Stone Manners Talent &
Literary (LA)*
6500 Wilshire Blvd Ste 550
Los Angeles, CA 90048-4950, USA

Jackson, Melvin (Football Player)
Green Bay Packers
4345 Enoro Dr
Los Angeles, CA 90008-4870, USA

Jackson, Michael (Actor, Choreographer,
Musician, Producer)
c/o Staff Member *Cunningham Escott
Slevin & Doherty (NY)*
257 Park Ave S Rm 950
New York, NY 10010-7304, USA

Jackson, Michael (Football Player)
Seattle Seahawks
14207 128th Pl NE
Kirkland, WA 98034-1575, USA

Jackson, Mick (Director)
1349 Berea Pl
Pacific Palisades, CA 90272-2602, USA

Jackson, Mike (Baseball Player)
Philadelphia Phillies
805 11th Ave Apt 2H
Paterson, NJ 07514-1012, USA

Jackson, Mike (Baseball Player)
Philadelphia Phillies
9410 Cypresswood Dr
Spring, TX 77379-6916, USA

Jackson, Milt (Football Player)
San Francisco 49ers
100 McMindes Ct
Roseville, CA 95747-5853, USA

Jackson, Monte C (Football Player)
Los Angeles Rams
7646 Westbrook Ave
San Diego, CA 92139-4006, USA

Jackson, Neil (Actor)
c/o Staff Member *IFA Talent Agency*
8730 W Sunset Blvd Ste 490
Los Angeles, CA 90069-2248, USA

Jackson, Noah (Football Player)
Chicago Bears
1640 Millburne Rd
Lake Forest, IL 60045-4106, USA

Jackson, O'Shea (Ice Cube) (Actor,
Director, Musician)
c/o Staff Member *CubeVision*
2900 Olympic Blvd
Santa Monica, CA 90404-4127, USA

Jackson, Pervis (Musician)
Buddy Allen Mgmt
3750 Hudson Manor Ter # 3ag
Bronx, NY 10463-1126, USA

Jackson, Peter (Director)
c/o Ken Kamins *Key Creatives*
9595 Wilshire Blvd Ste 800
Beverly Hills, CA 90212-2508, USA

Jackson, Phil (Coach)
c/o Marty Adelstein *Original Film*
284 N Saltair Ave
Los Angeles, CA 90049-2913, USA

Jackson, Philip (Actor)
Markham & Froggatt
Julian House
4 Windmill St
London W1P 1HF, UNITED KINGDOM
(UK)

Jackson, Philip D (Phil) (Basketball Player, Coach)
Los Angeles Lakers
1111 S Figueroa St
Staples Center
Los Angeles, CA 90015-1300, USA

Jackson, R Graham (Architect)
Calhoun Tungate Jackson Dill Architects
6200 Savoy Dr
Houston, TX 77036-3300, USA

Jackson, Randy (Musician, Reality TV Star)
Dream Merchant 21 Entertainment
4000 Warner Blvd Ste 700
Burbank, CA 91522-0001, USA

Jackson, Randy B (Football Player)
Chicago Bears
747 Musago Run
Lake Mary, FL 32746-2209, USA

Jackson, Randy J (Football Player)
Buffalo Bills
4449 Auburn St
Bel Aire, KS 67220-1805, USA

Jackson, Ransom (Baseball Player)
Chicago Cubs
250 Hunnicutt Dr
Athens, GA 30606-1708, USA

Jackson, Rebbie (Music Group, Musician, Songwriter, Writer)
4641 Hayvenhurst Ave
Encino, CA 91436-3251, USA

Jackson, Reggie (Baseball Player)
Kansas City A's
305 Amador Ave
Seaside, CA 93955-4725, USA

Jackson, Richard A (Religious Leader)
North Phoenix Baptist Church
5757 N Central Ave
Phoenix, AZ 85012-1397, USA

Jackson, Richard Lee
1815 Butler Ave Apt 120
Los Angeles, CA 90025-5462, USA

Jackson, Richard S (Richie) (Football Player)
Oakland Raiders
6000 Kingston Ct
All Pro Inc
New Orleans, LA 70131-5557, USA

Jackson, Rickey (Football Player)
New Orleans Saints
PO Box 655
Pahokee, FL 33476-0655, USA

Jackson, Rickey A (Football Player)
325 S Barfield Hwy
Pahokee, FL 33476-1929, USA

Jackson, Ron (Baseball Player)
Chicago White Sox
210 Raintree Cir
Kalamazoo, MI 49006-4165, USA

Jackson, Ron (Baseball Player)
California Angels
515 White Rd
Fayetteville, GA 30214-1211, USA

Jackson, Ronald Shannon (Musician)
Worldwide Jazz
1128 Broadway # 425
New York, NY 10010, USA

Jackson, Roy Lee (Baseball Player)
New York Mets
8269 Lee Road 54
Auburn, AL 36830-8222, USA

Jackson, Ryan (Baseball Player)
Florida Marlins
5354 Cork Oak St
Sarasota, FL 34232-3054, USA

Jackson, Samuel L (Actor)
15030 Ventura Blvd # 710
Sherman Oaks, CA 91403-5470, USA

Jackson, Shar (Actor)
c/o Neil Stearns *Don Buchwald & Associates Inc (LA)*
6500 Wilshire Blvd Ste 2200
Los Angeles, CA 90048-4942, USA

Jackson, Sheldon (Football Player)
Buffalo Bills
4466 Teresita Ct
Chino, CA 91710-3929, USA

Jackson, Sherry (Actor)
800 N Lucia Ave # A
Redondo Beach, CA 90277-2233, USA

Jackson, Shirley Ann (Educator, Physicist)
Rensselaer Polytechnic Institute
President's Office
Troy, NY 12180, USA

Jackson, Sonny (Baseball Player)
Houston Colt 45's
117 Palm Bay Dr Apt B
Palm Beach Gardens, FL 33418-5790, USA

Jackson, Steve (Football Player)
Houston Oilers
43752 Lees Mill Sq
Leesburg, VA 20176-3821, USA

Jackson, Steve (Football Player)
Washington Redskins
1153 Bergen Pkwy Ste M
Evergreen, CO 80439-9501, USA

Jackson, Stonewall (Music Group, Musician, Songwriter, Writer)
6007 Cloverland Dr
Brentwood, TN 37027-7607, USA

Jackson, Stoney (Actor)
3151 Cahuenga Blvd W Ste 310
Los Angeles, CA 90068-1768, USA

Jackson, Terry (Football Player)
New York Giants
22 Robin Rd
Norfolk, MA 02056-1731, USA

Jackson, Thomas Penfield (Judge)
US District Court
333 Constitution Ave NW Ste 4400
Washington, DC 20001-2837, USA

Jackson, Thomas (Tom) (Football Player, Sportscaster)
ESPN-TV
935 Middle St
Sports Dept Espn Plaza
Bristol, CT 06010-1000, USA

Jackson, Tim (Football Player)
Dallas Cowboys
6501 White Oak Dr
Rowlett, TX 75089-7441, USA

Jackson, Tito (Music Group, Musician)
2467 Taylor Ave
Corona, CA 92882-6980, USA

Jackson, Tre (Football Player)
Miami Dolphins
680 Harrison Ave
Peekskill, NY 10566-2219, USA

Jackson, Trina (Swimmer)
9271 Saltwater Way
Jacksonville, FL 32256-9606, USA

Jackson, Tyoka (Football Player)
Miami Dolphins
1 Rams Way
Earth City, MO 63045-1523, USA

Jackson, Verdell (Baseball Player)
Memphis Red Sox
413 Lincoln St
Venice, IL 62090-1117, USA

Jackson, Victoria (Actor, Comedian)
c/o Kim Dorr *Defining Artists*
10 Universal City Plz Ste 2000
Universal City, CA 91608-1074, USA

Jackson, Vincent E (Bo) (Baseball Player, Football Player)
PO Box 158
Mobile, AL 36601-0158, USA

Jackson, Wanda (Music Group, Musician)
Wanda Jackson Enterprises
8200 S Pennsylvania Ave
Oklahoma City, OK 73159-5202, USA

Jackson, Waverly (Football Player)
Indianapolis Colts
1231 Halifax St
South Hill, VA 23970-2319, USA

Jackson, Wilbur (Football Player)
San Francisco 49ers
PO Box 1571
Ozark, AL 36361-1571, USA

Jackson, Willie (Football Player)
Jacksonville Jaguars
PO Box 12643
Gainesville, FL 32604-0643, USA

Jackson Hoye, Rose (Actor)
c/o Staff Member *Haldeman Business Management*
1137 2nd St
Santa Monica, CA 90403-5011, USA

Jacob, Francois (Nobel Prize Laureate)
15 Rue de Conde
Paris 75006, FRANCE

Jacob, Irene (Actor)
Nicole Cann
1 Rue Alfred du Vigny
Paris 75008, FRANCE

Jacob, John E (Activist)
National Urban League
120 Wall St Fl 7
New York, NY 10005-3900, USA

Jacob, Katerina (Actor)
Agentur Doris Mattes
Merzstr 14
Munich 81679, GERMANY

Jacob, Stanley W (Doctor)
1055 SW Westwood Ct
Portland, OR 97239-2708, USA

Jacobi, Derek G (Actor)
International Creative Mgmt
76 Oxford St
London W1N OAX, UNITED KINGDOM
(UK)

Jacobi, Lou (Actor)
240 Central Park S
New York, NY 10019-1457, USA

Jacobs, Allen (Football Player)
Green Bay Packers
3050 Tolcate Ln
Salt Lake City, UT 84121-1545, USA

Jacobs, Cam (Football Player)
Tampa Bay Buccaneers
Dream Homes Of The First Coast SR 207
And I-95, Ext 94
Saint Augustine, FL 32085, USA

Jacobs, Dave (Football Player)
New York Jets
8388 Glen Eagle Dr
Manlius, NY 13104-9445, USA

Jacobs, Forrest (Baseball Player)
Philadelphia Athletics
509 Crestview Dr
Milford, DE 19963-2903, USA

Jacobs, Harry (Football Player)
Boston Patriots
108 Lenora Dr
Hamburg, NY 14075-4710, USA

Jacobs, Irwin M (Business Person)
Qualcomm Inc
5775 Morehouse Dr
San Diego, CA 92121-1714, USA

Jacobs, Jack H (War Hero)
Bankers Trust Co
1 Appold St
London EC2A 2HE, UNITED KINGDOM
(UK)

Jacobs, Jake (Baseball Player)
Washington Senators
1626 Terra Ceia Bay Cir
Palmetto, FL 34221-5947, USA

Jacobs, Jim (Writer)
International Creative Mgmt
40 W 57th St Ste 1800
New York, NY 10019-4001, USA

Jacobs, Julien I (Judge)
US Tax Court
400 2nd St NW
Washington, DC 20217-0002, USA

Jacobs, Katie (Producer, Writer)
c/o David O'Connor *Creative Artists Agency LCC (CAA-LA)*
2000 Avenue Of The Stars
Los Angeles, CA 90067-4700, USA

Jacobs, Lawrence-Hilton (Actor)
PO Box 67905
Los Angeles, CA 90067-0905, USA

Jacobs, Marc (Designer, Fashion Designer)
403 Bleeker St
New York, NY 10014, USA

Jacobs, Norman J (Publisher)
Century Publishing Co
990 Grove St
Evanston, IL 60201-4302, USA

Jacobs, Proverb (Football Player)
Philadelphia Eagles
4369 Detroit Ave
Oakland, CA 94619-1603, USA

Jacobs, Tim (Football Player)
Cleveland Browns
7306 Finns Ln
Lanham, MD 20706-1214, USA

Jacobs, Wilfred E (General, Governor)
Government House
Saint John's
Antigua, ANTIGUA & BARBUDA

Jacobs-Badini, Jane (Baseball Player)
1854 4th St
Cuyahoga Falls, OH 44221-3802, USA

Jacobs-Murk, Janet (Baseball Player)
899 Olentangy Rd
Franklin Lakes, NJ 07417-2811, USA

Jacobsen, Casey (Basketball Player)
Phoenix Suns
201 E Jefferson St
Phoenix, AZ 85004-2412, USA

Jacobsen, Peter (Golfer)
9400 SW Barnes Rd Ste 550
Portland, OR 97225-6690, USA

Jacobson, A Thurl (Geophysicist, Physicist)
7955 W Innsbrook Ct
Boise, ID 83704-4487, USA

Jacobson, D D (Bowler)
8261 Rees St
Playa Del Rey, CA 90293-7823, USA

Jacobson, Herbert L (Diplomat, Journalist)
Apartado 160
Escazu, COSTA RICA

Jacobson, Nina
c/o Staff Member *Creative Artists Agency LCC (CAA-LA)*
2000 Avenue Of The Stars
Los Angeles, CA 90067-4700, USA

Jacobson, Peter (Actor)
c/o Staff Member *Innovative Artists (LA)*
1505 10th St
Santa Monica, CA 90401-2805, USA

Jacobson, Peter Marc (Actor, Producer, Writer)
c/o Staff Member *New York Nick*
5750 Wilshire Blvd
Los Angeles, CA 90036-3697, USA

Jacobson, Scott (Actor)
c/o Staff Member *Creative Artists Agency LCC (CAA-LA)*
2000 Avenue Of The Stars
Los Angeles, CA 90067-4700, USA

Jacoby, Billy
PO Box 46324
Los Angeles, CA 90046-0324, USA

Jacoby, Brook (Baseball Player)
Atlanta Braves
21825 N Dobson Rd
Scottsdale, AZ 85255-4404, USA

Jacoby, Joe (Football Player)
Washington Redskins
Joe Jacoby Jeep/Eagle/Chrysler 510 Frost Ave
Warrenton, VA 20186, USA

Jacoby, Laura
PO Box 46324
Los Angeles, CA 90046-0324, USA

Jacoby, Lowell E (Admiral)
Director Defense Intelligence Agency
Washington, DC 20340-0001, USA

Jacoby, Scott (Actor)
PO Box 461100
Los Angeles, CA 90046-9100, USA

Jacome, Jason (Baseball Player)
New York Mets
5115 N Camino Esplendora
Tucson, AZ 85718-6226, USA

Jacot, Christopher (Actor)
c/o Ted Schachter *Schachter Entertainment*
1157 S Beverly Dr Fl 2
Los Angeles, CA 90035-1119, USA

Jacot, Michele (Skier)
Residence du Brevent
74 Chamonix, FRANCE

Jacott, Carlos (Actor)
c/o JB Roberts *Thruline Entertainment*
9250 Wilshire Blvd Ground Fl
Beverly Hills, CA 90210, USA

Jacox, Kendyl (Football Player)
San Diego Chargers
647 Shadyway Dr
Dallas, TX 75232-4821, USA

Jacques, Russell (Artist)
48701 Shady View Dr
Palm Desert, CA 92260-6730, USA

Jacquez, Pat (Baseball Player)
Chicago White Sox
4430 Annandale Dr
Stockton, CA 95219-1782, USA

Jacquez, Thomas (Baseball Player)
Philadelphia Phillies
4430 Annandale Dr
Stockton, CA 95219-1782, USA

Jacuzzi, Roy (Business Person)
Jacuzzi Whirlpool Bath
2121 N California Blvd
Walnut Creek, CA 94596-3572, USA

Jadakiss (Artist, Music Group, Musician)
International Creative Mgmt
8942 Wilshire Blvd # 219
Beverly Hills, CA 90211-1908, USA

Jade
c/o Staff Member *Diva Central Inc*
7510 W Sunset Blvd Ste 1445
Los Angeles, CA 90046-3408, USA

Jade, Samantha (Musician)
c/o Staff Member *Jive Records*
137 W 25th St
New York, NY 10001-7216, USA

Jadot, Jean L O (Religious Leader)
Ave de l'Atlantique 71-B-12
Brussels 1150, BELGIUM

Jae, Jana
PO Box 35736
Tulsa, OK 74153, USA

Jaeckel, Paul (Baseball Player)
Chicago Cubs
328 W 7th St
Claremont, CA 91711-4313, USA

Jaeckin, Just (Director)
8 Villa Mequillet
Neuilly/Seine 92200, FRANCE

Jaeger, Andrea (Tennis Player)
Kids Stuff Foundation
256 Rancho Milagro Way
Silver Lining Ranch
Hesperus, CO 81326-8750, USA

Jaeger, Jeff T (Football Player)
Cleveland Browns
3026 Sahalee Dr W
Sammamish, WA 98074-6304, USA

Jaenicke, Hannes
Goetherstr. 17
Munich D-80336, GERMANY

Jaffe, Herold W (Doctor)
Centers for Disease Control
1600 Clifton Rd NE
Atlanta, GA 30329-4018, USA

Jaffe, Robert L (Physicist)
Massachusetts Institute of Technology
Physics Dept
Cambridge, MA 02139, USA

Jaffe, Stanley R (Director, Producer)
Lean Building
10202 Washington Blvd
Culver City, CA 90232-3119, USA

Jaffe, Susan (Ballerina)
American Ballet Theatre
890 Broadway
New York, NY 10003-1278, USA

Jaffrey, Saeed (Actor, Bollywood, Comedian)
503 Sejal New Link Road
Andheri
Bombay, MS 400 058, INDIA

Jagan, Janet (President)
65 Plantation Bel Air
East Coast Demerara
Georgetown, GUYANA

Jagdeo, Bharrat (Prime Minister)
President's Office
Brickham
New Garden & South Sts
Georgetown, GUYANA

Jagendort, Andre T (Doctor)
455 Savage Farm Dr
Ithaca, NY 14850-6522, USA

Jager, Thomas (Tom) (Swimmer)
745 4th Ave E
Kalispell, MT 59901-5345, USA

Jager, Tom
64 Ramble Wood Blvd
Tijeras, NM 87059-8004, USA

Jagge, Finn Christian (Skier)
Michelets Vei 108
Stabekk 1320, NORWAY

Jagged Edge (Music Group)
c/o Nancy Josephson *Endeavor Agency LLC (LA)*
8942 Wilshire Blvd
Beverly Hills, CA 90211-1908, USA

Jagger, Bianca (Actor, Model)
530 Park Ave # 18D
New York, NY 10065-8015, USA

Jagger, Mick (Musician)
c/o Alix Gucovsky *Special Artists Agency*
9465 Wilshire Blvd Ste 890
Beverly Hills, CA 90212-2607, USA

Jagland, Thorbjoern (Prime Minister)
Stortinget
Karl Johans Gate 22
Oslo 0026, NORWAY

Jaglom, Henry (Director)
9165 W Sunset Blvd Ste 300
Los Angeles, CA 90069-3195, USA

Jagr, Jaromir (Hockey Player)
c/o Pat Brisson *Creative Artists Agency LCC (CAA-LA)*
2000 Avenue Of The Stars
Los Angeles, CA 90067-4700, USA

Jaguares (Music Group)
c/o Staff Member *BMG*
1540 Broadway
New York, NY 10036-4074, USA

Jaha, John (Baseball Player)
Milwaukee Brewers
2506 NW 24th Cir
Camas, WA 98607-8011, USA

Jahan, Marine (Actor, Dancer)
Media Artists Group
6300 Wilshire Blvd Ste 1470
Los Angeles, CA 90048-5200, USA

Jaheim (Musician)
Diane Mill
100 Evergreen Pl # 402
East Orange, NJ 07018, USA

Jahn, Helmut (Architect)
Murphy/Jahn
35 E Wacker Dr
Chicago, IL 60601-2157, USA

Jahn, Sigmund (Astronaut, General, Misc)
Fontanestr 35
Strausberg 15344, GERMANY

Jaidah, Ali Mohammed (Government Official)
Qatar Petroleum Corp
PO Box 3212
Doha, QATAR

Jaime, Bergman
8383 Wilshire Blvd Ste 550
Beverly Hills, CA 90211-2417, USA

Jaitley, Celina (Beauty Pageant Winner)
c/o Staff Member *Miss Universe Organization, The*
1370 Avenue Of The Americas Fl 16
New York, NY 10019-4602, USA

Jakeman, Seth (Musician)
c/o Staff Member *Paradigm (Monterey)*
509 Hartnell St
Monterey, CA 93940-2825, USA

Jakes, Bishop T D (Musician, Writer)
c/o Staff Member *Creative Artists Agency LCC (CAA-LA)*
2000 Avenue Of The Stars
Los Angeles, CA 90067-4700, USA

Jakes, T D (Religious Leader)
Potter's House
6777 W Kiest Blvd
Dallas, TX 75236-3006, USA

Jakes, Van (Football Player)
Kansas City Chiefs
305 Worthing Ln
McDonough, GA 30253-4244, USA

Jaki, Stanley L (Misc, Physicist)
PO Box 167
Princeton, NJ 08542-0167, USA

Jakobs, Marco (Athlete)
Oststr 1B
Unna 59427, GERMANY

Jakobson, Maggie (Actor)
Writers & Artists
360 N Crescent Dr Bldg North
Beverly Hills, CA 90210-6818, USA

Jakobson, Max (Government Official, Journalist)
Rahapajankatu 3B 17
Helsinki 16 00160, FINLAND

Jakosits, Michael (Misc)
Karlsbergstr 140
Homburg/Saar 66424, GERMANY

Jakowenko, George (Football Player)
Oakland Raiders
5 Aberdeen Dr
West Nyack, NY 10994-1301, USA

Jakub, Lisa (Actor)
Metropolitan Talent Agency
4500 Wilshire Blvd Fl 2
Los Angeles, CA 90010-3858, USA

Jalal, Farida (Actor, Bollywood)
3B Nandini Unik Housing Society
Opp Bon Bon J P Road Andheri
Mumbai, MS 400058, INDIA

Jalbert, Pierre
2642 N Beverly Glen Blvd
Los Angeles, CA 90077-2528, USA

Jamail, Joseph D Jr (Attorney, Attorney General, General)
Jamail & Kolius
500 Dallas St Ste 3434
Houston, TX 77002-4802, USA

Jamal, Ahmad (Music Group, Musician)
Brad Simon Organization
122 E 57th St # 300
New York, NY 10022-2623, USA

Jambor, Agi (Music Group, Musician)
1616 Bolton St
Baltimore, MD 21217-4316, USA

James, Anthony (Actor)
CNA Assoc
1875 Century Park E Ste 2250
Los Angeles, CA 90067-2563, USA

James, Bill (Baseball Player, Writer)
74 Naples Rd
Brookline, MA 02446-5751, USA

James, Bob (Baseball Player)
Montreal Expos
15844 Cindy Ct
Canyon Country, CA 91387-1881, USA

James, Boney (Musician)
c/o Staff Member *Paradigm (Monterey)*
509 Hartnell St
Monterey, CA 93940-2825, USA

James, Charlie (Baseball Player)
St Louis Cardinals
3303 Tanglewood Way
Fulton, MO 65251-3981, USA

James, Charmayne (Misc)
Gold Buckle Ranch
2100 N Highway 360 Ste 1207
Grand Prairie, TX 75050-1033, USA

James, Cheryl (Salt) (Artist, Music Group, Musician)
Famous Artists Agency
250 W 57th St
New York, NY 10107-0001, USA

James, Chris (Baseball Player)
Philadelphia Phillies
1252 County Road 2712
Alto, TX 75925-5964, USA

James, Claudis (Football Player)
Green Bay Packers
6767 Presidential Dr
Jackson, MS 39213-2427, USA

James, Cleo (Baseball Player)
Los Angeles Dodgers
PO Box 9970
Moreno Valley, CA 92552-1970, USA

James, Clifton (Actor)
500 W 43rd St Apt 25D
New York, NY 10036-4336, USA

James, Clive V L (Journalist, Misc)
P F D
Drury House
34-43 Russell St
London WC2B 5HA, UNITED KINGDOM
(UK)

James, Craig (Football Player)
New England Patriots
12714 W Fm 455
Celina, TX 75009-3959, USA

James, D Clayton (Historian)
106 Wagon Wheel Trl
Moneta, VA 24121-3328, USA

James, Dalton
303 N Buena Vista St Apt 209
Burbank, CA 91505-3686, USA

James, Delvin (Baseball Player)
Tampa Bay Devil Rays
RR 7 Box 6180
Nacogdoches, TX 75965, USA

James, Dion (Baseball Player)
Milwaukee Brewers
5 Shelter Point Ct
Sacramento, CA 95831-1415, USA

James, Don (Coach, Football Coach)
7047 Chanticleer Ave SE
Snoqualmie, WA 98065-9785, USA

James, Donald M (Business Person)
Vulcan Materials Co
1200 Urban Center Dr
Birmingham, AL 35242-2545, USA

James, Duncan (Musician)
c/o Staff Member *Concorde Intl Artists Ltd*
101 Shepherds Bush Rd
London W6 7LP, UNITED KINGDOM
(UK)

James, Duncan (Musician)
c/o Staff Member *BMG (UK)*
Bedford House
6979 Fulham High Street
London SW6 3JW, UNITED KINGDOM
(UK)

James, Etta (Music Group, Musician)
16409 Sally Ln
Riverside, CA 92504-5629, USA

James, Forrest H (Fob) Jr (Governor)
39 Alabama Rd N
Lehigh Acres, FL 33936-6809, USA

James, G Larry (Athlete, Track Athlete)
Stockton State College
Atheletic Dept
Pomona, NJ 08240, USA

James, Geraldine (Actor)
Julian Belfarge
46 Albermarle St
London W1X 4PP, UNITED KINGDOM
(UK)

James, Godfrey
The Shack Western Rd. Pevensey Bay
E. Sussex, ENGLAND

James, Jesse (Actor)
Coast to Coast Talent
3350 Barham Blvd
Los Angeles, CA 90068-1404, USA

James, John (Actor)
PO Box 9
Cambridge, NY 12816-0009, USA

James, John W (Football Player)
Atlanta Falcons
23108 NE 69th Ave
Melrose, FL 32666-6330, USA

James, Johnny (Baseball Player)
New York Yankees
6037 E Larkspur Dr
Scottsdale, AZ 85254-4444, USA

James, Joni (Music Group, Musician)
PO Box 7027
Westchester, IL 60154, USA

James, Kate (Model)
Men/Women Model Inc
199 Lafayette St
New York, NY 10012-4003, USA

James, Kevin (Actor, Comedian)
c/o Adam Venit *Endeavor Agency LLC (LA)*
9601 Wilshire Blvd Fl 3
Beverly Hills, CA 90210-5204, USA

James, Larry D (Astronaut)
AFELM
Uss Space Command
Peterson Air Force Base, CO 80914, USA

James, LeBron (Basketball Player)
GAP Communications
1667 E 40th St Ste 2B
Cleveland, OH 44103-2343, USA

James, Leela (Musician)
c/o Staff Member *Paradigm (Monterey)*
509 Hartnell St
Monterey, CA 93940-2825, USA

James, Lionel (Football Player)
San Diego Chargers
199 Woodbury Dr
Sterrett, AL 35147-8144, USA

James, Mike (Baseball Player)
California Angels
115 Austin Ct
Mary Esther, FL 32569-1396, USA

James, Oliver (Actor, Musician)
c/o JoAnne Colonna *Brillstein-Grey Entertainment*
9150 Wilshire Blvd Ste 350
Beverly Hills, CA 90212-3453, USA

James, P D (Writer)
Elaine Greene Ltd
37A Goldhawk Road
London W12 8QQ, UNITED KINGDOM
(UK)

James, Paul (Actor, Producer)
c/o Staff Member *HGTV/Home & Garden Television*
9721 Sherrill Blvd
Knoxville, TN 37932-3330, USA

James, Po (Football Player)
Philadelphia Eagles
1421 E Sherman St
Hammond, IN 46320-2208, USA

James, Ralph
205 S Arnaz Dr Apt 4
Beverly Hills, CA 90211-2881, USA

James, Rick (Baseball Player)
Chicago Cubs
302 W 23rd St Ste B
Panama City, FL 32405-7620, USA

James, Robert (Football Player)
Buffalo Bills
1511 N Highland Ave
Murfreesboro, TN 37130-2204, USA

James, Robert (Bob) (Music Group, Musician, Songwriter, Writer)
Monterey International
200 W Superior St Ste 202
Chicago, IL 60610-3554, USA

James, Roland (Football Player)
New England Patriots
19 Spring Ln
Sharon, MA 02067-2240, USA

James, Ryan (Actor)
c/o TJ Stein *Stein Entertainment Group*
11271 Ventura Blvd # 477
Studio City, CA 91604-3136, USA

James, Sheila (Actor)
3201 Pearl St
Santa Monica, CA 90405-3106, USA

James, Sheryl (Journalist)
Saint Petersburg Times
490 1st Ave S
Editorial Dept
Saint Petersburg, FL 33701-4223, USA

James, Skip (Baseball Player)
San Francisco Giants
7716 W 72nd Ter
Overland Park, KS 66204-1807, USA

James, Sonny (Music Group, Musician, Songwriter, Writer)
McFadden Artists
818 18th Ave S
Nashville, TN 37203-6663, USA

James, Stanislaus A (General, Governor)
Government House
Morue
Castries, SAINT LUCIA

James, Steve (Director, Producer, Writer)
Corner of the Sky Entertainment
1635 N Cahuenga Blvd Fl 6
Los Angeles, CA 90028-6201, USA

James, Tommy (Football Player)
Detroit Lions
1615 Wales Rd NE
Massillon, OH 44646-4167, USA

James, Tommy (Music Group, Musician)
Aura Entertainment
PO Box 4354
Clifton, NJ 07012-8354, USA

James, Toran (Football Player)
San Diego Chargers
RR 3 Box 14-13
Ahoskie, NC 27910, USA

James of Holland Park, Phyllis D (Writer)
Elaine Green Ltd
37A Goldhawk Road
London W12 SQQ, UNITED KINGDOM
(UK)

James-Roadman, Charmayne (Misc)
General Delivery
Clayton, NM 88415-9999, USA

Jameson, Elizabeth M (Betty) (Golfer)
1425 S Congress Ave Apt 268
Boynton Beach, FL 33426-6384, USA

Jameson, Jenna (Adult Film Star)
c/o Sarah Perkins *Club Jenna Inc*
8360 E Via De Ventura # F110 # 258
Scottsdale, AZ 85258-3172, USA

Jameson, Louise
18-21 Jermyn St.
London, ENGLAND SW1Y 6HP, UNITED KINGDOM (UK)

Jameson, Paulene
7 Warrington Gardens
London, ENGLAND W9 2QB, UNITED KINGDOM (UK)

Jamieson, Janet (Baseball Player)
PO Box 3094
Lynnwood, WA 98046-3094, USA

Jamieson, John K (Business Person)
10313 Stanley Cir
Minneapolis, MN 55437-2518, USA

The Celebrity Black Book 2008

Jamiroquai
151 El Camino Dr
Beverly Hills, CA 90212-2704, USA

Jamison, Antawn (Basketball Player)
Dallas Mavericks
2909 Taylor St
Dallas, TX 75226-1909, USA

Jamison, Jayne (Publisher)
Redbook Magazine
224 W 57th St
New York, NY 10019-3200, USA

Jamison, Mae
PO Box 580317
Houston, TX 77258-0317, USA

Jamison, Milo
1231 Tennyson St
Manhattan Beach, CA 90266-6956, USA

Jammeh, Yahya A J J (Misc)
President's Office
State House
Banjul, GAMBIA

Jammer, Quentin (Football Player)
San Diego Chargers
4020 Murphy Canyon Rd
San Diego, CA 92123-4407, USA

Jampolsky, Gerald (Writer)
Celestial Arts
PO Box 7123
Berkeley, CA 94707-0123, USA

Jan & Dean
221 Main St Ste P
Huntington Beach, CA 92648-8119, USA

Janakaraj (Actor)
8 H D Raja Street
Teynampet
Chennai, TN 600 018, INDIA

Janaki, Sowcar (Actor, Bollywood)
13 Cenetop Road
2nd Street
Chennai, TN 600018, INDIA

Jance, J A (Writer)
Avon/William Morrow
1350 Avenue Of The Americas
New York, NY 10019-4702, USA

Jancik, Bobby (Football Player)
Houston Oilers
114 5th St SE Apt 501E
Minneapolis, MN 55414-1161, USA

Jancso, Miklos (Director)
Solyom Laszio Utca 17
Budapest II 1022, HUNGARY

Janda, Krystyna (Actor)
Teatr Powszechny
Ul Zamoyskiego 20
Warsaw, POLAND

Jande, Marine (Actor)
Gilla Roos
16 W 22nd St Ste 303
3rd Floor
New York, NY 10010-5825, USA

Jane, Thomas (Actor)
c/o Ed Limato *International Creative Management (ICM-LA)*
10250 Constellation Blvd
Los Angeles, CA 90067-6200, USA

Janeski, Gerry (Baseball Player)
Chicago White Sox
28901 Via Buena Vis
San Juan Capistrano, CA 92675-5554, USA

Janet, Ernest (Football Player)
Chicago Bears
21838 SE 275th St
Maple Valley, WA 98038-3249, USA

Janeway, Michael C (Editor)
Northwestern University
Fisk Hall
Evanston, IL 60201, USA

Janeway, Richard (Doctor)
PO Box 188
Blowing Rock, NC 28605-0188, USA

Janik, Tom (Football Player)
Denver Broncos
RR 2 Box 49A
Falls City, TX 78113, USA

Janikowski, Bruce (Football Player)
Kansas City Chiefs
2716 W 112th St
Shawnee Mission, KS 66211-3084, USA

Janikowski, Sebastian (Football Player)
Oakland Raiders
3250 Hertlein Pl
Castro Valley, CA 94546-2900, USA

Janis, Byron (Music Group, Musician)
Columbia Artists Mgmt Inc
1790 Broadway Fl 6
New York, NY 10019-1412, USA

Janis, Conrad (Actor, Music Group, Musician)
1434 N Genesee Ave
Los Angeles, CA 90046-3930, USA

Janis, Elizabeth (Actor)
c/o Michael Greenwald *Don Buchwald & Associates Inc (LA)*
6500 Wilshire Blvd Ste 2200
Los Angeles, CA 90048-4942, USA

Janis, Ryan (Actor)
c/o TJ Stein *Stein Entertainment Group*
11271 Ventura Blvd # 477
Studio City, CA 91604-3136, USA

Janitz, John A (Business Person)
Textron Inc
40 Westminster St
Providence, RI 02903-2503, USA

Jankins, Corey (Baseball Player)
Bowman
456 S Church St Apt J1
Lexington, SC 29072-3342, USA

Jankowska-Cieslak, Jadwiga (Actor)
Film Polski
Ul Mazewiecka 6/8
Warsaw 00-950, POLAND

Jankowski, Gene F (Television Host)
American Film Institute
901 15th St NW # 700
Washington, DC 20005-2327, USA

Jankowski, Peter (Producer)
c/o Staff Member *Wolf Films Inc (LA)*
100 Universal City Plz Bldg 2252
Universal City, CA 91608-1002, USA

Jannazzo, Izzy (Boxer)
6924 62nd Ave
Flushing, NY 11379-1120, USA

Janney, Allison (Actor)
c/o Chris Henze *Thruline Entertainment*
9250 Wilshire Blvd Ground Fl
Beverly Hills, CA 90210, USA

Janney, Craig H (Hockey Player)
3 Overhill Rd
Enfield, CT 06082-5643, USA

Janov, Arthur (Philanthropist, Psychic)
1205 Abbot Kinney Blvd
Venice, CA 90291-3315, USA

Janowicz, Josh (Actor)
c/o Darren Goldberg *1 Management*
9000 W Sunset Blvd Ph 1550
West Hollywood, CA 90069-1838, USA

Janowitz, Gundula (Opera Singer)
3072 Kasten
75, AUSTRIA

Janowski, Marek (Conductor)
I M G Artists
3 Burlington Lane
Chiswick
London W4 2TH, UNITED KINGDOM (UK)

Jansante, Val (Football Player)
Pittsburgh Steelers
201 Frye Ave
Bentleyville, PA 15314-1305, USA

Janseen, Daniel (Business Person)
Solvay & Cie
33 Rue du Prince Albert
Brussels 1050, BELGIUM

Janseen, Famke (Actor, Model)
Creative Artists Agency
9830 Wilshire Blvd
Beverly Hills, CA 90212-1804, USA

Jansen, Daniel E (Dan) (Speed Skater)
PO Box 3354
Mooresville, NC 28117-3354, USA

Jansen, Jim (Actor)
c/o Martin Gage *Gage Group, The (LA)*
14724 Ventura Blvd Ste 505
Sherman Oaks, CA 91403-3505, USA

Jansen, Jon (Football Player)
c/o Staff Member *Washington Redskins*
21300 Redskin Park Dr
Ashburn, VA 20147-6100, USA

Jansen, Larry (Baseball Player)
New York Giants
3207 NW Highway 47
Forest Grove, OR 97116-8631, USA

Jansen, Raymond A (Publisher)
Newsday Inc
235 Pinelawn Rd
Melville, NY 11747-4250, USA

Jansons, Mariss (Conductor)
I M G Artists
3 Burlington Lane
Chiswick
London W4 2TH, UNITED KINGDOM (UK)

Janssen, Dani
2220 Avenue Of The Stars Apt 2803
Los Angeles, CA 90067-5686, USA

Janssen, Famke (Actor, Model)
c/o Peter Levine *Creative Artists Agency LCC (CAA-LA)*
2000 Avenue Of The Stars
Los Angeles, CA 90067-4700, USA

Janssen, Frances (Baseball Player)
4311 Mayflower Dr
Lafayette, IN 47909-3473, USA

Jantz, Richard (Misc)
University of Tennessee
Anthropology Dept
Knoxville, TN 37996-0001, USA

January, Don (Golfer)
4139 Sicily Dr
Frisco, TX 75034, USA

January, Lois (Actor)
PO Box 1233
Beverly Hills, CA 90213-1233, USA

Jany, Alexandre (Alex) (Swimmer)
104 Blvd Livon
Marseille 13007, FRANCE

Janzen, Edmund (Religious Leader)
General Conference of Mennonite Brethren
8000 W 21st St N
Wichita, KS 67205-1744, USA

Janzen, Lee (Golfer)
9088 Point Cypress Dr
Orlando, FL 32836-5476, USA

Janzen, Marty (Baseball Player)
Toronto Blue Jays
2955 Kaufmann Ave Apt 223
Dubuque, IA 52001-1658, USA

Jaqua, Jon (Football Player)
Washington Redskins
34320 McKenzie View Dr
Eugene, OR 97408-9205, USA

Jaquess, Pete (Football Player)
Houston Oilers
631 Cunningham Ln
El Cajon, CA 92019-3504, USA

Jardine, Al
PO Box 36
Big Sur, CA 93920-0036, USA

Jarecki, Andrew (Director, Musician, Producer)
c/o Staff Member *Hit the Ground Running Films*
200 W 57th St Ste 1304
New York, NY 10019-3211, USA

Jarman Jr, Claude (Actor)
11 Dos Encinas
Orinda, CA 94563-4115, USA

Jarmoluk, Mike (Football Player)
Chicago Bears
5878 NW 96th Ln
Ocala, FL 34482-7312, USA

Jarmusch, Jim (Director)
Exoskeleton Inc
208 E 6th St
New York, NY 10003-8207, USA

Jaroncyk, Ryan (Baseball Player)
Bowman
2923 Roseann Ave
Escondido, CA 92027-5306, USA

Jarostchuk, Ilia (Football Player)
St Louis Cardinals
4 Macarthur Rd
Wellesley, MA 02482-4422, USA

Jarre, Maurice A (Composer, Musician)
27011 Sea Vista Dr
Malibu, CA 90265-4434, USA

Jarreau, Al (Musician)
c/o Brett Steinberg *Creative Artists Agency LCC (CAA-LA)*
2000 Avenue Of The Stars
Los Angeles, CA 90067-4700, USA

Jarrell, Tom
77 W 66th St
New York, NY 10023-6201, USA

Jarrett, Dale (Race Car Driver)
1510 46th Ave NE
Hickory, NC 28601-8421, USA

The Celebrity Black Book 2008

Jarrett, Keith (Composer, Musician)
Stephen Cloud
PO Box 4774
Santa Barbara, CA 93140-4774, USA

Jarrett, Ned
3182 Ninth Tee Dr
Newton, NC 28658-8725, USA

Jarrett, Ned M (Race Car Driver)
Ned Jarrett Enterprises
RR 1 Box 160
Newton, NC 28658, USA

Jarrett, Will (Editor)
Dallas Times Herald
Herald Square
Editorial Dept
Dallas, TX 75215, USA

Jarrier, Jean-Pierre
17 bd. Larvotto
Monte Carlo, MONACO

Jarrott, Charles (Director)
4314 Marina City Dr Unit 418
Marina Del Rey, CA 90292-5814, USA

Jarryd, Anders (Tennis Player)
Maaneskoldsgatan 37
Lidkoping 531 00, SWEDEN

Jars of Clay (Music Group)
c/o Staff Member Creative Artists Agency LCC (CAA-LA)
2000 Avenue Of The Stars
Los Angeles, CA 90067-4700, USA

Jaru the Damaja (Musician)
William Morris Agency
1325 Avenue Of The Americas
New York, NY 10019-6091, USA

Jaruzelski, Wojciech (General, President)
Biuro Bylego
Al Jerozolimskie 91
Warsaw 02-001, POLAND

Jarvi, Neeme (Conductor)
PO Box 305
Sea Bright, NJ 07760-0305, USA

Jarvi, Paavo (Conductor)
Cincinnati Symphony
1241 Elm St
Music Hall
Cincinnati, OH 45202-7531, USA

Jarvis, Bruce (Football Player)
Buffalo Bills
4153 Issaquah Pine Lake Rd SE
Sammamish, WA 98075-6243, USA

Jarvis, Curtis (Football Player)
Tampa Bay Buccaneers
401 Albert Dr
Gardendale, AL 35071-2588, USA

Jarvis, Doug (Hockey Player)
812 Crane Dr
Coppell, TX 75019-5944, USA

Jarvis, Graham
15351 Via De Las Olas
Pacific Palisades, CA 90272-4648, USA

Jarvis, Kevin (Baseball Player)
Cincinnati Reds
1486 Willowbrooke Cir
Franklin, TN 37069-7200, USA

Jarvis, Lucy
171 W 57th St
New York, NY 10019-2203, USA

Jarvis, Martin
2-4 Noel St.
London, ENGLAND W1V 3RB, UNITED KINGDOM (UK)

Jarvis, Pat (Baseball Player)
Atlanta Braves
4201 Providence Ln
Tucker, GA 30084-2630, USA

Jarvis, Ray (Baseball Player)
Boston Red Sox
15 Higgins St Apt 106
Smithfield, RI 02917-4033, USA

Jarvis, Ray (Football Player)
Atlanta Falcons
18320 Taywood Cir Apt 102
Brookfield, WI 53045-5681, USA

Jason, Harvey
1280 Sunset Plaza Dr
Los Angeles, CA 90069-1245, USA

Jason, Sybil (Actor)
19200 Salt Lake Pl
Northridge, CA 91326-2345, USA

Jason & deMarco (Music Group)
c/o Staff Member RJN Music!
8033 W Sunset Blvd # 574
West Hollywood, CA 90046-2401, USA

Jason Shane, Scott
c/o Paulo Andres LINK Talent Group
4741 Laurel Canyon Blvd Ste 106
Valley Village, CA 91607-5907, USA

Jasper, Edward (Football Player)
Philadelphia Eagles
110 N Price St
Troup, TX 75789-1429, USA

Jasrai, Puntsagiin (Prime Minister)
Prime Minister's Office
Ulan Bator, MONGOLIA

Jaster, Larry (Baseball Player)
St Louis Cardinals
1105 Mill Creek Dr
Saint Johns, FL 32259-8973, USA

Jastremski, Chet (Swimmer)
1920 E 3rd St
Bloomington, IN 47401-3739, USA

Jastrow, Terry L (Director)
13201 Old Oak Ln
Los Angeles, CA 90049-2501, USA

Jastrow II, Kenneth M (Business Person)
Temple-Inland Inc
303 S Temple Dr
Diboll, TX 75941-2419, USA

Jata, Paul (Baseball Player)
Detroit Tigers
9276 SE 130th Loop
Summerfield, FL 34491-9451, USA

Jathar, Anjali (Actor, Bollywood)
Anand Ashram 1st Floor Building 22
Pandita Rambai Road Gamdevi
Mumbai, MS 400007, INDIA

Jatoi, Ghulan Mustafa (Prime Minister)
Jatoi House
18 Khayaban-E-Shamsheer Housing #V
Karachi, PAKISTAN

Jauron, Dick M (Coach, Football Coach, Football Player)
Detroit Lions
602 Wharton Dr
Lake Forest, IL 60045-4827, USA

Javan, Ali (Physicist)
12 Hawthome St
Cambridge, MA 02138, USA

Javed, Miandad Khan (Cricketer)
Pakistani Crciket Control Board
Gaddafi Stadium
Lahore, PAKISTAN

Javerbaum, David (Writer)
c/o Staff Member 3 Arts Entertainment Inc
9460 Wilshire Blvd Fl 7
Beverly Hills, CA 90212-2713, USA

Javier Galvan Y Fama (Music Group)
c/o Staff Member Sony Music Miami
605 Lincoln Rd Fl 7
Miami Beach, FL 33139-2900, USA

Javierre Ortas, Antonio M Cardinal (Religious Leader)
Via Rusticucci 13
Rome 00193, ITALY

Jaworski, Marian Cardinal (Religious Leader)
Mytropolycha Kuria Latynskoho
Ploscha Katedraina 1
29008, UKRAINE

Jaworski, Ron
8 Silver Hill Ln
Voorhees, NJ 08043-4732, USA

Jaworski, Ronald V (Ron) (Football Player, Sportscaster)
Los Angeles Rams
200 Golfview Dr
Blackwood, NJ 08012-5553, USA

Jax, Garth (Football Player)
Dallas Cowboys
4124 E Hazelwood St
Phoenix, AZ 85018-3747, USA

Jay, Joey (Baseball Player)
Milwaukee Braves
7209 Battenwood Ct
Tampa, FL 33615-2023, USA

Jay, Ken (Musician)
Andy Gould Mgmt
9100 Wilshire Blvd Ste 400W
Beverly Hills, CA 90212-3464, USA

Jay, Natalie
6230 Wilshire Blvd # 153
Los Angeles, CA 90048-5104, USA

Jay, Peter (Government Official)
Hensington Farmhouse
Woodstock
Oxon OX20 1LH, UNITED KINGDOM (UK)

Jay, Ricky (Actor)
Simone
1790 Broadway Ste 1000
New York, NY 10019-1412, USA

Jay, Tony (Actor)
c/o Staff Member Pakula/King & Associates
9229 W Sunset Blvd Ste 315
Los Angeles, CA 90069-3403, USA

Jay & The Americans
1045 Pomme De Pin Ln
New Port Richey, FL 34655-5627, USA

Jay & The Techniques
4250 Aia South #D-11
St Augustine, FL 32080, USA

Jaya Pradha (Actor, Bollywood)
202 Juhu Princes Juhu Beach
Juhu
Bombay, MS 400 049, INDIA

Jayabharathi (Actor, Bollywood)
75 4th Cross Street
Loghia Colony Saligramam
Chennai, TN 600093, INDIA

Jayachitra (Actor, Bollywood)
Lynwood Avenue 9 Lady Madhavan Nair Road
Mahalingapuram Gandhi Nagar
Chennai, TN 600093, INDIA

Jayamalini (Actor, Bollywood)
1 1st Mail Road
Thirunagar
Chennai, TN 600026, INDIA

Jayanthi (Actor, Bollywood)
873 19th Main Bana Shankari
II Stage
Bangalore, KA 500070, INDIA

Jayapradha (Actor, Bollywood)
1 Hindi Prachara Sabha Road
T Nagar
Chennai, TN 600017, INDIA

Jayasudha (Actor, Bollywood)
Veenas Colony
9-13 II Street
Chennai, TN 600018, INDIA

Jaymes, Terry (Radio Personality)
c/o Staff Member The Lex & Terry Morning Radio Network
11700 Central Pkwy
Jacksonville, FL 32224-2600, USA

Jayne, Billy
8521 Nash Dr
Los Angeles, CA 90046-7705, USA

Jayston, Michael (Actor)
Michael Whitehall
125 Gloucester Road
London SW7 4TE, UNITED KINGDOM (UK)

Jazz Crusaders, The (Music Group)
Universal
225 W 57th St Fl 5
New York, NY 10019-2136, USA

Jazzyfatnastees (Music Group)
c/o Staff Member Paradigm (Monterey)
509 Hartnell St
Monterey, CA 93940-2825, USA

Jbara, Gregory (Actor)
c/o Marilyn Szatmary SMS Talent Inc
8730 W Sunset Blvd Ste 440
Los Angeles, CA 90069-2277, USA

JBJ (Musician)
Q Prime
729 7th Ave Rm 1600
New York, NY 10019-6880, USA

Jean (Royalty)
Grand Ducal Palace
PB 331
2013, LUXEMBOURG

Jean, Gloria (Actor, Musician)
3844 W Channel Islands Blvd # 166
Oxnard, CA 93035-4001, USA

Jean, Wyclef (Musician)
c/o Sara Ramaker Paradigm (LA)
360 N Crescent Dr
North Bldg
Beverly Hills, CA 90210-6820, USA

Jean-Baptiste, Marianne (Actor)
Innovative Artists
1505 10th St
Santa Monica, CA 90401-2805, USA

Jean-Paul, Gaultier (Designer, Fashion Designer)
Jean-Paul Gaultier SA
70 Galerie Vivienne
Paris 75002, FRANCE

Jeangerard, Robert (Bob) (Basketball Player)
1930 Belmont Ave
San Carlos, CA 94070-4731, USA

Jeanmaire, ZiZi (Actor, Ballerina)
Ballets Roland Petit
20 Blvd Gabes
Marseilles 13008, FRANCE

Jeanrenaud, Joan (Musician)
Kronos Quartet
1235 9th Ave
San Francisco, CA 94122-2306, USA

Jecha, Ralph (Football Player)
Chicago Bears
717 Vinewood Ave
Willow Springs, IL 60480-1523, USA

Jee, Elizabeth (Actor)
Commercials Unlimited
190 N Canon Dr Ste 302
Beverly Hills, CA 90210-5314, USA

Jee, Rupert (Business Person)
Hello Deli
213 W 53rd St
New York, NY 10019-5805, USA

Jeetendra (Actor, Bollywood)
Plot No 26 Greater Bombay Co-Op
Society
Gulmohar Cross Road No 5 JVPD Scheme
Mumbai, MS 400049, INDIA

Jeffcoat, Don (Actor)
c/o Staff Member The House of
Representatives
211 S Beverly Dr Ste 208
Beverly Hills, CA 90212-3879, USA

Jeffcoat, Hal (Baseball Player)
Chicago Cubs
4016 W Wisconsin Ave
Tampa, FL 33616-1136, USA

Jeffcoat, James W (Jim) (Football Player)
Dallas Cowboys
5135 Summit Hill Dr
Dallas, TX 75287-7537, USA

Jeffcoat, Mike (Baseball Player)
Cleveland Indians
7003 Jeffcoat Ln
Pine Bluff, AR 71603-4372, USA

Jefferies, Gregg (Baseball Player)
New York Mets
7806 Bernal Ave
Pleasanton, CA 94588-7050, USA

Jeffers, Eve Jihan (Actor)
c/o Staff Member William Morris Agency
(WMA-LA)
1 William Morris Pl
Beverly Hills, CA 90212-4261, USA

Jeffers, Patrick (Football Player)
Denver Broncos
5810 Buckpasser Cv
Austin, TX 78746-1450, USA

Jeffers, Rusty (Athlete)
PO Box 30081
Phoenix, AZ 85046-0081, USA

Jefferson, George (Athlete, Track Athlete)
9414 Petit Cir
Ventura, CA 93004-2213, USA

Jefferson, James (Football Player)
Seattle Seahawks
11220 NE 53rd St
Kirkland, WA 98033-7595, USA

Jefferson, Jesse (Baseball Player)
Baltimore Orioles
1421 Railroad Ave
Midlothian, VA 23113-4330, USA

Jefferson, John (Football Player)
San Diego Chargers
43590 Merchant Mill Ter
Leesburg, VA 20176-8228, USA

Jefferson, Margo (Journalist)
New York Times
229 W 43rd St
Editorial Dept
New York, NY 10036-3959, USA

Jefferson, Reggie (Baseball Player)
Cincinnati Reds
2693 Miccosukee Rd
Tallahassee, FL 32308-5412, USA

Jefferson, Richard (Basketball Player)
New Jersey Nets
390 Murray Hill Pkwy
East Rutherford, NJ 07073-2109, USA

Jefferson, Roy (Football Player)
Pittsburgh Steelers
8813 Queen Elizabeth Blvd
Annandale, VA 22003-4247, USA

Jefferson, Stan (Baseball Player)
New York Mets
2420 Hunter Ave Apt 3E
Bronx, NY 10475-5644, USA

Jefferson, Thad (Football Player)
Houston Oilers
PO Box 1552
Rialto, CA 92377-1552, USA

Jefferson Starship (Music Group)
c/o Staff Member Mission Control
15030 Ventura Blvd # 541
Sherman Oaks, CA 91403-5470, USA

Jeffires, Haywood (Football Player)
Houston Oilers
3818 Hanberry Ln
Pearland, TX 77584-4951, USA

Jeffory, Dawn (Actor)
c/o Network Solutions
PO Box 447
Herndon, VA 20172-0447, USA

Jeffre, Justin (Musician)
DAS Communications
83 Riverside Dr
New York, NY 10024-5713, USA

Jeffrey, Arthur F (War Hero)
752 Juniper Glen Ct
Ballwin, MO 63021-7330, USA

Jeffrey, Richard C (Misc)
55 Patton Ave
Princeton, NJ 08540-5251, USA

Jeffreys, Anne (Actor)
18915 Nordhoff St Ste 5
Northridge, CA 91324-3790, USA

Jeffries, Chris (Basketball Player)
Toronto Raptors
Air Canada Center
40 Bay St
Toronto, ON M5J 2NB, CANADA

Jeffries, Doug (Adult Film Star)
c/o Staff Member Diva Central Inc
7510 W Sunset Blvd Ste 1445
Los Angeles, CA 90046-3408, USA

Jeffries, Herb (Musician)
Flaming-O Productions
44489 Town Center Way
Palm Desert, CA 92260-2723, USA

Jeffries, Jared (Basketball Player)
Washington Wizards
601 F St NW
Mci Centre
Washington, DC 20004-1605, USA

Jeffries, Lionel (Actor, Director)
International Creative Mgmt
76 Oxford St
London, ENGLAND W1N 0AX, UNITED
KINGDOM (UK)

Jelen, Ben (Musician)
c/o Staff Member Maverick Recording Co
(LA)
3300 Warner Blvd
Burbank, CA 91505-4632, USA

Jelesky, Tom (Football Player)
Philadelphia Eagles
9556 W 1160 N
Demotte, IN 46310-9634, USA

Jelic, Chris (Baseball Player)
New York Mets
33 Allegheny Ave Apt 5
Cuddy, PA 15031-9763, USA

Jelks, Greg
Philadelphia Phillies
615 Bay Springs Rd
Centre, AL 35960-1212, USA

Jelley, Thomas (Football Player)
Pittsburgh Steelers
200 Tabernacle Rd
Black Mountain, NC 28711-7733, USA

Jellicoe, George P J R (Government
Official)
Tidcombe Manor
Tidcombe near Marlborough
Wilts SN8 2SL, UNITED KINGDOM (UK)

Jeltz, Steve (Baseball Player)
Philadelphia Phillies
10211 Ura Ln
Denver, CO 80260-6360, USA

Jem (Musician)
c/o Staff Member ATO Records
157 Chambers St Fl 12
New York, NY 10007-1015, USA

Jemison, Antawn (Basketball Player)
Washington Wizards
601 F St NW
Mci Centre
Washington, DC 20004-1605, USA

Jemison, Eddie (Actor)
c/o Gleb Klioner Schachter Entertainment
1157 S Beverly Dr Fl 2
Los Angeles, CA 90035-1119, USA

Jemison, Theodore J (Religious Leader)
National Bapist Convention USA
1620 Whites Creek Pike
Nashville, TN 37207, USA

Jencks, William P (Misc)
11 Revere St
Lexington, MA 02420-4419, USA

Jendresen, Erik (Writer)
CAA
9830 Wilshire Blvd
Beverly Hills, CA 90212-1804, USA

Jenes Jr, Theodore G (General)
809 169th Pl SW
Lynnwood, WA 98037-3307, USA

Jeni, Richard (Comedian)
c/o Staff Member Agency for the
Performing Arts (APA-LA)
405 S Beverly Dr
Beverly Hills, CA 90212-4416, USA

Jenifer, Franklyn G (Educator)
University of Texas at Dallas
President's Office
Richardson, TX 75081, USA

Jenke, Noel (Football Player)
Minnesota Vikings
17665 Bonnie Ln
Brookfield, WI 53045-7800, USA

Jenkin of Roding, Patrick F (Government
Official)
703 Howard House
Dolphin Square
London SW1V 3PQ, UNITED KINGDOM
(UK)

Jenkins, Alfred le Sesne (Diplomat)
PO Box 586
Stalsama High Knob
Front Royal, VA 22630-0013, USA

Jenkins, Bill (Grumpy) (Misc)
Jenkins Competition
153 Pennsylvania Ave
Malvern, PA 19355-2419, USA

Jenkins, Carter (Actor)
c/o Staff Member Amsel Eisenstadt &
Frazier Inc
5055 Wilshire Blvd Ste 865
Los Angeles, CA 90036-6109, USA

Jenkins, Charlie (Athlete, Track Athlete)
Once Rca Dome
Indianapolis, IN 46225, USA

Jenkins, Daniel (Actor)
S M S Talent
8730 W Sunset Blvd Ste 440
Los Angeles, CA 90069-2277, USA

Jenkins, David W (Figure Skater)
5947 S Atlanta Ave
Tulsa, OK 74105-7545, USA

Jenkins, Dean (Hockey Player)
405 Great Rd Apt 10
Acton, MA 01720-4026, USA

Jenkins, Don (Football Player)
Baltimore Colts
49 W Main St
Frostburg, MD 21532-1640, USA

Jenkins, Don J (War Hero)
3783 Bowling Green Rd
Morgantown, KY 42261-8205, USA

Jenkins, Ed (Football Player)
Miami Dolphins
1750 Washington St Ste B1
Boston, MA 02118-1831, USA

Jenkins, Ferguson (Baseball Player)
Philadelphia Phillies
41913 N Signal Hill Ct
Phoenix, AZ 85086-1919, USA

Jenkins, Fletcher (Football Player)
Baltimore Colts
2347 S J St
Tacoma, WA 98405-3831, USA

Jenkins, Geoff (Baseball Player)
Colorado Rockies
6683 E Judson Rd
Paradise Valley, AZ 85253-4369, USA

Jenkins, George (Designer, Director)
2402 4th St Apt 10
Santa Monica, CA 90405-3668, USA

Jenkins, Hayes Alan (Figure Skater)
3183 Regency Pl
Westlake, OH 44145-6735, USA

Jenkins, Izel (Football Player)
Philadelphia Eagles
5106 Masters Ln N
Wilson, NC 27896-9136, USA

Jenkins, James (Baseball Player)
Cincinnati Indianapolis Clowns
630 Malcolm X Blvd
New York, NY 10037-1247, USA

Jenkins, Jerry B (Writer)
Tyndale House Publishers
PO Box 80
351 Executive Dr
Wheaton, IL 60189-0080, USA

Jenkins, Kackie (Butch) (Actor)
PO Box 541G
Fairview, NC 28730, USA

Jenkins, Ken (Actor)
c/o Chris Schmidt *Paradigm (LA)*
360 N Crescent Dr
North Bldg
Beverly Hills, CA 90210-6820, USA

Jenkins, Kerry (Football Player)
New York Jets
5492 Scout Trace Ln
Birmingham, AL 35244-3912, USA

Jenkins, Kris (Football Player)
Carolina Panthers
309 E Morehead St Apt 622
Charlotte, NC 28202-2310, USA

Jenkins, Loren (Journalist)
Washington Post
Editorial Dept
1150 15th St NW
Washington, DC 20071-0001, USA

Jenkins, Marilyn (Baseball Player)
1511 Van Auken St SE
Grand Rapids, MI 49508-2511, USA

Jenkins, Mark (Writer)
c/o Staff Member *HarperCollins Publishers*
10 E 53rd St Fl 17
New York, NY 10022-5244, USA

Jenkins, Patty (Director, Writer)
c/o Brad Wyman *Junction Films*
415 N Camden Dr
Beverly Hills, CA 90210-4410, USA

Jenkins, Paul (Artist)
Image Terrae
PO Box 6833
Yorkville Station
New York, NY 10128, USA

Jenkins, Richard (Actor)
c/o Staff Member *Gersh Agency, The (LA)*
232 N Canon Dr
Beverly Hills, CA 90210-5302, USA

Jenkins, Robert (Football Player)
Los Angeles Rams
2878 Fieldview Ter
San Ramon, CA 94583-1900, USA

Jenkins, Stephan (Musician)
Eric Godtland Mgmt
5715 Claremont Ave # C
Oakland, CA 94618-1279, USA

Jenner, Brody (Reality TV Star)
c/o Spencer Pratt *Innovator Management*
8899 Beverly Blvd Ste 629
Los Angeles, CA 90048-2448, USA

Jenner, Bruce (Athlete)
c/o Evan Morgenstein *PMG Sports*
700 Evanvale Ct
Cary, NC 27518-2806, USA

Jenney, Lucinda
1505 10th St
Santa Monica, CA 90401-2805, USA

Jennings, Bill (Baseball Player)
St Louis Browns
7065 Foxcroft Dr
Affton, MO 63123-1648, USA

Jennings, Dave (Football Player)
New York Giants
1 Briarcliff Rd
Upper Saddle River, NJ 07458-1401, USA

Jennings, Delbert O (War Hero)
2503 Aspinwall Rd NW
Olympia, WA 98502-1567, USA

Jennings, Doug
Oakland A's
3030 Canterbury Dr
Boca Raton, FL 33434-3348, USA

Jennings, Garth (Director)
c/o Frank Wuliger *Gersh Agency, The (LA)*
232 N Canon Dr
Beverly Hills, CA 90210-5302, USA

Jennings, Jason (Baseball Player)
Colorado Rockies
5274 Monterey Dr
Frisco, TX 75034-4087, USA

Jennings, Keith (Football Player)
Dallas Cowboys
3424 W Torreys Peak Dr
Superior, CO 80027-4638, USA

Jennings, Ken (Actor)
c/o Staff Member *JEOPARDY!*
10202 Washington Blvd
Culver City, CA 90232-3119, USA

Jennings, Lyfe (Musician)
c/o Staff Member *Sony/Columbia/CBS Records*
550 Madison Ave
New York, NY 10022-3211, USA

Jennings, Lynn (Athlete, Track Athlete)
17 Cushing Rd
Newmarket, NH 03857-1720, USA

Jennings, Richard (Football Player)
Oakland Raiders
6499 Park Riviera Way
Sacramento, CA 95831-1053, USA

Jennings, Robert B (Doctor)
Duke University
Medical Center
Pathology Dept
Durham, NC 27710-0001, USA

Jennings, Robert Y (Judge)
61 Bridle Way
Grantchester
Cambridge CB3 9NY, UNITED
KINGDOM (UK)

Jennings, Robin (Baseball Player)
Chicago Cubs
7773 Shootingstar Dr
Springfield, VA 22152-3105, USA

Jennings, Shooter (Musician)
c/o Staff Member *Paradigm (Monterey)*
509 Hartnell St
Monterey, CA 93940-2825, USA

Jennings, Stanford (Football Player)
Cincinnati Bengals
215 Jasmine Way
Alpharetta, GA 30004-4254, USA

Jennings, Will (Songwriter, Writer)
Gorfaine/Schwartz
4111 W Alameda Ave Ste 509
Burbank, CA 91505-4171, USA

Jenrette, Richard H (Business Person)
67 E 93rd St
New York, NY 10128-1331, USA

Jens, Salome (Actor)
Badgley Connor Talent
1680 Vine St Ste 1016
Los Angeles, CA 90028-8800, USA

Jens, Walter (Writer)
Sonnenstr 5
Tubingen, GERMANY

Jensen, Arthur R (Misc)
3330 S Lake Dr
Kelseyville, CA 95451-9042, USA

Jensen, Bob (Football Player)
Chicago Rockets
72420 Morningstar Rd
Rancho Mirage, CA 92270-4072, USA

Jensen, Dan
PO Box 567
Greendale, WI 53129-0567, USA

Jensen, Debra (Model)
31441 Santa Margarita Pkwy # 322
Rancho Santa Margarita, CA 92688-1836, USA

Jensen, Derrick (Football Player)
Oakland Raiders
147 Downing St
Panama City, FL 32413-3650, USA

Jensen, Elwood V (Misc)
Karolinska Institute
Medical Nutrition Dept
Huddinge 141 86, SWEDEN

Jensen, James (Misc)
Brigham Young University
Geology Dept
Provo, UT 84602, USA

Jensen, Jerry (Football Player)
Carolina Panthers
2714 86th St SE
Everett, WA 98208-3548, USA

Jensen, Jim (Football Player)
Miami Dolphins
8244 NW 9th St
Plantation, FL 33324-1208, USA

Jensen, Jim D (Football Player)
Dallas Cowboys
239 Habitat Cir
Windsor, CO 80550-6197, USA

Jensen, Karen (Actor)
9363 Wilshire Blvd # 212
Beverly Hills, CA 90210, USA

Jensen, Luke (Tennis Player)
370 Ferry Lndg NW
Atlanta, GA 30328-3539, USA

Jensen, Marcus (Baseball Player)
San Francisco Giants
19550 N Grayhawk Dr Unit 1134
Scottsdale, AZ 85255-3987, USA

Jensen, Maren (Actor)
Kessler Schneider Co
15260 Ventura Blvd Ste 1040
Sherman Oaks, CA 91403-5345, USA

Jensen, Roger W (Senator)
3542 Pennyroyal Rd
Port Charlotte, FL 33953-4606, USA

Jensen, Ryan (Baseball Player)
San Francisco Giants
4070 Petersen Ln
West Valley, UT 84120-3256, USA

Jensen Jr, James W (Cinematographer)
28853 Garnet Hill Ct
Agoura Hills, CA 91301-2130, USA

Jeremiah, David E (Admiral)
2898 Melanie Ln
Oakton, VA 22124-1809, USA

Jeremy, Ron (Adult Film Star)
c/o Staff Member *Coast II Coast Entertainment (LA)*
3350 Wilshire Blvd Ste 1200
Los Angeles, CA 90010-1836, USA

Jericho, Chris (Y2J) (Wrestler)
c/o Staff Member *World Wrestling Entertainment (WWE)*
1241 E Main St
Stamford, CT 06902-3520, USA

Jerkens, H Allen (Horse Racer)
9509 242nd St
Floral Park, NY 11001-3906, USA

Jermann, David (Artist)
2 Union St
Sparkill, NY 10976, USA

Jernberg, Sixten (Skier)
Fritidsby 780
Lima 7806, SWEDEN

Jernigan, Tamara E (Tammy) (Astronaut)
4268 Brindisi Pl
Pleasanton, CA 94566-2238, USA

Jerusalem, Siegfried (Opera Singer)
Sudring 9
Eckental 90542, GERMANY

Jervey, Travis (Football Player)
Green Bay Packers
747 Glossy Ibis Ln
Kiawah Island, SC 29455-5912, USA

Jerzembeck, Mike (Baseball Player)
New York Yankees
22011 Hartland Ave
Queens Village, NY 11427-1227, USA

Jessamy, Charles (Football Player)
New York Giants
1836 S Shenandoah St
Los Angeles, CA 90035-4327, USA

Jessee, Michael A (Financier)
Federal Home Loan Bank
1 Financial Ctr
Boston, MA 02111-2621, USA

Jessie, Ron (Football Player)
Detroit Lions
202 17th St Apt B
Huntington Beach, CA 92648-8426, USA

Jessie, Tim (Football Player)
Washington Redskins
155 Cedar Ave
Shepherdsville, KY 40165-6465, USA

Jessup, Bill (Football Player)
San Francisco 49ers
3342 Bradbury Rd Unit 14
Los Alamitos, CA 90720-4369, USA

Jestadt, Garry (Baseball Player)
Montreal Expos
9495 E San Salvador Dr Ste 100
Scottsdale, AZ 85258-5553, USA

Jester, Virgil (Baseball Player)
Boston Braves
8130 Raleigh Pl
Westminster, CO 80031-4317, USA

Jet (Actor)
c/o Staff Member *Creative Artists Agency LCC (CAA-LA)*
2000 Avenue Of The Stars
Los Angeles, CA 90067-4700, USA

Jeter, Derek (Athlete, Baseball Player)
c/o Team Member *New York Yankees*
Yankee Stadium
161st St & River Ave
Bronx, NY 10451, USA

Jeter, Gary M (Football Player)
New York Giants
13276 Danbury Ct Apt 206
North Royalton, OH 44133-7468, USA

Jeter, John (Baseball Player)
Pittsburgh Pirates
4717 Murdock Ave
Bronx, NY 10466-1011, USA

Jeter, Perry (Football Player)
Chicago Bears
772 Lincoln Blvd
Steubenville, OH 43952-3256, USA

Jeter, Robert D (Bob) (Football Player)
Green Bay Packers
7147 S Paxton Ave
Chicago, IL 60649-2523, USA

Jeter, Shawn (Baseball Player)
Chicago White Sox
4287 Walford St
Columbus, OH 43224-2342, USA

Jeter, Tommy (Football Player)
Philadelphia Eagles
14 Slate Path Dr
Spring, TX 77382-2009, USA

Jeter, Tony (Football Player)
Pittsburgh Steelers
71 S Orange Ave
South Orange, NJ 07079-1715, USA

Jethro Tull (Music Group)
c/o Staff Member *William Morris Agency (WMA-LA)*
1 William Morris Pl
Beverly Hills, CA 90212-4261, USA

Jets, The (Music Group)
Lustig Talent Enterprises
PO Box 770850
Orlando, FL 32877-0850, USA

Jetsons (Music Group)
Signature Entertainment
5727 Topanga Canyon Blvd Apt 3
Woodland Hills, CA 91367-4847, USA

Jett, Brent W (Astronaut)
5509 Crawford St
Houston, TX 77004-7119, USA

Jett, Jack E (Television Host)
c/o Len Evans *Project Publicity*
312 W 53rd St
New York, NY 10019-5743, USA

Jett, James (Football Player)
Oakland Raiders
PO Box 430
Kearneysville, WV 25430-0430, USA

Jett, Joan (Musician)
Blackheart Records Group
636 Broadway
New York, NY 10012-2607, USA

Jett, John (Football Player)
Dallas Cowboys
18521 Northumberland Hwy
Reedville, VA 22539-3412, USA

Jetton, Paul (Football Player)
Cincinnati Bengals
417 S Canyonwood Dr
Dripping Springs, TX 78620-4286, USA

Jeunet, Jean-Pierre (Director)
International Creative Mgmt
8942 Wilshire Blvd # 219
Beverly Hills, CA 90211-1908, USA

Jevanord, Oystein (Musician)
Bandana Mgmt
11 Elvaston Place
#300
London SW7 5QC, UNITED KINGDOM (UK)

Jewell, Buddy (Musician)
c/o Staff Member *William Morris Agency (WMA-TN)*
1600 Division St Ste 300
Nashville, TN 37203-2755, USA

Jewell, Geri (Actor)
c/o Staff Member *Kazarian/Spencer & Assoc (LA)*
11969 Ventura Blvd
Box 7409 Fl 3
Studio City, CA 91604-2630, USA

Jewett, Robert (Football Player)
Chicago Bears
991 N Shore Dr
Springport, MI 49284-9414, USA

Jewison, Norman F (Actor, Director, Producer, Writer)
c/o Staff Member *Yorktown Productions Ltd*
18 Gloucester Ln
Floor 5
Toronto, ON M4Y 1L5, CANADA

Jewitt-Beckett, Christine (Baseball Player)
PO Box 126
Stewart Valley, SK S0N 2P0, CANADA

Jhabvala, Ruth Prawer (Writer)
400 E 52nd St
New York, NY 10022-6404, USA

Jhene (Musician)
c/o Chris Stokes *Ultimate Group, The*
848 N La Cienega Blvd Ste 201
West Hollywood, CA 90069-6600, USA

Jhulka, Ayesha (Actor, Bollywood)
102 Tirupati Apartments
7 Bungalows Versova Andheri (W)
Mumbai, MS 400061, INDIA

Jia, Li (Misc)
Duke University
Medical Center
Hematology Dept
Durham, NC 27708-0001, USA

Jiahua, Zou (Government Official)
Communist Party Central Committee
Jhong Nan Hai
Beijing, CHINA

Jiang, Tian (Musician)
Columbia Artists Mgmt Inc
1790 Broadway Fl 6
New York, NY 10019-1412, USA

Jiang, Tiefeng (Artist)
Fingerhut Gallery
690 Bridgeway
Sausalito, CA 94965-2251, USA

Jiang, Zemin (President)
Central Military Commitee
Zhonganahai
Beijing, CHINA

Jiles, Dwayne (Football Player)
Philadelphia Eagles
3712 Churchill Ct
Plano, TX 75075-6119, USA

Jiles, Pam (Athlete, Track Athlete)
2623 Wisteria St
New Orleans, LA 70122-6041, USA

Jillian, Ann (Actor)
PO Box 57739
Sherman Oaks, CA 91413-2739, USA

Jim & Jesse
PO Box 27
Gallatin, TN 37066, USA

Jimenez, Carlos (Architect)
Jimenez Architectural Design Studio
1116 Willard St
Houston, TX 77006-1238, USA

Jimenez, Flaco (Misc)
DeLeon Artists
4031 Panama Ct
Piedmont, CA 94611-4930, USA

Jimenez, Manny (Baseball Player)
Kansas City A's
24003 Colmar Ln
Murrieta, CA 92562-1978, USA

Jimenez, Nicario (Artist)
5531 Teak Wood Dr
Naples, FL 34119-2515, USA

Jimenez Pons, Eduardo (Writer)
c/o Gabriel Blanco *Gabriel Blanco Iglesias (Mexico)*
Rio Balsas 35-32
Colonia Cuauhtemoc
DF 06500, MEXICO

Jiminez, Miguel (Baseball Player)
Oakland A's
128 Post Ave
New York, NY 10034-3432, USA

Jimmy, Jimmy
44 Harton Way Kings Heath
Birmingham, ENGLAND 146 PF, UNITED KINGDOM (UK)

Jimmy Eat World (Music Group)
GAS
722 Seward St
Los Angeles, CA 90038-3504, USA

Jimmy Jam
9830 Wilshire Blvd
Beverly Hills, CA 90212-1804, USA

Jin, Svoboda (Director)
Na Balkane 120
Prague 3, CZECH REPUBLIC

Jindrak, Mark (Wrestler)
2355 Reyer Rd
Auburn, NY 13021, USA

Jirsa, Ron (Coach)
University of Georgia
Athletic Dept
Athens, GA 30613, USA

Jiscke, Martin C (Educator)
Iowa State University
President's Office
Ames, IA 50011-0001, USA

Jive Bunny
5-7 Sixth Williams St Parthgate
So. Yorkshire, ENGLAND S62 6EP, UNITED KINGDOM (UK)

Joanou, Phil (Director)
Creative Artists Agency
9830 Wilshire Blvd
Beverly Hills, CA 90212-1804, USA

Job, Brian (Swimmer)
PO Box 70427
Sunnyvale, CA 94086-0427, USA

Jobe, Frank W (Doctor)
Kerlan-Jobe Orthopedic Clinic
501 E Hardy St Ste 200
Inglewood, CA 90301-4057, USA

Jobert, Marlene
8-10 blvd. de Courcelles
Paris 75008, FRANCE

Jobko, William (Football Player)
Los Angeles Rams
770 Fawn Ct
Loganville, GA 30052-3270, USA

Jobrani, Maz (Actor)
c/o Mitchell Stubbs *Mitchell K Stubbs & Assoc (MKS)*
8695 Washington Blvd Ste 204
Culver City, CA 90232-7419, USA

Jobs, Steven P (Business Person, Producer)
Apple Computer
1 Infinite Loop
Cupertino, CA 95014-2084, USA

Jocketty, Walt (Baseball Player)
St Louis Cardinals
1210 Lay Rd
Saint Louis, MO 63124-1872, USA

Jodat, Jim (Football Player)
Los Angeles Rams
25032 Mammoth Cir
El Toro, CA 92630-2515, USA

Jodie, Brett (Baseball Player)
New York Yankees
1359 Corley Mill Rd
Lexington, SC 29072-7635, USA

Joe (Musician)
c/o Staff Member *Jive Records*
137 W 25th St
New York, NY 10001-7216, USA

Joe, Billy (Football Player)
Denver Broncos
3129 Obrien Dr
Tallahassee, FL 32309-2754, USA

Joe, William (Billy) (Football Player)
Florida A&M University
Athletic Dept
Tallahassee, FL 32307, USA

Joel, Billy (Musician, Songwriter, Writer)
c/o Staff Member *Artists Group Intl (AGI)*
150 E 58th St # 19
New York, NY 10155-0002, USA

Joel, Richard M (Educator)
Yeshiva University
500 W 185th St
President's Office
New York, NY 10033-3299, USA

Joelson, Tsianina (Actor)
c/o Sherry Marsh *Marsh Entertainment*
12444 Ventura Blvd Ste 203
Studio City, CA 91604-2409, USA

Joens, Michael (Writer)
c/o Natasha Kern *Natasha Kern Literary Agency*
PO Box 2908
Portland, OR 97208-2908, USA

Joey Z (Musician)
Agency Group Ltd
1775 Broadway Ste 515
New York, NY 10019-1903, USA

Joffee, Roland V (Director, Producer)
Nomad
10351 Santa Monica Blvd Ste 402
Los Angeles, CA 90025-6937, USA

Jofre, Eder (Boxer)
Alamo de Ministero Rocha
Azevedo 373 C Cesar 21-15
Sao Paulo, BRAZIL

Jogis, Chris (Athlete)
7 Birch Rd
Larchmont, NY 10538-1526, USA

Johannesen, Lena (Athlete)
PO Box 325
Culver City, CA 90232-0325, USA

Johannsen, Jake (Actor, Comedian)
c/o Pam Ellis Ellis Talent Group
4705 Laurel Canyon Blvd Ste 300
Valley Village, CA 91607-5901, USA

Johannsson, Kristian (Opera Singer)
Herbert Breslin
119 W 57th St Ste 1505
New York, NY 10019-2401, USA

Johansen, David (Musician)
Agency Group Ltd
1775 Broadway Ste 515
New York, NY 10019-1903, USA

Johansen, Iris (Writer)
Bantam Books
1540 Broadway
New York, NY 10036-4039, USA

Johansen, John M (Architect)
Johansen & Bhavnani
821 Broadway
New York, NY 10003-4658, USA

Johanson, Donald C (Misc)
Arizona State University
Human Origins Institute
Tempe, AZ 85287-0001, USA

Johanson, Erika (Writer)
c/o Gabriel Blanco Gabriel Blanco
Iglesias (Mexico)
Rio Balsas 35-32
Colonia Cuauhtemoc
DF 06500, MEXICO

Johanson, Sue (Actor, Talk Show Host)
c/o Staff Member Sunday Night Sex Show
42 Pardee Ave
Toronto, ON M6K 3H5, CANADA

Johanssen, David
9200 W Sunset Blvd Ste 900
Los Angeles, CA 90069-3604, USA

Johansson, Kathy (Model)
PO Box 13923
Tucson, AZ 85732-3923, USA

Johansson, Ove (Football Player)
Philadelphia Eagles
3511 Goodfellow Ln
Amarillo, TX 79121-1613, USA

Johansson, Paul (Actor)
Gilbertson & Kincaid Mgmt
1330 4th St
Santa Monica, CA 90401-1302, USA

Johansson, Scarlett (Actor)
c/o Scott Lambert William Morris Agency
(WMA-LA)
1 William Morris Pl
Beverly Hills, CA 90212-4261, USA

John, Caspar (Admiral)
Trethewey
Mousehole Penzance
Cornwall, UNITED KINGDOM (UK)

John, David D (Misc)
7 Cyncoed Ave
Cardiff, WALES CF2 6ST, UNITED
KINGDOM (UK)

John, Elton (Musician, Songwriter, Writer)
c/o Staff Member Twenty-First Artists Ltd
(UK)
1 Blythe Rd
London W14 OHG, UNITED KINGDOM
(UK)

John, Gottfried (Actor)
Elisabethweg 4
Utting D-86919, GERMANY

John, Tommy (Baseball Player)
Cleveland Indians
6202 Seton House Ln
Charlotte, NC 28277-4524, USA

John, Tylyn (Model)
813 Harbor Blvd # 133
W Sacramento, CA 95691-2201, USA

Johnny & The Hurricanes
195 Hannum Ave
Rossford, OH 43460-1109, USA

Johns, Bibi
D-82049
Pullach, GERMANY

Johns, Cindy (Actor)
PO Box 369
Arlington, TX 76004-0369, USA

Johns, Daniel (Musician)
John Watson Mgmt
PO Box 281
Sunny Hills, NSW 2010, AUSTRALIA

Johns, Doug (Baseball Player)
Oakland A's
1131 SW 72nd Ave
Plantation, FL 33317-4125, USA

Johns, Freeman (Football Player)
Los Angeles Rams
906 Sally Cir
Wichita Falls, TX 76301-7230, USA

Johns, Glynis (Actor)
2051 N Highland Ave
Los Angeles, CA 90068-3238, USA

Johns, Jasper (Artist)
97 Low Rd # 642
Sharon, CT 06069, USA

Johns, Lori (Race Car Driver)
4418 Congressional Dr
Corpus Christi, TX 78413-2624, USA

Johns, Marcus (Actor)
c/o Sharon Lane Lane Management Group
13017 Woodbridge St
Studio City, CA 91604-1431, USA

Johns, Milton (Actor)
78 Temple Sheen Rd
London SW14 7RJ, ENGLAND

Johns, Stratford
29 Mostyn Rd. Merton Park
London, ENGLAND SW19 3LL, UNITED
KINGDOM (UK)

Johnson, Adam (Baseball Player)
Minnesota Twins
13513 Creekside Dr
Oklahoma City, OK 73131-1294, USA

Johnson, Addison (Cartoonist)
King Features Syndicate
888 7th Ave Ste 201
New York, NY 10106-0201, USA

Johnson, Alex (Baseball Player)
Philadelphia Phillies
18425 Bretton Dr
Detroit, MI 48223-1311, USA

Johnson, Alexz (Actor)
c/o Staff Member William Morris Agency
(WMA-LA)
1 William Morris Pl
Beverly Hills, CA 90212-4261, USA

Johnson, Allen (Athlete, Track Athlete)
Octagon
1751 Pinnacle Dr Ste 1500
McLean, VA 22102-3833, USA

Johnson, Alonzo (Football Player)
New Orleans Saints
PO Box 134
Stanley, NC 28164-0134, USA

Johnson, Amy Jo (Actor)
c/o Staff Member Burstein Company, The
15304 W Sunset Blvd Ste 208
Pacific Palisades, CA 90272-3656, USA

Johnson, Andreas (Musician)
c/o Staff Member United Stage Artist
PO Box 11029
Stockholm S-10061, SWEDEN

Johnson, Andy (Football Player)
New England Patriots
PO Box 6828
Athens, GA 30604-6828, USA

Johnson, Anne-Marie (Actor)
2522 Silver Lake Ter
Los Angeles, CA 90039-2608, USA

Johnson, Anthony (Football Player)
Indianapolis Colts
752 Peppervine Ave
Jacksonville, FL 32259-5272, USA

Johnson, Art (Baseball Player)
Boston Bees
23 Hemlock Dr
Holden, MA 01520-1617, USA

Johnson, Arte (Actor, Comedian)
2725 Bottlebrush Dr
Los Angeles, CA 90077-2009, USA

Johnson, Ashley (Actor)
Untitled Entertainment
8436 W 3rd St Ste 650
Los Angeles, CA 90048-4131, USA

Johnson, Bart (Baseball Player)
Chicago White Sox
904 Indian Boundary Dr
Westmont, IL 60559-1079, USA

Johnson, Batsey L (Designer, Fashion
Designer)
Betsey Johnson Co
127 E 9th St Ste 703
Los Angeles, CA 90015-1737, USA

Johnson, Ben (Baseball Player)
Chicago Cubs
112 Locksley Dr
Greenwood, SC 29649-9185, USA

Johnson, Betsey (Designer, Fashion
Designer)
c/o Staff Member Betsey Johnson
498 7th Ave Fl 21
New York, NY 10018-6798, USA

Johnson, Beverly (Actor, Model)
c/o Nancy Chaidez Nancy Chaidez &
Associates
6399 Wilshire Blvd Ste 424
Los Angeles, CA 90048-5716, USA

Johnson, Bill (Actor)
c/o Mike Pruitt Actors Clearinghouse
501 N 1H35
Austin, TX 78702, USA

Johnson, Bill (Baseball Player)
Chicago Cubs
14 Rankin Rd
Newark, DE 19711-4851, USA

Johnson, Bill (Football Player)
Cleveland Browns
3399 Hartwood Rd
Cleveland Heights, OH 44112-3027, USA

Johnson, Billy (Baseball Player)
New York Yankees
2903 Lake Forest Dr
Augusta, GA 30909-3025, USA

Johnson, Bob (Baseball Player)
Texas Rangers
265 Quari St
Aurora, CO 80011-8339, USA

Johnson, Bob (Football Player)
Cincinnati Bengals
165 Magnolia Ave
Cincinnati, OH 45246-4506, USA

Johnson, Bob D (Baseball Player)
New York Mets
255 Nunan St
Jacksonville, OR 97530-9699, USA

Johnson, Bob W (Baseball Player)
Kansas City A's
1474 Barclay St
Saint Paul, MN 55106-1406, USA

Johnson, Brian (Baseball Player)
San Diego Padres
7595 E Placita Vista Del Bosque
Tucson, AZ 85715-3651, USA

Johnson, Brian (Musician)
11 Leominster Road
Morden
Surrey SA4 6HN, UNITED KINGDOM
(UK)

Johnson, Brooks (Coach)
Stanford University
Athletic Dept
Stanford, CA 94305, USA

Johnson, Bryce (Actor)
c/o Theodore B Gekis Gekis Management
4217 Verdugo View Dr
Los Angeles, CA 90065-4317, USA

Johnson, Butch (Football Player)
9719 Red Oakes Dr
Highlands Ranch, CO 80126-3595, USA

Johnson, Carl (Football Player)
New Orleans Saints
8818 S Shannon Dr
Tempe, AZ 85284-3528, USA

Johnson, Carolyn Dawn (Musician,
Songwriter, Writer)
RPM Mgmt
209 10th Ave S Ste 229
Nashville, TN 37203-0721, USA

Johnson, Cecil (Football Player)
Tampa Bay Buccaneers
1481 NW 103rd St Apt 260
Miami, FL 33147-1409, USA

Johnson, Chad (Football Player)
Cincinnati Bengals
1051 NW 44th St
Miami, FL 33127-2552, USA

Johnson, Charles (Baseball Player)
Chicago American Giants
7832 S Vernon Ave
Chicago, IL 60619-2812, USA

Johnson, Charles L (Charley) (Football Player)
St Louis Cardinals
PO Box 1312
Mesilla, NM 88046-1312, USA

Johnson, Charles R (Writer)
University of Washington
English Dept
Seattle, WA 98105, USA

Johnson, Charlie W (Football Player)
San Francisco 49ers
1400 Willow Ave
Louisville, KY 40204-2506, USA

Johnson, Chris (Actor)
c/o Staff Member *Roklin Management*
8530 Wilshire Blvd Ste 550
Beverly Hills, CA 90211-3133, USA

Johnson, Chuck (Football Player)
Denver Broncos
1203 N Avenue M
Freeport, TX 77541-3611, USA

Johnson, Clark
9560 Wilshire Blvd # 516
Beverly Hills, CA 90212-2427, USA

Johnson, Claude A (Lady Bird) (Ex-First Lady, First Lady)
Lbj Ranch
Stonewall, TX 78671, USA

Johnson, Claude (Juan) (Musician)
Mars Talent
27 L Ambiance Ct
Bardonia, NY 10954-1421, USA

Johnson, Connie (Baseball Player)
Kansas City Monarchs
1900 E 54th St
Kansas City, MO 64130-3301, USA

Johnson, Cornelius (Football Player)
Baltimore Colts
603 Dale St
Highland Springs, VA 23075-1611, USA

Johnson, Courtney (Misc)
408 Tharp Dr
Moraga, CA 94556-2529, USA

Johnson, Curley (Football Player)
Dallas Texans
5512 Wedgefield Rd
Granbury, TX 76049-4411, USA

Johnson, Curt (Producer, Writer)
c/o Evan Corday *Evolution Entertainment (LA)*
901 N Highland Ave
Los Angeles, CA 90038-2412, USA

Johnson, Curtis (Baseball Player)
Kansas City Monarchs
PO Box B-188
St Rose, LA 70087, USA

Johnson, Curtis (Football Player)
Miami Dolphins
2015 Calumet Ave
Toledo, OH 43607-1608, USA

Johnson, Dale (Actor)
c/o Staff Member *LA Models/LA Talent Agency*
7700 W Sunset Blvd Fl 1st
Los Angeles, CA 90046-3913, USA

Johnson, Dane (Baseball Player)
Chicago White Sox
PO Box 465 Stn Main
Medicine Hat, AB T1A 7G2, CANADA

Johnson, Darrell (Baseball Player)
St Louis Browns
3870 Meadow Wood Dr
El Dorado Hills, CA 95762-7545, USA

Johnson, Daryl (Football Player)
Boston Patriots
126 Merrimac St
Newburyport, MA 01950-2446, USA

Johnson, Dave (Baseball Player)
Baltimore Orioles
3202 Woodhollow Cir
Abilene, TX 79606-4211, USA

Johnson, Dave (Baseball Player)
Pittsburgh Pirates
7101 Mount Vista Rd
Kingsville, MD 21087-1728, USA

Johnson, Dave (Misc)
United Garment Workers
4207 Lebanon Pike
Hermitage, TN 37076-1231, USA

Johnson, Davey (Baseball Player)
Baltimore Orioles
1064 Howell Branch Rd
Winter Park, FL 32789-1004, USA

Johnson, David Cay (Journalist)
New York Times
229 W 43rd St
Editorial Dept
New York, NY 10036-3959, USA

Johnson, David (Dave) (Athlete, Track Athlete)
Azusa Pacific University
PO Box 2713
Azusa, CA 91702, USA

Johnson, David G (Economist)
1700 E 56th St Apt 1306
Chicago, IL 60637-1934, USA

Johnson, David W (Business Person)
Campbell Soup Co
1 Campbell Pl
Camden, NJ 08103-1799, USA

Johnson, Demetrios (Football Player)
Detroit Lions
840 Garonne Dr
Ballwin, MO 63021-5656, USA

Johnson, Dennis (Football Player)
Buffalo Bills
675 Maple Ave
Teaneck, NJ 07666-1832, USA

Johnson, Dennis W (Basketball Player)
15003 Chuparosa St
Victorville, CA 92394-2035, USA

Johnson, DerMarr (Basketball Player)
Phoenix Suns
201 E Jefferson St
Phoenix, AZ 85004-2412, USA

Johnson, Dick (Baseball Player)
Chicago Cubs
5001 E Main St Lot 762
Mesa, AZ 85205-8172, USA

Johnson, Don (Actor)
c/o Jason Newman *Untitled Entertainment (LA)*
331 N Maple Dr Fl 3
Beverly Hills, CA 90210-3827, USA

Johnson, Dwayne (The Rock) (Actor)
c/o Darren Statt *United Talent Agency (UTA)*
9560 Wilshire Blvd Ste 500
Beverly Hills, CA 90212-2401, USA

Johnson, Dwight (Football Player)
Philadelphia Eagles
1812 King Cole Dr
Waco, TX 76705-2753, USA

Johnson, Earl (Bowler)
3625 Woody Ln
Minnetonka, MN 55305-4265, USA

Johnson, Earl (Football Player)
New Orleans Saints
340 S Keech St
Daytona Beach, FL 32114-4622, USA

Johnson, Earvin
9100 Wilshire Blvd # 1060
Beverly Hills, CA 90212-3401, USA

Johnson, Edward (Eddie) (Basketball Player)
6133 N 61st Pl
Paradise Valley, AZ 85253-4209, USA

Johnson, Emma (Misc)
Columbia Artists Mgmt Inc
1790 Broadway Fl 6
New York, NY 10019-1412, USA

Johnson, Eric (Actor)
c/o Jai Khanna *Brillstein-Grey Entertainment*
9150 Wilshire Blvd Ste 350
Beverly Hills, CA 90212-3453, USA

Johnson, Eric (Musician)
Joe Priesnitz Artist Mgmt
PO Box 5249
Austin, TX 78763-5249, USA

Johnson, Erik (Baseball Player)
San Francisco Giants
PO Box 2989
San Ramon, CA 94583-7989, USA

Johnson, Ernest (Baseball Player)
Kansas City Monarchs
3106 Bowdoin St
Des Moines, IA 50313-4613, USA

Johnson, Ernie (Baseball Player)
Boston Braves
6350 Polo Club Dr
Cumming, GA 30040-6597, USA

Johnson, Ervin (Basketball Player)
Minnesota Timberwolves
600 1st Ave N
Target Center
Minneapolis, MN 55403-1416, USA

Johnson, Essex (Football Player)
Cincinnati Bengals
1633 E Dimondale Dr
Carson, CA 90746-2914, USA

Johnson, Ezra (Football Player)
Green Bay Packers
2542 Greenfield Ln
Jonesboro, GA 30236-6196, USA

Johnson, Farnham (Football Player)
Chicago Rockets
190 Beech Ave
Winfield, AL 35594, USA

Johnson, Frank (Baseball Player)
San Francisco Giants
1151 Cypress Hill Ln
Stockton, CA 95206-6245, USA

Johnson, Frank (Basketball Player, Coach)
10929 Pebble Run Dr
Silver Spring, MD 20902-3684, USA

Johnson, Gary (Baseball Player)
Anaheim Angels
485 Canyon Oaks Dr Apt F
Oakland, CA 94605-3859, USA

Johnson, Gary (Football Player)
San Diego Chargers
1620 Fullerton St Apt 1314
Shreveport, LA 71107-6415, USA

Johnson, Gary L (Football Player)
450 Oliver Rd
Haughton, LA 71037-8942, USA

Johnson, Georgann (Actor)
218 Glenroy Pl
Los Angeles, CA 90049-2420, USA

Johnson, George (Golfer)
T & J Ventures
PO Box 1038
Lewisville, NC 27023-1038, USA

Johnson, Graham R (Musician)
83 Fordwych Road
London NW2 3TL, UNITED KINGDOM (UK)

Johnson, Gregory C (Astronaut)
19200 Space Center Blvd Apt 2213
Houston, TX 77058-3858, USA

Johnson, Hailey Noelle (Actor)
c/o Staff Member *TalentWorks (LA)*
3500 W Olive Ave Ste 1400
Burbank, CA 91505-5512, USA

Johnson, Hansford T (General)
USAA Capital Corp
9800 Fredericksburg Rd
San Antonio, TX 78284-8899, USA

Johnson, Harold (Boxer)
6101 Morris St
Philadelphia, PA 19144-3763, USA

Johnson, Haynes B (Journalist)
George Washington University
Communications Studies Ctr
Washington, DC 20052-0001, USA

Johnson, Holly (Musician)
Lustig Talent
PO Box 770850
Orlando, FL 32877-0850, USA

Johnson, Howard (Baseball Player)
Detroit Tigers
8597 SE Coconut St
Hobe Sound, FL 33455-2914, USA

Johnson, Ian (Journalist)
Wall Street Journal
200 Liberty St
Editorial Dept
New York, NY 10281-0084, USA

Johnson, J Bradley (Brad) (Football Player)
185 Woodland Way
Athens, GA 30606-4349, USA

Johnson, J J
648 Broadway # 703
New York, NY 10012-2301, USA

Johnson, J Seward (Artist)
Sculpture Foundation
2525 Michigan Ave Ste A6
Santa Monica, CA 90404-4031, USA

Johnson, Jack (Musician)
c/o Tom Chauncey *Partisan Arts*
PO Box 5085
Larkspur, CA 94977-5085, USA

Johnson, James A (Financier)
Federal National Mortgage Assn
3900 Wisconsin Ave NW
Washington, DC 20016-2806, USA

Johnson, James E (Johnnie) (War Hero)
Stables
Hargate Hall Buxton
Derbyshire SK17 8TA, UNITED
KINGDOM (UK)

Johnson, Jamie (Actor, Director, Producer)
Wise and Good Film
217 2nd Ave Apt 1
New York, NY 10003-2705, USA

Johnson, Jannette (Skier)
PO Box 901
Sun Valley, ID 83353-0901, USA

Johnson, Jason (Baseball Player)
Pittsburgh Pirates
PO Box 238
Santa Clara, UT 84765-0238, USA

Johnson, Jason (Football Player)
Indianapolis Colts
7673 Bluebird Ct
Brownsburg, IN 46112-8302, USA

Johnson, Jay (Actor, Comedian)
c/o Staff Member *William Morris Agency*
(WMA-LA)
1 William Morris Pl
Beverly Hills, CA 90212-4261, USA

Johnson, Jay Kenneth (Actor)
c/o Jeff Morrone *Jeff Morrone*
Management
9350 Wilshire Blvd Ste 224
Beverly Hills, CA 90212-3204, USA

Johnson, Jeff (Baseball Player)
New York Yankees
424 N Hardee St
Durham, NC 27703-2254, USA

Johnson, Jenna (Coach, Swimmer)
University of Tennessee
PO Box 15016
Athletic Dept
Knoxville, TN 37901-5016, USA

Johnson, Jerald Penny (Actor)
Susan Smith
1344 N Wetherly Dr
Los Angeles, CA 90069-1817, USA

Johnson, Jerome L (Admiral)
Navy-Marine Corps Releif Society
801 N Randolph St
Arlington, VA 22203, USA

Johnson, Jerry (Baseball Player)
Philadelphia Phillies
16670 Espola Rd
Poway, CA 92064-1630, USA

Johnson, Jesse (Football Player)
New York Jets
3308 Forest Hill Ave
Richmond, VA 23225-3434, USA

Johnson, Jimmie (Race Car Driver)
Jimmie Johnson Racing
PO Box 5599
Concord, NC 28027-1509, USA

Johnson, Jimmy (Cartoonist)
United Feature Syndicate
200 Madison Ave
New York, NY 10016-3911, USA

Johnson, Jimmy (Football Player)
San Francisco 49ers
656 Amaranth Blvd
Mill Valley, CA 94941-2605, USA

Johnson, Joanna (Actor)
c/o Staff Member *William Morris Agency*
(WMA-LA)
1 William Morris Pl
Beverly Hills, CA 90212-4261, USA

Johnson, Joe (Baseball Player)
Atlanta Braves
14 Evergreen Rd
Plainville, MA 02762-1902, USA

Johnson, Joe (Basketball Player)
c/o Staff Member *Atlanta Hawks*
101 Marietta St NW Ste 1900
Centennial Tower
Atlanta, GA 30303-2771, USA

Johnson, Johari (Actor)
H W A Talent
3500 W Olive Ave Ste 1400
Burbank, CA 91505-5512, USA

Johnson, John (Football Player)
San Francisco 49ers
133 Plymouth Dr
Lagrange, GA 30240-8537, USA

Johnson, John H (Football Player)
Chicago Bears
330 S Michigan Ave Apt 1606
Chicago, IL 60604-4453, USA

Johnson, John Henry (Football Player)
San Francisco 49ers
3463 Glendon Ave
Los Angeles, CA 90034-5418, USA

Johnson, Johnny (Football Player)
Phoenix Cardinals
929 Delaware Ave
Santa Cruz, CA 95060-6403, USA

Johnson, Jonathan (Baseball Player)
Texas Rangers
7 Alverston Ct
Irmo, SC 29063-8262, USA

Johnson, Joseph (Football Player)
New York Giants
166 Homestead Hills Cir
Winston Salem, NC 27103-6446, USA

Johnson, Junior (Race Car Driver)
1100 Glen Oaks Dr
Hamptonville, NC 27020-8279, USA

Johnson, Keith (Misc)
Woodworkers of America Union
1622 N Lombard St
Portland, OR 97217-5534, USA

Johnson, Ken (Baseball Player)
Kansas City A's
121 Myrtlewood Dr
Pineville, LA 71360-4325, USA

Johnson, Ken (Baseball Player)
St Louis Cardinals
326 Brookfield St
Wichita, KS 67206-1901, USA

Johnson, Kenneth (Football Player)
Green Bay Packers
536 E 169th St
Carson, CA 90746-1105, USA

Johnson, Kenneth (Football Player)
New York Giants
1334 NW 42nd St
Miami, FL 33142-4812, USA

Johnson, Kenny (Actor)
c/o Josh Katz *United Talent Agency (UTA)*
9560 Wilshire Blvd Ste 500
Beverly Hills, CA 90212-2401, USA

Johnson, Kermit (Football Player)
San Francisco 49ers
3259 Lincoln Ave
Altadena, CA 91001, USA

Johnson, Kevin (Baseball Player,
Sportscaster)
NBC-TV
30 Rockefeller Plz Ste 270E
Sports Dept
New York, NY 10112-0299, USA

Johnson, Keyshawn (Football Player)
c/o Staff Member *Dallas Cowboys*
1 Cowboys Pkwy
Irving, TX 75063-4999, USA

Johnson, Lamar (Baseball Player)
Chicago White Sox
4105 Sangre Trl
Arlington, TX 76016-2972, USA

Johnson, Lamont (Director)
935 Mesa Rd
Monterey, CA 93940-4611, USA

Johnson, Lance (Baseball Player)
St Louis Cardinals
5712 Foxfire Rd
Mobile, AL 36618-2653, USA

Johnson, Larry (Baseball Player)
Cleveland Indians
4733 Lee Rd Apt 101
Cleveland, OH 44128-3766, USA

Johnson, Larry D (Basketball Player)
c/o Staff Member *Kansas City Chiefs*
1 Arrowhead Dr
Kansas City, MO 64129-1651, USA

Johnson, Laura
1917 Weepah Way
Los Angeles, CA 90046-7722, USA

Johnson, Laurie (Composer)
Priority House
Camp Hill Stanmore
Middx HA7 3JQ, UNITED KINGDOM
(UK)

Johnson, Lee (Football Player)
Houston Oilers
1173 McDaniel Ct
Alpine, UT 84004-1231, USA

Johnson, Leon (Football Player)
New York Jets
813 Vine Arden Rd
Morganton, NC 28655-2758, USA

Johnson, Leshon (Football Player)
Green Bay Packers
PO Box 957
Haskell, OK 74436-0957, USA

Johnson, Lou (Baseball Player)
Kansas City Monarchs
4532 Valley Ridge Ave
Los Angeles, CA 90008-4827, USA

Johnson, Luci Baines
Lbj Ranch
Stonewall, TX 78701, USA

Johnson, Lynn-Holly (Actor)
Cavaleri
178 S Victory Blvd Ste 205
Burbank, CA 91502-2881, USA

Johnson, Marc (Musician)
A Train Mgmt
PO Box 29242
Oakland, CA 94604-9242, USA

Johnson, Margaret (Baseball Player)
625 Country Club Dr SE Apt 1D
Rio Rancho, NM 87124, USA

Johnson, Mark (Baseball Player)
Pittsburgh Pirates
40 Helen Ave
Rye, NY 10580-2447, USA

Johnson, Mark (Baseball Player)
Chicago White Sox
5818 E Palma Lane
Anaheim, CA 92807, USA

Johnson, Mark (Boxer)
1204 Howison Pl SW
Washington, DC 20024-4132, USA

Johnson, Mark Steven (Actor, Director,
Writer)
c/o Richard Lovett *Creative Artists Agency*
LCC (CAA-LA)
2000 Avenue Of The Stars
Los Angeles, CA 90067-4700, USA

Johnson, Marvin (Boxer)
5452 Turfway Cir
Indianapolis, IN 46228-2094, USA

Johnson, Maurice (Football Player)
Philadelphia Eagles
112 Mountainview Rd
Mount Laurel, NJ 08054-4729, USA

Johnson, Michael (Musician)
Buddy Lee
38 Music Sq E Ste 200
Nashville, TN 37203-4304, USA

Johnson, Michael D (Athlete, Track
Athlete)
Gold Medal Mgmt
1750 14th St
Boulder, CO 80302-6332, USA

Johnson, Mike (Baseball Player)
San Diego Padres
27632 N 42nd St
Cave Creek, AZ 85331-6614, USA

Johnson, Mike (Baseball Player)
Baltimore Orioles
165 Michaels Ct
Jupiter, FL 33458-8165, USA

Johnson, Mitchell (Football Player)
Dallas Cowboys
2764 Unicorn Ln NW
Washington, DC 20015-2234, USA

Johnson, Monica (Writer)
Innovative Artists
1505 10th St
Santa Monica, CA 90401-2805, USA

Johnson, Monte (Football Player)
Oakland Raiders
425 Laurel Chase Ct NW
Atlanta, GA 30327-4655, USA

Johnson, Nate (Football Player)
New York Yankees
846 W Chestnut St
Freeport, IL 61032-4951, USA

Johnson, Neil (Basketball Player)
821 Plymouth Ln
Virginia Beach, VA 23451-5926, USA

Johnson, Nicholas (Lawyer, Writer)
PO Box 1876
Iowa City, IA 52244-1876, USA

Johnson, Norm (Football Player)
400 Peachtree Industrial Blvd # 1615
Suwanee, GA 30024-6989, USA

Johnson, Norm (Football Player)
Seattle Seahawks
8523 NW Anderson Hill Rd
Silverdale, WA 98383-9353, USA

Johnson, Norma Holloway (Judge)
US District Court
333 Constitution Ave NW Ste 4400
Washington, DC 20001-2837, USA

Johnson, Norman (Musician)
Paramount Entertainment
PO Box 12
Far Hills, NJ 07931-0012, USA

Johnson, Ora J (Religious Leader)
General Assn of General Baptists
100 Stinson Dr
Poplar Bluff, MO 63901-8736, USA

Johnson, Paul (Hockey Player)
1719 Yale Ave
Burley, ID 83318-2242, USA

Johnson, Paul B (Historian)
Coach House
Over Stowey near Bridgewater
Somerset TA5 1HA, UNITED KINGDOM
(UK)

Johnson, Penny
121 N San Vicente Blvd
Beverly Hills, CA 90211-2303, USA

Johnson, Pete (Football Player)
Cincinnati Bengals
6304 Misty Cove Ln
Columbus, OH 43231-1689, USA

Johnson, R E (Misc)
Train Dispatchers Assn
1370 Ontario St Ste 1040
Cleveland, OH 44113-1736, USA

Johnson, Rafer L (Actor, Athlete, Track Athlete)
4217 Woodcliff Rd
Sherman Oaks, CA 91403-4339, USA

Johnson, Ralph (Baseball Player)
Birmingham Black Barons
2168 Telhurst St SW
Atlanta, GA 30310-1114, USA

Johnson, Ralph E (Architect)
Perkins & Will
330 N Wabash Ave Ste 3600
Chicago, IL 60611-3757, USA

Johnson, Randy (Baseball Player)
Montreal Expos
8404 N El Maro Cir
Paradise Valley, AZ 85253-2600, USA

Johnson, Randy (Baseball Player)
c/o Team Member *New York Yankees*
Yankee Stadium
161st St & River Ave
Bronx, NY 10451, USA

Johnson, Randy (Baseball Player)
Atlanta Braves
2427 Timber Creek Ln
Escondido, CA 92027-6749, USA

Johnson, Raylee (Football Player)
San Diego Chargers
3267 Wittman Way
San Diego, CA 92173-2890, USA

Johnson, Raymond Edward
167 Grieb Rd
Wallingford, CT 06492-2511, USA

Johnson, Richard
18-21 Jermyn St.
London, ENGLAND SW1Y 6NB, UNITED
KINGDOM (UK)

Johnson, Rob (Football Player)
Jacksonville Jaguars
26635 Aracena Dr
Mission Viejo, CA 92691-5105, USA

Johnson, Robert (Business Person)
c/o Staff Member *BET - Black
EntertainmentTelevision (DC)*
1235 W St NE
Washington, DC 20018-1101, USA

Johnson, Robert L (Business Person)
Black Entertainment TV
1900 W Pl NE
Washington, DC 20018-1230, USA

Johnson, Ron (Baseball Player)
Kansas City Royals
428 S Male Ave
Compton, CA 90220, USA

Johnson, Ronald A (Ron) (Football Player)
Cleveland Browns
226 Summit Ave
Summit, NJ 07901-2202, USA

Johnson, Rondin (Baseball Player)
Kansas City Royals
3620 SW 102nd St
Seattle, WA 98146-3623, USA

Johnson, Rontrez (Baseball Player)
Kansas City Royals
2733 Colonial Blvd Apt 104
Fort Myers, FL 33907-1639, USA

Johnson, Roy (Misc)
Roofers & Waterproofers Union
1125 17th St NW
Washington, DC 20036-4707, USA

Johnson, Russ (Baseball Player)
US Olympic Team
9121 Cockerham Rd
Denham Springs, LA 70726-2255, USA

Johnson, Russell (Actor)
Professor's Place
PO Box 1198
Bainbridge Island, WA 98110, USA

Johnson, Shannon (Basketball Player)
Connecticut Sun
Mohegan Sun Arena
Uncasville, CT 06382, USA

Johnson, Sheila (Business Person)
Washington Mystics
401 9th St NW
Washington, DC 20004-2128, USA

Johnson, Shelly W (Cinematographer)
970 Jimeno Rd
Santa Barbara, CA 93103-2060, USA

Johnson, Sonia (Activist)
3318 2nd St S
Arlington, VA 22204-1709, USA

Johnson, Stan (Baseball Player)
Chicago White Sox
56 Morningside Dr
Daly City, CA 94015-4509, USA

Johnson, Steve (Basketball Player)
9715 SW Quail Post Rd
Portland, OR 97219-6363, USA

Johnson, Syl (Musician, Songwriter, Writer)
Blue Sky Artists
761 Washington Ave N
Minneapolis, MN 55401-1101, USA

Johnson, Taj
170 N Rexford Dr
Beverly Hills, CA 90210-5406, USA

Johnson, Thomas (Baseball Player)
Philadelphia Stars
15107 Interlachen Dr Apt 324
Silver Spring, MD 20906-5629, USA

Johnson, Thomas C (Tom) (Hockey Player)
16 Spartina Place
West Falmouth, MA 02574, USA

Johnson, Tim (Baseball Player)
Milwaukee Brewers
603 Crawford St
Clay Center, KS 67432-2627, USA

Johnson, Tim (Football Player)
Washington Redskins
21300 Redskin Park Dr
Ashburn, VA 20147-6100, USA

Johnson, Tim (Football Player)
Pittsburgh Steelers
6418 Cartmel Ln
Windermere, FL 34786-5423, USA

Johnson, Timothy (Correspondent, Doctor)
c/o Staff Member *Good Morning America (NY)*
147 Columbus Ave Fl 6
Abc
New York, NY 10023-6503, USA

Johnson, Tom (Baseball Player)
Minnesota Twins
2700 Knox Ave N
Minneapolis, MN 55411-1246, USA

Johnson, Tre (Football Player)
Washington Redskins
680 Harrison Ave
Peekskill, NY 10566-2219, USA

Johnson, Undra (Football Player)
New Orleans Saints
244 Coventry Dr
Bridgeport, WV 26330-9251, USA

Johnson, Van (Actor)
Studio Artists
12402 Blossomwood Dr
Austin, TX 78727-5302, USA

Johnson, Vance (Football Player)
Denver Broncos
PO Box 370781
Denver, CO 80237-0781, USA

Johnson, Vaughan (Football Player)
New Orleans Saints
4915 Arendell St Apt 253
Morehead City, NC 28557-2687, USA

Johnson, Vaughan M (Football Player)
New Orleans Saints
5800 Airline Hwy
Metairie, LA 70003-3876, USA

Johnson, Vic (Baseball Player)
Boston Red Sox
3169 Venus Ave
Eau Claire, WI 54703-0920, USA

Johnson, Vickie (Basketball Player)
c/o Staff Member *New York Liberty*
2 Penn Plz Fl 22
New York, NY 10121-2299, USA

Johnson, Vinnie (Basketball Player)
5236 Elmsgate Dr
Orchard Lake, MI 48324, USA

Johnson, Virginia (Ballerina)
133 W 71st St
New York, NY 10023-3834, USA

Johnson, Virginia E (Doctor)
Johnson Assoc
800 Holland Rd
Ballwin, MO 63021-7200, USA

Johnson, Wallace (Baseball Player)
Montreal Expos
PO Box M618
Gary, IN 46401, USA

Johnson, Walter (Football Player)
Houston Oilers
22361 Rye Rd
Shaker Heights, OH 44122-3041, USA

Johnson, Warren (Race Car Driver)
PO Box 1357
Buford, GA 30515-8357, USA

Johnson, Warren C (Misc)
946 Bellclaire Ave SE
Grand Rapids, MI 49506-3104, USA

Johnson, Wendy (Race Car Driver)
126 Red Brook Ln
Mooresville, NC 28117-8801, USA

Johnson, William A (Billy White Shoes) (Football Player)
Houston Oilers
3701 Whitney Pl
Duluth, GA 30096-3170, USA

Johnson, William B (Business Person)
Ritz-Carlton Hotels
4445 Willard Ave Ste 800
Chevy Chase, MD 20815-3699, USA

Johnson, William H (Football Player)
New York Giants
522 E Pleasant Grove Rd
Montgomery, AL 36105-6110, USA

Johnson, William L (Football Player)
San Francisco 49ers
14538 New Hampton Pl
Fort Myers, FL 33912-7010, USA

Johnson, William R (Business Person)
H J Heinz Co
PO Box 57
Pittsburgh, PA 15230-0057, USA

Johnson, William W (Football Player)
Boston Patriots
20 Mohawk Rd
Canton, MA 02021-1254, USA

Johnson, Zach (Golfer)
c/o Staff Member *Pro Golfers Assoc of America (PGA)*
100 Avenue Of The Champions
Palm Beach Gardens, FL 33418-3653, USA

Johnson-Goodman, Mamie (Baseball Player)
Indianapolis Clowns
623 14th St NE
Washington, DC 20002-5413, USA

Johnson III, Joseph E (Doctor, Physicist)
Philadelphian
2401 Pennsylvania Ave Apt 15C44
Philadelphia, PA 19130-3050, USA

Johnson Jr, Benjamin S (ben) (Athlete, Track Athlete)
Ed Futerman
2 Saint Clair Ave E
#1500
Toronto, ON M4T 2R1, CANADA

Johnson Jr, Ernie (Sportscaster)
TNT-TV
1050 Techwood Dr NW
Sports Department
Atlanta, GA 30318-5604, USA

Johnson Jr, G Griffith (Government Official)
300 Locust Ave
Annapolis, MD 21401-3329, USA

Johnson Jr, Johnnie (Football Player)
Los Angeles Rams
PO Box 114
La Grange, TX 78945-0114, USA

Johnson Jr, Manuel H (Economist, Government Official)
Johnson Smick Int'l
888 16th St NW Ste 740
Washington, DC 20006-4107, USA

Johnson-Noga, Arlene
1923 7th Ave E
Regina, SK S4N 4M7, CANADA

Johnson Pucci, Gail (Swimmer)
2132 Ward Dr
Walnut Creek, CA 94596-5731, USA

Johnston, Alastair (Misc)
International Mgmt Group
75490 Fairway Dr
Indian Wells, CA 92210-8423, USA

Johnston, Allen H (Religious Leader)
Bishop's House
3 Wymer Terrace
PO Box 21
Hamilton, NEW ZEALAND

Johnston, Brian (Football Player)
New York Giants
236 Hideaway Ln
Mooresville, NC 28117-8402, USA

Johnston, Bruce (Musician)
International Creative Mgmt
8942 Wilshire Blvd # 219
Beverly Hills, CA 90211-1908, USA

Johnston, Freedy (Musician, Songwriter, Writer)
Morebarn Music
30 Hillcrest Ave
Morristown, NJ 07960-5090, USA

Johnston, Gerald A (Business Person)
McDonnell Douglas Corp
PO Box 516
Saint Louis, MO 63166-0516, USA

Johnston, Gerald E (Business Person)
Clorox Co
1221 Broadway
Oakland, CA 94612-1888, USA

Johnston, Harold S (Misc)
285 Franklin St
Harrisonburg, VA 22801-4018, USA

Johnston, J Bennett Jr (Senator)
Johnston Assoc
900 19th St NW Ste 800
Washington, DC 20006-2127, USA

Johnston, Jamie (Actor)
c/o Norbert Abrams *Noble Kaplan Agency*
1260 Yonge St Fl 2
Toronto, ON M4T 1W6, CANADA

Johnston, Joel (Baseball Player)
Kansas City Royals
1318 Meadowview Dr # M
Pottstown, PA 19464-1937, USA

Johnston, John Dennis (Actor)
S D B Partners
1801 Avenue Of Stars Ste 902
Los Angeles, CA 90067-5981, USA

Johnston, Ken
6300 Wilshire Blvd Ste 2110
Los Angeles, CA 90048-5282, USA

Johnston, Kristen (Actor)
c/o Judy Hofflund *Hofflund/Polone*
9465 Wilshire Blvd Ste 890
Beverly Hills, CA 90212-2607, USA

Johnston, Lynn (Cartoonist)
Universal Press Syndicate
4520 Main St
Kansas City, MO 64111-1876, USA

Johnston, Mark (Football Player)
Houston Oilers
5604 Southwest Pkwy Apt 3535
Austin, TX 78735-6278, USA

Johnston, Oliver (Animator)
986 High Country Dr
Port Angeles, WA 98362-7472, USA

Johnston, Rex D (Baseball Player, Football Player)
Pittsburgh Pirates
11372 Weatherby Rd
Los Alamitos, CA 90720-3035, USA

Johnston, Sabrina
c/o Staff Member *Diva Central Inc*
7510 W Sunset Blvd Ste 1445
Los Angeles, CA 90046-3408, USA

Johnston, Tom (Musician)
PO Box 359
Sonoma, CA 95476-0359, USA

Johnston-Forbes, Cathy (Golfer)
Ladies Pro Golf Assn
100 International Golf Dr
Daytona Beach, FL 32124-1082, USA

Johnston Jr, S K (Business Person)
Coca-Cola Enterprises
2500 Windy Ridge Pkwy SE
Atlanta, GA 30339-5677, USA

Johnston McKay, Marry H (Astronaut)
University of Tennessee
Space Institute
Tullahoma, TN 37388, USA

Johnstone, Jay (Baseball Player)
California Angels
853 Chapea Rd
Pasadena, CA 91107-5656, USA

Johnstone, John (Baseball Player)
Florida Marlins
9330 Clubside Cir Unit 3305
Sarasota, FL 34238-3367, USA

Johnstone Jr, John W (Business Person)
467 Carter St
New Canaan, CT 06840-5015, USA

Joiner, Rusty (Actor, Athlete, Model)
c/o Marc Chancer *Origin Talent Agency*
4705 Laurel Canyon Blvd Ste 306
Studio City, CA 91607-5940, USA

Joiner Jr, Charles (Charlie) (Coach, Football Coach, Football Player)
Houston Oilers
2254 Moore St
San Diego, CA 92110-3015, USA

Jolas, Betsy M (Composer)
Nat Superieur Musique Conservatoire
209 Ave Jaures
Paris 75019, FRANCE

Joli, France (Musician)
c/o Staff Member *Diva Central Inc*
7510 W Sunset Blvd Ste 1445
Los Angeles, CA 90046-3408, USA

Joliceur, David (Musician)
Famous Artists Agency
250 W 57th St
New York, NY 10107-0001, USA

Jolie, Angelina
c/o Geyer Kosinski *Media Talent Group*
9200 W Sunset Blvd Ste 810
W Hollywood, CA 90069-3603, USA

Jolitz, Evan (Football Player)
Cincinnati Bengals
15 Old Kimball Rd
Brooklyn, CT 06234-1414, USA

Jolley, Gordon (Football Player)
Detroit Lions
1459 Navajo Dr
St George, UT 84790-7728, USA

Jolley, Lewis (Football Player)
Houston Oilers
2715 Rosegate Ln
Charlotte, NC 28270-0764, USA

Jolley, Willie (Motivational Speaker)
PO Box 55459
Washington, DC 20040-5459, USA

Jolly, E Grady (Judge)
US Court of Appeals
245 E Capitol St
Eastland Courthouse
Jackson, MS 39201-2409, USA

Jolly, Ken (Football Player)
Kansas City Chiefs
159 Bon Aire Dr
Dallas, TX 75218-1034, USA

Jolovitz, Jenna (Actor, Writer)
c/o Staff Member *Creative Artists Agency LCC (CAA-LA)*
2000 Avenue Of The Stars
Los Angeles, CA 90067-4700, USA

Jomdt, L daniel (Business Person)
Walgreen Co
200 Wilmot Rd
Deerfield, IL 60015-4681, USA

Jon-Jules, Danny (Actor)
BBC Information - Artist Mail
PO Box 1116
Belfast B3Z 7AJ, UNITED KINGDOM (UK)

Jonas, Don (Football Player)
Chicago Bears
1831 Seneca Blvd
Winter Springs, FL 32708-5534, USA

Jonathan, Wesley (Actor)
c/o Steve Caserta *Sanders/Armstrong Management*
2120 Colorado Ave Ste 120
Santa Monica, CA 90404-3561, USA

Jones, Aaron (Football Player)
Pittsburgh Steelers
7677 Torino Ct
Orlando, FL 32835-8195, USA

Jones, Al (Baseball Player)
Chicago White Sox
1339 Brussels St
San Francisco, CA 94134-2224, USA

Jones, Alex S (Journalist)
1 Waterhouse St Apt 61
Cambridge, MA 02138-3612, USA

Jones, Alfred (Boxer)
19303 Patton St
Detroit, MI 48219-2530, USA

Jones, Allen (Artist)
41 Charterhouse Square
London EC1M 6EA, UNITED KINGDOM (UK)

Jones, Andruw (Baseball Player)
c/o Staff Member *Atlanta Braves*
PO Box 4064
Turner Field
Atlanta, GA 30302-4064, USA

Jones, Angus T (Actor)
c/o Wendi Green *Abrams Artists Agency (LA)*
9200 W Sunset Blvd Ph 11
Los Angeles, CA 90069-3601, USA

Jones, Antonia (Actor)
Buzz Halliday
8899 Beverly Blvd Ste 620
Los Angeles, CA 90048-2428, USA

Jones, Arthur (Inventor)
MedX
1155 NE 77th St
Ocala, FL 34479-8314, USA

Jones, Asjha (Basketball Player)
Connecticut Sun
Mohegan Sun Arena
Uncasville, CT 06382, USA

Jones, Barry (Baseball Player)
Pittsburgh Pirates
411 S Morton Ave
Centerville, IN 47330-1429, USA

Jones, Ben (Baseball Player)
New York Black Yankees
1323 Tewkesbury Pl NW
Washington, DC 20012-2921, USA

Jones, Ben J (Prime Minister)
Victoria St
Greenville
Saint Andrew's, GRENADA

Jones, Bert (Football Player)
Baltimore Colts
PO Box 248
Simsboro, LA 71275-0248, USA

Jones, Bob (Baseball Player)
Colorado Rockies
32 Elm St
Rutherford, NJ 07070-1263, USA

Jones, Bobby (Baseball Player)
Texas Rangers
413 S Zurich Ave
Tulsa, OK 74112-1406, USA

Jones, Bobby (Baseball Player)
New York Mets
10222 N Whitney Ave
Fresno, CA 93730-4742, USA

Jones, Bobby (Basketball Player)
7413 Valleybrook Rd
Charlotte, NC 28270-6548, USA

Jones, Booker T (Musician)
Rosebud Agency
PO Box 170429
San Francisco, CA 94117-0429, USA

Jones, Brent M (Football Player, Sportscaster)
San Francisco 49ers
756 El Pintado Rd
Danville, CA 94526-1407, USA

Jones, Bryn Terfel (Opera Singer)
Harlequin Agency
203 Fidlas Road
Cardiff, WALES CF4 5NA, UNITED KINGDOM (UK)

Jones, Carnetta (Actor)
CunninghamEscottDipene
10635 Santa Monica Blvd Ste 130
Los Angeles, CA 90025-8306, USA

Jones, Cedric (Football Player)
New England Patriots
18 Hollow Wood Ln # C
Greenwich, CT 06831-5002, USA

Jones, Charles W (Misc)
Brotherhood of Boilermakers
753 S 8th St
Kansas City, KS 66105, USA

Jones, Charlie (Sportscaster)
8080 El Paseo Grande
La Jolla, CA 92037-3284, USA

Jones, Cherry (Actor)
William Morris Agency
151 El Camino Dr
Beverly Hills, CA 90212-2775, USA

Jones, Chipper (Baseball Player)
c/o Staff Member *Atlanta Braves*
PO Box 4064
Turner Field
Atlanta, GA 30302-4064, USA

Jones, Chris (Baseball Player)
Houston Astros
1821 Westward Ho Cir
El Cajon, CA 92021-3721, USA

Jones, Chris (Baseball Player)
Cincinnati Reds
1312 E Thunderhill Pl
Phoenix, AZ 85048-6200, USA

Jones, Chris T (Football Player)
Philadelphia Eagles
19360 E Country Club Dr
Aventura, FL 33180-4817, USA

Jones, Christopher (Chris) (Actor, Artist)
PO Box 15714
C/O Sherry Dodd
Beverly Hills, CA 90209-1714, USA

Jones, Christopher Michael (Actor, Dancer)
c/o Justine Hunt *Hines and Hunt Entertainment*
1213 W Magnolia Blvd
Burbank, CA 91506-1829, USA

Jones, Claude Earl (Actor)
Henderson/Hogan
8285 W Sunset Blvd Ste 1
West Hollywood, CA 90046-2420, USA

Jones, Cleon (Baseball Player)
New York Mets
751 Edwards St
Mobile, AL 36610-3334, USA

Jones, Clinton (Football Player)
Minnesota Vikings
22368 Lavender Bell Ln
Woodland Hls, CA 91367-7229, USA

Jones, Cobi (Soccer Player)
501 N Edinburgh Ave
Los Angeles, CA 90048-2309, USA

Jones, Courtney J L (Figure Skater)
National Skating Assn
15-27 Gee St
London EC1V 3RE, UNITED KINGDOM (UK)

Jones, Dalton (Baseball Player)
Boston Red Sox
8485 N Parkland Dr
Baton Rouge, LA 70806-4814, USA

Jones, Damon (Football Player)
Jacksonville Jaguars
12690 Copper Springs Rd
Jacksonville, FL 32246-5143, USA

Jones, Dan (Football Player)
Cincinnati Bengals
5150 SW 20th St
Plantation, FL 33317-5410, USA

Jones, Daniel (Writer)
c/o Staff Member *The New York Times Company*
230 W 41st St Ste 1300
New York, NY 10036-7207, USA

Jones, Dante (Football Player)
Chicago Bears
326 Partridge Run Dr
Duncanville, TX 75137-3133, USA

Jones, Darryl (Baseball Player)
New York Yankees
PO Box 5132
State Farm Insurance
Conneaut Lake, PA 16316-5132, USA

Jones, Darryl (Musician)
Rascoff/Zysblat
110 W 57th St # 300
New York, NY 10019-3319, USA

Jones, Daryll (Football Player)
Green Bay Packers
74 Everglade Rd
Daviston, AL 36256-6400, USA

Jones, David A (Business Person)
Humana Corp
500 W Main St
Louisville, KY 40202-4268, USA

Jones, David D (Football Player)
Oakland Raiders
109 Crawford St
East Orange, NJ 07018-1810, USA

Jones, David (Davy) (Musician)
c/o Staff Member *Cunningham Escott Slevin & Doherty (LA)*
10635 Santa Monica Blvd Ste 130
Los Angeles, CA 90025-8306, USA

Jones, David (Deacon) (Football Player)
Los Angeles Rams
715 S Canyon Mist Ln
Anaheim, CA 92808-1433, USA

Jones, Davy (Race Car Driver)
TRW Racing
2000 Jaguar Dr
Valparaiso, IN 46383, USA

Jones, Dax (Baseball Player)
San Francisco Giants
10021 W Suddard Pl
Beach Park, IL 60087-1717, USA

Jones, Deacon (Baseball Player)
Chicago White Sox
1015 Goldfinch Ave
Sugar Land, TX 77478-3452, USA

Jones, Dean (Actor, Musician)
PO Box 570276
Tarzana, CA 91357-0276, USA

Jones, Denise (Musician)
TBA Artists Mgmt
300 10th Ave S
Nashville, TN 37203-4125, USA

Jones, Dick (Actor)
PO Box 7716
Northridge, CA 91327-7716, USA

Jones, Don (Football Player)
New York Jets
8446 Wren Creek Dr
Charlotte, NC 28269-6176, USA

Jones, Donell (Musician)
c/o Staff Member *Pyramid Entertainment Group*
377 Rector Pl Apt 21A
New York, NY 10280-1439, USA

Jones, Donta (Football Player)
Pittsburgh Steelers
6043 Legacy Cir
Charlotte, NC 28277-8116, USA

Jones, Doug (Actor)
c/o Staff Member *OmniPop Inc (LA)*
4605 Lankershim Blvd Ste 201
North Hollywood, CA 91602-1874, USA

Jones, Doug (Baseball Player)
Milwaukee Brewers
129 E Navilla Pl
Covina, CA 91723-3023, USA

Jones, Dwight (Basketball Player)
17122 Silverthome Lane
Spring, TX 77379, USA

Jones, E Edward (Religious Leader)
Baptist Convention of America
777 S R L Thornton Fwy
Dallas, TX 75203-2901, USA

Jones, E Fay (Architect)
Fay Jones/Maurice Jennings Architects
619 W Dickson St
Fayetteville, AR 72701-5017, USA

Jones, Earl (Athlete, Track Athlete)
15114 Petroskey Ave
Detroit, MI 48238, USA

Jones, Earl (Football Player)
Atlanta Falcons
3127 Seiler Ct
Naperville, IL 60565-4424, USA

Jones, Ed (Football Player)
Dallas Cowboys
1 Lost Valley Dr
Dallas, TX 75234-6465, USA

Jones, Eddie (Actor)
Gage Group
14724 Ventura Blvd Ste 505
Sherman Oaks, CA 91403-3505, USA

Jones, Eddie (Basketball Player)
3400 Paddock Rd
Weston, FL 33331-3520, USA

Jones, Edgar (Football Player)
Chicago Bears
410 Dean St Apt 1
Scranton, PA 18509-1306, USA

Jones, Edith H (Judge)
US Court of Appeals
515 Rusk St Ste 12015
Houston, TX 77002-2605, USA

Jones, Elvin R (Musician)
DL Media
PO Box 2728
Bala Cynwyd, PA 19004-6728, USA

Jones, Ernest (Football Player)
Seattle Seahawks
17410 SW 109th Ave
Miami, FL 33157-4042, USA

Jones, Etta
160 Goldsmith Ave
Newark, NJ 07112-2001, USA

Jones, Evan (Actor)
c/o Susan Curtis *Curtis Talent Management*
9607 Arby Dr
Beverly Hills, CA 90210-1202, USA

Jones, Freddie (Football Player)
San Diego Chargers
4919 Newton St
Bladensburg, MD 20710-2317, USA

Jones, Gary (Baseball Player)
New York Yankees
475 S Westridge Cir
Anaheim, CA 92807-3733, USA

Jones, Gary (Football Player)
Pittsburgh Steelers
1410 Ten Mile Dr
Cedar Hill, TX 75104-6239, USA

Jones, Gemma (Actor)
Conway Van Gelder Robinson
18-21 Jermyn St
London SW1Y 6NB, UNITED KINGDOM (UK)

Jones, George (Football Player)
Pittsburgh Steelers
4419 Cleveland Ave Apt 4
San Diego, CA 92116-3911, USA

Jones, Glenn (Musician)
Universal Attractions
145 W 57th St # 1500
New York, NY 10019-2220, USA

Jones, Gordon (Football Player)
Tampa Bay Buccaneers
18919 Fishermans Bend Dr
Lutz, FL 33558-9756, USA

Jones, Grace (Actor, Model, Musician)
Denis Vaughan Mgmt
PO Box 28286
#700
London, NY N21 3WT, UNITED KINGDOM (UK)

Jones, Greg (Football Player)
Washington Redskins
2331 S Frenton Dr
Lakewood, CO 80227, USA

Jones, Greg (Skier)
PO Box 500
Tahoe City, CA 96145-0500, USA

Jones, Gregory M (Football Player)
Buffalo Bills
3203 Kirby Ln
Walnut Creek, CA 94598-3908, USA

Jones, Griff Rhys (Actor, Producer, Writer)
c/o Staff Member *TalkBack Productions*
20-21 Newman St
London W1T 1PG, UNITED KINGDOM (UK)

Jones, Gwyneth (Opera Singer)
PO Box 556
Zurich 8037, SWITZERLAND

Jones, Hal (Baseball Player)
Cleveland Indians
4125 Palmyra Rd
Los Angeles, CA 90008-2445, USA

Jones, Hassan (Football Player)
Minnesota Vikings
2885 Sarah Dr
Clearwater, FL 33759-2010, USA

Jones, Hayes W (Athlete, Track Athlete)
1040 James K Blvd
Pontiac, MI 48341-1826, USA

Jones, Henry (Hank) (Musician)
Joel Chriss
300 Mercer St Apt 3J
New York, NY 10003-6732, USA

Jones, Homer C (Football Player)
New York Giants
408 S Texas St
Pittsburg, TX 75686-1538, USA

Jones, Horace (Football Player)
Oakland Raiders
7925 Hobart Ave
Pensacola, FL 32534-4030, USA

Jones, Howard (Musician, Songwriter, Writer)
Entourage Talent Associates
133 W 25th St
New York, NY 10001-7206, USA

Jones, Jack (Musician)
75825 Osage Trl
Indian Wells, CA 92210-8511, USA

Jones, Jacques (Baseball Player)
Minnesota Twins
347 Saint Rita Ct
San Diego, CA 92113-2092, USA

Jones, James (Football Player)
Dallas Cowboys
1009 Hunters Creek Dr
Carrollton, TX 75007-1111, USA

Jones, James (Football Player)
Cleveland Browns
PO Box 22694
Kansas City, MO 64113-0694, USA

Jones, James C (Football Player)
Chicago Bears
2 Odyssey Dr
Tinley Park, IL 60477-4842, USA

Jones, James Earl (Actor)
c/o Staff Member *Lagnese, Peyrot & Mucci*
5750 Wilshire Blvd Ste 580
Los Angeles, CA 90036-3695, USA

Jones, James L (Jack) (Misc)
74 Ruskin Park House
Champion Hill
London SE5, UNITED KINGDOM (UK)

Jones, James R Jr (Football Player)
Detroit Lions
16057 Tampa Palms Blvd W # 262
Tampa, FL 33647-2001, USA

Jones, Jamie (Musician)
MPI Talent
9255 W Sunset Blvd Ste 407
Los Angeles, CA 90069-3302, USA

Jones, Janet (Actor)
9100 Wilshire Blvd Ste 1000W
Beverly Hills, CA 90212-3463, USA

Jones, January (Actor)
c/o Lisa Hallerman *United Talent Agency (UTA)*
9560 Wilshire Blvd Ste 500
Beverly Hills, CA 90212-2401, USA

Jones, Jason (Baseball Player)
Texas Rangers
1125 Oakview Dr SE
Smyrna, GA 30080-7917, USA

Jones, Jeff (Baseball Player)
Oakland A's
51 Emmons Ct
Wyandotte, MI 48192-2553, USA

Jones, Jeff (Baseball Player)
Cincinnati Reds
311 White Horse Pike
Haddon Heights, NJ 08035-1704, USA

Jones, Jeff (Coach)
University of Virginia
Athletic Dept
Charlottesville, VA 22903, USA

Jones, Jeffrey (Actor)
7336 Santa Monica Blvd # 691
West Hollywood, CA 90046-6616, USA

Jones, Jenny (Comedian)
600 Plumtree Rd
Barrington, IL 60010, USA

Jones, Jermaine (Football Player)
New York Jets
1172 Larry St
Opelousas, LA 70570, USA

Jones, Jerrauld C (Jerry) (Misc)
Dallas Cowboys
1 Cowboys Pkwy
Irving, TX 75063-4999, USA

Jones, Jerrell Corron (J-Kwon) (Musician)
c/o Staff Member *So So Def Recordings Inc*
1350 Spring St NW Ste 750
Atlanta, GA 30309-2870, USA

Jones, Jill Marie (Actor)
c/o Peggy Rudman *Identity Talent Agency (ID)*
9107 Wilshire Blvd Ste 450
Beverly Hills, CA 90210-5535, USA

Jones, Jimmie (Football Player)
New York Jets
2658 Unicorn Ct
Herndon, VA 20171-2425, USA

Jones, Jimmy (Baseball Player)
San Diego Padres
3054 Newcastle Dr
Dallas, TX 75220-1636, USA

Jones, Joe (Football Player)
Cleveland Browns
1413 Scott Ct
Irving, TX 75060-3703, USA

Jones, John E (Football Player)
New York Jets
19610 100th Ave NE
Bothell, WA 98011-2318, USA

Jones, John Marshall
1801 Avenue Of The Stars Ste 307
Los Angeles, CA 90067-5905, USA

Jones, John Paul (Musician)
Opium Arts
49 Portland Road
London W11 4LJ, UNITED KINGDOM (UK)

Jones, Kelly (Musician)
Marsupial Mgmt
Home Farm
Welfor Newbury
Berkshire RG20 8HR, UNITED KINGDOM (UK)

Jones, Ken (Football Player)
Buffalo Bills
4455 Porter Rd
Niagara Falls, NY 14305-3309, USA

Jones, Kenneth V (Actor)
PRS
29/33 Berners St
London W1P 4AA, ENGLAND

Jones, Kim (Football Player)
New Orleans Saints
1396 Madison Ave Apt 150
Loveland, CO 80537-3218, USA

Jones, L Q (Actor)
2144 1/2 N Cahuenga Blvd
Los Angeles, CA 90068-2708, USA

Jones, Larry (Basketball Player)
1442 Cottingham Ct W
Columbus, OH 43209-3144, USA

Jones, Leilani (Actor)
Writers & Artists
360 N Crescent Dr Bldg North
Beverly Hills, CA 90210-6818, USA

Jones, LeRoi (Imamu Amiri Baraka) (Writer)
State University of New York
Afro American Studies Dept
Stony Brook, NY 11794-0001, USA

Jones, Lyle V (Misc)
RR 7
Pittsboro, NC 27312, USA

Jones, Lynn (Baseball Player)
Detroit Tigers
9959 Dicksonburg Rd
Conneautville, PA 16406-1817, USA

Jones, Malia (Actor, Athlete)
Henderson & Romo Inc.
10 Universal City Plz # 20
Universal City, CA 91608-1009, USA

Jones, Mandana (Actor)
CAM
19 Denmark Street
London WC2H 8NA, ENGLAND

Jones, Marcus (Baseball Player)
Oakland A's
20375 Longbay Dr
Yorba Linda, CA 92887-3250, USA

Jones, Marcus (Football Player)
Tampa Bay Buccaneers
18701 Pepper Pike
Lutz, FL 33558-5315, USA

Jones, Marilyn (Actor)
Kaplan-Stahler Agency
8383 Wilshire Blvd Ste 923
Beverly Hills, CA 90211-2408, USA

Jones, Marvin (Baseball Player)
Kansas City Monarchs
4134 12th St
Ecorse, MI 48229-1224, USA

Jones, Marvin (Football Player)
New York Jets
536 N Biscayne River Dr
Miami, FL 33169-6632, USA

Jones, Marvin M (Football Player)
8891 NW 193rd St
Hialeah, FL 33018-6256, USA

Jones, Maxine (Musician)
East West Records
75 Rockefeller Plz # 1200
New York, NY 10019-6908, USA

Jones, Merlakia (Basketball Player)
Cleveland Rockers
1 Center Ct
Gund Arena
Cleveland, OH 44115-4001, USA

Jones, Mick (Musician)
Hard to Handle Mgmt
16501 Ventura Blvd Ste 602
Encino, CA 91436-2072, USA

Jones, Mickey (Actor, Musician)
Lichtman/Salners
15865 Royal Haven Pl
Sherman Oaks, CA 91403-4724, USA

Jones, Mike (Baseball Player)
Kansas City Royals
44 Almeria Ave
Jacksonville, FL 32211-7601, USA

Jones, Mike (Musician)
c/o Staff Member *Warner Bros*
4000 Warner Blvd
Burbank, CA 91522-0002, USA

Jones, Mike A (Football Player)
Oakland Raiders
1843 E 76th St
Kansas City, MO 64132-2150, USA

Jones, Nasir (Nas) (Actor, Musician, Producer, Writer)
c/o Evan Tripoli *International Creative Management (ICM-LA)*
10250 Constellation Blvd
Los Angeles, CA 90067-6200, USA

Jones, Nathaniel R (Judge)
US Court of Appeals
425 Walnut St
US Courthouse
Cincinnati, OH 45202-3923, USA

Jones, Norah (Musician)
c/o Katherine McVicker *International Music Network (IMN)*
278 Main St
Gloucester, MA 01930-6022, USA

Jones, Odell (Baseball Player)
Pittsburgh Pirates
5831 Opal Ave
Palmdale, CA 93552-3967, USA

Jones, Orlando (Actor)
c/o Blair Belcher *United Talent Agency (UTA)*
9560 Wilshire Blvd Ste 500
Beverly Hills, CA 90212-2401, USA

Jones, P J (Race Car Driver)
Patrick Racing
8431 Georgetown Rd
Indianapolis, IN 46268-5628, USA

Jones, Parnelli (Race Car Driver)
20550 Earl St
Torrance, CA 90503-3012, USA

Jones, Patrick (Actor)
c/o Staff Member *Martin Weiss Management*
PO Box 5656
Santa Monica, CA 90409-5656, USA

Jones, Preston (Football Player)
Philadelphia Eagles
116 Hamilton Dr
Anderson, SC 29621-1558, USA

Jones, Quincy (Actor, Musician, Producer)
c/o Staff Member *Quincy Jones Media Group*
3800 Barham Blvd Fl 5
Los Angeles, CA 90068-1008, USA

Jones, Randy (Baseball Player)
San Diego Padres
2638 Cranston Dr
Escondido, CA 92025-7338, USA

Jones, Rashida (Actor, Musician)
1606 Rosecrans Ave Bldg 4A Fl 3
Manhattan Beach, CA 90266, USA

Jones, Rebecca (Actor)
c/o Gabriel Blanco *Gabriel Blanco Iglesias (Mexico)*
Rio Balsas 35-32
Colonia Cuauhtemoc
DF 06500, MEXICO

Jones, Rebinhak (Actor)
Writers & Artists
360 N Crescent Dr Bldg North
Beverly Hills, CA 90210-6818, USA

Jones, Reginald V (Physicist)
8 Queen's Terrace
Aberdeen AB1 1XL, SCOTLAND

Jones, Renee (Actor)
256 S Robertson Blvd # 700
Beverly Hills, CA 90211-2811, USA

Jones, Richard T (Actor)
Endeavor Talent Agency
9701 Wilshire Blvd Ste 1000
Beverly Hills, CA 90212-2010, USA

Jones, Richard Timothy
584 Broadway Rm 1009
New York, NY 10012-5239, USA

Jones, Rick (Baseball Player)
Boston Red Sox
1834 Weston Cir
Orange Park, FL 32003-8045, USA

Jones, Rickie Lee (Musician, Songwriter, Writer)
476 Broome St Ste 6A
New York, NY 10013-2275, USA

Jones, Robert (Football Player)
Dallas Cowboys
728 Barton Creek Blvd
Austin, TX 78746-4142, USA

Jones, Robert (K C) (Basketball Player, Coach)
13405 NW Spirit Ct W
Silverdale, WA 98383-9507, USA

Jones, Rod (Football Player)
Tampa Bay Buccaneers
205 Oleander Dr
Desoto, TX 75115-1470, USA

Jones, Roger (Football Player)
Tampa Bay Buccaneers
712 Trebor Dr
Goodlettsville, TN 37072-2935, USA

Jones, Ron (Baseball Player)
Philadelphia Phillies
2316 Chapman St
Seguin, TX 78155-1612, USA

Jones, Rosie (Golfer)
4895 High Point Rd NE
Atlanta, GA 30342-2340, USA

Jones, Ross (Baseball Player)
New York Mets
350 SE Mizner Blvd Apt 1411
Boca Raton, FL 33432-6053, USA

Jones, Rulon K (Football Player)
Denver Broncos
3753 E 4100 N
Eden, UT 84310, USA

Jones, Ruppert (Baseball Player)
Kansas City Royals
18766 Bernardo Center Ste 114-A
San Diego, CA 92128, USA

Jones, Sean (Football Player)
Oakland Raiders
257 Orange Rd
Montclair, NJ 07042-4433, USA

Jones, Selwyn (Football Player)
Cleveland Browns
11216 Grimes Ave
Pearland, TX 77584-5524, USA

Jones, Sherman (Baseball Player)
San Francisco Giants
3736 Weaver Dr
Kansas City, KS 66104-3763, USA

Jones, Shirley (Actor, Musician)
c/o Deborah Zucker *Ingels Entertainment*
Suite One Productions
16400 Ventura Blvd Ste 335
Encino, CA 91436-2196, USA

Jones, Simon (Actor)
Innovative Artists
1505 10th St
Santa Monica, CA 90401-2805, USA

Jones, Sir Charles
Hep'me Records
3947 Coxs Ferry Rd
Bolton, MS 39041-9519, USA

Jones, Spike (Football Player)
Houston Oilers
3612 Club Dr NW
Kennesaw, GA 30144-2019, USA

Jones, Stacy (Baseball Player)
Baltimore Orioles
1777 Ponderosa Rd
Attalla, AL 35954-5653, USA

Jones, Stan (Football Player)
Chicago Bears
10581 Pierson Cir
Broomfield, CO 80021-3523, USA

Jones, Stephen (Lawyer)
Jones & Wyatt
PO Box 472
Enid, OK 73702-0472, USA

Jones, Stephen J M (Designer, Fashion Designer)
36 Great Queen St
London WC1E 6BT, UNITED KINGDOM (UK)

Jones, Steve (Baseball Player)
Chicago White Sox
8116 Kingsdale Dr
Knoxville, TN 37919-7005, USA

Jones, Steve (Basketball Player)
2871 NE Alameda St
Portland, OR 97212-1621, USA

Jones, Steve (Football Player)
Buffalo Bills
12774 Fee Fee Rd
Saint Louis, MO 63146-4402, USA

Jones, Steve (Golfer)
3150 Graf St Apt 5
Bozeman, MT 59715-7129, USA

Jones, Steve (Musician)
Solo Agency
55 Fulham High St
London SW6 3JJ, UNITED KINGDOM (UK)

Jones, Steven (Physicist)
Brigham Young University
Physics Dept
Provo, UT 84602, USA

Jones, Tamala (Actor)
c/o Lena Roklin *Roklin Management*
8530 Wilshire Blvd Ste 550
Beverly Hills, CA 90211-3133, USA

Jones, Taylor (Cartoonist)
Times-Mirror Syndicate
Times-Mirror Square
Los Angeles, CA 90053, USA

Jones, Tebucky (Football Player)
New England Patriots
PO Box 769
Farmington, CT 06034-0769, USA

Jones, Terry (Animator, Director)
Python Pictures
34 Thistlewaite Road
London E5 QQQ, UNITED KINGDOM (UK)

Jones, Terry (Musician)
TBA Artists Mgmt
300 10th Ave S
Nashville, TN 37203-4125, USA

Jones, Thomas D (Astronaut)
2026 Beacon Heights Dr
Reston, VA 20191-4847, USA

Jones, Thomas V (Business Person)
1050 Moraga Dr
Los Angeles, CA 90049-1621, USA

Jones, Tim (Baseball Player)
Saint Louis Cardinals
30 Chicot Dr
Maumelle, AR 72113-5801, USA

Jones, Tim (Baseball Player)
Pittsburgh Pirates
6204 Green Eyes Way
Orangevale, CA 95662-4115, USA

Jones, Todd B G (Baseball Player)
4205 Mays Bend Rd
Pell City, AL 35128-7136, USA

Jones, Tom (Musician)
c/o Dick Alen *William Morris Agency (WMA-LA)*
1 William Morris Pl
Beverly Hills, CA 90212-4261, USA

Jones, Tommy Lee (Actor)
c/o Michael Cooper *William Morris Agency (WMA-LA)*
1 William Morris Pl
Beverly Hills, CA 90212-4261, USA

Jones, Tracy (Baseball Player)
Cincinnati Reds
101 Harbor Green Dr Apt 602
Bellevue, KY 41073-1155, USA

Jones, Trevor (Composer)
46 Ave Road Highgate
London N6 5DR, UNITED KINGDOM (UK)

Jones, Tyler Patrick (Actor)
c/o Staff Member *Martin Weiss Management*
PO Box 5656
Santa Monica, CA 90409-5656, USA

Jones, Victor P (Football Player)
Tampa Bay Buccaneers
14524 Harvington Dr
Huntersville, NC 28078-2215, USA

Jones, Victor T (Football Player)
Houston Oilers
2204 Skiles Dr
Plano, TX 75075-7454, USA

Jones, Vinnie (Actor)
c/o Nick Styne *Creative Artists Agency LCC (CAA-LA)*
2000 Avenue Of The Stars
Los Angeles, CA 90067-4700, USA

Jones, Volus
625 S Griffith Park Dr
Burbank, CA 91506-3001, USA

Jones, Wali (Basketball Player)
PO Box 3642
Winter Haven, FL 33885-3642, USA

Jones, Wallace (Wah-Wah) (Basketball Player)
512 Chinoe Rd
Lexington, KY 40502-2402, USA

Jones, Walter (Football Player)
St Louis Cardinals
RR 1 Box 128
Carrollton, AL 35447, USA

Jones, Walter Emanuel (Actor)
K & K Entertainment
1498 W Sunset Blvd
Los Angeles, CA 90026-3471, USA

Jones, Wayne (Actor, Comedian)
Smooth Man Productions
206 Belmont Dr
Palatka, FL 32177-6402, USA

Jones, Wesley (Architect)
Holt Hinshaw Jones
320 Florida St
San Francisco, CA 94110-1411, USA

Jones, William A (Dub) (Football Player)
Brooklyn Dodgers
904 Glendale Dr
Ruston, LA 71270-2346, USA

Jones, Willie D (Football Player)
Buffalo Bills
4440 Hidden Orchard Ln
Indianapolis, IN 46228-3023, USA

Jones-Doxey, Marilyn (Baseball Player)
6201 Rowena Dr
Palmetto, FL 34221, USA

Jones Girls, The
PO Box 6010
761
Sherman Oaks, CA 91413-6010, USA

Jones III, June S (Coach, Football Coach, Football Player)
Atlanta Falcons
2600 Campus Rd
University Of Hawaii Athletic Dept
Honolulu, HI 96822-2205, USA

Jones III, Samuel L (Actor)
c/o Staff Member *Abrams Artists Agency (LA)*
9200 W Sunset Blvd Ph 11
Los Angeles, CA 90069-3601, USA

Jones Jr, James L (General)
Supreme Allied Commander
Supreme Headquarters
APO, AE 09705, USA

Jones Jr, Roy (Boxer, Sportscaster)
c/o Darren Prince *Prince Marketing Group*
454 Prospect Ave # 74
West Orange, NJ 07052, USA

Jong, Erica
121 Davis Hill Rd
Weston, CT 06883-2015, USA

Jonrowe, Dee Dee (Athlete)
PO Box 272
Willow, AK 99688-0272, USA

Jonsen, Albert R (Doctor)
University of Washington
Med School
Medical Ethics Dept
Seattle, WA 98195-0001, USA

Jonson, Johnny (Football Player)
PO Box 4283
Mooresville, NC 28117-4283, USA

Jonsson, Jorgen (Hockey Player)
Anaheim Mighty Ducks
2000 E Gene Autry Way
Anaheim, CA 92806-6143, USA

Jonze, Spike (Actor, Director)
c/o Staff Member *Atom Films*
114 Sansome St Fl 10
San Francisco, CA 94104-3803, USA

Joop, Wolfgang (Designer, Fashion Designer)
Joop
Harvestehuder Weg 22
Hamburg 20149, GERMANY

Joost, Edwin D (Eddie) (Baseball Player)
Cincinnati Reds
7021 S Shingle Rd
Shingle Springs, CA 95682-9729, USA

Joosten, Kathryn (Actor)
Schiowitz/Clay/Rose
1680 Vine St Ste 614
Los Angeles, CA 90028-8833, USA

Jopling, T Michael (Government Official)
Ainderby Hall
Thirsk
North Yorks YO7 4HZ, UNITED
KINGDOM (UK)

Jordan, Anthony (Football Player)
Phoenix Cardinals
38 Albemarle St
Rochester, NY 14613-1402, USA

Jordan, Brian (Baseball Player)
c/o Tamara Wilson *Wyntersweet Entertainment*
PO Box 4745
Atlanta, GA 30302-4745, USA

Jordan, Brian (Football Player)
Atlanta Falcons
1050 Bedford Gardens Dr
Alpharetta, GA 30022-6276, USA

Jordan, Bud (Business Person)
c/o Staff Member *Paramount Pictures*
5555 Melrose Ave
The Crosby Bldg
Los Angeles, CA 90038-3197, USA

Jordan, Buford (Football Player)
New Orleans Saints
11 Acadia St
Kenner, LA 70065-1001, USA

Jordan, Charles M (Designer)
PO Box 8330
Rancho Santa Fe, CA 92067-8330, USA

Jordan, Claudia (Actor, Television Host)
c/o Staff Member *Style Network*
5750 Wilshire Blvd
Los Angeles, CA 90036-3697, USA

Jordan, Curtis (Football Player)
Tampa Bay Buccaneers
5617 Villa Dr
Lubbock, TX 79412-3213, USA

Jordan, Darin (Football Player)
Pittsburgh Steelers
44 Connell Dr
Stoughton, MA 02072-3708, USA

Jordan, Don (Boxer)
5100 2nd Ave
Los Angeles, CA 90043-1951, USA

Jordan, Don D (Business Person)
Reliant Energy
1111 Louisiana St
Houston, TX 77002-5230, USA

Jordan, Eddie (Basketball Player, Coach)
Washington Wizards
601 F St NW
Mci Centre
Washington, DC 20004-1605, USA

Jordan, Glenn (Director)
9401 Wilshire Blvd Ste 700
Beverly Hills, CA 90212-2944, USA

Jordan, Hamilton (Actor)
The Harry Walker Agency Inc
355 Lexington Ave Fl 21
New York, NY 10017-6603, USA

Jordan, I King (Educator)
Gallaudet University
800 Florida Ave NE
President's Office
Washington, DC 20002-3695, USA

Jordan, Kathy (Tennis Player)
114 Walter Hays Dr
Palo Alto, CA 94303-2923, USA

Jordan, Kevin (Baseball Player)
Philadelphia Phillies
678 Cherrydale Dr
Lafayette Hill, PA 19444-2327, USA

Jordan, Lamont (Football Player)
New York Jets
1407 Alberta Dr
Forestville, MD 20747-1902, USA

Jordan, Larry R (General)
Deputy Commander In Chief
US Army Europe/7Th Army
APO, AE 09014, USA

Jordan, Laura (Actor)
c/o Matthew Lesher *Lesher Entertainment Inc*
1134 S Cloverdale Ave
Los Angeles, CA 90019-6737, USA

Jordan, Le Roy
2425 Burbank St
Dallas, TX 75235-3128, USA

Jordan, Leander (Football Player)
Carolina Panthers
5021 Oxfordshire Rd
Waxhaw, NC 28173-7324, USA

Jordan, Lee Roy (Football Player)
Dallas Cowboys
7710 Caruth Blvd
Dallas, TX 75225-8103, USA

Jordan, Leslie (Actor)
c/o Billy Miller *Billy Miller Management*
8322 Ridpath Dr
Los Angeles, CA 90046-7710, USA

Jordan, Mary (Journalist)
Washington Post
Editorial Dept
1150 15th St NW
Washington, DC 20071-0001, USA

Jordan, Michael J (Athlete, Basketball Player)
c/o Staff Member *Jump Inc*
676 N Michigan Ave Ste 2930
Chicago, IL 60611-2861, USA

Jordan, Neil (Director, Writer)
c/o Staff Member *William Morris Agency (WMA-LA)*
1 William Morris Pl
Beverly Hills, CA 90212-4261, USA

Jordan, Neil P (Director)
6 Sorrento Terrace
Dalkey
County Dublin, IRELAND

Jordan, Niles (Baseball Player)
Philadelphia Phillies
1114 Metcalf St
Sedro Woolley, WA 98284-1510, USA

Jordan, Payton (Coach)
3775 Modoc Rd Apt 264
Santa Barbara, CA 93105-5433, USA

Jordan, Randy (Football Player)
Los Angeles Raiders
9520 Hollow Tree Dr
Lincoln, NE 68512-9533, USA

Jordan, Ricardo (Baseball Player)
Toronto Blue Jays
722 N Highland Ave
Tarpon Springs, FL 34688-8944, USA

Jordan, Ricky (Baseball Player)
Cleveland Indians
11472 Ghirardelli Ct
Gold River, CA 95670-7864, USA

Jordan, Scott (Baseball Player)
Cleveland Indians
1530 Carroll Dr NW Ste 103
Atlanta, GA 30318-3600, USA

Jordan, Shelby (Football Player)
New England Patriots
29208 Posey Way
Rancho Palos Verdes, CA 90275-4629, USA

Jordan, Stanley (Musician)
SJ Productions
16845 N 29th Ave # 2000
Phoenix, AZ 85053-3053, USA

Jordan, Steve (Football Player)
Indianapolis Colts
581 W San Marcos Dr
Chandler, AZ 85225-9555, USA

Jordan, Tom (Baseball Player)
Chicago White Sox
2909 S Wyoming Ave
Roswell, NM 88203-2374, USA

Jordan Jr, Vernon E (Civil Rights Activist)
Lazard Freres
30 Rockefeller Plz Fl 59
New York, NY 10112-5900, USA

Jordanaires, The
4619 220th Pl
Bayside, NY 11361-3650, USA

Jordanova, Vera (Actor, Model)
c/o Alix Gucovsky *Special Artists Agency*
9465 Wilshire Blvd Ste 890
Beverly Hills, CA 90212-2607, USA

Jorden, Tim (Football Player)
Phoenix Cardinals
11402 N 26th Pl
Scottsdale, AZ 85260, USA

Jordensen, Anker (Prime Minister)
Borgbjergvej 1
Copenhagen, SV 2450, DENMARK

Jordenson, Dale W (Economist)
1010 Memorial Dr Apt 14C
Cambridge, MA 02138-4858, USA

Jordison, Joey (Musician)
c/o Staff Member *Gersh Agency, The (NY)*
41 Madison Ave Fl 33
New York, NY 10010-2202, USA

Jorgensen, Mike (Baseball Player)
New York Mets
1820 Harbor Mill Dr
Fenton, MO 63026-2653, USA

Jorgensen, Terry (Baseball Player)
Minnesota Twins
1493 S Sugar Bush Rd
Luxemburg, WI 54217-9311, USA

Jorginho (Soccer Player)
Rua Levi Carreiro 420
Barra de Tijuca, BRAZIL

Jose, Felix (Baseball Player)
Oakland A's
11 Broadway Apt 2
Bayonne, NJ 07002-3430, USA

Jose, Jose (Musician)
Fanny Schatz Mgmt
Melchor Ocampo 309
Mexico City, DF CP 11590, MEXICO

Jose, Lind (Baseball Player)
Pittsburgh Pirates
18 Villa Santa
Dorado, PR 00646, USA

Josefowicz, Leila (Musician)
I M G Artists
420 W 45th St
New York, NY 10036-3503, USA

Joseph, Curtis (Hockey Player)
Newport Sports Mgmt
601-201 City Centre
Mississauga, ON L5B 2T4, CANADA

Joseph, Daryl J (Astronaut)
615 Peachtree Ct
Campbell, CA 95008-6353, USA

Joseph, James (Football Player)
Philadelphia Eagles
3811 Flintwood Ln
Opelika, AL 36804-7613, USA

Joseph, Jeffrey
400 S Beverly Dr Ste 102
Beverly Hills, CA 90212-4403, USA

Joseph, Stephen (Doctor)
New York City Health Department
125 Worth St
New York, NY 10013-4006, USA

Joseph, William (Football Player)
New York Giants
Giants Stadium
East Rutherford, NJ 07073, USA

Joseph III, Joseph E (Doctor)
University of Michigan
Taubman Center
Ann Arbor, MI 48109, USA

Josephine, Charlotte (Royalty)
Grand Ducal Palace
Luxembourg, LUXEMBOURG

Josephs, Wilfred (Composer)
4 Grand Union Walk
Kentish Town Rd Camden Town
London NW1 9LP, UNITED KINGDOM (UK)

Josephson, Brian D (Nobel Prize Laureate)
Cavendish Laboratory
Madingley Road
Cambridge CB3 0HE, UNITED KINGDOM (UK)

Josephson, Eriand (Actor)
Royal Dramatic Theater
Nybroplan
Box 5037
Stockholm 10241, SWEDEN

Josephson, Karen (Swimmer)
1923 Junction Dr
Concord, CA 94518-3361, USA

Josephson, Lester (Josey) (Football Player)
Los Angeles Rams
5388 N Genernatas Dr
Tucson, AZ 85704, USA

Josephson, Sarah (Swimmer)
1923 Junction Dr
Concord, CA 94518-3361, USA

Joshi, Indira (Actor)
c/o Staff Member *BBC Artist Mail*
PO Box 1116
Belfast BT2 7AJ, UNITED KINGDOM
(UK)

Joshi, Pallavi (Actor, Bollywood, Talk
Show Host)
23 Shefalee Makrand Soc
Veer Savarkar Rd Mahim
Bombay, MS 400016, INDIA

Joshua, Von (Baseball Player)
Los Angeles Dodgers
22580 Indianwood Dr
South Lyon, MI 48178-9417, USA

Jospin, Lionel R (Prime Minister)
Haute-Garonne Conseil
Place Saint Etienne
Toulouse Cedex 31090, FRANCE

Jostyn, Jennifer (Actor)
c/o Staff Member *Abrams Artists Agency
(LA)*
9200 W Sunset Blvd Ph 11
Los Angeles, CA 90069-3601, USA

Joswick, Robert (Football Player)
Miami Dolphins
10902 Wilson Ave
Alta Loma, CA 91737-2438, USA

Jothilakshmi (Actor, Bollywood)
32 Sarangapani Street
T Nagar
Chennai, TN 600017, INDIA

Jothimeena (Actor, Bollywood)
32 Sarangapani Street
T Nagar
Chennai, TN 600017, INDIA

Joubert, Beverly (Photographer)
National Geographic Magazine
17th & M Sts NW
Washington, DC 20036, USA

Joubert, Brian (Figure Skater)
Federation Francaise des Sports De Glace
35 rue Felicien David
Paris 75016, FRANCE

Joubert, Dereck (Photographer)
National Geographic Magazine
17th & M Sts NW
Washington, DC 20036, USA

Joulwan, George A (General)
1348 19th Rd S
Arlington, VA 22202-1637, USA

Jourdain Jr, Michel (Race Car Driver)
Team Rahal
4601 Lyman Dr
Hilliard, OH 43026-1249, USA

Jourdan, Louis (Actor)
c/o Staff Member *Abramson & Company*
15250 Ventura Blvd Ste 403
Sherman Oaks, CA 91403-3216, USA

Journell, Jimmy (Baseball Player)
Saint Louis Cardinals
40 S 4th St Apt 318
Memphis, TN 38103-5234, USA

Journey (Music Group)
c/o Staff Member *Azoffmusic
Management*
1100 Glendon Ave Ste 2000
Los Angeles, CA 90024-3524, USA

Jovanovich, Peter W (Publisher)
MacMillan
1177 Avenue Of The Americas # 1965
New York, NY 10036-2714, USA

Jovanovski, Ed (Hockey Player)
260 W Coconut Palm Rd
Boca Raton, FL 33432-7914, USA

Jovovich, Milla (Actor, Model, Musician)
c/o Staff Member *Creature Entertainment*
11766 Wilshire Blvd Ste 1610
Los Angeles, CA 90025-6565, USA

Jow, Melise (Actor)
c/o Glenn Hughes III *Gem Entertainment
Group*
2530 Wilshire Blvd Fl 3
Santa Monica, CA 90403-4643, USA

Joyce, Andrea (Correspondent,
Sportscaster)
Arts & Entertainment
235 E 45th St
New York, NY 10017-3354, USA

Joyce, Delvin (Football Player)
New York Giants
RR 10 Box 111
Martinsville, VA 24112, USA

Joyce, Dick (Baseball Player)
Kansas City A's
406 Versailles Dr
Cary, NC 27511-6013, USA

Joyce, Don (Football Player)
Chicago Cardinals
5200 Pathways Ave Unit 302
Saint Paul, MN 55110-6556, USA

Joyce, Elaine (Actor)
10745 Chalon Rd
Los Angeles, CA 90077-3301, USA

Joyce, James (Baseball Player)
9785 SW 167th Pl
Beaverton, OR 97007-8705, USA

Joyce, Joan (Golfer)
22856 Marbella Cir
Boca Raton, FL 33433-3802, USA

Joyce, John T (Misc)
Bricklayers & Allied Craftsmen
815 15th St NW
Washington, DC 20005, USA

Joyce, Matt (Football Player)
Arizona Cardinals
6330 E Wilshire Dr
Scottsdale, AZ 85257-1122, USA

Joyce, Mike (Baseball Player)
Chicago White Sox
1609 Whitman Ln
Wheaton, IL 60187-7445, USA

Joyce, Tom (Artist)
21 Likely Rd
Santa Fe, NM 87508-5963, USA

Joyce, William (Artist, Writer)
3302 Centenary Blvd
Shreveport, LA 71104-4504, USA

Joyce, William H (Business Person)
Union Carbide
39 Old Ridgebury Rd Ste 1
Danbury, CT 06810-5100, USA

Joyeux, Odette
1 rue Seguier
Paris 75006, FRANCE

Joyner, Alrederick (Al) (Athlete, Track
Athlete)
CMG World Wide
9229 W Sunset Blvd Ste 900
10th Fl Penthouse
West Hollywood, CA 90069-3410, USA

Joyner, Mark (Business Person, Writer)
Mark Joyner Inc
7426 Cherry Ave # 210-150
Fontana, CA 92336-4221, USA

Joyner, Michelle (Actor)
Paradigm Agency
10100 Santa Monica Blvd Ste 2500
Los Angeles, CA 90067-4116, USA

Joyner, Tom (Radio Personality)
PO Box 630495
Irving, TX 75063-0128, USA

Joyner-Kersee, Jacqueline (Jackie)
(Athlete, Track Athlete)
JJK Assoc
PO Box 69047
Saint Louis, MO 63169-0047, USA

Jozwiak, Brian J (Coach, Football Coach,
Football Player)
Kansas City Chiefs
203 Ruby Lake Ln
Winter Haven, FL 33884-3267, USA

Ju, Ming (Artist)
28 Lane 460
Chih Shan Road Section 2
Taipei, TAIWAN

Ju-Ju (Musician)
Agency Group Ltd
1775 Broadway Ste 515
New York, NY 10019-1903, USA

Juanes (Musician)
c/o Julissa Garcia *William Morris Agency
(WMA-LA)*
1 William Morris Pl
Beverly Hills, CA 90212-4261, USA

Juantorena Danger, Alberto (Athlete,
Track Athlete)
National Institute for Sports
Sports City
Havana, CUBA

Juby, Marcus L (Religious Leader)
Reformed Church of Latter-Day Saints
801 E 23rd St S
Independence, MO 64055-1609, USA

Juckes, Gordon W (Misc)
1475 Avenue B
Big Pine Key, FL 33043, USA

Judd, Ashley (Actor)
c/o Staff Member *Endeavor Agency LLC
(LA)*
9601 Wilshire Blvd Fl 3
Beverly Hills, CA 90210-5204, USA

Judd, Cledus T
707 18th Ave S
Nashville, TN 37203-3214, USA

Judd, Cris (Actor, Choreographer)
c/o Graham Kaye *Creative Management
Group (CMG)*
8522 National Blvd Ste 108
Culver City, CA 90232-2454, USA

Judd, Howard L (Misc)
University of California
Medical Center
Ob-Gyn Dept
Los Angeles, CA 90024, USA

Judd, Jackie (Correspondent)
ABC-TV
77 W 66th St
News Dept
New York, NY 10023-6201, USA

Judd, Mike (Baseball Player)
Los Angeles Dodgers
9805 Shadow Rd
La Mesa, CA 91941-4154, USA

Judd, Naomi
Naomi's New Morning
74 Trinity Pl Rm 806
Lightworks Producing Group
New York, NY 10006-2033, USA

Judd, Wynonna (Musician)
William Morris Agency
151 El Camino Dr
Beverly Hills, CA 90212-2775, USA

Juden, Jeff (Baseball Player)
Houston Astros
8684 SW 55th St
Cooper City, FL 33328-4322, USA

Judge, Christopher (Actor)
c/o Staff Member *Cunningham Escott
Slevin & Doherty (LA)*
10635 Santa Monica Blvd Ste 130
Los Angeles, CA 90025-8306, USA

Judge, George (Economist)
University of California
Economics Dept
Berkeley, CA 94720-0001, USA

Judge, Mike (Animator)
Three Arts Entertainment
9460 Wilshire Blvd Ste 700
Beverly Hills, CA 90212-2713, USA

Judkins, Jeff (Basketball Player, Coach)
3471 S 3570 E
Salt Lake City, UT 84109-3243, USA

Judson, Howie (Baseball Player)
Chicago White Sox
239 Fairway Cir
Winter Haven, FL 33881-8742, USA

Judson, William (Football Player)
Miami Dolphins
652 Sinclair Way
Jonesboro, GA 30238-7962, USA

Jue, Bhawoh (Football Player)
Green Bay Packers
129 E River Dr
De Pere, WI 54115-3781, USA

Juenger, David (Football Player)
Chicago Bears
790 Cliffside Dr
Chillicothe, OH 45601-2902, USA

Juergensen, Heather (Actor)
c/o Peg Donegan *Framework
Entertainment (LA)*
9057 Nemo St # C
W Hollywood, CA 90069-5511, USA

Jugnauth, Anerood (Prime Minister)
La Caverne 1
Vacoas, MAURITIUS

Juhl, Finn (Designer)
Kratvaenget 15
Chartottenlund 2920, DENMARK

Jules, Gary (Musician)
c/o Staff Member *Paradigm (Monterey)*
509 Hartnell St
Monterey, CA 93940-2825, USA

Julian, Fred (Football Player)
New York Titans
730 Strawberry Valley Ave NW
Comstock Park, MI 49321-9600, USA

Julian, Janet (Actor)
Borinstein Oreck Bogart
3172 Dona Susana Dr
Studio City, CA 91604-4356, USA

Julian, Jonathan (Actor)
c/o Susan Nathe *Nathe & Associates*
8281 Melrose Ave Ste 200
Los Angeles, CA 90046-6890, USA

Julian II, Alexander (Designer, Fashion Designer)
Alexander Julian Inc
PO Box 60
Georgetown, CT 06829-0060, USA

Julien, Max (Actor)
3580 Avenida Del Sol
Studio City, CA 91604-4018, USA

Julius, DeAnne (Economist)
Bank of England
Threadneedle St
London EC2R 8AH, UNITED KINGDOM (UK)

Jullen, Claude (Coach)
Montreal Canadiens
1260 de la Gauchetiere W
Montreal, PQ H3B 5E8, CANADA

Juma, Kevin (Football Player)
Seattle Seahawks
9220 Vancouver Dr NE
Lacey, WA 98516-6038, USA

Jump 5 (Music Group)
c/o Staff Member *Jeff Roberts & Associates*
3050 Business Park Cir Ste 301
Goodlettsville, TN 37072-3588, USA

Jumper, John P (General)
Chief Of Staff
Hqusaf Pentagon
Washington, DC 20330-0001, USA

Junck, Mary (Publisher)
Baltimore Sun
501 N Calvert St
Baltimore, MD 21202-3604, USA

Juncker, Jean-Claude (Prime Minister)
Hotel de Bourgogne
4 Rue de la Congregation
2910, LUXEMBOURG

Jung, Ernst (Writer)
8815 Lagenensligen/Wiltingen
GERMANY

Jung, Richard (Misc)
Waldhofstr 42
Freiburg 71691, GERMANY

Junge, Eric (Baseball Player)
Philadelphia Phillies
27 Claremont Ave
Rye, NY 10580-2503, USA

Junger, Gil (Director)
Creative Artists Agency
9830 Wilshire Blvd
Beverly Hills, CA 90212-1804, USA

Junger, Sebastian (Writer)
United Talent Agency
9560 Wilshire Blvd Ste 500
Beverly Hills, CA 90212-2401, USA

Jungman, Eric (Actor)
c/o Staff Member *Leslie Allan-Rice Management*
7524 Mulholland Dr
Los Angeles, CA 90046-1239, USA

Jungueira, Bruno (Race Car Driver)
2127 Brickell Ave Apt 3105
Miami, FL 33129-2105, USA

Junior, Ester J (E J) (Football Player)
St Louis Cardinals
911 W Summit St
Bolivar, MO 65613-1021, USA

Junior Balaiya (Actor)
3 Melgai Vaniyagar Street
Vadapalani
Chennai, TN 600 026, INDIA

Junior Varsity (Music Group)
Victory Records
346 N Justine St Ste 504
Chicago, IL 60607-1021, USA

Junker, Steve (Football Player)
Detroit Lions
5660 Julmar Dr
Cincinnati, OH 45238-1908, USA

Junkin, Abner (Football Player)
Buffalo Bills
5 Lakeside Ln
Newport, AR 72112-3948, USA

Junkin, Trey (Football Player)
Buffalo Bills
300 Wren St
Winnfield, LA 71483-2662, USA

Junor, Daisy (Baseball Player)
402-111 Lockwood Rd
Regina, SK S4S 3G5, CANADA

Juppe, Alain
57 rue de Varenne
Paris F-75007, FRANCE

Juppe, Alain M (Prime Minister)
Mairie
Place Pey-Berland
Bordeaux Cedex 33077, FRANCE

Jur, Jeffrey (Cinematographer)
10615 Northvale Rd
Los Angeles, CA 90064-4357, USA

Jurak, Ed (Baseball Player)
Boston Red Sox
3650 S Walker Ave
San Pedro, CA 90731-6046, USA

Juran, Nathan
197 Desert Lakes Dr
Rancho Mirage, CA 92270-4053, USA

Jurasik, Peter (Actor)
969 1/2 Manzanita St
Los Angeles, CA 90029-3009, USA

Jurevicius, Joe (Football Player)
New York Giants
4626 Avenue Longchamps
Lutz, FL 33558-5342, USA

Jurewicz, Mike (Baseball Player)
New York Yankees
13804 Evergreen Ct
Apple Valley, MN 55124-9257, USA

Jurgens, Dan
5033 Green Farms Rd
Edina, MN 55436-1091, USA

Jurgens, Udo
Carmenstr. 25
Zurich CH-8032, SWITZERLAND

Jurgensen, Karen (Editor)
USA Today
Editorial Dept
1000 Wilson Blvd
Arlington, VA 22229-0001, USA

Jurgensmeier-Carroll, Margaret (Baseball Player)
5245 Rowena Dr
Roscoe, IL 61073-7221, USA

Jurich, Tom (Football Player)
New Orleans Saints
University Of Louisville Attn Athletic Department
Louisville, KY 40292-0001, USA

Juriga, James (Football Player)
Denver Broncos
3001 Easton Pl
Saint Charles, IL 60175-5610, USA

Jurinac, Sena (Opera Singer)
State Opera House
Opernring 2
Vienna 1010, AUSTRIA

Jurkewicz, Walt (Football Player)
Detroit Lions
5441 Ligurian Dr
San Jose, CA 95138-2325, USA

Jurkovic, Mirko (Football Player)
Chicago Bears
68520 Garver Lake Rd
Edwardsburg, MI 49112-9404, USA

Jurow, Martin
5833 Berkshire Ln
Dallas, TX 75209-2403, USA

Just, Joe (Baseball Player)
Cincinnati Reds
7001 W Rawson Ave
Franklin, WI 53132-8113, USA

Just, Walter (Publisher)
Milwaukee Journal
333 W State St
Milwaukee, WI 53203-1309, USA

Just, Ward S (Writer)
36 Ave Junot
Paris, FRANCE

Just Jinger (Music Group)
c/o Staff Member *Paradigm (Monterey)*
509 Hartnell St
Monterey, CA 93940-2825, USA

Justice, David (Baseball Player)
Atlanta Braves
15260 Ventura Blvd Ste 2100
Sherman Oaks, CA 91403-5360, USA

Justice, Donald R (Writer)
338 Rocky Shore Dr
Iowa City, IA 52246-3836, USA

Justice, Victoria (Actor)
c/o Mitchell Gossett *Cunningham Escott Slevin & Doherty (LA)*
10635 Santa Monica Blvd Ste 130
Los Angeles, CA 90025-8306, USA

Justice, William
3832 Chanson Dr
Los Angeles, CA 90043-1602, USA

Justin, Kerry (Football Player)
Seattle Seahawks
13331 W Marlette Ct
Litchfield Park, AZ 85340-5377, USA

Justman, Seth (Musician)
Nick Ben-Meir
652 N Doheny Dr
Los Angeles, CA 90069-5526, USA

Jutze, Skip (Baseball Player)
St Louis Cardinals
3395 Zephyr Ct
Wheat Ridge, CO 80033-5967, USA

Juvenile (Musician)
c/o Staff Member *International Creative Management (ICM-LA)*
10250 Constellation Blvd
Los Angeles, CA 90067-6200, USA

K Bagyaraj (Actor)
Off 1 Kuppusamy Street
T Nagar
Chennai, TN 600 017, INDIA

K Balaji (Actor)
58 Pantheon Road
Egmore
Chennai, TN 600 008, INDIA

K Balasing (Actor)
86/2 Maddox Street Choolai
Chennai, TN 600 112, INDIA

K Bapaiah (Bollywood, Director)
15 Seethamma Colony 3rd Cross Road
Alwarpet
Madras, TN 600 017, INDIA

K-Ci & JoJo (Music Group)
c/o Dennis Ashley *Creative Artists Agency LCC (CAA-LA)*
2000 Avenue Of The Stars
Los Angeles, CA 90067-4700, USA

K Prabakaran (Actor)
23-C North Boag Road
T Nagar
Chennai, TN 600 017, INDIA

Ka Shing, Li (Business Person)
Li Ka Shing Foundation
7/F Cheung Kong Center
2 Queens Road Central
HONG KONG

Kaake, Jeff (Actor)
2533 N Carson St # 3105
Carson City, NV 89706-0147, USA

Kaas, Carmen (Model)
Men/Women Model Inc
199 Lafayette St # 700
New York, NY 10012-4003, USA

Kaas, Jon H (Psychic)
Vanderbilt University
Psychology Dept
Nashville, TN 37240-0001, USA

Kaas, Patrica (Musician)
Talent Sorcier
3 Rue des Petites-Ecuries
Paris 75010, FRANCE

Kaat, Jim (Baseball Player)
Washington Senators
PO Box 1130
Port Salerno, FL 34992-1130, USA

Kab, Vyto (Football Player)
Philadelphia Eagles
4 Sugar Hill Rd
Kinnelon, NJ 07405-2137, USA

Kabakov, Ilya (Artist)
Gladstone Gallery
525 W 52nd St
New York, NY 10019-5074, USA

Kabat-Zinn, Jon (Writer)
Sounds True, Inc
413 S Arthur Ave
Louisville, CO 80027-3013, USA

Kabbah, Ahmad Tejan (President)
President's Office
State House
Independence Ave
Freetown, SIERRA LEONE

Kabila, Joseph (General, President)
President's Office
Mont Ngaliema
Kinshaha, CONGO DEMOCRATIC
REPUBLIC

Kabua, Imata (President)
President's Office
Cabinet Building
PO Box 2
Majuro, MARSHALL ISLANDS

Kaci (Musician)
c/o Jim Morey *Morey Management Group*
1100 Glendon Ave Ph 1
Los Angeles, CA 90024-3526, USA

Kaczmarek, Jane (Actor)
Innovative Artists
1505 10th St
Santa Monica, CA 90401-2805, USA

Kadafi, Moammar
Bab el Aziziya
Tripoli, LIBYA

Kadanoff, Leo P (Physicist)
5421 S Cornell Ave
Chicago, IL 60615-5646, USA

Kadare, Ismael (Writer)
63 Blvd Saint-Michel
Paris 75005, FRANCE

Kadela, Dave (Football Player)
Atlanta Falcons
9413 Culross Ct
Dublin, OH 43017-9685, USA

Kadenyuk, Leonld K (Cosmonaut)
Potchta Kosmonavtov
Moskovskoi Oblasti
Syvisdny Goroduk 141160, RUSSIA

Kadher, Pakkoda (Actor)
9 Ponmana Semmal Street
M G R Nagar
Chennai, TN 600 078, INDIA

Kadish, Michael S (Mike) (Football Player)
Buffalo Bills
7941 Sudbury Ln SE
Ada, MI 49301-9356, USA

Kadish, Ronald T (Ron) (General)
Director
Missile Defense Agency
Washington, DC 20301-0001, USA

Kadison, Joshua (Musician, Songwriter, Writer)
Nick Bode
1265 Electric Ave
Venice, CA 90291-3397, USA

Kadziel, Ron (Football Player)
New England Patriots
2492 Creek Dr
Park City, UT 84060-6866, USA

Kaelin, Kato
6404 Wilshire Blvd Ste 950
Los Angeles, CA 90048-5529, USA

Kaestle, Carl F (Historian)
35 Charlesfield St
Providence, RI 02906-1114, USA

Kafelnikov, Yevgeny A (Tennis Player)
Int'l Mgmt Group
26 Riverside Dr
Rumson, NJ 07760-1048, USA

Kafentzis, Mark (Football Player)
Cleveland Browns
1305 Perkins Ave
Richland, WA 99354-3106, USA

Kaftan, George (Basketball Player)
2591 Lantern Light Way
Manasquan, NJ 08736-2247, USA

Kagan, Daryn
Washington Speakers Bureau
1663 Prince St
Alexandria, VA 22314-2818, USA

Kagan, Daryn (Correspondent)
Cable News Network
1050 Techwood Dr NW
News Dept
Atlanta, GA 30318-5604, USA

Kagan, Henri Boris (Misc)
University Paris-Sud
Institut de Chimie Moleculaire
Orsay 91405, FRANCE

Kagan, Jeremy Paul (Director)
2024 N Curson Ave
Los Angeles, CA 90046-2210, USA

Kagen, David (Actor)
6457 Firmament Ave
Van Nuys, CA 91406-6219, USA

Kagge, Erling (Skier)
Munkedamsveien 86
Oslo 0270, NORWAY

Kahan, Richard (Actor)
c/o Elena Kirschner *Lucas Talent Inc*
Sun Tower Floor 7
100 W Pender St
Vancouver, BC V6B 1R8, CANADA

Kahane, Jeffrey (Musician)
I M G Artists
420 W 45th St
New York, NY 10036-3503, USA

Kahin, Brian (Educator)
Harvard University
Information Infrastructure Project
Cambridge, MA 02138, USA

Kahler, Robert (Football Player)
Green Bay Packers
5500 Salem Square Dr N
Palm Harbor, FL 34685-1146, USA

Kahler, Royal (Football Player)
Pittsburgh Steelers
13116 Durango Dr
Amarillo, TX 79111-1454, USA

Kahlil, Aisha (Musician)
Sweet Honey Agency
PO Box 600099
Newtonville, MA 02460-0001, USA

Kahn, Alfred E (Economist, Government Official)
308 N Cayuga St
Ithaca, NY 14850-4209, USA

Kahn, Chaka (Actor)
c/o Staff Member *William Morris Agency (WMA-LA)*
1 William Morris Pl
Beverly Hills, CA 90212-4261, USA

Kahn, David R (Publisher)
New Yorker Magazine
4 Times Sq
Publisher's Office
New York, NY 10036-6592, USA

Kahn, Harold (Business Person)
Montgomery Ward Co
822 Montgomery Ave Ste 204
Narberth, PA 19072-1946, USA

Kahn, Joseph (Director, Writer)
c/o Staff Member *HSI Entertainment*
3630 Eastham Dr
Culver City, CA 90232-2411, USA

Kahn, Robert E (Scientist)
909 Lynton Pl
McLean, VA 22102-2113, USA

Kahn, Roger (Writer)
280 Marcotte Rd
Kingston, NY 12401-8318, USA

Kahne, Kasey (Race Car Driver)
Kasey Kahne Fan Club
PO Box 342
Enumclaw, WA 98022-0342, USA

Kahneman, Daniel (Nobel Prize Laureate)
41 Adams Dr
Princeton, NJ 08540-5401, USA

Kai, Teanna (Adult Film Star)
c/o Staff Member *Atlas Multimedia Inc*
9035 Independence Ave
Canoga Park, CA 91304-1743, USA

Kaifu, Toshiki (Prime Minister)
House of Representatives
Diet
Tokyo 100, JAPAN

Kaimer, Karl (Football Player)
New York Titans
3 Kerr Ave
Lavallette, NJ 08735-2138, USA

Kain, Karin A (Dancer)
National Ballet of Canada
470 Queens Quay
Toronto, ON M5V 3K4, CANADA

Kain, Khalil (Actor)
c/o Staff Member *Envision Entertainment*
9255 W Sunset Blvd Ste 500
West Hollywood, CA 90069-3301, USA

Kainer, Don (Baseball Player)
Texas Rangers
1923 Sieber Dr
Houston, TX 77017-6201, USA

Kaiser, A Dale (Misc)
832 Santa Fe Ave
Stanford, CA 94305-1023, USA

Kaiser, Bob (Baseball Player)
Cleveland Indians
8 Independence Way
Southampton, NJ 08088-9047, USA

Kaiser, Cecil (Baseball Player)
Homestead Grays
16890 Santa Rosa Dr Apt 1
Detroit, MI 48221-2629, USA

Kaiser, Don (Baseball Player)
Chicago Cubs
2901 E 12th St
Ada, OK 74820-7259, USA

Kaiser, George B (Financier)
Bank of Oklahoma
PO Box 2300
Bank Of Oklahoma Tower
Tulsa, OK 74102-2300, USA

Kaiser, Jason (Football Player)
Kansas City Chiefs
3885 Cheyenne Pl
Sedalia, CO 80135-8931, USA

Kaiser, Jeff (Baseball Player)
Oakland A's
26227 James Dr
Grosse Ile, MI 48138-2172, USA

Kaiser, Ken (Baseball Player)
56 Holley Sue Ln
Rochester, NY 14626-1170, USA

Kaiser, Michael (Misc)
Kennedy Center for Performing Arts
Washington, DC 20011, USA

Kaiser, Natasha (Athlete, Track Athlete)
2601 Hickman Rd
Des Moines, IA 50310-5550, USA

Kaiser, Suki (Actor)
c/o Pam Winter *Gary Goddard Agency*
10 Saint Mary Street #305
Toronto, ON M4Y 1P9, CANADA

Kaiser, Tim (Producer)
c/o Scott Schwartz *Vision Art Management*
9200 W Sunset Blvd Ph 1
Los Angeles, CA 90069-3601, USA

Kaiserman, William (Designer, Fashion Designer)
29 W 56th St
New York, NY 10019-3902, USA

Kaji, Gautam S (Financier)
World Bank Group
1818 H St NW
Washington, DC 20433-0002, USA

Kajol (Actor)
Usha Kiran
Altamount Road
Mumbai, MS 400026, INDIA

Kakhidze, Djansug I (Conductor)
Leselidze St 18
Tbilisi 380005, GEORGIA

Kakutani, Michiko (Journalist)
New York Times
229 W 43rd St
Editorial Dept
New York, NY 10036-3959, USA

Kalafat, Ed (Basketball Player)
1814 Pinehurst Ave
Saint Paul, MN 55116-2117, USA

Kalam, A P J Abdul (President)
President's Office
Bharat ka Rashtrapati Bhavan
New Delhi, New Delhi 110004, INDIA

Kalangis, Ike (Financier)
Boafmen's Sunwest
303 Roma Ave NW
Albuquerque, NM 87102-2219, USA

Kalas, Harry (Sportscaster)
Philadelphia Philies
3308 Chatham Pl
Media, PA 19063-4313, USA

Kalas, Todd (Baseball Player, Sportscaster)
Tampa Bay Devil Rays
9417 Cavendish Dr Apt 108
Tampa, FL 33626-5173, USA

Kalashnikov, Mikhail T (Designer, General)
A O Izhmash
426006 Izhevsk
Udmurtia Republic, RUSSIA

Kalb, Marvin (Correspondent, Educator)
Harvard University
Shorenstein Center
79 Jf Kennedy St
Cambridge, MA 02138, USA

Kalem, Toni (Actor)
House of Representatives
211 S Beverly Dr Ste 208
Beverly Hills, CA 90212-3879, USA

Kalember, Patricia (Actor)
Innovative Artists
1505 10th St
Santa Monica, CA 90401-2805, USA

Kalen, Herbert D (War Hero)
General Delivery
Angel Fire, NM 87710-9999, USA

Kaler, Jamie (Actor)
c/o Sheila Wenzel *Innovative Artists (LA)*
1505 10th St
Santa Monica, CA 90401-2805, USA

Kalichstein, Joseph (Musician)
I C M Artists
40 W 57th St
New York, NY 10019-4001, USA

Kalikow, Peter S (Publisher)
H J Kalikow Co
101 Park Ave
New York, NY 10178-0075, USA

kalina, Mike (Chef)
Travelin Gourmet Show
1320 Braddock Pl
Pbs-Tv
Alexandria, VA 22314-1692, USA

kalina, Richard (Artist)
44 King St
New York, NY 10014-4960, USA

Kaline, Albert W (Al) (Baseball Player)
Detroit Tigers
3613 York Ct
Bloomfield Hills, MI 48301-2058, USA

Kalis, Todd A (Football Player)
Minnesota Vikings
900 Bayview Ct
Cranberry Twp, PA 16066-3424, USA

Kalish, Martin (Misc)
School Administrators Federation
853 Broadway
New York, NY 10003-4703, USA

Kalitta, Connie (Race Car Driver)
American International Airways
804 Willow Run Airport
Ypsilanti, MI 48198-0899, USA

Kallaugher, Kevin (Kall) (Cartoonist)
Baltimore Sun
501 N Calvert St
Editorial Dept
Baltimore, MD 21202-3604, USA

Kallen, Jackie
c/o Daniel A (Dan) Strone *Trident Media Group LLC*
41 Madison Ave Fl 36
New York, NY 10010-2257, USA

Kallen, Kitty (Musician)
35 Winthrop Place
Englewood, NJ 07631, USA

Kallir, Lilian (Musician)
Columbia Artists Mgmt Inc
1790 Broadway Fl 6
New York, NY 10019-1412, USA

Kallman, Gerhard M (Architect)
Kallman McKinnell Wood
939 Boylston St
Boston, MA 02115-3192, USA

Kalloniatis, Anthony (Actor, Comedian, Composer, Director)
c/o Barry Katz *New Wave Entertainment (LA)*
2660 W Olive Ave
Burbank, CA 91505-4525, USA

Kalmanir, Thomas (Football Player)
Los Angeles Rams
425 E Shelldrake Cir
Fresno, CA 93730-1230, USA

Kalmbach, Herbert
1056 Santiago Dr
Newport Beach, CA 92660-5728, USA

Kalpokas, Donald (Prime Minister)
Prime Minister's Office
PO Box 110
Port Vila, VANUATA

Kalu, Ndukwe (Football Player)
Philadelphia Eagles
1910 Quiet Hollow Dr
Fresno, TX 77545-7539, USA

Kalule, Ayub (Boxer)
Palle Skjulet
Bagsvaert 12
Copenhagen 2880, DENMARK

Kalyagin, Aleksander A (Actor)
1905 Goda Str 3
#91
Moscow 123100, RUSSIA

Kamal, Gray (Musician)
William Morris Agency
1325 Avenue Of The Americas
New York, NY 10019-6091, USA

Kamali, Norma (Designer, Fashion Designer)
OMO Norma Kamali
11 W 56th St
New York, NY 10019-3902, USA

Kamana, John III (Football Player)
Los Angeles Rams
2319 Kapahu St
Honolulu, HI 96813-1433, USA

Kamano, Stacy (Actor)
c/o Staff Member *Amsel Eisenstadt & Frazier Inc*
5055 Wilshire Blvd Ste 865
Los Angeles, CA 90036-6109, USA

Kamarck, Martin A (Financier)
Export-Import Bank
811 Vermont Ave NW
Washington, DC 20571-0002, USA

Kamb, Alexander (Misc)
300 Alberta Way
Hillsborough, CA 94010-7148, USA

Kamel, Stanley (Actor)
Irv Schechter
9300 Wilshire Blvd # 410
Beverly Hills, CA 90212-3213, USA

Kamen, Dean (Inventor)
15 W Wind Dr
Bedford, NH 03110-5610, USA

Kamenshek, Dottie (Baseball Player)
78287 Brookhaven Ln
Palm Desert, CA 92211-2735, USA

Kamensky, Valeri (Hockey Player)
4 Bermuda Lake Dr
West Palm Beach, FL 33418-4583, USA

Kamesh, Kamala (Actor, Bollywood)
4F 3rd Block
Shanthi Towers 88 ArcotRoad Vadapalani
Chennai, TN 600026, INDIA

Kamieniecki, Scott (Baseball Player)
New York Yankees
7800 Somerhill Ln
Clarkston, MI 48348-4383, USA

Kamin, Blair (Critic)
Chicago Tribune
435 N Michigan Ave
Editorial Dept
Chicago, IL 60611-4024, USA

Kaminir, Lisa (Actor)
Ellis Talent Group
14241 N Maple Dr #207
Sherman Oaks, CA 91423, USA

Kaminski, Janusz Z (Cinematographer)
23801 Calabasas Rd Ste 2004
Calabasas, CA 91302-1565, USA

Kaminski, Larry (Football Player)
Denver Broncos
31423 State Highway 3 NE
Poulsbo, WA 98370-9373, USA

Kaminski, Marek (Misc)
Ul Dickmana 14/15
Gdansk 80-339, POLAND

Kaminsky, Arthur C (Lawyer)
Athletes & Artists
888 7th Ave Ste 3700
New York, NY 10106-3799, USA

Kaminsky, Walter (Misc)
Hamburg University
Martin-Luther-King Platz 6
Hamburg 20146, GERMANY

Kamisar, Yale (Educator, Lawyer)
2910 Daleview Dr
Ann Arbor, MI 48105-9684, USA

Kamm, Henry (Journalist)
New York Times
229 W 43rd St
Editorial Dept
New York, NY 10036-3959, USA

Kammen, Michael G (Historian)
Cornell University
McGraw Hall
History Dept
Ithaca, NY 14853, USA

Kammerer, Carl (Football Player)
San Francisco 49ers
6941 Brooks Rd
Highland, MD 20777-9540, USA

Kamoze, Ini (Musician)
Famous Artists Agency
250 W 57th St
New York, NY 10107-0001, USA

Kampa, Robert (Football Player)
Buffalo Bills
2001 Jennifer Dr
Aptos, CA 95003-2840, USA

Kampelman, Max M (Diplomat, Government Official)
3154 Highland Pl NW
Washington, DC 20008-3241, USA

Kampman, Aaron (Football Player)
Green Bay Packers
2887 Moose Creek Trl
Green Bay, WI 54313-3251, USA

Kamprad, Ingvar (Business Person)
IKEA Customer Relations
9930 Franklin Square Dr
Baltimore, MD 21236-4902, USA

Kamu, Okko T
Calle Mozart 7
Rancho Domingo
Benalmedina Pueblo 29369, SPAIN

Kan, Yuet Wai (Misc)
20 Yerba Buena Ave
San Francisco, CA 94127-1544, USA

Kanaga (Actor)
33 1st Mall Road
R A Puram
Chennai, TN 600028, INDIA

Kanakaredes, Melina (Actor)
c/o Bill Butler *Gersh Agency, The (NY)*
41 Madison Ave Fl 33
New York, NY 10010-2202, USA

Kanal, Tony (Musician, Songwriter, Writer)
Rebel Waltz Inc
31652 2nd Ave
Laguna Beach, CA 92651-8244, USA

Kanaly, Steve (Actor)
4663 Grand Ave
Ojai, CA 93023-9309, USA

Kanamori, Hiroo (Physicist)
California Institute of Technology
Geophysics Dept
Pasadena, CA 91125-0001, USA

Kanan, Sean
c/o Kim Matuka *Online Talent Group aka OTG Talent*
276 5th Ave Rm 204
New York, NY 10001-4565, USA

Kananln, Roman G (Architect)
Join-Stock Mosprojekt
13/14 1 Brestkaya Str
Moscow 125190, RUSSIA

Kancheli, Giya A (Georgy) (Composer)
Tovstonogov Str 6
Tbilisi 380064, GEORGIA

Kandel, Eric R (Nobel Prize Laureate)
9 Sigma Pl
Bronx, NY 10471-1215, USA

Kander, John H (Composer)
B M I
8730 W Sunset Blvd Ste 300
Los Angeles, CA 90069-2276, USA

Kane, Andy (Handy Andy) (Actor)
c/o Staff Member *David Anthony Promotions*
PO Box 286
Warrington
Cheshire WA2 8GA, UNITED KINGDOM (UK)

Kane, Big Daddy (Musician)
c/o Staff Member *Coast II Coast Entertainment (LA)*
3350 Wilshire Blvd Ste 1200
Los Angeles, CA 90010-1836, USA

Kane, Carol (Actor)
c/o Elise Konialian *Untitled Entertainment (NY)*
322 8th Ave Ste 601
New York, NY 10001-6715, USA

Kane, Christian (Actor)
c/o Stacy Boniello *The Firm*
9465 Wilshire Blvd Fl 6
Beverly Hills, CA 90212-2605, USA

Kane, John C (Business Person)
Cardinal Health
7000 Cardinal Pl
Dublin, OH 43017-1092, USA

Kane, Kelly (Actor)
D H Talent
1800 N Highland Ave # 300
Los Angeles, CA 90028-4527, USA

Kane, Khalil (Actor)
c/o Staff Member *Envision Entertainment*
9255 W Sunset Blvd Ste 500
West Hollywood, CA 90069-3301, USA

Kane, Nick (Musician)
AstroMedia
1620 16th Ave S
Nashville, TN 37212-2908, USA

Kane, Richard (Football Player)
Detroit Lions
2525 Greensboro Pt
Reno, NV 89509-5708, USA

Kane Elson, Marion (Swimmer)
4669 Badger Rd
Santa Rosa, CA 95409-2632, USA

Kanehl, Rod (Baseball Player)
New York Mets
2186 N Starr Rd
Palm Springs, CA 92262-3034, USA

Kanell, Danny (Football Player)
New York Giants
4632 Sea Grape Dr
Laud By Sea, FL 33308-3524, USA

Kanew, Jeffery R (Director)
Gersh Agency
232 N Canon Dr
Beverly Hills, CA 90210-5302, USA

Kang, Dong-Suk (Musician)
Clarion/Seven Muses
47 Whitehall Park
London N19 3TW, UNITED KINGDOM
(UK)

Kang, Sung (Actor)
c/o Scott Schachter *International Creative
Management (ICM-LA)*
10250 Constellation Blvd
Los Angeles, CA 90067-6200, USA

Kangas-Brody, Jennifer (Golfer)
2929 Margate Ln
East Lansing, MI 48823-9709, USA

Kango, Mayuri (Actor, Bollywood)
21 Kala Pathar Gokul Paradise
Thakur Complex Kandivili (E)
Mumbai, MS 400101, INDIA

Kanicki, James (Football Player)
Cleveland Browns
4590 Schramling Rd
Tackle Hill Farm
Pierpont, OH 44082-9712, USA

Kanievska, Marek (Director)
International Creative Mgmt
8942 Wilshire Blvd # 219
Beverly Hills, CA 90211-1908, USA

Kanin, Fay (Writer)
653 Palisades Beach Rd
Santa Monica, CA 90402-2605, USA

Kann, Peter R (Business Person, Journalist,
Publisher)
Dow Jones Co
200 Liberty St
New York, NY 10281-0083, USA

Kann, Stan
570 N Rossmore Ave
Los Angeles, CA 90004-2465, USA

Kannadasan, Vishali (Actor, Bollywood)
29/1 1st Cross Street
Chinmaya Nagar
Chennai, TN 600011, INDIA

Kannaiah, Ennathe (Actor)
RP Block No8 Llyods Colony
Royapet
Chennai, TN 600 014, INDIA

Kanne, Michael S (Judge)
US Court of Appeals
PO Box 1340
Lafayette, IN 47902-1340, USA

Kannenberg, Bernd (Athlete, Track
Athlete)
Sportschule
Sonthofen/Aligau 87527, GERMANY

Kanouse, Lyle (Actor)
c/o Staff Member *Gage Group, The (LA)*
14724 Ventura Blvd Ste 505
Sherman Oaks, CA 91403-3505, USA

Kanovitz, Howard (Artist)
361 N Sea Mecox Rd
Southampton, NY 11968-2829, USA

Kansas (Musician)
c/o Staff Member *Creative Artists Agency
LCC (CAA-LA)*
2000 Avenue Of The Stars
Los Angeles, CA 90067-4700, USA

Kansch, Heather (Artist)
Knowle
Rundlerohy Newton Abbot
Devon TQ12 2PJ, UNITED KINGDOM
(UK)

Kanter, Hal (Producer, Writer)
Hecox Horn Wheeler
4730 Woodman Ave
Sherman Oaks, CA 91423-2400, USA

Kanter, Paul (Musician)
Ron Rainey Mgmt
315 S Beverly Dr Ste 407
Beverly Hills, CA 90212-4301, USA

Kantor, Michael (Mickey) (Secretary)
2709 Olive Ave NW
Washington, DC 20007-3326, USA

Kantor, Secy Mickey
5019 Klingle St NW
Washington, DC 20016-2653, USA

Kantrowitz, Adrian (Doctor)
70 Gallogly Rd
Lake Angelus, MI 48326-1227, USA

Kantrowitz, Arthur R (Physicist)
4 Downing Rd
Hanover, NH 03755-1902, USA

Kanwaljit (Actor, Bollywood)
B-1001 Abhishek Apts
Juhu Versova Link Road 4 Bungalows
Andheri (W)
Mumbai, MS 400053, INDIA

Kanwar, Anita (Actor, Bollywood)
501A Anisha Apartments Yari Road
Versova Andheri
Mumbai, MS 400061, INDIA

Kanwar, Raj (Bollywood, Director,
Filmmaker, Producer)
6 Mewawala Building Haidery House
Next To Arrow Studio Vakola Masjid
Santacruz (E)
Bombay, MS 400 055, INDIA

Kao, Archie (Actor)
Gold Marshak Liedtke
3500 W Olive Ave Ste 1400
Burbank, CA 91505-5512, USA

Kapadia, Asif (Actor, Director, Writer)
c/o Steve Rabineau *William Morris
Agency (WMA-LA)*
9601 Wilshire Blvd Fl 3
Beverly Hills, CA 90210-5204, USA

Kapadia, Dimple (Actor, Bollywood)
201-A Vastu Bldg
Military Rd Juhu
Mumbai, MS 400049, INDIA

Kapanen, Sami (Hockey Player)
104 Royal Pine Court
Cary, NC 27511, USA

Kapele, John (Football Player)
Pittsburgh Steelers
45-543 Paleka Rd
Kaneohe, HI 96744-3448, USA

Kapelos, John (Actor)
c/o Kathy Carter *Axiom Management*
16302 Crowne Brook Cir
Franklin, TN 37067-1673, USA

Kapioitas, John (Business Person)
ITT Sheraton Corp
1111 Westchester Ave
West Harrison, NY 10604-3525, USA

Kaplan, Gabriel
9551 Hidden Valley Rd
Beverly Hills, CA 90210-1311, USA

Kaplan, Jonathan S (Director)
4323 Ben Ave
Studio City, CA 91604-1704, USA

Kaplan, Justin (Writer)
PO Box 219
Truro, MA 02666-0219, USA

Kaplan, Ken (Football Player)
Tampa Bay Buccaneers
8313 N Fremont Ave
Tampa, FL 33604-2707, USA

Kaplan, Marvin (Actor)
PO Box 1522
Burbank, CA 91507-1522, USA

Kaplan, Nathan O (Misc)
8587 La Jolla Scenic Dr N
La Jolla, CA 92037-2142, USA

Kapler, Gabe (Baseball Player)
c/o Staff Member *Boston Red Sox*
Fenway Park
4 Yawkey Way
Boston, MA 02215-3496, USA

Kaplon, Al (Actor)
2899 Agoura Rd Ste 172
Westlake Village, CA 91361-3218, USA

Kaplow, Herbert E (Correspondent)
211 N Van Buren St
Falls Church, VA 22046-3654, USA

Kapnek, Emily (Actor)
c/o Staff Member *Creative Artists Agency
LCC (CAA-LA)*
2000 Avenue Of The Stars
Los Angeles, CA 90067-4700, USA

Kapono, Jason (Basketball Player)
c/o Staff Member *Miami Heat*
601 Biscayne Blvd
American Airlines Arena
Miami, FL 33132-1801, USA

Kapoor, Anil (Actor, Bollywood)
31 Shringar, Presidency Society
7th Road JVPD Scheme
Mumbai, MS 400049, INDIA

Kapoor, Anish (Artist)
33 Coleherne Road
London SW10, UNITED KINGDOM (UK)

Kapoor, Kareena (Actor, Bollywood)
2-B/110/1201 Excellency 4th Cross Road
Lokhandwala Complex Andheri(W)
Mumbai, MS 400058, INDIA

Kapoor, Karishma (Actor, Bollywood)
2B Excellency 1101/1201
4th Cross Road, Lokhandwala Complex
Andheri (W)
Mumbai, MS 400048, INDIA

Kapoor, Karisma (Actor, Bollywood)
2B Excellency 1101 1201 4th Cross Road
Lokhandwala Complex
Bombay, MS 400 058, INDIA

Kapoor, Rajiv (Actor, Bollywood,
Director, Filmmaker, Producer)
R K Studios
Chembur
Bombay, MS 400 071, INDIA

Kapoor, Randhir (Actor, Bollywood,
Director, Producer)
R K Studios
Chembur
Bombay, MS 400 071, INDIA

Kapoor, Ravi (Actor)
c/o Matthew Lesher *Lesher Entertainment
Inc*
1134 S Cloverdale Ave
Los Angeles, CA 90019-6737, USA

Kapoor, Rishi (Actor, Bollywood)
27 Krishna Raj
Pali Hill Bandra
Mumbai, MS 400058, INDIA

Kapoor, Sanjay (Actor, Bollywood)
18 Arjun Magnum Bungalows
Lokhandwala Complex Andheri (W)
Mumbai, MS 400053, INDIA

Kapoor, Shakti (Actor, Bollywood,
Comedian)
Palm Beach 7th Floor Gandhigram Road
Juhu
Bombay, MS 400 049, INDIA

Kapoor, Shammi (Actor, Bollywood)
2 Blue Heaven Malabar Hill
Mt Pleasant Rd
Mumbai, MS 400006, INDIA

Kapoor, Shashi (Actor, Bollywood)
112 Atlas Apartments
Harkness Road
Bombay, MS 400 006, INDIA

Kapp, Joseph (Joe) (Coach, Football
Coach, Football Player)
Minnesota Vikings
PO Box 1973
Los Gatos, CA 95031-1973, USA

Kappu, Satyen (Actor, Bollywood)
201 Canvera J P Road
Versova Andheri
Bombay, MS 400 061, INDIA

Kapriski, Valerie
10 Ave. George V
Paris F-75008, FRANCE

Kaprisky, Valerie (Actor)
Artmedia
20 Ave Rapp
Paris 75007, FRANCE

Kapter, Alex (Football Player)
Cleveland Browns
2508 Haymarket St
Thousand Oaks, CA 91362-5322, USA

Kapture, Mitzi (Actor)
c/o Staff Member *Innovative Artists (LA)*
1505 10th St
Santa Monica, CA 90401-2805, USA

Kapur, Shekhar (Actor, Bollywood,
Director, Filmmaker, Producer)
42 Sheetal A B Nair Road
Juhu
Bombay, MS 400 049, INDIA

kar-Wai, Wong (Director)
c/o Peter Schwartzman *Jeff Morrone
Management*
9350 Wilshire Blvd Ste 224
Beverly Hills, CA 90212-3204, USA

Karageorghis, Vassos (Misc)
Foundation Anastasios Leventis
28 Sofoulis St
Nicosia, CYPRUS

Karamanov, Alemdar S (Composer)
Voykova Str 2
#4
Simferopol, Crimea, UKRAINE

Karamatic, George (Football Player)
Washington Redskins
982 Donald Way
Santa Maria, CA 93455-5019, USA

Karan, Donna (Designer, Fashion
Designer)
Donna Karan Co
550 7th Ave
New York, NY 10018-3203, USA

Karapati, Gyorgy (Misc)
Il Liva Utca 1
Budapest 1025, HUNGARY

Karath, Kym
40 Halsey Dr
Old Greenwich, CT 06870-1226, USA

Karathanasis, Sotirios K (Scientist)
Harvard Medical School
25 Shattuck St
Boston, MA 02115-6092, USA

Karatz, Bruce E (Business Person)
Kaufman & Broad Home
10990 Wilshire Blvd Fl 8th
Los Angeles, CA 90024-3918, USA

Karbacher, Bernd
Hufnagelstrasse 13
Munich D-80686, GERMANY

Karchner, Matt (Baseball Player)
Chicago White Sox
211 Duval St
Berwick, PA 18603-2120, USA

Kardashian, Kim (Actor, Reality TV Star)
c/o Jonathan Perry *United Talent Agency
(UTA)*
9560 Wilshire Blvd Ste 500
Beverly Hills, CA 90212-2401, USA

Kardashian, Robert
76201 Via Mariposa
Indian Wells, CA 92210-8706, USA

Karelskaya, Rimma K (Ballerina)
Bolshoi Theater
Teatralnaya Pl 1
Moscow 103009, RUSSIA

Karen, James
4455 Los Feliz Blvd Apt 807
Los Angeles, CA 90027-2138, USA

Karieva, Bernara (Ballerina)
Navoi Opera Theater
28 M K Otaturk St
Tashkent 700029, UZBEKISTAN

Karim, Reef (Actor)
c/o Staff Member *Select Artists Ltd (CA-
Westside Office)*
1138 12th St Apt 1
Santa Monica, CA 90403-5459, USA

Karim-Lamrani, Mohammed (Prime
Minister)
Rue du Mont Saint Michel
Anfa Superieur
Casablanca 21300, MOROCCO

Karimov, Islam M (President)
President's Office
Uzbekistansky Prosp 45
Tashkent, UZBEKISTAN

Karin, Anna (Actor)
Greene Assoc
7080 Hollywood Blvd Ste 1017
Los Angeles, CA 90028-6937, USA

Karina, Anna (Actor)
Artmedia
20 Ave Rapp
Paris 75007, FRANCE

Kariya, Paul (Hockey Player)
2493 Aquasanta
Tustin, CA 92782-1104, USA

karkovice, Ron (Baseball Player)
Chicago White Sox
108 Grace Ave
Kissimmee, FL 34747-5033, USA

Karl, George (Coach)
10936 N Port Washington Rd
Mequon, WI 53092-5031, USA

Karl, Jan
5555 Melrose Ave # L
Los Angeles, CA 90038-3989, USA

karl, Scott (Baseball Player)
Milwaukee Brewers
4503 Salisbury Dr
Carlsbad, CA 92010-2869, USA

Karle, Isabelia (Misc)
6304 Lakeview Dr
Falls Church, VA 22041-1309, USA

Karle, Jerome (Nobel Prize Laureate)
6304 Lakeview Dr
Falls Church, VA 22041-1309, USA

Karlen, John (Actor)
PO Box 1195
Santa Monica, CA 90406-1195, USA

Karlin, Ben (Producer, Writer)
c/o Staff Member *3 Arts Entertainment Inc*
9460 Wilshire Blvd Fl 7
Beverly Hills, CA 90212-2713, USA

Karlin, Fred
1187 Coast Village Rd # 1-339
Montecito, CA 93108-2737, USA

Karling, John S (Misc)
1219 Tuckaho Ln
West Lafayette, IN 47906-2334, USA

Karlis, Rich (Football Player)
Denver Broncos
13807 E Greenwood Dr
Aurora, CO 80014-3919, USA

Karloff, Sara
PO Box 2424
Rancho Mirage, CA 92270-1087, USA

Karlson, Phil
3094 Patricia Ave
Los Angeles, CA 90064-4534, USA

Karlsson, Lena (Musician)
MOB Agency
6404 Wilshire Blvd # 807
Los Angeles, CA 90048-5501, USA

Karlstad, Geir (Speed Skater)
Hamarveien 5A
Fjellhamar 1472, NORWAY

Karlzen, Mary (Musician, Songwriter,
Writer)
Little Big Man
155 Avenue Of The Americas Rm 700
New York, NY 10013-1507, USA

Karmanos Jr, Peter (Business Person)
Compuware Corp
1 Campus Martius
Detroit, MI 48226-5099, USA

Karmazin, Mike (Football Player)
New York Yankees
56 Lincoln St
Winthrop, MA 02152-2176, USA

Karmi, Ram (Architect)
Karmi Architects
17 Kaplan St
Tel Aviv 64734, ISRAEL

Karmi-Melamede, Ada (Architect)
Karmi Architects
17 Kaplan St
Tel Aviv 64734, ISRAEL

Karn, Richard (Actor)
Special Artists Agency
9465 Wilshire Blvd Ste 880
Beverly Hills, CA 90212-2607, USA

Karnad, Girish (Actor)
Silver Cascade Mount Mary Road
Bandra
Bombay, MS 400 050, INDIA

Karnes, David K (Senator)
Kutak Rock
1650 Farnam St Fl 3
Omaha Building
Omaha, NE 68102-2103, USA

Karnofsky, Sonny (Football Player)
Philadelphia Eagles
262 W Calle McCleary
Green Valley, AZ 85614-3717, USA

Karnow, Stanley (Historian)
10850 Spring Knoll Dr
Potomac, MD 20854-1550, USA

Karolyi, Bela (Coach)
478 Forest Service 200 Rd
Huntsville, TX 77340, USA

Karon, Jan (Writer)
7060 Esmont Farm
Esmont, VA 22937-1818, USA

Karp, Richard M (Scientist)
University of Washington
Computer Science Dept
Seattle, WA 98195-0001, USA

karp, Ryan (Baseball Player)
Philadelphia Phillies
1 Winterberry Ln
Medway, MA 02053-6209, USA

Karpatkin, Rhonda H (Publisher)
Consumer Reports Magazine
101 Truman Ave
Yonkers, NY 10703-1044, USA

Karpinski, Keith (Football Player)
Detroit Lions
9461 Clewley Rd
Lachine, MI 49753-9683, USA

Karpluk, Erin (Actor)
c/o Staff Member *ROAR LLC*
9701 Wilshire Blvd Ste 850
Beverly Hills, CA 90212-2032, USA

Karplus, Martin (Misc)
Harvard University
Chemistry Dept
Cambridge, MA 02138, USA

Karpov, Anatoly (Misc)
International Peace Fund
Prechistenka 10
Moscow, RUSSIA

Karpowich, Ed (Football Player)
Pittsburgh Steelers
PO Box 177
Fallon, NV 89407-0177, USA

Karr, Mary (Writer)
Syracuse University
English Dept
Syracuse, NY 13244-0001, USA

Karras, Alexander G (Alex) (Actor,
Football Player)
Detroit Lions
13400 Riverside Dr Ste 308
Sherman Oaks, CA 91423-2541, USA

Karras, John (Football Player)
Chicago Cardinals
123 Acacia Cir Apt 612
Indian Head Park, IL 60525-9098, USA

Karras, Louis (Football Player)
Washington Redskins
736 Island Way Apt 805
Clearwater Beach, FL 33767-1818, USA

Karras, Ted (Football Player)
Pittsburgh Steelers
1122 N Shelby St
Gary, IN 46403-1447, USA

Karros, Eric P (Baseball Player)
Los Angeles Dodgers
6212 Madra Ave
San Diego, CA 92120-3908, USA

Karsay, Steve (Baseball Player)
Oakland A's
845 United Nations Plz Apt 39D
New York, NY 10017-3533, USA

Karstens, George (Football Player)
Detroit Lions
9425 Kingston Dr
Bradenton, FL 34210-1830, USA

Kartheiser, Vincent (Actor)
c/o Evan Hainey *Untitled Entertainment
(LA)*
331 N Maple Dr Fl 3
Beverly Hills, CA 90210-3827, USA

Kartz, Keith (Football Player)
Denver Broncos
19232 E Hinsdale Ln
Centennial, CO 80016-2147, USA

Karusseit, Ursula (Actor)
Volksbunne
Rasa Luxemburg Platz
Berlin 10178, GERMANY

Karvan, Claudia (Actor, Musician)
c/o Robyn Gardiner *RGM Associates
(Australia)*
PO Box 128
Surry Hills NSW 2010, AUSTRALIA

Karwales, Jack (Football Player)
Chicago Cardinals
1116 Church St
Glenview, IL 60025-2929, USA

Karyo, Tcheky (Actor)
c/o Steve Chasman *Ace Media*
1411 5th St Ste 405
Santa Monica, CA 90401-2417, USA

Karzai, Hamid (Prime Minister)
Prime Minister's Office
Shar Rahi Sedarat
Kabul, AFGHANISTAN

Kasabian, Kamera (Musician)
c/o Staff Member *Paradigm (Monterey)*
509 Hartnell St
Monterey, CA 93940-2825, USA

Kasaks, Sally Frame (Business Person)
Ann Taylor Stores
142 W 57th St
New York, NY 10019-3399, USA

Kasaronov, Alexei (Hockey Player)
153 Eagle Rock Way
Montclair, NJ 07042-1621, USA

The Celebrity Black Book 2008

Kasarova, Vesselina (Opera Singer)
Columbia Artists Mgmt Inc
1790 Broadway Fl 6
New York, NY 10019-1412, USA

Kasatkina, Natalya R (Ballerina, Choreographer)
Saint Karietny Riad
H 5/10 B 37
Moscow 103006, RUSSIA

Kasay, John (Football Player)
Seattle Seahawks
8812 Covey Rise Ct
Charlotte, NC 28226-2649, USA

Kasch, Cody (Actor)
c/o Staff Member *International Creative Management (ICM-LA)*
10250 Constellation Blvd
Los Angeles, CA 90067-6200, USA

Kasch, Max (Actor)
c/o Staff Member *Abrams Artists Agency (LA)*
9200 W Sunset Blvd Ph 11
Los Angeles, CA 90069-3601, USA

Kasdan, Lawrence (Actor, Director, Producer, Writer)
c/o Staff Member *Kasdan Pictures*
9220 W Sunset Blvd Ste 108
West Hollywood, CA 90069-3500, USA

Kasem, Casey (Actor, Entertainer)
138 N Mapleton Dr
Los Angeles, CA 90077-3536, USA

Kasem, Jean (Actor)
138 N Mapleton Dr
Los Angeles, CA 90077-3536, USA

Kasem, Kerri (Actor)
c/o Steve Rohr *Rohr Talent Public Relations*
1901 Avenue Of The Stars Ste 365
Los Angeles, CA 90067-6025, USA

Kaser, Helmut A (Misc)
Hitzigweg 11
Zurich 8032, SWITZERLAND

Kasha, Al (Composer, Musician)
458 N Oakhurst Dr Apt 102
Beverly Hills, CA 90210-5701, USA

Kashkashian, Kim (Musician)
Musicians Corporate Mgmt
PO Box 825
Highland, NY 12528-0825, USA

Kashthuri (Actor, Bollywood)
4 Kashthuri Ranga Road
Chennai, TN 600018, INDIA

Kaskey, Raymond J (Artist)
Portlandia Productions
PO Box 25658
Portland, OR 97298-0658, USA

Kasko, Eddie (Baseball Player)
St Louis Cardinals
32 Major Ginter Ct
Richmond, VA 23227-3349, USA

Kason, Corinne (Actor)
Lovell Assoc
7095 Hollywood Blvd Ste 1006
Los Angeles, CA 90028-8912, USA

Kasovitz, Mathieu (Actor)
Cineart
36 Rue de Ponthieu
Paris 75008, FRANCE

Kasparaitis, Darius (Hockey Player)
48 Steers Ave
Northport, NY 11768-1541, USA

Kasparaltis, Darius
170 Fairway Landings Dr
Canonsburg, PA 15317-9567, USA

Kasparov, Garri (Misc)
Russian Chess Federation
Luzhnetskaya 8
Moscow 119270, RUSSIA

Kasper, Steve (Coach, Hockey Player)
6 Swan Ln
Andover, MA 01810-2844, USA

Kasper, Walter Cardinal (Religious Leader)
Via dell Erba 1
Rome 00193, ITALY

Kasperek, Dick (Football Player)
St Louis Cardinals
824 S County Line Rd
Hinsdale, IL 60521-4554, USA

Kaspszyk, Jacek (Conductor)
Teatr Wielu
Pl Teatrainy 1
Warsaw 00-077, POLAND

Kasrashvili, Makvala (Opera Singer)
Bolshoi Theater
Teatralnaya Pl 1
Moscow 103009, RUSSIA

Kass, Carmen (Model)
City Models
Rue Jean Mermoz
Paris 75008, FRANCE

Kass, Danny (Skier)
PO Box 8549
Mammoth Lakes, CA 93546-8549, USA

Kass, Leon R (Misc)
1150 17th St NW # Ae1
Washington, DC 20036-4603, USA

Kass, Patricia
B.P. 203
Illkirch F-06700, FRANCE

Kassebaum, Nancy Landon (Senator)
US Embassy
Unit 45004 Box 200
APO, AP 96337-5004, USA

Kassebaum-Baker, Nancy (Ex-Senator, Senator)
PO Box 8
Huntsville, TN 37756-0008, USA

Kassell, Carl (Correspondent)
National Public Radio
635 Massachusetts Ave NW
Washington, DC 20001-3753, USA

Kassir, John (Actor, Producer, Writer)
c/o Staff Member *Stone Manners Talent & Literary (LA)*
6500 Wilshire Blvd Ste 550
Los Angeles, CA 90048-4950, USA

Kassorla, Irene C (Doctor)
908 N Roxbury Dr
Beverly Hills, CA 90210-3020, USA

Kassulke, Karl O (Football Player)
Minnesota Vikings
3030 McCarthy Rdg
Eagan, MN 55121-1907, USA

Kastner, Elliott (Producer)
Winkast Films
Pinewood Studios
Iver Heath
Iver SL0 0NH, UNITED KINGDOM (UK)

Kastner, Peter (Actor)
459 Broadway
Cambridge, MA 02138-4125, USA

Kasyanov, Mikhail M (Prime Minister)
Prime Minister's Office
Kremlin
Staraya Pl 4
Moscow 103132, RUSSIA

Kata, Matt (Baseball Player)
Arizona Diamondbacks
2 Stafford Pl
Yardley, PA 19067-1036, USA

Katchik, Joe (Football Player)
New York Titans
25 Forty Oaks Rd
Whitehouse Station, NJ 08889-3121, USA

Katchor, Ben (Cartoonist)
Little Brown
3 Center Plz
Boston, MA 02108-2084, USA

Kates, Kimberley (Actor)
David Talent
116 S Gardner St
Los Angeles, CA 90036-2718, USA

Kates, Kimberly
3500 W Olive Ave Ste 1400
Burbank, CA 91505-5512, USA

Kates, Robert W (Misc)
1081 Bar Harbor Rd
Trenton, ME 04605-6017, USA

Kathadi, Ramamurthi (Actor)
4 Krishna Avenue
C V Raman Road
Chennai, TN 600 006, INDIA

Katims, Jason (Producer)
c/o Staff Member *Creative Artists Agency LCC (CAA-LA)*
2000 Avenue Of The Stars
Los Angeles, CA 90067-4700, USA

Katims, Milton (Conductor, Musician)
Fairway Estales
8001 Sand Point Way NE
Seattle, WA 98115-8112, USA

Katin, Peter R (Musician)
Maureen Lunn
Top Farm Parish Lane
Hedgerley
Bucks SL2 3JH, UNITED KINGDOM (UK)

Katrina & The Waves
45 Belvoir Rd. Cambridge
Cambridgeshire, ENGLAND CB4 1JH,
UNITED KINGDOM (UK)

Katritzky, Alan R (Misc)
1221 SW 21st Ave
Gainesville, FL 32601-8417, USA

Katsav, Moshe (President)
President's Office
3 Hanassi
Jerusalem 92188, ISRAEL

Katsoudas, Stella (Musician, Songwriter, Writer)
Ashley Talent
2002 Hogback Rd Ste 20
Ann Arbor, MI 48105-9736, USA

Katt, Nicky (Actor)
c/o John Carrabino *John Carrabino Management*
5900 Wilshire Blvd Ste 406
Los Angeles, CA 90036-5015, USA

Katt, William (Actor)
5860 Le Sage Ave
Woodland Hills, CA 91367-5902, USA

Kattan, Chris (Comedian)
c/o Staff Member *Endeavor Agency LLC (LA)*
9601 Wilshire Blvd Fl 3
Beverly Hills, CA 90210-5204, USA

Kattan, Mohammed Imad (Architect)
PO Box 950846
Amman 11195, JORDAN

Katz, Abraham (Diplomat)
US Council for International Business
1212 Avenue Of The Americas
New York, NY 10036-1689, USA

Katz, Alex (Artist)
435 W Broadway
New York, NY 10012-5902, USA

Katz, Cindy
Badgley Connor Talent Agency
1680 Vine St Ste 1016
Los Angeles, CA 90028-8800, USA

Katz, Douglas J (Doug) (Admiral)
1530 Gordon Cove Dr
Annapolis, MD 21403-5004, USA

Katz, Harold (Misc)
Philadelphia 76ers
3601 S Broad St
1st Union Center
Philadelphia, PA 19148-5287, USA

Katz, Hilda (Artist)
915 W End Ave Apt 5D
New York, NY 10025-3503, USA

Katz, Jonathan (Actor, Animator, Comedian)
Creative Artists Agency
9830 Wilshire Blvd
Beverly Hills, CA 90212-1804, USA

Katz, Michael (Misc)
1 Griggs Ln
Chappaqua, NY 10514-1404, USA

Katz, Omri (Actor)
JH Productions
23679 Calabasas Rd # 333
Calabasas, CA 91302-1502, USA

Katz, Ross (Producer)
c/o Staff Member *United Talent Agency (UTA)*
9560 Wilshire Blvd Ste 500
Beverly Hills, CA 90212-2401, USA

Katz, Samuel L (Misc)
1917 Wildcat Creek Rd
Chapel Hill, NC 27516-9786, USA

Katz, Simon (Musician)
Searles
Chapel
26A Munster St
London SW6 4EN, UNITED KINGDOM (UK)

Katz, Tonnie L (Editor)
Orange Country Register
625 N Grand Ave
Editorial Dept
Santa Ana, CA 92701-4347, USA

katz, Vera (Politician)
Mayor's Office
1221 SW 4th Ave # 340
City Hall
Portland, OR 97204-1904, USA

Katzenbach, Nicolas
5073 Province Line Rd
Princeton, NJ 08540-7522, USA

Katzenberg, Jeffrey (Business Person)
c/o Staff Member *DreamWorks SKG*
100 Universal City Plz
Universal City, CA 91608-1002, USA

Katzenmayer, Travis (Baseball Player)
562 N Overland
Mesa, AZ 85207-6670, USA

Katzenmoyer, Andy (Football Player)
New England Patriots
859 W Main St
Westerville, OH 43081-1224, USA

Katzir, Ephraim (President)
Weizmann Institute of Science
PO Box 26
Rehovot, ISRAEL

Katzur, Klaus (Swimmer)
Robert-Siewart-Str 76
Chemnitz 0912, GERMANY

Kauffman, Marta (Producer, Writer)
c/o Staff Member *Bright Kauffman Crane Productions*
4000 Warner Blvd Bldg 160 # 750
Burbank, CA 91522-0001, USA

Kaufman, Adam (Actor)
c/o JB Roberts *Thruline Entertainment*
9250 Wilshire Blvd Ground Fl
Beverly Hills, CA 90210, USA

Kaufman, Bob (Ajax) (Basketball Player)
1677 Rivermist Dr SW
Lilburn, GA 30047-2451, USA

Kaufman, Charlie (Writer)
c/o Staff Member *United Talent Agency (UTA)*
9560 Wilshire Blvd Ste 500
Beverly Hills, CA 90212-2401, USA

Kaufman, Curt (Baseball Player)
New York Yankees
308 Hillway Dr
Glenwood, IA 51534-1210, USA

Kaufman, Dan S (Misc)
University of Wisconsin
Medical School
Hematology Dept
Madison, WI 53706, USA

Kaufman, Donald (Writer)
c/o Staff Member *United Talent Agency (UTA)*
9560 Wilshire Blvd Ste 500
Beverly Hills, CA 90212-2401, USA

Kaufman, Henry (Financier)
Henry Kaufman Co
65 E 55th St
New York, NY 10022-3219, USA

Kaufman, Joan (Baseball Player)
1111 Crystal Spg
San Antonio, TX 78258-6909, USA

Kaufman, Moises (Director)
c/o Patty Detroit *International Creative Management (ICM-LA)*
10250 Constellation Blvd
Los Angeles, CA 90067-6200, USA

Kaufman, Napolean (Football Player)
Oakland Raiders
1913 Via Di Salerno
Pleasanton, CA 94566-2121, USA

Kaukonen, Jorma (Misc)
Agency Group Ltd
1775 Broadway Ste 515
New York, NY 10019-1903, USA

Kausalya (Actor)
15 A-2 Akshar
Palace Road
Bangalore, KA 52, INDIA

Kaushal, Kamini (Actor, Bollywood, Dancer)
B2 Anita Mt Pleasant Road
Malabar Hill
Bombay, MS 400 006, INDIA

Kaushik, Satish (Actor, Bollywood, Comedian, Director, Filmmaker)
1/124 Park View Zakaria Agadi Nagar
Yari Road Versova Andheri
Bombay, MS 400 061, INDIA

Kavana (Musician)
Tony Denton Promotions
19 S Molton Ln
Mayfair
London, England W1K 5LE, UNITED KINGDOM (UK)

kavanaugh, Kenneth W (Ken) (Football Player)
Chicago Bears
4907 Palm Aire Dr
Sarasota, FL 34243-3718, USA

Kavandi, Janet L (Astronaut)
3907 Park Circle Way
Houston, TX 77059-3019, USA

Kavelaars, Ingrid (Actor)
c/o Staff Member *Silver Massetti & Szatmary (SMS-NY)*
145 W 45th St # 1204
New York, NY 10036-4008, USA

Kaveri (Actor, Bollywood)
114 4th Street
New Britania Nagar
Chennai, TN 600087, INDIA

Kaviya (Actor, Bollywood)
Santhi Apts
Kumaran Colony 9th Street
Chennai, TN 600026, INDIA

Kavner, Julie (Actor)
c/o Paul Martino *International Creative Management (ICM-NY)*
40 W 57th St
New York, NY 10019-4001, USA

Kavovit, Andrew (Actor)
c/o Staff Member *TalentWorks (LA)*
3500 W Olive Ave Ste 1400
Burbank, CA 91505-5512, USA

Kawakubo, Rei (Designer, Fashion Designer)
Comme des Garcons
5-11-5 Minamiaoyana
Minatoku
Tokyo, JAPAN

Kawalerowicz, Jersy (Director, Writer)
Ul Marconich 5m 21
Warsaw 02-954, POLAND

Kawawa, Rashidi M (Prime Minister)
Ministry of Defense
Dar es Salaam
TANZANIA

Kay, Charles
18 Epple Rd.
London, ENGLAND SW6, UNITED KINGDOM (UK)

Kay, Dianne (Actor)
1565 Calle Del Estribo
Pacific Palisades, CA 90272-2009, USA

Kay, Jason (Jay) (Musician)
c/o Staff Member *William Morris Agency (WMA-LA)*
1 William Morris Pl
Beverly Hills, CA 90212-4261, USA

Kay, John (Musician)
Elite Management Corp
2211 Norfolk St Ste 760
Houston, TX 77098-4033, USA

Kay, Vanessa (Actor)
c/o Staff Member *Comedy Central (LA)*
2049 Century Park E # 4170
Los Angeles, CA 90067-3101, USA

Kay, William H (Football Player)
Houston Oilers
4266 Waterston Courtyard
Evans, GA 30809-5036, USA

Kaye, Davie A
1044 Ironwork Pass
Vancouver, BC V6H 3P1, CANADA

Kaye, Jonathan (Golfer)
328 W El Camino Dr
Phoenix, AZ 85021-5525, USA

Kaye, Judy (Actor, Musician)
Bret Adams
448 W 44th St
New York, NY 10036-5220, USA

Kaye, Lila
47 Courtfield Rd. #9
London, ENGLAND SW7 4DB, UNITED KINGDOM (UK)

Kaye, Melvina
PO Box 6085
Burbank, CA 91510-6085, USA

Kaye, Thorsten (Actor)
c/o Staff Member *International Creative Management (ICM-LA)*
10250 Constellation Blvd
Los Angeles, CA 90067-6200, USA

Kaye, Tony (Misc)
Sun Artists
9 Hillgate St
London W8 7SP, UNITED KINGDOM (UK)

Kaysen, Carl (Economist)
41 Holden St
Cambridge, MA 02138-2038, USA

Kayser, Elmer L (Historian)
2921 34th St NW
Washington, DC 20008-3510, USA

Kaz (Artist)
c/o Staff Member *Fantagraphics Books*
7563 Lake City Way NE
Seattle, WA 98115-4218, USA

Kazan, Lainie (Actor, Musician)
9903 Santa Monica Blvd # 283
Beverly Hills, CA 90212-1606, USA

Kazankina, Tatyana (Athlete, Track Athlete)
Hoshimina St
111211
Saint Petersburg, RUSSIA

Kazanski, Ted (Baseball Player)
Philadelphia Phillies
850 Stephenson Hwy Ste 400
Troy, MI 48083-1163, USA

Kazarnovskaya, Lubov Y (Opera Singer)
Hohenbergstr 50
Vienna 1120, AUSTRIA

Kazer, Beau
139A N San Fernando Blvd
Burbank, CA 91502, USA

Kazmaier, Dick
261 Park Ln
Concord, MA 01742-1621, USA

Kazmaier Jr, Richard W (Dick) (Football Player)
24 Dockside Ln
Box 29
Key Largo, FL 33037-5267, USA

KC & The Sunshine Band (Music Group)
c/o Staff Member *William Morris Agency (WMA-LA)*
1 William Morris Pl
Beverly Hills, CA 90212-4261, USA

Keach, James (Actor)
Metropolitan Talent Agency
4500 Wilshire Blvd Fl 2
Los Angeles, CA 90010-3858, USA

Keach, Stacy (Actor)
101 N Robertson Blvd Ste 200
Beverly Hills, CA 90211-2191, USA

Keady, Gene (Coach)
Purdue University
Mackey Arena
West Lafayette, IN 47907, USA

Keaggy, Phil (Musician)
2175 Oak Hill Dr
C/O Robin Mawdsley
Murfreesboro, TN 37130-2007, USA

Keagle, Greg (Baseball Player)
Detroit Tigers
11 Wolcott Dr
Horseheads, NY 14845-1012, USA

Kealey, Steve (Baseball Player)
California Angels
1080 1700 Ave
Abilene, KS 67410-6321, USA

Kean, Jane
c/o Staff Member *Pierce & Shelly*
13775A Mono Way # 220
Sonora, CA 95370-8813, USA

Kean, Laurel (Golfer)
11783 Puma Path
Venice, FL 34292-4125, USA

Kean, Thomas H (Educator, Governor)
Drew University
36 Madison Ave
President's Office
Madison, NJ 07940-1493, USA

Keanan, Staci (Actor)
Bill Rogin Management
427 N Canon Dr Ste 215
Beverly Hills, CA 90210-4840, USA

Keane (Musician)
c/o Staff Member *Island Records*
825 8th Ave
New York, NY 10019-7472, USA

Keane, Bill (Cartoonist)
5815 E Joshua Tree Ln
Paradise Valley, AZ 85253-3409, USA

Keane, Dolores (Musician)
D K Entertainments
Caherlistrane, Galway, IRELAND

Keane, Glen (Animator)
Walt Disney Studios
Animation Dept
500 S Buena Vista St
Burbank, CA 91521-0001, USA

The Celebrity Black Book 2008

Keane, James
612 Lighthouse Ave # 220
Pacific Grove, CA 93950-2615, USA

Keane, James P (Football Player)
Chicago Bears
505 Front St
McHenry, IL 60050-5508, USA

Keane, John B
37 William St
Listowel County Kerry, IRELAND

Keane, John M (Jack) (General)
Vice Chief Of Staff Hqusa
Pentagon
Washington, DC 20310-0001, USA

Keane, Kerrie (Actor)
S D B Partners
1801 Avenue Of Stars Ste 902
Los Angeles, CA 90067-5981, USA

Keane, Roy M (Soccer Player)
Manchester United
Busby Way
Old Trafford
Manchester M16 0RA, UNITED
KINGDOM (UK)

Keane, Sean (Misc)
Macklam Feldman Mgmt
1505 W 2nd Ave
#200
Vancouver, BC V6H 3Y4, CANADA

Keane, William
4526 Wilshire Blvd
Los Angeles, CA 90010-3801, USA

Kear, David (Misc)
34 W End
Ohope, NEW ZEALAND

Kearney, Bob (Baseball Player)
San Francisco Giants
2285 Riverbend Dr
Benton Harbor, MI 49022-6919, USA

Kearney, Jim (Football Player)
Detroit Lions
7340 Leavenworth Rd
Washington High School
Kansas City, KS 66109-1226, USA

Kearney, Tim (Football Player)
Cincinnati Bengals
2144 Dartmouth Gate Ct
Ballwin, MO 63011-5436, USA

Kearns, Austin (Athlete, Baseball Player)
Cincinnati Reds
719 Haverhill Dr
Lexington, KY 40503-3426, USA

Kearns, Dennis M (Hockey Player)
605 King Georges Way
West Vancouver, BC V7S 1S2, CANADA

Kearns, Thomas (Football Player)
New York Giants
121 Bay Colony Dr
Fort Lauderdale, FL 33308-2024, USA

Kearse, Amalya L (Judge)
US Court of Appeals
Foley Square
US Courthouse
New York, NY 10007, USA

Kearse, Jevon (Football Player)
Tennessee Titans
3750 Madison Ave
Fort Myers, FL 33916-1218, USA

Keathley, George (Director)
Missouri Repertory Theater
4949 Cherry St
Kansas City, MO 64110-2229, USA

Keating, Bill (Football Player)
Denver Broncos
4810 S Lafayette Ln
Englewood, CO 80113-7011, USA

Keating, Charles (Actor)
Don Buchwald
10 E 44th St
New York, NY 10017-3654, USA

Keating, Chris (Football Player)
Buffalo Bills
741 Canton Ave
Milton, MA 02186-3121, USA

Keating, Dominic (Actor)
c/o Staff Member *Integrated Films &
Management*
1041 N Formosa Ave
Santa Monica Bldg W #17
W Hollywood, CA 90046-6703, USA

Keating, Edward (Photographer)
New York Times
229 W 43rd St
Editorial Dept
New York, NY 10036-3959, USA

Keating, Henry (H R F) (Writer)
35 Northumberland Place
London W2 5AS, UNITED KINGDOM
(UK)

Keating, Paul (Royalty)
31 Bligh St Level 2
Sydney 2000, AUSTRALIA

Keating, Paul J (Prime Minister)
Keating Assoc-War Mgmt
Bushy Park Road
57 Meadowbank
Dublin, IRELAND

Keating, Ronan (Musician)
Carol Assoc-War Mgmt
Bushy Park Rd
57 Meadowbank
Dublin, IRELAND

Keating, Thomas A (Football Player)
Buffalo Bills
3725 W St NW
Washington, DC 20007-1714, USA

Keating II, Francis A (Frank) (Governor)
American Life Insurers Council
101 Constitution Ave NW Ste 700W
Washington, DC 20001-2146, USA

Keatley, Greg (Baseball Player)
Kansas City Royals
140 Rockridge Ct
Lexington, SC 29072-7970, USA

Keaton, Curtis (Football Player)
Cincinnati Bengals
1667 Lynnhurst Rd
Columbus, OH 43229-2639, USA

Keaton, Diane (Actor, Director, Producer)
c/o Adam Venit *Endeavor Agency LLC
(LA)*
9601 Wilshire Blvd Fl 3
Beverly Hills, CA 90210-5204, USA

Keaton, Joshua (Josh) (Actor)
c/o Brian Wilkins *Wilkins Management*
901 N Highland Ave
Los Angeles, CA 90038-2412, USA

Keaton, Michael (Actor)
11901 Santa Monica Blvd # 547
Los Angeles, CA 90025-2767, USA

Keats, Donald H (Composer)
University of Denver
Music School
Denver, CO 80208-0001, USA

Keats, Ele (Actor)
c/o Rob D'Avola *Identity Talent Agency
(ID)*
9107 Wilshire Blvd Ste 450
Beverly Hills, CA 90210-5535, USA

Keb Mo (Musician, Songwriter, Writer)
Monterey International
200 W Superior St Ste 202
Chicago, IL 60610-3554, USA

Kebble (Kebbel), Arielle (Actor)
c/o Martin Berneman *Martin Berneman
Management*
211 S Beverly Dr Ste 208
Beverly Hills, CA 90212-3879, USA

Kebede, Liya (Model)
IMG Models
304 Park Ave S # 1200
New York, NY 10010-4301, USA

Kebich, Vyacheslau F (Prime Minister)
National Assembly
K Marksa Str 38
Dom Urada
Minsk 220016, BELARUS

Keck, Donald B (Inventor)
2877 Chequers Cir
Big Flats, NY 14814-9610, USA

Keck Jr, Herman (Religious Leader)
Calvary Grace Christian Church of Faith
US Box 4266
Norton Afb, CA 92409, USA

Kecman, Dan (Football Player)
Boston Patriots
4408 Shadynook St
West Mifflin, PA 15122-2261, USA

Kedah (King)
Istana Anak Bukit
Alor Setar, Kedah Darul Aman,
MALAYSIA

Kedes, Maureen (Actor)
Tisherman Agency
6767 Forest Lawn Dr Ste 101
Los Angeles, CA 90068-1050, USA

Kee, John P (Musician)
Covenant Agency
123 California Ave Apt 116
Santa Monica, CA 90403-3560, USA

Keeble, Jerry (Football Player)
San Francisco 49ers
PO Box 367
Dunnigan, CA 95937-0367, USA

Keeble, John (Musician)
International Talent Group
729 7th Ave Rm 1600
New York, NY 10019-6880, USA

Keedy, Pat (Baseball Player)
California Angels
6308 Mountainview Cir
Gardendale, AL 35071-2088, USA

Keefe, Adam (Basketball Player)
15933 Alcima Ave
Pacific Palisades, CA 90272-2405, USA

Keefe, Mike (Cartoonist)
Denver Post
PO Box 1709
Editorial Dept
Denver, CO 80201-1709, USA

Keefer, Don (Actor)
4146 Allott Ave
Sherman Oaks, CA 91423-4302, USA

Keeffe, Bernard (Conductor)
153 Honor Oak Road
London SE23 3RN, UNITED KINGDOM
(UK)

Keegan, Andrew (Actor)
c/o Barry McPherson *Agency for the
Performing Arts (APA-LA)*
405 S Beverly Dr
Beverly Hills, CA 90212-4416, USA

Keegan, John (Historian)
Manor House
Kilmington near Warminster
Wilts BA12 6RD, UNITED KINGDOM
(UK)

Keehne, Virginya (Actor)
Craig Mgmt
125 S Sycamore Ave
Los Angeles, CA 90036-2938, USA

Keel Jr, Alton G (Business Person,
Diplomat)
Atlantic Partners
2891 South River Rd
Stanardsville, VA 22973-2416, USA

Keeler, Don
24000 Jensen Dr
West Hills, CA 91304-3011, USA

Keeler, William H Cardinal (Religious
Leader)
National Conference of Catholic Bishops
3211 4th St NE
Washington, DC 20017-1104, USA

Keeley, Robert V (Diplomat)
3814 Livingston St NW
Washington, DC 20015-2803, USA

Keeling, Charles D (Musician)
Scripps Oceanography Institute
9500 Gilman Dr
Ritler Hall
La Jolla, CA 92093-5004, USA

Keeling, Rex (Football Player)
Cincinnati Bengals
510 Country Club Dr
Gadsden, AL 35901-5804, USA

Keelor, Greg (Musician)
ArtisDirect
1601 Cloverfield Blvd # 400
Santa Monica, CA 90404-4082, USA

Keen, Robert Earl (Musician, Songwriter)
Rosetta
PO Box 2186
Bandera, TX 78003-2186, USA

Keen, Sam (Misc, Writer)
16331 Norrbom Rd
Sonoma, CA 95476-4783, USA

Keena, Monica (Actor)
c/o Heather Reynolds *One Entertainment
(NY)*
12 W 57th St Ph
New York, NY 10019-3900, USA

Keenan, Joseph D (Misc)
2727 29th St NW
Washington, DC 20008-5503, USA

Keenan, Maynard James (Musician)
c/o Staff Member *Virgin Records (NY)*
304 Park Ave S Fl 5
New York, NY 10010-4316, USA

Keenan, Mike (Misc)
550 NE 21st Ave Apt 13
Deerfield Beach, FL 33441-3809, USA

Keene, Bob (Football Player)
Detroit Lions
W Laurel Lane
Etowah, NC 28729, USA

Keene, Donald L (Educator)
Columbia University
Language Dept
Kent Hall
New York, NY 10027, USA

Keene, Tommy (Musician, Songwriter, Writer)
Black Park Mgmt
PO Box 107
Sunbury, NC 27979-0107, USA

Keene Cherot, Kyera (Actor)
c/o Staff Member *Creative Artists Agency LCC (CAA-LA)*
2000 Avenue Of The Stars
Los Angeles, CA 90067-4700, USA

Keenen, Mary Jo
9200 W Sunset Blvd Ste 1130
Los Angeles, CA 90069-3606, USA

Keener, Catherine (Actor)
c/o Leslie Siebert *Gersh Agency, The (LA)*
232 N Canon Dr
Beverly Hills, CA 90210-5302, USA

Keener, Jeff (Baseball Player)
St Louis Cardinals
2107 Dewey St
Murphysboro, IL 62966-2451, USA

Keener, Joe (Baseball Player)
Montreal Expos
26849 Lompoc Ave
Barstow, CA 92311, USA

Keenlyside, Simon (Opera Singer)
Columbia Artists Mgmt Inc
1790 Broadway Fl 6
New York, NY 10019-1412, USA

Keeny Jr, Spurgeon M (Misc)
3600 Albernarle St NW
Washington, DC 20008, USA

Keerthana, K (Actor, Bollywood)
71 A Kamarajar Salai
R A Puram
Chennai, TN 600028, INDIA

Keeslar, Matt (Actor)
c/o Staff Member *Stone Manners Talent & Literary (LA)*
6500 Wilshire Blvd Ste 550
Los Angeles, CA 90048-4950, USA

Keesling, Barbara (Writer)
c/o Staff Member *Random House Publicity*
1745 Broadway
New York, NY 10019-4343, USA

Keeton, Durwood (Football Player)
New England Patriots
1372 Diamond Gate Pl
El Paso, TX 79936-7841, USA

Keeton, Rickey (Baseball Player)
Milwaukee Brewers
3433 Stathem Ave
Cincinnati, OH 45211-5723, USA

Keezer, Geoff (Misc)
DL Media
PO Box 2728
Bala Cynwyd, PA 19004-6728, USA

Kegel, Oliver (Athlete)
Am Bogen 23
Berlin 13589, GERMANY

Keggi, Caroline (Golfer)
1248 Sunningdale Ln
Ormond Beach, FL 32174-1402, USA

Keibler, Stacey (Actor, Wrestler)
c/o Nick Reed *International Creative Management (ICM-LA)*
10250 Constellation Blvd
Los Angeles, CA 90067-6200, USA

Keibler, Stacy (Wrestler)
c/o Staff Member *World Wrestling Entertainment (WWE)*
1241 E Main St
Stamford, CT 06902-3520, USA

Keightley, David N (Historian)
University of California
History Dept
Berkeley, CA 94720-0001, USA

Keillor, Garrison E (Correspondent, Writer)
A Prairie Home Companion
611 Frontenac Pl
Saint Paul, MN 55104-7660, USA

Keim, Betty Lou
10642 Arnel Pl
Chatsworth, CA 91311-2501, USA

Keim, Jenny (Swimmer)
R O'Brien
1 Hall Of Fame Dr
Swimming Hall Of Fame
Fort Lauderdale, FL 33316-1611, USA

Keita, Ibrahaim Boubakar (Prime Minister)
Prime Minister's Office
BP97
Bamako, MALI

Keita, Salif (Composer, Musician)
International Music Network
278 S Main St #400
Gloucester, MA 01930, USA

Keitel, Harvey (Actor)
c/o Staff Member *Goatsingers, The*
443 Greenwich St # 4B
New York, NY 10013-1702, USA

Keith, Louis (Doctor)
333 E Superior St # 476
Chicago, IL 60611-2654, USA

Keith, Penelope (Actor)
66 Berkeley House
Hay Hill
London SW3, UNITED KINGDOM (UK)

Keith, Toby (Musician)
c/o Adena Chawke *Greenlight Management*
315 S Beverly Dr Ste 300
Beverly Hills, CA 90212-4309, USA

Keith Rennie, Callum (Actor)
c/o Staff Member *Agency for the Performing Arts (APA-LA)*
405 S Beverly Dr
Beverly Hills, CA 90212-4416, USA

Keithley, Gary (Football Player)
St Louis Cardinals
1801 W Westhill Dr
Cleburne, TX 76033-5952, USA

Kekalainen, Jarmo (Hockey Player)
145 Hillcrest Rd
Needham, MA 02492-3941, USA

kekich, Mike (Baseball Player)
Los Angeles Dodgers
5314 Canada Vista Pl NW
Albuquerque, NM 87120-2412, USA

Kelcher, Louie J (Football Player)
San Diego Chargers
10204 Carlotta Cv
Austin, TX 78733-1542, USA

Keleti, Agnes (Misc)
Wingate Institute for Physical Education & Sport
Matanya 42902, ISRAEL

Kelis (Musician)
c/o Staff Member *Solo Agency Ltd (UK)*
55 Fulham High St
London SW6 3JJ, UNITED KINGDOM (UK)

Kelis, Kid 'N Play (Music Group)
1650 Broadway Ste 508
New York, NY 10019-6833, USA

Kelker-Kelly, Robert
5 Tate Ave # 15
Piermont, NY 10968, USA

Kell, Everett (Baseball Player)
Philadelphia Athletics
PO Box 10113
Conway, AR 72034-0001, USA

Kell, George C (Baseball Player)
PO Box 158
Swifton, AR 72471-0158, USA

Kellagher, Bill (Football Player)
Chicago Rockets
17254 Valley Dr
Lewes, DE 19958-4035, USA

Kellar, Mark (Football Player)
Minnesota Vikings
3537 W Fuller St
Edina, MN 55410-2361, USA

Kellaway, Roger (Composer)
Pat Phillips Mgmt
520 E 81st St Ph C
New York, NY 10028-7045, USA

Kelleher, Bill (Journalist)
New York Times
229 W 43rd St
Editorial Dept
New York, NY 10036-3959, USA

Kelleher, Erhard (Misc)
Sudliche Munchneustr 6A
Grunwald 82031, GERMANY

Kelleher, Herbert D (Business Person)
144 Thelma Dr
San Antonio, TX 78212-2516, USA

Kelleher, Mick (Baseball Player)
St Louis Cardinals
1451 Alamo Pintado Rd
Solvang, CA 93463-9757, USA

Keller, Cord (Producer)
c/o Staff Member *Innovative Artists (LA)*
1505 10th St
Santa Monica, CA 90401-2805, USA

Keller, Hal (Baseball Player)
Washington Senators
241 Madrona Ter
Sequim, WA 98382-6804, USA

Keller, Jason (Race Car Driver)
Progressive Motorsports
177 Knob Hill Rd
Mooresville, NC 28117-6847, USA

Keller, John (Basketball Player)
2100 24th St
Great Bend, KS 67530-2547, USA

Keller, Kris (Baseball Player)
Detroit Tigers
2496 Oakview Dr
Jacksonville, FL 32246-2462, USA

Keller, Larry (Football Player)
New York Jets
3050 Bluebonnet Blvd
Brenham, TX 77833-9046, USA

Keller, Leonard B (War Hero)
6555 Baxley Rd
Milton, FL 32570-6431, USA

Keller, Martha (Actor)
Lemonstr 9
Munich 81679, GERMANY

Keller, Marthe
5 rue St. Dominique
Paris 75007, FRANCE

Keller, Mary Page (Actor)
c/o Staff Member *SMS Talent Inc*
8730 W Sunset Blvd Ste 440
Los Angeles, CA 90069-2277, USA

Keller, Rita (Baseball Player)
6410 Westchester St
Portage, MI 49024-3276, USA

Keller, Ron (Baseball Player)
Minnesota Twins
PO Box 3267
Cashiers, NC 28717-3267, USA

Keller, Thomas (Chef)
French Laundry
6540 Washington St
Yountville, CA 94599-1315, USA

Kellerman, Ernie (Football Player)
Cleveland Browns
90 Glenview Dr
Aurora, OH 44202-8219, USA

Kellerman, Faye (Writer)
Karpfinger Agency
357 W 20th St
New York, NY 10011-3379, USA

Kellerman, Jonathan S (Writer)
Karpfinger Agency
357 W 20th St
New York, NY 10011-3379, USA

Kellerman, Max (Actor, Sportscaster)
c/o Staff Member *I, Max*
10201 W Pico Blvd Bldg 101
Fox Sports Television Group
Los Angeles, CA 90064-2606, USA

Kellerman, Sally (Actor)
7944 Woodrow Wilson Dr
Los Angeles, CA 90046-1216, USA

Kellermeyer, Doug (Football Player)
Houston Oilers
1416 Glasgow Ln
Keller, TX 76248-8225, USA

Kelley, Allen (Al) (Basketball Player)
5900 Longleaf Dr
Lawrence, KS 66049-5801, USA

Kelley, Bill (Football Player)
Green Bay Packers
6446 US Highway 69 S
Lone Oak, TX 75453-2242, USA

Kelley, Brian (Football Player)
New York Giants
98 Constitution Way
Basking Ridge, NJ 07920-2961, USA

Kelley, David E (Producer, Writer)
David Kelley Productions
10201 W Pico Blvd
Los Angeles, CA 90064-2606, USA

Kelley, Dean (Basketball Player)
5900 Longleaf Dr
Lawrence, KS 66049-5801, USA

Kelley, Donald R (Historian)
45 Jefferson Ave
New Brunswick, NJ 08901-1737, USA

Kelley, Dwight (Football Player)
Philadelphia Eagles
1006 Clubview Blvd N
Columbus, OH 43235-1222, USA

Kelley, Earl A (Basketball Player)
21430 Windmere Lane
Tremont, IL 61566, USA

Kelley, Gaynor N (Business Person)
Perkin-Elmer Corp
710 Bridgeport Ave
Shelton, CT 06484-4794, USA

Kelley, Gordon (Football Player)
San Francisco 49ers
3101 S Ocean Blvd Apt 126
Highland Beach, FL 33487-2573, USA

Kelley, Harold H (Psychic)
21634 Rambla Vis
Malibu, CA 90265-5126, USA

Kelley, John A (Marathon) (Athlete, Track Athlete)
136 Cedar Hill Road
East Dennis, MA 02641, USA

Kelley, Jon (Television Host)
c/o Staff Member *Extra (LA)*
1840 Victory Blvd
Telepictures Productions
Glendale, CA 91201-2558, USA

Kelley, Kitty (Writer)
1228 Eton Ct NW
Washington, DC 20007-3240, USA

Kelley, Malcolm David (Actor)
c/o Staff Member *ESI Networking*
6310 San Vicente Blvd Ste 340
Los Angeles, CA 90048-5499, USA

Kelley, Manon
PO Box 315
Bellmore, NY 11710-0315, USA

Kelley, Mike (Artist)
2472 Eastman Ave # 35-36
Ventura, CA 93003-7709, USA

Kelley, Nathalie (Actor)
c/o Megan Silverman *Endeavor Agency LLC (LA)*
9601 Wilshire Blvd Fl 3
Beverly Hills, CA 90210-5204, USA

Kelley, Paul X (General)
1600 N Oak St Apt 1619
Arlington, VA 22209-2769, USA

Kelley, Rich (Basketball Player)
314 Raymundo Dr
Woodside, CA 94062-4129, USA

Kelley, Sheila (Actor)
524 Lorraine Blvd
Los Angeles, CA 90020-4732, USA

Kelley, Steve (Cartoonist)
San Diego Union
350 Camino De La Reina
Editorial Dept
San Diego, CA 92108-3003, USA

Kelley, Thomas G (War Hero)
600 Washington St Ste 1100
Boston, MA 02111-1704, USA

Kelley, William G (Business Person)
Consolidated Stores
1105 N Market St
Wilmington, DE 19801-1216, USA

Kellin, Kevin (Football Player)
Tampa Bay Buccaneers
3100 Walnut St NE
Saint Petersburg, FL 33704-2349, USA

Kellman, Barnet (Director)
c/o Staff Member *Jackoway Tyerman Wertheimer Austen Mandelbaum & Morris*
1888 Century Park E Fl 18
Los Angeles, CA 90067-1702, USA

Kellner, Catherine (Actor)
c/o Michael Lazo *Paradigm (LA)*
360 N Crescent Dr
North Bldg
Beverly Hills, CA 90210-6820, USA

Kellner, Deborah (Actor)
c/o Jessica (Pilch) Samuel *Sanders/ Armstrong Management*
10250 Constellation Blvd
Los Angeles, CA 90067-6200, USA

Kellner, Walt (Baseball Player)
Philadelphia Athletics
3737 N Tucson Blvd
Tucson, AZ 85716-1040, USA

Kellogg, Clark (Basketball Player, Sportscaster)
5423 Medallion Dr E
Westerville, OH 43082-8691, USA

Kellogg, Jeffrey (Baseball Player)
22900 Cherry Hill Ct
Mattawan, MI 49071-9562, USA

Kellogg, Mike (Football Player)
Denver Broncos
7497 Tabor St
Arvada, CO 80005-3283, USA

Kellogg, Vivian (Baseball Player)
105 W Mill Pond Dr
Brooklyn, MI 49230-8506, USA

Kellogg, William S (Business Person)
Kohl's Corp
N56W17000 Ridgewood Dr
Menomonee Falls, WI 53051-5660, USA

Kellogg Jr, Allan J (War Hero)
250 Iiihau St
Kailua, HI 96734, USA

Kellum, Marv (Football Player)
Pittsburgh Steelers
235 Jamaica Ave
Pittsburgh, PA 15229-1748, USA

Kelly, Annesse (Bowler)
2912 Cape Verde Ln
Las Vegas, NV 89128-7236, USA

Kelly, Barbara
5 Kidderpore Ave.
London, ENGLAND NW3 7SX, UNITED KINGDOM (UK)

Kelly, Bob (Baseball Player)
Chicago Cubs
9 Mohawk Dr
Niantic, CT 06357, USA

Kelly, Brendan (Actor)
c/o Staff Member *Allman/Rea Management*
141 S Barrington Ave Ste E
Los Angeles, CA 90049-3314, USA

Kelly, Brian (Football Player)
Tampa Bay Buccaneers
939 Harbour Bay Dr Apt 5102
Tampa, FL 33602-5738, USA

Kelly, Bryan (Baseball Player)
Detroit Tigers
8012 Rose Ave
Orlando, FL 32810-2630, USA

Kelly, Chris
21/22 Poland St.
London, ENGLAND W1V 3DD, UNITED KINGDOM (UK)

Kelly, Clinton
c/o Staff Member *The Learning Channel (TLC)*
7700 Wisconsin Ave
Bethesda, MD 20814-3578, USA

Kelly, Dale (Baseball Player)
Toronto Blue Jays
3417 Quail Meadows Dr
Santa Maria, CA 93455-2477, USA

Kelly, Daniel-Hugh (Actor)
Innovative Artists
1505 10th St
Santa Monica, CA 90401-2805, USA

Kelly, David (Actor)
535 King St. #219
The Plaza
London, ENGLAND SW10 0SZ, UNITED KINGDOM (UK)

Kelly, David Patrick (Actor)
c/o Staff Member *Paradigm (LA)*
360 N Crescent Dr
North Bldg
Beverly Hills, CA 90210-6820, USA

Kelly, Dean Lennox (Actor)
c/o Staff Member *Scott Marshall Partners Ltd*
54 Poland St #9
London W1F 7NJ, UNITED KINGDOM (UK)

Kelly, Donald P (Business Person)
DP Kelly Assoc
701 Harger Rd Ste 190
Oak Brook, IL 60523-1490, USA

Kelly, Eamon M (Educator)
3122 Octavia St
New Orleans, LA 70125-4936, USA

Kelly, Elisworth (Artist)
PO Box 1708
Chatham, NY 12037, USA

Kelly, Ellison (Football Player)
New York Giants
110 Eglinton Ave W
Toronto, ON M4R 1A3, CANADA

Kelly, Henry
10 Clorane Gardens
London, ENGLAND NW3 7PR, UNITED KINGDOM (UK)

Kelly, James E (Jim) (Football Player)
Buffalo Bills
44 Hillsboro Dr
Orchard Park, NY 14127-3434, USA

Kelly, James M (Jim) (Astronaut)
14634 Graywood Grove Ln
Houston, TX 77062-2130, USA

Kelly, Jean Louisa (Actor)
c/o Sally Ware *Gersh Agency, The (NY)*
41 Madison Ave Fl 33
New York, NY 10010-2202, USA

Kelly, Jeff (Football Player)
Atlanta Falcons
6437 Munke Rd
La Grange, TX 78945-5836, USA

Kelly, Jerry (Golfer)
723 Wilder Dr
Madison, WI 53704-6011, USA

Kelly, Jim (Actor)
c/o Leigh Castle *Castle-Hill Talent Agency*
1101 S Orlando Ave
Los Angeles, CA 90035-2511, USA

Kelly, Jim (Football Player)
Pittsburgh Steelers
1 Regency Ct
Marlton, NJ 08053-4243, USA

Kelly, Joanne (Actor)
c/o Staff Member *Burstein Company, The*
15304 W Sunset Blvd Ste 208
Pacific Palisades, CA 90272-3656, USA

Kelly, John (Musician)
EMI America Records
6920 W Sunset Blvd
Los Angeles, CA 90028-7010, USA

Kelly, John D (Football Player)
Washington Redskins
816 NE 18th Ave Apt 4
Fort Lauderdale, FL 33304-3005, USA

Kelly, John H (Diplomat)
International Equity Partners
1808 Over Lake Dr SE Ste D
Conyers, GA 30013-6608, USA

Kelly, Kevin (Baseball Player)
1311 Quarterpath Ct
Richmond, TX 77469-6502, USA

Kelly, Leonard P (Red) (Hockey Player)
30 Dunvegan
Toronto, ON M4V 2P6, CANADA

Kelly, Leroy (Football Player)
Cleveland Browns
115 Eastbrook Ln
Willingboro, NJ 08046-2224, USA

Kelly, Lisa Robin (Actor)
c/o Dan Baron *Agency for the Performing Arts (APA-LA)*
405 S Beverly Dr
Beverly Hills, CA 90212-4416, USA

Kelly, Mark E (Astronaut)
2121 Barrington Dr
League City, TX 77573, USA

Kelly, Mike (Baseball Player)
Atlanta Braves
9951 Kyle St
Los Alamitos, CA 90720-2236, USA

Kelly, Mike (Football Player)
Cincinnati Bengals
7941 David Kenney Farm Rd
Huntersville, NC 28078-8730, USA

Kelly, Minka (Actor)
c/o Aron Giannini *The Collective*
9100 Wilshire Blvd # 700 W
Beverly Hills, CA 90212-3401, USA

Kelly, Moira (Actor)
2329 Rodeo Dr
Austin, TX 78727-3402, USA

Kelly, Morgan (Actor)
c/o Tina Petro *Epic Talent*
3451 St. Laurent #400
Montreal, PQ H2X 2T6, CANADA

Kelly, Paul (Musician, Songwriter)
c/o Staff Member *Paradigm (Monterey)*
509 Hartnell St
Monterey, CA 93940-2825, USA

Kelly, Raymond (Misc)
Police Commissioner's Office
1 Police Plz
New York, NY 10038-1403, USA

Kelly, Richard (Rich) (Director, Writer)
c/o John Campisi *Creative Artists Agency
LCC (CAA-LA)*
2000 Avenue Of The Stars
Los Angeles, CA 90067-4700, USA

Kelly, Robert (Football Player)
Los Angeles Dons
5380 N 750 E
Hamlet, IN 46532-9531, USA

Kelly, Robert (R Kelly) (Artist, Musician,
Songwriter, Writer)
c/o Jeff Frasco *Creative Artists Agency
LCC (CAA-LA)*
2000 Avenue Of The Stars
Los Angeles, CA 90067-4700, USA

Kelly, Roberto (Baseball Player)
New York Yankees
510 Franklin Dr
Arlington, TX 76011-2244, USA

Kelly, Roz
5161 Riverton Ave Apt 105
N Hollywood, CA 91601-3943, USA

Kelly, Scott J (Astronaut)
2121 Barrington Dr
League City, TX 77573, USA

Kelly, Thomas (Football Player)
Tampa Bay Buccaneers
14524 La Mesa Dr
La Mirada, CA 90638-4026, USA

Kelly, Van (Baseball Player)
San Diego Padres
11 Beauregard Dr
Spencer, NC 28159-1957, USA

Kelly III, Thomas J (Journalist)
Sanatoga Branch
PO Box 2208
Pottstown, PA 19464, USA

Kelm, Larry (Football Player)
Los Angeles Rams
67 Driftoak Cir
The Woodlands, TX 77381-6632, USA

Kelman, Arthur (Misc)
2150 Center Ave Apt 20E
Fort Lee, NJ 07024-5805, USA

Kelman, James (Writer)
Weidenfeld-Nicolson
Upper Saint Martin's Lane
London WC2H 9EA, UNITED KINGDOM
(UK)

Kelsey, David (Actor)
c/o Staff Member *Select Artists Ltd (CA-
Westside Office)*
1138 12th St Apt 1
Santa Monica, CA 90403-5459, USA

Kelsey, Frances O (Misc)
Federal Drug Administration
5600 Fishers Ln
Rockville, MD 20852-1750, USA

Kelsey, Linda (Actor)
400 S Beverly Dr Ste 101
Beverly Hills, CA 90212-4403, USA

Kelso, Bill (Baseball Player)
Los Angeles Angels
136 NE Briarcliff Rd
Kansas City, MO 64116-4512, USA

Kelso, Mark (Football Player)
Buffalo Bills
897 Luther Rd
East Aurora, NY 14052-9764, USA

Kelso II, Frank B (Admiral)
7794 Turlock Rd
Springfield, VA 22153-2331, USA

kelton, David (Baseball Player)
Chicago Cubs
515 Rivers Rd
West Point, GA 31833, USA

Kem (Music Group)
c/o Staff Member *Paradigm (Monterey)*
509 Hartnell St
Monterey, CA 93940-2825, USA

Kemal, Yashar (Writer)
PK14 Basinkoy
Istanbul, TURKEY

Kemmerer, Beatrice (Baseball Player)
6437 Carter St
Bremen, IN 46506, USA

Kemmerer, Russ (Baseball Player)
Boston Red Sox
6335 Colebrook Dr
Indianapolis, IN 46220-4205, USA

Kemp, Gary (Musician)
International Talent Group
729 7th Ave Rm 1600
New York, NY 10019-6880, USA

Kemp, Jack
1776 I St NW Ste 800
Washington, DC 20006-3706, USA

Kemp, Jeff (Football Player)
Los Angeles Rams
22101 NE 66th Pl
Redmond, WA 98053-2337, USA

Kemp, Jeremy (Actor)
Marina Martin
12/13 Poland St
London W1V 3DE, UNITED KINGDOM
(UK)

Kemp, John F (Jack) (Football Player)
Pittsburgh Steelers
7904 Greentree Rd
Bethesda, MD 20817-1302, USA

Kemp, Martin (Musician)
Mission Control
Business Center
Lower Road
London SE16 2XB, UNITED KINGDOM
(UK)

Kemp, Ross (Actor)
EastEnders
BBC Elstree Centre
Clarendon Road
Borehamwood, Herts UK WD6 1JF,
UNITED KINGDOM (UK)

Kemp, Shawn T (Basketball Player)
1700 E 13th St Apt 12T
Cleveland, OH 44114-3218, USA

Kemp, Steve (Baseball Player)
Detroit Tigers
27150 Pacific Heights Dr
Mission Viejo, CA 92692-5035, USA

Kemper, Randolph E (Randy) (Designer,
Fashion Designer)
Randy Kemper Corp
530 Fashion Ave # 1400
New York, NY 10018-4878, USA

Kemper, Victor J (Cinematographer)
Gersh Agency
232 N Canon Dr
Beverly Hills, CA 90210-5302, USA

Kemper II, David W (Financier)
Commerce Bancshares
1000 Walnut St
Kansas City, MO 64106-2145, USA

Kempf, Cecil J (Admiral)
831 Olive Ave
Coronado, CA 92118-2525, USA

Kempf, Florian (Football Player)
Houston Oilers
8039 Pine Rd # 1
Philadelphia, PA 19111-1808, USA

Kempinska, Charles (Football Player)
Los Angeles Chargers
925 State St
Natchez, MS 39120-3577, USA

Kempner, Walter (Misc)
1505 Virginia Ave
Durham, NC 27705-3118, USA

Ken, Baird (Hockey Player)
California Golden Seals
Lot 4 Berry Bay
White Lake, MB R0B 1M0, CANADA

Kenan, Sean
77 W 66th St
New York, NY 10023-6201, USA

Kendal, Felicity (Actor)
Chatto & Linnit
Prince of Wales Coventry St
London W1V 7FE, UNITED KINGDOM
(UK)

Kendall, Donald M (Business Person)
PepsiCo Inc
Anderson Hill Road
Purchase, NY 10577, USA

Kendall, Fred (Baseball Player)
San Diego Padres
612 John St
Manhattan Beach, CA 90266-5837, USA

Kendall, Jason (Baseball Player)
Pittsburgh Pirates
692 Chautauqua Blvd
Pacific Palisades, CA 90272-4408, USA

Kendall, Jeannie (Musician)
Joe Taylor Artist Agency
2802 Columbine Pl
Nashville, TN 37204-3104, USA

Kendall, Pete (Football Player)
Arizona Cardinals
PO Box 888
Phoenix, AZ 85001-0888, USA

Kendall, Skip (Golfer)
4516 Burke St
Orlando, FL 32814-6017, USA

Kendall, Tom (Race Car Driver)
International Motor Sports Assn
1394 Broadway Ave
Braselton, GA 30517-2909, USA

Kendall, Tony
Via G. Talombini 12
Rome 00156, ITALY

Kenders, Al (Baseball Player)
Philadelphia Phillies
8744 Matilija Ave
Van Nuys, CA 91402-3320, USA

Kendler, Bob (Misc)
US Handball Assn
4101 Dempster St
Skokie, IL 60076-2152, USA

Kendrena, Ken (Baseball Player)
4235 Stone Mountain Dr
Chino Hills, CA 91709-6155, USA

Kendrick, Anna (Actor)
c/o Staff Member *Endeavor Agency LLC
(LA)*
9601 Wilshire Blvd Fl 3
Beverly Hills, CA 90210-5204, USA

Kendrick, Rodney (Composer, Musician)
Carolyn McClair
410 W 53rd St Apt 128C
New York, NY 10019-5629, USA

Keneally, Thomas M (Writer)
24 Serpentine
Bilgola Beach, NSW 2107, AUSTRALIA

Keneley, Matt (Football Player)
San Francisco 49ers
25142 Sandia Ct
Laguna Hills, CA 92653-5606, USA

Kener, Kira (Adult Film Star)
Vivid Entertainment
15127 Califa St
Van Nuys, CA 91411-3021, USA

Kenerson, John (Football Player)
Los Angeles Rams
4949 S Cottage Grove Ave Apt 602
Chicago, IL 60615-2647, USA

Kenilorea, Peter (Prime Minister)
Kalala House
PO Box 535 Honiara
Guadacanal, SOLOMON ISLANDS

Kenn, Michael L (Mike) (Football Player)
Atlanta Falcons
360 Bardolier
Alpharetta, GA 30022-5129, USA

Kenna, Edward (War Hero)
121 Coleraine Road
Hamilton, VIC 3300, AUSTRALIA

Kennan, Brian (Musician)
PO Box 770850
Lustig Talent
Orlando, FL 32877-0850, USA

Kennard, George (Football Player)
New York Giants
13852 N 45th Pl
Phoenix, AZ 85032-5527, USA

Kennard, William (Bill) (Government
Official)
Carlyie Group
1001 Pennsylvania Ave NW
Washington, DC 20004-2505, USA

Kenne, Leslie F (General)
Deputy Cofs For Warfighting Integration
Hqusa Pentagon
Washington, DC 20310-0001, USA

Kennedy, Adam (Baseball Player)
Anaheim Angels
131 S Cerro Vista Way
Anaheim, CA 92807-3512, USA

Kennedy, Alan D (Business Person)
Tupperware Corp
PO Box 2353
Orlando, FL 32802-2353, USA

Kennedy, Anthony M (Judge)
US Supreme Court
1 1st St NE
Washington, DC 20543-0002, USA

Kennedy, Claudia J (General)
William Morris Agency
151 El Camino Dr
Beverly Hills, CA 90212-2775, USA

Kennedy, Coenelia G (Judge)
US Court of Appeals
US Court House
231 W Lafayette Blvd
Detroit, MI 48226-2700, USA

Kennedy, Cortez (Football Player)
Seattle Seahawks
121 Gary Lynn Dr
Osceola, AR 72370-1709, USA

Kennedy, D James (Religious Leader)
Coral Ridge Presbyterian Church
5554 N Federal Hwy
Fort Lauderdale, FL 33308-3209, USA

Kennedy, Dan (Business Person, Writer)
Kennedy Inner Circle Inc
5818 N 7th St Ste 103
Phoenix, AZ 85014-5810, USA

Kennedy, David M (Historian)
Stanford University
History Dept
Stanford, CA 94305, USA

Kennedy, David M (Secretary)
3838 Ruth Dr
Salt Lake City, UT 84124-2327, USA

Kennedy, Donald (Educator)
Stanford University
International Studies Institute
Stanford, CA 94305, USA

Kennedy, Dwayne (Comedian)
c/o Staff Member *International Creative Management (ICM-LA)*
10250 Constellation Blvd
Los Angeles, CA 90067-6200, USA

Kennedy, Edward (Ted) (Politician)
2400 Jfk Building
Boston, MA 02203, USA

Kennedy, James C (Business Person)
Cox Enterprises
1400 Lake Hearn Dr NE
Atlanta, GA 30319-1418, USA

Kennedy, Jamie (Actor)
c/o Staff Member *Jamie Kennedy Experiment, The*
5555 Melrose Ave
Los Angeles, CA 90038-3989, USA

Kennedy, Jim (Baseball Player)
St Louis Cardinals
13940 SW Lisa Ln
Beaverton, OR 97005-4315, USA

Kennedy, Jimmy (Football Player)
Saint Louis Rams
901 N Broadway
Saint Louis, MO 63101-2800, USA

Kennedy, Joey D (Joe) Jr (Journalist)
1635 11th Pl S
Birmingham, AL 35205-5907, USA

Kennedy, John (Baseball Player)
Washington Senators
2 Rodney Rd
Peabody, MA 01960-3517, USA

Kennedy, John Milton (Actor)
5711 Reseda Blvd # 204
Tarzana, CA 91356-2201, USA

Kennedy, Junior (Baseball Player)
Cincinnati Reds
6601 Eucalyptus Dr Spc 215
Bakersfield, CA 93306-6844, USA

Kennedy, Kathleen (Producer)
c/o Staff Member *Kennedy/Marshall Company, The*
619 Arizona Ave
Santa Monica, CA 90401-1609, USA

Kennedy, Kenoy (Football Player)
Denver Broncos
16275 O Conner Ave
Forney, TX 75126-7572, USA

Kennedy, Kevin (Television Host)
c/o Staff Member *Best Damned Sports Show Period, The*
10201 W Pico Blvd
Fox Sports Net
Los Angeles, CA 90064-2606, USA

Kennedy, Lee (Business Person)
Equifax Inc
1550 Peachtree St NE
Atlanta, GA 30309-2468, USA

Kennedy, Leon Isaac (Actor)
859 N Hollywood Way # 384
Burbank, CA 91505-2814, USA

Kennedy, Lincoln (Football Player)
Atlanta Falcons
PO Box 920431
Norcross, GA 30010-0431, USA

kennedy, M Peter (Figure Skater)
7650 SE 41st St
Mercer Island, WA 98040-3437, USA

Kennedy, Mimi (Actor)
Agency for Performing Arts
405 S Beverly Dr Ste 500
Beverly Hills, CA 90212-4425, USA

Kennedy, Nigel (Musician)
Russels
Regency House
1-4 Warwick St
London W1R 5WB, UNITED KINGDOM (UK)

Kennedy, Page (Actor)
c/o Judy Page *Mitchell K Stubbs & Assoc (MKS)*
8695 Washington Blvd Ste 204
Culver City, CA 90232-7419, USA

Kennedy, Paul M (Historian)
409 Humphrey St
New Haven, CT 06511-3710, USA

Kennedy, Randall L (Educator, Lawyer)
Harvard University
Law School
Cambridge, MA 02138, USA

Kennedy, Ray F (Business Person)
Masco Corp
21001 Van Born Rd
Taylor, MI 48180-1300, USA

Kennedy, Robert F Jr (Lawyer)
Pace Environmental Litigation Clinic
78 N Broadway
Pace University School Of Law
White Plains, NY 10603-3710, USA

Kennedy, Robert H (Football Player)
New York Yankees
4906 N 76th Pl
Scottsdale, AZ 85251-1507, USA

Kennedy, T Lincoin (Football Player)
3917 Spring Garden Place #1
Spring Valley, CA 91977, USA

Kennedy, Terrence E (Terry) (Baseball Player)
c/o Staff Member *San Diego Surf Dawgs*
7080 Donlon Way Ste 109
Dublin, CA 94568-2788, USA

Kennedy, Theodore S (Teeder) (Hockey Player)
22 Lakeside Place W
Port Colbome, ON L3K 6B1, CANADA

Kennedy, William J (Football Player)
Detroit Lions
16383 Ronnie Ln
Livonia, MI 48154-2249, USA

Kennedy, William J (Writer)
New York State Writers Institute
Washington Ave
Albany, NY 12222-0001, USA

Kennedy, X Joseph (X J) (Writer)
22 Revere St
Lexington, MA 02420-4424, USA

Kennedy-Powell, Kathleen (Judge)
Los Angeles Municipal Court
110 N Grand Ave
Los Angeles, CA 90012-3001, USA

Kennedy Schlossberg, Caroline (Writer)
The John F Kennedy Presidential Library & Museum
Columbia Point
Boston, MA 02125, USA

kenner, Kevin (Musician)
Columbia Artists Mgmt Inc
1790 Broadway Fl 6
New York, NY 10019-1412, USA

Kennerly, David Hume (Journalist)
1015 18th St
Santa Monica, CA 90403-4435, USA

Kenney, Art (Baseball Player)
Boston Bees
3 Timber Ln
North Reading, MA 01864-3016, USA

Kenney, Jerry (Baseball Player)
New York Yankees
1980 Harrison Ave
Beloit, WI 53511-3048, USA

Kenney, Stephen F (Steve) (Football Player)
Philadelphia Eagles
1105 Silver Oaks Ct
Raleigh, NC 27614-9359, USA

Kenney, William P (Football Player)
Kansas City Chiefs
2808 SW Arthur Dr
Lees Summit, MO 64082-4062, USA

Kennibrew, Dee Dee (Musician)
Superstars Unlimited
PO Box 371371
Las Vegas, NV 89137-1371, USA

Kenniff, Sean (Doctor)
6 Madison Ln # 2
Carle Place, NY 11514-1064, USA

Kennison, Eddie (Football Player)
Kansas City Chiefs
1 Arrowhead Dr
Kansas City, MO 64129-1651, USA

Kenny, Shannon (Actor)
c/o Staff Member *Burstein Company, The*
15304 W Sunset Blvd Ste 208
Pacific Palisades, CA 90272-3656, USA

Kenny, Shirley Strum (Educator)
State University of New York
President's Office
Stony Brook, NY 11794-0001, USA

Kenny, Yvonne (Opera Singer)
I M G Artists
3 Burlington Lane
Chiswick
London W4 2TH, UNITED KINGDOM (UK)

Kenny G (Musician)
Turner Management Group
9200 W Sunset Blvd Ste 600
West Hollywood, CA 90069-3196, USA

Kenseth, Matt (Race Car Driver)
Matt Kenseth Fan Club
200 Highway 12 And 18
Cambridge, WI 53523-9276, USA

Kensit, Patsy (Actor, Musician)
14 Lambton Place Nottinghill
London W11 2SH, UNITED KINGDOM (UK)

Kent, Allegra (Ballerina)
New York City Ballet
Lincoln Center Plaza
New York, NY 10023, USA

Kent, Arthur (Correspondent)
2184 Torringford St
Torrington, CT 06790-2540, USA

Kent, (Edward G N P Patrick) (Misc)
York House
Saint James's Place
London SW1, UNITED KINGDOM (UK)

Kent, Heather Paige
c/o Staff Member *Untitled Entertainment (LA)*
331 N Maple Dr Fl 3
Beverly Hills, CA 90210-3827, USA

Kent, Jean (Actor)
London Mgmt
2-4 Noel St
London W1V 3RB, UNITED KINGDOM (UK)

Kent, Jeff (Baseball Player)
Toronto Blue Jays
550 Chaparral Ct
Altadena, CA 91001-3859, USA

Kent, Joey (Football Player)
Tennessee Titans
6409 Eric St NW
Huntsville, AL 35810-1605, USA

Kent, Jonathan (Director)
International Creative Mgmt
76 Oxford St
London W1N 0AX, UNITED KINGDOM (UK)

Kent, Julie (Ballerina)
American Ballet Theatre
890 Broadway
New York, NY 10003-1278, USA

Kent, Marjorie
1169 Mary Cir
La Verne, CA 91750-4210, USA

Kent, Peter (Misc)
43 Trinity Court Gray's Inn Road
London WC1, UNITED KINGDOM (UK)

Kent, Steve (Baseball Player)
Tampa Bay Devil Rays
10750 SW 11th St Apt 6
Miami, FL 33174-2511, USA

Kentner, Louis (Musician)
1 Mallord St
London SW3, UNITED KINGDOM (UK)

Kentucky Headhunters
PO Box 1895
Glasgow, KY 42142-1895, USA

Kenty, Hilmer (Boxer)
Escot Boxing
19260 Bretton Dr
Detroit, MI 48223-1364, USA

Kenworthy, Dick (Baseball Player)
Chicago White Sox
5551 Rue Royale Apt D
Indianapolis, IN 46227-1960, USA

Kenya, Wendi (Actor)
Michael Forman Management
409 N Camden Dr Ste 205
Beverly Hills, CA 90210-4423, USA

Kenyon, Mel (Race Car Driver)
2645 S 25 W
Lebanon, IN 46052-9748, USA

Kenzie, Leila
151 El Camino Dr
Beverly Hills, CA 90212-2704, USA

Kenzo (Designer, Fashion Designer)
3 Place des Victories
Paris 75001, FRANCE

Keobouphan, Sisavat (Prime Minister)
Premier's Office
Vientiane, LAOS

Keoghan, Phil (Television Host)
c/o Staff Member *International Creative Management (ICM-LA)*
10250 Constellation Blvd
Los Angeles, CA 90067-6200, USA

Keohane, Nannerl O (Educator)
Duke University
President's Office
Durham, NC 27704, USA

Keoke, Kimo (Actor)
612 1/2 N Spaulding Ave
Los Angeles, CA 90036-1838, USA

Keon, David M (Dave) (Hockey Player)
115 Brackenwood Rd
Palm Beach Gardens, FL 33418-9065, USA

Keough, Donald R (Financier)
200 Galleria Pkwy SE Ste 970
Atlanta, GA 30339-5945, USA

Keough, Harry J (Coach, Soccer Player)
7325 Rainor Ct
Saint Louis, MO 63116-3051, USA

Keough, Joe (Baseball Player)
Oakland A's
110 Binham Hts
Shavano Park, TX 78249-2056, USA

Keough, Lainey (Designer, Fashion Designer)
42 Dawson St
Dublin 2, IRELAND

Keough, Marty (Baseball Player)
Boston Red Sox
6874 E Nightingale Star Cir
Scottsdale, AZ 85266-7044, USA

Keough, Matt (Baseball Player)
Oakland A's
6281 Southfront Rd
Livermore, CA 94551-8215, USA

Kepcher, Carolyn (Reality TV Star)
c/o Staff Member *The Apprentice*
725 5th Ave
The Trump Co
New York, NY 10022-2519, USA

Kepshire, Kurt (Baseball Player)
St Louis Cardinals
141 Folino Dr
Bridgeport, CT 06606-1013, USA

Ker, Crawford (Football Player)
Dallas Cowboys
214 Harbor View Ln
Largo, FL 33770-4007, USA

Ker, Joshua (Football Player)
Indianapolis Colts
2927 Lakeshore Dr
Muskegon, MI 49441, USA

Kerbow, Randall (Football Player)
Houston Oilers
10122 Lost Hollow Ln
Missouri City, TX 77459-2494, USA

Kercher, Dick (Football Player)
Detroit Lions
3205 May Cir SE
Rio Rancho, NM 87124-7402, USA

Kercheval, Ken (Actor)
Stephany Hurkos
11935 Kling St Apt 10
Valley Village, CA 91607-5406, USA

Kercheval, Ralph (Football Player)
Brooklyn Dodgers
1220 Richmond Rd
Lexington, KY 40502-1614, USA

Kerdyk, Tracy (Golfer)
441 Valencia Ave Apt 401
Coral Gables, FL 33134-5782, USA

Kerekorian, Kirk (Business Person)
MGM/UA Communications
2500 Broadway
Santa Monica, CA 90404-3065, USA

Kerekou, Mathieu A (General, President)
President's Office
Boite Postale
Cotonou 2020, BENIN

Keresztes, K Sandor (Architect)
Fo Utca 44/50
Budapest 1011, HUNGARY

Kerfeld, Charlie (Baseball Player)
Houston Astros
250 Vallombrosa Ave Ste 200
Chico, CA 95926-3976, USA

Kern, Bill (Baseball Player)
Kansas City A's
625 W Green St
Allentown, PA 18102-1601, USA

Kern, Ericca
3972 Barranca Pkwy # J-321
Irvine, CA 92606-1204, USA

Kern, Geof (Photographer)
1355 Conant St
Dallas, TX 75207-6005, USA

Kern, Jim (Baseball Player)
Cleveland Indians
6009 Amberwood Ct
Arlington, TX 76016-1001, USA

Kern, Joey (Actor)
c/o Staff Member *Paradigm (LA)*
360 N Crescent Dr
North Bldg
Beverly Hills, CA 90210-6820, USA

Kern, Rex W (Football Player)
Baltimore Colts
2816 Avenida De Autlan
Camarillo, CA 93010-7471, USA

Kernek, George (Baseball Player)
St Louis Cardinals
16423 Cotton Gin Ave
Wayne, OK 73095-3172, USA

Kerns, Joanna (Actor)
c/o Susan Landau *Thompson Street Entertainment*
754 N Kilkea Dr
Los Angeles, CA 90046-7006, USA

Kerns, Sandra
620 Resolano Dr
Pacific Palisades, CA 90272-3032, USA

Kerr, Allen (Musician)
419 Carrington St
Adelaide, SA 5000, AUSTRALIA

Kerr, Brooke (Actor)
c/o Staff Member *Innovative Artists (LA)*
1505 10th St
Santa Monica, CA 90401-2805, USA

Kerr, Buddy (Baseball Player)
New York Giants
341 Grove St
Oradell, NJ 07649-2229, USA

Kerr, Cristie (Golfer)
8367 SW 137th Ave
Miami, FL 33183-4045, USA

Kerr, Edward
9701 Wilshire Blvd Fl 10
Beverly Hills, CA 90212-2010, USA

Kerr, Graham (Writer)
Kerr Corp
1020 N Sunset Dr
Camano Island, WA 98282-6665, USA

Kerr, John
16130 Ventura Blvd Ste 650
Encino, CA 91436-2543, USA

Kerr, John G (Actor)
2975 Monterey Rd
San Marino, CA 91108-1735, USA

Kerr, John G (Red) (Basketball Player, Coach, Sportscaster)
8700 W Bryn Mawr Ave # 600so
Chicago, IL 60631-3512, USA

Kerr, Judy (Actor)
4139 Tujunga Ave
Studio City, CA 91604-3065, USA

Kerr, Pat (Designer, Fashion Designer)
Pat Kerr Inc
200 Wagner Pl
Memphis, TN 38103-3617, USA

Kerr, Philip (Writer)
AP Watts Agents
20 John St
London WC1N 2DR, UNITED KINGDOM (UK)

Kerr, Tim (Coach, Hockey Player)
Power Play Really
2528 Dune Dr
Avalon, NJ 08202, USA

Kerr, William T (Business Person)
Meredith Corp
1716 Locust St
Des Moines, IA 50309-3023, USA

Kerr Jr, Donald M (Physicist)
Science Applications International
1241 Cave St
La Jolla, CA 92037-3602, USA

Kerrey, J Robert (Bob) (Governor)
New School University
66W E 12th St
President's Office
New York, NY 10003, USA

Kerrick, Donald L (General)
Deputy Assistant National Security Agency
Fort George C Meade, MD 20755, USA

Kerrigan, Joseph T (Joe) (Baseball Player)
Montreal Expos
450 Forest Ln
North Wales, PA 19454-2478, USA

Kerrigan, Marguerite (Baseball Player)
12179 94th St
Largo, FL 33773-4306, USA

Kerrigan, Nancy (Figure Skater)
C/O Jerry Solomon
40 Salem St # 101
Lynnfield, MA 01940-2673, USA

Kerrigan, Pamela (Golfer)
7082 Torrey Pines Cir
Port Saint Lucie, FL 34986-3200, USA

Kerry, Alexandra (Actor)
c/o Staff Member *TalentWorks (LA)*
3500 W Olive Ave Ste 1400
Burbank, CA 91505-5512, USA

Kerry, Bob (Ex-Senator, Senator)
7602 Pacific St
Omaha, NE 68114-5405, USA

Kersee, Bob
1034 S Brentwood Blvd Ste 1530
Saint Louis, MO 63117-1215, USA

Kersey, Jerome (Basketball Player)
Milwaukee Bucks
1001 N 4th St
Bradley Center
Milwaukee, WI 53203-1312, USA

Kersey, Merritt (Football Player)
Philadelphia Eagles
17 Ballance Mill Rd
Nottingham, PA 19362-9507, USA

Kersey, Paul (Actor)
c/o Staff Member *TalentWorks (LA)*
3500 W Olive Ave Ste 1400
Burbank, CA 91505-5512, USA

Kersh, David (Musician)
Mark Hybner Entertainment
PO Box 223
Shiner, TX 77984-0223, USA

Kershaw, Doug (Musician)
RR 1 Box 34285
Weld County Road 47
Eaton, CO 80615, USA

Kershaw, Sammy (Musician)
Sammy Kershaw Music
817 18th Ave S
Nashville, TN 37203-3218, USA

Kershner, Irvin (Director)
Somers Teitelbaum David
8840 Wilshire Blvd # 200
Beverly Hills, CA 90211-2606, USA

Kersten, Wally (Football Player)
Los Angeles Rams
4604 Longfellow Ave
Minneapolis, MN 55407-3638, USA

Kertesz, Imre (Nobel Prize Laureate)
Northwestern University Press
625 Colfax St
Evanston, IL 60208-4210, USA

Kerwin, Brian (Actor)
Paradigm Agency
200 W 57th St Ste 900
New York, NY 10019-3211, USA

Kerwin, Irene (Baseball Player)
610 W Albany Ave
Peoria, IL 61604-1506, USA

Kerwin, Joseph P (Astronaut)
10411 River Rd
College Station, TX 77845-6719, USA

Kerwin, Lance (Actor)
PO Box 1708
Kapaa, HI 96746-5708, USA

Kerwin, Larkin (Physicist)
2166 Bourboniere Park
Sillery, PQ G1T 1B4, CANADA

Keseday, Robert (Football Player)
St Louis Cardinals
57 Linden Ave
Park Ridge, NJ 07656-1254, USA

Keser, Dean (Football Player)
Philadelphia Eagles
202 Rod Cir
Middletown, MD 21769-7826, USA

Keshishian, Alek
450 N Rossmore Ave # 608
Los Angeles, CA 90004-2406, USA

Kesner, Jillian (Actor)
William Carroll Agency
11360 Brill Dr
Studio City, CA 91604-3103, USA

Kessinger, Donald E (Don) (Baseball Player)
Chicago Cubs
907 Cumberland Rdg
Oxford, MS 38655-9231, USA

Kessinger, Keith (Baseball Player)
Cincinnati Reds
4517 Clubhouse Dr
Jonesboro, AR 72401-8153, USA

Kessler, Alice & Ellen
Nymphenburger Str. 86
Munich D-80636, GERMANY

Kessler, David A (Doctor, Government Official)
University of California
Med School
Dean's Office
San Francisco, CA 94143-0001, USA

Kessler, Glenn (Producer, Writer)
c/o Staff Member *Creative Artists Agency LCC (CAA-LA)*
2000 Avenue Of The Stars
Los Angeles, CA 90067-4700, USA

Kessler, Robert (Bob) (Basketball Player)
14 Twin Pines Rd
Hilton Head, SC 29928-2911, USA

Kessler, Ron (Writer)
William Morris Agency
151 El Camino Dr
Beverly Hills, CA 90212-2775, USA

Kessler, Stephen
1120 S. Ridgley Dr.
Los Angeles, CA 90019, USA

Kessler, Todd (Producer, Writer)
c/o Staff Member *Creative Artists Agency LCC (CAA-LA)*
2000 Avenue Of The Stars
Los Angeles, CA 90067-4700, USA

Kester, Rick (Baseball Player)
Atlanta Braves
PO Box 623
Gardnerville, NV 89410-0623, USA

Kestner, Boyd (Actor)
Mirisch Agency
1801 Century Park E Ste 1801
Los Angeles, CA 90067-2320, USA

Ketchum, Dave
2318 Waterby St
Westlake Village, CA 91361-1834, USA

Ketchum, Hal (Musician)
c/o Staff Member *The Bobby Roberts Company Inc*
PO Box 1547
Goodlettsville, TN 37070-1547, USA

Ketchum, Rai (Musician, Songwriter, Writer)
602 Wayside Dr
Wimberley, TX 78676-5151, USA

Ketola-Lacamera, Helen (Baseball Player)
907 New York St
Edgewater, FL 32132-2373, USA

Ketterle, Wolfgang (Nobel Prize Laureate)
25 Bellingham Dr
Chestnut Hill, MA 02467-3246, USA

Kettle, Roger (Cartoonist)
King Features Syndicate
888 7th Ave Ste 201
New York, NY 10106-0201, USA

Keves, Gyorgy (Architect)
Keves es Epitesztarsai Rt
Melinda Utca 21
Budapest 1121, HUNGARY

Kevorkian, Jack (Doctor)
4870 Lockhart St
West Bloomfield, MI 48323-2533, USA

Key, Keegan Michael (Actor)
c/o Joel Zadak *Principato/Young Management*
9665 Wilshire Blvd Ste 500
Beverly Hills, CA 90212-2312, USA

Key, Larry (Football Player)
Tampa Bay Buccaneers
9661 60th St
Christ Gospel Church Attn: Church Administartions
Pinellas Park, FL 33782-3206, USA

Key, Sean (Football Player)
Dallas Cowboys
4637 Chapel Creek Dr
Plano, TX 75024-6852, USA

Key, Ted (Cartoonist)
1694 Glenhardie Rd
Wayne, PA 19087-1004, USA

Key, Wade (Football Player)
Philadelphia Eagles
PO Box 857
Hondo, TX 78861-0857, USA

Keyes, Daniel (Writer)
222 NW 69th St
Boca Raton, FL 33487-2389, USA

Keyes, Evelyn (Actor)
765 Hot Springs Rd
Santa Barbara, CA 93108-1106, USA

Keyes, Leroy (Football Player)
Philadelphia Eagles
6156 Pleasant Ave
Pennsauken, NJ 08110-3537, USA

Keymah, T'Keyah Crystal (Actor)
121 N San Vicente Blvd
Beverly Hills, CA 90211-2303, USA

Keynes, Skander (Actor)
c/o Brian Swardstrom *Endeavor Agency LLC (LA)*
9601 Wilshire Blvd Fl 3
Beverly Hills, CA 90210-5204, USA

Keys, Alicia (Musician, Songwriter, Writer)
c/o Jeff Robinson *MBK Entertainment*
240 W 35th St Fl 18
New York, NY 10001-2506, USA

Keys, Brady (Football Player)
Pittsburgh Steelers
2931 Banchory Rd
Winter Park, FL 32792-4501, USA

Keys, Ronald E (General)
Psc 813 Box 1
Commander In Chief Allied Forces South Europe
FPO, AE 09620-1000, USA

Keyser, Brian (Baseball Player)
Chicago White Sox
233 Summer Glenn Way
Central Point, OR 97502-8617, USA

Keyser, Richard L (Business Person)
WW Grainger Inc
100 Grainger Pkwy
Lake Forest, IL 60045-5201, USA

Keyser Jr, F Ray (Governor)
64 Warner Ave
Proctor, VT 05765-1322, USA

Keysey, Ken
RR 8 Box 477
Pleasant Hill, OR 97401, USA

Keyworth, Jon (Football Player)
Denver Broncos
7238 Corduroy Ct
Matthews, NC 28105-6792, USA

Khabibulin, Nikolai (Hockey Player)
6451 E El Maro Cir
Paradise Valley, AZ 85253-2622, USA

Khajag, Barsamian (Religious Leader)
Armenian Church of America
630 2nd Ave
Eastern Diocese
New York, NY 10016-4806, USA

Khaled (Musician)
Firstars Mgmt
14724 Ventura Blvd Ph
Sherman Oaks, CA 91403-3513, USA

Khali, Simbi (Actor)
Innovative Artists
1505 10th St
Santa Monica, CA 90401-2805, USA

Khalifa, Sam (Baseball Player)
Pittsburgh Pirates
741 E 6th St
Tucson, AZ 85719-5003, USA

Khalifa, Sheikh Hamad bin Isa al (Misc)
Rifa's Palace
Manama, BAHARIN

Khalifa, Sheikh Khalifa bin Sulman al (Prime Minister)
Prime Minister's Office
Government House
Manama, BAHARIN

Khalifa-al-Thani, Hamad Bin (Prime Minister, Prince)
Royal Palace
PO Box 923
Doha, QATAR

Khalil, Christel (Actor)
c/o Meredith Fine *Coast to Coast Talent Group*
3350 Barham Blvd
Los Angeles, CA 90068-1404, USA

Khalil, Cristel (Actor)
c/o Staff Member *Young and the Restless, The*
7800 Beverly Blvd Ste 3305
Los Angeles, CA 90036-2112, USA

Khalil, Mustafa (Prime Minister)
9A El Maahad El Swisry St
Zamalek
Cairo, EGYPT

Khamenei, Hojatolislam Sayyed Ali (President)
Religious Leader's Office
Teheran, IRAN

Khamtai, Siphandon (Prime Minister)
Prime Minister's Office
Council of Ministers
Vientiane, LAOS

Khan, Aamir (Actor, Bollywood)
c/o David Greenblatt *Key Creatives*
9595 Wilshire Blvd Ste 800
Beverly Hills, CA 90212-2508, USA

Khan, Abdulla (Actor)
20/1 Arch Bishop Avenue
Boat Club Road
Chennai, TN 600 018, INDIA

Khan, Ali Akbar (Composer)
Gregory DiGiovine Mgmt
121 Jordan St
San Rafael, CA 94901-3919, USA

Khan, Alia (Designer)
Asian Andaz Inc
40 E 34th St Rm 1719
New York, NY 10016-4501, USA

Khan, Amjad Ali (Composer)
3 Sadhna Enclave
Panchsheel Park
New Delhi, New Delhi 110 017, INDIA

Khan, Arbaaz (Actor, Bollywood)
3 Galaxy Apts BJ Road
Band Stand Bandra
Mumbai, MS 400050, INDIA

Khan, Ayub (Actor, Bollywood)
Xavier House 2nd Floor
St Peter Colony Bandra (W)
Mumbai, MS 400050, INDIA

Khan, Chaka (Actor, Musician)
c/o Jeff Frasco *Creative Artists Agency LCC (CAA-LA)*
2000 Avenue Of The Stars
Los Angeles, CA 90067-4700, USA

Khan, Fardeen (Actor, Bollywood)
Sunshine Jassawala Wadi
Juhu Road Juhu
Mumbai, MS 400049, INDIA

Khan, Feroz (Actor, Bollywood, Director, Filmmaker, Producer)
Sunshine Jussawala Wadi
Juhu Church Road
Mumbai, MS 400049, INDIA

Khan, Gulam Ishaq (Ex-President, President)
3B University Town
Jamrud Road
Peshawar, PAKISTAN

Khan, Inamullah (Religious Leader)
Muslim Congress
D26 Block 8
Gulshan-E_Iqbal
Karachi 75300, PAKISTAN

Khan, Jemima (Heir/Heiress)
c/o Staff Member *UNICEF*
Africa House
64-78 Kingsway
London WC2B 6NB, UNITED KINGDOM
(UK)

Khan, Kader (Actor, Bollywood)
102 Raj Kamal
2nd Hasnabad Lane Santacruz
Mumbai, MS 400054, INDIA

Khan, Niazi Imran (Cricketer)
Shankat Khanum Memorial Trust
29 Shah Jamai
Lahore 546000, PAKISTAN

Khan, Prince Sadruddin Aga
Collonge-Bellerive CH-1245,
SWITZERLAND

Khan, Princess Yasmin
146 Central Park W
New York, NY 10023-2005, USA

Khan, Salman (Actor, Bollywood)
3 Galaxy Apartments BJ Road
Band Stand Bandra
Mumbai, MS 400050, INDIA

Khan, Sanjay (Actor, Bollywood, Director,
Producer)
Sanjay House 11 Silver Beach A B Nair
Road
Juhu
Bombay, MS 400 049, INDIA

Khan, Shahbaaz (Actor, Bollywood)
GB6 Agha Khan Baug
Versova Andheri
Bombay, MS 400 061, INDIA

Khan, Shahrukh (Actor, Bollywood)
Unit One
St.-Ulrichs-Weg 3
Gauting-KÝnigswiesen 82131
GERMANY

Khan, Sohail (Actor, Bollywood, Director,
Producer)
4 Coral Reef 55 Chimbai Road
Bandra (W)
Mumbai, MS 400050, INDIA

Khan, The Aga IV
Aiglemont
Gouvieux F-60270, FRANCE

Khanh, Emanuelle (Designer, Fashion
Designer)
Emanuelle Khanh International
45 Ave Victor Hugo
Paris 75116, FRANCE

Khanna, Akshaye (Actor, Bollywood)
13/C Elplaza
Little Gibs Road Malabar Hill
Mumbai, MS 400026, INDIA

Khanna, Amit (Actor, Bollywood)
301 Sea Star Near Holiday Inn
Balraj Sahni Marg
Mumbai, MS 400049, INDIA

Khanna, Mukesh (Actor, Bollywood,
Director)
3 Parijat 95
Marine Drive
Bombay, MS 400 002, INDIA

Khanna, Rahul (Actor, Bollywood)
12/18 V.P. Road
C.P. Tank Mumbai 4
Mumbai, MS 400004, INDIA

Khanna, Rajesh (Actor, Bollywood)
Ashirwad 2 Carter Road
Bandra
Bombay, MS 400 050, INDIA

Khanna, Rinke (Actor, Bollywood)
201-A Vastu Bldg
Military Rd Juhu
Mumbai, MS 400049, INDIA

khanna, Twinkle (Actor, Bollywood)
Samudra Mahal Birla Lane
Juhu
Mumbai, MS 400049, INDIA

Khanna, Vinod (Actor, Bollywood)
11 Palazo 13th Flr Behind WIAA
Malabar Hill
Mumbai, MS 400006, INDIA

Khanzadian, Vahan (Opera Singer)
3604 Broadway Apt 2N
New York, NY 10031-3200, USA

Kharbanda, Kulbhushan (Actor)
501 Silver Cascade Mount Mary Road
Bandra
Bombay, MS 400 050, INDIA

Khariton, Yuli B (Physicist)
Nuclear Energy Center
Arsamas 16
Nizhy Novgorog Region, RUSSIA

Khashoggi, Adnan
Box 6
Riyadh, SAUDI ARABIA

Khashoggi, Adnan M (Business Person)
La Baraka
Marbella, SPAIN

Khatami, Mohammad (Politician,
President)
President's Office
Dr Ali Shariati Ave
Teheran, IRAN

Khavin, Vladimir Y (Architect)
Glavmosarchitectura
Mayakovsky Square 1
Moscow 103001, RUSSIA

Khayat, Edward (Eddie) (Coach, Football
Coach, Football Player)
Washington Redskins
7813 Haydenberry Cv
Nashville, TN 37221-4675, USA

Khayat, Robert (Educator)
University of Mississippi
Chancellor's Office
University, MS 38677, USA

Khayat, Robert (Football Player)
Washington Redskins
PO Box 667
Oxford, MS 38655-0667, USA

Kheel, Theodore W (Misc)
280 Park Ave
New York, NY 10017-1216, USA

Kher, Anupam (Actor, Bollywood)
402 Marina
Juhu Tara Road Juhu Beach
Mumbai, MS 400049, INDIA

Khitty (Actor)
E3 Sea Brook Apartments 4th C'Ward
Road
Valmigi Nagar Thiruvanmiyur
Chennai, TN 600 041, INDIA

Khokhlov, Boris (Dancer)
Myaskovsky St 11-13
#102
Moscow 121019, RUSSIA

Khondji, Darius (Cinematographer)
International Creative Mgmt
8942 Wilshire Blvd # 219
Beverly Hills, CA 90211-1908, USA

Khorana, Har Gobind (Nobel Prize
Laureate)
1573 Cambridge St Apt 304
Cambridge, MA 02138-4379, USA

Khorkina, Svetlana (Gymnast, Olympic
Athlete)
Russian Gymnastics Federation
Lujnetskaya Nabereynaya 8
Moscow 119270, RUSSIA

Khotan (Musician)
c/o Gabriel Blanco *Gabriel Blanco
Iglesias (Mexico)*
Rio Balsas 35-32
Colonia Cuauhtemoc
DF 06500, MEXICO

Khouna, Sheikh El Afia Quid Mohamed
(Prime Minister)
Prime Minister's Office
Nouakchott, MAURITANIA

Khourl, Callie (Director)
International Creative Mgmt
8942 Wilshire Blvd # 219
Beverly Hills, CA 90211-1908, USA

Khrennikov, Tikhon N (Composer)
Plotnikov Per 10/28
#19
Moscow 121200, RUSSIA

Khristenko, Viktor (Prime Minister)
Prime Minister's Office
Kremlin
Staraya Pl 4
Moscow 103132, RUSSIA

Khruschev, Sergei
PO Box 1948
Providence, RI 02912-1948, USA

Khush, Gurdev S (Scientist)
Int'l Rice Research Institute
PO Box 933
Manila 1099, PHILIPPINES

Khvorostovsky, Dimitri A (Opera Singer)
Elen Victorova
Mosfilmovskaya 26
#5
Moscow, RUSSIA

Kiana (Talk Show Host)
ESPN 2
935 Middle St
Bristol, CT 06010-1000, USA

Kiarostaml, Abbas (Director)
Zeitgeist Films
247 Centre St # 200
New York, NY 10013-3216, USA

Kibaki, Mwai (President)
President's Office
Harambee House
Harambee Ave
Nairobi, KENYA

Kibler, John (Baseball Player)
2701 El Camino Real # 205
Palo Alto, CA 94306-1713, USA

Kibrick, Anne (Educator)
130 Seminary Ave # 312
Auburndale, MA 02466-2651, USA

Kibrick, Sidney
10490 Wilshire Blvd Apt 1901
Los Angeles, CA 90024-4649, USA

Kichel III, Walter (Editor)
Fortune Magazine
1291 Avenue Of The Americas
Editorial Dept
New York, NY 10019, USA

Kid Rock (Musician)
c/o Erin Culley-LaChapelle *Creative Artists
Agency LCC (CAA-LA)*
2000 Avenue Of The Stars
Los Angeles, CA 90067-4700, USA

Kidd, Billy
2305 Mount Werner Cir
Steamboat Springs, CO 80487-9023, USA

Kidd, Dylan (Director)
c/o Staff Member *Creative Artists Agency
LCC (CAA-LA)*
2000 Avenue Of The Stars
Los Angeles, CA 90067-4700, USA

Kidd, Jason (Basketball Player)
c/o Staff Member *New Jersey Nets*
390 Murray Hill Pkwy
E Rutherford, NJ 07073-2109, USA

Kidd, Jodie (Model)
c/o Staff Member *IMG Models*
304 Park Ave S Fl 12
New York, NY 10010-4301, USA

Kidd, John (Football Player)
Buffalo Bills
4204 Moorland Dr
Midland, MI 48640-1906, USA

Kidd, Michael (Choreographer, Dancer)
1614 Old Oak Rd
Los Angeles, CA 90049-2506, USA

Kidd, Sue (Baseball Player)
51 17th St
Logansport, IN 46947-2842, USA

Kidder, Margot (Actor)
Noble Caplan Abrams Agency
1260 Yonge St 2nd Fl
Toronto, ON M4T 1W6, CANADA

Kidder Lee, Barbara (Skier)
1308 W Highland Ave
Phoenix, AZ 85013-2425, USA

Kidjo, Angelique (Musician)
Primary Talent
2-12 Petonville Road
London N1 9PL, UNITED KINGDOM
(UK)

Kidman, Nicole (Actor)
c/o Kevin Huvane *Creative Artists Agency
LCC (CAA-LA)*
2000 Avenue Of The Stars
Los Angeles, CA 90067-4700, USA

Kiecker, Dana (Baseball Player)
Boston Red Sox
4104 Prairie Ridge Rd
Saint Paul, MN 55123-1625, USA

Kiedis, Anthony (Musician)
c/o Staff Member *United Talent Agency
(UTA)*
9560 Wilshire Blvd Ste 500
Beverly Hills, CA 90212-2401, USA

Kiefer, Adolph G (Coach, Swimmer)
42125 N Hunt Club Rd
Wadsworth, IL 60083-9264, USA

Kiefer, Mark (Baseball Player)
Milwaukee Brewers
1182 Old Fashion Way
Garden Grove, CA 92840, USA

Kiefer, Steve (Baseball Player)
Oakland A's
1182 Old Fashion Way
Garden Grove, CA 92840, USA

Kiehl, Marina (Skier)
Hermie-Bland Str 11
Munich 81545, GERMANY

Kiehl, Stuart (Cinematographer)
4193 Concord Ave
Santa Rosa, CA 95407-6507, USA

Kiel, John (Football Player)
Tampa Bay Buccaneers
12100 Pebblepointe Pass
Carmel, IN 46033-9678, USA

Kiel, Richard (Actor)
c/o Steve (Sr) Stevens *The Stevens Group*
14011 Ventura Blvd # 201
Sherman Oaks, CA 91423-3533, USA

Kielty, Bob (Baseball Player)
Minnesota Twins
21504 Appaloosa Ct
Canyon Lake, CA 92587-7628, USA

Kiely, John (Baseball Player)
Detroit Tigers
118 Oregon St
East Bridgewater, MA 02333-1762, USA

Kiely, Mark
9255 W Sunset Blvd Ste 620
Los Angeles, CA 90069-3303, USA

Kier, Udo (Actor)
c/o Richard Schwartz *Richard Schwartz Management*
2934 1/2 N Beverly Glen Cir # 107
Los Angeles, CA 90077-1724, USA

Kiermayer, Susanne (Misc)
Amthofplatz 5
Kirchberg 94259, GERMANY

Kieschnick, Brook (Baseball Player)
Chicago Cubs
201 Evans Ave
San Antonio, TX 78209-3721, USA

Kieschnick, Brooks (Baseball Player)
c/o Staff Member *Houston Astros*
501 Crawford St
Astros Field
Houston, TX 77002-2113, USA

Kiesel, Theresia (Athlete, Track Athlete)
Stifterstr 24
Truan 4050, AUSTRIA

Kiewel, Jeff (Football Player)
Atlanta Falcons
637 Industrial Park Rd
Evans, GA 30809, USA

Kiggens, Lisa (Golfer)
1504 Club View Dr
Bakersfield, CA 93309-3541, USA

Kihn, Greg (Musician)
Riot Mgmt
55 Santa Clara Ave Ste 120
Oakland, CA 94610-1375, USA

Kiick, James F (Jim) (Football Player)
2900 S University Dr Apt 9112
Davie, FL 33328-1409, USA

Kikuchi, Rinko (Actor)
c/o Staff Member *Creative Artists Agency LCC (CAA-LA)*
2000 Avenue Of The Stars
Los Angeles, CA 90067-4700, USA

Kikutake, Kiyonori (Architect)
1-11-15 Otsuka
Bunkyoku, Tokyo, JAPAN

Kilar, Wojciech (Composer)
Ul Ksciuszki 165
Katowice 40-524, POLAND

Kilbey, Steven (Musician)
Globeshine
101 Chamberlayne Road
London NW10 3ND, UNITED KINGDOM (UK)

Kilborn, Craig (Talk Show Host)
c/o Shani Rosenzweig-Maydew *United Talent Agency (UTA)*
9560 Wilshire Blvd Ste 500
Beverly Hills, CA 90212-2401, USA

Kilbourne, Wendy (Actor)
9300 Wilshire Blvd # 410
Beverly Hills, CA 90212-3213, USA

Kilburn, Terry (Actor)
Meadowbrook Theatre
Oakland University
Walton & Squirrel
Rochester, MI 48309, USA

Kilcher, Jewel (Musician, Songwriter)
c/o Irving Azoff *AA Music Management*
1100 Glendon Ave Ste 2000
Los Angeles, CA 90024-3524, USA

Kilcher, Q'Orianka (Actor)
c/o Carlyne Grager *Dramatic Artists Agency*
50 16th Ave
Kirkland, WA 98033-4909, USA

Kiley, Ariel (Actor)
c/o Gene Parseghian *Untitled Entertainment (NY)*
322 8th Ave Ste 601
New York, NY 10001-6715, USA

Kilgallon, Robert D (Scientist)
662 Park Ave
Meadville, PA 16335-1743, USA

Kilgore, Al (Cartoonist)
21655 113th Dr
Queens Village, NY 11429-2617, USA

Kilgore, Jon (Football Player)
Los Angeles Rams
2422 Glen Oaks Ct NE
Atlanta, GA 30345-3928, USA

Kilgus, Paul (Baseball Player)
Texas Rangers
2102 Smallhouse Rd
Bowling Green, KY 42104-3266, USA

Kilian, Thomas J (Business Person)
Conseco Inc
PO Box 1957
Carmel, IN 46082-1957, USA

Kilius, Marika (Figure Skater)
Postfach 201151
Dreieich 63271, GERMANY

Kilkenny, Mike (Baseball Player)
Detroit Tigers
274 Holland St W
Bradford, ON L3Z 1J1, CANADA

Killebrew, Harmon (Baseball Player)
PO Box 14550
Scottsdale, AZ 85267-4550, USA

Killeen, Denise (Golfer)
803 Golden Wood Trce
Canton, GA 30114-6572, USA

Killeen, Evans (Baseball Player)
Kansas City A's
208 Collins Ave Apt 2-C
Mount Vernon, NY 10552, USA

Killens, Terry (Football Player)
Houston Oilers
4721 Malland Creek Dr
Mason, OH 45040, USA

Killett, Charlie (Football Player)
New York Giants
PO Box 573
Paris, TN 38242-0573, USA

Killinger, Kerry K (Financier)
Washington Mutual Inc
1201 3rd Ave Ste 100
Seattle, WA 98101-3042, USA

Killip, Christopher D (Photographer)
Harvard University
24 Quincy St
Visual Studies Dept
Cambridge, MA 02138-3804, USA

Killorin, Pat (Football Player)
Pittsburgh Steelers
8304 Partridgeberry Dr
Baldwinsville, NY 13027-8946, USA

Killy, Jean-Claude (Skier)
Villa Les 13 Chemin Bellefontaine
Cologny-GE 1223, SWITZERLAND

Kilmer, Billy
111 S Saint Joseph St
South Bend, IN 46601-1901, USA

Kilmer, Val (Actor)
c/o John Burnham *International Creative Management (ICM-LA)*
10250 Constellation Blvd
Los Angeles, CA 90067-6200, USA

Kilmer, William O (Billy) (Football Player)
San Francisco 49ers
1853 Monte Carlo Way #36
Coral Springs, FL 33071, USA

Kilmore, Chris (Musician)
ArtistDirect
1601 Cloverfield Blvd # 400
Santa Monica, CA 90404-4082, USA

Kilner, Kevin (Actor)
Innovative Artists
1505 10th St
Santa Monica, CA 90401-2805, USA

Kilpatrick, Eric
6330 Simpson Ave Apt 3
N Hollywood, CA 91606-3427, USA

Kilpatrick, Kwame (Politician)
Mayor's Office
2 Woodward Ave
City-County Building
Detroit, MI 48226-3453, USA

Kilrain, Susan L (Astronaut)
625 Cedar Ln
Virginia Beach, VA 23452-1805, USA

Kilrea, Brian (Coach, Hockey Player)
2192 Saunderson Dr
Ottawa, ON K1G 2G4, CANADA

Kilroy, Bucko (Football Player)
Eagles-Steelers Combine
89 South St
Foxboro, MA 02035-1714, USA

Kilts, James M (Business Person)
Gillette Co
Prudential Tower Building
Boston, MA 02199, USA

Kilzer, Louis C (Lon) (Journalist)
Minneapolis-Saint Paul Star-Tribune
425 Portland Ave
Minneapolis, MN 55488-1511, USA

Kim, Byung Hyun (Baseball Player)
Arizona Diamondbacks
2037 N Chestnut
Mesa, AZ 85213-2274, USA

Kim, Daniel Dae (Actor)
c/o Steven Siebert *Lighthouse Entertainment*
409 N Camden Dr Ste 202
Beverly Hills, CA 90210-4423, USA

Kim, Jacqueline (Actor)
Innovative Artists
1505 10th St
Santa Monica, CA 90401-2805, USA

Kim, Jaegwon (Misc)
Brown University
Philosophy Dept
Providence, RI 02912-0001, USA

Kim, Nelli V (Gymnast)
2480 Cobblehill
#A Alocove
Woodbury, MN 55125, USA

Kim, Peter S (Misc)
Whitehead Institute
9 Cambridge Ctr
Cambridge, MA 02142-1479, USA

Kim, Stephan Sou-hwan Cardinal
(Religious Leader)
Archbishop's House
2 Ka 1 Myong Dong Chungku
Seoul 100, SOUTH KOREA

Kim, Yoon-jin (Actor)
c/o Staff Member *William Morris Agency (WMA-LA)*
1 William Morris Pl
Beverly Hills, CA 90212-4261, USA

Kim, Young Sam (President)
Sangdo-dong 7-6
Tongjakku
Seoul, SOUTH KOREA

Kim, Young Uck (Musician)
Columbia Artists Mgmt Inc
1790 Broadway Fl 6
New York, NY 10019-1412, USA

Kim, Yunjin (Actor)
c/o Esther Chang *William Morris Agency (WMA-LA)*
1 William Morris Pl
Beverly Hills, CA 90212-4261, USA

Kim II, Jong (President)
President's Office
Central Committee
Pyongyang, NORTH KOREA

kim II, Jong P (Prime Minister)
Prime Minister's Office
77 Sejong-no
Chongnoku
Seoul, SOUTH KOREA

Kimball, Bobby (Musician)
World Entertainment Assoc
297101 Kinderkamack Road #128
Oradell, NJ 07649, USA

Kimball, Bruce (Football Player)
New York Giants
41 Spring Rd
Rye, NH 03870-2449, USA

Kimball, Cheyenne (Musician)
c/o Staff Member *Sony Music International*
550 Madison Ave Fl 6
New York, NY 10022-3211, USA

Kimball, Christopher (Chef)
Public Broadcasting SYstem
1320 Braddock Pl
Alexandria, VA 22314-1692, USA

Kimball, Dick (Coach)
1540 Waltham Dr
Ann Arbor, MI 48103-5631, USA

Kimball, Ward
8910 Ardendale Ave
San Gabriel, CA 91775-1906, USA

Kimball, Warren F (Historian)
2540 Otter Ln
Johns Island, SC 29455-6104, USA

Kimball-Purdham, Mary Ellen (Baseball Player)
PO Box 9
Irons, MI 49644-0009, USA

Kimber, William (Football Player)
New York Giants
7801 Point Meadows Dr Unit 3102
Jacksonville, FL 32256-9145, USA

Kimble, Warren (Artist)
RR 3 Box 1038
Brandon, VT 05733, USA

Kimbrough, Charles (Actor, Musician)
255 Amalfi Dr
Santa Monica, CA 90402-1125, USA

Kimbrough, Elbert (Football Player)
Los Angeles Rams
45340 Medicine Bow Ct
Fremont, CA 94539-6639, USA

Kimbrough, Will (Musician)
Cedar Creek Music
164 Dove Creek Rd
Frankfort, KY 40601-8945, USA

Kimery, James L (Misc)
Veterans of Foreign Wars
405 W 34th St
Kansas City, MO 64111, USA

Kimm, Bruce (Baseball Player)
Detroit Tigers
3168 121st St
Amana, IA 52203-8046, USA

Kimmel, Jerry (Football Player)
New York Giants
1411 Colesville Rd
Harpursville, NY 13787-1430, USA

Kimmel, Jimmy (Comedian, Television Host, Writer)
Jimmy Kimmel Live
6834 Hollywood Blvd Ste 600
Hollywood, CA 90028-6135, USA

Kimmelman, Michael (Critic)
New York Times
229 W 43rd St
Editorial Dept
New York, NY 10036-3959, USA

Kimmins, Kenneth (Actor)
c/o Staff Member *Burstein Company, The*
15304 W Sunset Blvd Ste 208
Pacific Palisades, CA 90272-3656, USA

Kims of Comedy (Comedian)
c/o Staff Member *Paradigm (Monterey)*
509 Hartnell St
Monterey, CA 93940-2825, USA

Kimura, Doreen (Psychic)
211 Madison Ave
Toronto, ON M5R 2S6, CANADA

Kimura, Kazuo (Designer)
Japan Design Foundation
2-2 Cenba Chuo
Higashiku
Osaka 541, JAPAN

Kinard, Billy (Football Player)
Cleveland Browns
3609 Gann Rd SW
Fort Payne, AL 35967-8422, USA

Kinard, Terry (Football Player)
New York Giants
90 Spring Valley Xing
Covington, GA 30016-8247, USA

Kincaid, Aron (Actor)
Coast to Coast Talent
3350 Barham Blvd
Los Angeles, CA 90068-1404, USA

Kincaid, Jamaica (Writer)
College Road
North Bennington, VT 05257, USA

Kinchen, Brian (Football Player)
Miami Dolphins
19052 E Pinnacle Cir
Baton Rouge, LA 70810-7996, USA

Kinchen, Todd W (Football Player)
Los Angeles Rams
5854 Menlo Dr
Baton Rouge, LA 70808-5047, USA

Kinchla, Chan (Musician)
ArtistDirect
1601 Cloverfield Blvd # 400
Santa Monica, CA 90404-4082, USA

Kincses, Veronika (Opera Singer)
Hungarian State Opera
Andrassy Ulca 22
Budapest 1061, HUNGARY

Kind, Danielle (Actor)
C/O Micheline Watson
Take One Talent Management Inc
PO Box 20019
Ottawa, ON K1N 9N5, CANADA

Kind, Richard (Actor)
c/o Arlene Forster *Forster-Delaney Entertainment*
12533 Woodgreen St
Los Angeles, CA 90066-2723, USA

Kind, Roslyn (Actor, Musician)
Scott Stander
13707 Riverside Dr # 201
Sherman Oaks, CA 91423, USA

Kindall, Jerry (Baseball Player)
Chicago Cubs
7220 E Grey Fox Ln
Tucson, AZ 85750-1377, USA

Kinder, Melvyn (Psychic)
1951 San Ysidro Dr
Beverly Hills, CA 90210-1555, USA

Kinder, Richard D (Business Person)
Enron Corp
PO Box 1188
Houston, TX 77251-1188, USA

Kinderman, Keith (Football Player)
San Diego Chargers
5837 Bradfordville Rd
Tallahassee, FL 32309-6613, USA

Kindig, Howard (Football Player)
San Diego Chargers
8740 Bayside Ave
Baton Rouge, LA 70806-7947, USA

Kindle, Greg (Football Player)
St Louis Cardinals
7606 Heron Park Ct
Humble, TX 77396-2222, USA

Kindler, Klaus
Am Berg 6
Schwietenkirchen D-85301, GERMANY

Kindred, David A (Writer)
Atlanta Constitution
72 Marietta St NW
Editorial Dept
Atlanta, GA 30303-2899, USA

Kiner, Ralph M (Baseball Player, Sportscaster)
Pittsburgh Pirates
200 Bradley Pl Apt 204
Palm Beach, FL 33480-3765, USA

Kiner, Steve (Football Player)
Dallas Cowboys
112 N Ole Hickory Trl
Carrollton, GA 30117-3509, USA

King, Alan (Actor, Producer, Writer)
c/o Lisa Gallant *International Creative Management (ICM-LA)*
10250 Constellation Blvd
Los Angeles, CA 90067-6200, USA

King, Albert (Basketball Player)
88 Sturbridge Cir
Wayne, NJ 07470-8402, USA

King, Alton (Baseball Player)
Detroit Motor City Giants
8226 Esper St
Detroit, MI 48204-3120, USA

King, Angelo (Football Player)
Dallas Cowboys
1300 Ponderosa Pine Ln
Carrollton, TX 75007-1028, USA

King, B B (Musician)
c/o Staff Member *MCA Records (LA)*
2220 Colorado Ave
Santa Monica, CA 90404-3506, USA

King, Ben E (Musician)
Smiling Clown Music
PO Box 1097
Teaneck, NJ 07666-1097, USA

King, Benjamin (Actor)
c/o Peter Principato *Principato/Young Management*
9665 Wilshire Blvd Ste 500
Beverly Hills, CA 90212-2312, USA

King, Bernard (Basketball Player)
307 Jupiter Hills Dr
Duluth, GA 30097-5900, USA

King, Bernard (Football Player)
Cincinnati Bengals
1708 N State Road 7
Hollywood Christian School Athletic Dept
Hollywood, FL 33021-4507, USA

King, Betsy (Golfer)
7418 E Alta Sierra Dr
Scottsdale, AZ 85266-1887, USA

King, Billy Jean (Tennis Player)
World Team Tennis
250 Park Ave S # 900
New York, NY 10003-1402, USA

King, Bruce (Governor)
16735 Lew Allen Cir
Riverside, CA 92518-2909, USA

King, Cammie (Actor)
511 Cypress St
Fort Bragg, CA 95437-5417, USA

King, Cammie Conlon
c/o Staff Member *Pierce & Shelly*
13775A Mono Way # 220
Sonora, CA 95370-8813, USA

King, Carlos (Football Player)
Pittsburgh Steelers
107 S Corncrib Ct
Cary, NC 27513-5407, USA

King, Carole (Musician)
c/o Staff Member *Paradigm (Monterey)*
509 Hartnell St
Monterey, CA 93940-2825, USA

King, Carolyn Dineen (Judge)
US Court of Appeals
515 Rusk St Ste 12015
US Courthouse
Houston, TX 77002-2605, USA

King, Cheryl (Actor)
CLInc Talent
843 N Sycamore Ave
Los Angeles, CA 90038-3316, USA

King, Chick (Baseball Player)
Detroit Tigers
4036 Highway 54
Paris, TN 38242-6335, USA

King, Claude (Musician)
House of Talent
9 Lucy Ln
Sherwood, AR 72120-3612, USA

King, Clyde E (Baseball Player)
Brooklyn Dodgers
103 Stratford Rd
Goldsboro, NC 27534-8971, USA

King, Colbert (Journalist)
Washington Post
Editorial Dept
1150 15th St NW
Washington, DC 20071-0001, USA

King, Dana (Correspondent)
CBS-TV
524 W 57th St
News Dept
New York, NY 10019-2924, USA

King, David A (Misc)
Masters Lodge
Downing College
Cambridge CB2 1DQ, UNITED KINGDOM (UK)

King, David J (Football Player)
San Diego Chargers
4177 Chapel Lake Dr
Decatur, GA 30034-3568, USA

King, Dennis (Artist)
3857 26th St
San Francisco, CA 94131-2007, USA

King, Derek (Hockey Player)
23233 N Pima Rd Ste 113
Scottsdale, AZ 85255-8387, USA

King, Dexter Scott (Misc)
M L King Nonviolent Social Change Center
449 Auburn Ave NE
Atlanta, GA 30312-1503, USA

King, Don
Don King Productions
968 Pinehurst Dr
Las Vegas, NV 89109-1569, USA

King, Donald W (Football Player)
Cleveland Browns
1621 Fox Hall Rd
Savannah, GA 31406-5005, USA

King, Ed (Football Player)
Buffalo Bills
405 River Oak Way
Phenix City, AL 36867-1306, USA

King, Ed (Football Player)
Cleveland Browns
9903 North Blvd
Cleveland, OH 44108-3429, USA

King, Edward J (Governor)
A J Lane Co
1500 Worcester Rd
Framingham, MA 01702-8999, USA

King, Elizabeth (Betsy) (Golfer)
General Delivery
Limekiln, PA 19535-9999, USA

King, Eric (Baseball Player)
Detroit Tigers
1063 Stanford Dr
Simi Valley, CA 93065-4952, USA

King, Erik (Actor)
c/o Staff Member *Burstein Company, The*
15304 W Sunset Blvd Ste 208
Pacific Palisades, CA 90272-3656, USA

King, Evelyn
1560 Broadway # 1308
New York, NY 10036-1518, USA

King, Evelyn (Champagne) (Musician)
Nationwide Entertainment
2756 N Green Valley Pkwy
Henderson, NV 89014-2120, USA

King, Francis H (Writer)
19 Gordon Place
London W8 4JE, UNITED KINGDOM
(UK)

King, Frank (Baseball Player)
Negro Baseball Leagues
415 E Rhinehill Rd SE
Atlanta, GA 30315-7403, USA

King, G Stephen (Football Player)
New England Patriots
45 Chipping Stone Rd
North Attleboro, MA 02760-4485, USA

King, George (Basketball Player)
109 Clubhouse Ln Apt 295
Naples, FL 34105-2922, USA

King, Gordon (Football Player)
New York Giants
2641 Highwood Dr
Roseville, CA 95661-7916, USA

King, Graham (Producer)
c/o Staff Member *Initial Entertainment Group*
3000 Olympic Blvd Bldg 2 Ste 1550
Santa Monica, CA 90404-5073, USA

King, Hall (Baseball Player)
Houston Astros
828 Geneva Dr
Oviedo, FL 32765-9503, USA

King, Hogue Maxine (Mick) (Swimmer)
US Air Force Academy
PO Box 155
USAF Academy, CO 80840-0155, USA

King, Horace (Football Player)
Detroit Lions
3230 Salem Dr
Rochester Hills, MI 48306-2931, USA

King, Jaime (Actor, Model)
c/o Paul Brown *Flutie Entertainment (NY)*
6500 Wilshire Blvd
Los Angeles, CA 90048-4920, USA

King, James A (Opera Singer)
Columbia Artists Mgmt Inc
1790 Broadway Fl 6
New York, NY 10019-1412, USA

King, James B (Editor)
Seattle Times
1120 John St
Editorial Dept
Seattle, WA 98109-5321, USA

King, James C (General)
Director
National Imagery/Mapping Agency
Chantilly, VA 22021, USA

King, James (Jaime) (Actor)
c/o Staff Member *Creative Artists Agency LCC (CAA-LA)*
2000 Avenue Of The Stars
Los Angeles, CA 90067-4700, USA

King, Jean
5510 Cahuenga Blvd
N Hollywood, CA 91601-2919, USA

King, Jeff (Baseball Player)
Pittsburgh Pirates
3510 Big Swamp Creek Rd
Wisdom, MT 59761-9706, USA

King, Jeff (Misc)
PO Box 48
Denali National Park, AK 99755-0048,
USA

King, Jim (Baseball Player)
Chicago Cubs
720 Stokenbury Rd
Elkins, AR 72727-3214, USA

King, Joe (Football Player)
Cincinnati Bengals
3114 Dahlia Dr
Dallas, TX 75216-7720, USA

King, Jonathan
1 Wyndham Yard
London, ENGLAND W1H 1AR, UNITED
KINGDOM (UK)

King, Kaki (Musician)
c/o Staff Member *Paradigm (Monterey)*
509 Hartnell St
Monterey, CA 93940-2825, USA

King, Kathryn (Katie) (Hockey Player)
6 Birchwood Rd
Salem, NH 03079-3406, USA

King, Kent Masters (Actor)
c/o Richard Schwartz *Richard Schwartz Management*
2934 1/2 N Beverly Glen Cir # 107
Los Angeles, CA 90077-1724, USA

King, Kevin (Baseball Player)
Seattle Mariners
RR 1 Box 107
Braggs, OK 74423-9739, USA

King, Lamar (Football Player)
Seattle Seahawks
1453 Browning Dr
Essex, MD 21221-4337, USA

King, Larry (Journalist, Talk Show Host)
Larry King Live
1 Time Warner Ctr Rm 802D
New York, NY 10019-6038, USA

King, Linden (Football Player)
San Diego Chargers
PO Box 798
Nicasio, CA 94946-0798, USA

King, Mary-Claire (Misc)
University of Washington
Medical School
Genetics Dept
Seattle, WA 98195-0001, USA

King, Mervyn A (Economist)
Bank of England
Threadneedle St
London EC2R 8AH, UNITED KINGDOM
(UK)

King, Michael (Business Person)
King World Productions
12400 Wilshire Blvd
Los Angeles, CA 90025-1019, USA

King, Michael (Business Person)
c/o Staff Member *King World Productions Inc (LA)*
2401 Colorado Ave Ste 110
Santa Monica, CA 90404-3577, USA

King, Michael Patrick (Producer, Writer)
c/o Staff Member *Jackoway Tyerman Wertheimer Austen Mandelbaum & Morris*
1888 Century Park E Fl 18
Los Angeles, CA 90067-1702, USA

King, Morgana (Actor, Musician)
Subrena Artists
330 W 56th St Apt 18M
New York, NY 10019-4222, USA

King, Nellie (Baseball Player)
Pittsburgh Pirates
3890 Bigelow Blvd Apt 405
Pittsburgh, PA 15213-1158, USA

King, Patsy
6/70 Hawksburn Rd South Yarra
Victoria 3141, AUSTRALIA

King, Perry (Actor)
3647 Wrightwood Dr
Studio City, CA 91604-3947, USA

King, Phillip (Artist)
Bernard Jackson Gallery
14A Clifford St
London W1X 1RF, UNITED KINGDOM
(UK)

King, R Stacey (Basketball Player)
5340 Prairie Xing
Long Grove, IL 60047-5215, USA

King, Ray (Baseball Player)
Chicago Cubs
290 E Cercado Ln
Litchfield Park, AZ 85340-4229, USA

King, Regina (Actor)
c/o Chuck James *Gersh Agency, The (LA)*
232 N Canon Dr
Beverly Hills, CA 90210-5302, USA

King, Richard L (Business Person)
Albertson's Inc
250 Parkcenter Blvd
Boise, ID 83726-0001, USA

King, Roger (Business Person)
King World Productions
12400 Wilshire Blvd
Los Angeles, CA 90025-1019, USA

King, Shaun (Athlete, Football Player)
Tampa Bay Buccaneers
1646 41st St S
Saint Petersburg, FL 33711-2710, USA

King, Stephen (Writer)
c/o Rand Holston *Creative Artists Agency LCC (CAA-LA)*
2000 Avenue Of The Stars
Los Angeles, CA 90067-4700, USA

King, Ted (Actor, Musician)
c/o Staff Member *Paradigm (LA)*
360 N Crescent Dr
North Bldg
Beverly Hills, CA 90210-6820, USA

King, Thea (Musician)
16 Milverton Road
London NW6 7AS, UNITED KINGDOM
(UK)

King, Thomas J (Tom) (Government Official)
House of Commons
Westminster
London SW1A 0AA, UNITED KINGDOM
(UK)

King, W David (Coach)
Calgary Flames
PO Box 1540
Station M
Calgary, AB T2P 3B9, CANADA

King, Zalman (Director)
308 Alta Ave
Santa Monica, CA 90402-2730, USA

King III, Martin Luther (Activist)
Southern Christian Leadership
600 W Peachtree St NW Ste 2200
Atlanta, GA 30308-3629, USA

King Jr, Woodie (Producer)
417 Convent Ave
New York, NY 10031-4213, USA

King Kong (Actor)
77 Sastri Street
Kaveri Nagar Saidapet
Chennai, TN 600 015, INDIA

King Sisters
10275 S 2505 E
Sandy, UT 84092-4464, USA

Kingdom, Roger (Athlete, Track Athlete)
146 S Fairmount St Apt 1
Pittsburgh, PA 15206-3580, USA

Kingery, Ellsworth (Football Player)
Chicago Cardinals
501 Auburn Ave
Monroe, LA 71201-5303, USA

Kingery, Mike (Baseball Player)
Kansas City Royals
51923 298th St
Grove City, MN 56243-4305, USA

Kingery, Wayne (Football Player)
Baltimore Colts
1045 Walters St Apt 411
Lake Charles, LA 70607-4686, USA

Kinglsey, Ben (Actor)
International Creative Mgmt
76 Oxford St
London W1N 0AX, UNITED KINGDOM
(UK)

Kingman, Brian (Baseball Player)
Oakland A's
5801 W Osborn Rd
Phoenix, AZ 85031-3241, USA

Kingman, Dave (Baseball Player)
San Francisco Giants
PO Box 209
Glenbrook, NV 89413-0209, USA

Kingrea, Richard O (Football Player)
Cleveland Browns
102 N Bayview St
Fairhope, AL 36532-2505, USA

Kings Norton, (Harold R Cox) (Engineer, Scientist)
Westcote House
Chipping Campden
Glos, UNITED KINGDOM (UK)

Kings of Convenience (Music Group)
c/o Staff Member *Paradigm (Monterey)*
509 Hartnell St
Monterey, CA 93940-2825, USA

Kingsley, Ben (Actor)
c/o Chris Andrews *Creative Artists Agency LCC (CAA-LA)*
2000 Avenue Of The Stars
Los Angeles, CA 90067-4700, USA

Kingsley, Patricia
371 Alma Real Dr
Pacific Palisades, CA 90272-4416, USA

Kingsmen, The
1720 N Ross St
Santa Ana, CA 92706-3605, USA

Kingsriter, Doug (Football Player)
Minnesota Vikings
3118 Saint Johns Dr
Dallas, TX 75205-2938, USA

Kingston, Alex (Actor)
c/o Lorrie Bartlett *Gersh Agency, The (LA)*
232 N Canon Dr
Beverly Hills, CA 90210-5302, USA

Kingston, Kenny
11561 Dona Dorotea Dr
Studio City, CA 91604-4250, USA

Kingston, Mark
47 Courtfield Rd. #9
London, ENGLAND SW7 4DB, UNITED KINGDOM (UK)

Kingston, Maxine Hong (Writer)
University of California
English Dept
Berkeley, CA 94720-0001, USA

Kingston Trio, The
9410 S 46th St
Phoenix, AZ 85044-7512, USA

Kinkade, Thomas (Artist)
Media Arts Group
900 Lightpost Way # 100
Morgan Hill, CA 95037-2869, USA

Kinkel, Klaus (Government Official)
Auswartigen Amt
Adenauerallee 101
Bonn 53113, GERMANY

Kinks, The
29 Ruston Mews
London, ENGLAND W11 1RB, UNITED KINGDOM (UK)

Kinley, Heather (Musician)
Epic Records
1211 S Highland Ave
Los Angeles, CA 90019-1734, USA

Kinley, Jennifer (Musician)
Epic Records
1211 S Highland Ave
Los Angeles, CA 90019-1734, USA

Kinley's, The
PO Box 128501
Nashville, TN 37212-8501, USA

Kinmont, Boothe Jill (Skier)
310 Sunland Dr
Rr1 Box 11
Bishop, CA 93514-7002, USA

Kinmont, Jill
310 Sunland Dr
Bishop, CA 93514-7002, USA

Kinmont, Kathleen (Actor)
9929 Sunset Blvd #310
Los Angeles, CA 90069, USA

Kinnamon, Bill (Baseball Player)
8211 Annwood Rd
Seminole, FL 33777-2022, USA

Kinnan, Timothy A (General)
US Military Representative
NATO Blvd Leopold III
Brussels 1110, BELGIUM

Kinnear, Dominic (Coach)
San Jose Earthquakes
100 N Almaden Ave
San Jose, CA 95110-2437, USA

Kinnear, Greg (Actor, Comedian)
2280 Mandeville Canyon Rd
Los Angeles, CA 90049-1827, USA

Kinnear III, James W (Business Person)
Ten Standard Forum
PO Box 120
Stamford, CT 06904-0120, USA

Kinnebrew, Larry (Football Player)
Cincinnati Bengals
216 Kingston Ave NE
Rome, GA 30161-5628, USA

Kinney, Dallas (Journalist)
13010 Silver Sands Dr
Fort Myers, FL 33913-6934, USA

Kinney, Dennis (Baseball Player)
Cleveland Indians
PO Box 304
Schnecksville, PA 18078-0304, USA

Kinney, Kathy (Actor)
10061 Riverside Dr # 777
Toluca Lake, CA 91602-2560, USA

Kinney, Matt (Athlete, Baseball Player)
Minnesota Twins
23 Fieldstone Dr
Bangor, ME 04401-3279, USA

Kinney, Steve (Football Player)
Chicago Bears
1714 Merrill Loop
San Jose, CA 95124-5814, USA

Kinney, Taylor (Actor)
Empire Talent Agency
468 N Camden Dr # 301H
Beverly Hills, CA 90210-4507, USA

Kinney, Terry (Actor)
Gersh Agency
232 N Canon Dr
Beverly Hills, CA 90210-5302, USA

Kinnock, Neil G (Government Official)
European Communities Commission
200 Rue de Loi
Brussels 1049, BELGIUM

Kinnunen, Mike (Baseball Player)
Minnesota Twins
5818 McKinley Pl N
Seattle, WA 98103-5711, USA

Kinscherf, Carl (Football Player)
New York Giants
18 Jackson Ave
Gladstone, NJ 07934-2117, USA

Kinsella, John P (Swimmer)
PO Box 3067
Sumas, WA 98295-3067, USA

Kinsella, Thomas (Writer)
Killalane
Laragh
County Wicklow, IRELAND

Kinsella, W P
PO Box 3067
Sumas, WA 98295-3067, USA

Kinsella, William Patrick (W P) (Writer)
1952-152A St
#216
Surrey, BC V4A 9T2, CANADA

Kinser, Steve (Race Car Driver)
Steve Kinser Racing
280 E Smithville Rd
Bloomington, IN 47401-9251, USA

Kinsey, James L (Misc)
Rice University
Natural Sciences School
Houston, TX 77005, USA

Kinshofer-Guthlein, Christa (Skier)
Munchnerstr 44
Rosenheim 83026, GERMANY

Kinski, Nastassja (Actor, Model)
1000 Bel Air Rd
Los Angeles, CA 90077-3012, USA

Kinsley, Michael E (Correspondent, Editor)
14150 NE 20th St # 527
Bellevue, WA 98007-3700, USA

Kinsman, Brent (Actor)
c/o Staff Member *AKA Talent Agency*
6310 San Vicente Blvd Ste 200
Los Angeles, CA 90048-5488, USA

Kinsman, Shane (Actor)
c/o Staff Member *AKA Talent Agency*
6310 San Vicente Blvd Ste 200
Los Angeles, CA 90048-5488, USA

Kinsman, T James (Jim) (War Hero)
111 Howe Rd E
Toledo, WA 98591-9204, USA

Kintner, William R (Scientist)
Foreign Policy Research Institute
3508 Market St
Philadelphia, PA 19104-3311, USA

Kinzer, Matt (Baseball Player)
St Louis Cardinals
6717 Sweetbrier Dr
Fort Wayne, IN 46814-4564, USA

KioKio (DJ)
c/o Staff Member *Diva Central Inc*
7510 W Sunset Blvd Ste 1445
Los Angeles, CA 90046-3408, USA

Kiper Jr, Mel (Sportscaster)
ESPN-TV
935 Middle St
Sports Dept Espn Plaza
Bristol, CT 06010-1000, USA

Kipketer, Wilson (Athlete, Track Athlete)
Atletik Forbund Idraettens Hus
Brondby Stadion 20
Brondby 2605, DENMARK

Kiplinger, Austin H (Publisher)
Montevideo
1680 River Road
Poolesville, MD 20837, USA

Kipp, Fred (Baseball Player)
Brooklyn Dodgers
6613 W 126th Ter
Klc
Overland Park, KS 66209-2599, USA

Kipper, Bob (Baseball Player)
California Angels
117 Tuscany Way
Greer, SC 29650-4070, USA

Kipper, Thornton (Baseball Player)
Philadelphia Phillies
8780 E McKellips Rd Lot 340
Scottsdale, AZ 85257-4802, USA

Kiraly, Charles F (Karch) (Coach, Volleyball Player)
c/o Staff Member *Simon & Schuster*
1230 6th Ave
New York, NY 10020-1586, USA

Kirby, Bruce (Actor)
629 N Orlando Ave Apt 3
West Hollywood, CA 90048-2193, USA

Kirby, Durwood (Writer)
PO Box 3454
Fort Myers, FL 33918-3454, USA

Kirby, Jack (Football Player)
Green Bay Packers
PO Box 206
Los Olivos, CA 93441-0206, USA

Kirby, Jim (Baseball Player)
Chicago Cubs
520 Lohman Rd
Mount Juliet, TN 37122-4005, USA

Kirby, Luke (Actor)
c/o Eunice Lee *Creative Artists Agency LCC (CAA-LA)*
2000 Avenue Of The Stars
Los Angeles, CA 90067-4700, USA

Kirby, Pete
PO Box 1734
Madison, TN 37116-1734, USA

Kirby, Ronald H (Architect)
PO Box 337
Melville
Johannesburg 2109, SOUTH AFRICA

Kirby, Terry (Football Player)
Miami Dolphins
113 Kirby Ln
Tabb, VA 23693-2532, USA

Kirby, Wayne (Baseball Player)
Cleveland Indians
113 Kirby Ln
Yorktown, VA 23693-2532, USA

Kirby, Will (Reality TV Star)
c/o Staff Member *Metropolitan*
4500 Wilshire Blvd Fl 2
Los Angeles, CA 90010-3858, USA

Kirchbach, Gunar (Athlete)
Georgi-Dobrowoiski-Ste 10
Furstenwalde 15517, GERMANY

Kirchenbauer, Bill
3800 Barham Blvd
Los Angeles, CA 90068-1008, USA

Kirchhoff, Ulrich (Misc)
Hoven 258
Rosendahl 48720, GERMANY

Kirchiro, Bill (Football Player)
Baltimore Colts
9889 Fleming Ave
Bethesda, MD 20814-2145, USA

Kirchner, Leon (Composer, Conductor)
Harvard University
Music Dept
Cambridge, MA 02138, USA

Kirchner, Mark (Athlete)
Hauptstr 74A
Scheibe-Alsbach 98749, GERMANY

Kirchner, Nestor (President)
Casa de Gobierno
Balcarce 50
Buenos Aires 1064, ARGENTINA

Kirchschlager, Angelika (Opera Singer)
Mastrioanni Assoc
161 W 61st St Apt 17E
New York, NY 10023-7460, USA

Kirgo, George (Actor, Writer)
178 N Carmelina Ave
Los Angeles, CA 90049-2737, USA

Kiriazis, Nick (Actor)
c/o Staff Member *Pakula/King & Associates*
9229 W Sunset Blvd Ste 315
Los Angeles, CA 90069-3403, USA

Kirilenko, Maria (Tennis Player)
c/o Staff Member *Women's Tennis Association (WTA (US))*
1 Progress Plz Ste 1500
St Petersburg, FL 33701-4335, USA

Kirk, Bill (Baseball Player)
Kansas City A's
16 Timber Villa
Elizabethtown, PA 17022-9424, USA

Kirk, Claude R Jr (Governor)
Kirk Co
1180 Gator Trl
West Palm Beach, FL 33409-2043, USA

Kirk, James (Actor)
c/o Tyman Stewart *Characters Talent Agency, The (Toronto)*
8 Elm St 3rd FL
Toronto, ON M5G 1G7, CANADA

Kirk, Justin (Actor)
c/o Bill Butler *Gersh Agency, The (NY)*
41 Madison Ave Fl 33
New York, NY 10010-2202, USA

Kirk, Ken (Football Player)
Chicago Bears
202 Milford St Apt 201
Tupelo, MS 38801-4691, USA

Kirk, Rahsaan Roland (Musician)
Atlantic Records
9229 W Sunset Blvd Ste 900
Los Angeles, CA 90069-3410, USA

Kirk, Thomas B (Physicist)
Brookhaven National Laboratory
2 Center St
Physics Dept
Upton, NY 11973-9700, USA

Kirk Jr, Walton (Walt) (Basketball Player)
2355 Coventry Park # B202
Dubuque, IA 52001-3066, USA

Kirkby, Emma (Musician)
Consort of Music
54A Leamington Road Villas
London W11 1HT, UNITED KINGDOM (UK)

Kirkconnell, Clare
PO Box 63
Rutherford, CA 94573-0063, USA

Kirkeby, Per (Artist)
Margarete Roeder Gallery
545 Broadway
New York, NY 10012-3921, USA

Kirkland, Gelsey (Ballerina)
500 Mount Tailac Ct
Roseville, CA 95747-8028, USA

Kirkland, Levon (Football Player)
Pittsburgh Steelers
18200 Town Harbour Rd
Cornelius, NC 28031-7775, USA

Kirkland, Lori (Producer)
c/o Staff Member *Roklin Management*
8530 Wilshire Blvd Ste 550
Beverly Hills, CA 90211-3133, USA

Kirkland, Mike (Musician)
Bob Flick Productions
300 Vine St Ste 14
Seattle, WA 98121-1465, USA

Kirkland, Sally (Actor)
c/o Michael Greene *Greene & Associates*
190 N Canon Dr Ste 200
Beverly Hills, CA 90210-5319, USA

Kirkland, Willie (Baseball Player)
San Francisco Giants
19374 Northrop St
Detroit, MI 48219-5500, USA

Kirkman, Rick (Cartoonist)
King Features Syndicate
888 7th Ave Ste 201
New York, NY 10106-0201, USA

Kirkpatrick, Ed (Baseball Player)
Los Angeles Angels
24791 Via Larga
Laguna Niguel, CA 92677-1933, USA

Kirkpatrick, Maggie (Actor)
Shanahan Mgmt
PO Box 1509
Darlinghurst, NSW 1300, AUSTRALIA

Kirkpatrick, Ralph (Musician)
Old Quarry
Guilford, CT 06437, USA

Kirkreit, Daron (Baseball Player)
1548 Langham Ter
Lake Mary, FL 32746-1971, USA

Kirkup, James (Writer)
British Monomarks
BM-Box 2780
London WC1V 6XX, UNITED KINGDOM (UK)

Kirkwood, Craig (Actor)
c/o Staff Member *Levine Management*
9028 W Sunset Blvd # Ph1
Los Angeles, CA 90069-1846, USA

Kirkwood, Don (Baseball Player)
California Angels
455 W Elmwood Ave
Clawson, MI 48017-1231, USA

Kirllenko, Andrei (Basketball Player)
Utah Jazz
301 W South Temple
Delta Center
Salt Lake City, UT 84101-1216, USA

Kirner, Gary (Football Player)
San Diego Chargers
22 Pegasus Dr
Trabuco Canyon, CA 92679-5122, USA

Kirouac, Lou (Football Player)
New York Giants
3630 Chattahoochee Ct
Duluth, GA 30096-3210, USA

Kirrane, John (Jack) (Hockey Player)
3 Centre St
Brookline, MA 02446, USA

Kirrene, Joe (Baseball Player)
Chicago White Sox
2557 Kilpatrick Ct
San Ramon, CA 94583-1726, USA

Kirsch, Stan
275 S Beverly Dr Ste 215
Beverly Hills, CA 90212-5002, USA

Kirschke, Travis (Football Player)
Detroit Lions
10196 Crooked Stick Trl
Lone Tree, CO 80124-8510, USA

Kirschner, Carl (Educator)
Rutgers State University College
President's Office
New Brunswick, NJ 08093, USA

kirschner, David (Actor)
c/o Staff Member *William Morris Agency (WMA-LA)*
1 William Morris Pl
Beverly Hills, CA 90212-4261, USA

Kirschstein, Ruth L (Doctor)
National Institute of Health
9000 Rockville Pike
Bethesda, MD 20892-0002, USA

Kirsebom, Vendela (Model)
c/o Staff Member *Ford Models (NY)*
111 5th Ave Fl 9
New York, NY 10003-1005, USA

Kirsh, Stan (Actor)
Kritzer
12200 W Olympic Blvd Ste 400
Los Angeles, CA 90064-1047, USA

Kirshbaum, Laurence J (Publisher)
Warner Books
Rockefeller Center
Time-Life Building
New York, NY 10020, USA

Kirshbaum, Ralph (Musician)
Columbia Artists Mgmt Inc
1790 Broadway Fl 6
New York, NY 10019-1412, USA

Kirshner, Irwin
9200 W Sunset Blvd # 401
Los Angeles, CA 90069-3502, USA

Kirshner, Mia (Actor)
c/o Daniel (Danny) Sussman *Brillstein-Grey Entertainment*
9150 Wilshire Blvd Ste 350
Beverly Hills, CA 90212-3453, USA

Kirszenstein, Szewinska Irena (Athlete, Track Athlete)
Ul Bagno 5m 80
Warsaw 00-112, POLAND

Kisabaka, Lisa (Athlete, Track Athlete)
Franz-Hitze-Str 22
Leverkusen 51372, GERMANY

Kiselak, Mike (Football Player)
Dallas Cowboys
316 Cimarron Trl
Irving, TX 75063-4598, USA

Kiser, Garland (Baseball Player)
Cleveland Indians
267 Carr Dr
Blountville, TN 37617-4608, USA

Kiser, Terry (Actor)
Innovative Artists
1505 10th St
Santa Monica, CA 90401-2805, USA

Kishida, Kyoko
7-5-34-801 Akasada Miatuku
Tokyo, JAPAN

Kishlansky, Mark A (Historian)
Harvard University
History Dept
Cambridge, MA 02138, USA

Kisio, Kelly (Hockey Player)
Birch Cliff
Bentley, AB T0C 0J0, CANADA

Kison, Bruce E (Baseball Player)
Pittsburgh Pirates
1403 Riverside Circle
Bradenton, FL 34209, USA

Kisor, Henry (Writer)
2800 Harrison St
Evanston, IL 60201-1218, USA

KISS (Music Group)
c/o Mitch Rose *Creative Artists Agency LCC (CAA-LA)*
2000 Avenue Of The Stars
Los Angeles, CA 90067-4700, USA

Kissel-Lafser, Audrey (Baseball Player)
9506 Port Dr
Affton, MO 63123-6530, USA

Kissell, Ed (Football Player)
Pittsburgh Steelers
40 Sebbins Pond Dr
Bedford, NH 03110-6630, USA

Kissin, Evgeni I (Musician)
Harold Holt
31 Sinclair Rd
London W14 0NS, UNITED KINGDOM (UK)

Kissinger, Henry A (Nobel Prize Laureate, Secretary)
350 Park Ave
New York, NY 10022-6022, USA

Kissling, Conny (Skier)
Hubel
Messen 3254, SWITZERLAND

Kistler, Darci (Ballerina)
New York City Ballet
Lincoln Center Plaza
New York, NY 10023, USA

Kitaen, Tawny (Actor)
Talent Group
5670 Wilshire Blvd Ste 820
Los Angeles, CA 90036-5613, USA

Kitaj, R B (Artist)
Mariborough Fine Art
6 Albermarle St
London W1, UNITED KINGDOM (UK)

Kitano, Takeshi (Actor, Director)
Office Kitano
5-4-14 Akasaka Minataku
Tokyo 107-0052, JAPAN

Kitaro (Composer, Musician)
GLP Huetteldorferstra 259
Vienna
1140, AUSTRIA

Kitayenko, Dmitri G (Conductor)
Chalet Kalimor
Botterens 1652, SWITZERLAND

Kitbunchu, M Michael Cardinal (Religious Leader)
122 Soi Naaksuwan
Thanon Nonsi Yannawa
Bangkok 10120, THAILAND

Kitchen, Michael (Actor)
International Creative Mgmt
76 Oxford St
London W1N 0AX, UNITED KINGDOM (UK)

Kite, Greg (Basketball Player)
3060 Seigneury Dr
Windermere, FL 34786-8353, USA

Kite, Tom (Golfer)
6000 Long Champ Ct
Austin, TX 78746-1106, USA

Kithune, Robert K U (Admiral)
1597 Haleloke St
Hilo, HI 96720-1571, USA

Kitna, John (Football Player)
18898 Bella Vista Ct
Northville, MI 48168-3534, USA

Kitsch, Taylor (Actor)
c/o Stephanie Simon *Untitled Entertainment (LA)*
331 N Maple Dr Fl 3
Beverly Hills, CA 90210-3827, USA

Kitson, Syd (Football Player)
Green Bay Packers
3 Frost Ln
New Providence, NJ 07974-1246, USA

Kitsos, Chris (Baseball Player)
Chicago Cubs
1219 Anchor Dr
Mobile, AL 36693-4501, USA

Kitt, A J (Skier)
2437 N Franklin Ave
Louisville, CO 80027-1216, USA

Kitt, Eartha (Actor, Musician)
c/o Andrew Freedman *Andrew Freedman PR LLC*
1717 Ferrari Dr
Beverly Hills, CA 90210-1603, USA

Kittel, Charles (Physicist)
University of California
Physics Dept
Berkeley, CA 94720-0001, USA

Kittinger Jr, Joseph W (Joe) (Misc)
608 Mariner Way
Altamonte Springs, FL 32701-5434, USA

Kittle, Ronald D (Ron) (Baseball Player)
Chicago White Sox
1840 Tour Trce
Chesterton, IN 46304-3465, USA

Kittles, Kerry (Basketball Player)
New Jersey Nets
390 Murray Hill Pkwy
East Rutherford, NJ 07073-2109, USA

Kittles, Tory (Actor)
c/o Matt Luber *Nine Yards Entertainment*
8530 Wilshire Blvd Fl 5
Beverly Hills, CA 90211-3102, USA

Kitzhaber, John A (Governor)
Oregon Health & Science University
Evidence Based Policy
Portland, OR 97201, USA

Kiyosaki, Kim (Business Person, Writer)
CASHFLOW Technologies Inc
4330 N Civic Center Plz Ste 100
Scottsdale, AZ 85251-3529, USA

Kiyosaki, Robert T (Business Person, Writer)
CASHFLOW Technologies Inc
4330 N Civic Center Plz Ste 100
Scottsdale, AZ 85251-3529, USA

Kizer, Carolyn A (Writer)
University of Arizona
English Dept
Tucson, AZ 85271, USA

Kizim, Leonid D (Cosmonaut)
Mojaysky Military School
Russian Space Forces
Saint Petersburg, RUSSIA

Kjer, Bodil (Actor)
Vestre Pavilion Frydenlund
Frydenlund Alle 19
Vedbaek 2950, DENMARK

Kjus, Lasse (Skier)
Rugdeveien 2C
Siggerud 1404, NORWAY

Klabunde, Charles S (Artist)
68 W 3rd St
New York, NY 10012-1029, USA

Klages, Fred (Baseball Player)
Chicago White Sox
7 Silkbay Pl
The Woodlands, TX 77382-1604, USA

Klammer, Franz (Skier)
Mooswald 22
Fresach/Ktn 9712, AUSTRIA

Klaplisch, Cedric (Director)
Cineart
36 Rue de Ponthieu
Paris 75008, FRANCE

Klares, John (Bowler)
1760 N Decatur Blvd Apt 10
Las Vegas, NV 89108-2249, USA

Klas, Eri (Conductor)
Nurme 54
Tallinn 0016, ESTONIA

Klasnic, John (Football Player)
Brooklyn Dodgers
924 Highland Ave
McKeesport, PA 15133-3920, USA

Klassen, Danny (Baseball Player)
Arizona Diamondbacks
8072 Kiawah Trce
Port Saint Lucie, FL 34986-3023, USA

Klaus, Billy (Baseball Player)
Boston Braves
PO Box 662
Valle Crucis, NC 28691-0662, USA

Klaus, Bobby (Baseball Player)
Cincinnati Reds
10661 Gabacho Dr
San Diego, CA 92124-1404, USA

Klaus, Deita (Actor)
c/o Staff Member *Digigraphics/Dream Girl World*
4650 Libbit Ave
Encino, CA 91436-2122, USA

Klaus, Vaclav (Politician, President)
c/o Staff Member *Kancelar Prezidenta Republiky (Czech Republic)*
Hradecek
Prague 1 119 08, CZECH REPUBLIC

Klausing, Chuck (Coach, Football Coach)
2115 Lazor St
Indiana, PA 15701-3463, USA

Klawitter, Tom (Baseball Player)
Minnesota Twins
2506 Kenwood Mill Rd
Janesville, WI 53545, USA

Klaxons (Music Group)
c/o Staff Member *Paradigm (Monterey)*
509 Hartnell St
Monterey, CA 93940-2825, USA

Klebba, Martin (Actor)
c/o Staff Member *The Stevens Group*
14011 Ventura Blvd # 201
Sherman Oaks, CA 91423-3533, USA

Klebe, Giselher (Composer)
Bruchstr 16
Detmold 32756, GERMANY

Klecko, Joseph E (Joe) (Football Player)
New York Jets
105 Stella Ln
Aston, PA 19014-2741, USA

Klees, Christian (Misc)
Eutiner Sportschutzen
Schutzenweg 26
Eutin 23701, GERMANY

Kleihues, Josef P (Architect)
Schlickweg 4
Berlin 14129, GERMANY

Klein, Alex (Misc)
Columbia Artists Mgmt Inc
1790 Broadway Fl 6
New York, NY 10019-1412, USA

Klein, Calvin R (Designer, Fashion Designer)
c/o Staff Member *Calvin Klein Inc*
200 Madison Ave
Phillips-Van Heusen Corporation
New York, NY 10016-3903, USA

Klein, Chris (Actor)
c/o Cynthia Pett-Dante *Brillstein-Grey Entertainment*
9150 Wilshire Blvd Ste 350
Beverly Hills, CA 90212-3453, USA

Klein, Danny (Musician)
Nick Ben-Meir
652 N Doheny Dr
Los Angeles, CA 90069-5526, USA

Klein, David (Misc)
National Child Health Institute
9000 Rockville Pike
Bethesda, MD 20892-0001, USA

Klein, Edward
c/o Daniel A (Dan) Strone *Trident Media Group LLC*
41 Madison Ave Fl 36
New York, NY 10010-2257, USA

Klein, Emilee (Golfer)
9930 Sweetleaf St
Orlando, FL 32827-6862, USA

Klein, Herbert G (Government Official, Publisher)
Copley Press
350 Camino De Reina
San Diego, CA 92108, USA

Klein, Jennifer (Producer)
c/o Carlos Goodman *Bloom Hergott Deimer Rosenthall La Violette*
9200 W Sunset Blvd Ste 1200
Los Angeles, CA 90069-3607, USA

Klein, Jenny
201 S Capitol Ave Ste 430
Indianapolis, IN 46225-1026, USA

Klein, Jess (Musician, Songwriter, Writer)
Drake Assoc
177 Woodland Ave
Westwood, NJ 07675-3218, USA

Klein, Joe (Journalist, Writer)
Newsweek Magazine
251 W 57th St
Editorial Dept
New York, NY 10019-1802, USA

Klein, Joel (Educator, Government Official, Lawyer)
NY City Schools
110 Livingston St
Chancellor's Office
Brooklyn, NY 11201-5011, USA

Klein, Lawrence R (Nobel Prize Laureate)
1400 Waverly Rd Apt B35
Gladwyne, PA 19035-1260, USA

Klein, Lester A (Doctor)
Scripps Clinic
10666 N Torrey Pines Rd
Urology Dept
La Jolla, CA 92037-1092, USA

Klein, Marci (Director, Producer, Writer)
c/o Jeffrey Jacobs *Creative Artists Agency LCC (CAA-LA)*
2000 Avenue Of The Stars
Los Angeles, CA 90067-4700, USA

Klein, Naomi (Producer, Writer)
Klein Lewis Productions
PO Box 67746 280 Spadina Ave
Toronto, ON M5T 3B0, CANADA

Klein, Perry (Football Player)
Atlanta Falcons
30760 Broad Beach Rd
Malibu, CA 90265-2613, USA

Klein, Richard J (Football Player)
Chicago Bears
609 E 2nd St
Pana, IL 62557-1446, USA

Klein, Robert (Entertainer)
c/o Rory Rosegarten *Conversation Company*
1044 Northern Blvd Ste 304
Roslyn, NY 11576-1589, USA

Klein, Robert O (Bob) (Football Player)
Los Angeles Rams
15933 Alcima Ave
Pacific Palisades, CA 90272-2405, USA

Klein Borkow, Dana (Producer)
c/o Staff Member *William Morris Agency (WMA-LA)*
1 William Morris Pl
Beverly Hills, CA 90212-4261, USA

Kleindienst, Richard
3103 W Crestview Dr
Prescott, AZ 86305-5001, USA

Kleine, Joseph (Joe) (Baseball Player)
4819 Stony Ford Dr
Dallas, TX 75287-7214, USA

Kleinert, Harold E (Doctor)
225 Abraham Flexner Way
Louisville, KY 40202-1882, USA

Kleinfeld, Andrew J (Judge)
US Court of Appeals
250 Cushman St
Courthouse Square
Fairbanks, AK 99701-4640, USA

Kleinman, Arthur M (Psychic)
Harvard University
Anthropology Dept
Cambridge, MA 02138, USA

Kleinrock, Leonard (Scientist)
318 N Rockingham Ave
Los Angeles, CA 90049-2636, USA

Kleinsasser, Jim (Football Player)
Minnesota Vikings
5955 3rd St SE
Carrington, ND 58421-8804, USA

Kleinsmith, Bruce (Cartoonist)
PO Box 325
Aromas, CA 95004-0325, USA

Kleiser, Randal (Director)
3050 Runyon Canyon Rd
Los Angeles, CA 90046-1347, USA

Klemm, Adrian (Football Player)
New England Patriots
2931 Plaza Del Amo Unit 115
Torrance, CA 90503-9331, USA

Klemm, Jay (Baseball Player)
1605 Airy Hill Ct Unit D
Crofton, MD 21114-2723, USA

Klemmer, John (Musician)
Boardman
10548 Clearwood Ct
Los Angeles, CA 90077-2019, USA

Klemp, Cardinal Jozef
Kolski U1Miodowa 17
Warsaw PL-00-583, POLAND

Klemperer, William (Misc)
53 Shattuck Rd
Watertown, MA 02472-1310, USA

Klemt, Becky (Lawyer)
Pence & MacMilan
PO Box 1285
Laramie, WY 82073-1285, USA

Klensch, Elsa
1050 Techwood Dr NW
Atlanta, GA 30318-5604, USA

Kleppe, Thomas S (Secretary)
7100 Darby Rd
Bethesda, MD 20817-2914, USA

Klesko, Ryan A (Baseball Player)
c/o Staff Member *San Diego Padres*
100 Park Blvd
San Diego, CA 92101-7405, USA

Klesla, Rotislav (Hockey Player)
Columbus Blue Jackts
200 W Nationwide Blvd
Arena
Columbus, OH 43215-2564, USA

Klett, Peter (Musician)
11410 NE 124th St # 627
Kirkland, WA 98034-4305, USA

Kleven, Jay (Baseball Player)
New York Mets
118 Via Boisa
San Lorenzo, CA 94580, USA

Klever, Rocky (Football Player)
New York Jets
3829 W 42nd Ave
Anchorage, AK 99517-2752, USA

Kley Minnis, Chaney (Actor)
c/o Brady McKay *Saffron Management*
9171 Wilshire Blvd Ste 441
Beverly Hills, CA 90210-5516, USA

Klick, Jim (Football Player)
Miami Dolphins
4001 E Lake Estates Dr
Davie, FL 33328-3072, USA

Klicullen, Bob (Football Player)
Chicago Bears
400 E Division St
Pilot Point, TX 76258-4510, USA

Kliks, Rudolf R (Architect)
Russian Chamber of Commerce
UI Kuibysheva 6
Moscow, RUSSIA

Klim, Michael (Swimmer)
177 Bridge Road
Richmond, VIC 3121, AUSTRALIA

Klima, Petr (Hockey Player)
5002 Avenue Avignon
Lutz, FL 33558-2825, USA

Klimchock, Lou (Baseball Player)
Kansas City A's
8876 S Myrtie Ave
Tempe, AZ 85284, USA

Klimek, Tony (Football Player)
Chicago Cardinals
17730 Brook Hill Dr
Orland Park, IL 60467-7524, USA

Klimke, Reiner (Misc)
Krumme Str 3
Munster 48143, GERMANY

Klimkowski, Ron (Baseball Player)
New York Yankees
117 Candy Ln
Syosset, NY 11791-4911, USA

Klimuk, Pyotr I (Cosmonaut)
Potchta Kosmonavtov
Moskovskoi Oblasti
Syvisdny Goroduk 141160, RUSSIA

Kline, Bobby (Baseball Player)
Washington Senators
6656 31st Way S
Saint Petersburg, FL 33712-5404, USA

Kline, Jeff (Producer, Writer)
c/o Staff Member *Endeavor Agency LLC* (LA)
9601 Wilshire Blvd Fl 3
Beverly Hills, CA 90210-5204, USA

Kline, Kevin D (Actor)
c/o Judy Hofflund *Hofflund/Polone*
9465 Wilshire Blvd Ste 890
Beverly Hills, CA 90212-2607, USA

Kline, Owen (Actor)
c/o Staff Member *William Morris Agency (WMA-LA)*
1 William Morris Pl
Beverly Hills, CA 90212-4261, USA

Kline, Richard (Actor)
c/o Harry Gold *TalentWorks (LA)*
3500 W Olive Ave Ste 1400
Burbank, CA 91505-5512, USA

Kline, Steve (Baseball Player)
New York Yankees
532 N Knights Bridge Rd
Canby, OR 97013-3339, USA

Kline, Steve (Baseball Player)
Cleveland Indians
258 Trutt Rd
Winfield, PA 17889-9304, USA

Kline-Randall, Maxine (Baseball Player)
3751 Milnes Rd
Hillsdale, MI 49242-9313, USA

Klingbeil, Chuck (Football Player)
Miami Dolphins
51977 Bootjack Rd
Lake Linden, MI 49945-9765, USA

Klingenbeck, Scott (Baseball Player)
Baltimore Orioles
6230 Kincora Ct
Cincinnati, OH 45233-4458, USA

Klingensmith, Michael J (Publisher)
Entertainment Weekly Magazine
Rockefeller Center
New York, NY 10020, USA

Klingler, David (Football Player)
Cincinnati Bengals
2206 Shelby Park Dr
Katy, TX 77450-6600, USA

Klingman, Lynzee (Actor)
c/o Staff Member *United Talent Agency (UTA)*
9560 Wilshire Blvd Ste 500
Beverly Hills, CA 90212-2401, USA

Klinsmann, Jurgen (Soccer Player)
3419 Via Lido # 600
Newport Beach, CA 92663-3908, USA

Klitbo, Cynthia (Actor)
c/o Staff Member *Televisa*
Blvd Adolfo Lopez Mateos 232
Colonia San Angel INN
DF CP 01060, MEXICO

Klitschko, Wladimir (Boxer)
Am Stradtrand 2
Hamburg 22047, GERMANY

Kllesmet, Robert B (Misc)
Union of Police Assns
815 16th St NW # 307
Washington, DC 20006-4101, USA

Klosowski, Dolores (Baseball Player)
14254 Farnsworth Dr
Sterling Heights, MI 48312-4352, USA

Klosterman, Bruce (Football Player)
Denver Broncos
14194 Deerfield Ct
Dubuque, IA 52003-9414, USA

Klotz, H Louis (Red) (Basketball Player, Coach)
114 S Osborne Ave
Margate City, NJ 08402-2530, USA

Klotz, Irving M (Misc)
1500 Sheridan Rd Unit 7D
Wilmette, IL 60091-1844, USA

Klotz, John S (Football Player)
New York Titans
729 E 25th St
Chester, PA 19013-5229, USA

Klous, Patricia (Actor)
2539 Benedict Canyon Dr
Beverly Hills, CA 90210-1020, USA

Kloves, Steve (Director, Writer)
c/o David O'Connor *Creative Artists Agency LCC (CAA-LA)*
2000 Avenue Of The Stars
Los Angeles, CA 90067-4700, USA

Kluer, Duane (Basketball Player, Coach)
252 Francis Avenue Ct
Terre Haute, IN 47804-5101, USA

Klug, Aaron (Nobel Prize Laureate)
70 Cavendish Ave
Cambridge CB1 40T, UNITED KINGDOM (UK)

Kluge, John W (Business Person)
Metromedia Co
1 Meadowlands Plz Ste 300
East Rutherford, NJ 07073-2152, USA

Kluger, Richard (Writer)
William Morris Agency
151 El Camino Dr
Beverly Hills, CA 90212-2775, USA

Klugh, Earl (Musician)
c/o Staff Member *Richard De La Font Agency*
4845 S Sheridan Rd Ste 505
Tulsa, OK 74145-5719, USA

Klum, Heidi (Model, Producer)
c/o Richard Weitz *Endeavor Agency LLC* (LA)
9601 Wilshire Blvd Fl 3
Beverly Hills, CA 90210-5204, USA

Klutka, Nick (Football Player)
Buffalo Bisons
2505 Alamosa Dr
Santa Fe, NM 87505-5213, USA

Klutts, Mickey (Baseball Player)
New York Yankees
6136 Maple Ave
Lake Isabella, CA 93240-9706, USA

Klymaxx (Music Group)
c/o Staff Member *Diva Central Inc*
7510 W Sunset Blvd Ste 1445
Los Angeles, CA 90046-3408, USA

Klyn, Vincent
4200 Ocean View Dr
Malibu, CA 90265-2822, USA

Klyszewski, Waclaw (Architect)
UI Gomoslaska 16m 15A
Warsaw 00-432, POLAND

Kmak, Joe (Baseball Player)
Milwaukee Brewers
1021 Hatteras Ct
Foster City, CA 94404-3546, USA

Kmetko, Steve
5670 Wilshire Blvd Ste 200
Los Angeles, CA 90036-5611, USA

Knackert, Brent (Baseball Player)
Seattle Mariners
16802 Leafwood Cir
Huntington Beach, CA 92647-4851, USA

Knafelc, Gary (Football Player)
Chicago Cardinals
2147 Burley Ave
Clermont, FL 34711-5744, USA

Knafelc, Greg (Football Player)
New Orleans Saints
612 Chantilly Rue
Green Bay, WI 54301-1432, USA

Knape, Lindberg Ulrike (Swimmer)
Drostvagen 7
Karlskoga 691 33, SWEDEN

Knapp, Charles B (Educator)
Aspen Institute
1333 New Hampshire Ave NW
Washington, DC 20036-1511, USA

Knapp, Chris (Baseball Player)
Chicago White Sox
788 Rich Dr
Oviedo, FL 32765-6447, USA

Knapp, Cleon T (Publisher)
Talewood Corp
10100 Santa Monica Blvd Ste 2000
Los Angeles, CA 90067-4134, USA

Knapp, Jennifer (Musician)
Creative Artists Agency
9830 Wilshire Blvd
Beverly Hills, CA 90212-1804, USA

Knapp, John W (Educator, General)
Virginia Military Institute
Superintendent's Office
Lexington, VA 24450, USA

Knapp, Lindsay (Football Player)
Kansas City Chiefs
5704 Fairfax Ave
Minneapolis, MN 55424-1559, USA

Knapp, Stefan (Artist)
Sandhills
Godalming
Surrey, UNITED KINGDOM (UK)

Knaus, William (Doctor)
George Washington University
Medical Center
Washington, DC 20052-0001, USA

Knauss, Hans (Skier)
Fastenberg 60
Schladming 8970, AUSTRIA

Kneale, R Bryan C (Artist)
10A Muswell Road
London N10 2BG, UNITED KINGDOM
(UK)

Knebel, John A (Secretary)
1418 Labumum St
McLean, VA 22101, USA

Knepper, Robert (Actor)
c/o Staff Member *Peter Strain & Associates Inc (LA)*
5455 Wilshire Blvd Ste 1812
Los Angeles, CA 90036-4268, USA

Knepper, Robert W (Bob) (Baseball Player)
San Francisco Giants
9400 Wade Blvd Apt 1515
Frisco, TX 75035-6534, USA

Kness, Richard M (Opera Singer)
240 Central Park S Apt 16M
New York, NY 10019-1460, USA

Kneuer, Cameo (Misc)
Starshape by Cameo
2554 Lincoln Blvd #640
Venice, CA 90291, USA

Knicely, Alan (Baseball Player)
Houston Astros
PO Box 433
Dayton, VA 22821-0433, USA

Knief, Gayle (Football Player)
Boston Patriots
1825 Birchwood Cir
Waukee, IA 50263-8194, USA

Knievel, Evel (Actor)
7600 River Mist Ct
Las Vegas, NV 89113-6609, USA

Knievel, Robbie (Actor, Motorcycle Race, Motorcycle Racer)
Zucker Media Group
1080 West Erwing Place #302
Seattle, WA 98119, USA

Knight, Andrew S B (Editor, Publisher)
News International
PO Box 495
Virginia St
London W1 9XY, UNITED KINGDOM
(UK)

Knight, Beverley (Musician)
c/o Staff Member *International Talent Booking (ITB - UK)*
27A Floral St Fl 3
Covent Garden
London WC2E 9, UNITED KINGDOM
(UK)

Knight, Billy (Basketball Player)
6375 Massey Manor Ln W
Memphis, TN 38120-1400, USA

Knight, Brandon (Baseball Player)
New York Yankees
2003 Spyglass Trl E Apt E
Oxnard, CA 93036-2761, USA

Knight, Brian (Baseball Player)
1123 Stuart St
Helena, MT 59601-2138, USA

Knight, C Ray (Baseball Player)
Cincinnati Reds
2308 Tara Dr
Albany, GA 31721-9111, USA

Knight, Charles F (Business Person)
Emerson Electric Co
8000 W Florissant Ave
Box 41000
Saint Louis, MO 63136-1415, USA

Knight, Chris (Musician, Songwriter, Writer)
Rick Alter Mgmt
1018 17th Ave S Ste 12
Nashville, TN 37212-2219, USA

Knight, Christopher (Actor)
c/o Neil Stearns *Don Buchwald & Associates Inc (LA)*
6500 Wilshire Blvd Ste 2200
Los Angeles, CA 90048-4942, USA

Knight, Curt (Football Player)
Washington Redskins
7230 Rio Flora Pl
Downey, CA 90241-2030, USA

Knight, David (Football Player)
New York Jets
2600 Farm Rd
Alexandria, VA 22302-2821, USA

Knight, Douglas M (Educator)
773 Greenwood Ave
Glencoe, IL 60022-1514, USA

Knight, Gladys (Musician)
c/o Staff Member *William Morris Agency (WMA-LA)*
1 William Morris Pl
Beverly Hills, CA 90212-4261, USA

Knight, Jean (Musician)
Ken Keene Artists
PO Box 1875
Gretna, LA 70054-1875, USA

Knight, Jonathan (Musician)
90 Apple St
Essex, MA 01929-1229, USA

Knight, Jordan (Musician)
c/o Frederick Levy *Management 101*
5527 1/2 Cahuenga Blvd
North Hollywood, CA 91601, USA

Knight, Marion (Suge) (Actor, Musician, Producer)
c/o Mickey Freiberg *Acme Talent & Literary (LA)*
4727 Wilshire Blvd Ste 333
Los Angeles, CA 90010-3874, USA

Knight, Michael E
1344 Lexington Ave
New York, NY 10128-1507, USA

Knight, Philip H (Business Person)
Nike Inc
1 SW Bowerman Dr
Beaverton, OR 97005-0979, USA

Knight, Robert M (Bobby) (Basketball Player, Coach)
Texas Tech University
Athletic Dept
Lubbock, TX 79409, USA

Knight, Shirley (Actor)
1548 N Orange Dr
Los Angeles, CA 90028, USA

Knight, Steve (Football Player)
Indianapolis Colts
4503 Bevington Ln Apt A
Indianapolis, IN 46240-4478, USA

Knight, Steve (Writer)
c/o Staff Member *Creative Artists Agency LCC (CAA-LA)*
2000 Avenue Of The Stars
Los Angeles, CA 90067-4700, USA

Knight, Summer
PO Box 9786
Marina Del Rey, CA 90295-2186, USA

Knight, T R (Actor)
c/o Staff Member *Gersh Agency, The (LA)*
232 N Canon Dr
Beverly Hills, CA 90210-5302, USA

Knight, Tom (Football Player)
Anzona Cardinals
PO Box 888
Phoenix, AZ 85001-0888, USA

Knight, Trevor (Adult Film Star)
c/o Staff Member *Diva Central Inc*
7510 W Sunset Blvd Ste 1445
Los Angeles, CA 90046-3408, USA

Knight, Wayne (Actor)
c/o Staff Member *Agency for the Performing Arts (APA-LA)*
405 S Beverly Dr
Beverly Hills, CA 90212-4416, USA

Knight, Wendi (Adult Film Star)
c/o Staff Member *Atlas Multimedia Inc*
9035 Independence Ave
Canoga Park, CA 91304-1743, USA

Knightley, Keira (Actor)
c/o Adam Isaacs *Endeavor Agency LLC (LA)*
9601 Wilshire Blvd Fl 3
Beverly Hills, CA 90210-5204, USA

Knightlinger, Lauren (Actor)
c/o Peter Principato *Principato/Young Management*
9665 Wilshire Blvd Ste 500
Beverly Hills, CA 90212-2312, USA

Knights, Dave (Musician)
195 Sandycombe Road
Kew TW9 2EW, UNITED KINGDOM
(UK)

Knobbs, Brian
14804 58th St.
North Clearwater, FL 34620, USA

Knoblauch, E Charles (Chuck) (Baseball Player)
Minnesota Twins
101 Westcott St Unit 1105
Houston, TX 77007-7048, USA

Knoff, Kurt (Football Player)
Washington Redskins
11121 Bluestem Ln
Eden Prairie, MN 55347-4732, USA

Knoll, Andrew H (Misc)
Harvard University
26 Oxford St
Botanical Museum
Cambridge, MA 02138-2902, USA

Knoll, Jozsef (Misc)
Semmelweis Medical University
Pharmacology Dept
Budapest 1089, HUNGARY

Knopf, Sascha (Actor, Model)
c/o Edward G (Eddie) Horowitz *Creative Management Group (CMG)*
8522 National Blvd Ste 108
Culver City, CA 90232-2454, USA

Knopfler, David (Musician)
Damage Mgmt
16 Lambton Place
London W11 2SH, UNITED KINGDOM
(UK)

Knopfler, Mark (Musician)
Paul Crockford Mgmt
37 Ruston Mews
London W11 1RB, UNITED KINGDOM
(UK)

Knopoff, Leon (Physicist)
University of California
Geophysics Institute
Los Angeles, CA 90024, USA

Knorr, Micah (Football Player)
Dallas Cowboys
2127 Bluebell
Forney, TX 75126-6353, USA

Knorr, Randy (Baseball Player)
Toronto Blue Jays
12134 Bishopsford Dr
Tampa, FL 33626-1319, USA

Knostman, Richard (Dick) (Basketball Player)
3960 Schooner Rdg
Alpharetta, GA 30005-4296, USA

Knott, Eric (Baseball Player)
Arizona Diamondbacks
1107 Hyacinth Ave
Sebring, FL 33875-8059, USA

Knotts, Gary (Baseball Player)
Florida Marlins
18 Covey Rd
Decatur, AL 35603-6021, USA

Knowles, Beyonce (Actor, Musician)
c/o Mathew Knowles *Music World Entertainment*
9255 W Sunset Blvd # 200
Los Angeles, CA 90069-3309, USA

Knowles, Darold (Baseball Player)
Baltimore Orioles
2322 Dora Dr
Clearwater, FL 33765-2719, USA

Knowles, Jeremy R (Misc)
67 Francis Ave
Cambridge, MA 02138-1911, USA

Knowles, Solange (Actor, Musician)
c/o Staff Member *Creative Artists Agency LCC (CAA-LA)*
2000 Avenue Of The Stars
Los Angeles, CA 90067-4700, USA

Knowles, William S (Nobel Prize Laureate)
PO Box 71
Kelly, WY 83011-0071, USA

Knowlton, Steve R (Skier)
Palmer Yeager Assoc
6600 E Hampden Ave # 210
Denver, CO 80224-3045, USA

Knowlton, William A (General)
4800 Fillmore Ave Apt 452
Alexandria, VA 22311-5055, USA

Knox, Bill (Football Player)
Chicago Bears
7836 Forest Ave
Gary, IN 46403-2139, USA

Knox, Chuck
11220 NE 53rd St
Kirkland, WA 98033-7505, USA

Knox, Elmer (Baseball Player)
Atlanta Black Crackers
838 Haven St SE
Atlanta, GA 30315-6857, USA

Knox, John (Baseball Player)
Detroit Tigers
1413 Thames Dr
Plano, TX 75075-2734, USA

Knox, Kenny (Golfer)
3813 Dills Rd
Monticello, FL 32344-4699, USA

Knox, Terence (Actor)
c/o Staff Member *The House of Representatives*
211 S Beverly Dr Ste 208
Beverly Hills, CA 90212-3879, USA

Knoxville, Johnny (Actor)
c/o Steve Alexander *Creative Artists Agency LCC (CAA-LA)*
2000 Avenue Of The Stars
Los Angeles, CA 90067-4700, USA

Knudsen, Arthur G (Skier)
5111 Wright Ave Apt 104
Racine, WI 53406-4592, USA

Knudsen, Erik (Actor)
c/o Staff Member *Burstein Company, The*
15304 W Sunset Blvd Ste 208
Pacific Palisades, CA 90272-3656, USA

Knudsen, Kurt (Baseball Player)
Detroit Tigers
5155 Patti Jo Dr
Carmichael, CA 95608-0968, USA

Knudson, Mark (Baseball Player)
Houston Astros
881 W 100th Ave
Northglenn, CO 80260-6255, USA

Knudson, Thomas J (Journalist)
Sacramento Bee
21st & Q Sts
Editorial Dept
Sacramento, CA 95816, USA

Knudson Jr, Alfred G (Misc)
Institute for Cancer Research
7701 Burholme Ave
Philadelphia, PA 19111-2437, USA

Knussen, S Oliver (Composer)
Harrison/Parrott
12 Penzance Place
London W11 4PA, UNITED KINGDOM (UK)

Knuth, Donald E (Scientist)
Stanford University
Computer Sciences Dept
Gates Building
Stanford, CA 94305, USA

Knutson, Gene (Football Player)
Green Bay Packers
61288 Lenawee Rd
Cassopolis, MI 49031-9428, USA

Knutson, Ronald (Religious Leader)
Free Lutheran Congregations Assn
402 W 11th St
Canton, SD 57013, USA

Koart, Matt (Football Player)
Green Bay Packers
122 Sonora Ave
Danville, CA 94526-3834, USA

Koba, Jeff
8899 Beverly Blvd Ste 705
Los Angeles, CA 90048-2448, USA

Koback, Nick (Baseball Player)
Pittsburgh Pirates
71 Hopmeadow St Apt 9A-1
Weatogue, CT 06089-9635, USA

Kobashigawa, Yeiki (War Hero)
85-120 Mill St
Waianae, HI 96793, USA

Kobel, Kevin (Baseball Player)
Milwaukee Brewers
7650 E Williams Dr Unit 1072
Scottsdale, AZ 85255-4810, USA

Kober, Jeff (Actor)
4544 Ethel Ave
Studio City, CA 91604-1002, USA

Koblik, Steven (Educator)
Huntington Library & Art Gallery
1151 Oxford Rd
San Marino, CA 91108-1218, USA

Koch, Alan (Baseball Player)
Detroit Tigers
1714 Pebble Creek Dr
Prattville, AL 36066-7206, USA

Koch, Bill
PO Box 1011
Kula, HI 96790-1011, USA

Koch, Billy (Baseball Player)
Toronto Blue Jays
1939 Scarlett Ave
North Port, FL 34289-9400, USA

Koch, David
740 Park Ave # 45
New York, NY 10021-4251, USA

Koch, Desmond (Des) (Athlete, Football Player, Track Athlete)
23296 Gilmore St
Canoga Park, CA 91307-3426, USA

Koch, Ed (Artist)
1211 NW Ogden Ave
Bend, OR 97701-1513, USA

Koch, Edward I (Politician)
WEVD
333 7th Ave Fl 14
The Voice Of Reason
New York, NY 10001-5004, USA

Koch, Gary (Golfer)
2934 W Lawn Ave
Tampa, FL 33611-1647, USA

Koch, Gregory M (Greg) (Football Player)
Green Bay Packers
4412 Darsey St
Bellaire, TX 77401-5607, USA

Koch, James V (Educator)
Old Dominion University
President's Office
Norfolk, VA 23529-0001, USA

Koch, Marianne
Am Hohenberg 27
Tutzing D-82327, GERMANY

Koch, Pete (Football Player)
Cincinnati Bengals
866 W 16th St
Newport Beach, CA 92663-2802, USA

Koch, Peter (Actor)
c/o Staff Member *Fly Trap, The*
900 E 1st St
Los Angeles, CA 90012-4032, USA

Koch, William (Bill) (Skier)
PO Box 115
Ashland, OR 97520-0004, USA

Koch, William I (Bill) (Business Person, Yachtsman)
Oxbow Corp
1601 Forum Pl
West Palm Beach, FL 33401-8101, USA

Koch Jr, Howard (Producer)
Producers Guild of America
8530 Wilshire Blvd Ste 450
Beverly Hills, CA 90211-3115, USA

Kocharian, Robert (President, Prime Minister)
President's Office
Marshal Bagramian Prosp 19
Yerevan 375010, ARMENIA

Kocherga, Anatoli I (Opera Singer)
Gogolevskaya 37/2/47
Kiev 254053, RUSSIA

Kochi, Jay K (Misc)
4372 Faculty Ln
Houston, TX 77004-6601, USA

Kochman, Roger (Football Player)
Buffalo Bills
521 Beverly Blvd
Upper Darby, PA 19082-3615, USA

Kocourek, Dave (Football Player)
Los Angeles Chargers
1170 Cara Ct
Marco Island, FL 34145-4518, USA

Kocsis, Zoltan (Composer, Musician)
Narcisa Ulca 29
Budapest 1126, HUNGARY

Kodba, Joe (Football Player)
Baltimore Colts
4287 Latifee Ct
Swartz Creek, MI 48473-1710, USA

Kodes, Jan (Tennis Player)
Na Berance 18
Prague 6/Dejvioe 160 00, CZECH REPUBLIC

Kodjoe, Boris (Actor, Model)
c/o Maani Golesorkhi *Bluestone Entertainment*
5639 Vista Del Monte Ave
Van Nuys, CA 91411-3356, USA

Koecher, Dick (Baseball Player)
Philadelphia Phillies
3310 Grand Cypress Dr Apt 102
Naples, FL 34119-7979, USA

Koegel, Pete (Baseball Player)
Milwaukee Brewers
301 The Birches
Saugerties, NY 12477-5249, USA

Koegel, Warren (Football Player)
Oakland Raiders
1273 N Fraser St
Coastal Carolina University
Georgetown, SC 29440-2853, USA

Koehler, Horst (Financier)
International Monetary Fund
700 19th St NW
Washington, DC 20431-0002, USA

Koehler, Horst (President)
Bundeskanzlerant
Schlossplatz 1
Berlin 10178, GERMANY

Koehn, Phyllis (Baseball Player)
1532 Darby Ct
Batavia, IL 60510-1613, USA

Koelle, George B (Misc)
3300 Darby Rd Apt 3310
Haverford, PA 19041-7701, USA

Koelling, Brian (Baseball Player)
Cincinnati Reds
20230 Augusta Dr
Lawrenceburg, IN 47025-7370, USA

Koen, Karleen (Writer)
Random House
1745 Broadway # B1
New York, NY 10019-4305, USA

Koenekamp, Fred (Cinematographer)
9756 Shoshone Ave
Northridge, CA 91325-1831, USA

Koenig, Brad (Model)
c/o Staff Member *Ford Models (NY)*
111 5th Ave Fl 9
New York, NY 10003-1005, USA

Koenig, Walter (Actor)
PO Box 4395
North Hollywood, CA 91617-0395, USA

Koepfer, Karl (Football Player)
Detroit Lions
2017 Waters Edge Dr
Westlake, OH 44145-6603, USA

Koepke, Andreas
441 av. du Prado B.P. 124
Marseilles Cedex 08 F-13267, FRANCE

Koepp, David (Director, Writer)
Hofflund-Polone
9465 Wilshire Blvd Ste 420
Beverly Hills, CA 90212-2603, USA

Koester, Helmut H K E (Misc)
12 Flintlock Rd
Lexington, MA 02420-1704, USA

Koetter, Dirk (Coach, Football Coach)
Arizona State University
Athletic Dept
Tempe, AZ 85287-0001, USA

Kofler, Matt (Football Player)
Buffalo Bills
1284 Hardin Dr
El Cajon, CA 92020-7213, USA

Kogan, Pavel L (Conductor, Musician)
Bryusov Per 8/10
Moscow 103009, RUSSIA

Kogan, Theo (Actor, Musician)
Wilhelmina Creative Mgmt
300 Park Ave S # 200
New York, NY 10010-5313, USA

Kogen, Jay (Producer)
c/o Staff Member *Endeavor Agency LLC (LA)*
9601 Wilshire Blvd Fl 3
Beverly Hills, CA 90210-5204, USA

Koger, Gene (Baseball Player)
Indianapolis Clowns
285 Koger Rd
Reidsville, NC 27320-9555, USA

Kohan, David (Producer)
c/o Staff Member *Will & Grace*
4024 Radford Ave
Bungalow 3
Studio City, CA 91604-2101, USA

Kohde-Kilsch, Claudia (Tennis Player)
Elsa-Brandstrom-Str 22
Saarbrucken 66119, GERMANY

Kohl, Ernest (Musician)
c/o Staff Member *Diva Central Inc*
7510 W Sunset Blvd Ste 1445
Los Angeles, CA 90046-3408, USA

The Celebrity Black Book 2008

Kohl, Helmut (Politician)
CDU/CSU
Maurestr 85
Berlin 10117, GERMANY

Kohlbrand, Joe (Football Player)
New Orleans Saints
3709 Indian River Dr
Cocoa, FL 32926-8705, USA

Kohler, Jurgen (Soccer Player)
Borussia Dortmund
Postfach 100509
Dortmund 44005, GERMANY

Kohli, Armaan (Actor, Bollywood)
44 Union Park Chembur
Mumbai, MS 400071, INDIA

Kohli, Raj Kumar (Bollywood, Director, Filmmaker, Producer)
Behind Lido Cinema
Juhu Road
Bombay, MS 400 049, INDIA

Kohlmeier, Ryan (Baseball Player)
Baltimore Orioles
301 Vine St
Cottonwood Falls, KS 66845-9812, USA

Kohlsaat, Peter (Cartoonist)
420 N 5th St Ste 707
Minneapolis, MN 55401-1372, USA

Kohn, A Eugene (Architect)
Kohn Pedersen Fox Assoc
111 W 57th St
New York, NY 10019-2211, USA

Kohn, Walter (Nobel Prize Laureate)
236 La Vista Grande
Santa Barbara, CA 93103-2819, USA

Kohrs, Bob (Football Player)
Pittsburgh Steelers
2910 E Nance St
Mesa, AZ 85213-1647, USA

Koib, Thomas Claudia A (Coach, Swimmer)
Stanford University
Athletic Dept
Stanford, CA 94305, USA

Koirala, manicha (Actor, Bollywood)
302 Beachwood Towers, Yari Road
Versova
Andheri (W), Mumbai 400061, INDIA

Koivu, Saku (Hockey Player)
2200-201 Portage Ave
Winnipeg, MB R3B 3L3, CANADA

Koizumi, Junichiro (Prime Minister)
Prime Minister's Office
1-6-1 Negatoicho
Chiyodaku, Tokyo 100, JAPAN

Kojac, George (Swimmer)
33 Arboles Del Norte
Fort Pierce, FL 34951-2877, USA

Kojis, Don (Basketball Player)
7652 Stevenson Way
San Diego, CA 92120-2229, USA

Kok Oudegeest, Mary (Swimmer)
Escuela Nacional de Natacion
Izarra
Alava, SPAIN

Kokkonen, Elissa Lee (Musician)
Columbia Artists Mgmt Inc
1790 Broadway Fl 6
New York, NY 10019-1412, USA

Kokonin, Vladimir (Opera Singer)
Bolshoi Theater
Teatralnaya Pl 1
Moscow 103009, RUSSIA

Kokosalaki, Sophia (Designer, Fashion Designer)
c/o Staff Member *Sophia Kokosalaki*
3/138 Long Acre
Convent Garden
London, England, UNITED KINGDOM (UK)

Kokotakis, Nick
9229 W Sunset Blvd Ste 315
Los Angeles, CA 90069-3403, USA

Kola, Joey (Comedian)
c/o Staff Member *William Morris Agency (WMA-LA)*
1 William Morris Pl
Beverly Hills, CA 90212-4261, USA

Kolakowski, Leszek (Misc)
77 Hamilton Road
Oxford OX2 7QA, UNITED KINGDOM (UK)

Kolanko, Mary Lou (Baseball Player)
3109 W Henry Ave
Tampa, FL 33614-5924, USA

Kolb, Brandon (Baseball Player)
Cincinnati Reds
2043 Pin Oak Pl
Danville, CA 94506-2119, USA

Kolb, Danny (Baseball Player)
Texas Rangers
205 S Main St
Walnut, IL 61376, USA

Kolb, Gary (Baseball Player)
St Louis Cardinals
5143 Hopewell Dr
Cross Lanes, WV 25313-1784, USA

Kolb, Jon (Football Player)
Pittsburgh Steelers
32 Lee Ave
Grove City, PA 16127-4648, USA

Kolber, Suzy (Sportscaster)
ESPN-TV
Sports Dept
Espn Plaza 935 Middle St
Bristol, CT 06010, USA

Kolbert, Kathryn (Lawyer)
Center for Reproductive Law & Policy
120 Wall St
New York, NY 10005-3904, USA

Kolden, Scott
8743 Quakertown Ave
Northridge, CA 91324-3229, USA

Kolehmainen, Mikko (Athlete)
Poppelitie 18
Mikkeli 50130, FINLAND

Kolen, Mike (Football Player)
Miami Dolphins
1613 Manchester Ln
Birmingham, AL 35243-4862, USA

Kolesar, Robert (Football Player)
Cleveland Browns
5003 Lincoln Ave
Cleveland, OH 44134-1866, USA

Kolff, Willem J (Inventor)
510 35th St
Port Townsend, WA 98368-5055, USA

Kolinsky, Sue (Producer)
c/o Staff Member *Innovative Artists (LA)*
1505 10th St
Santa Monica, CA 90401-2805, USA

Kollar, Bill (Football Player)
Cincinnati Bengals
1 Rams Way
Earth City, MO 63045-1523, USA

Kollas, Konstantinos V (Prime Minister)
124 Vassil Sophias St
Ampelokipi
Athens, GREECE

Kollek, Mayor Teddy
22 Jaffa Rd.
Jerusalem, ISRAEL

Koller, Dagmar
Naglergasse 2
Vienna A-1010, AUSTRIA

Koller, William C (Misc)
University of Kansas
Medical School
Neurology Dept
Kansas City, KS 66160-0001, USA

Kollner, Eberhard (Cosmonaut)
An der Trainierbahn 7
Neuenhagen 115366, GERMANY

Kollo, Rene (Opera Singer)
Opera et Concert
Maximillianstr 22
Munich 80539, GERMANY

Kolodner, Richard D (Scientist)
Dana-Forber Cancer Institute
44 Bynner St
Boston, MA 02130, USA

Kolodziewjski, Chris (Football Player)
Pittsburgh Steelers
1123 Sandalwood Dr
Lawrenceville, GA 30043-4621, USA

Kolpakova, Irina A (Ballerina)
American Ballet Theatre
890 Broadway
New York, NY 10003-1278, USA

Kolstad, Hal (Baseball Player)
Boston Red Sox
15149 Bel Escou Dr
San Jose, CA 95124-5032, USA

Kolsti, Paul (Cartoonist)
Dallas News
Communications Center
Editorial Dept
Dallas, TX 75211, USA

Kolta, Lajos (Cinematographer, Director)
c/o Staff Member *Gersh Agency, The (LA)*
232 N Canon Dr
Beverly Hills, CA 90210-5302, USA

Kolvenbach, Peter-Hans (Religious Leader)
Borgo Santo Spirito 5
CP 6139
Rome 00195, ITALY

Kolzig, Olaf (Hockey Player)
10931 E Bahia Dr
Scottsdale, AZ 85255-9091, USA

Komal (Royalty)
Royal Palace
Narayanhiti
Durbag Marg
Kathmandu, NEPAL

Koman, Bill (Football Player)
Baltimore Colts
5 Upper Ladue Rd
Saint Louis, MO 63124-1677, USA

Koman, Michael (Writer)
c/o Staff Member *International Creative Management (ICM-LA)*
10250 Constellation Blvd
Los Angeles, CA 90067-6200, USA

Komarkova, Vera (Misc)
University of Colorado
Instaar
Boulder, CO 80302, USA

Komenich, Kim (Journalist)
111 Cornelia Ave
Mill Valley, CA 94941-1807, USA

Komenich, Nadia (Gymnast)
The Bart Conner Gymnastics Academy
PO Box 720217
Norman, OK 73070-4166, USA

Kometani, Pam (Golfer)
4342 Kilauea Ave
Honolulu, HI 96816-5113, USA

Kominsky, Cheryl (Bowler)
Ladies Professional Bowling Tour
7200 Harrison Ave # 7171
Rockford, IL 61112-1017, USA

Komleva, Gabriela T (Ballerina)
Fontanka River 116
#34
Saint Petersburg 198005, RUSSIA

Komlo, Jeff (Football Player)
Detroit Lions
1617 Oak Hill Rd
Chester Springs, PA 19425-1111, USA

Komlos, Peter (Musician)
Torokvesz Ulca 94
Budapest 1025, HUNGARY

Komminsk, Brad (Baseball Player)
Atlanta Braves
688 Fallside Ln
Westerville, OH 43081-5003, USA

Kompara, John (Football Player)
Los Angeles Chargers
13030 Coldwater Loop
Clermont, FL 34711-8014, USA

Konare, Alpha Oumar (President)
President's Office
BP
Bamako, MALI

Koncar, Mark (Football Player)
Green Bay Packers
447 N Alpine Blvd
Alpine, UT 84004-1264, USA

Konchalovsky, Andrei (Director)
Creative Artists Agency
9830 Wilshire Blvd
Beverly Hills, CA 90212-1804, USA

Kondakova, Elena V (Cosmonaut)
Scientific Industrial Assn
Ulica Lenina 4A
Kallningrad 141070, RUSSIA

Kondratiyeva, Maria V (Ballerina)
Bolshoi Theater
Teatralnaya Pt1
Moscow 103009, RUSSIA

Kondria, John (Football Player)
Pittsburgh Steelers
599 Collier Rd
Uniontown, PA 15401-6877, USA

Konerko, Paul (Baseball Player)
Los Angeles Dodgers
11623 E Bloomfield Dr
Scottsdale, AZ 85259-2749, USA

Konieczny, Doug (Baseball Player)
Houston Astros
9503 Dundalk St
Spring, TX 77379-4314, USA

Konik, George (Hockey Player)
1027 Savannah Rd
Eagan, MN 55123-1543, USA

Koniszewski, John (Football Player)
Washington Redskins
207 Eleanor St
Peckville, PA 18452-1205, USA

Konitz, Lee (Musician)
Bennett Morgan
RR 376 Box 1282
Wappingers Falls, NY 12590, USA

Konner, Lawrence (Larry) (Writer)
c/o Tom Strickler *Endeavor Agency LLC*
(LA)
9601 Wilshire Blvd Fl 3
Beverly Hills, CA 90210-5204, USA

Kononenko, Oleg D (Cosmonaut)
Potchta Kosmoriavtov
Moskovskoi Oblasti
Syvisdny Goroduk 141160, RUSSIA

Konopasek, Ed (Football Player)
Green Bay Packers
2336 Meadowledge Ct
De Pere, WI 54115-8690, USA

Konrad, Dorothy
10650 Missouri Ave Apt 2
Los Angeles, CA 90025-4815, USA

Konrad, John H (Astronaut)
Hughes Space-Communications Group
PO Box 92919
Los Angeles, CA 90009-2919, USA

Konrad, Rob (Football Player)
Miami Dolphins
6600 N Andrews Ave Ste 130
Fort Lauderdale, FL 33309-2188, USA

Konsalik, Heinz
Aegidienberg
Bad Honnef D-53604, GERMANY

Konstantinidis, Aris (Architect)
4 Vasilissis Sofias Blvd
Athens 106 74, GREECE

Konstantinov, Vladimir (Hockey Player)
15 Windsor Pl
Essex Fells, NJ 07021-1710, USA

Konuszewski, Dennis (Baseball Player)
Pittsburgh Pirates
3054 Yorkshire Dr
Bay City, MI 48706-9244, USA

Konyukhov, Fedor F (Misc)
Tourism/Sports Union
Studeniy Proyezd 7
Moscow 129282, RUSSIA

Konz, Kenny (Football Player)
Cleveland Browns
12787 Greenbower St NE
Alliance, OH 44601-8862, USA

Kooks, The (Music Group)
c/o Staff Member *Paradigm (Monterey)*
509 Hartnell St
Monterey, CA 93940-2825, USA

Kool & The Gang (Music Group)
c/o Staff Member *J Bird Entertainment
Agency*
4905 S Atlantic Ave
Ponce Inlet, FL 32127-7311, USA

Kool Moe Dee
151 El Camino Dr
Beverly Hills, CA 90212-2704, USA

Koolhaas, Rem (Architect)
Metropolitan Architecture
Heer Bokelweg 149
Rotterdam 3032, THE NETHERLANDS

Koolman, Olindo (Governor)
Governor's Office
Oranjestad, ARUBA

Koonce, Graham (Baseball Player)
Oakland A's
1833 Whispering Pines Dr
Julian, CA 92036, USA

Koons, Jeff (Artist)
600 Broadway
New York, NY 10012-3206, USA

Koontz, Dean R (Writer)
PO Box 9529
Newport Beach, CA 92658-9529, USA

Koop, C Everett (Doctor)
3 Ivy Pointe Way
Hanover, NH 03755-1407, USA

Kooper, Al (Musician)
Legacy Records
550 Madison Ave # 1700
New York, NY 10022-3211, USA

Koopman, A Ton G M (Conductor)
Meerweg 23
BC Bussu 1405, THE NETHERLANDS

Koopmans-Kint, Cor (Swimmer)
Pacific Sands C'Van Park
Nambucca Heads, NSW 2448,
AUSTRALIA

Kooser, Ted (Writer)
1820 Branched Oak Rd
Garland, NE 68360-9303, USA

Koosman, Jerry (Baseball Player)
New York Mets
2483 State Road 35
Osceola, WI 54020-4216, USA

Kopacz, George (Baseball Player)
Atlanta Braves
14150 Somerset Ct
Orland Park, IL 60467-1142, USA

Kopay, Dave (Football Player)
San Francisco 49ers
113 S Larchmont Blvd
Los Angeles, CA 90004-3708, USA

Kopell, Bernie (Actor)
19413 Olivos Dr
Tarzana, CA 91356-4403, USA

Kopeloff, Eric (Director)
c/o Staff Member *William Morris Agency
(WMA-LA)*
1 William Morris Pl
Beverly Hills, CA 90212-4261, USA

Kopelson, Arnold (Producer)
901 N Roxbury Dr
Beverly Hills, CA 90210-3019, USA

Kopervas, Gary (Cartoonist)
King Features Syndicate
888 7th Ave Ste 201
New York, NY 10106-0201, USA

Kopins, Karen (Actor)
Sutton Barth Vennari
145 S Fairfax Ave Ste 310
Los Angeles, CA 90036-2176, USA

Kopit, Arthur (Writer)
240 W 98th St Apt 11B
New York, NY 10025-5516, USA

Koplan, Jeffrey (Misc)
Emory University
Academic Health Affairs Dept
Atlanta, GA 30322-0001, USA

Koplitz, Howie (Baseball Player)
Detroit Tigers
623 Boyd St
Oshkosh, WI 54901-4634, USA

Koplove, Mike (Baseball Player)
Arizona Diamondbacks
39 Festival Dr
Voorhees, NJ 08043-4325, USA

Kopolsky, Ken
151 El Camino Dr
Beverly Hills, CA 90212-2704, USA

Kopp, Jeff (Football Player)
Miami Dolphins
9409 Hannahs Mill Dr Apt 403
Owings Mills, MD 21117-6855, USA

Kopp, Wendy (Misc)
Teach for America Foundation
315 W 36th St Fl 6
New York, NY 10018-6532, USA

Koppe, Joe (Baseball Player)
Milwaukee Braves
7887 Beatrice
Westland, MI 48185-2507, USA

Koppel, Ted (Correspondent)
c/o Staff Member *Nightline*
1717 Desales St NW
Washington, DC 20036-4401, USA

Koppelman, Chaim (Artist)
498 Broome St
New York, NY 10013-2213, USA

Koppelman, Charles (Business Person)
c/o Staff Member *Martha Stewart Living
Omnimedia Inc*
20 W 43rd St Fl 25
New York, NY 10036-7400, USA

Kopper, Hilmar (Financier)
Deutsche Bank AG
Taunusanlage 12
Frankfurt/Main 60325, GERMANY

Koppes, Peter (Musician)
Globeshine
101 Chamberlayne Road
London NW10 3ND, UNITED KINGDOM
(UK)

Koppikar, Isha (Actor)
c/o Staff Member *Canyon Entertainment*
PO Box 256
Palm Springs, CA 92263-0256, USA

Kopple, Barbara J (Director)
Cabin Creek Films
155 Avenue Of The Americas
New York, NY 10013-1507, USA

Kopra, Timothy L (Astronaut)
2518 Lakeside Dr
Seabrook, TX 77586-3392, USA

Koptchak, Sergei (Opera Singer)
Robert Lombardo
61 W 62nd St Apt 6F
Harkness Plaza
New York, NY 10023-7017, USA

Koralek, Paul G (Architect)
7 Chalcot Road
#1
London NW1 8LH, UNITED KINGDOM
(UK)

Korben (Musician)
c/o Staff Member *Pop Idol (Fremantle
Media)*
2700 Colorado Ave Ste 450
Santa Monica, CA 90404-3599, USA

Korcheck, Steve (Baseball Player)
Washington Senators
6424 98th St E
Bradenton, FL 34202-9769, USA

Kord, Kazimierz (Conductor)
Filharmonia Narodowa
Ul Jasna 5
Warsaw 00-950, POLAND

Korda, Maria
304 N Screenland Dr
Burbank, CA 91505-3805, USA

Korda, Michael V (Writer)
Simon & Schuster/Pocket/Summit
1230 Avenue Of The Americas
New York, NY 10020-1513, USA

Korda, Petr (Tennis Player)
4909 61st Avenue Dr W
Bradenton, FL 34210-4041, USA

Korec Jan, Chryzostom Cardinal
(Religious Leader)
Biskupstvo Nitra
PP 46A
Nitra 95050, SLOVAKIA

Koreeda, Hirokazu (Director)
Directors' Guild of Japan
3-2 5F
Maruyamacho
Shibuya, Tokyo 150-0044, JAPAN

Koren, Edward B (Cartoonist)
New Yorker Magazine
4 Times Sq
Editorial Dept
New York, NY 10036-6592, USA

Koren, Steve (Producer, Writer)
c/o Staff Member *Creative Artists Agency
LCC (CAA-LA)*
2000 Avenue Of The Stars
Los Angeles, CA 90067-4700, USA

Korf, Mia (Actor)
Paradigm Agency
10100 Santa Monica Blvd Ste 2500
Los Angeles, CA 90067-4116, USA

Korince, George (Baseball Player)
Detroit Tigers
50 Lakeshore Rd
St Catharines, ON L2N 6P8, CANADA

Korjus, Tapio (Athlete, Track Athlete)
General Delivery
Lapua, FINLAND

Korman, Harvey (Actor, Comedian)
1136 Stradella Rd
Los Angeles, CA 90077-2610, USA

Korman, Maxime Carlot (Prime Minister)
Prime Minister's Office
PO Box 110
Port Vila, VANUATU

Kormann, Peter (Gymnast)
US Olympic Committee
1 Olympic Plz
Colorado Springs, CO 80909-5760, USA

Korn (Music Group)
c/o Staff Member *William Morris Agency
(WMA-LA)*
1 William Morris Pl
Beverly Hills, CA 90212-4261, USA

Kornberg, Arthur (Nobel Prize Laureate)
365 Golden Oak Dr
Portola Valley, CA 94028-7732, USA

Kornberg, Hannah (Actor)
c/o Staff Member *Williams Unlimited*
5010 Buffalo Ave
Sherman Oaks, CA 91423-1414, USA

Kornheiser, Tony (Sportscaster, Writer)
Washington Post
Editorial Dept
1150 15th St NW
Washington, DC 20071-0001, USA

Korowi, Wiwa (Governor)
Government House
Konedobu
Box 79
Port Moresby, Boroko, PAPUA NEW
GUINEA

Korpan, Richard (Business Person)
Florida Progress Corp
100 Central Ave
Saint Petersburg, FL 33701-3324, USA

Kors, R J (Football Player)
New York Jets
956 Gardenia Way
Corona Del Mar, CA 92625-1546, USA

Korsantiya, Alexander (Musician)
Columbia Artists Mgmt Inc
1790 Broadway Fl 6
New York, NY 10019-1412, USA

Kortas, Ken (Football Player)
St Louis Cardinals
466 Brooks Ln
Simpsonville, KY 40067-7419, USA

Korte, Steven J (Football Player)
New Orleans Saints
137 Dunleith Ln
Mandeville, LA 70471-1908, USA

Korvald, Lars (Prime Minister)
Vinkelgaten 6
Mjondalen 3050, NORWAY

Korver, Kelvin (Football Player)
Oakland Raiders
16934 Pella St
Adams, NE 68301-7790, USA

Korver, Kyle (Basketball Player)
c/o Staff Member *Philadelphia 76ers*
3601 S Broad St
1st Union Center
Philadelphia, PA 19148-5287, USA

Korzun, Valery G (Cosmonaut)
Potchta Kosmoriavtov
Moskovskoi Oblasti
Syvisdny Goroduk 14, RUSSIA

Kosar Jr, Bernie J (Football Player)
Cleveland Browns
2672 Riviera Mnr
Weston, FL 33332-3422, USA

Kosc, Greg (Baseball Player)
3465 Hunting Run Rd
Medina, OH 44256-8200, USA

Kosco, Andy (Baseball Player)
Minnesota Twins
3166 Howell Dr
Youngstown, OH 44514-2459, USA

Kosens, Terry (Football Player)
Minnesota Vikings
69 Lumur Dr
Sayville, NY 11782-1605, USA

Koshalek, Richard (Director)
Museum of Contemporary Art
250 S Grand Ave
Los Angeles, CA 90012-3021, USA

Koshiba, Masatoshi (Nobel Prize Laureate)
University of Tokyo
7-3-1 Hongo
Nunkyoku, Tokyo 113-8654, JAPAN

Koshiro IV, Matsumoto (Actor, Dancer)
Kabukiza Theatre
12-15-4 Ginza
Chuoku, Tokyo 104, JAPAN

Koshland Jr, Daniel E (Misc)
3991 Happy Valley Rd
Lafayette, CA 94549-2423, USA

Kosins, Gary (Football Player)
Chicago Bears
PO Box 340072
Dayton, OH 45434-0072, USA

Koski, Bill (Baseball Player)
Pittsburgh Pirates
1120 Valencia Ct
Modesto, CA 95350-4665, USA

Koskie, Corey (Baseball Player)
Minnesota Twins
161 Primrose Ln
Hamel, MN 55340-3603, USA

Koskoff, Sarah (Actor)
c/o Judy Page *Mitchell K Stubbs & Assoc
(MKS)*
8695 Washington Blvd Ste 204
Culver City, CA 90232-7419, USA

Koslo, Paul
PO Box 407
Lake Hughes, CA 93532-0407, USA

Koslofski, Kevin (Baseball Player)
Kansas City Royals
521 E Washington St
Maroa, IL 61756-9239, USA

Koslow, Lauren (Actor)
Michael Bruno
13576 Cheltenham Dr
Sherman Oaks, CA 91423-4818, USA

Kosner, Edward A (Editor)
Esquire Magazine
1790 Broadway Ste 1300
Editorial Dept
New York, NY 10019-1412, USA

Koss, Johann Olav (Speed Skater)
Dagaliveien 21
Oslo 0387, NORWAY

Koss, John C (Inventor)
Koss Corp
4129 N Port Washington Rd
Milwaukee, WI 53212-1029, USA

Koss, Stein (Football Player)
Kansas City Chiefs
5219 N Casa Blanca Dr # 31
Paradise Valley, AZ 85253-6201, USA

Kostadinova, Stefka (Athlete, Track
Athlete)
Rue Anghel Kantchev 4
Sofia 1000, BULGARIA

Kostal, Irwin
3149 Dona Susana Dr
Studio City, CA 91604-4357, USA

Kostelic, Janica (Skier)
Ski Association
Trg Sportova 11
Zagreb 1000, CROATIA

Koster, Steven J (Cinematographer)
26881 Goya Cir
Mission Viejo, CA 92691-6108, USA

Kostiuk, Mike (Football Player)
Cleveland Rams
24663 Beierman Ave
Warren, MI 48091-1716, USA

Kostner, Isolde (Skier)
General Delivery
Hortisei BZ, ITALY

Kostro, Frank (Baseball Player)
Detroit Tigers
36 Steele St Ste 20
Denver, CO 80206-5711, USA

Kosugi, Kane (Actor)
c/o Lou Pitt *Pitt Group, The*
9465 Wilshire Blvd Ste 480
Beverly Hills, CA 90212-2603, USA

Kosuth, Joseph (Artist)
591 Broadway
New York, NY 10012-3232, USA

Kotarski, Mike (Baseball Player)
31 Grove St
Lexington, MA 02420-1623, USA

Kotcheff, W Theodore (Ted) (Director)
Ted Kotcheff Productions
13451 Firth Dr
Beverly Hills, CA 90210-1118, USA

Koteas, Elias (Actor)
c/o Staff Member *Endeavor Agency LLC
(LA)*
9601 Wilshire Blvd Fl 3
Beverly Hills, CA 90210-5204, USA

Koterba, Jeff (Cartoonist)
Omaha World Herald
Editorial Dept
14th & Dodge St Wichita
Omaha, NE 68102, USA

Kotil, Ariene (Baseball Player)
13045 S 70th Ct
Palos Heights, IL 60463-2107, USA

Kotite, Richard E (Rich) (Coach, Football
Coach, Football Player)
New York Giants
241 Fanning St
Staten Island, NY 10314-5309, USA

Kotlarek, Gene (Skier)
4910 Walking Horse Pt
Colorado Springs, CO 80923-1110, USA

Kotlarek, George (Skier)
330 N Arlington Ave Apt 512
Duluth, MN 55811-5127, USA

Kotlayakov, Vladimir M (Geophysicist,
Physicist)
Geography Institute
Staromonetny per 29
Moscow 109017, RUSSIA

Kotsay, Mark (Baseball Player)
Florida Marlins
2947 Flint Ridge Ct
Reno, NV 89511-5327, USA

Kotsonis, Ieronymous (Religious Leader)
Archdiocese of Athens
Hatzichristou 8
Athens 402 53212, GREECE

Kottke, Leo (Musician, Songwriter)
c/o Staff Member *Paradigm (Monterey)*
509 Hartnell St
Monterey, CA 93940-2825, USA

Kotto, Yaphet (Actor, Director, Producer,
Writer)
c/o Staff Member *Diverse Talent Group*
1875 Century Park E Ste 2250
Los Angeles, CA 90067-2563, USA

Kotto, Yaphet F (Actor)
Artists Group
1650 Broadway Ste 610
New York, NY 10019-6833, USA

Kotulak, Ronald (Editor)
Chicago Tribune
435 N Michigan Ave
Editorial Dept
Chicago, IL 60611-4024, USA

Kotz, John (Basketball Player)
PO Box 7900
Madison, WI 53707-7900, USA

Kotzky, Alex S (Cartoonist)
20317 56th Ave
Oakland Gardens, NY 11364-1641, USA

Kouchner, Bernard (Doctor)
L'Action d'Humanitaire
8 Ave de Segur
Paris 75350, FRANCE

Koudelka, Josef (Photographer)
Magnum Photos
Moreland Bldgs
23 Old St
London EC1V 9HL, UNITED KINGDOM
(UK)

Koufax, Sandy (Baseball Player)
c/o Staff Member *Los Angeles Dodgers
(LA Dodgers)*
1000 Elysian Park Ave
Los Angeles, CA 90012-1112, USA

Kounen, Jan (Actor, Director, Producer,
Writer)
c/o Robert Newman *International Creative
Management (ICM-LA)*
10250 Constellation Blvd
Los Angeles, CA 90067-6200, USA

Kournikova, Anna (Tennis Player)
c/o Lisa Jacobsen *United Talent Agency
(UTA)*
9560 Wilshire Blvd Ste 500
Beverly Hills, CA 90212-2401, USA

Kovacevich, Richard M (Financier)
Wells Fargo Co
420 Montgomery St
San Francisco, CA 94163-0001, USA

Kovacevich, Stephen (Conductor,
Musician)
Van Walsum Mgmt
4 Addison Bridge Place
London W14 8XP, UNITED KINGDOM
(UK)

Kovach, Bill (Editor)
Harvard University
Nieman Fellows Program
Cambridge, MA 02138, USA

Kovacic, Ernst (Musician)
Ingpen & Williams
14 Kensington Court
London W8 5DN, UNITED KINGDOM
(UK)

Kovacic-Ciro, Zdravko (Misc)
JP Kamova 57
Rijeka 51000, SERBIA-MONTENEGRO

Kovack, Nancy
27 Oakmont Dr
Los Angeles, CA 90049-1901, USA

Kovacs, Andras (Director)
Magyar Jakobinusok Ter 2/3
Budapest 1122, HUNGARY

Kovacs, Denes (Musician)
Iranyi Utca 12
Budapest V, HUNGARY

Kovacs, Mijou
Sieberinger-Str. 92
Vienna 1030, AUSTRIA

Kovai, Anuradha (Actor)
2 23rd Street Amirtha Apartments
Nanganallur
Chennai, TN 600 061, INDIA

Kovai, Sarala (Actor, Bollywood)
80 Nevkatesh Nagar I Street
Dhasaratha Puram
Chennai, TN 600093, INDIA

Kovalchick-Roark, Dorothy (Golfer)
112 Maridale Dr
West Monroe, LA 71291-2350, USA

Kovalchuk, Ilya (Hockey Player)
SFX Sports
220 W 42nd St
New York, NY 10036-7200, USA

Kovalchuk, Ilya (Hockey Player)
c/o Staff Member *Atlanta Thrashers*
101 Marietta St NW Ste 1900
Centennial Tower
Atlanta, GA 30303-2771, USA

Kovalenko, Alexei (Hockey Player)
1 Trimont Ln Apt 2000A
Pittsburgh, PA 15211-1279, USA

Kovalenok, Vladimir S (Cosmonaut, General)
3 Ap 22
Hovanskaya St
Moscow 129515, RUSSIA

Kovalev, Alexei (Hockey Player)
4 Kassel Ct
Mamaroneck, NY 10543-4261, USA

Kovatch, John P (Football Player)
Cleveland Rams
619 Willowglen Rd
Santa Barbara, CA 93105-2437, USA

Kove, Martin (Actor)
23616 Fambrough St
Newhall, CA 91321-3455, USA

Kowalczyk, Ed (Musician)
Freedman & Smith
350 W End Ave Apt 1
New York, NY 10024-6818, USA

Kowalczyk, Jozef (Religious Leader)
Nuncjatura Apostolska
Al Ch Szucha 12
#163
Warsaw 00-582, POLAND

Kowalczyk, Walt (Football Player)
Philadelphia Eagles
144 W Maryknoll Rd
Rochester Hills, MI 48309-1938, USA

Kowalkowski, Robert (Football Player)
Detroit Lions
2410 Correll Dr
Lake Orion, MI 48360-2258, USA

Kowalkowski, Scott (Football Player)
Philadelphia Eagles
3995 Kelsey Rd
Lake Orion, MI 48360-2516, USA

Kowalski, Ted (Musician)
GEMS
PO Box 1031
Montrose, CA 91021-1031, USA

Kowalski, Walter
PO Box 67
Reading, MA 01867-0167, USA

Kowitz, Brian (Baseball Player)
Atlanta Braves
7218 Park Heights Ave
Pikesville, MD 21208-5474, USA

Koy, Ernie (Football Player)
New York Giants
PO Box 6
Kenney, TX 77452-0006, USA

Koy, Ted (Football Player)
Oakland Raiders
3501 Williams Dr
Georgetown, TX 78628-2421, USA

Koyama, Debbie (Golfer)
118 Tranquila Dr
Camarillo, CA 93012-5174, USA

Koz, Dave (Musician)
5850 W 3rd St # 307
Los Angeles, CA 90036-2862, USA

Kozak, Harley Jane (Actor)
21336 Colina Dr
Topanga, CA 90290, USA

Kozak, Julie (Journalist)
Extra c/o Warner Bros
4000 Warner Blvd
Burbank, CA 91522-0001, USA

Kozak, Scott (Football Player)
Houston Oilers
18617 S Grasle Rd
Oregon City, OR 97045-8898, USA

Kozakov, Mikhail M (Actor, Director)
Mayakovsky Theater
B Nikitskaya Str 17
Moscow 103009, RUSSIA

Kozar, Al (Baseball Player)
Washington Senators
5966 Bay Hill Cir
Lake Worth, FL 33463-6569, USA

Kozeev, Konstantin (Cosmonaut)
Potchta Kosmonavtov
Moskovskoi Oblasti
Syvisdny Goroduk 141160, RUSSIA

Kozena, Magdalena (Opera Singer)
Narodni Divadio
Dvorakova 11
Brno 60000, CZECH REPUBLIC

Kozer, Sarah (Actor)
8383 Wilshire Blvd Ste 510
C/O Ric Tanner
Beverly Hills, CA 90211-2404, USA

Kozinski, Alex (Judge)
US Court of Appeals
125 S Grand Ave
Pasadena, CA 91105-1652, USA

Kozlova, Anna (Swimmer)
c/o Staff Member *Premier Management Group*
700 Evanvale Ct
Cary, NC 27518-2806, USA

Kozlova, Valentina (Ballerina)
New York City Ballet
Lincoln Center Plaza
New York, NY 10023, USA

Kozlowiecki, Adam Cardinal (Religious Leader)
PO Box 50003
Ridgeway 15101, ZAMBIA

Kozlowski, Ben (Baseball Player)
Texas Rangers
9083 Briarwood Dr
Seminole, FL 33772-2810, USA

Kozlowski, Brian (Football Player)
New York Giants
3030 Sugarloaf Club Dr
Duluth, GA 30097-3701, USA

Kozlowski, Glen (Football Player)
Chicago Bears
18095 W Timber Ln
Grayslake, IL 60030-1936, USA

Kozlowski, Linda (Actor)
18 Marshall Crescent
Beacon Hill, NSW 2060, AUSTRALIA

Kozlowski, Mike (Football Player)
Miami Dolphins
10867 NW 9th Ct
Plantation, FL 33324-7330, USA

Kozol, Jonathan (Writer)
PO Box 145
Byfield, MA 01922-0145, USA

Kraatz, Victor (Figure Skater)
Connecticut Skating Center
300 Alumni Rd
Newington, CT 06111-1865, USA

Kraayeveld, Dave (Football Player)
Seattle Seahawks
10515 124th Ave NE
Kirkland, WA 98033-4628, USA

Krabbe, Jeroen (Actor)
Van Eeghaustraat 107
Amsterdam, EZ 1071, THE
NETHERLANDS

Krabbe, Katrin
Jahnstadion Schwedenstr. 25
Neubrandenburg D-17033, GERMANY

Krabbe-Zimmermann, Katrin (Athlete, Track Athlete)
Dorfstr 9
Pinnow 17091, GERMANY

Krackow, Jurgen (Business Person)
Schumannstr 100
Dusseldorf 40237, GERMANY

Kraemer, Harry J (Business Person)
Baxter International
1 Baxter Pkwy
Deerfield, IL 60015-4634, USA

Kraemer, Joe (Baseball Player)
Chicago Cubs
3212 NE 401st Cir
La Center, WA 98629-5241, USA

Kraft, Craig A (Artist)
931 R St NW
Washington, DC 20001-4109, USA

Kraft, Greg (Golfer)
14820 Rue De Bayonne Apt 302
Clearwater, FL 33762-3029, USA

Kraft, Leo A (Composer)
45 Hill Park Ave Apt 3E
Great Neck, NY 11021-3717, USA

Kraft, Robert (Composer)
4722 Noeline Ave
Encino, CA 91436-2106, USA

Kraft, Robert (Football Executive)
c/o Staff Member *New England Patriots*
60 Washington St
Gillette Stadium - RR 1
Foxboro, MA 02035-1388, USA

Kraft, Robert P (Physicist)
University of California
Lick Observatory
Santa Cruz, CA 95064, USA

Kragen, Greg (Football Player)
Denver Broncos
301 Livoma Heights Rd
Alamo, CA 94507, USA

Kragen, Ken
240 Baroda Dr
Los Angeles, CA 90077, USA

Krahl, Jim (Football Player)
New York Giants
514 Rolling Mill Dr
Sugar Land, TX 77478-3072, USA

Krainev, Vladimir V (Musician)
Staatiche Hochschule fur Musik
Walderseestr 100
Hanover, GERMANY

Krainin, Julian (President)
Krainin Productions
25211 Summerhill Ln
Stevenson Ranch, CA 91381-2262, USA

Krajicek, Richard (Tennis Player)
Octagon
1751 Pinnacle Dr Ste 1500
McLean, VA 22102-3833, USA

Krakau, Merv (Football Player)
Buffalo Bills
706 Prairie St
Guthrie Center, IA 50115-1711, USA

Krakoski, Joe (Football Player)
Washington Redskins
1359 Garden Wall Cir
Reston, VA 20194-1979, USA

Krakoski, Joe (Football Player)
Washington Redskins
908 Harold Dr
Incline Village, NV 89451-9057, USA

Krakowski, Jane (Actor, Musician)
Borinstein Oreck Bogart
3172 Dona Susana Dr
Studio City, CA 91604-4356, USA

Krall, Diana (Musician)
c/o Staff Member *William Morris Agency (WMA-LA)*
1 William Morris Pl
Beverly Hills, CA 90212-4261, USA

Krall, Gerald (Football Player)
Detroit Lions
9242 Mandell Rd
Perrysburg, OH 43551-3913, USA

Kraly, Steve (Baseball Player)
New York Yankees
12 Davis Ave
Johnson City, NY 13790-3007, USA

Kramarsky, David (Director)
1336 Havenhurst Dr
West Hollywood, CA 90046-4511, USA

Kramer, Billy J (Musician)
Mars Talent
27 L Ambiance Ct
Bardonia, NY 10954-1421, USA

Kramer, Chris (Actor)
c/o Deb Dillistone *Lucas Talent Inc*
Sun Tower Floor 7
100 W Pender St
Vancouver, BC V6B 1R8, CANADA

Kramer, Clare (Actor)
c/o Darren Goldberg *1 Management*
9000 W Sunset Blvd Ph 1550
West Hollywood, CA 90069-1838, USA

Kramer, Eric Allan (Actor)
c/o Staff Member *The Artists Group Ltd
(LA)*
1650 Broadway Ste 610
New York, NY 10019-6833, USA

Kramer, Erik (Football Player)
Atlanta Falcons
5950 Kingham Ct
Agoura Hills, CA 91301-4436, USA

Kramer, Gerald L (Jerry) (Football Player)
Green Bay Packers
11768 W Chinden Blvd
Boise, ID 83714-1028, USA

Kramer, Jack
231 Glenroy Pl
Los Angeles, CA 90049-2419, USA

Kramer, Jim (Writer)
c/o Staff Member *3 Arts Entertainment Inc*
9460 Wilshire Blvd Fl 7
Beverly Hills, CA 90212-2713, USA

Kramer, Joel R (Editor)
Minneapolis Star Tribune
425 Portland Ave
Minneapolis, MN 55488-1511, USA

Kramer, Joey (Musician)
282 Pudding Hill Ln
Marshfield, MA 02050-3151, USA

Kramer, Kent (Football Player)
San Francisco 49ers
200 Troon Rd
McKinney, TX 75070-6783, USA

Kramer, Kyle (Football Player)
Cleveland Browns
821 N Orchard Ln
Dayton, OH 45434-7216, USA

Kramer, Larry (Activist, Writer)
Gay Men's Health Crisis
119 W 24th St
New York, NY 10011-1913, USA

Kramer, Paul
20023 Bernist Ave
Torrance, CA 90503-2103, USA

Kramer, Randy (Baseball Player)
Pittsburgh Pirates
PO Box 2001
Cedar Rapids, IA 52406-2001, USA

Kramer, Ronald J (Ron) (Football Player)
Green Bay Packers
PO Box 473
Fenton, MI 48430-0473, USA

Kramer, Stepfanie (Actor)
c/o Mark Teitelbaum *Teitelbaum Artists
Group*
8840 Wilshire Blvd # 200
Beverly Hills, CA 90211-2606, USA

Kramer, Steve
1126 N Hollywood Way # 203-A
Burbank, CA 91505-2527, USA

Kramer, Thomas (Tommy) (Football
Player)
Minnesota Vikings
16650 Huebner Rd Apt 1717
San Antonio, TX 78248-2322, USA

Kramer, Tom (Baseball Player)
Cleveland Indians
1065 Hamilton Ave
Cincinnati, OH 45231, USA

Kramer, Wayne (Musician)
Performers of the World
8901 Melrose Ave # 200
West Hollywood, CA 90069-5605, USA

Kramer-Hartman, Ruth (Golfer)
1100 Limekiln Road
Limekiln, PA 19535, USA

Kramnik, Vladimir (Misc)
Russian Chess Federation
Luchnetskaya 8
Moscow 119270, RUSSIA

Kranek, Ernst
623 W Chino Canyon Rd
Palm Springs, CA 92262-2701, USA

Kranepool, Ed (Baseball Player)
New York Mets
177 High Pond Dr
Jericho, NY 11753-2806, USA

Krantz, Judith (Writer)
166 Groverton Pl
Los Angeles, CA 90077-3732, USA

Kranz, Eugene (Gene) (Scientist)
1108 Shady Oak Ln
Dickinson, TX 77539-3327, USA

Kranz, Fran (Actor)
c/o Rebecca (Becca) Kovacik *Hofflund/
Polone*
9465 Wilshire Blvd Ste 890
Beverly Hills, CA 90212-2607, USA

Kranz, Ken (Football Player)
Green Bay Packers
N57W24143 N Sycamore Cir
Sussex, WI 53089-5160, USA

Krapek, Karl (Business Person)
United Technologies Corp
United Technologies Building
Hartford, CT 06101, USA

Krasinski, John (Actor)
c/o James Suskin *James Suskin
Management*
2 Charlton St Apt 5K
New York, NY 10014-4917, USA

Krasniqi, Luan (Boxer)
Oschlewg 10
Rottweil 78628, GERMANY

Krasnoff, Eric (Business Person)
Pall Corp
2200 Northern Blvd
Greenvale, NY 11548-1289, USA

Krasny, Yuri (Artist)
Sloane Gallery
1612 17th St
Oxford Office Building
Denver, CO 80202-1204, USA

Kratch, Bob (Football Player)
New York Giants
10685 County Road 24
Watertown, MN 55388-9324, USA

Kratochvilova, Jarmila (Athlete, Track
Athlete)
Goleuv Jenikov
582 82, CZECH REPUBLIC

Kratzert, Bill (Golfer)
7470 Founders Way
Ponte Vedra Beach, FL 32082-1914, USA

Kraus, Peter
Kaiserplatz 7
Munich D-80803, GERMANY

Krause, Brian (Actor)
c/o Leland LaBarre *Diverse Talent Group*
1875 Century Park E Ste 2250
Los Angeles, CA 90067-2563, USA

Krause, Chester L (Publisher)
Krause Publications
700 E State St
Iola, WI 54990-0002, USA

Krause, Dieter (Athlete)
Karl-Marx-Allee 21
Berlin 1017, GERMANY

Krause, Larry (Football Player)
Green Bay Packers
1109 Wimbleton Way
Waunakee, WI 53597-1825, USA

Krause, Paul J (Football Player)
Washington Redskins
18099 Judicial Way N
Lakeville, MN 55044-7105, USA

Krause, Peter (Actor)
c/o Peter Levine *Creative Artists Agency
LCC (CAA-LA)*
2000 Avenue Of The Stars
Los Angeles, CA 90067-4700, USA

Krause, Richard M (Misc)
4000 Cathedral Ave NW Apt 413B
Washington, DC 20016-5268, USA

Kraushaar, Sitke (Athlete)
Friedr-Ludwig-Jahn-Str 34
Sonneberg 02692, GERMANY

Kraushaar, William L (Physicist)
27 Stoney Creek Rd
Scarborough, ME 04074-8385, USA

Krauss, Alison (Musician)
c/o Staff Member *Shore Fire Media*
32 Court St Ste 1600
Brooklyn, NY 11201-4441, USA

Krauss, Lawrence M (Physicist)
Case Western Reserve University
Physics Dept
Cleveland, OH 44106, USA

Krausse, Lew (Baseball Player)
Kansas City A's
12811 NE 186th St
Holt, MO 64048-8956, USA

Krausse, Stefan (Athlete)
Kart-Zink-Str 2
Ilmenau 96883, GERMANY

Krauthammer, Charles (Writer)
Washington Post Writers Group
1150 15th St NW
Washington, DC 20071-0001, USA

Kravchuk, Igor (Hockey Player)
Florida Partners
1 Panther Pkwy
Sunrise, FL 33323-5315, USA

Kravec, Ken (Baseball Player)
Chicago White Sox
6752 Taeda Dr
Sarasota, FL 34241-9152, USA

Kravitch, Phyllis A (Judge)
US Court of Appeals
56 Forsyth St NW
Atlanta, GA 30303-2295, USA

Kravits, Jason
6310 San Vicente Blvd Ste 520
Los Angeles, CA 90048-5421, USA

Kravitz, Danny (Baseball Player)
Pittsburgh Pirates
RR 1 Box 1119
Dushore, PA 18614-9353, USA

Kravitz, Lenny (Musician, Songwriter,
Writer)
c/o Craig Fruin *H.K. Management*
1100 Glendon Ave Ste 1100
Los Angeles, CA 90024-3515, USA

Krawczyk, Ray (Baseball Player)
Pittsburgh Pirates
67 Cloudcrest
Aliso Viejo, CA 92656-1323, USA

Krawitz, Jan (Filmmaker)
Bldg L20 Stanford University
Stanford, CA 94305, USA

Krayer, Otto H (Misc)
4140 E Cooper St
Tucson, AZ 85711-3463, USA

Krayzelburg, Lenny (Swimmer)
Octagon
1751 Pinnacle Dr Ste 1500
McLean, VA 22102-3833, USA

Krayzle, Bone (Musician)
Creative Artists Agency
9830 Wilshire Blvd
Beverly Hills, CA 90212-1804, USA

Kreamcheck, John (Football Player)
Chicago Bears
2508 N Villa Ln
McHenry, IL 60051-2975, USA

Krebbs, John (Race Car Driver)
3232 Amoruso Way
Diamond Ridge
Roseville, CA 95747-9786, USA

Krebs, Edwin G (Nobel Prize Laureate)
3835 E McGraw St
Seattle, WA 98112-2428, USA

Krebs, Robert D (Business Person)
Burlington North/Santa Fe
2650 Lou Menk Dr
Fort Worth, TX 76131-2830, USA

Krebs, Susan (Actor)
4704 Tobias Ave
Sherman Oaks, CA 91403-2825, USA

Kredel, Elmar Maria (Religious Leader)
Obere Karolinenstra 5
Bamber 96033, GERMANY

Kregel, Kevin R (Astronaut)
2601 Bay Shore Dr
Seabrook, TX 77586-1690, USA

Krehbiel, Frederick A (Business Person)
Molex Inc
2222 Wellington Ct
Lisle, IL 60532-1682, USA

Krehbiel, John Hammond (Business
Person)
Molex Inc.
2222 Wellington Ct
Lisle, IL 60532-1682, USA

Kreider, Steve (Football Player)
Cincinnati Bengals
350 Harrow Ln
Blue Bell, PA 19422-3110, USA

Kreischer, Bert (Musician)
c/o Staff Member *Paradigm (Monterey)*
509 Hartnell St
Monterey, CA 93940-2825, USA

Kreitling, Richard (Football Player)
Cleveland Browns
12121 Vonn Rd
Largo, FL 33774-3401, USA

Krejc, Otomar
Kubisova 26
Praha 8 CZ-18200, CZECH REPUBLIC

krels, Jason (Soccer Player)
Dallas Burn
14800 Quorum Dr Ste 300
Dallas, TX 75254-1442, USA

Krementz, Jill (Photographer)
620 Sagg Main St
Sagaponack, NY 11962, USA

Kremer, Andrea (Sportscaster)
ESPN-TV
Sports Dept
Espn Plaza 935 Middle St
Bristol, CT 06010, USA

Kremer, Gidon (Musician)
I C M Artists
40 W 57th St
New York, NY 10019-4001, USA

Kremer, Howard (Comedian)
c/o Staff Member *International Creative
Management (ICM-LA)*
10250 Constellation Blvd
Los Angeles, CA 90067-6200, USA

Kremer, Ken (Football Player)
Kansas City Chiefs
7312 N Nevada Ave
Parkville, MO 64152-1190, USA

kremers, James (Baseball Player)
Atlanta Braves
9525 S 95th East Ave
Tulsa, OK 74133-6164, USA

Kremmel, Jim (Baseball Player)
Texas Rangers
524 W 18th Ave
Spokane, WA 99203-2011, USA

Kremser, Karl (Football Player)
Miami Dolphins
12204 SW 109th Ct
Miami, FL 33176-4576, USA

Krenchicki, Wayne (Baseball Player)
Baltimore Orioles
2524 Hawthorne Dr
Beloit, WI 53511-2338, USA

Krenk, Mitch (Football Player)
Chicago Bears
1822 4th Ave
Nebraska City, NE 68410-1822, USA

Krens, Thomas (Misc)
Solomon R Guggenheim Museum
1071 5th Ave
New York, NY 10128-0112, USA

Krenwinkel, Patricia
#W8314 Bed #Ma11U Ca Inst. For
Women16756 Chino Corona
Frontera, CA 91720, USA

Krenz, Jan (Composer, Conductor)
Filharmonia Narodowa
Ul Jasna 5
Warsaw, POLAND

Kreppel, Paul
14300 Killion St
Sherman Oaks, CA 91401-5108, USA

Kreps, David M (Economist)
Stanford University
Graduate Business School
Stanford, CA 94305, USA

Kreps, Juanita M (Secretary)
1407 W Pettigrew St
Durham, NC 27705, USA

Krerowicz, Mark (Football Player)
Cleveland Browns
1425 Luscombe Dr
Toledo, OH 43614-2618, USA

Kresa, Kent (Business Person)
Northrop Grumman Corp
1840 Century Park E
Los Angeles, CA 90067-2101, USA

Kresge, Chris (Golfer)
834 Trailwood Dr
Apopka, FL 32712-3217, USA

Kreskin (Misc)
444 2nd St
Pitcairn, PA 15140, USA

Kress, Charlie (Baseball Player)
Cincinnati Reds
1705 Pine St Apt 112
Sandpoint, ID 83864-2044, USA

Kressley, Carson (Television Host)
c/o Staff Member *Queer Eye for the
Straight Guy*
119 Braintree St
Boston, MA 02134-1628, USA

Kretchmer, Arthur (Editor)
Playboy Magazine
680 N Lake Shore Dr
Editorial Dept
Chicago, IL 60611-4546, USA

Kretlow, Lou (Baseball Player)
Detroit Tigers
3302 Goldfinch Ln
Enid, OK 73703-1424, USA

Kretschmann, Thomas (Director)
c/o Staff Member *United Talent Agency
(UTA)*
9560 Wilshire Blvd Ste 500
Beverly Hills, CA 90212-2401, USA

Kreuger, Rick (Baseball Player)
Boston Red Sox
7269 21st Ave
Jenison, MI 49428-7779, USA

Kreuk, Kristin (Actor)
c/o Russ Mortensen *Pacific Artists
Management*
1404-510 W Hastings St
Vancouver, BC V6B 1L8, CANADA

Kreuter, Chad (Baseball Player)
Texas Rangers
78955 Carmel Cir
La Quinta, CA 92253, USA

Kreutz, Olin (Football Player)
Chicago Bears
1373 Honokahua St
Honolulu, HI 96825-3024, USA

Kreutzer, Frank (Baseball Player)
Chicago White Sox
921 Windwhisper Ln
Annapolis, MD 21403-3486, USA

Kreutzmann, Bill (Musician)
PO Box 1073
San Rafael, CA 94915-1073, USA

Kreuzer, Lisa
Bavariaring 32
Munich D-80336, GERMANY

Kreviazuk, Chantal (Musician, Songwriter)
c/o Staff Member *Paradigm (Monterey)*
509 Hartnell St
Monterey, CA 93940-2825, USA

Krevis, Al (Football Player)
Cincinnati Bengals
1 Springbrook Rd
Auburn, MA 01501-3114, USA

Krevlazuk, Chantel
1505 W. 2nd Ave. #200
Vancouver, BC V6H 3Y4, CANADA

Kribel, Joel (Golfer)
26254 N 46th St
Phoenix, AZ 85050-8510, USA

Kricfalusi (Kricfaluci), John K (Actor,
Director, Writer)
c/o Staff Member *Endeavor Agency LLC
(LA)*
9601 Wilshire Blvd Fl 3
Beverly Hills, CA 90210-5204, USA

Krick, Jaynie (Baseball Player)
1522 Azalea Dr
Arlington, TX 76013-3609, USA

Krickstein, Aaron (Tennis Player)
7559 Fairmont Ct
Boca Raton, FL 33496-5902, USA

Krieg, Arthur M (Misc)
University of Iowa
Medical College
Immunology Dept
Iowa City, IA 52242, USA

Krieger, Robbie (Musician, Songwriter,
Writer)
3011 Ledgewood Dr
Los Angeles, CA 90068-1959, USA

Krier, Leon (Architect)
16 Belsize Park
London NW3, UNITED KINGDOM (UK)

Kriewald, Doug (Football Player)
Chicago Bears
5031 Snow Mesa Dr
Fort Collins, CO 80528-8590, USA

Kriewaldt, Clint (Football Player)
Detroit Lions
2705 Beacon Hill Dr Apt 104
Auburn Hills, MI 48326-3755, USA

Krige, Alice (Actor)
2875 Barrymore Dr
Malibu, CA 90265-2959, USA

Krikalev, Sergei K (Cosmonaut)
Potchta Kosmonavtov
Moskovskoi Oblasti
Syvisdny Goroduk 141160, RUSSIA

Krimm, John (Football Player)
New Orleans Saints
2565 Abington Rd
Upper Arlington, OH 43221-3003, USA

Kripke, Saul A (Misc)
Princeton University
Philosophy Dept
Princeton, NJ 08544-0001, USA

Krisher, Bill (Football Player)
Pittsburgh Steelers
5915 Over Downs Dr
Dallas, TX 75230-4044, USA

Krishnamurthy, Suchithra (Actor,
Bollywood)
402A Leela Apartments
Cuerpark Co-op Society Yari Road
Andheri (W)
Mumbai, MS 400061, INDIA

Krishnan, Ramya (Actor, Bollywood)
7 Lakshmi Sri Street
Janaki Nagar
Chennai, TN 600087, INDIA

Kristel, Sylvia (Actor)
Edrick/Rich Mgmt
2400 Whitman Pl
Los Angeles, CA 90068-2464, USA

Kristen, Marta (Actor)
c/o Joel Kleinman *Baier/Kleinman
International*
3575 Cahuenga Blvd W Ste 500
Los Angeles, CA 90068-1344, USA

Kristiansen, Ingrid (Athlete, Track Athlete)
Nils Collett Vogts Vei 51B
Oslo, 0765, NORWAY

Kristiansen, Kjeld Kirk (Business Person,
Educator)
Lego Group
Billund 7190, DENMARK

Kristien, Dale
691 Country Club Dr
Burbank, CA 91501-1121, USA

Kristina Sisco, Kristina (Actor)
c/o Staff Member *Cohen/Thomas Agency*
1888 N Crescent Heights Blvd
Los Angeles, CA 90069-1647, USA

Kristof, Kathy M (Writer)
Los Angeles Times
202 W 1st St
Editorial Dept
Los Angeles, CA 90012-4105, USA

Kristof, Nicholas D (Journalist)
New York Times
229 W 43rd St
Editorial Dept
New York, NY 10036-3959, USA

Kristoff, Joe (Bowler)
4290 Meadowview Ct
Columbus, OH 43224-1927, USA

Kristofferson, Kris (Actor, Musician,
Songwriter, Writer)
c/o Brian Bunnin *International Creative
Management (ICM-LA)*
10250 Constellation Blvd
Los Angeles, CA 90067-6200, USA

Kristol, Irving (Editor, Scientist)
Public Interest Magazine
1112 16th St NW
Washington, DC 20036-4823, USA

Kristol, William
6625 Jill Ct
McLean, VA 22101-1613, USA

krivda, Rick (Baseball Player)
San Diego Padres
112 Dolores Dr
Irwin, PA 15642-5519, USA

Kriwet, Heinz (Business Person)
Thyssen AG
August-Thyssen-Str 1
Dusseldorf 40211, GERMANY

Krizmanich, Jack (Actor)
c/o Mara Santino *Kazarian/Spencer &
Assoc (LA)*
11969 Ventura Blvd
Box 7409 Fl 3
Studio City, CA 91604-2630, USA

Kroeger, Gary (Actor, Comedian)
10474 Santa Monica Blvd Ste 380
Los Angeles, CA 90025-6943, USA

Kroemer, Herbert (Nobel Prize Laureate)
University of California
Electrical/Computer Eng Dept
Santa Barbara, CA 93106-0001, USA

Krofft, Marty (Actor, Misc, Producer)
Sid & Marty Krofft Pictures
4024 Radford Ave
C/O Cbs Studio Center
Studio City, CA 91604-2101, USA

Krofft, Sid (Misc)
7710 Woodrow Wilson Dr
Los Angeles, CA 90046-1212, USA

Kroft, Steve (Correspondent)
c/o Staff Member *60 Minutes*
524 W 57th St
Cbs News
New York, NY 10019-2930, USA

Krol, John Cardinal
222 N 17th St
Philadelphia, PA 19103-1202, USA

Kroll, Alexander S (Alex) (Football Player)
New York Titans
581 Whalley Rd
Charlotte, VT 05445-9531, USA

Kroll, Gary (Baseball Player)
Philadelphia Phillies
9038 E 40th St
Tulsa, OK 74145-3713, USA

Kroll, Lucien (Architect)
Ave Louis Berlaimont 20
Boite 9
Brussels 1160, BELGIUM

Kroll, Robert L (Football Player)
Green Bay Packers
PO Box 8563
Maitland, FL 32751, USA

Kroll, Sylvio
Tranitzer Str. 8
Cottbus D-03048, GERMANY

Kromm, Bob (Coach)
Detroit Red Wings
600 Civic Center Dr
Joe Louis Arena
Detroit, MI 48226-4419, USA

Kromm, Richard (Rich) (Coach, Hockey Player)
35469 Banbury Rd
Livonia, MI 48152-2843, USA

Kronberger, Petra (Skier)
Ellmautal 37
Pfarrwerfen 5452, AUSTRIA

Krone, Julie (Jockey)
Jay Hovdey
100 Broadway # 700
Daily Racing Form
New York, NY 10005-1983, USA

Kroner, Gary (Football Player)
Denver Broncos
7330 Buckingham Ct
Boulder, CO 80301-6409, USA

Kroon, Marc (Baseball Player)
San Diego Padres
3940 E Sahuaro Dr
Phoenix, AZ 85028-3444, USA

Kropfelder, Nicholas (Soccer Player)
13803 Lighthouse Ave
Ocean City, MD 21842-4565, USA

Kroto, Harold W (Nobel Prize Laureate)
Sussex University
Chemistry Dept
Falmer
Brighton BN1 9QJ, UNITED KINGDOM (UK)

KRS-One (Musician)
Famous Artists Agency
250 W 57th St
New York, NY 10107-0001, USA

Krsnich, Rocky (Baseball Player)
Chicago White Sox
5701 W 92nd St
Shawnee Mission, KS 66207-2442, USA

Krstic, Nenad (Basketball Player)
New Jersy Nets
390 Murray Hill Pkwy
East Rutherford, NJ 07073-2109, USA

Kruckei, Marie (Baseball Player)
52128 Woodbridge Dr
South Bend, IN 46635, USA

Kruczek, Mike (Football Player)
Pittsburgh Steelers
1833 E San Carlos Pl
Chandler, AZ 85249-1840, USA

Krueger, Anne O (Economist)
Stanford University
Economics Dept
Stanford, CA 94305, USA

Krueger, Bill (Baseball Player)
Oakland A's
30132 SE Redmond Fall City Rd
Fall City, WA 98024-7104, USA

Krueger, Charles A (Charlie) (Football Player)
San Francisco 49ers
44 Regency Dr
Clayton, CA 94517-1729, USA

Krueger, James G (Misc)
Rockefeller University
1230 York Ave
Medical Center
New York, NY 10065-6399, USA

Krueger, Kurt
1221 La Collina Dr
Beverly Hills, CA 90210-2633, USA

Krueger, Robert C (Bob) (Diplomat, Senator)
US Embassy-Burundi
State Department
2201 C St NW
Washington, DC 20522-0001, USA

Krueger, Rolf (Football Player)
St Louis Cardinals
PO Box 638
Wallis, TX 77485-0638, USA

Krug, Chris (Baseball Player)
Chicago Cubs
PO Box 1350
Wildomar, CA 92595-1350, USA

Krug, Gary (Baseball Player)
Chicago Cubs
1327 Baylor Dr
Colorado Springs, CO 80909-3301, USA

Krug, Manfred
Rankestr. 9
Berlin D-10789, GERMANY

Kruger, Christiane
Waldschmidtstr. 16
Starnberg 82319, GERMANY

Kruger, Diane (Actor, Model)
c/o Christopher Lockhart *International Creative Management (ICM-LA)*
10250 Constellation Blvd
Los Angeles, CA 90067-6200, USA

Kruger, Hardy
PO Box 2450
Palm Springs, CA 92263-2450, USA

Kruger, Hardy (Actor)
L Von dem Knesebeck
Maximilianstr 23
Munich 80539, GERMANY

Kruger, Mike
Gorch-Fock-Kehre 9
Quickborn D-25451, GERMANY

Kruger, Pit (Actor)
Geleitstr 10
Frankfurt/Main 60599, GERMANY

Krugman, Paul R (Economist)
70 Lambert Dr
Princeton, NJ 08540-2319, USA

Kruk, John (Baseball Player)
San Diego Padres
21 Pheasant Dr
Mount Laurel, NJ 08054-5302, USA

krukow, Mike (Baseball Player)
Chicago Cubs
6094 Madbury Ct
San Luis Obispo, CA 93401-8244, USA

Krulwich, Robert (Correspondent)
CBS-TV
524 W 57th St
News Dept
New York, NY 10019-2924, USA

Krumholtz, David (Actor)
c/o Jeff Golenberg *The Collective*
9100 Wilshire Blvd # 700 W
Beverly Hills, CA 90212-3401, USA

Krumrie, Tim (Football Player)
c/o Staff Member *Kansas City Chiefs*
1 Arrowhead Dr
Kansas City, MO 64129-1651, USA

Krupa, Joanna (Actor)
c/o Tom Harrison *Diverse Talent Group*
1875 Century Park E Ste 2250
Los Angeles, CA 90067-2563, USA

Krupa, Joe (Football Player)
Pittsburgh Steelers
PO Box 1356
North Riverside, IL 60546-0756, USA

Kruschen, Jack
PO Box 10143
Canoga Park, CA 91309-1143, USA

Kruse, Earl J (Misc)
Roofers/Waterproofers/Allied Workers
1125 17th St NW
Washington, DC 20036-4707, USA

Kruse, Martin (Religious Leader)
Prinz-Friedrich-Leopold-Str 14
Berlin 14219, GERMANY

Krusiec, Michelle (Actor)
c/o Staff Member *Himber Entertainment Inc*
15760 Ventura Blvd Ste 700
Encino, CA 91436-3016, USA

Kryhoski, Dick (Baseball Player)
New York Yankees
18855 Warwick St
Beverly Hills, MI 48025-4068, USA

Krypreos, Nick (Hockey Player)
9209 Copenhaven Dr
Potomac, MD 20854, USA

Krzyzewski, Michael W (Mike) (Coach)
Duke University
Cameron Indoor Stadium
Athletic Dept
Durham, NC 27706, USA

Ksionzyk, John (Football Player)
Los Angeles Rams
1106 Washington St
Olean, NY 14760-2128, USA

KT Tunstall (Musician)
c/o Staff Member *Paradigm (Monterey)*
509 Hartnell St
Monterey, CA 93940-2825, USA

Kubala, Ray (Football Player)
Denver Broncos
5 Meandering Way
Round Rock, TX 78664-9619, USA

Kuban, Bob (Musician)
17626 Lasiandra Dr
Chesterfield, MO 63005-4912, USA

Kubasov, Valeri N (Cosmonaut)
Potchta Kosmonavtov
Moskovskoi Oblasti
Syvisdny Goroduk 141160, RUSSIA

Kubasov, Valery
141-160 Svyossdy Gorodok
Potchta Kosmonavtov, RUSSIA

Kubek, Anthony C (Tony) (Baseball Player, Sportscaster)
New York Yankees
685 Smokey Lake Dr
Phelps, WI 54554-9314, USA

Kubenka, Jeff (Baseball Player)
Los Angeles Dodgers
6935 Fm 957
Schulenburg, TX 78956-5091, USA

Kuberski, Robert (Football Player)
Green Bay Packers
13 Forwood Dr
Garnet Valley, PA 19061-1215, USA

Kubiak, Gary (Coach, Football Coach, Football Player)
Denver Broncos
PO Box 37415
Houston, TX 77237-7415, USA

Kubik, Brad (Football Player)
Indianapolis Colts
4855 S Tanager Ave
Battlefield, MO 65619-8301, USA

Kubin, Larry (Football Player)
Washington Redskins
315 Cannery Ln
Forest Hill, MD 21050-3066, USA

Kubiszyn, Jack (Baseball Player)
Cleveland Indians
2306 University Blvd
Tuscaloosa, AL 35401-1580, USA

Kublak, Ted (Baseball Player)
Kansas City A's
16443 Mountain Shadow Ln
Ramona, CA 92065-6926, USA

Kubski, Gil (Baseball Player)
California Angels
4542 Scenario Dr
Huntington Beach, CA 92649-2221, USA

Kucan, Milan (President)
President's Office
Erjavcera 17
Ljubljana 61000, SLOVENIA

Kucek, Jack (Baseball Player)
Chicago White Sox
8220 Blue Heron Ln
Canfield, OH 44406-9134, USA

Kucera, Frantisek (Hockey Player)
Pittsburg Penguins
66 Mario Lemieux Pl
Mellon Arena
Pittsburgh, PA 15219-3504, USA

Kuchar, Matt (Golfer)
121 Plantation Cir
Ponte Vedra, FL 32082-3921, USA

Kuchma, Leonid D (President)
President's Office
Bankova Str 11
Kiev 252011, UKRAINE

Kuchta, Frank (Football Player)
Washington Redskins
5021 Fairlawn Rd
Lyndhurst, OH 44124-1124, USA

Kucinich, Dennis
12217 Milan Ave
Cleveland, OH 44111-4550, USA

Kucinich, Dennis J (Misc)
14518 Drake Rd
Cleveland, OH 44136-7932, USA

Kucks, Johnny (Baseball Player)
New York Yankees
15 Oakland St
Hillsdale, NJ 07642-1846, USA

Kuczek, Steve (Baseball Player)
Boston Braves
769 Sacandaga Rd
Scotia, NY 12302-6028, USA

Kuczynski, Betty (Bowler)
4515 Prescott Ave
Lyons, IL 60534-1960, USA

Kud (Musician)
Agency Group Ltd
1775 Broadway Ste 515
New York, NY 10019-1903, USA

Kudelka, James A (Choreographer, Dancer)
National Ballet of Canada
470 Queens Quay W
Toronto, ON M5V 3K4, CANADA

Kudelski, Bob (Hockey Player)
64 Diamond Basin Rd
Cody, WY 82414, USA

Kuder, Mary (Artist)
Kuder Art Studio
539 Navahopi Rd
Sedona, AZ 86336-4007, USA

Kudlow, Lawrence (Television Host)
Kudlow & Company
900 Sylvan Ave
Cnbc
Englewood Cliffs, NJ 07632-3312, USA

Kudrna, Julius (Athlete)
Sekaninova 36
Prague 2 120 00, CZECH REPUBLIC

Kudrow, Lisa (Actor)
c/o Adam Venit *Endeavor Agency LLC (LA)*
9601 Wilshire Blvd Fl 3
Beverly Hills, CA 90210-5204, USA

Kuebler, David (Opera Singer)
Haydn Rawstron
36 Station Road
London SE20 7BQ, UNITED KINGDOM (UK)

Kuechenberg, Robert J (Bob) (Football Player)
Miami Dolphins
2519 SW 30th Ter
Fort Lauderdale, FL 33312-4729, USA

Kuechenberg, Rudy (Football Player)
Chicago Bears
2841 NW 73rd Ave
Hollywood, FL 33024-2733, USA

Kuehl, Ryan (Football Player)
Washington Redskins
10409 Masters Ter
Potomac, MD 20854-3862, USA

Kuehn, Art (Football Player)
Seattle Seahawks
19520 NE 185th St
Woodinville, WA 98077-5403, USA

Kuehn, Enrico (Athlete)
BSD
An der Schiessstatte 4
Berchtesgaden 83471, GERMANY

Kuehne, Kelli (Golfer)
7211 Oakbluff Dr
Dallas, TX 75254-2736, USA

Kuerten, Gustavo (Tennis Player)
Octagon
1751 Pinnacle Dr Ste 1500
McLean, VA 22102-3833, USA

Kufeldt, James (Business Person)
Winn-Dixie Stores
5050 Edgewood Ct
Jacksonville, FL 32254-1665, USA

Kufuor, John Agyekum (President)
Chairman's Office
Castle
PO Box 1627
Accra, GHANA

Kugler, Pete (Football Player)
San Francisco 49ers
9984 Whitetail Ln
Littleton, CO 80127-6104, USA

Kuhaulua, Fred (Baseball Player)
California Angels
89-203 Uaiakahiki Pl
Walanae, HI 96792, USA

Kuhaulua, Jesse (Wrestler)
Azumazeki Stable
4-6-4 Higashi Komagata
Ryogoku
Tokyo, JAPAN

Kuhlman, Ron (Actor)
5738 Willis Ave
Van Nuys, CA 91411-3327, USA

Kuhlmann, Kathleen M (Opera Singer)
Int'l Management Group
G Paris
54 Ave Marceau
Paris 75008, FRANCE

Kuhlmann-Wilsdorf, Doris (Physicist)
University of Virginia
Materials Science Dept
Charlottesville, VA 22901, USA

Kuhn, Bowie (Baseball Player)
Baseball Commissioner's Office
11 Shinnicock Road
Quogue, NY 11959, USA

Kuhn, Gustav (Conductor)
6343 Ere
AUSTRIA

Kuhn, Kenny (Baseball Player)
Cleveland Indians
12011 Schussing Way
Truckee, CA 96161-6209, USA

Kuhn, Stephen L (Steve) (Composer, Musician)
Berkeley Agency
2608 9th St
Berkeley, CA 94710-2550, USA

Kuhweide, Wilhelm
10031 E Buckskin Trl
Scottsdale, AZ 85255-2338, USA

Kuiper, Duane (Baseball Player)
Cleveland Indians
PO Box 24308
San Francisco, CA 94124-0308, USA

Kukoc, Toni (Basketball Player)
1850 Hybernia Dr
Highland Park, IL 60035, USA

Kulbacki, Joseph (Football Player)
Buffalo Bisons
9419 S Hill Rd
Boston, NY 14025, USA

Kuleshov, Valery (Musician)
Musicians Corporate Mgmt
PO Box 825
Highland, NY 12528-0825, USA

Kulich, Vladimir (Actor)
c/o Jeff Goldberg *Jeff Goldberg Management*
817 Monte Leon Dr
Beverly Hills, CA 90210-2629, USA

Kulikov, Viktor G (Misc)
Ministry of Defense
Myasnitskaya Str 37
Moscow 10100, RUSSIA

Kulka, Konstanty A (Musician)
Filharmonia Narodowa
Ul Jasna 5
Warsaw 00-007, POLAND

Kulkarni, Mamta (Actor, Bollywood)
D Wing 7th Floor 701 RC Complex
Versova Yari Road
Mumbai, MS 400061, INDIA

Kumanyika, Shiriki K (Misc)
University of Illinois
Nutrition/Dietetics Dept
Chicago, IL 60607, USA

Kumar, Akshay (Actor, Bollywood)
203 A Wing Benzer
Lokhandwala Complex Andheri (W)
Mumbai, MS 400053, INDIA

Kumar, Ashok (Actor, Bollywood)
47 Union Park Chembur
Mumbai, MS 400071, INDIA

Kumar, Dilip (Actor, Bollywood)
34/B Palli Hill
Nargis Dutt Road Bandra (W)
Mumbai, MS 400050, INDIA

Kumar, Kiran (Actor)
Jeevan Kiran S V Road
Bandra
Bombay, MS 400 050, INDIA

Kumar, Manoj (Actor, Director, Filmmaker, Producer)
Lakshmi Villa Grount Floor-45
Tagore Road Santacruz (W)
Bombay, MS 400 054, INDIA

Kumar, Mehul (Bollywood, Director, Filmmaker, Producer)
302 Atlantic J P Road
Seven Bangalows Andheri
Bombay, MS 400 061, INDIA

Kumar, Mohan (Bollywood, Director, Filmmaker)
Prem Sagar 'B' Linking Road
Khar
Bombay, MS 400 052, INDIA

Kumar, Rajendra (Actor, Bollywood, Director, Filmmaker, Producer)
Dimple 7 Pali Hill
Bandra
Bombay, MS 400 050, INDIA

Kumar, Sanjay (Business Person)
Computer Associates Int'l
1 Ca Plz
Islandia, NY 11749-7001, USA

Kumar, Sarath (Actor)
16 Rajamannaar Saalai
Thyagaraya Nagar
Chennai, TN 600 017, INDIA

Kumaratunga, Chandrika B (President)
President's Office
Republic Square
Sri Jayewardenepura Kotte
SRI LANKA

Kumbernuss, Astrid (Athlete, Track Athlete)
Neubrandenburg Jahnstadion
Schwedenstr 25
Neubrandenburg 17033, GERMANY

Kumble, Roger (Actor, Director, Writer)
c/o Marty Bowen *United Talent Agency (UTA)*
9560 Wilshire Blvd Ste 500
Beverly Hills, CA 90212-2401, USA

Kume, Mike (Baseball Player)
Kansas City A's
6810 Woodard Rd
Andover, OH 44003-9638, USA

Kumerow, Eric (Football Player)
Miami Dolphins
736 Fairview Ln
Bartlett, IL 60103-4566, USA

Kumin, Maxine W (Writer)
Joppa Road
Warner, NH 03278, USA

Kummer, Glenn F (Business Person)
Fleetwood Enterprises
3125 Myers St
Riverside, CA 92503-5544, USA

Kump, Ernest J (Architect)
Villa Boecklin
Jupiterstr 15
Zurich 8032, SWITZERLAND

Kundera, Milan (Writer)
Gallimard
5 Rue Sebastien-Bottin
Paris 75007, FRANCE

Kundla, John A (Basketball Player, Coach)
4519 Zenith Ave N
Minneapolis, MN 55422-1447, USA

Kunerth, Mark J (Producer, Writer)
c/o Ted Chervin *Broder Webb Chervin Silbermann Agency, The (BWCS)*
10250 Constellation Blvd Ste P
Los Angeles, CA 90067-6213, USA

Kunes, Ellen (Editor)
Oprah Magazine
224 W 57th St # 900
New York, NY 10019-3200, USA

Kung, Hans (Misc)
Waldhauserstr 23
Tubingen 72076, GERMANY

Kung, Patrick C (Misc)
T Cell Sciences
119 4th Ave
Needham, MA 02494-2725, USA

Kunis, Mila (Actor)
c/o Susan Curtis *Curtis Talent Management*
9607 Arby Dr
Beverly Hills, CA 90210-1202, USA

Kunitz, Matt (Producer)
c/o Staff Member *William Morris Agency (WMA-LA)*
1 William Morris Pl
Beverly Hills, CA 90212-4261, USA

Kunkel, Jeff (Baseball Player)
Texas Rangers
4921 County Road 605
Burleson, TX 76028-1155, USA

Kunkel, Louis M (Misc)
Children's Hospital
300 Longwood Ave
Boston, MA 02115-5737, USA

Kunkel-Huff, Anna (Baseball Player)
9220 E Fairway Blvd Apt C136
Sun Lakes, AZ 85248-6579, USA

Kunkle, John F (Religious Leader)
Evangelical Methodist Church
3000 W Kellogg Dr
Wichita, KS 67213-2204, USA

Kunnert, Kevin (Basketball Player)
8286 SW Qilderland Court
Tigard, OR 97224, USA

Kunstmann, Doris
Alexander Lamonstrasse 9
Munich D-81679, GERMANY

Kuntz, Rusty (Baseball Player)
Chicago White Sox
6541 E 83rd Pl
Tulsa, OK 74133-4159, USA

Kunz, George J (Football Player)
Atlanta Falcons
8215 Bermuda Rd
Las Vegas, NV 89123-2213, USA

Kunz, Lee (Football Player)
Chicago Bears
4096 Youngfield St
Wheat Ridge, CO 80033-3862, USA

Kunzel, Erich Jr (Conductor)
TRM Mgmt
825 S Lazelle St
Columbus, OH 43206-2021, USA

Kunzu, Hari (Writer)
EP Dutton
375 Hudson St
New York, NY 10014-3658, USA

Kupcinet, Kari (Actor)
1660 Mill Trl
Highland Park, IL 60035-1502, USA

Kupfer, Carl (Misc)
National Eye Institute
9000 Rockville Pike
Bethesda, MD 20892-0001, USA

Kupfer, Harry (Director)
Komische Oper
Behrenstr 55-57
Berlin 10117, GERMANY

Kupferberg, Sabine (Ballerina)
Dans Theater 3
Scheldoldoekshaven 60
Gravenhage, EN 2511, THE NETHERLANDS

Kupp, Craig (Football Player)
Phoenix Cardinals
609 S 31st Ave
Yakima, WA 98902-4009, USA

Kupp, Jacob (Jake) (Football Player)
Dallas Cowboys
4801 Snowmountain Rd
Yakima, WA 98908-2848, USA

Kupper, William P Jr (Publisher)
Business Week
1221 Avenue Of The Americas
New York, NY 10020-1095, USA

Kupperman, Joel
PO Box 672
Mansfield Center, CT 06250-0672, USA

Kuranari, Tadashi (Government Official)
2-18-12 Daita
Setangayaku
Tokyo 155, JAPAN

Kurant, Willy (Cinematographer)
Lyons Sheldon Agency
800 S Robertson Blvd Ste 6
Los Angeles, CA 90035-1635, USA

Kuras, Ellen M (Cinematographer)
54 Summit St
Nyack, NY 10960-3726, USA

Kurasov, Georgy (Artist)
4/2 Inzenernaja St
Saint Petersburg 191011, RUSSIA

Kureishi, Hanif (Writer)
81 Comeragh Road
London W14 9HS, UNITED KINGDOM (UK)

Kurek, Ralph (Football Player)
Chicago Bears
2913 N Burling St # 3
Chicago, IL 60657-6553, USA

Kurisko, Jamie (Football Player)
New York Jets
337 Hill Ave
Montgomery, NY 12549-2052, USA

Kuriyama, Chiaki (Actor)
c/o Staff Member *Crystal Sky Entertainment*
10203 Santa Monica Blvd Fl 5
Los Angeles, CA 90067-6405, USA

Kurkova, Karolina (Model)
DNA Model Mgmt
520 Broadway Fl 11
New York, NY 10012-4436, USA

Kurland, Robert A (Bob) (Basketball Player)
1024 Kings Crown Dr
Sanibel, FL 33957-4910, USA

Kurlander, Tom
1801 Avenue Of The Stars Ste 902
Los Angeles, CA 90067-5981, USA

Kurnick, Howie (Football Player)
Cincinnati Bengals
2339 Bretton Dr
Cincinnati, OH 45244-3729, USA

Kurokawa, Kisho (Architect)
Aoyama Building
#11F 1-2-3 Kita Aoyama
Minatoku, Tokyo, JAPAN

Kurosaki, Ryan (Baseball Player)
St Louis Cardinals
2024 Fairmont Dr
Benton, AR 72015-3163, USA

Kurrat, Kiaus-Dieter (Athlete, Track Athlete)
Am Hochwald 30
28460
Klemmachow 1453, GERMANY

Kurri, Jarri (Hockey Player)
Colorado Avalanche
1000 Chopper Cir
Pepsi Center
Denver, CO 80204-5805, USA

Kurtag, Gyorgy (Composer)
Lihego V3
Veroce 2621, HUNGARY

Kurtenbach, Orland J (Hockey Player)
119-15500 Rosemary Heights Crescent
Surrey, BC V3S 0K1, CANADA

Kurth, Wallace (Wally) (Actor, Musician)
2143 N Valley Dr
Manhattan Beach, CA 90266-2247, USA

Kurtis, Bill (Television Host)
c/o Staff Member *Kurtis Productions*
400 W Erie St Ste 500
Chicago, IL 60610-4041, USA

Kurtis, Dalene (Actor)
c/o Juliette Harris *It Girl Public Relations*
3763 Eddingham Ave
Calabasas, CA 91302-5835, USA

Kurtz, Hal (Baseball Player)
Cleveland Indians
511 Flat Iron Square Rd
Church Hill, MD 21623-1269, USA

Kurtz, Swoosie (Actor)
320 Central Park W
New York, NY 10025-7659, USA

Kurtzberg, Joanne (Physicist)
Duke University
Medical Center
Durham, NC 27708-0001, USA

Kurtze, Andrew (Business Person)
Sprint PCS Group
PO Box 11315
Kansas City, MO 64112-0315, USA

Kurtzman, Katy (Actor, Director)
c/o Staff Member *Lynn Production & Mgmt*
20411 Chapter Dr
Woodland Hills, CA 91364-5612, USA

Kurupt (Musician)
William Morris Agency
151 El Camino Dr
Beverly Hills, CA 90212-2775, USA

Kurys, Sophie (Baseball Player)
8301 E Fairmount Ave
Scottsdale, AZ 85251-4835, USA

Kurzweil, Raymond (Inventor)
Kurzwell Applied Intelligence
411 Waverly Oaks Rd
Waltham, MA 02452-8448, USA

Kusama, Karyn (Director)
Endeavor Talent Agency
9701 Wilshire Blvd Ste 1000
Beverly Hills, CA 90212-2010, USA

Kusatsu, Clyde (Actor)
Paradign Agency
10100 Santa Monica Blvd Ste 2500
Los Angeles, CA 90067-4116, USA

Kuschak, Metropolitan Andrei (Religious Leader)
Ukranian Orthodox Church in America
3 Davenport Ave
New Rochelle, NY 10805-3442, USA

Kush, Rod (Football Player)
Buffalo Bills
11010 Highway 6
Gretna, NE 68028-8000, USA

Kushboo (Actor, Bollywood)
20/1 Arch Bshap
Mithyas Ave Boat Club Road
Chennai, TN 600018, INDIA

Kushell, Lisa (Actor)
c/o Staff Member *Abrams Artists Agency (LA)*
9200 W Sunset Blvd Ph 11
Los Angeles, CA 90069-3601, USA

Kushner, Harold S (Writer)
145 Hartford St
Natick, MA 01760-3125, USA

Kushner, Robert E (Artist)
DC Moore Gallery
724 5th Ave
New York, NY 10019-4106, USA

Kuske, Kevin (Athlete)
BSD
An der Schlessstatte 4
Berchtesgaden 83471, GERMANY

Kuslck, Craig (Baseball Player)
Minnesota Twins
14228 Garrett Ave
Apple Valley, MN 55124-8453, USA

Kusnyer, Art (Baseball Player)
Chicago White Sox
6598 Taeda Dr
Sarasota, FL 34241-9145, USA

Kusturica, Emir (Actor, Director, Musician, Writer)
Fondazione Culturale Edison
Largo VIII Marzo, 9
Parma 43100, ITALY

Kutcher, Ashton (Actor, Producer)
c/o Staff Member *Katalyst Films*
6430 W Sunset Blvd Ste 1400
Los Angeles, CA 90028-8003, USA

Kutcher, Randy (Baseball Player)
San Francisco Giants
3016 Purple Sage Ln
Palmdale, CA 93550-7972, USA

Kuti, Fela (Musician)
Rosebud Agency
PO Box 170429
San Francisco, CA 94117-0429, USA

Kutner, Malcom J (Mal) (Football Player)
Chicago Cardinals
4121 Mojave Dr
Granbury, TX 76049-5253, USA

Kutner, Rob (Writer)
c/o Staff Member *Kaplan-Stahler-Gumer Agency*
8383 Wilshire Blvd Ste 923
Beverly Hills, CA 90211-2408, USA

Kuttner, Stephan G (Historian)
2270 Le Conte Ave #601
Berkeley, CA 94709, USA

Kutty, Padmini (Actor, Bollywood)
33 1st Street Kamdar Nagar
Nungambakkam
Chennai, TN 600034, INDIA

Kutyna, Donald J (General)
4818 Kenyon Ct
Colorado Springs, CO 80917-3615, USA

Kutyna, Marty (Baseball Player)
Kansas City A's
2255 NW 14th St
Delray Beach, FL 33445-2610, USA

Kutz, Mae
140 Buckingham Ct
Goodlettsville, TN 37072-2146, USA

Kutzler, Jerry (Baseball Player)
Chicago White Sox
8415 27th Ave
Kenosha, WI 53143-6232, USA

Kuykendall, Fulton (Football Player)
Atlanta Falcons
1497 Rucker Cir
Woodstock, GA 30188-2133, USA

Kuykendall, John W (Educator)
Davidson College
President's Office
Davidson, NC 28036, USA

Kuzava, Bob (Baseball Player)
Cleveland Indians
1118 Vinewood St
Wyandotte, MI 48192-4945, USA

Kuziel, Bob (Football Player)
New Orleans Saints
3375 Walnut Dr
Ellicott City, MD 21043-4351, USA

Kuzman, John (Football Player)
Chicago Cardinals
17 Osborne Ter
Wayne, NJ 07470-4368, USA

Kuznetsoff, Alexel (Musician)
Columbia Artists Mgmt Inc
1790 Broadway Fl 6
New York, NY 10019-1412, USA

Kuzyk, Mimi (Actor)
Artists Agency
1180 S Beverly Dr Ste 301
Los Angeles, CA 90035-1154, USA

Kwalick, Thaddeus J (Ted) (Football Player)
San Francisco 49ers
755 Purdue Ct
Santa Clara, CA 95051-5527, USA

Kwan, Jennie (Actor)
Innovative Artists
1505 10th St
Santa Monica, CA 90401-2805, USA

Kwan, Michelle (Figure Skater)
c/o Staff Member *Champions on Ice*
3500 W 80th St
Tom Collins Enterprises Inc
Minneapolis, MN 55431-1068, USA

Kwan, Nancy (Actor)
Marlin
252 7th Ave Apt 9P
New York, NY 10001-7340, USA

Kwanten, Ryan (Actor)
c/o Joel Lubin *Creative Artists Agency LCC (CAA-LA)*
2000 Avenue Of The Stars
Los Angeles, CA 90067-4700, USA

Kwapis, Ken (Comedian)
c/o Staff Member *Writers and Artists Group Intl (LA)*
8383 Wilshire Blvd Ste 550
Beverly Hills, CA 90211-2417, USA

Kwasniewski, Aleksander (President)
Kancelaria Prezydenta RP
Ul Wiejska 4/8
Warsaw 00-902, POLAND

Kweller, Ben (Musician)
c/o Staff Member *Paradigm (Monterey)*
509 Hartnell St
Monterey, CA 93940-2825, USA

Kwolek, Stephanie L (Inventor)
312 Spalding Rd
Wilmington, DE 19803-2422, USA

Kwouk, Burt (Actor)
Diamond Mgmt
31 Percey St
London W1T 2DD, UNITED KINGDOM (UK)

Kyle, Aaron (Football Player)
Dallas Cowboys
7810 Morrell Ln
Durham, NC 27713-6667, USA

Kyle, David L (Business Person)
ONEOK Inc
PO Box 871
100 W 5th St
Tulsa, OK 74102-0871, USA

Kyles, Cedric (The Entertainer) (Actor, Comedian, Producer, Writer)
c/o Gordon Bobb *Del, Shaw, Moonves, Tanaka & Finkelstein*
2120 Colorado Ave Ste 200
Santa Monica, CA 90404-3561, USA

Kylian, Jiri (Dancer)
Dance Theatre
Scheldeldoekshaven 60
Gravenhage, EN 2511, THE NETHERLANDS

Kyo, Machiko (Actor)
Olimpia Copu
6-35 JinguMae
Shibuyaku
Tokyo, JAPAN

Kysar, Jeff (Football Player)
Oakland Raiders
570 June St
Rialto, CA 92376-5729, USA

L

La Costeba, Banda (Music Group)
c/o Staff Member *BMG*
1540 Broadway
New York, NY 10036-4074, USA

La Fong, Michelle
3855 Shore Pkwy Apt 1D
Brooklyn, NY 11235-1053, USA

La Frenais, Ian (Director, Producer, Writer)
c/o Bruce Kaufman *Broder Webb Chervin Silbermann Agency, The (BWCS)*
10250 Constellation Blvd Ste P
Los Angeles, CA 90067-6213, USA

La Lanne, Jack
430 Quintana Rd # 151
Morro Bay, CA 93442-1948, USA

La Ley (Music Group)
c/o Staff Member *United Talent Agency (UTA)*
9560 Wilshire Blvd Ste 500
Beverly Hills, CA 90212-2401, USA

La Mura, Mark
6399 Wilshire Blvd Ste 414
Los Angeles, CA 90048-5716, USA

La Oreja de Van Gogh (Music Group)
c/o Staff Member *Sony Music Miami*
605 Lincoln Rd Fl 7
Miami Beach, FL 33139-2900, USA

La Placa, Alison
4526 Wilshire Blvd
Los Angeles, CA 90010-3801, USA

La Rue, Danny
57 Gr. Cumberland Pl
London, ENGLAND W1M 7LJ, UNITED KINGDOM (UK)

La Rue, Eva (Actor, Television Host)
c/o Staff Member *Style Network*
5750 Wilshire Blvd
Los Angeles, CA 90036-3697, USA

La Rue, Florence
4300 Louise Ave
Encino, CA 91316-3916, USA

Laakso, Eric (Football Player)
Miami Dolphins
300 N Palm Aire Dr Apt 707
Pompano Beach, FL, USA

Laatasi, Kamuta (Prime Minister)
Prime Minister's Office
Vaiaku
Funafuti, TUVALU

Labaff, Ernie (Misc)
Aluminum Brick Glass Workers Union
3362 Hollenberg Dr
Bridgeton, MO 63044-2432, USA

LaBeef, Sleepy (Musician)
14469 E Highway 264
Lowell, AR 72745-9212, USA

LaBelle, Patti (Musician)
c/o Staff Member *Richard De La Font Agency*
4845 S Sheridan Rd Ste 505
Tulsa, OK 74145-5719, USA

LaBeouf, Shia (Actor)
c/o John Crosby *John Crosby Management*
1310 N Spaulding Ave
Los Angeles, CA 90046-4010, USA

Labeque, Katia (Musician)
Columbia Artists Mgmt Inc
1790 Broadway Fl 6
New York, NY 10019-1412, USA

Labeque, Marielle (Musician)
Columbia Artists Mgmt Inc
1790 Broadway Fl 6
New York, NY 10019-1412, USA

Labine, Clement W (Clem) (Baseball Player)
Brooklyn Dodgers
2970 Mendon Rd Apt 64
Cumberland, RI 02864-3454, USA

Labine, Tyler (Actor)
c/o Jason Heyman *Creative Artists Agency LCC (CAA-LA)*
2000 Avenue Of The Stars
Los Angeles, CA 90067-4700, USA

Labiosa, David (Actor)
Artist's Agency
1180 S Beverly Dr Ste 301
Los Angeles, CA 90035-1154, USA

Labonte, Bobby (Race Car Driver)
403 Interstate Dr
Archdale, NC 27263-3162, USA

Laborde, Alden J (Business Person)
63 Oriole St
New Orleans, LA 70124-4517, USA

Labounty, Matt (Football Player)
San Francisco 49ers
360 W 17th Ave
Eugene, OR 97401-3859, USA

Labrador, Honey (Actor, Television Host)
c/o Bradley Bernstein *Fast Track Management*
736 N Alta Vista Blvd
Los Angeles, CA 90046-7602, USA

Labre, Yvon (Hockey Player)
7812 Tilmont Ave
Parkville, MD 21234-5539, USA

LaBute, Neil (Director, Writer)
Sanford Gross
6715 Hollywood Blvd # 236
Los Angeles, CA 90028-4627, USA

Labyorteaux, Matthew (Actor)
167 W 72nd St Apt 3F
New York, NY 10023-3253, USA

Labyorteaux, Patrick (Actor)
8447 Wilshire Blvd Ste 206
Beverly Hills, CA 90211-3207, USA

Lacey, Bob (Baseball Player)
Oakland A's
7623 E Decatur St
Mesa, AZ 85207-5728, USA

Lacey, Chonn (Football Player)
New Orleans Saints
1314 W Ontario St
Philadelphia, PA 19140-5220, USA

Lacey, Deborah (Actor)
1801 Avenue Of Stars # 1250
Los Angeles, CA 90067-5902, USA

Lacey, Jeff (Boxer)
Gary Shaw Productions LLC
33 Divan Way
Wayne, NJ 07470-5201, USA

Lach, Elmer J (Hockey Player)
89 Bayview Ave
Pointe Claire, PQ M9S 5C4, CANADA

Lachance, Michael (Mike) (Race Car Driver)
183 Sweetmans Ln
Millstone Township, NJ 08535-8107, USA

LaChapelle, David (Photographer)
Simon & Schuster/Pocket/Summit
1230 Avenue Of The Americas
New York, NY 10020-1513, USA

Lachapelle, Sean (Football Player)
Los Angeles Rams
8724 Lodestone Cir
Elk Grove, CA 95624-2520, USA

Lachemann, Marcel E (Baseball Player)
Oakland A's
PO Box 587
Penryn, CA 95663-0587, USA

Lachemann, Rene (Baseball Player)
Kansas City A's
7500 E Boulders Pkwy Unit 66
Scottsdale, AZ 85266-1212, USA

Lachey, Drew (Musician)
c/o Staff Member *The Artists Group*
1650 Broadway Ste 610
New York, NY 10019-6833, USA

Lachey, James M (Jim) (Football Player)
San Diego Chargers
1445 Roxbury Rd Apt G
Columbus, OH 43212-3211, USA

Lachey, Nick (Musician)
c/o Colton Gramm *Brillstein-Grey Entertainment*
9150 Wilshire Blvd Ste 350
Beverly Hills, CA 90212-3453, USA

Lachhiman, Gurung (War Hero)
Village Dahakhani
Village Development Conmelle
Ward 4, Chitwan, NEPAL

Lachowicz, Al (Baseball Player)
Texas Rangers
310 Roosevelt Ave
Mc Kees Rocks, PA 15136-2408, USA

Lacina, Corbin (Football Player)
Buffalo Bills
40 Sunny Side Ln
Sunfish Lake, MN 55118-4718, USA

Lackey, Brad (Race Car Driver)
Badco
35 Monument Plaza
Pleasant Hill, CA 94523, USA

Laclavere, Georges (Physicist)
53 Ave de Breteuil
Paris 75007, FRANCE

Laclotte, Michel R (Director)
10 Bis Rue du Pre-aux-Clerc
Paris 75007, FRANCE

Lacock, Pete (Baseball Player)
Chicago Cubs
10019 Mackey Cir
Shawnee Mission, KS 66212-3461, USA

Lacombe, Henri (Oceanographer)
20 Bis Ave de Lattre de Tassigny
Bourg-la-Reine 92340, FRANCE

Lacorte, Frank (Baseball Player)
Atlanta Braves
1667 El Dorado Dr
Gilroy, CA 95020-3754, USA

Lacoss, Mike (Baseball Player)
Cincinnati Reds
PO Box 44033
Lemon Cove, CA 93244-0033, USA

Lacoste, Catherine (Golfer)
Calle B6
#4 El Soto de la Moraleja Alcobendas
Madrid, SPAIN

Lacroix, Andre J (Hockey Player)
6770 Oakwood Dr
Oakland, CA 94611-1152, USA

LaCroix, Christian
73 rue du Faubourg-St.-Honore
Paris F-75008, FRANCE

Lacroix, Christian M M (Designer,
Fashion Designer)
73 Rue du Faubourg Saint Honore
Paris 75008, FRANCE

Lacrosse, Dave (Football Player)
Pittsburgh Steelers
1712 Harmon Rd
Conshohocken, PA 19428-1205, USA

Lacy, Alan (Business Person)
Sears Roebuck Co
3333 Beverly Rd
Hoffman Estates, IL 60179-0001, USA

Lacy, Kerry (Baseball Player)
Boston Red Sox
124 County Road 713
Higdon, AL 35979-6123, USA

Lacy, Lee (Baseball Player)
Los Angeles Dodgers
4424 Webster St
Oakland, CA 94609-2131, USA

Ladd, Alana
1420 Moraga Dr
Los Angeles, CA 90049-1648, USA

Ladd, Cheryl (Actor)
c/o Jay Schwartz *JDS Public Relations*
3151 Cahuenga Blvd W Ste 220
Los Angeles, CA 90068-1749, USA

Ladd, David (Actor)
9212 Hazen Dr
Beverly Hills, CA 90210-1827, USA

Ladd, Diane (Actor)
3860 Grand Ave
Ojai, CA 93023-8350, USA

Ladd, Ernie (Football Player)
San Diego Chargers
106 Jackson St
Franklin, LA 70538-5431, USA

Ladd, Jordan (Actor)
c/o Staff Member *Jeff Morrone
Management*
9350 Wilshire Blvd Ste 224
Beverly Hills, CA 90212-3204, USA

Ladd, Margaret (Actor)
444 21st St
Santa Monica, CA 90402-2436, USA

Ladd, Pete (Baseball Player)
Houston Astros
239 Town Farm Rd
New Gloucester, ME 04260-4438, USA

Ladd Jr, Alan
706 N Arden Dr
Beverly Hills, CA 90210-3512, USA

Laden, Nina B
6750 26th Ave NW
Seattle, WA 98117-5828, USA

Laderman, Exra (Composer)
Yale University
Music School
New Haven, CT 06520, USA

Ladewig, Marion (Bowler)
Ladies Professional Bowling Tour
7200 Harrison Ave # 7171
Rockford, IL 61112-1017, USA

Ladin, Eric (Actor)
c/o Joanne Halpern *Halpern & Associates*
12304 Santa Monica Blvd Ste 104
Los Angeles, CA 90025-2586, USA

Ladygo, Pete (Football Player)
Pittsburgh Steelers
708 Summit Ave # 1
Hagerstown, MD 21740-6359, USA

Laettner, Christian (Basketball Player)
c/o Staff Member *Washington Wizards*
601 F St NW
Mci Center
Washington, DC 20004-1605, USA

Laettnew, Christian D (Basketball Player)
1225 Church Rd
Angola, NY 14006-8831, USA

Lafata, Joe (Baseball Player)
New York Giants
25284 Saint Christopher St
Harrison Township, MI 48045-3725, USA

Laffer, Arthur (Doctor)
5375 Exec Sq #330
La Jolla, CA 92037, USA

Laffer, Arthur B (Economist)
24255 Pacific Coast Hwy
Malibu, CA 90263-3999, USA

Lafferty, James (Actor)
c/o Eric Nelson *Jaymes & Company*
12444 Ventura Blvd Ste 103
Studio City, CA 91604-2409, USA

Laffite, Jacques
Technopole de la Nievre
Magny Cours F-58470, FRANCE

LaFleur, Art (Actor)
c/o Joel King *Pakula/King & Associates*
9229 W Sunset Blvd Ste 315
Los Angeles, CA 90069-3403, USA

Lafleur, David (Football Player)
Dallas Cowboys
3900 Thompson Rd
Sulphur, LA 70665-8901, USA

Lafleur, Greg (Football Player)
St Louis Cardinals
2911 Rene Beauregard Ave
Baton Rouge, LA 70820-5712, USA

Lafleur, Guy D (Hockey Player)
14 Place du Molin
L'Ile-Bizard, PQ H9E 1N2, CANADA

Lafley, Alan G (Business Person)
Procter & Gamble Co
1 Procter And Gamble Plz
Cincinnati, OH 45202-3393, USA

LaFontaine, Don (Actor, Producer, Writer)
c/o Staff Member *Tisherman Agency Inc*
6767 Forest Lawn Dr Ste 101
Los Angeles, CA 90068-1050, USA

Lafontaine, Oskar (Government Official)
Landtag Saarland
Postfach 101833
Saarbrucken 66018, GERMANY

LaFontaine, Patrick (Pat) (Hockey Player)
3 Beach Dr
Lloyd Harbor, NY 11743-9766, USA

LaFosse, Robert (Choreographer)
New York City Ballet
Lincoln Center Plaza
New York, NY 10023, USA

Lafrancois, Roger (Baseball Player)
Boston Red Sox
64 Aspinook St
Jewett City, CT 06351-1802, USA

LaFrentz, Raef (Basketball Player)
22683 SW 96th Dr
Tualatin, OR 97062-7399, USA

Lafton, James D (Football Player)
15487 Mesquite Tree Trl
Poway, CA 92064-2286, USA

Laga, Mike (Baseball Player)
Detroit Tigers
838 Route 6
Shohola, PA 18458-3507, USA

Lagarde, Tom (Basketball Player)
135 Rivington St
New York, NY 10002-2415, USA

Lagasse, Emeril (Chef, Television Host)
c/o Staff Member *Food Network, The*
75 9th Ave
New York, NY 10011-7006, USA

Lagattuta, Bill (Correspondent)
CBS-TV
7800 Beverly Blvd
News Dept
Los Angeles, CA 90036-2112, USA

Lageman, Jeff (Football Player)
New York Jets
2907 Forest Cir
Jacksonville, FL 32257-5617, USA

Lagerberg, Bengt (Musician)
Motor SE
Gotabergs Gatan 2
Gothenburg 400 14, SWEDEN

Lagerfeld, Karl (Designer, Fashion
Designer)
14 Blvd de la Madeleine
Paris 75008, FRANCE

Lagerfelt, Caroline (Actor)
8730 W Sunset Blvd Ste 480
Los Angeles, CA 90069-2277, USA

Laghi, Pio Cardinal (Religious Leader)
Catholic Education Congregation
Piazza Pio XII 3
Rome 00193, ITALY

Lago, David (Actor)
c/o Staff Member *Young and the Restless,
The*
7800 Beverly Blvd Ste 3305
Los Angeles, CA 90036-2112, USA

Lagod, Chet (Football Player)
New York Giants
7016 Rocky Trl
Chattanooga, TN 37421-5213, USA

Lagoo, Shreeram (Actor, Bollywood)
3 Gold Mist 36 Carter Road
Bandra
Bombay, MS 400 050, INDIA

Lagos, Richard (President)
President's Office
Palacio de la Monedo
Santiago, CHILE

Lagrand, Morris (Football Player)
Kansas City Chiefs
4419 Ellenwood Ave
Saint Louis, MO 63116-1521, USA

Lagrossa, Stephanie (Reality TV Star)
c/o Jamie Lopez
3400 Beacon Ave S
The Actors Group
Seattle, WA 98144-6702, USA

Lagrow, Lerrin (Baseball Player)
Detroit Tigers
12271 E Turquoise Ave
Scottsdale, AZ 85259-5105, USA

Laguardia, Ernesto (Actor)
c/o Gabriel Blanco *Gabriel Blanco
Iglesias (Mexico)*
Rio Balsas 35-32
Colonia Cuauhtemoc
DF 06500, MEXICO

Laguna, Frederica de (Misc)
10 S Bryn Mawr Ave
Quadrangle
Bryn Mawr, PA 19010-3213, USA

Laguna, Ismael (Boxer)
Panama Zona 6
Entrega General
PANAMA

LaHaye, Tim (Writer)
Tyndale House Publishers
PO Box 80
351 Executive Dr
Wheaton, IL 60189-0080, USA

Lahbib, Simone (Actor)
c/o Staff Member *Ken McReddie Ltd*
Paurelle House
91 Regent St
London W1R7TB, UNITED KINGDOM
(UK)

Lahey, Pat (Football Player)
Chicago Rockets
308 Happ Rd Apt 406
Northfield, IL 60093-3462, USA

Lahiri, Jhumpa (Writer)
Houghton Mifflin
222 Berkeley St # 700
Boston, MA 02116-3748, USA

Lahood, Mike (Football Player)
Los Angeles Rams
1416 N Autumn Ln
Peoria, IL 61604-4605, USA

Lahoud, Joe (Baseball Player)
Boston Red Sox
90 Tinker Hill Rd
New Preston Marble Dale,
CT 06777-1415, USA

Lahould, Emile (President)
Presidential Palace
Baabda
Beirut, LEBANON

Lahti, Christine (Actor, Director)
237 S Burlingame Ave
Los Angeles, CA 90049-3702, USA

Lahti, Jeff (Baseball Player)
St Louis Cardinals
4632 Tyler Dr
Hood River, OR 97031-9742, USA

Lai, Francis (Composer)
23 Rue Franklin
Paris 75016, FRANCE

Laidlaw, Scott (Football Player)
Dallas Cowboys
28 Colonel Winstead Dr
Brentwood, TN 37027-8936, USA

Lail, Leah (Actor)
c/o Staff Member *Diverse Talent Group*
1875 Century Park E Ste 2250
Los Angeles, CA 90067-2563, USA

Laimbeer, Bill (Basketball Player)
4310 S Bay Dr
Orchard Lake, MI 48323-1500, USA

Laine, Cleo (Musician)
Acker's Int'l Jazz
53 Cambridge Mansions
London SW11 4RX, UNITED KINGDOM
(UK)

Laine, Dame Cleo
The Old Rectory Wavendon
Milton Keynes, ENGLAND MK17 8LT,
UNITED KINGDOM (UK)

Laine, Sarah (Actor)
c/o Eric Black *Anonymous Content (CA)*
3532 Hayden Ave
Culver City, CA 90232-2413, USA

Laingen, L Bruce (Diplomat)
5627 Old Chester Rd
Bethesda, MD 20814-1035, USA

Laird, Bruce (Football Player)
Baltimore Colts
20 Stone Ridge Ct
Baltimore, MD 21239-1339, USA

Laird, Gerald (Baseball Player)
Texas Rangers
8891 Mac Alpine Rd
Garden Grove, CA 92841-2321, USA

Laird, Melvin R (Business Person,
Secretary)
1730 Rhode Island Ave NW Ste 406
Washington, DC 20036-3134, USA

Laird, Peter (Cartoonist)
Teenage Mutant Ninja Turtles
PO Box 417
Haydenville, MA 01039-0417, USA

Laird, Ron
4706 Diane Dr
Ashtabula, OH 44004-4636, USA

Laitman, Jeffrey (Misc)
Mount Sinai Medical Center
Anatomy Dept
1 Lavy Place
New York, NY 10029, USA

LaJoie, Randy (Race Car Driver)
Phoenix Racing
195 Jones Rd
Spartanburg, SC 29307-5448, USA

Lajole, Bill (Baseball Player)
Detroit Tigers
456 Yacht Harbor Dr
Osprey, FL 34229-9744, USA

Lake, Carnell A (Football Player)
Pittsburgh Steelers
PO Box 55048
Irvine, CA 92619-5048, USA

Lake, Don (Actor, Writer)
c/o Gayle Divine *Divine Management*
3822 Latrobe St
Los Angeles, CA 90031-1446, USA

Lake, Greg (Musician)
Asia
9 Hillgate St
London W8 7SP, UNITED KINGDOM
(UK)

Lake, Oliver E (Musician)
DL Media
PO Box 2728
Bala Cynwyd, PA 19004-6728, USA

Lake, Ricki (Actor, Talk Show Host)
c/o Joan Hyler *Hyler Management*
3000 Olympic Blvd Bldg 5 Ste 2250
Santa Monica, CA 90404-5073, USA

Lake, Sanoe (Actor)
c/o Staff Member *Jet Set Talent Agency*
2160 Alzanida De La Playa
La Jolla, CA 92037, USA

Lake, Steve (Baseball Player)
Chicago Cubs
7402 N 177th Ave
Waddell, AZ 85355-9320, USA

Laker, Fredrick A (Business Person)
Princess Tower West Sunrise
Box F207 Freeport
Grand Bahamas, BAHAMAS

Laker, Jim (Cricketer)
Oak End
9 Portlinscale Road Putney
London SW15, UNITED KINGDOM (UK)

Laker, Tim (Baseball Player)
Montreal Expos
673 Azure Hills Dr
Simi Valley, CA 93065-5518, USA

Lakes, Gary (Opera Singer)
I C M Artists
40 W 57th St
New York, NY 10019-4001, USA

Lakes, Roland (Football Player)
San Francisco 49ers
2334 20th St
San Pablo, CA 94806-3508, USA

Lakin, Christine (Actor)
c/o Amy Abell *Innovative Artists (LA)*
1505 10th St
Santa Monica, CA 90401-2805, USA

Lakner, Yehoshua (Composer)
Postfach 7851
Luceme 7 6000, SWITZERLAND

Lakoue, Enoch Devant (Prime Minister)
Prime Minister's Office
Bangui, CENTRAL AFRICAN REPUBLIC

Lalaine (Actor)
c/o Beverly Strong *Anonymous Content
(CA)*
9350 Wilshire Blvd Ste 224
Beverly Hills, CA 90212-3204, USA

LaLanne, Jack (Misc)
c/o Staff Member *William Morris Agency
(WMA-LA)*
1 William Morris Pl
Beverly Hills, CA 90212-4261, USA

Laliberte, Guy (Misc)
Cirque de Soleil
8400 2nd Ave
Montreal, PQ H1Z 4M6, CANADA

Laliberte-Bourque, Andree (Director)
Musee du Quebec
1 Ave Wolfe-Montcalm
Quebec, PQ G1R 5H3, CANADA

Lalime, Patrick (Hockey Player)
Saint Louis Blues
1401 Clark Ave
Sawis Center
Saint Louis, MO 63103-2700, USA

Lalitha, Devi (Actor, Bollywood)
23 Karaneeswar Koil Street
Saidapet
Chennai, TN 600015, INDIA

Lall, Leah (Actor)
Writers & Artists
360 N Crescent Dr Bldg North
Beverly Hills, CA 90210-6818, USA

Lally, Bob (Football Player)
Green Bay Packers
18 Cartwright Dr
Princeton Junction, NJ 08550-1928, USA

Lalonde, Donny
2554 Lincoln Blvd # 729
Venice, CA 90291-5082, USA

Lalonde, Larry (Musician)
Figurehead Mgmt
3470 19th St
San Francisco, CA 94110-1740, USA

Lama, Dalai (Nobel Prize Laureate,
Religious Leader)
Office of His Holiness the Dalai Lama
Thekchen Choeling
PO McLeod Ganj
Himachai, Pradesh, INDIA

Lamabe, Jack (Baseball Player)
Pittsburgh Pirates
16224 Antietam Ave
Baton Rouge, LA 70817-3148, USA

Lamacchia, Al (Baseball Player)
St Louis Browns
13515 Vista Bonita
San Antonio, TX 78216-2203, USA

Lamar, Dwight (Bo) (Basketball Player)
103 Claire St
Lafayette, LA 70507-4803, USA

LaMarr, Phil (Actor, Comedian)
c/o Staff Member *Sanders/Armstrong
Management*
2120 Colorado Ave Ste 120
Santa Monica, CA 90404-3561, USA

Lamas, A J (Actor)
c/o Ryan Daly *Kazarian/Spencer & Assoc
(LA)*
11969 Ventura Blvd
Box 7409 Fl 3
Studio City, CA 91604-2630, USA

Lamas, Lorenzo (Actor)
c/o David Shapira *David Shapira &
Associates*
193 N Robertson Blvd
Beverly Hills, CA 90211-2103, USA

Lamb, Allan J (Cricketer)
Lamb Assoc
4 Saint Giles St
#400
Northampton NN1 1JB, UNITED
KINGDOM (UK)

Lamb, Brad (Football Player)
Buffalo Bills
6460 Chase Dr
Mentor, OH 44060-3606, USA

Lamb, David (Baseball Player)
Tampa Bay Devil Rays
821 Jensen St
Livermore, CA 94550-3630, USA

Lamb, Dennis (Diplomat)
19 Rue de Franqueville
Paris 75016, FRANCE

Lamb, John (Baseball Player)
Pittsburgh Pirates
Sharon Valley Road
Sharon, CT 06069, USA

Lamb, Ray (Baseball Player)
Los Angeles Dodgers
3 Corte Tallista
San Clemente, CA 92673-6863, USA

Lamb Jr, Willis E (Nobel Prize Laureate)
315 Red Rock Dr
Sedona, AZ 86351-9534, USA

Lamberg, Adam (Actor)
c/o Stephanie Davis *3 Arts Entertainment
Inc*
9460 Wilshire Blvd Fl 7
Beverly Hills, CA 90212-2713, USA

Lambert, Christophe (Actor)
9 Ave Trempley
C/Lui
Geneva 1209, SWITZERLAND

Lambert, Christopher (Actor, Producer,
Writer)
c/o Gerry Harrington *Brillstein-Grey
Entertainment*
9150 Wilshire Blvd Ste 350
Beverly Hills, CA 90212-3453, USA

Lambert, Dion (Football Player)
New England Patriots
11157 Sunburst St
Lake View Terrace, CA 91342-6628, USA

Lambert, Frank (Football Player)
Pittsburgh Steelers
9009 Lyndon Lakes Pl
Louisville, KY 40242-4538, USA

Lambert, Jerry
PO Box 25371
Charlotte, NC 28229-5371, USA

Lambert, John H (Jack) (Football Player)
Pittsburgh Steelers
318 Gaiser Rd
Worthington, PA 16262-4810, USA

Lambert, L W
RR 1
Olin, NC 28860, USA

Lambert, Mary M (Director)
International Creative Mgmt
8942 Wilshire Blvd # 219
Beverly Hills, CA 90211-1908, USA

Lambert, Phyllis (Architect)
Centre d'Architecture
1920 Rue Baile
Montreal, PQ H3H 2S6, CANADA

Lambert, Sheila (Basketball Player)
Charlotte Sting
333 E Trade St
Charlotte, NC 28202-2331, USA

Lamberti, Pasquale (Football Player)
New York Titans
8 Wellington Ave
Everett, MA 02149-1818, USA

Lambiel, Stephane (Figure Skater)
c/o Staff Member *Champions on Ice*
3500 W 80th St
Tom Collins Enterprises Inc
Minneapolis, MN 55431-1068, USA

Lambro, Phillip (Composer)
Trigram Music
1888 Century Park E # 10
Los Angeles, CA 90067-1702, USA

Lambros, Andy
9310 Topanga Canyon Blvd # 125
Chatsworth, CA 91311-5713, USA

Lambsdorff, Otto (Government Official)
Strasschensweg 7
Bon 53113, GERMANY

Lamelin, Stephanie (Actor)
c/o Staff Member *Writers and Artists Group Intl (LA)*
8383 Wilshire Blvd Ste 550
Beverly Hills, CA 90211-2417, USA

Lamm, Julie
PO Box B
Aspen, CO 81612-7402, USA

Lamm, Richard D (Ex-Governor, Governor)
University of Denver
Public Policy Center
Denver, CO 80208-0001, USA

Lamm, Robert (Musician)
Air Tight Mgmt
115 West Rd
Winchester Center, CT 06098-2323, USA

Lammers, Esmee (Director, Writer)
Features Creative Mgmt
Entrepotdok 76A
Amsterdam, AD 101, THE NETHERLANDS

Lammons, Pete (Football Player)
New York Jets
5006 E Fallen Bough Dr
Houston, TX 77041-7887, USA

Lamonica, Darryl (Football Player)
8796 N 6th St
Fresno, CA 93720-1711, USA

Lamonica, Roberto de (Artist)
Rua Anibal de Mendanca 180
AP 202
Rio de Janeiro, RJ ZC-37, BRAZIL

Lamont, Gene W (Baseball Player)
Detroit Tigers
5194 Siesta Woods Dr
Sarasota, FL 34242-1457, USA

Lamont, Norman S H (Government Official)
Balli Group PLC
5 Stanhope Gate
London W1Y 5LA, UNITED KINGDOM (UK)

Lamontagne, Donald A (General)
Commander
Air University
Maxwell Air Force Base, AL 36112, USA

LaMontagne, Ray (Musician)
c/o Staff Member *Paradigm (Monterey)*
509 Hartnell St
Monterey, CA 93940-2825, USA

LaMorte, Robia (Actor)
c/o Rob D'Avola *Identity Talent Agency (ID)*
9107 Wilshire Blvd Ste 450
Beverly Hills, CA 90210-5535, USA

LaMotta, Jake (Boxer)
400 E 57th St
New York, NY 10022-3019, USA

LaMotta, Vikki (Model)
PO Box 152
Deerfield Beach, FL 33443-0152, USA

Lamoureux, Robert
29 Bd. d'Aulteuil
Bologne 92100, FRANCE

Lamp, Dennis (Baseball Player)
Chicago Cubs
22751 El Prado Apt 4303
Rancho Santa Margarita, CA 92688-3829, USA

Lamp, Jeff (Basketball Player)
4971 Credit River Dr
Savage, MN 55378-4610, USA

Lampa, Rachael
25 Music Sq W
Nashville, TN 37203-3205, USA

Lampard, Frank (Soccer Player)
Chelsea Football Club
Stamford Bridge
Fulham Road
London SW6 1HS, UNITED KINGDOM (UK)

Lampard, Keith (Baseball Player)
Houston Astros
842 NE 74th Ave
Portland, OR 97213-6233, USA

Lamparski, Richard (Writer)
216 N Milpas St Apt G
Santa Barbara, CA 93103-3241, USA

Lampert, Edward S (Business Person)
ESL Investments Inc
200 Greenwich Ave Ste 3
Greenwich, CT 06830-2506, USA

Lampert, Zohra (Actor)
Don Buchwald
6500 Wilshire Blvd Ste 2200
Los Angeles, CA 90048-4942, USA

Lamphear, Dan (Football Player)
Houston Oilers
669 Bent Ridge Ln
Barrington, IL 60010-6604, USA

Lampkin, Tom (Baseball Player)
Cleveland Indians
3810 SE 153rd Ct
Vancouver, WA 98683-5313, USA

Lampley, Jim (Sportscaster)
3325 Caminito Daniella
Del Mar, CA 92014-4155, USA

Lamplugh, Ian (Baseball Player)
1830 Fairburn Dr
Victoria, BC V8N 1P9, CANADA

Lampton, Michael (Astronaut)
University of California
Space Science Laboratory
Berkeley, CA 94720-0001, USA

Lanbros, Andy
9040 Topanga Canyon Blvd # 200
West Hills, CA 91304-1435, USA

Lancaster, Les (Baseball Player)
Chicago Cubs
PO Box 22012
Mesa, AZ 85277-2012, USA

Lancaster, Penny (Actor)
c/o Staff Member *Special Artists Agency*
9465 Wilshire Blvd Ste 890
Beverly Hills, CA 90212-2607, USA

Lancaster, Sarah (Actor)
c/o Amanda Glazer *Kohner Agency, The*
9300 Wilshire Blvd Ste 555
Beverly Hills, CA 90212-3211, USA

Lance, Bert
PO Box 637
Calhoun, GA 30703-0637, USA

Lance, Dirk (Musician)
ArtistDirect
1601 Cloverfield Blvd # 400
Santa Monica, CA 90404-4082, USA

Lance, Gary (Baseball Player)
Kansas City Royals
212 Sunset Cir
Prosperity, SC 29127-8426, USA

Lancelotti, Rick (Baseball Player)
San Diego Padres
5190 Thompson Rd
Clarence, NY 14031-1127, USA

Land, Tammi
c/o Staff Member *Osbrink Talent Agency*
4343 Lankershim Blvd # 100
North Hollywood, CA 91602-2705, USA

Landaker, Dave (Baseball Player)
Topps
3593 Buffum St
Simi Valley, CA 93063-3215, USA

Landau, Irvin (Editor)
Consumer Reports Magazine
101 Truman Ave
Editorial Dept
Yonkers, NY 10703-1044, USA

Landau, Jacob (Artist)
2 Pine Dr
Roosevelt, NJ 08555, USA

Landau, Juliet (Actor)
c/o David Sweeney *Sweeney Management*
8755 Lookout Mountain Ave
Los Angeles, CA 90046-1861, USA

Landau, Martin (Actor)
c/o Harry Gold *TalentWorks (LA)*
3500 W Olive Ave Ste 1400
Burbank, CA 91505-5512, USA

Landeau, Aleksia (Actor)
c/o Melisa Spamer *Domain*
4526 Wilshire Blvd
Los Angeles, CA 90010-3801, USA

Landecker, John Records
MAGIC 104.3 WJMK
180 N Stetson Ave Ste 900
Prudential 2 Building
Chicago, IL 60601-6728, USA

Lander, Benjamin (Educator)
American University
President's Office
Washington, DC 20016, USA

Lander, David L (Actor)
c/o Staff Member *Arlene Thornton & Associates*
12711 Ventura Blvd Ste 490
Studio City, CA 91604-2477, USA

Landers, Andy (Coach)
University of Georgia
Athletic Dept
Athens, GA 30602, USA

Landers, Audrey (Actor, Musician)
4048 Las Palmas Way
Sarasota, FL 34238-4530, USA

Landers, Judy (Actor)
Media Artists Group
6300 Wilshire Blvd Ste 1470
Los Angeles, CA 90048-5200, USA

Landers, Robert (Golfer)
PO Box 497
Azle, TX 76098-0497, USA

Landes, David S (Historian)
24 Highland St
Cambridge, MA 02138-2210, USA

Landes, Michael
10100 Santa Monica Blvd Ste 2500
Los Angeles, CA 90067-4116, USA

Landestoy, Rafael (Baseball Player)
Los Angeles Dodgers
3121 SW 140th Ave
Miami, FL 33175-6504, USA

Landeta, Sean (Football Player)
New York Giants
PO Box 422
Manhasset, NY 11030-0422, USA

Landey, Nina (Actor)
c/o Staff Member *Bauman Redanty & Shaul Agency*
5757 Wilshire Blvd Ste 473
Los Angeles, CA 90036-3632, USA

Landgrebe, Ludrun
Goethstr. 17
Munich D-80336, GERMANY

Landi, Sal (Actor)
c/o Craig Mobbs *AKA Talent Agency*
6310 San Vicente Blvd Ste 200
Los Angeles, CA 90048-5488, USA

Landis, Bill (Baseball Player)
Kansas City A's
625 E Sycamore Dr
Hanford, CA 93230, USA

Landis, Jim (Baseball Player)
Chicago White Sox
203 Alchemy Way
Napa, CA 94558-7214, USA

Landis, John D (Director)
c/o Aaron Kaplan *Kaplan/Perrone Entertainment*
10202 Washington Blvd
Astaire Bldg, Suite #3003
Culver City, CA 90232-3119, USA

Lando, Joe (Actor)
c/o Staff Member *Metropolitan*
4500 Wilshire Blvd Fl 2
Los Angeles, CA 90010-3858, USA

Landon, Howard C R (Writer)
Chateau de Foncoussieres
Rabastens
Tarn 81800, FRANCE

Landon, Jennifer (Actor)
c/o Jamie Freed *The Collective*
8530 Wilshire Blvd Fl 5
Beverly Hills, CA 90211-3102, USA

Landon, Tina (Actor, Choreographer)
c/o Staff Member *McDonald/Selznick Assoc (MSA)*
1611A N El Centro Ave
Hollywood, CA 90028, USA

Landon Jr, Michael (Actor, Director, Producer, Writer)
c/o Mark Lichtman *Shapiro-Lichtman Talent Agency*
1333 Beverly Green Dr
Los Angeles, CA 90035-1018, USA

Landreaux, Ken (Baseball Player)
California Angeles
608 Leonard St
Montebello, CA 90640-1514, USA

Landres, Paul
5343 Amestoy Ave
Encino, CA 91316-2613, USA

Landreth, Larry (Baseball Player)
Montreal Expos
116 W 66th St Apt 39H
Stratford, ON N5A 2W8, CANADA

Landrieu, Mary (Senator)
7523 N Jefferson Place Cir
Baton Rouge, LA 70809-7644, USA

Landrieu, Moon (Secretary)
4301 S Prieur St
New Orleans, LA 70125-5125, USA

Landrith, Hobie (Baseball Player)
Cincinnati Reds
1462 Nome Ct
Sunnyvale, CA 94087-4264, USA

Landrum, Bill (Baseball Player)
Cincinnati Reds
715 Sharpe Rd
Columbia, SC 29203-9347, USA

Landrum, Ced (Baseball Player)
Chicago Cubs
2425 Hillview Dr
Fort Worth, TX 76119-2722, USA

Landrum, Joe (Baseball Player)
Brooklyn Dodgers
715 Sharpe Rd
Columbia, SC 29203-9347, USA

Landrum, Mike (Football Player)
Atlanta Falcons
88 Raybourn Rd
Sumrall, MS 39482-3926, USA

Landrum, Tito (Baseball Player)
St Louis Cardinals
160 W 66th St Apt 39H
New York, NY 10023-6564, USA

Landry, Ali (Actor, Model)
c/o Paul Santana *Agency for the Performing Arts (APA-LA)*
405 S Beverly Dr
Beverly Hills, CA 90212-4416, USA

Landry, Gregory P (Greg) (Coach, Football Coach, Football Player)
Detroit Lions
133 Melanie Ln
Troy, MI 48098-1707, USA

Landsburg, Valerie (Actor)
22745 Chamera Ln
Topanga, CA 90290-4006, USA

Landsee, Robert (Football Player)
Philadelphia Eagles
PO Box 628128
Middleton, WI 53562-8128, USA

Landy, Bernard (Government Official)
Government du Quebec
885 Grand Allee Est
Quebec, PQ GLA 1A2, CANADA

Landzaat, Andre
7500 Devista Dr
Los Angeles, CA 90046-1712, USA

Lane, Abbe (Actor, Musician)
444 N Faring Rd
Los Angeles, CA 90077-3519, USA

Lane, Barry (Golfer)
I M G
1360 E 9th St Ste 100
Cleveland, OH 44114-1730, USA

Lane, Cristy (Musician)
PO Box 654
Madison, TN 37116-0654, USA

Lane, Diane (Actor)
c/o Joan Hyler *Hyler Management*
3000 Olympic Blvd Bldg 5 Ste 2250
Santa Monica, CA 90404-5073, USA

Lane, Dick (Baseball Player)
Chicago White Sox
2717 Legend Dr
Las Vegas, NV 89134-8829, USA

Lane, Garcia (Football Player)
Kansas City Chiefs
154 E Boston Ave
Youngstown, OH 44507-1743, USA

Lane, John R (Jack) (Misc)
San Francisco Museum of Modem Art
151 3rd St
San Francisco, CA 94103-3107, USA

Lane, Johnny
5048 Casa Dr
Tarzana, CA 91356-4422, USA

Lane, Kenneth Jay (Designer, Fashion Designer)
Kenneth Jay Lane Inc
20 W 37th St Fl 9
New York, NY 10018-7367, USA

Lane, Lilas (Actor)
c/o Peter Kluge *Impact Artists Group LLC*
244 N California St
Burbank, CA 91505-3505, USA

Lane, MacArthur (Football Player)
St Louis Cardinals
3238 Knowland Ave
Oakland, CA 94619-2630, USA

Lane, Malcolm D (Misc)
5607 Roxbuy Place
Baltimore, MD 21209, USA

Lane, Marv (Baseball Player)
Detroit Tigers
40164 Gulliver Dr
Sterling Heights, MI 48310-1729, USA

Lane, Matthew (Golfer)
Links Mmg
5068 W Plano Pkwy Ste 256
Plano, TX 75093-4441, USA

Lane, Max (Football Player)
New England Patriots
79 Bond St
Gloucester, MA 01930-4925, USA

Lane, Melvin B (Publisher)
99 Tallwood Ct
Menlo Park, CA 94027-6431, USA

Lane, Mike (Cartoonist)
Baltimore Sun
501 N Calvert St
Editorial Dept
Baltimore, MD 21202-3604, USA

Lane, Nathan (Actor, Musician)
Creative Artists Agency
9830 Wilshire Blvd
Beverly Hills, CA 90212-1804, USA

Lane, Skip (Football Player)
New York Jets
76 Hillspoint Rd
Allied Commercial Property Group
Westport, CT 06880-5111, USA

Lane Jr, Lawrence W (Diplomat, Publisher)
3000 Sand Hill Rd # 215
Menlo Park, CA 94025-7113, USA

Lane of St Ippollitts, Geoffrey D (Judge)
Royal Courts of Justice
Strand
London WC2A 2LL, UNITED KINGDOM (UK)

Lanegan, Mark (Musician)
Helter Skelter Plaza
535 Kings Road
London SW1O 0S, UNITED KINGDOM (UK)

Laneuville, Eric (Actor)
5138 W Slauson Ave
Los Angeles, CA 90056-1641, USA

Laney, James T (Diplomat, Educator)
2015 Grand Prix Dr NE
Atlanta, GA 30345-3931, USA

Lang, Belinda (Actor)
Ken McReddie
91 Regent St
London W1R 7TB, UNITED KINGDOM (UK)

Lang, Chip (Baseball Player)
Montreal Expos
132 Westminster Dr
Pittsburgh, PA 15229-3165, USA

Lang, Don (Baseball Player)
Cincinnati Reds
150 Shelley Cir
Ventura, CA 93003-5522, USA

Lang, Ed (Photographer)
Elysium Growth Press
16255 Ventura Blvd Ste 515
Encino, CA 91436-2310, USA

Lang, Gene (Football Player)
Denver Broncos
11526 Azalea Trce
Gulfport, MS 39503-8398, USA

Lang, George C (War Hero)
3786 Clark St
Seaford, NY 11783-2101, USA

Lang, Helmut (Designer, Fashion Designer)
Michele Morgan
184 Rue Saint-Maur
Paris 75010, FRANCE

Lang, Jack (Government Official)
Mairie
Blois 41000, FRANCE

Lang, Jack (Writer)
Jack Lang Assoc
4 Barry Dr
East Northport, NY 11731-1307, USA

Lang, Jonny (Musician)
Blue Sky Artists
761 Washington Ave N
Minneapolis, MN 55401-1101, USA

Lang, June (Actor)
12756 Kahlenberg Ln
North Hollywood, CA 91607-2919, USA

Lang, Katherine Kelly (Actor, Model)
The Bold and The Beautiful'
7800 Beverly Blvd Ste 3371
Bell-Phillip Television Productions Inc
Los Angeles, CA 90036-2112, USA

Lang, KD (Actor, Musician)
c/o Staff Member *Direct Management Group*
947 N La Cienega Blvd Ste G
Los Angeles, CA 90069-4700, USA

Lang, Kenard (Football Player)
Washington Redskins
1781 Oakbrook Dr
Longwood, FL 32779-3168, USA

Lang, Le-Lo (Football Player)
Denver Broncos
18925 E Progress Ln
Centennial, CO 80015-4862, USA

Lang, Margie (Baseball Player)
44830 N Zorrillo Dr
New River, AZ 85087-7170, USA

Lang, Pearl (Choreographer, Dancer)
382 Central Park W
New York, NY 10025-6054, USA

Lang, Stephen (Actor)
c/o Susan Calogerakis *Thruline Entertainment*
9250 Wilshire Blvd Ground Fl
Beverly Hills, CA 90210, USA

Langbo, Arnold G (Business Person)
Kellogg Co
1 Kellogg Sq
PO Box 3599
Battle Creek, MI 49017-3517, USA

Langdon, Brooke
1180 S Beverly Dr Ste 608
Los Angeles, CA 90035-1158, USA

Langdon, Harry (Photographer)
PO Box 16816
Beverly Hills, CA 90209-2816, USA

Langdon, Michael
34 Arnham Ct. Grand Ave.
Hove E. Sussex, ENGLAND, UNITED KINGDOM (UK)

Langdon, Sue Ane (Actor)
24115 Long Valley Rd
Hidden Hills, CA 91302-1249, USA

Lange, Allison
3500 W Olive Ave Ste 1400
Burbank, CA 91505-5512, USA

Lange, Andre (Athlete)
BSD
An der Schiessstatte 4
Berchtesgaden 83471, GERMANY

Lange, Artie (Actor)
c/o Peter Principato *Principato/Young Management*
9665 Wilshire Blvd Ste 500
Beverly Hills, CA 90212-2312, USA

Lange, Bonnie
PO Box 3827
Beverly Hills, CA 90212-0827, USA

The Celebrity Black Book 2008

Lange, Detective Tom
12021 Wilshire Blvd # 846
Los Angeles, CA 90025-1206, USA

Lange, Dick (Baseball Player)
California Angels
39744 Salvatore Dr
Sterling Heights, MI 48313-5165, USA

Lange, Jessica (Actor)
c/o Staff Member *Creative Artists Agency LCC (CAA-LA)*
2000 Avenue Of The Stars
Los Angeles, CA 90067-4700, USA

Lange, Niklaus
4526 Wilshire Blvd
Los Angeles, CA 90010-3801, USA

Lange, Ted (Actor)
c/o Staff Member *Schiowitz/Clay/Ankrum & Ross FKA Talent Syndicate, The*
1680 Vine St Ste 614
Los Angeles, CA 90028-8833, USA

Lange, Thomas (Athlete)
ratzeburger Ruderclub
Domhof 57
Ratzeburg 23909, GERMANY

Langehorne, Reggie (Football Player)
Cleveland Browns
12260 Smiths Neck Rd
Carrollton, VA 23314-3802, USA

Langella, Frank (Actor)
108 Sunlit Dr W
Santa Fe, NM 87508-9382, USA

Langen, Christoph (Athlete)
BC Onterhaching
Ottobrunner Str 16
Unterhaching 82008, GERMANY

Langencamp, Reather (Actor)
156 F St SE
Washington, DC 20003-2603, USA

Langenkamp, Heather (Actor)
c/o Harrison Cheung *Harrison Cheung & Associates*
11617 Natrona Dr
Austin, TX 78759-4123, USA

Langer, A J (Actor)
c/o Staff Member *McKeon-Valeo-Myones Management*
9100 Wilshire Blvd Ste 350W
Beverly Hills, CA 90212-3437, USA

Langer, Alois A (Inventor)
111 Saddlebrook Dr
Harrison City, PA 15636-1413, USA

Langer, Bernhard (Golfer)
1120 SW 21st Ln
Boca Raton, FL 33486-6722, USA

Langer, James J (Jim) (Football Player)
Miami Dolphins
14280 Wolfram St NW
Ramsey, MN 55303-4563, USA

Langer, James S (Physicist)
1130 Las Canoas Ln
Santa Barbara, CA 93105-2331, USA

Langer, Robert (Doctor)
Massachusetts Institute of Technology
Chem Engineer Dept
Cambridge, MA 02139, USA

Langer, Robert S (Engineer, Inventor)
Massachusetts Institute of Technology
Engineering Dept
Cambridge, MA 02139, USA

Langerhans, Ryan (Baseball Player)
Atlanta Braves
PO Box 1026
Round Rock, TX 78680-1026, USA

Langevin, Dave (Hockey Player)
1090 W Circle Ct
Saint Paul, MN 55118-4148, USA

Langevin, Jim (Politician)
Jim Langevin for Congress
181 Knight St Ste A
Warwick, RI 02886-1296, USA

Langford, Rick (Baseball Player)
Pittsburgh Pirates
8330 9th Avenue Ter NW
Bradenton, FL 34209-9678, USA

Langham, C Antonio (Football Player)
Cleveland Browns
PO Box 232
Town Creek, AL 35672-0232, USA

Langham, Franklin (Golfer)
PO Box 3428
Peachtree City, GA 30269-7428, USA

Langham, Michael (Director)
Julliard School
144 W 66th St
Drama Division
New York, NY 10023, USA

Langham, Wallace (Actor)
10264 Rochester Ave
Los Angeles, CA 90024-5331, USA

Langham, Wally (Actor)
c/o Josh Katz *United Talent Agency (UTA)*
9560 Wilshire Blvd Ste 500
Beverly Hills, CA 90212-2401, USA

Langley, H Desmond A (General, Governor)
Governor's Office
11 Langton Hill
Pembroke
Hamilton HM 13, BERMUDA

Langley, Roger (Skier)
Broad St
Barre, MA 01005, USA

Langlois, Lisa (Actor)
House of Representatives
211 S Beverly Dr Ste 208
Beverly Hills, CA 90212-3879, USA

Langlois, Paul (Musician)
Management Trust
219 Dufferin St
#309B
Toronto, ON M5K 3J1, CANADA

Langlois Jr, Albert (Hockey Player)
2473 Crest View Dr
Los Angeles, CA 90046-1406, USA

Langston, J William (Doctor)
Parkinson's Foundation
2444 Moorpark Ave
San Jose, CA 95128, USA

Langston, Mark E (Baseball Player)
Seattle Mariners
56 Golden Eagle
Irvine, CA 92603-0309, USA

Langston, Murray (Actor, Comedian)
Entertainment Alliance
PO Box 4734
Santa Rosa, CA 95402-4734, USA

Langton, Brooke (Actor)
c/o Staff Member *United Talent Agency (UTA)*
9560 Wilshire Blvd Ste 500
Beverly Hills, CA 90212-2401, USA

Langway, Rod C (Hockey Player)
3613 Brook Rd
Richmond, VA 23227-4529, USA

Lanier, Chris (Artist)
c/o Staff Member *Fantagraphics Books*
7563 Lake City Way NE
Seattle, WA 98115-4218, USA

Lanier, H Max (Baseball Player)
St Louis Cardinals
11250 SW 186th Cir
Dunnellon, FL 34432-4528, USA

Lanier, Hal (Baseball Player)
San Francisco Giants
3270 Countryside View Dr
Saint Cloud, FL 34772-7050, USA

Lanier, Harold C (Hal) (Misc)
19380 SW 90th Lane Rd
Dunnellon, FL 34432-2753, USA

Lanier, Rimp (Baseball Player)
Cleveland Indians
4515 E Frontenac Dr
Cleveland, OH 44128-5004, USA

Lanier, Willie E (Football Player)
Kansas City Chiefs
2911 E Brigstock Rd
Midlothian, VA 23113-3905, USA

Lanier Jr, Robert J (Bob) (Basketball Player, Coach)
National Basketball Assn
645 5th Ave
Teamup Program
New York, NY 10022-5986, USA

Lanker, Brian (Journalist)
1993 Kimberly Dr
Eugene, OR 97405-5849, USA

Lankford, Frank (Baseball Player)
Los Angeles Dodgers
104 Lakeview Ave NE
Atlanta, GA 30305-3725, USA

Lankford, Paul (Football Player)
Miami Dolphins
3838 Biggin Church Rd W
Jacksonville, FL 32224-7984, USA

Lankford, Ray (Baseball Player)
St Louis Cardinals
15 Terry Hill Ln
Saint Louis, MO 63131-2422, USA

Lanois, Daniel (Actor, Musician)
c/o Staff Member *Paradigm (Monterey)*
509 Hartnell St
Monterey, CA 93940-2825, USA

LanSala, James (Misc)
Amalgamated Transit Union
5025 Wisconsin Ave NW
Washington, DC 20016-4139, USA

Lansbury, Angela (Actor, Musician)
c/o Staff Member *Corymore Productions*
9171 Wilshire Blvd Ste 400
Beverly Hills, CA 90210-5516, USA

Lansbury, David (Actor)
Don Buchwald
6500 Wilshire Blvd Ste 2200
Los Angeles, CA 90048-4942, USA

Lansdale, Joe R
113 Timber Ridge Dr
Nacogdoches, TX 75961, USA

Lansdowne, J Fenwick (Artist)
941 Victoria Ave
Victoria, BC V8S 4N6, CANADA

Lansford, Alex (Football Player)
Philadelphia Eagles
PO Box 905
Lampasas, TX 76550-0007, USA

Lansford, Camey (Baseball Player)
California Angels
1701 Homestead Rd
Santa Clara, CA 95050-5257, USA

Lansford, Jody (Baseball Player)
San Diego Padres
5730 San Lorenzo Dr
San Jose, CA 95123-2967, USA

Lansford, Mike (Football Player)
Los Angeles Rams
6200 E Canyon Rim Rd Ste 205
Anaheim, CA 92807-4340, USA

Lansing, Mike (Baseball Player)
Montreal Expos
9691 Sun Meadow St
Highlands Ranch, CO 80129-6925, USA

Lansing, Sherry L (Producer)
10741 Levico Way
Los Angeles, CA 90077-1918, USA

Lanter, Matt (Actor)
c/o Faras Rabadi *Emerald Talent Group*
6464 W Sunset Blvd
Los Angeles, CA 90028-8001, USA

Lanvin, Bernard (Designer, Fashion Designer)
22 Rue du Faubourg Saint Honore
Paris 70008, FRANCE

Lanz, David (Musician)
c/o *Narada*
4650 N Port Washington Rd
Milwaukee, WI 53212-1077, USA

Lanza, Charles (Football Player)
Pittsburgh Steelers
19 Snowberry Ct
Cockeysville, MD 21030-1954, USA

Lanza, Suzanne
345 N Maple Dr Ste 397
Beverly Hills, CA 90210-3856, USA

Laoretti, Larry (Golfer)
712 Baytree Dr
Titusville, FL 32780-2310, USA

LaPaglia, Anthony (Actor)
c/o Julie Silverman-Yorn *The Firm*
9465 Wilshire Blvd Fl 6
Beverly Hills, CA 90212-2605, USA

LaPaglia, Jonathan
1505 10th St
Santa Monica, CA 90401-2805, USA

Lapaine, Daniel (Actor)
Envision Entertainment
409 Santa Monica Blvd
Santa Monica, CA 90401-2378, USA

Lapalme, Paul (Baseball Player)
Pittsburgh Pirates
167 Smith St
Leominster, MA 01453-2155, USA

Laperriere, J Jacques H (Coach, Hockey Player)
1983 Nice Chomedey Estate
Laval, PQ H7S 1G5, CANADA

Lapham, Bill (Football Player)
Philadelphia Eagles
136 S 52nd St
West Des Moines, IA 50265-2895, USA

Lapham, Dave (Football Player)
Cincinnati Bengals
8254 Sunfish Ln
Maineville, OH 45039-8978, USA

Lapham, Lewis H (Editor)
Harper's Magazine
666 Broadway Fl 11
Editorial Dept
New York, NY 10012-2317, USA

Lapidus, Alan (Architect)
Lapidus Assoc
43 W 61st St
New York, NY 10023-7607, USA

Lapidus, Edmond (Ted) (Designer, Fashion Designer)
66 Blvd Maurice-Barres
Neuilly-sur-Seine 92200, FRANCE

Lapierre, Dominique (Historian)
Les Bignoles
Ramatuelle 83350, FRANCE

Lapine, James E (Director, Writer)
c/o George Lane *Creative Artists Agency (CAA-NY)*
162 5th Ave Fl 6
New York, NY 10010-6047, USA

Lapira, Liza (Actor)
c/o Tom Harrison *Diverse Talent Group*
1875 Century Park E Ste 2250
Los Angeles, CA 90067-2563, USA

Lapka, Myron (Football Player)
New York Giants
4129 Gertrude St
Simi Valley, CA 93063-2925, USA

Lapka, Ted (Football Player)
Washington Redskins
20337 Hellenic Dr
Olympia Fields, IL 60461-1419, USA

LaPlaca, Alison (Actor)
1614 Argyle Ave
Hollywood, CA 90028-6408, USA

LaPlanche, Rosemary (Actor)
13914 Hartsook St
Sherman Oaks, CA 91423-1210, USA

LaPlante, Lynda (Writer)
Random House
1745 Broadway # B1
New York, NY 10019-4305, USA

Lapli, John (General)
Governor General's House
Box 252
Honiara, GUADACANAL SOLOMON ISLANDS

Lapoint, Dave (Baseball Player)
Milwaukee Brewers
PO Box 348
Glens Falls, NY 12801-0348, USA

Lapointe, Guy
4568 E. des Bousquets
Augustin, PQ 6A3 1C4, CANADA

Laport, Osvaldo (Actor)
c/o Staff Member *Telefe - Argentina*
Pavon 2444 (C1248AAT)
Buenos Aires, ARGENTINA

LaPorte, Danny (Race Car Driver)
949 Via Del Monte
Palos Verdes Estates, CA 90274-1615, USA

Laposata, Joseph S (General)
Battle Monuments Commission
20 Massachusetts
Washington, DC 20314-0001, USA

Lapotaire, Jane (Actor)
92 Oxford Gardens
#C
London W10, UNITED KINGDOM (UK)

Lappalainen, Markku (Musician)
Island Def Jam Records
8920 W Sunset Blvd # 200
Los Angeles, CA 90069-1812, USA

Lappas, Steve (Coach)
Villanova University
Athletic Dept
Villanova, PA 19085, USA

Lappe, Frances Moore (Writer)
989 Market St
San Francisco, CA 94103-1708, USA

Laprade, Edgar (Hockey Player)
12 Shuniah St.
Thunder Bay, ON P7A 2Y8, CANADA

LaPraed, Ronald (Ron) (Musician)
Management Assoc
1920 Benson Ave
Saint Paul, MN 55116-3214, USA

Laquer, Walter (Historian)
Georgetown University
1800 K St NW
Strategic Studies
Washington, DC 20006-2202, USA

Lara, Brian C (Cricketer)
West Indies Cricket Club
PO Box 616
Saint John's, ANTIGUA & BARBUDA

Lara, Claude Autant
66 rue Lepic
Paris 75018, FRANCE

Lara, Joe (Actor)
c/o Peter Giagni *Peter Giagni Management*
8981 W Sunset Blvd Ste 103
West Hollywood, CA 90069-1850, USA

Laragh, John H (Doctor, Educator)
435 E 70th St
New York, NY 10021-5342, USA

Laraki, Azeddine (Prime Minister)
Islamic Conference
Kilo 6
Mecca Road
Jeddah 21411, SAUDI ARABIA

Laraway, Jack (Football Player)
Buffalo Bills
4268 Mallard Cv
Avon, OH 44011-3227, USA

Lardner Jr, George (Journalist)
Washington Post
Editorial Dept
1150 15th St NW
Washington, DC 20071-0001, USA

Lardon, Brad (Golfer)
17334 Sioux Springs Dr
College Station, TX 77845-4589, USA

Lardy, Henry A (Misc)
1829 Thorstrand Rd
Madison, WI 53705-1052, USA

Laredo, Jaime (Musician)
Harold Holt
31 Sinclair Road
London W14 0NS, UNITED KINGDOM (UK)

Laredo, Ruth (Musician)
I C M Artists
40 W 57th St
New York, NY 10019-4001, USA

Larena, John (Designer)
c/o Staff Member *Mirisch Agency*
1801 Century Park E Ste 1801
Los Angeles, CA 90067-2320, USA

Laresca, Vincent (Actor)
c/o Staff Member *Writers and Artists Group Intl (LA)*
8383 Wilshire Blvd Ste 550
Beverly Hills, CA 90211-2417, USA

Larionov, Igor (Hockey Player)
Detroit Red Wings
600 Civic Center Dr
Joe Louis Arena
Detroit, MI 48226-4419, USA

Lark, Maria (Actor)
c/o Staff Member *Frontier Booking International*
1560 Broadway # 1110
New York, NY 10036-1518, USA

Larker, Norm (Baseball Player)
Los Angeles Dodgers
4701 E Village Rd
Long Beach, CA 90808-1548, USA

Larkin, Andy (Baseball Player)
Florida Marlins
2844 E Flower St
Gilbert, AZ 85298-5754, USA

Larkin, Barry (Baseball Player)
Cincinnati Reds
5410 Osprey Isle Ln
Orlando, FL 32819-4015, USA

Larkin, Barry L (Baseball Player)
3348 Brinton Trl
Cincinnati, OH 45241-4811, USA

Larkin, Gene (Baseball Player)
Minnesota Twins
9496 Abbott Ct
Eden Prairie, MN 55347-2817, USA

Larkin, Pat (Baseball Player)
San Francisco Giants
23400 Canzonet St
Woodland Hills, CA 91367-6013, USA

Larkin, Patty (Musician, Songwriter, Writer)
SRO Artists
6629 University Ave Ste 206
Middleton, WI 53562-3037, USA

Larkin, Sheila
9229 W Sunset Blvd Ste 311
Los Angeles, CA 90069-3403, USA

Larkin, Stephen (Baseball Player)
Cincinnati Reds
9178 Solon Dr
Cincinnati, OH 45242-4616, USA

Larmore, Jennifer (Opera Singer)
I C M Artists
40 W 57th St
New York, NY 10019-4001, USA

Larner, Stevan (Cinematographer)
1209 Ballard Canyon Rd
Solvang, CA 93463-9716, USA

Laro, David (Judge)
US Tax Court
400 2nd St NW
Washington, DC 20217-0002, USA

Larocca, Greg (Baseball Player)
San Diego Padres
20808 N 27th Ave Apt 2042
Phoenix, AZ 85027-3217, USA

Larocha, Dave (Baseball Player)
California Angels
RR 4 Box 3
Fort Scott, KS 66701, USA

LaRoche, Philippe (Skier)
Club de Ski Acrobatique
Lac Beauport, PQ G0A 20Q, CANADA

LaRocque, Gene R (Government Official)
5015 Macomb St NW
Washington, DC 20016-2609, USA

Laroque, Michele (Actor)
Artmedia
20 Ave Rapp
Paris 75007, FRANCE

LaRosa, Julius (Musician)
67 Sycamore Ln
Irvington, NY 10533-1933, USA

Larose, Claude D (Hockey Player)
5060 NW 54th St
Coconut Creek, FL 33073-3713, USA

Larose, Dan (Football Player)
Detroit Lions
4873 N Raymond Rd
Luther, MI 49656-9503, USA

Larose, John (Baseball Player)
Boston Red Sox
99 Roland St
Cumberland, RI 02864-5515, USA

Larose, Vic (Baseball Player)
Chicago Cubs
2823 E Turquoise Dr
Phoenix, AZ 85028-4424, USA

Larouch, Pierre
116 Lancaster Ave
Pittsburgh, PA 15228-2354, USA

LaRouche, Lyndon
15820 Round Top Lane
Round Hill, VA 20141, USA

Larouche, Pierre (Hockey Player)
112 Vanderbilt Dr
Pittsburgh, PA 15243-1323, USA

LaRouche Jr, Lyndon H (Politician)
18520 Round Top Ln
Round Hill, VA 20141-2052, USA

Larrieux, Amel (Musician)
Bliss Life
2114 Pico Blvd # B
Santa Monica, CA 90405-1718, USA

Larroquette, John (Actor)
c/o Staff Member *Brillstein-Grey Entertainment*
9150 Wilshire Blvd Ste 350
Beverly Hills, CA 90212-3453, USA

Larry, Wendy (Coach)
Old Dominion University
Athletic Dept
Norfolk, VA 23529-0001, USA

Larry Sanitsky, Larry Sanitsky (Producer)
c/o Nancy Josephson *Endeavor Agency LLC (LA)*
8942 Wilshire Blvd
Beverly Hills, CA 90211-1908, USA

Larsen, Art (Tennis Player)
203 Lorraine Blvd
San Leandro, CA 94577-2724, USA

Larsen, Blaine (Musician)
c/o Staff Member *Paradigm (Monterey)*
509 Hartnell St
Monterey, CA 93940-2825, USA

Larsen, Bruce (Editor)
Vancouver Sun
2250 Granville St
Vancouver, BC V6H 3G2, CANADA

Larsen, Don J (Baseball Player)
St Louis Browns
PO Box 2863
Hayden Lake, ID 83835-2863, USA

Larsen, Gary L (Football Player)
Los Angeles Rams
4317 San Juan St NE
Lacey, WA 98516-6277, USA

Larsen, Libby (Composer)
2205 Kenwood Pkwy
Minneapolis, MN 55405-2329, USA

Larsen, Paul E (Religious Leader)
Evangelical Convenant Church
5101 N Francisco Ave
Chicago, IL 60625-3676, USA

Larsen, Ralph S (Business Person)
Johnson & Johnson
1 Johnson And Johnson Plz
New Brunswick, NJ 08933-0002, USA

Larson, April U (Religious Leader)
Evangelical Lutheran Church
PO Box 4900
Rochester, MN 55903-4900, USA

Larson, Brandon (Baseball Player)
Cincinnati Reds
8922 Rich Way
San Antonio, TX 78251-2971, USA

Larson, Brie (Actor)
c/o Anne Woodward *Saffron Management*
9171 Wilshire Blvd Ste 441
Beverly Hills, CA 90210-5516, USA

Larson, Charles R (Chuck) (Admiral)
591 Coover Rd
Annapolis, MD 21401-6921, USA

Larson, Dan (Baseball Player)
Houston Astros
797 Oxen St
Paso Robles, CA 93446-4656, USA

Larson, Darrell
8380 Melrose Ave Ste 207
Los Angeles, CA 90069-5498, USA

Larson, Eric (Publisher)
TV Guide Magazine
100 Matsonford Road
Wayne, PA 19080-0001, USA

Larson, Gary (Cartoonist)
Universal Press Syndicate
4520 Main St
Kansas City, MO 64111-1876, USA

Larson, Gerald (Jerry Lacy) (Actor)
c/o Staff Member *Sutton Barth & Vennari Inc*
145 S Fairfax Ave Ste 310
Los Angeles, CA 90036-2176, USA

Larson, Greg (Football Player)
New York Giants
PO Box 393
Nisswa, MN 56468-0393, USA

Larson, Jack (Actor)
449 N Skyewiay Rd
Los Angeles, CA 90049-2844, USA

Larson, Jay (Musician)
c/o Staff Member *Paradigm (Monterey)*
509 Hartnell St
Monterey, CA 93940-2825, USA

Larson, Jill (Actor)
Innovative Artists
1505 10th St
Santa Monica, CA 90401-2805, USA

Larson, Kent (Adult Film Star)
c/o Staff Member *Diva Central Inc*
7510 W Sunset Blvd Ste 1445
Los Angeles, CA 90046-3408, USA

Larson, Kurt (Football Player)
Indianapolis Colts
N57W35564 Misty Ter
Oconomowoc, WI 53066-2410, USA

Larson, Lance (Swimmer)
41 Balboa Cvs
Newport Beach, CA 92663-3226, USA

Larson, Lyndon (Football Player)
Baltimore Colts
4117 E Encanto St
Mesa, AZ 85205-5121, USA

Larson, Paul (Football Player)
Chicago Cardinals
3718 W Harding Rd
Turlock, CA 95380-9217, USA

Larson, Peter N (Business Person)
Brunswick Corp
1 N Field Ct
Lake Forest, IL 60045-4811, USA

Larson, Reed
14334 Fairway Dr
Eden Prairie, MN 55344-1955, USA

Larson, Shana (Producer, Writer)
c/o Lucy Stille *Paradigm (LA)*
360 N Crescent Dr
North Bldg
Beverly Hills, CA 90210-6820, USA

Larson, William H (Football Player)
San Francisco 49ers
1365 Redwood Dr
Windsor, CO 80550-4603, USA

Larson, Wolf (Actor)
10600 Holman Ave Apt 1
Los Angeles, CA 90024-5931, USA

Larsson, Dean (Golfer)
Advantage International
1751 Pinnacle Dr Ste 1500
Mc Lean, VA 22102-3833, USA

Larsson, Lars-Eric
Master Ernsts gata 6A
Helsingborg S-25435, SWEDEN

Larsson, Magnus
Pier House Strand on the Green Chiswick
London, ENGLAND W4, UNITED
KINGDOM (UK)

Larter, Al
6100 Wilshire Blvd Ste 1170
Los Angeles, CA 90048-5116, USA

Larter, Ali (Actor)
c/o Michael Bircumshaw *Water Street Management*
5225 Wilshire Blvd Ste 615
Los Angeles, CA 90036-4350, USA

LaRue, Chi Chi (Comedian)
c/o Staff Member *Diva Central Inc*
7510 W Sunset Blvd Ste 1445
Los Angeles, CA 90046-3408, USA

LaRue, Florence (Actor, Musician)
Sterling Winters
10877 Wilshire Blvd # 15
Los Angeles, CA 90024-4341, USA

Larue, Jason (Baseball Player)
Cincinnati Reds
3237 Hawthorne
Spring Branch, TX 78070-6424, USA

Larue, Renee (Adult Film Star)
c/o Staff Member *Atlas Multimedia Inc*
9035 Independence Ave
Canoga Park, CA 91304-1743, USA

LaRussa, Tony (Baseball Player)
Kansas City A's
338 Golden Meadow Pl
Alamo, CA 94507-2711, USA

LaRusso, Vincent
419 Park Ave S Rm 1009
New York, NY 10016-8410, USA

Lary, Frank S (Baseball Player)
Detroit Tigers
11813 Baseball Dr
Northport, AL 35475-4908, USA

Lary, R Yale (Football Player)
Detroit Lions
6366 Lansdale Rd
Fort Worth, TX 76116-1622, USA

Las Ketchup (Music Group)
c/o Staff Member *Sony Music Miami*
605 Lincoln Rd Fl 7
Miami Beach, FL 33139-2900, USA

LaSalle, Denise (Musician)
CAI Entertainment Agency
PO Box 9267
Jackson, MS 39286-9267, USA

LaSalle, Eriq (Actor, Director)
PO Box 2369
Beverly Hills, CA 90213-2369, USA

Lasardo, Robert (Actor)
c/o Staff Member *SMS Talent Inc*
8730 W Sunset Blvd Ste 440
Los Angeles, CA 90069-2277, USA

Lascher, David (Actor)
c/o Staff Member *Untitled Entertainment (LA)*
331 N Maple Dr Fl 3
Beverly Hills, CA 90210-3827, USA

LaScola, Judith (Artist)
Compositions Gallery
317 Sutter St
San Francisco, CA 94108-4301, USA

Lash, Bill (Skier)
17438 Bothell Way NE Apt C305
Bothell, WA 98011-1965, USA

Lash, Jim (Football Player)
Minnesota Vikings
597 Van Everett Ave
Akron, OH 44306-2418, USA

Lashar, Tim (Football Player)
Chicago Bears
4056 Nicole Pl
Norman, OK 73072-1758, USA

Lasher, Fred (Baseball Player)
Minnesota Twins
N9596 County Road K
Merrillan, WI 54754-8038, USA

Lasker, Dee Dee (Golfer)
1665 Chamisal Ct
Carlsbad, CA 92011-5031, USA

Lasker, Greg (Football Player)
New York Giants
319 E Pine Ave
West Lafayette, IN 47906-4885, USA

Laskey, Bill (Baseball Player)
San Francisco Giants
4312 N Holland Sylvania Rd Apt 203
Toledo, OH 43623-4702, USA

Laskey, Bill (Football Player)
Buffalo Bills
PO Box 734
3257 N Manitou Trail
Leland, MI 49654-0734, USA

Laskey, Frank (Football Player)
New York Giants
584 Battle Branch Vista Dr
Franklin, NC 28734-8548, USA

Laslavic, Jim (Football Player)
Detroit Lions
648 A Ave
Coronado, CA 92118-2205, USA

Lasorda, Tommy (Baseball Player)
Brooklyn Dodgers
1473 W Maxzim Ave
Fullerton, CA 92833-4611, USA

Lassally, Walter (Cinematographer)
6 Ladbroke Gardens
London W11 2PT, UNITED KINGDOM
(UK)

Lasse, Richard S (Football Player)
Pittsburgh Steelers
111 Windcrest Ct
Beaver Falls, PA 15010-1178, USA

Lasser, Louise (Actor, Comedian)
200 E 71st St Apt 20C
New York, NY 10021-5153, USA

Lasseter, John (Animator, Director)
c/o Staff Member *Pixar Animation Studios*
1200 Park Ave
Emeryville, CA 94608-3677, USA

Lassetter, Don (Baseball Player)
St Louis Cardinals
PO Box 326
Lyon, MS 38645-0326, USA

Lassez, Sarah (Actor)
Innovative Artists
1505 10th St
Santa Monica, CA 90401-2805, USA

Lassick, Sydney
2734 Bellevue Ave
Los Angeles, CA 90026-3882, USA

Lassiter, Amanda (Basketball Player)
Minnesota Lunx
600 1st Ave N
Target Center
Minneapolis, MN 55403-1400, USA

Lassiter, Isaac (Football Player)
Denver Broncos
2812 Rawson St
Oakland, CA 94619-3348, USA

Lassiter, Kwamie (Football Player)
Arizona Cardinals
1222 W Sunrise Pl
Chandler, AZ 85248-3741, USA

Last, James (Musician)
Schone Aussicht 16
Hamburg 22085, GERMANY

Laster, Danny B (Scientist)
Hruska Meal Animal Research Center
PO Box 166
Clay Center, NE 68933-0166, USA

Laszlo, Andrew (Cinematographer)
15838 Magnolia Blvd
Encino, CA 91436-1513, USA

Lateef, Yusef (Composer, Musician)
Rhino Records
10635 Santa Monica Blvd
Los Angeles, CA 90025-8300, USA

Latham, Bill (Baseball Player)
New York Mets
4001 Edgeview Cir
Trussville, AL 35173-3292, USA

Latham, Chris (Baseball Player)
Minnesota Twins
6331 Buzz Aldrin Dr
Las Vegas, NV 89149-1389, USA

Latham, Louise (Actor)
300 Hot Springs Rd
Santa Barbara, CA 93108-2038, USA

Lathan, Sanaa (Actor)
c/o Philip Grenz *William Morris Agency*
(WMA-LA)
1 William Morris Pl
Beverly Hills, CA 90212-4261, USA

Lathan, Stan (Director, Producer, Writer)
c/o Staff Member *Simmons Lathan Media*
Group
6100 Wilshire Blvd Ste 1111
Los Angeles, CA 90048-5198, USA

Lathiere, Bernard (Business Person)
Airbus Industries
5 Ave de Villiers
Paris 75017, FRANCE

Lathon, Lamar L (Football Player)
Houston Oilers
3711 Poplar Springs Dr
Missouri City, TX 77459-6722, USA

Latimer, Don (Football Player)
Denver Broncos
562 S Kalispell Way
Aurora, CO 80017-2112, USA

Latimore (Musician)
Rodgers Redding
1048 Tattnall St
Macon, GA 31201-1537, USA

Latimore, Joseph
1505 10th St
Santa Monica, CA 90401-2805, USA

Latin, Jerry (Football Player)
St Louis Cardinals
5253 Linden Rd Apt 10316
Rockford, IL 61109-5854, USA

Latman, Barry (Baseball Player)
Chicago White Sox
1206 San Julian Dr
San Marcos, CA 92078-4807, USA

Latortue, Gerard (Prime Minister)
Prime Minister's Office
Palais Ministeres
Port-au-Prince, HAITI

LaTourette, John E (Educator)
218 S Deerview Cir
Prescott, AZ 86303-5705, USA

Lattimore, Brian (Football Player)
Indianapolis Colts
1790 Santa Blas Walk Apt 503
Saint Louis, MO 63138-1950, USA

Lattimore, Kenny
151 El Camino Dr
Beverly Hills, CA 90212-2704, USA

Lattisaw, Stacy (Musician)
Walter Reeder Productions
PO Box 27641
Philadelphia, PA 19118-0641, USA

Lattlmore, Kenny (Musician)
Rhythm Jazz Entertainment Group
4465 Don Milagro Dr
Los Angeles, CA 90008-2831, USA

Lattner, John J (Johnny) (Football Player)
Pittsburgh Steelers
1700 Riverwoods Dr Apt 503
Melrose Park, IL 60160-1617, USA

Lattner, Johnny
933 Wenonah Ave
Oak Park, IL 60304-1810, USA

Latzke, Paul (Football Player)
San Diego Chargers
53 Pasatiempo Dr
Santa Cruz, CA 95060-1806, USA

Lauda, Andreas-Nikolaus (Niki) (Race Car Driver)
San Costa de Baix
Santa Eulalia
Ibiza, SPAIN

Lauda, Niki
San Costa de Baix
Santa Eularia des Riu (Ibiza) E-07840,
SPAIN

Lauder, Leonard A (Business Person)
Estee Lauder Companies
767 5th Ave
New York, NY 10153-0003, USA

Lauder, Ronald (Business Person)
Estee Lauder Companies
767 5th Ave
New York, NY 10153-0003, USA

Lauer, Andrew (Actor)
3018 3rd St
Santa Monica, CA 90405-5410, USA

Lauer, Andy (Actor)
c/o Andrea Pett-Joseph *Brillstein-Grey*
Entertainment
9150 Wilshire Blvd Ste 350
Beverly Hills, CA 90212-3453, USA

Lauer, Martin (Athlete, Track Athlete)
Hardstr 41
Lauf 77886, GERMANY

Lauer, Matt (Correspondent)
c/o Staff Member *Today Show, The*
30 Rockefeller Plz # 374E
New York, NY 10112-0015, USA

Laufenberg, Brandon (Football Player)
Washington Redskins
500 Saint Laurent Ct
Southlake, TX 76092-5874, USA

Laughlin, John (Actor)
Laughlin Enterprises
13116 Albers St
Sherman Oaks, CA 91401-6002, USA

Laughlin, Lori (Actor)
c/o Joanna (Joanie) Burstein *Burstein*
Company, The
15304 W Sunset Blvd Ste 208
Pacific Palisades, CA 90272-3656, USA

Laughlin, Robert B (Nobel Prize Laureate)
Stanford University
Physics Dept
Stanford, CA 94305, USA

Laughlin, Teresa (TC) (Actor, Designer)
TC Laughlin Design Group Inc
8 Larchmont Ave
Larchmont, NY 10538-4220, USA

Laughlin, Tom
PO Box 840
Moorpark, CA 93020-0840, USA

Laukkanen, Janne (Hockey Player)
Tampa Bay Lightning
401 Channelside Dr
Ice Palace
Tampa, FL 33602-5400, USA

Laumer, Keith
PO Box 972
Brookside, FL 33512, USA

Lauper, Cyndi (Musician, Songwriter, Writer)
c/o Tim Curtis *William Morris Agency*
(WMA-LA)
1 William Morris Pl
Beverly Hills, CA 90212-4261, USA

Laurance, Dale (Business Person)
Occidental Petroleum
10889 Wilshire Blvd
Los Angeles, CA 90024-4201, USA

Laurance, Matthew (Actor)
1951 Hillcrest Rd
Los Angeles, CA 90068-3116, USA

Laure, Carole (Actor, Musician)
Cineart
36 Rue de Ponthieu
Paris 75008, FRANCE

Lauren, Ralph (Designer, Fashion Designer)
Polo Ralph Lauren Corp
650 Madison Ave Fl C1
New York, NY 10022-1062, USA

Lauren, Tammy (Actor)
Gage Group
14724 Ventura Blvd Ste 505
Sherman Oaks, CA 91403-3505, USA

Laurents, Arthur (Writer)
PO Box 582
Quogue, NY 11959-0582, USA

Laurer, Joanie (Chyna) (Actor, Wrestler)
c/o Staff Member *Identity Talent Agency*
(ID)
9107 Wilshire Blvd Ste 450
Beverly Hills, CA 90210-5535, USA

Lauria, Dan (Actor)
c/o Harry Gold *TalentWorks (LA)*
3500 W Olive Ave Ste 1400
Burbank, CA 91505-5512, USA

Lauricella, Francis E (Hank) (Football Player)
Dallas Texans
1200 S Clearview Pkwy Ste 1166
Harahan, LA 70123-2378, USA

Lauridsen, Morten (Composer, Musician)
University of Southern California
Music Dept
Los Angeles, CA 90089-0001, USA

Laurie, Greg (Religious Leader)
Harvest Christian Fellowship Church
6115 Arlington Ave
Riverside, CA 92504-1911, USA

Laurie, Hugh (Actor, Comedian, Writer)
c/o Brandt Joel *Creative Artists Agency*
LCC (CAA-LA)
2000 Avenue Of The Stars
Los Angeles, CA 90067-4700, USA

Laurie, Piper (Actor)
2118 Wilshire Blvd # 931
Santa Monica, CA 90403-5784, USA

Lauro, Lindore (Football Player)
Chicago Cardinals
111 Scott Dr
New Castle, PA 16105-3101, USA

Lautenberg, Frank (Senator)
506 Hart Senate Office Bldg.
Washington, DC 20510-0001, USA

Lautenschlaeger, Fred (Football Player)
New York Giants
612 Breton Pl
Arnold, MD 21012-1536, USA

Lauter, Ed (Actor)
9165 W Sunset Blvd Ste 202
Los Angeles, CA 90069-3195, USA

Lauterbur, Paul C (Nobel Prize Laureate)
2702 Holcomb Dr
Urbana, IL 61802-7777, USA

Lauterstein, Alex (DJ)
c/o Staff Member *Diva Central Inc*
7510 W Sunset Blvd Ste 1445
Los Angeles, CA 90046-3408, USA

Lautner, Georges C (Director)
9 Chemin des Basses Ribes
Grasse 06130, FRANCE

Lautner, Taylor (Actor)
c/o Steve Simon *Landis-Simon*
Productions Talent Management
8899 Beverly Blvd Ste 815
West Hollywood, CA 90048-2452, USA

Lauzerique, George (Baseball Player)
Kansas City A's
601 Oleaster Ave
Wellington, FL 33414-8197, USA

Lavalliere, Mike (Baseball Player)
Philadelphia Phillies
216 81st St W
Bradenton, FL 34209-2154, USA

Lave, Lester B (Economist)
1008 Devonshire Rd
Pittsburgh, PA 15213-2914, USA

Laveikin, Aleksandr I (Cosmonaut)
Potchta Kosmonavtov
Moskovskoi Oblasti
Syvisdny Goroduk 141160, RUSSIA

Lavelle, Gary (Baseball Player)
San Francisco Giants
1100 Worthington Ct
Virginia Beach, VA 23464-5855, USA

Lavelli, Dante B J (Football Player)
Cleveland Rams
23273 Pheasant Ln # 11
Westlake, OH 44145-4358, USA

Lavender, Jay (Producer)
c/o Staff Member *Principato/Young*
Management
9665 Wilshire Blvd Ste 500
Beverly Hills, CA 90212-2312, USA

Lavender, Joseph (Football Player)
Philadelphia Eagles
1215 Alma St
Glendale, CA 91202-2014, USA

Laventhol, Henry L (Hank) (Artist)
445 Heritage Hls Unit F
Somers, NY 10589-1941, USA

Laver, Rod
PO Box 4798
Hilton Head Island, SC 29938-4798, USA

Lavery, Sean (Dancer)
New York City Ballet
Lincoln Center Plaza
New York, NY 10023, USA

Lavi, Daliah (Actor)
Dahlienweg 2
Herdecke 58313, GERMANY

Lavigne, Avril (Musician, Songwriter)
c/o Ian Volke *Nettwerk Management (Canada)*
1850 W Second Ave
Vancouver, BC V6J 4R3, CANADA

Lavin, Bernice E (Business Person)
Alberto-Culver
2525 Armitage Ave
Melrose Park, IL 60160-1163, USA

Lavin, Leonard H (Business Person)
Alberto-Culver
2525 Armitage Ave
Melrose Park, IL 60160-1163, USA

Lavin, Linda (Actor, Musician)
c/o Staff Member *Lavin Entertainment Group*
411 S Front St
Wilmington, NC 28401-5011, USA

Laviolette, Peter (Coach, Hockey Player)
3400 Spartina Ct
Raleigh, NC 27606-4843, USA

Lavoine, Marc (Actor)
c/o Staff Member *ArtMedia*
20 av Rapp
Paris 75007, FRANCE

Lavoir, Jennifer
PO Box 846
Merrimack, NH 03054-0846, USA

Lavon, Peaches (Musician)
c/o Janice Gaffney *Butterscotch Castle*
8118 Vantage Ave
North Hollywood, CA 91605-1437, USA

LaVorgna, Adam (Actor)
c/o Beverly Strong *Anonymous Content (CA)*
9350 Wilshire Blvd Ste 224
Beverly Hills, CA 90212-3204, USA

Lavrosky, Mikhail L (Ballerina)
Voznesesenky Per 16/4
#7
Moscow 103009, RUSSIA

Lavrov, Kyrill Y (Actor)
Michurinskaya 1
#36
Saint Petersburg 197046, RUSSIA

Law, Bernard F Cardinal (Religious Leader)
Saint Mary Major Basilica
00120, VATICAN CITY

Law, John Phillip
1339 Miller Dr
Los Angeles, CA 90069-1419, USA

Law, Jude (Actor)
c/o Scott Melrose *Endeavor Agency LLC (LA)*
9601 Wilshire Blvd Fl 3
Beverly Hills, CA 90210-5204, USA

Law, Ron (Baseball Player)
Cleveland Indians
3 Mountainview Rd
Greenwood Village, CO 80111-1736, USA

Law, Rudy (Baseball Player)
Los Angeles Dodgers
4841 Lennox Blvd
Inglewood, CA 90304-2109, USA

Law, Ty (Football Player)
New England Patriots
10862 Hawks Vista St
Plantation, FL 33324-8206, USA

Law, Vance (Baseball Player)
Pittsburgh Pirates
1682 N 1950 W
Provo, UT 84604-1177, USA

Law, Vern (Baseball Player)
Pittsburgh Pirates
1718 N 1050 W
Provo, UT 84604-1159, USA

Lawford, Christopher
1 Sutton Pl S
New York, NY 10022-2471, USA

Lawler, Jerry
5190 Walnut Grove Rd
Memphis, TN 38117-2876, USA

Lawler, Kate (Reality TV Star)
c/o Staff Member *Channel 4 Television Corporation*
124 Horseferry Road
London SW1P 2, UNITED KINGDOM (UK)

Lawless, Burton (Football Player)
Dallas Cowboys
2035 Oak Glen Dr
Mc Gregor, TX 76657-3455, USA

Lawless, Lucy (Actor)
c/o Scott Melrose *Endeavor Agency LLC (LA)*
9601 Wilshire Blvd Fl 3
Beverly Hills, CA 90210-5204, USA

Lawless, Tim (Baseball Player)
Cincinnati Reds
1238 Laura St
Casselberry, FL 32707-2764, USA

Lawn, John C (Lawyer)
New York Yankees
Yankee Stadium
161st St & River Ave
Bronx, NY 10451, USA

Lawrence, Andrea Mead
PO Box 43
Mammoth Lakes, CA 93546-0043, USA

Lawrence, Andrew (Actor)
c/o Adam Asherson *The Firm*
9465 Wilshire Blvd Fl 6
Beverly Hills, CA 90212-2605, USA

Lawrence, Bill (Writer)
c/o Staff Member *Broder Webb Chervin Silbermann Agency, The (BWCS)*
10250 Constellation Blvd Ste P
Los Angeles, CA 90067-6213, USA

Lawrence, Braxton Janice (Basketball Player)
Cleveland Rockers
1 Center Ct
Gund Arena
Cleveland, OH 44115-4001, USA

Lawrence, Brian (Baseball Player)
San Diego Padres
8880 San Diego Drive
San Diego, CA 93010, USA

Lawrence, Carol (Actor)
12337 Ridge Cir
Los Angeles, CA 90049-1183, USA

Lawrence, Cynthia (Opera Singer)
Herbert Breslin
119 W 57th St Ste 1505
New York, NY 10019-2401, USA

Lawrence, David Jr (Publisher)
Miami Herald
1 Herald Plz
Miami, FL 33132-1693, USA

Lawrence, Don (Football Player)
Washington Redskins
12620 Cedar St
Shawnee Mission, KS 66209-3167, USA

Lawrence, Francis (Actor)
c/o Gretchen Bruggeman-Rush *Hansen, Jacobson, Teller, Hoberman, Newman, Warren, Sloane & Richman, LLP*
450 N Roxbury Dr Fl 8
Beverly Hills, CA 90210-4222, USA

Lawrence, Francis (Director)
c/o David Naylor *David Naylor & Associates*
6535 Santa Monica Blvd
Los Angeles, CA 90038-1407, USA

Lawrence, Francis L (Educator)
Rutgers University
President's Office
New Brunswick, NJ 08903, USA

Lawrence, Henry (Football Player)
Oakland Raiders
PO Box 614
Pro Athlete Marketing
Beaver Falls, PA 15010-0614, USA

Lawrence, James (Loz) (Musician)
PO Box 33
Pontypool, Gwent NP4 6YU, UNITED KINGDOM (UK)

Lawrence, Jim (Baseball Player)
Cleveland Indians
225 Haddington St
Caledonia, ON N3W 1G1, CANADA

Lawrence, Joseph (Joey) (Actor)
c/o Staff Member *Himber Entertainment Inc*
15760 Ventura Blvd Ste 700
Encino, CA 91436-3016, USA

Lawrence, Kent (Football Player)
Philadelphia Eagles
150 Charter Ct
Athens, GA 30605-4628, USA

Lawrence, Linda
4926 Commonwealth Ave
La Canada, CA 91011-2514, USA

Lawrence, Marjie
13 Glenhurst Ave.
London, ENGLAND NW5, UNITED KINGDOM (UK)

Lawrence, Martin (Actor, Comedian)
c/o Staff Member *3-J Entertainment*
3209 S General Wainwright Dr
Lake Charles, LA 70615-8166, USA

Lawrence, Matthew (Actor)
c/o Staff Member *William Morris Agency (WMA-LA)*
1 William Morris Pl
Beverly Hills, CA 90212-4261, USA

Lawrence, Nigel (Musician)
c/o Staff Member *Paradigm (Monterey)*
509 Hartnell St
Monterey, CA 93940-2825, USA

Lawrence, Patricia
33 St. Luke's St.
London, ENGLAND SW3, UNITED KINGDOM (UK)

Lawrence, Richard D (General)
7301 Valbum Dr
Austin, TX 78731, USA

Lawrence, Robert S (Physicist)
4000 N Charles St Apt 1112
Highfield House
Baltimore, MD 21218-1737, USA

Lawrence, Rolland (Football Player)
Atlanta Falcons
317 Sugarcreek Dr
Franklin, PA 16323-5641, USA

Lawrence, Russell
7800 Beverly Blvd # 3305
Los Angeles, CA 90036-2112, USA

Lawrence, Sean (Baseball Player)
Pittsburgh Pirates
336 S Poplar Ave
Elmhurst, IL 60126-3565, USA

Lawrence, Sharon (Actor)
c/o Staff Member *Stone Manners Talent & Literary (LA)*
6500 Wilshire Blvd Ste 550
Los Angeles, CA 90048-4950, USA

Lawrence, Steve (Musician)
944 Pinehurst Dr
Las Vegas, NV 89109-1569, USA

Lawrence, Tracy (Musician, Songwriter, Writer)
c/o Staff Member *William Morris Agency (WMA-LA)*
1 William Morris Pl
Beverly Hills, CA 90212-4261, USA

Lawrence, Vicki (Actor, Musician)
6000 Lido Ln
Long Beach, CA 90803-4105, USA

Lawrence, Wendy B (Astronaut)
National Reconnaissance Office
14675 Lee Rd
Chantilly, VA 20151-1715, USA

Laws, Hubert
1078 S Ogden Dr
Los Angeles, CA 90019-6501, USA

Laws, Ronnie (Musician)
Pyramid Entertainment
89 5th Ave Ste 700
New York, NY 10003-3020, USA

Lawson, Bianca (Actor)
c/o Karynne Tencer *Tencer & Associates PR*
9777 Wilshire Blvd Ste 1005
Beverly Hills, CA 90212-1901, USA

Lawson, Denis (Actor, Director, Writer)
c/o Staff Member *Yakety Yak*
8 Bloomsbury Sq
London WC1A 2UA, UNITED KINGDOM (UK)

Lawson, Doyle (Musician)
c/o Staff Member *Paradigm (Monterey)*
509 Hartnell St
Monterey, CA 93940-2825, USA

Lawson, Kara (Basketball Player)
c/o Staff Member *Sacramento Monarchs*
1 Sports Pkwy
Arco Arena
Sacramento, CA 95834-2300, USA

Lawson, Ken (Ken L) (Actor)
c/o Staff Member *Agency West Entertainment*
6255 W Sunset Blvd Ste 908
Hollywood, CA 90028-7410, USA

Lawson, Leigh (Actor)
P F D Drury House
34-43 Russell St
London WC2B 5HA, UNITED KINGDOM (UK)

Lawson, Maggie (Actor)
c/o Ellen Meyer *Ellen Meyer Entertainment*
8899 Beverly Blvd Ste 612
Los Angeles, CA 90048-2429, USA

Lawson, Nigella (Chef, Writer)
EI Television
5750 Wilshire Blvd
Los Angeles, CA 90036-3697, USA

Lawson, Odell (Football Player)
Boston Patriots
2626 Garcitas Crk
Richmond, TX 77469-1961, USA

Lawson, Richard (Actor)
8840 Wilshire Blvd # 200
Beverly Hills, CA 90211-2606, USA

Lawson, Richard L (General)
6910 Clifton Rd
Clifton, VA 20124-1524, USA

Lawson, Steve (Baseball Player)
Texas Rangers
PO Box 5630
Brookings, OR 97415-0120, USA

Lawson, Twiggy (Actor, Model, Writer)
c/o Maureen Vincent *Peters Fraser & Dunlop (PFD - UK)*
Drury House
34-43 Russell St
London WC2B 5HA, UNITED KINGDOM (UK)

Lawson, William (Baseball Player)
8800 E McClellan St
Tucson, AZ 85710-4419, USA

Lawson of Blaby, Nigel (Government Official)
32 Sutherland Walk
London SE17, UNITED KINGDOM (UK)

Lawston, Marlene (Actor)
c/o Victoria Kress *Don Buchwald & Associates Inc (NY)*
10 E 44th St
New York, NY 10017-3601, USA

Lawton, Liam (Musician)
GM Publicity
86 Haddington Rd
Ballsbridge, Dublin 4
IRELAND

Lawton, Marcus (Baseball Player)
New York Yankees
110 Connie Dr
Gulfport, MS 39503-3254, USA

Lawton, Mary (Cartoonist)
Chronicle Features
901 Mission St
San Francisco, CA 94103-2905, USA

Lawton, Matthew (Matt) (Baseball Player)
Minnesota Twins
27264 Highway 67
Saucier, MS 39574-9020, USA

Lawton, Robert B (Educator)
Loyola Marymount University
President's Office
Los Angeles, CA 90045, USA

Lawwill, Theodore (Misc)
7609 Tallwood Rd
Prospect, KY 40059-9416, USA

Lax, John (Hockey Player)
3 Greendale Ln
Harwich, MA 02645, USA

Lax, Melvin (Physicist)
12 High St
Summit, NJ 07901-2413, USA

Laxalt, Paul D (Ex-Governor, Ex-Senator, Governor, Senator)
801 Pennsylvania Ave NW Ste 750
Washington, DC 20004-2670, USA

Laxmikant, Berde (Actor, Bollywood)
105 Nirakar B-Wing
1st Floor Kalyan Complex Yari Road
Versova Andheri
Bombay, MS 400061, INDIA

Laxton, Bill (Baseball Player)
Philadelphia Phillies
261 Mansion Ave
Audubon, NJ 08106-1529, USA

Laxton, Brett (Baseball Player)
Oakland A's
606 SW Elwood Dr
Lees Summit, MO 64081-2716, USA

Lay, Donald P (Judge)
US Court of Appeals
316 Robert St N
Saint Paul, MN 55101-1495, USA

Layevska, Anna (Actor)
c/o Staff Member *Televisa*
Blvd Adolfo Lopez Mateos 232
Colonia San Angel INN
DF CP 01060, MEXICO

Layman, Jason (Football Player)
Houston Oilers
163 New Center Rd
Sevierville, TN 37876-2167, USA

Layne, Hilly (Baseball Player)
Washington Senators
101 Woodcliff Cir
Signal Mountain, TN 37377-3142, USA

Layne, Jerry (Baseball Player)
2323 Cypress Gardens Blvd
Winter Haven, FL 33884-2120, USA

Layton, Les (Baseball Player)
New York Giants
8780 E McKellips Rd Lot 27
Scottsdale, AZ 85257-4809, USA

Layzie, Bone (Musician)
Creative Artists Agency
9830 Wilshire Blvd
Beverly Hills, CA 90212-1804, USA

Lazar, Danny (Baseball Player)
Chicago White Sox
8444 Oakwood Ave
Munster, IN 46321-1915, USA

Lazar, Laurence (Religious Leader)
Romanian Orthodox Episcopate
2522 Grey Tower Rd
Jackson, MI 49201-9120, USA

Lazard, Justin
9350 Wilshire Blvd Ste 324
Beverly Hills, CA 90212-3206, USA

Lazarev, Alexander N
Christopher Tennant Artists
39 Taderna ROad
#2
London SW10 0PY, UNITED KINGDOM (UK)

Lazaroff, Barbara
805 N Sierra Dr
Beverly Hills, CA 90210-2644, USA

Lazarus, Mell (Cartoonist)
Creators Syndicate
5777 W Century Blvd Ste 700
Los Angeles, CA 90045-9023, USA

Lazarus, Shelly (Business Person)
Ogilvy & Mather Worldwide
309 W 49th St
New York, NY 10019-7399, USA

Lazear, Edward P (Economist)
277 Old Spanish Trl
Portola Valley, CA 94028-8129, USA

Lazenby, George (Actor)
c/o Staff Member *Hervey/Grimes Talent Agency*
10561 Missouri Ave Apt 2
Los Angeles, CA 90025-5940, USA

Lazetich, Bill (Football Player)
Cleveland Rams
3840 Rimrock Rd Apt 2100
Billings, MT 59102-0153, USA

Lazetich, Pete (Football Player)
San Diego Chargers
185 Martin St
Reno, NV 89509-2827, USA

Lazier, Buddy (Race Car Driver)
Dreyer & Reinbold Racing
9375 Whitley Dr
Indianapolis, IN 46240-1349, USA

Lazlo, Viktor
56 rue de Lisbonne
Paris F-75008, FRANCE

Lazorko, Jack (Baseball Player)
Milwaukee Brewers
1360 Meandering Way
Rockwall, TX 75087-2309, USA

Lazuktin, Alexander I (Cosmonaut)
Potcha Kosmonavtov
Moskovskoi Oblasti
Syvisdny Goroduk 141160, RUSSIA

Lazure, Gabrielle (Actor)
Cineart
36 Rue de Ponthieu
Paris 75008, FRANCE

Le Bon, Yasmin (Model)
c/o Staff Member *Ford Models (NY)*
111 5th Ave Fl 9
New York, NY 10003-1005, USA

Le Duc, Anh (General, President)
President's Office
Hoang Hoa Tham
Hanoi, VIETNAM

Le Mat, Paul
6300 Wilshire Blvd Ste 1460
Los Angeles, CA 90048-5200, USA

Le Prevost, Nicholas
43A Princess Rd. Regents Park
London, ENGLAND NW1 8JS, UNITED KINGDOM (UK)

Le Prevost, Nigel
43A Princess Rd.
London, ENGLAND W1, UNITED KINGDOM (UK)

Le Rosa, Stefan (Actor)
c/o Staff Member *Nickelodeon UK*
PO Box 6425
LONDON W1A 6UR, UNITED KINGDOM (UK)

Le Vert
110-112 Lantoga Rd. #D
Wayne, PA 19087, USA

Lea, Charles W (Charlie) (Baseball Player)
Montreal Expos
3064 Mistwood Cv S
Collierville, TN 38017-8921, USA

Lea, Nicholas (Actor)
c/o Adam Levine *Anthem Entertainment*
6100 Wilshire Blvd Ste 1170
Los Angeles, CA 90048-5116, USA

Leach, Henry C (Admiral)
Wonston Lea
Winchester, Hants SO21 3LS, UNITED KINGDOM (UK)

Leach, Jalal (Baseball Player)
San Francisco Giants
3718 Phillip Island Rd
W Sacramento, CA 95691-5939, USA

Leach, Penelope (Misc)
3 Tanza Lane
London NW3 2UA, UNITED KINGDOM (UK)

Leach, Rick (Baseball Player)
Detroit Tigers
593 Layman Creek Cir
Grand Blanc, MI 48439-1384, USA

Leach, Robin (Entertainer, Producer, Television Host)
c/o Staff Member *Leach Entertainment Enterprises Inc*
122 E 42nd St Rm 1518
New York, NY 10168-1599, USA

Leach, Rosemary (Actor)
Felix de Wolfe
51 Maida Vale
London W9 1SD, UNITED KINGDOM (UK)

Leach, Sheryl (Animator)
Lyons Group
300 E Bethany Dr
Allen, TX 75002-3802, USA

Leach, Terry (Baseball Player)
New York Mets
2135 SW Locks Rd
Stuart, FL 34997-7011, USA

Leachman, Cloris (Actor)
c/o Steven Vail *Vanguard Talent Management*
1155 N La Cienega Blvd Apt 502
Los Angeles, CA 90069-2437, USA

Leadbetter, Kelly (Golfer)
9606 Tavistock Ct
Orlando, FL 32827-7018, USA

Leader, George M (Governor)
Country Meadows
830 Cherry Dr
Hershey, PA 17033-3402, USA

Leader, Tom (Architect)
537 Golden Gate Ave
Richmond, CA 94801-3709, USA

Leadon, Bernie (Musician)
Joe's Garage
4405 Belmont Park Ter
Nashville, TN 37215-3609, USA

Leaf, Alexander (Physicist)
5 Sussex Rd
Winchester, MA 01890-3846, USA

Leaf, Ryan (Football Player)
San Diego Chargers
4401 S Coulter St Apt 2312
Amarillo, TX 79109-5069, USA

Leahy, Bob (Football Player)
Pittsburgh Steelers
2701 Rosedale Dr
Monroe, LA 71201-3068, USA

Leahy, Pat (Baseball Player)
1350 Dazet Rd
Yakima, WA 98908-9600, USA

Leahy, Patrick (Senator)
433 Russell Senate Office Bldg
Washington, DC 20510-0001, USA

Leahy, Patrick J (Pat) (Football Player)
New York Jets
717 Chamblee Ln
Saint Louis, MO 63141-7324, USA

Leak, Jennifer (Actor)
James D'Auria Associates
PO Box 2219
Amagansett, NY 11930-2219, USA

Leak, Justice (Actor)
c/o Staff Member *People Store*
645 Lambert Dr NE
Atlanta, GA 30324-4125, USA

Leake, Brett (Comedian)
3561 Leatherwood Ln
Maidens, VA 23102-2025, USA

Leaks, Roosevelt Jr (Football Player)
Baltimore Colts
11525 Glen Falloch Ct
Austin, TX 78754-5807, USA

Leal, Sharon (Actor, Musician)
c/o Staff Member *Edmonds Management*
1635 N Cahuenga Blvd Fl 5
Los Angeles, CA 90028-6201, USA

Leandros, Vicky
Postfach 31 28
Kiel D-24030, GERMANY

LeAnn, Summer (Actor)
c/o Rebecca Wood *Triple Threat*
7070 W Sunset Blvd Ste 126
Los Angeles, CA 90028-7521, USA

Lear, Evelyn (Opera Singer)
414 Sailboat Cir
Weston, FL 33326-1506, USA

Lear, Norman M (Director, Producer, Writer)
c/o Staff Member *Act III Productions*
100 N Crescent Dr Ste 250
Beverly Hills, CA 90210-5451, USA

Learned, Michael (Actor)
1600 N Beverly Dr
Beverly Hills, CA 90210-2316, USA

Leary, Denis (Actor, Comedian)
c/o Stephen (Steve) Small *Paradigm (LA)*
360 N Crescent Dr
North Bldg
Beverly Hills, CA 90210-6820, USA

Leary, Tim (Baseball Player)
New York Mets
1766 Michael Ln
Pacific Palisades, CA 90272-2037, USA

Leatherdale, Douglas W (Business Person)
Saint Paul Companies
385 Washington St
Saint Paul, MN 55102-1396, USA

Leaud, Jean-Pierre (Actor)
Artmedia
20 Ave Rapp
Paris 75007, FRANCE

Leavell, Chuck (Musician)
Charlane Plantation
665 Charlane Dr
Dry Branch, GA 31020-5256, USA

Leavenworth, Scotty (Actor)
c/o Susan Curtis *Curtis Talent Management*
9607 Arby Dr
Beverly Hills, CA 90210-1202, USA

Leaves (Music Group)
c/o Staff Member *Paradigm (Monterey)*
509 Hartnell St
Monterey, CA 93940-2825, USA

Leavitt, Michael O (Government Official, Governor)
Environmental Protection Agency
401 M St SW
Washington, DC 20460-0003, USA

Leavitt, Phil (Musician)
GEMS
PO Box 1031
Montrose, CA 91021-1031, USA

Leavy, Edward (Judge)
US Court of Appeals
700 SW 6th Ave Ste 211
Portland, OR 97204-1434, USA

Lebadang (Artist)
Circle Gallery
303 E Wacker Dr
Chicago, IL 60601-5212, USA

LeBaron, Eddie
400 Capitol Mall Ste 1700
Sacramento, CA 95814-4419, USA

LeBaron, Edward W (Eddie) Jr (Football Player)
Washington Redskins
7524 Pineridge Ln
Fair Oaks, CA 95628-4854, USA

LeBeau, Becky
9461 Charleville Blvd # 602
Beverly Hills, CA 90212-3017, USA

LeBeau, C Richard (Dick) (Coach, Football Player)
Detroit Lions
10405 Stone Ct
Cincinnati, OH 45242-5128, USA

LeBeauf, Sabrina (Actor)
735 Kappock St Apt 6F
Bronx, NY 10463-4629, USA

Lebedev, Valentin V (Cosmonaut)
Potcha Kosmonavtov
Moskovskoi Oblasti
Syvisdny Goroduk 141160, RUSSIA

LeBel, B Harper (Football Player)
Seattle Seahawks
3379 Scadlock Ln
Sherman Oaks, CA 91403-4914, USA

LeBel, Robert (Bob) (Misc)
25 Rue Saint Pierre
Cite de Chambly, PQ J3L 1L7, CANADA

Leberman, Robert (Football Player)
Baltimore Colts
General Delivery
Center Lovell, ME 04016-9999, USA

Lebis, Attilo (Choreographer, Dancer)
Opera de Paris
120 Rue Lyon
Paris 75012, FRANCE

LeBlanc, Christian
12840 Moorpark St Apt 106
Studio City, CA 91604-1363, USA

LeBlanc, Matt (Actor)
c/o Staff Member *Fort Hill Productions*
4000 Warner Blvd Bldg 138 Rm 1102
Burbank, CA 91512, USA

LeBlanc, Sherri (Ballerina)
New York City Ballet
Lincoln Center Plaza
New York, NY 10023, USA

LeBoeuf, Raymond W (Business Person)
PPG Industries
1 Ppg Pl
Pittsburgh, PA 15272-0001, USA

LeBon, Simon (Musician, Songwriter, Writer)
c/o Staff Member *DD Productions*
93A Westbourne Park Villas
London W2 5ED, UNITED KINGDOM (UK)

Lebowitz, Fran (Writer)
Random House
1745 Broadway # B1
New York, NY 10019-4305, USA

Leboyer, Frederick (Physicist)
Georges Borchardt
136 E 57th St
New York, NY 10022-2707, USA

LeBrock, Kelly (Actor, Model)
Bartels Co
PO Box 57593
Sherman Oaks, CA 91413-2593, USA

Lebron, Juan (Baseball Player)
Bowman
PO Box 242
Arroyo, PR 00714-0242, USA

LeBrun, Christopher M (Artist)
Marlborough Fine Art
6 Albermarle St
London W1X 4BY, UNITED KINGDOM (UK)

LeCarre, John (Writer)
9 Gainsborough Gardens
London NW3 1BJ, UNITED KINGDOM (UK)

LeCavalier, Vincent (Hockey Player)
c/o Staff Member *Tampa Bay Lightning*
401 Channelside Dr
Ice Palace
Tampa, FL 33602-5400, USA

Lechter, Sharon L (Writer)
Cashflow Technologies
4330 N Civic Center Plz
Scottsdale, AZ 85251-3528, USA

Leckonby, William (Football Player)
Brooklyn Dodgers
1311 Santee Mill Rd
Bethlehem, PA 18017-1111, USA

LeClair, James M (Jim) (Football Player)
Cincinnati Bengals
32 4th Ave NE
Mayville, ND 58257-1226, USA

Leclair, Jim (Football Player)
Denver Broncos
600 Plymouth Way
Burlingame, CA 94010-2733, USA

LeClerc, Jean (Actor)
19 W 44th St Ste 1500
New York, NY 10036-6101, USA

Leclerc, Roger (Football Player)
Chicago Bears
257 Elm St
Agawam, MA 01001-2444, USA

LeClere, Jennifer
5601 Navigation Blvd
Houston, TX 77011-1105, USA

LeClezio, Jean-Marie (Writer)
Editions Gallimard
5 Rue Sebastien-Bottin
Paris 75007, FRANCE

Lecomte, Benoit (Swimmer)
Cross Atlantic Swimming Challenge
3005 S Lamar Blvd # D109-353
Austin, TX 78704-8864, USA

Leconte, Henri (Tennis Player)
IMG
Pier House
Strand-on-Green
Chiswick, London W4 3NN, UNITED KINGDOM (UK)

Leconte, Patrice (Director)
William Morris Agency
151 El Camino Dr
Beverly Hills, CA 90212-2775, USA

Lecount, Terry (Football Player)
San Francisco 49ers
1288 Branchfield Ct
Riverdale, GA 30296-2148, USA

Lecroy, Matt (Baseball Player)
Minnesota Twins
410 Brown Ave
Belton, SC 29627-1504, USA

Ledbetter, Monte (Football Player)
Houston Oilers
340 Sawgrass Dr
Valdosta, GA 31602-1477, USA

Ledee, Ricky (Baseball Player)
New York Yankees
D29 Ext Carmen
Salinas, PR 00751-2208, USA

Leder, Philip (Scientist)
Howard Hughes Med Institute
4000 Jones Bridge Rd
Chevy Chase, MD 20815-6789, USA

Lederberg, Joshua (Nobel Prize Laureate)
Rockefeller University
1230 York Ave
President's Office
New York, NY 10065-6399, USA

Lederer, Howard (Misc)
c/o Staff Member *Kolyma Corporation*
Full Tilt Poker
62 Lloyd G Smith Blvd
Oranjestad, AW, ARUBA

Lederman, Leon M (Nobel Prize Laureate)
3101 S Dearborn St
Chicago, IL 60616-2852, USA

Ledesma, Aaron (Baseball Player)
New York Mets
2446 Douglas St
Union City, CA 94587-1865, USA

Ledford, Brandy (Actor)
c/o Staff Member *Marshak/Zachary Company, The*
8840 Wilshire Blvd Fl 1
Beverly Hills, CA 90211-2606, USA

Ledford, Frank F Jr (General)
Southwest Biomed Research Foundation
PO Box 760549
San Antonio, TX 78245-0549, USA

Ledford, Judith
11365 Ventura Blvd Ste 100
Studio City, CA 91604-3148, USA

Ledger, Heath (Actor)
c/o Steve Alexander *Creative Artists Agency LCC (CAA-LA)*
2000 Avenue Of The Stars
Los Angeles, CA 90067-4700, USA

Ledley, Robert S (Inventor)
17000 Melbourne Dr
Laurel, MD 20707-2796, USA

Ledoyen, Virginie (Actor, Model)
c/o Don Spradlin *Essential Talent Management*
6464 W Sunset Blvd Ste 760
Los Angeles, CA 90028-8006, USA

Leduc-Alverson, Noella (Baseball Player)
5 Leonard Ave
Leonardo, NJ 07737-1536, USA

Ledyard, Courtney (Football Player)
New York Jets
419 Miller Ave
Freeport, NY 11520-6112, USA

Lee, Alexandra (Actor)
Sanders Armstrong Management
2120 Santa Monica Blvd Ste 120
Santa Monica, CA 90404, USA

Lee, Amy (Musician)
c/o Dennis Rider *Dennis Rider Management*
931 Hilldale Ave
West Hollywood, CA 90069-4404, USA

Lee, Andy Scott (Musician)
c/o Staff Member *Pop Idol (Fremantle Media)*
2700 Colorado Ave Ste 450
Santa Monica, CA 90404-3599, USA

Lee, Ang (Director)
c/o Victoria Metzger *Creative Artists Agency LCC (CAA-LA)*
2000 Avenue Of The Stars
Los Angeles, CA 90067-4700, USA

Lee, Anthonia W (Amp) (Football Player)
San Francisco 49ers
990 Brickyard Rd
Chipley, FL 32428-4346, USA

Lee, Bertram M (Misc)
Denver Nugglets
1000 Chopper Cir
Pepsi Center
Denver, CO 80204-5805, USA

Lee, Beverly
10100 Santa Monica Blvd Ste 2490
Los Angeles, CA 90067-4144, USA

Lee, Beverly (Musician)
Bevi Corp
PO Box 100
Clifton, NJ 07015-0100, USA

Lee, Bill (Baseball Player)
Boston Red Sox
305 Common View Dr
Craftsbury, VT 05826-9779, USA

Lee, Bob (Baseball Player)
Los Angeles Angels
2110 Casper Dr
Lake Havasu City, AZ 86406-8143, USA

Lee, Bobby (Actor)
c/o Staff Member *Gersh Agency, The (LA)*
232 N Canon Dr
Beverly Hills, CA 90210-5302, USA

Lee, Brandon (Adult Film Star)
c/o Staff Member *Diva Central Inc*
7510 W Sunset Blvd Ste 1445
Los Angeles, CA 90046-3408, USA

Lee, Brenda (Musician)
c/o Staff Member *Paradigm (Monterey)*
509 Hartnell St
Monterey, CA 93940-2825, USA

Lee, Butch (Basketball Player)
1322 Teller Ave
Bronx, NY 10456-1603, USA

Lee, Carl (Football Player)
Minnesota Vikings
PO Box 1000 Campus Box 181
West Virginia State College
Institute, WV 25112-1000, USA

Lee, Catherine J (Artist)
PO Box 132
Condon, OR 97823-0132, USA

Lee, Chang-Rae (Writer)
International Creative Mgmt
40 W 57th St Ste 1800
New York, NY 10019-4001, USA

Lee, Charles R (Business Person)
GTE Corp
1255 Corporate Dr
Irving, TX 75038-2518, USA

Lee, Christopher F C (Actor)
c/o Jean Diamond *London Management*
2-4 Noel St
London W1V 3RB, UNITED KINGDOM (UK)

Lee, Cliff (Baseball Player)
Cleveland Indians
602 S Neeley St
Benton, AR 72015, USA

Lee, Corey (Baseball Player)
Texas Rangers
702 Joyner St
Clayton, NC 27520-2838, USA

Lee, David (Baseball Player)
Colorado Rockies
56 Terrace Dr
Pittsburgh, PA 15205-4312, USA

Lee, David (Director, Writer)
Jim Preminger Agency
10866 Wilshire Blvd Fl 10
Los Angeles, CA 90024-4350, USA

Lee, David A (Football Player)
Baltimore Colts
2518 N Waverly Dr
Bossier City, LA 71111-5940, USA

Lee, David H (Astronomer, Writer)
Plenum Publishing Group
233 Spring St
New York, NY 10013-1522, USA

Lee, David L (Business Person)
Global Crossing Ltd
Wessex House
45 Reid St
Hamilton, HM 12, BERMUDA

Lee, David M (Nobel Prize Laureate)
Comell University
Clark Hall
Physics Dept
Ithaca, NY 14853, USA

Lee, Derek (Baseball Player)
Minnesota Twins
5230 Hyland Hills Ave Unit 1311
Sarasota, FL 34241-7154, USA

Lee, Derrek (Athlete, Baseball Player)
c/o Staff Member *Chicago Cubs*
1060 W Addison St
Wrigley Field
Chicago, IL 60613-4397, USA

Lee, Dickey (Musician)
Mars Talent
27 L Ambiance Ct
Bardonia, NY 10954-1421, USA

Lee, Don (Baseball Player)
Detroit Tigers
9101 E Palm Tree Dr
Tucson, AZ 85710-8626, USA

Lee, Dr Henry (Misc)
c/o Staff Member *Prometheus Books*
59 John Glenn Dr
Amherst, NY 14228-2197, USA

Lee, Dwight (Football Player)
San Francisco 49ers
PO Box 480397
New Haven, MI 48048-0397, USA

Lee, Edward (Football Player)
Detroit Lions
1781 Verbena St NW
Washington, DC 20012-1048, USA

Lee, Edward (Writer)
Necro Publications/Bedlam Press
PO Box 540298
Orlando, FL 32854-0298, USA

Lee, Eunice (Musician)
Columbia Artists Mgmt Inc
1790 Broadway Fl 6
New York, NY 10019-1412, USA

Lee, Geddy (Musician)
Macklam Feldman Mgmt
1505 W 2nd Ave
#200
Vancouver, BC V6H 3Y4, CANADA

Lee, Grandma (Actor, Comedian)
Lee Strong
626 Staffordshire Dr
Jacksonville, FL 32225, USA

Lee, H Douglas (Educator)
Stetson University
President's Office
Deland, FL 32720, USA

Lee, Harper (Writer)
McIntosh & Otis
353 Lexington Ave Rm 1500
New York, NY 10016-0941, USA

Lee, Homer & The Braschler's
PO Box 1408
Branson, MO 65615-1408, USA

Lee, Howard V (War Hero)
529 King Arthur Dr
Virginia Beach, VA 23464-2235, USA

Lee, Jack R (Football Player)
Houston Oilers
6306 Mid Pines Dr
Jack Lee Interests Inc
Houston, TX 77069-1346, USA

Lee, Jared B (Cartoonist)
Jared B Lee Studio
2942 Hamilton Rd
Lebanon, OH 45036-8857, USA

Lee, Jason (Actor)
c/o Sharon Sheinwold *United Talent Agency (UTA)*
9560 Wilshire Blvd Ste 500
Beverly Hills, CA 90212-2401, USA

Lee, Jenny (Golfer)
1705 Canyon Edge Dr
Austin, TX 78733-2000, USA

Lee, Joe (Business Person)
Darden Restaurants
5900 Lake Ellenor Dr
Orlando, FL 32809-4634, USA

Lee, Johnny (Musician, Songwriter, Writer)
WIFT Mgmt
2317 Pecan St
Dickinson, TX 77539-4949, USA

Lee, Jon (Actor, Musician)
c/o Staff Member *S Club 7*
9830 Wilshire Blvd
Creative Artists Agency Lcc (Caa-La)
Beverly Hills, CA 90212-1804, USA

Lee, Jonna (Actor)
8721 W Sunset Blvd Ste 103
Los Angeles, CA 90069-2271, USA

Lee, Julia (Actor)
c/o Staff Member *Privilege Talent Agency*
PO Box 260860
Encino, CA 91426-0860, USA

Lee, Kathy
204 River Edge Lane
Seiverville, TN 37862, USA

Lee, Keith (Basketball Player)
11653 Metz Pl
Eads, TN 38028-6912, USA

Lee, Kuan Yew (Prime Minister)
Senoir Minister's Office
Istana Annexe
Istana
Singapore 0923, SINGAPORE

Lee, Laron (Baseball Player)
St Louis Cardinals
8150 Warren Ct
Granite Bay, CA 95746-9576, USA

Lee, Larry (Football Player)
Detroit Lions
2826 Tall Oaks Ct Apt 12
Auburn Hills, MI 48326-4151, USA

Lee, Laura
155 N Beverwyck Rd Pmb 245
Lake Hiawatha, NJ 07034, USA

Lee, Laurie Ann (Baseball Player)
19528 Cohasset St
Reseda, CA 91335-2436, USA

Lee, Lela (Actor)
c/o Staff Member *The Artists Group Ltd (LA)*
1650 Broadway Ste 610
New York, NY 10019-6833, USA

Lee, London
1650 Broadway Ste 1410
New York, NY 10019-6833, USA

Lee, Malcolm D (Actor, Director, Writer)
c/o Adam Kanter *Creative Artists Agency LCC (CAA-LA)*
2000 Avenue Of The Stars
Los Angeles, CA 90067-4700, USA

Lee, Mark (Baseball Player)
San Diego Padres
130 N Rosemont St
Amarillo, TX 79106-5214, USA

Lee, Mark (Baseball Player)
Kansas City Royals
3580 Brunswick Dr
Colorado Springs, CO 80920-7338, USA

Lee, Mark (Football Player)
Green Bay Packers
3610 208th St SE
Bothell, WA 98021-7023, USA

Lee, Mark C (Astronaut)
4574 Bishops Ct
Middleton, WI 53562-2326, USA

Lee, Michele
830 Birchwood Dr
Los Angeles, CA 90024-2502, USA

Lee, Mike (Baseball Player)
Cleveland Indians
1790 Calmin Dr
Fallbrook, CA 92028-4303, USA

Lee, Natasha (Actor, Dancer, Model)
c/o Staff Member *Don Capo Entertainment*
Ste 5 South Bank Terrace
Surbiton
Surrey KT6 6DG, UNITED KINGDOM (UK)

Lee, Patrick (Golfer)
Links Mmg
5068 W Plano Pkwy Ste 256
Plano, TX 75093-4441, USA

Lee, Raphael C (Doctor)
Massachusetts Institute Technology
Engineering Dept
Cambridge, MA 02139, USA

Lee, Robert M (Football Player)
Minnesota Vikings
363 Parker Ave
San Francisco, CA 94118-4235, USA

Lee, Ron (Basketball Player)
35788 Woodridge Ct
Farmington Hills, MI 48335-2206, USA

Lee, Ronnie (Football Player)
Miami Dolphins
139 Shady Trl
Mc Gregor, TX 76657-3768, USA

Lee, RonReaco
c/o Brett Carella *Lab, The*
5540 Hollywood Blvd # 200
Hollywood, CA 90028-6808, USA

Lee, Ruta (Actor)
2623 Laurel Canyon Blvd
Los Angeles, CA 90046-1106, USA

Lee, Samuel (Sammy) (Coach)
16537 Harbour Ln
Huntington Beach, CA 92649-2105, USA

Lee, Sandra (Chef, Television Host)
Sandra Lee Semi-Homemade
1453A 14th St # 126
Santa Monica, CA 90404-2703, USA

Lee, Shannon (Actor)
c/o John Elias *Three Twins Entertainment, Inc*
PO Box 100210
Staten Island, NY 10310-0210, USA

Lee, Sheryl (Actor)
William Morris Agency
151 El Camino Dr
Beverly Hills, CA 90212-2775, USA

Lee, Spike (Director)
c/o Staff Member *40 Acres & A Mule Filmworks Inc (NY)*
124 Dekalb Ave
Brooklyn, NY 11217-1200, USA

Lee, Stan (Cartoonist, Publisher)
Marvel Entertainment
1440 S Sepulveda Blvd # 114
Los Angeles, CA 90025-3458, USA

Lee, Steven (Television Host)
c/o Staff Member *Travel Channel*
1 Discovery Pl
Silver Spring, MD 20910-3354, USA

Lee, Sung Hi (Actor)
c/o Staff Member *TalentWorks (LA)*
3500 W Olive Ave Ste 1400
Burbank, CA 91505-5512, USA

Lee, Terry (Baseball Player)
Cincinnati Reds
143 Wedgewood Dr
Eugene, OR 97404-5909, USA

Lee, Tommy (Musician)
c/o Carl Stubner *Sanctuary Artist Management (UK)*
Sanctuary House
45-53 Sinclair Road
London W14 0NS, UNITED KINGDOM (UK)

Lee, Tony (Actor)
c/o Dave Phillips *Edmonds Management*
1635 N Cahuenga Blvd Fl 5
Los Angeles, CA 90028-6201, USA

Lee, Travis (Baseball Player)
Arizona Diamondbacks
985 Via Colinas
Westlake Village, CA 91362-5051, USA

Lee, Tsung-Dao (Nobel Prize Laureate)
25 Claremont Ave
New York, NY 10027-6813, USA

Lee, Vernon R (Religious Leader)
Wyatt Baptist Church
4621 W Hillsboro St
El Dorado, AR 71730-6768, USA

Lee, Vincent (Baseball Player)
Baltimore Black Sox
3228 Avondale Ave
Baltimore, MD 21215-4702, USA

Lee, William Gregory (Actor)
c/o Jeff Witjas *Agency for the Performing Arts (APA-NY)*
888 7th Ave
New York, NY 10106-0001, USA

Lee, Willie James (Baseball Player)
Kansas City Monarchs
400 5th Way
Birmingham, AL 35214-5706, USA

Lee, Yuan T (Nobel Prize Laureate)
Academy Sinica
Nankang
Taipei 11529, TAIWAN

Lee, Zeph (Football Player)
Denver Broncos
7417 1/2 S Normandie Ave
Los Angeles, CA 90044-2468, USA

Lee-Dries, Dolores (Baseball Player)
HC 78 Box 125X
Deming, NM 88030, USA

Lee-Harmon, Annabelle (Baseball Player)
960 Senate St
Costa Mesa, CA 92627-3332, USA

Leech, Beverly
9150 Wilshire Blvd Ste 175
Beverly Hills, CA 90212-3450, USA

Leech, Richard (Opera Singer)
Thea Dispeker Artists
59 E 54th St
New York, NY 10022-4256, USA

Leek, Gene (Baseball Player)
Cleveland Indians
4055 Hamilton St Apt 5
San Diego, CA 92104-6108, USA

Leek, Sybil (Misc)
Prentice-Hall
RR 9W
Englewood Cliffs, NJ 07632, USA

Leen, Bill (Musician)
William Morris Agency
1600 Division St Ste 300
Nashville, TN 37203-2755, USA

Leeper, Dave (Baseball Player)
Kansas City Royals
7730 Briarglen Loop Unit D
Stanton, CA 90680-4128, USA

Leerhsen, Erica (Actor)
c/o Staff Member *Principal Entertainment (LA)*
1964 Westwood Blvd Ste 400
Los Angeles, CA 90025-4695, USA

Leese, Howard (Musician)
219 2nd Ave N # 333
Seattle, WA 98109, USA

Leestma, David C (Astronaut)
4314 Lake Grove Dr
Seabrook, TX 77586-4114, USA

Leetch, Brian
29 Stratton Dr
Cheshire, CT 06410-3140, USA

Leetch, Brian J (Hockey Player)
225 W 83rd St
New York, NY 10024-4952, USA

Leetsma, David C
2101 Nasa Pkwy
Houston, TX 77058-3607, USA

Leetzow, Max (Football Player)
Denver Broncos
6590 S Williams Cir E
Centennial, CO 80121-2737, USA

Leeuwenburg, Jay (Football Player)
Chicago Bears
6268 S Coventry Ln W
Littleton, CO 80123-6756, USA

Leeves, Jane (Actor)
c/o Staff Member *3 Arts Entertainment Inc*
9460 Wilshire Blvd Fl 7
Beverly Hills, CA 90212-2713, USA

Lefcourt, Peter (Actor)
c/o Staff Member *Creative Artists Agency LCC (CAA-LA)*
2000 Avenue Of The Stars
Los Angeles, CA 90067-4700, USA

Lefebvre, Bill (Baseball Player)
Boston Red Sox
7349 Ulmerton Rd Lot 1379
Largo, FL 33771-4859, USA

Lefebvre, Jim (Baseball Player)
Los Angeles Dodgers
10160 E Whispering Wind Dr
Scottsdale, AZ 85255-3007, USA

Lefebvre, Joe (Baseball Player)
New York Yankees
10 Shore View Dr
Bow, NH 03304-4116, USA

Lefferts, Craig (Baseball Player)
Chicago Cubs
1818 Emerson Park Dr
Knoxville, TN 37922, USA

Leflore, Ron (Baseball Player)
Detroit Tigers
6263 93rd Ter Apt 4206
Pinellas Park, FL 33782-4640, USA

Leforce Jr, Clyde (Football Player)
Detroit Lions
715 Spring Ln
Bristow, OK 74010-1846, USA

Leftwich, Byron (Football Player)
Jacksonville Jaguars
1 Alltel Stadium Pl
Jacksonville, FL 32202-1917, USA

Leftwich, Phil (Baseball Player)
California Angels
1443 Rainbow Forest Dr
Lynchburg, VA 24502-3098, USA

Legace, Jean-Guy (Hockey Player)
126 Casa Grande Ln
Santa Rosa Beach, FL 32459-3162, USA

LeGault, Lance (Actor)
c/o Staff Member *Tisherman Agency Inc*
6767 Forest Lawn Dr Ste 101
Los Angeles, CA 90068-1050, USA

Legend, John (Actor, Musician)
c/o Dennis Ashley *Creative Artists Agency LCC (CAA-LA)*
2000 Avenue Of The Stars
Los Angeles, CA 90067-4700, USA

Leggett, Earl (Football Player)
Chicago Bears
PO Box 1204
Raymond, MS 39154-1204, USA

Legette, Burnie (Football Player)
New England Patriots
1118 Doyle Pl
Colorado Springs, CO 80915-2327, USA

Legette, Tyrone (Football Player)
New Orleans Saints
1304 Hancock St
Columbia, SC 29205-4850, USA

Legg, Greg (Baseball Player)
Philadelphia Phillies
412 Jenna Kay Dr
Archbald, PA 18403-1583, USA

Leggat, Ashley (Actor)
c/o Staff Member *Walt Disney Co, The (Buena Vista Motion Picture Group)*
500 S Buena Vista St
Ink And Paint Building Rm230
Burbank, CA 91521-0001, USA

Legge, Michael (Actor)
c/o Staff Member *Hatton McEwan*
PO Box 37385
London N1 7XF, UNITED KINGDOM (UK)

Leggett, Anthony J (Nobel Prize Laureate)
607 W Pennsylvania Ave
Urbana, IL 61801-4818, USA

Leggett, Jay (Actor, Producer, Writer)
c/o Lenore Zerman *Liberman/Zerman Management*
252 N Larchmont Blvd Ste 200
Los Angeles, CA 90004-3754, USA

Legien, Waldemar (Athlete)
Ul Grottgera 10
Bytom 41-902, POLAND

Legorreta, Vilchis Ricardo (Architect)
Palacio de Versalles
#285A
C Lomas Reforma
Mexico City 11020, MEXICO

Legrand, Michel (Composer, Musician)
c/o Staff Member *Kraft-Engel Management*
15233 Ventura Blvd Ste 200
Sherman Oaks, CA 91403-2244, USA

Legrande, Larry (Baseball Player)
Memphis Red Sox
1331 Leon St NW
Roanoke, VA 24017-6011, USA

Legree, Lance (Football Player)
New York Giants
4697 N Highway 52
Saint Stephen, SC 29479, USA

Legris, Manuel C (Ballerina)
National Theater of Paris Opera
8 Rue Scribe
Paris 75009, FRANCE

LeGros, James (Actor)
I F A Talent Agency
8730 W Sunset Blvd Ste 490
Los Angeles, CA 90069-2248, USA

LeGuin, Ursula K (Writer)
3321 NW Thurman St
Portland, OR 97210-1226, USA

Leguizamo, John (Actor, Comedian,
Producer, Writer)
c/o Staff Member *Rebel Films*
1 Worth St Fl 2
New York, NY 10013-2930, USA

Lehane, Dennis (Writer)
1412 Jackson Rd
Kerrville, TX 78028-3906, USA

Lehew, Jim (Baseball Player)
Baltimore Orioles
3086 Fairview Rd
Grantsville, MD 21536-2239, USA

Lehman, I Robert (Scientist)
895 Cedro Way
Palo Alto, CA 94305-1002, USA

Lehman, Jeffrey (Educator)
Cornell University
President's Office
Ithaca, NY 14853, USA

Lehman, Ken (Baseball Player)
Brooklyn Dodgers
3463 Renee Dr
Sedro Woolley, WA 98284-8812, USA

Lehman, Kristen (Actor)
c/o Perry Zimel *Oscars Abrams Zimel &
Associates*
438 Queen St E
Toronto, ON M5A 1T4, CANADA

Lehman, Manny (DJ)
c/o Len Evans *Project Publicity*
312 W 53rd St
New York, NY 10019-5743, USA

Lehman, Tom (Golfer)
9820 E Thompson Peak Pkwy Unit 704
Scottsdale, AZ 85255-6656, USA

Lehmann, Edie (Actor)
24844 Malibu Rd
Malibu, CA 90265-4617, USA

Lehmann, Erich L (Misc)
Research Statistics Group
Education Testing Service
Princeton, NJ 08541-0001, USA

Lehmann, Karl Cardinal (Religious Leader)
Bischofliches Ordinariat
PF 1560
Bischofsplatz 2
Mainz 55116, GERMANY

Lehmann, Michael (Director)
Creative Artists Agency
9830 Wilshire Blvd
Beverly Hills, CA 90212-1804, USA

Lehmberg, Stanford E (Historian)
1005 Calle Largo
Santa Fe, NM 87501-1068, USA

Lehmkuhl, Reichen (Model, Reality TV
Star, Writer)
c/o Ryan Daly *Kazarian/Spencer & Assoc
(LA)*
11969 Ventura Blvd
Box 7409 Fl 3
Studio City, CA 91604-2630, USA

Lehn, Jean Marie
21 rue d'Oslo
Strasbourg F-67000, FRANCE

Lehn, Jean-Marie P (Nobel Prize Laureate)
Louis Pasteur Universite
4 Rue Blaise Pascal
Strasbourg 67008, FRANCE

Lehninger, Albert L (Misc)
15020 Tanyard Rd
Sparks, MD 21152-9752, USA

Lehr, John (Actor, Producer, Writer)
c/o Staff Member *William Morris Agency
(WMA-LA)*
1 William Morris Pl
Beverly Hills, CA 90212-4261, USA

Lehrer, Jim (Journalist)
The NewsHour with Jim Lehrer
3620 27th St S
Arlington, VA 22206-2350, USA

Lehrer, Thomas A (Tom) (Comedian,
Musician)
University of California
Cowell College
Santa Cruz, CA 95064, USA

Lehrer, Tom
11 Sparks St
Cambridge, MA 02138-4711, USA

Lehrman, Logan (Actor)
c/o Joseph (Joe) Rice *Abrams Artists
Agency (LA)*
9200 W Sunset Blvd Ph 11
Los Angeles, CA 90069-3601, USA

Lehtinen, Dexter (Attorney, Attorney
General, General, Government Official)
US Attorney's Office
155 S Miami Ave
Justice Dept
Miami, FL 33130-1617, USA

Lehtinen, Jere (Hockey Player)
622 Stratford Ln
Coppell, TX 75019-6129, USA

Leibel, Rudolph (Misc)
464 Riverside Dr # 95
New York, NY 10027-6822, USA

Leiber, Jerry (Songwriter, Writer)
Leiber & Stoller Ent
9000 W Sunset Blvd
West Hollywood, CA 90069-5801, USA

Leibman, Ron (Actor)
c/o Staff Member *Agency for the
Performing Arts (APA-LA)*
405 S Beverly Dr
Beverly Hills, CA 90212-4416, USA

Leibovitz, Annie (Artist)
c/o Staff Member *Doubleday/
RandomHouse*
1745 Broadway
New York, NY 10019-4305, USA

Leibovitz, Mitchell G (Business Person)
Pep Boys-Manny Moe & Jack
3111 W Allegheny Ave
Philadelphia, PA 19132-1116, USA

Leifer, Carol (Actor, Comedian)
Brillstein/Grey
9150 Wilshire Blvd Ste 350
Beverly Hills, CA 90212-3453, USA

Leiferkus, Sergei P (Opera Singer)
5 The Paddocks
Abberbury Road
Iffley, Oxford OX4 4ET, UNITED
KINGDOM (UK)

Leifheit, Sylvia (Model)
Agentur Reed
Treppendorfer Weg 13
Berlin 12527, GERMANY

Leigeb, Brian (Football Player)
Indianapolis Colts
2528 N Wisner Ave
White Cloud, MI 49349-9478, USA

Leigh, Barbara
PO Box 246
Los Angeles, CA 90078-0246, USA

Leigh, Charlie (Football Player)
Cleveland Browns
PO Box 12931
Albany, NY 12212-2931, USA

Leigh, Danni (Musician)
c/o Bridget Bauer *Bismeaux Productions*
PO Box 463
Austin, TX 78767-0463, USA

Leigh, Jennifer Jason (Actor)
c/o Greg Clark *Untitled Entertainment
(LA)*
331 N Maple Dr Fl 3
Beverly Hills, CA 90210-3827, USA

Leigh, Mike (Director)
Thin Man Films
9 Greek St
Soho
London W1D 4DQ, UNITED KINGDOM
(UK)

Leigh, Mitch (Composer)
29 W 57th St # 1000
New York, NY 10019-3406, USA

Leigh, Regina (Musician)
Bobby Roberts
3050 Business Park Cir Ste 303
Goodlettsville, TN 37072-3588, USA

Leigh, Tara (Actor)
c/o Staff Member *William Morris Agency
(WMA-LA)*
1 William Morris Pl
Beverly Hills, CA 90212-4261, USA

Leighton, GB (Musician)
c/o Staff Member *Paradigm (Monterey)*
509 Hartnell St
Monterey, CA 93940-2825, USA

Leighton, Laura (Actor)
c/o Paul Santana *Agency for the
Performing Arts (APA-LA)*
405 S Beverly Dr
Beverly Hills, CA 90212-4416, USA

Leija, James (Jesse) (Boxer)
154 Octavia Pl
San Antonio, TX 78214-1236, USA

Leiker, Tony (Football Player)
Green Bay Packers
411 E 21st St
Hays, KS 67601-2805, USA

Leimkuehler, Paul (Business Person, Skier)
351 Darbys Run
Bay Village, OH 44140-2968, USA

Leinart, Matt (Actor)
c/o Steve Lashever *Creative Artists Agency
LCC (CAA-LA)*
2000 Avenue Of The Stars
Los Angeles, CA 90067-4700, USA

Leiper, Dave (Baseball Player)
Oakland A's
13082 N 103rd St
Scottsdale, AZ 85260-7272, USA

Leister, John (Baseball Player)
Boston Red Sox
304 Devon Dr
Saint Louis, MI 48880-9427, USA

Leisure, David (Actor)
26358 Woodlark Ln
Valencia, CA 91355-3518, USA

Leitch, Donovan
8794 Lookout Mountain Ave
Los Angeles, CA 90046-1859, USA

Leitch, Matthew (Actor)
c/o Colleen Schlegel *Innovative Artists
(LA)*
1505 10th St
Santa Monica, CA 90401-2805, USA

Leiter, Alois T (Al) (Baseball Player)
New York Yankees
2660 Riviera Mnr
Weston, FL 33332-3422, USA

Leiter, Mark (Baseball Player)
New York Yankees
110 Pine St
Toms River, NJ 08753-6822, USA

Leitner, Patric-Fritz (Athlete)
BSD
An der Schiessstatte 4
Berchtesgaden 83471, GERMANY

Leitso, Tyron (Actor)
c/o Deb Dillistone *Lucas Talent Inc*
Sun Tower Floor 7
100 W Pender St
Vancouver, BC V6B 1R8, CANADA

Leitzel, Joan (Educator)
University of Nebraska
President's Office
Lincoln, NE 68588, USA

Leius, Scott (Baseball Player)
Minnesota Twins
12620 42nd Pl N
Minneapolis, MN 55442-2344, USA

Lejohn, Don (Baseball Player)
Los Angeles Dodgers
154 Edwards St
Brownsville, PA 15417-9316, USA

Lekakis, Paul (Musician)
c/o Staff Member *Diva Central Inc*
7510 W Sunset Blvd Ste 1445
Los Angeles, CA 90046-3408, USA

Lekang, Anton (Skier)
47 Pratt St
Winsted, CT 06098-2025, USA

Lelbrandt, Charlie (Baseball Player)
Cincinnati Reds
1235 Stuart Rdg
Alpharetta, GA 30022-6364, USA

Lelliott, Jeremy (Actor)
c/o Joan Green *Joan Green Management*
1836 Courtney Ter
Los Angeles, CA 90046-2106, USA

LeLouch, Claude (Director)
15 Ave Hoche
Paris 75008, FRANCE

Lelyveld, Joseph (Editor)
New York Times
229 W 43rd St
Editorial Dept
New York, NY 10036-3959, USA

Lemaire, Jacques G (Coach, Hockey
Player)
803 Riviera Dunes Way
Palmetto, FL 34221-7125, USA

Lemanczyk, Dave (Baseball Player)
Detroit Tigers
24 Lehigh Ct
Rockville Centre, NY 11570-2016, USA

Lemaster, Denny (Baseball Player)
Milwaukee Braves
4833 Carlene Way SW
Lilburn, GA 30047-4705, USA

Lemaster, Frank (Football Player)
Philadelphia Eagles
PO Box 159
Birchrunville, PA 19421-0159, USA

Lemaster, Johnnie (Baseball Player)
San Francisco Giants
372 4th St
Paintsville, KY 41240, USA

Lemay, Dick (Baseball Player)
San Francisco Giants
1741 N Holland Ln
Wichita, KS 67212-6242, USA

LeMay-Doan, Michelle (Speed Skater)
Landmark Sport Group
277 Richmond St W
Toronto, ON M5V 1X1, CANADA

Lembeck, Helaine (Actor)
Conan Carroll & Associates
11350 Ventura Blvd Ste 200
Studio City, CA 91604-3140, USA

Lembeck, Michael (Actor, Director)
23852 Pacific Coast Hwy # 355
Malibu, CA 90265-4876, USA

Lemche, Kris (Actor)
c/o Brian Wilkins *Wilkins Management*
901 N Highland Ave
Los Angeles, CA 90038-2412, USA

Lemek, Ray (Football Player)
Washington Redskins
36536 Center Ridge Rd
North Ridgeville, OH 44039-2843, USA

Lemelson, Jerome H (Inventor)
48 Parkside Dr
Princeton, NJ 08540-4813, USA

LeMesurier, John (Actor)
56 Barron's Keep
London W14, UNITED KINGDOM (UK)

Lemieux, Claude (Hockey Player)
6008 N Saguaro Rd
Paradise Valley, AZ 85253-4223, USA

Lemieux, Jocelyn (Hockey Player)
1123 Sandhurst Ct
Buffalo Grove, IL 60089-6822, USA

Lemieux, Joseph H (Business Person)
Owens-Illinois Inc
1 Sea Gate
Toledo, OH 43666-0001, USA

LeMieux, Kathryn (Cartoonist)
King Features Syndicate
888 7th Ave Ste 201
New York, NY 10106-0201, USA

Lemieux, Mario (Hockey Player)
630 Academy Ave
Sewickley, PA 15143-1172, USA

Lemieux, Raymond U (Misc)
7602 119th St
Edmonton, AB T6G 1W3, CANADA

Lemke, Mark A (Baseball Player)
Atlanta Braves
3 Olena Dr
Whitesboro, NY 13492-2103, USA

Lemme, Steve (Comedian)
c/o Staff Member *United Talent Agency (UTA)*
9560 Wilshire Blvd Ste 500
Beverly Hills, CA 90212-2401, USA

Lemmerman, Bruce (Football Player)
Atlanta Falcons
621 Silverado Way
Eagle Point, OR 97524-9011, USA

Lemmon, Chris (Actor)
80 Murray Dr
South Glastonbury, CT 06073-2435, USA

Lemmons, Kasi (Director, Writer)
8605 Appian Way
Los Angeles, CA 90046-7730, USA

Lemon, Don (Baseball Player)
603 Peeksville Rd
Locust Grove, GA 30248-3142, USA

Lemon, Lynn
2220 Shady Grove Dr
Bedford, TX 76021-4421, USA

Lemon, Peter C (War Hero)
6245 Viewfield Hts
Colorado Springs, CO 80919-3747, USA

Lemon Jelly (Music Group)
c/o Staff Member *Paradigm (Monterey)*
509 Hartnell St
Monterey, CA 93940-2825, USA

Lemonds, Dave (Baseball Player)
Chicago Cubs
5029 Jackson Dr
Charlotte, NC 28269-1910, USA

Lemongelio, Mark (Baseball Player)
Houston Astros
13437 S 47th St
Phoenix, AZ 85044-4833, USA

Lemonheads
1775 Broadway Ste 433
New York, NY 10019-1903, USA

Lemons, Abe
4314 Saint Thomas Dr
Oklahoma City, OK 73120-8320, USA

Lemos, Richie (Boxer)
18658 Klum Pl
Rowland Heights, CA 91748-4850, USA

Lemper, Ute (Actor, Dancer, Musician)
Les Visiteurs du Soir
40 Rue de la Folie Regnault
Paris 75011, FRANCE

Lenahan, Edward P (Publisher)
Fortune Magazine
Rockefeller Center
New York, NY 10020, USA

Lenard, Jo (Baseball Player)
38 S Walworth Ave
Williams Bay, WI 53191-9741, USA

Lenard, Michael B (Misc)
US Olympic Committee
1 Olympic Plz
Colorado Springs, CO 80909-5760, USA

Lenard, Voshon (Basketball Player)
Denver Nuggets
1000 Chopper Cir
Pepsi Center
Denver, CO 80204-5805, USA

Lendl, Ivan (Tennis Player)
400 5 1/2 Mile Rd
Goshen, CT 06756-1032, USA

Lenfant, Claude J M (Physicist)
PO Box 83027
Gaithersburg, MD 20883-3027, USA

Lengies, Vanessa (Actor)
c/o Daniel (Danny) Sussman *Brillstein-Grey Entertainment*
9150 Wilshire Blvd Ste 350
Beverly Hills, CA 90212-3453, USA

L'Engle, Madeleine (Writer)
924 W End Ave
New York, NY 10025-3534, USA

Lenhardt, Don (Baseball Player)
St Louis Browns
13317 Woodlake Village Ct W
Saint Louis, MO 63141-6071, USA

Lenich, Bill (Football Player)
Milwaukee Chiefs
545 Bambury Way
Kirkwood, MO 63122-1142, USA

Lenihan, Brian J (Government Official)
24 Park View
Castleknock
County Dublin, IRELAND

Leningrad CowboysBMG Ariola
Steinhauser Str. 3
Munich D-81677, GERMANY

Lenk, Maria (Swimmer)
Rua Cupertino Durao 16
Leblon
Rio de Janeiro 22441, BRAZIL

Lenk, Thomas (Artist)
Gemeinde Braunsbach
Schloss Tierberg 7176, GERMANY

Lenk, Tom (Actor)
c/o Michael Valeo *McKeon-Valeo-Myones Management*
9100 Wilshire Blvd Ste 350W
Beverly Hills, CA 90212-3437, USA

Lenkaitis, William E (Football Player)
San Diego Chargers
26 Rose Court Way
East Walpole, MA 02032-1185, USA

Lennie, Angus (Actor)
Jean Drysdale
15 Pembroke Gardens
London W8, UNITED KINGDOM (UK)

Lennix, Harry (Actor)
c/o Staff Member *Creative Artists Agency LCC (CAA-LA)*
2000 Avenue Of The Stars
Los Angeles, CA 90067-4700, USA

Lennon, Bob (Baseball Player)
New York Giants
8 Dudley Ln
Dix Hills, NY 11746-6504, USA

Lennon, Diane (Musician)
1984 State Highway 165
Branson, MO 65616-8936, USA

Lennon, Janet (Musician)
1984 State Highway 165
Branson, MO 65616-8936, USA

Lennon, Julian (Musician, Songwriter, Writer)
30 Ives St
London SW3 2ND, UNITED KINGDOM (UK)

Lennon, Kathy (Musician)
Overlook Dr #10
Branson, MO 65616, USA

Lennon, Patrick (Baseball Player)
Seattle Mariners
716 Pinewood Dr
Whiteville, NC 28472-3828, USA

Lennon, Peggy (Musician)
1984 State Highway 165
Branson, MO 65616-8936, USA

Lennon, Richard G (Religious Leader)
Archdiocese of Boston
2121 Commonwealth Ave
Boston, MA 02135-3193, USA

Lennon, Sean (Musician)
Dakota Hotel
1 W 72nd St
New York, NY 10023-3486, USA

Lennon, Thomas (Actor)
c/o Lee Gabler *Creative Artists Agency LCC (CAA-LA)*
2000 Avenue Of The Stars
Los Angeles, CA 90067-4700, USA

Lennon Sisters
1984 State Highway 165
Branson, MO 65616-8936, USA

Lennox, Annie (Musician)
c/o Jeff Frasco *Creative Artists Agency LCC (CAA-LA)*
2000 Avenue Of The Stars
Los Angeles, CA 90067-4700, USA

Lennox, William Jr (Educator, General)
Superintendent
US Military Academy
West Point, NY 10996, USA

Lenny, Rick H. (Business Person)
Hershey Foods
100 Crystal A Dr
Hershey, PA 17033-9702, USA

Leno, Jay (Actor, Comedian, Talk Show Host)
c/o Staff Member *NBC Studios*
3000 W Alameda Ave
Burbank, CA 91523-0001, USA

Lenoir, William B (Astronaut)
Space Flight & Station Office
Nasa Hq
Code M/S
Washington, DC 20546-0001, USA

Lenska, Rula (Actor, Model)
David Daley Assoc
586A Kings Road
London SW6 2DX, UNITED KINGDOM (UK)

Lentine, Jim (Baseball Player)
St Louis Cardinals
1066 Calle Del Cerro Unit 1411
San Clemente, CA 92672-6075, USA

Lenton, Lisbeth (Athlete, Olympic Athlete)
Australian Swimming Inc
Unit 12/7 Beissel Street
Canberra, Belconnen 2617, AUSTRALIA

Lenz, Bethany Joy (Joie) (Actor)
c/o Elena Deutsch *Envoy Entertainment*
3656 Dellvale Pl
Encino, CA 91436-4144, USA

Lenz, Kay (Actor)
5916 Filaree Hts
Malibu, CA 90265-3721, USA

Lenz, Kim (Musician, Songwriter, Writer)
Mark Pucia Media
5000 Oak Bluff Ct
Atlanta, GA 30350-1069, USA

Lenz, Rick (Actor)
12955 Calvert St
Van Nuys, CA 91401-3206, USA

Lenzi, Mark (Misc)
3524 S Burks Ct
Bloomington, IN 47401-8464, USA

Leo, Melissa (Actor)
c/o Staff Member *Altman, Greenfield & Selvaggi*
11766 Wilshire Blvd Ste 1610
Los Angeles, CA 90025-6565, USA

Leon
1180 S Beverly Dr Ste 608
Los Angeles, CA 90035-1158, USA

Leon, Carlos
4519 Cockerham Dr
Los Angeles, CA 90027-1223, USA

Leon, Eddie (Baseball Player)
Cleveland Indians
6241 E Vista Del Canon
Tucson, AZ 85750-1038, USA

Leon, Kenny (Actor, Business Person, Director)
True Colors Theatre Company
659 Auburn Ave NE Apt 257
Atlanta, GA 30312-1981, USA

Leon, Melina (Musician)
c/o Staff Member *Sony Music Miami*
605 Lincoln Rd Fl 7
Miami Beach, FL 33139-2900, USA

Leon, Valerie (Actor)
Essanay Ltd
2 Conduit St
London W1R 9TG, UNITED KINGDOM (UK)

Leonard, Bill (Football Player)
Baltimore Colts
928 Meadow Ln
Schenectady, NY 12309-6529, USA

Leonard, Bob (Slick) (Basketball Player, Coach)
1241 Hillcrest Dr
Carmel, IN 46033-2343, USA

Leonard, Dennis P (Baseball Player)
Kansas City Royals
4102 SW Evergreen St
Blue Springs, MO 64015-9713, USA

Leonard, Elmore (Writer)
2192 Yarmouth Rd
Bloomfield Village, MI 48301-2339, USA

Leonard, Hugh (Writer)
6 Rossaun Pilot View
Dalkey
County Dublin, IRELAND

Leonard, James (Football Player)
Tampa Bay Buccaneers
RR 332 Box 349
Mullica Hill, NY 10862, USA

Leonard, Jeffrey (Baseball Player)
Los Angeles Dodgers
1626 N Felton St
Philadelphia, PA 19151-3438, USA

Leonard, Joanne (Photographer)
University of Michigan
Art Dept
Ann Arbor, MI 48109, USA

Leonard, Joe (Motorcycle Race, Motorcycle Racer, Race Car Driver)
Motorsports Hall of Fame
PO Box 194
Novi, MI 48376-0194, USA

Leonard, Joshua (Actor)
c/o Staff Member *Innovative Artists (LA)*
1505 10th St
Santa Monica, CA 90401-2805, USA

Leonard, Mark (Baseball Player)
San Francisco Giants
22042 Hibiscus Dr
Cupertino, CA 95014-0109, USA

Leonard, Ray C (Sugar Ray) (Boxer)
c/o Christopher Barrett *Metropolitan*
4500 Wilshire Blvd Fl 2
Los Angeles, CA 90010-3858, USA

Leonard, Robert Sean (Actor)
14 Bergen Ave
Waldwick, NJ 07463-1919, USA

Leonard, Wayne (Business Person)
Entergy Corp
10055 Grogans Mill Rd # 5A
The Woodlands, TX 77380-1059, USA

Leonard-Linehan, Rhoda (Baseball Player)
84 Bruce Rd
Norwood, MA 02062-3103, USA

Leonetti, John R (Cinematographer)
5251 Genesta Ave
Encino, CA 91316-2617, USA

Leonetti, Matthew (Cinematographer)
1362 Bella Oceana Vis
Pacific Palisades, CA 90272-2359, USA

Leong, Page (Actor)
C N A Assoc
1925 Century Park E Ste 750
Los Angeles, CA 90067-2708, USA

Leonhard, Dave (Baseball Player)
Baltimore Orioles
87 Corning St
Beverly, MA 01915-3732, USA

Leonhart, William (Diplomat)
119 Oak Ter
Lake Bluff, IL 60044-2717, USA

Leoni, Tea (Actor)
c/o Jimmy Miller *Mosaic Media Group*
24 Music Sq W Fl 1
Nashville, TN 37203-6661, USA

Leonov, Aleksei A (Cosmonaut, General)
Alfa Capital
Acad Sakharov Prospect 12
Moscow 107078, RUSSIA

Leonskaja, Elisabeth (Musician)
Columbia Artists Mgmt Inc
1790 Broadway Fl 6
New York, NY 10019-1412, USA

Leopold, Bobby (Football Player)
San Francisco 49ers
801 Beckleymeade Ave Apt 1116
Dallas, TX 75232-5225, USA

Leopold, Tom (Comedian)
c/o Staff Member *Gersh Agency, The (LA)*
232 N Canon Dr
Beverly Hills, CA 90210-5302, USA

Lepcio, Ted (Baseball Player)
Boston Red Sox
263 Greenlodge St
Dedham, MA 02026-6400, USA

LePelley, Guernsey (Cartoonist, Editor)
35 Saint Germain St
Boston, MA 02115-3216, USA

LePichon, Xavier (Geophysicist, Physicist)
Ecole Normale Superieure
24 Rue Lhomond
Paris 75005, FRANCE

Leppard, Raymond J
Indianapolis Symphony
32 E Washington St Ste 600
Indianapolis, IN 46204-3585, USA

Lepperd, Thomas (Baseball Player)
5962 Wistful Vista Dr
West Des Moines, IA 50266-2864, USA

Leppert, Don (Baseball Player)
Pittsburgh Pirates
9226 Rami Ave
Columbus, OH 43240-2158, USA

Leppert, Don (Baseball Player)
Baltimore Orioles
1630 Epping Forest Dr
Southaven, MS 38671-8849, USA

Lepsis, Matt (Football Player)
Denver Broncos
326 Paragon Way
Castle Rock, CO 80108-9017, USA

Lerach, William (Bill) (Attorney, Attorney General, General)
Milberg Weiss Hynes Lerach
1600 Broadway # 1800
San Diego, CA 92101-5715, USA

L'Erario, Joe
7700 Wisconsin Ave
Bethesda, MD 20814-3578, USA

Lerch, Randy (Baseball Player)
Philadelphia Phillies
19490 Monterey St
Morgan Hill, CA 95037-2606, USA

Lerche, Sondre (Musician)
c/o Staff Member *Paradigm (Monterey)*
509 Hartnell St
Monterey, CA 93940-2825, USA

Lerchen, George (Baseball Player)
Detroit Tigers
354 E Rose Ave
Garden City, MI 48135-2645, USA

Lerner, Michael (Actor)
Innovative Artists
1505 10th St
Santa Monica, CA 90401-2805, USA

LeRoux, Francois (Opera Singer)
I M G Artists
3 Burlington Lane
Chiswick
London W4 2TH, UNITED KINGDOM (UK)

Leroy, Emarlos (Football Player)
Jacksonville Jaguars
10135 Gate Pkwy N
Jacksonville, FL 32246-8274, USA

LeRoy, Gloria (Actor)
Shelly & Pierce
13775A Mono Way # 220
Sonora, CA 95370-8813, USA

Leroy, Philippe
77 rue Pigalle
Paris F-75009, FRANCE

Lersch, Barry (Baseball Player)
Philadelphia Phillies
2280 S Jasper Way Apt B
Aurora, CO 80013-1199, USA

Lesane, Jimmy (Football Player)
Chicago Bears
3629 Coronado Rd
Baltimore, MD 21244-3848, USA

Lesar, David (Business Person)
Halliburton Co
500 N Akard St
Lincoln Plaza
Dallas, TX 75201-3302, USA

Leschin, Luisa (Producer, Writer)
c/o Staff Member *William Morris Agency (WMA-LA)*
1 William Morris Pl
Beverly Hills, CA 90212-4261, USA

Lesco, Lisa (Actor)
2006 S Canfield Ave
Los Angeles, CA 90034-1111, USA

Lesh, Phil (Musician)
PO Box 1073
San Rafael, CA 94915-1073, USA

Leshana, David C (Educator)
8246 E Hoverland Rd
Scottsdale, AZ 85255-3908, USA

Lesher, Brian (Baseball Player)
Oakland A's
10015 E Mountain View Rd
Scottsdale, AZ 85258-5221, USA

Leshnock, Don (Baseball Player)
Detroit Tigers
289 Carlin Ct W
Columbus, OH 43230-1608, USA

Leskanic, Court (Baseball Player)
Colorado Rockies
2032 Alaqua Dr
Longwood, FL 32779-3116, USA

Lesko, Matthew (Writer)
HiRise Promotions Inc
1555 N Dearborn Pkwy Fl 25
C/O Kim McCoy
Chicago, IL 60610-1448, USA

Lesley, Brad (Baseball Player)
Cincinnati Reds
5235 Kester Ave Apt 207
Sherman Oaks, CA 91411-4076, USA

Leslie, Aleen
1700 Lexington Rd
Beverly Hills, CA 90210-2810, USA

Leslie, Fred W (Astronaut)
317 Inverness Dr SW
Huntsville, AL 35802-4511, USA

Leslie, Joan (Actor)
2228 N Catalina St
Los Angeles, CA 90027-1127, USA

Leslie, Lisa (Basketball Player, Model)
5200 Shenandoah Ave
Los Angeles, CA 90056-1035, USA

Leslie, Robbie (DJ)
c/o Staff Member *Diva Central Inc*
7510 W Sunset Blvd Ste 1445
Los Angeles, CA 90046-3408, USA

Lesnar, Brock (Wrestler)
c/o Staff Member *World Wrestling Entertainment (WWE)*
1241 E Main St
Stamford, CT 06902-3520, USA

Lesnie, Andrew (Cinematographer)
c/o Wayne Fitterman *United Talent Agency (UTA)*
9560 Wilshire Blvd Ste 500
Beverly Hills, CA 90212-2401, USA

Lesser, Len (Actor)
934 N Evergreen St
Burbank, CA 91505-2713, USA

Lessing, Doris M (Writer)
11 Kingscroft Road
#3
London NW2 3QE, UNITED KINGDOM (UK)

Lester, Adrian (Actor)
c/o Staff Member *Seven Summits Pictures & Management*
8906 W Olympic Blvd Ground Floor
Beverly Hills, CA 90211, USA

Lester, Darrell G (Football Player)
3721 Echo Trl
Fort Worth, TX 76109-3432, USA

Lester, Ketty (Actor, Musician)
5931 Comey Ave
Los Angeles, CA 90034-2213, USA

Lester, Mark (Actor)
Carlton Clinic
1 Carlton St
Cheltenham
Glou GLS2 6AG, UNITED KINGDOM
(UK)

Lester, Mark L (Director)
17268 Camino Yatasto
Pacific Palisades, CA 90272, USA

Lester, Richard
River Lane Petersham
Surrey, ENGLAND, UNITED KINGDOM
(UK)

Lester, Tim (Football Player)
Los Angeles Rams
1160 Bream Dr
Alpharetta, GA 30004-4411, USA

Lester, Tom
c/o Gary Moore *Gary Moore Management*
55 Karen Dr
Greenville, SC 29607-1207, USA

Lester of Herne Hill, Anthony P
(Attorney, Attorney General, General)
Blackstone Chambers
Blackstone House
Temple
London EC4Y 9BW, UNITED KINGDOM
(UK)

Lesure, James (Actor)
c/o Vincent Cirrincione *Vincent Cirrincione Associates*
1516 N Fairfax Ave
Los Angeles, CA 90046-2608, USA

Letarte, Pierre (Cinematographer)
551 W Pinacle
Albercom, PQ J0E 1B0, CANADA

Letbetter, R Steve (Business Person)
Reliant Energy
1111 Louisiana St
Houston, TX 77002-5230, USA

Lethem, Jonathan (Writer)
Doubleday Press
1540 Broadway
New York, NY 10036-4039, USA

Letlow, W R (Russ) (Football Player)
1876 Thelma Dr
San Luis Obispo, CA 93405-6238, USA

Letner, Robert (Football Player)
Buffalo Bills
6515 Patty Ln
Harrison, TN 37341-6987, USA

Leto, Jared (Actor)
c/o Josh Lieberman *Creative Artists Agency LCC (CAA-LA)*
2000 Avenue Of The Stars
Los Angeles, CA 90067-4700, USA

Letscher, Matt (Actor)
c/o Sandy Joseph *SLJ Management*
8336 De Longpre Ave
Los Angeles, CA 90069-2602, USA

Letsie III (King)
Royal Palace
PO Box 524
Maseru, LESOTHO

Lett, Leon (Football Player)
Dallas Cowboys
4959 Cape Coral Dr
Dallas, TX 75287-7234, USA

Letterle, Daniel (Actor)
c/o Geordie Frey *GEF Entertainment*
122 N Clark Dr Apt 401
West Hollywood, CA 90048-6315, USA

Letterman, David (Comedian, Talk Show Host)
Late Show with David Letterman
1697 Broadway Fl 11
Cbs
New York, NY 10019-5904, USA

Lettermen, The
9255 W Sunset Blvd Ste 407
Los Angeles, CA 90069-3302, USA

Leung, Ken (Actor)
c/o Rachel Shapiro *Jeff Morrone Management*
9350 Wilshire Blvd Ste 224
Beverly Hills, CA 90212-3204, USA

Leuwerik, Ruth
Zuccalistr. 31
Munich D-80639, GERMANY

Levangie, Gigi (Writer)
c/o David Lubliner *William Morris Agency (WMA-LA)*
1 William Morris Pl
Beverly Hills, CA 90212-4261, USA

LeVay, Simon (Scientist)
970 Palm Ave
West Hollywood, CA 90069-4072, USA

Levchenko, Alexander
141 Sryosdny Gorodok
Potchta Kosmonavtov, RUSSIA

Levellers (Music Group)
c/o Staff Member *Paradigm (Monterey)*
509 Hartnell St
Monterey, CA 93940-2825, USA

Levene, Ben (Artist)
Royal Academy of Arts
Piccadilly
London W1V 2LP, UNITED KINGDOM
(UK)

Levenick, Dave (Football Player)
Atlanta Falcons
13947 Northridge Dr
Holly, MI 48442-8231, USA

Levens, Dorsey (Football Player)
Green Bay Packers
2070 Meadowsweet Dr
Green Bay, WI 54313-5447, USA

Levenseller, Mike (Football Player)
Buffalo Bills
1570 SW Wadleigh Dr
Pullman, WA 99163-2049, USA

Levenstein, John (Comedian)
c/o Staff Member *International Creative Management (ICM-LA)*
10250 Constellation Blvd
Los Angeles, CA 90067-6200, USA

Leveque, Michel (Politician)
Minister of State's Office
BP 522
Monaco Cedex 98015, MONACO

Lever, Johny (Actor, Bollywood, Comedian)
151/152 Oxford Tower Yamuna Nagar
Lokhandwala Complex Andheri
Bombay, MS 400 058, INDIA

Leverington, Shelby
1801 Avenue Of The Stars # 1250
Los Angeles, CA 90067-5902, USA

Levert, Eddie (Musician)
Associated Booking Corp
PO Box 2055
New York, NY 10021-0051, USA

Levesque, Joanna (JoJo) (Musician)
c/o Brian Bunnin *International Creative Management (ICM-LA)*
10250 Constellation Blvd
Los Angeles, CA 90067-6200, USA

Levesque, Paul Michael (Wrestler)
c/o Kevin Volchok *Endeavor Agency LLC (LA)*
9601 Wilshire Blvd Fl 3
Beverly Hills, CA 90210-5204, USA

Levi, Wayne (Golfer)
17 Ironwood Rd
New Hartford, NY 13413-3902, USA

Levi, Yoel
Askonas Holt Ltd
27 Chancery Lane
London WC2A 1PF, UNITED KINGDOM
(UK)

Levi, Zachary (Actor)
c/o Joan Hyler *Hyler Management*
3000 Olympic Blvd Bldg 5 Ste 2250
Santa Monica, CA 90404-5073, USA

Levi-Montalcini, Rita (Nobel Prize Laureate)
Cell Biology Institute
Piazzale Aldo Moro 7
Rome 00185, ITALY

Levi-Strauss, Claude (Misc)
2 Rue des Marronniers
Paris 75016, FRANCE

LeVias, Jerry (Football Player)
Houston Oilers
3322 Chris Dr
Houston, TX 77063-6230, USA

Levin, Drake (Musician)
Paradise Artists
108 E Matilija St
Ojai, CA 93023-2639, USA

Levin, Harvey
6922 Hollywood Blvd # 415
Hollywood, CA 90028-6117, USA

Levin, Ira (Writer)
1172 Park Ave
New York, NY 10128-1213, USA

Levin, Richard C (Educator)
Yale University
President's Office
New Heaven, CT 06520, USA

Levin, Tony (Musician)
c/o Staff Member *Agency Group Ltd, The (NY)*
1775 Broadway Ste 515
New York, NY 10019-1903, USA

Levine, Adam (Music Group, Musician)
c/o Robert Norman *Creative Artists Agency LCC (CAA-LA)*
2000 Avenue Of The Stars
Los Angeles, CA 90067-4700, USA

Levine, Al (Baseball Player)
Chicago White Sox
10916 E Paradise Dr
Scottsdale, AZ 85259-7007, USA

Levine, David (Artist)
161 Henry St
Brooklyn, NY 11201-2565, USA

Levine, Ellen R (Editor)
Good Housekeeping Magazine
959 8th Ave
New York, NY 10019-3737, USA

Levine, Irving R (Correspondent)
Lynn University
International Studies/Economics Dept
Boca Raton, FL 33431, USA

Levine, Jack (Artist)
68 Morton St
New York, NY 10014-4021, USA

Levine, James
Boston Symphony Orchestra
301 Massachusetts Ave
Boston, MA 02115-4557, USA

Levine, Jerry
1505 10th St
Santa Monica, CA 90401-2805, USA

Levine, Ken (Writer)
c/o Staff Member *Broder Webb Chervin Silbermann Agency, The (BWCS)*
10250 Constellation Blvd Ste P
Los Angeles, CA 90067-6213, USA

Levine, Michael (Business Person)
Levine Communications
1180 S Beverly Dr Ste 301
Los Angeles, CA 90035-1154, USA

Levine, Philip (Writer)
4549 N Van Ness Blvd
Fresno, CA 93704-3727, USA

Levine, Rachmiel (Misc)
614 Walnut St
Newtonville, MA 02460-2462, USA

Levine, S Robert (Business Person)
Cabletron Systems
PO Box 5005
Rochester, NH 03866-5005, USA

Levine, Samm (Actor)
c/o Staff Member *3 Arts Entertainment Inc*
9460 Wilshire Blvd Fl 7
Beverly Hills, CA 90212-2713, USA

Levine, Sol (Activist)
30 Powell St
Brookline, MA 02446-3921, USA

Levine, Ted (Actor)
c/o Robbi Kass *RK Management*
209 N Canon Dr
Beverly Hills, CA 90210-5301, USA

Levingston, Cliff (Basketball Player)
Denver Nuggets
1000 Chopper Cir
Pepsi Center
Denver, CO 80204-5805, USA

Levingstone, Ken (Government Official)
House of Commons
Westminster
London SW1A 0AA, UNITED KINGDOM
(UK)

Levinsohn, Gary (Producer)
c/o Staff Member *Mutual Film Company*
650 N Bronson Ave
Clinton Bldg
Los Angeles, CA 90004-1404, USA

Levinson, Barry (Actor, Director, Producer, Writer)
c/o Staff Member *Levinson/Fontanta Company, The*
185 Broome St
New York, NY 10002-3901, USA

Levinson, Chris (Writer)
c/o Staff Member *Endeavor Agency LLC (LA)*
9601 Wilshire Blvd Fl 3
Beverly Hills, CA 90210-5204, USA

Levinson, Jay Conrad (Business Person, Writer)
Guerilla Marketing Intl
3700 S Westport Ave # 2994
Sioux Falls, SD 57106-6360, USA

Levinson, Sanford V (Attorney, Attorney General, Educator, General)
3410 Windsor Rd
Austin, TX 78703-2248, USA

Levis, Jesse (Baseball Player)
Cleveland Indians
1219 Highland Ave
Fort Washington, PA 19034-1605, USA

Levis, Patrick (Actor)
c/o Staff Member *TalentWorks (LA)*
3500 W Olive Ave Ste 1400
Burbank, CA 91505-5512, USA

Levitas, Andrew (Actor)
Metropolitan Talent Agency
4500 Wilshire Blvd Fl 2
Los Angeles, CA 90010-3858, USA

Levitt, Arthus Jr (Financier, Government Official)
Carlyle Group
1001 Pennsylvania Ave NW Ste 220S
Washington, DC 20004-2525, USA

Levitt, Chad (Football Player)
Oakland Raiders
104 Towanda Ave
Melrose Park, PA 19027-2932, USA

Levitt, Gene
9200 W Sunset Blvd Ph 25
Los Angeles, CA 90069-3601, USA

Levitt, George (Misc)
82 Via Del Corso
Palm Beach Gardens, FL 33418-3773, USA

LeVox, Gary (Musician)
LBG Media
1228 Pineview Ln
Nashville, TN 37211-7422, USA

Levrault, Allen (Baseball Player)
Milwaukee Brewers
18 Milk Ave
Westport, MA 02790-3714, USA

Levy, Clifford J (Journalist)
New York Times
229 W 43rd St
Editorial Dept
New York, NY 10036-3959, USA

Levy, David (Government Official)
New Way Party
Knesset
Kiryat Ben Gurion
Jerusalem 91950, ISRAEL

Levy, Ed (Baseball Player)
Philadelphia Phillies
5701 NW 88th Ave Ste 360
Tamarac, FL 33321-4400, USA

Levy, Eugene (Actor, Director)
c/o David (Dave) Becky *3 Arts Entertainment Inc*
9460 Wilshire Blvd Fl 7
Beverly Hills, CA 90212-2713, USA

Levy, Kenneth (Business Person)
KLA-Tencor Corp
160 Rio Robles
San Jose, CA 95134-1813, USA

Levy, Leonard W (Historian)
1025 Timberline Ter
Ashland, OR 97520-3436, USA

Levy, Mariana (Actor)
c/o Staff Member *Televisa*
Blvd Adolfo Lopez Mateos 232
Colonia San Angel INN
DF CP 01060, MEXICO

Levy, Marv (Coach)
National Organization of Professional Athletes
1806 Watermere Ln
Windermere, FL 34786-6121, USA

Levy, Marvin David (Composer)
Sheldon Sofer Mgmt
130 W 56th St
New York, NY 10019-3866, USA

Levy, Michael R (Publisher)
Texas Monthly Magazine
PO Box 1569
Austin, TX 78767-1569, USA

Levy, Peter (Cinematographer)
International Creative Mgmt
8942 Wilshire Blvd # 219
Beverly Hills, CA 90211-1908, USA

Levy, Shawn (Actor, Director)
c/o Staff Member *The Firm*
9465 Wilshire Blvd Fl 6
Beverly Hills, CA 90212-2605, USA

Lewallyn, Dennis (Baseball Player)
Los Angeles Dodgers
2900 Breckenridge Dr
Pensacola, FL 32526-2903, USA

Lewinsky, Monica (Designer, Fashion Designer)
c/o Staff Member *BWR (BWR-LA)*
9100 Wilshire Blvd Fl 6
West Tower
Beverly Hills, CA 90212-3401, USA

LeWinter, Nancy Nadler (Publisher)
Esquire Magazine
1790 Broadway Ste 1300
New York, NY 10019-1412, USA

Lewis, Aaron (Musician)
Staind/Elektra Records
75 Rockefeller Plz
New York, NY 10019-6908, USA

Lewis, Al (Grandpa) (Actor)
PO Box 277
New York, NY 10044-0205, USA

Lewis, Albert R (Football Player)
Kansas City Chiefs
3532 Macedonia Rd
Centreville, MS 39631-3634, USA

Lewis, Allen (Government Official)
Beaver Lodge
Mom PO Box 1076
Castries, Sanit Lucia, WEST INDIES

Lewis, Ananda (Correspondent)
c/o Staff Member *Insider, The*
5555 Melrose Ave
Stage 26
Los Angeles, CA 90038-3989, USA

Lewis, Andrew L (Drew) (Business Person, Secretary)
PO Box 70
Lederach, PA 19450-0070, USA

Lewis, Anthony (Writer)
New York Times
2 Faneuil Hall Sq
Editorial Dept
Boston, MA 02109, USA

Lewis, Barbara (Musician)
Hello Stranger Productions
PO Box 300488
Fern Park, FL 32730-0488, USA

Lewis, Bernard (Historian)
Princeton University
Near Eastern Studies Dept
Princeton, NJ 08544-0001, USA

Lewis, Bill (Coach, Football Coach)
Georgia Institute of Technology
Athletic Dept
Atlanta, GA 30332-0001, USA

Lewis, Bobby (Musician)
Lustig Talent
PO Box 770850
Orlando, FL 32877-0850, USA

Lewis, Buddy (Baseball Player)
Washington Senators
PO Box 788
Gastonia, NC 28053-0788, USA

Lewis, Carl (Actor)
c/o Staff Member *William Morris Agency (WMA-LA)*
1 William Morris Pl
Beverly Hills, CA 90212-4261, USA

Lewis, Charlotte (Basketball Player)
2814 N Sheridan Rd
Peoria, IL 61604-2716, USA

Lewis, Clea (Actor)
1659 S Highland Ave
Los Angeles, CA 90019-5540, USA

Lewis, Colby (Baseball Player)
Texas Rangers
14800 Orchard Crest Ave
Bakersfield, CA 93314-9280, USA

Lewis, Crystal (Musician)
Proper Mgmt
PO Box 150867
Nashville, TN 37215-0867, USA

Lewis, Cynthia R (Publisher)
Harper's Bazaar
1770 Broadway
New York, NY 10019, USA

Lewis, D D (Football Player)
Dallas Cowboys
1624 Northcrest Dr
Plano, TX 75075-8749, USA

Lewis, Damian (Actor)
Markham & Froggalt
Julian House
4 Windmill St
London W1P 1HF, UNITED KINGDOM (UK)

Lewis, Damione (Football Player)
Saint Louis Rams
9115 Drayton Ln
Fort Mill, SC 29707-5848, USA

Lewis, Dan (Football Player)
Detroit Lions
460 S Park St
Detroit, MI 48215-4108, USA

Lewis, Darren (Baseball Player)
Oakland A's
2212 Rosemount Ln
San Ramon, CA 94582-5719, USA

Lewis, Darren (Football Player)
Chicago Bears
641 Seabeach Rd
Dallas, TX 75232-4842, USA

Lewis, Dave (Coach, Hockey Player)
22583 Heatherbridge Lane
Northville, MN 48167, USA

Lewis, David Levering (Writer)
Rutgers University
History Dept
East Rutherford, NJ 08903, USA

Lewis, David R (Football Player)
Cincinnati Bengals
406 142nd St
Ocean City, MD 21842-5602, USA

Lewis, Dawnn (Actor)
c/o Staff Member *Gage Group, The (LA)*
14724 Ventura Blvd Ste 505
Sherman Oaks, CA 91403-3505, USA

Lewis, Emmanuel (Manny) (Actor)
c/o Gregory (Greg) Mayo *Orange Grove Group Inc*
12178 Ventura Blvd Ste 205
Studio City, CA 91604-2540, USA

Lewis, Frank (Football Player)
Pittsburgh Steelers
118 Presque Isle Dr
Houma, LA 70363-3828, USA

Lewis, Garry (Football Player)
Oakland Raiders
1000 Alcorn Dr # 737
Lorman, MS 39096-7500, USA

Lewis, Gary (Musician)
701 Balin Court
Nashville, TN 37221, USA

Lewis, Gary W (Football Player)
Green Bay Packers
10 N Farm Road 144
Mount Pleasant, TX 75455-8809, USA

Lewis, Geoffrey (Actor)
William Morris Agency
151 El Camino Dr
Beverly Hills, CA 90212-2775, USA

Lewis, Grady (Basketball Player)
8926 W Topeka Dr
Peoria, IL 61615, USA

Lewis, Huey (Actor, Musician)
c/o Carol Stair *Bob Brown Management*
PO Box 779
Mill Valley, CA 94942-0779, USA

Lewis, J L (Golfer)
2504 Orleans Dr
Cedar Park, TX 78613-4727, USA

Lewis, Jamal (Football Player)
Baltimore Ravens
PO Box 1416
Randallstown, MD 21133-1410, USA

Lewis, Jason (Actor)
c/o Alissa Vradenburg *Untitled Entertainment (LA)*
331 N Maple Dr Fl 3
Beverly Hills, CA 90210-3827, USA

Lewis, Jazsmin
c/o Daniel (Dan) Spilo *Artistry Management*
525 Westbourne Dr
West Hollywood, CA 90048-1913, USA

Lewis, Jeff (Football Player)
Denver Broncos
RR 2 Box 189
Greentop, MO 63546-9730, USA

Lewis, Jenifer
PO Box 5617
Beverly Hills, CA 90209-5617, USA

Lewis, Jenna (Reality TV Star)
c/o Juliette Harris *It Girl Public Relations*
3763 Eddingham Ave
Calabasas, CA 91302-5835, USA

Lewis, Jermaine (Football Player)
Octagon
1751 Pinnacle Dr Ste 1500
McLean, VA 22102-3833, USA

Lewis, Jerry (Actor, Comedian, Director)
1701 Waldman Ave
Las Vegas, NV 89102-2428, USA

Lewis, Jerry Lee (Composer, Musician)
JKL Enterprise
PO Box 384
Nesbit, MS 38651-0384, USA

Lewis, Jim (Baseball Player)
San Diego Padres
3481 Sargent St
La Verne, CA 91750-3427, USA

Lewis, Jim (Baseball Player)
Seattle Mariners
5311 Hansel Ave Apt D12
Orlando, FL 32809-3415, USA

Lewis, Johnny (Baseball Player)
St Louis Cardinals
810 Tara Cir
Cantonment, FL 32533-9700, USA

Lewis, Jon Peter (Musician, Reality TV Star)
PO Box 533
Newbury Park, CA 91319-0533, USA

Lewis, Judy
71359 Cypress Dr
Rancho Mirage, CA 92270-3553, USA

Lewis, Juliette (Actor)
c/o Brandy Lewis *BL Management*
3330 Barham Blvd Ste 208
Hollywood, CA 90068-1445, USA

Lewis, Karen (Writer)
c/o James Sarnoff *The Sarnoff Company Inc*
10 Universal City Plz Ste 2000
Universal City, CA 91608-1074, USA

Lewis, Kenneth D (Financier)
Bank of America Corp
100 N Tryon St
Charlotte, NC 28255-0001, USA

Lewis, Kevin (Football Player)
New York Giants
4417 Roy St
Orlando, FL 32812-7350, USA

Lewis, Lennox (Boxer)
Panix Promotions
99 Middlesex St
London E1 7DA, UNITED KINGDOM
(UK)

Lewis, Marcia
700 New Hampshire Ave NW
Washington, DC 20037-2407, USA

Lewis, Mark (Baseball Player)
Cleveland Indians
1753 Cleveland Ave
Hamilton, OH 45013-5114, USA

Lewis, Mark (Football Player)
Green Bay Packers
PO Box 11021
Spring, TX 77391-1021, USA

Lewis, Marvin (Coach, Football Coach)
Cincinnati Bengals
1 Paul Brown Stadium
Cincinnati, OH 45202-3492, USA

Lewis, Mary (Christianni Brand) (Writer)
88 Maida Vale
London W9, UNITED KINGDOM (UK)

Lewis, Matthew (Actor)
c/o Sarah Spear *Curtis Brown Ltd*
Hay Market House 28/29
Hay Market Fl 4
London SW1 Y45, UNITED KINGDOM
(UK)

Lewis, Michael (Writer)
W W Norton
500 5th Ave
New York, NY 10110-0054, USA

Lewis, Mike (Football Player)
Atlanta Falcons
3350 Blodgett St
Houston, TX 77004-6305, USA

Lewis, Mo (Football Player)
New York Jets
3280 Northside Pkwy NW Apt 314
Atlanta, GA 30327-2260, USA

Lewis, Monica (Musician)
Lang
1100 Alta Loma Rd Apt 16A
Los Angeles, CA 90069-2441, USA

Lewis, Peter B (Business Person)
Progressive Corp
32854 Sorrento Ln
Avon Lake, OH 44012-2386, USA

Lewis, Phill (Actor)
c/o Gregg A Klein *Abrams Artists Agency (LA)*
9200 W Sunset Blvd Ph 11
Los Angeles, CA 90069-3601, USA

Lewis, Ramsey (Composer, Musician)
c/o Staff Member *APA Talent and Literary Agency*
9200 W Sunset Blvd
Los Angeles, CA 90069-3502, USA

Lewis, Rashard (Basketball Player)
Seattle SuperSonics
1201 3rd Ave Ste 1000
Seattle, WA 98101-3038, USA

Lewis, Ray (Football Player)
Baltimore Ravens
1421 Connestee Rd
Lakeland, FL 33805-3348, USA

Lewis, Richard (Actor, Comedian)
8001 Hemet Pl
Los Angeles, CA 90046-2117, USA

Lewis, Richard J (Producer)
c/o Staff Member *Writers and Artists Group Intl (LA)*
8383 Wilshire Blvd Ste 550
Beverly Hills, CA 90211-2417, USA

Lewis, Richie (Baseball Player)
Baltimore Orioles
13209 E County Road 700 S
Losantville, IN 47354-9514, USA

Lewis, Ron (Football Player)
San Francisco 49ers
12821 Haverford Rd W Apt 1
Jacksonville, FL 32218-4879, USA

Lewis, Russell T (Business Person, Publisher)
New York Times Co
229 W 43rd St
New York, NY 10036-3959, USA

Lewis, Scott (Baseball Player)
California Angels
2584 Fairway Dr
Costa Mesa, CA 92627-1312, USA

Lewis, Shaznay (Musician)
c/o Staff Member *Concorde Intl Artists Ltd*
101 Shepherds Bush Rd
London W6 7LP, UNITED KINGDOM
(UK)

Lewis, Sherman (Football Player)
New York Jets
45822 Bristol Cir
Novi, MI 48377-3900, USA

Lewis, Tim (Football Player)
Green Bay Packers
9105 Clerkenwell Dr
Waxhaw, NC 28173-6786, USA

Lewis, Vaughan A (Prime Minister)
United Workers Party
1 Riverside Road
Castries, SAINT LUCIA

Lewis, Vicki (Actor, Comedian)
Special Artists Agency
9465 Wilshire Blvd Ste 880
Beverly Hills, CA 90212-2607, USA

Lewis, Victor (Musician)
Joanne Klein
130 W 28th St
New York, NY 10001-6151, USA

Lewis III, Leo (Football Player)
Minnesota Vikings
10116 Ivywood Ct
Eden Prairie, MN 55347-4543, USA

Lewiston, Denis C (Cinematographer)
13700 Tahiti Way # 24
Marina Del Rey, CA 90292-6584, USA

Lewit-Nirenberg, Julie (Publisher)
Mademoiselle Magazine
350 Madison Ave
New York, NY 10017-3700, USA

LeWitt, Sol (Artist)
20 Pratt St
Chester, CT 06412-1307, USA

Ley, La (Musician)
c/o Staff Member *Creative Artists Agency LCC (CAA-LA)*
2000 Avenue Of The Stars
Los Angeles, CA 90067-4700, USA

Ley, Terry (Baseball Player)
New York Yankees
2620 1st St
Baker City, OR 97814-2007, USA

Leyden, Paul (Actor)
c/o Rhonda Price *Gersh Agency, The (NY)*
41 Madison Ave Fl 33
New York, NY 10010-2202, USA

Leygue, Louis Georges (Artist)
6 Rue de Docteur Blanche
Paris 75016, FRANCE

Leyland, James R (Jim) (Baseball Player)
261 Tech Rd
Pittsburgh, PA 15205-1734, USA

Leyritz, James J (Jim) (Baseball Player)
495 Vinegarten Dr
Cincinnati, OH 45255-5204, USA

Leyritz, Jim (Baseball Player)
New York Yankees
6511 Rodeo Dr
Southwest Ranches, FL 33330-3600, USA

Leyton, John (Actor, Musician)
53 Keyes House
Dolphin Square
London SW1V 3NA, UNITED KINGDOM
(UK)

Leyva, Nicholas T (Nick) (Baseball Player)
1098 Tilghman Rd
Chesterbrook, PA 19087-5878, USA

Lezcano, Carlos (Baseball Player)
Chicago Cubs
415 W Boxelder Pl
Chandler, AZ 85225-7114, USA

Lezcano, Sixto (Baseball Player)
Milwaukee Brewers
7828 Bardmoor Hill Cir
Orlando, FL 32835-8158, USA

LFO (Musician)
Evolution Talent Agency
1776 Broadway Fl 15
New York, NY 10019-2002, USA

L'Hermitte, Thierry (Actor)
ICE 3
13 Rue Yves-Toudic
Paris 75010, FRANCE

Li, Gong (Actor, Model)
Xi'an Film Studio
Xi'an City
Shaanxi Province, CHINA

Li, Jet (Actor)
c/o Steve Chasman *Ace Media*
1411 5th St Ste 405
Santa Monica, CA 90401-2417, USA

Li, Keyu (Designer, Fashion Designer)
21 Gong-Jian Hutong
Di An-Men
Beijing 100009, CHINA

Li, Lanqing (Government Official)
Communist Party Central Committee
Zhong Nan Hai
Beijing, CHINA

Li, Peng (President)
Communist Party Central Committee
Zhong Nan Hai
Beijing, CHINA

Liacouras, Peter J (Educator)
Temple University
President's Office
Philadelphia, PA 19122, USA

Liaklev, Reidar (Speed Skater)
2770 Jaren
NORWAY

Liars (Music Group)
c/o David T Viecelli *Billions Corporation, The*
833 W Chicago Ave Ste 101
Chicago, IL 60622-8408, USA

Liars Inc (Music Group)
c/o Staff Member *Foodchain Records*
6464 W Sunset Blvd Ste 920
Los Angeles, CA 90028-8011, USA

Libano Christo, Carlos A (Activist, Writer)
Rua Atibaia 420
Sao Paulo 01235-010, BRAZIL

Liber, Jon (Baseball Player)
Pittsburgh Pirates
2805 Churchbell Ct
Mobile, AL 36695-2528, USA

Liberace, Dora
1775 E Tropicana Ave
Las Vegas, NV 89119-6529, USA

Libertini, Richard (Actor)
2313 McKinley Ave
Venice, CA 90291-4623, USA

Liberty, Richard
225 SW 6th St
Dania, FL 33004-3943, USA

Libeskind, Daniel (Architect)
Studio Daniel Libeskund
Windscheidstr 18
Berlin 10627, GERMANY

Libran, Frankie (Baseball Player)
San Diego Padres
100 Calle Principe Apt 1
Mayaguez, PR 00680-3545, USA

Libutti, Frank (General, Misc)
New York City Deputy Commissioner's Office
Police Plaza
New York, NY 10038, USA

Licad, Cecile (Musician)
Columbia Artists Mgmt Inc
1790 Broadway Fl 6
New York, NY 10019-1412, USA

Lichfield, Earl of (Photographer)
Lichfield Studios
133 Oxford Gardens
London W10 6NE, UNITED KINGDOM (UK)

Licht, Jeremy (Actor)
4355 Clybourn Ave
Toluca Lake, CA 91602-2906, USA

Licht, Louis (Scientist)
Ecoltree
3017 Valley View Ln NE
North Liberty, IA 52317-9538, USA

Lichtenberg, Byron K (Astronaut)
5701 Impala South Rd
Athens, TX 75752-6053, USA

Lichtenberger, H W (Business Person)
Praxair Inc
39 Old Ridgebury Rd
Danbury, CT 06810-5109, USA

Lichtenstein, Harvey (Music Group)
Brooklyn Academy of Music
30 Lafayette Ave
Brooklyn, NY 11217-1486, USA

Lick, Dennis A (Football Player)
Chicago Bears
6140 S Knox Ave
Chicago, IL 60629-5424, USA

Lickert, John (Baseball Player)
Boston Red Sox
PO Box 279
North Scituate, RI 02857-0279, USA

Lickliter, Frank (Golfer)
8111 Seven Mile Dr
Ponte Vedra Beach, FL 32082-3110, USA

Licon, Jeffrey (Actor)
c/o Katie Mason *Paradigm (LA)*
360 N Crescent Dr
North Bldg
Beverly Hills, CA 90210-6820, USA

Lidback, Jenny (Golfer)
1130 Graystone Xing
Alpharetta, GA 30005-7436, USA

Liddell, Chuck (Athlete, Wrestler)
c/o Jervis Cole *Zinkin Entertainment & Sports Management*
5 E River Park Pl W Ste 203
Fresno, CA 93720-1557, USA

Liddell, Dave (Baseball Player)
New York Mets
2631 Preakness Way
Norco, CA 92860-4201, USA

Liddy, Edward M (Business Person)
Allstate Corp
2775 Sanders Rd
Allstate Plaza
Northbrook, IL 60062-6127, USA

Liddy, G Gordon (Actor)
9112 Riverside Dr
Fort Washington, MD 20744-6863, USA

Lidge, Brad (Baseball Player)
Houston Astros
447 N Gate Stone
Houston, TX 77007-8341, USA

Lidov, Arthur (Artist)
Pleasant Ridge Rd
Poughquag, NY 12570, USA

Lidstrom, Nicklas (Hockey Player)
47725 Bellagio Dr
Northville, MI 48167-9803, USA

Liebensteuin, Todd (Football Player)
Washington Redskins
4486 Chain O Lakes Rd
Eagle River, WI 54521-8856, USA

Lieber, Larry (Cartoonist)
King Features Syndicate
888 7th Ave Ste 201
New York, NY 10106-0201, USA

Lieber, Paul (Actor)
Margrit Polak Mgmt
1411 Carroll Ave
Los Angeles, CA 90026-5111, USA

Lieber, Rob (Writer)
c/o Staff Member *International Creative Management (ICM-LA)*
10250 Constellation Blvd
Los Angeles, CA 90067-6200, USA

Lieberman, Joseph I (Senator)
Senate Hart Office Bldg #Sh-706
Washington, DC 20510-0001, USA

Lieberman, Wendy
PO Box 5617
Beverly Hills, CA 90209-5617, USA

Lieberman, William S (Misc)
Metropolitan Museum of Art
5th Ave & 82nd St
New York, NY 10028, USA

Liebert, Ottmar (Musician)
Jones & O'Malley
10123 Camarillo St
Toluca Lake, CA 91602, USA

Lieberthai, Mike (Baseball Player)
Philadelphia Phillies
1740 Larkfield Ave
Westlake Village, CA 91362-4245, USA

Lieberthal, Michael S (Mike) (Baseball Player)
1750 Larkfield Ave
Westlake Village, CA 91362, USA

Liebeskind, John (Doctor)
University of California Medical Center
Surgery Dept
Los Angeles, CA 90024, USA

Liebesman, Jonathan (Director)
c/o David Gardner *Current Entertainment*
9200 W Sunset Blvd
West Hollywood, CA 90069-3502, USA

Liebman, David (Musician)
2206 Brislin Rd
Stroudsburg, PA 18360-8623, USA

Liebowitz, Fran
205 W 57th St
New York, NY 10019-2105, USA

Liebrich, Barbara (Baseball Player)
16608 N 51st St
Scottsdale, AZ 85254-1063, USA

Liefeld, Rob (Cartoonist)
Image Comics
1942 University Ave Ste 305
Berkeley, CA 94704-1073, USA

Lien, Chan (Prime Minister)
Prime Minister's Office
1 Chunghsiano East Road
Sec 1
Taipei, TAIWAN

Lien, Jennifer (Actor)
c/o Staff Member *Abrams Artists Agency (LA)*
9200 W Sunset Blvd Ph 11
Los Angeles, CA 90069-3601, USA

Lienas, Winston (Baseball Player)
California Angels
Apartado #92
Santiago, DOMINICAN REPUBLIC

Lienhard, William (Bill) (Basketball Player)
1320 Lawrence Ave
Lawrence, KS 66049-2938, USA

Liepa, Andris (Ballerina)
Bryusov Per 17
#12
Moscow 103009, RUSSIA

Liepa, Iisa (Ballerina)
Bryusov Per 17
#12
Moscow 103009, RUSSIA

Liepmann, Hans W (Engineer, Physicist)
55 Haverstock Road
La Canada-Flintridge, CA 91011, USA

Lietzke, Bruce (Golfer)
PO Box 177
Larue, TX 75770-0177, USA

Lifehouse (Music Group)
c/o Staff Member *Creative Artists Agency (CAA-Nashville)*
3310 W End Ave Fl 5
Nashville, TN 37203-1028, USA

Lifeson, Alex (Musician)
Macklam Feldman Mgmt
1505 W 2nd Ave
#200
Vancouver, BC V6H 3Y4, CANADA

Lifford, Tina (Actor)
c/o Mark Armstrong *Sanders/Armstrong Management*
2120 Colorado Ave Ste 120
Santa Monica, CA 90404-3561, USA

Lifvendahl, Harold R (Publisher)
Orlando Sentinel
633 N Orange Ave
Orlando, FL 32801-1349, USA

Ligarde, Sebastian (Actor)
c/o Staff Member *Televisa*
Blvd Adolfo Lopez Mateos 232
Colonia San Angel INN
DF CP 01060, MEXICO

Light, John (Actor)
CAA
9830 Wilshire Blvd
Beverly Hills, CA 90212-1804, USA

Light, Judith (Actor)
c/o Bob Gersh *Gersh Agency, The (LA)*
232 N Canon Dr
Beverly Hills, CA 90210-5302, USA

Lightfoot, Gordon (Musician, Songwriter, Writer)
That's Entertainment
1711 Lawrence Rd # 101
Franklin, TN 37069-1703, USA

Lightfoot, Leonard
446 S Orchard Dr
Burbank, CA 91506-2738, USA

Lightner, Candy (Activist)
22653 Pacific Coast Hwy # 289
Malibu, CA 90265-5096, USA

Ligon, Tom
227 Waverly Pl
New York, NY 10014-2407, USA

Ligouri, James A (Educator)
Iona College
President's Office
New Rochelle, NY 10801, USA

Ligtenberg, Kerry (Baseball Player)
Atlanta Braves
9274 Albright Ct
Inver Grove, MN 55077-4546, USA

Likens, Peter W (Educator)
Lehigh University
President's Office
Bethlehem, PA 18020, USA

Lil' Cease (Musician)
Famous Artists Agency
250 W 57th St
New York, NY 10107-0001, USA

Lil' J (Actor, Musician, Television Host)
c/o Staff Member *Thruline Entertainment*
9250 Wilshire Blvd Ground Fl
Beverly Hills, CA 90210, USA

Lil Jon (Musician)
c/o Charles King *William Morris Agency (WMA-LA)*
1 William Morris Pl
Beverly Hills, CA 90212-4261, USA

Lil' Kim (Musician)
c/o Mark Cheatham *International Creative Management (ICM-NY)*
40 W 57th St
New York, NY 10019-4001, USA

Lil' Romeo (Musician)
c/o Michael Menchel *Relevant Entertainment Group (LA)*
12300 Wilshire Blvd Ste 420
Los Angeles, CA 90025-1061, USA

Liles, Kevin (Business Person)
75 Rockefeller Plz Fl 32
New York, NY 10019-6908, USA

Lilja, George (Football Player)
Los Angeles Rams
35 Steepleview Dr
Hudson, OH 44236-2299, USA

Lill, John R (Musician)
Harold Holt
31 Sinclair Road
London W14 0NS, UNITED KINGDOM
(UK)

Lillard, Bill (Baseball Player)
Philadelphia Athletics
750 Black Oak Ln
Nipomo, CA 93444-8822, USA

Lillard, Bill (Bowler)
5418 Imogene St
Houston, TX 77096-2206, USA

Lillard, Matthew (Actor)
c/o Jimmy Miller *Mosaic Media Group*
24 Music Sq W Fl 1
Nashville, TN 37203-6661, USA

Lillee, Dennis K (Cricketer)
Swan Sport
PO Box 158
Byron Bay, NSW 2481, AUSTRALIA

Lilley, Chris (Actor)
RGM Associates
c/o Sharne MacDonald
PO Box 128
Surry Hills NSW 2010, AUSTRALIA

Lilley, James R (Diplomat)
2801 New Mexico Ave NW Apt 407
Washington, DC 20007-3929, USA

Lilliquist, Derek (Baseball Player)
Atlanta Braves
426 33rd Ave SW
Vero Beach, FL 32968-3122, USA

Lillis, Bob (Baseball Player)
Los Angeles Dodgers
5107 Cherry Tree Ln
Orlando, FL 32819-3848, USA

Lillis, Charles M (Business Person)
MediaOne Group
188 Iverness Dr W
Englewood, CO 80112, USA

Lillix (Music Group)
c/o Staff Member *SL Feldman &
Associates*
1505 W 2nd Ave #200
Vancouver, BC V6H 3Y4, CANADA

Lilly, Evangeline (Actor)
c/o Hylda Queally *Creative Artists Agency
LCC (CAA-LA)*
2000 Avenue Of The Stars
Los Angeles, CA 90067-4700, USA

Lilly, Kristine (Athlete, Soccer Player)
c/o Team Member *Boston Breakers*
200 Highland Ave Ste 400
Needham, MA 02494-3019, USA

Lilly, Robert L (Bob) (Football Player)
Dallas Cowboys
104 Aster Cir
Georgetown, TX 78633-4537, USA

Lilly, Ted (Baseball Player)
Montreal Expos
208 NE Monroe Cir N Apt 305
St Petersburg, FL 33702-7570, USA

Lilly, Theodore (Baseball Player)
Montreal Expos
PO Box 257
Bass Lake, CA 93604-0257, USA

Lillywhite, Verl (Football Player)
San Francisco 49ers
1828 N Barkley
Mesa, AZ 85203-2702, USA

Lim, Kwan Hi
1660 Piikoi St
Honolulu, HI 96822-2719, USA

Lima, Adriana (Actor)
c/o Staff Member *DNA Model
Management*
520 Broadway Fl 11
New York, NY 10012-4436, USA

Lima, Devin
LFO/BMG Records
8750 Wilshire Blvd
Beverly Hills, CA 90211-2713, USA

Lima, Jose (Baseball Player)
Detroit Tigers
8012 Wiles Rd # 7
Coral Springs, FL 33067-2072, USA

Lima, Jose (Baseball Player)
Carr Janico Km 12 1/2
#61
Santigo, DOMINICAN REPUBLIC

Lima, Luis (Opera Singer)
1950 Redondela Dr
Rancho Palos Verdes, CA 90275-1028,
USA

Liman, Doug (Director, Producer, Writer)
c/o Adam Kanter *Creative Artists Agency
LCC (CAA-LA)*
2000 Avenue Of The Stars
Los Angeles, CA 90067-4700, USA

Limato, Ed
456 S Plymouth Blvd
Los Angeles, CA 90020-4708, USA

Limbaugh, Rush (Radio Personality)
Premiere Radio Networks, Inc
15260 Ventura Blvd
Sherman Oaks, CA 91403-5307, USA

Limbrick, Garrett (Football Player)
Miami Dolphins
2123 4th St
Hempstead, TX 77445-6922, USA

Lime, Yvonne (Actor)
Fedderson
6135 E McDonald Dr
Paradise Valley, AZ 85253-5222, USA

Limelighters, The
11761 E Speedway Blvd
Tucson, AZ 85748-2017, USA

Limmer, Lou (Baseball Player)
Philadelphia Athletics
231 Medford Ct Unit A
Manalapan, NJ 07726-4433, USA

Limos, Tiffany (Actor)
c/o Staff Member *Paradigm (LA)*
360 N Crescent Dr
North Bldg
Beverly Hills, CA 90210-6820, USA

Lin, Bridget (Actor)
8 Fei Ngo Shan Road
Kowloon
Hong Kong, CHINA

Lin, Ching-Hsia (Actor)
Taiwan Cinema-Drama Assn
196 Chunghua Road
10/F Sec 1
Taipei, TAIWAN

Lin, Cho-Laing
473 W End Ave # 15A
New York, NY 10024-4934, USA

Lin, Cho-Liang (Musician)
Hilliard School
60 Lincoln Center Plz
New York, NY 10023-6588, USA

Lin, Maya Ying (Architect, Artist)
Sidney Janis Gallery
120 E 75th St # 6A
New York, NY 10021-3240, USA

Lin, Tsung-Yi (Misc)
6287 MacDonald St
Vancouver, BC V6N 1E7, CANADA

Lincoln, Andrew (Actor)
c/o Staff Member *International Creative
Management (ICM-UK)*
Oxford House
76 Oxford St
London W1N 0AX, UNITED KINGDOM
(UK)

Lincoln, Howard (Baseball Player)
Seattle Mariners
6 Holly Hill Dr
Mercer Island, WA 98040-5326, USA

Lincoln, Jeremy (Football Player)
Chicago Bears
71 Broadway Apt 20A
New York, NY 10006-2612, USA

Lincoln, Keith P (Football Player)
San Diego Chargers
550 SE Crestview St
Pullman, WA 99163-2257, USA

Lincoln, Lar Park
8899 Beverly Blvd Ste 510
Los Angeles, CA 90048-2449, USA

Lincoln, Michael (Baseball Player)
Minnesota Twins
8269 Moss Oak Ave
Citrus Heights, CA 95610-0763, USA

Lind, DeDe
PO Box 1712
Boca Raton, FL 33429-1712, USA

Lind, Don L (Astronaut)
51 N 376 E
Smithfield, UT 84335-1111, USA

Lind, Joan (Athlete)
240 Euclid Ave
Long Beach, CA 90803-6020, USA

Lind, Juha (Hockey Player)
Montreal Canadiens
1260 de la Gauchetiere W
Montreal, PQ H3B 5E8, CANADA

Lind, Marshall L (Educator)
University of Alaska Southeast
Chancellor's Office
Janeau, AK 99801, USA

Lind, Sarah (Actor)
c/o Staff Member *Lucas Talent Inc*
Sun Tower Floor 7
100 W Pender St
Vancouver, BC V6B 1R8, CANADA

Lindahl, George III (Business Person)
Union Pacific Resources
PO Box 1330
Houston, TX 77251-1330, USA

Lindahl, Virgil (Football Player)
New York Giants
10315 W Kingswood Cir
Sun City, AZ 85351-1940, USA

Lindbeck, Assar (Economist)
50 Ostermalmsgatan
Stockholm 114 26, SWEDEN

Lindbeck, Em (Baseball Player)
Detroit Tigers
210 Hillcrest Dr
Kewanee, IL 61443-3424, USA

Lindberg, Chad (Actor)
c/o Staff Member *Michael Black
Management*
9701 Wilshire Blvd Ste 1000
Beverly Hills, CA 90212-2010, USA

Lindbergh, Reeve (Writer)
Simon and Schuster, Inc
1230 Avenue Of The Americas Fl Conc1
New York, NY 10020-1586, USA

Lindelind, Liv (Model)
PO Box 1029
Frazier Park, CA 93225-1029, USA

Lindell, Heather (Actor)
c/o Alan Ellsweig *Metropolitan*
4500 Wilshire Blvd Fl 2
Los Angeles, CA 90010-3858, USA

Lindell, Rian (Football Player)
Seattle Seahawks
712 NE 157th Ct
Vancouver, WA 98684-8734, USA

Lindelof, Damon (Producer, Writer)
c/o Ted Miller *Creative Artists Agency
LCC (CAA-LA)*
2000 Avenue Of The Stars
Los Angeles, CA 90067-4700, USA

Lindeman, Jim (Baseball Player)
St Louis Cardinals
2278 S Scott St
Des Plaines, IL 60018-3147, USA

Linden, Hal (Actor)
c/o Staff Member *Stone Manners Talent &
Literary (NY)*
900 Broadway Ste 803
New York, NY 10003-1229, USA

Linden, Walt (Baseball Player)
Boston Braves
4432 Harvey Ave
Western Springs, IL 60558-1645, USA

Lindenlaub, Karl W (Cinematographer)
3021 Nichols Canyon Rd
Los Angeles, CA 90046-1242, USA

Lindenmann, Tony (Bowler)
35096 Jefferson Ave Apt 216
Harrison Township, MI 48045-3275, USA

Linder, Kate (Actor)
c/o Sandra Siegal *Siegal Company, The*
9025 Wilshire Blvd Ste 400
Beverly Hills, CA 90211-1828, USA

Lindes, Hal (Musician)
Damage Mgmt
16 Lambton Place
London W11 2SH, UNITED KINGDOM
(UK)

Lindh, Hilary (Skier)
PO Box 33036
Juneau, AK 99803-3036, USA

Lindholm, Ingvar
Hringe Hages Vag 33
Ronninge 14400, SWEDEN

Lindig, Bill M (Business Person)
Sysco Corp
1390 Enclave Pkwy
Houston, TX 77077-2099, USA

Lindley, Christina (Model)
Lindley Enterprises
114 Rhine Dr
Madison, TN 37115-3561, USA

Lindley, John W (Cinematographer)
PO Box 351
15332 Antioch St
Pacific Palisades, CA 90272-0351, USA

Lindley, Leta (Golfer)
104 Alegria Way
Palm Beach Gardens, FL 33418-1722,
USA

Lindner, Carl (Baseball Player)
Cincinnati Reds
8455 Shawnee Run Rd
Cincinnati, OH 45243, USA

Lindner, William G (Misc)
Transport Workers Union
80 W End Ave
New York, NY 10023-6399, USA

Lindo, Delroy (Actor)
c/o Brian Swardstrom *Endeavor Agency
LLC (LA)*
9601 Wilshire Blvd Fl 3
Beverly Hills, CA 90210-5204, USA

Lindon, Vincent (Actor)
Artmedia
20 Ave Rapp
Paris 75007, FRANCE

Lindros, Eric (Hockey Player)
411 Glencaim Ave
Toronto, ON M5N 1V4, CANADA

Lindroth, Eric (Misc)
13151 Dufresne Pl
San Diego, CA 92129-2383, USA

Lindsay, Everett (Football Player)
Minnesota Vikings
10416 Whitestone Rd
Raleigh, NC 27615-1236, USA

Lindsay, Jack (Writer)
56 Maids Causeway
Cambridge, UNITED KINGDOM (UK)

Lindsay, Mark (Musician, Songwriter,
Writer)
Mars Talent
27 L Ambiance Ct
Bardonia, NY 10954-1421, USA

Lindsay, Mort
6970 Fernhill Dr
Malibu, CA 90265-4239, USA

Lindsay, R B Theodore (Ted) (Hockey
Player)
2598 Invitational Dr
Oakland, MI 48363-2453, USA

Lindsay, Robert (Actor, Musician)
Felix de Wolfe
1 Robert St
Adelphi
London WC2N 6BH, UNITED KINGDOM
(UK)

Lindsay, Robert V (Financier)
PO Box 1454
Millbrook, NY 12545-1454, USA

Lindsay, William (Baseball Player)
Hilldale Stars
1208 S 57th St
Philadelphia, PA 19143-3909, USA

Lindsey, Bill (Baseball Player)
Chicago White Sox
3646 NE 5th Ter
Ocala, FL 34479-2331, USA

Lindsey, Dale (Football Player)
Cleveland Browns
4020 Murphy Canyon Rd
San Diego, CA 92123-4407, USA

Lindsey, Doug (Baseball Player)
Philadelphia Phillies
2410 Silver Spur Ln
Leander, TX 78641-7883, USA

Lindsey, James E (Football Player)
Minnesota Vikings
1165 E Joyce Blvd
Fayetteville, AR 72703-5183, USA

Lindsey, Rodney (Baseball Player)
Detroit Tigers
610 Comanchee Dr Lot 43
Opelika, AL 36804-6500, USA

Lindsey, Steven W (Astronaut)
14702 Dawn Vale Dr
Houston, TX 77062-2106, USA

Lindsey, Tracy
651 N Kilkea Dr
Los Angeles, CA 90048-2213, USA

Lindsley, Blake (Actor)
Gold Marshak Liedtke
3500 W Olive Ave Ste 1400
Burbank, CA 91505-5512, USA

Lindsley, Donald B (Physicist)
517 11th St
Santa Monica, CA 90402-2901, USA

Lindstrand, Per (Misc)
Thunder & Colt
Maesbury Road
Oswestry, Shropshire SY10 8HA, UNITED
KINGDOM (UK)

Lindstrom, Charlie (Baseball Player)
Chicago White Sox
PO Box 486
Atlanta, IL 61723-0486, USA

Lindstrom, Chris (Football Player)
Cincinnati Bengals
70 Dudley Hill Rd
Dudley, MA 01571-5924, USA

Lindstrom, David (Football Player)
San Diego Chargers
13209 Woodson St
Shawnee Mission, KS 66209-3817, USA

Lindstrom, Jack (Cartoonist)
United Feature Syndicate
200 Madison Ave
New York, NY 10016-3911, USA

Lindstrom, Jon (Actor)
Artists Group
1650 Broadway Ste 610
New York, NY 10019-6833, USA

Lindvall, Angela (Actor, Model)
c/o Brett Norensberg *Gersh Agency, The
(LA)*
232 N Canon Dr
Beverly Hills, CA 90210-5302, USA

Lindvall, Olle (Doctor)
University of Lund
Medical Cell Research Dept
Lund 23362, SWEDEN

Lindwall, Raymond R (Cricketer)
3 Wentworth Court
Endeavour St Mt Ommaney
Brisbane, QLD 4074, AUSTRALIA

Line, Bill (Football Player)
Chicago Bears
7103 Criner Rd SE
Huntsville, AL 35802-1944, USA

Line, Lorie (Musician)
Lorie Line
222 Minnetonka Ave S
Wayzata, MN 55391-1717, USA

Linear
2139 N University Dr # 348
Coral Springs, FL 33071-6134, USA

Linebrink, Scott (Baseball Player)
San Francisco Giants
PO Box 862
Taylor, TX 76574-0862, USA

Lineger, Jerry
2101 Nasa Pkwy
Houston, TX 77058-3607, USA

Lineker, Gary W (Soccer Player)
Markee UK
6 Saint George St
Nottingham NG1 3BE, UNITED
KINGDOM (UK)

Linenger, Jerry M (Astronaut)
550 S Stoney Point Rd
Suttons Bay, MI 49682-9575, USA

Lines, Dick (Baseball Player)
Washington Senators
1716 Pebble Beach Ln
Lady Lake, FL 32159-2238, USA

Liney, John (Cartoonist)
King features Syndicate
888 7th Ave Ste 201
New York, NY 10106-0201, USA

Ling (Model)
I M G Models
304 Park Ave S # 1200
New York, NY 10010-4301, USA

Ling, Bai (Actor)
c/o Sara Ramaker *Paradigm (LA)*
360 N Crescent Dr
North Bldg
Beverly Hills, CA 90210-6820, USA

Ling, Lisa (Correspondent)
c/o Staff Member *William Morris Agency
(WMA-LA)*
1 William Morris Pl
Beverly Hills, CA 90212-4261, USA

Ling, Sergei S (Prime Minister)
Prime Minister's Office
Pl Nezavisimosti
Minsk 220010, BELARUS

Lingenfelter, Bob (Football Player)
Cleveland Browns
53144 865 Rd
Plainview, NE 68769-2505, USA

Lingmerth, Goran (Football Player)
Cleveland Browns
3216 NE 4th St
Pompano Beach, FL 33062-5007, USA

Lingner, Adam (Football Player)
Kansas City Chiefs
70 Stoughton Ln
Orchard Park, NY 14127-2084, USA

Linhart, Anton (Football Player)
New Orleans Saints
13 Summer Run Ct
Timonium, MD 21093-4346, USA

Linhart, Cart (Baseball Player)
Detroit Tigers
2647 Delmar Ave
Granite City, IL 62040-3439, USA

Linhart, Toni (Football Player)
New Orleans Saints
13 Summer Run Ct
Lutherville Timonium, MD 21093-4346,
USA

Liniak, Cole (Baseball Player)
Chicago Cubs
1752 Morgans Ave
San Marcos, CA 92078-1045, USA

Liniger, Dave (Business Person)
RE/MAX International Inc
5075 S Syracuse St
Denver, CO 80237-2712, USA

Link, Arthur A (Governor)
2201 Grimsrud Dr
Bismarck, ND 58501, USA

Linke, Paul (Actor)
Zealous Artists
139 S Beverly Dr Ste 225
Beverly Hills, CA 90212-3028, USA

Linkert, Lo (Cartoonist)
Singer Media Corp
9541 Lenore Dr
Garden Grove, CA 92841-4925, USA

Linklater, Richard (Director, Writer)
Creative Artists Agency
9830 Wilshire Blvd
Beverly Hills, CA 90212-1804, USA

Linklatter, Hamish
800 S Robertson Blvd
Los Angeles, CA 90035-1606, USA

Linkletter, Art (Entertainer)
1100 Bel Air Rd
Los Angeles, CA 90077-3014, USA

Linkletter, John A (Editor)
Popular Mechanics Magazine
224 W 57th St
Editorial Dept
New York, NY 10019-3200, USA

Linkletter, Nicole (Model)
c/o Staff Member *Ford Models (NY)*
111 5th Ave Fl 9
New York, NY 10003-1005, USA

Linley, Cody (Actor)
c/o Jamie Freed *The Collective*
8530 Wilshire Blvd Fl 5
Beverly Hills, CA 90211-3102, USA

Linn, Jack (Football Player)
Indianapolis Colts
6250 Half Mile Rd
Theodore, AL 36582-2721, USA

Linn, Richard (Judge)
US Court of Appeals
717 Madison Pl NW
Washington, DC 20439-0001, USA

Linn, Teri Ann (Actor)
Sutton Barth Vennari
145 S Fairfax Ave Ste 310
Los Angeles, CA 90036-2176, USA

Linn-Baker, Mark (Actor)
27702 Fairweather St
Canyon Country, CA 91351-2925, USA

Linne, Aubrey (Football Player)
Baltimore Colts
4606 Lanham St
Midland, TX 79705-3213, USA

Linne, Larry (Football Player)
New England Patriots
15779 Silverado Ct
Fort Myers, FL 33908-2408, USA

Linnehan, Richard M (Astronaut)
16802 Hartwood Way
Houston, TX 77058-2305, USA

Linney, Laura (Actor)
c/o Aleen Keshishian *Brillstein-Grey
Entertainment*
9150 Wilshire Blvd Ste 350
Beverly Hills, CA 90212-3453, USA

The Celebrity Black Book 2008

Linnin, Chris (Football Player)
New York Giants
1037 Purple Sage Loop
Castle Rock, CO 80104-7846, USA

Linowitz, Sol M (Diplomat)
2230 California St NW # 4B
Washington, DC 20008-3936, USA

Linsalata, Joe (Baseball Player)
4017 Washington St
Hollywood, FL 33021-7349, USA

Linseman, Ken (Hockey Player)
1070 Ocean Blvd
Hampton, NH 03842-1500, USA

Linskey, Mike (Baseball Player)
Bowman
18826 Polo Meadow Dr
Humble, TX 77346-8121, USA

Linson, Art (Director, Producer)
Art Linson Productions
Warner Bros
4000 Warner Blvd
Burbank, CA 91522-0001, USA

Lint, Royce (Baseball Player)
St Louis Cardinals
6814 SE Jack Rd
Milwaukie, OR 97222-2834, USA

Lintel, Michelle (Actor)
c/o Staff Member *William Morris Agency
(WMA-LA)*
1 William Morris Pl
Beverly Hills, CA 90212-4261, USA

Linteris, Gregory T (Astronaut)
US Commerce Dept
Fire Science Division
Gaithersburg, MD 20899-0001, USA

Linton, Doug (Baseball Player)
Toronto Blue Jays
201 Ellison St
Rochester, NY 14609-4047, USA

Lintz, Larry (Baseball Player)
Montreal Expos
5969 Silver Shadow Cir
Sacramento, CA 95823-6960, USA

Linville, Joanne (Actor)
345 N Maple Dr # 302
Beverly Hills, CA 90210-3869, USA

Linz, Alex D (Actor)
Innovative Artists
1505 10th St
Santa Monica, CA 90401-2805, USA

Linz, Phil (Baseball Player)
New York Yankees
20 Rocky Raplds Rd
Stamford, CT 06903, USA

Linzy, Frank (Baseball Player)
San Francisco Giants
RR 2 Box 39-5
Coweta, OK 74429, USA

Lioeanjie, Rene (Misc)
National Maritime Union
1150 17th St NW
Washington, DC 20036-4603, USA

Lionetti, Donald M (General)
4517 W Rosemere Rd
Tampa, FL 33609-4209, USA

Liotta, Ray (Actor)
c/o Beth Holden-Garland *Untitled
Entertainment (LA)*
331 N Maple Dr Fl 3
Beverly Hills, CA 90210-3827, USA

Lipa, Elisabeta (Athlete)
Str Reconstructiei 1
#78
Bucharest, ROMANIA

Lipetri, Angelo (Baseball Player)
Philadelphia Phillies
150 Yoakum Ave
Farmingdale, NY 11735-5034, USA

Lipinski, Ann Marie (Journalist)
Chicago Tribune
435 N Michigan Ave
Editorial Dept
Chicago, IL 60611-4024, USA

Lipinski, Tara (Actor, Figure Skater)
PO Box 1487
Sugar Land, TX 77487-1487, USA

Lipman, Maureen (Actor, Writer)
c/o Staff Member *Talking Concepts*
19 Bird Street
Lichfield
Staffordshire WS13 6PW, UNITED
KINGDOM (UK)

Lipnicki, Jonathan (Actor)
c/o Staff Member *Cunningham Escott
Slevin & Doherty (LA)*
10635 Santa Monica Blvd Ste 130
Los Angeles, CA 90025-8306, USA

Lipovsek, Marjana (Opera Singer)
Artists Mgmt Zurich
Rutistr 52
Zurich-Gockhausen 8044, SWITZERLAND

Lippard, Stephen J (Misc)
975 Memorial Dr Apt 602
Cambridge, MA 02138-5803, USA

Lippett, Ronnie (Football Player)
New England Patriots
PO Box 1338
Easton, MA 02334-1338, USA

Lippincott, Philip E (Business Person)
Campbell Soup Co
Campbell Place
Cemden, NJ 08103, USA

Lipporien, Paavo Tapio (Prime Minister)
Premier's Office
Snellmaninkatu 1
Helsinki 00170, FINLAND

Lipps, Lisa
2251 N Rampart Blvd # 355
Las Vegas, NV 89128-7640, USA

Lipps, Louis (Football Player)
Pittsburgh Steelers
PO Box 614
Pro Athlete Marketing
Beaver Falls, PA 15010-0614, USA

Lipscomb, William N Jr (Nobel Prize
Laureate)
142 Garden St
Cambridge, MA 02138-6725, USA

Lipset, Seymour M (Misc)
900 N Strafford St #2131
Arlington, VA 22203, USA

Lipsett, Mortimer B (Physicist)
National Institute of Health
9000 Rockville Pike
Bethesda, MD 20892-0002, USA

Lipshutz, Bruce H (Misc)
University of California
Chemistry Dept
Santa Barbara, CA 93106-0001, USA

Lipski, Bob (Baseball Player)
Cleveland Indians
1 Snook St
Scranton, PA 18505-2865, USA

Lipson, D Herbert (Publisher)
Philadelphia Magazine
1500 Walnut St
Philadelphia, PA 19102-3523, USA

Lipton, Holly
1021 16th Ave S
Nashville, TN 37212-2302, USA

Lipton, James (Actor, Producer, Television
Host)
Inside the Actors Studio
30 Avenue D Apt 14E
New York, NY 10009-7047, USA

Lipton, Martin (Attorney, Attorney
General, General)
Wachtell Lipton Rosen Katz
51 W 52nd St
New York, NY 10019-6150, USA

Lipton, Peggy
c/o Belle Zwerdling *Progressive Artists
Agency*
400 S Beverly Dr Ste 216
Beverly Hills, CA 90212-4404, USA

Lipton, Robert
9300 Wilshire Blvd # 410
Beverly Hills, CA 90212-3213, USA

Liquor, Shirley Q (Comedian)
c/o Staff Member *Diva Central Inc*
7510 W Sunset Blvd Ste 1445
Los Angeles, CA 90046-3408, USA

Liquori, Marty
2915 NW 58th Blvd
Gainesville, FL 32606-8517, USA

Lis, Joe (Baseball Player)
Philadelphia Phillies
4055 Secretariat Dr
Newburgh, IN 47630-2215, USA

Lisa, Lisa (Musician)
Talent Consultants International
105 Shad Row Ste B
Piermont, NY 10968-3001, USA

Lisa, Mona
8860 Corbin Ave # 185
Northridge, CA 91324-3309, USA

Lisa Lisa
1560 Broadway # 1308
New York, NY 10036-1518, USA

Lisbe, Mike (Writer)
c/o Brian Sher *International Creative
Management (ICM-LA)*
10250 Constellation Blvd
Los Angeles, CA 90067-6200, USA

Lisch, Russell (Football Player)
St Louis Cardinals
206 Country Club Ln
Belleville, IL 62223-1910, USA

Liscio, Patti (Golfer)
7803 Glenneagle Dr
Dallas, TX 75248-2335, USA

Liscio, Tony (Football Player)
Dallas Cowboys
7803 Glenneagle Dr
Dallas, TX 75248-2335, USA

Lisi, Virna (Actor)
Via di Filomarino 4
Rome, ITALY

Lisitsa, Valentina (Musician)
Columbia Artists Mgmt Inc
1790 Broadway Fl 6
New York, NY 10019-1412, USA

Liska, Stephen
8688 Hollywood Blvd
Los Angeles, CA 90069-1416, USA

Liss, Joe (Actor)
c/o Scott Howard *Howard Entertainment*
10850 Wilshire Blvd Ste 1260
Los Angeles, CA 90024-4337, USA

Lissie (Musician)
c/o Staff Member *Paradigm (Monterey)*
509 Hartnell St
Monterey, CA 93940-2825, USA

Lissner, Stephane (Opera Singer)
Theatre du Chatelet
2 Rue Eduouard Colonne
Paris 75001, FRANCE

List, Peyton (Actor)
c/o Staff Member *As The World Turns*
1268 E 14th St
Jc Studios
Brooklyn, NY 11230-5241, USA

List, Robert F (Governor)
1660 Catalpa Ln
Reno, NV 89511-7563, USA

Listach, Pat (Baseball Player)
Milwaukee Brewers
PO Box 2012
Natchitoches, LA 71457-2012, USA

Lister, Alton (Basketball Player)
233 Hudson Bay
Alameda, CA 94502-7908, USA

Lister Jr, Tommy (Tiny Zeus) (Actor)
c/o Ryan Martin *Agency for the
Performing Arts (APA-LA)*
405 S Beverly Dr
Beverly Hills, CA 90212-4416, USA

Listopad, Ed (Football Player)
Chicago Cardinals
6719 Roberts Ave
Dundalk, MD 21222-1053, USA

Listowel, Earl of (William F Hare)
(Government Official)
10 Downshire Hill
London NW3, UNITED KINGDOM (UK)

Lithgow, John (Actor)
c/o Rick Kurtzman *Creative Artists Agency
LCC (CAA-LA)*
2000 Avenue Of The Stars
Los Angeles, CA 90067-4700, USA

Littell, Mark (Baseball Player)
Kansas City Royals
27358 N 88th Ln
Peoria, AZ 85383-4853, USA

Littenberg, Barbara (Architect)
Peterson/Littenberg Achitecture
13 E 66th St
New York, NY 10065-5801, USA

Litterell, Brian (Musician)
The Firm
9100 Wilshire Blvd Ste 100W
Beverly Hills, CA 90212-3435, USA

Little, Anthony (Gordine) (Musician)
Mars Talent
27 L Ambiance Ct
Bardonia, NY 10954-1421, USA

Little, Big Tiny
3985 W Taft Dr
Spokane, WA 99208-4870, USA

Little, Bryan (Baseball Player)
Montreal Expos
4766 Tiffany Park Cir
Bryan, TX 77802-5822, USA

Little, Carole (Designer, Fashion Designer)
Carole Little Inc
PO Box 77917
Los Angeles, CA 90007, USA

Little, Chad (Race Car Driver)
5400 Little Pkwy
Sherrills Ford, NC 28673-9114, USA

Little, Charles L (Misc)
United Transportation Union
14600 Detroit Ave
Cleveland, OH 44107-4250, USA

Little, Dwight H (Director)
Creative Artists Agency
9830 Wilshire Blvd
Beverly Hills, CA 90212-1804, USA

Little, Everett (Football Player)
Tampa Bay Buccaneers
5219 Kingsbury St
Houston, TX 77021-3724, USA

Little, Floyd D (Football Player)
Denver Broncos
33207 Pacific Hwy S
Federal Way, WA 98003-6442, USA

Little, George (Football Player)
Miami Dolphins
1805 Powers St
McKeesport, PA 15132-5150, USA

Little, Jack (Football Player)
Baltimore Colts
2816 Speegle Rd
Waco, TX 76712-2621, USA

Little, Jeff (Baseball Player)
St Louis Cardinals
5711 County Road 169
Genoa, OH 43430, USA

Little, Larry C (Coach, Football Player)
San Diego Chargers
14761 SW 169th Ln
Miami, FL 33187-1745, USA

Little, Mark (Baseball Player)
St Louis Cardinals
518 Gilbert Dr
Edwardsville, IL 62025-5300, USA

Little, Milton (Musician)
Camil Productions
6606 Solitary Ave
Las Vegas, NV 89110, USA

Little, Rich (Actor, Comedian)
c/o David Martin *David Martin Management*
13849 Riverside Dr
Sherman Oaks, CA 91423-2426, USA

Little, Robert A (Chef)
49 Firth St
London W1V 5TE, UNITED KINGDOM
(UK)

Little, Scott (Baseball Player)
Pittsburgh Pirates
1321 Rosebud Dr
Jackson, MO 63755-1086, USA

Little, Steven (Musician)
Premier Talent
3 E 54th St # 1100
New York, NY 10022-3108, USA

Little, Tasmin E (Musician)
harold Holt
31 Sinclair Road
London W14 0NS, UNITED KINGDOM
(UK)

Little, Tawny
5515 Melrose Ave
Los Angeles, CA 90038-3149, USA

Little, Tawny Godin (Beauty Pageant Winner, Entertainer)
17941 Sky Park Cir Ste F
Irvine, CA 92614-4375, USA

Little, W Grady (Misc)
130 National Dr
Pinehurst, NC 28374-8165, USA

Little, William (Baseball Player)
Kansas City Monarchs
4889 Horn Lake Rd
Memphis, TN 38109-6625, USA

Little Anthony (Gourdine)
27 L Ambiance Ct
Bardonia, NY 10954-1421, USA

Little Big Town (Music Group)
c/o Risha Rodgers *Creative Artists Agency (CAA-Nashville)*
3310 W End Ave Fl 5
Nashville, TN 37203-1028, USA

Little Eva
1161 NW 76th Ave
Plantation, FL 33322-5120, USA

Little JJ (Actor)
c/o Charles King *William Morris Agency (WMA-LA)*
1 William Morris Pl
Beverly Hills, CA 90212-4261, USA

Little Man Tate (Music Group)
c/o Staff Member *Paradigm (Monterey)*
509 Hartnell St
Monterey, CA 93940-2825, USA

Little Ones, The (Music Group)
c/o Staff Member *Paradigm (Monterey)*
509 Hartnell St
Monterey, CA 93940-2825, USA

Little Richard (Musician)
c/o Staff Member *Richard De La Font Agency*
4845 S Sheridan Rd Ste 505
Tulsa, OK 74145-5719, USA

Little River Band
9850 Sandalfoot Blvd # 458
Boca Raton, FL 33428-6645, USA

Littlefield, John (Baseball Player)
St Louis Cardinals
1935 Ramar Rd
Bullhead City, AZ 86442-6949, USA

Littlefield, Warren (Producer)
c/o Staff Member *Littlefield Company, The*
5555 Melrose Ave
Cooper #115
Los Angeles, CA 90038-3989, USA

Littleford, Beth (Actor)
c/o Karen Forman *Metropolitan*
4500 Wilshire Blvd Fl 2
Los Angeles, CA 90010-3858, USA

Littlejohn, Dennis (Baseball Player)
San Francisco Giants
6813 Klamath Way Apt D
Bakersfield, CA 93309-7899, USA

Littler, Gene (Golfer)
PO Box 1949
Rancho Santa Fe, CA 92067-1949, USA

Littles, Gene (Basketball Player)
Denver Nuggets
1000 Chopper Cir
Pepsi Center
Denver, CO 80204-5805, USA

Littleton, Harvey K (Artist)
RR 1 Box 843
Spruce Pine, NC 28777, USA

Littleton, Larry (Baseball Player)
Cleveland Indians
1076 Dunbarton Trce NE
Atlanta, GA 30319-2674, USA

Littman, Jonathan (Producer)
c/o Staff Member *Creative Artists Agency LCC (CAA-LA)*
2000 Avenue Of The Stars
Los Angeles, CA 90067-4700, USA

Litton, Andrew
IMG Artists
Media House
3 Burlington Lane
London W4 2TH, UNITED KINGDOM
(UK)

Litton, Drew (Cartoonist, Editor)
Rocky Mountain News
101 W Colfax Ave # 500
Editorial Dept
Denver, CO 80202-5315, USA

Litton, Greg (Baseball Player)
San Francisco Giants
4296 Brighton Dr
Pensacola, FL 32504-4928, USA

Littrell, Gary L (War Hero)
4302 Belle Vista Dr
St Pete Beach, FL 33706-3825, USA

Littrell, Jack (Baseball Player)
Philadelphia Athletics
7510 Floydsburg Rd
Crestwood, KY 40014-9297, USA

Litwhiler, Danny (Baseball Player)
Philadelphia Phillies
1099 N McMullen Booth Rd Apt 124
Clearwater, FL 33759-3452, USA

Liu, Lucy (Actor)
c/o Jason Weinberg *Untitled Entertainment (LA)*
331 N Maple Dr Fl 3
Beverly Hills, CA 90210-3827, USA

Liu, Matthew Stephen
10635 Santa Monica Blvd Ste 130
Los Angeles, CA 90025-8306, USA

Liu, Nancy
9057C Nemo St
W Hollywood, CA 90069, USA

Liut, Mike (Hockey Player)
888 Ann St
Birmingham, MI 48009-1728, USA

Livage, Jacques (Misc)
College de France
11 Place M Berthelot
Paris Cedex 05 75231, FRANCE

Live (Music Group)
c/o Staff Member *Paradigm (Monterey)*
509 Hartnell St
Monterey, CA 93940-2825, USA

Lively, Blake (Actor)
c/o Alex Yarosh *Gersh Agency, The (LA)*
232 N Canon Dr
Beverly Hills, CA 90210-5302, USA

Lively, Bud (Baseball Player)
Cincinnati Reds
8605 Esslinger Ct SE
Huntsville, AL 35802-3640, USA

Lively, Eric (Actor)
c/o Andrea Pett-Joseph *Brillstein-Grey Entertainment*
9150 Wilshire Blvd Ste 350
Beverly Hills, CA 90212-3453, USA

Lively, Penelope M (Writer)
c/o David Higham Associates
5-8 Lower John Street
London W1R 4HA, UNITED KINGDOM
(UK)

Lively, Robyn (Actor)
William Morris Agency
151 El Camino Dr
Beverly Hills, CA 90212-2775, USA

Livermore, Ann (Business Person)
Hewlett-Packard Co
300 Hanover St
Palo Alto, CA 94304, USA

Livers, Virgil (Football Player)
Chicago Bears
313 Clearview Ave
Bowling Green, KY 42101-3613, USA

Living Colour
6201 W Sunset Blvd # 329
Hollywood, CA 90028, USA

Livingston, Andrew (Football Player)
Chicago Bears
650 E Century Ave
Gilbert, AZ 85296-1118, USA

Livingston, Barry (Actor)
11310 Blix St
North Hollywood, CA 91602-1209, USA

Livingston, Bruce (Football Player)
Dallas Cowboys
511 25th Ave W
Bradenton, FL 34205-8264, USA

Livingston, Cliff (Football Player)
New York Giants
4682 Deer Forest Ave
Las Vegas, NV 89139-7642, USA

Livingston, Dale (Football Player)
Cincinnati Bengals
PO Box 122
Alanson, MI 49706-0122, USA

Livingston, James E (General, War Hero)
3146 Pignatelli Cres
Mount Pleasant, SC 29466-8059, USA

Livingston, Mike (Football Player)
Kansas City Chiefs
8181 Monrovia St
Shawnee Mission, KS 66215-2728, USA

Livingston, Robert L Jr (Politician)
Livingston Group
499 S Capitol St SW Ste 600
Washington, DC 20003-4037, USA

Livingston, Ron (Actor)
Rigberg Roberts Rugolo
1180 S Beverly Dr Ste 601
Los Angeles, CA 90035-1158, USA

Livingston, Shaun (Basketball Player)
Los Angeles Clippers
1111 S Figueroa St
Staples Center
Los Angeles, CA 90015-1300, USA

Livingston, Stanley (Actor)
PO Box 1782
Studio City, CA 91614-0782, USA

Livingston, Warren (Football Player)
Dallas Cowboys
308 E Malibu Dr
Tempe, AZ 85282-5304, USA

Livingstone, Bob (Football Player)
Chicago Rockets
1625 Bluebird Ln
Munster, IN 46321-3322, USA

Livingstone, Scott (Baseball Player)
Detroit Tigers
1303 Pecos Dr
Southlake, TX 76092-5915, USA

Livinston (Actor)
45 Thackers Street
Pursawakkam
Chennai, TN 600 084, INDIA

Lizalde, Enrique (Actor)
c/o Staff Member *Televisa*
Blvd Adolfo Lopez Mateos 232
Colonia San Angel INN
DF CP 01060, MEXICO

Lizarazo, Carolina (Actor)
c/o Gabriel Blanco *Gabriel Blanco
Iglesias (Mexico)*
Rio Balsas 35-32
Colonia Cuauhtemoc
DF 06500, MEXICO

Lizaso, Saul (Actor)
c/o Staff Member *Televisa*
Blvd Adolfo Lopez Mateos 232
Colonia San Angel INN
DF CP 01060, MEXICO

Ljungberg, Freddie (Model, Soccer Player)
c/o Staff Member *Calvin Klein Inc*
200 Madison Ave
Phillips-Van Heusen Corporation
New York, NY 10016-3903, USA

LL Cool J (Actor, Musician)
c/o Jason Barrett *Alchemy Entertainment*
9229 W Sunset Blvd Ste 720
Los Angeles, CA 90069-3407, USA

Llaca, Patricia (Actor)
c/o Staff Member *TV Azteca*
Periferico Sur 4121
Colonia Fuentes del Pedregal
DF CP 14141, MEXICO

Llamosa, Carlos (Soccer Player)
New England Revolution
1 Patriot Pl
Cmgi Field
Foxboro, MA 02035-1388, USA

Llewellyn, John A (Astronaut)
University of South Florida
4202 E Fowler Ave
Tampa, FL 33620-9951, USA

Llewellyn, Robert (Actor, Writer)
c/o Maureen Vincent *Peters Fraser &
Dunlop (PFD - UK)*
Drury House
34-43 Russell St
London WC2B 5HA, UNITED KINGDOM
(UK)

Llewelyn, Doug
8075 W 3rd St # 303
Los Angeles, CA 90048-4318, USA

Llosa, Mario Vargas (Writer)
Las Magnolias 295
6 Piso
Barranco, Lima 4, PERU

Lloyd, Arroyn (Actor)
c/o Michael Bircumshaw *Water Street
Management*
5225 Wilshire Blvd Ste 615
Los Angeles, CA 90036-4350, USA

Lloyd, Charles (Composer, Musician)
Joel Chriss
300 Mercer St Apt 3J
New York, NY 10003-6732, USA

Lloyd, Christopher (Actor)
Managemint
PO Box 491246
Los Angeles, CA 90049-9246, USA

Lloyd, Clive H (Cricketer)
Harefield
Harefield Dr
Wilmslow, Cheshire SK9 1NJ, UNITED
KINGDOM (UK)

Lloyd, Dave (Football Player)
Cleveland Browns
24432 County Road 3107
Gladewater, TX 75647-8842, USA

Lloyd, Earl (Basketball Player, Coach)
PO Box 1976
Crossville, TN 38558-1976, USA

Lloyd, Emily (Actor)
Malcolm Sheddon Mgmt
1 Charlotte Square
London W1P 1DH, UNITED KINGDOM
(UK)

Lloyd, Eric (Actor)
c/o Mark Schumacher *Schumacher
Management*
9255 W Sunset Blvd Ste 727
Los Angeles, CA 90069-3304, USA

Lloyd, Geoffrey E R (Misc)
2 Prospect Row
Cambridge CB1 1DU, UNITED
KINGDOM (UK)

Lloyd, Georgina (Writer)
Bantam Books
1540 Broadway
New York, NY 10036-4039, USA

Lloyd, Graeme (Baseball Player)
Milwaukee Brewers
1695 Barrabool Road RMB Gnarwarre
Victoria 3221, AUSTRALIA

Lloyd, Jake (Actor)
Osbrink Talent
4343 Lankershim Blvd # 100
North Hollywood, CA 91602-2705, USA

Lloyd, Kathleen (Actor)
House of Representatives
211 S Beverly Dr Ste 208
Beverly Hills, CA 90212-3879, USA

Lloyd, Madison (Actor)
Osbrink Talent
4343 Lankershim Blvd # 100
North Hollywood, CA 91602-2705, USA

Lloyd, Norman (Actor)
1813 Old Ranch Rd
Los Angeles, CA 90049-2206, USA

Lloyd, Robert A (Opera Singer)
67B Fortis Green
London SE1 9HL, UNITED KINGDOM
(UK)

Lloyd, Sabrina (Actor)
Paradigm Agency
10100 Santa Monica Blvd Ste 2500
Los Angeles, CA 90067-4116, USA

Lloyd, Sam (Actor)
c/o Staff Member *Stone Manners Talent &
Literary (LA)*
6500 Wilshire Blvd Ste 550
Los Angeles, CA 90048-4950, USA

Lloyd, Sue (Actor)
Barry Burnett
31 Coventry St
London W1V 8AS, UNITED KINGDOM
(UK)

Lloyd, Walt (Cinematographer)
22287 Mulholland Hwy # 393
Calabasas, CA 91302-5157, USA

Llyod, Tony (Baseball Player)
Birmingham Black Barons
6536 Cherokee Dr
Fairfield, AL 35064-1703, USA

Lo, Ismael (Musician)
Mad Minute Music
5-7 Rue Paul Bert
Saint Ouen 93400, FRANCE

Lo Bianco, Tony
c/o Staff Member *Artists Only
Management*
10203 Santa Monica Blvd
Los Angeles, CA 90067-6405, USA

Loach, Ken C (Director)
c/o Staff Member *Sixteen Films*
187 Wardour St
Floor 2
London W1F 8ZB, ENGLAND

Loach, Kenneth (Ken) (Director)
Parallax Pictures
7 Denmark St
London WC2H 8LS, UNITED KINGDOM
(UK)

Loaiza, Esteban A (Baseball Player)
779 Florida St
Imperial Beach, CA 91932-2276, USA

Loalza, Esteban (Baseball Player)
Pittsburgh Pirates
1404 Lands End Ct
Southlake, TX 76092-4224, USA

Lobdell, Frank (Artist)
Pier 70
San Francisco, CA 94102, USA

Lobel, Bruno
Ramering 41
Heldenstein 84431, GERMANY

Lobenstein, William (Football Player)
Denver Broncos
3272 Deerfield Rd
Deerfield, WI 53531-9733, USA

Lobkowicz, Nicholas (Misc)
Katholische Universitat
Eichstatt 85071, GERMANY

Loc, Tone
7932 Hillside Ave
Los Angeles, CA 90046-2122, USA

Loc, Tone (Music Group)
c/o Staff Member *Entertainment Artists*
2409 21st Ave S Ste 100
Nashville, TN 37212-5317, USA

Local, Ivars Godmanis (Prime Minister)
Brivibus Bluv 36
Riga, PDP 226170, LATVIA

Locane, Amy (Actor)
c/o Staff Member *Don Buchwald &
Associates Inc (LA)*
6500 Wilshire Blvd Ste 2200
Los Angeles, CA 90048-4942, USA

Locatelli, Paul L (Educator)
Santa Clara University
President's Office
Santa Clara, CA 95053-0001, USA

Loceff, Michael (Producer)
c/o Staff Member *Roklin Management*
8530 Wilshire Blvd Ste 550
Beverly Hills, CA 90211-3133, USA

Locher, Dick
435 N Michigan Ave
Chicago, IL 60611-4066, USA

Lochhead, Kenneth C (Artist)
35 Wilton Crescent
Ottawa, ON K1S 2T4, CANADA

Lochner, Philip R Jr (Business Person,
Government Official)
Time Warner Inc
75 Rockefeller Plz
New York, NY 10019-6990, USA

Lochner, Rudi
Hofreitstr. 15
Schonau D-83471, GERMANY

Lock, Don (Baseball Player)
Washington Senators
11725 W Alderny Ct Unit 42
Wichita, KS 67212-6510, USA

Lockbaum, Gordie (Football Player)
35 Brookshire Rd
Worcester, MA 01609-1251, USA

Locke, Bruce (Actor)
5670 Wilshire Blvd Ste 820
Los Angeles, CA 90036-5613, USA

Locke, Charlie (Baseball Player)
Baltimore Orioles
1560 Haven Hills Rd
Poplar Bluff, MO 63901-2749, USA

Locke, Kimberley (Actor, Musician)
PO Box 45378
Los Angeles, CA 90045-0378, USA

Locke, Larry (Baseball Player)
Cleveland Indians
155 Eighty Acres Rd Apt 2
Dunbar, PA 15431-2275, USA

Locke, Ron (Baseball Player)
New York Mets
15 Lewiston Ave
West Kingston, RI 02892-1131, USA

Locke, Sonda (Actor)
c/o Staff Member *David Shapira &
Associates*
193 N Robertson Blvd
Beverly Hills, CA 90211-2103, USA

Locke, Sondra (Actor)
7465 Hillside Ave
Los Angeles, CA 90046-2228, USA

Locke, Tembi (Actor)
c/o Bob McGowan *McGowan
Management*
8733 W Sunset Blvd Ste 103
W Hollywood, CA 90069-2241, USA

Locke-Bonney, Spencer (Actor)
c/o Sharon Lane *Lane Management Group*
13017 Woodbridge St
Studio City, CA 91604-1431, USA

Locker, Bob (Baseball Player)
Chicago White Sox
1561 Rancho View Rd
Lafayette, CA 94549-2236, USA

Lockerman, Brad
300 S Raymond Ave Ste 11
Pasadena, CA 91105-2639, USA

Lockett, Kevin (Football Player)
Kansas City Chiefs
1319 W Xyler St
Tulsa, OK 74127-2717, USA

Lockett, Lester (Baseball Player)
Birmingham Black Barons
1366 W Fullerton Ave
Imperial Nursing Home
Chicago, IL 60614-2129, USA

Lockhart, Anne (Actor)
191 Upper Lake Rd
Lake Sherwood, CA 91361-5137, USA

Lockhart, Eugene (Football Player)
Dallas Cowboys
2215 High Country Dr
Carrollton, TX 75007-1701, USA

Lockhart, James
105 Woodcock Hill
Harrow, Middx HA3 0JJ, UNITED
KINGDOM (UK)

Lockhart, June (Actor)
c/o Staff Member *Agency for the
Performing Arts (APA-LA)*
405 S Beverly Dr
Beverly Hills, CA 90212-4416, USA

Lockhart, Keith
Boston Pops Orchestra
301 Massachusetts Ave
Symphony Hall
Boston, MA 02115-4557, USA

Lockhart, Keith (Baseball Player)
San Diego Padres
3330 McKinley Point Dr
Dacula, GA 30019-1599, USA

Lockhart, Paul S (Astronaut)
3142 Pleasant Cove Ct
Houston, TX 77059-3232, USA

Lockington, David
Cramer/Marder Artists
3436 Springhill Rd
Lafayette, CA 94549-2535, USA

Locklear, Gene (Baseball Player)
Cincinnati Reds
1811 Penasco Rd
El Cajon, CA 92019-3708, USA

Locklear, Heather (Actor)
c/o Iris Grossman *International Creative
Management (ICM-LA)*
10250 Constellation Blvd
Los Angeles, CA 90067-6200, USA

Locklin, Hank
PO Box 117
Brewton, AL 36427-0117, USA

Locklin, Stu (Baseball Player)
Cleveland Indians
224 Paseo Del Volcan SW Trir 43
Albuquerque, NM 87121, USA

Lockman, Whitey (Baseball Player)
New York Giants
8787 E Mountain View Rd Apt 1102
Scottsdale, AZ 85258-6231, USA

Lockwood, Gary (Actor)
1065 E Loma Alta Dr
Altadena, CA 91001-1507, USA

Lockwood, Scott (Football Player)
New England Patriots
1995 E Coalton Rd Apt 44-103
Superior, CO 80027-4428, USA

Lockwood, Skip (Baseball Player)
Kansas City A's
47 John Druce Ln
Wrentham, MA 02093-1390, USA

Locorriere, Dennis (Musician)
P.O. Box 4444
Worthing BN11 3WJ, SUSSEX

Loder, Kurt (Journalist, Television Host)
c/o Staff Member *MTV News*
1515 Broadway Fl 29
New York, NY 10036-8901, USA

Lodge, David
8 Sydney Rd.
Richmond Surrey, ENGLAND, UNITED
KINGDOM (UK)

Lodge, David John (Writer)
University of Birmingham
English Dept
Birmingham B15 2TT, UNITED
KINGDOM (UK)

Lodge, Roger (Actor, Television Host)
c/o Michelle Bega *Rogers & Cowan PR*
8687 Melrose Ave Ste G700
Pacific Design Center
Los Angeles, CA 90069-5721, USA

Lodigiani, Dario (Baseball Player)
Philadelphia Athletics
745 Lathrop St
Napa, CA 94558-5117, USA

Lodise, Peter
1130 S Flower St Apt 421
Los Angeles, CA 90015-2144, USA

Lodish, Mike (Football Player)
Buffalo Bills
1600 Trailwood Path
Bloomfield Hills, MI 48301-1733, USA

Loe, Harald A (Doctor)
National Dental Research Institute
9000 Rockville Pike
Bethesda, MD 20892-0001, USA

Loeb, Jerome T (Business Person)
May Department Stores
611 Olive St
Saint Louis, MO 63101-1756, USA

Loeb, John L Jr (Diplomat, Financier)
1 Rockefeller Plz # 2500
New York, NY 10020-2003, USA

Loeb, Lisa (Musician, Songwriter, Writer)
c/o Jenna Adler *Creative Artists Agency
LCC (CAA-LA)*
2000 Avenue Of The Stars
Los Angeles, CA 90067-4700, USA

Loeb, Marshall R (Editor)
31 Montrose Rd
Scarsdale, NY 10583-1129, USA

Loehr, Bet (Actor)
c/o Staff Member *Coast to Coast Talent
Group*
3350 Barham Blvd
Los Angeles, CA 90068-1404, USA

Loehr, Bret (Actor)
c/o Staff Member *Coast to Coast Talent
Group*
3350 Barham Blvd
Los Angeles, CA 90068-1404, USA

Loengard, John (Photographer)
20 W 86th St
New York, NY 10024-3604, USA

Loepfe, Richard (Football Player)
Chicago Cardinals
9301 N 76th St
Milwaukee, WI 53223-1074, USA

Loes, Billy (Baseball Player)
Brooklyn Dodgers
3308 84th St
Jackson Heights, NY 11372-1539, USA

Loewen, James W (Historian)
Catholic University
History Dept
Washington, DC 20064-0001, USA

Loewer, Carlton (Baseball Player)
Philadelphia Phillies
332 Carl Loewer Rd
Eunice, LA 70535-2735, USA

Lofgren, Nils (Musician, Songwriter,
Writer)
Vision Music
8012 Old Georgetown Rd
Bethesda, MD 20814-2427, USA

Lofton, Cirroc (Actor)
c/o Staff Member *Innovative Artists (LA)*
1505 10th St
Santa Monica, CA 90401-2805, USA

Lofton, Fred C (Religious Leader)
Progressive National Baptist Convention
601 50th St NE
Washington, DC 20019-5498, USA

Lofton, James (Baseball Player)
Boston Red Sox
14103 Cerise Ave Apt 18
Hawthorne, CA 90250-8843, USA

Lofton, James D (Football Player)
Green Bay Packers
13177 Via Mesa Dr
San Diego, CA 92129-2287, USA

Lofton, Kenneth (Kenny) (Baseball Player)
Houston Astros
PO Box 68473
Tucson, AZ 85737-8473, USA

Logan, Chuck (Football Player)
Pittsburgh Steelers
2526 Lawndale Ave
Evanston, IL 60201-1158, USA

Logan, Daniel (Actor)
c/o Mitchell Gossett *Cunningham Escott
Slevin & Doherty (LA)*
10635 Santa Monica Blvd Ste 130
Los Angeles, CA 90025-8306, USA

Logan, David R (Football Player)
Cleveland Browns
5875 S Dry Creek Ct
Greenwood Village, CO 80121-1709,
USA

Logan, Dick (Football Player)
Green Bay Packers
475 Chapple Hill Dr NE
North Canton, OH 44720-1775, USA

Logan, Don (Publisher)
Time Inc
Rockefeller Center
Time-Life Building
New York, NY 10020, USA

Logan, Ernie (Football Player)
Cleveland Browns
609 Francis Ct
Spring Lake, NC 28390-3006, USA

Logan, Jack (Musician)
William Morris Agency
1325 Avenue Of The Americas
New York, NY 10019-6091, USA

Logan, James K (Judge)
US Court of Appeals
PO Box 790
1 Patrons Plaza
Olathe, KS 66051-0790, USA

Logan, Jerry (Football Player)
Baltimore Colts
112 Guinevere Ct
Weatherford, TX 76086-5910, USA

Logan, John (Producer, Writer)
c/o David O'Connor *Creative Artists
Agency LCC (CAA-LA)*
2000 Avenue Of The Stars
Los Angeles, CA 90067-4700, USA

Logan, John (Johnny) (Baseball Player)
Boston Braves
6115 W Cleveland Ave
Milwaukee, WI 53219-2653, USA

Logan, Marc (Football Player)
Cincinnati Bengals
PO Box 11886
Lexington, KY 40578-1886, USA

Logan, Melissa (Musician)
K Records
924 Jefferson St SE # 101
Olympia, WA 98501, USA

Logan, Phyllis
47 Courtfield Rd. #9
London, ENGLAND SW7 4DB, UNITED
KINGDOM (UK)

Logan, Randy (Football Player)
Philadelphia Eagles
1122 Willow St
Norristown, PA 19401-3832, USA

Logan, Rayford W (Historian)
3001 Veazey Ter NW
Washington, DC 20008-5454, USA

Loges, Stephan (Opera Singer)
Van Walsum Mgmt
4 Addison Bridge Place
London W14 8XP, UNITED KINGDOM
(UK)

Loggia, Robert (Actor)
544 Bellagio Ter
Los Angeles, CA 90049-1709, USA

Loggins, Kenny (Musician, Songwriter,
Writer)
c/o Brett Steinberg *Creative Artists Agency
LCC (CAA-LA)*
2000 Avenue Of The Stars
Los Angeles, CA 90067-4700, USA

Logston, Cory A
26329 Torreypines Dr
Newhall, CA 91321-2231, USA

Logue, Donal (Actor)
c/o Staff Member *Principal Entertainment
(LA)*
1964 Westwood Blvd Ste 400
Los Angeles, CA 90025-4695, USA

Loh, John M (Mike) (General)
125 Captaine Graves
Williamsburg, VA 23185-8906, USA

Lohan, Lindsay (Actor)
c/o Jason Weinberg *Untitled
Entertainment (LA)*
331 N Maple Dr Fl 3
Beverly Hills, CA 90210-3827, USA

Lohan, Sinead (Musician, Songwriter,
Writer)
Pat Egan Sound
Merchant's Court
24 Merchant's Quay
Dublin, IRELAND

Lohman, Alison (Actor)
c/o Rick Kurtzman *Creative Artists Agency LCC (CAA-LA)*
2000 Avenue Of The Stars
Los Angeles, CA 90067-4700, USA

Lohmann, Katie (Actor)
c/o Michael Zanuck *Zanuck, Passon and Pace, Inc*
28035 Dorothy Dr Ste 120
Atrium #102
Agoura Hills, CA 91301-4918, USA

Lohr, Aaron (Actor)
c/o Staff Member *Savage Agency*
6212 Banner Ave
Los Angeles, CA 90038-2802, USA

Lohr, Bob (Golfer)
8225 Breeze Cove Ln
Orlando, FL 32819-5078, USA

Lohrke, Jack (Baseball Player)
New York Giants
2817 Lucena Dr
San Jose, CA 95132-2244, USA

Loiola, Jose (Volleyball Player)
3521 Maple Ave
Manhattan Beach, CA 90266-3509, USA

Loisel, John S (War Hero)
2504 Overcreek Dr
Richardson, TX 75080-1915, USA

Loiselie, Rich (Baseball Player)
Pittsburgh Pirates
11182 W Alvarado Rd
Avondale, AZ 85392-5067, USA

Lokanc, Joe (Football Player)
Chicago Cardinals
2666 E 73rd St Apt SE
Chicago, IL 60649-2798, USA

Loken, Kristanna (Actor)
c/o Miles Levy *James/Levy/Jacobson Management*
3500 W Olive Ave Ste 1470
Burbank, CA 91505-5514, USA

Lokey, Lorey (Business Person)
Business Wire
44 Montgomery St Fl 39
San Francisco, CA 94104-4602, USA

Lokoloko, Tore (Governor)
PO Box 5622
Port Moresby, PAPUA NEW GUINEA

Lolich, Michael S (Mickey) (Baseball Player)
Detroit Tigers
6252 Robin Hl
Washington, MI 48094-2186, USA

Lolich, Ron (Baseball Player)
Chicago White Sox
7055 SW Dogwood Pl
Portland, OR 97225-1571, USA

Lolita
Grossgmain
- A-5084, AUSTRIA

Lollar, Tim (Baseball Player)
New York Yankees
16626 W Bayaud Dr
Golden, CO 80401-6577, USA

Lollobrigida, Gina (Actor)
Via Appia Antica 223
Rome 00178, ITALY

Lom, Herbert (Actor)
London Mgmt
2-4 Noel St
London W1V 3RB, UNITED KINGDOM
(UK)

Loman, Doug (Baseball Player)
Milwaukee Brewers
25 Lincoln St
Bakersfield, CA 93305-3412, USA

Lomas, Mark (Football Player)
New York Jets
PO Box 17781
Irvine, CA 92623-7781, USA

Lomasney, Steve (Baseball Player)
Boston Red Sox
620 SE 21st Ter
Cape Coral, FL 33990-2521, USA

Lomax, Melanie
5900 Wilshire Blvd
Los Angeles, CA 90036-5013, USA

Lomax, Michael (Educator)
United Negro Fund
500 E 62nd St
New York, NY 10065-8314, USA

Lomax, Neil V (Football Player)
St Louis Cardinals
13090 Knaus Rd
Lake Oswego, OR 97034-1590, USA

Lombard, George (Baseball Player)
Atlanta Braves
2275 Rhinehill Rd SE
Atlanta, GA 30315-7413, USA

Lombard, Karina (Actor, Model)
EOS Entertainment Corporation
1209 N Orange St
Wilmington, DE 19801-1120, USA

Lombard, Louise
P F D Drury House
34-43 Russell St
London WC2B 5HA, UNITED KINGDOM
(UK)

Lombardi, John V (Educator)
University of Florida
President's Office
Gainesville, FL 32611, USA

Lombardi, Leigh (Actor)
c/o Staff Member *Abrams Artists Agency (NY)*
275 7th Ave Fl 26
New York, NY 10001-6708, USA

Lombardi, Phil (Baseball Player)
New York Yankees
9640 Etiwanda Ave
Northridge, CA 91325-1719, USA

Lombardo, John (Musician)
Agency for Performing Arts
405 S Beverly Dr Ste 500
Beverly Hills, CA 90212-4425, USA

Lombardozzi, Steve (Baseball Player)
Minnesota Twins
64 Willowbrook Dr
Auburn, NY 13021, USA

Lombreglio, Ralph (Writer)
Doubleday Press
1540 Broadway
New York, NY 10036-4039, USA

Lomma, Jonathan
1120 S Washington Ave
Scranton, PA 18505-1532, USA

Lommi, Tony (Musician)
Red Light Communications
3305 Lobban Pl
Charlottesville, VA 22903-7069, USA

Lomon, Kevin (Baseball Player)
New York Mets
24955 Blaylock Ln
Cameron, OK 74932-2041, USA

Lonborg, James R (Jim) (Baseball Player)
Boston Red Sox
498 First Parish Rd
Scituate, MA 02066-3201, USA

Lonchakov, Yuri V (Cosmonaut)
Potcha Kosmonavtov
Moskovskoi Oblasti
Syvisdny Goroduk 141160, RUSSIA

London, Antonio (Football Player)
Detroit Lions
404 SW Atlantic St
Tullahoma, TN 37388-4409, USA

London, Irving M (Physicist)
Harvard-MIT Health Sciences
77 Massachusetts Ave
Cambridge, MA 02139-4301, USA

London, Jason (Actor)
c/o Adam Levine *Anthem Entertainment*
6100 Wilshire Blvd Ste 1170
Los Angeles, CA 90048-5116, USA

London, Jeremy (Actor)
c/o Andrea Pett-Joseph *Brillstein-Grey Entertainment*
9150 Wilshire Blvd Ste 350
Beverly Hills, CA 90212-3453, USA

London, Lauren (Actor)
c/o Staff Member *William Morris Agency (WMA-LA)*
1 William Morris Pl
Beverly Hills, CA 90212-4261, USA

London, Lisa (Actor, Model)
8949 W Sunset Blvd Ste 201
Los Angeles, CA 90069-1806, USA

London, Rick (Cartoonist)
c/o Staff Member *Artistic Licensing Agency*
126 Oriole St Apt 409
Hot Springs, AR 71901-3087, USA

Lone, John (Actor)
Levine Thall Plotkin
1740 Broadway
New York, NY 10019-4396, USA

Loneker, Keith (Football Player)
Los Angeles Rams
56 W Lincoln Ave
Roselle Park, NJ 07204-1358, USA

Lonergan, Kenneth (Writer)
c/o Staff Member *William Morris Agency (WMA-LA)*
1 William Morris Pl
Beverly Hills, CA 90212-4261, USA

Lonestar (Music Group)
c/o Gary Borman *Borman Entertainment*
1250 6th St Ste 401
Santa Monica, CA 90401-1638, USA

Lonetto, Sarah (Baseball Player)
26560 Burg Rd Apt 132
Warren, MI 48089-3594, USA

Long, Anthony A (Educator)
1088 Telvin St
Albany, CA 94706, USA

Long, Bill (Baseball Player)
Chicago White Sox
7699 Dimmick Rd
Cincinnati, OH 45241-1166, USA

Long, Bob (Baseball Player)
Pittsburgh Pirates
5172 Poplar Springs Rd
Ringgold, GA 30736-5707, USA

Long, Bob (Football Player)
Green Bay Packers
3695 Stonebrook Ct
Brookfield, WI 53005-2265, USA

Long, Bob (Football Player)
Los Angeles Rams
1413 W Via De La Gloria
Green Valley, AZ 85614-5007, USA

Long, Bob (Football Player)
Buffalo Bills
PO Box 245
Ashland, PA 17921-0245, USA

Long, Carl (Baseball Player)
Birmingham Black Barons
401 Duggins Dr
Kinston, NC 28501-8211, USA

Long, Charles F (Chuck) II (Football Player)
2425 N Macarthur Blvd
Oklahoma City, OK 73127-1605, USA

Long, Dale W (Publisher)
Working Woman Magazine
342 Madison Ave
New York, NY 10173-0002, USA

Long, Dallas (Athlete, Track Athlete)
PO Box 355
Whitefish, MT 59937-0355, USA

Long, Dave (Football Player)
St Louis Cardinals
4890 W Spoonhill Dr
Tucson, AZ 85742, USA

Long, David L (Publisher)
Sports Illustrated Magazine
Rockefeller Center
New York, NY 10020, USA

Long, Dennis (Denny) (Soccer Player)
RR 5
Poplar Bluff, MO 63901, USA

Long, Elizabeth Valk (Publisher)
Time Magazine
Rockefeller Center
New York, NY 10020, USA

Long, Geoff (Baseball Player)
St Louis Cardinals
11 Flower Ct
Lakeside Park, KY 41017-2102, USA

Long, Grant (Basketball Player)
8501 Morton Taylor Rd
Belleville, MI 48111-5313, USA

Long, Howie (Actor, Football Player, Sportscaster)
c/o Jack Gilardi *International Creative Management (ICM-LA)*
10250 Constellation Blvd
Los Angeles, CA 90067-6200, USA

Long, Joan D (Producer)
La Burrage Place
Lindfield, NSW 2070, AUSTRALIA

Long, Joey (Baseball Player)
San Diego Padres
5541 Kiser Lake Rd
Conover, OH 45317-9643, USA

Long, Justin (Actor)
c/o David Guillod *United Talent Agency (UTA)*
9560 Wilshire Blvd Ste 500
Beverly Hills, CA 90212-2401, USA

Long, Mark (Reality TV Star)
c/o Staff Member *MTV Networks (LA)*
2600 Colorado Ave
Santa Monica, CA 90404-3519, USA

Long, Matthew (Matt) (Actor)
c/o Rick Kurtzman *Creative Artists Agency LCC (CAA-LA)*
2000 Avenue Of The Stars
Los Angeles, CA 90067-4700, USA

Long, Mel (Football Player)
Cleveland Browns
837 Imani Cir
Toledo, OH 43604-8425, USA

Long, Nia (Actor)
c/o Wes Stevens *VOX Inc*
5670 Wilshire Blvd Ste 820
Los Angeles, CA 90036-5613, USA

Long, Richard (Artist)
Old School
Lower Failand
Bristol BS8 3SL, UNITED KINGDOM (UK)

Long, Rien (Football Player)
Tennessee Titans
460 Great Circle Rd
Nashville, TN 37228-1404, USA

Long, Robert (Misc)
University of California
Paleontology Museum
Berkeley, CA 94720-0001, USA

Long, Robert M (Business Person)
Longs Drug Stores
141 N Civic Dr
Walnut Creek, CA 94596-3815, USA

Long, Ryan (Baseball Player)
Kansas City Royals
2021 Stonecrest Way
Pearland, TX 77581-6462, USA

Long, Scott (Actor, Reality TV Star)
c/o Staff Member *Big Brother*
12925 Riverside Dr Fl 4
Arnold Shapiro Productions
Sherman Oaks, CA 91423-5264, USA

Long, Sharon R (Scientist)
Standard University
Biological Sciences Dept
Stanford, CA 94305, USA

Long, Shelley (Actor)
15237 W Sunset Blvd
Pacific Palisades, CA 90272-3690, USA

Long, Terrance (Baseball Player)
New York Mets
8337 Marsh Pointe Dr
Montgomery, AL 36117-7409, USA

Long, Tim (Football Player)
San Francisco 49ers
1594 John Ridge Dr
Collierville, TN 38017-8658, USA

Long, William Ivey (Designer)
International Creative Mgmt
40 W 57th St Ste 1800
New York, NY 10019-4001, USA

Long-View (Music Group)
c/o Staff Member *Paradigm (Monterey)*
509 Hartnell St
Monterey, CA 93940-2825, USA

Longdon, Johnny
5401 W Palmer Dr
Banning, CA 92220-5149, USA

Longet, Claudine (Actor)
Ronald D Austin
6000 E Hopkins
Aspen, CO 81611, USA

Longfield, William (Business Person)
CR Bard Inc
730 Central Ave
New Providence, NJ 07974-1199, USA

Longley, Clint (Football Player)
Dallas Cowboys
13602 Camino De Oro Ct
Corpus Christi, TX 78418-6910, USA

Longley, Luc (Basketball Player)
New York Knicks
2 Penn Plz
Madison Square Garden
New York, NY 10121-1703, USA

Longmire, Tony (Baseball Player)
Philadelphia Phillies
PO Box 5304
Cottonwood, CA 96022, USA

Longmuir, Alan (Musician)
27 Preston Grange
Preston Pans E
Lothian, SCOTLAND

Longmuir, Derek (Musician)
27 Preston Grange
Preston Pans E
Lothian, SCOTLAND

Longo, Lenny (Musician)
Texas Sounds
PO Box 1644
Dickinson, TX 77539-1644, USA

Longo, Robert (Artist)
Longo Studio
224 Centre St
New York, NY 10013-3619, USA

Longo, Tom (Football Player)
New York Giants
2 Donna Ln
Wayne, NJ 07470-2711, USA

Longo, Tony
24 Westwind St
Marina Del Rey, CA 90292-7135, USA

Longoria, Eva (Actor)
c/o Staff Member *Desperate Housewives*
2300 W Riverside Dr
Abc Television
Burbank, CA 91506-2976, USA

Longuet-Higgins, H Christopher (Misc)
Sussex University
Exper Psych Lab
Falmer, Brighton BN1 9QG, UNITED KINGDOM (UK)

Longwell, Ryan (Football Player)
Green Bay Packers
17570 Bearpath Trl
Eden Prairie, MN 55347-3488, USA

Lonneke (Model)
Pauline's Talent Corp
379 W Broadway # 502
New York, NY 10012-5121, USA

Lonnett, Joe (Baseball Player)
Philadelphia Phillies
126 Duncan Cir
Beaver, PA 15009-9660, USA

Lonow, Claudia (Comedian)
c/o Staff Member *International Creative Management (ICM-LA)*
10250 Constellation Blvd
Los Angeles, CA 90067-6200, USA

Lonsbrough, Porter Anita (Swimmer)
6 Rivendell Gardens
Tettendall
Wolverhampton WV6 8SY, UNITED KINGDOM (UK)

Lonsdale, Gordon C (Cinematographer)
4513 W 10600 N
Highland, UT 84003-9552, USA

Lonsdale, Laurie (Writer)
49 Lighthouse St
Whitby, ON L1N 9R9, CANADA

Lonsdale, Michael
25 rue de General-Foy
Paris F-75008, FRANCE

Look, Bruce
Minnesota Twins
4298 Maitland Rd
Williamsburg, MI 49690-9575, USA

Look, Dean (Baseball Player)
Chicago White Sox
80 Victorian Hills Dr
Okemos, MI 48864-3160, USA

Lookinland, Mike (Actor)
PO Box 9968
Salt Lake City, UT 84109-0968, USA

Loomis, Rod
5114 Vineland Ave
North Hollywood, CA 91601-3814, USA

Loon (Musician)
c/o Michael (Mike) Esterman *Esterman Entertainment*
214 Park Rd
Riva, MD 21140-1224, USA

Looney, Donald L (Don) (Football Player)
Philadelphia Eagles
PO Box 3103
Midland, TX 79702-3103, USA

Looney, Shelley (Hockey Player)
31 Beaman Ln
North Falmouth, MA 02556, USA

Looney, William R III (General)
Commander
Electronic Systems Center
Hanscom Air Force Base, MA 01731, USA

Looper, Aaron (Baseball Player)
Seattle Mariners
1700 Blake Way
Ada, OK 74820-8586, USA

Looper, Braden (Baseball Player)
St Louis Cardinals
442 Shadow Creek Dr
Palos Heights, IL 60463-2912, USA

Loose, A Mohan (Actor)
15A/4 Kesavaperumal East Street
Chennai, TN 600 004, INDIA

Loose, John W (Business Person)
Coming Corp
Houghton Park
Corning, NY 14831-0001, USA

Looseleaf, Victoria
144 S Doheny Dr Apt 304
Los Angeles, CA 90048-2939, USA

Lopardo, Frank (Opera Singer)
7 Suzanne B Ct
Massapequa, NY 11758-7300, USA

Lopasky, William (Football Player)
San Francisco 49ers
Huntsville Ceasetown Road
Dallas, PA 18612, USA

Lopata, Stan (Baseball Player)
Philadelphia Phillies
2239 Leisure World
Mesa, AZ 85206-5384, USA

Lopatka, Art (Baseball Player)
St Louis Cardinals
815 Leicester Rd Apt 113
Elk Grove Vlg, IL 60007-7303, USA

Lopert, Tanya (Actor)
Cineart
36 Rue de Pnthieu
Paris 75008, FRANCE

Lopes, Davey (Baseball Player)
Los Angeles Dodgers
17762 Vineyard Ln
Poway, CA 92064-1061, USA

Lopes, David E (Davey) (Baseball Player)
17762 Vineyard Ln
Poway, CA 92064-1061, USA

Lopes, Lisa
1505 10th St
Santa Monica, CA 90401-2805, USA

Lopez, Adamari (Actor)
c/o Staff Member *Telemundo*
2470 W 8th Ave
Hialeah, FL 33010-2000, USA

Lopez, Albie (Baseball Player)
Cleveland Indians
2887 E Palo Verde Ct
Gilbert, AZ 85296-9418, USA

Lopez, Areliano Oswaldo (General, President)
Servico Aereo de Honduras
Apdo 129
Tegucigalpa, DC, HONDURAS

Lopez, Arturo (Baseball Player)
New York Yankees
16056 English Oaks Ave Apt C
Bowie, MD 20716-3355, USA

Lopez, Danny (Little Red) (Boxer)
16531 Aquamarine Ct
Chino Hills, CA 91709-4644, USA

Lopez, Felipe (Baseball Player)
Toronto Blue Jays
110 Blue Ravine Rd Ste 105
Folsom, CA 95630-4712, USA

Lopez, George (Actor, Comedian)
c/o Steve Smooke *Creative Artists Agency LCC (CAA-LA)*
2000 Avenue Of The Stars
Los Angeles, CA 90067-4700, USA

Lopez, Hector (Athlete, Baseball Player)
Kansas City A's
11415 Faldo Ct
Hudson, FL 34667, USA

Lopez, Israel (Cachao) (Musician)
c/o Staff Member *Paradigm (Monterey)*
509 Hartnell St
Monterey, CA 93940-2825, USA

Lopez, Javier (Baseball Player)
Atlanta Braves
466 Morgan Pl
Decatur, GA 30032-3250, USA

Lopez, Javier (Baseball Player)
Colorado Rockies
1002 Capistrano Ct
College Station, TX 77845-7920, USA

Lopez, Javy (Baseball Player)
c/o Staff Member *Baltimore Orioles*
333 W Camden St
Oriole Park
Baltimore, MD 21201-2435, USA

Lopez, Jennifer (Actor, Musician)
c/o Simon Fields *Nuyorican Productions*
1100 Glendon Ave Ste 920
Los Angeles, CA 90024-3513, USA

Lopez, Lourdes (Ballerina)
New York City Ballet
Lincoln Center Plaza
New York, NY 10023, USA

Lopez, Luis (Baseball Player)
San Diego Padres
3550 S Stonegate Cir Apt 208
New Berlin, WI 53151-9527, USA

Lopez, Luis (Baseball Player)
Los Angeles Dodgers
636 40th St
Brooklyn, NY 11232-3108, USA

Lopez, Lynda (Television Host)
c/o Staff Member *Style Network*
5750 Wilshire Blvd
Los Angeles, CA 90036-3697, USA

Lopez, Marga (Actor)
c/o Staff Member *Televisa*
Blvd Adolfo Lopez Mateos 232
Colonia San Angel INN
DF CP 01060, MEXICO

Lopez, Maria (Judge)
c/o Staff Member *Rebel Entertainment Partners Inc*
5700 Wilshire Blvd Ste 456
Los Angeles, CA 90036-3648, USA

Lopez, Mario (Actor, Television Host)
c/o Mark Schulman *3 Arts Entertainment Inc*
9460 Wilshire Blvd Fl 7
Beverly Hills, CA 90212-2713, USA

Lopez, Nancy (Golfer)
2308 Tara Dr
Albany, GA 31721-9111, USA

Lopez, Perry
8520 Sherwood Dr
Los Angeles, CA 90069-4719, USA

Lopez, Priscilla (Actor)
Writers & Artists
360 Park Ave # 16
New York, NY 10022-5909, USA

Lopez, Raul (Basketball Player)
Utah Jazz
301 W South Temple
Delta Center
Salt Lake City, UT 84101-1216, USA

Lopez, Robert S (Historian)
41 Richmond Ave
New Haven, CT 06515-2013, USA

Lopez, Rodrigo (Baseball Player)
Baltimore Orioles
333 W Camden St
Oriole Park
Baltimore, MD 21201-2435, USA

Lopez, Sal (Actor, Musician)
c/o Ivan De Paz *Arenas Entertainment*
100 N Crescent Dr
Garden Level
Beverly Hills, CA 90210-5408, USA

Lopez, Sergi (Actor)
c/o Staff Member *International Creative Management (ICM-LA)*
10250 Constellation Blvd
Los Angeles, CA 90067-6200, USA

Lopez, Trini (Actor, Musician)
1139 Abrigo Rd
Palm Springs, CA 92262-4101, USA

Lopez-Alegria, Michael E (Astronaut)
1919 Tangle Press Court
Houston, TX 77062, USA

Lopez-Cobos, Jesus
Terry Harrison Mgmt
1 Clarendon Court
Charlbury, Oxon OX7 3PS, UNITED KINGDOM (UK)

Lopez-Garcia, Antonio (Artist)
Marlborough Fine Art
6 Albermarle St
London W1, UNITED KINGDOM (UK)

Lopez Rodriguez, Nicolas de J Cardinal (Religious Leader)
Archdiocese of Santo Domingo
Santo Domingo, AP 186, DOMINICAN REPUBLIC

Lopez Tarso, Ignacio (Actor)
c/o Staff Member *Televisa*
Blvd Adolfo Lopez Mateos 232
Colonia San Angel INN
DF CP 01060, MEXICO

Lopez Trujillo, Alfonso Cardinal (Religious Leader)
Arzobispado
Calle 57 N 48-28
Medellin, COLOMBIA

Loquasto, Santo (Designer)
Paradigm Agency
10100 Santa Monica Blvd Ste 2500
Los Angeles, CA 90067-4116, USA

Lorant, Stefan
215 W Mountain Rd
Lenox, MA 01240, USA

Lorca, Valeria (Actor)
c/o Staff Member *Telefe - Argentina*
Pavon 2444 (C1248AAT)
Buenos Aires, ARGENTINA

Lorch, George A (Business Person)
Armstrong World
313 W Liberty St
Lancaster, PA 17603-2798, USA

Lorch, Karl (Football Player)
Washington Redskins
92-861 Palailai St
Kapolei, HI 96707-1239, USA

Lord, Albert L (Business Person)
SLM Holding Corp
11600 Sallie Mae Dr
Reston, VA 20193-0001, USA

Lord, Lance W (General)
Commander
US Space Command
Peterson Air Force Base, CO 80914, USA

Lord, M G (Cartoonist, Editor)
Newsday
235 Pinelawn Rd
Editorial Dept
Melville, NY 11747-4250, USA

Lord, Marjorie (Actor)
1110 Maytor Pl
Beverly Hills, CA 90210-2600, USA

Lord, Peter (Animator, Director)
Aardman Animations
Gas Ferry Road
Bristol BS1 6UN, UNITED KINGDOM (UK)

Lord, Walter
116 E 68th St
New York, NY 10065-5955, USA

Lord, Winston (Diplomat)
740 Park Ave
New York, NY 10021-4251, USA

Lords, Traci
c/o Staff Member *Juliet Green Management*
9025 Wilshire Blvd Ste 400
Beverly Hills, CA 90211-1828, USA

Loree, Brad (Actor)
c/o Brenda Wong *TalentCo*
111 Water St #308
Vancouver, BC V6B 1A7, CANADA

Loren, Sophia (Actor)
c/o Leonard Hirshan *Leonard Hirshan Management*
9171 Wilshire Blvd Ste 400
Beverly Hills, CA 90210-5516, USA

Lorentz, Jim (Hockey Player)
2555 Staley Rd
Grand Island, NY 14072-2040, USA

Lorenz, Edward N (Scientist)
Massachusetts Institute of Technology
Earth Sciences Dept
Cambridge, MA 02139, USA

Lorenz, Lee (Cartoonist)
PO Box 131
Easton, CT 06612-0131, USA

Lorenz, Robert (Producer)
c/o Staff Member *Malpaso Productions*
4000 Warner Bros Ste 101 Bldg 81
Burbank, CA 91522-0001, USA

Lorenzen, Fred (Race Car Driver)
906 Burr Oak Ct
Oak Brook, IL 60523-1514, USA

Lorenzo, Blas (Actor)
PO Box 2127
Los Angeles, CA 90078-2127, USA

Lorenzoni, Andrea (Astronaut)
Via B Vergine del Carmelo 168
Rome 00144, ITALY

Loretta, Mark (Baseball Player)
Milwaukee Brewers
PO Box 9505
Rancho Santa Fe, CA 92067-4505, USA

Loria, Christopher (Gus) (Astronaut)
102 Sea Mist Dr
League City, TX 77573-6928, USA

Loria, Jeffrey (Baseball Player)
Florida Marlins
44 Cocoanut Row Unit 407-B
Palm Beach, FL 33480-4069, USA

Lorick, Tony (Football Player)
Baltimore Colts
349 Burney Ln
Kerrville, TX 78028-8074, USA

Loring, Gloria (Actor, Musician)
PO Box 1243
Cedar Glen, CA 92321-1243, USA

Loring, John R (Artist)
350 W 43rd St Apt 36E
New York, NY 10036-6478, USA

Loring, Lisa (Actor)
Genesis Creations
1815 Via Capri
Chula Vista, CA 91913-1523, USA

Loring, Lynn (Actor)
4910 Petit Ave
Encino, CA 91436-1131, USA

Loriod, Yvonne (Musician)
Bureau de Concerts
7 Rue de Richepanse
Paris 75008, FRANCE

Lorius, Claude (Scientist)
Glaciologies Laboratoire
Rue Moliere
Saint-Martin d'Heres 38402, FRANCE

Lorraine, Andrew (Baseball Player)
California Angels
10436 E Acoma Dr
Scottsdale, AZ 85255-1711, USA

Lorring, Joan
345 E 68th St
New York, NY 10065-5656, USA

Lorscheider, Aloisio Cardinal (Religious Leader)
Guna Metropolitana
CP 05 Tone Basilica
Aparecida, SP 12570-000, BRAZIL

Lortie, Louis (Musician)
Cramer/Marder Artists
3436 Springhill Rd
Lafayette, CA 94549-2535, USA

Los, Marinus (Misc)
American Cyanamid Corp
4201 Quakebridge Road
Princeton Junction, NJ 08550, USA

Los Lagos, Banda (Music Group)
c/o Staff Member *Sony Music Miami*
605 Lincoln Rd Fl 7
Miami Beach, FL 33139-2900, USA

Los Lobos (Music Group)
c/o Staff Member *Paradigm (Monterey)*
509 Hartnell St
Monterey, CA 93940-2825, USA

Los Lonely Boys (Music Group)
Loophole Entertainment
PO Box 162045
Austin, TX 78716-2045, USA

Los Mauricios (Writer)
c/o Staff Member *Gabriel Blanco Iglesias (Colombia)*
Dg 127A #20-36
Conjunto Plenitud, Apto 132
Bogota, COLOMBIA

Los Rabanes (Music Group)
c/o Staff Member *Sony Music Miami*
605 Lincoln Rd Fl 7
Miami Beach, FL 33139-2900, USA

Los Sementales de Nuevo Leon (Music Group)
c/o Staff Member *Sony Music Miami*
605 Lincoln Rd Fl 7
Miami Beach, FL 33139-2900, USA

Losch, Jack (Football Player)
Green Bay Packers
1606 Kaiser Ave
Williamsport, PA 17702-7015, USA

Loscutoff, James (Jim) (Basketball Player, Coach)
166 Jenkins Rd
Andover, MA 01810-2304, USA

Lost Boys
1775 Broadway Ste 433
New York, NY 10019-1903, USA

Lostprophets (Music Group)
c/o Staff Member *Sony Music International*
550 Madison Ave Fl 6
New York, NY 10022-3211, USA

Lothamer, Ed (Football Player)
San Diego Chargers
14545 W 183rd St
Olathe, KS 66062-9192, USA

Lott, Felicity A (Opera Singer)
Kunstleragentur Raab & Bohm
Plankengasse 7
Vienna 1010, AUSTRIA

Lott, John (Football Player)
Pittsburgh Steelers
3373 E Nolan Dr
Chandler, AZ 85249-3611, USA

Lott, Ronald M (Ronnie) (Sportscaster)
Fox-TV
PO Box 900
Sports Dept
Beverly Hills, CA 90213-0900, USA

Lott, Ronnie (Football Player)
San Francisco 49ers
11342 Canyon View Cir
Cupertino, CA 95014-4838, USA

Lott, Thomas (Football Player)
St Louis Cardinals
PO Box 940585
Plano, TX 75094-0585, USA

Lott, Trent (Senator)
3100 Pascagoula St
Pascagoula, MS 39567-4215, USA

Lotti, Helmut
Bevrijdingstraat 39
Turnhout 2300, BELGIUM

Lotz, Anne Graham (Religious Leader)
AnGel Ministries
3246 Lewis Farm Rd
Raleigh, NC 27607-6723, USA

Louchiey, Corey (Football Player)
Buffalo Bills
8 Misty Creek Ln
Greenville, SC 29611-7718, USA

Loucks, Scott (Baseball Player)
Houston Astros
1801 Viola Dr
Sierra Vista, AZ 85635-2149, USA

Loucks, Vernon R Jr (Business Person)
Baxter International
1 Baxter Pkwy
Deerfield, IL 60015-4634, USA

Louderback, Tom (Football Player)
Philadelphia Eagles
PO Box 6879
Oakland, CA 94603-0879, USA

Loudon, Rodney (Physicist)
3 Gaston St
East Bergholt
Colchester, Essex CO7 6SD, UNITED KINGDOM (UK)

Louganis, Greg
c/o Evan Morgenstein *PMG Sports*
700 Evanvale Ct
Cary, NC 27518-2806, USA

Loughery, Kevin (Basketball Player, Coach)
4474 Club Dr NE
Atlanta, GA 30319-1122, USA

Loughlin, Mary Anne (Correspondent)
WTBS-TV News Dept
1050 Techwood Dr NW
Atlanta, GA 30318-5604, USA

Loughran, James
34 Cleveden Dr
Glasgow G12 0RX, SCOTLAND

Louis, Jin Luxian (Religious Leader)
Shesshan Catholic Seminary
Beijing, CHINA

Louis, Murray (Choreographer, Dancer)
Nikolais/Louis Foundation
375 W Broadway
New York, NY 10012-4324, USA

Louis-Dreyfus, Julia (Actor, Comedian)
c/o Judy Hofflund *Hofflund/Polone*
9465 Wilshire Blvd Ste 890
Beverly Hills, CA 90212-2607, USA

Louis-Dreyfus, Robert L M (Business Person)
Adidas AG
Adi Dassier Str 2
Herzogenaurach 91702, GERMANY

Louisa, Maria (Model)
Next Model Mgmt
23 Watts St
New York, NY 10013, USA

Louise, Tina (Actor, Musician)
310 E 46th St Apt 18T
New York, NY 10017-3029, USA

Louiso, Todd (Actor)
S M S Talent
8730 W Sunset Blvd Ste 440
Los Angeles, CA 90069-2277, USA

Louisy, C Pearlette (Governor)
Governer General's House
Morne
Castries, SAINT LUCIA

Loukas, Angelo (Football Player)
Buffalo Bills
1535 Robin Rd
Bannockburn, IL 60015-1852, USA

Loun, Don (Baseball Player)
Washington Senators
9095 Wexford Dr
Vienna, VA 22182-2152, USA

Lounge, John
555 Forge River Rd # 150
Webster, TX 77598-4369, USA

Lounge, John M (Mike) (Astronaut)
4002 Park Thicket
Houston, TX 77058-1222, USA

Lourdusamy, D Simon Cardinal (Religious Leader)
Palazzo dei Convertendi
64 Via della Conciliazione
Rome 00193, ITALY

Lourie, Alan D (Judge)
US Court of Appeals
717 Madison Pl NW
Washington, DC 20439-0001, USA

Louris, Gary (Musician, Songwriter, Writer)
Sussman Assoc
1222 16th Ave S Fl 3
Nashville, TN 37212-2926, USA

Lousma, Jack R (Astronaut)
2722 Roseland Dr
Ann Arbor, MI 48103-2137, USA

Loutfy, All (Prime Minister)
29 Ahmed Hesmat St
Zamalek
Cairo, EGYPT

Louvier, Alain (Composer)
53 Ave Victor Hugo
Boulogne-Billancourt 92100, FRANCE

Louvin, Charlie (Musician, Songwriter, Writer)
2851 Sainville Rd
Manchester, TN 37355-6338, USA

Lovano, Joe (Composer)
International Music Network
278 S Main St #400
Gloucester, MA 01930, USA

Love, Alexis
PO Box 491205
Los Angeles, CA 90049-9205, USA

Love, Ben H (Misc)
1327 Anna Ct
Boy Scouts Of America
Cedar Park, TX 78613-4022, USA

Love, Courtney (Musician, Songwriter, Writer)
c/o Staff Member *Special Artists Agency*
9465 Wilshire Blvd Ste 890
Beverly Hills, CA 90212-2607, USA

Love, Darlene (Actor, Musician)
Greater Talent
437 5th Ave Fl 7
New York, NY 10016-2205, USA

Love, Davis III (Golfer)
PO Box 30959
Sea Island, GA 31561-0959, USA

Love, Duval (Football Player)
Los Angeles Rams
8985 Yuba River Ave
Fountain Valley, CA 92708-6346, USA

Love, Faizon (Actor)
c/o Ben Feigin *Nine Yards Entertainment*
8530 Wilshire Blvd Fl 5
Beverly Hills, CA 90211-3102, USA

Love, Gael (Editor)
Connoisseur Magazine
1790 Broadway
Editorial Dept
New York, NY 10019-1412, USA

Love, Ian (Musician)
c/o Staff Member *Paradigm (Monterey)*
509 Hartnell St
Monterey, CA 93940-2825, USA

Love, Loni (Actor, Comedian)
c/o Staff Member *Power Entertainment*
9100 Wilshire Blvd # 700
Beverly Hills, CA 90212-3401, USA

Love, Michael D (Mike) (Musician)
PO Box 7800
Incline Village, NV 89452-7800, USA

Love, Mike
24563 Ebelden Ave
Santa Clarita, CA 91321-3745, USA

Love, Randy (Football Player)
St Louis Cardinals
2202 Fairlands Dr
Garland, TX 75040-1158, USA

Love, Sean (Football Player)
Tampa Bay Buccaneers
121 Hunter St
Tamaqua, PA 18252-2405, USA

Love, Stan (Basketball Player)
1950 Egan Way
Lake Oswego, OR 97034-2728, USA

Love, Stanley G (Astronaut)
4315 Indian Sunrise Ct
Houston, TX 77059-5582, USA

Love & Rockets (Music Group)
4 The Lakes Bushey
Hertfordshire, ENGLAND WD2 1HS, UNITED KINGDOM (UK)

Lovelace, Vance (Baseball Player)
California Angels
5608 12th Ave S
Tampa, FL 33619-3756, USA

Lovelady, Edwin (Football Player)
New York Giants
2707 Glenwood Pkwy
Chattanooga, TN 37404-1712, USA

Loveless, Patty (Musician, Songwriter, Writer)
c/o Staff Member *William Morris Agency (WMA-LA)*
1 William Morris Pl
Beverly Hills, CA 90212-4261, USA

Lovell, Jacqueline
8707 Shirley Ave
Northridge, CA 91324-3410, USA

Lovell, James A, Jr (Astronaut)
Lovell Communications
PO Box 49
Lake Forest, IL 60045-0049, USA

Lovell, Marilyn
7840 Torreyson Dr
Los Angeles, CA 90046-1229, USA

Lovellette, Clyde E (Basketball Player)
319 Maple St
Munising, MI 49862-1042, USA

Lovelock, James E (Inventor, Scientist)
Coombe Mill
Saint Giles-on-Heath
Launceston, Cornwall PL 15 9RY, UNITED KINGDOM (UK)

Lover, Ed (Actor)
c/o Staff Member *The Artists Group Ltd (LA)*
1650 Broadway Ste 610
New York, NY 10019-6833, USA

Lover, Seth (Engineer, Inventor)
4 Village Dr
Saint Louis, MO 63146-5346, USA

Loverboy
1505 W. 2nd St. #200
Vancouver, BC V6H 3Y4, CANADA

Loverne, David (Football Player)
New York Jets
2307 Amber Falls Dr
Rocklin, CA 95765-4200, USA

Lovetere, John (Football Player)
Los Angeles Rams
PO Box 2901
Lebanon, TN 37088-2901, USA

Lovett, Lyie (Musician, Songwriter, Writer)
Haber Corp
1016 17th Ave S # 1
Nashville, TN 37212-2202, USA

Lovett, Lyle (Musician)
c/o Staff Member *Paradigm (Monterey)*
509 Hartnell St
Monterey, CA 93940-2825, USA

Lovett, Ruby (Musician)
Myers Media
PO Box 378
Canton, NY 13617, USA

Lovett, Steve (Actor)
c/o Steve Lovett *Lovett Management*
1327 Brinkley Ave
Los Angeles, CA 90049-3619, USA

Loviglio, Jay (Baseball Player)
Philadelphia Phillies
23 3rd Ave
East Islip, NY 11730-2015, USA

Loville, Derek (Football Player)
Seattle Seahawks
635 Head St
San Francisco, CA 94132-2809, USA

Lovin' Spoonful
Duryea Entertainment
35 White Birch Rd
Ridgefield, CT 06877-5620, USA

Lovine, Vicki
c/o Daniel A (Dan) Strone *Trident Media Group LLC*
41 Madison Ave Fl 36
New York, NY 10010-2257, USA

Loving, Candy (Actor, Model)
c/o Staff Member *Playboy Enterprises Inc*
680 N Lake Shore Dr Ste 1500
Chicago, IL 60611-4455, USA

Lovins, Amory B (Physicist)
Hypercar Inc
220 Cody Ln
Basalt, CO 81621-9106, USA

Lovitz, Jon (Actor, Comedian, Producer, Writer)
c/o Jason Shapiro *United Talent Agency (UTA)*
9560 Wilshire Blvd Ste 500
Beverly Hills, CA 90212-2401, USA

Lovrich, Pete (Baseball Player)
Kansas City A's
19626 Beechnut Dr
Mokena, IL 60448-9333, USA

Lovullo, Torey (Baseball Player)
Detroit Tigers
16825 Bajio Rd
Encino, CA 91436-3522, USA

Lovuolo, Frank (Football Player)
New York Giants
6 Pleasant Ct
Binghamton, NY 13905-1516, USA

Low, Francis E (Physicist)
7102 Plantation Ln
Rockville, MD 20852-4421, USA

Low, G David (Astronaut)
Orbital Science Group
21839 Atlantic Blvd
Sterling, VA 20166-6850, USA

Low, Stephen (Diplomat)
2855 Tilden St NW
Washington, DC 20008-3820, USA

Low Stars (Music Group)
c/o Staff Member *Paradigm (Monterey)*
509 Hartnell St
Monterey, CA 93940-2825, USA

Lowder, Kyle (Actor)
c/o Michael Meltzer *Michael Meltzer & Associates*
12207 Riverside Dr Apt 208
Valley Village, CA 91607-3821, USA

Lowdermilk, R Kirk (Football Player)
Minnesota Vikings
9475 Apollo Rd NE
Kensington, OH 44427, USA

Lowe, Barry
31S. Audley St.
London, ENGLAND W1, UNITED KINGDOM (UK)

Lowe, Chad (Actor)
c/o David Rose *Innovative Artists (LA)*
1505 10th St
Santa Monica, CA 90401-2805, USA

Lowe, Chan (Cartoonist, Editor)
Fort Lauderdale Sun-Sentinel
200 E Olas Blvd
Fort Lauderdale, FL 33301, USA

Lowe, Crystal (Actor, Model)
Characters Talent Agency
8 Elm Street
Toronto, ON M5G 1G&, CANADA

Lowe, Derek (Baseball Player)
Boston Red Sox
15401 Old Wedgewood Ct
Fort Myers, FL 33908-7207, USA

Lowe, Derek C (Baseball Player)
Boston Red Sox
Fenway Park
4 Yawkey Way
Boston, MA 02215-3496, USA

Lowe, Gary (Football Player)
Washington Redskins
16940 Lauderdale Ave
Beverly Hills, MI 48025-5549, USA

Lowe, Kevin (Coach, Hockey Player)
Edmonton Oilers
11230 110th St
Edmonton, AB T5G 3H7, CANADA

Lowe, Lloyd (Football Player)
Chicago Bears
8805 Deerwood Dr
Rowlett, TX 75088-4809, USA

Lowe, Nick (Musician, Songwriter, Writer)
MVO Ltd
307 7th Ave Rm 807
New York, NY 10001-6066, USA

Lowe, Paul (Football Player)
Los Angeles Chargers
3906 Marine View Ave
San Diego, CA 92113-4331, USA

Lowe, Rob (Actor)
15030 Ventura Blvd # 710
Sherman Oaks, CA 91403-5470, USA

Lowe, Sean (Baseball Player)
St Louis Cardinals
9948 County Road 2469
Royse City, TX 75189-5246, USA

Lowe, Sidney (Basketball Player, Coach)
2631 Wallingford Rd
Winston Salem, NC 27101-1923, USA

Lowe, Stephanie (Golfer)
2004 Delancey Dr
Norman, OK 73071-3872, USA

Lowe, Woodrow (Coach, Football Player)
San Diego Chargers
282 Grande View Pkwy
Maylene, AL 35114-6073, USA

Lowell, Charlie (Musician)
Flood Burnstead McCready McCarthy
1700 Hayes St Ste 304
Nashville, TN 37203-3014, USA

Lowell, Christopher (Television Host)
Christopher Lowell Inc
12200 W Olympic Blvd Ste 460
Los Angeles, CA 90064-1055, USA

Lowell, Michael A (Mike) (Baseball Player)
New York Yankees
620 Santurce Ave
Coral Gables, FL 33143-6360, USA

Lowell, Scott
6500 Wilshire Blvd Ste 2200
Los Angeles, CA 90048-4942, USA

Lowenstein, Evan (Actor, Musician)
c/o Billy Lazarus *United Talent Agency (UTA)*
9560 Wilshire Blvd Ste 500
Beverly Hills, CA 90212-2401, USA

Lowenstein, Jaron (Actor, Musician)
c/o Billy Lazarus *United Talent Agency (UTA)*
9560 Wilshire Blvd Ste 500
Beverly Hills, CA 90212-2401, USA

Lowenstein, Louis (Attorney, Attorney General, Educator, General)
5 Oak Ln
Larchmont, NY 10538-3917, USA

Lowery, Corey (Musician)
Agency Group Ltd
1775 Broadway Ste 515
New York, NY 10019-1903, USA

Lowery, Nick (Football Player)
New England Patriots
30616 W 98th St
De Soto, KS 66018-9311, USA

Lowery, Terrell (Baseball Player)
Chicago Cubs
3565 Antigua Pl
W Sacramento, CA 95691-5822, USA

Lowitsch, Klaus
Am Hochacker 51
Munich D-81827, GERMANY

Lowman, Frank A (Financier)
Federal Home Loan Bank
2 Townsite Plaza
Topeka, KS 66603, USA

Lown, Bernard (Doctor)
Lown Cardiovascular Group
21 Longwood Ave
Brookline, MA 02446-5239, USA

Lown, Turk (Baseball Player)
Chicago Cubs
1106 Van Buren St
Pueblo, CO 81004-2832, USA

Lowry, Lois (Writer)
205 Brattle St
Cambridge, MA 02138-3345, USA

Lowry, Mark
MLP Inc
PO Box 1405
Hendersonville, TN 37077-1405, USA

Lowry, Noah (Baseball Player)
San Francisco Giants
181 N Encinal Ave
Ojai, CA 93023-2119, USA

Loy, Frank E (Misc)
Marshall German Fund
11 Dupont Cir NW
Washington, DC 20036-1207, USA

Loy, James M (Admiral, Government Official)
Transportation Security Administration
400 7th St SW
Washington, DC 20590-0001, USA

Loynd, Mike (Baseball Player)
Texas Rangers
19 Randall Dr
Short Hills, NJ 07078-1957, USA

Lozada, Johnny (Actor)
c/o Staff Member *Televisa*
Blvd Adolfo Lopez Mateos 232
Colonia San Angel INN
DF CP 01060, MEXICO

Lozado, Willie (Baseball Player)
Milwaukee Brewers
4407 Sunrise Ct
Sellersburg, IN 47172-9248, USA

Lozano, Conrad (Musician)
Gold Mountain
3575 Cahuenga Blvd W Ste 450
Los Angeles, CA 90068-1364, USA

Lozano, Ignacio E Jr (Editor)
La Opinion
700 S Flower St Ste 3000
Los Angeles, CA 90017-4217, USA

Lozano, Karyme (Actor)
c/o Ivan De Paz *Arenas Entertainment*
100 N Crescent Dr
Garden Level
Beverly Hills, CA 90210-5408, USA

Lozano, Silvia (Choreographer)
Ballet Folklorico
31 Esq Con Riva Palacio
Mexico City, DF, MEXICO

Lozano Barragan, Javier Cardinal (Religious Leader)
Health Care Workers Assistance
Via Conciliazione 3
Rome 00193, ITALY

Lu, Edward T (Ed) (Astronaut)
18222 Bal Harbour Dr
Houston, TX 77058-4311, USA

Lu, Lisa
1737 N Orange Grove Ave
Los Angeles, CA 90046-2131, USA

Lu, Qihui (Artist)
100-301
398 Xin-Pei Road
Xin-Zuan, Shanghai, CHINA

Lualdi, Antonella
via Cassia Antica 35
Rome, ITALY

Lubanski, Ed (Bowler)
5326 Christi Dr
Warren, MI 48091-4195, USA

Lubbers, Ruud F M (Prime Minister)
Lambertweg 4
Rotterdam, RA 3062, THE NETHERLANDS

Lubezki, Emmanuel (Cinematographer)
Broder Kurland Webb Uffner
10250 Constellation Blvd
Los Angeles, CA 90067-6200, USA

Lubich, Bronko (Wrestler)
3146 Whitemarsh Cir
Dallas, TX 75234-2239, USA

Lubich, Silvia Chiara (Misc)
Focolare Movement
306 Via di Frascati
Rocca di Papa, RM 00040, ITALY

Lubin, Arthur
5737 Newcastle Ave
Encino, CA 91316-1054, USA

Lubin, Steven (Musician)
State University of New York
School Of Arts
Purchase, NY 10577, USA

Lubischer, Steve (Football Player)
Miami Dolphins
6 Fiore Ct
Oceanport, NJ 07757-1405, USA

Lubotsky, Mark (Musician)
Overtoom 329 III
Amsterdam, JM 1054, THE NETHERLANDS

Lubovitch, Lar (Choreographer, Dancer)
Lar Lubovitch Dance Co
229 W 42nd St Fl 8
New York, NY 10036-7205, USA

Lubratich, Steve (Baseball Player)
California Angels
24 Sackett Rd
Lee, NH 03861-6616, USA

Lubs, Herbert A (Scientist)
5133 SW 71st Pl
Miami, FL 33155-5639, USA

Lubys, Bronislovas (Prime Minister)
Prime Minister's Office
Tuo-Vaizganto 2
Vilnius, LITHUANIA

Luc, Tone (Actor, Musician)
Headline Talent
1650 Broadway Ste 508
New York, NY 10019-6833, USA

Lucado, Max
19595 W 1H 10
San Antonio, TX 78257, USA

Lucaro, Carlos (Judge)
US Court of Appeals
1929 Stout St
Denver, CO 80294-0003, USA

Lucas, Aubrey K (Educator)
University of Southern Mississippi
President's Office
Hattiesburg, MS 39406-0001, USA

Lucas, Cornel (Photographer)
57 Addison Road
London W148JJ, UNITED KINGDOM
(UK)

Lucas, Craig (Director, Producer, Writer)
c/o Staff Member *Gersh Agency, The (LA)*
232 N Canon Dr
Beverly Hills, CA 90210-5302, USA

Lucas, Gary (Baseball Player)
San Diego Padres
1511 High St
Rice Lake, WI 54868-1874, USA

Lucas, George (Business Person, Director, Producer)
c/o Staff Member *LucasFilm Ltd*
5858 Lucas Valley Rd
Nicasio, CA 94946-9703, USA

Lucas, Jacklyn H (Jack) (War Hero)
75 Elks Lake Rd
Hattiesburg, MS 39401-8636, USA

Lucas, Josh (Actor)
c/o Scott Wexler *3 Arts Entertainment Inc*
9460 Wilshire Blvd Fl 7
Beverly Hills, CA 90212-2713, USA

Lucas, Ken (Football Player)
Seattle Seahawks
1108 Stamps Cv
Cleveland, MS 38732-4014, USA

Lucas, Matt (Actor, Writer)
TROIKA
74 Clerkenwell Rd 3rd Fl
London EC1M52A, UNITED KINGDOM
(UK)

Lucas, Maurice (Basketball Player, Coach)
5691 Bonita Rd
Lake Oswego, OR 97035-3217, USA

Lucas, Ray (Football Player)
New England Patriots
7 Quaker Hill Rd
Jackson, NJ 08527-4814, USA

Lucas, Richard J (Richie) (Football Player)
Pittsburgh Steelers
712 Tussey Ln
State College, PA 16801-7826, USA

Lucas, Robert E Jr (Nobel Prize Laureate)
5448 S East View Park Apt 3
Chicago, IL 60615-5929, USA

Lucas, William (Government Official)
Justice Department
Constitution & 10th NW
Washington, DC 20530-0001, USA

Lucca, Lou (Baseball Player)
Topps
10211 Willow Bend Cir Apt 1B
Charlotte, NC 28210-8424, USA

Lucca, Tony (Actor)
c/o Staff Member *Burstein Company, The*
15304 W Sunset Blvd Ste 208
Pacific Palisades, CA 90272-3656, USA

Lucchesi, Frank
3027 Glasgow Dr
Arlington, TX 76015-2228, USA

Lucchesini, Andrea (Musician)
Arts Management Group
1133 Broadway Ste 1025
New York, NY 10010-7985, USA

Lucci, Mike (Football Player)
Cleveland Browns
3184 Middlebelt Rd
W Bloomfield, MI 48323-1937, USA

Lucci, Susan (Actor)
16 Carteret Pl
Garden City, NY 11530-1542, USA

Lucci, Vince Sr (Bowler)
1182 Queens Way
West Chester, PA 19382, USA

Luce, Derrel (Football Player)
Baltimore Colts
4112 Green Oak Dr
Waco, TX 76710-1440, USA

Luce, Henry III (Publisher)
Mill Hill Road
Mill Neck, NY 11765, USA

Luce, Lew (Football Player)
Washington Redskins
850 Symphony Isles Blvd
Ruskin, FL 33572-2764, USA

Luce, R Duncan (Misc)
20 Whitman Ct
Irvine, CA 92617-4057, USA

Luce, Richard N (Governor)
Governor's Office
Convent, GIBRALTAR

Luce, William (Bill) (Writer)
PO Box 370
Depoe Bay, OR 97341-0370, USA

Lucebert (Artist, Writer)
Boendermakerhof 10
Bergen N-H, TB 1861, THE
NETHERLANDS

Lucero (Musician)
c/o Staff Member *Sony Music Miami*
605 Lincoln Rd Fl 7
Miami Beach, FL 33139-2900, USA

Lucey, Dorothy (Actor, Correspondent, Television Host)
c/o Staff Member *Good Day Live*
20th Century Fox Television
10201 W Pico Blvd Blg 88 Rm 29
Los Angeles, CA 90035, USA

Luchko, Klara S (Actor)
Kotelmicheskaya Nab 1/15 Korp B
#308
Moscow 109240, RUSSIA

Lucid, Shannon W (Astronaut, Physicist)
1622 Gunwale Rd
Houston, TX 77062-4538, USA

Lucier, Lou (Baseball Player)
Boston Red Sox
579 Highland St
Northbridge, MA 01534-1113, USA

Lucio, Shannon (Actor)
c/o Adam Sher *William Morris Agency
(WMA-LA)*
1 William Morris Pl
Beverly Hills, CA 90212-4261, USA

Luck, Frank (Athlete)
Lerchenweg 9
Springstille 98587, GERMANY

Luckenbill, Laurence
PO Box 636
Cross River, NY 10518-0636, USA

Luckhurst, Mick (Football Player)
Atlanta Falcons
103 Pierrepont Isle
Duluth, GA 30097-5908, USA

Luckinbill, Laurence (Actor)
RR 3
Katonah, NY 10536, USA

Luckinbill, Lawrence (Actor)
PO Box 330
Georgetown, CT 06829-0330, USA

Luckinbill, Thad (Actor)
c/o Staff Member *Young and the Restless, The*
7800 Beverly Blvd Ste 3305
Los Angeles, CA 90036-2112, USA

Lucking, William (Actor)
c/o Staff Member *Twentieth Century Artists*
15760 Ventura Blvd Ste 700
Encino, CA 91436-3016, USA

Luckovich, Mike (Cartoonist, Editor)
Atlanta Constitution
72 Marietta St NW
Editorial Dept
Atlanta, GA 30303-2899, USA

Lucky, Lillian (Baseball Player)
243 Owens St
Niles, MI 49120-4150, USA

Lucky, Mike (Football Player)
Dallas Cowboys
4156 N Morning Dove Cir
Mesa, AZ 85207-1194, USA

Luczo, Stephen J (Business Person)
Seagate Technology
920 Disc Dr
Scotts Valley, CA 95066-4542, USA

Luddy, Barbara
119 Sultan Ave
Capitol Heights, MD 20743-1954, USA

Luder, Owen H (Architect)
Communication in Construction
2 Smith Square
London SW1P 3H5, UNITED KINGDOM
(UK)

Ludes, John T (Business Person)
Fortune Brands Inc
300 Tower Pkwy
Lincolnshire, IL 60069-3665, USA

Luding-Rothenburger, Christa (Speed Skater)
Dresdener Eisspot-Club
Pieschener Allee 1
Dresden 01067, GERMANY

Ludlum, Robert (Actor)
c/o Ben Smith *International Creative Management (ICM-LA)*
10250 Constellation Blvd
Los Angeles, CA 90067-6200, USA

Ludwick, Eric (Baseball Player)
St Louis Cardinals
10183 Whispy Willow Way
Las Vegas, NV 89135-2089, USA

Ludwick, Ryan (Baseball Player)
Texas Rangers
10183 Whispy Willow Way
Las Vegas, NV 89135-2089, USA

Ludwig, Christa (Opera Singer)
Calliopie
162 Chemin du Santon
Mougins 06250, FRANCE

Ludwig, George H (Physicist)
215 Aspen Trl
Winchester, VA 22602-1404, USA

Ludwig, Ken (Writer)
c/o Peter Franklin *William Morris Agency
(WMA-NY)*
1325 Avenue Of The Americas
New York, NY 10019-6026, USA

Luebber, Steve (Baseball Player)
Minnesota Twins
3302 Moorhead Dr
Joplin, MO 64804-5323, USA

Luebbers, Larry (Baseball Player)
Cincinnati Reds
844 Isaac Shelby Cir E
Frankfort, KY 40601-8806, USA

Lueck, Bill (Football Player)
Green Bay Packers
13440 W Camelback Rd
Litchfield Park, AZ 85340, USA

Luecken, Rick (Baseball Player)
Kansas City Royals
2902 Fontana Dr
Houston, TX 77043-1305, USA

Luft, Joey
108 E Matilija St
Ojai, CA 93023-2639, USA

Luft, Lorna (Actor, Musician)
Stiletto Entertainment
8295 S La Cienega Blvd
C/O Garry Kief
Inglewood, CA 90301-1521, USA

Lugar, Richard (Senator)
7841 Old Dominion Dr
McLean, VA 22102-2425, USA

Lugbill, Jon (Athlete)
American Cance Assn
7432 Alban Station Blvd Ste B232
Springfield, VA 22150-2321, USA

Luger, Lex
52B49 Uford Hwy.
Atlanta, GA 30340, USA

Lugo, Julio (Baseball Player)
Houston Astros
440 Neptune Ave Apt 120
Brooklyn, NY 11224-4455, USA

Lugo, Richard (Actor)
Official International Fan Club
PO Box 6079
Bellingham, WA 98227-6079, USA

Lugosi Jr, Bela
520 N Central Ave Ste 800
Glendale, CA 91203-3962, USA

Luhn, Nolan (Football Player)
Green Bay Packers
1400C Zillock Rd Ofc
San Benito, TX 78586-7852, USA

Luhrmann, Baz (Director, Producer)
c/o Staff Member *Bazmark Inq (AUS)*
PO Box 430
Kings Cross
NSW 2011, AUSTRALIA

Lui, Stephen
10635 Santa Monica Blvd Ste 130
Los Angeles, CA 90025-8306, USA

Luisetti, Hank
131 Winchester Ct
Foster City, CA 94404-3540, USA

Luisi, James
22562 Seaver Ct
Santa Clarita, CA 91350-1389, USA

Lujack, John C (Johnny) (Football Player)
Chicago Bears
3700 N Harrison St
Davenport, IA 52806-5905, USA

Lujan, Fernando (Actor)
c/o Staff Member *TV Azteca*
Periferico Sur 4121
Colonia Fuentes del Pedregal
DF CP 14141, MEXICO

Lujan, Manuel Jr (Secretary)
Manuel Lujan Agencies
PO Box 3727
Albuquerque, NM 87190-3727, USA

Lukachyk, Robert (Baseball Player)
Montreal Expos
14706 Beacon Hill Ct
Midlothian, VA 23112-2320, USA

Lukas, D Wayne (Coach)
5242 Katella Ave Ste 103
Los Alamitos, CA 90720-2861, USA

Lukashenko, Aleksandr (President)
President's Office
JK Marks St 38
Minsk 220016, BELARUS

Lukasiewicz, Mark (Baseball Player)
Anaheim Angels
8035 Fir Dr
Clay, NY 13041-8646, USA

Lukather, Steve (Musician)
Fitzgerald-Hartley
34 N Palm St
Ventura, CA 93001-2635, USA

Luke (Musician)
Richard Walters
1800 Argyle Ave # 408
Los Angeles, CA 90028-5253, USA

Luke, Derek (Actor)
651N N Kilkea Dr
Los Angeles, CA 90048, USA

Luke, John A Jr (Business Person)
Westvaco Corp
299 Park Ave
New York, NY 10171-0009, USA

Luke, Matt (Baseball Player)
New York Yankees
2467 Middlesex Pl
Fullerton, CA 92835-3121, USA

Luke, Steve (Football Player)
Green Bay Packers
812 Bluffview Dr
Columbus, OH 43235-1728, USA

Luken, Tom (Football Player)
Philadelphia Eagles
8036 Cast A Way
Mason, OH 45040-8365, USA

Lukens, Max L (Business Person)
Baker Hughes Inc
3900 Essex Ln
Houston, TX 77027-5133, USA

Luketic, Robert (Actor)
c/o Staff Member *Mosaic Media Group*
24 Music Sq W Fl 1
Nashville, TN 37203-6661, USA

Lukin, Matt (Musician)
Legends of 21st Century
7 Trinity Row
Florence, MA 01062-1931, USA

Lukkarinen, Marjut (Skier)
Lohja Ski Team
Lohja, FINLAND

Lula da Silva, Luis Ignacio (President)
Palacio do Planotto
Praca dos 3 Poderas
Brasilia, DF 70 150, BRAZIL

Lulabel & Scottie
PO Box 171132
Nashville, TN 37217-8132, USA

Lulu (Actor, Musician)
CIA
101 Shepherds Bush
Concorde House
London W6 7LP, UNITED KINGDOM
(UK)

Lum, Mike (Baseball Player)
Atlanta Braves
3476 Cochise Dr SE
Atlanta, GA 30339-4324, USA

Lumbly, Carl (Actor)
8721 W Sunset Blvd Ste 205
Los Angeles, CA 90069-2272, USA

Lumenti, Ralph (Baseball Player)
Washington Senators
9 Tomaso Rd
Milford, MA 01757-2224, USA

Lumet, Sidney (Director)
Amjen Entertainment
1 W 81st St # 4D
New York, NY 10024-6048, USA

Lumley, Joanna (Actor)
International Creative Mgmt
76 Oxford St
London W1N 0AX, UNITED KINGDOM
(UK)

Lumley, John L (Physicist)
743 Snyder Hill Rd
Ithaca, NY 14850-8708, USA

Lumme, Jyrki (Hockey Player)
Toronto Maple Leafs
40 Bay St
Toronto, ON M5J 2K2, CANADA

Lumpe, Jerry (Baseball Player)
New York Yankees
732 S Pearson Dr
Springfield, MO 65809-1613, USA

Lumpkin, Norman (Baseball Player)
Atlanta Black Crackers
155 Hyacinth Ave NW
Atlanta, GA 30314-1215, USA

Lumpp, Raymond (Ray) (Basketball Player)
21 Hewlett Dr
East Williston, NY 11596-2003, USA

Lumsden, David J
Melton House
Soham, Cambridgeshire, UNITED
KINGDOM (UK)

Luna, Barbara (Actor)
18026 Rodarte Way
Encino, CA 91316-4370, USA

Luna, Diego (Actor)
c/o Elyse Scherz *Endeavor Agency LLC
(LA)*
9601 Wilshire Blvd Fl 3
Beverly Hills, CA 90210-5204, USA

Luna, Robert (Football Player)
San Francisco 49ers
4844 Byrd Ln
College Grove, TN 37046-9261, USA

Luna-Hill, Betty (Baseball Player)
19887 Red Feather Rd
Apple Valley, CA 92307-5514, USA

Lunar, Fernando (Baseball Player)
Atlanta Braves
1508 Campbell Pl
Alamogordo, NM 88310-4832, USA

Lunatics, St (Musician)
c/o Staff Member *Team Lunatics (MO)*
4246 Forest Park Ave Ste 2C
Saint Louis, MO 63108-2811, USA

Lund, Bill (Football Player)
Cleveland Rams
77 S Franklin St
Chagrin Falls, OH 44022-3212, USA

Lund, Don (Baseball Player)
Brooklyn Dodgers
1000 S State St
Ann Arbor, MI 48109-2201, USA

Lund, Gordon (Baseball Player)
Cleveland Indians
1602 S Harvard Ave
Arlington Heights, IL 60005-3517, USA

Lund, Katia (Director)
c/o Sandra Lucchesi *Gersh Agency, The
(LA)*
232 N Canon Dr
Beverly Hills, CA 90210-5302, USA

Lunday, James (Actor)
c/o Staff Member *The Learning Channel
(TLC)*
7700 Wisconsin Ave
Bethesda, MD 20814-3578, USA

Lunday, Kenneth (Football Player)
New York Giants
1419 W Locust St
Durant, OK 74701-3458, USA

Lundberg, Anders (Misc)
Goteberg University
Physiology Dept
Box 33033
Goteborg 40 033, SWEDEN

Lundberg, Fred Borre (Skier)
Skogbrynet 11
Bardu, 9250, NORWAY

Lunden, Joan (Actor, Producer, Writer)
Celebrity Consultants LLC
3340 Ocean Park Blvd Ste 3030
Santa Monica, CA 90405-3217, USA

Lundgren, Dolph (Actor)
c/o Michael (Mike) Jelline *International
Creative Management (ICM-LA)*
10250 Constellation Blvd
Los Angeles, CA 90067-6200, USA

Lundgren, Terry (Business Person)
Federated Department Stores
151 W 34th St
New York, NY 10001-2101, USA

Lundholm, Mark (Actor, Comedian)
c/o Staff Member *William Morris Agency
(WMA-LA)*
1 William Morris Pl
Beverly Hills, CA 90212-4261, USA

Lundi, Monika
Viktoriastr. 24
Munich D-80803, GERMANY

Lundquist, Dave (Baseball Player)
San Diego Padres
714 12th Ave NE
Hickory, NC 28601-2707, USA

Lundquist, Gus (Misc)
5100 John D Ryan Blvd Apt 616
San Antonio, TX 78245-3535, USA

Lundquist, Steve (Swimmer)
PO Box 1545
Stockbridge, GA 30281-8545, USA

Lundquist, Verne (Sportscaster)
NBC-TV
30 Rockefeller Plz Ste 270E
Sports Dept
New York, NY 10112-0299, USA

Lundsledt, Tom (Baseball Player)
Chicago Cubs
PO Box 409
Ephraim, WI 54211-0409, USA

Lundy, Carmen (Musician)
Abby Hoffer
223 1/2 E 48th St
New York, NY 10017, USA

Lundy, Jessica (Actor)
c/o Staff Member *Metropolitan*
4500 Wilshire Blvd Fl 2
Los Angeles, CA 90010-3858, USA

Lundy, Lamar (Football Player)
New York Giants
825 S 11th St
Richmond, IN 47374-6334, USA

Lundy, Victor A (Architect)
Victor A Lundy Assoc
701 Mulberry Ln
Bellaire, TX 77401-3805, USA

Luner, Jaime (Actor)
Martin Hurwitz
427 N Canon Dr Ste 215
Beverly Hills, CA 90210-4840, USA

Luner, Jamie (Actor)
c/o Martin Berneman *Martin Berneman
Management*
211 S Beverly Dr Ste 208
Beverly Hills, CA 90212-3879, USA

Lunghi, Cherie (Actor)
Yakety Yak
8A Bloomsbury Square
London WC1A 2NE, UNITED KINGDOM
(UK)

Lunka, Zoltan (Boxer)
Weinheimer Str 2
Schriesheim 69198, GERMANY

Lunn, Bob (Golfer)
PO Box 1495
Woodbridge, CA 95258-1495, USA

The Celebrity Black Book 2008

Lunney, Glenn (Scientist)
United Space Alliance
1150 Gemini St
Houston, TX 77058-2708, USA

Lunsford, Scott (Actor)
c/o Robert Yaffee *Infinity Management*
PO Box 492032
Los Angeles, CA 90049-8032, USA

Lunsford, Trey (Baseball Player)
San Francisco Giants
3955 Nail Rd
Southaven, MS 38672-6739, USA

Lupberger, Edwin A (Business Person)
Entergy Corp
10055 Grogans Mill Rd # 5A
The Woodlands, TX 77380-1059, USA

Lupica, Mike (Writer)
55 Runningbrook Ln
New Canaan, CT 06840-6547, USA

Luplen, Tony (Baseball Player)
Boston Red Sox
PO Box 351
Norwich, VT 05055-0351, USA

Luplow, Al (Baseball Player)
Cleveland Indians
4250 Lakecress Dr E
Saginaw, MI 48603-1687, USA

Lupo, Benedetto (Musician)
Gerhild Baron Mgmt
Dombacher Str 41/III/3
Vienna 1170, AUSTRIA

Lupo, Frank (Producer, Writer)
c/o Stephen Marks *Evolution Entertainment (LA)*
901 N Highland Ave
Los Angeles, CA 90038-2412, USA

LuPone, Patti (Actor, Musician)
c/o Staff Member *Innovative Artists (LA)*
1505 10th St
Santa Monica, CA 90401-2805, USA

Lupu, Radu (Musician)
Terry Harrison Mgmt
3 Clarendon Court
Charlbury, Oxon OX7 3PS, UNITED KINGDOM (UK)

Lupus, Peter (Actor)
2401 S 24th St # 110
Phoenix, AZ 85034-6806, USA

Lurie, Alison (Writer)
Cornell University
English Dept
Ithaca, NY 14850, USA

Lurie, Ranan R (Cartoonist, Editor)
Cartoonnews International
PO Box 698
Greenwich, CT 06836-0698, USA

Lurtsema, Bob (Football Player)
New York Giants
16920 Judicial Rd
Lakeville, MN 55044-8975, USA

Lusader, Scott (Baseball Player)
Detroit Tigers
4169 Bold Mdws
Oakland Township, MI 48306-4701, USA

Lush, Mike (Football Player)
Indianapolis Colts
910 Rebecca Ln
Orefield, PA 18069-8842, USA

Lusha, Masiela (Actor)
c/o Staff Member *Jeff Morrone Management*
9350 Wilshire Blvd Ste 224
Beverly Hills, CA 90212-3204, USA

Lusis, Janis (Athlete, Track Athlete)
Vesetas 8-3
Riga, 1013, LATVIA

Lusk, Herbert (Football Player)
Philadelphia Eagles
71 Palomar Real
Campbell, CA 95008-4206, USA

Lusteg, Booth (Football Player)
Buffalo Bills
18297 NW 6th St
Pembroke Pines, FL 33029-3677, USA

Lustig, Aaron (Actor)
c/o Staff Member *The House of Representatives*
211 S Beverly Dr Ste 208
Beverly Hills, CA 90212-3879, USA

Lustig, William
1441 N Ogden Dr
Los Angeles, CA 90046-3906, USA

Lustiger, Jean-Marie Cardinal (Religious Leader)
Maison Dioceine
8 Rue de la Ville-l'Eveque
Paris 75008, FRANCE

Lutes, Eric (Actor)
Artists Group
1650 Broadway Ste 610
New York, NY 10019-6833, USA

Luther, Bobbi Sue (Actor, Model)
c/o Jerry Shandrew *Shandrew Public Relations*
1050 S Stanley Ave
Los Angeles, CA 90019-6634, USA

Luther, Ed (Football Player)
San Diego Chargers
30486 Le Prt
Laguna Niguel, CA 92677-5537, USA

Lutt, Jorg-Uwe Prof
Mensing-Str 17
Flensburg D-24937, GERMANY

Luttig, J Michael (Judge)
US Appeals Court
200 S Washington St
Alexandria, VA 22314-5405, USA

Luttrell, Rachel (Actor)
c/o Staff Member *SMS Talent Inc*
8730 W Sunset Blvd Ste 440
Los Angeles, CA 90069-2277, USA

Lutz, Bob (Tennis Player)
101 Via Ensueno
San Clemente, CA 92672-2456, USA

Lutz, Joe (Baseball Player)
St Louis Browns
1411 Quail Dr
Sarasota, FL 34231-3563, USA

Lutz, Joleen (Actor)
H David Moss
733 Seward St Ph
Los Angeles, CA 90038-3503, USA

Lutz, Kellan (Actor)
c/o Staff Member *Kazarian/Spencer & Assoc (LA)*
11969 Ventura Blvd
Box 7409 Fl 3
Studio City, CA 91604-2630, USA

Lutz, Mark (Actor)
c/o Nancy LeFeaver *LeFeaver Talent Management Ltd*
2 College St #202
Toronto, ON M5G 1K3, CANADA

Lutz, Robert A (Business Person)
3600 Green Ct Ste 720
Ann Arbor, MI 48105-1570, USA

Luuloa, Kelth (Baseball Player)
Anaheim Angels
29126 Old Wrangler Road
Riverside, CA 91790, USA

LuValle, James (Athlete, Track Athlete)
1174 Los Altos Ave Apt 160
Los Altos, CA 94022-1062, USA

Luxon, Benjamin M (Opera Singer)
Mazet
Relubbus Lane
Saint Hillary
Penzance, Cornwall TR20 9DS, UNITED KINGDOM (UK)

Luyendyk, Arie (Race Car Driver)
12494 N 116th St
Scottsdale, AZ 85259-2704, USA

Luyties, Ricci (Volleyball Player)
Assn of Volleyball Pros
330 Washington Blvd # 400
Marina Del Rey, CA 90292-5141, USA

Luz, Franc
606 N Larchmont Blvd Ste 309
Los Angeles, CA 90004-1309, USA

Luzhkov, Yuri M (Politician)
Government of Moscow
Tverskaya Str 13
Moscow 103032, RUSSIA

Luzi, Mario (Writer)
Via Belle Riva 20
Florence 50136, ITALY

Luzinski, Ryan (Baseball Player)
1429 Valhalla Dr
Denver, NC 28037-5457, USA

Lyakhov, Vladimir A (Cosmonaut)
Potcha Kosmonavtov
Moskovskoi Oblasti
Syvisdny, Goroduk 141160, RUSSIA

Lyden, Mitch (Baseball Player)
Florida Marlins
227 Shore Ct
Lauderdale By The Sea, FL 33308-5030, USA

Lydon, James (Jimmy) (Actor)
3538 Lomacitas Ln
Bonita, CA 91902-1105, USA

Lydon, John (Johnny Rotten) (Musician)
31962 Pacific Coast Hwy
Malibu, CA 90265-2506, USA

Lydon, Malcolm (Astronaut)
1429 Jaudon Road
Dover, FL 33527, USA

Lydy, Scott (Baseball Player)
Oakland A's
2856 E Fountain St
Mesa, AZ 85213-5445, USA

Lye, Mark (Golfer)
4484 Wayside Dr
Naples, FL 34119-8404, USA

Lyfe (Musician)
c/o Staff Member *Sony/Columbia/CBS Records*
550 Madison Ave
New York, NY 10022-3211, USA

Lyle, Garry (Football Player)
Chicago Bears
222 Beach Dr NE
Saint Petersburg, FL 33701-3414, USA

Lyle, Kami (Musician, Songwriter, Writer)
DS Mgmt
2814 12th Ave S Ste 202
Nashville, TN 37204-2513, USA

Lyle, Sandy (Golfer)
4905 Duck Creek Ln # 450
Ponte Vedra Beach, FL 32082-3023, USA

Lyle, Sparky (Baseball Player)
Boston Red Sox
17 Signal Hill Dr
Voorhees, NJ 08043-2948, USA

Lyles, A C
2115 Linda Flora Dr
Los Angeles, CA 90077-1408, USA

Lyles, Leonard (Football Player)
Baltimore Colts
2315 Cross Hill Rd
Louisville, KY 40206-2809, USA

Lyles, Lester (Football Player)
New York Jets
6315 14th St NW
Washington, DC 20011-8003, USA

Lyles, Lester L (Les) (General)
Commander Air Material Command
Wright-Patterson Air Force, OH 45433, USA

Lyman, Arthur
508 Kaanini St
Hilo, HI 96720-2751, USA

Lyman, Dorothy
c/o Staff Member *Stone Manners Talent & Literary (LA)*
6500 Wilshire Blvd Ste 550
Los Angeles, CA 90048-4950, USA

Lyman, Richard W (Educator)
Stanford University
Education School
Stanford, CA 94305, USA

Lymon, Frankie
1650 Broadway Ste 508
New York, NY 10019-6833, USA

Lympany, Moura (Musician)
Transart
8 Bristol Gardens
London W9 2JG, UNITED KINGDOM (UK)

Lyn, Mai
190 W Kern Ave
Mc Farland, CA 93250-1349, USA

Lynch, Allen J (War Hero)
438 Belle Plaine Ave
Gurnee, IL 60031-2902, USA

Lynch, Claire
1 Camp St
Cambridge, MA 02140-1103, USA

Lynch, Dan (Cartoonist, Editor)
Fort Wayne-Journal-Gazette
600 W Main St
Editorial Dept
Fort Wayne, IN 46802-1408, USA

Lynch, David (Director)
c/o Staff Member *Creative Artists Agency LCC (CAA-LA)*
2000 Avenue Of The Stars
Los Angeles, CA 90067-4700, USA

Lynch, David K (Director)
PO Box 93624
Los Angeles, CA 90093-0624, USA

Lynch, Ed (Baseball Player)
New York Mets
5940 SW 120th St
Miami, FL 33156-5758, USA

Lynch, Edele (Musician)
Clintons
55 Drury Lane
Covent Garden
London WC2B 5SQ, UNITED KINGDOM
(UK)

Lynch, James E (Jim) (Football Player)
Kansas City Chiefs
1009 W 67th St
Kansas City, MO 64113-1916, USA

Lynch, Jane (Actor)
c/o Gabrielle Krengel *Domain*
9229 W Sunset Blvd Ste 415
West Hollywood, CA 90069-3404, USA

Lynch, Jennifer (Actor)
1894 El Cerrito Pl
Los Angeles, CA 90068-3781, USA

Lynch, Jerry (Baseball Player)
Pittsburgh Pirates
4840 Chamblee Dunwoody Rd
Atlanta, GA 30338-5606, USA

Lynch, Jessica (Beauty Pageant Winner)
c/o Staff Member *Miss New York City
Scholarship Organization*
35 E 19th St
2nd Floor
New York, NY 10003-1313, USA

Lynch, Jessica (War Hero)
Knopf
1745 Broadway
New York, NY 10019-4305, USA

Lynch, John Carroll (Actor)
c/o James Suskin *James Suskin
Management*
2 Charlton St Apt 5K
New York, NY 10014-4917, USA

Lynch, Keavy (Musician)
Clintons
55 Drury Lane
Covent Garden
London WC2B 5SQ, UNITED KINGDOM
(UK)

Lynch, Kelly (Actor, Model)
c/o Eric Black *Anonymous Content (CA)*
3532 Hayden Ave
Culver City, CA 90232-2413, USA

Lynch, Peg
304 11th St Box 339
Becket, MA 01223, USA

Lynch, Peter S (Financier)
27 State St
Boston, MA 02109-2706, USA

Lynch, Richard (Actor)
Richard Sindell
1910 Holmby Ave Apt 1
Los Angeles, CA 90025-5936, USA

Lynch, Richard (Dick) (Football Player)
Washington Redskins
203 Manor Rd
Flushing, NY 11363-1129, USA

Lynch, Sandra L (Judge)
US Appeals Court
McCormack Federal Building
Boston, MA 02109, USA

Lynch, Shane (Musician)
Carol Assoc-War Mgmt
Bushy Park Road
57 Meadowbank
Dublin, IRELAND

Lynch, Stephen (Comedian)
c/o Staff Member *William Morris Agency
(WMA-LA)*
1 William Morris Pl
Beverly Hills, CA 90212-4261, USA

Lynch, Thomas C (Admiral)
751 Eagle Farm Rd
Villanova, PA 19085-2035, USA

Lynde, Janice (Actor)
c/o David Moore *Moore Artist's
Management*
310 Washington Blvd Ste 117
Marina Del Rey, CA 90292-5164, USA

Lyndon, Frank (Musician)
Paramount Entertainment
PO Box 12
Far Hills, NJ 07931-0012, USA

Lyne, Adrian
9876 Beverly Grove Dr
Beverly Hills, CA 90210-2120, USA

Lyngstad, Anni-Frida (Musician,
Songwriter, Writer)
Mono Music
Sodra Brobaeken 41A
Stockholm 111 49, SWEDEN

Lynley, Carol (Actor)
Don gerler
3349 Cahuenga Blvd W Ste 1
Los Angeles, CA 90068-1379, USA

Lynn, Anthony (Football Player)
Denver Broncos
1508 Brook Ln
Celina, TX 75009-2279, USA

Lynn, Betty
2203 Ridge Crest Ln
Mount Airy, NC 27030-2486, USA

Lynn, Cheryl (Actor, Musician)
PO Box 667
Smithtown, NY 11787-0667, USA

Lynn, Frederic M (Fred) (Baseball Player)
Boston Red Sox
7336 El Fuerte St
Carlsbad, CA 92009-6409, USA

Lynn, Ginger (Adult Film Star)
c/o Staff Member *Atlas Multimedia Inc*
9035 Independence Ave
Canoga Park, CA 91304-1743, USA

Lynn, Greg (Architect)
University of California
Architecture School
Los Angeles, CA 90024, USA

Lynn, James T (Secretary)
6 Sunset Cay Rd
Key Largo, FL 33037-3726, USA

Lynn, Johnnie (Football Player)
New York Jets
5 Wood Valley Ct
Reisterstown, MD 21136-4629, USA

Lynn, Jonathan (Director)
Holflund/Polane
9465 Wilshire Blvd Ste 420
Beverly Hills, CA 90212-2603, USA

Lynn, Loretta (Musician, Songwriter,
Writer)
General Delivery
Hurricane Mills, TN 37078-9999, USA

Lynn, Meredith Scott (Actor)
Rigberg Roberts Rugolo
1180 S Beverly Dr Ste 601
Los Angeles, CA 90035-1158, USA

Lynn, Salomon Janet (Figure Skater)
PO Box 1026
Haymarket, VA 20168-8026, USA

Lynn, Therese
PO Box 6057
Hoboken, NJ 07030-7201, USA

Lynn, Vera (Actor, Musician)
Ditchling, Sussex, UNITED KINGDOM
(UK)

Lynn Chadwick, Aimee (Actor)
c/o Melanie Sharp-Snyder *Sharp Talent*
117 N Orlando Ave
Los Angeles, CA 90048-3403, USA

Lynne, Bobbe
22732 Foothill Rd. #6
Hayward, CA 94541, USA

Lynne, Gillian (Choreographer, Dancer)
Lean-2 Productions
18 Rutland St
Knightsbridge
London SW7 1EF, UNITED KINGDOM
(UK)

Lynne, Gloria (Musician)
Subrena Artists
330 W 56th St Apt 18M
New York, NY 10019-4222, USA

Lynne, Jeff (Musician)
Not Lame Recording Company
PO Box 2266
Fort Collins, CO 80522-2266, USA

Lynne, Shelby (Musician, Songwriter,
Writer)
c/o Staff Member *William Morris Agency
(WMA-LA)*
1 William Morris Pl
Beverly Hills, CA 90212-4261, USA

Lynskey, Melanie (Actor)
c/o Susan Smith *Susan Smith Company,
The*
1344 N Wetherly Dr
Los Angeles, CA 90069-1817, USA

Lynyrd Skynyrd (Music Group)
c/o Staff Member *William Morris Agency
(WMA-TN)*
1600 Division St Ste 300
Nashville, TN 37203-2755, USA

Lyon, Brandon (Baseball Player)
Toronto Blue Jays
1244 Morning Sun Dr
Salt Lake City, UT 84123-4862, USA

Lyon, Lisa (Actor, Athlete)
Jungle Gym
PO Box 585
Santa Monica, CA 90406-0585, USA

Lyon, Sue (Actor)
1244 Havenhurst Dr
West Hollywood, CA 90046-4911, USA

Lyon, William (Business Person, General)
William Lyon Co
4490 Von Karman Ave
Newport Beach, CA 92660-2000, USA

Lyonne, Natasha (Actor)
c/o Ben Feigin *Nine Yards Entertainment*
8530 Wilshire Blvd Fl 5
Beverly Hills, CA 90211-3102, USA

Lyons, Barry (Baseball Player)
New York Mets
1079 Frank P Corso St
Biloxi, MS 39530-1922, USA

Lyons, Bill (Baseball Player)
St Louis Cardinals
811 Tomahawk
Heyworth, IL 61745-9309, USA

Lyons, Curt (Baseball Player)
Cincinnati Reds
124 Virginia Dr
Richmond, KY 40475-8631, USA

Lyons, Ed (Baseball Player)
Washington Senators
8799 Center Grove Church Rd
Clemmons, NC 27012-9149, USA

Lyons, Elena (Actor)
c/o David Sweeney *Sweeney
Management*
8755 Lookout Mountain Ave
Los Angeles, CA 90046-1861, USA

Lyons, Hersh (Baseball Player)
St Louis Cardinals
7900 Dunbarton Ave
Los Angeles, CA 90045-1035, USA

Lyons, James A Jr (Admiral)
9481 Piney Mountain Rd
Warrenton, VA 20186-7441, USA

Lyons, Jeffrey
205 W 57th St
New York, NY 10019-2105, USA

Lyons, Jennifer (Actor)
c/o Brian McCabe *The McCabe Group*
8285 W Sunset Blvd Ste 1
West Hollywood, CA 90046-2420, USA

Lyons, Lamar (Football Player)
Oakland Raiders
3726 Bluff Pl
San Pedro, CA 90731-7006, USA

Lyons, Marty (Football Player)
New York Jets
8 White Pine Ct
Smithtown, NY 11787-1199, USA

Lyons, Mitchell W (Mitch) (Football
Player)
Atlanta Falcons
8344 Woodcrest Dr NE
Rockford, MI 49341-8507, USA

Lyons, Phyllis
9171 Wilshire Blvd Ste 441
Beverly Hills, CA 90210-5516, USA

Lyons, Robert F
1801 Avenue Of Stars # 1250
Los Angeles, CA 90067-5902, USA

Lyons, Steve (Baseball Player)
Boston Red Sox
301 2nd St
Hermosa Beach, CA 90254-4662, USA

Lyons, Steve (Correspondent)
Fox-TV
205 W 67th St
Sports Dept
New York, NY 10021, USA

Lyons, Thomas L (Football Player)
Denver Broncos
2814 Drummond Pt SE
Atlanta, GA 30339-5332, USA

Lysacek, Evan (Figure Skater)
Toyota Sports Center
555 N Nash St
El Segundo, CA 90245-2818, USA

Lysander, Rick (Baseball Player)
Oakland A's
12667 Gaillon Ct
San Diego, CA 92128-6179, USA

Lysiak, Tom (Hockey Player)
1050 Cedar Grove Rd
Buckhead, GA 30625-1818, USA

Lyst, John H (Editor)
Indianapolis Star
307 N Pennsylvania St
Editorial Dept
Indianapolis, IN 46204-1899, USA

Lythgoe, Nigel (Producer)
c/o Staff Member *Creative Artists Agency LCC (CAA-LA)*
2000 Avenue Of The Stars
Los Angeles, CA 90067-4700, USA

Lytle, Jason
c/o Staff Member *Paradigm (Monterey)*
509 Hartnell St
Monterey, CA 93940-2825, USA

Lytle, Matt (Football Player)
Carolina Panthers
4602 Irish Creek Rd
Bernville, PA 19506-8346, USA

Lytle, Rob (Football Player)
Denver Broncos
1829 Buckland Ave
Fremont, OH 43420-3503, USA

Lyttle, Jim (Baseball Player)
New York Yankees
751 Camino Lakes Cir
Boca Raton, FL 33486-6961, USA

Lyttle, Kevin (Musician)
c/o Michael (Mike) Esterman *Esterman Entertainment*
214 Park Rd
Riva, MD 21140-1224, USA

Lyubimov, Alexey B (Musician)
Klimentovskiy Per 9
#12
Moscow, RUSSIA

Lyubimov, Yuri P (Actor, Director)
Tanganka Theater
Chkalova Str 76
Moscow, RUSSIA

Lyubshin, Stanislav A (Actor)
Vernadskogo Prosp 123
#171
Moscow 117571, RUSSIA

M

M, Banumathi (Actor, Bollywood)
15 Poes Road
4th Street
Chennai, TN 600018, INDIA

M Karthik (Actor)
2 Kasthuri Ranga 1st Road
Teynampet
Chennai, TN 600 018, INDIA

M2M (Music Group)
c/o Staff Member *Creative Artists Agency LCC (CAA-LA)*
2000 Avenue Of The Stars
Los Angeles, CA 90067-4700, USA

Ma, Tzi (Actor)
Greene & Associates
526 N Larchmont Blvd Ste 201
Los Angeles, CA 90004-1300, USA

Ma, Yo Yo (Musician)
c/o Staff Member *International Creative Management (ICM-LA)*
10250 Constellation Blvd
Los Angeles, CA 90067-6200, USA

Ma, Yo-Yo (Musician)
Askonas Holt Ltd
27 Chancery Lane
London WC2A 1PF, UNITED KINGDOM (UK)

Maarleveld, John (Football Player)
Tampa Bay Buccaneers
42 Carlton Pl
Rutherford, NJ 07070-1120, USA

Maas, Alex
6962 Wildlife Rd
Malibu, CA 90265-4309, USA

Maas, Bill (Football Player)
Kansas City Chiefs
653 NE Shoreline Dr
Lees Summit, MO 64064-1382, USA

Maas, Kevin (Baseball Player)
New York Yankees
PO Box 21019
Castro Valley, CA 94546-9019, USA

Maas, William T (Bill) (Football Player)
PO Box 2175
Lees Summit, MO 64063-7175, USA

Maathai, Wangari (Activist, Misc)
Green Belt Movement
PO Box 67545
Nairobi, KENYA

Maazel, Lorin V (Conductor, Musician)
New York Philharmonic
10 Lincoln Center Plz
Avery Fisher Hall
New York, NY 10023-6970, USA

Mabe, Bob (Baseball Player)
St Louis Cardinals
339 Georges Ln Lot 7
Blairs, VA 24527-1070, USA

Mabe, Manabu (Artist)
Rua das Canjeranas 321
Jabaquara
Sao Paulo, SP, BRAZIL

Mabius, Eric (Actor)
c/o Geordie Frey *GEF Entertainment*
122 N Clark Dr Apt 401
West Hollywood, CA 90048-6315, USA

Mably, Luke (Actor)
c/o Stephanie Ritz *Endeavor Agency LLC (NY)*
23 Watts St Fl 6
New York, NY 10013, USA

Mabon, Lee (Baseball Player)
Indianapolis Clowns
2084 Vollintine Ave
Memphis, TN 38107-4700, USA

Mabra, Ron (Football Player)
Atlanta Falcons
155 Thornton Ct
Fayetteville, GA 30214-3830, USA

Mabrey, Sunny (Actor)
c/o Chris Schmidt *Paradigm (LA)*
360 N Crescent Dr
North Bldg
Beverly Hills, CA 90210-6820, USA

Mabrey, Vicki (Correspondent, Journalist)
c/o Staff Member *Nightline*
1717 Desales St NW
Washington, DC 20036-4401, USA

Mabry, John (Baseball Player)
St Louis Cardinals
715 Bellerive Manor Dr
Saint Louis, MO 63141-6084, USA

Mabus, Raymond E Jr (Governor)
PO Box 200
Jackson, MS 39205, USA

Mac, Bernie (Actor, Comedian)
c/o Marty Bowen *United Talent Agency (UTA)*
9560 Wilshire Blvd Ste 500
Beverly Hills, CA 90212-2401, USA

Mac, Fleetwood (Music Group)
c/o Staff Member *Agency for the Performing Arts (APA-LA)*
405 S Beverly Dr
Beverly Hills, CA 90212-4416, USA

Mac, Robert
9242 Beverly Blvd Ste 200
Beverly Hills, CA 90210-3731, USA

Mac Mohan (Actor)
Gulam Cottage Four Bungalows
Andheri
Bombay, MS 400 058, INDIA

Mac Quayle (DJ)
c/o Staff Member *Diva Central Inc*
7510 W Sunset Blvd Ste 1445
Los Angeles, CA 90046-3408, USA

MacAfee, Ken (Football Player)
51 Canterbury Ln
Needham, MA 02492-3201, USA

Macafee Sr, Ken (Football Player)
New York Giants
26 W Elm Ter
Brockton, MA 02301-3629, USA

Macapagal-Arroyo, Gloria (President)
Malacanang Palace
JP Laurel St
Metro Manila 100, PHILIPPINES

MacArthur, Ellen (World Record Holder)
Offshore Challenges Events
Whitegates
Arctic Rd
Cowes, Isle of Wight PO31 7PG, UNITED KINGDOM (UK)

MacArthur, James
74092 Covered Wagon Trl
Palm Desert, CA 92260-5604, USA

MacArthur, Robb (Reality TV Star)
c/o Staff Member *Boy Meets Boy*
299 Queen Street West
Toronto, ON M5V 2Z5, CANADA

Macat, Julio G (Cinematographer)
Gersh Agency
232 N Canon Dr
Beverly Hills, CA 90210-5302, USA

Macauley, Edward C (Easy Ed) (Basketball Player)
13277 Barrett Chase Cir
Ballwin, MO 63021-3825, USA

MacAvoy, Paul W (Economist)
2 Laurel St
Etna, NH 03750-3315, USA

MacBeth, Lois
4095 Athenia Way
Los Angeles, CA 90043, USA

Macchio, Ralph (Actor)
c/o Jennifer Levine *Untitled Entertainment (LA)*
331 N Maple Dr Fl 3
Beverly Hills, CA 90210-3827, USA

MacCorkindale, Simon (Actor)
James Sharkey
21 Golden Square
London W1R 3PA, UNITED KINGDOM (UK)

MacCormac, Richard C (Architect)
9 Heneage St
London E1 5LJ, UNITED KINGDOM (UK)

Maccormack, Frank (Baseball Player)
Detroit Tigers
2 Schmidts Pl
Secaucus, NJ 07094-4110, USA

MacCormack, Jean F (Educator)
University of Massachusetts
President's Office
Boston, MA 02125, USA

MacDermid, Paul (Hockey Player)
81 Lakeland Dr
Sauble Beach, ON N0H 2G0, CANADA

MacDermot, Galt (Composer)
12 Silver Lake Rd
Macdermot Assoc
Staten Island, NY 10301-3013, USA

MacDiarmid, Alan G (Nobel Prize Laureate)
635 Drexel Ave
Drexel Hill, PA 19026-3816, USA

Macdissi, Peter (Actor)
c/o Staff Member *Acme Talent & Literary (LA)*
4727 Wilshire Blvd Ste 333
Los Angeles, CA 90010-3874, USA

MacDonald, Adam (Actor)
c/o Staff Member *Characters Talent Agency, The (Toronto)*
8 Elm St 3rd FL
Toronto, ON M5G 1G7, CANADA

Macdonald, Bob (Baseball Player)
Toronto Blue Jays
522 Harbor Grove Cir
Safety Harbor, FL 34695-4977, USA

MacDonald, C Parker (Hockey Player)
3 Miller Rd
Northford, CT 06472-1424, USA

MacDonald, Charles (War Hero)
RR 5 Box C77
Definiak Springs, FL 32433, USA

MacDonald, Jeffrey (Doctor)
#00131-177 Fed Corr Inst 27072 Ballston
Sheridan, OR 97378, USA

MacDonald, Julien (Designer, Fashion Designer)
c/o Staff Member *Julien MacDonald*
Haydens Place
247A Portobello Road
London, England W11 1LT, UNITED KINGDOM (UK)

Macdonald, Mark (Football Player)
Minnesota Vikings
19178 Echo Ln
Farmington, MN 55024-9184, USA

Macdonald, Norm (Actor, Comedian)
c/o Marc Gurvitz *Brillstein-Grey Entertainment*
9150 Wilshire Blvd Ste 350
Beverly Hills, CA 90212-3453, USA

MacDonald, Ryan
5000 Delita Pl
Woodland Hills, CA 91364-2436, USA

MacDowell, Andie (Actor)
c/o Risa Shapiro *International Creative Management (ICM-LA)*
10250 Constellation Blvd
Los Angeles, CA 90067-6200, USA

Macek, Don (Football Player)
San Diego Chargers
3615 Monte Real
Escondido, CA 92029-7911, USA

MacFadyen, Angus (Actor)
International Creative Mgmt
8942 Wilshire Blvd # 219
Beverly Hills, CA 90211-1908, USA

Macfadyen, Matthew (Actor)
c/o Hylda Queally *Creative Artists Agency LCC (CAA-LA)*
2000 Avenue Of The Stars
Los Angeles, CA 90067-4700, USA

Macfariane, Mike (Baseball Player)
Kansas City Royals
7421 Woodside Dr
Stockton, CA 95207-1554, USA

MacFarlane, Luke (Actor)
c/o Peter Kiernan *Management 360*
9111 Wilshire Blvd
Beverly Hills, CA 90210-5508, USA

MacFarlane, Seth (Actor, Director, Writer)
c/o Richard Weitz *Endeavor Agency LLC (LA)*
9601 Wilshire Blvd Fl 3
Beverly Hills, CA 90210-5204, USA

MacGowan, Shane (Musician)
Free Trade Agency
Chapel Place
Rivington St
London EC2A 3DQ, UNITED KINGDOM (UK)

MacGraw, Ali (Actor)
c/o Laina Cohn *Relativity Management*
8899 Beverly Blvd Ste 510
Los Angeles, CA 90048-2449, USA

MacGregor, Ian K (Government Official)
Castleton House
Lochgilphead
Argyll, SCOTLAND

MacGregor, Jeff
151 El Camino Dr
Beverly Hills, CA 90212-2704, USA

MacGregor, Joanna C (Musician)
Columbia Artists Mgmt Inc
1790 Broadway Fl 6
New York, NY 10019-1412, USA

MacGregor, Katherine (Actor)
1900 Vine St Apt 306
Los Angeles, CA 90068-3979, USA

Macha, Kenneth H (Ken) (Baseball Player)
Pittsburgh Pirates
6934 Berkshire Dr
Export, PA 15632-8946, USA

Macha, Mike (Baseball Player)
Atlanta Braves
PO Box 3844
Victoria, TX 77903-3844, USA

Machado, Justina (Actor)
c/o Danielle Allman *Allman/Rea Management*
141 S Barrington Ave Ste E
Los Angeles, CA 90049-3314, USA

Machado, Mario
5750 Briarcliff Rd
Los Angeles, CA 90068-3633, USA

Machado, Robert (Athlete, Baseball Player)
Chicago White Sox
9095 Misty Creek Dr
Sarasota, FL 34241-8581, USA

Macharski, Franciszak Cardinal (Religious Leader)
Metropolita Krakowski
Ul Franciszkanska 3
Krakow 31-004, POLAND

Machemehl, Chuck (Baseball Player)
Cleveland Indians
2005 Machemehl Rd
Brenham, TX 77833-6695, USA

Machemer, Dave (Baseball Player)
California Angels
2159 Alpine Ct
Stevensville, MI 49127-9554, USA

Machlis, Gail (Cartoonist)
Chronicle Features
150 4th St # 695
San Francisco, CA 94103-3048, USA

Machover, Tod (Composer)
Massachusetts Institute of Technology Media Laboratory
Cambridge, MA 02139, USA

Macht, Gabriel (Actor)
c/o Staff Member *Management 360*
9111 Wilshire Blvd
Beverly Hills, CA 90210-5508, USA

Macht, Stephen (Actor)
248 S Rodeo Dr
Beverly Hills, CA 90212-3804, USA

Machurek, Mike (Football Player)
Detroit Lions
1650 N Interlachen Way
Meridian, ID 83646-1017, USA

Macias, Eduardo R (Director)
c/o Gabriel Blanco *Gabriel Blanco Iglesias (Mexico)*
Rio Balsas 35-32
Colonia Cuauhtemoc
DF 06500, MEXICO

Macias, Jose (Athlete, Baseball Player)
c/o Staff Member *Montreal Expos*
4549 Avenue Pierre de Coubertin
Montreal, PQ H1V 3N7, CANADA

Macinnis, Allan (Al) (Hockey Player)
710 Hamptons Lane
Chesterfield, MO 63017, USA

MacIntosh, Craig (Cartoonist)
3403 W 28th St
Minneapolis, MN 55416-4302, USA

MacIntosh, Sir Cameron
1 Bedford Sq.
London, ENGLAND WC1B 3RA, UNITED KINGDOM (UK)

MacIntyre, Colin (Musician)
c/o Staff Member *Paradigm (Monterey)*
509 Hartnell St
Monterey, CA 93940-2825, USA

Macintyre, Marguerite (Actor)
c/o Donna Massetti *SMS Talent Inc*
8730 W Sunset Blvd Ste 440
Los Angeles, CA 90069-2277, USA

Macio (Musician)
c/o Staff Member *Paradigm (Monterey)*
509 Hartnell St
Monterey, CA 93940-2825, USA

Macionis, John (Swimmer)
25 Washington Ln Apt 607
Wyncote, PA 19095-1407, USA

Mack, Allison (Actor)
c/o Sheila Wenzel *Innovative Artists (LA)*
1505 10th St
Santa Monica, CA 90401-2805, USA

Mack, Cedric (Football Player)
St Louis Cardinals
116 Chestnut St
Lake Jackson, TX 77566-5526, USA

Mack, Connie (Congressman)
Friends of Connie Mack
5100 S Cleveland Ave Ste 318 # 388
Fort Myers, FL 33907-2191, USA

Mack, J Kevin (Football Player)
Cleveland Browns
7402 Greenwood Lake Dr
Sugar Land, TX 77479, USA

Mack, Lonnie (Musician)
Concerted Efforts
59 Parsons St
West Newton, MA 02465-2137, USA

Mack, Quinn (Baseball Player)
Seattle Mariners
13708 Felson St
Cerritos, CA 90703-8938, USA

Mack, Rico (Football Player)
Pittsburgh Steelers
1200 R D Mack Rd
Statham, GA 30666-3140, USA

Mack, Rodney (Wrestler)
c/o Staff Member *World Wrestling Entertainment (WWE)*
1241 E Main St
Stamford, CT 06902-3520, USA

Mack, Shane (Baseball Player)
San Diego Padres
2032 Nightrider Dr
Las Vegas, NV 89134-2573, USA

Mack, Thomas I (Tom) (Football Player)
Los Angeles Rams
6268 N Willard Ave
San Gabriel, CA 91775-2548, USA

Mack, Tony (Baseball Player)
California Angels
8214 E McDonald Dr
Scottsdale, AZ 85250-6218, USA

Mack, Tremain (Football Player)
Cincinnati Bengals
3604 Rock Creek Dr
Tyler, TX 75707-1634, USA

Mack, Warner (Musician)
National Talent Agency
2260 E Apple Ave
Muskegon, MI 49442-4369, USA

Mack, William (Football Player)
Pittsburgh Steelers
51910 N Shoreham Ct
South Bend, IN 46637-1357, USA

Mack 10 (Musician)
c/o Staff Member *Famous Artists Agency*
250 W 57th St # 821
New York, NY 10107-0001, USA

Mackall, Michelle (Golfer)
2057 Oxford Ave
Cardiff By The Sea, CA 92007-1719, USA

Mackanin, Pete (Baseball Player)
Texas Rangers
4029 Bee Ridge Rd # 5017
Sarasota, FL 34233-2549, USA

Mackay, David (Director)
Gersh Agency
232 N Canon Dr
Beverly Hills, CA 90210-5302, USA

Mackay, Harvey (Writer)
Mackay Envelope Corp
2100 Elm St SE
Minneapolis, MN 55414-2597, USA

Mackbee, Earsell (Football Player)
Minnesota Vikings
9742 Russell Ave S
Minneapolis, MN 55431-2469, USA

Macke, Richard C (Admiral)
1887 Alaweo St
Honolulu, HI 96821-1343, USA

MacKenney, Tamara
4935 Parkers Mill Rd
Lexington, KY 40513-9760, USA

MacKenzie, Benjamin (Actor)
c/o Staff Member *Management 360*
9111 Wilshire Blvd
Beverly Hills, CA 90210-5508, USA

Mackenzie, Eric (Baseball Player)
Kansas City A's
2002 James East
Bright Grove, ON NON 1CO, CANADA

Mackenzie, Gordy (Baseball Player)
Kansas City A's
36535 Micro Racetrack Rd
Fruitland Park, FL 34731-5163, USA

MacKenzie, J C
3500 W Olive Ave Ste 1400
Burbank, CA 91505-5512, USA

Mackenzie, Jeremy J G (General)
Royal Hospital
Chelsea
London Sw3 4SR, UNITED KINGDOM (UK)

MacKenzie, John L (Director)
International Creative Mgmt
8942 Wilshire Blvd # 219
Beverly Hills, CA 90211-1908, USA

Mackenzie, Ken (Baseball Player)
Milwaukee Braves
15 Fair St
Guilford, CT 06437-2601, USA

MacKenzie, Patch
3500 W Olive Ave Ste 1400
Burbank, CA 91505-5512, USA

MacKenzie, Peter (Actor)
c/o Michael Greene *Greene & Associates*
190 N Canon Dr Ste 200
Beverly Hills, CA 90210-5319, USA

Mackenzie, Warren (Artist)
8695 68th St N
Stillwater, MN 55082-7310, USA

Mackerras, A Charles M
10 Hamilton Terrace
London NW8 9UG, UNITED KINGDOM (UK)

Mackey, Cindy (Golfer)
1190 Millstone Run
Bogart, GA 30622-3062, USA

Mackey, John (Football Player)
Baltimore Colts
1198 Pacific Coast Hwy # D506
Seal Beach, CA 90740-6251, USA

Mackey, Kyle (Football Player)
St Louis Cardinals
PO Box 156
Arp, TX 75750-0156, USA

Mackey, Rick (Misc)
5938 Four Mile Rd
Nanana, AK 99760, USA

Mackie, Anthony (Actor)
c/o Jason Spire *Inspire Entertainment*
252 7th Ave Apt 7Z
New York, NY 10001-7336, USA

MacKinnon, Catherine (Lawyer)
University of Michigan
Law School
Ann Arbor, MI 48109, USA

MacKinnon, Gillies (Director)
c/o Patty Detroit *International Creative Management (ICM-LA)*
10250 Constellation Blvd
Los Angeles, CA 90067-6200, USA

MacKinnon, Roderick (Nobel Prize Laureate)
545 W End Ave
New York, NY 10024-2713, USA

Mackinnon, Simmone (Actor)
c/o Staff Member *David Shapira & Associates*
193 N Robertson Blvd
Beverly Hills, CA 90211-2103, USA

Mackintosh, Cameron A (Producer)
Cameron Mackintosh Ltd
1 Bedford Sq
London WC1B 3RA, UNITED KINGDOM (UK)

Mackintosh, Steven (Actor)
c/o Staff Member *Yakety Yak*
8 Bloomsbury Sq
London WC1A 2UA, UNITED KINGDOM (UK)

Macklin, David (Actor)
5410 Wilshire Blvd # 227
Los Angeles, CA 90036-4216, USA

Macknowski, Stephen (Athlete)
462 Kimball Ave
Yonkers, NY 10704-2329, USA

Mackowlak, Rob (Baseball Player)
Pittsburgh Pirates
9462 W 159th Ave
Lowell, IN 46356-7028, USA

Mackrides, William (Football Player)
Philadelphia Eagles
23 Roberts Rd
Newtown Square, PA 19073-2011, USA

MacLachian, Kyle (Actor)
Industry Entertainment
955 Carrillo Dr Ste 300
Los Angeles, CA 90048-5400, USA

MacLachlan, Janet
1919 Taft Ave
Los Angeles, CA 90068-3620, USA

MacLachlan, Kyle (Actor)
c/o Brad Lefler *Management 360*
9111 Wilshire Blvd
Beverly Hills, CA 90210-5508, USA

MacLachlan, Patricia (Writer)
21 Unquomonk Rd
Williamsburg, MA 01096-9718, USA

MacLaine, Shirley (Actor)
c/o Carol Bodie *International Creative Management (ICM-LA)*
10250 Constellation Blvd
Los Angeles, CA 90067-6200, USA

MacLean, Don (Basketball Player)
216 Los Padres Dr
Thousand Oaks, CA 91361-1333, USA

MacLean, Doug (Coach)
448 W Nationwide Blvd Apt 401
Columbus, OH 43215-2396, USA

MacLean, Steven G (Astronaut)
Astronaut Program
6767 Rt de Aeroport
Saint-Hubert, PQ J3Y 8Y9, CANADA

MacLean-Ross, Lucella (Baseball Player)
401-5107 47th Street
Lloydminster, AB T9V 0G1, CANADA

MacLeish, Rick (Hockey Player)
5612 Bay Ave
Ocean City, NJ 08226-1000, USA

Maclennan, Robert A R (Government Official)
74 Abingdon Villas
London W8 6XB, UNITED KINGDOM (UK)

Macleod, Bill (Baseball Player)
Boston Red Sox
14 Heritage Way
Marblehead, MA 01945-2332, USA

MacLeod, Gavin (Actor)
1877 Michael Ln
Pacific Palisades, CA 90272-2040, USA

MacLeod, John (Coach)
4610 E Fanfol Dr
Phoenix
Phoenix, AZ 85028-5206, USA

Macleod, Tom (Football Player)
Green Bay Packers
RR 5 Box 431
Spokane, WA 99208, USA

MacLeond, Lewis
BBC Scotland Queen Margaret Dr.
Glasgow G12 8DG, SCOTLAND

Maclin, Lonnie (Baseball Player)
St Louis Cardinals
9635 Meeks Blvd
Saint Louis, MO 63132-1507, USA

MacMahon, Brian (Misc)
89 Warren St
Needham, MA 02492-3115, USA

MacMahon, Julian (Actor)
c/o Stephanie Davis *3 Arts Entertainment Inc*
9460 Wilshire Blvd Fl 7
Beverly Hills, CA 90212-2713, USA

MacMillan, Shannon (Soccer Player)
Portland University
Athletic Dept
Portland, OR 97203, USA

MacNamara, William
PO Box 25148
Farmington, NY 14425-0148, USA

Macnee, Patrick (Actor)
PO Box 1853
Rancho Mirage, CA 92270-1081, USA

MacNeil, Cornell H (Opera Singer)
Columbia Artists Mgmt Inc
1790 Broadway Fl 6
New York, NY 10019-1412, USA

MacNeil, Rita
4950 Yonge St. #2400
Toronto, ON M2N 6K1, CANADA

Macneil, Robert
356 W 58th St
New York, NY 10019-1804, USA

MacNichol, Peter (Actor)
International Creative Mgmt
8942 Wilshire Blvd # 219
Beverly Hills, CA 90211-1908, USA

MacNicol, Peter (Actor)
c/o Ron West *Thruline Entertainment*
9250 Wilshire Blvd Ground Fl
Beverly Hills, CA 90210, USA

Macomber, Debbie
PO Box 1458
Port Orchard, WA 98366-0110, USA

Macomber, Dick (Jockey)
6720 NW 28th Ter
Fort Lauderdale, FL 33309-1320, USA

Macomber, George B H (Skier)
1 Design Center Pl Ste 600
Boston, MA 02210-2349, USA

Macosko, Anna (Golfer)
304 Earl Dr
Kerrville, TX 78028-7019, USA

Macphail, Andy (Baseball Player)
Chicago Cubs
1080 Sunset Rd
Winnetka, IL 60093-3625, USA

Macpherson, Daniel (Actor)
c/o Staff Member *Morrissey Management*
77 Glebe Point Road
Sydney NSW 2037, AUSTRALIA

MacPherson, Duncan I (Cartoonist, Editor)
Toronto Star
Editorial Dept
1 Yonge St
Toronto, ON M5E 1E6, CANADA

Macpherson, Elle (Model)
c/o Staff Member *Storm Model Management Limited*
5 Jubilee Place Fl 5
London SW3 3TD, UNITED KINGDOM (UK)

Macpherson, Harry (Baseball Player)
Boston Braves
971 Vista Bay Blvd
Englewood, FL 34223, USA

Macpherson, Wendy (Bowler)
PO Box 93433
Henderson, NV 89009-3433, USA

MacQuitty, Jonathan (Inventor)
Abingworth Mgmt Inc
3000 Sand Hill Rd Ste 41355
Menlo Park, CA 94025-7113, USA

Macrae, Scott (Baseball Player)
Cincinnati Reds
1164 Forest Brook Ct
Marietta, GA 30068-2827, USA

MacRae, Sheila (Actor, Musician)
666 W End Ave # 10H
New York, NY 10025-7357, USA

MacTavish, Craig (Coach, Hockey Player)
3 Quail Hollow Ct
Voorhees, NJ 08043-2800, USA

Maculan, Tim (Actor)
c/o Barbara Lawrence *Opus Entertainment*
5225 Wilshire Blvd Ste 905
Los Angeles, CA 90036-4353, USA

Macwhorter, Keith (Baseball Player)
Boston Red Sox
9 Manning St
Providence, RI 02906, USA

Macy, Bill
10130 Angelo Cir
Beverly Hills, CA 90210-2701, USA

Macy, Kyle (Basketball Player)
3320 Overbrook Dr
Lexington, KY 40502-3352, USA

Macy, William H (Actor)
c/o Kenneth Gross *Kenneth H Gross Management*
7919 W Sunset Blvd Fl 2
Los Angeles, CA 90046-3357, USA

Maczuzak, John (Football Player)
Kansas City Chiefs
9070 Lucia Ln
Irwin, PA 15642-4913, USA

Madball
1115 46th Rd Apt 4E
Long Island City, NY 11101-5348, USA

Maddalena, Julie (Actor)
c/o Staff Member *Tisherman Agency Inc*
6767 Forest Lawn Dr Ste 101
Los Angeles, CA 90068-1050, USA

Maddaloni, Martin J (Misc)
Plumbing & Pipe Fitting Union
901 Massachusetts Ave NW
Washington, DC 20001-4307, USA

Madden, Benji (Musician)
c/o Staff Member *Creative Artists Agency LCC (CAA-LA)*
2000 Avenue Of The Stars
Los Angeles, CA 90067-4700, USA

Madden, D S (Religious Leader)
American Baptist Assn
4605 N State Line Ave
Texarkana, TX 75503-2916, USA

Madden, Dave (Actor)
1009 Flora Parke Dr
Saint Johns, FL 32259-4255, USA

Madden, David (Writer)
Louisiana State University
US Civil War Center
Baton Rouge, LA 70803-0001, USA

Madden, Diane (Dancer)
Trisha Brown Dance Co
211 W 61st St
New York, NY 10023-7832, USA

Madden, Joel (Musician)
c/o Brian Greenbaum *Creative Artists Agency LCC (CAA-LA)*
2000 Avenue Of The Stars
Los Angeles, CA 90067-4700, USA

Madden, John (Director)
c/o Michael Peretzian *Creative Artists Agency LCC (CAA-LA)*
2000 Avenue Of The Stars
Los Angeles, CA 90067-4700, USA

Madden, John E (Coach, Football Coach, Football Player, Sportscaster)
5955 Coronado Ln
Pleasanton, CA 94588-8518, USA

Madden, John P (Director)
William Morris Agency
52/53 Poland Place
London W1F 7LX, UNITED KINGDOM (UK)

Madden, Mike (Baseball Player)
Houston Astros
4733 Frankfort Way
Denver, CO 80239-5922, USA

Madden, Morris (Baseball Player)
Detroit Tigers
105 Jennings St
Laurens, SC 29360-3317, USA

Maddix, Raydell (Baseball Player)
Indianapolis Clowns
3724 E North Bay St
Tampa, FL 33610-7959, USA

Maddock, Robert (Football Player)
Chicago Cardinals
3541 Geranium Ave
Corona Del Mar, CA 92625-1673, USA

Maddox, Elliott (Baseball Player)
Detroit Tigers
980 Coral Ridge Dr Apt 104
Coral Springs, FL 33071-4148, USA

Maddox, Garry (Baseball Player)
San Francisco Giants
312 Wynne Ln
Penn Valley, PA 19072-1338, USA

Maddox, Jerry (Baseball Player)
Atlanta Braves
3141 N Driftwood St
Orange, CA 92865-1101, USA

Maddox, Lester (Ex-Governor, Governor)
3155 Johnson Ferry Rd
Marietta, GA 30062-5656, USA

Maddox, Mark (Football Player)
Buffalo Bills
1020 E Mountain Vista Dr
Phoenix, AZ 85048-1904, USA

Maddox, Robert (Football Player)
Cincinnati Bengals
7612 Coison Dr
Louisville, KY 40220, USA

Maddux, Greg (Baseball Player)
Chicago Cubs
36 Innisbrook Ave
Las Vegas, NV 89113-1225, USA

Maddux, Mike (Baseball Player)
Philadelphia Phillies
7100 Doe Ave
Las Vegas, NV 89117-1504, USA

Maddy, Penelope Jo (Misc)
University of California
Philosophy Dept
Irvine, CA 92717, USA

Mader, Gunther (Skier)
Am Brenner 28
Gries 6156, AUSTRIA

Mader, Rebecca (Actor)
c/o Craig Shapiro *Innovative Artists (LA)*
1505 10th St
Santa Monica, CA 90401-2805, USA

Maderos, George (Football Player)
San Francisco 49ers
12 Spinnaker Way
Chico, CA 95926-1627, USA

Madfai, Kahtan al (Architect)
22 Vassileos Constantinou
Athens 11635, GREECE

Madhavi (Actor, Bollywood)
21/C Neha Ave
Juhu Tara Road
Mumbai, MS 400049, INDIA

Madhoo (Actor, Bollywood)
Krishna Kutir
Sagarika Society Juhu Tara Road
Bombay, MS 400049, INDIA

Madhubala (Actor, Bollywood)
Krishna Kutir
1 Juhu Tara Road
Mumbai, MS 400049, INDIA

Madi, Ferenc (President)
Egyetem Ter 1-3
Budapest 1364, HUNGARY

Madigan, Amy (Actor)
22031 Carbon Mesa Rd
Malibu, CA 90265-5008, USA

Madigan, John W (Business Person,
Publisher)
Tribune Co
435 N Michigan Ave Ste 1800
Chicago, IL 60611-4030, USA

Madigan, Kathleen (Comedian)
c/o Staff Member *Gersh Agency, The (LA)*
232 N Canon Dr
Beverly Hills, CA 90210-5302, USA

Madigan, Martha (Photographer)
Tyler School of Art Beech & Penrose Aves
Philadelphia, PA 19126, USA

Madigan, Sam (Football Player)
3685 Heron Ridge Ln
Weston, FL 33331-3711, USA

Madio, James (Actor)
c/o Melisa Spamer *Domain*
4526 Wilshire Blvd
Los Angeles, CA 90010-3801, USA

Madison, Holly (Model, Reality TV Star)
Playboy Mansion
10236 Charing Cross Rd
Los Angeles, CA 90024-1815, USA

Madison, Sarah Danielle (Actor)
c/o Connie Tavel *Forward Entertainment*
9255 W Sunset Blvd Ste 805
Los Angeles, CA 90069-3305, USA

Madison, Scotty (Baseball Player)
Detroit Tigers
5397 Thornapple Ln NW
Acworth, GA 30101-7886, USA

Madlock, Bill (Baseball Player)
2124 Churchill Ct
Highland Park, IL 60035-1609, USA

Madonna (Actor, Dancer, Musician,
Songwriter)
c/o Guy Oseary *Maverick Films*
331 N Maple Dr Fl 2
Beverly Hills, CA 90210-3827, USA

Madrazo, Ignacio N (Doctor)
Av Paseo de la Reforma
#476 1er Piso
Col Juarez CP, DF 6698, MEXICO

Madrid, Alex (Baseball Player)
Milwaukee Brewers
PO Box 1974
Saint Johns, AZ 85936-1974, USA

Madrugada (Music Group)
c/o Staff Member *Paradigm (Monterey)*
509 Hartnell St
Monterey, CA 93940-2825, USA

Madsen, Loren (Artist)
426 Broome St
New York, NY 10013-3251, USA

Madsen, Michael (Actor)
c/o Chuck Binder *Binder & Associates*
1465 Lindacrest Dr
Beverly Hills, CA 90210-2519, USA

Madsen, Virgina (Actor)
c/o Katie Rhodes *Untitled Entertainment
(LA)*
331 N Maple Dr Fl 3
Beverly Hills, CA 90210-3827, USA

Madson, Michael (Actor)
The Firm
9100 Wilshire Blvd Ste 100W
Beverly Hills, CA 90212-3435, USA

Madson, Ryan (Baseball Player)
Philadelphia Phillies
149 E Edgerfield Dr
Summerville, SC 29483, USA

Madura, Ricardo (President)
Casa Presidencial
Blvd Juan Pablo II
Tegucigalpa, HONDURAS

Mae, Vanessa (Musician)
Mel Bush
Stratford Saye
20 Wellington Rd
Bournemouth BH8 8JN, UNITED
KINGDOM (UK)

Maedizossian, Prefate Moushegh
(Religious Leader)
Armenian Apostolic Church
4401 Russell Ave
Los Angeles, CA 90027-4416, USA

Maegte, Richard L (Dick) (Football Player)
4047 Aberdeen Way
Houston, TX 77025-2305, USA

Maestri, Hector (Baseball Player)
Washington Senators
581 SW 89th Ct
Miami, FL 33174-2338, USA

Maestro, Johnny (Musician)
PO Box 309M
Bay Shore, NY 11706, USA

Maestro, Mia (Actor)
c/o Pam Kohl *3 Arts Entertainment Inc*
9460 Wilshire Blvd Fl 7
Beverly Hills, CA 90212-2713, USA

Maffay, Peter
Klenzestr. 1
Tutzing D-82327, GERMANY

Maffett, Debra
1525 McGavock St
Nashville, TN 37203, USA

Maffia, Roma (Actor)
c/o Staff Member *Stone Manners Talent &
Literary (LA)*
6500 Wilshire Blvd Ste 550
Los Angeles, CA 90048-4950, USA

Magadan, Dave (Baseball Player)
New York Mets
4505 W North A St
Tampa, FL 33609-2028, USA

Magallanes, Ever (Baseball Player)
Cleveland Indians
18312 W Banff Ln
Surprise, AZ 85388-7655, USA

Magaw, John W (Government Official,
Lawyer)
Transportation Security Administration
400 7th St SW
Washington, DC 20590-0001, USA

Magaziner, Henry J (Architect)
1504 South St
Philadelphia, PA 19146-1636, USA

Magee, Andy (Golfer)
6100 E Huntress Dr
Paradise Valley, AZ 85253-4217, USA

Magee, Dave (Race Car Driver)
5S350 Deer Ridge Path
Big Rock, IL 60511-9777, USA

Magee, Wendell (Baseball Player)
Philadelphia Phillies
1552 Nola Rd NE
Brookhaven, MS 39601, USA

Maggard, Dave (Athlete, Track Athlete)
University of Houston
Athletic Dept
Houston, TX 77204-0001, USA

Maggart, Brandon (Actor)
8730 W Sunset Blvd Ste 480
Los Angeles, CA 90069-2277, USA

Maggart, Garett (Actor)
c/o Staff Member *SDB Partners Inc*
1801 Avenue Of The Stars Ste 902
Los Angeles, CA 90067-5981, USA

Maggert, Jeff (Golfer)
62 W Bracebridge Cir
The Woodlands, TX 77382-2539, USA

Maggette, Corey (Basketball Player)
Los Angeles Clippers
1111 S Figueroa St
Staples Center
Los Angeles, CA 90015-1300, USA

Magic Numbers, The (Music Group)
c/o Staff Member *Paradigm (Monterey)*
509 Hartnell St
Monterey, CA 93940-2825, USA

Magill, Frank J (Judge)
US Court of Appeals
657 2nd Ave N
Federal Building
Fargo, ND 58102-4727, USA

Magilton, Gerald E (Jerry) (Astronaut)
Marlin Marietta Astro Space
100 Campus Dr
Newtown, PA 18940-1784, USA

Maginnes, John (Golfer)
612 Topwater Ln
Greensboro, NC 27455-3458, USA

Magistretti, Vico (Architect)
Via Conservatorio 20
Milan, ITALY

Magnante, Mike (Baseball Player)
Kansas City Royals
5305 Via Quinto
Newbury Park, CA 91320-6937, USA

Magnus, Edie (Correspondent)
NBC-TV
30 Rockefeller Plz Ste 270E
News Dept
New York, NY 10112-0299, USA

Magnus, Robert (General)
Deputy CofS Programs/Resources
Hqusmc
2 Navy St
Washington, DC 20380-0001, USA

Magnus, Sandra H (Sandy) (Astronaut)
3477 Vinings North Trl SE
Smyrna, GA 30080-4581, USA

Magnuson, Ann
1317 Maltman Ave
Los Angeles, CA 90026-6224, USA

Magnussen, Karen
2852 Thorndiff Dr.
N. Vancouver, BC V7R 285, CANADA

Magoon, Bob (Misc)
1688 Meridian Ave
Miami Beach, FL 33139-2710, USA

Magowan, Peter (Baseball Player)
San Francisco Giants
2100 Washington St
San Francisco, CA 94109-2845, USA

Magrane, Joe (Baseball Player)
St Louis Cardinals
705 Guisando De Avila
Tampa, FL 33613-5204, USA

Magrann, Tom (Baseball Player)
Cleveland Indians
910 N 31st Ct
Hollywood, FL 33021-5509, USA

Magri, Charles G (Charlie) (Boxer)
345 Bethnal Green Road
Bethnal Green
London E2 6LG, UNITED KINGDOM
(UK)

Magrini, Pete (Baseball Player)
Boston Red Sox
2402 Rancho Cabeza Dr
Santa Rosa, CA 95404-2326, USA

Magruder, Chris (Baseball Player)
Texas Rangers
1740 Leisure Ln
Yakima, WA 98908-9224, USA

Magsamen, Sandra (Artist, Writer)
Orchard Books/Scholastic
557 Broadway
New York, NY 10012-3962, USA

Maguire, Adrian E (Jockey)
Jockey Club
42 Portman Square
London W1H 0EM, UNITED KINGDOM
(UK)

Maguire, Les (Musician)
Barry Collins
21A Cliftown Road
Southend-on-Sea
Essex SS1 1AB, UNITED KINGDOM (UK)

Maguire, Michael (Actor)
Epstein-Wyckoff
280 S Beverly Dr Ste 400
Beverly Hills, CA 90212-3904, USA

Maguire, Paul L (Football Player,
Sportscaster)
707 Ocean Blvd
Isle Of Palms, SC 29451-2136, USA

Maguire, Richard W (Cinematographer)
26 Condesa Rd
Santa Fe, NM 87508-9153, USA

Maguire, Tobey (Actor)
c/o Staff Member *Maguire Entertainment*
9220 W Sunset Blvd Ste 300
Los Angeles, CA 90069-3503, USA

Maguson, Keith A (Hockey Player)
265 King Muir Rd
Lake Forest, IL 60045-2034, USA

Magyar, Derek (Actor)
c/o Staff Member *Wilkins Management*
12200 W Olympic Blvd Ste 400
Los Angeles, CA 90064-1047, USA

Mahaffey, Arthur (Art) (Baseball Player)
Philadelphia Phillies
PO Box 1212
Allentown, PA 18105-1212, USA

Mahaffey, Valerie (Actor)
Kazarian/Spencer
11365 Ventura Blvd Ste 100
Studio City, CA 91604-3148, USA

Mahaffey, Valerio
121 N San Vicente Blvd
Beverly Hills, CA 90211-2303, USA

Mahal, Taj (Musician, Songwriter, Writer)
Bill Graham Mgmt
PO Box 429094
San Francisco, CA 94142-9094, USA

Mahalingam, Gemini (Actor)
47 Harrington Road
Chennai, TN 600 031, INDIA

Mahan, Art (Baseball Player)
Philadelphia Phillies
418 Glenmore Ave
Elkins Park, PA 19027-1841, USA

Mahan, Hunter (Golfer)
5336 Corinthian Bay Dr
Plano, TX 75093-4122, USA

Mahan, Larry
PO Box 41
Camp Verde, TX 78010-0041, USA

Mahan, Lawrence (Larry) (Rodeo Rider)
4771 Fruitland Rd
Sunset, TX 76270-6511, USA

Maharidge, Date D (Writer)
Stanford University
Communications Dept
Stanford, CA 94305, USA

Maharishi Mahesh Yogi (Religious Leader)
Maharishi University
Institute Of World Leadership
Fairfield, IA 52556, USA

Mahay, Ron (Baseball Player)
Boston Red Sox
19 Sutton Pl
East Windsor, NJ 08520-1716, USA

Maher, Bill (Talk Show Host)
c/o Marc Gurvitz *Brillstein-Grey
Entertainment*
9150 Wilshire Blvd Ste 350
Beverly Hills, CA 90212-3453, USA

Maher, Sean
c/o Staff Member *Gersh Agency, The (LA)*
232 N Canon Dr
Beverly Hills, CA 90210-5302, USA

Maheswari (Actor, Bollywood)
9 North Ave
Sree Nagar Colony Saidapet
Chennai, TN 600015, INDIA

Maheu, Robert
3523 Cochise Ln
Las Vegas, NV 89169-3307, USA

Mahlberg, Greg (Baseball Player)
Texas Rangers
5100 N Placita Del Lazo
Tucson, AZ 85750-1535, USA

Mahler, Mickey (Baseball Player)
Atlanta Braves
7911 Quirt St
San Antonio, TX 78227-2636, USA

Mahler, Rick (Baseball Player)
Atlanta Braves
12667 SE Old Cypress Dr # 5
Hobe Sound, FL 33455-7923, USA

Mahogany, Kevin (Actor, Musician)
Ted Kurland
173 Brighton Ave
Boston, MA 02134-2003, USA

Mahomes, Patrick (Baseball Player)
Minnesota Twins
PO Box 1025
Lindale, TX 75771-1025, USA

Mahon, Sean (Actor)
c/o Staff Member *The McCabe Group*
8285 W Sunset Blvd Ste 1
West Hollywood, CA 90046-2420, USA

Mahoney, David L (Business Person)
McKesson HBOX Inc
1 Post St
San Francisco, CA 94104-5277, USA

Mahoney, Jim (Baseball Player)
Boston Red Sox
150 Sycamore Ter
Glen Rock, NJ 07452-1907, USA

Mahoney, John (Actor)
c/o Staff Member *International Creative
Management (ICM-NY)*
40 W 57th St
New York, NY 10019-4001, USA

Mahoney, Marle (Baseball Player)
207 Birdsall St
Houston, TX 77007-8107, USA

Mahoney, Mike (Baseball Player)
Chicago Cubs
4412 98th St
Urbandale, IA 50322-1362, USA

Mahony, Cardinal Roger
1531 W 9th St
Los Angeles, CA 90015-1112, USA

Mahood, Beverly (Musician)
c/o Staff Member *Paquin Entertainment
Agency*
110 Bond St
Toronto, ON M5B 1X8, CANADA

Mahorn, Rick (Basketball Player)
3091 Mapleridge Ct
Rochester Hills, MI 48309-4505, USA

Mahovlich, Francis W (Frank) (Hockey
Player)
2-954 Ave ROad
Toronto, ON M5P 2K8, CANADA

Mahre, Phil
PO Box 100
Park City, UT 84060-0100, USA

Mahre, Phillip (Phil) (Skier)
70 Roza View Dr
Yakima, WA 98901-9390, USA

Mahre, Steve (Skier)
7610 W Chestnut Ave
Yakima, WA 98908-1553, USA

Maida, Adam J Cardinal (Religious
Leader)
Archdiocese of Detroit
1234 Washington Blvd
Detroit, MI 48226-1800, USA

Maida, Raine (Musician)
c/o Staff Member *Paradigm (Monterey)*
509 Hartnell St
Monterey, CA 93940-2825, USA

Maiden-Naccarato, Jeanne (Bowler)
1 N Stadium Way Apt 4
Tacoma, WA 98403-3154, USA

Maier, Hermann (Skier)
Reitdorf 116
Flachau 5542, AUSTRIA

Maier, Pauline R (Historian)
60 Larchwood Dr
Cambridge, MA 02138-4639, USA

Maier, Sepp (Soccer Player)
Parkstr 62
Anzing 84405, GERMANY

Mailho, Emil (Baseball Player)
Philadelphia Athletics
566 Scott St
Fremont, CA 94539-5208, USA

Mailhouse, Robert (Actor)
c/o Staff Member *Stone Manners Talent &
Literary (LA)*
6500 Wilshire Blvd Ste 550
Los Angeles, CA 90048-4950, USA

Mailinvaud, Edmond (Economist)
42 Ave de Saxe
Paris 75007, FRANCE

Maillard, Carol (Musician)
Sweet Honey Agency
PO Box 600099
Newtonville, MA 02460-0001, USA

Maiman, Theodore H (Ted) (Inventor)
15A Alberni St
Vancouver, BC V6G 3N7, CANADA

Maines, Natalie (Musician)
c/o Simon Renshaw *Strategics Artist
Management*
1100 Glendon Ave Ste 1000
Los Angeles, CA 90024-3514, USA

Maisel, Jay (Photographer)
190 Bowery
New York, NY 10012-4203, USA

Maisel, Sherman J (Economist)
2164 Hyde St
San Francisco, CA 94109-1788, USA

Maisenberg, Olega (Musician)
In Der Gugl 9
Klostemeuburg, AUSTRIA

Maisky, Mischa M (Musician)
Columbia Artists Mgmt Inc
1790 Broadway Fl 6
New York, NY 10019-1412, USA

Maisnik, Kathy
260 S Beverly Dr Ste 308
Beverly Hills, CA 90212-3814, USA

Maisonneuve, Brian (Soccer Player)
Columbus Crew
2121 Volman Ave
Columbus, OH 43211, USA

Maitland, Beth (Actor)
Epstein-Wyckoff
280 S Beverly Dr Ste 400
Beverly Hills, CA 90212-3904, USA

Majdarzavyn, Ganzorig (Cosmonaut)
Academy of Sciences
Peace Ave 54B
Ulan Bator 51, MONGOLIA

Majerle, Dan (Basketball Player)
c/o Staff Member *Phoenix Suns*
201 E Jefferson St
Phoenix, AZ 85004-2412, USA

Majerus, Rick (Basketball Player, Coach)
ESPN-TV Sports Dept
935 Middle St
Espn Plaza
Bristol, CT 06010-1000, USA

Majoli, Iva (Tennis Player)
27 Framingham Ln
Pittsford, NY 14534-1047, USA

Major, Clarence L (Writer)
University of California
English Dept
Voorhies Hall
Davis, CA 95616, USA

Major, John (Prime Minister)
8 Stuckley Road
Huntingdon, Cambs, UNITED KINGDOM
(UK)

Majoras, Deborah (Government Official)
Federal Trade Commission
Pennsylvania Ave & 6th St NW
Washington, DC 20580-0001, USA

Majorino, Tina (Actor)
c/o Abby Bluestone *Innovative Artists (LA)*
1505 10th St
Santa Monica, CA 90401-2805, USA

Majors, Austin
Major Minors
3940 Laurel Canyon Blvd # 177
Studio City, CA 91604-3709, USA

Majors, John I (Johnny) (Coach, Football Coach, Football Player)
4207 Beechwood Rd
Knoxville, TN 37920-6011, USA

Majors, Lee (Actor)
c/o Staff Member *Shapiro-Lichtman Talent Agency*
1333 Beverly Green Dr
Los Angeles, CA 90035-1018, USA

MajorSundararajan (Actor)
9 Pooram Prakash Rao Street
Balaji Nagar Royapeta
Chennai, TN 600 014, INDIA

Majumder, Shaun (Musician)
c/o Staff Member *Paradigm (Monterey)*
509 Hartnell St
Monterey, CA 93940-2825, USA

Makarov, Askold A (Dancer)
Plutalova Str 18-4
Saint Petersburg 197136, RUSSIA

Makarov, Sergei (Hockey Player)
Professional Sports Services
4072 Teale Ave
San Jose, CA 95117-3432, USA

Makarova, Inna V (Actor)
Ukrainian Blvd 11
Moscow 121059, RUSSIA

Makarova, Natalia R (Ballerina)
Herbert Breslin
119 W 57th St Ste 1505
New York, NY 10019-2401, USA

Make Good Your Escape (Music Group)
c/o Staff Member *Paradigm (Monterey)*
509 Hartnell St
Monterey, CA 93940-2825, USA

Makeba, Miriam (Musician)
Sadiane Corp
350 5th Ave Ste 7412
New York, NY 10118-7412, USA

Makhalina, Yufia (Ballerina)
Kirov Ballet Theater
1 Pl Iskusstr
Saint Petersburg 190000, RUSSIA

Makings, Elizabeth (Golfer)
10063 E San Bernardo Dr
Scottsdale, AZ 85258-5665, USA

Makinson, Jessica (Comedian)
c/o Staff Member *OmniPop Inc (LA)*
4605 Lankershim Blvd Ste 201
North Hollywood, CA 91602-1874, USA

Makk, Karoly (Director)
Hanoczy Jeno Utca 15
Budapest 1022, HUNGARY

Makkena, Wendy (Actor)
c/o Craig Dorfman *Blueprint Management*
5670 Wilshire Blvd Ste 2525
Los Angeles, CA 90036-5647, USA

Mako (Actor)
6477 Peppertree Ln
Somis, CA 93066-9758, USA

Mako, C Gene (Tennis Player)
430 S Burnside Ave Apt Mc
Los Angeles, CA 90036-5319, USA

Makowski, Tom (Baseball Player)
Detroit Tigers
6686 Omphalius Rd # 2
Colden, NY 14033-9763, USA

Maksimoya, Yekaterina S (Ballerina)
Bolshoi Theater
Teatrainsya Pl 1
Moscow 103009, RUSSIA

Maksudian, Mike (Baseball Player)
Toronto Blue Jays
12148 E San Simeon Dr
Scottsdale, AZ 85259-6049, USA

Maksymiuk, Jerzy
Hoza 5A m 13
Warsaw 00-528, POLAND

Maktoum, Shaikh Maktoum bin Rashid al- (Prime Minister)
Royal Palace
PO Box 899
Abu Dhabi, UNITED ARAB EMIRATES

Malach-Webb, Kay (Baseball Player)
3257 Louisville Rd
Louisville, TN 37777-3732, USA

Malahide, Patrick (Actor)
International Creative Mgmt
76 Oxford St
London W1N 0AX, UNITED KINGDOM (UK)

Malakar, Sanjaya (Musician, Reality TV Star)
c/o Staff Member *American Idol*
7800 Beverly Blvd # 251
Los Angeles, CA 90036-2112, USA

Malakhov, Vladimir (Hockey Player)
10225 Collins Ave Apt 302
Bal Harbour, FL 33154-1400, USA

Malakian, Daron (Musician)
Velvet Hammer
9911 W Pico Blvd # 350
Los Angeles, CA 90035-2703, USA

Malandrino, Catherine (Designer, Fashion Designer)
468 Broome St
New York, NY 10013-2611, USA

Malanowski-Marlowe, Jean (Baseball Player)
100 Smallacombe Dr # 205-24
Scranton, PA 18508-2650, USA

Malaska, Mark (Baseball Player)
Tampa Bay Devil Rays
3823 Cumberland Dr
Youngstown, OH 44515-4610, USA

Malavoy, Christopher
9 sq. de Montsouris
Paris F-75014, FRANCE

Malaysia Vasudevan (Actor)
5 Kaman Street SFI Apts
6-B Samiyar Matt
Chennai, TN 600 024, INDIA

Malchow, Tom
1 Olympic Plz
Colorado Springs, CO 80909-5780, USA

Malco, Romany (Actor)
c/o Michael Greene *Greene & Associates*
190 N Canon Dr Ste 200
Beverly Hills, CA 90210-5319, USA

Malcolm, George J (Musician)
99 Wimbledon Hill Road
London SW19 4BE, UNITED KINGDOM (UK)

Maldacena, Juan (Physicist)
Harvard University
Physics Dept
Cambridge, MA 02138, USA

Malden, Karl (Actor)
1845 Mandeville Canyon Rd
Los Angeles, CA 90049-2222, USA

Maldini, Paolo (Coach, Soccer Player)
AC Milan
Via Turati 3
Milan 20221, ITALY

Maldonado, Candy (Baseball Player)
Los Angeles Dodgers
HC 2 Box 16800
Arecibo, PR 00612-9396, USA

Malee, Chompoo (Designer, Fashion Designer)
Hino & Malee Inc
3701 N Ravenswood Ave
Chicago, IL 60613-3553, USA

Maleeva, Katerina (Tennis Player)
Mladostr 1 #45
NH 14
Sofia 1174, BULGARIA

Maleeva-Fragniere, Manuela (Tennis Player)
Bourg-Dessous 28
La Tour de Peitz 1814, SWITZERLAND

Malek, Rami (Actor)
c/o Kyle Fritz *Kyle Fritz Management*
6325 Heather Dr
Los Angeles, CA 90068-1633, USA

Malenchenko, Yuri I (Cosmonaut)
Potcha Kosmonavtov
Moskovskoi Oblasti
Syvisdny Goroduk 141160, RUSSIA

Maler, Jim (Baseball Player)
Seattle Mariners
1758 NE 177th St
North Miami Beach, FL 33162-1510, USA

Malerba, Franco E (Astronaut)
Via Cantore 10
Genova 16149, ITALY

Malerba, Luigi
Via Tro Millina 31
Rome, CA, ITALY

Malfitano, Catherine (Opera Singer)
Columbia Artists Mgmt Inc
1790 Broadway Fl 6
New York, NY 10019-1412, USA

Malhotra, Harmesh (Bollywood, Director, Filmmaker, Producer)
32A Sunset Heights 59 Pali Hill
Nargis Dutt Road Bandra
Bombay, MS 400 050, INDIA

Malice (Musician)
Star Trak/Arista Records
888 7th Ave # 3800
New York, NY 10106-0001, USA

Malick, Terrence
7920 W Sunset Blvd
Los Angeles, CA 90046-3300, USA

Malick, Wendie (Actor, Model)
Innovative Artists
1505 10th St
Santa Monica, CA 90401-2805, USA

Malicky, Neal (Educator)
Baldwin-Wallace College
President's Office
Berea, OH 44017, USA

Malielegaoi, Tuilaepa Sailele (Prime Minister)
Prime Minister's Office
PO Box L1861
Vailima, Apia, SAMOA

Malik, Art (Actor)
18 Sydney Mews
London SW3 6HL, UNITED KINGDOM (UK)

Malina, Josh
2262 Cloverfield Blvd
Santa Monica, CA 90405-1821, USA

Malina, Joshua (Actor)
c/o Staff Member *Innovative Artists (LA)*
1505 10th St
Santa Monica, CA 90401-2805, USA

Malinger, Ross
6212 Banner Ave
Los Angeles, CA 90038-2802, USA

Malini, Hema (Actor, Bollywood)
17 Jai Hind Society
12th Road Juhu Scheme
Mumbai, MS 400049, INDIA

Malinin, Mike (Musician)
Atlas/Third Rail Entertainment
9200 W Sunset Blvd
West Hollywood, CA 90069-3502, USA

Malinosky, Tony (Baseball Player)
Brooklyn Dodgers
5540 W 5th St Spc 60
Oxnard, CA 93035-4872, USA

Maliozzi, Ray (Talk Show Host)
PBS
1320 Braddock Pl
Alexandria, VA 22314-1692, USA

Maliozzi, Tom (Talk Show Host)
PBS
1320 Braddock Pl
Alexandria, VA 22314-1692, USA

Maliponte, Adrianna (Opera Singer)
Gorlinsky Promotions
35 Darer
London W1, UNITED KINGDOM (UK)

Malizia, Mike (Golfer)
2750 NW Windermere Dr
Jensen Beach, FL 34957, USA

Malkhov, Vladimir (Ballerina)
American Baliet Theatre
890 Broadway
New York, NY 10003-1278, USA

Malkin, Evgenl (Hockey Player)
Pittsburgh Penguins
66 Mario Lemieux Pl
Mellon Arena
Pittsburgh, PA 15219-3504, USA

Malkin, Laurence (Writer)
c/o Josh Kesselman *Jericho Entertainment*
2121 Avenue Of The Stars Ste 2900
Los Angeles, CA 90067-5057, USA

Malkmus, Bobby (Baseball Player)
Milwaukee Braves
400 Wallingford Ter
Union, NJ 07083-7328, USA

Malkovich, John (Actor)
c/o Staff Member *Mr Mudd*
5225 Wilshire Blvd Ste 604
Los Angeles, CA 90036-4350, USA

Mallary, Robert (Artist)
PO Box 97
Conway, MA 01341-0097, USA

Mallea, Eduardo (Writer)
Posadas 1120
Buenos Aires, ARGENTINA

Mallet, W George (Governor)
Governor General's Office
Morne, Castries, SAINT LUCIA

Mallett, Jerry (Baseball Player)
Boston Red Sox
7610 Forest Park Dr
Beaumont, TX 77707-1626, USA

Mallette, Alfred J (General)
7040 Quail Hill Rd
Charlotte, NC 28210-5104, USA

Mallette, Brian (Baseball Player)
Milwaukee Brewers
3012 Gilder Rd
Glenwood, GA 30428-2202, USA

Mallette, Mai (Baseball Player)
Brooklyn Dodgers
15 Barratts Chapel Ct
Durham, NC 27705-1311, USA

Malley, Kenneth C (Admiral)
136 Riverside Rd
Edgewater, MD 21037-1405, USA

Mallick, Dan (Misc)
42045 Tilton Dr
Quartz Hill, CA 93536-7321, USA

Mallicoat, Rob (Baseball Player)
Houston Astros
2050 SE Larson Ct
Hillsboro, OR 97123-5304, USA

Mallon, Meg (Golfer)
5105 N Ocean Blvd Apt C
Ocean Ridge, FL 33435-7087, USA

Mallory, Carole (Actor)
2300 5th Ave
New York, NY 10037-1610, USA

Mallory, Glynn C Jr (General)
19221 Heather Frst
San Antonio, TX 78258-3820, USA

Mallory, Sheldon (Baseball Player)
Oakland A's
21353 Old North Church Rd
Frankfort, IL 60423-3016, USA

Malloy, Bob (Baseball Player)
Texas Rangers
1904 San Carlos Ave
Allen, TX 75002-2626, USA

Malloy, Edward A (Educator)
University of Notre Dame
President's Office
Notre Dame, IN 46556, USA

Malloy, Marty (Baseball Player)
Atlanta Braves
2030 SW 100th St
Trenton, FL 32693-5530, USA

Malloy, Robert (Pete Hamil) (Actor, Writer)
c/o Staff Member *International Creative Management (ICM-LA)*
10250 Constellation Blvd
Los Angeles, CA 90067-6200, USA

Malloy, Tommy
1687 Amsterdam Ave
Merrick, NY 11566-2516, USA

Malloys, The (Music Group)
c/o Staff Member *Creative Artists Agency LCC (CAA-LA)*
2000 Avenue Of The Stars
Los Angeles, CA 90067-4700, USA

Malo, Raul (Musician, Songwriter, Writer)
c/o Mario Tirado *Creative Artists Agency (CAA-NY)*
162 5th Ave Fl 6
New York, NY 10010-6047, USA

Maloff, Sam (Designer)
PO Box 8051
Alta Loma, CA 91701-0051, USA

Malone, Arthur L (Art) (Football Player)
1619 E Carmen St
Tempe, AZ 85283-4145, USA

Malone, Beverly L (Misc)
American Nurses Assn
Maryland Ave SW
Washington, DC 20202-0001, USA

Malone, Brendan (Coach)
Indiana Pacers
125 S Pennsylvania St
Conseco Fieldhouse
Indianapolis, IN 46204-3610, USA

Malone, Chuck (Baseball Player)
Philadelphia Phillies
310 Liberty St
Marked Tree, AR 72365-2209, USA

Malone, Dorothy (Actor)
PO Box 7287
Dallas, TX 75209-0287, USA

Malone, Eddie (Baseball Player)
Chicago White Sox
10450 Wine Palm Rd Apt 5721
Fort Myers, FL 33966-5762, USA

Malone, Jena (Actor)
c/o Allison Band *United Talent Agency (UTA)*
9560 Wilshire Blvd Ste 500
Beverly Hills, CA 90212-2401, USA

Malone, John (Business Person)
Liberty Media
12300 Liberty Blvd
Englewood, CO 80112-7009, USA

Malone, Karl
301 W South Temple
Salt Lake City, UT 84101-1216, USA

Malone, Moses (Basketball Player)
c/o Staff Member *San Antonio Spurs*
100 Montana St
Alamodome
San Antonio, TX 78203-1031, USA

Malone, Patricia (Business Person)
c/o Staff Member *Gucci America*
50 Hartz Way
Secaucus, NJ 07094-2420, USA

Malone, Shannon (Actor, Television Host)
c/o Jerry Shandrew *Shandrew Public Relations*
1050 S Stanley Ave
Los Angeles, CA 90019-6634, USA

Maloney, Jim (Baseball Player)
Cincinnati Reds
7027 N Teilman Ave # 102
Fresno, CA 93711-0589, USA

Maloney, Sean (Baseball Player)
Milwaukee Brewers
4601 E Skyline Dr Apt 1205
Tucson, AZ 85718-1660, USA

Maloof, Gavin (Business Person)
c/o Staff Member *Sacramento Kings*
1 Sports Pkwy
Arco Arena
Sacramento, CA 95834-2301, USA

Malrena, Oswaldo (Baseball Player)
Chicago Cubs
160 E 6th Pl
Mesa, AZ 85201-5068, USA

Maltbie, Roger (Golfer)
179 Longmeadow Dr
Los Gatos, CA 95032-5655, USA

Maltin, Leonard (Correspondent)
c/o Staff Member *Entertainment Tonight (ET)*
5555 Melrose Ave
Mae West Bldg Fl 2
Los Angeles, CA 90038-3989, USA

Maly, Arturo (Actor)
c/o Staff Member *Telefe - Argentina*
Pavon 2444 (C1248AAT)
Buenos Aires, ARGENTINA

Malzone, Frank (Baseball Player)
Boston Red Sox
16 Aletha Rd
Needham, MA 02492-4302, USA

Mamas & The Papas, The
61 Purchase St Ste 2
Rye, NY 10580-3059, USA

Mambo, Kevin
3500 W. Olympic Blvd. #1400
Burbank, CA 91505, USA

Mamet, David (Actor, Director, Producer, Writer)
c/o Jeff Berg *International Creative Management (ICM-LA)*
10250 Constellation Blvd
Los Angeles, CA 90067-6200, USA

Mamoa, Jason (Actor)
c/o Jeff Witjas *Agency for the Performing Arts (APA-NY)*
888 7th Ave
New York, NY 10106-0001, USA

Mana (Music Group)
c/o Staff Member *Creative Artists Agency LCC (CAA-LA)*
2000 Avenue Of The Stars
Los Angeles, CA 90067-4700, USA

Manahan, Austin (Baseball Player)
Bowman
5936 E Phelps Rd
Scottsdale, AZ 85254-9223, USA

Manatt, Charles T
4814 Woodway Ln NW
Washington, DC 20016-3243, USA

Manchester, Melissa
5440 Corbin Ave
Tarzana, CA 91356-2927, USA

Mancina, Mark (Actor)
c/o Staff Member *Gorfaine/Schwartz Agency Inc*
4111 W Alameda Ave Ste 509
Burbank, CA 91505-4171, USA

Mancini, Ray (Actor)
12524 Indianapolis St
Los Angeles, CA 90066-1512, USA

Mancuso, Frank (Baseball Player)
St Louis Browns
5126 Cripple Creek Dr
Houston, TX 77017-6005, USA

Mancuso, Nick (Actor)
c/o Joel Dean *TalentWorks (LA)*
9200 W Sunset Blvd Ste 900
Los Angeles, CA 90069-3604, USA

Mancuso Jr, Frank (Producer)
c/o Staff Member *FGM Entertainment*
201 N Canon Dr # 328
Beverly Hills, CA 90210, USA

Mandan, Robert
247 S Beverly Dr # 102
Beverly Hills, CA 90212-3830, USA

Mandel, Howie (Comedian)
c/o Michael Rotenberg *3 Arts Entertainment Inc*
9460 Wilshire Blvd Fl 7
Beverly Hills, CA 90212-2713, USA

Mandel, Johnny
28946 Cliffside Dr
Malibu, CA 90265-4212, USA

Mandel, Loring
555 W 57th St Ste 1230
New York, NY 10019-2925, USA

Mandela, N Winnie Madikizela (Activist)
Orlando West
Soweto
Johannesburg, SOUTH AFRICA

Mandela, Nelson R (Politician)
Private Bag X70000
Houghton 2041, SOUTH AFRICA

Mandelbaum, Michael (Writer)
Basic Books
387 Park Ave S Fl 12
New York, NY 10016-8810, USA

Mandella, Lenora (Baseball Player)
2921 Chester St
McKeesport, PA 15132-1825, USA

Manders, Hal (Baseball Player)
Detroit Tigers
PO Box 149
Dallas Center, IA 50063-0149, USA

Mandich, Jim (Football Player)
Miami Dolphins
16101 Aberdeen Way
Miami Lakes, FL 33014-6566, USA

Mandrell, Barbara (Musician)
c/o Staff Member *Creative Artists Agency LCC (CAA-LA)*
2000 Avenue Of The Stars
Los Angeles, CA 90067-4700, USA

Mandvi, Aasif (Actor)
c/o Lillian LaSalle *LaSalle Holland*
141 W 28th St Rm 300
New York, NY 10001-6187, USA

Mandylor, Costas (Actor)
c/o Cynthia Campos-Greenberg *Atlas Entertainment*
6100 Wilshire Blvd Ste 1170
Los Angeles, CA 90048-5116, USA

Mandylor, Louis (Actor)
c/o Karen Forman *Metropolitan*
4500 Wilshire Blvd Fl 2
Los Angeles, CA 90010-3858, USA

Mane, Tyler (Actor)
c/o Staff Member *Miller & Company Management*
427 N Canon Dr Ste 215
Beverly Hills, CA 90210-4840, USA

Manetti, Larry
4615 Winnetka
Woodland Hills, CA 91364, USA

Mangan, Jim (Baseball Player)
Pittsburgh Pirates
6878 Trinidad Dr
San Jose, CA 95120-2057, USA

Mangelsdorff, AlbertEmil-
Claar-Str. 23
Frankfurt/Main 60322, GERMANY

Manges, Mark (Football Player)
St Louis Cardinals
13199 5th Ave
Cumberland, MD 21502-5567, USA

Mangieri, Dino (Football Player)
Kansas City Chiefs
108 Lamport Blvd
Staten Island, NY 10305-3629, USA

Mangione, Chuck (Musician)
476 Hampton Blvd
Rochester, NY 14612-4227, USA

Mangold, James Allen (Director,
Producer, Writer)
c/o Staff Member *Tree Line Films*
1708 Berkeley St
Santa Monica, CA 90404-4105, USA

Mangual, Angel (Baseball Player)
Pittsburgh Pirates
1406 R Del Valle
Ponce, PR 00728, USA

Mangual, Pepe (Baseball Player)
Montreal Expos
2325 Calle Tabonuco
Ponce, PR 00716-2712, USA

Mangum, John (Football Player)
Chicago Bears
150 Sherwood Ln
Brandon, MS 39042, USA

Mangum, John (Football Player)
Boston Patriots
508 10th Ave SE
Magee, MS 39111-3820, USA

Mangum, Jonathan (Actor)
c/o Staff Member *Shapiro/West &
Associates*
141 El Camino Dr Ste 205
Beverly Hills, CA 90212-2718, USA

Mangum, Kris (Football Player)
Carolina Panthers
20 Clearwater Pt
Petal, MS 39465-8649, USA

Manheim, Camryn (Actor, Producer,
Writer)
c/o Maryellen Mulcahy *Framework
Entertainment (LA)*
9057 Nemo St # C
W Hollywood, CA 90069-5511, USA

Maniaci, Joe (Football Player)
Brooklyn Dodgers
3215 Rankin Ave
Windsor, ON N9E 3C2, CANADA

Manic Street Preachers (Music Group)
c/o Staff Member *Paradigm (Monterey)*
509 Hartnell St
Monterey, CA 93940-2825, USA

Manigault-Stallworth, Omarosa (Actor,
Reality TV Star)
c/o Jenny Delaney *Forster-Delaney
Entertainment*
12533 Woodgreen St
Los Angeles, CA 90066-2723, USA

Manilow, Barry (Musician)
c/o Gary Kief *STILETTO Entertainment*
8295 S La Cienega Blvd
Inglewood, CA 90301-1521, USA

Manisha, Koirala (Actor, Bollywood)
302 Beachwood Towers
Yari Road Versova Andher (W)
Mumbai, MS 400061, INDIA

Mankiewicz, Frank
The Wyoming Columbia Rd. NW
Washington, DC 20009, USA

Mankiewicz, Tom
1609 Magnetic Ter
Los Angeles, CA 90069-1149, USA

Mankiller, Wilma P (Activist)
c/o Staff Member *Cherokee Nation*
PO Box 948
Tahlequah, OK 74465-0948, USA

Mankowitz, Wolf
Ahakista County Cork
Kilcrohane 11, IRELAND

Mankowski, Phil (Baseball Player)
Detroit Tigers
2280 Southwestern Blvd
Buffalo, NY 14224-4423, USA

Manley, Elizabeth (Figure Skater)
Marco Enterprises
74830 Velie Way # A
Palm Desert, CA 92260-1964, USA

Manley, Leon (Football Player)
Green Bay Packers
1207 Knollpark Cir
Austin, TX 78758-3815, USA

Manlikova, Hana
Vymolova 8
Prague 5 15000, CZECH REPUBLIC

Mann, Almee (Musician, Songwriter,
Writer)
Michael Hausman Mgmt
511 Avenue Of The Americas # 197
New York, NY 10011-8436, USA

Mann, Barry (Composer)
1010 Laurel Way
Beverly Hills, CA 90210-2305, USA

Mann, Carol (Golfer)
6 Cape Chestnut Dr
The Woodlands, TX 77381-2978, USA

Mann, Catherine
9417 Spruce Tree Cir
Bethesda, MD 20814-1654, USA

Mann, Charles (Football Player)
Washington Redskins
1518 Night Shade Ct
Vienna, VA 22182-7301, USA

Mann, David W (Religious Leader)
10550 S 200 W
Columbia City, IN 46725-9618, USA

Mann, Delbert (Director, Producer)
Caroline Productions
556 S Ogden Dr
Los Angeles, CA 90036-3229, USA

Mann, Dick (Motorcycle Race,
Motorcycle Racer)
American Motorcycle Assn
13515 Yarmouth Dr
Pickerington, OH 43147-8273, USA

Mann, Errol (Football Player)
Detroit Lions
5521 Bonanza Pl
Missoula, MT 59808-9386, USA

Mann, Gabriel (Actor)
c/o Michael McConnell *Innovative Artists
(LA)*
8730 W Sunset Blvd Ste 490
Los Angeles, CA 90069-2248, USA

Mann, Garbriel (Actor)
United Talent Agency
9560 Wilshire Blvd Ste 500
Beverly Hills, CA 90212-2401, USA

Mann, H Thompson (Swimmer)
23 Pleasant St Apt 501
Newburyport, MA 01950-2634, USA

Mann, Jim (Baseball Player)
New York Mets
197 N Franklin St
Holbrook, MA 02343-1111, USA

Mann, Johnny (Composer, Conductor)
78516 Gorman Lane
Indio, CA 92203, USA

Mann, Kelly (Baseball Player)
Atlanta Braves
PO Box 34296
Los Angeles, CA 90034-0296, USA

Mann, Leslie (Actor)
c/o Scott Melrose *Endeavor Agency LLC
(LA)*
9601 Wilshire Blvd Fl 3
Beverly Hills, CA 90210-5204, USA

Mann, Manfred (Misc)
EMI Records
43 Brook Green
London W6 7EF, UNITED KINGDOM
(UK)

Mann, Marvin L (Business Person)
Lexmark International
740 W New Circle Road
Lexington, KY 40550-0001, USA

Mann, Michael K (Actor, Director,
Producer, Writer)
c/o Staff Member *Forward Pass Inc*
12233 W Olympic Blvd Ste 340
Los Angeles, CA 90064-1039, USA

Mann, Monroe (Actor, Producer, Writer)
Monroe Mann, Inc
PO Box 3674
New York, NY 10163-3674, USA

Mann, Robert (Football Player)
Detroit Lions
515 SW Hampton Ct
Port Saint Lucie, FL 34986-2022, USA

Mann, Shelley I (Swimmer)
1301 S Scott St # 638S
Arlington, VA 22204-6205, USA

Mann, Terrence V (Actor)
138 W 118th St Apt 3B
New York, NY 10026-1814, USA

Manners, Miss
1651 Harvard St NW
Washington, DC 20009-3702, USA

Mannheim Steamroller (Music Group)
9120 Mormon Bridge Rd
Omaha, NE 68152-1937, USA

Manning, Eli (Athlete, Football Player)
c/o Staff Member *New Orleans Saints*
5800 Airline Dr
Metairie, LA 70003-3876, USA

Manning, Jane (Opera Singer)
2 Wilton Square
London N1, UNITED KINGDOM (UK)

Manning, Jim (Baseball Player)
Minnesota Twins
41 Fox Run Dr
Weaverville, NC 28787-8307, USA

Manning, Peyton (Athlete, Football Player)
c/o Staff Member *Indianapolis Colts*
7001 W 56th St
Indianapolis, IN 46254-9698, USA

Manning, Richard E (Rick) (Baseball
Player)
Cleveland Indians
12151 New Market
Chesterland, OH 44026-2041, USA

Manning, Susanne (Musician)
c/o Staff Member *Pop Idol (Fremantle
Media)*
2700 Colorado Ave Ste 450
Santa Monica, CA 90404-3599, USA

Manning, Taryn (Actor, Musician)
c/o Theresa Peters *William Morris Agency
(WMA-LA)*
1 William Morris Pl
Beverly Hills, CA 90212-4261, USA

Manning, Wade (Football Player)
Dallas Cowboys
5133 Malaya St
Denver, CO 80249-8548, USA

Manoa, Tim (Football Player)
Cleveland Browns
15332 Howe Rd
Cleveland, OH 44136-5324, USA

Manoff, Dinah (Actor)
Innovative Artists
1505 10th St
Santa Monica, CA 90401-2805, USA

Manoogian, RIchard A (Business Person)
Masco Corp
2100 Van Born Road
Taylor, MI 48180, USA

Manor, Brison (Football Player)
Denver Broncos
285 Spruce St
Bridgeton, NJ 08302-3347, USA

Manorama (Actor, Bollywood)
5 Neelagandan Street
T Nagar
Chennai, TN 600017, INDIA

Manos, Sam (Football Player)
Cincinnati Bengals
1424 E Normandy Blvd
Deltona, FL 32725-8408, USA

Manoukian, Don (Football Player)
Oakland Raiders
5405 Mae Anne Ave
Reno, NV 89523-1813, USA

Manrique, Fred (Baseball Player)
Toronto Blue Jays
1775 SW 2nd Ave
Boca Raton, FL 33432-7230, USA

Mansell, Kevin (Business Person)
Kohl's Corp
N56W17000 Ridgewood Dr
Menomonee Falls, WI 53051-5660, USA

Mansell, Nigel (Race Car Driver)
Nigel Mansell Racing
Brands Hatch
Longfield, Kent DA3 8NG, UNITED
KINGDOM (UK)

Manser, Michael J (Architect)
Morton House
Chiswick Mall
London W4 2PS, UNITED KINGDOM
(UK)

Mansfield, Mike (Ex-Senator, Senator)
1101 Pennsylvania Ave NW Ste 900
Washington, DC 20004-2514, USA

Mansfield, Peter (Nobel Prize Laureate)
Notingham University
Physics Dept
Nottingham NG7 2RD, UNITED
KINGDOM (UK)

Mansfield, Von (Football Player)
Philadelphia Eagles
3600 W 203rd St
Rich Central High School
Olympia Fields, IL 60461-1025, USA

Mansfield-Kelley, Marie (Baseball Player)
9 Eastland Rd
Jamaica Plain, MA 02130-4616, USA

Mansholt, Sicco L (Government Official)
Oosteinde 16
Wapserveen, HB 8351, THE
NETHERLANDS

Manson, Dave (Hockey Player)
Dallas Stars
2601 Avenue Of The Stars Ste 100
Starcenter
Frisco, TX 75034-9016, USA

Manson, Marilyn (Musician)
c/o Rick Roskin *Creative Artists Agency
LCC (CAA-LA)*
2000 Avenue Of The Stars
Los Angeles, CA 90067-4700, USA

Manson, Shirley (Musician)
Borman Entertainment
1250 6th St Ste 401
Santa Monica, CA 90401-1638, USA

Mansour, Nicole (Actor)
c/o Michael Eisenstadt *Amsel Eisenstadt &
Frazier Inc*
5055 Wilshire Blvd Ste 865
Los Angeles, CA 90036-6109, USA

Mansouri, Lotfi (Actor)
San Francisco Opera House
301 Van Ness Ave
San Francisco, CA 94102-4509, USA

Mantee, Paul (Actor)
Flick East-West
9057 Nemo St # A
West Hollywood, CA 90069-5511, USA

Mantegna, Joe (Actor)
PO Box 7304
103
North Hollywood, CA 91603-7304, USA

Mantei, Matt (Baseball Player)
Florida Marlins
4709 Chicago Path
Stevensville, MI 49127-9356, USA

Mantel, Hillary M (Writer)
AM Heath
79 Saint Martin's Lane
London WC2N 4AA, UNITED KINGDOM
(UK)

Mantello, Joe (Director)
Writers & Artists
360 Park Ave # 16
New York, NY 10022-5909, USA

Mantenuto, Michael (Actor)
c/o Kim Hodgert *Creative Artists Agency
LCC (CAA-LA)*
2000 Avenue Of The Stars
Los Angeles, CA 90067-4700, USA

Mantha, Mo
8423 Tally Ho Rd
Lutherville, MD 21093-4725, USA

Mantha, Moe (Hockey Player)
1538 Scio Ridge Rd
Ann Arbor, MI 48103-8991, USA

Manthra (Actor, Bollywood)
5-A Block 2 Vijay Shanti Apts
Arcot Road Vadapalani
Chennai, TN 600026, INDIA

Mantilla, Felix (Baseball Player)
Milwaukee Braves
6973 N Tacoma St
Milwaukee, WI 53224-4759, USA

Mantley, John
4121 Longridge Ave
Sherman Oaks, CA 91423-4335, USA

Manto, Jeff (Baseball Player)
Cleveland Indians
802 3rd Ave
Bristol, PA 19007-3222, USA

Mantooth, Randolph (Actor)
c/o Staff Member *Stone Manners Talent &
Literary (LA)*
6500 Wilshire Blvd Ste 550
Los Angeles, CA 90048-4950, USA

Mantranga, Jonah (Musician)
c/o Staff Member *Paradigm (Monterey)*
509 Hartnell St
Monterey, CA 93940-2825, USA

Mantreola, Patricia
c/o Staff Member *BMG*
1540 Broadway
New York, NY 10036-4074, USA

Manucci, Dan (Football Player)
Buffalo Bills
1208 W Sand Dune Dr
Gilbert, AZ 85233-5615, USA

Manuel, Barry (Baseball Player)
Texas Rangers
805 Oak St
Mamou, LA 70554-2715, USA

Manuel, Charles F (Chuck) (Baseball
Player)
2931 Plantation Rd
Winter Haven, FL 33884-1233, USA

Manuel, Jerry (Baseball Player)
Detroit Tigers
4023 Greenview Dr
El Dorado Hills, CA 95762-7620, USA

Manuel, Lionel (Football Player)
New York Giants
827 E Cedar Dr
Chandler, AZ 85249-3319, USA

Manuel, Robert (Actor)
La Maison du Buisson
22-26 Rue Jules Regnier
Plaisir 78370, FRANCE

Manuelidis, Laura (Misc)
Yale University Medical School
Neuropathology Dept
New Haven, CT 06520, USA

Manusky, Greg (Football Player)
Washington Redskins
4939 Eastbourne Ct
San Jose, CA 95138-2124, USA

Manville, Dick (Baseball Player)
Boston Braves
1436 Lake Francis Dr
Apopka, FL 32712-2007, USA

Manwaring, Kirt (Baseball Player)
San Francisco Giants
20 Prospect Rdg
Horseheads, NY 14845-7988, USA

Manwaring, Kurt D (Baseball Player)
20 Prospect Rdg
Horseheads, NY 14845-7988, USA

Manz, Wolfgang (Musician)
Pasteuralle 55
Hanover 30655, GERMANY

Manza, Ralph
550 Hygeia Ave
Encinitas, CA 92024-2601, USA

Manzanero, Armando (Musician)
Pro Art
Paz Soidan 170
Of 903
San Isidro, Lima 27, PERU

Manzanillo, Josias (Baseball Player)
Boston Red Sox
274 Kennebec St
Mattapan, MA 02126-1106, USA

Manzarek, Ray (Musician)
Goldman & Knell
1801 Century Park E Ste 2160
Los Angeles, CA 90067-2343, USA

Manzi, Catello (Horse Racer)
1 Hickory Ln
Freehold, NJ 07728-1588, USA

Manzini, Baptiste (Football Player)
Philadelphia Eagles
903 Amelia St
Belle Vernon, PA 15012-2203, USA

Manzo, Joe (Football Player)
Detroit Lions
121 Riverside Ave Apt 1006
Medford, MA 02155-4649, USA

Manzoni, Giacomo (Composer)
Viale Papiniano 31
Milan 20123, ITALY

Mapes, Cliff
PO Box 872
Pryor, OK 74362-0872, USA

Maples, Marla (Actor)
c/o Staff Member *United Talent Agency
(UTA)*
9560 Wilshire Blvd Ste 500
Beverly Hills, CA 90212-2401, USA

Mapother, William (Actor)
c/o Staff Member *Diverse Talent Group*
1875 Century Park E Ste 2250
Los Angeles, CA 90067-2563, USA

Mara, Adele (Actor, Dancer)
1928 Mandeville Canyon Rd
Los Angeles, CA 90049-2225, USA

Mara, Ratu Sir Kamisese K T (President)
11 Ballery Road
Suva, FIJI

Marachuk, Steve
568 Hana Hwy
Paia, HI 96779-9732, USA

Maradona, Diego
Brandsen 805
Capital Federal 1161, ARGENTINA

Marak, Paul (Baseball Player)
Atlanta Braves
1211 Comanche Trl
Alamogordo, NM 88310-4010, USA

Maramorosch, Karl (Scientist)
1050 George St
New Brunswick, NJ 08901-1012, USA

Marangi, Gary (Football Player)
Buffalo Bills
26 Morton St
Port Jefferson Station, NY 11776-4013,
USA

Maraniss, David (Journalist)
Washington Post
Editorial Dept
1150 15th St NW
Washington, DC 20071-0001, USA

Maratos, Terry (Actor)
c/o Staff Member *Cage Group, The*
14724 Ventura Blvd Ste 505
Sherman Oaks, CA 91403-3505, USA

Maratos-Flier, Elfetheria (Doctor)
Joslin Diabetes Center
1 Joslin Pl
Boston, MA 02215-5394, USA

Marber, Patrick (Writer)
Judy Daish
2 Saint Charles Place
London W10 6EG, UNITED KINGDOM
(UK)

Marbury, Stephon (Basketball Player)
c/o Staff Member *New York Knicks*
4 Penn Plz
Madison Square Garden
New York, NY 10121-0004, USA

Marbut, Robert G (Publisher)
Argyle Communications
100 NE Loop #1400
San Antonio, TX 78216, USA

Marc, Alessandra (Opera Singer)
Columbia Artists Mgmt Inc
1790 Broadway Fl 6
New York, NY 10019-1412, USA

Marceau, Sophie (Actor)
Artmedia
20 Ave Rapp
Paris 75007, FRANCE

Marcelino, Mario
1418 N Highland Ave # 102
Los Angeles, CA 90028-7611, USA

March, Forbes (Actor)
c/o Staff Member *Innovative Artists (LA)*
1505 10th St
Santa Monica, CA 90401-2805, USA

March, Jane (Actor, Model)
Storm Model Mgmt
5 Jubilee Place
#100
London SW3 3TD, UNITED KINGDOM
(UK)

March, Joan
Whale Rock Ranch Rd.
Ojai, CA 93023, USA

March, Little Peggy (Musician)
Cape Entertainment
8432 NW 31st Ct
Sunrise, FL 33351-8901, USA

March, Peggy
1161 NW 76th Ave
Plantation, FL 33322-5120, USA

March, Stephanie (Actor)
c/o Carrie Byalick *I/D PR (NY)*
155 Spring St Fl 6
New York, NY 10012-5208, USA

Marchand, Guy
40 rue Francois 1er
Paris F-75008, FRANCE

Marchette, Josh
6500 Wilshire Blvd Ste 2200
Los Angeles, CA 90048-4942, USA

Marchetti, Gino J (Football Player)
Baltimore Colts
324 Devon Way
West Chester, PA 19380-6825, USA

Marchetti, Leo V (Misc)
Fraternal Order of Police
5615 Belair Rd
Baltimore, MD 21206-3619, USA

Marchibroda, Ted (Football Player)
Pittsburgh Steelers
90 Orchard Point Dr
Weems, VA 22576-2648, USA

Marchinko, Jhoni (Producer)
c/o Staff Member *United Talent Agency (UTA)*
9560 Wilshire Blvd Ste 500
Beverly Hills, CA 90212-2401, USA

Marchiol, Ken (Football Player)
New Orleans Saints
4705 S Helena Way
Aurora, CO 80015-1709, USA

Marchionne, Sergio (Business Person)
Fiat SpA
Via Nizza 250
Turin 10126, ITALY

Marchisano, Francesco Cardinal
(Religious Leader)
Cancelleria Apostolica Palazzo
Plazza Cancelleria 1
Rome 00186, ITALY

Marchlewski, Frank (Football Player)
Los Angeles Rams
428 Toledo Dr
Lower Burrell, PA 15068-3315, USA

Marchuk, Yevhen K (Prime Minister)
Verkovna Rada
M Hrushevskoho Str 5
Kiev 252008, UKRAINE

Marciano, David (Actor)
c/o Staff Member *Don Buchwald & Associates Inc (LA)*
6500 Wilshire Blvd Ste 2200
Los Angeles, CA 90048-4942, USA

Marciano, Rob (Anchor)
c/o Staff Member *CNN (Atlanta)*
1 Cnn Ctr NW
PO Box 105366
Atlanta, GA 30303-2762, USA

Marcikic, Ivan (Inventor, Physicist)
Geneva University
24 Rue du General Dufour
Geneva 1211, SWITZERLAND

Marcil, Vanessa (Actor)
c/o Adena Chawke *Greenlight Management*
1505 10th St
Santa Monica, CA 90401-2805, USA

Marcille (Pigford), Eva (Model, Reality TV Star)
c/o Staff Member *Abrams Artists Agency (LA)*
9200 W Sunset Blvd Ph 11
Los Angeles, CA 90069-3601, USA

Marcinkevicius, Iustinus M (Writer)
Mildos Str 33
#6
Vilnius 232055, LITHUANIA

Marcis, Dave (Race Car Driver)
Marcis Auto Racing
PO Box 645
Skyland, NC 28776-0645, USA

Marcis, Dave (Race Car Driver)
71 Beadle Road
Arden, NC 28704, USA

Marco, Gian (Musician)
c/o Staff Member *Creative Artists Agency LCC (CAA-LA)*
2000 Avenue Of The Stars
Los Angeles, CA 90067-4700, USA

Marcol, Czeslaw C (Chester) (Football Player)
gr
PO Box 466
Dollar Bay, MI 49922-0466, USA

Marcontell, Ed (Football Player)
St Louis Cardinals
PO Box 884
Rusk, TX 75785-0884, USA

Marcos (Musician)
East West America Records
75 Rockefeller Plz
New York, NY 10019-6908, USA

Marcos, Imelda
Leyte Providencia Dept
Tolosa Leyte, PHILIPPINES

Marcotte, Don (Hockey Player)
12 Cote St
Amesbury, MA 01913-3804, USA

Marcovicci, Andrea (Actor, Musician)
Donald Smith Promotions
1640 E 48th St #14U
New York, NY 10017, USA

Marcucci, Bob
10600 Holman Ave
Los Angeles, CA 90024-5960, USA

Marcum, Art (Writer)
c/o Staff Member *Nine Yards Entertainment*
8530 Wilshire Blvd Fl 5
Beverly Hills, CA 90211-3102, USA

Marcus, Bernard (Business Person)
Home Depot Inc
2455 Paces Ferry Rd SE
Atlanta, GA 30339-1834, USA

Marcus, Jurgen
Pestalozzistr. 23a
Munich D-80469, GERMANY

Marcus, Ken (Photographer)
6916 Melrose Ave
Los Angeles, CA 90038-3306, USA

Marcus, Rudolph A (Nobel Prize Laureate)
331 S Hill Ave
Pasadena, CA 91106-3405, USA

Marcus, Ruth B (Misc)
311 Saint Ronan St
New Haven, CT 06511-2328, USA

Marcus, Trula M (Actor)
The Agency
1800 Avenue Of The Stars Ste 400
Los Angeles, CA 90067-4206, USA

Mardall, Cyril L (Architect)
5 Boyne Terrace Mews
London W11 3LR, UNITED KINGDOM (UK)

Marden, Brice (Artist)
6 Saint Lukes Pl
New York, NY 10014-3974, USA

Marder, Barry
c/o Daniel A (Dan) Strone *Trident Media Group LLC*
41 Madison Ave Fl 36
New York, NY 10010-2257, USA

Marderian, Greg (Football Player)
Atlanta Falcons
10133 Crebs Ave
Northridge, CA 91324-1304, USA

Mardones, Benny (Musician)
Tony Cee
PO Box 410
Utica, NY 13503-0410, USA

Mare, Olindo (Football Player)
Miami Dolphins
1711 SE 13th St
Fort Lauderdale, FL 33316-2215, USA

Maree, Sydney (Athlete, Track Athlete)
2 Braxton Rd
Bryn Mawr, PA 19010-1029, USA

Maren, Elizabeth (Actor)
3126 Oakcrest Dr
Los Angeles, CA 90068-1856, USA

Maren, Jerry
3126 Oakcrest Dr
Los Angeles, CA 90068-1856, USA

Marentette, Leo (Baseball Player)
Detroit Tigers
33606 Beechwood St
Westland, MI 48185-3002, USA

Margal, Albert M (Prime Minister)
8 Hornsey Rise Gardens
London N19, UNITED KINGDOM (UK)

Margalit, Israela (Musician)
Columbia Artists Mgmt Inc
1790 Broadway Fl 6
New York, NY 10019-1412, USA

Margarita, Henry R (Football Player)
Chicago Bears
4 Drury Ln
Stoneham, MA 02180-3205, USA

Margeot, Jean Cardinal (Religious Leader)
Bonne Terre
Vacoas, MAURITIUS

Margera, Brandon (Bam) (Actor, Producer, Writer)
2 Grey Hawk Ln
Thornton, PA 19373-2000, USA

Margerum, Ken (Football Player)
Chicago Bears
University Of California
2200 University Ave # Dept
Berkeley, CA 94720-0001, USA

Margison, Richard (Opera Singer)
George Martynuk
352 7th Ave
New York, NY 10001-5012, USA

Margo, Philip (Musician)
American Mgmt
19948 Mayall St
Chatsworth, CA 91311-3522, USA

Margoliash, Emmanuel (Scientist)
554 Oakdale Ave
Glencoe, IL 60022-2043, USA

Margolin, Phillip (Writer)
c/o Jean V Naggar *Jean Naggar Literary Agency*
216 E 75th St Ste 1E
New York, NY 10021-2921, USA

Margolin, Stuart (Actor)
Three Owl Productions
Box 478
Ganges, BC V0S 1E0, CANADA

Margolis, Cindy (Actor, Model)
c/o Michael (Mike) Esterman *Esterman Entertainment*
214 Park Rd
Riva, MD 21140-1224, USA

Margolis, Lawrence S (Judge)
US Claims Court
717 Madison Pl NW
Washington, DC 20439-0001, USA

Margolyes, Miriam (Actor)
c/o Staff Member *Peters Fraser & Dunlop (PFD - UK)*
Drury House
34-43 Russell St
London WC2B 5HA, UNITED KINGDOM (UK)

Margoneri, Joe (Baseball Player)
New York Giants
341 Turkeytown Rd
West Newton, PA 15089-1850, USA

Margoyles, Miriam (Actor)
P F D Drury House
34-43 Russell St
London WC2B 5HA, UNITED KINGDOM (UK)

Margrave, John L (Misc)
4511 Verone St
Bellaire, TX 77401-5513, USA

Margrethe II (Royalty)
Amalienborg Palace
Copenhgen K 1257, DENMARK

Margulies, Donald (Writer)
Yale University
English Dept
New Haven, CT 06520, USA

Margulies, James H (Jimmy) (Cartoonist, Editor)
Hackensack Record
150 River St
Editorial Dept
Hackensack, NJ 07601-7110, USA

Margulies, Julianna (Actor)
c/o Aleen Keshishian *Brillstein-Grey Entertainment*
9150 Wilshire Blvd Ste 350
Beverly Hills, CA 90212-3453, USA

Mariago, Cesare
19 788 Citadel Dr.#120
Pt. Coquitlam, BC V3C 6G, CANADA

Mariam, Mengistu Haile (President)
PO Box 1536
Gunhill Enclave
Harare, ZIMBABWE

Mariategui, Sandro (Prime Minister)
Ave Ramirez Gaston 375
Miraflores, Lima, PERU

Marie, Aurelius J B L (President)
Zicack
Portsmouth, DOMINICAN REPUBLIC

Marie, Constance (Actor)
c/o Staff Member *Kass & Stokes Management*
9229 W Sunset Blvd Ste 504
Los Angeles, CA 90069-3405, USA

Marie, Lisa (Actor, Model)
c/o Staff Member *William Morris Agency (WMA-LA)*
1 William Morris Pl
Beverly Hills, CA 90212-4261, USA

Marie, Princess (Royalty)
Schloss Vaduz
Vaduz 9490, LIECHTENSTEIN

Marie, Rose (Actor)
c/o Leanna Levy *Cassell-Levy Inc*
843 N Sycamore Ave
Los Angeles, CA 90038-3391, USA

Marie, Teena (Musician)
c/o Staff Member *Richard De La Font Agency*
4845 S Sheridan Rd Ste 505
Tulsa, OK 74145-5719, USA

Marienthal, Eli (Actor)
c/o Lisa Gallant *International Creative Management (ICM-LA)*
10250 Constellation Blvd
Los Angeles, CA 90067-6200, USA

Marienthal, Eric (Musician)
15030 Ventura Blvd # 710
Sherman Oaks, CA 91403-5470, USA

Marillion (Musician)
c/o Staff Member *Paradigm (Monterey)*
509 Hartnell St
Monterey, CA 93940-2825, USA

Marilyn
33-34 Cleveland St.
London, ENGLAND W1, UNITED KINGDOM (UK)

Marimow, William K (Journalist)
1942 Panama St
Philadelphia, PA 19103-6610, USA

Marin, Christian
27 rue de Richelieu
Paris F-75001, FRANCE

Marin, Jack (Basketball Player)
3909 Regent Rd
Durham, NC 27707-5311, USA

Marin, Maguy (Choreographer)
Compagnie Maguy Marin
Place Salvador Allende
Creteil 94000, FRANCE

Marin, Richard A (Cheech) (Actor, Comedian)
c/o Ben Feigin *Nine Yards Entertainment*
8530 Wilshire Blvd Fl 5
Beverly Hills, CA 90211-3102, USA

Marinaro, Ed (Football Player)
Minnesota Vikings
1466 N Doheny Dr
Los Angeles, CA 90069-1143, USA

Marinin, Maxim (Figure Skater)
c/o Staff Member *Champions on Ice*
3500 W 80th St
Tom Collins Enterprises Inc
Minneapolis, MN 55431-1068, USA

Marino, Dan (Football Player)
c/o Staff Member *Miami Dolphins*
7500 SW 30th St
Davie, FL 33314-1020, USA

Marino, Ken (Actor)
I F A Talent Agency
8730 W Sunset Blvd Ste 490
Los Angeles, CA 90069-2248, USA

Marinovich, Marv (Football Player)
Oakland Raiders
Prowess Tech 29961
1/2 Santa Margarita Pkwy
Rancho Santa Margari, CA 92688, USA

Marinovich, Todd (Football Player)
Oakland Raiders
132 E Balboa Blvd
Newport Beach, CA 92661-1118, USA

Marinus, Martin
Postbus 724
AS Gouda 2800, THE NETHERLANDS

Mario (Musician)
c/o Staff Member *J Records (Division of BMG Entertainment)*
745 5th Ave Fl 6
New York, NY 10151-0099, USA

Mario, Ernest (Business Person)
ALZA Corp
1950 Charleston Rd
Mountain View, CA 94043-1218, USA

Marion, Brock E (Football Player)
Dallas Cowboys
10 NW 42nd St
Ocala, FL 34475-1503, USA

Marion, Frank (Football Player)
New York Giants
15920 SW 99th Ct
Miami, FL 33157-1615, USA

Marion, Fred (Football Player)
New England Patriots
2725 Canoe Creek Rd
Saint Cloud, FL 34772-6502, USA

Marion, Martin W (Marty) (Baseball Player)
St Louis Cardinals
8 Forcee Ln
Saint Louis, MO 63124-1245, USA

Marion, Shawn (Basketball Player)
Phoenix Suns
201 E Jefferson St
Phoenix, AZ 85004-2412, USA

Mariotti, Ray (Editor)
Austin American-Statesman
166 E Riverside Dr
Editorial Dept
Austin, TX 78704, USA

Maris, Ada
10100 Santa Monica Blvd Ste 2500
Los Angeles, CA 90067-4116, USA

Marisol (Artist)
Marlborough Gallery
40 W 57th St
New York, NY 10019-4069, USA

Mariucci, Steve (Coach, Football Coach)
Detroit Lions
222 Republic Dr
Allen Park, MI 48101-3650, USA

Mariye, Lily (Director, Writer)
c/o Staff Member *Bauman Redanty & Shaul Agency*
5757 Wilshire Blvd Ste 473
Los Angeles, CA 90036-3632, USA

Mark, Albert J (Beauty Pageant Winner)
Miss American Pageant
1325 Broadway
Atlantic City, NJ 08401, USA

Mark, Bruce (Artist, Ballerina, Director)
Boston Ballet Co
19 Clarendon St
Boston, MA 02116-6100, USA

Mark, Greg (Football Player)
Miami Dolphins
2920 Washington St
Miami, FL 33133-3825, USA

Mark, Hans M (Educator, Government Official, Physicist)
1715 Scenic Dr
Austin, TX 78703, USA

Mark, Marky
63 Pilgrim Rd
Braintree, MA 02184-6003, USA

Mark, Mary Ellen (Photographer)
143 Price St
New York, NY 10012, USA

Mark, Reuben (Business Person)
Colgate-Palmolive Co
300 Park Ave
New York, NY 10022-7499, USA

Mark, Robert (Government Official, Lawyer)
Esher
Surrey KT10 8LU, UNITED KINGDOM (UK)

Mark Green, Mark
c/o *Brewco Motorsports Inc*
PO Box 3453
Dana Point, CA 92629-8453, USA

Markaryants, Vladimir S (Government Official)
Council of Ministers
Yerevan, ARMENIA

Markbreit, Jerry (Football Player)
NFL Referee
9739 Keystone Ave
Skokie, IL 60076-1136, USA

Marken, William R (Editor)
Sunset Magazine
80 Willow Rd
Editorial Dept
Menlo Park, CA 94025-3691, USA

Marker, Steve (Musician)
Borman Entertainment
1250 6th St Ste 401
Santa Monica, CA 90401-1638, USA

Markey, Lucille P (Misc)
18 Lagorce Cir
La Gorce Island
Miami Beach, FL 33141-4520, USA

Markham, Dale (Football Player)
New York Giants
613 Stafford Rd
Janesville, WI 53546-1918, USA

Markham, Monte (Actor)
PO Box 607
Malibu, CA 90265-0607, USA

Markie, Biz (Musician)
c/o Staff Member *Paradigm (Monterey)*
509 Hartnell St
Monterey, CA 93940-2825, USA

Markland, Jeff (Football Player)
Pittsburgh Steelers
1331 W Cinnabar Ave
Phoenix, AZ 85021-2251, USA

Markle, Peter F (Director)
7510 W Sunset Blvd # 509
Los Angeles, CA 90046-3408, USA

Markovich, Mark (Football Player)
San Diego Chargers
9825 N Townsend Dr
Peoria, IL 61615-1389, USA

Markowitz, Barry (Cinematographer)
225 W 83rd St Apt 20G
New York, NY 10024-4964, USA

Markowitz, Harry M (Nobel Prize Laureate)
1010 Turquoise St Ste 245
San Diego, CA 92109-1266, USA

Markowitz, Michael (Artist)
23rd Street Gallery
3747 23rd St
San Francisco, CA 94114-3407, USA

Markowitz, Robert (Director, Producer)
11521 Amanda Dr
Studio City, CA 91604-4144, USA

Marks, Chandler
PO Box 184
Franklin, TN 37065-0184, USA

Markstein, Gary (Cartoonist, Editor)
Milwaukee Journal
333 W State St
Editorial Dept
Milwaukee, WI 53203-1309, USA

Markwart, Nevin (Hockey Player)
210 Cushing Hill Rd
Hanover, MA 02339-1192, USA

Marley, Damian (Musician)
c/o Staff Member *William Morris Agency (WMA-LA)*
1 William Morris Pl
Beverly Hills, CA 90212-4261, USA

Marley, Ziggy (Musician, Songwriter, Writer)
Jack's Hill
Kingston, JAMAICA

Marlin, Sterling (Race Car Driver)
995 Mahon Rd
Columbia, TN 38401-8808, USA

Marlow, Jean
32 Exeter Rd.
London, ENGLAND NW2, UNITED KINGDOM (UK)

Marlowe, Scott
6399 Wilshire Blvd Ste 414
Los Angeles, CA 90048-5716, USA

Marm, Walter J Jr (War Hero)
PO Box 2017
Fremont, NC 27830-1217, USA

Marnie, Larry (Coach, Football Coach)
Arizona State University
Athletic Dept
Tempe, AZ 85287-0001, USA

Marohn, William D (Business Person)
Whirlpool Corp
2000 N State St
RR 63
Benton Harbor, MI 49022, USA

Marolewski, Fred (Baseball Player)
St Louis Cardinals
15705 W Waterford Ln
Manhattan, IL 60442-8160, USA

Maron, Marc (Comedian)
c/o Staff Member *United Talent Agency (UTA)*
9560 Wilshire Blvd Ste 500
Beverly Hills, CA 90212-2401, USA

Marone, Lou (Baseball Player)
Pittsburgh Pirates
10851 Carbet Pl
San Diego, CA 92124-2042, USA

Maroney, Daniel V Jr (Misc)
Amalgamated Transil Union
5025 Wisconsin Ave NW
Washington, DC 20016-4139, USA

Maroney, Kelli (Actor)
Peter Strain
5455 Wilshire Blvd Ste 1812
Los Angeles, CA 90036-4268, USA

Maroon 5 (Actor, Music Group)
c/o Erin Culley-LaChapelle *Creative Artists Agency LCC (CAA-LA)*
2000 Avenue Of The Stars
Los Angeles, CA 90067-4700, USA

Maroth, Mike (Baseball Player)
Detroit Tigers
12566 Aldershot Ln
Windermere, FL 34786-6610, USA

Marotte, Carl
438 Queen E
Toronto, ON M5A 1, CANADA

Marotte, J Gilles (Hockey Player)
1759 Notre Dameo
Victoriaville, PQ G6A 7M4, CANADA

Maroulis, Constantine (Musician)
c/o Staff Member *American Idol*
7800 Beverly Blvd # 251
Los Angeles, CA 90036-2112, USA

Marquand, Christian
45 rue de Bellechasse
Paris F-75007, FRANCE

Marquardt, Bridget (Model, Reality TV Star)
Playboy Mansion
10236 Charing Cross Rd
Los Angeles, CA 90024-1815, USA

Marques, Gabriel Garcia
Fuego 144
Pedregal de San Angel Mexico DF, MEXICO

Marques, Maria Elena
Nubes 723 Pedregal
Mexico DF, MEXICO

Marquette, Chris (Actor)
c/o Holly Williams *Williams Unlimited*
5010 Buffalo Ave
Sherman Oaks, CA 91423-1414, USA

Marquez, Alfonso (Baseball Player)
4102 S Skyline Ct
Gilbert, AZ 85297-9668, USA

Marquez, Raul -
14611 Maisemore Rd
Houston, TX 77015-1772, USA

Marquis, Bob (Baseball Player)
Cincinnati Reds
3755 Delaware St Apt 303
Beaumont, TX 77706-7934, USA

Marquis, Jason (Baseball Player)
Atlanta Braves
3558 Piedmont Rd NE
Atlanta, GA 30305-1513, USA

Marquis, Roger (Baseball Player)
Baltimore Orioles
5 Lindbergh Ave
Holyoke, MA 01040-1905, USA

Marraccini, Matt (Actor)
c/o Cynthia Campos-Greenberg *Anthem Entertainment*
6100 Wilshire Blvd Ste 1170
Los Angeles, CA 90048-5116, USA

Marrero, Eli (Baseball Player)
St Louis Cardinals
10230 SW 64th St
Miami, FL 33173-2807, USA

Marriner, Neville
Academy Saint Martin in Fields
Raine St
London E1 9RG, UNITED KINGDOM (UK)

Marriott, Craig (Actor)
c/o Staff Member *Nickelodeon UK*
PO Box 6425
LONDON W1A 6UR, UNITED KINGDOM (UK)

Marriott, Evan (Reality TV Star)
c/o Michael (Mike) Esterman *Esterman Entertainment*
214 Park Rd
Riva, MD 21140-1224, USA

Marriott, J Willard Jr (Business Person)
Marriott International
10400 Fernwood Rd
Bethesda, MD 20817-1102, USA

Marriott, Richard E (Business Person)
Host Marriott Corp
10400 Fernwood Rd
Bethesda, MD 20817-1118, USA

Marro, Anthony J (Editor)
Newsday
235 Pinelawn Rd
Editorial Dept
Melville, NY 11747-4250, USA

Marron, Donald B (Financier)
UBS PaineWebber
1285 6th Ave
New York, NY 10019-6096, USA

Marrone, Doug (Football Player)
Miami Dolphins
Georgia Tech 150 Bobby Dodd Way
Attn Athletic Dept
Atlanta, GA 30313, USA

Marrow, Tracy (Ice T) (Musician)
c/o Staff Member *United Talent Agency (UTA)*
9560 Wilshire Blvd Ste 500
Beverly Hills, CA 90212-2401, USA

Mars, Forrest E. Jr. (Business Person)
Mars Inc
6885 Elm St
McLean, VA 22101-6031, USA

Mars, Kenneth (Actor)
International Creative Mgmt
8942 Wilshire Blvd # 219
Beverly Hills, CA 90211-1908, USA

Marsalis, Branford (Composer, Musician)
Wilkins Mgmt
323 Broadway
Cambridge, MA 02139-1801, USA

Marsalis, James (Football Player)
Kansas City Chiefs
101 Royal Oak Ln
Kathleen, GA 31047-2149, USA

Marsalis, Wynton (Composer, Musician)
Management Ark
116 Village Blvd Ste 200
Princeton, NJ 08540-5700, USA

Marschall, Marita (Actor)
Agentur Alexander
Lamontstr 9
Munich 81679, GERMANY

Marsden, Bernie (Musician)
Int'l Talent Booking
27A Floral St
#300
London WC2E 9DQ, UNITED KINGDOM (UK)

Marsden, Freddie (Musician)
Barry Collins
21A Cliftown Road
Southend-on-Sea
Essex SS1 1AB, UNITED KINGDOM (UK)

Marsden, Gerald (Gerry) (Musician)
Barry Collins
21A Cliftown Rd
Southend-on-Sea
Essex SS1 1AB, UNITED KINGDOM (UK)

Marsden, James (Actor)
c/o Andrea Pett-Joseph *Brillstein-Grey Entertainment*
9150 Wilshire Blvd Ste 350
Beverly Hills, CA 90212-3453, USA

Marsden, Jason (Actor)
c/o Staff Member *Cunningham Escott Slevin & Doherty (LA)*
10635 Santa Monica Blvd Ste 130
Los Angeles, CA 90025-8306, USA

Marsden, Matthew (Actor)
c/o Staff Member *Creative Artists Agency LCC (CAA-LA)*
2000 Avenue Of The Stars
Los Angeles, CA 90067-4700, USA

Marsden, Roy (Actor)
London Mgmt
2-4 Noel St
London W1V 3RB, UNITED KINGDOM (UK)

Marsh, Brad (Hockey Player)
Ottawa Senators
1000 Palladium Dr
Kanata, ON K2V 1A4, CANADA

Marsh, Carol
7 Leicester Pl. #100
London, ENGLAND WC2H 7B1, UNITED KINGDOM (UK)

Marsh, Frank (Baseball Player)
Birmingham Black Barons
806 Palmetto Street Apt C
Mobile, AL 36603, USA

Marsh, Fred (Baseball Player)
Cleveland Indians
14632 Hereford Rd
Corry, PA 16407-8944, USA

Marsh, Graham (Golfer)
112 Pga Tour Blvd
Ponte Vedra Beach, FL 32082-3046, USA

Marsh, Henry (Athlete, Track Athlete)
General Delivery
Bountiful, UT 84010-9999, USA

Marsh, Jean (Actor)
c/o Staff Member *London Management*
2-4 Noel St
London W1V 3RB, UNITED KINGDOM (UK)

Marsh, Jodie (Model)
c/o Staff Member *Page 3*
News International Newspapers Ltd
1 Virginia St
London E98 1XY, UNITED KINGDOM (UK)

Marsh, Julian (DJ)
c/o Staff Member *Diva Central Inc*
7510 W Sunset Blvd Ste 1445
Los Angeles, CA 90046-3408, USA

Marsh, Kym (Musician)
c/o Staff Member *Safe Management*
111 Guildford Rd
Lightwater
Surrey GU18 5RA, UNITED KINGDOM (UK)

Marsh, Linda (Actor)
170 W End Ave Apt 22P
New York, NY 10023-5414, USA

Marsh, Little Peggy
8236 NW 9th St
Plantation, FL 33324-1208, USA

Marsh, Marian (Actor)
PO Box 1
Palm Desert, CA 92261-0001, USA

Marsh, Michael (Mike) (Athlete, Track Athlete)
2425 Holly Hall St # 152
Houston, TX 77054-3968, USA

Marsh, Mike
2847 Indian Trail Dr.
Missouri City, TX 77489, USA

Marsh, Miles L (Business Person)
Fort James Corp
1919 S Broadway
Green Bay, WI 54304-4905, USA

Marsh, Randy (Baseball Player)
3023 Winterbourne Rd
Edgewood, KY 41017-9683, USA

Marsh, Robert T (Business Person, General)
6659 Avignon Blvd
Falls Church, VA 22043-1724, USA

Marsh, Thomas (Baseball Player)
Philadelphia Phillies
3460 Canal Ave
Toledo, OH 43609, USA

Marsh of Mannington, Richard W (Government Official)
House of Lords
Westminster
London SW1A 0PW, UNITED KINGDOM (UK)

Marshal-Green, Logan (Actor)
c/o Nicholas Frenkel *3 Arts Entertainment Inc*
9460 Wilshire Blvd Ste 700
Beverly Hills, CA 90212-2713, USA

Marshall, Albert L (Ben) (Hockey Player)
9603 166th Street Ct E
Puyallup, WA 98375-2203, USA

Marshall, Amanda (Actor)
Macklam Feldman Mgmt
1505 W 2nd Ave
#200
Vancouver, BC V6H 3Y4, CANADA

Marshall, Amanda (Musician)
c/o Rob Light *Creative Artists Agency LCC (CAA-LA)*
2000 Avenue Of The Stars
Los Angeles, CA 90067-4700, USA

Marshall, Amanda (Reality TV Star)
c/o Staff Member *Bachelor, The*
15301 Ventura Blvd Bldg E
Sherman Oaks, CA 91403-5885, USA

Marshall, Arthur (Football Player)
Denver Broncos
4821 Rocky Shoals Cir
Evans, GA 30809-7042, USA

Marshall, Barry J (Scientist)
Queen Elizabeth II Med Center
Nedlands, WA 6009, AUSTRALIA

Marshall, Brian (Musician)
Agency Group
1776 Broadway Ste 430
New York, NY 10019-2002, USA

Marshall, Carolyn M (Religious Leader)
United Methodist Church
204 N Newlin St
Veedersburg, IN 47987-1358, USA

Marshall, Charles (Football Player)
New York Jets
4605 Preston Bend Dr
Arlington, TX 76016-1970, USA

Marshall, Charlie (Baseball Player)
St Louis Cardinals
1 Radcliffe Ct
Wilmington, DE 19804-1346, USA

Marshall, Clarence (Baseball Player)
New York Yankees
27642 Susan Beth Way Unit I
Saugus, CA 91350-1797, USA

Marshall, Dale Rogers (Educator)
Whealon COllege
President's Office
Norton, MA 02766, USA

Marshall, Dave (Baseball Player)
San Francisco Giants
4802 E Centralia St
Long Beach, CA 90808-1312, USA

Marshall, David (Football Player)
Cleveland Browns
2740 Towne Village Dr
Duluth, GA 30097-7614, USA

Marshall, Donyell (Basketball Player)
12440 SE 27th St
Kent, WA 98030, USA

Marshall, Ed (Football Player)
Cincinnati Bengals
4820 Delwood St Apt D2
Corpus Christi, TX 78413-5103, USA

Marshall, F Ray (Secretary)
PO Box Y
Austin, TX 78713-8925, USA

Marshall, Frank W (Filmmaker, Producer)
Kennedy/Marshall Co
650 N Bronson Ave # 100
Los Angeles, CA 90004-1404, USA

Marshall, Garry K (Actor, Director)
c/o Staff Member *Henderson Productions*
4252 W Riverside Dr
Burbank, CA 91505-4145, USA

Marshall, James (Actor)
1833 Rulgers Dr
Thousands Oaks, CA 91360, USA

Marshall, James L (Jim) (Football Player)
Minnesota Vikings
7250 York Ave S Apt 101
Minneapolis, MN 55435-4419, USA

Marshall, Jim (Baseball Player)
Baltimore Orioles
19700 N 76th St Apt 1119
Scottsdale, AZ 85255-4787, USA

Marshall, Jim C (Football Player)
New Orleans Saints
5258 Brookleigh Dr
Jackson, MS 39272-6009, USA

Marshall, Keith (Baseball Player)
Kansas City Royals
RR 1
Woodhull, NY 14898, USA

Marshall, Ken (Actor)
Marshall Artists
345 N Maple Dr # 302
Beverly Hills, CA 90210-3869, USA

Marshall, Kris (Actor)
c/o Claire Maroussas *International Creative Management (ICM-UK)*
Oxford House
76 Oxford St
London W1N OAX, UNITED KINGDOM (UK)

Marshall, Kristal (Wrestler)
c/o Staff Member *World Wrestling Entertainment (WWE)*
1241 E Main St
Stamford, CT 06902-3520, USA

Marshall, Larry (Football Player)
Kansas City Chiefs
4605 SW Hickory Ln
Blue Springs, MO 64015-4524, USA

Marshall, Leonard (Football Player)
New York Giants
21756 Marigot Dr
Boca Raton, FL 33428-4826, USA

Marshall, Margaret A (Opera Singer)
Woodside
Main St
Gargunnock, Stirling FKS 3BP, SCOTLAND

Marshall, Michael A (Mike) (Baseball Player)
Albany-Colonie Diamond Dogs
Heritage Park
Albany, PA 12211, USA

Marshall, Michael G (Mike) (Baseball Player)
Detroit Tigers
38313 Vinson Ave
Zephyrhills, FL 33542-5946, USA

Marshall, Mike
4436 Plum St
Zephyrhills, FL 33542-7846, USA

Marshall, Mike (Baseball Player)
Los Angeles Dodgers
12 Madoch Ct
Deer Park, IL 60010-3708, USA

Marshall, Patricia
807 N Alpine Dr
Beverly Hills, CA 90210-2901, USA

Marshall, Paula (Actor)
1505 10th St
Santa Monica, CA 90401-2805, USA

Marshall, Penny (Actor, Director)
c/o Staff Member *Parkway Productions*
7095 Hollywood Blvd Ste 1009
Hollywood, CA 90028-8912, USA

Marshall, Peter (Television Host)
16714 Oak View Dr
Encino, CA 91436-3238, USA

Marshall, Rob (Director)
Gendler & Kelly
450 N Roxbury Dr
Beverly Hills, CA 90210-4232, USA

Marshall, Scott (Actor, Director)
c/o Staff Member *Creative Artists Agency LCC (CAA-LA)*
2000 Avenue Of The Stars
Los Angeles, CA 90067-4700, USA

Marshall, Theda (Baseball Player)
708 E Phillips Dr N
Littleton, CO 80122-2864, USA

Marshall, W W (Bones) (General, War Hero)
1517 Ehupua Pl
Honolulu, HI 96821-1468, USA

Marshall, Whit (Football Player)
Philadelphia Eagles
2218 Riada Dr NW
Atlanta, GA 30305-3916, USA

Marshall, Wilber B (Football Player)
Chicago Bears
4553 Sir Page Ln
Titusville, FL 32796-1444, USA

Marshall, Willard
204 Main St
Fort Lee, NJ 07024-5702, USA

Marshall of Knightsbridge, Colin M (Business Person)
British Airways
Heathrow Airport
Hounslow
Middx TW6 2JA, UNITED KINGDOM (UK)

Marshall Tucker Band
100 W Putnam Ave
Greenwich, CT 06830-5342, USA

Marsters, James (Actor)
c/o Staff Member *Himber Entertainment Inc*
15760 Ventura Blvd Ste 700
Encino, CA 91436-3016, USA

Marston, Joshua (Director, Writer)
c/o Cliff Roberts *William Morris Agency (WMA-LA)*
1 William Morris Pl
Beverly Hills, CA 90212-4261, USA

Marston, Natalie Elizabeth (Actor)
c/o Darryl Marshak *Marshak/Zachary Company, The*
8840 Wilshire Blvd Fl 1
Beverly Hills, CA 90211-2606, USA

Marston, Nathanial (Actor)
c/o Staff Member *Donegan Entertainment*
129 W 27th St
New York, NY 10001-6206, USA

Marston, Nathaniel (Actor)
c/o Staff Member *One Life to Live*
56 W 66th St
New York, NY 10023-6225, USA

Marta, Lynn
4342 Lankershim Blvd
North Hollywood, CA 91602-2745, USA

Marte, Judy (Actor)
c/o Michael Cooper *William Morris Agency (WMA-LA)*
1 William Morris Pl
Beverly Hills, CA 90212-4261, USA

Martel, Arlene (Actor)
2109 S Wilbur Ave
Walla Walla, WA 99362-9048, USA

Martell, Donna
PO Box 3335
Granada Hills, CA 91394-0335, USA

Martens, Wilfried (Prime Minister)
Europese Volkspartij
16 Rue de la Victoire
Brussels 1060, BELGIUM

Martha, Paul (Football Player)
Pittsburgh Steelers
110 Riding Trail Ln
Pittsburgh, PA 15215-1500, USA

Marti, Benita (Actor)
c/o Staff Member *Select Artists Ltd (CA-Valley Office)*
PO Box 4359
Burbank, CA 91503-4359, USA

Martika (Musician)
Entertainment Artists
2409 21st Ave S Ste 100
Nashville, TN 37212-5317, USA

Martin, Aaron (Football Player)
Los Angeles Rams
3605 Seth Ct
Springdale, MD 20774-5408, USA

Martin, Agnes B (Artist)
414 Placilas Road
Taos, NM 87571, USA

Martin, Al (Baseball Player)
Pittsburgh Pirates
11000 N 77th Pl Unit 1005
Scottsdale, AZ 85260-5599, USA

Martin, Alastair B (Misc)
Bessemer Trust Co
630 5th Ave
New York, NY 10111-0100, USA

Martin, Albert C (Architect)
Albert C Martin Assoc
811 W 7th St Ste 800
Los Angeles, CA 90017-3419, USA

Martin, Amos (Football Player)
Minnesota Vikings
209 Townepark Cir Ste 100
Louisville, KY 40243-2323, USA

Martin, Andrea (Actor)
c/o Staff Member *Innovative Artists (LA)*
1505 10th St
Santa Monica, CA 90401-2805, USA

Martin, Ann (Correspondent)
KCBS-TV
6121 W Sunset Blvd
News Dept
Los Angeles, CA 90028-6493, USA

Martin, Ann M (Writer)
c/o Staff Member *Scholastic Entertainment*
557 Broadway
New York, NY 10012-3999, USA

Martin, Babe (Baseball Player)
St Louis Browns
4438 E Fort Lowell Rd
Tucson, AZ 85712-1107, USA

Martin, Billy (Football Player)
Chicago Bears
6740 Polo Dr
Cumming, GA 30040-5725, USA

Martin, Billy (Musician)
c/o Brian Greenbaum *Creative Artists Agency LCC (CAA-LA)*
2000 Avenue Of The Stars
Los Angeles, CA 90067-4700, USA

Martin, Blanche (Football Player)
New York Titans
2022 Lindy Dr
Lansing, MI 48917-9726, USA

Martin, Boyce F Jr (Judge)
US Court of Appeals
601 W Broadway
US Courthouse
Louisville, KY 40202-2238, USA

Martin, Brian (Athlete)
777 San Antonio Rd Apt 132
Palo Alto, CA 94303-4858, USA

Martin, Casey
PO Box 109601
Palm Beach Gardens, FL 33410-9601, USA

Martin, Chris (Actor)
c/o Paul Nicholls *Artistry Management*
525 Westbourne Dr
West Hollywood, CA 90048-1913, USA

Martin, Chris (Musician)
Network Mgmt
1650 W 2nd Ave
Vancouver, BC V6J 4R3, CANADA

Martin, Christy (Boxer)
1203 Foxtree Trl
Apopka, FL 32712-3030, USA

Martin, Curtis (Football Player)
New York Jets
1000 Fullon Ave
Hempstead, NY 11550, USA

Martin, Dave (Chef)
c/o Staff Member *Magical Elves Inc*
453 S Spring St
Los Angeles, CA 90013-2013, USA

Martin, Dave (Football Player)
Kansas City Chiefs
9306 E Berry Ave
Greenwood Village, CO 80111-3509,
USA

Martin, David (Correspondent)
CBS-TV
2020 M St NW
News Dept
Washington, DC 20036-3304, USA

Martin, Demetri (Comedian)
c/o Staff Member *International Creative
Management (ICM-LA)*
10250 Constellation Blvd
Los Angeles, CA 90067-6200, USA

Martin, Denise B (Editor)
MOney Magazine
Editorial Dept
Time-Life Building
New York, NY 10020, USA

Martin, Dewey
1371 E. Ave. De Los Arboles
Thousand Oaks, CA 91360, USA

Martin, Dick (Actor, Comedian)
30765 Pacific Coast Hwy # 103
Malibu, CA 90265-3646, USA

Martin, Don (Coach, Football Coach,
Football Player)
New England Patriots
1220 Harbor Bay Pkwy
Oakland Raiders Attn Coaching Staff
Alameda, CA 94502-6501, USA

Martin, Doug (Golfer)
1406 Meadowlake Way
Union, KY 41091-7118, USA

Martin, Duane (Actor)
Paul Konner
9300 Wilshire Blvd Ste 555
Beverly Hills, CA 90212-3211, USA

Martin, Ed (Baseball Player)
Philadelphia Stars
6666 Brookmont Ter Apt 407
Nashville, TN 37205-4622, USA

Martin, Ed F (Actor)
c/o Staff Member *Talent Syndicate, LLC,
The (LA)*
1680 Vine St Ste 614
Los Angeles, CA 90028-8833, USA

Martin, Edward H (Admiral)
729 Guadalupe Ave
Coronado, CA 92118-2314, USA

Martin, Eric (Football Player)
New Orleans Saints
111 Windfall Pl
Clinton, MS 39056-6072, USA

Martin, Eric Band
PO Box 5952
San Francisco, CA 94101, USA

Martin, Gene (Baseball Player)
Washington Senators
133 Winchester Dr
Leesburg, GA 31763-5064, USA

Martin, George (Football Player)
New York Giants
50 Cheshire Ln
Ringwood, NJ 07456-2743, USA

Martin, Greg (Musician)
Mitchell Fox Mgmt
212 3rd Ave N Ste 301
Nashville, TN 37201-1632, USA

Martin, Gregory S (General)
Commander
US Air Forces Europe
Ramstein Air Base
APO, AE 09094, USA

Martin, Helen
1440 N Fairfax Ave Apt 109
West Hollywood, CA 90046-3939, USA

Martin, Henry R (Cartoonist)
1382 Newtown Langhorne Rd # G206
Newtown, PA 18940-2401, USA

Martin, J C (Baseball Player)
Chicago White Sox
112 Oakmont Ct
Advance, NC 27006-7097, USA

Martin, Jacques (Coach)
Florida Panthers
1 Panther Pkwy
Sunrise, FL 33323-5315, USA

Martin, James G (Governor)
Carolina Medical Center
PO Box 32861
Charlotte, NC 28232-2861, USA

Martin, Jeanne
613 N Linden Dr
Beverly Hills, CA 90210-3223, USA

Martin, Jerry (Baseball Player)
Philadelphia Phillies
109 Chelton Ct
Columbia, SC 29212-8522, USA

Martin, Jesse L (Actor)
c/o Bob McGowan *McGowan
Management*
8733 W Sunset Blvd Ste 103
W Hollywood, CA 90069-2241, USA

Martin, Joe (Cartoonist)
Weederman Grafix
C/O Neatly Chiseled Features
1870 Loramoor Lane
Lake Geneva, WI 53147, USA

Martin, John H (Educator)
JHM Corp
3930 Rca Blvd # 3240
Palm Beach Gardens, FL 33410-4267,
USA

Martin, Judith (Miss Manners) (Journalist)
1651 Harvard St NW
Washington, DC 20009-3702, USA

Martin, Kellie (Actor)
5918 Van Nuys Blvd
Van Nuys, CA 91401-3623, USA

Martin, Kelvin (Football Player)
Dallas Cowboys
1008 Briar Ridge Dr
Keller, TX 76248-8369, USA

Martin, Kenyon (Basketball Player)
Denver Nuggets
1000 Chopper Cir
Pepsi Center
Denver, CO 80204-5805, USA

Martin, LeRoy (Government Official,
Lawyer)
Chicago Police Dept
Superintendent's Office
Chicago, IL 60602, USA

Martin, Lynn M (Secretary)
171 Willabay Dr
Williams Bay, WI 53191-9673, USA

Martin, Maria (Actor)
c/o Staff Member *Select Artists Ltd (CA-
Valley Office)*
PO Box 4359
Burbank, CA 91503-4359, USA

Martin, Marsha P (Financier)
Farm Credit Administration
1501 Farm Credit Dr
McLean, VA 22102-5090, USA

Martin, Max
c/o Staff Member *Innovative Artists (LA)*
1505 10th St
Santa Monica, CA 90401-2805, USA

Martin, Medeski (Musician)
c/o Staff Member *Paradigm (Monterey)*
509 Hartnell St
Monterey, CA 93940-2825, USA

Martin, Mike (Baseball Player)
US Olympic Team
1006 Lovers Leap Rd
Kingston Springs, TN 37082-9269, USA

Martin, Millicent (Actor, Musician)
London Mgmt
2-4 Noel St
London W1V 3RB, UNITED KINGDOM
(UK)

Martin, Morrie (Baseball Player)
Brooklyn Dodgers
1786 Pottery Rd
Washington, MO 63090-4189, USA

Martin, Nan (Actor)
33604 Pacific Coast Hwy
Malibu, CA 90265-2311, USA

Martin, Paul (Baseball Player)
Pittsburgh Pirates
1529 33rd St
San Diego, CA 92102-1609, USA

Martin, Paul (Government Official)
Finance Department
140 O'Connor St
Ottawa, ON K1A 0G5, CANADA

Martin, Preston (Financier, Government
Official)
1130 N Lake Shore Dr Apt 4E
Chicago, IL 60611-1048, USA

Martin, R Bruce (Misc)
University of Virginia
Chemistry Dept
Charlottesville, VA 22903, USA

Martin, Ray (Baseball Player)
Boston Braves
383 Adams St
Quincy, MA 02169-1703, USA

Martin, Renie (Baseball Player)
Kansas City Royals
509 Little Eagle Ct
Valrico, FL 33594-3973, USA

Martin, Ricky (Musician)
c/o Allison Winkler *Creative Artists
Agency LCC (CAA-LA)*
2000 Avenue Of The Stars
Los Angeles, CA 90067-4700, USA

Martin, Rod (Football Player)
Oakland Raiders
312 Highland Ave Apt A
Manhattan Beach, CA 90266-6437, USA

Martin, Ronald D (Editor)
Atlanta Journal-Constitution
72 Marietta St NW
Editorial Dept
Atlanta, GA 30303-2899, USA

Martin, Rudolf (Actor)
c/o Amanda Glazer *Kohner Agency, The*
9300 Wilshire Blvd Ste 555
Beverly Hills, CA 90212-3211, USA

Martin, Rudolph (Actor)
c/o Staff Member *Treusch/Erickson
Associates*
8955 Norma Pl
Los Angeles, CA 90069-4818, USA

Martin, Sandy (Actor)
CNA Assoc
1875 Century Park E Ste 2250
Los Angeles, CA 90067-2563, USA

Martin, Sir George
Lynhurst Road Hampstead
London, ENGLAND NW3 5NG, UNITED
KINGDOM (UK)

Martin, Stater N (Basketball Player)
4119 Placid St
Houston, TX 77022-4127, USA

Martin, Steve (Actor, Comedian,
Producer, Writer)
c/o Staff Member *Martin/Stein Company,
The*
1528 N Curson Ave
Los Angeles, CA 90046-2804, USA

Martin, Sylvia Wene (Bowler)
2701 Clark Towers Ct Apt 125
Las Vegas, NV 89102-5855, USA

Martin, Todd (Tennis Player)
156 Coach Lamp Way
Ponte Vedra Beach, FL 32082-1904, USA

Martin, Tom (Baseball Player)
Houston Astros
8001 Surf Dr
Panama City, FL 32408-8530, USA

Martin, Tony (Actor, Musician)
10724 Wilshire Blvd Apt 1406
Los Angeles, CA 90024-4473, USA

Martin, Tony (Football Player)
Miami Dolphins
1198 B Green Rd
Boston, GA 31626-2010, USA

Martin, Victor Hugo (Actor)
c/o Staff Member *TV Azteca*
Periferico Sur 4121
Colonia Fuentes del Pedregal
DF CP 14141, MEXICO

Martin, Wayne (Football Player)
New Orleans Saints
25 Chateau Mouton Dr
Kenner, LA 70065-1902, USA

Martin Chase, Deborah (Debra)
(Producer)
c/o Staff Member *William Morris Agency
(WMA-LA)*
1 William Morris Pl
Beverly Hills, CA 90212-4261, USA

Martindale, Wink (Entertainer, Musician)
5744 Newcastle Ln
Calabasas, CA 91302-3117, USA

Martines, Alessandra (Actor)
c/o Francois-Xavier Molin *ArtMedia*
20 av Rapp
Paris 75007, FRANCE

Martinez, A (Actor)
PO Box 6387
Malibu, CA 90264-6387, USA

Martinez, Alfredo (Baseball Player)
California Angels
2346 Thomas St
Los Angeles, CA 90031-2820, USA

Martinez, Ana Maria (Opera Singer)
JF Mastroianni
151 W 51st St # 17E
New York, NY 10019-6019, USA

Martinez, Anais (Musician)
Univision Music Group
5820 Canoga Ave Ste 300
Woodland Hills, CA 91367-6564, USA

Martinez, Angela (Television Host)
c/o Staff Member *Abrams Artists Agency (LA)*
9200 W Sunset Blvd Ph 11
Los Angeles, CA 90069-3601, USA

Martinez, Angie (Musician)
WMA
151 El Camino Dr
Beverly Hills, CA 90212-2704, USA

Martinez, Billy Joe (Actor)
c/o Linda McAlister *Linda McAlister Talent*
100 Oak Ln
Waxahachie, TX 75167-8412, USA

Martinez, Buck (Baseball Player)
Kansas City Royals
10315 Long Beach Blvd
Long Beach Township, NJ 08008-3135, USA

Martinez, Carmelo (Baseball Player)
Chicago Cubs
32 Brisas Del Plata
Dorado, PR 00646-5118, USA

Martinez, Conchita (Tennis Player)
511 Westminster Dr
Cardiff-By-The-Sea, CA 92007, USA

Martinez, Constantino (Tino) (Baseball Player)
c/o Team Member *New York Yankees*
Yankee Stadium
161st St & River Ave
Bronx, NY 10451, USA

Martinez, Daniel J (Artist)
University of California
Studio Art Dept
Irvine, CA 92717, USA

Martinez, Dave (Baseball Player)
Chicago Cubs
3315 Enterprise Rd E
Safety Harbor, FL 34695-5307, USA

Martinez, Edgar (Baseball Player)
Seattle Mariners
PO Box 53490
Bellevue, WA 98015-3490, USA

Martinez, Fred (Baseball Player)
California Angels
2346 Thomas St
Los Angeles, CA 90031-2820, USA

Martinez, Greg (Baseball Player)
Milwaukee Brewers
1596 Palora Ave
Las Vegas, NV 89169-2504, USA

Martinez, J Dennis (Baseball Player)
Baltimore Orioles
9400 SW 63rd Ct
Miami, FL 33156-1817, USA

Martinez, Jorge (Actor)
c/o Staff Member *Telefe - Argentina*
Pavon 2444 (C1248AAT)
Buenos Aires, ARGENTINA

Martinez, Jose (Baseball Player)
Pittsburgh Pirates
14601 SW 33rd Ct
Miramar, FL 33027-3729, USA

Martinez, Marty (Baseball Player)
Minnesota Twins
748 N 23rd West Ave
Tulsa, OK 74127-5203, USA

Martinez, Natalie (Actor)
c/o Sean Fay *Imparato Fay Management*
1126 Roxbury Dr
Los Angeles, CA 90035-1031, USA

Martinez, Olivier (Actor)
Artmedia
20 Ave Rapp
Paris 75007, FRANCE

Martinez, Patrice (Actor)
c/o Staff Member *Select Artists Ltd (CA-Valley Office)*
PO Box 4359
Burbank, CA 91503-4359, USA

Martinez, Pedro (Baseball Player)
Los Angeles Dodgers
3029 Birkdale
Weston, FL 33332-1813, USA

Martinez, Pedro A (Baseball Player)
186 Fairmount Ave
Hyde Park, MA 02136-3506, USA

Martinez, Ramon J (Baseball Player)
Los Angeles Dodgers
3029 Birkdale
Weston, FL 33332-1813, USA

Martinez, Robert (Bob) (Government Official, Governor)
4647 W San Jose St
Tampa, FL 33629-6542, USA

Martinez, Silvio (Baseball Player)
Chicago White Sox
8321 Cornish Ave Apt 2
Elmhurst, NY 11373-3753, USA

Martinez, Tippy (Baseball Player)
New York Yankees
1524 Dellsway Rd
Towson, MD 21286-5901, USA

Martinez Somalo, Eduardo Cardinal (Religious Leader)
Palazzo delle Congregazioni
Piazza Pio XII 3
Rome 00193, ITALY

Martini, Carlo Maria Cardinal (Religious Leader)
Palazzo Arcivescovile
Piazza Fontana 2
Milan 20122, ITALY

Martini, Max (Actor, Director, Writer)
c/o Lorrie Bartlett *Gersh Agency, The (LA)*
232 N Canon Dr
Beverly Hills, CA 90210-5302, USA

Martinkovic, John (Football Player)
Green Bay Packers
1001 Ernst Dr
Green Bay, WI 54304-2205, USA

Martino, Al (Actor, Musician)
927 N Rexford Dr
Beverly Hills, CA 90210-2910, USA

Martino, Frank D (Misc)
Chemical Workers Union
1799 Akron Peninsula Rd # 300
Akron, OH 44313-4847, USA

Martino, Pat (Composer, Musician)
2318 S 16th St
Philadelphia, PA 19145-4310, USA

Martino, Renato R Cardinal (Religious Leader)
Justice & Peace Curia
Piazzo S Calisto 16
Vatican City 00120, VATICAN CITY

Martins, Joao Carlos (Musician)
Musicians Corporate Mgmt
PO Box 825
Highland, NY 12528-0825, USA

Martins, Peter (Ballerina, Dancer, Director)
New York City Ballet
Lincoln Center Plaza
New York, NY 10023, USA

Martinson, Leslie
2288 Coldwater Canyon Dr
Beverly Hills, CA 90210-1756, USA

Martlin, Marlee (Actor)
10340 Santa Monica Blvd
Los Angeles, CA 90025-6904, USA

Marton, Eva (Opera Singer)
Opera et Concert
Maximilianstr 22
Munich 80539, GERMANY

Martone, Lino (Musician)
c/o Gabriel Blanco *Gabriel Blanco Iglesias (Mexico)*
Rio Balsas 35-32
Colonia Cuauhtemoc
DF 06500, MEXICO

Marts, Lonnie (Football Player)
Kansas City Chiefs
13650 Bromley Point Dr
Jacksonville, FL 32225-2635, USA

Marty, Martin E (Misc)
175 E Delaware Pl Apt 8508
Chicago, IL 60611-7750, USA

Marty, Mike (Coach, Football Coach)
Saint Louis Rams
901 N Broadway
Saint Louis, MO 63101-2800, USA

Martyn, Bob (Baseball Player)
Kansas City A's
9984 NW Leahy Rd
Portland, OR 97229-6350, USA

Martz, Gary (Baseball Player)
Kansas City Royals
525 Sage Hills Dr
Wenatchee, WA 98801-2466, USA

Martz, Randy (Baseball Player)
Chicago Cubs
211 Hi Pointe Pl
East Alton, IL 62024-1641, USA

Martzke, Rudy (Writer)
USA Today
1000 Wilson Blvd
Editorial Dept
Arlington, VA 22209-3927, USA

Marusha
Kaiser-Friedrich-Str. 41
Berlin D-10627, GERMANY

Marusin, Yury M (Opera Singer)
Mariinsky Theater
Teatralnaya Pl 1
Saint Petersburg, RUSSIA

Maruyama, Karen (Actor)
c/o Staff Member *Halpern & Associates*
12304 Santa Monica Blvd Ste 104
Los Angeles, CA 90025-2586, USA

Marvaso, Tommy (Football Player)
New York Jets
2 W Melrose St
Chevy Chase, MD 20815-4244, USA

Marve, Eugene (Football Player)
Buffalo Bills
4516 W Lamb Ave
Tampa, FL 33629-6530, USA

Marvel, Elizabeth (Actor)
c/o Staff Member *William Morris Agency (WMA-LA)*
1 William Morris Pl
Beverly Hills, CA 90212-4261, USA

Marvelettes, The (Music Group)
9936 Majorca Pl
Boca Raton, FL 33434-3714, USA

Marx, Gilda (Designer, Fashion Designer)
Gilda Marx Industries
11755 Exposition Blvd
Los Angeles, CA 90064-1338, USA

Marx, Greg (Football Player)
Atlanta Falcons
536 Cadieux Rd
Grosse Pointe, MI 48230, USA

Marx, Gyorgy (Physicist)
Fehervari Utca 119
Budapest 1119, HUNGARY

Marx, Jeffrey A (Journalist)
Lexington Herald-Leader
Editorial Dept
Main & Midland
Lexington, KY 40507, USA

Marx, Richard (Musician, Songwriter, Writer)
c/o Wayne Isaak
514 Broadway Apt 4H
New York, NY 10012-4427, USA

Marx, Timothy (Producer)
c/o Staff Member *International Creative Management (ICM-LA)*
10250 Constellation Blvd
Los Angeles, CA 90067-6200, USA

Mary Mary (Music Group)
c/o Bryan Myers *Creative Artists Agency (CAA-Nashville)*
3310 W End Ave Fl 5
Nashville, TN 37203-1028, USA

Maryland, Russell (Football Player)
Dallas Cowboys
1330 Eagle Bnd
Southlake, TX 76092-9406, USA

Marzano, John (Baseball Player)
Boston Red Sox
1224 S 11th St
Philadelphia, PA 19147-5032, USA

Marzich, Andy (Bowler)
1421 Cravens Ave Apt 318
Torrance, CA 90501-2734, USA

Marzio, Peter C (Director)
Houston Museum of Fine Arts
PO Box 6826
1001 Bissonnet
Houston, TX 77265-6826, USA

Marzoli, Andrea (Misc)
Berkeley Geochronolgoy Center
2455 Ridge Rd
Berkeley, CA 94709-1211, USA

Mas, Adrian (Actor)
c/o Gabriel Blanco *Gabriel Blanco Iglesias (Mexico)*
Rio Balsas 35-32
Colonia Cuauhtemoc
DF 06500, MEXICO

Masak, Ron (Actor)
5440 Shirley Ave
Tarzana, CA 91356-2941, USA

Masakayan, Liz (Volleyball Player)
2864 Palomino Cir
La Jolla, CA 92037-7066, USA

Masako, Princess (Royalty)
Imperial Palace
1-1 Chiyoda-ku
Tokyo, JAPAN

Masaoka, Onan (Baseball Player)
Los Angeles Dodgers
1323 Auwae Rd
Hilo, HI 96720-6906, USA

Mascaras, Mil
200 W 16th St # 10
New York, NY 10011-6165, USA

Masco, Judit
Paseo De Gracia 67 Pral. IA
Barcelona 08008, SPAIN

Mascolo, Joseph (Actor)
c/o Staff Member *Bold and The Beautiful, The*
7800 Beverly Blvd # 3371
Los Angeles, CA 90036-2112, USA

Mase (Musician)
c/o Staff Member *Interscope Records (NY)*
1790 Broadway
New York, NY 10019-1412, USA

Masefield, J Thorold (Governor)
Government House
11 Langton Hill
Pembroke HM13, BERMUDA

Masekela, Hugh (Musician)
Peformers of the World
8901 Melrose Ave # 200
West Hollywood, CA 90069-5605, USA

MaShay, Pepper (Actor, Musician)
c/o Staff Member *Diva Central Inc*
7510 W Sunset Blvd Ste 1445
Los Angeles, CA 90046-3408, USA

Mashburn, Jesse (Athlete, Track Athlete)
8520 S Pennsylvania Ave
Oklahoma City, OK 73159-5226, USA

Mashkov, Vladimir L (Actor)
Oleg Tabakov Theater
Chaokygina Str 12A
Moscow, RUSSIA

Mashore, Clyde (Baseball Player)
Cincinnati Reds
PO Box 1023
Livingston, TX 77351-0018, USA

Mashore, Damon (Baseball Player)
Oakland A's
1519 Heather Dr
Concord, CA 94521-3039, USA

Masiello, Tony (Politician)
Mayor's Office
City Hall
65 Niagara Square
Buffalo, NY 14202-3331, USA

Masire, Q Ketumile J (President)
PO Box 70
Gaborone, BOTSWANA

Maske, Henry (Boxer)
Sauerland Promotion
Hochstadenstr 1-3
Cologne 50674, GERMANY

Maslansky, Paul (Director, Filmmaker, Producer)
Henry Barnberger
10866 Wilshire Blvd # 1000
Los Angeles, CA 90024-4300, USA

Masloff, Sophie (Politician)
Mayor's Office
414 Grant St
City-County Building
Pittsburgh, PA 15219-2426, USA

Maslowski, Matt (Football Player)
Los Angeles Rams
22281 Destello
Mission Viejo, CA 92691-1525, USA

Mason, Anthony (Basketball Player)
7818 Sawyer Brown Rd
Nashville, TN 37221-1215, USA

Mason, B John (Misc)
64 Christchurch Road
East Sheen
London SW14, UNITED KINGDOM (UK)

Mason, Bobbie Ann (Writer)
PO Box 518
Lawrenceburg, KY 40342-0518, USA

Mason, Brent (Musician)
Mercury Records
54 Music Sq E Ste 300
Nashville, TN 37203-4386, USA

Mason, Dave (Football Player)
New England Patriots
1560 Polo Run Ter
Green Bay, WI 54313-6190, USA

Mason, Dave (Musician, Songwriter, Writer)
3130 E Ojai Ave
Ojai, CA 93023-9319, USA

Mason, Derrick (Football Player)
Tennessee Titans
2402 Long Ridge Rd
Reisterstown, MD 21136-5679, USA

Mason, Desmond (Basketball Player)
Milwaukee Bucks
1001 N 4th St
Bradley Center
Milwaukee, WI 53203-1312, USA

Mason, Don (Baseball Player)
San Francisco Giants
8 Fawn Rd
South Yarmouth, MA 02664-1808, USA

Mason, Glen (Coach, Football Coach)
University of Minnesota
Athletic Dept
Minneapolis, MN 55455, USA

Mason, Hank (Baseball Player)
Kansas City Monarchs
3801 Brook Rd
Richmond, VA 23227-4101, USA

Mason, Jackie (Actor, Comedian)
World According to Me
146 W 57th St # 68D
New York, NY 10019-3301, USA

Mason, James Appreciation Society
PO Box 3552
London, ENGLAND SWl9 3QH, UNITED KINGDOM (UK)

Mason, Jim (Baseball Player)
Washington Senators
11410 Queens Way
Theodore, AL 36582-8312, USA

Mason, Larry B (War Hero)
826 Cinebar Rd
Cinebar, WA 98533-9732, USA

Mason, Laurence (Actor)
c/o Mara Santino *Kazarian/Spencer & Assoc (LA)*
11969 Ventura Blvd
Box 7409 Fl 3
Studio City, CA 91604-2630, USA

Mason, Lindsey (Football Player)
Oakland Raiders
3 Elwell Ct
Randallstown, MD 21133-4307, USA

Mason, Marilyn
27 Glen Oak Ct
Medford, OR 97504-7671, USA

Mason, Marsha (Actor)
c/o Michael Black *Michael Black Management*
9701 Wilshire Blvd Ste 1000
Beverly Hills, CA 90212-2010, USA

Mason, Mike (Baseball Player)
Texas Rangers
2711 Piper Ridge Ln
Excelsior, MN 55331-7803, USA

Mason, Monica (Ballerina)
Royal Opera House
Convent Garden
Bow St
London WC2, UNITED KINGDOM (UK)

Mason, Nick (Musician)
Agency Group
370 City Road
London EC1V 2QA, UNITED KINGDOM (UK)

Mason, Roger (Baseball Player)
Detroit Tigers
4587 Stover Rd
Bellaire, MI 49615-9046, USA

Mason, Ron (Coach)
Michigan State University
Athletic Dept
East Lansing, MI 48224, USA

Mason, Stephen (Musician)
Flood Bumstead McCready McCarthy
1700 Hayes St Ste 304
Nashville, TN 37203-3014, USA

Mason, Stephen (Musician, Songwriter, Writer)
Evolution Talent
1776 Broadway Ste 1500
New York, NY 10019-2002, USA

Mason, Steve (Musician)
Agency Group Ltd
370 City Road
London EC1V 2QA, UNITED KINGDOM (UK)

Mason, Sully
4043 Irving Pl
Culver City, CA 90232, USA

Mason, Tom (Actor)
870 Heights Pl
Oyster Bay, NY 11771, USA

Mason, Tommy (Football Player)
Minnesota Vikings
240 S Orange Acres Dr
Anaheim, CA 92807-3617, USA

Mason, Vince (Musician)
Famous Artists Agency
250 W 57th St
New York, NY 10107-0001, USA

Mason, Willy (Musician)
c/o Staff Member *Paradigm (Monterey)*
509 Hartnell St
Monterey, CA 93940-2825, USA

Mason Dixon
PO Box 214
Flint, TX 75762-0214, USA

Mason of Barnsley, Roy (Government Official)
12 Victoria Ave
Barnsley
South Yorks S7O 2BH, UNITED KINGDOM (UK)

Masri, Tahir Nashat (Prime Minister)
PO Box 5550
Amman, JORDAN

Mass, Jochen (Race Car Driver)
RTL-Sportredaktion
Cologne 50570, GERMANY

Mass, Wayne (Football Player)
Chicago Bears
71 Eagle Vw
Durango, CO 81303-6686, USA

Massa, Felipe (Race Car Driver)
c/o Staff Member *Jaguar Racing Ltd*
Bradbourne Drive
Tilbrook
Milton Keynes MK7 8BJ, UNITED KINGDOM (UK)

Massa, Gordon (Baseball Player)
Chicago Cubs
8255 Bonanza Ln
Cincinnati, OH 45255-2504, USA

Massari, Lea
Viale Parioli 59
Rome I-00197, ITALY

Masse, Bill (Baseball Player)
US Olympic Team
2501 Amherst Ct Apt 25A
Boynton Beach, FL 33436-9017, USA

Massen, Osa
10501 Wilshire Blvd Unit 704
Los Angeles, CA 90024-6321, USA

Massengale, Don (Golfer)
715 W Davis St
Conroe, TX 77301-2704, USA

Masset, Andrew
11635 Huston St
N Hollywood, CA 91601-4315, USA

Massey, Anna (Actor)
Markham and Froggatt
Julian House
4 Windmill St
London W1P 1HF, UNITED KINGDOM (UK)

Massey, Athena
PO Box 6180
Beverly Hills, CA 90212-1180, USA

Massey, Debbie (Golfer)
PO Box 116
Cheboygan, MI 49721-0116, USA

Massey, Robert (Football Player)
New Orleans Saints
6101 Corktree Ct
Charlotte, NC 28212-1912, USA

Massey, Vincent (Misc)
University of Michigan
Biochemistry Dept
Ann Arbor, MI 48109, USA

Massey, Waiter E (Educator, Physicist)
Morehouse College
830 Westview Dr SW
President's Office
Atlanta, GA 30314-3776, USA

Massie, Robert K (Writer)
52 W Clinton Ave
Irvington, NY 10533-2130, USA

Massimino, Michael J (Astronaut)
15814 Elk Park Ln
Houston, TX 77062-4775, USA

Massimino, Rollie (Coach)
18578 Es Ferland Court
Jupiter, FL 33469, USA

Mast, Dick (Golfer)
1081 Greenside Ct
Forest, VA 24551-2356, USA

Mast, Rick (Race Car Driver)
390 E Midland Trl
Lexington, VA 24450-5703, USA

Masteller, Dan (Baseball Player)
Minnesota Twins
159111 Aldersyde Dr
Shaker Heights, OH 44120, USA

Masters, Alfreda
1045 S Cloverdale Ave Apt 2A
Los Angeles, CA 90019-6735, USA

Masters, Ben
8730 W Sunset Blvd Ste 480
Los Angeles, CA 90069-2277, USA

Masters, Billy (Football Player)
Buffalo Bills
501 SW Silverspur Cir
Lees Summit, MO 64081-2482, USA

Masters, Geoff (Tennis Player)
De Lorain St
Wavell Heights, QLD 4012, AUSTRALIA

Masters, Norm (Football Player)
Green Bay Packers
2249 Chestnut Hill Drive
Bloomfield Hills, MI 48013, USA

Masters, Roy
8780 Venice Blvd # 34036
Los Angeles, CA 90034-3224, USA

Masterson, Christopher (Chris) Kennedy (Actor)
c/o Staff Member *United Talent Agency (UTA)*
9560 Wilshire Blvd Ste 500
Beverly Hills, CA 90212-2401, USA

Masterson, Connie (Golfer)
4004 Island Bay Cir
Sanford, FL 32771-6344, USA

Masterson, Danny (Actor)
c/o Staff Member *United Talent Agency (UTA)*
9560 Wilshire Blvd Ste 500
Beverly Hills, CA 90212-2401, USA

Masterson, Fay
PO Box 5617
Beverly Hills, CA 90209-5617, USA

Masterson, Forrest (Football Player)
Chicago Bears
310 W Broad St
Louisville, OH 44641-1314, USA

Masterson, Mary Stuart (Actor)
c/o Staff Member *Don Buchwald & Associates Inc (LA)*
6500 Wilshire Blvd Ste 2200
Los Angeles, CA 90048-4942, USA

Masterson, Peter (Director, Producer, Writer)
1165 5th Ave # 15A
New York, NY 10029-6931, USA

Masterson, Sean (Actor, Writer)
c/o Melanie Truhett *Messina Baker/ Entertainment*
955 Carrillo Dr Ste 100
Los Angeles, CA 90048-5400, USA

Masterson, Valerie (Opera Singer)
Music International
13 Ardilaun Road
London N5 2QR, UNITED KINGDOM (UK)

Masterson, Walt (Baseball Player)
Washington Senators
4515 Carteret Dr
Trent Woods, NC 28562-7209, USA

Maston, Le'shai (Football Player)
Houston Oilers
7856 Overridge Dr
Dallas, TX 75232-4316, USA

Mastracchio, Richard A
1910 Hillside Oak Ln
Houston, TX 77062-3663, USA

Mastracchio, Richard A (Rick) (Astronaut)
4410 Pine Blossom Trl
Houston, TX 77059-3144, USA

Mastrangelo, Carlo (Musician)
Paramount Entertainment
PO Box 12
Far Hills, NJ 07931-0012, USA

Mastrantonio, Mary Elizabeth (Actor, Musician)
International Creative Mgmt
8942 Wilshire Blvd # 219
Beverly Hills, CA 90211-1908, USA

Mastrogiacomo, Gina (Actor)
Pakula/King
9229 W Sunset Blvd Ste 315
Los Angeles, CA 90069-3403, USA

Mastroianni, Chiara (Actor)
P F D Drury House
34-43 Russell St
London WC2B 5HA, UNITED KINGDOM (UK)

Masur, Kurt
Leipzing Gweandhausorchester
Augustusplatz 8
Leipzig 04109, GERMANY

Masur, Richard (Actor)
10340 Santa Monica Blvd
Los Angeles, CA 90025-6904, USA

Masurok, Yuri (Opera Singer)
Bolshoi Theater
Teatralnaya Pl 1
Moscow 103009, RUSSIA

Mata'aho (Royalty)
Royal Palace
PO Box 6
Nuku'alofa, TONGA

Matalin, Mary (Journalist, Talk Show Host, Writer)
Gaslight Inc
424 S Washington St
Alexandria, VA 22314-3630, USA

Matarazza, Heather (Actor)
Agency for Performing Arts
405 S Beverly Dr Ste 500
Beverly Hills, CA 90212-4425, USA

Matarazzo, Heather (Actor)
c/o Robert Flutie *Flutie Entertainment (NY)*
270 Lafayette St Ste 1400
New York, NY 10012-3364, USA

Matarazzo, Len (Baseball Player)
Philadelphia Athletics
2715 Carlisle St
New Castle, PA 16105-1714, USA

Matchbox 20 (Music Group)
c/o Staff Member *Creative Artists Agency LCC (CAA-LA)*
2000 Avenue Of The Stars
Los Angeles, CA 90067-4700, USA

Matchett, Kari (Actor)
c/o Tom Chasin *Chasin Agency, The*
8899 Beverly Blvd Ste 716
Los Angeles, CA 90048-2449, USA

Matchetts, John (Hockey Player)
2415 N Chelton Rd
Colorado Springs, CO 80909-1350, USA

Matchick, Tom (Baseball Player)
Detroit Tigers
7700 Pilliod Rd
Holland, OH 43528-8077, USA

Matenopoulos, Debbie (Actor, Producer)
c/o Jeff Morrone *Jeff Morrone Management*
9350 Wilshire Blvd Ste 224
Beverly Hills, CA 90212-3204, USA

Mateo, Guillermo (Athlete, Baseball Player)
c/o Staff Member *Montreal Expos*
4549 Avenue Pierre de Coubertin
Montreal, PQ H1V 3N7, CANADA

Matesa, Zlatko (Prime Minister)
Prime Minister's Office
Jordanovac 71
Zagreb 41000, CROATIA

Matheny, Jim (Football Player)
Chicago Cardinals
16 San Bernardino Ave
Ventura, CA 93004-1131, USA

Matheny, Mike (Baseball Player)
Milwaukee Brewers
2034 Joes Way
Chesterfield, MO 63005-6545, USA

Mather, Chuck (Football Player)
Chicago Bears
10725 Thatcher Way
Duluth, GA 30097-5711, USA

Mather, John C (Misc)
Goddard Space Flight
G85 Code
Greenbelt, MD 20771-0001, USA

Mathers, Frank (Hockey Player)
32 Oakglade Dr
Hummelstown, PA 17036-9516, USA

Mathers, Jerry (Actor)
Boutique
10 Universal City Plz Ste 2000
Universal City, CA 91608-1074, USA

Mathers, Marshall (Eminem) (Musician)
c/o David Schiff *Schiff Company*
9465 Wilshire Blvd Ste 480
Beverly Hills, CA 90212-2603, USA

Matherson, Tim (Actor, Director)
246 Miramar Ave
Montecito, CA 93108-2628, USA

Matheson, Don
10275 1/2 Missouri Ave
Los Angeles, CA 90025, USA

Matheson, Richard
PO Box 81
Woodland Hills, CA 91365-0081, USA

Matheson, Tim (Actor, Director)
c/o Michael Nilon *Creative Artists Agency LCC (CAA-LA)*
2000 Avenue Of The Stars
Los Angeles, CA 90067-4700, USA

Mathews, Byron (Baseball Player)
557 Golfwood Dr
Ballwin, MO 63021-6316, USA

Mathews, F David (Secretary)
6050 Mad River Rd
Dayton, OH 45459-1508, USA

Mathews, Greg (Baseball Player)
St Louis Cardinals
1752 Craig Rd
Saint Louis, MO 63146-4710, USA

Mathews, Harlan (Senator)
420 Hunt Club Rd
Nashville, TN 37221-4310, USA

Mathews, Nelson (Baseball Player)
Chicago Cubs
211 E Crestview Dr
Columbia, IL 62236-1203, USA

Mathews, Ray (Football Player)
Pittsburgh Steelers
PO Box 108
Harrisville, PA 16038-0108, USA

Mathews, Sheila
21554 Pacific Coast Hwy
Malibu, CA 90265-5207, USA

Mathews, T J (Baseball Player)
St Louis Cardinals
10802 Vemoa Dr
Las Vegas, NV 89141-3836, USA

Mathews, Terry (Baseball Player)
Texas Rangers
1132 Belgard Bnd
Boyce, LA 71409-9216, USA

Mathias, Bob
7469 E Pine Ave
Fresno, CA 93727-9520, USA

Mathias, Carl (Baseball Player)
Cleveland Indians
567 Long Ln
Oley, PA 19547-9009, USA

Mathias, Charles McC Jr (Financier, Senator)
3808 Leland St
Chevy Chase, MD 20815-4902, USA

Mathias, William (Composer)
Y Graigwen Cadnant Road
Menai Bridge
Anglesey, Gwynedd WALES LL59, UNITED KINGDOM (UK)

Mathieson, John (Director)
c/o Spyros Skouras *The Skouras Agency*
1149 3rd St Fl 3
Santa Monica, CA 90403-7201, USA

Mathieu, Georges V A (Artist)
125 Ava de Makakoff
Paris 75116, FRANCE

Mathieu, Mireille
12 rue du Bois de Boulogne
Neuilly F-92200, FRANCE

Mathieu, Philip (Musician)
Lindy S MArtin Mgmt
5 Loblolly Ct
Executive Suite
Pinehurst, NC 28374-9349, USA

Mathilde, Princess (Royalty)
Koninklijk Palace
Rue de Brederode
Brussels 1000, BELGIUM

Mathis, Bill (Football Player)
New York Titans
43 Paces West Dr NW
Atlanta, GA 30327-2744, USA

Mathis, Clint (Soccer Player)
New York/New Jersey MetroStars
1 Harmon Plz # 300
Secaucus, NJ 07094-2803, USA

Mathis, Edith (Opera Singer)
Ingpen & Williams
14 Kensington Court
London W8 5DN, UNITED KINGDOM
(UK)

Mathis, Johnny (Musician)
Rojon Productions
1612 W Olive Ave Ste 305
Burbank, CA 91506-2463, USA

Mathis, Ron (Baseball Player)
Houston Astros
2922 Kismet Ln
Houston, TX 77043-1322, USA

Mathis, Samantha (Actor)
7536 Sunnywood Ln
Los Angeles, CA 90046-1248, USA

Mathis, Terance (Football Player)
New York Jets
1335 Portmarnock Dr
Alpharetta, GA 30005-6968, USA

Mathis Jr, Buster
4409 Carol Ave SW
Wyoming, MI 49519-4519, USA

Mathison, Cameron (Actor)
c/o Staff Member Innovative Artists (LA)
1505 10th St
Santa Monica, CA 90401-2805, USA

Mathison, Melissa (Writer)
655 Macculloch Dr
Los Angeles, CA 90049-2024, USA

Matias, John (Baseball Player)
Chicago White Sox
98-1616 Hoolauae St
Aiea, HI 96701-1801, USA

Matkevich, Mark (Actor)
*c/o Staff Member Glasser/Black
Management*
283 Cedarhurst Ave
Cedarhurst, NY 11516-1671, USA

Matlack, Jon (Baseball Player)
New York Mets
192 Cleveland Rd
Johnsburg, NY 12843-2802, USA

Matlack-Sagrati, Ruth (Baseball Player)
925 Rock Hill Rd
Quakertown, PA 18951-3215, USA

Matlin, Marlee (Actor, Producer)
c/o Staff Member Solo One Productions
8205 Santa Monica Blvd # 1279
West Hollywood, CA 90046-5977, USA

Matlock, Glen (Musician)
Solo Agency
55 Fulham High St
London SW6 3JJ, UNITED KINGDOM
(UK)

Matlock, Jack F Jr (Diplomat)
940 Princeton Kingston Rd
Princeton, NJ 08540-4128, USA

Matlock, John (Football Player)
New York Jets
127 Seagrape Dr Apt 102
Jupiter, FL 33458-7885, USA

Matola, Sharon (Misc)
Belize Zoo & Tropical Education Center
PO Box 1787
Belize City, BELIZE

Matondkar, Urmila (Actor, Bollywood)
93/14 Sangam Lokhandwala Road
Andheri (W)
Mumbai, MS 400058, INDIA

Matorin, Vladimir A (Opera Singer)
Ulansky Per 21 Korp 1
#53
Moscow 103045, RUSSIA

Matranga, Dave (Baseball Player)
Houston Astros
303 N Park Ln
Orange, CA 92867-7642, USA

Matricaria, Ronald (Business Person)
Saint Jude Medical Inc
1 Lillehei Plz
Saint Paul, MN 55117-1799, USA

Matsch, Richard P (Judge)
US District Court
1929 Stout St
Denver, CO 80294-0003, USA

Matsik, George A (Business Person)
Ball Corp
10 Longs Peak Dr
Broomfield, CO 80021-2510, USA

Matson, April (Actor)
*c/o Jennifer Millar Abrams Artists Agency
(LA)*
9200 W Sunset Blvd Ph 11
Los Angeles, CA 90069-3601, USA

Matson, J Randel (Randy) (Athlete, Track
Athlete)
1002 Park Pl
College Station, TX 77840-3008, USA

Matson, Oliver G (Ollie) (Athlete,
Football Player, Track Athlete)
Chicago Cardinals
1319 S Hudson Ave
Los Angeles, CA 90019-3014, USA

Matson, Pat (Football Player)
Denver Broncos
3660 Eagle St Apt L
San Diego, CA 92103-3986, USA

Matson, Randy
1002 Park Pl
College Station, TX 77840-3008, USA

Matsos, Arch (Football Player)
Buffalo Bills
1410 Coventry Close St
East Lansing, MI 48823-2419, USA

Matsuda, Naomi (Actor)
c/o Staff Member AKA Talent Agency
6310 San Vicente Blvd Ste 200
Los Angeles, CA 90048-5488, USA

Matsuda, Seiko (Actor, Musician)
Propaganda Films Mgmt
1741 Ivar Ave
Los Angeles, CA 90028-5105, USA

Matsui, Keiko (Musician)
Ted Kurland
173 Brighton Ave
Boston, MA 02134-2003, USA

Matsui, Kosei (Artist)
Ibaraki-ken
Kasama-shi
Kasama 350, JAPAN

Matsumoto, Shigeharu (Writer)
International House of Japan
11-16 Roppongi
Minatuku
Tokyo, JAPAN

Matsushita, Hiro (Race Car Driver)
14772 Ridgeboro Pl
Tustin, CA 92780-6666, USA

Matta, del Meskin (Religious Leader)
Deir el Makarios Monastery
Cairo, EGYPT

Matte, Thomas R (Tom) (Football Player)
Baltimore Colts
11309 Old Carriage Rd
Glen Arm, MD 21057-9422, USA

Mattea, Kathy (Actor, Musician)
*c/o Staff Member William Morris Agency
(WMA-LA)*
1 William Morris Pl
Beverly Hills, CA 90212-4261, USA

Mattei, Frank (Musician)
Joe Taylor Mgmt
PO Box 1017
Turnersville, NJ 08012-0837, USA

Matter, Niall (Actor)
*c/o Trina Allen Pacific Artists
Management*
1404-510 W Hastings St
Vancouver, BC V6B 1L8, CANADA

Mattes, Eva (Actor)
Agentur Carola Studlar
Neurieder Str
#1C
Planegg 92152, GERMANY

Mattes, Ron (Football Player)
Seattle Seahawks
1718 Moreland Wood Trl NW
Concord, NC 28027-8093, USA

Mattes, Troy (Baseball Player)
Montreal Expos
2932 Lexington St
Sarasota, FL 34231-6118, USA

Mattesich, Rudi (Skier)
General Delivery
Troy, VT 05868-9999, USA

Matthes, Roland (Swimmer)
Luitpoldstr 35A
Marktheidenfeld 97828, GERMANY

Matthes, Ulrich (Actor)
Kuno-Fischer-Str 14
Berlin 14057, GERMANY

Matthew, Catriona (Golfer)
I M G
Pler House Strand on the Green
Chiswick
London W4 3NN, UNITED KINGDOM
(UK)

Matthews, Alvin (Football Player)
Green Bay Packers
19541 Diablo Dr
Pflugerville, TX 78660-5088, USA

Matthews, Bill (Football Player)
New England Patriots
32 Olde Farm Rd
South Easton, MA 02375-1438, USA

Matthews, Bo (Football Player)
San Diego Chargers
10053 Vine Ct
Denver, CO 80229-2385, USA

Matthews, Bruce R (Football Player)
Houston Oilers
6423 Oilfield Rd
Sugar Land, TX 77479-9603, USA

Matthews, Carys (Musician)
MRM Productions
5 Kirby St
London EC1N 8TS, UNITED KINGDOM
(UK)

Matthews, Chris (Television Host)
The Chris Matthews Show
4001 Nebraska Ave NW
Nbc Enterprises
Washington, DC 20016-2733, USA

Matthews, Dakin (Actor)
c/o Staff Member The McCabe Group
8285 W Sunset Blvd Ste 1
West Hollywood, CA 90046-2420, USA

Matthews, Dave (Music Group, Musician)
c/o Staff Member IFA Talent Agency
8730 W Sunset Blvd Ste 490
Los Angeles, CA 90069-2248, USA

Matthews, DeLane (Actor)
Don Buchwald
5500 Wilshire Blvd # 2200
Los Angeles, CA 90036-3802, USA

Matthews, Denise (Vanity) (Model,
Musician, Religious Leader)
Egangelist Denise Matthews
39279 Paseo Padre Pkwy # 214
Fremont, CA 94538, USA

Matthews, Gary (Baseball Player)
San Diego Padres
4653 Willens Ave
Woodland Hills, CA 91364-3812, USA

Matthews, Gary (Baseball Player)
San Francisco Giants
1542 W Jackson Blvd
Chicago, IL 60607-5304, USA

Matthews, Ian (Musician)
Geoffrey Blumenauer
11846 Balboa Blvd # 204
Granada Hills, CA 91344-2753, USA

Matthews, Liesel (Actor)
*c/o Staff Member Creative Artists Agency
LCC (CAA-LA)*
2000 Avenue Of The Stars
Los Angeles, CA 90067-4700, USA

Matthews, Mike (Baseball Player)
St Louis Cardinals
976 Spirea
Howell, MI 48843-6872, USA

Matthews, Pat Stanley (Actor)
210 Stanton St
Walla Walla, WA 99362-2058, USA

Matthews, Robert C O (Economist)
Clare College
Cambridge
CB2 1TL, UNITED KINGDOM (UK)

Matthews, Shane (Football Player)
Chicago Bears
10727 SW 27th Ave
Gainesville, FL 32607-1237, USA

Matthews, Vincent (Vince) (Athlete, Track
Athlete)
6755 193rd Ln
Fresh Meadows, NY 11365-4034, USA

Matthews, W Clay Jr (Football Player)
Cleveland Browns
6068 Canterbury Dr
Agoura Hills, CA 91301-4131, USA

Matthies, Nina (Coach, Volleyball Player)
Pepperdine University
Athletic Dept
Malibu, CA 90265, USA

Matthiessen, Peter (Writer)
Bridge Lane
Sagaponack, NY 11962, USA

Mattick, Bobby (Baseball Player)
Chicago Cubs
14500 N Frank Lloyd Wright Blvd
Scottsdale, AZ 85260-8822, USA

Mattila, Karita M (Opera Singer)
45B Croxley Road
London W9 3HJ, UNITED KINGDOM
(UK)

Mattingly, Donald A (Don) (Baseball
Player)
New York Yankees
11825 Darmstadt Rd
Evansville, IN 47725-9542, USA

Mattingly, Mack F (Senator)
4315 10th St
East Beach
Saint Simons Island, GA 31522-3004,
USA

Mattingly, Thomas K II (Admiral,
Astronaut)
Rocket Development Co
1501 Quail St # 102
Newport Beach, CA 92660-2726, USA

Mattlace, Len (Golfer)
12802 Hunt Club Rd N
Jacksonville, FL 32224-7654, USA

Mattox, Gus (Adult Film Star)
c/o Staff Member *Diva Central Inc*
7510 W Sunset Blvd Ste 1445
Los Angeles, CA 90046-3408, USA

Mattson, Riley (Football Player)
Washington Redskins
3900 SW 75th Ave
Portland, OR 97225-2731, USA

Mattson, Robin (Actor)
Stan Kamens Mgmt
7772 Torreyson Dr
Los Angeles, CA 90046-1227, USA

Mattson, Walter E (Publisher)
New York Times Co
229 W 43rd St
New York, NY 10036-3959, USA

Mattson-Baumgart, Jacqueline (Baseball
Player)
4814 W Fillmore Dr
West Allis, WI 53219-2364, USA

Matula, Rick (Baseball Player)
Atlanta Braves
1817 Chapel Hts
Wharton, TX 77488-4459, USA

Matuszak, Marv (Football Player)
Pittsburgh Steelers
3054 Mill Grove Ter
Dacula, GA 30019-5019, USA

Matuszek, Len (Baseball Player)
Philadelphia Phillies
10326 Deerfield Rd
Cincinnati, OH 45242-5105, USA

Matuza, Albert (Football Player)
Chicago Bears
131 Paul Rd
Morrisville, PA 19067-4855, USA

Matz, Johanna
Opernring 4
Vienna 1010, AUSTRIA

Matzdorf, Pat (Athlete, Track Athlete)
1252 Bainbridge Dr
Naperville, IL 60563-2065, USA

Mauban, Maria
4 sq. Vitruve
Paris 75020, FRANCE

Mauch, Billy & Bobby
538 W Northwest Hwy Unit C
Palatine, IL 60067-8695, USA

Maugham, R H (Religious Leader)
Christian & Missionary Alliance
PO Box 35000
Colorado Springs, CO 80935-3500, USA

Maughan, Deryck (Financier)
Citigroup Inc
399 Park Ave
New York, NY 10022-4699, USA

Mauinier, Thierry
3 rue Yves-Carriou
Marnes-la-Coquette 92430, FRANCE

Maulden, Jerry L (Business Person)
Entergy Corp
10055 Grogans Mill Rd # 5A
The Woodlands, TX 77380-1059, USA

Mauldin, William H (Cartoonist)
Loomis-Watkins Agency
150 E 35th St
New York, NY 10016-4102, USA

Maule, Brad (Actor)
c/o Hank Hedland *Opus Entertainment*
5225 Wilshire Blvd Ste 905
Los Angeles, CA 90036-4353, USA

Maumenee, Alfred E (Misc)
1700 Hillside Rd
Stevenson, MD 21153-0662, USA

Maupin, Armistead (Writer)
584 Castro St # 528
San Francisco, CA 94114-2512, USA

Maura, Carmen (Actor)
GRPC SL
Calle Fuencarral 17
Madrid 28004, SPAIN

Maurer, Andy (Football Player)
Atlanta Falcons
30 Perrydale Ave
Medford, OR 97501-2037, USA

Maurer, Dave (Baseball Player)
San Diego Padres
884 Saint Moritz
Victoria, MN 55386-3700, USA

Maurer, Gilbert C (Publisher)
Hearst Corp
300 W 57th St Fl 42
New York, NY 10019-3790, USA

Maurer, Rob (Baseball Player)
Texas Rangers
6240 Oak Hill Rd
Evansville, IN 47711-6759, USA

Maurer, Robert D (Inventor)
2572 W 28th Ave
Eugene, OR 97405-1456, USA

Mauresmo, Amelie (Amy) (Tennis Player)
Athleteline
2 rue du chemin vert
Clichy 92110, FRANCE

Maurey, Nicole
21 chemin Vauillons
Marly-le-Roi 78160, FRANCE

Mauriac, Claude (Writer)
24 Quai de Bethune
Paris 75004, FRANCE

Mauriello, Ralph (Baseball Player)
Los Angeles Dodgers
4241 Persimmon St
Moorpark, CA 93021-3515, USA

Maurier, Claire
Il rue de la Montague-le-Breuil
Epinay Orge 91360, FRANCE

Maurin, Laurence (Skier)
PO Box 1980
West Bend, WI 53095-7980, USA

Mauro, Carmen (Baseball Player)
Chicago Cubs
5545 Marconl Ave Apt 118
Carmichael, CA 95608, USA

Mauroy, Pierre (Prime Minister)
17-19 Rue Voltaire
Lille 59800, FRANCE

Maurstad, Toralv (Actor, Director)
National Theatre
Storlingsgt 15
Osto 1, NORWAY

Mauser, Tim (Baseball Player)
Philadelphia Phillies
1321 Saxony Rd
Fort Worth, TX 76116-1658, USA

Mauz, Henry H (Hank) Jr (Admiral)
1608 Viscaino Rd
Pebble Beach, CA 93953-3303, USA

Maven, Max
PO Box 3819
La Mesa, CA 91944-3819, USA

Mavericks, The (Music Group)
c/o Staff Member *Asgard Promotions*
125 Pkwy
Regents Park
London NW1 7PS, UNITED KINGDOM
(UK)

Mavis, Bob (Baseball Player)
Detroit Tigers
300 Markwood Dr
Little Rock, AR 72205-2412, USA

Mawae, Kevin J (Football Player)
Seattle Seahawks
478 Cotton Ln
Franklin, TN 37069-4122, USA

Mawby, Russell G (Misc)
WK Kellogg FOundation
1 Michigan Ave E
Battle Creek, MI 49017-4012, USA

Max, Peter (Artist)
118 Riverside Dr
New York, NY 10024-3708, USA

Maxa, Rudy (Television Host)
c/o Staff Member *Public Broadcasting
Service (PBS)*
1320 Braddock Pl
Alexandria, VA 22314-1692, USA

Maxcy, Brian (Baseball Player)
Detroit Tigers
8 Azalea Ln
Amory, MS 38821-8700, USA

Maxey, Caty (Designer)
c/o Staff Member *Mirisch Agency*
1801 Century Park E Ste 1801
Los Angeles, CA 90067-2320, USA

Maxey, Virginia
16414 Pick Pl
Riverside, CA 92504-5645, USA

Maxi, Fumihiko (Architect)
5-16-22 Higashi Gotanda
Shinagawaku
Tokyo, JAPAN

Maxie, Brett (Football Player)
New Orleans Saints
10251 Blue Palm St
Plantation, FL 33324-8262, USA

Maxie, Larry (Baseball Player)
Atlanta Braves
296 Verdugo Way
Upland, CA 91786-7138, USA

Maximova, Ekaterina (Ballerina)
Bolshoi Theater
Teatralnaya Pi 1
Moscow 103009, RUSSIA

Maxson, Alvin (Football Player)
New England Patriots
17500 E Brown Cir
Aurora, CO 80013-2193, USA

Maxson, Robert (Educator)
California State University
President's Office
Long Beach, CA 90840-0001, USA

Maxvill, Dal (Baseball Player)
St Louis Cardinals
1115 Eagle Creek Rd
Chesterfield, MO 63005-6606, USA

Maxwell (Musician)
c/o Staff Member *Shore Fire Media*
32 Court St Ste 1600
Brooklyn, NY 11201-4441, USA

Maxwell, Arthur E (Oceanographer)
PO Box 31249
Santa Fe, NM 87594-1249, USA

Maxwell, Cedric (Cornbread) (Basketball
Player)
WEEI Sports Radio
116 Huntington Ave
Boston, MA 02116-5749, USA

Maxwell, Charlie (Baseball Player)
Boston Red Sox
730 Mapleview Dr
Paw Paw, MI 49079-1185, USA

Maxwell, Dobie (Comedian)
333 W North Ave # 343
Chicago, IL 60610-1293, USA

Maxwell, Frank (Politician)
Federation of TV-Radio Artists
260 Madison Ave
New York, NY 10016-2401, USA

Maxwell, Ian (Publisher)
Eaton Terrace
London SW1, UNITED KINGDOM (UK)

Maxwell, Jacqui (Actor)
c/o Staff Member *Untitled Entertainment
(LA)*
331 N Maple Dr Fl 3
Beverly Hills, CA 90210-3827, USA

Maxwell, Jason (Baseball Player)
Chicago Cubs
1821 Brockton Pi
Franklin, TN 37064, USA

Maxwell, Kevin F H (Publisher)
Hill Burn
Hailey near Wallingford
Oxford OX10 6AD, UNITED KINGDOM
(UK)

Maxwell, Robert D (War Hero)
1001 SE 15th St Unit 44
Bend, OR 97702-2351, USA

Maxwell, Ron (Director)
c/o Adam Shulman *The Firm*
9465 Wilshire Blvd Fl 6
Beverly Hills, CA 90212-2605, USA

Maxwell, Ronald F (Ron) (Director,
Writer)
c/o Staff Member *Person to Person Films*
200 Fogg Mountain Ln
Flint Hill, VA 22627-1842, USA

Maxwell, Tommy (Football Player)
Baltimore Colts
1634 Rockview Dr
Granbury, TX 76049-5733, USA

May, Arthur (Architect)
Kohn Pedersen Fox Assoc
111 W 57th St
New York, NY 10019-2211, USA

May, Bob (Golfer)
420 Grand Augusta Ln
Las Vegas, NV 89144-4300, USA

May, Briane (Musician, Songwriter,
Writer)
Old Bakehouse
16A High St Barnes
London SW13, UNITED KINGDOM (UK)

May, Carlos (Baseball Player)
Chicago White Sox
6102 Amherst Pl
Matteson, IL 60443-1988, USA

May, Darrell (Baseball Player)
Atlanta Braves
747 Minthome Rd
Rogue River, OR 97537, USA

May, Dave (Baseball Player)
Baltimore Orioles
124 Madison Dr
Newark, DE 19711-4406, USA

May, Deborah (Actor)
Artists Agency
1180 S Beverly Dr Ste 301
Los Angeles, CA 90035-1154, USA

May, Deems (Football Player)
San Diego Chargers
5616 Hillingdon Rd
Charlotte, NC 28226-7389, USA

May, Derrick (Baseball Player)
Chicago Cubs
2 Jaymar Blvd
Newark, DE 19702-2877, USA

May, Don (Basketball Player)
1128 Colwick Dr
Dayton, OH 45420-2206, USA

May, Donald
733 Seward St
Los Angeles, CA 90038-3503, USA

May, Elaine (Actor, Director)
William Morris Agency
151 El Camino Dr
Beverly Hills, CA 90212-2775, USA

May, Joe (Misc)
General Delivery
Thorne Bay, AK 99919-9999, USA

May, Lee (Baseball Player)
Cincinnati Reds
2272 4th Place Cir NE # NE
Birmingham, AL 35215-3808, USA

May, Lee A (Baseball Player)
5593 Hill Dale Dr
Cincinnati, OH 45213, USA

May, Mark (Football Player)
Washington Redskins
3557 E Minton St
Mesa, AZ 85213-1748, USA

May, Mark E (Football Player,
Sportscaster)
Mark May Salisbury Ford
1902 N Salisbury Blvd
Salisbury, MD 21801-3335, USA

May, Mathilda (Actor)
Artmedia
20 Ave Rapp
Paris 75007, FRANCE

May, Milt (Baseball Player)
Pittsburgh Pirates
2200 Manatee Ave W
Bradenton, FL 34205-5430, USA

May, Misty (Volleyball Player)
Irvine Valley College
5500 Irvine Center Dr
Irvine, CA 92618-0300, USA

May, Ralphie (Actor, Comedian,
Producer, Writer)
c/o Staff Member *Parallel Entertainment*
9255 W Sunset Blvd Ste 1040
Los Angeles, CA 90069-3307, USA

May, Rudy (Baseball Player)
California Angels
8090 N Augusta St
Fresno, CA 93720-2031, USA

May, Scott (Baseball Player)
Texas Rangers
1630 Raven Cir Unit H
Estes Park, CO 80517-9477, USA

May, Scott G (Basketball Player)
2001 E Hillside Dr
Bloomington, IN 47401-6203, USA

May, Torsten (Boxer)
Sauerland Promotion
Hans-Bockler-Str 163
Hurth 50354, GERMANY

Mayaki, Ibrahim Hassane (Prime Minister)
Prime Minister's Office
State House
Niamey, NIGER

Mayall, John (Composer, Musician)
Monterey International
200 W Superior St Ste 202
Chicago, IL 60610-3554, USA

Mayall, Rik (Actor, Comedian)
Brunskill Mgmt
169 Queen's Gate
London SW7 5HE, UNITED KINGDOM
(UK)

Mayasich, John E (Hockey Player)
2250 Riverwood Pl
Saint Paul, MN 55104-5646, USA

Mayberry, Jermane (Football Player)
Philadelphia Eagles
111 Post Oak
Floresville, TX 78114-6703, USA

Mayberry, John C (Baseball Player)
Houston Astros
11115 W 121st Ter
Overland Park, KS 66213-1945, USA

Mayberry, Tony (Football Player)
Tampa Bay Buccaneers
15704 Cochester Rd
Tampa, FL 33647-1100, USA

Maydan, Dan (Business Person)
Applied Materials
3050 Bowers Ave
Santa Clara, CA 95054-3298, USA

Mayer, Chip
4601 Willis Ave Apt 210
Sherman Oaks, CA 91403-2623, USA

Mayer, Christian (Skier)
Siedlerweg 18
Finkelstein 9884, AUSTRIA

Mayer, Ed (Baseball Player)
Philadelphia Athletics
440 Oakland Ave
Corte Madera, CA 94925, USA

Mayer, Gene (Tennis Player)
115 South St
Glen Dale, MD 20769, USA

Mayer, H Robert (Judge)
US Court of Appeals
717 Madison Pl NW
Washington, DC 20439-0001, USA

Mayer, John (Musician, Songwriter,
Writer)
c/o Rob Light *Creative Artists Agency LCC
(CAA-LA)*
2000 Avenue Of The Stars
Los Angeles, CA 90067-4700, USA

Mayer, Joseph E (Physicist)
2345 Via Siena
La Jolla, CA 92037-3933, USA

Mayer, Martin J (Admiral)
Deputy CinC
116 Lake View Pkwy
Joint Forces Command
Suffolk, VA 23435-2659, USA

Mayer, P Augustin Cardinal (Religious
Leader)
Ecclesia Dei
Vatican City 00120, VATICAN CITY

Mayer, Phil
RR 9 Box 715M
Yakima, WA 98901, USA

Mayer, Travis (Skier)
37050 Williams St
Steamboat Springs, CO 80487, USA

Mayes, Alonzo (Football Player)
Chicago Bears
3000 SE 56th St
Oklahoma City, OK 73135-1620, USA

Mayes, David (Football Player)
Cleveland Browns
3018 Kingsley Rd
Shaker Heights, OH 44122-2816, USA

Mayes, Derrick (Football Player)
Green Bay Packers
4425 Brown Rd
Indianapolis, IN 46226-3147, USA

Mayes, Rueben (Football Player)
New Orleans Saints
610 SE Edge Knoll Dr
Pullman, WA 99163-2447, USA

Mayes, Wendell
1504 Bel Air Rd
Los Angeles, CA 90077-3022, USA

Mayfair, Billy (Golfer)
PO Box 25844
Scottsdale, AZ 85255-0114, USA

Mayfield, Corey (Football Player)
Tampa Bay Buccaneers
210 Tournament Rd
Tyler, TX 75702-6649, USA

Mayfield, Jeremy (Race Car Driver)
Everham Motorsports
320 Aviation Dr
Statesville, NC 28677-2509, USA

Mayhew, Lauren (Actor)
c/o David Eisenberg *Protege
Entertainment*
710 E Angeleno Ave
Burbank, CA 91501-2213, USA

Mayhew, Patrick B B (Government
Official)
House of Lords
Westminster
London SW1A 0PW, UNITED KINGDOM
(UK)

Maynard, Andrew (Boxer)
Mike Trainer
3922 Fairmont Ave
Bethesda, MD 20814, USA

Maynard, Brad (Football Player)
Tampa Bay Buccaneers
4915 Rfd
Long Grove, IL 60047-8227, USA

Maynard, Mimi (Actor)
Badgley Connor Talent
1680 Vine St Ste 1016
Los Angeles, CA 90028-8800, USA

Mayne, Brent (Baseball Player)
Kansas City Royals
3535 E Pacific Coast Street Apt 8
Corona Del Mar, CA 92625, USA

Mayne, D Roger (Photographer)
Colway Manor
Colway Lane
Lyme Regis, Dorset DT7 3HD, UNITED
KINGDOM (UK)

Mayne, Kenny (Sportscaster)
ESPN-TV
935 Middle St
Sports Dept Espn Plaza
Bristol, CT 06010-1000, USA

Mayne, Thomas (Architect)
Morphosis Architects
2041 Colorado Ave
Santa Monica, CA 90404-3415, USA

Maynor, Asa
PO Box 1641
Beverly Hills, CA 90213-1641, USA

Maynor, Stephanie (Golfer)
6213 Three Apple Downs
Columbia, MD 21045-7419, USA

Mayo, Eddie (Baseball Player)
New York Giants
39663 Surreyfield Way
Leesburg, VA 20175-6920, USA

Mayo, Jackie (Baseball Player)
Philadelphia Phillies
719 Maple Ave
Youngstown, OH 44512, USA

Mayock, Michael (Football Player)
New York Giants
607 Georges Ln
Ardmore, PA 19003-1905, USA

Mayor, Zaragoza Federico (Government
Official)
UNESCO
7 Place de Fonteroy
Paris 75352, FRANCE

Mayotte, Timothy S (Tim) (Tennis Player)
SFX Sports Group
2665 S Bayshore Dr Ste 602
Miami, FL 33133-5402, USA

Mayron, Melanie (Actor, Director)
1435 N Ogden Dr
Los Angeles, CA 90046-3906, USA

Mays, Alvoid (Football Player)
Washington Redskins
3903 Cape Vista Dr
Bradenton, FL 34209-6725, USA

Mays, Damon (Football Player)
Washington Redskins
5763 W Bloomfield Rd
Glendale, AZ 85304-1832, USA

Mays, Jayma (Actor)
c/o Steven Levy *Framework Entertainment (LA)*
9057 Nemo St # C
W Hollywood, CA 90069-5511, USA

Mays, Jeryn (Actor)
Amaysment Enterprises
28318 Birdie St
Moreno Valley, CA 92555-6358, USA

Mays, Joe (Baseball Player)
Minnesota Twins
17556 Bearpath Trl
Eden Prairie, MN 55347-3488, USA

Mays, Lowry (Business Person)
Clear Channel Communications
200 Concord Plz
San Antonio, TX 78216-6943, USA

Mays, Lyle (Musician)
Ted Kurland
173 Brighton Ave
Boston, MA 02134-2003, USA

Mays, Rueben
7306 172nd St SW
Edmonds, WA 98026-5121, USA

Mays, Willie (Baseball Player)
The San Francisco Giants
24 Willie Mays Plz
San Francisco, CA 94107-2199, USA

Maysey, Matt (Baseball Player)
Montreal Expos
14910 W Victoria Xing
Lockport, IL 60441-6293, USA

Mayweather, Floyd Jr (Boxer)
4720 Laguna Vista St
Las Vegas, NV 89147-6043, USA

Mazach, John J (Admiral)
5423 Grist Mill Woods Way
Alexandria, VA 22309-1592, USA

Mazar, Debi (Actor)
c/o Peg Donegan *Framework Entertainment (LA)*
9057 Nemo St # C
W Hollywood, CA 90069-5511, USA

Mazaroski, William S (Bill) (Baseball Player)
281 Walton Tea Room Rd
Greensburg, PA 15601-6406, USA

Maznicki, Frank (Football Player)
Chicago Bears
2 Coaches Ct
West Warwick, RI 02893, USA

Mazor, Stanley (Stan) (Inventor)
FTI/Teklicon
3031 Tisch Way
San Jose, CA 95128-2541, USA

Mazowiecki, Tadeusz (Prime Minister)
Sejm RP Ul Qiekska 4/6/8
Warsaw 00-902, POLAND

Mazur, Jay J (Misc)
Industrial Textile Employees Needletrades
1710 Broadway
New York, NY 10019-5254, USA

Mazur, Monet (Actor)
c/o Marsha McManus *Principal Entertainment (LA)*
1964 Westwood Blvd Ste 400
Los Angeles, CA 90025-4695, USA

Mazursky, Paul (Director)
c/o Larry Shapiro *Nine Yards Entertainment*
8530 Wilshire Blvd Fl 5
Beverly Hills, CA 90211-3102, USA

Mazza, Valeria (Model)
Riccardo Ga
8/10 Via Revere
Milan 20123, ITALY

Mazzanti, Geno (Football Player)
Baltimore Colts
4188 E Highway 82
Lake Village, AR 71653-6057, USA

Mazzanti, Jerry (Football Player)
Philadelphia Eagles
1712 S Lakeshore Dr
Lake Village, AR 71653-1573, USA

Mazzara, Glen (Producer)
c/o Staff Member *Creative Artists Agency LCC (CAA-LA)*
2000 Avenue Of The Stars
Los Angeles, CA 90067-4700, USA

Mazzarello, Marcelo (Actor)
c/o Staff Member *Telefe - Argentina*
Pavon 2444 (C1248AAT)
Buenos Aires, ARGENTINA

Mazzello, Joseph (Actor)
46691 Mission Blvd # 536
Fremont, CA 94539-7994, USA

Mazzetti, Tim (Football Player)
Atlanta Falcons
2609 W 118th St
Leawood, KS 66211-3035, USA

Mazzie, Marin (Actor, Musician)
J Michael Bloom
233 Park Ave S # 1000
New York, NY 10003-1606, USA

Mazzilli, Lee L (Baseball Player)
New York Mets
67 Stonehedhe Dr S
Greenwich, CT 06831, USA

Mazzo, Kay (Ballerina)
American Ballet School
144 W 66th St
New York, NY 10023, USA

Mazzola, Anthony T (Editor)
Town & Country Magazine
1790 Broadway
Editorial Dept
New York, NY 10019-1412, USA

Mba, Casimir Oye (Prime Minister)
Prime Minister's Office
Boile Postale 546
Libreville, GABON

Mbasogo, Teodoro Obiang Nguema (President)
President's Office
Malabo, EQUATORIAL GUINEA

Mbeki, Thabo (President)
President's Office
Union Buildings
Pretoria 0001, SOUTH AFRICA

M'Bow, Amadou-Mahtar (Government Official)
BP 5276
Dakar-Fann, SENEGAL

McAdams, Carl (Football Player)
New York Jets
HC 82 Box 526
Atoka, OK 74525, USA

McAdams, Rachel (Actor)
c/o Alix Gucovsky *Special Artists Agency*
9465 Wilshire Blvd Ste 890
Beverly Hills, CA 90212-2607, USA

McAdoo, Robert A (Bob) (Basketball Player, Coach)
16710 SW 82nd Ave
Village Of Palmetto Bay, FL 33157-3792, USA

McAfee, George (Football Player)
Chicago Bears
2600 Croasdaile Farm Pkwy Bldg D
Durham, NC 27705-1303, USA

McAfee, Ken
51 Canterbury Ln
Needham, MA 02492-3201, USA

McAleese, Mary P (President)
President's Office
Baile Athe Cliath 8
Dublin, IRELAND

McAleese, Peter (Producer)
c/o Lisa Helsing Lenhoff *Lenhoff & Lenhoff*
830 Palm Ave
West Hollywood, CA 90069-4009, USA

McAleney, Ed (Football Player)
Tampa Bay Buccaneers
981 Shore Rd
Cape Elizabeth, ME 04107-1908, USA

McAlister, Chris (Football Player)
Baltimore Ravens
259 W Duarte Rd # H
Monrovia, CA 91016, USA

McAlister, James E (Athlete, Football Player, Track Athlete)
155 Glorieta St
Pasadena, CA 91103-3018, USA

McAlpine, Donald M (Cinematographer)
377 Placer Creek Ln
Henderson, NV 89014-4560, USA

McAnally, Ernie (Baseball Player)
Montreal Expos
PO Box 942
Mount Pleasant, TX 75456-0942, USA

McAnally, Mac (Musician, Songwriter)
c/o Staff Member *Paradigm (Monterey)*
509 Hartnell St
Monterey, CA 93940-2825, USA

McAnany, Jim (Baseball Player)
Chicago White Sox
11518 Poema Pl Unit 102
Chatsworth, CA 91311-1147, USA

McAndrew, Jarnie (Baseball Player)
Milwaukee Brewers
16007 Davis Rd Apt 1013
Fort Myers, FL 33908-2947, USA

McAndrew, Jim (Baseball Player)
New York Mets
16540 E El Lago Blvd Unit 41
Fountain Hills, AZ 85268-4732, USA

McAndrew, Tracey (Nell) (Actor, Model)
c/o Staff Member *Adult Model SEM Group*
98 Cockfosters Rd
Barnet
Hertfordshirt EN4 0DP, UNITED KINGDOM (UK)

McArdle, Andrea (Actor, Musician)
Edd Kalehoff
14 Shady Glen Ct
New Rochelle, NY 10805-1806, USA

McArthur, Alex (Actor)
10435 Wheatland Ave
Sunland, CA 91040-1249, USA

McArthur, Kevin (Football Player)
New York Jets
3817 Meredith Ln
Mesquite, TX 75180-5017, USA

McArthur, William S (Bill) Jr (Astronaut)
14503 Sycamore Lake Rd
Houston, TX 77062-2245, USA

McAuliffe, Dennis P (General)
9076 Belvoir Woods Pkwy
Fort Belvoir, VA 22060-2702, USA

McAuliffe, Dick (Baseball Player)
Detroit Tigers
32 Worthington Dr
Farmington, CT 06032-1493, USA

McAvoy, James (Actor)
c/o Ruth Young *Peters Fraser & Dunlop (PFD - UK)*
Drury House
34-43 Russell St
London WC2B 5HA, UNITED KINGDOM (UK)

McAvoy, Tom (Baseball Player)
Washington Senators
2 Clinton Ct
Stillwater, NY 12170-1306, USA

McBain, Diane (Actor)
20185 Canyon View Dr # 1
Canyon Country, CA 91351-5734, USA

McBain, Ed (Writer)
324 Main Ave
PO Box 339
Norwalk, CT 06851, USA

McBath, Mike (Football Player)
Buffalo Bills
5044 Sailwind Cir
Orlando, FL 32810-1839, USA

McBean, Al (Baseball Player)
Pittsburgh Pirates
PO Box 4475
St Thomas, VI 00801, USA

McBee, Rives (Golfer)
1504 Canyon Oaks Dr
Irving, TX 75061-2116, USA

McBride, Bake (Baseball Player)
St Louis Cardinals
4077 Reliant Cir
Owensboro, KY 42301-0024, USA

McBride, Chi (Actor)
United Talent Agency
9560 Wilshire Blvd Ste 500
Beverly Hills, CA 90212-2401, USA

McBride, Jeff
4185 Paradise Rd Apt 2081
Las Vegas, NV 89169-6508, USA

McBride, Jon A (Astronaut)
Image Development Group
1018 Kanawha Blvd E Ste 901
Charleston, WV 25301-2800, USA

McBride, Ken (Baseball Player)
Chicago White Sox
3446 Cypress Cir
Westlake, OH 44145-4409, USA

McBride, Martina (Musician)
c/o Bruce Allen *SL Feldman & Associates*
1505 W 2nd Ave #200
Vancouver, BC V6H 3Y4, CANADA

McBride, Oscar (Football Player)
Arizona Cardinals
PO Box 247
Chiefland, FL 32644-0247, USA

McBride, Patricia (Ballerina)
Sharon Wagner Artists
150 W End Ave
New York, NY 10023-5702, USA

Mcbride, Susan (Writer)
8712 Garden Ct
Brentwood, MO 63144-1830, USA

McBride, William J (Misc)
Gorse Lodge
Ballyclare
County Antrim BT39 9DE, NORTHERN
IRELAND

McBroom, Amanda (Musician,
Songwriter, Writer)
167 Fairview Rd
Ojai, CA 93023-9537, USA

McCabe, Bryan (Hockey Player)
c/o Staff Member *Toronto Maple Leafs*
Air Canada Centre
40 Bay St #400
Toronto, ON M5J 2X2, CANADA

McCabe, Frank (Basketball Player)
6712 N White Fir Dr
Edwards, IL 61528-9424, USA

McCabe, Joe (Baseball Player)
Minnesota Twins
3003 Gulf Shore Blvd N Apt 904
Naples, FL 34103-3969, USA

McCabe, John (Musician)
Novello Co
8/9 Firth St
London W1V 5TZ, UNITED KINGDOM
(UK)

McCabe, Marcia
Ansonia Sta
1990 Broadway # 417
New York, NY 10023, USA

McCabe, Patrick (Writer)
Picador
Macmillan Books
25 Eccleston Place
London SW1W 9NF, UNITED KINGDOM
(UK)

McCabe, Zia (Musician)
Mongui Mgmt
PO Box 5908
Portland, OR 97228-5908, USA

McCafferty, Donald F (Don) Jr (Coach,
Football Coach)
167 E Shore Rd
Halesite, NY 11743-1128, USA

McCaffrey, Barry R (General)
506 Crown View Dr
Alexandria, VA 22314-4806, USA

McCaffrey, Mike (Football Player)
Buffalo Bills
4370 Fruitvale Ave
Bakersfield, CA 93308-3934, USA

McCain, Bob (Football Player)
Brooklyn Dodgers
606 1/2 W Henry St
Greenwood, MS 38930-5325, USA

McCain, Edwin (Songwriter, Writer)
c/oMelissa Simmons
PO Box 1267
Harrington Management
Decatur, GA 30031-1267, USA

McCain, John (Politician)
U.S. Senate
241 Russell
Senate Office Bldg
Washington, DC 20510-0001, USA

McCall, Brian (Baseball Player)
Chicago White Sox
550 Tremont Ave
Greensburg, PA 15601-4263, USA

McCall, Davina (Actor)
c/o Staff Member *John Noel Management*
10A Belmont St
Floor 2
London NW1 8HH, UNITED KINGDOM
(UK)

McCall, Don (Football Player)
New Orleans Saints
16830 Kingsbury St Apt 131
Granada Hills, CA 91344-6465, USA

McCall, John (Baseball Player)
Boston Red Sox
8043 E Ragweed Dr
Tucson, AZ 85710-8580, USA

McCall, Larry (Baseball Player)
New York Yankees
RR 5 Box 354
Candler, NC 28715, USA

McCall, Mitzi (Actor)
Epstein-Wyckoff
280 S Beverly Dr Ste 400
Beverly Hills, CA 90212-3904, USA

McCall, Reese (Football Player)
Baltimore Colts
4913 Richard M Scrushy Pkwy
Fairfield, AL 35064-1454, USA

McCall, Robert T (Artist)
4816 E Moonlight Way
Paradise Valley, AZ 85253-2926, USA

McCall Smith, Alexander (Writer)
c/o Staff Member *Random House*
1540 Broadway
New York, NY 10036-4039, USA

McCallany, Holt (Actor)
Agency for Performing Arts
9220 W Sunset Blvd # 900
Los Angeles, CA 90069-3501, USA

McCallister, Blaine (Golfer)
8030 Pebble Creek Ln W
Ponte Vedra Beach, FL 32082-3102, USA

McCallum, David (Actor)
Hilary Gagan
Caprice House
3 New Burlington St
London W1X 1FE, UNITED KINGDOM
(UK)

McCallum, John
1740 Pittwater Rd.
Bayview NSW 2104, AUSTRALIA

McCallum, Napolean (Football Player)
Oakland Raiders
314 Doe Run Cir
Henderson, NV 89012-2700, USA

McCambridge, Mercedes (Astronaut)
210932 Pleasant Park Dr
Conifer, CO 80433, USA

McCament, Randy (Baseball Player)
San Francisco Giants
17338 N Del Webb Blvd
Sun City, AZ 85373-1951, USA

McCandless, Bruce (Doctor)
21852 Pleasant Park Rd
Conifer, CO 80433-6802, USA

McCanlies, Tim (Director, Producer,
Writer)
c/o Lindsay Williams *The Gotham Group
Inc*
9255 W Sunset Blvd Ste 515
Los Angeles, CA 90069-3301, USA

McCann, Chuck (Actor, Comedian)
2941 Briar Knoll Dr
Los Angeles, CA 90046-1122, USA

McCann, David A (Publisher)
Town & Country Magazine
1700 Broadway
New York, NY 10019-5905, USA

McCann, Les (Composer, Musician)
DeLeon Artists
4031 Panama Ct
Piedmont, CA 94611-4930, USA

McCann, Lila (Musician)
c/o Rick Shipp *William Morris Agency
(WMA-TN)*
1600 Division St Ste 300
Nashville, TN 37203-2755, USA

McCann, Michelle
1200 Singer Dr
West Palm Beach, FL 33404-2765, USA

McCants, Keith (Football Player)
Tampa Bay Buccaneers
5323 Forest Park Dr
Mobile, AL 36618-2421, USA

McCardell, Keenan (Football Player)
Cleveland Browns
4918 Newpoint Dr
Fresno, TX 77545-9200, USA

McCarren, Larry (Football Player)
Green Bay Packers
520 W Chickadee Ln
Green Bay, WI 54313-5039, USA

McCarrick, Theodore E Cardinal
(Religious Leader)
Archdiocesan Pastoral Center
5001 Eastern Ave
Washington, DC 20017, USA

McCarron, Chris
PO Box 861
Sierra Madre, CA 91025-0861, USA

McCarron, Christopher (Chris) (Jockey)
Dun Roamin
318 N Terrace View Dr
Monrovia, CA 91016-1570, USA

McCarron, Douglas J (Misc)
Carpenters/Joiners Brotherhood
101 Connecticut Ave NW
Washington, DC 20001, USA

McCarron, Scott (Golfer)
15569 Topspin Way
Rancho Murieta, CA 95683-8810, USA

McCarry, Charles (Writer)
Random House
1745 Broadway # B1
New York, NY 10019-4305, USA

McCartan, Jack (Hockey Player)
15504 Almond Ln
Eden Prairie, MN 55347-2554, USA

McCarter Sisters
PO Box 121551
Nashville, TN 37212-1551, USA

McCarthy, Andrew (Actor)
c/o Emily Gerson Saines *Brookside Artists
Management (NY)*
250 W 57th St Ste 2303
New York, NY 10107-2399, USA

McCarthy, Bill (Football Player)
Boston Yankees
1640 Walnut Ave
Winter Park, FL 32789-2036, USA

McCarthy, David (Baseball Player)
Minnesota Twins
110 Waldo Ave
Piedmont, CA 94611-3943, USA

McCarthy, Dennis (Composer)
Vangelos Mgmt
15233 Ventura Blvd Ste 200
Sherman Oaks, CA 91403-2244, USA

McCarthy, Dennis M (General)
Commander Forces Reserve
Hqusmc
2 Navy St
Washington, DC 20380-0001, USA

McCarthy, Greg (Baseball Player)
Seattle Mariners
256 Pennsylvania Ave
Bridgeport, CT 06610-1820, USA

McCarthy, Jenny (Actor)
c/o Erwin More *William Morris Agency
(WMA-LA)*
1 William Morris Pl
Beverly Hills, CA 90212-4261, USA

McCarthy, John (Scientist)
Stanford University
Computer Science Dept
Stanford, CA 94305, USA

McCarthy, Julianna (Actor)
Stone Manners
6500 Wilshire Blvd Ste 550
Los Angeles, CA 90048-4950, USA

McCarthy, Kevin (Actor)
14854 Sutton St
Sherman Oaks, CA 91403-4145, USA

McCarthy, Lin
233 N Swall Dr
Beverly Hills, CA 90211-1712, USA

McCarthy, Mary Frances (Educator,
Writer)
Trinity College
English Dept
Washington, DC 20017, USA

McCarthy, Melissa (Actor)
Gilmore Girls
4000 Warner Blvd Bldg 2222
Burbank, CA 91522-0001, USA

McCarthy, Nobu
9229 W Sunset Blvd Ste 311
Los Angeles, CA 90069-3403, USA

McCarthy, Norma
818385 Mead Lane Slu Box 9063
Victorville, CA 92392, USA

McCarthy, Shawn (Football Player)
New England Patriots
300 N Lakeshore Rd
Payson, AZ 85541-6220, USA

McCarthy, Timothy
8686 Butterfield Ln
Orland Park, IL 60462-1492, USA

McCarthy, Tom (Baseball Player)
Boston Red Sox
PO Box 38
Limington, ME 04049-0038, USA

McCarthy, tom (Director)
c/o Staff Member *Gersh Agency, The (LA)*
232 N Canon Dr
Beverly Hills, CA 90210-5302, USA

McCarthy, Tony (Songwriter, Writer)
29/33 Berners Road
London W1P 4AA, UNITED KINGDOM
(UK)

McCartney, Heather Mills (Activist)
MPL Communications Ltd
1 Soho Square
London, W1V 6BQ, ENGLAND

McCartney, Jesse (Actor)
c/o Mara Glauberg *Cunningham Escott
Slevin & Doherty (NY)*
257 Park Ave S Rm 950
New York, NY 10010-7304, USA

McCartney, Paul (Musician, Songwriter,
Writer)
c/o Staff Member *Paul Freundlich
Associates Media*
451 Greenwich St Rm 503
New York, NY 10013-1757, USA

McCartney, Stella (Designer, Fashion
Designer)
13 Rue Turbigo
Paris 75002, FRANCE

McCarty, Chris
9105 Carmelita Ave Apt 101
Beverly Hills, CA 90210-3543, USA

McCarty, Darren (Athlete)
c/o Staff Member *Detroit Red Wings*
600 Civic Center Dr
Joe Luis Arena
Detroit, MI 48226-4419, USA

McCarty, Mary (Baseball Player)
9455 N Genesee Rd
Mount Morris, MI 48458-9734, USA

McCarty, Mickey (Football Player)
Kansas City Chiefs
4803 Mistletoe Rd
Pasadena, TX 77505-2144, USA

McCarver, J Timothy (Tim) (Baseball
Player, Sportscaster)
118 County Line Rd
Bryn Mawr, PA 19010-3108, USA

McCarver, Shonna
13280 Northwest Fwy # F-252
Houston, TX 77040-6029, USA

McCarver, Tim (Baseball Player)
San Francisco Giants
5825 Riegels Harbor Rd
Sarasota, FL 34242-1779, USA

McCary, Michael (Musician)
Southpaw Entertainment
1710 N Fuller Ave Apt 323
Los Angeles, CA 90046-3064, USA

McCashin, Constance (Actor)
66 Fountain St
West Newton, MA 02465-3023, USA

McCaskill, Kirk E (Baseball Player)
California Angels
PO Box 451
Rancho Santa Fe, CA 92067-0451, USA

McCatty, Steve (Baseball Player)
Oakland A's
1075 Woodbriar Dr
Oxford, MI 48371-6069, USA

McCauley, Barry (Opera Singer)
598 Ridgewood Rd
Oradell, NJ 07649-2104, USA

McCauley, William F (Admiral)
570 Margarita Ave
Coronado, CA 92118, USA

McCay, Peggy (Actor)
2714 Carmar Dr
Los Angeles, CA 90046-1009, USA

McChesney, Robert (Bob) (Writer)
1103 S Douglas Ave
Urbana, IL 61801-4934, USA

McCkorkle, Kevin
c/o Peter Kluge *Impact Artists Group LLC*
244 N California St
Burbank, CA 91505-3505, USA

McClain, Cady (Actor)
c/o Staff Member *All My Children*
500 S Buena Vista St
Burbank, CA 91521-0001, USA

McClain, Charly (Musician)
John Lentz
PO Box 198888
Nashville, TN 37219-8888, USA

McClain, Dewey (Football Player)
Atlanta Falcons
1032 Flagg Way
Lawrenceville, GA 30044-3354, USA

McClain, Eugene (Baseball Player)
Philadelphia Stars
828 W 8th St
Chester, PA 19013-3712, USA

McClain, Joe (Baseball Player)
Washington Senators
1370 Milligan Hwy
Johnson City, TN 37601-5518, USA

McClain, Katrina (Basketball Player)
1907 Carlton St
North Charleston, SC 29405-5811, USA

McClairen, Jack (Cy) (Coach, Football
Coach)
Pittsburgh Steelers
1337 Idlewild Dr
Daytona Beach, FL 32114-1614, USA

McClanahan, Brent (Football Player)
Minnesota Vikings
1100 Sayword Ct
Bakersfield, CA 93312-5750, USA

McClanahan, Randy (Football Player)
Oakland Raiders
8107 W Via Del Sol
Peoria, AZ 85383-2142, USA

McClanahan, Robert (Rob) (Hockey
Player)
1462 Hunter Dr
Wayzata, MN 55391-9658, USA

McClanahan, Rue (Actor)
c/o Barbara Lawrence *Opus Entertainment*
5225 Wilshire Blvd Ste 905
Los Angeles, CA 90036-4353, USA

McClard, Bill (Football Player)
San Diego Chargers
149 N Pleasant Ridge Dr
Rogers, AR 72756-0702, USA

McClarnon, Zahn (Actor)
c/o Staff Member *Amsel Eisenstadt &
Frazier Inc*
5055 Wilshire Blvd Ste 865
Los Angeles, CA 90036-6109, USA

McClary, Thomas (Tom) (Musician)
Management Assoc
1920 Benson Ave
Saint Paul, MN 55116-3214, USA

McClatchy, Kevin (Baseball Player)
Pittsburgh Pirates
4858 Ellsworth Ave
Pittsburgh, PA 15213-2805, USA

McCleary, Norris (Football Player)
Kansas City Chiefs
115 Ferguson Dr
Kings Mountain, NC 28086-9727, USA

McCleery, Finnis D (War Hero)
616 N Jackson St
San Angelo, TX 76901-2520, USA

McClellan, Mike (Football Player)
Philadelphia Eagles
1801 Longbranch Ct
Arlington, TX 76012-5723, USA

McClellan, Paul (Baseball Player)
San Francisco Giants
1648 Andover Ln
Lincoln, CA 95648-8454, USA

McClellan, Scott (Government Official)
White House
1600 Pennsylvania Ave NW
Washington, DC 20500-0004, USA

McClelland, David C (Psychic)
81 Washington Ave
Cambridge, MA 02140-2716, USA

McClelland, Melissa (Musician)
c/o Staff Member *Paradigm (Monterey)*
509 Hartnell St
Monterey, CA 93940-2825, USA

McClelland, Tim (Baseball Player)
5405 Woodlans Ave
West Des Moines, IA 50266, USA

McClenathan, Cory (Race Car Driver)
MBNA Motorsports
1945 W Commonwealth Ave Ste A
Fullerton, CA 92833-3036, USA

McClendon, Lloyd (Baseball Player)
Cincinnati Reds
1082 Mission Hills Ct
Chesterton, IN 46304-9605, USA

McClendon, Reiley (Actor)
c/o Staff Member *Fenton-Kritzer
Entertainment*
8840 Wilshire Blvd Fl 3
Beverly Hills, CA 90211-2606, USA

McClendon, Sarah
3133 Connecticut Ave NW Apt 215
Washington, DC 20008-5105, USA

McClendon, Skip (Football Player)
Cincinnati Bengals
16844 Forrer St
Detroit, MI 48235, USA

McClendon, Willie (Football Player)
Chicago Bears
575 Cativo Dr SW
Atlanta, GA 30311-2107, USA

McClinic, Nath (Baseball Player)
Cleveland Buckeyes
1405 Bobo St SE
Rome, GA 30161-6425, USA

McClintock, Eddie (Actor)
c/o Ric Beddingfield *Beddingfield
Company, The*
9255 W Sunset Blvd Ste 920
Los Angeles, CA 90069-3306, USA

McClintock, Jessica (Designer, Fashion
Designer)
Jessica McClintock Co
1400 16th St
San Francisco, CA 94103-5181, USA

McClinton, Curtis (Football Player)
Dallas Texans
1020 N Rutland St
Wichita, KS 67206-3823, USA

McCloskey, J Michael (Misc)
Sierra Club
85 2ns St #200
San Francisco, CA 94105, USA

McCloskey, Jack (Basketball Player)
Minnesota Timberwolves
600 1st Ave N
Target Center
Minneapolis, MN 55403-1416, USA

McCloskey, Jim (Activist)
221 Witherspoon St
Princeton, NJ 08542-3215, USA

McCloskey, Leigh
6032 Philip Ave
Malibu, CA 90265-3747, USA

McCloskey, Mike (Football Player)
Houston Oilers
108 Summer Ridge Dr
Lansdale, PA 19446-6707, USA

McCloskey, Rep (Politician)
580 Mountain Home Rd
Woodside, CA 94062-2515, USA

McCloskey, Robert J (Diplomat)
111 Hesketh St
Chevy Chase, MD 20815-4222, USA

McCloskey-Rogers, Gloria (Baseball
Player)
PO Box 512
Macon, MO 63552-0512, USA

McCloud, Tyrus (Football Player)
Baltimore Ravens
2850 NW 8th St
Pompano Beach, FL 33069-2139, USA

McCloughan, Dave (Football Player)
Indianapolis Colts
2501 W 36th St
Loveland, CO 80538-5334, USA

McCloughan, Kent (Football Player)
Oakland Raiders
2241 Woody Creek Cir
Loveland, CO 80538-5333, USA

McClung, Seth (Baseball Player)
Tampa Bay Devil Rays
RR 2 Box 176
Lewisburg, WV 24901-9319, USA

McClure, Bob (Baseball Player)
Kansas City Royals
PO Box 842
Salem, VA 24153-0842, USA

McClure, Donald S (Misc)
23 Hemlock Cir
Princeton, NJ 08540-5405, USA

McClure, Kandyse (Actor)
c/o Richard Lucas *Lucas Talent Inc*
Sun Tower Floor 7
100 W Pender St
Vancouver, BC V6B 1R8, CANADA

McClure, Marc
1420 Beaudry Blvd
Glendale, CA 91208-1708, USA

McClure, Molly
12456 Ventura Blvd Ste 1
Studio City, CA 91604-2484, USA

McClure, Tane (Actor)
Don Gerler
3349 Cahuenga Blvd W Ste 1
Los Angeles, CA 90068-1379, USA

McClurg, Edie
9229 W Sunset Blvd Ste 315
Los Angeles, CA 90069-3403, USA

McClurkin, Donnie (Musician)
c/o Staff Member *Covenant Agency, The*
123 California Ave Apt 116
Santa Monica, CA 90403-3560, USA

McCole Bartusiak, Skye (Actor)
c/o Melissa Berger *Cunningham Escott Slevin & Doherty (LA)*
10635 Santa Monica Blvd Ste 130
Los Angeles, CA 90025-8306, USA

McColl, Bill (Football Player)
Chicago Bears
5166 Chelsea St
La Jolla, CA 92037-7908, USA

McCollum, Andy (Football Player)
New Orleans Saints
3933 Autumn Farms Dr
Pacific, MO 63069-2517, USA

McColm, Matt (Actor)
c/o Bob Read *ReBar Management*
10061 Riverside Dr # 722
Toluca Lake, CA 91602-2560, USA

McColms, Matt (Actor)
c/o Staff Member *Agency for the Performing Arts (APA-LA)*
405 S Beverly Dr
Beverly Hills, CA 90212-4416, USA

McComb, Jeremy (Musician)
c/o Staff Member *Paradigm (Monterey)*
509 Hartnell St
Monterey, CA 93940-2825, USA

McComb, Joanne (Baseball Player)
105 Nottingham Rd
Bloomsburg, PA 17815-3021, USA

McConaughey, Matthew (Actor)
c/o Gus Gustawes *J.K. Livin'*
238 S Lasky Dr
Beverly Hills, CA 90212-3615, USA

McConkey, Jim C (Cinematographer)
505 W 54th St # Ph-12
New York, NY 10019-5056, USA

McConkey, Phil (Football Player)
New York Giants
1599 Coast Walk
La Jolla, CA 92037-3731, USA

McConnell, Harden M (Misc)
Stanford University
Chemistry Dept
Stanford, CA 94305, USA

McConnell, John P (Business Person)
Worthington Industries
1205 Dearborn Dr
Columbus, OH 43085-4769, USA

McConnell, Page (Musician)
c/o Staff Member *Paradigm (Monterey)*
509 Hartnell St
Monterey, CA 93940-2825, USA

McConnell, Robert M G (Rob) (Musician)
Thomas Cassidy
11761 E Speedway Blvd
Tucson, AZ 85748-2017, USA

McConville, Frank (Misc)
Union of Plant Guard Workers of America
25510 Kelly Rd
Roseville, MI 48066-4932, USA

McCoo, Marilyn
2639 Lavery Ct Ste 5
Newbury Park, CA 91320-2275, USA

McCook, John (Actor)
10245 Briarwood Dr
Los Angeles, CA 90077-2521, USA

McCool, Bill (Baseball Player)
Cincinnati Reds
9250 SE 121st Loop
Summerfield, FL 34491-9477, USA

McCord, Bob (Hockey Player)
11540 N Donley Dr
Parker, CO 80138-8027, USA

McCord, Clinton (Baseball Player)
Baltimore Elite Giants
1821 Knowles St
Nashville, TN 37208-2438, USA

McCord, Darris (Football Player)
Detroit Lions
6160 W Surrey Rd
Bloomfield Hills, MI 48301-1661, USA

McCord, Gary (Golfer)
8620 E Thompson Peak Pkwy
Scottsdale, AZ 85255-9141, USA

McCord, Kent
c/o Staff Member *Tisherman Agency Inc*
6767 Forest Lawn Dr Ste 101
Los Angeles, CA 90068-1050, USA

McCord, Quentin (Football Player)
Atlanta Falcons
20014 Sugarloaf Reserve Dr
Duluth, GA 30097-5214, USA

McCormack, Catherine (Actor)
c/o Adam Isaacs *United Talent Agency (UTA)*
9560 Wilshire Blvd Ste 500
Beverly Hills, CA 90212-2401, USA

McCormack, Don (Baseball Player)
Philadelphia Phillies
866 Glenfield Dr
Palm Harbor, FL 34684-3218, USA

McCormack, Eric (Actor)
c/o Staff Member *Big Cattle Productions*
4370 Tujunga Ave Ste 130
Studio City, CA 91604-2769, USA

McCormack, Mary (Actor)
PO Box 67335
Los Angeles, CA 90067-0335, USA

McCormack, Mike (Football Player)
New York Yankees
265 Bouquet Canyon Dr
Palm Desert, CA 92211-3202, USA

McCormack, Patty
c/o Kurt Patino *LINK Talent Group*
4741 Laurel Canyon Blvd Ste 106
Valley Village, CA 91607-5907, USA

McCormack, Will (Actor)
c/o Greg Clark *Untitled Entertainment (LA)*
331 N Maple Dr Fl 3
Beverly Hills, CA 90210-3827, USA

McCormick, Carolyn (Actor)
Bresler Kelly Assoc
11500 W Olympic Blvd Ste 510
Los Angeles, CA 90064-1527, USA

McCormick, John (Football Player)
Minnesota Vikings
2615 Oak Dr Unit 34
Lakewood, CO 80215-7168, USA

McCormick, Kelly
PO Box 250
Seal Beach, CA 90740-0250, USA

McCormick, Maureen (Actor, Musician)
c/o Wes Stevens *VOX Inc*
5670 Wilshire Blvd Ste 820
Los Angeles, CA 90036-5613, USA

McCormick, Mike (Baseball Player)
New York Giants
1600 Morganton Rd Lot U9
Pinehurst, NC 28374-6859, USA

McCormick, Pat (Swimmer)
PO Box 250
Seal Beach, CA 90740-0250, USA

McCormick, Richard (Educator)
Rutgers State University
President's Office
East Rutherford, NJ 08903, USA

McCormick, Tim (Basketball Player)
2500 Leroy Ln
West Bloomfield, MI 48324-2234, USA

McCormick, Tom (Football Player)
Los Angeles Rams
397 Wehmeyer Loop
Mountain Home, AR 72653-6656, USA

McCormick, Walter (Football Player)
San Francisco 49ers
2150 N Peppertree Ct
Visalia, CA 93291-8878, USA

McCorvey, Norma
12730 Thomas Sumpter St.
San Antonio, TX 78223, USA

McCouch, Grayson
c/o Dan Baron *Agency for the Performing Arts (APA-LA)*
405 S Beverly Dr
Beverly Hills, CA 90212-4416, USA

McCourt, James (Actor, Television Host)
c/o Staff Member *Princess Productions*
Whiteley's Centre
151 Queensway
London W2 4SB, UNITED KINGDOM (UK)

McCoury, Del (Musician)
c/o Staff Member *Paradigm (Monterey)*
509 Hartnell St
Monterey, CA 93940-2825, USA

McCovey, Willie (Baseball Player)
San Francisco Giants
PO Box 620342
Woodside, CA 94062-0342, USA

McCowen, Sir Alec
3 Goodwin's Ct. St. Martin's Lane
London, ENGLAND WG2, UNITED KINGDOM (UK)

McCoy, Benny (Baseball Player)
Detroit Tigers
3932 Omaha St SW
Grandville, MI 49418-1867, USA

McCoy, Charlie (Musician)
PO Box 50455
Nashville, TN 37205-0455, USA

McCoy, Dave (Misc)
Mammoth Mountain Chairlifts
PO Box 24
Mammoth Lakes, CA 93546-0024, USA

McCoy, John B (Financier)
Corillian
3400 NW John Olsen Pl
Hillsboro, OR 97124-5808, USA

McCoy, Larry (Baseball Player)
5758 Highway 139
Greenway, AR 72430-7045, USA

McCoy, Mark
7120 Hawthorn Ave Apt 18
Los Angeles, CA 90046-3280, USA

McCoy, Matt (Actor)
Artists Agency
1180 S Beverly Dr Ste 301
Los Angeles, CA 90035-1154, USA

McCoy, Mike (Football Player)
Green Bay Packers
2224 Cotton Gin Row
Jefferson, GA 30549-8819, USA

McCoy, Neal (Musician)
c/o Greg Oswald *William Morris Agency (WMA-TN)*
1600 Division St Ste 300
Nashville, TN 37203-2755, USA

McCoy, Sandra (Actor)
c/o Staff Member *Metropolitan*
4500 Wilshire Blvd Fl 2
Los Angeles, CA 90010-3858, USA

McCoy, Tony (Football Player)
Indianapolis Colts
PO Box 616382
Orlando, FL 32861-6382, USA

McCrabb, Les (Baseball Player)
Philadelphia Athletics
433 S Kinzer Ave # 26
New Holland, PA 17557-9360, USA

McCracken, Jeff
15760 Ventura Blvd Ste 1730
Encino, CA 91436-3048, USA

McCracken, Paul W (Economist, Government Official)
2564 Hawthorne Road
Ann Arbor, MI 48104, USA

McCracken, Quinton (Baseball Player)
Colorado Rockies
11308 E Autumn Sage Dr
Scottsdale, AZ 85255-8949, USA

McCrane, Paul (Actor)
VOX
5670 Wilshire Blvd Ste 820
Los Angeles, CA 90036-5613, USA

McCrary, Darius (Actor)
c/o Stephen Rice *Diverse Talent Group*
1875 Century Park E Ste 2250
Los Angeles, CA 90067-2563, USA

McCrary, Joel (Actor)
c/o Holly Shelton *Stone Manners Talent & Literary (LA)*
6500 Wilshire Blvd Ste 550
Los Angeles, CA 90048-4950, USA

McCrary, Michael (Football Player)
Seattle Seahawks
9907 Chase Hill Ct
Vienna, VA 22182-1427, USA

McCrary, Prentice (Football Player)
New England Patriots
5414 E Dolphin Cir
Mesa, AZ 85206-2225, USA

McCraw, Tommy (Baseball Player)
Chicago White Sox
3142 SE Monte Vista Ct
Port Saint Lucie, FL 34952-6062, USA

McCray, Nikki (Basketball Player)
288 S Center St Apt 6
Collierville, TN 38017-3028, USA

McCray, Rodney (Baseball Player)
Chicago White Sox
20273 Faust Ave
Detroit, MI 48219-1514, USA

McCrea, Jody
Country Rd. 395 Box 195
Hondo, NM 89336, USA

McCready, Mike (Musician)
Annie Ohayon Media Relations
525 Broadway # 600
New York, NY 10012-4411, USA

McCreary, Tex
PO Box 405
Mill Neck, NY 11765-0405, USA

McCrills, John W (Writer)
McCrillis & Eldredge Insurance
17 Depot St
Newport, NH 03773-1533, USA

McCrimmon, Brad (Hockey Player)
Atlanta Thrashers Philips Arena
13 South Ave SE
Atlanta, GA 30315, USA

McCrory, Glenn (Boxer)
Holborn 35 Station Road
County Durham, UNITED KINGDOM
(UK)

McCrory, Milton (Milt) (Boxer)
Escot Boxing Enterprises
19244 Bretton Dr
Detroit, MI 48223-1364, USA

McCrudden, Ian (Actor)
Margrit Polak Mgmt
1411 Carroll Ave
Los Angeles, CA 90026-5111, USA

McCullers, Lance (Baseball Player)
San Diego Padres
3309 Hoedt Rd
Tampa, FL 33618-1611, USA

McCulley, Michael J (Astronaut)
44 Live Oak Bnd
Bay City, TX 77414-9153, USA

McCullin, Donald (Don) (Photographer)
Holly Hill House
Batcombe Shepton Mallet
Somerset BA4 6BL, UNITED KINGDOM
(UK)

McCulloch, Ed (Race Car Driver)
1397 Cherry Tree Rd
Avon, IN 46123-7103, USA

McCulloch, Frank W (Educator, Lawyer)
5604 Kirkside Dr
Chevy Chase, MD 20815-7112, USA

McCulloch (McCullough), Bruce (Actor)
c/o Marty Bowen *United Talent Agency*
(UTA)
9560 Wilshire Blvd Ste 500
Beverly Hills, CA 90212-2401, USA

McCullough, Bob (Football Player)
Denver Broncos
11111 NE 38th Pl
Bellevue, WA 98004-7622, USA

McCullough, Colleen (Writer)
PO Box 333
Norfolk Island, NSW 2899, AUSTRALIA

McCullough, David (Actor)
c/o Staff Member *Creative Artists Agency
LCC (CAA-LA)*
2000 Avenue Of The Stars
Los Angeles, CA 90067-4700, USA

McCullough, David (Writer)
Janklow & Nesbit Assoc
445 Park Ave # 1300
New York, NY 10022-2606, USA

McCullough, Earl (Athlete, Football
Player, Track Athlete)
2108 Santa Fe Ave
Long Beach, CA 90810-3546, USA

McCullough, Julian (Musician)
c/o Staff Member *Paradigm (Monterey)*
509 Hartnell St
Monterey, CA 93940-2825, USA

McCullough, Kimberly
9229 W Sunset Blvd Ste 315
Los Angeles, CA 90069-3403, USA

McCullough, Shanna
7920 Alabama Ave
Canoga Park, CA 91304-4907, USA

McCullough, Wayne (Boxer)
9972 Shady Glade Ct
Las Vegas, NV 89148-1687, USA

McCullum, Sam (Football Player)
Minnesota Vikings
7701 88th Pl SE
Mercer Island, WA 98040-5746, USA

McCully, Kilmer (Doctor)
Veteran Affairs Med Center
Davis Park
Pathology Dept
Providence, RI 02908, USA

McCumber, Mark (Golfer, Sportscaster)
53 Ponte Vedra Blvd
Ponte Vedra Beach, FL 32082-1311, USA

McCune, Lisa (Actor)
c/o Staff Member *RGM Associates
(Australia)*
PO Box 128
Surry Hills NSW 2010, AUSTRALIA

McCurdy, Cindy (Golfer)
18 Cottage Dr
Newnan, GA 30265-5513, USA

McCurdy, Jennette (Actor)
Voltronix
PO Box 6355
Marcus McCurdy
Garden Grove, CA 92846-6355, USA

McCurry, Jeff (Baseball Player)
Pittsburgh Pirates
3635 Underwood St
Houston, TX 77025-1905, USA

McCurry, Margaret (Architect)
Tigerman McCurry Architects
444 N Wells St Ste 200
Chicago, IL 60610-4522, USA

McCurry, Mike (Journalist, Politician)
Cable News Network
1050 Techwood Dr NW
News Dept
Atlanta, GA 30318-5604, USA

McCusker, Jim (Football Player)
Chicago Cardinals
209 N Main St
Jamestown, NY 14701-5209, USA

McCutcheon, Dayton (Football Player)
Cleveland Browns
901 Golden Springs Dr # F-G
Diamond Bar, CA 91765-1181, USA

McCutcheon, Lawrence (Football Player)
Los Angeles Rams
19981 Weems Ln
Huntington Beach, CA 92646-3835, USA

McCutcheon, Linda (Publisher)
AARP Publications
Director's Office
601 E St NW
Washington, DC 20049-0001, USA

McCutcheon, Martine (Musician)
P F D Drury House
34-43 Russell St
London WC2B 5HA, UNITED KINGDOM
(UK)

McDaniel, James (Actor)
c/o Craig Shapiro *Innovative Artists (LA)*
1505 10th St
Santa Monica, CA 90401-2805, USA

McDaniel, John (Cinematographer,
Musician, Producer)
c/o Glenn Daniels *Glenn Daniels Arts
Management*
56 Warren St Apt 5E
New York, NY 10007-1097, USA

McDaniel, John (Football Player)
Cincinnati Bengals
608 Andalusia Trl
Desoto, TX 75115-6310, USA

McDaniel, Lecharls (Football Player)
Washington Redskins
12844 Starwood Ln
San Diego, CA 92131-4210, USA

McDaniel, Lindy
RR 2 Box 353A
Hollis, OK 73550, USA

McDaniel, Lyndail D (Lindy) (Baseball
Player)
St Louis Cardinals
1095 Meadow Hill Dr
Lavon, TX 75166-1262, USA

McDaniel, Mel (Musician, Songwriter,
Writer)
106 Cranwill Dr
Hendersonville, TN 37075-2804, USA

McDaniel, Randall C (Football Player)
Minnesota Vikings
20405 Manor Rd
Excelsior, MN 55331-9470, USA

McDaniel, Terry (Baseball Player)
New York Mets
10326 N Central St
Kansas City, MO 64155-3527, USA

McDaniel, Terry (Football Player)
Oakland Raiders
4825 S Washington Rd
Saginaw, MI 48601-7205, USA

McDaniel, Xavier (Basketball Player)
2 Oakmist Ct
Blythewood, SC 29016-8707, USA

McDaniels, Darryl (Darryl M) (Music
Group, Musician)
Entertainment Artists
2409 21st Ave S Ste 100
Nashville, TN 37212-5317, USA

McDavid, Ray (Baseball Player)
San Diego Padres
1245 Market St Apt 1348
San Diego, CA 92101-7358, USA

McDermott, Alice (Writer)
Farrar Straus Giroux
19 Union Sq W Fl 11
New York, NY 10003-3304, USA

McDermott, Brian
27 Upper Berkeley St.
London, ENGLAND W1, UNITED
KINGDOM (UK)

McDermott, Dean (Actor)
c/o Ted Schachter *Schachter
Entertainment*
1157 S Beverly Dr Fl 2
Los Angeles, CA 90035-1119, USA

McDermott, Dylan (Actor)
c/o Judy Hofflund *Hofflund/Polone*
9465 Wilshire Blvd Ste 890
Beverly Hills, CA 90212-2607, USA

McDermott, Edward A (Government
Official)
875 E Camino Real
Lake House South
Boca Raton, FL 33432-6356, USA

McDermott, R Terrance (Terry) (Speed
Skater)
5078 Chain Bridge Rd
Bloomfield Hills, MI 48304-3727, USA

McDermott, Shane
200 W 57th St Ste 900
New York, NY 10019-3211, USA

McDermott, Terry (Baseball Player)
Los Angeles Dodgers
7205 Sunlight Peak Dr NE
Rio Rancho, NM 87144-7508, USA

McDevitt, Danny (Baseball Player)
Brooklyn Dodgers
2274 Salem Rd SE Ste 106
Conyers, GA 30013-2097, USA

McDiarmid, Ian (Actor)
Wood Lane
London W12 7RJ, UNITED KINGDOM
(UK)

McDill, Allen (Baseball Player)
Kansas City Royals
1024 Evergreen Dr
Arkadelphia, AR 71923-2934, USA

McDivitt, James
9146 Cherry Ave
Rapid City, MI 49676-9669, USA

McDivitt, James A (Jim) (Astronaut,
General)
3530 E Calle Puerta De Acero
Tucson, AZ 85718-6000, USA

McDole, Ron (Football Player)
St Louis Cardinals
2083 Lockes Mill Rd
Berryville, VA 22611-3931, USA

McDonagh, Martin (Writer)
Creative Artists Agency
9830 Wilshire Blvd
Beverly Hills, CA 90212-1804, USA

McDonald, Alvin B (Ab) (Hockey Player)
419 Thompson Dr
Winnipeg, MB R3J 3E7, CANADA

McDonald, Audra (Actor, Musician)
Gersh Agency
232 N Canon Dr
Beverly Hills, CA 90210-5302, USA

McDonald, Ben (Baseball Player)
Baltimore Orioles
General Delivery
Denham Springs, LA 70726-9999, USA

McDonald, Bruce (Director, Producer)
c/o Bill Douglass *Paradigm (LA)*
360 N Crescent Dr
North Bldg
Beverly Hills, CA 90210-6820, USA

McDonald, Christopher
c/o Daniel (Danny) Sussman *Brillstein-Grey Entertainment*
9150 Wilshire Blvd Ste 350
Beverly Hills, CA 90212-3453, USA

McDonald, Country Joe (Musician)
PO Box 7054
Berkeley, CA 94707-0054, USA

McDonald, Darnell (Football Player)
Tampa Bay Buccaneers
13551 Bentley Cir
Woodbridge, VA 22192-4336, USA

McDonald, Dave (Baseball Player)
New York Yankees
2545 SE 3rd St
Pompano Beach, FL 33062-5401, USA

McDonald, David L (Admiral)
PO Box 45214
Jacksonville, FL 32232-5214, USA

McDonald, Devon (Football Player)
Indianapolis Colts
425 E 25th St
Paterson, NJ 07514-2306, USA

McDonald, Donzell (Baseball Player)
New York Yankees
3353 W Monterey St
Chandler, AZ 85226-2337, USA

McDonald, Forrest (Historian)
PO Box 155
Coker, AL 35452-0155, USA

McDonald, Gregory C (Writer)
Arthur Greene
101 Park Ave Rm 2607
New York, NY 10178-2602, USA

McDonald, Jiggs (Sportscaster)
8331 Arborfield Ct
Fort Myers, FL 33912-4684, USA

McDonald, Jim (Baseball Player)
Boston Red Sox
3767 Stirrup Dr
Kingman, AZ 86409-2943, USA

McDonald, Joe
17337 Ventura Blvd Ste 208
Encino, CA 91316-3992, USA

McDonald, John (Baseball Player)
Cleveland Indians
11 Nelson Dr
East Lyme, CT 06333-1146, USA

McDonald, Keith (Baseball Player)
St Louis Cardinals
5162A E Greensboro Ln
Anaheim, CA 92807, USA

McDonald, Kevin Hamilton (Actor, Writer)
c/o Kevin McDonald *Celebrity Connection*
2208 Patricia Ave
Los Angeles, CA 90064-2318, USA

McDonald, Lanny (Hockey Player)
CHA
2424 University NW
Calgary, AB T2N 3Y9, CANADA

McDonald, Michael (Musician, Songwriter, Writer)
c/o Staff Member *Vector Management*
1607 17th Ave S
Nashville, TN 37212-2812, USA

McDonald, Mike (Football Player)
Los Angeles Rams
1067 E Angeleno Ave
Burbank, CA 91501-1420, USA

McDonald, Paul (Football Player)
Cleveland Browns
1815 Tradewinds Ln
Newport Beach, CA 92660-3810, USA

McDonald, Ricardo (Football Player)
Cincinnati Bengals
1916 Fairlawn St
Pittsburgh, PA 15221-1504, USA

McDonald, Richie (Musician)
PO Box 128648
Nashville, TN 37212, USA

McDonald, Thomas F (Tommy) (Football Player)
Philadelphia Eagles
537 W Valley Forge Rd
King Of Prussia, PA 19406-1568, USA

McDonald, Tim (Football Player)
St Louis Cardinals
10851 N Maple Ave
Fresno, CA 93730-3501, USA

McDonell, R Terry (Editor)
US Weekly
1290 Avenue Of The Americas
Editorial Dept
New York, NY 10104-0295, USA

McDonnell, John F (Business Person)
McDonnell Douglas Corp
PO Box 516
Saint Louis, MO 63166-0516, USA

McDonnell, Mary (Actor)
PO Box 6010-540
Sherman Oaks, CA 91413, USA

McDonnell, Patrick (Cartoonist)
King Features Syndicate
888 7th Ave Ste 201
New York, NY 10106-0201, USA

McDonough, Mary (Actor)
6858 Cantaloupe Ave
Van Nuys, CA 91405-4148, USA

McDonough, Neal (Actor)
c/o Glenn Rigberg *Rigberg-Rugolo Entertainment*
1180 S Beverly Dr Ste 601
Los Angeles, CA 90035-1158, USA

McDonough, Sean (Sportscaster)
ABC-TV
77 W 66th St
Sports Dept
New York, NY 10023-6201, USA

McDonough, William (Architect)
410 E Water St
Charlottesville, VA 22902-5276, USA

McDonough, William J (Financier)
Public Company Accounting Oversight Board
1666 K St NW Fl 8-9
Washington, DC 20006-1250, USA

McDorman, Jake (Actor)
c/o Jennifer Millar *Abrams Artists Agency (LA)*
9200 W Sunset Blvd Ph 11
Los Angeles, CA 90069-3601, USA

McDormand, Frances (Actor)
c/o Brian Swardstrom *Endeavor Agency LLC (LA)*
9601 Wilshire Blvd Fl 3
Beverly Hills, CA 90210-5204, USA

McDormond, Frances
333 W End Ave Apt 12C
New York, NY 10023-8132, USA

McDougal, Bob (Football Player)
Green Bay Packers
8300 SW 62nd Ct
South Miami, FL 33143-8008, USA

McDougal, Mike (Hockey Player)
2892 Tanglewood Dr
Kimball, MI 48074-1535, USA

McDougal, Susan
350 S Grand Ave Ste 3900
Los Angeles, CA 90071-3480, USA

McDougald, Gil
10 Warren Ave
Spring Lake, NJ 07762-1216, USA

McDougald, Gilbert J (Gil) (Baseball Player)
New York Yankees
2005 Mill Pond Ct
Wall Township, NJ 07719-3660, USA

McDougale, Stockar (Football Player)
Detroit Lions
15 Bradford Ct
Dearborn, MI 48126-4170, USA

McDougall, Charles (Writer)
c/o Staff Member *Industry Entertainment*
955 Carrillo Dr Ste 300
Los Angeles, CA 90048-5400, USA

McDougall, Ian (Producer)
c/o Staff Member *Gersh Agency, The (LA)*
232 N Canon Dr
Beverly Hills, CA 90210-5302, USA

McDougall, Walter A (Historian)
University of Pennsylvania
History Dept
Philadelphia, PA 19104, USA

McDowell, Bubba (Football Player)
Houston Oilers
6353 Richmond Ave
Houston, TX 77057-5964, USA

McDowell, Frank (Doctor)
100 N Kalaheo Place #F
Kailua Kona, HI 96734, USA

McDowell, Jack (Baseball Player)
Chicago White Sox
2530 Crawford Ave Ste 307
Evanston, IL 60201-4972, USA

McDowell, Malcolm (Actor)
Markham & Froggatt
Julian House
4 Windmill St
London W1P 1HF, UNITED KINGDOM (UK)

McDowell, Oddlbe (Baseball Player)
Texas Rangers
5240 SW 18th St
West Park, FL 33023-3157, USA

McDowell, Roger (Baseball Player)
New York Mets
58 Robinwood Pl
Jackson, MS 39211-2405, USA

McDowell, Ronnie (Musician)
PO Box 53
Portland, TN 37148-0053, USA

McDowell, Samuel E (Sam) (Baseball Player)
Cleveland Indians
12902 Brown Bark Trl
Clermont, FL 34711-7646, USA

McDuffie, George (Football Player)
Detroit Lions
819 Independence Rd
Toledo, OH 43607-2529, USA

McDuffie, Otis J (O J) (Football Player)
Miami Dolphins
1333 NW 121st Ave
Plantation, FL 33323-2438, USA

McDuffie, Robert (Musician)
Columbia Artists Mgmt Inc
1790 Broadway Fl 6
New York, NY 10019-1412, USA

McDyess, Antonio (Basketball Player)
410 Thompson Ave
Quitman, MS 39355-2215, USA

McEldowney, Brooke (Cartoonist)
United Feature Syndicate
200 Madison Ave
New York, NY 10016-3911, USA

McElhenny, Hugh (Football Player)
San Francisco 49ers
3013 Via Venezia
Henderson, NV 89052-3802, USA

McElhone, Natascha (Actor)
Creative Artists Agency
9830 Wilshire Blvd
Beverly Hills, CA 90212-1804, USA

McElhorne, Natascha (Artist)
c/o Staff Member *International Creative Management (ICM-LA)*
10250 Constellation Blvd
Los Angeles, CA 90067-6200, USA

McElligott, Sarah (Actor)
c/o Tom Chasin *Chasin Agency, The*
8899 Beverly Blvd Ste 716
Los Angeles, CA 90048-2449, USA

McElmury, Jim (Hockey Player)
9122 78th St S
Cottage Grove, MN 55016-2211, USA

McElroy, Chuck (Baseball Player)
Philadelphia Phillies
1049 Nederland Ave
Port Arthur, TX 77640-4338, USA

McElroy, Hugh (Football Player)
Arizona Cardinals
3899 Fonville Ave
Beaumont, TX 77705-2207, USA

McElroy, Reggie (Football Player)
New York Jets
RR 1 Box 109A
Preston, MO 65732-9743, USA

McElroy, Vann (Football Player)
Los Angeles Raiders
524 Private Road 4450
Uvalde, TX 78801-1194, USA

McEnaney, Will (Baseball Player)
Cincinnati Reds
1055 SW 3rd St
Boca Raton, FL 33486-4553, USA

McEnery, Peter (Actor)
International Creative Agency
76 Oxford St
London W1N 0AX, UNITED KINGDOM (UK)

McEnroe, John (Tennis Player)
23712 Malibu Colony Rd
Malibu, CA 90265-4636, USA

McEntee, Gerald W (Politician)
State County Municipal Employees Union
1625 L St NW
Washington, DC 20036-5665, USA

McEntire, Reba (Musician)
c/o Narvel Blackstock *Starstruck Entertainment*
40 Music Sq W
Nashville, TN 37203-3206, USA

McEwan, Geraldine (Actor)
Marmont Mgmt
Langham House
302/8 Regent St
London W1R 5AL, UNITED KINGDOM
(UK)

McEwan, Ian R (Writer)
15 Park Town
Oxford OX2 6SN, UNITED KINGDOM
(UK)

McEwen, Bruce S (Scientist)
Rockefeller University
1230 York Ave
Immunology Dept
New York, NY 10065-6399, USA

McEwen, Craig (Football Player)
Washington Redskins
1610 Hilton Head Ct Apt 1265
El Cajon, CA 92019-4578, USA

McEwen, Mark (Correspondent)
CBS TV
51 W 52nd St
News Dept
New York, NY 10019-6119, USA

McEwen, Tom (Writer)
Tampa Tribune
202 S Parker St
Editorial Dept
Tampa, FL 33606-2395, USA

McEwing, Joe (Baseball Player)
St Louis Cardinals
630 Deerbrook Dr
Yardley, PA 19067-4537, USA

McFadden, Cynthia (Correspondent,
Journalist, Television Host)
c/o Staff Member *Nightline*
1717 Desales St NW
Washington, DC 20036-4401, USA

McFadden, Daniel L (Nobel Prize
Laureate)
41 Southampton Ave
Berkeley, CA 94707-2034, USA

McFadden, Davenia (Actor)
c/o Felicia Sager *Art Work Entertainment*
5900 Wilshire Blvd Ste 2150
Los Angeles, CA 90036-5021, USA

McFadden, Gates (Actor)
2332 E Allview Ter
Los Angeles, CA 90068-3021, USA

McFadden, Leon (Baseball Player)
Houston Astros
8617 S 10th Ave
Inglewood, CA 90305-2346, USA

McFadden, Mary J (Designer, Fashion
Designer)
240 W 35th St Ste 700
New York, NY 10001-2514, USA

McFadden, Paul (Football Player)
Philadelphia Eagles
7395 Christopher Dr
Youngstown, OH 44514-2563, USA

McFadden, Robert D (Journalist)
New York Times
229 W 43rd St
Editorial Dept
New York, NY 10036-3959, USA

McFadden-Rusynyk, Betty Jean (Baseball
Player)
7267 W 130th St
Parma, OH 44130-7814, USA

McFadin, Bud
1467 Albrecht Rd
Victoria, TX 77905-2613, USA

McFadin, Lewis P (Bud) (Football Player)
Los Angeles Rams
647 Springwood
Victoria, TX 77905-2580, USA

McFadyen, Angus (Actor)
c/o Tracy Brennan *Creative Artists Agency
LCC (CAA-LA)*
2000 Avenue Of The Stars
Los Angeles, CA 90067-4700, USA

McFarland, Anthony (Football Player)
Tampa Bay Buccaneers
7733 Still Lakes Dr
Odessa, FL 33556-2262, USA

McFarland, Jim (Football Player)
Buffalo Bills
5102 S 90th St
Lincoln, NE 68526-9627, USA

McFarland, Kay (Football Player)
San Francisco 49ers
7394 S Monaco St
Centennial, CO 80112-1528, USA

McFarland, Kirsten (Writer)
c/o Staff Member *International Creative
Management (ICM-LA)*
10250 Constellation Blvd
Los Angeles, CA 90067-6200, USA

McFarlane, Andrew (Actor)
c/o Staff Member *Jeff Morrone
Management*
9350 Wilshire Blvd Ste 224
Beverly Hills, CA 90212-3204, USA

McFarlane, Orlando (Baseball Player)
Pittsburgh Pirates
1021 Aviary Rd
Wellington, FL 33414-7928, USA

McFarlane, Robert C (Government
Official)
2010 Prospect St NW
Washington, DC 20037, USA

McFarlane, Todd (Cartoonist)
PO Box 12230
Tempe, AZ 85284-0038, USA

McFayden, Brian (Actor)
c/o Kenny Goodman *William Morris
Agency (WMA-LA)*
1 William Morris Pl
Beverly Hills, CA 90212-4261, USA

McFeeley, William S (Historian, Writer)
31 Concord Ave Apt 2
Cambridge, MA 02138-2339, USA

McFerrin, Bobby (Actor, Songwriter,
Writer)
Original Artists
826 Broadway # 400
New York, NY 10003-4826, USA

Mcfly (Music Group)
c/o Staff Member *Universal Music Group
(UMG - LA)*
2220 Colorado Ave
Santa Monica, CA 90404-3506, USA

McGaffigan, Andy (Baseball Player)
New York Yankees
6243 Forestwood Dr E
Lakeland, FL 33811-2402, USA

McGahee, Willis (Football Player)
Buffalo Bills
1 Bills Dr
Orchard Park, NY 14127-2237, USA

McGahern, John (Writer)
Faber & Faber
3 Queen Square
London WC1N 3AU, UNITED KINGDOM
(UK)

McGahey, James C (Misc)
Plant Guard Workers Union
25510 Kelly Rd
Roseville, MI 48066-4932, USA

McGann, Paul (Actor)
Marina Martin
12/13 Poland St
London W1V 3DE, UNITED KINGDOM
(UK)

McGarity, Vernon (War Hero)
6901 Andrews Rd
Bartlett, TN 38135-3010, USA

McGarity, Wane (Football Player)
Dallas Cowboys
4622 Lavender Ln
San Antonio, TX 78220-2511, USA

McGarrahan, Scott (Football Player)
Green Bay Packers
6636 W William Cannon Dr
Austin, TX 78735-8529, USA

McGarrigle, Anne (Musician)
Concerted Efforts
59 Parsons St
West Newton, MA 02465-2137, USA

McGarrigle, Kate (Musician)
Concerted Efforts
59 Parsons St
West Newton, MA 02465-2137, USA

McGarry, John (Football Player)
Green Bay Packers
5725 S Woodlawn Ave
Chicago, IL 60637-1602, USA

McGarry, Steve (Cartoonist)
United feature Syndicate
200 Madison Ave
New York, NY 10016-3911, USA

McGaw, Patrick (Actor)
Banner Entertainment
8265 W Sunset Blvd Ste 200
West Hollywood, CA 90046-2470, USA

McGeady, Sister Mary Rose (Activist)
Covenant House
460 W 41st St
New York, NY 10036-6898, USA

McGee, Ben (Football Player)
Pittsburgh Steelers
35 Castle Cv
Jackson, MS 39212-3448, USA

McGee, Henry
19 Sydney Mews
London, ENGLAND SW3 6HL, UNITED
KINGDOM (UK)

McGee, Michael B (Mike) (Football
Player)
St Louis Cardinals
2 Medical Park Rd Ste 502
University Of South California
Columbia, SC 29203-6876, USA

McGee, Pamela (Pam) (Basketball Player)
Los Angeles Sparks
1111 S Figueroa St
Staples Center
Los Angeles, CA 90015-1300, USA

McGee, Tim (Football Player)
Cincinnati Bengals
688 Riddle Rd Apt 1000F
Cincinnati, OH 45220-2642, USA

McGee, Tony (Football Player)
Chicago Bears
170 Tana Dr
Fayetteville, GA 30214-7539, USA

McGee, Vonetta
1801 Avenue Of The Stars Ste 902
Los Angeles, CA 90067-5981, USA

McGee, William M (Max) (Football
Player)
Green Bay Packers
19625 Chimo West St
Wayzata, MN 55391-3506, USA

McGee, Willie D (Baseball Player)
St Louis Cardinals
2081 Lupine Rd
Hercules, CA 94547-1104, USA

McGeever, John (Football Player)
Denver Broncos
3479 Norwich Dr
Birmingham, AL 35243-2128, USA

McGegan, Nicholas (Conductor)
Schwalbe Partners
170 E 61st St # 5N
New York, NY 10065-8551, USA

McGehee, Kevin (Baseball Player)
Baltimore Orioles
18 Melmoore Dr
Pineville, LA 71405-3108, USA

McGeorge, Missle (Golfer)
907 Meadow Ln
Southlake, TX 76092-8338, USA

McGeorge, Rich (Football Player)
Green Bay Packers
2200 Trail Wood Dr
Durham, NC 27705-1305, USA

McGhee, George C (Government Official)
36276 Mountville Rd
Middleburg, VA 20117-3308, USA

McGhee-Anderson, Kathleen (Producer)
c/o Staff Member *Creative Artists Agency
LCC (CAA-LA)*
2000 Avenue Of The Stars
Los Angeles, CA 90067-4700, USA

McGibbony, Charles (Football Player)
Brooklyn Tigers
714 5th Ave
Conway, AR 72032-5804, USA

McGiffin, Carol (Actor, Talk Show Host)
c/o Staff Member *ITV Network*
200 Gray's Inn Rd
London, CA WC1X 8HF, UNITED
KINGDOM (UK)

McGilberry, Randy (Baseball Player)
Kansas City Royals
2011 Ridgeline Dr
Mobile, AL 36695-4031, USA

McGill, Billy (Basketball Player)
5129 W 58th Pl
Los Angeles, CA 90056-1601, USA

McGill, Bruce (Actor)
c/o Scott Manners *Stone Manners Talent
& Literary (LA)*
6500 Wilshire Blvd Ste 550
Los Angeles, CA 90048-4950, USA

McGill, Bryant (Writer)
11C Lower Dorset St
Dubline 1, IRELAND

McGill, Jill (Golfer)
2609 S Quebeo St Apt 5
Denver, CO 80231, USA

McGill, Karmeeleyah (Football Player)
Cincinnati Bengals
1626 N Greenwood Ave
Clearwater, FL 33755, USA

McGill, Mike (Football Player)
Minnesota Vikings
8930 Louis Ct
Saint John, IN 46373-9708, USA

McGill, William J (Educator)
2624 Costebelle Dr
La Jolla, CA 92037-3516, USA

McGillin, Howard
151 El Camino Dr
Beverly Hills, CA 90212-2704, USA

McGillion, Paul (Actor)
c/o Jamie Levitt *Lauren Levitt & Associates Inc*
1525 W 8th St 3rd Fl
Vancouver, BC V6J 1T5, CANADA

McGillis, Kelly (Actor)
Kelly's Caribbean Bar & Grill
303 Whitehead St
Key West, FL 33040, USA

McGinest, Willie (Football Player)
New England Patriots
2211 Easy Ave
Long Beach, CA 90810-3534, USA

McGinley, John C (Actor)
Innovative Artists
1505 10th St
Santa Monica, CA 90401-2805, USA

McGinley, Ted (Actor)
c/o Adena Chawke *Greenlight Management*
315 S Beverly Dr Ste 300
Beverly Hills, CA 90212-4309, USA

McGinn, Bernard J (Misc)
5702 S Kenwood Ave
Chicago, IL 60637, USA

McGinn, Dan (Baseball Player)
Cincinnati Reds
1340 S 163rd St
Omaha, NE 68130-1417, USA

McGinnis, Dave (Coach, Football Coach)
Arizona Cardinals
PO Box 888
Phoenix, AZ 85001-0888, USA

McGinnis, George (Basketball Player)
11245 Marlin Rd
Indianapolis, IN 46239-8400, USA

McGinnis, Joe (Writer)
Janklow & Nesbit
445 Park Ave # 1300
New York, NY 10022-2606, USA

McGinnis, Russ (Baseball Player)
Texas Rangers
1110 N Judd Pl
Chandler, AZ 85226-8709, USA

McGinnis, Susan (Television Host)
c/o Staff Member *CBS News*
524 W 57th St
Viacom Inc
New York, NY 10019-2924, USA

McGinty, John J III (War Hero)
51 Barbara Ln
Hudson, NH 03051-3769, USA

McGirt, James (Buddy) (Boxer)
195 Suffolk Ave
Brentwood, NY 11717-4205, USA

McGlinchy, Kevin (Baseball Player)
Atlanta Braves
1927 Halifax Rd
Danville, VA 24540-5827, USA

McGlockin, Jon (Basketball Player)
5281 State Road 83
Hartland, WI 53029-9306, USA

McGlockton, Chester (Football Player)
Oakland Raiders
6930 S Perth St
Aurora, CO 80016-2340, USA

McGlothin, Pat (Baseball Player)
Brooklyn Dodgers
1454 Kenesaw Ave
Knoxville, TN 37919-7749, USA

McGlynn, Dennis (Race Car Driver)
Dover Downs Speedway
PO Box 843
Dover, DE 19903-0843, USA

McGlynn, Dick (Hockey Player)
17 Butternut Ave
Peabody, MA 01960-4603, USA

McGlynn, Pat (Musician)
27 Preston Grange
Preston Pans E
Lothian, SCOTLAND

McGoohan, Patrick (Actor)
523 Chapala Dr
Pacific Palisades, CA 90272-4430, USA

McGoon, Dwight C (Doctor)
211 2nd St NW Apt 2016
Rochester, MN 55901-3101, USA

McGovern, Elizabeth (Actor)
17319 Magnolia Blvd
Encino, CA 91316-2542, USA

McGovern, George S (Politician, Senator)
FAO
Via delle Terme di Carachkka
Rome 00100, ITALY

McGovern, Jim (Golfer)
384 Francis Ct
Oradell, NJ 07649-1308, USA

McGovern, Maureen (Actor, Musician)
MM Productions Inc
12087 Evergreen St NW
C/O Jennifer Howe
Minneapolis, MN 55448-2433, USA

McGovern, Rob (Football Player)
Kansas City Chiefs
419 E 57th St Apt 2D
New York, NY 10022-3060, USA

McGowan, Charles E (Religious Leader)
Presbyterian Church in America
1852 Century Pl NE
Atlanta, GA 30345-4305, USA

McGowan, Pat (Golfer)
PO Box 88
Southern Pines, NC 28388-0088, USA

McGowan, Rose (Actor)
c/o Jason Weinberg *Untitled Entertainment (LA)*
331 N Maple Dr Fl 3
Beverly Hills, CA 90210-3827, USA

McGrady, Michael (Actor)
c/o Staff Member *SDB Partners Inc*
1801 Avenue Of The Stars Ste 902
Los Angeles, CA 90067-5981, USA

McGrady, Tracy (Basketball Player)
Houston Rockets
1510 Polk St
Houston, TX 77002-1099, USA

McGrath, Doug (Director)
c/o Staff Member *International Creative Management (ICM-LA)*
10250 Constellation Blvd
Los Angeles, CA 90067-6200, USA

McGrath, Douglas (Actor, Director, Writer)
c/o Staff Member *Creative Artists Agency LCC (CAA-LA)*
2000 Avenue Of The Stars
Los Angeles, CA 90067-4700, USA

McGrath, Eugene R (Business Person)
Consolidated Edison
4 Irving Pl
New York, NY 10003-3598, USA

McGrath, James (Scientist)
Yale University
Genetics Dept
New Haven, CT 06520, USA

McGrath, Jeremy (Motorcycle Race, Motorcycle Racer)
American Motorcycle Assn
13515 Yarmouth Dr
Pickerington, OH 43147-8273, USA

McGrath, Judy (Business Person)
c/o Staff Member *MTV Networks (LA)*
2600 Colorado Ave
Santa Monica, CA 90404-3519, USA

McGrath, Mark (Musician, Television Host)
c/o Staff Member *Extra (LA)*
1840 Victory Blvd
Telepictures Productions
Glendale, CA 91201-2558, USA

McGrath, Mike (Bowler)
738 Colusa Ave
El Cerrito, CA 94530-3313, USA

McGraw, Jay (Writer)
c/o Staff Member *The Dr. Phil Show*
5555 Melrose Ave
Mae West Bldg
Los Angeles, CA 90038-3989, USA

McGraw, Mike (Football Player)
St Louis Cardinals
PO Box 529
Medicine Bow, WY 82329-0529, USA

McGraw, Phil (Dr. Phil) (Doctor, Talk Show Host)
c/o Staff Member *The Dr. Phil Show*
5555 Melrose Ave
Mae West Bldg
Los Angeles, CA 90038-3989, USA

McGraw, Robin (Writer)
c/o Staff Member *The Dr. Phil Show*
5555 Melrose Ave
Mae West Bldg
Los Angeles, CA 90038-3989, USA

McGraw, Thurman (Football Player)
749 Sandpiper Pt
Fort Collins, CO 80525-3111, USA

McGraw, Tim (Musician)
c/o Bryan Loucks *Creative Artists Agency LCC (CAA-LA)*
2000 Avenue Of The Stars
Los Angeles, CA 90067-4700, USA

McGraw, Tom (Baseball Player)
St Louis Cardinals
930 N Parkway Ave Apt K
Battle Ground, WA 98604, USA

McGraw III, Harold W (Business Person, Publisher)
McGraw-Hill Inc
1221 Avenue Of The Americas
New York, NY 10020-1095, USA

McGregor, Ewan (Actor)
c/o Brandt Joel *Creative Artists Agency LCC (CAA-LA)*
2000 Avenue Of The Stars
Los Angeles, CA 90067-4700, USA

McGregor, Keli (Baseball Player, Football Player, President)
Denver Broncos
14776 W Byers Pl
Golden, CO 80401-5170, USA

McGregor, Maurice (Doctor)
Royal Victoria Hospital
687 Pine Ave W
Montreal, PQ H3A 1A1, CANADA

McGregor, Scott H (Baseball Player)
Baltimore Orioles
1514 Providence Rd # A
Towson, MD 21286-1523, USA

McGrew, Larry (Football Player)
New England Patriots
1818 Short St
Berkeley, CA 94702-1525, USA

McGrew, Reggie (Football Player)
San Francisco 49ers
1247 Lakeside Dr Apt 2039
Sunnyvale, CA 94085-1008, USA

McGriff, Frederick S (Fred) (Baseball Player)
Toronto Blue Jays
16314 Millan De Avila
Tampa, FL 33613-1089, USA

McGriff, Hershel (Race Car Driver)
General Delivery
Green Valley, AZ 85622-9999, USA

McGriff, James H (Jimmy) Jr (Music Group, Musician)
Maxine Harvard
7942 W Bell Rd
Glendale, AZ 85308-8708, USA

McGriff, Lee (Football Player)
Tampa Bay Buccaneers
3501 W University Ave Ste A
Gainesville, FL 32607-2465, USA

McGriff, Tery (Baseball Player)
Cincinnati Reds
2905 Langston Dr
Fort Pierce, FL 34946-1180, USA

McGriff, Travis (Football Player)
Denver Broncos
5910 NW 19th Pl
Gainesville, FL 32605-3246, USA

McGriggs, Lamar (Football Player)
New York Giants
1209-115 Main St E
Hamilton, ON L8N 1G5, CANADA

McGruder, Aaron (Cartoonist)
Universal Press Syndicate
4520 Main St
Kansas City, MO 64111-1876, USA

McGuane III, Thomas F (Writer)
410 S 3rd Ave
Bozeman, MT 59715-5251, USA

McGuinn, Martin G (Financier)
Mellon Financial Corp
Mellon Bank Center
500 Grant St
Pittsburgh, PA 15258-0001, USA

McGuinn, Roger (Musician, Songwriter, Writer)
Elizabeth Rush Agency
82 Cumberland Ave
Verona, NJ 07044-2105, USA

McGuire, Allie
4 Tanglewood Ln
Winchester, MA 01890-3376, USA

McGuire, Betty (Actor)
H David Moss
733 Seward St Ph
Los Angeles, CA 90038-3503, USA

McGuire, Bill (Baseball Player)
Seattle Mariners
17209 L St
Omaha, NE 68135, USA

McGuire, Christine (Musician)
100 Rancho Cir
Las Vegas, NV 89107-4600, USA

McGuire, Dorothy (Musician)
100 Rancho Cir
Las Vegas, NV 89107-4600, USA

McGuire, Gene (Football Player)
New Orleans Saints
704 W 17th St
Lynn Haven, FL 32444-4213, USA

McGuire, Kevin E (Basketball Player)
20 Blue Jay Ln
North Oaks, MN 55127-2015, USA

Mcguire, Maeve
c/o Staff Member *Gage Group, The (LA)*
14724 Ventura Blvd Ste 505
Sherman Oaks, CA 91403-3505, USA

McGuire, Mickey (Baseball Player)
Baltimore Orioles
1521 Middle Park Dr
Dayton, OH 45414-1500, USA

McGuire, Patricia A (Educator)
Trinity College
President's Office
Washington, DC 20017, USA

McGuire, Phyllis (Musician)
100 Rancho Cir
Las Vegas, NV 89107-4600, USA

McGuire, Richard J (Dick) (Basketball Player, Coach)
17 Redwood Dr
Dix Hills, NY 11746-7727, USA

McGuire, Ryan (Baseball Player)
Montreal Expos
2 Spoon Ln
Trabuco Canyon, CA 92679-4924, USA

McGuire, Willard H (Misc)
National Education Assn
1201 16th St NW
Washington, DC 20036-3290, USA

McGuire, William Biff (Actor)
McKenrick
1443 Pandoza Ave
Los Angeles, CA 90024, USA

McGuire, William W (Business Person)
United HealthCare Corp
9900 Bren Rd E
Opus Center
Minnetonka, MN 55343-4402, USA

McGuire Sisters (Music Group)
c/o Stan Scottland *Stan Scottland Entertainment*
157 E 57th St Apt 18B
New York, NY 10022-2115, USA

McGwire, Mark (Athlete, Baseball Player)
c/o Harlan Werner *Sports Placement Service*
6671 W Sunset Blvd Ste 1521
Los Angeles, CA 90028-7123, USA

McHale, John (Baseball Player)
Detroit Tigers
2014 NW Royal Fem Ct
Palm City, FL 34990, USA

McHale, Kevin E (Basketball Player)
20 Blue Jay Ln
Saint Paul, MN 55127-2015, USA

McHattie, Stephen (Actor)
c/o Christopher (Chris) Wright *Christopher Wright Management*
3207 Winnie Dr
Los Angeles, CA 90068-1439, USA

McHattle, Stephen (Actor)
Macklam Feldman Mgmt
1505 W 2nd Ave
#200
Vancouver, BC V6H 3Y4, CANADA

McHenry, Donald F (Diplomat)
Georgetown University
Foreign Service School
Washington, DC 20057-0001, USA

McHenry, Vance (Baseball Player)
Seattle Mariners
2396 Brown St
Durham, CA 95938-9620, USA

McHugh, Heather (Writer)
University of Washington
English Dept
PO Box 35330
Seattle, WA 98195-0001, USA

McIlhenny, Don (Football Player)
Detroit Lions
8505 Edgemere Rd Apt 101
Dallas, TX 75225-3520, USA

Mcilvaine, Jim (Basketball Player)
811 Blaine Ave
Racine, WI 53405-2407, USA

McInally, Pat (Football Player)
Cincinnati Bengals
1026 White Sails Way
Corona Del Mar, CA 92625-1542, USA

McInerney, Jay (Actor, Writer)
c/o Doug MacLaren *International Creative Management (ICM-LA)*
10250 Constellation Blvd
Los Angeles, CA 90067-6200, USA

McInnis, Hugh (Football Player)
St Louis Cardinals
290 Rockwell Church Rd NE
Winder, GA 30680-3039, USA

McInnis, Marty (Hockey Player)
21 Peter Hobart Dr
Hingham, MA 02043-3751, USA

McIntosh, Bill (Golfer)
5263 SW Bimini Cir N
Palm City, FL 34990-1246, USA

Mcintosh, Bradley (Actor, Musician)
c/o Staff Member *S Club 7*
9830 Wilshire Blvd
Creative Artists Agency Lcc (Caa-La)
Beverly Hills, CA 90212-1804, USA

McIntyre, Guy (Football Player)
San Francisco 49ers
257 Arrowhead Way
Hayward, CA 94544-6649, USA

McIntyre, Joe (Actor)
c/o Gina Rugolo-Judd *Rigberg-Rugolo Entertainment*
1180 S Beverly Dr Ste 601
Los Angeles, CA 90035-1158, USA

McIntyre, Secedrick (Football Player)
Atlanta Falcons
4801 Tannery Ave
Tampa, FL 33624-4533, USA

McIver, Everett (Football Player)
New York Jets
6443 Applewhite Rd
Fayetteville, NC 28304-6039, USA

McIvor, Richard (Football Player)
St Louis Cardinals
PO Box 148
Fort Davis, TX 79734-0002, USA

McJulien, Paul (Football Player)
Green Bay Packers
12111 Gibbens Rd
Baton Rouge, LA 70807-1602, USA

McKagan, Duff Rose (Musician)
Big F D Entertainment
301 Artzona Ave #200
Santa Monica, CA 90401, USA

McKagen, Duff
8647 Edwin Dr
Los Angeles, CA 90046-1047, USA

McKay, Bob (Football Player)
Cleveland Browns
4110 Bluffridge Dr
Austin, TX 78759-7354, USA

McKay, Cody (Baseball Player)
Oakland A's
9702 E La Posada Cir
Scottsdale, AZ 85255-3716, USA

McKay, Dave (Baseball Player)
Minnesota Twins
9702 E La Posada Cir
Scottsdale, AZ 85255-3716, USA

McKay, David S (Scientist)
NASA
2101 Nasa Pkwy
Johnson Space Center
Houston, TX 77058-3691, USA

McKay, Gardner
1040 Lunalilo St Ph 2
Honolulu, HI 96822-5712, USA

McKay, Heather (Athlete)
48 Nesbitt Ave
Toronto, ON M4W 2G3, CANADA

McKay, Jim (Sportscaster)
Battlefield Farm
2805 Sheppard Rd
Monkton, MD 21111-1339, USA

McKay, John (Football Player)
Tampa Bay Buccaneers
4110 Bluffridge Dr
Austin, TX 78759-7354, USA

McKay, Mhairi (Golfer)
898 W Ashbourne Dr
Eagle, ID 83616-6433, USA

McKay, Peggy (Actor)
8811 Wonderland Ave
Los Angeles, CA 90046-1851, USA

Mckean, Jim (Baseball Player)
740 Sand Pine Dr NE
Saint Petersburg, FL 33703-3181, USA

McKean, Michael (Actor, Comedian)
c/o Harriet Sternberg *Harriet Sternberg Management*
4530 Gloria Ave
Encino, CA 91436-2718, USA

McKee, Bonnie (Musician)
15353 SE 49th Pl
Bellevue, WA 98006-3652, USA

McKee, Frank S (Misc)
United Steelworkers Union
5 Gateway Ctr
Pittsburgh, PA 15222, USA

McKee, Gina (Actor)
Rozane Vacca
8 Silver Place
London W1R 3LJ, UNITED KINGDOM (UK)

McKee, Kinnaird R (Admiral)
7100 Wheeler Park Cir
Easton, MD 21601-8448, USA

McKee, Lucky (Director)
9300 Wilshire Blvd Ste 555
Beverly Hills, CA 90212-3211, USA

McKee, Maria (Musician)
Eleven Thirty
449A Trollingwood Rd
Haw River, NC 27258-8750, USA

McKee, Rogers (Baseball Player)
Philadelphia Phillies
409 Forest Hill Dr
Shelby, NC 28150-5520, USA

McKee, Theodore A (Judge)
US Appeals Court
601 Market St Rm 22409
US Couthouse
Philadelphia, PA 19106-1715, USA

McKee, Todd (Actor)
611 N Flores St Apt 2
West Hollywood, CA 90048-2134, USA

McKeehan, Pat
PO Box 486
Louisville, TN 37777-0486, USA

McKeel, Walt (Baseball Player)
Boston Red Sox
7637 Nc Highway 58 N
Stantonsburg, NC 27883-8635, USA

McKeever, Marlin (Football Player)
Los Angeles Rams
4000 E 2nd St
Long Beach, CA 90803-5223, USA

McKellar, Danica (Actor)
c/o Staff Member *Don Buchwald & Associates Inc (LA)*
6500 Wilshire Blvd Ste 2200
Los Angeles, CA 90048-4942, USA

McKellen, Ian (Actor)
c/o Chris Andrews *Creative Artists Agency LCC (CAA-LA)*
2000 Avenue Of The Stars
Los Angeles, CA 90067-4700, USA

McKeller, Keith (Football Player)
Buffalo Bills
1972 Waccamaw Path
Winston Salem, NC 27127-9433, USA

McKelvey, Rob (Golfer)
c/o Staff Member *Pro Golfers Association (PGA) Tour*
112 Tpc Blvd
Ponte Vedra Beach, FL 32082, USA

McKenna, Andrew J (Business Person)
McDonald's Corp
1 McDonalds Plz
1 Kroc Dr
Oak Brook, IL 60523-1911, USA

McKenna, David (Dave) (Musician)
Thomas Cassidy
11761 E Speedway Blvd
Tucson, AZ 85748-2017, USA

McKenna, T P (Actor)
28 Claverley Grove
London N3 2DH, UNITED KINGDOM
(UK)

McKenna, Virginia (Actor)
8 Buckfast Court
Runcorn, Cheshire WA7 1QJ, UNITED
KINGDOM (UK)

McKenney, Donald H (Don) (Hockey
Player)
16 Edgewater Dr
Norton, MA 02766-2123, USA

McKennitt, Loreena (Musician)
c/o Staff Member *Helter Skelter (UK)*
535 Kings Rd
The Plaza
London SW10 0SZ, UNITED KINGDOM
(UK)

McKennitt, Lorena (Musician, Songwriter,
Writer)
Quinlan Road
PO Box 933
Stratford, ON N5A 7M3, CANADA

McKennon, Keith R (Business Person)
6079 N Paradise View Dr
Paradise Valley, AZ 85253-3828, USA

McKenzie, Andrew (Misc)
Leather Goods Plastics Novelty Union
265 W 14th St
New York, NY 10011-7103, USA

McKenzie, Benjamin (Actor)
c/o David Seltzer *Management 360*
9111 Wilshire Blvd
Beverly Hills, CA 90210-5508, USA

McKenzie, Constance
3360 Barham Blvd
Los Angeles, CA 90068-1473, USA

McKenzie, Dan P (Misc)
Bullard Labs
Madingley Rise
Madingley Road
Cambridge CB3 0EZ, UNITED KINGDOM
(UK)

McKenzie, Jacqueline (Actor)
c/o Brett Carella *Lab, The*
5540 Hollywood Blvd # 200
Hollywood, CA 90028-6808, USA

McKenzie, Julia
Kingston Richmond Park
Surrey, ENGLAND, UNITED KINGDOM
(UK)

McKenzie, Kevin (Ballerina)
American Ballet Theatre
890 Broadway
New York, NY 10003-1278, USA

McKenzie, Raleigh (Football Player)
Washington Redskins
715 Huntsman Pl
Herndon, VA 20170-3160, USA

McKenzie, Reggie (Football Player)
Los Angeles Raiders
5211 Pinnacle Dr
Knoxville, TN 37914-4331, USA

McKenzie, Reginald (Reggie) (Football
Player)
Buffalo Bills
1849 Campau Farms Cir
Detroit, MI 48207-5167, USA

McKenzie, Vashti (Religious Leader)
Payne Memorial Church
1714 Madison Ave # 16
Baltimore, MD 21217, USA

McKeon, Doug (Actor)
4644 Arriba Dr
Tarzana, CA 91356-4824, USA

McKeon, Joel (Baseball Player)
Chicago White Sox
1901 Pierce St Apt 7
Hollywood, FL 33020-4047, USA

McKeon, John A (Jack) (Baseball Player)
13453 Luna Dr
Redding, CA 96003-8919, USA

McKeon, Lindsey (Actor)
c/o Robbie Kass *Kass & Stokes
Management*
9229 W Sunset Blvd Ste 504
Los Angeles, CA 90069-3405, USA

McKeon, Matt (Soccer Player)
Kansas City Wizards
8900 State Line Rd
Leawood, KS 66206-1941, USA

McKeon, Nancy (Actor)
PO Box 6778
Burbank, CA 91510-6778, USA

McKeown, Bob (Correspondent)
CBS-TV
51 W 52nd St
News Dept
New York, NY 10019-6119, USA

McKeown, Fintan (Actor)
c/o Alan Saffron *Saffron Management*
9171 Wilshire Blvd Ste 441
Beverly Hills, CA 90210-5516, USA

McKeown, Les
27 Preston Grange Preston Pans
E. Lothian, SCOTLAND

McKeown, Leslie (Les) (Music Group,
Musician)
Brian Gannon Mgmt
PO Box 106
Rochdale, OL 16 4HW, UNITED
KINGDOM (UK)

McKeown, M Margaret (Judge)
US Court of Appeals
1010 5th Ave
US Courthouse
Seattle, WA 98104-1195, USA

McKernan, John R Jr (Governor)
77 Sanderson Rd
Cumberland Foreside, ME 04110-1436,
USA

McKey, Derrick (Basketball Player)
4243 Creekside Pass
Zionsville, IN 46077-9290, USA

McKibben, Mike (Football Player)
New York Jets
2523 Forest Brook Dr
Upper Saint Clair, PA 15241-2586, USA

McKibbin, Nikki (Musician)
c/o Staff Member *Fox Television Studios*
10201 W Pico Blvd Bldg 41
Los Angeles, CA 90064-2606, USA

McKidd, Kevin (Actor)
c/o Philip Grenz *William Morris Agency
(WMA-LA)*
1 William Morris Pl
Beverly Hills, CA 90212-4261, USA

McKiernan, David (General)
Commanding General
3rd Army
Atlanta, GA 30330-0001, USA

McKinley, Dennis (Football Player)
Arizona Cardinals
150 McKinley Rd
Mc Cool, MS 39108-4220, USA

McKinley, John (Misc)
952 Bloomfield Village Blvd
Auburn Hills, MI 48326-3572, USA

McKinley, Robin (Writer)
Writer's House
21 W 26th St
New York, NY 10010-1083, USA

McKinley-Uselmann, Therese (Baseball
Player)
1644 N Greenwood Ave
Park Ridge, IL 60068-1215, USA

McKinnely, Phil (Football Player)
Atlanta Falcons
585 Edgehill Pl
Alpharetta, GA 30022-7006, USA

McKinney, Gil (Actor)
c/o Julia Buchwald *Don Buchwald &
Associates Inc (LA)*
6500 Wilshire Blvd Ste 2200
Los Angeles, CA 90048-4942, USA

McKinney, Greg
1800 Avenue Of The Stars Ste 400
Los Angeles, CA 90067-4206, USA

McKinney, Kurt
9200 W Sunset Blvd Ste 1130
Los Angeles, CA 90069-3606, USA

McKinney, Mark (Actor)
c/o Staff Member *William Morris Agency
(WMA-LA)*
1 William Morris Pl
Beverly Hills, CA 90212-4261, USA

McKinney, Odis (Football Player)
New York Giants
23126 Collins St
Woodland Hills, CA 91367-4225, USA

McKinney, Rich (Baseball Player)
Chicago White Sox
2495 E Peterson Rd
Troy, OH 45373-7790, USA

McKinney, Royce (Football Player)
Buffalo Bills
1930 N Beech Daly Rd
Dearborn Heights, MI 48127-3462, USA

McKinney, Steve (Football Player)
Indianapolis Colts
335 County Road 201
Centerville, TX 75833-3406, USA

McKinney, Tamara
4935 Parkers Mill Rd
Lexington, KY 40513-9760, USA

McKinnie, Bryant (Football Player)
Minnesota Vikings
9520 Viking Dr
Eden Prairie, MN 55344-3898, USA

McKinnie, Silas (Football Player)
St Louis Cardinals
22875 Summer House Ct Apt 205
Novi, MI 48375-4582, USA

McKinnney, Kurt (Actor)
5003 Tilden Ave Unit 206
Sherman Oaks, CA 91423-1747, USA

McKinnney, Richard (Rick) (Athlete)
7659 Kavooras Dr
Sacramento, CA 95831-4207, USA

McKinnon, Bruce (Cartoonist, Editor)
Halifax Herald
Editorial Dept
PO Box 610
Halifax, NS B3J 2T2, CANADA

McKinnon, Dan (Hockey Player)
610 E River Dr
Warroad, MN 56763, USA

McKinnon, Dennis (Football Player)
Chicago Bears
1016 Adams St
North Chicago, IL 60064-1227, USA

McKinnon, Ray (Actor)
Judy Schoen
606 N Larchmont Blvd Ste 309
Los Angeles, CA 90004-1309, USA

McKinnon, Ronald (Football Player)
Arizona Cardinals
1063 Grand Oaks Dr
Bessemer, AL 35022-7237, USA

McKinny, Laura Hart
3224 Nottingham Rd
Winston Salem, NC 27104-1839, USA

McKissock, Gary S (General)
*Deputy CofS for Installations/Logistics
Hqusmc*
2 Navy St
Washington, DC 20380-0001, USA

McKnight, Brian (Musician, Songwriter,
Writer)
c/o Staff Member *William Morris Agency
(WMA-LA)*
1 William Morris Pl
Beverly Hills, CA 90212-4261, USA

McKnight, Clarence E Jr (General)
1624 Linway Park Dr
McLean, VA 22101-4149, USA

McKnight, Ira (Baseball Player)
Kansas City Monarchs
608 S Summit Dr Apt 1
South Bend, IN 46619-2436, USA

McKnight, James (Football Player)
Seattle Seahawks
16705 Berkshire Ct
Southwest Ranches, FL 33331-1331, USA

McKnight, Jeff (Baseball Player)
New York Mets
3296 Highway 92 W
Bee Branch, AR 72013-8937, USA

McKnight, Ted (Football Player)
Kansas City Chiefs
400 W 68th St
Kansas City, MO 64113-1919, USA

McKnight, Tony (Baseball Player)
Houston Astros
406 Dundee Rd
Texarkana, AR 71854-9768, USA

McKuen, Rod (Musician, Songwriter,
Writer)
PO Box 2783
Los Angeles, CA 90078-2783, USA

McKusick, Victor A (Scientist)
221 Morthway
Baltimore, MD 21218, USA

McKyer, Tim (Football Player)
San Francisco 49ers
12333 McAllister Park Dr
Charlotte, NC 28277-2503, USA

McLachlan, Craig
Box 176
Potts Point NSW 2011, AUSTRALIA

McLachlan, Sarah (Musician, Songwriter)
c/o Terry McBride *Nettwerk Productions*
1650 W 2nd Ave
Vancouver, BC V6J 4R3, CANADA

McLafferty, Fred W (Scientist)
103 Needham Pl
Ithaca, NY 14850-2120, USA

McLaglen, Andrew
PO Box 1056
Friday Harbor, WA 98250-1056, USA

McLain, Dennis D (Denny) (Baseball Player)
Detroit Tigers
4889 Mercer Rd
Pinckney, MI 48169-9387, USA

McLain, Kevin (Football Player)
Calico Enterprises
2551 State St Ste 222
Carlsbad, CA 92008-1682, USA

McLane, Drayton (Baseball Player)
Houston Astros
100 N Apache Dr
Temple, TX 76504-2863, USA

McLane, James P (Jimmy) Jr (Swimmer)
85 Pinckney St
Boston, MA 02114-4303, USA

McLaren, Sally
28 Berkeley Sq.
London, ENGLAND W1X 6HD, UNITED KINGDOM (UK)

McLaughlin, Ann Dore (Secretary)
Urban Institute of Washington
2100 M St NW
Washington, DC 20037-1264, USA

McLaughlin, Audrey (Government Official)
New Democratic Party
House of Commons
Ottawa, ON K1A 0A6, CANADA

McLaughlin, Byron (Baseball Player)
Seattle Mariners
7030 Alamitos Ave
San Diego, CA 92154-4764, USA

McLaughlin, Carol (Musician)
Columbia Artists Mgmt Inc
1790 Broadway Fl 6
New York, NY 10019-1412, USA

McLaughlin, Joey (Baseball Player)
Atlanta Braves
1611 S Troost Ave
Tulsa, OK 74120-6615, USA

McLaughlin, John (Football Player)
Tampa Bay Buccaneers
6038 Marina Pointe Court #207
Tampa, FL 33635, USA

McLaughlin, John (Government Official)
Central Intelligence Agency
Deputy Director's Office
Washington, DC 20505-0001, USA

McLaughlin, John J (Television Host)
The McLaughlin Group
1717 Rhode Island Ave NW Ste 640
Oliver Productions Inc
Washington, DC 20036-3025, USA

McLaughlin, Mike (Race Car Driver)
PO Box 45
Waterloo, NY 13165-0045, USA

McLean, A J (Actor, Musician)
c/o Staff Member *The Firm*
9465 Wilshire Blvd Fl 6
Beverly Hills, CA 90212-2605, USA

McLean, Barney (Skier)
9555 W 59th Ave Apt 303
Arvada, CO 80004-5396, USA

McLean, Don (Musician, Songwriter, Writer)
c/o Jim Lenz *Paradise Artists*
108 E Matilija St
Ojai, CA 93023-2639, USA

McLean, Greg (Director)
c/o Staff Member *Endeavor Agency LLC (LA)*
9601 Wilshire Blvd Fl 3
Beverly Hills, CA 90210-5204, USA

McLean, Rene (Musician)
Brad Simon Organization
122 E 57th St # 300
New York, NY 10022-2623, USA

McLean, Sally (Actor, Producer)
c/o Staff Member *Salmac Management*
PO Box 526
Mt Martha VIC 3934, AUSTRALIA

McLean, Scott (Football Player)
Dallas Cowboys
375 Bear Ln
Lake Placid, FL 33852-4411, USA

McLeland, Wayne (Baseball Player)
Detroit Tigers
6622 Beldart St
Houston, TX 77087-6510, USA

Mclellan, Zoe (Actor)
c/o Christopher Barrett *Metropolitan*
4500 Wilshire Blvd Fl 2
Los Angeles, CA 90010-3858, USA

McLemore, Dana (Football Player)
San Francisco 49ers
2908 Fairman St
Lakewood, CA 90712-3634, USA

McLemore, LaMonte (Musician)
Sterling/Winters
10877 Wilshire Blvd # 15
Los Angeles, CA 90024-4341, USA

McLemore, Mark (Baseball Player)
California Angels
533 S White Chapel Blvd
Southlake, TX 76092-7316, USA

McLeod, Ralph (Baseball Player)
Boston Bees
541 Ralph Talbot St
South Weymouth, MA 02190-3331, USA

McLeod, Robert D (Football Player)
Houston Oilers
600 Spring Creek Rd
Brenham, TX 77833-8159, USA

McLerie, Allyn Ann (Actor, Dancer)
3344 Campanil Dr
Santa Barbara, CA 93109-1017, USA

McLish, Cal (Baseball Player)
Brooklyn Dodgers
639 Timber Ln
Edmond, OK 73034-4631, USA

McLish, Rachel (Actor, Athlete)
c/o Ron Samuels *Ron Samuels Entertainment*
100 Wilshire Blvd Ste 750
Santa Monica, CA 90401-1100, USA

McIntosh, Joe (Baseball Player)
San Diego Padres
1011 Western Ave Ste 803
Seattle, WA 98104-1083, USA

McIntosh, Tim (Baseball Player)
Milwaukee Brewers
4325 E Norwich Ave
Fresno, CA 93726-2643, USA

McIntyre, Donald C (Opera Singer)
Foxhill Farm
Jackass Lane Keston Bromley
Kent BR2 6AN, UNITED KINGDOM (UK)

McMahan, Jack (Baseball Player)
Pittsburgh Pirates
131 Forest View Cir
Hot Springs, AR 71913-6557, USA

McMahon, Art (Football Player)
Boston Patriots
PO Box 292
Reading, MA 01867-0492, USA

McMahon, Ed (Entertainer, Television Host)
The Ed McMahon Show
10487 Sunland Blvd
Sunland, CA 91040-1905, USA

McMahon, James R (Jim) (Football Player)
Chicago Bears
34 Bridlewood Rd
Northbrook, IL 60062-4702, USA

McMahon, Jenna
PO Box 5033
Carmel By The Sea, CA 93921-5033, USA

McMahon, Julian (Actor)
c/o Stephanie Davis *3 Arts Entertainment Inc*
9460 Wilshire Blvd Fl 7
Beverly Hills, CA 90212-2713, USA

McMahon, Mike (Football Player)
Detroit Lions
313 Oak Grove Ct
Wexford, PA 15090-9570, USA

McMahon, Shane (Wrestler)
c/o Staff Member *World Wrestling Entertainment (WWE)*
1241 E Main St
Stamford, CT 06902-3520, USA

McMahon, Stephanie (Wrestler)
c/o Staff Member *World Wrestling Entertainment (WWE)*
1241 E Main St
Stamford, CT 06902-3520, USA

McMahon Jr, Vince (Actor, Producer, Writer)
1241 E Main St
Stamford, CT 06902-3520, USA

McMahon Sr, Vincent K (Misc)
47 Hurtingham Dr
Greenwich, CT 06831, USA

McMakin, John (Football Player)
Pittsburgh Steelers
3825 S Ave
Anacortes, WA 98221-3644, USA

McManus, Don (Actor)
c/o Staff Member *Principal Entertainment (LA)*
1964 Westwood Blvd Ste 400
Los Angeles, CA 90025-4695, USA

McManus, Jim (Baseball Player)
Kansas City A's
2352 Hopkins Mill Rd
Duluth, GA 30096-4524, USA

McManus, Michelle (Musician)
c/o Staff Member *Pop Idol (Fremantle Media)*
2700 Colorado Ave Ste 450
Santa Monica, CA 90404-3599, USA

McMartin, John (Actor, Musician)
Artists Agency
1180 S Beverly Dr Ste 301
Los Angeles, CA 90035-1154, USA

McMath, Jimmy (Baseball Player)
Chicago Cubs
3321 22nd St
Tuscaloosa, AL 35401-5203, USA

McMenamin, Mark (Misc)
Mount Holyoke College
Geology Dept
South Hadley, MA 01075, USA

McMichael, Greg (Baseball Player)
Atlanta Braves
11072 Peachcove Ct
Suwanee, GA 30024-6103, USA

McMichael, Steve D (Football Player)
New England Patriots
4250 N Marine Dr Apt 1027
Chicago, IL 60613-1757, USA

McMichen, Robert S (Misc)
International Typographical Union
PO Box 157
Colorado Springs, CO 80901-0157, USA

McMillan, Audray (Football Player)
Houston Oilers
1230 Hahlo St
Houston, TX 77020-7340, USA

McMillan, Caroline (Golfer)
5101 N Casa Blanca Dr Unit 206
Paradise Valley, AZ 85253-6987, USA

McMillan, Eddie (Football Player)
Los Angeles Rams
21524 73rd Pl W
Edmonds, WA 98026-7727, USA

McMillan, Erik (Football Player)
New York Jets
1746 Carissa Dr
Conyers, GA 30094-1126, USA

McMillan, Ernie (Football Player)
St Louis Cardinals
14816 Sycamore Manor Ct
Chesterfield, MO 63017-5535, USA

McMillan, Nate (Basketball Player, Coach)
2520 39th Ave E
Seattle, WA 98112-2542, USA

McMillan, Susan Carpenter
1744 Oak Ln
San Marino, CA 91108-1021, USA

McMillan, Terry (Writer)
PO Box 2408
Danville, CA 94526-7408, USA

McMillan, Tommy (Baseball Player)
Seattle Mariners
712 Spring Lake Rd
Thomasville, GA 31792-8605, USA

McMillan, William (Bill) (Misc)
1930 Sandstone Vista Ln
Encinitas, CA 92024-4247, USA

McMillen, C Thomas (Tom) (Basketball Player)
1167 Jeffrey Dr
Crofton, MD 21114-1316, USA

McMillian, Audray G (Football Player)
4015 Brightwood St
Missouri City, TX 77459-1814, USA

McMillian, Michael (Actor)
c/o Sandra Chang *Industry Entertainment*
955 Carrillo Dr Ste 300
Los Angeles, CA 90048-5400, USA

McMillin, James R (Football Player)
Denver Broncos
7985 Westview Dr
Lakewood, CO 80214-4541, USA

McMillon, Billy (Baseball Player)
Florida Marlins
1131 Shaws Fork Rd
Aiken, SC 29805-8596, USA

McMonagle, Donald R (Astronaut)
7737 E Shadow Vista Ct
Tucson, AZ 85750-0742, USA

McMorris, Jerry (Baseball Player)
Colorado Rockies
PO Box 217
Timnath, CO 80547-0217, USA

McMullen, Ken (Baseball Player)
Los Angeles Dodgers
10 Estaban Dr
Camarillo, CA 93010-1610, USA

McMurray, Jamie (Race Car Driver)
RWI Racing LLC
215 Milford Cir
Mooresville, NC 28117-7001, USA

McMurray, Sam
11500 W Olympic Blvd Ste 510
Los Angeles, CA 90064-1527, USA

McMurray, W Grant (Religious Leader)
Reorganized Church of Latter Day Saints
PO Box 1059
Independence, MO 64051-0559, USA

McMurtry, James (Musician, Songwriter, Writer)
High Road
751 Bridgeway # 300
Sausalito, CA 94965-2165, USA

McMurtry, Larry (Writer)
PO Box 552
Archer City, TX 76351-0552, USA

McMurty, Craig (Baseball Player)
Atlanta Braves
2835 Bottoms East Rd
Troy, TX 76579-3008, USA

McNab, Mercedes (Actor)
c/o Ilene Haller *Opus Entertainment*
5225 Wilshire Blvd Ste 905
Los Angeles, CA 90036-4353, USA

McNabb, Carl (Baseball Player)
Detroit Tigers
PO Box 203
Jasper, TN 37347-0203, USA

McNabb, Dexter (Football Player)
Green Bay Packers
673 Saint Marys St
De Pere, WI 54115-1069, USA

McNabb, Donovan (Football Player)
c/o Staff Member *Philadelphia Eagles*
1 Novacare Way
Philadelphia, PA 19145-5996, USA

McNair, Kelly (Actor)
c/o Staff Member *Greater Vision Artist*
9229 W Sunset Blvd Ste 320
Los Angeles, CA 90069-3403, USA

McNair, Robert E (Governor)
RR 2 Box 310
Columbia, SC 29212, USA

McNair, Steve (Football Player)
c/o Staff Member *Baltimore Ravens*
1 Winning Dr
Owings Mills, MD 21117-4776, USA

McNair, Sylvia (Opera Singer)
Kunstleragentur Raab & Bohm
Plankengasse 7
Vienna 1010, AUSTRIA

McNally, Kevin
162A Ladbrooke Grove
London, ENGLAND W10, UNITED KINGDOM (UK)

McNally, Stephen (Ste) (Musician)
Day Time
Crown House
225 Kensington High St
London W8 8SA, UNITED KINGDOM (UK)

McNamara, Bob (Baseball Player)
Philadelphia Athletics
4764 Dalea Pl
Oceanside, CA 92057-6136, USA

McNamara, Bob (Football Player)
Denver Broncos
4909 Prescott Cir
Edina, MN 55436-1011, USA

McNamara, Brian (Actor)
837 12th St Apt C
Santa Monica, CA 90403-5920, USA

McNamara, Eileen (Journalist)
Boston Globe
Editorial Dept
135 W T Morrissey Blvd
Dorchester, MA 02125, USA

McNamara, Jim (Baseball Player)
San Francisco Giants
15317 Surrey House Way
Centreville, VA 20120-1196, USA

McNamara, John F (Baseball Player)
1206 Beech Hill Rd
Brentwood, TN 37027-5530, USA

McNamara, Julianne L (Actor, Gymnast)
Barry Axelrod
2236 Encinitas Blvd Ste A
Encinitas, CA 92024-4353, USA

McNamara, Melissa (Golfer)
c/o Staff Member *Pro Golfers Association (PGA) Tour*
112 Tpc Blvd
Ponte Vedra Beach, FL 32082, USA

McNamara, Robert S (Secretary)
700 New Hampshire Ave NW # 101
Washington, DC 20037-2407, USA

McNamara, William (Actor)
c/o Frederick Levy *Management 101*
5527 1/2 Cahuenga Blvd
North Hollywood, CA 91601, USA

McNanie, Sean (Football Player)
Buffalo Bills
14915 Rancho Real
Del Mar, CA 92014-4213, USA

McNaught, Judith (Writer)
Pocket Books
1230 Avenue Of The Americas
New York, NY 10020-1586, USA

McNaughton, John D (Director)
1370 N Milwaukee Ave
Chicago, IL 60622-2149, USA

McNaughton, Robert F Jr (Scientist)
2511 15th St
Troy, NY 12180-1704, USA

McNeal, Donald (Don) (Football Player)
Miami Dolphins
3311 Toledo St
Coral Gables, FL 33134, USA

McNealy, Rusty (Baseball Player)
Oakland A's
3301 Bozeman St
Sacramento, CA 95838-4105, USA

McNealy, Scott G (Business Person)
901 San Antonio Rd
Sun Microsystems
Palo Alto, CA 94303-4900, USA

McNeeley, Big Jay (Misc)
Ray Lawrence
PO Box 1967
Studio City, CA 91614-0967, USA

McNeeley, Brother Jay
PO Box 1987
Studio City, CA 91614-0987, USA

McNeely, Jeff (Baseball Player)
Boston Red Sox
405 Everette St
Monroe, NC 28112-5622, USA

McNeely, Paulette
4518 Rodeo Ln Apt 2
Los Angeles, CA 90016-5641, USA

McNeice, Ian (Actor)
c/o Renee Jennett *Renee Jennett Management*
5757 Wilshire Blvd Ste 473
Los Angeles, CA 90036-3632, USA

McNeil, Clifton (Football Player)
Cleveland Browns
1001 Westbury Dr # 98
Mobile, AL 36609-3336, USA

McNeil, Emanuel (Football Player)
New England Patriots
2 University Ct Apt G17
Martin, TN 38237-4025, USA

McNeil, Frederick A (Fred) (Football Player)
9667 W Olympic Blvd Apt 5
Beverly Hills, CA 90212-3745, USA

McNeil, Freeman (Football Player)
New York Jets
52 Dunlop Rd
Huntington, NY 11743-3934, USA

McNeil, Gerald (Football Player)
Cleveland Browns
104 Summerwood Cv
San Marcos, TX 78666-2245, USA

McNeil, Kate (Actor)
1743 N Dillon St
Los Angeles, CA 90026-1113, USA

McNeil, Lori (Tennis Player)
Int'l Mgmt Group
1 Erieview Plz
1360 E 9th St #1300
Cleveland, OH 44114-1738, USA

McNeil, Ryan (Football Player)
Detroit Lions
4702 Avenue Q
Fort Pierce, FL 34947-7049, USA

McNeill, Robert Duncan (Actor)
Susan Smith
1344 N Wetherly Dr
Los Angeles, CA 90069-1817, USA

McNeill, W Donald (Don) (Tennis Player)
2165 15th Ave
Vero Beach, FL 32960-3435, USA

McNeish, Richard (Archaeologist)
Andover Archaeology Research Foundation
1 Woodland Rd
Andover, MA 01810-2111, USA

McNell, Rufus (Baseball Player)
Indianapolis Clowns
205 Heard St
Kinston, NC 28501-5850, USA

McNerney, David H (War Hero)
20322 New Moon Trl
Crosby, TX 77532-3513, USA

McNertney, Gerald (Baseball Player)
Chicago White Sox
1124 10th St
Nevada, IA 50201-1708, USA

McNichol, Brian (Baseball Player)
Chicago Cubs
15725 E Palisades Blvd
Fountain Hills, AZ 85268-3626, USA

McNorton, Bruce (Football Player)
Detroit Lions
PO Box 672
Bloomfield Hills, MI 48303-0672, USA

McNown, Cade (Football Player)
Chicago Bears
7540 Kentwood Ct
Gilroy, CA 95020-4741, USA

McNulty, Bill (Baseball Player)
Oakland A's
12210 172nd St E Apt G101
Puyallup, WA 98374-8825, USA

McPartlin, Ant (Television Host)
c/o Staff Member *Pop Idol (Fremantle Media)*
2700 Colorado Ave Ste 450
Santa Monica, CA 90404-3599, USA

McPartlin, Ryan (Actor)
c/o Miles Levy *James/Levy/Jacobson Management*
3500 W Olive Ave Ste 1470
Burbank, CA 91505-5514, USA

McPartlnad, Marian M (Musician)
Abby Hoffer
223 1/2 E 48th St
New York, NY 10017, USA

McPeak, Holly (Volleyball Player)
Association of Volleyball Professionals
6100 Center Dr Ste 900
Los Angeles, CA 90045-9207, USA

McPeak, Merrill A (Tony) (General)
123 Furnace St
Lake Oswego, OR 97034-3954, USA

McPhail, Coleman (Football Player)
Baltimore Colts
104 Flagstone Ct
Chapel Hill, NC 27517-8381, USA

McPhee, John A (Writer)
475 Drakes Corner Rd
Princeton, NJ 08540-7516, USA

McPhee, Katharine (Musician, Reality TV Star)
c/o Jason Weinberg *Untitled Entertainment (LA)*
331 N Maple Dr Fl 3
Beverly Hills, CA 90210-3827, USA

McPherson, Charles (Misc)
Joel Chriss
300 Mercer St Apt 3J
New York, NY 10003-6732, USA

McPherson, Don (Football Player)
Philadelphia Eagles
360 Huntington Ave
Boston, MA 02115-5005, USA

McPherson, Harry C Jr (Government Official)
10213 Montgomery Ave
Kensington, MD 20895-3325, USA

McPherson, James M (Historian)
15 Randall Rd
Princeton, NJ 08540-3609, USA

McPherson, John (Cartoonist)
Universal Press Syndicate
4520 Main St
Kansas City, MO 64111-1876, USA

McPherson, Leon (Musician)
c/o Staff Member *Pop Idol (Fremantle Media)*
2700 Colorado Ave Ste 450
Santa Monica, CA 90404-3599, USA

McPherson, M Peter (Educator)
Michigan State University
President's Office
East Lansing, MI 48824, USA

McPherson, Miles (Football Player)
San Diego Chargers
11360 Mandrake Pt
San Diego, CA 92131-3766, USA

McPherson, Rolf K (Religious Leader)
Church of Foursquare Gospel
1100 Glendale Blvd
Los Angeles, CA 90026-3203, USA

McQuagg, Sam (Race Car Driver)
8886 Hamilton Road
Midland, GA 31820, USA

McQuarters, R W (Football Player)
San Francisco 49ers
1548 E 54th St N
Tulsa, OK 74126-2811, USA

McQueen, Alexander (Designer, Fashion Designer)
House of Givenchy
3 Ave Saint George
Paris 75008, FRANCE

McQueen, Chad (Actor)
c/o Staff Member *MSI Entertainment*
9229 W Sunset Blvd Ste 710
Los Angeles, CA 90069-3407, USA

McQueen, Mike (Baseball Player)
Atlanta Braves
3206 Cameo Dr
Houston, TX 77080-3539, USA

McQueen, Neile
2323 Bowmont Dr
Beverly Hills, CA 90210-1808, USA

McQueen, Steven R (Actor)
c/o Staff Member *Everwood*
1000 W 2610 S
Salt Lake City, UT 84119-2434, USA

McQuilken, Kim (Football Player)
Atlanta Falcons
1050 Techwood Dr NW
Turner Broadcasting Sales Inc
Atlanta, GA 30318-5604, USA

McRae, Bennie (Football Player)
Chicago Bears
532 W 143rd St Apt 63
New York, NY 10031-6518, USA

McRae, Brian (Baseball Player)
Kansas City Royals
500 N 13th St Apt 8C
Saint Louis, MO 63103-1957, USA

McRae, Charles (Football Player)
Tampa Bay Buccaneers
PO Box 30257
Knoxville, TN 37930-0257, USA

McRae, Frank (Actor)
Marshak/Zachary Company
8840 Wilshire Blvd Fl 1
Beverly Hills, CA 90211-2606, USA

McRae, Harold O (Hal) (Baseball Player)
Cincinnati Reds
2431 Landings Cir
Bradenton, FL 34209-9675, USA

McRae, Tom (Musician)
c/o Staff Member *Paradigm (Monterey)*
509 Hartnell St
Monterey, CA 93940-2825, USA

McRaney, Gerald (Actor)
c/o Tim Stone *Stone Manners Talent & Literary (LA)*
6500 Wilshire Blvd Ste 550
Los Angeles, CA 90048-4950, USA

McRee, Lisa
327 N Orange Dr
Los Angeles, CA 90036-2613, USA

McReynolds, Jim & Jesse
PO Box 304
Gallatin, TN 37066-0304, USA

McReynolds, Kevin (Baseball Player)
San Diego Padres
7 Witry Ct
Little Rock, AR 72223-9176, USA

McReynolds, Madison (Actor)
c/o Bonnie Ventis *Kazarian/Spencer & Assoc (LA)*
11969 Ventura Blvd
Box 7409 Fl 3
Studio City, CA 91604-2630, USA

McRoy, Spike (Golfer)
15019 Collier Dr SE
Huntsville, AL 35803-3631, USA

McShane, Ian (Actor)
International Creative Mgmt
76 Oxford St
London W1N 0AX, UNITED KINGDOM (UK)

McShane, Jamie (Actor)
c/o Staff Member *Select Artists Ltd (CA-Westside Office)*
1138 12th St Apt 1
Santa Monica, CA 90403-5459, USA

McShane, Jennifer (Jenny) (Actor)
c/o Laura Pallas *Pallas Management*
12535 Chandler Blvd Apt 1
Valley Village, CA 91607-1934, USA

McShane, Michael (Actor)
c/o Maureen Vincent *Peters Fraser & Dunlop (PFD - UK)*
Drury House
34-43 Russell St
London WC2B 5HA, UNITED KINGDOM (UK)

McShann, James C (Jay) (Musician)
Ozark Talent
718 Schwarz Rd
Lawrence, KS 66049-4506, USA

McSorley, Gerard (Actor)
c/o Staff Member *Lesher Entertainment Inc*
1134 S Cloverdale Ave
Los Angeles, CA 90019-6737, USA

McSwain, Chuck (Football Player)
Dallas Cowboys
PO Box 603
Caroleen, NC 28019-0603, USA

McSwain, Rod (Football Player)
New England Patriots
5393 Stonewood Dr
Hickory, NC 28602-5578, USA

McSweeney, Alex
c/o Staff Member *EastEnders*
1 Mortimer St
London W1T 3JA, UNITED KINGDOM (UK)

McTeer, Janet (Actor)
Propaganda Films Mgmt
1741 Ivar Ave
Los Angeles, CA 90028-5105, USA

McTeer, Robert D Jr (Financier, Government Official)
Federal Reserve Bank
2200 N Pearl St
Dallas, TX 75201-2272, USA

McTeigue, James (Director)
c/o Lawrence Mattis *Circle of Confusion LLC (NY)*
10723 71st Rd # 300
Forest Hills, NY 11375-4707, USA

McTiernan, John C (Director)
The Firm
9100 Wilshire Blvd Ste 100W
Beverly Hills, CA 90212-3435, USA

McVeigh, John (Football Player)
Seattle Seahawks
1404 W Beach Dr
Panama City, FL 32401-1927, USA

McVicar, Daniel (Actor)
1704 Oak St
Santa Monica, CA 90405-4804, USA

McVie, Christine (Musician, Songwriter, Writer)
406 Poplar Dr
Wilmette, IL 60091-2731, USA

McVie, John (Musician, Songwriter, Writer)
Boulevard Mgmt
21731 Ventura Blvd Ste 300
Woodland Hills, CA 91364-1851, USA

McVie, Tom (Hockey Player)
Boston Bruins
1 Fleetcenter Pl Ste 250
Boston, MA 02114-1390, USA

McWashington, Shawn (Football Player)
Kansas City Chiefs
3400 S King St
Seattle, WA 98144-2653, USA

McWethy, John F (Correspondent)
4850 Meredith Way Apt 304
Boulder, CO 80303-9105, USA

McWherter, Ned R (Governor)
321 Linden St
Dresden, TN 38225-1418, USA

McWhirter, Jillian (Actor)
PO Box 6308
Beverly Hills, CA 90212-1308, USA

McWilliam, Edward (Artist)
8A Holland Villas Road
London W14 8DP, UNITED KINGDOM (UK)

McWilliams, Brian (Misc)
Longshoremen/Warehousemen Union
1188 Franklin St
San Francisco, CA 94109-6800, USA

McWilliams, Caroline (Actor)
Premiere Artists
1875 Century Park E Ste 2250
Los Angeles, CA 90067-2563, USA

McWilliams, David (Football Executive, Football Player)
University of Texas
Athletic Dept
Austlin, TX 78712, USA

McWilliams, Fleming (Musician)
Michael Dixon Mgmt
119 Pebble Creek Rd
Franklin, TN 37064-5525, USA

McWilliams, John (Football Player)
Arizona Cardinals
4540 E Blue Spruce Ln
Gilbert, AZ 85298-4637, USA

McWilliams, Larry (Baseball Player)
Atlanta Braves
4102 Beckley Ct
Colleyville, TX 76034-4670, USA

McWilliams, Larry (Baseball Player)
New York Yankees
7079 S Columbine Way
Centennial, CO 80122-1844, USA

McWilliams, Robert H (Judge)
US COurt of Appeals
1929 Stout St
US Courthouse
Denver, CO 80294-0003, USA

MDO (Music Group)
c/o Staff Member *Sony Music Miami*
605 Lincoln Rd Fl 7
Miami Beach, FL 33139-2900, USA

Me First And The Gimme Gimmes (Music Group)
c/o Staff Member *Fat Wreck Chords*
PO Box 193690
San Francisco, CA 94119-3690, USA

Meacham, Mildred (Baseball Player)
4027 Winedale Ln
Charlotte, NC 28205-4524, USA

Meacham, Rusty (Baseball Player)
Detroit Tigers
1906 Eden Glen Ln
Pearland, TX 77581-1700, USA

Mead, Amber (Actor)
c/o Courtney Kivowitz *Benderspink*
110 S Fairfax Ave Ste 350
Los Angeles, CA 90036-2179, USA

Mead, Charlie (Baseball Player)
New York Giants
7482 Svl Box
Victorville, CA 92395-5157, USA

Mead, John (Football Player)
New York Giants
401 Westwood Dr Apt 2
Sister Bay, WI 54234-9262, USA

Mead, Shepherd (Writer)
53 Rivermead Court
London SW6 3RY, UNITED KINGDOM (UK)

Meade, Carl J (Astronaut)
5711 Blenveneda Terrace
Palmdale, CA 93551, USA

Meade, Glenn (Writer)
Saint Martin's Press
175 5th Ave
New York, NY 10010-7848, USA

Meade, Julia
1010 5th Ave
New York, NY 10028-0130, USA

Meador, Eddie D (Ed) (Football Player)
Los Angeles Rams
1135 Padgetts Hill Rd
Natural Bridge, VA 24578-4147, USA

Meador, Vaughn
1096 Middle Two Rock Rd
Petaluma, CA 94952-3601, USA

Meadows, Bernard W (Artist)
34 Belsize Grove
London NW3, UNITED KINGDOM (UK)

Meadows, Brian (Baseball Player)
Florida Marlins
208 Palos Verdes Dr
Troy, AL 36079-1701, USA

Meadows, Jayne (Actor)
16185 Woodvale Rd
Encino, CA 91436-3448, USA

Meadows, Loule (Baseball Player)
Houston Astros
110 Heavens Ln
Maysville, NC 28555-9479, USA

Meadows, Stephen (Actor)
1760 Courtney Ave
Los Angeles, CA 90046-2103, USA

Meadows, Tim (Actor, Comedian)
c/o Staff Member *Brillstein-Grey Entertainment*
9150 Wilshire Blvd Ste 350
Beverly Hills, CA 90212-3453, USA

Meads, Dave (Baseball Player)
Houston Astros
3220 Cypress Way
Santa Rosa, CA 95405-7512, USA

Meads, Johnny (Football Player)
Houston Oilers
9419 Pine Lilly Ct
Navarre, FL 32566-2865, USA

Meagher, Mary T (Swimmer)
404 Vanderwall
Peachtree City, GA 30269-3335, USA

Meals, Gerald (Baseball Player)
2164 Shamrock Arbor Dr
Salem, OH 44460-7639, USA

Meamber, Tim (Football Player)
Minnesota Vikings
3410 Grant St
Vancouver, WA 98660-1823, USA

Meaney, Colm (Actor)
11921 Laurel Hills Rd
Studio City, CA 91604-3726, USA

Meaney, Kevin (Actor, Comedian)
28 Beech Ln
Tarrytown, NY 10591-3002, USA

Means, Natrone J (Football Player)
San Diego Chargers
14221 Timbergreen Dr
Huntersville, NC 28078-0608, USA

Means, Russell (Activist)
444 Crazy Horse Dr
Porcupine, SD 57772, USA

Meara, Anne (Actor, Comedian)
c/o Staff Member *Innovative Artists (LA)*
1505 10th St
Santa Monica, CA 90401-2805, USA

Meares, Pat (Baseball Player)
Minnesota Twins
8405 Bridlewood St
Wichita, KS 67206-4408, USA

Mears, Casey (Race Car Driver)
Chip Ganassi Racing
600 E Laburnum Ave
Richmond, VA 23222-2207, USA

Mears, Gary (Musician)
12170 County Road 215
Tyler, TX 75707-5710, USA

Mears, Roger Sr (Race Car Driver)
PO Box 520
Terrell, NC 28682-0520, USA

Mears, Walter R (Journalist)
Associated Press
2021 K St NW
Editorial Dept
Washington, DC 20006-1082, USA

Meat, Loaf (Actor, Musician)
Solo Agency
252-260 Regent St
#100
London W1B 3BX, UNITED KINGDOM (UK)

Mecchi, Irene (Actor)
c/o Staff Member *Endeavor Agency LLC (LA)*
9601 Wilshire Blvd Fl 3
Beverly Hills, CA 90210-5204, USA

Mecham, Evan (Governor)
Mecham Pontiac-AMC-Renault
4510 W Glendale Ave
Glendale, AZ 85301-2809, USA

Meche, Gil (Baseball Player)
Seattle Mariners
105 Lefleur Cir
Lafayette, LA 70503-5826, USA

Mechlowicz, Scott (Actor)
c/o Eric Kranzler *Management 360*
9111 Wilshire Blvd
Beverly Hills, CA 90210-5508, USA

Mechoso, Julio Oscar (Actor)
c/o Staff Member *Gage Group, The (LA)*
14724 Ventura Blvd Ste 505
Sherman Oaks, CA 91403-3505, USA

Meciar, Vladimir (Prime Minister)
Urad Vlady SR
Nam Slobody 1
Bratislava 81370, SLOVAKIA

Mecir, Jim (Baseball Player)
Seattle Mariners
21219 Creekside Dr
Kildeer, IL 60047-7847, USA

Mecir, Miloslav (Tennis Player)
Julova 1
Bratislava 83101, CZECH REPUBLIC

Mecklenburg, Karl (Football Player)
Denver Broncos
6372 S Zenobia Ct
Littleton, CO 80123-6740, USA

Medak, Peter (Director)
1355 N Laurel Ave Apt 9
West Hollywood, CA 90046-4629, USA

Medaris, J Bruce (General)
PO Box 415
Fern Park, FL 32751, USA

Medavoy, Mike (Producer)
c/o Staff Member *Phoenix Pictures*
10202 Washington Blvd
Frankovich Bldg
Culver City, CA 90232-3119, USA

Medcalf, Kim (Actor)
London Mgmt
2-4 Noel St
London W1V 3RB, UNITED KINGDOM (UK)

Meddick, Jim (Cartoonist)
United Feature Syndicate
200 Madison Ave
New York, NY 10016-3911, USA

Medeiros, Glenn (Musician)
PO Box 8
Lawai, HI 96765-0008, USA

Medeiros, Ray (Baseball Player)
Cincinnati Reds
313 San Miguel Ave
San Mateo, CA 94403-2957, USA

Medgyessy, Peter (Prime Minister)
Prime Minister's Office
Kossuth Lajos Ter 1-3
Budapest 1055, HUNGARY

Mediate, Rocco (Golfer)
2338 Immokalee Rd
Pmb 136
Naples, FL 34110-1445, USA

Medich, George (Baseball Player)
New York Yankees
2206 Ridgevue Ave
Aliquippa, PA 15001-4252, USA

Medina, Luis (Baseball Player)
Cleveland Indians
16015 S 1st St
Phoenix, AZ 85048-2001, USA

Medina, Patricia (Actor)
10787 Wilshire Blvd Apt 1503
Los Angeles, CA 90024-4475, USA

Medina, Rafael (Baseball Player)
Florida Marlins
18322 NW 68th Ave
Hialeah, FL 33015-3423, USA

Medina Estevez, Jorge Arturo Cardinal (Religious Leader)
Congregation for Divine Worship
Vatican City 00120, VATICAN CITY

Medley, Bill (Musician)
c/o Staff Member *William Morris Agency (WMA-LA)*
1 William Morris Pl
Beverly Hills, CA 90212-4261, USA

Medley, Charles R O (Artist)
Charterhouse
Charterhouse Square
London EC1M 6AN, UNITED KINGDOM (UK)

Medrano, Frank (Actor)
c/o Kathy Carter *Axiom Management*
16302 Crowne Brook Cir
Franklin, TN 37067-1673, USA

Medress, Henry (Musician)
Brothers Mgmt
141 Dunbar Ave
Fords, NJ 08863-1551, USA

Medved, Aleksandr V (Wrestler)
Central Soviet Sports Federation
Skatertny p 4
Moscow, RUSSIA

Medved, Ron (Football Player)
Philadelphia Eagles
6790 161st Ave SE Unit A
Bellevue, WA 98006-5691, USA

Medvedev, Andrei (Tennis Player)
6352 Ellmau
Tirol, AUSTRIA

Medvin, Scott (Baseball Player)
Pittsburgh Pirates
22900 Center Ridge Rd Apt 419
Rocky River, OH 44116-3093, USA

Medwin, Michael (Actor)
International Creative Mgmt
76 Oxford St
London W1N 0AX, UNITED KINGDOM (UK)

Meehan, Thomas E (Musician, Writer)
Obtuse Road
Brook House
Newtown, CT 06470, USA

Meehl, Paul E (Misc)
1544 E River Ter
Minneapolis, MN 55414-3646, USA

Meek, Jeffrey
c/o Ann Geddes *Geddes Agency, The*
8430 Santa Monica Blvd Ste 200
Los Angeles, CA 90069-4253, USA

Meeker, Howie (Hockey Player, Sportscaster)
979 Dickenson Way
Parksville, BC V9P 1Z7, CANADA

Meeks, Aaron (Actor)
c/o Staff Member *Showtime Networks (LA)*
10880 Wilshire Blvd Ste 1600
Los Angeles, CA 90024-4117, USA

Meeks, Bob (Football Player)
Denver Broncos
2223 S Quentin Way Apt 201
Aurora, CO 80014-6323, USA

Meeks, Bryant (Football Player)
Pittsburgh Steelers
1332 Wade Hampton Rd
Dublin, GA 31021-0831, USA

Meeks, Sammy (Baseball Player)
Washington Senators
4963 Helene Rd
Memphis, TN 38117-6739, USA

Meeler, Phil (Baseball Player)
Detroit Tigers
102 Pine St
Knightdale, NC 27545-9443, USA

Meely, Cliff (Basketball Player)
3240 Iris Ave Apt 204
Boulder, CO 80301-1969, USA

Meena (Actor, Bollywood)
58 Second Street
Venkatesh Nagar
Chennai, TN 600093, INDIA

Meese (Music Group)
c/o Staff Member *Paradigm (Monterey)*
509 Hartnell St
Monterey, CA 93940-2825, USA

Meese, Edwin III (Attorney, Attorney General, General)
1075 Spring Hill Rd
McLean, VA 22102-2304, USA

Meester, Brad (Football Player)
Jacksonville Jaguars
7644 Chipwood Ln
Jacksonville, FL 32256-2338, USA

Meester, Leighton (Actor)
c/o Staff Member *Abrams Artists Agency (LA)*
9200 W Sunset Blvd Ph 11
Los Angeles, CA 90069-3601, USA

Meeuwsen, Terry (Religious Leader, Television Host)
c/o Staff Member *700 Club*
Christian Broadcasting Network
977 Centerville Turnpike
Virginia Beach, VT 23463, USA

Meggysey, Dave (Football Player)
St Louis Cardinals
2528 Benvenue Ave
Berkeley, CA 94704-3031, USA

Megnot, Roya (Actor)
House of Representatives
211 S Beverly Dr Ste 208
Beverly Hills, CA 90212-3879, USA

Meher, Bill (Comedian, Correspondent)
Agency for Performing Arts
405 S Beverly Dr Ste 500
Beverly Hills, CA 90212-4425, USA

Mehl, Lance A (Football Player)
New York Jets
44920 Kacsmar Estates Dr
Saint Clairsville, OH 43950-9454, USA

Mehra, Prakash (Bollywood, Director, Filmmaker, Producer)
30 Sumeet Bangalow 11th Road
JVPD Scheme
Bombay, MS 400 049, INDIA

Mehra, Smirti (Golfer)
4038 Greystone Dr
Clermont, FL 34711-7197, USA

Mehrabian, Robert (Educator)
Carnegie Mellon University
President's Office
Pittsburgh, PA 15206, USA

Mehta, Shailesh J (Business Person)
Providian Financial Corp
201 Mission St
San Francisco, CA 94105-1831, USA

Mehta, Sujata (Actor, Bollywood)
56 Dev Chhaya Tardeo Haji Ali Road
Tardeo
Bombay, MS 400 034, INDIA

Mehta, Ved (Writer)
139 E 79th St
New York, NY 10075-0324, USA

Mehta, Zubin (Conductor)
Israel Philharmonic
1 Huberman St
Tel Aviv 61112, ISRAEL

Mehta (Metha) Saltzman, Deepa (Director, Editor, Producer, Writer)
Echo Lake Entertainment
421 S Beverly Dr Fl 8
Beverly Hills, CA 90212-4408, USA

Meier, Richard A (Architect)
Richard Meier Partners
475 10th Ave Fl 6
New York, NY 10018-9721, USA

Meier, Shad (Football Player)
Tennessee Titans
4001 Skyline Dr
Nashville, TN 37215-2318, USA

Meier, Waltraud (Opera Singer)
Festspielhugel 3
Bayreuth 95445, GERMANY

Meilinger, Steve (Football Player)
Washington Redskins
719 Camino Rd
Lexington, KY 40502-2776, USA

Meinwald, Jerrold (Misc)
Cornell University
Chemistry Dept
Ithaca, NY 14853, USA

Meinyk, Steve (Golfer)
5015 Pirates Cove Rd
Jacksonville, FL 32210-8309, USA

Meirelles, Fernando (Director, Producer)
c/o Staff Member *Endeavor Agency LLC (LA)*
9601 Wilshire Blvd Fl 3
Beverly Hills, CA 90210-5204, USA

Meirelles, Priscilla (Model)
Carousel Productions, Inc
8 San Manuel St., Capitol
Pasig City, Metro Manila 1603, PHILIPPINES

Meisel, Stephen (Photographer)
1271 Avenue Of The Americas
New York, NY 10020-1300, USA

Meiselas, Susan (Photographer)
256 Mott St
New York, NY 10012-3482, USA

Meisner, Greg (Football Player)
Los Angeles Rams
419 Glenmeade Rd
Greensburg, PA 15601-1170, USA

Meisner, Joachim Cardinal (Religious Leader)
Archbishop's Diocese
Marzellenstr 32
Cologne 50668, GERMANY

Meisner, Randy (Musician)
3706 Eureka Dr
Studio City, CA 91604-3104, USA

Meissner, Kimmie (Figure Skater)
Office of Public Relations
105 E Main St
The Academy Building
Newark, DE 19716-0799, USA

Meja (Musician)
Basic Music Mgmt
Norrtullsgatan 51
Stockholm 113 45, SWEDEN

Mejdani, Rexhep (President)
President's Office
Keshilli i Ministrave
Tirana, ALBANIA

Mejia, Hipolito (President)
Palacio Nacional
Calle Moises Garcia
Santo Domingo, DOMINICAN REPUBLIC

Mejia, Jorge Maria Cardinal (Religious Leader)
Biblioteca Apostolica Vaticina
Vatican City 00120, VATICAN CITY

Mejia, Paul R (Ballerina, Choreographer)
Fort Worth Ballet
6848 Green Oaks Rd
Fort Worth, TX 76116, USA

Mejias, Roman (Baseball Player)
Pittsburgh Pirates
27325 Terrytown Rd
Sun City, CA 92586-5220, USA

Mekka, Eddie (Actor)
Cosden Morgan
129 W Wilson St Ste 202
Costa Mesa, CA 92627-1586, USA

Melamed, Lisa
151 El Camino Dr
Beverly Hills, CA 90212-2704, USA

Melamld, Aleksandr (Artist)
Ronald Freeman Fine Arts
31 Mercer St
New York, NY 10013-2595, USA

Melander, Jon (Football Player)
New England Patriots
8255 Kelzer Pond Dr
Victoria, MN 55386-4500, USA

Melanie (Musician, Songwriter, Writer)
53 Baymont St # 5
Clearwater Beach, FL 33767-1705, USA

Melato, Mariangela (Actor)
Carol Levi Co
Via Giuseppe Pisanelli
Rome 00196, ITALY

Melcher, John (Senator)
2519 Wylie Ave
Missoula, MT 59802-3260, USA

Melchionni, Bill (Basketball Player)
115 Whitehall Blvd
Garden City, NY 11530-2725, USA

Melchior, Ib (Writer)
8228 Marmont Ln
Los Angeles, CA 90069-1624, USA

Melchoir, Tracy Lindsay
c/o Michael Bruno *The Michael Bruno Group*
13576 Cheltenham Dr
Sherman Oaks, CA 91423-4818, USA

Mele, Sam (Baseball Player)
Boston Red Sox
340 Adams St
Quincy, MA 02169-1702, USA

Melendez, A J (Musician)
c/o Staff Member *American Idol*
7800 Beverly Blvd # 251
Los Angeles, CA 90036-2112, USA

Melendez, Bill (Animator)
Bill Melendez Productions
13400 Riverside Dr Ste 201
Sherman Oaks, CA 91423-2501, USA

Melendez, John (Musician)
c/o Staff Member *Paradigm (Monterey)*
509 Hartnell St
Monterey, CA 93940-2825, USA

Melendez, Kiki (Musician)
c/o Staff Member *Paradigm (Monterey)*
509 Hartnell St
Monterey, CA 93940-2825, USA

Melendez, Lisette (Musician)
Famous Artists Agency
250 W 57th St
New York, NY 10107-0001, USA

Melendez, Ron
12533 Woodgreen St
Los Angeles, CA 90066-2723, USA

Meler, Dave (Baseball Player)
Minnesota Twins
523 W Stuart Ave
Fresno, CA 93704-1430, USA

Meler, Raymond (Photographer)
Raymond Meier Photography
532 Broadway Fl 8
New York, NY 10012-3939, USA

Melhuse, Adam (Baseball Player)
Los Angeles Dodgers
245 Almond St
San Luis Obispo, CA 93405-2301, USA

Melinda (Artist)
M Entertainment
120 E Flamingo Rd
Las Vegas, NV 89109, USA

Mellanby, Scott (Hockey Player)
2548 Town And Country Ln
Saint Louis, MO 63131-1121, USA

Mellekas, John (Football Player)
Chicago Bears
498 Broadway
Newport, RI 02840-1440, USA

Mellencamp, John (Musician, Songwriter, Writer)
c/o Jeremy Plager *Creative Artists Agency LCC (CAA-LA)*
2000 Avenue Of The Stars
Los Angeles, CA 90067-4700, USA

Mellers, Wilfrid H (Composer, Writer)
Oliver Sheldon House
17 Aldwark
York YO1 2BX, UNITED KINGDOM (UK)

Melles, Carl
Grunbergstr 4
Vienna 1130, AUSTRIA

Melling, O R (Writer)
C/O Geraldine Whlean
26 Wolfe Tone Square E
Bray, Co Wicklow, IRELAND

Mellinkoff, Sherman M (Educator, Physicist)
University of California
Med Center
10833 Leconte Ave
Los Angeles, CA 90095-0001, USA

Mello, Jim (Football Player)
Boston Yankees
5133 E Emerald Cir
Mesa, AZ 85206-2870, USA

Mello, Tamara (Actor)
Abrams Artists
9200 W Sunset Blvd Ste 1125
Los Angeles, CA 90069-3610, USA

Mellons, Ken (Musician)
c/o Staff Member *Buddy Lee Attractions Inc*
38 Music Sq E Ste 200
Nashville, TN 37203-4304, USA

Mellor, John W (Economist)
John Mellor Assoc
801 Pennsylvania Ave NW Apt Ph18
Washington, DC 20004-2672, USA

Mellor, Thomas (Tom) (Hockey Player)
63 Spoonhill Ave
Marlborough, MA 01752-2500, USA

Melnick, Bruce E (Astronaut)
Boeing Aerospace
PO Box 21233
Kennedy Space Center, FL 32815-0233, USA

Melnick, Daniel (Producer)
1123 Sunset Hills Rd
Los Angeles, CA 90069-1756, USA

Melniker, Benjamin (Producer)
Batfilm Productions
123 W 44th St # 10-K
New York, NY 10036-4012, USA

Melnikov, Vitaly V (Director)
Svetianovsky Proyezd 105
#20
Saint Petersburg 195269, RUSSIA

Melody (Musician)
c/o Staff Member *Sony Music Miami*
605 Lincoln Rd Fl 7
Miami Beach, FL 33139-2900, USA

Meloni, Christopher (Actor)
c/o William Butler *Gersh Agency, The (NY)*
41 Madison Ave Fl 33
New York, NY 10010-2202, USA

Melrose, Barry J (Coach, Hockey Player)
ESPN-TV
Sports Dept
Espn Plaza 935 Middle St
Bristol, CT 06010, USA

Melroy, Pamela A (Astronaut)
3910 Valley Green Ct
Houston, TX 77059-5556, USA

Melton, Bill (Baseball Player)
Chicago White Sox
333 E 35th St
Chicago, IL 60616-3951, USA

Melton, Dave (Baseball Player)
Kansas City A's
10253 Richwood Dr
Cupertino, CA 95014-3360, USA

Melton, Sid (Actor)
PO Box 57933
Sherman Oaks, CA 91413-2933, USA

Meltzer, Allan L (Economist)
Camegie Mellon University
Economics Dept
Pittsburgh, PA 15260, USA

Meluskey, Mitch (Baseball Player)
Houston Astros
26 Meadowbrook Rd
Yakima, WA 98903-9505, USA

Melvill, Michael W (Astronaut)
24120 Jacaranda Dr
Tehachapi, CA 93561-8309, USA

Melvin, Allan (Actor)
271 N Bowling Green Way
Los Angeles, CA 90049-2815, USA

Melvin, Bob (Baseball Player)
Detroit Tigers
5637 E Canyon Ridge North Dr
Cave Creek, AZ 85331-9319, USA

Melvin, Donnie
45 Overlook Ter
New York, NY 10033-2218, USA

Melvin, Murray
Joy Jameson
Plaza
535 Kings Road
London SW10 OSZ, UNITED KINGDOM (UK)

Melvoin, Wendy
c/o Renata Kanclerz *Girl Brothers*
9454 Wilshire Blvd Ste 711
Beverly Hills, CA 90212-2910, USA

Melzack, Ronald (Misc)
51 Banstead Road
Montreal, PQ H4X 1P1, CANADA

Members, Swollen (Musician)
c/o Staff Member *Agency Group Ltd, The (NY)*
1775 Broadway Ste 515
New York, NY 10019-1903, USA

Memmelaar, Dale (Football Player)
Chicago Cardinals
13 Manor Dr
Washingtonville, NY 10992-1632, USA

Men, Baha (Music Group)
Evolution Talent
1776 Broadway Fl 15
New York, NY 10019-2002, USA

Men Women & Children (Music Group)
c/o Staff Member *Paradigm (Monterey)*
509 Hartnell St
Monterey, CA 93940-2825, USA

Menafee, Cornell (Football Player)
Green Bay Packers
403 Elm Ct
Opelika, AL 36801-6423, USA

Menaker, Mitchell G
5062 Isleworth Country Club Dr
Windermere, FL 34786-8920, USA

Menand, Louis (Historian, Writer)
New Yorker Magazine
4 Times Sq
Editorial Dept
New York, NY 10036-6592, USA

Menard, Marc (Actor)
Infinite Artists
10 - 206 E 6th Ave
Vancouver, BC V5T 1J8, CANADA

Menard, Renry W (Misc)
Scripps Institute of Oceanography
Geology Dept
La Jolla, CA 92093, USA

Mench, Kevin (Baseball Player)
Texas Rangers
414 Saint Regis Dr
Newark, DE 19711-6107, USA

Menchu Tum, Rigoberta (Nobel Prize Laureate)
UN Working Group on Indigenous Populations
Un Plaza
New York, NY 10017, USA

Mencia, Carlos (Actor)
c/o *Hollywood Center Studios*
1040 N Las Palmas Ave
9 East
Los Angeles, CA 90038-2409, USA

Mendenhall, John (Football Player)
New York Giants
PO Box 532
Cullen, LA 71021-0532, USA

Mendenhall, Ken (Football Player)
Baltimore Colts
1708 S Rankin St
Edmond, OK 73013-5128, USA

Mendes, Eva (Actor)
c/o David Seltzer *Management 360*
9111 Wilshire Blvd
Beverly Hills, CA 90210-5508, USA

Mendes, Sam (Director)
Donmar Warehouse
41 Earlham St
London WC2H 9LD, UNITED KINGDOM (UK)

Mendez, Lucia (Actor)
c/o Staff Member *TV Azteca*
Periferico Sur 4121
Colonia Fuentes del Pedregal
DF CP 14141, MEXICO

Mendoza, June (Artist)
34 Inner Park Road
London SW19 6DD, UNITED KINGDOM (UK)

Mendoza, Linda (Director)
c/o Staff Member *Creative Artists Agency LCC (CAA-LA)*
2000 Avenue Of The Stars
Los Angeles, CA 90067-4700, USA

Mendoza, Mike (Baseball Player)
Houston Astros
14207 S 20th St
Phoenix, AZ 85048-4519, USA

Mendoza, Minnie (Baseball Player)
Minnesota Twins
2070 SW 57th Ct
Miami, FL 33155-2237, USA

Mendoza, Ramiro (Athlete, Baseball Player)
New York Yankees
18706 Pepper Pike
Lutz, FL 33558-5303, USA

Mendoza, Reynol (Baseball Player)
2408 2nd St
Eagle Pass, TX 78852-4119, USA

Mendte, Larry
330 Bob Hope Dr.
Burbank, CA 91523-0001, USA

Menechino, Frank (Baseball Player)
Oakland A's
522 Arlene St
Staten Island, NY 10314-3818, USA

Menendez, Erik
Calif. Correctional Inst.
#1878449 Csp-Sac.
Box 290066
Represa, CA 95671-0066, USA

Menendez, Lyle
#1887106 Cci-Box 1031
Tehachapi, CA 93581, USA

Menendez, Tony (Baseball Player)
Cincinnati Reds
18730 NW 48th Ct
Miami Gardens, FL 33055-2536, USA

Meneses, Alex (Actor)
c/o Cindy Ambers *Verve Entertainment*
6140 Washington Blvd
Culver City, CA 90232-7465, USA

Meneses, Antonio (Musician)
Columbia Artists Mgmt Inc
1790 Broadway Fl 6
New York, NY 10019-1412, USA

Menez, Bernard
119 Blvd. de Grenelle
Paris 75015, FRANCE

Mengatti, John
8322 Beverly Blvd Ste 200
Los Angeles, CA 90048-2664, USA

Mengers, Sue
938 Bel Air Rd
Los Angeles, CA 90077-3010, USA

Menges, Chris (Cinematographer, Director)
Harmony Pictures
420 S Beverly Dr # 1-100
Beverly Hills, CA 90212-4426, USA

Menhart, Paul (Baseball Player)
Toronto Blue Jays
725 Kelsall Dr
Richmond Hill, GA 31324-7707, USA

Menheer-Zoromapal, Marie (Baseball Player)
8871 Lake Marion Creek Rd
Haines City, FL 33844-2004, USA

Menichetti, Roberto (Designer, Fashion Designer)
3 Loc Monteleto
Gubbio, ITALY

Menke, Denis (Baseball Player)
Milwaukee Braves
1246 Berkshire Ln
Tarpon Springs, FL 34688-7626, USA

Menken, Alan (Composer)
Shukat Co
670 W End Ave Apt 8A
New York, NY 10025-7327, USA

Mennea, Pietro (Athlete, Track Athlete)
Via Cassia 1041
Rome 00189, ITALY

Meno, Chorepiscopus John (Religious Leader)
263 Elm Ave
Teaneck, NJ 07666-2323, USA

Menon, Mambillikalathil G K (Physicist)
C-63 Tarang Apts
Mother Dairy Road
Patparganj, Delhi 110092, INDIA

Menounos, Maria (Actor, Correspondent)
c/o Staff Member *Access Hollywood*
Nbc
3000 W Alameda Ave Trailer E
Burbank, CA 91523-0001, USA

Mensah, Peter (Actor)
c/o Staff Member *Stone Manners Talent & Literary (LA)*
6500 Wilshire Blvd Ste 550
Los Angeles, CA 90048-4950, USA

Menshov, Vladimir V (Actor, Director)
3D Tverskaya-Yamskaya 52
Moscow 125047, RUSSIA

Menudo
2895 Biscayne Blvd # 455
Miami, FL 33137-4537, USA

Menzel, Idina (Actor, Musician)
c/o Bonnie Bernstein *Endeavor Agency LLC (NY)*
152 W 57th St Fl 25
New York, NY 10019-3310, USA

Menzel, Jiri (Director)
Studio 89
Kratky Film Jindrisska 34
Prague 1 112 07, CZECH REPUBLIC

Menzies, Heather (Actor)
PO Box 1645
Park City, UT 84060-1645, USA

Menzies, Peter G Jr (Cinematographer)
903 Tahoe Blvd # 802
Incline Village, NV 89451, USA

Meola, Eric (Photographer)
535 Greenwich St
New York, NY 10013-1004, USA

Meola, Tony (Soccer Player)
488 Forest St
Kearny, NJ 07032-3623, USA

Meoli, Christian (Actor)
c/o Staff Member *Lichtman/Salners Company*
15865 Royal Haven Pl
Sherman Oaks, CA 91403-4724, USA

Meoll, Rudy (Baseball Player)
California Angels
8150 E Oak Ridge Cir
Anaheim, CA 92808-1941, USA

Merbold, Ulf (Astronaut)
Am Sonnenhang 4
Siegburg 53721, GERMANY

Mercado, Orlando (Baseball Player)
Seattle Mariners
PO Box 1465
Arecibo, PR 00613-1465, USA

Mercante, Arthur (Referee)
596 Pacing Way
Westbury, NY 11590-6675, USA

Merced, Orlando (Baseball Player)
Pittsburgh Pirates
1246 W Stone Meadow Way
Springfield, MO 65810-1609, USA

Mercein, Chuck (Football Player)
New York Giants
746 Mamaroneck Ave Apt 1320
Mamaroneck, NY 10543-1989, USA

Mercer, Marian (Actor, Musician)
5250 Colodny Dr Apt 13
Agoura Hills, CA 91301-2657, USA

Mercer, Mark (Baseball Player)
Texas Rangers
10607 Penn Ave S
Minneapolis, MN 55431-3445, USA

Mercer, Mike (Football Player)
Minnesota Vikings
64463 McGrath Rd
Bend, OR 97701-8830, USA

Mercer, Ron (Basketball Player)
San Antonio Spurs
1 Sbc Center Pkwy
Alamodome
San Antonio, TX 78219-3604, USA

Mercer, Toby (Artist)
Mercer Studios
316 E Reserve Dr
Kalispell, MT 59901-6647, USA

Merchant, Andy (Baseball Player)
Boston Red Sox
Bates Lake Road
Malcolm, AL 36556, USA

Merchant, Natalie (Musician, Songwriter, Writer)
c/o Christopher Dalston *Creative Artists Agency LCC (CAA-LA)*
2000 Avenue Of The Stars
Los Angeles, CA 90067-4700, USA

Merchant, Stephen (Actor, Director, Producer, Writer)
c/o Duncan Hayes *Peters Fraser & Dunlop (PFD - UK)*
Drury House
34-43 Russell St
London WC2B 5HA, UNITED KINGDOM (UK)

Mercker, Kent (Baseball Player)
Atlanta Braves
5340 Mulrfield Ct
Dublin, OH 43017, USA

Mercurio, Nicole (Actor)
Innovative Artists
1505 10th St
Santa Monica, CA 90401-2805, USA

Mercurio, Paul (Actor, Musician)
Beyond Films
53-55 Brisbane St Surreyhills
Sydney, NSW 2010, AUSTRALIA

Mercurio, Steven
Columbia Artists Mgmt Inc
1790 Broadway Fl 6
New York, NY 10019-1412, USA

Mercurio, Tara (Actor)
c/o Aaron Ray *Nine Yards Entertainment*
8530 Wilshire Blvd Fl 5
Beverly Hills, CA 90211-3102, USA

Meredith, Don (Football Player)
Dallas Texans
PO Box 597
Santa Fe, NM 87504-0597, USA

Meredith, James H (Misc)
929 Meadowbrook Rd
Jackson, MS 39206-5945, USA

Meredith, Richard (Hockey Player)
6520 Ridgeview Dr
Edina, MN 55439-1235, USA

Meredith, William (Writer)
Connecticut College
PO Box 1498
New London, CT 06320, USA

Merigan Jr, Thomas C (Scientist)
148 Goya Rd
Portola Valley, CA 94028-7307, USA

Merila, Mark (Baseball Player)
US Olympic Team
11819 Westview Pkwy
San Diego, CA 92126-8540, USA

Meritano, Lorena (Actor)
c/o Gabriel Blanco *Gabriel Blanco Iglesias (Mexico)*
Rio Balsas 35-32
Colonia Cuauhtemoc
DF 06500, MEXICO

Meriweather, Joe C (Basketball Player)
5816 NW 64th Ter
Kansas City, MO 64151, USA

Meriweather, Lee (Actor, Beauty Pageant Winner)
12139 Jeanette Pl
Granada Hills, CA 91344-2336, USA

Meriwether, Chick (Baseball Player)
2409 Seifried St
Nashville, TN 37208-1344, USA

Meriwether, Lee (Actor)
c/o Scott Stander *Scott Stander & Associates*
13701 Riverside Dr Ste 201
Sherman Oaks, CA 91423-2447, USA

Merkens, Guido (Football Player)
Houston Oilers
2301 S Millbend Dr Apt 405
Spring, TX 77380-1754, USA

Merkerson, S Epatha (Actor)
c/o Craig Dorfman *Blueprint Management*
5670 Wilshire Blvd Ste 2525
Los Angeles, CA 90036-5647, USA

Merkin, Daphne (Writer)
c/o Staff Member *The New York Times Company*
230 W 41st St Ste 1300
New York, NY 10036-7207, USA

Merle, Carole (Skier)
Chalet La Calette
Super-Sauze 04400, FRANCE

Merletti, Lewis C (Lawyer)
Cleveland Browns
76 Lou Groza Blvd
Berea, OH 44017-1269, USA

Merlin, Jan (Actor)
347 N California St
Burbank, CA 91505-3508, USA

Merlo, James L (Football Player)
New Orleans Saints
1547 E Starpass Dr
Fresno, CA 93730-3448, USA

Merloni, Lou (Baseball Player)
Boston Red Sox
29 Wild Hunter Rd
Dennis, MA 02638-1114, USA

Merlyn-Rees, Merlyn (Government Official)
House of Lords
Westminster
London SW1A 0PW, UNITED KINGDOM (UK)

Mero, Rena (Sable) (Actor, Model, Wrestler)
760 Valley Stream Dr
Geneva, FL 32732-9231, USA

Meron, Neil (Producer)
c/o Staff Member *William Morris Agency (WMA-LA)*
1 William Morris Pl
Beverly Hills, CA 90212-4261, USA

Merovich, Pete (Soccer Player)
945 Spruce St
Pittsburgh, PA 15234-2127, USA

Merow, James F (Judge)
US Claims Court
717 Madison Pl NW
Washington, DC 20439-0001, USA

Merrells, Jason (Actor)
c/o Nicola Richards *QVoice*
8 Kings St
London WC2E 8HN, UNITED KINGDOM (UK)

Merrick, Dawn
8281 Melrose Ave Ste 200
Los Angeles, CA 90046-6890, USA

Merrifield, R Bruce (Nobel Prize Laureate)
43 Mezzine Dr
Cresskill, NJ 07626, USA

Merrill, Casey (Football Player)
Green Bay Packers
78395 Avenue 41
Bermuda Dunes, CA 92203-1008, USA

Merrill, Catherine (Artist)
Old Church Pottery
1456 Florida St
San Francisco, CA 94110-4812, USA

Merrill, Dina (Actor)
Sue Siegel
405 E 54th St Apt 12A
New York, NY 10022-5126, USA

Merrill, John O (Architect)
101 Gardner Pl
Colorado Springs, CO 80906-3314, USA

Merrill, Mark (Football Player)
New York Jets
782 Mimosa Ln
New Brighton, MN 55112-2520, USA

Merrill, Stephen E (Steve) (Governor)
562 Main St
Farmington, NH 03835, USA

Merriman, Brent (Baseball Player)
Minnesota Twins
907 N Cobblestone St
Gilbert, AZ 85234-8742, USA

Merriman, Lloyd (Baseball Player)
Cincinnati Reds
645 E Champlain Dr Apt 104
Fresno, CA 93730-1292, USA

Merriman, Randy
PO Box 70025
Houston, TX 77270-0025, USA

Merriman, Ryan (Actor)
c/o Hylda Queally *Creative Artists Agency LCC (CAA-LA)*
2000 Avenue Of The Stars
Los Angeles, CA 90067-4700, USA

Merriman, Ryan (Actor)
Jamieson
PO Box 710025
Houston, TX 77271-0025, USA

Merriman, Ryan (Actor)
c/o Vincent Cirrincione *Vincent Cirrincione Associates*
1516 N Fairfax Ave
Los Angeles, CA 90046-2608, USA

Merritt, Chris (Opera Singer)
George M Martynuk
352 7th Ave
New York, NY 10001-5012, USA

Merritt, David (Football Player)
Miami Dolphins
479 Hartford Dr
Nutley, NJ 07110-3944, USA

Merritt, Gilbert S (Judge)
US Court of Appeals
701 Broadway
US Courthouse
Nashville, TN 37203-3944, USA

Merritt, Jack N (General)
US Army Assn
2425 Wilson Blvd Ste 100
Arlington, VA 22201-3320, USA

Merritt, James J (Jim) (Baseball Player)
Minnesota Twins
833 Sandwagon Cir
Hemet, CA 92544-1891, USA

Merritt, Lloyd (Baseball Player)
St Louis Cardinals
4703 Wild Iris Dr Apt 301
Myrtle Beach, SC 29577-8718, USA

Merritt, Tift (Musician)
c/o Staff Member *High Road Touring*
751 Bridgeway Fl 3
Sausalito, CA 94965-2174, USA

Merriweather, Mike (Football Player)
Pittsburgh Steelers
PO Box 8351
Stockton, CA 95208-0351, USA

Merrow, Susan (Misc)
Sierra Club
85 2nd St Ste 200
San Francisco, CA 94105-3488, USA

Merson, Michael (Government Official)
World Health Organization
Ave Appia
Geneva 27 1211, SWITZERLAND

Merten, Lauri (Golfer)
105 Foulk Rd
Wilmington, DE 19803-3740, USA

Mertens, Alan (Misc)
PacWest Racing Group
150 Gasoline Aly
Indianapolis, IN 46222-3965, USA

Mertens, Jerry (Football Player)
San Francisco 49ers
465 Woodside Dr
Woodside, CA 94062-2375, USA

Merton, Robert C (Nobel Prize Laureate)
Harvard University
Business School
Boston, MA 02163, USA

Mertz, Edwin T (Misc)
1504 Via Delta Scala
Henderson, NV 89052, USA

Mertz, Francis J (Educator)
Farleigh Dickinson University
President's Office
Teaneck, NJ 07666, USA

Merullo, Lennie (Baseball Player)
Chicago Cubs
159 Summer Ave
Reading, MA 01867-2825, USA

Merullo, Matt (Baseball Player)
Chicago White Sox
8 Fox Run Rd
Madison, CT 06443-2052, USA

Merwin, John D (Governor)
PO Box 1029
Hudson, OH 44236-6229, USA

Merwin, William Stanley (Writer)
Farleigh Dickinson University Press
285 Madison Ave
Madison, NJ 07940-1099, USA

Merz, Curt (Football Player)
Dallas Texans
1111 W Seminole St
Springfield, MO 65807-2551, USA

Merz, Suzanne (Sue) (Hockey Player)
5 Douglas Dr
Greenwich, CT 06831-3612, USA

Mesa, Carlos (President)
President's Office
Palacio de Gobierno
Plaza Murilla
La Paz, BOLIVIA

Mesa, Jose (Baseball Player)
Baltimore Orioles
13173 SW 51st St
Miramar, FL 33027-5522, USA

Meschery, Tom (Basketball Player)
PO Box 1297
Truckee, CA 96160-1297, USA

Meselson, Matthew S (Misc)
Harvard University
Fairchild Biochemistry Laboratories
Cambridge, MA 02138, USA

Mesereau, Thomas (Lawyer)
1875 Century Park E
Los Angeles, CA 90067-2501, USA

Meseroll, Mark (Football Player)
New Orleans Saints
450 Roger Dr
Salisbury, NC 28147-8878, USA

Mesguich, Daniel (Actor, Director)
Agence Monita Derrieux
17-21 Rue Duret
Paris 75116, FRANCE

Mesic, Stipe (President)
Presidential Palace
Pantovcak 241
Zagreb 10000, CROATIA

Mesina Stanley, Dianne (Producer)
c/o Staff Member *United Talent Agency (UTA)*
9560 Wilshire Blvd Ste 500
Beverly Hills, CA 90212-2401, USA

Meskill, Thomas J (Governor, Judge)
218 Stony Mill Ln
East Berlin, CT 06023-1042, USA

Mesner, Bruce (Football Player)
Buffalo Bills
3178 NW 60th St
Boca Raton, FL 33496-3323, USA

Mesnil Du Buisson, Robert
(Archaeologist)
Chateau de Champobert
Par Exmes
Orne 61310, FRANCE

Messager, Annette (Artist)
146 Blvd Camelinat
Colombier-Fontaine 92240, FRANCE

Messenger, Melinda (Model)
Arcadia Mgmt
2-3 Golden Square
London W1R 3AD, UNITED KINGDOM
(UK)

Messer, Dale (Football Player)
San Francisco 49ers
5449 N Brooks Ave
Fresno, CA 93711-2914, USA

Messer, Thomas M (Misc)
1105 Park Ave
New York, NY 10128-1200, USA

Messerschmid, Ernst (Astronaut)
Universitat Stuttgart
Pfaffenwaldring 31
Stuttgart 70569, GERMANY

Messerschmidt, J Alexander (Andy)
(Baseball Player)
200 Lagunita Dr
Soquel, CA 95073-9594, USA

Messersmith, Andy (Baseball Player)
California Angels
200 Lagunita Dr
Soquel, CA 95073-9594, USA

Messier, Mark (Hockey Player)
c/o Staff Member *New York Rangers*
2 Pennsylvania Plaza
New York, NY 10121, USA

Messier, Mark D (Hockey Player)
205 W 57th St
New York, NY 10019-2105, USA

Messina, Jo Dee (Musician, Songwriter, Writer)
c/o Greg Oswald *William Morris Agency (WMA-TN)*
1600 Division St Ste 300
Nashville, TN 37203-2755, USA

Messing, Debra (Actor)
c/o Molly Madden *3 Arts Entertainment Inc*
9460 Wilshire Blvd Fl 7
Beverly Hills, CA 90212-2713, USA

Messner, Heinrich (Heini) (Skier)
Huebenweg 11
Steinach 6150, AUSTRIA

Messner, Johnny (Actor)
c/o Mel McKeon *McKeon-Valeo-Myones Management*
9100 Wilshire Blvd Ste 350W
Beverly Hills, CA 90212-3437, USA

Messner, Reinhold (Mountaineer)
Schloss Juval
Kastelbell, Tschars 39040, ITALY

Mestrik, Frank (Football Player)
St Louis Cardinals
730 Eagles Mere Ct
Alpharetta, GA 30005-4233, USA

Meszaros, Maria (Director)
Malfilm Studio
Lumumba Utca 174
Budapest 1149, HUNGARY

Metallica (Musician)
c/o Staff Member *Q Prime Inc*
729 7th Ave Fl 16
New York, NY 10019-6831, USA

Metcalf, Eric Q (Football Player)
Cleveland Browns
7465 S 114th St
Seattle, WA 98178-3163, USA

Metcalf, John (Writer)
128 Lewis St
Ottawa, ON K2P 0S7, CANADA

Metcalf, Joseph III (Admiral)
4658 Charleston Ter NW
Washington, DC 20007-1900, USA

Metcalf, Laurie (Actor)
c/o Staff Member *International Creative Management (ICM-LA)*
10250 Constellation Blvd
Los Angeles, CA 90067-6200, USA

Metcalf, Mark (Actor)
c/o Staff Member *Peter Strain & Associates Inc (LA)*
5455 Wilshire Blvd Ste 1812
Los Angeles, CA 90036-4268, USA

Metcalf, Shelby (Coach)
Texas A & M University
Athletic Dept
College Station, TX 77843-0001, USA

Metcalf, Terrance R (Terry) (Football Player)
St Louis Cardinals
5112 S Fountain St
Seattle, WA 98178-2114, USA

Metcalf, Tom (Baseball Player)
New York Yankees
1390 Wisconsin River Dr
Port Edwards, WI 54469-1042, USA

Metcalfe, Burt
11800 Brookdale Ln
Studio City, CA 91604-4203, USA

Metcalfe, Jesse (Actor)
c/o Craig Gartner *Endeavor Agency LLC (LA)*
9601 Wilshire Blvd Fl 3
Beverly Hills, CA 90210-5204, USA

Metcalfe, Robert M (Scientist)
Polaris Venture Partners
1000 Winter St Ste 3350
Waltham, MA 02451-1437, USA

Metesh, Bernice (Baseball Player)
1210 Kelly Ave
Joliet, IL 60435-4251, USA

Metheny, Pat
c/o Staff Member *Endeavor Agency LLC (LA)*
9601 Wilshire Blvd Fl 3
Beverly Hills, CA 90210-5204, USA

Metheny, Patrick B (Pat) (Composer, Musician)
Ted Kurland
173 Brighton Ave
Boston, MA 02134-2003, USA

Metrano, Art (Actor)
131 N Croft Ave Apt 402
Los Angeles, CA 90048-3472, USA

Metric (Music Group)
c/o Staff Member *Paradigm (Monterey)*
509 Hartnell St
Monterey, CA 93940-2825, USA

Metro, Charlie (Baseball Player)
Detroit Tigers
7890 Indiana St
Arvada, CO 80007-7123, USA

Metrolis, Norma (Baseball Player)
175 Sea Dunes Dr
Melbourne Beach, FL 32951-3313, USA

Mette-Marit, Princess (Royalty)
Det Kongelige
Slottet Drammensvein 1
Oslo 0010, NORWAY

Metzelaars, Pete (Football Player)
Seattle Seahawks
292 Point Carpenter Rd
Fort Mill, SC 29707-6875, USA

Metzenbaum, Howard M (Senator)
Consumer Federation of America
1424 16th St NW
Washington, DC 20036-2211, USA

Metzger, Butch (Baseball Player)
San Francisco Giants
PO Box 22037
Sacramento, CA 95822-0037, USA

Metzger, Henry (Misc)
3410 Taylor St
Chevy Chase, MD 20815-4024, USA

Metzger, Roger (Baseball Player)
Chicago Cubs
3560 Bluebonnet Blvd
Brenham, TX 77833-7180, USA

Metzig, Bill (Baseball Player)
Chicago White Sox
221 Chuck Wagon Rd
Lubbock, TX 79404-1903, USA

Metzler, Jim
6300 Wilshire Blvd Ste 2110
Los Angeles, CA 90048-5282, USA

Meulens, Hensley (Baseball Player)
New York Yankees
Kaya Cupldo 7
Curacao, NETHERLANDS ANTILLES

Mewes, Jason (Actor)
c/o Andrew Weitz *Endeavor Agency LLC (LA)*
9601 Wilshire Blvd Fl 3
Beverly Hills, CA 90210-5204, USA

Mey, Reinhard
Sigismundkorso 63
Berlin D-13465, GERMANY

Mey, Uwe-Jens (Speed Skater)
Vulkanstr 22
Berlin 10367, GERMANY

Meyer, Alejandra (Actor)
c/o Staff Member *Televisa*
Blvd Adolfo Lopez Mateos 232
Colonia San Angel INN
DF CP 01060, MEXICO

Meyer, Armin H (Diplomat)
6624 Rannoch Rd
Bethesda, MD 20817-5411, USA

Meyer, Bess
PO Box 5617
Beverly Hills, CA 90209-5617, USA

Meyer, Bob (Baseball Player)
New York Yankees
PO Box 3024
Mission Viejo, CA 92690-1024, USA

Meyer, Breckin (Actor)
Brillstein/Grey
9150 Wilshire Blvd Ste 350
Beverly Hills, CA 90212-3453, USA

Meyer, Brian (Baseball Player)
Houston Astros
33 Bank St
Medford, NJ 08055-2635, USA

Meyer, Dan (Baseball Player)
Detroit Tigers
9610 Davona Dr
San Ramon, CA 94583-3704, USA

Meyer, Daniel J (Business Person)
Milacron Inc
2090 Florence Ave
Cincinnati, OH 45206-2455, USA

Meyer, Debbie
PO Box 2076
Carmichael, CA 95609-2076, USA

Meyer, Dina (Actor)
2804 6th St
Santa Monica, CA 90405-4340, USA

Meyer, Edward C (General)
1101 S Arlington Ridge Rd Apt 1116
Arlington, VA 22202-1929, USA

Meyer, Jerome J (Business Person)
Tektronix Inc
26600 SW Parkway Ave
Wilsonville, OR 97070-9297, USA

Meyer, Joey (Baseball Player)
Milwaukee Brewers
392 Kaimake Loop
Kailua, HI 96734-2019, USA

Meyer, John (Football Player)
Houston Oilers
2085 Lost Dauphin Rd
De Pere, WI 54115-1605, USA

Meyer, Joyce (Writer)
PO Box 655
Fenton, MO 63026-0655, USA

Meyer, Karl H (Misc)
642 Wyndham Rd
Teaneck, NJ 07666-1825, USA

Meyer, Lawrence H (Economist,
Government Official)
Federal Reserve Board
20th & Constitution NW
Washington, DC 20551-0001, USA

Meyer, Nicholas (Director)
Creative Artists Agency
9830 Wilshire Blvd
Beverly Hills, CA 90212-1804, USA

Meyer, Robert K (Misc)
3 Rawlings Place
Fadden, ACT 2904, AUSTRALIA

Meyer, Ron (Football Player)
Pittsburgh Steelers
628 18th St
Windom, MN 56101-1102, USA

Meyer, Scott (Baseball Player)
Oakland A's
9311 E Calle De Valle Dr
Scottsdale, AZ 85255-4303, USA

Meyer-Petrovic, Anna (Baseball Player)
1125 N Nema Ave
Tucson, AZ 85712-4723, USA

Meyer Reyes, Deborah E (Debbie)
(Swimmer)
PO Box 2076
Carmichael, CA 95609-2076, USA

Meyerowitz, Joel (Photographer)
817 W End Ave
New York, NY 10025-5370, USA

Meyerriecks, Jeffrey (Director, Musical
Director)
Lindy Martin Mgmt
5 Loblolly Ct
Pinehurst, NC 28374-9349, USA

Meyers, Anne Akiko (Musician)
ICM Artists
40 W 57th St
New York, NY 10019-4001, USA

Meyers, Ari (Actor)
c/o Holly Lebed *Holly Lebed Personal
Management*
10535 Wilshire Blvd Apt 808
Los Angeles, CA 90024-4556, USA

Meyers, Augie (Musician)
Encore Talent
2137 Zercher Rd
San Antonio, TX 78209-1194, USA

Meyers, Chad (Baseball Player)
Chicago Cubs
816 Summit Ridge Dr
Papillion, NE 68046-8096, USA

Meyers, David (Director)
c/o Oren Koules *Evolution Entertainment
(LA)*
901 N Highland Ave
Los Angeles, CA 90038-2412, USA

Meyers, David (Dave) (Basketball Player)
40629 Carmelina Circle
Temecula, CA 92591, USA

Meyers, Josh (Comedian)
c/o Staff Member *William Morris Agency
(WMA-LA)*
1 William Morris Pl
Beverly Hills, CA 90212-4261, USA

Meyers, Krystal (Musician)
5902 Parham Rd
Franklin, TN 37064-9220, USA

Meyers, Nancy (Director)
c/o Staff Member *Waverly Films/Nancy
Meyers Productions*
10202 Washington Blvd
Crawford Bldg
Culver City, CA 90232-3119, USA

Meyers, Seth (Actor, Comedian)
c/o Staff Member *William Morris Agency
(WMA-LA)*
1 William Morris Pl
Beverly Hills, CA 90212-4261, USA

Meyer's Drysdale, Ann E (Basketball
Player, Sportscaster)
6621 Doral Dr
Huntington Beach, CA 92648-6129, USA

Meyerson, Martin (Educator)
2016 Spruce St
Philadelphia, PA 19103-6524, USA

Meyfarth, Ulrike
Friedensweg 59
Wesseling D-50389, GERMANY

Meyfarth, Ulrike Nasse (Athlete, Track
Athlete)
Buschweg 53
Odenthal 51519, GERMANY

Meyjes, Menno (Director, Producer,
Writer)
c/o Staff Member *Casarotto Ramsay &
Associates Ltd (UK)*
National House
60-66 Wardour Street
London W1V 4ND, UNITED KINGDOM
(UK)

Meysel, Inge
Sudstrand 13
Bullenhausen D-21217, GERMANY

Mezentseva, Galina (Ballerina)
Kirov Ballet Theatre
1 Ploshchad Iskusstr
Saint Petersburg, RUSSIA

Mfume, Kweisi (Misc)
NAACP
PO Box 1557
President's Office
Baltimore, MD 21203-1557, USA

MGMT (Music Group)
c/o Staff Member *Paradigm (Monterey)*
509 Hartnell St
Monterey, CA 93940-2825, USA

Miadich, Bart (Baseball Player)
Anaheim Angels
17841 Hillside Dr
Lake Oswego, OR 97034-7525, USA

Mialik, Larry (Football Player)
Atlanta Falcons
100 Wisconsin Ave Apt 900
Madison, WI 53703-4169, USA

Miami Sound Machine
6205 Bird Rd
Miami, FL 33155-4823, USA

Miano, Rich (Football Player)
New York Jets
7168 Makaa St
Miano Sports Bar
Honolulu, HI 96825-3103, USA

Micech, Phil (Football Player)
Minnesota Vikings
3029 N 91st St
Milwaukee, WI 53222-4620, USA

Miceli, Danny (Baseball Player)
Pittsburgh Pirates
8037 Hook Cir
Orlando, FL 32836-5340, USA

Miceli, Joe
189 Vanderbilt Ave
Brentwood, NY 11717-2518, USA

Micell, Justine (Actor)
Don Buchwald
6500 Wilshire Blvd Ste 2200
Los Angeles, CA 90048-4942, USA

Micelotta, Mickey (Baseball Player)
Philadelphia Phillies
3266 Jog Park Dr # 11
Greenacres, FL 33467-2014, USA

Michael (King)
Villa Serena
77 Chemin Louis-Degallier
Versoix-Geneva 1290, SWITZERLAND

Michael, Alum E (Government Official)
National Assembly for Wales
Cardiff Bay
Cardiff, WALES CF99 1NA, UNITED
KINGDOM (UK)

Michael, Archbishop (Religious Leader)
Antiochian Orthodox Christian Church
358 Mountain Rd
Englewood, NJ 07631-3727, USA

Michael, Bob (Politician)
1029 N Glenwood Ave
Peoria, IL 61606-1007, USA

Michael, Eugene R (Gene) (Misc)
49 Union Ave
Upper Saddle River, NJ 07458-2024, USA

Michael, ex-King
77 Chemin Louis Degallier
Versoix 1290, SWITZERLAND

Michael, Gary G (Business Person)
Alberston's Inc
250 E Parkcenter Blvd
Boise, ID 83706-3999, USA

Michael, Gene (Baseball Player)
Pittsburgh Pirates
49 Union Ave
Upper Saddle River, NJ 07458-2024, USA

Michael, George (Musician, Songwriter,
Writer)
c/o Brandt Joel *Creative Artists Agency
LCC (CAA-LA)*
2000 Avenue Of The Stars
Los Angeles, CA 90067-4700, USA

Michael, Gregory (Actor)
c/o Mitchell Gossett *Cunningham Escott
Slevin & Doherty (LA)*
10635 Santa Monica Blvd Ste 130
Los Angeles, CA 90025-8306, USA

Michael, Kevin (Musician)
c/o Staff Member *Paradigm (Monterey)*
509 Hartnell St
Monterey, CA 93940-2825, USA

Michael, Prince & Princess of Kent
Kensington Palace
London, ENGLAND W8 5AF, UNITED
KINGDOM (UK)

Michael Carroll, Jason (Musician)
c/o Staff Member *Creative Artists Agency
(CAA-Nashville)*
3310 W End Ave Fl 5
Nashville, TN 37203-1028, USA

Michaels, Al
47 W 66th St
New York, NY 10023-6201, USA

Michaels, Alan R (Al) (Sportscaster)
ABC-TV
77 W 66th St
Sports Dept
New York, NY 10023-6201, USA

Michaels, Beverly
11921 Weddington St
N Hollywood, CA 91607-2853, USA

Michaels, Brett (Musician)
c/o Staff Member *Agency for the
Performing Arts (APA-NY)*
888 7th Ave
New York, NY 10106-0001, USA

Michaels, Eugene H (Misc)
Alzheimer's Disease Research
15825 Shady Grove Rd
Rockville, MD 20850-4008, USA

Michaels, Fern (Writer)
1006 S Main St
Summerville, SC 29483-4231, USA

Michaels, James W (Editor)
Forbes Magazine
60 5th Ave
Editorial Dept
New York, NY 10011-8868, USA

Michaels, Jason (Baseball Player)
Philadelphia Phillies
10412 Carroll Cove Pl
Tampa, FL 33612-6520, USA

Michaels, Lorne (Producer, Writer)
Broadway Video
1619 Broadway Fl 9
New York, NY 10019-7463, USA

Michaels, Louis A (Lou) (Football Player)
Los Angeles Rams
69 Grace St
Swoyersville, PA 18704-3040, USA

Michaels, Marilyn
185 W End Ave
New York, NY 10023-5539, USA

Michaels, Michael
1640 S Sepulveda Blvd Ste 218
Los Angeles, CA 90025-7535, USA

Michaels, Shawn (Wrestler)
c/o Staff Member *World Wrestling Entertainment (WWE)*
1241 E Main St
Stamford, CT 06902-3520, USA

Michaels, Tammy Lynn (Actor)
c/o Marcel Pariseau *True Public Relations*
6725 W Sunset Blvd Ste 570
Los Angeles, CA 90028-7180, USA

Michaels, Walter (Walt) (Coach, Football Coach, Football Player)
Green Bay Packers
282 Michaels Rd
Shickshinny, PA 18655-4142, USA

Michaelsen, Kari (Actor)
Kazarian/Spencer
11365 Ventura Blvd Ste 100
Studio City, CA 91604-3148, USA

Michaelson, Ingrid (Musician)
c/o Staff Member *Paradigm (Monterey)*
509 Hartnell St
Monterey, CA 93940-2825, USA

Michalak, Chris (Baseball Player)
Arizona Diamondbacks
14747 W Hickory Ave
Lemont, IL 60439-7903, USA

Michaleczewski, Dariusz (Boxer)
Universum Box-Promotion
Am Stadtrand 27
Hamburg 22047, GERMANY

Michalik, Art (Football Player)
San Francisco 49ers
33400 Gafford St
Wildomar, CA 92595-8293, USA

Michalka, Alyson (Actor, Musician)
c/o David M Rudy *Crysis Management*
3800 Barham Blvd Ste 409
Los Angeles, CA 90068-1042, USA

Michalka, Amanda (Musician)
c/o David M Rudy *Crysis Management*
3800 Barham Blvd Ste 409
Los Angeles, CA 90068-1042, USA

Michals, Duane (Photographer)
109 E 19th St
New York, NY 10003-9603, USA

Micheaux, Nicki (Actor)
c/o Staff Member *MBST Entertainment*
345 N Maple Dr Ste 200
Beverly Hills, CA 90210-3860, USA

Micheel, Shaun (Golfer)
3100 Kenney Dr
Germantown, TN 38139-8041, USA

Michel, Alex (Reality TV Star)
PO Box 46605
Los Angeles, CA 90046-0605, USA

Michel, F Curtis (Astronaut)
2101 University Blvd
Houston, TX 77030-1218, USA

Michel, Hartmut (Nobel Prize Laureate)
Max-Planck Institut
Heinrich-Hoffmann-Str 7
Frankfort 60528, GERMANY

Michel, Jean-Louis (Oceanographer, Scientist)
IFREMER
Center de Toulon
La Seyne dur Mer, Toulon 83500, FRANCE

Michel, Mike (Football Player)
Miami Dolphins
378 Drexel Ave
Ventura, CA 93003-2329, USA

Michel, Paul R (Judge)
US Court of Appeals
717 Madison Pl NW
Washington, DC 20439-0001, USA

Michele, Chrisette (Musician)
c/o Staff Member *Paradigm (Monterey)*
509 Hartnell St
Monterey, CA 93940-2825, USA

Michele, Michael (Actor)
PMK Public Relations
700 N San Vicente Blvd Ste G910
West Hollywood, CA 90069-5061, USA

Michele, Yvette
250 W 57th St # 821
New York, NY 10107-0001, USA

Micheler, Elisabeth (Athlete)
Gruntenstr 45
Augsburg 86163, GERMANY

Michell, Keith (Actor)
Chatto & Linnit
Prince of Wales
Coventry St
London W1V 7FE, UNITED KINGDOM (UK)

Michell, Roger (Director)
Duncan Heath
Paramount House
162 Wardour
London, W1V 3AT, UNITED KINGDOM (UK)

Michelle, Candice (Actor, Model)
c/o Jeff Donaldson *Pacific Talent & Models*
1926 S Pacific Coast Hwy Ste 201
Redondo Beach, CA 90277-6145, USA

Michelle, Sheley (Actor)
c/o Mike Simpson *William Morris Agency (WMA-LA)*
1 William Morris Pl
Beverly Hills, CA 90212-4261, USA

Michelmore, Guy
72 Goldsmith Ave.
London, ENGLAND W3 6HN, UNITED KINGDOM (UK)

Michelmore, Lawrence (Government Official)
4924 Sentinel Dr
Bethesda, MD 20816-3590, USA

Michels, John (Football Player)
Green Bay Packers
4544 Alveo Rd
La Canada Flintridge, CA 91011-3703, USA

Michels, John (Football Player)
Philadelphia Eagles
504 Matterhorn Dr
Gatlinburg, TN 37738-6422, USA

Michels, Rinus (Coach, Football Coach)
Hotel Breitenbacher Hof
H-Heine-Allee 36
Dusseldorf 40213, GERMANY

Michener, Charles D (Misc)
1706 W 2nd St
Lawrence, KS 66044-1016, USA

Michie, Donald (Scientist)
6 Inveralmond Grove
Cramond
Edinburg EH4 6RA, SCOTLAND

Michiko (Royalty)
Imperial Palace
1-1 Chiyoda-ku
Tokyo 100, JAPAN

Michnik, Adam (Editor)
Czerha 8/10
Warsaw 00732, POLAND

Michos, Anastas N (Cinematographer)
Gersh Agency
232 N Canon Dr
Beverly Hills, CA 90210-5302, USA

Mickal, Abe (Football Player, Physicist)
774 Topaz St
New Orleans, LA 70124-3624, USA

Mickell, Darren (Football Player)
Kansas City Chiefs
9250 Chelsea Dr
Miramar, FL 33025-3803, USA

Mickelson, Ed (Baseball Player)
St Louis Cardinals
1532 Charlemont Dr
Chesterfield, MO 63017-4604, USA

Mickelson, Phil (Golfer)
c/o Staff Member *Pro Golfers Assoc of America (PGA)*
100 Avenue Of The Champions
Palm Beach Gardens, FL 33418-3653, USA

Mickens, Glenn (Baseball Player)
Brooklyn Dodgers
5920 Kini Pl
Kapaa, HI 96746-8938, USA

Mickey, Joey (Football Player)
Dallas Cowboys
6213 Canyon Dr
Oklahoma City, OK 73105-6415, USA

Middendorf, Dave (Football Player)
Cincinnati Bengals
PO Box 525
Port Orchard, WA 98366-0525, USA

Middendorf, J William II (Diplomat, Secretary)
565 W Main Rd
Little Compton, RI 02837-1131, USA

Middendorf, Tracy (Actor)
PO Box 480410
Los Angeles, CA 90048-1410, USA

Middle of the Road
18 Irvine Dr. Linwood
Refrewshire, ENGLAND, UNITED KINGDOM (UK)

Middlebrook, Jason (Baseball Player)
San Diego Padres
3309 Glenview Ave
Austin, TX 78703-1446, USA

Middlebrooks, Charley (Baseball Player)
Indianapolis Clowns
528 Rigby St NE
Marietta, GA 30063-0001, USA

Middlebrooks, Willie (Football Player)
Denver Broncos
18775 SW 78th Ct
Cutler Bay, FL 33157-7404, USA

Middleton, Dave (Football Player)
Detroit Lions
Too Ill To Sign Autographs
USA

Middleton, Mike (Model)
Louisa Models
Ebersberger Str 9
Munich 81679, GERMANY

Middleton, Rick (Hockey Player)
PO Box 1161
Hampton, NH 03843-1161, USA

Middleton, Terdell (Football Player)
Green Bay Packers
1893 Prospect St
Memphis, TN 38106-7645, USA

Middleton-Gentry, Ruth (Baseball Player)
28 Grandview Heights
Hamilton, IN 46742, USA

Midkiff, Dale (Actor)
c/o Staff Member *Innovative Artists (LA)*
1505 10th St
Santa Monica, CA 90401-2805, USA

Midler, Bette (Actor, Musician)
c/o Rob Light *Creative Artists Agency LCC (CAA-LA)*
2000 Avenue Of The Stars
Los Angeles, CA 90067-4700, USA

Midnight Fish
Samlandstr. 32
Munich D-81825, GERMANY

Midnight Oil
Box 186 Glebe
Sydney NSW 2037, AUSTRALIA

Midori (Musician)
Midori Foundation
850 7th Ave Ste 705
New York, NY 10019-5230, USA

Miechur, Thomas F (Misc)
Cement & Allied Workers Union
2500 Brickdale
Elk Grove Village, IL 60007, USA

Mieczko, A J (Hockey Player)
295 Central Park W Apt 9G
New York, NY 10024-3023, USA

Mielke, Gary (Baseball Player)
Texas Rangers
1718 Orchid Dr S
North Mankato, MN 56003-1435, USA

Mientkiewicz, Doug (Baseball Player)
c/o Staff Member *Kansas City Royals*
1 Royal Way
Kauffman Studios
Kansas City, MO 64129-1695, USA

Mierkowicz, Ed (Baseball Player)
Detroit Tigers
7530 Macomb St Apt 1A
Grosse Ile, MI 48138-1522, USA

Mieske, Matt (Baseball Player)
Milwaukee Brewers
2199 E Bombay Rd
Midland, MI 48642-8351, USA

Mieszkowski, Ed (Football Player)
Brooklyn Dodgers
10251 S Spaulding Ave
Evergreen Park, IL 60805-3761, USA

Mieto, Juha (Skier)
General Delivery
Mieto, FINLAND

Migenes, Julia (Opera Singer)
Artists Group
1650 Broadway Ste 610
New York, NY 10019-6833, USA

Miggins, Larry (Baseball Player)
St Louis Cardinals
2405 Kingston St
Houston, TX 77019-6603, USA

Mighty Clouds of Joy
PO Box 570815
Tarzana, CA 91357-0815, USA

Mighty Mighty Bosstones (Music Group)
c/o Staff Member *Paradigm (Monterey)*
509 Hartnell St
Monterey, CA 93940-2825, USA

Migliazzo, Paul (Football Player)
Chicago Bears
605 W 68th Ter
Kansas City, MO 64113-1954, USA

Mignola, Mike (Cartoonist)
Dark Horse Publishing
10956 SE Main St
Portland, OR 97216, USA

Miguel, Luis (Musician)
William Morris Agency
1325 Avenue Of The Americas
New York, NY 10019-6091, USA

Mihaly, Andras (Composer)
Verhalom Ter 9B
Budapest II 1025, HUNGARY

Mihm, Chris (Basketball Player)
Celeland Cavallers
1 Center Ct
Gund Arena
Cleveland, OH 44115-4001, USA

Mihok, Dash (Actor)
Handprint Entertainment
1100 Glendon Ave Ste 1000
Los Angeles, CA 90024-3514, USA

Mike-Mayer, Istvan (Steve) (Football Player)
San Francisco 49ers
681 Lincoln Ave
Glen Rock, NJ 07452-2519, USA

Mike-Mayer, Nicholas (Nick) (Football Player)
Atlanta Falcons
681 Lincoln Ave
Glen Rock, NJ 07452-2519, USA

Mike Rizzo, Mike (DJ)
c/o Staff Member *Diva Central Inc*
7510 W Sunset Blvd Ste 1445
Los Angeles, CA 90046-3408, USA

Mikell, George
23 Shuttleworth Rd
London, ENGLAND SW11, UNITED KINGDOM (UK)

Mikeska, Russ (Football Player)
Atlanta Falcons
148 Phoenix Dr
Eatonton, GA 31024-5635, USA

Mikhalchenko, Alla A (Ballerina)
Malaya Gruzinskaya St 12/18
Moscow 123242, RUSSIA

Mikhalkov, Nikita (Director)
Maly Kozikhinksy Per 4
#16-17
Moscow 103001, RUSSIA

Mikhalkov-Konchalovsky, Andrei S (Director)
Malaya Gruzinskaya 28 #130
Moscow 123557, RUSSIA

Miki, Minouri (Composer)
1-11-6 Higashi Nogawa
Komae-shi
Tokyo 201, JAPAN

Mikita, Valerie (Actor)
c/o Staff Member *The Stevens Group*
14011 Ventura Blvd # 201
Sherman Oaks, CA 91423-3533, USA

Mikkelsen, A Verner (Vern) (Basketball Player, Golfer)
17715 Breconville Rd
Wayzata, MN 55391, USA

Mikkelsen, Mads (Actor)
Ulrich Moller Jorgensen
Art Management ApS
Peblinge Dossering 18 2200
DENMARK

Mikkelsen, Pete (Baseball Player)
New York Yankees
141501 W North River Rd
Prosser, WA 99350-8225, USA

Miklich, William (Football Player)
New York Giants
Highway 106
Dousman, WI 53118, USA

Miklos, Arpad (Adult Film Star)
c/o Staff Member *Diva Central Inc*
7510 W Sunset Blvd Ste 1445
Los Angeles, CA 90046-3408, USA

Miko, Isabella (Actor)
c/o Kesha Williams *Melanie Greene Management & Productions*
425 N Robertson Blvd
West Hollywood, CA 90048-1735, USA

Miko, Izabella (Actor)
Evolution Talent
1776 Broadway Ste 1500
New York, NY 10019-2002, USA

Mikolajewski, Pete (Football Player)
San Diego Chargers
2520 Singing Vista Way
El Cajon, CA 92019-2740, USA

Miksis, Eddie (Baseball Player)
Brooklyn Dodgers
3906 Whitman Rd
Huntingdon Valley, PA 19006-2353, USA

Mikulski, Barbara (Senator)
1201 Pemberton Dr
Salisbury, MD 21801-2497, USA

Mikva, Abner J (Judge)
442 New Jersey Ave SE
Washington, DC 20003-4008, USA

Milacki, Bob (Baseball Player)
Baltimore Orioles
1873 Martinique Dr
Lake Havasu City, AZ 86406-9232, USA

Milan, Don (Football Player)
Green Bay Packers
PO Box 126
Gardnerville, NV 89410-0126, USA

Milandro, Kristina
2518 Cardigan Ct
Los Angeles, CA 90077-1337, USA

Milano, Alyssa (Actor)
c/o Joan Hyler *Hyler Management*
3000 Olympic Blvd Bldg 5 Ste 2250
Santa Monica, CA 90404-5073, USA

Milano, Fred (Musician)
Paramount Entertainment
PO Box 12
Far Hills, NJ 07931-0012, USA

Milbourne, Larry (Baseball Player)
Houston Astros
9020 Hillcrest Rd
Pittsburgh, PA 15237-4715, USA

Milbrett, Tiffeny (Soccer Player)
US Soccer Federation
1801 S Prairle Ave
Chicago, IL 60616, USA

Milburn, Darryl (Football Player)
Detroit Lions
270 E Harding St
Baton Rouge, LA 70802-7323, USA

Milburn, Glyn (Football Player)
Denver Broncos
515 S Kilei Rd Apt C502
Kihei, HI 96753, USA

Milbury, Mike (Coach, Hockey Player)
98 Claydon Rd
Garden City, NY 11530-1807, USA

Milchan, Arnon (Producer)
c/o Staff Member *New Regency Productions*
10201 W Pico Blvd Bldg 12
Los Angeles, CA 90064-2606, USA

Milchin, Mike (Baseball Player)
Minnesota Twins
13651 Glynshel Dr
Winter Garden, FL 34787-5001, USA

Mildren, L Jack Jr (Football Executive, Football Player)
Baltimore Colts
1701 Guilford Ln
Nichols Hills, OK 73120-1013, USA

Miles, Aaron (Baseball Player)
Chicago White Sox
1716 San Jose Drive
Davenport, IA 52807, USA

Miles, Carl (Baseball Player)
Philadelphia Athletics
5 Miller Dr
Columbia, MO 65201-5420, USA

Miles, Darius (Basketball Player)
Cleveland Cavaliers
1 Center Ct
Gund Arena
Cleveland, OH 44115-4001, USA

Miles, Don (Baseball Player)
Los Angeles Dodgers
22335 Baneberry Rd
Magnolia, TX 77355-3548, USA

Miles, Eddie (Football Player)
Pittsburgh Steelers
8575 Atlas Cir
Inver Grove Heights, MN 55077-3639, USA

Miles, Jim (Baseball Player)
Washington Senators
134 Moores Creek Rd
Maben, MS 39750-5532, USA

Miles, Joanna (Actor)
2062 Vine St
Los Angeles, CA 90068-3928, USA

Miles, John (Baseball Player)
Chicago American Giants
4130 Treehouse Dr
San Antonio, TX 78222-3510, USA

Miles, John R (Jack) (Writer)
3568 Mountain View Ave
Pasadena, CA 91107-4616, USA

Miles, John W (Geophysicist, Physicist)
26800 Academy Dr Apt 30
Palos Verdes Peninsula, CA 90274-3975, USA

Miles, Josephine (Writer)
2275 Virginia St
Berkeley, CA 94709-1617, USA

Miles, Mark (Misc, Tennis Player)
Assn of Tennis Pros
200 Tournament Players Road
Ponte Vedra Beach, FL 32082, USA

Miles, Sarah (Actor)
Chithurst Manor
Trotton near Petersfield
Hants GU31 5EU, UNITED KINGDOM (UK)

Miles, Sylvia (Actor)
240 Central Park S
New York, NY 10019-1457, USA

Miles, Vera (Actor)
PO Box 1599
Palm Desert, CA 92261-1599, USA

Miles-Clark, Jearl (Athlete, Track Athlete)
J J Clark
University Of Florida
Athletic Dept
Gainsville, FL 32611, USA

Milgram, Stanley (Doctor)
City Universtiy of New York
Graduate Center
New York, NY 10036, USA

Milhoan, Michael (Actor)
c/o Staff Member *Sanders/Armstrong Management*
2120 Colorado Ave Ste 120
Santa Monica, CA 90404-3561, USA

Milian, Christina (Actor)
c/o Johnny Wright *Wright Entertainment Group (WEG)*
424 E Central Blvd
Orlando, FL 32801-1923, USA

Milian, Marilyn (Judge)
c/o Staff Member *People's Court, The*
4113 Radford Ave
Studio City, CA 91604-2105, USA

Milicevic, Ivana (Actor, Model)
c/o Staff Member *United Talent Agency (UTA)*
9560 Wilshire Blvd Ste 500
Beverly Hills, CA 90212-2401, USA

Milinchik, Joe (Football Player)
Detroit Lions
9329 Barker Rd
New Hill, NC 27562-9795, USA

Militello, Sam (Baseball Player)
New York Yankees
3217 W Saint John St
Tampa, FL 33607-2127, USA

Milius, John F (Director, Writer)
888 Linda Flora Dr
Los Angeles, CA 90049-1629, USA

Milken, Michael R (Financier, Philanthropist)
4543 Tara Dr
Encino, CA 91436-3217, USA

Milla, Roger (Soccer Player)
Federation Camerounaise de Football
BP 1116
Yaounde, CAMEROON

Millan, Cesar (Misc)
Dog Psychology Center
PO Box 54069
Los Angeles, CA 90054-0069, USA

Millan, Felix (Baseball Player)
Atlanta Braves
G16 Calle Camarero
Carolina, PR 00987-8523, USA

Millar, Kevin (Baseball Player)
Florida Marlins
5290 Berwick Dr
Beaumont, TX 77706-2578, USA

Millar, Miles (Writer)
c/o Staff Member *Millar/Gough Ink*
3800 Barham Blvd Ste 503
Los Angeles, CA 90068-1042, USA

Millard, Keith (Football Player)
Minnesota Vikings
3739 Oakhurst Way
Dublin, CA 94568-8834, USA

Millbern, David (Actor)
c/o Staff Member *Barry Krost Management*
9465 Wilshire Blvd Ste 430
Beverly Hills, CA 90212-2613, USA

Millcic, Darko (Basketball Player)
Detroit Pistons
2 Championship Dr
Palace
Auburn Hills, MI 48326-1753, USA

Millegan, Eric (Actor)
c/o Peter Young *Don Buchwald & Associates Inc (LA)*
1902 Coldwater Canyon Dr
Beverly Hills, CA 90210-1731, USA

Millen, Hugh (Football Player)
Los Angeles Rams
6836 Cascade Ave SE
Snoqualmie, WA 98065-9725, USA

Millen, Matt G (Football Executive, Football Player)
Oakland Raiders
862 Durham Rd
Riegelsville, PA 18077, USA

Miller, Alan (Football Player)
Boston Patriots
3118 Erie Dr
Orchard Lake, MI 48324-1512, USA

Miller, Alan (Journalist)
Los Angeles Times
202 W 1st St
Editorial Dept
Los Angeles, CA 90012-4105, USA

Miller, Alice (Golfer)
2 Log Church Rd
Wilmington, DE 19807-1724, USA

Miller, Allan (Actor)
Douglas Gorman Rothacker Wilhelm
1501 Broadway Ste 703
New York, NY 10036-5505, USA

Miller, Andre (Basketball Player)
Denver Nuggets
1000 Chopper Cir
Pepsi Center
Denver, CO 80204-5805, USA

Miller, Ben (Actor, Producer)
c/o Staff Member *International Creative Management (ICM-UK)*
Oxford House
76 Oxford St
London W1N OAX, UNITED KINGDOM (UK)

Miller, Bill (Football Player)
Dallas Texans
701 Belden Ct
St Augustine, FL 32086-6821, USA

Miller, Billy (Football Player)
Denver Broncos
465 Cosmos Court
Westlake, CA 91362, USA

Miller, Bob (Baseball Player)
Detroit Tigers
1702 Kelm Trl
Saint Charles, IL 60174, USA

Miller, Bob (Baseball Player)
Philadelphia Phillies
17397 Glenmore
Detroit, MI 48240-2127, USA

Miller, Bode (Skier)
63 Eastern Valley Road
Franconia, NH 03580, USA

Miller, Brad (Basketball Player)
Sacramento Kings
1 Sports Pkwy
Arco Arena
Sacramento, CA 95834-2301, USA

Miller, Bruce (Baseball Player)
San Francisco Giants
2126 Parkland Dr
Fort Wayne, IN 46825-3929, USA

Miller, Buddy (Musician)
Mark Pucci Media
5000 Oak Bluff Ct
Atlanta, GA 30350-1069, USA

Miller, C Arden (Doctor)
350 Carolina Meadows Villa
Chapel Hill, NC 27517-7549, USA

Miller, C Ray (Religious Leader)
United Brethren in Christ
302 Lake St
Huntington, IN 46750-1264, USA

Miller, Calvin (Football Player)
New York Giants
1602 Fairfield Dr
Stillwater, OK 74074-2331, USA

Miller, Carl (Football Player)
Dallas Cowboys
PO Box 773
Crowley, TX 76036-0773, USA

Miller, Charles D (Business Person)
Avery Dennison Corp
150 N Orangge Grove Blvd
Pasadena, CA 91103, USA

Miller, Cheryl (Actor)
c/o Staff Member *Fisherman Agency Inc*
6767 Forest Lawn Dr Ste 101
Los Angeles, CA 90068-1050, USA

Miller, Cheryl D (Basketball Player, Coach)
3206 Ellington Dr
Los Angeles, CA 90068-1741, USA

Miller, Chris (Football Player)
Atlanta Falcons
2114 Elkhorn Dr
Eugene, OR 97408-1203, USA

Miller, Christa (Actor)
K&H
1212 Avenue Of The Americas # 3
New York, NY 10036-1602, USA

Miller, Christine Cook (Judge)
US Claims Court
717 Madison Pl NW
Washington, DC 20439-0001, USA

Miller, Coco (Basketball Player)
Washington Mystics
601 F St NW
McI Center
Washington, DC 20004-1605, USA

Miller, Corey (Football Player)
New York Giants
2528 Crofton Way
Columbia, SC 29223-2299, USA

Miller, Corky (Baseball Player)
Cincinnati Reds
1115 7th St
Calimesa, CA 92320-1013, USA

Miller, Damian (Baseball Player)
Minnesota Twins
N1276 Wuensch Rd
La Crosse, WI 54601-2655, USA

Miller, Dan (Musician)
Trans Continental Records
7380 W Sand Lake Rd # 350
Orlando, FL 32819-5248, USA

Miller, Darrell (Baseball Player)
California Angels
21159 Via Alisa
Yorba Linda, CA 92887-2510, USA

Miller, David (Cartoonist)
167 Tremont St
Rehoboth, MA 02769-2818, USA

Miller, Denise (Actor, Producer)
c/o Richard Sindell *Bob Waters Agency*
9301 Wilshire Blvd Ste 300
Beverly Hills, CA 90210-6119, USA

Miller, Dennis (Actor, Comedian)
c/o Brad Grey *Brillstein-Grey Entertainment*
9150 Wilshire Blvd Ste 350
Beverly Hills, CA 90212-3453, USA

Miller, Denny (Actor)
9612 Gavin Stone Ave
Las Vegas, NV 89145-8626, USA

Miller, Dyar (Baseball Player)
Baltimore Orioles
8816 Admirals Bay Dr
Indianapolis, IN 46236-9292, USA

Miller, Eddie (Baseball Player)
Texas Rangers
5014 Hartnett Ave
Richmond, CA 94804-4749, USA

Miller, Eddie (Football Player)
Indianapolis Colts
1503 Summerwood Dr
Clarkston, GA 30021-3096, USA

Miller, Elizabeth C (Doctor, Educator)
1822 Masters Ln
Madison, WI 53719-4440, USA

Miller, Eugene A (Financier)
Comerica Inc
500 Woodward Ave
Detroit, MI 48226-5480, USA

Miller, Frank (Actor, Writer)
c/o Staff Member *Shapiro-Lichtman Talent Agency*
1333 Beverly Green Dr
Los Angeles, CA 90035-1018, USA

Miller, Frank (Cartoonist)
Dark House Publishing
10956 SE Main St
Milwaukie, OR 97222-7644, USA

Miller, Fred (Football Player)
St Louis Rams
1920 S 3rd St Apt 59
Waco, TX 76706-2612, USA

Miller, Fred D (Football Player)
Baltimore Colts
4535 Black Rock Rd
Upperco, MD 21155-9544, USA

Miller, Gabrielle (Actor)
c/o Staff Member *Corner Gas*
PO Box 9
Station O
Scarborough, ON M4A 2M9, CANADA

Miller, George A (Doctor)
2221 Windrow Dr
Princeton, NJ 08540-5021, USA

Miller, George D (General)
20 Phillips Pond Rd
Natick, MA 01760-5643, USA

Miller, George T (Kennedy) (Director)
30 Orwell St
King's Cross
Sydney, NSW 2011, AUSTRALIA

Miller, Glenn Birthplace Society
PO Box 61
Clarinda, IA 51632-0061, USA

Miller, Glenn (Orchestra)
605 Crescent Executive Ct # 300
Lake Mary, FL 32746-2100, USA

Miller, Glenn Society
18 Crendon St.
High Wycombe, Bucks. ENGLAND, UNITED KINGDOM (UK)

Miller, Harvey R (Attorney, Attorney General, General)
Weil Gotshal Manges
797 5th Ave
New York, NY 10065, USA

Miller, J Ronald (Religious Leader)
Int'l Community Churches Council
21116 Washington Pkwy
Frankfort, IL 60423-3112, USA

Miller, James C III (Government Official)
Citizens for Sound Economy
1250 H St NW
Washington, DC 20005-3952, USA

Miller, Jamir (Football Player)
Phoenix Cardinals
331 Grenadine Way
Hercules, CA 94547-2048, USA

Miller, Jeff
1301 Spring Oaks Cir
Houston, TX 77055-4703, USA

Miller, Jeremy (Actor)
5255 Vesper Ave
Sherman Oaks, CA 91411-4011, USA

Miller, Jerry (Admiral)
Smithsonian Institution Press
750 9th St NW # 4300
Washington, DC 20560-0011, USA

Miller, Jim (Football Player)
San Francisco 49ers
PO Box 863
Ripley, MS 38663-0863, USA

Miller, Jody (Musician)
PO Box 413
Blanchard, OK 73010-0413, USA

Miller, Joel McKinnon (Actor)
c/o Michael Greene *Greene & Associates*
190 N Canon Dr Ste 200
Beverly Hills, CA 90210-5319, USA

Miller, John (Baseball Player)
New York Yankees
5105 River Ave Apt A
Newport Beach, CA 92663-2436, USA

Miller, John (Baseball Player)
Baltimore Orioles
13443 Old Annapolis Rd
Mount Airy, MD 21771-7732, USA

Miller, John (Baseball Player)
Washington Senators
1890 N Highway 37 Access
George West, TX 78022-3677, USA

Miller, John (Correspondent)
ABC-TV
77 W 66th St
News Dept
New York, NY 10023-6201, USA

Miller, Johnny (Football Player)
Washington Redskins
94 Beach St
Revere, MA 02151-5006, USA

Miller, Johnny Lee
8730 W Sunset Blvd Ste 490
Los Angeles, CA 90069-2248, USA

Miller, Jon (Baseball Player, Sportscaster)
San Francisco Giants
201 Nevada Ave
Moss Beach, CA 94038, USA

Miller, Jonathan (Director)
63 Gloucester Crescent
London NW1, UNITED KINGDOM (UK)

Miller, Josh (Football Player)
Pittsburgh Steelers
16 Summer Heights Dr
Franklin, MA 02038-2365, USA

Miller, Joyce D (Misc)
Amalgamated Clothing & Textile Workers
1710 Broadway Frnt 3
New York, NY 10019-5254, USA

Miller, Julie (Musician, Songwriter, Writer)
Mark Pucci Media
5000 Oak Bluff Ct
Atlanta, GA 30350-1069, USA

Miller, Justin (Baseball Player)
Toronto Blue Jays
2646 Dalemead St
Torrance, CA 90505-7027, USA

Miller, Keith (Baseball Player)
New York Mets
1161 Saint Andrews
Highland, MI 48357-4757, USA

Miller, Keith (Baseball Player)
Philadelphia Phillies
1831 W Alamosa Dr
Terrell, TX 75160-0811, USA

Miller, Keith H (Governor)
3705 Arctic Blvd
Anchorage, AK 99503-5774, USA

Miller, Kelly (Basketball Player)
Indiana Fever
125 S Pennsylvania St
Conseco Fieldhouse
Indianapolis, IN 46204-3610, USA

Miller, Kenny
5312 Eagle Lake Dr
Palm Beach Gardens, FL 33418-1539, USA

Miller, Kristen (Actor)
Lighthouse
409 N Camden Dr Ste 202
Beverly Hills, CA 90210-4423, USA

Miller, Kurt (Baseball Player)
Florida Marlins
1511 Iroquois Cir
Carrollton, TX 75007-6264, USA

Miller, Lajos (Opera Singer)
Balogh Adam Utca 28
Budapest 1026, HUNGARY

Miller, Larry (Actor, Comedian)
Spivak Entertainment
11845 W Olympic Blvd # 1125
Los Angeles, CA 90064-1149, USA

Miller, Larry (Baseball Player)
Los Angeles Dodgers
10045 N 36th St
Phoenix, AZ 85028-3942, USA

Miller, Larry (Football Player)
Minnesota Vikings
3 Cour De La Reine
Palos Hills, IL 60465-2405, USA

Miller, Larry H (Misc)
Utah Jazz
301 W South Temple
Delta Center
Salt Lake City, UT 84101-1216, USA

Miller, Lawrence (Larry) (Basketball Player)
1300 Paddock Dr
Raleigh, NC 27609-5493, USA

Miller, Lemmie (Baseball Player)
Los Angeles Dodgers
14N693 Getzelman Rd
Hampshire, IL 60140-8255, USA

Miller, Lennox (Athlete, Track Athlete)
2120 Pinecrest Dr
Altadena, CA 91001-2121, USA

Miller, Lenore (Misc)
Retail/Wholesale/Department Store Union
30 E 29th St
New York, NY 10016-7925, USA

Miller, Linda G
242 Conway Ave
Los Angeles, CA 90024-2602, USA

Miller, Marisa (Actor, Model)
c/o Craig Schneider *Pinnacle PR*
8265 W Sunset Blvd Ste 201
West Hollywood, CA 90046-2470, USA

Miller, Mark (Football Player)
Buffalo Bills
6020 Poling Rd
Elida, OH 45807-9492, USA

Miller, Mark (Musician)
Sawyer Brown Inc
5200 Old Hardling Road
Franklin, TN 37064, USA

Miller, Mark-Thomas
280 S Beverly Dr Ste 400
Beverly Hills, CA 90212-3904, USA

Miller, Marvin J (Director)
211 E 70th St Apt 32G
New York, NY 10021-5210, USA

Miller, Matt (Baseball Player)
Detroit Tigers
4501 83rd St
Lubbock, TX 79424-4240, USA

Miller, Matt (Football Player)
Cleveland Browns
15 Highgate Cir
Ithaca, NY 14850-1429, USA

Miller, Michael (Football Player)
New York Giants
116 E McClellan St
Flint, MI 48505-4224, USA

Miller, Mike (Basketball Player)
Memphis Grizzlies
191 Beale St
Memphis, TN 38103-3715, USA

Miller, Mildred (Opera Singer)
PO Box 110108
Pittsburgh, PA 15232-0608, USA

Miller, Mitch (Conductor, Director, Musical Director)
345 W 58th St
New York, NY 10019-1145, USA

Miller, Mulgrew (Musician)
3725 Farmersville Rd
Easton, PA 18045-2300, USA

Miller, Nate (Boxer)
1214 Allengrove St
Philadelphia, PA 19124-2904, USA

Miller, Nicole J (Designer, Fashion Designer)
780 Madison Ave
New York, NY 10065-6108, USA

Miller, Nolan (Designer, Fashion Designer)
Nolan Miller Collection
241 S Robertson Blvd
Beverly Hills, CA 90211-2810, USA

Miller, Norm (Baseball Player)
Houston Astros
43 Columbia Crest Pl
Spring, TX 77382-1331, USA

Miller, Oliver (Basketball Player)
2912 S Meadow Dr
Fort Worth, TX 76133-7214, USA

Miller, Omar Benson (Actor)
c/o Stephen Tenenbaum *MBST Entertainment*
345 N Maple Dr Ste 200
Beverly Hills, CA 90210-3860, USA

Miller, Paul (Baseball Player)
Pittsburgh Pirates
252 Redbud Ln
Batavia, IL 60510-3623, USA

Miller, Paul (Football Player)
Los Angeles Rams
14686 Old Hammond Hwy # 118
Baton Rouge, LA 70816-1235, USA

Miller, Penelope Ann (Actor)
United Talent Agency
9560 Wilshire Blvd Ste 500
Beverly Hills, CA 90212-2401, USA

Miller, Percy (Master P) (Actor, Musician)
c/o Michael Menchel *Relevant Entertainment Group (LA)*
12300 Wilshire Blvd Ste 420
Los Angeles, CA 90025-1061, USA

Miller, Peter North (Business Person)
Dawson House
5 Jewry St
London EC3N 2EX, UNITED KINGDOM (UK)

Miller, Randy (Baseball Player)
Baltimore Orioles
22523 Oak Mist Ln
Katy, TX 77494-2256, USA

Miller, Raymond (Baseball Player)
Indianapolis Clowns
13534 Covered Bridge Rd
Lowell, MI 49331-9085, USA

Miller, Reginald W (Reggie) (Basketball Player)
14301 E 113th St
Fortville, IN 46040-9660, USA

Miller, Rick (Baseball Player)
Boston Red Sox
28548 F B Fowler Ct
Bonita Springs, FL 34135-0400, USA

Miller, Robert M (Football Player)
Detroit Lions
8475 Knox Rd
Clarkston, MI 48348-1721, USA

Miller, Robert N (Red) (Coach, Football Coach)
3841 S Narcissus Way
Denver, CO 80237-1239, USA

Miller, Rod (Baseball Player)
Brooklyn Dodgers
40 Mogul Mountain Dr
Reno, NV 89523-9615, USA

Miller, Ron (Football Player)
Los Angeles Rams
6392 Washington
Youngville, CA 94599, USA

Miller, Scott (Football Player)
Miami Dolphins
26432 Charford Way
Lake Forest, CA 92630-6520, USA

Miller, Shannon (Gymnast)
505 Lancaster St Apt 10ab
Jacksonville, FL 32204-4136, USA

Miller, Shawn (Football Player)
Los Angeles Rams
3070 W Old Highway Rd
Morgan, UT 84050-9307, USA

Miller, Sienna (Actor)
c/o Dallas Smith *Peters Fraser & Dunlop (PFD - UK)*
Drury House
34-43 Russell St
London WC2B 5HA, UNITED KINGDOM (UK)

Miller, Stanley L (Misc)
University of California
Chemistry Dept
La Jolla, CA 92093, USA

Miller, Stephanie (Television Host)
22647 Ventura Blvd # 1005
Woodland Hills, CA 91364-1416, USA

Miller, Steve (Director, Musical Director, Musician, Songwriter, Writer)
PO Box 12680
Seattle, WA 98111-4680, USA

Miller, Stuart L (Stu) (Baseball Player)
St Louis Cardinals
3701 Ocaso Ct
Cameron Park, CA 95682-8961, USA

Miller, Tangi (Actor)
c/o Staff Member *Gersh Agency, The (LA)*
232 N Canon Dr
Beverly Hills, CA 90210-5302, USA

Miller, Terry (Football Player)
Buffalo Bills
9015 W 2nd Ave
Stillwater, OK 74074-6775, USA

Miller, Tom (Football Player)
Philadelphia Eagles
430 Grant St Apt 240
De Pere, WI 54115-2161, USA

Miller, Travis (Baseball Player)
Minnesota Twins
8339 US Route 35 W
Eaton, OH 45320-9641, USA

Miller, Trever (Baseball Player)
Detroit Tigers
1015 Osburn Hollow Rd
Arrington, TN 37014-9114, USA

Miller, Ty (Actor)
David Shapira
193 N Robertson Blvd
Beverly Hills, CA 90211-2103, USA

Miller, Valarie Rae
3500 W Olive Ave Ste 1400
Burbank, CA 91505-5512, USA

Miller, Wade (Baseball Player)
Houston Astros
12 Woods Way
Reading, PA 19610-1199, USA

Miller, Warren (Photographer)
505 Pler Ave
Hermosa Beach, CA 90254, USA

Miller, Wentworth (Actor)
c/o Peter Kiernan Management 360
9111 Wilshire Blvd
Beverly Hills, CA 90210-5508, USA

Miller, Wiley (Cartoonist)
8 Granite Heights Rd
Kennebunkport, ME 04046-5262, USA

Miller, William (Baseball Player)
PO Box 2681
Aptos, CA 95001-2681, USA

Miller, Willie T (Football Player)
Cleveland Browns
308 Martin Dr
Birmingham, AL 35215-1180, USA

Miller, Zell (Government Official)
McKenna Long & Aldridge
303 Peachtree St NE Ste 5300
Atlanta, GA 30308-3265, USA

Miller-Lawrence, Christa (Actor)
Wolf/Kasteler PR
132 S Rodeo Dr Ste 300
Beverly Hills, CA 90212-2415, USA

Millett, Kate (Writer)
20 Old Overlook Rd
Poughkeepsie, NY 12603-6220, USA

Millett, Lewis L (War Hero)
Korean War Memorial Patriotic Hall
1816 S Figueroa St # 700
Los Angeles, CA 90015-3422, USA

Millette, Joe (Baseball Player)
Philadelphia Phillies
759 Solana Dr
Lafayette, CA 94549-5206, USA

Millhauser, Steven (Writer)
235 Caroline St
Saratoga Springs, NY 12866-3505, USA

Milliken, Bob (Baseball Player)
Brooklyn Dodgers
1875 Southwood Ln
Clearwater, FL 33764-2467, USA

Millionaire, Tony (Artist)
c/o Staff Member Fantagraphics Books
7563 Lake City Way NE
Seattle, WA 98115-4218, USA

Millman, Dan (Writer)
PO Box 6148
San Rafael, CA 94903-0148, USA

Millman, Irving (Inventor)
310 Windsor Cir
Cherry Hill, NJ 08002-2423, USA

Millo, Aprile E (Opera Singer)
Columbia Artists Mgmt Inc
1790 Broadway Fl 6
New York, NY 10019-1412, USA

Milloy, Lawyer (Football Player)
Buffalo Bills
1 Bills Dr
Orchard Park, NY 14127-2237, USA

Mills, Alan (Baseball Player)
New York Yankees
1811 Bellgrove St
Lakeland, FL 33805-2523, USA

Mills, Alley (Actor)
444 Carroll Canal
Venice, CA 90291-4682, USA

Mills, Bill (Baseball Player)
Philadelphia Athletics
4344 Commercial St
Port Charlotte, FL 33953-5945, USA

Mills, Billy (Athlete, Track Athlete)
c/o Staff Member Billy Mills Speakers Bureau, The
7760 Winding Way # 723
Fair Oaks, CA 95628-5735, USA

Mills, Brad (Baseball Player)
Montreal Expos
3025 E Birch Ave
Visalia, CA 93292-6822, USA

Mills, Curtis (Athlete, Track Athlete)
328 Lake St
Lufkin, TX 75904, USA

Mills, Dick (Baseball Player)
Boston Red Sox
11445 E Via Linda Ste 2
Scottsdale, AZ 85259-2654, USA

Mills, Donna (Actor)
c/o Joel Dean TalentWorks (LA)
3500 W Olive Ave Ste 1400
Burbank, CA 91505-5512, USA

Mills, Eddie
9200 W Sunset Blvd Ste 1130
Los Angeles, CA 90069-3606, USA

Mills, Erie (Opera Singer)
John J Miller
801 W 18th St #20
New York, NY 10033, USA

Mills, Ernie (Football Player)
Pittsburgh Steelers
5763 NE 34th St
Silver Springs, FL 34488-1887, USA

Mills, Frank (Composer, Musician)
Rocklands Talent
PO Box 1282
Peterborough, ON K9L 7H5, CANADA

Mills, John Henry (Football Player)
Houston Oilers
755 Bahia Cir
Ocala, FL 34472-8831, USA

Mills, Jordan
6500 Wilshire Blvd Ste 2200
Los Angeles, CA 90048-4942, USA

Mills, Judson (Actor)
2401 W Olive Ave Ste 290
Burbank, CA 91506-2666, USA

Mills, Kyle (Writer)
William Morris Agency
151 El Camino Dr
Beverly Hills, CA 90212-2775, USA

Mills, Mike (Musician)
REM/Athens Ltd
PO Box 8032
Athens, GA 30603-8032, USA

Mills, Pete (Football Player)
Buffalo Bills
27 Langfield Dr
Buffalo, NY 14215-3321, USA

Mills, Samuel D (Sam) Jr (Football Player)
9 Precedent Pl
Manalapan, NJ 07726-8670, USA

Mills, Stephanie (Actor, Musician)
Associated Booking Corp
PO Box 2055
New York, NY 10021-0051, USA

Mills, Terry (Basketball Player)
Indiana Pacers
125 S Pennsylvania St
Conseco Fieldhouse
Indianapolis, IN 46204-3610, USA

Millwood, Kevin A (Baseball Player)
Atlanta Braves
300 Leesville Ave
Bessemer City, NC 28016-8528, USA

Milmoe, Caroline (Actor)
Nigel Martin-Smith
41 S King St
Manchester M2 6DE, UNITED KINGDOM (UK)

Milnar, Al (Baseball Player)
Cleveland Indians
11415 Mourning Dove Pl
Painesville, OH 44077-9337, USA

Milne, Brian (Football Player)
Cincinnati Bengals
15314 Willy Rd
Union City, PA 16438, USA

Milner, Anthony F D (Composer)
147 Heythorp St
Southfields
London SW18 5BT, UNITED KINGDOM (UK)

Milner, Brian (Baseball Player)
Toronto Blue Jays
1202 Thistle Hill Trl
Weatherford, TX 76087-4977, USA

Milner, Brian (Baseball Player)
Houston Astros
536 N Grand
Mesa, AZ 85201-5031, USA

Milner, Eddie (Baseball Player)
Cincinnati Reds
491 Stambaugh Ave
Columbus, OH 43207-2565, USA

Milner, Martin (Actor)
3106 Azahar St
Carlsbad, CA 92009-8362, USA

Milnes, Sherrill E (Opera Singer)
Herbert Barrett
266 W 37th St Fl 20
New York, NY 10018-6648, USA

Milo, Sandra
Viale Liegi 42
Rome I-00198, ITALY

Milongo, Andre (Prime Minister)
Union for Democracy & Republic
Brazzaville, CONGO REPUBLIC

Milos, Sofia (Actor)
c/o Scott Zimmerman Untitled Entertainment (LA)
331 N Maple Dr Fl 3
Beverly Hills, CA 90210-3827, USA

Milow, Keith (Artist)
32 W 20th St
New York, NY 10011-4207, USA

Milsap, Ronnie (Musician, Songwriter, Writer)
c/o Ron Merlino Columbia Artists Mgmt Inc
1790 Broadway Fl 6
New York, NY 10019-1412, USA

Milsome, Doug (Cinematographer)
Simth/Gosnell/Nicholson
PO Box 1156
Studio City, CA 91614-0156, USA

Milstead, Charles (Football Player)
Houston Oilers
10043 Meadow Lake Ln
Houston, TX 77042-2915, USA

Milstead, Rod (Football Player)
San Francisco 49ers
11815 Brookeville Landing Ct
Bowie, MD 20721-4502, USA

Milstein, Elliott (Educator)
American University
President's Office
Washington, DC 20016, USA

Milton, DeLisha (Basketball Player)
Los Angeles Sparks
1111 S Figueroa St
Staples Center
Los Angeles, CA 90015-1300, USA

Milton, Eric (Baseball Player)
Minnesota Twins
14581 Jonathan Harbour Dr
Fort Myers, FL 33908-2802, USA

Milva
9 via Gabrio Serbelloni
Milan I-20122, ITALY

Mimbs, Michael (Baseball Player)
Philadelphia Phillies
2761 Mimbs Rd
Alamo, GA 30411-2502, USA

Mimoun, Alain (Athlete, Track Athlete)
27 Ave Edouard-Jenner
Champigny-sur-Marne 94500, FRANCE

Mims, Chris (Football Player)
San Diego Chargers
11175 Forestview Ln
San Diego, CA 92131-1351, USA

Mims, Madeline Manning (Athlete, Track Athlete)
7477 E 48th St # 83-4
Tulsa, OK 74145-6679, USA

Min, Gao (Misc)
Olympic Committee
9 Tuyuguan
Beijing, CHINA

Minarcin, Rudy (Baseball Player)
Cincinnati Reds
1037 1st St
Vandergrift, PA 15690-1007, USA

Minarik, Henry (Football Player)
Pittsburgh Steelers
1001 N Linda Ln
Lake City, MI 49651-9227, USA

Mincer, Jacob (Economist)
448 Riverside Dr
New York, NY 10027-6819, USA

Mincher, Don (Baseball Player)
Washington Senators
5605 Criner Rd SE
Huntsville, AL 35802-1858, USA

Minchey, Nate (Baseball Player)
Boston Red Sox
1212 Ramble Creek Dr
Pflugerville, TX 78660-2155, USA

Mincy, Charles (Football Player)
Kansas City Chiefs
1142 W 79th St
Los Angeles, CA 90044-3508, USA

Mincy, Purnell (Baseball Player)
Philadelphia Stars
127 W 96th St Apt 160
New York, NY 10025-6427, USA

Mindel, Lee F (Architect)
Shelton Mindel Assoc
56 W 22nd St Fl 12
New York, NY 10010-7279, USA

Mindell, Earl (Writer)
Hay House
PO Box 5100
Carlsbad, CA 92018-5100, USA

Minds, Simple (Music Group)
c/o Staff Member *Solo Agency Ltd (UK)*
55 Fulham High St
London SW6 3JJ, UNITED KINGDOM
(UK)

Minear, Tim (Director, Writer)
c/o Lawrence Shuman *Shuman Company*
3815 Hughes Ave Fl 4
Culver City, CA 90232-2715, USA

Minehan, Cathy E (Financier, Government
Official)
Federal Reserve Bank
600 Atlantic Ave
Boston, MA 02210-2204, USA

Miner, Roger J (Judge)
US Court of Appeals
445 Broadway Ste 414
Albany, NY 12207-2926, USA

Miner, Steve (Director)
1137 2nd St Ste 103
Santa Monica, CA 90403-5069, USA

Minervini, Craig (Baseball Player)
Florida Marlins
229 Cameron Dr
Weston, FL 33326-3515, USA

Mineta, Norman Y (Secretary)
Transportation Department
400 7th St SW
Washington, DC 20590-0001, USA

Minetto, Craig (Baseball Player)
Oakland A's
1809 Lakeshore Dr
Lodi, CA 95242-4230, USA

Ming, Tsai (Chef)
Food Network
1180 Avenue Of The Americas Ste 1200
New York, NY 10036-8401, USA

Ming-Na, Wen (Actor)
c/o Andy Cohen *International Creative
Management (ICM-LA)*
10250 Constellation Blvd
Los Angeles, CA 90067-6200, USA

Mingenbach, Louise (Designer)
c/o Wayne Fitterman *United Talent
Agency (UTA)*
9560 Wilshire Blvd Ste 500
Beverly Hills, CA 90212-2401, USA

Minghella, Anthony (Director)
Judy Daish
2 Saint Charles Place
London W10 6EG, UNITED KINGDOM
(UK)

Mingo, Gene (Football Player)
Denver Broncos
5701 E Colorado Ave
Denver, CO 80224-2102, USA

Mingori, Steve (Baseball Player)
Cleveland Indians
8841 N Congress Ave Apt 637
Kansas City, MO 64153-1914, USA

Mingus, Charles
484 W 43rd St Apt 43S
New York, NY 10036-6327, USA

Minh, Tran (Choreographer, Dancer)
2014 NE 47th Ave
Portland, OR 97213-2016, USA

Miniefield, Kevin (Football Player)
Chicago Bears
1030 Lakehurst Rd
Waukegan, IL 60085-8232, USA

Minisi, Anthony S (Skip) (Football Player)
New York Giants
300 Continental Ln
Paoli, PA 19301-2043, USA

Mink, Rep (Politician)
PO Box 50144
Honolulu, HI 96850-5544, USA

Minka (Adult Film Star)
USP Entertainment Inc
8635 W Sahara Ave # 564
Las Vegas, NV 89117-5858, USA

Minkoff, Rob (Director)
Creative Artists Agency
9830 Wilshire Blvd
Beverly Hills, CA 90212-1804, USA

Minnelli, Liza (Actor, Musician)
c/o Jonathan Howard *Innovative Artists
(LA)*
1505 10th St
Santa Monica, CA 90401-2805, USA

Minner, Paul (Baseball Player)
Brooklyn Dodgers
558 Race St
Harrisburg, PA 17104-1646, USA

Minnick, Don (Baseball Player)
Washington Senators
215 Bernard Rd
Rocky Mount, VA 24151-2243, USA

Minniear, Randy (Football Player)
New York Giants
739 Westport Rd
Easton, CT 06612-1537, USA

Minnifield, Frank (Football Player)
Cleveland Browns
4809 Chaffey Ln
Lexington, KY 40515-1166, USA

Minnillo, Vanessa (Actor, Television Host)
c/o Staff Member *Entertainment Tonight
(ET)*
5555 Melrose Ave
Mae West Bldg Fl 2
Los Angeles, CA 90038-3989, USA

Minogue, Dannii (Musician)
Melissa LeGear Management
C/O Melissa LeGear
329 Montague St
Albert Park, Victoria 3206, AUSTRALIA

Minogue, Kylie (Actor, Musician)
c/o Robert Marsala *Bauer Company, The*
9300 Wilshire Blvd Ph
Beverly Hills, CA 90212-3213, USA

Minor, Blas (Baseball Player)
Pittsburgh Pirates
7139 Dean St
Winton, CA 95388-9766, USA

Minor, Claudie (Football Player)
Denver Broncos
730 17th St Ste 520
The Premier Companies
Denver, CO 80202-3539, USA

Minor, Damon (Baseball Player)
San Francisco Giants
1709 Kamber Ter
Edmond, OK 73003-2386, USA

Minor, Kory (Football Player)
Carolina Panthers
1402 W Farlington St
West Covina, CA 91790-3354, USA

Minor, Lincoln (Football Player)
New Orleans Saints
720 Carrollwood Village Dr
Gretna, LA 70056-6001, USA

Minor, Michael
280 S Beverly Dr Ste 400
Beverly Hills, CA 90212-3904, USA

Minor, Rickey (Director, Musical Director)
c/o Staff Member *William Morris Agency
(WMA-LA)*
1 William Morris Pl
Beverly Hills, CA 90212-4261, USA

Minor, Ronald R (Religious Leader)
Pentecostal Church of God
4901 Pennsylvania Ave
Joplin, MO 64804-4947, USA

Minor, Ryan (Baseball Player)
Baltimore Orioles
1709 Kamber Ter
Edmond, OK 73003-2386, USA

Minor, Shane (Musician)
ESP Mgmt
838 N Doheny Dr Apt 302
West Hollywood, CA 90069-4849, USA

Minor, Travis (Football Player)
Miami Dolphins
300 Three Islands Blvd Apt 1A
Hallandale Beach, FL 33009-2826, USA

Minoso, Minnle (Baseball Player)
Cleveland Indians
324 W 35th St
Chicago, IL 60616, USA

Minow, Newton N (Government Official)
179 E Lake Shore Dr # 15W
Chicago, IL 60611-1340, USA

Minshall, Jim (Baseball Player)
Pittsburgh Pirates
225 Mary Ingles Hwy
Melbourne, KY 41059-8217, USA

Minshew, Alicia (Actor)
c/o Seth Greenky *Green Key Mgmt (NY)*
251 W 89th St Apt 4A
New York, NY 10024-1713, USA

Minsky, Marvin L (Scientist)
Massachusetts Institute of Technology
Computer Sci Dept
Cambridge, MA 02139, USA

Minter, Barry (Football Player)
Chicago Bears
2626 Garcitas Crk
Richmond, TX 77469-1961, USA

Minter, Cedric (Football Player)
New York Jets
5653 E Bay Trail Ct
Boise, ID 83716-7031, USA

Minter, Kelly (Actor)
Marshak Wyckoff
280 S Beverly Dr Ste 400
Beverly Hills, CA 90212-3904, USA

Minter, Kristin (Actor)
c/o Charles Silver *SMS Talent Inc*
8730 W Sunset Blvd Ste 440
Los Angeles, CA 90069-2277, USA

Minter, Mike (Football Player)
Carolina Panthers
3661 Richwood Cir
Kannapolis, NC 28081-6704, USA

Mintoff, Dominic (Prime Minister)
Olives
Xintill St
Tarxien, MALTA

Minton, Greg (Baseball Player)
San Francisco Giants
4434 E Camelback Rd Unit 127
Phoenix, AZ 85018-2835, USA

Minton, Yvonne F (Opera Singer)
Ingpen & Williams
26 Wadham Road
London SW15 2LR, UNITED KINGDOM
(UK)

Mintz, Shiomo (Musician)
I C M Artists
40 W 57th St
New York, NY 10019-4001, USA

Mintz, Steve (Baseball Player)
San Francisco Giants
128 Forest Hills Dr
Leland, NC 28451-9744, USA

Minutelli, Gino (Baseball Player)
Cincinnati Reds
3305 Foxtrot Ct
Spring Hill, TN 37174-7116, USA

Miou-Miou (Actor)
VMA
20 Ave Rapp
Paris 75008, FRANCE

Mir, Isabelle (Skier)
Saint-Lary 65170, FRANCE

Mira, George (Football Player)
San Francisco 49ers
19225 SW 128th Ct
Miami, FL 33177-4222, USA

Mirabella, Grace (Editor, Publisher)
Mirabella Magazine
200 Madison Ave
New York, NY 10016-3903, USA

Mirabella, Paul (Baseball Player)
Texas Rangers
125 Jenks Rd
Morristown, NJ 07960, USA

Mirabelli, Doug (Baseball Player)
San Francisco Giants
9788 Edgewood Ave
Traverse City, MI 49684-8173, USA

Miracles, The
141 Dunbar Ave
Fords, NJ 08863-1551, USA

Miranda, Christianne (Musician,
Songwriter, Writer)
c/o Staff Member *Kult Records*
38 W 36th St Fl 3
New York, NY 10018-8078, USA

Miranda, Patricia (Wrestler)
Stanford Wrestling - Department of Athletics
Stanford University
Arrillaga Family Sports Center
Stanford, CA 94305, USA

Miranda, Willie
5502 Whitwood Rd
Baltimore, MD 21206-3748, USA

Mirer, Rick
11220 NE 53rd St
Kirkland, WA 98033-7505, USA

Miriciolu, Nelly (Opera Singer)
53 Midhurst Ave
Muswell Hill
London N10, UNITED KINGDOM (UK)

Mirikitani, Janice (Writer)
Glide Memorial United Methodist Church
330 Ellis St
San Francisco, CA 94102-2735, USA

Mirisch, Walter M (Producer)
647 Warner Ave
Los Angeles, CA 90024-2566, USA

Mirkerevic, Dragen (Prime Minister)
Premier's Office
Vojvode Putnkia 3
Sarajevo 71000, BOSNIA-HERZEGOVINA

Mirkin, David (Actor, Director)
c/o David Gersh *Gersh Agency, The (LA)*
232 N Canon Dr
Beverly Hills, CA 90210-5302, USA

Mironov, Boris (Hockey Player)
New York Rangers
2 Penn Plz
Madison Square Garden
New York, NY 10121-1703, USA

Mironov, Dmitri (Hockey Player)
Anaheim Mighty Ducks
2000 E Gene Autry Way
Anaheim, CA 92806-6143, USA

Mironov, Yevgeniy V (Actor)
Oleg Tabajiv Theater
Chaokygina Str 12A
Moscow, RUSSIA

Mirra, Dave (Athlete)
Wasserman Media Group, LLC
12100 W Olympic Blvd Ste 400
Los Angeles, CA 90064-1052, USA

Mirren, Helen (Actor)
c/o Fred Specktor *Creative Artists Agency LCC (CAA-LA)*
2000 Avenue Of The Stars
Los Angeles, CA 90067-4700, USA

Mirrlees, James A (Nobel Prize Laureate)
Trinity College
Economics Dept
Cambridge CB2 1TQ, UNITED KINGDOM (UK)

Mirzoev, Akbar (Prime Minister)
Prime Minister's Office
Dushaube, TAJIKISTAN

Mischak, Bob (Football Player)
New York Giants
73 Brookwood Rd Unit 12
Orinda, CA 94563-3310, USA

Mischka, Badgley (Designer, Fashion Designer)
525 7th Ave Fl 14
New York, NY 10018-4901, USA

Mischka, James (Designer, Fashion Designer)
Badgley Mischka
525 Fashion Ave
New York, NY 10018-4901, USA

Mischke, Carl H (Religious Leader)
1034 Buena Vista Dr
Sun Prairie, WI 53590-2031, USA

Misersky, Antje (Athlete)
Grenzgraben 3A
Stutzerbach 98714, GERMANY

Misiano, Christopher (Director)
c/o Staff Member *Creative Artists Agency LCC (CAA-LA)*
2000 Avenue Of The Stars
Los Angeles, CA 90067-4700, USA

Misiano, Vincent (Director)
c/o Glen Bickel *Creative Artists Agency LCC (CAA-LA)*
2000 Avenue Of The Stars
Los Angeles, CA 90067-4700, USA

Misraki, Paul
35 av. Bugeaud
Paris F-75116, FRANCE

Miss Teen USA
6420 Wilshire Blvd
Los Angeles, CA 90048-5502, USA

Missing Persons
11935 Laurel Hills Rd
Studio City, CA 91604-3726, USA

Mistler, John (Football Player)
New York Giants
3111 E Desert Flower Ln
Phoenix, AZ 85048-8331, USA

Mistral, Fernanda (Actor)
c/o Staff Member *Telefe - Argentina*
Pavon 2444 (C1248AAT)
Buenos Aires, ARGENTINA

Mistry, Jimi (Actor)
c/o Staff Member *Endeavor Agency LLC (LA)*
9601 Wilshire Blvd Fl 3
Beverly Hills, CA 90210-5204, USA

Misuraca, Mike (Baseball Player)
Milwaukee Brewers
2203 Kingsbridge Ct
San Dimas, CA 91773-3723, USA

Miszak, Anna Cepinska (Beauty Pageant Winner)
c/o Staff Member *Miss World Ltd*
21 Golden Sq
London W1R 3PA, UNITED KINGDOM (UK)

Mitchell, Aaron (Football Player)
Dallas Cowboys
1701 Broadway
Seattle Central College Attn Athletic Dept
Seattle, WA 98122-2413, USA

Mitchell, Andrea (Correspondent)
2710 Chain Bridge Rd NW
Washington, DC 20016-3404, USA

Mitchell, Betsy (Swimmer)
Laurel High School
1 Lyman Cir
Athletic Dept
Cleveland, OH 44122-2110, USA

Mitchell, Beverley (Actor)
c/o Barry McPherson *Agency for the Performing Arts (APA-LA)*
405 S Beverly Dr
Beverly Hills, CA 90212-4416, USA

Mitchell, Beverly (Actor)
c/o Staff Member *Forster-Delaney Entertainment*
12533 Woodgreen St
Los Angeles, CA 90066-2723, USA

Mitchell, Bobby (Baseball Player)
Los Angeles Dodgers
13887 Torrey Bella Ct
San Diego, CA 92129-4628, USA

Mitchell, Bobby (Football Player)
Cleveland Browns
2121 George Halas Dr NW
Professional Football Hof
Canton, OH 44708-2630, USA

Mitchell, Bobby (Golfer)
435 Wimbish Dr
Danville, VA 24541-5823, USA

Mitchell, Brian (Actor)
5307 Wilkinson Ave Apt 20B
Valley Village, CA 91607-2464, USA

Mitchell, Brian K (Football Player)
New York Giants
Giants Stadium
East Rutherford, NJ 07073, USA

Mitchell, Brian Stokes (Actor, Musician)
243 W 98th St Apt 5C
New York, NY 10025-5566, USA

Mitchell, Charlie (Baseball Player)
Boston Red Sox
5017 Hasty Dr
Nashville, TN 37211-5345, USA

Mitchell, Craig (Baseball Player)
Oakland A's
PO Box 174
Elk, CA 95432-0174, USA

Mitchell, Dale (Football Player)
San Francisco 49ers
1960 Witham Dr
Woodland, CA 95776-9345, USA

Mitchell, Darryl (Actor)
William Morris Agency
151 El Camino Dr
Beverly Hills, CA 90212-2775, USA

Mitchell, Daryl 'Chill' (Actor)
c/o Jenny Delaney *William Morris Agency (WMA-LA)*
1 William Morris Pl
Beverly Hills, CA 90212-4261, USA

Mitchell, Don (Actor)
4139 S Cloverdale Ave
Los Angeles, CA 90008-1034, USA

Mitchell, Donald (Football Player)
Tennessee Titans
5620 Minner Dr
Beaumont, TX 77708-4515, USA

Mitchell, Eddy
40 av. Sainte Foy
Neuilly 92200, FRANCE

Mitchell, Edgar D (Astronaut)
PO Box 540037
Greenacres, FL 33454-0037, USA

Mitchell, Elizabeth (Actor)
c/o Ben Levine *Evolution Entertainment (LA)*
10585 Santa Monica Blvd Ste 120
Los Angeles, CA 90025-4984, USA

Mitchell, Freddie (Football Player)
Philadelphia Eagles
PO Box 1626
Lakeland, FL 33802-1626, USA

Mitchell, George J (Senator)
c/o Staff Member *Walt Disney Company, The*
500 S Buena Vista St
Burbank, CA 91521-0001, USA

Mitchell, Harris A (War Hero)
2701 Dees St
San Marcos, TX 78666-5074, USA

Mitchell, Jack (Photographer)
1413 Live Oak St
New Smyrna Beach, FL 32168-7740, USA

Mitchell, James (Actor)
320 W 66th St
New York, NY 10023-6304, USA

Mitchell, James Fitzallen (Royalty)
Premier's Office
Kingstown
Saint Vincent, SAINT VINCENT & GRENADINES

Mitchell, Jeff (Football Player)
Baltimore Ravens
14747 Ballantyne Country Club Dr
Charlotte, NC 28277-2716, USA

Mitchell, Jeff (Golfer)
360 Troon Way
Half Moon Bay, CA 94019-2297, USA

Mitchell, Jessie (Baseball Player)
Birmingham Black Barons
124 Dugan Ave Apt A
Birmingham, AL 35214-5182, USA

Mitchell, Jim H (Football Player)
Detroit Lions
120 Twin Creek Ter
Forest, VA 24551-1328, USA

Mitchell, Jim R (Football Player)
Atlanta Falcons
PO Box 1283
Shelbyville, TN 37162-1283, USA

Mitchell, John (Baseball Player)
Detroit Stars
1708 Castleberry Way
Birmingham, AL 35214-4826, USA

Mitchell, John Cameron (Actor, Director)
c/o Patrick Herold *International Creative Management (ICM-NY)*
40 W 57th St
New York, NY 10019-4001, USA

Mitchell, Joni (Musician)
c/o Sam Feldman *SL Feldman & Associates*
1505 W 2nd Ave #200
Vancouver, BC V6H 3Y4, CANADA

Mitchell, Keith (Baseball Player)
Atlanta Braves
731 S 42nd St
San Diego, CA 92113-1813, USA

Mitchell, Keith C (Prime Minister)
Ministerial Complex 6th Fl
Botanical Gardens
Saint George's, GRENADA

Mitchell, Kel (Actor)
c/o Staff Member *Nine Yards Entertainment*
8530 Wilshire Blvd Fl 5
Beverly Hills, CA 90211-3102, USA

Mitchell, Ken (Football Player)
Atlanta Falcons
4665 Hall Rd
Orlando, FL 32817-1201, USA

Mitchell, Kenneth (Actor)
c/o Stephen (Steve) Small *Paradigm (LA)*
360 N Crescent Dr
North Bldg
Beverly Hills, CA 90210-6820, USA

Mitchell, Kevin (Baseball Player)
New York Mets
3867 Ocean View Blvd
San Diego, CA 92113-1736, USA

Mitchell, Kim
41 Britain St. #305
Toronto, ON M5A 1R, CANADA

Mitchell, Larry (Baseball Player)
Philadelphia Phillies
1040 Preston Ave
Charlottesville, VA 22903-2109, USA

Mitchell, Leona (Opera Singer)
Columbia Artists Mgmt Inc
1790 Broadway Fl 6
New York, NY 10019-1412, USA

Mitchell, Leroy (Football Player)
Boston Patriots
6598 N Pinewood Dr
Parker, CO 80134-6356, USA

Mitchell, Lydell D (Football Player)
Baltimore Colts
702 Reservoir St
Baltimore, MD 21217-4632, USA

Mitchell, Mack (Football Player)
Cleveland Browns
1200 Maynard St
Diboll, TX 75941-2602, USA

Mitchell, Michael (Actor)
c/o Abby Bluestone *Innovative Artists (LA)*
1505 10th St
Santa Monica, CA 90401-2805, USA

Mitchell, Mike (Director)
c/o Staff Member *Endeavor Agency LLC (LA)*
9601 Wilshire Blvd Fl 3
Beverly Hills, CA 90210-5204, USA

Mitchell, Pat (Politician)
Public Broadcasting System
1320 Braddock Pl
Alexandria, VA 22314-1692, USA

Mitchell, Paul (Baseball Player)
Baltimore Orioles
23 Carr Rd
Berlin, MA 01503-1116, USA

Mitchell, Pete (Football Player)
Jacksonville Jaguars
100 Paddock Pl
Ponte Vedra Beach, FL 32082-3957, USA

Mitchell, Radha (Actor)
c/o Rick Ax *Gold Coast Management*
1023 1/2 Abbot Kinney Blvd
Venice, CA 90291-5536, USA

Mitchell, Rick (DJ)
c/o Staff Member *Diva Central Inc*
7510 W Sunset Blvd Ste 1445
Los Angeles, CA 90046-3408, USA

Mitchell, Robert (Baseball Player)
Cleveland Buckeyes
2009 Elmwood Ave
Tampa, FL 33605-6625, USA

Mitchell, Roger (Director)
Creative Artists Agency
9830 Wilshire Blvd
Beverly Hills, CA 90212-1804, USA

Mitchell, Roger (Football Player)
Green Bay Packers
500 E Chaminade Dr
Chaminade-Madonna College Prep
Hollywood, FL 33021-5853, USA

Mitchell, Roland (Football Player)
Buffalo Bills
PO Box 5701
Lake Charles, LA 70606-5701, USA

Mitchell, Roscoe E Jr (Composer, Musician)
SRO Artists
6629 University Ave Ste 206
Middleton, WI 53562-3037, USA

Mitchell, Russ (Correspondent, Television Host)
c/o Staff Member *CBS Weekend Evening News*
524 W 57th St Fl 8
New York, NY 10019-2930, USA

Mitchell, Sam (Basketball Player, Coach)
Toronto Raptors
Air Canada Center
40 Bay St
Toronto, ON M5J 2N8, CANADA

Mitchell, Sasha (Actor)
Flick East-West
9057A Nemo St # A
West Hollywood, CA 90069, USA

Mitchell, Scott (Football Player)
5060 Franklin Rd
Bloomfield Hills, MI 48302-2614, USA

Mitchell, Shareen (Actor)
J Michael Bloom
9255 W Sunset Blvd Ste 710
Los Angeles, CA 90069-3304, USA

Mitchell, Sharon
1122 White Rock Dr
Dixon, IL 61021-9049, USA

Mitchell, Shirley
10635 Santa Monica Blvd Ste 130
Los Angeles, CA 90025-8306, USA

Mitchell, Steve (Actor)
c/o Staff Member *Select Artists Ltd (CA-Westside Office)*
1138 12th St Apt 1
Santa Monica, CA 90403-5459, USA

Mitchell, Susan (Writer)
Florida Atlantic University
English Dept
Boca Raton, FL 33431, USA

Mitchell, Tom (Football Player)
Oakland Raiders
1421 SW 49th Ter
Cape Coral, FL 33914-6934, USA

Mitchell, Vernessa (Musician)
c/o Staff Member *Diva Central Inc*
7510 W Sunset Blvd Ste 1445
Los Angeles, CA 90046-3408, USA

Mitchell, Warren
28 Sheldon Ave.
London, ENGLAND N6, UNITED KINGDOM (UK)

Mitchum, Carrie (Actor)
Camden ITG Talent
1501 Main St Ste 204
Venice, CA 90291-3699, USA

Mithun, Chakraborty (Actor, Bollywood)
Monarch Hotel
Ooty, TN, INDIA

Mitinger, Bob (Football Player)
San Diego Chargers
1368 S Atherton St
Mitinger And Engle Law Office
State College, PA 16801-6203, USA

Mitra, Rhona (Actor)
c/o Courtney Kivowitz *Benderspink*
110 S Fairfax Ave Ste 350
Los Angeles, CA 90036-2179, USA

Mitrione, Matt (Football Player)
New York Giants
729 Toddsbury Ln
Richmond, IN 47374-7152, USA

Mitsotakis, Constantine (Prime Minister)
1 Aravantinou St
Athens 106 74, GREECE

Mitsoula, Jana (Actor)
Collingwood Management Inc
c/o Dylan Thomas Collingwood
#300 - 100 West Pender St
Vancouver, BC V6B 1R8, CANADA

Mitta, Aleksander N (Director)
Malaya Gruzinskaya Str 28
#105
Moscow 123557, RUSSIA

Mittal, Lakshmi (Business Person)
LNM Group
15th Floor
Hofplein 20
Rotterdam 3032, THE NETHERLANDS

Mittermaier, Rosi
Winklmoosalm
Reit im Winkl D-83242, GERMANY

Mittermaier-Neureuther, Rosi (Skier)
Winkelmoosalm
Reit Im Winkel 83242, GERMANY

Mittermayer, Tatjana (Skier)
Bucha 2A
Lenggries, GERMANY

Mitterwald, George (Baseball Player)
Minnesota Twins
1721 Murdock Blvd
Orlando, FL 32825-5644, USA

Mitts, Heather (Soccer Player)
US Soccer/ Heather Mitts
18400 Avalon Blvd Ste 500
Carson, CA 90746-2183, USA

Mitz, Alonzo (Football Player)
Seattle Seahawks
2609 NE 4th St Apt 216
Renton, WA 98056-4053, USA

Mitzelfeld, Jim (Journalist)
969 N Lebanon St
Arlington, VA 22205-1455, USA

Mivelaz, Betty (Bowler)
6671 Shadygrove St
Tujunga, CA 91042-3348, USA

Mix, Bryant (Football Player)
Houston Oilers
37 Greenwood Plantation Rd
Natchez, MS 39120-8946, USA

Mix, Ronald J (Ron) (Football Player)
Los Angeles Chargers
2317 Camino Recodo
San Diego, CA 92107, USA

Mix, Steve (Basketball Player)
25743 Willowbend Road
Newtown, PA 18940, USA

Mix Master Mike (DJ)
c/o Staff Member *Agency Group Ltd, The (UK)*
361-373 City Road
London EC1V 1PQ, UNITED KINGDOM (UK)

Mixon, Billy (Football Player)
San Francisco 49ers
4145 Woodvale St
Jackson, MS 39211-6541, USA

Mixon, J Wayne (Governor)
2219 Demeron Rd
Tallahassee, FL 32308-0943, USA

Mixon, Ken (Football Player)
Miami Dolphins
12741 Kapok Ln
Davie, FL 33330-5201, USA

Miyamura, Hiroshi H (War Hero)
659 Kaimalino St
Kailua, HI 96734-1616, USA

Miyazaki, Hayao (Animator)
Studio Ghibli
1-4-25 Kajinocho
Koganeishi 184, JAPAN

Miyazawa, Kiichi (Prime Minister)
6-34-1 Jingu-Mae
Shibuyaku
Tokyo 150, JAPAN

Miyori, Kim (Actor)
Susan Smoth
121A N San Vicente Blvd
Beverly Hills, CA 90211-2303, USA

Mize, John D (War Hero)
112 Sunset Dr
Belmond, IA 50421-1733, USA

Mize, Larry (Golfer)
106 Graystone Ct
Columbus, GA 31904-4300, USA

Mize, Ola L (War Hero)
211 Hartwood Dr
Gadsden, AL 35901-6228, USA

Mizerock, John (Baseball Player)
Houston Astros
PO Box 580
Punxsutawney, PA 15767-0580, USA

Mizrahi, Isaac (Fashion Designer, Television Host)
c/o Staff Member *Style Network*
5750 Wilshire Blvd
Los Angeles, CA 90036-3697, USA

Mizzy, Vic
2170 Stradella Rd
Los Angeles, CA 90077-2325, USA

Mkapa, Benjamin William (President)
President's Office
State House
PO Box 9120
Dar es Salaam, TANZANIA

Mlicki, Dave (Baseball Player)
Cleveland Indians
5350 Reserve Dr
Dublin, OH 43017-8404, USA

Mlkvy, Bill (Basketball Player)
586 Linton Hill Rd
Newtown, PA 18940-1204, USA

Mmahat, Kevin (Baseball Player)
New York Yankees
5500 Erlanger Rd
Kenner, LA 70065-1534, USA

Mnookin, Robert H (Attorney, Attorney General, Educator, General)
10 Follen St
Cambridge, MA 02138-3503, USA

Mnouchkine, Ariane (Director)
Theater du Soleil
Cartoucherie
Paris 75012, FRANCE

Moakler, Shanna (Actor, Model, Reality TV Star)
c/o Michael Greenwald *Don Buchwald & Associates Inc (LA)*
6500 Wilshire Blvd Ste 2200
Los Angeles, CA 90048-4942, USA

Moates, Dave (Baseball Player)
Texas Rangers
7924 24th Ave W
Bradenton, FL 34209-5233, USA

Moats, David (Journalist)
Rutland Herald
PO Box 668
Editorial Dept
Rutland, VT 05702-0668, USA

Mobb Deep (Music Group)
c/o Staff Member *Interscope Records (NY)*
1790 Broadway
New York, NY 10019-1412, USA

Mobley, Cuttino (Basketball Player)
c/o Staff Member *Los Angeles Clippers*
1111 S Figueroa St
Los Angeles, CA 90015-1300, USA

Mobley, Mary Ann (Actor, Beauty Pageant Winner)
2751 Hutton Dr
Beverly Hills, CA 90210-1215, USA

Mobley, Rudy (Football Player)
Baltimore Colts
RR 3
Ahoskie, NC 27910, USA

Mobley, Singor (Football Player)
Dallas Cowboys
2123 US Highway 80 E
Mesquite, TX 75150-5549, USA

Mobley, William H (Educator)
1507 Bamfield Cv
Round Rock, TX 78665-5607, USA

Moby (Musician)
c/o Staff Member *MVO Ltd*
307 7th Ave Rm 807
New York, NY 10001-6066, USA

Moceanu, Dominique (Gymnast)
Brown's Gymnastics Metro
4676 McLeod Road
Orlando, FL 32811, USA

Mochrie, Colin (Actor)
385 Adelaide St W
Toronto, ON M5V 1S4, CANADA

Mochrie Pepper, Dorothy (Dottie) (Golfer)
15 Blazing Star Trl
Landrum, SC 29356-3305, USA

Mockett, Cathy (Golfer)
1601 Antigua Way
Newport Beach, CA 92660-4345, USA

Mocumbi, Pascoal (Prime Minister)
Prime Minister's Office
Avenida Julius Nyerere 1780
Maputo, MOZAMBIQUE

Moczynski, Betty (Baseball Player)
5209 Lakeside Dr
Greendale, WI 53129-1924, USA

Modano, Mike (Hockey Player)
c/o Staff Member *Dallas Stars*
2601 Avenue Of The Stars Ste 100
Frisco, TX 75034-9016, USA

Modell, Arthur B (Football Executive)
Baltimore Ravens
Ravens Stadium
11001 Russell St
Baltimore, MD 21230, USA

Modell, Frank (Cartoonist)
295 Central Park W Apt 11E
New York, NY 10024-3023, USA

Modern Talking
Modern Talking Fan Club
56200 Hoehr-Grenzhausen
GERMANY

Modernaires, The
11761 E Speedway Blvd
Tucson, AZ 85748-2017, USA

Modine, Matthew (Actor, Director, Producer, Writer)
c/o Elise Konialian *Untitled Entertainment (NY)*
322 8th Ave Ste 601
New York, NY 10001-6715, USA

Modrow, Hans (Prime Minister)
Frankfurter Tor 6
Berlin 10243, GERMANY

Modrzejewski, Robert J (War Hero)
4725 Oporto Ct
San Diego, CA 92124-2446, USA

Modzelewski, Ed (Football Player)
Pittsburgh Steelers
PO Box 4207
Sedona, AZ 86340-4207, USA

Modzelewski, Richard B (Dick) (Football Player)
Washington Redskins
1 Pier Pt
New Bern, NC 28562-8820, USA

Moe (Music Group)
c/o Staff Member *Paradigm (Monterey)*
509 Hartnell St
Monterey, CA 93940-2825, USA

Moe, Douglas E (Doug) (Basketball Player)
13 Arnold Palmer
San Antonio, TX 78257-1722, USA

Moe, Thomas S (Tommy) (Skier)
1556 Hidden Ln
Anchorage, AK 99501-4916, USA

Moe, Tommy
2138 Churchill Dr
Anchorage, AK 99517-1389, USA

Moe-Humphreys, Karen (Swimmer)
505 Augusta Dr
Moraga, CA 94556-3004, USA

Moegle, Dick (Football Player)
San Francisco 49ers
4047 Aberdeen Way
Houston, TX 77025-2305, USA

Moehler, Brian (Baseball Player)
Detroit Tigers
4492 Belvedere Pl SE
Marietta, GA 30067-4066, USA

Moeller, Chad (Baseball Player)
Minnesota Twins
11058 E Raintree Dr
Scottsdale, AZ 85255-1809, USA

Moeller, Chuck (Actor)
c/o Chuck Binder *Binder & Associates*
1465 Lindacrest Dr
Beverly Hills, CA 90210-2519, USA

Moeller, Dennis (Baseball Player)
Kansas City Royals
2324 Ridgemont Dr
Birmingham, AL 35244-1219, USA

Moeller, Dennis (Inventor)
25 Cobbie Ridge Dr
Chapel Hill, NC 27516, USA

Moeller, Joe (Baseball Player)
Los Angeles Dodgers
130 30th St # A
Hermosa Beach, CA 90254-2371, USA

Moeller, Ralf (Actor)
c/o Chuck Binder *Binder & Associates*
1465 Lindacrest Dr
Beverly Hills, CA 90210-2519, USA

Moeller, Ron (Baseball Player)
Baltimore Orioles
6248 Eagles Lake Dr
Cincinnati, OH 45248-6852, USA

Moellering, John H (General)
50130 Manly
Chapel Hill, NC 27517-8565, USA

Moennig, Katherine (Actor)
c/o Jennifer Wiley *Framework Entertainment (NY)*
129 W 27th St Fl 12
New York, NY 10001-6206, USA

Moffat, Donald (Actor)
151 El Camino Dr
Beverly Hills, CA 90212-2704, USA

Moffat, Katherine (Kitty) (Actor)
Henderson/Hogan
8285 W Sunset Blvd Ste 1
West Hollywood, CA 90046-2420, USA

Moffatt, John
59A Warrington St.
London, ENGLAND W9, UNITED KINGDOM (UK)

Moffatt, Katy (Musician, Songwriter, Writer)
PO Box 334
O Fallon, IL 62269-0334, USA

Moffet, Jane (Baseball Player)
228 Sequoyah Dr
Waynesville, NC 28785-9436, USA

Moffett, D W (Actor)
Three Arts Entertainment
9460 Wilshire Blvd Ste 700
Beverly Hills, CA 90212-2713, USA

Moffett, James R (Business Person)
Freeport-McMoRan Inc
1615 Poydras St
New Orleans, LA 70112-1254, USA

Moffett, Randy (Actor)
110 Lakeover Dr
Athens, GA 30607-2046, USA

Moffett, Tim (Football Player)
Los Angeles Raiders
115 County Road 213
Oxford, MS 38655-8855, USA

Moffitt, Randy (Baseball Player)
San Francisco Giants
1725 Baltic Ave
Prescott, AZ 86301-6501, USA

Mofford, Rose (Governor)
330 W Maryland Ave Unit 104
Phoenix, AZ 85013-1340, USA

Moford, Herb (Baseball Player)
St Louis Cardinals
PO Box 12
Minerva, KY 41062-0012, USA

Mogae, Festus G (President)
President's Office
State House
Private Bag 001
Gaborone, BOTSWANA

Mogenburg, Dietmar (Athlete, Track Athlete)
Alter Garfen 34
Leverkusen 51371, GERMANY

Mogilevsky, Evgeny (Musician)
Columbia Artists Mgmt Inc
1790 Broadway Fl 6
New York, NY 10019-1412, USA

Mogilny, Alexander (Hockey Player)
Int'l Management Group
801 6th St SW
Calgary, AB T2P 3V8, CANADA

Mohacsi, Mary (Bowler)
15445 Sunset St
Livonia, MI 48154-3215, USA

MoHair (Music Group)
c/o Staff Member *Paradigm (Monterey)*
509 Hartnell St
Monterey, CA 93940-2825, USA

Mohammed VI (King)
Royal Palais
Rabat, MOROCCO

Mohan (Actor, Bollywood)
8 Mylai Ranganathan Street
T Nagar
Chennai, TN 600017, INDIA

Mohler, Mike (Baseball Player)
Oakland A's
1627 S Shirley Ave
Gonzales, LA 70737-3917, USA

Mohmand, Abdul Ahad (Cosmonaut)
Potchta Kosmonavtov
Moskovkoi Oblasti
Syvlsdny Goroduk 141160, RUSSIA

Mohn, Reinhard (Business Person, Publisher)
Bertelsmann AG
Carl-Bertelsmann-Str 256
Guetersloh 33311, GERMANY

Mohoney, J Daniel (Judge)
US Court of Appeals
40 Foley Sq
New York, NY 10007-1561, USA

Mohoney, John (Actor)
International Creative Mgmt
8942 Wilshire Blvd # 219
Beverly Hills, CA 90211-1908, USA

Mohoney, Roger (Cartoonist)
King Features Syndicate
888 7th Ave Ste 201
New York, NY 10106-0201, USA

Mohony, Roger Cardinal (Religious Leader)
Archdiocese of Los Angeles
3424 Wilshire Blvd
Los Angeles, CA 90010-2241, USA

Mohorcic, Dale (Baseball Player)
Texas Rangers
15501 Rockside Rd
Maple Heights, OH 44137-3948, USA

Mohr, Chris (Football Player)
Tampa Bay Buccaneers
PO Box 1232
Thomson, GA 30824-1232, USA

Mohr, Dustan (Baseball Player)
Minnesota Twins
103 Parkwood Dr
Hattiesburg, MS 39402-2217, USA

Mohr, Jay (Actor, Comedian)
c/o Barry Katz *New Wave Entertainment
(LA)*
2660 W Olive Ave
Burbank, CA 91505-4525, USA

Mohr, Todd (Musician)
Morris Bliessner
1658 York St
Denver, CO 80206-1410, USA

Mohri, Mamoru (Astronaut)
NASDA
2-1-2 Sengen
Tukubashi
Ibaraki 305, JAPAN

Moine, Marc Forne (President)
President's Office
Casa de la Valle
Andorra la Vella, ANDORRA

Moir, Richard (Actor)
Shanahan Mgmt
PO Box 1509
Darlinghurst, NSW 1300, AUSTRALIA

Moisan, Bill (Baseball Player)
Chicago Cubs
PO Box 41
Newton, NH 03858-0041, USA

Moiseyev, Igor A (Choreographer,
Director)
Moiseyev Dance Co
20 Triumfalnaya Pl
Moscow, RUSSIA

Mojsiejenko, Ralf (Football Player)
San Diego Chargers
11334 Baldwin Rd
Bridgman, MI 49106-9727, USA

Mokri, Amir (Cinematographer)
Montana Artists
625 Montana Ave # 200
Santa Monica, CA 90403-1409, USA

Mokrzynski, Jerzy (Architect)
Ul Marszalkowska 140 m 18
Warsaw 00 061, POLAND

Mol, Gretchen (Actor)
1964 Westwood Blvd Ste 400
Los Angeles, CA 90025-4695, USA

Molden, Alex (Football Player)
New Orleans Saints
2406 Lexington Village Ln
Colorado Springs, CO 80916-2672, USA

Moldofsky, Philip J (Scientist)
Fox Chase Cancer Center
7701 Burholme Ave
Philadelphia, PA 19111-2497, USA

Mole, Fenton (Baseball Player)
New York Yankees
738 Glen Eagle Ct
Danville, CA 94526-6209, USA

Moler, Jason (Baseball Player)
Ted Williams
2918 Ranch Road 620 N Apt 281
Austin, TX 78734-2269, USA

Molina, Alfred (Actor)
Hyler Mgmt
25 Sea Colony Dr
Santa Monica, CA 90405-5495, USA

Molina, Gabe (Baseball Player)
Baltimore Orioles
2181 E 119th Pl
Northglenn, CO 80233-1305, USA

Molina, Islay (Baseball Player)
Oakland A's
15226 SW 111th St
Miami, FL 33196-4522, USA

Molina, Mario J (Nobel Prize Laureate)
PO Box 12406
La Jolla, CA 92039-2406, USA

Molinaro, Al (Actor)
1530 Arboles Dr
Glendale, CA 91207-1204, USA

Molinaro, Bob (Baseball Player)
Detroit Tigers
1 Harbourside Dr Apt 2312
Delray Beach, FL 33483-5170, USA

Molitor, Paul L (Baseball Player, Coach)
Milwaukee Brewers
748 Lake Point Dr
Chanhassen, MN 55317-9284, USA

Molko, Brian (Musician)
Immediate Business Management
2-4 Lambton Pl
London W11 2SH, UNITED KINGDOM
(UK)

Moll, Georgia
229A v. Pineta Sacchetti
Rome, CA, ITALY

Moll, Kurt (Opera Singer)
Voigtelstr 22
Cologne 50933, GERMANY

Moll, Richard (Actor)
1119 Amalfi Dr
Pacific Palisades, CA 90272-4031, USA

Molla, Jordi (Actor)
Kuranda Movies SL
Calle Segre 14
Madrid 28002, SPAIN

Moller, Andreas (Soccer Player)
Borussia Dortmund
Postfach 100509
Dortmund 44005, GERMANY

Moller, Frank (Athlete)
Sportclub Berlin
Weissenseer Weg 51-55
Berlin 13051, GERMANY

Moller, Gunnar
6 Cloverdale Rd.
London, ENGLAND NW2, UNITED
KINGDOM (UK)

Moller, Hans (Artist)
2207 W Allen St
Allentown, PA 18104-4327, USA

Moller, Paul (Engineer, Inventor)
Moller International
1222 Research Park Dr
Davis, CA 95618-4849, USA

Moller-Gladisch, Silke (Athlete, Track
Athlete)
Lange Str 6
Rostock 18055, GERMANY

Mollo-Christiansen, Erik L
(Oceanographer)
10 Barberry Rd
Lexington, MA 02421-8026, USA

Molloy, Bryan B (Inventor)
7948 Beaumont Green Pl
Indianapolis, IN 46250-1663, USA

Molloy, Irene
PO Box 5617
Beverly Hills, CA 90209-5617, USA

Molloy, Matt (Musician)
Macklam Feldman Mgmt
1505 W 2nd Ave
#200
Vancouver, BC V6H 3Y4, CANADA

Moloney, Janel (Actor)
c/o Staff Member *Gersh Agency, The (LA)*
232 N Canon Dr
Beverly Hills, CA 90210-5302, USA

Moloney, Michael (Actor, Reality TV Star)
c/o Staff Member *Extreme Makeover:
Home Edition*
9255 W Sunset Blvd Ste 1100
Endemol Entertainment USA
Los Angeles, CA 90069-3308, USA

Moloney, Paddy (Musician)
Macklam Feldman Mgmt
1505 W 2nd Ave
#200
Vancouver, BC V6H 3Y4, CANADA

Moloney, Rich (Baseball Player)
Chicago White Sox
125 Mallard Way
Waltham, MA 02452-8117, USA

Molyneux, Juan Pablo (Architect)
J P Molyneux Studio
29 E 69th St
New York, NY 10021-4917, USA

Mom Rajawong, Sirikit Kitiyarara
(Royalty)
Royal Residence
Chirtalad a Villa
Bangkok, THAILAND

Momaday, N Scott (Writer)
University of Arizona
English Dept
Tucson, AZ 85721-0001, USA

Momoa, Jason (Actor)
c/o Jeff Witjas *Agency for the Performing
Arts (APA-NY)*
888 7th Ave
New York, NY 10106-0001, USA

Momper, ex-Mayor Walter
Fichtestr. 15
Berlin D-10967, GERMANY

Momsen, Robert (Football Player)
Detroit Lions
4730 Glendale Ave Apt 102
Toledo, OH 43614-1974, USA

Momsen, Taylor (Musician)
c/o Staff Member *Abrams Artists Agency
(LA)*
9200 W Sunset Blvd Ph 11
Los Angeles, CA 90069-3601, USA

Monacelli, Amieto (Bowler)
Professional Bowlers Assn
719 2nd Ave Ste 701
Seattle, WA 98104-1747, USA

Monaco, Kelly (Actor)
c/o Staff Member *General Hospital*
500 S Buena Vista St
Burbank, CA 91521-0001, USA

Monaco, Ray (Football Player)
Washington Redskins
950 Smith St
Providence, RI 02908-2717, USA

Monaghan, Dominic (Actor)
c/o Brian Young *Untitled Entertainment
(LA)*
331 N Maple Dr Fl 3
Beverly Hills, CA 90210-3827, USA

Monaghan, Kris (Golfer)
54 Golf Course Dr
Ranchos De Taos, NM 87557-7914, USA

Monaghan, Marjorie
121 N San Vicente Blvd
Beverly Hills, CA 90211-2303, USA

Monaghan, Michelle (Actor)
c/o Frank Frattaroli *Widescreen
Management*
270 Lafayette St Ste 402
New York, NY 10012-3327, USA

Monaghan, Thomas L
3001 Earhart Rd
Ann Arbor, MI 48105, USA

Monahan, Dan (Actor)
c/o Helene Sokol *Cuzzins Management*
499 N Canon Dr
Beverly Hills, CA 90210-4842, USA

Monahan, David (Actor, Director)
c/o Staff Member *Metropolitan*
4500 Wilshire Blvd Fl 2
Los Angeles, CA 90010-3858, USA

Monahan, Pat (Musician)
Jon Landau
158 Rowayton Ave
Norwalk, CT 06853-1442, USA

Monahan, Rinty (Baseball Player)
Philadelphia Athletics
165 83rd St
Brooklyn, NY 11209-4309, USA

Monahan, Shane (Baseball Player)
Seattle Mariners
624 Stickley Oak Way
Woodstock, GA 30189-3781, USA

Monan, J Donald (Educator)
Boston College
President's Office
Chestnut Hill, MA 02167, USA

Monbouquette, William C (Bill) (Baseball
Player)
Boston Red Sox
46 Doonan St
Medford, MA 02155-1333, USA

Monchak, Al (Baseball Player)
Philadelphia Phillies
7414 8th Ave W
Bradenton, FL 34209-3425, USA

Moncrieff, Karen (Actor)
c/o Brad Gross *Brad Gross Agency, The*
6715 Hollywood Blvd # 236
Los Angeles, CA 90028-4627, USA

Mond, Philip (Photographer)
PO Box 8906
Fort Lauderdale, FL 33310-8906, USA

Mondale, Eleanor
282 Edge Of Woods Rd
Southampton, NY 11968-2513, USA

Mondale, Walter F (President, Senator,
Vice President)
50 S 6th St Ste 1500
Minneapolis, MN 55402-1498, USA

Mondavi, Robert G (Business Person)
Robert Mondavi Winery
7801 St Helena Highways
Oakville, CA 94562, USA

Monday, Rick (Baseball Player)
Kansas City A's
811 Gayfeather Ln
Vero Beach, FL 32963-2048, USA

Monday, Robert J (Rick) (Baseball Player, Sportscaster)
811 Gayleather Lane
Vero Beach, FL 32963, USA

Mondesi, Raul (Athlete, Baseball Player)
Los Angeles Dodgers
1169 Old Phillips Rd
Glendale, CA 91207-1153, USA

Monds, Wonderful (Baseball Player)
Fleer
665 NW Fairhaven Dr
Port Saint Lucie, FL 34983-1079, USA

Monduzzi, Dino Cardinal (Religious Leader)
Via Monfe della Farina 64
Rome 00186, ITALY

Moneo, J Fafael (Architect)
Calle Mino 5
Madrid 28002, SPAIN

Monet, Daniella (Actor)
c/o Jennifer Miller *Abrams Artists Agency (LA)*
9200 W Sunset Blvd Ph 11
Los Angeles, CA 90069-3601, USA

Money, Don (Baseball Player)
Philadelphia Phillies
282 Old Forest Rd
Vineland, NJ 08360-1667, USA

Money, Eddie (Musician)
International Creative Mgmt
40 W 57th St Ste 1800
New York, NY 10019-4001, USA

Money, John W (Misc)
2104 E Madison St
Baltimore, MD 21205-2337, USA

Money, Ken (Astronaut)
DCIEM
1133 Sheppard Ave W
#2000
Downsview, ON M3M 3B9, CANADA

Moneyham, Bill (Baseball Player)
Oakland A's
5731 White Crane Rd
Atwater, CA 95301-8573, USA

Monfort, Avery (Football Player)
Chicago Cardinals
PO Box 84
Twain Harte, CA 95383-0084, USA

Monge, Sid (Baseball Player)
California Angels
716 5th Ave
Chula Vista, CA 91910-5408, USA

Monger, Matt (Football Player)
New York Jets
1306 N Douglas Dr
Claremore, OK 74017-4623, USA

Monica (Musician)
Rowdy/Arista Records
8750 Wilshire Blvd # 300
Beverly Hills, CA 90211-2713, USA

Monicelli, Mario (Director)
Via del Babuino 135
Rome 00137, ITALY

Monin, Clarence V (President)
Locomotive Engineers Brotherhood
1370 Ontario St
Cleveland, OH 44113-1702, USA

Moniz, Wendy (Actor)
c/o Nancy Sanders *Sanders/Armstrong Management*
2120 Colorado Ave Ste 120
Santa Monica, CA 90404-3561, USA

Monk, Arthur (Art) (Football Player, Sportscaster)
Washington Redskins
10896 Lake Windermere Dr
Great Falls, VA 22066-1528, USA

Monk, Debra (Actor)
Gage Group
315 W 57th St Frnt 4H
New York, NY 10019-3158, USA

Monk, Meredith J (Choreographer, Composer)
House Foundation for Arts
131 Varick St
New York, NY 10013-1410, USA

Monk, Quincy (Football Player)
New York Giants
104 White Oak Blvd # 104
Jacksonville, NC 28546-4539, USA

Monk, Sophie (Actor)
c/o Josh Pollack *Agency for the Performing Arts (APA-LA)*
405 S Beverly Dr
Beverly Hills, CA 90212-4416, USA

Monk Jr, Thelonious
173 Brighton Ave
Boston, MA 02134-2003, USA

Monkees, The (Music Group)
c/o Staff Member *Primary Talent International (UK)*
2-12 Pentonville Rd Fl 5
London N1 9PL, UNITED KINGDOM (UK)

Monkey See-Monkey Do
Feurigstr. 16
Berlin D-10827, GERMANY

Monreal Luque, Alberto (Government Official)
Eurotabac Monte Esquinza 28
Madrid 28010, SPAIN

Monroe, A L (Mike) (Misc)
International Brotherhood pf Painters
1750 New York Ave NW
Washington, DC 20006-5301, USA

Monroe, Betty (Actor)
c/o Staff Member *TV Azteca*
Periferico Sur 4121
Colonia Fuentes del Pedregal
DF CP 14141, MEXICO

Monroe, Craig (Baseball Player)
Texas Rangers
4123 Lynn Dr
Texarkana, TX 75503-2816, USA

Monroe, Larry (Baseball Player)
Chicago White Sox
725 N Hundley St
Hoffman Estates, IL 60169-4559, USA

Monroe, Meredith (Musician)
c/o Rachel Shapiro *Jeff Morrone Management*
9350 Wilshire Blvd Ste 224
Beverly Hills, CA 90212-3204, USA

Monroe, Mircea (Actor)
c/o Tiffany Kuzon *Evolution Entertainment (LA)*
901 N Highland Ave
Los Angeles, CA 90038-2412, USA

Monroe, Richard (Publisher)
Atlanta Journal-Constitution
72 Marietta St NW
Atlanta, GA 30303-2899, USA

Monroe, Zach (Baseball Player)
New York Yankees
1 Sandalwood Ln
Bartonville, IL 61607-2145, USA

Monson, Dan (Basketball Player, Coach)
University of Minnesota
Bierman Athletic Building
Minneapolis, MN 55455, USA

Monsters, The (Music Group)
c/o Staff Member *Paradigm (Monterey)*
509 Hartnell St
Monterey, CA 93940-2825, USA

Mont, Tommy (Football Player)
Washington Redskins
15414 W Sky Hawk Dr
Sun City, AZ 85375-6511, USA

Montag, Heidi (Reality TV Star)
c/o Spencer Pratt *Innovator Management*
8899 Beverly Blvd Ste 629
Los Angeles, CA 90048-2448, USA

Montagna, Joe
10415 Sarah St
Toluca Lake, CA 91602-1511, USA

Montagnier, Luc (Scientist)
Institut Pasteur
25 Rue du Docteur
Paris Cedux 15 75015, FRANCE

Montague, Ashley
321 Cherry Hill Rd
Princeton, NJ 08540-7617, USA

Montague, Diana (Opera Singer)
91 Saint Martin's Lane
London WC2, UNITED KINGDOM (UK)

Montague, Ed (Baseball Player)
1521 Cherrywood Dr
San Mateo, CA 94403-3903, USA

Montague, John (Baseball Player)
Montreal Expos
6001 Vineyard Ln
Montgomery, AL 36117-5003, USA

Montague, Lee (Actor)
Conway Van Gelder Robinson
18-21 Jermyn St
London SW1Y 6NB, UNITED KINGDOM (UK)

Montague-Smith, Patrick W (Editor)
Brereton
197 Park Road
Kingston-upon-Thames
Surrey, UNITED KINGDOM (UK)

Montalban, Paolo (Actor)
c/o Staff Member *Talent Entertainment Group*
9111 Wilshire Blvd
Beverly Hills, CA 90210-5508, USA

Montalban, Ricardo (Actor)
c/o Tim Curtis *William Morris Agency (WMA-LA)*
1 William Morris Pl
Beverly Hills, CA 90212-4261, USA

Montalbano, Chuck (Golfer)
4725 Farmdale Ave
North Hollywood, CA 91602-1109, USA

Montana, Claude (Designer, Fashion Designer)
131 Rue Saint-Denis
Paris 75001, FRANCE

Montana Jr, Joseph C (Joe) (Football Player)
San Francisco 49ers
9000 Franz Valley Rd
Calistoga, CA 94515-9552, USA

Montanez, Willie (Baseball Player)
California Angels
HC 5 Box 52020
Caguas, PR 00725-9201, USA

Montano, Sumalee (Actor)
c/o Kim Dorr *Defining Artists*
10 Universal City Plz Ste 2000
Universal City, CA 91608-1074, USA

Montazeri, Ayatollah Hussein Ali (Religious Leader)
Madresseh Faizieh
Qom, IRAN

Monte, Chante
William Morris Agency (WMA-NY)
1325 Avenue Of The Americas
New York, NY 10019-6026, USA

Montefusco, John (Baseball Player)
San Francisco Giants
PO Box 3508
Lake Havasu City, AZ 86405-3508, USA

Monteiro, Antonio M (President)
President's Office
Cia de la Republica
Sao Tiago Praia, CAPE VERDE

Monteith, Kelly
PO Box 11669
Knoxville, TN 37939-1669, USA

Monteleone, Rich (Baseball Player)
Seattle Mariners
2515 W Fern St
Tampa, FL 33614-4217, USA

Montermini, Andrea (Race Car Driver)
434 E Main St
Brownsburg, IN 46112-1419, USA

Montero, Gabriela (Musician)
c/o Staff Member *Paradigm (Monterey)*
509 Hartnell St
Monterey, CA 93940-2825, USA

Montero, Pablo (Actor)
c/o Staff Member *Televisa*
Blvd Adolfo Lopez Mateos 232
Colonia San Angel INN
DF CP 01060, MEXICO

Monterola, Pablo (Musician)
c/o Staff Member *BMG*
1540 Broadway
New York, NY 10036-4074, USA

Montevecchi, Liliane (Musician)
Buzz Halliday
8899 Beverly Blvd Ste 620
Los Angeles, CA 90048-2428, USA

Montez, Chris
6671 W Sunset Blvd Ste 1502
Hollywood, CA 90028-7235, USA

Montgomerie, Colin S (Golfer)
Int'l Mgmt group
1360 E 9th St Ste 100
Cleveland, OH 44114-1782, USA

Montgomery, Alton (Football Player)
Denver Broncos
925 Meriwether St # B
Griffin, GA 30224-4025, USA

Montgomery, Anthony (Actor)
c/o Jerry Shandrew *Shandrew Public Relations*
1050 S Stanley Ave
Los Angeles, CA 90019-6634, USA

The Celebrity Black Book 2008

Montgomery, Belinda (Actor)
Epstein-Wyckoff
280 S Beverly Dr Ste 400
Beverly Hills, CA 90212-3904, USA

Montgomery, Bob (Baseball Player)
Boston Red Sox
2 Parkway Dr
Saugus, MA 01906-1957, USA

Montgomery, Chuck (Actor)
c/o Staff Member *Don Buchwald &
Associates Inc (LA)*
6500 Wilshire Blvd Ste 2200
Los Angeles, CA 90048-4942, USA

Montgomery, Cleo (Football Player)
Cincinnati Bengals
404 Dakota Trl
Irving, TX 75063-4547, USA

Montgomery, David (Photographer)
11 Edith Grove #B
London SW10, UNITED KINGDOM (UK)

Montgomery, Delmonico (Football Player)
Indianapolis Colts
3011 Pecan Way Ct
Richmond, TX 77469-6902, USA

Montgomery, Dorothy (Baseball Player)
2621 Berkley Dr
Chattanooga, TN 37415-5701, USA

Montgomery, Eddie (Musician)
Hallmark Direction
713 18th Ave S
Nashville, TN 37203-3214, USA

Montgomery, Grady (Baseball Player)
Baltimore Elite Giants
11904 Fort Washington Rd
Fort Washington, MD 20744-5908, USA

Montgomery, James P (Jim) (Coach,
Swimmer)
1537 Bella Vista Dr
Dallas, TX 75218-3510, USA

Montgomery, Jeff (Baseball Player)
Cincinnati Reds
2713 W 116th St
Leawood, KS 66211-3025, USA

Montgomery, John Michael (Musician)
c/o Mark Roeder *William Morris Agency
(WMA-TN)*
1600 Division St Ste 300
Nashville, TN 37203-2755, USA

Montgomery, John W (Misc)
2 Rue de Rome
Starsbourg 67000, FRANCE

Montgomery, Lisa Kennedy (Actor)
Game Show Network
10202 Washington Blvd
Culver City, CA 90232-3119, USA

Montgomery, Marv (Football Player)
Denver Broncos
1509 S Macon St
Aurora, CO 80012-5140, USA

Montgomery, Melba (Musician)
Joe Taylor Artist Agency
2802 Columbine Pl
Nashville, TN 37204-3104, USA

Montgomery, Mike (Basketball Player,
Coach)
Golden State Warriors
1001 Broadway
Oakland, CA 94607-4019, USA

Montgomery, Mike (Football Player)
San Diego Chargers
4224 High Star Ln
Dallas, TX 75287-6624, USA

Montgomery, Monty (Baseball Player)
Kansas City Royals
807 Corn Tassel Trl
Martinsville, VA 24112-5601, USA

Montgomery, Poppy (Actor)
Mindel/Donigan
9057C Nemo St # C
West Hollywood, CA 90069, USA

Montgomery, Ray (Baseball Player)
Houston Astros
3107 S Webber Ct
Pearland, TX 77584-9418, USA

Montgomery, Steve (Baseball Player)
Oakland A's
3262 Avenida Del Alba
Carlsbad, CA 92009-9535, USA

Montgomery, Wilbert N (Football Player)
Philadelphia Eagles
45990 Tournament Dr
Northville, MI 48168-8498, USA

Montgomery Jr, Dan (Actor)
c/o Karyn Spencer *Peter Strain &
Associates Inc (LA)*
5455 Wilshire Blvd Ste 1812
Los Angeles, CA 90036-4268, USA

Montiel, H Pierre
102 W 73rd St
New York, NY 10023-3047, USA

Montler, Mike (Football Player)
Boston Patriots
479 Tiara Vista Dr
Grand Junction, CO 81503-8716, USA

Montminy, Marc R (Scientist)
Salk Institute
10100 N Torrey Pines Rd
La Jolla, CA 92037, USA

Montoya, Al (Hockey Player)
New York Rangers
2 Penn Plz
Madison Square Garden
New York, NY 10121-1703, USA

Montoya, Juan (Race Car Driver)
Williams Grand Prix
Grove
Wontage, Oxfordshire OX12 0D0,
UNITED KINGDOM (UK)

Montoyo, Jose Carlos (Baseball Player)
Montreal Expos
1611 SW Pancoast St
Port Saint Lucie, FL 34987-2002, USA

Montreull, Allan (Baseball Player)
Chicago Cubs
2016 Laurel Ave
Gretna, LA 70056-5232, USA

Montross, Eric (Basketball Player)
4668 S Nc Highway 150
Lexington, NC 27295-8026, USA

Montsho, Este (Musician)
William Morris Agency
1325 Avenue Of The Americas
New York, NY 10019-6091, USA

Montvidas, Edgaras (Opera Singer)
Van Walsum Mgmt
4 Addison Bridge Place
London W14 8XP, UNITED KINGDOM
(UK)

Montville, Leigh (Writer)
Boston Globe
Editorial Dept
135 Wt Morrissey Blvd
Dorchester, MA 02125, USA

Monty, Harry
1600 N Bronson Ave Apt 17
Hollywood, CA 90028-6598, USA

Monty Q (DJ)
c/o Staff Member *Diva Central Inc*
7510 W Sunset Blvd Ste 1445
Los Angeles, CA 90046-3408, USA

Moock, Joe (Baseball Player)
New York Mets
12432 Pecos Ave
Greenwell Springs, LA 70739-3039, USA

Moodle, Janice (Golfer)
29551 Indian Ridge Cv
Westlake, OH 44145-6417, USA

Moody, Eric (Baseball Player)
Texas Rangers
336 Gleneagle Cir
Irmo, SC 29063-8432, USA

Moody, James (Musician)
BPR
230 12th St # 118
Miami Beach, FL 33139-4603, USA

Moody, Keith M (Football Player)
Buffalo Bills
4632 Riverview Ct
Tracy, CA 95377-8288, USA

Moody, Lynne (Actor)
8708 Skyline Dr
Los Angeles, CA 90046-1422, USA

Moody, Micky (Musician)
Int'l Talent Booking
27A Floral St #300
London WC2E 9DQ, UNITED KINGDOM
(UK)

Moody, Ritchie (Baseball Player)
1321 Orchardview Ct
Dayton, OH 45458-9682, USA

Moody, Ron (Actor)
Eric Glass
28 Berkeley Square
London W1X 6HD, UNITED KINGDOM
(UK)

Moody Blues (Music Group)
c/o Robert Norman *Creative Artists
Agency LCC (CAA-LA)*
2000 Avenue Of The Stars
Los Angeles, CA 90067-4700, USA

Moody-Luckhurst, Terri (Golfer)
c/o Staff Member *Pro Golfers Association
(PGA) Tour*
112 Tpc Blvd
Ponte Vedra Beach, FL 32082, USA

Moog, Andy (Hockey Player)
530 Rolling Hills Rd
Coppell, TX 75019-4049, USA

Moomaw, Donn D (Football Player)
3124 Corda Dr
Los Angeles, CA 90049-1104, USA

Moon, Philip
449 N Highland Ave
Los Angeles, CA 90036-2627, USA

Moon, Sun Myung (Religious Leader)
Unification Church
4 W 43rd St
New York, NY 10036-7499, USA

Moon, Wallace W (Wally) (Baseball
Player)
St Louis Cardinals
702 Ellen Lee Ct
Bryan, TX 77802-1146, USA

Moon, Wally
1415 Angelina Cir
College Station, TX 77840-4952, USA

Moon, Warren (Football Player)
PO Box 22388
Houston, TX 77227-2388, USA

Mooney, Ed (Football Player)
Detroit Lions
4105 63rd St
Lubbock, TX 79413-5023, USA

Mooney, John (Musician)
Intrepid Artists
1300 Baxter St Ste 405
Midtown Plaza
Charlotte, NC 28204-3081, USA

Mooney, Michael J (Educator)
Lewis & Clark College
President's Office
Portland, OR 97219, USA

Mooney, Michael P (Mike) (Football
Player)
San Diego Chargers
4801 Diane Ave
Mount Airy, MD 21771-8923, USA

Moonves, Leslie (Business Person,
Producer)
CBS-TV
51 W 52nd St
New York, NY 10019-6119, USA

Moordyukova, Nonna V (Actor)
Rublevskoye Shosse 34
Korp 2 #549
Moscow 121609, RUSSIA

Moore, Abra (Musician)
Haber Corp
16830 Ventura Blvd Ste 501
Encino, CA 91436-1731, USA

Moore, Ann S (Publisher)
People Magazine
Publisher's Office
Time & Life Building
New York, NY 10020, USA

Moore, Arch A Jr (Governor)
PO Box 250
Moundsville, WV 26041-0250, USA

Moore, Archie (Baseball Player)
New York Yankees
201 Courtland Rd
Indiana, PA 15701-3202, USA

Moore, Arthur (Misc)
Sheet Metal Workers Int'l Assn
1750 New York Ave NW
Washington, DC 20006-5386, USA

Moore, Balor (Baseball Player)
Montreal Expos
6301 Almeda Rd Apt 717
Houston, TX 77021-1087, USA

Moore, Barry (Baseball Player)
Washington Senators
6702 Conifer Cir
Indian Trail, NC 28079-7588, USA

Moore, Benjamin (Artist)
3123 39th Place S
Seattle, WA 98144, USA

Moore, Billie (Coach)
2247 Meadow Ln
Fullerton, CA 92831-2122, USA

Moore, Billy (Baseball Player)
Montreal Expos
419 N Astell Ave
West Covina, CA 91790-1803, USA

Moore, Bob (Baseball Player)
San Francisco Giants
2500 Wellington Rd
Los Angeles, CA 90016-3034, USA

Moore, Bobby (Baseball Player)
Kansas City Royals
3703 Hyde Park Ave
Cincinnati, OH 45209-2321, USA

Moore, Booker (Football Player)
Buffalo Bills
2539 Stevenson St
Flint, MI 48504-3309, USA

Moore, Brad (Baseball Player)
Philadelphia Phillies
3135 Challenger Point Dr
Loveland, CO 80538-7222, USA

Moore, Brandon (Football Player)
New England Patriots
15010 S 47th St
Phoenix, AZ 85044-6889, USA

Moore, Brent (Football Player)
Green Bay Packers
137 Wild Horse Valley Rd
Novato, CA 94947-3615, USA

Moore, Bud (Race Car Driver)
4 Duck Ln
Isle Of Palms, SC 29451-2501, USA

Moore, Chante (Musician, Songwriter, Writer)
Artistic Control
1350 Spring St NW Ste 700
Atlanta, GA 30309-2874, USA

Moore, Charles Jr (Athlete, Track Athlete)
10 Barclay St
New York, NY 10007-2705, USA

Moore, Charlie (Baseball Player)
Milwaukee Brewers
342 County Road 276
Cullman, AL 35057-4976, USA

Moore, Chessie
PO Box 1516
Palatka, FL 32178-1516, USA

Moore, Chris (Producer)
c/o Staff Member *LivePlanet*
2644 30th St
Santa Monica, CA 90405-3060, USA

Moore, Christina (Actor)
c/o Staff Member *Gersh Agency, The (LA)*
232 N Canon Dr
Beverly Hills, CA 90210-5302, USA

Moore, Christy (Musician)
It's a Gas Mgmt
1184 Fischer Blvd Ste 2B
Toms River, NJ 08753-3089, USA

Moore, Darryl (Football Player)
Washington Redskins
503 High St
Minden, LA 71055-3698, USA

Moore, Dave (Football Player)
c/o Team Member *Tampa Bay Buccaneers*
1 Bucaneer Place
Tampa, FL 33607, USA

Moore, Demi (Actor)
c/o Jason Weinberg *Untitled Entertainment (LA)*
331 N Maple Dr Fl 3
Beverly Hills, CA 90210-3827, USA

Moore, Derrick (Football Player)
Detroit Lions
3164 Jackson Creek Dr
Stockbridge, GA 30281-5688, USA

Moore, Dick (Cartoonist)
Dick Moore Assoc
1560 Broadway
New York, NY 10036-1518, USA

Moore, Dickie
150 W End Ave Apt 26C
New York, NY 10023-5743, USA

Moore, Dorothy (Musician)
Sirius Entertainment
13531 Claimont Way #8
Oregon City, OR 97045, USA

Moore, Earl
215 W End Blvd
Winston Salem, NC 27101, USA

Moore, Eric P (Football Player)
New York Giants
2225 Lindsay Ln
Florissant, MO 63031-5626, USA

Moore, Gary (Baseball Player)
Los Angeles Dodgers
7985 Roundrock Rd
Dallas, TX 75248-5341, USA

Moore, George E (Doctor)
12048 Black Hawk Dr
Conifer, CO 80433-7137, USA

Moore, Henry (Football Player)
New York Giants
2200 Pleasure Dr
Benton, AR 72019-6365, USA

Moore, Herman J (Football Player)
Detroit Lions
265 Mount Hermon Cir
Danville, VA 24540-5227, USA

Moore, J Jeremy (General)
Lloyds Bank
Cox's & King's Branch
7 Pall Mall
London SW1, UNITED KINGDOM (UK)

Moore, Jackie (Baseball Player)
Detroit Tigers
2721 Laurel Valley Ln
Arlington, TX 76006-4019, USA

Moore, Jackie (Musician)
T-Best Talent Agency
508 Honey Lake Ct
Danville, CA 94506-1237, USA

Moore, Jacqueline (Wrestler)
c/o Staff Member *World Wrestling Entertainment (WWE)*
1241 E Main St
Stamford, CT 06902-3520, USA

Moore, James E Jr (General)
18940 Joaquin Ct
Salinas, CA 93908-9609, USA

Moore, Jeffrey B (Football Player)
Los Angeles Rams
2090 Dogwood Estates Cv
Germantown, TN 38139-5620, USA

Moore, Jerald (Football Player)
St Louis Rams
3539 N Macgregor Way
Houston, TX 77004-8003, USA

Moore, Jerry (Football Player)
Chicago Bears
401 Ivory Dr
Little Rock, AR 72205-2640, USA

Moore, Joe
2410 Memorial Dr # 3C
Bryan, TX 77802-2851, USA

Moore, John (Director, Producer, Writer)
c/o Rowena Arquelles *Creative Artists Agency LCC (CAA-LA)*
2000 Avenue Of The Stars
Los Angeles, CA 90067-4700, USA

Moore, John W (Educator)
Indiana State University
President's Office
Terre Haute, IN 47809-0001, USA

Moore, Julianne (Actor)
c/o Evelyn O'Neill *Management 360*
9111 Wilshire Blvd
Beverly Hills, CA 90210-5508, USA

Moore, Junior (Baseball Player)
Atlanta Braves
3728 Wall Ave
Richmond, CA 94804-3346, USA

Moore, Kelvin (Baseball Player)
Oakland A's
75 Stoney Point Ter
Covington, GA 30014-7070, USA

Moore, Kelvin (Football Player)
Cincinnati Bengals
1564 W 110th Pl
Los Angeles, CA 90047-4915, USA

Moore, Ken (Football Player)
New York Giants
7497 SE Jamestown Ter
Hobe Sound, FL 33455-5879, USA

Moore, Kenya (Actor)
c/o Staff Member *Cunningham Escott Slevin & Doherty (LA)*
10635 Santa Monica Blvd Ste 130
Los Angeles, CA 90025-8306, USA

Moore, Kerwin (Baseball Player)
Oakland A's
18137 Goddard St
Detroit, MI 48234-4404, USA

Moore, Leonard E (Lenny) (Football Player)
Baltimore Colts
8815 Stonehaven Rd
Randallstown, MD 21133-4223, USA

Moore, LeRoi (Musician)
Red Light Mgmt
PO Box 520
Crozet, VA 22932-0520, USA

Moore, Leroy (Football Player)
Buffalo Bills
842 Golf Dr Apt 201
Pontiac, MI 48341-2385, USA

Moore, Lorrie (Writer)
University of Wisconsin
English Dept
Madison, WI 53706, USA

Moore, Lucille (Baseball Player)
6450 Miami Cir
South Bend, IN 46614-6480, USA

Moore, Malcolm A S (Scientist)
Memorial Sloan-Dettering Cancer Center
1275 York Ave
New York, NY 10065-6007, USA

Moore, Mandy (Actor, Musician)
c/o Jon Leshay *The Firm*
9465 Wilshire Blvd Fl 6
Beverly Hills, CA 90212-2605, USA

Moore, Manfred (Football Player)
San Francisco 49ers
1672 Buckingham Rd
Los Angeles, CA 90019-5903, USA

Moore, Mary (Baseball Player)
4225 Lake Grove Ct
White Lake, MI 48383-1528, USA

Moore, Mary Tyler (Actor)
c/o Allison Band *United Talent Agency (UTA)*
9560 Wilshire Blvd Ste 500
Beverly Hills, CA 90212-2401, USA

Moore, McNeil (Football Player)
Chicago Bears
1212 Woodlawn Dr
Center, TX 75935-3030, USA

Moore, Melanie
3500 W Olive Ave Ste 920
Burbank, CA 91505-5514, USA

Moore, Melba (Actor, Musician)
Artist Services Inc
1017 O St NW # B
Washington, DC 20001-4229, USA

Moore, Melissa Anne (Actor)
PO Box 55
Versailles, KY 40383-0055, USA

Moore, Michael (Director)
c/o Staff Member *Dog Eat Dog Films Inc*
430 W 14th St Ste 401
New York, NY 10014-1037, USA

Moore, Michael K (Mike) (Prime Minister)
World Trade Organization
154 Rue Lausanne
Geneva 21 1211, SWITZERLAND

Moore, Michael (Mike) (Attorney, Attorney General, General)
Attorney General's Office
PO Box 220
Jackson, MS 39205-0220, USA

Moore, Mike (Baseball Player)
Seattle Mariners
1472 E Calle De Caballos
Tempe, AZ 85284-2406, USA

Moore, Moulty (Football Player)
Miami Dolphins
5781 S Sable Cir
Margate, FL 33063-5697, USA

Moore, Nathanlel (Nat) (Football Player)
Miami Dolphins
20041 E Oakmont Dr
Hialeah, FL 33015-2048, USA

Moore, Otis (Baseball Player)
Pittsburgh Pirates
2923 178th Dr Apt 3
Hammond, IN 46323, USA

Moore, Patrick (Astronomer, Writer)
Farthings
39 West St
Selsey, Sussex PO20 9AAD, UNITED KINGDOM (UK)

Moore, Patrick (Golfer)
19607 Valiant Way
Cornelius, NC 28031-6362, USA

Moore, Rachel (Actor, Model)
c/o Staff Member *Xposure Public Relations*
8271 Melrose Ave Ste 110
Los Angeles, CA 90046-6800, USA

Moore, Ralph (Musician)
Denon Records
135 W 50th St # 1915
New York, NY 10020-1201, USA

Moore, Red (Baseball Player)
Atlanta Black Crackers
2450 Perry Blvd NW
Atlanta, GA 30318-8809, USA

Moore, Richard (Actor)
London Mgmt
2-4 Noel St
London W1V 3RB, UNITED KINGDOM
(UK)

Moore, Richard W (Dickie) (Hockey
Player)
4955 Clemin Saint Francois
Saint Laurent, PQ 1P3, CANADA

Moore, Rob (Football Player)
New York Jets
14239 S 8th St
Phoenix, AZ 85048-4435, USA

Moore, Robert A (Football Player)
Atlanta Falcons
1906 E Gate Dr
Stone Mountain, GA 30087-1947, USA

Moore, Robert R (Football Player)
Oakland Raiders
20 Sally Ann Rd
Orinda, CA 94563-3525, USA

Moore, Roger (Actor)
London Management
2-4 Noel St
London W1V 3RB, UNITED KINGDOM
(UK)

Moore, Roger (Actor, Director, Producer)
c/o Geneva Bray *GVA Talent Agency Inc*
9229 W Sunset Blvd Ste 320
Los Angeles, CA 90069-3403, USA

Moore, Ron (Football Player)
Phoenix Cardinals
5730 Oakwood St
Spencer, OK 73084, USA

Moore, Ronald D (Producer, Writer)
c/o Staff Member *Creative Artists Agency
LCC (CAA-LA)*
2000 Avenue Of The Stars
Los Angeles, CA 90067-4700, USA

Moore, Sam (Musician)
I'ma Da Wife Enterprises
7119 E Shea Blvd # 109-436
Scottsdale, AZ 85254-6107, USA

Moore, Scotty (Musician)
4104 Blueberry Hill Rd
Nashville, TN 37218-3519, USA

Moore, Shawn (Football Player)
Denver Broncos
573 Brookfield Dr
Centreville, MD 21617-2397, USA

Moore, Shemar (Actor)
15030 Ventura Blvd # 710
Sherman Oaks, CA 91403-5470, USA

Moore, Tamara
Phoenix Mercury
201 E Jefferson St
American West Arena
Phoenix, AZ 85004-2412, USA

Moore, Toby (Actor)
c/o Staff Member *Sanders/Armstrong
Management*
2120 Colorado Ave Ste 120
Santa Monica, CA 90404-3561, USA

Moore, Tom (Football Player)
Green Bay Packers
1038 Forest Harbor Dr
Hendersonville, TN 37075-9649, USA

Moore, Tommy (Baseball Player)
New York Mets
5235 Thompson Rd
Clarence, NY 14031-1130, USA

Moore, Trey (Baseball Player)
Montreal Expos
5128 Bellerive Bend Dr
College Station, TX 77845-4477, USA

Moore, Zeke (Football Player)
Houston Oilers
3422 Prudence Dr
Houston, TX 77045-5718, USA

Moore (Paxson), Melanie Deanne (Actor)
c/o Melisa Spamer *Domain*
4526 Wilshire Blvd
Los Angeles, CA 90010-3801, USA

Moore-Warner, Eleanor (Baseball Player)
2172 Kinney Ave NW
Grand Rapids, MI 49534-1160, USA

Moore-Watkins, Pauline (Actor)
4077 Sunset Dr Apt 202
Lake Oswego, OR 97035-4391, USA

Moorehead, Emery (Football Player)
New York Giants
1005 Sussex Dr
Northbrook, IL 60062-3328, USA

Moorehouse, Adrian
St. Helier Bradford Rd. Bringley
W. York., ENGLAND BD16 1PA, UNITED
KINGDOM (UK)

Moorer, Allison (Actor, Musician,
Songwriter, Writer)
TKO Artist Mgmt
2303 21st Ave S Fl 3
Nashville, TN 37212-4947, USA

Moorer, Llana (MC Lyte) (Musician)
Sunni Gyrl Inc
PO Box 691394
Los Angeles, CA 90069-9394, USA

Mooring, John (Football Player)
New York Jets
1901 Pat Booker Rd
Universal City, TX 78148-3438, USA

Moorman, Mo (Football Player)
Kansas City Chiefs
9641 Shelbyville Rd
Simpsonville, KY 40067-6506, USA

Moorse, Kiki (Musician)
K Records
924 Jefferson St SE # 101
Olympia, WA 98501, USA

MOP (Music Group)
c/o Staff Member *Interscope Records (NY)*
1790 Broadway
New York, NY 10019-1412, USA

Mora, Danny (Actor)
c/o Staff Member *Acme Talent & Literary
(LA)*
4727 Wilshire Blvd Ste 333
Los Angeles, CA 90010-3874, USA

Mora, Gene (Cartoonist)
United Feature Syndicate
200 Madison Ave
New York, NY 10016-3911, USA

Mora, Jim
6928 Saints Dr
Metairie, LA 70003, USA

Mora, Melvin (Baseball Player)
New York Mets
2205 Warwick Way Ste 200
Marriottsville, MD 21104-1632, USA

Mora, Philippe (Director)
Altman Co
9255 W Sunset Blvd Ste 901
Los Angeles, CA 90069-3306, USA

Mora, Sergio (Reality TV Star)
c/o Staff Member *The Contender*
Nbc Entertainment
3000 W. Alameda Ave #5366
Burbank, CA 91523-0001, USA

Mora Gramunt, Gabriel (Architect)
Passtage Sant Felip
12 Bis
Barcelona 08006, SPAIN

Mora Jr, James E (Jim) (Coach, Football
Coach)
Atlanta Falcons
4400 Falcon Pkwy
Flowery Branch, GA 30542-3176, USA

Morabito, Rocky (Journalist,
Photographer)
3036 Gilmore St
Jacksonville, FL 32205, USA

Morabito, Tim (Football Player)
Cincinnati Bengals
PO Box 152
Garnerville, NY 10923-0152, USA

Moraga, David (Baseball Player)
Montreal Expos
608 Peach Ct
Suisun City, CA 94534-1522, USA

Morahan, Christopher T (Director)
Highcombe
Devil's Punchbowl
Thursley
Godalming, Surrey GU8 6NS, UNITED
KINGDOM (UK)

Morales, Esai (Actor)
c/o Steven Muller *Innovative Artists (LA)*
1505 10th St
Santa Monica, CA 90401-2805, USA

Morales, Esal (Actor)
7527 Woodrow Wilson Dr
Los Angeles, CA 90046-1324, USA

Morales, Jose M (Baseball Player)
Oakland A's
17411 Fosgate Rd
Montverde, FL 34756-3002, USA

Morales, P Pablo (Swimmer)
University of Nebraska
Athletic Dept
Lincoln, NE 68588, USA

Morales, Rich (Baseball Player)
Chicago White Sox
1650 Rosita Rd
Pacifica, CA 94044-4431, USA

Morales, Willie (Baseball Player)
Baltimore Orioles
5001 W Camino Del Desierto
Tucson, AZ 85745-9119, USA

Moran, Al (Baseball Player)
New York Mets
34134 Banbury St
Farmington Hills, MI 48331-2216, USA

Moran, Bill (Baseball Player)
Chicago White Sox
200 Shore Dr
Portsmouth, VA 23701-1241, USA

Moran, Billy (Baseball Player)
Cleveland Indians
107 Emerling Ln
Peachtree City, GA 30269-3220, USA

Moran, Carl (Baseball Player)
Chicago White Sox
200 Shore Dr
Portsmouth, VA 23701-1241, USA

Moran, John (Religious Leader)
Missionary Church
PO Box 9127
Fort Wayne, IN 46899-9127, USA

Moran, Julie (Entertainer, Sportscaster)
Creative Artists Agency
9830 Wilshire Blvd
Beverly Hills, CA 90212-1804, USA

Moran, Nick (Actor)
c/o Jai Khanna *Brillstein-Grey
Entertainment*
9150 Wilshire Blvd Ste 350
Beverly Hills, CA 90212-3453, USA

Moran, Pauline
275 Kensington Rd.
London, ENGLAND SW1 6BY, UNITED
KINGDOM (UK)

Moran, Richard J (Rich) (Football Player)
Green Bay Packers
7252 Mimosa Dr
Carlsbad, CA 92011-5149, USA

Moran, Sean (Football Player)
Buffalo Bills
15539 W 75th Pl
Arvada, CO 80007-7957, USA

Moran, Tommy (Actor)
c/o Staff Member *Creative Artists Agency
LCC (CAA-LA)*
2000 Avenue Of The Stars
Los Angeles, CA 90067-4700, USA

Moran, Tony (DJ)
c/o Len Evans *Project Publicity*
312 W 53rd St
New York, NY 10019-5743, USA

Morandini, Mickey (Baseball Player)
Philadelphia Phillies
290 E Tratebas Rd
Chesterton, IN 46304-2556, USA

Moranis, Rick (Actor)
c/o Staff Member *William Morris Agency
(WMA-LA)*
1 William Morris Pl
Beverly Hills, CA 90212-4261, USA

Morante, Laura (Actor)
Carol Levi Co
Via Giuseppe Pisanelli
Rome 00196, ITALY

Morasca, Jenna (Reality TV Star)
M Morasca
6027 Belle Terre Ct
Bridgeville, PA 15017-3459, USA

Morast, Daniel J (Misc)
International Wildlife Coalition
634 N Falmouth Hwy
North Falmouth, MA 02556-9998, USA

Morath, Max (Musician)
Producers Inc
1186 N 56th St
Tampa, FL 33617, USA

Morauta, Mekere (Prime Minister)
Premier's Office
Marea Haus
Walgani
Port Moresby, PAPUA NEW GUINEA

Moravec, Ivan (Musician)
Cramer/Marder Artists
3436 Springhill Rd
Lafayette, CA 94549-2535, USA

Morceli, Noureddine (Athlete, Track Athlete)
Youth & Sports Ministry
3 Rue Mohamed Belouizdad
Algiers, ALGERIA

Morcott, Southwood J (Business Person)
Dana Corp
PO Box 1000
Toledo, OH 43697-1000, USA

Mordecai, Mike (Baseball Player)
Atlanta Braves
9155 Nesbit Ferry Rd Unit 64
Alpharetta, GA 30022-5534, USA

Mordillo, Guillermo (Cartoonist)
Haye Top Present
Oberweg 8
Unterhacing 82008, GERMANY

Mordkovitch, Lydia (Musician)
25B Belsize Ave
London NW3 3BL, UNITED KINGDOM
(UK)

More, Camilla (Actor)
Sharon Kemp
477 S Robertson Blvd # 204
Beverly Hills, CA 90211, USA

Moreau, Doug (Football Player)
Miami Dolphins
5875 Highland Rd
Baton Rouge, LA 70808-6559, USA

Moreau, Jeanne (Actor)
Agence Intertalent
5 Rue Clemont Marot
Paris 75008, FRANCE

Moreau, Marguerite (Actor)
c/o Nikki Marish *Edmonds Management*
1635 N Cahuenga Blvd Fl 5
Los Angeles, CA 90028-6201, USA

Moreau, Sylvie
11 av. Corentin Cariou
Paris 75019, FRANCE

Morehead, Dave (Baseball Player)
Boston Red Sox
13872 Glenmere Dr
Santa Ana, CA 92705-2812, USA

Morehead, Seth (Baseball Player)
Philadelphia Phillies
8675 Grover Pl
Shreveport, LA 71115-2709, USA

Moreino, Joe (Football Player)
New York Jets
25 Gemini Dr
East Providence, RI 02914-4069, USA

Moreira, Airto (Musician)
A Train Mgmt
PO Box 29242
Oakland, CA 94604-9242, USA

Morejon, Dan (Baseball Player)
Cincinnati Reds
22625 SW 207th Ave
Miami, FL 33170-4846, USA

Moreland, Keith (Baseball Player)
Philadelphia Phillies
1515 Oak Dr
Lewisville, TX 75028-3608, USA

Morelli, Oscar (Actor)
c/o Staff Member *Televisa*
Blvd Adolfo Lopez Mateos 232
Colonia San Angel INN
DF CP 01060, MEXICO

Morello, Tom (Musician)
GAS Entertainment
8935 Lindblade St
Culver City, CA 90232-2438, USA

Morelos, Lisette (Actor)
c/o Staff Member *Televisa*
Blvd Adolfo Lopez Mateos 232
Colonia San Angel INN
DF CP 01060, MEXICO

Moreno, Azucar (Music Group)
c/o Staff Member *Sony Music Miami*
605 Lincoln Rd Fl 7
Miami Beach, FL 33139-2900, USA

Moreno, Catalina Sandino (Actor)
c/o Staff Member *Creative Artists Agency LCC (CAA-LA)*
2000 Avenue Of The Stars
Los Angeles, CA 90067-4700, USA

Moreno, Isabel (Actor)
c/o Gabriel Blanco *Gabriel Blanco Iglesias (Mexico)*
Rio Balsas 35-32
Colonia Cuauhtemoc
DF 06500, MEXICO

Moreno, Jaime (Musician)
New York/New Jersey Mtrostars
1 Harmon Plz # 300
Secaucus, NJ 07094-2803, USA

Moreno, Jaime (Race Car Driver)
252 Montclaire Dr
Weston, FL 33326, USA

Moreno, Jorge (Musician)
c/o Staff Member *Creative Artists Agency LCC (CAA-LA)*
2000 Avenue Of The Stars
Los Angeles, CA 90067-4700, USA

Moreno, Jose Elias (Actor)
c/o Staff Member *Televisa*
Blvd Adolfo Lopez Mateos 232
Colonia San Angel INN
DF CP 01060, MEXICO

Moreno, Lea
4739 Lankershim Blvd
N Hollywood, CA 91602-1803, USA

Moreno, Moses (Football Player)
Chicago Bears
11627 Lakeside Ave
Lakeside, CA 92040-1614, USA

Moreno, Rita (Actor)
Leonard Gordon
7027 Devon Way
Berkeley, CA 94705-1722, USA

Moresco, Robert (Actor, Director, Producer, Writer)
c/o Chris Silbermann *Broder Webb Chervin Silbermann Agency, The (BWCS)*
10250 Constellation Blvd Ste P
Los Angeles, CA 90067-6213, USA

Moresco, Tim (Football Player)
Green Bay Packers
2413 Pond Rd
Duluth, GA 30096-6002, USA

Moret, Rogelio (Baseball Player)
Boston Red Sox
HC 1
PO Box 5225
Guaynabo, PR 00971, USA

Moretti, Fabrizio (Musician)
MVO Ltd
370 7th Ave # 807
New York, NY 10001-3912, USA

Moretz, Chloe (Actor)
c/o Pam Kohl *3 Arts Entertainment Inc*
9460 Wilshire Blvd Fl 7
Beverly Hills, CA 90212-2713, USA

Morey, Bill (Actor)
Kazarian/Spencer
11365 Ventura Blvd Ste 100
Studio City, CA 91604-3148, USA

Morfogen, George (Actor)
c/o Staff Member *Gersh Agency, The (LA)*
232 N Canon Dr
Beverly Hills, CA 90210-5302, USA

Morgado, Arnold (Football Player)
Kansas City Chiefs
1750 Kaahumanu St Apt 53-C
Pearl City, HI 96782, USA

Morgan, Barbara R (Astronaut)
15602 River Maple Ln
Houston, TX 77062-4766, USA

Morgan, Bob
175 Lakeshore Dr
Asheville, NC 28804-2340, USA

Morgan, Bobby (Baseball Player)
Brooklyn Dodgers
3004 Stonybrook Rd
Oklahoma City, OK 73120-5716, USA

Morgan, Chad (Actor)
c/o Staff Member *Burstein Company, The*
15304 W Sunset Blvd Ste 208
Pacific Palisades, CA 90272-3656, USA

Morgan, Cindy
280 S Beverly Dr Ste 400
Beverly Hills, CA 90212-3904, USA

Morgan, Craig (Musician)
c/o Staff Member *Neostar Management*
2 S University Dr Ste 325
Plantation, FL 33324-3307, USA

Morgan, Dan (Football Player)
Carolina Panthers
1915 Funny Cide Dr
Waxhaw, NC 28173-8299, USA

Morgan, Debbi (Actor)
Mitchell K Stubbs
8695 Washington Blvd Ste 204
Culver City, CA 90232-7419, USA

Morgan, Debelah (Musician)
DAS Communications
83 Riverside Dr
New York, NY 10024-5713, USA

Morgan, Donald M (Cinematographer)
15826 Mayall St
North Hills, CA 91343-1415, USA

Morgan, Elaine
24 Aberford Rd. Mt. Ash
Glamorgan, ENGLAND, UNITED KINGDOM (UK)

Morgan, Gil (Golfer)
PO Box 806
Edmond, OK 73083-0806, USA

Morgan, Glen (Director, Producer, Writer)
c/o Marty Adelstein *Original Film*
284 N Saltair Ave
Los Angeles, CA 90049-2913, USA

Morgan, Harry (Actor)
13172 Boca De Canon Ln
Los Angeles, CA 90049-2220, USA

Morgan, James C (Business Person)
Applied Materials
3050 Bowers Ave
Santa Clara, CA 95054-3298, USA

Morgan, James N (Economist)
1217 Bydding Rd
Ann Arbor, MI 48103-3103, USA

Morgan, Jane (Musician)
27740 Pacific Coast Hwy
Malibu, CA 90265-4341, USA

Morgan, Jaye P (Actor, Musician)
1185 La Grange Ave
Newbury Park, CA 91320-5316, USA

Morgan, Jeffrey Dean (Actor)
c/o Richard Lewis *Geddes Agency, The*
8430 Santa Monica Blvd Ste 200
Los Angeles, CA 90069-4253, USA

Morgan, Joe (Baseball Player)
Houston Colt 45's
3523 Country Club Pl
Danville, CA 94506-5879, USA

Morgan, Joseph (Actor)
c/o Staff Member *International Creative Management (ICM-LA)*
10250 Constellation Blvd
Los Angeles, CA 90067-6200, USA

Morgan, Joseph M (Joe) (Baseball Player)
Milwaukee Braves
15 Oak Hill Dr
Walpole, MA 02081-2713, USA

Morgan, Kevin (Baseball Player)
New York Mets
205 Yearling Rd Apt A
Duson, LA 70529-3118, USA

Morgan, Kim (Actor)
Artists Group
1650 Broadway Ste 610
New York, NY 10019-6833, USA

Morgan, Lewis R (Judge)
US Court of Appeals
25 Elmtree Dr
Sharpsburg, GA 30277-1946, USA

Morgan, Marabel (Writer)
Total Woman Inc
1300 NW 167th St
Miami, FL 33169-5787, USA

Morgan, Michael (Scientist)
Wellcome Trust
183 Euston Road
London NW1 2BE, UNITED KINGDOM
(UK)

Morgan, Michele (Actor, Musician)
5 Rue Jacques Dulud
Neuillysur-Seine 92200, FRANCE

Morgan, Mike (Baseball Player)
c/o Staff Member *Arizona Diamondbacks*
401 E Jefferson St
Bank One Ballpark
Phoenix, AZ 85004-2438, USA

Morgan, Mike (Cartoonist)
Creators Syndicate
5777 W Century Blvd Ste 1700
Los Angeles, CA 90045-5671, USA

Morgan, Mike (Football Player)
Chicago Bears
14383 Carey Rd
Baker, LA 70714, USA

Morgan, Robert B (Senator)
PO Box 377
Lillington, NC 27546, USA

Morgan, Shelly Taylor (Actor)
Pakula/King
9229 W Sunset Blvd Ste 315
Los Angeles, CA 90069-3403, USA

Morgan, Stanley D (Football Player)
New England Patriots
PO Box 383048
Germantown, TN 38183-3048, USA

Morgan, Tracy (Actor, Comedian)
c/o David (Dave) Becky *3 Arts*
Entertainment Inc
9460 Wilshire Blvd Fl 7
Beverly Hills, CA 90212-2713, USA

Morgan, Trevor (Actor)
c/o Beverly Strong *Anonymous Content*
(CA)
9350 Wilshire Blvd Ste 224
Beverly Hills, CA 90212-3204, USA

Morgan, W Jason (Misc)
Princton University
Geophysic Dept
Princeton, NJ 08544-0001, USA

Morgan, Walter T J (Misc)
57 Woodbury Dr
Sutton
Surrey, UNITED KINGDOM (UK)

Morgan, William N (Architect)
William Morgan Architects
220 E Forsyth St
Jacksonville, FL 32202-3320, USA

Morgan Chad
4526 Wilshire Blvd
Los Angeles, CA 90010-3801, USA

Morganna (Entertainer, Model)
PO Box 20281
Columbus, OH 43220-0281, USA

Morgenson, Gretchen (Journalist)
New York Times
229 W 43rd St
Editorial Dept
New York, NY 10036-3959, USA

Morgenstern, Maia (Actor)
c/o Catherine Davray *Catherine Davray*
Agency
16 bis rue de l'Abbe de l'Epee
Paris 75005, FRANCE

Morgenthau, Robert M (Attorney,
Attorney General, General)
1085 Park Ave
New York, NY 10128-1168, USA

Morgenweck, Henry Charles (Baseball
Player)
33 Bogert St
Teaneck, NJ 07666-4903, USA

Morgridge, John P (Business Person)
Cisco Systems
170 W Tasan Dr
San Jose, CA 95134, USA

Morhardt, Moe (Baseball Player)
Chicago Cubs
182 Williams Ave
Winsted, CT 06098-1120, USA

Mori, Hanae (Designer, Fashion Designer)
Hanae Mori Haute Couture
17-19 Ave Montaigne
Paris, 75008, FRANCE

Mori, Yoshiro (Prime Minister)
Prime Minister's Office
1-6-1 Nagatoicho
Chiyodaku
Tokyo 100, JAPAN

Moriarty, Evelyn
6251 Coldwater Canyon Ave Unit 102
N Hollywood, CA 91606-3001, USA

Moriarty, Michael (Actor)
200 W 58th St # 3B
New York, NY 10019-1432, USA

Moriarty, Mike (Baseball Player)
Baltimore Orioles
5 E Oleander Dr
Mount Laurel, NJ 08054-3601, USA

Moriarty, Phillip (Phil) (Coach)
12 Vista De Laguna
Fort Pierce, FL 34951-2826, USA

Moriarty, Tom (Football Player)
Atlanta Falcons
28800 Fairmount Blvd
Cleveland, OH 44124-4542, USA

Moriarty-Gentile, Cathy (Actor)
c/o Brian Liebman *Liebman Entertainment*
25 E 21st St Ph
New York, NY 10010-6226, USA

Morimoto, Masaharu
105 Hudson St
New York, NY 10013-2331, USA

Morin, Jim (Cartoonist, Editor)
Miami Herald
Herald Plaza
Editorial Dept
Miami, FL 33101, USA

Morin, Lee M E (Astronaut)
10 Marys Creek Ln
Friendswood, TX 77546-3492, USA

Morin, Milt (Football Player)
Cleveland Browns
45 N Maple St Rear B
Hadley, MA 01035-9768, USA

Morison, Patricia (Actor, Musician)
Craig Mgmt
125 S Sycamore Ave
Los Angeles, CA 90036-2938, USA

Morissette, Alanis (Musician, Songwriter,
Writer)
c/o Staff Member *Creative Artists Agency*
LCC (CAA-LA)
2000 Avenue Of The Stars
Los Angeles, CA 90067-4700, USA

Moritz, Brett (Football Player)
Tampa Bay Buccaneers
613 Cameron Ridge Ct
Parkton, MD 21120-8906, USA

Moritz, Louisa
405 S Cliffwood Ave
Los Angeles, CA 90049-3827, USA

Moriyama, Raymond (Architect)
32 Daveport Road
Toronto, ON 1H3, CANADA

Mork, Truis (Musician)
Harrison/Parrott
12 Penzance Place
London W11 4PA, UNITED KINGDOM
(UK)

Morkis, Dorothy (Horse Racer)
17 Farm St
Dover, MA 02030-2303, USA

Morlan, John (Baseball Player)
Pittsburgh Pirates
2348 Salem Ave
Grove City, OH 43123-1832, USA

Morland, David (Golfer)
5531 Oxford Moor Blvd
Windermere, FL 34786-7012, USA

Morley, Joanne (Golfer)
I M G
Pier House Strand on the Ocean
Chiswick
London W4 3NN, UNITED KINGDOM
(UK)

Morley, Lawrence W (Geophysicist,
Physicist)
90 Hemlock St
Saint Thomas, ON N5R 1X9, CANADA

Morley, Malcolm (Artist)
Pace Gallery
32 E 57th St
New York, NY 10022-2530, USA

Morley, W I (Editor)
London Free Press
369 York St
London, ON N6A 4G1, CANADA

Morman, Alvin (Baseball Player)
Houston Astros
1512 Poplar Ridge Rd
Fuquay Varina, NC 27526-7782, USA

Mormon, Russ (Baseball Player)
Chicago White Sox
34W002 Cherry Ln
Geneva, IL 60134-4104, USA

Mornell, Sara
9300 Wilshire Blvd Ste 555
Beverly Hills, CA 90212-3211, USA

Morning After Girls, The (Music Group)
c/o Staff Member *Paradigm (Monterey)*
509 Hartnell St
Monterey, CA 93940-2825, USA

Morningwood (Music Group)
Anton Brooks
Bad Moon PR
19 B All Saints Rd
London W11 1HE, UNITED KINGDOM
(UK)

Moroder, Giorgio (Composer)
1880 Century Park E Ste 900
Los Angeles, CA 90067-1610, USA

Morogiello, Dan (Baseball Player)
Baltimore Orioles
99 Distillery Rd
Whitehouse Station, NJ 08889-3005, USA

Moronko, Jeff (Baseball Player)
Cleveland Indians
3903 Bartons Ct
Sugar Land, TX 77479-1941, USA

Moroski, Mike (Football Player)
Atlanta Falcons
1214 Pine Ln
Davis, CA 95616-1700, USA

Morozov, Akexei (Hockey Player)
Pittsburgh Penguins
Mellon Arena
66 Mario Lemieux Placa
Pittsburgh, PA 15219, USA

Morozov, Vladimir M (Opera Singer)
Kirov Opera
Mariinsky Theater
Reatralnaya 1
Saint Petersburg, RUSSIA

Morphet, David
101 Honor Oak Rd.
London, ENGLAND SE23 3LB, UNITED
KINGDOM (UK)

Morphine
48 Laight St
New York, NY 10013-2016, USA

Morrall, Earl (Football Player)
San Francisco 49ers
2751 68th St SW
Naples, FL 34105-7235, USA

Morretti, Tobias (Actor)
ZBF Agentur
Ordensmeisterstr 15-16
Berling 12099, GERMANY

Morrice, Norman A (Ballerina,
Choreographer)
Royal Ballet
Covent Garden
Bow St
London WC2E 9DD, UNITED KINGDOM
(UK)

Morricone, Ennio (Composer)
Viale delle Letteratura
#30
Rome 00144, ITALY

Morris, Betty (Bowler)
225 Lemming Dr
Reno, NV 89523-9662, USA

Morris, Byron (Bam) (Football Player)
Pittsburgh Steelers
251 NE 4th St
Cooper, TX 75432-1833, USA

Morris, Colleen
8271 Melrose Ave Ste 110
Los Angeles, CA 90046-6800, USA

Morris, Danny (Baseball Player)
Minnesota Twins
4498 State Route 505 S
Horse Branch, KY 42349-9584, USA

Morris, Desmond (Doctor)
78 Danbury Rd
Oxford, ENGLAND

Morris, Dick
64 Twin Lakes Rd
South Salem, NY 10590-1009, USA

Morris, Donnie Joe (Football Player)
Kansas City Chiefs
1414 NW 13th Ave
Amarillo, TX 79107-1604, USA

Morris, Doug (Business Person)
c/o Staff Member *Universal Music Group*
(UMG - LA)
2220 Colorado Ave
Santa Monica, CA 90404-3506, USA

Morris, Dwaine (Football Player)
Philadelphia Eagles
4002 Kilkenny Dr
Baton Rouge, LA 70814-7525, USA

Morris, Edmund (Educator, Writer)
222 Central Park S # 14A
New York, NY 10019-1408, USA

Morris, Errol (Director)
Endeavor Talent Agency
9701 Wilshire Blvd Ste 1000
Beverly Hills, CA 90212-2010, USA

Morris, Eugene (Mercury) (Football
Player)
Miami Dolphins
11315 SW 243rd Ter
Homestead, FL 33032-7125, USA

Morris, Gary (Musician)
Gary Morris Productions
PO Box 176
Chromo, CO 81128-0176, USA

Morris, George A (Football Player)
San Francisco 49ers
720 Fair Oaks Mnr NW
Atlanta, GA 30327-4365, USA

Morris, Hal (Baseball Player)
New York Yankees
1111 Macarthur Blvd
Munster, IN 46321-3005, USA

Morris, Jack (Baseball Player)
Detroit Tigers
7993 100th St N
Saint Paul, MN 55110-1445, USA

Morris, James P (Opera Singer)
Colbert Artists
111 W 57th St
New York, NY 10019-2236, USA

Morris, Jan (Writer)
Trefan Morys
Llanystumdwy
Criccieth, Gwymedd WALES, UNITED
KINGDOM (UK)

Morris, Jason (Athlete)
16 Gail St
Chelmsford, MA 01824-3510, USA

Morris, Jenny (Musician)
Artist & Event Mgmt
PO Box 537
Randwick, NSW 2031, AUSTRALIA

Morris, Jim (Baseball Player)
Tampa Bay Devil Rays
5975 Indigo Sky Dr
Frisco, TX 75034, USA

Morris, John (Baseball Player)
Philadelphia Phillies
5538 E Paradise Ln
Scottsdale, AZ 85254-1165, USA

Morris, John (Baseball Player)
St Louis Cardinals
2645 Elm Dr
North Bellmore, NY 11710-1303, USA

Morris, Johnny (Football Player)
Chicago Bears
753 Shoreline Rd
Lake Barrington, IL 60010-3825, USA

Morris, Jon (Football Player)
Boston Patriots
10 Berkeley Ct
Bluffton, SC 29910-4839, USA

Morris, Julian (Actor)
c/o Jai Khanna *Brillstein-Grey
Entertainment*
9150 Wilshire Blvd Ste 350
Beverly Hills, CA 90212-3453, USA

Morris, Julianne (Actor)
c/o Staff Member *Pakula/King &
Associates*
9229 W Sunset Blvd Ste 315
Los Angeles, CA 90069-3403, USA

Morris, Kathryn (Actor)
c/o David (Dave) Fleming *Mosaic Media
Group*
24 Music Sq W Fl 1
Nashville, TN 37203-6661, USA

Morris, Keith (Musician)
International Creative Mgmt
8942 Wilshire Blvd # 219
Beverly Hills, CA 90211-1908, USA

Morris, Larry (Artist)
105 N Union St # 4
Alexandria, VA 22314-3217, USA

Morris, Lawrence C (Larry) (Football
Player)
Los Angeles Rams
4737 Upper Berkshire Rd
Flowery Branch, GA 30542-3692, USA

Morris, Marianne (Golfer)
4013 Lisa Ln
Middletown, OH 45042-2832, USA

Morris, Mark W (Choreographer)
Mark Morris Dance Group
3 Lafayette Ave # 504
Brooklyn, NY 11217-1415, USA

Morris, Matt (Baseball Player)
St Louis Cardinals
397 Old Jupiter Beach Rd
Jupiter, FL 33477-5034, USA

Morris, Mitch (Actor)
c/o Benjamin Tappan *Bauer Company,
The*
9300 Wilshire Blvd Ph
Beverly Hills, CA 90212-3213, USA

Morris, Nathan (Musician)
Southpaw Entertainment
1710 N Fuller Ave Apt 323
Los Angeles, CA 90046-3064, USA

Morris, Oswald (Ossie)
(Cinematographer)
Holbrook Church St
Fontmell Magna
Shaftesbury SP7 0NY, UNITED
KINGDOM (UK)

Morris, Phil (Actor)
704 Strand
Manhattan Beach, CA 90266, USA

Morris, Reginald H (Cinematographer)
255 Bambaugh Circle #308
Scarborough, ON M1W 3T6, CANADA

Morris, Robert (Artist)
Hunter College
Art Dept
New York, NY 10021, USA

Morris, Ronald (Ron) (Athlete, Track
Athlete)
330 S Reese Pl
Burbank, CA 91506-2724, USA

Morris, Sarah Ann (Actor)
c/o Staff Member *TalentWorks (LA)*
3500 W Olive Ave Ste 1400
Burbank, CA 91505-5512, USA

Morris, Seth Irvin (Architect)
2 Waverly Ct
Houston, TX 77005-1842, USA

Morris, Shellee
6117 Highway 135
Lake City, AR 72437-8851, USA

Morris, Wanya (Musician)
c/o Staff Member *Creative Artists Agency
LCC (CAA-LA)*
2000 Avenue Of The Stars
Los Angeles, CA 90067-4700, USA

Morris, Warren (Baseball Player)
Pittsburgh Pirates
401 W Dem Dr
Alexandria, LA 71303-7011, USA

Morris, Wayna (Musician)
Southpaw Entertainment
1710 N Fuller Ave Apt 323
Los Angeles, CA 90046-3064, USA

Morris, Wayne (Football Player)
St Louis Cardinals
5715 Old Ox Rd
Dallas, TX 75241-2118, USA

Morris, Wingerter Pam (Swimmer)
PO Box 14381
New Bern, NC 28561-4381, USA

Morrison, Christopher (Mink) (Director)
c/o Staff Member *International Creative
Management (ICM-LA)*
10250 Constellation Blvd
Los Angeles, CA 90067-6200, USA

Morrison, Dan (Baseball Player)
7069 Key Haven Rd Apt 401
Seminole, FL 33777-3856, USA

Morrison, Darryl (Football Player)
Washington Redskins
703 Brigadier Ct SE
Leesburg, VA 20175-4450, USA

Morrison, Don (Football Player)
New Orleans Saints
PO Box 432
Wolfe City, TX 75496-0432, USA

Morrison, Felton (Baseball Player)
Philadelphia Stars
3860 N Bouvier St
Philadelphia, PA 19140-3528, USA

Morrison, Fred (Football Player)
Chicago Bears
38189 Greywalls Dr
Murrieta, CA 92562-3058, USA

Morrison, Ian (Scotty) (Misc)
Kennisis Lake
RR 1 PO Box 314
Haliburton, ON K0M 1S0, CANADA

Morrison, James (Actor)
c/o Darryl Marshak *Marshak/Zachary
Company, The*
8840 Wilshire Blvd Fl 1
Beverly Hills, CA 90211-2606, USA

Morrison, Jennifer (Actor)
c/o Peter Kiernan *Management 360*
9111 Wilshire Blvd
Beverly Hills, CA 90210-5508, USA

Morrison, Jim (Baseball Player)
Philadelphia Phillies
8715 11th Avenue Pl NW
Bradenton, FL 34209-9661, USA

Morrison, Mark (Musician)
Atlantic Records
1290 Avenue Of The Americas
New York, NY 10104-0184, USA

Morrison, Robert S (Bob) (Business
Person)
Quaker Oats Co
PO Box 049001
Quaker Tower
Chicago, IL 60604-9001, USA

Morrison, Shelley (Actor)
c/o Staff Member *Marshak/Zachary
Company, The*
8840 Wilshire Blvd Fl 1
Beverly Hills, CA 90211-2606, USA

Morrison, Temuera (Actor)
c/o Staff Member *Abrams Artists Agency
(LA)*
9200 W Sunset Blvd Ph 11
Los Angeles, CA 90069-3601, USA

Morrison, Toni (Nobel Prize Laureate)
185 Nassau St
Princeton, NJ 08542-7007, USA

Morrison, Van (Musician, Songwriter,
Writer)
c/o Paul Charles *Asgard Promotions*
125 Parkway
Regents Park
London NW1 7PS, UNITED KINGDOM
(UK)

Morrison-Gamberdella, Ester (Baseball
Player)
3179 Pleasant Creek Rd
Rogue River, OR 97537-9803, USA

Morriss, Guy (Football Player)
Philadelphia Eagles
University Of Kentucky
Attn Athletic Dept
Lexington, KY 40506-0001, USA

Morrissette, Billy (Actor, Director, Writer)
c/o Brian Inerfeld *Protocol Entertainment
(LA)*
8899 Beverly Blvd Ste 600
Los Angeles, CA 90048-2429, USA

Morrissey (Music Group, Songwriter,
Writer)
MVO Ltd
307 7th Ave Rm 807
New York, NY 10001-6066, USA

Morrissey, Bill (Musician, Songwriter,
Writer)
c/o Staff Member *Creative Artists Agency
LCC (CAA-LA)*
2000 Avenue Of The Stars
Los Angeles, CA 90067-4700, USA

Morrissey, David (Actor)
c/o Melanie Greene *Melanie Greene
Management & Productions*
425 N Robertson Blvd
West Hollywood, CA 90048-1735, USA

Morrissey, Jim (Football Player)
Chicago Bears
48 Fox Trl
Lincolnshire, IL 60069-4012, USA

Morrissey, Neil (Actor)
c/o Staff Member *International Creative
Management (ICM-LA)*
10250 Constellation Blvd
Los Angeles, CA 90067-6200, USA

Morrone, Joe (Coach, Football Coach)
University of Connecticut
Athletic Dept
Storrs Mansfield, CT 06269-0001, USA

Morrow, Bobby
18512 Minor Rd
San Benito, TX 78586-7039, USA

Morrow, Bobby Joe (Athlete, Track
Athlete)
PO Box 9
Beeville, TX 78104-0009, USA

Morrow, Bruce (Cousin Brucie)
(Entertainer, Radio Personality)
SIRIUS Satellite Radio
1221 Avenue Of The Americas Fl 19
New York, NY 10020-1001, USA

Morrow, Harold (Football Player)
Minnesota Vikings
3390 US Highway 82
Maplesville, AL 36750-5112, USA

Morrow, Joshua (Actor)
c/o Staff Member *Young and the Restless,
The*
7800 Beverly Blvd Ste 3305
Los Angeles, CA 90036-2112, USA

Morrow, Kenneth (Ken) (Hockey Player)
39 Crystal Dr
Warwick, RI 02889, USA

Morrow, Mari (Actor)
Abrams-Rubaloff Lawrence
5700 Wilshire Blvd Ste 456
Los Angeles, CA 90036-3648, USA

Morrow, Rob (Actor)
Hofflund/Polone
9465 Wilshire Blvd Ste 420
Beverly Hills, CA 90212-2603, USA

Morse, Barry (Actor)
71 Charles St E
#506
Toronto, ON M4Y 2T3, CANADA

Morse, David (Actor)
Yvette Bikoff
1040 1st Ave # 1126
New York, NY 10022-2991, USA

Morse, David (Musician)
Agency for Performing Arts
405 S Beverly Dr Ste 500
Beverly Hills, CA 90212-4425, USA

Morse, David E (Publisher)
Christian Science Monitor
1 Norway St
Publisher's Office
Boston, MA 02115-3195, USA

Morse, Helen (Actor)
147 King St #A
Sydney, NSW 2000, AUSTRALIA

Morse, John (Golfer)
9291 17 Mile Rd
Marshall, MI 49068-9755, USA

Morse, Natalie (Actor)
William Morris Agency
52/53 Poland Place
London W1F 7LX, UNITED KINGDOM
(UK)

Morse, Philip M (Physicist)
126 Wildwood St
Winchester, MA 01890-2308, USA

Morse, Ray
989 NW Spruce Ave Apt 207
Corvallis, OR 97330-2173, USA

Morse, Robert (Actor)
13830 Davana Ter
Sherman Oaks, CA 91423-4216, USA

Morse, Steve (Football Player)
Pittsburgh Steelers
32743 Weybridge St
Fulshear, TX 77441-4132, USA

Mortensen, Chris (Sportscaster)
ESPN-TV
935 Middle St
Sports Dept Espn Plaza
Bristol, CT 06010-1000, USA

Mortensen, J D (Doctor)
Cardipulmonics Inc
5060 Amelia Earhart Dr
Salt Lake City, UT 84116-2853, USA

Mortensen, Viggo (Actor)
c/o Staff Member *Endeavor Agency LLC
(LA)*
9601 Wilshire Blvd Fl 3
Beverly Hills, CA 90210-5204, USA

Mortier, Gerard (Opera Singer)
Saizburg Festpiele
Hofstallgasse 1
Saizburg 5020, AUSTRIA

Mortimer, Barrett Angela (Tennis Player)
Oaks
Coombe Hill
Kingston-on-Thames, Surrey, UNITED
KINGDOM (UK)

Mortimer, Emily (Actor)
c/o Aleen Keshishian *Brillstein-Grey
Entertainment*
9150 Wilshire Blvd Ste 350
Beverly Hills, CA 90212-3453, USA

Mortimer, John C (Writer)
Turville Heath Cottage
Henley-on-Thames
Oxon, UNITED KINGDOM (UK)

Mortimer, Kenneth P (Educator)
University of Hawaii Manoa
President's Office
Honolulu, HI 96822, USA

Mortita, Pat (Noriyuki) (Actor)
6399 Wilshire Blvd # 444
Los Angeles, CA 90048-5703, USA

Morton, Alicia (Actor)
c/o Staff Member *William Morris Agency
(WMA-LA)*
1 William Morris Pl
Beverly Hills, CA 90212-4261, USA

Morton, Bruce A (Correspondent)
Cable News Network
820 1st St NE
News Dept
Washington, DC 20002-4243, USA

Morton, Bubba (Baseball Player)
Detroit Tigers
18501 SE 424th St
Enumclaw, WA 98022-8534, USA

Morton, Craig (Football Player)
Dallas Cowboys
9850 N 73rd St Unit 2037
Scottsdale, AZ 85258-1032, USA

Morton, Guy (Baseball Player)
Boston Red Sox
567 Femdale Ave
Vermilion, OH 44089, USA

Morton, Joe (Actor)
Judy Schoen
605 N Larchmont Blvd # 309
Los Angeles, CA 90004, USA

Morton, John (Football Player)
San Francisco 49ers
39991 Purmice Dr
Cassel, CA 96016, USA

Morton, Johnnie (Football Player)
2911 Oakwood Ln
Torrance, CA 90505-7121, USA

Morton, Kevin (Baseball Player)
Boston Red Sox
26 Glen Ave
Norwalk, CT 06850, USA

Morton, Samantha (Actor)
Conway Van Gelder Robinson
18-21 Jermyn St
London SW1Y 6NB, UNITED KINGDOM
(UK)

Morukov, Boris V (Cosmonaut)
Potcha Kosmonavtov
Moskovskoi Oblasti
Syvisdny Goroduk 141160, RUSSIA

Morze, Frank (Football Player)
San Francisco 49ers
PO Box 9097
Incline Village, NV 89452-9097, USA

Mosbacher, Robert A (Secretary)
Mosbacher Energy Co
712 Main St Ste 2200
Houston, TX 77002-3206, USA

Moschen, Michael (Artist)
PO Box 178
Cornwall Bridge, CT 06754-0178, USA

Moschitta Jr, John
11601 Dunstan Way Apt 206
Los Angeles, CA 90049-4300, USA

Moschitto, Ross (Baseball Player)
New York Yankees
1633 SW Harbour Isles Cir
Port Saint Lucie, FL 34986-3405, USA

Moscow, David (Actor)
c/o Robert Stein *Robert Stein Management*
345 N Maple Dr Ste 317
Beverly Hills, CA 90210-3856, USA

Mosebar, Donald H (Don) (Football
Player)
Oakland Raiders
1713 Walnut Ave
Manhattan Beach, CA 90266-5016, USA

Moseby, Lloyd (Baseball Player)
Toronto Blue Jays
9140 Los Lagos Cir S
Granite Bay, CA 95746-5842, USA

Mosel, Tad (Writer)
149 E Side Dr
PO Box 249
Concord, NH 03301-5410, USA

Moseley, Bill (Actor)
c/o Peter Young *Don Buchwald &
Associates Inc (LA)*
1902 Coldwater Canyon Dr
Beverly Hills, CA 90210-1731, USA

Moseley, Jonny (Skier)
167 Trinidad Dr
Tiburon, CA 94920-1037, USA

Moseley, Mark (Football Player)
Philadelphia Eagles
7250 Middle Rd
Middletown, VA 22645-2121, USA

Moseley, Roy
152 Ivor Ct Gloucester Pl.
London, ENGLAND NW1, UNITED
KINGDOM (UK)

Moseley, T Michael (Buzz) (General)
Vice Cheif Of Staff
Hqusaf Pentagon
Washington, DC 20330-0001, USA

Moseley, William (Actor)
c/o David Guillod *United Talent Agency
(UTA)*
9560 Wilshire Blvd Ste 500
Beverly Hills, CA 90212-2401, USA

Moselle, Dominic (Football Player)
Cleveland Browns
2019 Hammond Ave
Superior, WI 54880-2751, USA

Moser, Barry (Misc)
115 Pantry Rd
North Hatfield, MA 01066, USA

Moser, Donald B (Don) (Editor)
Smithsonian Magazine
Editorial Dept
900 Jefferson SW
Washington, DC 20560-0001, USA

Moser, Rick (Football Player)
Pittsburgh Steelers
1616 Esplanade Apt 10
Redondo Beach, CA 90277-5261, USA

Moser, Thomas (Opera Singer)
Lies Askonas
6 Henrietta St
London WC2E 8LA, UNITED KINGDOM
(UK)

Moser-Proll, Annemarie (Skier)
Moser Cafe-Bar
#92
Kleinari 115 5602, AUSTRIA

Moses, Albert
15 Overstone Rd
Harpenden Herts., ENGLAND AL5 5PN,
UNITED KINGDOM (UK)

Moses, Billy E
409 N Camden Dr Ste 202
Beverly Hills, CA 90210-4423, USA

Moses, Ed
1 Olympic Plz
Colorado Springs, CO 80909-5780, USA

Moses, Edwin C (Track Athlete)
1184 Daventry Way NE
Atlanta, GA 30319-4547, USA

Moses, Gerry (Baseball Player)
Boston Red Sox
9 Raymond Ct
Georgetown, MA 01833-1852, USA

Moses, Haven C (Football Player)
Buffalo Bills
1140 Cherokee St Unit 640
Denver, CO 80204-3684, USA

Moses, John (Baseball Player)
Seattle Mariners
2133 E Lake Sammamish Pl SE
Issaquah, WA 98075-7439, USA

Moses, Kim (Producer)
c/o Staff Member *William Morris Agency
(WMA-LA)*
1 William Morris Pl
Beverly Hills, CA 90212-4261, USA

Moses, Mark (Actor)
c/o Suzanne (Sue) Wohl *TalentWorks (LA)*
3500 W Olive Ave Ste 1400
Burbank, CA 91505-5512, USA

Moses, Rick (Actor, Musician)
Calder Agency
19919 Redwing St
Woodland Hills, CA 91364-2620, USA

Moses, Robert (Bob) (Activist, Educator)
99 Bishop Allen Dr
Cambridge, MA 02139-3428, USA

Moses, Yolanda T (Educator)
City College of New York
President's Office
New York, NY 10031, USA

Moshammer, Rudolph
Maximilianstr. 14
Munich D-80539, GERMANY

Mosher, Gregory D (Director, Producer)
Lincoln Center Theater
150 W 165th St
New York, NY 10023, USA

Moshinsky, Elijah (Opera Singer)
28 Kidbrooke Groove
London SE3 0LG, UNITED KINGDOM
(UK)

Mosimann, Anton (Chef)
Mosimann's
11B W Halkin St
London SW1X 8JL, UNITED KINGDOM
(UK)

Mosisilli, Pakalitha (Prime Minister)
Chairman's Office
Military Council
PO Box 527
Maseru 100, LESOTHO

Moskau, Paul (Baseball Player)
Cincinnati Reds
5041 N Apache Hills Trl
Tucson, AZ 85750-5912, USA

Moskow, Michael (Financier, Government Official)
Federal Reserve Bank
230 S Lasalle St
Chicago, IL 60604-1413, USA

Moskowitz, Robert (Artist)
81 Leonard St
New York, NY 10013-3436, USA

Mosler, John (Football Player)
Denver Broncos
12604 Cambridge Rd
Leawood, KS 66209-1327, USA

Mosley, Brian (Actor)
After Dinner
Saga Court
S Heath G Missenden
Bucks HP16 9QQ, UNITED KINGDOM (UK)

Mosley, J Brooke (Religious Leader)
1604 Foulkeways
Gwynedd, PA 19436-1033, USA

Mosley, Max R (Race Car Driver)
Int'l Automobile Fed
2 Chermin Blandonnet
Geneva 1215, SWITZERLAND

Mosley, Mike (Football Player)
Buffalo Bills
109 Heritage Hill Rd
Wimberley, TX 78676-5632, USA

Mosley, Norm (Football Player)
Pittsburgh Steelers
1056 53rd St S
Birmingham, AL 35222-4038, USA

Mosley, Roger E (Actor)
4470 W Sunset Blvd # 107-342
Los Angeles, CA 90027-6302, USA

Mosley, Russ (Football Player)
Green Bay Packers
5577 Cherry Tree Cir
Blytheville, AR 72315-3862, USA

Mosley, Walter (Writer)
c/o Rosalie Swedlin *Industry Entertainment*
955 Carrillo Dr Ste 300
Los Angeles, CA 90048-5400, USA

Mosoke, Kintu (Prime Minister)
Prime Minister's Office
PO Box 341
Kampala, UGANDA

Mosquera, Julio (Baseball Player)
Toronto Blue Jays
1419 Stone Creek Dr
Tarpon Springs, FL 34689-3045, USA

Moss, Carrie-Anne (Actor)
c/o Staff Member *William Morris Agency (WMA-LA)*
1 William Morris Pl
Beverly Hills, CA 90212-4261, USA

Moss, Cynthia (Misc)
African Wildlife Foundation
Mara Road
PO Box 48177
Nairobi, KENYA

Moss, Damian (Baseball Player)
Atlanta Braves
1877 Ga Highway 19 S
Dublin, GA 31021-1480, USA

Moss, Eddie (Football Player)
St Louis Cardinals
15404 Eagle Estates Ct
Florissant, MO 63034, USA

Moss, Elisabeth (Actor)
United Talent Agency
9560 Wilshire Blvd Ste 500
Beverly Hills, CA 90212-2401, USA

Moss, Elza (Religious Leader)
Primitive Advent Christian Church
273 Frame Rd
Elkview, WV 25071-9626, USA

Moss, Eric Owen (Architect)
8557 Higuera St
Culver City, CA 90232-2535, USA

Moss, Geoffrey (Cartoonist)
315 E 68th St
New York, NY 10065-5692, USA

Moss, Jon
64 Knighton Park Rd
London, ENGLAND SE26 5RL, UNITED KINGDOM (UK)

Moss, Kate (Model)
c/o Staff Member *Storm Model Management Limited*
5 Jubilee Place Fl 5
London SW3 3TD, UNITED KINGDOM (UK)

Moss, Les (Baseball Player)
St Louis Browns
420 Tullis Ave
Longwood, FL 32750-5535, USA

Moss, Paige (Actor)
c/o Staff Member *Marshak/Zachary Company, The*
8840 Wilshire Blvd Fl 1
Beverly Hills, CA 90211-2606, USA

Moss, Perry (Football Player, Golfer)
2187 Deercroft Dr
Viera, FL 32940-6349, USA

Moss, Randy (Football Player)
c/o Team Member *Oakland Raiders*
1220 Harbor Bay Pkwy
Alameda, CA 94502-6570, USA

Moss, Roland (Football Player)
Baltimore Colts
411 Camelot Dr
Salisbury, NC 28144-9416, USA

Moss, Ronn (Actor)
2401 Nottingham Ave
Los Angeles, CA 90027-1036, USA

Moss, Santana (Football Player)
New York Jets
18619 SW 50th Ct
Miramar, FL 33029-6245, USA

Moss, Shirley (Artist)
Moss Studios
PO Box 18104
Anaheim, CA 92817-8104, USA

Moss, Stirling
46 Shepherd St. Mayfair
London, ENGLAND W1Y 8JN, UNITED KINGDOM (UK)

Moss, Tegan (Actor)
c/o Clayton Mathis *Envision Entertainment*
9255 W Sunset Blvd Ste 500
West Hollywood, CA 90069-3301, USA

Moss, Zefross (Football Player)
Indianapolis Colts
126 Kensington Dr
Madison, AL 35758-7844, USA

Mossbauer, Rudolf L (Nobel Prize Laureate)
Stumpflingstr 6A
Grunwald 82031, GERMANY

Mosser, Jonell (Musician)
Phil Mayo Co
PO Box 304
Bomoseen, VT 05732-0304, USA

Mossi, Don (Baseball Player)
Cleveland Indians
23250 Canyon Ln
Caldwell, ID 83607-7709, USA

Mossman, Doug
999 Kalapaki St
Honolulu, HI 96825-2707, USA

Most, Don (Actor)
6643 Buttonwood Ave
Oak Park, CA 91377-1326, USA

Most, Donny
280 S Beverly Dr Ste 400
Beverly Hills, CA 90212-3904, USA

Mostardo, Rich (Football Player)
Cleveland Browns
3376 Summit Rd
Ravenna, OH 44266-9015, USA

Mostert, Dutch (Artist)
93696 Mallard Ln
North Bend, OR 97459-8407, USA

Mostow, Jonathan (Director)
c/o Ken Stovitz *Creative Artists Agency LCC (CAA-LA)*
2000 Avenue Of The Stars
Los Angeles, CA 90067-4700, USA

Mota, Andres (Baseball Player)
Houston Astros
3395 Tareco Dr
Los Angeles, CA 90068-1527, USA

Mota, Jose (Baseball Player)
San Diego Padres
3395 Tareco Dr
Los Angeles, CA 90068-1527, USA

Mota, Manny (Baseball Player)
San Francisco Giants
3395 Tareco Dr
Los Angeles, CA 90068-1527, USA

Mota, Ross (Athlete, Track Athlete)
R Teatro 194 4 Esq
Porto 4100, PORTUGAL

Mote, Bobby (Rodeo Rider)
20840 NW Kachina Ave
Redmond, OR 97756-9226, USA

Mote, Kelley (Football Player)
Detroit Lions
41121 Ocean View Dr
Avon, NC 27915, USA

Moten, Mike (Football Player)
Arizona Cardinals
706 Loomis Ave
Daytona Beach, FL 32114-4724, USA

Mother Mother (Music Group)
c/o Staff Member *Paradigm (Monterey)*
509 Hartnell St
Monterey, CA 93940-2825, USA

Mothersbaugh, Mark
8760 W Sunset Blvd
West Hollywood, CA 90069-2206, USA

Motion, Andrew (Writer)
University of East Anglia
English Dept
Norwich NR4 7TJ, UNITED KINGDOM (UK)

Motion City Soundtrack (Music Group)
Asquared Management
2336 W Belmont Ave
Chicago, IL 60618-6423, USA

Motley, Darryl (Baseball Player)
Kansas City Royals
2847 Hertha Ave
Orlando, FL 32826-3329, USA

Motley, Isolde (Editor)
Life Magazine
Editorial Dept
Time-Life Building
New York, NY 10020, USA

Motley Crue (Music Group)
c/o Staff Member *Artist Group International (NY)*
150 E 58th St Fl 19
New York, NY 10155-1900, USA

Motorhead (Music Group)
98 Puddleton Cres Poole
Dorset, ENGLAND, UNITED KINGDOM (UK)

Mott, John C (Football Player)
New York Jets
215 Thistledown Ln
Hamilton, MT 59840-9153, USA

Mott, Steve (Football Player)
Detroit Lions
7018 N Highfield Dr
Birmingham, AL 35242-7239, USA

Mott, Stewart R (Politician)
515 Madison Ave
New York, NY 10022-5403, USA

Motta, Dick (Coach)
PO Box 4
Fish Haven, ID 83287-0004, USA

Mottelson, Ben R (Nobel Prize Laureate)
Nordita
Blegdamsvei 17
Copenhagen 2100, DENMARK

Mottola, Chad (Baseball Player)
Cincinnati Reds
6479 Lake Pembroke Pl
Orlando, FL 32829-7620, USA

Mottola, Greg (Director, Writer)
c/o Staff Member *United Talent Agency (UTA)*
9560 Wilshire Blvd Ste 500
Beverly Hills, CA 90212-2401, USA

Mottola, Thomas (Tommy) (Business Person)
c/o Staff Member *Casablanca Records*
8255 W Sunset Blvd
West Hollywood, CA 90046-2417, USA

Motton, Curt (Baseball Player)
Baltimore Orioles
19903 Quiet Valley Ct
Parkton, MD 21120-8917, USA

Motulsky, Amo G (Scientist)
4347 53rd Ave NE
Seattle, WA 98105-4938, USA

Motyka, Christopher (Actor)
c/o Staff Member *Bobby Ball Talent Agency*
4605 Lankershim Blvd Ste 721
North Hollywood, CA 91602-1878, USA

Motz, Diana Gribbon (Judge)
US Appeals Court
101 W Lombard St
Baltimore, MD 21201-2605, USA

Motzfeldt, Jonathan (Prime Minister)
Greenland Home Rule Government
PO Box 1015
Nuuk 3900, GREENLAND

Mouawad, Jerry (Director)
Imago Theater
PO Box 15182
Portland, OR 97293-5182, USA

Mould, Bob (Musician, Songwriter, Writer)
High Road
751 Bridgeway # 300
Sausalito, CA 94965-2165, USA

Moulder-Brown, John
193 Wardour St.
London, ENGLAND W1V 3FA, UNITED KINGDOM (UK)

Moulds, Eric (Football Player)
Buffalo Bills
5295 Briercliff Dr
Hamburg, NY 14075-3449, USA

Mouli (Actor, Bollywood)
12 Srinivasa Ave
Chennai, TN 600028, INDIA

Moulton, Sara (Chef, Television Host)
c/o Staff Member *Food Network, The*
75 9th Ave
New York, NY 10011-7006, USA

Mounsey, Tara (Hockey Player)
24 E Sugar Ball Rd
Concord, NH 03301-5803, USA

Mounsey, Yvonne (Ballerina)
Westside School of Ballet
1711 Stewart St
Santa Monica, CA 90404-4021, USA

Mount, Anson (Actor)
William Morris Agency
1325 Avenue Of The Americas
New York, NY 10019-6091, USA

Mount, Rick (Basketball Player)
904 Hopkins Rd
Lebanon, IN 46052-1436, USA

Mount, Thomas H (Tom) (Producer)
c/o Staff Member *Mount Film Company*
9245 Cordell Dr
Los Angeles, CA 90069-1753, USA

Mountcastle Jr, Vernon B (Misc)
6605 Walnutwood Cir
Baltimore, MD 21212-1214, USA

Mourning, Alonzo (Basketball Player)
3525 Anchorage Way
Coconut Grove, FL 33133-5923, USA

Mouse, Mickey (Club)
PO Box 10200
Lake Buena Vista, FL 32830-0200, USA

Mouskouri, Nana
12 rue Gutenberg
Boulogne F-92100, FRANCE

Moussier, Sabine (Actor)
c/o Staff Member *Televisa*
Blvd Adolfo Lopez Mateos 232
Colonia San Angel INN
DF CP 01060, MEXICO

Moustaki, Georges (Musician)
PolyGram Records
20 Rue des Fosses-Saint-Jacques
Paris 75005, FRANCE

Mouton, James (Baseball Player)
Houston Astros
1416 South Ave
Sacramento, CA 95838-4522, USA

Mouton, Leslie (Journalist)
1333 Northland Dr
Mendota Heights, MN 55120-1141, USA

Mouton, Lyle (Baseball Player)
Chicago White Sox
4101 Auston Way
Palm Harbor, FL 34685-4014, USA

Movessian, Victoria (Viki) (Hockey Player)
17 Webb St
Lexington, MA 02420-2219, USA

Movita
2766 Motor Ave
Los Angeles, CA 90064-3436, USA

Mowat, Farley M (Writer)
18 King St
Port Hope, ON L1A 2R4, CANADA

Mowatt, Ezekial (Football Player)
New York Giants
245 Prospect Ave Apt 2B
Hackensack, NJ 07601-2571, USA

Mower, Patrick (Actor)
c/o Staff Member *Burnett Granger & Assoc*
Prince of Wales Theatre
31 Coventy St
London W1D 6AS, UNITED KINGDOM (UK)

Mowerson, Robert (Swimmer)
2601 Kenzle Terrace #324
Minneapolis, MN 55418, USA

Mowrey, Caitlin (Actor)
c/o Staff Member *William Morris Agency (WMA-LA)*
1 William Morris Pl
Beverly Hills, CA 90212-4261, USA

Mowrey, Dude (Musician)
Joe Taylor Artist Agency
2802 Columbine Pl
Nashville, TN 37204-3104, USA

Mowry, Tahj (Actor)
c/o Staff Member *DRM Management*
PO Box 5009
Woodland Hills, CA 91365-5009, USA

Mowry, Tamera (Actor, Producer)
c/o Christopher Barrett *Metropolitan*
4500 Wilshire Blvd Fl 2
Los Angeles, CA 90010-3858, USA

Mowry, Tia (Actor)
c/o Darlene Mowry *DRM Management*
PO Box 5009
Woodland Hills, CA 91365-5009, USA

Moxey, John Llewellyn (Director)
Shapiro-Lichtman
1333 Beverly Green Dr
Los Angeles, CA 90035-1018, USA

Moyer, Jamie (Baseball Player)
Chicago Cubs
2550 40th Ave W
Seattle, WA 98199-3112, USA

Moyer, Ken (Football Player)
Cincinnati Bengals
3896 Magma Ct
Mason, OH 45040-2896, USA

Moyer, Paul (Correspondent)
12742 Highwood St
Los Angeles, CA 90049-2624, USA

Moyers, Bill D (Correspondent)
151 Central Park W
New York, NY 10023-1514, USA

Moyet, Alison (Musician)
Primary Talent
2-12 Petonville Road
London N1 9PL, UNITED KINGDOM (UK)

Moyle, Allan (Director, Writer)
Becsey Wisdom Kalajian
849 S Wooster St Apt 7
Los Angeles, CA 90035-1792, USA

Moynahan, Bridget (Actor, Model)
c/o Patrick Whitesell *Endeavor Agency LLC (LA)*
9601 Wilshire Blvd Fl 3
Beverly Hills, CA 90210-5204, USA

Moynihan, Christopher (Actor)
c/o Staff Member *OmniPop Inc (LA)*
4605 Lankershim Blvd Ste 201
North Hollywood, CA 91602-1874, USA

Moynihan, Colin B (Government Official)
Crown Reach
16 Grosvenor Road
London SW1V 3JV, UNITED KINGDOM (UK)

Moyroud, Louis M (Inventor)
202 Grove Way
Delray Beach, FL 33444-2920, USA

Mphahele, Ezekiel (Writer)
5444 Zone 5
Pimville
Johannesburg, SOUTH AFRICA

Mr, Cheeks (Musician)
Agency Group Ltd
1775 Broadway Ste 515
New York, NY 10019-1903, USA

Mr Blackwell (Designer, Fashion Designer)
531 S Windsor Blvd
Los Angeles, CA 90020-4715, USA

Mr T (Actor)
15208 La Maida St
Sherman Oaks, CA 91403, USA

Mraz, Jason (Musician, Songwriter)
c/o Bill Silva *Bill Silva Management*
8225 Santa Monica Blvd
West Hollywood, CA 90046-5912, USA

Mrkonic, George (Football Player)
Philadelphia Eagles
5712 Lowell St
Shawnee Mission, KS 66202-2248, USA

Mrosko, Robert (Football Player)
Houston Oilers
14853 Thompson Ave
Middlefield, OH 44062-9589, USA

Mroudjae, Ali (Prime Minister)
BP 58 Rond Point Gobadjou
Moroni, COMOROS

Mrozinski, Ron (Baseball Player)
Philadelphia Phillies
8 Autumn Ln
Hackettstown, NJ 07840-4703, USA

Msuya, Cleopa D (Prime Minister)
Prime Minister's Office
PO Box 980
Dodoma, TANZANIA

Mswati III (King)
Royal Palace
PO Box 1
Mbabane, SWAZILAND

Mu'all, Sheikh Rashid bin Ahmed al (Politician)
Ruler's Place
Umm Al Quwain
UNITED ARAB EMIRATES

Mubarak, Muhammad Hosni (General, President)
Presidential Palace
Abdeen
Cairo, EGYPT

Muccino, Gabriele (Director, Writer)
c/o Ken Stovitz *Creative Artists Agency LCC (CAA-LA)*
2000 Avenue Of The Stars
Los Angeles, CA 90067-4700, USA

Mucha, Barb (Golfer)
5922 Crystal View Dr
Orlando, FL 32819-4207, USA

Mucke, Manuela (Athlete)
Charlottenstr 13
Berlin 10315, GERMANY

Muckensturm, Jerry (Football Player)
Chicago Bears
4209 Hickory Ln
Jonesboro, AR 72401-8430, USA

Muckler, John (Coach)
Ottawa Senators
1000 Palladium Dr
Kanata, ON K2V 1A4, CANADA

Mudd, Howard E (Coach, Football Player)
San Francisco 49ers
1776 E 106th St
Carmel, IN 46032-4002, USA

Mudd, Jodie (Golfer)
3512 Mildred Dr
Louisville, KY 40216-4341, USA

Mudd, Roger
7167 Old Dominion Dr
McLean, VA 22101-2705, USA

Mudge-Cato, Nancy (Baseball Player)
23019 County Road 1
Elk River, MN 55330-9437, USA

Mudra, Darrell (Coach, Football Coach)
424 Tiger Hammock Rd
Crawfordville, FL 32327-1470, USA

Mudrock, Phil (Baseball Player)
Chicago Cubs
2548 E 6600 S
Salt Lake City, UT 84121-2346, USA

Mudvayne (Music Group)
c/o Chuck Toler *Anger Management*
6907 University Ave # 199
Middleton, WI 53562-2767, USA

Muehlheuser, Frank (Football Player)
Boston Yankees
780 County Road 579
Pittstown, NJ 08867-5152, USA

Muelhaupt Jr, Chuck (Football Player)
Buffalo Bills
4111 Tonawanda Dr
Des Moines, IA 50312-2911, USA

Muelier, Charles W (Business Person)
Ameren Corp
1901 Chouteau Ave
Saint Louis, MO 63103-3003, USA

Mueller, Bill (Baseball Player)
San Francisco Giants
11868 Charlemagne Dr
Maryland Heights, MO 63043-1506, USA

Mueller, Don (Baseball Player)
New York Giants
11224 Mueller Ln
Maryland Heights, MO 63043, USA

Mueller, Gordy (Baseball Player)
Boston Red Sox
7115 Wheeler Park Cir
Easton, MD 21601-8448, USA

Mueller, Les (Baseball Player)
Detroit Tigers
PO Box 294
Millstadt, IL 62260-0294, USA

Mueller, Vance (Football Player)
Los Angeles Raiders
8141 Damico Dr
El Dorado Hills, CA 95762-5482, USA

Mueller, Willard (Baseball Player)
Milwaukee Brewers
2320 Tolbert Ln
West Bend, WI 53090-1234, USA

Mueller-Bajda, Dolores (Baseball Player)
2913 N Linder Ave
Chicago, IL 60641-4812, USA

Mueller-Stahl, Armin (Actor)
c/o ZBF
Ordensmeisterstr. 15-16
Berlin D-12099, GERMANY

Muellner, William (Football Player)
Chicago Cardinals
727 Sherwood Rd
La Grange Park, IL 60526-1545, USA

Muench, David (Photographer)
PO Box 30500
Santa Barbara, CA 93130-0500, USA

Muetterties, Earl L (Misc)
University of California
Chemistry Dept
Berkeley, CA 94720-0001, USA

Muetzelfeldt, Bruno (Religious Leader)
Lutheran World Federation
150 Rt de Femey
Geneva 20 1211, SWITZERLAND

Muffett, Billy (Baseball Player)
St Louis Cardinals
1145 Finks Hideaway Rd
Monroe, LA 71203-2425, USA

Mugabe, Robert G (President)
President's Office
Munhumutapa Bldg
Samora Machel Ave
Harare, ZIMBABWE

Mugler, Thierry (Designer, Fashion
Designer)
4-6 Rue Aux Ours
Paris 75003, FRANCE

Muhammad, Elijah
7351 S Stony Island Ave
Chicago, IL 60649-3106, USA

Muhammad, Wallace D (Religious
Leader)
American Muslim Mission
7351 S Stony Island Ave
Chicago, IL 60649-3106, USA

Muir, Roger
10 Druid Hill Ave
Methuen, MA 01844-3210, USA

Muir DeGraad, Karen (Swimmer)
Applebosch State Hospital
Ozwatini
Natal, SOUTH AFRICA

Muirhead, Brian (Astronomer, Scientist)
Jet Propulsion Laboratory
4800 Oak Grove Dr
Pasadena, CA 91109-8001, USA

Muirsheil of Kilmacolm, Viscount
(Government Official)
Knapps
Kilmacolm
Renfrewshire, SCOTLAND

Mujica, Aylin (Actor)
c/o Staff Member TV Azteca
Periferico Sur 4121
Colonia Fuentes del Pedregal
DF CP 14141, MEXICO

Mukaddam, Ali (Actor)
c/o Yanick Landry Edward G Agency
19 Isabella St
Toronto, ON M4Y 1M7, CANADA

Mukai, Chiaki Naito (Astronaut)
15836 Seahorse Dr # 253
Houston, TX 77062-6222, USA

Mukhamedov, Irek J (Ballerina)
Royal Ballet
Covent Garden Bow St
London WC2E 9DD, UNITED KINGDOM
(UK)

Mukherjee, Bharati (Writer)
130 Rivoli St
San Francisco, CA 94117-4341, USA

Mukherjee, Hrishikesh (Bollywood,
Director, Filmmaker, Producer)
123A Anupama Carter Road
Bandra
Bombay, MS 400 050, INDIA

Mukherjee, Rani (Actor, Bollywood)
B/405 Shakti Apartments
Kaylan Complex Yari Road Versova
Mumbai, MS 400061, INDIA

Mulari, Tarja (Speed Skater)
Motion Oy
Vanhan Mankkaantie 33
Espoo 02180, FINLAND

Mulcahy, Anne
Xerox Corp
800 Long Ridge Rd
Stamford, CT 06902-1288, USA

Mulcahy, J Patrick (Business Person)
Raiston Purina Co
Checkerboard Square
Saint Louis, MO 63164-0001, USA

Mulcahy, Russell (Director)
Agency For Performing Arts
405 S Beverly Dr Ste 500
Beverly Hills, CA 90212-4425, USA

Muldaur, Diana (Actor)
20 Cummings Way
Edgartown, MA 02539, USA

Muldaur, Maria (Musician, Songwriter,
Writer)
Piedmont Talent
PO Box 680006
Charlotte, NC 28216-0001, USA

Mulder, Karen (Model)
*c/o Staff Member Elite Model
Management (NY)*
111 E 22nd St
New York, NY 10010-5400, USA

Mulder, Mark (Baseball Player)
*c/o Staff Member Saint Louis Cardinals (St
Louis Cardinals)*
250 Stadium Plz
Saint Louis, MO 63102, USA

Muldoon, Leslie L (Doctor)
Oregon Health Sciences University
Neurology Dept
Portland, OR 97201, USA

Muldoon, Patrick (Actor, Model)
11030 Ventura Blvd Ste 3
Studio City, CA 91604-3571, USA

Muldoon, Paul B (Writer)
Princeton University
Creative Writing Program
Princeton, NJ 08544-0001, USA

Muldowney, Dominic J (Composer)
Royal National Theater
Music Dept
South Bank
London SE1 1PX, UNITED KINGDOM
(UK)

Mulgrew, Kate (Actor)
Marie Ambrosino Mgmt
12740 Pacific Ave Apt 5
Los Angeles, CA 90066-4238, USA

Mulhern, Matt (Actor)
Gold Marshak Liedtke
3500 W Olive Ave Ste 1400
Burbank, CA 91505-5512, USA

Mulhern, Sinead (Opera Singer)
Van Walsum Mgmt
4 Addison Bridge Place
London W14 8XP, UNITED KINGDOM
(UK)

Mulholland, Terry (Baseball Player)
San Francisco Giants
4011 E Claremont St
Paradise Valley, AZ 85253-3901, USA

Mulis, Kary B (Nobel Prize Laureate)
Vyrex
2519 Avenida De La Palaya
La Jolla, CA 92037, USA

Mulitalo, Edwin (Football Player)
Baltimore Ravens
110 Santa Barbara Ave
Daly City, CA 94014-1045, USA

Mulkerin, Ted (Writer)
*c/o Staff Member Endeavor Agency LLC
(LA)*
9601 Wilshire Blvd Fl 3
Beverly Hills, CA 90210-5204, USA

Mulkey, Chris (Actor)
Paradigm Agency
10100 Santa Monica Blvd Ste 2500
Los Angeles, CA 90067-4116, USA

Mulkey-Robertson, Kim (Basketball
Player, Coach)
Baylor University
Athletic Dept
Waco, TX 76798, USA

Mull, Martin (Actor)
338 S Chadbourne Ave
Los Angeles, CA 90049-3709, USA

Mullady, Tom (Football Player)
New York Giants
2855 Crooked Oak Dr
Germantown, TN 38138-7614, USA

Mullally, Megan (Actor, Musician)
*c/o Dannielle Thomas Untitled
Entertainment (LA)*
331 N Maple Dr Fl 3
Beverly Hills, CA 90210-3827, USA

Mullan, Peter (Writer)
*c/o Staff Member International Creative
Management (ICM-LA)*
10250 Constellation Blvd
Los Angeles, CA 90067-6200, USA

Mullane, Richard M (Mike) (Astronaut)
1301 Las Lomas Rd NE
Albuquerque, NM 87106-4527, USA

Mullaney, Mark (Football Player)
Minnesota Vikings
13490 Essex Ct
Eden Prairie, MN 55347-1710, USA

Mullany, Mitch (Television Host)
*c/o Barry Katz New Wave Entertainment
(LA)*
2660 W Olive Ave
Burbank, CA 91505-4525, USA

Mullavy, Greg
1818 Thayer Ave Apt 303
Los Angeles, CA 90025-4965, USA

Mullen, Ford (Baseball Player)
Philadelphia Phillies
1841 Trosper Rd SW Trlr 8
Tumwater, WA 98512, USA

Mullen, Josep P (Joey) (Hockey Player)
126 Fieldgate Dr
Pittsburgh, PA 15241, USA

Mullen, Larry Jr (Musician)
Principle Mgmt
30-32 Sir John Rogerson Quay
Dublin 2, IRELAND

Mullen, Michael G (Admiral)
Vice Chief Of Naval Operations
Hqusn Pentagon
Washington, DC 20350-0001, USA

Mullen, Nicole (Musician)
*c/o Staff Member Creative Artists Agency
LCC (CAA-LA)*
2000 Avenue Of The Stars
Los Angeles, CA 90067-4700, USA

Mullen, Rodney (Skateboarder)
c/o Staff Member HarperCollins Publishers
10 E 53rd St Fl 1
New York, NY 10022-5244, USA

Mullen, Scott (Baseball Player)
Kansas City Royals
1105 13th St
Port Royal, SC 29935-1950, USA

Mullen, Tom (Football Player)
New York Giants
107 Greenbriar Ridge Ct
Saint Louis, MO 63122-3355, USA

Muller, Egon (Motorcycle Race,
Motorcycle Racer)
Dorfstr 17
Rodenbek, Kiel 24247, GERMANY

Muller, Elisabeth
. Feld 14
Sempach/Lu 6204, SWITZERLAND

Muller, Gerd (Soccer Player)
Neuestr 21
Munich 81479, GERMANY

Muller, Jennifer (Choreographer, Dancer)
Muller/Works Foundation
131 W 24th St
New York, NY 10011-1942, USA

Muller, Jorg (Race Car Driver)
Insert Motorsport
Fassoldshof 1
Mainleus 95336, GERMANY

Muller, K ALex (Nobel Prize Laureate)
IBM Research Laboratory
Saumerstr 4
Ruschlikon 8803, SWITZERLAND

Muller, Lillian (Actor, Model)
PO Box 20029-414
Encino, CA 91416, USA

Muller, Lisel (Writer)
LSU Press
PO Box 25053
Baton Rouge, LA 70894-5053, USA

Muller, Marcia (Writer)
Mysterious Press
1271 6th Ave
Warner Books
New York, NY 10020-1300, USA

Muller, Michel (Actor, Writer)
c/o Celine Kamina *ArtMedia*
20 av Rapp
Paris 75007, FRANCE

Muller, Peter (Architect)
PO Box 545
Clare, SA 5453, AUSTRALIA

Muller, Peter (Skier)
Haldenstr 18
Adliswil 8134, SWITZERLAND

Muller, Robby (Cinematographer)
Smith/Gosnell/Nicholson
PO Box 1156
Studio City, CA 91614-0156, USA

Muller, Robert (Misc)
Federal Bureau of Investigation
9th & Pennsylvania NW
Washington, DC 20535-0001, USA

Muller, Steven (Educator)
21st Century Foundation
919 18th St NW Ste 800
Washington, DC 20006-5509, USA

Muller-Stahl, Armin (Actor)
Gartenweg 31
Sierksdorf 23730, GERMANY

Muller-Westernhagen, Marius
Mittelweg 69
Hamburg D-20149, GERMANY

Mulley of Manor Park, Frederick W
(Government Official)
House of Lords
Westminster
London SW1A 0PW, UNITED KINGDOM
(UK)

Mulligan, Gerry (Writer)
c/o Staff Member *3 Arts Entertainment Inc*
9640 Wilshire Blvd Fl 7
Beverly Hills, CA 90212-2713, USA

Mulligan, Robert P (Director)
JV Broffman
5150 Wilshire Blvd # 505
Los Angeles, CA 90036-4302, USA

Mulligan, Sean (Baseball Player)
San Diego Padres
24474 Eastgate Dr
Diamond Bar, CA 91765-4626, USA

Mulligan, Wayne (Football Player)
St Louis Cardinals
2410 The Haul Over
Johns Island, SC 29455-6103, USA

Mulliken, William (Bill) (Swimmer)
4216 N Keeler Ave
Chicago, IL 60641-2271, USA

Mullin, Chris (Baseball Player)
116 Laurelwood Dr
Danville, CA 94506-1408, USA

Mullin, J Stanley (Skier)
Sheppard Mullin Richter Hampton
333 S Hope St
Los Angeles, CA 90071-1448, USA

Mullin, Leo F (Business Person)
Delta Air Lines
Hartsfield International Airport
Atlanta, GA 30320, USA

Mulliniks, Rance (Baseball Player)
California Angels
2614 S Peppertree St
Visalia, CA 93277-5507, USA

Mullins, Eric (Football Player)
Houston Oilers
3249 Parkwood Dr
Houston, TX 77021-1136, USA

Mullins, Fran (Baseball Player)
Chicago White Sox
9226 Ritenour Ct
Lone Tree, CO 80124-8971, USA

Mullins, Gerry (Football Player)
Pittsburgh Steelers
1108 Mohawk Rd
Mc Donald, PA 15057-2552, USA

Mullins, Greg (Baseball Player)
Milwaukee Brewers
PO Box 443
Florahome, FL 32140-0443, USA

Mullins, Jeffrey (Jeff) (Basketball Player)
8866 N Sea Oaks Way Apt 202
Vero Beach, FL 32963-4195, USA

Mullins, Larry (Model)
U2
30-32 Sir John Rogerson's Quarry
Dublin, IRELAND

Mullins, Shawn (Musician, Songwriter, Writer)
High Road
751 Bridgeway # 300
Sausalito, CA 94965-2165, USA

Mullova, Viktoria Y (Musician)
Askonas Holt Ltd
27 Chancery Lane
London WC2A 1PF, UNITED KINGDOM
(UK)

Mulloy, Gardner (Tennis Player)
800 NW 9th Ave
Miami, FL 33136-3006, USA

Mulroney, Dermot (Actor)
c/o Steven Huvane *PMK/HBH Public Relations (PMK-LA)*
700 N San Vicente Blvd Ste G910
West Hollywood, CA 90069-5061, USA

Mulroney, Kieran
6100 Wilshire Blvd Ste 1170
Los Angeles, CA 90048-5116, USA

Mulroney, M Brian (Prime Minister)
47 Forden Crescent
Westmount, PQ H3Y 2Y5, CANADA

Muluzi, Bakili (President)
President's Office
Private Bag 301
Capitol City
Lilongwe 3, MALAWI

Mulva, James J (Business Person)
Conoco/Philips Inc
600 N Dairy Ashford St
Houston, TX 77079-1175, USA

Mulvey, Grant (Hockey Player)
491 S Hampshire Ave
Elmhurst, IL 60126-4105, USA

Mulvoy, Mark (Editor, Publisher)
Sports Illustrated Magazine
Rockefeller Center
New York, NY 10020, USA

Mumba, Samantha (Actor, Musician)
Polydor Records
1 Sussex Place
London W6 9XT, UNITED KINGDOM
(UK)

Mumley, Nick (Football Player)
New York Titans
1432 Audubon Dr
Columbus, IN 47203-1432, USA

Mumphord, Lloyd (Football Player)
Miami Dolphins
2316 Mumphord St
Victoria, TX 77901-7750, USA

Mumphrey, Jerry (Baseball Player)
St Louis Cardinals
7709 Fm 850
Tyler, TX 75705-2135, USA

Mumy, Bill (Actor)
11333 Moor Park St
PO Box 433
Studio City, CA 91602-2618, USA

Mumy, Liliana (Actor)
c/o Meredith Fine *Coast to Coast Talent Group*
3350 Barham Blvd
Los Angeles, CA 90068-1404, USA

Muna, Solomon Tandeng (Prime Minister)
PO Box 15 Mbengwi
Mono Division
North West Province, CAMEROON

Munchak, Michael A (Mike) (Football Player)
Houston Oilers
9155 Saddlebow Dr
Brentwood, TN 37027-6060, USA

Muncrief, Kevin (Golfer)
939 S Flood Ave
Norman, OK 73069-4504, USA

Mundae, Misty (Actor)
PO Box 447
Ringwood, NJ 07456-0447, USA

Mundell, Robert A (Nobel Prize Laureate)
35 Claremont Ave
New York, NY 10027-6815, USA

Mundy, Carl E Jr (General)
9308 Ludgale Dr
Alexandria, VA 22309, USA

Munitz, Barry A (Educator)
California State University Syetem
400 Golden Shore
Long Beach, CA 90802, USA

Muniz, Frankie (Actor)
c/o Michael Rotenberg *3 Arts Entertainment Inc*
9460 Wilshire Blvd Fl 7
Beverly Hills, CA 90212-2713, USA

Muniz, Manuel (Baseball Player)
Philadelphia Phillies
PO Box 6301
Caguas, PR 00726-6301, USA

Munk, Peter (Business Person)
Barrick Gold Corp
200 Bay St
Toronto, ON M5J 2J3, CANADA

Munk, Walter H (Geophysicist, Physicist)
9530 La Jolta Shores
La Jolla, CA 92037, USA

Munn, Allison (Actor)
c/o Steve Caserta *Sanders/Armstrong Management*
2120 Colorado Ave Ste 120
Santa Monica, CA 90404-3561, USA

Munn, Olivia (Talk Show Host)
c/o Loch Powell *Leverage Management*
3030 Pennsylvania Ave
Santa Monica, CA 90404-4112, USA

Munninghoff, Scott (Baseball Player)
Philadelphia Phillies
886 Laverty Ln
Cincinnati, OH 45230-3558, USA

Munos, Maria (Television Host)
c/o Staff Member *Entertainment Tonight (ET)*
5555 Melrose Ave
Mae West Bldg Fl 2
Los Angeles, CA 90038-3989, USA

Munoz, Bobby (Baseball Player)
New York Yankees
9040 NW 20th St
Pembroke Pines, FL 33024-3211, USA

Munoz, M Anthony (Football Player, Sportscaster)
Cincinnati Bengals
6529 Irwin Simpson Rd
Mason, OH 45040-9285, USA

Munoz, Mike (Baseball Player)
Los Angeles Dodgers
1000 Carroll Meadows Ct
Southlake, TX 76092-3830, USA

Munro, Alice (Writer)
PO Box 1133
Clinton, ON N0M 1L0, CANADA

Munro, Caroline (Admiral)
PO Box 2589
London W1A 3NQ, UNITED KINGDOM
(UK)

Munro, Dana G (Diplomat)
PO Box 317
Media, PA 19063-0317, USA

Munro, Ian (Editor)
Annals of Internal Medicine
34 Beacon St
Editorial Dept
Boston, MA 02108-1415, USA

Munro, J Richard (Publisher)
Time Warner Inc
Rockefeller Plaza
New York, NY 10020, USA

Munro, Lochlyn (Actor)
International Creative Mgmt
8942 Wilshire Blvd # 219
Beverly Hills, CA 90211-1908, USA

Munro, Peter (Baseball Player)
Toronto Blue Jays
4025 Gramercy St
Houston, TX 77025-1108, USA

Munsel, Patrice (Opera Singer)
PO Box 472
Schroon Lake, NY 12870-0472, USA

Munsey, Nelson (Football Player)
Baltimore Colts
12190 Cuyamaca College Dr E Unit 1212
El Cajon, CA 92019-4353, USA

Munson, Eric (Baseball Player)
Detroit Tigers
1574 W Yellowstone Way
Chandler, AZ 85248-4864, USA

Munson, John (Musician)
Monterey Peninsula Artists
509 Hartnell St
Monterey, CA 93940-2825, USA

Muntyan, Mikhail (Opera Singer)
16 N Iorga Str
#13
Chisnau 277012, MOLDOVA

Muppets, The
c/o Staff Member *Jim Henson Company (LA)*
1416 N La Brea Ave
Hollywood, CA 90028-7506, USA

Mura, Steve (Baseball Player)
San Diego Padres
31892 Old Oak Rd
Trabuco Canyon, CA 92679-3245, USA

Murad, Ferid (Nobel Prize Laureate)
2121 W Holcombe Blvd
Houston, TX 77030-3303, USA

Murad, Raza (Actor, Bollywood)
B 104 Mayfair Raviraj Oberoi Complex
Near Lakxmi Industrial Estate New Link
Road Andheri
Bombay, MS 400 058, INDIA

Muradov, Sakhat A (Government Official)
Turkmenistan Mejlis
17 Gogol St
Ashkhabad 744017, TURKMENISTAN

Murakami, Masanori (Baseball Player)
San Francisco Giants
1-4-15-1506 Nisho Ohi Shinagawa-KU
Tokyo 140-0015, JAPAN

Murakami, Ryu (Writer)
Kodansha Books
2-12-21 Otowa
Bunkyoku
Tokyo 112-8001, JAPAN

Murali (Actor, Bollywood)
3-77th Street
Chennai, TN 600083, INDIA

Muraliyev, Amangeldy (Prime Minister)
Prime Minister's Office
Ul Perromayskaya 57
Bishkek, KYRGYZSTAN

Muransky, Ed (Football Player)
Los Angeles Raiders
16221 Villarreal De Avila
Tampa, FL 33613-1083, USA

Muratova, Kira G (Director)
Proletarsjy Blvd 14B
#15
Odessa 270015, RUSSIA

Murayama, Makio (Scientist)
5010 Benton Ave
Bethesda, MD 20814-2804, USA

Murayama, Tomiichi (Prime Minister)
3-2-2 Chiyomachi Oita
Oita 870, JAPAN

Murcer, Bobby R (Baseball Player)
New York Yankees
5808 Chestnut Ct
Edmond, OK 73025-2513, USA

Murchison, Ira (Athlete, Track Athlete)
10113 S Sangamon St
Chicago, IL 60643-2228, USA

Murchison, Lee (Football Player)
Dallas Cowboys
1976 E Mariposa Rd
Stockton, CA 95205-7736, USA

Murciano, Jr, Enrique (Actor)
c/o Ilene Feldman *IFA Talent Agency*
8730 W Sunset Blvd Ste 490
Los Angeles, CA 90069-2248, USA

Murdoch, Murray (Hockey Player)
190 Dessa Dr
Hamden, CT 06517-2108, USA

Murdoch, Robert J (Bob) (Coach, Hockey Player)
410 11th Ave S
Cranbrook, BC V1C 2P9, CANADA

Murdoch, Rupert (Publisher)
News America Publishing
1211 Avenue Of The Americas
New York, NY 10036-8701, USA

Murdoch, Stuart (Musician, Songwriter, Writer)
Legends of 21st Century
7 Trinity Row
Florence, MA 01062-1931, USA

Murdock, David H (Business Person)
10900 Wilshire Blvd Ste 1600
Los Angeles, CA 90024-6538, USA

Murdock, George (Actor)
5733 Sunfield Ave
Lakewood, CA 90712-1823, USA

Murdock, George P (Doctor)
Wynnewood Plaza #107
Wynnewood, PA 19096, USA

Murdock, Guy (Football Player)
Houston Oilers
106 Medinah Ln
Tower Lakes, IL 60010-1350, USA

Murdock, Shirley (Musician)
Millennium Entertainment Group
1319 5th Ave N
Nashville, TN 37208-2725, USA

Muresan, Georghe (Actor, Basketball Player)
New Jersey Nets
390 Murray Hill Pkwy
East Rutherford, NJ 07073-2109, USA

Murff, Red (Baseball Player)
Milwaukee Braves
5401 Hollytree Dr Apt 1301
Tyler, TX 75703-3467, USA

Muris, Timothy (Government Official)
Federal Trade Commission
Pennsylvania Ave & 6th St NW
Washington, DC 20580-0001, USA

Muris, Timothy J (Educator, Government Official)
George Mason University
Law School
Fairfax, VA 22030, USA

Murphey, Michael Martin (Musician, Songwriter, Writer)
Wildfire Productions
1105 16th Ave S Ste D
Nashville, TN 37212-2327, USA

Murphy, Ben (Actor)
2690 Rambla Pacifico St
Malibu, CA 90265-3423, USA

Murphy, Bill (Football Player)
Boston Patriots
6411 SW 25th St
Excel Communications
Miramar, FL 33023-2829, USA

Murphy, Billy (Baseball Player)
New York Mets
7511 44th St W Apt 21
University Place, WA 98466-3771, USA

Murphy, Bob (Baseball Player, Sportscaster)
New York Mets
220 Coral Cay Ter
Palm Beach Gardens, FL 33418-4003, USA

Murphy, Bob (Golfer)
11910 N Lake Dr
Boynton Beach, FL 33436-5556, USA

Murphy, Brian
265 Liverpool Rd
London, ENGLAND N1 1LX, UNITED KINGDOM (UK)

Murphy, Brittany (Actor)
c/o Staff Member *Media Talent Group*
9200 W Sunset Blvd Ste 810
W Hollywood, CA 90069-3603, USA

Murphy, Calvin J (Basketball Player)
43 Sterling St
Sugar Land, TX 77479-2934, USA

Murphy, Carolyn (Model)
I M G Models
304 Park Ave S # 1200
New York, NY 10010-4301, USA

Murphy, Caryle M (Journalist)
Washington Post
Editorial Dept
1150 15th St NW
Washington, DC 20071-0001, USA

Murphy, Charles Q (Actor)
c/o Lorrie Bartlett *Gersh Agency, The (LA)*
232 N Canon Dr
Beverly Hills, CA 90210-5302, USA

Murphy, Charles S (Government Official)
100 Bluff View Dr Apt 503C
Belleair Bluffs, FL 33770-1376, USA

Murphy, Cillian (Actor)
c/o Staff Member *United Talent Agency (UTA)*
9560 Wilshire Blvd Ste 500
Beverly Hills, CA 90212-2401, USA

Murphy, Dale (Baseball Player)
Atlanta Braves
467 Aspen Ridge Ln
Alpine, UT 84004-1223, USA

Murphy, Dan (Baseball Player)
San Diego Padres
19661 Symeron Rd
Apple Valley, CA 92307-4736, USA

Murphy, Danny (Baseball Player)
Chicago Cubs
5030 Champion Blvd # 6226
Boca Raton, FL 33496-2473, USA

Murphy, Diana E (Judge)
US Court of Appeals
300 S 4th St
Minneapolis, MN 55415-1320, USA

Murphy, Dick (Baseball Player)
Cincinnati Reds
6890 Connie Dr
Avon, IN 46123-8532, USA

Murphy, Donna (Actor, Musician)
Gerson Saines
250 W 57th St Ste 2303
New York, NY 10107-2399, USA

Murphy, Dwayne (Baseball Player)
Oakland A's
1811 S Karen Dr
Chandler, AZ 85286-6350, USA

Murphy, Ed (Basketball Player, Coach)
University of Mississippi
Smith Coliseum
University, MS 38677, USA

Murphy, Eddie (Actor, Comedian)
c/o Jim Wiatt *William Morris Agency (WMA-LA)*
1 William Morris Pl
Beverly Hills, CA 90212-4261, USA

Murphy, Erin (Actor)
c/o Staff Member *James/Levy/Jacobson Management*
3500 W Olive Ave Ste 1470
Burbank, CA 91505-5514, USA

Murphy, Lawrence T (Larry) (Hockey Player)
927 S Bates St
Birmingham, MI 48009-1974, USA

Murphy, Mark (Football Player)
Washington Redskins
736 Michigan Ave
Evanston, IL 60202-2512, USA

Murphy, Mark H (Musician)
Prince/SF Productions
1450 Southgate Ave Apt 206
Daly City, CA 94015-4021, USA

Murphy, Mark S (Football Player)
Green Bay Packers
1020 Ruby St NW
Hartville, OH 44632-9651, USA

Murphy, Michael
9830 Wilshire Blvd
Beverly Hills, CA 90212-1804, USA

Murphy, Michael Martin
4077 State Hwy. 68
Rancho De Taos, NM 87557, USA

Murphy, Michael R (Judge)
US Court of Appeals
125 S State St
Federal Building
Salt Lake City, UT 84138-1102, USA

Murphy, Mike (Coach, Hockey Player)
317 15th St
Manhattan Beach, CA 90266-4605, USA

Murphy, Peter (Musician)
c/o Staff Member *11 Eleven Management*
1284 Arthur Linsmer
Montreal, PQ H4N 3E3, CANADA

Murphy, Raymond D (War Hero)
4677 Sutton St NW
Albuquerque, NM 87114-4239, USA

Murphy, Reg (Editor, Publisher)
National Geographic Society
1145 17th St NW
Washington, DC 20036-4688, USA

Murphy, Richard W (Diplomat)
16 Sutton Pl # 9A
New York, NY 10022-3057, USA

Murphy, Rob (Baseball Player)
Cincinnati Reds
44 S Sewalls Point Rd
Sewalls Point, FL 34996-6728, USA

Murphy, Rosemary (Actor)
220 E 73rd St
New York, NY 10021-4319, USA

Murphy, Ryan (Director, Producer, Writer)
c/o Kevin Huvane *Creative Artists Agency LCC (CAA-LA)*
2000 Avenue Of The Stars
Los Angeles, CA 90067-4700, USA

Murphy, Sean (Golfer)
1004 June Pl
Lovington, NM 88260-4521, USA

Murphy, Terry (Entertainer)
Sherry Ingram
3575 Cahuenga Blvd W Ste 600
Los Angeles, CA 90068-1345, USA

Murphy, Thomas (Tom) (Writer)
4 Garville Road
Dublin 6, IRELAND

Murphy, Tom (Baseball Player)
California Angels
26561 Via Sacramento
Capistrano Beach, CA 92624-1337, USA

Murphy, Troy (Basketball Player)
404 W Mountain Rd
Sparta, NJ 07871-3532, USA

Murphy-O'Connor, Cormac Cardinal
(Religious Leader)
Archbishop's House
Ambrosden Ave
London SW1P 1QJ, UNITED KINGDOM
(UK)

Murray, Albert L (Writer)
45 W 132nd St
New York, NY 10037-3101, USA

Murray, Andy (Hockey Player)
Los Angeles Kings
1111 S Figueroa St
Staples Center
Los Angeles, CA 90015-1300, USA

Murray, Anne (Musician)
Box 69030
12 St. Clair Ave East
Toronto, ON M4T 1K0, CANADA

Murray, Anne (Opera Singer)
Helge Rudolf Augstein
Sebastianplatz 3
Munich 80331, GERMANY

Murray, Bill (Actor, Comedian)
c/o David Nochimson *Ziffren Brittenham Branca Fischer Gilbert-Lurie, Stiffman & Cook*
1801 Century Park W
Los Angeles, CA 90067-6409, USA

Murray, Brain Doyle (Actor)
Abrams Artists
9200 W Sunset Blvd Ste 1125
Los Angeles, CA 90069-3610, USA

Murray, Bruce C (Scientist)
Jet Propulsion Laboratory
4800 Oak Grove Dr
Pasadena, CA 91109-8001, USA

Murray, Bryan C (Hockey Player)
2215 NE 32nd Ave
Fort Lauderdale, FL 33305-1856, USA

Murray, Calvin (Baseball Player)
San Francisco Giants
17434 Courtney Pine Cir
Spring, TX 77379-8505, USA

Murray, Chad Michael (Actor)
15030 Ventura Blvd # 710
Sherman Oaks, CA 91403-5470, USA

Murray, Charles A (Scientist)
American Enterprise Institute
1150 17th St NW
Washington, DC 20036-4670, USA

Murray, Charles P Jr (War Hero)
5906 Northridge Rd
Columbia, SC 29206-4336, USA

Murray, Cherry A (Business Person, Physicist)
Lucent technologies
700 Mountain Ave
New Providence, NJ 07974-1208, USA

Murray, Chris (Misc)
IBM T J Watson Research Center
PO Box 218
Yorktown Heights, NY 10598-0218, USA

Murray, Dale (Baseball Player)
Montreal Expos
RR 2 Box 1850
Yorktown, TX 78164, USA

Murray, Dan (Baseball Player)
New York Mets
4312 W 78th St
Prairie Village, KS 66208-4352, USA

Murray, Dan (Football Player)
Indianapolis Colts
9 Washington Rd
Ogdensburg, NJ 07439-1036, USA

Murray, Dave (Musician)
Sanctuary Music Mgmt
82 Bishop's Bridge Road
London W2 6BB, UNITED KINGDOM
(UK)

Murray, David K (Musician)
Joel Chriss
300 Mercer St Apt 3J
New York, NY 10003-6732, USA

Murray, Devon (Actor)
PO Box 814
Maynooth
Co. Kildare, IRELAND

Murray, Don (Actor)
1201 La Patera Canyon Rd
Goleta, CA 93117, USA

Murray, Doug (Cartoonist)
Marvel Comic Group
10 E 40th St Rm 900
New York, NY 10016-0201, USA

Murray, Eddie C (Baseball Player)
Baltimore Orioles
15319 Saddleback Rd
Canyon Country, CA 91387-4704, USA

Murray, Edward P (Eddie) (Football Player)
Detroit Lions
1070 Forest Bay Dr
Waterford, MI 48328-4284, USA

Murray, Elizabeth (Artist)
Paula Cooper Gallery
534 W 21st St
New York, NY 10011-2812, USA

Murray, Glenn (Baseball Player)
Philadelphia Phillies
41 W End St
Manning, SC 29102-2021, USA

Murray, Heath (Baseball Player)
San Diego Padres
1212 Stonyridge Ave
Troy, OH 45373-1548, USA

Murray, Joe (Football Player)
Los Angeles Rams
12900 Ridgemoor Dr
Prospect, KY 40059-8195, USA

Murray, Joel
PO Box 5617
Beverly Hills, CA 90209-5617, USA

Murray, John E Jr (Educator)
Duquesne University
President's Office
Pittsburgh, PA 15282-0001, USA

Murray, Jonathan (Producer)
c/o Staff Member *Bunim/Murray Productions Inc*
6007 Sepulveda Blvd
Van Nuys, CA 91411-2502, USA

Murray, Joseph E (Nobel Prize Laureate)
108 Abbott Rd
Wellesley Hills, MA 02481-6104, USA

Murray, Keith (Artist, Musician)
Famous Artists Agency
250 W 57th St
New York, NY 10107-0001, USA

Murray, Larry (Baseball Player)
New York Yankees
2851 Redwood Pkwy Apt 906
Vallejo, CA 94591-8656, USA

Murray, Margaret (Baseball Player)
1320 S Desert Meadows Cir Apt 3109
Green Valley, AZ 85614-1832, USA

Murray, Maritza (Artist)
c/o David Sweeney *Sweeney Management*
8755 Lookout Mountain Ave
Los Angeles, CA 90046-1861, USA

Murray, Matt (Baseball Player)
Atlanta Braves
109 Greenwood Ave
Swampscott, MA 01907-2124, USA

Murray, Michael (Musician)
4436 Zeller Rd
Columbus, OH 43214-2620, USA

Murray, Neil (Musician)
Int'l Talent Booking
27A Floral St
#300
London WC2E 9DQ, UNITED KINGDOM
(UK)

Murray, Peg (Actor)
800 Light House Ln
Southold, NY 11971, USA

Murray, Rich (Baseball Player)
San Francisco Giants
435 E 108th St
Los Angeles, CA 90061-2507, USA

Murray, Sean
8436 W 3rd St Ste 740
Los Angeles, CA 90048-4130, USA

Murray, Terence R (Terry) (Hockey Player)
Philadelphia Flyers
3601 S Broad St
1st Union Center
Philadelphia, PA 19148-5297, USA

Murray, Terrence (Terry) (Financier)
Fleet Boston Corp
1 Federal Corp
Boston, MA 02110, USA

Murray, Timothy V (Architect)
444 Springfield Road
Ottawa, ON K1M 0K4, CANADA

Murray, Tracy (Basketball Player)
4337 Marina City Dr
Marina Del Rey, CA 90292-5813, USA

Murray, Ty (Rodeo Rider)
1660 Private Road 1213
Stephenville, TX 76401-6215, USA

Murray-Leslie, Alex (Musician)
K Records
924 Jefferson St SE # 101
Olympia, WA 98501, USA

Murray of Epping Forest, Lionel (Len)
(Misc)
29 Crescent
Loughton
Essex 1G10 4PY, UNITED KINGDOM
(UK)

Murrell, Ivan (Baseball Player)
Houston Colt.45's
316 SE Inwood Ave
Port Saint Lucie, FL 34984-5113, USA

Murro, Noam (Director)
c/o Staff Member *Management 360*
9111 Wilshire Blvd
Beverly Hills, CA 90210-5508, USA

Murtagh, Kate (Actor)
19557 Tribune St
Northridge, CA 91326-2247, USA

Murukarni, Masanori (Baseball Player)
1-4-15-1506 Nisho Ohi Shinagawaku
Tokyo 140-0015, JAPAN

Musa, Said (Prime Minister)
Prime Minister's Office
East Bloc
Belmopan, BELIZE

Musabayev, Talgat A (Cosmonaut)
Potcha Kosmonavtov
Moskovskoi Oblasti
Syvisdny Goroduk 141160, RUSSIA

Musante, Tony (Actor)
38 Bedford St
New York, NY 10014-4413, USA

Musberger, Brent
47 W 66th St
New York, NY 10023-6201, USA

Musburger, Brent (Sportscaster)
286 Locha Dr
Jupiter, FL 33458-7733, USA

Muscarello, Carl
720 NW 71st Ave
Plantation, FL 33317-1125, USA

Muse (Music Group)
c/o Natasha Anderson *Agency Group Ltd, The (UK)*
361-373 City Road
London EC1V 1PQ, UNITED KINGDOM
(UK)

Muse, William V (Educator)
Auburn University
President's Office
Auburn University, AL 36849-0001, USA

Muser, Tony (Baseball Player)
Boston Red Sox
11222 Martha Ann Dr
Los Alamitos, CA 90720-2956, USA

Museveni, Yoweri K (President)
President's Office
PO Box 7108
Kampala, UGANDA

Musgrave, Bill (Football Player)
San Francisco 49ers
4062 Leprechan Way
Duluth, GA 30097-8147, USA

Musgrave, F Story (Astronaut)
8572 Sweetwater Trl
Kissimmee, FL 34747-1519, USA

Musgrave, Mandy (Actor)
c/o Adam Levine *Anthem Entertainment*
6100 Wilshire Blvd Ste 1170
Los Angeles, CA 90048-5116, USA

Musgrave, R Kenton (Judge)
US Court of International Trade
1 Federal Plz
New York, NY 10278-0001, USA

Musgrave, Spain (Football Player)
Washington Redskins
9727 Mount Pisgah Rd Apt 811
Silver Spring, MD 20903-2011, USA

Musgrave, Ted (Race Car Driver)
175 Lakeside Dr E
Port Orange, FL 32128-6620, USA

Musgrave, Thea (Composer)
Virginia Opera Assn
PO Box 2580
Norfolk, VA 23501-2580, USA

Musgraves, Dennis (Baseball Player)
New York Mets
RR 4
Centralia, MO 65240, USA

Musharraf, Parvez (President)
President's Office
Aiwan-e-Sadr
Mall & Mayo Roads
Islamabad, PAKISTAN

Mushok, Mike (Musician)
William Morris Agency
151 El Camino Dr
Beverly Hills, CA 90212-2775, USA

Musial, Stan (Baseball Player)
St Louis Cardinals
85 Trent Dr
Saint Louis, MO 63124-1032, USA

Music, The (Music Group)
c/o Staff Member *Paradigm (Monterey)*
509 Hartnell St
Monterey, CA 93940-2825, USA

Musiol, Bogdan (Athlete)
Fitness-Studio
Talstr 50
Zella-Mehlis 98544, GERMANY

Musiq (Musician)
Def Soul Records
825 8th Ave # 2700
New York, NY 10019-7416, USA

Musiq Soulchild (Music Group)
c/o Staff Member *Paradigm (Monterey)*
509 Hartnell St
Monterey, CA 93940-2825, USA

Musker, John (Animator, Director)
Walt Disney Productions
500 S Buena Vista St
Burbank, CA 91521-0001, USA

Musonge, Pater Mafani (Prime Minister)
Prime Minister's Office
Yaounde, BP 1057, CAMEROON

Mussa, Michael (Economist)
International Monetary Fund
700 19th St NW
Washington, DC 20431-0002, USA

Musselman, Jeff (Baseball Player)
Toronto Blue Jays
1842 Port Timmin Pl
Newport Beach, CA 92680, USA

Musselman, Ron (Baseball Player)
Seattle Mariners
5313 Autumn Dr
Wilmington, NC 28409-5701, USA

Mussill, Barney (Baseball Player)
Philadelphia Phillies
912 Moorland Dr
Grosse Pointe Woods, MI 48236-1131, USA

Mussina, Mike (Baseball Player)
Baltimore Orioles
1302 Spruce St
Montoursville, PA 17754-2116, USA

Musso, John (Football Player)
Chicago Bears
242 E 3rd St
Hinsdale, IL 60521-4221, USA

Mussolini, Alessandra (Government Official)
Italian Social Movement (MSI)
Chamber of Deputies
Rome 00100, ITALY

Must (Music Group)
c/o Staff Member *Wind-up Records*
72 Madison Ave Fl 8
New York, NY 10016-8731, USA

Mustaine, Dave (Musician)
ESP Mgmt
838 N Doheny Dr Apt 302
West Hollywood, CA 90069-4849, USA

Mustalov, Abdulkhashim M (Prime Minister)
Government House
Tashkent 700008, UZBEKISTAN

Mustan, Abbas (Actor, Bollywood)
119 Haveliwala Building 1st Floor
E R Road
Mumbai, MS 400003, INDIA

Muster, Brad (Football Player)
Chicago Bears
Santa Rosa Junior College
1501 Mendocino Ave Attn Football Program
Santa Rosa, CA 95401, USA

Muster, Thomas (Tennis Player)
370 Felter Ave
Hewlett, NY 11557-1132, USA

Mustin, Henry C (Admiral)
2347 S Rolle St
Arlington, VA 22202, USA

Mustonen, Olli (Composer, Musician)
Shuman Assoc
120 W 58th St Apt 8D
New York, NY 10019-2126, USA

Mutchie, Marjorie Ann
1169 Mary Cir
La Verne, CA 91750-4210, USA

Mutchnick, Max (Producer)
c/o Staff Member *Will & Grace*
4024 Radford Ave
Bungalow 3
Studio City, CA 91604-2101, USA

Muteba II, Ronald Muwenda (King)
Royal Palace
Kampala, UGANDA

Muth, Ellen (Actor)
c/o Barbara Gale *Envoy Entertainment*
3656 Dellvale Pl
Encino, CA 91436-4144, USA

Muth, Rene (Coach)
Pennsylvania State University
Athletic Dept
University Park, PA 16802, USA

Muthu, Kumari (Actor)
A-6 53 South West Boag Road
T Nagar
Chennai, TN 600 017, INDIA

Muti, Ornella (Actor)
33 Via Porta de Pinta
Bergamo 24100, ITALY

Muti, Riccardo
Via Corti Alle Mura 25
Ravenna 48100, ITALY

Muti, Richard
via Corti alle Mura 25
Ravenna 48100, ITALY

Mutis, Jeff (Baseball Player)
Cleveland Indians
630 E Wyoming St
Allentown, PA 18103-3536, USA

Mutombo, Dikembe (Basketball Player)
1300 Valley Rd
Villanova, PA 19085-2124, USA

Mutscheller, Jim (Football Player)
Baltimore Colts
12350 Rosslare Ridge Rd Unit 102
Lutherville Timonium, MD 21093-8233, USA

Mutschler, Carlfried (Architect)
E7
7
Mannheim 68159, GERMANY

Mutter, Anne-Sophie (Musician)
Effnerstr 48
Munich 81925, GERMANY

Mutter, Carol A (General)
Women Marines Assn
PO Box 8405
Falls Church, VA 22041-8405, USA

Muxworthy, Jake (Actor)
c/o Staff Member *United Talent Agency (UTA)*
9560 Wilshire Blvd Ste 500
Beverly Hills, CA 90212-2401, USA

Muzorewa, Abel T (Religious Leader)
PO Box 353
Borrowdale
Harare, ZIMBABWE

Mwanawasa, Levy P (President)
President's Office
State House
PO Box 135
Lusaka, ZAMBIA

Mwinyi, Ali Hassam (President)
President's Office
State House
PO Box 9120
Dar es Salaam, TANZANIA

My Chemical Romance (Music Group)
Eyeball Records
Eyeball Records
Kearny, NJ 07032, USA

Mya (Actor, Musician)
c/o Mark Winkler *United Talent Agency (UTA)*
9560 Wilshire Blvd Ste 500
Beverly Hills, CA 90212-2401, USA

Myer, Steve (Football Player)
Seattle Seahawks
423 E Mead Dr
Chandler, AZ 85249-5331, USA

Myers, A Maurice (Business Person)
Waste Management Inc
1001 Fannin St Ste 4000
Houston, TX 77002-6711, USA

Myers, Anne M (Religious Leader)
Church of the Brethren
1451 Dundee Ave
Elgin, IL 60120-1694, USA

Myers, Barton (Architect)
Barton Myers Assoc
9348 Civic Center Dr
Beverly Hills, CA 90210-3624, USA

Myers, Billie
PO Box 12198
Miami, FL 33101-2198, USA

Myers, Brett (Baseball Player)
Philadelphia Phillies
385 Summerset Dr
Saint Johns, FL 32259-8885, USA

Myers, Cynthia (Actor, Model)
PO Box 10
Llano, CA 93544-0010, USA

Myers, Danny (Race Car Driver)
Childress Racing
PO Box 1189
Industrial Dr
Welcome, NC 27374-1189, USA

Myers, Dee Dee (Actor, Writer)
c/o Ari Greenburg *Endeavor Agency LLC (LA)*
9601 Wilshire Blvd Fl 3
Beverly Hills, CA 90210-5204, USA

Myers, Dwight (Heavy D)
c/o Kevin Volchock *Endeavor Agency LLC (LA)*
9601 Wilshire Blvd Fl 3
Beverly Hills, CA 90210-5204, USA

Myers, Frank (Football Player)
Minnesota Vikings
3874 Woodhollow Dr Apt 410
Euless, TX 76040-7473, USA

Myers, Greg (Baseball Player)
Toronto Blue Jays
640 Westborough Ln
Riverside, CA 92506-7549, USA

Myers, Jack (Football Player)
Philadelphia Eagles
25 Biltmore Ln
Menlo Park, CA 94025-6686, USA

Myers, Jack D (Physicist)
University of Pittsburg
1291 Scaife Hall
Pittsburgh, PA 15261-2012, USA

Myers, Jimmy (Baseball Player)
Baltimore Orioles
7857 Sandywood Ln
Memphis, TN 38133-2868, USA

Myers, Lisa (Correspondent)
NBC-TV
4001 Nebraska Ave NW
News Dept
Washington, DC 20016-2733, USA

Myers, Margaret J (Dee Dee)
(Government Official)
Equal Time Show
1233 20th St NW Ste 302
Cbs-Tv
Washington, DC 20036-2482, USA

Myers, Mike (Actor, Comedian)
c/o Peter Levine *Creative Artists Agency LCC (CAA-LA)*
2000 Avenue Of The Stars
Los Angeles, CA 90067-4700, USA

Myers, Mike (Baseball Player)
Florida Marlins
337 High Ridge Way
Castle Rock, CO 80108-3422, USA

Myers, Norman (Scientist)
Upper Meadow Old Road
Headington
Oxford OX3 8SZ, UNITED KINGDOM
(UK)

Myers, Randy (Baseball Player)
New York Mets
15525 NE Caples Rd
Brush Prairie, WA 98606-8504, USA

Myers, Reginald R (War Hero)
PO Box 803
Annandale, VA 22003-0803, USA

Myers, Richard (Scientist)
Stanford University
Human Genome Center
Stanford, CA 94305, USA

Myers, Richard B (Dick) (General)
Chairman Joint Chiefs Of Staff
Pentagon
Washington, DC 20318-0001, USA

Myers, Richie (Baseball Player)
Chicago Cubs
521 Pony Trl
Mount Shasta, CA 96067-9063, USA

Myers, Rochelle (Writer)
3827 California St
San Francisco, CA 94118-1501, USA

Myers, Rod (Baseball Player)
Chicago Cubs
761 Davis St
Rockford, IL 61107-3145, USA

Myers, Roderick (Baseball Player)
Kansas City Royals
1816 S 3rd St
Conroe, TX 77301-5131, USA

Myers, Russell (Cartoonist)
Tribune Media Services
435 N Michigan Ave Ste 1500
Chicago, IL 60611-4012, USA

Myers, Terry Jo (Golfer)
11592 Timberline Cir
Fort Myers, FL 33966-5701, USA

Myers, Tikalsky Linda (Skier)
RR 5 Box 2651
Santa Fe, NM 87506, USA

Myers, Tom (Football Player)
New Orleans Saints
1815 Seven Maples Dr
Kingwood, TX 77345-1711, USA

Myers, Walter Dean (Photographer)
Scholastic Press
555 Broadway
New York, NY 10012-3919, USA

Myers Jr, Harry J (Publisher)
46 W Ranch Trl
Morrison, CO 80465-9504, USA

Myerson, Bess (Actor, Beauty Pageant
Winner, Lawyer)
3 E 71st St # 9A
New York, NY 10021-4154, USA

Myerson, Harvey (Attorney, Attorney
General, General)
Finley Kumble Wagner Assoc
425 Park Ave
New York, NY 10022-3506, USA

Myerson, Jacob M (Diplomat, Economist)
2 Rue Lucien-Gaulard
Paris 75018, FRANCE

Myette, Aaron (Baseball Player)
Chicago White Sox
14277 101a Ave
Surrey, BC V0B 2G2, CANADA

Myhre, Wencke
Im Vendla 22
Nesoya N-1315, NORWAY

Myles, Alannah (Musician)
Miracle Prestige
1 Water Lane
Camden Town
London NW1 8N2, UNITED KINGDOM
(UK)

Myles, Eve (Actor)
c/o *Torchwood Production Office*
BBC Television Centre
Cardiff, Wales, UNITED KINGDOM (UK)

Myles, Sophia (Actor)
c/o Staff Member *Personal Management
Company*
425 N Robertson Blvd
West Hollywood, CA 90048-1735, USA

Myre, Philippe (Phil) (Hockey Player)
101 Rue Dugas
Joliette, PQ J6E 4G7, CANADA

Myrick, Bob (Baseball Player)
New York Mets
32 Troon
Hattiesburg, MS 39401-8629, USA

Myrick, Daniel (Director)
Artisan Entertainment
2700 Colorado Ave
Santa Monica, CA 90404-3553, USA

Myrin, Arden (Actor)
c/o Steve Caserta *Sanders/Armstrong
Management*
2120 Colorado Ave Ste 120
Santa Monica, CA 90404-3561, USA

Myrtle, Chip (Football Player)
Denver Broncos
6010 S Lima Way
Englewood, CO 80111-5813, USA

Mysen, Bjorn O (Misc)
Camegie Institution
5221 Broad Branch Rd NW
Washington, DC 20015, USA

Myslinski, Tom (Football Player)
Washington Redskins
504 W Sycamore St
Rome, NY 13440-2631, USA

Mysterio, Rey (Wrestler)
Rey Mysterio Inc
PO Box 6039
Anaheim, CA 92816-0039, USA

Mystic (Musician)
WMA
151 El Camino Dr
Beverly Hills, CA 90212-2704, USA

Mystics
88 Amador St
Staten Island, NY 10303-1709, USA

Mystikal (Musician)
c/o Staff Member *International Creative
Management (ICM-LA)*
10250 Constellation Blvd
Los Angeles, CA 90067-6200, USA

N Chandra (Bollywood, Director,
Filmmaker, Producer)
Ankush 1 Belscot Units Lokhandwala
Complex
Andheri Linking Road Andheri
Bombay, MS 400 058, INDIA

Na-Ming
9903 Santa Monica Blvd # 575
Beverly Hills, CA 90212-1606, USA

Nabe, Ricky (Actor)
c/o Staff Member *Envision Entertainment*
9255 W Sunset Blvd Ste 500
West Hollywood, CA 90069-3301, USA

Naber, Jofin P (Swimmer)
PO Box 50107
Pasadena, CA 91115-0107, USA

Naber, John
PO Box 50107
Pasadena, CA 91115-0107, USA

Nabers, Drayton Jr (Business Person)
Protective Life Corp
2801 Highway 280 S
Birmingham, AL 35223-2488, USA

Nabhoiz, Chris (Baseball Player)
Montreal Expos
602 Kenwood Dr
Pottsville, PA 17901-9197, USA

Nabokov, Evgeni (Hockey Player)
San Jose Sharks
525 W Santa Clara St
San Jose Arena
San Jose, CA 95113-1500, USA

Nabors, Jim (Actor, Musician)
PO Box 10364
Honolulu, HI 96816-0364, USA

Nabors, Richard (Football Player)
1625 Brighton Ct
Beaumont, TX 77706-3220, USA

Naccarato, Vin (Musician)
Paramount Entertainment
PO Box 12
Far Hills, NJ 07931-0012, USA

Nachamkin, Boris (Basketball Player)
350 E 62nd St Apt 5J
New York, NY 10065-8261, USA

Nachmansohn, David (Misc)
560 Riverside Dr
New York, NY 10027-3202, USA

Nada Surf (Music Group)
c/o Staff Member *Paradigm (Monterey)*
509 Hartnell St
Monterey, CA 93940-2825, USA

Nadal, Rafael (Tennis Player)
c/o Staff Member *ATP Tour*
201 Atp Tour Blvd
Ponte Vedra Beach, FL 32082-3211, USA

Nader, Michael (Actor)
28 E 10th St
New York, NY 10003-6201, USA

Nader, Ralph (Activist)
1600 20th St NW
Washington, DC 20009-1001, USA

Nadiya (Actor, Bollywood)
A Block Door No 23
Anna Nagar
Chennai, TN 600102, INDIA

Nadon, Branden (Actor)
PMG Management
1118 Homer St 228
Vancouver, BC V6B 6L5, CANADA

Naehring, Tim (Baseball Player)
Boston Red Sox
7300 Pinehurst Dr
Cincinnati, OH 45244-3272, USA

Naeole, Chris (Football Player)
New Orleans Saints
1314 Charter Ct E
Jacksonville, FL 32225-2658, USA

Nafziger, Dana A (Football Player)
Tampa Bay Buccaneers
251 El Dorado Way
Pismo Beach, CA 93449-1535, USA

Nagakura, Saburo (Misc)
2-7-13 Higashicho
Kichijoji
Musashino, Tokyo 1800002, JAPAN

Nagano, Kent G
Van Walsum Mgmt
4 Addison Bridge Place
London W14 8XP, UNITED KINGDOM
(UK)

Nagarjuna (Actor, Bollywood)
29 Kasturi Rangan Rd
Alwarpet
Madras, TN 600018, INDIA

Nagashima, Shigeo (Baseball Player)
3-29-19 Denenchofu
Ohtaku
Tokyo 145, JAPAN

Nagel, Craig (Football Player)
New England Patriots
222 Woodcrest Dr
Loveland, OH 45140-7772, USA

Nagel, Sidney R (Physicist)
4913 S Kimbark Ave
Chicago, IL 60615-2954, USA

Nagel, Steven R (Astronaut)
16923 Cottonwood Way
Houston, TX 77059-3102, USA

Nagel, Thomas (Misc)
New York University
40 Washington Sq S
Law School
New York, NY 10012-1005, USA

Nagelson, Rusty (Baseball Player)
Cleveland Indians
4 Carriage Ct
Little Rock, AR 72211-2280, USA

Nagesh (Actor)
127 St Marys Road
Chennai, TN 600 018, INDIA

Naghma (Actor, Bollywood)
23 A Kalpak Aspen 1st Floor
Perry Cross Road Bandra
Bombay, MS 400 050, INDIA

Nagle, Browning (Football Player)
New York Jets
1153 Willow Bend Cv
Collierville, TN 38017-3479, USA

Nagler, Gern (Football Player)
Chicago Cardinals
73595 Agave Ln
Palm Desert, CA 92260-6685, USA

Nagma (Actor, Bollywood)
43 IInd Street
Navarathna Gardens Ekkaduthangal
Chennai, TN 600017, INDIA

Nagra, Parminder (Actor)
ARG
4 Great Portland St
London W1W 8PA, UNITED KINGDOM
(UK)

Nagy, Charles (Baseball Player)
Cleveland Indians
PO Box 102
Rancho Santa Fe, CA 92067-0102, USA

Nagy, Mike (Baseball Player)
Boston Red Sox
8 Indian Trl
Bronx, NY 10465-3813, USA

Nagy, Stanislaw Cardinal (Religious
Leader)
Priests of Sacred Heart
Via Casale S Piov 20
Rome 00126, ITALY

Nagy, Steve (Baseball Player)
Pittsburgh Pirates
2205 NE Ridgewood Dr
Poulsbo, WA 98370-8529, USA

Nahan, Stu (Sportscaster)
11274 Canton Dr
Studio City, CA 91604-4154, USA

Naharin, Ohad (Choreographer)
Dance Theater
Scheldeldoekshaven 60
Gravenhage, EN 2511, THE
NETHERLANDS

Nahem, Sam (Baseball Player)
Brooklyn Dodgers
1024 Willow Ave Apt 1
Hoboken, NJ 07030-3119, USA

Naifeh, Steven W (Writer)
335 Sumter St SE
Aiken, SC 29801-4661, USA

Nail, Jimmy
76 Oxford St.
London, ENGLAND W1N 0AX, UNITED
KINGDOM (UK)

Naimoli, Vincent (Baseball Player)
Tampa Bay Devil Rays
16616 Villalenda De Avila
Tampa, FL 33613-5200, USA

Naipaul, V S (Nobel Prize Laureate)
Aitken & Stone Ltd
29 Fernshaw Road
London SW10 0TG, UNITED KINGDOM
(UK)

Nair, Mira (Director)
Mirabai Films
5 E 16th St Fl 12
New York, NY 10003-3112, USA

Naisbitt, John (Writer)
Spittelauer Platz 5A3A
Vienna 1090, AUSTRIA

Naish, Bronwen (Musician)
Moelfre Xwm Pennant
Gamdolbenmaen
Gwunedd
North Wales, WALES LL5 9AX, UNITED
KINGDOM (UK)

Najarian, John S (Doctor)
University of Minnesota
Health Center
Surgery Dept
Minneapolis, MN 55455, USA

Najee (Musician)
Associated booking Corp
PO Box 2055
New York, NY 10021-0051, USA

Najera, Eduardo (Basketball Player)
c/o Staff Member *Dallas Mavericks*
2909 Taylor St
Dallas, TX 75226-1909, USA

Najimy, Kathy (Actor)
c/o Robert (Bob) Levinson *International
Creative Management (ICM-LA)*
10250 Constellation Blvd
Los Angeles, CA 90067-6200, USA

Nakama, Keo (Swimmer)
1344 9th Ave
Honolulu, HI 96816-2615, USA

Nakasone, Yasuhiro (Prime Minister)
3-22-7 Kamikitazawa
Setagayaku
Tokyo, JAPAN

Naked, Bif (Musician)
Crazed Mgmt
PO Box 356
Jamison, PA 18929-0356, USA

Naktenis, Pete (Baseball Player)
Philadelphia Athletics
132 Royal Palm Way
Palm Beach, FL 33480-4254, USA

Nalder, Eric C (Journalist)
Seattle Times
1120 John St
Editorial Dept
Seattle, WA 98109-5321, USA

Nalen, Thomas (Football Player)
Denver Broncos
9281 E Hidden Hill Ct
Lone Tree, CO 80124-5416, USA

Nalick, Anna (Musician)
Lippman Entertainment
23586 Calabasas Rd Ste 208
Calabasas, CA 91302-1361, USA

Nalinikanth (Actor)
413 29th Street
6th Sector
Chennai, TN 600 078, INDIA

Nall, Benita Krista (Actor)
c/o Staff Member *Main Title Entertainment*
5225 Wilshire Blvd Ste 500
Los Angeles, CA 90036-4349, USA

Nall, N Anita (Swimmer)
PO Box 872505
Tempe, AZ 85287-0001, USA

Nam, Leonardo (Actor)
c/o Staff Member *Overbrook
Entertainment*
450 N Roxbury Dr Fl 4
Beverly Hills, CA 90210-4232, USA

Namaliu, Rabbie L (Prime Minister)
PO Box 6655
National Capital District
Boroko, PAPUA NEW GUINEA

Namath, Joseph W (Joe) (Actor, Football
Player)
c/o Harlan Werner *Sports Placement
Service*
6671 W Sunset Blvd Ste 1521
Los Angeles, CA 90028-7123, USA

Nambiar, M N (Actor)
4 6th Street
Gopalapuram
Chennai, TN 600 086, INDIA

Nambu, Yoichiro (Physicist)
5535 S University Ave
Chicago, IL 60637-1521, USA

Nance, John J (Writer)
4512 8th Ave
West Tacoma, WA 98466, USA

Nance, Robin
5757 Wilshire Blvd Ste 510
Los Angeles, CA 90036-3629, USA

Nance, Shane (Baseball Player)
Milwaukee Brewers
3403 Harbour Breeze Ln
Pearland, TX 77584-7958, USA

Nance, Todd (Musician)
Brown Cat Inc
400 Foundry St
Athens, GA 30601-2623, USA

Nancy, Ted L
c/o Daniel A (Dan) Strone *Trident Media
Group LLC*
41 Madison Ave Fl 36
New York, NY 10010-2257, USA

Nanne, Louis V (Lou) (Hockey Player)
6982 Tupa Dr
Edina, MN 55439-1641, USA

Nanni, Gianna
Carmenstr. 12
Zurich CH-8032, SWITZERLAND

Nantucket
250 N Kepler Rd
Deland, FL 32724-4712, USA

Nantz, Jim (Sportscaster)
CBS-TV
51 W 52nd St
Sports Dept
New York, NY 10019-6119, USA

Napier, Charles (Actor)
Star Route Box 60H
Caliente, CA 93518, USA

Napier, Hugo
2207 N Beachwood Dr
Los Angeles, CA 90068-2903, USA

Napier, James (Actor)
c/o Staff Member *Auckland Actors*
PO Box 56460
Dominion Road
Auckland, NEW ZEALAND

Napier, John (Designer)
MLR Douglas House
16-18 Douglas St
London SW1P 4PB, UNITED KINGDOM
(UK)

Napier, Wilfrid F Cardinal (Religious
Leader)
Archbishop's House
154 Gordon Road
Greyville 4023, SOUTH AFRICA

Naples, Al (Baseball Player)
St Louis Browns
99 Nickerson Rd
Orleans, MA 02653-3314, USA

Napolean, Danny (Baseball Player)
New York Mets
116 Oliver Ave
Trenton, NJ 08618-2831, USA

Napoles, Jose (Boxer)
Cerrada De Tizapan 9-303 Ediciov
Codigo Postel
Mexico City 06080, MEXICO

Naponic, Robert (Football Player)
Houston Oilers
10807 Timberglen Dr
Houston, TX 77024-6808, USA

Naragon, Hal (Baseball Player)
Cleveland Indians
1521 Hagey Dr
Barberton, OH 44203-7724, USA

Narain, Nicole (Actor)
8033 W Sunset Blvd # 224
West Hollywood, CA 90046-2401, USA

Naranjo, Lazaro (Baseball Player)
Pittsburgh Pirates
10906 NW 1st Ln
Miami, FL 33172-3667, USA

Naranjo, Monica (Musician)
c/o Staff Member *Sony Music Miami*
605 Lincoln Rd Fl 7
Miami Beach, FL 33139-2900, USA

Narasimhan, V L (Actor)
9-6 L I C Staff Quarters
K K Nagar
Chennai, TN 600 078, INDIA

Narducci, Katherine
2843 Waterbury Ave
Bronx, NY 10461-6150, USA

Narducci, Tim (Musician)
Artists Group International
9560 Wilshire Blvd Ste 400
Beverly Hills, CA 90212-2416, USA

Narita, Hiro (Cinematographer)
2262 Magnolia Ave
Petaluma, CA 94952-1631, USA

Narita, Richard
8831 W Sunset Blvd # 304
Los Angeles, CA 90069, USA

Narizzano, Silvio (Cas) (Director)
Al Parker
55 Park Lane
London W1Y 3DD, UNITED KINGDOM
(UK)

Narleski, Ray (Baseball Player)
Cleveland Indians
1183 Chews Landing Rd
Laurel Springs, NJ 08021-2805, USA

Narron, Jerry (Baseball Player)
New York Yankees
216 W Wilson St
Smithfield, NC 27577-5133, USA

Naruhito (Royalty)
Imperial Palaca
1-1 Chiyoda
Chiyoda-ku
Tokyo, JAPAN

Narvekar, Prabhakar R (Financier)
International Monetary Fund
700 19th St NW
Washington, DC 20431-0002, USA

Narz, Jack (Television Host)
1906 Beverly Pl
Beverly Hills, CA 90210, USA

NAS (Musician)
c/o Staff Member *Richard De La Font
Agency*
4845 S Sheridan Rd Ste 505
Tulsa, OK 74145-5719, USA

Nasclemento, Milton (Musician,
Songwriter, Writer)
Tribo Producoes
Av A Lombardi 800
Rio de Janeiro 22 640-000, BRAZIL

Naseeruddin, Shah (Actor, Bollywood)
204 Sand Pebbles
Perry X Road Bandra
Mumbai, MS 400050, INDIA

Nash, Charles F (Cotton) (Baseball Player, Basketball Player)
Chicago White Sox
600 Summershade Cir
Lexington, KY 40502-2723, USA

Nash, Chris (Actor)
c/o Staff Member *Commercial Talent Agency*
9255 W Sunset Blvd Ste 505
West Hollywood, CA 90069-3301, USA

Nash, David (Artist)
Capel Rhiw Blanau
Flestiniog
Gwynedd Wales, WALES LL41 3NT,
UNITED KINGDOM (UK)

Nash, Graham W (Musician, Songwriter, Writer)
PO Box 838
Hanalei, HI 96714-0838, USA

Nash, Jamia Simone (Actor)
c/o Staff Member *Carson-Adler Agency*
250 W 57th St Ste 2030
New York, NY 10107-2013, USA

Nash, Jim (Baseball Player)
Kansas City A's
4383 White Surrey Dr NW
Kennesaw, GA 30144-5106, USA

Nash, Joe (Football Player)
Seattle Seahawks
29 Vermont St
West Roxbury, MA 02132-2336, USA

Nash, John F Jr (Nobel Prize Laureate)
Princeton University
Economics Department
Fine Hall
Princeton, NJ 08544-0001, USA

Nash, Johnny (Musician, Songwriter, Writer)
Legacy Records
550 Madison Ave # 1700
New York, NY 10022-3211, USA

Nash, Keisha
344 E 59th St
New York, NY 10022-1593, USA

Nash, Kevin (Wrestler)
c/o Staff Member *World Wrestling Entertainment (WWE)*
1241 E Main St
Stamford, CT 06902-3520, USA

Nash, Leigh (Musician)
c/o Staff Member *Paradigm (Monterey)*
509 Hartnell St
Monterey, CA 93940-2825, USA

Nash, Niecy (Actor, Television Host)
c/o Staff Member *Principato/Young Management*
9665 Wilshire Blvd Ste 500
Beverly Hills, CA 90212-2312, USA

Nash, Noreen (Actor)
4990 Puesta Del Sol St
Malibu, CA 90265-2512, USA

Nash, Richard
19323 Oxnard St
Tarzana, CA 91356-1122, USA

Nash, Rick (Hockey Player)
c/o Staff Member *Columbus Blue Jackets*
200 W Nationwide Blvd Unit 1
Nationwide Arena
Columbus, OH 43215-2564, USA

Nash, Steve (Basketball Player)
c/o Staff Member *BDA Sports Management (BDA-CA)*
822 Ashley Ln # A
Walnut Creek, CA 94597-3271, USA

Naslund, Markus (Hockey Player)
Mike Gillis Assoc
154 Earl St
Kingston, ON K7L 2H2, CANADA

Naslund, Mats (Hockey Player)
6963 Progressona
SWITZERLAND

Naslund, Ron (Hockey Player)
2600 Cheyenne Cir
Minnetonka, MN 55305-2309, USA

Nasr, Seyyed Hossein (Misc)
George Washington University
Gelman Library
Washington, DC 20052-0001, USA

Nasser, Jacques A (Business Person)
One Equity Partners
1st National Plaza
Chicago, IL 60607, USA

Nasser M (Actor)
245 Guhan Street
Kamakoti Nagar Valasarawakkam
Chennai, TN 600 087, INDIA

Nastase, Ilie (Tennis Player)
Calea Plevnei 14
Bucarest, HUNGARY

Nastu, Phil (Baseball Player)
San Francisco Giants
119 Austin St
Bridgeport, CT 06604-5440, USA

Nat, Marie-Jose
10 rue Royale
Paris 75008, FRANCE

Natal, Bob (Baseball Player)
Montreal Expos
3913 Cockrill Dr
McKinney, TX 75070-2413, USA

Natali, Vincenzo (Director)
c/o Philip Raskind *Endeavor Agency LLC (LA)*
9601 Wilshire Blvd Fl 3
Beverly Hills, CA 90210-5204, USA

Natalicio, Diana S (Educator)
University Of Texas At El Paso
President's Office
El Paso, TX 79968-0001, USA

Natalie (Musician)
c/o Staff Member *Motown Records (NY)*
1755 Broadway Fl 6
New York, NY 10019-3768, USA

Nater, Swen (Basketball Player)
1116 Pioneer St
Enumclaw, WA 98022-2656, USA

Nath, Alok (Actor, Bollywood)
901 Skydeck Oshiwara Complex
Off New Link Road Andheri
Mumbai, MS 400061, INDIA

Nathan, David G (Physicist)
Dana-Farber Cancer Institute
44 Binney St
Boston, MA 02115-6084, USA

Nathan, Joe (Baseball Player)
San Francisco Giants
2512 N 10th St
Phoenix, AZ 85006-1054, USA

Nathan, Joseph A (Business Person)
Compuware Corp
1 Campus Martius
Detroit, MI 48226-5099, USA

Nathan, S R (President)
President's Office
Orchard Road
Istana
Singapore 0922, SINGAPORE

Nathan, Tony C (Coach, Football Coach, Football Player)
Miami Dolphins
15110 Dunbarton Pl
Miami Lakes, FL 33016-1415, USA

Nathaniel (Popp), Bishop (Religious Leader)
Romanian Orthodox Episcopate
2522 Grey Tower Rd
Jackson, MI 49201-9120, USA

Nathanson, Jeff (Writer)
c/o Staff Member *United Talent Agency (UTA)*
9560 Wilshire Blvd Ste 500
Beverly Hills, CA 90212-2401, USA

Nathanson, Roy (Musician)
Brad Simon Organization
122 E 57th St # 300
New York, NY 10022-2623, USA

Nathman, John B (Admiral)
Commander Naval Air Force Pacific
Nas North Island
San Diego, CA 92135, USA

Nation, Joey (Baseball Player)
Chicago Cubs
8701 Cindy Rd
Oklahoma City, OK 73132-3110, USA

Natividad, Charles
Star Rt Box 60H
Caliente, CA 93518, USA

Natividad, Kitten
5917 Oak Ave # 148
Temple City, CA 91780-2028, USA

Natkin, Robert (Artist)
24 Mark Twain Ln
West Redding, CT 06896-2227, USA

Naton, Pete (Baseball Player)
Pittsburgh Pirates
4136 Split Rock Rd
Camillus, NY 13031-8704, USA

Natori, Josie C (Designer, Fashion Designer)
Natori Co
40 E 34th St
New York, NY 10016-4501, USA

Natowich, Andrew (Football Player)
Washington Redskins
24 Lexington Ave
Brattleboro, VT 05301-6626, USA

Natsios, Andrew (Government Official)
US International Development Agency
320 21st St NW
Washington, DC 20523-0002, USA

Natt, Calvin (Basketball Player)
4475 S Eagle Cir
Aurora, CO 80015-1333, USA

Natter, Robert J (Admiral)
Commander
Atlantic Fleet
Norfolk, VA 23551-0001, USA

Nattiel, Ricky (Football Player)
Denver Broncos
835 NW 119th St
Gainesville, FL 32606-0449, USA

Natural (Musician)
Official International Fan Club
PO Box 5097
Bellingham, WA 98227-5097, USA

Naude, C F Beyers (Religious Leader)
26 Hoylake Road
Greenside 2193, SOUTH AFRICA

Naudet, Jules (Producer)
c/o Staff Member *William Morris Agency (WMA-LA)*
1 William Morris Pl
Beverly Hills, CA 90212-4261, USA

Nauert, Paul (Baseball Player)
1201 Steeple Run
Lawrenceville, GA 30043-6354, USA

Naughton, David (Actor)
14955 Dickens St Apt 208
Sherman Oaks, CA 91403-3428, USA

Naughton, James
8942 Wilshire Blvd
Beverly Hills, CA 90211-1908, USA

Naughton, Laurie (Actor)
c/o Bruce Smith *OmniPop Inc (LA)*
4605 Lankershim Blvd Ste 201
North Hollywood, CA 91602-1874, USA

Naughton, Naturi (Musician)
Pyramid Entertainment
89 5th Ave Ste 700
New York, NY 10003-3020, USA

Naulis, Willie (Basketball Player)
Chuck & Willie's Auto Agency
13900 Hawthorne Blvd
Hawthorne, CA 90250-7002, USA

Naulty, Dan (Baseball Player)
Minnesota Twins
8447 Hackamore Rd
Littleton, CO 80125-7974, USA

Naum-Parker, Dorothy (Baseball Player)
2620 Bridlecreek Ln
Galesburg, IL 61401-5547, USA

Nauman, Bruce L (Artist)
4630 Rising Hill Rd
Altadena, CA 91001-3748, USA

Naumoff, Paul (Football Player)
Detroit Lions
932 Mohawk St
Columbus, OH 43206-2633, USA

Nause, Martha (Golfer)
13206 Patterson Trail
Minocqua, WI 54548, USA

Nava, Gregory (Director)
International Creative Mgmt
8942 Wilshire Blvd
Beverly Hills, CA 90211-1908, USA

Navaira, Emilio
15L El Camino Dr.
Beverly Hills, CA 90212, USA

Naval, Deepti (Actor, Bollywood)
603 Oceanic Seven Bungalows
Versova Andheri
Mumbai, MS 400061, INDIA

Navarez, Alfred (Musician)
MPI Talent
9255 W Sunset Blvd Ste 407
Los Angeles, CA 90069-3302, USA

Navarro, Dave (Musician)
c/o Larrisa Friend *Sanctuary Artist Management (LA)*
9255 W Sunset Blvd # 200
Los Angeles, CA 90069-3309, USA

Navarro, Emilio (Baseball Player)
Cuban Stars
97 Calle Torre
Ponce, PR 00730-3655, USA

Navarro, Guillermo J (Cinematographer)
Lyons Sheldon Prosnit Agency
800 S Robertson Blvd Ste 6
Los Angeles, CA 90035-1635, USA

Navarro, Jalme (Baseball Player)
Milwaukee Brewers
8100 Oak Park Rd
Orlando, FL 32819-3266, USA

Navarro, Tito (Baseball Player)
New York Mets
556 Calle Creuz
San Juan, PR 00923-1826, USA

Navas, Bibiana (Actor)
c/o Gabriel Blanco *Gabriel Blanco Iglesias (Mexico)*
Rio Balsas 35-32
Colonia Cuauhtemoc
DF 06500, MEXICO

Navasky, Victor S (Editor, Publisher)
33 W 67th St
New York, NY 10023-6224, USA

Navis, Hannibal (Football Player)
Carolina Panthers
4616 Rustling Woods Dr
Denver, NC 28037-5600, USA

Navon, Itzhak (President)
Education & Culture Ministry
Hakiria
Jerusalem, ISRAEL

Navratilova, Martina (Tennis Player)
Int'l Mgmt group
1 Erieview Plz
1360 E 9th St #1300
Cleveland, OH 44114-1738, USA

Naylor, Gloria (Writer)
One Way Productions
638 2nd St
Brooklyn, NY 11215-2602, USA

Naymenko, Gregg (Athlete)
2695 E Katella Ave
Anaheim, CA 92806-5904, USA

Naymick, Mike (Baseball Player)
Cleveland Indians
8334 Berwick Way
Stockton, CA 95210-2612, USA

Nazam, Hisham (Government Official)
Ministry of Petroleum & Mineral Resources
Riyadh, SAUDI ARABIA

Nazarbayev, Nursultan A (President)
President's Office
Pl Respublik
Astana 480091, KAZAKHSTAN

Nazario, Ednita (Musician)
c/o Staff Member *Sony Music Miami*
605 Lincoln Rd Fl 7
Miami Beach, FL 33139-2900, USA

Nazario, Sonia (Journalist)
Los Angeles Times
202 W 1st St
Editorial Dept
Los Angeles, CA 90012-4105, USA

Ndayizeye, Domitien (President)
President's Office
Bujumbura, BURUNDI

Ndegeocello, Me'Shell (Musician)
Monetary Peninsula Artists
509 Hartnell St
Monterey, CA 93940-2825, USA

Ndegeocello, Michelle (Musician)
c/o Staff Member *Paradigm (Monterey)*
509 Hartnell St
Monterey, CA 93940-2825, USA

Ndimira, Pascal Firmin (Prime Minister)
Prime Minister's Office
Bujumbura, BURUNDI

N'Dour, Youssou (Musician)
Konzertagentur Berthold Seliger
Nonnengasse 15
Fulda 36037, GERMANY

Ne Yo (Musician)
c/o Staff Member *Island Def Jam Music Group*
825 8th Ave Fl 28
New York, NY 10019-7416, USA

Neagle, Denny (Baseball Player)
Minnesota Twins
16254 Sandstone Dr
Morrison, CO 80465-2163, USA

Neal, Blaine (Baseball Player)
Florida Marlins
256 Dowdy Dr
Gibbstown, NJ 08027-1175, USA

Neal, Diane (Actor)
c/o Tina Thor *TMT Entertainment Group*
648 Broadway # 1002
New York, NY 10012-2301, USA

Neal, Doris (Baseball Player)
1212 Stoeber Ave Rear
Sarasota, FL 34232-2136, USA

Neal, Dylan (Actor)
Pakula/King
9229 W Sunset Blvd Ste 315
Los Angeles, CA 90069-3403, USA

Neal, Edwin (Actor)
501 W Powell Ln
Austin, TX 78753-5978, USA

Neal, Elise (Actor)
3626 Oakfield Dr
Sherman Oaks, CA 91423-4448, USA

Neal, Fred (Curly) (Basketball Player)
PO Box 915415
Longwood, FL 32791-5415, USA

Neal, James (Basketball Player)
803 Medora Dr
Greer, SC 29650-4751, USA

Neal, James F (Attorney, Attorney General, General)
Neal & Harwell
3rd National Bank Building #800
Nashville, TN 37219, USA

Neal, Lloyd (Basketball Player)
8640 SE Causey Ave
Portland, OR 97266, USA

Neal, Lorenzo (Football Player)
New Orleans Saints
777 S Orange Ave
Fresno, CA 93702-3401, USA

Neal, Patricia (Actor)
45 E End Ave Apt 4C
New York, NY 10028-7980, USA

Neal, Philip M (Business Person)
Avery Dennison Corp
150 N Orange Grove Blvd
Pasadena, CA 91103-3534, USA

Neal, Scott (Actor)
c/o Staff Member *Jonathan Altaras Assoc Ltd*
11 Garrick Street
Covent Garden
London WC2E 9AT, UNITED KINGDOM (UK)

Neal, T Daniel (Dan) (Football Player)
Baltimore Colts
711 Homestead Blvd
Louisville, KY 40207-3630, USA

Neale, Gary L (Business Person)
Northern Indiana Service
801 E 86th Ave
Merrillville, IN 46410-6271, USA

Nealon, Kevin (Actor, Comedian)
c/o Marc Gurvitz *Brillstein-Grey Entertainment*
9150 Wilshire Blvd Ste 350
Beverly Hills, CA 90212-3453, USA

Nealy, Eddie (Basketball Player)
702 Lightstone Dr
San Antonio, TX 78258-2305, USA

Neame, Christopher (Actor)
Borinstein Oreck Bogart
3172 Dona Susana Dr
Studio City, CA 91604-4356, USA

Neame, Ronald (Director)
Kimridge Corp
2317 Kimridge Rd
Beverly Hills, CA 90210-1830, USA

Near, Holly (Actor, Musician, Songwriter, Writer)
PO Box 236
Ukiah, CA 95482-0236, USA

Nearing, Merna (Baseball Player)
21079 W Good Hope Rd Apt D-1
Lannon, WI 53046, USA

Neary, Martin G J (Musician)
2 Little Cloister
Westminster Abbey
London SW1P 3PL, UNITED KINGDOM (UK)

Nebel, Dorothy Hoyt (Skier)
5340 Balfor Dr
Virginia Beach, VA 23464-2441, USA

Neblett, Carol (Opera Singer)
Sardos Artists
180 W End Ave
New York, NY 10023-4902, USA

Nebout, Claire (Actor)
Artmedia
20 Ave Rapp
Paris 75007, FRANCE

Necciai, Ron (Baseball Player)
Pittsburgh Pirates
6261 Overlook Ln
Belle Vernon, PA 15012-3928, USA

Nechaev, Victor (Hockey Player)
6820 La Presa Dr
San Gabriel, CA 91775-1110, USA

Neck, Tommy (Football Player)
Chicago Bears
2107 Marie Pl
Monroe, LA 71201-3413, USA

Ned, Derrick (Football Player)
New Orleans Saints
430 Charles St
Eunice, LA 70535-4904, USA

Nedeljakova, Barbara (Actor)
Beverly Hecht Agency
3500 W Olive Ave Ste 1180
C/O Robert Depp
Burbank, CA 91505-4651, USA

Nederlander, James M (Producer)
Netherlander Organization
810 7th Ave
New York, NY 10019-5818, USA

Nedney, Joe (Football Player)
Miami Dolphins
121 Lauren Cir
Scotts Valley, CA 95066-3836, USA

Nedomansky, Vaclav (Hockey Player)
57 Cresta Verde Dr
Rolling Hills Estates, CA 90274-5476, USA

Nedorost, Vaclav (Hockey Player)
Florida Panthers
1 Panther Pkwy
Sunrise, FL 33323-5315, USA

Nedved, Petr (Hockey Player)
Edmonton Oilers
11230 110th St
Edmonton, AB T5G 3H7, CANADA

Needham, Connie (Actor)
2241 Watermarke Pl
Irvine, CA 92612-7692, USA

Needham, Hal (Director)
Laura Lizer Assoc
PO Box 46609
Los Angeles, CA 90046-0609, USA

Needham, James J (Business Person)
97 Coopers Farm Rd Unit 1
Southampton, NY 11968-4066, USA

Needham, Tracey (Actor)
Badgley Connor Talent
1680 Vine St Ste 1016
Los Angeles, CA 90028-8800, USA

Needham, Tracy
9229 W Sunset Blvd Ste 311
Los Angeles, CA 90069-3403, USA

Needleman, Jacob (Misc)
841 Wawona Ave
Oakland, CA 94610-1250, USA

Neel, Troy (Baseball Player)
Oakland A's
PO Box 1582
El Campo, TX 77437-1582, USA

Neeleman, David (Business Person)
jetBlue Airways Corp
80-02 Kew Gardens Floor 4
New York, NY 11415, USA

Neelu (Actor)
G-5 Madhuram Flats Ururalagat Kuppam
5th Avenue
Besant Nagar
Chennai, TN 600 090, INDIA

Neely, Cam (Hockey Player)
76 Davison Dr
Lincoln, MA 01773-2216, USA

Neely, Ralph E (Football Player)
Dallas Cowboys
6943 Sperry St
Dallas, TX 75214-2855, USA

Neely Jr, Mark E (Historian)
Oxford University Press
198 Madison Ave Fl 9
New York, NY 10016-4308, USA

Neeman, Cal (Baseball Player)
Chicago Cubs
93 Champagne Dr
Lake Saint Louis, MO 63367-1604, USA

Ne'eman, Yuval (Physicist)
Tel-Aviv University
Physics/Astronomy Dept
Tel-Aviv 69978, ISRAEL

Neeson, Liam (Actor)
c/o Steven Arcieri *Arcieri & Associates Inc*
305 Madison Ave Ste 2315
New York, NY 10165-5015, USA

Nef, John U (Historian)
2726 N St NW
Washington, DC 20007-3323, USA

Nef, Sonia (Skier)
Halten 345
Grub 9035, SWITZERLAND

Neff, Bob (Football Player)
Miami Dolphins
2 Crestview
Athens, TX 75751-2932, USA

Neff, Francine I (Government Official)
PO Box 1498
Pena Blanca, NM 87041-1498, USA

Neff, William D (Psychic)
2080 Hideaway Ct
Morris, IL 60450-9601, USA

Negishi, Takashi (Economist)
2-10-5-301 Motoazabu
Minatoku
Tokyo 106, JAPAN

Negoesco, Stephen (Coach)
University of San Francisco
Athletic Dept
San Francisco, CA 94117, USA

Negray, Ron (Baseball Player)
Brooklyn Dodgers
587 W Nimisila Rd
Akron, OH 44319-4616, USA

Negri Sembilan, Yang Di-Pertuan Besar (President)
Yang Di-Pertuan Agong's Residence
Serembam, MALAYSIA

Negron, Chuck (Musician)
Mitch Schneider Organization
14724 Ventura Blvd Ste 710
Sherman Oaks, CA 91403-3520, USA

Negron, Taylor
8447 Wilshire Blvd Ste 206
Beverly Hills, CA 90211-3207, USA

Negroponte, John D (Diplomat)
US State Department
2201 C St NW
Washington, DC 20520-0099, USA

Negus, Fred (Football Player)
Chicago Bears
865 Acorn Rdg
Whitewater, WI 53190-2959, USA

Nehamas, Alexander (Misc)
Princeton University
Philosophy Dept
Princeton, NJ 08544-0001, USA

Nehemiah, Renaldo (Football Player)
San Francisco 49ers
1751 Pinnacle Dr Ste 1500
Mc Lean, VA 22102-3833, USA

Neher, Erwin (Nobel Prize Laureate)
Domane 11
Bovenden 37120, GERMANY

Nehmer, Meinhard (Athlete)
Vamkevitz
Altenkirchen 18556, GERMANY

Neibauer, Gary (Baseball Player)
Atlanta Braves
146 Delta Ave
Bismarck, ND 58504-6655, USA

Neibhors, William (Football Player)
Boston Patriots
1904 Chippendale Dr SE
Huntsville, AL 35801-1309, USA

Neid, Silvia (Soccer Player)
Betramstr 18
Frankfurt/Main 60320, GERMANY

Neidert, John (Football Player)
Cincinnati Bengals
4731 Placid Cir
Sarasota, FL 34231-6486, USA

Neidich, Charles (Musician)
Colbert Artists
111 W 57th St
New York, NY 10019-2236, USA

Neidlinger, Jim (Baseball Player)
Los Angeles Dodgers
139 Sunset Dr
Burlington, VT 05408-1910, USA

Neiger, Al (Baseball Player)
Philadelphia Phillies
213 Pinehurst Rd
Wilmington, DE 19803-3125, USA

Neighbors, William (Billy) (Football Player)
1904 Chippendale Dr SE
Huntsville, AL 35801-1309, USA

Neil, Andrew F (Editor)
Glenbum Enterprises
PO Box 584
London SW7 3QY, UNITED KINGDOM (UK)

Neil, Hildegarde (Actor)
Vernon Conway
5 Spring St
London W2 3RA, UNITED KINGDOM (UK)

Neil, Ray (Baseball Player)
Ethiopian Clowns
250 N Wells Ave Apt 511
Benton Harbor, MI 49022, USA

Neil, Vince (Musician)
c/o Staff Member *Fisher Films LLC*
14359 Miramar Pkwy # 246
Miramar, FL 33027-4134, USA

Neill, Mary Gardner (Director)
Seattle Art Museum
Volunteer Park
Seattle, WA 98112, USA

Neill, Mike (Baseball Player)
Oakland A's
17 Cape May Pt
Greensboro, NC 27455-1363, USA

Neill, Noel (Actor)
331 Sage Ln
Santa Monica, CA 90402-1119, USA

Neill, Rolfe (Publisher)
Charlotte News-Observer
600 S Tryon St
Charlotte, NC 28202-1842, USA

Neill, Sam (Actor)
c/o Chris Andrews *Creative Artists Agency LCC (CAA-LA)*
2000 Avenue Of The Stars
Los Angeles, CA 90067-4700, USA

Neill, William M (Football Player)
New York Giants
19 Nicholas Dr
Butler, NJ 07405-2742, USA

Neils, Steve (Football Player)
St Louis Cardinals
1329 Waterford Rd
Woodbury, MN 55125-2366, USA

Neilson-Bell, Sandra (Swimmer)
3101 Mistyglen Cir
Austin, TX 78746-7811, USA

Neiman, LeRoy (Artist)
c/o Gail Parenteau *Parenteau Guidance*
132 E 35th St # 3J
New York, NY 10016-3892, USA

Neinas, Charles M (Chuck) (Misc)
5344 Westridge Dr
Boulder, CO 80301-6501, USA

Neis, Reagan Dale (Actor)
c/o Staff Member *William Morris Agency (WMA-LA)*
1 William Morris Pl
Beverly Hills, CA 90212-4261, USA

Neizvestny, Ernst I (Artist)
81 Grand St
New York, NY 10013-2256, USA

Nelkin, Stacey
2770 Hutton Dr
Beverly Hills, CA 90210-1216, USA

Nelligan, Kate (Actor)
Innovative Artists
1505 10th St
Santa Monica, CA 90401-2805, USA

Nellis, William J (Physicist)
Lawrence Livermore Laboratory
7000 East Ave
Livermore, CA 94550-9698, USA

Nellssen, Roelof J (Financier, Government Official)
PO Box 552
AN Laren 1250, THE NETHERLANDS

Nelms, Michael (Mike) (Football Player)
Washington Redskins
10411 James Monroe Hwy
Champion Chevrolet
Culpeper, VA 22701-8028, USA

Nelsen, Bill (Football Player)
Pittsburgh Steelers
13512 Dornoch Dr
Orlando, FL 32828-8802, USA

Nelson
15003 Greenleaf St
Sherman Oaks, CA 91403-4006, USA

Nelson, Al (Football Player)
Philadelphia Eagles
660 Boas St Apt 918
Harrisburg, PA 17102-1323, USA

Nelson, Andy (Football Player)
Baltimore Colts
12251 Manor Rd
Glen Arm, MD 21057-9542, USA

Nelson, Bill (Football Player)
Los Angeles Rams
PO Box 9235
Pahrump, NV 89060-9235, USA

Nelson, Bob (Baseball Player)
Baltimore Orioles
10830 Wallbrook Dr
Dallas, TX 75238-2943, USA

Nelson, Bry (Baseball Player)
Boston Red Sox
11 Campden Hill Rd
Sherwood, AR 72120-6536, USA

Nelson, Cailin (Physicist)
Lawrence Livermore Laboratory
7000 East Ave
Livermore, CA 94550-9698, USA

Nelson, Charles L (Football Player)
Los Angeles Rams
3028 162nd Pl SE
Mill Creek, WA 98012-7848, USA

Nelson, Charlie (Baseball Player)
US Olympic Team
11205 Kinsley St
Eden Prairie, MN 55344-1826, USA

Nelson, Cordner (Misc)
USA Track & Field
4341 Starlight Dr
Indianapolis, IN 46239-1473, USA

Nelson, Craig Richard (Actor)
Borinstein Oreck Bogart
3172 Dona Susana Dr
Studio City, CA 91604-4356, USA

Nelson, Craig T (Actor)
c/o Connie Tavel *Forward Entertainment*
9255 W Sunset Blvd Ste 805
Los Angeles, CA 90069-3305, USA

Nelson, Cynthia (Cindy) (Skier)
PO Box 1699
0171 Larkspur Lane
Vail, CO 81658-1699, USA

Nelson, Darrin (Football Player)
215 Marianne Ct
Mountain View, CA 94040-3283, USA

Nelson, Dave (Baseball Player)
Cleveland Indians
12213 Clubhouse Dr
Bradenton, FL 34202-2098, USA

Nelson, David A (Judge)
US Court of Appeals
425 Walnut St
Courthouse Building
Cincinnati, OH 45202-3923, USA

Nelson, David O (Actor, Director)
c/o Staff Member *Nine Yards Entertainment*
8530 Wilshire Blvd Fl 5
Beverly Hills, CA 90211-3102, USA

Nelson, Deborah (Journalist)
Seattle Times
1120 John St
Editorial Dept
Seattle, WA 98109-5321, USA

Nelson, Dennis (Football Player)
Baltimore Colts
6098 E 2370 St
Kewanee, IL 61443-8529, USA

Nelson, Derrie (Football Player)
San Diego Chargers
7790 S Marian Rd
Hastings, NE 68901-7564, USA

Nelson, Donald A (Nellie) (Basketball Player, Coach)
Dallas Mavericks
2909 Taylor St
Dallas, TX 75226-1909, USA

Nelson, Dorothy W (Judge)
US Court of Appeals
125 S Grand Ave
Pasadena, CA 91105-1652, USA

Nelson, Drew (Actor)
c/o Staff Member *Select Artists Ltd (CA-Westside Office)*
1138 12th St Apt 1
Santa Monica, CA 90403-5459, USA

Nelson, Ed (Actor)
7647 Westlake Rd
Sterlington, LA 71280-3231, USA

Nelson, Ed (Football Player)
Pittsburgh Steelers
PO Box 614
Pro Athelete Marketing
Beaver Falls, PA 15010-0614, USA

Nelson, Gene (Baseball Player)
New York Yankees
4724 Birchfield Loop
Spring Hill, FL 34609-0634, USA

Nelson, George D (Astronaut)
AAAS Project
1200 New York Ave NW Ste 100
Washington, DC 20005-3929, USA

Nelson, Glen D (Business Person)
Medtronic Inc
7000 Central Ave NE
Minneapolis, MN 55432-3576, USA

Nelson, Gunnar
13030 Valleyheart Dr Apt 105
Studio City, CA 91604-1960, USA

Nelson, Jameer (Basketball Player)
Orlando Magic
8701 Maitland Summit Blvd
Waterhouse Center
Orlando, FL 32810-5915, USA

Nelson, James E (Religious Leader)
Baha i Faith
536 Sheridan Rd
Wilmette, IL 60091-2891, USA

Nelson, Jamie (Baseball Player)
Seattle Mariners
3990 24th Ave N
St Petersburg, FL 33713-3406, USA

Nelson, Jeff (Baseball Player)
Seattle Mariners
8335 Hyde Ct S
Cottage Grove, MN 55016-3229, USA

Nelson, Jerry E (Astronomer, Physicist)
University of California
Astronomy Dept
Berkeley, CA 94720-0001, USA

Nelson, Jim (Baseball Player)
Pittsburgh Pirates
5732 Lonsdale Dr
Sacramento, CA 95822-2428, USA

Nelson, Jimmy
10404 Greenhaven Pkwy
Brecksville, OH 44141-1625, USA

Nelson, Joe (Baseball Player)
Atlanta Braves
1816 San Antonio Ave
Alameda, CA 94501-4125, USA

Nelson, John Allen (Actor)
c/o Cynthia Booth *Agency Group Ltd, The (LA)*
1880 Century Park E Ste 711
Los Angeles, CA 90067-1618, USA

Nelson, John R (Misc)
1111 Hermann Dr Unit 19A
Houston, TX 77004-6930, USA

Nelson, John W
Astrid Schoerke
Monckebergallee 41
Hanover 30453, GERMANY

Nelson, Judd (Actor)
409 N Camden Dr Ste 202
Beverly Hills, CA 90210-4423, USA

Nelson, Judith (Opera Singer)
2600 Buena Vista Way
Berkeley, CA 94708-1930, USA

Nelson, Karl (Football Player)
New York Giants
58 Woodland Rd
Montvale, NJ 07645-1333, USA

Nelson, Kent C (Business Person)
United Parcel Service
55 Glenlake Pkwy NE
Atlanta, GA 30328-3498, USA

Nelson, Kirsten (Actor)
c/o Megan Schumacher *Himber Entertainment Inc*
15760 Ventura Blvd Ste 700
Encino, CA 91436-3016, USA

Nelson, Larry (Golfer)
421 Oakmont Cir SE
Marietta, GA 30067-4819, USA

Nelson, Lee (Football Player)
St Louis Cardinals
4178 Summit Way
Marietta, GA 30066-2364, USA

Nelson, Marilyn Carlson (Business Person)
Carlson Companies
PO Box 59159
Carlson Parkway
Minneapolis, MN 55459-8200, USA

Nelson, Mary (Baseball Player)
4222 Katrina Ln
San Antonio, TX 78222-2712, USA

Nelson, Matthew
12344 Moorpark St Unit 4
Studio City, CA 91604-1277, USA

Nelson, Mel (Baseball Player)
St Louis Cardinals
27420 Fisher St
Highland, CA 92346-3251, USA

Nelson, Ralph A (Misc)
Carle Foundation Hospital
611 W Park St Ste 1
Urbana, IL 61801-2512, USA

Nelson, Richard (Baseball Player)
104 Montgomery Ln
Perryville, AR 72126-8114, USA

Nelson, Ricky (Baseball Player)
Seattle Mariners
16441 S 46th Pl
Phoenix, AZ 85048-0138, USA

Nelson, Rob (Baseball Player)
Oakland A's
312 Alta Vista Ave
South Pasadena, CA 91030-3502, USA

Nelson, Robert L (Football Player)
Buffalo Bills
14711 Copperfield Pl
Wayzata, MN 55391-2503, USA

Nelson, Rocky (Baseball Player)
St Louis Cardinals
PO Box 35
Portsmouth, OH 45662-0035, USA

Nelson, Scott (Baseball Player)
811 Overlook Dr
Coshocton, OH 43812-9107, USA

Nelson, Shane (Football Player)
Buffalo Bills
559 Carmel Dr
Sandia, TX 78383-5678, USA

Nelson, Terry (Football Player)
Los Angeles Rams
3393 Highway 51 N
Arkadelphia, AR 71923-8584, USA

Nelson, Tex (Baseball Player)
Baltimore Orioles
10830 Wallbrook Dr
Dallas, TX 75238-2943, USA

Nelson, Thomas G (Judge)
US Court of Appeals
550 W Fort St
Boise, ID 83724-0101, USA

Nelson, Tim Blake (Actor)
c/o Mara Buxbaum *I/D PR (NY)*
155 Spring St Fl 6
New York, NY 10012-5208, USA

Nelson, William (Bill) (Astronaut, Senator)
Florida Insurance Dept
200 E Gaines St
Tallahassee, FL 32399-6502, USA

Nelson, Willie (Musician, Songwriter, Writer)
c/o David Snyder *William Morris Agency (WMA-LA)*
1 William Morris Pl
Beverly Hills, CA 90212-4261, USA

Nelson Jr, J Bryon (Golfer)
RR 2 Box 5
Fairway Ranch Litsey Road
Roanoke, TX 76262, USA

Nelson-Walker, Doris (Baseball Player)
7887 N 16th St Unit 129
Phoenix, AZ 85020-4453, USA

Nemchinov, Sergei (Hockey Player)
53 Walker Ave
Rye, NY 10580-1219, USA

Nemcova, Petra (Model)
c/o Rob Shuter *The Shuter Group*
470 W 24th St Apt 15C
New York, NY 10011-1238, USA

Nemec, Corin (Actor)
859 N Hollywood Way # 104
Burbank, CA 91505-2814, USA

Nemecek, Bohumil (Boxer)
V Zahradkach 30
Usti Nad Labem 400 00, CZECH REPUBLIC

Nemelka, Richard (Basketball Player)
1949 Sunridge Dr
Sandy, UT 84093-7045, USA

Nemeth, Miklos (Prime Minister)
European Reconstruction Bank
1 Exchange Square
London EC2A 2EH, UNITED KINGDOM (UK)

Nemov, AlekseiRGF
Lujnetskaya Nabereunaya 8
Moscow 119.270, RUSSIA

Nemov, Alexei (Gymnast)
Gymnastics Federation
Lujnetskaya Nabereynaya 8
Moscow 119270, RUSSIA

Nen, Dick (Baseball Player)
Los Angeles Dodgers
6152 Killarney Ave
Garden Grove, CA 92845-2730, USA

Nen, Robb (Baseball Player)
Texas Rangers
8 S View
Trabuco Canyon, CA 92679-5376, USA

Nenez, Clemente (Baseball Player)
6433 Blackberry Pl
Riverside, CA 92505-2205, USA

Nennerman, Richard A (Editor)
PO Box 992
East Brunswick, NJ 08816-0992, USA

Nenninger, Eric (Actor)
c/o Lena Roklin *Roklin Management*
8530 Wilshire Blvd Ste 550
Beverly Hills, CA 90211-3133, USA

Nepoleon (Actor)
12/5 Sandilya Apartments Jagathambal Colony
II Street Royapettah
Chennai, TN 600 014, INDIA

Nepote, Jean (Lawyer, Misc)
26 Rue Armengaud
92210 Saint-Cloud
Hauts-de-Seine, FRANCE

N*E*R*D (Music Group)
c/o Staff Member *Paradigm (Monterey)*
509 Hartnell St
Monterey, CA 93940-2825, USA

Nerette, Joseph (Judge, President)
Supreme Court
Chief Justice's Office
Port-au-Prince, HAITI

Neri, Francesca (Actor)
c/o Brian Gersh *Blue Train Entertainment*
798 Brooktree Rd
Pacific Palisades, CA 90272-3901, USA

Nerl, Manuel (Artist)
greg Kucera Gallery
212 3rd Ave S
Seattle, WA 98104-2608, USA

Nerl Vela, Rodolfo (Astronaut)
Playa Copacabana 131
Col Marte
Mexico City, DF 08830, MEXICO

Nerlove, Marc L (Economist)
University of Maryland
Agricultural/Resource Economics
College Park, MD 20742-0001, USA

Nerman, Maxens (Actor)
Continent II
62, Rue des Grands Champs
Paris 75020, FRANCE

Nero, Franco ((Actor)
c/o Camilla Fluxman-Pines *Muse Management*
429 Santa Monica Blvd Ste 520
Santa Monica, CA 90401-3401, USA

Nero, Haley (Actor)
c/o Staff Member *Charlie's Talent Agency*
1350 Old Skokie Rd Ste 202
Highland Park, IL 60035-3058, USA

Nero, Peter (Musician)
202 Hidden Acres Ln
Media, PA 19063-1666, USA

Nerud, John (Misc)
19 Pound Hollow Rd
Glen Head, NY 11545-2209, USA

Nery, Carl (Football Player)
Pittsburgh Steelers
239 Ryan Dr
Pittsburgh, PA 15220-1915, USA

Nesbit, Jamar (Football Player)
Carolina Panthers
4083 Richmond Park Dr E
Jacksonville, FL 32224-2223, USA

Nesbitt, James (Actor)
c/o Staff Member *Yakety Yak*
8 Bloomsbury Sq
London WC1A 2UA, UNITED KINGDOM
(UK)

Nesbitt-Wisham, Mary (Baseball Player)
PO Box 194
Hollister, FL 32147-0194, USA

Neserovic, Radoslav (Basketball Player)
San Antonio Spurs
1 Sbc Center Pkwy
Alamodome
San Antonio, TX 78219-3604, USA

Nesher, Avi (Director)
Gersh Agency
232 N Canon Dr
Beverly Hills, CA 90210-5302, USA

Nesic, Alex (Actor)
c/o Staff Member *Principato/Young Management*
9665 Wilshire Blvd Ste 500
Beverly Hills, CA 90212-2312, USA

Nesmith, Michael (Mike) (Musician)
Videoranch
1793 Catalina St
Seaside, CA 93955-3546, USA

Nespral, Jackie (Correspondent)
NBC-TV
30 Rockefeller Plz Ste 270E
News Dept
New York, NY 10112-0299, USA

Ness, Norman F (Physicist)
9 Wilkinson Dr
Landenberg, PA 19350-9359, USA

Ness, Rick (Musician)
Metropolitan Entertainment Group
2 Penn Plz Rm 1500
New York, NY 10121-1590, USA

Nessen, Ronald H (Ron) (Correspondent, Government Official)
6409 Walhonding Rd
Bethesda, MD 20816-2264, USA

Nesterenko, Eric (Hockey Player)
2395 Bald Mountain Rd
Vail, CO 81657-4605, USA

Nesterenko, Evgeny Y (Opera Singer)
Fruzenskaya Nab 24 Korp 1
#178
Moscow 119146, RUSSIA

Netherland, Joseph H (Business Person)
FMC Corp
200 E Randolph St
Chicago, IL 60601-6801, USA

Netherton, Tom (Musician)
Germantown Performing Arts Centre
1801 Exeter Rd
Germantown, TN 38138-2934, USA

Nett, Robert B (War Hero)
5417 Kessington Dr
Columbus, GA 31907-1830, USA

Nettles, Doug (Football Player)
Baltimore Colts
13105 Quail Creek Ct
Silver Spring, MD 20904-3588, USA

Nettles, Graig (Baseball Player)
Minnesota Twins
4255 Parris Dr
Lenoir City, TN 37772-3947, USA

Nettles, Jennifer (Musician)
c/o Staff Member *Gail Gellman Management*
23852 Pch #920
Malibu, CA 90265, USA

Nettles, Jim (Baseball Player)
Minnesota Twins
4632 N Darien Dr
Tacoma, WA 98407-1212, USA

Nettles, Jim (Football Player)
Philadelphia Eagles
3817 Mandeville Canyon Rd
Los Angeles, CA 90049-1027, USA

Nettles, John (Actor)
Saraband Assoc
265 Liverpool Road
London N1 1LX, UNITED KINGDOM
(UK)

Nettles, Morris (Baseball Player)
California Angels
551 1/2 San Juan Ave
Venice, CA 90291-5643, USA

Nettleton, Lois (Actor)
Susan Mann
29738 Strawberry Hill Dr
Agoura Hills, CA 91301-4087, USA

Neu, Mike (Baseball Player)
Oakland A's
134 Macalvey Dr
Martinez, CA 94553-5851, USA

Neubert, Keith
10000 Santa Monica Blvd # 305
Los Angeles, CA 90067, USA

Neufeld, Elizabeth F (Misc)
University of California
Medical School
Biology Dept
Los Angeles, CA 90024, USA

Neufeld, Ray (Hockey Player)
RE/MAX Real Estate
3919 Henderson Highway
Winnipeg, MB R2G 1P4, CANADA

Neufeld, Ryan (Football Player)
Dallas Cowboys
625 Spring Hill Dr
Morgan Hill, CA 95037-4814, USA

Neugebauer, Marcia (Physicist)
7519 S Elliot Ln
Tucson, AZ 85747-9627, USA

Neugebauer, Nick (Baseball Player)
Milwaukee Brewers
101 S Sahuaro Dr
Gilbert, AZ 85233-5927, USA

Neuharth, Allen H (Publisher)
Freedom Dorum
1101 Wilson Blvd
Arlington, VA 22209-2265, USA

Neuhaus, Max (Artist, Composer)
350 5th Ave Ste 3304
New York, NY 10118-3304, USA

Neuhaus, Richard J (Religious Leader)
Center on Religion & Society
152 Madison Ave
New York, NY 10016-5424, USA

Neuhauser, Duncan V B (Misc)
2655 N Park Blvd
Cleveland Heights, OH 44106-3622, USA

Neuheisel, Richard (Rick) (Coach, Football Coach, Football Player)
San Diego Chargers
2109 E Balboa Dr
Tempe, AZ 85282-4006, USA

Neumann, Wolfgang (Opera Singer)
Opera et Concert
Maximilianstr 22
Munich 80539, GERMANY

Neumark, Julie
900 E 1st St Apt 314
Los Angeles, CA 90012-4039, USA

Neumeier, Dan (Baseball Player)
Chicago White Sox
N2635 County Road V
Lodi, WI 53555-1568, USA

Neumeler, John (Choreographer)
Hamburg Ballet
54 Caspar-Voght-Str
Hamburg 20535, GERMANY

Neumeyer, Bobby (Producer)
Creative Artists Agency
9830 Wilshire Blvd
Beverly Hills, CA 90212-1804, USA

Neuner, Doris (Athlete)
6024 Innsbruck
AUSTRIA

Neuwelt, Edward A (Misc)
Oregon Health Sciences University
Neurology Dept
Portland, OR 97201, USA

Neuwirth, Bebe (Actor, Dancer, Musician)
c/o Brian Mann *International Creative Management (ICM-LA)*
10250 Constellation Blvd
Los Angeles, CA 90067-6200, USA

Nevett, Elijah (Football Player)
New Orleans Saints
931 30th St N
Bessemer, AL 35020-3565, USA

Nevil, Bobbie
20 Manchester Sq
London W1M 5AE, ENGLAND

Neville, Aaron (Musician)
1090 Millwood Ct
Brentwood, TN 37027-8478, USA

Neville, Arthel (Correspondent, Television Host)
1840 Victory Blvd
Glendale, CA 91201-2558, USA

Neville, Bill (Cartoonist)
506 Oakdale Rd
Jamestown, NC 27282-9214, USA

Neville, John (Actor, Director)
139 Winnett Ave
Toronto, ON M6C 3L7, CANADA

Neville, Katherine (Writer)
PO Box 788
Warrenton, VA 20188-0788, USA

Neville, Robert C (Misc)
Boston University
Theology School
Boston, MA 02215, USA

Neville, Thomas O (Football Player)
Boston Patriots
PO Box 11175
Montgomery, AL 36111-0175, USA

Nevin, Brooke (Actor)
c/o Suzanne (Sue) Wohl *TalentWorks (LA)*
3500 W Olive Ave Ste 1400
Burbank, CA 91505-5512, USA

Nevin, Phil (Baseball Player)
Houston Astros
18795 Heritage Dr
Poway, CA 92064-6643, USA

Nevins, Claudette (Actor)
Gold Marshak Liedtke
3500 W Olive Ave Ste 1400
Burbank, CA 91505-5512, USA

Nevinson, Nancy
23 Mill Close Fishbourne
Chichester, ENGLAND, UNITED KINGDOM (UK)

New Edition (Music Group)
c/o Staff Member *International Creative Management (ICM-LA)*
10250 Constellation Blvd
Los Angeles, CA 90067-6200, USA

New Grass Revival
PO Box 128037
Nashville, TN 37212-8037, USA

New Order
72 Chancellor's Rd.
London, ENGLAND W6 9SG, UNITED KINGDOM (UK)

New Radicals
c/o Staff Member *MCA Records (LA)*
2220 Colorado Ave
Santa Monica, CA 90404-3506, USA

New Rascals, The
PO Box 1821
Ojai, CA 93024-1821, USA

New Riders of the Purple Sage
PO Box 3773
San Rafael, CA 94912-3773, USA

New Song (Music Group)
c/o Staff Member *VanLiere-Wilcox*
251 2nd Ave S
Franklin, TN 37064-2659, USA

New York Yankees
Yankee Stadium
161st & River
Bronx, NY 10451, USA

Newbern, George (Actor)
Entertainment Tavel
9255 W Sunset Blvd Ste 805
West Hollywood, CA 90069-3305, USA

Newberry, Jeremy (Football Player)
San Francisco 49ers
1225 Almondwood Dr
Antioch, CA 94509-5170, USA

Newberry, Thomas (Tom) (Football Player)
Los Angeles Rams
224 Tarpon St
Tavernier, FL 33070-2534, USA

Newbigging, William (Publisher)
Edmonton Journal
10006 101st St
Edmonton, AB T5J 2S6, CANADA

Newborn, Ira (Composer)
Vangelos Mgmt
15233 Ventura Blvd Ste 200
Sherman Oaks, CA 91403-2244, USA

Newburn, George
PO Box 5617
Beverly Hills, CA 90209-5617, USA

Newcomb, Gerry (Artist)
7029 17th Ave NW
Seattle, WA 98117-5551, USA

Newcomb, Jonathan (Publisher)
35 Pierrepont St
Brooklyn, NY 11201-3359, USA

Newcomb, Mike (Radio Personality)
OnSecondThought
4927 E Palo Brea Ln
Cave Creek, AZ 85331-5995, USA

Newcombe, Don (Baseball Player)
Newark Eagles
20200 Cantara St Unit 404D
Kappy Lyons
Canoga Park, CA 91306-1877, USA

Newcome, John
PO Box 310469
New Braunfels, TX 78131-0469, USA

Newcomer, Carrie (Musician)
PO Box 5653
Bloomington, IN 47407-5653, USA

Newell, Horner E (Physicist)
2567 Nicky Ln
Alexandria, VA 22311-1311, USA

Newell, James
20519 Rodax St
Canoga Park, CA 91306-1530, USA

Newell, Mike (Actor, Director, Producer)
c/o Duncan Heath *International Creative
Management (ICM-UK)*
Oxford House
76 Oxford St
London W1N OAX, UNITED KINGDOM
(UK)

Newell, Peter F (Pete) (Coach)
16078 Via Viajera
Rancho Santa Fe, CA 92091-4328, USA

Newell, Tom (Baseball Player)
Philadelphia Phillies
9525 Cordoba Blvd
Sparks, NV 89441-5569, USA

Newfield, Heidi (Musician)
Creative Artists Agency
9830 Wilshire Blvd
Beverly Hills, CA 90212-1804, USA

Newfield, Marc (Baseball Player)
Seattle Mariners
5591 Selkirk Dr
Huntington Beach, CA 92649-4830, USA

Newgard, Christopher (Misc)
Southwestern Medical Center
Biochemistry Dept
Dallas, TX 75237, USA

Newhan, David (Baseball Player)
San Diego Padres
2678 Harvest Crest Ln
Corona, CA 92881-3572, USA

Newhart, Bob (Actor, Comedian)
c/o Leanne Coronel *Endeavor Agency LLC
(LA)*
9601 Wilshire Blvd Fl 3
Beverly Hills, CA 90210-5204, USA

Newhauser, Don (Baseball Player)
Boston Red Sox
321 Sheryl Dr
Deltona, FL 32738-8441, USA

Newhouse, Bob
6847 Truxton Dr
Dallas, TX 75231-5717, USA

Newhouse, Donald E (Publisher)
Advance Publications
950 W Fingerboard Rd
Staten Island, NY 10305-1453, USA

Newhouse, Fred
816 Bantry Way
Benicia, CA 94510-3804, USA

Newhouse, Fredrick (Fred) (Athlete, Track
Athlete)
3003 Pine Lake Trl
Houston, TX 77068-1435, USA

Newhouse Jr, Samuel I (Publisher)
Advance Publications
950 W Fingerboard Rd
Staten Island, NY 10305-1453, USA

Newkirk (Anastacia), Anastacia
(Musician)
c/o Simon Renshaw *Strategics Artist
Management*
1100 Glendon Ave Ste 1000
Los Angeles, CA 90024-3514, USA

Newland, Bob (Football Player)
New Orleans Saints
3895 Vine Maple St
Eugene, OR 97405-4494, USA

Newlin, Mike (Basketball Player)
1414 Horseshoe Dr
Sugar Land, TX 77478-3464, USA

Newman, Al (Baseball Player)
Montreal Expos
1044 La Roda Ct
Ontario, CA 91762-6105, USA

Newman, Al (Baseball Player)
Tampa Bay Devil Rays
24 Rice Loop
Pineville, LA 71405, USA

Newman, Alec (Actor)
c/o Laina Cohn *Relativity Management*
8899 Beverly Blvd Ste 510
Los Angeles, CA 90048-2449, USA

Newman, Anthony (Conductor, Musician)
I C M Artists
40 W 57th St
New York, NY 10019-4001, USA

Newman, Barry (Actor)
c/o Michael Greene *Greene & Associates*
190 N Canon Dr Ste 200
Beverly Hills, CA 90210-5319, USA

Newman, David (Composer)
Agency for Performing Arts
405 S Beverly Dr Ste 500
Beverly Hills, CA 90212-4425, USA

Newman, David(Fathead) (Musician)
Maxine Harvard
7942 W Belt Road
Glendale, AZ 85308, USA

Newman, Edward K (Ed) (Football Player)
Miami Dolphins
10100 SW 140th St
Miami, FL 33176-6685, USA

Newman, Edwin
870 United Nations Plz Apt 16D
New York, NY 10017-1824, USA

Newman, James H (Astronaut)
18583 Martinique Dr
Houston, TX 77058-4213, USA

Newman, Jeff (Baseball Player)
Oakland A's
10133 N 103rd St
Scottsdale, AZ 85258-4953, USA

Newman, Jimmy C (Musician, Songwriter,
Writer)
RR 2
Christiana, TN 37037, USA

Newman, Johnny (Basketball Player)
Dallas Mavericks
2909 Taylor St
Dallas, TX 75226-1909, USA

Newman, Jon O (Judge)
US Court of Appeals
450 Main St Rm 218
Hartford, CT 06103-3018, USA

Newman, Joseph M (Director)
2319 Magnolia St
Simi Valley, CA 93065-2636, USA

Newman, Kevin (Correspondent)
ABC-TV
77 W 66th St
News Dept
New York, NY 10023-6201, USA

Newman, Laraine (Actor, Comedian)
c/o Staff Member *TalentWorks (LA)*
3500 W Olive Ave Ste 1400
Burbank, CA 91505-5512, USA

Newman, Michael (Actor)
Morgan Agency
1200 N Doheny Dr
Los Angeles, CA 90069-1723, USA

Newman, Nanette (Actor)
Seven Pines Wentworth
Surrey GU25 4QP, UNITED KINGDOM
(UK)

Newman, Oscar (Architect)
Community Design Analysis Institute
66 Clover Dr
Great Neck, NY 11021-1030, USA

Newman, Paul (Actor)
c/o Toni Howard *International Creative
Management (ICM-NY)*
40 W 57th St
New York, NY 10019-4001, USA

Newman, Pauline (Judge)
US Court of Appeals
717 Madison Pl NW
Washington, DC 20439-0001, USA

Newman, Phyllis (Actor, Musician)
Gage Group
315 W 57th St Frnt 4H
New York, NY 10019-3158, USA

Newman, Randy (Musician, Songwriter)
c/o Staff Member *Paradigm (Monterey)*
509 Hartnell St
Monterey, CA 93940-2825, USA

Newman, Ray (Baseball Player)
Chicago Cubs
1260 Malibu Ln
Myrtle Beach, SC 29577-6342, USA

Newman, Terence (Football Player)
Dallas Cowboys
1 Cowboys Pkwy
Irving, TX 75063-4999, USA

Newman, Thomas (Actor)
Badgley Connor Talent
1680 Vine St Ste 1016
Los Angeles, CA 90028-8800, USA

Newman, Thomas (Composer)
Gorfaine/Schwartz
4111 W Alameda Ave Ste 509
Burbank, CA 91505-4171, USA

Newmar, Julie (Actor)
204 S Carmelina Ave
Los Angeles, CA 90049-3952, USA

News, Huey Lewis & The (Music Group)
c/o Staff Member *Paradigm (Monterey)*
509 Hartnell St
Monterey, CA 93940-2825, USA

Newsom, David (Actor)
Innovative Artists
1505 10th St
Santa Monica, CA 90401-2805, USA

Newsom, David D (Diplomat)
500 Crestwood Dr Apt 2504
Charlottesville, VA 22903-4883, USA

Newsome, Billy (Football Player)
Baltimore Colts
PO Box 8401
Jacksonville, TX 75766-8401, USA

Newsome, Gavin (Misc)
Mayor's Office
400 S Van Ness Ave
City Hall
San Francisco, CA 94103-3630, USA

Newsome, Harry (Football Player)
Pittsburgh Steelers
531 Manor Rd
Cheraw, SC 29520, USA

Newsome, Ozzie (Football Player)
Cleveland Browns
6 Padonia Woods Ct
Cockeysville, MD 21030-1744, USA

Newsome, Timothy A (Football Player)
Dallas Cowboys
7005 Quartermile Ln
Dallas, TX 75248-1447, USA

Newsome, Vince (Football Player)
Los Angeles Rams
5308 Woodnote Ln
Columbia, MD 21044-5707, USA

Newson, Warren (Baseball Player)
Chicago White Sox
13232 Padre Ave
Keller, TX 76248-1826, USA

Newsted, Jason (Musician)
205 Alamo View Pl
Walnut Creek, CA 94595-2600, USA

Newton, Becki (Actor)
c/o Matthew Lesher *Lesher Entertainment
Inc*
1134 S Cloverdale Ave
Los Angeles, CA 90019-6737, USA

Newton, C M (Coach)
200 W 2nd St Unit 300
Lexington, KY 40507-1123, USA

Newton, Christopher (Director)
22 Prideaux St
Niagara-on-the-Lake, ON L0S 1J0,
CANADA

Newton, John Haymes (Actor)
c/o Staff Member *Pakula/King &
Associates*
9229 W Sunset Blvd Ste 315
Los Angeles, CA 90069-3403, USA

Newton, Jon (Business Person)
American General Corp
2929 Allen Pkwy
Houston, TX 77019-2155, USA

Newton, Juice (Musician, Songwriter,
Writer)
OJ Mgmt
4321 Reyes Dr
Tarzana, CA 91356-5127, USA

Newton, Nate (Football Player)
Dallas Cowboys
1921 White Oak Clearing
Southlake, TX 76092-6929, USA

Newton, Robert L (Football Player)
Chicago Bears
11500 NE 76th St # A-353
Vancouver, WA 98662-3901, USA

Newton, Roger (Scientist)
Esperion Therapeutics
695 Kms Pl
3621 S State St
Ann Arbor, MI 48108-1657, USA

Newton, Thandie (Actor)
c/o Joe Libonati *I/D PR (LA)*
8409 Santa Monica Blvd
West Hollywood, CA 90069-4209, USA

Newton, Thomas
9229 W Sunset Blvd Ste 311
Los Angeles, CA 90069-3403, USA

Newton, Tom (Football Player)
New York Jets
169 Park Rd
Rochester, NY 14622-1217, USA

Newton, Wayne (Actor, Musician)
Wayne Newton Mgmt
6730 S Pecos Rd
Las Vegas, NV 89120-2812, USA

Newton-John, Olivia (Actor, Musician)
c/o Mark Hartley *Fitzgerald-Hartley*
34 N Palm St # 100
Ventura, CA 93001-2635, USA

Ney, Edward N (Business Person, Diplomat)
Burson-Marsteller
230 Park Ave S
New York, NY 10003-1566, USA

Neyelova, Marina M (Actor)
Potapovsky Per 12
Moscow 117333, RUSSIA

Neyra, Gianella (Actor)
c/o Staff Member *Telefe - Argentina*
Pavon 2444 (C1248AAT)
Buenos Aires, ARGENTINA

Nezelek, Andy (Baseball Player)
5707 Long Cove Rd
Midlothian, VA 23112-2450, USA

Nezhat, Camran (Misc)
Fertility/Endocrinology Ctr
5555 Peachtree Dunwoody Rd NE
Atlanta, GA 30342-1703, USA

Nguema, Tedoro Obiang (President)
President's Office
Malabo
EQUATORIAL GUINEA

Nguyen, Dat (Football Player)
Dallas Cowboys
3610 Spears Rd
Houston, TX 77066-4117, USA

Nguyen, Dustin (Actor)
1051 S Dunsmuir Ave
Los Angeles, CA 90019-6755, USA

Nguyen, Navia (Actor)
c/o Michael Greenwald *Don Buchwald & Associates Inc (LA)*
6500 Wilshire Blvd Ste 2200
Los Angeles, CA 90048-4942, USA

Nguyen, Scotty (Misc)
c/o Staff Member *Poker Royalty, LLC*
8367 W Flamingo Rd Ste 102
Las Vegas, NV 89147-4150, USA

Niarhos, Gus (Baseball Player)
New York Yankees
563 Kimberton Rd
Phoenixville, PA 19460-4745, USA

Nicastro, Michelle
1800 Avenue Of The Stars Ste 400
Los Angeles, CA 90067-4206, USA

Nicaud, Philippe
104 rue des Sablons
Mareil-Marly 78750, FRANCE

Niccol, Andrew (Director, Producer, Writer)
c/o Ken Stovitz *Creative Artists Agency LCC (CAA-LA)*
2000 Avenue Of The Stars
Los Angeles, CA 90067-4700, USA

Nichol, Joseph McGinty (McG) (Musician, Producer, Writer)
c/o Staff Member *Wonderland Sound and Vision*
8739 W Sunset Blvd
W Hollywood, CA 90069-2205, USA

Nicholas, Alison (Golfer)
Pat Darby The Flat
Badgar Farm House
Badgar near Wolverhampton WV6 7IS, UNITED KINGDOM (UK)

Nicholas, Denise (Actor)
932 S Longwood Ave
Los Angeles, CA 90019-1752, USA

Nicholas, Don (Baseball Player)
Chicago White Sox
12311 Chase St
Garden Grove, CA 92845-2109, USA

Nicholas, Eric (Writer)
c/o Staff Member *Gersh Agency, The (LA)*
232 N Canon Dr
Beverly Hills, CA 90210-5302, USA

Nicholas, Henry (Misc)
Hospital & Health Care Union
330 W 42nd St Ste 1905
New York, NY 10036-6902, USA

Nicholas, J D (Musician)
Management Assoc
1920 Benson Ave
Saint Paul, MN 55116-3214, USA

Nicholas, Peter M (Business Person)
Boston Scientific Corp
1 Boston Scientific Pl
Natick, MA 01760-1537, USA

Nicholas, Thomas Ian (Actor)
Osbrink Talent
4343 Lankershim Blvd # 100
North Hollywood, CA 91602-2705, USA

Nicholas Jr, Nicholas J (Publisher)
Pluggers Inc
1000 SW Broadway # 1850
Portland, OR 97205-3035, USA

Nicholas(Smisko), Bishop (Religious Leader)
American Carpatho
312 Garfield St
Johnstown, PA 15906-2122, USA

Nicholls, Craig (Musician)
Winterman-Goldstein
17 Holdsworth St
Newton, NSW 2042, AUSTRALIA

Nicholls, Paul (Actor)
c/o Darren Statt *United Talent Agency (UTA)*
9560 Wilshire Blvd Ste 500
Beverly Hills, CA 90212-2401, USA

Nichols, Austin (Actor)
c/o Amy Slomovits *Joan Green Management*
1836 Courtney Ter
Los Angeles, CA 90046-2106, USA

Nichols, Bobby (Golfer)
8681 Glenlyon Ct
Fort Myers, FL 33912-2408, USA

Nichols, Carl (Baseball Player)
Baltimore Orioles
4531 S Van Ness Ave
Los Angeles, CA 90062-1938, USA

Nichols, Dorothy L (Financier)
Farm Credit Administration
1501 Farm Credit Dr
McLean, VA 22102-5090, USA

Nichols, Hamilton J (Football Player)
Chicago Cardinals
11015 Kirkmead Dr
Houston, TX 77089-3116, USA

Nichols, Joe (Musician)
c/o Staff Member *Creative Artists Agency (CAA-Nashville)*
3310 W End Ave Fl 5
Nashville, TN 37203-1028, USA

Nichols, John (Writer)
c/o Staff Member *The New Press*
38 Greene St Fl 4
New York, NY 10013-2505, USA

Nichols, Kenwood C (Business Person)
Champion Int'l Corp
1 Champion Plz
Stamford, CT 06921-6001, USA

Nichols, Kyra (Ballerina)
Peter Diggins Assoc
133 W 71st St
New York, NY 10023-3834, USA

Nichols, Larry (Designer)
Moleculon Research Corp
139 Main St
Cambridge, MA 02142-1530, USA

Nichols, Lorrie (Bowler)
1251 Lexington Dr
Algonquin, IL 60102-2065, USA

Nichols, Marisol (Actor)
206 S Brand Blvd
Glendale, CA 91204-1310, USA

Nichols, Mark (Football Player)
Detroit Lions
5905 Penn Station Ln
Bakersfield, CA 93311-9016, USA

Nichols, Mike (Comedian, Director)
Friends in Deed Inc
594 Broadway Rm 706
New York, NY 10012-3257, USA

Nichols, Nichelle (Actor)
23281 Leonora Dr
Woodland Hills, CA 91367-6038, USA

Nichols, Peter R (Writer)
Alan Brodie
211 Piccadilly
London W1V 9LD, UNITED KINGDOM (UK)

Nichols, Rachel (Actor)
c/o Peter Kiernan *Management 360*
9111 Wilshire Blvd
Beverly Hills, CA 90210-5508, USA

Nichols, Reld (Baseball Player)
Boston Red Sox
721 Country View Ct
Birmingham, AL 35215-2129, USA

Nichols, Rod (Baseball Player)
Cleveland Indians
PO Box 64
Kannapolis, NC 28082-0064, USA

Nichols, Stephen (Actor)
11664 National Blvd # 116
Los Angeles, CA 90064-3802, USA

Nicholson, Bruce
PO Box 2573
Georgetown, SC 29442-2573, USA

Nicholson, Dave (Baseball Player)
Baltimore Orioles
527 Spring St
Roselle, IL 60172, USA

Nicholson, Jack (Actor)
c/o Sandy Bresler *Bresler Kelly & Associates*
11500 W Olympic Blvd Ste 352
Los Angeles, CA 90064-1525, USA

Nicholson, Jim (Football Player)
Kansas City Chiefs
91-845 Kauwili St
Ewa Beach, HI 96706-2854, USA

Nicholson, Jim (Government Official, Secretary)
412 Russell Senate Office Building
Washington, DC 20510-0001, USA

Nicholson, Julianne (Actor)
939 8th Ave Apt 609
New York, NY 10019-4204, USA

Nicholson, Kathrin
9057A Nemo St
W Hollywood, CA 90069, USA

Nichting, Chris (Baseball Player)
Texas Rangers
300 University Ln Apt 116
Batavia, OH 45103-2711, USA

Nickel, Elbert (Football Player)
Pittsburgh Steelers
2624 Evercrest Ct
Naperville, IL 60564-4624, USA

Nickel Creek (Music Group)
c/o Staff Member *William Morris Agency (WMA-TN)*
1600 Division St Ste 300
Nashville, TN 37203-2755, USA

Nickelback (Music Group)
c/o Natasha Anderson *Agency Group Ltd, The (UK)*
361-373 City Road
London EC1V 1PQ, UNITED KINGDOM (UK)

Nickerson, Hardy O (Football Player)
Pittsburgh Steelers
8716 Longview Club Dr
Waxhaw, NC 28173-6696, USA

Nickerson Jr, Donald A (Religious Leader)
Episcopal Church
815 2nd Ave
New York, NY 10017-4594, USA

Nickla, Ed (Football Player)
Chicago Bears
21 Ida Ln
North Babylon, NY 11703-1403, USA

Nicklaus, Gary
112 Tpc Blvd.
Ponte Vedra Beach, FL 32082, USA

Nicklaus, Jack W (Golfer)
Golden Bear Sports Management
11760 US Highway 1 Ste 500
North Palm Beach, FL 33408-3088, USA

Nickle, Doug (Baseball Player)
Philadelphia Phillies
19440 Victoria Ct Apt R2
Sonoma, CA 95476-3829, USA

Nicks, John A W (Misc)
Ice Capades Chalet
13211 Brooks Dr # A
Baldwin Park, CA 91706, USA

Nicks, Regina (Musician)
Bobby Roberts
3050 Business Park Cir Ste 303
Goodlettsville, TN 37072-3588, USA

Nicks, Stevie (Musician, Songwriter, Writer)
H K Mgmt
9200 W Sunset Blvd Ste 530
Los Angeles, CA 90069-3509, USA

Nickson, Julia (Actor)
Elkins Entertainment
8306 Wilshire Blvd # 438
Beverly Hills, CA 90211-2304, USA

Nicol, Steve (Coach, Football Coach)
New England Revolution
1 Patriot Pl
Cmgi Field
Foxboro, MA 02035-1388, USA

Nicol-Fox, Helen (Baseball Player)
432 E Cornell Dr
Tempe, AZ 85283-1908, USA

Nicolaou, Kyriacos Costa (Misc)
Scripps Research Institute
10550 N Torrey Pines Rd
La Jolla, CA 92037-1000, USA

Nicole
Im Pfarrwittum 1
Nohfelden D-66625, GERMANY

Nicolet, Aurele (Musician)
Hans Ulrich Schmid
Postfach 1617
Hanover 30016, GERMANY

Nicolet, Danielle (Actor)
c/o Paul Santana *Agency for the Performing Arts (APA-LA)*
405 S Beverly Dr
Beverly Hills, CA 90212-4416, USA

Nicoletti Susi
Goethegasse
Vienna 1 A-1010, AUSTRIA

Nicollier, Claude (Astronaut)
18710 Martinique Dr
Houston, TX 77058-4218, USA

Nicolucci, Guy (Writer)
c/o Staff Member *Gersh Agency, The (LA)*
232 N Canon Dr
Beverly Hills, CA 90210-5302, USA

Nicora, Attilio Cardinal (Religious Leader)
Patrimony of Apostolic See
Palazzo Apostolico
00120, VATICAN CITY

Nicosia, Steve (Baseball Player)
Pittsburgh Pirates
1404 NW 103rd Ave
Plantation, FL 33322, USA

Nieberg, Lars (Misc)
Gestit Waldershausen
Homberg 35315, GERMANY

Nied, David (Baseball Player)
Atlanta Braves
PO Box 836
Grand Prairie, TX 75050, USA

Niedenfuer, Tom (Baseball Player)
Los Angeles Dodgers
3933 Losillias Dr
Sarasota, FL 34238-4537, USA

Nieder, William H (Bill) (Athlete, Track Athlete)
PO Box 310
Mountain Ranch, CA 95246-0310, USA

Niederhoffer, Victor (Misc)
Niederhoffer Cross Zeckhauser
757 3rd Ave
New York, NY 10017-2013, USA

Niedermayer, Scott (Hockey Player)
49 Belcourt Dr
Newport Beach, CA 92660-4214, USA

Niedernhuber, Barbara (Athlete)
Schwarzeckstr 58
Ramsau 83486, GERMANY

Niehaus, Dave (Sportscaster)
Seattle Mariners
PO Box 4100
Safeco Field
Seattle, WA 98194-0100, USA

Niehaus, David (Baseball Player)
Seattle Mariners
18406 NW Montreux Dr
Issaquah, WA 98027-7817, USA

Niehaus, Lennie (Composer)
Robert Light Agency
6404 Wilshire Blvd Ste 1225
Los Angeles, CA 90048-5550, USA

Niehaus, Ralph (Football Player)
Cleveland Rams
114 Siebenthaler Ave
Cincinnati, OH 45215-3716, USA

Niehaus, Steve (Football Player)
Seattle Seahawks
114 Siebenthaler Ave
Cincinnati, OH 45215-3716, USA

Niekro, Joe (Baseball Player)
Chicago Cubs
2707 S Fairway Dr
Plant City, FL 33566-0919, USA

Niekro, Lance (Baseball Player)
San Francisco Giants
634 Peninsular Dr
Lakeland, FL 33813-4523, USA

Niekro, Phil (Baseball Player)
Milwaukee Braves
6382 Nichols Rd
Flowery Branch, GA 30542-2619, USA

Niel, Steve (Actor)
c/o Laura Walsh *Central Artists*
3310 W Burbank Blvd # A
Burbank, CA 91505-2230, USA

Nielsen, Brigitte (Actor, Model)
c/o Staff Member *L M Management (Italy)*
c/o Studio Lele Mora
viale Monza 9
Milan 20125, ITALY

Nielsen, Connie (Actor)
c/o Estelle Lasher *Principal Entertainment (LA)*
1964 Westwood Blvd Ste 400
Los Angeles, CA 90025-4695, USA

Nielsen, Gifford (Football Player)
Houston Oilers
10 Sarahs Cv
Sugar Land, TX 77479-2449, USA

Nielsen, Jerry (Baseball Player)
New York Yankees
4631 Kewanee St
Fair Oaks, CA 95628-6219, USA

Nielsen, Leslie (Actor)
c/o Sandy Bresler *Bresler Kelly & Associates*
11500 W Olympic Blvd Ste 352
Los Angeles, CA 90064-1525, USA

Nielsen, Milt (Baseball Player)
Cleveland Indians
215 N Power Rd Unit 194
Mesa, AZ 85205-8442, USA

Nielsen, Rick (Musician)
Monterey Peninsula Artists
509 Hartnell St
Monterey, CA 93940-2825, USA

Nielsen, Scott (Baseball Player)
New York Yankees
2898 Valley View Ave
Salt Lake City, UT 84117-5550, USA

Niemann, Randy (Baseball Player)
Houston Astros
1585 SW Harbour Isles Cir
Port Saint Lucie, FL 34986-3403, USA

Niemann-Stirnemann, Gunda (Speed Skater)
Postfach 503
Erfurt 99010, GERMANY

Niemeyer, Paul V (Judge)
US Court of Appeals
101 W Lombard St
Baltimore, MD 21201-2605, USA

Niemi, Lisa (Actor)
Flick East-West
9057 Nemo St # A
West Hollywood, CA 90069-5511, USA

Niemiec-Konwinski, Dolly (Baseball Player)
1821 Spring Meadow Ct SE
Caledonia, MI 49316-9154, USA

Nieminen, Toni (Skier)
Landen Kanava 99
vesijarvenkatu 74
Lahti 15140, FINLAND

Nierman, Leonardo (Artist)
Amsterdam 43 PH
Mexico City 11 DF, MEXICO

Nies, Eric (Actor, Model, Reality TV Star)
c/o Staff Member *Bunim/Murray Productions Inc*
6007 Sepulveda Blvd
Van Nuys, CA 91411-2502, USA

Nieson, Chuck (Baseball Player)
Minnesota Twins
14408 Edgewood Ave
Savage, MN 55378-2872, USA

Nieto, Adriana (Actor)
c/o Staff Member *Televisa*
Blvd Adolfo Lopez Mateos 232
Colonia San Angel INN
DF CP 01060, MEXICO

Nieto, Tom (Baseball Player)
St Louis Cardinals
22446 Eagles Watch Dr
Land O Lakes, FL 34639-6759, USA

Nieuwendyk, Joe (Hockey Player)
11784 NW 69th Pl
Parkland, FL 33076-3322, USA

Nieves, Juan (Baseball Player)
Milwaukee Brewers
1676 Calle 22 SW
San Juan, PR 00921-1238, USA

Nieves, Melvin (Baseball Player)
Atlanta Braves
PO Box 87
Southern Pines, NC 28388-0087, USA

Nigam, Anjul (Actor)
c/o Lisa DiSante-Frank *Greene & Associates*
190 N Canon Dr Ste 200
Beverly Hills, CA 90210-5319, USA

Nigh, George P (Educator, Governor)
University of Central Oklahoma
100 N University Dr
Edmond, OK 73034-5209, USA

Nighswander, Nicholas (Football Player)
Buffalo Bills
PO Box 46
Burgoon, OH 43407-0046, USA

Night Ranger (Music Group)
c/o Staff Member *Paradigm (Monterey)*
509 Hartnell St
Monterey, CA 93940-2825, USA

Nightingale, Maxine
c/o Staff Member *Diva Central Inc*
7510 W Sunset Blvd Ste 1445
Los Angeles, CA 90046-3408, USA

Nighy, Bill (Actor)
c/o Chris Andrews *Creative Artists Agency LCC (CAA-LA)*
2000 Avenue Of The Stars
Los Angeles, CA 90067-4700, USA

Nigrelli, Ross F (Misc)
29 Barracuda Rd
East Quogue, NY 11942-4915, USA

Nihalani, Govind (Director, Filmmaker, Producer)
139 Aradhana Behind Bhavishya Nidhi Bandra (E)
Bombay, MS 400 051, INDIA

Niinimaa, Janne (Hockey Player)
2200-201 Portage Ave
Winnipeg, MB R3B 3L3, CANADA

Nikkanen, Kurt (Musician)
Columbia Artists Mgmt Inc
1790 Broadway Fl 6
New York, NY 10019-1412, USA

Niklas, Jan
Konigsberger Str. 20
Munich D-81927, GERMANY

Nikolishin, Andrei (Hockey Player)
105 Bloomfield Ave
Hartford, CT 06105-1008, USA

Niland, John H (Football Player)
Dallas Cowboys
16058 Chalfont Ct
Dallas, TX 75248-3547, USA

Niles, John (Composer, Musician)
Magic Wing Music
PO Box 222
West Linn, OR 97068-0222, USA

Niles, Nicholas H (Publisher)
Sporting News Publishing Co
1212 N Lindbergh Blvd
Saint Louis, MO 63132, USA

Niles, Prescott (Musician)
Artists & Audience Entertainment
PO Box 35
Pawling, NY 12564-0035, USA

Niles, Thomas M T (Diplomat)
National Defense Hdqs Library
101 C By Dr
Ottawa, ON K1A 0K2, CANADA

Nilsen, Reed (Football Player)
Detroit Lions
1078 S 1400 W
Salt Lake City, UT 84104-3233, USA

Nilsmark, Catrin (Golfer)
187 Commodore Dr
Jupiter, FL 33477-4007, USA

Nilsson, David (Baseball Player)
Milwaukee Brewers
9100 E Raintree Dr
Scottsdale, AZ 85260-2762, USA

Nilsson, Inger
Box 12710
Stockholm 11294, SWEDEN

Nilsson, Lennart (Photographer)
Pantheon Books
201 E 50th St
New York, NY 10022-7703, USA

Nimmo, Dirk (Actor)
Michael Whitehall
125 Gloucester Road
London SW7 4TE, UNITED KINGDOM
(UK)

Nimmons, Ernest (Baseball Player)
Indianapolis Clowns
1509 Paine St
Lorain, OH 44052-3253, USA

Nimoy, Leonard (Actor, Director,
Photographer)
c/o Bob Gersh *Gersh Agency, The (LA)*
232 N Canon Dr
Beverly Hills, CA 90210-5302, USA

Nimri, Najwa (Actor, Musician)
c/o Staff Member *Kuranda Management
Intl*
Santo Angel, 84
Madrid 28043, SPAIN

Nimziki, Joe (Director)
Paradigm Agency
10100 Santa Monica Blvd Ste 2500
Los Angeles, CA 90067-4116, USA

Nine Black Alps (Music Group)
c/o Staff Member *Paradigm (Monterey)*
509 Hartnell St
Monterey, CA 93940-2825, USA

Nine Inch Nails (NIN) (Music Group)
c/o Staff Member *Helter Skelter (UK)*
535 Kings Rd
The Plaza
London SW10 0SZ, UNITED KINGDOM
(UK)

Ninedays (Music Group)
c/o Staff Member *Epic Records Group*
550 Madison Ave
New York, NY 10022-3211, USA

Nininger, Harvey H (Misc)
PO Box 420
Sedona, AZ 86339-0420, USA

Ninowski, Jim (Football Player)
Cleveland Browns
2715 Melcombe Cir Apt 302
Troy, MI 48084-3453, USA

Nipar, Yvette (Actor)
Irv Schechter
9300 Wilshire Blvd # 410
Beverly Hills, CA 90212-3213, USA

Nipon, Albert (Designer, Fashion
Designer)
Leslie Faye Co
1400 Broadway Rm 1600
Albert Nipon Div
New York, NY 10018-5200, USA

Nipp, Maury (Football Player)
Philadelphia Eagles
631 E Michelle St
West Covina, CA 91790-5146, USA

Nipper, Al (Baseball Player)
Boston Red Sox
401 White Birch Valley Ct
Chesterfield, MO 63017-2457, USA

Nippert, Merlin (Baseball Player)
Boston Red Sox
1015 N Michigan Ave
Mangum, OK 73554-1820, USA

Nirenberg, Marshall W (Nobel Prize
Laureate)
10005 Gary Rd
Potomac, MD 20854-4110, USA

Nirmala, Sister (Religious Leader)
Missionaries of Charity
54A Lower Circular Road
Kolkata, WB 700016, INDIA

Nirosha (Actor, Bollywood)
3 Paul Appasamy Street
T Nagar
Chennai, TN 600017, INDIA

Nirvana
151 El Camino Dr
Beverly Hills, CA 90212-2704, USA

Nisbet, Robert A (Activist, Historian)
6131 Purple Aster Ln NE
Albuquerque, NM 87111-8082, USA

Nisby, John (Football Player)
Pittsburgh Steelers
6339 Saint Andrews Dr
Stockton, CA 95219-1861, USA

Nischwitz, Ron (Baseball Player)
Detroit Tigers
17 S Saint Clair St Ste 330
Dayton, OH 45402-2178, USA

Nishizawa, Junichi (Engineer, Inventor)
Semiconductor Research Institute
Kawauchi
Aobaku
Sendai 9800862, JAPAN

Nishizuka, Yasutomi (Physicist)
Kobe University
7-5-1 Kusunokichochuoki
Kobe 650-0017, JAPAN

Nishkian, Byron (Skier)
150 4th St Ph
San Francisco, CA 94103-3048, USA

Niskanen Jr, William A (Economist,
Government Official)
Cato Institute
1000 Massachusetts Ave NW # 6
Washington, DC 20001-5401, USA

Nispel, Marcus (Director)
c/o Staff Member *Endeavor Agency LLC
(LA)*
9601 Wilshire Blvd Fl 3
Beverly Hills, CA 90210-5204, USA

Nissalke, Tom (Coach)
4569 Thousand Oaks Dr
Salt Lake City, UT 84124-3963, USA

Nissen, Steve (Doctor)
817 Hanover Rd
Gates Mills, OH 44040-9602, USA

Nithya (Actor, Bollywood)
37 Palayakaran Street
Chennai, TN 600024, INDIA

Nitkowski, C J (Baseball Player)
Cincinnati Reds
205 Townsend Ln
Alpharetta, GA 30004-2553, USA

Nittmann, David (Artist)
PO Box 19065
Boulder, CO 80308-2065, USA

Nittmo, Bjorn (Football Player)
New York Giants
201 E Jefferson St
Phoenix, AZ 85004-2412, USA

Nitty Gritty Dirt Band (Music Group)
c/o Staff Member *Paradigm (Monterey)*
509 Hartnell St
Monterey, CA 93940-2825, USA

Nitzkowski, Monte (Coach)
7041 Seat Circle
Huntington Beach, CA 92648, USA

Niven, Barbara
9300 Wilshire Blvd # 410
Beverly Hills, CA 90212-3213, USA

Niven, Kip (Actor)
9000 W Sunset Blvd Ste 801
Los Angeles, CA 90069-5808, USA

Niven, Laurence (Larry) (Writer)
11874 Macoda Ln
Chatsworth, CA 91311-1271, USA

Niven Jr, David
1457 Blue Jay Way
Los Angeles, CA 90069-1212, USA

Nivola, Alessandro (Actor)
c/o Eric Kranzler *Management 360*
9111 Wilshire Blvd
Beverly Hills, CA 90210-5508, USA

Niwa, Gail (Musician)
Siegel Artist Mgmt
1416 Hinman Ave
Evanston, IL 60201-5324, USA

Niwano, Nikkyo (Religious Leader)
Rissho Kosel-Kai
2-11-1 Wada Suginamiku
Tokyo 166, JAPAN

Nix, Doyle (Football Player)
Green Bay Packers
710 E 4th St
Weatherford, TX 76086-1844, USA

Nix, Emery (Football Player)
New York Giants
RR 4 Box 385
Blanco, TX 78606, USA

Nix, Garth (Writer)
Harper Collins
77 - 85 Fulham palace road
London W12 8ER, UNITED KINGDOM
(UK)

Nix, John L (Football Player)
San Francisco 49ers
2278 Lindsey Ct
Fallbrook, CA 92028-5304, USA

Nix, Kent (Football Player)
Pittsburgh Steelers
2732 Colonial Pkwy
Fort Worth, TX 76109-1211, USA

Nix, Matt (Writer)
c/o Staff Member *Endeavor Agency LLC
(LA)*
9601 Wilshire Blvd Fl 3
Beverly Hills, CA 90210-5204, USA

Nixon, Agnes (Producer, Writer)
774 Conestoga Rd
Bryn Mawr, PA 19010-1257, USA

Nixon, Cynthia (Actor)
c/o Emily Gerson Saines *Brookside Artists
Management (NY)*
250 W 57th St Ste 2303
New York, NY 10107-2399, USA

Nixon, Donell (Baseball Player)
Seattle Mariners
6401 Chadbourn Hwy
Chadbourn, NC 28431-1613, USA

Nixon, Gary (Motorcycle Race,
Motorcycle Racer)
Gary Nixon Enterprises
2408 Carroll Mill Rd
Phoenix, MD 21131-1104, USA

Nixon, Jeff (Football Player)
Buffalo Bills
549 Linwood Ave
Buffalo, NY 14209-1403, USA

Nixon, Marni (Actor, Musician)
Agency for Performing Arts
405 S Beverly Dr Ste 500
Beverly Hills, CA 90212-4425, USA

Nixon, Norm
607 Marguerita Ave
Santa Monica, CA 90402-1919, USA

Nixon, Otis (Baseball Player)
New York Yankees
1015 Leadenhall St
Alpharetta, GA 30022-8491, USA

Nixon, Russ (Baseball Player)
Cleveland Indians
4265 N Tee Pee Ln
Las Vegas, NV 89129-2628, USA

Nixon, Sam (Musician)
c/o Staff Member *Pop Idol (Fremantle
Media)*
2700 Colorado Ave Ste 450
Santa Monica, CA 90404-3599, USA

Nixon, Torran (Football Player)
San Francisco 49ers
3265 Thorn St
San Diego, CA 92104-4754, USA

Nixon, Trot (Baseball Player)
Boston Red Sox
1023 Ocean Ridge Dr
Wilmington, NC 28405-5287, USA

Niyazov, Saparmurad (President)
President's Office
Karl Marx Str 24
Ashkabad 744017, TURKMENISTAN

Nizhalgal, Raviee (Actor)
4 Sriram Nagar North Street
Chennai, TN 600 018, INDIA

Niziolek, Robert (Football Player)
Detroit Lions
206 W Brome Ave
Lafayette, CO 80026-1738, USA

Niznik, Stephanie (Actor)
c/o Staff Member *Niad Management*
15030 Ventura Blvd Ste 19 Ste 860
Sherman Oaks, CA 91403-2444, USA

NKOTB (New Kids on the Block)
27 Dudley St
Roxbury, MA 02119-3522, USA

No Doubt (Music Group)
c/o Jim Guerinot *Rebel Waltz Inc*
31652 2nd Ave
Laguna Beach, CA 92651-8244, USA

Noah, John (Hockey Player)
3315 W Prairiewood Dr S
Fargo, ND 58103-4666, USA

Noah, Max W (General)
820 Arcturus On Potomac
Alexandria, VA 22308-1301, USA

Noah, Yannick (Coach, Tennis Player)
20 Rue Billancourt
Boulogne 92100, FRANCE

Noakes, Michael (Artist)
146 Hamilton Terrace
Saint John's Wood
London NW8 9UX, UNITED KINGDOM
(UK)

Nobile, Leo (Football Player)
Washington Redskins
109 Cottonwood Ct
Coraopolis, PA 15108-2605, USA

Nobilo, Frank (Golfer)
Int'l Mgmt Group
1360 E 9th St Ste 100
Cleveland, OH 44114-1782, USA

Nobis, Thomas H (Tommy) Jr (Football
Executive, Football Player)
Atlanta Falcons
40 S Battery Pl NE
Atlanta, GA 30342-2443, USA

Noble, Adrian K (Director)
Royal Shakespeare Co
Barbican Theater
London EC2Y 8BQ, UNITED KINGDOM
(UK)

Noble, Brandon (Football Player)
Dallas Cowboys
2154 Ferncroft Ln
Chester Springs, PA 19425-3846, USA

Noble, Brian D (Football Player)
Green Bay Packers
2912 Nikki Lee Ct
Green Bay, WI 54313-9235, USA

Noble, Chelsea (Actor)
c/o Court Coursey *Red Wall Management*
9255 W Sunset Blvd Ste 727
Los Angeles, CA 90069-3304, USA

Noble, James (Actor)
113 Ledgebrook Dr
Norwalk, CT 06854-1070, USA

Noble, John (Actor)
c/o Nicolas Bernheim *Seven Summits
Pictures & Management*
8906 W Olympic Blvd Ground Floor
Beverly Hills, CA 90211, USA

Noble, Karen (Golfer)
160 Riverside Blvd Apt 5G
New York, NY 10069-0703, USA

Noble, Ross (Actor, Comedian)
c/o Staff Member *Real Talent
Management (UK)*
24 Goodge St
London W1T 2QF, UNITED KINGDOM
(UK)

Noblitt, Niles L (Business Person)
Biomet Inc
PO Box 587
Airport Industrial Park
Warsaw, IN 46581-0587, USA

Noboa, Gustavo (Educator, President)
Palacio de Gobierno
Garcia Moreno, Quito 1043, ECUADOR

Noce, Paul (Baseball Player)
Chicago Cubs
913 W Maumee St
Adrian, MI 49221-1915, USA

Nock, George (Football Player)
New York Jets
1025 Nine North Dr Ste H
Alpharetta, GA 30004-3951, USA

Nodell, Mart (Cartoonist)
117 Lake Irene Dr
West Palm Beach, FL 33411-2266, USA

Noe, Vergilius Cardinal (Religious Leader)
Piazza della Citta Leonina 1
Rome 00193, ITALY

Noel, Chris
6815 Lake Ave
West Palm Beach, FL 33405-4525, USA

Noel, Monique (Actor, Model)
PO Box 232058
Encinitas, CA 92023-2058, USA

Noel, Philip W (Governor)
345 Channel Vw Unit 105
Warwick, RI 02889-6520, USA

Nofsinger, Terry (Football Player)
Pittsburgh Steelers
21 Windsor Ct
Bountiful, UT 84010-8079, USA

Noguchi, Soichi (Astronaut)
NASA
2101 Nasa Pkwy
Johnson Space Center
Houston, TX 77058-3691, USA

Noguchi, Thomas (Doctor)
1110 Avoca Ave
Pasadena, CA 91105-3405, USA

Nogulich, Natalia (Actor)
11841 Kiowa Ave Apt 7
Los Angeles, CA 90049-6016, USA

Noji, Minae (Actor)
c/o Steven Jensen *The Independent Group
LLC*
8721 W Sunset Blvd Ste 105
Los Angeles, CA 90069-2271, USA

Nojima, Minoru (Musician)
John Gingrich Mgmt
PO Box 515
New York, NY 10023, USA

Nolan, Christopher (Writer)
c/o Dan Aloni *Creative Artists Agency
LCC (CAA-LA)*
2000 Avenue Of The Stars
Los Angeles, CA 90067-4700, USA

Nolan, Deanna (Basketball Player)
Detroit Shock
2 Championship Dr
Palace
Auburn Hills, MI 48326-1753, USA

Nolan, Gary (Baseball Player)
Cincinnati Reds
97 Acacia Ave
Oroville, CA 95966-3658, USA

Nolan, Graham
162 Godfrey Ter
East Aurora, NY 14052-2040, USA

Nolan, Joe (Baseball Player)
New York Mets
9515 Alix Dr
Saint Louis, MO 63123-7101, USA

Nolan, Jonathan (Writer)
c/o Keya Khayatian *United Talent Agency
(UTA)*
9560 Wilshire Blvd Ste 500
Beverly Hills, CA 90212-2401, USA

Nolan, Kathleen
250 W 57th St # 703
New York, NY 10107-0001, USA

Nolan, Kathleen (Kathy) (Actor)
c/o Staff Member *The House of
Representatives*
211 S Beverly Dr Ste 208
Beverly Hills, CA 90212-3879, USA

Nolan, Michelle (Actor)
c/o Rebecca (Becca) Kovacik *Hofflund/
Polone*
9465 Wilshire Blvd Ste 890
Beverly Hills, CA 90212-2607, USA

Nolan, Richard C (Dick) (Coach, Football
Player)
New York Giants
4 Gentry Ct
Trophy Club, TX 76262-5526, USA

Nolan, Ted (Coach, Hockey Player)
269 Queen St E
Sault Sainte Marie, ON P6A 1Y9,
CANADA

Nolan, Thomas B (Scientist)
2219 California St NW
Washington, DC 20008-3917, USA

Nolan, Tom
1335 N Ontario St
Burbank, CA 91505-1910, USA

Noland, Kenneth C (Artist)
PO Box 359
Port Clyde, ME 04855-0359, USA

Nolasco, Amaury (Actor)
c/o Samantha Crisp *Kohner Agency, The*
9300 Wilshire Blvd Ste 555
Beverly Hills, CA 90212-3211, USA

Nold, Dick (Baseball Player)
Washington Senators
715 Athens St
San Francisco, CA 94112-3513, USA

Noles, Dickie (Baseball Player)
Philadelphia Phillies
51 Hidden Valley Rd
Aston, PA 19014-2531, USA

Nolin, Gena Lee (Actor)
c/o David Rose *Innovative Artists (LA)*
1505 10th St
Santa Monica, CA 90401-2805, USA

Nolte, Claudia (Government Official)
Mulgarten 28
Ilmenau 98693, GERMANY

Nolte, Eric (Baseball Player)
San Diego Padres
682 Seville Dr
Hemet, CA 92543-2665, USA

Nolte, Nick (Actor)
c/o Joel Lubin *Creative Artists Agency
LCC (CAA-LA)*
2000 Avenue Of The Stars
Los Angeles, CA 90067-4700, USA

Nolting, Paul F (Religious Leader)
Church of Lutheran Confession
620 E 50th St
Loveland, CO 80538-1838, USA

Nomellini, Leo
520 Saint Claire Dr
Palo Alto, CA 94306-3050, USA

Nomina, Tom (Football Player)
Denver Broncos
731 N County Road 19 E
Loveland, CO 80537-4401, USA

Nomo, Hideo (Baseball Player)
Los Angeles Dodgers
10380 Wilshire Blvd Apt 202
Los Angeles, CA 90024-4741, USA

Nool, Erki (Athlete, Track Athlete)
Regati 1
Tallinn 11911, ESTONIA

Noonan, Chris (Actor)
c/o Staff Member *Creative Artists Agency
LCC (CAA-LA)*
2000 Avenue Of The Stars
Los Angeles, CA 90067-4700, USA

Noonan, Danny (Football Player)
Dallas Cowboys
1 Cowboys Pkwy
Irving, TX 75063-4999, USA

Noonan, John T Jr (Judge)
US Court of Appeals
95 7th St
Court Building
San Francisco, CA 94103-1518, USA

Noonan, Karl (Football Player)
Miami Dolphins
7149 Oxford Hunt Dr
Stanley, NC 28164-6803, USA

Noonan, Patrick F (Misc)
3553 Hamlet Pl
Chevy Chase, MD 20815-4822, USA

Noonan, Peggy (Writer)
Reagan Books
10 E 53rd St
New York, NY 10022-5244, USA

Noonan, Robert W Jr (General)
Deputy Chief of Stafff for Intelligence
Hqusa
Pentagon
Washington, DC 20310-0001, USA

Noonan, Timothy J (Business Person)
Rite Aid Corp
30 Hunter Ln
Camp Hill, PA 17011-2410, USA

Noone, Kathleen (Actor)
130 W 42nd St Ste 1804
New York, NY 10036-7902, USA

Noone, Nora Jane (Actor)
c/o Staff Member *International Creative
Management (ICM-UK)*
Oxford House
76 Oxford St
London W1N OAX, UNITED KINGDOM
(UK)

Noone, Peter (Actor, Musician)
9265 Robin Dr
Los Angeles, CA 90069-1146, USA

Noor, Queen
Baab al-Salem Palace
Amman, JORDAN

Noor Al-Hussein (Royalty)
Royal Palace
Amman, JORDAN

Noppenberg, John (Football Player)
Pittsburgh Steelers
5850 SW 100th St
Miami, FL 33156-2017, USA

Norcross, Clayton
951 Galloway St
Pacific Palisades, CA 90272-3850, USA

Nordbrook, Tim (Baseball Player)
Baltimore Orioles
70 Open Gate Ct
Nottingham, MD 21236-1681, USA

Nordenberg, Mark A (Educator)
University of Pittsburgh
President's Office
Pittsburgh, PA 15261-0001, USA

Nordenstrom, Bjorn (Doctor)
Karolinska Institute
Radiology Dept
Stockholm, SWEDEN

Nordhagen, Wayne (Baseball Player)
Chicago White Sox
25538 Baker Pl
Stevenson Ranch, CA 91381-1509, USA

Nordheim, Arne (Composer)
Wergelandsveien 2
Oslo 0167, NORWAY

Nordlander, Mattias (Musician)
MOB Agency
6404 Wilshire Blvd Ste 505
Los Angeles, CA 90048-5507, USA

Nordli, Odvar (Prime Minister)
Sanveien 4
Ottestad 2312, NORWAY

Nordling, Jeffrey
100 Universal City Plaza Bldg. 507#3D
Universal City, CA 91608, USA

Nordquist, Helen (Baseball Player)
PO Box 474
Alton, NH 03809-0474, USA

Nordquist, Mark (Football Player)
Philadelphia Eagles
3495 Seacrest Dr
Carlsbad, CA 92008-2039, USA

Nordsieck, Kenneth H (Astronaut)
University of Wisconsin
Space Astronomy Laboratory
Madison, WI 53706, USA

Noren, Irv (Baseball Player, Basketball
Player)
Washington Senators
3154 Camino Crest Dr
Oceanside, CA 92056-3613, USA

Noren, Lars (Writer)
Ostermalmsgatan 33
Stockholm 11426, SWEDEN

Norgard, Erik C (Football Player)
Houston Oilers
404 Winterthur Way
Littleton, CO 80129-5662, USA

Noriander, John (Basketball Player)
801 9th St N Apt 102
Virginia, MN 55792-2393, USA

Noriega, Carlos I (Astronaut)
13710 Shadow Falls Ct
Houston, TX 77059-3502, USA

Noriega, Eduardo (Actor)
c/o Staff Member *Televisa*
Blvd Adolfo Lopez Mateos 232
Colonia San Angel INN
DF CP 01060, MEXICO

Noriega, John (Baseball Player)
Cincinnati Reds
2 E Monticello Dr
Kaysville, UT 84037-2801, USA

Noriega, Victor (Actor)
c/o Staff Member *Televisa*
Blvd Adolfo Lopez Mateos 232
Colonia San Angel INN
DF CP 01060, MEXICO

Norman, Chris (Musician)
Denis Vaughan Mgmt
PO Box 28286
London N21 3WT, UNITED KINGDOM
(UK)

Norman, ChrisNL-
Venlo 5902 MA, THE NETHERLANDS

Norman, Dan (Baseball Player)
New York Mets
2011 Borrego Dr Apt 27
Barstow, CA 92311-6753, USA

Norman, Edie Jo (Bowler)
3544 Mariner Blvd
Spring Hill, FL 34609-2487, USA

Norman, Fred (Baseball Player)
Kansas City A's
1621 De Armand Ave
Cincinnati, OH 45239-4805, USA

Norman, Gregory J (Greg) (Golfer)
Great White Shark Enterprises
501 N Highway A1A
Jupiter, FL 33477-4577, USA

Norman, Jessye (Musician)
L'Orchidee
PO Box South
Crugers, NY 10521, USA

Norman, Joe (Football Player)
Seattle Seahawks
1526 Saunders Dr
Wooster, OH 44691-1558, USA

Norman, Ken (Basketball Player)
19020 Kelzie Ave
Homewood, IL 60430, USA

Norman, Marsha (Writer)
Abrams
275 7th Ave Fl 26
New York, NY 10001-6708, USA

Norman, Michael (Astronomer, Physicist)
University of California
Astronomy Dept
La Jolla, CA 90293, USA

Norman, Monty (Composer)
PRS
29/33 Berners St
London W1P 4AA, UNITED KINGDOM
(UK)

Norman, Nelson (Baseball Player)
Texas Rangers
3867 Jonathans Way
Boynton Beach, FL 33436-8524, USA

Norman, Pettis (Football Player)
Dallas Cowboys
1430 Bar Harbor Cir
Dallas, TX 75232-3010, USA

Norman, Steve (Musician)
International Talent Group
729 7th Ave Rm 1600
New York, NY 10019-6880, USA

Norman, Todd (Football Player)
Seattle Seahawks
27517 Via Montoya
San Juan Capistrano, CA 92675-5364,
USA

**Norodom Sihanouk, Prince Samdech
Preah** (King)
Khemarindra Palace
Phnom Penh, CAMBODIA

Norona, David (Actor)
c/o Staff Member *Kohner Agency, The*
9300 Wilshire Blvd Ste 555
Beverly Hills, CA 90212-3211, USA

Norrington, Roger A C
Camerata Academica Salzburg
Bergstr 22
Salzburg 5020, AUSTRIA

Norris, Alan E (Judge)
US Court of Appeals
85 Marconi Blvd
US Courthouse
Columbus, OH 43215-2823, USA

Norris, Chuck (Actor)
c/o Erik Kritzer *Fenton-Kritzer
Entertainment*
8840 Wilshire Blvd Fl 3
Beverly Hills, CA 90211-2606, USA

Norris, Darran (Actor)
c/o Staff Member *International Creative
Management (ICM-LA)*
10250 Constellation Blvd
Los Angeles, CA 90067-6200, USA

Norris, David Owen (Musician)
Aughton Rise
Collingbourne
Kingston Wilts SN8 3SA, UNITED
KINGDOM (UK)

Norris, James R Jr (Misc)
University of Chicago
5735 S Ellis Ave
Chemistry Dept
Chicago, IL 60637-1403, USA

Norris, Jim (Baseball Player)
Cleveland Indians
6375 Oak Hollow Dr
Burleson, TX 76028-2839, USA

Norris, John (Journalist, Television Host)
c/o Staff Member *MTV News*
1515 Broadway Fl 29
New York, NY 10036-8901, USA

Norris, Michele (Correspondent)
ABC-TV
5010 Creston St
News Dept
Hyattsville, MD 20781-1216, USA

Norris, Mike (Baseball Player)
Oakland A's
407 Perkins St Apt 105B
Oakland, CA 94610-4763, USA

Norris, Paul J (Business Person)
WR Grace Co
7500 Grace Dr
Columbia, MD 21044-4029, USA

Norris, Terry (Boxer)
Don King Productions
968 Pinehurst Dr
Las Vegas, NV 89109-1569, USA

Norris, Tim (Golfer)
1604 Little Kitten Ave
Manhattan, KS 66503-7500, USA

Norris, William A (Judge)
US COurt of Appeals
312 N Spring St Ste G33
Los Angeles, CA 90012-4711, USA

Norseth, Mike (Football Player)
Cincinnati Bengals
9774 Jameson Point Cv
Sandy, UT 84092-4200, USA

Norstrom, Mattais (Actor)
Los Angeles Kings
1111 S Figueroa St
Los Angeles, CA 90015-1300, USA

Norstrom, Mattias (Hockey Player)
3516 Amherst Ave
Dallas, TX 75225-7419, USA

North, Andy (Golfer)
3289 High Point Rd
Madison, WI 53719, USA

North, Billy (Baseball Player)
Chicago Cubs
5523 106th Ave NE
Kirkland, WA 98033-7413, USA

North, Chandra (Model)
Women Model Mgmt
107 Greene St # 200
New York, NY 10012-3803, USA

North, Douglass C (Nobel Prize Laureate)
7569 Homestead Rd
Benzonia, MI 49616-9520, USA

North, J J
PO Box 614
Bloomfield, NJ 07003-0614, USA

North, Jay (Actor)
290 NE 1st Ave
Lake Butler, FL 32054-1202, USA

North, Oliver L (General, Government
Official, Television Host)
c/o Staff Member *Fox News Channel (NY)*
1211 Avenue Of The Americas
Level C1
New York, NY 10036-8701, USA

Northam, Jeremy (Actor)
c/o Chris Andrews *Creative Artists Agency
LCC (CAA-LA)*
2000 Avenue Of The Stars
Los Angeles, CA 90067-4700, USA

Northcutt, Dennis (Football Player)
Cleveland Browns
26596 Oakdale Canyon Ln
Canyon Country, CA 91387-8125, USA

Northey, Scott (Baseball Player)
Kansas City Royals
9920 Bankside Dr
Roswell, GA 30076-3735, USA

Northrop, Wayne (Actor)
37900 Road 800
Raymond, CA 93653-9714, USA

Northrup, Jim (Baseball Player)
Detroit Tigers
3450 Saddle Rdg
Highland, MI 48357-2536, USA

Northrup, Wayne
21919 Canon Dr
Topanga, CA 90290-4336, USA

Northrup, MD, Christiane (Writer)
Empowering Women's Wisdom
PO Box 199
Yarmouth, ME 04096-0199, USA

Northtrip, Richard A (Misc)
Cement & Allied Workers Union
2500 Brickdale
Elk Grove Village, IL 60007, USA

Northway, Douglas (Doug) (Swimmer)
3239 E 3rd St
Tucson, AZ 85716-4231, USA

Norton, Corin (Actor)
c/o Staff Member *Bruce Heller and
Associates*
3272 Motor Ave Suites F & G
Los Angeles, CA 90039, USA

Norton, Edward (Actor)
c/o Brian Swardstrom *Endeavor Agency
LLC (LA)*
9601 Wilshire Blvd Fl 3
Beverly Hills, CA 90210-5204, USA

Norton, Gale (Secretary)
Interior Department
1849 C St NW
Washington, DC 20240-0001, USA

Norton, Graham (Actor)
c/o Staff Member *Talk Back Management*
20-21 Newman St
London W1T 1PG, UNITED KINGDOM
(UK)

Norton, Greg (Baseball Player)
Chicago White Sox
312 Windchime Dr
Danville, CA 94506-1110, USA

Norton, James A (Football Player)
San Francisco 49ers
2550 S Ellsworth Rd Unit 13
Mesa, AZ 85209-1198, USA

Norton, James C (Football Player)
Houston Oilers
PO Box 495997
Garland, TX 75049-5997, USA

Norton, James J (Misc)
Graphic Communications International
1900 L St NW Fl 8
Washington, DC 20036-5022, USA

Norton, Jeff (Hockey Player)
1701 E Las Olas Blvd # 1
Fort Lauderdale, FL 33301-2441, USA

Norton, Jerry (Football Player)
Philadelphia Eagles
6901 Chevy Chase Ave
Dallas, TX 75225-2416, USA

Norton, Peter (Designer)
225 Arizona Ave # 200W
Santa Monica, CA 90401-1243, USA

Norton, Phil (Baseball Player)
Chicago Cubs
677 County Road 3772
Queen City, TX 75572-7947, USA

Norton, Rick (Football Player)
Miami Dolphins
901 W Mahoney St
Plant City, FL 33563-4435, USA

Norton, Tom (Baseball Player)
Minnesota Twins
4900 Southwood Dr
Sheffield Lake, OH 44054-1559, USA

Norton, Virginia (Bowler)
11706 Mindanao St
Cypress, CA 90630-5662, USA

Norvell, Jay (Football Player)
Chicago Bears
2166 Clinton Ave
Alameda, CA 94501-4945, USA

Norville, Deborah (Television Host)
PO Box 426
Mill Neck, NY 11765-0426, USA

Norvind, Nailea (Actor)
c/o Staff Member *Televisa*
Blvd Adolfo Lopez Mateos 232
Colonia San Angel INN
DF CP 01060, MEXICO

Norwood, Brandy (Brandy) (Actor,
Musician)
c/o Erwin More *William Morris Agency
(WMA-LA)*
1 William Morris Pl
Beverly Hills, CA 90212-4261, USA

Norwood, Ray J (Actor, Musician)
c/o Staff Member *Defining Artists*
10 Universal City Plz Ste 2000
Universal City, CA 91608-1074, USA

Norwood, Scott (Football Player)
Buffalo Bills
42923 Shelbourne Sq
Chantilly, VA 20152-2097, USA

Norwood, Willie (Baseball Player)
Minnesota Twins
225 Gunsmoke Dr
Diamond Bar, CA 91765-1257, USA

Nosbusch, Desiree
Mohrengasse 18
Hohenems A-6845, AUSTRIA

Nosek, Randy (Baseball Player)
Detroit Tigers
15485 Knobhill Dr
Linden, MI 48451-8716, USA

Noseworthy, Jack
955 Carrillo Dr Ste 300
Los Angeles, CA 90048-5400, USA

Nossal, Gustav J V (Doctor)
46 Fellows St
Kew, VIC 3101, AUSTRALIA

Nosseck, Noel (Director)
1435 San Ysidro Dr
Beverly Hills, CA 90210-2108, USA

Nossek, Joe (Baseball Player)
Minnesota Twins
630 Sunrise Dr
Amherst, OH 44001-1659, USA

Notaro, Phyllis (Bowler)
20284 Brant Angota Road
Angola, NY 14006, USA

Notebaert, Richard (Business Person)
Quest Communications
1801 California St
Denver, CO 80202-2658, USA

Noth, Christopher (Actor)
c/o Mark Armstrong *Sanders/Armstrong
Management*
2120 Colorado Ave Ste 120
Santa Monica, CA 90404-3561, USA

Nothstein, Marty
1 Olympic Plz
Colorado Springs, CO 80909-5780, USA

Notkins, Abner L (Scientist)
National Institute of Dental Research
9000 Rockville Pike
Bethesda, MD 20892-0001, USA

Noto, Lucio A (Business Person)
Mobil Corp
3225 Gallows Rd
Fairfax, VA 22037-0002, USA

Nott, John W F (Government Official)
Hillsdown Holdings PLC
32 Hampstead High St
London NW3 1QD, UNITED KINGDOM
(UK)

Nottbart, Don (Baseball Player)
Milwaukee Braves
219 Round Pond Rd
East Wakefield, NH 03830-3854, USA

Nottebohm, Andreas (Artist)
Mentzstr 44
Mulheim An Der Ruhr, GERMANY

Nottingham, Don (Football Player)
Baltimore Colts
5750 NE 36th Avenue Rd
Ocala, FL 34479-1990, USA

Nottingham, Robert
4348 Coldwater Canyon Ave Apt B
Studio City, CA 91604-5016, USA

Nouhak, Phoumsavanh (President)
President's Office
Presidential House
Vientiane, LAOS

Nouri, Michael (Actor)
Burnstein
15304 W Sunset Blvd Ste 208
Pacific Palisades, CA 90272-3656, USA

Noury, Alain
Soyans s/Crest
26400, FRANCE

Nouvel, Jean (Architect)
Architectures Jean Nouvel
10 Cite d'Angouleme
Paris 75011, FRANCE

Nova, Heather
Box 3704
London, ENGLAND W4 4ZN, UNITED
KINGDOM (UK)

Nova, Nikki (Actor)
PO Box 431
4331 E Baseline Road # B 105
Gilbert, AZ 85299-0431, USA

Novack, K J (Business Person)
America Online
22000 Aol Way
Dulles, VA 20166-9302, USA

Novack, William
3 Ashton Ave
Newton, MA 02459-1526, USA

Novak, B J (Actor, Comedian, Writer)
c/o Staff Member *Brillstein-Grey
Entertainment*
9150 Wilshire Blvd Ste 350
Beverly Hills, CA 90212-3453, USA

Novak, David C (Business Person)
Tricon Global Restaurants
1441 Gardiner Ln
Louisville, KY 40213-1914, USA

Novak, Jack (Football Player)
Cincinnati Bengals
308 River Chase Ct
Georgetown, TX 78628-5314, USA

Novak, John R (Inventor)
Engelhard Corp
101 Wood Ave S
Automotive Emissions Systems
Iselin, NJ 08830-2703, USA

Novak, Kim (Actor)
c/o Staff Member *William Morris Agency
(WMA-LA)*
1 William Morris Pl
Beverly Hills, CA 90212-4261, USA

Novak, Michael (Misc)
American Enterprise Institute
1150 17th St NW
Washington, DC 20036-4670, USA

Novak, Pablo (Actor)
c/o Staff Member *Telefe - Argentina*
Pavon 2444 (C1248AAT)
Buenos Aires, ARGENTINA

Novak, Popper Ilona (Swimmer)
Il Orso Utca 23
Budapest, HUNGARY

Novak, Robert (Correspondent, Writer)
1750 Pennsylvania Ave NW # 1312
Washington, DC 20006-4502, USA

Novarina, Maurice P J (Architect)
52 Rue Raynouard
Paris 75116, FRANCE

Novelli, William (Misc)
American Association of Retired Persons
601 E St NW
Washington, DC 20049-0002, USA

Novello, Antonia C (Misc)
5438 Coral Ridge Dr
Grand Blanc, MI 48439-9522, USA

Novello, Don
PO Box 245
Fairfax, CA 94978-0245, USA

Novello, Don (Fr Guido Sarducci) (Actor,
Comedian)
Elizabeth Rush Agency
82 Cumberland Ave
Verona, NJ 07044-2105, USA

Noveskey, Matt (Musician)
Ashley Talent
2002 Hogback Rd Ste 20
Ann Arbor, MI 48105-9736, USA

Novoa, Rafael (Actor)
c/o Staff Member *TV Caracol*
Calle 76 #11 - 35
Piso 10AA
Bogota DC 26484, COLOMBIA

Novosel, Michael J (War Hero)
10 Doral Dr
Shalimar, FL 32579-1612, USA

Novoselsky, Brent (Football Player)
Chicago Bears
405 Marvins Way
Buffalo Grove, IL 60089-6419, USA

Novotna, Jana (Tennis Player)
7834 Montvale Way
McLean, VA 22102-2028, USA

Novotny, Dave (Musician)
Helter Skelter Plaza
535 Kings Road
London SW10 0S, UNITED KINGDOM
(UK)

Nowak, Lisa M (Astronaut)
17123 Parsley Hawthome Court
Houston, TX 77059, USA

Nowak, Peter (Coach, Soccer Player)
DC United
14120 Newbrook Dr
Chantilly, VA 20151-2273, USA

Nowatzke, Tom (Football Player)
Detroit Lions
4335 Diuble Rd
Ann Arbor, MI 48103-9606, USA

Nowicki, Tom (Actor)
c/o Staff Member *Davis Management*
4111 Lankershim Blvd
Studio City, CA 91602-2828, USA

Nowinksi, Christopher (Wrestler)
c/o Staff Member *World Wrestling
Entertainment (WWE)*
1241 E Main St
Stamford, CT 06902-3520, USA

Nowitzki, Dirk (Basketball Player)
c/o Staff Member *Dallas Mavericks*
2909 Taylor St
Dallas, TX 75226-1909, USA

Nowra, Louis (Writer)
Level 18 Plaza 11
500 Oxford St
Bondi Junction, NSW 2011, AUSTRALIA

Noxon, Marti (Writer)
c/o Staff Member *Endeavor Agency LLC
(LA)*
9601 Wilshire Blvd Fl 3
Beverly Hills, CA 90210-5204, USA

Noyce, Phillip (Director)
Cresswell
163 Brougham St
Woolloomooloo
Sydney 2011, AUSTRALIA

Noyd, R Allen (Religious Leader)
General Council
1294 Rutledge Rd
Christian Church
Transfer, PA 16154-2226, USA

Noyes, Albert Jr (Misc)
5102 Fairview Dr
Austin, TX 78731-5426, USA

Noyori, Ryoji (Nobel Prize Laureate)
135-417 Shinden
Umemoricho
Nisshin, Aichi 470-0132, JAPAN

Nozieres, Philippe P G F (Physicist)
15 Route d Saint Nizier
Seyssins 38180, FRANCE

Nri, Cyril (Actor)
Bosun House
1 Deer Park Road
Merton
London SW19 3TL, UNITED KINGDOM
(UK)

Nsengiyremeye, Dismas (Prime Minister)
Prime Minister's Office
Kigali, RWANDA

Nsibanbi, Apolo (Prime Minister)
Premier's Office
International Conference Center
Kampala, UGANDA

Ntombi (Royalty)
Royal Residence
PO Box 1
Lobamba, SWAZILAND

Ntoutoume, Jean-Francois (Prime Minister)
Prime Minister's Office
BP 546
Libreville, GABON

Nuami, Sheikh Humaid bin Rashid an- (King, Royalty)
Royal Palaca
PO Box 1
Ajman, UNITED ARAB EMIRATES

Nubla, Malou (Journalist)
KPIX TV
855 Battery St
San Francisco, CA 94111-1503, USA

Nucci, Danny (Actor)
Gold Marshak Liedtke
3500 W Olive Ave Ste 1400
Burbank, CA 91505-5512, USA

Nucci, Leo (Opera Singer)
I C M Artists
40 W 57th St
New York, NY 10019-4001, USA

Nugent, Eddie
PO Box 1266
New York, NY 10150-1266, USA

Nugent, Nelle (Producer)
Foxboro Entertainment
133 E 58th St Ste 301
New York, NY 10022-1168, USA

Nugent, Ted (Musician)
4008 W Michigan Ave
Jackson, MI 49202-1829, USA

Nujoma, Sam S (President)
President's Office
State House
Mugabe Ave
Windhoek 9000, NAMIBIA

Numan, Gary (Musician, Songwriter, Writer)
86 Staines Road
Wraysbury
N Staines, Middlesex TW19 5A, UNITED KINGDOM (UK)

Numminen, Teppo (Hockey Player)
3422 E Palo Verde Dr
Paradise Valley, AZ 85253-5015, USA

Nunez, Abraham (Baseball Player)
Pittsburgh Pirates
2505 Fox Hollow Dr
Pittsburgh, PA 15237-3833, USA

Nunez, Edwin (Baseball Player)
Seattle Mariners
2481 E Stephens Pl
Chandler, AZ 85225-4144, USA

Nunez, Miguel Angel Jr (Actor)
c/o Patricia (Patty) Woo TalentWorks (LA)
3500 W Olive Ave Ste 1400
Burbank, CA 91505-5512, USA

Nunez, Victor (Director)
Paul Kohner
9300 Wilshire Blvd Ste 555
Beverly Hills, CA 90212-3211, USA

Nunez, Vladimir (Baseball Player)
Arizona Diamondbacks
18053 SW 139th Pl
Miami, FL 33177-2792, USA

Nunley, Frank (Football Player)
San Francisco 49ers
24632 Olive Tree Ln
Los Altos Hills, CA 94024-6424, USA

Nunley, Jeremy (Football Player)
Houston Oilers
476 Oak Hill Dr
Estill Springs, TN 37330-4205, USA

Nunn, Howie (Baseball Player)
St Louis Cardinals
204 S Depot St
Pilot Mountain, NC 27041-8528, USA

Nunn, Sam (Ex-Senator, Senator)
75 14th St NE Unit 4810
Atlanta, GA 30309-7623, USA

Nunn, Teri (Musician)
MOB Agency
6404 Wilshire Blvd Ste 505
Los Angeles, CA 90048-5507, USA

Nunn, Trevor R (Director)
Royal National Theater
South Bank
London SE1 9PX, UNITED KINGDOM
(UK)

Nunnally, Jon (Baseball Player)
Kansas City Royals
1380 Old Quarry Rd Apt 2
Ringgold, VA 24586-3056, USA

Nunnari, Talmadge (Baseball Player)
Montreal Expos
7101 Joy St Apt A8
Pensacola, FL 32504-6480, USA

Nunnery, R B (Football Player)
Dallas Texans
3276 Claude Smith Rd
Magnolia, MS 39652-9534, USA

Nurding, Louise (Actor)
42 Colwith Road
London, ENGLAND W6 9EY, UNITED KINGDOM (UK)

Nurse, Paul M (Nobel Prize Laureate)
Clare Hall Laboratories
Cell Cycle Control Lab
Herts EN6 3LD, UNITED KINGDOM (UK)

Nussbaum, Danny (Actor)
Conway Van Gelder RObinson
18-21 Jermyn St
London SW1Y 6NB, UNITED KINGDOM (UK)

Nussbaum, Joe (Actor, Director, Writer)
c/o Adriana Alberghetti Endeavor Agency LLC (LA)
9601 Wilshire Blvd Fl 3
Beverly Hills, CA 90210-5204, USA

Nussbaum, Karen (Misc)
9-5 National Working Women Assn
231 W Wisconsin Ave Apt 900
Milwaukee, WI 53203-2306, USA

Nussbaum, Martha C (Misc)
University of Chicago
111 E 60th St
Law School
Chicago, IL 60637-2105, USA

Nussiein-Volhard, Christiane (Nobel Prize Laureate)
Max Planck Biology Institute
Spenmannstr 35/III
Tubingen 72076, GERMANY

Nussmeier, Doug (Football Player)
New Orleans Saints
28493 SW Meadows Loop
Wilsonville, OR 97070-6779, USA

Nutini, Paolo (Musician)
Atlantic Records UK
Electric Lighting Station
46 Kensington Ct
Londo W8 5DA, UNITED KINGDOM (UK)

Nutt, Jim (Artist)
1035 Greenwood Ave
Wilmette, IL 60091-1753, USA

Nutter, Alice (Musician)
Doug Smith Assoc
PO Box 1151
London W3 8ZJ, UNITED KINGDOM (UK)

Nutter, Buzz (Football Player)
Baltimore Colts
9180 Crescent Ln
La Plata, MD 20646-2815, USA

Nutter, David (Director)
Shapiro-Lichtman
1333 Beverly Green Dr
Los Angeles, CA 90035-1018, USA

Nutting, Ed (Football Player)
Cleveland Browns
607 Ashford Pkwy
Atlanta, GA 30338-5534, USA

Nutting, Wallace H (General)
PO Box 96
Biddeford Pool, ME 04006-0096, USA

Nutzie, Futzie (Artist, Cartoonist)
PO Box 325
Aromas, CA 95004-0325, USA

Nuwer, Hank (Journalist, Writer)
PO Box 21
Waldron, IN 46182-0021, USA

Nuxhall, Joe (Baseball Player)
Cincinnati Reds
5706 Lindenwood Ln
Fairfield, OH 45014-3565, USA

Nuxhall, Joseph H (Joe) (Baseball Player)
5706 Lingenwood Lane
Fairfield, OH 45014, USA

Nuyen, France (Actor)
c/o Budd Burton Moss Shapiro-Lichtman Talent Agency
1333 Beverly Green Dr
Los Angeles, CA 90035-1018, USA

Nuzorewa, Abel Tendekayi (Prime Minister)
United African National Council
40 Charter Road
Harare, ZIMBABWE

Nyad, Diana (Sportscaster, Swimmer)
Uptown Racquet Club
151 E 86th St
New York, NY 10028-2106, USA

Nyberg, Frederik (Skier)
Kaptensgatan 2C
Froson 832 00, SWEDEN

Nyberg, Karen L (Astronaut)
2518 Lakeside Lndg
Seabrook, TX 77586-8313, USA

Nye, Bill
401 Mercer St
Seattle, WA 98109-4640, USA

Nye, Blaine (Football Player)
Dallas Cowboys
1200 Bay Laurel Dr
Menlo Park, CA 94025-5871, USA

Nye, Erie (Business Person)
Texas Utilities Co
1601 Bryan St
Energy Plaza
Dallas, TX 75201-3430, USA

Nye, Rich (Baseball Player)
Chicago Cubs
7510 W North Ave
Elmwood Park, IL 60707-4140, USA

Nye, Robert (Writer)
Thomfield
Kingsland
Ballinghassig, County Cork, IRELAND

Nye, Ryan (Baseball Player)
Philadelphia Phillies
General Delivery
Cameron, OK 74932-9999, USA

Nyers, Dick (Football Player)
Baltimore Colts
4055 N Riverside Dr
Columbus, IN 47203-1118, USA

Nyers, Rezso (Secretary)
Ozgida Utca 22/A
Budapest 1025, HUNGARY

Nygaard, Richard L (Judge)
US Court of Appeals
717 State St
1st National Bank Building
Erie, PA 16501-1341, USA

Nyland, William L (General)
Assistant Commander In Chief Hqsmc
2 Navy St
Washington, DC 20380-0001, USA

Nyman, Chris (Baseball Player)
Chicago White Sox
1700 Happy Creek Rd
Front Royal, VA 22630-6438, USA

Nyman, Jerry (Baseball Player)
Chicago White Sox
PO Box 5
Smithfield, UT 84335-0005, USA

Nyman, Michael L (Composer, Musician)
Michael Nyman Ltd
PO Box 430
High Wycombe HP13 5QT, UNITED KINGDOM (UK)

Nyman, Nyls (Baseball Player)
Chicago White Sox
PO Box 236
Susanville, CA 96130-0236, USA

Nyquist, Ryan (Athlete)
%Stephen Astephen
1545 Faraday Ave
The Familie
Carlsbad, CA 92008-7319, USA

Nystrom, Bob (Hockey Player)
475 Berry Hill Road
Oyster Bay, NY 11771, USA

Nystrom, Joakim (Tennis Player)
Torsgatan 194
Skellefteaa 931 00, SWEDEN

Nystrom, Lee (Football Player)
Green Bay Packers
18411 Priory Ave
Minnetonka, MN 55345-2459, USA

Nyvell, Vic (Football Player)
New Orleans Saints
PO Box 159C
Kilgore, TX 75663, USA

O, Karen (Musician)
Yeah Yeah Yeahs
249 Metropolitan Ave
Brooklyn, NY 11211-4009, USA

O??????, Tommy (Director)
c/o Staff Member *William Morris Agency (WMA-LA)*
1 William Morris Pl
Beverly Hills, CA 90212-4261, USA

O' Sullivan, Thaddeus (Director)
c/o Anthony Jones *Peters Fraser & Dunlop (PFD - UK)*
Drury House
34-43 Russell St
London WC2B 5HA, UNITED KINGDOM (UK)

O Town
7380 W Sand Lake Rd # 350
Orlando, FL 32819-5248, USA

O-Town (Music Group)
Official International Fan Club
PO Box 5488
Bellingham, WA 98227-5488, USA

Oak Ridge Boys (Music Group)
c/o Staff Member *William Morris Agency (WMA-TN)*
1600 Division St Ste 300
Nashville, TN 37203-2755, USA

Oakes, Don (Football Player)
Philadelphia Eagles
101 Aftons Meadow Rd
Vinton, VA 24179-9701, USA

Oakes, James L (Judge)
US Court of Appeals
PO Box 696
Brattleboro, VT 05302-0696, USA

Oakes, Summer Rayne (Model)
59 Grand St
Brooklyn, NY 11211-4110, USA

Oakley, Charles (Basketball Player)
Washington Wizards
601 F St NW
Mci Centre
Washington, DC 20004-1605, USA

OAR (Music Group)
Red Light Management
PO Box 1467
Charlottesville, VA 22902-1467, USA

Oasis
54 Linhope St.
London, ENGLAND NW1 6HL, UNITED KINGDOM (UK)

Oates, Adam R (Hockey Player)
1480 S County Rd
Osterville, MA 02655-1544, USA

Oates, Bart S (Football Player, Sportscaster)
New York Giants
1 Silverbrook Dr
Morristown, NJ 07960-8002, USA

Oates, John (Musician, Songwriter, Writer)
Creative Artists Agency
9830 Wilshire Blvd
Beverly Hills, CA 90212-1804, USA

Oates, Joyce Carol (Writer)
John Hawkins
71 W 23rd St Ste 1600
New York, NY 10010-4185, USA

Oats, Carleton (Football Player)
Oakland Raiders
2475 Dundee Ct
San Leandro, CA 94577-6014, USA

Oatway, Devin
10635 Santa Monica Blvd Ste 130
Los Angeles, CA 90025-8306, USA

Obama, Barack (Politician)
Obama for Illinois
PO Box 802799
Democrat For U.S. Senate 2004
Chicago, IL 60680-2799, USA

Obando, Bravo Miguel Cardinal (Religious Leader)
Arzobispado
Apartado 3050
Managua, NICARAGUA

Obando, Sherman (Baseball Player)
Baltimore Orioles
7037 Coral Cove Dr
Orlando, FL 32818-2866, USA

O'Bannon, Dan (Director)
Agency For Performing Arts
405 S Beverly Dr Ste 500
Beverly Hills, CA 90212-4425, USA

O'Bannon, Ed (Basketball Player)
11930 Agnes St
Cerritos, CA 90703-6902, USA

O'Bard, Ronnie (Football Player)
San Diego Chargers
27121 Puerta Del Oro
Mission Viejo, CA 92691-4421, USA

Obasanjo, Olusegun (General, President)
President's Office
State House
Ribadu Road Ikoyi
Lagos, NIGERIA

Obato, Gyo (Architect)
Helimuth Obato Kassabaum
1 Metropolitan Sq Ste 600
Saint Louis, MO 63102-2733, USA

Obee, Duncan (Football Player)
4488 283rd St
Toledo, OH 43611-1864, USA

Obeid, Atef (Prime Minister)
Prime Minister's Office
PO Box 191
1 Majlis El-Shaab St
Cairo, EGYPT

Obeidallah, Dean (Comedian)
338 E 70th St Apt 3A
New York, NY 10021-8682, USA

Obeidat, Ahmad Abdul-Majeed (Prime Minister)
Law & Arbitration Center
PO Box 926544
Amman, JORDAN

Oben, Roman (Football Player)
New York Giants
11476 Creekstone Ln
San Diego, CA 92128-6325, USA

Oberding, Mark (Basketball Player)
4131 Cliff Oaks St
San Antonio, TX 78229-3536, USA

Oberg, Margo (Misc)
Koloa
RR 1 Box 73
Kaui, HI 96756, USA

Oberg, Tom (Football Player)
Denver Broncos
280 Avery St
Ashland, OR 97520-2202, USA

Oberkfell, Ken (Baseball Player)
St Louis Cardinals
1335 W Welsford Dr
Spring, TX 77386-2599, USA

Oberlin, David W (Government Official)
800 Independence Ave SW # 814
Washington, DC 20591-0001, USA

Obermeyer, Klaus F (Designer, Fashion Designer)
Sport Obermeyer
115 Atlantic
Aspen, CO 81611-2502, USA

Obermueller, Wes (Baseball Player)
Kansas City Royals
2191 Port Talbot Pl
Coralville, IA 52241-3445, USA

Oberoi, Vivek (Actor, Bollywood)
5 Kartar Kunj Golden Beach
Ruia Park Juhu
Mumbai, MS 400 0049, INDIA

O'Berry, Mike (Baseball Player)
Boston Red Sox
194 County Road 266
Cullman, AL 35057-4846, USA

Oberst, Conner
c/o Brian Young *Untitled Entertainment (LA)*
331 N Maple Dr Fl 3
Beverly Hills, CA 90210-3827, USA

O'Boyle, Maureen (Entertainer)
30 Rockefeller Plz # 820E
New York, NY 10112-0015, USA

Obradors, Jacqueline (Actor)
c/o Ryan Martin *Agency for the Performing Arts (APA-LA)*
405 S Beverly Dr
Beverly Hills, CA 90212-4416, USA

O'Bradovich, Ed (Football Player)
Chicago Bears
235 N Smith St Apt 207
Palatine, IL 60067-8503, USA

Obradovich, James R (Jim) (Football Player)
New York Giants
2436 Silverstrand Ave
Hermosa Beach, CA 90254-2663, USA

O'Bradovich, Jim (Baseball Player)
Houston Astros
1101 S Miramar Ave Apt 203
Indialantic, FL 32903-3450, USA

Obraztsova, Elena V (Opera Singer)
Bolshoi Theater
Teatralnaya Pl 1
Moscow 103009, RUSSIA

Obregon, Alejandro (Artist)
Apartado Aereo 37
Barranquilla, COLOMBIA

Obregon, Ana (Actor)
Paul Kohner
9300 Wilshire Blvd Ste 555
Beverly Hills, CA 90212-3211, USA

O'Brian, Hugh (Actor)
Hugh O'Brian Youth Foundation
10880 Wilshire Blvd Ste 410
Los Angeles, CA 90024-4187, USA

O'Brian, Richard (Actor)
Jonathan Alparas
27 Floral St
London C2E 9DP, UNITED KINGDOM (UK)

O'Brian-Cooke, Penny (Baseball Player)
307-1335 East 27th St
North Vancouver, BC V7J 1S6, CANADA

O'Brien, Austin (Actor)
Gersh Agency
232 N Canon Dr
Beverly Hills, CA 90210-5302, USA

O'Brien, Bill (Football Player)
Detroit Lions
1253 Flamingo
Wixom, MI 48393-1506, USA

O'Brien, Bob (Baseball Player)
Los Angeles Dodgers
2303 E Acacia Ave Apt 148
Fresno, CA 93726-0302, USA

O'Brien, Brian (Physicist)
PO Box 166
Woodstock, CT 06281-0166, USA

O'Brien, Carl (Cubby) (Actor)
2530 Independence Ave Apt 2J
Bronx, NY 10463-6236, USA

O'Brien, Cathy (Athlete, Track Athlete)
19 Foss Farm Rd
Durham, NH 03824-2927, USA

O'Brien, Charlie (Baseball Player)
Oakland A's
4932 E 38th Pl
Tulsa, OK 74135-5529, USA

O'Brien, Conan (Comedian, Talk Show Host)
Late Night with Conan O'Brien
30 Rockefeller Plz
901 West
New York, NY 10112-0015, USA

O'Brien, Conor Cruise (Diplomat, Writer)
Whitewater
Howth Summit
Dublin, IRELAND

O'Brien, Cubby
2839 N Surrey Dr
Carrollton, TX 75006-4800, USA

O'Brien, Dan (Baseball Player)
St Louis Cardinals
2656 McKelvey Rd
Maryland Heights, MO 63043-1639, USA

O'Brien, Dave (Football Player)
304 Newbury St # 349
Boston, MA 02115-2839, USA

O'Brien, David (Football Player)
Minnesota Vikings
66 Emerson Rd
Watertown, MA 02472-1606, USA

O'Brien, Ed (Musician)
Nasty Little Man
72 Spring St # 1100
New York, NY 10012-4019, USA

O'Brien, Eddie (Baseball Player)
Pittsburgh Pirates
522 Alder St Apt 101
Edmonds, WA 98020-3494, USA

O'Brien, Edna (Writer)
Wylie Agency
52 Knightsbridge
London SW1X 7JP, UNITED KINGDOM
(UK)

O'Brien, G Dennis (Educator)
PO Box 510
Middlebury, VT 05753-0510, USA

O'Brien, George H Jr (War Hero)
2001 Douglas Ave
Midland, TX 79701-4059, USA

O'Brien, Gregory M (Educator)
University of New Orleans
Chancellor's Office
New Orleans, LA 70148-0001, USA

O'Brien, Jim (Basketball Player, Coach)
Philadelphia 76er's
3601 S Broad St
1 Union Center
Philadelphia, PA 19148-5287, USA

O'Brien, Jim (Football Player)
Baltimore Colts
413 Bethany St
Thousand Oaks, CA 91360-2025, USA

O'Brien, John (Writer)
2 Columbine Placa
Delran, NJ 08075, USA

O'Brien, John T (Johnny) (Baseball Player,
Basketball Player)
Pittsburgh Pirates
7712 18th Ave NE
Seattle, WA 98115-4426, USA

O'Brien, Keith M P Cardinal (Religious
Leader)
Archdiocese
113 Whitehouse Loan
Edinburgh EH9 1BB, SCOTLAND

O'Brien, Kenneth J (Ken) Jr (Football
Player)
New York Jets
201 Manhattan Ave
Manhattan Beach, CA 90266-6439, USA

O'Brien, M Vincent (Coach, Horse Racer)
Ballydoyle House
Cashel
County Tipperary, IRELAND

O'Brien, Margaret (Actor)
1250 La Peresa Dr
Thousand Oaks, CA 91362-2229, USA

O'Brien, Mark (Business Person)
Pulte Corp
33 Bloomfield Hills Pkwy
Bloomfield Hills, MI 48304-2944, USA

O'Brien, Maureen (Actor)
Kate Feast
Primrose Hill Studios
Fitzroy Road
London NW1 8TR, UNITED KINGDOM
(UK)

O'Brien, Miles (Television Host)
c/o Staff Member *CNN (NY)*
1 Time Warner Ctr
New York, NY 10019-6038, USA

O'Brien, Pat (Sportscaster, Television
Host)
c/o Staff Member *International Creative
Management (ICM-LA)*
10250 Constellation Blvd
Los Angeles, CA 90067-6200, USA

O'Brien, Pete (Baseball Player)
Texas Rangers
5509 Montclair Dr
Colleyville, TX 76034-5028, USA

O'Brien, Peter
397 Riley St.
Surry Hills NSW 2010, AUSTRALIA

O'Brien, Richard (Composer, Songwriter,
Writer)
TimeWarp
1 Elm Grove
Hildenborough
Tonbridge Kent TN11 9HE, UNITED
KINGDOM (UK)

O'Brien, Ron (Coach)
6044 Strafford Oaks Dr
Sebring, FL 33875-4779, USA

O'Brien, Scott (Football Player)
Green Bay Packers
12690 Overlook Mountain Dr
Charlotte, NC 28216-6726, USA

O'Brien, Soledad (Television Host)
c/o Staff Member *CNN (NY)*
1 Time Warner Ctr
New York, NY 10019-6038, USA

O'Brien, Syd (Baseball Player)
Boston Red Sox
6570 Richard Ave
Placerville, CA 95667-9452, USA

O'Brien, Thomas H (Financier)
PNC Bank Corp
249 5th Ave Ste 1200
1 Pnc Center
Pittsburgh, PA 15222-2707, USA

O'Brien, Thomas M (Financier)
North Side Savings Bank
185 W 23st St
Bronx, NY 10463, USA

O'Brien, Tim (Athlete, Track Athlete)
17 Partridge Lane
Boxford, MA 01921, USA

O'Brien, Tina (Actor)
c/o Martin Spencer *Creative Artists
Agency LCC (CAA-LA)*
2000 Avenue Of The Stars
Los Angeles, CA 90067-4700, USA

O'Brien, Trever (Actor)
c/o Faras Rabadi *Emerald Talent Group*
6464 W Sunset Blvd
Los Angeles, CA 90028-8001, USA

O'Brien, Trevor (Actor)
Gersh Agency
232 N Canon Dr
Beverly Hills, CA 90210-5302, USA

O'Brien, W Parry (Athlete, Track Athlete)
3415 Alginet Dr
Encino, CA 91436, USA

O'Bryan, Sean (Actor)
c/o Staff Member *Alan Siegel
Entertainment*
345 N Maple Dr Ste 375
Beverly Hills, CA 90210-5942, USA

Obst, Lynda (Producer)
c/o Staff Member *Lynda Obst Productions*
5555 Melrose Ave # 210
Los Angeles, CA 90038-3989, USA

O'Callaghan, Donald N (Mike)
(Governor)
Las Vegas Sun
2275 Corporate Cir Ste 300
Henderson, NV 89074-7745, USA

O'Callahan, John (Football Player)
Seattle Seahawks
361A La Perle Ln
Costa Mesa, CA 92627-3757, USA

O'Callahan, John (Jack) (Hockey Player)
101 Linden Ave
Glencoe, IL 60022-2144, USA

Ocampo Uria, Adriana C (Scientist)
*National Aeronautics/Space
Administration*
300 E St SW
Washington, DC 20456-0001, USA

O'Caroll, Sinead (Musician)
Clintons
55 Drury Lane
Covent Garden
London WC2B 5SQ, UNITED KINGDOM
(UK)

Ocasek, Ric (Musician, Songwriter,
Writer)
Elektra Records
75 Rockefeller Plz
New York, NY 10019-6908, USA

Occhipinti, Andrea (Actor)
Carol Levi Co
Via Giuseppe Pisanelli
Rome 00196, ITALY

Ocean, Billy (Musician)
Laura Jay Enterprises
32 Willesden Lane
London NW6 7ST, UNITED KINGDOM
(UK)

Ocean Colour Scene (Music Group)
c/o Staff Member *Paradigm (Monterey)*
509 Hartnell St
Monterey, CA 93940-2825, USA

Oceansize (Music Group)
c/o Staff Member *Paradigm (Monterey)*
509 Hartnell St
Monterey, CA 93940-2825, USA

Ochirbat, Punsalmaagiyn (President)
Tengeriin Tsag Co
Olympic St 14
Ulan Bator, MONGOLIA

Ochman, Wieslaw (Opera Singer)
Ul Miaczynska 46B
Warsaw 02-637, POLAND

Ochoa, Alex (Baseball Player)
New York Mets
8325 NW 158th Ter
Miami Lakes, FL 33016-6604, USA

Ochoa, Ellen (Astronaut)
4515 Sterling Wood Way
Houston, TX 77059-3153, USA

Ochoa, Lorena (Golfer)
Ochoa Sports Management
413 Interamerica Blvd Ste 14 # 222
C/O Alejandro Ochoa
Laredo, TX 78045-7926, USA

Ochoa, Raymond (Actor)
c/o Robin Spitzer *Origin Talent Agency*
4705 Laurel Canyon Blvd Ste 306
Studio City, CA 91607-5940, USA

Ockels, Wubbo (Astronaut)
ESTEC
Postbus 299
Noordwijk, AG 2200, THE
NETHERLANDS

O'connell, Charlie (Actor)
c/o Barry McPherson *Agency for the
Performing Arts (APA-LA)*
405 S Beverly Dr
Beverly Hills, CA 90212-4416, USA

O'Connell, Deirdre (Actor)
c/o Martin Berneman *Martin Berneman
Management*
211 S Beverly Dr Ste 208
Beverly Hills, CA 90212-3879, USA

O'Connell, Jerry (Actor)
c/o Michael Rotenberg *3 Arts
Entertainment Inc*
9460 Wilshire Blvd Fl 7
Beverly Hills, CA 90212-2713, USA

O'Connell, Maura (Musician)
Maura O'Connell Mgmt
4222 Lindawood Dr
Nashville, TN 37215-3208, USA

O'Connell, Patricia (Hitchcock)
3835 E Thousand Oaks Blvd # 435
Westlake Village, CA 91362-3637, USA

O'Conner, Tom
1 The Stiles Ormskirk
Lancashire, ENGLAND L39 3QG,
UNITED KINGDOM (UK)

O'Connolly, James (Astronaut)
1305 Lafayette Dr
Alexandria, VA 22308-1107, USA

O'Connolly, James (Director)
61 Edith Grove
London SW10, UNITED KINGDOM (UK)

O'Connor, Bill (Football Player)
New York Yanks
1905-40 Richview Rd
Toronto, ON M9A 5C1, CANADA

O'Connor, Brian (Baseball Player)
Pittsburgh Pirates
3054 Inwood Dr
Cincinnati, OH 45241-3101, USA

O'Connor, Bryan D
305 Lafayette Dr
Alexandria, VA 22308, USA

O'Connor, Derrick (Actor)
c/o Michael Greene *Greene & Associates*
190 N Canon Dr Ste 200
Beverly Hills, CA 90210-5319, USA

O'Connor, Des
23 Eyot Gardens
London, ENGLAND W6 9TR, UNITED
KINGDOM (UK)

O'Connor, Edmund F (General)
1169 Ironsides Ave
Melbourne, FL 32940-6735, USA

O'Connor, Frances (Actor)
c/o Staff Member *Creative Artists Agency LCC (CAA-LA)*
2000 Avenue Of The Stars
Los Angeles, CA 90067-4700, USA

O'Connor, Gavin (Director)
United Talent Agency
9560 Wilshire Blvd Ste 500
Beverly Hills, CA 90212-2401, USA

O'Connor, Glynnis (Actor)
c/o Staff Member *Bauman Redanty & Shaul Agency*
5757 Wilshire Blvd Ste 473
Los Angeles, CA 90036-3632, USA

O'Connor, J Dennis (Educator)
Smithsonlan Institution
Provost's Office
Washington, DC 20560-0001, USA

O'Connor, Jack (Baseball Player)
Minnesota Twins
PO Box 430
Yucca Valley, CA 92286-0430, USA

O'Connor, Mark (Musician)
CM Mgmt
5749 Lanyan Dr
Woodland Hills, CA 91367, USA

O'Connor, Martin J (Religious Leader)
Palazzo San Carlo
Vatican City 00120, VATICAN CITY

O'Connor, Maryanne (Basketball Player)
60 Romanock Pl
Fairfield, CT 06825-7240, USA

O'Connor, Patrick (Actor)
c/o Staff Member *Select Artists Ltd (CA-Westside Office)*
1138 12th St Apt 1
Santa Monica, CA 90403-5459, USA

O'Connor, Patrick D (Pat) (Director)
International Creative Mgmt
76 Oxford St
London W1N 0AX, UNITED KINGDOM (UK)

O'Connor, Renee (Actor)
c/o Staff Member *Grant Management*
1158 26th St # 414
Santa Monica, CA 90403-4698, USA

O'Connor, Sandra Day (Judge)
US Supreme Court
1 1st St NE
Washington, DC 20543-0002, USA

O'Connor, Sinead (Musician, Songwriter)
c/o Staff Member *Paradigm (Monterey)*
509 Hartnell St
Monterey, CA 93940-2825, USA

O'Connor, Thom (Artist)
Moss Road
Voorheesville, NY 12186, USA

O'Connor, Tim (Actor)
PO Box 458
Nevada City, CA 95959-0458, USA

O'Connor, Zeke (Football Player)
New York Yanks
Sir Edmund Hillary Foundation 222 Jarvis St
Toronto, ON M5B 2B8, CANADA

O'Conor, John (Musician)
Columbia Artists Mgmt Inc
1790 Broadway Fl 6
New York, NY 10019-1412, USA

O'Day, Alan (Musician, Songwriter, Writer)
Talent Consultants International
105 Shad Row Ste B
Piermont, NY 10968-3001, USA

ODB (Musician)
Famous Artists Agency
250 W 57th St
New York, NY 10107-0001, USA

Oddsson, David (Prime Minister)
Prime Minister's Office
Stjo'maaroshusio
Reykjavik 150, ICELAND

Odegard, Vickie (Golfer)
112 Ashford Dr
Bridgeport, WV 26330-1138, USA

Odelein, Selmar (Hockey Player)
Farm
Quill Lake, SK S0A 3E0, CANADA

O'Dell, Billy (Baseball Player)
Baltimore Orioles
225 Odell Rd
Newberry, SC 29108-9250, USA

Odell, Bob H (Coach, Football Coach, Football Player)
911 Stenton Pl
Ocean City, NJ 08226-4343, USA

Odell, Deborah (Actor)
c/o Staff Member *Characters Talent Agency, The (Toronto)*
8 Elm St 3rd FL
Toronto, ON M5G 1G7, CANADA

O'Dell, Jennifer (Actor)
3500 W Olive Ave Ste 920
Burbank, CA 91505-5514, USA

O'Dell, Nancy
c/o Staff Member *Access Hollywood*
Nbc
3000 W Alameda Ave Trailer E
Burbank, CA 91523-0001, USA

Odell, Noel E (Mountaineer, Scientist)
5 Dean Court
Cambridge, UNITED KINGDOM (UK)

O'Dell, Stewart (Football Player)
Washington Redskins
3532 State Road 144
Mooresville, IN 46158, USA

O'Dell, Tawni (Writer)
Viking Press
375 Hudson St
New York, NY 10014-3658, USA

O'Dell, Tony
417 N Griffith Park Dr
Burbank, CA 91506-2031, USA

Oden, Derrick (Football Player)
Philadelphia Eagles
1805 S Barkley Dr
Mobile, AL 36606-1151, USA

Odenkirk, Bob (Actor)
c/o Bernie Brillstein *Brillstein-Grey Entertainment*
9150 Wilshire Blvd Ste 350
Beverly Hills, CA 90212-3453, USA

Odermatt, Robert A (Architect)
140 Camino Don Miguel
Orinda, CA 94563-1710, USA

Odessa, Devon (Actor)
Writers & Artists
360 N Crescent Dr Bldg North
Beverly Hills, CA 90210-6818, USA

Odetta (Musician)
Douglas Yeager Productions
300 W 55th St
New York, NY 10019-5151, USA

Odjig, Daphne (Artist)
102 Foresbrook Place
Penticton, BC V2A 7N4, CANADA

Odle, Phil (Football Player)
Detroit Lions
691 W 650 S
Orem, UT 84058-6065, USA

Odom, Cliff (Football Player)
Cleveland Browns
6708 Marthas Vineyard Dr
Arlington, TX 76001-5508, USA

Odom, Jason (Football Player)
Tampa Bay Buccaneers
11506 Joshuas Bend Dr
Tampa, FL 33612-5071, USA

Odom, John Lee (Blue Moon) (Baseball Player)
Kansas City A's
10343 Slater Ave Apt 204
Fountain Valley, CA 92708-4783, USA

Odom, Lamar (Basketball Player)
Los Angeles Lakers
1111 S Figueroa St
Staples Center
Los Angeles, CA 90015-1300, USA

Odom, Steve (Football Player)
Green Bay Packers
1482 Lincoln St
Berkeley, CA 94702-1247, USA

Odom, William E (General)
5112 38th St NW
Washington, DC 20016-4204, USA

Odomes, Nathaniel B (Nate) (Football Player)
Buffalo Bills
900 Quail Creek Dr
Columbus, GA 31907-6536, USA

Odoms, Riley M (Football Player)
Denver Broncos
834 1/2 Staffordshire Rd
Stafford, TX 77477, USA

O'Donahue, Pat (Football Player)
San Francisco 49ers
1524 Wheeler Rd Unit D
Madison, WI 53704-7048, USA

O'Donnell, Annie (Actor)
Capital Artists
6404 Wilshire Blvd Ste 950
Los Angeles, CA 90048-5529, USA

O'Donnell, Charles (Chuck) (Bowler)
7354 Forest Haven Est
Saint Louis, MO 63123-2101, USA

O'Donnell, Chris (Actor)
c/o Jason Weinberg *Untitled Entertainment (LA)*
331 N Maple Dr Fl 3
Beverly Hills, CA 90210-3827, USA

O'Donnell, Daniel (Musician)
c/o Staff Member *Public Broadcasting Service (PBS)*
1320 Braddock Pl
Alexandria, VA 22314-1692, USA

O'Donnell, George (Baseball Player)
Pittsburgh Pirates
70 Crusaders Rd
Springfield, IL 62704-5207, USA

O'Donnell, James Michael (Baseball Player)
204 N Diamond St
Clifton Heights, PA 19018-1507, USA

O'Donnell, Joe (Football Player)
Buffalo Bills
447 Bodley Cres
Milan, MI 48160-1206, USA

O'Donnell, John J (Misc)
Air Line Pilots Assn
1625 Massachusetts Ave NW
Washington, DC 20036-2212, USA

O'Donnell, Keir (Actor)
c/o Tom Parziale *Visionary Entertainment*
1558 N Stanley Ave
West Hollywood, CA 90046-2711, USA

O'Donnell, Lawrence (Producer, Writer)
c/o Chris Silbermann *Broder Webb Chervin Silbermann Agency, The (BWCS)*
10250 Constellation Blvd Ste P
Los Angeles, CA 90067-6213, USA

O'Donnell, Mark (Writer)
202 Riverside Dr Apt 8E
New York, NY 10025-7280, USA

O'Donnell, Neil K (Football Player)
Pittsburgh Steelers
PO Box 403
New Vernon, NJ 07976-0403, USA

O'Donnell, Rosie (Actor)
c/o Nancy Josephson *Endeavor Agency LLC (LA)*
9601 Wilshire Blvd Fl 3
Beverly Hills, CA 90210-5204, USA

O'Donnell, William (Bill) (Horse Racer)
569 Penn Est
East Stroudsburg, PA 18301-9062, USA

O'Donoghue, John (Baseball Player)
Kansas City A's
5246 Far Oak Cir
Sarasota, FL 34238-3304, USA

O'Donoghue, Neil (Football Player)
Buffalo Bills
1118 Flushing Ave
Clearwater, FL 33764-4906, USA

O'Dowd, Anna Mae (Baseball Player)
3000 Carefree Blvd Apt E-15
Fort Myers, FL 33917-7135, USA

O'Driscoll, Martha (Actor)
22 Indian Creek Island Rd
Indian Creek Village, FL 33154-2904, USA

Odrowski, Gerry
Box 126
Trout Creek, ON P0H 2L0, CANADA

Oduber, Nelson O (Prime Minister)
Movimenti Electoral di Pueblo
Curnana 84
Oranjestad, ARUBA

Oe, Kenzaburo (Nobel Prize Laureate)
585 Seijo-Machi
Setagayaku
Tokyo, JAPAN

Oedekerk, Steve (Director)
William Morris Agency
151 El Camino Dr
Beverly Hills, CA 90212-2775, USA

Oefelein, William A (Astronaut)
1205 Hawkhill Dr
Friendswood, TX 77546-7811, USA

Oelkers, Bryan (Baseball Player)
Minnesota Twins
3404 Taylor Ave
Bridgeton, MO 63044-3055, USA

Oenish, Dean (Doctor)
Preventive Medical Research Institute
900 Bridgeway # 204
Sausalito, CA 94965-2100, USA

Oester, Ron (Baseball Player)
Cincinnati Reds
3780 Nine Mile-Tobasco Rd
Cincinnati, OH 45255-5232, USA

Oetiker, Phil (Cinematographer)
422 10th St
Brooklyn, NY 11215-4009, USA

O'Farrill, Orlando (Baseball Player)
Philadelphia Stars
Villa Rafaela Herrera Casa A-30
Managua, NICARAGUA

Offerdahl, John A (Football Player)
Miami Dolphins
2749 NE 37th Dr
Fort Lauderdale, FL 33308-6326, USA

Offerman, Jose (Baseball Player)
Los Angeles Dodgers
819 E Cypress Ave
Burbank, CA 91501-1305, USA

Offerman, Jose A (Baseball Player)
Ed 81
Urb Anscaona Moscoso
San Pedro de Marcos, DOMINICAN REPUBLIC

Office, Rowland (Baseball Player)
Atlanta Braves
1028 Lake Glen Way
Sacramento, CA 95822-3224, USA

Offishall, Kardinal (Musician)
c/o Staff Member *MCA Records (LA)*
2220 Colorado Ave
Santa Monica, CA 90404-3506, USA

Offspring (Music Group)
c/o Staff Member *Rebel Waltz Inc*
31652 2nd Ave
Laguna Beach, CA 92651-8244, USA

Ogato, Sadako (Government Official)
United Nations Office for Refugees
CP 2500
Geneva 2 1211, SWITZERLAND

Ogden, Joanne (Baseball Player)
200 1/2 W Cypress St
Glendale, CA 91204-2660, USA

Ogden, Jonathan (Jon) (Football Player)
Baltimore Ravens
Ravens Stadium
11001 Russell St
Baltimore, MD 21230, USA

Ogden, Ray (Football Player)
St Louis Cardinals
188 Anderson Dr
Brunswick, GA 31520-1610, USA

Ogea, Chad (Baseball Player)
Cleveland Indians
418 Bonarbridge Dr
Baton Rouge, LA 70808-8166, USA

Ogi, Adolf (President)
Bundesiause-Nord
Kochergasse 10
Berne 3003, SWITZERLAND

Ogier, Bulle (Actor)
Artmedia
20 Ave Rapp
Paris 75007, FRANCE

Ogier, Maurice (Baseball Player)
4612 Senac Dr
Metairie, LA 70003-2706, USA

Ogilvie, Kelvin K (Educator)
Po Box 307
Canning, NS B0P 1X0, CANADA

Ogilvie, Lana (Model)
Company Models
17 Little West 12th St Ste 333
New York, NY 10014-1311, USA

Ogilvy, Ian (Actor)
Julian Belfarge
46 Albermarle St
London W1X 4PP, UNITED KINGDOM (UK)

Ogle, Brett (Golfer)
Advantage International
1751 Pinnacle Dr Ste 1500
Mc Lean, VA 22102-3833, USA

Oglesby, Alfred L (Football Player)
Miami Dolphins
111 Pendelton Place Cir
Sugar Land, TX 77479-5061, USA

Oglive, Benjamin A (Ben) (Baseball Player)
1012 E Sandpiper Dr
Tempe, AZ 85283-2021, USA

O'Grady, Gail (Actor)
c/o Alan lezman *Shelter Entertainment*
9255 W Sunset Blvd Ste 1010
Los Angeles, CA 90069-3307, USA

O'Grady, Scott
3519 Wallingford Ave N Apt 2
Seattle, WA 98103-9057, USA

O'Grady, Sean (Boxer)
Adoreable Promotions
PO Box 9
Bay City, MI 48707-0009, USA

Ogrin, David (Golfer)
1927 Club Xing
New Braunfels, TX 78130-2453, USA

Ogrodnick, John (Hockey Player)
37034 Aldgate Ct
Farmington Hills, MI 48335-5402, USA

Ogunleye, Adewale (Football Player)
Miami Dolphins
19113 NW 23rd Ct
Pembroke Pines, FL 33029-5336, USA

Oh, Sadaharu (Baseball Player)
Fukuoka Dorne Daiei Hawks
6F 2-2-2 Jigyohama
Chuo-Ku Fukouka 810, JAPAN

Oh, Sandra (Actor)
c/o Staff Member *Grey's Anatomy*
500 S Buena Vista St
Burbank, CA 91521-0001, USA

Oh, Soon Teck
5091 N Fresno St Ste 130
Fresno, CA 93710-7617, USA

O?Hagan, Andrew (Editor, Writer)
c/o Staff Member *UNICEF*
Africa House
64-78 Kingsway
London WC2B 6NB, UNITED KINGDOM (UK)

Ohalloran, Greg (Baseball Player)
Florida Marlins
1021 Hedge Dr
Mississauga, ON L4Y-1G3, CANADA

O'Hara, Catherine (Actor, Comedian)
c/o Marc Gurvitz *Brillstein-Grey Entertainment*
9150 Wilshire Blvd Ste 350
Beverly Hills, CA 90212-3453, USA

O'Hara, Jamie
1025 16th Ave S Ste 200
Nashville, TN 37212-2328, USA

O'Hara, Jenny (Actor)
8663 Wonderland Ave
Los Angeles, CA 90046-1452, USA

O'Hara, Terrence J (Director)
Armstrong/Hirsch
1888 Century Park E Ste 1800
Los Angeles, CA 90067-1722, USA

O'Hare, Denis (Actor)
c/o Staff Member *Innovative Artists (LA)*
1505 10th St
Santa Monica, CA 90401-2805, USA

O'Hare, Michael (Actor)
E/W
280 S Beverly Dr Ste 400
Beverly Hills, CA 90212-3904, USA

Ohl, Don (Basketball Player)
2 E Lockhaven Ct
Edwardsville, IL 62025-3703, USA

Ohlsson, Garrick (Musician)
International Creative Mgmt
8942 Wilshire Blvd # 219
Beverly Hills, CA 90211-1908, USA

Ohlund, Mattias (Hockey Player)
Vancouver Canucks
800 Griffiths Way
Vancouver, BC V6B 6G1, CANADA

Ohman, Jack (Cartoonist, Editor)
Portland Oregonian
1320 SW Broadway
Editorial Dept
Portland, OR 97201-3411, USA

Ohman, Will (Baseball Player)
Chicago White Sox
8663 E Thunderbird Cir
Parker, CO 80134-5722, USA

Ohme, Kevin (Baseball Player)
St Louis Cardinals
806 Starlifter Ln
Valrico, FL 33594-2978, USA

Ohno, Apolo Anton (Speed Skater)
c/o Janey Miller *Janey Miller Management*
1937 Norwood Ave
Boulder, CO 80304-1327, USA

O'Horgan, Thomas F (Tom) (Composer, Director)
Carl Goldstein
9951 Seacrest Cir Apt 201
Boynton Beach, FL 33437-3848, USA

Ohoven, Ute-Henriette (Misc)
c/o Staff Member *United Nations Educational, Scientific and Cultural Organization (UNESCO)*
7, place de Fontenoy
75352
Paris 07 SP, FRANCE

Ohrner, Tommy
Ortlinderstr. 6
Munich D-81927, GERMANY

Ohtani, Monshu Roshin (Religious Leader)
Horikawa-Dori
Hanayachosagaru Shimogyoku
Kyoto 600, JAPAN

O'Hurley, John (Actor)
11661 San Vicente Blvd Ste 307
Los Angeles, CA 90049-5111, USA

Ohyama, Heilchiro (Conductor)
6305 Via Cabrera
La Jolla, CA 92037-5836, USA

Oimeon, Casper (Skier)
540 S Mountain Ave
Ashland, OR 97520-3242, USA

Oingo Boingo
3236 Prlmera Ave.
Los Angeles, CA 90068, USA

Oistrakh, Igor D (Musician)
Novolesnaya Str 3
Korp 2 #10
Moscow, RUSSIA

Oiter, Bailey (President)
President's Office
Palikia
Pohnepei FM
Kolonia 96941, MICRONESIA

Oja, Kim (Actor)
c/o Staff Member *Gage Group, The (LA)*
14724 Ventura Blvd Ste 505
Sherman Oaks, CA 91403-3505, USA

Ojala, Kirt (Baseball Player)
Florida Marlins
1902 Forest Lake Dr SE
Grand Rapids, MI 49546-8234, USA

Ojeda, Augle (Baseball Player)
Chicago Cubs
9402 Dorothy Ave
South Gate, CA 90280-5106, USA

Ojeda, Bob (Baseball Player)
Boston Red Sox
9241 Allano Way
Santee, CA 92071-2202, USA

Ojeda, Miguel (Baseball Player)
c/o Staff Member *San Diego Padres*
100 Park Blvd
San Diego, CA 92101-7405, USA

Ojukwu, Chukwuerneka O (General, President)
Vilaska Lodge
29 Queen's Dr
Ikoyi
Lagos State, NIGERIA

Oka, Masi (Actor)
c/o Paulo Andres *LINK Talent Group*
4741 Laurel Canyon Blvd Ste 106
Valley Village, CA 91607-5907, USA

Oka, Takeshi (Misc)
1463 E Park Pl
Chicago, IL 60637-1835, USA

Okabe, Noroki (Architect, Engineer)
Kansai Airport
1 Banchi Senshu-Kuko Kita
Izumisanoshi
Osake 549, JAPAN

Okafor, Emeka (Basketball Player)
Charlotte Bobcats
333 E Trade St
Charlotte, NC 28202-2331, USA

Okamoto, Ayako (Golfer)
22627 Ladeene Ave
Torrance, CA 90505-3438, USA

Okamura, Arthur (Artist)
210 Kale St
Bolinas, CA 94924, USA

O'Keefe, Jeremiah J Sr (War Hero)
PO Box 430
Ocean Springs, MS 39566-0430, USA

O'Keefe, Jodi Lyn (Actor)
c/o Staff Member *Vincent Cirrincione Associates*
1516 N Fairfax Ave
Los Angeles, CA 90046-2608, USA

O'Keefe, Jodie Lyn (Actor)
J Michael Bloom
9255 W Sunset Blvd Ste 710
Los Angeles, CA 90069-3304, USA

O'Keefe, Michael (Actor)
5850 W 3rd St # 144
Los Angeles, CA 90036-2862, USA

O'Keefe, Miles (Actor)
c/o Alexandra Karrys *Divine Management*
117 N Orlando Ave
Los Angeles, CA 90048-3403, USA

O'Keefe, Paul
225 W 83rd St # 9-5
New York, NY 10024-4952, USA

O'Keefe, Sean (Government Official)
national Aviation/Space Administration
300 E St SW
Washington, DC 20024-3202, USA

Okhotnikoff, Nikolai P (Opera Singer)
Canal Griboedova 109
#13
Saint Petersburg 190068, RUSSIA

Okobi, Chukky (Football Player)
Pittsburgh Steelers
600 Georgetowne Ct
Wexford, PA 15090-8666, USA

Okogie, Anthony Olubunmi Cardinal
(Religious Leader)
Archdiocese
PO Box 8
19 Catholic Mission St
Lagos, NIGERIA

Okolowicz, Jeff (Musician)
Living Eye Productions
PO Box 12956
Rochester, NY 14612-0956, USA

Okolowicz, Ted (Musician)
Living Eye Productions
PO Box 12956
Rochester, NY 14612-0956, USA

Okonedo, Sophie (Actor)
c/o Staff Member *International Creative Management (ICM-LA)*
10250 Constellation Blvd
Los Angeles, CA 90067-6200, USA

Okoniewski, Steve (Football Player)
Buffalo Bills
222 S Oakland Ave
Oconto Falls, WI 54154-1617, USA

O'Koren, Mike (Basketball Player)
Washington Wizards
601 F St NW
Mcl Centre
Washington, DC 20004-1605, USA

Okoye, Christian E (Football Player)
Kansas City Chiefs
10082 Big Pine Dr
Alta Loma, CA 91737-4247, USA

Okrie, Len (Baseball Player)
Washington Senators
2636 Burke Ln
Fayetteville, NC 28306-2629, USA

Okubo, Susumu (Physicist)
1209 East Ave
Rochester, NY 14607-2336, USA

Okuda, Hiroshi (Business Person)
Toyota Motor Corp
1 Toyotacho
Toyota City
Aichi Prefecture 471, JAPAN

Okumura, Tomohiro (Musician)
Jecklin Assoc
2717 Nichols Ln
Davenport, IA 52803-3620, USA

Olafsson, Olafur J (Publisher)
Sony Electronics Publishing USA
9 W 57th St
New York, NY 10019-2701, USA

Olah, George A (Nobel Prize Laureate)
2252 Gloaming Way
Beverly Hills, CA 90210-1717, USA

Olander, Ed (War Hero)
61 Fox Farms Rd
Florence, MA 01062-1334, USA

Olander, Jim (Baseball Player)
Milwaukee Brewers
8421 S Triangle R Ranch Pl
Vail, AZ 85641-8719, USA

Olander, Jimmy (Musician)
Dreamcatcher Artists Mgmt
2908 Poston Ave
Nashville, TN 37203-1312, USA

Olandt, Ken (Actor)
Gold Marshak Liedtke
3500 W Olive Ave Ste 1400
Burbank, CA 91505-5512, USA

Olay, Ruth
2700 Neilson Way Apt 736
Santa Monica, CA 90405-4017, USA

Olazabel, Jose Maria (Golfer)
Sergio Gomez
Apartado 26
San Sebastian E-20080, SPAIN

Olberman, Bob (Football Player)
Kansas City Chiefs
4486 Dobbs Xing
Marietta, GA 30068-2714, USA

Olbermann, Keith (Sportscaster, Television Host)
c/o Staff Member *MSNBC (NJ)*
Nbc/One Microsoft Corporation
1 Msnc Plaza
Secaucus, NJ 07094, USA

Olczyk, Ed (Coach, Hockey Player)
Pittsburgh Penguins
66 Mario Lemieux Pl
Mellon Arena
Pittsburgh, PA 15219-3504, USA

Old Crow Medicine Show (Music Group)
c/o Staff Member *Paradigm (Monterey)*
509 Hartnell St
Monterey, CA 93940-2825, USA

Oldenburg, Claes T (Artist)
556 Broome St
New York, NY 10013-1517, USA

Oldenburg, Richard E (Director)
447 E 57th St
New York, NY 10022-3064, USA

Oldendorf, William (Doctor)
University of California
Medical Center
Neurology Dept
Los Angeles, CA 90024, USA

Older, Charles (Chuck) (War Hero)
930 Thayer Ave
Los Angeles, CA 90024-3314, USA

Olderman, Murray (Writer)
832 Inverness Dr
Rancho Mirage, CA 92270-1451, USA

Oldershaw, Kelsey (Actor)
c/o Darren Goldberg *1 Management*
9000 W Sunset Blvd Ph 1550
West Hollywood, CA 90069-1838, USA

Oldfield, Bruce (Designer, Fashion Designer)
27 Beauchamp Place
London SW3, UNITED KINGDOM (UK)

Oldfield, Mike (Actor, Composer, Director)
c/o Staff Member *Air-Edel (UK)*
18 Rodmarton Street
London W1H 3F, UNITED KINGDOM (UK)

Oldfield, Sally (Musician)
Global Artists Mgmt
Willy-Brandt-Str 39
Erftstadt 50374, GERMANY

Oldham, D Ray (Football Player)
Baltimore Colts
1096 Harbor Landing Dr
Soddy Daisy, TN 37379-5755, USA

Oldham, John (Baseball Player)
Cincinnati Reds
1845 Anne Way
San Jose, CA 95124-6137, USA

Oldham, John (Basketball Player, Coach)
2127 Sycamore Dr
Bowling Green, KY 42104-3868, USA

Oldham, Tasha (Director)
c/o Jerry Shandrew *Shandrew Public Relations*
1050 S Stanley Ave
Los Angeles, CA 90019-6634, USA

Oldham, Todd (Designer, Fashion Designer)
120 Wooster St
New York, NY 10012-5200, USA

Oldis, Bob (Baseball Player)
Washington Senators
306 Virginia Dr
Iowa City, IA 52245-1639, USA

Oldman, Gary (Actor, Director)
c/o Douglas Urbanski *Douglas Management*
9713 Santa Monica Blvd Ste 218
Beverly Hills, CA 90210-4217, USA

Olds, Bill (Football Player)
Baltimore Colts
7414 Pohick Rd
Lorton, VA 22079-1518, USA

Olds, Gabriel
PO Box 120551
Nashville, TN 37212-0551, USA

Olds, Robin (Football Player, War Hero)
PO Box 1478
Steamboat Springs, CO 80477, USA

Olds, Walter (Wally) (Hockey Player)
37296 Pincherry Rd
Cohasset, MN 55721-2069, USA

O'Leary, Brian T (Astronaut)
1993 S Kihei Rd # 21200
Kihei, HI 96753-7834, USA

O'Leary, Dan (Football Player)
Buffalo Bills
3300 W 159th St
Cleveland, OH 44111-1946, USA

O'Leary, George (Coach, Football Coach)
Central Florida University
Athletic Dept
Orlando, FL 32918, USA

O'Leary, Hazel R (Secretary)
Energy Department
1000 Independence Ave SW
Washington, DC 20585-0001, USA

O'Leary, John (Actor)
Gage Group
14724 Ventura Blvd Ste 505
Sherman Oaks, CA 91403-3505, USA

O'Leary, Marrissa (Actor)
c/o Staff Member *Select Artists Ltd (CA-Valley Office)*
PO Box 4359
Burbank, CA 91503-4359, USA

O'Leary, Matthew (Actor)
c/o Brian Swardstrom *Endeavor Agency LLC (LA)*
9601 Wilshire Blvd Fl 3
Beverly Hills, CA 90210-5204, USA

O'Leary, Michael (Actor)
38 Prospect Ave
Montclair, NJ 07042-1915, USA

O'Leary, Troy (Baseball Player)
Milwaukee Brewers
1060 W Norwood St
Rialto, CA 92377-8220, USA

O'Leary, William (Actor)
House of Representatives
211 S Beverly Dr Ste 208
Beverly Hills, CA 90212-3879, USA

Oleksy, Jozef (Prime Minister)
Ul Wiktorii Wiedenskiej 5 M 4
Warsaw 02-954, POLAND

Olerich, Dave (Football Player)
San Francisco 49ers
2138 Wellesley St
Palo Alto, CA 94306-1335, USA

Olerud, John (Baseball Player)
Toronto Blue Jays
1310 180th Ave NE
Bellevue, WA 98008-3232, USA

Olesz, Rostislav (Hockey Player)
Florida Panthers
1 Panther Pkwy
Sunrise, FL 33323-5315, USA

Olevsky, Julian (Musician)
68 Blue Hills Rd
Amherst, MA 01002-2220, USA

Oleynik, Larisa (Actor)
c/o Staff Member *Savage Agency*
6212 Banner Ave
Los Angeles, CA 90038-2802, USA

Oliceira, Ana Cristina (Actor)
c/o Cliff Gilbert-Lurie *Ziffren Brittenham Branca Fischer Gilbert-Lurie, Stiffman & Cook*
1801 Century Park W
Los Angeles, CA 90067-6409, USA

Olin, Ken (Actor)
Endeavor Talent Agency
9701 Wilshire Blvd Ste 1000
Beverly Hills, CA 90212-2010, USA

Olin, Lena (Actor)
Industry Entertainment
955 Carrillo Dr Ste 300
Los Angeles, CA 90048-5400, USA

Olin, Lina (Actor)
c/o Staff Member *Industry Entertainment*
955 Carrillo Dr Ste 300
Los Angeles, CA 90048-5400, USA

Olinger, Marilyn (Baseball Player)
6451 Far Hills Ave
Dayton, OH 45459-2725, USA

Olinski, Harry (Football Player)
Washington Redskins
3205 Furman Blvd
Louisville, KY 40220-1949, USA

Oliphant, Patrick B (Cartoonist)
Universal Press Syndicate
4520 Main St
Kansas City, MO 64111-1876, USA

Oliphant, Randall (Business Person)
Barrick Gold Corp
200 Bay St
Toronto, ON M5J 2J3, CANADA

Olitski, Jules (Artist)
PO Box 440
Marlboro, VT 05344-0440, USA

Oliu, Ingrid (Actor)
c/o Staff Member *Cunningham Escott Slevin & Doherty (LA)*
10635 Santa Monica Blvd Ste 130
Los Angeles, CA 90025-8306, USA

Oliva, L Jay (Educator)
New York University
President's Office
New York, NY 10012, USA

Oliva, Sergio (Misc)
Oliva's Gym
7383 N Rogers Ave
Chicago, IL 60626-1524, USA

Oliva, Tony (Baseball Player)
Minnesota Twins
212 Spring Valley Dr
Minneapolis, MN 55420-5540, USA

Olivares, Ed (Baseball Player)
St Louis Cardinals
HC 2 Box 12887
San German, PR 00683, USA

Olivares, Omar (Baseball Player)
St Louis Cardinals
90 Alton Rd Apt 804
Miami Beach, FL 33139-6707, USA

Olivas, John D (Astronaut)
2618 Sunset Blvd
Houston, TX 77005-2440, USA

Olive, Jason (Actor, Model)
c/o Staff Member *Kazarian/Spencer & Assoc (LA)*
11969 Ventura Blvd
Box 7409 Fl 3
Studio City, CA 91604-2630, USA

Oliveira, Elmar (Musician)
Cramer/Marder Artists
3436 Springhill Rd
Lafayette, CA 94549-2535, USA

Oliveira, Nathan J (Artist)
785 Santa Maria Ave
Palo Alto, CA 94305-8439, USA

Oliver, Albert (Al) (Baseball Player)
Pittsburgh Pirates
PO Box 1466
Portsmouth, OH 45662-1466, USA

Oliver, Bob (Baseball Player)
Pittsburgh Pirates
1716 G St
Rio Linda, CA 95673-4534, USA

Oliver, Christian (Actor)
7211 Mulholland Dr
Los Angeles, CA 90068-2031, USA

Oliver, Clancy (Football Player)
Pittsburgh Steelers
233 Springview
Irvine, CA 92620-1970, USA

Oliver, Covey T (Attorney, Attorney General, Diplomat, General)
Ingleton-On-Miles
RR 1 Box 194
Easton, MD 21601, USA

Oliver, Daniel (Government Official)
Heritage Foundation
214 Massachusetts Ave NE
Washington, DC 20002-4999, USA

Oliver, Darren (Baseball Player)
Texas Rangers
1804 Larkspur Ct
Southlake, TX 76092-3572, USA

Oliver, Dave (Baseball Player)
Cleveland Indians
1709 Timberlake Cir
Lodi, CA 95242-4283, USA

Oliver, Dean (Race Car Driver)
21386 Notus Rd
Greenleaf, ID 83626-8940, USA

Oliver, Gene (Baseball Player)
St Louis Cardinals
2805 35th St
Rock Island, IL 61201-5635, USA

Oliver, Hubie (Football Player)
Philadelphia Eagles
136 Blake St
Elyria, OH 44035-5422, USA

Oliver, Jamie (Chef)
15 Barmbles
Bishops Storford
Herts CM23 4PX, UNITED KINGDOM (UK)

Oliver, Joe (Baseball Player)
Cincinnati Reds
4540 Foreland Pl
Orlando, FL 32812-1935, USA

Oliver, Louis (Football Player)
Miami Dolphins
5082 SW 167th Ave
Miramar, FL 33027-4910, USA

Oliver, Mary (Writer)
Molly Malone Cook Agency
PO Box U
Sweet Briar, VA 24595-1071, USA

Oliver, Murray C (Hockey Player)
5505 McGuire Rd
Minneapolis, MN 55439-1342, USA

Oliver, Nate (Baseball Player)
Los Angeles Dodgers
4403 Oak Hill Rd
Oakland, CA 94605-4632, USA

Oliver, Pam (Sportscaster)
Fox-TV
205 W 67th St
Sports Dept
New York, NY 10021, USA

Oliver, Ron (Director, Writer)
c/o Mark Itkin *William Morris Agency (WMA-LA)*
1 William Morris Pl
Beverly Hills, CA 90212-4261, USA

Oliver, Winslow (Football Player)
Carolina Panthers
2027 Summerall Ct
Richmond, TX 77469-6737, USA

Oliveres, Rubin
PO Box 113
Montebello, CA 90640-0113, USA

Olivia (Musician)
c/o Staff Member *Interscope Records (LA) - Main*
2220 Colorado Ave
Santa Monica, CA 90404-3506, USA

Olivo, Joey (Boxer)
9628 Poinciana St
Pico Rivera, CA 90660-4242, USA

Olivor, Jane (Music Group, Musician)
Ed Keane
32 Saint Edward Rd
Boston, MA 02128-1263, USA

Olkewicz, Neal (Football Player)
Washington Redskins
17717 Crystal Spring Ter
Ashton, MD 20861-3605, USA

Olkewicz, Walter (Actor)
Gold Marshak Liedtke
3500 W Olive Ave Ste 1400
Burbank, CA 91505-5512, USA

Ollom, Jim (Baseball Player)
Minnesota Twins
10916 27th Ave SE
Everett, WA 98208-7807, USA

Olmedo, Alex (Tennis Player)
5067 Woodley Ave
Encino, CA 91436-1472, USA

Olmo, Luis (Baseball Player)
Brooklyn Dodgers
620 Figueroa Street
Santurce, PR 00907, USA

Olmos, Edward James (Actor)
c/o Steve Tellez *Creative Artists Agency LCC (CAA-LA)*
2000 Avenue Of The Stars
Los Angeles, CA 90067-4700, USA

Olmstead, Matt (Producer)
c/o Staff Member *International Creative Management (ICM-LA)*
10250 Constellation Blvd
Los Angeles, CA 90067-6200, USA

Olmsted, Al
St Louis Cardinals
1008 Pinecone Trl
Florissant, MO 63031-7436, USA

Olney, Claude W (Educator)
Olney 'A' Seminars
PO Box 686
Scottsdale, AZ 85252-0686, USA

O'Loughlin, Gerald
PO Box 340832
Arleta, CA 91334-0832, USA

O'Loughlin, Gerald S (Actor)
23388 Mulholland Dr # 204
Woodland Hills, CA 91364-2733, USA

Olowaonkandi, Michael (Basketball Player)
c/o Staff Member *Los Angeles Clippers*
1111 S Figueroa St
Los Angeles, CA 90015-1300, USA

Olowokandi, Michael (Basketball Player)
Minnesota Timberwolves
600 1st Ave N
Target Center
Minneapolis, MN 55403-1416, USA

Olsavsky, Bill (Football Player)
Dallas Texans
132 Walnut Ave
Saint Clairsville, OH 43950-1702, USA

Olsavsky, Jerry (Football Player)
Pittsburgh Steelers
92 Lake Shore Dr
Youngstown, OH 44511-3552, USA

Olsen, Andrew (Baseball Player)
451 93rd Ave N
Saint Petersburg, FL 33702-3147, USA

Olsen, Ashley (Actor)
c/o Staff Member *DualStar Entertainment*
3760 Robertson Blvd # 2
Culver City, CA 90232-2319, USA

Olsen, David A (Financier)
Marsh & McLennan Co
1166 Avenue Of The Americas
New York, NY 10036-2728, USA

Olsen, Eric Christian (Actor)
c/o Ellen Meyer *Ellen Meyer Entertainment*
8899 Beverly Blvd Ste 612
Los Angeles, CA 90048-2429, USA

Olsen, Gregory (Astronaut, Business Person)
Sensors Unlimited
3490 US Route 1 Building 12
Princeton, NJ 08540, USA

Olsen, Kaitlin (Actor)
c/o Amy Slomovits *Joan Green Management*
1836 Courtney Ter
Los Angeles, CA 90046-2106, USA

Olsen, Kenneth H (Inventor)
111 Powder Mill Rd
Maynard, MA 01754-1482, USA

Olsen, Kevin (Ballerina)
Florida Marlins
3353 Dales Dr
Norco, CA 92860-2281, USA

Olsen, Mary Kate (Actor)
c/o Staff Member *DualStar Entertainment*
3760 Robertson Blvd # 2
Culver City, CA 90232-2319, USA

Olsen, Merlin J (Actor, Football Player, Sportscaster)
Los Angeles Rams
PO Box 3148
Park City, UT 84060-3148, USA

Olsen, Olaf (Archaeologist)
Strevelsiovedvej 2
Alro
Oder 8300, DENMARK

Olsen, Paul E (Misc)
Columbia University
Lamont-Doherty Geological Laboratory
New York, NY 10027, USA

Olsen, Phil (Football Player)
Los Angeles Rams
112 Hitching Post Rd
Bozeman, MT 59715-8027, USA

Olsen, Robert C Jr (Admiral, Educator)
US Coast Guard Academy
Superintendent's Office
New London, CT 06320, USA

Olsen, Stanford (Opera Singer)
Columbia Artists Mgmt Inc
1790 Broadway Fl 6
New York, NY 10019-1412, USA

Olshwanger, Ron (Journalist,
Photographer)
1447 Meadowside Dr
Saint Louis, MO 63146-4914, USA

Olson, Allen I (Governor)
631 Broken Arrow Rd
Chanhassen, MN 55317-9569, USA

Olson, Benji (Football Player)
Tinnessee Titans
2211 Old Natchez Trce
Franklin, TN 37069-1904, USA

Olson, Greg (Baseball Player)
Minnesota Twins
18592 Saint Mellion Pl
Eden Prairie, MN 55347-3487, USA

Olson, Gregg (Baseball Player)
Baltimore Orioles
1996 Port Nelson Pl
Newport Beach, CA 92660-6618, USA

Olson, Harold (Football Player)
Buffalo Bills
1622 Holly Springs Rd NE
Marietta, GA 30062-2829, USA

Olson, James (Actor)
250 W 57th St Ste 803
New York, NY 10107-0800, USA

Olson, Karl (Baseball Player)
Boston Red Sox
PO Box 1897
Zephyr Cove, NV 89448-1897, USA

Olson, Mancur (Economist)
4316 Clagett Pine Way
University Park, MD 20782-1141, USA

Olson, Mark (Economist, Government
Official)
Federal Reserve Board
20th St & Constitution Ave
Washington, DC 20551-0001, USA

Olson, Mark (Musician, Songwriter,
Writer)
Sussman Assoc
1222 16th Ave S Fl 3
Nashville, TN 37212-2926, USA

Olson, Nancy (Actor)
945 N Alpine Dr
Beverly Hills, CA 90210-2946, USA

Olson, R Lute (Basketball Player, Coach)
University of Arizona
McKate Memorial Center
Tucson, AZ 85721-0001, USA

Olson, Richard E (Business Person)
Champion Int'l Corp
1 Champion Plz
Stamford, CT 06921-6001, USA

Olson, Weldon (Hockey Player)
2623 Goldenrod Ln
Findlay, OH 45840-1025, USA

Olssen, Lance (Football Player)
San Francisco 49ers
5222 E Timberwood Dr
Newburgh, IN 47630-3014, USA

Olsson, Ann (Ann-Margret) (Actor,
Dancer, Musician)
c/o Alan Margulies *AM Productions &
Management*
8899 Beverly Blvd Ste 713
Los Angeles, CA 90048-2450, USA

Olstead, Renee
3013 Fountain View Dr Ste 240
Houston, TX 77057-6120, USA

Olszewski, Jan F (Prime Minister)
Biuro Poselskie
Al Ujazdowskie 13
Warsaw 00-567, POLAND

Olwine, Ed (Baseball Player)
Atlanta Braves
223 Spanish Lakes Dr
Nokomis, FL 34275-1534, USA

Olyphant, Timothy (Actor)
William Morris Agency
151 El Camino Dr
Beverly Hills, CA 90212-2775, USA

Omakuchi, Narasimhann (Actor)
24 Vasudevapuram
Besant Road
Chennai, TN 600 005, INDIA

O'Malley, Jim (Football Player)
Denver Broncos
238 S Berryline Cir
Spring, TX 77381-4824, USA

O'Malley, Joe (Football Player)
Pittsburgh Steelers
656 Sugar Creek Trl SE
Conyers, GA 30094-3808, USA

O'Malley, Mike (Actor)
Creative Artists Agency
9830 Wilshire Blvd
Beverly Hills, CA 90212-1804, USA

O'Malley, Peter (Baseball Player)
326 S Hudson Ave
Los Angeles, CA 90020-4804, USA

O'Malley, Robert E (War Hero)
PO Box 775
Goldthwaite, TX 76844-0775, USA

O'Malley, Sean Patrick (Religious Leader)
Archdiocese of Boston
2121 Commonwealth Ave
Brighton, MA 02135-3193, USA

O'Malley, Susan (Misc)
Washington Wizards
601 F St NW
Mcl Centre
Washington, DC 20004-1605, USA

O'Malley, Thomas D (Business Person)
Tosco Corp
1700 E Putnam Ave # 500
Old Greenwich, CT 06870-1321, USA

O'Malley, Tom (Baseball Player)
San Francisco Giants
10 Carriage Sq
Montoursville, PA 17754, USA

Oman, Qaboos Bin Said Sultan of
The Palace
Muscat, OMAN

Omar, Chamassi Said (Prime Minister)
Prime Minister's Office
BP 421
Moroni, COMOROS

Omar & The Howlers
PO Box 93
Austin, TX 78767-0093, USA

O'Mara, Jason (Actor)
c/o Michael (Mike) Jelline *International
Creative Management (ICM-LA)*
10250 Constellation Blvd
Los Angeles, CA 90067-6200, USA

O'Mara, Kate (Actor)
Michael Ladkin Mgmt
1 Duchess St
#1
London W1N 3DE, UNITED KINGDOM
(UK)

O'Mara, Mark (Coach, Horse Racer)
6882 NW 65th Ter
Parkland, FL 33067-1442, USA

O'Meara, Jo (Actor, Musician)
c/o Staff Member *S Club 7*
9830 Wilshire Blvd
Creative Artists Agency Lcc (Caa-La)
Beverly Hills, CA 90212-1804, USA

O'Meara, Mark (Golfer)
9705 Lake Isleworth Ct
Windermere, FL 34786-8919, USA

O'Meara, Peter (Actor)
c/o Staff Member *ROAR LLC*
9701 Wilshire Blvd Ste 850
Beverly Hills, CA 90212-2032, USA

O'Mears, Mark (Golfer)
6312 Deacon Cir
Windermere, FL 34786-8938, USA

Omidyar, Pierre (Business Person)
eBay
2145 Hamilton Ave
San Jose, CA 95125-5905, USA

Onanian, Edward (Religious Leader)
Diocese of Armenian Church
630 2nd Ave
New York, NY 10016-4806, USA

Onassis, Athina (Heir/Heiress)
88 av Foch
Paris F-75116, FRANCE

Ondaatje, Michael (Writer)
Glendon College
English Dept
2275 Bayview
Toronto, ON M4N 3M6, CANADA

Ondetti, Miguel A
79 Hemlock Cir
Princeton, NJ 08540-5405, USA

Ondrasik, John (Musician, Songwriter)
c/o Staff Member *Paradigm (Monterey)*
509 Hartnell St
Monterey, CA 93940-2825, USA

Ondricek, Miroslav (Cinematographer)
Nad Pomnikem 1
Prague 5, Smichow 15200, CZECH
REPUBLIC

ONeal, Alexander (Musician)
c/o *Eminence Leisure*
18-24 John St
Luton LU1 2JE, UNITED KINGDOM (UK)

O'Neal, E Stan (Financier)
Merrill Lynch Co
2 Vesey St
World Financial Center
New York, NY 10007, USA

O'Neal, Griffin (Actor)
14209 Riverside Dr
Van Nuys, CA 91423-2364, USA

O'Neal, Jamie (Musician, Songwriter,
Writer)
Fitzgerald Hartley
19078 Wedgewood Ave
Nashville, TN 37212, USA

O'Neal, Jermaine (Basketball Player)
c/o Staff Member *Indiana Pacers*
125 S Pennsylvania St
Conseco Fieldhouse
Indianapolis, IN 46204-3610, USA

O'Neal, Leslie C (Football Player)
San Diego Chargers
5617 Adobe Falls Rd Unit A
San Diego, CA 92120-4654, USA

O'Neal, Patrice (Musician)
c/o Staff Member *Paradigm (Monterey)*
509 Hartnell St
Monterey, CA 93940-2825, USA

O'Neal, Randy (Baseball Player)
Detroit Tigers
524 Rambling Drive Cir
Wellington, FL 33414, USA

O'Neal, Ryan (Actor)
21368 Pacific Coast Hwy
Malibu, CA 90265-5203, USA

O'Neal, Shaquille (Actor, Basketball
Player)
c/o Staff Member *Miami Heat*
601 Biscayne Blvd
American Airlines Arena
Miami, FL 33132-1801, USA

O'Neal, Steve (Football Player)
New York Jets
2914 Coronado Dr
College Station, TX 77845-7716, USA

O'Neal, Tatum (Actor)
c/o Brian Young *Untitled Entertainment
(LA)*
331 N Maple Dr Fl 3
Beverly Hills, CA 90210-3827, USA

O'Neil, Edward W (Football Player)
Detroit Lions
6691 Aiken Rd
Lockport, NY 14094-9648, USA

O'Neil, John (Baseball Player, Coach)
Philadelphia Phillies
220 Southwestern Dr Apt 131
Lakewood, NY 14750-2142, USA

O'Neil, Lawrence (Director)
International Creative Mgmt
8942 Wilshire Blvd # 219
Beverly Hills, CA 90211-1908, USA

O'Neil, Ron
10100 Santa Monica Blvd Ste 2500
Los Angeles, CA 90067-4116, USA

O'Neil, Susie (Athlete, Swimmer)
177 Bridge Road
Richmond, Vic 3121, AUSTRALIA

O'Neil, Tricia (Actor)
David Shapira
193 N Robertson Blvd
Beverly Hills, CA 90211-2103, USA

O'Neil, Warren (Baseball Player)
Detroit Stars
258 Terrace Park
Rochester, NY 14619-2443, USA

O'Neill, Brian (Hockey Player)
2600-1800 McGill College Ave
Montreal, PQ H3A 3J6, CANADA

O'Neill, Ed (Actor)
c/o Marc Gurvitz *Brillstein-Grey
Entertainment*
9150 Wilshire Blvd Ste 350
Beverly Hills, CA 90212-3453, USA

O'Neill, Jennifer (Actor, Model)
(615) 463-3126
PO Box 40707
Nashville, TN 37204-0707, USA

O'Neill, Kevin (Football Player)
Detroit Lions
1363 Masters Dr
Metamora, MI 48455-8701, USA

O'Neill, Michael (Actor)
c/o Staff Member *Mitchell K Stubbs & Assoc (MKS)*
8695 Washington Blvd Ste 204
Culver City, CA 90232-7419, USA

O'Neill, Michael J (Editor)
23 Cayuga Rd
Scarsdale, NY 10583-6941, USA

O'Neill, Paul (Baseball Player)
Cincinnati Reds
7785 Hartford Hill Ln
Cincinnati, OH 45242-4347, USA

O'Neill, Paul H (Secretary)
3 Von Lent Pl
Pittsburgh, PA 15232-1444, USA

O'Neill, Susan (Susie) (Swimmer)
207 Kent St
#1800
Sydney, NSW 2000, AUSTRALIA

O'Neill, Terence P (Terry) (Photographer)
8 Warwick Ave
London W2 1XB, UNITED KINGDOM (UK)

O'Neill, William A (Governor)
PO Box 360
East Hampton, CT 06424-0360, USA

O'Neill of Bengarve, O Sylvia (Misc)
NewHam College
Cambridge CB3 9DF, UNITED KINGDOM (UK)

Onesti, Larry (Football Player)
Houston Oilers
5476 E James Rd
Bloomington, IN 47408-9402, USA

Onetto, Victoria (Actor)
c/o Staff Member *Telefe - Argentina*
Pavon 2444 (C1248AAT)
Buenos Aires, ARGENTINA

Onkotz, Dennis H (Football Player)
New York Jets
270 Walker Dr
State College, PA 16801-7097, USA

Onodi, Henrietta (Gymnast)
Gymnastic Federation
Magyar Toma Szovetseg
Budapest 1143, HUNGARY

O'Nora, Brian (Baseball Player)
4294 Maureen Dr
Youngstown, OH 44511-1014, USA

Onorati, Peter
c/o Kay Liberman *Liberman/Zerman Management*
252 N Larchmont Blvd Ste 200
Los Angeles, CA 90004-3754, USA

Ontiveros, Lupe (Actor)
c/o Staff Member *Mitchell K Stubbs & Assoc (MKS)*
8695 Washington Blvd Ste 204
Culver City, CA 90232-7419, USA

Ontiveros, Steve (Baseball Player)
Oakland A's
9970 E Charter Oak Rd
Scottsdale, AZ 85260-5138, USA

Ontkean, Michael (Actor)
PO Box 51
Kilauea, HI 96754-0051, USA

Onufriyenko, Yuri I (Astronaut, Misc)
Potchta Kosmonavtov
Moskovskoi Oblasti
Syvisdny Goroduk 141160, RUSSIA

Oorvasi (Actor, Bollywood)
117 Solai Krishnan Street
Janaki Nagar
Chennai, TN 600087, INDIA

Oosterhouse, Carter (Television Host)
c/o Staff Member *Trading Spaces*
7700 Wisconsin Ave
The Learning Channel
Bethesda, MD 20814-3578, USA

Oosterhuis, Peter (Golfer)
Riviera County Club
1250 Capri Dr
Pacific Palisades, CA 90272-4099, USA

Oosterhuls, Peter (Golfer)
10687 E Fernwood Ln
Scottsdale, AZ 85262-3431, USA

Opalinski-Harrer, Janice (Volleyball Player)
Women's Pro Volleyball Assn
840 Apollo St Ste 204
El Segundo, CA 90245-4737, USA

Opasik, Jim (Artist)
1914 Beverly Rd
Baltimore, MD 21228-4227, USA

Ophula, Marcel
10 rue Ernst-Deloison
Neuilly 92200, FRANCE

Opie, John D (Business Person)
General Electric Co
3135 Easton Tpke
Fairfield, CT 06828-0001, USA

Oppel, Richard A (Editor)
Knight-Ridder
National Press Building
529 14th St NW
Washington, DC 20045-1000, USA

Oppenheim, Dennis A (Artist)
54 Franklin St
New York, NY 10013-4009, USA

Oppenheim, Irwin (Physicist)
140 Upland Rd
Cambridge, MA 02140-3623, USA

Oppenheim-Barnes, Saily (Government Official)
Quietways Highlands
Painswick
Glos, UNITED KINGDOM (UK)

Oppenheimer, Alan
1207 Beverly Green Dr
Beverly Hills, CA 90212-4105, USA

Oppenheimer, Deborah (Producer)
c/o Staff Member *United Talent Agency (UTA)*
9560 Wilshire Blvd Ste 500
Beverly Hills, CA 90212-2401, USA

Opry, Tonya
1525 E Noble Ave # 160
Visalia, CA 93292-3043, USA

Oquendo, Jose (Baseball Player)
New York Mets
13219 Selma Rd
De Soto, MO 63020-5242, USA

O'Quinn, John M (Attorney, Attorney General, General)
O'Quinn Kerensky McAnich
440 Louisiana St
2300 Lyric Center
Houston, TX 77002-1639, USA

O'Quinn, Terry (Actor)
Innovative Artists
1505 10th St
Santa Monica, CA 90401-2805, USA

Oquist, Mike (Baseball Player)
Baltimore Orioles
1910 Raton Ave
La Junta, CO 81050-3427, USA

Orange, Walter (Clyde) (Music Group, Musician)
Management Assoc
1920 Benson Ave
Saint Paul, MN 55116-3214, USA

Oravetz, Ernie (Baseball Player)
Washington Senators
4417 W Paul Ave
Tampa, FL 33611-3321, USA

Orbach, Raymond L (Educator)
3001 Veazey Ter NW Apt 525
Washington, DC 20008-5401, USA

Orbelian, Konstantin A (Composer)
Demirchyan Str 27 #12
Yerevan 3750002, ARMENIA

Orbit, William (Musician)
c/o Staff Member *Creative Artists Agency LCC (CAA-LA)*
2000 Avenue Of The Stars
Los Angeles, CA 90067-4700, USA

Ord, Maren
Frontside Management Group
1187 W 16th Ave
Vancouver, BC V6H 1S8, CANADA

Ord, Robert L (Bob) III (General)
3020 Ribera Rd
Carmel, CA 93923-9724, USA

Ordonez, Magglio (Baseball Player)
c/o Staff Member *Detroit Tigers*
2100 Woodward Ave
Comerica Park
Detroit, MI 48201-3474, USA

Ordonez, Rey (Baseball Player)
New York Mets
1000 SE 9th Ave
Hialeah, FL 33010-5810, USA

Ordovos, Jose M (Scientist)
Tufts University
Nutrition Research Center
Medford, MA 02155, USA

Orduna, Joe (Football Player)
New York Giants
15 Grant
Irvine, CA 92620-3354, USA

Ordway, Frederick I III (Writer)
2401 N Taylor St
Arlington, VA 22207-4021, USA

O'Ree, William E (Willie) (Hockey Player)
7961 Anders Cir
La Mesa, CA 91942-2304, USA

O'Reilly, Anthony (Business Person)
HJ Heinz Co
PO Box 57
Pittsburgh, PA 15230-0057, USA

O'Reilly, Bill (Television Host)
c/o Staff Member *Fox News Channel (NY)*
1211 Avenue Of The Americas
Level C1
New York, NY 10036-8701, USA

O'Reilly, Cyril (Actor)
Stone Manners
6500 Wilshire Blvd Ste 550
Los Angeles, CA 90048-4950, USA

O'Reilly, Terry (Coach, Hockey Player)
PO Box 5544
Salisbury, MA 01952-0544, USA

Oremans, Miriam (Tennis Player)
Octagon
1751 Pinnacle Dr Ste 1500
McLean, VA 22102-3833, USA

Orend, Jack R
1808 N Van Ness Ave
Hollywood, CA 90028-5674, USA

Orendi, Ron
6323 Salem Park Cir
Mechanicsburg, PA 17050-2839, USA

Orenduff, J Michael (Educator)
New Mexico State University
President's Office
Las Cruces, NM 88003, USA

Orenstein, Andrew (Producer)
c/o Staff Member *United Talent Agency (UTA)*
9560 Wilshire Blvd Ste 500
Beverly Hills, CA 90212-2401, USA

Oreskaband (Music Group)
c/o Staff Member *Paradigm (Monterey)*
509 Hartnell St
Monterey, CA 93940-2825, USA

Oresko, Nicholas (War Hero)
4 Tenakill Park E Apt 109
Cresskill, NJ 07626-2061, USA

Orgad, Ben-Zion (Composer)
14 Bloch St
Tel-Aviv 64161, ISRAEL

Organ, H Bryan (Artist)
Stables
Marston Trussel near Market Harborough
Leics LE16 9TX, UNITED KINGDOM (UK)

Orgy (Music Group)
c/o Staff Member *Creative Artists Agency LCC (CAA-LA)*
2000 Avenue Of The Stars
Los Angeles, CA 90067-4700, USA

Oriard, Michael (Football Player)
Kansas City Chiefs
3010 NW McKinley Dr
Corvallis, OR 97330-1138, USA

Orie, Kevin (Baseball Player)
Chicago Cubs
997 Centennial Dr
West Chester, PA 19382-2352, USA

O'Riordan, Dolores (Musician)
Sendyk Leonard
532 Colorado Ave
Santa Monica, CA 90401-2408, USA

Orland, Frank J (Doctor)
519 Jackson Blvd
Forest Park, IL 60130-1807, USA

Orlando, Bo (Football Player)
Houston Oilers
1360 Armstrong Rd
Bethlehem, PA 18017-1002, USA

Orlando, Geoarge J (Misc)
Distillery Wine & Allied Workers
219 Paterson Ave
Little Falls, NJ 07424-1657, USA

Orlando, Tony (Music Group, Musician)
Brokaw Co
9255 W Sunset Blvd Ste 804
Los Angeles, CA 90069-3305, USA

Orleans, Joan (Musician)
PO Box 2596
New York, NY 10009-8923, USA

Orlenko, Oksana (Actor)
c/o Staff Member *Sharp Entertainment*
1515 Broadway
New York, NY 10036-8901, USA

Orlich, Dan (Football Player)
Green Bay Packers
1030 Porter Cir
Reno, NV 89509-2349, USA

Orlov, Yuri
Cornell Univ. Newman Lab.
Ithaca, NY 14853, USA

Orman, Suze (Business Person,
Correspondent, Writer)
Suze Orman Financial Group
2000 Powell St Ste 1605
Emeryville, CA 94608-1861, USA

Orme, Stanley (Government Official)
8 Northwood Grove
Sale
Cheshire M33 3DZ, UNITED KINGDOM
(UK)

Ormond, Brian (Musician)
c/o Staff Member *Pop Idol (Fremantle
Media)*
2700 Colorado Ave Ste 450
Santa Monica, CA 90404-3599, USA

Ormond, Julia (Actor)
Marmont Mgmt
Langham House
302/8 Regent St
London W1R 5AL, UNITED KINGDOM
(UK)

Ormond, Paul (Business Person)
Manor Care Inc
333 N Summit St Ste 100
Toledo, OH 43604-2617, USA

Oropesa, Eddie (Baseball Player)
Philadelphia Phillies
15757 SW 102nd St
Miami, FL 33196-5420, USA

Orosco, Jesse (Baseball Player)
New York Mets
PO Box 503610
San Diego, CA 92150-3610, USA

O'Ross, Ed (Actor)
c/o Staff Member *Whitaker Agency, The*
4924 Vineland Ave
N Hollywood, CA 91601-3847, USA

Orosz, Tom (Football Player)
Miami Dolphins
425 1/2 5th St
Fairport Harbor, OH 44077-5629, USA

O'Rourke, Charles C (Football Player)
220 Bedford St Apt 7A
Bridgewater, MA 02324-3123, USA

O'Rourke, Charlie (Baseball Player)
St Louis Cardinals
15612 N Little Spokane Dr
Spokane, WA 99208-8527, USA

O'Rourke, Tom (Actor)
c/o Staff Member *Law & Order: SVU*
100 Universal City Plz Bldg 2252
Universal City, CA 91608-1002, USA

Orr, Bobby
2 Open Space Dr
Sandwich, MA 02563-3100, USA

Orr, Christopher (Actor)
c/o Staff Member *3 Arts Entertainment Inc*
9460 Wilshire Blvd Fl 7
Beverly Hills, CA 90212-2713, USA

Orr, David A (Business Person)
Home Farm House Shackleford
Godalming
Surrey GU8 6AH, UNITED KINGDOM
(UK)

Orr, James E (Football Player)
Pittsburgh Steelers
3104 Glynn Ave
Brunswick, GA 31520, USA

Orr, John (Johnny) (Coach)
5736 Gallery Ct
West Des Moines, IA 50266-6629, USA

Orr, Kay S (Governor)
1425 H St
Lincoln, NE 68508-3759, USA

Orr, Louis (Coach)
1333 Pine Valley Dr
Bowling Green, OH 43402-5207, USA

Orr, Terrence S (Dancer)
American Ballet Theatre
890 Broadway
New York, NY 10003-1278, USA

Orr, Terry (Football Player)
Washington Redskins
2710 Kellogg Ave
Dallas, TX 75216-3250, USA

Orr-Cahall, Christina (Director)
Norton Gallery of Art
1451 S Olive Ave
West Palm Beach, FL 33401-7198, USA

Orr-Ewing, Hamish (Business Person)
Fox Mill
Purton near Swindon
Wilts SN5 9EF, UNITED KINGDOM (UK)

Orr III, James E (Business Person)
UNUMProvident Corp
2211 Congress St
Portland, ME 04122-0002, USA

Orrall, Robert Ellis (Musician)
3 E 54th St # 1400
New York, NY 10022-3108, USA

Orrico, Stacie (Musician)
Forefront Records
230 Franklin Rd Bldg 2A
Franklin, TN 37064-2290, USA

Orser, Brian (Figure Skater)
1600 James Naismith Dr
Gloucester, ON L1B 5N4, CANADA

Orser, Leland (Actor)
c/o Kami Putnam *Endeavor Agency LLC
(LA)*
232 N Canon Dr
Beverly Hills, CA 90210-5302, USA

Orsin, Raymond (Cartoonist)
Cleveland Plain Dealer
1801 Superior Ave E
Cleveland, OH 44114-2198, USA

Orsini, Myrna J (Artist)
Orsini Studios
4411 N 7th St
Tacoma, WA 98406-3507, USA

Orsino, John (Baseball Player)
San Francisco Giants
6141 Terra Mere Cir
Boynton Beach, FL 33437-4920, USA

Orsulak, Joe (Baseball Player)
Pittsburgh Pirates
29 Keansburg Rd
Parsippany, NJ 07054-3508, USA

Orta, Jorge (Baseball Player)
Chicago White Sox
1201 Heather Hill Cres
Flossmoor, IL 60422-1425, USA

Ortega, Amancio (Business Person)
Edificio Inditex
Industria de Diseno Textil
Avenida de la Diputacion
La Coruna, Arteixo 15142, SPAIN

Ortega, Bill (Baseball Player)
St Louis Cardinals
8121 NW 197th St
Hialeah, FL 33015-6344, USA

Ortega, Gaspar
38 Branhaven Dr
East Haven, CT 06513-2005, USA

Ortega, Jeannie (Musician)
Hollywood Records
500 S Buena Vista St
Burbank, CA 91521-0002, USA

Ortega, Keith (Football Player)
Chicago Bears
142 Lucille St
Lake Charles, LA 70601-8423, USA

Ortega, Kenny (Actor, Choreographer,
Director, Producer)
c/o Andy Patman *Paradigm (LA)*
360 N Crescent Dr
North Bldg
Beverly Hills, CA 90210-6820, USA

Ortega, Manuel (Actor)
c/o Staff Member *Telefe - Argentina*
Pavon 2444 (C1248AAT)
Buenos Aires, ARGENTINA

Ortega, Phil (Baseball Player)
Los Angeles Dodgers
4031 Altura Dr
Oceanside, CA 92056-4356, USA

Ortega, Ralph (Football Player)
Atlanta Falcons
10465 SW 124th St
Miami, FL 33176-4721, USA

Ortega Saavedra, Daniel (President)
Frente Sandinista de Liberacion National
Managua, NICARAGUA

Ortega y Alamino, Jaime Cardinal
(Religious Leader)
Apartado 594
Calle Habana 152
Havana 10100, CUBA

Ortenberg, Arthur (Business Person)
Liz Claiborne Inc
1441 Broadway
New York, NY 10018-2088, USA

Ortenzio, Frank (Baseball Player)
Kansas City Royals
2357 Oak St
Jacksonville, FL 32204, USA

Ortiz, Alejo (Actor)
c/o Staff Member *Telefe - Argentina*
Pavon 2444 (C1248AAT)
Buenos Aires, ARGENTINA

Ortiz, Ana (Actor)
c/o Gayle Max *Blue Max Management*
1802 N Kenmore Ave
Los Angeles, CA 90027-4008, USA

Ortiz, Cristina (Musician)
Harrison/Parrott
12 Penzance Place
London W11 4PA, UNITED KINGDOM
(UK)

Ortiz, Dave (Actor)
c/o Maani Golesorkhi *Bluestone
Entertainment*
5639 Vista Del Monte Ave
Van Nuys, CA 91411-3356, USA

Ortiz, Domingo (Misc)
Brown Cat Inc
400 Foundry St
Athens, GA 30601-2623, USA

Ortiz, Javier (Baseball Player)
Houston Astros
19520 SW 39th Ct
Miramar, FL 33029-2736, USA

Ortiz, Junior (Baseball Player)
Pittsburgh Pirates
PO Box 213
Humacao, PR 00792-0213, USA

Ortiz, Louis (Baseball Player)
1683 La Verde Dr
San Marcos, CA 92078-5223, USA

Ortiz, Luis (Baseball Player)
Boston Red Sox
6408 Rogers Dr
North Richland Hills, TX 76180-4807,
USA

Ortiz, Manuel
1 Hall Of Fame Dr
Canastota, NY 13032-1175, USA

Ortiz, Ramon (Baseball Player)
c/o Staff Member *Anaheim Angels*
2000 E Gene Autry Way
Edison Field
Anaheim, CA 92806-6143, USA

Ortiz, Russ (Baseball Player)
San Francisco Giants
4040 E McLellan Rd Unit 13
Mesa, AZ 85205-3105, USA

Ortiz, Tito (Athlete)
19744 Beach Blvd # 245
Huntington Beach, CA 92648-2988, USA

Ortiz Jr, Frank V (Diplomat)
663 Garcia St
Santa Fe, NM 87505-2857, USA

Ortlieb, Patrick (Skier)
Hotel Montana
Obertech
Lech 6764, AUSTRIA

Ortmann, Charles (Football Player)
Pittsburgh Steelers
4 River Birch Ln
Savannah, GA 31411-2847, USA

Ortner, Bev (Bowler)
PO Box 436
Odebolt, IA 51458-0436, USA

Ortolani, Riz
Via Aurelia km 23 400
Torrimpietra I-00050, ITALY

Orton, Beth (Musician)
c/o Beth Holden-Garland *Untitled Entertainment (LA)*
331 N Maple Dr Fl 3
Beverly Hills, CA 90210-3827, USA

Orton, John (Baseball Player)
California Angels
1437 S 58th St
Mesa, AZ 85206-6775, USA

Orton, Kyle (Football Player)
c/o Staff Member *Chicago Bears*
1000 Football Dr
Lake Forest, IL 60045-4829, USA

Orton, Randy (Wrestler)
c/o Staff Member *World Wrestling Entertainment (WWE)*
1241 E Main St
Stamford, CT 06902-3520, USA

Oruche, Phina (Actor)
c/o Staff Member *Bauman Redanty & Shaul Agency*
5757 Wilshire Blvd Ste 473
Los Angeles, CA 90036-3632, USA

Oruviral, Krishna Rao (Actor)
4/1 Vellala Street
Kodambakkam
Chennai, TN 600 024, INDIA

Orvick, George M (Religious Leader)
Evangelical Lutheran Synod
6 Browns Ct
Mankato, MN 56001-6121, USA

Orvis, Herb (Football Player)
Detroit Lions
1475 Abbey Ln
Lafayette, OR 97127-9180, USA

Ory, Meghan (Actor)
c/o Staff Member *Pacific Artists Management*
1404-510 W Hastings St
Vancouver, BC V6B 1L8, CANADA

Osborn, Danny (Baseball Player)
Chicago White Sox
7620 Knox Ct
Westminster, CO 80030-4540, USA

Osborn, David V (Dave) (Football Player)
Minnesota Vikings
18067 Judicial Way S
Lakeville, MN 55044-8895, USA

Osborn, Jim (Football Player)
Chicago Bears
4 Canyon Ct
Algonquin, IL 60102-6306, USA

Osborn, Kassidy (Musician)
LGB Media
1228 Pineview Ln
Nashville, TN 37211-7422, USA

Osborn, Kelsi (Musician)
LGB Media
1228 Pineview Ln
Nashville, TN 37211-7422, USA

Osborn, Kristyn (Musician, Songwriter, Writer)
LGB Media
1228 Pineview Ln
Nashville, TN 37211-7422, USA

Osborn, William A (Financier)
Northern Trust Corp
50 S Lasalle St
Chicago, IL 60675-0001, USA

Osborne, Barrie M (Director, Producer)
c/o Staff Member *Emerald City Productions*
9777 Wilshire Blvd Ste 550
Beverly Hills, CA 90212-1905, USA

Osborne, Bobo (Baseball Player)
Detroit Tigers
3309 Rough Creek Dr
Woodstock, GA 30189-6137, USA

Osborne, Burl (Editor, Publisher)
Dallas Morning News
Communications Center
Editorial Dept
Dallas, TX 75211, USA

Osborne, Burl (Religious Leader)
Salvation Army
799 Bloomfield Ave
Verona, NJ 07044-1367, USA

Osborne, Donovan (Baseball Player)
St Louis Cardinals
1510 Big Valley Way
Reno, NV 89521-6141, USA

Osborne, Jeffrey (Musician, Songwriter, Writer)
Entertainment Artists
2409 21st Ave S Ste 100
Nashville, TN 37212-5317, USA

Osborne, Joan (Musician, Songwriter)
c/o Staff Member *Paradigm (Monterey)*
509 Hartnell St
Monterey, CA 93940-2825, USA

Osborne, Mary Pope (Writer)
Random House
1745 Broadway # B1
New York, NY 10019-4305, USA

Osborne, Richard (Football Player)
Philadelphia Eagles
418 Tango Dr
San Antonio, TX 78216-3564, USA

Osborne, Tom (Football Player)
Washington Redskins
5400 Trotter Rd
Lincoln, NE 68516-3419, USA

Osborne Brothers (Musician)
c/o Staff Member *Billy Deaton Talent*
1214 16th Ave S
Nashville, TN 37212-2902, USA

Osbourne, Jack (Reality TV Star)
c/o Staff Member *Sharon Osbourne Management*
8899 Beverly Blvd Ste 905
Los Angeles, CA 90048-2427, USA

Osbourne, Kelly (Musician)
c/o Staff Member *Sharon Osbourne Management*
8899 Beverly Blvd Ste 905
Los Angeles, CA 90048-2427, USA

Osbourne, Ozzy (Musician, Songwriter, Writer)
c/o Sharon Osbourne *Sharon Osbourne Management*
8899 Beverly Blvd Ste 905
Los Angeles, CA 90048-2427, USA

Osbourne, Sharon (Business Person)
c/o Ariel (Ari) Emanuel *Endeavor Agency LLC (LA)*
9601 Wilshire Blvd Fl 3
Beverly Hills, CA 90210-5204, USA

Osburn, Pat (Baseball Player)
Cincinnati Reds
208 64th Street Ct NW
Bradenton, FL 34209-1625, USA

Osby, Greg (Musician)
Bridge Agency
35 Clark St Apt A5
Brooklyn, NY 11201-2374, USA

O'Scannlain, Diarmuld F (Judge)
US Court of Appeals
700 SW 6th Ave Ste 211
Pionner Courthouse
Portland, OR 97204-1434, USA

Oscar Scheld, Eusebio Cardinal (Religious Leader)
Archdiocese
Rua Benjamin Constant 23/502
Rio de Janeiro 20241, BRAZIL

Oseary, Guy (Producer)
c/o Staff Member *Maverick Films*
331 N Maple Dr Fl 2
Beverly Hills, CA 90210-3827, USA

Osgood, Charles E (Educator)
30 E Main St
Champaign, IL 61820-3629, USA

Osgood, Charlie (Baseball Player)
Brooklyn Dodgers
3 S Meadow Vig #22
Carver, MA 02330, USA

Osgood, Chris (Hockey Player)
6382 Pembrook Dr
Westland, MI 48185-7759, USA

O'Shea, Kevin (Basketball Player, Coach)
87 Aquauista Way
San Francisco, CA 94131, USA

O'Shea, Milo (Actor)
Bancroft Hotel
40 W 72nd St Apt 17A
New York, NY 10023-4192, USA

O'Shea, Terry (Football Player)
Pittsburgh Steelers
1034 Quincy Dr
Greensburg, PA 15601-1128, USA

Osheroff, Douglas D (Nobel Prize Laureate)
75 Ranch Rd
Woodside, CA 94062-4809, USA

Oshima, Nagisa (Director)
Oshima Productions
2-15-7 Arasaka
Minatoku
Tokyo, JAPAN

Oshodin, Willie (Football Player)
Denver Broncos
8134 Murray Hill Dr
Fort Washington, MD 20744-4416, USA

Osiecki, Sandy (Football Player)
Kansas City Chiefs
11 Bryan Cir
Seymour, CT 06483-3676, USA

Osik, Keith (Baseball Player)
Pittsburgh Pirates
5 Pal Ct
Shoreham, NY 11786-2352, USA

Osima, Nagisa
4-11-5 Kugenuma-Matsugaoka
Fujisawa-Shi 251, JAPAN

Osinski, Dan (Baseball Player)
Kansas City A's
9723 W Amber Tri
Sun City, AZ 85351, USA

Oslin, K T (Musician)
Moress-Nanas-Hart
704 18th Ave S
Nashville, TN 37203-3215, USA

Osman, Mat (Musician)
Interceptor Enterprises
98 White Lion St
London N1 9PF, UNITED KINGDOM (UK)

Osmar, Dean (Misc)
PO Box 32
Clam Gulch, AK 99568-0032, USA

Osment, Emily (Actor)
c/o Staff Member *Coast to Coast Talent Group*
3350 Barham Blvd
Los Angeles, CA 90068-1404, USA

Osment, Haley Joel (Actor)
c/o Meredith Fine *Coast to Coast Talent Group*
3350 Barham Blvd
Los Angeles, CA 90068-1404, USA

Osmond, Cliff (Actor, Director)
630 Bienveneda Ave
Pacific Palisades, CA 90272-3337, USA

Osmond, Donny (Actor, Musician, Producer, Writer)
PO Box 7122
Branson, MO 65615-7122, USA

Osmond, Ken (Actor)
9863 Wornom Ave
Sunland, CA 91040-1535, USA

Osmond, Marie (Actor, Musician)
c/o Staff Member *William Morris Agency (WMA-LA)*
1 William Morris Pl
Beverly Hills, CA 90212-4261, USA

Osmond Boys
PO Box 7122
Branson, MO 65615-7122, USA

Osnes, Larry G (Educator)
Hamline University
President's Office
Saint Paul, MN 55104, USA

Osorio, Jorge Federico (Musician)
Columbia Artists Mgmt Inc
1790 Broadway Fl 6
New York, NY 10019-1412, USA

Oss Jr, Arnold (Hockey Player)
8012 Pennsylvania Rd
Bloomington, MN 55438-1135, USA

Ossana, Diana
151 El Camino Dr
Beverly Hills, CA 90212-2704, USA

Ost, Friedheim (Government Official)
Heiersmauer 59
Paderborn 33098, GERMANY

Ostaseski, Frank (Director)
Zen Hospice Project
273 Page St
San Francisco, CA 94102-5616, USA

Osteen, Claude W (Baseball Player)
Cincinnati Reds
624 Brent Dr
Arlington, TX 76012-3520, USA

Osteen, Darrell (Baseball Player)
Cincinnati Reds
69902 Van Gogh Rd
Cathedral City, CA 92234-8936, USA

Osteen Jr, H M (Financier)
Bankers First Corp
1 10th St
Augusta, GA 30901-0100, USA

Oster, Bill (Baseball Player)
Philadelphia Athletics
56 Little Neck Rd
Centerport, NY 11721-1617, USA

Osterhage, Jeff (Actor)
210 N Cordova St Apt D
Burbank, CA 91505-3419, USA

Osteroth, Alexander
Steinsdorfstr. 20
Munich 80538, GERMANY

Ostertag, Greg (Basketball Player)
1603 W 15th St Apt C202
Lawrence, KS 66044-3839, USA

Ostheim, Michael (Model)
Louisa Models
Ebersberger Str 9
Munich 81679, GERMANY

Ostin, Michael (Business Person)
DreamWorks SKG
1000 Flower St
Glendale, CA 91201-3007, USA

Ostin, Mo (Business Person)
Dreamworks SKG
100 Universal City Plz
Music Div
Universal City, CA 91608-1002, USA

Osting, Jimmy (Baseball Player)
San Diego Padres
139 Briscoe Ln
Taylorsville, KY 40071-9665, USA

Ostman, Arnold (Conductor)
Haydn Rawstron
36 Station Road
London SE20 7BQ, UNITED KINGDOM
(UK)

Ostos, Javier (Swimmer)
FINA
Isabel La Catolica 13
Desp 401-2
Mexico City 1, DF, MEXICO

Ostriker, Jeremiah P (Physicist)
33 Philip Dr
Princeton, NJ 08540-5409, USA

Ostrom, John H (Misc)
52 Hillhouse Rd
Goshen, CT 06756-1001, USA

Ostroski, Gerald (Football Player)
Buffalo Bills
6926 E 115th Pl S
Bixby, OK 74008-8248, USA

Ostrosky, Beth (Actor, Model)
c/o Staff Member *Don Buchwald &
Associates Inc (NY)*
10 E 44th St
New York, NY 10017-3601, USA

Ostrosky, David (Actor)
c/o Staff Member *Televisa*
Blvd Adolfo Lopez Mateos 232
Colonia San Angel INN
DF CP 01060, MEXICO

Ostrosser, Brian (Baseball Player)
New York Mets
27 Chelsea Cres
Stoney Creek, ON L8E 5R7, CANADA

Ostrum, Peter (Actor)
6065 Duncan Rd
Glenfield, NY 13343-4021, USA

Ostwald, Martin (Educator)
408 Walnut Ln
Swarthmore, PA 19081-1137, USA

O'Sullevan, Peter J (Sportscaster, Writer)
37 Cranmer Court
London SW3 3HW, UNITED KINGDOM
(UK)

O'Sullivan, Gilbert (Musician)
Park Promotions
PO Box 651
Park Road
Oxford OX2 9RB, UNITED KINGDOM
(UK)

O'Sullivan, Peter (Editor)
Houston Post
4747 Southwest Fwy
Editorial Dept
Houston, TX 77027-6901, USA

O'Sullivan, Richard (Actor)
Al Mitchell
5 Anglers Lane
Kentish Town
London NW5 3DG, UNITED KINGDOM
(UK)

O'Sullivan, Sonia (Athlete, Track Athlete)
Kim McDonald
201 High St
Hampton Hill
Middx TW12 1NL, UNITED KINGDOM
(UK)

Osuna, Al (Baseball Player)
Houston Astros
8256 Via Rosa
Orlando, FL 32836-8789, USA

Osuna, Antonio (Baseball Player)
Los Angeles Dodgers
5139 Maplewood Ave
Los Angeles, CA 90004-1697, USA

Oswald, J Julian R (Admiral)
Naval Secretary
Victory Bldg
HM Naval Base
Portsmouth PO1 3LS, UNITED
KINGDOM (UK)

Oswald, Mark (Opera Singer)
Herbert Barrett
266 W 37th St Fl 20
New York, NY 10018-6648, USA

Oswald, Mark (Race Car Driver)
Championship Quest Motorsports
PO Box 99
Pfafftown, NC 27040-0099, USA

Oswald, Paul (Football Player)
Pittsburgh Steelers
521 Cambridge Ct
Alpharetta, GA 30005-4216, USA

Oswald, Stephen S (Astronaut)
NASA
2101 Nasa Pkwy
Johnson Space Center
Houston, TX 77058-3691, USA

Oswalt, Patton (Actor)
c/o Gregory (Greg) McKnight *Creative
Artists Agency LCC (CAA-LA)*
2000 Avenue Of The Stars
Los Angeles, CA 90067-4700, USA

Oswalt, Roy (Baseball Player)
Houston Astros
9280 Ms Highway 413
Weir, MS 39772-8947, USA

Oszajca, John (Musician)
Interscope Records
2220 Colorado Ave
Santa Monica, CA 90404-3506, USA

Otaka, Tadaaki (Conductor)
Harold Holt
31 Sinclair Road
London W14 0NS, UNITED KINGDOM
(UK)

Otellini, Paul (Business Person)
Intel Corp
2200 Mission College Blvd
Santa Clara, CA 95054-1549, USA

Oteri, Cheri (Actor, Comedian)
c/o Peg Donegan *Framework
Entertainment (LA)*
9057 Nemo St # C
W Hollywood, CA 90069-5511, USA

Otero, Ricky (Baseball Player)
New York Mets
350 W 48th St Apt 1E
New York, NY 10036-1360, USA

Othenin-Girard, Dominque (Director)
327 S Church Ln
Los Angeles, CA 90049-3057, USA

Otis, Amos J (Baseball Player)
New York Mets
588 Preakness Stakes St
Henderson, NV 89015-6948, USA

Otis, Carre (Actor, Model)
c/o Staff Member *Goldman/Knell Agency*
1801 Century Park E Ste 2160
Los Angeles, CA 90067-2343, USA

Otis, Glenn K (General)
Lake Shore Road
3401 RR 9
Peru, NY 12972, USA

Otis, James L (Jim) (Football Player)
New Orleans Saints
14795 Greenleaf Valley Dr
Chesterfield, MO 63017-5542, USA

Otis, Johnny (Musician, Songwriter,
Writer)
1226 E Altadena Dr
Altadena, CA 91001-2004, USA

Otman, Assed Mohamed (Prime Minister)
Villa Rissani
Route Oued Akrach
Souissi, Rabat, MOROCCO

O'Toole, Annette (Actor)
11936 Gorham Ave Apt 106
Los Angeles, CA 90049-5360, USA

O'Toole, Denny (Baseball Player)
Cincinnati Reds
3453 Ridgerwood Dr
Erlanger, KY 41018, USA

O'Toole, Jim (Baseball Player)
Cincinnati Reds
1010 Lanette Dr
Cincinnati, OH 45230-3616, USA

O'Toole, S Peter (Actor)
Chartwell Ink Management
7319 Beverly Blvd Ste 10
C/O Ross Brown
Los Angeles, CA 90036-2556, USA

Otstott, Charles P (General)
6152 Pohick Station Dr
Fairfax Station, VA 22039-1646, USA

Otsuki, Tamayo (Actor)
Patterson Assoc
20318 Hiawatha St
Chatsworth, CA 91311-2553, USA

Ott, Billy (Baseball Player)
Chicago Cubs
132 W Nyack Way
County Lock
West Nyack, NY 10994-2202, USA

Ott, Ed (Baseball Player)
Pittsburgh Pirates
1511 W Hamilton St
Allentown, PA 18102-4211, USA

Otten, Jim (Baseball Player)
Chicago White Sox
1417 N Forest
Mesa, AZ 85203-3903, USA

Ottey, Merlene
PO Box 120
Indianapolis, IN 46206, USA

Ottey-Page, Merlene (Athlete, Track
Athlete)
Jamaican Olympic Committee
Po Box 544
Kingston 10, JAMAICA

Otto, August J (Gus) (Football Player)
Oakland Raiders
14411 Open Meadow Ct W
Chesterfield, MO 63017-9627, USA

Otto, Bob (Football Player)
Dallas Cowboys
1713 Guthrie Dr
Las Vegas, NV 89117-9000, USA

Otto, Dave (Baseball Player)
Oakland A's
1383 Shady Ln
Wheaton, IL 60187-3722, USA

Otto, Frei (Architect)
Berghalde 19
7250 Leonberg
Warmbroun 71229, GERMANY

Otto, James E (Jim) (Football Player)
Oakland Raiders
0 Estates Dr
Auburn, CA 95602-9265, USA

Otto, Joel (Hockey Player)
77 Sunset Way SE
Calgary, AB T2X 3C1, CANADA

Otto, Kristin (Swimmer)
ZDF Sportedaktion
Postfach 4040
Mainz 55100, GERMANY

Otto, Michael (Business Person)
Spiegel Inc
3500 Lacey Rd Ste 200
Downers Grove, IL 60515-5423, USA

Otto, Miranda (Actor)
Shanahan Mgmt
PO Box 1509
Darlinghurst, NSW 1300, AUSTRALIA

Otto, Sylke (Athlete)
BSD
An der Schiessstatte 4
Berchtesgaden 83471, GERMANY

Otto Jr, A T (Misc)
Railroad Yardmasters Union
1411 Peterson Ave Ste 201
Park Ridge, IL 60068-5076, USA

Otwell, Ralph M (Editor)
34 Knox Cir
Evanston, IL 60201-1912, USA

Ouaido, Nassour Guelengdoussia (Prime
Minister)
Prime Minister's Office
N'Djamena, CHAD

Ouattara, Alassane D (Financier, Prime Minister)
International Monetary Fund
700 19th St NW # 12-300H
Washington, DC 20431-0001, USA

Oubre, Louis (Football Player)
New Orleans Saints
11008 Curran Blvd
New Orleans, LA 70127-1408, USA

Ouchi, William G (Educator)
University of California
Graduate Management School
Los Angeles, CA 90024, USA

Ouedraogo, Gerard Kango (Prime Minister)
01 BP 347
Ouagadougou, BURKINA FASO

Ouedraogo, Idrissa (Director)
FEPACI
01 BP 2524
Ouagadougou, BURKINA FASO

Ouedraogo, Kdre Desire (Prime Minister)
Prime Minister's Office
Parliament Building
Ouagadougou, BURKINA FASO

Ouellet, Joseph G N Cardinal (Religious Leader)
Archdiocese
34 Rue de l'Eveche E
CP 730
Rimouski, PQ G5L 7C7, CANADA

Ouellette, Phil (Baseball Player)
San Francisco Giants
7421 Poppy St
Corona, CA 92881-3739, USA

Our Lady Peace (Music Group)
c/o Staff Member *Paradigm (Monterey)*
509 Hartnell St
Monterey, CA 93940-2825, USA

Oureiro, Natalia (Musician)
c/o Staff Member *BMG*
1540 Broadway
New York, NY 10036-4074, USA

Ourisson, Guy (Misc)
10 Rue Geiler
Strasbourg 67000, FRANCE

Ousland, Borge (Skier)
Axel Huitfeldts V5
Oslo 1170, NORWAY

Outkast (Music Group)
c/o Charles King *William Morris Agency (WMA-LA)*
1 William Morris Pl
Beverly Hills, CA 90212-4261, USA

Outlar, Jesse (Writer)
116 Loblolly Cir
Peachtree City, GA 30269-2035, USA

Outlaw, Charles (Bo) (Basketball Player)
14815 River Ml
San Antonio, TX 78216-7817, USA

Outlaw, Jimmy (Baseball Player)
Cincinnati Reds
8872 County Road 34
Fairhope, AL 36532-7009, USA

Outlaw, Travis (Basketball Player)
Portland Trail Blazers
1 N Center Court St
Rose Garden
Portland, OR 97227-2102, USA

Outman, Tim (Artist)
57101 N Bank Rd
Mc Kenzie Bridge, OR 97413-9629, USA

OV7 (Music Group)
c/o Staff Member *Sony Music Miami*
605 Lincoln Rd Fl 7
Miami Beach, FL 33139-2900, USA

Ovchinikov, Vladmir P (Musician)
Manygate
13 Cotswold Mews
30 Battersea Square
London SW11 3RA, UNITED KINGDOM (UK)

Ovechkin, Alexander (Hockey Player)
Washington Capitals
601 F St NW
Mcl Center
Washington, DC 20004-1605, USA

Overall, Park (Actor)
PO Box 348
Pearblossom, CA 93553-0348, USA

Overath, Wolfgang
Auf dem Hummerich
Siegburg D-53721, GERMANY

Overbay, Lyle (Baseball Player)
Arizona Diamondbacks
1103 G St
Centralia, WA 98531-3211, USA

Overbeek, Jan T G (Misc)
Zweerslaan 35
Bilthoven, HN 3723, THE NETHERLANDS

Overgard, Robert M (Religious Leader)
Church of Lutheran Brethren
PO Box 655
Fergus Falls, MN 56538-0655, USA

Overgard, William (Cartoonist)
United Feature Syndicate
200 Madison Ave
New York, NY 10016-3911, USA

Overhauser, Albert W (Physicist)
236 Pawnee Dr
West Lafayette, IN 47906-2115, USA

Overhauser, Chad (Football Player)
Chicago Bears
8303 N Mo Pac Expy Ste 425B
Austin, TX 78759-8322, USA

Overleese, Joanne (Baseball Player)
849 Coach Blvd
La Jolla, CA 92037, USA

Overman, Ion
c/o Staff Member *GVA Talent Agency Inc*
9229 W Sunset Blvd Ste 320
Los Angeles, CA 90069-3403, USA

Overman, Larry E (Misc)
University of California
Chemistry Dept
Irvine, CA 92717, USA

Overmyer, Eric (Writer)
Yale University
English Dept
New Haven, CT 06520, USA

Overstreet, Paul (Musician, Songwriter, Writer)
White Horse Enterprises
475 Annex Ave
Nashville, TN 37209-2747, USA

Overstreet, Tommy (Musician, Songwriter, Writer)
PO Box 455
Brentwood, TN 37024-0455, USA

Overstreet, Will (Football Player)
Atlanta Falcons
106 Avondale Street
Jackson, MS 39216, USA

Overton, Kelly (Actor)
c/o Staff Member *Management 360*
9111 Wilshire Blvd
Beverly Hills, CA 90210-5508, USA

Overton, Rick (Actor)
c/o Staff Member *Don Buchwald & Associates Inc (LA)*
6500 Wilshire Blvd Ste 2200
Los Angeles, CA 90048-4942, USA

Overy, Mike (Baseball Player)
California Angels
3010 N 152nd Ln
Goodyear, AZ 85395-8636, USA

Ovitz, Michael S (Business Person)
457 N Rockingham Ave
Los Angeles, CA 90049-2637, USA

Ovshinsky, Stanford R (Engineer, Inventor)
Energy Conversion Devices
2956 Waterview Dr
Rochester Hills, MI 48309-3484, USA

Owchinko, Bob (Baseball Player)
San Diego Padres
14000 N 94th St Unit 1033
Scottsdale, AZ 85260-7776, USA

Owen, Clive (Actor)
c/o Jimmy Darmody *Creative Artists Agency LCC (CAA-LA)*
2000 Avenue Of The Stars
Los Angeles, CA 90067-4700, USA

Owen, Dave (Baseball Player)
Chicago Cubs
1921 Fm 3136
Cleburne, TX 76031-8792, USA

Owen, David A L (Government Official)
78 Narrow St
Limehouse
London E14 8BP, UNITED KINGDOM (UK)

Owen, Edwyn (Bob) (Hockey Player)
3630 SW Stratford Rd
Topeka, KS 66604-2544, USA

Owen, Henry (Diplomat)
Brookings Institute
1775 Massachusetts Ave NW
Washington, DC 20036-2103, USA

Owen, Larry (Baseball Player)
Atlanta Braves
804 White Pine St
New Carlisle, OH 45344-1125, USA

Owen, Michael (Soccer Player)
c/o Staff Member *Newcastle United FC*
Saint James Park
Newcastle-Tyne NE1 4ST, UNITED KINGDOM (UK)

Owen, Randy Y (Musician)
PO Box 529
Fort Payne, AL 35968, USA

Owen, Spike (Baseball Player)
Seattle Mariners
11211 Musket Rim St
Austin, TX 78738-6613, USA

Owen, Tom (Football Player)
San Francisco 49ers
PO Box 3
Albany, OK 74721-0003, USA

Owens, Al (Baseball Player)
Nashville Elite Giants
63 Bluff Ave
La Grange, IL 60525-2507, USA

Owens, Brig (Football Player)
Washington Redskins
6902 Lupine Ln
Mc Lean, VA 22101-1578, USA

Owens, Burgess (Football Player)
New York Jets
1430 Telegraph Rd
West Chester, PA 19380-1621, USA

Owens, Charles W (Tinker) (Football Player)
New Orleans Saints
2547 McGee Dr
Norman, OK 73072-6704, USA

Owens, Chris (Actor)
c/o Jerry Shandrew *Shandrew Public Relations*
1050 S Stanley Ave
Los Angeles, CA 90019-6634, USA

Owens, Cotton (Race Car Driver)
7605 White Ave
Spartanburg, SC 29303, USA

Owens, Dan (Football Player)
Detroit Lions
280 Selkirk Ln
Duluth, GA 30097-8043, USA

Owens, Dana (Queen Latifah) (Actor, Musician)
c/o Staff Member *Flavor Unit Entertainment*
155 Morgan St
Jersey City, NJ 07302-2932, USA

Owens, Darrick (Football Player)
Pittsburgh Steelers
610 Cypress St
Raceland, LA 70394-2817, USA

Owens, Eric (Baseball Player)
Cincinnati Reds
11873 Westview Pkwy
San Diego, CA 92126-8540, USA

Owens, Gary (Entertainer)
17856 Via Vallarta
Encino, CA 91316-4345, USA

Owens, Jackson (Baseball Player)
Chicago American Giants
138 E Kenwood Ave
Decatur, IL 62526-4350, USA

Owens, James D (Jim) (Coach, Football Coach, Football Player)
Baltimore Colts
PO Box 1749
8450 Mount Highway 35
Bigfork, MT 59911-1749, USA

Owens, Jayhawk (Baseball Player)
Colorado Rockies
2085 Kay Rd
Sardinia, OH 45171-9479, USA

Owens, Jim (Baseball Player)
Philadelphia Phillies
1426 Ramada Dr
Houston, TX 77062-5908, USA

Owens, Joe (Football Player)
San Diego Chargers
2754 Highway 13 N
Columbia, MS 39429-8634, USA

Owens, Kem (Musician)
c/o Staff Member *Motown Records (LA)*
6255 W Sunset Blvd Fl 18
Los Angeles, CA 90028-7419, USA

Owens, Lorenzo (Musician)
c/o Staff Member *Paradigm (Monterey)*
509 Hartnell St
Monterey, CA 93940-2825, USA

Owens, Luke (Football Player)
Baltimore Colts
3330 Warrensville Center Rd Apt 502
Shaker Heights, OH 44122-3791, USA

Owens, Mel (Football Player)
Los Angeles Rams
1230 Market St # 504
San Francisco, CA 94102-4801, USA

Owens, Morris (Football Player)
Miami Dolphins
3010 W Yorkshire Dr Apt 1114
Phoenix, AZ 85027-3919, USA

Owens, Rawleigh C (R C) (Football Player)
San Francisco 49ers
1533 Brookdale Way
Manteca, CA 95336-9159, USA

Owens, Rena (Actor, Model)
526 N Larchmont Blvd Ste 201
Los Angeles, CA 90004-1300, USA

Owens, Steve (Football Player)
Detroit Lions
4704 Harrogate Dr
Norman, OK 73072-3958, USA

Owens, Terrell (Football Player)
c/o Staff Member *Dallas Cowboys*
1 Cowboys Pkwy
Irving, TX 75063-4999, USA

Owens, Terry (Football Player)
San Diego Chargers
2524 Poovey Rd SE
Decatur, AL 35603-5624, USA

Owens, William A (Admiral)
510 Lake St S Apt B302
Kirkland, WA 98033-6486, USA

Owensby, Earl
1 Motion Picture Blvd
Shelby, NC 28152-1044, USA

Ownbey, Rick (Baseball Player)
New York Mets
1178 Newcastle Ct
Oceanside, CA 92056-6463, USA

Owsley, Douglas (Misc)
Smithsonian Institute
17th & M Sts NW
Washington, DC 20036, USA

Oxenberg, Catherine (Actor)
9461 Charleville Blvd # 380
Beverly Hills, CA 90212-3017, USA

Oyakawa, Yoshinobu (Yoshi) (Swimmer)
4171 Hutchinson Rd
Cincinnati, OH 45248-2219, USA

Oye, Erlend (Musician)
c/o Staff Member *Paradigm (Monterey)*
509 Hartnell St
Monterey, CA 93940-2825, USA

Oz, Amos (Writer)
Ben Gurion University
PO Box 653
Beer-Sheva 84195, ISRAEL

Oz, Frank R (Director)
c/o David O'Connor *Creative Artists Agency LCC (CAA-LA)*
2000 Avenue Of The Stars
Los Angeles, CA 90067-4700, USA

Ozaki, Masashi (Golfer)
Bridgestone Sports
14230 Lochridge Blvd Ste G
Covington, GA 30014-4953, USA

Ozaki, Satoshi (Physicist)
Brookhaven National Lab
2 Center St
Heavy Ion Collider
Upton, NY 11973-9700, USA

Ozark, Daniel L (Danny) (Misc)
PO Box 6666
Vero Beach, FL 32961-6666, USA

Ozawa, Ichiro (Government Official)
Daiichi Giia Kaikan
Nagatacho Chiyodaku
Tokyo 100, JAPAN

Ozawa, Seiji (Conductor)
Columbia Artists Mgmt Inc
1790 Broadway Fl 6
New York, NY 10019-1412, USA

Ozbek, Rifat (Designer, Fashion Designer)
Ozbek Ltd
18 Haunch of Venison Yard
London W1Y 1AF, UNITED KINGDOM (UK)

Ozio, David (Bowler)
6110 Barrington Ave
Beaumont, TX 77706-7381, USA

Ozolinsh, Sandis (Hockey Player)
Anaheim Mighty Ducks
2000 E Gene Autry Way
Anaheim, CA 92806-6143, USA

Ozomatli (Musician)
c/o Staff Member *Paradigm (Monterey)*
509 Hartnell St
Monterey, CA 93940-2825, USA

Ozsan, Hal (Actor)
c/o Staff Member *Overbrook Entertainment*
450 N Roxbury Dr Fl 4
Beverly Hills, CA 90210-4232, USA

Ozzie, Raymond (Ray) (Designer)
33 Harbor St
Manchester By The Sea, MA 01944-1461, USA

Paabo, Svante (Director)
Evolutionary Anthropology Inst
Deutscher Platz 6
Leipzig 04103, GERMANY

Paavola, Rodney (Hockey Player)
General Delivery
Hancock, MI 49930-9999, USA

Pablo Cruise
PO Box 770850
Orlando, FL 32877-0850, USA

Pacar, Johnny (Actor)
c/o Jeff Morrone *Jeff Morrone Management*
9350 Wilshire Blvd Ste 224
Beverly Hills, CA 90212-3204, USA

Pace, Darrell O (Athlete)
4394 Princeton Rd
Hamilton, OH 45011-9753, USA

Pace, Dominic (Actor)
c/o Staff Member *Shapiro-Lichtman Talent Agency*
1333 Beverly Green Dr
Los Angeles, CA 90035-1018, USA

Pace, Judy (Actor)
4139 S Cloverdale Ave
Los Angeles, CA 90008-1034, USA

Pace, Justin (Actor)
c/o Todd Justice *Venture IAB*
8285 W Sunset Blvd Ste 1
West Hollywood, CA 90046-2420, USA

Pace, Lee (Actor)
c/o Staff Member *Innovative Artists (LA)*
1505 10th St
Santa Monica, CA 90401-2805, USA

Pace, Orlando (Football Player)
St Louis Rams
355 Galahad Dr
Weldon Spring, MO 63304-5703, USA

Pace, Peter (General)
Vice Chairman
Joint Chiefs Of Staff Pentagon
Washington, DC 20318-0001, USA

Pacella, John (Baseball Player)
New York Mets
1500 Abbotsford Green Dr
Powell, OH 43065-8938, USA

Pacheco, Abel (President)
Casa Presidencial
Apdo 520-2010
San Jose 1000, COSTA RICA

Pacheco, Ferdie (Sportscaster)
4151 Gate Ln
Miami, FL 33137-3319, USA

Pacheco, Manuel T (Educator)
University of Arizona
President's Office
Tucson, AZ 85721-0001, USA

Pacillo, Pat (Baseball Player)
Cincinnati Reds
8 Rocky Glen Way
Lebanon, NJ 08833-4611, USA

Pacino, Al (Actor)
c/o Rick Nicita *Creative Artists Agency LCC (CAA-LA)*
2000 Avenue Of The Stars
Los Angeles, CA 90067-4700, USA

Paciorek, Jim (Baseball Player)
Milwaukee Brewers
9641 E Waters Edge Pl
Tucson, AZ 85749-7901, USA

Paciorek, John (Baseball Player)
Houston Colt.45's
8400 Huntington Dr
San Gabriel, CA 91775-1154, USA

Paciorek, Tom (Baseball Player)
Los Angeles Dodgers
2389 Broad Creek Dr
Stone Mountain, GA 30087-3755, USA

Packard, Kelly (Actor, Model)
19614 Mathilde Ln
Santa Clarita, CA 91350-3884, USA

Packard, Scott (Baseball Player)
135 Eastview Dr
Horseheads, NY 14845-2548, USA

Packer, A William (Billy) (Sportscaster)
Bazel Group
115 Penn Warren Dr Ste 300
Brentwood, TN 37027-5054, USA

Packer, James (Business Person)
Consolidated Press Holdings
54 Park St
Sydney NSW 2000, AUSTRALIA

Packwocd, Bob (Ex-Senator, Senator)
2201 Wisconsin Ave NW Ste C120
Washington, DC 20007-4114, USA

Pactwa, Joe (Baseball Player)
Kansas City Royals
4560 Trieste Dr
Carlsbad, CA 92010-3741, USA

Pacula, Joanna (Actor)
Chuck Binder
1465 Lindacrest Dr
Beverly Hills, CA 90210-2519, USA

Padalecki, Jared (Actor)
c/o Daniel (Dan) Spilo *Artistry Management*
525 Westbourne Dr
West Hollywood, CA 90048-1913, USA

Padalka, Gennadi I (Cosmonaut)
Potchta Kosmonavtov
Moskovskoi Oblasti
Syvisdny Goroduk 141160, RUSSIA

Paddock, John (Coach, Hockey Player)
1315 Penn Ave
Hershey, PA 17033-1844, USA

Padgett, Jason (Actor)
c/o Staff Member *GVA Talent Agency Inc*
9229 W Sunset Blvd Ste 320
Los Angeles, CA 90069-3403, USA

Padilla, Douglas (Doug) (Athlete, Track Athlete)
182 N 555 W
Orem, UT 84057-1937, USA

Padilla, Vicente (Baseball Player)
c/o Staff Member *Philadelphia Phillies*
3501 S Broad St
Veterans Stadium
Philadelphia, PA 19148, USA

Padjen, Gary (Football Player)
Baltimore Colts
9314 Tower Bridge Rd Apt B
Indianapolis, IN 46240-5434, USA

Padma-Nathan, Harin (Doctor)
1245 16th St Ste 312
Santa Monica, CA 90404-1239, USA

Padmini (Actor, Bollywood)
9 Palot Madhavan Road
Mahalingapuram
Chennai, TN 600034, INDIA

Paetkau, David (Actor)
c/o Martin Berneman *Martin Berneman Management*
5820 Wilshire Blvd Ste 200
Los Angeles, CA 90036-4587, USA

Paez, Jorge (Maromero) (Boxer)
233 Paulin Ave
Calexico, CA 92231-2615, USA

Paez, Richard A (Judge)
US Appellate Court
125 S Grand Ave
Court Building
Pasadena, CA 91105-1643, USA

Paffrath, Bob (Football Player)
Miami Seahawks
5250 SW Barclay Ct
Beaverton, OR 97005-3641, USA

Pafko, Andrew (Andy) (Baseball Player)
Chicago Cubs
1420 W Blackhawk Dr
Mount Prospect, IL 60056-3634, USA

Pagac, Fred (Football Player)
Chicago Bears
10261 Normandy Crst
Eden Prairie, MN 55347-4849, USA

Pagan, Dave (Baseball Player)
New York Yankees
504 10th Ave W
Nipawin, SK S0E 1E0, CANADA

Pagan, Jose (Athlete, Baseball Player)
San Francisco Giants
425 Maple Ln
Sebring, FL 33876-6318, USA

Pagan, Reo (Baseball Player)
Negro Baseball Leagues
280 Creekview Trl
Fayetteville, GA 30214-7230, USA

Paganelli, Robert P (Diplomat)
331 S Main St
Albion, NY 14411-1602, USA

Pagano, Lindsay (Musician)
Azoff Music
1100 Glendon Ave Ste 2000
Los Angeles, CA 90024-3524, USA

Page, Alan (Football Player)
Minnesota Vikings
1732 Knox Ave S
Minneapolis, MN 55403-2833, USA

Page, Alan C (Football Player, Judge)
PO Box 581254
Minneapolis, MN 55458-1254, USA

Page, Anita (Actor)
14840 Valerio St
Van Nuys, CA 91405-1819, USA

Page, Ashley (Choreographer, Dancer)
Royal Ballet
Covent Garden
Bow St
London WC2E 9DD, UNITED KINGDOM
(UK)

Page, Bettie
2641 S 53rd St
Kansas City, KS 66106-3365, USA

Page, Bettle (Model)
JL Swanson
PO Box 56176
Chicago, IL 60656-0176, USA

Page, Corey (Actor)
Agency for Performing Arts
405 S Beverly Dr Ste 500
Beverly Hills, CA 90212-4425, USA

Page, David (Artist)
3724 Greenmount Ave
Baltimore, MD 21218-1843, USA

Page, David C (Misc)
Whitehead Institute
9 Cambridge Ctr
Cambridge, MA 02142-1479, USA

Page, Ellen (Actor)
c/o Gabrielle (Gaby) Morgerman *William
Morris Agency (WMA-LA)*
1 William Morris Pl
Beverly Hills, CA 90212-4261, USA

Page, Erika (Actor)
Progressive Artists Agency
400 S Beverly Dr Ste 216
Beverly Hills, CA 90212-4404, USA

Page, Genevieve (Actor)
52 Rue de Vaugirard
Paris 75006, FRANCE

Page, Greg (Boxer)
Don King Promotions
968 Pinehurst Dr
Las Vegas, NV 89109-1569, USA

Page, Harrison (Actor)
S D B Partners
1801 Avenue Of Stars Ste 902
Los Angeles, CA 90067-5981, USA

Page, Kimberly (Actor)
c/o Staff Member *The Paradise Group*
8721 W Sunset Blvd Ste 209
Los Angeles, CA 90069-2272, USA

Page, Larry (Business Person, Engineer)
Google Inc
1600 Amphitheatre Pkwy # 41
Mountain View, CA 94043-1351, USA

Page, Michael (Misc)
PO Box 229
North Salem, NY 10560-0229, USA

Page, Mike (Baseball Player)
Atlanta Braves
599 Briarcliff Dr
Woodruff, SC 29388-2326, USA

Page, Mitchell (Baseball Player)
Oakland A's
484 Lake Park Ave # 162
Oakland, CA 94610-2730, USA

Page, Murriel (Basketball Player)
Washington Mystics
601 F St NW
Mci Center
Washington, DC 20004-1605, USA

Page, Oscar C (Educator)
Austin College
President's Office
Sherman, TX 75090, USA

Page, Patti (Actor, Musician)
404 Loma Larga Dr
Solana Beach, CA 92075-1719, USA

Page, Pierre (Coach, Hockey Player)
Anaheim Mighty Ducks
2000 E Gene Autry Way
Anaheim, CA 92806-6143, USA

Page, Sam (Actor)
c/o Staff Member *Roklin Management*
8530 Wilshire Blvd Ste 550
Beverly Hills, CA 90211-3133, USA

Page, Solomon (Football Player)
Dallas Cowboys
9302 Vista Cir
Irving, TX 75063-5060, USA

Page, Steven (Musician)
Nettwerk Mgmt
8730 Wilshire Blvd # 304
Beverly Hills, CA 90211-2716, USA

Page, Tim (Journalist)
Washington Post
Editorial Dept
1150 15th St NW
Washington, DC 20071-0001, USA

Pagel, Karl (Baseball Player)
Chicago Cubs
2698 N Ellis St
Chandler, AZ 85224-1777, USA

Pagel, Mike (Football Player)
Baltimore Colts
11981 Coopers Run
Strongsville, OH 44149-9260, USA

Paget, Debra (Actor)
411 Kari Ct
Houston, TX 77024-6804, USA

Pagett, Nicola (Actor)
22 Victoria Road
Mortlake
London SW14, UNITED KINGDOM (UK)

Paggi, Nicole (Actor)
c/o Felicia Sager *Art Work Entertainment*
5900 Wilshire Blvd Ste 2150
Los Angeles, CA 90036-5021, USA

Paglia, Camille (Educator, Writer)
University of the Arts
320 S Broad St
Humanities Dept
Philadelphia, PA 19102-4994, USA

Pagliaroni, Jim (Baseball Player)
Boston Red Sox
10388 Partridge Rd
Grass Valley, CA 95945-7449, USA

Pagliarulo, Michael T (Mike) (Baseball
Player)
New York Yankees
11 Fieldstone Dr
Winchester, MA 01890-3257, USA

Pagliei, Joe (Football Player)
Philadelphia Eagles
7 Pine Ridge Ct
Sewell, NJ 08080-3648, USA

Pagnozzi, Thomas A (Tom) (Baseball
Player)
St Louis Cardinals
2319 N Heather Cv
Fayetteville, AR 72701-2991, USA

Pagnucco, Chris (Football Player)
Detroit Lions
937 W Belden Ave
Chicago, IL 60614-3239, USA

Pagonis, William G (General)
202 Smalstig Rd
Evans City, PA 16033-3924, USA

Pahang (Misc)
Istana Abu Bakar
Pekan
Pahang, MALAYSIA

Pahlavi, Ashraf
12 Ave. Montaigne
Paris 75016, FRANCE

Pahukoa, Jeff (Football Player)
Los Angeles Rams
20191 Cape Coral Ln
Huntington Beach, CA 92646-8514, USA

Paich, David (Musician)
Fitzgerald-Hartley
34 N Palm St
Ventura, CA 93001-2635, USA

Paige, Betty
PO Box 56176
Chicago, IL 60656-0176, USA

Paige, Elaine (Actor, Musician)
DeWalden Court
85 New Cavendish St
London W1M 7RA, UNITED KINGDOM
(UK)

Paige, Janis (Actor)
1700 Rising Glen Rd
Los Angeles, CA 90069-1230, USA

Paige, Jennifer (Musician, Songwriter,
Writer)
Evolution Talent
1776 Broadway Ste 1500
New York, NY 10019-2002, USA

Paige, Peter (Actor)
c/o Suzanne (Sue) Wohl *TalentWorks (LA)*
3500 W Olive Ave Ste 1400
Burbank, CA 91505-5512, USA

Paige, Rod (Secretary)
Education Department
400 Maryland Ave SW
Washington, DC 20202-0001, USA

Paige, Stephone (Football Player)
Kansas City Chiefs
5586 Lilyview Way
Elk Grove, CA 95757-2836, USA

Paik, Kun Woo (Musician)
Worldwide Artists
12 Rosebery
Thomton Heath
Surrey CR7 8PT, UNITED KINGDOM
(UK)

Pailes, William A (Astronaut)
411 S Cedar Ridge Cir
Robinson, TX 76706-5681, USA

Paine, Chris
c/o Eddie Michaels *Insignia Public
Relations*
9255 W Sunset Blvd Ste 920
Los Angeles, CA 90069-3306, USA

Paine, Horner (Football Player)
Chicago Rockets
1105 W York Ave
Enid, OK 73703-7104, USA

Paine, John (Musician)
Bob Flick Productions
300 Vine St Ste 14
Seattle, WA 98121-1465, USA

Paintal (Actor, Bollywood, Comedian)
B 103 Sun Swept Lokhandwala Complex
Andheri
Bombay, MS 400 058, INDIA

Painter, John Mark (Musician)
Michael Dixon Mgmt
119 Pebble Creek Rd
Franklin, TN 37064-5525, USA

Painter, Lance (Baseball Player)
Colorado Rockies
8028 N Santa Monica Blvd
Milwaukee, WI 53217-2968, USA

Paire-Davis, Lavonne (Baseball Player)
15847 Marlin Pl
Van Nuys, CA 91406-5019, USA

Paisley, Brad (Musician)
c/o Rob Beckham *William Morris Agency
(WMA-TN)*
1600 Division St Ste 300
Nashville, TN 37203-2755, USA

Paisley, Ian R K (Politician)
Parsonage
17 Cyprus Ave
Belfast BT5 5NT, NORTHERN IRELAND

Pak, Charles (Scientist)
University of Texas
Health Sciences Center
Dallas, TX 75235, USA

Pak, Se Ri (Golfer)
8836 Elliotts Ct
Orlando, FL 32836-5027, USA

Pakeledinaz, Martin (Designer)
Gersh Agency
232 N Canon Dr
Beverly Hills, CA 90210-5302, USA

Paksas, Rolandus (Prime Minister)
President's Office
Gediminas 53
Vilnius 232026, LITHUANIA

The Celebrity Black Book 2008

Palacios, Rey (Baseball Player)
Kansas City Royals
160 Heberton Ave Apt 4H
Staten Island, NY 10302-1463, USA

Palade, George E (Nobel Prize Laureate)
University of California
Cellular & Molecular
La Jolla, CA 92093, USA

Paladecki, Jared (Actor)
Gilmore Girls
4000 Warner Blvd Bldg 2222
Burbank, CA 91522-0001, USA

Palagyi, Mike (Baseball Player)
Washington Senators
167 14th St
Conneaut, OH 44030-1805, USA

Palahniuk, Chuck (Writer)
c/o Howard Sanders *United Talent Agency (UTA)*
9560 Wilshire Blvd Ste 500
Beverly Hills, CA 90212-2401, USA

Palance, Holly
2753 Roscomare Rd
Los Angeles, CA 90077-1632, USA

Palastra Jr, Joseph T (General)
RR 1 Box 267
Myrtle, MO 65778-9726, USA

Palatella, Lou (Football Player)
San Francisco 49ers
1532 Kennewick Dr
Sunnyvale, CA 94087-4158, USA

Palau, Doug (Producer)
c/o Staff Member *Endeavor Agency LLC (LA)*
9601 Wilshire Blvd Fl 3
Beverly Hills, CA 90210-5204, USA

Palau, Luis (Misc)
1500 NW 167th Pl
Beaverton, OR 97006-7342, USA

Palazzari, Doug (Hockey Player)
4370 Dynasty Dr
Colorado Springs, CO 80918-6133, USA

Palazzi, Lou (Football Player)
New York Giants
6400 Windcrest Dr Apt 826
Plano, TX 75024-3059, USA

Paldridge, Curt (Football Player)
Seattle Seahawks
2820 Country Club Ln
Dekalb, IL 60115-4922, USA

Palekar, Amol (Actor, Bollywood, Director)
Chire Bandee
10th N S Road JVPD Scheme
Mumbai, MS 400049, INDIA

Palelei, Lonnie (Football Player)
Pittsburgh Steelers
1808 SW Chief Cir
Blue Springs, MO 64015-5420, USA

Palermo, Stephen M (Steve) (Baseball Player)
5102 W 143rd Ter
Overland Park, KS 66224-3746, USA

Palesh, Shirley (Baseball Player)
120 Grand Ave Apt 213
Wausau, WI 54403-7202, USA

Paleta, Ludwika (Actor)
c/o Staff Member *Televisa*
Blvd Adolfo Lopez Mateos 232
Colonia San Angel INN
DF CP 01060, MEXICO

Paley, Albert R (Artist)
Paley Studio
25 N Washington St
Rochester, NY 14614-1110, USA

Paley, Grace (Writer)
PO Box 112
Thetford, VT 05074-0112, USA

Palias, Cecile (Actor)
P F D
Drury House
34-43 Russell St
London WC2B 5HA, UNITED KINGDOM (UK)

Palillo, Ron (Actor)
Spotlight
322 Bowling Green
New York, NY 10274, USA

Palin, Michael (Actor, Writer)
Gurnby Corp
68A Delancey St
Camden Town
London NW1 7RY, UNITED KINGDOM (UK)

Pall, Donn (Baseball Player)
Chicago White Sox
154 Wellington Dr
Bloomingdale, IL 60108-3011, USA

Pall, Gloria (Actor, Model)
12814 Victory Blvd
North Hollywood, CA 91606-3013, USA

Pall, Olga (Skier)
Fahrenweg 28
Absam 6060, AUSTRIA

Palladino, Eric (Actor)
341 N Van Ness Ave
Los Angeles, CA 90004-1523, USA

Palladino, Erik (Actor)
c/o Tiffany Kuzon *Evolution Entertainment (LA)*
901 N Highland Ave
Los Angeles, CA 90038-2412, USA

Palladino, Vincent (Misc)
National Assn of Postal Supervisors
1727 King St
Alexandria, VA 22314-2700, USA

Pallavi (Actor, Bollywood)
14A Directors Colony
Kodambakkam
Chennai, TN 600024, INDIA

Palli, Anne-Marie (Golfer)
4510 N Alta Haclenda Dr
Phoenix, AZ 85018, USA

Palm, Mike (Baseball Player)
Boston Red Sox
21 Riverview Pl
Scituate, MA 02066-1215, USA

Palm, Siegfried
Gerhild Baron Mgmt
Dombacher Str 41/III/3
Vienna 1170, AUSTRIA

Palmeiro, Orlando (Baseball Player)
Anaheim Angels
11991 SW 103rd Ter
Miami, FL 33186-2654, USA

Palmeiro, Rafael C (Baseball Player)
c/o Staff Member *Baltimore Orioles*
333 W Camden St
Oriole Park
Baltimore, MD 21201-2435, USA

Palmer, Arnold D (Golfer)
9000 Bay Hill Blvd
Orlando, FL 32819-4880, USA

Palmer, Betsy (Actor)
PO Box 55
Disney, OK 74340-0055, USA

Palmer, Byron
7044 Los Tilos Rd
Los Angeles, CA 90068-3109, USA

Palmer, C R (Business Person)
Rowan Companies
2800 Post Oak Blvd Ste 5450
Transco Tower
Houston, TX 77056-6127, USA

Palmer, Carl (Musician)
Asia
9 Hillgate St
London W8 7SP, UNITED KINGDOM (UK)

Palmer, Carson (Football Player)
Cincinnati Bengals
25052 Adelanto Dir
Laguna Niguel, CA 92677, USA

Palmer, Dave R (Educator, General)
4531 Blue Ridge Dr
Belton, TX 76513-4906, USA

Palmer, David (Baseball Player)
Montreal Expos
61 Sherman Ave
Glens Falls, NY 12801-2708, USA

Palmer, David (Football Player)
Minnesota Vikings
527 Carlton Pl
Birmingham, AL 35214-1331, USA

Palmer, Dean (Baseball Player)
Texas Rangers
3907 W Millers Bridge Rd
Tallahassee, FL 32312-1054, USA

Palmer, Derrell (Football Player)
New York Yankees
900 Jennifer Ct
Cleburne, TX 76033-5931, USA

Palmer, Geoffrey (Actor)
Marmont Mgmt
Langham House
302/8 Regent St
London W1R 5AL, UNITED KINGDOM (UK)

Palmer, Geoffrey W R (Prime Minister)
63 Roxburgh St
Mount Victoria
Wellington, NEW ZEALAND

Palmer, Gery (Football Player)
Kansas City Chiefs
6411 E Irish Pl
Centennial, CO 80112-2404, USA

Palmer, Gregg
5726 Graves Ave
Encino, CA 91316-1441, USA

Palmer, Gretchen
15301 Ventura Blvd # 345
Sherman Oaks, CA 91403-3102, USA

Palmer, Jesse (Football Player, Reality TV Star)
c/o Staff Member *San Francisco 49ers*
4949 Centennial Blvd
Santa Clara, CA 95054-1229, USA

Palmer, Jim (Baseball Player, Sportscaster)
Baltimore Orioles
239 Sanford Ave
Palm Beach, FL 33480-3619, USA

Palmer, Keke (Actor)
c/o Staff Member *Coast to Coast Talent Group*
3350 Barham Blvd
Los Angeles, CA 90068-1404, USA

Palmer, Lowell (Baseball Player)
Philadelphia Phillies
PO Box 5253
El Dorado Hills, CA 95762-0005, USA

Palmer, Mitch (Football Player)
Tampa Bay Buccaneers
14420 Cypress Pt
Poway, CA 92064-6600, USA

Palmer, Patsy (Actor)
c/o Staff Member *International Artistes Limited*
Holborn Hall - 4th Floor
193-7 High Holborn
London WC1V 7BD, UNITED KINGDOM (UK)

Palmer, Peter (Actor)
216 Kingsway Dr
Temple Terrace, FL 33617-4823, USA

Palmer, Ralph (Baseball Player)
Chicago American Giants
844 48th St SE
Grand Rapids, MI 49508-4718, USA

Palmer, Reginald Oswald (Governor)
Government House
Saint George's, GRENADA

Palmer, Richard H (Football Player)
Miami Dolphins
14420 Cypress Pt
Poway, CA 92064-6600, USA

Palmer, Sandra (Golfer)
498 Peralta Ave
Long Beach, CA 90803-2218, USA

Palmer, Scott (Football Player)
New York Jets
7408 Lady Suzannes Ct
Austin, TX 78729-7793, USA

Palmer, William R (Publisher)
Detroit News
615 W Lafayette Blvd
Detroit, MI 48226-3142, USA

Palmieri, Eddie (Musician)
Berkeley Agency
2608 9th St Ste 301
Berkeley, CA 94710-2556, USA

Palmieri, Paul (Religious Leader)
Church of Jesus Christ
6th & Lincoln Sts
Monongahela, PA 15063, USA

Palminteri, Chazz (Actor)
375 Greenwich St
New York, NY 10013-2376, USA

Palmisano, Samuel J (Business Person)
IBM Corp
1 N Castle Dr
Armonk, NY 10504-1784, USA

Palmquist, Ed (Baseball Player)
Los Angeles Dodgers
2475 Southside Rd
Grants Pass, OR 97527-8981, USA

Palms, John M (Educator)
University of South Carolina
President's Office
Columbia, SC 29208-0001, USA

The Celebrity Black Book 2008

Palomeque, Lincoln (Actor)
c/o Staff Member *TV Caracol*
Calle 76 #11 - 35
Piso 10AA
Bogota DC 26484, COLOMBIA

Palomino, Carlos (Boxer)
14242 Burbank Blvd # 8
Sherman Oaks, CA 91401-4937, USA

Paltrow, Gwyneth (Actor)
c/o Rick Kurtzman *Creative Artists Agency LCC (CAA-LA)*
2000 Avenue Of The Stars
Los Angeles, CA 90067-4700, USA

Paltrow, Jake (Director)
c/o John Lesher *Endeavor Agency LLC (LA)*
9601 Wilshire Blvd Fl 3
Beverly Hills, CA 90210-5204, USA

Palumba, Joe (Football Player)
927 Old Garth Rd
Charlottesville, VA 22901-1937, USA

Palumbo, Sam (Football Player)
Cleveland Browns
5176 Case Ave
Lyndhurst, OH 44124-1012, USA

Palys, Stan (Baseball Player)
Philadelphia Phillies
RR 6 Box 6119
Moscow, PA 18444-9045, USA

Pampanini, Sylvana
Via Flaminia 322
Rome I-00196, ITALY

Pampling, Rod (Golfer)
4709 Rangewood Dr
Flower Mound, TX 75028-1695, USA

Pan, Hong (Actor)
Omei Film Studio
Tonghui Menwai
Chengdu City, Sichuan Province, CHINA

Panabaker, Danielle (Actor)
c/o Staff Member *Noble Media Group Inc*
53 Sunrise Creek Rd
Superior, MT 59872-9746, USA

Panabaker, Kay (Actor)
c/o Staff Member *Endeavor Agency LLC (LA)*
9601 Wilshire Blvd Fl 3
Beverly Hills, CA 90210-5204, USA

Panafieu, Bernard L A Cardinal (Religious Leader)
Archdiocese
14 Place du Colonel-Edon
Marseille Cedex 07 13284, FRANCE

Pancake, Sam (Actor)
c/o Joel King *Pakula/King & Associates*
9229 W Sunset Blvd Ste 315
Los Angeles, CA 90069-3403, USA

Pancholi, Aditya (Actor, Bollywood)
Hattes Bungalow
Gandhigram Road Juhu
Mumbai, MS 400049, INDIA

Panday, Basdeo (Prime Minister)
Premier's Office
Eric Williams Plaza
Port of Spain, TRINIDAD & TOBAGO

Pandey, Chunky (Actor, Bollywood)
1 A/B Monisha Apartments
St Andrews Road Bandra
Mumbai, MS 400050, INDIA

Pandian (Actor)
185/6 Bharatidasan Street
Baskar Colony
Chennai, TN 600 093, INDIA

Pandian, Arun (Actor)
2A Bajaj Apartment
Nandanam
Chennai, TN 600 035, INDIA

Panelli, John (Football Player)
Detroit Lions
17549 Kirkshire Ave
Beverly Hills, MI 48025-3265, USA

Panetierre, Hayden (Actor)
c/o Emily Gerson Saines *Brookside Artists Management (NY)*
250 W 57th St Ste 2303
New York, NY 10107-2399, USA

Panetta, Leon E (Government Official)
15 Panetta Rd
Carmel Valley, CA 93924-9452, USA

Pang, May
1619 3rd Ave Apt 9D
New York, NY 10128-3937, USA

Pang, Qing (Figure Skater)
c/o Staff Member *Champions on Ice*
3500 W 80th St
Tom Collins Enterprises Inc
Minneapolis, MN 55431-1068, USA

Panhofer, Walter (Musician)
Erdbergstr 35/9
Vienna 1030, AUSTRIA

Panic, Milan (Business Person, Prime Minister)
1050 Arden Rd
Pasadena, CA 91106-4004, USA

Panichas, George A (Writer)
PO Box Ab
College Park, MD 20741-3025, USA

Panish, Morton B (Misc)
52 Baldwin Rd
Freeport, ME 04032-6485, USA

Pankey, Irv (Football Player)
348 Walker St
Aberdeen, MD 21001-3543, USA

Pankin, Stuart (Actor)
1288 Bienveneda Ave
Pacific Palisades, CA 90272-2317, USA

Pankovits, Jim (Baseball Player)
Houston Astros
2834 Queensland Dr
Richmond, VA 23294-5249, USA

Pankow, James (Musician)
3874 Puerco Canyon Rd
Malibu, CA 90265-4504, USA

Pankow, John (Actor)
Gersh Agency
232 N Canon Dr
Beverly Hills, CA 90210-5302, USA

Panni, Marcello (Composer)
3 Piazza Borghese
Rome 00186, ITALY

Panofsky, Wolfgang K H (Physicist)
25671 Chapin Rd
Los Altos Hills, CA 94022-3413, USA

Panos, Joe (Football Player)
Philadelphia Eagles
3355 Bradee Rd
Brookfield, WI 53005-2729, USA

Panov, Valery M (Ballerina)
Carson Office
119 W 57th St # 903
New York, NY 10019-2303, USA

Panozzo, Chuck (Musician)
c/o Sterling Bacon *TBA Artist Management (Atlanta)*
1111 Alderman Dr Ste 285
Alpharetta, GA 30005-5433, USA

Panther, Jim (Baseball Player)
Oakland A's
7936 Tiger Palm Way
Fort Myers, FL 33966-6447, USA

Pantoja, Arnie (Actor)
c/o Julie Balfour *AKA Talent Agency*
6310 San Vicente Blvd Ste 200
Los Angeles, CA 90048-5488, USA

Pantoliano, Joe (Joey Pants) (Actor)
c/o Lisa Hallerman *United Talent Agency (UTA)*
9560 Wilshire Blvd Ste 500
Beverly Hills, CA 90212-2401, USA

Pantotiano, Joe (Actor)
600 Willow Ave Apt 3
Hoboken, NJ 07030-6919, USA

Panza dl Blumo, Giuseppe (Misc)
PO Box 3183
Lugano 6901, SWITZERLAND

Paola (Royalty)
Koninklijk Palais
Rue de Brederode
Brussels 1000, BELGIUM

Paolini, Christopher (Writer)
c/o Staff Member *Random House*
1540 Broadway
New York, NY 10036-4039, USA

Paolo, Connor (Actor)
c/o Ellen Gilbert *Abrams Artists Agency (LA)*
9200 W Sunset Blvd Ph 11
Los Angeles, CA 90069-3601, USA

Paolozzi, Eduardo L (President)
107 Dovehouse
London SW3 6JZ, UNITED KINGDOM (UK)

Papa, Greg (Baseball Player)
Oakland A's
11 San Andreas Dr
Danville, CA 94506-2035, USA

Papa, John (Baseball Player)
Baltimore Orioles
29 Philip Dr
Shelton, CT 06484-5130, USA

Papa, Tom (Comedian)
c/o Staff Member *William Morris Agency (WMA-LA)*
1 William Morris Pl
Beverly Hills, CA 90212-4261, USA

Papa Doo Run Run
PO Box 255
Cupertino, CA 95015-0255, USA

Papa Roach (Music Group)
c/o Staff Member *Creative Artists Agency LCC (CAA-LA)*
2000 Avenue Of The Stars
Los Angeles, CA 90067-4700, USA

Papach, George (Football Player)
Pittsburgh Steelers
5454 S Hohman Ave
Hammond, IN 46320-1931, USA

Papadopoulos, Tassos (President)
Presidential Palace
5 Ioannis Ceridos St
Nicosia, CYPRUS

Papale, Vince (Football Player)
Philadelphia Eagles
2219 S 15th St
Philadelphia, PA 19145-3920, USA

Papamichael, Phedon M (Cinematographer)
Innovative Artists
1505 10th St
Santa Monica, CA 90401-2805, USA

Papas, Irene (Actor)
38 Xenokratous St
Athens 106 76, GREECE

Papathanassiou, Aspassia (Actor)
38 Xenokratous St
Athens 106 76, GREECE

Papazian, Marty (Actor)
c/o Tom Chasin *Chasin Agency, The*
8899 Beverly Blvd Ste 716
Los Angeles, CA 90048-2449, USA

Pape, Ken (Baseball Player)
Texas Rangers
2617 Green Creek St
San Antonio, TX 78232, USA

Papi, Stan (Baseball Player)
St Louis Cardinals
1111 W Sierra Madre Ave
Fresno, CA 93705-0433, USA

Papis, Max (Race Car Driver)
30212 Tomas
Rancho Santa Margarita, CA 92688-2122, USA

Papit, Johnny (Football Player)
Washington Redskins
29 Sellers Ave
Lexington, VA 24450-1930, USA

Pappalardo, Salvatore Cardinal (Religious Leader)
Arcibescovado
Via Matteo Bonello 2
Palermo 90134, ITALY

Pappano, Antonio
Royal Opera House
Covent Garden
Bow St
London WC2E 9DD, UNITED KINGDOM (UK)

Pappas, Brenden (Golfer)
5770 SW 42nd Pl
Ocala, FL 34474-9516, USA

Pappas, Deane (Golfer)
3225 W Orange Country Club Dr
Winter Garden, FL 34787-5304, USA

Pappas, Erik (Baseball Player)
Chicago Cubs
2545 W 11th Street
Chicago, IL 60655, USA

Pappas, George (Bowler)
21108 Blakely Shores Dr
Cornelius, NC 28031-6606, USA

Pappas, Milt (Baseball Player)
Baltimore Orioles
502 Highlington Ct
Beecher, IL 60401-3576, USA

Pappenheimer, John R (Physicist)
66 Sherman St Apt 113
Cambridge, MA 02140-3528, USA

Pappin, James J (Jim) (Hockey Player)
48947 Greasewood Ln
Palm Desert, CA 92260-6836, USA

Paquette, Craig (Baseball Player)
Oakland A's
1500 Garden Valley Dr
Glencoe, MO 63038-1488, USA

Paquin, Anna (Actor)
1503 Ventura Blvd #710
Sherman Oaks, CA 91403, USA

Paradis, Vanessa (Actor, Model, Musician)
c/o Staff Member *Agence Marceline Lenoir*
14 rue Lincoln
Paris 75008, FRANCE

Paradise, Bob (Hockey Player)
1303 Beechwood Pl
Saint Paul, MN 55116-2202, USA

Parado, Alejandra (Actor)
c/o Gabriel Blanco *Gabriel Blanco Iglesias (Mexico)*
Rio Balsas 35-32
Colonia Cuauhtemoc
DF 06500, MEXICO

Parahia, Murray (Musician)
I M G Artists
420 W 45th St
New York, NY 10036-3503, USA

Paraseghian, Ara
51767 Oakbrook Ct
Granger, IN 46530-8731, USA

Parazaider, Walter (Musician)
Front Line Mgmt
8900 Wilshire Blvd Ste 300
Beverly Hills, CA 90211-1959, USA

Parazynski, Scott E (Astronaut)
2015 Wroxton Rd
Houston, TX 77005-1654, USA

Parcells, Duane C (Bill) (Coach, Football Coach)
c/o Staff Member *Dallas Cowboys*
1 Cowboys Pkwy
Irving, TX 75063-4999, USA

Pardee, Arthur B (Misc)
15 Buzzards Bay Ave
Woods Hole, MA 02543-1105, USA

Pardee, Jack (Coach)
PO Box 272
Gause, TX 77857-0272, USA

Pardes, Herbert (Misc)
15 Claremont Ave # 93
New York, NY 10027-6809, USA

Pardo, Al (Baseball Player)
Baltimore Orioles
908 Hillary Cir
Lutz, FL 33548-5052, USA

Pardo, Don (Correspondent)
NBC-TV
30 Rockefeller Plz Ste 270E
News Dept
New York, NY 10112-0299, USA

Pardo, Jimmy (Comedian)
c/o Staff Member *OmniPop Inc (LA)*
4605 Lankershim Blvd Ste 201
North Hollywood, CA 91602-1874, USA

Pardue, Kip (Actor)
c/o Jason Newman *Untitled Entertainment (LA)*
331 N Maple Dr Fl 3
Beverly Hills, CA 90210-3827, USA

Pare, Jessica (Actor)
c/o Nick Frenkel *3 Arts Entertainment (NY)*
9460 Wilshire Blvd Ste 700
Beverly Hills, CA 90212-2713, USA

Pare, Michael (Actor)
c/o Staff Member *David Shapira & Associates*
193 N Robertson Blvd
Beverly Hills, CA 90211-2103, USA

Paredes, Marisa (Actor)
Alsira Maroto Garcia
Gran Via 63
#3 Izda
Madrid 28013, SPAIN

Parekh, Asha (Actor, Bollywood)
Azad Road
Juhu
Mumbai, MS 400049, INDIA

Parent, Gail
2001 Mandeville Canyon Rd
Los Angeles, CA 90049-2226, USA

Parent, Mark (Baseball Player)
San Diego Padres
PO Box 591
Cottonwood, CA 96022-0591, USA

Parent, Monique (Actor, Model)
PO Box 3458
Ventura, CA 93006-3458, USA

Paret, Peter (Historian, Writer)
Institute for Advanced Studies
Historical Studies School
Princeton, NJ 08540, USA

Paretsky, Sara N (Writer)
1504 E 53rd St # 302
Chicago, IL 60615-4503, USA

Parfit, Derek A (Misc)
All Souls College
Philosophy Dept
Oxford OX1 4AL, UNITED KINGDOM (UK)

Parfitt, Judy
8383 Wilshire Blvd Ste 550
Beverly Hills, CA 90211-2417, USA

Parham, Gus (Football Player)
Philadelphia Eagles
Taylor Made Office Systems 4294 El Camino Real
Los Altos, CA 94022, USA

Parilla, Lana (Actor)
c/o Staff Member *Windfall*
3000 W Alameda Ave
Burbank, CA 91523-0001, USA

Parillaud, Anne (Actor)
Artmedia
20 Ave Rapp
Paris 75007, FRANCE

Parilli, Babe (Football Player)
Green Bay Packers
8060 E Girard Ave Apt 218
Denver, CO 80231-4414, USA

Parilli, Vito (Babe) (Coach, Football Coach, Football Player)
8060 E Girard Ave Apt 218
Denver, CO 80231-4414, USA

Paris, Brandon (Actor)
Official International fan Club
PO Box 16045
1199 Lynn Valley Road
North Vancouver, BC V7J 2P0, CANADA

Paris, Bubba (Football Player)
San Francisco 49ers
40 Darlington Cv
Jackson, TN 38305-7561, USA

Paris, Kelly (Baseball Player)
St Louis Cardinals
1515 Redwood Cir
Thousand Oaks, CA 91360-6336, USA

Paris, Mica (Musician)
Richard Walters
1800 Argyle Ave # 408
Los Angeles, CA 90028-5253, USA

Paris, Twila (Musician, Songwriter, Writer)
Proper Mgmt
PO Box 150867
Nashville, TN 37215-0867, USA

Parise, Louis (Misc)
National Maritime Union
1125 15th St NW
Washington, DC 20005-2702, USA

Parise, Robert L (Basketball Player)
20 Stonybrook Rd Apt 1
Framingham, MA 01702-5997, USA

Parise, Ronald A (Astronaut)
15419 Good Hope Rd
Silver Spring, MD 20905-4129, USA

Parise, Vanessa (Actor)
c/o Lara Rosenstock *Lara Rosenstock Management*
8371 Blackburn Ave Apt 1
Los Angeles, CA 90048-4245, USA

Parisot, Dean (Director)
c/o Staff Member *3 Arts Entertainment Inc*
9460 Wilshire Blvd Fl 7
Beverly Hills, CA 90212-2713, USA

Parisse, Annie (Actor)
c/o Kami Putnam *Endeavor Agency LLC (LA)*
232 N Canon Dr
Beverly Hills, CA 90210-5302, USA

Parizeau, Jacques (Politician)
88 Grand Alle Est
Quebec, PQ G1A 1A2, CANADA

Park, Alyssa (Musician)
Columbia Artists Mgmt Inc
1790 Broadway Fl 6
New York, NY 10019-1412, USA

Park, Chan Ho (Baseball Player)
Los Angeles Dodgers
1800 O Henry Ct
Arlington, TX 76006-2673, USA

Park, Charles R (Physicist)
5325 Stanford Dr
Nashville, TN 37215-4233, USA

Park, D Bradford (Brad) (Coach, Hockey Player)
20 Stanley Rd
Lynnfield, MA 01940-1732, USA

Park, Ernie (Football Player)
San Diego Chargers
3160 Private Road 1101
Clyde, TX 79510-4905, USA

Park, Grace (Golfer)
c/o Evan Hainey *Untitled Entertainment (LA)*
331 N Maple Dr Fl 3
Beverly Hills, CA 90210-3827, USA

Park, Linda (Actor)
c/o Ro Diamond *SDB Partners Inc*
1801 Avenue Of The Stars Ste 902
Los Angeles, CA 90067-5981, USA

Park, Linkin (Musician)
c/o Rob McDermott *The Firm*
9465 Wilshire Blvd Fl 6
Beverly Hills, CA 90212-2605, USA

Park, Merle F (Ballerina)
Royal Ballet School
144 Talgarth Road
London W14 9DE, UNITED KINGDOM (UK)

Park, Nicholas W (Nick) (Animator, Director)
Aardvark Animation
Gas Ferry Road
Bristol B51 6UN, UNITED KINGDOM (UK)

Park, Patrick (Musician)
c/o Staff Member *Paradigm (Monterey)*
509 Hartnell St
Monterey, CA 93940-2825, USA

Park, Ray (Actor)
c/o Michael Greenwald *Don Buchwald & Associates Inc (LA)*
6500 Wilshire Blvd Ste 2200
Los Angeles, CA 90048-4942, USA

Park, Reg
Box 1002-Morningside 2057 Sandton
Gauteng, SOUTH AFRICA

Park, Steve (Race Car Driver)
1675 Coddle Creek Hwy
Mooresville, NC 28115, USA

Parke, Dorothy (Actor)
c/o Staff Member *AKA Talent Agency*
6310 San Vicente Blvd Ste 200
Los Angeles, CA 90048-5488, USA

Parke, Evan Dexter (Actor)
c/o Don Spradlin *Essential Talent Management*
6399 Wilshire Blvd Ste 400
Los Angeles, CA 90048-5716, USA

Parkening, Christopher (Musician)
IMG Artists
420 W 45th St
New York, NY 10036-3503, USA

Parker, Ace (Baseball Player)
Philadelphia Athletics
210 Snead Fairway
Portsmouth, VA 23701-1641, USA

Parker, Alan W (Director)
Parker Film Co
Pinewood Studios
Iver Heath
Bucks SL0 0NH, UNITED KINGDOM (UK)

Parker, Anthony (Basketball Player)
Orlando Magic
8701 Maitland Summit Blvd
Waterhouse Center
Orlando, FL 32810-5915, USA

Parker, Anthony (Football Player)
Indianapolis Colts
1054 E Geneva Dr
Tempe, AZ 85282-3805, USA

Parker, Artimus (Football Player)
Philadelphia Eagles
4231 47th St
Sacramento, CA 95820-4034, USA

Parker, Bob (Skier)
408 Camino Don Miguel
Santa Fe, NM 87505-5948, USA

Parker, Brant J (Cartoonist)
901 Glenwood Blvd
Waynesboro, VA 22980-3409, USA

Parker, Caryl Mack (Musician)
Scream Marketing
PO Box 120053
Nashville, TN 37212-0053, USA

Parker, Chris (Actor)
Elstree Centre
Clarendon Road
Borehamwood
Herts WD6 1JF, UNITED KINGDOM (UK)

Parker, Christian (Baseball Player)
New York Yankees
10101 Mesa Arriba Ave NE
Albuquerque, NM 87111-4962, USA

Parker, Christopher (Actor)
Shepherd Mgmt
13 Radnor Walk
London SW3 4BP, UNITED KINGDOM (UK)

Parker, Clay (Baseball Player)
Seattle Mariners
1112 Charwood Ln
Hixson, TN 37343-2816, USA

Parker, Corey (Actor)
Muse Mgmt
429 Santa Monica Blvd # 520
Santa Monica, CA 90401-3401, USA

Parker, Craig (Actor)
c/o Joe Smith *International Creative Management (ICM-LA)*
10250 Constellation Blvd
Los Angeles, CA 90067-6200, USA

Parker, Dave (Baseball Player)
Pittsburgh Pirates
4036 Oak Tree Ct
Loveland, OH 45140-1090, USA

Parker, Denise (Athlete)
4801 Wallace Ln
Salt Lake City, UT 84117, USA

Parker, Eleanor (Actor)
2195 S La Paz Way
Palm Springs, CA 92264-9529, USA

Parker, Ervin (Football Player)
Buffalo Bills
1311 12th Ave S Apt B201
Seattle, WA 98144-7426, USA

Parker, Ervin (Football Player)
Cleveland Browns
RR 4 Box 83-2
Broken Bow, OK 74728-9463, USA

Parker, Eugene N (Physicist)
1323 Evergreen Rd
Homewood, IL 60430-3410, USA

Parker, Fess (Actor, Musician)
Fess Parker Winery
PO Box 908
Los Olivos, CA 93441-0908, USA

Parker, Franklin (Writer)
Western Carolina University
Education & Psychology Dept
Cullowhee, NC 28723, USA

Parker, George M (Misc)
Glass Workers Union
1440 S Byrne Road
Toledo, OH 43614, USA

Parker, Harry (Baseball Player)
St Louis Cardinals
6049 Havenview Dr
Mechanicsville, VA 23111-7507, USA

Parker, Jack D (Jackie) (Football Player)
10623 65 Ave NW
Edmonton, AB T6H 1V5, CANADA

Parker, James T (Jim) (Football Player)
1902 Cedar Circle Dr
Catonsville, MD 21228-3741, USA

Parker, Jameson (Actor)
Stone Manners
6500 Wilshire Blvd Ste 550
Los Angeles, CA 90048-4950, USA

Parker, Lara (Actor)
PO Box 1254
Topanga, CA 90290-1254, USA

Parker, Larry (Football Player)
Kansas City Chiefs
711 Spirit Lake Dr
Bakersfield, CA 93312-2925, USA

Parker, Lu
12222 Vance Jackson Rd Apt 734
San Antonio, TX 78230-5941, USA

Parker, Maceo (Musician)
Central Entertainment Services
109 W Newark Ave
Wildwood, NJ 08260-1038, USA

Parker, Mary-Louise (Actor)
c/o Gene Parseghian *Untitled Entertainment (NY)*
322 8th Ave Ste 601
New York, NY 10001-6715, USA

Parker, Molly (Actor)
Macklam Feldman Mgmt
1505 W 2nd Ave
#200
Vancouver, BC V6H 3Y4, CANADA

Parker, Nate (Actor)
c/o Sara Ramaker *Paradigm (LA)*
360 N Crescent Dr
North Bldg
Beverly Hills, CA 90210-6820, USA

Parker, Nathanial
10100 Santa Monica Blvd Ste 2500
Los Angeles, CA 90067-4116, USA

Parker, Nathaniel (Actor)
Markham & Froggatt
Julian House
4 Windmill St
London W1P 1HF, UNITED KINGDOM (UK)

Parker, Nicole (Actor)
c/o Stephen Hirsh *Gersh Agency, The (NY)*
41 Madison Ave Fl 33
New York, NY 10010-2202, USA

Parker, Noelle
9300 Wilshire Blvd Ste 555
Beverly Hills, CA 90212-3211, USA

Parker, Oliver
76 Oxford St.
London, ENGLAND W1N 0AX, UNITED KINGDOM (UK)

Parker, Olivia (Photographer)
Robert Klein
38 Newbury St # 400
Boston, MA 02116-3210, USA

Parker, Orlando (Football Player)
New York Jets
4402 Chatham Pl
Montgomery, AL 36108-4902, USA

Parker, Paula Jai (Actor)
c/o Leonard Torgan *Leverage Management*
1610 Broadway
Santa Monica, CA 90404-2792, USA

Parker, Ray Jr (Musician)
Performers of the World
8901 Melrose Ave # 200
West Hollywood, CA 90069-5605, USA

Parker, Rick (Baseball Player)
San Francisco Giants
2641 NE 74th St
Gladstone, MO 64119-5349, USA

Parker, Riddick (Football Player)
Seattle Seahawks
11226 NE 68th St Apt 212-B
Kirkland, WA 98033-7181, USA

Parker, Robert A R (Astronaut)
Jet Propulsion Laboratory
4800 Oak Grove Dr
Pasadena, CA 91109-8001, USA

Parker, Robert B (Writer)
555 W 57th St Ste 1230
New York, NY 10019-2925, USA

Parker, Sarah Jessica (Actor, Producer)
c/o Kevin Huvane *Creative Artists Agency LCC (CAA-LA)*
2000 Avenue Of The Stars
Los Angeles, CA 90067-4700, USA

Parker, Scott (Motorcycle Race, Motorcycle Racer)
6096 Grand Blanc Rd
Swartz Creek, MI 48473-9441, USA

Parker, T Jefferson (Writer)
William Morris Agency
151 El Camino Dr
Beverly Hills, CA 90212-2775, USA

Parker, Tony (Basketball Player)
San Antonio Spurs
1 Sbc Center Pkwy
Alamodome
San Antonio, TX 78219-3604, USA

Parker, Trey (Animator, Writer)
c/o Gabrielle (Gaby) Morgerman *William Morris Agency (WMA-LA)*
1 William Morris Pl
Beverly Hills, CA 90212-4261, USA

Parker, Vaughn (Football Player)
San Diego Chargers
2500 6th Ave Apt 107
San Diego, CA 92103-6629, USA

Parker, Wes (Baseball Player)
Los Angeles Dodgers
1237 Villa Woods Dr
Pacific Palisades, CA 90272-3953, USA

Parker, Willie (Football Player)
Buffalo Bills
9327 Kai Dr
Beach City, TX 77520-2333, USA

Parker-Bowles, Camilla (Royalty)
Clarence House
Stable Yard Gate
London SW1, UNITED KINGDOM (UK)

Parkhill, Barry (Basketball Player)
3429 Cesford Grange
Keswick, VA 22947-9127, USA

Parkhurst, Heather
8383 Wilshire Blvd # 954
Beverly Hills, CA 90211-2412, USA

Parkhurst, Heather Elizabeth (Actor)
8491 W Sunset Blvd # 440
West Hollywood, CA 90069-1911, USA

Parkins, Barbara
6399 Wilshire Blvd Ste 414
Los Angeles, CA 90048-5716, USA

Parkinson, Bradford W (Business Person)
2780 Volley Cir
Meadow Vista, CA 95722, USA

Parkinson, Michael
c/o PFD
Drury House
34/43 Russell St
London WC2B 5HA, UNITED KINGDOM (UK)

Parkinson, Robert
20 Kingston Lane Teddington
Middlesex, ENGLAND, UNITED KINGDOM (UK)

Parkinson, Robert L Jr (Business Person)
Abbott Laboratories
100 Abbott Park Rd
Abbott Park, IL 60064-3500, USA

Parkinson, Roger P (Publisher)
Minneapolis Star Tribune
425 Portland Ave
Minneapolis, MN 55488-1511, USA

Parks, Andrew
1830 Grace Ave
Los Angeles, CA 90028-4916, USA

Parks, David W (Dave) (Football Player)
6629 Southpoint Dr
Dallas, TX 75248-2221, USA

Parks, Derek (Baseball Player)
Minnesota Twins
6562 Starstone Pl
Rancho Cucamonga, CA 91739-2024, USA

Parks, Maxie (Athlete, Track Athlete)
4545 E Norwich Ave
Fresno, CA 93726-2726, USA

Parks, Michael (Actor)
11684 Ventura Blvd # 476
Studio City, CA 91604-2699, USA

Parks, Michael (Editor)
Los Angeles Times
202 W 1st St
Editorial Dept
Los Angeles, CA 90012-4105, USA

Parks, Suzan-Lori (Misc)
William Morris Agency
151 El Camino Dr
Beverly Hills, CA 90212-2775, USA

Parks, Van Dyke (Composer)
267 S Arden Blvd
Los Angeles, CA 90004-3718, USA

Parks, Wally (Misc)
National Hot Rod Assn
2023 E Financial Way
Glendora, CA 91741, USA

Parks-Young, Barbara (Baseball Player)
5078 Edinboro Ln
Wilmington, NC 28409-8518, USA

Parlavecchio, Chet (Football Player)
Green Bay Packers
52 Oak St
Hornell, NY 14843-1949, USA

Parlen, Megan (Actor)
c/o Staff Member *Cunningham Escott Slevin & Doherty (LA)*
10635 Santa Monica Blvd Ste 130
Los Angeles, CA 90025-8306, USA

Parmalee, Bernie (Football Player)
Miami Dolphins
14695 Heatherton Dr
Granger, IN 46530-4212, USA

Parmenter, Charles S (Misc)
Indiana University
Chemistry Dept
Bloomington, IN 47405, USA

Parmer, Jim (Football Player)
Philadelphia Eagles
2311 S County Road 1120
Midland, TX 79706-4942, USA

Parmet, Philip (Cinematographer)
1080 S Hayworth Ave
Los Angeles, CA 90035-2602, USA

Parnell, Chris (Actor)
c/o Jimmy Miller *Mosaic Media Group*
24 Music Sq W Fl 1
Nashville, TN 37203-6661, USA

Parnell, Lee Roy (Musician)
PO Box 23451
Nashville, TN 37202-3451, USA

Parnell, LeRoy
PO Box 23451
Nashville, TN 37202-3451, USA

Parnell, Mel (Baseball Player)
Boston Red Sox
700 Turquoise St
New Orleans, LA 70124-3541, USA

Parnell, Peter (Writer)
c/o Staff Member *United Talent Agency (UTA)*
9560 Wilshire Blvd Ste 500
Beverly Hills, CA 90212-2401, USA

Parnevik, Jesper (Golfer)
17553 SE Conch Bar Ave
Jupiter, FL 33469-1709, USA

Parodi, Starr (Musician)
c/o Staff Member *Evolution Music Partners*
9100 Wilshire Blvd
East Tower #201
Beverly Hills, CA 90212-3401, USA

Paronto, Chad (Baseball Player)
Baltimore Orioles
617 Benedict Rd
Pittsfield, MA 01201-2899, USA

Parque, Jim (Baseball Player)
Chicago White Sox
4109 Crystal Ridge Dr SE
Puyallup, WA 98372-5214, USA

Parr, Carolyn Miller (Judge)
US Tax Court
400 2nd St NW
Washington, DC 20217-0002, USA

Parr, Jerry S
4529 38th St NW
Washington, DC 20016-1827, USA

Parr, Ralph S (War Hero)
14831 Heather Valley Way
Houston, TX 77062-2337, USA

Parr, Robert G (Misc)
701 Kenmore Rd
Chapel Hill, NC 27514-2019, USA

Parra, Derek (Speed Skater)
US Speedskating
PO Box 18370
Salt Lake City, UT 84118-0370, USA

Parrella, John (Football Player)
Buffalo Bills
8161 Regency Dr
Pleasanton, CA 94588-3136, USA

Parrett, Jeff (Baseball Player)
Montreal Expos
722 Seattle Dr
Lexington, KY 40503-2127, USA

Parrett, William (Business Person)
Deloitte Touche Tohmatsu
433 Country Club Rd
New Canaan, CT 06840-3604, USA

Parrilla, Lana
c/o Barbara Gale *Envoy Entertainment*
3656 Dellvale Pl
Encino, CA 91436-4144, USA

Parris, Fred (Musician)
Paramount Entertainment
PO Box 12
Far Hills, NJ 07931-0012, USA

Parris, Gary (Football Player)
San Diego Chargers
5170 9th St
Vero Beach, FL 32966-2841, USA

Parris, Steve (Baseball Player)
Pittsburgh Pirates
22942 Judith Dr
Plainfield, IL 60586-9653, USA

Parrish, Bernard J (Bernie) (Football Player)
Cleveland Browns
140 A Torns Creek Road
Eastanollee, GA 30538, USA

Parrish, Hunter (Actor)
c/o Staff Member *Cunningham Escott Slevin & Doherty (LA)*
10635 Santa Monica Blvd Ste 130
Los Angeles, CA 90025-8306, USA

Parrish, Lance M (Baseball Player)
Detroit Tigers
5141 Via Samuel
Yorba Linda, CA 92886-4527, USA

Parrish, Larry A (Baseball Player)
Montreal Expos
234 Green Haven Ln W
Dundee, FL 33838-4112, USA

Parrish, Lemar (Football Player)
Cincinnati Bengals
733 Schumate Chapel Rd
Jefferson City, MO 65109-0515, USA

Parrot, Andrew
Jonathan Wentworth
10 Fiske Pl Ste 530
Mount Vernon, NY 10550-3211, USA

Parrott, Ian
Abermad nr. Aberystwyth
Dyfed Wales, ENGLAND SY 23 4RS, UNITED KINGDOM (UK)

Parrott, Mike (Baseball Player)
Baltimore Orioles
PO Box 1264
Lyons, CO 80540-1264, USA

Parry, Craig (Golfer)
5139 Latrobe Dr
Windermere, FL 34786-8916, USA

Parry, Ken (Actor)
c/o Linda Kremer *Billy Marsh Drama Ltd*
174-178 North Gower Street
London NW1 2NB, UNITED KINGDOM (UK)

Parry, Robert T (Financier)
11362 Barranca Rd
Santa Rosa Valley, CA 93012-9227, USA

Parseghian, Ara (Coach, Football Coach, Sportscaster)
51767 Oakbridge Court
Granger, IN 46539, USA

Parseghian, Gregory (Business Person)
Federal Home Loan Mortgage
8200 Jones Branch Dr
McLean, VA 22102-3107, USA

Parshall, George W (Misc)
2401 Pennsylvania Ave Apt 714
Wilmington, DE 19806-1410, USA

Parsky, Gerald L (Attorney, Attorney General, General)
Aurora Capital Partners
1800 Century Park E
Los Angeles, CA 90067-1501, USA

Parsons, Alan (Musician)
Agency Group Ltd
1775 Broadway Ste 515
New York, NY 10019-1903, USA

Parsons, Benny (Race Car Driver)
2049 Country Club Dr
Port Orange, FL 32128-6853, USA

Parsons, Bill (Baseball Player)
Milwaukee Brewers
16209 S 1st St
Phoenix, AZ 85048-2006, USA

Parsons, Bob (Football Player)
Chicago Bears
1292 Thorndale Ln
Hawthorn Woods, IL 60047-2795, USA

Parsons, Casey (Baseball Player)
Seattle Mariners
17214 E Galactica Ct
Greenacres, WA 99016-7766, USA

Parsons, David (Choreographer)
Parsons Dance Foundation
476 Broadway
New York, NY 10013-2621, USA

Parsons, Estelle (Actor)
924 W End Ave Apt T5
New York, NY 10025-3543, USA

Parsons, John T (Inventor)
1456 Brigadoon Ct
Traverse City, MI 49686-5922, USA

Parsons, Karyn (Actor)
c/o Matthew Lesher *Lesher Entertainment Inc*
1134 S Cloverdale Ave
Los Angeles, CA 90019-6737, USA

Parsons, Nicholas (Actor)
Susan Shaper
174/178 N Gower St
London NW1 2NB, UNITED KINGDOM (UK)

Parsons, Phil (Race Car Driver)
18801 Coveside Ln
Cornelius, NC 28031-5250, USA

Parsons, Richard D (Business Person, Financier)
c/o Staff Member *Time Warner Inc*
75 Rockefeller Plz
New York, NY 10019-6990, USA

Parsons, Tom (Baseball Player)
Pittsburgh Pirates
7106 Lorraine Ave NW
North Canton, OH 44720-8832, USA

Parsons-Zipay, Suzanne (Baseball Player)
2310 Englewood Rd
Englewood, FL 34223-6333, USA

Part, Arvo (Composer)
Universal Editions
Warwick House
9 Warrick St
London W1R 5RA, UNITED KINGDOM (UK)

Partee, Barbara H (Educator)
50 Hobart Ln
Amherst, MA 01002-1321, USA

Partee, Dennis (Football Player)
San Diego Chargers
400 N Bolivar St
Marshall, TX 75670-3311, USA

Parten, Ty (Football Player)
Cincinnati Bengals
41121 N Prosperity Way
Anthem, AZ 85086-1510, USA

Partlow, Hope (Musician)
c/o Staff Member *Virgin Records (NY)*
304 Park Ave S Fl 5
New York, NY 10010-4316, USA

Parton, Dolly (Actor, Musician, Songwriter, Writer)
c/o Teresa Hughes *Inca Hoots*
PO Box 150307
Nashville, TN 37215-0307, USA

Parton, Stella (Musician)
PO Box 120871
Nashville, TN 37212-0871, USA

Partridge, Derek
96 Broadway Bexley Heath
Kent, ENGLAND DA6 7DE, UNITED KINGDOM (UK)

Partridge, John A (Architect)
20 Old Pye St
Westminster
London SW1, UNITED KINGDOM (UK)

Partridge, Rick (Football Player)
New Orleans Saints
707 Reeder Rd
Paramus, NJ 07652-3721, USA

Parvanov, Georgi (President)
President's Office
2 Dondukov Blvd
Sofia 1123, BULGARIA

Pasanella, Giovanni (Architect)
Pasanella & Klein
330 W 42nd St
New York, NY 10036-6902, USA

Pasanella, Marco (Designer)
Pasanella Co
45 W 18th St
New York, NY 10011-4609, USA

Pasarell, Charles (Tennis Player)
78200 Miles Ave
Indian Wells, CA 92210-6803, USA

Pascal, Adam (Actor)
c/o Staff Member *Paradigm (LA)*
360 N Crescent Dr
North Bldg
Beverly Hills, CA 90210-6820, USA

Pascal, Francoise
89 Riverview Gardens
London, ENGLAND SW12 9RA, UNITED KINGDOM (UK)

Pascal, Olivia
Merzstr. 14
Munich D-81679, GERMANY

Paschal, Doug (Football Player)
Minnesota Vikings
4600 Coburn Ct
Charlotte, NC 28277-2553, USA

Paschall, Bill (Baseball Player)
Kansas City Royals
7926 Windspray Dr
Summerfield, NC 27358-9715, USA

Paschall, Jim (Race Car Driver)
RR 2 Box 450
Denton, NC 27239, USA

Paschke, Melanie (Athlete, Track Athlete)
Asseweg 2
Braunschweig 38124, GERMANY

Pasco, Richard (Actor)
Michael Whitehall
125 Gloucester Road
London SW7 4TE, UNITED KINGDOM
(UK)

Pascoal, Hermeto (Musician)
Brasil Universo Prod
RVN Vitor Guisard 209
Rio de Janerio 21832, BRAZIL

Pascual, Camilo (Baseball Player)
Washington Senators
7741 SW 32nd St
Miami, FL 33155-2611, USA

Pascual, Carlos (Baseball Player)
Washington Senators
2540 SW 92nd Ct
Miami, FL 33165-8139, USA

Pascual, Luis (Director)
Theatre de l'Europe
1 Place Paul Claudel
Paris 75006, FRANCE

Pasdar, Adrian (Actor)
c/o Staff Member *Special Artists Agency*
9465 Wilshire Blvd Ste 890
Beverly Hills, CA 90212-2607, USA

Pashnick, Larry (Baseball Player)
Detroit Tigers
506 Highland St
Wyandotte, MI 48192-2433, USA

Pasik, Mario (Actor)
c/o Staff Member *Telefe - Argentina*
Pavon 2444 (C1248AAT)
Buenos Aires, ARGENTINA

Pasillas, Jose (Musician)
ArtistDirect
109000 Wilshire Blvd #1400
Los Angeles, CA 90024, USA

Paskai, Laszio Cardinal (Religious Leader)
Uri Utca 62
Budapest 1014, HUNGARY

Paskvan, George (Football Player)
Green Bay Packers
1313 Gentry Ave N
Saint Paul, MN 55128-5722, USA

Pasley, Kevin (Baseball Player)
Los Angeles Dodgers
2701 Lancaster Dr
Sun City Center, FL 33573-6517, USA

Pasmore, E J Victor (Artist)
Dar Gamri
Gudja, MALTA

Pasqua, Dan (Baseball Player)
New York Yankees
45 Silo Ridge Rd E
Orland Park, IL 60467-7327, USA

Pasquale, Steven (Actor)
c/o Staff Member *Overbrook
Entertainment*
450 N Roxbury Dr Fl 4
Beverly Hills, CA 90210-4232, USA

Pasqualini, Tony (Actor)
Marc Bass Agency, Inc
9255 W Sunset Blvd Ste 727
West Hollywood, CA 90069-3304, USA

Pasqualoni, Paul (Coach, Football Coach)
Syracuse University
Athletic Dept
Syracuse, NY 13244-0001, USA

Pasquesi, Anthony (Football Player)
Chicago Cardinals
463 E Clubview Ct
Addison, IL 60101-2998, USA

Pasquin, John R (Director, Filmmaker,
Producer)
Creative Artists Agency
9830 Wilshire Blvd
Beverly Hills, CA 90212-1804, USA

Pass, Patrick (Football Player)
New England Patriots
4 Spruce Pond Rd
Franklin, MA 02038-2500, USA

Passarelli, Pasquale (Wrestler)
Ander Froschlache 23
Munster 4400, GERMANY

Passavant, Jon (Model)
c/o Staff Member *Major Model
Management*
381 Park Ave S Rm 150
New York, NY 10016-8806, USA

Passer, Ivan (Director)
Creative Road Corp
8281 Melrose Ave Ste 300
Los Angeles, CA 90046-6891, USA

Passions, The
141 Dunbar Ave
Fords, NJ 08863-1551, USA

Passmore, John A (Misc)
6 Jansz Crescent
Manuka, ACT 2603, AUSTRALIA

Pasternak, Michael (Actor)
c/o Michael Bloom *Marc Bass Agency Inc*
9255 W Sunset Blvd Ste 727
West Hollywood, CA 90069-3304, USA

Pasternak, Reagan (Actor)
c/o Staff Member *Noble Kaplan Agency*
1260 Yonge St Fl 2
Toronto, ON M4T 1W6, CANADA

Pastomicky, Cliff (Baseball Player)
Kansas City Royals
120 Hourglass Dr
Venice, FL 34293-6055, USA

Pastor, Amy Wynn (Actor)
c/o Staff Member *Discover Networks*
1 Discovery Pl
Silver Spring, MD 20910-3354, USA

Pastore, Vincent (Actor)
c/o Bob McGowan *McGowan
Management*
8733 W Sunset Blvd Ste 103
W Hollywood, CA 90069-2241, USA

Pastorini, Dante (Football Player)
Houston Oilers
17021 Running Ridge Rd
Washington, TX 77880-6651, USA

Pastrana, Arango Andres (President)
Palacio de Narino
Plaza de Bolivar
Carrera 8A
Bogota, DE, COLOMBIA

Pastrana, Travis (Athlete)
c/o Staff Member *Familie, The*
1545 Faraday Ave
Carlsbad, CA 92008-7319, USA

Pataki, Governor George E (Politician)
State Capitol
Albany, NY 12224, USA

Patane, Giuseppe
Holbeinstr 6
Munich 81679, GERMANY

Patasse, Ange-Felix (President)
Palais de Renaissance
Bangui, CENTRAL AFRICAN REPUBLIC

Patat, Frederic (Misc)
Faculte de Medecine
2 Bis Blvd Tonnelle
Tours Cedex 37032, FRANCE

Pate, Bob (Baseball Player)
Montreal Expos
17509 Nauset Ct
Carson, CA 90746-1639, USA

Pate, Jerry (Golfer)
5 Hyde Park Rd
Pensacola, FL 32503-5830, USA

Pate, Michael (Actor)
OAM
130 Jenson Road
Wadalba, NSW 2259, AUSTRALIA

Pate, Rupert (Football Player)
Chicago Cardinals
428 Shadowbrook Dr
Burlington, NC 27215-4775, USA

Pate, Steve (Golfer)
1034 Brookview Ave
Westlake Village, CA 91361-1623, USA

Patek, Freddie (Baseball Player)
Pittsburgh Pirates
227 Willow St
Sealy, TX 77474-4201, USA

Patekar, Nana (Actor, Bollywood)
304 Sheetal Apna Ghar Society
Samarth Nagar Andheri
Mumbai, MS 400053, INDIA

Patel, Anuradha (Actor, Bollywood)
1001D Abhishek Apartments
Juhu Versova Road Andheri
Mumbai, MS 400058, INDIA

Patel, C Kumar N (Inventor)
1171 Roberto Ln
Los Angeles, CA 90077-2302, USA

Patel, Piyush (Business Person)
Cabletron Systems
35 Industrial St
Rochester, NY 14614, USA

Patera, Dennis (Football Player)
San Francisco 49ers
61535 S Highway 97 # 9512
Bend, OR 97702-2154, USA

Patera, George (Football Player)
Baltimore Colts
7305 172nd St SW
Edmonds, WA 98026-5121, USA

Patera, John A (Jack) (Coach, Football
Coach, Football Player)
Baltimore Colts
82 Osprey Dr
Cle Elum, WA 98922, USA

Patera, Ken (Athlete)
6932 Stratford Draw
Saint Paul, MN 55125-2413, USA

Patera, Pavel (Hockey Player)
Minnesota Wild
175 Kellogg Blvd W
Xcel Enegy Arena
Saint Paul, MN 55102-1206, USA

Paterno, Joe
830 McKee St
State College, PA 16803-3632, USA

Paterra, Greg (Football Player)
Atlanta Falcons
305 Douglas Ave
Elizabeth, PA 15037-1724, USA

Paterra, Herb (Football Player)
Buffalo Bills
3696 Woodmonte Dr
Rochester, MI 48306-4799, USA

Paterson, Bill (Actor)
Kerry Gardner
15 Kensington High St
London W8 5NP, UNITED KINGDOM
(UK)

Pathon, Jerome (Football Player)
Indianapolis Colts
4827 Eagles Watch Ln
Indianapolis, IN 46254-9531, USA

Patillo, Maria
6300 Wilshire Blvd Ste 2110
Los Angeles, CA 90048-5282, USA

Patinkin, Mandy (Actor, Musician)
c/o Iris Grossman *International Creative
Management (ICM-LA)*
10250 Constellation Blvd
Los Angeles, CA 90067-6200, USA

Patitz, Tatjana (Model)
Elite Model Management
111 E 22nd St Rm 200
New York, NY 10010-5414, USA

Patkau, John (Architect)
Patkau Architects
560 Beaty St
#L110
Vancouver, BC V6B 2L3, CANADA

Patrese, Ricardo (Race Car Driver)
Via Umberto 1
Padova 35100, ITALY

Patriarco, Earie (Opera Singer)
I C M Artists
40 W 57th St
New York, NY 10019-4001, USA

Patric, Jason (Actor, Producer)
c/o Eric Gold *Mosaic Media Group*
24 Music Sq W Fl 1
Nashville, TN 37203-6661, USA

Patrick, Bronswell (Baseball Player)
Milwaukee Brewers
3202 Morton Ln
Greenville, NC 27834-4930, USA

Patrick, Craig (Coach, Hockey Player)
Pittsburgh Penguins
66 Mario Lemieux Pl
Mellon Arena
Pittsburgh, PA 15219-3504, USA

Patrick, Dan (Sportscaster)
ESPN-TV
935 Middle St
Sports Dept Espn Plaza
Bristol, CT 06010-1000, USA

Patrick, Danica (Race Car Driver)
Rahal Letterman
4601 Lyman Dr
Hilliard, OH 43026-1249, USA

Patrick, Frank (Football Player)
Green Bay Packers
5689 SW 98th St
Denton, NE 68339-3346, USA

Patrick, Marcus (Actor)
c/o Staff Member *Gar Lester Agency*
4130 Cahuenga Blvd Ste 108
Toluca Lake, CA 91602-2848, USA

Patrick, Mary Anthony
56 Copsterhill Rd.Oldham
Manchester, ENGLAND, UNITED
KINGDOM (UK)

Patrick, Mike (Football Player)
New England Patriots
PO Box 7755
Diberville, MS 39540-7721, USA

Patrick, Nicholas J M (Astronaut)
15923 Mesa Verde Dr
Houston, TX 77059-6439, USA

Patrick, Pat (Misc)
Patrick Racing
8431 Green Town Road #400
Indianapolis, IN 46234, USA

Patrick, Richard (Musician)
Filter
3300 Warner Blvd
Warner Bros Records
Burbank, CA 91505-4632, USA

Patrick, Robert (Actor)
2700 La Cuesta Dr
Los Angeles, CA 90046-1339, USA

Patrick, Ruth (Educator)
Academy of Natural Sciences
19th & Parkway
Philadelphia, PA 19103, USA

Patrick, Tara Leigh (Carmen Electra)
(Actor, Model, Music Group)
c/o Stephanie Simon *Untitled
Entertainment (LA)*
331 N Maple Dr Fl 3
Beverly Hills, CA 90210-3827, USA

Patrick, Thomas M (Business Person)
Peoples Energy Corp
130 E Randolph St
Chicago, IL 60601-6302, USA

Patrick, Tom
Heimeranstr. 51
Munich D-80339, GERMANY

Patrick, Wayne (Football Player)
Buffalo Bills
329 Peppertree Dr
Amherst, NY 14228-2955, USA

Patrone, Shana
209 10th Ave S Ste 229
Nashville, TN 37203-0721, USA

Patten, Christopher F (Governor)
Coutts Co
Campbells Office
440 STrand
London WC2R 0QS, UNITED KINGDOM
(UK)

Patten, Joel (Football Player)
Cleveland Browns
13415 Marble Rock Dr
Chantilly, VA 20151-2482, USA

Patterson, Bob (Baseball Player)
San Diego Padres
26 10th St SW
Hickory, NC 28602-2630, USA

Patterson, Carly (Gymnast)
Worki Gymnastics Academy
1937 W Parker Rd
Plano, TX 75023-7503, USA

Patterson, Corey (Baseball Player)
Chicago Cubs
1558 Halisport Lake Dr NW
Kennesaw, GA 30152-4072, USA

Patterson, Danny (Baseball Player)
Texas Rangers
13944 E Yucca St
Scottsdale, AZ 85259-4638, USA

Patterson, Daryl (Baseball Player)
Detroit Tigers
20145 Tollhouse Rd
Clovis, CA 93619-9760, USA

Patterson, Dave (Baseball Player)
Los Angeles Dodgers
8425 Evanston Ave
Raytown, MO 64138-3346, USA

Patterson, Don (Football Player)
Detroit Lions
1558 Halisport Lake Dr NW
Kennesaw, GA 30152-4072, USA

Patterson, Elvis V (Football Player)
New York Giants
3939 Alberta St
Houston, TX 77021-4009, USA

Patterson, Francine G (Penny) (Misc)
Gorilla Foudation
PO Box 620-640
Woodside, CA 94062, USA

Patterson, Gary (Cartoonist)
Patterson International
25208 Malibu Rd
Malibu, CA 90265-4635, USA

Patterson, Gil (Baseball Player)
New York Yankees
16119 Belle Meade Blvd
Odessa, FL 33556-3309, USA

Patterson, James (Business Person, Writer)
J Walter Thompson
466 Lexington Ave Fl 6
New York, NY 10017-3113, USA

Patterson, Jarrod (Baseball Player)
Detroit Tigers
405 6th St N
Clanton, AL 35045-2823, USA

Patterson, Jeff (Baseball Player)
New York Yankees
27825 Tamara Dr
Yorba Linda, CA 92887-5843, USA

Patterson, John (Baseball Player)
San Francisco Giants
2659 E Jade Pl
Chandler, AZ 85286-2697, USA

Patterson, John (Baseball Player)
Arizona Diamondbacks
2709 Country Club Dr
Orange, TX 77630-2142, USA

Patterson, John M (Governor)
Court of Judiciary
PO Box 30155
Montgomery, AL 36103, USA

Patterson, Katerine (Writer)
70 Wildersburg Cmn
Barre, VT 05641-9761, USA

Patterson, Ken (Baseball Player)
Chicago White Sox
6723 Fish Pond Rd
Waco, TX 76710-2503, USA

Patterson, Lorna (Actor)
23852 Pacific Coast Hwy # 355
Malibu, CA 90265-4876, USA

Patterson, Marne (Actor)
c/o Matthew Lesher *Lesher Entertainment
Inc*
1134 S Cloverdale Ave
Los Angeles, CA 90019-6737, USA

Patterson, Melody (Actor)
MILLER SPECIALTIES
141 Sunny Ln
Branson West, MO 65737-9606, USA

Patterson, Michael (Financier)
JP Morgan Chase
270 Park Ave Fl 12
New York, NY 10017-7924, USA

Patterson, Mike (Baseball Player)
Oakland A's
19306 Chamblee Ave
Cerritos, CA 90703-6751, USA

Patterson, Neva
2498 Mandeville Canyon Rd
Los Angeles, CA 90049-1236, USA

Patterson, Percival J (Prime Minister)
Prime Minister's Office
1 Devon Road
PO Box 272
Kingston 6, JAMAICA

Patterson, Reggie (Baseball Player)
Chicago White Sox
7748 S Crest Tri
Bessemer, AL 35022, USA

Patterson, Richard North (Writer)
PO Box 183
West Tisbury, MA 02575-0183, USA

Patterson, Robert M (War Hero)
907 Ironwood Dr
Henderson, KY 42420-4866, USA

Patterson, Ross (Actor)
c/o Staff Member *Paradigm (LA)*
360 N Crescent Dr
North Bldg
Beverly Hills, CA 90210-6820, USA

Patterson, Scott (Actor)
c/o Laina Cohn *Relativity Management*
8899 Beverly Blvd Ste 510
Los Angeles, CA 90048-2449, USA

Patterson, Shawn (Football Player)
Green Bay Packers
15711 E Avenida Del Ville Ct
Chandler, AZ 85249, USA

Patterson, Willie (Baseball Player)
New York Cubans
409 Tuscaloosa Ave SW Apt 7
Birmingham, AL 35211-1457, USA

Pattillo, Linda (Correspondent)
Cable News Network
820 1st St NE
News Dept
Washington, DC 20002-4243, USA

Pattin, Marty (Baseball Player)
California Angels
3401 Sweetgrass Ct
Lawrence, KS 66049-4245, USA

Pattison, Mark (Football Player)
Los Angeles Rams
3828 48th Ave NE
Seattle, WA 98105-5227, USA

Patton, Antwon (Big Boi) (Artist, Music
Group, Musician)
c/o Charles King *William Morris Agency
(WMA-LA)*
1 William Morris Pl
Beverly Hills, CA 90212-4261, USA

Patton, Donovan (Actor)
c/o Staff Member *Glasser/Black
Management*
283 Cedarhurst Ave
Cedarhurst, NY 11516-1671, USA

Patton, Gene (Baseball Player)
Boston Barves
60 S 17th Ave
Coatesville, PA 19320-2566, USA

Patton, Jerry (Football Player)
Minnesota Vikings
219 N 12th St
Saginaw, MI 48601-1718, USA

Patton, Marvcus (Football Player)
Buffalo Bills
12994 Wyckland Dr
Clifton, VA 20124-2053, USA

Patton, Mel
2312 Via Del Aquacate
Fallbrook, CA 92028-9697, USA

Patton, Paula (Actor, Director)
c/o James Lassiter *Overbook
Entertainment*
450 N Roxbury Dr Fl 4
Beverly Hills, CA 90210-4232, USA

Patton, Tom (Baseball Player)
Baltimore Orioles
807 Reservoir Rd
Honey Brook, PA 19344-1334, USA

Patton, Will (Actor)
520 Washington Blvd # 903
Marina Del Rey, CA 90292, USA

Patty, Edward
14 Ave. de Jurigoz
Lausanne 1006, SWITZERLAND

Patty, J Edward (Budge) (Tennis Player)
La Mame
14 Ave de Jurigoz
Lausanne 1006, SWITZERLAND

Patty, Sandi
c/o Staff Member *Richard De La Font
Agency*
4845 S Sheridan Rd Ste 505
Tulsa, OK 74145-5719, USA

Patty, Sandi (Music Group, Musician)
Anderson Group
PO Box 6
Pendleton, IN 46064-0006, USA

Patu, Saul (Football Player)
Tennessee Titans
10234 Renton Ave S
Seattle, WA 98178-2347, USA

Patulski, Walter G (Walt) (Football
Player)
Buffalo Bills
420 Kimber Rd
Syracuse, NY 13224-1836, USA

Patz, Arnall (Doctor)
Johns Hopkins Hospital
Wilmer Eye Institute
600 N Wolfe
Baltimore, MD 21287-0001, USA

Patzaichin, Ivan (Athlete)
SC Sportiv Unirea Tricolor
Soseaua Stefan Cel Mare 9
Bucharest, ROMANIA

Patzak, PeterJosef
Schottlgasse 23
Klosterneuburg A-3400, AUSTRIA

Patzakis, Michele (Opera Singer)
Kunstleragentur Raab & Bohrn
Plandengasse 7
Vienna 1010, AUSTRIA

Pauk, Gyorgy (Musician)
27 Armitage Road
London NW11, UNITED KINGDOM (UK)

Paul, Aaron (Actor)
c/o Loch Powell *Leverage Management*
1610 Broadway
Santa Monica, CA 90404-2792, USA

Paul, Adrian (Actor)
15030 Ventura Blvd # 710
Sherman Oaks, CA 91403-5470, USA

Paul, Alan (Music Group, Musician)
Columbia/CBS Records
1801 Century Park W
Los Angeles, CA 90067-6409, USA

Paul, Alexandra (Actor)
c/o Daniel Sladek *Daniel Sladek
Entertainment Corporation*
8306 Wilshire Blvd # 510
Beverly Hills, CA 90211-2304, USA

Paul, Billy (Musician)
8215 Winthrop St
Philadelphia, PA 19136-1914, USA

Paul, Christi (Correspondent)
Cable News Network
1050 Techwood Dr NW
News Dept
Atlanta, GA 30318-5604, USA

Paul, Don (Football Player)
Los Angeles Rams
20100 Delita Dr
Woodland Hills, CA 91364-3519, USA

Paul, Don Michael (Actor, Director)
c/o Marc Korman *United Talent Agency
(UTA)*
9560 Wilshire Blvd Ste 500
Beverly Hills, CA 90212-2401, USA

Paul, Henry (Music Group, Musician)
Vector Mgmt
1607 17th Ave S
Nashville, TN 37212-2812, USA

Paul, Jarrad (Actor)
c/o JC Spink *Benderspink*
110 S Fairfax Ave Ste 350
Los Angeles, CA 90036-2179, USA

Paul, John Michael (Actor)
c/o Marc Korman *United Talent Agency
(UTA)*
9560 Wilshire Blvd Ste 500
Beverly Hills, CA 90212-2401, USA

Paul, Josh (Baseball Player)
Chicago White Sox
5682 Delano Ave
San Diego, CA 92120-2906, USA

Paul, Les (Inventor, Musician)
78 Deerhaven Rd
Mahwah, NJ 07430-2717, USA

Paul, Markus (Football Player)
Chicago Bears
PO Box 423041
Kissimmee, FL 34742-3041, USA

Paul, Mike (Baseball Player)
Cleveland Indians
5121 N Circulo Sobrio
Tucson, AZ 85718-6037, USA

Paul, Oakenfold (Musician)
PO Box 19788
London SW15 2FT, UNITED KINGDOM
(UK)

Paul, Robert (Figure Skater)
10675 Rochester Ave
Los Angeles, CA 90024-5009, USA

Paul, Vinnie (Musician)
Concrete Mgmt
361 W Broadway # 200
New York, NY 10013-2209, USA

Paul, Whitney (Football Player)
Kansas City Chiefs
6802 Thornwild Rd
Missouri City, TX 77489-2649, USA

Paul, Wolfgang (Soccer Player)
Postfach 1324
Olsberg-Bigge 59939, GERMANY

Paul & Paula
7251 Lowell Dr # 200
Overland Park, KS 66204-1840, USA

Paula, Alejandro F (Jandi) (Prime
Minister)
Primier's Office
Fort Amsterdam 17
Willemstad, NETHERLANDS ANTILLES

Paulauskas, Arturas (President)
President's Office
Gediminas 53
Vilnius 232026, LITHUANIA

Paulette, Pauley (Actor)
c/o Jeff Kolodny *William Morris Agency
(WMA-LA)*
1 William Morris Pl
Beverly Hills, CA 90212-4261, USA

Pauley, Jane (Correspondent)
c/o Staff Member *William Morris Agency
(WMA-NY)*
1325 Avenue Of The Americas
New York, NY 10019-6026, USA

Paulk, Jeff (Football Player)
Atlanta Falcons
7751 S Bonarden Ln
Tempe, AZ 85284-1569, USA

Paulo (DJ)
c/o Staff Member *Diva Central Inc*
7510 W Sunset Blvd Ste 1445
Los Angeles, CA 90046-3408, USA

Pauls, Raymond (Composer, Music
Group, Musician)
Veidenbaum Str 41/43 #26
Riga 226001, LATVIA

Paulsen, Robert (Rob) (Artist, Voice Over
Artist)
c/o Staff Member *Sutton Barth & Vennari
Inc*
145 S Fairfax Ave Ste 310
Los Angeles, CA 90036-2176, USA

Paulson, Carl (Golfer)
8211 Tibet Butler Dr
Windermere, FL 34786-5614, USA

Paulson, Dainard (Football Player)
New York Titans
2904 Main St
Union Gap, WA 98903-1756, USA

Paulson, Dennis (Golfer)
1721 Aryana Dr
Encinitas, CA 92024-1282, USA

Paulson, Richard L (Business Person)
Potlatch Corp
601 W Riverside Ave
Spokane, WA 99201-0621, USA

Paulson, Sarah (Actor)
c/o Joan Hyler *Hyler Management*
3000 Olympic Blvd Bldg 5 Ste 2250
Santa Monica, CA 90404-5073, USA

Paultz, Billy (Basketball Player)
7049 Spout Springs Rd
Flowery Branch, GA 30542-5538, USA

Paulusma, Polly (Musician)
c/o Staff Member *Paradigm (Monterey)*
509 Hartnell St
Monterey, CA 93940-2825, USA

Paup, Bryce E (Football Player)
1112 Moraine Way
Green Bay, WI 54303-9400, USA

Paupua, Tomasi (General, Governor)
Governor General's Office
Government House
Vaiaku
Funafuti, TUVALU

Pausini, Laura (Musician)
c/o Staff Member *Creative Artists Agency
LCC (CAA-LA)*
2000 Avenue Of The Stars
Los Angeles, CA 90067-4700, USA

Pavan, Marisa (Actor)
4 Allee des Brouillards
Paris 75018, FRANCE

Pavano, Carl (Baseball Player)
Montreal Expos
7900 Fairway Ln
West Palm Beach, FL 33412-2411, USA

Paven, Corey
2515 McKinney Ave # 10
Dallas, TX 75201-1908, USA

Paver, Michelle (Writer)
ILRM LLC
186 Bickenhall Mansions
London W1U 6BX, UNITED KINGDOM
(UK)

Pavia, Ria
3500 W Olive Ave Ste 1400
Burbank, CA 91505-5512, USA

Pavin, Corey (Golfer)
4332 Gilbert Ave
Dallas, TX 75219-2908, USA

Pavlas, David (Baseball Player)
Chicago Cubs
PO Box 1224
Shiner, TX 77984-1224, USA

Pavletic, Viaiko (President)
Presidential Palace
Pantovcak 241
Zagreb 10000, CROATIA

Pavletich, Don (Baseball Player)
Cincinnati Reds
13645 Adelaide Ln
Brookfield, WI 53005-4965, USA

Pavlik, Roger (Baseball Player)
Texas Rangers
622 Beaver Bend Rd
Houston, TX 77037-2004, USA

Pavlovic, Aleksandar (Basketball Player)
Utah Jazz
301 W South Temple
Delta Center
Salt Lake City, UT 84101-1216, USA

Pavlow, Muriel
2 Conduit St.
London, ENGLAND W1R 9TG, UNITED
KINGDOM (UK)

Pawelczyk, James A (Jim) (Astronaut)
NASA
2101 Nasa Pkwy
Johnson Space Center
Houston, TX 77058-3691, USA

Pawlowski, John (Baseball Player)
Chicago White Sox
257 Mill Branch Way
North Augusta, SC 29860-8622, USA

Pawlowski, Stan (Baseball Player)
Cleveland Indians
413 Maryjoe Way
Warrington, PA 18976-1695, USA

Paxman, Jeremy
56 Wood Lane
London, ENGLAND W12 7RJ, UNITED
KINGDOM (UK)

Paxon, L William (Bill) (Misc)
Akin Gump Strauss Hauer Feld
1333 New Hampshire Ave NW
Washington, DC 20036-1564, USA

Paxson, Jim (Basketball Player)
Cleveland Cavaliers
1 Center Ct
Gund Arena
Cleveland, OH 44115-4001, USA

Paxson, John (Basketball Player, Misc)
125 Boardman Ct
Lake Bluff, IL 60044-2454, USA

Paxson, Melanie (Actor)
c/o Staff Member *Brady Brannon & Rich*
5670 Wilshire Blvd Ste 820
Los Angeles, CA 90036-5613, USA

Paxton, Bill (Actor)
c/o Brian Swardstrom *Endeavor Agency
LLC (LA)*
9601 Wilshire Blvd Fl 3
Beverly Hills, CA 90210-5204, USA

Paxton, John (Editor)
Saint Martin's Press
175 5th Ave
New York, NY 10010-7848, USA

Paxton, Mike (Baseball Player)
Boston Red Sox
897 Deloach Ln
Collierville, TN 38017-6933, USA

Paxton, Sara (Actor)
c/o TJ Stein *Stein Entertainment Group*
1351 N Crescent Heights Blvd Apt 312
West Hollywood, CA 90046-4549, USA

Paxton, Tom (Music Group, Musician,
Songwriter, Writer)
Fleming Tamulevich Assoc
733 N Main St
Ann Arbor, MI 48104-1030, USA

Payette, Julie (Astronaut)
Space Agency
Rockliffe Base
Ottawa, ON K1A 1A1, CANADA

Paymer, David (Actor)
327 19th St
Santa Monica, CA 90402-2409, USA

Payne, Alexander (Actor, Director,
Producer, Writer)
c/o David Lonner *William Morris Agency
(WMA-LA)*
1 William Morris Pl
Beverly Hills, CA 90212-4261, USA

Payne, Alexaner (Writer)
c/o Staff Member *Endeavor Agency LLC (LA)*
9601 Wilshire Blvd Fl 3
Beverly Hills, CA 90210-5204, USA

Payne, Allen (Actor)
c/o Tom Harrison *Diverse Talent Group*
1875 Century Park E Ste 2250
Los Angeles, CA 90067-2563, USA

Payne, Anthony E (Composer)
2 Wilton Square
London N1 3DL, UNITED KINGDOM
(UK)

Payne, Barbara (Baseball Player)
15897 W Desert Meadow Dr
Surprise, AZ 85374-5636, USA

Payne, Bruce (Actor)
c/o Gordon Gilbertson *Gilbertson-Kincaid Management*
1334 3rd Street Promenade Ste 201
Santa Monica, CA 90401-1320, USA

Payne, Dougie (Musician)
Wildlife Entertainment
21 Heathmans Road
London SW6 4TJ, UNITED KINGDOM
(UK)

Payne, Freda (Music Group, Musician)
c/o Staff Member *Diva Central Inc*
7510 W Sunset Blvd Ste 1445
Los Angeles, CA 90046-3408, USA

Payne, Harry C (Educator)
Williams College
President's Office
Williamstown, MA 01267, USA

Payne, Henry (Cartoonist, Editor)
Detroit News
615 W Lafayette Blvd
Editorial Dept
Detroit, MI 48226-3142, USA

Payne, Julie (Actor)
c/o Staff Member *Pakula/King & Associates*
9229 W Sunset Blvd Ste 315
Los Angeles, CA 90069-3403, USA

Payne, Keith (War Hero)
2 Saint Bee's Ave
Bucasia, QLD 4740, AUSTRALIA

Payne, Ken (Football Player)
Green Bay Packers
307 W 108th Pl
Chicago, IL 60628-3344, USA

Payne, Ladell (Educator)
Randolph-Macon College
President's Office
Ashland, VA 23005, USA

Payne, Rod (Football Player)
Cincinnati Bengals
9622 Stonemasters Dr
Loveland, OH 45140-6209, USA

Payne, Scherrie-
433 N Camden Dr Ste 400
Beverly Hills, CA 90210-4408, USA

Payne, Seth (Football Player)
Jacksonville Jaguars
1765 Beach Ave
Atlantic Beach, FL 32233-5838, USA

Payne, Waylon (Actor, Musician)
c/o Ben Feigin *Nine Yards Entertainment*
8530 Wilshire Blvd Fl 5
Beverly Hills, CA 90211-3102, USA

Pays, Amanda (Actor)
c/o Staff Member *Personal Management Company*
425 N Robertson Blvd
West Hollywood, CA 90048-1735, USA

Payton, Benjamin F (Educator)
Tuskegee Institute
President's Office
Tuskegee, AL 36088, USA

Payton, Christian (Actor)
c/o Staff Member *William Morris Agency (WMA-LA)*
1 William Morris Pl
Beverly Hills, CA 90212-4261, USA

Payton, Eddie (Football Player)
Cleveland Browns
118 Woodland Hills Blvd
Madison, MS 39110-7820, USA

Payton, Gary (Basketball Player)
c/o Staff Member *Miami Heat*
601 Biscayne Blvd
American Airlines Arena
Miami, FL 33132-1801, USA

Payton, Gary E (Astronaut)
10140 Community Ln
Fairfax Station, VA 22039-2529, USA

Payton, Jay (Baseball Player)
New York Mets
3545 Mount Prospect Cir
Raleigh, NC 27614-7588, USA

payton, khary (Actor)
c/o Theodore B Gekis *Gekis Management*
4217 Verdugo View Dr
Los Angeles, CA 90065-4317, USA

Payton, Melvin (Basketball Player)
17310 River Ave
Noblesville, IN 46062-8526, USA

Payton, Nicholas (Musician)
Management Ark
116 Village Blvd Ste 200
Princeton, NJ 08540-5700, USA

Payton, Sean (Football Player)
Chicago Bears
Dallas Cowboys
1 Cowboys Pkwy Attn: Coaching Staff
Irving, TX 75063, USA

Pazienda, Vinnie
64 Waterman Ave
Cranston, RI 02910-4522, USA

Pazienza, Vinny (Boxer)
c/o Darren Prince *Prince Marketing Group*
454 Prospect Ave # 74
West Orange, NJ 07052, USA

Pazik, Mike (Baseball Player)
Minnesota Twins
8413 Comanche Ct
Bethesda, MD 20817-4533, USA

PC Quest
PO Box 720423
Norman, OK 73070-4310, USA

Peþa, Elizabeth (Actor)
c/o Staff Member *Rigberg-Rugolo Entertainment*
1180 S Beverly Dr Ste 601
Los Angeles, CA 90035-1158, USA

Peace, Larry (Football Player)
Brooklyn Dodgers
5278 S Hardwood Ter
Lecanto, FL 34461-9253, USA

Peace, Terry (Actor)
PO Box 74
Allison Park, PA 15101-0074, USA

Peace, Warren (Baseball Player)
Newark Eagles
27921 Nc Highway 903
Robersonville, NC 27871-8904, USA

Peaches & Herb
1560 Broadway # 1308
New York, NY 10036-1518, USA

Peacock, Andrew S (Government Official)
30 Monomeath Ave
Canterbury, VIC 3126, AUSTRALIA

Peacocke, Arthur R (Misc)
Society of Ordained Scientists
11 Summer St
St Mark's Rectory
Augusta, ME 04330-5128, USA

Peake, Don (Musician)
c/o Mike Rosen *Working Artists Agency*
13525 Ventura Blvd
Sherman Oaks, CA 91423-3801, USA

Peake, James B (General)
5109 Leesburg Pike
Sergeon General US Army
Falls Church, VA 22041-3215, USA

Peaker, E J (Actor)
4935 Densmore Ave
Encino, CA 91436-1537, USA

Peaks, Clarence (Football Player)
Philadelphia Eagles
2500 Knights Rd Apt 3-2
Creekside Apartments
Bensalem, PA 19020-3413, USA

Peaks, Pandora (Adult Film Star)
Photo Clubs
6011 Winterpointe Ln Apt 201
Raleigh, NC 27606-2278, USA

Pear, Dave (Football Player)
Baltimore Colts
3126 199th Ave SE
Sammamish, WA 98075-9652, USA

Pearce, Guy (Actor)
Shanahan Mgmt
PO Box 1509
Darlinghurst, NSW 1300, AUSTRALIA

Pearce, Jacqueline (Actor)
Rhubarb Personal Mgmt
6 Langley St #41
London WC2H 9JA, UNITED KINGDOM
(UK)

Pearce, Jim (Baseball Player)
Washington Senators
224 Clyde Pearce Rd
Zebulon, NC 27597-7779, USA

Pearce, Josh (Baseball Player)
St Louis Cardinals
2607 Draper Rd
Yakima, WA 98903-9216, USA

Pearce, Richard I (Director)
Bauer Co
9465 Wilshire Blvd
Beverly Hills, CA 90212-2612, USA

Pearcy, James W (Football Player)
Chicago Rockets
PO Box 609
Cobbs Creek, VA 23035-0609, USA

Pearl Jam (Musician)
c/o Donald (Don) Muller *Creative Artists Agency LCC (CAA-LA)*
2000 Avenue Of The Stars
Los Angeles, CA 90067-4700, USA

Pearlman, Rhea (Actor)
c/o Stan Rosenfield *Stan Rosenfield & Associates Ltd*
2029 Century Park E Ste 1190
Los Angeles, CA 90067-2931, USA

Pearlstein, Philip (Artist)
361 W 36th St
New York, NY 10018-6408, USA

Pearlstine, Norman (Editor)
Time Warner Inc
Rockefeller Plaza
Magazines Division
New York, NY 10020, USA

Pears, David F (Misc)
7 Sandford Road
Littlemore
Oxford OX4 4PU, UNITED KINGDOM
(UK)

Pearson, Albie (Baseball Player)
Washington Senators
55473 Oak Hi
La Quinta, CA 92253, USA

Pearson, Barry (Football Player)
Pittsburgh Steelers
85 Westledge Rd
West Simsbury, CT 06092-2327, USA

Pearson, Corey (Actor)
c/o Colton Gramm *Original Film*
284 N Saltair Ave
Los Angeles, CA 90049-2913, USA

Pearson, David
PO Box 8099
Spartanburg, SC 29305-8099, USA

Pearson, Drew (Football Player)
Dallas Cowboys
3721 Mount Vernon Way
Plano, TX 75025-3729, USA

Pearson, Durk
PO Box 1067
Hollywood, FL 33022, USA

Pearson, Jason (Baseball Player)
San Diego Padres
2373 Sunset Dr
Freeport, IL 61032-8348, USA

Pearson, Jayice (Football Player)
Kansas City Chiefs
721 SW Winterhill Ln
Lees Summit, MO 64081-2676, USA

Pearson, Larry (Race Car Driver)
12015 Lazy Willow Ln
Charlotte, NC 28273-6720, USA

Pearson, Lindell (Football Player)
Detroit Lions
5512 NW 114th St
Oklahoma City, OK 73162-3745, USA

Pearson, Preston (Football Player)
Baltimore Colts
9104 Moss Farm Ln
Dallas, TX 75243-7429, USA

Pearson, Terry (Baseball Player)
Detroit Tigers
3010 Wisteria Ln
Northport, AL 35473-8165, USA

Pearson-Tesseine, Dolly (Baseball Player)
1510A Canterbury Trl
Mount Pleasant, MI 48858-4002, USA

Pease, Patsy (Actor)
15432 Hartland St
Van Nuys, CA 91406-5216, USA

Peasgood, Julie (Actor)
c/o Staff Member *NCI Management Ltd*
51 Queen Ann Street
Floor 2
London W1G 9HS, UNITED KINGDOM
(UK)

Peatros, Maurice (Baseball Player)
Homestead Grays
8633 Copper Mine Ave
Las Vegas, NV 89129-7630, USA

Peay, Francis (Football Player)
New York Giants
PO Box 53877
Indianapolis, IN 46253-0877, USA

Peck, Austin (Actor)
c/o Lena Roklin *Roklin Management*
8530 Wilshire Blvd Ste 550
Beverly Hills, CA 90211-3133, USA

Peck, Ethan (Actor)
Buchwald Talent Group, LLC
6500 Wilshire Blvd Ste 2200
Los Angeles, CA 90048-4942, USA

Peck, J Eddie (Actor)
c/o Kim Dorr *Defining Artists*
10 Universal City Plz Ste 2000
Universal City, CA 91608-1074, USA

Peck, Josh (Actor)
c/o Staff Member *Metropolitan*
4500 Wilshire Blvd Fl 2
Los Angeles, CA 90010-3858, USA

Peck, M Scott (Writer)
RR 1
New Preston Marble Bliss Road
Washington Depot, CT 06793, USA

Peck, Tom
PO Box 249
Mc Connellsburg, PA 17233-0249, USA

Pecota, Bill (Baseball Player)
Kansas City Royals
332 NE Warrington Ct
Lees Summit, MO 64064-1605, USA

Pederson, Stu (Baseball Player)
Los Angeles Dodgers
45 Alannah Ct
Palo Alto, CA 94303-3009, USA

Pedre, Jorge (Baseball Player)
Kansas City Royals
7894 Bellflower Dr
Buena Park, CA 90620, USA

Pedrigue, Al (Baseball Player)
New York Mets
1702 E Saint Apollonia St
Tucson, AZ 85713-7400, USA

Peebles, Danny (Football Player)
Tampa Bay Buccaneers
12205 Fieldmist Dr
Raleigh, NC 27614-7539, USA

Peeler, Anthony (Basketball Player)
c/o Staff Member *Minnesota Timberwolves*
600 1st Ave N
Target Center
Minneapolis, MN 55403-1416, USA

Peeples, Nathaniel (Baseball Player)
Kansas City Monarchs
1275 Neptune St
Memphis, TN 38106-3311, USA

Peeples, Nia (Actor)
c/o Staff Member *Innovative Artists (LA)*
1505 10th St
Santa Monica, CA 90401-2805, USA

Peet, Amanda (Actor)
c/o Eric Kranzler *Management 360*
9111 Wilshire Blvd
Beverly Hills, CA 90210-5508, USA

Peet, Lizzie (Actor)
952 Maltman Ave Apt 108
Los Angeles, CA 90026-2754, USA

Peete, Calvin (Golfer)
128 Garden Gate Dr
Ponte Vedra Beach, FL 32082-3668, USA

Peete, Rodney (Football Player, Television Host)
c/o Staff Member *Best Damned Sports Show Period, The*
10201 W Pico Blvd
Fox Sports Net
Los Angeles, CA 90064-2606, USA

Peets, Brian (Football Player)
Seattle Seahawks
9500 Alta Mesa Rd
Wilton, CA 95693-9647, USA

Pegg, Simon (Actor)
c/o Hylda Queally *Creative Artists Agency LCC (CAA-LA)*
2000 Avenue Of The Stars
Los Angeles, CA 90067-4700, USA

Peggy, Baby (Montgomery)
7220 Durango Cir
Carlsbad, CA 92011-5114, USA

Pegler, Luke (Actor)
c/o Will Ward *ROAR LLC*
9701 Wilshire Blvd Fl 8
Beverly Hills, CA 90212-2008, USA

Pegram, Erric (Football Player)
Atlanta Falcons
2408 Keystone Dr
McKinney, TX 75070-7106, USA

Peguero, Julio (Baseball Player)
Philadelphia Phillies
1500 State Road 1
Socorro, NM 87801-5093, USA

Pegues, Steve (Baseball Player)
Cincinnati Reds
362 Presidents Dr
Pontotoc, MS 38863-2322, USA

Peguese, Willis (Football Player)
Houston Oilers
Hialeah-Miami Lakes High School 7977
W 12th Ave
Hialeah, FL 33014, USA

Pei, I M
600 Madison Ave
New York, NY 10022-1615, USA

Peirce, Kimberly Ane (Kim) (Director, Editor, Producer, Writer)
c/o Elizabeth (Beth) Swofford *Creative Artists Agency LCC (CAA-LA)*
2000 Avenue Of The Stars
Los Angeles, CA 90067-4700, USA

Peirse, Sarah (Actor)
c/o Dallas Smith *Peters Fraser & Dunlop (PFD - UK)*
Drury House
34-43 Russell St
London WC2B 5HA, UNITED KINGDOM
(UK)

Peizerat, Gwendal (Figure Skater)
c/o Staff Member *Champions on Ice*
3500 W 80th St
Tom Collins Enterprises Inc
Minneapolis, MN 55431-1068, USA

Pelaez, Alex (Baseball Player)
San Diego Padres
1501 Oleander Ave
Chula Vista, CA 91911-5623, USA

Pelaez, Juan (Actor)
c/o Staff Member *Televisa*
Blvd Adolfo Lopez Mateos 232
Colonia San Angel INN
DF CP 01060, MEXICO

Peldon, Ashley (Actor)
c/o Pamela Wagner *Metropolitan*
4500 Wilshire Blvd Fl 2
Los Angeles, CA 90010-3858, USA

Peldon, Courtney (Actor)
c/o Chuck Binder *Binder & Associates*
1465 Lindacrest Dr
Beverly Hills, CA 90210-2519, USA

Pele (Athlete, Soccer Player)
Rua Riachuelo 121-3
Andar-Fones 34-1633/35
Santos SP, BRAZIL

Pelfrey, Raymond (Football Player)
Green Bay Packers
1301 Summit St
Portsmouth, OH 45662-3719, USA

Pelikan, Lisa
PO Box 57593
Sherman Oaks, CA 91413-2593, USA

Pell, Claybourne (Ex-Senator, Senator)
45 Ledge Rd
Newport, RI 02840-4257, USA

Pellagrini, Eddie (Baseball Player)
Boston Red Sox
103 Webb St
Weymouth, MA 02188-2719, USA

Pellegrini, Bob
567 Roslaire Dr
Hummelstown, PA 17036-9165, USA

Pellegrini, Margaret
5018 N 61st Ave
Glendale, AZ 85301-7310, USA

Pellegrini, Robert (Football Player)
Philadelphia Eagles
1731 Route 9 Unit 97
Ocean View, NJ 08230-1388, USA

Pellegrino, Mark (Actor)
c/o Staff Member *Handprint Entertainment*
1100 Glendon Ave Ste 1000
Los Angeles, CA 90024-3514, USA

Pelley, Scott (Correspondent)
c/o Staff Member *20/20*
147 Columbus Ave
Abc
New York, NY 10023-6503, USA

Pellicano, Anthony
9200 W Sunset Blvd # 322
Los Angeles, CA 90069-3502, USA

Pellow, Kit (Baseball Player)
Kansas City Royals
2965 Long Bend Rd
Galena, MO 65656-4865, USA

Pellow, Marti (Musician)
c/o Staff Member *Solo Agency Ltd (UK)*
55 Fulham High St
London SW6 3JJ, UNITED KINGDOM
(UK)

Pelluer, Steve (Football Player)
Dallas Cowboys
1306 177th Ave NE
Bellevue, WA 98008-3208, USA

Pelphrey, Tom (Actor)
c/o Cyrena Esposito *Cyrena Esposito Management*
437 W 48th St Apt D
New York, NY 10036-1285, USA

Peltier, Dan (Baseball Player)
Texas Rangers
239 Lapp Rd
Clifton Park, NY 12065-6012, USA

Peltier, Leonard
PO Box 583
Lawrence, KS 66044-0583, USA

Peluce, Meeno
2713 N Keystone St
Burbank, CA 91504-1602, USA

Pelzer, Dave
PO Box 1846
Rancho Mirage, CA 92270-1081, USA

Pember, Dave (Baseball Player)
Milwaukee Brewers
8832 Mallow Dr
Knoxville, TN 37922-8004, USA

Pemberton, Brock (Baseball Player)
New York Mets
1402 N Elm St
Owasso, OK 74055-4926, USA

Pena, Alejandro (Baseball Player)
Los Angeles Dodgers
12635 Etris Rd
Roswell, GA 30075-1039, USA

Pena, Carlos (Baseball Player)
Texas Rangers
440 North Ave Apt 126
Haverhill, MA 01830-1531, USA

Pena, Federico Secy
3517 Sterling Ave
Alexandria, VA 22304-1834, USA

Pena, Jim (Baseball Player)
San Francisco Giants
3228 E Silverwood Dr
Phoenix, AZ 85048-7257, USA

Pena, Jose
A. Flores #1116 NTE C Jiquilpan
Los Mochia Sinoloa, MEXICO

Pena, Michael (Actor)
c/o Staff Member *Art Work Entertainment*
5900 Wilshire Blvd Ste 2150
Los Angeles, CA 90036-5021, USA

Pena, Orlando (Baseball Player)
Cincinnati Reds
1750 W 46th St Apt 416
Hialeah, FL 33012-2849, USA

Pena, Robert (Football Player)
Cleveland Browns
77 John Parker Rd
East Falmouth, MA 02536-5116, USA

Penaranda, Jairo (Football Player)
Los Angeles Rams
2023 Lloyd Ctr
Portland, OR 97232-1314, USA

Penchion, Bob (Football Player)
Buffalo Bills
315 County Road 266
Town Creek, AL 35672-3939, USA

Pender, Mel
4910 Karls Gate Dr
Marietta, GA 30068-1629, USA

Pendergrass, Teddy (Athlete)
1505 Flat Rock Rd
Penn Valley, PA 19072-1227, USA

Pendleton, Austin
155 E 76th St
New York, NY 10021-2810, USA

Pendleton, Terry (Baseball Player)
332 Grassmeade Way
Snellville, GA 30078-7782, USA

Penfold, James (Model)
c/o Staff Member *DNA Model Management*
520 Broadway Fl 11
New York, NY 10012-4436, USA

Penghlis, Thaao (Actor)
c/o Christopher Barrett *Metropolitan*
4500 Wilshire Blvd Fl 2
Los Angeles, CA 90010-3858, USA

Penguins, The
24210 E East Fork Rd Spc 9
Azusa, CA 91702-6249, USA

Penhaligon, Susan
109 Jermyn St
London, ENGLAND SW1, UNITED KINGDOM (UK)

Peniche, Arturo (Actor)
c/o Staff Member *Televisa*
Blvd Adolfo Lopez Mateos 232
Colonia San Angel INN
DF CP 01060, MEXICO

Penick, Trevor (Musician)
Trans Continental Records
7380 W Sand Lake Rd # 350
Orlando, FL 32819-5248, USA

Penikett, Tahmoh (Actor)
c/o Deb Dillistone *Lucas Talent Inc*
Sun Tower Floor 7
100 W Pender St
Vancouver, BC V6B 1R8, CANADA

Peniston, Ce Ce
250 W 57th St # 821
New York, NY 10107-0001, USA

Peniston, CeCe (Musician)
c/o Staff Member *Diva Central Inc*
7510 W Sunset Blvd Ste 1445
Los Angeles, CA 90046-3408, USA

Penn, Arthur H (Director)
William Morris Agency
151 El Camino Dr
Beverly Hills, CA 90212-2775, USA

Penn, Chris (Football Player)
Kansas City Chiefs
PO Box 123
S Coffeyville, OK 74072-0123, USA

Penn, Irving (Photographer)
Irving Penn Studio
89 5th Ave
New York, NY 10003-3020, USA

Penn, Jesse (Football Player)
Dallas Cowboys
8420 Wildcreek Dr
Plano, TX 75025-4150, USA

Penn, (Jillette) (Comedian)
William Morris Agency
151 El Camino Dr
Beverly Hills, CA 90212-2775, USA

Penn, Kal (Actor)
c/o Daniel (Dan) Spilo *Artistry Management*
525 Westbourne Dr
West Hollywood, CA 90048-1913, USA

Penn, Sean (Actor, Director)
c/o Brian Gersh *Blue Train Entertainment*
798 Brooktree Rd
Pacific Palisades, CA 90272-3901, USA

Penn, Shannon (Baseball Player)
Detroit Tigers
1548 Jonathan Ave # 2
Cincinnati, OH 45207-1449, USA

Penn & Teller (Comedian, Live Show)
c/o Jennifer Craig *Gersh Agency, The (LA)*
232 N Canon Dr
Beverly Hills, CA 90210-5302, USA

Pennacchio, Len A (Misc)
Stanford University
Human Genome Center
Stanford, CA 94305, USA

Pennario, Leonard (Musician)
Columbia Artists Mgmt Inc
1790 Broadway Fl 6
New York, NY 10019-1412, USA

Pennebaker, Ed (Artist)
428 County Road 9351
Green Forest, AR 72638-9764, USA

Pennell, Larry
15516 W Sunset Blvd Apt 101
Pacific Palisades, CA 90272-3542, USA

Penner, Jonathan (Actor)
Writers & Artists
360 N Crescent Dr Bldg North
Beverly Hills, CA 90210-6818, USA

Pennington, Ann
701 N Oakhurst Dr
Beverly Hills, CA 90210-3532, USA

Pennington, Art (Baseball Player)
Chicago American Giants
922 5th St SE Apt E5
Cedar Rapids, IA 52401-2440, USA

Pennington, Brad (Baseball Player)
Baltimore Orioles
7220 E State Road 160
Salem, IN 47167-7856, USA

Pennington, Chad (Athlete, Football Player)
c/o Team Member *New York Jets*
1000 Fulton Ave
Hempstead, NY 11550-1030, USA

Pennington, Janice (Actor, Model)
PO Box 11402
Beverly Hills, CA 90213-4402, USA

Pennington, Julia
PO Box 5617
Beverly Hills, CA 90209-5617, USA

Pennington, Michael (Actor)
Marmont Mgmt
Langham House
302/8 Regent St
London W1R 5AL, UNITED KINGDOM (UK)

Pennington, T Durwood (Football Player)
Dallas Texans
480 Peninsula Rd
Gainesville, GA 30506-1705, USA

Pennington, Ty (Actor)
Extreme Lock and Key Productions
1149 S Gower St #10
Los Angeles, CA 90038, USA

Pennison, Jay (Football Player)
Houston Oilers
3007 W Autumn Run Cir
Sugar Land, TX 77479-2624, USA

Pennock, Chris (Actor)
25150 1/2 Malibu Rd
Malibu, CA 90265-4639, USA

Pennock of Norton, Raymond (Business Person)
Morgan Grenfell Group
23 Great Winchester St
London EC2P 2AX, UNITED KINGDOM (UK)

Penny, Brad (Baseball Player)
Florida Marlins
13758 NW 19th St
Pembroke Pines, FL 33028, USA

Penny, Joe (Actor)
c/o Deborah Miller *Deborah Miller & Company Management*
427 N Canon Dr Ste 215
Beverly Hills, CA 90210-4840, USA

Penny, Roger P (Business Person)
Bethlehem Steel
1 E Broad St Ste 210
Bethlehem, PA 18018-5951, USA

Penny, Sudney (Actor)
Baker/Winokur/Ryder
9100 Wilshire Blvd # 600
Beverly Hills, CA 90212-3401, USA

Penny, Sydney (Actor)
c/o Bob McGowan *McGowan Management*
8733 W Sunset Blvd Ste 103
W Hollywood, CA 90069-2241, USA

Pennyfeather, Will (Baseball Player)
Pittsburgh Pirates
31 S 2nd Ave Apt 8B
Mount Vernon, NY 10550-3429, USA

Penny's
3220 Altura Ave Apt 106
La Crescenta, CA 91214-3304, USA

Pennywell, Carlos (Football Player)
New England Patriots
3729 Clover Dr
Arcadia, LA 71001-3628, USA

Pennywell, Robert (Football Player)
Atlanta Falcons
1523 Staring Ln
Baton Rouge, LA 70810-1458, USA

Penot, Jacques
9 rue de l'Isly
Paris F-75008, FRANCE

Penrose, Craig R (Football Player)
Denver Broncos
1609 Camino Way
Woodland, CA 95695-5517, USA

Penske, Roger S (Race Car Driver)
Penske Racing
200 Penske Way
Mooresville, NC 28115-8022, USA

Penson, Paul (Baseball Player)
Philadelphia Phillies
711 Lake Of The Frst
Bonner Springs, KS 66012-9543, USA

Pentecost, Del (Actor)
c/o Staff Member *Paradigm (LA)*
360 N Crescent Dr
North Bldg
Beverly Hills, CA 90210-6820, USA

Penthouse Pets
277 Park Ave
New York, NY 10172-0003, USA

Pentland, Alex P (Scientist)
Massachusetts Institute of Technology
Media Laboratory
Cambridge, MA 02139, USA

Pentz, Gene (Baseball Player)
Detroit Tigers
207 Rainbow Dr
Johnstown, PA 15904-2253, USA

Penzias, Arno A (Nobel Prize Laureate)
AT & T Bell Laboratories
600 Mountain Ave
New Providence, NJ 07974-2008, USA

People, Village (Musician)
c/o Staff Member *William Morris Agency (WMA-LA)*
1 William Morris Pl
Beverly Hills, CA 90212-4261, USA

Peoples, David (Golfer)
6115 S Hampshire Ct
Windermere, FL 34786-5623, USA

Peoples, John (Physicist)
Fermi Nat Acceleration Lab
PO Box 500
Cdf Collaboration
Batavia, IL 60510-5011, USA

Peoples, Woodrow (Woody) (Football Player)
San Fransisco 49ers
1810 Eulaula Ave
Birmingham, AL 35208, USA

Pepitone, Joseph A (Joe) (Baseball Player)
New York Yankees
32 Lois Ln
Farmingdale, NY 11735-6003, USA

Peplinski, Jim (Hockey Player)
Peplinski Auto Leasing
212 Meridian Road NE
Calgary, AB T2A 2N6, CANADA

Peppas, June (Baseball Player)
1700 NE Indian River Dr Apt 302
Jensen Beach, FL 34957-5860, USA

Pepper, Barry (Actor)
Paul Kohner
9300 Wilshire Blvd Ste 555
Beverly Hills, CA 90212-3211, USA

Pepper, Cynthia
219 Friendly Ct
Henderson, NV 89052-5660, USA

Pepper, Don (Baseball Player)
Detroit Tigers
7 Beckenham Ln
Greenville, SC 29609-6023, USA

Pepper, Dottie (Golfer)
c/o Staff Member *Ladies Pro Golf Association (LPGA)*
100 International Golf Dr
Daytona Beach, FL 32124-1082, USA

Pepper, Dottle (Golfer)
131 Echo Dr
Jupiter, FL 33458-7735, USA

Pepper, Gene (Football Player)
Washington Redskins
105 Park Ridge Dr
O Fallon, MO 63366-1087, USA

Pepper, Laurin (Baseball Player)
Pittsburgh Pirates
8932 Davis St
Ocean Springs, MS 39564-3633, USA

Peppers, Julius (Football Player)
c/o Staff Member *Carolina Panthers*
800 S Mint St
Ericsson Stadium
Charlotte, NC 28202-1640, USA

Peppler, Mary Jo (Volleyball Player)
Coast Volleyball Club
11526 Sorrento Valley Rd
San Diego, CA 92121-1346, USA

Perabo, Piper (Actor)
c/o Tina Thor *TMT Entertainment Group*
648 Broadway # 1002
New York, NY 10012-2301, USA

Perak, Sultan of (King)
Sultan's Palace
Istana Bukit Serene
Kula Lumpur, MALAYSIA

Perakis, Nicos
Isabellastr. 19
Munich D-80798, GERMANY

Peralta, Ricardo (Astronaut)
Ingeneria Instituto
Ciudad Universitaria
Mexico City, DF 04510, MEXICO

Peranoski, Ron (Baseball Player)
Los Angeles Dodgers
3805 Indian River Dr E
Vero Beach, FL 32963-1404, USA

Perayra, Marianela (Television Host)
c/o Michael (Mike) Esterman *Esterman Entertainment*
214 Park Rd
Riva, MD 21140-1224, USA

Percival, Lance (Actor)
PVA 2 High St
Westbury-on-Trim
Bristol BS9 3DU, UNITED KINGDOM (UK)

Percival, Mac (Football Player)
Chicago Bears
6710 Flowermound Dr
Sugar Land, TX 77479-6000, USA

Percival, Troy E (Baseball Player)
28920 Greick Dr
Moreno Valley, CA 92555, USA

Perconte, Jack (Baseball Player)
Los Angeles Dodgers
6197 Hinterlong Ct
Lisle, IL 60532-2818, USA

Percy, Charles H (Ex-Senator, Senator)
10450 Lottsford Rd Apt 5014
Bowie, MD 20721-3301, USA

Perdue, Will (Basketball Player)
3332 SE Salmon St
Portland, OR 97214-4267, USA

Perec, Marie-Jose (Athlete, Track Athlete)
Federacion d'Athletisme
10 Rue du Fg Poissonniere
Paris 75480, FRANCE

Peregrym, Missy
c/o Jai Khanna *Brillstein-Grey Entertainment*
9150 Wilshire Blvd Ste 350
Beverly Hills, CA 90212-3453, USA

Pereira, Aristides M (President)
PO Box 172
Praia, CAPE VERDE

Pereira, Jose (Baseball Player)
Baltimore Elite Giants
1738 Lexington Ave Apt 12H
New York, NY 10029-3520, USA

Perelman, Ronald O (Business Person)
MacAndrews & Forbes
35 E 62nd St
New York, NY 10065-8014, USA

Perelman, Vadim (Director)
c/o Simon Millar *The Firm*
9465 Wilshire Blvd Fl 6
Beverly Hills, CA 90212-2605, USA

Perenyi, Miklos (Musician)
Erdoalja Utca 1/B
Budapest 1037, HUNGARY

Peres, Shimon (Nobel Prize Laureate)
Aenot Law House
8 Shaul Hamelech Blvd
Tel Aviv 64733, ISRAEL

Peretokin, Mark (Dancer)
Bolshoi Theater
Teatralnaya Pl 1
Moscow 103009, RUSSIA

Perez, Atanasio (Baseball Player)
1717 N Bayshore Dr Apt 2735
Miami, FL 33132-1163, USA

Perez, Chris (Musician)
Big FD Entertainment
301 Arizona Ave Ste 200
Santa Monica, CA 90401-1364, USA

Perez, Danny (Baseball Player)
Milwaukee Brewers
319 Kensington Lake Cir Apt C-1
Brandon, FL 33511-3871, USA

Perez, Eddie (Baseball Player)
c/o Staff Member *Atlanta Braves*
PO Box 4064
Turner Field
Atlanta, GA 30302-4064, USA

Perez, Eduardo (Baseball Player)
California Angels
113 Calle Las Flores
Santurce, PR 00911-2298, USA

Perez, George (Baseball Player)
Pittsburgh Pirates
218 S Dewey Ave
Newbury Park, CA 91320-5075, USA

Perez, Hugo (Soccer Player)
22018 Newbridge Dr
Lake Forest, CA 92630-6511, USA

Perez, Luiz (Louie) (Musician)
Gold Mountain
3575 Cahuenga Blvd W Ste 450
Los Angeles, CA 90068-1364, USA

Perez, Marty (Baseball Player)
California Angels
30 Willowick Dr
Lithonia, GA 30038-1722, USA

Perez, Mike (Baseball Player)
St Louis Cardinals
800 Kylewood Pl
Ballwin, MO 63021-4796, USA

Perez, Odalis A (Baseball Player)
Los Angeles Dodgers
1000 Elysian Park Ave
Stadium
Los Angeles, CA 90012-1199, USA

Perez, Oliver (Baseball Player)
c/o Staff Member *Pittsburgh Pirates*
115 Federal St
Pnc Park
Pittsburgh, PA 15212-5740, USA

Perez, Pascual (Baseball Player)
Pittsburgh Pirates
7021 NW 70th St
Parkland, FL 33067-1486, USA

Perez, Rosie (Actor)
c/o Jason Weinberg *Untitled Entertainment (LA)*
331 N Maple Dr Fl 3
Beverly Hills, CA 90210-3827, USA

Perez, Scott (Cartoonist)
DC Comics
1700 Broadway
New York, NY 10019-5914, USA

Perez, Timothy Paul (Actor)
Badgley Connor Talent
1680 Vine St Ste 1016
Los Angeles, CA 90028-8800, USA

Perez, Tony (Baseball Player)
Cincinnati Reds
113 Calle Las Flores Apt B
San Juan, PR 00911-2298, USA

Perez, Vincent (Actor)
Artmedia
20 Ave Rapp
Paris 75007, FRANCE

Perez-Brown, Maria (Producer)
c/o Staff Member *William Morris Agency (WMA-LA)*
1 William Morris Pl
Beverly Hills, CA 90212-4261, USA

Perez de Cuellar, Javier (General, Secretary)
Avenida A Miro Quesada
Lima 1071, PERU

Perez Esquivel, Adolfo (Nobel Prize Laureate)
Servicio Paz y Justicia
Piedras 730
Buenos Aires 1070, ARGENTINA

Perez Fernandez, Pedro (Government Official)
PSOE
Ferraz 68 y 70
Madrid 28008, SPAIN

Perez Limon, Iyari (Actor)
c/o Mitchell Stubbs *Mitchell K Stubbs & Assoc (MKS)*
8695 Washington Blvd Ste 204
Culver City, CA 90232-7419, USA

Perezchica, Tony (Baseball Player)
San Francisco Giants
79220 Victoria Dr
La Quinta, CA 92253-4274, USA

Pergine, John (Football Player)
Los Angeles Rams
5 Jody Dr
Plymouth Meeting, PA 19462-2625, USA

Perick, Christof (Conductor)
Kaylor Mgmt
130 W 57th St Apt 8G
New York, NY 10019-3311, USA

Perishers, The (Music Group)
c/o Staff Member *Paradigm (Monterey)*
509 Hartnell St
Monterey, CA 93940-2825, USA

Perisho, Matt (Baseball Player)
Anaheim Angels
1462 W Cardinal Way
Chandler, AZ 85286-4379, USA

Periyar, Dasan (Actor)
30 Muthaiappa Street
Shenoy Nagar
Chennai, TN 600 030, INDIA

Perkins, Broderick (Baseball Player)
San Diego Padres
10024 Jacoby Rd
Spring Valley, CA 91977-6509, USA

Perkins, Bruce (Football Player)
Tampa Bay Buccaneers
19014 E Ryan Rd
Queen Creek, AZ 85242-6877, USA

Perkins, Cecil (Baseball Player)
New York Yankees
711 Cushwa Rd
Martinsburg, WV 25403-1228, USA

Perkins, Dan (Baseball Player)
Minnesota Twins
7720 SW 61st Ave
South Miami, FL 33143-5016, USA

Perkins, Donald A (Football Player)
Dallas Cowboys
808 Vassar Dr NE
Albuquerque, NM 87106-2726, USA

Perkins, Edward J (Diplomat)
State Department
2201 C St NW
Washington, DC 20520-0099, USA

Perkins, Elivs (Musician)
c/o Staff Member *Paradigm (Monterey)*
509 Hartnell St
Monterey, CA 93940-2825, USA

Perkins, Elizabeth (Actor)
c/o Leslie Siebert *Gersh Agency, The (LA)*
232 N Canon Dr
Beverly Hills, CA 90210-5302, USA

Perkins, John M (Activist)
1655 St Charles St
Jackson, MS 39209-5404, USA

Perkins, Johnny (Football Player)
New York Giants
5320 Fairway Cir
Granbury, TX 76049-5184, USA

Perkins, Kathleen Rose (Actor)
c/o Devon Jackson *Trademark Talent*
4758 Allott Ave
Sherman Oaks, CA 91423-2403, USA

Perkins, Kendrick (Basketball Player)
Boston Celtics
151 Merrimac St # 1
Boston, MA 02114-4714, USA

Perkins, Lucian (Journalist)
3103 17th St NW
Washington, DC 20010-2701, USA

Perkins, Millie (Actor)
2511 Canyon Dr
Los Angeles, CA 90068-2415, USA

Perkins, Oz
7720 W Sunset Blvd
Los Angeles, CA 90046-3962, USA

Perkins, Tex (Musician)
Stack/Polydor Records
70 Universal City Plz
Universal City, CA 91608-1011, USA

Perkins, W Ray (Coach, Football Coach, Football Player)
Baltimore Colts
57 Honors Ln
Hattiesburg, MS 39402-7100, USA

Perkins Jr, Lawrence B (Architect)
Perkins Eastman Partners
437 5th Ave
New York, NY 10016-2205, USA

Perkoff, Gerald T (Doctor)
1300 Torrey Pines Dr
Columbia, MO 65203-4826, USA

Perkowski, Harry (Baseball Player)
Cincinnati Reds
211 McGinnis St
Beckley, WV 25801-5725, USA

Perks, Craig (Golfer)
321 Thibodeaux Dr
Lafayette, LA 70503-4444, USA

Perl, Frank J (Cinematographer)
5020 Biloxi Ave
North Hollywood, CA 91601-4140, USA

Perl, Martin L (Nobel Prize Laureate)
3737 El Centro St
Palo Alto, CA 94306-2642, USA

Perle, George (Composer)
Queens College
Music Dept
Flushing, NY 11367, USA

Perley, James (Misc)
American Assn of University Professors
1012 14th St NW
Washington, DC 20005-3465, USA

Perlich, Max (Actor)
c/o Staff Member *Metropolitan*
4500 Wilshire Blvd Fl 2
Los Angeles, CA 90010-3858, USA

Perlick-Keating, Edythe (Baseball Player)
3051 S Palm Aire Dr Bldg 34
Pompano Beach, FL 33069-4277, USA

Perlman, Itzhak (Conductor, Musician)
I M G Artists
420 W 45th St
New York, NY 10036-3503, USA

Perlman, Jon (Baseball Player)
Chicago Cubs
3225 Bryn Mawr Dr
Dallas, TX 75225-7646, USA

Perlman, Lawrence (Business Person)
Ceridian Corp
3311 E Old Shakopee Rd
Minneapolis, MN 55425-1640, USA

Perlman, Phil
439 S Catalina Ave Apt 102
Pasadena, CA 91106-3343, USA

Perlman, Rhea (Actor)
PO Box 491246
Los Angeles, CA 90049-9246, USA

Perlman, Ron (Actor)
Kritzer Entertainment
12200 W Olympic Blvd Ste 400
Los Angeles, CA 90064-1047, USA

Perlozzo, Sam (Baseball Player)
Minnesota Twins
18101 Emerald Bay St
Tampa, FL 33647-3316, USA

Perls, Tom (Misc)
2 Harrington Ln
Weston, MA 02493-1355, USA

Perme, Len (Baseball Player)
Chicago White Sox
3350 D St
Hayward, CA 94541-4590, USA

Perner, Wolfgang (Athlete)
Schildlehen 29
ramsau-D 8972, AUSTRIA

Pernice, Tom Jr (Golfer)
38390 Shoal Creek Dr
Murrieta, CA 92562-3069, USA

Pero, Perry R (Financier)
Northern Trust Corp
50 S La Salle St
Chicago, IL 60675-0001, USA

Peron, Isabelita Martinez de (President)
Moreto 3
Los Jeronimos
Madrid 28014, SPAIN

Perot, Pete (Football Player)
Philadelphia Eagles
2401 Hillside Rd
Ruston, LA 71270-2093, USA

Perot, Ross H (Business Person)
c/o Staff Member *Perot Group*
2300 W Plano Pkwy
Plano, TX 75075-8427, USA

Perot Jr, Henry Ross (Business Person)
c/o Staff Member *Perot Group*
2300 W Plano Pkwy
Plano, TX 75075-8427, USA

Perranoski, Ron
3805 Indian River Dr
Vero Beach, FL 32963-1404, USA

Perreau, Gigi (Actor)
5841 Cantaloupe Ave
Van Nuys, CA 91401-4311, USA

Perreault, Gilbert (Gil) (Hockey Player)
4 Rue de la Serenite
Victoriaville, PQ G6P 6S2, CANADA

Perreault, Pete (Football Player)
New York Jets
7540 Sunshine Skyway Ln S
Saint Petersburg, FL 33711-5115, USA

Perrella, James E (Business Person)
Ingersoll-Rand Co
155 Chestnut Ridge Rd
Montvale, NJ 07645-1115, USA

Perretta, Ralph (Football Player)
San Diego Chargers
1305 Calle Scott
Encinitas, CA 92024-5532, USA

Perrette, Pauley (Actor)
c/o Jeff Kolodny *William Morris Agency
(WMA-LA)*
1 William Morris Pl
Beverly Hills, CA 90212-4261, USA

Perrier, Mireille (Actor)
Cineart
36 Rue de Ponthieu
Paris 75008, FRANCE

Perrin, Benny (Football Player)
St Louis Cardinals
2509 Burningtree Dr SE
Decatur, AL 35603-5138, USA

Perrin, Lonnie (Football Player)
Denver Broncos
7809 Green St
Clinton, MD 20735-1973, USA

Perrin, Philippe (Astronaut)
11923 Mighty Redwood Dr
Houston, TX 77059-5542, USA

Perrine, Valerie (Actor)
c/o Staff Member *Bensky Entertainment*
15030 Ventura Blvd # 343
Sherman Oaks, CA 91403-5470, USA

Perrineau Jr, Harold (Actor)
c/o Ryan Martin *Agency for the
Performing Arts (APA-LA)*
405 S Beverly Dr
Beverly Hills, CA 90212-4416, USA

Perrineau Jr, Harry (Actor)
Creative Artists Agency
9830 Wilshire Blvd
Beverly Hills, CA 90212-1804, USA

Perron, Jean (Coach)
5 Thomas Mellon Cir
San Francisco, CA 94134-2501, USA

Perrotta, Tom (Writer)
Saint Martin's Press
175 5th Ave
New York, NY 10010-7848, USA

Perry, Anne (Writer)
Turn Vawr
Seafield Postmahomack
Rosshire IV20 1RE, SCOTLAND

Perry, Barbara
6926 La Presa Dr
Los Angeles, CA 90068-3103, USA

Perry, Barry W (Business Person)
Engelhard Corp
101 Wood Ave S
Iselin, NJ 08830-2703, USA

Perry, Bob (Baseball Player)
Los Angeles Angels
621 Fox Chase Vig
New Bern, NC 28562, USA

Perry, Chan (Baseball Player)
Cleveland Indians
788 NE County Road 353
Mayo, FL 32066-5450, USA

Perry, Charles O (Artist)
20 Shorehaven Rd
Norwalk, CT 06855-2807, USA

Perry, Chris (Golfer)
170 Valley Run Dr
Powell, OH 43065-9454, USA

Perry, Darren (Football Player)
Pittsburgh Steelers
6451 Pinehurst Ln
Mason, OH 45040-2051, USA

Perry, Ed (Football Player)
Miami Dolphins
1583 SW 161st Ave
Pembroke Pines, FL 33027-5140, USA

Perry, Felton (Actor)
PO Box 931359
Los Angeles, CA 90093-1359, USA

Perry, Fletcher (Joe) (Football Player)
1644 E Chicago St
Chandler, AZ 85225-5796, USA

Perry, Gaylord J (Baseball Player)
San Francisco Giants
PO Box 489
Spruce Pine, NC 28777-0489, USA

Perry, Gerald (Baseball Player)
Atlanta Braves
1348 Waterford Green Close
Marietta, GA 30068-2919, USA

Perry, Gerald (Football Player)
Denver Broncos
2940 Dell Dr
Columbia, SC 29209-4906, USA

Perry, Gerald E (Football Player)
Detroit Lions
336 5th St
Manhattan Beach, CA 90266-5712, USA

Perry, Herbert (Baseball Player)
Cleveland Indians
353 SW Lincoln Rd
Mayo, FL 32066-4030, USA

Perry, James E (Jim) (Baseball Player)
Cleveland Indians
2608 S Ridgeview Way
Sioux Falls, SD 57105-4220, USA

Perry, Jeff (Actor)
2029 Century Park E Ste 1060
Los Angeles, CA 90067-2919, USA

Perry, Joe (Musician, Songwriter, Writer)
c/o Staff Member *Paradigm (Monterey)*
509 Hartnell St
Monterey, CA 93940-2825, USA

Perry, John Bennett (Actor)
Judy Schoen
606 N Larchmont Blvd Ste 309
Los Angeles, CA 90004-1309, USA

Perry, John R (Misc)
Stanford University
Language & Information Study Center
Stanford, CA 94305, USA

Perry, Kenny (Golfer)
418 Quail Ridge Rd
Franklin, KY 42134-9650, USA

Perry, Leon (Football Player)
New York Giants
RR 1 Box 195A
Gloster, MS 39638, USA

Perry, Luke (Actor)
c/o Steve Himber *Himber Entertainment
Inc*
15760 Ventura Blvd Ste 700
Encino, CA 91436-3016, USA

Perry, Matthew (Actor)
c/o Peter Levine *Creative Artists Agency
LCC (CAA-LA)*
2000 Avenue Of The Stars
Los Angeles, CA 90067-4700, USA

Perry, Michael Dean (Football Player)
Cleveland Browns
PO Box 221771
Charlotte, NC 28222-1771, USA

Perry, Nickolas (Director, Writer)
William Morris Agency
151 El Camino Dr
Beverly Hills, CA 90212-2775, USA

Perry, Pat (Baseball Player)
St Louis Cardinals
1115 W Franklin St
Taylorville, IL 62568-2037, USA

Perry, Rachel (Actor)
c/o Staff Member *Envision Entertainment*
9255 W Sunset Blvd Ste 500
West Hollywood, CA 90069-3301, USA

Perry, Rod (Football Player)
Los Angeles Rams
PO Box 532551
Indianapolis, IN 46253-2551, USA

Perry, Ruth (Prime Minister)
Prime Minister's Office
Capitol Hill
Monrovia, LIBERIA

Perry, Scott (Football Player)
Cincinatti Bengals
3708 S Dolphin St
San Pedro, CA 90731-6020, USA

Perry, Steve (Director, Producer)
c/o Staff Member *DH1 Studios*
8730 W Sunset Blvd Fl 6
West Hollywood, CA 90069-2210, USA

Perry, Steve (Musician)
c/o Staff Member *William Morris Agency (WMA-LA)*
1 William Morris Pl
Beverly Hills, CA 90212-4261, USA

Perry, Todd (Football Player)
Chicago Bears
13805 Brittle Rd
Alpharetta, GA 30004-3577, USA

Perry, Troy D (Religious Leader)
Metropolitan Churches Fellowship
5300 Santa Monica Blvd
Los Angeles, CA 90029-1131, USA

Perry, Tyler (Actor, Producer, Writer)
c/o Charles King *William Morris Agency (WMA-LA)*
1 William Morris Pl
Beverly Hills, CA 90212-4261, USA

Perry, Vernon (Football Player)
Houston Oilers
PO Box 842201
Houston, TX 77284-2201, USA

Perry, William A (Football Player)
Chicago Bears
349 Kershaw St NE
Aiken, SC 29801-4432, USA

Perry, Wilmont (Football Player)
New Orleans Saints
1757 W River Rd
Franklinton, NC 27525-8293, USA

Perry, Yvonne (Actor)
As World Turns Show
524 W 57th St
Cbs-Tv
New York, NY 10019-2930, USA

Perryman, Jill
4 Hillside Crescent
Gooseberry Hill 6076 W Aus,
AUSTRALIA

Perryman, Jim (Football Player)
Buffalo Bills
2345 Southwood Dr
Pittsburgh, PA 15241-3344, USA

Perryman, Robert (Football Player)
New England Patriots
PO Box 8543
Haverhill, MA 01835-0985, USA

Perschy, Maria
Maxingstr. 30
Vienna 1130, AUSTRIA

Persoff, Nahemiah (Actor)
5670 Moonstone Beach Dr
Cambria, CA 93428-2210, USA

Persoff, Nehemiah (Actor)
5847 Tampa Ave
Tarzana, CA 91356, USA

Person, Chuck (Basketball Player)
Cleveland Cavaliers
1 Center Ct
Gund Arena
Cleveland, OH 44115-4001, USA

Person, Robert (Baseball Player)
New York Mets
25 Bellerive Acres
Saint Louis, MO 63121-4328, USA

Person, Wesley (Basketball Player)
PO Box 481
Brantley, AL 36009-0481, USA

Persons, Peter (Golfer)
1153 Saint Andrews Dr
Macon, GA 31210-4760, USA

Persson, Goeran (Prime Minister)
Statsradsberedningen
Rosenbad 4
Stockholm 103 33, SWEDEN

Persson, Nina (Musician)
Motor SE
Gotabergs Gatan 2
Gothenburg 400 14, SWEDEN

Persson, Stefan (Business Person)
Sverige H & M Hennes & Mauritz AB
Sverigekontoret
Stockholm SE-106 38, SWEDEN

Persuaders, The
225 W 57th St Ste 500
New York, NY 10019-2136, USA

Pertucceli, Valeria (Actor)
c/o Staff Member *Telefe - Argentina*
Pavon 2444 (C1248AAT)
Buenos Aires, ARGENTINA

Pertwee, Bill
25 Whitehall
London, ENGLAND SW1A 2BS, UNITED KINGDOM (UK)

Pervical, Troy (Baseball Player)
California Angels
2127 Century Ave
Riverside, CA 92506-4653, USA

Perzanowski, Stan (Baseball Player)
Chicago White Sox
3250 173rd St
Hammond, IN 46323-2763, USA

Perzigian, Jerry (Producer, Writer)
c/o Joseph Cohen *Creative Artists Agency LCC (CAA-LA)*
2000 Avenue Of The Stars
Los Angeles, CA 90067-4700, USA

Pescatelli, Tammy (Actor)
c/o Douglas Edley *Gersh Agency, The (LA)*
232 N Canon Dr
Beverly Hills, CA 90210-5302, USA

Pesce, P J (Director, Writer)
c/o Jordan Bayer *Original Artists (LA)*
9465 Wilshire Blvd Ste 324
Beverly Hills, CA 90212-2602, USA

Pesch, Doro & Warlock
Box 8721
Dusseldorf 1 D-(W) 4000, GERMANY

Pesci, Joe (Actor)
c/o Melissa Prophet *Melissa Prophet Management*
4321 Matilija Ave Apt 21
Sherman Oaks, CA 91423-3672, USA

Pescia, Lisa (Actor)
Epstein-Wyckoff
280 S Beverly Dr Ste 400
Beverly Hills, CA 90212-3904, USA

Pescow, Donna (Actor)
8267 Paseo Canyon Dr
Malibu, CA 90265, USA

Pesek, Libor (Conductor)
I M G Artists
Media House
3 Burlington Lane
London W4 2TH, UNITED KINGDOM (UK)

Pesky, Johnny (Baseball Player)
Boston Red Sox
25 Parsons Dr
Swampscott, MA 01907-2929, USA

Pesonen, Richard (Football Player)
Green Bay Packers
765 Pine Hills Pl
The Villages, FL 32162-1617, USA

Pestana, Simon (Actor)
c/o Staff Member *Telefe - Argentina*
Pavon 2444 (C1248AAT)
Buenos Aires, ARGENTINA

Pestka, Sidney (Misc)
Robert Wood Johnson Medical School
675 Hoes Ln W
Piscataway, NJ 08854-8021, USA

Pet Shop Boys (Music Group)
c/o Staff Member *Creative Artists Agency LCC (CAA-LA)*
2000 Avenue Of The Stars
Los Angeles, CA 90067-4700, USA

Petagine, Roberto (Baseball Player)
Houston Astros
2495 Provence Cir
Weston, FL 33327-1303, USA

Peter, Barton (Actor)
c/o Staff Member *The Artists Agency (LA)*
1180 S Beverly Dr Ste 301
Los Angeles, CA 90035-1154, USA

Peter, Jason (Football Player)
Carolina Panthers
11611 Secretariat Dr
Walton, NE 68461-9804, USA

Peter, Paul & Mary
121 Mount Hermon Way
Ocean Grove, NJ 07756-1443, USA

Peter, Valentine J (Educator, Religious Leader)
Father Flanagan's Boys Home
Boys Town, NE 68010, USA

Peter II, Edward C (General)
4 Herons Nest
Savannah, GA 31410-3332, USA

Peterdi, Gabor (Artist)
108 Highland Ave
Norwalk, CT 06853-1315, USA

Peterek, Jeff (Baseball Player)
Milwaukee Brewers
1547 Echo Valley Dr
Niles, MI 49120-8738, USA

Peterman, Donald W (Cinematographer)
Gersh Agency
232 N Canon Dr
Beverly Hills, CA 90210-5302, USA

Peterman, Melissa (Actor)
c/o Staff Member *Reba*
10201 W Pico Blvd Bldg 38 Rm 125
Los Angeles, CA 90064-2606, USA

Peters, Andy (Television Host)
c/o Staff Member *BBC Artist Mail*
PO Box 1116
Belfast BT2 7AJ, UNITED KINGDOM (UK)

Peters, Anthony L (Tony) (Football Player)
2402 Boston St
Muskogee, OK 74401-5233, USA

Peters, Barbara (Director)
1118 Magnolia Blvd
North Hollywood, CA 91601, USA

Peters, Bernadette (Actor, Musician)
c/o Jeff Hunter *William Morris Agency (WMA-NY)*
1325 Avenue Of The Americas
New York, NY 10019-6026, USA

Peters, Bob (Coach)
Bernidji State University
Athletic Dept
Bernidji, MN 56601, USA

Peters, Caleigh (Musician)
c/o Siri Garber *Platform Public Relations*
2133 Holly Dr
Los Angeles, CA 90068-2851, USA

Peters, Chris (Baseball Player)
Pittsburgh Pirates
6091 Irishtown Rd
Bethel Park, PA 15102-2343, USA

Peters, Clarke (Actor)
c/o Staff Member *Writers and Artists Group Intl (NY)*
19 W 44th St Ste 1000
New York, NY 10036-6101, USA

Peters, Dan (Musician)
Legends of 21st Century
7 Trinity Row
Florence, MA 01062-1931, USA

Peters, Emmitt (Dog Sled Racer)
General Delivery
Ruby, AK 99768-9999, USA

Peters, Even (Actor)
c/o Megan Silverman *Endeavor Agency LLC (LA)*
9601 Wilshire Blvd Fl 3
Beverly Hills, CA 90210-5204, USA

Peters, Floyd (Coach, Football Coach, Football Player)
Baltimore Colts
1895 Hidden Meadows Dr
Reno, NV 89502-8755, USA

Peters, Gary C (Baseball Player)
Chicago White Sox
7121 N Serenoa Dr
Sarasota, FL 34241-9271, USA

Peters, Gordon
20 Elm Tree Ave.
Ester Surrey, ENGLAND, UNITED KINGDOM (UK)

Peters, Gretchen (Musician, Songwriter, Writer)
Gretchen Peters Management
PO Box 331242
Nashville, TN 37203-7512, USA

Peters, Jon (Producer)
9941 Tower Ln
Beverly Hills, CA 90210-2129, USA

Peters, Maria Liberia (Prime Minister)
Prime Minister's Office
Fort Amsterdam
Willemstad, NETHERLANDS ANTILLES

Peters, Marjorie (Baseball Player)
4081 S 122nd St
Greenfield, WI 53228-1823, USA

Peters, Mary (Athlete, Track Athlete)
Willowtree Cottage
River Road
Dunmurray, Belfast, NORTHERN IRELAND

Peters, Mike (Cartoonist)
PO Box 957
Bradenton, FL 34206-0957, USA

Peters, Ray (Baseball Player)
Milwaukee Brewers
106 Cifuentes Way
Hot Springs Village, AR 71909-7421, USA

Peters, Rick (Actor)
c/o Gabrielle Krengel *Domain*
4526 Wilshire Blvd
Los Angeles, CA 90010-3801, USA

Peters, Ricky (Baseball Player)
Detroit Tigers
1534 W Comstock Dr
Chandler, AZ 85224-1855, USA

Peters, Roberta (Actor, Opera Singer)
19356 Cedar Glen Dr
Boca Raton, FL 33434-5129, USA

Peters, Steve (Baseball Player)
St Louis Cardinals
1524 SW 123rd St
Oklahoma City, OK 73170-4935, USA

Peters, Tom (Business Person)
Tom Peters Group
555 Hamilton Ave
Palo Alto, CA 94301-2015, USA

Peters, Volney (Football Player)
Chicago Cardinals
325 Lancaster Rd
Walnut Creek, CA 94595-1760, USA

Peters Jr, House
1202 Borden Rd Sp #91
Escondido, CA 92026, USA

Petersdorf, Robert G (Physicist)
8001 Sand Point Way NE Apt C71
Seattle, WA 98115-6382, USA

Petersen, Byron (Scientist)
University of Pittsburgh
Medical Center
Pittsburgh, PA 15260, USA

Petersen, Chris (Baseball Player)
Colorado Rockies
125 Razorbill Ct
Orlando, FL 32828-8418, USA

Petersen, Jan (Government Official)
Utenriksdepatementet
Postboks 8114 Dep
Oslo 0032, NORWAY

Petersen, Kurt (Football Player)
Dallas Cowboys
5520 Linmore Ln
Plano, TX 75093-7619, USA

Petersen, Niels Helveg (Government Official)
Drosselvej 72
Frederiksberg 2000, DENMARK

Petersen, Pat
1634 Veteran Ave
Los Angeles, CA 90024-5517, USA

Petersen, Paul (Actor, Musician)
A Minor Consideration
14530 S Denker Ave
Gardena, CA 90247-2323, USA

Petersen, Raymond J (Publisher)
Hearst Corp
300 W 57th St Fl 42
New York, NY 10019-3790, USA

Petersen, Robert E (Publisher)
Petersen Publishing Co
6420 Wilshire Blvd # 100
Los Angeles, CA 90048-5502, USA

Petersen, Stewart
PO Box 64
Cokeville, WY 83114-0064, USA

Petersen, Ted (Football Player)
Pittsburgh Steelers
323 Ridge Point Cir Apt 32A
Bridgeville, PA 15017-1566, USA

Petersen, William L (Actor, Producer)
c/o Staff Member *High Horse Films*
25135 Anza Dr
Stage 5
Santa Clarita, CA 91355-3416, USA

Petersen, Wolfgang (Director)
c/o Staff Member *Radiant Productions*
914 Montana Ave Fl 2
Santa Monica, CA 90403-1505, USA

Petersmark, Brett (Football Player)
Houston Oilers
2082 Pennsbury Ln
Hanover Park, IL 60133-6715, USA

Peterson, Adam (Baseball Player)
Chicago White Sox
6401 NE 144th St
Vancouver, WA 98686-2016, USA

Peterson, Anthony (Football Player)
San Fransisco 49ers
1974 Montrose Dr
Atlanta, GA 30344-3003, USA

Peterson, Buddy (Baseball Player)
Chicago White Sox
9764 White Pine Way
Elk Grove, CA 95624-4427, USA

Peterson, Buzz (Coach)
University of Tennessee
Athletic Dept
Knoxville, TN 37996-0001, USA

Peterson, Cal (Football Player)
Dallas Cowboys
22646 Ingomar St
Canoga Park, CA 91304-4622, USA

Peterson, Cassandra (Elvira) (Actor, Writer)
Queen B Productions
PO Box 38246
Los Angeles, CA 90038-0246, USA

Peterson, David C (Journalist)
4805 Pinehurst Ct
Pleasant Hill, IA 50327-0959, USA

Peterson, Debbi (Musician)
Bangles Mall
PO Box 180
1341 Fullerton Ave
Chicago, IL 60690-0180, USA

Peterson, Donald H
427 Pebblebrook Dr
Seabrook, TX 77586-6012, USA

Peterson, Elly (Activist)
1515 M St NW
Washington, DC 20005, USA

Peterson, Forrest J (Misc)
17 Collins Meadow Dr
Georgetown, SC 29440, USA

Peterson, Fred I (Fritz) (Baseball Player)
New York Yankees
PO Box 802
Dubuque, IA 52004-0802, USA

Peterson, Harding (Baseball Player)
Pittsburgh Pirates
2822 Sherbrooke Ln Apt C
Palm Harbor, FL 34684-2545, USA

Peterson, John (Wrestler)
457 19th Ave
Comstock, WI 54826-9746, USA

Peterson, Kyle (Baseball Player)
Milwaukee Brewers
13253 Hamilton St
Omaha, NE 68154-5293, USA

Peterson, Lars (Doctor)
Sahlgrenska University Hospital
Surgery Dept
Goteborg 413 45, SWEDEN

Peterson, Maggie
3310 W Warm Springs Rd
Las Vegas, NV 89118-5229, USA

Peterson, Michael (Football Player)
Indianapolis Colts
PO Box 904
Alachua, FL 32616-0904, USA

Peterson, Michael (Musician)
1103 17th Ave S
Falcon/Goodman Mgmt
Nashville, TN 37212-2203, USA

Peterson, Morris (Basketball Player)
Toronto Raptors
Air Canada Center
40 Bay St
Toronto, ON M5J 2N8, CANADA

Peterson, Oscar E (Composer, Musician)
Regal Recordings
2421 Hammond Road
Mississauga, ON L5K 1T3, CANADA

Peterson, Paul E (Scientist)
5 Midland Rd
Wellesley, MA 02482-6927, USA

Peterson, Peter G (Business Person, Financier, Secretary)
Blackstone Group
345 Park Ave
New York, NY 10154-0191, USA

Peterson, Russell W (Governor)
11 E Mozart Dr
Wilmington, DE 19807-1942, USA

Peterson, Seth (Actor)
3424 Blair Dr
Los Angeles, CA 90068-1412, USA

Peterson, Sid (Baseball Player)
St Louis Browns
3516 Cranbrook Ln
Wichita Falls, TX 76308-1402, USA

Peterson, Steven (Architect)
Peterson/Littenberg Architecture
131 E 66th St
New York, NY 10065-6129, USA

Peterson, Todd (Football Player)
Arizona Cardinals
3249 Chatham Rd NW
Atlanta, GA 30305-1101, USA

Peterson, Vicki (Musician)
Bangles Mall
1341 W Fullerton Ave
Box 180
Chicago, IL 60614-2362, USA

Peterson, Walter R (Educator, Governor)
PO Box 3100
Peterborough, NH 03458-3100, USA

Peterson, William L (Actor)
United Talent Agency
9560 Wilshire Blvd Ste 500
Beverly Hills, CA 90212-2401, USA

Peterson, William W (Football Player)
Cincinatti Bengals
13536 Mijo Ln
Lakeside, CA 92040-4824, USA

Peterson-Fox, Betty Jean (Baseball Player)
PO Box 280
110 E North St
Wyanet, IL 61379-0280, USA

Peterson-Parker, Katie (Golfer)
527 Henkel Cir
Winter Park, FL 32789-5127, USA

Petherbridge, Edward (Actor)
Jonathan Altaras
13 Shorts Gardens
London WC2H 9AT, UNITED KINGDOM (UK)

Petievich, Gerald (Producer, Writer)
c/o Brian Lipson *Endeavor Agency LLC (LA)*
9601 Wilshire Blvd Fl 3
Beverly Hills, CA 90210-5204, USA

Petit, Philippe (Misc)
Cathedral of Saint John the Devine
1047 Amsterdam Ave
New York, NY 10025-1798, USA

Petit, Roland (Dancer)
20 Blvd Gabes
Marseilles 13008, FRANCE

Petitbon, John (Football Player)
Dallas Texans
3804 N Labarre Rd
Metairie, LA 70002-1817, USA

Petitbon, Richie (Football Player)
Chicago Bears
9628 Percussion Way
Vienna, VA 22182-3334, USA

Petitgout, Luke (Football Player)
New York Giants
5221 S Nichol St
Tampa, FL 33611-4178, USA

Petke, Mike (Soccer Player)
DC United
14120 Newbrook Dr
Chantilly, VA 20151-2273, USA

Petkovsek, Mark (Baseball Player)
Texas Rangers
5575 Duff St
Beaumont, TX 77706-6307, USA

Peto, Richard (Misc)
Radcliffe Infirmary
Harkness Building
Oxford, ON OX2 6HE, UNITED KINGDOM (UK)

Petra, Yvon (Tennis Player)
Residence du Prieure
Saint Germain en Laye 78100, FRANCE

Petralli, Geno (Baseball Player)
Toront Blue Jays
119 Laser Ln
Weatherford, TX 76087-4006, USA

Petras, Ernestine (Baseball Player)
5 Greenwood Ave
Haskell, NJ 07420-1417, USA

Petrassi, Gottfredovia
Ferdinando di Savola 3
Rome 00196, ITALY

Petrenko, Victor (Figure Skater)
c/o Staff Member *Champions on Ice*
3500 W 80th St
Tom Collins Enterprises Inc
Minneapolis, MN 55431-1068, USA

Petrenko, Viktor (Figure Skater)
International Skating Center
PO Box 577
Simsbury, CT 06070-0577, USA

Petrey, Dan
1808 Cartlen Dr
Placentia, CA 92870-2734, USA

Petri, Michala (Musician)
Nordskraenten 3
Kokkedal 2980, DENMARK

Petri, Nina (Actor)
Agentur Carola Studlar
Agnesstr 47
Munich 80798, GERMANY

Petrich, Bob (Football Player)
San Diego Chargers
1391 Silverberry Ct
El Cajon, CA 92019-2835, USA

Petrick, Ben (Baseball Player)
Colorado Rockies
5320 SE Pine St
Hillsboro, OR 97123-7683, USA

Petrie, Geoff (Basketball Player)
Sacramento Kings
1 Sports Pkwy
Arco Arena
Sacramento, CA 95834-2301, USA

Petrocelli, Americo P (Rico) (Baseball Player)
37 Green Heron Ln
Nashua, NH 03062-2239, USA

Petrocelli, Daniel (Attorney, Attorney General, General)
Mitchell Silverberg Krupp
11377 W Olympic Blvd
Los Angeles, CA 90064-1625, USA

Petrone, Shana (Musician)
Creative Artists Agency
3310 W End Ave Ste 500
Nashville, TN 37203-1087, USA

Petroni, Michael (Director)
United Talent Agency
9560 Wilshire Blvd Ste 500
Beverly Hills, CA 90212-2401, USA

Petronio, Stephen (Choreographer, Dancer)
95 Saint Marks Pl
New York, NY 10009-5110, USA

Petroske, John (Hockey Player)
PO Box 366
Side Lake, MN 55781-0366, USA

Petrov, Andrei P (Composer)
Petrovskaya Str 42
#75
Saint Petersburg 197046, RUSSIA

Petrov, Nikolai A (Musician)
Kutuzovsky Prosp 26
#23
Moscow 121165, RUSSIA

Petrovic, Tim (Golfer)
12708 Tradition Dr
Dade City, FL 33525-8240, USA

Petrovich, George (Football Player)
Chicago Cardinals
3300 Joyce Dr
Fort Worth, TX 76116-6424, USA

Petrovics, Emil (Composer)
Attila Utca 29
Budapest 1013, HUNGARY

Petrovsky, Daniel J (General)
Commanding General
Un Command Korea
APO, AE 96343, USA

Petsko, Gregory A (Misc)
8 Jason Rd
Belmont, MA 02478-3129, USA

Pett, Joel (Cartoonist)
Lexington Herald-Leader
1010 W New Circle Rd
Lexington, KY 40511, USA

Pettee, Roger (Football Player)
Dallas Cowboys
210 S Obrien St
Tampa, FL 33609-3526, USA

Pettengill, Gordon H (Physicist)
Massachusetts Institute of Technology
Space Research Ctr
Cambridge, MA 02139, USA

Petterson, Donald K (Diplomat)
American Embassy Khartoum #63900
APO, AE 09829, USA

Pettersson, Carl (Golfer)
2208 Oak Lawn Way
Wake Forest, NC 27587-4700, USA

Pettibon, Raymond (Artist)
Michael Kohn Gallery
920 Colorado Ave
Santa Monica, CA 90401-2717, USA

Pettibon, Richard A (Richie) (Football Player)
9628 Percussion Way
Vienna, VA 22182-3334, USA

Pettibone, Jay (Baseball Player)
Minnesota Twins
5112 Via Marcos
Yorba Linda, CA 92887-2530, USA

Petties, Neal (Football Player)
Baltimore Colts
767 Jewell Dr
San Diego, CA 92113-2731, USA

Pettiet, Christopher
9255 W Sunset Blvd Ste 620
Los Angeles, CA 90069-3303, USA

Pettigrew, Antonio (Athlete, Track Athlete)
Saint Augustine's College
Athletic Dept
Raleigh, NC 27610, USA

Pettigrew, Gary (Football Player)
Philadelphia Eagles
1107 W 33rd Ave
Spokane, WA 99203-1403, USA

Pettigrew, L Eudora (Educator)
State University of New York
President's Office
Old Westbury, NY 11568, USA

Pettijohn, Francis J (Misc)
11630 Glen Arm Rd # V51
Glen Arm, MD 21057-9403, USA

Pettinato, Rachelle (Actor)
c/o Staff Member *Select Artists Ltd (CA-Westside Office)*
1138 12th St Apt 1
Santa Monica, CA 90403-5459, USA

Pettini, Joe (Baseball Player)
San Francisco Giants
112 Logan Ct
Bethany, WV 26032-2016, USA

Pettis, Gary (Baseball Player)
California Angels
3129 Crestline Ct
Antioch, CA 94531-6640, USA

Pettit, Bob (Basketball Player)
7 Garden Ln
New Orleans, LA 70124-1024, USA

Pettit, Donald R (Astronaut)
2014 Country Ridge Dr
Houston, TX 77062-3636, USA

Pettit, Paul (Baseball Player)
Pittsburgh Pirates
928 Sarazen St
Hemet, CA 92543, USA

Pettite, Andrew E (Andy) (Baseball Player)
2310 W Lawther Dr
Deer Park, TX 77536-6053, USA

Pettitte, Andy (Baseball Player)
New York Yankees
2222 W Lawther Dr
Deer Park, TX 77536-6060, USA

Petty, Kyle (Race Car Driver)
135 Longfield Dr
Mooresville, NC 28115-7342, USA

Petty, Lori (Actor)
c/o Craig Schneider *Pinnacle PR*
8265 W Sunset Blvd Ste 201
West Hollywood, CA 90046-2470, USA

Petty, Richard L (Race Car Driver)
Petty Enterprises
311 Branson Mill Rd
Randleman, NC 27317-8008, USA

Petty, Tom (Musician, Songwriter, Writer)
c/o Tony Dimitriades *East End Management*
12441 Ventura Ct
Studio City, CA 91604-2417, USA

Pettyfer, Alex (Actor)
c/o Adam Isaacs *United Talent Agency (UTA)*
9560 Wilshire Blvd Ste 500
Beverly Hills, CA 90212-2401, USA

Pettyjohn, Adam (Baseball Player)
Detroit Tigers
717 Westwood Dr
Exeter, CA 93221-1438, USA

Pevec, Katja (Actor)
c/o Staff Member *Creative Management Group*
3815 Hughes Ave Fl 3
Culver City, CA 90232-2715, USA

Pevey, Marty (Baseball Player)
Montreal Expos
158 Nightwind Trce
Acworth, GA 30101-5981, USA

Peviani, Bob (Football Player)
New York Giants
25262 Northrup Dr
Laguna Hills, CA 92653-5223, USA

Peyroux, Madeline (Musician, Songwriter, Writer)
Bumstead Productions
PO Box 158
Station E
Toronto, ON M6H 4E2, CANADA

Peyser, Penny (Actor)
Epstein-Wyckoff
280 S Beverly Dr Ste 400
Beverly Hills, CA 90212-3904, USA

Peyton, Brad (Director)
c/o Staff Member *Endeavor Agency LLC (LA)*
9601 Wilshire Blvd Fl 3
Beverly Hills, CA 90210-5204, USA

Peyton of Yeovil, John W W (Government Official)
Old Malt House
Hinton Saint George
Somerset TA17 8SE, UNITED KINGDOM (UK)

Pezzano, Chuck (Writer)
27 Mountainside Ter
Clifton, NJ 07013-1107, USA

Pfaff, Judy (Artist)
Holly Solomon Gallery
175 E 79th St # 2B
New York, NY 10075-0432, USA

Pfann, George R (Coach, Football Coach, Football Player)
120 Warwick Pl
Ithaca, NY 14850-1731, USA

Pfeiffer, Dedee (Actor, Model)
c/o Scott Henderson *William Morris Agency (WMA-LA)*
1 William Morris Pl
Beverly Hills, CA 90212-4261, USA

Pfeiffer, Doug (Editor)
PO Box 1806
Big Bear Lake, CA 92315-1806, USA

Pfeiffer, Michelle (Actor)
c/o Kevin Huvane *Creative Artists Agency LCC (CAA-LA)*
2000 Avenue Of The Stars
Los Angeles, CA 90067-4700, USA

Pfeiffer, Norman (Architect)
Hardy Holzman Pfeiffer
811 W 7th St
Los Angeles, CA 90017-3408, USA

Pfeil, Bobby (Baseball Player)
New York Mets
2922 Snowbrook Ct
Stockton, CA 95219-6513, USA

Pfeil, Mark (Golfer)
2565 Chelsea Rd
Palos Verdes Estates, CA 90274-4309, USA

Pfister, Dan (Baseball Player)
Kansas City A's
1436 NW 9th St
Dania, FL 33004-2332, USA

Pflug, Jo Ann (Actor)
PO Box 3292
Jupiter, FL 33469-1004, USA

Pfund, Lee (Baseball Player)
Brooklyn Dodgers
130 Windsor Park Dr Apt C214
Carol Stream, IL 60188-1998, USA

Pfund, Randy (Coach)
Miami Heat
601 Biscayne Blvd
American Airlines Arena
Miami, FL 33132-1801, USA

Phair, Liz (Actor, Musician, Songwriter)
c/o Jason Weinberg *Untitled Entertainment (LA)*
331 N Maple Dr Fl 3
Beverly Hills, CA 90210-3827, USA

Pham, Tuan (Cosmonaut)
4C-1000-Soc Son
Hanoi, VIETNAM

Pham Dinh Tung, Paul J Cardinal (Religious Leader)
Archdiocese
Toa Tong Giam Muc
Pho Nha Chung
Hanoi 40, VIETNAM

Pham Minh Man, Jean-Baptiste Cardinal
(Religious Leader)
Toa Tonggiam Muc
180 Nguyen Dink Chieu
Thanh-Pho Ho Chi Minh, VIETNAM

Phan, Dat (Actor, Comedian)
c/o Gayle Divine *Divine Management*
3822 Latrobe St
Los Angeles, CA 90031-1446, USA

Phan, Van Khai (Prime Minister)
Prime Minister's Office
Hoang Hoa Thum St
Hanoi, VIETNAM

Phantog (Mountaineer)
Wuxi Sports & Physical Culture Comm
Jiagnsu, CHINA

Phelan, Jim (Basketball Player, Coach)
16579 Old Emmitsburg Rd
Emmitsburg, MD 21727-8927, USA

Phelps, Brian
1265 Coldwater Canyon Dr
Beverly Hills, CA 90210-2419, USA

Phelps, Doug (Musician)
Mitchell Fox Mgmt
212 3rd Ave N Ste 301
Nashville, TN 37201-1632, USA

Phelps, Edmund S (Economist)
45 E 89th St
New York, NY 10128-1251, USA

Phelps, James (Actor)
JOP Project
PO Box 9765
Coldfield
Sutton B75 5XB, UNITED KINGDOM
(UK)

Phelps, Jaycie (Gymnast)
Cincinnati Gymnastics Academy
3635 Woodridge Blvd
Fairfield, OH 45014-8521, USA

Phelps, Josh (Baseball Player)
Toront Blue Jays
1503 Regal Mist Loop
Trinity, FL 34655-4974, USA

Phelps, Kelly Joe (Musician)
Fleming/Tamulevich Assoc
733 N Main St # 35
Ann Arbor, MI 48104-1030, USA

Phelps, Ken (Baseball Player)
Kansas City Royals
6030 E Foothill Dr N
Paradise Valley, AZ 85253-3070, USA

Phelps, Michael (Swimmer)
c/o Staff Member *Octagon (VA)*
1751 Pinnacle Dr Ste 1500
McLean, VA 22102-3833, USA

Phelps, Oliver (Actor)
c/o Staff Member *JOP Project*
PO Box 9765
Sutton Coldfield B75 5XB, UNITED
KINGDOM (UK)

Phelps, Richard (Athlete)
c/o Staff Member *ESPN (Main)*
935 Middle St
Espn Plaza
Bristol, CT 06010-1000, USA

Phelps, Richard F (Digger) (Coach)
ESPN-TV
Sports Dept
Espn Plaza 935 Middle St
Bristol, CT 06010, USA

Phelps, Tommy (Baseball Player)
Florida Marlins
3710 Whitehall Dr Apt 202
West Palm Beach, FL 33401-1057, USA

Phelps, Travis (Baseball Player)
Tampa Bay Devil Rays
PO Box 514
Wheaton, MO 64874-0514, USA

Phelps Jr, Ashton (Publisher)
New Orleans Times-Picayune
3800 Howard Ave
New Orleans, LA 70125-1429, USA

Phenix, Perry Lee (Football Player)
Tennesse Titans
4849 Frankford Rd Apt 715
Dallas, TX 75287-5309, USA

Phifer, Mekhi (Actor)
c/o John Fogelman *William Morris
Agency (WMA-LA)*
1 William Morris Pl
Beverly Hills, CA 90212-4261, USA

Phifer, Roman Z (Football Player)
Los Angeles Rams
PO Box 83215
Los Angeles, CA 90083-0215, USA

Philaret, Patriarch (Religious Leader)
10 Osvobozdeniya St
Minsk 22004, BELARUS

Philbin, Gerry (Football Player)
New York Jets
9976 Marsala Way
Delray Beach, FL 33446-9727, USA

Philbin, Joy
101 W 67th St Apt 51A
New York, NY 10023-5953, USA

Philbin, Regis (Television Host)
Live with Regis and Kelly
7 Lincoln Sq Fl 5
Wabc-Tv
New York, NY 10023-6201, USA

Philbrick, Denise (Golfer)
5364 Carnegie Loop
Livermore, CA 94550-7136, USA

Philcox, Todd (Football Player)
Cincinatti Bengals
1201 1st St N Apt 703
Jacksonville Beach, FL 32250-8205, USA

Philip (Prince)
Buckingham Palace
London SW1A 1AA, UNITED KINGDOM
(UK)

Philip, HRH Prince
Buckingham Palace
London, ENGLAND SW1, UNITED
KINGDOM (UK)

Philip, Primate (Religious Leader)
Antiochian Orthodox Christian Church
358 Mountain Rd
Englewood, NJ 07631-3727, USA

Philipp, Stephanie (Model)
Agentur Margit de la Berg
Icking-Isartal 82057, GERMANY

Philippe, Crown Prince (Royalty)
Koninklijk Palais
Rue de Brederode
Brussels 1000, BELGIUM

Philippoussis, Mark (Tennis Player)
Octagon
1751 Pinnacle Dr Ste 1500
McLean, VA 22102-3833, USA

Philipps, Busy (Actor)
c/o Staff Member *3 Arts Entertainment Inc*
9460 Wilshire Blvd Fl 7
Beverly Hills, CA 90212-2713, USA

Philips, Chuck (Journalist)
Los Angeles Times
202 W 1st St
Editorial Dept
Los Angeles, CA 90012-4105, USA

Philips, Emo (Actor)
c/o Staff Member *OmniPop Inc (LA)*
4605 Lankershim Blvd Ste 201
North Hollywood, CA 91602-1874, USA

Philips, Gena (Actor, Producer)
c/o Erik Kritzer *Fenton-Kritzer
Entertainment*
8840 Wilshire Blvd Fl 3
Beverly Hills, CA 90211-2606, USA

Philips, Gina (Actor)
c/o Erik Kritzer *Fenton-Kritzer
Entertainment*
8840 Wilshire Blvd Fl 3
Beverly Hills, CA 90211-2606, USA

Philips, Jeanne (Writer)
c/o Lee Gabler *Creative Artists Agency
LCC (CAA-LA)*
2000 Avenue Of The Stars
Los Angeles, CA 90067-4700, USA

Philley, Dave (Baseball Player)
Chicago White Sox
1336 E Polk St
Paris, TX 75460-7460, USA

Phillippe, Ryan (Actor)
c/o David Schiff *Schiff Company*
9465 Wilshire Blvd Ste 480
Beverly Hills, CA 90212-2603, USA

Phillips, Anthony (Musician, Songwriter,
Writer)
Solo Agency
55 Fulham High St
London SW6 3JJ, UNITED KINGDOM
(UK)

Phillips, Bijou (Actor, Model, Musician)
c/o Brian Young *Untitled Entertainment
(LA)*
331 N Maple Dr Fl 3
Beverly Hills, CA 90210-3827, USA

Phillips, Bill
Muscle Media
444 Corporate Cir
Golden, CO 80401, USA

Phillips, Bobbie (Actor)
The Kelly Agency
3001 Heavenly Ridge St
Thousand Oaks, CA 91362-1178, USA

Phillips, Brandon (Baseball Player)
Cleveland Indians
586 Rowland Rd
Stone Mountain, GA 30083-4573, USA

Phillips, Caryl (Writer)
Amherst College
English Dept
Amherst, MA 01002, USA

Phillips, Chynna (Actor, Musician)
1007 Montana Ave # 230
Santa Monica, CA 90403-1603, USA

Phillips, Damon (Baseball Player)
Cincinnati Reds
1006 Oakchase Ct
Azle, TX 76020-2550, USA

Phillips, Davey (Baseball Player)
12 Upper Whitmoor Dr
Weldon Spring, MO 63304-0541, USA

Phillips, Ed (Baseball Player)
St Louis Cardinals
8878 County Road 414
Hannibal, MO 63401, USA

Phillips, Emo (Comedian)
Harbour Agency
63 William St
#300
East Sydney, NSW 1022, AUSTRALIA

Phillips, Ethan (Actor)
4212 W McFarlane Ave
Burbank, CA 91505-4018, USA

Phillips, Gersha (Designer)
c/o Staff Member *Paradigm (LA)*
360 N Crescent Dr
North Bldg
Beverly Hills, CA 90210-6820, USA

Phillips, Grace (Actor)
c/o Staff Member *Framework
Entertainment (LA)*
9057 Nemo St # C
W Hollywood, CA 90069-5511, USA

Phillips, Grant Lee (Musician)
c/o Staff Member *Paradigm (Monterey)*
509 Hartnell St
Monterey, CA 93940-2825, USA

Phillips, Harvey (Misc)
TubaRanch
4769 S Harrell Rd
Bloomington, IN 47401-9028, USA

Phillips, Howard (Misc)
Conservative Caucus
47 West St
Boston, MA 02111-1219, USA

Phillips, Jack (Baseball Player)
New York Yankees
721 May Rd # 2
Potsdam, NY 13676-3244, USA

Phillips, James (Red) (Football Player)
1948 Wicker Point Rd
Alexander City, AL 35010-6504, USA

Phillips, Jason (Baseball Player)
New York Mets
9926 Greenalder Cv N
Cordova, TN 38016-0661, USA

Phillips, Jeffrey
8436 W 3rd St Ste 740
Los Angeles, CA 90048-4130, USA

Phillips, Jess (Football Player)
Cincinatti Bengals
2820 San Antonio St
Beaumont, TX 77701-8036, USA

Phillips, Jim (Football Player)
Los Angeles Rams
67 Lakeview Dr Unit 10D
Alexander City, AL 35010-6292, USA

Phillips, Joe (Football Player)
Minnesota Vikings
425 Barker Ave
Oregon City, OR 97045-3449, USA

Phillips, John (Coach)
University of Tulsa
Athletic Dept
Tulsa, OK 74104, USA

Phillips, John L (Astronaut)
4422 Cedar Ridge Trl
Houston, TX 77059-3116, USA

Phillips, Joseph C
8730 W Sunset Blvd Ste 480
Los Angeles, CA 90069-2277, USA

Phillips, Julianne (Actor)
2227 Mandeville Canyon Rd
Los Angeles, CA 90049-1826, USA

Phillips, Kate (Writer)
Houghton Mifflin
222 Berkeley St # 700
Boston, MA 02116-3748, USA

Phillips, Kevin (Actor)
c/o Beverly Strong *Anonymous Content (CA)*
3532 Hayden Ave
Culver City, CA 90232-2413, USA

Phillips, Kirk (Football Player)
Dallas Cowboys
2103 E Alma Ave
Sherman, TX 75090-4008, USA

Phillips, Kristie (Gymnast)
610 1st Ave
Asbury Park, NJ 07712-5906, USA

Phillips, Lawrence (Football Player)
St Louis Rams
9527 Langdon Ave
North Hills, CA 91343-2102, USA

Phillips, Leslie (Actor)
Storm Artists Mgmt
47 Brewer St
London W1R 3FD, UNITED KINGDOM (UK)

Phillips, Lou Diamond (Actor)
c/o JB Roberts *Thruline Entertainment*
9250 Wilshire Blvd Ground Fl
Beverly Hills, CA 90210, USA

Phillips, Loyd (Football Player)
Chicago Bears
General Delivery
Springdale, AR 72764-9999, USA

Phillips, Mackenzie (Actor)
S D B Partners
1801 Avenue Of Stars Ste 902
Los Angeles, CA 90067-5981, USA

Phillips, Mel (Football Player)
San Fransisco 49ers
6368 Milk Wagon Ln
Miami Lakes, FL 33014-6083, USA

Phillips, Michelle
c/o Annie Schwartz *Origin Talent Agency*
4705 Laurel Canyon Blvd Ste 306
Studio City, CA 91607-5940, USA

Phillips, Mike (Baseball Player)
San Francisco Giants
3322 Ridgefield St
Irving, TX 75062-4157, USA

Phillips, Norma (Activist)
Mothers Against Drunk Driving
PO Box 819100
Dallas, TX 75381, USA

Phillips, Peter C B (Economist)
PO Box 208281
New Haven, CT 06520-8281, USA

Phillips, Phil (Musician, Songwriter, Writer)
PO Box 105
Jennings, LA 70546-0105, USA

Phillips, Princess Zara (Royalty)
Gatcombe Park
Minchinhampton
Stroud GL6 9AT, UNITED KINGDOM (UK)

Phillips, Richard (Baseball Player)
Kansas City Monarchs
343 Tazor St NW
Atlanta, GA 30314-2716, USA

Phillips, Ricky (Musician)
c/o Sterling Bacon *TBA Artist Management (Atlanta)*
1111 Alderman Dr Ste 285
Alpharetta, GA 30005-5433, USA

Phillips, Sam (Musician, Songwriter, Writer)
Prager & Fenton
12424 Wilshire Blvd Ste 1000
Los Angeles, CA 90025-1071, USA

Phillips, Scott (Musician)
Agency Group
1776 Broadway Ste 430
New York, NY 10019-2002, USA

Phillips, Sean
153 Petherton Rd. Highbury
London, ENGLAND N5 2RS, UNITED KINGDOM (UK)

Phillips, Sian (Actor)
8 Alexa Court
78 Lexham Gardens
London, ENGLAND W8 6JL, UNITED KINGDOM (UK)

Phillips, Stone (Correspondent)
c/o Staff Member *Dateline NBC*
30 Rockefeller Plz Ste 270E
Nbc News
New York, NY 10112-0299, USA

Phillips, Susan M (Financier, Government Official)
Federal Reserve Board
20th St & Constitution NW
Washington, DC 20551-0001, USA

Phillips, Tari (Basketball Player)
New York Liberty
2 Penn Plz
Madison Square Garden
New York, NY 10121-1703, USA

Phillips, Taylor (Baseball Player)
Milwaukee Braves
594 Mein Mitchell Rd
Hiram, GA 30141-5810, USA

Phillips, Teresa (Basketball Player, Coach)
Tennessee State University
Athletic Dept
Nashville, TN 37209, USA

Phillips, Todd (Actor, Director, Producer, Writer)
c/o Todd Feldman *Creative Artists Agency LCC (CAA-LA)*
2000 Avenue Of The Stars
Los Angeles, CA 90067-4700, USA

Phillips, Tony (Baseball Player)
Oakland A's
13341 E Cochise Rd
Scottsdale, AZ 85259-5442, USA

Phillips, Wade (Coach, Football Coach)
San Diego Chargers
4020 Murphy Canyon Rd
San Diego, CA 92123-4407, USA

Phillips, Warren H (Publisher)
Bridge Works Publications
PO Box 1798
Bridgehampton, NY 11932-1798, USA

Phillips, Wendy (Actor)
1642 Westwood Blvd # 300
Los Angeles, CA 90024-5643, USA

Phillips, William D (Nobel Prize Laureate)
13409 Chestnut Oak Dr
Gaithersburg, MD 20878-3541, USA

Phillips Jr, J Dixon (Judge)
US Court of Appeals
100 Europa Dr
Chapel Hill, NC 27517-2357, USA

Phillopusis, Mark (Tennis Player)
c/o Staff Member *Octagon (VA)*
1751 Pinnacle Dr Ste 1500
McLean, VA 22102-3833, USA

Philyaw, Charles (Football Player)
Oakland Raiders
3929 Eileen Ln
Shreveport, LA 71109-1921, USA

Phipps, Michael E (Mike) (Football Player)
Cleveland Browns
2748 NE 25th St
Lighthouse Point, FL 33064-8308, USA

Phipps, Sam
2346 Walgrove Ave
Los Angeles, CA 90066-3504, USA

Phish (Music Group)
c/o Staff Member *Paradigm (Monterey)*
509 Hartnell St
Monterey, CA 93940-2825, USA

Phoebus, Thomas H (Tom) (Baseball Player)
Baltimore Orioles
2822 SW Lakemont Pl
Palm City, FL 34990-6094, USA

Phoenic, Robin (Musician)
Nine Inch Nails
63 Main St
Cold Spring, NY 10516-3014, USA

Phoenix, Joaquin (Actor)
c/o Iris Burton *Iris Burton Agency*
201 N Crescent Dr Apt 319
Beverly Hills, CA 90210-6181, USA

Phoenix, Steve (Baseball Player)
Oakland A's
11212 Horizon Hills Dr
El Cajon, CA 92020-8231, USA

Phoenix, Summer (Actor)
c/o Nick Frenkel *3 Arts Entertainment (NY)*
9460 Wilshire Blvd Ste 700
Beverly Hills, CA 90212-2713, USA

Pianalto, Sandra (Financier)
Federal Reserve Bank
1455 E 6th St
Cleveland, OH 44114-2566, USA

Piano, Renzo (Architect, Nobel Prize Laureate)
Renzo Piano Building Workshop
Via Rubens 29
Genoa 16158, ITALY

Piatkowski, Eric (Basketball Player)
Houston Rockets
2 Greenway Plz
Toyota Center
Houston, TX 77046-0297, USA

Piatt, Adam (Baseball Player)
Oakland A's
1808 SE 37th Ter
Cape Coral, FL 33904-5036, USA

Piatt, Doug (Baseball Player)
Montreal Expos
29 L St
Beaver, PA 15009-1520, USA

Piazza, Michale J (Mike) (Baseball Player)
Los Angeles Dodgers
9595 Wilshire Blvd Ste 1010
Beverly Hills, CA 90212-2510, USA

Picard, Alexandre (Hockey Player)
Columbus Blue Jackets
200 W Nationwide Blvd
Arena
Columbus, OH 43215-2564, USA

Picard, Robert
31831 Grand River Ave Unit 55
Farmington, MI 48336-4147, USA

Picardo, Robert (Actor)
Don Buchwald
6500 Wilshire Blvd Ste 2200
Los Angeles, CA 90048-4942, USA

Picasso, Paloma (Actor, Designer)
Quintana Ron Ltd
291A Brompton Road
London SW3 2DY, UNITED KINGDOM (UK)

Picatto, Alexandra (Actor)
c/o Kari Estrin *Paradigm (LA)*
360 N Crescent Dr
North Bldg
Beverly Hills, CA 90210-6820, USA

Piccard, Bertrand (Misc)
Media Impact
Rue de Lausanne 42
Geneva 1201, SWITZERLAND

Piccard, Jacques E J (Scientist)
Place d'Armes
Cully 1096, SWITZERLAND

Picciolo, Rob (Baseball Player)
Oakland A's
11773 Invierno Dr
San Diego, CA 92124-2814, USA

Picco, Giandomenico
1 United Nations Plz
New York, NY 10017-3515, USA

Piccoli, Camille (Actor)
Cineart
36 Rue de Ponthieu
Paris 75008, FRANCE

Piccoli, Michel (Actor)
11 Rue des Lions Saint Paul
Paris 75004, FRANCE

Piccolo, Bill (Football Player)
New York Giants
10003 Blossom Ln
Twinsburg, OH 44087-1089, USA

Piccone, Lou (Football Player)
New York Jets
49 S Youngs Rd
Williamsville, NY 14221-7024, USA

Piccone, Robin (Designer, Fashion Designer)
Piccone Apparel Corp
1424 Washington Blvd
Venice, CA 90291, USA

Picerni, Paul (Actor)
PO Box 88
Llano, CA 93544-0088, USA

Pichardo, Hipolito (Baseball Player)
Kansas City Royals
21218 Saint Andrews Blvd Apt 305
Boca Raton, FL 33433-2449, USA

Piche, Ron (Baseball Player)
Milwaukee Braves
128-100 Rue de Gaspe
Verdun, PQ H3E 1E5, CANADA

Pichler, Joseph A (Business Person)
Kroger Co
1014 Vine St
Cincinnati, OH 45202-1100, USA

Pick, Amelie (Actor)
Artmedia
20 Ave Rapp
Paris 75007, FRANCE

Pickard, Nancy (Writer)
7258 Mastin St
Shawnee, KS 66203-4606, USA

Pickel, Bill (Football Player)
9 Autumn Ridge Rd
South Salem, NY 10590-1103, USA

Pickens, Bruce (Football Player)
Atlanta Falcons
2811 Wickeford Mill Dr
Buford, GA 30519-7611, USA

Pickens, Carl M (Football Player)
Cincinatti Bengals
623 Terrace Ave
Murphy, NC 28906, USA

Pickens, Jo Ann (Opera Singer)
Norman McCann Artists
56 Lawrie Park Gardens
London SE26 6XJ, UNITED KINGDOM
(UK)

Pickens, Robert (Football Player)
Chicago Bears
6701 S Crandon Ave # 21B
Chicago, IL 60649-1274, USA

Pickens Jr, James (Actor)
c/o Staff Member *Grey's Anatomy*
500 S Buena Vista St
Burbank, CA 91521-0001, USA

Pickens Jr, T Boone (Business Person)
1 Woodstone St
Amarillo, TX 79106-4151, USA

Pickering, Byron (Artist)
6919 NE Highland Dr
Lincoln City, OR 97367, USA

Pickering, Calvin (Baseball Player)
Baltimore Orioles
201 Tanglewood Pl Apt 305
Tampa, FL 33617, USA

Pickering, Donald
Back Court Manor House
Eastleach Glos, ENGLAND, UNITED
KINGDOM (UK)

Pickering, Jeff (Cartoonist)
King Features Syndicate
888 7th Ave Ste 201
New York, NY 10106-0201, USA

Pickering, Thomas R (Business Person,
Diplomat)
Boeing Corp
PO Box 3707
Seattle, WA 98124-2207, USA

Pickett, Cindy (Actor)
662 N Van Ness Ave Ste 305
Los Angeles, CA 90004-1555, USA

Pickett, Jay
24801 Eilat St
Woodland Hills, CA 91367-1036, USA

Pickett, Rex
c/o Daniel A (Dan) Strone *Trident Media
Group LLC*
41 Madison Ave Fl 36
New York, NY 10010-2257, USA

Pickett, Ricky (Baseball Player)
Arizona Diamondbacks
1017 Wood Ridge Dr
Azle, TX 76020-3759, USA

Pickett, Ryan (Football Player)
Saint Louis Rams
901 N Broadway
Saint Louis, MO 63101-2800, USA

Pickford, Kevin (Baseball Player)
San Diego Padres
6006 N Harcourt Dr
Coeur D Alene, ID 83815-8473, USA

Pickford, Mary Foundation
9171 Wilshire Blvd # 512
Beverly Hills, CA 90210-5530, USA

Pickitt, John L (General)
38 Sunrise Point Rd
Lake Wylie, SC 29710-9230, USA

Pickler, John M (General)
Director Army Staff
Hqusa Pentagon
Washington, DC 20310-0001, USA

Pickler, Kellie (Reality TV Star)
c/o Staff Member *American Idol*
7800 Beverly Blvd # 251
Los Angeles, CA 90036-2112, USA

Pickles, Christina (Actor)
137 S Westgate Ave
Los Angeles, CA 90049-4222, USA

Pickles, Vivian
91 Regent St.
London, ENGLAND W1R 8RU, UNITED
KINGDOM (UK)

Pickren, Bradley (Actor)
c/o Philip Marcus *Kazarian/Spencer &
Assoc (LA)*
11969 Ventura Blvd
Box 7409 Fl 3
Studio City, CA 91604-2630, USA

Pickren, Spencer (Actor)
c/o Philip Marcus *Kazarian/Spencer &
Assoc (LA)*
11969 Ventura Blvd
Box 7409 Fl 3
Studio City, CA 91604-2630, USA

Pickup, Ronald
54 Crouch Hall Rd.
London, ENGLAND N8 8HG, UNITED
KINGDOM (UK)

Pico, Jeff (Baseball Player)
Chicago Cubs
613 Texas St
Antioch, CA 94509-3638, USA

Picone, Mario (Baseball Player)
New York Giants
8876 Bay 16th St
Brooklyn, NY 11214-5902, USA

Picoult, Jodi (Writer)
38 Goodfellow Rd
Hanover, NH 03755-4800, USA

Pictor, Bruce (Musician)
Variety Artists
793 Higuera St Ste 6
San Luis Obispo, CA 93401-0500, USA

Pidgeon, Rebecca (Actor)
Julian Belfarge
46 Albermarle St
London W1X 4PP, UNITED KINGDOM
(UK)

Piech, Ferdinand (Business Person)
Volkswagenwerk AG
Braunschweiger Str 63
Schwulper 38179, GERMANY

Pied Pipers, The
25 Cobble Creek Dr # 91
Tannersville, PA 18372, USA

Piekarski, Julie (Actor)
Phoenix Productions
#301-100 Donwood Drive
Winnipeg, MB R2G 0W1, CANADA

Piel, Jonathan (Editor)
Scientific American Magazine
415 Madison Ave
New York, NY 10017-1111, USA

Pienaar, Jacobus F (Misc)
Rugby Football Union
PO Box 99
Newlands, 7725, SOUTH AFRICA

Piene, Otto (Artist)
383 Old Ayer Rd
Groton, MA 01450-1823, USA

Pieper, Marjorie (Baseball Player)
2434 W Gardenia Dr RR 2
Citrus Springs, FL 34434-4848, USA

Pierce, Adrienne (Musician)
c/o Staff Member *Paradigm (Monterey)*
509 Hartnell St
Monterey, CA 93940-2825, USA

Pierce, Chester M (Psychic)
17 Prince St
Jamaica Plain, MA 02130-2725, USA

Pierce, David Hyde (Actor)
c/o Marilyn Szatmary *SMS Talent Inc*
8730 W Sunset Blvd Ste 440
Los Angeles, CA 90069-2277, USA

Pierce, Ed (Baseball Player)
Kansas City Royals
962 Bidwell Rd
San Dimas, CA 91773-1566, USA

Pierce, Jack (Baseball Player)
Atlanta Braves
1002 Cortez St
Laredo, TX 78040-6237, USA

Pierce, Jeff (Baseball Player)
Boston Red Sox
1046 Lantern Ln
Circle Pines, MN 55014-1335, USA

Pierce, Jeffrey (Actor)
c/o Gary Pearl *Pearl Pictures &
Management*
10956 Weyburn Ave Ste 200
Los Angeles, CA 90024-2835, USA

Pierce, Jill (Actor)
Extreme Team Productions
15941 Harlem Ave # 319
Tinley Park, IL 60477-1609, USA

Pierce, John (Musician)
c/o Staff Member *Paradigm (Monterey)*
509 Hartnell St
Monterey, CA 93940-2825, USA

Pierce, Jonathan (Musician)
Muse Assoc
330 Franklin Rd # 135-8
Brentwood, TN 37027-3280, USA

Pierce, Lincoln (Cartoonist)
United Feature Syndicate
200 Madison Ave
New York, NY 10016-3911, USA

Pierce, Paul (Basketball Player)
Boston Celtics
151 Merrimac St # 1
Boston, MA 02114-4714, USA

Pierce, Stack (Actor)
Haeggstrom Office
11288 Ventura Blvd # 620
Studio City, CA 91604-3187, USA

Pierce, Tamora (Writer)
612 Westcott St
Syracuse, NY 13210-2536, USA

Pierce, Tony (Baseball Player)
Kansas City A's
6119 Brittany Ct
Columbus, GA 31909-4247, USA

Pierce, W William (Billy) (Baseball
Player)
Detroit Tigers
1321 Baileys Crossing Dr
Lemont, IL 60439-8540, USA

Pierce, Wendell (Actor)
c/o Staff Member *Paradigm (LA)*
360 N Crescent Dr
North Bldg
Beverly Hills, CA 90210-6820, USA

Pierce-Roberts, Tony (Cinematographer)
1 Princes Garden
London W5 1SD, UNITED KINGDOM
(UK)

Pierces, The (Music Group)
c/o Staff Member *Paradigm (Monterey)*
509 Hartnell St
Monterey, CA 93940-2825, USA

Piercy, Marge (Writer)
PO Box 1473
Wellfleet, MA 02667-1473, USA

Pieri, Damon (Football Player)
New York Jets
1120 W Tuckey Ln
Phoenix, AZ 85013-1049, USA

Pierpoint, Eric (Actor)
2199 Topanga Skyline Dr
Topanga, CA 90290-4050, USA

Pierpoint, Robert (Correspondent)
CBS-TV
2020 M St NW
News Dept
Washington, DC 20036-3304, USA

Pierre, Andrew J (Scientist)
Carnegie Endowment for Peace
1779 Massachusetts Ave NW Ste 1
Washington, DC 20036-2128, USA

Pierre, Juan (Baseball Player)
c/o Staff Member *Florida Marlins*
2269 Dan Marino Blvd
Miami Gardens, FL 33056-2600, USA

Pierre of Normandy, Abbe (Activist,
Religious Leader)
La Halte d'Emmaus
Esteville 76690, FRANCE

Pierro, Bill (Baseball Player)
Pittsburgh Pirates
1751 74th St
Brooklyn, NY 11204-5616, USA

Piers, Julie (Golfer)
5019 SW Hammock Creek Dr
Palm City, FL 34990-7909, USA

Piersall, James A (Jimmy) (Baseball
Player)
1105 Oakview Dr
Wheaton, IL 60187-3026, USA

Pierson, Frank R (Director, Writer)
20536 Seaboard Rd
Malibu, CA 90265-5352, USA

Pierson, Geoff (Actor)
Ambrosio/Mortimer
165 W 46th St
New York, NY 10036-2501, USA

Pierson, Kate (Musician)
Direct Management Group
947 N La Cienega Blvd # 2
Los Angeles, CA 90069-4782, USA

Pierson, Marcus (Artist)
Outwest
7216 Washington St NE Ste A
Albuquerque, NM 87109-4514, USA

Pierson, Pete (Football Player)
Tampa Bay Buccaneers
19130 Beckett Dr
Odessa, FL 33556-2274, USA

Pierzynski, Anthony J (AJ) (Baseball Player)
Minnesota Twins
8990 Darlene Dr
Orlando, FL 32836-5828, USA

Pietrangeli, Nicola (Tennis Player)
Via Eustachio Manfredi
Rome 15, ITALY

Pietrangelo, Frank (Hockey Player)
11 Buttonwood Lane
Avon, CT 06001, USA

Pietrus, Mickael (Basketball Player)
Golden State Warriors
1001 Broadway
Oakland, CA 94607-4019, USA

Pietruski Jr, John M (Business Person)
27 Paddock Ln
Colts Neck, NJ 07722-1266, USA

Pietrzak, Jim (Football Player)
New York Giants
9800 4th St N Ste 400
Saint Petersburg, FL 33702-2464, USA

Pietrzykowski, Zbigniew (Boxer)
Ul Gomicza 5
Bielsko-Blata 43-409, POLAND

Pietz, Amy (Actor)
c/o Scott Howard *Howard Entertainment*
10850 Wilshire Blvd Ste 1260
Los Angeles, CA 90024-4337, USA

Pifferini, Bob Sr (Football Player)
Detroit Lions
4160 Jade St Spc 65
Capitola, CA 95010-3922, USA

Piggott, Lester K (Jockey)
Beech Tree House
Tostock Bury Saint Edmonds
Suffolk 1P20 9NY, UNITED KINGDOM
(UK)

Pignatano, Joe (Baseball Player)
Brooklyn Dodgers
150 78th St
Brooklyn, NY 11209-2914, USA

Pigott, Mark C (Business Person)
PACCAR Inc
777 106th Ave NE
Bellevue, WA 98004-5027, USA

Pigott-Smith, Tim (Actor)
P F D Drury House
34-43 Russell St
London WC2B 5HA, UNITED KINGDOM
(UK)

Pihos, Peter L (Pete) (Football Player)
Philadelphia Eagles
2755 Winslow Ln
Winston Salem, NC 27103-5738, USA

Pikaizen, Viktor A (Musician)
Chekhova Str 31/22
#37
Moscow, RUSSIA

Pike, Gary (Musician)
10031 Benares Pl
Sun Valley, CA 91352-4207, USA

Pike, Jim (Musician)
MPI Talent Agency
9255 W Sunset Blvd Ste 407
Los Angeles, CA 90069-3302, USA

Pike, Rosamund (Actor)
c/o Dallas Smith *Peters Fraser & Dunlop
(PFD - UK)*
Drury House
34-43 Russell St
London WC2B 5HA, UNITED KINGDOM
(UK)

Pikser, Jeremy (Actor)
c/o Margaret Riley *Margaret Riley
Management*
1041 N Formosa Ave
West Hollywood, CA 90046-6703, USA

Pilarcik, Al (Baseball Player)
Kansas City A's
PO Box 185
Saint John, IN 46373-0185, USA

Pilarczyk, Daniel E (Religious Leader)
100 E 8th St
Cincinnati, OH 45202-2129, USA

Pileggi, Mitch (Actor)
c/o Joel King *Pakula/King & Associates*
9229 W Sunset Blvd Ste 315
Los Angeles, CA 90069-3403, USA

Pileggi, Nicholas (Writer)
Creative Artists Agency
9830 Wilshire Blvd
Beverly Hills, CA 90212-1804, USA

Pilic, Nicki (Tennis Player)
DTB
Otto-Fleck-Schneise 8
Frankfurt/Maim 60528, GERMANY

Piligian, Craig (Producer)
c/o Staff Member *William Morris Agency
(WMA-LA)*
1 William Morris Pl
Beverly Hills, CA 90212-4261, USA

Pilkey, Dav (Writer)
Scholastic Press
555 Broadway
New York, NY 10012-3919, USA

Pilkey, Dave (Writer)
7406 Summer Trail Dr
Sugar Land, TX 77479-6232, USA

Pilkis, Simon J (Physicist)
State University of New York
Health Sciences Center
Stony Brook, NY 11794-0001, USA

Pill, Alison (Actor)
c/o Joanna (Joanie) Burstein *Burstein
Company, The*
15304 W Sunset Blvd Ste 208
Pacific Palisades, CA 90272-3656, USA

Pilla, Anthony M (Religious Leader)
Catholic Bishops National Conference
3211 4th St NE
Washington, DC 20017-1104, USA

Pillath, Roger (Football Player)
Los Angeles Rams
N3623 Lepinsky Rd
Peshtigo, WI 54157-9403, USA

Piller, Zach (Football Player)
Tennese Titans
3907 Dunleer Ct
Tallahassee, FL 32309-2630, USA

Pillers, Lawrence (Football Player)
New York Jets
4305 Handing Moss Rd
Jackson, MS 39206, USA

Pillette, Duane (Baseball Player)
New York Yankees
404 Lily Ann Way
San Jose, CA 95123-5948, USA

Pilliod Jr, Charles J (Business Person,
Diplomat)
49 Twin Oaks Rd # 2
Akron, OH 44313-6819, USA

Pillow, Ray (Musician)
Joe Taylor Artist Agency
2802 Columbine Pl
Nashville, TN 37204-3104, USA

Pillsbury, Edmund P (Director)
3601 Potomac Ave
Fort Worth, TX 76107-1722, USA

Pilotdrift (Music Group)
c/o Staff Member *Paradigm (Monterey)*
509 Hartnell St
Monterey, CA 93940-2825, USA

Pilote, Pierre P (Hockey Player)
25 Mary Jane
Elmwood, ON L0L 2PO, CANADA

Pilska, Paul (Opera Singer)
George M Martynuk
352 7th Ave
New York, NY 10001-5012, USA

Pilson, Neal H (Producer)
CBS-TV
51 W 52nd St
Sports Dept
New York, NY 10019-6119, USA

Pimenta, Simon Ignatius Cardinal
(Religious Leader)
Archbishop's House
21 Nathalal Parekh Marg
Mumbai, MS 400 039, INDIA

Pinal, Silvia
Av. de las Fuentas 629 Pedregal de San
Angel
Mexico DF, MEXICO

Pincay, Laffit
PO Box 250
Lexington, KY 40588-0250, USA

Pinchak, Jimmy (Jax) (Actor)
c/o Staff Member *Agency for the
Performing Arts (APA-LA)*
405 S Beverly Dr
Beverly Hills, CA 90212-4416, USA

Pinchot, Bronson (Actor)
10061 Riverside Dr
Toluca Lake, CA 91602-2560, USA

Pinckney, Ed (Basketball Player)
3350 SW 27th Ave Apt 1202
Miami, FL 33133-5326, USA

Pinckney, Sandra (Chef, Television Host)
c/o Staff Member *Food Network, The*
75 9th Ave
New York, NY 10011-7006, USA

Pinder, Cyril (Football Player)
Philadelphia Eagles
7137 S Luella Ave
Chicago, IL 60649-2511, USA

Pinder, Michael (Mike) (Misc)
Moody Blues
53-55 High St
Cobham
Surrey KT11 3DP, UNITED KINGDOM
(UK)

Pine, Chris (Actor)
c/o John Carrabino *John Carrabino
Management*
5900 Wilshire Blvd Ste 406
Los Angeles, CA 90036-5015, USA

Pine, Courtney (Musician)
Elizabeth Rush Agency
82 Cumberland Ave
Verona, NJ 07044-2105, USA

Pine, Philip
3972 Acapulco Ave
Las Vegas, NV 89121-6104, USA

Pine, Robert (Actor)
4212 Ben Ave
Studio City, CA 91604-2021, USA

Pineau-Valencienne, Didler (Business
Person)
Schneider
64/70 J Baptiste Clement
Boulogne-Billancourt 92646, FRANCE

Pineda, Salvador (Actor)
c/o Staff Member *TV Azteca*
Periferico Sur 4121
Colonia Fuentes del Pedregal
DF CP 14141, MEXICO

Pinero, Joel (Baseball Player)
c/o Staff Member *Seattle Mariners*
PO Box 4100
Safeco Field
Seattle, WA 98194-0100, USA

Pines, Alexander (Misc)
University of California
Chemistry Dept
Hildebrand Hall
Berkeley, CA 94720-0001, USA

Pinette, John
c/o Staff Member *International Creative
Management (ICM-LA)*
10250 Constellation Blvd
Los Angeles, CA 90067-6200, USA

Ping Lu, Kun (Misc)
Beth Israel Deaconess Medical Center
3300 Brookline Ave
Boston, MA 02215, USA

Pingel, John S (Football Player)
80 Celestial Way Apt 203
Juno Beach, FL 33408-2328, USA

Pinger, Mark (Swimmer)
5201 Orduna Dr Apt 6
Coral Gables, FL 33146-2655, USA

Piniella, Louis V (Lou) (Baseball Player)
Baltimore Orioles
1005 Taray De Avila
Tampa, FL 33613-1045, USA

Pink (Musician)
c/o Dana Sims *William Morris Agency
(WMA-LA)*
1 William Morris Pl
Beverly Hills, CA 90212-4261, USA

Pinkel, Donald P (Misc)
275 Martene Dr
San Luis Obispo, CA 93405, USA

Pinkel, Gary (Coach, Football Coach)
University of Missouri
Athletic Dept
Columbia, MO 64211, USA

Pinkett, Allen (Football Player)
Houston Oilers
2026 Tuam St
Houston, TX 77004-1349, USA

Pinkett Smith, Jada (Actor)
c/o Miguel Melendez *Overbrook Entertainment*
450 N Roxbury Dr Fl 4
Beverly Hills, CA 90210-4232, USA

Pinkham Jr, Daniel R (Composer)
150 Chilton St
Cambridge, MA 02138-1227, USA

Pinkins, Tonya (Actor)
Innovative Artists
1505 10th St
Santa Monica, CA 90401-2805, USA

Pinkston, Ryan (Actor)
c/o Staff Member *MBST Entertainment*
345 N Maple Dr Ste 200
Beverly Hills, CA 90210-3860, USA

Pinkston, Todd (Football Player)
1 Novacare Way
Philadelphia, PA 19145-5900, USA

Pinmonkey (Music Group)
c/o Staff Member *William Morris Agency (WMA-TN)*
1600 Division St Ste 300
Nashville, TN 37203-2755, USA

Pinney, Ray (Football Player)
Pittsburgh Steelers
6529B NE Windermere Rd
Seattle, WA 98105-2057, USA

Pinnock, Trevor (Conductor, Musician)
35 Gloucester Crescent
London NW1 7DL, UNITED KINGDOM (UK)

Pino, Danny (Actor)
c/o Staff Member *The Firm*
9465 Wilshire Blvd Fl 6
Beverly Hills, CA 90212-2605, USA

Pinos, Carmen (Architect)
Av Diagonal 490
#3/2
Barcelona 08006, SPAIN

Pinsky, Drew (Dr Drew) (Actor)
c/o Staff Member *William Morris Agency (WMA-LA)*
1 William Morris Pl
Beverly Hills, CA 90212-4261, USA

Pinsky, Robert N (Writer)
Boston University
236 Bay State Rd
Creative Writing Dept
Boston, MA 02215-1403, USA

Pinson, Julie (Actor)
13576 Cheltenham Dr
Sherman Oaks, CA 91423-4818, USA

Pinson, Vada
710 31st St
Oakland, CA 94609-2925, USA

Pintauro, Danny (Actor)
FHL
10667 Adamsong Ave
Las Vegas, NV 89135-2025, USA

Pinter, Harold (Writer)
Judy Daish
2 Saint Charles Place
London W10 6EG, UNITED KINGDOM (UK)

Pintilie, Lucian (Director)
44 Mihail Kogalniceanu Blvd
Bucharest, ROMANIA

Pintscher, Matthias (Composer)
Van Walsum Mgmt
4 Addison Bridge Place
London W14 8XP, UNITED KINGDOM (UK)

Piovanelli, Silvano Cardinal (Religious Leader)
Piazzi S Giovanni 3
Florence 50129, ITALY

Piper, Billie (Actor)
c/o Connie Tavel *Forward Entertainment*
9255 W Sunset Blvd Ste 805
Los Angeles, CA 90069-3305, USA

Piper, Jacki (Actor)
Lengford Assoc
17 Westfields Ave
Barnes
London SW13 0AT, UNITED KINGDOM (UK)

Piper, Rowdy Roddy (Actor, Wrestler)
Flying Noodles Inc.
13110 SW Whitmore Rd
Roderic Toombs
Hillsboro, OR 97123-9073, USA

Pipes, Leah (Actor)
c/o Rob D'Avola *Identity Talent Agency (ID)*
9107 Wilshire Blvd Ste 450
Beverly Hills, CA 90210-5535, USA

Pipes, R Byron (Educator)
4509 Sugar Maple Dr
Lafayette, IN 47905-4617, USA

Pipettes, The (Music Group)
c/o Staff Member *Paradigm (Monterey)*
509 Hartnell St
Monterey, CA 93940-2825, USA

Pippard, A Brian (Physicist)
30 Porson Road
Cambridge CB2 2EU, UNITED KINGDOM (UK)

Pippen, Scottie (Basketball Player)
Chicago Bulls
1901 W Madison St
United Center
Chicago, IL 60612-2459, USA

Pippig, Uta (Athlete, Track Athlete)
4279 Niblick Dr
Longmont, CO 80503-8326, USA

Piquet, Nelson (Race Car Driver)
Autodromo
SEN/CDPM
Rua da Gasolina #01
Brasilia, DF 7007-400, BRAZIL

Pirae, Marcus Jean (Actor)
c/o Tom Parziale *Visionary Entertainment*
1558 N Stanley Ave
West Hollywood, CA 90046-2711, USA

Piraro, Dan (Cartoonist)
United Feature Syndicate
200 Madison Ave
New York, NY 10016-3911, USA

Pirates of the Mississippi
PO Box 17087
Nashville, TN 37217-0087, USA

Pirelli, Leopoldo (Business Person)
Via Gaetano Negri 10
Milan 20123, ITALY

Pires, Alexandre (Musician)
c/o Staff Member *BMG*
1540 Broadway
New York, NY 10036-4074, USA

Pires, Mary Joao (Musician)
Columbia Artists Mgmt Inc
1790 Broadway Fl 6
New York, NY 10019-1412, USA

Pires, Pedro V R (General, Prime Minister)
PAICV
CP 22
Praia
Santiago, CAPE VERDE

Pires de Miranda, Pedro (Government Official)
Avenida da India 10
Lisbon 1300, PORTUGAL

Pirkl, Greg (Baseball Player)
Seattle Mariners
6822 Emerald Bay Ln
Indianapolis, IN 46237-5063, USA

Pirner, Dave (Musician, Songwriter, Writer)
Monterey Peninsula Artists
509 Hartnell St
Monterey, CA 93940-2825, USA

Piro, Stephanie (Cartoonist)
PO Box 605
Hampton, NH 03843-0605, USA

Pirok, Pauline (Baseball Player)
13636 86th Ave
Orland Park, IL 60462-1612, USA

Pirri, Jim
9300 Wilshire Blvd Ste 555
Beverly Hills, CA 90212-3211, USA

Pirtle, Gerry (Baseball Player)
Montreal Expos
4420 Prescott Ct
Flower Mound, TX 75028-2077, USA

Pisarkiewicz, Steve (Football Player)
St Louis Cardinals
1601 Johns Lake Rd Apt 1121
Clermont, FL 34711-6666, USA

Pischetsrider, Bernd (Business Person)
Bayerishe Motoren Werke
Petuelring 130
Munich 80788, GERMANY

Pisciotta, Marc (Baseball Player)
Chicago Cubs
867 Village Greene NW
Marietta, GA 30064-4749, USA

Piscopo, Joe (Actor, Comedian)
c/o Michael Eisenstadt *Amsel Eisenstadt & Frazier Inc*
5055 Wilshire Blvd Ste 865
Los Angeles, CA 90036-6109, USA

Pisier, Marie-France ((Actor)
Gaumont International
30 Ave Charles de Gaulle
Neuilly 92200, FRANCE

Piskula, Grace (Baseball Player)
415 Cherry Hill Dr
Racine, WI 53406-3523, USA

Pisoni, Jim (Baseball Player)
St Louis Browns
5500 Promise Land Dr
Frisco, TX 75035-7600, USA

Pister, Karl S (Educator)
University of California
Chancellor's Office
Santa Cruz, CA 95064, USA

Pistone, Tom (Race Car Driver)
12536 Caldwell Rd
Charlotte, NC 28213-3808, USA

Pitchford, Dean
1701 Queens Ct
Los Angeles, CA 90069-1431, USA

Pitcock, Joan (Golfer)
341 E Lester Ave
Fresno, CA 93720-1615, USA

Pithart, Petr (Government Official)
Senate
Vakdstejnske Nam 4
Prague 118 11, CZECH REPUBLIC

Pitillo, Maria (Actor)
William Morris AGency
151 El Camino Dr
Beverly Hills, CA 90212-2775, USA

Pitino, Richard (Rick) (Coach)
University of Louisville
Crawford Gym
Louisville, KY 40292-0001, USA

Pitko, Alex (Baseball Player)
Philadelphia Phillies
2689 Sports Village Loop # 12
Pinetop, AZ 85935-8159, USA

Pitlock, Skip (Baseball Player)
San Francisco Giants
215 Prospect St
Seguin, TX 78155-6018, USA

Pitman, Jennifer S (Race Car Driver)
Weathercock House
Upper Lamboum Hungerford
Berks RG17 8QT, UNITED KINGDOM (UK)

Pitoc, J P
1836 Courtney Ter
Los Angeles, CA 90046-2106, USA

Pitoc, John Paul (Actor)
c/o Staff Member *Don Buchwald & Associates Inc (LA)*
6500 Wilshire Blvd Ste 2200
Los Angeles, CA 90048-4942, USA

Pitou Zimmerman, Penny (Skier)
560 Sanborn Rd
Sanbornton, NH 03269-2401, USA

Pitt, Brad
c/o Staff Member *Plan B*
9150 Wilshire Blvd Ste 350
Beverly Hills, CA 90212-3453, USA

Pitt, Eugene (Musician)
Paramount Entertainment
PO Box 12
Far Hills, NJ 07931-0012, USA

Pitt, Ingrid (Actor)
Langford
17 Westfields Ave
London SW13 0AT, UNITED KINGDOM (UK)

Pitt, William
9 rue Jean Mermoz
Paris F-75008, FRANCE

Pittaro, Chris (Baseball Player)
Detroit Tigers
42 Pintinalli Dr
Trenton, NJ 08619-1558, USA

Pittenger, Mark F (Scientist)
Osrins Therapeutics
2001 Aliceanna St
Baltimore, MD 21231-3043, USA

Pittman, Charles (Basketball Player)
16286 N 29th Dr
Phoenix, AZ 85053-3004, USA

Pittman, Danny (Football Player)
New York Giants
University Of Wyoming Attn: Alumni
Association
Laramie, WY 82071, USA

Pittman, Joe (Baseball Player)
Houston Astros
809 McKinnon Dr
Columbus, GA 31907-6508, USA

Pittman, Michael (Football Player)
Arizona Cardinals
11239 Blacksmith Dr
Tampa, FL 33626-2675, USA

Pittman, R F (Publisher)
Tampa Tribune
202 S Parker St
Tampa, FL 33606-2395, USA

Pittman, Richard A (War Hero)
5380 Dehesa Rd
El Cajon, CA 92019-1807, USA

Pittman Jr, James A (Misc)
5 Ridge Dr
Birmingham, AL 35213-3631, USA

Pitts, Frank (Football Player)
Kansas City Chiefs
8249 S Laredo Ave
Baton Rouge, LA 70811-4055, USA

Pitts, Gaylen (Baseball Player)
Oakland A's
214 Rocky Bluff Ln
Mountain Home, AR 72653-7186, USA

Pitts, Greg
8383 Wilshire Blvd Ste 550
Beverly Hills, CA 90211-2417, USA

Pitts, Hugh (Football Player)
Los Angeles Rams
3612 Short St
Greenville, TX 75401-3900, USA

Pitts, John (Football Player)
Buffalo Bills
4899 W Tyson St
Chandler, AZ 85226-2909, USA

Pitts, Robert (R C) (Basketball Player)
12655 E Millburn Ave
Baton Rouge, LA 70815-6827, USA

Pitts, Ron (Football Player)
Buffalo Bills
3811 Davids Rd
Agoura Hills, CA 91301-3643, USA

Pitts, Ron (Sportscaster)
Fox TV
205 W 67th St
Sports Dept
New York, NY 10021, USA

Pitts, Tyrone S (Religious Leader)
Progressive National Baptist Convention
601 50th St NE
Washington, DC 20019-5498, USA

Pittsley, Jim (Baseball Player)
Kansas City Royals
5 Old Woods Rd
Du Bois, PA 15801-8711, USA

Pivec, Dave (Football Player)
Los Angeles Rams
219 Ashland Rd
Cockeysville, MD 21030-1901, USA

Piven, Jeremy (Actor)
c/o Tracy Brennan *Creative Artists Agency*
LCC (CAA-LA)
2000 Avenue Of The Stars
Los Angeles, CA 90067-4700, USA

Piza, Arthur Luiz de (Artist)
16 Rue Dauphine
Paris 75006, FRANCE

Pizarro, Artur (Musician)
Muscians Corporate Mgmt
PO Box 825
Highland, NY 12528-0825, USA

Pizarro, Juan (Baseball Player)
Milwaukee Braves
2262 Ave Borinquen
Santurce, PR 00915-4421, USA

Piziou, Peter
16 Belsize Park
London, ENGLAND NW3 4ES, UNITED
KINGDOM (UK)

Pizzo, Angelo (Director, Producer, Writer)
c/o David Greenblatt *Key Creatives*
9595 Wilshire Blvd Ste 800
Beverly Hills, CA 90212-2508, USA

PJ & Duncan
PO Box 122Ashford
Kent, ENGLAND TN27 9BZ, UNITED
KINGDOM (UK)

Place, Mary Kay (Actor)
2739 Motor Ave
Los Angeles, CA 90064-3441, USA

Placebo (Music Group)
Elevator Lady Ltd
4 South Street
Epsom
Surrey KT18 7PF, UNITED KINGDOM
(UK)

Plachta, Leonard E (Educator)
Central Michigan University
President's Office
Mount Pleasant, MI 48859-0001, USA

Placido, Michele
. 5200 via San Cornelia
Formello-RM 00060, ITALY

Pladson, Gordon (Baseball Player)
Houston Astros
19087 87a Ave
Surrey, BC V4N 3G5, CANADA

Plager, Robert B (Bob) (Coach, Hockey
Player)
362 Branchport Dr
Chesterfield, MO 63017-2902, USA

Plager, S Jay (Judge)
US Court of Appeals
7171 Madison Place NW
Washington, DC 20439-0001, USA

Plain, Belva (Writer)
Houghton Mifflin
215 Park Ave S Fl 12
New York, NY 10003-1621, USA

Plainic, Zoran (Basketball Player)
New Jersey Nets
390 Murray Hill Pkwy
East Rutherford, NJ 07073-2109, USA

Plakson, Suzie (Actor)
302 N La Brea Ave # 363
Los Angeles, CA 90036-2518, USA

Plan B (Music Group)
c/o Staff Member *Paradigm (Monterey)*
509 Hartnell St
Monterey, CA 93940-2825, USA

Plana, Tony (Actor)
c/o Staff Member *Agency for the
Performing Arts (APA-NY)*
888 7th Ave
New York, NY 10106-0001, USA

Planchon, Roger (Director, Writer)
Teatre National Populaire
8 Pl Lazare Goujon
Villeurbanne 69627, FRANCE

Planinc, Milka (Prime Minister)
Fed Exec Council
Bul Lenjina 2
Novi Belgrad 11075, SERBIA-
MONTENEGRO

Plank, Doug (Football Player)
Chicago Bears
12622 E Paradise Dr
Scottsdale, AZ 85259-3455, USA

Plank, Eddie (Baseball Player)
San Francisco Giants
6112 W Okanogan Ct
Spokane, WA 99208, USA

Plank, Raymond (Business Person)
Apache Corp
2000 Post Oak Blvd
Houston, TX 77056-4400, USA

Plank, Scott
151 El Camino Dr
Beverly Hills, CA 90212-2704, USA

Plano, Richard J (Physicist)
PO Box 5306
Somerset, NJ 08875-5306, USA

Plant, Robert (Musician, Songwriter,
Writer)
Trinifold Mgmt
12 Oval Road
London NW1 7DH, UNITED KINGDOM
(UK)

Plante, Bruce (Cartoonist)
Chattanooga Times
100 E 11th St Ste 400
Editorial Dept
Chattanooga, TN 37402-4214, USA

Plante, William M (Correspondent)
CBS-TV
2020 M St NW
News Dept
Washington, DC 20036-3304, USA

Plantenberg, Erik (Baseball Player)
Seattle Mariners
1420 NW Gilman Blvd Ste 2615
Issaquah, WA 98027-5394, USA

Plantier, Phil (Baseball Player)
Boston Red Sox
16208 Oak Creek Trl
Poway, CA 92064-1704, USA

Plantu (Cartoonist)
Le Monde
Editorial Dept
21 Bis Rue Claude Bernard
Paris 75005, FRANCE

Planutis, Jerry (Football Player)
Washington Redskins
3776 Stadium Dr
Bridgman, MI 49106-9789, USA

Plaskett, Thomas G (Business Person)
5215 N O Connor Blvd Ste 1070
Irving, TX 75039-3738, USA

Plater-Zyberk, Elizabeth M (Architect)
Duany & Plater-Zyberk Architects
1023 SW 25th Ave
Miami, FL 33135-4824, USA

Platini, Michel
90 av. des Champs-Elysees
Paris F-75008, FRANCE

Platinli, Michel (Soccer Player)
World Cup Organization
17-21 Ave Gen Mangin
Paris Cedex 75024, FRANCE

Platinum Blonde
Box 1223 Sta. F
Toronto, ON M4Y 2T, CANADA

Platon, Nicolas (Archaeologist)
Leof Alexandras 126
Athens 11471, GREECE

Platov, Yevgeni (Dancer)
Connecticut Skating Center
300 Alumni Rd
Newington, CT 06111-1865, USA

Platt, David (Soccer Player)
FourFourTwo
52 Victoria Street
McMahons Point NSW 2060, AUSTRALIA

Platt, Howard
9200 W Sunset Blvd Ste 1130
Los Angeles, CA 90069-3606, USA

Platt, Kenneth A (Doctor)
11435 Quivas Way
Westminster, CO 80234-2620, USA

Platt, Lewis E (Lew) (Business Person)
Hewlett-Packard Co
3000 Hanover St
Palo Alto, CA 94304-1185, USA

Platt, Nicholas (Diplomat)
131 E 69th St
New York, NY 10021-5158, USA

Platt, Oliver (Actor)
c/o Michelle Bohan *Endeavor Agency LLC*
(LA)
1 William Morris Pl
Beverly Hills, CA 90212-4261, USA

Platters
2756 N Green Valley Pkwy # 449
Henderson, NV 89014-2120, USA

Plavinsky, Dmitri P (Artist)
Arbat Str 51
Kotp 2 #97
Moscow 121002, RUSSIA

Playboy Playmates
2112 Broadway
Santa Monica, CA 90404-2912, USA

Player, Gary J (Golfer)
11390 N Jog Rd Ste 100
Palm Beach Gardens, FL 33418-1755,
USA

Player, Scott (Football Player)
Arizona Cardinals
1583 W Saltsage Dr
Phoenix, AZ 85045-1712, USA

Playten, Alice (Actor)
33 5th Ave
New York, NY 10003-4338, USA

Pleasant, Anthony (Football Player)
Cleveland Browns
17249 Connor Quay Ct
Cornelius, NC 28031-6503, USA

Pleasant, Reggie (Football Player)
Atlanta Falcons
8270 Milford Plantation Rd
Pinewood, SC 29125-9249, USA

Pleau, Lawrence W (Larry) (Coach,
Hockey Player)
650 Spyglass Summit Dr
Chesterfield, MO 63017-2143, USA

Pleis, Bill (Baseball Player)
Minnesota Twins
3835 Little Country Rd
Parrish, FL 34219-9274, USA

Plemons, Jesse (Actor)
c/o Staff Member *Simmons & Scott
Entertainment*
4110 W Burbank Blvd
Burbank, CA 91505-2121, USA

Plenty, Patty
1350 E Flamingo Rd Ste 150
Las Vegas, NV 89119-5225, USA

Plesac, Dan (Baseball Player)
Milwaukee Brewers
245 White Thorne Ln
Valparaiso, IN 46383-9785, USA

Pleshette, John (Actor)
2643 Creston Dr
Los Angeles, CA 90068-2207, USA

Pleshette, Suzanne (Actor)
c/o Joel Dean *TalentWorks (LA)*
3500 W Olive Ave Ste 1400
Burbank, CA 91505-5512, USA

Pless, Rance (Baseball Player)
Kansas City A's
5528 Asheville Hwy
Greeneville, TN 37743-2287, USA

Pletcher, Eidon (Cartoonist)
210 Canberra Ct
Slidell, LA 70458-1520, USA

Pletnev, Mikhail V (Musician)
Starpkonyushenny Per 33
#16
Moscow, RUSSIA

Plews, Herb (Baseball Player)
Washington Senators
350 Ponca Pl
Boulder, CO 80303-3802, USA

Plimpton, Calvin H (Doctor)
Downstate Medical Center
450 Clarkson Ave
Brooklyn, NY 11203-2098, USA

Plimpton, Martha (Actor)
502 Park Ave # 15G
New York, NY 10022-1108, USA

Plisetskaya, Maiya M (Ballerina)
Tverskaya 25/9
#31
Moscow 103050, RUSSIA

Plodinec, Tim (Baseball Player)
St Louis Cardinals
23251 Gilmore St
West Hills, CA 91307-3427, USA

Ploeger, Kurt (Football Player)
Dallas Cowboys
304 2nd Ave SW
Pipestone, MN 56164-1508, USA

Plotkin, Stanley A (Musician)
3940 Delancey St
Philadelphia, PA 19104-4107, USA

Plott, Charles R (Economist)
881 El Campo Dr
Pasadena, CA 91107-5565, USA

Plough, Thomas (Educator)
North Dakota State University
President's Office
Fargo, ND 58105, USA

Plowden, David (Photographer, Writer)
609 Cherry St
Winnetka, IL 60093-2614, USA

Plowright, Joan A (Actor)
Malthouse
Horsham Road Ashurst Steying
West Sussex BN44 3AR, UNITED
KINGDOM (UK)

Plowright, Joan A (Opera Singer)
83 Saint Mark's Ave
Salisbury
Wilts SP1 3DW, UNITED KINGDOM
(UK)

Pluhar, Erika
Huschkagasse 5
Vienna A-1190, AUSTRIA

Plum, Milton R (Milt) (Football Player)
Cleveland Browns
1104 Oakside Ct
Raleigh, NC 27609-3596, USA

Plum, Ted (Football Player)
Buffalo Bills
17 Laurel Hill Dr
Cherry Hill, NJ 08003-2658, USA

Plumb, Eve (Actor)
c/o Staff Member *Edwards & Associates*
5455 Wilshire Blvd Ste 1614
Los Angeles, CA 90036-4205, USA

Plumer, Patricia (PattiSue) (Athlete, Track
Athlete)
USA Track & Field
4341 Starlight Dr
Indianapolis, IN 46239-1473, USA

Plummer, Amanda (Actor)
160 Prince St Apt 2
New York, NY 10012-5340, USA

Plummer, Bill (Baseball Player)
Chicago Cubs
137 E Main St
Missoula Osprey Baseball Club Attn
Managers Office
Missoula, MT 59802-4421, USA

Plummer, Christopher (Actor, Musician)
49 Wampum Hill Rd Ste 480
Weston, CT 06883-1228, USA

Plummer, Gary (Football Player)
San Diego Chargers
10374 Rue Chamberry
San Diego, CA 92131-2212, USA

Plummer, Glenn (Actor)
c/o Staff Member *Innovative Artists (LA)*
1505 10th St
Santa Monica, CA 90401-2805, USA

Plummer, Scotty
909 Parkview Ave
Lodi, CA 95242-2347, USA

Plummer, Stephen B (General)
Deputy To Assistant Secretary
Hqusaf Pentagon
Washington, DC 20330-0001, USA

Plunk, Eric (Baseball Player)
Oakland A's
9500 Pats Point Dr
Corona, CA 92883-5068, USA

Plunkett, Jim
New Orleans Saints
51 Kilroy Way
Atherton, CA 94027-5405, USA

Plunkett, Maryann
10 E 44th St
New York, NY 10017-3601, USA

Plunkett, Warren (Football Player)
Cleveland Rams
25150 N Windy Walk Dr Unit 30
Scottsdale, AZ 85255-8106, USA

Plus One (Music Group)
c/o Teresa Davis *Paradigm (Nashville)*
124 12th Ave S Ste 410
Nashville, TN 37203-3170, USA

Plushenko, Evgeni (Figure Skater)
c/o Staff Member *Champions on Ice*
3500 W 80th St
Tom Collins Enterprises Inc
Minneapolis, MN 55431-1068, USA

Ply, Bobby (Football Player)
Dallas Texans
8616 Ash Ave
Raytown, MO 64138-3431, USA

Plympton, Jeff (Baseball Player)
Boston Red Sox
8 Robin St
Plainville, MA 02762-1522, USA

Plyushch, Ivan S (Misc)
Verkhovna Rada
M Hrushevskoho 5
Kiev 252019, UKRAINE

PM Dawn
14 E 4th St
New York, NY 10012-1155, USA

Poch, Terri (Wrestler)
c/o Staff Member *World Wrestling
Entertainment (WWE)*
1241 E Main St
Stamford, CT 06902-3520, USA

Pochman, Owen (Football Player)
New York Giants
7405 91st Ave SE
Mercer Island, WA 98040-5805, USA

Pocklington, Peter H (Misc)
Edmonton Oilers
11230 110th St
Edmonton, AB T5G 3H7, CANADA

Pocoroba, Biff (Baseball Player)
Atlanta Braves
7002 Deshon Ridge Dr
Lithonia, GA 30058-2973, USA

POD (Music Group)
c/o Staff Member *Paradigm (Monterey)*
509 Hartnell St
Monterey, CA 93940-2825, USA

Podell, Eyal (Actor)
c/o Samantha Crisp *Kohner Agency, The*
9300 Wilshire Blvd Ste 555
Beverly Hills, CA 90212-3211, USA

Poderoso, Gozo (Musician)
c/o Staff Member *William Morris Agency
(WMA-LA)*
1 William Morris Pl
Beverly Hills, CA 90212-4261, USA

Podesta, John (Government Official)
White House
1600 Pennsylvania Ave NW
Washington, DC 20500-0004, USA

Podesta, Rosanna
Via Bartolomeo Ammannati 8
Rome I-00197, ITALY

Podesta, Rossana (Actor)
Via Bartolomeo Ammanatti 8
Rome 00187, ITALY

Podeswa, Jeremy (Director, Writer)
c/o Jennifer Levine *Untitled Entertainment
(LA)*
331 N Maple Dr Fl 3
Beverly Hills, CA 90210-3827, USA

Podewell, Cathy (Actor)
17328 S Crest Dr
Los Angeles, CA 90035, USA

Podhoretz, Norman (Editor, Writer)
Commentary Magazine
165 E 56th St
Editorial Dept
New York, NY 10022-2709, USA

Podkopayeva, Lilia
Rue des Oeuches 10
Moutier CP 350 374, SWITZERLAND

Podolak, Edward J (Ed) (Football Player)
Kansas City Chiefs
2227 Emma Rd
Basalt, CO 81621-8326, USA

Podoley, Jim (Football Player)
Washington Redskins
3818 12th St NE
State Farm Ins
Washington, DC 20017-2630, USA

Podolski, Lukas (Soccer Player)
Norbert Pflipen
Heinz-Nixdorf-Strasse 33
MÝnchengladbach 41179, GERMANY

Podres, John J (Johnny) (Baseball Player)
Brooklyn Dodgers
1 Colonial Ct
Queensbury, NY 12804-1912, USA

Podsednik, Scott (Baseball Player)
c/o Staff Member *Chicago White Sox*
333 W 35th St
Comiskey Park
Chicago, IL 60616-3651, USA

Poe (Musician, Songwriter, Writer)
Creative Artists Agency
9830 Wilshire Blvd
Beverly Hills, CA 90212-1804, USA

Poe, Gregory (Designer, Fashion
Designer)
Dutch Courage
1950 S Santa Fe Ave
Los Angeles, CA 90021-2928, USA

Poe, Johnnie (Football Player)
New Orleans Saints
924 Donald F McHenry Pl
East Saint Louis, IL 62201-1046, USA

Poe, Richard
10 Prospect Park SW Apt 17
Brooklyn, NY 11215-5937, USA

Poehler, Amy (Actor, Comedian)
Three Arts Entertainment
9460 Wilshire Blvd Ste 700
Beverly Hills, CA 90212-2713, USA

Poepping, Mike (Baseball Player)
Minnesota Twins
10581 Lake Rd
Pierz, MN 56364-7117, USA

Poesy, Clemence (Actor)
c/o Hylda Queally *Creative Artists Agency
LCC (CAA-LA)*
2000 Avenue Of The Stars
Los Angeles, CA 90067-4700, USA

Poff, John (Baseball Player)
Philadelphia Phillies
2786 Mishler Rd
Mio, MI 48647-9505, USA

Pogorelich, Ivo (Musician)
Kantor Concert Mgmt
67 Teignmouth Road
London NW2 4EA, UNITED KINGDOM
(UK)

Pogrebin, Letty Cottin (Activist, Editor, Writer)
33 W 67th St
New York, NY 10023-6224, USA

Pogue, Donald W (Judge)
IS International Trade Court
1 Federal Plz
New York, NY 10278-0001, USA

Pogue, William R (Astronaut)
4 Cromer Dr
Bella Vista, AR 72715-5318, USA

Pohl, Dan (Golfer)
3424 E Suncrest Ct
Phoenix, AZ 85044-3506, USA

Pohl, Don (Golfer)
3424 E Suncrest Ct
Phoenix, AZ 85044-3506, USA

Pohl, Frederick
855 S Harvard Dr
Palatine, IL 60067-7026, USA

Pohlad, Carl (Baseball Player)
Minnesota Twins
470 Ferndale Rd S
Wayzata, MN 55391, USA

Poimboeuf, Lance (Football Player)
Dallas Cowboys
309 Fairfield Dr
Thibodaux, LA 70301-3721, USA

Poindexter, Alan G (Astronaut)
2389 Calypso Ln
League City, TX 77573-2796, USA

Poindexter, Anthony (Football Player)
Baltimore Ravens
RR 3 Box 128
Forest, VA 24551, USA

Poindexter, Buster (Musician)
Agency Group Ltd
1775 Broadway Ste 515
New York, NY 10019-1903, USA

Poindexter, Christian H (Business Person)
Constellation Energy Group
39 W Lexington St
Baltimore, MD 21201-3979, USA

Poindexter, John M (Admiral, Government Official)
10 Barrington Fare
Rockville, MD 20850-3001, USA

Point of Grace (Music Group)
Blanton Harrell Cooke & Corzine
5250 Virginia Way Ste 110
Brentwood, TN 37027-7575, USA

Pointer, Anita (Musician)
12060 Crest Ct
Beverly Hills, CA 90210-1348, USA

Pointer, Bonnie (Musician)
T-Best Talent Agency
508 Honey Lake Ct
Danville, CA 94506-1237, USA

Pointer, Noel (Musician)
Headline Talent
1650 Broadway Ste 508
New York, NY 10019-6833, USA

Pointer, Priscilla (Actor)
c/o Staff Member *William Morris Agency (WMA-LA)*
1 William Morris Pl
Beverly Hills, CA 90212-4261, USA

Pointer, Priscilla (Musician)
213 16th St
Santa Monica, CA 90402-2215, USA

Pointer, Ruth (Musician)
William Morris AGency
151 El Camino Dr
Beverly Hills, CA 90212-2775, USA

Pointer Sisters (Music Group)
c/o Jim Morey *Morey Management Group*
1100 Glendon Ave Ph 1
Los Angeles, CA 90024-3526, USA

Poirier, Anne
32 rue Lenine
Ivry F-94200, FRANCE

Poirier, Patrick
32 rue Lenine
Ivry F-94200, FRANCE

Poison (Music Group)
c/o Staff Member *Agency for the Performing Arts (APA-LA)*
405 S Beverly Dr
Beverly Hills, CA 90212-4416, USA

Poitier, Sidney (Actor)
c/o Staff Member *Verdon-Cedric Productions*
PO Box 2639
Beverly Hills, CA 90213-2639, USA

Polaha, Kris (Actor)
c/o Nick Frenkel *3 Arts Entertainment (NY)*
9460 Wilshire Blvd Ste 700
Beverly Hills, CA 90212-2713, USA

Polamalu, Troy (Football Player)
Pittsburgh Steelers
3400 S Water St
Pittsburgh, PA 15203-2349, USA

Polanco, Placido (Baseball Player)
Milwaukee Brewers
9494 SW 125th Ter
Miami, FL 33176-5051, USA

Polanski, Roman (Director)
c/o Jeff Berg *International Creative Management (ICM-LA)*
10250 Constellation Blvd
Los Angeles, CA 90067-6200, USA

Polansky, Abraham
135 S McCarty Dr Ph 4
Beverly Hills, CA 90212-2257, USA

Polansky, Mark (Astronaut)
2010 Hillside Oak Ln
Houston, TX 77062-3642, USA

Polanyi, John C (Nobel Prize Laureate)
142 Collier St
Toronto, ON M4W 1M3, CANADA

Polchinski, Joseph G (Physicist)
University of California
Physics Institute
Santa Barbara, CA 93106-0001, USA

Polcovich, Kevin (Baseball Player)
Pittsburgh Pirates
3 Beardsley St
Auburn, NY 13021-2809, USA

Pole, Dick (Baseball Player)
Boston Red Sox
21012 Whitlock Dr
Dearborn Heights, MI 48127-2648, USA

Poledouris, Basil (Composer)
Kraft-Benjamin-Engel
15233 Ventura Blvd Ste 200
Sherman Oaks, CA 91403-2244, USA

Poleshchuk, Alexander F (Cosmonaut)
Potchta Kosmonavtov Moskovskoi Oblasti
Syvisdny Goroduk 141160, RUSSIA

Poletiek, Noah (Actor)
c/o Staff Member *Protege Entertainment*
710 E Angeleno Ave
Burbank, CA 91501-2213, USA

Poletto, Severino Cardinal (Religious Leader)
Via Arcivescovado 12
Torino 10121, ITALY

Polgar, Laszlo (Opera Singer)
Abel Jeno Utca 12
Budapest 1113, HUNGARY

Polic, Henry II (Actor)
Sutton Barth Vennari
145 S Fairfax Ave Ste 310
Los Angeles, CA 90036-2176, USA

Police, The
194 Kensington Park Rd.
London, ENGLAND W11 2ES, UNITED KINGDOM (UK)

Polish, Mark (Actor, Producer, Writer)
c/o Sean Elliott *Endeavor Agency LLC (LA)*
9601 Wilshire Blvd Fl 3
Beverly Hills, CA 90210-5204, USA

Polish, Michael (Director)
Endeavor Talent Agency
9701 Wilshire Blvd Ste 1000
Beverly Hills, CA 90212-2010, USA

Polishchuk, Oleksiy (Figure Skater)
c/o Staff Member *Champions on Ice*
3500 W 80th St
Tom Collins Enterprises Inc
Minneapolis, MN 55431-1068, USA

Polito, Jon (Actor)
c/o Staff Member *Writers and Artists Group Intl (LA)*
8383 Wilshire Blvd Ste 550
Beverly Hills, CA 90211-2417, USA

Politte, Cliff (Baseball Player)
St Louis Cardinals
6306 Sprig Oak Ct Apt C
Saint Louis, MO 63128-4336, USA

Politz, Henry A (Judge)
US Court of Appeals
500 Fannin St
Shreveport, LA 71101-3023, USA

Polk, Steven R (General)
Vice Commander
Pacific Air Forces
Hickam Air Force Base, HI 96853, USA

Polke, Sigmar (Artist)
Michael Werner
4 E 77th St # 200
New York, NY 10075-1727, USA

Polkinghome, John C (Physicist)
Queen's College
Cambridge University
Cambridge CB3 9ET, UNITED KINGDOM (UK)

Poll, Martin H (Producer)
Martin Poll Productions
8961 W Sunset Blvd # E
Los Angeles, CA 90069-1807, USA

Pollack, Andrea (Swimmer)
SSV
Postfach 420140
Kassel 34070, GERMANY

Pollack, Daniel (Musician)
University of Southern California
Music Dept
Los Angeles, CA 90089-0001, USA

Pollack, Frank (Football Player)
San Francisco 49ers
1063 Morse Ave
Sunnyvale, CA 94089-4619, USA

Pollack, Jim (Actor)
Ericka Wain
1418 N Highland Ave # 102
Los Angeles, CA 90028-7611, USA

Pollack, Joseph (Misc)
Insurance Workers Union
1017 12th St NW
Washington, DC 20005-4054, USA

Pollack, Kevin (Actor)
c/o Annett Wolf *Wolf Kasteler Van Iden & Associates (LA)*
335 N Maple Dr Ste 351
Beverly Hills, CA 90210-3860, USA

Pollack, Sam (Misc)
6811 Monkland Ave
Montreal, PQ H4B 1J2, CANADA

Pollack, Sydney (Actor, Director)
c/o Staff Member *Mirage Enterprises (LA)*
9220 W Sunset Blvd
West Hollywood, CA 90069-3501, USA

Pollak, Kevin (Actor, Comedian)
Calm Down Productions
1360 N Crescent Heights Blvd
West Hollywood, CA 90046-4553, USA

Pollak, Lisa (Journalist)
Baltimore Sun
501 N Calvert St
Editorial Dept
Baltimore, MD 21202-3604, USA

Pollan, Tracy (Actor)
Baker/Winokur/Ryder
9100 Wilshire Blvd # 600
Beverly Hills, CA 90212-3401, USA

Pollard, Bob (Football Player)
New Orleans Saints
8987 Washington Blvd
Beaumont, TX 77707-2814, USA

Pollard, Frank (Football Player)
Pittsburgh Steelers
1526 N 12th St
Waco, TX 76707-2320, USA

Pollard, Jonathan
Federal Reformatory
Marion, IL 62959, USA

Pollard, Marcus (Football Player)
Indianapolis Colts
17279 NE 120th Way
Redmond, WA 98052-2339, USA

Pollard, Michael J (Actor)
520 S Burnside Ave Apt 12A
Los Angeles, CA 90036-3956, USA

Pollard, Scott (Basketball Player)
Indiana Pacers
125 S Pennsylvania St
Conseco Fieldhouse
Indianapolis, IN 46204-3610, USA

Pollard, Su
24 Denmark St.
London, ENGLAND WC2H 8NA, UNITED KINGDOM (UK)

Polle, David R (Misc)
Nashville Predators
501 Broadway
Nashville, TN 37203-3932, USA

Polle, Norman R (Bud) (Coach, Hockey Player)
1509-2004 Fullerton Ave
North Vancouver, BC V7P 3G8, CANADA

Pollen, Arabella R H (Designer, Fashion Designer)
Canham Mews
#8 Canham Road
London W3 7SR, UNITED KINGDOM (UK)

Polley, Dale (Ballerina)
New York Yankees
107 Redding Rd
Georgetown, KY 40324-1078, USA

Polley, Eugene J (Inventor)
202 W Berkshire Ave
Lombard, IL 60148-1549, USA

Polley, Sarah (Actor)
10 Mary St
#308
Toronto, ON M4Y 1P9, CANADA

Pollin, Abe (Baseball Player)
Centre Group
Capital Centre
1 Truman Dr
Landover, MD 20785, USA

Pollini, Maurizio (Musician)
RESIA
Via Manzoni 31
Milan 20120, ITALY

Pollitt-Deschaine, Alice (Baseball Player)
9140 Silver Strand Rd
Levering, MI 49755-9103, USA

Pollock, Alex J (Business Person)
Federal Home Loan Bank
111 E Wacker Dr
Chicago, IL 60601-4361, USA

Pollock, Michael P (Admiral)
Ivy House
Churchstoke Montgomery
Powys, WALES SY15 6DU, UNITED KINGDOM (UK)

Polnter, Aaron (Baseball Player)
Houston Colt .45's
4902 N Scenic View Ln
Tacoma, WA 98407-1365, USA

Polo, Ana Maria (Actor)
c/o Staff Member *Telemundo*
2470 W 8th Ave
Hialeah, FL 33010-2000, USA

Polo, Teri (Actor)
c/o Bob McGowan *McGowan Management*
8733 W Sunset Blvd Ste 103
W Hollywood, CA 90069-2241, USA

Polo, Terri (Actor)
c/o Staff Member *United Talent Agency (UTA)*
9560 Wilshire Blvd Ste 500
Beverly Hills, CA 90212-2401, USA

Polofsky, Gordon (Football Player)
Chicago Cardinals
8815 Gatwick Dr
Concord, TN 37922-6098, USA

Polone, Gavin (Producer)
c/o Staff Member *Endeavor Agency LLC (LA)*
9601 Wilshire Blvd Fl 3
Beverly Hills, CA 90210-5204, USA

Poloni, John (Baseball Player)
Texas Rangers
1714 Polo Club Dr
Tarpon Springs, FL 34689-8013, USA

Polowski, Larry (Football Player)
Seattle Seahawks
365 E Brookhollow Dr
Boise, ID 83706-6730, USA

Polozkova, Lidia P (Speed Skater)
Solianka Str 14/2
Moscow 109240, RUSSIA

Polshak, James Stewart (Architect)
James Polshak Partners
320 W 134th St # 800
New York, NY 10030, USA

Polson, John (Actor)
c/o Robyn Gardiner *RGM Associates (Australia)*
PO Box 128
Surry Hills NSW 2010, AUSTRALIA

Polyakov, Valeri V (Cosmonaut)
Health Ministry
Choroshevskoye Chaussee 76A
Moscow 123007, RUSSIA

Polyakov, Valery
141 160 Zvezdny Gorodok
Moscow Obl, RUSSIA

Polynice, Olden (Basketball Player)
PO Box 220339
Newhall, CA 91322-0339, USA

Polyphonic Spree, The (Music Group)
c/o Staff Member *Paradigm (Monterey)*
509 Hartnell St
Monterey, CA 93940-2825, USA

Pomers, Scarlett (Actor)
c/o Siri Garber *Platform Public Relations*
2133 Holly Dr
Los Angeles, CA 90068-2851, USA

Pommier, Jean-Bernard (Musician)
2 Chemin des Cotes de Montmoiret
Lausanne 1012, SWITZERLAND

Pomodora, Arnaldo (Artist)
Via Vigevano 5
Milan 20144, ITALY

Pompedda, Mario Francesco Cardinal (Religious Leader)
Palazzo della Cancelleria
Plazza della Cancelleria 1
Rome 00186, ITALY

Pompeo, Ellen (Actor)
c/o Staff Member *Grey's Anatomy*
500 S Buena Vista St
Burbank, CA 91521-0001, USA

Ponazecki, Joe (Actor)
Don Buchwald
10 E 44th St
New York, NY 10017-3654, USA

Ponce, Carlos (Baseball Player)
Milwaukee Brewers
590 Kingsbury Ct
Wellington, FL 33414-3919, USA

Ponce, Carlos (Musician)
c/o Staff Member *William Morris Agency (WMA-LA)*
1 William Morris Pl
Beverly Hills, CA 90212-4261, USA

Ponce, Enrile Juan (Government Official)
2305 Morado St
Dasmarinas Village Makati
Metro Manila, PHILIPPINES

Ponce, LuAnne (Actor)
Gold Marshak Liedtke
3500 W Olive Ave Ste 1400
Burbank, CA 91505-5512, USA

Ponce, Ponce
13501 Delano St
Van Nuys, CA 91401-3033, USA

Ponce, Walter (Musician)
Columbia Artists Mgmt Inc
1790 Broadway Fl 6
New York, NY 10019-1412, USA

Poncino, Larry (Baseball Player)
2954 N Calle Ladera
Tucson, AZ 85715-3202, USA

Pond, Matt (Musician)
c/o Staff Member *Paradigm (Monterey)*
509 Hartnell St
Monterey, CA 93940-2825, USA

Ponder, Dave (Football Player)
Dallas Cowboys
1818 Sandalwood Ln
Grapevine, TX 76051-7344, USA

Poni-Tails, The
PO Box 262
Carteret, NJ 07008-0262, USA

Pons, B Stanley (Misc)
University of Utah
Chemistry Dept
Eyring Building
Salt Lake City, UT 84112, USA

Pons, Juan (Opera Singer)
Herbert Breslin
119 W 57th St Ste 1505
New York, NY 10019-2401, USA

Pont, John (Coach, Football Coach)
482 White Oak Dr
Oxford, OH 45056-9272, USA

Pontes, Marcos (Astronaut)
16807 Soaring Forest Dr
Houston, TX 77059-4002, USA

Ponti, Cario (Producer)
Palazzo Colonna
1 Piazza d'Ara Coell 1
Rome, ITALY

Ponti, Michael (Musician)
Heubergstr 32
Eschenlohe 83565, GERMANY

Pontius, Chris (Actor, Writer)
c/o Beth Holden-Garland *Untitled Entertainment (LA)*
331 N Maple Dr Fl 3
Beverly Hills, CA 90210-3827, USA

Pontois, Noella-Chantal (Ballerina)
25 Rue de Maubeuge
Paris 75009, FRANCE

Ponty, Jean-Luc (Composer, Musician)
Monterey Peninsula Artists
509 Hartnell St
Monterey, CA 93940-2825, USA

Pony, Trick (Music Group)
c/o Staff Member *Creative Artists Agency (CAA-Nashville)*
3310 W End Ave Fl 5
Nashville, TN 37203-1028, USA

Ponzini, Anthony (Actor)
Gold Marshak Liedtke
3500 W Olive Ave Ste 1400
Burbank, CA 91505-5512, USA

Ponzlov, Frederick (Writer)
c/o Staff Member *Careyes Entertainment*
9000 W Sunset Blvd Ste 800
Los Angeles, CA 90069-5808, USA

Pooja, Bhatt (Actor, Bollywood)
601 Kyle More Apartments
Behind Mehboob Studios Bandra(W)
Mumbai, MS 400050, INDIA

Pook, Chris (Race Car Driver)
Championship Auto Racing
5350 Lakeview Parkway South Dr
Indianapolis, IN 46268-5129, USA

Pool, David (Football Player)
Buffalo Bills
460 Vista Glen Dr
Cincinnati, OH 45246-2366, USA

Pool, John L (Doctor)
4104 Corbin Hall Ln
Fredericksburg, VA 22408-9534, USA

Poole, Bob (Football Player)
San Francisco 49ers
7802 Shadyvilla Ln
Houston, TX 77055, USA

Poole, Brian (Musician)
67 Tower Drive
Neath Hill
Milton Keynes MK14 6JX, UNITED KINGDOM (UK)

Poole, David J (Artist)
Trinity Flint Bam
Weston Lane
Petersfield Hants GU32 3NN, UNITED KINGDOM (UK)

Poole, G Barney (Football Player)
213 E Railroad Ave N
Gloster, MS 39638, USA

Poole, George B (Football Player)
New York Yankees
PO Box 278
Gloster, MS 39638-0278, USA

Poole, Jim (Baseball Player)
Los Angeles Dodgers
605 Falls Lake Dr
Alpharetta, GA 30022-8059, USA

Poole, Keith (Football Player)
New Orleans Saints
2027 E Teakwood Pl
Chandler, AZ 85249-3508, USA

Poole, Larry (Football Player)
Cleveland Browns
15803 Sea Oats Pl
Tampa, FL 33624-1629, USA

Poole, Nathan (Football Player)
Cincinnati Bengals
8686 Longwood St
San Diego, CA 92126-3654, USA

Poole, Oliver (Football Player)
New York Yankees
PO Box 184
Gloster, MS 39638-0184, USA

Poole, Ray (Baseball Player)
Philadelphia Athletics
1495 Beagle Club Rd
Salisbury, NC 28146-2013, USA

Poole, Ray (Football Player)
New York Giants
214 Country Club Rd
Oxford, MS 38655-2606, USA

Poole, Tyrone (Football Player)
Carolina Panthers
3415 Rivers Call Blvd
Atlanta, GA 30339-5662, USA

Poole, William (Government Official)
Federal Reserve Bank
411 Locust St
Saint Louis, MO 63102-2034, USA

Pooley, Don (Golfer)
5251 N Camino Sumo
Tucson, AZ 85718-6047, USA

Poons, Larry (Artist)
PO Box 115
Islamorada, FL 33036-0115, USA

Poornam, Viswanatha (Actor)
7 Lodi Khan Street
T Nagar
Chennai, TN 600 017, INDIA

Poot, Marcel
Ave. Louis Lepoutre 72
Brussels 1060, BELGIUM

Pop, Iggy (Actor, Musician, Songwriter, Writer)
MVO Ltd
307 7th Ave Rm 807
New York, NY 10001-6066, USA

Popcorn, Faith (Writer)
Brain Reserve
1 Dag Hammarskjold Plz
885 Second Avenue Fl 16
New York, NY 10017-2201, USA

Pope, Bucky (Football Player)
Los Angeles Rams
7 Bunker Hill Dr
Washington Crossing, PA 18977-1415, USA

Pope, Carly (Actor)
Handprint Entertainment
1100 Glendon Ave Ste 1000
Los Angeles, CA 90024-3514, USA

Pope, Eddie (Soccer Player)
New York/New Jersey MetroStars
1 Harmon Plz # 300
Secaucus, NJ 07094-2803, USA

Pope, Edwin (Writer)
Miami Herald Editorial Dept
1 Herald Plz
Miami, FL 33132-1609, USA

Pope, Everett P (War Hero)
54 Governors Way Apt 704
Topsham, ME 04086-1430, USA

Pope, Marguez P (Football Player)
PO Box 470487
San Francisco, CA 94147-0487, USA

Pope, Monsanto (Football Player)
Denver Broncos
312 13th St NW Apt 10
Charlottesville, VA 22903-2754, USA

Pope, Odeon (Musician)
Brad Simon Organization
122 E 57th St # 300
New York, NY 10022-2623, USA

Pope, Willie (Baseball Player)
Homestead Grays
7616 Bennett St
Pittsburgh, PA 15208-1602, USA

Pope Jr, Clarence C (Religious Leader)
Fort Worth Episcopal Church Diocese
6300 Ridlea Place
Fort Worth, TX 76116, USA

Popiel, Poul P (Hockey Player)
2501 Peppermill Ridge Dr
Chesterfield, MO 63005-6707, USA

Popoff, A Jay (Musician)
Sepetys Entertainment
1223 Wilshire Blvd # 804
Santa Monica, CA 90403-5400, USA

Popoff, Frank P (Business Person)
Dow Chemical
2030 Dow Center
Midland, MI 48674-0001, USA

Popov, Aleksandr (Swimmer)
Swimming Assn
Sports House
Maitland Road #7
Hackett 2602, AUSTRALIA

Popov, Leonid I (Cosmonaut)
Potchta Kosmonavtov Moskovskoi Oblasti
Syvisdny Goroduk 141160, RUSSIA

Popovac, Gwynn (Artist)
17270 Robin Rdg
Sonora, CA 95370-8108, USA

Popovich, Gregg (Coach)
San Antonio Spurs
1 Sbc Center Pkwy
Alamodome
San Antonio, TX 78219-3604, USA

Popovich, Milt (Football Player)
Chicago Cardinals
810 N Hoback St
Helena, MT 59601-3883, USA

Popovich, Paul (Baseball Player)
Chicago Cubs
2604 Woodlawn Rd
Northbrook, IL 60062-5951, USA

Popovich, Pavel R (Cosmonaut)
AIUS-Agroressurs
VNIZ
Bolshevitskij Per 11
Moscow 101000, RUSSIA

Popowich, Paul (Actor)
c/o Staff Member *GVA Talent Agency Inc*
9229 W Sunset Blvd Ste 320
Los Angeles, CA 90069-3403, USA

Popp, Nathaniel (Religious Leader)
Romanian Orthodox Episcopate
PO Box 309
Grass Lake, MI 49240-0309, USA

Poppe, Nils
Fredriksdale Theaterin Domsten
Helsingborg 25590, SWEDEN

Popper, John (Musician)
ArtistDirect
1601 Cloverfield Blvd # 400
Santa Monica, CA 90404-4082, USA

Popplewell, Anna (Actor)
c/o Staff Member *Sasha Leslie Management*
34 Pember Rd
London NW10 5LS, UNITED KINGDOM (UK)

Poquette, Tom (Baseball Player)
Kansas City Royals
2821 Hallie Ln
Eau Claire, WI 54703-0942, USA

Porcaro, Jeff
5247 Twin Oaks Rd
Hidden Hills, CA 91302-2417, USA

Porcaro, Steve (Composer)
13596 Contour Dr
Sherman Oaks, CA 91423-4702, USA

Porcaro, Steve (Musician)
Fitzgerald-Hartley
34 N Palm St
Ventura, CA 93001-2635, USA

Porch, Colleen (Actor)
c/o Vincent Cirrincione *Vincent Cirrincione Associates*
1516 N Fairfax Ave
Los Angeles, CA 90046-2608, USA

Porcher, Robert (Football Player)
c/o Staff Member *Detroit Lions*
222 Republic Dr
Allen Park, MI 48101-3650, USA

Porfilio, John C (Judge)
US Court of Appeals
1919 Stout St
Denver, CO 80294, USA

Porizkova, Paulina (Actor, Model)
c/o Staff Member *Paradigm (LA)*
360 N Crescent Dr
North Bldg
Beverly Hills, CA 90210-6820, USA

Pork Tornado (Music Group)
c/o Staff Member *Paradigm (Monterey)*
509 Hartnell St
Monterey, CA 93940-2825, USA

Porras, German (Director)
c/o Staff Member *Gabriel Blanco Iglesias (Colombia)*
Dg 127A #20-36
Conjunto Plenitud, Apto 132
Bogota, COLOMBIA

Porretta, Matthew (Actor)
Damage Mgmt
10 Southwick Mews
London W2, UNITED KINGDOM (UK)

Port, Chris (Football Player)
New Orleans Saints
452 Walnut St
New Orleans, LA 70118-4932, USA

Portale, Carl (Publisher)
Elle Magazine
1633 Broadway
Hachette Filipacchi
New York, NY 10019-6741, USA

Porteous, Peter
Glencot Parkside Cheam
Surrey, ENGLAND SM3 8BS, UNITED KINGDOM (UK)

Porter, Alison
112 S Almont Dr
Los Angeles, CA 90048-2911, USA

Porter, Andrew (Baseball Player)
Nashville Elite Giants
4881 Linscott Pl Apt 1
Los Angeles, CA 90016-5422, USA

Porter, Billy (Musician)
William Morris AGency
151 El Camino Dr
Beverly Hills, CA 90212-2775, USA

Porter, Bo (Baseball Player)
Chicago Cubs
1226 N Teal Estates Cir
Fresno, TX 77545-9676, USA

Porter, Daryl (Football Player)
Detroit Lions
9053 W Sunrise Blvd
Plantation, FL 33322-5218, USA

Porter, David H (Educator)
Skidmore College
President's Office
Saratoga Springs, NY 12866, USA

Porter, Gail (Actor)
Rabbit Vocal Management
18 Broad Wick St 2nd Fl
London W1F 8HS, UNITED KINGDOM (UK)

Porter, Howard (Basketball Player)
1034 Iglehart Ave
Saint Paul, MN 55104-5428, USA

Porter, Jack (Football Player)
San Diego Chargers
1027 County Road 1530
Rush Springs, OK 73082-2416, USA

Porter, Jean
3945 Westfall Dr
Encino, CA 91436-3709, USA

Porter, Jody (Musician)
MOB Agency
6404 Wilshire Blvd Ste 505
Los Angeles, CA 90048-5507, USA

Porter, Joey (Football Player)
c/o Staff Member *Pittsburgh Steelers*
3400 S Water St
Pittsburgh, PA 15203-2349, USA

Porter, Kalan (Musician, Reality TV Star)
c/o Joanne Setterington *BMG Canada Inc*
190 Liberty St #100
Toronto, ON M6K 3L5, CANADA

Porter, Lee (Golfer)
1604 Birch Ln
Greensboro, NC 27408-6500, USA

Porter, Marina Oswald
1850 W Fm 550
Rockwall, TX 75032-8186, USA

Porter, Rick
943 Hartzell St
Pacific Palisades, CA 90272-3819, USA

Porter, Ricky (Football Player)
Detroit Lions
5800 Airline Dr
Metairie, LA 70003-3876, USA

Porter, Rufus (Football Player)
Seattle Seahawks
20403 Amberlight Ln
Katy, TX 77450-5049, USA

Porter, Scott (Actor)
c/o Staff Member *Gersh Agency, The (NY)*
41 Madison Ave Fl 33
New York, NY 10010-2202, USA

Porter, Terry (Basketball Player, Coach)
Milwaukee Bucks
1001 N 4th St
Bradley Center
Milwaukee, WI 53203-1312, USA

Porter-King, Mary Bea (Golfer)
6412 Kalama Rd
Kapaa, HI 96746-8633, USA

Porterfield, Ellary Hume (Actor)
c/o Marv Dauer *Marv Dauer Management*
11661 San Vicente Blvd Ste 104
Los Angeles, CA 90049-5150, USA

Porterfield, Garry (Football Player)
Dallas Cowboys
7621 S Harvard Pl
Tulsa, OK 74136-8000, USA

Portes, Richard D (Economist)
Economic Policy Centre
90-98 Goswell Road
London EC1V 7RR, UNITED KINGDOM (UK)

Portilla, Jose (Football Player)
Atlanta Falcons
3520 Mystic Dr
Buford, GA 30519-7060, USA

Portillo, Alfonso (President)
President's Office
Palacio Nacional
Guatemala City, GUATEMALA

Portis, Charles (Writer)
7417 Kingwood Rd
Little Rock, AR 72207-1734, USA

Portis, Clinton (Football Player)
c/o Staff Member *Washington Redskins*
21300 Redskin Park Dr
Ashburn, VA 20147-6100, USA

Portisch, Lajos (Misc)
Chess Federation
Nephadsereg Utca 10
Budapest 1055, HUNGARY

Portishead (Music Group)
High Road Touring
751 Bridgeway Fl 3
Sausalito, CA 94965-2174, USA

Portland, Rene (Coach)
Pennsylvania State University
Greenberg Complex
University Park, PA 16802, USA

Portman, Natalie (Actor)
c/o Aleen Keshishian *Brillstein-Grey Entertainment*
9150 Wilshire Blvd Ste 350
Beverly Hills, CA 90212-3453, USA

Portman, Rachel (Composer)
PRS
29/33 Berners St
London W1P 4AA, UNITED KINGDOM (UK)

Portman Jr, John C (Architect)
Charles Portman Assoc
225 Peachtree St NE Ste 220
Atlanta, GA 30303-1727, USA

Porto, James (Photographer)
601 W 26th St Rm 1321
New York, NY 10001-1134, USA

Portwich, Ramona (Athlete)
KC Limmer
Stockhardweg 3
Hanover 30453, GERMANY

Posada, Jorge R (Baseball Player)
c/o Team Member *New York Yankees*
Yankee Stadium
161st St & River Ave
Bronx, NY 10451, USA

Poschl, Hanno
Singerstr. 13/15
Vienna 1010, AUSTRIA

Posehn, Brian (Comedian)
c/o Staff Member *William Morris Agency (WMA-LA)*
1 William Morris Pl
Beverly Hills, CA 90212-4261, USA

Poses, Frederic M (Business Person)
AlliedSignal Inc
PO Box 4000
Morristown, NJ 07962-4000, USA

Posey, Parker (Actor)
c/o Frank Frattaroli *Widescreen Management*
270 Lafayette St Ste 402
New York, NY 10012-3327, USA

Posner, Richard A (Judge)
US Court of Appeals
219 S Dearborn St
Chicago, IL 60604-1874, USA

Posner, Vladimir
1125 16th St NW
Washington, DC 20036-4801, USA

Posokhin, Mikhail M (Architect)
Mosproyekt-2
2 Brestskaya Str 5
Moscow 123056, RUSSIA

Post, Avery D (Religious Leader)
80 Lyme Rd Apt 246
Hanover, NH 03755-1246, USA

Post, Markie (Actor)
c/o Staff Member *Lesher Entertainment Inc*
1134 S Cloverdale Ave
Los Angeles, CA 90019-6737, USA

Post, Mike (Composer)
Mike Post Productions
1007 W Olive Ave
Burbank, CA 91506-2211, USA

Post, Richard (Football Player)
San Diego Chargers
1812 Rickey Canyon Rd
Rice, WA 99167-9754, USA

Post, Sandra (Golfer)
Ladies Pro Golf Assn
100 International Golf Dr
Daytona Beach, FL 32124-1082, USA

Post, Ted (Director)
Norman Blumenthal
11030 Santa Monica Blvd
Los Angeles, CA 90025-7530, USA

Post, William (Business Person)
Pinnacle West Capital
400 E Van Buren St
PO Box 52132
Phoenix, AZ 85004-0673, USA

Post III, Glen F (Business Person)
Centurytel Inc
100 Century Park Dr
Monroe, LA 71203, USA

Postema, Pam (Baseball Player)
519 Landmark Ln
Henderson, NV 89002-9636, USA

Poster, Steve (Cinematographer)
Smith/Gosnell/Nicholson
PO Box 1156
Studio City, CA 91614-0156, USA

Postlethwaite, Pete (Actor)
Markham & Froggatt
Julian House
4 Windmill St
London W1P 1HF, UNITED KINGDOM (UK)

Postlewait, Kathy (Golfer)
111 Saint Johns Landing Dr
Winter Springs, FL 32708-6501, USA

Postus, Al (Football Player)
Pittsburgh Steelers
411 N Middletown Rd # B-108
Media, PA 19063-4422, USA

Poteat, Hank (Football Player)
Pittsburgh Steelers
4107 Buxmont Rd
Marlton, NJ 08053-8510, USA

Potente, Franka (Actor)
Presseburo Sohela Emani
Etterschlager Str 60
Steinebach 82237, GERMANY

Pothan, Pratap (Actor)
8-C Peninsula Apartments
Tailers Road Kilpauk
Chennai, TN 600 010, INDIA

Poti, Tom (Hockey Player)
103 Alvarado Ave
Worcester, MA 01604-1151, USA

Potrykus, Ingo (Scientist)
Eidgenossische Tech Hochshule
Plant Sci Dept
Zurich 8093, SWITZERLAND

Potter, Carol (Actor)
151 El Camino Dr
Beverly Hills, CA 90212-2704, USA

Potter, Chris (Actor)
565 Orwell St
Missigauga, ON L5A 2W4, CANADA

Potter, Chris (Musician)
Joel Chriss
300 Mercer St Apt 3J
New York, NY 10003-6732, USA

Potter, Cindy
1189 Ragley Hall Rd NE
Atlanta, GA 30319, USA

Potter, Cynthia (Cindy) (Sportscaster, Swimmer)
1188 Ragley Hall Rd NE
Atlanta, GA 30319-2512, USA

Potter, Dan M (Religious Leader)
21 Forest Dr
Albany, NY 12205-2521, USA

Potter, Grace (Musician)
c/o Staff Member *Paradigm (Monterey)*
509 Hartnell St
Monterey, CA 93940-2825, USA

Potter, Huntington (Scientist)
Harvard Medical School
25 Shattuck St
Boston, MA 02115-6092, USA

Potter, John (Government Official)
US Postal Service
475 Lenfant Plz SW
Washington, DC 20260-0004, USA

Potter, Monica (Actor)
c/o David Guillod *United Talent Agency (UTA)*
9560 Wilshire Blvd Ste 500
Beverly Hills, CA 90212-2401, USA

Potter, Nelson (Business Person)
Fleetwood Enterprises
3125 Myers St
Riverside, CA 92503-5544, USA

Potter, Philip A (Religious Leader)
3A York Castle Ave
Kingston 6, JAMAICA

Potter, Scott (Baseball Player)
1637 Cordova Ave
Daytona Beach, FL 32117-1708, USA

Potter, Steve (Football Player)
Miami Dolphins
750 SE 7th Ave
Pompano Beach, FL 33060-9502, USA

Pottinger, Stanley (Writer)
William Morris Agency
151 El Camino Dr
Beverly Hills, CA 90212-2775, USA

Pottios, Myron J (Mike) (Football Player)
71569 Sahara Rd
Rancho Mirage, CA 92270-4324, USA

Pottruck, David S (Financier)
Charles Schwab Co
101 Montgomery St
San Francisco, CA 94104-4175, USA

Potts, Annie (Actor)
c/o Staff Member *Forward Entertainment*
9255 W Sunset Blvd Ste 805
Los Angeles, CA 90069-3305, USA

Potts, Cliff (Actor)
PO Box 131
Topanga, CA 90290-0131, USA

Potts, Erwin (Business Person)
McClatchy Newspapers
2100
Sacramento, CA 95816, USA

Potts, MC
818 18th Ave S
Nashville, TN 37203-6663, USA

Potts, Roosevelt (Football Player)
Indianapolis Colts
2800 Crystal St Apt J-4
Anderson, IN 46012-1446, USA

Potts, Tony (Television Host)
c/o Staff Member *Access Hollywood*
Nbc
3000 W Alameda Ave Trailer E
Burbank, CA 91523-0001, USA

Potvin, Denis (Hockey Player)
6820 NW 101st Ter
Parkland, FL 33076-2921, USA

Potvin, Felix (Hockey Player)
Boston Bruins
1 Fleetcenter Pl Ste 250
Boston, MA 02114-1390, USA

Potvin, Jean R (Hockey Player)
24 Longwood Dr
Huntington Station, NY 11746-4716, USA

Pouget, Ely (Actor)
Writers & Artists
360 N Crescent Dr Bldg North
Beverly Hills, CA 90210-6818, USA

Pough, Ernest (Football Player)
Pittsburgh Steelers
2141 Buckman St
Jacksonville, FL 32206-4124, USA

Poul, Alan (Producer)
c/o Staff Member *United Talent Agency (UTA)*
9560 Wilshire Blvd Ste 500
Beverly Hills, CA 90212-2401, USA

Poulin, Dave (Coach, Hockey Player)
16771 Orchard Ridge Ct
Granger, IN 46530-5916, USA

Poullain, Frankie (Musician)
c/o Sue Whitehouse *Whitehouse Management*
PO Box 43829
London NW6 3PJ, UNITED KINGDOM (UK)

Pound, Richard W D (Misc)
87 Arlington Ave
Westmount, PQ H3Y 2W5, CANADA

Pound, Robert V (Physicist)
87 Pinehurst Rd
Belmont, MA 02478-1502, USA

Pound, The Dog
8942 Wilshire Blvd
Beverly Hills, CA 90211-1908, USA

Pounder, C C H (Actor)
Susan Smith
1344 N Wetherly Dr
Los Angeles, CA 90069-1817, USA

Poundstone, Paula (Actor, Comedian)
c/o David Snyder *William Morris Agency (WMA-LA)*
1 William Morris Pl
Beverly Hills, CA 90212-4261, USA

Poupard, Paul Cardinal (Religious Leader)
Pontificium Consilium Pro Dialogo
00120, VATICAN CITY

Pousette, Lena (Actor)
Atkins Assoc
8040 Ventura Canyon Ave
Panorama City, CA 91402-6313, USA

Poussaint, Alvin F (Educator)
Judge Baker Guidance Center
295 Longwood Ave
Boston, MA 02115, USA

Povich, Maury (Talk Show Host)
Maury
15 Penn Plz Ste 74
Hotel Pennsylvania/Grand Ballroom
New York, NY 10001-2016, USA

Powe, Karl (Football Player)
Dallas Cowboys
PO Box 13293
Mobile, AL 36663-0293, USA

Powell, A J Philip (Architect)
16 Little Boltons
London SW10, UNITED KINGDOM (UK)

Powell, Andre (Football Player)
New York Giants
N50W16962 Maple Crest Ln
Menomonee Falls, WI 53051-6689, USA

Powell, Art (Football Player)
Philadelphia Eagles
25221 Via Lido
Laguna Niguel, CA 92677-7307, USA

Powell, Billy (Musician)
Vector Mgmt
1607 17th Ave S
Nashville, TN 37212-2812, USA

Powell, Brittany
145 S Fairfax Ave Ste 310
Los Angeles, CA 90036-2176, USA

Powell, Brittney (Actor, Model)
Amset Eisenstadt Frazier
5055 Wilshire Blvd Ste 860
Los Angeles, CA 90036-6108, USA

Powell, Cecil (Misc)
220 Villa Verde Dr SE
Rio Rancho, NM 87124-1341, USA

Powell, Charley (Football Player)
San Fransisco 49ers
4119 Aralia Rd
Altadena, CA 91001-3701, USA

Powell, Clifton (Actor)
c/o Christopher Black *Opus Entertainment*
5225 Wilshire Blvd Ste 905
Los Angeles, CA 90036-4353, USA

Powell, Colin L (General, Secretary)
1317 Ballantrae Farm Dr
McLean, VA 22101-3028, USA

Powell, Dick (Baseball Player)
Baltimore Elite Giants
2864 Hunt Valley Dr
Glenwood, MD 21738-9639, USA

Powell, James R (Inventor)
Plus Ultra Technologies
180 Harbor Rd
Stony Brook, NY 11790-2006, USA

Powell, Jesse (Football Player)
Miami Dolphins
3507 77th Dr
Lubbock, TX 79423-1213, USA

Powell, Jesse (Musician)
Pyramid Entertainment
89 5th Ave Ste 700
New York, NY 10003-3020, USA

Powell, John (Composer)
Kraft-Benjamin-Engel
15233 Ventura Blvd Ste 200
Sherman Oaks, CA 91403-2244, USA

Powell, John G (Athlete, Track Athlete)
John Powell Assoc
10445 Mary Ave
Cupertino, CA 95014-1348, USA

Powell, John W (Boog) (Baseball Player)
Boog's Barbeque
333 W Camden St
Baltimore, MD 21201-2435, USA

Powell, Joseph L (Jody) (Government Official, Journalist)
Powell Tate
700 13th St NW Ste 1000
Washington, DC 20005-5926, USA

Powell, Marvin (Football Player)
New York Jets
5441 8th Ave
Los Angeles, CA 90043-2517, USA

Powell, Michael K (Government Official)
Federal Communications Commission
1919 M St NW
Washington, DC 20036-3521, USA

Powell, Michael (Mike) (Athlete, Track Athlete)
Team Powell
PO Box 8000-354
Alta Loma, CA 91701, USA

Powell, Mike
1751 Pinnacle Dr Ste 1500
McLean, VA 22102-3833, USA

Powell, Monroe (Musician)
Personality Presents
880 E Sahara Ave Ste 101
Las Vegas, NV 89104-3008, USA

Powell, Nicole (Basketball Player)
Charlotte Sting
333 E Trade St
Charlotte, NC 28202-2331, USA

Powell, Randolph
2644 Highland Ave
Santa Monica, CA 90405-4402, USA

Powell, Robert (Actor)
10 Pond Place
London W12 7RJ, UNITED KINGDOM (UK)

Powell, Sandy (Designer)
London Mgmt
2-4 Noel St
London W1V 3RB, UNITED KINGDOM (UK)

Powell, Susan (Actor)
6333 Bryn Mawr Dr
Los Angeles, CA 90068-2808, USA

Powell, William (Baseball Player)
Birmingham Black Barons
5516 Avenue I
Birmingham, AL 35208-3011, USA

Powell III, Earl A (Rusty) (Misc)
National Gallery of Art
Constitution Ave & 4th St NW
Washington, DC 20565-0001, USA

Powell Jr, D Duane (Cartoonist)
215 S McDowell St
Raleigh, NC 27601-1331, USA

Power, Dave (Actor)
c/o Steven Siebert *Lighthouse Entertainment*
409 N Camden Dr Ste 202
Beverly Hills, CA 90210-4423, USA

Power, J D (Dave) (Business Person)
J D Power Associates
2625 Townsgate Rd
Westlake Village, CA 91361-5751, USA

Power, Romina(Brindise)
I-72020 Cellino
San Marco, ITALY

Power, Udana
1962 N Beachwood Dr Apt 202
Los Angeles, CA 90068-4073, USA

Powers, Alexandra (Actor)
United Talent Agency
9560 Wilshire Blvd Ste 500
Beverly Hills, CA 90212-2401, USA

Powers, Clyde (Football Player)
New York Giants
6020 NW Williams Ave
Lawton, OK 73505-1317, USA

Powers, James B (Religious Leader)
American Baptist Assn
4605 N State Line Ave
Texarkana, TX 75503-2916, USA

Powers, Ross (Skier)
PO Box 657
South Londonderry, VT 05155-0657, USA

Powers, Stefanie (Actor)
Bartels Co
PO Box 57593
Sherman Oaks, CA 91413-2593, USA

Powers, Warren (Football Player)
Denver Broncos
3909 Lausanne Rd
Randallstown, MD 21133-4511, USA

Powers, Warren A (Football Player)
Oakland Raiders
14742 Thornbird Manor Pkwy
Chesterfield, MO 63017-2497, USA

Powlus, Ron (Football Player)
Philadelphia Eagles
1012 Ruthann Dr
Berwick, PA 18603-2426, USA

Powter, Daniel (Musician)
c/o Staff Member *Paradigm (Monterey)*
509 Hartnell St
Monterey, CA 93940-2825, USA

Poynter, Dougie (Musician)
c/o Staff Member *Universal Music Group (UMG - LA)*
2220 Colorado Ave
Santa Monica, CA 90404-3506, USA

Poza, Jorge (Actor)
c/o Staff Member *Televisa*
Blvd Adolfo Lopez Mateos 232
Colonia San Angel INN
DF CP 01060, MEXICO

Pozderac, Phil (Football Player)
Dallas Cowboys
2193 Carmel Dr
Carrollton, TX 75006-2814, USA

Pozdnykova, Tatyana (Athlete, Track Athlete)
4151 NW 43rd St
Gainesville, FL 32606-4582, USA

Pozsgay, Imre (Government Official)
Parliament Buildings
Kossuth Lajos Ter 1
Budapest 1055, HUNGARY

Prabhu (Actor)
16 Chevaliea Sivaji Ganesan Salai
T Nagar
Chennai, TN 600 017, INDIA

Prada, Aura Helena (Actor)
c/o Gabriel Blanco *Gabriel Blanco Iglesias (Mexico)*
Rio Balsas 35-32
Colonia Cuauhtemoc
DF 06500, MEXICO

Prada, Miuccia (Designer, Fashion Designer)
Prada SPA
Via Andrea Maffei 2
Milan 20154, ITALY

Praed, Michael
11500 W Olympic Blvd Ste 510
Los Angeles, CA 90064-1527, USA

Prager, Dennis (Radio Personality)
18455 Burbank Blvd Ste 407
Tarzana, CA 91356-6651, USA

Pran (Actor, Bollywood)
25 Union Park
Khar
Bombay, MS 400 052, INDIA

Prance, Ghilean T (Misc)
Kew Royal Botanic Gardens
Richmond
Surrey TW9 3AE, UNITED KINGDOM (UK)

Prange, Laurie
1519 Sargent Pl
Los Angeles, CA 90026, USA

Pras (Musician)
DAS Communications
83 Riverside Dr
New York, NY 10024-5713, USA

Prasanna (Actor)
C4 Cauvery Apartments
14 Brindavanam Street
Chennai, TN 600 004, INDIA

Prashanth (Actor)
No 40 North Usman Road
Thiagaraja Nagar
Chennai, TN 600 017, INDIA

Pratchett, Terry (Writer)
Colin Smythe
PO Box 67981
Gerrards Cross
Bucks SL9 8XA, UNITED KINGDOM (UK)

Prather, Joan (Actor)
31647 Sea Level Dr
Malibu, CA 90265-2633, USA

Pratiwi, Sudarmono (Astronaut)
Jalan Pegangsaan
Timur
Jakarta 16, INDONESIA

Pratt, Awadagin (Musician)
Cramer/Marder Artists
3436 Springhill Rd
Lafayette, CA 94549-2535, USA

Pratt, Chris (Actor)
c/o Marni Goldman *Abrams Artists Agency (LA)*
9200 W Sunset Blvd Ph 11
Los Angeles, CA 90069-3601, USA

Pratt, Judson
8745 Oak Park Ave
Northridge, CA 91325-3211, USA

Pratt, Keri Lynn (Actor)
c/o Steve Caserta *Sanders/Armstrong Management*
2120 Colorado Ave Ste 120
Santa Monica, CA 90404-3561, USA

Pratt, Kyla (Actor)
c/o Steve Simon *Landis-Simon Productions Talent Management*
8899 Beverly Blvd Ste 815
West Hollywood, CA 90048-2452, USA

Pratt, Kyle (Actor)
c/o Staff Member *Acme Talent & Literary (LA)*
4727 Wilshire Blvd Ste 333
Los Angeles, CA 90010-3874, USA

Pratt, Mary (Baseball Player)
1428 Quincy Shore Dr
Quincy, MA 02169-2333, USA

Pratt, Robert (Football Player)
Baltimore Colts
320 Greenway Ln
Richmond, VA 23226-1632, USA

Pratt, Roger (Cinematographer)
10 Nightingale Lane
Hornsey
London N8 7QU, UNITED KINGDOM (UK)

Pratt, Vicky
1930 Yonge St. #1155
Toronto, ON M4A 1, CANADA

Pratt, Victoria (Actor)
c/o Staff Member *Gilbertson-Kincaid Management*
1334 3rd Street Promenade Ste 201
Santa Monica, CA 90401-1320, USA

Prchlik, John (Football Player)
Detroit Lions
128 Brokenwood Ln
Crossville, TN 38558-7713, USA

Preas, George (Football Player)
Baltimore Colts
2220 Carolina Ave SW Apt 302
Roanoke, VA 24014-1798, USA

Preate Jr, Ernest D (Attorney, Attorney General, General, Government Official)
Attorney General's Office
4th & Walnut
Harrisburg, PA 17120-0001, USA

Prebola, Gene (Football Player)
Denver Broncos
24 Hayward Rd
Sparta, NJ 07871-3119, USA

Precourt, Charles J (Astronaut)
1960 Shoshone Dr
Ogden, UT 84403-4655, USA

Predock, Antoine (Architect)
Antoine Predock Architect
300 12th St
Northwest Albuquerque, NM 87102, USA

Preece, Steve (Football Player)
New Orleans Saints
2723 NW Monte Vista Ter
Portland, OR 97210-3338, USA

Pregerson, Harry (Judge)
US Court of Appeals
21800 Oxnard St
Woodland Hills, CA 91367-3633, USA

Pregulman, Merv (Football Player)
Green Bay Packers
44 S Crest Rd
Chattanooga, TN 37404-4005, USA

Prejean, Patrick
B5 135 Poissonniere
Paris F-75002, FRANCE

Preki (Soccer Player)
Kansas City Wizards
8900 State Line Rd
Leawood, KS 66206-1941, USA

Premice, Josephine
755 W End Ave
New York, NY 10025-6238, USA

Prendergast, Alan (Journalist)
c/o Staff Member *William Morris Agency (WMA-LA)*
1 William Morris Pl
Beverly Hills, CA 90212-4261, USA

Prentice, Dean S (Hockey Player)
13-220 Salisbury Ave
Cambridge, ON N1S 1K5, CANADA

Prentiss, Lee
122 Middlesex St.
London, ENGLAND El 7HY, UNITED KINGDOM (UK)

Prentiss, Paula (Actor, Comedian)
719 Foothill Rd
Beverly Hills, CA 90210-3437, USA

Prepon, Laura (Actor)
c/o Staff Member *United Talent Agency (UTA)*
9560 Wilshire Blvd Ste 500
Beverly Hills, CA 90212-2401, USA

Prescott, John L (Government Official)
365 Saltshouse Road
Sutton-on-Hull
North Humberside, UNITED KINGDOM (UK)

Presle, Micheline (Actor)
6 Rue Antoine Dubois
Paris 75006, FRANCE

Presley, Brian (Actor)
c/o Nikki Joel *International Creative Management (ICM-LA)*
10250 Constellation Blvd
Los Angeles, CA 90067-6200, USA

Presley, Lisa-Marie (Musician)
c/o Staff Member *Special Artists Agency*
9465 Wilshire Blvd Ste 890
Beverly Hills, CA 90212-2607, USA

Presley, Priscilla (Actor)
1167 Summit Dr
Beverly Hills, CA 90210-2251, USA

Presley, Priscilla (Actor, Producer, Writer)
c/o Staff Member *William Morris Agency (WMA-LA)*
1 William Morris Pl
Beverly Hills, CA 90212-4261, USA

Presley, Reg (Musician)
Stan Green
PO Box 4
Dartmouth
Devon TQ6 0YD, UNITED KINGDOM (UK)

Presley, Richard (Musician)
William Morris Agency
151 El Camino Dr
Beverly Hills, CA 90212-2775, USA

Presnell, Harve (Actor, Musician)
Abrams Artists
9200 W Sunset Blvd Ste 1125
Los Angeles, CA 90069-3610, USA

Press, Bill (Correspondent)
Cable News Network
1050 Techwood Dr NW
News Dept
Atlanta, GA 30318-5604, USA

Press, Frank (Physicist)
2500 Virginia Ave NW # 616
Washington, DC 20037-1902, USA

Pressel, Morgan (Golfer)
9266 Legare St
Boca Raton, FL 33434-5905, USA

Pressey, Paul (Basketball Player, Coach)
8415 N Indian Creek Pkwy
Milwaukee, WI 53217-2343, USA

Pressler, H Paul (Attorney, Attorney General, General, Judge)
3711 San Felipe St Unit 9J
Houston, TX 77027-4048, USA

Pressler, Larry L (Senator)
2812 Davis Ave
Alexandria, VA 22302-2507, USA

Pressler, Menahem M J (Musician)
Melvin Kaplan
115 College St Ste 4
Burlington, VT 05401-8428, USA

Pressley, Robert (Race Car Driver)
6 Forestdale Dr
Asheville, NC 28803-1811, USA

Pressly, Jaime (Actor, Model)
c/o Dar Rollins *International Creative Management (ICM-LA)*
10250 Constellation Blvd
Los Angeles, CA 90067-6200, USA

Pressman, Edward R (Producer)
Edward Pressman Films
130 El Camino Dr
Beverly Hills, CA 90212-2705, USA

Pressman, Lawrence (Actor)
15033 Encanto Dr
Sherman Oaks, CA 91403-4409, USA

Pressman, Michael (Director)
William Morris Agency
151 El Camino Dr
Beverly Hills, CA 90212-2775, USA

Pressman, Sally (Actor)
c/o Staff Member *Abrams Artists Agency (LA)*
9200 W Sunset Blvd Ph 11
Los Angeles, CA 90069-3601, USA

Presswood, Henry (Baseball Player)
Cincinnati Buckeyes
1445 W 71st Pl
Chicago, IL 60636-3961, USA

Presta, Peter (DJ)
c/o Len Evans *Project Publicity*
312 W 53rd St
New York, NY 10019-5743, USA

Prestel, Jim (Football Player)
Cleveland Browns
6150 N Hurricane Ct
Parker, CO 80134-5704, USA

Preston, Cynthia (Actor)
c/o Charles Silver *SMS Talent Inc*
8730 W Sunset Blvd Ste 440
Los Angeles, CA 90069-2277, USA

Preston, Duncan
46 Hilltop House Hornsey Lane
London, ENGLAND N6 5NW, UNITED KINGDOM (UK)

Preston, J A (Actor)
Paradigm Agency
10100 Santa Monica Blvd Ste 2500
Los Angeles, CA 90067-4116, USA

Preston, Johhny
PO Box 1875
Gretna, LA 70054-1875, USA

Preston, Johnny (Musician)
Ken Keene Artists
PO Box 1875
Gretna, LA 70054-1875, USA

Preston, Kelly (Actor)
c/o Joel Stevens *Joel Stevens Entertainment*
206 S Brand Blvd
Glendale, CA 91204-1310, USA

Preston, Mike (Actor)
House of Representatives
211 S Beverly Dr Ste 208
Beverly Hills, CA 90212-3879, USA

Preston, Ray (Football Player)
San Diego Chargers
12885 Prairie Dog Ave
San Diego, CA 92129-2213, USA

Preston, Simon J (Musician)
Little Hardwick
Langton Green Tunbridge Wells
Kent TN3 OEY, UNITED KINGDOM (UK)

Prestridge, Luke (Football Player)
Denver Broncos
1919 Post Oak Park Dr Apt 1113
Houston, TX 77027-3313, USA

Pretre, Georges (Conductor)
Chateau de Vaudricourt
A Naves
Par Casters 81100, FRANCE

Pretty Ricky (Music Group)
c/o Staff Member *Atlantic Records (LA)*
9229 W Sunset Blvd
Los Angeles, CA 90069-3402, USA

Prettyman, Tristan (Musician)
c/o Staff Member *Paradigm (Monterey)*
509 Hartnell St
Monterey, CA 93940-2825, USA

Preus, David W (Religious Leader)
2481 Como Ave
Saint Paul, MN 55108-1445, USA

Previn, Andre G (Musician)
180 W 80th St # 206
New York, NY 10024-6301, USA

Previn, Dory (Musician, Songwriter, Writer)
2533 Zorada Dr
Los Angeles, CA 90046-1747, USA

Previn Andre
180 W 80th St # 206
New York, NY 10024-6301, USA

Previte, Richard (Business Person)
Advanced Micro Devices
1 Amd Pl
PO Box 3453
Sunnyvale, CA 94085-3905, USA

Prevost, Josette (Actor)
Tisherman Agency
6767 Forest Lawn Dr Ste 101
Los Angeles, CA 90068-1050, USA

Prew, William A (Business Person, Swimmer)
30600 Telegraph Rd Ste 3110
Bingham Farms, MI 48025-4589, USA

Pribilinec, Jozef (Athlete, Track Athlete)
Moyzesova 75
Lutila 966 22, SLOVAKIA

Price, Alan (Musician, Songwriter, Writer)
Lustig Talent
PO Box 770850
Orlando, FL 32877-0850, USA

Price, Antony (Designer, Fashion Designer)
468 Kings Road
London SW1, UNITED KINGDOM (UK)

Price, Charles W (Football Player)
Detroit Lions
9709 Orlando Ave Apt A
Lubbock, TX 79423-3992, USA

Price, Elex (Football Player)
New Orleans Saints
2833 Newport St
Jackson, MS 39213-5335, USA

Price, Ferne (Baseball Player)
720 E Mary Ln
Terre Haute, IN 47802-4617, USA

Price, Frank (Misc)
Price Entertainment
2425 Olympic Blvd
Santa Monica, CA 90404-4030, USA

Price, Frederick K C (Religious Leader)
Crenshaw Christian Church
7901 S Vermont Ave
Los Angeles, CA 90044-3500, USA

Price, George C (Prime Minister)
House of Representatives
Belmopan, BELIZE

Price, Hillary (Cartoonist)
221 Pine St # 4G3
Florence, MA 01062-1267, USA

Price, James G (Doctor)
12205 Mohawk Rd
Leawood, KS 66209-2137, USA

Price, James K
19 Lacresta Dr
Florence, KY 41042-9635, USA

Price, Katie (Jordan) (Actor, Model)
Katie Price Fan Club
P.O. Box PO1 5036
Crowhurst Road
Brighton, East Sussex BN1 8AR, UNITED KINGDOM (UK)

Price, Kelly (Musician)
JL Ent
18653 Ventura Blvd # 340
Tarzana, CA 91356-4103, USA

Price, Larry C (Journalist)
930 S Garfield St
Denver, CO 80209-5006, USA

Price, Lindsay (Actor)
3033 Vista Crest Dr
Los Angeles, CA 90068-1824, USA

Price, Lloyd (Musician, Songwriter, Writer)
95 Horseshoe Hill Rd
Pound Ridge, NY 10576-1636, USA

Price, Lonny (Actor)
c/o Joy Gorman *Anonymous Content (CA)*
3532 Hayden Ave
Culver City, CA 90232-2413, USA

Price, M V Leontyne (Opera Singer)
9 Vandam St
New York, NY 10013-1215, USA

Price, Marc (Actor)
8444 Magnolia Dr
Los Angeles, CA 90046-1932, USA

Price, Margaret B (Opera Singer)
Ulf Tornqvist
Sankt Eriksgatan 100
Stockholm 113 31, SWEDEN

Price, Marvin (Baseball Player)
Chicago American Giants
10753 S Normal Ave
Chicago, IL 60628-3203, USA

Price, Megyn (Actor)
c/o Staff Member *United Talent Agency (UTA)*
9560 Wilshire Blvd Ste 500
Beverly Hills, CA 90212-2401, USA

Price, Mike (Coach, Football Coach)
University of Texas
Athletic Dept
El Paso, TX 79968-0001, USA

Price, Mitchell (Football Player)
Cincinatti Bengals
3935 Thousand Oaks Dr Apt 1506
San Antonio, TX 78217-1877, USA

Price, Molly (Actor)
c/o Stephen Hirsch *Gersh Agency, The (NY)*
41 Madison Ave Fl 33
New York, NY 10010-2202, USA

Price, Noel (Hockey Player)
21 Windeyer Crescent
Kanata, ON K2K 2P6, CANADA

Price, Paul B (Physicist)
1056 Overlook Rd
Berkeley, CA 94708-1712, USA

Price, Peerless (Football Player)
Buffalo Bills
5658 Legends Club Cir
Braselton, GA 30517-6029, USA

Price, Ray (Musician)
c/o Staff Member *The Bobby Roberts Company Inc*
PO Box 1547
Goodlettsville, TN 37070-1547, USA

Price, Reynolds (Writer)
PO Box 99014
Durham, NC 27708-9014, USA

Price, S H (Publisher)
Newsweek Inc
251 W 57th St
New York, NY 10019-1846, USA

Price, Terry (Football Player)
Chicago Bears
59 Fieldstone Dr
South Glastonbury, CT 06073-3717, USA

Price, W Mark (Basketball Player)
Georgia Institute of Technology
Athletic Dept
Atlanta, GA 30332-0001, USA

Price, Willard D (Misc)
PO Box 2783
Laguna Hills, CA 92654-2783, USA

Price-Bunch, Ashil (Golfer)
1629 Country Club Dr
Morristown, TN 37814-3316, USA

Price II, Charles H (Business Person, Diplomat)
1 W Armour Blvd Ste 300
Kansas City, MO 64111-2087, USA

Prichard, Peter S (Editor)
USA Today
1000 Wilson Blvd
Editorial Dept
Arlington, VA 22209-3927, USA

Priddy, Nancy (Actor)
11223 Sunshine Ter
Studio City, CA 91604-3123, USA

Pride, Charley (Baseball Player)
Memphis Red Sox
3198 Royal Ln Ste 204
Dallas, TX 75229-6921, USA

Pride, Charlie (Musician)
CECCA Productions
PO Box 670507
Dallas, TX 75367-0507, USA

Pride, Dicky (Golfer)
PO Box 844
Windermere, FL 34786-0844, USA

Pride, Lynn (Basketball Player)
Minnesota Lynx
600 1st Ave N
Target Center
Minneapolis, MN 55403-9802, USA

Pride, Mack (Baseball Player)
Kansas City Monarchs
3305 Pierce St
Wheat Ridge, CO 80033-6333, USA

Pridemore, Tom (Football Player)
Atlanta Falcons
3935 Poplar Springs Rd
Gainesville, GA 30507-8618, USA

Pridy, Todd (Baseball Player)
3430 Scenic Dr
Napa, CA 94558-4239, USA

Priesand, Sally J (Religious Leader)
32 Fernwood Dr
Asbury Park, NJ 07712-8713, USA

Priest, Judas (Musician)
c/o Staff Member *International Talent Booking (ITB - UK)*
27A Floral St Fl 3
Covent Garden
London WC2E 9, UNITED KINGDOM (UK)

Priest, Maxi (Musician)
Virgin Records
150 5th Ave Frnt 3
New York, NY 10011-4311, USA

Priest, Steve (Musician)
DCM International
296 Nether St
Finchley
London N3 1RJ, UNITED KINGDOM (UK)

Priestley, Jason (Actor)
c/o JB Roberts *Thruline Entertainment*
9250 Wilshire Blvd Ground Fl
Beverly Hills, CA 90210, USA

Priestley, Jr, Thomas (Director, Photographer)
c/o Jay Gilbert *Broder Webb Chervin Silbermann Agency, The (BWCS)*
10250 Constellation Blvd Ste P
Los Angeles, CA 90067-6213, USA

Prieto, Rodrigo (Cinematographer)
2926 Nicada Dr
Los Angeles, CA 90077-2026, USA

Primatesta, Raul Francisco Cardinal (Religious Leader)
Arzobispado
Ave H Irigoyen 98
Cordoba 5000, ARGENTINA

Primeau, Keith (Hockey Player)
2 Danforth Dr
Voorhees, NJ 08043-3947, USA

Primis, Lance R (Publisher)
New York Times Co
229 W 43rd St
New York, NY 10036-3959, USA

Primrose, Neil (Musician)
Wildlife Entertainment
21 Heathmans Road
London SW6 4TJ, UNITED KINGDOM (UK)

Primus, Barry
2735 Creston Dr
Los Angeles, CA 90068-2209, USA

Prince (Musician)
c/o Staff Member *Paisley Park Enterprises*
7801 Audubon Rd
Chanhassen, MN 55317-8205, USA

Prince, Charles (Chuck) (Financier)
Citigroup Inc
399 Park Ave
New York, NY 10022-4699, USA

Prince, Clayton
3500 W Olive Ave Ste 1400
Burbank, CA 91505-5512, USA

Prince, Faith (Actor, Musician)
Innovative Artists
1505 10th St
Santa Monica, CA 90401-2805, USA

Prince, Harold S (Hal) (Director, Producer)
Harold Prince Organization
10 Rockefeller Plz Ste 1104
New York, NY 10020-1903, USA

Prince, Jonathan
526 N Camden Dr
Beverly Hills, CA 90210-3202, USA

Prince, Karim
3313 1/2 Barham Blvd
Los Angeles, CA 90068-1450, USA

Prince, Larry L (Business Person)
Genuine Parts Co
2999 Cir 75 Pkwy
Atlanta, GA 30339-3050, USA

Prince, Tayshaun (Basketball Player)
Detroit Pistons
2 Championship Dr
Palace
Auburn Hills, MI 48326-1753, USA

Prince Alwaleed
Citibank
Gefinor Center Block E 6th Fl
PO Box 113-5794
Rue Clemenceau, Beirut, LEBANON

Prince-Bythewood, Gina (Director, Producer, Writer)
c/o Jeanne Williams *Creative Artists Agency LCC (CAA-LA)*
2000 Avenue Of The Stars
Los Angeles, CA 90067-4700, USA

Prince Jr, Gregory S (Educator)
Hampshire College
President's Office
Amherst, MA 01003, USA

Prince William (Prince)
Clarence House
London SW1A 1BA, UNITED KINGDOM
(UK)

Princess Ann Claire (Actor, Musician, Royalty)
c/o Staff Member *Love Is In The Heir*
5750 Wilshire Blvd
E! Entertainment Television
Los Angeles, CA 90036-3697, USA

Princess Beatrice (Royalty)
Buckingham Palace
London SW1A 1AA, UNITED KINGDOM
(UK)

Princess Eugenie (Royalty)
Buckingham Palace
London SW1A 1AA, UNITED KINGDOM
(UK)

Principal, Victoria (Actor)
120 S Spalding Dr Ste 205
Beverly Hills, CA 90212-1840, USA

Principe, Dom (Football Player)
New York Giants
300 N Highway A1A Apt E303
Jupiter, FL 33477-4542, USA

Principi, Anthony (Secretary)
Veteran Affairs Department
810 Vermont Ave NW
Washington, DC 20420-0001, USA

Prine, Andrew (Actor)
3364 Longridge Ave
Sherman Oaks, CA 91423, USA

Prine, John (Musician, Songwriter, Writer)
Al Bunetta Mgmt
33 Music Sq W Ste 102B
Nashville, TN 37203-6607, USA

Pringle, Joan (Actor)
Gold Marshak Liedtke
3500 W Olive Ave Ste 1400
Burbank, CA 91505-5512, USA

Pringley, Mike (Football Player)
Detroit Lions
709 Gilchrist Ave
Linden, NJ 07036-1210, USA

Prinosil, David (Athlete)
TC Wolfsberg
Am Schanzl 3
Amberg 92224, GERMANY

Prinze Jr, Freddie (Actor)
c/o Aleen Keshishian *Brillstein-Grey Entertainment*
9150 Wilshire Blvd Ste 350
Beverly Hills, CA 90212-3453, USA

Prinzi, Frank (Cinematographer)
571 W 113th St # 24
New York, NY 10025, USA

Prioleau, Pierson (Football Player)
San Fransisco 49ers
2221 Santee River Rd
Alvin, SC 29479-3844, USA

Prior, Anthony (Football Player)
New York Jets
3861 Lofton Pl
Riverside, CA 92501-1809, USA

Prior, Maddy (Musician)
Park Promotions
PO Box 651
Park Road
Oxford OX2 9RB, UNITED KINGDOM
(UK)

Prior of Brampton, James M L
(Government Official)
36 Morpeth Mansions
London SW1, UNITED KINGDOM (UK)

Priory, Richard B (Business Person)
Duke Energy Co
526 S Church St
Charlotte, NC 28202-1802, USA

Pritchard, Barry (Musician)
Lustig Talent
PO Box 770850
Orlando, FL 32877-0850, USA

Pritchard, David E (Physicist)
Massachusetts Institute of Technology
Physics Dept
Cambridge, MA 02139, USA

Pritchard, Michael (Football Player)
Atlanta Falcons
1041 Collingtree St
Las Vegas, NV 89145-8513, USA

Pritchard, Ron (Football Player)
Houston Oilers
690 E Park Ave
Gilbert, AZ 85234-5894, USA

Pritchett, James (Actor)
53 W 74th St
New York, NY 10023-2484, USA

Pritchett, Kelvin (Football Player)
Detroit Lions
4765 Guilford Forest Dr SW
Atlanta, GA 30331-7395, USA

Pritchett, Matt (Cartoonist)
London Daily Telegraph
181 Marsh Wall
London E14 9SR, UNITED KINGDOM
(UK)

Pritchett, Sir Victor
12 Regent's Park Terrace
London, ENGLAND NW1, UNITED
KINGDOM (UK)

Pritchett, Stanley (Football Player)
Miami Dolphins
523 Monteagle Trce
Stone Mountain, GA 30087-4937, USA

Pritchett, Wes (Football Player)
Buffalo Bills
1194 Brookgate Way NE
Atlanta, GA 30319-2877, USA

Pritha, Saratha (Actor, Bollywood)
2 1st Main Road
West Shenoy Nagar
Chennai, TN 600030, INDIA

Prithiveeraj (Bablu) (Actor)
146 Anna Nagar (West)
Chennai, TN 600 040, INDIA

Pritikin, Greg (Actor)
c/o Shawn Hopkins *Catch 23 Entertainment (C23)*
385 Monroe St
Denver, CO 80206-4444, USA

Pritkin, Roland I (Doctor)
4128 Grove Ave
Stickney, IL 60402-4435, USA

Pritko, Steve (Football Player)
New York Giants
328 Chanticlair Dr
Apex, NC 27502-9623, USA

Pritzker, Robert A (Business Person)
Marmon Group
225 W Washington St Ste 1900
Chicago, IL 60606-3562, USA

Pritzker, Thomas (Business Person)
Hyatt Corp
200 W Madison St
Chicago, IL 60606-3414, USA

Prix, Wolf (Architect)
Coop Himmelblau
3526 Beethoven St
Los Angeles, CA 90066-3039, USA

Probst, Jeff (Talk Show Host)
c/o Sean Perry *Endeavor Agency LLC (LA)*
9601 Wilshire Blvd Fl 3
Beverly Hills, CA 90210-5204, USA

Prochazka, Martin (Hockey Player)
Toronto Maple Leafs
40 Bay St
Toronto, ON M5J 2K2, CANADA

Prochnow, Jurgen (Actor)
c/o Staff Member *International Creative Management (ICM-LA)*
10250 Constellation Blvd
Los Angeles, CA 90067-6200, USA

Prock, Markus (Athlete)
6142 Mieders
AUSTRIA

Proclaimers, The (Music Group)
c/o Staff Member *Braw Music Management*
31 Hartington Pl
Edinburgh
Lothian EH10 4LF, UNITED KINGDOM
(UK)

Procol Harum
195 Sandycombe Rd.
Kew, ENGLAND TW9 2EW, UNITED
KINGDOM (UK)

Procter, Emily (Actor)
c/o Scott Fedro *Lone Star Entertainment*
139 S Beverly Dr Ste 314
Beverly Hills, CA 90212-3040, USA

Proctor, Charles N (Skier)
100 Lockwood Ln Apt 238
Scotts Valley, CA 95066-3959, USA

Proctor, David (Baseball Player)
Bowman
5517 SW 23rd St
Topeka, KS 66614-1727, USA

Proctor, Dewey (Football Player)
New York Yanks
905 Myrtle St
Mullins, SC 29574-4109, USA

Proctor, James (Baseball Player)
Indianapolis Clowns
2 Westmoreland Pl
Saint Louis, MO 63108-1228, USA

Prodi, Romano (Prime Minister)
European Communities Commission
200 Rue de la Loi
Brussels, BELGIUM

Prodigy
205 Vickarage Hill Benfleet
Essex, ENGLAND SS7 1PF, UNITED
KINGDOM (UK)

Prodigy (Musician)
Maverick Records
3300 Warner Blvd
Burbank, CA 91505-4632, USA

Proehl, Ricky (Football Player)
Phoenix Cardinals
3504 Bromley Wood Ln
Greensboro, NC 27410-2181, USA

Professor, Griff (Musician)
William Morris Agency
151 El Camino Dr
Beverly Hills, CA 90212-2775, USA

Profit, Gene (Football Player)
New England Patriots
6116 Nightshade Ct
Rockville, MD 20852-3409, USA

Project 86 (Music Group)
c/o Staff Member *Paradigm (Monterey)*
509 Hartnell St
Monterey, CA 93940-2825, USA

Pronger, Chris (Hockey Player)
29 Blue Grass
Irvine, CA 92603-0412, USA

Pronovost, R Marcel (Hockey Player)
4620 Dali Court
Windsor, ON N9G 2MB, CANADA

Proops, Greg (Actor)
c/o Melanie Truhett *Messina Baker/ Entertainment*
955 Carrillo Dr Ste 100
Los Angeles, CA 90048-5400, USA

Prophet, Billy (Musician)
Paramount Entertainment
PO Box 12
Far Hills, NJ 07931-0012, USA

Prophet, Elizabeth Clare (Religious
Leader)
Church Universal & Triumphant
PO Box A
Livingston, MT 59047, USA

Prophet, Ronnie
1227 Saxon Dr
Nashville, TN 37215-4426, USA

Propp, Brian (Hockey Player)
2320 Riverton Rd
Cinnaminson, NJ 08077-3719, USA

Props, Rene (Actor)
Agency for Performing Arts
405 S Beverly Dr Ste 500
Beverly Hills, CA 90212-4425, USA

Prosky, Robert (Actor)
309 9th St SE
Washington, DC 20003-2116, USA

Prospal, Vaclav (Hockey Player)
Anaheim Mighty Ducks
2000 E Gene Autry Way
Anaheim, CA 92806-6143, USA

Prospal, Vactav (Hockey Player)
Tampa Bay Lighting
401 Channelside Dr
Ice Palace
Tampa, FL 33602-5400, USA

Prosper, Sandra (Actor)
c/o Staff Member *Mitchell K Stubbs & Assoc (MKS)*
8695 Washington Blvd Ste 204
Culver City, CA 90232-7419, USA

Prosser, C Ladd (Misc)
101 W Windsor Rd # 2106
Urbana, IL 61802-6663, USA

Prosser, James (Musician)
Refugee Mgmt
209 10th Ave S Ste 347
Nashville, TN 37203-0762, USA

Prosser, Robert (Religious Leader)
Cumberland Presbyterian Church
1978 Union Ave
Memphis, TN 38104-4134, USA

Prost, Alain M P (Race Car Driver)
Prost-Grand-Prix
7 Ave Eugene Freyssinet
Guyancourt 78286, FRANCE

Prost, Sharon (Judge)
US Court of Appeals
717 Madison Pl NW
Washington, DC 20439-0001, USA

Protopopov, Oleg (Figure Skater)
Chalet Hubel
Grindelwald 3818, SWITZERLAND

Prouix, E Annie (Writer)
PO Box 230
Centennial, WY 82055-0230, USA

Prout, Bob (Football Player)
Oakland Raiders
23102 N Shepard Rd
Chillicothe, IL 61523-9035, USA

Prout, Brian (Musician)
Oreamcatcher Artists Mgmt
2908 Poston Ave
Nashville, TN 37203-1312, USA

Proval, David (Actor)
c/o Andrew Howard *Incognito Management*
9440 Santa Monica Blvd Ste 302
Beverly Hills, CA 90210-4614, USA

Provence, Andrew (Football Player)
Atlanta Falcons
224 Providence Rd
Fayetteville, GA 30215-2844, USA

Provenza, Paul (Actor)
c/o Peter Golden *Golden Entertainment West*
10921 Wilshire Blvd
Los Angeles, CA 90024-3906, USA

Provine, Dorothy (Actor)
8832 Ferncliff Ave NE
Bainbridge Island, WA 98110-2907, USA

Provost, Jon
627 Montclair Dr
Santa Rosa, CA 95409-2833, USA

Prowse, David (Actor)
Spotlight
7 Lelcester Place
London WC2H 7BP, UNITED KINGDOM (UK)

Proyas, Alex (Director)
International Creative Mgmt
8942 Wilshire Blvd # 219
Beverly Hills, CA 90211-1908, USA

Prudden, Bonnie (Misc)
PO Box 65240
Tucson, AZ 85728-5240, USA

Prudhomme, Don (Race Car Driver)
1232 Distribution Way
Vista, CA 92081-8816, USA

Prudhomme, Paul (Chef)
2424 Chartres St
New Orleans, LA 70117-8607, USA

Pruett, Harold
8904 Wonderland Ave
Los Angeles, CA 90046-1854, USA

Pruett, Jeanne (Musician, Songwriter, Writer)
Joe Taylor Artists Agency
2802 Columbine Pl
Nashville, TN 37204-3104, USA

Pruett, Scott (Race Car Driver)
9743 W Bray Creek St
Star, ID 83669-5815, USA

Pruitt, Gregory D (Greg) (Football Player)
Cleveland Browns
13851 Larchmere Blvd
Cleveland, OH 44120-1349, USA

Pruitt, James (Football Player)
Miami Dolphins
PO Box 244483
Boynton Beach, FL 33424-4483, USA

Pruitt, Jason (Baseball Player)
Topps
320 Clark Drive Apt 101
Summerfield, NC 27358, USA

Pruitt, Michael(Mike) (Football Player)
Cleveland Browns
472 S Mumaugh Rd
Lima, OH 45804-3530, USA

Pruitt Jr, Basil A (Doctor)
US Army Institute of Surgical Research
Fort Sam Houston, TX 78234, USA

Prunariu, Dumitru D (Cosmonaut)
Str Sf Spiridon 12
#4
Bucharest 70231, ROMANIA

Prunskiene, Kazimiera (Politician)
Lithuanian-European Institute
Vilnius St 45-13
Vilnius 2001, LITHUANIA

Prusiner, Stanley B (Nobel Prize Laureate)
University of California
Biochemistry Dept
San Francisco, CA 94143-0001, USA

Pryce, Jonathan (Actor, Musician)
Julian Belfarge
46 Albermarle St
London, ENGLAND W1X 4PP, UNITED KINGDOM (UK)

Pryce, Travor (Football Player)
Denver Broncos
13655 Broncos Pkwy
Englewood, CO 80112-4150, USA

Pryor, David H (Senator)
712 S 6 1/2 St
Paragould, AR 72450-5005, USA

Pryor, Hubert (Editor, Publisher)
3560 S Ocean Blvd Apt 607
Palm Beach, FL 33480-5773, USA

Pryor, Nicholas (Actor)
S D B Partners
1801 Avenue Of Stars Ste 902
Los Angeles, CA 90067-5981, USA

Pryor, Peter P (Editor)
Daily Variety
5700 Wilshire Blvd Ste 120
Editorial Dept
Los Angeles, CA 90036-5804, USA

Pryor, Rain (Actor, Producer)
PryorKindlin Productions
2809 Saint Paul St # 2
Baltimore, MD 21218-4312, USA

Przybilla, Joel (Basketball Player)
Milwaukee Bucks
1001 N 4th St
Bradley Center
Milwaukee, WI 53203-1312, USA

Psaltis, Jim (Football Player)
Chicago Cardinals
23115 Samuel St Apt 23
Torrance, CA 90505-3850, USA

Psycho, Les (Musician)
Agency Group Lts
1775 Broadway Ste 515
New York, NY 10019-1903, USA

Ptacek, Bob (Football Player)
Cleveland Browns
648 Deptford Ave
Dayton, OH 45429-5941, USA

Ptacek, Louis (Misc)
University of Utah
Howard Hughes Institute
Salt Lake City, UT 84112, USA

Ptak, Frank (Business Person)
Illinois Tool Works
3600 W Lake Ave
Glenview, IL 60026-5811, USA

Ptashne, Mark S (Misc)
Harvard University
Biochemistry Dept
Cambridge, MA 02138, USA

Puapua, Tomasi (Governor)
Governor General's Office
Vaiaku
Funafuti, TUVALU

Public Enemy
c/o Staff Member *William Morris Agency (WMA-LA)*
1 William Morris Pl
Beverly Hills, CA 90212-4261, USA

Pucci, Ben (Football Player)
Buffalo Bisons
8502 Timber West St
San Antonio, TX 78250-4209, USA

Pucci, Bert (Publisher)
Los Angeles Magazine
1888 Century Park E
Los Angeles, CA 90067-1702, USA

Puck, Wolfgang (Chef)
Wolfgang Puck Worldwide Inc
100 N Crescent Dr Ste 100
Beverly Hills, CA 90210-5447, USA

Puckett, Gary (Musician, Songwriter, Writer)
10710 Seminole Blvd Ste 3
Largo, FL 33778-3316, USA

Puddle of Mud (Music Group)
c/o Staff Member *Geffen Records*
2220 Colorado Ave
Santa Monica, CA 90404-3506, USA

Puemer, John P (Publisher)
Chicago Tribune
435 N Michigan Ave
Chicago, IL 60611-4024, USA

Puenzo, Luis A (Director)
Cinematografia Nacional Instituto
Lima 319
Buenos Aires 1073, ARGENTINA

Puerner, John P (Publisher)
Los Angeles Times
202 W 1st St
Editorial Dept
Los Angeles, CA 90012-4105, USA

Puett, Tommy (Actor)
16621 Cerulean Ct
Chino Hills, CA 91709-4690, USA

Puetz, Garry (Football Player)
Ney York Jets
1779 Robinson Rd
Dahlonega, GA 30533-6119, USA

Pugacheva, Alia B (Musician)
State Variety Theater
Bersenevskaya Nab 20/2
Moscow 109072, RUSSIA

Pugh, Larry (Football Player)
RR 4
New Castle, PA 16101, USA

Pugh, Tim (Baseball Player)
Cincinnati Reds
1806 S Madison Blvd
Bartlesville, OK 74006-6936, USA

Pugh Jr, Jethro (Football Player)
Gifts Inc
329 E Colorado Blvd
Dallas, TX 75203-1213, USA

Pugsley, Don (Actor)
Lichtman/Salners
15865 Royal Haven Pl
Sherman Oaks, CA 91403-4724, USA

Puhl, Terry (Baseball Player)
Houston Astros
331 W Alkire Lake Dr
Sugar Land, TX 77478-3511, USA

Puig, Rich (Baseball Player)
New York Mets
2809 Albion Ave
Orlando, FL 32833-4330, USA

Pujats, Janis Cardinal (Religious Leader)
Metropolijas Jurija
Maza Pils Iela 2/A
Riga 1050, LATVIA

Pujol, Laetitia (Ballerina)
Paris Opera Ballet
Place de l'Opera
Paris 75009, FRANCE

Pujol I Soley, Jordi (Politician)
Generalitat Palau
Placa Sant Jaume S/N
Barcelona 2, SPAIN

Pujols, Albert (Baseball Player)
St Louis Cardinals
13229 Autumn Trails Ct
Saint Louis, MO 63141-3210, USA

Pujols, Luis B (Baseball Player)
Houston Astros
3867 Jonathans Way
Boynton Beach, FL 33436-8524, USA

Pulcini, Robert (Director)
c/o Staff Member *Creative Artists Agency LCC (CAA-LA)*
2000 Avenue Of The Stars
Los Angeles, CA 90067-4700, USA

Pulford, Robert J (Bob) (Hockey Player)
78 Coventry Rd
Northfield, IL 60093-3117, USA

Puljic, Vinko Cardinal (Religious Leader)
Nadbiskupski Ordinarijat
Kaptol 7
Sarajevo 71000, BOSNIA-HERZEGOVINA

Pullen, Melanie Clark (Actor)
c/o Staff Member *Julian Belfrage & Associates*
Adam House
14 New Burlington St
London W1S 3BQ, UNITED KINGDOM (UK)

Pulli, Frank (Baseball Player)
1981 Downing Pl
Palm Harbor, FL 34683-5727, USA

Pulliam, Harvey (Baseball Player)
Kansas City Royals
160 Lake Destiny Trl
Altamonte Springs, FL 32714-3455, USA

Pulliam, Keisha Knight (Actor)
PO Box 866
Teaneck, NJ 07666-0866, USA

Pullman, Bill (Actor)
c/o JJ Harris *One Entertainment (LA)*
12 W 57th St Ph
New York, NY 10019-3900, USA

Pullman, Philip (Writer)
24 Templar Road
Oxford OX2 8LT, UNITED KINGDOM
(UK)

Pulp (Music Group)
c/o Staff Member *Paradigm (Monterey)*
509 Hartnell St
Monterey, CA 93940-2825, USA

Pulsipher, Bill (Baseball Player)
New York Mets
1986 SW Certosa Rd
Port Saint Lucie, FL 34953-1393, USA

Pulver, Liselotte (Actor)
Villa Bip
Kanton Vaudois
Perroy 1166, SWITZERLAND

Punk, Daft (Composer, Writer)
c/o Staff Member *Primary Talent
International (UK)*
2-12 Pentonville Rd Fl 5
London N1 9PL, UNITED KINGDOM
(UK)

Punsley, Bernard (Actor)
1415 Granvia Altamira
Palos Verdes Estates, CA 90274-2130,
USA

Punto, Nick (Baseball Player)
Philadelphia Phillies
27756 Soller # 35
Mission Viejo, CA 92692-1165, USA

Puppa, Daren (Hockey Player)
4526 Cheval Blvd
Lutz, FL 33558-5331, USA

Puppies, The
15476 NW 77th Ct # 286
Miami Lakes, FL 33016-5823, USA

Pupunu, Alfred (Football Player)
San Diego Chargers
13343 Akagi Ln
Draper, UT 84020-8216, USA

Purcell, Dominic (Actor)
c/o Staff Member *Untitled Entertainment
(NY)*
322 8th Ave Ste 601
New York, NY 10001-6715, USA

Purcell, Herman (Baseball Player)
Cleveland Buckeyes
1031 Cass Ave SE
Grand Rapids, MI 49507-1119, USA

Purcell, James N (Government Official)
6 Chateau-Banquet
Geneva 1202, SWITZERLAND

Purcell, Lee (Actor)
11101 Provence Ln
Tujunga, CA 91042-1263, USA

Purcell, Patrick B (Publisher)
Boston Herald
1 Herald St
Boston, MA 02118, USA

Purcell, Philip J (Financier)
Morgan Stanley Co
1585 Broadway
New York, NY 10036-8293, USA

Purcell, Sarah (Actor)
6525 Esplanade
Playa Del Rey, CA 90293-7521, USA

Purcell, William (Physicist)
Northwestern University
Astrophysics Dept
Evanston, IL 60208-0001, USA

Purdee, Nathan (Actor)
56 W 66th St
New York, NY 10023-6225, USA

Purdin, John (Baseball Player)
Los Angeles Dodgers
4928 Signature Dr Apt 101
Myrtle Beach, SC 29579-0979, USA

Purdom, Edmund (Actor)
Via Isonzo 42/C
Rome 00198, ITALY

Purdy, Alfred (Writer)
Harbour Publishing
PO Box 219
Madeira Park, BC V0N 2H0, CANADA

Purdy, James (Writer)
236 Henry St
Brooklyn, NY 11201-4280, USA

Purdy, Ted (Golfer)
141 W Boca Raton Rd
Phoenix, AZ 85023-6250, USA

Pure Reason Revolution (Music Group)
c/o Staff Member *Paradigm (Monterey)*
509 Hartnell St
Monterey, CA 93940-2825, USA

Purefoy, James (Actor)
International Creative Mgmt
76 Oxford St
London W1N 0AX, UNITED KINGDOM
(UK)

Pureifory, David (Football Player)
Green Bay Packers
6250 Textile Rd
Ypsilanti, MI 48197-8962, USA

Puri, Om (Actor)
703 Trishul II Seven Bangalows
Versova Andheri
Bombay, MS 400 061, INDIA

Purim, Flora (Musician)
A Train Mgmt
PO Box 29242
Oakland, CA 94604-9242, USA

Purkey, Robert T (Bob) (Baseball Player)
Pittsburgh Pirates
5559 Steeplechase Ct
Bethel Park, PA 15102-4501, USA

Purl, Linda (Actor)
Shelly & Pierce
13775A Mono Way # 220
Sonora, CA 95370-8813, USA

Purnell, Frank (Football Player)
Green Bay Packers
PO Box 1387
Seaside, CA 93955-1387, USA

Purpura, Dominick P (Scientist)
Albert Einstein College of Medicine
1300 Morris Park Ave
Bronx, NY 10461-1975, USA

Purtzer, Tom (Golfer)
9828 E Desert Cove Ave
Scottsdale, AZ 85260-6220, USA

Purves, William (Financier)
87 Chester Square
London SW1W 9HT, UNITED KINGDOM
(UK)

Purvis, Jeff (Race Car Driver)
Jeff Purvis Racing Club
900 Providence Blvd
Clarksville, TN 37042-4477, USA

Purvis, Jeff (Race Car Driver)
4106 Roberta Rd
Concord, NC 28027, USA

Puryear, Martin (Artist)
Nancy Drysdale Gallery
700 New Hampshire Ave NW # 917
Washington, DC 20037-2407, USA

Pusha, T (Musician)
Star Trax/Arista Records
888 7th Ave # 3800
New York, NY 10106-0001, USA

Pushelberg, Glenn (Designer)
Yabu Pushelberg
55 Booth Ave
Toronto, ON M4M 2M3, CANADA

Puskarioc, Joseph (Baseball Player)
429 35th St
McKeesport, PA 15132-7226, USA

Pussycat Dolls (Music Group)
c/o Jeff Haddad *Jeff Haddad Management*
317 S Swall Dr
Beverly Hills, CA 90211-3611, USA

Putch, John (Actor)
3972 Sunswept Dr
Studio City, CA 91604-2330, USA

Putilin, Nikolai G (Opera Singer)
Mariinsky Theater
Teatralnaya Square 1
Saint Petersburg 190000, RUSSIA

Putin, Vladimir V (President)
President's Office
Kremlin
Staraya Pl 4
Moscow 103132, RUSSIA

Putman, Earl (Football Player)
Chicago Cardinals
PO Box 18091
Munds Park, AZ 86017-8091, USA

Putman, Ed (Baseball Player)
Chicago Cubs
257 N Forestdale Ave
Covina, CA 91723-2412, USA

Putman, Pat (Baseball Player)
Texas Rangers
2311 Carrell Rd
Fort Myers, FL 33901-8012, USA

Putnam, Ashley (Opera Singer)
Maurice Mayer
201 W 54th St Apt 1C
New York, NY 10019-5520, USA

Putnam, David (Actor, Producer)
c/o Staff Member *Enigma Productions*
429 Santa Monica Blvd Ste 700
Santa Monica, CA 90401-3435, USA

Putnam, Duane (Football Player)
Los Angeles Rams
1545 Magnolia Ave
Ontario, CA 91762-5335, USA

Putnam, Hilary W (Misc)
116 Winchester Rd
Arlington, MA 02474-2139, USA

Puttnam, David T (Producer)
Engima Productions
29A Tufton St
London SW1P 3QL, UNITED KINGDOM
(UK)

Putz, J J (Baseball Player)
Seattle Mariners
4039 Butler Ct
Trenton, MI 48183-3927, USA

Putzier, Jeb (Football Player)
Denver Broncos
5305 Pocahontas St
Bellaire, TX 77401-4822, USA

Puyana, Rafael (Musician)
88 Rue de Grenelle
Paris 75007, FRANCE

Pyavko, Vladislav I (Opera Singer)
Bryusov Per 2/14
#27
Moscow 103009, RUSSIA

Pyburn, Jack (Football Player)
Miami Dolphins
1197 Peachtree St NE Ste 533A
Atlanta, GA 30361-3508, USA

Pyburn, Jim (Baseball Player)
Baltimore Orioles
259 Longview Dr
Jasper, AL 35504-3715, USA

Pye, Eddie (Baseball Player)
Los Angeles Dodgers
307 Polk St
Columbia, TN 38401-4453, USA

Pye, William B (Artist)
43 Hambalt Road
Clapham
London SW4 9EQ, UNITED KINGDOM
(UK)

Pyeatt, Johnny (Football Player)
Denver Broncos
19122 E Via De Arboles
Queen Creek, AZ 85242-4039, USA

Pyecha, John (Baseball Player)
Chicago Cubs
107 Nottingham Dr
Chapel Hill, NC 27517-6569, USA

Pyfrom, Shawn (Actor)
c/o Liza Anderson *Warren Cowan &
Associates PR*
8899 Beverly Blvd Ste 919
Los Angeles, CA 90048-2436, USA

Pyle, Andy (Musician)
Larry Page
29 Ruston Mews
London W11 1RB, UNITED KINGDOM
(UK)

Pyle, Ewald (Baseball Player)
St Louis Browns
17648 SE 117th Cir
Summerfield, FL 34491-7860, USA

Pyle, Michael J (Mike) (Football Player)
Chicago Bears
2436 Saranac Ct
Glenview, IL 60026-1042, USA

Pyle, Missi (Actor)
c/o Staff Member *Paradigm (LA)*
360 N Crescent Dr
North Bldg
Beverly Hills, CA 90210-6820, USA

Pyle, Missy (Actor)
Paradigm Agency
10100 Santa Monica Blvd Ste 2500
Los Angeles, CA 90067-4116, USA

Pyle, Palmer (Football Player)
Baltimore Colts
2487 Potter Rd E
Traverse City, MI 49686-8572, USA

Pym of Sandy, Francis L (Government Official)
Everton Park
Sandy
Beds SG19 2DE, UNITED KINGDOM (UK)

Pyne, George F (Football Player)
Boston Patriots
123 Congress St
Milford, MA 01757-2006, USA

Pyne, Natasha (Actor)
Kate Feast
Primrose Hill Studios
Fitzroy Road
London NW1 8TR, UNITED KINGDOM (UK)

Pyne, Stephen J (Historian, Writer)
Arizona State University
History Dept
Tempe, AZ 85287-0001, USA

Pyott, David E I (Business Person)
Allergan Inc
2525 Dupont Dr
Irvine, CA 92612-1599, USA

Python, Monty
34 Thistlewaite Rd.
London, ENGLAND E5 0QQ, UNITED KINGDOM (UK)

Pyznarski, Tim (Baseball Player)
San Diego Padres
10716 Austin Ave
Chicago Ridge, IL 60415-2224, USA

Q, Maggie (Actor)
c/o Mick Sullivan *Creative Artists Agency LCC (CAA-LA)*
2000 Avenue Of The Stars
Los Angeles, CA 90067-4700, USA

Q-Tip
9830 Wilshire Blvd
Beverly Hills, CA 90212-1804, USA

Qabas ibn Sa'id al Sa'id (King)
Royal Palace
PO Box 252
Muscat, OMAN

Qarase, Laisenia (Prime Minister)
Prime Minister's Office
6 Berkeley Crescent
Suva
VITI LEVU, FIJI

Qasimi, Sheikh Saqr bin Muhammad al (President)
Ruler's Palace
Ras Al Khaimah
UNITED ARAB EMIRATES

Qasimi, Sheikh Sultan bin Muhammad al (President)
Ruler's Palace
Sharjah, UNITED ARAB EMIRATES

Qi, Shu (Actor)
c/o Steve Chasman *Ace Media*
1411 5th St Ste 405
Santa Monica, CA 90401-2417, USA

Qin, Shaobo (Actor)
c/o Don Hughes *IAI Presentations*
PO Box 4
Pismo Beach, CA 93448-0004, USA

QT, Megan (Model)
Phil-Flash Media
352 N Birch St Apt 1
Manteno, IL 60950-1301, USA

Quackenbush, Bill
54 Danielle Ct
Lawrenceville, NJ 08648-1452, USA

Quade, John (Actor)
Alex Brewis
12429 Laurel Terrace Dr
Studio City, CA 91604-2402, USA

Quaerna, Jerry (Football Player)
Detroit Lions
1211 Pheasant Ct
Lake Geneva, WI 53147-1077, USA

Quaid, Dennis (Actor)
c/o George Freeman *William Morris Agency (WMA-LA)*
1 William Morris Pl
Beverly Hills, CA 90212-4261, USA

Quaid, Randy (Actor)
c/o David DeCamillo *Gersh Agency, The (LA)*
232 N Canon Dr
Beverly Hills, CA 90210-5302, USA

Quaintance, Rachel (Comedian)
c/o Staff Member *OmniPop Inc (LA)*
4605 Lankershim Blvd Ste 201
North Hollywood, CA 91602-1874, USA

Qualife, Pete (Musician)
Larry Page
29 Ruston Mews
London W11 1RB, UNITED KINGDOM (UK)

Qualls, DJ (Actor)
c/o Josh Katz *United Talent Agency (UTA)*
9560 Wilshire Blvd Ste 500
Beverly Hills, CA 90212-2401, USA

Qualls, Jim (Baseball Player)
Chicago Cubs
410 N County Road 950
Sutter, IL 62373-5021, USA

Qualters, Tom (Baseball Player)
Philadelphia Phillies
236 Lake Rd
Somerset, PA 15501-1644, USA

Quandt, Richard E (Economist)
162 Springdale Rd
Princeton, NJ 08540-4948, USA

Quann, Megan (Swimmer)
Thomas Quann
8421 Woodland Ave E
Puyallup, WA 98371-6557, USA

Quant, Mary (Designer, Fashion Designer)
Mary Quant Ltd
3 Ives St
London SW3 2NE, UNITED KINGDOM (UK)

Quantrill, Paul (Baseball Player)
Boston Red Sox
334 E Lake Rd
Palm Harbor, FL 34685-2427, USA

Quarashi (Musician)
c/o Staff Member *Creative Artists Agency LCC (CAA-LA)*
2000 Avenue Of The Stars
Los Angeles, CA 90067-4700, USA

Quaresma, Rhonda Lee (Misc)
PO Box 22033
Kingston, ON K7M 8S5, CANADA

Quarles, Shelton (Football Player)
Tampa Bay Buccaneers
17019 Candeleda De Avila
Tampa, FL 33613-5213, USA

Quarrie, Donald (Don) (Athlete, Track Athlete)
Jamaican Amateur Athletic Assn
PO Box 272
Kingston 5, JAMAICA

Quarry, Robert (Actor)
11032 Moor Park St # A3
North Hollywood, CA 91602-3451, USA

Quarshie, Hugh (Actor)
PO Box 20092
London NW2 6FJ, UNITED KINGDOM (UK)

Quarterflash
5410 SW Macadam Ave Ste 280
Portland, OR 97239-3825, USA

Quarterman, Saundra (Actor)
c/o Staff Member *Stone Manners Talent & Literary (LA)*
6500 Wilshire Blvd Ste 550
Los Angeles, CA 90048-4950, USA

Quasha, Alan G (Business Person)
Hanover Direct Inc
1509 Harbor Blvd
Weehawken, NJ 07086, USA

Quasthoff, Thomas (Musician)
Cramer/Marser Artists
3436 Springhill Rd
Lafayette, CA 94549-2535, USA

Quatro, Suzi (Musician, Songwriter, Writer)
Jive
4 Pasteur Courtyard Whittle Road
Corby
Norths, FL NN17 5DX, UNITED KINGDOM (UK)

Quayle, Anna (Actor)
CDA
47 Courtfield Road
London, ENGLAND SW7 4DB, UNITED KINGDOM (UK)

Quayle, Dan (Ex-Vice President)
7001 N Scottsdale Rd Ste 2010
Scottsdale, AZ 85253-3644, USA

Quayle, Jenny (Actor)
c/o Staff Member *Michelle Braidman Assoc*
Lower John St Fl 3 #10/11
London W1F 9EB, UNITED KINGDOM (UK)

Quayle, Marilyn Tucker
2929 E Camelback Rd Ste 124
Phoenix, AZ 85016-4425, USA

Quddus (Television Host)
c/o Michael (Mike) Esterman *Esterman Entertainment*
214 Park Rd
Riva, MD 21140-1224, USA

Queen, Billy (Baseball Player)
Milwaukee Braves
1616 E Perry St
Gastonia, NC 28054-5840, USA

Queen, Ida (Musician)
Traditional Arts Services
16045 36th Ave NE
Lake Forest Park, WA 98155-6623, USA

Queen, Jeff (Football Player)
San Diego Chargers
1367 Temple Heights Dr
Oceanside, CA 92056-2210, USA

Queen, Konga (Actor, Wrestler)
PO Box 5050
Carson, CA 90749-5050, USA

Queen, Mel (Baseball Player)
Cincinnati Reds
430 Quintana Rd # 116
Morro Bay, CA 93442-1948, USA

Queens of the Stone Age (Music Group)
c/o Staff Member *Creative Artists Agency LCC (CAA-LA)*
2000 Avenue Of The Stars
Los Angeles, CA 90067-4700, USA

Queensryche (Music Group)
c/o Staff Member *Monterey Peninsula Artists (Chicago)*
200 W Superior St Ste 202
Chicago, IL 60610-3554, USA

Queffelec, Anne (Musician)
15 Ave Corneille
Maisons-Laffittle 78600, FRANCE

Queler, Eve (Conductor)
Opera Orchestra of New York
239 W 72nd St Apt 2R
New York, NY 10023-2734, USA

Quellmatz, Udo (Athlete)
Friedhofstr 10
Omgolstandt 85049, GERMANY

Quenneville, Joel (Coach, Hockey Player)
39 Cherry Hills Farm Dr
Englewood, CO 80113-7113, USA

Quenzrd, Nathalie (Actor)
Cineart
36 Rue de Ponthieu
Paris 75008, FRANCE

Query, Jeff (Football Player)
Green Bay Packers
93 Woodlily Pl
Spring, TX 77382-1254, USA

Quester, Hugues (Actor)
Cineart
36 Rue de Ponthieu
Paris 75008, FRANCE

Questlove (Musician)
Motown Records
6255 W Sunset Blvd
Los Angeles, CA 90028-7403, USA

Questrom, Allen I (Business Person)
J C Penney Co
6501 Legacy Dr
Plano, TX 75024-3698, USA

Quezada, Milly (Musician)
c/o Staff Member *Sony Music Miami*
605 Lincoln Rd Fl 7
Miami Beach, FL 33139-2900, USA

Quezada Toruno, Rodolfo Cardinal
(Religious Leader)
Archdiocese
7A Avenida 6-21
Zona 1
Guatemala City 01001, GUATEMALA

Quick, Clarence E (Musician, Songwriter, Writer)
376 Quincy St
Brooklyn, NY 11216-1502, USA

Quick, Diana (Actor)
39 Seymour Walk
London SW10, UNITED KINGDOM (UK)

Quick, James E (Jim) (Actor)
PO Box 12760
Scottsdale, AZ 85267-2760, USA

Quick, Michael A (Mike) (Football Player)
Philadelphia Eagles
13 Slab Branch Ct
Marlton, NJ 08053-5407, USA

Quick, Rebecca (Talk Show Host)
900 Sylvan Ave
Squawk Box
Englewood Cliffs, NJ 07632-3312, USA

Quick, Richard (Coach, Swimmer)
Stanford University
Athletic Dept
Stanford, CA 94305, USA

Quicksilver (Music Group)
c/o Staff Member *Paradigm (Monterey)*
509 Hartnell St
Monterey, CA 93940-2825, USA

Quie, Albert H (Al) (Governor)
4209 Christy Ln
Hopkins, MN 55345-3001, USA

Quiet Riot
2002 Hogback Rd Ste 20
Ann Arbor, MI 48105-9736, USA

Quigley, Austin E (Educator)
Columbia College
President's Office
New York, NY 10027, USA

Quigley, Dana (Golfer)
Crestwood Country Club
90 Wheeler St
Rehoboth, MA 02769-1110, USA

Quigley, Joan
1055 California St # 14
San Francisco, CA 94108-2203, USA

Quigley, Linnea (Actor)
2608-1 N. Ocean Blvd #126
Pompano Beach, FL 33062, USA

Quigley, Philip J (Phil) (Business Person)
Pacific Telesis Group
130 Keamy St
San Francisco, CA 94108, USA

Quik, D J (Musician)
International Creative Mgmt
8942 Wilshire Blvd # 219
Beverly Hills, CA 90211-1908, USA

Quilici, Frank (Baseball Player)
Minnesota Twins
3413 E 126th St
Burnsville, MN 55337-3440, USA

Quill, Leonard W (Financier)
Wilmington Trust Corp
1100 N Market St
Rodney Square N
Wilmington, DE 19801-1281, USA

Quill, Timothy E (Activist)
University of Rochester
Medical & Dentistry School
Rochester, NY 14642-0001, USA

Quillan, Frederick (Fred) (Football Player)
San Francisco 49ers
2924 Bailey Ln
Eugene, OR 97401-6926, USA

Quinlan, Kathleen (Actor)
PO Box 861
Rockaway, OR 97136-0861, USA

Quinlan, Maeve (Actor)
c/o Staff Member *Main Title Entertainment*
5225 Wilshire Blvd Ste 500
Los Angeles, CA 90036-4349, USA

Quinlan, Maive
1123 N Flores St
W Hollywood, CA 90069-2967, USA

Quinlan, Tom (Baseball Player)
Toronto Blue Jays
1061 Sterling St S
Maplewood, MN 55119-5972, USA

Quinlan, William D (Bill) (Football Player)
Cleveland Browns
393 Mount Vernon St
Lawrence, MA 01843-3103, USA

Quinn, Aidan (Actor)
c/o Staff Member *Framework Entertainment (LA)*
9057 Nemo St # C
W Hollywood, CA 90069-5511, USA

Quinn, Aileen (Actor)
400 Madison Ave Fl 20
New York, NY 10017-8911, USA

Quinn, Anthony (Actor, Director, Producer)
c/o Johnnie Planco *Untitled Entertainment (NY)*
322 8th Ave Ste 601
New York, NY 10001-6715, USA

Quinn, Brady (Football Player)
c/o Team Member *Cleveland Browns*
76 Lou Groza Blvd
Berea, OH 44017-1269, USA

Quinn, Brandon (Actor)
c/o Ben Feigin *Nine Yards Entertainment*
8530 Wilshire Blvd Fl 5
Beverly Hills, CA 90211-3102, USA

Quinn, Brian (Coach, Soccer Player)
San Jose Earthquakes
100 N Almaden Ave
San Jose, CA 95110-2437, USA

Quinn, Carmel (Musician)
Jane Mathers Mgmt
230 W Summit Ave # 1
Haddonfield, NJ 08033-3703, USA

Quinn, Colin (Actor, Comedian)
c/o Jimmy Miller *Mosaic Media Group*
24 Music Sq W Fl 1
Nashville, TN 37203-6661, USA

Quinn, Colleen (Actor)
Bauman Assoc
5750 Wilshire Blvd # 473
Los Angeles, CA 90036-3697, USA

Quinn, Danny (Actor)
Don Buchwald
6500 Wilshire Blvd Ste 2200
Los Angeles, CA 90048-4942, USA

Quinn, David W (Business Person)
Centex Corp
2728 N Harwood St
Dallas, TX 75201-1591, USA

Quinn, DeClan (Cinematographer)
22 Cherry Ave
Cornwall On Hudson, NY 12520-1506, USA

Quinn, Ed (Actor)
Endeavor Talent Agency
9701 Wilshire Blvd Ste 1000
Beverly Hills, CA 90212-2010, USA

Quinn, Francesco (Actor)
3910 Woodcliff Rd
Sherman Oaks, CA 91403-5054, USA

Quinn, Freddy
Am Pfeilshof 35
Hamburg D-22393, GERMANY

Quinn, Glenn (Actor)
Sanders Armstrong Management
2120 Colorado Ave Ste 120
Santa Monica, CA 90404-3561, USA

Quinn, J B Patrick (Pat) (Coach, Hockey Player)
Toronto Maple Leals
40 Bay St
Toronto, ON M5J 2K2, CANADA

Quinn, Jane Bryant (Journalist)
Newsweek Magazine
251 W 57th St
Editorial Dept
New York, NY 10019-1802, USA

Quinn, Jim (Misc)
675 S Sierra Ave Unit 32
Solana Beach, CA 92075-3232, USA

Quinn, John C (Editor)
365 S Atlantic Ave
Cocoa Beach, FL 32931-2719, USA

Quinn, Mark (Baseball Player)
Kansas City Royals
1941 Terrebonne Ave
San Dimas, CA 91773-1334, USA

Quinn, Martha (Actor, Model)
11684 Ventura Blvd # 453
Studio City, CA 91604-2699, USA

Quinn, Mike (Football Player)
Pittsburgh Steelers
10703 Del Monte Dr
Houston, TX 77042-2326, USA

Quinn, Sally (Journalist)
3014 N St NW
Washington, DC 20007-3404, USA

Quinn, Stephen (Football Player)
Houston Oilers
RR 1 Box 163
Mount Sterling, IL 62353-9765, USA

Quinn, William F (Governor)
4340 Pahoa Ave Apt 13C
Honolulu, HI 96816-5023, USA

Quinones, John (Correspondent)
c/o Staff Member *20/20*
147 Columbus Ave
Abc
New York, NY 10023-6503, USA

Quinones, Luis (Baseball Player)
Oakland A's
U47 Calle 27
Ponce, PR 00728-4409, USA

Quinones, Rey (Baseball Player)
Boston Red Sox
216 Calle Ronda
San Juan, PR 00926-2351, USA

Quintal, Stephane (Hockey Player)
1356A La Fontaine
Montreal, PQ H2L 1T5, CANADA

Quintana, Chela (Golfer)
Ladies Pro Golf Assn
100 International Golf Dr
Daytona Beach, FL 32124-1082, USA

Quinto, Zachary (Actor)
c/o Eric Black *Anonymous Content (CA)*
3532 Hayden Ave
Culver City, CA 90232-2413, USA

Quirico, Rafael (Baseball Player)
Philadelphia Phillies
4422 W Rogers Ave
Tampa, FL 33611-5630, USA

Quiring, Frederic (Actor)
Cineart
36 Rue de Ponthieu
Paris 75008, FRANCE

Quirk, Art (Baseball Player)
Baltimore Orioles
2 Ensign Ln
Stonington, CT 06378-2944, USA

Quirk, James P (Jamie) (Baseball Player)
Kansas City Royals
310 W 123rd Ter
Kansas City, MO 64145-1186, USA

Quirk, Michael J (War Hero)
1700 Kit Ln
Navarre, FL 32566, USA

Quiroga, Elena (Writer)
Agencia Balcells
Diagonal 580
Barcelona 08021, SPAIN

Quiroga, Jorge (Tuto) (President)
President's Office
Palacio de Gobierno
Plaza Murllia
La Paz, BOLIVIA

Quist, Janet (Model)
13446 Poway Rd # 239
Poway, CA 92064-4714, USA

Quitones, John (Correspondent)
ABC-TV
77 W 66th St
News Dept
New York, NY 10023-6201, USA

Quivar, Florence (Opera Singer)
Columbia Artists Mgmt Inc
1790 Broadway Fl 6
New York, NY 10019-1412, USA

Quivers, Robin (Actor, Entertainer, Radio Personality, Talk Show Host)
c/o Staff Member *Don Buchwald & Associates Inc (LA)*
6500 Wilshire Blvd Ste 2200
Los Angeles, CA 90048-4942, USA

Qulgley, Brett (Golfer)
127 Sandpiper Cir
Jupiter, FL 33477-8434, USA

Qulgley, Dana (Golfer)
2670 Tecumseh Dr
West Palm Beach, FL 33409-7421, USA

Qureia, Ahmed (Prime Minister)
Prime Minister's Office
Gara City
Gaza Strip
Palestine, ISRAEL

R E M (Music Group)
170 College Ave
Athens, GA 30601-2805, USA

R M A, Bharathimohan (Actor)
31/8 Madley Lind Street
T Nagar
Chennai, TN 600 017, INDIA

R Pandiarajan (Actor)
18 Sivasailam Street
T Nagar
Chennai, TN 600 017, INDIA

R Partheepan (Actor)
Veerappa Nagar
Chennai, TN 600 093, INDIA

Raab, Marc (Football Player)
Washington Redskins
8500 Sea Pines Pl
McKinney, TX 75070-8412, USA

Raabe, Brian (Baseball Player)
Minnesota Twins
38760 Kost Tri
North Branch, MN 55056, USA

Raabe, Max (Opera Singer)
Klimperkasten
Thuyring 63
Berlin 12101, GERMANY

Raabe, Meinhardt
PO Box 913
Penney Farms, FL 32079-0913, USA

Raaj Kumar, Puru (Actor, Bollywood)
57 Worli Sea Face
Bombay, MS 400 018, INDIA

Raakhee (Actor, Bollywood)
Muktangan Sarojini Naidu Road
Santacruz
Bombay, MS 400 054, INDIA

Raaurn, Gustav (Skier)
PO Box 700
Mercer Island, WA 98040-0700, USA

Raba, Robert (Football Player)
New York Jets
16066 Acre St
North Hills, CA 91343-4822, USA

Rabb, Johnny (Baseball Player)
San Francisco Giants
1942 W Manchester Ave
Los Angeles, CA 90047-2923, USA

Rabe, Charlie (Baseball Player)
Cincinnati Reds
6059 E Sierra Blance St
Mesa, AZ 85215, USA

Rabe, Pamela (Actor)
Shanahan Mgmt
PO Box 1509
Darlinghurst, NSW 1300, AUSTRALIA

Rabin, Trevor (Composer)
Kraft-Benjamin-Engel
15233 Ventura Blvd Ste 200
Sherman Oaks, CA 91403-2244, USA

Rabinovitch, Benton S (Misc)
12530 42nd Ave NE
Seattle, WA 98125-4621, USA

Rabinow, Jacob (Engineer, Inventor)
6920 Selkirk Dr
Bethesda, MD 20817-4750, USA

Rabinowitz, Dorothy (Journalist)
Wall Street Journal
200 Liberty St
Editorial Dept
New York, NY 10281-0084, USA

Rabinowitz, Harry (Composer, Conductor)
11 Mead Road
Cranleigh
Surrey GU6 7BG, UNITED KINGDOM
(UK)

Rabinowitz, Jesse C (Misc)
University of California
Molecular & Cell Biology Dept
Berkeley, CA 94720-0001, USA

Rabkin, Mitchell T (Doctor)
Beth Israel Deaconess Medical Center
330 Brookline Ave
Boston, MA 02215-5491, USA

Raby, Stuart (Physicist)
Ohio State University
Physics Dept
Columbus, OH 43210, USA

Racan, Ivica (Prime Minister)
Prime Minister's Office
Jordanovac 71
Zagreb 41000, CROATIA

Racette, Patricia (Opera Singer)
Columbia Artists Mgmt Inc
1790 Broadway Fl 6
New York, NY 10019-1412, USA

Rachal, Latorio (Football Player)
San Diego Chargers
3266 Golden Ave
Long Beach, CA 90806-1208, USA

Rachin, Julian (Musician)
Columbia Artists Mgmt Inc
1790 Broadway Fl 6
New York, NY 10019-1412, USA

Rachins, Alan (Actor)
130 N Beachwood Dr
Los Angeles, CA 90004-3822, USA

Racicot, Marc F (Governor)
901 15th St S Apt 201
Arlington, VA 22202-5031, USA

Racimo, Victoria (Actor)
Marion Rosenberg
PO Box 69826
West Hollywood, CA 90069-0826, USA

Rackers, Neil (Football Player)
Cincinnati Bengals
945 Shady Path Ct
Saint Peters, MO 63376-3898, USA

Rackley, Derek (Football Player)
Atlanta Falcons
5659 Legends Club Cir
Braselton, GA 30517-6029, USA

Rackley, Marv (Baseball Player)
Brooklyn Dodgers
512 S Bibb St
Westminster, SC 29693-2134, USA

Raczka, Mike (Baseball Player)
Oakland A's
72 Foley Dr
Southington, CT 06489-4400, USA

Radachowsky, George (Football Player)
Indianapolis Colts
87 Merrimac St
Danbury, CT 06810-6463, USA

Radcliffe, Daniel (Actor)
c/o Staff Member *Artists Rights Group Talent (ARG)*
4 Great Portland St
London W1W 8PA, UNITED KINGDOM
(UK)

Raddatz, Carl
Stalluponer Allee 54
Berlin 14055, GERMANY

Rade, John (Football Player)
Atlanta Falcons
611 Deertrail Dr
Hailey, ID 83333-8731, USA

Rademacher, Bill (Football Player)
New York Jets
5409 Maple Rdg
Haslett, MI 48840-8651, USA

Rademacher, Ingo (Actor)
S D B Partners
1801 Avenue Of Stars Ste 902
Los Angeles, CA 90067-5981, USA

Rademacher, Pete
5585 River Styx Rd
Medina, OH 44256-8786, USA

Rademacher, T Peter (Pete) (Boxer)
5585 River Styx Rd
Medina, OH 44256-8786, USA

Rader, Dave (Baseball Player)
San Francisco Giants
2114 Oakwood Dr
Bakersfield, CA 93304-5434, USA

Rader, Douglas L (Doug) (Baseball Player)
Houston Astros
3332 SE Court Dr
Stuart, FL 34997-6012, USA

Rader, Randall R (Judge)
US Appeals Court
717 Madison Pl NW
Washington, DC 20439-0001, USA

Rader, Stanley
360 Waverly Dr
Pasadena, CA 91105-1820, USA

Rader-Duval, Dean (Actor)
c/o Staff Member *Don Gerler Agency*
3349 Cahuenga Blvd W Ste 1
Los Angeles, CA 90068-1379, USA

Radford, Mark (Basketball Player)
3423 NE 22nd Ave
Portland, OR 97212-2432, USA

Radford, Michael (Director)
38 Rickering Mews
London W2 5AD, UNITED KINGDOM
(UK)

Radha Ravi (Actor)
23 Poes Road
Teynampet
Chennai, TN 600 018, INDIA

Radhika (Actor, Bollywood)
3 Paul Appasamy Street
Abhirampuram
Chennai, TN 600018, INDIA

Radigan, Terry (Musician, Songwriter, Writer)
Frank Callan Corp
6039 Robin Hill Rd
Nashville, TN 37205-3227, USA

Radinsky, Scott (Baseball Player)
Chicago White Sox
2974 Santiago St
Westlake Village, CA 91362-3737, USA

Radiohead (Music Group)
c/o Staff Member *Creative Artists Agency LCC (CAA-LA)*
2000 Avenue Of The Stars
Los Angeles, CA 90067-4700, USA

Radisic, Zivko (President)
President's Office
Marsala Titz 7
Sarajevo 71000, BOSNIA-HERZEGOVINA

Radke, Brad W (Baseball Player)
Minnesota Twins
501 Mandalay Ave Apt 1010
Clearwater Beach, FL 33767-1714, USA

Radko, Christopher (Artist)
PO Box 536
Elmsford, NY 10523-0536, USA

Radloff, Wayne (Football Player)
Atlanta Falcons
106 Wedgefield Dr
Hilton Head Island, SC 29926-2260, USA

Radlosky, Robert (Baseball Player)
Minnesota Twins
1219 W Broward St
Lantana, FL 33462-3013, USA

Radmanovic, Vladimir (Basketball Player)
Seattle SuperSonics
1201 3rd Ave Ste 1000
Seattle, WA 98101-3038, USA

Radmanovich, Ryan (Baseball Player)
Seattle Mariners
205-337 6 Ave NE
Calgary, AB T2E 0M1, CANADA

Radner, Roy (Economist)
30711 Overlook Run
Buena Vista, CO 81211-9836, USA

Radnor, Josh (Actor)
c/o Rhonda Price *Gersh Agency, The (NY)*
41 Madison Ave Fl 33
New York, NY 10010-2202, USA

Radojevic, Danilo (Dancer)
American Ballet Theatre
890 Broadway
New York, NY 10003-1278, USA

Radosevich, George (Football Player)
Baltimore Colts
414 Shaffer Ave
Elizabeth, PA 15037-1840, USA

Radtke, Jack (Baseball Player)
Brooklyn Dodgers
1828 Bridgeview Blvd Apt 116
Twin Falls, ID 83301-3057, USA

Raduege Jr, Harry D (General)
Director
Defense Information Systems Agency
Arlington, VA 22204, USA

Radwanski, George (Editor)
Toronto Star
Editorial Dept
1 Yonge St
Toronto, ON M5E 1E6, CANADA

Rae, Cassidy (Actor)
SDB Partners Inc
1801 Avenue Of The Stars Ste 902
C/O Ro Diamond
Los Angeles, CA 90067-5981, USA

Rae, Charlotte (Actor)
10790 Wilshire Blvd Apt 903
Los Angeles, CA 90024-4478, USA

Rae, Chris
122 Holland Park Ave.
London, ENGLAND W11 4UA, UNITED
KINGDOM (UK)

Rae, Mike (Football Player)
Oakland Raiders
18541 Auburn Ave
Santa Ana, CA 92705-2704, USA

Rae, Patricia (Actor)
c/o Marianne Golan *Marianne Golan Management*
6528 W 6th St
Los Angeles, CA 90048-4716, USA

Rae, Robert K (Bob) (Politician)
Goodman Phillips Vineberg
250 Yonge St
Toronto, ON M5B 2M6, CANADA

Rae Westley, Jennifer (Actor)
c/o Staff Member *da Vinci Talent*
919 Marie Anne Est
Montreal, PQ H2J 2B2, CANADA

Raekwon (Musician)
Famous Artists Agency
250 W 57th St
New York, NY 10107-0001, USA

Raether, Hal (Baseball Player)
Philadelphia Athletics
6105 Lincoln Dr Apt 133
Minneapolis, MN 55436-1619, USA

Rafalski, Brian (Hockey Player)
New Jersey Devils
Continental Arena
50 RR 120 N
East Rutherford, NJ 07073, USA

Rafelson, Bob (Director)
1543 Dog Team Road
1022 Palm Ave. #3
New Haven, VT 05472, USA

Raffarin, Jean-Pierre (Prime Minister)
Premier's Office
Hotel Matignon
57 Rue de Varenne
Paris 75000, FRANCE

Rafferty, Thomas M (Tom) (Football Player)
Dallas Cowboys
1526 Mount Gilead Rd
Roanoke, TX 76262-7358, USA

Raffo, Al (Baseball Player)
Philadelphia Phillies
330 Pleasant View Cir
Jasper, TN 37347-7242, USA

Rafikov, Mars Z (Cosmonaut)
Ul M Gorkova 59
KV 44
Almaty 480 002, KAZAKHSTAN

Rafko, Kaye Lani Rae
4932 Frary Ln
Monroe, MI 48161-9708, USA

Rafsanjani, Hashemi (Ex-President, President)
Ali Shariati Ave
Tehran, IRAN

Rafsanjani, Hojatoleslam H (President)
Expediency Council of Islamic Order
Majilis
Teheran, IRAN

Rafshoon, Gerald
3028 Q St NW
Washington, DC 20007-3080, USA

Rafter, Patrick (Tennis Player)
PO Box 1235
North Sydney, NSW 2059, AUSTRALIA

Raftery, S Frank (Misc)
Painters & Allied Trades Union
1750 New York Ave NW Ste 501
Washington, DC 20006-5301, USA

Ragavendar (Actor)
2-C Palace View Apartments
788 Santhome High Road
Chennai, TN 600 028, INDIA

Rage Against The Machine (Musician)
c/o Staff Member *Creative Artists Agency LCC (CAA-LA)*
2000 Avenue Of The Stars
Los Angeles, CA 90067-4700, USA

Raggi, Florencia (Actor)
c/o Staff Member *Telefe - Argentina*
Pavon 2444 (C1248AAT)
Buenos Aires, ARGENTINA

Raggio, Lisa
9300 Wilshire Blvd # 410
Beverly Hills, CA 90212-3213, USA

Ragglo, Brady (Baseball Player)
St Louis Cardinals
2971 Roundrock Ct
Reno, NV 89511-5328, USA

Raghavan, V S (Actor)
6 School View Road
Mandavelli
Chennai, TN 600 028, INDIA

Raghavi (Actor, Bollywood)
18 Crescent Park Road
T Nagar
Chennai, TN 600017, INDIA

Raghuvaran (Actor)
D-1 Ist Floor Anandsree Apartments
32 Hindi Prachar Saba Street
Chennai, TN 600 017, INDIA

Ragin, Derek Lee (Opera Singer)
Colbert Artists
111 W 57th St
New York, NY 10019-2236, USA

Ragin, John S (Actor)
5706 Briarcliff Rd
Los Angeles, CA 90068, USA

Ragland, Tom (Baseball Player)
Washington Senators
20201 Greenlawn St
Detroit, MI 48221-1187, USA

Raglin, Floyd (Football Player)
Miami Dolphins
2701 Alister Ave
Tustin, CA 92782-0934, USA

Rago, Pablo (Actor)
c/o Staff Member *Telefe - Argentina*
Pavon 2444 (C1248AAT)
Buenos Aires, ARGENTINA

Ragogna, Mike (Musician, Producer)
3975 Meier St Apt 201
Los Angeles, CA 90066-4187, USA

Ragsdale, William (Actor)
Innovative Artists
1505 10th St
Santa Monica, CA 90401-2805, USA

Ragunas, Vincent (Football Player)
Pittsburgh Steelers
4201 W Grace St
Richmond, VA 23230-3803, USA

Rahal, Bobby
4601 Lyman Dr
Hilliard, OH 43026-1249, USA

Rahlves, Daron (Skier)
PO Box 333
Truckee, CA 96160-0333, USA

Rahm, Kevin (Actor)
3 Arts Entertainment
9460 Wilshire Blvd Ste 700
Beverly Hills, CA 90212-2713, USA

Rahman Khan, Ataur (Prime Minister)
Bangladesh Jatiya League
500 A Dhanmondi R/A
Road 7
Dhaka, BANGLADESH

Rahul, Roy (Actor, Bollywood)
502 Gildar Villa
17 Master Vinayak X Road Bandra
Mumbai, MS 400050, INDIA

Rahzel (Musician)
Agency Group Ltd
1775 Broadway Ste 515
New York, NY 10019-1903, USA

Rai, Aishwarya (Actor, Bollywood)
c/o Staff Member *Canyon Entertainment*
PO Box 256
Palm Springs, CA 92263-0256, USA

Rai, Rajeev (Bollywood, Director, Filmmaker, Producer)
22 Sonmarg Nepean Sea Road
Bombay, MS 400 006, INDIA

Rai, Rajiv (Bollywood, Director, Producer)
B-11 Commerce Center
Tardeo
Mumbai, MS 400034, INDIA

Raible, Steve (Football Player)
Seattle Seahawks
2721 1st Ave Apt 1002
Seattle, WA 98121-3521, USA

Raich, Eric (Baseball Player)
Cleveland Indians
3963 Edward Dr
Brunswick, OH 44212-1509, USA

Raichle, Marcus E (Doctor)
Washington University
Medical School
Neurology Dept
Saint Louis, MO 63130, USA

Raider-Wexler, Victor (Actor)
c/o Staff Member *Stone Manners Talent & Literary (LA)*
6500 Wilshire Blvd Ste 550
Los Angeles, CA 90048-4950, USA

Raikkonen, Kimi (Race Car Driver)
c/o Staff Member *Formula Management Ltd*
PO Box 222
Borehamwood
Herts WD6 3FJ, UNITED KINGDOM (UK)

Railsback, Steve (Actor)
11684 Ventura Blvd # 581
Studio City, CA 91604-2699, USA

Raimi, Sam (Director)
c/o Staff Member *Ghost House Pictures*
10202 Washington Blvd
David Lean Bldng # 100
Culver City, CA 90232-3119, USA

Raimi, Ted
252 N Larchmont Blvd Ste 200
Los Angeles, CA 90004-3754, USA

Raimond, Jean-Bernard (Government Official)
Servier SA
22 Rue Garnier
Neuilly-sur-Seine 92200, FRANCE

Raimondi, Ben (Football Player)
New York Yankees
5 Grandview Dr
Holmdel, NJ 07733-2007, USA

Raimondi, Ruggero (Opera Singer)
M Gromof
140 Bis Rue Lecourbe
Paris 75015, FRANCE

Rain, Misty
PO Box 67
Lakewood, CA 90714-0067, USA

Raine, Craig A (Writer)
New College
English Dept
Oxford OX1 3BN, UNITED KINGDOM (UK)

Raine, Gillian
13 Billing Rd.
London, ENGLAND SW10, UNITED KINGDOM (UK)

Rainer, Luise (Actor)
54 Eaton Square
London SW1, UNITED KINGDOM (UK)

Rainer, Wali (Football Player)
Cleveland Browns
4715 Monaco Dr
Sandston, VA 23150-3205, USA

Raines, Cristina
6399 Wilshire Blvd Ste 414
Los Angeles, CA 90048-5716, USA

Raines, Franklin D (Financier, Government Official)
Federal National Mortgage Assn
3900 Wisconsin Ave NW
Washington, DC 20016-2806, USA

Raines, Mike (Football Player)
San Francisco 49ers
112 Lupine Dr
Jacksonville, FL 32259-5406, USA

Raines, Timothy (Tim) (Baseball Player)
1242 St Albans Loop
Lake Mary, FL 32746-1978, USA

Rainey, Matt (Journalist)
Star-Ledger
1 Star Ledger Plz
Editorial Dept
Newark, NJ 07102-1291, USA

Rainey, Wayne (Race Car Driver)
1660 Akron Peninsula Rd Ste 201
Akron, OH 44313-5192, USA

Rains, Dan (Football Player)
Chicago Bears
2509 Wigwam Rd
Aliquippa, PA 15001-4340, USA

Raintano, Natalie (Actor)
c/o Staff Member *Artists Only Management*
10203 Santa Monica Blvd
Los Angeles, CA 90067-6405, USA

Rainwater, G L (Business Person)
Ameren Corp
1901 Chouteau Ave
Saint Louis, MO 63103-3003, USA

Rainwater, Gregg (Actor)
PO Box 291836
Los Angeles, CA 90029-8836, USA

Rainwater, Keech (Musician)
Borman Entertainment
1222 16th Ave S Ste 23
Nashville, TN 37212-2926, USA

Rainwater, Marvin (Musician)
36968 295th St
Aitkin, MN 56431-4374, USA

Raitt, Bonnie L (Musician, Songwriter, Writer)
c/o Staff Member *Paradigm (Monterey)*
509 Hartnell St
Monterey, CA 93940-2825, USA

Raj, Prakash (Actor)
183 Bharathidasan Street
Baskar Colony Virugambakka
Chennai, TN 600 092, INDIA

Raja (Actor)
6 Ranjith Road
Kotturpuram
Chennai, TN 600 085, INDIA

Rajasulochana (Actor, Bollywood)
70 G N Chetty Road
T Nagar
Chennai, TN 600017, INDIA

Rajat, Kapoor (Actor, Bollywood)
Unit No 140 Andheri Indl Est
Off Veera Desai Road Andheri (W)
Mumbai, MS 400053, INDIA

Rajeev (Actor)
12/V Ambedkar Street Gandhi Nagar
Saligramam
Chennai, TN 600 093, INDIA

Rajeevi (Actor, Bollywood)
32 Raman Street
T Nagar
Chennai, TN 600017, INDIA

Rajendran, S S (Actor)
3/3 Eldams Road
Chennai, TN 600 018, INDIA

Rajesh (Actor)
7 Kannappa Salai
Ashok Nagar
Chennai, TN 600 083, INDIA

Rajinikanth (Actor)
18 Raghava Veera Avenue
Poes Garden
Chennai, TN 600 086, INDIA

Rajkiran (Actor, Bollywood)
145/5 North Boag Road
T Nagar
Chennai, TN 600017, INDIA

Rajna, Thomas (Composer, Musician)
10 Wyndover Road
Claremont
Cape 7700, SOUTH AFRICA

Rajnikant (Actor, Bollywood)
18 Ragava Veera Avenue
Poes Garden
Madras, TN 600 086, INDIA

Rajskub, Mary Lynn (Actor)
c/o Adam Venit *Endeavor Agency LLC (LA)*
9601 Wilshire Blvd Fl 3
Beverly Hills, CA 90210-5204, USA

Rakestraw, Larry (Football Player)
Chicago Bears
2462 Welford Ct
Suwanee, GA 30024-3130, USA

Rakhmonov, Emomali (President)
President's Office
Supreme Soviet
Dushanbe, TAJIKISTAN

Raki, Laya (Actor)
Atkins Assoc
8040 Ventura Canyon Ave
Panorama City, CA 91402-6313, USA

Rakim (Musician)
Padell Nadell Fine Wineberger
156 W 56th St # 400
New York, NY 10019-3800, USA

Rakoczy, Gregg (Football Player)
Cleveland Browns
8709 Hidden Green Ln
Tampa, FL 33647-2271, USA

Rakotomavo, Pascal (Prime Minister)
Prime Minister's Office
Mahazoarivo
Antananarivo, MADAGASCAR

Rakowski, Mieczyslaw F (Prime Minister)
Miesiecznik Dzis
Ul Poznanska 3
Warsaw 00-680, POLAND

Rales, Steven M (Business Person)
Danaher Corp
1250 24th St NW
Washington, DC 20037-1124, USA

Rall, Gunther (War Hero)
Schmalschlagerstr 17
Bad Reichenhall 83435, GERMANY

Rall, J Edward (Doctor)
3947 Baltimore St
Kensington, MD 20895-3913, USA

Rall, Ted (Cartoonist)
Chronicle Features
901 Mission St
San Francisco, CA 94103-2905, USA

Rall, Tommy (Actor)
Kathleen Schultz & Assoc
6442 Coldwater Canyon Ave Ste 206
North Hollywood, CA 91606-1137, USA

Ralph, Christopher (Actor)
c/o Paul Nicholls *Artistry Management*
525 Westbourne Dr
West Hollywood, CA 90048-1913, USA

Ralph, Richard P (Governor)
Governor's Office
Government House
Stanley, FALKLAND ISLANDS

Ralston, Bob
17027 Tennyson Pl
Granada Hills, CA 91344-1225, USA

Ralston, Dennis (Tennis Player)
2005 San Vicente Dr
Concord, CA 94519, USA

Ralston, John R (Coach, Football Coach, Football Player)
8245 Claret Ct
San Jose, CA 95135-1415, USA

Ralston, Steve (Soccer Player)
New England Revolution
1 Patriot Pl
Cmgi Field
Foxboro, MA 02035-1388, USA

Ram, C Venkata (Doctor)
Texas Southwestern Medical Center
5323 Harry Hines Blvd
Dallas, TX 75390-7200, USA

Rama IX (King)
Chitralada Villa
Bangakok, THAILAND

Rama Rau, Santha (Writer)
496 Leedsville Rd
Amenia, NY 12501-5820, USA

Ramage, Rob (Hockey Player)
16127 Wilson Manor Dr
Chesterfield, MO 63005-4583, USA

Ramahata, Victor (Prime Minister)
PO Box 6004
Antanarivo 101, MADAGASCAR

Ramamurthy, Sendhil (Actor)
c/o David Lederman *Innovative Artists (LA)*
1505 10th St
Santa Monica, CA 90401-2805, USA

Raman, Priya (Actor, Bollywood)
Plot No 69
Part II VGP Sea View Palavakkam
Chennai, TN 600041, INDIA

Raman, Ragha (Actor, Bollywood)
Flat 202 II Floor
167 Eldams Road Teynampet
Chennai, TN 600018, INDIA

Ramaphosa, M Cyril (Government Official)
New Africa Investments
PO Box 782922
Sandton 2416, SOUTH AFRICA

Ramarajan (Actor)
1 Ramakrishna Street
T Nagar
Chennai, TN 600 017, INDIA

Ramasami, V. K. (Actor, Bollywood)
26 Tilak Street
T Nagar
Chennai, TN 600017, INDIA

Ramazzotti, Eros (Musician)
Via Vittoria Colonna
Milan I-20149, ITALY

Ramba (Actor)
44/1 Navaneethammal Street
Saligramam
Chennai, TN 600 093, INDIA

Ramba (Actor, Bollywood)
184 Bharathidasan Salai
Baskaran Colony Saligramam
Chennai, TN 600092, INDIA

Rambahadur, Limbu (War Hero)
Box 420
Bandar Seri Begawan
Negara Brunei Darussalam, BRUNEI

Rambert, Charles J J (Architect)
179 Rue de Courcelles
Paris 75017, FRANCE

Rambin, Leven (Actor)
c/o Rhonda Price *Gersh Agency, The (NY)*
41 Madison Ave Fl 33
New York, NY 10010-2202, USA

Rambis, Kurt (Basketball Player, Coach)
20 Chatham
Manhattan Beach, CA 90266-7225, USA

Rambo, David L (Religious Leader)
Christian & Missionary Alliance
PO Box 35000
Colorado Springs, CO 80935-3500, USA

Rambo, John (Athlete, Track Athlete)
1847 Myrtle Ave
Long Beach, CA 90806-5613, USA

Rambola, Tony (Musician)
William Morris Agency
151 El Camino Dr
Beverly Hills, CA 90212-2775, USA

Ramey, Louis (Actor, Comedian)
c/o Staff Member *William Morris Agency (WMA-LA)*
1 William Morris Pl
Beverly Hills, CA 90212-4261, USA

Ramey, Samuel E (Opera Singer)
320 Central Park W
New York, NY 10025-7659, USA

Ramgoolam, Navinchandra (Prime Minister)
85 Sir Seewilsagur Ramgoolam St
Port Louis, MAURITIUS

Ramgoolam, Seewosagur (Prime Minister)
85 Desforges St
Port Louis, MAURITIUS

Ramirez, Aramis (Baseball Player)
c/o Staff Member *Chicago Cubs*
1060 W Addison St
Wrigley Field
Chicago, IL 60613-4397, USA

Ramirez, Carolina (Actor)
c/o Gabriel Blanco *Gabriel Blanco Iglesias (Mexico)*
Rio Balsas 35-32
Colonia Cuauhtemoc
DF 06500, MEXICO

Ramirez, Dania (Actor, Producer)
c/o Jeff Morrone *Jeff Morrone Management*
9350 Wilshire Blvd Ste 224
Beverly Hills, CA 90212-3204, USA

Ramirez, Edgar (Actor)
c/o Elyse Scherz *Endeavor Agency LLC (LA)*
9601 Wilshire Blvd Fl 3
Beverly Hills, CA 90210-5204, USA

Ramirez, Efren (Actor)
c/o Staff Member *James/Levy/Jacobson Management*
3500 W Olive Ave Ste 1470
Burbank, CA 91505-5514, USA

Ramirez, Manny (Baseball Player)
c/o Staff Member *Boston Red Sox*
Fenway Park
4 Yawkey Way
Boston, MA 02215-3496, USA

Ramirez, Michael P (Mike) (Cartoonist)
Los Angeles Times
202 W 1st St
Editorial Dept
Los Angeles, CA 90012-4105, USA

Ramirez, Pedro J (Editor)
El Mundo
Calle Pradillo 42
Madrid 28002, SPAIN

Ramirez, Raul (Tennis Player)
Avenida Ruiz
65 Sur Ensenada
Baja California, MEXICO

Ramirez, RaulAvenida Ruiz
65 Sur Ensenada
Baja California, MEXICO

Ramirez, Sara (Actor)
c/o Staff Member *Mitchell K Stubbs & Assoc (MKS)*
8695 Washington Blvd Ste 204
Culver City, CA 90232-7419, USA

Ramirez, Twiggy (Musician)
Mitch Schenlder Organization
14724 Ventura Blvd Ste 710
Sherman Oaks, CA 91403-3520, USA

Ramirez Vazquez, Pedro (Architect)
Ave de la Fuentes 170
Mexico City, DF 01900, MEXICO

Ramis, Harold (Actor, Director)
160 Euclid Ave
Glencoe, IL 60022-2107, USA

Rammstein (Music Group)
c/o Staff Member *Nasty Little Man*
110 Greene St Ste 605
New York, NY 10012-3838, USA

Ramo, Simon (Business Person)
9200 W Sunset Blvd # 401
West Hollywood, CA 90069-3502, USA

Ramon, Haim (Government Official)
Knesset
Jerusalem 91010, ISRAEL

Ramone, Phil
3301 Barham Blvd Ste 201
Los Angeles, CA 90068-1358, USA

Ramones, The (Music Group)
c/o Gary Kurfirst *Kurfirst/Blackwell Management*
601 W 26th St Fl 11
New York, NY 10001-1101, USA

Ramos, Constance (Connie) (Actor, Reality TV Star)
c/o Staff Member *Extreme Makeover: Home Edition*
9255 W Sunset Blvd Ste 1100
Endemol Entertainment USA
Los Angeles, CA 90069-3308, USA

Ramos, Del (Musician)
Variety Artists
793 Higuera St Ste 6
San Luis Obispo, CA 93401-0500, USA

Ramos, Diego (Actor)
c/o Gabriel Blanco *Gabriel Blanco Iglesias (Mexico)*
Rio Balsas 35-32
Colonia Cuauhtemoc
DF 06500, MEXICO

Ramos, Fidel (President)
Malacanang Palace
Manila, PHILIPPINES

Ramos, Jorge (Actor)
c/o Staff Member *Univision*
605 3rd Ave Fl 12
New York, NY 10158-1299, USA

Ramos, Mando (Boxer)
1252 W Park Western Dr Unit 91
San Pedro, CA 90732-2294, USA

Ramos, Mel (Artist)
5941 Ocean View Dr
Oakland, CA 94618-1842, USA

Ramos, Monica (Musician)
MNW Records Group
PO Box 535
Taby 183 25, SWEDEN

Ramos, Rudy
280 S Beverly Dr Ste 400
Beverly Hills, CA 90212-3904, USA

Ramos, Sarah (Actor)
c/o Staff Member *Abrams Artists Agency (LA)*
9200 W Sunset Blvd Ph 11
Los Angeles, CA 90069-3601, USA

Ramos, Tab (Soccer Player)
William Morris Agency
151 El Camino Dr
Beverly Hills, CA 90212-2775, USA

Ramos-Horta, Jose (Nobel Prize Laureate)
Rua Sao Lazoro 16
#1
Lisbon 1150, PORTUGAL

Ramos Jr, Hilario (Larry) (Musician)
Variety Artists
793 Higuera St Ste 6
San Luis Obispo, CA 93401-0500, USA

Rampling, Charlotte (Actor)
c/o Elisabeth Tanner *ArtMedia*
20 av Rapp
Paris 75007, FRANCE

Ramsay, Anne
PO Box 5617
Beverly Hills, CA 90209-5617, USA

Ramsay, Bruce
9150 Wilshire Blvd Ste 350
Beverly Hills, CA 90212-3453, USA

Ramsay, Craig (Coach, Hockey Player)
9701 NW 58th Ct
Parkland, FL 33076-1829, USA

Ramsay, Gordon (Chef)
Gordon Ramsay Holding Ltd
1 Catherine Place
London sw1e6dx, UNITED KINGDOM
(UK)

Ramsay, John T (Jack) (Coach)
444 Ridgeway Rd
Lake Oswego, OR 97034-3823, USA

Ramsay, Keshu (Director, Filmmaker, Producer)
Maharaja Surajmal 'C'
New Versova Link Road Andheri
Bombay, MS 400 058, INDIA

Ramsay, Laymon (Baseball Player)
Chicago American Giants
2417 Princeton Ave SW
Birmingham, AL 35211-3144, USA

Ramsay, Wayne (Hockey Player)
General Delivery
Oak River, MB R0K 1T0, CANADA

Ramsbottom, Nancy (Golfer)
2216 Parkers Hill Dr
Maidens, VA 23102-2243, USA

Ramsey, Chuck (Football Player)
New York Jets
17519 Marvel Rd
Lenior City, TN 37772, USA

Ramsey, David (Actor)
c/o Staff Member *Agency for the Performing Arts (APA-LA)*
405 S Beverly Dr
Beverly Hills, CA 90212-4416, USA

Ramsey, Derrick (Football Player)
Oakland Raiders
1801 Barwick Dr
Lexington, KY 40505-2546, USA

Ramsey, Garrard S (Buster) (Football Player)
613 Georgia Ave
Signal Mountain, TN 37377-1813, USA

Ramsey, Gerrard (Football Player)
Chicago Cardinals
4102 US Highway 411 S
Maryville, TN 37801-9148, USA

Ramsey, John (Misc)
Campaign Headquarters
PO Box 243
Cheboygan, MI 49721-0243, USA

Ramsey, Knox (Football Player)
Chicago Cardinals
10544 Pontofino Cir
Trinity, FL 34655-7084, USA

Ramsey, Laura (Actor)
c/o Michael Katcher *Creative Artists Agency LCC (CAA-LA)*
2000 Avenue Of The Stars
Los Angeles, CA 90067-4700, USA

Ramsey, Logan
12923 Killion St
Sherman Oaks, CA 91401-5421, USA

Ramsey, Mary (Musician)
Agency for Performing Arts
405 S Beverly Dr Ste 500
Beverly Hills, CA 90212-4425, USA

Ramsey, Michael (Mike) (Hockey Player)
445 W 79th St
Chanhassen, MN 55317-4505, USA

Ramsey, Nate (Football Player)
Philadelphia Eagles
1938 Cambridge St
Philadelphia, PA 19130-1508, USA

Ramsey, Ray (Football Player)
1612 Sequoria Dr
Chatham, IL 62629, USA

Ramsey, Ray (Musician, Songwriter, Writer)
Elbchaussee 118
Hamburg 22763, GERMANY

Ramsey, Tom (Football Player)
New England Patriots
5435 E Otero Dr
Centennial, CO 80122-3875, USA

Ramsey, Wes (Actor)
c/o Edward G (Eddie) Horowitz *Creative Management Group (CMG)*
8522 National Blvd Ste 108
Culver City, CA 90232-2454, USA

Ramsey, William E (Admiral)
825 Bayshore Dr
Pensacola, FL 32507-3470, USA

Ramsey Jr, Frank V (Basketball Player, Coach)
363 Buckner Ridge Ln
Madisonville, KY 42431, USA

Ramsey Jr, Norman F (Nobel Prize Laureate)
24 Monmouth Ct
Brookline, MA 02446-5634, USA

Ramson, Eason (Football Player)
St Louis Cardinals
1000 Claudia Ct Apt 39
Antioch, CA 94509-3440, USA

Ran, Shulamit (Composer)
University of Chicago
5845 S Ellis Ave
Music Dept
Chicago, IL 60637-1476, USA

Rana, Ashutosh (Actor, Bollywood)
23 Bharat Petroleum Colony
Aziz Baug Chembur
Mumbai, MS 400074, INDIA

Ranaldo, Alyson (Actor)
c/o Tamara Houston *Sanctuary Artist Management (LA)*
9255 W Sunset Blvd # 200
Los Angeles, CA 90069-3309, USA

Rancic, Bill (Reality TV Star)
c/o Jason Burns *Gersh Agency, The (LA)*
232 N Canon Dr
Beverly Hills, CA 90210-5302, USA

Rand, Marvin (Photographer)
Marvin Rand Assoc
1310 Abbot Kinney Blvd
Venice, CA 90291-3758, USA

Rand, Reese Mary (Athlete, Track Athlete)
6650 Los Gatos Rd
Atascadero, CA 93422-3608, USA

Rand, Robert W (Educator)
Good Samaritan Hospital
Neurosciences Institute
Los Angeles, CA 90017, USA

Randa, Joe (Baseball Player)
W236N1150 Archery Dr
Waukesha, WI 53188-1718, USA

Randall, Alice (Writer)
c/o Staff Member *Creative Artists Agency LCC (CAA-LA)*
2000 Avenue Of The Stars
Los Angeles, CA 90067-4700, USA

Randall, Carolyn D (Judge)
US Court of Appeals
515 Rusk St Ste 12015
Houston, TX 77002-2605, USA

Randall, Claire (Religious Leader)
9965 W Royal Oak Rd Apt 1214
Sun City, AZ 85351-6116, USA

Randall, Frankie (Boxer)
355 Fish Hatchery Rd # 2
Morristown, TN 37813, USA

Randall, Jon (Musician)
Joe's Garage
4405 Belmont Park Ter
Nashville, TN 37215-3609, USA

Randall, Josh (Actor)
I F A Talent Agency
8730 W Sunset Blvd Ste 490
Los Angeles, CA 90069-2248, USA

Randall, Rebel (Actor)
Women United Int'l
PO Box 1405
Riverside, CA 92502-1405, USA

Randall, Tom (Football Player)
Dallas Cowboys
2521 Park Vista Cir
Ames, IA 50014-4568, USA

Randazzo, Anthony (Baseball Player)
2936 Scenic Cir
Las Cruces, NM 88011, USA

Randazzo, Mike (Actor, Talk Show Host)
Michael Essany Show
3469 W Stones Crossing Rd
C/O Mike Randazzo
Greenwood, IN 46143-8564, USA

Randi, James (Misc)
12000 NW 8th St
Plantation, FL 33325-1406, USA

Randie, John (Football Player)
PO Box 489
Harrisonburg, VA 22803-0489, USA

Randle, Betsy
9300 Wilshire Blvd Ste 555
Beverly Hills, CA 90212-3211, USA

Randle, Ervin (Football Player)
Tampa Bay Buccaneers
209 Wellington Rd
Irving, TX 75063-4293, USA

Randle, John (Football Player)
c/o Staff Member *Seattle Seahawks*
11220 NE 53rd St
Kirkland, WA 98033-7595, USA

Randle, Lynda (Musician)
5565 NW Barry Rd
PO Box 236
Kansas City, MO 64154-1408, USA

Randle, Tate (Football Player)
Houston Oilers
495 Koebig Rd
Seguin, TX 78155-0327, USA

Randle, Theresa (Actor)
c/o Tammy Rosen *Melanie Greene Management & Productions*
425 N Robertson Blvd
West Hollywood, CA 90048-1735, USA

Randle, Ulmo (Sonny) (Football Player)
St Louis Cardinals
PO Box 487
Harrisonburg, VA 22803-0487, USA

Randolph, A Raymond (Judge)
US Court of Appeals
333 Constitution Ave NW
Washington, DC 20001-2866, USA

Randolph, Alvin (Football Player)
San Francisco 49ers
319 Roble Ave
Redwood City, CA 94061-3732, USA

Randolph, Carl (Musician)
David Levin Mgmt
200 W 57th St Ste 308
New York, NY 10019-3211, USA

Randolph, Jackson H (Business Person)
Cinergy Corp
139 E 4th St
Cincinnati, OH 45202-4003, USA

Randolph, Joyce
295 Central Park W Apt 18A
New York, NY 10024-3024, USA

Randolph, Judson G (Doctor)
111 Michigan Ave NW
Washington, DC 20010-2978, USA

Randolph, Sam (Golfer)
1305 Briar Ridge Dr
Keller, TX 76248-8376, USA

Randolph, Willie L (Baseball Player)
715 Jenney Trl
Franklin Lakes, NJ 07417-2907, USA

Randolph, Zach (Basketball Player)
Portland Trail Blazers
1 N Center Court St
Rose Garden
Portland, OR 97227-2102, USA

Randrup, Michael (Misc)
10 Fairlawn Road
Lythamst Annes
Lancashire FY8 5PT, UNITED KINGDOM (UK)

Rands, Bernard (Composer)
Harvard University
Music Dept
Cambridge, MA 02138, USA

Ranford, William (Bill) (Hockey Player)
Coquitlam Express
633 Poirier St
Coquitlam, BC V3J 6B1, CANADA

Ranganathan, Suman (Actor, Bollywood)
Gilder Building
Turner Road Bandra
Mumbai, MS 400050, INDIA

Rangel, Charles B (Politician)
74 W 132nd St
New York, NY 10037-3313, USA

Ranger, Doug (Songwriter, Writer)
New Frontier Mgmt
1921 Broadway
Nashville, TN 37203-2719, USA

Rani (Actor, Bollywood)
Anubhav Apts
Arunachalam Road
Chennai, TN 600083, INDIA

Rania (Royalty)
Royal Palace
Amman, JORDAN

Raniers, Massimo
via Giovanni Battista Tiepolo 34
Rome 00196, ITALY

Ranis, Gustav (Economist)
7 Mulberry Rd
Woodbridge, CT 06525-1716, USA

Ranjani (Actor, Bollywood)
78/a Moubrews Road
Alwarpet
Chennai, TN 600018, INDIA

Ranjeet (Actor, Bollywood)
14 Silver Beach A B Nair Road
Juhu
Bombay, MS 400 049, INDIA

Ranki, Dezso (Musician)
OrdogoromLejto 11/B
Budapest 1112, HUNGARY

Rankin, Chris (Actor)
c/o Staff Member *Ken McReddie Ltd*
Paurelle House
91 Regent St
London W1R7TB, UNITED KINGDOM (UK)

Rankin, Judy (Golfer)
2715 Racquet Club Dr
Midland, TX 79705-7432, USA

Rankin, Kenny (Musician, Songwriter, Writer)
Absolute Artists
530 Howard St Ste 200
San Francisco, CA 94105-3018, USA

Rankin Jr, Alfred M (Business Person)
NACCO Industries
5875 Landerbrook Dr Ste 300
Mayfield Heights, OH 44124-4069, USA

Rankine, Terry (Architect)
Cambridge Seven Assoc
1050 Massachusetts Ave
Cambridge, MA 02138-5359, USA

Ranks, Shabba (Musician)
Epic Records
550 Madison Ave # 2500
New York, NY 10022-3211, USA

Ranney, Helen M (Doctor)
6229 La Jolla Mesa Dr
La Jolla, CA 92037-6332, USA

Ransdell, Gary (Educator)
Western Kentucky University
President's Office
Bowling Green, KY 42101, USA

Ransey, Kelvin (Basketball Player)
3195 Monterey Dr
Tupelo, MS 38801-6817, USA

Ransom, Derrick (Football Player)
Kansas City Chiefs
6521 Sparrowood Ct
Indianapolis, IN 46236-8122, USA

Ransome, Prunella
59 Frith St.
London, ENGLAND W1, UNITED KINGDOM (UK)

Rantel, Al (Radio Personality)
c/o Staff Member *International Creative Management (ICM-LA)*
10250 Constellation Blvd
Los Angeles, CA 90067-6200, USA

Rao, Ashok (Actor)
28 17th Cross Malleswaram
Bangalore, KA, INDIA

Rao, C N Ramchandra (Misc)
JNC President's House
Indian Science Institute
Bangalore, KA 560012, INDIA

Rao, T Rama (Actor, Bollywood, Director, Filmmaker, Producer)
No 14 1st Balaji Street Balaji Avenue
T Nagar
Madras, TN 600 017, INDIA

Rapaport, Michael (Actor)
c/o Suzan Bymel *Management 360*
9111 Wilshire Blvd
Beverly Hills, CA 90210-5508, USA

Raper, Kenneth B (Misc)
602 N Segoe Rd
Madison, WI 53705-3113, USA

Raphael (Actor)
Kaduri Agency
16125 NE 18th Ave
North Miami Beach, FL 33162-4749, USA

Raphael, Fredric M (Writer)
Largadeile
Saint Lauraent la Vallee
Belves 24170, FRANCE

Raphael, Sally Jessy (Entertainer)
c/o Steve Tellez *Creative Artists Agency LCC (CAA-LA)*
2000 Avenue Of The Stars
Los Angeles, CA 90067-4700, USA

Raposo, Greg (Musician)
PO Box 434
Glen Head, NY 11545-0434, USA

Rapp, Anthony (Actor)
c/o Elise Konialian *Untitled Entertainment (NY)*
322 8th Ave Ste 601
New York, NY 10001-6715, USA

Rappeneau, Jean-Paul (Director)
24 Rue Henri Barbusse
Paris 75005, FRANCE

Rapping 4-Tay (Musician)
Richard Walters
1800 Argyle Ave # 408
Los Angeles, CA 90028-5253, USA

Rappuoli, Rino (Scientist)
Sclavo Research Center
Via Fiorentina 1
Siena 53100, ITALY

Rapson, Ralph (Architect)
1 Seymour Ave SE
Minneapolis, MN 55414-3521, USA

Rapuano, Ed (Baseball Player)
10815 Japonica Ct
Boca Raton, FL 33498-4839, USA

Rare, Vanessa (Actor)
c/o Staff Member *Auckland Actors*
PO Box 56460
Dominion Road
Auckland, NEW ZEALAND

Rarick, Cindy (Golfer)
1625 N Via Dorado
Tucson, AZ 85715-4724, USA

Rasa Don (Musician)
William Morris Agency
1325 Avenue Of The Americas
New York, NY 10019-6091, USA

Rasby, Walter (Football Player)
Pittsburgh Steelers
6413 Brookbury Ct
Charlotte, NC 28226-6131, USA

Rascal Flatts (Music Group)
c/o Charles Dorris *William Morris Agency (WMA-TN)*
1600 Division St Ste 300
Nashville, TN 37203-2755, USA

Rasche, David (Actor)
687 Grove Ln
Santa Barbara, CA 93105-2449, USA

Rascon, Alfred V (War Hero)
10397 Derby Dr
Laurel, MD 20723-5743, USA

Rash, Steve (Director)
Broder Kurland Webb Uffner
10250 Constellation Blvd
Los Angeles, CA 90067-6200, USA

Rashad, Phylicia (Actor)
25 Magnolia Ave
Mount Vernon, NY 10553-1209, USA

Rasheeda (Musician)
International Creative Mgmt
8942 Wilshire Blvd # 219
Beverly Hills, CA 90211-1908, USA

Rashid, Karim (Designer)
357 W 17th St
New York, NY 10011-5060, USA

Rasi (Actor, Bollywood)
28B Main Road
Zakkaria Colony Saligramam
Chennai, TN 600094, INDIA

Raskin, Alex (Journalist)
Los Angeles Times
202 W 1st St
Editorial Dept
Los Angeles, CA 90012-4105, USA

Raskin, David (Composer)
Robert Light
6404 Wilshire Blvd
Los Angeles, CA 90048-5501, USA

Rasley, Rocky (Football Player)
Detroit Lions
1918 S Mills Ave Apt 4
Lodi, CA 95242-4475, USA

Rasmussen, Anders Fogh (Prime Minister)
prins Jorgens Gard 11
Copenhagen K 2000, DENMARK

Rasmussen, Poul Nyrup (Prime Minister)
Aliegade 6A
Frederiksberg 2000, DENMARK

Rasmussen, Randy (Football Player)
Pittsburgh Steelers
3990 114th Ln NW
Coon Rapids, MN 55433-2506, USA

Rasmussen, Randy (Football Player)
New York Jets
81 Grumman Hill Rd
Wilton, CT 06897-4508, USA

Rasmussen, Wayne (Football Player)
Detroit Lions
9000 E Maple St
Brandon, SD 57005-1026, USA

Raspberry, Larry (Musician)
Craig Nowag Attractions
6037 Haddington Cv
Memphis, TN 38119-7423, USA

Raspberry, William J (Journalist)
Washington Post
Editorial Dept
1150 15th St NW
Washington, DC 20071-0001, USA

Rassas, Nick (Football Player)
Atlanta Falcons
PO Box 227
Moose, WY 83012-0227, USA

Rasuk, Victor (Actor)
c/o Staff Member *Washington Square Arts (LA)*
1041 N Formosa Ave
Writers Bldg #305
West Hollywood, CA 90046-6703, USA

Ratchford, Jeremy (Actor)
Paradigm Agency
10100 Santa Monica Blvd Ste 2500
Los Angeles, CA 90067-4116, USA

Ratelle, J G Y Jean (Hockey Player)
1200 Salem St Apt 111
Lynnfield, MA 01940-1595, USA

Rather, Bo (Football Player)
Miami Dolphins
7728 La Jessica Cir
Kalamazoo, MI 49009-7542, USA

Rather, Dan (Correspondent, Television Host)
Dan Rather Reports
130 W 42nd St Ste 850
Hdnet
New York, NY 10036-7804, USA

Rathke, Henrich K M H (Religious Leader)
Schleifmuhlenweg 11
Schwering 19061, GERMANY

Rathman, Tom (Football Player)
San Francisco 49ers
2762 Bloomfield Crossing
Bloomfield, MI 48304-1711, USA

Rathmann, George B (Business Person)
ICOS Corp
22021 20th Ave SE
Bothell, WA 98021-4406, USA

Rathmann, Jim (Race Car Driver)
14 Marina Isles Blvd # 14G
Indian Harbour Beach, FL 32937-5372, USA

Rathnam, Mani (Bollywood, Director)
3 First Cross Road
Venus Colony
Alwarpet, Madras 600018, INDIA

Ratigan, Brian (Football Player)
Indianapolis Colts
743 26th St
Manhattan Beach, CA 90266-2366, USA

Ratkowski, Ray (Football Player)
Boston Patriots
PO Box 2736
Hyannis, MA 02601-7736, USA

Ratleff, Ed (Basketball Player)
4202 Paseo De Oro
Cypress, CA 90630-3420, USA

Ratliff, Don (Football Player)
Philadelphia Eagles
9048 Bay Hill Blvd
Orlando, FL 32819-4880, USA

Ratliff, Theo (Basketball Player)
Portland Trail Blazers
1 N Center Court St
Rose Garden
Portland, OR 97227-2102, USA

Ratner, Brett (Director)
c/o Staff Member *Rat Entertainment/Rat TV*
9255 W Sunset Blvd Ste 310
Los Angeles, CA 90069-3313, USA

Ratner, Ellen
6127 Glen Tower St
Los Angeles, CA 90068-2254, USA

Ratner, Helmer (Director)
Creative Artists Agency
9830 Wilshire Blvd
Beverly Hills, CA 90212-1804, USA

Ratner, Mark A (Misc)
615 Greenleaf Ave
Glencoe, IL 60022-1745, USA

Ratnoff, Oscar D (Doctor)
1801 Chestnut Hills Dr
Cleveland, OH 44106-4643, USA

Rato, Rodrigo (Government Official)
International Monetary Fund
700 19th St NW
Washington, DC 20431-0002, USA

Ratser, Dmitri (Musician)
Naxim Gershunoff
1401 NE 9th St Apt 38
Fort Lauderdale, FL 33304-4412, USA

Ratsiraka, Didier (Admiral, President)
President's Office
Iavoloha
Antananarivo, MADAGASCAR

RATT
1818 Illion St
San Diego, CA 92110-1313, USA

Ratt (Music Group)
WBS, Inc
11684 Ventura Blvd # 675
Studio City, CA 91604-2699, USA

Ratterman, George (Football Player)
Buffalo Bisons
4751 E Costilla Ave Apt 115
Centennial, CO 80122-2393, USA

Rattle, Simon D (Conductor)
Frank Salomon
201 W 54th St Apt 1C
New York, NY 10019-5520, USA

Rattner, Steven (Business Person)
Quadrangle Group LLC
375 Park Ave
New York, NY 10152-0002, USA

Ratushinskaya, Irina B (Writer)
Vargius Publishing House
Kuzakova Str 18
Moscow 107005, RUSSIA

Ratzenberger, John (Actor)
Shelter Entertainment
9255 W Sunset Blvd Ste 1010
Los Angeles, CA 90069-3307, USA

Ratzinger, Joseph A Cardinal (Religious Leader)
Palazzo del S Uffizio II
Rome 00193, ITALY

Rau, Doug
RR 1 Box 154A
Columbus, TX 78934, USA

Rau, Johannes (Politician, President)
Haroldstr 2
Dusseldorf 47057, GERMANY

Rauch, John (Johnny) (Coach, Football Coach, Football Player)
New York Yankees
30 Tads Trl
Oldsmar, FL 34677-2318, USA

Rauch, Siegfried
Weilheimerstr. 6
Untersochering D-82395, GERMANY

Rauner-Harrington, Helen (Baseball Player)
2027 Kentucky Ave
Fort Wayne, IN 46805-4442, USA

Raup, David M (Musician)
423 Johnson Dr
Washington Island, WI 54246-9169, USA

Rauschenberg, Robert (Artist)
381 Lafayette St
New York, NY 10003-7022, USA

Rautio, Nina (Opera Singer)
Herbert Breslin
119 W 57th St Ste 1505
New York, NY 10019-2401, USA

Ravalec, Blanche (Actor)
Babette Pouget
6 Square Villaret de Joyeuse
Paris 75017, FRANCE

Ravali (Actor, Bollywood)
159 Thirupathi Nagar
Valasaravakkam
Chennai, TN 600087, INDIA

Ravalomanana, Marc (President)
President's Office
Iavoloha
Antananarivo, MADAGASCAR

Raveena, Tondon (Actor, Bollywood)
Nippon Society
Juhu Church
Mumbai, MS 400049, INDIA

Raven, Eddy (Musician, Songwriter, Writer)
Great American Talent
PO Box 2476
Hendersonville, TN 37077-2476, USA

Raven, Peter H (Misc)
Missouri Botanical Garden
PO Box 299
Saint Louis, MO 63166-0299, USA

Ravensberg, Robert (Football Player)
Chicago Cardinals
636 Sherwood Dr
Saint Louis, MO 63119-3754, USA

Raver, Kim (Actor)
c/o Richard Jackson *Innovative Artists (NY)*
235 Park Ave S Fl 7
New York, NY 10003-1405, USA

Ravitch, Diane S (Historian)
New York University
Washington Place
Press Building
New York, NY 10003, USA

Ravony, Francisque (Prime Minister)
Union des Forces Vivas Democratiques
Antananarivo, MADAGASCAR

Ravotti, Eric (Football Player)
Pittsburgh Steelers
6000 Christopher Wren Dr Apt 117
Wexford, PA 15090-7364, USA

Rawail, Rahul (Bollywood, Director, Filmmaker, Producer)
B103 Kailash Juhu Church Road
Juhu
Bombay, MS 400 049, INDIA

Rawal, Paresh (Actor, Bollywood, Comedian)
11 Sea Breeze Apartments 12th Road
JVPD Scheme
Bombay, MS 400 049, INDIA

Rawat, Navi (Actor)
c/o Amy Slomovits *Joan Green Management*
1836 Courtney Ter
Los Angeles, CA 90046-2106, USA

Rawis, Betsy (Golfer)
501 Country Club Dr
Wilmington, DE 19803-2430, USA

Rawlings, Adrian (Actor)
Ken McReddie Ltd
91 Regent St
London W1R 7TB, ENGLAND

Rawlins, V Lane (Educator)
Washington State University
President's Office
Pullman, WA 99164-0001, USA

Rawlinson, Chris (Athlete, Olympic Athlete)
Trafford Athletic Club
Longford Park Stadium
Ryebank Road
Chorlton Cum Hardy, Manchester M21 9TA, UNITED KINGDOM (UK)

Rawlinson of Ewell, Peter A G (Government Official)
Wardour Castle
Tisbury
Wilts SP3 6RH, UNITED KINGDOM (UK)

Rawls, Betsy
4613 Sylvanus Dr
Wilmington, DE 19803-4813, USA

Rawls, Elizabeth E (Betsy) (Golfer)
501 Country Club Dr
Wilmington, DE 19803-2430, USA

Rawls, Sam (Cartoonist)
King Features Syndicate
888 7th Ave Ste 201
New York, NY 10106-0201, USA

Ray, Alexa (Actor)
The Agency
1800 Avenue Of Stars Ste 400
Los Angeles, CA 90067-4206, USA

Ray, Amy (Musician, Songwriter, Writer)
Russell Carter Artist Mgmt
315 W Ponce De Leon Ave Ste 756
Decatur, GA 30030-2497, USA

Ray, Anthony L (Sir Mix-A-Lot) (Artist, Musician)
Richard Walters
PO Box 2789
Toluca Lake, CA 91610-0789, USA

Ray, Darrol (Football Player)
New York Jets
13000 Doriath Way
Oklahoma City, OK 73170-2108, USA

Ray, David (Football Player)
Los Angeles Rams
6962 Bridgewater Dr
Huntington Beach, CA 92647-4023, USA

Ray, Edward J (Educator)
Oregon State University
President's Office
Corvallis, OR 97331, USA

Ray, Fred Olen (Director)
PO Box 3563
Van Nuys, CA 91407-3563, USA

Ray, Jimmy (Musician)
Nineteen Music/Mgmt
35-37 Parkgate Road
London SW11 4NP, UNITED KINGDOM
(UK)

Ray, John (Football Player)
Indianapolis Colts
10 Ranger Ln
Charleston, WV 25309-8980, USA

Ray, Lisa (Actor)
c/o Martin Johnson *Victory Productions*
9663 Santa Monica Blvd # 7700
Beverly Hills, CA 90210-4303, USA

Ray, Marguerite (Actor)
1329 N Vista St Apt 106
Los Angeles, CA 90046-4833, USA

Ray, Rachael (Chef)
16 E 34th St Fl 14
New York, NY 10016-4360, USA

Ray, Robert D (Governor)
Blue Cross/Blue Shield of Iowa
636 Grand Ave
Des Moines, IA 50309-2502, USA

Ray, Ronald E (War Hero)
2670 Saint Andrews Blvd
Tarpon Springs, FL 34688-6339, USA

Ray, Sugar
c/o Staff Member *Pinnacle Entertainment*
30 Glenn St
White Plains, NY 10603-3254, USA

Ray, Terry (Football Player)
Atlanta Falcons
42559 Angel Wing Way
Ashburn, VA 20148-5635, USA

Raybon, Marty (Musician)
Hallmark Direction
713 18th Ave S
Nashville, TN 37203-3214, USA

Raycroft, Andrew (Hockey Player)
c/o Staff Member *Toronto Maple Leafs*
Air Canada Centre
40 Bay St #400
Toronto, ON M5J 2X2, CANADA

rayder, franki (Model)
Why Not
via Zenale, 9
Milano 20123, ITALY

Raydon, Curt (Baseball Player)
Pittsburgh Pirates
PO Box 5124
Jasper, TX 75951-7701, USA

Raye, Lisa (Actor)
c/o Staff Member *Agency West
Entertainment*
4401 Wilshire Blvd # 250
Los Angeles, CA 90010-3703, USA

Rayford, Floyd (Baseball Player)
Baltimore Orioles
11701 Pointe Cir
Fort Myers, FL 33908-2161, USA

Rayhal, Bobby
934A Crescent Blvd
Glen Ellyn, IL 60137, USA

RayJ (Actor, Musician)
c/o Michael (Mike) Esterman *Esterman
Entertainment*
214 Park Rd
Riva, MD 21140-1224, USA

Rayl, Jim (Basketball Player)
201 W Boulevard
Kokomo, IN 46902-2154, USA

Raymer, Cory (Football Player)
Washington Redskins
46629 Hampshire Station Dr
Sterling, VA 20165-7395, USA

Raymo, Maureen (Misc)
Boston University
Geology Dept
Boston, MA 02215, USA

Raymond, Corey (Football Player)
New York Giants
106 Carter St
New Iberia, LA 70560-6214, USA

Raymond, Guy (Actor)
550 Erskine Dr
Pacific Palisades, CA 90272-4247, USA

Raymond, Kenneth N (Misc)
University of California
Chemistry Dept
Berkeley, CA 94720-0001, USA

Raymond, Lee R (Business Person)
Exxon Corp
5959 Las Colinas Blvd
Irving, TX 75039-2298, USA

Raymond, Lisa (Tennis Player)
Octagon
1751 Pinnacle Dr Ste 1500
McLean, VA 22102-3833, USA

Raymond, Paula (Actor)
PO Box 86
Beverly Hills, CA 90213-0086, USA

Raymond, Ralph (Coach)
USA Softball
1 Olympia Plaza
Colorado Springs, CO 80909, USA

Raymond, Usher (Actor, Musician)
Usher's New Look Inc
2775 Cruse Rd Ste 901
C/O Shawn H Wilson
Lawrenceville, GA 30044-7143, USA

Raymonde, Tania (Actor)
c/o Katie Rhodes *Untitled Entertainment
(LA)*
331 N Maple Dr Fl 3
Beverly Hills, CA 90210-3827, USA

Rayner, Chuck
116-5710 201st St.
Langley, BC V3A 8A6, CANADA

Raynor, Bruce (Politician)
Unite
275 7th Ave Fl 11
New York, NY 10001-6708, USA

Raynr (Hubbard), David (Actor, Director,
Producer, Writer)
c/o Stuart Fry *Endeavor Agency LLC (LA)*
9601 Wilshire Blvd Fl 3
Beverly Hills, CA 90210-5204, USA

Raz, Kavi (Actor)
Dale Garrick
8831 W Sunset Blvd # 402
Los Angeles, CA 90069, USA

Raz B (Actor, Musician)
c/o Michael (Mike) Esterman *Esterman
Entertainment*
214 Park Rd
Riva, MD 21140-1224, USA

Raza, S Atiq (Business Person)
Advanced Micro Devices
1 Amd Pl
Sunnyvale, CA 94085-3905, USA

**Razafindratandra, Armand Gaetan
Cardinal** (Religious Leader)
Archeveche
Andohalo
Antananarivo 101, MADAGASCAR

Razanamasy, Guy (Prime Minister)
Prime Minister's Office
Mahazoarivo
Antananarivo, MADAGASCAR

Raziano, Barry (Baseball Player)
Kansas City Royals
1315 4th St
Kenner, LA 70062-7311, USA

Razorlight (Music Group)
Universal Music Operations
364-366 Kensington High St
London W14 8NS, UNITED KINGDOM
(UK)

Re, Giovanni Battsti Cardinal (Religious
Leader)
Palazzo delle Congregazioni
Piazza Pio XII #10
Rome 00193, ITALY

Rea, Peggy (Actor)
10331 Riverside Dr Apt 204
Toluca Lake, CA 91602-2455, USA

Rea, Stephen (Actor)
861 Sutherland Ave
London W9, UNITED KINGDOM (UK)

Read, Amy (Golfer)
7622 Fall Creek Bnd
Humble, TX 77396-3460, USA

Read, James (Actor)
3713 Hitchcock Ranch Rd
Santa Barbara, CA 93105-3177, USA

Read, Nicolas (Actor)
c/o Carlo Capomazza *Capocom
Entertainment*
8970 Norma Pl
Los Angeles, CA 90069-4819, USA

Read, Richard (Journalist)
Portland Oregonian
1320 SW Broadway
Editorial Dept
Portland, OR 97201-3411, USA

Read, Sister Joel (Educator)
Alvermo College
PO Box 343922
President's Office
Milwaukee, WI 53234-3922, USA

Read-Martin, Dolly
30765 Pacific Coast Hwy # 103
Malibu, CA 90265-3646, USA

Readdy, William F (Bill) (Astronaut)
NASA
2101 Nasa Pkwy
Johnson Space Center
Houston, TX 77058-3691, USA

Ready, Randy (Baseball Player)
Milwaukee Brewers
15835 El Camino Entrada
Poway, CA 92064-2161, USA

Reagan, Bernice Johnson (Musician)
American University
History Dept
Washington, DC 20016, USA

Reagan, Michael
The Michael Reagan
PO Box 6061-405
Sherman Oaks, CA 91412, USA

Reagan, Nancy D (Actor, First Lady)
10880 Wilshire Blvd Ste 870
Los Angeles, CA 90024-4109, USA

Reagan Jr, Ron (Television Host)
c/o Staff Member *MSNBC (NJ)*
Nbc/One Microsoft Corporation
1 Msnc Plaza
Secaucus, NJ 07094, USA

Reagor, Montae (Football Player)
Denver Broncos
1511 Drexel Dr
Waxahachie, TX 75165-4409, USA

Real, Roxanne (Musician)
Headline Talent
1650 Broadway Ste 508
New York, NY 10019-6833, USA

Reality, Maxim (Musician)
Midi Mgmt
Jenkins Lane
Great Hallinsbury
Essex CM22 7QL, UNITED KINGDOM
(UK)

Ream, Charles (Football Player)
Cleveland Rams
1412 Snowmass Rd
Columbus, OH 43235-2130, USA

Reamon, Tommy (Football Player)
Kansas City Chiefs
709 Galahad Dr
Newport News, VA 23608-1807, USA

Reams, Leroy (Baseball Player)
Philadelphia Phillies
6140 E 17th St
Oakland, CA 94621-4108, USA

Rearden, Kenny
568 Grosvenor Ave.
Westmount, PQ H3Y 4Z3, CANADA

Reardon, Jeffrey J (Jeff) (Baseball Player)
New York Mets
5 Marlwood Ln
Palm Beach Gardens, FL 33418-6805,
USA

Reardon, John (Actor)
c/o Murray Gibson *Characters Talent
Agency, The (Toronto)*
8 Elm St 3rd FL
Toronto, ON M5G 1G7, CANADA

Reaser, Elizabeth (Actor)
c/o Staff Member *Gersh Agency, The (LA)*
232 N Canon Dr
Beverly Hills, CA 90210-5302, USA

Reason, Rex (Actor)
Roadside Productions
20105 Rhapsody Rd
Walnut, CA 91789-3533, USA

Reason, Rhodes
PO Box 503
Gladstone, OR 97027-0503, USA

Reasons, Gary P (Football Player)
New York Giants
17029 Hardwood Pl
Edmond, OK 73012-9121, USA

Reaux, Angelina (Opera Singer)
Herbert Breslin
119 W 57th St Ste 1505
New York, NY 10019-2401, USA

Reaves, Ken (Football Player)
Atlanta Falcons
413 Oakside Dr SW
Atlanta, GA 30331-3724, USA

Reaves, Shawn (Actor)
c/o Claudia Black *Glasser/Black
Management*
283 Cedarhurst Ave
Cedarhurst, NY 11516-1671, USA

Reaves, Stephanie (Race Car Driver)
PO Box 55
Bar Mills, ME 04004-0055, USA

Reaves, T Johnson (John) (Coach, Football
Coach, Football Player)
Philadelphia Eagles
5716 Bayshore Blvd
Tampa, FL 33611-4726, USA

Reavis, Dave (Football Player)
Pittsburgh Steelers
5495 S Newport Cir
Greenwood Village, CO 80111-1601,
USA

Rebagliati, Ross
1 Erieview Plz # 1300
Cleveland, OH 44114-1738, USA

Rebardo, Joe (Musician)
Billy Paul Mgmt
8215 Winthrop St
Philadelphia, PA 19136-1914, USA

Rebekah (Musician)
Int'l Talent Booking
27A Floral St
#300
London WC2E 9DQ, UNITED KINGDOM
(UK)

Rebel, Art (Baseball Player)
Philadelphia Phillies
4147 Alpine Rd
Land O Lakes, FL 34639-4053, USA

Rebel Emergency (Music Group)
c/o Staff Member *Paradigm (Monterey)*
509 Hartnell St
Monterey, CA 93940-2825, USA

Reberger, Frank (Baseball Player)
Chicago Cubs
439 Sunset View Ln
Hope, ID 83836-9845, USA

Rebhorn, James (Actor)
145 W 45th St # 1204
New York, NY 10036-4008, USA

Reboulet, Jeff (Baseball Player)
Minnesota Twins
3776 Grand Oak Tri
Dayton, OH 45440, USA

Rebowe, Rusty (Football Player)
New Orleans Saints
656 Pine St
Norco, LA 70079-2136, USA

Rebroff, Ivan
Agil Anagire
Skopelos/Magnisias, GREECE

Recchi, Mark (Hockey Player)
Pittsburgh Penguins
66 Mario Lemieux Pl
Mellon Arena
Pittsburgh, PA 15219-3504, USA

Recher, Dave (Football Player)
Philadelphia Eagles
970 E Devon Dr
Gilbert, AZ 85296-3620, USA

Rechichar, Albert (Bert) (Football Player)
Cleveland Browns
141 W McClain Rd
Belle Vernon, PA 15012-3507, USA

Rechin, Bill (Cartoonist)
North American Syndicate
235 E 45th St
New York, NY 10017-3305, USA

Rechter, Yacov (Architect)
150 Arlozorov St
Tel Aviv 62098, ISRAEL

Reckell, Peter (Actor)
PO Box 2704-462
Huntington Beach, CA 92647, USA

Reckless Kelly (Music Group)
c/o Staff Member *Paradigm (Monterey)*
509 Hartnell St
Monterey, CA 93940-2825, USA

Rector, Jeff (Actor)
10748 Aqua Vista St
North Hollywood, CA 91602-3207, USA

Rector, Milton G (Misc)
*National Council on Crime &
Delinquency*
288 Monroe Ave
River Edge, NJ 07661-1316, USA

Red-Horse, Valerie (Actor, Director,
Producer, Writer)
Red-Horse Productions
6028 Calvin Ave
Tarzana, CA 91356-1115, USA

Red Hot Chili Peppers (Music Group)
c/o Marlene Tsuchii *Creative Artists
Agency LCC (CAA-LA)*
2000 Avenue Of The Stars
Los Angeles, CA 90067-4700, USA

Redbone, Leon (Musician)
Red Shark Inc
2169 Aquetong Rd
New Hope, PA 18938-1148, USA

Redd, Glen (Football Player)
New Orleans Saints
4526 W 1500 N
Ogden, UT 84404-9097, USA

Redd, Michael (Basketball Player)
Milwaukee Bucks
1001 N 4th St
Bradley Center
Milwaukee, WI 53203-1312, USA

Redden, Barry (Football Player)
Los Angeles Rams
22503 Diamond Shore Ct
Katy, TX 77450-8053, USA

Reddicliffe, Steven (Editor)
TV Guide Magazine
Editorial Dept
100 Matsonford Road
Wayne, PA 19080-0001, USA

Redding, Juli
PO Box 1806
Beverly Hills, CA 90213-1806, USA

Redding, Tim (Baseball Player)
Houston Astros
70 Greenway Blvd
Churchville, NY 14428-9205, USA

Reddy, D Raj (Scientist)
Robotics Institute
Carnegie-Mellon University
Pittsburgh, PA 15213, USA

Reddy, Helen (Musician)
c/o Stacey Testro *Stacey Testro
International*
8265 W Sunset Blvd Ste 100
West Hollywood, CA 90046-2433, USA

Redfern, Pete (Baseball Player)
Minnesota Twins
12516 Haddon Ave
Sylmar, CA 91342-3636, USA

Redfield, James (Actor, Producer, Writer)
c/o Hampton Roads Publishing
1125 Stoney Ridge Rd
Charlottesville, VA 22902-8719, USA

Redfield, Joe (Baseball Player)
California Angels
307 Glenview Cir
Woodway, TX 76712-3141, USA

Redford, Paul (Producer, Writer)
c/o Staff Member *Broder Webb Chervin
Silbermann Agency, The (BWCS)*
10250 Constellation Blvd Ste P
Los Angeles, CA 90067-6213, USA

Redford, Robert (Actor, Director)
c/o Jill Cutler *Creative Artists Agency LCC
(CAA-LA)*
2000 Avenue Of The Stars
Los Angeles, CA 90067-4700, USA

Redgrave, Corin (Actor)
Kate Feast
Primrose Hill Studios
Fitzroy Road
London NW1 8TR, UNITED KINGDOM
(UK)

Redgrave, Jemma (Actor)
Conway Van Gelder Robinson
18-21 Jermyn St
London SW1Y 6NB, UNITED KINGDOM
(UK)

Redgrave, Lynn (Actor)
P F D Drury House
34-43 Russell St
London WC2B 5HA, UNITED KINGDOM
(UK)

Redgrave, Vanessa (Actor)
c/o Staff Member *Gavin Barker Assoc*
2D Wimpole St
London W1G 0EB, UNITED KINGDOM
(UK)

Redick, JJ (Basketball Player)
Duke Athletic Dept
PO Box 90555
Durham, NC 27708-0555, USA

Redman (Musician)
International Creative Mgmt
8942 Wilshire Blvd # 219
Beverly Hills, CA 90211-1908, USA

Redman, Amanda (Actor)
c/o Staff Member *Lip Service Casting Ltd*
4 Kingly St, Soho
London W1B 5PE, UNITED KINGDOM
(UK)

Redman, Dewey (Composer, Musician)
Joel Chriss
300 Mercer St Apt 3J
New York, NY 10003-6732, USA

Redman, Joshua (Composer, Musician)
Wilkins Mgmt
323 Broadway
Cambridge, MA 02139-1801, USA

Redman, Joyce (Actor)
P F D Drury House
34-43 Russell St
London WC2B 5HA, UNITED KINGDOM
(UK)

Redman, Magdalen (Baseball Player)
N7780 Vicksburg Way Apt D
Oconomowoc, WI 53066-2016, USA

Redman, Mark (Baseball Player)
Minnesota Twins
Davie, FL 33328, USA

Redman, Michele (Golfer)
3410 Queensland Ln N
Minneapolis, MN 55447-1153, USA

Redman, Richard C (Football Player)
San Diego Chargers
1000 Warren Ave N
Seattle, WA 98109-3655, USA

Redman, Richard C (Rick) (Football
Player)
153 Prospect St
Seattle, WA 98109-3749, USA

Redman, Susle (Golfer)
137 SW Sarasota Ave
Port Saint Lucle, FL 34952, USA

Redmann, Teal (Actor)
c/o Amy Abell *Innovative Artists (LA)*
1505 10th St
Santa Monica, CA 90401-2805, USA

Redmon, Glenn (Baseball Player)
San Francisco Giants
8509 Dee Cir
Riverview, FL 33569-4728, USA

Redmond, Marge (Actor)
Abrams Artists
9200 W Sunset Blvd Ste 1125
Los Angeles, CA 90069-3610, USA

Redmond, Markus (Actor)
Writers & Artists
360 N Crescent Dr Bldg North
Beverly Hills, CA 90210-6818, USA

Redmond, Michael E (Mickey) (Hockey
Player)
30699 Harlincin Ct
Franklin, MI 48025-1521, USA

Redmond, Mike (Baseball Player)
Florida Marlins
1391 SW 52nd Ave
Plantation, FL 33317-5533, USA

Redmond, Rudy (Football Player)
Atlanta Falcons
17091 Melrose St
Southfield, MI 48075-4260, USA

Redmond, Wayne (Baseball Player)
Detroit Tigers
180 60 Sussex Drive
Detroit, MI 48235, USA

Rednikova, Yekaterina (Actor)
358 N Gardner St
C/O Larry Hummel
Los Angeles, CA 90036-5721, USA

Redpath, Jean (Musician)
Sunny Knowe
Promenade
Leven, Fife, SCOTLAND

Redstone, Summer M (Business Person)
Viacom Inc
1515 Broadway
New York, NY 10036-8901, USA

Redstone, Sumner (Business Person)
c/o Staff Member *Viacom Entertainment Group*
5555 Melrose Ave
Los Angeles, CA 90038-3989, USA

Redus, Gary (Baseball Player)
Cincinnati Reds
2202 Mallard Ln SE
Decatur, AL 35601-6759, USA

Redwine, Jarvis J (Football Player)
Minnesota Vikings
2707 W 79th St
Inglewood, CA 90305-1033, USA

Redwine, Tim
3518 Cahuenga Blvd W # 200
Los Angeles, CA 90068, USA

Reece, Beasley (Football Player, Sportscaster)
Dallas Cowboys
17 Stirling Way
Lumberton, NJ 08048-5207, USA

Reece, Bob (Baseball Player)
Montreal Expos
3106 Castlewood Cir
Pollock Pines, CA 95726-9522, USA

Reece, Daniel (Danny) (Football Player)
Tampa Bay Buccaneers
24610 S Avalon Blvd
Wilmington, CA 90744-1023, USA

Reece, Gabrielle (Gabby) (Model, Volleyball Player)
c/o Christopher Gough Gough *Creative Artists Agency LCC (CAA-LA)*
2000 Avenue Of The Stars
Los Angeles, CA 90067-4700, USA

Reece, John (Football Player)
St Louis Rams
5927 Cape Hatteras Dr
Houston, TX 77041-5911, USA

Reece, Thomas L (Business Person)
Dover Corp
280 Park Ave
New York, NY 10017-1215, USA

Reed, Alvin (Football Player)
Houston Oilers
3910 Abbeywood Dr
Pearland, TX 77584-4943, USA

Reed, Andre D (Football Player)
Buffalo Bills
PO Box 9383
Rancho Santa Fe, CA 92067-4383, USA

Reed, Ben
151 El Camino Dr
Beverly Hills, CA 90212-2704, USA

Reed, Bill (Baseball Player)
Boston Braves
11807 Primwood Dr
Houston, TX 77070-2354, USA

Reed, Bob (Baseball Player)
Detroit Tigers
42519 Lake Hospitality Ln
Altoona, FL 32702-9584, USA

Reed, Brandy (Basketball Player)
Phoenix Mercury
201 E Jefferson St
American West Arena
Phoenix, AZ 85004-2412, USA

Reed, Brian (Musician, Songwriter, Writer)
Turner Management Group
9200 W Sunset Blvd Ste 600
West Hollywood, CA 90069-3196, USA

Reed, Darren (Baseball Player)
New York Mets
8101 Santa Ana Rd
Ventura, CA 93001-9723, USA

Reed, Eddie (Baseball Player)
Memphis Red Sox
708 8th Ave S
Great Falls, MT 59405-2052, USA

Reed, Eric (Musician)
Joel Chriss
300 Mercer St Apt 3J
New York, NY 10003-6732, USA

Reed, Herb (Musician)
Platters Mgmt
990 Massachusetts Ave
Arlington, MA 02476-4532, USA

Reed, Jack (Baseball Player)
New York Yankees
PO Box 728
Tougaloo, MS 39174-0728, USA

Reed, Jeff (Baseball Player)
Minnesota Twins
259 Sunrise Dr
Elizabethton, TN 37643-6459, USA

Reed, Jerry (Actor, Musician, Songwriter, Writer)
Jerry Lee Enterprises
PO Box 3586
Brentwood, TN 37024-3586, USA

Reed, Jerry (Baseball Player)
Philadelphia Phillies
505 Enka Lake Rd
Candler, NC 28715-9246, USA

Reed, Jody (Baseball Player)
Boston Red Sox
17299 Solie Rd
Odessa, FL 33556-1943, USA

Reed, Joe (Football Player)
San Francisco 49ers
5214 70th St
Lubbock, TX 79424-2018, USA

Reed, John H (Governor)
410 O St NW
Washington, DC 20024, USA

Reed, John S (Financier)
Citigroup Inc
399 Park Ave
New York, NY 10022-4699, USA

Reed, Johnny (Musician)
Jackson Artists
7251 Lowell Dr # 200
Overland Park, KS 66204-1840, USA

Reed, Kira
PO Box 251255
Los Angeles, CA 90025-9755, USA

Reed, Lou (Musician, Songwriter, Writer)
Three Artist Mgmt
2550 Laurel Pass
Los Angeles, CA 90046-1404, USA

Reed, Margaret
524 W 57th St # 5330
New York, NY 10019-2930, USA

Reed, Mark A (Doctor)
Yale University
Electrical Engineering Dept
PO Box 2157
New Haven, CT 06520, USA

Reed, Nikki (Actor)
c/o Booh Schut *Booh Schut Company*
11365 Sunshine Ter
Studio City, CA 91604-3141, USA

Reed, Oscar (Football Player)
Minnesota Vikings
700 Elizabeth Ln
Minneapolis, MN 55411-3340, USA

Reed, Pamela (Actor)
Innovative Artists
1505 10th St
Santa Monica, CA 90401-2805, USA

Reed, Peyton (Actor, Composer, Director, Producer, Writer)
c/o Staff Member *Creative Artists Agency LCC (CAA-LA)*
2000 Avenue Of The Stars
Los Angeles, CA 90067-4700, USA

Reed, Ralph (Religious Leader)
1801 Sara Dr Ste L
Chesapeake, VA 23320-2647, USA

Reed, Rex (Critic)
Dakota Hotel
1 W 72nd St Apt 86
New York, NY 10023-3425, USA

Reed, Richard A (Rick) (Baseball Player)
Pittsburgh Pirates
9604 County Road 107 Unit 7
Proctorville, OH 45669-8023, USA

Reed, Richard J (Misc)
University of Washington
Atmospheric Sciences Dept
Seattle, WA 98195-0001, USA

Reed, Rick (Baseball Player)
4938 Crestone Way
Rochester, MI 48306-1682, USA

Reed, Robert (Football Player)
Minnesota Vikings
1700 Western Ave # 1
Nortel
Albany, NY 12203-4302, USA

Reed, Ronald L (Ron) (Baseball Player, Basketball Player)
Atlanta Braves
2613 Cliffview Dr SW
Lilburn, GA 30047-4794, USA

Reed, Shanna (Actor)
1327 Brinkley Ave
Los Angeles, CA 90049-3619, USA

Reed, Steve (Baseball Player)
San Francisco Giants
5335 Pine Ridge Rd
Golden, CO 80403-8030, USA

Reed, Thomas C (Government Official)
Quaker Hill Development Corp
PO Box 2240
Healdsburg, CA 95448-2240, USA

Reed, Tony (Football Player)
Kansas City Chiefs
4551 W 107th St
Applebee's Attn: Human Resources Dept
Overland Park, KS 66207-4037, USA

Reed, Walter
3400 Paul Sweet Rd Unit B209
Santa Cruz, CA 95065-1552, USA

Reed Jr, Alan
3455 Laurelvale Dr
Studio City, CA 91604-4135, USA

Reed Jr, Willis (Baseball Player, Coach)
New Orleans Hornets
1250 Poydras St # 19
New Orleans Arena
New Orleans, LA 70113-1804, USA

Reeds, Mark (Hockey Player)
7823 Cardinal Ridge Ct
Saint Louis, MO 63119-5014, USA

Reedus, Norman (Actor, Model)
c/o Brian Wilkins *Wilkins Management*
12200 W Olympic Blvd Ste 400
Los Angeles, CA 90064-1047, USA

Reel & Reel
Box 480 High Wycombe
Bucks., ENGLAND PH12 4LH, UNITED KINGDOM (UK)

Rees, Andrew (Opera Singer)
Van Walsum Mgmt
4 Addison Bridge Place
London W14 8XP, UNITED KINGDOM (UK)

Rees, Angharad (Actor)
James Sharkey
21 Golden Square
London W1R 3PA, UNITED KINGDOM (UK)

Rees, Dai (Designer, Fashion Designer)
c/o Staff Member *Dai Rees*
6 Blackstock Mews
Blackstock Road
London, England N42BT, UNITED KINGDOM (UK)

Rees, Eberhard (Physicist)
69 Revere Way
Huntsville, AL 35801-2847, USA

Rees, Jed (Actor)
c/o Staff Member *Elizabeth Hodgson Mgmt Group*
525 Seymour St #550
Vancouver, BC V6B 3H7, CANADA

Rees, John (Musician)
TPA
PO Box 124
Round Corner, NSW 2158, AUSTRALIA

Rees, Norma S (Educator)
California State University
President's Office
Hayward, CA 94546, USA

Rees, Roger (Actor)
Innovative Artists
1505 10th St
Santa Monica, CA 90401-2805, USA

Rees-Jones, Trevor
Oswestry
Shropshire, ENGLAND, UNITED KINGDOM (UK)

Rees Jr, Clifford H (Ted) (General)
1620 Mayflower Ct Apt B414
Winter Park, FL 32792-2571, USA

Rees-Mogg of Hinton Bleweet, William (Publisher)
3 Smith Square
London SW1, UNITED KINGDOM (UK)

Reese, Della (Actor, Musician)
Lett/Reese International Productions
1910 Bel Air Rd
Los Angeles, CA 90077-2727, USA

Reese, Eddie (Coach, Swimmer)
University of Texas
Athletic Dept
Austin, TX 78712, USA

Reese, Guy (Football Player)
Dallas Cowboys
16301 Ledgemont Ln Apt 204
Addison, TX 75001-5977, USA

Reese, Ike (Football Player)
c/o Staff Member *Atlanta Falcons*
4400 Falcon Pkwy
Flowery Branch, GA 30542-3176, USA

Reese, Izell (Football Player)
Dallas Cowboys
4037 Thessa Cv NE
Roswell, GA 30075-5750, USA

Reese, Miranda (Ballerina)
New York City Ballet
Lincoln Center Plaza
New York, NY 10023, USA

Reese, Pokey (Baseball Player)
Cincinnati Reds
12416 Sylvan Oak Way
Charlotte, NC 28273-4728, USA

Reese, Rich (Baseball Player)
Minnesota Twins
PO Box 2339
Carefree, AZ 85377-2339, USA

Reese, Steve (Football Player)
New York Jets
1146 Parkwood Trce
Stone Mountain, GA 30083-2485, USA

Reeser, Autumn (Actor)
c/o Staff Member *Identity Talent Agency
(ID)*
9107 Wilshire Blvd Ste 450
Beverly Hills, CA 90210-5535, USA

Reeves, Bryant (Basketball Player)
memphis Grizzlies
191 Beale St
Memphis, TN 38103-3715, USA

Reeves, Dan (Football Player)
Dallas Cowboys
785 W Conway Dr NW
Atlanta, GA 30327-3633, USA

Reeves, Diane
PO Box 66
Englishtown, NJ 07726-0066, USA

Reeves, Julie
PO Box 300
Russell, KY 41169-0300, USA

Reeves, Keanu (Actor)
c/o Erwin Stoff *3 Arts Entertainment Inc*
9460 Wilshire Blvd Fl 7
Beverly Hills, CA 90212-2713, USA

Reeves, Martha (Musician)
Mars Talent
27 L Ambiance Ct
Bardonia, NY 10954-1421, USA

Reeves, Melissa
6520 Platt Ave # 634
West Hills, CA 91307-3218, USA

Reeves, Perrey (Actor)
Prophet
1640 S Sepulveda Blvd Ste 218
Los Angeles, CA 90025-7535, USA

Reeves, Phil (Actor)
c/o Staff Member *Bauman Redanty &
Shaul Agency*
5757 Wilshire Blvd Ste 473
Los Angeles, CA 90036-3632, USA

Reeves, Richard (Misc)
Universal Press Syndicate
4520 Main St
Kansas City, MO 64111-1876, USA

Reeves, Ronna
5114 Albert Dr
Brentwood, TN 37027-6810, USA

Reeves, Saskia (Actor)
Markham & Froggatt
Julian House
4 Windmill St
London W1P 1HF, UNITED KINGDOM
(UK)

Reeves, Scott (Actor)
6520 Platt Ave # 634
West Hills, CA 91307-3218, USA

Reeves, Walter (Football Player)
Phoenix Cardinals
PO Box 231313
Montgomery, AL 36123-1313, USA

Regalado, Rudy (Baseball Player)
Cleveland Indians
PO Box 475
Borrego Springs, CA 92004-0475, USA

Regalbuto, Joe
724 24th St
Santa Monica, CA 90402-3138, USA

Regan, Brian (Actor, Comedian)
Conversation Co
697 Middle Neck Rd
Great Neck, NY 11023-1216, USA

Regan, Donald T
240 McLaws Cir Ste 142
Williamsburg, VA 23185-6429, USA

Regan, Gerald A (Government Official)
PO Box 828
Station B
Ottawa, ON K1P 5P9, CANADA

Regan, Judith (Talk Show Host, Writer)
Regan Media
10 E 53rd St
18th Fl
New York, NY 10022-5244, USA

Regan, Larry (Hockey Player)
4A-260 Metcalfe St
Ottawa, ON K2P 1R6, CANADA

Regan, Laura (Actor)
c/o Staff Member *TMT Entertainment
Group*
648 Broadway # 1002
New York, NY 10012-2301, USA

Regan, Philip R (Phil) (Baseball Player)
Detroit Tigers
1375 108th St SW
Byron Center, MI 49315-8607, USA

Regazzoni, Clay (Race Car Driver)
Via Monzoni 13
Lugano 6900, SWITZERLAND

Regehr, Duncan (Actor)
2501 Main St
Santa Monica, CA 90405, USA

Regen, Elizabeth (Actor)
c/o Mark Measures *Abrams Artists Agency
(LA)*
9200 W Sunset Blvd Ph 11
Los Angeles, CA 90069-3601, USA

Reger, Nate (Writer)
c/o Staff Member *International Creative
Management (ICM-LA)*
10250 Constellation Blvd
Los Angeles, CA 90067-6200, USA

Reggiani, Serge (Actor, Musician)
Charley Marouani
4 Ave Hoche
Paris 75008, FRANCE

Reggio, Godfrey (Director)
Regional Education Institute
PO Box 2404
Santa Fe, NM 87504-2404, USA

Regina, Paul
2911 Canna St
Thousand Oaks, CA 91360-1418, USA

Regine (Business Person)
502 Park Ave
New York, NY 10022-1108, USA

Regis, John (Athlete, Track Athlete)
67 Fairby Road
London SE12, UNITED KINGDOM (UK)

Regner, Tom (Football Player)
Houston Oilers
2231 Big Trail Cir
Reno, NV 89521-8957, USA

Regnier, Charles (Actor, Director)
Neherstr 7
Munich 81675, GERMANY

Rehberg, Scott (Football Player)
New England Patriots
1120 Kittiwake Dr
Venice, FL 34285-6614, USA

Rehder, Tom (Football Player)
New England Patriots
181 Rim Rock Rd
Nipomo, CA 93444, USA

Rehm, Diane (Radio Personality)
c/o Staff Member *National Public Radio
(NPR)*
635 Massachusetts Ave NW
Washington, DC 20001-3753, USA

Rehm, Jack D (Publisher)
19 Neponset Ave # 9A
Old Saybrook, CT 06475-3107, USA

Rehm Jr, Daniel R (War Hero)
1043 Del Norte St
Houston, TX 77018-1422, USA

Rehn, Trista (Reality TV Star)
1640 S Sepulveda Blvd Ste 216
Los Angeles, CA 90025-7535, USA

Rehr, Frank (Cartoonist)
United Feature Syndicate
200 Madison Ave
New York, NY 10016-3911, USA

Rehrer-Carteaux, Rita (Baseball Player)
3210 Kenwood Ave
Fort Wayne, IN 46805-2932, USA

Reich, Charles A (Educator, Lawyer)
Crown Publishers
225 Park Ave S
New York, NY 10003-1604, USA

Reich, Frank M (Football Player)
Buffalo Bills
9020 Arrington Manor Pl
Charlotte, NC 28277-7824, USA

Reich, Herm (Baseball Player)
Washington Senators
PO Box 1292
Bonsall, CA 92003-1292, USA

Reich, Jason (Writer)
c/o Staff Member *Kaplan-Stahler-Gumer
Agency*
8383 Wilshire Blvd Ste 923
Beverly Hills, CA 90211-2408, USA

Reich, John (Director)
724 Bohemia Pkwy
Sayville, NY 11782-3300, USA

Reich, Robert B (Secretary)
1230 Bonita Ave
Berkeley, CA 94709-1923, USA

Reich, Steve M (Composer)
Nonesuch Records
75 Rockefeller Plz
New York, NY 10019-6908, USA

Reichardt, Bill (Football Player)
Green Bay Packers
2935 Sioux Ct
Des Moines, IA 50321-1427, USA

Reichardt, Rick (Baseball Player)
Los Angeles Angels
2605 NW 90th Ter
Gainesville, FL 32606-6742, USA

Reichel, Robert (Hockey Player)
Toronto Maple Leafs
40 Bay St
Toronto, ON M5J 2K2, CANADA

Reichenbach, Mike (Football Player)
Philadelphia Eagles
2230 Cloverly Cir
Jamison, PA 18929-1555, USA

Reichert, Dan (Baseball Player)
Kansas City Royals
445 Cornell Dr
Turlock, CA 95382-0502, USA

Reichert, Jack F (Business Person)
580 Douglas Dr
Lake Forest, IL 60045-3342, USA

Reichert, Tanja (Actor)
Pacific Artists
1404-510 W Hastings St
Vancouver, BC V6B 1L8, CANADA

Reichl, Ruth M (Editor)
Gourmet Magazine
4 Times Sq
Editorial Dept
New York, NY 10036-6563, USA

Reichman, Fred (Artist)
1235 Stanyan St
San Francisco, CA 94117-3816, USA

Reichow, Garet N (Football Player)
Detroit Lions
PO Box 822
Tesuque, NM 87574-0822, USA

Reid, Andy (Coach, Football Coach)
Philadelphia Eagles
1 Novacare Way
Philadelphia, PA 19145-5996, USA

Reid, Antonio (L.A.) (Producer)
c/o Staff Member *Hitco Music Publishing*
500 Bishop St NW Ste A4
Atlanta, GA 30318-4380, USA

Reid, Daphne Maxwell (Actor)
10520 Wilshire Blvd Apt 1507
Los Angeles, CA 90024-7603, USA

Reid, Don S (Musician, Songwriter,
Writer)
American Major Talent
8747 Highway 304
Hernando, MS 38632-8445, USA

Reid, Dorice (Baseball Player)
1165 Via Santa Paulo
Vista, CA 92081-6332, USA

Reid, Elliott
11201 Ventura Blvd
Studio City, CA 91604-3136, USA

Reid, Frances (Actor)
235 Oceano Dr
Los Angeles, CA 90049-4123, USA

Reid, Harold W (Musician, Songwriter,
Writer)
American Major Talent
8747 Highway 304
Hernando, MS 38632-8445, USA

Reid, J R (Basketball Player)
121 Cemetary St
Chester, SC 29706-1620, USA

Reid, Jesse (Baseball Player)
San Francisco Giants
2641 Carey Station Rd
Greensboro, GA 30642-2625, USA

Reid, Joe (Football Player)
Detroit Lions
651 Shady Hollow St
Houston, TX 77056-1635, USA

Reid, Michael B (Mike) (Composer,
Football Player)
Cincinnati Bengals
825 Overton Ln
Nashville, TN 37220-1515, USA

Reid, Mike (Football Player)
Philadelphia Eagles
PO Box 362
Pacolet, SC 29372-0362, USA

Reid, Mike (Golfer)
935 E 80 N
Orem, UT 84097-4978, USA

Reid, Norman R (Misc)
50 Brabourne Rise
Park Langley Beckenham
Kent, UNITED KINGDOM (UK)

Reid, Ogden
Ophir Hill
Purchase, NY 10577, USA

Reid, Robert (Basketball Player, Coach)
Washington Wizards
601 F St NW
Mcl Centre
Washington, DC 20004-1605, USA

Reid, Robert (Skier)
Dixfield Health Care Center
Dixfield, ME 04224, USA

Reid, Scott (Baseball Player)
Philadelphia Phillies
PO Box 50669
Phoenix, AZ 85076-0669, USA

Reid, Stephen E (Steve) (Doctor, Football
Player)
1784 Locust St
Des Plaines, IL 60018-2234, USA

Reid, Tara (Actor)
c/o Jack Ketsoyan *PMK/HBH Public
Relations (PMK-LA)*
700 N San Vicente Blvd Ste G910
West Hollywood, CA 90069-5061, USA

Reid, Terry (Musician)
Blumenauer
PO Box 343
Burbank, CA 91503-0343, USA

Reid, Tim (Actor, Director)
1 New Millennium Dr
Petersburg, VA 23805-8907, USA

Reid, William J (Football Player)
San Francisco 49ers
315 Ramona St
Palo Alto, CA 94301-1440, USA

Reidy, Carolyn K (Publisher)
Simon & Schuster
1230 Avenue Of The Americas
New York, NY 10020-1586, USA

Reifsnyder, Robert H (Bob) (Football
Player)
New York Titans
4 Helm Ct
Berlin, MD 21811-1836, USA

Reightler Jr, Kenneth S (Astronaut)
1602 Honeysuckle Ridge Ct
Annapolis, MD 21401-6425, USA

Reihner, George (Football Player)
Houston Oilers
1010 Electric St
Scranton, PA 18509-1951, USA

Reilly, Charles Nelson (Actor, Director)
c/o Robert Malcolm *The Artists Group Ltd
(LA)*
1650 Broadway Ste 610
New York, NY 10019-6833, USA

Reilly, Gabrielle (Model)
14117 W 53rd Ter
Shawnee, KS 66216-5149, USA

Reilly, Jennifer
345 N Maple Dr Ste 397
Beverly Hills, CA 90210-3856, USA

Reilly, John (Actor)
335 N Maple Dr # 3360
Beverly Hills, CA 90210-3857, USA

Reilly, John C (Actor)
United Talent Agency
9560 Wilshire Blvd Ste 500
Beverly Hills, CA 90212-2401, USA

Reilly, Kevin (Football Player)
Philadelphia Eagles
Webster Farms 1141 Webster Dr
Wilmington, DE 19803, USA

Reilly, Mike (Football Player)
Los Angeles Rams
708 Loretto Ct
Dubuque, IA 52003-7813, USA

Reilly, William K (Government Official)
Stanford University
International Studies Institute
Stanford, CA 94305, USA

Reilly II, James F (Astronaut)
15903 Lake Lodge Dr
Houston, TX 77062-4745, USA

Reimer, Dennis J (Denny) (General)
PO Box 889
Mipt
Oklahoma City, OK 73101-0889, USA

Reimer, Kevin (Baseball Player)
Texas Rangers
1206 West Salmon Arm Road
Enderby, BC VOE 1VO, CANADA

Reimer, Roland (Religious Leader)
mennonite Brethren Churches Conference
8000 W 21st St N
Wichita, KS 67205-1744, USA

Reimers, Bruce (Football Player)
Cincinnati Bengals
2206 W River Dr
Humboldt, IA 50548-2638, USA

Reina (Musician)
c/o Staff Member *Diva Central Inc*
7510 W Sunset Blvd Ste 1445
Los Angeles, CA 90046-3408, USA

Reincke, Heinz
Hof 38
Mondsee A-5310, AUSTRIA

Reineck, Thomas (Athlete)
Graf-Bernadotte-Str 4
Essen 45133, GERMANY

Reinemund, Steven S (Business Person)
Pepsi Co Inc
700 Anderson Hill Rd
Purchase, NY 10577-1444, USA

Reiner, Carl (Actor, Director)
c/o George Shapiro *Shapiro/West &
Associates*
141 El Camino Dr Ste 205
Beverly Hills, CA 90212-2718, USA

Reiner, ex-DA Ira
1290 Sunset Plaza Dr
Los Angeles, CA 90069-1245, USA

Reiner, John (Cartoonist)
Parade Magazine
750 3rd Ave
Editorial Dept
New York, NY 10017-2703, USA

Reiner, Rob (Actor, Director)
c/o Staff Member *Castle Rock
Entertainment*
335 N Maple Dr # 135
Beverly Hills, CA 90210-3857, USA

Reinfeldt, Mike (Football Player)
Oakland Raiders
1204 Waterstone Blvd
Franklin, TN 37069-7208, USA

Reinhard, Bill (Football Player)
Los Angeles Dons
43683 Old Troon Ct
Indio, CA 92201-8910, USA

Reinhard, Robert R (Bob) (Football
Player)
37230 Soap Creek Rd
Corvallis, OR 97330-9376, USA

Reinhardt, John E (Diplomat)
3154 Gracefield Rd Apt 417
Silver Spring, MD 20904-0808, USA

Reinhardt, Stephen R (Judge)
US Court of Appeals
312 N Spring St Ste G33
Los Angeles, CA 90012-4711, USA

Reinharz, Jehuda (Educator)
Brandeis University
President's Office
Waltham, MA 02254, USA

Reinhold, Judge (Actor, Director)
Paradigm Agency
10100 Santa Monica Blvd Ste 2500
Los Angeles, CA 90067-4116, USA

Reinking, Ann (Actor, Dancer, Director)
International Creative Mgmt
40 W 57th St Ste 1800
New York, NY 10019-4001, USA

Reinsdorf, Jerry (Baseball Player)
Chicago White Sox
40 E Elm St
Chicago, IL 60611-1016, USA

Reis, Tommy (Baseball Player)
Philadelphia Phillies
15456 SW 15th Terrace Rd
Ocala, FL 34473-8862, USA

Reiser, Jerry (Architect)
28 S Washington Ave
Dobbs Ferry, NY 10522-1807, USA

Reiser, Paul (Actor, Producer, Writer)
c/o Peter Safran *The Safran Company*
2000 Avenue Of The Stars Ste 600N
Los Angeles, CA 90067-4708, USA

Reiser, Rock
9014 Melrose Ave
W Hollywood, CA 90069-5610, USA

Reisman, Garrett E (Astronaut)
1715 Hedgecroft Dr
Seabrook, TX 77586, USA

Reiss, Howard (Misc)
16656 Oldham St
Encino, CA 91436-3706, USA

Reisz, Michael (Actor)
c/o Staff Member *William Morris Agency
(WMA-LA)*
1 William Morris Pl
Beverly Hills, CA 90212-4261, USA

Reiter, Mario (Skier)
Hauselweg 5
Rankweil 6830, AUSTRIA

Reiter, Thomas (Astronaut)
Europe Astronaut Center
Linder Hohe
Box 906096
Cologne 51127, GERMANY

Reith, Brian (Baseball Player)
Cincinnati Reds
4222 Mayflower Dr
Lafayette, IN 47909-3490, USA

Reitman, Ivan (Director, Producer)
900 Cold Springs Rd
Montecito, CA 93108-1009, USA

Reitman, Joe (Actor)
c/o Suzanne (Sue) Wohl *TalentWorks (LA)*
3500 W Olive Ave Ste 1400
Burbank, CA 91505-5512, USA

Reitsma, Chris (Baseball Player)
Cincinnati Reds
5474 Chanteclaire
Sarasota, FL 34235-0941, USA

Reitz, Bruce (Doctor)
Johns Hopkins Hospital
600 N Wolfe St
Baltimore, MD 21287-0005, USA

Reitz, Ken (Baseball Player)
St Louis Cardinals
1704 Carbine Ln
Saint Charles, MO 63303-1104, USA

ReK (Artist)
Rek's World
PO Box 1484
Southampton, PA 18966-0832, USA

Rekar, Bryan (Baseball Player)
Colorado Rockies
4326 Waterville Ave
Wesley Chapel, FL 33543-7037, USA

Rekha (Actor, Bollywood)
Sea Springs Bungalow 2
Band Stand Bandra
Mumbai, MS 400050, INDIA

Reklow, Jesse (Cartoonist)
2415 College Ave Apt 20
Berkeley, CA 94704-2458, USA

Relaford, Desmond (Baseball Player)
Philadelphia Phillies
12483 Highview Dr
Jacksonville, FL 32225-5725, USA

Relch, Steve (Baseball Player)
US Olympic Team
28 Scofield Hill Rd
Washington Depot, CT 06794-1012, USA

Reliford, Charlie (Baseball Player)
1509 Cypress St
Ashland, KY 41101-3624, USA

Relman, Arnold S (Doctor, Editor)
New England Journal of Medicine
860 Winter St Ste 2
Waltham, MA 02451-1412, USA

Remar, James (Actor)
409 N Camden Dr Ste 202
Beverly Hills, CA 90210-4423, USA

Rembert, Johnny (Football Player)
New England Patriots
1415 Indian Woods Dr
Neptune Beach, FL 32266-3149, USA

Remedios, Alberto T (Opera Singer)
21 Lanhill Road
London W9 2BS, UNITED KINGDOM
(UK)

Remedy
225 Crossroads Blvd # 107
Carmel, CA 93923-8674, USA

Remek, Vladimir (Cosmonaut)
Veletrzni 17
Prague 7 17000, CZECH REPUBLIC

Remigino, Lindy (Athlete, Track Athlete)
22 Paris Ln
Newington, CT 06111-1628, USA

Remington, Deborah W (Artist)
309 W Broadway
New York, NY 10013-5325, USA

Remini, Leah (Actor)
c/o Harry Gold *TalentWorks (LA)*
3500 W Olive Ave Ste 1400
Burbank, CA 91505-5512, USA

Remlinger, Mike (Baseball Player)
San Francisco Giants
5320 E Palo Verde Dr
Paradise Valley, AZ 85253-5158, USA

Remmerswaal, Win (Baseball Player)
Boston Red Sox
Doktor Van Praag St 16
Wassenaar, THE NETHERLANDS

Remmert, Dennis (Football Player)
Buffalo Bills
3933 Briarwood Dr
Cedar Falls, IA 50613-7508, USA

Remnick, David (Writer)
c/o Robert (Bob) Bookman *Creative Artists Agency LCC (CAA-LA)*
2000 Avenue Of The Stars
Los Angeles, CA 90067-4700, USA

Remnick, David J (Editor, Writer)
257 W 86th St # 11A
New York, NY 10024-3105, USA

Remo, Ken
121 S Orange Dr
Los Angeles, CA 90036-3012, USA

Rempt, Rodney (Admiral, Educator)
Superintendent
US Naval Academy
Annapolis, MD 21402, USA

Remy, Gerald P (Jerry) (Baseball Player)
California Angels
33 Viles St
Weston, MA 02493-1743, USA

Renard, Mercedes (Actor)
c/o Staff Member *International Creative Management (ICM-LA)*
10250 Constellation Blvd
Los Angeles, CA 90067-6200, USA

Renaud, Line (Musician)
5 Rue du Bois-de-Boulogne
Paris 75116, FRANCE

Renault, Dennis (Cartoonist)
Sacramento Bee
21st & Q Sts
Editorial Dept
Sacramento, CA 95816, USA

Renbourn, John (Musician)
Folklore Inc
1671 Appian Way
Santa Monica, CA 90401-3258, USA

Rendall, Mark (Actor)
c/o Staff Member *Artist Management Inc*
464 King St E
Toronto, ON M5A 1L7, CANADA

Rendell, Majorie O (Judge)
US Court of Appeals
601 Market St
US Courthouse
Philadelphia, PA 19106-1790, USA

Rendell, Ruth
Nusstead's Polstead Suffolk
Colchester, ENGLAND CO6 5DN,
UNITED KINGDOM (UK)

Rendell of Barbergh, Ruth B (Writer)
Nussteads Polstead
Suffolk
Colchester CO6 5DN, UNITED
KINGDOM (UK)

Rene, France-Albert (President)
President's Office
State House
Victoria
Mahe, SEYCHELLES

Reneau, Daniel D (Educator)
Louisiana Tech University
President's Office
Ruston, LA 71272-0001, USA

Renee Clunie, Michelle (Actor)
Abrams Artists
9200 W Sunset Blvd Ste 1125
Los Angeles, CA 90069-3610, USA

Renfrew of Kaimsthorn, Andrew C (Archaeologist)
McDonald Archaeological Institute
Downing St
Cambridge CB2 3ER, UNITED KINGDOM
(UK)

Renfro, Brad (Actor)
c/o Ben Feigin *Nine Yards Entertainment*
8530 Wilshire Blvd Fl 5
Beverly Hills, CA 90211-3102, USA

Renfro, Melvin L (Mel) (Football Player)
Dallas Cowboys
4120 International Pkwy Ste 1150
Renfro Bridge Foundation
Carrollton, TX 75007-1959, USA

Renfro, Mike (Football Player)
Houston Oilers
PO Box 93073
Southlake, TX 76092-1073, USA

Renfroe, Jay (Producer)
c/o Staff Member *Renegade 83 Entertainment*
5700 Wilshire Blvd
6th Floor
Los Angeles, CA 90036-3659, USA

Renfroe, Laddie (Baseball Player)
Chicago Cubs
236 Hickory Ln
Batesville, MS 38606-9339, USA

Rengel, Mike (Football Player)
New Orleans Saints
1782 Montane Dr E
Golden, CO 80401, USA

Renger, Annemarie (Government Official)
Bundestag
Bundestag
Platz der Republik 1
Berlin 11011, GERMANY

Renick, Jesse (Cab) (Basketball Player, Coach)
2656 SE Washington Blvd
Bartlesville, OK 74006-7614, USA

Renick, Rick (Baseball Player)
Minnesota Twins
7320 Hawkins Rd
Sarasota, FL 34241-9375, USA

Renier, Jeremie (Actor)
Artmedia
20 Ave Rapp
Paris 75007, FRANCE

Reniff, Hal (Baseball Player)
New York Yankees
648 E 6th St
Ontario, CA 91764-1821, USA

Renk, Silke (Athlete, Track Athlete)
Erhard-Hubner-Str 13
Halle/S 06132, GERMANY

Renko, Steven (Steve) (Baseball Player)
PO Box 3566
West Palm Beach, FL 33402-3566, USA

Renna, Eugene A (Business Person)
Mobil Corp
3225 Gallows Rd
Fairfax, VA 22037-0002, USA

Renne, Paul (Misc)
Berkeley Geochronology Center
2445 Ridge Rd
Berkeley, CA 94709, USA

Rennebohm, J Fred (Misc)
Holbeinstr 58
Berlin 12203, GERMANY

Rennebohm, J Fred (Religious Leader)
Congregational Christian Churches Assn
PO Box 1620
Oak Creek, MI 53154, USA

Renner, Jeremy (Actor)
c/o Beth Holden-Garland *Untitled Entertainment (LA)*
331 N Maple Dr Fl 3
Beverly Hills, CA 90210-3827, USA

Rennert, Dutch (Baseball Player)
2560 46th Rd
Walkers Glen
Vero Beach, FL 32966-2053, USA

Rennert, Gunther (Director, Opera Singer)
Holbeinstr 58
Berlin 12203, GERMANY

Renney, Tom (Coach)
New York Rangers
2 Penn Plz
Madison Square Garden
New York, NY 10121-1703, USA

Renni, Gino (Actor)
c/o Staff Member *Telefe - Argentina*
Pavon 2444 (C1248AAT)
Buenos Aires, ARGENTINA

Reno, Jack
PO Box 1001
Florence, KY 41022-1001, USA

Reno, Janet (Attorney, Attorney General, General)
11200 N Kendall Dr
Miami, FL 33176-1108, USA

Reno, Jean (Actor)
c/o Amy Guenther *Gateway Management Partners*
5225 Wilshire Blvd Ste 702
Los Angeles, CA 90036-4351, USA

Reno, William H (General)
2706 S Ives St
Arlington, VA 22202-2372, USA

Renoth, Heldi (Skier)
Lercheckerweg 23
Berchtesgaden 83471, GERMANY

Rense, Paige (Editor)
Architectural Digest
5900 Wilshire Blvd
Editorial Dept
Los Angeles, CA 90036-5013, USA

Renteria, Edgar (Baseball Player)
1408 N West Shore Blvd Ste 512
Tampa, FL 33607-4539, USA

Rentie, Caesar (Football Player)
Chicago Bears
2243 Elderoaks Ln
Dallas, TX 75232-3310, USA

Rentmeester, Co (Photographer)
PO Box 1562
Westhampton Beach, NY 11978-7562,
USA

Renton of Mount Harry, R Timothy (Government Official)
House of Lords
Westminster
London SW1A 0PW, UNITED KINGDOM
(UK)

Rentzel, Lance (Football Player)
Minnesota Vikings
12104 Monument Dr Ste 354
Lance Rentzel Productions
Fairfax, VA 22033-4053, USA

Rentzel, T Lance (Football Player)
Trust Data Corp
159 Almanden Blvd #500
San Jose, CA 95113, USA

Rentzepis, Peter M (Misc)
University of California
Chemistry Dept
Irvine, CA 92717, USA

Renucci, Robin
64 rue Condorcet
Paris 75009, FRANCE

Renvall, Johan (Dancer)
American Ballet Theatre
890 Broadway
New York, NY 10003-1278, USA

Renyi, Thomas A (Financier)
Bank of New York
1 Wall St
New York, NY 10286-0001, USA

Repeta, Nina (Actor)
Gage Group
14724 Ventura Blvd Ste 505
Sherman Oaks, CA 91403-3505, USA

Repin, Vadim V (Musician)
Eckholdtweg 2A
Lubeck 23566, GERMANY

Rerych, Stephen (Steve) (Swimmer)
445 Biltmore Ave
Asheville, NC 28801-4565, USA

Resch, Alexander (Athlete)
BSD
An der Schiessstatte 4
Berchtesgaden 83471, GERMANY

Rescher, Nicholas (Misc)
1033 Milton St
Pittsburgh, PA 15218-1228, USA

Rescigno, Nicola (Conductor)
Robert Lombardo
61 W 62nd St Apt 6F
New York, NY 10023-7017, USA

Resin, Dan (Actor)
Don Buchwald
6500 Wilshire Blvd Ste 2200
Los Angeles, CA 90048-4942, USA

Resnais, Alain (Director)
70 Rue des Plantes
Paris 75014, FRANCE

Resnik, Regina (Opera Singer)
American Guild of Musical Arts
1430 Broadway Rm 1404
New York, NY 10018-3382, USA

Ressler, Glenn E (Football Player)
Baltimore Colts
1524 Woodcreek Dr
Mechanicsburg, PA 17055-6766, USA

Ressler, Robert
PO Box 187
Spotsylvania, VA 22553-0187, USA

Restani, Jane A (Judge)
US Court of International Trade
1 Federal Plz
New York, NY 10278-0001, USA

Restani, Kevin (Basketball Player)
16 Lyndhurst Dr
San Francisco, CA 94132-2017, USA

Restic, Joe (Football Player)
Philadelphia Eagles
18 Penny Ln
Milford, MA 01757-1516, USA

Restless Heart (Music Group)
*c/o Staff Member Agency for the
Performing Arts (APA-Nashville)*
3017 Poston Ave
Nashville, TN 37203-1313, USA

Retherford, Dave (Football Player)
Tampa Bay Buccaneers
2609 W Watrous Ave
Tampa, FL 33629-5346, USA

Retore, Guy (Director)
Theatre de l'Est Parislen
159 Ave Gambetta
Paris 75020, FRANCE

Retton, Mary Lou (Gymnast)
203 Fairmeadow Cir
Houston, PA 15342-1069, USA

Retzer, Otto W (Director)
Justinus-Kerner-Str 10
Munich 80686, GERMANY

Retzlaff, Palmer (Pete) (Football Player)
Philadelphia Eagles
669 New Rd
Gilbertsville, PA 19525-9613, USA

Reuben, Gloria (Actor)
William Morris Agency
15030 Ventura Blvd # 710
Sherman Oaks, CA 91403-5470, USA

Reubens, Paul (Actor, Comedian)
c/o Kelly Bush I/D PR (LA)
8409 Santa Monica Blvd
West Hollywood, CA 90069-4209, USA

Reuschel, Ricky E (Rick) (Baseball Player)
PO Box 143
Renfrew, PA 16053-0143, USA

Reuss, Jerry (Baseball Player)
350 SW 1st St
Des Moines, IA 50309-4631, USA

Reusser, Ken L (War Hero)
17345 SW Reusser Ct
Aloha, OR 97007-8772, USA

Reutemann, Carlos
San Martin 3233
Santa Fe, ARGENTINA

Reuter, Edzard (Business Person)
Daimler-benz AG
Postfach 800230
Stuttgart 70546, GERMANY

Reutershan, Randy (Football Player)
Pittsburgh Steelers
4 Indian Field Ct
Mahwah, NJ 07430-2243, USA

Reutersward, Carl Fredrik (Artist)
6 Rue Montilieu
Bussigny/Lausanne 1030, SWITZERLAND

Revathi (Actor, Bollywood)
7 1st Crescent Road
GandhiNagar Adyar
Chennai, TN 600020, INDIA

Reveiz, Fuad (Football Player)
Miami Dolphins
2160 Lakeside Centre Way Ste 250
Knoxville, TN 37922-0201, USA

Revell, Graeme (Composer)
APRA
PO Box 567
Crow's Nest, NSW 2065, AUSTRALIA

Revere, Paul (Musician)
Paradise Artists
108 E Matilija St
Ojai, CA 93023-2639, USA

Reverho, Christine (Actor)
Artmedia
20 Ave Rapp
Paris 75007, FRANCE

Revill, Clive (Actor)
15029 Encanto Dr
Sherman Oaks, CA 91403-4409, USA

Revs, The (Music Group)
c/o Staff Member Paradigm (Monterey)
509 Hartnell St
Monterey, CA 93940-2825, USA

Rex (Musician)
Concrete Mgmt
361 W Broadway # 200
New York, NY 10013-2209, USA

Rex, Simon (Sebastian) (Actor, Television Host)
c/o Matt Luber Nine Yards Entertainment
8530 Wilshire Blvd Fl 5
Beverly Hills, CA 90211-3102, USA

Rey, Paola (Actor)
*c/o Gabriel Blanco Gabriel Blanco
Iglesias (Mexico)*
Rio Balsas 35-32
Colonia Cuauhtemoc
DF 06500, MEXICO

Rey, Reynaldo (Actor, Comedian, Writer)
Starwil Talent
433 N Camden Dr Ste 400
Beverly Hills, CA 90210-4408, USA

Reyes, Judy (Actor)
c/o Staff Member Paradigm (LA)
360 N Crescent Dr
North Bldg
Beverly Hills, CA 90210-6820, USA

Reyes, Sandra (Actor)
c/o Staff Member TV Caracol
Calle 76 #11 - 35
Piso 10AA
Bogota DC 26484, COLOMBIA

Reyes Jr, Ernie
12561 Willard St
N Hollywood, CA 91605-1244, USA

Reymundo, Alex (Comedian)
c/o Alex D'Andrea Edmonds Management
1635 N Cahuenga Blvd Fl 5
Los Angeles, CA 90028-6201, USA

Reynold, Catherine B (Business Person)
Catherine B Reynolds Foundation
PO Box 11346
McLean, VA 22102-9346, USA

Reynolds, Alastair (Writer)
P F D Drury House
34-43 Russell St
London WC2B 5HA, UNITED KINGDOM (UK)

Reynolds, Albert (Prime Minister)
Mount Carmel House
Dublin Road
Longford, IRELAND

Reynolds, Anna (Opera Singer)
Peesten 9
Kasendorf 95359, GERMANY

Reynolds, Burt (Actor, Director)
PO Box 3288
Tequesta, FL 33469-1004, USA

Reynolds, David S (Historian, Writer)
16 Linden Ln
Old Westbury, NY 11568-1610, USA

Reynolds, Dean (Correspondent)
ABC-TV
5010 Creston St
News Dept
Hyattsville, MD 20781-1216, USA

Reynolds, Debbie (Actor, Musician)
c/o Staff Member William Morris Agency (WMA-LA)
1 William Morris Pl
Beverly Hills, CA 90212-4261, USA

Reynolds, Ed (Football Player)
New England Patriots
173 Moyer Rd
Stoneville, NC 27048-8462, USA

Reynolds, Gene (Actor, Producer)
2034 Castilian Dr
Los Angeles, CA 90068-2609, USA

Reynolds, Glenn F (Inventor)
242 Edgewood Ave
Westfield, NJ 07090-3918, USA

Reynolds, Harry (Butch) (Athlete, Track Athlete)
Advantage International
1025 Thomas Jefferson St NW # 450
Washington, DC 20007-5201, USA

Reynolds, J Guy (Admiral)
1605 Fox Hunt Court
Alexandria, VA 22307, USA

Reynolds, Jack (Football Player)
Los Angeles Rams
11480 SW 102nd St
Miami, FL 33176-2588, USA

Reynolds, Jamai (Football Player)
Green Bay Packers
PO Box 10628
Green Bay, WI 54307-0628, USA

Reynolds, Jamal (Football Player)
Cleveland Browns
76 Lou Groza Blvd
Berea, OH 44017-1269, USA

Reynolds, James (Actor)
1925 Hanscom Dr
South Pasadena, CA 91030-4009, USA

Reynolds, James (Baseball Player)
708 Highpoint Dr
Rocky Hill, CT 06067-1088, USA

Reynolds, Jerry O (Coach)
Sacramento Kings
1 Sports Pkwy
Arco Arena
Sacramento, CA 95834-2301, USA

Reynolds, Jim (Football Player)
Miami Seahawks
2200 Elkoa's St
Selma, AL 36701, USA

Reynolds, John R (Educator, Physicist)
University of California
Physics Dept
Berkeley, CA 94720-0001, USA

Reynolds, Kevin
151 El Camino Dr
Beverly Hills, CA 90212-2704, USA

Reynolds, Patti
PO Box 530
Fontana, WI 53125-0530, USA

Reynolds, R Shane (Baseball Player)
2205 Warwick Way Ste 200
Marriottsville, MD 21104-1632, USA

Reynolds, Rachel (Actor, Model)
c/o Staff Member Price Is Right, The
2700 Colorado Ave Fl 4
Santa Monica, CA 90404-3553, USA

Reynolds, Randolph N (Business Person)
Reynolds Metal Co
6603 W Broad St
6601 Broad St
Richmond, VA 23230-1723, USA

Reynolds, Richard V (General)
Commander Aeronautical Systems
Wright-Patterson Air Force, OH 45433, USA

Reynolds, Ricky (Football Player)
Tampa Bay Buccaneers
12728 Tradition Dr
Dade City, FL 33525-8240, USA

Reynolds, Robert (Musician)
AristoMedia
1620 16th Ave S
Nashville, TN 37212-2908, USA

Reynolds, Ryan (Actor)
c/o Jonathan Perry United Talent Agency (UTA)
9560 Wilshire Blvd Ste 500
Beverly Hills, CA 90212-2401, USA

Reynolds, Sheldon (Musician)
Great Scott Productions
4750 Lincoln Blvd Apt 229
Marina Del Rey, CA 90292-6991, USA

Reynolds, Star Jones (Talk Show Host)
c/o Jim Griffin William Morris Agency (WMA-NY)
1325 Avenue Of The Americas
New York, NY 10019-6026, USA

Reynolds, W Ann (Educator)
City University of New York
Chancellor's Office
New York, NY 10021, USA

Reynolds Booth, Nancy (Skier)
3197 Padaro Ln
Carpinteria, CA 93013-1115, USA

Reynolds Jr, Thomas A (Lawyer)
Winston & Strawn
45 W Wacker Dr
1 First National Plaza
Chicago, IL 60601, USA

Reza, Yasmina (Actor, Writer)
Marta Andras
14 Rue des Sablons
Paris 75116, FRANCE

Reznor, Trent (Musician)
c/o Staff Member *Interscope Records (LA)
- Main*
2220 Colorado Ave
Santa Monica, CA 90404-3506, USA

Rhames, Ving (Actor)
1158 26th St # 549
Santa Monica, CA 90403-4698, USA

Rhea, Caroline (Actor, Comedian)
c/o Jonathan Howard *Innovative Artists
(LA)*
1505 10th St
Santa Monica, CA 90401-2805, USA

Rhea, Floyd (Football Player)
Chicago Cardinals
12 Rivo Alto Canal
Long Beach, CA 90803-4036, USA

Rheams, Leonta (Football Player)
New England Patriots
1712 W Jackson St
Tyler, TX 75701-1209, USA

Rheaume, Manon (Hockey Player)
University of Minnesota
Athletic Dept
Duluth, MN 55812, USA

Rhett, Alicia (Actor)
PO Box 700
Charleston, SC 29402-0700, USA

Rhett, Errict (Football Player)
Tampa Bay Buccaneers
6 NW 108th Ter
Plantation, FL 33324-1560, USA

Rhimes, Shonda (Actor, Producer, Writer)
Shondaland
4151 Prospect Ave
Los Feliz Tower 4th Fl
Los Angeles, CA 90027-4524, USA

Rhind-Tutt, Julian (Actor)
c/o Staff Member *Peters Fraser & Dunlop
(PFD - UK)*
Drury House
34-43 Russell St
London WC2B 5HA, UNITED KINGDOM
(UK)

Rhinehart, Coby (Football Player)
Arizona Cardinals
8209 Meadow Rd Apt 1140
Dallas, TX 75231-3644, USA

Rhines, Peter B (Oceanographer)
5753 61st Ave NE
Seattle, WA 98105-2037, USA

Rhoads, George (Artist)
1478 Mecklenburg Rd
Ithaca, NY 14850-9301, USA

Rhoads, James B (Misc)
1300 Fox Run Trl
Platte City, MO 64079-7640, USA

Rhoden, Richard A (Rick) (Baseball
Player)
8009 Whisper Lake Ln E
Ponte Vedra, FL 32082-3114, USA

Rhodes, Cynthia (Actor, Dancer)
15260 Ventura Blvd Ste 2100
Sherman Oaks, CA 91403-5360, USA

Rhodes, Donnelly (Actor)
Gold Marshak Liedtke
3500 W Olive Ave Ste 1400
Burbank, CA 91505-5512, USA

Rhodes, Dusty
240 Datura St
Henderson, NV 89074, USA

Rhodes, Frank H T (Educator)
Cornell University
Snee Hall
Geology Dept
Ithaca, NY 14853, USA

Rhodes, Harry (Baseball Player)
Chicago American Giants
743 E 72nd St Apt 1
Chicago, IL 60619-1232, USA

Rhodes, Lou (Musician)
c/o Staff Member *Paradigm (Monterey)*
509 Hartnell St
Monterey, CA 93940-2825, USA

Rhodes, Mark (Musician)
c/o Staff Member *Pop Idol (Fremantle
Media)*
2700 Colorado Ave Ste 450
Santa Monica, CA 90404-3599, USA

Rhodes, Nick (Musician)
DD Productions
93A Westbourne Park Villas
London W2 5ED, UNITED KINGDOM
(UK)

Rhodes, Philip (Musician)
William Morris Agency
1600 Division St Ste 300
Nashville, TN 37203-2755, USA

Rhodes, Ray (Coach, Football Coach,
Football Player)
Ney York Giants
25812 NE 4th Pl
Sammamish, WA 98074-3419, USA

Rhodes, Richard L (Writer)
Janklow & Nesbit
445 Park Ave # 1300
New York, NY 10022-2606, USA

Rhodes, Tom (Actor, Comedian)
William Morris Agency
151 El Camino Dr
Beverly Hills, CA 90212-2775, USA

Rhodes, Zandra (Designer, Fashion
Designer)
79-85 Bermondsey St
London SE1 3XF, UNITED KINGDOM
(UK)

Rhome, Gerald B (Jerry) (Coach, Football
Coach, Football Player)
Dallas Cowboys
3883 Morning Meadow Ln
Buford, GA 30519-4383, USA

Rhone, Earnest (Football Player)
Miami Dolphins
3603 Potomac Ave
Texarkana, TX 75503-3519, USA

Rhone, Earriest C (Ernie) (Football Player)
3603 Potomac Ave
Texarkana, TX 75503-3519, USA

Rhone, Sylvia (Business Person)
Elektra Entertainment Group
75 Rockefeller Plz
15th Floor
New York, NY 10019-6908, USA

Rhyan, Dick (Golfer)
111 Camp Dr
Georgetown, TX 78633-4874, USA

Rhymer, Don (Writer)
c/o David Kramer *United Talent Agency
(UTA)*
9560 Wilshire Blvd Ste 500
Beverly Hills, CA 90212-2401, USA

Rhymes, Busta (Musician)
c/o Staff Member *Violator Music &
Management*
36 W 25th St
New York, NY 10010-2706, USA

Rhymes, Buster (Football Player)
Minnesota Vikings
17120 NW 37th Ave
Miami Gardens, FL 33056-4112, USA

Rhys, Matthew (Actor)
c/o Suzan Bymel *Management 360*
9111 Wilshire Blvd
Beverly Hills, CA 90210-5508, USA

Rhys, Paul (Actor)
Gersh Agency
232 N Canon Dr
Beverly Hills, CA 90210-5302, USA

Rhys, Phillip (Actor)
c/o Staff Member *3 Arts Entertainment Inc*
9460 Wilshire Blvd Fl 7
Beverly Hills, CA 90212-2713, USA

Rhys-Davies, John (Actor)
c/o Staff Member *Agency for the
Performing Arts (APA-LA)*
405 S Beverly Dr
Beverly Hills, CA 90212-4416, USA

**Rhys-Jones, HRH Sophie (Duchess of
Wessex)**
Bagshot Park
Surrey, ENGLAND GUl9 5PN, UNITED
KINGDOM (UK)

Rhys-Meyer, Jonathan
Velvets Town House Butteront
County Cork, IRELAND

Rhys-Meyers, Jonathan (Actor)
c/o Sharon Sheinwold *United Talent
Agency (UTA)*
9560 Wilshire Blvd Ste 500
Beverly Hills, CA 90212-2401, USA

Rhythm Syndicate
6255 W Sunset Blvd # 2100
Los Angeles, CA 90028-7403, USA

Ri Jong Ok (President, Vice President)
Vice President's Office
Pyongyang, NORTH KOREA

Ribas Reig, Oscar (Government Official)
Governmental Offices
Andorra la Vella, ANDORRA

Ribbons, Rosie (Musician)
c/o Staff Member *Pop Idol (Fremantle
Media)*
2700 Colorado Ave Ste 450
Santa Monica, CA 90404-3599, USA

Ribbs, Willy T (Race Car Driver)
2343 Ribbs Ln
San Jose, CA 95116-2147, USA

Ribeau, Sidney A (Educator)
Bowling Green State University
President's Office
Bowling Green, OH 43403-0001, USA

Ribeiro, Alfonso (Actor)
19122 Halsted St
Northridge, CA 91324-1716, USA

Ribeiro, Andre (Race Car Driver)
Tasman Motor Spoerts Group
4192 Weaver Ct S
Hilliard, OH 43026, USA

Ribeiro, Ignacio (Designer, Fashion
Designer)
Clements Ribejro Ltd
48 S Molton St
London W1X 1HE, UNITED KINGDOM
(UK)

Ribisi, Giovanni (Actor)
c/o William Choi *Management 360*
9111 Wilshire Blvd
Beverly Hills, CA 90210-5508, USA

Ribisi, Marissa (Actor)
4121 Wilshire Blvd Apt 415
Los Angeles, CA 90010-3525, USA

Ricard, Alan (Football Player)
Baltimore Ravens
4711 Winterset Way Apt 7
Owings Mills, MD 21117-4746, USA

Ricardo, Benny (Football Player)
Buffalo Bills
3012 Harding Way
Costa Mesa, CA 92626-2846, USA

Ricardo Y Alberto (Music Group)
c/o Staff Member *Sony Music Miami*
605 Lincoln Rd Fl 7
Miami Beach, FL 33139-2900, USA

Ricca, Jim (Football Player)
Washington Redskins
55 Whittingham Cir
Sterling, VA 20165-6236, USA

Ricci, Christina (Actor)
c/o Aleen Keshishian *Brillstein-Grey
Entertainment*
9150 Wilshire Blvd Ste 350
Beverly Hills, CA 90212-3453, USA

Ricci, Ruggiero (Musician)
2930 E Delhi Rd
Ann Arbor, MI 48103-9007, USA

Ricciarelli, Katia (Opera Singer)
Via Magellana 2
Corsica 20097, ITALY

Rice, Alex (Actor)
c/o Ryan Revel *Imparato Fay Management*
1126 Roxbury Dr
Los Angeles, CA 90035-1031, USA

Rice, Andy (Football Player)
Kansas City Chiefs
801 N Main St
Hallettsville, TX 77964-2321, USA

Rice, Anne (Writer)
c/o Staff Member *Creative Artists Agency
LCC (CAA-LA)*
2000 Avenue Of The Stars
Los Angeles, CA 90067-4700, USA

Rice, Bobby G
505 Canton Pass
Madison, TN 37115-5449, USA

Rice, Buddy (Race Car Driver)
Team Rahal
4601 Lyman Dr
Hilliard, OH 43026-1249, USA

Rice, Condoleeza (Government Official)
US Department of State
2201 C St NW
Washington, DC 20520-0099, USA

Rice, Condoleezza (Government Official)
National Security Council
1600 Pennsylvania Ave NW
Washington, DC 20500-0003, USA

Rice, Damien (Musician)
c/o Staff Member *Paradigm (Monterey)*
509 Hartnell St
Monterey, CA 93940-2825, USA

Rice, Elizabeth (Actor)
c/o Steven (Steve) Warren *Hansen,
Jacobson, Teller, Hoberman, Newman,
Warren, Sloane & Richman, LLP*
450 N Roxbury Dr Fl 8
Beverly Hills, CA 90210-4222, USA

Rice, Gene D (Religious Leader)
Church of God
PO Box 2430
Cleveland, TN 37320-2430, USA

Rice, Gigi (Actor)
14951 Alva Dr
Pacific Palisades, CA 90272-4402, USA

Rice, Glen
9492 Doral Blvd
Miami, FL 33178, USA

Rice, James E (Jim) (Baseball Player)
35 Bobby Jones Dr
Andover, MA 01810-2880, USA

Rice, James R (Geophysicist, Physicist)
Harvard University
Applied Science Division
Cambridge, MA 02138, USA

Rice, Jerry (Football Player)
c/o Staff Member *Denver Broncos*
13655 Broncos Pkwy
Englewood, CO 80112-4150, USA

Rice, John (Baseball Player)
2666 E 73rd St Apt 12W
Chicago, IL 60649-2732, USA

Rice, Ken (Football Player)
Buffalo Bills
10619 Big Canoe
Big Canoe, GA 30143-5130, USA

Rice, Norman B (Politician)
Mayor's Office
600 4th Ave
Municipal Building
Seattle, WA 98104-1822, USA

Rice, Ron (Football Player)
Detroit Lions
22880 Twyckingham Way
Southfield, MI 48034-6260, USA

Rice, Simeon (Football Player)
1360 E 9th St
Cleveland, OH 44114-1737, USA

Rice, Stuart A (Misc)
5517 S Kimbark Ave
Chicago, IL 60637-1618, USA

Rice, Thomas M (Physicist)
Theoretische Physik
ETH-Hoggerberg
Zurich, 8093, SWITZERLAND

Rice, Timothy M B (Tim) (Musician)
Chiltens
France-Hill Dr Camberley
Surrey GU153-30A, UNITED KINGDOM
(UK)

Rice-Hughes, Donna
PO Box 888
Fairfax, VA 22030-0888, USA

Rich, Adam (Actor)
4814 Lemona Ave
Sherman Oaks, CA 91403-2010, USA

Rich, Adrienne (Writer)
Stanford University
English Dept
Stanford, CA 94305, USA

Rich, Alexander (Misc)
2 Walnut Ave
Cambridge, MA 02140-2707, USA

Rich, Allan (Actor)
225 E 57th St
New York, NY 10022-2822, USA

Rich, Christopher (Actor)
Bresler Kelly Assoc
11500 W Olympic Blvd Ste 510
Los Angeles, CA 90064-1527, USA

Rich, Claude
18 Chemin de la Butte
Orgeval F-78630, FRANCE

Rich, Clayton (Doctor)
University of Oklahoma
Health Services Center
Oklahoma City, OK 73190-0001, USA

Rich, Denise (Musician)
IGD Music & Media
785 5th Ave
New York, NY 10022-1608, USA

Rich, Elaine
500 S Sepulveda Blvd
Los Angeles, CA 90049-3540, USA

Rich, Frank H (Critic, Writer)
New York Times
229 W 43rd St
Editorial Dept
New York, NY 10036-3959, USA

Rich, Herb (Football Player)
Baltimore Colts
6617 Ellwood Ct
Nashville, TN 37205-3929, USA

Rich, John
2501 Colorado Ave Ste 350
Santa Monica, CA 90404-3583, USA

Rich, Katie
1O100 Santa Monica Blvd. #2490
Los Angeles, CA 90067, USA

Rich, Lee (Business Person)
Lee Rich Productions
75 Rockefeller Plz
Warner
New York, NY 10019-6908, USA

Rich, Matty
9560 Wilshire Blvd Ste 500
Beverly Hills, CA 90212-2401, USA

Rich, Mike (Writer)
c/o Billy Rose *United Talent Agency
(UTA)*
9560 Wilshire Blvd Ste 500
Beverly Hills, CA 90212-2401, USA

Rich, The Tony Project
14724 Ventura Blvd Ste 410
Sherman Oaks, CA 91403-3504, USA

Rich, Tony (Musician)
Prestige
220 E 23rd St Ste 303
New York, NY 10010-4676, USA

Richard, Cliff (Musician)
Harley House
Portsmouth Road Box 46C
Esher
Surrey KT10 9AA, UNITED KINGDOM
(UK)

Richard, Deb (Golfer)
125 Hidden Cove Ln
Ponte Vedra Beach, FL 32082-2154, USA

Richard, Henri (Hockey Player)
905-4300 Place de Cageux
Ile Paton Laval, PQ H7W 4Z3, CANADA

Richard, Ivor S (Government Official)
11 South Square
Gray's Inn
London WC1R 5EU, UNITED KINGDOM
(UK)

Richard, James Rodney (J R) (Baseball
Player)
5134 Bungalow Ln
Houston, TX 77048-2706, USA

Richard, Pierre
6 rue de Vieux-Moulin
Droue-sur-Drouette 28230, FRANCE

Ri'chard, Robert (Actor)
c/o Michael Goldman *Michael Goldman
Management*
11818 Laurel Hills Rd
Studio City, CA 91604-3723, USA

Richard, Ruth (Baseball Player)
880 Allentown Rd
Sellersville, PA 18960-1000, USA

Richard, Wendy
5 Denmark St.
London, ENGLAND WCl 8LP, UNITED
KINGDOM (UK)

Richard III, Oliver G (Business Person)
Columbia Energy Group
200 Civic Center Dr
Columbus, OH 43215-4157, USA

Richards, Ariana (Actor)
Don Buchwald
6500 Wilshire Blvd Ste 2200
Los Angeles, CA 90048-4942, USA

Richards, Bobby (Football Player)
Philadelphia Eagles
2881 Fairplay Rd
Rutledge, GA 30663-2000, USA

Richards, Brad (Hockey Player)
60 Ladoga Ave
Tampa, FL 33606-3804, USA

Richards, Curvin (Football Player)
Dallas Cowboys
9535 Fairdale Ln
Houston, TX 77063-3841, USA

Richards, David R (Football Player)
San Diego Chargers
4209 San Carlos St
Dallas, TX 75205-2049, USA

Richards, Denise (Actor)
c/o Stephanie Simon *Untitled
Entertainment (LA)*
331 N Maple Dr Fl 3
Beverly Hills, CA 90210-3827, USA

Richards, Emelie
PO Box 7052
Arlington, VA 22207-0052, USA

Richards, Evan
1800 Avenue Of The Stars Ste 400
Los Angeles, CA 90067-4206, USA

Richards, Frederic M (Misc)
69 Andrews Rd
Guilford, CT 06437-3715, USA

Richards, Golden (Football Player)
Dallas Cowboys
7274 Winesap Ct
Salt Lake City, UT 84121-4439, USA

Richards, Howard (Football Player)
Dallas Cowboys
Psc 98 Box 30
APO, AE 09830-0001, USA

Richards, I Vivian A (Viv) (Cricketer)
West Indian Cricket Board
PO Box 616
Saint John's, ANTIGUA & BARBUDA

Richards, J August (Actor)
PO Box 99
China Spring, TX 76633-0099, USA

Richards, J R (Musician)
William Morris Agency
1325 Avenue Of The Americas
New York, NY 10019-6091, USA

Richards, James B (Football Player)
Ney York Jets
733 Vanderbilt Ave
Virginia Beach, VA 23451-3632, USA

Richards, Kim (Actor)
10326 Orion Ave
Los Angeles, CA 90064, USA

Richards, Lou
2467 Brighton Dr. #2-B
Valencia, CA 91355, USA

Richards, Mark (Misc)
755 Hunter St
Newcastle, NSW 2302, AUSTRALIA

Richards, Michael (Actor, Comedian)
c/o Staff Member *Untitled Entertainment
(NY)*
322 8th Ave Ste 601
New York, NY 10001-6715, USA

Richards, Paul G (Misc)
Lamont-Doherty Geological Observatory
Palisades, NY 10964, USA

Richards, Paul W (Astronaut)
NASA
2101 Nasa Pkwy
Johnson Space Center
Houston, TX 77058-3691, USA

Richards, Perry (Football Player)
Pittsburgh Steelers
25835 Continental Cir # 4
Taylor, MI 48180-3134, USA

Richards, Renee (Tennis Player)
1604 Union St
San Francisco, CA 94123-4507, USA

Richards, Rex E (Misc)
13 Woodstock Close
Oxford OX2 8DB, UNITED KINGDOM
(UK)

Richards, Richard N (Astronaut)
NASA
2101 Nasa Pkwy
Johnson Space Center
Houston, TX 77058-3691, USA

Richards, Robert E (Bob) (Athlete, Track
Athlete)
1616 Estates Dr
Waco, TX 76712-2208, USA

Richards, Stephanie (Actor)
H David Moss
733 Seward St Ph
Los Angeles, CA 90038-3503, USA

Richards, Viv (Cricketer)
c/o Staff Member *West Indies Cricket Club*
PO Box 616
St John's, ANTIGUA & BARBUDA

Richards, Warren J
PO Box 2496
Salt Lake City, UT 84110-2496, USA

Richardson, Al (Football Player)
Atlanta Falcons
3003 Mary Ashley Ct SE
Conyers, GA 30013-6419, USA

Richardson, Ashley (Model)
Ford Model Agency
142 Greene St # 400
New York, NY 10012-3236, USA

Richardson, Bill
799 United Nations Plz
New York, NY 10017-3505, USA

Richardson, Bill (Secretary)
1000 Independence Ave SW
Washington, DC 20585-0001, USA

Richardson, Bucky (Football Player)
Houston Oilers
9015 Stones Throw Ln
Missouri City, TX 77459-2990, USA

Richardson, Cameron (Actor)
c/o Staff Member *United Talent Agency (UTA)*
9560 Wilshire Blvd Ste 500
Beverly Hills, CA 90212-2401, USA

Richardson, Cheryl (Actor)
749 Fair Oaks Dr
Alamo, CA 94507-1457, USA

Richardson, Damien (Football Player)
Carolina Panthers
30 Adolph Sutro Ct Apt 102
San Francisco, CA 94131-1165, USA

Richardson, Dan (Musician)
Agency Group Ltd
1775 Broadway Ste 515
New York, NY 10019-1903, USA

Richardson, Donna (Misc)
Anchor Bay Entertainment
2401 W Big Beaver Rd Ste 200
Troy, MI 48084-3306, USA

Richardson, Dorothy (Dot) (Misc)
USC Medical Center
1200 N State St # Gh3900
Los Angeles, CA 90089-0123, USA

Richardson, Earl (Educator)
Morgan State University
President's Office
Baltimore, MD 21202, USA

Richardson, Eliot
1100 Crest Ln
McLean, VA 22101-1815, USA

Richardson, Eric (Football Player)
Buffalo Bills
509 Ely Blvd S
Petaluma, CA 94954-3813, USA

Richardson, Gloster (Football Player)
Kansas City Chiefs
9143 S Euclid Ave
Chicago, IL 60617-3749, USA

Richardson, Gordon W H (Financier)
Morgan Stanley
25 Cabot Square
Canary Wharf
London E14 4QA, UNITED KINGDOM (UK)

Richardson, Grady (Football Player)
Washington Redskins
5804 La Jolla Way
Cypress, CA 90630-3210, USA

Richardson, Greg (Boxer)
382 Camden Ave
Youngstown, OH 44505-4845, USA

Richardson, Hamilton (Tennis Player)
870 United Nations Plz
New York, NY 10017-1807, USA

Richardson, Huey (Football Player)
Pittsburgh Steelers
1288 Skyhaven Rd SE
Atlanta, GA 30316-2606, USA

Richardson, Jack (Artist)
12171 Sunset Ave
Grass Valley, CA 95945-8512, USA

Richardson, Jake (Actor)
c/o Meredith Fine *Coast to Coast Talent Group*
3350 Barham Blvd
Los Angeles, CA 90068-1404, USA

Richardson, Jason (Basketball Player)
Golden State Warriors
1001 Broadway
Oakland, CA 94607-4019, USA

Richardson, Jeffrey (Baseball Player)
California Angels
12663 N Gentle Rain Dr
Marana, AZ 85658-4394, USA

Richardson, Jerry (Football Player)
Los Angeles Rams
3200 Fleetwood Dr Apt 14
Amarillo, TX 79109-3218, USA

Richardson, Joely (Actor)
c/o Carol Bodie *International Creative Management (ICM-LA)*
10250 Constellation Blvd
Los Angeles, CA 90067-6200, USA

Richardson, John (Football Player)
Miami Dolphins
2064 Antares Ct
Westlake Village, CA 91361-2076, USA

Richardson, John T (Educator)
2233 N Kenmore Ave
Chicago, IL 60614-3547, USA

Richardson, Kevin Michael (Actor)
c/o Anita Haeggstrom *Haeggstrom Office, The*
11288 Ventura Blvd # 620
Studio City, CA 91604-3187, USA

Richardson, LaTanya (Actor, Producer)
c/o Staff Member *Paradigm (LA)*
360 N Crescent Dr
North Bldg
Beverly Hills, CA 90210-6820, USA

Richardson, Linda (Opera Singer)
Van Walsum Mgmt
4 Addison Bridge Place
London W14 8XP, UNITED KINGDOM (UK)

Richardson, Midge T (Editor)
Seventeen Magazine
850 3rd Ave
Editorial Dept
New York, NY 10022-6222, USA

Richardson, Mike (Football Player)
Chicago Bears
1619 W Caldwell St
Compton, CA 90220-4333, USA

Richardson, Mike W (Football Player)
Houston Oilers
2015 Pebble Beach Ct
Richardson, TX 75082-3219, USA

Richardson, Miranda (Actor)
Kerry Gardner Mgmt
7 Saint George's Square
London SW1V 2HX, UNITED KINGDOM (UK)

Richardson, Natasha (Actor)
c/o Chris Andrews *Creative Artists Agency LCC (CAA-LA)*
2000 Avenue Of The Stars
Los Angeles, CA 90067-4700, USA

Richardson, Nolan (Coach)
2539 E Joyce Blvd
Fayetteville, AR 72703-4553, USA

Richardson, Patricia (Actor)
149 S Barrington Ave # 510
Los Angeles, CA 90049-3310, USA

Richardson, Quentin (Basketball Player)
Los Angeles Clippers
1111 S Figueroa St
Staples Center
Los Angeles, CA 90015-1300, USA

Richardson, Robert (Cinematographer)
Skouras Agency
725 Arizona Ave Ste 406
Santa Monica, CA 90401-1736, USA

Richardson, Robert C (Nobel Prize Laureate)
4 Hunter Ln
Ithaca, NY 14850-9662, USA

Richardson, Robert C (Bobby) (Baseball Player)
47 Adams Ave
Sumter, SC 29150-4037, USA

Richardson, Sam (Artist)
4121 Sequoyah Rd
Oakland, CA 94605-4539, USA

Richardson, W Franklyn (Religious Leader)
National Baptist Convention
52 S 6th Ave
Mount Vernon, NY 10550-3005, USA

Richardson, Willam C (Educator)
W K Kellogg Foundation
1 Michigan Ave E
Battle Creek, MI 49017-4012, USA

Richardson, Willie (Football Player)
Baltimore Colts
5928 Waverly Dr
Jackson, MS 39206-2503, USA

Richardson of Lee, John S (Doctor)
Windcutter
Lee
North Devon EX34 8LW, UNITED KINGDOM (UK)

Richardson-Whitfield, Salli (Actor)
c/o Craig Dorfman *Blueprint Management*
5670 Wilshire Blvd Ste 2525
Los Angeles, CA 90036-5647, USA

Richardt, Mike (Baseball Player)
Texas Rangers
5286 W Richert Ave
Fresno, CA 93722-9152, USA

Richer, Stephane (Hockey Player)
New Jersey Devils
Continental Arena
50 RR 120 N
East Rutherford, NJ 07073, USA

Richert, Nate (Actor)
c/o Iris Burton *Iris Burton Agency*
201 N Crescent Dr Apt 319
Beverly Hills, CA 90210-6181, USA

Richert, Pete (Baseball Player)
Los Angeles Dodgers
80 La Cerra Dr
Rancho Mirage, CA 92270-3811, USA

Richeson, Ray (Football Player)
Chicago Hornets
1348 Willoughby Rd
Birmingham, AL 35216-2906, USA

Richey, Cliff (Tennis Player)
2936 Cumberland Dr
San Angelo, TX 76904-6163, USA

Richey, Jennifer (Actor)
Bobby Ball Talent
4605 Lankershim Blvd Ste 721
North Hollywood, CA 91602-1878, USA

Richey, Nancy (Tennis Player)
2936 Cumberland Dr
San Angelo, TX 76904-6163, USA

Richey, Wade (Football Player)
San Francisco 49ers
720 Patin Rd
Carencro, LA 70520-5206, USA

Richie, Bob (Baseball Player)
Detroit Tigers
1835 Meadowvale Way
Sparks, NV 89431-2949, USA

Richie, Lionel (Musician, Songwriter, Writer)
c/o Kevin Huvane *Creative Artists Agency LCC (CAA-LA)*
2000 Avenue Of The Stars
Los Angeles, CA 90067-4700, USA

Richie, Nicole (Heir/Heiress, Reality TV Star)
c/o Jonathan Perry *United Talent Agency (UTA)*
9560 Wilshire Blvd Ste 500
Beverly Hills, CA 90212-2401, USA

Richie, Shane (Actor)
c/o Phil Dale *Qdos Entertainment*
8 King St
Covent Garden
London WC2 8HN, UNITED KINGDOM (UK)

Riching, Julian (Actor)
c/o Staff Member *Gary Goddard Agency*
10 Saint Mary Street #305
Toronto, ON M4Y 1P9, CANADA

Richman, Caryn (Actor)
1805 Via Arriba
Palos Verdes Estates, CA 90274-1236, USA

Richman, Jonathan (Actor, Musician)
High Road
751 Bridgeway # 300
Sausalito, CA 94965-2165, USA

Richman, Peter Mark (Actor)
5114 Del Moreno Dr
Woodland Hills, CA 91364-2426, USA

Richmond, Branscombe (Actor)
5706 Calvin Ave
Tarzana, CA 91356-1109, USA

Richmond, Julius B (Doctor)
PO Box 996
West Tisbury, MA 02575-0996, USA

Richmond, Mitch (Basketball Player)
25374 Prado De La Felicidad
Calabasas, CA 91302-3649, USA

Richmond, Tequan (Actor)
c/o Staff Member *Nancy Chaidez & Associates*
6399 Wilshire Blvd Ste 424
Los Angeles, CA 90048-5716, USA

Richt, Mark (Coach, Football Coach)
University of Georgia
PO Box 1472
Athletic Dept
Athens, GA 30603-1472, USA

Richter, Al (Baseball Player)
Boston Red Sox
PO Box 41
Virginia Beach, VA 23458-0041, USA

Richter, Andy (Actor, Comedian)
c/o Tim Sarkes *Brillstein-Grey Entertainment*
9150 Wilshire Blvd Ste 350
Beverly Hills, CA 90212-3453, USA

Richter, Burton (Nobel Prize Laureate)
Stanford University
Linear Accelerator Center
PO Box 4349
Stanford, CA 94309, USA

Richter, Frank (Football Player)
Denver Broncos
711 N Slappey Blvd
Albany, GA 31701-1452, USA

Richter, Gerhard (Artist)
Bismarckstr 50
Cologne 50672, GERMANY

Richter, Hans
In der Wasserschopp 43
Heppenheim D-64646, GERMANY

Richter, James A (Jim) (Football Player)
8620 Bournemouth Dr
Raleigh, NC 27615-2008, USA

Richter, Jason James (Actor)
United Talent Agency
9560 Wilshire Blvd Ste 500
Beverly Hills, CA 90212-2401, USA

Richter, Leslie A (Les) (Football Player)
Los Angeles Rams
1405 Via Vallarta
Riverside, CA 92506-3663, USA

Richter, Michael T (Mike) (Hockey Player)
c/o Staff Member *New York Rangers*
2 Pennsylvania Plaza
New York, NY 10121, USA

Richter, Pat V (Football Executive, Football Player)
Washington Redskins
833 Kings Way
Madison, WI 53704-6046, USA

Richwine, Maria (Actor)
Abrams-Rubaloff Lawrence
5700 Wilshire Blvd Ste 456
Los Angeles, CA 90036-3648, USA

Ricker, Robert S (Religious Leader)
Baptists Conference
2002 Arlington Heights Rd
Arlington Heights, IL 60005-4193, USA

Ricketts, Dave (Baseball Player)
St Louis Cardinals
12860 Polo Parc Dr
Saint Louis, MO 63146-1504, USA

Ricketts, Jeff (Actor)
c/o Michael Greene *Greene & Associates*
190 N Canon Dr Ste 200
Beverly Hills, CA 90210-5319, USA

Ricketts, Tom (Football Player)
Pittsburgh Steelers
720 Warrendale Bayne Rd
Wexford, PA 15090-7492, USA

Rickles, Don (Actor, Comedian)
10249 Century Woods Dr
Los Angeles, CA 90067-6312, USA

Rickman, Alan (Actor)
Creative Artists Agency
9830 Wilshire Blvd
Beverly Hills, CA 90212-1804, USA

Ricks, Mikhael (Football Player)
San Diego Chargers
PO Box 41
506 N Texas
Anahuac, TX 77514-0041, USA

Rickter, Alicia (Actor)
c/o Staff Member *Innovative Artists (LA)*
1505 10th St
Santa Monica, CA 90401-2805, USA

Rico, Alfredo (Baseball Player)
Kansas City A's
7720 Ensign Ave
Sun Valley, CA 91352-4451, USA

Ricoeur, Paul (Misc)
18 Rue Henri Marrou
Chatenay Malabry 92290, FRANCE

Ridder, Eric (Publisher)
Piping Rock Road
Locust Valley, NY 11560, USA

Ridder, P Anthony (Business Person, Publisher)
Knight-Ridder Inc
50 W San Fernando St
San Jose, CA 95113-2429, USA

Riddick, Frank A Jr (Physicist)
150 Broadway St Apt 709
New Orleans, LA 70118-7603, USA

Riddick, Steven (Steve) (Athlete, Track Athlete)
7601 Crittenden St Apt F2
Philadelphia, PA 19118-3225, USA

Riddles, Libby (Dog Sled Racer)
PO Box 15253
Fritz Creek, AK 99603-6253, USA

Ride, Sally K (Astronaut)
California Space Institute
PO Box 221
9500 Gilman Dr
La Jolla, CA 92038-0221, USA

Rider, Amy (Actor)
c/o Staff Member *Diverse Talent Group*
1875 Century Park E Ste 2250
Los Angeles, CA 90067-2563, USA

Rider, Isaiah (J R) (Basketball Player)
PO Box 121R
Montchanin, DE 19710, USA

Rider, Thomas J (Tom) (Governor, Secretary)
Homeland Security Department
Washington, DC 20528-0001, USA

Riders In The Sky
38 Music Sq E Ste 300
Nashville, TN 37203-4396, USA

Riders of the Purple Sage
PO Box 1987
Studio City, CA 91614-0987, USA

Ridge, Houston (Football Player)
San Diego Chargers
7027 Benson Ave
San Diego, CA 92114-5908, USA

Ridgeley, Andrew (Musician)
8800 W Sunset Blvd # 401
Los Angeles, CA 90069-2105, USA

Ridgeway, Angle (Golfer)
c/o Staff Member *Pro Golfers Association (PGA) Tour*
112 Tpc Blvd
Ponte Vedra Beach, FL 32082, USA

Ridgeway, Frank (Cartoonist)
King Features Syndicate
888 7th Ave Ste 201
New York, NY 10106-0201, USA

Ridgle, Elston (Football Player)
San Francisco 49ers
5317 Wilkinson Ave
Studio City, CA 91607-2412, USA

Ridgley, Bob (Actor)
20th Century Artists
4605 Lankershim Blvd Ste 305
North Hollywood, CA 91602-1875, USA

Ridgway, Brunilde S (Archaeologist)
Bryn Mawr College
Archaeology Dept
Bryn Mawr, PA 19010, USA

Ridings, Tag (Golfer)
2040 Bantry Dr
Roanoke, TX 76262-9001, USA

Ridker, Paul (Doctor)
Brigham & Women's Hospital
75 Francis St
Boston, MA 02115-6106, USA

Ridlehuber, Preston (Football Player)
Atlanta Falcons
720 Serramonte Dr
Marietta, GA 30068-4674, USA

Ridlon, James A (Football Player)
San Francisco 49ers
8006 E Lake Rd
Cazenovia, NY 13035, USA

Ridnour, Luke (Basketball Player)
Seattle SuperSonics
1201 3rd Ave Ste 1000
Seattle, WA 98101-3038, USA

Ridzik, Steve (Baseball Player)
Philadelphia Phillies
7008 11th Ave W
Bradenton, FL 34209-4066, USA

Riedel, Deborah (Opera Singer)
Columbia Artists Mgmt Inc
1790 Broadway Fl 6
New York, NY 10019-1412, USA

Riedel, Lars (Athlete, Track Athlete)
LAC Chemnitz
Reichenhainer Str 154
Chemnitz 09125, GERMANY

Riedlbauch, Vaclav (Composer)
Revolucni 6
Prague 1 110 00, CZECH REPUBLIC

Riedling, John (Baseball Player)
Cincinnati Reds
14321 Draft Horse Ln
Wellington, FL 33414-1020, USA

Rieger, Max (Skier)
Innsbrucker Str 12
Mittenwald 82481, GERMANY

Riegert, Peter (Actor)
c/o John S Kelly *Bresler Kelly & Associates*
11500 W Olympic Blvd Ste 352
Los Angeles, CA 90064-1525, USA

Riegger, John (Golfer)
768 Tossa De Mar Ave
Henderson, NV 89002-6536, USA

Riegle, Donald W Jr (Senator)
352 S Saginaw St
Flint, MI 48502-1927, USA

Riegle, Gene (Coach, Horse Racer)
1162 Fort Jefferson Ave
Greenville, OH 45331-1044, USA

Riehle, Richard (Actor)
Abrams Artists
9200 W Sunset Blvd Ste 1125
Los Angeles, CA 90069-3610, USA

Rieker, Richard (Baseball Player)
5337 Foxshire Ct
Orlando, FL 32819-3824, USA

Rienstra, John (Football Player)
Pittsburgh Steelers
5056 Briscoglen Dr
Colorado Springs, CO 80906-8612, USA

Riepe, James S (Business Person)
T Rowe Price Assoc
100 E Pratt St
Baltimore, MD 21202-1090, USA

Ries, Christopher D (Artist)
Keelersburg Road
Tunkhannock, PA 18657, USA

Ries-Zillmer, Ruth (Baseball Player)
133 Adeline St
Walworth, WI 53184, USA

Riese, Randall
5859 W 3rd St
Los Angeles, CA 90036-2838, USA

Riesenberg, Doug (Football Player)
New York Giants
25068 Starr Creek Rd
Corvallis, OR 97333-9576, USA

Riesgo, Nikco (Baseball Player)
Montreal Expos
607 8th Ave
Shenandoah, IA 51601-1939, USA

Riess, Adam (Astronomer, Physicist)
Space Telescope Science Institute
3700 San Martin Dr
Baltimore, MD 21218-2463, USA

Riessen, Marty (Tennis Player)
PO Box 5444
Santa Barbara, CA 93150-5444, USA

Rieu, Andre (Musician)
Polygram Holland
Mozartlaan 25
Hilversum, CM 1217, THE NETHERLANDS

Rieves, Charles (Football Player)
Oakland Raiders
3107 Long Bay Ct
Houston, TX 77059-3720, USA

Rife, Rikki
520 Washington Blvd # 924
Marina Del Rey, CA 90292, USA

Riff
PO Box 7257
Paterson, NJ 07509-7257, USA

Rifkin, Jeremy (Activist, Writer)
1660 L St NW Ste 216
Washington, DC 20036-5642, USA

Rifkin, Ron (Actor, Musician)
c/o Raelle Koota *Anonymous Content (NY)*
8522 National Blvd Ste 101
Culver City, CA 90232-2454, USA

Rifkind, Joshua (Conductor, Musician)
100 Montgomery St
Cambridge, MA 02140-1725, USA

Rigali, Justin F Cardinal (Religious Leader)
Archdiocese
222 N 17th St
Philadelphia, PA 19103-1202, USA

Rigby, Amy (Musician, Songwriter, Writer)
Press Network
1229 17th Ave S
Nashville, TN 37212-2801, USA

Rigby, Brad (Baseball Player)
Oakland A's
1317 Ballentyne Pl
Apopka, FL 32703-6870, USA

Rigby, Cathy
110 E Wilshire Ave Ste 200
Fullerton, CA 92832-1956, USA

Rigby, Jean P (Opera Singer)
Harold Holt
31 Sinclair Road
London W14 0NS, UNITED KINGDOM
(UK)

Rigby, McCoy Cathy (Actor, Gymnast)
McCoy/Rigby Entertainment
110 E Wilshire Ave Ste 200
Fullerton, CA 92832-1956, USA

Rigby, Randall Jr (General)
Deputy Cg
US Army Training/Doctrine Command
Fort Monroe, VA 23651, USA

Rigdon, Paul (Baseball Player)
Cleveland Indians
10738 Fall Creek Dr E
Jacksonville, FL 32222-1379, USA

Rigg, Diana (Actor)
London Mgmt
2-4 Noel St
London W1V 3RB, UNITED KINGDOM
(UK)

Rigg, Rebecca (Actor)
June Cann Mgmt
110 Queen St
Woollahra, NSW 2025, AUSTRALIA

Riggan, Jerrod (Baseball Player)
New York Mets
903 Selkirk Place
Brewster, WA 98812, USA

Riggio, Leonard (Business Person)
Barnes & Noble Inc
122 5th Ave
New York, NY 10011-5693, USA

Riggle, Bob (Football Player)
Atlanta Falcons
55 Waynesburg Rd
Washington, PA 15301-3224, USA

Riggleman, James D (Jim) (Baseball Player)
14950 Gulf Blvd Apt 1003
Madeira Beach, FL 33708-2047, USA

Riggs, Adam (Baseball Player)
Los Angeles Dodgers
26 Pebble Hollow Ct
Spring, TX 77381-4803, USA

Riggs, Gerald (Football Player)
2574 Bright Ct
Decatur, GA 30034-2245, USA

Riggs, Lorrin A (Misc)
80 Lyme Rd Apt 104
Hanover, NH 03755-1229, USA

Riggs, Thron (Football Player)
Boston Yankees
2645 E Southern Ave Apt A496
Tempe, AZ 85282-7791, USA

Righetti, Amanda (Actor)
c/o Staff Member *MBST Entertainment*
345 N Maple Dr Ste 200
Beverly Hills, CA 90210-3860, USA

Righetti, David A (Dave) (Baseball Player)
New York Yankees
552 Magdalena Ave
Los Altos Hills, CA 94024-5233, USA

Right Said Fred
PO Box 891135
Edam ZJ, THE NETHERLANDS

Righteous Bros (Music Group)
c/o Staff Member *William Morris Agency (WMA-LA)*
1 William Morris Pl
Beverly Hills, CA 90212-4261, USA

Rightnowar, Ron (Baseball Player)
Milwaukee Brewers
8926 Stonybrook Blvd
Sylvania, OH 43560-8906, USA

Rights, Graham H (Religious Leader)
Moravian Church Southern Province
459 S Church St
Winston Salem, NC 27101-5314, USA

Rijker, Lucia (Actor)
c/o Harlan Werner *Sports Placement Service*
6671 W Sunset Blvd Ste 1521
Los Angeles, CA 90028-7123, USA

Rijo, Jose (Baseball Player)
New York Yankees
2127 Brickell Ave Apt 2101
Miami, FL 33129-2146, USA

Rikaart, Greg (Actor)
c/o Kyle Fritz *Kyle Fritz Management*
6325 Heather Dr
Los Angeles, CA 90068-1633, USA

Riker, Albert J (Misc)
2760 E 8th St
Tucson, AZ 85716-4712, USA

Riker, Robin (Actor)
c/o Staff Member *Don Buchwald & Associates Inc (LA)*
6500 Wilshire Blvd Ste 2200
Los Angeles, CA 90048-4942, USA

Riklis, Meshulam (Business Person)
Riklis Family Corp
2901 Las Vegas Blvd S
Las Vegas, NV 89109-1933, USA

Riles, Ernest (Baseball Player)
Milwaukee Brewers
221 Asante Dr
Ellenwood, GA 30294-3187, USA

Riley, Bill (Hockey Player)
286 Buckingham Ave
Riverview, NB E1B 2P2, CANADA

Riley, Bridget L (Artist)
Mayor Rowan Gallery
31A Bruton Place
London W1X 7A8, UNITED KINGDOM
(UK)

Riley, Chris (Golfer)
2289 Surrey Meadows Ave
Henderson, NV 89052-2335, USA

Riley, Forbes (Actor)
c/o Staff Member *Cohen Entertainment*
532 N Croft Ave
West Hollywood, CA 90048-2546, USA

Riley, George (Baseball Player)
Chicago Cubs
2738 S Sheridan St
Philadelphia, PA 19148-4825, USA

Riley, Gerald (Jerry) (Dog Sled Racer)
General Delivery
Nenana, AK 99760-9999, USA

Riley, H John Jr (Business Person)
Cooper Industries
600 Travis St
Houston, TX 77002-3009, USA

Riley, Jack (Actor)
House of Representatives
211 S Beverly Dr Ste 208
Beverly Hills, CA 90212-3879, USA

Riley, James (Football Player)
Miami Dolphins
2201 Cardinal Dr
Edmond, OK 73013-7635, USA

Riley, James C (General)
Commanding General
V Corps
APO, AE 09079, USA

Riley, Jeannie C (Musician)
906 Granville Rd
Franklin, TN 37064-2067, USA

Riley, John P (Jack) (Coach, Hockey Player)
PO Box 1302
Marstons Mills, MA 02648-5302, USA

Riley, Ken (Football Player)
Cincinnati Bengals
1865 E Gibbons St
Bartow, FL 33830-6712, USA

Riley, Lee (Football Player)
Detroit Lions
1511 Yarbro Ln
Paducah, KY 42003-0281, USA

Riley, Matt (Baseball Player)
Baltimore Orioles
8008 Sacramento St
Fair Oaks, CA 95628-7527, USA

Riley, Michael
9200 W Sunset Blvd Ste 900
Los Angeles, CA 90069-3604, USA

Riley, Mike (Coach, Football Coach)
Oregon State University
Athletic Dept
Corvallis, OR 97331, USA

Riley, Pat
180 Arvida Pkwy
Miami, FL 33156-2313, USA

Riley, Richard D (Misc)
16 Boathouse Rd
Laconia, NH 03246-1949, USA

Riley, Ruth (Athlete)
3777 Lapeer Rd
Auburn Hills, MI 48326-1733, USA

Riley, Steve (Football Player)
Minnesota Vikings
7 Via Cancion
San Clemente, CA 92673-6907, USA

Riley, Teddy (Musician, Songwriter, Writer)
Future Enterprise Records
70 Universal City Plz
Universal City, CA 91608-1011, USA

Riley, Terry M (Composer, Musician)
Shri Moonshine Ranch
13699 Moonshine Rd
Camptonville, CA 95922-9713, USA

Riley, Victor (Football Player)
Kansas City Chiefs
136 Sandy Oak Ln
Gaston, SC 29053-8775, USA

Riley, William Jay (Judge)
US Court of Appeals
PO Box 307
Federal Bldg
Omaha, NE 68101-0307, USA

Rilling, Helmuth
Int'l Bach Academy
Johann-Sebastian-Bach-Platz
Stuttgart 70178, GERMANY

Rimando, Nick (Soccer Player)
DC United
2400 East Capitol St, SE
Rfk Stadium
Washington, DC 20003, USA

Rimer, Jeff (Sportscaster)
9916 Morris Dr
Dublin, OH 43017-8859, USA

Rimes, LeAnn (Musician)
c/o Alix Gucovsky *Special Artists Agency*
9465 Wilshire Blvd Ste 890
Beverly Hills, CA 90212-2607, USA

Rimington, Dave (Football Player)
Cincinnati Bengals
125 W 110th St Apt 5A
New York, NY 10026-4274, USA

Rimington, Stella (Government Official)
PO Box 1604
London SW1P 1XB, UNITED KINGDOM
(UK)

Rimmel, James E (Religious Leader)
Evangetical Presbyterian Church
26049 5 Mile Rd
Detroit, MI 48239-3235, USA

Rinaldi, Kathy (Tennis Player)
Advantage International
1025 Thomas Jefferson St NW # 450
Washington, DC 20007-5201, USA

Rinaldo, Benjamin (Skier)
Ski World
2680 Buena Park Dr
North Hollywood, CA 91604, USA

Rincon, Andy (Baseball Player)
St Louis Cardinals
5425 Los Toros Ave
Pico Rivera, CA 90660-3038, USA

Rincon, Ricardo (Baseball Player)
c/o Staff Member *Oakland Athletics*
7000 Coliseum Way
Oakland, CA 94621-1992, USA

Rinearson, Peter M (Journalist)
Seattle Times
1120 John St
Editorial Dept
Seattle, WA 98109-5321, USA

Rineer, Jeff (Baseball Player)
Baltimore Orioles
325 W Charlotte St
Millersville, PA 17551-9515, USA

Rinehart, Kenneth (Misc)
University of Illinois
Chemistry Dept
Urbana, IL 61801, USA

Rines, Robert H (Inventor)
17 Ripley Rd
Belmont, MA 02478-1246, USA

Ringadoo, Veerasamy (President)
Corner of Farquhar & Sir Celicourt
Antelme Sts
Quatre-Bornes, MAURITIUS

Ringer, Jennifer (Ballerina)
New York City Ballet
Lincoln Center Plaza
New York, NY 10023, USA

Ringer, Robert J (Publisher, Writer)
Stratford Press
1880 Century Park E
Los Angeles, CA 90067-1600, USA

Ringling Brothers Barnum & Bailey Circus
8607 Westwood Cir
Vienna, VA 22182, USA

Ringo, James S (Jim) (Football Player)
Green Bay Packers
408 Montross Ct
Chesapeake, VA 23323-7018, USA

Ringwald, Molly (Actor)
c/o Greg Clark *Untitled Entertainment (LA)*
331 N Maple Dr Fl 3
Beverly Hills, CA 90210-3827, USA

Rini, Mary (Baseball Player)
37592 Charter Oaks Blvd
Clinton Township, MI 48036-2422, USA

Rinker, Larry (Golfer)
1615 Woodland Ave
Winter Park, FL 32789-2774, USA

Rinker, Lee (Golfer)
Signature Sports
4150 Olson Memorial Hwy Ste 110
Minneapolis, MN 55422-4804, USA

Rinna, Lisa (Actor)
c/o Staff Member *United Talent Agency (UTA)*
9560 Wilshire Blvd Ste 500
Beverly Hills, CA 90212-2401, USA

Rinser, Luise
via di Marino 49
Rocca di Papa I-00040, ITALY

Rintoul, David
91 Regent St.
London, ENGLAND W1R 7TB, UNITED KINGDOM (UK)

Rintoul, Steve (Golfer)
17506 Osprey Manor Way
Lithia, FL 33547-5044, USA

Rintzler, Marius A (Opera Singer)
Friedingstr 18
Dusseldorf 40625, GERMANY

Riordan, ex-Mayor Richard
141 N Bristol Ave
Los Angeles, CA 90049-2601, USA

Riordan, Marjorie
1833 Pelham Ave
Los Angeles, CA 90025-4713, USA

Riordan, Mike (Basketball Player)
Riordan's Saloon
26 Market Space
Annapolis, MD 21401-1894, USA

Riordan, Richard J (Politician)
141 N Bristol Ave
Los Angeles, CA 90049-2601, USA

Rios, Alberto (Writer)
Arizona State University
English Dept
Tempe, AZ 85287-0001, USA

Rios, Alexis (Baseball Player)
Yale Field
252 Derby Ave
West Haven, CT 06516-1046, USA

Rios, Danny (Baseball Player)
New York Yankees
2523 W 9th Ln
Hialeah, FL 33010-1225, USA

Rios, Marcelo (Tennis Player)
Int'l Mgmt Group
Via Augusta 200
#400
Barcelona 08021, SPAIN

Rios, Montt Efrain (General, President)
6A Avenida A 3-18 Zona 1
Guatamela City, GUATEMALA

Rios, Osvaldo (Actor)
c/o Staff Member *TV Caracol*
Calle 76 #11 - 35
Piso 10AA
Bogota DC 26484, COLOMBIA

Riotta, Vincent (Actor)
c/o Staff Member *Scott Marshall Partners Ltd*
54 Poland St #9
London W1F 7NJ, UNITED KINGDOM (UK)

Ripa, Kelly (Actor)
Live with Regis and Kelly
7 Lincoln Sq Fl 5
Wabc-Tv
New York, NY 10023-6201, USA

Ripert, Eric (Chef)
Le Bernardin
787 7th Ave Fl Conc1
New York, NY 10019-6018, USA

Ripken, Billy (Baseball Player)
Baltimore Orioles
900 Mount Soma Ct
Fallston, MD 21047-1935, USA

Ripken, Calvin E (Cal) Jr (Baseball Player)
1427 Clarkview Rd Ste 100
Baltimore, MD 21209-0030, USA

Ripley, Alice (Actor, Musician)
Douglas Gorman ROthacker Wilhelm
1501 Broadway Ste 703
New York, NY 10036-5505, USA

Rippelmeyer, Ray (Baseball Player)
Washington Senators
104 Eagle Ct
Waterloo, IL 62298-3158, USA

Rippey, Rodney Allan (Actor)
3941 Veselich Ave # 4-251
Los Angeles, CA 90039-1461, USA

Rippey, Rodney Allen
3939 Veselich Ave # 351
Los Angeles, CA 90039-1460, USA

Ripple, Kenneth F (Judge)
US Court of Appeals
204 S Main St
South Bend, IN 46601-2122, USA

Rippley, Steve (Baseball Player)
3900 Galt Ocean Dr Apt 1406
Fort Lauderdale, FL 33308-6606, USA

Risebrough, Doug (Coach, Hockey Player)
5809 Schaefer Rd
Edina, MN 55436-1115, USA

Risen, Arnie (Basketball Player)
3217 Bremerton Rd
Pepper Pike, OH 44124-5346, USA

Risen, Arnold (Arnie) (Basketball Player)
3217 Bremerton Rd
Pepper Pike, OH 44124-5346, USA

Risher, Alan (Football Player)
Tampa Bay Buccaneers
15814 Chantilly Ave
Baton Rouge, LA 70817-2405, USA

Risien, Cody L (Football Player)
Cleveland Browns
12060 Lake Ave Apt 401
Lakewood, OH 44107-1865, USA

Risinger, Earlene (Baseball Player)
334 Aurora St SE
Grand Rapids, MI 49507-3124, USA

Risk, Thomas N (Financier)
10 Belford Place
Edinburgh EH4 3DH, SCOTLAND

Riske, David (Baseball Player)
Cleveland Indians
2302 Great Elk Dr
Henderson, NV 89052-7069, USA

Risley, Bill (Baseball Player)
Montreal Expos
1160 Prim Rose Cir
Greenwood, AR 72936-3066, USA

Rispoli, Michael (Actor)
c/o Staff Member *Gersh Agency, The (LA)*
232 N Canon Dr
Beverly Hills, CA 90210-5302, USA

Rissmiller, Ray (Football Player)
Philadelphia Eagles
114 Iken Cir
Goose Creek, SC 29445-7148, USA

Rist, Robbie
PO Box 867
Woodland Hills, CA 91365-0867, USA

Ristorucci, Lisa (Actor)
Progressive Artists Agency
400 S Beverly Dr Ste 216
Beverly Hills, CA 90212-4404, USA

Ritcher, James A (Jim) (Football Player)
Buffalo Bills
8620 Boumemouth Dr
Raleigh, NC 27615, USA

Ritchie, Daniel L (Educator, Television Host)
University of Denver
Chancellor's Office
Denver, CO 80208-0001, USA

Ritchie, Guy (Director)
c/o Staff Member *SKA Films*
2nd Floor, 6 Salem Rd
London W2 4BU, UNITED KINGDOM (UK)

Ritchie, Ian (Architect)
110 Three Colt St
London E14 8A2, UNITED KINGDOM (UK)

Ritchie, Jay (Baseball Player)
Boston Red Sox
8275 Highway 52
Rockwell, NC 28138-8545, USA

Ritchie, Jill (Actor)
c/o Staff Member *Rigberg-Rugolo Entertainment*
1180 S Beverly Dr Ste 601
Los Angeles, CA 90035-1158, USA

Ritchie, Jim (Artist)
Adelson Galleries
19 E 82nd St
Mark Hotel
New York, NY 10028-0302, USA

Ritchie, John H (Architect)
Mount Heswall
Wirrai L60 4RD, UNITED KINGDOM (UK)

Ritchie, Jon (Football Player)
c/o Staff Member *Philadelphia Eagles*
1 Novacare Way
Philadelphia, PA 19145-5996, USA

Ritchie, Todd (Baseball Player)
Minnesota Twins
114 Hulan Dr
Kerens, TX 75144-6046, USA

Ritchie, Wally (Baseball Player)
Philadelphia Phillies
5 Wheatstone Farm
Ladera Ranch, CA 92694-1034, USA

Ritchie Family, The
4100 W Flagler St Ste B2
Coral Gables, FL 33134-1640, USA

Ritchson, Alan (Actor)
c/o Ryan Martin *Agency for the Performing Arts (APA-LA)*
405 S Beverly Dr
Beverly Hills, CA 90212-4416, USA

Ritenour, Lee (Composer, Musician)
11808 Dorothy St Apt 108
Los Angeles, CA 90049-5469, USA

Ritger, Dick (Bowler)
804 Valley View Dr
River Falls, WI 54022-2724, USA

Rittenhouse, Lenore (Golfer)
295 Bellhaven Dr
Carthage, NC 28327-7133, USA

Ritter, C Dowd (Financier)
AmSouth Bancorp
1900 5th Ave N
Amsouth Sonat Tower
Birmingham, AL 35203-2667, USA

Ritter, Huntley (Actor)
c/o Staff Member *Agency for the Performing Arts (APA-LA)*
405 S Beverly Dr
Beverly Hills, CA 90212-4416, USA

Ritter, Jason (Actor)
c/o Joanna (Joanie) Burstein *Burstein Company, The*
15304 W Sunset Blvd Ste 208
Pacific Palisades, CA 90272-3656, USA

Ritter, Krysten (Actor)
c/o David Lederman *Innovative Artists (LA)*
1505 10th St
Santa Monica, CA 90401-2805, USA

Ritter, Lawrence (Baseball Player)
424 W End Ave Apt 6D
New York, NY 10024-5777, USA

Ritter, Reggie (Baseball Player)
Cleveland Indians
1564 Estep Rd
Donaldson, AR 71941-8987, USA

Ritts, Jim (Golfer, Television Host)
Ladies Pro Golf Assn
100 International Golf Dr
Daytona Beach, FL 32124-1082, USA

Rittwage, Jim (Baseball Player)
Cleveland Indians
23931 Columbus Rd
Bedford, OH 44146-2969, USA

Ritz, David
c/o Daniel A (Dan) Strone *Trident Media Group LLC*
41 Madison Ave Fl 36
New York, NY 10010-2257, USA

Ritz, Kevin (Baseball Player)
Detroit Tigers
836 N 6th St
Cambridge, OH 43725-1400, USA

Ritzenhaler, Henry Leon
1617 Pearson Rd
Paradise, CA 95969-6029, USA

Ritzman, Alice (Golfer)
614 S Foys Lake Dr
Kalispell, MT 59901-7440, USA

Riutta, Ernest R (Admiral)
Commander
Coast Guard Island
US Coast Guard Pacific
Alameda, CA 94501, USA

Riva, Emmanuelle
37 rue de la Harpe
Paris F-75005, FRANCE

Rivaldo (Soccer Player)
AC Milan
Via Turati 3
Milan 20221, ITALY

Rivas, Daniel Louis (Actor)
c/o Paul Santana *Agency for the Performing Arts (APA-LA)*
405 S Beverly Dr
Beverly Hills, CA 90212-4416, USA

Rivas, Gonzalo (Actor)
c/o Staff Member *Televisa*
Blvd Adolfo Lopez Mateos 232
Colonia San Angel INN
DF CP 01060, MEXICO

Rivas Montaño, Hanna (Actor)
c/o Staff Member *Televisa*
Blvd Adolfo Lopez Mateos 232
Colonia San Angel INN
DF CP 01060, MEXICO

Rivera, Ana Liz (Actor)
c/o Staff Member *Televisa*
Blvd Adolfo Lopez Mateos 232
Colonia San Angel INN
DF CP 01060, MEXICO

Rivera, Angelica (Actor)
c/o Staff Member *Televisa*
Blvd Adolfo Lopez Mateos 232
Colonia San Angel INN
DF CP 01060, MEXICO

Rivera, Chita (Actor, Dancer, Musician)
c/o Staff Member *William Morris Agency (WMA-LA)*
1 William Morris Pl
Beverly Hills, CA 90212-4261, USA

Rivera, Geraldo (Journalist, Television Host)
c/o Staff Member *Fox News Channel (NY)*
1211 Avenue Of The Americas
Level C1
New York, NY 10036-8701, USA

Rivera, Gina
PO Box 5617
Beverly Hills, CA 90209-5617, USA

Rivera, Jerry (Musician)
c/o Staff Member *BMG*
1540 Broadway
New York, NY 10036-4074, USA

Rivera, Jim (Baseball Player)
St Louis Browns
2311 Abbey Dr Apt 7
Fort Wayne, IN 46835-3150, USA

Rivera, Jose (Producer, Writer)
c/o Rick Berg *Neverland Films*
9229 W Sunset Blvd Ste 615
Los Angeles, CA 90069-3406, USA

Rivera, Luis (Baseball Player)
Montreal Expos
16 Calle Lazaro Ramos
Cidra, PR 00739-3424, USA

Rivera, Lupillo (Music Group)
c/o Staff Member *Sony Music Miami*
605 Lincoln Rd Fl 7
Miami Beach, FL 33139-2900, USA

Rivera, Mariano (Baseball Player)
New York Yankees
147 Anderson Hill Rd
Purchase, NY 10577-2007, USA

Rivera, Ron (Football Player)
Chicago Bears
14420 Rancho Del Prado Trl
San Diego, CA 92127-3866, USA

Rivera Carrera, Norberto Cardinal (Religious Leader)
Curia Arzobispal
Aptdo Postal 24-4-33
Mexico City, DF 06700, MEXICO

Rivero, Jorge (Actor)
H David Moss
733 Seward St Ph
Los Angeles, CA 90038-3503, USA

Rivers, Glenn (Doc) (Basketball Player, Coach)
5 Isle Of Sicily
Winter Park, FL 32789-1505, USA

Rivers, Jamie (Football Player)
St Louis Cardinals
4006 Lindell Blvd
Saint Louis, MO 63108-3202, USA

Rivers, Joan (Comedian, Producer)
PO Box 49774
Los Angeles, CA 90049-0774, USA

Rivers, Johnny (Musician, Songwriter, Writer)
3141 Coldwater Canyon Ln
Beverly Hills, CA 90210-1250, USA

Rivers, Marcellus (Football Player)
New York Giants
12003 Eden Ln
Frisco, TX 75034-1146, USA

Rivers, Melissa (Talk Show Host)
c/o Tim Curtis *William Morris Agency (WMA-LA)*
1 William Morris Pl
Beverly Hills, CA 90212-4261, USA

Rivers, Mickey (Baseball Player)
California Angels
350 NW 48th St
Miami, FL 33127-2459, USA

Rivers, Philip (Football Player)
San Diego Chargers
4020 Murphy Canyon Rd
San Diego, CA 92123-4407, USA

Rivers, Reggie (Football Player)
Denver Broncos
5003 E Weaver Pl
Centennial, CO 80121-3520, USA

Riverside, Vincent
c/o Melanie Sharp-Snyder *Sharp Talent*
117 N Orlando Ave
Los Angeles, CA 90048-3403, USA

Rives, Don (Football Player)
Chicago Bears
603 E Garfield Ave
Morton, TX 79346-4106, USA

Rivest, Ronald (Scientist)
Massachusetts Institute of Technology
77 Massachusetts Ave Technology
Cambridge, MA 02139-4307, USA

Rivette, Jacques (Director)
20 Blvd de la Bastille
Paris 75012, FRANCE

Riviere, Marie
5 rue Edmond Gondinet
Paris 75013, FRANCE

Rivlin, Alice M (Government Official)
2842 Chesterfield Pl NW
Washington, DC 20008-1015, USA

Rizzo, Jack (Football Player)
New York Giants
1105 Forest Trails Dr
Castle Rock, CO 80108-8280, USA

Rizzo, Joe (Football Player)
Denver Broncos
6131 Dorsett Pl
Wilmington, NC 28403-0128, USA

Rizzo, Patti (Golfer)
2455 Provence Cir
Weston, FL 33327-1303, USA

Rizzo, Rizzo (DJ)
c/o Len Evans *Project Publicity*
312 W 53rd St
New York, NY 10019-5743, USA

Rizzo, Todd (Baseball Player)
Chicago White Sox
7 Williamsburg Ct
Sewell, NJ 08080-3230, USA

Rizzo-Depardon, Patti (Golfer)
1008 SE 5th Ct
Ft Lauderdale, FL 33301-3004, USA

Rizzotti, Jennifer (Basketball Player, Coach)
University of Hartford
Athletic Dept
West Hartford, CT 06117, USA

Roa, Joe (Baseball Player)
Cleveland Indians
677 E Brickley Ave
Hazel Park, MI 48030-1270, USA

Roa Bastos, Augusto (Writer)
Berutti 2828
Martinez
Buenos Aires, ARGENTINA

Roach, Jason (Baseball Player)
New York Mets
11031 Louson Pl
Raleigh, NC 27614-6729, USA

Roach, Jay (Director)
International Creative Mgmt
8942 Wilshire Blvd # 219
Beverly Hills, CA 90211-1908, USA

Roach, John (Football Player)
Chicago Cardinals
4101 San Carlos St
Dallas, TX 75205-2047, USA

Roach, Mel (Baseball Player)
Milwaukee Braves
4131 Southaven Rd
Richmond, VA 23235-1026, USA

Roach, Steve (Musician)
Hearts of Space
PO Box 5916
Sausalito, CA 94966-5916, USA

Roache, Linus (Actor)
c/o Staff Member *Endeavor Agency LLC (LA)*
9601 Wilshire Blvd Fl 3
Beverly Hills, CA 90210-5204, USA

Roaches, Carl (Football Player)
Houston Oilers
1314 Twining Oaks Ln
Missouri City, TX 77489-2110, USA

Roaf, William L (Willie) (Football Player)
New Orleans Saints
1900 E 38th Ave
Pine Bluff, AR 71601-7280, USA

Roan, Michael (Football Player)
Houston Oilers
11275 Green Valley Rd
Sebastopol, CA 95472-9771, USA

Roan, Oscar (Football Player)
Cleveland Browns
9 Pringle Ln
Rockwall, TX 75087-8004, USA

Roark, Terry P (Educator)
1752 Edward Dr
Laramie, WY 82072-2331, USA

Roarke, Mike (Baseball Player)
Detroit Tigers
11 Roseview Dr
Cranston, RI 02920-3124, USA

Roath, Stephen D (Business Person)
Longs Drug Stores
141 N Civic Dr
Walnut Creek, CA 94596-3815, USA

Robards, Jake
350 Willow St
Southport, CT 06890-1430, USA

Robards, Sam (Actor)
Rigberg Roberts Rugolo
1180 S Beverly Dr Ste 601
Los Angeles, CA 90035-1158, USA

Robb, Annasophia (Actor)
c/o Mitchell Gossett *Cunningham Escott Slevin & Doherty (LA)*
10635 Santa Monica Blvd Ste 130
Los Angeles, CA 90025-8306, USA

Robb, David (Actor)
William Morris Agency
151 El Camino Dr
Beverly Hills, CA 90212-2775, USA

Robb, Doug (Musician)
c/o Jenna Adler *Creative Artists Agency LCC (CAA-LA)*
2000 Avenue Of The Stars
Los Angeles, CA 90067-4700, USA

Robb, Lynda Johnson
612 Chain Bridge Rd
McLean, VA 22101-1810, USA

Robb, Walter L (Business Person, Inventor)
1358 Ruffner Rd
Niskayuna, NY 12309-2500, USA

Robbe-Grillet, Alain (Director, Writer)
18 Blvd Maillot
Neuilly-sur-Seine 92200, FRANCE

Robbers on High Street (Music Group)
c/o Staff Member *Paradigm (Monterey)*
509 Hartnell St
Monterey, CA 93940-2825, USA

Robbie, Seymour
9980 Liebe Dr
Beverly Hills, CA 90210-1037, USA

Robbie, Timothy J (Tim) (Football Executive)
Miami Dolphins
7500 SW 30th St
Davie, FL 33314-1020, USA

Robbins, Amy (Actor)
c/o Staff Member *Artists Rights Group (ARG London)*
4 Great Portland St
London W1W 8PA, UNITED KINGDOM (UK)

Robbins, Austin (Football Player)
Oakland Raiders
4627 Hilltop Ter SE
Washington, DC 20019-7837, USA

Robbins, Barret (Football Player)
Oakland Raiders
26186 Shadow Rock Ln
Valencia, CA 91381-0654, USA

Robbins, Brian (Director)
7743 Woodrow Wilson Dr
Los Angeles, CA 90046-1211, USA

Robbins, Bruce (Baseball Player)
Detroit Tigers
19311 Morrison Way
Noblesville, IN 46060-1173, USA

Robbins, Deanna (Actor)
630 N Keystone St
Burbank, CA 91506-1922, USA

Robbins, Doug (Baseball Player)
US Olympic Team
7655 W Randolph County Line
Williamsburg, IN 47393-9500, USA

Robbins, Jane (Actor)
Scott Marshall Mgmt
44 Perry Road
London W3 7NA, UNITED KINGDOM (UK)

Robbins, Kelly (Golfer)
1025 Lincoln Dr
Weidman, MI 48893-9365, USA

Robbins, Lizz (Model)
c/o Michael (Mike) Esterman *Esterman Entertainment*
214 Park Rd
Riva, MD 21140-1224, USA

Robbins, Mary
PO Box 641032
Miami, FL 33164-1032, USA

Robbins, Randy (Athlete, Football Player)
Denver Broncos
1131 E Valle Vista Dr
Nogales, AZ 85621-1229, USA

Robbins, Tim (Actor, Director)
c/o Rick Kurtzman *Creative Artists Agency LCC (CAA-LA)*
2000 Avenue Of The Stars
Los Angeles, CA 90067-4700, USA

Robbins, Tom (Writer)
PO Box 338
La Conner, WA 98257-0338, USA

Robbins, Tony (Writer)
Jennifer Martinez
9888 Carroll Centre Rd
San Diego, CA 92126-4579, USA

Robbins, Tootie (Football Player)
St Louis Cardinals
6712 W Shannon St
Chandler, AZ 85226-1669, USA

Robby Krieger Band (Music Group)
c/o Sammy Boyd *dv8 Entertainment & Productions*
208 Main St Ste 202
Asbury Park, NJ 07712-7033, USA

Robelot, Jane (Correspondent)
CBS-TV
51 W 52nd St
News Dept
New York, NY 10019-6119, USA

Robens of Woldingham, Alfred (Educator, Government Official)
2 Laleham Abbey
Staines, Middx TW18 1SZ, UNITED KINGDOM (UK)

Roberge, Bert (Baseball Player)
Houston Astros
267 Sunderland Dr
Auburn, ME 04210-9232, USA

Roberson, Antoinette (Musician)
c/o Staff Member *Diva Central Inc*
7510 W Sunset Blvd Ste 1445
Los Angeles, CA 90046-3408, USA

Roberson, Irvin (Bo) (Athlete, Football Player, Track Athlete)
San Diego Chargers
820 N Raymond Ave Apt 47
Pasadena, CA 91103-3151, USA

Roberson, James (Football Player)
Houston Oilers
417 Labarre Ct
Saint Johns, FL 32259-4024, USA

Roberson, James W (Cinematographer)
PO Box 121013
Big Bear Lake, CA 92315-8948, USA

Roberson, Kevin (Baseball Player)
Chicago Cubs
1565 E North Port Rd
Decatur, IL 62526-2823, USA

Roberson, Sid (Baseball Player)
Milwaukee Brewers
132 Tulip Tree Ct
Jupiter, FL 33458-7179, USA

Robert, Jacques F (Attorney, Attorney General, General)
14 Villa Saint-Georges
Antony 92160, FRANCE

Robert, Rene (Hockey Player)
4020 Rue Savard
Troie Rivieres, PQ G8Y 4B8, CANADA

Roberts, Alfredo (Football Player)
Kansas City Chiefs
20406 Donegal Ln
Strongsville, OH 44149-0960, USA

Roberts, Bernard (Musician)
Uwchlaw'r Coed
Llanbedr
Gwynedd, WALES LL45 2NA, UNITED KINGDOM (UK)

Roberts, Bert C Jr (Business Person)
MCI WorldCom Inc
500 Clinton Blvd
Clinton, MS 39056, USA

Roberts, Beverly
30912 Ariana Ln
Laguna Niguel, CA 92677-2786, USA

Roberts, Bill (Football Player)
Green Bay Packers
5901 Amy Dr
Minneapolis, MN 55436-1933, USA

Roberts, Brad (Musician)
Macklam Feldman Mgmt
1505 W 2nd Ave
#200
Vancouver, BC V6H 3Y4, CANADA

Roberts, Brian L (Business Person)
Comcast
1500 Market St Fl 33E
Philadelphia, PA 19102-4782, USA

Roberts, Bruce (Musician, Songwriter, Writer)
c/o Staff Member *Gorfaine/Schwartz Agency Inc*
4111 W Alameda Ave Ste 509
Burbank, CA 91505-4171, USA

Roberts, Cecil (Misc)
United Mine Workers
8315 Lee Hwy Fl 5
Fairfax, VA 22031-2215, USA

Roberts, Corrine (Cookie) (Correspondent)
5315 Bradley Blvd
Bethesda, MD 20814-1244, USA

Roberts, Danny (Reality TV Star)
c/o Staff Member *Bunim/Murray Productions Inc*
6007 Sepulveda Blvd
Van Nuys, CA 91411-2502, USA

Roberts, David (Dave) (Athlete, Track Athlete)
14310 SW 73rd Ave
Archer, FL 32618-2914, USA

Roberts, Dee (Artist)
2012 N 19th St
Boise, ID 83702-0821, USA

Roberts, Doris (Actor)
c/o Michael R Cannata *Swimma Productions Inc (SPI)*
1840 S Elena Ave Ste 200
Redondo Beach, CA 90277-5717, USA

Roberts, Emma (Actor)
c/o David Sweeney *Sweeney Management*
8755 Lookout Mountain Ave
Los Angeles, CA 90046-1861, USA

Roberts, Eric (Actor)
c/o Mark Teitelbaum *Teitelbaum Artists Group*
8840 Wilshire Blvd # 200
Beverly Hills, CA 90211-2606, USA

Roberts, Eugene L Jr (Educator)
New York Times
229 W 43rd St
Editorial Dept
New York, NY 10036-3959, USA

Roberts, Gary (Hockey Player)
Wooden Sticks
PO Box 848 Station Main
Uxbridge, PM L9P 1N2, CANADA

Roberts, Gene (Football Player)
New York Giants
10803 E 49 Highway
Independence, MO 64055, USA

Roberts, Gordon R (War Hero)
445 Ward Koebel Rd
Oregonia, OH 45054-9468, USA

Roberts, Gregory David (Writer)
c/o Staff Member *United Talent Agency (UTA)*
9560 Wilshire Blvd Ste 500
Beverly Hills, CA 90212-2401, USA

Roberts, H Edward (Ed) (Designer)
Bleckley Memorial Hospital
145 E Peacock St
Cochran, GA 31014-7846, USA

Roberts, Jake
PO Box 3859
Stamford, CT 06905, USA

Roberts, James A (Jim) (Coach, Hockey Player)
137 Ridgecrest Dr
Chesterfield, MO 63017-2653, USA

Roberts, John (Director)
c/o Staff Member *International Creative Management (ICM-UK)*
Oxford House
76 Oxford St
London W1N OAX, UNITED KINGDOM (UK)

Roberts, John (Judge)
US Supreme Court
1st St NE
Washington, DC 20543-0001, USA

Roberts, John D (Misc)
California Institute of Technology
Chemistry Dept
Pasadena, CA 91125-0001, USA

Roberts, John D (J D) (Coach, Football Player)
6708 Trevi Ct
Oklahoma City, OK 73116-2604, USA

Roberts, Julia (Actor)
c/o Richard Lovett *Creative Artists Agency LCC (CAA-LA)*
2000 Avenue Of The Stars
Los Angeles, CA 90067-4700, USA

Roberts, Julie (Musician)
c/o Staff Member *Universal Music Group (TN)*
60 Music Sq E
Nashville, TN 37203-4325, USA

Roberts, Kenny (Motorcycle Race, Motorcycle Racer)
KR Marketing
419 Medina Rd
Medina, OH 44256-9619, USA

Roberts, Kevin (Business Person)
Saatchi & saatchi Worldwide
375 Hudson St
New York, NY 10014-3658, USA

Roberts, Lawrence G (Scientist)
Caspian Networks
101 University Ave Ste 100
Palo Alto, CA 94301-1638, USA

Roberts, Leonard (Actor)
c/o Todd Sharp *Bedlam Media*
9299 Sunset Blvd #810
Beverly Hills, CA 90069, USA

Roberts, Leonard (Business Person)
Tandy Corp
100 Throckmorton St
Fort Worth, TX 76102-2870, USA

Roberts, Loren (Golfer)
8429 Orchard Hill Dr
Germantown, TN 38138-6297, USA

Roberts, Louie
2401 12th Ave S
Nashville, TN 37204-2415, USA

Roberts, Lynn
42 Vespers Way
Okatie, SC 29909-6216, USA

Roberts, M Brigitte (Writer)
Atkins & Stone
29 Fernshaw Road
London SW10 0TG, UNITED KINGDOM
(UK)

Roberts, Marcus (Musician)
Columbia Artists Mgmt Inc
1790 Broadway Fl 6
New York, NY 10019-1412, USA

Roberts, Michael
76 Oxford St.
London, ENGLAND W1N OAX, UNITED
KINGDOM (UK)

Roberts, Michael D (Actor)
Renna Management
501 W Glenoaks Blvd # 446
Glendale, CA 91202-2896, USA

Roberts, Nora (Writer)
19239 Burnside Bridge Rd
Keedysville, MD 21756-1603, USA

Roberts, Oral (Misc)
Oral Roberts University
7777 S Lewis Ave
Tulsa, OK 74171-0001, USA

Roberts, Pernell (Actor)
20395 Seaboard Rd
Malibu, CA 90265-5347, USA

Roberts, R Michael (Scientist)
2213 Hominy Branch Ct
Columbia, MO 65201-6113, USA

Roberts, Rachel (Actor, Model)
c/o Staff Member *Models 1*
12 Macklin Street
Covent Gardens
London WC2B 5SZ, UNITED KINGDOM
(UK)

Roberts, Ralph J (Business Person)
Comcast Corp
1500 Market St
Philadelphia, PA 19102-2196, USA

Roberts, Richard J (Nobel Prize Laureate)
New England Biolabs
32 Tozer Rd
Beverly, MA 01915-5599, USA

Roberts, Richard L (Educator)
Oral Roberts University
President's Office
7777 S Lewis Ave
Tulsa, OK 74171-0001, USA

Roberts, Rick
9150 Wilshire Blvd Ste 350
Beverly Hills, CA 90212-3453, USA

Roberts, Robin (Baseball Player)
504 Terrace Hill Dr
Tampa, FL 33617-3850, USA

Roberts, Robin (Sportscaster, Television
Host)
c/o Staff Member *Good Morning America
(NY)*
147 Columbus Ave Fl 6
Abc
New York, NY 10023-6503, USA

Roberts, Stanley (Basketball Player)
1192 Congaree Rd
Hopkins, SC 29061-9704, USA

Roberts, Steven
5315 Bradley Blvd
Bethesda, MD 20814-1244, USA

Roberts, Tanya (Actor)
c/o Staff Member *The Artists Group Ltd
(LA)*
1650 Broadway Ste 610
New York, NY 10019-6833, USA

Roberts, Thomas (Anchor)
c/o Staff Member *CNN (Atlanta)*
1 Cnn Ctr NW
PO Box 105366
Atlanta, GA 30303-2762, USA

Roberts, Tim (Football Player)
Houston Oilers
3930 Minnow Rd
Rex, GA 30273-1536, USA

Roberts, Tony (Actor)
970 Park Ave # 8N
New York, NY 10028-0324, USA

Roberts, Trish (Basketball Player)
218 Carver Dr
Monroe, GA 30655-1814, USA

Roberts, Walter (Football Player)
Cleveland Browns
268 Kenbrook Cir
San Jose, CA 95111-3262, USA

Roberts, William H (Football Player)
New York Giants
18520 NW 67th Ave # 141
Hialeah, FL 33015-3302, USA

Roberts, Xavier (Business Person,
Designer)
PO Box 1438
Cleveland, GA 30528-0027, USA

Robertson, Alvin C (Basketball Player)
3 Bimam Oaks
San Antonio, TX 78248, USA

Robertson, Belinda (Designer, Fashion
Designer)
BR Cashmere
22 Palmerston Place
Edinburgh EH12 5AL, SCOTLAND

Robertson, Bob (Football Player)
Brooklyn Dodgers
411 Belle Monti Ct
Aptos, CA 95003-5208, USA

Robertson, Cliff (Actor)
c/o Jack Gilardi *International Creative
Management (ICM-LA)*
10250 Constellation Blvd
Los Angeles, CA 90067-6200, USA

Robertson, Dale (Actor)
PO Box 850707
Yukon, OK 73085-0707, USA

Robertson, Davis (Dancer)
Joffrey Ballet
70 E Lake St Ste 1300
Chicago, IL 60601-7458, USA

Robertson, DeWayne (Football Player)
New York Jets
1000 Fulton Ave
Hempstead, NY 11550-1030, USA

Robertson, Georgina (Model)
Compagny
270 Lafayette St Ste 1400
New York, NY 10012-3364, USA

Robertson, Gordon (Religious Leader,
Television Host)
c/o Staff Member *700 Club*
Christian Broadcasting Network
977 Centerville Turnpike
Virginia Beach, VT 23463, USA

Robertson, Isiah (Football Player)
Los Angeles Rams
PO Box 1405
Mabank, TX 75147-1405, USA

Robertson, Jamie Robbie (Actor,
Musician, Producer)
c/o Staff Member *Creative Artists Agency
LCC (CAA-LA)*
2000 Avenue Of The Stars
Los Angeles, CA 90067-4700, USA

Robertson, Jenny (Actor)
Shelter Entertainment
9255 W Sunset Blvd Ste 1010
Los Angeles, CA 90069-3307, USA

Robertson, Kathleen (Actor)
c/o Staff Member *Jeff Morrone
Management*
9350 Wilshire Blvd Ste 224
Beverly Hills, CA 90212-3204, USA

Robertson, Kimmy (Actor)
Commercials Unlimited
190 N Canon Dr Ste 302
Beverly Hills, CA 90210-5314, USA

Robertson, Lisa
1365 Enterprise Dr
West Chester, PA 19380-5959, USA

Robertson, Marcus A (Football Player)
Houston Oilers
3218 Cypress Point Dr
Missouri City, TX 77459-3634, USA

Robertson, Oscar
621 Tusculum Ave
Cincinnati, OH 45226-1771, USA

Robertson, Pat (Religious Leader,
Television Host)
c/o Staff Member *700 Club*
Christian Broadcasting Network
977 Centerville Turnpike
Virginia Beach, VT 23463, USA

Robertson, Robbie (Musician, Songwriter,
Writer)
323 14th St
Santa Monica, CA 90402-2113, USA

Robes, Ernest C (Bill) (Skier)
3 Mile Road
Etna, NH 03750, USA

Robie, Carl (Swimmer)
2525 Sunnybrook Dr
Sarasota, FL 34239-4729, USA

Robinowitz, Joseph R (Editor, Publisher)
TV Guide Magazine
Editorial Dept
100 Matsonford Road
Wayne, PA 19080-0001, USA

Robins, Lee N (Scientist)
Washington University
Medical School
Psychiatry Dept
Saint Louis, MO 63110, USA

Robinson, Alexia
3500 W Olive Ave Ste 920
Burbank, CA 91505-5514, USA

Robinson, Andrew (Actor)
2671 Byron Pl
Los Angeles, CA 90046-1021, USA

Robinson, Ann (Actor)
1357 Elysian Park Dr
Los Angeles, CA 90026-3407, USA

Robinson, Anne (Actor, Entertainer)
Penrose Media
19 Victoria Grove
London W8 5RW, UNITED KINGDOM
(UK)

Robinson, Arthur H (Misc)
7707 N Brookline Dr Apt 302
Madison, WI 53719-3526, USA

Robinson, Bo (Football Player)
Detroit Lions
PO Box 2323
Coppell, TX 75019-8323, USA

Robinson, Brooks (Baseball Player)
PO Box 1168
Baltimore, MD 21203-1168, USA

Robinson, Bumper (Actor)
14135 Regina Dr
Rancho Cucamonga, CA 91739-5117,
USA

Robinson, Charles
10000 Santa Monica Blvd # 305
Los Angeles, CA 90067, USA

Robinson, Charles Knox
10637 Burbank Blvd
N Hollywood, CA 91601-2512, USA

Robinson, Chip (Race Car Driver)
3034 Lake Forest Dr
Augusta, GA 30909-3081, USA

Robinson, Chris (Actor)
Mitch Schneider Organization
14724 Ventura Blvd Ste 710
C/O Todd Brodginski
Sherman Oaks, CA 91403-3520, USA

Robinson, Chris (Director)
c/o Peter Safran *The Safran Company*
2000 Avenue Of The Stars Ste 600N
Los Angeles, CA 90067-4708, USA

Robinson, Chris (Musician)
c/o Staff Member *Paradigm (Monterey)*
509 Hartnell St
Monterey, CA 93940-2825, USA

Robinson, Clarence (Arnie) (Athlete,
Track Athlete)
2904 Ocean View Blvd
San Diego, CA 92113-1336, USA

Robinson, Cliff (Basketball Player)
98 S Bardsbrook Cir
Spring, TX 77382-2858, USA

Robinson, Clifford (Basketball Player)
PO Box 3357
San Ramon, CA 94583-8357, USA

Robinson, Daniel (Baseball Player)
10889 Dauphine St
Shreveport, LA 71106-8524, USA

Robinson, David M (Basketball Player)
c/o Staff Member *San Antonio Spurs*
100 Montana St
Alamodome
San Antonio, TX 78203-1031, USA

Robinson, Dawn (Musician)
William Morris Agency
151 El Camino Dr
Beverly Hills, CA 90212-2775, USA

Robinson, Dwight P (Financier)
Government National Mortgage Assn
451 7th St SW
Washington, DC 20410-0001, USA

Robinson, Elizabeth
12706 E Pacific Cir # 202
Aurora, CO 80014, USA

Robinson, Emily (Musician)
c/o Staff Member *Creative Artists Agency
LCC (CAA-LA)*
2000 Avenue Of The Stars
Los Angeles, CA 90067-4700, USA

Robinson, Emily Erwin (Football Player)
Atlanta Falcons
4400 Falcon Pkwy
Flowery Branch, GA 30542-3176, USA

Robinson, Fatima
Fatima
8306 Wilshire Blvd
Pmb 833
Beverly Hills, CA 90211-2304, USA

Robinson, Flynn (Basketball Player)
11875 Manor Dr # 1
Hawthorne, CA 90250-2950, USA

Robinson, Frank (Baseball Player)
15557 Aqua Verde Dr
Los Angeles, CA 90077-1503, USA

Robinson, Frank (Football Player)
Cincinnati Bengals
15401 E Wyoming Dr Unit C
Aurora, CO 80017-4727, USA

Robinson, Gerald (Football Player)
Minnesota Vikings
4708 Scarborough Pl
Stone Mountain, GA 30087-4104, USA

Robinson, Glenn (Basketball Player,
Coach)
Franklin & Marshall College
Athletic Dept
Lancaster, PA 17604, USA

Robinson, Jacob (Baseball Player)
Chicago American Giants
1300 Giddings Ave SE
Grand Rapids, MI 49506-3216, USA

Robinson, James (Baseball Player)
Philadelphia Stars
65 W 96th St Apt 22G
New York, NY 10025-6533, USA

Robinson, Janice (Musician)
c/o Staff Member *Diva Central Inc*
7510 W Sunset Blvd Ste 1445
Los Angeles, CA 90046-3408, USA

Robinson, Jay (Actor)
13757 Milbank St
Sherman Oaks, CA 91423-2966, USA

Robinson, Jerry (Football Player)
Philadelphia Bengals
1408 Fairoaks Ct
Merced, CA 95340-2341, USA

Robinson, John A (Coach, Football
Coach)
6991 Goldstone Rd
Carlsbad, CA 92009-1711, USA

Robinson, Johnny N (Football Player)
Dallas Texans
3209 S Grand St
Monroe, LA 71202-5225, USA

Robinson, Keith (Actor)
c/o Staff Member *Stone Manners Talent &
Literary (LA)*
6500 Wilshire Blvd Ste 550
Los Angeles, CA 90048-4950, USA

Robinson, Keith (Musician)
c/o Staff Member *Paradigm (NY)*
360 Park Ave S Fl 16
New York, NY 10010-1716, USA

Robinson, Kenneth (Government Official)
12 Grove Terrace
London NW5, UNITED KINGDOM (UK)

Robinson, Koren (Football Player)
Seattle Seahawks
12 Henry Ave
Belmont, NC 28012-3930, USA

Robinson, Larry (Coach, Hockey Player)
10709 Winding Stream Way
Bradenton, FL 34212-5255, USA

Robinson, Laura (Actor)
Henderson/Hogan
8285 W Sunset Blvd Ste 1
West Hollywood, CA 90046-2420, USA

Robinson, Leon (Leon) (Actor, Producer)
c/o Staff Member *Rigberg-Rugolo
Entertainment*
1180 S Beverly Dr Ste 601
Los Angeles, CA 90035-1158, USA

Robinson, Madeleine
63 av. de Chillon
Territet-Veytaux D1820, SWITZERLAND

Robinson, Marcus (Football Player)
Chicago Bears
PO Box 1924
Fort Valley, GA 31030-1924, USA

Robinson, Mark (Football Player)
Kansas City Chiefs
303 Pennsylvania Ave
Palm Harbor, FL 34683-5222, USA

Robinson, Mary (President)
Aras an Uachtarain
Phoenix Park
Dublin 8, IRELAND

Robinson, Matt (Football Player)
New York Jets
12374 Mandarin Rd
Jacksonville, FL 32223-1892, USA

Robinson, Nichole (Actor)
c/o Tiffany Kuzon *Evolution Entertainment
(LA)*
901 N Highland Ave
Los Angeles, CA 90038-2412, USA

Robinson, Patrick (Designer, Fashion
Designer)
Ann Klein Co
11 W 42nd St Ste 2300
New York, NY 10036-8002, USA

Robinson, Patrick (Football Player)
Cincinnati Bengals
3875 N Advantage Way Dr Apt 104
Memphis, TN 38128-7239, USA

Robinson, Paul (Football Player)
Cincinnati Bengals
1303 W 26th St
Safford, AZ 85546-3721, USA

Robinson, Paul Michael
11300 W Olympic Blvd Ste 610
Los Angeles, CA 90064-1643, USA

Robinson, Rachel (Actor, Reality TV Star)
c/o Staff Member *Bunim/Murray
Productions Inc*
6007 Sepulveda Blvd
Van Nuys, CA 91411-2502, USA

Robinson, Rafael (Football Player)
Seattle Seahawks
6203 Wynbrook Dr
Randolph, NJ 07869-1287, USA

Robinson, Randall
1744 R St NW
Washington, DC 20009-2410, USA

Robinson, Rich (Musician)
c/o Staff Member *Paradigm (Monterey)*
509 Hartnell St
Monterey, CA 93940-2825, USA

Robinson, Richard D (Dave) (Football
Player)
Green Bay Packers
406 S Rose Blvd
Akron, OH 44320-1308, USA

Robinson, Robinson (Director)
c/o Peter Safran *The Safran Company*
2000 Avenue Of The Stars Ste 600N
Los Angeles, CA 90067-4708, USA

Robinson, Rumeal (Basketball Player)
Detroit Pistons
2 Championship Dr
Palace
Auburn Hills, MI 48326-1753, USA

Robinson, Sammy (Baseball Player)
Detroit Stars
503 Umatilla St SE
Grand Rapids, MI 49507-1218, USA

Robinson, Shaun (Correspondent)
c/o Staff Member *Access Hollywood*
Nbc
3000 W Alameda Ave Trailer E
Burbank, CA 91523-0001, USA

Robinson, Shawna (Race Car Driver)
Performance One
545 Pitts School Rd NW # C
Concord, NC 28027, USA

Robinson, Shelton (Football Player)
Seattle Seahawks
18725 20th Dr SE
Bothell, WA 98012-8721, USA

Robinson, Stacy (Football Player)
New York Giants
2409 Starcrest Dr
Silver Spring, MD 20904-5459, USA

Robinson, Stephen K (Astronaut)
2405 Airline Dr
Friendswood, TX 77546-5509, USA

Robinson, T Wayne
PO Box 249
Mc Connellsburg, PA 17233-0249, USA

Robinson, Tony (Football Player)
Washington Redskins
728 Efferson St
Tallahassee, FL 32303-5321, USA

Robinson, V Gene (Religious Leader)
Saint Paul's Church
21 Centre St
Concord, NH 03301-6301, USA

Robinson, Wendy Raquel (Actor)
c/o Patty Woo *HWA Talent*
3500 W Olive Ave Ste 1400
Burbank, CA 91505-5512, USA

Robinson, William (Smokey) (Musician,
Producer, Songwriter, Writer)
c/o Staff Member *William Morris Agency
(WMA-LA)*
1 William Morris Pl
Beverly Hills, CA 90212-4261, USA

Robinson, Zuleikha (Actor)
c/o Daniel (Dan) Spilo *Artistry
Management*
525 Westbourne Dr
West Hollywood, CA 90048-1913, USA

Robinson of Woolwich, John (Religious
Leader)
Trinity College
Cambridge CB2 1TQ, UNITED
KINGDOM (UK)

Robinson-Peete, Holly (Actor)
11964 Crest Pl
Beverly Hills, CA 90210-1341, USA

Robisch, Dave (Basketball Player)
1401 Guemes Ct
Springfield, IL 62702-6400, USA

Robiskie, Terry (Football Player)
Oakland Raiders
333 Las Olas Way Apt 910
Fort Lauderdale, FL 33301-4300, USA

Robison, Bruce (Musician, Songwriter,
Writer)
Artists Envoy Agency
1016 16th Ave S Apt 101
Nashville, TN 37212-2315, USA

Robison, Charlie (Musician, Songwriter)
c/o Staff Member *Paradigm (Monterey)*
509 Hartnell St
Monterey, CA 93940-2825, USA

Robison, Paula (Musician)
Matthew Sprizzo
18 Allison Ave
Staten Island, NY 10306-2806, USA

Robison, Tommy (Football Player)
Green Bay Packers
4102 Adams Rd
Milton, FL 32571-9331, USA

Robitaille, Luc (Hockey Player)
13801 Ventura Blvd
Sherman Oaks, CA 91423-3603, USA

Robl, Harold (Football Player)
Chicago Cardinals
W1089 County Road C
Gleason, WI 54435-9472, USA

Robles, Jorge (Actor)
c/o Staff Member *Televisa*
Blvd Adolfo Lopez Mateos 232
Colonia San Angel INN
DF CP 01060, MEXICO

Robles, Marisa (Musician)
38 Luttrll Ave
London SW15 6PE, UNITED KINGDOM
(UK)

Robles, Mike (Producer)
ICM
8942 Wilshire Blvd
Beverly Hills, CA 90211-1908, USA

Roboz, Zsuzsi (Artist)
6 Bryanston Court
George St
London W1H 7HA, UNITED KINGDOM
(UK)

Robson, Bryan (Soccer Player)
Middlesbrough FC
Riverside Stadium
Midds
Cleveland TS3 6RS, UNITED KINGDOM
(UK)

Robson, Wade (Actor, Dancer, Musician, Producer)
c/o Eddy Yablans *International Creative Management (ICM-LA)*
10250 Constellation Blvd
Los Angeles, CA 90067-6200, USA

Robuchon, Joel (Chef)
Societe de Gestion Culinaire
67 Blvd du Gen M Valin
Paris 75015, FRANCE

Robustelli, Andrew R (Andy) (Football Player)
Los Angeles Rams
30 Spring St
Stamford, CT 06901-1701, USA

Robyn (Musician)
Lifeline
73C Saint Charles Square
London W10 6EJ, UNITED KINGDOM
(UK)

Rocard, Michel L L (Prime Minister)
Hotel de Ville
63 Rue M Berteaux
Conflans-Sainte-Honorine 78700, FRANCE

Rocca, Constantino (Golfer)
Golf Products International
5719 Lake Lindero Dr
Agoura Hills, CA 91301-1444, USA

Rocca, Mo (Correspondent)
c/o Staff Member *Creative Artists Agency LCC (CAA-LA)*
2000 Avenue Of The Stars
Los Angeles, CA 90067-4700, USA

Rocca, Peter (Swimmer)
534 Hazel Ave
San Bruno, CA 94066-4228, USA

Rocco, Alex (Actor)
20518 Pacific Coast Hwy
Malibu, CA 90265-5402, USA

Rocco, Rinaldo (Actor)
Carol Levi Co
Via Giuseppe Pisanelli
Rome 00196, ITALY

Rocha, Enrique (Actor)
c/o Staff Member *Televisa*
Blvd Adolfo Lopez Mateos 232
Colonia San Angel INN
DF CP 01060, MEXICO

Rocha, Ephraim (Red) (Basketball Player, Coach)
4970 SW Hollyhock Cir
Corvallis, OR 97333-1773, USA

Rocha, Kali (Actor)
c/o Katie Rhodes *Untitled Entertainment (LA)*
331 N Maple Dr Fl 3
Beverly Hills, CA 90210-3827, USA

Rochberg, George (Composer)
3500 West Chester Pike # Ch118
Newtown Square, PA 19073-4101, USA

Roche, Alden (Football Player)
Denver Broncos
1082 Farragut St
New Orleans, LA 70114-2810, USA

Roche, Anthony D (Tony) (Tennis Player)
5 Kapiti St
Saint Ives, NSW 2075, AUSTRALIA

Roche, Brian (Football Player)
San Diego Chargers
1358 Oak Tree Cir
Chino Hills, CA 91709-2231, USA

Roche, E Kevin (Architect)
Roche Dinkeloo Assoc
20 Davis St
Hamden, CT 06517-3599, USA

Roche, George A (Financier)
T Rowe Price Assoc
100 E Pratt St
Baltimore, MD 21202-1090, USA

Roche, James G (Secretary)
Air Force Department
Secretary's Office
Pentagon
Washington, DC 20310-0001, USA

Rochefort, Jean (Actor)
Le Chene Rogneaux
Grosvre 078125, FRANCE

Rochester, Paul (Football Player)
Dallas Texans
218 Evans Dr
Jacksonville, FL 32250-2631, USA

Rochon, Debbie (Actor)
PO Box 1299
New York, NY 10009-8958, USA

Rochon, Lela (Actor)
Gersh Agency
232 N Canon Dr
Beverly Hills, CA 90210-5302, USA

Rock (Actor, Wrestler)
World Wrestling Entertainment
1241 E Main St
Titan Towers
Stamford, CT 06902-3520, USA

Rock, Angela (Volleyball Player)
4771 Vista Ln
San Diego, CA 92116-2535, USA

Rock, Chris (Actor, Comedian, Director, Writer)
c/o Eric Gold *Mosaic Media Group*
4024 Radford Ave Bldg 3
Studio City, CA 91604-2101, USA

Rock, Tony (Comedian)
c/o Staff Member *William Morris Agency (WMA-LA)*
1 William Morris Pl
Beverly Hills, CA 90212-4261, USA

Rock, Walt (Football Player)
San Francisco 49ers
1030 Highams Ct
Woodbridge, VA 22191-1445, USA

Rockburne, Dorothea G (Artist)
140 Grand St
New York, NY 10013-3127, USA

Rockefeller, Laurance S (Misc)
Rockefeller Bros Fund
30 Rockefeller Plz # 5600
New York, NY 10112-0015, USA

Rockefeller, Sharon Percy
1940 Shepherd St NW
Washington, DC 20011, USA

Rockenbach, Lyle (Football Player)
Detroit Lions
25 State Road 13 # E9-E11
Jacksonville, FL 32259-2842, USA

Rocker, David (Football Player)
Los Angeles Rams
465 Belle Dr
Fayetteville, GA 30214-2703, USA

Rocker, John (Baseball Player)
1223 Manor Oaks Ct
Atlanta, GA 30338-2756, USA

Rockett, Rikki (Musician)
H K Mgmt
9200 W Sunset Blvd Ste 530
Los Angeles, CA 90069-3509, USA

Rockford, Jim (Football Player)
San Diego Chargers
1829 Camden St
Springfield, IL 62702-3201, USA

Rockwell, Martha (Coach, Skier)
Dartmouth College
PO Box 9
Hanover, NH 03755-0009, USA

Rockwell, Nancy (Baseball Player)
54658 County Road 101
Elkhart, IN 46514-8967, USA

Rockwell, Robert
18428 Coastline Dr
Malibu, CA 90265-5707, USA

Rockwell, Sam (Actor)
9 Desbrosses St Rm 200
New York, NY 10013-1701, USA

Rockwood, Marcia (Editor)
Reader's Digest
Editorial Dept
PO Box 100
Pleasantville, NY 10572-0001, USA

Rodan, Jay (Actor)
c/o Staff Member *William Morris Agency (WMA-LA)*
1 William Morris Pl
Beverly Hills, CA 90212-4261, USA

Roday, James (Actor, Writer)
c/o Stephen Hirsh *Gersh Agency, The (NY)*
41 Madison Ave Fl 33
New York, NY 10010-2202, USA

Rodd, Marcia (Actor)
11738 Moorpark St Apt C
Studio City, CA 91604-2116, USA

Roddam, Franc (Director)
William Morris Agency
52/53 Poland Place
London W1F 7LX, UNITED KINGDOM
(UK)

Roddick, Andy (Tennis Player)
c/o Collin Smeeton *SFX Sports*
5335 Wisconsin Ave NW Ste 850
Washington, DC 20015-2052, USA

Rodenhauser, Mark (Football Player)
Chicago Bears
1451 Charlotte Hwy
York, SC 29745-8947, USA

Roderick, Brande (Actor, Model)
c/o Darren Prince *Prince Marketing Group*
454 Prospect Ave # 74
West Orange, NJ 07052, USA

Rodgers, Anton
The White House Lower Basildon
Berkshire, ENGLAND, UNITED
KINGDOM (UK)

Rodgers, Del (Football Player)
Green Bay Packers
3112 Yosemite Park Way
Elk Grove, CA 95758-4687, USA

Rodgers, Derrick (Football Player)
Miami Dolphins
5550 SW 192nd Ter
Southwest Ranches, FL 33332-3333, USA

Rodgers, Jimmie
42230 Sandy Bay Rd
Bermuda Dunes, CA 92203-1394, USA

Rodgers, Johnny (Football Player)
San Diego Chargers
2011 Wirt St
Omaha, NE 68110-2051, USA

Rodgers, Michael (Actor)
c/o Adam Levine *Anthem Entertainment*
6100 Wilshire Blvd Ste 1170
Los Angeles, CA 90048-5116, USA

Rodgers, Paul (Musician)
Work Hard PR
19D Pinhold Road
London SW16 5GD, UNITED KINGDOM
(UK)

Rodgers, Phil (Golfer)
Eddle Elias Enterprises
3641 Bay Hill Dr
Akron, OH 44333-9227, USA

Rodin, Judith S (Educator)
35 Hillhouse Ave
New Haven, CT 06511-3703, USA

Rodman, Dennis (Athlete)
c/o Darren Prince *Prince Marketing Group*
454 Prospect Ave # 74
West Orange, NJ 07052, USA

Rodrigues, Blenvenido (Baseball Player)
Chicago American Giants
PO Box 42
Santa Isabel, PR 00757-0042, USA

Rodriguez, Adam (Actor)
c/o Abe Hoch *Magus Entertainment*
9107 Wilshire Blvd Ste 650
Beverly Hills, CA 90210-5544, USA

Rodriguez, Alexander E (Alex) (Baseball Player)
New York Yankees
Yankee Stadium
161st St & River Ave
Bronx, NY 10451, USA

Rodriguez, Anthony (Golfer)
13602 Summer Glen Dr
San Antonio, TX 78247-3510, USA

Rodriguez, Eduardo (President)
President's Office
Palacio de Gobierno
Plaza Murilla
La Paz, BOLIVIA

Rodriguez, Freddie (Actor)
c/o Staff Member *Innovative Artists (LA)*
1505 10th St
Santa Monica, CA 90401-2805, USA

Rodriguez, Freddy (Actor)
c/o Robbie Kass *Kass & Stokes Management*
9229 W Sunset Blvd Ste 504
Los Angeles, CA 90069-3405, USA

Rodriguez, Genesis (Actor)
c/o Staff Member *Select Artists Ltd (CA-Valley Office)*
PO Box 4359
Burbank, CA 91503-4359, USA

Rodriguez, Hector (Baseball Player)
New York Cubans
Taxistas Reg 92 Zona 6 Lote 75 Num
Cancun
Quintana Roo, MEXICO

Rodriguez, Ivan (Pudge) (Baseball Player)
c/o Staff Member *Detroit Tigers*
2100 Woodward Ave
Comerica Park
Detroit, MI 48201-3474, USA

Rodriguez, Jai (Television Host)
c/o Staff Member *Queer Eye for the
Straight Guy*
119 Braintree St
Boston, MA 02134-1628, USA

Rodriguez, Javier (Actor)
c/o Staff Member *Select Artists Ltd (CA-
Valley Office)*
PO Box 4359
Burbank, CA 91503-4359, USA

Rodriguez, Johnny
PO Box 23162
Nashville, TN 37202-3162, USA

Rodriguez, Jose Luis (El Puma) (Musician)
c/o Staff Member *BMG*
1540 Broadway
New York, NY 10036-4074, USA

Rodriguez, Juan (Chi Chi) (Athlete)
Eddie Elias Enterprises
3916 Clock Pointe Trl Ste 101
Stow, OH 44224-2932, USA

Rodriguez, Michelle (Actor)
c/o CeCe Yorke *True Public Relations*
6725 W Sunset Blvd Ste 570
Los Angeles, CA 90028-7180, USA

Rodriguez, Paul (Actor)
c/o Staff Member *International Creative
Management (ICM-LA)*
10250 Constellation Blvd
Los Angeles, CA 90067-6200, USA

Rodriguez, Ramon (Actor)
c/o Allan Grifka *The Collective*
9100 Wilshire Blvd # 700 W
Beverly Hills, CA 90212-3401, USA

Rodriguez, Robert (Director, Producer)
c/o Robert Newman *International Creative
Management (ICM-LA)*
10250 Constellation Blvd
Los Angeles, CA 90067-6200, USA

Roe, Bill (Football Player)
Dallas Cowboys
9931 E Ohio Ave
Denver, CO 80247-1958, USA

Roe, Elwin
3003 Gleghorn St
West Plains, MO 65775-1869, USA

Roe, John (Baseball Player)
704 Masala Dr Apt A
Orlando, FL 32818-7463, USA

Roe, Preacher (Baseball Player)
St Louis Cardinals
3003 Gleghorn St
West Plains, MO 65775-1869, USA

Roe, Tommy
PO Box 26037
Minneapolis, MN 55426-0037, USA

Roebuck, Daniel
PO Box 3462
Burbank, CA 91508-3462, USA

Roebuck, Ed (Baseball Player)
Brooklyn Dodgers
3434 Warwood Rd
Lakewood, CA 90712-3751, USA

Roedel, Herb (Football Player)
Oakland Raiders
4810 201st St
Flushing, NY 11364-1012, USA

Roeg, Nicolas
14 Courtnell St
London, ENGLAND W2 5BX, UNITED
KINGDOM (UK)

Roemer, Sarah (Actor, Model)
c/o Staff Member *Roklin Management*
8530 Wilshire Blvd Ste 550
Beverly Hills, CA 90211-3133, USA

Roenick, Jeremy (Hockey Player)
c/o Staff Member *Los Angeles Kings*
1111 S Figueroa St
Los Angeles, CA 90015-1300, USA

Roenicke, Gary (Baseball Player)
Montreal Expos
14152 Greenwood Ct
Nevada City, CA 95959, USA

Roenicke, Ron (Baseball Player)
Los Angeles Dodgers
2212 Avenida Las Ramblas
Chino Hills, CA 91709-1362, USA

Roesler, Mike (Baseball Player)
Cincinnati Reds
12033 Fallen Leaf Ct
Fort Wayne, IN 46845-8992, USA

Roethlisberger, Ben (Football Player)
c/o Staff Member *Pittsburgh Steelers*
3400 S Water St
Pittsburgh, PA 15203-2349, USA

Roffe-Barker, Melanie (Director)
c/o Staff Member *Don Capo
Entertainment*
Ste 5 South Bank Terrace
Surbiton
Surrey KT6 6DG, UNITED KINGDOM
(UK)

Roffe-Barker, Nigel (Director, Producer,
Writer)
c/o Staff Member *Don Capo
Entertainment*
Ste 5 South Bank Terrace
Surbiton
Surrey KT6 6DG, UNITED KINGDOM
(UK)

Rogan, Joe (Comedian)
c/o Staff Member *United Talent Agency
(UTA)*
9560 Wilshire Blvd Ste 500
Beverly Hills, CA 90212-2401, USA

Rogas, Dan (Football Player)
Detroit Lions
2352 Evalon St
Beaumont, TX 77702-1310, USA

Rogen, Seth
522 S Genesee Ave
Los Angeles, CA 90036-3241, USA

Roger, John (Religious Leader)
John Roger Foundation
2101 Wilshire Blvd
Santa Monica, CA 90403-5744, USA

Rogers, Amerie M M (Musician)
c/o Richard Murphy *International Creative
Management (ICM-NY)*
40 W 57th St
New York, NY 10019-4001, USA

Rogers, Bill (Golfer)
710 Patterson Ave
San Antonio, TX 78209-5637, USA

Rogers, Dennis (Athlete)
c/o Staff Member *Big Machine Media*
404 E 76th St Apt 5K
New York, NY 10021-1411, USA

Rogers, George (Football Player)
New Orleans Saints
1007 Lofty Pine Dr
Columbia, SC 29212-2037, USA

Rogers, Greg (Writer)
PO Box 3637
McAlester, OK 74502-3637, USA

Rogers, Jane
1485 S Beverly Dr Apt 8
Los Angeles, CA 90035-3021, USA

Rogers, Joy
4141 W Kling St Apt 3
Burbank, CA 91505-3309, USA

Rogers, Kenny (Baseball Player)
Texas Rangers
403 Bryn Mdws
Southlake, TX 76092-9405, USA

Rogers, Kenny (Musician)
c/o Debbie Cross *Kenny Rogers Inc*
2910 Poston Ave
Nashville, TN 37203-1312, USA

Rogers, Kevin (Baseball Player)
San Francisco Giants
604 Douglas Ave
Cleveland, MS 38732-2026, USA

Rogers, Lamarr (Baseball Player)
1240 Spring Green Ln
Burnsville, MN 55306-6413, USA

Rogers, Melody
2051 Nichols Canyon Rd
Los Angeles, CA 90046-1727, USA

Rogers, Mimi (Actor)
c/o Staff Member *Millbrook Farm
Productions*
11693 San Vicente Blvd # 241
Los Angeles, CA 90049-5105, USA

Rogers, Paul (Actor)
9 Hillside Gardens
London, ENGLAND N6 5SU, UNITED
KINGDOM (UK)

Rogers, Peter (Producer)
Peter Rogers Productions
52 Queen Anne St
London W1M 0LA, UNITED KINGDOM
(UK)

Rogers, Reg (Actor)
c/o Emily Gerson Saines *Overbrook
Entertainment*
450 N Roxbury Dr Fl 4
Beverly Hills, CA 90210-4232, USA

Rogers, Shorty
PO Box 1711
Bellingham, WA 98227-1711, USA

Rogers, Stephen D (Steve) (Baseball
Player)
3746 S Madison Ave
Tulsa, OK 74105-3016, USA

Rogers, Steve (Baseball Player)
Montreal Expos
2 Lenape Ln
Princeton Junction, NJ 08550-1817, USA

Rogers, Suzanne (Actor)
11266 Canton Dr
Studio City, CA 91604-4154, USA

Rogers, Tracy (Football Player)
Kansas City Chiefs
1011 Tam O Shanter Dr
Bakersfield, CA 93309-2451, USA

Rogers, Wayne (Actor)
11828 La Grange Ave
Los Angeles, CA 90025-5212, USA

Rogge, Jacques (Misc)
Int'l Olympic Committee
Chateau de Vidy
Lausanne 1007, SWITZERLAND

Roggeman, Tom (Football Player)
Chicago Bears
51267 Pembridge Ct
Granger, IN 46530-8306, USA

Roggenburk, Garry (Baseball Player)
Minnesota Twins
33550 Streamview Dr
Avon, OH 44011-2597, USA

Roggin, Fred
3000 W Alameda Ave
Burbank, CA 91523-0001, USA

Rogin, Gilbert L (Editor)
21 W 10th St Apt 5A
New York, NY 10011-8771, USA

Rogodzinski, Mike (Baseball Player)
Philadelphia Phillies
1 Emlyn Ct
Laurel Springs, NJ 08021-4871, USA

Rogoff, Ilan (Musician)
Apdo 1098
Palma de Mallorca 07080, SPAIN

Rogow, Stan (Producer)
c/o Staff Member *International Creative
Management (ICM-LA)*
10250 Constellation Blvd
Los Angeles, CA 90067-6200, USA

Rogue Wave (Music Group)
c/o Staff Member *Paradigm (Monterey)*
509 Hartnell St
Monterey, CA 93940-2825, USA

Rohde, Bruce (Business Person)
ConAgra Inc
1 Conagra Dr
Omaha, NE 68102-5003, USA

Rohde, Dave (Baseball Player)
Houston Astros
1707 Port Barmouth Pl
Newport Beach, CA 92660-5314, USA

Rohde, David (Journalist)
Chrsitian Science Monitor
1 Norway St
Editorial Dept
Boston, MA 02115-3195, USA

Rohde, Kristen (Actor)
c/o Staff Member *Gersh Agency, The (LA)*
232 N Canon Dr
Beverly Hills, CA 90210-5302, USA

Rohde, Len (Football Player)
San Francisco 49ers
324 Alta Vista Ave
Los Altos, CA 94022-2103, USA

Rohini (Actor, Bollywood)
D-1 Ist Floor Anandsree Apartments
32 Hindi Prachara Saba Street
Chennai, TN 600017, INDIA

Rohlander, Uta (Athlete, Track Athlete)
Liebigstr 9
Leuna 06237, GERMANY

Rohm, Elisabeth (Actor)
c/o Daniel (Danny) Sussman *Brillstein-Grey Entertainment*
9150 Wilshire Blvd Ste 350
Beverly Hills, CA 90212-3453, USA

Rohmer, Eric (Director)
Films du Losange
22 Ave Pierre-de-Serbie
Paris 75116, FRANCE

Rohn, Dan (Baseball Player)
Chicago Cubs
9247 W Long Lake Rd
Alpena, MI 49707-9382, USA

Rohn, Jim (Motivational Speaker)
Jim Rohn International
2835 Exchange Blvd Ste 200
Southlake, TX 76092-9192, USA

Rohner, Clayton
6924 Treasure Trl
Los Angeles, CA 90068-1838, USA

Rohner, Georges (Artist)
Galerie Framond
3 Rue des Saints Peres
Paris 75006, FRANCE

Rohr, Bill (Baseball Player)
Boston Red Sox
1780 Tustin Ct
San Jacinto, CA 92583-2302, USA

Rohr, James E (Financier)
PNC Bank Corp
249 5th Ave Ste 1200
1 Pnc Plaza
Pittsburgh, PA 15222-2707, USA

Rohr, Les (Baseball Player)
New York Mets
1508 Wicks Ln
Billings, MT 59105-4412, USA

Rohrer, Heinrich (Nobel Prize Laureate)
IBM Research Laboratory
Saumerstr 4
Ruschilkon 8803, SWITZERLAND

Rohrer, Jeff (Football Player)
Dallas Cowboys
3201 Executive Cir
Dallas, TX 75234-3764, USA

Rohrmeier, Dan (Baseball Player)
Seattle Mariners
4240 W Fork Rd
Cincinnati, OH 45247-7568, USA

Roig, Tony (Baseball Player)
Washington Senators
24125 E Lakeridge Dr
Liberty Lake, WA 99019-9612, USA

Roizman, Owen (Cinematographer)
17533 Magnolia Blvd
Encino, CA 91316, USA

Roja (Actor)
12 43rd Street
6th Avenue Ashok Nagar
Chennai, TN 600 083, INDIA

Roja (Actor, Bollywood)
8 Saravana Mudali Street
T.Nagar
Chennai, TN 600017, INDIA

Rojas, Mel (Baseball Player)
Montreal Expos
15645 Collins Ave Apt 802
North Miami Beach, FL 33160-4790, USA

Rojas, Nydia (Musician)
Silverlight Entertainment
9171 Wilshire Blvd Ste 426
Beverly Hills, CA 90210-5516, USA

Rojas, Octavio R (Cookie) (Baseball Player)
Cincinnati Reds
19195 Mystic Pointe Dr Apt 3002
Aventura, FL 33180-4502, USA

Rojcewicz, Susan (Sue) (Basketball Player)
48 Elena Cir
San Rafael, CA 94903-3342, USA

Rojo, Ana Patricia (Actor)
c/o Staff Member *Televisa*
Blvd Adolfo Lopez Mateos 232
Colonia San Angel INN
DF CP 01060, MEXICO

Rojo, Gustavo (Actor)
c/o Staff Member *Televisa*
Blvd Adolfo Lopez Mateos 232
Colonia San Angel INN
DF CP 01060, MEXICO

Roker, Al (Entertainer)
c/o Staff Member *Al Roker Productions*
250 W 57th St # 1514
New York, NY 10107-0001, USA

Rokk, Marika
Mozartstr. 15
Baden A-2500, AUSTRIA

Rokke, Ervin J (General)
810 Dolan Dr
Monument, CO 80132-2219, USA

Roland, Ed (Musician, Songwriter, Writer)
Spivak Entertainment
11845 W Olympic Blvd # 1125
Los Angeles, CA 90064-1149, USA

Roland, Jim (Baseball Player)
Minnesota Twins
1802 Arbor Way Dr
Shelby, NC 28150-6166, USA

Roland, Johnny E (Coach, Football Player)
St Louis Cardinals
8701 S Hardy Dr
Tempe, AZ 85284-2800, USA

Rolandi, Gianna (Opera Singer)
Columbia Artists Mgmt Inc
1790 Broadway Fl 6
New York, NY 10019-1412, USA

Rolen, Scott B (Baseball Player)
Philadelphia Phillies
11711 N Pennsylvania St Ste 250
Carmel, IN 46032-4560, USA

Roles-Williams, Barbara (Figure Skater)
3790 Leisure Ln
Las Vegas, NV 89103-2323, USA

Rolfe, Dale
365 Hughson St.
Gravenhurst, ON P1P 1G8, CANADA

Rolfe, Johnson Anthony (Opera Singer)
I C M Artists
40 W 57th St
New York, NY 10019-4001, USA

Rolison, Nathan (Baseball Player)
Florida Marlins
89 Bridgefield Ct
Hattiesburg, MS 39402-8689, USA

Rolle, Butch (Football Player)
Buffalo Bills
17822 NW 15th St
Pembroke Pines, FL 33029-3134, USA

Rolle, Dave (Football Player)
Denver Broncos
1107 Woodmount Ct
Denton, TX 76209-1424, USA

Roller, David E (Football Player)
Ney York Giants
1404 Bristol Pkwy
Alpharetta, GA 30022-1080, USA

Rollin, Betty (Correspondent, Writer)
67 Park Ave
New York, NY 10016-2557, USA

Rollins, Ed
c/o Staff Member *William Morris Agency (WMA-LA)*
1 William Morris Pl
Beverly Hills, CA 90212-4261, USA

Rollins, Henry (Actor)
7615 Hollywood Blvd
Los Angeles, CA 90046-2709, USA

Rollins, Henry (Musician, Songwriter, Writer)
Three Artists Mgmt
14260 Ventura Blvd Ste 201
Sherman Oaks, CA 91423-2734, USA

Rollins, James (Jimmy) (Baseball Player)
Philadelphia Phillies
1137 Rosewood Way
Alameda, CA 94501-5635, USA

Rollins, John (Golfer)
8703 Playground Ct
Richmond, VA 23237-2378, USA

Rollins, Kenneth (Kenny) (Basketball Player)
Gardens
220 Hibiscus Way
Parrish, FL 34219-9074, USA

Rollins, Kenny
2370 Bryant Rd
Lexington, KY 40509, USA

Rollins, Rich (Baseball Player)
Minnesota Twins
214 Melody Dr
Copley, OH 44321-1152, USA

Rollins, Sonny
193 Brighton Ave
Boston, MA 02134, USA

Rollins, Theodore W (Sonny) (Composer, Musician)
RR 9G
Germantown, NY 12526, USA

Rollins, Wayne (Tree) (Basketball Player, Coach)
2107 Westover Reserve Blvd
Windermere, FL 34786-6216, USA

Rolls, Damian (Baseball Player)
Tampa Bay Devil Rays
2341 Messenger Cir
Safety Harbor, FL 34695-5520, USA

Roloff, Matt
23985 NW Grossen Dr
Hillsboro, OR 97124-8149, USA

Roloson, Dwayne (Hockey Player)
Minnesota Wild
175 Kellogg Blvd W
Xcel Energy Arena
Saint Paul, MN 55102-1206, USA

Rolston, Holmes III (Misc)
Colorado State University
Philosophy Dept
Fort Collins, CO 80523-0001, USA

Rolston, Matthew (Photographer)
Venus Entertainment
3630 Eastham Dr
Culver City, CA 90232-2411, USA

Roman, Bill (Baseball Player)
Detroit Tigers
1720 Yale Ct
Lake Forest, IL 60045-5117, USA

Roman, Dan (Baseball Player)
10313 Arran Ct
Huntersville, NC 28078-7021, USA

Roman, John (Football Player)
New York Jets
13 Mendham Rd
Bernardsville, NJ 07924, USA

Roman, Joseph (Misc)
Glass & Ceramic Workers Union
556 E Town St
Columbus, OH 43215-4802, USA

Roman, Lauren
170 Flanders Drakestown Rd
Flanders, NJ 07836-4014, USA

Roman, Petre (Prime Minister)
Str Gogol 2
Sector 1
Bucharest, ROMANIA

Roman, Phil
10635 Riverside Dr
Toluca Lake, CA 91602-2341, USA

Roman, Ric
2967 E 3rd St
Los Angeles, CA 90033-4108, USA

Roman Holiday
Box 475
London, ENGLAND, UNITED KINGDOM (UK)

Romanek, Mark (Director)
c/o Staff Member *Creative Artists Agency LCC (CAA-LA)*
2000 Avenue Of The Stars
Los Angeles, CA 90067-4700, USA

Romanenko, Roman Y (Cosmonaut)
Polchta Kosmonavtov
Moskovskoi Oblasti
Syvisdny Goroduk 141160, RUSSIA

Romanenko, Yuri V (Cosmonaut)
Polchta Kosmonavtov
Moskovskoi Oblasti
Syvisdny Goroduk 141160, RUSSIA

Romanick, Ron (Baseball Player)
California Angels
15709 E Cervantes Ct
Fountain Hills, AZ 85268-1820, USA

Romanik, Steve (Football Player)
Chicago Bears
805 Pleasant Ave
Millville, NJ 08332-4525, USA

Romaniszyn, Jim (Football Player)
Cleveland Browns
619 Amy Lee Cir
Port Orange, FL 32127-7542, USA

Romano, Christy Carlson (Actor)
c/o Staff Member *Brillstein-Grey Entertainment*
9150 Wilshire Blvd Ste 350
Beverly Hills, CA 90212-3453, USA

Romano, Jason (Baseball Player)
Texas Rangers
3523 Heards Ferry Dr
Tampa, FL 33618-2922, USA

Romano, John (Misc)
212 Valley Rd
Merion Station, PA 19066-1543, USA

Romano, Johnny (Baseball Player)
Chicago White Sox
160 W Pago Pago Dr
Naples, FL 34113-8616, USA

Romano, Larry (Actor)
Gold Marshak Liedtke
3500 W Olive Ave Ste 1400
Burbank, CA 91505-5512, USA

Romano, Pete (Cinematographer)
HydroFlex Inc
5335 McConnell Ave
Los Angeles, CA 90066-7025, USA

Romano, Ray (Actor, Comedian, Producer, Writer)
c/o Rory Rosegarten *Conversation Company*
1044 Northern Blvd Ste 304
Roslyn, NY 11576-1589, USA

Romano, Roberta (Attorney, Educator)
Yale University
127 Wall St
Law School
New Haven, CT 06511-8918, USA

Romano, Tom (Baseball Player)
Montreal Expos
1266 Penora St
Depew, NY 14043-4512, USA

Romano, Umberto (Artist)
162 E 83rd St
New York, NY 10028-1901, USA

Romanos, John J (Jack) Jr (Publisher)
Pocket Books
1230 Avenue Of The Americas
New York, NY 10020-1586, USA

Romanov, Pyotr V (Government Official)
Communist Party
Bolshoy Komsomlsky Per 8/7
Moscow 10100, RUSSIA

Romanov, Stephanie (Actor)
c/o Staff Member *Diverse Talent Group*
1875 Century Park E Ste 2250
Los Angeles, CA 90067-2563, USA

Romansky, Monroe J (Doctor)
5600 Wisconsin Ave
Chevy Chase, MD 20815-4405, USA

Romantics, The
1924 Spring St
Paso Robles, CA 93446-1620, USA

Romanus, Richard (Actor)
Chasin Agency
8899 Beverly Blvd Ste 716
Los Angeles, CA 90048-2449, USA

Romanus, Robert (Actor)
c/o Melanie Sharp-Snyder *Sharp Talent*
117 N Orlando Ave
Los Angeles, CA 90048-3403, USA

Romario (Soccer Player)
Fluminense FC
Rua Alvaro Chaves 41
Rio de Janiero 22231-200, BRAZIL

Romashin, Anatoliy V (Actor)
Vspolny Per 16 Korp 1
#60
Moscow 103101, RUSSIA

Romatowski, Jenny (Baseball Player)
678 Channing Dr
Palm Harbor, FL 34684-3911, USA

Romby, Bob (Baseball Player)
Baltimore Elite Giants
38 Holman Mill Rd
Cumberland, VA 23040-2804, USA

Rome, Jim (Actor)
c/o Jeffrey Jacobs *Creative Artists Agency LCC (CAA-LA)*
2000 Avenue Of The Stars
Los Angeles, CA 90067-4700, USA

Rome, Stan (Football Player)
Kansas City Chiefs
4489 Green Island Rd
Valdosta, GA 31602-0870, USA

Romelfanger, Charles (Misc)
Pattern Makers League
4106 34th Ave
Moline, IL 61265-5501, USA

Romer, Roy R (Governor)
Los Angeles School District
333 S Beaudry Ave
Los Angeles, CA 90017-1466, USA

Romer, Suzanne F C (Prime Minister)
Prime Minister's Office
Willemstad, Curacao, NETHERLANDS ANTILLES

Romero, Angel (Musician)
Thea Dispeker Artists
59 E 54th St
New York, NY 10022-4256, USA

Romero, Celino (Musician)
Columbia Artists Mgmt Inc
1790 Broadway Fl 6
New York, NY 10019-1412, USA

Romero, Danny Jr (Boxer)
800 Salida Sandia SW
Albuquerque, NM 87105-7607, USA

Romero, Ed (Baseball Player)
Milwaukee Brewers
1380 Wood Row Way
Wellington, FL 33414-9082, USA

Romero, George
c/o Staff Member *Gersh Agency, The (LA)*
232 N Canon Dr
Beverly Hills, CA 90210-5302, USA

Romero, Mandy (Baseball Player)
San Diego Padres
19280 SW 216th St
Miami, FL 33170-1214, USA

Romero, Ned (Actor)
19438 Lassen St
Northridge, CA 91324-1121, USA

Romero, Pepe (Musician)
Frank Salomon
201 W 54th St Apt 1C
New York, NY 10019-5520, USA

Romero, Richard (Actor)
c/o Staff Member *Select Artists Ltd (CA-Valley Office)*
PO Box 4359
Burbank, CA 91503-4359, USA

Romijn, Rebecca (Actor, Model)
c/o Molly Madden *3 Arts Entertainment Inc*
9460 Wilshire Blvd Fl 7
Beverly Hills, CA 90212-2713, USA

Romine, Alton (Football Player)
Chicago Bears
286 Highway 79
Phil Campbell, AL 35581-6314, USA

Romine, Kevin (Baseball Player)
Boston Red Sox
8750 Rogue River Ave
Fountain Valley, CA 92708-5517, USA

Rominger, Kent V (Astronaut)
2714 Bridgeport Ave
Salt Lake City, UT 84121-5603, USA

Rommel, Ex-Mayor Manfred
Eduard-Steinle-Str 60
Stuttgart D-70619, GERMANY

Rommelaere-Manning, Martha (Baseball Player)
503-3252 Glasgow Ave
Victoria, BC V8X 1M2, CANADA

Romo, Daniela (Actor)
c/o Staff Member *Televisa*
Blvd Adolfo Lopez Mateos 232
Colonia San Angel INN
DF CP 01060, MEXICO

Romonosky, John (Baseball Player)
St Louis Cardinals
5090 Bixby Rd
Groveport, OH 43125-9564, USA

Rompre, Robert (Hockey Player)
316 W Maple Ave
Beaver Dam, WI 53916-1614, USA

Ron, Moo-hyun (President)
President's Office
Chong Wa Dae
1 Sejong-no
Seoul, SOUTH KOREA

Ronaldo, Cristiano (Soccer Player)
c/o Staff Member *Manchester United PLC*
Sir Matt Busby Way
Old Trafford
Manchester M160RA, UNITED KINGDOM (UK)

Ronan, Marc (Baseball Player)
St Louis Cardinals
104 Evonshire Dr
Arkadelphia, AR 71923-5449, USA

Rondon, Gil (Baseball Player)
Houston Astros
216 Cond Anaida Gardens
Ponce, PR 00731, USA

Ronettes, The
855 E Twain Ave # 123411
Las Vegas, NV 89169-0819, USA

Roney, Matt (Baseball Player)
Detroit Tigers
1809 Nighthawk Ct
Edmond, OK 73034-6110, USA

Roney, Paul H (Judge)
US Court of Appeals
100 1st Ave S
Saint Petersburg, FL 33701-4379, USA

Ronney, Paul D (Astronaut)
613 Ranchito Rd
Monrovia, CA 91016-3733, USA

Ronning, Cliff (Hockey Player)
316 Newton Dr
RR 3
Penticton, BC V2A 8Z5, CANADA

Ronningen, Jon (Wrestler)
Mellomasveien 132
Trollasen 1414, NORWAY

Rono, Peter (Athlete, Track Athlete)
Mount Saint Mary's College
Athletic Dept
Emmitsburg, MD 21727, USA

Ronson, Len
2006 SW Eastwood Ave
Gresham, OR 97080-5751, USA

Ronstadt, Linda (Musician)
c/o Sheldon (Shelly) Schultz *Trident Media Group LLC*
41 Madison Ave Fl 36
New York, NY 10010-2257, USA

Roocroft, Amanda (Opera Singer)
Ingpen & Williams
26 Wadham Road
London SW15 2LR, UNITED KINGDOM (UK)

Roof, Gene (Baseball Player)
St Louis Cardinals
175 Spring Valley Dr
Paducah, KY 42003-8894, USA

Roof, Michael (Actor)
c/o Staff Member *3 Arts Entertainment Inc*
9460 Wilshire Blvd Fl 7
Beverly Hills, CA 90212-2713, USA

Roof, Phil (Baseball Player)
Milwaukee Braves
7350 US Highway 45
Boaz, KY 42047, USA

Rook, Susan (Correspondent)
Cable News Network
1050 Techwood Dr NW
News Dept
Atlanta, GA 30318-5604, USA

Rooker, Jim (Baseball Player)
Detroit Tigers
2378 Windchime Dr
Jacksonville, FL 32224-2016, USA

Rooker, Michael (Actor)
275 S Beverly Dr Ste 215
Beverly Hills, CA 90212-5002, USA

Roomes, Rolando (Baseball Player)
Chicago Cubs
11520 E Pratt Ave
Mesa, AZ 85212-1949, USA

Rooney, Andrew A (Andy) (Correspondent)
PO Box 48
Rensselaervle, NY 12147-0048, USA

Rooney, Daniel M (Football Executive)
940 N Lincoln Ave
Pittsburgh, PA 15233-1814, USA

Rooney, Jim (Soccer Player)
New England Revolution
1 Patriot Pl
Cmgi Field
Foxboro, MA 02035-1388, USA

Rooney, Joe Don (Musician)
LGB Media
1228 Pineview Ln
Nashville, TN 37211-7422, USA

Rooney, Kevin (Actor)
c/o Staff Member *Metropolitan*
4500 Wilshire Blvd Fl 2
Los Angeles, CA 90010-3858, USA

Rooney, Mickey (Actor, Director, Writer)
c/o Robert Malcolm *The Artists Group Ltd (LA)*
1650 Broadway Ste 610
New York, NY 10019-6833, USA

Rooney, Pat (Baseball Player)
Montreal Expos
4825 Lighthouse Dr
Racine, WI 53402-2666, USA

Rooney, Patrick W (Business Person)
Cooper Tire & Rubber Co
Lima & Western Aves
Findlay, OH 45840, USA

Rooney, Wayne (Soccer Player)
c/o Staff Member *Manchester United PLC*
Sir Matt Busby Way
Old Trafford
Manchester M160RA, UNITED KINGDOM (UK)

Roopenian, Mark (Football Player)
Buffalo Bills
358 Charles River Rd
Watertown, MA 02472-2737, USA

Rooper, Jemima (Actor)
c/o Andrew Rogers *Paradigm (LA)*
360 N Crescent Dr
North Bldg
Beverly Hills, CA 90210-6820, USA

Roos, Don (Actor, Producer)
c/o Steve Rabineau *William Morris Agency (WMA-LA)*
9601 Wilshire Blvd Fl 3
Beverly Hills, CA 90210-5204, USA

Rooster (Music Group)
c/o Staff Member *BMG*
1540 Broadway
New York, NY 10036-4074, USA

Rooster, The Red
PO Box 3859
Stamford, CT 06905, USA

Root, Bonnie
8383 Wilshire Blvd Ste 550
Beverly Hills, CA 90211-2417, USA

Root, Jim (Football Player)
Chicago Cardinals
1540 Linkside Dr
Orange Park, FL 32003-7767, USA

Root, Stephen (Steven) (Actor)
c/o Chris Schmidt *Paradigm (LA)*
360 N Crescent Dr
North Bldg
Beverly Hills, CA 90210-6820, USA

Roots, Melvin H (Misc)
Plasters & Cement Workers Union
1125 17th St NW
Washington, DC 20036-4707, USA

Roots, The (Music Group)
c/o Staff Member *William Morris Agency (WMA-LA)*
1 William Morris Pl
Beverly Hills, CA 90212-4261, USA

Roper, Dee Dee (Spinderella) (Musician)
Nest Plateau Records
1650 Broadway Ste 1130
New York, NY 10019-6833, USA

Roper, John (Baseball Player)
Cincinnati Reds
519 John Roper Ave
Raeford, NC 28376-2211, USA

Roper, John (Football Player)
Chicago Bears
4213 Alice St
Houston, TX 77021-4903, USA

Rorem, Ned (Composer, Writer)
PO Box 764
Nantucket, MA 02554-0764, USA

Rorty, Richard M (Misc)
402 Peacock Dr
Charlottesville, VA 22903-9725, USA

Rosa, John (Educator, General)
Citadel
President's Office
Charleston, SC 29409-0001, USA

Rosa, Robi Draco (Composer, Musician, Producer)
Tanner Mainstain Assoc
10866 Wilshire Blvd # 10000
Los Angeles, CA 90024-4300, USA

Rosa, Rosa
6640 W Sunset Blvd # 110
Los Angeles, CA 90028-7104, USA

Rosado, Eduardo (Opera Singer)
Calle 3
Ave Cupules 112A Col G Giberes
Menda, Yucatan 97070, MEXICO

Rosales, Jenny (Golfer)
265 S Vine St
Anaheim, CA 92805-4128, USA

Rosamund, John
4 Dean's Yard
London, ENGLAND SW1P, UNITED KINGDOM (UK)

Rosand, David (Historian)
560 Riverside Dr
New York, NY 10027-3202, USA

Rosario, Jimmy (Baseball Player)
San Francisco Giants
200 Calle 6
Bayamon, PR 00959-4800, USA

Rosario, Mel (Baseball Player)
Baltimore Orioles
205 Round Tree Ct
Egg Harbor Township, NJ 08234-7910, USA

Rosario, Santiago (Baseball Player)
Kansas City A's
HC 1 Box 7982
Guayanilla, PR 00656, USA

Rosas, Cesar (Musician, Songwriter, Writer)
Monterey International
200 W Superior St Ste 202
Chicago, IL 60610-3554, USA

Rosato, Genesia (Ballerina)
Royal Ballet
Covent Garden
Bow St
London WC2E 9DD, UNITED KINGDOM (UK)

Rosato, Tony (Actor, Writer)
c/o Staff Member *Don Capo Entertainment*
Ste 5 South Bank Terrace
Surbiton
Surrey KT6 6DG, UNITED KINGDOM (UK)

Rosberg, Keke (Race Car Driver)
7 Rue Gabian
Monte Carlo 9800, MONACO

Rosburg, Bob (Golfer)
49425 Avenida Club La Quinta
La Quinta, CA 92253-2703, USA

Roschkov, Victor (Cartoonist, Editor)
Toronto Star
Editorial Dept
1 Yonge St
Toronto, ON M5E 1E5, CANADA

Rose, Axl (Musician, Songwriter, Writer)
c/o Rob Light *Creative Artists Agency LCC (CAA-LA)*
2000 Avenue Of The Stars
Los Angeles, CA 90067-4700, USA

Rose, Barry (Football Player)
Denver Broncos
507 Southside Dr
Woodville, WI 54028-9532, USA

Rose, Bernard (Director, Producer, Writer)
c/o Jenne Casarotto *Casarotto Ramsay & Associates Ltd (UK)*
National House
60-66 Wardour Street
London W1V 4ND, UNITED KINGDOM (UK)

Rose, Bobby (Baseball Player)
California Angels
9595 Wilshire Blvd Ste 1010
Beverly Hills, CA 90212-2510, USA

Rose, Brian (Baseball Player)
Boston Red Sox
5 Ashland St
South Dartmouth, MA 02748-3211, USA

Rose, Carol (Attorney, Educator)
Yale University
127 Wall St
Law School
New Haven, CT 06511-8918, USA

Rose, Charles (Charlie) (Television Host)
Charlie Rose Inc
731 Lexington Ave
New York, NY 10022-1331, USA

Rose, Chris (Television Host)
c/o Staff Member *Best Damned Sports Show Period, The*
10201 W Pico Blvd
Fox Sports Net
Los Angeles, CA 90064-2606, USA

Rose, Clarence (Golfer)
405 Walnut Creek Dr
Goldsboro, NC 27534-8995, USA

Rose, Cristine (Actor)
Paradigm Agency
10100 Santa Monica Blvd Ste 2500
Los Angeles, CA 90067-4116, USA

Rose, Don (Baseball Player)
New York Mets
16254 Palomino Mesa Way
San Diego, CA 92127-4445, USA

Rose, Donovan (Football Player)
Kansas City Chiefs
103 Lenox Ct
Yorktown, VA 23693-5501, USA

Rose, George (Football Player)
Minnesota Vikings
161 Baywood Cir
Brunswick, GA 31525-8585, USA

Rose, H Michael (General)
Coldstream Guards
Wellington Barracks
London SW1E 6HQ, UNITED KINGDOM (UK)

Rose, Jalen (Basketball Player)
Toronto Raptors
Air Canada Center
40 Bay St
Toronto, ON M5J 2N8, CANADA

Rose, Jamie (Actor)
c/o Staff Member *Marshak/Zachary Company, The*
8840 Wilshire Blvd Fl 1
Beverly Hills, CA 90211-2606, USA

Rose, Joe (Football Player)
Miami Dolphins
3293 SW 138th Way
Davie, FL 33330-4664, USA

Rose, Katy (Musician)
c/o Staff Member *Paradigm (Monterey)*
509 Hartnell St
Monterey, CA 93940-2825, USA

Rose, Ken (Football Player)
New York Jets
1736 Bronzewood Ct
Thousand Oaks, CA 91320-4546, USA

Rose, Lee (Director, Producer)
c/o Staff Member *Broder Webb Chervin Silbermann Agency, The (BWCS)*
10250 Constellation Blvd Ste P
Los Angeles, CA 90067-6213, USA

Rose, Marie (Actor)
6916 Chisholm Ave
Van Nuys, CA 91406-5111, USA

Rose, Matthew (Business Person)
Burlington North/Santa Fe
2650 Lou Menk Dr
Fort Worth, TX 76131-2830, USA

Rose, Murray (Swimmer)
77 Berry Level 3
North Sydney, NSW 2060, AUSTRALIA

Rose, Pete (Baseball Player)
Cincinnati Reds
13348 Chandler Blvd
Sherman Oaks, CA 91401-5323, USA

Rose, Pete Jr (Baseball Player)
Cincinnati Reds
3921 Legendary Ridge Ln
Cleves, OH 45002-2395, USA

Rose, Peter E (Pete) (Baseball Player)
8144 Glades Rd
Boca Raton, FL 33434-4064, USA

Rose, Peter H (Business Person)
Krytek Corp
2 Centennial Dr
Peabody, MA 01960-7911, USA

Rose, Richard (Scientist)
Bennochy
1 E Abercromby St
Helensburgh, Dunbartonshire G84 7SP, SCOTLAND

Rose, Shayna (Actor)
Rough Diamond Productions
1424 N Kings Rd
C/O Bill Kravitz
Los Angeles, CA 90069-1908, USA

Rose, Sherrie (Actor, Model)
1758 Laurel Canyon Blvd
Los Angeles, CA 90046-2134, USA

Rosecrans, James (Football Player)
New York Jets
210 Houston Ave
Syracuse, NY 13224-1754, USA

Rosegarten, Rory (Producer)
c/o Staff Member *William Morris Agency (WMA-LA)*
1 William Morris Pl
Beverly Hills, CA 90212-4261, USA

Roselle, David P (Educator)
14 Laurel Ridge Rd
Wilmington, DE 19807-1322, USA

Roselli, Jimmy
64 Division Ave
Levittown, NY 11756-2999, USA

Rosellini, Albert D (Governor)
5936 6th Ave S
Seattle, WA 98108-3302, USA

Rosema, Roger (Football Player)
St Louis Cardinals
6081 Champagne Ct SE
Grand Rapids, MI 49546-6430, USA

Roseman, Saul (Scientist)
8206 Cranwood Ct
Baltimore, MD 21208-1822, USA

Rosemont, Romy (Actor)
c/o Staff Member *Don Buchwald & Associates Inc (LA)*
6500 Wilshire Blvd Ste 2200
Los Angeles, CA 90048-4942, USA

Rosen, Albert (Al) (Conductor)
Corbett Arts Mgmt
2101 California St Apt 2
San Francisco, CA 94115-2801, USA

Rosen, Albert L (Al) (Baseball Player)
15 Mayfair Dr
Rancho Mirage, CA 92270-2586, USA

Rosen, Beatrice (Actor)
c/o Brandt Joel *Creative Artists Agency LCC (CAA-LA)*
2000 Avenue Of The Stars
Los Angeles, CA 90067-4700, USA

Rosen, Charles W (Musician)
101 W 78th St
New York, NY 10024-6717, USA

Rosen, Harold A (Engineer, Inventor)
Rosen Electrical Equipment
8226 Whittier Blvd
Pico Rivera, CA 90660-2584, USA

Rosen, Milton W (Engineer, Physicist)
5610 Alta Vista Rd
Bethesda, MD 20817-3512, USA

Rosen, Nathaniel (Musician)
4555 Henry Hudson Pkwy Apt 1110
Bronx, NY 10471-3840, USA

Rosenbaum, Edward E (Physicist)
333 NW 23rd Ave
Portland, OR 97210-3403, USA

Rosenbaum, Michael (Actor)
c/o Jeff Golenberg *The Collective*
9100 Wilshire Blvd # 700 W
Beverly Hills, CA 90212-3401, USA

Rosenberg, Alan
PO Box 5617
Beverly Hills, CA 90209-5617, USA

Rosenberg, Craig (Director, Writer)
c/o Staff Member *The Firm*
9465 Wilshire Blvd Fl 6
Beverly Hills, CA 90212-2605, USA

Rosenberg, Howard (Misc)
5859 Larboard Ln
Agoura Hills, CA 91301-1422, USA

Rosenberg, Joel C (Writer)
Beverly Rykerd Public Relations
17915 Woodhaven Dr
C/O Beverly Rykerd
Colorado Springs, CO 80908-1381, USA

Rosenberg, Michael (Producer)
c/o Staff Member *Imagine Entertainment*
9465 Wilshire Blvd Fl 7
Beverly Hills, CA 90212-2606, USA

Rosenberg, Pierre M (Director)
Musee du Louvre
34-36 Quai du Louvre
Paris 75068, FRANCE

Rosenberg, Scott (Writer)
c/o David O'Connor *Creative Artists Agency LCC (CAA-LA)*
2000 Avenue Of The Stars
Los Angeles, CA 90067-4700, USA

Rosenberg, Steven A (Doctor)
10104 Iron Gate Rd
Potomac, MD 20854-4728, USA

Rosenberg, Stuart (Director)
1984 Coldwater Canyon Dr
Beverly Hills, CA 90210-1731, USA

Rosenberg, Tina (Writer)
New School for Social Research
World Policy Institute
New York, NY 10011, USA

Rosenblath, Marshall N (Physicist)
2311 Via Siena
La Jolla, CA 92037-3933, USA

Rosenblatt, Dana (Boxer)
39 Cleveland Rd
Chestnut Hill, MA 02467-1417, USA

Rosenblum, Robert (Educator)
New York University
Fine Arts Dept
New York, NY 10003, USA

Rosenbluth, Leonard (Lennie) (Basketball Player)
19461 La Serena Dr
Fort Myers, FL 33967-0528, USA

Rosenbohm, Jim (Baseball Player)
9513 Bedford Ave
Omaha, NE 68134-4607, USA

Rosenburg, Saul A (Doctor)
Stanford University
Oncology Division
Stanford, CA 94305, USA

Rosendahl, Heidemarie (Heide) (Athlete, Track Athlete)
Burscheider Str 426
Leverkusen 51381, GERMANY

Rosenfeld, Arnold S (Editor)
Cox Newspapers
PO Box 105720
Atlanta, GA 30348-5720, USA

Rosenfeld, Isadore (Physicist)
Warner Books
1271 Avenue Of The Americas
New York, NY 10020-1300, USA

Rosenfels, Sage (Football Player)
Miami Dolphins
110 Ferndale St
Bellaire, TX 77401-5325, USA

Rosenfield, John Max (Educator)
165 Chestnut St Apt 313
Brookline, MA 02445-7592, USA

Rosengarten, David (Writer)
PO Box 20459
New York, NY 10025-1520, USA

Rosenman, Leonard (Composer)
Elizabeth Dworkin
PO Box 248
Bedford Hills, NY 10507-0248, USA

Rosenmeyer, Grant (Actor)
c/o Staff Member *DreamWorks SKG*
100 Universal City Plz
Universal City, CA 91608-1002, USA

Rosenn, Max (Judge)
US Court of Appeals
197 S Main St
US Courthouse
Wilkes Barre, PA 18701-1500, USA

Rosenquist, James A (Artist)
PO Box 4
420 Broadway
Aripeka, FL 34679-0004, USA

Rosenstein, Samuel M (Judge)
US Court of International Trade
2200 S Ocean Ln
Fort Lauderdale, FL 33316-3836, USA

Rosenthal, Albert J (Attorney, Attorney General, Educator, General)
15 Oak Way
Scarsdale, NY 10583-1415, USA

Rosenhall, Amy Krouse (Writer)
Crown Publishing Group
1745 Broadway
New York, NY 10019-4305, USA

Rosenthal, David S (Director, Writer)
1801 Century Park E Ste 2160
Los Angeles, CA 90067-2343, USA

Rosenthal, Howard L (Scientist)
Princeton University
Politics Dept
Princeton, NJ 08544-0001, USA

Rosenthal, Jacob (Jack) (Journalist)
New York Times
229 W 43rd St
Editorial Dept
New York, NY 10036-3959, USA

Rosenthal, Mark D (Writer)
c/o Tom Strickler *Endeavor Agency LLC (LA)*
9601 Wilshire Blvd Fl 3
Beverly Hills, CA 90210-5204, USA

Rosenthal, Mike (Football Player)
New York Giants
6112 Every Sail Path
Clarksville, MD 21029-2904, USA

Rosenthal, Philip (Producer)
c/o Adam Berkowitz *Creative Artists Agency LCC (CAA-LA)*
2000 Avenue Of The Stars
Los Angeles, CA 90067-4700, USA

Rosenthal, Richard L (Rick) (Director, Producer)
c/o Staff Member *Whitewater Films*
2232 Cotner Ave
Los Angeles, CA 90064-1802, USA

Rosenthal, Robert J (Editor)
Philadelphia Inquirer
400 N Broad St
Editorial Dept
Philadelphia, PA 19130-4099, USA

Rosenthal, Tony (Artist)
173 E 73rd St
New York, NY 10021-3510, USA

Rosenzweig, Barney (Producer)
2311 Fisher Island Dr
Miami Beach, FL 33109-0086, USA

Rosenzweig, Mark R (Misc)
University of California
Psychology Dept
Tolman Hall
Berkeley, CA 94720-0001, USA

Rosenzweig, Robert M (Educator)
1462 Dana Ave
Palo Alto, CA 94301-3115, USA

Roses, Allen D (Doctor)
Duke University
Medical Center
Bryan Research Center
Durham, NC 27706, USA

Rosewall, Ken (Tennis Player)
Turramurra
111 Pentacost Ave
Sydney, NSW 2074, AUSTRALIA

Rosewoman, Michele (Musician)
Abby Hoffer
223 1/2 E 48th St
New York, NY 10017, USA

Roshan, Hrithik (Actor, Bollywood)
Filmkraft Mayur
Tilak Road Santa cruz (W)
Mumbai, MS 400054, INDIA

Roshan, Rakesh (Actor, Bollywood, Director, Producer)
Kavita 10th Road
JVPD Scheme
Mumbai, MS 400049, INDIA

Rosi, Francesco
Via Gregoriana 36
Rome 1-00187, ITALY

Rosin, Walter L (Religious Leader)
Lutheran Church Missouri Synod
1333 S Kirkwood Rd
Saint Louis, MO 63122-7295, USA

Rosinski, Edward J (Inventor)
2305 Arnold Ave
Yorkville, NY 13495-1802, USA

Roskill of Newtown, Eustace W (Judge)
New Court
Temple
London EC4, UNITED KINGDOM (UK)

Rosman, Mackenzie (Actor)
c/o Staff Member *7th Heaven*
5700 Wilshire Blvd Ste 575
Los Angeles, CA 90036-3768, USA

Ross, Al (Cartoonist)
2185 Bolton St
Bronx, NY 10462-1367, USA

Ross, Annie (Actor)
c/o Staff Member *The Artists Group Ltd (LA)*
1650 Broadway Ste 610
New York, NY 10019-6833, USA

Ross, Ben (Director)
United Talent Agency
9560 Wilshire Blvd Ste 500
Beverly Hills, CA 90212-2401, USA

Ross, Betsy (Sportscaster)
ESPN-TV
Sports Dept
Espn Plaza 935 Middle St
Bristol, CT 06010, USA

Ross, Brian (Correspondent)
c/o Staff Member *20/20*
147 Columbus Ave
Abc
New York, NY 10023-6503, USA

Ross, Charlotte (Actor)
c/o Paul Santana *Agency for the Performing Arts (APA-LA)*
405 S Beverly Dr
Beverly Hills, CA 90212-4416, USA

Ross, Chelcie (Actor)
c/o Staff Member *Geddes Agency, The*
8430 Santa Monica Blvd Ste 200
Los Angeles, CA 90069-4253, USA

Ross, Dan (Football Player)
Cincinnati Bengals
10 Manasquan Cir
Londonderry, NH 03053-2636, USA

Ross, David A (Director)
Whitney Museum of American Art
945 Madison Ave
New York, NY 10021-2790, USA

Ross, Diana (Actor, Musician)
c/o Mitch Rose *Creative Artists Agency LCC (CAA-LA)*
2000 Avenue Of The Stars
Los Angeles, CA 90067-4700, USA

Ross, Don (Athlete)
PO Box 981
Venice, CA 90294-0981, USA

Ross, Donald R (Judge)
US Court of Appeals
PO Box 307
Federal Building
Omaha, NE 68101-0307, USA

Ross, Douglas T (Scientist)
Softech Inc
2 Highwood Dr Ste 200
Tewksbury, MA 01876-1100, USA

Ross, Evan (Actor)
c/o Adam Griffin *The Collective*
331 N Maple Dr Fl 2
Beverly Hills, CA 90210-3827, USA

Ross, Fairbanks Anne (Swimmer)
10 Grandview Ave
Troy, NY 12180-2113, USA

Ross, Gary (Director)
Creative Artists Agency
9830 Wilshire Blvd
Beverly Hills, CA 90212-1804, USA

Ross, George (Reality TV Star)
c/o Staff Member *The Apprentice*
725 5th Ave
The Trump Co
New York, NY 10022-2519, USA

Ross, Heather (Musician)
HER Productions
6736 Breezy Palm Dr
Riverview, FL 33578-8802, USA

Ross, Herbert
8383 Wilshire Blvd Ste 550
Beverly Hills, CA 90211-2417, USA

Ross, Jeffrey (Jeff) (Actor)
c/o Steve Smooke *Creative Artists Agency
LCC (CAA-LA)*
2000 Avenue Of The Stars
Los Angeles, CA 90067-4700, USA

Ross, Jerry L (Astronaut)
NASA
2101 Nasa Pkwy
Johnson Space Center
Houston, TX 77058-3691, USA

Ross, Jim (Wrestler)
605 Shadow View Ct
Norman, OK 73072-4827, USA

Ross, Jimmy D (General)
4981 Maple Glen Pl
Sanford, FL 32771-7183, USA

Ross, John (Misc)
620 Sand Hill Rd Apt 405E
Palo Alto, CA 94304-2078, USA

Ross, Jonathan (Actor)
34/42 Cleveland St.
London, ENGLAND W1P 5SB, UNITED
KINGDOM (UK)

Ross, Jonathon (Actor, Producer, Writer)
Talking Concepts
19 Bird Street
Lichfield, Staffordshire WS13 6PW,
UNITED KINGDOM (UK)

Ross, Karie (Sportscaster)
ESPN-TV
Sports Dept
Espn Plaza 935 Middle St
Bristol, CT 06010, USA

Ross, Katharine
33050 Pacific Coast Hwy
Malibu, CA 90265-2300, USA

Ross, Kevin (Football Player)
Kansas City Chiefs
146 High St
Woodbury, NJ 08096-2304, USA

Ross, Louis (Football Player)
Buffalo Bills
4283 Booker St
Orlando, FL 32811-4662, USA

Ross, Marion (Actor)
c/o Jimmy Cota *The Artists Agency (LA)*
1180 S Beverly Dr Ste 301
Los Angeles, CA 90035-1154, USA

Ross, Rick (Musician)
c/o Staff Member *Island Def Jam Music
Group*
825 8th Ave Fl 28
New York, NY 10019-7416, USA

Ross, Robert J (Bobby) (Coach, Football
Coach)
US Millitary Academy
Athletic Dept
West Point, NY 10996, USA

Ross, Scott (Football Player)
New Orleans Saints
303 Lake View Dr # D
Montgomery, TX 77356-5782, USA

Ross, Stan
1410 N Gardner St
Los Angeles, CA 90046-4142, USA

Ross, Tracee Ellis (Actor)
c/o Jenean Glover *Screen Partners Inc*
9663 Santa Monica Blvd Ste 639
Beverly Hills, CA 90210-4303, USA

Ross, Willie (Football Player)
Buffalo Bills
1100 S Hamilton Ave
Chicago, IL 60612-4207, USA

Ross, Yolanda (Actor)
c/o Brian Liebman *Liebman Entertainment*
25 E 21st St Ph
New York, NY 10010-6226, USA

Rossdale, Gavin (Actor, Musician)
c/o Cynthia Pett-Dante *Brillstein-Grey
Entertainment*
9150 Wilshire Blvd Ste 350
Beverly Hills, CA 90212-3453, USA

Rosselli, Jimmy
344 Paterson Plank Rd
Jersey City, NJ 07307-1051, USA

Rossellini, Isabella (Actor)
c/o Gene Parseghian *Untitled
Entertainment (NY)*
322 8th Ave Ste 601
New York, NY 10001-6715, USA

Rossen, Carol
1119 23rd St Unit 8
Santa Monica, CA 90403-5732, USA

Rossi, Alice (Scientist)
34 Stagecoach Rd
Amherst, MA 01002-3527, USA

Rossi, Tony (Ray) (Actor)
c/o Kristene Wallis *Wallis Agency*
210 N Pass Ave Ste 205
Burbank, CA 91505-3936, USA

Rossi, Valentino (Motorcycle Race,
Motorcycle Racer)
Honda Europe Motorcycles
Via della Cecchignola 5-7
Rome 00143, ITALY

Rossio, Terry (Writer)
c/o Staff Member *Creative Artists Agency
LCC (CAA-LA)*
2000 Avenue Of The Stars
Los Angeles, CA 90067-4700, USA

Rossovich, Rick
PO Box 5617
Beverly Hills, CA 90209-5617, USA

Rossovich, Tim (Football Player)
Philadelphia Eagles
19811 Wildwood West Dr
Penn Valley, CA 95946-9547, USA

Rossum, Allen (Football Player)
Philadelphia Eagles
2520 Johnson Dr
Mesquite, TX 75181-4619, USA

Rossum, Emmy (Actor, Musician)
c/o Ara Keshishian *Creative Artists Agency
LCC (CAA-LA)*
2000 Avenue Of The Stars
Los Angeles, CA 90067-4700, USA

Rostenkowski, Dan (Politician)
1372 W Evergreen Ave
Chicago, IL 60622-2363, USA

Rostosky, Pete (Football Player)
Pittsburgh Steelers
637 E McMurray Rd
Canonsburg, PA 15317-3430, USA

Rostow, Walt
1 Wildwind Pt
Austin, TX 78746-2434, USA

Rote, Kyle
24700 Deepwater Point Dr Unit 14
St Michaels, MD 21663-2327, USA

Rote, Tobin
7590 Lighthouse Rd
Port Hope, MI 48468-9760, USA

Rote Jr, Kyle
6075 Poplar Ave Ste 920
Memphis, TN 38119-4717, USA

Roth, Andrea (Actor)
c/o Adam Levine *Anthem Entertainment*
6100 Wilshire Blvd Ste 1170
Los Angeles, CA 90048-5116, USA

Roth, David Lee (Musician)
c/o Staff Member *International Creative
Management (ICM-LA)*
10250 Constellation Blvd
Los Angeles, CA 90067-6200, USA

Roth, Eli (Producer, Writer)
c/o Staff Member *Raw Nerve Productions*
9 Desbrosses St Fl 2
New York, NY 10013-1701, USA

Roth, Ellaine (Baseball Player)
872 Goguac St W
Springfield, MI 49015-1737, USA

Roth, Eric (Writer)
c/o Staff Member *Creative Artists Agency
LCC (CAA-LA)*
2000 Avenue Of The Stars
Los Angeles, CA 90067-4700, USA

Roth, Matt
PO Box 5617
Beverly Hills, CA 90209-5617, USA

Roth, Philip (Writer)
c/o Andrew Wylie *The Andrew Wylie
Agency*
250 W 57th St Ste 2114
New York, NY 10107-2199, USA

Roth, Rachel (Actor)
c/o Justine Hunt *Hines and Hunt
Entertainment*
1213 W Magnolia Blvd
Burbank, CA 91506-1829, USA

Roth, Tim (Actor)
c/o Staci Wolfe *Polaris PR*
8135 W 4th St
2 Floor
Los Angeles, CA 90048-4415, USA

Rothemund, Marc (Director)
c/o Daniel J Talbot *International Creative
Management (ICM-LA)*
10250 Constellation Blvd
Los Angeles, CA 90067-6200, USA

Rothenberger, Anneliese (Opera Singer)
Quellenhof
Salenstein, TG 8268, SWITZERLAND

Rothery, Teryl (Actor)
c/o Staff Member *Twenty First Century
Artists*
501 - 825 Granville St
Vancouver, BC V6Z 1K9, CANADA

Rothman, John
9229 W Sunset Blvd Ste 710
Los Angeles, CA 90069-3407, USA

Rothrock, Cynthia
20670 Callon Dr
Topanga, CA 90290-3712, USA

Rotunno, Giuseppe
Via Crescenzio 58
Rome 00193, ITALY

Rouen, Tom (Football Player)
Denver Broncos
19947 N 84th Way
Scottsdale, AZ 85255-3974, USA

Rouillard, Richard
11750 W Sunset Blvd Apt 117
Los Angeles, CA 90049-2904, USA

Roundtree, Raleigh (Football Player)
San Diego Chargers
2001 Roosevelt Dr
Augusta, GA 30904-5021, USA

Roundtree, Richard (Actor)
c/o Staff Member *Stone Manners Talent &
Literary (LA)*
6500 Wilshire Blvd Ste 550
Los Angeles, CA 90048-4950, USA

Rountree, Mary (Baseball Player)
8204 NW 80th St
Tamarac, FL 33321-1627, USA

Rourke, Jim (Football Player)
Kansas City Chiefs
466 Plymouth St
Abington, MA 02351-1842, USA

Rourke, Mickey (Marielito) (Actor)
c/o Richard Konigsberg *International
Creative Management (ICM-LA)*
10250 Constellation Blvd
Los Angeles, CA 90067-6200, USA

Rouse, Curtis (Football Player)
Minnesota Vikings
301 Hampshire Ct
Clarksville, TN 37043-4661, USA

Rouse, Irving (Misc)
509 Rockavon Rd
Narberth, PA 19072-2318, USA

Rouse, Jeff
302 Gerber Dr
Fredericksburg, VA 22408-2920, USA

Rouse, Mitch (Actor)
c/o David (Dave) Becky *3 Arts Entertainment Inc*
9460 Wilshire Blvd Fl 7
Beverly Hills, CA 90212-2713, USA

Rousellot, John
2111 Wilson Blvd Ste 850
Arlington, VA 22201-3051, USA

Roush, Jack (Misc)
Roush Racing
122 Knob Hill Rd
Mooresville, NC 28117-6847, USA

Rouson, Lee (Football Player)
New York Giants
20 Main St
Flanders, NJ 07836-9112, USA

Roussel, Tom (Football Player)
Washington Redskins
13 Heron Ln
Mandeville, LA 70471-6739, USA

Roussell, Thierry
Villa Crystal
St. Moritz CH-7500, SWITZERLAND

Rousselot, Philippe (Cinematographer)
Gersh Agency
232 N Canon Dr
Beverly Hills, CA 90210-5302, USA

Rousset, Christophe (Musician)
Trawick Artists
1926 Broadway
New York, NY 10023-6915, USA

Roustabouts, The
PO Box 25371
Charlotte, NC 28229-5371, USA

Routh, Brandon (Actor)
c/o Stew Strunk *Main Title Entertainment*
5225 Wilshire Blvd Ste 500
Los Angeles, CA 90036-4349, USA

Routledge, Alison (Actor)
Marmont Mgmt
Langham House
302/8 Regent St
London W1R 5AL, UNITED KINGDOM (UK)

Routledge, Patricia (Actor)
c/o Staff Member *Marmont Management*
Langham House
308 Regent St
London W1B 3AT, UNITED KINGDOM (UK)

Roux, Albert H (Chef)
Le Gavroche
43 Upper Brook St
London W1Y 1PF, UNITED KINGDOM (UK)

Roux, Jean-Louis (Actor, Director)
4145 Blueridge Crescent
#2
Montreal, PQ H3H 1S7, CANADA

Roux, Michel A (Chef)
Waterside Inn
Ferry Road
Bray, Berks SL6 2AT, UNITED KINGDOM (UK)

Rove, Karl (Government Official)
White House
1600 Pennsylvania Ave NW
Washington, DC 20500-0004, USA

Rovick, Sheriff John
3531 Clifton Pl
Glendale, CA 91208-1350, USA

Rowan, Carl T
3116 Fessenden St NW
Washington, DC 20008-2029, USA

Rowan, Kelly
c/o Jennifer Goldhar *Characters Talent Agency, The (Toronto)*
8 Elm St 3rd FL
Toronto, ON M5G 1G7, CANADA

Rowden, William H (Admiral)
55 Pinewood Ct
Lancaster, VA 22503-2321, USA

Rowe, Alan
8 Sherwood Close
London, ENGLAND SW13, UNITED KINGDOM (UK)

Rowe, Bob (Football Player)
St Louis Cardinals
2564 Viola Gill Ln
Grover, MO 63040-1165, USA

Rowe, Brad (Actor)
1327 Brinkley Ave
Los Angeles, CA 90049-3619, USA

Rowe, Dave (Football Player)
New Orleans Saints
330 W Presnell St Apt 43
Asheboro, NC 27203-4700, USA

Rowe, John W (Business Person)
Unicom Corp
10 S Dearborn St Fl 45
Chicago, IL 60603-2398, USA

Rowe, John W (Business Person)
Aetna Inc
151 Farmington Ave
Hartford, CT 06156-0001, USA

Rowe, Maggie (Comedian)
c/o Staff Member *International Creative Management (ICM-LA)*
10250 Constellation Blvd
Los Angeles, CA 90067-6200, USA

Rowe, Mike (Television Host)
Pilgrim Films & Television Inc
4730 Woodman Ave Ste 300
Sherman Oaks, CA 91423-2406, USA

Rowe, Misty (Actor)
2193 River Rd
Egg Harbor Cy, NJ 08215-4745, USA

Rowe, Nicolas
52 Shaftesbury Ave
London, ENGLAND WlV 7DE, UNITED KINGDOM (UK)

Rowe, Patrick (Football Player)
Cleveland Browns
6259 Alderley St
San Diego, CA 92114-6715, USA

Rowe, Ray (Football Player)
Washington Redskins
11443 Westonhill Dr
San Diego, CA 92126-1450, USA

Rowe, Red
79 Margarita
Camarillo Springs, CA 93010, USA

Rowe, Sandra M (Editor)
Portland Oregonian
1320 SW Broadway
Editorial Dept
Portland, OR 97201-3411, USA

Rowe-Jackson, Debbie
435 N Roxbury Dr
Beverly Hills, CA 90210-5027, USA

Rowell, Victoria (Actor)
c/o Staff Member *Third Hill Entertainment*
195 S Beverly Dr Ste 400
Beverly Hills, CA 90212-3044, USA

Rowland, Betty (Dancer)
125 N Barrington Ave Apt 103
Los Angeles, CA 90049-2949, USA

Rowland, Brad (Football Player)
Chicago Bears
552 Rosebud Dr N
Lombard, IL 60148-6166, USA

Rowland, Dave
PO Box 121089
Nashville, TN 37212-1089, USA

Rowland, F Sherwood (Nobel Prize Laureate)
4807 Dorchester Rd
Corona Del Mar, CA 92625-2718, USA

Rowland, J David (Business Person)
National Westminster Bank
41 Lothbury
London EC2P 2BP, UNITED KINGDOM (UK)

Rowland, James A (General)
17 Pindari Ave
Mosman, NSW 2088, AUSTRALIA

Rowland, John W (Misc)
Amalgamated Transit Union
5025 Wisconsin Ave NW
Washington, DC 20016-4139, USA

Rowland, Justin (Football Player)
Chicago Bears
1919 NW Loop 410 Ste 200
San Antonio, TX 78213-2325, USA

Rowland, Kelly (Musician)
c/o Dennis Ashley *Creative Artists Agency LCC (CAA-LA)*
2000 Avenue Of The Stars
Los Angeles, CA 90067-4700, USA

Rowland, Landon H (Business Person)
Kansas City Southern
PO Box 219335
Kansas City, MO 64121-9335, USA

Rowland, Rodney (Actor, Model)
Booh Schut
11350 Ventura Blvd Ste 206
Studio City, CA 91604-3140, USA

Rowland, Troy (Producer)
c/o Susan Curtis *Curtis Talent Management*
9607 Arby Dr
Beverly Hills, CA 90210-1202, USA

Rowlands, Gena (Actor)
c/o Lou Pitt *Pitt Group, The*
9465 Wilshire Blvd Ste 480
Beverly Hills, CA 90212-2603, USA

Rowlands, Patsy
265 Liverpool Rd.
London, ENGLAND N1 1LX, UNITED KINGDOM (UK)

Rowlands, Sherry
5055 Seminary Rd
Alexandria, VA 22311-2034, USA

Rowley, Cynthia (Designer, Fashion Designer)
c/o Staff Member *IMG Models*
304 Park Ave S Fl 12
New York, NY 10010-4301, USA

Rowley, Elwood R (Football Player)
Pittsburgh Steelers
712 Southwick Ave
Clayton, NC 27527-6666, USA

Rowley, Janet D (Physicist)
5310 S University Ave
Chicago, IL 60615-5106, USA

Rowling, J K (Joanne Kathleen) (Writer)
c/o Staff Member *Christopher Little Literary Agency*
10 Eel Brook Studios
125 Moore Park Rd
London SW6 4PS, UNITED KINGDOM (UK)

Rowlinson, John S (Misc)
12 Pullens Field
Headington OX3 0BU, UNITED KINGDOM (UK)

Rowny, Edward L (General)
6200 Oregon Ave NW Apt 345
Washington, DC 20015-1542, USA

Rowser, John (Football Player)
Green Bay Packers
17564 Alta Vista Dr
Southfield, MI 48075-1936, USA

Roxburgh, Richard (Actor, Music Group)
c/o Eric Kranzler *Management 360*
9111 Wilshire Blvd
Beverly Hills, CA 90210-5508, USA

Roxette (Music Group)
c/o Staff Member *Official Roxette Fanclub*
PO Box 177
Capelle a/d IJssel NL-2900AD, THE NETHERLANDS

Roxton, Steve
6 Thornton Rd. Leytonstone
London, ENGLAND E11, UNITED KINGDOM (UK)

Roy (Misc)
Beyond Belief
1639 Valley Dr
Las Vegas, NV 89108-2002, USA

Roy, Arundhati (Writer)
Random House
1745 Broadway # B1
New York, NY 10019-4305, USA

Roy, James D (Financier)
Federal Hone Loan Bank
601 Grant St
Pittsburgh, PA 15219-4455, USA

Roy, John (Comedian)
c/o Staff Member *Metropolitan*
4500 Wilshire Blvd Fl 2
Los Angeles, CA 90010-3858, USA

Roy, Patricia (Baseball Player)
201 E Amkey Way
Ihsaa
Carmel, IN 46032-5170, USA

Roy, Rachel (Designer)
463 7th Ave Fl 16
New York, NY 10018-7604, USA

Roy, Reena (Actor, Bollywood)
Pam Villa D'Monte Park Road
Bandra
Bombay, MS 400 050, INDIA

Royal, Billy Joe (Musician, Songwriter, Writer)
1306 Patterson St
Morehead City, NC 28557-4100, USA

Royal, Darrell K (Coach, Football Coach, Football Player)
6204 Hawk Hill Dr
McKinney, TX 75071-7622, USA

Royals, Mark (Football Player)
St Louis Cardinals
9921 Menander Wood Ct
Odessa, FL 33556-2449, USA

Royce, Kenneth
3 Abbott's Close Andover
Hants., ENGLAND SP11 7NP, UNITED
KINGDOM (UK)

Royce, Mike (Comedian)
c/o Staff Member *United Talent Agency*
(UTA)
9560 Wilshire Blvd Ste 500
Beverly Hills, CA 90212-2401, USA

Roye, Orpheus (Football Player)
Pittsburgh Steelers
26403 Primrose Ln
Westlake, OH 44145-5491, USA

Roylance, Juanita (Baseball Player)
PO Box 282
Lorida, FL 33857-0282, USA

Roylance, Pamela
221 S Gale Dr Unit 403
Beverly Hills, CA 90211-5409, USA

Royo, Sanchez Aristides (President)
Morgan & Morgan
PO Box 1824
Panama City 1, PANAMA

Royster, Jeron K (Jerry) (Baseball Player)
1 Brewers Way
Milwaukee, WI 53214-3655, USA

Royster, Mazio (Football Player)
Tampa Bay Buccaneers
7348 Crimson Dr
Highland, CA 92346-5316, USA

Royston, Ed (Football Player)
New York Giants
22 8th Ave
Seaside Park, NJ 08752-1810, USA

Rozalla (Musician)
c/o Staff Member *Diva Central Inc*
7510 W Sunset Blvd Ste 1445
Los Angeles, CA 90046-3408, USA

Rozanov, Evgeny G (Architect)
Int'l Architecture Academy
Bolshara Dmitrovka 24
Moscow 103284, RUSSIA

Rozelle, Pete
PO Box 9686
Rancho Santa Fe, CA 92067-4686, USA

Rozhdestvensky, Gennady N (Musician)
Victor Hochhauser Ltd
4 Oak Hill Way
London NW3, UNITED KINGDOM (UK)

Rozhdestvensky, Valery I (Cosmonaut)
Potchta Kosmonavtov
Moskovskoi Oblasti
Syvisdny Goroduk 141160, RUSSIA

Rozier, Clifford (Basketball Player)
Toronto Raptors
Air Canada Center
40 Bay St
Toronto, ON M5J 2N8, CANADA

Rozier, Mike (Football Player)
Houston Oilers
9 Hidden Hollow Ln
Sicklerville, NJ 08081-3910, USA

Rozon, Tim
c/o Tina Petro *Epic Talent*
3451 St. Laurent #400
Montreal, PQ H2X 2T6, CANADA

Rozumek, Dave (Football Player)
Kansas City Chiefs
18 Old Rockingham Rd
Salem, NH 03079-2111, USA

Rozzell, Aubrey (Football Player)
Pittsburgh Steelers
PO Box 844
Quitman, MS 39355-0844, USA

Rubalcaba, Gonzalo (Musician)
Eardrums Music
5930 NW 201st St
Hialeah, FL 33015-4886, USA

Rubbia, Carlo (Nobel Prize Laureate)
CERN
Particle Physics Laboratory
Geneva 23 1211, SWITZERLAND

Ruben, Joseph P (Joe) (Director)
250 W 57th St Ste 1905
New York, NY 10107-1901, USA

Rubens, Larry (Football Player)
Green Bay Packers
12213 Ansley Ct
Knoxville, TN 37934-1525, USA

Rubenstein, Ann (Correspondent)
NBC-TV
30 Rockefeller Plz Ste 270E
News Dept
New York, NY 10112-0299, USA

Rubenstein, David (Business Person)
Carlyle Group
1001 Pennsylvania Ave NW Ste 220S
Washington, DC 20004-2525, USA

Rubenstein, Edward (Physicist)
Stanford University Medical School
Surgery Dept
Stanford, CA 94305, USA

Rubiano, Saenz Pedro Cardinal (Religious
Leader)
Arzubispado
Carrera 7A N 10-20
Santafe de Bogota, DC 1, COLOMBIA

Rubick, Rob (Football Player)
Detroit Lions
1571 Stonewood Dr
Lapeer, MI 48446-4200, USA

Rubik, Erno (Inventor)
Rublik Erno
Varosmajor Utca 74
Budapest 1122, HUNGARY

Rubin, Amy (Actor)
Hervey/Grimes
PO Box 64249
Los Angeles, CA 90064-0249, USA

Rubin, Benjamin A (Inventor)
1329 173rd St
Hazel Crest, IL 60429-1921, USA

Rubin, Chanda
708 S Saint Antoine St
Lafayette, LA 70501-5740, USA

Rubin, Ellis (Lawyer)
4141 NE 2nd Ave Ste 203A
Miami, FL 33137-3539, USA

Rubin, Gloria (Actor)
c/o Leigh Brillstein *International Creative
Management (ICM-LA)*
10250 Constellation Blvd
Los Angeles, CA 90067-6200, USA

Rubin, Leigh (Cartoonist)
Creators Syndicate
5777 W Century Blvd Ste 700
Los Angeles, CA 90045-9023, USA

Rubin, Louis D Jr (Writer)
702 Gimghoul Rd
Chapel Hill, NC 27514-3811, USA

Rubin, Rick (Actor, Director, Musician,
Producer)
c/o Staff Member *American Recordings*
8920 W Sunset Blvd
Los Angeles, CA 90069-1812, USA

Rubin, Robert (Misc)
Massachusetts General Hospital
32 Fruit St
Boston, MA 02114-2620, USA

Rubin, Robert E (Financier, Secretary)
Citigroup Inc
399 Park Ave
New York, NY 10022-4699, USA

Rubin, Stephen E (Publisher)
Doubleday Co
1540 Broadway
New York, NY 10036-4039, USA

Rubin, Theodore I (Misc)
219 E 62nd St
New York, NY 10065-7685, USA

Rubin, Vanessa (Musician)
Joel Chriss
300 Mercer St Apt 3J
New York, NY 10003-6732, USA

Rubin, William (Misc)
Museum of Modern Art
11 W 53rd St
New York, NY 10019-5497, USA

Rubin-Vega, Daphne (Actor)
300 Park Ave S # 300
New York, NY 10010-5313, USA

Rubinek, Saul (Actor)
Gersh Agency
232 N Canon Dr
Beverly Hills, CA 90210-5302, USA

Rubinfeld, Daniel (Attorney, Educator)
University of California
Law School
Boalt Hall
Berkeley, CA 94720-0001, USA

Rubini, Cesare (Coach)
Federazione Italian Pallacanestro
Via Fogliano 15
Rome 00199, ITALY

Rubino, Frank A (Lawyer)
2601 S Bayshore Dr
Miami, FL 33133-5417, USA

Rubinoff, Marla (Actor)
c/o Staff Member *Commercial Talent
Agency*
9255 W Sunset Blvd Ste 505
West Hollywood, CA 90069-3301, USA

Rubinstein, John (Actor)
4417 Leydon Ave
Woodland Hills, CA 91364-4847, USA

Rubinstein, Zeida (Actor)
The Agency
1800 Avenue Of Stars Ste 400
Los Angeles, CA 90067-4206, USA

Rubinstein, Zelda
8730 W Sunset Blvd Ste 270
Los Angeles, CA 90069-2247, USA

Rubio, Maria
2238Blvd. Adolfo Lopez Mateo 5
Placopac San Angel
Mexico DF 01040, MEXICO

Rubio, Paulina (Musician)
c/o Rob Prinz *United Talent Agency
(UTA)*
9560 Wilshire Blvd Ste 500
Beverly Hills, CA 90212-2401, USA

Rubke, Karl (Football Player)
San Francisco 49ers
1650 Barnes Mill Rd Apt 1425
Marietta, GA 30062-7568, USA

Ruby & The Romantics
1650 Broadway Ste 508
New York, NY 10019-6833, USA

Rucci, Todd (Football Player)
New England Patriots
5 Southview Ln
Lititz, PA 17543-8205, USA

Ruccolo, Richard (Actor)
ER Talent
301 W 53rd St Apt 4K
New York, NY 10019-5768, USA

Ruch, Charles (Educator)
Boise State University
President's Office
Boise, ID 83725-0001, USA

Rucinsky, Martin (Hockey Player)
Vancouver Canucks
800 Griffiths Way
Vancouver, BC V6B 6G1, CANADA

Ruck, Alan (Actor)
Innovative Artists
1505 10th St
Santa Monica, CA 90401-2805, USA

Rucka, Leo (Football Player)
San Francisco 49ers
814 Crosby Dayton Rd
Crosby, TX 77532-5803, USA

Ruckelshaus, William D (Business Person,
Government Official)
PO Box 76
Medina, WA 98039-0076, USA

Rucker, Anja (Athlete, Track Athlete)
TUS Jena
Wollnitzer Str 42
Jena 07749, GERMANY

Rucker, Darius (Musician)
FishCo Mgmt
2519 Devine St
Columbia, SC 29205-2435, USA

Rucker, Michael (Football Player)
Carolina Panthers
5971 Rolling Ridge Dr
Kannapolis, NC 28081-6705, USA

Rucker, Reggie (Football Player)
Dallas Cowboys
4517 Saint Germain Blvd
Cleveland, OH 44128-6205, USA

Rucker, Reginald J (Reggie) (Football
Player)
3128 Richmond Rd
Beachwood, OH 44122-3249, USA

Rudbottom, Roy R Jr (Diplomat)
7831 Park Ln Apt 213A
Dallas, TX 75225-2045, USA

Rudd, Dwayne (Football Player)
Minnesota Vikings
PO Box 273309
Boca Raton, FL 33427-3309, USA

Rudd, Paul (Actor)
9465 Wilshire Blvd # 517
Beverly Hills, CA 90212-2612, USA

Rudd, Ricky (Race Car Driver)
124 Summerville Dr
Mooresville, NC 28115-7864, USA

Rudd, Xavier (Musician)
c/o Staff Member *Paradigm (Monterey)*
509 Hartnell St
Monterey, CA 93940-2825, USA

Ruddock, Donovan (Razor) (Boxer)
7379 NW 34th St
Lauderhill, FL 33319-4962, USA

Ruddy, Al
1601 Clear View Dr
Beverly Hills, CA 90210-2010, USA

Ruddy, Tim (Football Player)
Miami Dolphins
3885 Vale View Ln
Mead, CO 80542-4500, USA

Rudel, Julius
101 Central Park W # 11A
New York, NY 10023-4250, USA

Rudenstine, Neil L (Educator)
41 Armour Rd
Princeton, NJ 08540-3003, USA

Ruder, David S (Educator, Government Official)
Baker & McKenzie
130 E Randolph St
1 Prudential Plaza
Chicago, IL 60601-6342, USA

Rudi, Joseph O (Joe) (Baseball Player)
17667 Deer Park Loop
Baker City, OR 97814-8425, USA

Rudie, Evelyn (Actor)
Santa Monica Playhouse
7514 Hollywood Blvd
Los Angeles, CA 90046-2814, USA

Rudin, Scott (Filmmaker, Producer)
Scott Rudin Productions
120 W 45th St
New York, NY 10036-4041, USA

Rudis-Bestudik, Mary (Baseball Player)
4333 Deeboyar Ave
Lakewood, CA 90712-3703, USA

Rudman, Warren (Ex-Senator, Senator)
1615 L St NW Ste 1300
Washington, DC 20036-5668, USA

Rudman, Warren B (Senator)
327 10th St SE
Washington, DC 20003-2132, USA

Rudnay, Jack (Football Player)
Kansas City Chiefs
7219 Whipperwill Rd
Versailles, MO 65084-4033, USA

Rudner, Rita (Actor, Comedian)
c/o Staff Member *International Creative Management (ICM-LA)*
10250 Constellation Blvd
Los Angeles, CA 90067-6200, USA

Rudnick, Paul (Writer)
c/o Robert (Bob) Bookman *Creative Artists Agency LCC (CAA-LA)*
2000 Avenue Of The Stars
Los Angeles, CA 90067-4700, USA

Rudnick, Tim (Football Player)
Baltimore Colts
7311 N Octavia Ave
Chicago, IL 60631-4348, USA

Rudoff, Sheldon (Religious Leader)
Union of Orthodox Jewish Congregations
333 7th Ave
New York, NY 10001-5004, USA

Rudolph, Alan
15760 Ventura Blvd Fl 16
Encino, CA 91436-3027, USA

Rudolph, Alan S (Director)
International Creative Mgmt
8942 Wilshire Blvd # 219
Beverly Hills, CA 90211-1908, USA

Rudolph, Ben (Football Player)
New York Jets
561 E General Gorgas Dr
Mobile, AL 36617-3036, USA

Rudolph, Coleman (Football Player)
New York Jets
412 Billings Farm Ln
Canton, GA 30115, USA

Rudolph, Council (Football Player)
Houston Oilers
8310 Lago Vista Dr
Tampa, FL 33614-2769, USA

Rudolph, Frederick (Historian)
234 Ide Rd
Williamstown, MA 01267-2800, USA

Rudolph, Larry (Producer)
Diamond Park Entertainment
432 Park Ave S Fl 2
New York, NY 10016-8013, USA

Rudolph, Maya (Actor)
c/o Sharon Sheinwold *United Talent Agency (UTA)*
9560 Wilshire Blvd Ste 500
Beverly Hills, CA 90212-2401, USA

Rudometkin, John (Basketball Player)
6181 Wise Rd
Newcastle, CA 95658-9643, USA

Rudzinski, Paul (Football Player)
Green Bay Packers
3216 Delahaut St
Green Bay, WI 54301-1551, USA

Rudzinski, Witold (Composer)
Ul Narbutta 50 m 6
Warsaw 02-541, POLAND

Rue, Sara (Actor)
c/o Alan David *Alan David Management*
8840 Wilshire Blvd
Beverly Hills, CA 90211-2606, USA

Ruegamer, Grey (Football Player)
Miami Dolphins
PO Box 70155
Las Vegas, NV 89170-0155, USA

Ruehe, Volker (Government Official)
Bundesministerium Der Verteidigunj
Hardthoehe
Honn 53125, GERMANY

Ruehl, Mercedes (Actor)
c/o Jonathan Howard *Innovative Artists (LA)*
1505 10th St
Santa Monica, CA 90401-2805, USA

Ruelas, Gabriel (Gabe) (Boxer)
1119 S Hudson Ave
Los Angeles, CA 90019-1807, USA

Ruell, Aaron (Actor, Director, Writer)
c/o Staff Member *Brillstein-Grey Entertainment*
9150 Wilshire Blvd Ste 350
Beverly Hills, CA 90212-3453, USA

Ruether, Mike (Football Player)
St Louis Cardinals
23014 Gardner Dr
Alpharetta, GA 30004-2179, USA

Ruether, Rosemary R (Misc)
530 Mayflower Rd
Claremont, CA 91711-4237, USA

Ruettgers, Ken (Football Player)
Green Bay Packers
16897 Golden Stone Dr
Sisters, OR 97759-9696, USA

Ruettgers, Michael C (Business Person)
ECM Corp
35 Parkway Dr
Hopkinton, MA 01748, USA

Ruff, Howard J (Economist, Writer)
PO Box 441
Orem, UT 84059-0441, USA

Ruff, Lindy (Coach, Hockey Player)
5006 Winding Ln
Clarence, NY 14031-1500, USA

Ruffalo, Mark (Actor)
c/o Robert Stein *Robert Stein Management*
345 N Maple Dr Ste 317
Beverly Hills, CA 90210-3856, USA

Ruffin, Jimmy
102 Ryders Ln
East Brunswick, NJ 08816-1328, USA

Ruffini, Attilio (Government Official)
Camera dei Deputati
Via della Missione 10
Rome 00187, ITALY

Ruffo, Victoria (Actor)
c/o Staff Member *Televisa*
Blvd Adolfo Lopez Mateos 232
Colonia San Angel INN
DF CP 01060, MEXICO

Rufus
7250 Beverly Blvd Ste 200
Los Angeles, CA 90036-2560, USA

Ruge, John A (Cartoonist)
240 Bronxville Rd Apt B4
Bronxville, NY 10708-2800, USA

Rugolo, Pete
3955 Pacheco Dr
Sherman Oaks, CA 91403-4420, USA

Ruhman, Chris (Football Player)
San Francisco 49ers
6 Wyckham Cir
Spring, TX 77382-5829, USA

Ruivivar, Anthony Michael (Actor)
c/o Staff Member *Gersh Agency, The (LA)*
232 N Canon Dr
Beverly Hills, CA 90210-5302, USA

Ruiz, Jose Carlos (Actor)
c/o Staff Member *Televisa*
Blvd Adolfo Lopez Mateos 232
Colonia San Angel INN
DF CP 01060, MEXICO

Ruiz, Mark
201 S Capitol Ave Ste 430
Indianapolis, IN 46225-1026, USA

Ruiz, Rodrigo (Actor)
c/o Staff Member *Televisa*
Blvd Adolfo Lopez Mateos 232
Colonia San Angel INN
DF CP 01060, MEXICO

Rukavina, Terry (Baseball Player)
6676 Washington Cir
Franklin, OH 45005-5521, USA

Rule, Gordon (Football Player)
Green Bay Packers
716 Manchester Rd
Neenah, WI 54956-4910, USA

Rulli, Sebastian (Actor)
c/o Gabriel Blanco *Gabriel Blanco Iglesias (Mexico)*
Rio Balsas 35-32
Colonia Cuauhtemoc
DF 06500, MEXICO

Rummells, Dave (Golfer)
1820 Harbor Blvd
Kissimmee, FL 34744-6623, USA

Rumsey, Janet (Baseball Player)
7830 W County Road 80 N
Greensburg, IN 47240-7910, USA

Rumsfeld, Donald (Business Person)
Defense Department
Pentagon
Washington, DC 20301-0001, USA

Run D M C (Music Group)
250 W 57th St # 821
New York, NY 10107-0001, USA

Runager, Max (Football Player)
Philadelphia Eagles
PO Box 37971
Rock Hill, SC 29732-0534, USA

Rundgren, Todd (Musician)
Panacea Entertainment
2705 Glendower Rd
Los Angeles, CA 90027, USA

Runga, Bic (Musician)
c/o Staff Member *Paradigm (Monterey)*
509 Hartnell St
Monterey, CA 93940-2825, USA

Runge, Brian (Baseball Player)
1333 Via Isidro
Oceanside, CA 92056-5629, USA

Runge, Paul (Baseball Player)
8225 E County Dr
El Cajon, CA 92021-8826, USA

Runnels, Terri (Model, Wrestler)
11520 NW 8th Ln
Gainesville, FL 32606-0408, USA

Runnels, Tom (Football Player)
Washington Redskins
6111 Laredo Ct
Granbury, TX 76049-5220, USA

RunningWolf, Myrton (Actor)
c/o Tracy Mapes *Arlene Thornton & Associates*
12711 Ventura Blvd Ste 490
Studio City, CA 91604-2477, USA

Runrig
55 Wellington St.
Aberdeen AB2 1BX, SCOTLAND

Runyan, Jon (Football Player)
Houston Oilers
262 Mount Laurel Rd
Mount Laurel, NJ 08054, USA

Runyan, Marla
PO Box 120
Indianapolis, IN 46206, USA

Runyon, Jennifer (Actor)
5922 SW Amberwood Ave
Corvallis, OR 97333-2702, USA

RuPaul (Actor, Model, Musician)
RuCo Inc
332 Bleecker St # F22
New York, NY 10014-2980, USA

Rupp, Debra Jo (Actor)
c/o Stephen Hanks *Stephen Hanks Management*
252 N Larchmont Blvd Ste 200
Los Angeles, CA 90004-3754, USA

Ruprecht, Tom (Writer)
c/o Staff Member *3 Arts Entertainment Inc*
9460 Wilshire Blvd Fl 7
Beverly Hills, CA 90212-2713, USA

Rusedski, Greg (Tennis Player)
G-Force
PO Box 57
Caernarfon LL55 4WL, UNITED
KINGDOM (UK)

Rush (Music Group)
c/o Staff Member *Artist Group
International (NY)*
150 E 58th St Fl 19
New York, NY 10155-1900, USA

Rush, Barbara (Actor)
1709 Tropical Ave
Beverly Hills, CA 90210, USA

Rush, Deborah
PO Box 5617
Beverly Hills, CA 90209-5617, USA

Rush, Geoffrey (Actor)
c/o Staff Member *Creative Artists Agency
LCC (CAA-LA)*
2000 Avenue Of The Stars
Los Angeles, CA 90067-4700, USA

Rush, Jennifer
145 Central Park W
New York, NY 10023-2004, USA

Rush, Jerry (Football Player)
Detroit Lions
17536 Oak Dr
Detroit, MI 48221-2747, USA

Rush, Mathew (Adult Film Star)
c/o Staff Member *Diva Central Inc*
7510 W Sunset Blvd Ste 1445
Los Angeles, CA 90046-3408, USA

Rush, Merrilee (Musician)
C/O Wendy Kay
27 L Ambiance Ct
Mars Talent Agency Inc
Bardonia, NY 10954-1421, USA

Rush, Robert J (Football Player)
San Diego Chargers
8201 Scruggs Dr
Germantown, TN 38138-6119, USA

Rush, Rudy (Comedian)
c/o Staff Member *International Creative
Management (ICM-LA)*
10250 Constellation Blvd
Los Angeles, CA 90067-6200, USA

Rush, Sarah (Actor)
c/o Staff Member *Acme Talent & Literary
(LA)*
4727 Wilshire Blvd Ste 333
Los Angeles, CA 90010-3874, USA

Rush, Tom (Musician)
Maple Hill Productions Inc
PO Box 490
Wilson, WY 83014-0490, USA

Rushdie, A Salman (Writer)
Wylie Agency
42 Knightsbridge
London SW1S 7JR, UNITED KINGDOM
(UK)

Rushen, Patrice
PO Box 6278
Altadena, CA 91003-6278, USA

Rushing, Marion (Football Player)
Chicago Cardinals
358 Bathon Dr
Pinckneyville, IL 62274-3335, USA

Rusler, Robert
112 S Almont Dr
Los Angeles, CA 90048-2911, USA

Russ, Tim (Actor, Director, Writer)
c/o Gregg Edwards *Gem Entertainment
Group*
2530 Wilshire Blvd Fl 3
Santa Monica, CA 90403-4643, USA

Russek, David (Actor)
c/o Neil Koenigsberg *Koenigsberg
Management/ AsIS Productions*
316 N Rossmore Ave Apt 400
Los Angeles, CA 90004-2413, USA

Russell, Andy (Football Player)
Pittsburgh Steelers
PO Box 614
Pro Athlete Marketing
Beaver Falls, PA 15010-0614, USA

Russell, Betsy
13926 Magnolia Blvd
Sherman Oaks, CA 91423-1230, USA

Russell, Bing
229 E Gainsborough Rd
Thousand Oaks, CA 91360-5331, USA

Russell, Brenda (Actor, Musician)
c/o Seth Keller *SKM Artist Management*
PO Box 25906
Los Angeles, CA 90025-0906, USA

Russell, C Andrew (Football Player)
Pittsburgh Steelers
230 Glen Abbey Ct
Presto, PA 15142-1000, USA

Russell, Chuck (Director)
c/o Robert Stein *Paradigm (LA)*
360 N Crescent Dr
North Bldg
Beverly Hills, CA 90210-6820, USA

Russell, David O (Actor, Director,
Producer, Writer)
c/o John Lesher *Endeavor Agency LLC
(LA)*
9601 Wilshire Blvd Fl 3
Beverly Hills, CA 90210-5204, USA

Russell, Jack (Football Player)
New York Yankees
PO Box 16505
Fort Worth, TX 76162-0505, USA

Russell, Johnny
PO Box 37
Box
Hendersonville, TN 37077-0037, USA

Russell, Ken (Director)
c/o Staff Member *International Creative
Management (ICM-UK)*
Oxford House
76 Oxford St
London W1N 0AX, UNITED KINGDOM
(UK)

Russell, Ken (Football Player)
c/o Staff Member *Detroit Lions*
222 Republic Dr
Allen Park, MI 48101-3650, USA

Russell, Keri (Actor)
c/o Kenny Goodman *William Morris
Agency (WMA-LA)*
1 William Morris Pl
Beverly Hills, CA 90212-4261, USA

Russell, Kimberly
11617 Laurelwood Dr
Studio City, CA 91604-3818, USA

Russell, Kurt (Actor, Producer)
c/o Rick Nicita *Creative Artists Agency
LCC (CAA-LA)*
2000 Avenue Of The Stars
Los Angeles, CA 90067-4700, USA

Russell, Leonard (Football Player)
New England Patriots
497 Saint Louis Ave Apt 102
Long Beach, CA 90814-3363, USA

Russell, Lynne (Anchor, Designer)
Benevento Lampshade Co
880 Marietta Hwy # 630-273
Lynne Russell Unlimited Inc
Roswell, GA 30075-6755, USA

Russell, Mark
3201 33rd Pl NW
Washington, DC 20008-3304, USA

Russell, Ragina (Actor)
c/o Staff Member *Don Gerler Agency*
3349 Cahuenga Blvd W Ste 1
Los Angeles, CA 90068-1379, USA

Russell, T E
8271 Melrose Ave Ste 110
Los Angeles, CA 90046-6800, USA

Russell, Theresa (Actor)
c/o Scott Zimmerman *Untitled
Entertainment (LA)*
331 N Maple Dr Fl 3
Beverly Hills, CA 90210-3827, USA

Russell, Twan (Football Player)
Washington Redskins
11201 NW 8th St
Plantation, FL 33325-1508, USA

Russell, William (Actor)
Kate Feast
Primrose Hill Studios
Fitzroy Road
London NW1 8TR, UNITED KINGDOM
(UK)

Russert, Tim (Television Host)
Meet the Press
4001 Nebraska Ave NW
Nbc
Washington, DC 20016-2733, USA

Russi, Bernhard
6490 Andermatt
SWITZERLAND

Russo, Anthony (Director, Producer,
Writer)
c/o Staff Member *United Talent Agency
(UTA)*
9560 Wilshire Blvd Ste 500
Beverly Hills, CA 90212-2401, USA

Russo, James
8306 Wilshire Blvd # 438
Beverly Hills, CA 90211-2304, USA

Russo, Joe (Director, Producer, Writer)
c/o Staff Member *United Talent Agency
(UTA)*
9560 Wilshire Blvd Ste 500
Beverly Hills, CA 90212-2401, USA

Russo, John
218 Euclid Ave
Glassport, PA 15045-1331, USA

Russo, Patricia (Business Person)
Lucent Technologies Inc
600 Mountain Ave
New Providence, NJ 07974-2008, USA

Russo, Rene (Actor, Model)
c/o John Crosby *John Crosby Management*
1310 N Spaulding Ave
Los Angeles, CA 90046-4010, USA

Russo-Jones, Margaret (Baseball Player)
PO Box 421
Salisbury Center, NY 13454-0421, USA

Rutan, Elbert L (Burt) (Designer)
14329 Rutan Rd
Mojave, CA 93501-2118, USA

Rutan, Richard G (Dick) (Designer)
2833 Delmar Ave
Mojave, CA 93501-1113, USA

Rutgens, Joe (Football Player)
Washington Redskins
227 W Devlin St
Spring Valley, IL 61362-1923, USA

Ruth, Lauren (Cartoonist)
PO Box 200206
New Haven, CT 06520-0206, USA

Ruth, Mike (Football Player)
New England Patriots
85 Jenkins Rd
Andover, MA 01810-2318, USA

Rutherford, John S (Johnny) III (Race Car
Driver)
4819 Black Oak Ln
River Oaks, TX 76114, USA

Rutherford, Johnny (Race Car Driver)
4919 Black Oak Ln
River Oaks, TX 76114-2933, USA

Rutherford, Kelly (Actor)
10390 Santa Monica Blvd Ste 360
Los Angeles, CA 90025-6915, USA

Rutherford, Mike (Musician)
Solo Agency
55 Fulham High St
London SW6 3JJ, UNITED KINGDOM
(UK)

Rutigliano, Sam (Coach, Football Coach)
Liberty University
Athletic Dept
Lynchburg, VA 24506, USA

Rutkowski, Ed (Football Player)
Buffalo Bills
47 Brenton Ln
Hamburg, NY 14075-4327, USA

Rutland, Reggie (Football Player)
Minnesota Vikings
4265 Jailette Rd
Atlanta, GA 30349-1881, USA

Rutledge, Jeffrey R (Jeff) (Coach, Football
Coach, Football Player)
Los Angeles Rams
6102 W Gary Dr
Chandler, AZ 85226-1193, USA

Rutledge, Johnny (Football Player)
Arizona Cardinals
948 SW Avenue J
Belle Glade, FL 33430-4232, USA

Rutschman, Adolph (Ad) (Coach, Football
Coach)
2142 NW Pinehurst Dr
McMinnville, OR 97128-2426, USA

Ruttan, Susan (Actor)
c/o Christopher Black *Opus Entertainment*
5225 Wilshire Blvd Ste 905
Los Angeles, CA 90036-4353, USA

Rutter, John M (Composer)
Old Lacey's
Saint John's Church
Duxford, Cambridge, UNITED KINGDOM
(UK)

Ruttgers, Jurgen (Government Official)
BM fur Bildung/Technologie
Heinemannstr 2
Bonn 53175, GERMANY

Rutting, Barbara
Sommerholz 30
Neumarkt 5202, AUSTRIA

Ruttman, Joe
3 Knob Hill Rd.
Mooresville, NC 28115, USA

Ruud, Birger (Skier)
Munstersvei 20
Kongsberg 3600, NORWAY

Ruud, Sigmund (Skier)
Kirkeveien 57
Oslo 3, NORWAY

Ruud, Tom (Football Player)
Buffalo Bills
1821 S 33rd St
Lincoln, NE 68506-1905, USA

Ruuska, Percy Sylvia (Swimmer)
4216 College View Way
Carmichael, CA 95608, USA

Ruusuvuori, Aarno E (Architect)
Annankalu 15 B 10
Helsinki 12 00120, FINLAND

Ruutel, Arnold (President)
Koidula Str 3-5
Tallinn 0010, ESTONIA

Ruwe, Robert P (Judge)
US Tax Court
400 2nd St NW
Washington, DC 20217-0002, USA

Ruzek, Roger (Football Player)
Dallas Cowboys
921 Warwick St
Bedford, TX 76022-7856, USA

Ruzicka, Vladimir (Hockey Player)
17 Highland Ct
Needham, MA 02492-3149, USA

Ruznak, Josef (Director)
Writers & Artists
360 N Crescent Dr Bldg North
Beverly Hills, CA 90210-6818, USA

Ryan, Arthur F (Business Person)
Prudential Insurance
Prudential Plz
751 Broad St
Newark, NJ 07102-2992, USA

Ryan, Blanchard (Actor)
c/o Staff Member *Jeff Morrone
Management*
9350 Wilshire Blvd Ste 224
Beverly Hills, CA 90212-3204, USA

Ryan, Buddy
8701 S Hardy Dr
Tempe, AZ 85284-2800, USA

Ryan, Dave (Musician)
Agency Group Ltd
1775 Broadway Ste 515
New York, NY 10019-1903, USA

Ryan, Debbie (Comedian)
University of Virginia
PO Box 3785
Athletic Dept
Charlottesville, VA 22903-0785, USA

Ryan, Fran
4204 W Woodland Ave
Burbank, CA 91505-3758, USA

Ryan, Frank (Football Player)
Los Angeles Rams
PO Box 185
Grafton, VT 05146-0185, USA

Ryan, Jeri (Actor)
Nick Terzian Agency
1445 N Stanley Ave Fl 2
Los Angeles, CA 90046-4015, USA

Ryan, Kent (Football Player)
Detroit Lions
5550 W University Blvd
Dallas, TX 75209-5118, USA

Ryan, Lee (Musician)
c/o Staff Member *Concorde Intl Artists Ltd*
101 Shepherds Bush Rd
London W6 7LP, UNITED KINGDOM
(UK)

Ryan, Lisa (Religious Leader, Television Host)
c/o Staff Member *700 Club*
Christian Broadcasting Network
977 Centerville Turnpike
Virginia Beach, VT 23463, USA

Ryan, Lisa Dean (Actor)
c/o Staff Member *Pakula/King &
Associates*
9229 W Sunset Blvd Ste 315
Los Angeles, CA 90069-3403, USA

Ryan, Lynn (Nolan) Jr (Baseball Player)
Nolan Ryan Foundation
2925 S Bypass 35
Alvin, TX 77511, USA

Ryan, Marisa (Actor)
c/o Bob McGowan *McGowan
Management*
8733 W Sunset Blvd Ste 103
W Hollywood, CA 90069-2241, USA

Ryan, Mark (Actor)
Henderson Hogan
247 S Beverly Dr # 102
Beverly Hills, CA 90212-3830, USA

Ryan, Max (Actor)
c/o Erik Kritzer *Fenton-Kritzer
Entertainment*
8840 Wilshire Blvd Fl 3
Beverly Hills, CA 90211-2606, USA

Ryan, Meg (Actor)
c/o Suzan Bymel *Management 360*
9111 Wilshire Blvd
Beverly Hills, CA 90210-5508, USA

Ryan, Mitchell (Actor)
30355 Mulholland Hwy
Cornell, CA 91301-3117, USA

Ryan, Norbert R Jr (Admiral)
Cheif Of Naval Porsonnel
2 Navy Anx
2 Navy St
Washington, DC 20370-5240, USA

Ryan, Pat (Football Player)
New York Jets
6930 Old Kent Dr
Knoxville, TN 37919-7472, USA

Ryan, Patrick G (Business Person)
Aon Corp
200 East Randolf St
Chicago, IL 60601, USA

Ryan, Roz (Actor)
c/o Leanna Levy *Cassell-Levy Inc*
843 N Sycamore Ave
Los Angeles, CA 90038-3391, USA

Ryan, Ryan (Actor)
c/o Staff Member *Warner Bros Television
Production*
4000 Warner Blvd
Burbank, CA 91522-0001, USA

Ryan, Shawn (Producer)
c/o Staff Member *International Creative
Management (ICM-LA)*
10250 Constellation Blvd
Los Angeles, CA 90067-6200, USA

Ryan, Thomas M (Business Person)
CVS Corp
1 Cvs Dr
Woonsocket, RI 02895-6184, USA

Ryan, Tim E (Football Player)
Chicago Bears
1159 Calle Ventura
San Jose, CA 95120-5503, USA

Ryan, Timothy T (Tim) (Football Player)
Tampa Bay Buccaneers
4901 Sugar Creek Dr
Evansville, IN 47715-7744, USA

Ryan, Tom K (Cartoonist)
North American Syndicate
235 E 45th St
New York, NY 10017-3305, USA

Ryans, Larry (Football Player)
Tampa Bay Buccaneers
110 Brookfield Dr
Greenwood, SC 29646-8501, USA

Ryazanov, Eldar A (Director)
Bolshoi Tishinski Per 12 #70
Moscow 123557, RUSSIA

Rybkin, Ivan (Government Official)
National Security Council
4 Staraya Poischad
Moscow 103073, RUSSIA

Rybska, Agnieszka (Music Group,
Musician)
RPM Music Productions
48B W 10th St
New York, NY 10011, USA

Rychlec, Tom (Football Player)
Detroit Lions
71 Round Hill Rd
Southington, CT 06489-3645, USA

Ryckman, Billy (Football Player)
Atlanta Falcons
513 Doucet Rd
Lafayette, LA 70503-3557, USA

Ryczek, Dan (Football Player)
Washington Redskins
3714 Monitor Pl
Olney, MD 20832-2248, USA

Ryczek, Paul (Football Player)
Atlanta Falcons
9335 Scott Rd
Roswell, GA 30076-3416, USA

Rydal, Emma (Actor)
c/o Lucy Brazier *Peters Fraser & Dunlop
(PFD - UK)*
Drury House
34-43 Russell St
London WC2B 5HA, UNITED KINGDOM
(UK)

Rydalch, Ron (Football Player)
Chicago Bears
500 E Durfee St
Grantsville, UT 84029-9514, USA

Rydell, Bobby (Actor, Music Group,
Musician)
917 Bryn Mawr Ave
Penn Valley, PA 19072-1524, USA

Rydell, Christopher (Actor)
911 N Sweetzer Ave Apt C
Los Angeles, CA 90069-4368, USA

Rydell, Mark (Director)
Concourse Productions
3110 Main St Ste 220
Santa Monica, CA 90405-5353, USA

Ryder, Lisa (Actor)
Andromeda Productions
8651 E Lake Dr
Burnaby, BC V5A 4T7, CANADA

Ryder, Mitch (Music Group, Musician)
Entertainment Services Int'l
6400 Pleasant Park Dr
Chanhassen, MN 55317-8804, USA

Ryder, Nick (Football Player)
Detroit Lions
14 Ridgeway
Goshen, NY 10924-1408, USA

Ryder, Thomas O (Publisher)
Reader's Digest Assn
PO Box 100
Pleasantville, NY 10572-0100, USA

Ryder, Winona (Actor)
c/o Susan Calogerakis *Thruline
Entertainment*
9250 Wilshire Blvd Ground Fl
Beverly Hills, CA 90210, USA

Ryders, Ruff (Music Group)
c/o Staff Member *International Creative
Management (ICM-LA)*
10250 Constellation Blvd
Los Angeles, CA 90067-6200, USA

Rydze, Richard (Misc)
125 7th St
Pittsburgh, PA 15222-3410, USA

Ryerson, Ann
935 Gayley Ave
Los Angeles, CA 90024-2805, USA

Ryff, Frankie
2055 McGraw Ave
Bronx, NY 10462-8014, USA

Rykiel, Sonia F (Designer, Fashion
Designer)
175 Blvd Saint Germain
Paris 75006, FRANCE

Ryknow (Musician)
Agency Group Ltd
1775 Broadway Ste 515
New York, NY 10019-1903, USA

Rylance, Mark (Actor, Director)
Shakespeare's Globe
Southwark
London SE1, UNITED KINGDOM (UK)

Ryman, Robert T (Artist)
17 W 16th St
New York, NY 10011-6301, USA

Rymer, Charlie (Golfer)
1450 Spartan Ln
Athens, GA 30606-5326, USA

Rymer, Pamela Ann (Judge)
US Court of Appeals
125 S Grand Ave
Pasadena, CA 91105-1652, USA

Rynkiewicz, Mariusz (Artist, Misc)
12401 Alexander Rd
Everett, WA 98204-4715, USA

Rypdal, Terje (Musician)
PJP as
Utragata 16
Voss 5700, NORWAY

Rypien, Mark R (Football Player)
Washington Redskins
3811 E Bellerive Ln
Spokane, WA 99223-6188, USA

Rysanek, Leony
Altenbeuren D-88682, GERMANY

Ryumin, Valery V (Astronaut, Misc)
Potchta Kosmonavtov
Moskovskoi Oblasti
Syvsdny Goroduk 141160, RUSSIA

Ryun, James R (Jim) (Athlete, Track Athlete)
PO Box 62B
Lawrence, KS 66044, USA

Ryun, Jim
RR 3 Box 62B
Lawrence, KS 66044, USA

Ryzhkov, Nikolai I (Misc)
State Duma
Okhotny Ryad 1
Moscow 103009, RUSSIA

RZA (Artist, Music Group, Musician)
c/o Joe Carlone *The Firm*
9465 Wilshire Blvd Fl 6
Beverly Hills, CA 90212-2605, USA

Rzeznik, Johnny (Musician)
c/o Pat Magnarella *PMC*
5900 Wilshire Blvd Ste 1720
Los Angeles, CA 90036-5017, USA

S

S, Kimberley
c/o Staff Member *Diva Central Inc*
7510 W Sunset Blvd Ste 1445
Los Angeles, CA 90046-3408, USA

S, Kimberly (DJ)
c/o Len Evans *Project Publicity*
312 W 53rd St
New York, NY 10019-5743, USA

S Club 7 (Music Group)
c/o Staff Member *Creative Artists Agency LCC (CAA-LA)*
2000 Avenue Of The Stars
Los Angeles, CA 90067-4700, USA

S Jayaram (Actor)
7-Majestic Terrace 48 Arcot Road
Saligramam
Chennai, TN 600 098, INDIA

Saadiq, Raphael (Musician)
c/o Jeff Frasco *Creative Artists Agency LCC (CAA-LA)*
2000 Avenue Of The Stars
Los Angeles, CA 90067-4700, USA

Saakashvili, Mikhail (President)
President's Office
Rustaveli Prosp 29
Tbilsi 380008, GEORGIA

Saalfeld, Kelly (Football Player)
New York Giants
761 N 153rd Ave
Omaha, NE 68154-1807, USA

Saar, Bettye (Artist)
8074 Willow Glen Rd
Los Angeles, CA 90046-1617, USA

Saari, Roy A (Swimmer)
PO Box 7086
Mammoth Lakes, CA 93546-7086, USA

Saatchi, Charles (Business Person)
M&C Saatchi
36 Golden Square
London W1R 4EE, UNITED KINGDOM (UK)

Saatchi, Maurice (Business Person)
36 Golden Square
London W1R 4EE, UNITED KINGDOM (UK)

Sabah, Sheikh Saad al-Abdullah al-Salem (Prime Minister, Prince)
Prime Minister's Office
PO Box 4
Safat
Kuwait City 13001, KUWAIT

Saban, Haim (Producer)
c/o Staff Member *Saban Entertainment*
10960 Wilshire Blvd Fl 22
Los Angeles, CA 90024-3808, USA

Saban, Lou (Coach, Football Coach)
Cleveland Rams
177 Lake Laurel Dr
Dahlonega, GA 30533-6596, USA

Saban, Nick (Athlete)
Chowan College
Chowan College
Athletic Dept
Murfreesboro, NC 27855, USA

Sabara, Daryl (Actor)
Endeavor Talent Agency
9701 Wilshire Blvd Ste 1000
Beverly Hills, CA 90212-2010, USA

Sabathia, C C (Baseball Player)
c/o Staff Member *Cleveland Indians*
2401 Ontario St
Jacobs Field
Cleveland, OH 44115-4003, USA

Sabatini, Gabriela (Tennis Player)
c/o Staff Member *Women's Tennis Association (WTA (UK))*
Bank Lane
Roehampton
London SW15 5XZ, UNITED KINGDOM (UK)

Sabatino, Joe (Actor)
c/o Greg Meyer *Acme Talent & Literary (LA)*
4727 Wilshire Blvd Ste 333
Los Angeles, CA 90010-3874, USA

Sabatino, Michael (Actor)
13538 Valleyheart Dr N
Sherman Oaks, CA 91423-3124, USA

Sabato, Ernesto (Writer)
Severino Langeri 3135
Santos Lugares, ARGENTINA

Sabato Jr, Antonio (Actor, Model)
c/o Jeff Frankel *Colden, McKuin, & Frankel*
141 El Camino Dr Ste 100
Beverly Hills, CA 90212-2717, USA

Sabb, Dwayne (Football Player)
New England Patriots
26 Marie Rd
Fords, NJ 08863-1306, USA

Sabbah, Michel (Religious Leader)
Latin Patriarch Office
PO Box 14152
Jerusalem, ISRAEL

Sabbatini, Rory (Golfer)
1605 Byron Nelson Pkwy
Southlake, TX 76092-9634, USA

Sabella, Ernie (Actor, Artist, Voice Over Artist)
c/o Staff Member *Gage Group, The (LA)*
14724 Ventura Blvd Ste 505
Sherman Oaks, CA 91403-3505, USA

Sabelle (Music Group, Musician, Songwriter, Writer)
Sarmast Entertainment
241 W 36th St Apt 2R
New York, NY 10018-7541, USA

Saberhagen, Bret W (Baseball Player)
5535 Amber Cir
Calabasas, CA 91302-3146, USA

Sabihy, Kyle (Actor)
c/o TJ Stein *Stein Entertainment Group*
11271 Ventura Blvd # 477
Studio City, CA 91604-3136, USA

Sabiston, David C Jr (Doctor)
622 Cedar Club Cir
Chapel Hill, NC 27517-7215, USA

Sabo, Christopher A (Chris) (Baseball Player)
7455 Stonemeadow Ln
Cincinnati, OH 45242-6305, USA

Sabo-Dusanko, Julie (Baseball Player)
7702 E Doubletree Ranch Rd Ste 150
Scottsdale, AZ 85258-2130, USA

Sabol, Steve (Business Person)
c/o Staff Member *NFL Films*
330 Fellowship Rd
Mount Laurel, NJ 08054-1201, USA

Sabuda, Robert (Writer)
155 W 72nd St Rm 401
New York, NY 10023-3250, USA

Saca, Elias Antonio (President)
Casa Presidencial Avda Cuba
Barrosan Jacinto
San Salvador, EL SALVADOR

Sacchi, Robert
203 N Gramercy Pl
Los Angeles, CA 90004-4021, USA

Sacco, Joe (Artist)
c/o Staff Member *Fantagraphics Books*
7563 Lake City Way NE
Seattle, WA 98115-4218, USA

Sacco, Michael (Misc)
Seafarers International Union
5201 Auth Way
Suitland, MD 20746-4275, USA

Saccone, Viviana (Actor)
c/o Staff Member *Telefe - Argentina*
Pavon 2444 (C1248AAT)
Buenos Aires, ARGENTINA

Sachar, Louis (Writer)
Foster Books/Farrar Straus Giroux
19 Union Sq W
New York, NY 10003-3304, USA

Sachdev, Asha (Actor, Bollywood)
18B Sunset Heights
59 Pali Hill Bandra
Mumbai, MS 40050, INDIA

Sachenbacher, Evi (Skier)
WSV Reit im Winkl
Rthausplatz 1
Reit im Winkl 83242, GERMANY

Sachin (Actor, Bollywood, Director, Filmmaker)
B609 Pearl Apartments 33 Swami Samarth Nagar
Cross Road No 3 Andheri
Bombay, MS 400 058, INDIA

Sachs, Andrew (Actor)
Richard Stone
2 Henrietta St
London WC2E 8PS, UNITED KINGDOM (UK)

Sachs, Gloria (Designer, Fashion Designer)
117 E 57th St
New York, NY 10022-2002, USA

Sachs, Gunter
101 E 63rd St
New York, NY 10065-7302, USA

Sachs, Jeffrey D (Economist)
Harvard University
International Development Institute
Cambridge, MA 02138, USA

Sachs, Richard (Doctor)
6 Saint Ronan Ter
New Haven, CT 06511-2315, USA

Sachs, William (Director)
3739 Montuso Pl
Encino, CA 91436-4001, USA

Sachu (Actor, Bollywood)
78 Sairam Colony
Alwarpet
Chennai, TN 600018, INDIA

Sack, Kevin (Journalist)
Los Angeles Times
202 W 1st St
Editorial Dept
Los Angeles, CA 90012-4105, USA

Sack, Steve (Cartoonist)
Minneapolis Star-Tribune
425 Portland Ave
Minneapolis, MN 55488-1511, USA

Sackheim, Daniel (Director, Editor, Producer)
c/o Chris Simonian *Creative Artists Agency LCC (CAA-LA)*
2000 Avenue Of The Stars
Los Angeles, CA 90067-4700, USA

Sackhoff, Kate (Actor)
c/o Staff Member *Envision Entertainment*
9255 W Sunset Blvd Ste 500
West Hollywood, CA 90069-3301, USA

Sackhoff, Katee (Actor)
c/o Leland LaBarre *Diverse Talent Group*
1875 Century Park E Ste 2250
Los Angeles, CA 90067-2563, USA

Sacks, Greg (Race Car Driver)
6092 Sabal Creek Blvd
Port Orange, FL 32128-7131, USA

Sacks, Jonathan H (Religious Leader)
735 High Road
London N12 0US, UNITED KINGDOM (UK)

Sacks, Oliver W (Doctor, Writer)
2 Horatio St Apt 3G
New York, NY 10014-1638, USA

Sacrinty, Nick (Football Player)
Chicago Bears
531 Dogwood Dr
Eden, NC 27288-5212, USA

Sadanah, Kamal (Actor, Bollywood)
Jal Kamal Plot 202
23rd Road Bandra
Mumbai, MS 400050, INDIA

Sadat, Jehan El- (Activist)
University of Maryland
Int'l Development Center
College Park, MD 20742-0001, USA

Sadat, Madame Jehan
Nw2310 Decatur Pl.
Washington, DC 20008, USA

Sade (Musician, Songwriter, Writer)
c/o Staff Member Creative Artists Agency
LCC (CAA-LA)
2000 Avenue Of The Stars
Los Angeles, CA 90067-4700, USA

Sadeckl, Raymond M (Ray) (Baseball Player)
4237 E Clovis Ave
Mesa, AZ 85206-1945, USA

Sadik, Nafis (Government Official)
United Nations Population Fund
220 E 42nd St
New York, NY 10017-5880, USA

Sadler, Elliott (Race Car Driver)
PO Box 871
Emporia, VA 23847-0871, USA

Sadler, William
10474 Santa Monica Blvd Ste 380
Los Angeles, CA 90025-6943, USA

Sadowski, Jonathan (Actor)
c/o Susan Yoo Edmonds Management
1635 N Cahuenga Blvd Fl 5
Los Angeles, CA 90028-6201, USA

Safdie, Moshe (Architect)
100 Rev Nazareno Properzi Way
Somerville, MA 02143-3740, USA

Safer, Morley (Correspondent)
c/o Staff Member 60 Minutes
524 W 57th St
Cbs News
New York, NY 10019-2930, USA

Saferight, Harry (Baseball Player)
2321 Wadebridge Rd
Midlothian, VA 23113-3839, USA

Saffiotti, Umberto (Doctor)
5114 Wissioming Rd
Bethesda, MD 20816-2259, USA

Safin, Marat (Tennis Player)
TC Weiden am Postkeller
Schirmitzer Weg
Weiden 92637, GERMANY

Safina, Alessandro (Opera Singer)
Interscope Records
2220 Colorado Ave
Santa Monica, CA 90404-3506, USA

Safire, William (Journalist, Writer)
6200 Elmwood Rd
Chevy Chase, MD 20815-6624, USA

Safka, Melanie (Musician)
Two Story Records, Inc
53 Baymont St
Clearwater, FL 33767-1705, USA

Safran Foer, Jonathan (Writer)
c/o Geoffrey Sanford Rabineau Wachter &
Sanford Literary
522 Wilshire Blvd Ste L
Santa Monica, CA 90401-1445, USA

Safuto, Dominick (Randy) (Music Group, Musician)
PO Box 656507
Fresh Meadows, NY 11365-6507, USA

Safuto, Frank (Music Group, Musician)
PO Box 656507
Fresh Meadows, NY 11365-6507, USA

Sagal, Jean (Actor)
Progressive Artists Agency
400 S Beverly Dr Ste 216
Beverly Hills, CA 90212-4404, USA

Sagal, Katey (Actor)
7095 Hollywood Blvd Ste 792
Los Angeles, CA 90028-8912, USA

Sagal, Liz
4526 Wilshire Blvd
Los Angeles, CA 90010-3801, USA

Sagansky, Jeff
145 Ocean Avenue Ext
Santa Monica, CA 90402-1211, USA

Sagapolutele, Pio (Football Player)
Cleveland Browns
PO Box 110
Bellevue, ID 83313-0110, USA

Sagar, Ramanand (Actor, Director, Filmmaker, Producer)
Natraj Studios 194 M V Road
Andheri (E)
Bombay, MS 400 069, INDIA

Sagdeev, Roald Z (Physicist)
Space Research Institute
Profsoyuznaya 84/32
Moscow B485 11780, RUSSIA

Sage, William (Actor)
Gersh Agency
232 N Canon Dr
Beverly Hills, CA 90210-5302, USA

Sagebrecht, Marianne (Actor)
Kaulbachstr 61
Ruckgeb
Munich 80539, GERMANY

Sagely, Floyd (Football Player)
San Francisco 49ers
0181 Wildflower Pl
Edwards, CO 81362, USA

Sagemiller, Melissa (Actor)
c/o Leslie Siebert Gersh Agency, The (LA)
232 N Canon Dr
Beverly Hills, CA 90210-5302, USA

Sager, Carole Bayer (Music Group, Musician, Songwriter, Writer)
10761 Bellagio Rd
Los Angeles, CA 90077-3731, USA

Sager, Craig (Sportscaster)
3064 Spring Hill Pkwy SE
Smyrna, GA 30080-4793, USA

Saget, Bob (Actor)
c/o Staff Member William Morris Agency
(WMA-LA)
1 William Morris Pl
Beverly Hills, CA 90212-4261, USA

Saglio, Laura (Actor)
Cineart
36 Rue de Ponthieu
Paris 75008, FRANCE

Sagnier, Ludivine (Actor)
c/o Elyse Scherz Endeavor Agency LLC
(LA)
9601 Wilshire Blvd Fl 3
Beverly Hills, CA 90210-5204, USA

Sagona, Katie (Actor)
Wilhelmina Creative Mgmt
300 Park Ave S # 200
New York, NY 10010-5313, USA

Sahagun, Elena (Actor)
Artists Agency
1180 S Beverly Dr Ste 301
Los Angeles, CA 90035-1154, USA

Sahara Hotnights (Music Group)
c/o Staff Member Paradigm (Monterey)
509 Hartnell St
Monterey, CA 93940-2825, USA

Sahgal, Ajay (Actor, Producer, Writer)
c/o Nicole Clemens International Creative
Management (ICM-LA)
10250 Constellation Blvd
Los Angeles, CA 90067-6200, USA

Sahgal, Nayantara (Writer)
181B Rajpur Road
Dehra Dun, Uttar Pradesh 248009, INDIA

Sahi, Deepa (Actor, Bollywood)
466 Laxmi Bhuvan Sardar Patel Road
Mumbai, MS 400004, INDIA

Sahl, Mort (Actor, Comedian)
1441 3rd Ave Apt 12C
New York, NY 10028-1976, USA

Sahm, Hans-Werner (Artist)
Zur Wasserburg 7
Bidingen
Schwab, GERMANY

Saidock, Tom (Football Player)
Philadelphia Eagles
20316 Old Colony Rd
Dearborn Heights, MI 48127-2758, USA

Sailer, Anton (Toni) (Skier)
Gundhabing 19
Kitzbuhl 6370, AUSTRIA

Sailer, Toni
Gundhabing 19
Kitzbuhel A-6370, AUSTRIA

Sailors, Kenny (Ken) (Basketball Player)
1614 Shoestring Rd
Gooding, ID 83330-5234, USA

Saimes, George (Football Executive, Football Player)
Buffalo Bills
2307 Beechmoor Dr NW
North Canton, OH 44720-5814, USA

Sain, John F (Johnny) (Baseball Player)
2S707 Avenue Latour
Oak Brook, IL 60523-1085, USA

Sain, Johnny
2 So. 707 Ave. Latour
Oakbrook, IL 60521, USA

Saindon, Pat (Football Player)
New Orleans Saints
105 King Arthur Pl
Alabaster, AL 35007-9111, USA

Sainsbury of Preston Candover, John D (Business Person)
J Sainsbury PLC
Stamford House
Stamford St
London SE1 9LL, UNITED KINGDOM (UK)

Sainsbury of Turville, David J (Business Person)
4 Charterhouse Mews
Charterhouse Square
London EC1M 6BB, UNITED KINGDOM (UK)

Saint, Crosbie E (General)
1116 N Pitt St
Alexandria, VA 22314-1455, USA

Saint, Eva Marie (Actor)
c/o Staff Member International Creative
Management (ICM-LA)
10250 Constellation Blvd
Los Angeles, CA 90067-6200, USA

Saint, Laurent Yves (Designer, Fashion Designer)
7 Rue Leonce Reynaud
Paris 75116, FRANCE

Saint, Silva (Adult Film Star)
c/o Staff Member Atlas Multimedia Inc
9035 Independence Ave
Canoga Park, CA 91304-1743, USA

Saint, Sylvia
Suze.net
26500 Agoura Rd # 389
Calabasas, CA 91302-1952, USA

Saint James, Sara
289 S Robertson Blvd # 259
Beverly Hills, CA 90211-2810, USA

Saint James, Susan (Actor)
c/o David Tenzer Creative Artists Agency
LCC (CAA-LA)
2000 Avenue Of The Stars
Los Angeles, CA 90067-4700, USA

Saint-Subber, Arnold (Producer)
116 E 64th St
New York, NY 10065-7307, USA

Sainte-Marie, Buffy (Music Group, Musician, Songwriter, Writer)
1191 Kuhio Highway
Kapaa, HI 96746, USA

Sainz, Salvador (Actor, Director)
Ave Prat de la Riba 43
Reus (Tarragona) 43201, SPAIN

Sajak, Pat (Game Show Host)
c/o Staff Member PAT Productions
10202 Washington Blvd
Dave Lean #230
Culver City, CA 90232-3119, USA

Sajawal, Aziz (Actor, Bollywood, Director, Filmmaker)
S303 Sameer Society JP Road
Seven Bungalows Andheri
Mumbai, MS 400058, INDIA

Sajko, Kristina (Model)
Karin Models
6 W 14th St # 300
New York, NY 10011-7505, USA

Sakamoto, Ryoichi (Composer)
Columbia Artists Mgmt Inc
1790 Broadway Fl 6
New York, NY 10019-1412, USA

Sakamoto, Soichi (Coach, Swimmer)
768 McCully St
Honolulu, HI 96826-3915, USA

Sakamura, Ken (Inventor)
University of Tokyo
Information Science Dept
Tokyo, JAPAN

Sakato, George T (War Hero)
6369 Katherine Way
Denver, CO 80221, USA

Sakharov, Alik (Cinematographer)
6050 Boulevard E Apt 4D
West New York, NJ 07093-3932, USA

Sakic, Joe (Hockey Player)
4785 S Franklin St
Englewood, CO 80113-5940, USA

Sakmann, Bert (Nobel Prize Laureate)
Max Planck Institute
Jehnstr 39
Heidelberg 69120, GERMANY

Saks, Gene (Actor, Director)
International Creative Mgmt
40 W 57th St Ste 1800
New York, NY 10019-4001, USA

Sala, Edoardo (Actor)
Carol Levi Co
Via Giuseppe Pisanelli
Rome 00196, ITALY

Sala, Oskar
Leistikowstr. 5
Berlin 14050, GERMANY

Sala, Richard (Cartoonist)
3131 College Ave
Berkeley, CA 94705-2740, USA

Salaam, Abdul (Football Player)
New York Jets
11153 Embassy Dr
Cincinnati, OH 45240-3005, USA

Salaam, Ephraim (Football Player)
Atlanta Falcons
8868 Chadbury Pl
Elk Grove, CA 95758-6214, USA

Salaam, Rashaan (Football Player)
Chicago Bears
8132 Brookhaven Rd
San Diego, CA 92114-7404, USA

Salac, Joe
2205 Avenue Coslee
Quebec, PQ GIL 4W7, CANADA

Salad Hassan, Abdikassim (President)
President's Office
People's Palace
Mogadishu, SOMALIA

Salamanca & Garcia (Writer)
c/o Gabriel Blanco *Gabriel Blanco Iglesias (Mexico)*
Rio Balsas 35-32
Colonia Cuauhtemoc
DF 06500, MEXICO

Salans, Lester B (Doctor)
Sandoz Research Institute
RR 10
Hanover, NJ 07936, USA

Salata, Paul (Football Player)
San Francisco 49ers
3723 Birch St Ste 11
Newport Beach, CA 92660-2614, USA

Salazar, Alberto (Athlete, Track Athlete)
Int'l Mgmt Group
1 Erieview Plz
1360 E 9th St #1300
Cleveland, OH 44114-1738, USA

Salazar, Arion (Musician)
Eric Godtland Mgmt
5715 Claremont Ave # C
Oakland, CA 94618-1279, USA

Salazar, Eliseo (Race Car Driver)
2310 Rippling Way S
Indianapolis, IN 46260-6570, USA

Saldana, Theresa (Actor)
c/o Kim Dorr *Defining Artists*
10 Universal City Plz Ste 2000
Universal City, CA 91608-1074, USA

Saldana, Zoe (Actor)
c/o Bill Butler *Gersh Agency, The (NY)*
41 Madison Ave Fl 33
New York, NY 10010-2202, USA

Saldanha, Carlos (Animator, Director)
c/o Staff Member *Blue Sky Studios*
44 S Broadway Fl 17
White Plains, NY 10601-4411, USA

Saldarini, Giovanni Cardinal (Religious Leader)
Archdiocese of Turin
Via dell'Archivescovado 12
Turin 10121, ITALY

Saldi, Jay (Football Player)
Dallas Cowboys
303 Donley Ct
Southlake, TX 76092-5940, USA

Sale, Jamie (Dancer)
12116 NW 128th St
Edmonton, AB T5L 1C3, CANADA

Saleh, Ali Abdullah (General, President)
President's Office
Zubairy St
Sana'a, YEMEN ARAB REPUBLIC

Saleh, Jaime H (Governor)
Fort Amsterdam 1
Willemstad
Curacao, NETHERLANDS ANTILLES

Salem, Dahlia (Actor)
c/o Adam Levine *Anthem Entertainment*
6100 Wilshire Blvd Ste 1170
Los Angeles, CA 90048-5116, USA

Salem, Harvey (Football Player)
Houston Oilers
25 Menlo Pl
Berkeley, CA 94707-1532, USA

Salem, Marc (Actor, Comedian)
William Morris Agency
151 El Camino Dr
Beverly Hills, CA 90212-2775, USA

Salemi, Sam (Football Player)
New York Yankees
2971 Delaware Ave
Kenmore, NY 14217-2353, USA

Salenger, Meredith (Actor)
Shelter Entertainment
9255 W Sunset Blvd Ste 1010
Los Angeles, CA 90069-3307, USA

Salerno, Al (Baseball Player)
1913 Tilden Ave
New Hartford, NY 13413-3106, USA

Salerno-Sonnenberg, Nadja (Musician)
Columbia Artists Mgmt Inc
1790 Broadway Fl 6
New York, NY 10019-1412, USA

Sales, Eugenio de Araujo Cardinal (Religious Leader)
Palacio Sao Joaquim
Rua Gloria 446
Rio de Janeiro RJ 20241-150, BRAZIL

Sales, Nykesha (Basketball Player)
Connecticut Sun
Mohegan Sun Arena
Uncasville, CT 06382, USA

Sales, Soupy (Actor, Comedian)
245 E 35th St
New York, NY 10016-4283, USA

Salgado, Michael (Musician)
c/o Staff Member *Sony Music Miami*
605 Lincoln Rd Fl 7
Miami Beach, FL 33139-2900, USA

Salgado, Sabastiano R (Photographer)
Instituto Terra
Fazenda Bulcao
Minas Gerais, BRAZIL

Saliba, Metropolitan Primate Philip (Religious Leader)
Antiochian Orthodox Christian Diocese
358 Mountain Rd
Englewood, NJ 07631-3798, USA

Saliers, Emily (Musician, Songwriter, Writer)
Russell Carter Artist Mgmt
567 Ralph McGill Blvd NE
Atlanta, GA 30312-1110, USA

Salim, Salim Ahmed (Prime Minister)
Organization of African Unity
PO Box 3243
Addis Ababa, ETHIOPIA

Salinas, Carmen (Actor)
c/o Staff Member *Televisa*
Blvd Adolfo Lopez Mateos 232
Colonia San Angel INN
DF CP 01060, MEXICO

Salinas, Jorge (Actor)
c/o Staff Member *Televisa*
Blvd Adolfo Lopez Mateos 232
Colonia San Angel INN
DF CP 01060, MEXICO

Salinas, Maria Elena (Actor)
c/o Staff Member *Univision*
605 3rd Ave Fl 12
New York, NY 10158-1299, USA

Salinas, Nora (Actor)
c/o Staff Member *Televisa*
Blvd Adolfo Lopez Mateos 232
Colonia San Angel INN
DF CP 01060, MEXICO

Salinger, Diane (Actor)
The Agency
1800 Avenue Of Stars Ste 400
Los Angeles, CA 90067-4206, USA

Salinger, Emmanuel (Actor)
Cineart
36 Rue de Ponthieu
Paris 75008, FRANCE

Salinger, Jerome David (J D) (Writer)
RR 3 Box 176
Comish Flat, NH 03745, USA

Salinger, Matt (Actor)
Bresler Kelly Assoc
11500 W Olympic Blvd Ste 510
Los Angeles, CA 90064-1527, USA

Salisbury, Benjamin (Actor)
c/o Staff Member *ICA Talent*
818 12th St Apt 9
Santa Monica, CA 90403-1727, USA

Salisbury, Sean (Football Player)
Indianapolis Colts
5823 Brushy Creek Trl
Dallas, TX 75252-2341, USA

Salkind, Ilya (Producer)
Pinewood Studios
Iverheath
Iver
Bucks SL0 0NH, UNITED KINGDOM (UK)

Salle, David (Artist)
Larry Gagosian Gallery
980 Madison Ave Ph
New York, NY 10075-1848, USA

Salles, Walter (Director, Producer)
c/o Staff Member *Endeavor Agency LLC (LA)*
9601 Wilshire Blvd Fl 3
Beverly Hills, CA 90210-5204, USA

Salley, John (Basketball Player, Television Host)
c/o Staff Member *Best Damned Sports Show Period, The*
10201 W Pico Blvd
Fox Sports Net
Los Angeles, CA 90064-2606, USA

Sallinen, Aulis H (Composer)
Runneberginkatu 37A
Helsinki 10 00100, FINLAND

Sallis, Peter (Actor)
Jonathan Altaras
13 Shorts Gardens
London WC2H 9AT, UNITED KINGDOM (UK)

Sally, Jerome (Football Player)
New York Giants
4107 Roxbury Ct
Columbia, MO 65203-6832, USA

Salminen, Matti (Opera Singer)
Mariedi Anders Artists
535 El Camino Del Mar
San Francisco, CA 94121-1099, USA

Salming, Borje (Hockey Player)
Borje Salming Assoc
Box 45438
Stockholm 104 31, SWEDEN

Salmon, Colin (Actor)
Markham & Froggatt
Julian House
4 Windmill St
London W1P 1HF, UNITED KINGDOM (UK)

Salmon, Tim
6061 E Sunnyside Dr
Scottsdale, AZ 85254-4977, USA

Salmon, Timothy J (Tim) (Baseball Player)
24767 Masters Cup Way
Valencia, CA 91355-2306, USA

Salmons, John (Basketball Player)
Philadelphia 76ers
3601 S Broad St
1st Union Center
Philadelphia, PA 19148-5287, USA

Salmons, Steve (Volleyball Player)
1717 N El Dorado Ave
Ontario, CA 91764-1115, USA

Salo, Mika (Race Car Driver)
TWI Formula One
Leafield
Whitney
Oxon OX8 5PF, UNITED KINGDOM (UK)

Salomon, Mikael (Cinematographer)
PO Box 2230
Los Angeles, CA 90078-2230, USA

Salomon, Sandy (Actor)
Cineart
36 Rue de Ponthieu
Paris 75008, FRANCE

Salonen, Brian (Football Player)
Dallas Cowboys
2801 S Russell St Ste 33
Missoula, MT 59801-7914, USA

Salonen, Esa-Pekka (Composer)
Los Angeles Philharmonic
135 N Grand Ave
Music Center
Los Angeles, CA 90012-3013, USA

Salonga, Lea (Actor, Music Group, Musician)
Writers & Artists
360 N Crescent Dr Bldg North
Beverly Hills, CA 90210-6818, USA

Salopek, Paul (Journalist)
Chicago Tribune
435 N Michigan Ave
Editorial Dept
Chicago, IL 60611-4024, USA

Salpeter, Edwin E (Physicist)
116 Westbourne Ln
Ithaca, NY 14850-2414, USA

Salt, Jennifer (Actor)
3742 Sheridge Dr
Sherman Oaks, CA 91403-5005, USA

Salt-N-Peppa
250 W 57th St # 821
New York, NY 10107-0001, USA

Salter, Bryant (Football Player)
San Diego Chargers
16810 SW 88th Ct
Palmetto Bay, FL 33157-4537, USA

Salter, Hans
3658 Woodhill Canyon Rd
Studio City, CA 91604-3658, USA

Saltpeter, Edwin E (Misc)
Cornell University
Physical Sciences Dept
Ithaca, NJ 14853, USA

Saltykov, Aleksey A (Director)
Institute Mosfilmosvsky
Per 4A #104
Moscow 119285, RUSSIA

Saltykov, Boris G (Economist, Government Official)
Bryusov Per 11
Moscow 103009, RUSSIA

Salva, Victor (Director)
c/o Staff Member *Gersh Agency, The (LA)*
232 N Canon Dr
Beverly Hills, CA 90210-5302, USA

Salvador, Henri
6 place Vendome
Paris 75001, FRANCE

Salvail, Eve (DJ)
c/o Len Evans *Project Publicity*
312 W 53rd St
New York, NY 10019-5743, USA

Salvatore, Adamo (Musician)
Tonight Music S.A.
Avenue Louise 522
Bruxelles 1050, BELGIUM

Salvay, Bennett (Composer)
Gorfaine/Schwartz
4111 W Alameda Ave Ste 509
Burbank, CA 91505-4171, USA

Salvino, Carmen (Bowler)
65 Stevens Dr
Schaumburg, IL 60173-2176, USA

Sam the Sham (Musician)
6123 Old Brunswick Rd
Arlington, TN 38002-5928, USA

Samaranch, Juan Antonio
Avenida Pau Casals 24
Barcelona E-08021, SPAIN

Samaranch Torello, Juan Antonio (Misc)
Avenida Pau Casals 24
Barcelona 6 08021, SPAIN

Samaras, Lucas (Artist, Photographer)
Pace Gallery
32 E 57th St
New York, NY 10022-2530, USA

Sambora, Richie (Music Group, Musician, Songwriter, Writer)
c/o CeCe Yorke *True Public Relations*
6725 W Sunset Blvd Ste 570
Los Angeles, CA 90028-7180, USA

Samios, Nicholas P (Misc, Physicist)
Brookhaven National Laboratory
2 Center St
Directors's Office
Upton, NY 11973-9700, USA

Samis, Phil
1509 Rue Sherbrooke O
Montreal, PQ H3G 1M1, CANADA

Sammartino, Bruno (Wrestler)
413 Goldsmith Rd
Pittsburgh, PA 15237-3723, USA

Sammie (Actor)
c/o Staff Member *Green Light Talent Agency*
PO Box 3172
Beverly Hills, CA 90212-0172, USA

Samms, Emma (Actor)
2934 1/2 N Beverly Glen Cir # 417
Los Angeles, CA 90077-1724, USA

Samoilova, Tatiana Y (Actor)
Spiridonyevsky Per 8/11
Moscow 103104, RUSSIA

Samotsvetov, Anatoly (Hockey Player)
Nashville Predators
501 Broadway
Nashville, TN 37203-3932, USA

Sampaio, Jorge (President)
President's Office
Palacio de Belem
Lisbon 1300, PORTUGAL

Sample, Joe (Musician)
Patrick Ralns Assoc
1255 5th Ave Apt 7J
New York, NY 10029-3848, USA

Sample, Steven B (Educator)
University of Southern California
President's Office
Los Angeles, CA 90089-0001, USA

Samples, Keith (Director, Producer, Writer)
c/o Rob Kenneally *Creative Artists Agency LCC (CAA-LA)*
2000 Avenue Of The Stars
Los Angeles, CA 90067-4700, USA

Sampleton, Lawrence (Football Player)
Philadelphia Eagles
2900 Bunny Run
Austin, TX 78746-1702, USA

Sampras, Pete (Tennis Player)
c/o Jill Smoller *William Morris Agency (WMA-LA)*
1 William Morris Pl
Beverly Hills, CA 90212-4261, USA

Sampson, Greg (Football Player)
Houston Oilers
1940 Camino Loma Verde
Vista, CA 92084-3601, USA

Sampson, Kelvin (Basketball Player, Coach)
University of Oklahoma
Lloyd Noble Complex
Norman, OK 73019-0001, USA

Sampson, Ralph L Jr (Basketball Player, Coach)
10831 W Broad St
Glen Allen, VA 23060-3311, USA

Sampson, Robert (Actor)
20th Century Artists
4605 Lankershim Blvd Ste 305
North Hollywood, CA 91602-1875, USA

Sams, Dean (Musician)
Borman Entertainment
1222 16th Ave S Ste 23
Nashville, TN 37212-2926, USA

Sams, Doris (Baseball Player)
715 Avenue A
Knoxville, TN 37920-4153, USA

Sams, Jeffrey D (Actor)
c/o Toni Benson *Third Hill Entertainment*
195 S Beverly Dr Ste 400
Beverly Hills, CA 90212-3044, USA

Sams, Judy (Golfer)
2603 Wells Ave
Sarasota, FL 34232-3954, USA

Sams, Russell (Actor)
c/o Staff Member *William Morris Agency (WMA-LA)*
1 William Morris Pl
Beverly Hills, CA 90212-4261, USA

Samuels, Chris (Football Player)
San Diego Chargers
18303 Oakhampton Dr
Houston, TX 77084-3260, USA

Samuels, Dale (Football Player)
Chicago Cardinals
7625 Highway X
Three Lakes, WI 54562-9267, USA

Samuels, Jack (Baseball Player)
16040 Leffingwell Rd Apt 25
Whittier, CA 90603-3120, USA

Samuels, Ron
PO Box 1690
Rancho Mirage, CA 92270-1058, USA

Samuelson, Pamela (Attorney, Attorney General, General)
University of California
Center For Law/Technology
Berkeley, CA 94720-0001, USA

Samuelson, Paul A (Nobel Prize Laureate)
94 Somerset St
Belmont, MA 02478-2010, USA

Samuelsson, Bengt I (Nobel Prize Laureate)
Karolinska Institute
Chemistry Dept
Stockholm 171 77, SWEDEN

Samuelsson, Kjell (Hockey Player)
5 Simsbury Dr
Voorhees, NJ 08043-3948, USA

Samuelsson, Ulf (Hockey Player)
37 W Hills Dr
Avon, CT 06001-2239, USA

San Basilio, Paloma (Music Group)
c/o Staff Member *Sony Music Miami*
605 Lincoln Rd Fl 7
Miami Beach, FL 33139-2900, USA

Sanabria, Marilyn (Actor)
c/o Laura Walsh *Central Artists*
3310 W Burbank Blvd # A
Burbank, CA 91505-2230, USA

Sanborn, David (Musician)
c/o Staff Member *International Creative Management (ICM-LA)*
10250 Constellation Blvd
Los Angeles, CA 90067-6200, USA

Sanches, Stacy (Model)
c/o Staff Member *Playboy Entertainment Group Inc*
2112 Broadway
Santa Monica, CA 90404-2912, USA

Sanchez, Eduardo (Director)
Artisan Entertainment
2700 Colorado Ave
Santa Monica, CA 90404-3553, USA

Sanchez, Emilio (Tennis Player)
Sabiono de Avena 28
Barcelona 46, SPAIN

Sanchez, Jose T Cardinal (Religious Leader)
Via Rusticucci 13
Rome 00193, ITALY

Sanchez, Juan (Pepe) (Basketball Player)
c/o Staff Member *Detroit Pistons*
2 Championship Dr
Palace
Auburn Hills, MI 48326-1753, USA

Sanchez, Kiele (Actor)
c/o Daniel (Dan) Spilo *Artistry Management*
525 Westbourne Dr
West Hollywood, CA 90048-1913, USA

Sanchez, Lupe (Football Player)
Pittsburgh Steelers
28870 Road 68
Visalia, CA 93277-9470, USA

Sanchez, Marco (Actor)
Stone Manners
6500 Wilshire Blvd Ste 550
Los Angeles, CA 90048-4950, USA

Sanchez, Monika (Actor)
c/o Gabriel Blanco *Gabriel Blanco Iglesias (Mexico)*
Rio Balsas 35-32
Colonia Cuauhtemoc
DF 06500, MEXICO

Sanchez, Pancho (Musician)
PO Box 59236
Norwalk, CA 90652-0236, USA

Sanchez, Pedro (Scientist)
Columbia University
Earth Institute
New York, NY 10027, USA

Sanchez, Pepe (Director)
c/o Staff Member *Gabriel Blanco Iglesias (Colombia)*
Dg 127A #20-36
Conjunto Plenitud, Apto 132
Bogota, COLOMBIA

Sanchez, Roselyn (Actor)
c/o Jeff Golenberg *The Collective*
9100 Wilshire Blvd # 700 W
Beverly Hills, CA 90212-3401, USA

Sanchez Azuara, Rocio (Actor)
c/o Staff Member *TV Azteca*
Periferico Sur 4121
Colonia Fuentes del Pedregal
DF CP 14141, MEXICO

Sanchez Gijon, Aitana (Actor)
Alsira Garcia Maroto
Gran Via 63 #3
Izda
Madrid 28013, SPAIN

Sanchez-Vicario, Arantxa (Tennis Player)
Sabino de Arana 28 #6-1A
Barcelona 08028, SPAIN

Sanchez-Vilella, Roberto (Governor)
414 Ave Munoz Rivera Stop 31 1/2 # 7A
San Juan, PR 00918-3356, USA

Sand, Paul (Actor)
Paradigm Agency
10100 Santa Monica Blvd Ste 2500
Los Angeles, CA 90067-4116, USA

Sand, Shauna
c/o Staff Member *Acme Talent & Literary (LA)*
4727 Wilshire Blvd Ste 333
Los Angeles, CA 90010-3874, USA

Sand, Todd (Figure Skater)
2973 Harbor Blvd # 468
Costa Mesa, CA 92626-3912, USA

Sanda, Dominique
201 rue du Faubourg St. Honore
Paris F-75008, FRANCE

Sander, Casey
c/o Jeffrey Leavitt *Leavitt Talent Group*
6404 Wilshire Blvd Ste 950
Los Angeles, CA 90048-5529, USA

Sander, Ian (Producer)
c/o Staff Member *William Morris Agency (WMA-LA)*
1 William Morris Pl
Beverly Hills, CA 90212-4261, USA

Sander, Jil (Designer, Fashion Designer)
Osterfeldstr 32-34
Hamburg 22529, GERMANY

Sander, Mark (Football Player)
Miami Dolphins
4930 NW 83rd Ave
Lauderhill, FL 33351-5553, USA

Sanderling, Kurt (Conductor)
Am Iderfenngraben 47
Berlin 13156, GERMANY

Sanderman, Bill (Football Player)
Dallas Cowboys
PO Box 203
Tahoma Meadows Bed And Breakfast
Homewood, CA 96141-0203, USA

Sanders, Barry (Football Player)
Pro Football Hall Of Fame
2121 George Halas Dr NW
Canton, OH 44708-2699, USA

Sanders, Beverly (Actor)
12218 Morrison St
Valley Village, CA 91607-3627, USA

Sanders, Bill (Cartoonist)
PO Box 661
Milwaukee, WI 53201-0661, USA

Sanders, Bobby (Baseball Player)
Birmingham Black Barons
12106 Soika Ave
Cleveland, OH 44120-3159, USA

Sanders, Charles A (Charlie) (Coach, Football Coach, Football Player)
Detroit Lions
3418 Palm Aire Ct
Rochester Hills, MI 48309-1040, USA

Sanders, Chris (Director)
c/o Rob Carlson *William Morris Agency (WMA-LA)*
1 William Morris Pl
Beverly Hills, CA 90212-4261, USA

Sanders, Daryl (Football Player)
Detroit Lions
9220 Shawnee Trl
Powell, OH 43065-5012, USA

Sanders, Deion L (Baseball Player, Football Player)
c/o Staff Member *Baltimore Ravens*
1 Winning Dr
Owings Mills, MD 21117-4776, USA

Sanders, Doug (Golfer)
8828 Sandringham Dr
Houston, TX 77024-5819, USA

Sanders, Eric D (Football Player)
Atlanta Falcons
9325 Tailey Cir
Duluth, GA 30097-2451, USA

Sanders, Frank (Football Player)
Arizona Cardinals
12310 Silver Cup Ct
Reisterstown, MD 21136-6481, USA

Sanders, Frank (Hockey Player)
670 Lade View Dr
Saint Paul, MN 55129, USA

Sanders, James (Baseball Player)
Kansas City Monarchs
1001 43rd Pl W
Birmingham, AL 35208-1402, USA

Sanders, Jay O (Actor)
165 W 46th St Ste 409
New York, NY 10036-2522, USA

Sanders, John M (Football Player)
New England Patriots
520 Old Whitfield Rd
Pearl, MS 39208-5512, USA

Sanders, Mariene (Correspondent)
WNET-TV
356 W 58th St
News Dept
New York, NY 10019-1804, USA

Sanders, Marlene
175 Riverside Dr
New York, NY 10024-1616, USA

Sanders, Orban (Football Player)
New York Yankees
3520 NW Ferris Ave
Lawton, OK 73505-6104, USA

Sanders, Pharoah (Musician)
Joel Chriss
300 Mercer St Apt 3J
New York, NY 10003-6732, USA

Sanders, Reggie
1764 Williamsburg Cir
Florence, SC 29506-6914, USA

Sanders, Robert J (Football Player)
Atlanta Falcons
412 Homestead Ave
Metairie, LA 70005-3208, USA

Sanders, Scott G (Baseball Player)
15910 Ventura Blvd Ste 1701
Encino, CA 91436-2816, USA

Sanders, Summer (Swimmer)
731 Martingale Ln
Park City, UT 84098-7559, USA

Sanders, Thomas (Football Player)
Chicago Bears
72 S Flore Pkwy
Vernon Hills, IL 60061, USA

Sanders, Thomas (Satch) (Basketball Player, Misc)
114 Fenway
Boston, MA 02115-3715, USA

Sanders, W J (Jerry) III (Business Person)
Advanced Micro Devices
1 Amd Pl
PO Box 3453
Sunnyvale, CA 94085-3905, USA

Sanderson, Cael (Wrestler)
Steve Sanderson
1380 Valley Hills Blvd
Heber City, UT 84032-1111, USA

Sanderson, Derek M (Hockey Player)
267 Manning St
Needham, MA 02492-3507, USA

Sanderson, Nikki (Actor)
c/o *Coronation Street*
Granada Studios, Quay St
Manchester M60 9EA, UNITED KINGDOM (UK)

Sanderson, Peter (Artist)
1105 Shell Gate Pl
Alameda, CA 94501-5949, USA

Sanderson, Reggie (Football Player)
Chicago Bears
160 Mara Ave
Ventura, CA 93004-1513, USA

Sanderson, Theresa (Tessa) (Athlete, Track Athlete)
Tee-Dee Promotion
Atles Center
Oxgate Lane
London NW2 7HU, UNITED KINGDOM (UK)

Sanderson, William (Actor)
4251 W Sarah St
Burbank, CA 91505-3815, USA

Sandeson, William S (Cartoonist, Editor)
2230 Muskoday Pass
Fort Wayne, IN 46809-1428, USA

Sandiford, L Erskine (Prime Minister)
Hillvista
Porters
Saint James, BARBADOS

Sandig, Curtis (Football Player)
Pittsburgh Steelers
2742 Pebble Breeze
San Antonio, TX 78232-4116, USA

Sandin, Bill (Inventor)
University of Illinois
Electronic Visualization Lab
Chicago, IL 60607, USA

Sandit, Tom (Athlete)
540 S Ashland Ave
La Grange, IL 60525-2811, USA

Sandler, Adam (Actor, Comedian)
c/o Staff Member *Happy Madison Productions*
10202 Washington Blvd
Judy Garland Bldg
Culver City, CA 90232-3119, USA

Sandler, Herbert M (Financier)
Golden West Financial
1901 Harrison St
Oakland, CA 94612-3546, USA

Sandler, Marion O (Financier)
Golden West Financial
1901 Harrison St
Oakland, CA 94612-3546, USA

Sandlund, Debra (Actor)
Innovative Artists
1505 10th St
Santa Monica, CA 90401-2805, USA

Sandoval, Arturo (Musician)
4706 Granada Blvd
Coral Gables, FL 33146-1250, USA

Sandoval, Hope (Music Group, Musician)
Rough Trade Mgmt
66 Golbarne Road
London W10 5PS, UNITED KINGDOM (UK)

Sandoval, Miguel (Actor)
Paradigm Agency
10100 Santa Monica Blvd Ste 2500
Los Angeles, CA 90067-4116, USA

Sandoval, Sonny (Musician)
East West America Records
75 Rockefeller Plz
New York, NY 10019-6908, USA

Sandoval Iniguez, Juan Cardinal (Religious Leader)
Morelos 244
San Pedro Tlaquepaque 45500, MEXICO

Sandow, Nick (Actor)
c/o Staff Member *Sweet Mud Group*
648 Broadway # 1002
New York, NY 10012-2301, USA

Sandre, Didier (Actor)
Agents Associes Beaume
201 Faubourg Saint Honore
Paris 75008, FRANCE

Sandrelli, Stefania (Actor)
TNA
Viale Parioli 41
Rome 00197, ITALY

Sandrich, Jay (Director)
2501 Colorado Ave Ste 350
Santa Monica, CA 90404-3583, USA

Sands, Julian (Actor)
1287 Ozeta Ter
Los Angeles, CA 90069-1835, USA

Sands, Tommy (Actor, Musician)
225 N Evergreen St # 301
Burbank, CA 91505-3925, USA

Sands-Ferguson, Sarah Jane (Baseball Player)
338 Rohrsburg Rd
Orangeville, PA 17859-9108, USA

Sandstrom, Sven (Financier)
World Bank Group
1818 H St NW
Washington, DC 20433-0002, USA

Sandstrom, Tomas (Hockey Player)
156 Iron Run Rd
Bethel Park, PA 15102-1081, USA

Sandusky, Alexander B (Alex) (Football Player)
Baltimore Colts
22 Floral Ave
Key West, FL 33040-6243, USA

Sandusky, John (Football Player)
Cleveland Browns
9630 NW 28th St
Hollywood, FL 33024-8501, USA

Sandusky, Mike (Football Player)
Pittsburgh Steelers
2786 Amberwood Ct
Naples, FL 34120-7520, USA

Sandvoss, Steve (Actor)
c/o Scott Zimmerman *Untitled Entertainment (LA)*
331 N Maple Dr Fl 3
Beverly Hills, CA 90210-3827, USA

Sandy, Baby (Sandra Magee)
6846 Haywood St
Tujunga, CA 91042-2850, USA

Sandy, Gary (Actor)
PO Box 818
Cynthiana, KY 41031-0818, USA

Sandy B (Musician)
Atlantic Entertainment Group
2922 Atlantic Ave Ste 200
Atlantic City, NJ 08401-6337, USA

Sandy Jr, Alomar (Baseball Player)
4635 Prestwick Xing
Westlake, OH 44145-5073, USA

Sanford, Ed (Hockey Player)
18 Clearwater Rd
Winchester, MA 01890-4011, USA

Sanford, Jack
2300 Presidential Way
West Palm Beach, FL 33401-1510, USA

Sanford, Leo (Football Player)
Chicago Cardinals
3044 Gorton St
Shreveport, LA 71119-3606, USA

Sanford, Lucius M (Football Player)
Buffalo Bills
8745 Carriage Hills Dr
Columbia, MD 21046, USA

Sanford, Meredith (Athlete)
2800 Highway 389
Starkville, MS 39759-8379, USA

Sanford, Richard M (Rick) (Football Player)
New England Patriots
335 Lemonts Rd
Chapin, SC 29036-9772, USA

Sangavi (Actor, Bollywood)
20 4th Street
Dr. Subraya Nagar Kodambakkam
Chennai, TN 600024, INDIA

Sangeetha (Actor, Bollywood)
26A Brindavan Apartments
Karumari Amman Koil Street Vadapalani
Chennai, TN 600026, INDIA

Sanger, David J (Musician)
Old Wesleyan Chapel
Embleton Near Cockermouth
Cumbria CA13 9YA, UNITED KINGDOM (UK)

Sanger, Frederick (Nobel Prize Laureate)
Far Leys Fen Lane
Swaffham Bulbeck
Cambridge CB5 0NJ, UNITED KINGDOM (UK)

Sanger, Stephan W (Business Person)
General Mills Inc
1 General Mills Blvd
PO Box 1113
Minneapolis, MN 55426-1348, USA

SanGiacomo, Laura (Actor)
15030 Ventura Blvd # 710
Sherman Oaks, CA 91403-5470, USA

Sangster, Jimmy (Writer)
1590 Lindercrest Dr
Beverly Hills, CA 90210, USA

Sangster, Thomas (Actor)
c/o Staff Member *Marcus & McCrimmon Management*
4 Fitzwarren Gardens
Highgate
London, UNITED KINGDOM (UK)

Sangueli, Andrei (Prime Minister)
Parliament House
Prosp 105
Kishineau 277073, MOLDOVA

Sanguinetti Cairolo, Julio Maria (President)
Partido Colorado
Andres Martinez Trueba 1271
Montevideo, URUGUAY

Sanha, Malam Bacai (President)
President's Office
Bissau, GUINEA-BISSAU

SanJuan, Olga (Actor)
O'Brien
12100 W Sunset Blvd # 2
Los Angeles, CA 90049-4143, USA

Sanjukta, Singh (Actor, Bollywood)
4th Floor Mona Apts
Breach Candy
Mumbai, MS 400036, INDIA

Sano, Roya A (Religious Leader)
United Methodist Church
PO Box 320
Nashville, TN 37202-0320, USA

Sanobar, Kabir (Actor, Bollywood)
402 Karan Building Yari Road
Versova Andheri (W)
Mumbai, MS 400061, INDIA

Sansom, Bruce (Ballerina)
Royal Ballet
Convent Garden
Bow St
London WC2E 9DD, UNITED KINGDOM (UK)

Sansom, Chip (Cartoonist)
204 Long Beach Rd
Centerville, MA 02632-3534, USA

Sant, Alfred (Prime Minister)
National Labor Center
Mills End Road
Hannum, MALTA

Santa Rosa, Gilberto (Musician)
Universal Attractions
225 W 57th St Ste 500
New York, NY 10019-2136, USA

Santamaria, Eduardo (Actor)
c/o Gabriel Blanco *Gabriel Blanco Iglesias (Mexico)*
Rio Balsas 35-32
Colonia Cuauhtemoc
DF 06500, MEXICO

Santana, Carlos (Musician, Songwriter)
Santana Mgmt
121 Jordan St
San Rafael, CA 94901-3919, USA

Santana, Juelz (Musician)
269 Reichelt Rd Apt A
New Milford, NJ 07646-5297, USA

Santana, Manuel (Tennis Player)
International Tennis Hall of Fame
194 Bellevue Ave
Newport, RI 02840-3586, USA

Santer, Jacques (Misc)
69 Rue J P Huberty
1742, LUXEMBOURG

Santiago, Benito R (Baseball Player)
12503 NW 23rd St
Pembroke Pines, FL 33028-2540, USA

Santiago, Carlos (Baseball Player)
New York Cubans
7 Calle Archilla Cabrera
Mayaguez, PR 00680-3302, USA

Santiago, Daniel (Basketball Player)
c/o Staff Member *Phoenix Suns*
201 E Jefferson St
Phoenix, AZ 85004-2412, USA

Santiago, Eddie (Musician)
c/o Staff Member *Sony Music Miami*
605 Lincoln Rd Fl 7
Miami Beach, FL 33139-2900, USA

Santiago, Jose (Baseball Player)
New York Cubans
690 Calle Cesar Gonzalez Apt 2108
San Juan, PR 00918-3906, USA

Santiago, Tessie (Actor)
c/o Craig Shapiro *Innovative Artists (LA)*
1505 10th St
Santa Monica, CA 90401-2805, USA

Santiago-Hudson, Ruben (Actor)
Gersh Agency
232 N Canon Dr
Beverly Hills, CA 90210-5302, USA

Santo, Ron (Athlete, Baseball Player)
1721 Meadow Ln
Bannockburn, IL 60015-1844, USA

Santo & Johnny
217 Edgewood Ave
Clearwater, FL 33755-5702, USA

Santorelli, Frank (Actor)
c/o Mitch Smelkinson *Stone Meyer & Genow*
9665 Wilshire Blvd Ste 510
Beverly Hills, CA 90212-2312, USA

Santorini, Paul E (Engineer, Physicist)
PO Box 49
Athens, GREECE

Santoro, Rodrigo (Actor)
c/o John Fogelman *William Morris Agency (WMA-LA)*
1 William Morris Pl
Beverly Hills, CA 90212-4261, USA

Santos, Al (Actor)
c/o Staff Member *Don Buchwald & Associates Inc (LA)*
6500 Wilshire Blvd Ste 2200
Los Angeles, CA 90048-4942, USA

Santos, Bruno (Model)
c/o Staff Member *WHY NOT Model Agency*
via Zenale 9
Milano 20123, ITALY

Santos, Joe (Actor)
1444 Queens Rd
Los Angeles, CA 90069-1913, USA

Santos, Rey-Phillip (Actor)
c/o Staff Member *Dramatic Artists Agency*
50 16th Ave
Kirkland, WA 98033-4909, USA

Santos de Oliveira, Alessandra (Basketball Player)
Washington Mystics
601 F St NW
Mci Center
Washington, DC 20004-1605, USA

Sanz, Alejandro (Musician, Songwriter, Writer)
c/o Allison Winkler *Creative Artists Agency LCC (CAA-LA)*
2000 Avenue Of The Stars
Los Angeles, CA 90067-4700, USA

Sanz, Horatio (Actor)
c/o David (Dave) Becky *3 Arts Entertainment Inc*
9460 Wilshire Blvd Fl 7
Beverly Hills, CA 90212-2713, USA

Saper, Clifford (Doctor)
Beth Israel Hospital
330 Brookline Ave
Neurology Dept
Boston, MA 02215-5491, USA

Saperstein, David (Director, Producer, Writer)
c/o Staff Member *Fran Saperstein Organization*
Marina Del Rey, CA 90292, USA

Sapienza, Al
10474 Santa Monica Blvd Ste 380
W Los Angeles, CA 90025-6943, USA

Sapienza, Americo (Football Player)
New York Titans
6 Forenza Rd
Peabody, MA 01960-3732, USA

Saplenza, Al (Actor)
PO Box 691240
West Hollywood, CA 90069-9240, USA

Sapp, Bob (Actor, Wrestler)
c/o Staff Member *Writers and Artists Group Intl (LA)*
8383 Wilshire Blvd Ste 550
Beverly Hills, CA 90211-2417, USA

Sapp, Carolyn
1840 41st Ave # 102-227
Capitola, CA 95010-2513, USA

Sapp, Theron (Football Player)
Philadelphia Eagles
892 N Belair Rd
Evans, GA 30809-4222, USA

Sapp, Warren (Football Player)
c/o Team Member *Tampa Bay Buccaneers*
1 Bucaneer Place
Tampa, FL 33607, USA

Sara, Mia (Actor)
2311 Alto Oak Dr
Los Angeles, CA 90068-2509, USA

Sarachan, Dave (Coach, Soccer Player)
Chicago Fire
7000 S Harlem Ave
Bridgeview, IL 60455-1160, USA

Sarafian, Richard C (Actor, Director, Writer)
c/o Staff Member *Leavitt Talent Group*
6404 Wilshire Blvd Ste 950
Los Angeles, CA 90048-5529, USA

Sarah, Duchess of York
Birch Hall
Windlesham Surrey, ENGLAND GU2O 6BN, UNITED KINGDOM (UK)

Saraiva Martins, Jose Cardinal (Religious Leader)
Via Pancrazio Pfeiffer 10
Rome 00193, ITALY

Saralegui, Cristina (Correspondent)
c/o Staff Member *Creative Artists Agency LCC (CAA-LA)*
2000 Avenue Of The Stars
Los Angeles, CA 90067-4700, USA

Saramago, Jose (Writer)
Los Topes 3
35572 Tias/Lansarote
Canaries, SPAIN

Sarandon, Chris (Actor)
c/o Miles Levy *James/Levy/Jacobson Management*
3500 W Olive Ave Ste 1470
Burbank, CA 91505-5514, USA

Sarandon, Susan (Actor)
c/o Sam Cohn *International Creative Management (ICM-NY)*
40 W 57th St
New York, NY 10019-4001, USA

Saranya (Actor, Bollywood)
17A Rajaram Directors Colony
Kodambakkam
Chennai, TN 600024, INDIA

Saraste, Jukka-Pekka
Van Walsum Mgmt
4 Addison Bridge Place
London W14 8XP, UNITED KINGDOM (UK)

Sarazen-Smith, Dorothy (Baseball Player)
4774 Eagle Crest Dr
Madison, WI 53704-6426, USA

Sarbanes, Paul (Senator)
320 Suffolk Rd
Baltimore, MD 21218-2521, USA

Sarcev, Ursula
PO Box 25738
Los Angeles, CA 90025-0738, USA

Sare, Chris
21100 Erwin St
Woodland Hills, CA 91367-3712, USA

Sarfatl, Alain (Architect)
28 Rue Barbet du Jouy
Paris 75007, FRANCE

Sargent, Ben (Cartoonist, Editor)
Austin American-Statesman
166 E Riverside Dr
Austin, TX 78704, USA

Sargent, John T (Producer)
Hasley Lane
Watermill, NY 11976, USA

Sargent, Joseph (Director, Producer)
27242 Latigo Bay View Dr
Malibu, CA 90265-2865, USA

Sargent, Ronald L (Business Person)
Staples Inc
PO Box 9265
Framingham, MA 01701-9265, USA

Sargeson, Alan M (Misc)
National University
Chemistry Dept
Canberra, ACT 0200, AUSTRALIA

Sari, Gabriela (Actor)
c/o Staff Member *Telefe - Argentina*
Pavon 2444 (C1248AAT)
Buenos Aires, ARGENTINA

Saritha (Actor, Bollywood)
Karthik Apartments III Floor, No.46,
Vijayaraghava Road
T. Nagar
Chennai, TN 600017, INDIA

Sarkisian, Alex (Football Player)
1604 E 142nd St
East Chicago, IN 46312-3008, USA

Sarna, Craig (Hockey Player)
1375 Brown Rd S
Wayzata, MN 55391-9316, USA

Sarne, Tanya (Designer, Fashion Designer)
Ghost
Chapel 263 Kensal Road
London W10 5DB, UNITED KINGDOM (UK)

Sarner, Craig (Hockey Player)
1375 Brown Rd S
Wayzata, MN 55391-9316, USA

Sarni, Vincent A (Baseball Player, Misc)
Pittsburgh Pirates
115 Federal St
Pnc Park
Pittsburgh, PA 15212-5740, USA

Sarnoff, Liz (Actor)
c/o Staff Member *Creative Artists Agency LCC (CAA-LA)*
2000 Avenue Of The Stars
Los Angeles, CA 90067-4700, USA

Sarnoff, William (Publisher)
Warner Publishing Inc
1325 Avenue Of The Americas
New York, NY 10019-6026, USA

Sarojadevi (Actor, Bollywood)
351 4th Main Road
Sadasivanagar
Bangalore, KA 560080, INDIA

Sarosi, Imre (Coach, Swimmer)
1033 Bp Harrer Dal Utca 4
HUNGARY

Sarratt, Charles (Football Player)
Detroit Lions
5812 Oak Tree Rd
Edmond, OK 73025-2620, USA

Sarrazin, Michael (Actor)
9696 Culver Blvd Ste 203
Culver City, CA 90232-2754, USA

Sarsgaard, Peter (Actor)
c/o Tony Lipp *Creative Artists Agency LCC (CAA-LA)*
2000 Avenue Of The Stars
Los Angeles, CA 90067-4700, USA

Sartain, Gailard (Actor)
c/o Michael Livingston *The Artists Agency (LA)*
1180 S Beverly Dr Ste 301
Los Angeles, CA 90035-1154, USA

Sartzetakis, Christos (President)
Presidential Palace
7 Vas Georgiou B
Odos Zalokosta 10
Athens, GREECE

Sarven, Allan (Al Snow) (Wrestler)
c/o Staff Member *World Wrestling Entertainment (WWE)*
1241 E Main St
Stamford, CT 06902-3520, USA

Sarzo, Rudy
1155 N La Cienega Blvd Apt 506
Los Angeles, CA 90069-2437, USA

Sasaki, Kazuhiro (Baseball Player)
Seattle Mariners
PO Box 4100
Safeco Field
Seattle, WA 98194-0100, USA

Sasdy, Peter (Director)
Cleves
21 Matham Rd E
Molesey
Surrey KT8 0SX, ENGLAND

Sasikala (Actor, Bollywood)
D-10 Parsan Apartments
204 T.T.K. Road Alwarpet
Chennai, TN 600018, INDIA

Sassano, C E (Business Person)
Bausch & Lomb
1 Bausch And Lomb Pl
Rochester, NY 14604-2799, USA

Sassard, Jacqueline
54 av. Montaigne
Paris F-75008, FRANCE

Sasser, Clarence E (War Hero)
13414 Fm 521 Rd
Rosharon, TX 77583-6608, USA

Sasso, Will (Actor, Comedian)
InnerAct Entertainment
141 S Barrington Ave Ste E
Los Angeles, CA 90049-3314, USA

Sasson, Debra (Opera Singer)
Erlenhaupstr 10
Bensheim 64625, GERMANY

Sassoon, Beverly (Model)
1800 The Strand
Manhattan Beach, CA 90266-4527, USA

Sassoon, David (Designer, Fashion Designer)
Bellville Sassoon
18 Culford Gardens
London SW3 2ST, UNITED KINGDOM (UK)

Sassou-Nguesso, Denis (President)
President's Office
Brazzaville, CONGO REPUBLIC

Sastre, Ines (Actor)
c/o Staff Member *International Creative Management (ICM-LA)*
10250 Constellation Blvd
Los Angeles, CA 90067-6200, USA

Satanowski, Robert (Conductor)
Ul Madalinskiego 50/52 m 1
Warsaw 02-581, POLAND

Satcher, David (Misc)
Kaiser Family Foundation
2400 Sand Hill Rd
Menlo Park, CA 94025-6941, USA

Satcher, Leslie (Music Group, Musician, Songwriter, Writer)
Warner Bros Records
3300 Warner Blvd
Burbank, CA 91505-4694, USA

Satchwell, Brooke (Actor)
Darren Gray Management
2 Marston Lane
Portsmouth
Hampshire, England PO3 5TW, UNITED KINGDOM (UK)

Sather, Glen C (Coach, Hockey Player)
505 Buffalo St
Banff, AB T0L 0C0, CANADA

Sathiyaraj (Actor)
13-A Pirakathambal Street
Chennai, TN 600 034, INDIA

Sato, Kazuo (Economist)
300 E 71st St Apt 15H
New York, NY 10021-5245, USA

Satra, Sonia (Actor)
Innovative Artists
1505 10th St
Santa Monica, CA 90401-2805, USA

Satre, Philip G (Business Person)
Harrah's Entertainment
1023 Cherry Rd
Memphis, TN 38117-5423, USA

Satriani, Joe (Music Group, Musician)
Joe Satriani Music
PO Box 429094
San Francisco, CA 94142-9094, USA

Satterfield, Paul (Actor)
PO Box 6945
Beverly Hills, CA 90212-6945, USA

Satterwhite, Howard (Football Player)
New York Jets
3418 Action Ln
San Antonio, TX 78210-3402, USA

Satturno, William (Archaeologist)
University of New Hampshire
Archaeology Dept
Durham, NH 03824, USA

Saturday, Jeff (Football Player)
Indianapolis Colts
2437 Londonberry Blvd
Carmel, IN 46032-8219, USA

Saud, Prince Sultan Bin Abdulaziz al (Government Official)
Defense Ministry
PO Box 26731
Airport Road
Riyadh 11165, SAUDI ARABIA

Saudek, Jan (Photographer)
Blodkova 6
Prague 3 130 00, CZECH REPUBLIC

Sauer, Craig (Football Player)
Atlanta Falcons
6926 Pagenkopf Rd
Maple Plain, MN 55359-8725, USA

Sauer, George H Jr (Football Player)
New York Jets
3625 Macarthur Dr
Waco, TX 76708-1743, USA

Sauer, Hank
207 Vallejo Ct
Millbrae, CA 94030-2835, USA

Sauer, Louis (Architect)
3472 Marlowe St
Montreal, PQ H4A 2L7, CANADA

Sauer, Richard J (Educator)
National 4-H Council
7100 Connecticut Ave
Bethesda, MD 20815-4999, USA

Sauerlander, Willibald P W (Historian)
Zentralinstitut fyr Kunstgeschichte
Meiserstr 10
Munich 80333, GERMANY

Sauers, Gene (Golfer)
9 Judsons Ct
Savannah, GA 31410-1060, USA

Saul, April (Journalist)
Philadelphia Inquirer
400 N Broad St
Editorial Dept
Philadelphia, PA 19130-4099, USA

Saul, Bill (Football Player)
Baltimore Colts
Emerald Tavern 8300 Harford Rd
Parkville, MD 21234, USA

Saul, John
Robin Straus
229 E 79th St
New York, NY 10075-0866, USA

Saul, John (Writer)
Grade A Entertainment
368 N La Cienega Blvd
Los Angeles, CA 90048-1949, USA

Saul, John W III (Writer)
The Firm
9100 Wilshire Blvd Ste 100W
Beverly Hills, CA 90212-3435, USA

Saul, Ralph S (Business Person)
1400 Waverly Rd Apt B145
Gladwyne, PA 19035-1264, USA

Saul, Ron (Football Player)
Houston Oilers
RR 3 Box 227
Charles Town, WV 25414, USA

Saul, Stephanie (Journalist)
Newsday
235 Pinelawn Rd
Editorial Dept
Melville, NY 11747-4250, USA

Sauli, Daniel (Actor)
c/o Staff Member *The Firm*
9465 Wilshire Blvd Fl 6
Beverly Hills, CA 90212-2605, USA

Sauls, Don (Religious Leader)
Pentecostal Free Will Baptist Church
PO Box 1568
Dunn, NC 28335-1568, USA

Saum, Sherri (Actor)
c/o Jerry Shandrew *Shandrew Public Relations*
1050 S Stanley Ave
Los Angeles, CA 90019-6634, USA

Saunders, Doug
43 Saint Kitts
Dana Point, CA 92629-4130, USA

Saunders, George (Writer)
Random House
1745 Broadway # B1
New York, NY 10019-4305, USA

Saunders, George L Jr (Attorney, Attorney General, General)
179 E Lake Shore Dr
Chicago, IL 60611-1340, USA

Saunders, Jennifer (Actor)
P F D
Drury House
34-43 Russell St
London WC2B 5HA, UNITED KINGDOM (UK)

Saunders, John (Cartoonist)
King Features Syndicate
888 7th Ave Ste 201
New York, NY 10106-0201, USA

Saunders, John (Sportscaster)
ESPN-TV
Sports Dept
Espn Plaza 935 Middle St
Bristol, CT 06010, USA

Saunders, John R (Race Car Driver)
Watkins Glen Speedway
PO Box 500F
Watkins Glen, NY 14891, USA

Saunders, Lori (Actor)
Lori's Friends
99 La Vuelta Rd
Santa Barbara, CA 93108-2621, USA

Saunders, Phil (Flip) (Basketball Player, Coach)
Minnesota Timberwolves
600 1st Ave N
Target Center
Minneapolis, MN 55403-1416, USA

Saunders, Rachel
203 Bocage Dr
Dothan, AL 36303-2944, USA

Saunders, Townsend (Wrestler)
733 Chantilly Dr
Sierra Vista, AZ 85635-4733, USA

Saura, Carlos (Director)
Antonio Duran
Calle Arturo Soria 52
#Edif 2 1-5A
Madrid 28027, SPAIN

Sauter, Cory (Football Player)
Detroit Lions
3333 Centerpoint Pkwy Apt 217
Pontiac, MI 48341-3159, USA

Sauve, Robert (Bob) (Hockey Player)
Jandec Inc
803-3080 Boul le Carrefour
Laval, PQ H7T 2R5, CANADA

Savage, Adam (Television Host)
1000 Universal Studios Blvd
Universal Cty, CA 91608-1008, USA

Savage, Ann (Actor)
1541 N Hayworth Ave Apt 203
Los Angeles, CA 90046-3333, USA

Savage, Ben (Actor)
c/o Staff Member *Abrams Artists Agency (LA)*
9200 W Sunset Blvd Ph 11
Los Angeles, CA 90069-3601, USA

Savage, Chad (Adult Film Star)
c/o Staff Member *Diva Central Inc*
7510 W Sunset Blvd Ste 1445
Los Angeles, CA 90046-3408, USA

Savage, Chantay (Music Group, Musician)
Famous Artists Agency
250 W 57th St
New York, NY 10107-0001, USA

Savage, Fred (Actor)
c/o Andy Elkin *Creative Artists Agency LCC (CAA-LA)*
2000 Avenue Of The Stars
Los Angeles, CA 90067-4700, USA

Savage, John (Actor)
5584 Bonneville Rd
Hidden Hills, CA 91302-1201, USA

Savage, Michael (Radio Personality)
PO Box 141000
Nashville, TN 37214-1000, USA

Savage, Randy Macho Man
7650 Bayshore Dr # 10038
Treasure Island, FL 33706-3530, USA

Savage, Rick (Musician)
Q Prime Mgmt
729 7th Ave Rm 1400
New York, NY 10019-6889, USA

Savage, Stephanie (Producer, Writer)
c/o Staff Member *Wonderland Sound and Vision*
8739 W Sunset Blvd
W Hollywood, CA 90069-2205, USA

Savage, Tracie
6212 Banner Ave
Los Angeles, CA 90038-2802, USA

Savage Garden
9255 W Sunset Blvd Ste 411
W Hollywood, CA 90069-3302, USA

Saval, Dany
131 rue de l'Universite
Paris 75007, FRANCE

Savant, Doug (Actor)
c/o Kay Liberman *Liberman/Zerman Management*
252 N Larchmont Blvd Ste 200
Los Angeles, CA 90004-3754, USA

Savard, Denis (Hockey Player)
Chicago Blackhawks
1901 W Madison St
United Center
Chicago, IL 60612-2459, USA

Savard, Serge A (Hockey Player)
1790 Ch du Golf
RR 1
Saint Bruno, PQ J3V 4P6, CANADA

Savary, Jerome (Director)
Theatre National de Chaillot
1 Place du Trocadero
Paris 75116, FRANCE

Savchenko, Arkadly M (Opera Singer)
8-358 Storozhovskaya Str
Minsk 220002, BELARUS

Save Ferris (Music Group)
c/o Staff Member *Epic Records Group*
550 Madison Ave
New York, NY 10022-3211, USA

Saveleva, Lyudmila M (Actor)
Tverskaya Str 19
#76
Moscow 103050, RUSSIA

Saverson, Henry (Baseball Player)
Detroit Stars
1726 Benjamin Ave NE
Grand Rapids, MI 49505-5434, USA

Saves the Day (Music Group)
c/o Jeff Hanson *Jeff Hanson Management & Promotions*
2813 S Hiawassee Rd Ste 307
Orlando, FL 32835-6690, USA

Savident, John (Actor)
c/o Staff Member *Coronation Street*
Granada Television
Quay Street
Manchester M60 9EA, UNITED KINGDOM (UK)

Savidge, Jennifer (Actor)
c/o Staff Member *TalentWorks (LA)*
3500 W Olive Ave Ste 1400
Burbank, CA 91505-5512, USA

Savile, David
28 Colomb St.
London, ENGLAND SW10 9EW, UNITED KINGDOM (UK)

Saville, Curtis (Misc)
Rfd Box 44
West Charleston, VT 05872, USA

Saville, Fleur (Actor)
c/o Staff Member *Auckland Actors*
PO Box 56460
Dominion Road
Auckland, NEW ZEALAND

Saville, Kathleen (Misc)
Rfd Box 44
West Charleston, VT 05872, USA

Savini, Tom
311 Taylor St
Pittsburgh, PA 15224-1862, USA

Savinykh, Viktor P (Misc)
Moscow State University
Gorochovskii 4
Moscow 103064, RUSSIA

Savitskaya, Svetalana Y (Misc)
Russian Association
Khovanskaya Str 3
Moscow 129515, RUSSIA

Savitsky, George M (Football Player)
Philadelphia Eagles
350 E Seabright Rd
Ocean City, NJ 08226-4505, USA

Savitt, Dick
19 E 80th St
New York, NY 10075-0117, USA

Savoy, Gene
643 Ralston St
Reno, NV 89503-4436, USA

Savoy, Guy (Chef)
101 Blvd Pereire
Paris 75017, FRANCE

Savre, Danielle (Actor)
c/o Wendi Niad *Niad Management*
15030 Ventura Blvd Ste 19 Ste 860
Sherman Oaks, CA 91403-2444, USA

Savvina, Iya S (Actor)
Bolshaya
Grunzinskaya St 12 #43
Moscow 123242, RUSSIA

Saw, Maung (General, Prime Minister)
Prime Minister's Office
Yangon, MYANMAR

Sawa, Devon (Actor)
7201 Melrose Ave Ste 202
Los Angeles, CA 90046-7654, USA

Sawalha, Julia (Actor)
P F D
Drury House
34-43 Russell St
London WC2B 5HA, UNITED KINGDOM (UK)

Sawalha, Nadia (Talk Show Host)
BBC
Broadcasting House
Portland Place
London, UK W1A 1AA, UNITED KINGDOM (UK)

Sawallisch, Wolfgang (Conductor, Musician)
Hinterm Bichi 2
Grassau 83224, GERMANY

Sawyer, Amos (President)
President's Office
Executive Mansion
PO Box 9001
Monrovia, LIBERIA

Sawyer, Charles H (Misc)
466 Tuallitan Rd
Los Angeles, CA 90049-1941, USA

Sawyer, Daine (Correspondent)
147 Columbus Ave # 300
New York, NY 10023-6503, USA

Sawyer, Elton (Race Car Driver)
Akins Motorsports
PO Box 4300
Mooresville, NC 28117-2300, USA

Sawyer, Forrest (Correspondent)
NBC-TV
30 Rockefeller Plz Ste 270E
News Dept
New York, NY 10112-0299, USA

Sawyer, James L (Misc)
Leather Workers Union
11 Peabody Sq Ste 4
Peabody, MA 01960-5600, USA

Sawyer, John (Football Player)
Houston Oilers
23637 Sunnyside Ln
Zachary, LA 70791-6118, USA

Sawyer, Ken (Football Player)
Cincinnati Bengals
667 Violet Ave Lot 36
Hyde Park, NY 12538-1951, USA

Sawyer, Paul (Race Car Driver)
Richmond International Raceway
PO Box 9257
Richmond, VA 23227-0257, USA

Sawyer, Robert E (Religious Leader)
Moravian Church Southern Province
459 S Church St
Winston Salem, NC 27101-5314, USA

Sawyer, Talance (Football Player)
Minnesota Vikings
6150 Brookhaven Dr
Bastrop, LA 71220-1878, USA

Sawyer Brown (Music Group)
c/o Staff Member *Paradigm (Nashville)*
124 12th Ave S Ste 410
Nashville, TN 37203-3170, USA

Sax, Stephen L (Steve) (Baseball Player)
201 Wesley Ct
Roseville, CA 95661-7913, USA

Sax, Steve
201 Wesley Ct
Roseville, CA 95661-7913, USA

Saxbe, William H (Attorney, Attorney
General, General, Senator)
4600 N Ocean Blvd Ste 200
Boynton Beach, FL 33435-7365, USA

Saxe, Adrian (Artist)
4835 N Figueroa St
Los Angeles, CA 90042-4408, USA

Saxon, David S (Physicist)
1008 Hilts Ave
Los Angeles, CA 90024-3215, USA

Saxon, Edward (Producer)
c/o Staff Member *Creative Artists Agency
LCC (CAA-LA)*
2000 Avenue Of The Stars
Los Angeles, CA 90067-4700, USA

Saxon, James E (Football Player)
Kansas City Chiefs
RR 3 Box 34X
Beaufort, SC 29906, USA

Saxon, James E (Jimmy) (Football Player)
1 Mulberry Ln
West Lake Hills, TX 78746-4321, USA

Saxon, John (Actor)
2432 Banyan Dr
Los Angeles, CA 90049-1240, USA

Saxon, Mike (Football Player)
Dallas Cowboys
660 W Peninsula Dr
Coppell, TX 75019-6801, USA

Saxton, Brian (Football Player)
New York Giants
177 Van Houten Ave
Wyckoff, NJ 07481-2421, USA

Saxton, Jimmy (Football Player)
Dallas Texans
1 Mulberry Ln
West Lake Hills, TX 78746-4321, USA

Saxton, Johnny (Boxer)
1710 4th Ave N
Crystal Palms
Lake Worth, FL 33460-2808, USA

Saxton, Shirley Childress (Music Group,
Musician)
Sweet Honey Agency
PO Box 600099
Newtonville, MA 02460-0001, USA

Say, Peggy
438 Lake Shore Dr.
Cadiz, KY 42211, USA

Sayed, Mostafa Amr El (Misc)
579 Westover Dr NW
Atlanta, GA 30305-3537, USA

Sayer, Leo (Music Group, Musician,
Songwriter, Writer)
Mission Control
Business Center
Lower Road
London SE16 2XB, UNITED KINGDOM
(UK)

Sayers, E Roger (Educator)
University of Alabama
President's Office
Tuscaloosa, AL 35487-0001, USA

Sayers, Gale (Football Player)
Chicago Bears
1313 N Ritchie Ct Apt 407
Chicago, IL 60610-2153, USA

Saykally, Richard J (Misc)
University of California
Chemistry Dept
Latimer Hall
Berkeley, CA 94720-0001, USA

Sayles, John T (Director)
210 13th St
Hoboken, NJ 07030-4435, USA

Sayre, Anne
1268 E 14th St
Brooklyn, NY 11230-5241, USA

Sazio, Ralph (Football Player)
Brooklyn Dodgers
4005 Gulf Shore Blvd N Apt 1107
Naples, FL 34103-2674, USA

Sbarge, Raphael
4526 Wilshire Blvd
Los Angeles, CA 90010-3801, USA

Sbranti, Ron (Football Player)
Denver Broncos
2925 Roosevelt Ln
Antioch, CA 94509-5040, USA

Scaasi, Arnold (Designer, Fashion
Designer)
16 E 52nd St
New York, NY 10022-5306, USA

Scacchi, Greta (Actor)
P F D
Drury House
34-43 Russell St
London WC2B 5HA, UNITED KINGDOM
(UK)

Scaduto, Al (Cartoonist)
571 Swanson Cres
Milford, CT 06461-2735, USA

Scafa, Bob (Baseball Player)
US Olympic Team
2090 Milton Ave
Park Ridge, IL 60068-2320, USA

Scaggs, Boz (Musician)
9460 Wilshire Blvd Ste 310
Beverly Hills, CA 90212-2710, USA

Scaggs, William R (Boz) (Music Group,
Musician, Songwriter, Writer)
H K Mgmt
9200 W Sunset Blvd Ste 530
Los Angeles, CA 90069-3509, USA

Scagliotti-Smith, Allison (Actor)
c/o Staff Member *Osbrink Talent Agency*
4343 Lankershim Blvd # 100
North Hollywood, CA 91602-2705, USA

Scales, Charlie (Football Player)
Pittsburgh Steelers
4035 Vistaview St
West Mifflin, PA 15122-2134, USA

Scales, Dwight (Football Player)
Los Angeles Rams
6112 Roosevelt Cir NW
Huntsville, AL 35810-1634, USA

Scales, Greg (Football Player)
New Orleans Saints
4118 Carnation Dr
Winston Salem, NC 27105-3219, USA

Scales, Hurles (Football Player)
Chicago Bears
600 N Adams St
Amarillo, TX 79107-5068, USA

Scales, Prunella (Actor)
Conway Van Gelder Robinson
18-21 Jermyn St
London SW1Y 6NB, UNITED KINGDOM
(UK)

Scalia, Jack (Actor)
c/o Alan Ellsweig *Metropolitan*
4500 Wilshire Blvd Fl 2
Los Angeles, CA 90010-3858, USA

Scalia, Justice Antonin (Judge)
US Supreme Court
1 1st St NE
Washington, DC 20543-0002, USA

Scalia, Pietro (Actor, Director, Editor,
Producer)
c/o Spyros Skouras *The Skouras Agency*
1149 3rd St Fl 3
Santa Monica, CA 90403-7201, USA

Scalians, Bret (Musician)
Media Five Entertainment
3005 Brodhead Read #170
Bethlehem, PA 18020, USA

Scalzitti, Will (Baseball Player)
19321 SW 61st St
Ft Lauderdale, FL 33332-3354, USA

Scalzo, Tony (Music Group, Musician)
Russell Carter Artists
567 Ralph McGill Blvd NE
Atlanta, GA 30312-1110, USA

Scaminace, Joseph M (Business Person)
Sherwin-Williams Co
101 W Prospect Ave
Cleveland, OH 44115-1075, USA

Scancarelli, Jim (Cartoonist)
Mark J Cohen
PO Box 1892
Santa Rosa, CA 95402-1892, USA

Scandiuzzi, Roberto (Opera Singer)
Opera et Concert
Maximilianstr 22
Munich 80539, GERMANY

Scanga, Italo (Artist)
7127 Olivetas Ave
La Jolla, CA 92037-5332, USA

Scanlan, Hugh P S (Misc)
23 Seven Stones Dr
Broadstairs
Kent, UNITED KINGDOM (UK)

Scarbath, John C (Jack) (Football Player)
Washington Redskins
736 Calvert Rd
Rising Sun, MD 21911-2332, USA

Scarber, Sam (Football Player)
San Diego Chargers
12209 Crewe St
North Hollywood, CA 91605-5609, USA

Scarborough, Joe (Senator)
575 Woodbine Dr
Pensacola, FL 32503-3239, USA

Scarborough, Jon (Television Host)
c/o Staff Member *MSNBC (NJ)*
Nbc/One Microsoft Corporation
1 Msnc Plaza
Secaucus, NJ 07094, USA

Scarbrough, W Carl (Misc)
Furniture Workers Union
1910 Air Lane Dr
Nashville, TN 37210-3810, USA

Scardelletti, Robert A (Misc)
Transportation Communications Union
3 Research Pl
Rockville, MD 20850-3279, USA

Scardino, Albert J (Journalist)
19 Empire House
Thurloe Place
London SW7 2RU, UNITED KINGDOM
(UK)

Scarf, Herbert E (Economist)
88 Blake Rd
Hamden, CT 06517-3402, USA

Scarface (Musician)
c/o Staff Member *American Talent Agency*
173 Main St
Ossining, NY 10562-4704, USA

Scarfe, Gerald A (Cartoonist)
10 Cheyne Walk
London SW3, UNITED KINGDOM (UK)

Scarfe, Jonathan
4739 Lankershim Blvd
N Hollywood, CA 91602-1803, USA

Scargill, Arthur (Misc)
National Union of Mineworkers
2 Huddersfield Road
Bamsley, UNITED KINGDOM (UK)

Scarpati, Joseph H (Football Player)
Philadelphia Eagles
32 Lexington Cir
Marlton, NJ 08053-3860, USA

Scarpelli, Glenn
3480 Barham Blvd Apt 320
Los Angeles, CA 90068-1469, USA

Scarpitto, Bob (Football Player)
San Diego Chargers
2836 Santa Cruz Ct
Merced, CA 95340-2672, USA

Scarry, Mike (Football Player)
Cleveland Rams
7430 Lake Breeze Dr Apt 104
Fort Myers, FL 33907-8058, USA

Scarwid, Diana (Actor)
PO Box 3614
Savannah, GA 31414-3614, USA

Scates, Al (Coach, Volleyball Player)
8433 Apple Hill Ct
Las Vegas, NV 89128-7635, USA

Scattini, Monica (Actor)
Carol Levi Co
Via Giuseppe Pisanelli
Rome 00196, ITALY

Scelba-Shorte, Mercedes (Reality TV Star)
c/o Staff Member *Ty Ty Baby Productions*
8346 W 3rd St # 650
Los Angeles, CA 90048-4311, USA

Schaaf-Behle, Petra
Am Rodeland 22
Willingen D-34508, GERMANY

Schaal, Richard (Actor)
612 Gulf Blvd # 9
Indian Rocks Beach, FL 33785-2666, USA

Schaal, Wendy (Actor)
Gage Group
14724 Ventura Blvd Ste 505
Sherman Oaks, CA 91403-3505, USA

Schaap, Dick
77 W 66th St
New York, NY 10023-6201, USA

Schabarum, Pete (Football Player)
San Francisco 49ers
46170 E Eldorado Dr
Indian Wells, CA 92210-8633, USA

Schacher, Mel (Musician)
Lustig Talent
PO Box 770850
Orlando, FL 32877-0850, USA

Schacht, Henry B (Business Person)
Lucent Technologies Inc
600 Mountain Ave
New Providence, NJ 07974-2008, USA

Schachter, Blanche (Baseball Player)
163 W 18th St Apt 3A
New York, NY 10011-4144, USA

Schachter, Steven (Director, Writer)
c/o Staff Member *Writers and Artists Group Intl (LA)*
8383 Wilshire Blvd Ste 550
Beverly Hills, CA 90211-2417, USA

Schachter-Shalomi, Zalman (Religious Leader)
Spiritual Eldering Institute
535 W South Boulder Rd Ste 240
Lafayette, CO 80026-2098, USA

Schachter Sisters
182-06 Midland Park Blvd.
Jamaica Estates, NY 11432, USA

Schade, Molly (Actor)
c/o Aron Giannini *The Collective*
9100 Wilshire Blvd # 700 W
Beverly Hills, CA 90212-3401, USA

Schadler, Jay (Correspondent)
c/o Staff Member *Primetime*
147 Columbus Ave
New York, NY 10023-6503, USA

Schadt, James P (Publisher)
Reader's Digest Assn
Readers Digest Rd
Pleasantville, NY 10570-7001, USA

Schaech, Johnathon (Actor)
c/o Chuck James *Gersh Agency, The (LA)*
232 N Canon Dr
Beverly Hills, CA 90210-5302, USA

Schaech, Jonathon (Actor, Musician, Producer, Writer)
c/o Staff Member *Chesapeake Films*
132B Industry Ln Ste 7
Forest Hill, MD 21050-3206, USA

Schaefer, Don (Football Player)
Philadelphia Eagles
286 Birch Pkwy
Wyckoff, NJ 07481-2831, USA

Schaefer, Ernst J (Scientist)
Tufts University
Nutrition Research Center
Medford, MA 02155, USA

Schaefer, George A Jr (Financier)
Fifth Third Bancorp
38 Fountain Square Plaza
Cincinnati, OH 45263-0001, USA

Schaefer, Henry F III (Misc)
University of Georgia
Computational Quantum Chemistry Center
Athens, GA 30602, USA

Schaefer, Molly (Publisher)
Town & Country Magazine
1700 Broadway
New York, NY 10019-5905, USA

Schaefer, Roberto (Cinematographer)
Innovative Artists
1505 10th St
Santa Monica, CA 90401-2805, USA

Schaefer, William D (Governor)
7184 Springhouse Ln
Baltimore, MD 21226-2200, USA

Schaeffer, Eric (Actor, Director)
Writers & Artists
360 N Crescent Dr Bldg North
Beverly Hills, CA 90210-6818, USA

Schaeffer, George
1040 Woodland Dr
Beverly Hills, CA 90210-2936, USA

Schaeffer, Leonard (Business Person)
WellPoint Health Networks
1 Wellpoint Way
Westlake Village, CA 91362-3893, USA

Schaefzel, John R (Writer)
2 Bay Tree Ln
Bethesda, MD 20816-1046, USA

Schaffel, Lewis (Basketball Player, Misc)
Miami Heat
601 Biscayne Blvd
American Airlines Arena
Miami, FL 33132-1801, USA

Schaffer, Eric (Music Group, Musician)
Kennedy Center for Performing Arts
Washington, DC 20011, USA

Schafrath, Dick (Football Player)
Cleveland Browns
196 Mapledale Ave
Mansfield, OH 44903-1867, USA

Schakper, Allison (Writer)
c/o Staff Member *Endeavor Agency LLC (LA)*
9601 Wilshire Blvd Fl 3
Beverly Hills, CA 90210-5204, USA

Schall, Alvin A (Judge)
US Appeals Court
717 Madison Pl NW
Washington, DC 20439-0001, USA

Schaller, Willie (Soccer Player)
3283 S Indiana St
Lakewood, CO 80228-5499, USA

Schallert, William (Actor)
14920 Ramos Pl
Pacific Palisades, CA 90272-4460, USA

Schally, Andrew V (Nobel Prize Laureate)
3801 Collins Ave
Miami Beach, FL 33140-3705, USA

Schama, Simon M (Historian, Writer)
Minda de Gunzburg European Studies Center
Adolphus Hall
Cambridge, MA 02138, USA

Schamehorn, Kevin (Hockey Player)
5536 Stoney Brook Rd
Kalamazoo, MI 49009-7703, USA

Schanberg, Sydney H (Journalist)
164 W 79th St Apt 12D
New York, NY 10024-6494, USA

Schank, Roger C (Doctor, Scientist)
Northwestern University
Learning Sciences Institute
Evanston, IL 60201, USA

Schankweiler, Scott (Football Player)
Buffalo Bills
11 Bartley Ct
Nottingham, MD 21236-2428, USA

Schanz, Heidi (Actor)
Gersh Agency
232 N Canon Dr
Beverly Hills, CA 90210-5302, USA

Schapp, Dick (Sportscaster)
ESPN-TV
Sports Dept
Espn Plaza 935 Middle St
Bristol, CT 06010, USA

Schar, Dwight (Business Person)
NVR Inc
11700 Plaza America Dr Ste 500
Reston, VA 20190-4792, USA

Scharansky, Natan (Activist, Scientist)
Trade & Industry Ministry
30 Rehov Agron
Jerusalem 91002, ISRAEL

Scharar, Erich (Athlete)
Grutstrasse 63
Herrliberg 8074, SWITZERLAND

Scharping, Rudolf (Government Official)
Wilhelmstr 5
Lahnstein 56112, GERMANY

Schatz, Howard (Photographer)
435 W Broadway Fl 2
New York, NY 10012-5902, USA

Schatzberg, Jerry N (Director)
International Creative Mgmt
8942 Wilshire Blvd # 219
Beverly Hills, CA 90211-1908, USA

Schatzman, Evry (Physicist)
11 Rue de l'Eglise
Domplerre
Maignelay-Montigny 60420, FRANCE

Schaudt, Martin (Athlete, Horse Racer)
Gerhardstr 10/2
Albstadt 72461, GERMANY

Schaufuss, Peter (Ballerina, Director)
Papoutsis Representation
18 Sundial Ave
London SE25 4BX, UNITED KINGDOM (UK)

Schaum, Greg (Football Player)
Dallas Cowboys
4303 Piney Park Rd
Perry Hall, MD 21128-9524, USA

Schayes, Adolph (Dolph) (Basketball Player)
PO Box 156
Syracuse, NY 13214-0156, USA

Schayes, Danny (Basketball Player)
PO Box 665
Windermere, FL 34786-0665, USA

Scheck, Barry (Attorney, Attorney General, Educator, General)
Yeshiva University
55 5th Ave
Law School
New York, NY 10003-4391, USA

Scheckter, Jody D (Race Car Driver)
39 Ave Princess Grace
Monte Carlo, MONACO

Schedeen, Anne (Actor)
Metropolitan Talent Agency
4500 Wilshire Blvd Fl 2
Los Angeles, CA 90010-3858, USA

Scheetz, Larry (Football Player)
Washington Redskins
3175 Grape Bay
Doylestown, PA 18902-1708, USA

Scheffler, Israel (Misc)
Harvard University
Larsen Hall
Cambridge, MA 02138, USA

Schefft, Jen (Actor, Reality TV Star)
c/o Staff Member *Bachelorette, The*
15301 Ventura Blvd Bldg E
Sherman Oaks, CA 91403-5885, USA

Scheibel, Arnold B (Doctor)
16231 Morrison St
Encino, CA 91436-1331, USA

Scheider, Roy (Actor)
c/o Jack Gilardi *International Creative Management (ICM-LA)*
10250 Constellation Blvd
Los Angeles, CA 90067-6200, USA

Schein, Philip S (Doctor)
6212 Robinwood Rd
Bethesda, MD 20817-6115, USA

Schekman, Randy W (Scientist)
Howard Hughes Institute
4000 Jones Bridge Rd
Chevy Chase, MD 20815-6789, USA

Schell, Catherine (Actor)
Postfach 800504
Cologne 51005, GERMANY

Schell, Jonathan (Journalist)
Newsday
235 Pinelawn Rd
Editorial Dept
Melville, NY 11747-4250, USA

Schell, Maximilian (Actor)
2323 S Beverly Glen Blvd Unit 3
Los Angeles, CA 90064-2591, USA

Schell, Maximillian (Actor, Director, Writer)
c/o Staff Member *The Blake Agency*
1333 Ocean Ave
Santa Monica, CA 90401-1023, USA

Schell, Ronnie
Angel City Talent
4741 Laurel Canyon Blvd Ste 101
Valley Village, CA 91607-5905, USA

Schellenbach, Kate (Musician)
Metropolitan Entertainment
2 Penn Plz # 2600
New York, NY 10121-0101, USA

Schellenberg, August (Actor)
Gold Marshak Liedtke
3500 W Olive Ave Ste 1400
Burbank, CA 91505-5512, USA

Schellhase, Dave (Basketball Player)
PO Box 48482
Tampa, FL 33646-0121, USA

Schelling, Thomas C (Economist)
University of Maryland
Economics Dept
College Park, MD 20742-0001, USA

Schellman, John A (Misc)
65 W 30th Ave # 508
Eugene, OR 97405-3373, USA

Schelmerding, Kirk (Misc, Race Car Driver)
Childress Racing
PO Box 1189
Industrial Dr
Welcome, NC 27374-1189, USA

Schemansky, Norbert (Misc)
24826 New York St
Dearborn, MI 48124-4485, USA

Schembechler, Bo
1904 Boulder Dr
Ann Arbor, MI 48104-4164, USA

Schembechler, Glenn E (Bo) Jr (Coach, Football Player)
1904 Boulder Dr
Ann Arbor, MI 48104-4164, USA

Schemling, Bill
PO Box 11308
Portland, OR 97211-0308, USA

Schenert, Turk (Football Player)
Cincinnati Bengals
239 Willow Ave
Pompton Lakes, NJ 07442-2443, USA

Schenk, Franziska (Speed Skater)
DSEG
Mensinger Str 68
Munich 80992, GERMANY

Schenkenberg, Markus (Actor, Model)
c/o Staff Member *Ford Models (Miami)*
311 Lincoln Rd Ste 205
Miami Beach, FL 33139-3150, USA

Schenker, Nathan (Football Player)
Cleveland Rams
26400 George Zeiger Dr Apt 116
Beachwood, OH 44122-7511, USA

Schenkkan, Robert F (Writer)
Dramatist Guild
1501 Broadway Ste 701
New York, NY 10036-5505, USA

Schenkman, Eric (Musician)
DAS Communications
84 Riverside Dr
New York, NY 10024-5723, USA

Schepisi, Fred (Director)
c/o Staff Member *William Morris Agency (WMA-LA)*
1 William Morris Pl
Beverly Hills, CA 90212-4261, USA

Schepisl, Frederic A (Director)
Film House
159 Eastern Road
South Melbourne, VIC 3205, AUSTRALIA

Scherbo, Vitaly
8308 Aqua Spray Ave
Las Vegas, NV 89128-7432, USA

Scherega, Harold A (Misc)
212 Homestead Ter
Ithaca, NY 14850-6220, USA

Scherer, Bernard (Football Player)
Green Bay Packers
PO Box 5201
Carmel By The Sea, CA 93921-5201, USA

Scherrer, Jean-Louis (Designer, Fashion Designer)
51 Ave du Montaigne
Paris 75008, FRANCE

Scherza, Chuck (Hockey Player)
51 Manistee St
Pawtucket, RI 02861-4011, USA

Scherzinger, Nicole (Actor, Musician)
c/o Marnie Sparer *Innovative Artists (LA)*
1505 10th St
Santa Monica, CA 90401-2805, USA

Scheuer, Paul J (Misc)
3271 Melemele Pl
Honolulu, HI 96822-1431, USA

Scheuring, Paul (Director)
c/o Staff Member *Endeavor Agency LLC (LA)*
9601 Wilshire Blvd Fl 3
Beverly Hills, CA 90210-5204, USA

Schevill, James (Writer)
1309 Oxford St
Berkeley, CA 94709-1424, USA

Schiavo, Mary (Activist, Government Official)
Ohio State University
Public Policy Dept
Columbus, OH 43210, USA

Schiavone, Carmine
3589 S Ocean Blvd Apt 137
Palm Beach, FL 33480-5734, USA

Schickel, Richard (Critic, Writer)
9051 Dicks St
Los Angeles, CA 90069-4808, USA

Schickele, Peter (Comedian, Composer)
International Creative Mgmt
40 W 57th St Ste 1800
New York, NY 10019-4001, USA

Schiebold, Hans (Artist)
13705 SW 118th Ct
Tigard, OR 97223-2857, USA

Schieffer, Bob (Correspondent, Television Host)
Face the Nation
Cbs
2020 Main St NW
Washington, DC 20036, USA

Schiff, Andras (Musician)
Shirley Kirshbaum
711 W End Ave Apt 5kn
New York, NY 10025-6843, USA

Schiff, Heinrich (Musician)
Astrid Schoerke
Monckegergallee 41
Hannover 30453, GERMANY

Schiff, John J Jr (Financier)
Cincinnati Financial Corp
6200 S Gilmore Rd
Fairfield, OH 45014-5141, USA

Schiff, Mark (Actor, Comedian)
Gail Stocker Presents
1025 N Kings Rd Apt 113
Los Angeles, CA 90069-6007, USA

Schiff, Richard (Actor)
524 Lorraine Blvd
Los Angeles, CA 90020-4732, USA

Schiff, Robin (Writer)
c/o Staff Member *Broder Webb Chervin Silbermann Agency, The (BWCS)*
10250 Constellation Blvd Ste P
Los Angeles, CA 90067-6213, USA

Schiffer, Claudia (Model)
c/o Lisa Jacobsen *United Talent Agency (UTA)*
9560 Wilshire Blvd Ste 500
Beverly Hills, CA 90212-2401, USA

Schiffer, Eric (Writer)
6965 El Camino Real Ste 105
Pmb 517
Carlsbad, CA 92009-4101, USA

Schiffer, Michael (Actor)
c/o David Greenblatt *Key Creatives*
9595 Wilshire Blvd Ste 800
Beverly Hills, CA 90212-2508, USA

Schiffner, Travis (Actor)
c/o Staff Member *Bohemia Entertainment Group*
8170 Beverly Blvd Ste 102
Los Angeles, CA 90048-4533, USA

Schiffrin, Andre (Publisher)
New Press
201 E 50th St
New York, NY 10022-7703, USA

Schifrin, Lalo (Composer)
710 N Hillcrest Rd
Beverly Hills, CA 90210-3517, USA

Schillebeeckx, Edward (Misc, Religious Leader)
Crossroad Publishing Co
575 Lexington Ave
New York, NY 10022-6102, USA

Schiller, Harvey W (Misc)
Turner Sports
1050 Techwood Dr NW
Atlanta, GA 30318-5604, USA

Schiller, Lawrence J (Director, Writer)
5430 Oakdale Ave
Woodland Hills, CA 91364-2611, USA

Schilling, Curtis (Curt) M (Baseball Player)
c/o Staff Member *Boston Red Sox*
Fenway Park
4 Yawkey Way
Boston, MA 02215-3496, USA

Schilling, Peter
Geiselgasteigstr. 76
Munich 81545, GERMANY

Schilling, William
626 N Valley St
Burbank, CA 91505-3147, USA

Schimberg, Henry R (Business Person)
Coca-Cola Enterprises
2500 Windy Ridge Pkwy SE
Atlanta, GA 30339-5677, USA

Schimberni, Mario (Business Person)
Armando Curcio Editore SpA
Via IV Novembre
Rome 00187, ITALY

Schindelholz, Lorenz (Athlete)
Hardstr 184
Herbetswil 4715, SWITZERLAND

Schindler, Steve (Football Player)
Denver Broncos
6109 Willow Springs Dr
Morrison, CO 80465-2133, USA

Schinkel, Kenneth (Ken) (Hockey Player)
19927 Beaulieu Ct
Fort Myers, FL 33908-4832, USA

Schino, Dominic (Producer)
c/o Staff Member *Magic Touch Records*
1215 36th Ave Apt 4E
Long Island City, NY 11106-4736, USA

Schipper, Ron (Coach, Football Coach)
1088 Fountain View Cir Unit 1
Holland, MI 49423-5620, USA

Schirinowskij, Wladmir
Sokolnitscheskij wal 38-114
Moscow 107113, RUSSIA

Schirripa, Steven R (Actor)
c/o Tim Stone *Stone Manners Talent & Literary (LA)*
6500 Wilshire Blvd Ste 550
Los Angeles, CA 90048-4950, USA

Schisgal, Murray J (Writer)
International Creative Mgmt
40 W 57th St Ste 1800
New York, NY 10019-4001, USA

Schissler, Les (Bowler)
3060 E Bridge St Lot 20
Brighton, CO 80601-2718, USA

Schlafly, Phyllis (Activist)
68 Fairmont Ave
Alton, IL 62002, USA

Schlag, Edward W (Misc)
Osterwaldstr 91
Munich 80805, GERMANY

Schlamme, Thomas (Actor)
c/o Rosalie Swedlin *Industry Entertainment*
955 Carrillo Dr Ste 300
Los Angeles, CA 90048-5400, USA

Schlatmann, Gert Jan
Oostzeedijk Gen 39a
Rotterdam NL 3062 WK, THE NETHERLANDS

Schlatter, Charlie (Actor)
638 Lindero Canyon Rd # 322
Oak Park, CA 91377-5457, USA

Schlatter, George
400 Robert Ln
Beverly Hills, CA 90210-2632, USA

Schleech, Russ (Misc)
21634 Paseo Maravia
Mission Viejo, CA 92692-4963, USA

Schlegel, Hans W (Astronaut)
DLR Astronaulenburo Linder Hohe
Postfach 906058
Cologne 51140, GERMANY

Schlegel, John P (Educator)
University of San Francisco
President's Office
San Francisco, CA 94117, USA

Schleich, Vic (Football Player)
New York Yankees
27 Valley Heights Dr
Williamsport, PA 17701-1922, USA

Schlein, Dov C (Financier)
Republic New York Corp
452 5th Ave
New York, NY 10018-2706, USA

Schlesinger, Adam (Music Group, Musician, Songwriter, Writer)
MOB Agency
6404 Wilshire Blvd Ste 505
Los Angeles, CA 90048-5507, USA

Schlesinger, Cory (Football Player)
Detroit Lions
36 Bradford Ct
Dearborn, MI 48126-4169, USA

Schlesinger, James R (Secretary)
Georgetown University
1800 K St NW Ste 400
Washington, DC 20006-2230, USA

Schlesinger, Laura (Radio Personality)
Premier Radio Network
15260 Ventura Blvd Ste 500
Sherman Oaks, CA 91403-5339, USA

Schlessinger, Laura (Doctor)
3201 Campanil Dr
Santa Barbara, CA 93109-1014, USA

Schleyer, Paul Von R (Misc)
Frederich-Alexander-Universtat
Henkestr 41
Erlangen 91469, GERMANY

Schlichtmann, Jan (Attorney, Attorney
General, General)
359 Hale St
Beverly, MA 01915, USA

Schlondorff, Volker (Director)
Studio Babelsberg
Postfach 900361
Potsdam 14439, GERMANY

Schloredt, Robert S (Bob) (Football
Player)
Nestle-Beich
1827 N 167th St
Shoreline, WA 98133-5505, USA

Schlossberg, Edwin (Writer)
*The John F Kennedy Presidential Library
& Museum*
Columbia Point
New York, NY 10002, USA

Schlossberg, Katie (Actor)
Talent Group
6300 Wilshire Blvd Ste 2100
Los Angeles, CA 90048-5282, USA

Schlossberg, Katle (Actor)
Talent Group
5670 Wilshire Blvd Ste 820
Los Angeles, CA 90036-5613, USA

Schlosser, Eric (Writer)
*c/o Houghton Mifflin Company Trade
Division*
222 Berkeley St
Adult Editorial, 8th Floor
Boston, MA 02116-3748, USA

Schlueter, Dale (Basketball Player)
15555 SW Harcourt Ter
Portland, OR 97224-5234, USA

Schluter, Poul H (Prime Minister)
Frederiksberg Allee 66
Frederiksberg C 1820, DENMARK

Schmautz, Bobby
15544 SE Webster Rd
Portland, OR 97267, USA

Schmeichel, Peter (Soccer Player)
Aston Villa
Villa Park
Trinity Road
Birmingham B6 6HE, UNITED KINGDOM
(UK)

Schmemann, Serge (Journalist)
New York Times
229 W 43rd St
Editorial Dept
New York, NY 10036-3959, USA

Schmid, Dave
17173 Rayen St
Northridge, CA 91325-2908, USA

Schmid, Kyle (Actor)
c/o Norbert Abrams Noble Kaplan Agency
1260 Yonge St Fl 2
Toronto, ON M4T 1W6, CANADA

Schmid, Rudi (Misc)
211 Woodland Rd
Kentfield, CA 94904-2631, USA

Schmid, Sigi (Coach, Soccer Player)
Los Angeles Galaxy
1010 Rose Bowl Dr
Pasadena, CA 91103, USA

Schmidgall, Jennifer (Hockey Player)
3640 Wooddale Ave S Unit 103
Minneapolis, MN 55416-5157, USA

Schmidly, David J (Educator)
Texas Tech University
President's Office
Lubbock, TX 79409, USA

Schmidt, Andreas (Opera Singer)
Fossredder 51
Hamburg 22359, GERMANY

Schmidt, Benno C Jr (Educator)
Edison Project
375 Park Ave
New York, NY 10152-0002, USA

Schmidt, Bob (Football Player)
New York Giants
10005 Sky View Way Apt 2106
Fort Myers, FL 33913-6606, USA

Schmidt, Dave (Baseball Player)
7172 N Serenoa Dr
Sarasota, FL 34241-9270, USA

Schmidt, Eric E (Business Person,
Engineer)
Google Inc
1600 Amphitheatre Pkwy # 41
Mountain View, CA 94043-1351, USA

Schmidt, Hank (Football Player)
San Francisco 49ers
4641 Mission Bell Ln
La Mesa, CA 91941-5450, USA

Schmidt, Harald (Athlete, Track Athlete)
Schulstr 11
Hasselroth 63594, GERMANY

Schmidt, Helmut (Misc)
Neuberger Weg 80
Hamburg 22419, GERMANY

Schmidt, Jason D (Baseball Player)
35 View Ridge Cir
Longview, WA 98632-5555, USA

Schmidt, Joe (Football Player)
29600 Northwestern Hwy
PO Box 2210
Southfield, MI 48034-1016, USA

Schmidt, John (Football Player)
2 Mayflower Rd
Glen Head, NY 11545-3120, USA

Schmidt, Joseph P (Joe) (Football Player)
Detroit Lions
226 Norcliff Dr
Bloomfield Hills, MI 48302-1556, USA

Schmidt, Kathryn (Kate) (Athlete, Track
Athlete)
1008 Dexter St
Los Angeles, CA 90042-2248, USA

Schmidt, Kenneth (Actor)
*c/o Staff Member Coast to Coast Talent
Group*
3350 Barham Blvd
Los Angeles, CA 90068-1404, USA

Schmidt, Mike (Baseball Player,
Motivational Speaker)
Playing Field Promotions
277 S Forest St
Denver, CO 80246-1148, USA

Schmidt, Milt (Hockey Player)
10 Logwood Dr #376
Westwood, MA 02090, USA

Schmidt, Ole (Composer, Conductor)
Puggaardsgade 17
Copenhagen 1573, DENMARK

Schmidt, Richard (Doctor)
University of Pennsylvania
3400 Spruce St
Philadelphia, PA 19104-4274, USA

Schmidt, Roy (Football Player)
New Orleans Saints
1844 Highpoint Rd
Snellville, GA 30078-2802, USA

Schmidt, Steve (Race Car Driver)
8560 E 30th St
Indianapolis, IN 46219-1423, USA

Schmidt, Terry (Football Player)
New Orleans Saints
16506 Blenheim Dr
Lutz, FL 33549-6810, USA

Schmidt, Timothy (Musician)
*c/o Staff Member Azoffmusic
Management*
1100 Glendon Ave Ste 2000
Los Angeles, CA 90024-3524, USA

Schmidt, William (Bill) (Athlete, Track
Athlete)
1809 Devonwood Ct
Knoxville, TN 37922-6233, USA

Schmidt, Wolfgang (Athlete, Track
Athlete)
Birkheckenstr 116B
Stuttgart 70599, GERMANY

Schmidt, Wolfgang (Opera Singer)
Kunstleragentur Raab & Bohm
Plankengasse 7
Vienna 1010, AUSTRIA

Schmidt-Nielsen, Knut (Doctor)
Kuke University
Zoology Dept
Durham, NC 27706, USA

Schmidt-Weitzman, Violet (Baseball
Player)
225 S Mill St
Mishawaka, IN 46544-2002, USA

Schmidtmer, Christiane (Actor, Model)
Postfach 120617
Heidelberg 69067, GERMANY

Schmidtt, Harrison (Ex-Senator, Senator)
PO Box 90730
Albuquerque, NM 87199-0730, USA

Schmiege, Marilyn (Opera Singer)
Opera et Concert
Maximilianstr 22
Munich 80539, GERMANY

Schmiegel, Klaus K (Inventor)
4507 Staughton Dr
Indianapolis, IN 46226-3127, USA

Schmiesing, Joe (Football Player)
St Louis Cardinals
19460 County 2
Sauk Centre, MN 56378-4624, USA

Schmit, Timothy B (Musician)
William Morris Agency
1325 Avenue Of The Americas
New York, NY 10019-6091, USA

Schmitt, Martin (Skier)
Muhleschweg 4
VA-Tannehim 78052, GERMANY

Schmitz, John A (Johnny) (Baseball
Player)
526 W Union Ave
Wausau, WI 54401, USA

Schmitz, Johnny (Baseball Player)
526 E Union Ave
Wausau, WI 54403-3365, USA

Schmoeller, David (Director)
3910 Woodhill Ave
Las Vegas, NV 89121-6245, USA

Schnabel, Julian (Artist, Director)
Pace Gallery
32 E 57th St
New York, NY 10022-2530, USA

Schnabel, Marco (Director)
c/o Simon Millar The Firm
9465 Wilshire Blvd Fl 6
Beverly Hills, CA 90212-2605, USA

Schnackenberg, Roy L (Artist)
1919 N Orchard St
Chicago, IL 60614-5159, USA

Schnarre, Monika (Actor, Model)
Alex Stevens
137 N Larchmont Blvd # 259
Los Angeles, CA 90004-3704, USA

Schnebli, Dolf (Architect)
Sudstr 45
Zurich 8008, SWITZERLAND

Schneck, Mike (Football Player)
Pittsburgh Steelers
110 Three Degree Road
Allison Park, PA 15101, USA

Schneer, Charles (Producer)
8 Ilchester Place
London W14 8AA, UNITED KINGDOM
(UK)

Schneider, Andrew (Journalist)
*c/o Richard Weitz Endeavor Agency LLC
(LA)*
9601 Wilshire Blvd Fl 3
Beverly Hills, CA 90210-5204, USA

Schneider, Bernd (Race Car Driver)
Team AMG Mercedes
Daimlerstr 1
Affalterbach 71563, GERMANY

Schneider, Dan (Producer, Writer)
*c/o Staff Member Endeavor Agency LLC
(LA)*
9601 Wilshire Blvd Fl 3
Beverly Hills, CA 90210-5204, USA

Schneider, Fred (Music Group, Musician,
Songwriter, Writer)
Direct Management Group
947 N La Cienega Blvd # 2
Los Angeles, CA 90069-4782, USA

Schneider, Helen
12L Church St
Washington Depot, CT 06777, USA

Schneider, Helge
Prinz-Regent-Str. 50-60
Bochum 44795, GERMANY

Schneider, Howie (Cartoonist)
United Feature Syndicate
200 Madison Ave
New York, NY 10016-3911, USA

Schneider, John (Actor, Musician)
c/o Staff Member *Stone Manners Talent & Literary (LA)*
6500 Wilshire Blvd Ste 550
Los Angeles, CA 90048-4950, USA

Schneider, Lew (Comedian, Producer)
c/o Staff Member *Everybody Loves Raymond*
4000 Warner Blvd Bldg 131
Burbank, CA 91522-0001, USA

Schneider, Maria
Associated International Management
Nederlander House 7 Great Russell Street
London WC1B 3NH, UNITED KINGDOM (UK)

Schneider, Mathieu (Hockey Player)
1311 6th St
Manhattan Beach, CA 90266-6041, USA

Schneider, Rob (Actor, Comedian)
c/o Staff Member *From Out of Nowhere*
2920 W Olive Ave Ste 204
Burbank, CA 91505-4548, USA

Schneider, Vreni (Skier)
Dorf
Elm 8767, SWITZERLAND

Schneider, William (Buzz) (Hockey Player)
5656 Turtle Lake Rd
Shoreview, MN 55126-4769, USA

Schneider, William G (Misc)
National Research Council
65 Whitemart Dr #2
Ottawa, ON K1L 8J9, CANADA

Schneiderman, David A (Editor, Publisher)
Village Voice
36 Cooper Sq
President's Office
New York, NY 10003-7149, USA

Schneiderman, Leon
1578 Topanga Skyline Dr
Topanga, CA 90290-4035, USA

Schneidman, Herm (Football Player)
1811 S 24th St # 5
Quincy, IL 62301-6950, USA

Schnelker, Bob (Coach)
Philadelphia Eagles
85 Silver Oaks Cir Apt 6102
Naples, FL 34119-4665, USA

Schnellbacher, Otto O (Basketball Player, Football Player)
New York Yankees
1815 SW Westwood Cir
Topeka, KS 66604-3269, USA

Schnelldorfer, Manfred (Figure Skater)
Seydlitzstr 55
Munich 80993, GERMANY

Schnellenberger, Howard (Coach, Football Coach)
5109 N Ocean Blvd Apt G
Ocean Ridge, FL 33435-7066, USA

Schnetzer, Stephen
448 W 44th St
New York, NY 10036-5205, USA

Schnitker, Mike (Football Player)
Denver Broncos
12397 Calfee Gulch Rd
Conifer, CO 80433-6406, USA

Schnittker, Richard (Dick) (Basketball Player)
2303 E Las Granadas
Green Valley, AZ 85614, USA

Schobel, Frank
Sterntalerstr. 16
Berlin D-12555, GERMANY

Schochet, Bob (Cartoonist)
6 Sunset Rd
Highland Mills, NY 10930, USA

Schock, Gina (Musician)
PO Box 720160
San Francisco, CA 94172-0160, USA

Schock, Ron (Hockey Player)
1360 Whalen Rd
Penfield, NY 14526-1918, USA

Schockemohle, Alwin (Horse Racer)
Munsterlandstr 51
Muhlen 49439, GERMANY

Schoelen, Jill (Actor)
Gold Marshak Liedtke
3500 W Olive Ave Ste 1400
Burbank, CA 91505-5512, USA

Schoellkopf, Carolyn Hunt
100 Crescent #1700
Dallas, TX 75201, USA

Schoen, Gerry (Baseball Player)
1717 Nero St
Metairie, LA 70005-1521, USA

Schoen, Max H (Doctor)
123 Wellfleet Cir
Folsom, CA 95630-6541, USA

Schoen, Tom (Football Player)
Cleveland Browns
437 W Belmont Ave Apt 13
Chicago, IL 60657-4756, USA

Schoenbaechler, Andreas (Skier)
Muhlrustistr 2
Affoltern a A 8910, SWITZERLAND

Schoenborn, Christoph Cardinal (Religious Leader)
Wollzeile 2
Vienna 1010, AUSTRIA

Schoenfeld, Gerald (Producer)
Shubert Organization Inc
225 W 44th St
New York, NY 10036-3907, USA

Schoenfeld, Jim (Coach, Hockey Player)
11745 E Cortez Dr
Scottsdale, AZ 85259-2605, USA

Schoenfield, Al (Misc, Swimmer)
75 Santa Rosa St
San Luis Obispo, CA 93405-1819, USA

Schoenfield, Dana (Swimmer)
7734 E Lakeview Trl
Orange, CA 92869-2446, USA

Schoenke, Raymond F (Football Player)
Dallas Cowboys
21151 Woodfield Rd
Laytonsville, MD 20882-4847, USA

Schoffer, Nicolas (Artist)
Villa Des Arts
15 Rue Hegesippe-Moreau
Paris 75018, FRANCE

Schofield, Annabel (Actor)
Special Artists Agency
9465 Wilshire Blvd Ste 880
Beverly Hills, CA 90212-2607, USA

Schofield, Dwight (Hockey Player)
5900 N Illinois St
Fairview Heights, IL 62208-2700, USA

Schofield, John (Actor, Producer)
c/o Pete Franciosa *United Talent Agency (UTA)*
9560 Wilshire Blvd Ste 500
Beverly Hills, CA 90212-2401, USA

Schofield, Phillip
56 Wood Lane
London, ENGLAND W12 7RJ, UNITED KINGDOM (UK)

Scholder, Fritz (Artist)
118 Cattletrack Road
Scottsdale, AZ 85251, USA

Scholes, Clarke (Swimmer)
1360 Somerset Ave
Grosse Pointe Park, MI 48230-1031, USA

Scholes, Myron S (Nobel Prize Laureate)
Stanford University
Graduate Business School
Stanford, CA 94305, USA

Schollander, Don
3576 Lakeview Blvd
Lake Oswego, OR 97035-5544, USA

Scholten, Jim (Music Group, Musician)
Sawyer Brown Inc
5200 Old Harding Rd
Franklin, TN 37064-9406, USA

Scholtz, Bob (Football Player)
Detroit Lions
6721 S 71st East Ave
Tulsa, OK 74133-1818, USA

Scholtz, Bruce (Football Player)
Seattle Seahawks
6607 Cypress Pt N
Austin, TX 78746-7104, USA

Scholz, Rupert (Government Official)
Postfach 1328
Bonn 1 5300, GERMANY

Scholz, Tom (Musician)
c/o Gail Parenteau *Parenteau Guidance*
132 E 35th St # 3J
New York, NY 10016-3892, USA

Schomberg, A Thomas (Artist)
4923 Snowberry Ln
Evergreen, CO 80439-5622, USA

Schon, Jan Hendrik (Inventor)
Lucent Technology Bell Laboratory
600 Mountain Ave
New Providence, NJ 07974-2008, USA

Schon, Kyra (Actor)
930 N Sheridan Ave
Pittsburgh, PA 15206-2261, USA

Schon, Neal (Musician)
Artists & Audience Entertainment
PO Box 35
Pawling, NY 12564-0035, USA

Schon, Neil (Musician)
c/o Staff Member *William Morris Agency (WMA-LA)*
1 William Morris Pl
Beverly Hills, CA 90212-4261, USA

Schone, Lydia
2020 Broadway
Santa Monica, CA 90404-2910, USA

Schonhuber, Franz (Correspondent)
Europaburo
Fraunhoferstr 23
Munich 80469, GERMANY

Schoofs, Mark (Journalist)
Village Voice
32 Cooper Sq
Editorial Dept
New York, NY 10003-7117, USA

Schools, Dave (Musician)
Brown Cat Inc
400 Foundry St
Athens, GA 30601-2623, USA

Schoomaker, Peter J (Pete) (General)
Chief Of Staff Hqusa
Pentagon
Washington, DC 20310-0001, USA

Schorer, Jane (Journalist)
Des Moines Register
PO Box 957
Editorial Dept
Des Moines, IA 50306-0957, USA

Schorr, Bill (Cartoonist)
United Feature Syndicate
200 Madison Ave
New York, NY 10016-3911, USA

Schorr, Daniel (Journalist, Writer)
3113 Woodley Rd NW
Washington, DC 20008-3449, USA

Schorske, Carl E (Historian, Writer)
45 Meadow Lks Apt 1
Hightstown, NJ 08520-3389, USA

Schott, Stephen (Baseball Player)
Oakland A's
12330 Hilltop Dr
Los Altos Hills, CA 94024-5218, USA

Schotte, Jan P Cardinal (Religious Leader)
Sinodo Dei Vescovi
00120, VATICAN CITY

Schou, Mogens (Doctor)
Aarhus University
Institute of Psychiatry
Aarhus, DENMARK

Schowalter, Edward R Jr (War Hero)
913 Bibb Ave # 312
Auburn, AL 36830-2715, USA

Schrader, Ken (Race Car Driver)
PO Box 325
East Flat Rock, NC 28726-0325, USA

Schrader, Maria (Actor)
c/o Davien Littlefield *Davien Littlefield Management*
33 W 67th St Ph
New York, NY 10023-6224, USA

Schrader, Paul (Actor, Director, Writer)
c/o Johnnie Planco *Untitled Entertainment (NY)*
322 8th Ave Ste 601
New York, NY 10001-6715, USA

Schrader, Paul J (Director, Writer)
9696 Culver Blvd Ste 203
Culver City, CA 90232-2754, USA

Schram, Bitty (Actor)
c/o Dan Baron *Agency for the Performing Arts (APA-LA)*
405 S Beverly Dr
Beverly Hills, CA 90212-4416, USA

Schramm, David (Actor)
3521 Berry Dr
Studio City, CA 91604-3882, USA

Schranz, Karl (Skier)
Hotel Garni
Saint Anton 6580, AUSTRIA

Schreiber, Adam (Football Player)
Seattle Seahawks
2520 River Summit Dr
Duluth, GA 30097-2255, USA

Schreiber, Avery
6399 Wilshire Blvd Ste 414
Los Angeles, CA 90048-5716, USA

Schreiber, Larry (Football Player)
San Francisco 49ers
388 Albion Ave
Woodside, CA 94062-3603, USA

Schreiber, Liev (Actor)
c/o Rick Kurtzman *Creative Artists Agency
LCC (CAA-LA)*
2000 Avenue Of The Stars
Los Angeles, CA 90067-4700, USA

Schreiber, Martin J (Governor)
2700 S Shore Dr # B
Milwaukee, WI 53207-2300, USA

Schreler, Peter (Conductor, Opera Singer)
Calberlastr 13
Dresdon 01326, GERMANY

Schremmer, Patty (Golfer)
714 Siesta Key Cir
Sarasota, FL 34242-1250, USA

Schremp, Bob (Football Player)
Los Angeles Chargers
PO Box 584
Bellflower, CA 90707-0584, USA

Schrempp, Jurgen E (Business Person)
Daimler-Chrysler AG
Plieningerstra
Stuttgart 70546, GERMANY

Schreyer, Cindy (Golfer)
18 Cottage Dr
Newnan, GA 30265-5513, USA

Schreyer, Edward R (General, Governor)
250 Wellington Crescent #401
Winnipeg, MB R3M 0B3, CANADA

Schrieber, Paul (Baseball Player)
9715 E Gary Rd
Scottsdale, AZ 85260-6225, USA

Schrieffer, John R (Nobel Prize Laureate)
Florida State University
1800 E Paul Dirac Dr
Tallahassee, FL 32310-3706, USA

Schrier, Eric W (Editor)
Reader's Digest
Editorial Dept
PO Box 100
Pleasantville, NY 10572-0001, USA

Schriesheim, Alan (Misc)
1440 N Lake Shore Dr Apt 31ac
Chicago, IL 60610-5927, USA

Schrimshaw, Nevin S (Doctor)
Sandwich Notch Farm
Thompton, NH 03223, USA

Schriner, David
3216 Upland Pl. NW
Calgary, AB, CANADA

Schrock, Richard R (Misc)
Massachusetts Institute of Technology
Chemistry Dept
Cambridge, MA 02139, USA

Schroder, Ernst A (Actor)
Podere Montalto
Castellina In Chianti
Siena 53011, ITALY

Schroder, Gerhard
Bundeskanzleramt
Berlin 11012, GERMANY

Schroder, Jochen
Postfach 10 23 46
Bochum D-44723, GERMANY

Schroder, Rick (Actor)
c/o Rebecca (Becca) Kovacik *Hofflund/
Polone*
9465 Wilshire Blvd Ste 890
Beverly Hills, CA 90212-2607, USA

Schrody, Eric (Everlast) (Actor, Musician)
c/o Irving Azoff *AA Music Management*
1100 Glendon Ave Ste 2000
Los Angeles, CA 90024-3524, USA

Schroeder, Barbet (Director, Producer)
8033 W Sunset Blvd # 51
West Hollywood, CA 90046-2401, USA

Schroeder, Carly (Actor)
c/o Staff Member *KWAC*
1875 Century Park E Ste 700
Century City, CA 90067-2508, USA

Schroeder, Gene (Football Player)
Chicago Bears
788 Eastbrook Ln
Crown Point, IN 46307-5013, USA

Schroeder, Gerhard (Misc)
Bundeskanzlerant
Willy-Brandt-Str 1
Berlin 10557, GERMANY

Schroeder, Jay (Football Player)
Washington Redskins
1849 S Paragon Dr
Saint George, UT 84790-6146, USA

Schroeder, Jim (Bowler)
3 Greenhaven Ter
Tonawanda, NY 14150-5503, USA

Schroeder, John (Golfer)
PO Box 2768
Del Mar, CA 92014-5768, USA

Schroeder, John H (Educator)
University of Wisconsin
Chancellor's Office
Milwaukee, WI 53211, USA

Schroeder, Kenneth L (Business Person)
KLA-Tencor Corp
160 Rio Robles
San Jose, CA 95134-1813, USA

Schroeder, Manfred R (Physicist)
Rieswartenweg 8
Gottingen 37073, GERMANY

Schroeder, Mary M (Judge)
US Court of Appeals
230 N 1st Ave
Phoenix, AZ 85003-1723, USA

Schroeder, Patricia S (Misc)
William Morris Agency
151 El Camino Dr
Beverly Hills, CA 90212-2775, USA

Schroeder, Paul W (Writer)
University of Illinois
810 S Wright St
History Dept
Urbana, IL 61801-3644, USA

Schroeder, Steven A (Doctor, Misc)
10 Paseo Mirasol
Bel Tiburon, CA 94920-2021, USA

Schroeder, Terry (Athlete, Coach)
4901 Lewis Rd
Agoura Hills, CA 91301-2453, USA

Schroll, William (Football Player)
Detroit Lions
1640 Oakley Dr
Baton Rouge, LA 70806-8623, USA

Schrom, Kenneth M (Ken) (Baseball
Player)
1002 Black Diamond Ct
Portland, TX 78374-4162, USA

Schroy, Ken (Football Player)
New York Jets
79 Russell Rd
Garden City, NY 11530-1933, USA

Schruefer, John J (Doctor)
Georgetown University Hospital
Ob-Gyn Dept
Washington, DC 20007, USA

Schuba, Beatrice (Trixi) (Figure Skater)
Giorgengasse 2/1/8
Vienna 1190, AUSTRIA

Schubb, Mark
9744 Wilshire Blvd Ste 308
Beverly Hills, CA 90212-1813, USA

Schubert, Eric (Football Player)
New York Giants
722 Homestead Ave
Maybrook, NY 12543-1308, USA

Schubert, Mark (Coach, Swimmer)
PO Box 479
Surfside, CA 90743-0479, USA

Schubert, Richard F (Misc)
6615 Madison McLean Dr
McLean, VA 22101-2902, USA

Schubert, Steve (Football Player)
New England Patriots
7 Douglas Dr
Candia, NH 03034-2304, USA

Schuck, Anett (Athlete)
Defoestry 6A
Leipzig 04159, GERMANY

Schuck, John (Actor)
1501 Broadway Ste 703
New York, NY 10036-5505, USA

Schueler, Jon R (Artist)
40 W 22nd St
New York, NY 10010-5806, USA

Schuenke, Donald J (Business Person)
Nortel Networks Corp
8200 Dixie Road
Brampton, ON L6T 5P6, CANADA

Schuerholz, John (Baseball Player)
Atlanta Braves
1025 Royal Dr
Canonsburg, PA 15317-5004, USA

Schuessel, Wolfgang (Misc)
Chancellor's Office
Ballhausplatz 2
Vienna 1014, AUSTRIA

Schuessler, Jack (Business Person)
Wendy's International
4288 W Dublin Granville Rd
Dublin, OH 43017-2093, USA

Schuh, Harry F (Football Player)
Oakland Raiders
2309 Massey Rd
Memphis, TN 38119-6516, USA

Schuh, Jeff (Football Player)
Cincinnati Bengals
5550 Vagabond Ln N
Minneapolis, MN 55446-1323, USA

Schuhmacher, John (Football Player)
Houston Oilers
6000 Reims Rd Apt 3006
Houston, TX 77036-3053, USA

Schul, Robert (Bob) (Athlete, Track
Athlete)
320 Wisteria Dr
Dayton, OH 45419-3553, USA

Schulberg, Budd
PO Box 707
Brookside
Westhampton Beach, NY 11978-0707,
USA

Schuler, Bill (Football Player)
New York Giants
201 Cahaba Park Cir Ste 400
Birmingham, AL 35242-8130, USA

Schuler, Carolyn (Swimmer)
26552 Via Del Sol
Mission Viejo, CA 92691-6125, USA

Schulhofer, Scotty (Misc)
PO Box 1581
Waynesville, NC 28786-1581, USA

Schull, Rebecca (Actor)
Writers & Artists
8383 Wilshire Blvd Ste 550
Beverly Hills, CA 90211-2417, USA

Schuller, Grete (Artist)
8 Barstow Rd Apt 7G
Great Neck, NY 11021-3547, USA

Schuller, Gunther (Composer, Conductor)
Margun Music
167 Dudley Rd
Newton Center, MA 02459-2830, USA

Schuller, Robert (Religious Leader)
Crystal Cathedral Ministries
12141 Lewis St
Garden Grove, CA 92840-4627, USA

Schult, Jurgen (Athlete, Track Athlete)
Drosselweg 6
Leuna 19069, GERMANY

Schulte, Greg (Baseball Player)
Arizona Diamondbacks
20723 N 56th Ave
Glendale, AZ 85308-6276, USA

Schulte, Richard (Football Player)
Buffalo Bills
1216 N Kenneth Pl
Chandler, AZ 85226-7210, USA

Schulters, Lance (Football Player)
San Francisco 49ers
594 Grant Ave
Roselle, NJ 07203-2911, USA

Schultz, Axel (Boxer)
Axel Schultz Mgmt
Kloetzrstr 15
Riesa 01587, GERMANY

Schultz, Bill (Football Player)
Indianapolis Colts
9954 Hidden Falls Cir
Fishers, IN 46037-4311, USA

Schultz, Dave (Hockey Player)
2051 Lucas Ln
Voorhees, NJ 08043-2568, USA

Schultz, Dave (Race Car Driver)
2365 Lazy River Ln
Fort Myers, FL 33905-2242, USA

Schultz, Dean (Financier)
Federal Home Laon Bank
1079 Hutchinson Rd
Walnut Creek, CA 94598-4543, USA

Schultz, Dwight (Actor)
Borinstein Oreck Bogart
3172 Dona Susana Dr
Studio City, CA 91604-4356, USA

Schultz, Flip (Comedian)
c/o Staff Member *International Creative Management (ICM-LA)*
10250 Constellation Blvd
Los Angeles, CA 90067-6200, USA

Schultz, Frederick H (Government Official)
PO Box 1200
Jacksonville, FL 32201-1200, USA

Schultz, Howard (Business Person)
Starbucks Corp
2401 Utah Ave S Ste 800
Seattle, WA 98134-1435, USA

Schultz, Howard H (Howie) (Baseball Player, Basketball Player)
1333 McKusick Road Ln N
Stillwater, MN 55082-4163, USA

Schultz, John (Football Player)
Denver Broncos
503 Skyline Dr
Vestal, NY 13850-5321, USA

Schultz, Kurt (Football Player)
Buffalo Bills
5075 Rockledge Dr
Clarence, NY 14031-2426, USA

Schultz, Michael A (Director)
Chrystalite Productions
PO Box 1940
Santa Monica, CA 90406-1940, USA

Schultz, Peter C (Inventor)
Heraeus Amersil Inc
3473 Satellite Blvd Ste 300
Duluth, GA 30096-4658, USA

Schultz, Peter G (Misc)
Salk Research Institute
10550 N Torrey Pines Rd
La Jolla, CA 92037-1000, USA

Schultz, Richard D (Misc)
US Olympic Committee
1 Olympic Plz
Colorado Springs, CO 80909-5760, USA

Schultze, Charles L (Government Official)
Brookings Institute
1775 Massachusetts Ave NW
Washington, DC 20036-2103, USA

Schulz, Axel
Zehmeplatz 10
Frankfurt/Oder D-15230, GERMANY

Schulz, Jody (Football Player)
Philadelphia Eagles
222 Schulz Ln
Chester, MD 21619-2658, USA

Schulz, William (Editor)
Reader's Digest
Editorial Dept
PO Box 100
Pleasantville, NY 10572-0001, USA

Schulze, Matt (Actor)
Gersh Agency
232 N Canon Dr
Beverly Hills, CA 90210-5302, USA

Schulze, Paul (Actor)
c/o Staff Member *Kyle Fritz Management*
6325 Heather Dr
Los Angeles, CA 90068-1633, USA

Schulze, Richard M (Business Person)
Best Buy Co
7601 Penn Ave S
Minneapolis, MN 55423-3645, USA

Schumacher, Gregg (Football Player)
Los Angeles Rams
104 Surfview Dr Apt 2108
Palm Coast, FL 32137-2348, USA

Schumacher, Joel (Director)
Greenfield & Selvaggi
11766 Wilshire Blvd Ste 1610
Los Angeles, CA 90025-6565, USA

Schumacher, Kelly (Basketball Player)
Indiana Fever
125 S Pennsylvania St
Conseco Fieldhouse
Indianapolis, IN 46204-3610, USA

Schumacher, Kurt (Football Player)
New Orleans Saints
673 Northfield Ln
Harleysville, PA 19438-1698, USA

Schumacher, Michael (Race Car Driver)
Via Ascari 55-57
Maranello 40153, ITALY

Schumacher, Ralf (Race Car Driver)
Weber Mgmt
Trankestr 11
Stuttgart 70597, GERMANY

Schuman, Allan L (Business Person)
Ecolab Inc
370 Wabasha St N
Ecolab Center
Saint Paul, MN 55102-1349, USA

Schuman, Melissa (Actor)
c/o Nils Larsen *Elements Entertainment*
1635 N Cahuenga Blvd Fl 5
Los Angeles, CA 90028-6201, USA

Schuman, Tom (Musician)
Crosseyed Bear Productions
PO Box 435
Highland Mills, NY 10930-0435, USA

Schumann, Ralf (Misc)
Steomach 22
Stockheim 97640, GERMANY

Schur, Michael (Writer)
c/o Staff Member *3 Arts Entertainment Inc*
9460 Wilshire Blvd Fl 7
Beverly Hills, CA 90212-2713, USA

Schurmann, Petra (Swimmer)
Max-Emanuel-Str 7
Starnberg 82319, GERMANY

Schurr, Harry W (War Hero)
Cleveland Cavaliers
1178 Davis Dr
Fairborn, OH 45324-5614, USA

Schussler Florenza, Elisabeth (Misc, Writer)
Notre Dame University
Theology Dept
Notre Dame, IN 46556, USA

Schuster, Rudolf (President)
President's Office
Nam Slobody 1
Bratislava 91370, SLOVAKIA

Schute, Anja
Parkstr. 37
Erfstadt D-50374, GERMANY

Schutz, Klaus (Government Official)
9 Konstanzerstr
Berlin 10707, GERMANY

Schutz, Stephen (Artist)
Blue Mountain Arts Inc
PO Box 4549
Boulder, CO 80306-4549, USA

Schutz, Susan Polis (Writer)
Blue Mountain Arts Inc
PO Box 4549
Boulder, CO 80306-4549, USA

Schuur, Diane (Music Group, Musician)
Paul Canter Enterprises
33042 Ocean Rdg
Dana Point, CA 92629-1078, USA

Schwab, John J (Doctor)
21 Bradley Rd Apt 117
Woodbridge, CT 06525-2255, USA

Schwabb, Charles R (Financier)
Charles Scwab Co
101 Montgomery St
San Francisco, CA 94104-4175, USA

Schwantz, Jim (Football Player)
Chicago Bears
1047 W Chatham Dr
Palatine, IL 60067-5817, USA

Schwarthoff, Florian (Athlete, Track Athlete)
Fischweiher 51
Heppenheim 64646, GERMANY

Schwartz, Don (Football Player)
New Orleans Saints
19410 NE Redmond Rd
Redmond, WA 98053, USA

Schwartz, Jacob T (Scientist)
New York University
Courant Math Sciences Institute
New York, NY 10012, USA

Schwartz, Josh (Producer, Writer)
c/o Mike Bondesen *Fuse Entertainment*
1041 N Formosa Ave
Formosa Bldg #197
West Hollywood, CA 90046-6703, USA

Schwartz, Lloyd (Journalist)
27 Pennsylvania Ave
Somerville, MA 02145-2217, USA

Schwartz, Maxime (Misc)
Institut Pasteur
25-28 Rue du Docteur-Roux
Paris Cedex 15 75724, FRANCE

Schwartz, Melvin (Nobel Prize Laureate)
PO Box 5068
Ketchum, ID 83340-5068, USA

Schwartz, Neil
3044 Pearl Harbor Dr
Las Vegas, NV 89117-0925, USA

Schwartz, Norton A (General)
Commander
11th Air Force
Elmendorf Air Force Base, AK 99506, USA

Schwartz, Sherwood
1865 Carla Rdg
Beverly Hills, CA 90210-1936, USA

Schwartz, Stephen L (Composer, Music Group, Musician, Songwriter, Writer)
Chaplin Entertainment
545 8th Ave # 14
New York, NY 10018-4307, USA

Schwartz, Thomas A (General)
Commander
United Nations Command/Us Forces Korea
APO, AP 96205, USA

Schwartz, Tony (Misc)
455 W 56th St
New York, NY 10019-3601, USA

Schwartzman, Jason (Actor)
c/o Matthew (Matt) Labov *BWR (BWR-LA)*
9100 Wilshire Blvd Fl 6
West Tower
Beverly Hills, CA 90212-3401, USA

Schwartzman, John (Cinematographer)
Mirisch Agency
1801 Century Park E Ste 1801
Los Angeles, CA 90067-2320, USA

Schwartzman, Robert (Actor)
c/o Joanne Wiles *William Morris Agency (WMA-LA)*
1 William Morris Pl
Beverly Hills, CA 90212-4261, USA

Schwarz, Gerard R (Conductor)
New York Chamber Symphony
1395 Lexington Ave
New York, NY 10128-1612, USA

Schwarz, Hanna (Opera Singer)
Opera et Concert
Maximilianstr 22
Munich 80539, GERMANY

Schwarz, John H (Physicist)
California Institute of Technology
Physics Dept
Pasadena, CA 91125-0001, USA

Schwarz-Shilling, Christian (Government Official)
Post-Telecomm Ministry
Heinrich-von-Stephanstr 1
Bonn 53175, GERMANY

Schwarzbein, Diana (Doctor, Writer)
Health Communications
3201 SW 15th St
Deerfield Beach, FL 33442-8157, USA

Schwarzenegger, Arnold (Actor, Governor)
Governor's Office
State Capitol Building
Sacramento, CA 95814, USA

Schwarzkopf, H Norman (General)
Black Summit
302 Knights Run Ave Ste 910
Tampa, FL 33602-5979, USA

Schwarzman, Steve (Business Person)
Blackstone Group
345 Park Ave
New York, NY 10154-0191, USA

Schwebel, Stephen M (Judge)
PO Box 356
Woodstock, VT 05091-0356, USA

Schweder, John (Football Player)
Baltimore Colts
525 Barclay Dr
Bethlehem, PA 18017-3858, USA

Schwedes, Gerhard (Football Player)
New York Titans
PO Box 570
Clayton, NY 13624-0570, USA

Schwedes, Scott (Football Player)
Miami Dolphins
6871 Claret Cir
Fayetteville, NY 13066-1048, USA

Schweig, Eric (Actor)
Prime Talent
PO Box 5163
Vancouver, BC V7B 1M4, CANADA

Schweiger, Til (Actor)
Agentur Players
Sophienstr 21
Berlin 10178, GERMANY

Schweiker, Richard S (Secretary)
8890 Windy Ridge Way
McLean, VA 22102-1558, USA

Schweikert, J E (Religious Leader)
Old Roman Catholic Church
4200 N Kedvale Ave
Chicago, IL 60641-2215, USA

Schweikher, Paul (Architect)
3222 E Missouri Ave
Phoenix, AZ 85018-1431, USA

Schweinsteiger, Bastian (Soccer Player)
FC Bayern Munich
Attention Bastian Schweinsteiger
S"bener Strasse 51
Munich 81547, GERMANY

Schweitzer, Brian (Governor)
PO Box 5012
Helena, MT 59604-5012, USA

Schwertsik, Kurt (Composer)
Doblinger Music
Dorotheergasse 10
Vienna 1011, AUSTRIA

Schwery, Henry Cardinal (Religious Leader)
Bishoporic of Sion
CP 2068
Sion 2 1950, SWITZERLAND

schwimer, rusty (Actor)
c/o Scott Manners *Stone Manners Talent & Literary (LA)*
6500 Wilshire Blvd Ste 550
Los Angeles, CA 90048-4950, USA

Schwimmer, David (Actor)
c/o Peter Safran *The Safran Company*
2000 Avenue Of The Stars Ste 600N
Los Angeles, CA 90067-4708, USA

Schwinden, Ted (Governor)
401 N Fee St
Helena, MT 59601-4846, USA

Schwitters, Roy F (Physicist)
1718 Cromwell Hl
Austin, TX 78703-3307, USA

Schygulla, Hanna (Actor)
ZBF Agentur
Leopoldstr 19
Munich 80802, GERMANY

Scialfa, Patti
17 E 76th St
New York, NY 10021-1720, USA

Scialfa, Patty (Music Group, Musician)
c/o Staff Member *Sony Music International*
550 Madison Ave Fl 6
New York, NY 10022-3211, USA

Sciarra, John M (Football Player)
Philadelphia Eagles
4420 Woodleigh Ln
Flintridge, CA 91011-3541, USA

Sciascia, Leonardo
Viale Scaduto 10/B
Palermo 1-90144, ITALY

Scifres, Steve (Football Player)
Dallas Cowboys
2026 Northglen Dr
Colorado Springs, CO 80909-1629, USA

Sciole, Jennifer (Actor, Producer)
Result Talent Group
3341 1/2 Primera Ave
Los Angeles, CA 90068-1549, USA

Scioli, Brad (Football Player)
Indianapolis Colts
106 Steinbright Dr
Collegeville, PA 19426-3190, USA

Sciorra, Anabella (Actor)
Writers & Artists
360 N Crescent Dr Bldg North
Beverly Hills, CA 90210-6818, USA

Sciorra, Annabella (Actor)
c/o Jason Heyman *Creative Artists Agency LCC (CAA-LA)*
2000 Avenue Of The Stars
Los Angeles, CA 90067-4700, USA

Scioscia, Michael L (Mike) (Baseball Player)
1915 Falling Star Ave
Westlake Village, CA 91362-5284, USA

Scioscia, Mike
444 Fargo St
Thousand Oaks, CA 91360-1515, USA

Scirica, Anthony J (Judge)
US Court of Appeals
601 Market St
US Courthouse
Philadelphia, PA 19106-1790, USA

Scissor Sisters (Music Group)
c/o Staff Member *Paradigm (NY)*
360 Park Ave S Fl 16
New York, NY 10010-1716, USA

Sciutto, Nellie (Actor)
c/o Ted Schachter *Schachter Entertainment*
1157 S Beverly Dr Fl 2
Los Angeles, CA 90035-1119, USA

Scofield, Dean
12304 Santa Monica Blvd Ste 104
Los Angeles, CA 90025-2586, USA

Scofield, Dino (Actor)
3330 Barham Blvd Ste 103
Los Angeles, CA 90068-1476, USA

Scofield, John (Musician)
Ted Kurland
173 Brighton Ave
Boston, MA 02134-2003, USA

Scofield, Paul (Actor)
Gables
Balcombe
Sussex RH17 6ND, UNITED KINGDOM (UK)

Scofield, Richard M (Dick) (General)
3251 Country Club Pkwy
Castle Rock, CO 80108-9078, USA

Scoggins, Eric (Football Player)
San Francisco 49ers
3513 W 78th St
Inglewood, CA 90305-1205, USA

Scoggins, Matt (Swimmer)
4900 Calhoun Canyon Loop
Austin, TX 78735-6417, USA

Scoggins, Tracy (Actor)
c/o Staff Member *Bette Smith Management*
499 N Canon Dr
Beverly Hills, CA 90210-4842, USA

Scogin, Mack (Architect)
Scogin Elam Bray
1819 Peachtree Rd NE Ste 700
Atlanta, GA 30309-1849, USA

Scola, Angelo Cardinal (Religious Leader)
Archdiocese
S Marco 320/A
Venezia 30124, ITALY

Scola, Ettore (Director)
Via Bertoloni 1/E
Rome 00197, ITALY

Scolari, Peter (Actor)
c/o Staff Member *Peter Strain & Associates Inc (LA)*
5455 Wilshire Blvd Ste 1812
Los Angeles, CA 90036-4268, USA

Scolnick, Edward M (Doctor, Scientist)
1201 Magnolia Dr
Wayland, MA 01778-2848, USA

Scolnik, Glenn (Football Player)
Pittsburgh Steelers
301 Willowgate Dr
Indianapolis, IN 46260-1476, USA

Scooters, The
15190 Encanto Dr
Sherman Oaks, CA 91403-4410, USA

Score, Herbert J (Herb) (Baseball Player, Sportscaster)
12700 Lake Ave
Lakewood, OH 44107-1576, USA

Scorpions (Music Group)
c/o Nick Caris *Agency Group Ltd, The (NY)*
1775 Broadway Ste 515
New York, NY 10019-1903, USA

Scorsese, Martin (Director)
c/o Rick Yorn *The Firm*
9465 Wilshire Blvd Fl 6
Beverly Hills, CA 90212-2605, USA

Scorsese, Nicolette (Actor)
c/o Gregory (Greg) Mayo *Orange Grove Group Inc*
12178 Ventura Blvd Ste 205
Studio City, CA 91604-2540, USA

Scorupco, Izabella (Actor, Model, Music Group, Musician)
c/o Lena Roklin *Roklin Management*
8530 Wilshire Blvd Ste 550
Beverly Hills, CA 90211-3133, USA

Scott, Adam (Actor)
c/o Danielle Thomas *Untitled Entertainment (LA)*
331 N Maple Dr Fl 3
Beverly Hills, CA 90210-3827, USA

Scott, Adam (Golfer)
c/o Staff Member *Pro Golfers Assoc of America (PGA)*
100 Avenue Of The Champions
Palm Beach Gardens, FL 33418-3653, USA

Scott, Andy (Musician)
DCM International
296 Nether St
Finchley
London N3 1RJ, UNITED KINGDOM (UK)

Scott, Arthur (Football Player)
New York Titans
209 Lincoln Ave
Conshohocken, PA 19428-2529, USA

Scott, Ashley (Actor)
c/o Jonathan Perry *Original Film*
284 N Saltair Ave
Los Angeles, CA 90049-2913, USA

Scott, Bo (Football Player)
Cleveland Browns
1301 Fountain Ln Apt 1
Columbus, OH 43213, USA

Scott, Bobby (Football Player)
New Orleans Saints
801 McKinley Pointe Ln
Knoxville, TN 37934-1568, USA

Scott, Byron (Basketball Player, Coach)
405 Murray Hill Pkwy
East Rutherford, NJ 07073-2136, USA

Scott, Camilla
23773 Via Canon Unit 201
Newhall, CA 91321-4632, USA

Scott, Campbell (Actor)
c/o Clifford Stevens *Paradigm (NY)*
360 Park Ave S Fl 16
New York, NY 10010-1716, USA

Scott, Carlos (Football Player)
St Louis Cardinals
RR 1 Box 346
Hempstead, TX 77445, USA

Scott, Chad (Football Player)
Pittsburgh Steelers
18526 Reliant Dr
Gaithersburg, MD 20879-5421, USA

Scott, Charles (Charlie) (Basketball Player)
300 Chastain Manor Dr
Norcross, GA 30071-2186, USA

Scott, Chuck (Football Player)
Los Angeles Rams
875 Landover Xing
Suwanee, GA 30024-3045, USA

Scott, Clarence (Football Player)
Boston Patriots
3-17-6 NishiAzabu Regency Apt 202
Minato-ku, Tokyo, JAPAN

Scott, Clarence (Football Player)
Cleveland Browns
216 Sisson Ave NE
Atlanta, GA 30317-1422, USA

Scott, Clyde L (Smackover) (Athlete, Football Player, Track Athlete)
Philadelphia Eagles
12840 Rivercrest Dr
Little Rock, AR 72212-1446, USA

Scott, Coltin
195 S Beverly Dr Ste 400
Beverly Hills, CA 90212-3044, USA

Scott, Dale (Baseball Player)
1283 SW Cardinell Dr
Portland, OR 97201-3114, USA

Scott, Darnay (Football Player)
Cincinnati Bengals
18551 Patton St
Detroit, MI 48219-5202, USA

Scott, Dave (Football Player)
Atlanta Falcons
3151 Robindale Rd
Decatur, GA 30034-4962, USA

Scott, David
1300 Manhattan Ave Apt B
Manhattan Beach, CA 90266-4776, USA

Scott, David R (Astronaut)
Merces
30 Hackamore Ln Ste 1
Vc Johnson
Bell Canyon, CA 91307-1065, USA

Scott, Deborah L (Designer, Fashion Designer)
Gersh Agency
232 N Canon Dr
Beverly Hills, CA 90210-5302, USA

Scott, Dennis (Basketball Player)
5425 Palm Lake Cir
Orlando, FL 32819-3911, USA

Scott, Donovan (Actor)
Talent Group
6300 Wilshire Blvd Ste 2100
Los Angeles, CA 90048-5282, USA

Scott, Dougray (Actor)
P F D
Drury House
34-43 Russell St
London WC2B 5HA, UNITED KINGDOM
(UK)

Scott, Edward (Baseball Player)
Indianapolis Clowns
720 Kasserine Pass
Mobile, AL 36609-6430, USA

Scott, Eric
11934 River Grove Ct
Moorpark, CA 93021-3105, USA

Scott, Freddie (Musician)
Headline Talent
1650 Broadway Ste 508
New York, NY 10019-6833, USA

Scott, Freddie L (Football Player)
Baltimore Colts
PO Box 197
Coahoma, MS 38617-0197, USA

Scott, Gavin (Writer)
c/o Jordan Bayer *Original Artists (LA)*
9465 Wilshire Blvd Ste 324
Beverly Hills, CA 90212-2602, USA

Scott, Geoffrey
1126 N Hollywood Way # 203-A
Burbank, CA 91505-2527, USA

Scott, George (Baseball Player)
1216 Fair Park Blvd
Harlingen, TX 78550-2324, USA

Scott, Gloria Dean Randle (Educator)
Bennett College
President's Office
Greensboro, NC 27401, USA

Scott, H Lee Jr (Business Person)
Wal-Mart Stores
702 SW 8th St
Bentonville, AR 72712-6209, USA

Scott, Herbert (Football Player)
Dallas Cowboys
605 Rawhide Ct
Plano, TX 75023-4753, USA

Scott, Jack (Music Group, Musician, Songwriter, Writer)
34039 Coachwood Dr
Sterling Heights, MI 48312-5617, USA

Scott, Jacob E (Jake) Jr (Football Player)
Miami Dolphins
PO Box 857
Hanalei, HI 96714-0857, USA

Scott, Jacqueline (Actor)
Lichtman/Salners
15865 Royal Haven Pl
Sherman Oaks, CA 91403-4724, USA

Scott, James (Football Player)
Chicago Bears
10127 Chisholm Trl
Dallas, TX 75243-2511, USA

Scott, Jane (Critic)
Cleveland Plain Dealer
1801 Superior Ave E
Cleveland, OH 44114-2198, USA

Scott, Jean Bruce (Actor)
144 N Westerly Dr
Los Angeles, CA 90048, USA

Scott, Jerry (Cartoonist)
Creators Syndicate
5777 W Century Blvd Ste 700
Los Angeles, CA 90045-9023, USA

Scott, Jill (Musician)
Rhythm Jazz Entertainment
4465 Don Milagro Dr
Los Angeles, CA 90008-2831, USA

Scott, Jimmy (Music Group, Musician)
J's Way Jazz
175 Prospect St #20D
East Orange, NJ 07017, ITALY

Scott, John (Football Player)
Buffalo Bills
1583 N Ellen Ave
Decatur, IL 62526-3718, USA

Scott, Josey (Music Group, Musician)
Helter Skelter
Plaza
535 Kings Road
London SW10 0S, UNITED KINGDOM
(UK)

Scott, Judson
10000 Santa Monica Blvd # 305
Los Angeles, CA 90067, USA

Scott, Kathryn Leigh (Actor)
3236 Bennett Dr
Los Angeles, CA 90068-1702, USA

Scott, Kevin B (Football Player)
San Diego Chargers
2335 Cascade St
Milpitas, CA 95035-7807, USA

Scott, Klea (Actor)
Talent Entertainment Group
9111 Wilshire Blvd
Beverly Hills, CA 90210-5508, USA

Scott, Larry (Athlete)
148 N Main St
Kaysville, UT 84037-1951, USA

Scott, Lary R (Business Person)
Carolina Freight Corp
PO Box 1000
Cherryville, NC 28021-1000, USA

Scott, Lew (Football Player)
Denver Broncos
4 Osprey Ct
Streamwood, IL 60107-2813, USA

Scott, Lindsay (Football Player)
New Orleans Saints
214 N Troupe St
Valdosta, GA 31601-5738, USA

Scott, Lizabeth (Actor)
8277 Hollywood Blvd
Los Angeles, CA 90069-1611, USA

Scott, Melody Thomas (Actor)
12068 Crest Ct
Beverly Hills, CA 90210-1354, USA

Scott, Michael W (Mike) (Baseball Player)
28355 Chat Dr
Laguna Niguel, CA 92677-1384, USA

Scott, Patricia (Baseball Player)
40 Huey Dr
Walton, KY 41094-1022, USA

Scott, Paul (Writer)
33 Drumsheugh Gardens
Edinburgh, SCOTLAND

Scott, Pippa (Actor)
10850 Wilshire Blvd # 250
Los Angeles, CA 90024-4305, USA

Scott, Randy (Football Player)
Green Bay Packers
1440 Woodland Lake Dr
Snellville, GA 30078-2097, USA

Scott, Ray (Basketball Player, Coach)
Colonial Life Insurance
33200 Schoolcraft Rd
Livonia, MI 48150-1643, USA

Scott, Richard U (Dick) (Football Player)
3369 Upland Ct
Adamstown, MD 21710-9665, USA

Scott, Ridley (Director)
Scott Free
42/44 Beak St
London W1R 3DA, UNITED KINGDOM
(UK)

Scott, Robert (Baseball Player)
New York Black Yankees
236 W Grand St
Elizabeth, NJ 07202-1284, USA

Scott, Robert L Jr (War Hero, Writer)
PO Box 2469
Warner Robins, GA 31099-2469, USA

Scott, Robert W (Educator, Governor)
North Carolina Community College System
200 W Jones St
Raleigh, NC 27603-1378, USA

Scott, Sean (Football Player)
Dallas Cowboys
3217 Boise St
Berkeley, CA 94702-2607, USA

Scott, Seann William (Actor)
c/o Staff Member *Identity Films*
100 Universal City Plz
Bungalow 4144
Universal City, CA 91608-1002, USA

Scott, Shelby (Misc)
American Federation of TV/Radio Artists
260 Madison Ave
New York, NY 10016-2401, USA

Scott, Stephen (Musician)
Bridge Agency
35 Clark St Apt A5
Brooklyn, NY 11201-2374, USA

Scott, Steven M (Steve) (Athlete, Track Athlete)
4106 La Portalada Dr
Carlsbad, CA 92010-2805, USA

Scott, Stuart
c/o Staff Member *ESPN (Main)*
935 Middle St
Espn Plaza
Bristol, CT 06010-1000, USA

Scott, Thomas C (Tom) (Football Player)
3259 Kirkwood Court
Keswick, VA 22947, USA

Scott, Todd (Football Player)
Minnesota Vikings
5605 Avenue P
Galveston, TX 77551-5028, USA

Scott, Tom (Football Player)
Cincinnati Bengals
1012 Peed Dr Apt 8
Greenville, NC 27834-7063, USA

Scott, Tom (Football Player)
Philadelphia Eagles
3359 Kirkwood Ct
Keswick, VA 22947-9138, USA

Scott, Tom (Musician)
Performers of the World
8901 Melrose Ave # 200
West Hollywood, CA 90069-5605, USA

Scott, Tom Everett (Actor)
United Talent Agency
9560 Wilshire Blvd Ste 500
Beverly Hills, CA 90212-2401, USA

Scott, Tony (Director)
Totem Productions
8009 Santa Monica Blvd
West Hollywood, CA 90046-5008, USA

Scott, W Richard (Misc)
940 Lathrop Pl
Stanford, CA 94305-1060, USA

Scott, Walter (Football Player)
New England Patriots
1991 Edgefield Rd
Trenton, SC 29847-2435, USA

Scott, Willard (Television Host)
c/o Staff Member *NBC Television (NY)*
30 Rockefeller Plz Ste 270E
New York, NY 10112-0299, USA

Scott, Willard W Jr (Educator, General)
9115 McNair Dr
Alexandria, VA 22309-3315, USA

Scott, William Lee
c/o Staff Member *Sager Management*
260 S Beverly Dr Ste 205
Beverly Hills, CA 90212-3812, USA

Scott, Willie (Football Player)
Kansas City Chiefs
1123 Long St
Newberry, SC 29108-4231, USA

Scott, Winston E (Astronaut)
PO Box 1192
Cape Canaveral, FL 32920-1192, USA

Scott Brown, Denise (Architect)
Venturi Scott Brown Assoc
4236 Main St
Philadelphia, PA 19127-1603, USA

Scott Kay, Dominic (Actor)
c/o Rich Hueners *Paradigm (LA)*
360 N Crescent Dr
North Bldg
Beverly Hills, CA 90210-6820, USA

Scott Thomas, Kristin (Actor)
c/o Judy Hofflund *Hofflund/Polone*
9465 Wilshire Blvd Ste 890
Beverly Hills, CA 90212-2607, USA

Scotti, Benjamin (Football Player)
Washington Redskins
715 N Beverly Dr
Beverly Hills, CA 90210-3321, USA

Scotti, Nick (Actor, Musician)
c/o Elise Konialian *Untitled Entertainment (NY)*
322 8th Ave Ste 601
New York, NY 10001-6715, USA

Scotto, Renato
61 W 62nd St Apt 6F
New York, NY 10023-7017, USA

Scottoline, Lisa (Writer)
Harper Collins Publishers
10 E 53rd St Fl Cellar2
New York, NY 10022-5076, USA

Scotty K (DJ)
c/o Staff Member *Diva Central Inc*
7510 W Sunset Blvd Ste 1445
Los Angeles, CA 90046-3408, USA

Scouler, Angela (Actor)
Daly Gagan
60 Old Brompton Road
London SW7 3LQ, UNITED KINGDOM
(UK)

Scovell, Nell (Producer)
c/o Staff Member *William Morris Agency
(WMA-LA)*
1 William Morris Pl
Beverly Hills, CA 90212-4261, USA

Scowcroft, Brent (General, Government
Official)
350 Park Ave # 2600
New York, NY 10022-6022, USA

Scrafford, Kirk (Football Player)
Cincinnati Bengals
19400 US Highway 93 N
Florence, MT 59833-5914, USA

Scranton, Nancy (Golfer)
15820 Sanctuary Dr
Tampa, FL 33647-1075, USA

Scranton, William W (Governor)
PO Box 116
Dalton, PA 18414-0116, USA

Scratch (Artist, Musician)
William Morris Agency
1325 Avenue Of The Americas
New York, NY 10019-6091, USA

Scream3 (Music Group)
c/o Staff Member *Wind-up Records*
72 Madison Ave Fl 8
New York, NY 10016-8731, USA

Scribner, Bucky (Football Player)
Green Bay Packers
512 Georgina Ave
Santa Monica, CA 90402-1912, USA

Scribner, Rick (Race Car Driver)
8904 Amerigo Ave
Orangevale, CA 95662-4612, USA

Scrimm, Angus (Actor)
PO Box 5193
North Hollywood, CA 91616-5193, USA

Scrimshaw, Nevin S (Doctor)
PO Box 330
Sandwich Mountain Farm
Campton, NH 03223-0330, USA

Scripps, Charles E (Publisher)
10 Grandin Ln
Cincinnati, OH 45208-3304, USA

Scroggins, Tracy (Football Player)
Detroit Lions
2026 Willow Leaf Dr
Rochester Hills, MI 48309-3730, USA

Scruggs, Earl (Musician, Songwriter,
Writer)
774 Elysian Road
Nashville, TN 37204, USA

Scruggs, Eugene (Baseball Player)
Detroit Stars
618 Dawson Ter NW
Huntsville, AL 35811-1782, USA

Scruggs, Randy (Musician)
c/o Staff Member *Creative Artists Agency
(CAA-Nashville)*
3310 W End Ave Fl 5
Nashville, TN 37203-1028, USA

Scudamore, Peter (Jockey)
Mucky Cottage Grangehill
Naunton Cheltenham
Glos GL54 3AY, UNITED KINGDOM
(UK)

Scudero, Joe (Football Player)
Washington Redskins
2534 N Railroad Way
Hernando, FL 34442-2988, USA

Scull, Angel (Baseball Player)
1875 NW 132nd St
Miami, FL 33167-1538, USA

Scully, John (Football Player)
Atlanta Falcons
3500 Bankview Dr
Joliet, IL 60431-4804, USA

Scully, Sean P (Artist)
Timothy Taylor Gallery
1 Bruton Place
London W1X 7AB, UNITED KINGDOM
(UK)

Scully, Vin (Sportscaster)
c/o Staff Member *Los Angeles Dodgers
(LA Dodgers)*
1000 Elysian Park Ave
Los Angeles, CA 90012-1112, USA

Scully-Power, Paul D (Astronaut)
Civil Aviation Safety Authority
Box 2005
Canberra, ACT 2600, AUSTRALIA

Sculthorpe, Peter J (Composer)
91 Holdsworth St
Woollahra, NSW 2025, AUSTRALIA

Scutaro, Marco (Baseball Player)
c/o Staff Member *Oakland Athletics*
7000 Coliseum Way
Oakland, CA 94621-1992, USA

Scutt, Der (Architect)
Der Scutt Architect
44 W 28th St
New York, NY 10001-4212, USA

Sczurek, Stan (Football Player)
Cleveland Browns
689 Beaver Ridge Trl
Broadview Heights, OH 44147-1972,
USA

Seabra, Verissimo Correia (General,
President)
President's Office
Bissau, GUINEA-BISSAU

Seabron, Malcolm (Football Player)
Houston Oilers
10418 Cliffwood Dr
Houston, TX 77035-3702, USA

Seacrest, Ryan (Radio Personality, Reality
TV Star, Television Host)
c/o Staff Member *Ryan Seacrest
Productions*
5750 Wilshire Blvd Fl 4th
Los Angeles, CA 90036-7201, USA

Seaforth-Hayes, Susan (Actor)
4528 Beck Ave
North Hollywood, CA 91602-1904, USA

Seaga, Edward P G (Prime Minister)
24-26 Grenada Crescent
New Kingston
Kingston 5, JAMAICA

Seagal, Steven (Actor)
c/o Staff Member *Steamroller Productions
Inc*
1438 N Gower St Ste 70 Rm 222
Hollywood, CA 90028-8358, USA

Seagrave, Jocelyn (Actor)
c/o Gregg Steiner *Perspective Film*
15030 Ventura Blvd
Sherman Oaks, CA 91403-5470, USA

Seagraves, Ralph (Race Car Driver)
RR 10 Box 413
Winston Salem, NC 27127, USA

Seagren, Bob
1 Hoosier Dome
Indianapolis, IN 46225-1052, USA

Seagren, Robert L (Bob) (Athlete, Track
Athlete)
21902 Velicata St
Woodland Hills, CA 91364-3114, USA

Seagrove, Jenny (Actor)
Marmont Mgmt
Langham House
302/8 Regent St
London W1R 5AL, UNITED KINGDOM
(UK)

Seal (Musician)
c/o Mitch Rose *Creative Artists Agency
LCC (CAA-LA)*
2000 Avenue Of The Stars
Los Angeles, CA 90067-4700, USA

Seal, Paul (Football Player)
New Orleans Saints
21599 Hidden Rivers Dr N
Southfield, MI 48075-6110, USA

Seale, Bobby (Politician)
Cafe Society
302 W Chelten Ave
Philadelphia, PA 19144-3805, USA

Seale, John C (Cinematographer)
Mirisch Agency
1801 Century Park E
Los Angeles, CA 90067-2302, USA

Seale, Sam (Football Player)
Oakland Raiders
1818 Da Gama Ct
Escondido, CA 92026-1729, USA

Seals, Brady
2100 W End Ave # 1000
Nashville, TN 37203-5200, USA

Seals, Dan (Music Group, Musician,
Songwriter, Writer)
Morningstar Productions
153 Sanders Ferry Rd
Hendersonville, TN 37075-3626, USA

Seals, George (Football Player)
Washington Redskins
1101 1st St Unit 204
Coronado, CA 92118-1496, USA

Seals, Ray (Football Player)
Tampa Bay Buccaneers
664 NW Shaw Gln
Lake City, FL 32055-0408, USA

Seals & Croft (Music Group)
c/o Staff Member *4STAR Entertainment
LLC*
1675 York Ave Apt 32C
New York, NY 10128-6905, USA

Seaman, Christopher (Conductor)
25 Westfield Dr
Glasgow G52 2SG, SCOTLAND

Seaman, David (Soccer Player)
Arsenal London
Avenell Road
Highbury
London N5 1BU, UNITED KINGDOM
(UK)

Sean Paul (Musician)
c/o Cara Lewis *William Morris Agency
(WMA-NY)*
1325 Avenue Of The Americas
New York, NY 10019-6026, USA

Searchers, The
2514 Build America Dr
Hampton, VA 23666-3223, USA

Searcy, Leon (Football Player)
Pittsburgh Steelers
3841 Biggin Church Rd W
Jacksonville, FL 32224-7985, USA

Searcy, Nick (Actor)
c/o Lara Nesburn *Abrams Artists Agency
(LA)*
9200 W Sunset Blvd Ph 11
Los Angeles, CA 90069-3601, USA

Searfoss, Richard A (Astronaut)
24480 Silver Creek Way
Tehachapi, CA 93561-8399, USA

Searle, Jackie
7214 Chestwood Dr.
Tujunga, CA 91042, USA

Searle, John R (Misc)
109 Yosemite Road
Berkeley, CA 94707, USA

Searle, Ronald (Animator, Cartoonist)
Elaine McMahon Agency
329 Avenue E Apt 8
Bayonne, NJ 07002-4635, USA

Sears, Paul B (Misc)
17 Las Milpas
Taos, NM 87571, USA

Sears, Victor W (Vic) (Football Player)
Philadelphia Eagles
112 Mallard Glen Cir
Winston Salem, NC 27106-2591, USA

Sears, Dr, William
34761 Doheny Pl
Capistrano Beach, CA 92624-1713, USA

Sease, Marvin
Malaco Music Group
PO Box 9287
Jackson, MS 39286-9287, USA

Seaver, Tom (Baseball Player)
1761 Diamond Mountain Rd
Calistoga, CA 94515-9672, USA

Seavey, David (Cartoonist, Editor)
USA Today
1000 Wilson Blvd
Editorial Dept
Arlington, VA 22209-3927, USA

Seaward, Tracey (Producer)
c/o Staff Member *International Creative
Management (ICM-LA)*
10250 Constellation Blvd
Los Angeles, CA 90067-6200, USA

Seaward, Tracy (Producer)
c/o Staff Member *International Creative
Management (ICM-UK)*
Oxford House
76 Oxford St
London W1N OAX, UNITED KINGDOM
(UK)

Seay, Mark (Football Player)
San Diego Chargers
2866 Muscupiabe Dr
San Bernardino, CA 92405-3060, USA

Seay, Virgil (Football Player)
Washington Redskins
5611 Fort Corloran Dr
Burke, VA 22015-2112, USA

Sebaldt, Maria
Geranienstr. 3
Grunwald D-82031, GERMANY

Sebastian, Cuthbert (General, Governor)
Governor General's House
Basseterre, SAINT KITTS & NEVIS

Sebastian, John (Musician)
Lustig Talent
PO Box 770850
Orlando, FL 32877-0850, USA

Sebastiani, Sergio Cardinal (Religious Leader)
Palazzo delle Congregazioni
Lardo del Colonnato 3
Rome 00193, ITALY

Sebek, Nick (Football Player)
Washington Redskins
3233 Rachelle Dr
North Tonawanda, NY 14120-1459, USA

Sebestyen, Marta (Music Group, Musician)
Konzertgentur Berthold Seliger
Nonnengasse 15
Fulda 36037, GERMANY

Sebold, Alice (Writer)
c/o Staff Member *Steven Barclay Agency*
12 Western Ave
Petaluma, CA 94952-2907, USA

Secada, Jon (Musician)
c/o Jorge Pinos *William Morris Agency (WMA-LA)*
1 William Morris Pl
Beverly Hills, CA 90212-4261, USA

Seck, Idrissa (Prime Minister)
Prime Minister's Office
Ave Leopold Sedar Senghor
Dakar, SENEGAL

Secor, Kyle (Actor)
Brillstein/Grey
9150 Wilshire Blvd Ste 350
Beverly Hills, CA 90212-3453, USA

Secord, Al (Hockey Player)
950 Ginger Ct
Southlake, TX 76092-6063, USA

Secord, John (Music Group, Musician)
Making Texas Music
PO Box 1013
Old Putnam Bank Building
Putnam, TX 76469-1013, USA

Secord, Richard V (General)
Computerized Thermal Imaging
1719 W 2800 S
Ogden, UT 84401-3263, USA

Secrest, Charles (Baseball Player)
215 Orchard Grove Ave
Lewistown, PA 17044, USA

Secret GardenContinental AS, Marcus
Thranesgate 2b
Oslo 0473, NORWAY

Secrets, No (Music Group)
Official International Fan Club
PO Box 5247
Bellingham, WA 98227-5247, USA

Secules, Scott (Football Player)
Miami Dolphins
1007 Hawkins Wood Ln
Midlothian, VA 23114-4577, USA

Seda, Jon (Actor)
c/o Staff Member *Anthem Entertainment*
6100 Wilshire Blvd Ste 1170
Los Angeles, CA 90048-5116, USA

Sedaka, Neil (Musician)
Sedaka Music
201 E 66th St Apt 3N
New York, NY 10065-6454, USA

Sedaris, Amy (Actor)
c/o Jonathan Bluman *Paradigm (LA)*
360 N Crescent Dr
North Bldg
Beverly Hills, CA 90210-6820, USA

Sedaris, David (Comedian, Writer)
Steven Barclay Agency
12 Western Ave
Petaluma, CA 94952-2907, USA

Seddon, M Rhea
1709 Shagbark Trl
Murfreesboro, TN 37130-1136, USA

Seddon, Margaret Rhea (Astronaut)
1709 Shagbark Trl
Murfreesboro, TN 37130-1136, USA

Sedelmaier, J Josef (Joe) (Animator, Director)
Sedelmaier Film Productions
858 W Armitage Ave # 267
Chicago, IL 60614-4370, USA

Sedgman, Frank (Tennis Player)
28 Bolton Ave
Hampton, VIC 3188, AUSTRALIA

Sedgwick, Kyra (Actor)
15030 Ventura Blvd # 710
Sherman Oaks, CA 91403-5470, USA

Sedgworth, Bill
1811 Volusia Ave
Daytona Beach, FL 32114, USA

Sedney, Jules (Prime Minister)
Maystreet 24
Paramaribo, SURINAME

Sedoris, Chris (Football Player)
Washington Redskins
7500 Turner Ridge Rd
Crestwood, KY 40014-8951, USA

Seduction (Music Group)
c/o Staff Member *Diva Central Inc*
7510 W Sunset Blvd Ste 1445
Los Angeles, CA 90046-3408, USA

Sedykh, Yuri G (Athlete, Track Athlete)
Russian Light Athletics Federation
Luzhnetskaya Nab 8
Moscow, RUSSIA

See, Carolyn (Writer)
17339 Tramonto Dr Apt 303
Pacific Palisades, CA 90272-3149, USA

Seear, Beatrice N S (Government Official)
189B Kennington Road
London SE11 6ST, UNITED KINGDOM (UK)

Seegal, Denise (Business Person)
Liz Claiborne Inc
1441 Broadway
New York, NY 10018-2088, USA

Seeger, Michael
PO Box 1592
Lexington, VA 24450-1592, USA

Seeger, Pete (Music Group, Musician, Songwriter, Writer)
PO Box 431
Dutchess Junction
Beacon, NY 12508-0431, USA

Seehorn, Rhea (Actor)
c/o Randi Ross *Epstein Wyckoff & Assoc (LA)*
280 S Beverly Dr Ste 400
Beverly Hills, CA 90212-3904, USA

Seelenfreund, Alan (Business Person)
McKesson HBOC Inc
1 Post St
San Francisco, CA 94104-5277, USA

Seeler, Uwe (Soccer Player)
HSV
Rothenbaumchaussee 125
Hamburg 20149, GERMANY

Seeley, Andrew (Actor, Musician)
c/o Staff Member *TalentWorks (LA)*
3500 W Olive Ave Ste 1400
Burbank, CA 91505-5512, USA

Seeling, Angelle (Motorcycle Race, Motorcycle Racer)
Star Performance Suzuki Racing Team
PO Box 1240
Americus, GA 31709, USA

Seely, Jeannie (Music Group, Musician, Songwriter, Writer)
c/o Staff Member *Tessier-Marsh Talent*
505 Canton Pass
Madison, TN 37115-5449, USA

Seelye, Talcott W (Diplomat)
5510 Pembroke Rd
Bethesda, MD 20817-6300, USA

Seema (Actor, Bollywood)
25 Madhavan Nair Road
Mahalingapuram
Chennai, TN 600034, INDIA

Seether (Music Group)
c/o Staff Member *Wind-up Records*
72 Madison Ave Fl 8
New York, NY 10016-8731, USA

Seffrin, John R (Misc)
American Cancer Society
1599 Clifton Ter NE
Atlanta, GA 30307, USA

Sega, Ronald M (Astronaut, Engineer)
711 Staters Lane #B
Alexandria, VA 22314, USA

Segal, Erich (Writer)
Wolfson College
English School
Oxford OX2 6UD, UNITED KINGDOM (UK)

Segal, Fred (Designer, Fashion Designer)
Fred Segal Jeans
8100 Melrose Ave
Los Angeles, CA 90046-7012, USA

Segal, George (Actor)
c/o Douglas Urbanski *Douglas Management*
9713 Santa Monica Blvd Ste 218
Beverly Hills, CA 90210-4217, USA

Segal, Jason (Actor)
c/o Staff Member *United Talent Agency (UTA)*
9560 Wilshire Blvd Ste 500
Beverly Hills, CA 90212-2401, USA

Segal, Jonathan
PO Box 3059
Tel Aviv 61030, ISRAEL

Segal, Michael
27 Cyprus Ave Finchley
London, ENGLAND N3 1SS, UNITED KINGDOM (UK)

Segal, Peter (Director)
William Morris Agency
151 El Camino Dr
Beverly Hills, CA 90212-2775, USA

Segal, Uri
MA Artists Mgmt
28 Sheffield Terrace
London W8 7NA, UNITED KINGDOM (UK)

Segall, Pamela
1450 S Robertson Blvd
Los Angeles, CA 90035-3402, USA

Seganti, Paolo (Actor)
PFD
Drury House
34-43 Russell St
London W8 7NA, UNITED KINGDOM (UK)

Segel, Jason (Actor, Producer, Writer)
c/o Stacy Abrams *Abrams Artists Agency (LA)*
9200 W Sunset Blvd Ph 11
Los Angeles, CA 90069-3601, USA

Seger, Bob (Music Group, Musician, Songwriter, Writer)
Capitol Records
1750 Vine St
Los Angeles, CA 90028-5274, USA

Seger, Shea (Music Group, Musician)
Helter Skelter
Plaza
535 Kings Road
London SW10 0S, UNITED KINGDOM (UK)

Segerstam, Leif S (Composer)
Garvey & Ivor
59 Lansdowne Place
Hove BN3 1FL, UNITED KINGDOM (UK)

Segui, David V (Baseball Player)
13421 Leavenworth Rd
Kansas City, KS 66109-3351, USA

Segui, Diego P (Baseball Player)
7520 King St Apt J
Shawnee Mission, KS 66214-1251, USA

Segura, Francisco (Pancho) (Tennis Player)
Rancho La Costa Hotel & Spa
7690 Camino Real
Carlsbad, CA 92009, USA

Segura, Pancho
La Costa Hotel
Costa Del Mar Rd
Carlsbad, CA 92009, USA

Seguso, Robert (Tennis Player)
Advantage International
1025 Thomas Jefferson St NW # 450
Washington, DC 20007-5201, USA

Sehorn, Jason (Football Player)
New York Giants
3460 Marjorie Way
Sacramento, CA 95820-1952, USA

Seibou, Ali (General, President)
Chairman's Office
National Orientation Higher Council
Niamey, NIGER

Seidel, Kelly
8441 Balboa Blvd Apt 36
Northridge, CA 91325-4096, USA

Seidel, Martie (Music Group, Musician)
Senior Mgmt
9465 Wilshire Blvd Fl 6
Beverly Hills, CA 90212-2605, USA

Seidelman, Susan (Director)
Michael Shedler
225 W 34th St Ste 1012
New York, NY 10122-1012, USA

Seidenberg, Ivan G (Business Person)
1095 Avenue Of The Americas
Bell Atlantic Corp
New York, NY 10036-6797, USA

Seidman, L William (Business Person, Government Official)
1025 Connecticut Ave NW Ste 800
Washington, DC 20036-5419, USA

Seifert, George G (Coach, Football Coach, Sportscaster)
1908 Bay Flat Rd
Bodega Bay, CA 94923, USA

Seifert, Mike (Football Player)
Cleveland Browns
N5610 Lac Verde Cir
Green Lake, WI 54941-9702, USA

Seigenthaler, John L (Television Host)
c/o Staff Member *MSNBC (NJ)*
Nbc/One Microsoft Corporation
1 Msnc Plaza
Secaucus, NJ 07094, USA

Seigner, Emmanuelle (Actor)
Artmedia
20 Ave Rapp
Paris 75007, FRANCE

Seigner, Mathilde (Actor)
Artmedia
20 Ave Rapp
Paris 75007, FRANCE

Seignoret, Clarence H A (President)
24 Cork St
Roseau, DOMINICAN REPUBLIC

Seiko
9200 W Sunset Blvd # Ph-15
W Hollywood, CA 90069-3502, USA

Seilacher, Adolf (Geophysicist, Physicist)
Yale University
Geology/Geophysics Laboratory
New Haven, CT 06520, USA

Seinfeld, Jerry (Actor, Comedian)
c/o George Shapiro *Shapiro/West & Associates*
141 El Camino Dr Ste 205
Beverly Hills, CA 90212-2718, USA

Seiple, Larry (Football Player)
Miami Dolphins
1361 W Golfview Dr
Pembroke Pines, FL 33026-3112, USA

Seitz, Frederick (Educator, Politician)
Rockefeller University
1230 York Ave
Physics Dept
New York, NY 10065-6399, USA

Seitz, Raymond G H (Diplomat)
Lehman Brothers International
1 Broadgate
London EC2M 7HA, UNITED KINGDOM (UK)

Seiwald, Robert J (Inventor)
59 Burnside Ave
San Francisco, CA 94131-2904, USA

Seixas, E Victor (Vic) Jr (Tennis Player)
8 Harbor Point Dr Apt 207
Mill Valley, CA 94941-3241, USA

Seixas, Vic
8 Harbor Point Dr Apt 207
Mill Valley, CA 94941-3241, USA

Seizinger, Katja (Skier)
Rudolf-Epp-Str 48
Eberbach 69412, GERMANY

Seka
1122 White Rock Dr
Dixon, IL 61021-9049, USA

Sela, Michael (Doctor, Misc)
Weizmann Science Institute
Immunology Dept
Rehovot 76100, ISRAEL

Selanne, Teemu (Hockey Player)
31731 Madre Selva Ln
Trabuco Canyon, CA 92679-3613, USA

Selby, David (Actor)
International Creative Mgmt
8942 Wilshire Blvd # 219
Beverly Hills, CA 90211-1908, USA

Selby, Philip (Composer)
Hill Cottage
Via 1 Maggio 93
Rignano Flaminio
Rome 00068, ITALY

Seldes, Marian
210 Central Park S
New York, NY 10019-1428, USA

Seldin, Donald W (Doctor)
Texas Southwestern Medical Center
5323 Harry Hines Blvd
Dallas, TX 75390-7200, USA

Sele, Aaron H (Baseball Player)
5796 NE Gunderson Rd
Poulsbo, WA 98370-8820, USA

Seles, Monica (Tennis Player)
2895 Dick Wilson Dr
Sarasota, FL 34240-8729, USA

Seley, Jason (Artist)
Cornell University
Art Dept
Ithaca, NY 14853, USA

Self, Bill (Basketball Player, Coach)
University of Kansas
Athletic Dept
Allen Fieldhouse
Lawrence, KS 66045-0001, USA

Self, Clarence (Football Player)
Chicago Cardinals
7430 Lake Breeze Dr Apt 509
Fort Myers, FL 33907-8060, USA

Selfridge, Andy (Football Player)
Buffalo Bills
3400 Dunscroft Ct
Keswick, VA 22947-9141, USA

Selig, Bud (Baseball Player, Misc)
Baseball Commissioner's Office
1480 E Standish Pl
Bayside, WI 53217-1958, USA

Selig-Prieb, Wendy (Baseball Player)
Milwaukee Brewers
6620 N Lake Dr
Milwaukee, WI 53217-4245, USA

Seliger, Mark (Photographer)
3 Center Plz
Little Brown
Boston, MA 02108-2003, USA

Seligman, Martin E P (Doctor)
University of Pennsylvania
Psychology Dept
Philadelphia, PA 19104, USA

Selkirk, George N (Government Official)
Rose Lawn Coppice
Wimborne
Dorset, UNITED KINGDOM (UK)

Selkoe, Dennis J (Doctor)
Brigham & Women's Hospital
221 Longwood Ave
Boston, MA 02115-5817, USA

Sellars, Peter (Director)
Creative Artists Agency
9830 Wilshire Blvd
Beverly Hills, CA 90212-1804, USA

Selldorf, Annabelle (Architect)
Selldorf Architects
62 White St
New York, NY 10013-3593, USA

Selleca, Connie (Actor)
15050 Ventura Blvd # 916
Sherman Oaks, CA 91403-2441, USA

Selleck, Tom (Actor)
c/o Nina Nisenholtz *N2N Entertainment*
1230 Montana Ave Apt 203
Santa Monica, CA 90403-5987, USA

Seller, Peg (Coach, Swimmer)
72 Monkswood Crescent
Newmarket, ON L3Y 2K1, CANADA

Sellers, Franklin (Religious Leader)
Reformed Episcopal Church
2001 Frederick Rd
Baltimore, MD 21228-5511, USA

Sellers, Goldie (Football Player)
San Diego Chargers
13425 Braun Rd
Golden, CO 80401-1646, USA

Sellers, Larry (Actor)
c/o Vaughn Hart *Vaughn Hart & Associates*
8899 Beverly Blvd
Los Angeles, CA 90048-2412, USA

Sellers, Michael (Actor, Producer, Writer)
c/o Staff Member *Quantum Entertainment*
209 E Alameda Ave Ste 203
Burbank, CA 91502-2674, USA

Sellers, Piers J (Astronaut)
16011 Craighurst Dr
Houston, TX 77059-6424, USA

Sellers, Ron F (Football Player)
Boston Patriots
4109 Hickory Dr
Palm Beach Gardens, FL 33418-3901, USA

Sellers, Victoria
1927 Vista Del Mar St
Hollywood, CA 90068-4004, USA

Sellick, Phyllis (Musician)
Beverly House
29A Ranelagh Ave
Barnes SW13 0BN, UNITED KINGDOM (UK)

Selmon, Dewey W (Football Player)
Tampa Bay Buccaneers
2725 S Berry Rd
Norman, OK 73072-6908, USA

Selmon, Lee Roy (Football Player)
Tampa Bay Buccaneers
15350 Amberty Dr #624
Tampa, FL 33647, USA

Selmon, Lucious (Coach, Football Player)
Jacksonville Jaguars
1 Alltel Stadium Pl
Jacksonville, FL 32202-1917, USA

Selten, Reinhard (Nobel Prize Laureate)
Hardtweg 23
Konigswinter 53639, GERMANY

Seltz, Rolland (Basketball Player)
3328 Oswego Heights Road
Shoreview, MN 55126, USA

Seltzer, David (Director, Producer, Writer)
c/o Dan Aloni *Creative Artists Agency LCC (CAA-LA)*
2000 Avenue Of The Stars
Los Angeles, CA 90067-4700, USA

Selverstone, Katy (Actor)
c/o Jason Priluck *Agency Group Ltd, The (LA)*
1880 Century Park E Ste 711
Los Angeles, CA 90067-1618, USA

Selvy, Franklin D (Frank) (Basketball Player)
305 Honey Horn Dr
Simpsonville, SC 29681, USA

Selya, Bruce M (Judge)
US Court of Appeals
US Courthouse
Providence, RI 02903, USA

Selzer, Richard (Doctor, Writer)
6 Saint Ronan Ter
New Haven, CT 06511-2315, USA

Selznick, Albie
2800 Nielsen Way
Santa Monica, CA 90405, USA

Semak, Michael W (Photographer)
1796 Spruce Hill Road
Pickering, ON L1V 1S4, CANADA

Sembello, Michael (Musician, Songwriter, Writer)
Talent Consultants International
105 Shad Row Ste B
Piermont, NY 10968-3001, USA

Sembier, Melvin F (Diplomat)
Sembler Co
5858 Central Ave
Saint Petersburg, FL 33707-1716, USA

Semel, David (Director)
c/o Staff Member *3 Arts Entertainment Inc*
9460 Wilshire Blvd Fl 7
Beverly Hills, CA 90212-2713, USA

Semel, Terry (Business Person)
Yahoo! Inc
701 First Ave
Sunnyvale, CA 94089-1019, USA

Semenov, Anatoli (Hockey Player)
4136 Prairie Dunes Dr
Corona, CA 92883-0686, USA

Semenova, Juliana (Basketball Player)
Zalalela 4-35
Riga 1010, LATVIA

Semenyaka, Lyudmila (Ballerina)
Bolshoi Theater
Teatralnaya Pl 1
Moscow 103009, RUSSIA

Semiz, Teata (Bowler)
3131 Kennedy Blvd
North Bergen, NJ 07047-2379, USA

Semizorova, Nina L (Ballerina)
2 Zhukovskaya St
#8
Moscow, RUSSIA

Semkow, Jerzy G
Ul Dynasy 6 m 1
Warsaw 00-354, POLAND

Semler, Dean (Cinematographer, Director)
4260 Arcola Ave
Toluca Lake, CA 91602-2902, USA

Semmelrogge, Martin
Terhallestr. II
Munich D-81545, GERMANY

Sempe, Jean-Jacques (Cartoonist)
Editions Denoel
9 Rue du Cherche-Midi
Paris 75006, FRANCE

Semple, Robert B Jr (Journalist)
New York Times
229 W 43rd St
Editorial Dept
New York, NY 10036-3959, USA

Semyonov, Vladilen G (Ballerina)
15/17-504 Roubinshteina St
Saint Petersburg 191002, RUSSIA

Sen, Amartya K (Nobel Prize Laureate)
Trinity College
Economics Dept
Cambridge CB2 1TP, UNITED KINGDOM
(UK)

Sen, Dog (Musician)
William Morris Agency
151 El Camino Dr
Beverly Hills, CA 90212-2775, USA

Sen, Moon Moon (Actor)
Ruia Park Flat No 62 'B'
Juhu
Bombay, MS 400 049, INDIA

Sen, Mrinal (Director)
4E Motilal Nehru Road
Culcutta 700029, INDIA

Sen, Riya (Actor, Bollywood)
62-B Ruia Park
Juhu
Mumbai, MS 400049, INDIA

Sen, Sushmita (Actor, Bollywood)
6th Floor Beach Queen
Yari Road Versova Andheri (W)
Mumbai, MS 400061, INDIA

Sena, Dominic (Director)
c/o Robert Newman *International Creative
Management (ICM-LA)*
10250 Constellation Blvd
Los Angeles, CA 90067-6200, USA

Sena, Suzanne
6310 San Vicente Blvd Ste 200
Los Angeles, CA 90048-5488, USA

Sendak, Maurice
200 Chestnut Hill Rd
Ridgefield, CT 06877-1200, USA

Sendel, Peter (Athlete)
Zallaer Str 9
Oberhof 98599, GERMANY

Sendel, Sergio (Actor)
c/o Staff Member *Televisa*
Blvd Adolfo Lopez Mateos 232
Colonia San Angel INN
DF CP 01060, MEXICO

Senderens, Alain (Chef)
Restaurant Lucas Carton
9 Place de la Madeleine
Paris 75008, FRANCE

Sendlein, Robin (Football Player)
Minnesota Vikings
14737 E Mark Ln
Scottsdale, AZ 85262-7814, USA

Senff, Dina (Nida) (Swimmer)
DW Coutuner-Senff
Praam 122
Amstelveen 1186 TL, THE
NETHERLANDS

Senior, Peter (Golfer)
c/o Staff Member *Pro Golfers Association
(PGA) Tour*
112 Tpc Blvd
Ponte Vedra Beach, FL 32082, USA

Senn, Adam (Model)
c/o Staff Member *NEXT*
188 rue de Rivoli
Paris 75001, FRANCE

Sennewald, Robert W (General)
212 Wolfe St
Alexandria, VA 22314-3858, USA

Senser, Joe (Football Player)
Minnesota Vikings
Joe Senser's Sports Grill 4217 W 80th St
Bloomington, MN 55437, USA

Sensibaugh, Mike (Football Player)
Kansas City Chiefs
18414 Woodlands Terrace Dr
Glencoe, MO 63038-1829, USA

Sentelle, David B (Judge)
US Court of Appeals
333 Constitution Ave NW
Washington, DC 20001-2866, USA

Seow, Yit Kin (Musician)
8 North Terrace
London SW3 2BA, UNITED KINGDOM
(UK)

Sepe, Crescenzio Cardinal (Religious
Leader)
Piazza della Citta Leonina 9
Rome 00193, ITALY

Septimus, Jake (Producer)
c/o Staff Member *Creative Artists Agency
LCC (CAA-LA)*
2000 Avenue Of The Stars
Los Angeles, CA 90067-4700, USA

Sepulveda, Charlie (Musician)
Ralph Mercado Mgmt
568 Broadway Rm 608
New York, NY 10012-3260, USA

Serano, Greg (Actor)
c/o Erik Kritzer *Fenton-Kritzer
Entertainment*
8840 Wilshire Blvd Fl 3
Beverly Hills, CA 90211-2606, USA

Seraphin, Oliver (Prime Minister)
44 Green's Lane
Goodwill, DOMINICAN REPUBLIC

Serbedzija, Rade (Actor)
P F D
Drury House 34-43 Russell St
London WC2B 5HA, UNITED KINGDOM
(UK)

Serebrier, Jose (Composer)
20 Queensgate Gardens
London SW7 5LZ, UNITED KINGDOM
(UK)

Serebrov, Alexander A (Misc)
Potchta Kosmonavtov
Moskovskoi Oblasti
Syvisdny Goroduk 141160, RUSSIA

Serembus, John (Misc)
Upholsterers Union
25 N 4th St
Philadelphia, PA 19106-2104, USA

Serendipity Singers, The
349 S Main St
Wauconda, IL 60084-1966, USA

Sereno, Paul (Scientist)
University of Chicago
Paleontology Dept
Chicago, IL 60537, USA

Seresin, Michael (Cinematographer)
59 North Wharf Road
London W2 1LA, UNITED KINGDOM
(UK)

Sereys, Jacques
84 bd. Malesherbes
Paris F-75008, FRANCE

Sergei, Ivan (Actor)
c/o David DeCamillo *Gersh Agency, The
(LA)*
232 N Canon Dr
Beverly Hills, CA 90210-5302, USA

Serig, Jennifer (Designer, Fashion
Designer)
c/o Staff Member *Perception Public
Relations LLC*
3940 Laurel Cyn
Pmb 169
Studio City, CA 91604-3709, USA

Serious, Yahoo (Actor)
12/33 E Crescent St
McMahons Point, NSW 2060,
AUSTRALIA

Serkin, Peter A (Musician)
Manne Music College
150 W 85th St
New York, NY 10024-4402, USA

Serkis, Andy (Actor)
c/o Staff Member *Gersh Agency, The (LA)*
232 N Canon Dr
Beverly Hills, CA 90210-5302, USA

Sermon, Eric (Musician)
Richard Walters
1800 Argyle Ave # 408
Los Angeles, CA 90028-5253, USA

Serna, Assumpta (Actor)
8306 Wilshire Blvd # 438
Beverly Hills, CA 90211-2304, USA

Serna, Diego (Soccer Player)
Los Angeles Galaxy
1010 Rose Bowl Dr
Pasadena, CA 91103, USA

Serna, Pepe (Actor)
127 Ruby Ave
Newport Beach, CA 92662-1125, USA

Serota, Nicholas A (Director)
Tate Gallery
Millbank
London SW1P 4RG, UNITED KINGDOM
(UK)

Serra, Eduardo (Cinematographer)
4344 Promenade Way Unit 209
Marina Del Rey, CA 90292-6291, USA

Serra, Pablo (Writer)
c/o Gabriel Blanco *Gabriel Blanco
Iglesias (Mexico)*
Rio Balsas 35-32
Colonia Cuauhtemoc
DF 06500, MEXICO

Serra, Richard (Artist)
173 Duane St
New York, NY 10013-3334, USA

Serrano, Diego (Actor)
c/o Mel McKeon *McKeon-Valeo-Myones
Management*
9100 Wilshire Blvd Ste 350W
Beverly Hills, CA 90212-3437, USA

Serrano, Juan (Musician)
Prince/SF Productions
1450 Southgate Ave Apt 206
Daly City, CA 94015-4021, USA

Serrano, Nestor (Actor)
c/o Danielle Galiana-Allman *InnerAct
Entertainment*
141 S Barrington Ave Ste E
Los Angeles, CA 90049-3314, USA

Serratos, Christian (Actor)
c/o Robert Haas *Innovative Artists (LA)*
1505 10th St
Santa Monica, CA 90401-2805, USA

Serrauot, Michel
201 rue Du Faubourg-St.-Honore
Paris F-75008, FRANCE

Serreau, Coline (Director)
Artmedia
20 Ave Rapp
Paris 75007, FRANCE

Servan-Schreiber, Jean-Claude (Journalist)
147 Bis Rue d'Alesia
Paris 75014, FRANCE

SerVass, Cory J (Editor)
Saturday Evening Post Magazine
1100 Waterway Blvd
Indianapolis, IN 46202-2156, USA

Server, Josh (Actor)
c/o Staff Member *Amsel Eisenstadt &
Frazier Inc*
5055 Wilshire Blvd Ste 865
Los Angeles, CA 90036-6109, USA

Sesame Street
1 Lincoln Plz
New York, NY 10023-7129, USA

Sessions, John
4 Windmill St.
London, ENGLAND W1P 1HF, UNITED
KINGDOM (UK)

Sessions, William S (Judge)
112 E Pecan St Ste 2900
San Antonio, TX 78205-1549, USA

Sessler, Gerhard M (Inventor)
Fichtenstra 30B
Darmstadt 64285, GERMANY

Setari, Robert (Actor)
c/o Patty Stevens *Vessel Entertainment*
10989 Bluffside Dr Apt 3210
Studio City, CA 91604-4407, USA

Seter, Mordecai (Composer)
1 Kamy St
Ramat Aviv
Tel-Aviv, ISRAEL

Seth, Joshua (Actor)
c/o Staff Member *Sutton Barth & Vennari
Inc*
145 S Fairfax Ave Ste 310
Los Angeles, CA 90036-2176, USA

Seth, Oliver (Judge)
US Court of Appeals
PO Box 1
Santa Fe, NM 87504-0001, USA

Seth, Vikram (Writer)
Phoenix House
Orion House
5 Upper St
London WC2H 9EA, UNITED KINGDOM
(UK)

Sethi, Parmeet (Actor, Bollywood)
702/B-1 Sundervan
Off Lokhandwala Road Andheri (W)
Mumbai, MS 400053, INDIA

Settle, John (Football Player)
Atlanta Falcons
2626 Placid St
Fitchburg, WI 53711-5427, USA

Settle, Matthew (Actor)
c/o Beth Holden-Garland *Untitled Entertainment (LA)*
331 N Maple Dr Fl 3
Beverly Hills, CA 90210-3827, USA

Settles, Tawambi (Football Player)
Jacksonville Jaguars
4204 Rogers Rd
Chattanooga, TN 37411-3244, USA

Setzer, Brian (Music Group, Musician)
c/o Staff Member *William Morris Agency (WMA-LA)*
1 William Morris Pl
Beverly Hills, CA 90212-4261, USA

Setziol, LeRoy I (Roy) (Artist)
30450 SW Moriah Ln
Sheridan, OR 97378-9745, USA

Seubert, Rich (Football Player)
New York Giants
D1891 County Road C
Stratford, WI 54484-9330, USA

Seurer, Frank (Football Player)
Kansas City Chiefs
16168 S Brookfield St
Olathe, KS 66062-3927, USA

Sevastyanov, Vitayi I (Misc)
Potchta Kosmonavtov
Moskovskoi Oblasti
Syvisdny Goroduk 141160, RUSSIA

Seven, Johnny (Actor)
11213 McLennan Ave
Granada Hills, CA 91344-4242, USA

Sevendust (Music Group)
c/o Staff Member *TVT Records*
23 E 4th St Fl 3
New York, NY 10003-7028, USA

Severance, Joan (Actor)
c/o Joel Dean *TalentWorks (LA)*
9200 W Sunset Blvd Ste 900
Los Angeles, CA 90069-3604, USA

Severeid, Suzanne (Actor, Model)
PO Box 4171
Malibu, CA 90264-4171, USA

Severin, G Timothy (Tim) (Misc)
Inchy Bridge
Timoleague
County Cork, IRELAND

Severino, John C (Misc)
Prime Ticket Network
401 S Prairie St
Inglewood, CA 90301, USA

Severinsen, Carl H (Doc) (Musician)
11812 San Vicente Blvd Ste 200
Los Angeles, CA 90049-6622, USA

Severson, Jeff (Football Player)
Washington Redskins
20625 Sierra Elena
Murrieta, CA 92562-8817, USA

Sevier, Corey (Actor)
c/o Sheila Wenzel *Innovative Artists (LA)*
1505 10th St
Santa Monica, CA 90401-2805, USA

Sevigny, Chloe (Actor)
Brillstein/Grey
9150 Wilshire Blvd Ste 350
Beverly Hills, CA 90212-3453, USA

Sevilla, Carmen (Actor)
Plaza de Pablo Ruiz Picasso s/n Torre
Picasso Planto 36
Madrid 2800, SPAIN

Sevsec, Pedro (Actor)
c/o Staff Member *Telemundo*
2470 W 8th Ave
Hialeah, FL 33010-2000, USA

Sevy, Jeff (Football Player)
Chicago Bears
PO Box 2177
Loomis, CA 95650-2177, USA

Seward, George C (Attorney, Attorney General, General)
Seward & Kissel
1 Battery Park Plz
New York, NY 10004-1485, USA

Sewell, George (Actor)
Peter Charlesworth
68 Old Brompton Road
London SW7 3LQ, UNITED KINGDOM
(UK)

Sewell, Harley (Football Player)
Detroit Lions
104 W Lilly Ln
Arlington, TX 76010-5605, USA

Sewell, Rufus (Actor)
Julian Belfarge
46 Albemarle St
London W1X 4PP, UNITED KINGDOM
(UK)

Sewell, Steve (Football Player)
Denver Broncos
15918 E Crestridge Pl
Centennial, CO 80015-4219, USA

Seweryn, Andrzej (Actor)
Comedie Francaise
Place Colette
Paris 75001, FRANCE

Sex Pistols
c/o Mitch Schneider *Mitch Schneider Organization, The*
14724 Ventura Blvd Ste 710
Sherman Oaks, CA 91403-3520, USA

Sexsmith, Ron (Musician)
c/o Staff Member *Paradigm (Monterey)*
509 Hartnell St
Monterey, CA 93940-2825, USA

Sexson, Richie (Athlete, Baseball Player)
6539 170th Pl SE
Bellevue, WA 98006-6012, USA

Sexto, Camilo (Musician)
c/o Staff Member *BMG*
1540 Broadway
New York, NY 10036-4074, USA

Sexton, Brent (Actor)
c/o Staff Member *Greene & Associates*
190 N Canon Dr Ste 200
Beverly Hills, CA 90210-5319, USA

Sexton, Charlie (Musician)
Courage Artists
310 Water St
#201
Vancouver, BC V6B 1B6, CANADA

Sexton III, Brendan (Actor)
c/o Staff Member *Gersh Agency, The (LA)*
232 N Canon Dr
Beverly Hills, CA 90210-5302, USA

Seyferth, Dietmar (Misc)
Massachusetts Institute of Technology
Chemistry Dept
Cambridge, MA 02139, USA

Seyfried, Amanda (Actor)
c/o Harding Jones *GHJ Management*
405 E 54th St Apt 3H
New York, NY 10022-5176, USA

Seyler, Athene (Actor)
Coach House
26 Upper Mall Hammersmith
London W8, UNITED KINGDOM (UK)

Seymour, Cara (Actor)
c/o Vanessa Pereira *Artists Independent Management (LA)*
825 Nowita Pl
Venice, CA 90291-3836, USA

Seymour, Caroline (Actor)
Langford Assoc
17 Westfields Ave
London SW13 0AT, UNITED KINGDOM
(UK)

Seymour, Carolyn (Actor)
Chasin Agency
8899 Beverly Blvd Ste 716
Los Angeles, CA 90048-2449, USA

Seymour, Jane (Actor)
c/o Adam Levine *Anthem Entertainment*
6100 Wilshire Blvd Ste 1170
Los Angeles, CA 90048-5116, USA

Seymour, John (Senator)
77655 Iroquois Dr
Indian Wells, CA 92210-6130, USA

Seymour, Lesley Jane (Editor)
Redbook Magazine
224 W 57th St
Editorial Dept
New York, NY 10019-3200, USA

Seymour, Lynn (Ballerina)
Artistes in Action
16 Balderton St
London W1Y 1TF, UNITED KINGDOM
(UK)

Seymour, Paul (Football Player)
Buffalo Bills
4188 Shoals Dr
Okemos, MI 48864-3431, USA

Seymour, Richard (Football Player)
New England Patriots
1156 Cate Rd
Eastover, SC 29044-9550, USA

Seymour, Stephanie (Model)
c/o Peg Donegan *Framework Entertainment (LA)*
9057 Nemo St # C
W Hollywood, CA 90069-5511, USA

Seymour, Stephanie K (Judge)
US Court of Appeals
333 W 4th St
US Courthouse
Tulsa, OK 74103-3877, USA

Seynhaeve, Ingrid
111 E 22nd St Rm 200
New York, NY 10010-5414, USA

Sezer, Ahmet Necdet (President)
President's Office
Cumhurbaskanlgl Kosku
Cankaya
Ankara, TURKEY

Sfar, Rachid (Prime Minister)
278 Ave de Tervuren
Brussels 1150, BELGIUM

Sfeir, Nasrallah Pierre Cardinal (Religious Leader)
Patriarcat Maronite
Bkerke, LEBANON

Sgouros, Dimitris (Musician)
Tompazi 28 Str
Piraeus 18537, GREECE

Shack, Edward S P (Eddie) (Hockey Player)
508 Fairlawn Ave
North York, ON M5M 1V2, CANADA

Shack, William A (Misc)
2597 Hilgard Ave
Berkeley, CA 94709-1104, USA

Shackelford, Don (Football Player)
Atlanta Falcons
PO Box 1468
Lansdale, PA 19446, USA

Shackelford, Ted (Actor)
12305 Valleyheart Dr
Studio City, CA 91604-1643, USA

Shackouls, Bobby S (Business Person)
Burlington Resources
5051 Westheimer Rd
Houston, TX 77056-5622, USA

Shadic-Campbell, Lillian (Baseball Player)
61 Bloody Hill Rd
Craryville, NY 12521-5101, USA

Shadix, Glenn (Actor)
c/o Staff Member *Juliet Green Management*
9025 Wilshire Blvd Ste 400
Beverly Hills, CA 90211-1828, USA

Shadow (DJ)
Quannum Projects LLC
690 5th St # 208
San Francisco, CA 94107-1517, USA

Shadyac, Tom (Director)
United Talent Agency
9560 Wilshire Blvd Ste 500
Beverly Hills, CA 90212-2401, USA

Shafer, Martin (Business Person)
c/o Staff Member *Castle Rock Entertainment*
335 N Maple Dr # 135
Beverly Hills, CA 90210-3857, USA

Shafer, R Donald (Religious Leader)
Brethren in Christ Church
PO Box 290
Grantham, PA 17027-0290, USA

Shaffer, David H (Publisher)
MacMillan
1177 Avenue Of The Americas # 1965
New York, NY 10036-2714, USA

Shaffer, Paul (Music Group, Musician)
Panacea Entertainment
12020 Chandler Blvd # 300
North Hollywood, CA 91607-2189, USA

Shaffer, Peter (Writer)
Lantz
200 W 57th St Ste 503
New York, NY 10019-3211, USA

Shagari, Alhaji Shehu Usman Aliu
(President)
22 Shehu Crescent
PO Box 162 Adarawa
Sokoto State, NIGERIA

Shaggy (Musician)
c/o Christopher Dalston *Creative Artists Agency LCC (CAA-LA)*
2000 Avenue Of The Stars
Los Angeles, CA 90067-4700, USA

Shaggy (Radio Personality)
c/o Staff Member *WPKX*
1331 Main St Ste 4
Springfield, MA 01103-1621, USA

Shah, Idries (Writer)
AP Watt Ltd
26/28 Bedford Row
London WC1R 4HL, UNITED KINGDOM
(UK)

Shah, Satish (Actor, Bollywood, Comedian)
30A Anand Nagar
Forjeet Street
Bombay, MS 400 036, INDIA

Shahan, Gil (Musician)
ICM Artists
40 W 57th St
New York, NY 10019-4001, USA

Shahi, Sara (Actor)
c/o Jim Hess *Paradigm (LA)*
360 N Crescent Dr
North Bldg
Beverly Hills, CA 90210-6820, USA

Shahi, Sarah (Actor)
c/o Michael Greenwald *Don Buchwald & Associates Inc (LA)*
6500 Wilshire Blvd Ste 2200
Los Angeles, CA 90048-4942, USA

Shahmatova, Larissa (Musician)
Julliard Music School
Lincoln Center Plaza
New York, NY 10023, USA

Shaiman, Marc (Composer)
8476 Brier Dr
West Hollywood, CA 90046-1908, USA

Shake, Christi (Model)
Starr Entertainment
2518 Lodge Forest Dr
Baltimore, MD 21219-1911, USA

Shakespeare, Frank J Jr (Diplomat, Television Host)
303 Coast Blvd
La Jolla, CA 92037-4630, USA

Shakira (Musician)
c/o Mitch Rose *Creative Artists Agency LCC (CAA-LA)*
2000 Avenue Of The Stars
Los Angeles, CA 90067-4700, USA

Shakur, Kula
39A Gramercy Park N Apt 1C
New York, NY 10010-6312, USA

Shakurov, Sergei K (Actor)
Bibliotechnava Str 27
#94
Moscow 109544, RUSSIA

Shal-Houd, Tony
9560 Wilshire Blvd # 516
Beverly Hills, CA 90212-2427, USA

Shalala, Donna (Secretary)
University of Miami
President's Office
Coral Gables, FL 33124, USA

Shalamar
707 18th Ave S
Nashville, TN 37203-3214, USA

Shales, Thomas W (Journalist)
Washington Post
Editorial Dept
1150 15th St NW
Washington, DC 20071-0001, USA

Shales, Tom
1650 Kirby Rd
McLean, VA 22101-3209, USA

Shalets, Victoria (Actor)
c/o Angharad Wood *Artists Independent Management (LA)*
825 Nowita Pl
Venice, CA 90291-3836, USA

Shalhoub, Tony (Actor)
c/o Martin Lesak *Creative Artists Agency LCC (CAA-LA)*
2000 Avenue Of The Stars
Los Angeles, CA 90067-4700, USA

Shalikashvili, John M (Shali) (General)
55 Chapman Loop
Steilacoom, WA 98388-1731, USA

Shalim (Musician)
c/o Staff Member *Sony Music Miami*
605 Lincoln Rd Fl 7
Miami Beach, FL 33139-2900, USA

Shalit, Gene (Critic)
NBC-TV
30 Rockefeller Plz Ste 270E
News Dept
New York, NY 10112-0299, USA

Shamask, Ronaldus (Designer, Fashion Designer)
Moss Shamask
39 W 37th St
New York, NY 10018-6217, USA

Shamir, Yitzhak (Prime Minister)
Beit Amot Mishpat
8 Shaul Hamelech Blvd
Tel Aviv 64733, ISRAEL

Shamrock, Ken (Actor, Athlete, Wrestler)
c/o Jeremy Lappen *Triumph Entertainment*
7920 W Sunset Blvd Fl 2
Los Angeles, CA 90046-3300, USA

Shan Kuo-Hsi, Paul Cardinal (Religious Leader)
Bishop's House
125 Szu-Wie 3rd Road
Kaohsiung 80203, TAIWAN

Shanahan, Brendan (Hockey Player)
47 Saquatucket Bluffs Rd
Harwich Port, MA 02646-2510, USA

Shanahan, Mike (Coach, Football Coach)
Denver Broncos
13655 Broncos Pkwy
Englewood, CO 80112-4150, USA

Shand, Remy (Music Group, Musician, Songwriter, Writer)
Universal Records
2550 Victoria Park
Toronto, ON M2J 4A2, CANADA

Shandling, Garry (Actor, Comedian)
c/o Jimmy Miller *Mosaic Media Group*
24 Music Sq W Fl 1
Nashville, TN 37203-6661, USA

Shandrowsky, Alex (Misc)
Marine Engineer Beneficial Assn
444 N Capitol St NW
Washington, DC 20001-1512, USA

Shane, Bob (Music Group, Musician)
9410 S 46th St
Phoenix, AZ 85044-7512, USA

Shangri-La's, The
27 L Ambiance Ct
Bardonia, NY 10954-1421, USA

Shanice (Musician)
Richard Walters
1800 Argyle Ave # 408
Los Angeles, CA 90028-5253, USA

Shank, Bud
PO Box 948
Port Townsend, WA 98368-0004, USA

Shank, Clarence E (Bud) (Musician)
PO Box 70128
Tucson, AZ 85737-0028, USA

Shankar, Anoushka (Musician)
c/o Staff Member *International Creative Management (ICM-LA)*
10250 Constellation Blvd
Los Angeles, CA 90067-6200, USA

Shankar, Naren (Producer)
c/o Staff Member *CSI*
7800 Beverly Blvd
Los Angeles, CA 90036-2112, USA

Shankar, Ravi
17 Warden Ct Gowalia Tank Rd.
Bombay 36, INDIA

Shankley, Amelia
2-4 Noel St.
London, ENGLAND W1V 3RB, UNITED KINGDOM (UK)

Shankman, Adam (Comedian, Director)
c/o Staff Member *Brillstein-Grey Entertainment*
9150 Wilshire Blvd Ste 350
Beverly Hills, CA 90212-3453, USA

Shanks, Michael (Actor, Director, Writer)
c/o Ronda Cooper *Characters Talent Agency, The (Toronto)*
8 Elm St 3rd FL
Toronto, ON M5G 1G7, CANADA

Shanley, Jim (Football Player)
Green Bay Packers
4 Brookside Dr Apt D
Walla Walla, WA 99362, USA

Shanley, John Patrick (Director, Writer)
c/o Staff Member *Creative Artists Agency LCC (CAA-LA)*
2000 Avenue Of The Stars
Los Angeles, CA 90067-4700, USA

Shann, Robert (Football Player)
Philadelphia Eagles
56 Deer Run Ln
N Falmouth, MA 02556-2322, USA

Shannon (Music Group, Musician)
Big Mgmt
226 5th Ave
New York, NY 10001-7706, USA

Shannon (Musician)
c/o Staff Member *Diva Central Inc*
7510 W Sunset Blvd Ste 1445
Los Angeles, CA 90046-3408, USA

Shannon, Carver (Football Player)
Los Angeles Rams
6005 S La Cienega Blvd
Los Angeles, CA 90056-1523, USA

Shannon, Mem (Music Group, Musician, Songwriter, Writer)
Miasma Mgmt
1048 Hesper Ave
Metairie, LA 70005-1552, USA

Shannon, Michael (Actor)
c/o Staff Member *Endeavor Agency LLC (LA)*
9601 Wilshire Blvd Fl 3
Beverly Hills, CA 90210-5204, USA

Shannon, Michael E (Business Person)
Ecolab Inc
370 Wabasha St N
Ecolab Center
Saint Paul, MN 55102-1349, USA

Shannon, Molly (Actor, Comedian)
Innovative Artists
1505 10th St
Santa Monica, CA 90401-2805, USA

Shannon, Randy (Football Player)
Dallas Cowboys
7420 SW 107th Ave Apt 7-207
Miami, FL 33173-2970, USA

Shannon, Vicellous Reon (Actor)
c/o Staff Member *Talent Entertainment Group*
9111 Wilshire Blvd
Beverly Hills, CA 90210-5508, USA

Shantz, Robert C (Bobby) (Baseball Player)
152 E Mount Pleasant Ave
Ambler, PA 19002-4209, USA

Shanze, Michael
Fichtenweg 8
Feldafing D-82340, GERMANY

Shapar, Howard K (Government Official)
PO Box 30242
Bethesda, MD 20824-0242, USA

Shapiro, Dani (Writer)
Random House
1745 Broadway # B1
New York, NY 10019-4305, USA

Shapiro, Debbie (Actor)
Agency for Performing Arts
405 S Beverly Dr Ste 500
Beverly Hills, CA 90212-4425, USA

Shapiro, Harold T (Educator)
10 Campbelton Cir
Princeton, NJ 08540-3010, USA

Shapiro, Irwin I (Physicist)
17 Lantern Ln
Lexington, MA 02421-6029, USA

Shapiro, James (Doctor)
University of Alberta
114th St & 89th Ave
Edmonton, AB T6G 2M7, CANADA

Shapiro, Jim (Actor)
Legislative Office Building Room 4028
Hartford, CT 06106, USA

Shapiro, Joel E (Artist)
Pace Gallery
32 E 57th St
New York, NY 10022-2530, USA

Shapiro, Mary L (Government Official)
Securities & Exchange Commission
450 5th St NW
Washington, DC 20001-2739, USA

Shapiro, Maurice M (Physicist)
5809 Nicholson Ln Apt 801
Rockville, MD 20852-5710, USA

Shapiro, Mel (Writer)
University of California
Theater Film/Tv Dept
Los Angeles, CA 90024, USA

Shapiro, Neal (Horse Racer)
296 Sharon Rd
Trenton, NJ 08691-2313, USA

Shapiro, Richard & Esther
617 N Alta Dr
Beverly Hills, CA 90210-3503, USA

Shapley, Lloyd S (Economist, Mathematician)
University of California
Economics Dept
Los Angeles, CA 90024, USA

Sharapova, Maria (Tennis Player)
Int'l Mgmt Group
1 Erieview Plz
1360 E 9th St #1300
Cleveland, OH 44114-1738, USA

Share, Charlie (Chuck) (Basketball Player)
12922 Twin Meadows Ct
Saint Louis, MO 63146-1803, USA

Sharif, Omar (Actor)
BP 41
Bougival
Yvelines 78380, FRANCE

Sharipov, Sallzhan S (Cosmonaut)
Potchta Kosmonavtov
Moskovskoi Oblasti
Syvisdny Goroduk 141160, RUSSIA

Sharkey, Ed (Football Player)
New York Yankees
3615 Russell Rd
Centralia, WA 98531-1666, USA

Sharma, Barbara (Actor)
PO Box 29125
Los Angeles, CA 90029-0125, USA

Sharma, Kawal (Actor, Bollywood)
A 502 Janak Deep Seven Bangalows
Versova Andheri
Bombay, MS 400 049, INDIA

Sharma, Rakesh (Cosmonaut)
Hindustan Aeronautics
Bangalore, KA 560037, INDIA

Sharman, Helen (Cosmonaut)
12 Stratton Court
Adelade Road Surbiton
Surrey, UNITED KINGDOM (UK)

Sharman, Jim (Director)
M&L
49 Daringhurst St
Kings Cross, NSW 2100, AUSTRALIA

Sharmila (Actor, Bollywood)
5 Narsimhan 1st CrossStreet
B.N. Reddy Road T.Nagar
Chennai, TN 600017, INDIA

Sharmili (Actor, Bollywood)
5/A, Karnan Street
SVT Maligai Rangarajapuram
Chennai, TN 600024, INDIA

Sharockman, Ed (Football Player)
Minnesota Vikings
8955 Thomas Ln
Woodbury, MN 55125-7603, USA

Sharp, Dee Dee (Musician)
Cape Entertainment
8432 NW 31st Ct
Sunrise, FL 33351-8901, USA

Sharp, Don
80 Castelnau
London, ENGLAND SW13 9EX, UNITED KINGDOM (UK)

Sharp, Kevin (Musician)
Rising Star
1415 River Landing Way
Woodstock, GA 30188-5345, USA

Sharp, Lesley
76 Oxford St.
London, ENGLAND WIN OAX, UNITED KINGDOM (UK)

Sharp, Leslie (Actor)
International Creative Mgmt
8942 Wilshire Blvd # 219
Beverly Hills, CA 90211-1908, USA

Sharp, Linda K (Coach)
Phoenix Mercury
201 E Jefferson St
American West Arena
Phoenix, AZ 85004-2412, USA

Sharp, Marsha (Coach)
Texas Tech University
Athletic Dept
Lubbock, TX 79409, USA

Sharp, Mitchell W (Government Official)
33 Monkland Ave
Ottawa, ON K1S 1Y8, CANADA

Sharp, Phillip A (Nobel Prize Laureate)
36 Fairmont Ave
Newton, MA 02458-2506, USA

Sharp, Preston (Actor, Reality TV Star)
c/o Staff Member *Extreme Makeover: Home Edition*
9255 W Sunset Blvd Ste 1100
Endemol Entertainment USA
Los Angeles, CA 90069-3308, USA

Sharp, Richard L (Business Person)
Circuit City Group
9950 Mayland Dr
Richmond, VA 23233-1464, USA

Sharpe, Rochelle P (Journalist)
94 Dudley St # 2
Brookline, MA 02445-5937, USA

Sharpe, Shannon (Football Player)
867 Carlton Rdg NE
Atlanta, GA 30342-4346, USA

Sharpe, Sterling (Football Player)
Green Bay Packers
81 Running Fox Rd
Columbia, SC 29223-3052, USA

Sharpe, Thomas R (Tom) (Writer)
38 Tunwells Lane
Great Shelford
Cambridge CB2 5LJ, UNITED KINGDOM (UK)

Sharpe, William F (Nobel Prize Laureate)
PO Box 610
Los Altos, CA 94023-0610, USA

Sharpe Jr, Luis E (Football Player)
St Louis Cardinals
13418 S 38th Pl
Phoenix, AZ 85044-8202, USA

Sharper, Darren (Football Player)
Green Bay Packers
11613 Heverley Ct
Glen Allen, VA 23059-4829, USA

Sharper, Jamie (Football Player)
Baltimore Ravens
11613 Heverley Ct
Glen Allen, VA 23059-4829, USA

Sharpless, K Barry (Nobel Prize Laureate)
Scripps Research Institute
10650 N Torrey Pines Rd
La Jolla, CA 92037-1001, USA

Sharpton, Al (Activist, Religious Leader)
1941 Madison Ave Fl 2
New York, NY 10035-1822, USA

Sharqi, Sheikh Hamad bin Muhammad al (President)
Royal Palace
Emiri Court
PO Box 1
Fujairah, UNITED ARAB EMIRATES

Shatalov, Vladimir A (Cosmonaut)
Potchta Kosmonavtov
Moskovskoi Oblasti
Syvisdny Goroduk 141160, RUSSIA

Shatner, Melanie (Actor)
Henderson/Hogan
8285 W Sunset Blvd Ste 1
West Hollywood, CA 90046-2420, USA

Shatner, William (Actor)
c/o Harry Gold *TalentWorks (LA)*
3500 W Olive Ave Ste 1400
Burbank, CA 91505-5512, USA

Shatraw, David
c/o Staff Member *Stone Manners Talent & Literary (LA)*
6500 Wilshire Blvd Ste 550
Los Angeles, CA 90048-4950, USA

Shattuck, Kim (Musician)
International Creative Mgmt
40 W 57th St Ste 1800
New York, NY 10019-4001, USA

Shaud, Grant (Actor)
8738 Appian Way
Los Angeles, CA 90046-7733, USA

Shaud, John A (General)
Air Force Aid Society
241 18th St S Ste 202
Arlington, VA 22202-3409, USA

Shaughnessy, Charles (Actor)
c/o Joel Shire *Joel Shire Management*
211 S Beverly Dr Ste 208
Beverly Hills, CA 90212-3879, USA

Shavelson, Mel
11947 Sunshine Ter
N Hollywood, CA 91604-3708, USA

Shaver, Billy Joe (Musician, Songwriter, Writer)
435 N Martel Ave
Los Angeles, CA 90036-2513, USA

Shaver, Helen (Actor)
Innovative Artists
1505 10th St
Santa Monica, CA 90401-2805, USA

Shavers, Ernie (Boxer)
30 Doreen Ave Moretown Wirral
Merseyside CH46 6DN, UNITED KINGDOM (UK)

Shaw, Bernard (Correspondent)
7526 Heatherton Ln
Potomac, MD 20854-3222, USA

Shaw, Bryant (Football Player)
Dallas Cowboys
13832 Far Hills Ln
Dallas, TX 75240-3737, USA

Shaw, Carolyn Hagner (Publisher)
Social Register
2620 P St NW
Washington, DC 20007-3062, USA

Shaw, Dennis (Football Player)
Buffalo Bills
13646 Fairgate Dr
Poway, CA 92064-5836, USA

Shaw, Fiona (Actor)
International Creative Mgmt
76 Oxford St
London W1N 0AX, UNITED KINGDOM (UK)

Shaw, Jason (Actor, Model)
c/o Joanna (Joanie) Burstein *Burstein Company, The*
15304 W Sunset Blvd Ste 208
Pacific Palisades, CA 90272-3656, USA

Shaw, Jeffrey L (Jeff) (Baseball Player)
465 Carolyn Rd
Washington Court House,
OH 43160-2343, USA

Shaw, John H (Geophysicist, Physicist)
Harvard University
Geophysics Dept
Cambridge, MA 02138, USA

Shaw, Kenneth A (Educator)
Syracuse University
President's Office
Syracuse, NY 13244-0001, USA

Shaw, Kristen (Actor)
c/o Rich Siegel *Marathon Entertainment*
8060 Melrose Ave Fl 4th
Los Angeles, CA 90046-7038, USA

Shaw, Mariena (Musician)
Berkeley Agency
2608 9th St
Berkeley, CA 94710-2550, USA

Shaw, Martin (Actor)
204 Belswins Lane
Hemel
Hempstead, Herts, UNITED KINGDOM (UK)

Shaw, Pete (Football Player)
San Diego Chargers
25052 Pappas Rd
Ramona, CA 92065-4920, USA

Shaw, Robert (Football Player)
Dallas Cowboys
4013 Centenary Ave
Dallas, TX 75225-5430, USA

Shaw, Robert (Football Player)
Cleveland Rams
487 Old Coach Rd Apt D
Westerville, OH 43081-1392, USA

Shaw, Robert J (Bob) (Baseball Player)
2225 US Highway 1 #208
Tequesta, FL 33469, USA

Shaw, Run Run (Producer)
Shaw House
Lot 220 Clear Water Bar Road
Kowloon, Hong Kong, CHINA

Shaw, Scott (Journalist)
20771 Lake Rd
Cleveland, OH 44116-1335, USA

Shaw, Sedrick (Football Player)
New England Patriots
1007 Waller St
Austin, TX 78702-2632, USA

Shaw, Stan (Actor)
Innovative Artists
1505 10th St
Santa Monica, CA 90401-2805, USA

Shaw, Tim
5315 River Ave
Newport Beach, CA 92663-2208, USA

Shaw, Tommy (Musician, Songwriter, Writer)
c/o Sterling Bacon *TBA Artist Management (Atlanta)*
1111 Alderman Dr Ste 285
Alpharetta, GA 30005-5433, USA

Shaw, Vinessa (Actor)
Industry Entertainment
955 Carrillo Dr Ste 300
Los Angeles, CA 90048-5400, USA

Shaw, William L (Billy) (Football Player)
Buffalo Bills
3427 Old Rothell Rd
Toccoa, GA 30577-9436, USA

Shaw Jr, Brewster H (Astronaut)
3519 Rice Blvd
Houston, TX 77005-2937, USA

Shawkat, Alia (Actor)
c/o Lynn Reynolds *Shelter Entertainment*
9255 W Sunset Blvd Ste 1010
Los Angeles, CA 90069-3307, USA

Shawn, Wallace (Actor, Writer)
Gersh Agency
232 N Canon Dr
Beverly Hills, CA 90210-5302, USA

Shawyer, David
16 Rylett Rd.
London, ENGLAND W12, UNITED KINGDOM (UK)

Shay, Jerry (Football Player)
Minnesota Vikings
81 E Shasta St
Chula Vista, CA 91910-6127, USA

Shaye, Lin (Actor)
Paul Kohner
9300 Wilshire Blvd Ste 555
Beverly Hills, CA 90212-3211, USA

Shaye, Skyler (Actor)
c/o Staff Member *Artists Only Management*
10203 Santa Monica Blvd
Los Angeles, CA 90067-6405, USA

Shchedrin, Rodion K (Composer)
Tverskaya St
#31
Moscow 103050, RUSSIA

Shea, Charity (Actor)
c/o Staff Member *Anodyne Entertainment*
2151 Hillsboro Ave
Los Angeles, CA 90034-1120, USA

Shea, Eric (Actor)
27710 Jubilee Run Rd
Pearblossom, CA 93553-3439, USA

Shea, George Beverly
1300 Harmon Pl
Minneapolis, MN 55403-1925, USA

Shea, Jere (Actor)
SMS Talent
8730 W Sunset Blvd Ste 440
Los Angeles, CA 90069-2277, USA

Shea, John (Actor)
Mutant X
40 Carl Hall Road
Toronto, ON M3K 2B8, CANADA

Shea, Joseph F (Scientist)
15 Dogwood Rd
Weston, MA 02493-2403, USA

Shea, Judith (Artist)
Barbara Krakow Gallery
10 Newbury St Ste 5
Boston, MA 02116-3223, USA

Shea, Katt (Actor)
International Creative Mgmt
8942 Wilshire Blvd # 219
Beverly Hills, CA 90211-1908, USA

Shea, Pat (Football Player)
San Diego Chargers
1175 Evergreen Dr
Encinitas, CA 92024-3918, USA

Shea, Robert M (General)
Director Cmd Control Communications
Hqusmc 2 Navy St
Washington, DC 20380-0001, USA

Shea, Terry (Coach, Football Coach)
San Jose State University
Athletic Dept
San Jose, CA 95192-0001, USA

Shear, Jules (Musician, Songwriter, Writer)
Concerted Efforts
59 Parsons St
West Newton, MA 02465-2137, USA

Shear, Rhonda (Actor, Comedian, Model)
J Cast Productions
2550 Greenvalley Rd
Los Angeles, CA 90046-1438, USA

Sheard, Kiera Kiki (Musician)
c/o Staff Member *EMI Gospel*
PO Box 5085
Brentwood, TN 37024-5085, USA

Shearer, Al (Actor, Reality TV Star)
c/o Staff Member *Dolores Robinson Entertainment*
3815 Hughes Ave # 3
Culver City, CA 90232-2715, USA

Shearer, Alan (Soccer Player)
Newcastle United FC
Saint James Park
Newcastle-Tyne NE1 4ST, UNITED KINGDOM (UK)

Shearer, Bob (Golfer)
International Management Group
281 Clarence Street
2nd Floor
Sydney, NSW 2000, AUSTRALIA

Shearer, Harry (Actor, Comedian)
c/o Melanie Greene *Melanie Greene Management & Productions*
425 N Robertson Blvd
West Hollywood, CA 90048-1735, USA

Shearer, Peter M (Geophysicist, Physicist)
Scripps Oceanography Institute
Geophysics Dept
La Jolla, CA 92093, USA

Shearer, S Bradford (Brad) (Football Player)
Chicago Bears
1909B Lakeshore Dr # B
Austin, TX 78746-2904, USA

Shearin, Joe (Football Player)
Los Angeles Rams
3533 Stanford Ave
Dallas, TX 75225-7402, USA

Shearing, George A (Composer, Musician)
350 5th Ave Ste 6215
New York, NY 10118-6215, USA

Shearmur, Edward (Ed) (Composer, Musician)
c/o Staff Member *Gorfaine/Schwartz Agency Inc*
4111 W Alameda Ave Ste 509
Burbank, CA 91505-4171, USA

Shearsmith, Reece (Actor)
c/o Lorraine Hamilton *Hamilton Hodell Ltd*
66 - 68 Margaret St 5th Fl
London W1W 8SR, UNITED KINGDOM (UK)

SheDaisy (Music Group)
PO Box 120573
Nashville, TN 37212-0573, USA

Shedd, Kenny (Football Player)
Oakland Raiders
1928 Tioga Pass Way
Antioch, CA 94531-9054, USA

Sheed, Wilfrid J J (Writer)
General Delivery
Sag Harbor, NY 11963-9999, USA

Sheedy, Ally (Actor)
Don Buchwald
6500 Wilshire Blvd Ste 2200
Los Angeles, CA 90048-4942, USA

Sheehan, Doug (Actor)
Innovative Artists
1505 10th St
Santa Monica, CA 90401-2805, USA

Sheehan, Jeremiah J (Business Person)
Reynolds Metals Co
6603 W Broad St
6601 Broad St
Richmond, VA 23230-1723, USA

Sheehan, Neil (Journalist)
4505 Klingle St NW
Washington, DC 20016-3580, USA

Sheehan, Patrick (Golfer)
2913 Ashton Ter
Oviedo, FL 32765-7949, USA

Sheehan, Patty (Golfer)
c/o Staff Member *Ladies Pro Golf Association (LPGA)*
100 International Golf Dr
Daytona Beach, FL 32124-1082, USA

Sheehan, Susan (Writer)
4505 Klingle St NW
Washington, DC 20016-3580, USA

Sheehy, Timothy (Tim) (Hockey Player)
4 Boswell Ln
Southborough, MA 01772-1763, USA

Sheelor, Willie (Baseball Player)
Chicago American Giants
152 Beaumont Ave
Kannapolis, NC 28083-6501, USA

Sheen, Charles (Actor)
Jeffrey Ballard
4814 Lemara Ave
Sherman Oaks, CA 91403, USA

Sheen, Charlie (Actor)
15030 Ventura Blvd
Sherman Oaks, CA 91403-5470, USA

Sheen, Martin (Actor)
15030 Ventura Blvd # 710
Sherman Oaks, CA 91403-5470, USA

Sheen, Michael (Actor)
c/o Melanie Greene *Melanie Greene Management & Productions*
425 N Robertson Blvd
West Hollywood, CA 90048-1735, USA

Sheen, Ramon
6916 Dume Dr
Malibu, CA 90265-4227, USA

Sheer, Ireen
Yachthof B-22
Waldeck D-34513, GERMANY

Sheerer, Gary (Athlete)
1557 Country Club Dr
Los Altos Hills, CA 94024-5908, USA

Sheets, Ben (Baseball Player)
11234 George Lambert Rd
Saint Amant, LA 70774-4024, USA

Sheffer, Craig (Actor)
5699 Kanan Rd # 275
Agoura, CA 91301-3358, USA

Sheffield, Gary A (Baseball Player)
The Britto Agency
234 W 56th St Ph
New York, NY 10019-4302, USA

Sheffield, Johnny
834 1st Ave
Chula Vista, CA 91911-1451, USA

Sheffield, Lois (Baseball Player)
227 Jones St
Wellington, OH 44090-1062, USA

Sheffield, Tony (Baseball Player)
PO Box 164
Tullahoma, TN 37388-0164, USA

Sheffield, William J (Bill) (Governor)
PO Box 91476
Anchorage, AK 99509-1476, USA

Shefft, Jen (Reality TV Star)
c/o Michael (Mike) Esterman *Esterman Entertainment*
214 Park Rd
Riva, MD 21140-1224, USA

Shehee, Rashaan (Football Player)
Kansas City Chiefs
6120 Bay Club Ct
Bakersfield, CA 93312-6212, USA

Sheibler, Jim
PO Box 60
Venice, CA 90294-0060, USA

Sheik, Duncan (Musician, Songwriter, Writer)
Nonesuch Records
75 Rockefeller Plz
New York, NY 10019-6908, USA

Sheikh, Farooque (Actor, Bollywood)
Rafi Mansion 28th Road
Bandra
Mumbai, MS 400050, INDIA

Sheila E (Musician)
Ofoove Ent
1005 N Alfred St Apt 2
West Hollywood, CA 90069-4757, USA

Sheiner, David S (Actor)
1827 Veteran Ave Apt 19
Los Angeles, CA 90025-4567, USA

Sheinfeld, David (Composer)
112 Ash Way
San Rafael, CA 94903-2902, USA

Shelby, Carol (Race Car Driver)
19020 Anelo Ave
Gardena, CA 90248-4520, USA

Shelby, Carroll (Race Car Driver)
19020 Anelo Ave
Gardena, CA 90248-4520, USA

Shelby, Mark (Composer, Musician)
Thomas Cassidy
11761 E Speedway Blvd
Tucson, AZ 85748-2017, USA

Sheldon, Jack (Musician)
7095 Hollywood Blvd Ste 617
Los Angeles, CA 90028-8912, USA

Shell, Arthur (Art) (Coach, Football Coach, Football Player)
c/o Team Member *Oakland Raiders*
1220 Harbor Bay Pkwy
Alameda, CA 94502-6570, USA

Shell, Donnie (Football Player)
Pittsburgh Steelers
2945 Shandon Rd
Rock Hill, SC 29730-9521, USA

Shell, Todd (Football Player)
San Francisco 49ers
4222 E McLellan Cir Unit 15
Mesa, AZ 85205-3119, USA

Shellen, Stephen
615 Yonge St. #401
Toronto, ON M4Y I, CANADA

Shelley, Barbara (Actor)
Ken McReddie
91 Regent St
London W1R 7TB, UNITED KINGDOM (UK)

Shelley, Carole (Actor)
333 W 56th St
New York, NY 10019-3764, USA

Shelley, Howard G (Conductor, Musician)
38 Cholmeley Park
London N6 5ER, UNITED KINGDOM (UK)

Shelley, Rachel (Actor)
c/o Staff Member *Personal Management Company*
425 N Robertson Blvd
West Hollywood, CA 90048-1735, USA

Shelly, Randy (Actor)
c/o Ellen Gilbert *Abrams Artists Agency (LA)*
9200 W Sunset Blvd Ph 11
Los Angeles, CA 90069-3601, USA

Shelton, Abigail (Actor)
Dale Garrick
8831 W Sunset Blvd # 402
Los Angeles, CA 90069, USA

Shelton, Blake (Musician)
c/o Marc Dennis *William Morris Agency (WMA-TN)*
2100 W End Ave
Nashville, TN 37203-5200, USA

Shelton, Deborah (Actor)
c/o Marc Bass *Marc Bass Agency Inc*
9255 W Sunset Blvd Ste 727
West Hollywood, CA 90069-3304, USA

Shelton, L J (Football Player)
Arizona Cardinals
14844 S 30th St
Phoenix, AZ 85048-8714, USA

Shelton, Lonnie (Basketball Player)
860 S 8th Ave
Kingsburg, CA 93631, USA

Shelton, Marley (Actor)
c/o Stacy Boniello *The Firm*
9465 Wilshire Blvd Fl 6
Beverly Hills, CA 90212-2605, USA

Shelton, Peter (Architect)
Shelton Mindel Assoc
56 W 22nd St Fl 12
New York, NY 10010-7279, USA

Shelton, Richard (Football Player)
Denver Broncos
6367 Raw Hyde Trl N
Jacksonville, FL 32210-3821, USA

Shelton, Ricky Van (Musician, Songwriter, Writer)
PO Box 683
Lebanon, TN 37088-0683, USA

Shelton, Ron
2364 Hermits Gln
Los Angeles, CA 90046-1440, USA

Shelton, Ronald W (Director)
15200 Friends St
Pacific Palisades, CA 90272-4605, USA

Shelton, Samantha (Actor)
c/o Staff Member *Innovative Artists (LA)*
1505 10th St
Santa Monica, CA 90401-2805, USA

Shelton, William E (Educator)
Eastern Michigan University
President's Office
Ypsilanti, MI 48197, USA

Shen, Parry (Actor)
c/o Staff Member *Lichtman/Salners Company*
15865 Royal Haven Pl
Sherman Oaks, CA 91403-4724, USA

Shenandoah
PO Box 1547
Goodlettsville, TN 37070-1547, USA

Shenandoh, Joanne (Musician, Songwriter, Writer)
Oneida Nation Territory
PO Box 450
Oneida, NY 13421-0450, USA

Shenkman, Ben (Actor)
2 Charlton St Apt 5K
New York, NY 10014-4917, USA

Shepard, Dax (Actor, Reality TV Star)
c/o Greg Siegel *Endeavor Agency LLC (LA)*
9601 Wilshire Blvd Fl 3
Beverly Hills, CA 90210-5204, USA

Shepard, Devon (Producer, Writer)
c/o Staff Member *Agency for the Performing Arts (APA-LA)*
405 S Beverly Dr
Beverly Hills, CA 90212-4416, USA

Shepard, Jean (Musician)
Billy Deaton Talent
5811 Still Hollow Rd
Nashville, TN 37215-4819, USA

Shepard, Judy (Activist)
The Matthew Shepard Foundation
301 Thelma Dr # 512
Casper, WY 82609-2325, USA

Shepard, Kenny Wayne (Musician)
Ken Shephard Co
4361 Youree Dr # 200
Shreveport, LA 71105-3339, USA

Shepard, Kiki (Actor)
c/o Staff Member *Cunningham Escott Slevin & Doherty (LA)*
10635 Santa Monica Blvd Ste 130
Los Angeles, CA 90025-8306, USA

Shepard, Roger N (Psychic)
5775 Montclair Ave
Marysville, CA 95901-6820, USA

Shepard, Samuel K (Sam) (Actor, Writer)
c/o Jeff Melnick *Eighth Square Entertainment*
606 N Larchmont Blvd Ste 307
Los Angeles, CA 90004-1309, USA

Shepard, Vonda (Actor, Musician, Songwriter, Writer)
William Morris Agency
151 El Camino Dr
Beverly Hills, CA 90212-2775, USA

Sheperd, Ben (Musician)
Susan Silver Mgmt
6523 California Ave SW # 348
Seattle, WA 98136-1833, USA

Sheperd, Cybill (Actor, Model)
PO Box 261503
Encino, CA 91426-1503, USA

Sheperd, Elizabeth (Actor)
London Mgmt
2-4 Noel St
London W1V 3RB, UNITED KINGDOM (UK)

Sheperd, Morgan (Race Car Driver)
57 Rhody Creek Loop
Stuart, VA 24171-3011, USA

Shephard, Gillian P (Government Official)
House of Commons
Westminster
London SW1A 0AA, UNITED KINGDOM (UK)

Shepherd, Chris (Director, Writer)
c/o Staff Member *Slinky Pictures*
Old Truman Brewery
91 Brick Ln
London E16 QN, UNITED KINGDOM (UK)

Shepherd, Cybill (Actor)
c/o Judy Hofflund *Hofflund/Polone*
9465 Wilshire Blvd Ste 890
Beverly Hills, CA 90212-2607, USA

Shepherd, Gannon (Football Player)
Jacksonville Jaguars
5818 Alvaton Ct
Norcross, GA 30092-3901, USA

Shepherd, Kenny Wayne
4361 Youree Dr
Shreveport, LA 71105-3339, USA

Shepherd, Sherrie (Cartoonist)
United Feature Syndicate
200 Madison Ave
New York, NY 10016-3911, USA

Shepherd, William M (Astronaut)
18623 Prince William Ln
Houston, TX 77058-4224, USA

Shepherd (Sheperd), Sherri (Actor)
c/o Staff Member *Untitled Entertainment (LA)*
331 N Maple Dr Fl 3
Beverly Hills, CA 90210-3827, USA

Shepis, Tiffany
PO Box 1077
Venice, CA 90294-1077, USA

Sheppard, Alfred J (Business Person)
Court Mead
6 Guildown Ave Guilford
Surrey GU2 5HB, UNITED KINGDOM (UK)

Sheppard, Anna (Designer, Fashion Designer)
International Creative Mgmt
8942 Wilshire Blvd # 219
Beverly Hills, CA 90211-1908, USA

Sheppard, Bob (Baseball Player, Sportscaster)
2621 Park Ave
Baldwin, NY 11510-3645, USA

Sheppard, Jonathan (Misc)
287 Lamborntown Rd
West Grove, PA 19390-9237, USA

Sheppard, Julian (Comedian)
c/o Staff Member *Gersh Agency, The (LA)*
232 N Canon Dr
Beverly Hills, CA 90210-5302, USA

Sheppard, Mark (Actor)
c/o Staff Member *Stone Manners Talent & Literary (LA)*
6500 Wilshire Blvd Ste 550
Los Angeles, CA 90048-4950, USA

Sheppard, Mike (Coach, Football Coach)
University of New Mexico
Athletic Dept
Albuquerque, NM 87131-0001, USA

Sher, Antony (Actor)
Conway Van Gelder Robinson
18-21 Jermyn St
London SW1Y 6NB, UNITED KINGDOM (UK)

Shera, Mark (Actor)
PO Box 15717
Beverly Hills, CA 90209-1717, USA

Sherba, John (Musician)
Kronos Quartet
1235 9th Ave
San Francisco, CA 94122-2306, USA

Sherbedgia, Rade (Actor)
Innovative Artists
1505 10th St
Santa Monica, CA 90401-2805, USA

Sherer, Dave (Football Player)
Baltimore Colts
4212 Colgate Ave
Dallas, TX 75225-6603, USA

Sherffius, John (Cartoonist)
Saint Louis Post Dispatch
900 N Tucker Blvd
Editorial Dept
Saint Louis, MO 63101-1099, USA

Sheridan, Bonnie
18011 Martha St
Encino, CA 91316-1052, USA

Sheridan, Dave C (Actor, Writer)
c/o Daniel Rappaport *Management 360*
9111 Wilshire Blvd
Beverly Hills, CA 90210-5508, USA

Sheridan, Dinah (Actor)
International Creative Mgmt
76 Oxford St
London W1N 0AX, UNITED KINGDOM (UK)

Sheridan, Jamey (Actor)
c/o Scott Schachter *International Creative Management (ICM-LA)*
10250 Constellation Blvd
Los Angeles, CA 90067-6200, USA

Sheridan, Jim (Actor, Director, Producer, Writer)
c/o Staff Member *Creative Artists Agency LCC (CAA-LA)*
2000 Avenue Of The Stars
Los Angeles, CA 90067-4700, USA

Sheridan, Lisa (Actor)
c/o Staff Member *Burstein Company, The*
15304 W Sunset Blvd Ste 208
Pacific Palisades, CA 90272-3656, USA

Sheridan, Liz (Actor)
11333 Moorpark #427
West Hollywood, CA 91602, USA

Sheridan, Nicole (Adult Film Star)
c/o Staff Member *Atlas Multimedia Inc*
9035 Independence Ave
Canoga Park, CA 91304-1743, USA

Sheridan, Nicollette (Actor)
c/o Staff Member *Desperate Housewives*
2300 W Riverside Dr
Abc Television
Burbank, CA 91506-2976, USA

Sheridan, Rondell (Actor)
Gail Stocker Presents
1025 N Kings Rd Apt 113
Los Angeles, CA 90069-6007, USA

Sheridan, Tony (Musician)
Gems
PO Box 1031
Montrose, CA 91021-1031, USA

Sheriff, Haja (Actor)
20/1 Desikar Street
Chennai, TN 600 026, INDIA

Sherk, Jerry M (Football Player)
Cleveland Browns
1819 Bel Air Ter
Encinitas, CA 92024-5502, USA

Sherk, Kathy (Golfer)
Canadian Golf Hall of Fame
1333 Dorval Dr
Oakville, ON L6M 4G2, CANADA

Sherlock, Nancy J (Astronaut)
NASA
2101 Nasa Pkwy
Johnson Space Center
Houston, TX 77058-3691, USA

Sherlock-Currie, Nancy
2101 Nasa Pkwy
Houston, TX 77058-3607, USA

Sherman, Alex (Allie) (Coach, Football Coach, Football Player)
New York Off Track Betting Corp
1501 Broadway Ste 1000
New York, NY 10036-5505, USA

Sherman, Bobby (Actor, Musician)
1870 Sunset Plaza Dr
Los Angeles, CA 90069-1314, USA

Sherman, Cindy (Photographer)
Metro Pictures
519 W 24th St
New York, NY 10011-1104, USA

Sherman, Edgar A (Coach, Football Coach)
920 Sharon Valley Rd Apt 301
Newark, OH 43055-2874, USA

Sherman, Mike (Coach, Football Coach)
Green Bay Packers
PO Box 10628
Green Bay, WI 54307-0628, USA

Sherman, Richard M (Composer, Musician)
PO Box 17740
Beverly Hills, CA 90209-3740, USA

Sherman, Rod (Football Player)
Oakland Raiders
3410 Mira Vista Cir
San Jose, CA 95132-3123, USA

Sherman, Saul (Football Player)
Chicago Bears
175 E Delaware Pl Apt 6410
Chicago, IL 60611-7730, USA

Sherman-Palladino, Amy (Director, Producer, Writer)
c/o Rick Rosen *Endeavor Agency LLC (LA)*
9601 Wilshire Blvd Fl 3
Beverly Hills, CA 90210-5204, USA

Shernoff, William M (Attorney, Attorney General, General)
600 S Indian Hill Blvd
Claremont, CA 91711-5444, USA

Sherrard, Michael W (Mike) (Football Player)
Dallas Cowboys
5661 Colodny Dr
Agoura Hills, CA 91301-2217, USA

Sherrill, Jackie W (Coach, Football Coach)
Mississippi State University
Athletic Dept
Mississippi State, MS 39762, USA

Sherrin, Edward G (Ned) (Director)
4 Cornwall Mansions
Ashburnham Road
London SW10 0PE, UNITED KINGDOM (UK)

Sherrington, Georgina (Actor)
c/o Staff Member *JGM*
15 Lexham Mews
London W8 6JW, UNITED KINGDOM (UK)

Sherry, Lawrence (Larry) (Baseball Player)
22851 Hickory Hills Ave
Lake Forest, CA 92630-2966, USA

Sherry, Paul H (Religious Leader)
United Church of Christ
475 E Lockwood Ave
Saint Louis, MO 63119-3124, USA

Sherwin, Tim (Football Player)
Baltimore Colts
6 Mill Rd
Latham, NY 12110-1184, USA

Sherwood, Brad (Actor)
c/o Rich Super *Super Artists*
12021 Wilshire Blvd
Los Angeles, CA 90025-1206, USA

Sheshadri, Meenakshi (Actor, Bollywood)
601 Sheshadri Moonbeam
Union Park Khar (W)
Mumbai, MS 400052, INDIA

Shesol, Jeff (Cartoonist)
Creators Syndicate
5777 W Century Blvd Ste 700
Los Angeles, CA 90045-9023, USA

Shestakova, Tatyana B (Actor)
Maly Drama Theatre
Rubinstein St 18
Saint Petersburgh, RUSSIA

Shetty, Shilpa (Actor, Bollywood)
12 Dev Darshan
262 St Anthony Road Chembur
Mumbai, MS 400071, INDIA

Shetty, Sunil (Actor, Bollywood)
18/B Prithvi Apartments
Altamont Road
Mumbai, MS 400026, INDIA

Shevchenko, Arkady N (Politician)
Alfred Knopf/Ballantine/Fawcett Publishers
201 E 50th St
New York, NY 10022-7703, USA

Shi, David E (Educator)
Furman University
President's Office
Greenville, SC 29613-0001, USA

Shicoff, Neil (Opera Singer)
Opera et Concert
Maximilianstr 22
Munich 80539, GERMANY

Shields, Ben (Actor)
10965 Fruitland Dr Apt 102
Studio City, CA 91604-4601, USA

Shields, Billy (Football Player)
San Diego Chargers
12701 Treeridge Ter
Poway, CA 92064-6426, USA

Shields, Brooke (Actor, Model)
c/o Peter Safran *The Safran Company*
2000 Avenue Of The Stars Ste 600N
Los Angeles, CA 90067-4708, USA

Shields, Perry (Judge)
US Tax Court
400 2nd St NW
Washington, DC 20217-0002, USA

Shields, Robert (Misc)
Robert Shields Designs
PO Box 10024
Sedona, AZ 86339-8024, USA

Shields, Scott (Football Player)
Pittsburgh Steelers
3317 Kennelworth Ln
Bonita, CA 91902-1507, USA

Shields, Will H (Football Player)
Kansas City Chiefs
1 Arrowhead Dr
Kansas City, MO 64129-1651, USA

Shiely, John S (Business Person)
Briggs & Stratton
PO Box 702
Milwaukee, WI 53201-0702, USA

Shifty, Shellshock (Musician)
Q Prime
729 7th Ave Rm 1600
New York, NY 10019-6880, USA

Shigeta, James (Actor)
10635 Santa Monica Blvd Ste 130
Los Angeles, CA 90025-8306, USA

Shih, Wen Yann (Actor)
c/o Vincent Cirrincione *Vincent Cirrincione Associates*
1516 N Fairfax Ave
Los Angeles, CA 90046-2608, USA

Shikler, Aaron (Artist)
44 W 77th St
New York, NY 10024-5150, USA

Shiley, Newhouse Jean (Athlete, Track Athlete)
1100 Sunnybrae Ave
Chatsworth, CA 91311, USA

Shilton, Justin (Actor)
c/o Staff Member *Magnolia Entertainment*
9595 Wilshire Blvd Ste 601
Beverly Hills, CA 90212-2506, USA

Shilton, Peter (Soccer Player)
Hubbards Cottage
Bentley Lane
Maxstoke near Coleshill B46 2QR, UNITED KINGDOM (UK)

Shimada, Yoko
7245 Hillside Ave Apt 415
Los Angeles, CA 90046-2342, USA

Shimell, William (Opera Singer)
I M G Artists
3 Burlington Lane
Chiswick
London W4 2TH, UNITED KINGDOM (UK)

Shimerman, Armin (Actor)
Innovative Artists
1505 10th St
Santa Monica, CA 90401-2805, USA

Shimkis, Joanna
9255 Doheny Rd
Los Angeles, CA 90069-3201, USA

Shimkus, Joanna (Actor)
c/o Staff Member *Creative Artists Agency LCC (CAA-LA)*
2000 Avenue Of The Stars
Los Angeles, CA 90067-4700, USA

Shimono, Sab (Actor)
12711 Ventura Blvd Ste 440
Studio City, CA 91604-2456, USA

Shindle, Kate
2 Ocean Way Ste 1000
Atlantic City, NJ 08401-4111, USA

Shinefield, Henry R (Misc)
2240 Hyde St # 2
San Francisco, CA 94109-1509, USA

Shiner, Dick (Football Player)
Washington Redskins
19 Fox Trl
Gettysburg, PA 17325-7383, USA

Shinn, Christopher (Comedian)
c/o Staff Member *Gersh Agency, The (LA)*
232 N Canon Dr
Beverly Hills, CA 90210-5302, USA

Shinners, John (Football Player)
New Orleans Saints
N120W14985 Freistadt Rd
Germantown, WI 53022-2065, USA

Shinoda, Mike (Musician)
Artist Group International
9560 Wilshire Blvd Ste 400
Beverly Hills, CA 90212-2416, USA

Shiny Toy Guns (Music Group)
c/o Staff Member *Paradigm (Monterey)*
509 Hartnell St
Monterey, CA 93940-2825, USA

Shipkey, Jerry (Football Player)
Pittsburgh Steelers
PO Box 31259
Laughlin, NV 89028-1259, USA

Shipler, David K (Journalist)
4005 Thornapple St
Bethesda, MD 20815-5037, USA

Shipley, Walter V (Financier)
Chase Manhattan Corp
270 Park Ave
New York, NY 10017-2089, USA

Shipman, Clarie (Correspondent)
ABC-TV
77 W 66th St
News Dept
New York, NY 10023-6201, USA

Shipman, Kim (Golfer)
239 Texas Dr
Hideaway, TX 75771-5030, USA

Shipp, E R (Misc)
New York Daily News
220 E 42nd St
Editorial Dept
New York, NY 10017-5806, USA

Shipp, Jackie (Football Player)
Miami Dolphins
3117 Trails Ct
Norman, OK 73072-7459, USA

Shipp, Jerry (Basketball Player)
PO Box 370
Kingston, OK 73439-0370, USA

Shipp, John Wesley (Actor)
c/o Cindy Ambers *Verve Entertainment*
6140 Washington Blvd
Culver City, CA 90232-7465, USA

Shipp, William (Football Player)
New York Giants
3920 Camellia Dr
Mobile, AL 36693-2814, USA

Shirakawa, Hideki (Nobel Prize Laureate)
University of Tsukuba
Chemistry Dept
Sakura-Mura
Ibaraki 305, JAPAN

Shirayanagi, Peter Seiichi Cardinal
(Religious Leader)
Archbishop's House
3-16-15 Sekiguchi
Bunkyoku
Tokyo 112, JAPAN

Shire, David L (Composer)
19 Ludlow Ln
Palisades, NY 10964-1606, USA

Shire, Talia (Actor, Director)
10730 Bellagio Rd
Los Angeles, CA 90077-3730, USA

Shirelles, The
PO Box 100
Clifton, NJ 07015-0100, USA

Shirk, Gary (Football Player)
New York Giants
5419 Silchester Ln
Charlotte, NC 28215-5307, USA

Shirley, Al (Baseball Player)
716 Huntly Dr
Chesapeake, VA 23320-6649, USA

Shirley, George I (Opera Singer)
University of Michigan
Music School
Ann Arbor, MI 48109, USA

Shirley, J Dallas (Referee)
5324 Pommel Dr
Mount Airy, MD 21771-8124, USA

Shirley-Quirk, John S (Opera Singer)
6062 Red Clover Ln
Clarksville, MD 21029-1272, USA

Shirodkar, Namrata (Actor, Bollywood)
Venkatesh Vihar
7th Road Khar
Mumbai, MS 400052, INDIA

Shirodkar, Shilpa (Actor, Bollywood)
Venkatesh Vihar
4th Floor 7th Road Khar
Mumbai, MS 400050, INDIA

Shiver, Sanders (Football Player)
Baltimore Colts
9217 Christo Ct
Owings Mills, MD 21117-3596, USA

Shivers, Roy (Football Player)
St Louis Cardinals
2067 Hidden Hollow Ln
Henderson, NV 89012-3203, USA

Shivpuri, Himani (Actor)
16A/24 PGM Colony Poonam Nagar
Mahakali Caves Road Andheri (E)
Bombay, MS 400 093, INDIA

Shivpuri, Ritu (Actor, Bollywood)
12 Poonam 29/30 Pali Hill Union Bank
Khar
Bombay, MS 400 052, INDIA

Shlaudeman, Harry W (Diplomat)
7006 Pebble Beach Way
San Luis Obispo, CA 93401-8916, USA

Shlyapina, Galina A (Ballerina)
Bolshoi Theater
Teatralnaya Pl 1
Moscow 103009, RUSSIA

Shnayerson, Robert B (Editor)
118 Riverside Dr
New York, NY 10024-3708, USA

Shoals, Roger (Football Player)
Cleveland Browns
365 Righters Mill Rd
Gladwyne, PA 19035-1542, USA

Shobana (Actor, Bollywood)
77/5 Gulmohar Avenue
Velachery High Road
Chennai, TN 600032, INDIA

Shobana, Maganadhi (Actor, Bollywood)
A P 198
16th Street 2nd Sector
Chennai, TN 600078, INDIA

Shobert, Bubba (Race Car Driver)
8905 153rd St
Wolfforth, TX 79382-4305, USA

Shocked, Michelle (Musician)
Siddons Assoc
584 N Larchmont Blvd
Los Angeles, CA 90004-1306, USA

Shockey, Jeremy (Football Player)
c/o Team Member *New York Giants*
Giants Stadium
East Rutherford, NJ 07073, USA

Shockley, William (Actor)
6345 Balboa Blvd Ste 375
Encino, CA 91316-5238, USA

Shoecraft, John A (Misc)
Shoecraft Contracting Co
7430 E Stetson Dr
Scottsdale, AZ 85251-3566, USA

Shoeffling, Michael
PO Box 2563
Canyon Country, CA 91386-2563, USA

Shoemaker, Bill
250 W Main St # 1820
Lexington, KY 40507-1714, USA

Shoemaker, Craig (Actor)
c/o Rick Dorfman *Rick Dorfman Management*
450 W 15th St Ste 500
New York, NY 10011-7026, USA

Shoemaker, Robert M (General)
PO Box 768
Belton, TX 76513-0768, USA

Shoemaker, Sydney S (Misc)
104 Northway Rd
Ithaca, NY 14850-2241, USA

Shoemate, C Richard (Business Person)
Bestfoods
700 Sylvan Ave
International Plaza
Englewood Cliffs, NJ 07632-3150, USA

Shofner, Delbert M (Del) (Football Player)
1665 Del Mar Ave
San Marino, CA 91108-2621, USA

Shofner, James (Jim) (Football Player)
Cleveland Browns
9620 Champions Dr
Granbury, TX 76049-4447, USA

Shoji, Dave (Coach)
University of Hawaii
Athletic Dept
Hilo, HI 96720, USA

Shonekan, Ernest A O (President)
12 Alexander Ave
Ikoyi
Lagos, NIGERIA

Shonin, Georgi S (Cosmonaut, General)
Potchta Kosmonavtov
Moskovskoi Oblasti
Syvisdny Goroduk 141160, RUSSIA

Shonta, Charles J (Football Player)
Boston Patriots
37755 Westvale St
Romulus, MI 48174-4730, USA

Shoop, Ron
PO Box 92
Rural Valley, PA 16249-0092, USA

Shope, Allan (Architect)
Shope Reno Wharton
18 W Putnam Ave
Greenwich, CT 06830-5341, USA

Shore, David (Producer, Writer)
c/o Lawrence Shuman *Shuman Company*
3815 Hughes Ave Fl 4
Culver City, CA 90232-2715, USA

Shore, Howard (Actor, Composer, Musician)
Gortaine/Schwartz
13245 Riverside Dr Ste 450
Sherman Oaks, CA 91423-2172, USA

Shore, Pauly (Actor, Comedian)
c/o Staff Member *3 Arts Entertainment Inc*
9460 Wilshire Blvd Fl 7
Beverly Hills, CA 90212-2713, USA

Shore, Roberta
PO Box 71639
Salt Lake City, UT 84171-0639, USA

Shorr, Lonnie
707 18th Ave S
Nashville, TN 37203-3214, USA

Short, Columbus (Actor)
c/o Colton Gramm *Brillstein-Grey Entertainment*
9150 Wilshire Blvd Ste 350
Beverly Hills, CA 90212-3453, USA

Short, Martin (Actor, Comedian, Musician)
c/o Bernie Brillstein *Brillstein-Grey Entertainment*
9150 Wilshire Blvd Ste 350
Beverly Hills, CA 90212-3453, USA

Short, Nigel (Misc)
Daily Telegraph
Peterborough Court
Marsh Wall
London E14, UNITED KINGDOM (UK)

Short, Purvis (Basketball Player)
8111 Fondren Lake Dr
Houston, TX 77071-3610, USA

Short, Thomas C (Misc)
Theatrical Stage Employees Alliance
1515 Broadway
New York, NY 10036-8901, USA

Shorter, Frank (Athlete, Track Athlete)
558 Utica Ct
Boulder, CO 80304-0773, USA

Shorter, Wayne (Composer, Musician)
International Music Network
278 S Main St #400
Gloucester, MA 01930, USA

Shortridge, Steve (Actor)
1707 Clear View Dr
Beverly Hills, CA 90210-2012, USA

Shorts, Peter (Football Player)
New England Patriots
810 S Cedar Point Dr
Anaheim, CA 92808-1680, USA

Shostakovich, Maxim D (Musician)
PO Box 273
Jordanville, NY 13361-0273, USA

Shou, Robin (Actor)
Paradigm Agency
10100 Santa Monica Blvd Ste 2500
Los Angeles, CA 90067-4116, USA

Shoults, Paul (Football Player)
New York Bulldogs
530 Tanglewood Ln Apt 132
Mishawaka, IN 46545-2654, USA

Shout Out Louds (Music Group)
c/o Staff Member *Paradigm (Monterey)*
509 Hartnell St
Monterey, CA 93940-2825, USA

Show, Grant (Actor)
937 S Tremaine Ave
Los Angeles, CA 90019-1768, USA

Showalter, Buck
7501 Jefferson Ave
Century, FL 32535-2848, USA

Showalter, William N (Buck) III (Misc)
9736 Hathaway St
Dallas, TX 75220-2114, USA

Shower, Kathy (Actor, Model)
Provenca 23 1-1
Barcelona, SPAIN

Shraner, Kim (Actor)
c/o Robyn Friedman *Artist Management Inc*
464 King St E
Toronto, ON M5A 1L7, CANADA

Shreve, Anita (Writer)
c/o Sally Willcox *Creative Artists Agency LCC (CAA-LA)*
2000 Avenue Of The Stars
Los Angeles, CA 90067-4700, USA

Shreve, Susan R (Writer)
3506 35th St NW
Washington, DC 20016-3114, USA

Shribman, David M (Journalist)
Boston Globe
1130 Connecticut Ave NW
Editorial Dept
Washington, DC 20036-3943, USA

Shrimpton, Jean (Actor, Model)
Abbey Hotel Penzance
Cornwall, UNITED KINGDOM (UK)

Shriner, Kin (Actor)
Don Buchwald
6500 Wilshire Blvd Ste 2200
Los Angeles, CA 90048-4942, USA

Shriner, Wil (Entertainer)
5313 Quakertown Ave
Woodland Hills, CA 91364-3542, USA

Shriver, Anthony
100 SE 2nd St # 1990
Miami, FL 33131-2100, USA

The Celebrity Black Book 2008

Shriver, Bobby
501 Colorado Ave Ste 200
Santa Monica, CA 90401-2426, USA

Shriver, Duward F (Scientist)
1100 Colfax St
Evanston, IL 60201-2611, USA

Shriver, Eunice Kennedy (Business Person)
9109 Harnington Dr
Potomac, MD 20854, USA

Shriver, Loren J (Astronaut)
108 Charleston St
Friendswood, TX 77546-4928, USA

Shriver, Maria (Correspondent, Television Host)
c/o Richard Leibner *NS Bienstock Inc*
1740 Broadway Fl 24
New York, NY 10019-4382, USA

Shriver, Mark Kennedy
10015 Carter Rd
Bethesda, MD 20817, USA

Shriver, Pam
c/o Jill Smoller *William Morris Agency (WMA-LA)*
1 William Morris Pl
Beverly Hills, CA 90212-4261, USA

Shriver, R
1325 G St NW
Washington, DC 20005-3104, USA

Shriver Jr, R Sargent (Government Official)
Special Olympics Int'l
1133 19th St NW # 11
Washington, DC 20036-3604, USA

Shroff, Jackie (Actor, Bollywood)
1302 Le Pepeyon
Mount Mary Road Bandra
Mumbai, MS 400050, INDIA

Shrontz, Frank A (Business Person)
2949 81st Pl SE # P
Mercer Island, WA 98040-3059, USA

Shroud, Johnathan (Writer)
Laura Cecil Literary Agency
17 Alwyne Villas
London N1 2HG, UNITED KINGDOM (UK)

Shrowder, Lisa (Race Car Driver)
1650 E Golf Road
Schaumburg, IL 60196-0001, USA

Shroyer, Sonny (Actor)
12725 Ventura Blvd Ste F
Studio City, CA 91604-2437, USA

Shtalenkov, Mikhail (Hockey Player)
501 Broadway
Nashville, TN 37203-3932, USA

Shtokolov, Boris T (Opera Singer)
Mariinsky Theater
Teatralnaya Pl 1
Saint Petersburg, RUSSIA

Shuart, James M (Educator)
Hofstra University
President's Office
Hempstead, NY 11550, USA

Shue, Andrew (Actor)
c/o Jimmy Darmody *Creative Artists Agency LCC (CAA-LA)*
2000 Avenue Of The Stars
Los Angeles, CA 90067-4700, USA

Shue, Elisabeth (Actor)
c/o David Seltzer *Management 360*
9111 Wilshire Blvd
Beverly Hills, CA 90210-5508, USA

Shue, Gene (Coach)
4338 Redwood Ave Apt 303
Marina Del Rey, CA 90292-7648, USA

Shugart, Alan F (Inventor)
Seagate Technologies
920 Disc Dr
Scotts Valley, CA 95066-4542, USA

Shugart, Clyde (Football Player)
Washington Redskins
6368 Heronwalk Dr
Gulf Breeze, FL 32563-7024, USA

Shugarts, Bret (Football Player)
Pittsburgh Steelers
18823 Forest Bend Creek Way
Spring, TX 77379-5510, USA

Shukovsky, Joel (Writer)
Shukovsky-English Ent
4024 Radford Ave
Studio City, CA 91604-2101, USA

Shula, David D (Dave) (Coach, Football Player)
Baltimore Colts
10805 Indian Trl
Cooper City, FL 33328-5509, USA

Shula, Donald F (Don) (Coach, Football Coach, Football Player)
16 Indian Creek Island Rd
Indian Creek Village, FL 33154-2904, USA

Shula, Mike (Coach, Football Coach, Football Player)
Tampa Bay Buccaneers
13754 Bromley Point Dr
Jacksonville, FL 32225-2634, USA

Shuler, Heath (Football Player)
Washington Redskins
8550 Kingston Pike
Shuler Real Estate
Knoxville, TN 37919-5353, USA

Shuler, Mickey C (Football Player)
New York Jets
332 Belle Vista Dr
Marysville, PA 17053-9640, USA

Shuler Jr, Ellie G (Buck) (General)
32 Willow Ln
Alexander City, AL 35010, USA

Shulgin, Alexander (Scientist)
1483 Shulgin Rd
Lafayette, CA 94549-2226, USA

Shulman, Lawrence E (Scientist)
3726 Tudor Arms Ave
Baltimore, MD 21211-2245, USA

Shulock, John (Baseball Player)
4180 5th St SW
Vero Beach, FL 32968-3909, USA

Shumaker, John W (Educator)
University of Louisville
President's Office
Louisville, KY 40292-0001, USA

Shuman-Juransinski, Amy (Baseball Player)
424 Douglass St
Wyomissing, PA 19610-2906, USA

Shumate, John (Basketball Player, Coach)
1710 E Harwell Rd
Phoenix, AZ 85042-6882, USA

Shumate, Rachel (Actor)
c/o Sean Fay *Imparato Fay Management*
1126 Roxbury Dr
Los Angeles, CA 90035-1031, USA

Shut Up Stella (Music Group)
c/o Staff Member *Paradigm (Monterey)*
509 Hartnell St
Monterey, CA 93940-2825, USA

Shutt, Steve (Coach, Hockey Player)
Cimco Refrigeration
65 Villiers
Toronto, ON M5A 3S1, CANADA

Shuttleworth, Mark (Astronaut)
HBD Ventura Capital
PO Box 1159
Durbanville 7551, SOUTH AFRICA

Shuttz, George P
776 Dolores St
Stanford, CA 94305-8428, USA

Shy, Don (Football Player)
Pittsburgh Steelers
1645 Avenida Oceano
Oceanside, CA 92056-6948, USA

Shy, Les (Football Player)
Dallas Cowboys
512 N McClurg Ct Apt 3611
Chicago, IL 60611-4122, USA

Shyamalan, M Night (Director)
c/o Jeremy Zimmer *United Talent Agency (UTA)*
9560 Wilshire Blvd Ste 500
Beverly Hills, CA 90212-2401, USA

Shydner, Ritch (Comedian)
c/o Staff Member *Agency for the Performing Arts (APA-LA)*
405 S Beverly Dr
Beverly Hills, CA 90212-4416, USA

Shyer, Charles R (Director, Writer)
227 N Glenroy Ave
Los Angeles, CA 90049-2417, USA

Shys, The (Music Group)
c/o Staff Member *Paradigm (Monterey)*
509 Hartnell St
Monterey, CA 93940-2825, USA

Sia, Beau (Actor)
c/o Staff Member *Creative Artists Agency LCC (CAA-LA)*
2000 Avenue Of The Stars
Los Angeles, CA 90067-4700, USA

Siana (Model)
PO Box 4957
Virginia Beach, VA 23454-0957, USA

Siani, Michael J (Mike) (Football Player)
Oakland Raiders
9768 Leyland Dr Unit 11
Myrtle Beach, SC 29572-5553, USA

Sias, John B (Publisher)
Chronicle Publishing Co
901 Mission St
San Francisco, CA 94103-2905, USA

Sibbett, Jane (Actor)
c/o John Carrabino *John Carrabino Management*
5900 Wilshire Blvd Ste 406
Los Angeles, CA 90036-5015, USA

Sibley, Antoinette (Ballerina)
Royal Dancing Academy
36 Battersea Square
London SW11 3LT, UNITED KINGDOM (UK)

Sibley, David (Actor)
c/o Staff Member *Select Artists Ltd (CA-Westside Office)*
1138 12th St Apt 1
Santa Monica, CA 90403-5459, USA

Sicard, Pedro (Actor)
c/o Gabriel Blanco *Gabriel Blanco Iglesias (Mexico)*
Rio Balsas 35-32
Colonia Cuauhtemoc
DF 06500, MEXICO

Sichting, Jerry (Basketball Player)
3190 N Country Club Rd
Martinsville, IN 46151-7929, USA

Siddig, Alexander (Actor)
c/o Pippa Markham *Markham and Froggatt Agency*
4 Windmill St
London W1T 1HF, UNITED KINGDOM (UK)

Siddiqui, Farouge (Director, Filmmaker)
16/24 Old Collector Compound
Malvani Colony Gate No 5 Malad
Bombay, MS 400 095, INDIA

Siddle, Joseph (Baseball Player)
Kansas City Monarchs
5532 Bunch Rd
Summerfield, NC 27358-9084, USA

Siddons, Ann Rivers (Writer)
60 Church St
Charleston, SC 29401-2558, USA

Siddons, Anne R (Writer)
767 Vermont Road
Atlanta, GA 30319, USA

Sidenbladh, Goran (Architect)
Narvagen 23
Stockholm 114 60, SWEDEN

Sider, Harvey R (Religious Leader)
Brethren in Christ Church
PO Box 290
Grantham, PA 17027-0290, USA

Sidgmore, John (Business Person)
WorldCom
500 Clinton Center Dr
Clinton, MS 39056-5654, USA

Sidime, Lamine (Prime Minister)
Prime Minister's Office
Conakry, GUINEA

Sidlin, Murry (Conductor)
Catholic University
Music School
Washington, DC 20064-0001, USA

Sidney, Dainon (Football Player)
Tennessee Titans
605 Lakemeade Pt
Old Hickory, TN 37138-2588, USA

Sidney, Laurin
PO Box 105366
Atlanta, GA 30348-5366, USA

Sidransky, David (Doctor, Scientist)
Baylor Medical Center
1200 Moursund St
Houston, TX 77030-3404, USA

Sieber, Christopher (Actor)
c/o Richard Fisher *Abrams Artists Agency (NY)*
275 7th Ave Fl 26
New York, NY 10001-6708, USA

Siebert, Sonny
2583 Brush Creek Rd
Saint Louis, MO 63129-5601, USA

Siebert, Wilfred C (Sonny) (Baseball Player)
2555 Brush Creek Rd
Saint Louis, MO 63129-5601, USA

Siega, Marcos (Director)
c/o Staff Member *Endeavor Agency LLC (LA)*
9601 Wilshire Blvd Fl 3
Beverly Hills, CA 90210-5204, USA

Siegal, Bernard (Writer)
61 0X Bow Ln
Woodbridge, CT 06525, USA

Siegal, Jay (Music Group, Musician)
Brothers Mgmt
141 Dunbar Ave
Fords, NJ 08863-1551, USA

Siegal, John (Football Player)
Chicago Bears
Harvey's Bt
Harveys Lake, PA 18618, USA

Siegbahn, Kai M B (Nobel Prize Laureate)
University of Uppasala
Physics Institute
Box 530
Uppasala 75 121, SWEDEN

Siegel, Barry (Journalist)
Los Angeles Times
202 W 1st St
Editorial Dept
Los Angeles, CA 90012-4105, USA

Siegel, Bernie S (Doctor, Writer)
61 Oxbow Ln
Woodbridge, CT 06525-1525, USA

Siegel, Eric (Actor)
c/o Staff Member *Pure Arts Entertainment*
1925 Century Park E Ste 2320
Los Angeles, CA 90067-2724, USA

Siegel, Herbert J (Business Person)
Chris-Craft Industries
767 5th Ave
New York, NY 10153-0023, USA

Siegel, Ira T (Publisher)
16589 Senterra Dr
Delray Beach, FL 33484-6986, USA

Siegel, Janis (Musician)
International Creative Mgmt
40 W 57th St Ste 1800
New York, NY 10019-4001, USA

Siegel, Joel (Correspondent)
c/o Staff Member *Good Morning America (NY)*
147 Columbus Ave Fl 6
Abc
New York, NY 10023-6503, USA

Siegel, L Pendleton (Business Person)
Potlatch Corp
601 W Riverside Ave
Spokane, WA 99201-0621, USA

Siegel, Norman (Attorney)
Committee for Norman Siegel
260 Madison Ave
New York, NY 10016-2401, USA

Siegel, Robert C (Correspondent)
c/o Gregory (Greg) McKnight *Creative Artists Agency LCC (CAA-LA)*
2000 Avenue Of The Stars
Los Angeles, CA 90067-4700, USA

Siegert, Herb (Football Player)
Washington Redskins
PO Box 256
Pana, IL 62557-0256, USA

Siegert, Wayne (Football Player)
New York Yankees
401 E 4th St
Pana, IL 62557-1655, USA

Siegfried (Magician)
Beyond Belief
1639 Valley Dr
Las Vegas, NV 89108-2002, USA

Siegfried, Larry (Basketball Player)
4178 Covert Rd
Perrysville, OH 44864-9320, USA

Siemaszko, Casey (Actor)
Gersh Agency
232 N Canon Dr
Beverly Hills, CA 90210-5302, USA

Siemaszko, Nina (Actor)
c/o David Rose *Innovative Artists (LA)*
1505 10th St
Santa Monica, CA 90401-2805, USA

Sieminski, Chuck (Football Player)
San Francisco 49ers
5000 Village Way Apt 406
Marcus Hook, PA 19061-6857, USA

Siemon, Jeffrey G (Jeff) (Football Player)
Minnesota Vikings
5401 Londonderry Rd
Edina, MN 55436-1026, USA

Sienkiewicz, Troy (Football Player)
San Diego Chargers
186 Darcy Ave
Goose Creek, SC 29445-6664, USA

Siepi, Cesare (Opera Singer)
12095 Brookfield Club Dr
Roswell, GA 30075-1261, USA

Siering, Lauri (Swimmer)
3829 Rotterdam Ave
Modesto, CA 95356-0739, USA

Sierra, Jessica (Musician)
c/o *Network Solutions*
PO Box 447
Herndon, VA 20172-0447, USA

Sierra, Pedro (Baseball Player)
Indianapolis Clowns
11013 Horde St
Silver Spring, MD 20902-3617, USA

Sierra, Ruben A (Baseball Player)
c/o Staff Member *New York Mets*
12301 Roosevelt Ave
Shea Stadium
Flushing, NY 11368-1699, USA

Sierra, Rubin
Ed25 #2501 Jardines Selles
Rio Piedras, PR 00924, USA

Siers, Kevin (Cartoonist, Editor)
Charlotte Observer
600 S Tryon St
Editorial Dept
Charlotte, NC 28202-1842, USA

Sievers, Eric (Football Player)
San Diego Chargers
11550 Great Falls Way
Great Falls, VA 22066-1148, USA

Sievers, Roy E (Baseball Player)
11505 Bellefontaine Rd
Saint Louis, MO 63138-1706, USA

Sieverts, Thomas C W (Architect)
Buschstr 20
Bonn 53113, GERMANY

Sifford, Charlie (Golfer)
PO Box 43128
Highland Heights, OH 44143-0128, USA

Sific, Mokdad (Prime Minister)
Prime Minister's Office
Government Palais
Al-Moradia
Algiers, ALGERIA

Sigel, Beanie (Musician)
International Creative Mgmt
8942 Wilshire Blvd # 219
Beverly Hills, CA 90211-1908, USA

Sigel, Jay (Golfer)
1284 Farm Rd
Berwyn, PA 19312-2000, USA

Sigel, Tom (Cinematographer)
International Creative Mgmt
8942 Wilshire Blvd # 219
Beverly Hills, CA 90211-1908, USA

Sigholtz, Bob
5425 Shirley Ave
Tarzana, CA 91356-2910, USA

Sigler-Discala, Jamie-Lynn (Actor)
c/o Andrea Pett-Joseph *Brillstein-Grey Entertainment*
9150 Wilshire Blvd Ste 350
Beverly Hills, CA 90212-3453, USA

Sigman, Stan (Business Person)
Cingular Creative Mgmt
5565 Glenridge Connector NE
Atlanta, GA 30342-4756, USA

Signaigo, Joe (Football Player)
New York Yankees
1687 Bryn Mawr Cir
Germantown, TN 38138-2618, USA

Sigoloff, Sanford
320 N Cliffwood Ave
Los Angeles, CA 90049-2618, USA

Sigur Ros (Music Group)
c/o Staff Member *Paradigm (Monterey)*
509 Hartnell St
Monterey, CA 93940-2825, USA

Sigurdson, Sig (Football Player)
Baltimore Colts
2233 NW 59th St Apt 103
Seattle, WA 98107-3155, USA

Sigwart, Ulrich (Doctor)
Centre Hospitalier Universitaire Vaudois
Lausanne, SWITZERLAND

Siilasvuo, Ensio (General)
Castrenikatu 6A17
Helsinki 53 00530, FINLAND

Sikahema, Vai (Football Player)
St Louis Cardinals
28 Abington Rd
Mount Laurel, NJ 08054-4720, USA

Sikes, Alfred C (Government Official)
3214 Kirwans Neck Rd
Church Creek, MD 21622-1323, USA

Sikes, Cynthia (Actor)
250 Delfern Dr
Los Angeles, CA 90077-3543, USA

Sikharulidze, Anton (Figure Skater)
Ice House Skating Rink
111 Midtown Bridge Approac
Hackensack, NJ 07601-7505, USA

Sikich, Mike P (Football Player)
Cleveland Browns
702 Tudor Dr
Janesville, WI 53546-2001, USA

Sikking, James B (Actor)
258 S Carmelina Ave
Los Angeles, CA 90049-3957, USA

Sikma, Jack (Basketball Player)
8005 SE 28th St
Mercer Island, WA 98040-2911, USA

Silas, James (Basketball Player)
823 Congress Ave # 610
Austin, TX 78701-2405, USA

Silas, Paul (Basketball Player, Coach)
2463 Peninsula Shores Ct
Denver, NC 28037-7655, USA

Silatolu, Ratu Timoci (Prime Minister)
Prime Minister's Office
6 Berkeley Crescent
Suva
Viti Levu, FIJI

Silber, John R (Educator)
132 Carlton St
Brookline, MA 02446-4009, USA

Silberling, Bradley (Brad) (Director, Producer)
Creative Artists Agency
9830 Wilshire Blvd
Beverly Hills, CA 90212-1804, USA

Silberman, Laurence H (Diplomat, Judge)
US Court of Appeals
3rd & Constitution NW
Washington, DC 20001, USA

Silberstein, Diane Wichard (Publisher)
New Yorker Magazine
4 Times Sq
Publisher's Office
New York, NY 10036-6592, USA

Silbey, Robert J (Misc)
Massachusetts Institute of Technology
Chemistry Dept
Cambridge, MA 02139, USA

Sileo, Dan (Football Player)
Tampa Bay Buccaneers
5000 Culbreath Key Way Apt 1317
Tampa, FL 33611-3054, USA

Silja, Anja (Opera Singer)
Colbert Artists
111 W 57th St
New York, NY 10019-2236, USA

Silk (Artist, Musician)
Creative Artists Agency
9830 Wilshire Blvd
Beverly Hills, CA 90212-1804, USA

Silk, David (Dave) (Hockey Player)
4 Glen Ridge Ter
Norwell, MA 02061-1137, USA

Silla, Felix
8927 Snowden Ave
Arleta, CA 91331-6115, USA

Sillas, Karen (Actor)
PO Box 725
Wading River, NY 11792-0725, USA

Silliman, Michael B (Mike) (Basketball Player)
6602 Deep Creek Dr
Prospect, KY 40059-9441, USA

Sillitoe, Alan (Writer)
14 Ladbroke Terrace
London W11 3PG, UNITED KINGDOM (UK)

Sills, Douglas (Actor, Musician)
Gold Marshak Liedike
3500 W Olive Ave Ste 1400
Burbank, CA 91505-5512, USA

Sills, Stephen (Architect, Designer)
Sills Huniford Assoc
30 E 67th St
New York, NY 10065-6120, USA

Silva, Adele (Actor, Model)
c/o Staff Member *McLean-Williams Management*
212 Piccadilly
London W1H 9HG, UNITED KINGDOM (UK)

Silva, Daniel (Writer)
3512 Winfield Ln NW
Washington, DC 20007-2344, USA

Silva, Gilberto (Football Player)
Arsenal Stadium
Highbury
London N5 1BU, ENGLAND

Silva, Henry (Actor)
8747 Clifton Way Apt 305
Beverly Hills, CA 90211-2125, USA

Silva, Jackie (Volleyball Player)
Marcia Esposito
PO Box 931416
Los Angeles, CA 90093-1416, USA

Silva, Tom (Entertainer)
This Old House Show
PO Box 2284
South Burlington, VT 05407-2284, USA

Silva, Zack (Actor)
Valeo Entertainment
8265 W Sunset Blvd Ste 103
C/O Michael Dean Valeo
West Hollywood, CA 90046-2433, USA

Silver, Claudia (Producer)
c/o Staff Member *Writers and Artists Group Intl (LA)*
8383 Wilshire Blvd Ste 550
Beverly Hills, CA 90211-2417, USA

Silver, Edward J (Religious Leader)
Bible Way Church
5118 Clarendon Rd
Brooklyn, NY 11203-5329, USA

Silver, Horace (Composer, Musician)
Bridge Agency
35 Clark St Apt A5
Brooklyn, NY 11201-2374, USA

Silver, Jeffrey (Producer)
c/o Staff Member *Outlaw Productions*
9350 Civic Center Dr Ste 100
Beverly Hills, CA 90210-3629, USA

Silver, Joan Macklin (Director)
Silverfilm Productions
510 Park Ave # 9B
New York, NY 10022-1105, USA

Silver, Joel (Producer)
c/o Staff Member *Silver Pictures*
4000 Warner Blvd Bldg 90
Burbank, CA 91522-0001, USA

Silver, Michael B
9229 W Sunset Blvd Ste 315
Los Angeles, CA 90069-3403, USA

Silver, Ron (Actor)
c/o David Seltzer *Management 360*
9111 Wilshire Blvd
Beverly Hills, CA 90210-5508, USA

Silverchair
Box 15
Merewether NSW 2291, AUSTRALIA

Silverman, Al (Publisher)
411 E 53rd St
16H
New York, NY 10022-5106, USA

Silverman, Barry G (Judge)
US Court of Appeals
230 N 1st St
Phoenix, AZ 85004, USA

Silverman, Fred
1642 Mandeville Canyon Rd
Los Angeles, CA 90049-2524, USA

Silverman, Henry R (Business Person)
Cendant Corp
9 W 57th St
New York, NY 10019-2701, USA

Silverman, Jonathan (Actor)
c/o Beth Holden-Garland *Untitled Entertainment (LA)*
331 N Maple Dr Fl 3
Beverly Hills, CA 90210-3827, USA

Silverman, Kenneth E (Educator, Writer)
New York University
19 University Pl
English Dept
New York, NY 10003-4556, USA

Silverman, Sarah (Comedian)
c/o Judy Wixon-Darmody *Mosaic Media Group*
24 Music Sq W Fl 1
Nashville, TN 37203-6661, USA

Silvers, Robert (Artist)
Henry Holt
115 W 18th St
New York, NY 10011-4113, USA

Silverstein, Elliott (Director)
Gersh Agency
232 N Canon Dr
Beverly Hills, CA 90210-5302, USA

Silverstein, Joseph H (Conductor, Musician)
Utah Symphony Orchestra
123 W South Temple
Salt Lake City, UT 84101-1403, USA

Silverstone, Alicia (Actor)
c/o Staff Member *First Kiss Productions*
468 N Camden Dr # 200
Beverly Hills, CA 90210-4507, USA

Silverstone, Ben (Actor)
c/o Staff Member *London Management*
2-4 Noel St
London W1V 3RB, UNITED KINGDOM (UK)

Silvestre, Armando
Cerro Macultepec 273Col. Campestre Churubusco
Mexico DF, MEXICO

Silvestri, Alan A (Composer)
Gorfaine/Schwartz
4111 W Alameda Ave Ste 509
Burbank, CA 91505-4171, USA

Silvestri, Carl (Football Player)
St Louis Cardinals
330 W White Oak Way
Thiensville, WI 53092-6249, USA

Silvestrini, Achille Cardinal (Religious Leader)
Oriental Churches Congregation
Via Conciliazione 34
Rome 00193, ITALY

Silvia (Royalty)
Kungliga Slottet
Stottsbacken
Stockholm 111 30, SWEDEN

Silvstedt, Victoria (Actor, Model)
Andy Gould Mgmt
8484 Wilshire Blvd Ste 425
Beverly Hills, CA 90211-3235, USA

Sim, Gerald (Actor)
Associated Internationl Mgmt
7 Great Russell St
London W1D 1BS, UNITED KINGDOM (UK)

Sim, Sheila
Old Friars Richmond Greene
Surrey, ENGLAND, UNITED KINGDOM (UK)

Simanek, Robert E (War Hero)
25194 Westmoreland Dr
Farmington Hills, MI 48336-1270, USA

Simcoe, Anthony (Actor)
c/o Staff Member *Farscape*
PO Box 20726
New York, NY 10023-1488, USA

Sime, David W (Dave) (Athlete, Doctor, Track Athlete)
240 Harbor Dr
Key Biscayne, FL 33149-1218, USA

Simeon II (King, Prime Minister)
Prime Minister's Office
1 Dondukov Blvd
Sofia 1000, BULGARIA

Simeoni, Sara (Athlete, Track Athlete)
Via Castello Rivoli Veronese
Verona 37010, ITALY

Simhan, Meera (Actor)
Bamboo Management
17 Buccaneer St
C/O Heidi L Ifft
Marina Del Rey, CA 90292-5103, USA

Simic, Charles (Writer)
PO Box 192
Strafford, NH 03884-0192, USA

Simien, Tracy (Football Player)
Kansas City Chiefs
3219 Sumac Dr
Pearland, TX 77584-8069, USA

Simien, Wayne (Basketball Player)
c/o Staff Member *Miami Heat*
601 Biscayne Blvd
American Airlines Arena
Miami, FL 33132-1801, USA

Simitis, Costas (Prime Minister)
35 Akadanuas St
Athens 106 72, GREECE

Simkus, Arnold (Football Player)
New York Jets
4248 Chicago Rd
Warren, MI 48092-1471, USA

Simmel, Johannes Mario
Bohlgutsch 3
Zug CH-6300, SWITZERLAND

Simmonds, Kennedy A (Prime Minister)
PO Box 167
Earle Mome Development
Basseterre, SAINT KITTS & NEVIS

Simmons, Arthur (Baseball Player)
Kansas City Monarchs
27 158th Pl Apt 2W
Calumet City, IL 60409-4945, USA

Simmons, Bob (Football Player)
Kansas City Chiefs
16040 Chalfont Cir
Dallas, TX 75248-3544, USA

Simmons, Brian (Football Player)
Cincinnati Bengals
311 Sena Dr
Metairie, LA 70005-3343, USA

Simmons, Chelan (Actor)
c/o Staff Member *Pacific Artists Management*
1404-510 W Hastings St
Vancouver, BC V6B 1L8, CANADA

Simmons, Curtis T (Curt) (Baseball Player)
200 Park Rd
Ambler, PA 19002-1121, USA

Simmons, Dick
3215 E Silvercliff Cir
Prescott, AZ 86303-5708, USA

Simmons, Earl (DMX) (Actor, Musician)
c/o Charles King *William Morris Agency (WMA-LA)*
1 William Morris Pl
Beverly Hills, CA 90212-4261, USA

Simmons, Ed (Football Player)
Washington Redskins
PO Box 6632
Kennewick, WA 99336-0639, USA

Simmons, Floyd (Chunk) (Athlete, Track Athlete)
2330 Pembroke Ave Apt 8
Charlotte, NC 28207-2147, USA

Simmons, Gene (Musician)
c/o Staff Member *Gene Simmons Company, The*
PO Box 16075
Beverly Hills, CA 90209-2075, USA

Simmons, Henry (Actor)
c/o E Brian Dobbins *Principato/Young Management*
9665 Wilshire Blvd Ste 500
Beverly Hills, CA 90212-2312, USA

Simmons, Hubert (Baseball Player)
Baltimore Elite Giants
3247 Sonia Trl
Ellicott City, MD 21043-3273, USA

Simmons, J K (Actor)
c/o Staff Member *Gersh Agency, The (LA)*
232 N Canon Dr
Beverly Hills, CA 90210-5302, USA

Simmons, Jaason (Actor)
Gilbertson & Kincaid Mgmt
1330 4th St
Santa Monica, CA 90401-1302, USA

Simmons, Jason (Football Player)
Pittsburgh Steelers
2828 Spring St
Pittsburgh, PA 15210-2675, USA

Simmons, Jean (Actor)
636 Adelaide Dr
Santa Monica, CA 90402-1352, USA

Simmons, Jerry (Football Player)
Pittsburgh Steelers
2233 S King Dr
Chicago, IL 60616-1415, USA

Simmons, John E (Baseball Player, Basketball Player)
9 Lee Dr
Farmingdale, NY 11735-5407, USA

Simmons, Joseph (Artist, Musician)
Entertainment Artists
2409 21st Ave S Ste 100
Nashville, TN 37212-5317, USA

Simmons, Kimora Lee (Designer, Fashion Designer)
c/o Staff Member *Phat Fashions LLC*
512 Fashion Ave Rm 4300
New York, NY 10018-4743, USA

Simmons, Lionel J (Basketball Player)
108 Wellesley Ct
Mount Laurel, NJ 08054-5133, USA

Simmons, Richard (Actor, Misc, Producer)
Richard Simmons Inc
8899 Beverly Blvd Ste 506
Los Angeles, CA 90048-2447, USA

Simmons, Richard D (Publisher)
Int'l Herald Tribune
181 Ave Charles de Gaulie
Neuilly 92521, FRANCE

Simmons, Richard P (Business Person)
Allegheny Teledyne
1000 6 Ppg Place
Pittsburgh, PA 15222, USA

Simmons, Russell (Producer)
c/o Staff Member *Rush Communications*
512 Fashion Ave Rm 4300
New York, NY 10018-4743, USA

Simmons, Ruth (Educator)
Brown University
President's Office
Providence, RI 02912-0001, USA

Simmons, Shadia (Actor)
265 Ga Highway 30 W
Americus, GA 31719-8502, USA

Simmons, Stacey (Football Player)
Indianapolis Colts
1780 Harbor Dr
Clearwater, FL 33755-1828, USA

Simmons, Ted L (Baseball Player)
PO Box 26
Chesterfield, MO 63006-0026, USA

Simmons, Todd (Baseball Player)
39778 Pinedale Way
Murrieta, CA 92562-6719, USA

Simmons, Tony (Football Player)
San Diego Chargers
366 Grand Ave Apt 319
Oakland, CA 94610-4840, USA

Simmons, Vanessa (Model)
c/o Staff Member *Ford Models (LA)*
8826 Burton Way
Beverly Hills, CA 90211-1715, USA

Simmons, Victor (Football Player)
Dallas Cowboys
PO Box 2992
Chicago, IL 60690-2992, USA

Simms, Chris (Football Player)
c/o Team Member *Tampa Bay Buccaneers*
1 Bucaneer Place
Tampa, FL 33607, USA

Simms, Joan (Actor)
MGA
Southbank House
Black Prince Road
London SE1 7SJ, UNITED KINGDOM (UK)

Simms, Kimberley (Actor)
House of Representatives
211 S Beverly Dr Ste 208
Beverly Hills, CA 90212-3879, USA

Simms, Larry (Actor)
1043 Keeho Marina
Honolulu, HI 96819, USA

Simms, Philip (Phil) (Football Player, Sportscaster)
New York Giants
930 Old Mill Rd
Franklin Lakes, NJ 07417-1906, USA

Simms, Primate George Otto (Religious Leader)
62 Cypress Grove Road
Dublin 6, IRELAND

Simms, Willie (Baseball Player)
Kansas City Monarchs
4020 W 29th St
Los Angeles, CA 90018-2823, USA

Simollardes, Drew (Musician)
David Levin Mgmt
200 W 57th St Ste 308
New York, NY 10019-3211, USA

Simon, Bob (Correspondent)
c/o Staff Member *60 Minutes*
524 W 57th St
Cbs News
New York, NY 10019-2930, USA

Simon, Carly (Musician, Songwriter, Writer)
c/o Kerri Brusca *KB Management*
137 5th Ave Fl 8
New York, NY 10010-7141, USA

Simon, Corey (Football Player)
Philadelphia Eagles
9010 Winged Foot Dr
Tallahassee, FL 32312-4000, USA

Simon, David (Actor, Producer, Writer)
c/o Staff Member *Creative Artists Agency LCC (CAA-LA)*
2000 Avenue Of The Stars
Los Angeles, CA 90067-4700, USA

Simon, Dick (Race Car Driver)
Dick Simon Racing
701 S Girls School Rd
Indianapolis, IN 46231-3132, USA

Simon, George W (Astronaut)
PO Box 62
Sunspot, NM 88349-0062, USA

Simon, James (Football Player)
Detroit Lions
8501 SW 103rd Ave
Gainesville, FL 32608-7206, USA

Simon, John I (Critic)
New York Magazine
444 Madison Ave
Editorial Dept
New York, NY 10022-6999, USA

Simon, Josette (Actor)
Conway Van Gelder Robinson
18-21 Jermyn St
London SW1Y 6NB, UNITED KINGDOM (UK)

Simon, Neil (Writer)
c/o Staff Member *William Morris Agency (WMA-LA)*
1 William Morris Pl
Beverly Hills, CA 90212-4261, USA

Simon, Paul (Musician, Songwriter, Writer)
c/o Rob Light *Creative Artists Agency LCC (CAA-LA)*
2000 Avenue Of The Stars
Los Angeles, CA 90067-4700, USA

Simon, Roger M (Writer)
Baltimore Sun
1627 K St NW
Editorial Dept
Washington, DC 20006-1702, USA

Simon, Salem (Football Player)
Baltimore Ravens
2245 Sheridan Rd
Evanston, IL 60201-2918, USA

Simon, Sam
c/o Gary Cosay *United Talent Agency (UTA)*
9560 Wilshire Blvd Ste 500
Beverly Hills, CA 90212-2401, USA

Simon, Scott (Correspondent)
NBC-TV
30 Rockefeller Plz Ste 270E
News Dept
New York, NY 10112-0299, USA

Simone, Albert J (Educator)
Rochester Institute of Technology
President's Office
Rochester, NY 14623, USA

Simoneau, Mark (Football Player)
Atlanta Falcons
17 Waterview Dr
Sicklerville, NJ 08081-1683, USA

Simoneau, Yves
151 El Camino Dr
Beverly Hills, CA 90212-2704, USA

Simonini, Edward (Ed) (Football Player)
Baltimore Colts
3825 E 66th St
Tulsa, OK 74136-2820, USA

Simonis, Adrianus J Cardinal (Religious Leader)
Aartbisdom
BP 14019 Maliebaan
Utrecht, SB 3508, THE NETHERLANDS

Simonon, Paul (Musician)
Premier Talent
3 E 54th St # 1100
New York, NY 10022-3108, USA

Simonov, Yuriy I (Conductor)
Moscow Conservatory
Gertsema St 13
Moscow, RUSSIA

Simons, Elwyn L (Misc)
Duke University
3705 Erwin Rd
Primate Center
Durham, NC 27705-5031, USA

Simons, Lawrence B (Government Official)
Powell Goldstein Frazier
1001 Pennsylvania Ave NW
Washington, DC 20004-2505, USA

Simonsen, Renee (Actor, Model)
Ford Model Agency
142 Greene St # 400
New York, NY 10012-3236, USA

Simonson, Dave (Football Player)
Baltimore Colts
408 1st St SW
Austin, MN 55912-3254, USA

Simple Kid (Music Group)
c/o Staff Member *Paradigm (Monterey)*
509 Hartnell St
Monterey, CA 93940-2825, USA

Simple Plan (Music Group)
c/o Staff Member *Creative Artists Agency LCC (CAA-LA)*
2000 Avenue Of The Stars
Los Angeles, CA 90067-4700, USA

Simply Red (Music Group)
PO Box 20197
London W10 6YQ, UNITED KINGDOM (UK)

Simpson, Alan (Educator)
Yellow Gate Farm
Little Compton, RI 02837, USA

Simpson, Alan K (Senator)
1201 Sunshine Ave
PO Box 270
Cody, WY 82414-4228, USA

Simpson, Arnelle
11661 San Vicente Blvd # 632
Los Angeles, CA 90049-5103, USA

Simpson, Ashlee (Actor, Musician)
c/o Brandt Joel *Creative Artists Agency LCC (CAA-LA)*
2000 Avenue Of The Stars
Los Angeles, CA 90067-4700, USA

Simpson, Bill (Football Player)
Los Angeles Rams
5732 Huntley Ave
Garden Grove, CA 92845-2040, USA

Simpson, Carole (Correspondent)
ABC-TV
77 W 66th St
News Dept
New York, NY 10023-6201, USA

Simpson, Charles R (Judge)
US Tax Court
400 2nd St NW
Washington, DC 20217-0002, USA

Simpson, Geoffrey (Cinematographer)
PO Box 3194
Bellevue Hills, NSW 2023, AUSTRALIA

Simpson, Herbert (Baseball Player)
Birmingham Black Barons
1462 Farragut St
New Orleans, LA 70114-2818, USA

Simpson, Jason
11661 San Vicente Blvd # 632
Los Angeles, CA 90049-5103, USA

Simpson, Jessica (Musician)
c/o Rob Light *Creative Artists Agency LCC (CAA-LA)*
2000 Avenue Of The Stars
Los Angeles, CA 90067-4700, USA

Simpson, Jimmi (Actor)
Agency for the Performing Arts
485 Madison Ave
New York, NY 10022-5803, USA

Simpson, Joanne G (Scientist)
NASA/GSFC
Mail Code 912
Earth Sciences Center
Greenbelt, MD 20771-0001, USA

Simpson, Joe (Producer)
c/o Brandt Joel *Creative Artists Agency LCC (CAA-LA)*
2000 Avenue Of The Stars
Los Angeles, CA 90067-4700, USA

Simpson, Juliene Brazinski (Basketball Player)
PO Box 1267
Stroudsburg, PA 18360-4267, USA

Simpson, Keith (Football Player)
Seattle Seahawks
20710 Castle Bend Dr
Katy, TX 77450-4911, USA

Simpson, Louis A M (Writer)
7 Stony Rd
Stony Brook, NY 11790-1525, USA

Simpson, Orenthal James (OJ) (Actor, Football Player, Sportscaster)
Buffalo Bills
9450 SW 112th St
Miami, FL 33176-3648, USA

Simpson, Ralph (Basketball Player)
7578 S Duquesne Way
Aurora, CO 80016-1317, USA

Simpson, Scott (Golfer)
15778 Paseo Hermoso
Poway, CA 92064-2164, USA

Simpson, Stern Carol (Misc)
American Assn of University Professors
1012 14th St NW
Washington, DC 20005-3465, USA

Simpson, Suzi (Actor, Model)
24338 El Toro Rd # E315
Laguna Woods, CA 92637-2776, USA

Simpson, Terry (Coach)
Anaheim Mighty Ducks
2000 E Gene Autry Way
Anaheim, CA 92806-6143, USA

Simpson, Wayne K (Baseball Player)
330 E Collamer Dr
Carson, CA 90746-1139, USA

Simpson Sr, John F (Race Car Driver)
Mount Morris Star Route
Waynesburg, PA 15370, USA

Simpy Red (Music Group)
c/o Staff Member *Lee & Thompson*
15 St Christopher's Pl
London W1M 5HE, UNITED KINGDOM (UK)

Simran (Actor)
C/o Hotel Residency
Thyagaraya Nagar
Chennai, TN 600 017, INDIA

Sims, Barry (Football Player)
Oakland Raiders
19945 Summerridge Dr
Castro Valley, CA 94552-5322, USA

Sims, Billy R (Football Player)
Detroit Lions
PO Box 3147
Coppell, TX 75019-9147, USA

Sims, Darryl (Football Player)
Pittsburgh Steelers
PO Box 379
Mc Farland, WI 53558-0379, USA

Sims, Joan
17 Esmond Ct.Thackery St.
London, ENGLAND WE 5HB, UNITED KINGDOM (UK)

Sims, Keith (Football Player)
Miami Dolphins
2920 Luckle Rd
Weston, FL 33331, USA

Sims, Ken (Football Player)
St Louis Cardinals
4898 Converse Ave
East Saint Louis, IL 62207-2533, USA

Sims, Kenneth W (Football Player)
New England Patriots
PO Box 236
Kosse, TX 76653-0236, USA

Sims, Molly (Actor)
c/o Alissa Vradenburg *Untitled Entertainment (LA)*
331 N Maple Dr Fl 3
Beverly Hills, CA 90210-3827, USA

Sin, Jaime L Cardinal (Religious Leader)
121 Arzobispo St Entramuros
PO Box 132
Manila 10099, PHILIPPINES

Sinatra, Nancy (Actor, Musician)
7215 Williams Rd
Lansing, MI 48911-3036, USA

Sinatra, Ray
1234 8th Pl
Las Vegas, NV 89104-1555, USA

Sinbad (Actor, Comedian)
c/o Scott Simpson *Agency for the Performing Arts (APA-LA)*
405 S Beverly Dr
Beverly Hills, CA 90212-4416, USA

Sinceno, Kaseem (Football Player)
Philadelphia Eagles
168B Bradford Ct
Mount Laurel, NJ 08054, USA

Sinceros
25 Buliver St.Shephard's Bush
London, ENGLAND W12 8AR, UNITED KINGDOM (UK)

Sinclair, Clive M (Inventor)
Sinclair Research
7 York Central
70 York Way
London N1 9AG, UNITED KINGDOM (UK)

Sinclair, Harry (Director, Writer)
c/o Ken Kamins *International Creative Management (ICM-LA)*
10250 Constellation Blvd
Los Angeles, CA 90067-6200, USA

Sinclair, Joshua (Actor, Director, Producer, Writer)
c/o Staff Member *Sun Gateway Entertainment*
Taubenheimstr 30
70372, GERMANY

Sinclair, Michael (Football Player)
Seattle Seahawks
14215 Heidi Oaks Ln
Humble, TX 77396-3497, USA

Sindelar, Jerry
213 Prospect Hill Rd
Horseheads, NY 14845, USA

Sindelar, Joan (Baseball Player)
504 W Sunland Ave
Phoenix, AZ 85041-4822, USA

Sindelar, Joey (Golfer)
18 Prospect Rdg
Horseheads, NY 14845-7988, USA

Sinden, Donald A (Actor)
Rats Castle
Isle of Oxney
Kent TN30 7HX, UNITED KINGDOM (UK)

Sinden, Harry (Hockey Player)
9 Olde Village Dr
Winchester, MA 01890-2213, USA

Sinfelt, John H (Misc)
Exxon Research & Engineering
Clinton Township
RR 22E
Annadale, NJ 08801, USA

Singer, Bryan (Director)
c/o David Wirtschafter *William Morris Agency (WMA-LA)*
1 William Morris Pl
Beverly Hills, CA 90212-4261, USA

Singer, Lori (Actor)
Chuck Binder
1465 Lindacrest Dr
Beverly Hills, CA 90210-2519, USA

Singer, Marc (Actor)
11218 Canton Dr
Studio City, CA 91604-4154, USA

Singer, Maxine F (Educator)
5410 39th St NW
Washington, DC 20015-2902, USA

Singer, Peter A D (Misc)
Princeton University
Human Values Center
Princeton, NJ 08544-0001, USA

Singer, S Fred (Physicist)
4084 University Dr Ste 101
Fairfax, VA 22030-6803, USA

Singer, William R (Bill) (Baseball Player)
1119 Mallard Marsh Dr
Osprey, FL 34229-6810, USA

Singh, Amrita (Actor, Bollywood)
Bungalow 5
Lokhandwala Complex Andheri Link Road
Mumbai, MS 400058, INDIA

Singh, Archana Puran (Actor, Bollywood)
G426 Anjali Apartments
Seven Bungalows Anheri
Mumbai, MS 400061, INDIA

Singh, Bipin (Choreographer, Dancer)
Manipuri Nartanalaya
15A Bipin Pal Road
Kolkata, WB 700026, INDIA

Singh, Chandrachur (Actor, Bollywood)
6th Floor Oakland Park
Off Lokhandwala Complex Versova
Mumbai, MS 400049, INDIA

Singh, Dara (Actor, Bollywood)
Dara Villa Mamta Apartments
Ground Floor A. B. Nair Road Juhu
Mumbai, MS 400049, INDIA

Singh, Manmohan (Prime Minister)
Premier's Office
South Block
Safdarjung Road
New Delhi, Delhi 110011, INDIA

Singh, Tjinder (Musician)
Legends of 21st Century
7 Trinity Row
Florence, MA 01062-1931, USA

Singh, Vijay (Golfer)
1275 Ponte Vedra Blvd
Ponte Vedra Beach, FL 32082-4402, USA

Singh, Vishwanath Pratap (Prime Minister)
1 Teen Murti Marg
New Delhi, ND 110001, INDIA

Singletary, Daryl
1000 18th Ave S
Nashville, TN 37212-2105, USA

Singletary, Michael (Mike) (Football Player)
Chicago Bears
14982 Sobey Rd
Saratoga, CA 95070-6236, USA

Singletary, Tony (Director)
c/o Lee Dintsman *Agency for the Performing Arts (APA-LA)*
405 S Beverly Dr
Beverly Hills, CA 90212-4416, USA

Singleton, Chris (Football Player)
New England Patriots
301 E Redwood Ln
Phoenix, AZ 85048-3004, USA

Singleton, Doris
344 Dalehurst Ave
Los Angeles, CA 90024-2512, USA

Singleton, Isaac (Actor)
c/o Nadja Koglin *Richard Schwartz Management*
2934 1/2 N Beverly Glen Cir # 107
Los Angeles, CA 90077-1724, USA

Singleton, John D (Director, Producer, Writer)
New Deal Productions
5555 Melrose Ave
Los Angeles, CA 90038-3989, USA

Singleton, Kenneth W (Kenny) (Baseball Player)
10 Sparks Farm Rd
Sparks, MD 21152-9300, USA

Singleton, Margie (Musician)
PO Box 567
Hendersonville, TN 37077-0567, USA

Sinha, Mala (Actor)
8 Turner Road
Bandra
Bombay, MS 400 050, INDIA

Sinha, Shatrughan (Actor, Bollywood, Politician)
104 Green Star Apts Rizvi Complex
Sherly Rajan Road Bandra
Bombay, MS 400 050, INDIA

Sinise, Gary (Actor)
c/o Marc Gurvitz *Brillstein-Grey Entertainment*
9150 Wilshire Blvd Ste 350
Beverly Hills, CA 90212-3453, USA

Sinn, Pearl (Golfer)
132 21st Pl
Manhattan Beach, CA 90266-4402, USA

Sinner, George A (Governor)
101 3rd St N
Moorhead, MN 56560-1952, USA

Sinnott, John (Football Player)
Baltimore Colts
9 Primrose Ln
North Providence, RI 02904-3840, USA

Sinowatz, Fred (Government Official, Governor)
Loewelstr 18
Vienna 1010, AUSTRIA

Sinton, Nell (Artist)
484 Lake Park Ave # 189
Oakland, CA 94610-2730, USA

Sinyavskaya, Tamara I (Opera Singer)
Kunstleragentur Raab & Bohm
Plankengasse 7
Vienna 1010, AUSTRIA

Siouxsie & The Banshees
1325 Avenue Of The Americas
New York, NY 10019-6026, USA

Siouzsie, Sioux (Musician)
Helter Skelter
Plaza
535 Kings Road
London SW10 0S, UNITED KINGDOM (UK)

Sipchen, Bob (Journalist)
Los Angeles Times
202 W 1st St
Editorial Dept
Los Angeles, CA 90012-4105, USA

Sipe, Brian W (Football Player)
Cleveland Browns
1630 Luneta Dr
Del Mar, CA 92014-2435, USA

Siphandon, Khamtay (General, President)
President's Office
Vientiane, LAOS

Sipinen, Arto K (Architect)
Arkkitehtitoimistro Arto Sipinen Ky
Ahertajantie 3
Espoo 02100, FINLAND

Sippy, G P (Actor)
3/G Naaz Building
Lamington Road
Bombay, MS 400 004, INDIA

Sippy, Raj (Bollywood, Director, Filmmaker, Producer)
101 Jal Tarang Kishore Kumar Ganguly Marg
Juhu Tara Road
Bombay, MS 400 049, INDIA

Sippy, Ramesh (Bollywood, Director, Filmmaker, Producer)
379 Sathe House 14th Road
Khar
Bombay, MS 400 052, INDIA

Sippy Cups, The (Music Group)
c/o Staff Member *Paradigm (Monterey)*
509 Hartnell St
Monterey, CA 93940-2825, USA

Sir Douglas Quintet
59 Parsons St.
Newtonville, MA 02160, USA

Siragusa, Tony (Football Player)
Indianapolis Colts
349 Ashwood Ave
Kenilworth, NJ 07033-2056, USA

Siren, Heikki (Architect)
Tiirasaarentie 35
Heisinki 00200, FINLAND

Siren, Katri A H (Architect)
Tiirasaarentie 35
Heisinki 00200, FINLAND

Sirgo, Otto (Actor)
c/o Staff Member *Televisa*
Blvd Adolfo Lopez Mateos 232
Colonia San Angel INN
DF CP 01060, MEXICO

Sirhan, Sirhan
#B21014 Corcoran State Prison Box 8800
Corcoran, CA 93212, USA

Siri Singh Sahib (Religious Leader)
Sikh
PO Box 351149
Los Angeles, CA 90035-9549, USA

Sirico, Tony (Actor)
c/o Bob McGowan *McGowan Management*
8733 W Sunset Blvd Ste 103
W Hollywood, CA 90069-2241, USA

Sirikit (Royalty)
Chritrada Villa
Bangkok, THAILAND

Sirmon, Peter (Football Player)
Tennessee Titans
5255 McGavock Rd
Brentwood, TN 37027-5197, USA

Sirtis, Marina (Actor)
15030 Ventura Blvd # 710
Sherman Oaks, CA 91403-5470, USA

Sisco, Joseph J (Engineer, Government Official)
2702 Parkview Dr
Riva, MD 21140-1017, USA

Sisemore, Jerald G (Jerry) (Football Player)
Philadelphia Eagles
17301 Whippoorwill Trl
Leander, TX 78645-9734, USA

Sisk, John (Football Player)
Chicago Bears
7814 W Wisconsin Ave
Wauwatosa, WI 53213-3420, USA

Sislen, Myrna (Musician)
Lindy Martin Mgmt
5 Loblolly Ct
Pinehurst, NC 28374-9349, USA

Sisqo (Musician)
c/o Jason Priluck *Agency Group Ltd, The (LA)*
1880 Century Park E Ste 711
Los Angeles, CA 90067-1618, USA

Sissel (Musician)
Stageway Impressario
Skuteviksboder 11
Bergen 5035, NORWAY

Sissel, George A (Business Person)
Ball Corp
10 Longs Peak Dr
Broomfield, CO 80021-2510, USA

Sissi (Actor)
c/o Staff Member *Univision*
605 3rd Ave Fl 12
New York, NY 10158-1299, USA

Sisson, Scott (Football Player)
New England Patriots
902 Ravenwood Way
Canton, GA 30115-6421, USA

Sissons, Kimber (Actor)
412 Amaz Dr #204
Los Angeles, CA 90048, USA

Sister, Max (Designer, Fashion Designer)
Mount Everest Centre for Buddhist Studies
Kathmandu, NEPAL

Sister Hazel (Music Group)
c/o Staff Member *Sixthman*
158 Moreland Ave SE
Atlanta, GA 30316-1676, USA

Sister Sledge (Music Group)
c/o Staff Member *Tony Denton Promotions Limited (UK)*
19 South Molton Way
London W1K 5LE, UNITED KINGDOM (UK)

Sisters of Mercy
28 Kensington Church St.
London, ENGLAND W8 4EP, UNITED KINGDOM (UK)

Sisti, Sebastian D (Sibby) (Baseball Player)
38 Clifford Hts
Amherst, NY 14226, USA

Sisto, Jeremy (Actor)
Innovative Artists
1505 10th St
Santa Monica, CA 90401-2805, USA

Sistrunk, Manny (Football Player)
Washington Redskins
1601 Jarvis Ave
Oxon Hill, MD 20745-3243, USA

Sistrunk, Otis (Football Player)
Oakland Raiders
PO Box 372
Dupont, WA 98327-0372, USA

Sites, Brian (Actor)
c/o Staff Member *Innovative Artists (LA)*
1505 10th St
Santa Monica, CA 90401-2805, USA

Sites, James W (Producer)
American Legion Magazine
700 N Pennsylvania St
Indianapolis, IN 46204-1129, USA

Sithara (Actor, Bollywood)
556 I Floor
2nd Block 2nd Cross R T Nagar
Bangalore, KA 560032, INDIA

Sitkovetsky, Dmitry (Musician)
Columbia Artists Mgmt Inc
1790 Broadway Fl 6
New York, NY 10019-1412, USA

Sitter, Charles R (Business Person)
Exxon Corp
5959 Las Colinas Blvd
Irving, TX 75039-2298, USA

Sittler, Walter (Actor)
Agentur Heppeler
Seinstr 54
Munich 81667, GERMANY

Sivad, Darryl
400 S Beverly Dr Ste 101
Beverly Hills, CA 90212-4403, USA

Sivam, Peeli (Actor)
43 Parthasarathy Pettai
II Street
Chennai, TN 600 086, INDIA

Sivaranjani (Ooha) (Actor, Bollywood)
7 Vivekananda Nagar
Nesapakkam
Chennai, TN 600092, INDIA

Six Shooter
PO Box 53
Portland, TN 37148-0053, USA

Sixx
9255 W Sunset Blvd # 200
Los Angeles, CA 90069-3309, USA

Sixx, Nikki (Musician)
936 Vista Ridge Ln
Westlake Village, CA 91362-5612, USA

Siza, Alvaro (Architect)
Oporto University
Architecture School
Oporto, PORTUGAL

Sizemore, Matt (Adult Film Star)
c/o Staff Member *Diva Central Inc*
7510 W Sunset Blvd Ste 1445
Los Angeles, CA 90046-3408, USA

Sizemore, Tom (Actor)
United Talent Agency
9560 Wilshire Blvd Ste 500
Beverly Hills, CA 90212-2401, USA

Sizemore, Tom (Educator)
Brown University
Essential Schools Coalition
Providence, RI 02912-0001, USA

Sizova, Alla I (Ballerina)
Universal Ballet School
4301 Harewood Rd NE
Washington, DC 20017-1514, USA

Sjoberg, Patrik (Athlete, Track Athlete)
Hokegatan 17
Goteberg 416 66, SWEDEN

Skaggs, Jim (Football Player)
Philadelphia Eagles
421 Falcon Ridge Rd
Ellensburg, WA 98926-5037, USA

Skaggs, Ricky (Actor, Musician)
c/o Bobby Cudd *Paradigm (Nashville)*
124 12th Ave S Ste 410
Nashville, TN 37203-3170, USA

Skah, Khalid (Athlete, Track Athlete)
Boite Postale 2577
Fez, MOROCCO

Skala, Brian T (Actor)
c/o Staff Member *Osbrink Talent Agency*
4343 Lankershim Blvd # 100
North Hollywood, CA 91602-2705, USA

Skarsgard, J Stellan (Actor)
Hogersgatan 40
Stockholm 118 26, SWEDEN

Skarsgard, Stellan (Actor)
Hogbergsgatan 40 II
Stockholm S-118 26, SWEDEN

Skarsten, Rachel (Actor)
c/o Steve Lovett *Lovett Management*
1327 Brinkley Ave
Los Angeles, CA 90049-3619, USA

Skaugstad, Daryle (Football Player)
Houston Oilers
17216 NE 195th St
Woodinville, WA 98072, USA

Skayskal, Wayne
PO Box 191
Tampa, FL 33601-0191, USA

Skeels, Mark (Baseball Player)
1835 Hilton Head Rd
El Cajon, CA 92019-4472, USA

Skeen, Archie (Baseball Player)
2685 N 4275 W
Ogden, UT 84404-9074, USA

Skeeters, The (Music Group)
c/o Staff Member *Paradigm (Monterey)*
509 Hartnell St
Monterey, CA 93940-2825, USA

Skeggs, Leonard T Jr (Misc)
10212 Blair Ln
Kirtland, OH 44094-9514, USA

Skeie, Andris (Prime Minister)
Prime Minister's Office
Brivibus Bulv 36
Riga, PDP 226170, LATVIA

Skelton, Byron G (Judge)
US Court of Appeals
717 Madison Pl NW
Washington, DC 20439-0001, USA

Skerritt, Tom (Actor)
United Talent Agency
9560 Wilshire Blvd Ste 500
Beverly Hills, CA 90212-2401, USA

Skibbie, Lawrence F (General)
2309 S Queen St
Arlington, VA 22202-1550, USA

Skibinski, Joe (Football Player)
Cleveland Browns
1912 Pine St
Peru, IL 61354-1828, USA

Skibniewska, Halina (Architect)
Wydzlat Architektury Politechniki
Ul Koszykowa 55
Warsaw 00-659, POLAND

Skid Row (Music Group)
c/o Doc McGhee *McGhee Entertainment*
8730 W Sunset Blvd Ste 175
Los Angeles, CA 90069-2246, USA

Skinner, Frank (Actor, Writer)
Avalon Management Group Ltd
4a Exmoor Street
London, England W10 6BD, UNITED
KINGDOM (UK)

Skinner, Jane (Anchor)
c/o Staff Member *Fox News Channel (NY)*
1211 Avenue Of The Americas
Level C1
New York, NY 10036-8701, USA

Skinner, Jimmy (Coach, Hockey Player)
2860 Askin Ave
Windsor, ON N9E 3H9, CANADA

Skinner, Joel P (Baseball Player)
275 Pamilla Cir
Avon Lake, OH 44012-1973, USA

Skinner, Jonty (Coach, Swimmer)
University of Alabama
Athletic Dept
Tuscaloosa, AL 35487-0001, USA

Skinner, Mike (Musician)
attn: Christopher Evans
Stark House Farm
Goose Hill, Thatcham RG19 8AR,
UNITED KINGDOM (UK)

Skinner, Mike (Race Car Driver)
Mike Skinner Enterprises
221 Cessna Blvd
Daytona Beach, FL 32124, USA

Skinner, Robert R (Bob) (Baseball Player)
1576 Diamond St
San Diego, CA 92109-3050, USA

Skinner, Samuel K (Business Person, Secretary)
Commonwealth Edison
PO Box 767
1 First National Plaza
Chicago, IL 60690-0767, USA

Skinner, Sonny (Golfer)
114 Northlake Dr
Sylvester, GA 31791-3909, USA

Skinner, Val (Golfer)
44 Bridge Ave
Bay Head, NJ 08742-4747, USA

Skjelbreid, Ann-Elen (Athlete)
5640 Eikelandsosen
NORWAY

Skladany, Thomas E (Tom) (Football Player)
Detroit Lions
6666 Highland Lakes Pl
Westerville, OH 43082-8703, USA

Sklvorecky, Josef (Writer)
Erindale College
English Dept
Toronto, ON M5S 1A5, CANADA

Skoczen, Stan (Football Player)
Cleveland Rams
6368 Brecksville Rd
Seven Hills, OH 44131-3405, USA

Skol, Michael (Diplomat)
PO Box 596
Dennis, MA 02638-0596, USA

Skolimowski, Jerzy (Director)
Film Polski
Ul Mazowiecka 6/8
Warsaw 00-048, POLAND

Skolnick, Mark H (Scientist)
University of Utah
Medical Center
Genetics Dept
Salt Lake City, UT 84112, USA

Skoog, Meyer (Whitey) (Basketball Player, Coach)
35689 398th Ln
Saint Peter, MN 56082-4333, USA

Skopil Jr, Otto R (Judge)
US Court of Appeals
700 SW 6th Ave Ste 211
Pionner Courthouse
Portland, OR 97204-1434, USA

Skorich, Nick (Football Player)
Pittsburgh Steelers
9 Briarwood Ct
Columbus, NJ 08022-1102, USA

Skoronski, Bob (Football Player)
Green Bay Packers
3907 Signature Dr
Middleton, WI 53562-2388, USA

Skorupan, John P (Football Player)
Buffalo Bills
142 Crossing Ridge Trl
Cranberry Township, PA 16066-6512,
USA

Skotheim, Robert A (Misc)
2120 Place Rd
Port Angeles, WA 98363-9664, USA

Skou, Jens C (Nobel Prize Laureate)
Rislundvej 9
Risskov 8240, DENMARK

Skouras, Thanos (Economist)
8 Chlois St
Athens 145 62, GREECE

Skovhus, Bo (Opera Singer)
Balmer & Dixon Mgmt
Granitweg 2
Zurich 8006, SWITZERLAND

Skowron, Bill (Baseball Player)
1118 Beach Comber Dr
Schaumburg, IL 60193-3832, USA

Skowron, Moose
1118 Beach Comber Dr
Schaumburg, IL 60193-3832, USA

Skrebneski, Victor (Photographer)
1350 N Lasalle St
Chicago, IL 60610-1911, USA

Skrepenak, Greg (Football Player)
Oakland Raiders
Hyders Total Fitnbess Center 400 Middle
Rd
Nanticoke, PA 18634, USA

Skribble (DJ)
c/o Len Evans *Project Publicity*
312 W 53rd St
New York, NY 10019-5743, USA

Skrien, Dave (Football Player)
Philadelphia Eagles
445 Enchanted Dr
Mound, MN 55364, USA

Skrovan, Steve (Comedian)
c/o Staff Member *William Morris Agency (WMA-LA)*
1 William Morris Pl
Beverly Hills, CA 90212-4261, USA

Skrowaczewski, Stanislaw (Composer)
Minnesota Symphony
1111 Nicollet Mall
Minneapolis, MN 55403, USA

Skrypnk, Metropolitan Mstyslav S (Religious Leader)
Ukranian Orthodox Church
PO Box 445
South Bound Brook, NJ 08880-0445, USA

Skvorecky, Josef V (Writer)
487 Sackville St
Montreal, ON M4X 1T6, CANADA

Sky, Jennifer (Actor)
12533 Woodgreen St
Los Angeles, CA 90066-2723, USA

Skye, Azura (Actor)
c/o Dominique Appel *BWR (BWR-LA)*
9100 Wilshire Blvd Fl 6
West Tower
Beverly Hills, CA 90212-3401, USA

Skye, Ione (Actor)
8794 Lookout Mountain Ave
Los Angeles, CA 90046-1859, USA

Skyrms, Brian (Misc)
University of California
Philosophy Dept
Irvine, CA 92717, USA

Slaby, Lou (Football Player)
New York Giants
6 Elder Pl
Denville, NJ 07834-9312, USA

Slack, Reggie (Football Player)
Houston Oilers
5973 Queen St
Milton, FL 32570-3574, USA

Slade, Bernard N (Writer)
345 N Saltair Ave
Los Angeles, CA 90049-2914, USA

Slade, Chris (Football Player)
New England Patriots
4810 Ivy Ridge Dr SE Unit 201
Smyrna, GA 30080-6652, USA

Slade, Chris (Musician)
11 Leominster Road
Morden
Surrey SA4 6HN, UNITED KINGDOM
(UK)

Slade, Mark (Actor)
38 Joppa Rd
Worcester, MA 01602-2230, USA

Slade, Roy (Artist)
Cranbrook Academy Art Museum
PO Box 801
Bloomfield Hills, MI 48303-0801, USA

Slagle, James R
13630 Barryknoll Ln
Houston, TX 77079-5928, USA

Slaney, Mary Decker (Athlete, Track Athlete)
87141 Kellmore St
Eugene, OR 97402-9128, USA

Slash (Musician)
801 N Roxbury Dr
Beverly Hills, CA 90210-3017, USA

Slater, Bob (Baseball Player)
4322 Avenida Rio Del Oro
Yorba Linda, CA 92886-3011, USA

Slater, Christian (Actor)
c/o Perry Zimel *Oscars Abrams Zimel & Associates*
438 Queen St E
Toronto, ON M5A 1T4, CANADA

Slater, Helen (Actor)
1327 Brinkley Ave
Los Angeles, CA 90049-3619, USA

Slater, Jackie (Football Player)
Los Angeles Rams
PO Box 6411
Orange, CA 92863-6411, USA

Slater, Jock C K (John) (Admiral)
Naval Secretary
Victory Bldg
HM Naval Base
Portsmouth PO1 3LS, UNITED
KINGDOM (UK)

Slater, Kelly (Actor, Athlete)
SLAM Management
31652 2nd Ave
Laguna Beach, CA 92651-8244, USA

Slater, Mark (Football Player)
San Diego Chargers
10545 Rome Ave
Young America, MN 55397-9468, USA

Slater, Ryan
3500 W Olive Ave Ste 1400
Burbank, CA 91505-5512, USA

Slater, Suzanne
10000 Riverside Dr Ste 10
Toluca Lake, CA 91602-2537, USA

Slatkin, Leonard E (Conductor)
Washington National Symphony
Kennedy Center
Washington, DC 20011, USA

Slaton, Mike (Football Player)
Minnesota Vikings
7691 Park Village Rd
San Diego, CA 92129-4514, USA

Slaton, Tony (Football Player)
Los Angeles Rams
122 E Childs Ave
Merced, CA 95341-6346, USA

Slattery, John (Actor)
c/o Staff Member *Gersh Agency, The (LA)*
232 N Canon Dr
Beverly Hills, CA 90210-5302, USA

Slattvik, Simon (Athlete)
Bankgata 22
Lillehammer 2600, NORWAY

Slatzer, Robert F
PO Box 1075
Los Angeles, CA 90078-1075, USA

Slaughter (Music Group)
c/o Staff Member *Artist Representation & Management*
1257 Arcade St
Saint Paul, MN 55106-2022, USA

Slaughter, Frank (Doctor)
Box 14 Ortega Station
Jacksonville, FL 32210, USA

Slaughter, J Mack (Actor)
c/o Jeff Golenberg *The Collective*
9100 Wilshire Blvd # 700 W
Beverly Hills, CA 90212-3401, USA

Slaughter, John B (Educator)
Occidental College
President's Office
Los Angeles, CA 90041, USA

Slaughter, Mickey (Football Player)
Denver Broncos
1402 Mesa Ave
Ruston, LA 71270-2032, USA

Slaughter, Webster (Football Player)
Cleveland Browns
3706 Rory Ct
Missouri City, TX 77459-6662, USA

Slavin, Randall (Actor)
Gold Marshak Liedtke
3500 W Olive Ave Ste 1400
Burbank, CA 91505-5512, USA

Slavitt, David R (Writer)
35 West St Apt 5
Cambridge, MA 02139-1723, USA

Slay, Brandon (Wrestler)
6155 Lehman Dr
Colorado Springs, CO 80918-3456, USA

Sleater, Lou (Baseball Player)
St Louis Cardinals
12 Bandon Ct Unit 102
Timonium, MD 21093-7504, USA

Sledge, Leroy (Football Player)
Houston Oilers
6036 Golden Gate Cir
Dallas, TX 75241-5258, USA

Sledge, Percy (Musician)
c/o Terry Shields
9430 Palmetto Ln
Shreveport, LA 71118-4012, USA

Sleep, Wayne (Actor, Choreographer, Dancer)
22 Queensberry Mews West
London SW7 2DY, UNITED KINGDOM (UK)

Sleepy Jackson, The (Music Group)
c/o Staff Member Paradigm (Monterey)
509 Hartnell St
Monterey, CA 93940-2825, USA

Slegr, Jiri (Hockey Player)
Vancouver Canucks
800 Griffiths Way
Vancouver, BC V6B 6G1, CANADA

Slegr, Jirl (Hockey Player)
Boston Bruins
1 Fleetcenter Pl Ste 250
Boston, MA 02114-1390, USA

Slezak, Erika (Actor)
International Creative Mgmt
40 W 57th St Ste 1800
New York, NY 10019-4001, USA

Slichter, Charles P (Physicist)
61 Chestnut Ct
Champaign, IL 61822-7121, USA

Slichter, Jacob (Musician)
Monterey Peninsula Artists
509 Hartnell St
Monterey, CA 93940-2825, USA

Slick, Grace (Musician, Songwriter, Writer)
Bill Thompson Mgmt
5956 Kanan Dume Rd
Malibu, CA 90265-4027, USA

Slick, Rick (Musician)
Famous Artists Agency
250 W 57th St
New York, NY 10107-0001, USA

Sliger, Bernard F (Educator)
3341 E Lakeshore Dr
Tallahassee, FL 32312-1440, USA

Slightly Stoopid (Music Group)
c/o Staff Member Paradigm (Monterey)
509 Hartnell St
Monterey, CA 93940-2825, USA

Slim Helu, Carlos (Business Person)
Lago Alberto 366
Mexico, DF 11320, MEXICO

Slipknot (Musician)
c/o Staff Member Agency Group Ltd, The (NY)
1775 Broadway Ste 515
New York, NY 10019-1903, USA

Sliwa, Curtis
628 W 28th St
New York, NY 10001, USA

Sloan (Music Group)
c/o Staff Member Paradigm (Monterey)
509 Hartnell St
Monterey, CA 93940-2825, USA

Sloan, Amy (Actor)
c/o Marion Campbell TalentWorks (LA)
3500 W Olive Ave Ste 1400
Burbank, CA 91505-5512, USA

Sloan, David (Football Player)
Detroit Lions
10898 E Butherus Dr
Scottsdale, AZ 85255-1848, USA

Sloan, Ed (Musician)
216 Lincoln St
West Columbia, SC 29170-1812, USA

Sloan, Gerald E (Jerry) (Basketball Player, Coach)
300 S Washington St
Mc Leansboro, IL 62859-1141, USA

Sloan, Holly Goldberg (Director)
Sanford-Beckett-Skouras
1015 Gayley Ave # 300
Los Angeles, CA 90024-3413, USA

Sloan, Michael (Actor, Producer)
c/o Mickey Freiberg Acme Talent & Literary (LA)
4727 Wilshire Blvd Ste 333
Los Angeles, CA 90010-3874, USA

Sloan, P F (Musician, Songwriter, Writer)
All the Best
PO Box 164
Cedarhurst, NY 11516-0164, USA

Sloan, Stephen C (Steve) (Coach, Football Coach, Football Player)
University of Central Florida
Athletic Dept
Orlando, FL 32816-0001, USA

Sloan Jr, Robert B (Educator)
Bayor University
President's Office
Waco, TX 76798, USA

Sloane, Carol (Musician)
Magi Productions
705 Centre St # 300
Boston, MA 02130-2598, USA

Sloane, Lindsay (Actor)
Abrams Artists
9200 W Sunset Blvd Ste 1125
Los Angeles, CA 90069-3610, USA

Sloatman, Lala
11917 Vose St
N Hollywood, CA 91605-5750, USA

Slobodyanik, Alexander (Musician)
Columbia Artists Mgmt Inc
1790 Broadway Fl 6
New York, NY 10019-1412, USA

Slocombe, Douglas (Cinematographer)
London Mgmt
2-4 Noel St
London W1V 3RB, UNITED KINGDOM (UK)

Slocum, Heath (Golfer)
5640 Keystone Rd
Pensacola, FL 32504-8416, USA

Slocum, Ron (Baseball Player)
San Francisco Giants
4584 Mesa Blvd
Chino Hills, CA 91709-2705, USA

Slocumb, Reathcliff (Heath) (Baseball Player)
Chicago Cubs
1045 Arthur St
Uniondale, NY 11553-3103, USA

Slon, Steve (Editor)
AARP Magazine
601 E St NW
Washington, DC 20049-0001, USA

Slonimsky, Sergey M (Composer)
9 Kanal Griboedova
#97
Saint Petersburg, RUSSIA

Slosburg, Phil (Football Player)
Boston Yankees
201 Glen Ln
Elkins Park, PA 19027-1761, USA

Slotnick, Bernard (Publisher)
DC Comics Group
355 Lexington Ave
New York, NY 10017-6603, USA

Slotnick, Joey (Actor)
Gersh Agency
232 N Canon Dr
Beverly Hills, CA 90210-5302, USA

Slotnick, Mortimer H (Artist)
43 Amherst Dr
New Rochelle, NY 10804-1814, USA

Slotnick, R Nathan (Doctor)
825 Fairfax Ave
Norfolk, VA 23507-1914, USA

Slovan, Eric (Comedian)
c/o Staff Member William Morris Agency (WMA-LA)
1 William Morris Pl
Beverly Hills, CA 90212-4261, USA

Slover, Karl
504 Firetower Rd
Dublin, GA 31021-2642, USA

Slovin, Eric (Writer)
c/o Staff Member Principato/Young Management
9665 Wilshire Blvd Ste 500
Beverly Hills, CA 90212-2312, USA

Sloviter, Dolores K (Judge)
US Court of Appeals
601 Market St
US Courthouse
Philadelphia, PA 19106-1790, USA

Slowes, Charles (Baseball Player, Sportscaster)
Tampa Bay Devil Rays
3936 Mimosa Pl
Palm Harbor, FL 34685-3674, USA

Sloyan, James (Actor)
920 Kagawa St
Pacific Palisades, CA 90272-3833, USA

Sluman, Jeff (Golfer)
808 McKinley Ln
Hinsdale, IL 60521-4831, USA

Slusarski, Joe (Baseball Player)
Oakland A's
2904 Biscayne Dr
Springfield, IL 62707-6906, USA

Slutskaya, Irina (Figure Skater)
c/o Staff Member Champions on Ice
3500 W 80th St
Tom Collins Enterprises Inc
Minneapolis, MN 55431-1068, USA

Slutsky, Lorie A (Misc)
New York Community Trust
2 Park Ave Fl 3
New York, NY 10016-5602, USA

Sly, Darryl (Hockey Player)
Blue Mountain Chrysler
Highway 26
Collingwood, ON L9Y 1W6, CANADA

Smagala, Stan (Football Player)
Dallas Cowboys
13155 Meadow Hill Ln
Lemont, IL 60439-6743, USA

Smagorinsky, Joseph (Misc)
72 Gabriel Ct
Hillsborough, NJ 08844-1450, USA

Small, Aaron (Baseball Player)
Toronto Blue Jays
775 Loudon Rd
Loudon, TN 37774-6705, USA

Small, Brendan (Comedian)
c/o Tim Sarkes Brillstein-Grey Entertainment
9150 Wilshire Blvd Ste 350
Beverly Hills, CA 90212-3453, USA

Small, Gerald (Football Player)
Miami Dolphins
2081 Danvers Way
Sacramento, CA 95832-1180, USA

Small, Hank (Baseball Player)
Atlanta Braves
4715 Millbrook Dr NW
Atlanta, GA 30327-3548, USA

Small, Jim (Baseball Player)
Detroit Tigers
7960 Island Ct
Stanwood, MI 49346-8920, USA

Small, Lawrence W (Financier)
Smithsonian Institution
1000 Jefferson Dr SW
Washington, DC 20560-0009, USA

Small, Mark (Baseball Player)
Houston Astros
20088 Woden Ct NE
Poulsbo, WA 98370-8761, USA

Small, Mary
165 W 66th St
New York, NY 10023-6508, USA

Small, Marya (Actor)
CL Inc
843 N Sycamore Ave
Los Angeles, CA 90038-3316, USA

Small, Torrance (Football Player)
New Orleans Saints
66 Chateau Mouton Dr
Kenner, LA 70065-1903, USA

Small, William N (Admiral)
1605 Bluecher Ct
Virginia Beach, VA 23454-2501, USA

Smalley, Roy Jr (Baseball Player)
Texas Rangers
6319 Timber Trl
Edina, MN 55439-1049, USA

Smalley Sr, Roy (Baseball Player)
Chicago Cubs
256 Timber Trace Drive
Saint Albans, MO 63073, USA

Smallwood, Dwana (Dancer)
Alvin Ailey American Dance Foundation
211 W 61st St # 300
New York, NY 10023-7832, USA

Smallwood, Richard (Music Group, Musician)
Sierra Mgmt
1035 Bates Ct
Hendersonville, TN 37075-8864, USA

Smart, Amy (Actor)
c/o Elyse Scherz *Endeavor Agency LLC (LA)*
9601 Wilshire Blvd Fl 3
Beverly Hills, CA 90210-5204, USA

Smart, J D (Baseball Player)
Montreal Expos
1325 Lost Creek Blvd
Austin, TX 78746-6331, USA

Smart, Jean (Actor)
17351 Rancho St
Encino, CA 91316-3946, USA

Smart, Keith (Basketball Player, Coach)
5306 Asterwood Dr
Dublin, CA 94568-7718, USA

Smart, Pamela
#93G0356 Bedford Hills Corr. Fac.
Bedford Hills, NY 10507, USA

Smash Mouth (Musician)
c/o Robert Norman *Creative Artists Agency LCC (CAA-LA)*
2000 Avenue Of The Stars
Los Angeles, CA 90067-4700, USA

Smashing Pumpkins
9830 Wilshire Blvd
Beverly Hills, CA 90212-1804, USA

Smathers, George A (Senator)
Alred I Du Pont Building
169 E Flager St
Miami, FL 33131, USA

Smeal, Eleanor
900 N Stafford St Apt 1217
Arlington, VA 22203-1845, USA

Smeaton, Bruce
585 Nepean Hwy. Carrum
Victoria 3197, AUSTRALIA

Smedley, Geoffrey (Artist)
RR 3
Gambier Island
Gibsons, BC V0N 1V0, CANADA

Smedvig, Rolf (Musician)
Columbia Artists Mgmt Inc
1790 Broadway Fl 6
New York, NY 10019-1412, USA

Smeenge, Joel (Football Player)
New Orleans Saints
4366 Bass Creek Dr
Hudsonville, MI 49426-8602, USA

Smehlik, Richard (Hockey Player)
8824 Hearthstone Dr
East Amherst, NY 14051-2354, USA

Smerek, Don (Football Player)
Dallas Cowboys
1298 Valhalla Dr
Denver, NC 28037-5503, USA

Smerlas, Frederick C (Fred) (Football Player)
Buffalo Bills
11 Saddle Ridge Rd
Sudbury, MA 01776-2770, USA

Smid, Ladislav (Hockey Player)
Anaheim Mighty Ducks
2000 E Gene Autry Way
Anaheim, CA 92806-6143, USA

Smigel, Irwin (Doctor)
Smigel Research
635 Madison Ave
New York, NY 10022-1009, USA

Smigelsky, Dave (Football Player)
Atlanta Falcons
4332 Nesting Pl
Oakwood, GA 30566-3247, USA

Smiley, Don (Baseball Player, President)
Florida Marlins
3233 Huntington
Weston, FL 33332-1820, USA

Smiley, John (Baseball Player)
Pittsburgh Pirates
208 W 3rd Ave
Collegeville, PA 19426-2212, USA

Smiley, Rickey (Comedian)
c/o Staff Member *International Creative Management (ICM-LA)*
10250 Constellation Blvd
Los Angeles, CA 90067-6200, USA

Smiley, Tavis (Radio Personality, Television Host)
The Tavis Smiley Show
4401 W Sunset Blvd
Los Angeles, CA 90027-6017, USA

Smiley, Tommie B (Football Player)
Cincinnati Bengals
5340 Timberline Ln
Beaumont, TX 77706-7343, USA

Smirnoff, Yakov (Actor, Comedian)
c/o Staff Member *Richard De La Font Agency*
4845 S Sheridan Rd Ste 505
Tulsa, OK 74145-5719, USA

Smirnov, Nikolai I (Admiral)
Ministry of Defense
4 Staraya Pl
Moscow 103073, RUSSIA

Smith, Aaron (Football Player)
Pittsburgh Steelers
25 Laurel Rd
Bradfordwoods, PA 15015-1207, USA

Smith, Adrian (Basketball Player)
2829 Saddleback Dr
Cincinnati, OH 45244-3914, USA

Smith, Adrian (Musician)
Chipster Entertainment
1976 E High St Ste 101
Pottstown, PA 19464-3277, USA

Smith, Akili (Football Player)
Cincinnati Bengals
7771 Gribble St
San Diego, CA 92114-6018, USA

Smith, Al (Baseball Player)
1101 Ogilvie St
Bossier City, LA 71111-4639, USA

Smith, Al (Football Player)
Houston Oilers
15 Pembroke St
Sugar Land, TX 77479-2929, USA

Smith, Alexander J C (Financier)
Marsh & McLennan Co
1166 Avenue Of The Americas
New York, NY 10036-2728, USA

Smith, Alexis (Artist)
215 Windward Ave
Venice, CA 90291-3764, USA

Smith, Alice (Musician)
c/o Staff Member *Paradigm (Monterey)*
509 Hartnell St
Monterey, CA 93940-2825, USA

Smith, Allen D (Football Player)
Buffalo Bills
1220 Walker Dr Apt A
Decatur, GA 30030-5709, USA

Smith, Allison (Actor)
Innovative Artists
1505 10th St
Santa Monica, CA 90401-2805, USA

Smith, Amber (Actor, Model)
Shelter Entertainment
9255 W Sunset Blvd Ste 1010
Los Angeles, CA 90069-3307, USA

Smith, Ann (Tennis Player)
6901 E Chauncey Ln Apt 3015
Phoenix, AZ 85054-5134, USA

Smith, Anna Deavere (Actor)
Creative Artists Agency
9830 Wilshire Blvd
Beverly Hills, CA 90212-1804, USA

Smith, Anne Mollegen (Editor)
451 W 24th St
New York, NY 10011-1253, USA

Smith, Anthony W (Educator)
PO Box 573
Fontana, CA 92334-0573, USA

Smith, Antowain (Football Player)
Buffalo Bills
2121 Hepburn St Apt 917
Houston, TX 77054-3221, USA

Smith, April (Writer)
427 7th St
Santa Monica, CA 90402-1907, USA

Smith, Art (Chef)
c/o Evan Morgenstein *PMG Sports*
700 Evanvale Ct
Cary, NC 27518-2806, USA

Smith, Arthur K Jr (Educator)
5346 McCulloch Cir
Houston, TX 77056-6619, USA

Smith, Artie (Football Player)
San Francisco 49ers
3809 W 68th St
Stillwater, OK 74074-2428, USA

Smith, B (Television Host)
c/o Staff Member *B Smith With Style*
168 Park Ave
Harrison, NY 10528-4208, USA

Smith, Barbara (Business Person)
B. Smith Enterprises
1120 Avenue Of The Americas Fl 4
New York, NY 10036-6700, USA

Smith, Barry (Football Player)
Green Bay Packers
4048 Corkwood Ct
Palm Harbor, FL 34684-3608, USA

Smith, Barty (Football Player)
Green Bay Packers
2290 Dabney Rd
Richmond, VA 23230-3344, USA

Smith, Beau (Cartoonist)
PO Box 706
Flying Fist Ranch
Ceredo, WV 25507-0706, USA

Smith, Ben (Cartoonist)
King Features Syndicate
888 7th Ave Ste 201
New York, NY 10106-0201, USA

Smith, Ben (Coach, Hockey Player)
47 Norwood Hts
Gloucester, MA 01930-1212, USA

Smith, Ben (Football Player)
Philadelphia Eagles
1127 Riverbend Club Dr SE
Atlanta, GA 30339-2817, USA

Smith, Bennett W (Religious Leader)
Progressive National Baptist Convention
601 50th St NE
Washington, DC 20019-5498, USA

Smith, Bernie (Baseball Player)
Milwaukee Brewers
PO Box 513
Lutcher, LA 70071-0513, USA

Smith, Bill (Football Player)
Chicago Rockets
19 Woodcrest Dr
Lexington, NC 27295-1661, USA

Smith, Billy (Hockey Player)
8356 Quail Meadow Way
West Palm Beach, FL 33412-1505, USA

Smith, Billy Ray Jr (Football Player)
San Diego Chargers
14755 Caminito Porta Delgada
Del Mar, CA 92014-4307, USA

Smith, Bob (Baseball Player)
Boston Braves
221 Hackberry Ln
Aiken, SC 29803-2733, USA

Smith, Bob (Golfer)
PO Box 6511
Ventura, CA 93006-6511, USA

Smith, Bobby (Baseball Player)
Tampa Bay Devil Rays
2822 60th Ave
Oakland, CA 94605-1502, USA

Smith, Bobby (Hockey Player)
10800 E Cactus Rd Unit 46
Scottsdale, AZ 85259-2505, USA

Smith, Bobby Gene (Baseball Player)
St Louis Cardinals
1267 Tucker Rd Unit 15
Hood River, OR 97031-8601, USA

Smith, Brad (Musician)
Shapiro Co
9229 W Sunset Blvd Ste 607
Los Angeles, CA 90069-3406, USA

Smith, Brent (Football Player)
Miami Dolphins
258 Ridgewood Dr
Pontotoc, MS 38863-3532, USA

Smith, Brick (Baseball Player)
Seattle Mariners
4743 Amity Pl
Charlotte, NC 28212-5305, USA

Smith, Brooke (Actor)
1860 N Fuller Ave Apt 104
Los Angeles, CA 90046-2371, USA

Smith, Bruce W (Director)
c/o Staff Member *Jambalaya Studio*
111 N Maryland Ave # 300
Glendale, CA 91206-4238, USA

Smith, Bryn (Baseball Player)
Montreal Expos
1239 Highway 1
Santa Maria, CA 93455-5909, USA

Smith, C Reginald (Reggie) (Baseball Player)
22239 1/2 Erwin St
Woodland Hills, CA 91367-0946, USA

Smith, Calvin (Athlete, Track Athlete)
16703 Sheffield Park Dr
Lutz, FL 33549-6833, USA

Smith, Carl (Musician)
2510 Franklin Pike
Nashville, TN 37204-2714, USA

Smith, Carl R (General)
2345 S Queen St
Arlington, VA 22202-1550, USA

Smith, Carolyn Renee
PO Box 813
N Hollywood, CA 91603-0813, USA

Smith, Chad (Musician)
Q Prime
729 7th Ave Rm 1600
New York, NY 10019-6880, USA

Smith, Charles A (Bubba) (Actor, Football Player)
c/o V W (Chap) Chappell *Chappell Entertainment Corp*
214 N Griffin Dr
Casselberry, FL 32707-2965, USA

Smith, Charles Martin (Actor, Director)
980 Cedarcliff Ct
Westlake Village, CA 91362-5291, USA

Smith, Charlie E (Football Player)
Philadelphia Eagles
1906 Crescent Dr
Monroe, LA 71202-3024, USA

Smith, Charlie H (Football Player)
Oakland Raiders
14074 Skyline Blvd
Oakland, CA 94619-3622, USA

Smith, Chelsi
335 E San Augustine St
Deer Park, TX 77536-4185, USA

Smith, Chris (Baseball Player)
Montreal Expos
4206 Dawn Ln
Oceanside, CA 92056-4716, USA

Smith, Chris (Golfer)
208 S Bellerive Dr
Peru, IN 46970-8060, USA

Smith, Chris M (Football Player)
Kansas City Chiefs
1424 Martway Cir Apt A
Olathe, KS 66061-5820, USA

Smith, Chuck (Baseball Player)
Florida Marlins
10271 SW 9th Ln
Pembroke Pines, FL 33025-3584, USA

Smith, Chuck (Football Player)
Atlanta Falcons
1155 Havenbrook Ct
Suwanee, GA 30024-2877, USA

Smith, Clifford (Method Man) (Musician, Television Host)
c/o Shauna Garr *Native Productions*
1041 N Formosa Ave
West Hollywood, CA 90046-6703, USA

Smith, Clinton J (Clint) (Hockey Player)
501-1919 Bellview Ave
West Vancouver, BC V7V 1B7, CANADA

Smith, Connie (Music Group, Musician)
Gurley Co
1204B Cedar Ln
Nashville, TN 37212-5910, USA

Smith, Cotter (Actor)
15332 Antioch St # 800
Pacific Palisades, CA 90272-3628, USA

Smith, D Brooks (Judge)
US Court of Appeals
319 Washington St Ste 208
Penn Traffic Bldg
Johnstown, PA 15901-1624, USA

Smith, Dan (Baseball Player)
Texas Rangers
2305 Harvard Dr
Flower Mound, TX 75022-4864, USA

Smith, Dan (Baseball Player)
Montreal Expos
715 N Carbon St
Girard, KS 66743-1025, USA

Smith, Danny (Actor)
c/o Lisa Harrison *Endeavor Agency LLC (LA)*
9601 Wilshire Blvd Fl 3
Beverly Hills, CA 90210-5204, USA

Smith, Dante (Mos Def) (Actor, Musician)
c/o Sara Ramaker *Paradigm (LA)*
360 N Crescent Dr
North Bldg
Beverly Hills, CA 90210-6820, USA

Smith, Darden (Music Group, Musician, Songwriter, Writer)
AGF Entertainment
30 W 21st St # 700
New York, NY 10010-6905, USA

Smith, Darrin (Football Player)
Dallas Cowboys
7395 NW 19th Ct
Hollywood, FL 33024-1015, USA

Smith, Daryl (Baseball Player)
Kansas City Royals
3 Sunny Mills Ct
Randallstown, MD 21133-4449, USA

Smith, Daryle (Football Player)
Dallas Cowboys
6275 Country Club Dr
Huntington, WV 25705-2009, USA

Smith, Dave (Baseball Player)
California Angels
16330 Jersey Dr
Houston, TX 77040-2020, USA

Smith, Dave (Football Player)
Houston Oilers
7906 W 116th Ter
Overland Park, KS 66210-2527, USA

Smith, Dave (Football Player)
Pittsburgh Steelers
650 S 13th St # 123-20
Indiana, PA 15701-3566, USA

Smith, Dean E (Basketball Player, Coach)
University of North Carolina
PO Box 2126
Chapel Hill, NC 27515-2126, USA

Smith, Dennis (Football Player)
Denver Broncos
2450 Achilles Dr
Los Angeles, CA 90046-1626, USA

Smith, Derek (Football Player)
Washington Redskins
4949 Centennial Blvd
Santa Clara, CA 95054-1229, USA

Smith, Derek (Hockey Player)
201 Bramblewood Ln
East Amherst, NY 14051-2228, USA

Smith, Dick (Baseball Player)
Pittsburgh Pirates
1926 Norwood Ln
State College, PA 16803-1326, USA

Smith, Dick (Baseball Player)
Washington Senators
2615 Gates Rd
Lincolnton, NC 28092-7968, USA

Smith, Dick (Baseball Player)
New York Mets
6850 Downing Rd Spc 35
Central Point, OR 97502-3418, USA

Smith, Dick (Coach, Swimmer)
PO Box 1831
Dewey, AZ 86327-1831, USA

Smith, Donald L (Football Player)
Atlanta Falcons
3338 Pineview Dr
Holiday, FL 34691-9732, USA

Smith, Doug (Basketball Player)
21930 Winchester St
Southfield, MI 48076-4892, USA

Smith, Doug (Coach, Football Coach, Football Player)
University of Southern California
Heritage Hall
Los Angeles, CA 90089-0001, USA

Smith, Doug (Football Player)
New York Giants
25661 Pacific Crest Dr
Mission Viejo, CA 92692-5040, USA

Smith, Douglas (Doug) (Actor)
c/o Beverly Strong *Anonymous Content (CA)*
9350 Wilshire Blvd Ste 224
Beverly Hills, CA 90212-3204, USA

Smith, Dwight (Baseball Player)
Chicago Cubs
PO Box 98
Varnville, SC 29944-0098, USA

Smith, Dylan (Actor)
c/o Staff Member *TalentWorks (LA)*
3500 W Olive Ave Ste 1400
Burbank, CA 91505-5512, USA

Smith, Earl (Baseball Player)
Pittsburgh Pirates
2764 N Leonard Ave
Fresno, CA 93727-9720, USA

Smith, Ed (Football Player)
Green Bay Packers
PO Box 99
Alto, NM 88312-0099, USA

Smith, Elliot (Football Player)
San Diego Chargers
1343 Cadillac Dr
Jackson, MS 39213-4811, USA

Smith, Elmore (Basketball Player)
PO Box 241475
Cleveland, OH 44124-8475, USA

Smith, Emmett
1 Cowboys Pkwy
Irving, TX 75063-4924, USA

Smith, Eugene (Baseball Player)
Cincinnati Buckeyes
8337 Flora Ave
Saint Louis, MO 63114-6203, USA

Smith, F Dean (Athlete, Track Athlete)
PO Box 71
Breckenridge, TX 76424-0071, USA

Smith, Floyd (Hockey Player)
138 Stonehenge Dr
Orchard Park, NY 14127-2845, USA

Smith, Forry
3500 W Olive Ave Ste 1400
Burbank, CA 91505-5512, USA

Smith, Frank (Baseball Player)
Cincinnati Reds
PO Box 724
Malone, FL 32445-0724, USA

Smith, Frankie (Football Player)
Miami Dolphins
620 N Grayson St
Groesbeck, TX 76642-1157, USA

Smith, Frederick W (Business Person)
FDX Corp
942 S Shady Grove Rd
Memphis, TN 38120-4117, USA

Smith, G E
24 Thorndike St
Cambridge, MA 02141-1882, USA

Smith, G Elaine (Religious Leader)
American Baptist Churches USA
PO Box 851
Valley Forge, PA 19482-0851, USA

Smith, Gary (Hockey Player)
Villa Cortina
4451 Albert St #102
Burnaby, BC V5C 2G4, CANADA

Smith, George (Cartoonist)
Universal Press Syndicate
4520 Main St
Kansas City, MO 64111-1876, USA

Smith, Gerald (Misc)
World Tennis Assn
133 1st St NE
Saint Petersburg, FL 33701-3307, USA

Smith, Gerald C (Government Official)
2425 Tracy Pl NW
Washington, DC 20008-1628, USA

Smith, Greg (Baseball Player)
Chicago Cubs
27435 Hanes Rd E
Davenport, WA 99122-9443, USA

Smith, Gregory (Actor)
c/o Beverly Strong *Anonymous Content (CA)*
9350 Wilshire Blvd Ste 224
Beverly Hills, CA 90212-3204, USA

Smith, Gregory White (Writer)
129 1st Ave SW
Aiken, SC 29801-4862, USA

Smith, Hal (Baseball Player)
St Louis Cardinals
9514 Londonderry Ct
Fort Smith, AR 72908-9520, USA

Smith, Hal (Baseball Player)
Baltimore Orioles
637 Houston St
Columbus, TX 78934-2618, USA

Smith, Hal (Football Player)
Boston Patriots
PO Box 570517
Tarzana, CA 91357-0517, USA

Smith, Hamilton O (Nobel Prize Laureate)
13607 Hanover Pike
Reisterstown, MD 21136-4520, USA

Smith, Harry (Bowler)
580 E Cuyahoga Falls Ave
Akron, OH 44310-1540, USA

Smith, Harry (Correspondent)
c/o Staff Member *Early Show, The (NY)*
524 W 57th St
New York, NY 10019-2930, USA

Smith, Harry E (Black Jack) (Coach, Football Coach, Football Player)
Detroit Lions
805 Leawood Ter
Columbia, MO 65203-2729, USA

Smith, Hedrick L (Journalist)
4204 Rosemary St
Chevy Chase, MD 20815-5218, USA

Smith, Helen (Baseball Player)
2104 Turtle Run Dr Apt 6
Richmond, VA 23233-3673, USA

Smith, Hillary B
8730 W Sunset Blvd Ste 480
Los Angeles, CA 90069-2277, USA

Smith, Hulett C (Governor)
2105 Harper Rd
Beckley, WV 25801-2615, USA

Smith, Hunter (Football Player)
c/o Staff Member *Indianapolis Colts*
7001 W 56th St
Indianapolis, IN 46254-9698, USA

Smith, Ian
Gwenoro Farm
Shurugwi, ZIMBABWE

Smith, Ilan Mitchell
10460 Queens Blvd Apt 10C
Forest Hills, NY 11375-7306, USA

Smith, Ivor (Architect)
Station Officer's House
Prawle Pointe Kingsbridge
Devon TQ7 2BX, UNITED KINGDOM
(UK)

Smith, J D (Football Player)
Philadelphia Eagles
1615 County Road 204
Richland Springs, TX 76871, USA

Smith, J D Jr (Football Player)
Chicago Bears
3332 Florida St
Oakland, CA 94602-3808, USA

Smith, J Robert (Football Player)
Detroit Lions
6102 Timberlake Ct
Flower Mound, TX 75022-5627, USA

Smith, J T (Football Player)
Washington Redskins
10110 Planters Row Dr
Frisco, TX 75034-0255, USA

Smith, Jack (Baseball Player)
Los Angeles Dodgers
250 Doubles Dr
Covington, GA 30016-1736, USA

Smith, Jackie L (Football Player)
St Louis Cardinals
1566 Walpole Dr
Chesterfield, MO 63017-4615, USA

Smith, Jaclyn (Actor)
c/o Tom Burke *International Creative Management (ICM-LA)*
10250 Constellation Blvd
Los Angeles, CA 90067-6200, USA

Smith, Jacob (Actor)
c/o Elaine Lively *LA Entertainment*
1317 N San Fernando Blvd # 155
Burbank, CA 91504-4236, USA

Smith, James (Bonecrusher) (Boxer)
355 Keith Hills Rd
Lillington, NC 27546, USA

Smith, Jamie Renee (Actor)
c/o Pam Grimes *Hervey/Grimes Talent Agency*
10561 Missouri Ave Apt 2
Los Angeles, CA 90025-5940, USA

Smith, Jean (Baseball Player)
5351 S Lake Shore Dr
Harbor Springs, MI 49740-9109, USA

Smith, Jennifer M (Misc, Prime Minister)
Premier's Office
Cabinet Building
105 Front St
Hamilton, HM 12, BERMUDA

Smith, Jermaine (Football Player)
Green Bay Packers
1345 12th St
Augusta, GA 30901-3260, USA

Smith, Jerry (Judge)
US Court of Appeals
515 Rusk St Ste 12015
Houston, TX 77002-2605, USA

Smith, Jim (Baseball Player)
Pittsburgh Pirates
1730 S Arroyo Ln
Gilbert, AZ 85295-4815, USA

Smith, Jim (Football Player)
Pittsburgh Steelers
2639 Round Table Blvd
Lewisville, TX 75056-5723, USA

Smith, Jim Ray (Football Player)
Cleveland Browns
7049 Cliffbrook Dr
Dallas, TX 75254-7909, USA

Smith, Jimmy Lee (Football Player)
Dallas Cowboys
1302 Charter Ct E
Jacksonville, FL 32225-2658, USA

Smith, Joe (Basketball Player)
7639 Leafwood Dr
Norfolk, VA 23518-4536, USA

Smith, John (Actor)
c/o Ilene Feldman *IFA Talent Agency*
8730 W Sunset Blvd Ste 490
Los Angeles, CA 90069-2248, USA

Smith, John L (Coach, Football Coach)
Michigan State University
Daugherty Field House
East Lansing, MI 48824, USA

Smith, John M (Football Player)
New England Patriots
184 Centre St
Dover, MA 02030-2413, USA

Smith, John W (Wrestler)
5315 S Sangre Rd
Stillwater, OK 74074-2071, USA

Smith, Josh (Misc)
University of Pennsylvania
240 S 33rd St
Philadelphia, PA 19104-6316, USA

Smith, Justin (Football Player)
Cincinnati Bengals
968 Aristides Dr
Union, KY 41091-8261, USA

Smith, Karin
2300 Palisades Ave
Los Osos, CA 93402-3910, USA

Smith, Kathy (Misc)
PO Box 491433
Los Angeles, CA 90049-9433, USA

Smith, Katie (Basketball Player)
Minnesota Lynx
600 1st Ave N
Target Center
Minneapolis, MN 55403-9802, USA

Smith, Keely Shaye (Actor)
c/o John Ferriter *William Morris Agency (WMA-LA)*
1 William Morris Pl
Beverly Hills, CA 90212-4261, USA

Smith, Keith (Baseball Player)
New York Yankees
18024 Grace Ln Unit 103
Canyon Country, CA 91387-6485, USA

Smith, Keith (Baseball Player)
Texas Rangers
5823 13th St E
Bradenton, FL 34203-6819, USA

Smith, Kellita (Actor)
c/o Vincent Cirrincione *Vincent Cirrincione Associates*
1516 N Fairfax Ave
Los Angeles, CA 90046-2608, USA

Smith, Ken (Architect)
80 Warren St Apt 28
New York, NY 10007-1029, USA

Smith, Ken (Baseball Player)
Atlanta Braves
100 Lansdowne Blvd
Youngstown, OH 44506-1137, USA

Smith, Kenneth L (Baseball Player, Football Player)
Cleveland Browns
313 Ellen Dr
Deer Park, TX 77536-3534, USA

Smith, Kenny (Sportscaster)
c/o Staff Member *Turner Sports*
1 Cnn Ctr NW
Atlanta, GA 30303-2762, USA

Smith, Kerr (Actor)
c/o Jennifer Craig *Gersh Agency, The (LA)*
232 N Canon Dr
Beverly Hills, CA 90210-5302, USA

Smith, Kevin (Actor, Director, Producer, Writer)
c/o Staff Member *View Askew Productions Inc*
116 Broad St
Red Bank, NJ 07701-1962, USA

Smith, Kevin (Football Player)
Oakland Raiders
5928 Turtle Creek Dr
Plano, TX 75093-4338, USA

Smith, Kurtwood (Actor)
1146 N Central Ave # 521
Glendale, CA 91202-2506, USA

Smith, Lance (Football Player)
St Louis Cardinals
PO Box 948
Kannapolis, NC 28082-0948, USA

Smith, Larry (Basketball Player)
1767 Lakeside Dr
Vicksburg, MS 39180-9369, USA

Smith, Larry (Football Player)
Los Angeles Rams
3601 Bayshore Blvd
Tampa, FL 33629-8942, USA

Smith, Lauren Lee (Actor)
c/o Eric Black *Anonymous Content (CA)*
3532 Hayden Ave
Culver City, CA 90232-2413, USA

Smith, Laverne (Football Player)
Pittsburgh Steelers
2122 N Homestead St
Wichita, KS 67208-1872, USA

Smith, Lawrence Leighton
Louisville Symphony
611 W Main St
Louisville, KY 40202-2963, USA

Smith, Lee A (Baseball Player)
Atlanta Braves
2124 Highway 507
Castor, LA 71016-4069, USA

Smith, Leonard P (Football Player)
St Louis Cardinals
18053 Creek Hollow Rd
Baton Rouge, LA 70817-3304, USA

Smith, Lewis
8271 Melrose Ave Ste 110
Los Angeles, CA 90046-6800, USA

Smith, Liz (Writer)
c/o Joni Evans *William Morris Agency (WMA-LA)*
1 William Morris Pl
Beverly Hills, CA 90212-4261, USA

Smith, Lois (Actor)
Abrams Artists
420 Madison Ave # 1400
New York, NY 10017-1107, USA

Smith, Lonnie (Baseball Player)
Philadelphia Phillies
361 Ginger Cake Rd
Fayetteville, GA 30214-1037, USA

Smith, Loren A (Judge)
US Claims Court
717 Madison Pl NW
Washington, DC 20439-0001, USA

Smith, Lovie (Coach, Football Coach, Football Player)
Chicago Bears
1000 Football Dr
Lake Forest, IL 60045-4829, USA

Smith, M Elizabeth (Liz) (Writer)
160 E 38th St
New York, NY 10016-2651, USA

Smith, Madeline (Actor)
Joan Gray
Sunbury Island
Sunbury on Thames
Middx, UNITED KINGDOM (UK)

Smith, Maggie (Actor)
International Creative Mgmt
76 Oxford St
London W1N 0AX, UNITED KINGDOM
(UK)

Smith, Margaret (Producer, Writer)
c/o Jonathan Howard *Innovative Artists (LA)*
1505 10th St
Santa Monica, CA 90401-2805, USA

Smith, Margo (Musician, Songwriter, Writer)
Tristar Enterprises Inc
PO Box 3367
Brentwood, TN 37024-3367, USA

Smith, Marilynn (Golfer)
3784 N 162nd Ln
Goodyear, AZ 85395-8017, USA

Smith, Mark (Baseball Player)
Baltimore Orioles
713 W Duarte Rd # G105
Arcadia, CA 91007-7564, USA

Smith, Mark (Baseball Player)
Oakland A's
814 Beirs Mill Road
Rockville, MD 20850, USA

Smith, Marquis (Football Player)
Cleveland Browns
843 51st St
San Diego, CA 92114-1002, USA

Smith, Martha (Actor, Model)
9690 Heather Rd
Beverly Hills, CA 90210-1757, USA

Smith, Marvel (Football Player)
Pittsburgh Steelers
30 Waterfront Dr
Pittsburgh, PA 15222-4748, USA

Smith, Marvin (Smitty) (Musician)
Joel Chriss
300 Mercer St Apt 3J
New York, NY 10003-6732, USA

Smith, Melanie (Actor)
Innovative Artists
1505 10th St
Santa Monica, CA 90401-2805, USA

Smith, Michael Bailey (Actor)
c/o Alexandra Karrys *Divine Management*
117 N Orlando Ave
Los Angeles, CA 90048-3403, USA

Smith, Michael W (Musician, Songwriter, Writer)
c/o Staff Member *Creative Artists Agency (CAA-Nashville)*
3310 W End Ave Fl 5
Nashville, TN 37203-1028, USA

Smith, Mike (Baseball Player)
Cincinnati Reds
3226 Livingston Rd
Jackson, MS 39213-6106, USA

Smith, Mike (Baseball Player)
Toronto Blue Jays
6 Willett Pond Rd
Westwood, MA 02090-3417, USA

Smith, Mike (Baseball Player)
Baltimore Orioles
1417 E Locust St
Springfield, MO 65803-3841, USA

Smith, Mike (Cartoonist)
Las Vegas Sun
2275 Corporate Cir
Editorial Dept
Henderson, NV 89074-7719, USA

Smith, Mike (Football Player)
Miami Dolphins
619 Feamster Dr
Houston, TX 77022-2505, USA

Smith, Mike (Misc)
Names Project Foundation
310 Townsend St
San Francisco, CA 94107-1653, USA

Smith, Mindy (Musician, Songwriter, Writer)
Vanguard Records
2700 Pennsylvania Ave
Santa Monica, CA 90404-4066, USA

Smith, Moishe (Artist)
Utah State University
Art Dept
Logan, UT 84322-0001, USA

Smith, Myron (Football Player)
Dallas Cowboys
6604 Sandgate Dr
Arlington, TX 76002-5549, USA

Smith, Nate (Baseball Player)
Baltimore Orioles
6365 Tahoe Dr
Atlanta, GA 30349-4052, USA

Smith, Neil (Football Player)
Kansas City Chiefs
1601 NW Arrowhead Trl
Blue Springs, MO 64015-7291, USA

Smith, Nicholas (Actor)
10/11 Lower John St
London, ENGLAND W1R 3PE, UNITED KINGDOM (UK)

Smith, Noland (Football Player)
Kansas City Chiefs
4338 Watkins Dr
Jackson, MS 39206-4450, USA

Smith, O C
1650 Broadway Ste 508
New York, NY 10019-6833, USA

Smith, O Guinn (Athlete, Track Athlete)
2 Hawthorne Pl Apt 3P
Boston, MA 02114-2304, USA

Smith, Orin R (Business Person)
Engelhard Corp
101 Wood Ave S
Iselin, NJ 08830-2703, USA

Smith, Orlando (Tubby) (Coach)
University of Kentucky
Athletic Dept
Lexington, KY 40536-0001, USA

Smith, Osborne E (Ozzie) (Baseball Player)
PO Box 164
Saint Albans, MO 63073-0164, USA

Smith, Patti (Songwriter, Writer)
Primary Talent International Ltd
2-12 Pentonville Road
5th Fl
Sausalito, London N1 9PL, UNITED KINGDOM (UK)

Smith, Paul B (Designer, Fashion Designer)
Paul Smith Ltd
41/44 Floral St
Covent Garden
London WC2E 9DG, UNITED KINGDOM (UK)

Smith, Putter
318 Fairview Ave
South Pasadena, CA 91030-1715, USA

Smith, Quincy (Baseball Player)
Cleveland Buckeyes
715 S 14th St
Terre Haute, IN 47807, USA

Smith, Quinn (Actor)
1738 Whitley Ave
Hollywood, CA 90028-4809, USA

Smith, R Jackson (Swimmer)
122 Palmers Hill Rd Unit 3101
Stamford, CT 06902-2147, USA

Smith, Ralph (Cartoonist)
King Features Syndicate
888 7th Ave Ste 201
New York, NY 10106-0201, USA

Smith, Ralph (Football Player)
Philadelphia Eagles
PO Box 1406
McComb, MS 39649-1406, USA

Smith, Randy (Basketball Player)
1542 Amherst St
Buffalo, NY 14214-1923, USA

Smith, Ray E (Religious Leader)
Open Bible Standard Churches
2020 Bell Ave
Des Moines, IA 50315-1031, USA

Smith, Raymond W (Business Person, Financier)
Rothschild North America
1251 Avenue Of The Americas
New York, NY 10020-1104, USA

Smith, Rex (Actor)
16986 Encino Hills Dr
Encino, CA 91436-4008, USA

Smith, Richard A (Publisher)
Harcourt general
275 Washington St
Newton, MA 02458-1646, USA

Smith, Richard M (Editor)
Newsweek Magazine
251 W 57th St
Editorial Dept
New York, NY 10019-1802, USA

Smith, Ricky (Musician, Reality TV Star)
c/o Staff Member *American Idol*
7800 Beverly Blvd # 251
Los Angeles, CA 90036-2112, USA

Smith, Rico (Football Player)
Cleveland Browns
8976 Foothill Blvd # B7-389
Rancho Cucamonga, CA 91730-3400, USA

Smith, Riley (Actor)
c/o Abby Bluestone *Innovative Artists (LA)*
1505 10th St
Santa Monica, CA 90401-2805, USA

Smith, Robert B (Football Player)
Minnesota Vikings
1012 S Royal St
Bogalusa, LA 70427-5457, USA

Smith, Robert C (Editor)
TV Guide Magazine
Editorial Dept
100 Matsonford Road
Wayne, PA 19080-0001, USA

Smith, Robert C (Bob) (Senator)
9012 Rocky Lake Ct
Sarasota, FL 34238-4008, USA

Smith, Robert Gray (Graysmith) (Cartoonist)
San Francisco Chronicle
901 Mission St
San Francisco, CA 94103-2934, USA

Smith, Robert L (Football Player)
Buffalo Bills
426 Cape Lookout Dr
Corpus Christi, TX 78412-2636, USA

Smith, Robert Lee (Musician)
Speer Entertainment Services
PO Box 2620
McDonough, GA 30253-1738, USA

Smith, Robert S (Football Player)
Minnesota Vikings
5668 Harrison Ave
Maple Heights, OH 44137-3331, USA

Smith, Robyn (Jockey)
1155 San Ysidro Dr
Beverly Hills, CA 90210-2102, USA

Smith, Rod (Football Player)
New England Patriots
821 W 4th St
Charlotte, NC 28202-1103, USA

Smith, Roger (Actor)
2707 Benedict Canyon Dr
Beverly Hills, CA 90210-1024, USA

Smith, Roger Guenveur (Actor)
Wiliiam Morris Agency
151 El Camino Dr
Beverly Hills, CA 90212-2775, USA

Smith, Rolland (Correspondent)
CBS-TV
524 W 57th St
News Dept
New York, NY 10019-2924, USA

Smith, Ron (Football Player)
Los Angeles Rams
1804 Park Ave
Richmond, VA 23220-2821, USA

Smith, Ron (Football Player)
Los Angeles Rams
266 York St
Trussville, AL 35173-3224, USA

Smith, Ronnie Ray (Athlete, Track Athlete)
752 W Athens Blvd
Los Angeles, CA 90044-3921, USA

Smith, Royce (Football Player)
New Orleans Saints
404 S College St
Claxton, GA 30417-1820, USA

Smith, Russell (Musician)
LC Media
PO Box 965
Antioch, TN 37011-0965, USA

Smith, Shawnee (Actor)
c/o Brian Wilkins *Wilkins Management*
901 N Highland Ave
Los Angeles, CA 90038-2412, USA

Smith, Shelley (Actor)
4184 Colfax Ave
Studio City, CA 91604-2165, USA

Smith, Sherman (Football Player)
Seattle Seahawks
1421 Primrose Ln
Franklin, TN 37064-9333, USA

Smith, Shevin (Football Player)
Tampa Bay Buccaneers
10110 Farmingdale Pl
Tampa, FL 33624-5419, USA

Smith, Sid (Football Player)
Kansas City Chiefs
1939 Melody Ln
Richmond, TX 77469-2411, USA

Smith, Siniin (Volleyball Player)
Assn of Volleyball Pros
330 Washington Blvd # 400
Marina Del Rey, CA 90292-5141, USA

Smith, Sonny (Baseball Player)
Chicago American Giants
3549 N College Ave
Indianapolis, IN 46205-3733, USA

Smith, Stan
194 Bellevue Ave
Newport, RI 02840-3515, USA

Smith, Stanley R (Stan) (Tennis Player)
ProServe
1101 Woodrow Wilson Blvd #1800
Arlington, VA 22209, USA

Smith, Steve (Football Player)
Pittsburgh Steelers
1104 Lake Shore Dr N
Barrington, IL 60010-3427, USA

The Celebrity Black Book 2008

Smith, Steve (Producer)
c/o Staff Member *S&S Productions*
212 King St W #205
Toronto, ON M5H 1K5, CANADA

Smith, Steve A (Football Player)
Oakland Raiders
2717 Millwood Dr
Richardson, TX 75082-3832, USA

Smith, Steven (Misc)
National Rural Letter Carriers Assn
1630 Duke St
Alexandria, VA 22314-3467, USA

Smith, Steven D (Steve) (Basketball Player)
c/o Staff Member *Charlotte Bobcats*
333 E Trade St
Charlotte, NC 28202-2331, USA

Smith, Steven L (Astronaut)
15728 Lake Lodge Dr
Houston, TX 77062, USA

Smith, Susan
Leath Correctional Institution
2809 Airport Rd
Leath Correctional Institution
Greenwood, SC 29649-9212, USA

Smith, Taran (Actor)
Full Circle Mgmt
12665 Kling St
North Hollywood, CA 91604-1143, USA

Smith, Tasha (Actor)
Writers & Artists
360 N Crescent Dr Bldg North
Beverly Hills, CA 90210-6818, USA

Smith, Thomas (Football Player)
Buffalo Bills
RR 1 Box 198
Gates, NC 27937, USA

Smith, Tommie (Athlete, Football Player, Track Athlete)
Cincinnati Bengals
1800 Lilburn Stone Mountain Rd
Stone Mountain, GA 30087-1720, USA

Smith, Tony (Football Player)
Atlanta Falcons
PO Box 480234
Charlotte, NC 28269-5302, USA

Smith, Travian (Football Player)
Oakland Raiders
13941 County Road 2167D
Tatum, TX 75691-3214, USA

Smith, Vernice (Football Player)
Phoenix Cardinals
4347 Arajo Ct
Orlando, FL 32812-2854, USA

Smith, Vernon L (Nobel Prize Laureate)
801 N Monroe St Apt 501
Arlington, VA 22201-2371, USA

Smith, Vince (Musician)
Process Talent Management
439 Wiley Ave
Franklin, PA 16323-2834, USA

Smith, W Lawrence (Football Player)
Los Angeles Rams
3601 Bayshore Blvd
Tampa, FL 33629-8942, USA

Smith, Wallace B (Religious Leader)
Reorganized Church of Latter Day Saints
PO Box 1059
Independence, MO 64051-0559, USA

Smith, Walter (Designer, Engineer)
Microsoft Corp
1 Microsoft Way
Redmond, WA 98052-8300, USA

Smith, Walter H F (Oceanographer)
Nat'l Oceanic/Atmospheric Administration
Commerce Dept
Washington, DC 20230-0001, USA

Smith, Wayne (Football Player)
Detroit Lions
7730 S Bishop St
Chicago, IL 60620-4127, USA

Smith, Wilbur (Writer)
Charles Pick Constituency
3 Bryanston Place
#3
London W1H 7FN, UNITED KINGDOM (UK)

Smith, Will (Actor, Musician)
c/o James Lassiter *Overbook Entertainment*
450 N Roxbury Dr Fl 4
Beverly Hills, CA 90210-4232, USA

Smith, William (Actor)
3202 Anacapa St
Santa Barbara, CA 93105, USA

Smith, William D (Admiral)
7025 Fairway Oaks
Fayetteville, PA 17222-9416, USA

Smith, William Jay (Writer)
62 Luther Shaw Rd
RR 1 Box 151
Cummington, MA 01026, USA

Smith, William Y (General)
6541 Brooks Pl
Falls Church, VA 22044-1106, USA

Smith, Willie (Baseball Player)
Homestead Grays
607 Bradford St
Anniston, AL 36201-7305, USA

Smith, Willie (Football Player)
Baltimore Ravens
Ravens Stadium
11001 Russell St
Baltimore, MD 21230, USA

Smith, Yeardley (Actor)
Bresler Kelly Assoc
11500 W Olympic Blvd Ste 510
Los Angeles, CA 90064-1527, USA

Smith, Zadie (Writer)
Random House
1745 Broadway # B1
New York, NY 10019-4305, USA

Smith Court, Margaret (Tennis Player)
21 Lewanna Way
City Beach
Perth, WA 6010, AUSTRALIA

Smith Jr, John F (Jack) (Business Person)
General Motors Corp
100 Renaissance Ctr
Detroit, MI 48243-1114, USA

Smith Jr, Lonnie Liston (Musician)
Associated Booking Corp
PO Box 2055
New York, NY 10021-0051, USA

Smith Jr, William R (Lawyer)
PO Box 3239
1 Harbour Place
Tampa, FL 33601-3239, USA

Smith-McCulloch, Colleen (Baseball Player)
3-7168 Ash Cres
Vancouver, BC V6P 3K7, CANADA

Smith Osborne, Madolyn (Actor)
United Talent Agency
9560 Wilshire Blvd Ste 500
Beverly Hills, CA 90212-2401, USA

Smither, Beri (Model)
c/o Staff Member *Flutie Entertainment (NY)*
270 Lafayette St Ste 1400
New York, NY 10012-3364, USA

Smithers, William
2202 Anacapa St
Santa Barbara, CA 93105-3506, USA

Smithies, Oliver (Misc)
318 Urnstead Dr
Chapel Hill, NC 27516, USA

Smitrovich, Bill (Actor)
3512 Crownridge Dr
Sherman Oaks, CA 91403-4814, USA

Smitrovich, William (Actor)
c/o Steven Siebert *Lighthouse Entertainment*
409 N Camden Dr Ste 202
Beverly Hills, CA 90210-4423, USA

Smits, Jimmy (Actor)
El Sendero
PO Box 49922
Barrington Station
Los Angeles, CA 90049-0922, USA

Smogolski, Henry R (Financier)
Northwestern Savings & Loan
2300 N Western Ave
Chicago, IL 60647-3179, USA

Smokie
Box 2711
Venlo NL-5902 MA, THE NETHERLANDS

Smolan, Rick (Photographer)
Workman Publishers
225 Varick St Fl 9
New York, NY 10014-4381, USA

Smolinski, Mark (Football Player)
Baltimore Colts
3300 Country Club Rd
Petoskey, MI 49770-8211, USA

Smolka, James W (Misc)
PO Box 2123
Lancaster, CA 93539-2123, USA

Smoltz, John A (Baseball Player)
c/o Staff Member *Atlanta Braves*
PO Box 4064
Turner Field
Atlanta, GA 30302-4064, USA

Smoot, Fred (Football Player)
c/o Staff Member *Washington Redskins*
21300 Redskin Park Dr
Ashburn, VA 20147-6100, USA

Smoot, George F III (Physicist)
Lawrence Berkeley Laboratory
1 Cyclotron Rd
Berkeley, CA 94720-8099, USA

Smothers, Dick (Actor, Comedian)
6442 Coldwater Canyon Ave Ste 107B
North Hollywood, CA 91606-1137, USA

Smothers, Tom (Actor, Comedian)
6442 Coldwater Canyon Ave Ste 107B
North Hollywood, CA 91606-1137, USA

Smothers Brothers, The (Comedian)
c/o Staff Member *William Morris Agency (WMA-LA)*
1 William Morris Pl
Beverly Hills, CA 90212-4261, USA

Smuin, Michael (Ballerina, Choreographer)
Smuin Ballets
1314 34th Ave
San Francisco, CA 94122-1309, USA

Smulders, Cobie (Actor)
c/o Louise Spinner Ward *William Morris Agency (WMA-LA)*
1505 10th St
Santa Monica, CA 90401-2805, USA

Smurfit, Victoria
76 Oxford St.
London, ENGLAND W1N 0AX, UNITED KINGDOM (UK)

Smyl, Stan (Hockey Player)
202-130 W 5th St
North Vancouver, BC V7M 1J8, CANADA

Smyth, Charles P (Misc)
245 Prospect Ave
Princeton, NJ 08540-5303, USA

Smyth, Craig H (Historian)
PO Box 39
Cresskill, NJ 07626-0039, USA

Smyth, Joe (Music Group, Musician)
Sawyer Brown Inc
5200 Old Harding Rd
Franklin, TN 37064-9406, USA

Smyth, Patty (Musician)
23712 Malibu Colony Rd
Malibu, CA 90265-4636, USA

Smyth, Ryan (Hockey Player)
Newport Sports
601-201 City Centre Dr
Mississauga, ON L5B 2T4, CANADA

Smythe, Marcus
10635 Santa Monica Blvd Ste 130
Los Angeles, CA 90025-8306, USA

Snapcase
PO Box 711966
Salt Lake City, UT 84171-1966, USA

Snarr, Trevor (Actor)
5223 Spring Clover Dr
Salt Lake City, UT 84123-8416, USA

Snead, Jesse Caryle (J C) (Golfer)
PO Box 782170
Wichita, KS 67278-2170, USA

Snead, Norman B (Norm) (Football Player)
Washington Redskins
508 Veranda Way Apt C204
Naples, FL 34104-6049, USA

Snead, W T Sr (Religious Leader)
Baptist Convention Missionary
PO Box 1602
Los Angeles, CA 90001-0602, USA

Sneaker Pimps (Music Group)
c/o Staff Member *Paradigm (Monterey)*
509 Hartnell St
Monterey, CA 93940-2825, USA

Snedden, Stephen
1925 Century Park E Ste 750
Los Angeles, CA 90067-2708, USA

Sneddon, Bob (Football Player)
Washington Redskins
901 E 1140 S
Ogden, UT 84404-6448, USA

Sneed, Ed (Golfer)
4155 Nottinghill Gate Rd
Columbus, OH 43220-3942, USA

Sneed, Floyd (Musician)
McKenzie Accountancy
5171 Caliente St Unit 134
Las Vegas, NV 89119-2198, USA

Sneed, Joseph T (Judge)
US Court of Appeals
95 7th St
Court Building
San Francisco, CA 94103-1518, USA

Snelder, Richard L (Diplomat)
211 Central Park W
New York, NY 10024-6020, USA

Snell, Esmond E (Misc)
819 Tempted Ways Dr
Longmont, CO 80504-8467, USA

Snell, Matthews (Matt) (Football Player)
New York Jets
S C I Limited Inc 175 Clendenny Ave
Jersey City, NJ 07304, USA

Snell, Peter (Athlete, Track Athlete)
6452 Dunstan Ln
Dallas, TX 75214-2239, USA

Snell, Ray (Football Player)
Tampa Bay Buccaneers
10306 Councils Way
Tampa, FL 33617-4058, USA

Sneva, Tom (Race Car Driver)
3301 E Valley Vista Ln
Paradise Valley, AZ 85253-3739, USA

Sniadecki, Jim (Football Player)
San Francisco 49ers
3267 Congressional Cir
Fairfield, CA 94534-7869, USA

Snicket, Lemony (Writer)
Harper Collins Publishers
10 E 53rd St Fl Cellar2
New York, NY 10022-5076, USA

Snider, Dee (Musician)
Pooch
9511 Weldon Cir Apt 316
Fort Lauderdale, FL 33321-0922, USA

Snider, Edward M (Ed) (Hockey Player)
PO Box 25088
Philadelphia, PA 19147-0288, USA

Snider, Mike
PO Box 140710
Nashville, TN 37214-0710, USA

Snider, R Michael (Scientist)
Pfizer Pharmaceuticals
Eastern Point Road
Groton, CT 06340, USA

Snider, Todd (Music Group, Musician, Songwriter, Writer)
Al Bunneta Mgmt
33 Music Sq W Ste 102B
Nashville, TN 37203-6607, USA

Snidow, Ron (Football Player)
Washington Redskins
18742 Via San Marco
Irvine, CA 92603-3436, USA

Snipes, Wesley (Actor)
c/o David Schiff *Schiff Company*
9465 Wilshire Blvd Ste 480
Beverly Hills, CA 90212-2603, USA

Snitzier, Larry (Musician)
Lindy Martin Mgmt
5 Loblolly Ct
Pinehurst, NC 28374-9349, USA

Snodgrass, William D (Writer)
3061 Hughes Rd
Erieville, NY 13061-4128, USA

Snow (Artist, Musician, Songwriter, Writer)
Hype Music
2076 Sherobee Road #510
Mississauga, ON L5A 4C4, CANADA

Snow, Brittany (Actor)
c/o Katie Rhodes *Untitled Entertainment (LA)*
331 N Maple Dr Fl 3
Beverly Hills, CA 90210-3827, USA

Snow, Eric (Basketball Player)
Philadelphia 76ers
3601 S Broad St
1st Union Center
Philadelphia, PA 19148-5287, USA

Snow, John W (Secretary)
Treasury Department
1500 Pennsylvania Ave NW
Washington, DC 20220-0001, USA

Snow, Justin (Football Player)
Indianapolis Colts
8432 Sawgrass Dr
Indianapolis, IN 46234-1765, USA

Snow, Kate (Television Host)
c/o Staff Member *Good Morning America (NY)*
147 Columbus Ave Fl 6
Abc
New York, NY 10023-6503, USA

Snow, Mark (Composer)
Gorfaine/Schwartz
4111 W Alameda Ave Ste 509
Burbank, CA 91505-4171, USA

Snow, Michelle (Basketball Player)
c/o Staff Member *Houston Comets*
1510 Polk St
Houston, TX 77002-1099, USA

Snow, Percy L (Football Player)
Kansas City Chiefs
2010 48th St NE
Canton, OH 44705-3082, USA

Snow, Phoebe (Musician)
c/o Nina Nisenholtz *N2N Entertainment*
1230 Montana Ave Apt 203
Santa Monica, CA 90403-5987, USA

Snow, Richard F (Editor)
American Heritage Magazine
60 5th Ave
Editorial Dept
New York, NY 10011-8868, USA

Snow, Tony (Government Official)
White House Press Secretary
1600 Pennsylvania Ave NW
Washington, DC 20500-0003, USA

Snow Patrol (Music Group)
c/o Staff Member *Paradigm (Monterey)*
509 Hartnell St
Monterey, CA 93940-2825, USA

Snowden, Alison (Writer)
c/o Staff Member *Endeavor Agency LLC (LA)*
9601 Wilshire Blvd Fl 3
Beverly Hills, CA 90210-5204, USA

Snowden, Earl of (A C R Armstrong-Jones) (Photographer)
22 Launceston Place
London W8 5RL, UNITED KINGDOM (UK)

Snowden, Lisa (Model)
Susan Smith
121A N San Vincente Blvd
Beverly Hills, CA 90211, USA

Snowdon, Lord
22 Lauceston Pl
London, ENGLAND W1, UNITED KINGDOM (UK)

Snyder, Allan W (Scientist)
National University
Optical Science Center
Canberra, ACT 2601, AUSTRALIA

Snyder, Ben (Comedian)
c/o Staff Member *Gersh Agency, The (LA)*
232 N Canon Dr
Beverly Hills, CA 90210-5302, USA

Snyder, Bill (Coach, Football Coach)
Kansas State University
Athletic Dept
Manhattan, KS 66506, USA

Snyder, Daniel (Football Executive)
c/o Staff Member *Washington Redskins*
21300 Redskin Park Dr
Ashburn, VA 20147-6100, USA

Snyder, Dick (Basketball Player)
4621 E Mockingbird Ln
Paradise Valley, AZ 85253-2420, USA

Snyder, Evan (Doctor)
Harvard Medical School
25 Shattuck St
Boston, MA 02115-6092, USA

Snyder, Fonda (Actor)
c/o Staff Member *William Morris Agency (WMA-LA)*
1 William Morris Pl
Beverly Hills, CA 90212-4261, USA

Snyder, Gary S (Writer)
18442 Macnab Cypress Rd
Nevada City, CA 95959-8504, USA

Snyder, J Cory (Baseball Player)
468 N Loafer Dr
Payson, UT 84651-4535, USA

Snyder, Joan (Artist)
Hirschi & Adler Modern
21 E 70th St
New York, NY 10021-4907, USA

Snyder, Joshua (Actor)
c/o Gloria Hinojosa *Amsel Eisenstadt & Frazier Inc*
5055 Wilshire Blvd Ste 865
Los Angeles, CA 90036-6109, USA

Snyder, Liza
c/o Susan Smith *Susan Smith Company, The*
1344 N Wetherly Dr
Los Angeles, CA 90069-1817, USA

Snyder, Loren (Football Player)
Dallas Cowboys
7727 Via Cortona
San Diego, CA 92127-3824, USA

Snyder, Solomon H (Doctor)
3801 Canterbury Rd Unit 1001
Baltimore, MD 21218-2379, USA

Snyder, Suzanne (Actor)
Premiere Artists Agency
1875 Century Park E Ste 2250
Los Angeles, CA 90067-2563, USA

Snyder, Todd (Football Player)
Atlanta Falcons
850 S Valley Ln
Palatine, IL 60067-7185, USA

Snyder, William (Journalist)
508 Young St
Dallas, TX 75202-4808, USA

Snyder, William D (Journalist, Photographer)
Dallas Morning News
Communications Center
Editorial Dept
Dallas, TX 75265, USA

Snyder, Zack (Director, Writer)
c/o Todd Feldman *Creative Artists Agency LCC (CAA-LA)*
2000 Avenue Of The Stars
Los Angeles, CA 90067-4700, USA

Snyderman, Nancy (Doctor, Entertainer)
Leading Authorities Inc
1220 L St NW Ste 850
Washington, DC 20005-4095, USA

So, Linda (Model)
6130 W Tropicana Ave # 280
Las Vegas, NV 89103-4604, USA

So Solid Crew (Music Group)
c/o Staff Member *Mission Control Artists Agency*
50 City Business Centre
Lower Road
London SE16 2XB, UNITED KINGDOM (UK)

Soares, Mario A N L (President)
Rue Dr Joao Soares #2-3
Lisbon 1600, PORTUGAL

Sobel, Barry
9000 W Sunset Blvd Ste 1200
Los Angeles, CA 90069-5812, USA

Sobers, Garfield S (Gary) (Cricketer)
Cricket Board
9 Appleblossom
Petit Valley
Diego Martin, TRINIDAD & TOBAGO

Sobieski, Leelee (Actor)
c/o Staff Member *United Talent Agency (UTA)*
9560 Wilshire Blvd Ste 500
Beverly Hills, CA 90212-2401, USA

Soble, Ron (Actor)
Tyler Kjar
4637 Willowcrest Ave
North Hollywood, CA 91602-1464, USA

Sobule, Jill (Musician, Songwriter, Writer)
c/o Jonny (Jon) Podell *Podell Talent Agency LLC*
22 W 21st St Fl 9
New York, NY 10010-7095, USA

Sochor, James (Jim) (Coach, Football Coach)
1018 Kent Dr
Davis, CA 95616-0933, USA

Socolofsky, Shelley (Artist)
3285 Sumac Dr S
Salem, OR 97302-4080, USA

Sodano, Angelo Cardinal (Religious Leader)
Office of Secretary of State
Palazzo Apostolico
00120, VATICAN CITY

Soderbaum, Kristina
St.-Jakobs-platz 10 D-
Munich 80331, GERMANY

Soderberg, E Loren (Photographer)
PO Box 313
Sausalito, CA 94966-0313, USA

Soderbergh, Steven (Director)
c/o Staff Member *Section Eight Productions*
4000 Warner Blvd Bldg 15
Burbank, CA 91522-0001, USA

Soderstrom, Elisabeth (Opera Singer)
19 Hersbyvagen
Lidingo 181 42, SWEDEN

Soderstrom, Elizabeth
19 Jersbyvagen
Lidingo 181-42, SWEDEN

Sofaer, Abraham D (Lawyer)
120 Bryant St
Palo Alto, CA 94301, USA

Sofer, Rena (Actor)
Metropolitan Talent Agency
4500 Wilshire Blvd Fl 2
Los Angeles, CA 90010-3858, USA

Soffer, Jesse Lee (Actor)
c/o Marnie Sparer *Innovative Artists (LA)*
1505 10th St
Santa Monica, CA 90401-2805, USA

Sofie von Otter, Anne (Musician)
c/o Staff Member *International Creative Management (ICM-LA)*
10250 Constellation Blvd
Los Angeles, CA 90067-6200, USA

Softley, Iain (Director)
32A Camaby St
London, W1V 1PA, UNITED KINGDOM (UK)

Sohmer, Steve
2625 Larmar Rd
Los Angeles, CA 90068-2631, USA

Sohn Kee-Chung (Athlete, Track Athlete)
Korean Olympic Committee
International PO Box 1106
Seoul, SOUTH KOREA

Soklosky, Bing (Cinematographer)
4654 Cartwright Ave
Toluca Lake, CA 91602-1451, USA

Sokol, Marilyn (Actor)
24 W 40th St # 1700
New York, NY 10018-3904, USA

Sokoloff, Louis (Misc)
National Mental Health Institute
9000 Rockville Pike
Bethesda, MD 20892-0001, USA

Sokoloff, Marla (Actor)
The Firm
9100 Wilshire Blvd Ste 100W
Beverly Hills, CA 90212-3435, USA

Sokolosky, John (Football Player)
Detroit Lions
13240 Leech Dr
Sterling Heights, MI 48312-3253, USA

Sokolov, Grigory L (Musician)
Trawick Artists
1926 Broadway
New York, NY 10023-6915, USA

Sokolove, James G (Lawyer)
1 Boston Pl
Boston, MA 02108-4407, USA

Sokomanu, A George (President)
Mele Village
PO Box 1319
Port Villa, VANUATU

Sokurov, Alexander N (Director)
Smolenskaya Nab 4 #222
Saint Petersburg 199048, RUSSIA

Sol Hudson, Slash (Musician)
5664 Cahuenga Blvd # 246
N Hollywood, CA 91601-2103, USA

Solana Madariaga, Javier (Government Official)
European Union Foreign Office
Rue de la Loi
Brussels 1048, BELGIUM

Solano, Jose (Actor)
c/o Staff Member *The House of Representatives*
211 S Beverly Dr Ste 208
Beverly Hills, CA 90212-3879, USA

Solars, Stephen
241 Dover St
Brooklyn, NY 11235-3721, USA

Solberg, Magnar (Athlete)
Stabellvn 60
Trondheim 7000, NORWAY

Soleil, Stella (Music Group, Musician)
Kurfirst/Blackwell
350 W End Ave Apt 1A
New York, NY 10024-6818, USA

Soler, Juan (Actor)
c/o Staff Member *Televisa*
Blvd Adolfo Lopez Mateos 232
Colonia San Angel INN
DF CP 01060, MEXICO

Soleri, Paolo (Architect)
Cosanti Foundation
6433 E Doubletree Ranch Rd
Scottsdale, AZ 85253-1826, USA

Soles, Pamela Jayne (Actor)
c/o Jerry Pace *Zanuck, Passon and Pace, Inc*
4717 Van Nuys Blvd Ste 102
Atrium #102
Sherman Oaks, CA 91403-2150, USA

Solh, Rashid (Prime Minister)
Chambre of Deputes
Place de l'Etoile
Beirut, LEBANON

Solich, Frank (Coach, Football Coach)
University of Nebraska
Athletic Dept
Lincoln, NE 68588, USA

Solis, Christina
9300 Wilshire Blvd Ste 555
Beverly Hills, CA 90212-3211, USA

Sollscher, Goran (Musician)
Kunstleragentur Raab & Bohm
Plankengasse 7
Vienna 1010, AUSTRIA

Soloman, Anthony M (Financier)
535 Park Ave
New York, NY 10065-8167, USA

Soloman, Freddie (Football Player)
803 Turtle River Ct
Plant City, FL 33567-2474, USA

Solomon, Ariel (Football Player)
Pittsburgh Steelers
3142 5th St
Boulder, CO 80304-2504, USA

Solomon, Arthur K (Physicist)
27 Craigie St
Cambridge, MA 02138-3457, USA

Solomon, Bruce
3518 Cahuenga Blvd W # 316
Los Angeles, CA 90068, USA

Solomon, David H (Scientist)
3640 Dragonfly Dr Apt 202
Thousand Oaks, CA 91360-8445, USA

Solomon, Edward I (Misc)
Stanford University
Chemistry Dept
Stanford, CA 94305, USA

Solomon, Harold (Tennis Player)
Int'l Mgmt Group
1 Erieview Plz
1360 E 9th St #1300
Cleveland, OH 44114-1738, USA

Solomon, Jesse (Football Player)
Minnesota Vikings
401 SW Bunker St
Madison, FL 32340-1902, USA

Solomon, Richard H (Diplomat, Scientist)
US Institute for Peace
1200 17th St NW Ste 200
Washington, DC 20036-3011, USA

Solomon, Sophie (Musician)
c/o Staff Member *Paradigm (Monterey)*
509 Hartnell St
Monterey, CA 93940-2825, USA

Solomon, Susan (Misc)
National Oceanic & Atmospheric Admin
325 Broadway St
Boulder, CO 80305-3337, USA

Solomon, Yonty (Musician)
56 Canonbury Park N
London N1 2JT, UNITED KINGDOM (UK)

Solondz, Todd (Director, Writer)
Industry Entertainment
955 Carrillo Dr Ste 300
Los Angeles, CA 90048-5400, USA

Solovey, Sam (Actor)
c/o Staff Member *Ruth Webb Enterprises*
10580 Des Moines Ave
Northridge, CA 91326-2926, USA

Soloviyev, Vladimir A (Cosmonaut)
Khovanskaya Ui D 3
Kv 28
Moscow 129515, RUSSIA

Solovyev, Anatoli Y (Cosmonaut)
Potchta Kosmonavtov
Moskovskoi Oblasti
Syvisdny Goroduk 141160, RUSSIA

Solovyev, Sergei A (Director, Writer)
Akademika Pilyugina Str 8
Korp 1 #330
Moscow 11393, RUSSIA

Solow, Robert M (Nobel Prize Laureate)
528 Lewis Wharf
Boston, MA 02110-3920, USA

Soloway, Jill (Producer)
c/o Staff Member *International Creative Management (ICM-LA)*
10250 Constellation Blvd
Los Angeles, CA 90067-6200, USA

Solt, Ron (Football Player)
Indianapolis Colts
1200 Thornhurst Rd
Bear Creek Township, PA 18702-8212, USA

Soltan, Jerzy (Architect)
6 Shady Hill Sq
Cambridge, MA 02138-2036, USA

Soltau, Gordie (Football Player)
San Francisco 49ers
1290 Sharon Park Dr Apt 50
Menlo Park, CA 94025-7038, USA

Soltau, Gordon (Gordy) (Football Player)
1290 Sharon Park Dr
Menlo Park, CA 94025-7052, USA

Soltau, Gordy
1111 Hamilton Ave
Palo Alto, CA 94301-2217, USA

Soluna (Music Group)
c/o Staff Member *Creative Artists Agency LCC (CAA-LA)*
2000 Avenue Of The Stars
Los Angeles, CA 90067-4700, USA

Solvay, Jacques (Business Person)
Solvay Cie SA
Rue de Prince Albert 33
Brussels 1050, BELGIUM

Solymosi, Zoltan (Dancer)
Royal Ballet
Covent GArden
Bow St
London WC2E 9DD, UNITED KINGDOM (UK)

Solyom, Janos P (Musician)
Norr Malarstrand 54
VII
Stockholm 11220, SWEDEN

Solzhenitsyn, Ignat (Musician)
Columbia Artists Mgmt Inc
1790 Broadway Fl 6
New York, NY 10019-1412, USA

Somare, Michael T (Prime Minister)
Assembly House
Karan
Murik Lakes
East Sepik, PAPUA NEW GUINEA

Sombrotto, Vincent R (Misc)
National Letter Carriers Assn
100 Indiana Ave NW
Washington, DC 20001-2144, USA

Somerhalder, Ian (Actor)
c/o Alissa Vradenburg *Untitled Entertainment (LA)*
331 N Maple Dr Fl 3
Beverly Hills, CA 90210-3827, USA

Somers, Gwen (Actor, Model)
Alice Fries Agency
1927 Vista Del Mar St
Los Angeles, CA 90068-4004, USA

Somers, Suzanne (Actor)
MPI Talent Agency
9255 W Sunset Blvd Ste 407
Los Angeles, CA 90069-3302, USA

Somerset, Willie (Basketball Player)
PO Box 314
Monmouth Junction, NJ 08852-0314, USA

Somerville, Bonnie (Actor)
c/o Staff Member *McKeon-Valeo-Myones Management*
9100 Wilshire Blvd Ste 350W
Beverly Hills, CA 90212-3437, USA

Something Corporate (Music Group)
c/o Staff Member *Agency for the Performing Arts (APA-LA)*
405 S Beverly Dr
Beverly Hills, CA 90212-4416, USA

Sommars, Julie (Actor)
S D B Partners
1801 Avenue Of Stars Ste 902
Los Angeles, CA 90067-5981, USA

Sommaruga, Cornelio (Misc)
International Red Cross
19 Ave de la Paix
Genoa 1202, SWITZERLAND

Sommer, Elke (Actor)
Atzelaberger Str 46
Marloffstein D-91080, GERMANY

Sommerfeld, Kent (Sportscaster)
Milwaukee Brewers
13935 W Maria Dr
New Berlin, WI 53151-6891, USA

Sommers, Gordon L (Religious Leader)
Moravian Church Northem Province
1021 Center St
Bethlehem, PA 18018-2838, USA

Sommers, Joanie (Musician)
Xentel
900 SE 3rd Ave Ste 201
Fort Lauderdale, FL 33316-1118, USA

Sommers, Stephen (Director)
c/o John Fogelman *William Morris
Agency (WMA-LA)*
1 William Morris Pl
Beverly Hills, CA 90212-4261, USA

Sommore (Comedian)
c/o Staff Member *International Creative
Management (ICM-LA)*
10250 Constellation Blvd
Los Angeles, CA 90067-6200, USA

Somogyi, Jeannie R (Ballerina)
New York City Ballet
Lincoln Center Plaza
New York, NY 10023, USA

Somogyi, Jozsef (Artist)
Marton Utca 3/5
Budapest 1038, HUNGARY

Somorjai, Gabor A (Misc)
665 San Luis Rd
Berkeley, CA 94707-1725, USA

Sondeckis, Saulls (Conductor)
Ciurlionio 28
Vilnius, LITHUANIA

Sondheim, Stephen (Composer, Musician)
Stephen Sondheim Organization, The
265 Wollaton Vale
Wollaton, Nottingham NG8 2PX, UNITED
KINGDOM (UK)

Sondrini, Joe (Baseball Player)
Bowman
16712 Stockland Ct
Huntersville, NC 28078-6438, USA

Song, Brenda (Actor)
c/o Susan Curtis *Curtis Talent
Management*
9607 Arby Dr
Beverly Hills, CA 90210-1202, USA

Song, Xiaodong (Misc)
Columbia University
Lamont-Doherty Earth Observatory
New York, NY 10027, USA

Songz, Trey (Musician)
c/o Staff Member *Paradigm (Monterey)*
509 Hartnell St
Monterey, CA 93940-2825, USA

Sonja (Royalty)
Det Kongelige Slott
Drammensveien 1
Oslo 0010, NORWAY

Sonnenfeld, Barry (Director)
c/o Richard Lovett *Creative Artists Agency
LCC (CAA-LA)*
2000 Avenue Of The Stars
Los Angeles, CA 90067-4700, USA

Sonnenschein, Hugo F (Educator)
University of Chicago
President's Office
Chicago, IL 60637, USA

Sonnenschein, Klaus
Breisgauer Str. 15a
Berlin D-14129, GERMANY

Sonnier, Jo-El (Musician)
Entertainment Artists
2409 21st Ave S Ste 100
Nashville, TN 37212-5317, USA

Sons of the Desert (Music Group)
c/o Staff Member *William Morris Agency
(WMA-TN)*
1600 Division St Ste 300
Nashville, TN 37203-2755, USA

Sons of the Pioneers
117 Berms Cir Apt 4
Branson, MO 65616-3875, USA

Sonsini, Larry W (Lawyer)
Wilson Sonsini Goodrich Rosati
650 Page Mill Rd
Palo Alto, CA 94304-1050, USA

Sood, Veena (Actor, Producer)
c/o Robyn Friedman *Artist Management
Inc*
464 King St E
Toronto, ON M5A 1L7, CANADA

Soomekh, Bahar (Actor)
c/o Paul Kohner *Kohner Agency, The*
9300 Wilshire Blvd Ste 555
Beverly Hills, CA 90212-3211, USA

Sophia (Royalty)
Palacio de la Zarzuela
Madrid 28071, SPAIN

Sopko, Michael D (Business Person)
Inco Ltd
145 King St W
Toronto, ON M5H 4B7, CANADA

Sopkovic, Kay (Baseball Player)
6540 W Butler Dr Unit 62
Glendale, AZ 85302-4313, USA

Sorbo, Kevin (Actor)
c/o Staff Member *Nine Yards
Entertainment*
8530 Wilshire Blvd Fl 5
Beverly Hills, CA 90211-3102, USA

Sorel, Edward (Artist)
156 Franklin St
New York, NY 10013-2908, USA

Sorel, Jean (Actor)
Cineart
36 Rue de Ponthieu
Paris 75008, FRANCE

Sorel, Louise (Actor)
10808 Lindbrook Dr
Los Angeles, CA 90024-3007, USA

Sorensen, Jacki F (Misc)
Jacki's Inc
129 1/2 N Woodland Blvd Ste 5
Deland, FL 32720-4269, USA

Sorensen, Nick (Football Player)
St Louis Rams
305 Grandview Dr
Blacksburg, VA 24060-6222, USA

Sorensen, Theodore C (Attorney, Attorney
General, General, Government Official)
Paul Weiss Rifkind Assoc
1285 Avenue Of The Americas
New York, NY 10019-6031, USA

Sorenson, Dave (Basketball Player)
19000 Lake Rd Apt 723
Rocky River, OH 44116-1762, USA

Sorenson, Heidi (Actor, Model)
Shelly & Pierce
13775A Mono Way # 220
Sonora, CA 95370-8813, USA

Sorenson, Paul (Actor)
11802 Lindbrook Dr
Los Angeles, CA 90024, USA

Sorenson, Theodore
1285 Avenue Of The Americas
New York, NY 10019-6031, USA

Sorenstam, Annika (Golfer)
c/o Staff Member *International
Management Group (IMG Sports)*
1360 E 9th St Ste 100
Cleveland, OH 44114-1730, USA

Sorenstam, Charlotta (Golfer)
c/o Patrick Levine
1411 W Whitman Ct
Anthem, AZ 85086-3927, USA

Sorey, Revie (Football Player)
Chicago Bears
485 Saint Moritz Dr
Glen Ellyn, IL 60137-4320, USA

Sorgers, Jana (Athlete)
Potsdamer RG
An Der Pirschheide
Potsdam 14471, GERMANY

Soriano, Alfonso G (Baseball Player)
Texas Rangers
1000 Ballpark Way Ste 306
Arlington, TX 76011-5169, USA

Soriano, Edward (General)
Vice Commander
I Corps/Fort Lewis
Fort Lewis, WA 98433, USA

Sorkin, Aaron (Producer, Writer)
c/o Tracy Shaffer *PMK/HBH Public
Relations (PMK-LA)*
700 N San Vicente Blvd Ste G910
West Hollywood, CA 90069-5061, USA

Sorkin, Arleen (Actor)
623 S Beverly Glen Blvd
Los Angeles, CA 90024-2531, USA

Sorlie, Donald M (Misc)
14612 44th Avenue Ct NW
Gig Harbor, WA 98332-9048, USA

Sorokin, Peter P (Physicist)
5 Ashwood Rd
South Salem, NY 10590-1601, USA

Soros, George (Financier)
Soros Fund Mgmt
888 7th Ave # 3300
New York, NY 10106-0001, USA

Soroya, Princess
Ave. Montaigne
Paris 75008, FRANCE

Sorrento, Paul A (Baseball Player)
5918 Mont Blanc Pl NW
Issaquah, WA 98027-7859, USA

Sorsa, T Kalevi (Prime Minister)
Hakaniemenranta 16D
Helsinki 00530, FINLAND

Sorte, Maria (Actor)
c/o Staff Member *Televisa*
Blvd Adolfo Lopez Mateos 232
Colonia San Angel INN
DF CP 01060, MEXICO

Sortun, Henrik (Football Player)
St Louis Cardinals
6708 16th Ave NW
Seattle, WA 98117-5513, USA

Sorvino, Mira (Actor)
c/o Jean Fox *Fox-Albert Management*
88 Central Park W
New York, NY 10023-5209, USA

Sorvino, Paul (Actor)
8A1 Mountain View Dr
Gilbert, PA 18331, USA

Sosa, Samuel (Sammy) (Baseball Player)
c/o Staff Member *Baltimore Orioles*
333 W Camden St
Oriole Park
Baltimore, MD 21201-2435, USA

Sossaman, Shannyn (Actor)
c/o Staff Member *Dash Group, The*
550 N Larchmont Blvd Ste 201
Los Angeles, CA 90004-1318, USA

Sossamon, Lou (Football Player)
New York Yankees
6308 Exum Dr
West Columbia, SC 29169-7184, USA

Soter, Paul (Comedian)
c/o Staff Member *United Talent Agency
(UTA)*
9560 Wilshire Blvd Ste 500
Beverly Hills, CA 90212-2401, USA

Sotin, Hans (Opera Singer)
Schulheide 10
Bendestorf 21227, GERMANY

Sotirhos, Michael A (Diplomat)
American Embassy
A Leoforos Vassilissis Sofias 91
Athens 106 60, GREECE

Sotkilava, Zurab L (Opera Singer)
Bolshoi Theater
Teatralnaya Pi 1
Moscow 103009, RUSSIA

Soto, Gabriel (Actor)
c/o Staff Member *Televisa*
Blvd Adolfo Lopez Mateos 232
Colonia San Angel INN
DF CP 01060, MEXICO

Soto, Jock (Dancer)
New York City Ballet
Lincoln Center Plaza
New York, NY 10023, USA

Soto, Mario M (Baseball Player)
Joachs-Lachaustegui #42
Sur-Bani, DOMINICAN REPUBLIC

Soto, Talisa (Actor)
c/o Peg Donegan *Framework
Entertainment (LA)*
9057 Nemo St # C
W Hollywood, CA 90069-5511, USA

Sotomayor, Antonio (Artist)
3 Leroy Pl
San Francisco, CA 94109-4224, USA

Sotomayor Sanabria, Javier (Athlete,
Track Athlete)
Int'l Mgmt Group
1 Erieview Plz
1360 E 9th St #1300
Cleveland, OH 44114-1738, USA

Sottsass Jr, Ettore (Designer)
Via Manzoni 14
Milan 20121, ITALY

Souchak, Mike (Golfer)
79 Pelican Pl
Belleair, FL 33756-1512, USA

Souders, Cecil (Football Player)
Detroit Lions
1803 Channingway Court E
Reynoldsburg, OH 43068, USA

Soul, David (Actor, Musician)
Innovative Artists
1505 10th St
Santa Monica, CA 90401-2805, USA

Soul Asylum
955 Carrillo Dr Ste 300
Los Angeles, CA 90048-5400, USA

Soul II Soul (Music Group)
c/o Staff Member *Profile Artists Agency*
Unit 10, J Block
Tower Bridge Business Complex, 110
Clements Road
London SE16 4DG, UNITED KINGDOM
(UK)

Soulages, Pierre (Artist)
18 Rue des Trois-Portes
Paris 75005, FRANCE

SoulDecision (Music Group)
c/o Staff Member *SL Feldman &
Associates*
1505 W 2nd Ave #200
Vancouver, BC V6H 3Y4, CANADA

Sound Tribe Sector 9 (Music Group)
c/o Staff Member *Paradigm (Monterey)*
509 Hartnell St
Monterey, CA 93940-2825, USA

Soundarya (Actor, Bollywood)
Bangalore, KA, INDIA

Sousa, Mauricio de (Cartoonist)
Mauricio de Sousa Producoes
Rua do Curtume 745
Sao Paulo SP, BRAZIL

Soutar, Dave (Bowler)
6910 Chickasaw Falls Ave
Bradenton, FL 34203, USA

Soutar, Judy (Bowler)
3914 102nd Pl N
Clearwater, FL 33762-5404, USA

Soutendijk, Renee (Actor)
Marion Rosenberg
PO Box 69826
West Hollywood, CA 90069-0826, USA

Souter, David H (Judge)
US Supreme Court
1 1st St NE
Washington, DC 20543-0002, USA

South, Joe (Musician, Songwriter, Writer)
3051 Clairmont Rd NE
Atlanta, GA 30329-1601, USA

South, Mike
PO Box 1288
Tucker, GA 30085-1288, USA

Souther, J D (Musician, Songwriter, Writer)
8263 Hollywood Blvd
Los Angeles, CA 90069-1611, USA

Southern, Silas (Eddie) (Athlete, Track Athlete)
2006 Custer Pkwy
Richardson, TX 75080-3403, USA

Southern Belles
11150 W Olympic Blvd Ste 1100
Los Angeles, CA 90064-1822, USA

Southworth, Carrie (Actor)
c/o Staff Member *TalentWorks (LA)*
3500 W Olive Ave Ste 1400
Burbank, CA 91505-5512, USA

Souza, Francis N (Artist)
148 W 67th St
New York, NY 10023-5965, USA

Sova, Peter M (Cinematographer)
1492 Roses Brook Rd
South Kortright, NY 13842-2514, USA

Sovereign, Lady (Musician)
c/o Staff Member *Paradigm (Monterey)*
509 Hartnell St
Monterey, CA 93940-2825, USA

Sovern, Michael I (Educator)
Columbia University
435 W 116th St
Law School
New York, NY 10027-7237, USA

Sovey, William P (Business Person)
Newell Co
20 E Milwaukee St Ste 212
Janesville, WI 53545-3061, USA

Soward, R J (Football Player)
Jacksonville Jaguars
7660 Chipwood Ln
Jacksonville, FL 32256-2338, USA

Sowell, Arnold (Arnie) (Athlete, Track Athlete)
1647 Waterstone Ln # 1
Charlotte, NC 28262-3176, USA

Sowell, Thomas (Economist)
Stanford University
Hoover Institution
Stanford, CA 94305, USA

Sowells, Rich (Football Player)
New York Jets
6711 McCullum Rd
Missouri City, TX 77489-3430, USA

Sowers, Barbara (Baseball Player)
1191 Ricardo Ln
Punta Gorda, FL 33983-6122, USA

Soyer, David (Musician)
PO Box 307
Brattleboro, VT 05302-0307, USA

Soyinka, Wole (Nobel Prize Laureate)
University of Nevada
Creative Writing Dept
Las Vegas, NV 89154, USA

Soyster, Harry E (General)
4706 Duncan Dr
Annandale, VA 22003-4614, USA

Spaak, Catherine
Viale Parioli 59
Rome 00197, ITALY

Spacek, Jaroslav (Hockey Player)
Columbus Blue Jackets
200 W Nationwide Blvd
Arena
Columbus, OH 43215-2564, USA

Spacek, Sissy (Actor)
Beau Val Farm
Box 22 #640
Cobham, VA 22929, USA

Spacey, Kevin (Actor)
c/o Staff Member *Trigger Street
Productions*
755A N La Cienega Blvd
Los Angeles, CA 90069-5203, USA

Spaddky, Boris V (Misc)
State Committee for Sports
Skatertny Pereulok 4
Moscow, RUSSIA

Spade, David (Actor, Comedian)
c/o Marc Gurvitz *Brillstein-Grey
Entertainment*
9150 Wilshire Blvd Ste 350
Beverly Hills, CA 90212-3453, USA

Spade, Kate (Designer, Fashion Designer)
Public Relations Dept
48 W 25th St Fl 4
New York, NY 10010-2708, USA

Spader, James (Actor)
c/o Joe Funicello *International Creative
Management (ICM-LA)*
10250 Constellation Blvd
Los Angeles, CA 90067-6200, USA

Spafford, Eugene (Educator)
Purdue University
Education Research Center
West Lafayette, IN 47907, USA

Spagnola, John S (Football Player)
Philadelphia Eagles
414 Hillbrook Rd
Bryn Mawr, PA 19010-3634, USA

Spahn, Ryan (Actor)
c/o TJ Stein *Stein Entertainment Group*
11271 Ventura Blvd # 477
Studio City, CA 91604-3136, USA

Spahr, Charles E (Business Person)
800 Beach Rd
Vero Beach, FL 32963-3392, USA

Spain, Douglas (Actor)
Innovative Artists
1505 10th St
Santa Monica, CA 90401-2805, USA

Spalding, Leslie (Golfer)
1055 O Malley Dr
Billings, MT 59102-2524, USA

Spali, Timothy (Actor)
Markham & Froggatt
Julian House
4 Windmill St
London W1P 1HF, UNITED KINGDOM
(UK)

Spall, Timothy (Actor)
c/o Pippa Markham *Markham and
Froggatt Agency*
4 Windmill St
London W1T 1HF, UNITED KINGDOM
(UK)

Spanarkel, Jim (Basketball Player)
436 Edgewood Pl
Rutherford, NJ 07070-2662, USA

Spanger, Amy (Actor)
c/o Maureen Taran *New Wave
Entertainment (LA)*
2660 W Olive Ave
Burbank, CA 91505-4525, USA

Spani, Gary (Football Player)
Kansas City Chiefs
3920 NE Sequoia St
Lees Summit, MO 64064-1574, USA

Spanic, Gabriela (Actor)
c/o Staff Member *Televisa*
Blvd Adolfo Lopez Mateos 232
Colonia San Angel INN
DF CP 01060, MEXICO

Spanjers, Martin (Actor)
c/o Staff Member *8 Simple Rules for
Dating My Teenage Daughter*
Stage 6 Fl 5 Teenage Daughter
500 S Buena Vista
Burbank, CA 91521-0001, USA

Spano, Joe (Actor)
EC Assoc
10315 Woodley Ave Ste 110
Granada Hills, CA 91344-6900, USA

Spano, Robert (Musician)
c/o Staff Member *International Creative
Management (ICM-LA)*
10250 Constellation Blvd
Los Angeles, CA 90067-6200, USA

Spano, Vincent (Actor)
c/o Jo Kincaid *Gilbertson-Kincaid
Management*
1334 3rd Street Promenade Ste 201
Santa Monica, CA 90401-1320, USA

Sparks
106 N Buffalo St Ste 200
Warsaw, IN 46580-2755, USA

Sparks, Dana (Actor)
VOX
5670 Wilshire Blvd Ste 820
Los Angeles, CA 90036-5613, USA

Sparks, Hal (Actor, Comedian, Musician)
c/o Sherry Marsh *Marsh Entertainment*
12444 Ventura Blvd Ste 203
Studio City, CA 91604-2409, USA

Sparks, Hayley
5757 Wilshire Blvd # 512
Los Angeles, CA 90036-5810, USA

Sparks, Jordin (Musician)
c/o Staff Member *American Idol*
7800 Beverly Blvd # 251
Los Angeles, CA 90036-2112, USA

Sparks, Kylie (Actor)
c/o Myrna Lieberman *Myrna Lieberman
Management*
3001 Hollyridge Dr
Hollywood, CA 90068-1951, USA

Sparks, Mike (Referee)
c/o Staff Member *World Wrestling
Entertainment (WWE)*
1241 E Main St
Stamford, CT 06902-3520, USA

Sparks, Nicholas (Writer)
Warner Books
1271 Avenue Of The Americas
New York, NY 10020-1300, USA

Sparks, Phillippi (Football Player)
Green Bay Packers
3315 W Walter Way
Phoenix, AZ 85027-1084, USA

Sparks, Stephanie (Golfer)
48 Redwood Ln
Wheeling, WV 26003-4854, USA

Sparlis, Alexander (Al) (Football Player)
Green Bay Packers
HC 4 Box 243
Porterville, CA 93257-9706, USA

Sparv, Camilla (Actor)
957 Cole Ave
Los Angeles, CA 90038-2610, USA

Sparxxx, Bubba (Musician)
c/o Staff Member *Paradigm (Monterey)*
509 Hartnell St
Monterey, CA 93940-2825, USA

Spassky, Boris
Skatertny Pereulok 5
Moscow, CA, RUSSIA

Speakman-Pitt, William (War Hero)
Victoria Cross Assn
Old Admiralty Building
London SW1A 2BL, UNITED KINGDOM
(UK)

Speaks, Ruben L (Religious Leader)
African Methodist Episcopal Zion Church
PO Box 32843
Charlotte, NC 28232-2843, USA

Spear, Laurinda H (Architect)
Arquitectonica International
550 Brickell Ave # 200
Miami, FL 33131, USA

Spearman, Alvin (Baseball Player)
Chicago American Giants
635 E 49th St Apt 3
Chicago, IL 60615-1556, USA

Spearritt, Hannah (Actor, Musician)
c/o Jeb Brandon *Endeavor Agency LLC
(LA)*
9601 Wilshire Blvd Fl 3
Beverly Hills, CA 90210-5204, USA

Spears, Aries (Actor)
c/o Leigh Brillstein *International Creative
Management (ICM-LA)*
10250 Constellation Blvd
Los Angeles, CA 90067-6200, USA

Spears, Billie Jo (Musician)
PO Box 23470
Nashville, TN 37202-3470, USA

Spears, Britney (Actor, Musician)
c/o Jeff Kwatinetz *The Firm*
9465 Wilshire Blvd Fl 6
Beverly Hills, CA 90212-2605, USA

Spears, Ernest (Football Player)
New Orleans Saints
201 50th Ave Apt 24K
Long Island City, NY 11101-5782, USA

Spears, Jamie Lynn (Actor)
c/o Michael Katcher *Creative Artists
Agency LCC (CAA-LA)*
2000 Avenue Of The Stars
Los Angeles, CA 90067-4700, USA

Spears, Marcus (Football Player)
Chicago Bears
10402 Reading Rd
Richmond, TX 77469-7330, USA

Spears, William D (Football Player)
63 Waterbridge Pl
Ponte Vedra Beach, FL 32082-2323, USA

Specter, Arlen (Senator)
310 Spruce St
Scranton, PA 18503-1413, USA

Spector, Elisabeth (Lisa) (Government
Official)
Resolution Trust Corp
801 17th St NW
Washington, DC 20232-0001, USA

Spector, Phil (Business Person,
Songwriter, Writer)
686 S Arroyo Pkwy # 175
Pasadena, CA 91105-3233, USA

Spector, Ronnie (Musician)
Absolute Artists
8490 W Sunset Blvd Ste 403
West Hollywood, CA 90069-1926, USA

Speech (Artist)
William Morris Agency
1325 Avenue Of The Americas
New York, NY 10019-6091, USA

Speed, Horace (Baseball Player)
San Francisco Giants
2423 E Flower St
Phoenix, AZ 85016-7413, USA

Speed, Lake (Race Car Driver)
4027 Old Salisbury Concord Rd
Kannapolis, NC 28083-9699, USA

Speed, Lizz (Producer)
c/o Staff Member *Jackoway Tyerman
Wertheimer Austen Mandelbaum &
Morris*
1888 Century Park E Fl 18
Los Angeles, CA 90067-1702, USA

Speedman, Scott (Actor)
c/o Brian Swardstrom *Endeavor Agency
LLC (LA)*
9601 Wilshire Blvd Fl 3
Beverly Hills, CA 90210-5204, USA

Speedwagon, REO (Musician)
c/o Staff Member *Creative Artists Agency
LCC (CAA-LA)*
2000 Avenue Of The Stars
Los Angeles, CA 90067-4700, USA

Speer, Del (Football Player)
Cleveland Browns
17620 NW 40th Ave
Miami Gardens, FL 33055-3864, USA

Speer, Hugo (Actor)
c/o Staff Member *Artists Rights Group
(ARG London)*
4 Great Portland St
London W1W 8PA, UNITED KINGDOM
(UK)

Speers, Ted (Hockey Player)
61515 Brookway Dr
South Lyon, MI 48178-7056, USA

Spehr, Tim (Baseball Player)
Kansas City Royals
8524 Briargrove Dr
Waco, TX 76712-2305, USA

Speight, Lester (Rasta) (Actor)
c/o Staff Member *Endeavor Agency LLC
(LA)*
9601 Wilshire Blvd Fl 3
Beverly Hills, CA 90210-5204, USA

Speir, Chris
6114 E Montecito Ave
Scottsdale, AZ 85251-1936, USA

Speiser, Jerry (Musician)
TPA
PO Box 124
Round Corner, NSW, AUSTRALIA

Speler, Justin (Baseball Player)
c/o Staff Member *Colorado Rockies*
2001 Blake St
Coors Field
Denver, CO 80205-2000, USA

Spelke, Elizabeth S (Doctor)
Harvard University
Psychology Dept
Cambridge, MA 02138, USA

Spelling, Randy (Actor)
c/o Staff Member *Innovative Artists (LA)*
1505 10th St
Santa Monica, CA 90401-2805, USA

Spelling, Tori (Actor)
c/o Ruthanne Secunda *United Talent
Agency (UTA)*
9560 Wilshire Blvd Ste 500
Beverly Hills, CA 90212-2401, USA

Spellman, Alonzo R (Football Player)
Chicago Bears
1300 Marigold Way
Pflugerville, TX 78660-4137, USA

Spellman, John D (Governor)
7048 51st Ave NE
Seattle, WA 98115-6132, USA

Spelvin, Georgina
3121 Ledgewood Dr
Hollywood, CA 90068-1913, USA

Spence, A Michael (Nobel Prize Laureate)
768 Mayfield Ave
Stanford, CA 94305-1044, USA

Spence, Blake (Football Player)
New York Jets
14005 SW Teal Blvd Apt D
Beaverton, OR 97008-4305, USA

Spence, Bob (Baseball Player)
Chicago White Sox
3550 3rd Ave Apt 1C
San Diego, CA 92103-4901, USA

Spence, Dave (Misc)
Horseshores Union
RR 2 Box 71C
Englishtown, NJ 07726, USA

Spence, Gerry (Lawyer)
Spence Moriarity Schuster
15 South Jackson Street
Jackson, WY 83001, USA

Spence, Jonathan D (Historian, Writer)
691 Forest Rd
West Haven, CT 06516-7932, USA

Spence, Roger F (Religious Leader)
Reformed Episcopal Church
2001 Jackson St
Jackson, WY 83001, USA

Spence, Sebastian (Actor)
1005 Cambie St
Vancouver, BC V6B 5L7, CANADA

Spencer, Abigail (Actor)
c/o Staff Member *Principal Entertainment
(LA)*
1964 Westwood Blvd Ste 400
Los Angeles, CA 90025-4695, USA

Spencer, Bud (Actor)
Mistral Film Group
Via Archmede 24
Rome 00187, ITALY

Spencer, Chris
10100 Santa Monica Blvd Ste 2490
Los Angeles, CA 90067-4144, USA

Spencer, Danielle (Actor)
Robert Barnham Mgmt
432 Tygarah Road
Myocum, NSW 2481, AUSTRALIA

Spencer, Darryl (Football Player)
Atlanta Falcons
1473 Beechfern Dr
Melbourne, FL 32935-5989, USA

Spencer, Daryl (Baseball Player)
New York Giants
2740 Larkin St
Wichita, KS 67216-1258, USA

Spencer, Earl Charles
Althorpe House Gr. Brington
Northamptonshire, ENGLAND NN7 4HQ,
UNITED KINGDOM (UK)

Spencer, Elizabeth (Writer)
402 Longleaf Dr
Chapel Hill, NC 27517-3042, USA

Spencer, Elmore (Basketball Player)
1770 Foxlair Trail
Atlanta, GA 30349, USA

Spencer, F Gilman (Editor)
Denver Post
1560 Broadway
Editorial Dept
Denver, CO 80202-6000, USA

Spencer, Felton (Basketball Player)
New York Knicks
2 Penn Plz
Madison Square Garden
New York, NY 10121-1703, USA

Spencer, Frank Cole (Doctor, Educator)
560 1st Ave
New York, NY 10016-6402, USA

Spencer, George (Baseball Player)
New York Giants
8160 Hickory Ave
Galena, OH 43021-8508, USA

Spencer, Jesse (Actor)
c/o Robyn Gardiner *RGM Associates
(Australia)*
PO Box 128
Surry Hills NSW 2010, AUSTRALIA

Spencer, Jimmy (Football Player)
5331 Talavero Pl
Parker, CO 80134-2799, USA

Spencer, John (Athlete, Misc)
17 Knowles St
Radcliffe
Lancs M26 0DN, UNITED KINGDOM
(UK)

Spencer, Lara (Television Host)
c/o Staff Member *Insider, The*
5555 Melrose Ave
Stage 26
Los Angeles, CA 90038-3989, USA

Spencer, Marc (Radio Personality)
c/o Staff Member *WPKX*
1331 Main St Ste 4
Springfield, MA 01103-1621, USA

Spencer, Maurice (Football Player)
St Louis Cardinals
61 W 62nd St
New York, NY 10023-7015, USA

Spencer, Melvin J (Attorney, Attorney
General, General, Religious Leader)
5910 N Shawnee Ave
Oklahoma City, OK 73112-1627, USA

Spencer, Octavia (Actor)
c/o Michael Greene *Greene & Associates*
190 N Canon Dr Ste 200
Beverly Hills, CA 90210-5319, USA

Spencer, Roderick
602 Bay St
Santa Monica, CA 90405-1215, USA

Spencer, Sean (Baseball Player)
Seattle Mariners
3584 E Calistoga Ct
Port Orchard, WA 98366-4084, USA

Spencer, Shane (Baseball Player)
New York Yankees
2890 Conestoga Cir
Alpine, CA 91901-3189, USA

Spencer, Susan (Correspondent)
CBS-TV
2020 M St NW
News Dept
Washington, DC 20036-3304, USA

Spencer, Timothy (Tim) (Football Player)
San Diego Chargers
1435 Sherborne Ln
Powell, OH 43065-7604, USA

Spencer, Tom (Baseball Player)
Chicago White Sox
2021 E Conner Stra
Tucson, AZ 85719-3206, USA

Spencer, Tracie (Musician)
Rogers & Cowan
8687 Melrose Ave
West Hollywood, CA 90069-5701, USA

Spencer, Willie (Football Player)
Minnesota Vikings
1109 Johnson St SE
Massillon, OH 44646-8266, USA

Spencer-Churchill, Victor
6 Cumberland Geo. St.
London, ENGLAND W1, UNITED
KINGDOM (UK)

Spencer-Devlin, Muffin (Golfer)
1278 Glenneyre St Apt 155
Laguna Beach, CA 92651-3103, USA

Spender, Percy C (Judge)
Headingley House
11 Wellington St Woolhara
Sydney, NSW 2025, AUSTRALIA

Spenn, Fred (Baseball Player)
5201 Desoto Rd
Sarasota, FL 34235-3607, USA

Sperber Carter, Paula (Bowler)
9895 SW 96th St
Miami, FL 33176-2802, USA

Spergel, David (Misc)
Princeton University
Astrophysicist Dept
Princeton, NJ 08544-0001, USA

Sperling, Gene (Government Official,
Politician)
National Economic Council
1600 Pennsylvania Ave NW
Washington, DC 20506-0001, USA

Spero, Nancy
530 Laguardia Pl
New York, NY 10012-1427, USA

Sperring, Rob (Baseball Player)
Chicago Cubs
13302 Chriswood Dr
Cypress, TX 77429-2066, USA

Speth, George (Football Player)
Detroit Lions
10705 Footprint Ln
Port Richey, FL 34668-2713, USA

Speyrer, Cotton (Football Player)
Baltimore Colts
7905 San Felipe Blvd Apt 117
Austin, TX 78729-7638, USA

Spheeris, Penelope (Director)
PO Box 1128
Studio City, CA 91614-0128, USA

Spice
338 Foothill Rd
Beverly Hills, CA 90210-3631, USA

Spice 1 (Artist, Musician)
JL Entertainment
18653 Ventura Blvd # 340
Tarzana, CA 91356-4103, USA

Spice Girls
35 Parkgate Rd. #32 Ransome Dock
London, ENGLAND SW11 4NP, UNITED
KINGDOM (UK)

Spicer, Bob (Baseball Player)
Kansas City A's
423 McPhee Dr
Fayetteville, NC 28305-5129, USA

Spicer III, William E (Physicist)
620 Sand Hill Rd Apt 305E
Palo Alto, CA 94304-2610, USA

SPider Loc (Musician)
c/o Staff Member *Interscope Records (NY)*
1790 Broadway
New York, NY 10019-1412, USA

Spidia, Vladimir (Prime Minister)
Kancelar Presidenta Republiky
Hradecek
Prague 1 119 08, CZECH REPUBLIC

Spidlik, Tomas Cardinal (Religious Leader)
Society of Jesus
Borgo S Spirito 4
CP 6139
Rome-Prati 00195, ITALY

Spiegel, Henry W (Economist)
6848 Nashville Rd
Lanham Seabrook, MD 20706-3742, USA

Spiegelman, Art (Writer)
c/o Staff Member *Steven Barclay Agency*
12 Western Ave
Petaluma, CA 94952-2907, USA

Spieier, Patrick (Baseball Player)
6635 S 108th Ave
Omaha, NE 68137-4733, USA

Spielberg, David (Actor)
10537 Cushdon Ave
Los Angeles, CA 90064-3315, USA

Spielberg, Steven (Director, Producer)
c/o Staff Member *DreamWorks SKG*
100 Universal City Plz
Universal City, CA 91608-1002, USA

Spielman, C Christopher (Chris) (Football
Player, Sportscaster)
Detroit Lions
2094 Edgemont Rd
Columbus, OH 43212-1970, USA

Spier, Peter E (Artist)
PO Box 566
Shoreham, NY 11786-0566, USA

Spier, Wolfgang
Kaiserdamm 98
Berlin 14057, GERMANY

Spiers, Bill (Baseball Player)
Milwaukee Brewers
9233 Old State Rd
Cameron, SC 29030-8129, USA

Spiers, Judi
1-3 Charlotte St.
London, ENGLAND W1P 1HD, UNITED
KINGDOM (UK)

Spiers, Ronald I (Diplomat)
1176 Middletown Rd
South Londonderry, VT 05155-9143, USA

Spies, Joshua (Artist)
PO Box 90
Watertown, SD 57201-0090, USA

Spiezio, Ed (Baseball Player)
St Louis Cardinals
2027 Taller Rd
Morris, IL 60450-6831, USA

Spiezio, Scott (Baseball Player)
Oakland A's
2027 Taller Rd
Morris, IL 60450-6831, USA

Spikes, Cameron (Football Player)
St Louis Rams
3001 Fraternity Row # 132
College Station, TX 77845, USA

Spikes, Charlie (Baseball Player)
New York Yankees
531 N Border Dr
Bogalusa, LA 70427-3307, USA

Spikes, Jack E (Football Player)
Dallas Texans
9537 Highland View Dr
Dallas, TX 75238-1025, USA

Spikes, Takeo (Football Player)
Cincinnati Bengals
5005 Heatherwood Ct
Roswell, GA 30075-2285, USA

Spilde, Jenna (Model, Reality TV Star)
c/o Staff Member *The Sports Illustrated
Fresh Faces Competition*
Nbc Entertainment
3000 W Alameda Ave #5366
Burbank, CA 91523-0001, USA

Spilker, Angela
425 N Oakhurst Dr
Beverly Hills, CA 90210-3911, USA

Spiller, Michael A (Cinematographer)
2418 Roscornare Road
Los Angeles, CA 90077, USA

Spillner, Dan (Baseball Player)
San Diego Padres
18505 SE Newport Way Unit C113
Issaquah, WA 98027-9032, USA

Spilman, Harry (Baseball Player)
Cincinnati Reds
4423 Saint Phillips Rd S
Mount Vernon, IN 47620-9629, USA

Spin Doctors, The (Music Group)
c/o Staff Member *Paradigm (Monterey)*
509 Hartnell St
Monterey, CA 93940-2825, USA

Spindt, Capp (Inventor)
SRI International
333 Ravenswood Ave
Menlo Park, CA 94025-3493, USA

Spinella, Stephen (Actor)
William Morris Agency
1325 Avenue Of The Americas
New York, NY 10019-6091, USA

Spiner, Brent (Actor)
c/o Ben Press *Innovative Artists (LA)*
1505 10th St
Santa Monica, CA 90401-2805, USA

Spinetta, Jean-Cyril (Business Person)
Group Air France
45 Rue de Paris
Roissy CDG Cedex 95747, FRANCE

Spinetti, Victor (Actor)
15 Devonshire Place
Brighton
Sussex, UNITED KINGDOM (UK)

Spinks, Michael (Boxer)
Butch Lewis Productions
250 W 57th St Ste 311
New York, NY 10107-0311, USA

Spinks, Scipio (Baseball Player)
Houston Astros
14730 Eariswood Dr
Houston, TX 77083, USA

Spinners, The
65 W 55th St Apt 6C
New York, NY 10019-4917, USA

Spinotti, Dante (Cinematographer)
Smith/Gosnell/Nicholson
PO Box 1156
Studio City, CA 91614-0156, USA

Spires, Greg (Football Player)
New England Patriots
175 Centre St # 520
Quincy, MA 02169-8600, USA

Spiro, Lev L (Director)
c/o Staff Member *Endeavor Agency LLC
(LA)*
9601 Wilshire Blvd Fl 3
Beverly Hills, CA 90210-5204, USA

Spirtas, Kevin (Actor)
c/o Staff Member *Stone Manners Talent &
Literary (LA)*
6500 Wilshire Blvd Ste 550
Los Angeles, CA 90048-4950, USA

Spittka, Marko (Athlete)
Judo Club 90
Zielona-Gora-Str 9
Frankfurt/Ober 15230, GERMANY

Spitz, Mark A (Swimmer)
c/o Evan Morgenstein *PMG Sports*
700 Evanvale Ct
Cary, NC 27518-2806, USA

Spitzer, Robert (Doctor, Psychic)
Columbia University
Psychiatry School
New York, NY 10027, USA

Spivakov, Vladimr T (Musician)
Vspolny Per 17
#14
Moscow, RUSSIA

Spivey, Junior (Baseball Player)
Arizona Diamondbacks
PO Box 82621
Oklahoma City, OK 73148-0621, USA

Spivey, Sebron (Football Player)
Dallas Cowboys
435 Capitol View Dr
Columbus, OH 43203-1037, USA

Spizzirri, Angelo (Actor)
Metropolitan Talent Agency
4500 Wilshire Blvd Fl 2
Los Angeles, CA 90010-3858, USA

Splatt, Rachel (Race Car Driver)
12631 N Tatum Blvd
Phoenix, AZ 85032-7710, USA

Split Ends
136 New Kings Rd.
London, ENGLAND SW6, UNITED
KINGDOM (UK)

Splittorff Jr, Paul W (Baseball Player)
Kansas City Royals
4204 SW Hickory Ln
Blue Springs, MO 64015-4517, USA

Spohr, Arnold T (Director)
Royal Winnipeg Ballet
380 Graham Ave
Winnipeg, MB R3C 4K2, CANADA

Spoiler, The
3615 W Waters Ave # 110
Tampa, FL 33614-2783, USA

Spoljario, Paul (Baseball Player)
Toronto Blue Jays
13261 N 73rd Ave
Peoria, AZ 85381-6054, USA

Sponenburgh, Mark (Artist)
5562 NW Pacific Coast Hwy
Seal Rock, OR 97376-9619, USA

Spong, John S (Religious Leader)
24 Puddingdtone Road
Morris Plains, NJ 07950, USA

Spooner, John (Financier, Writer)
Houghton Miffin
222 Berkeley St # 700
Boston, MA 02116-3748, USA

Spoonhour, Charles (Charlie) (Coach)
University of Nevada
Athletic Dept
Las Vegas, NV 89154, USA

Spork, Shirley (Golfer)
73010 Somera Rd
Palm Desert, CA 92260-6032, USA

Sporkin, Stanley (Government Official, Judge)
US District Court
Courthouse
3rd & Constitution NW
Washington, DC 20001, USA

Sporleder, Gregory (Actor)
c/o Staff Member *Don Buchwald & Associates Inc (LA)*
6500 Wilshire Blvd Ste 2200
Los Angeles, CA 90048-4942, USA

Sposa, Mike (Golfer)
8317 Old Town Dr
Tampa, FL 33647-3335, USA

Spottiswoode, Roger (Director)
9696 Culver Blvd Ste 203
Culver City, CA 90232-2754, USA

Spottsville, Ray (Baseball Player)
Houston Eagles
PO Box 591
Colfax, LA 71417-0591, USA

Spound, Michael (Actor)
James/Levy/Jacobson
3500 W Olive Ave Ste 1470
Burbank, CA 91505-5514, USA

Spradlin, Danny (Football Player)
Dallas Cowboys
1011 Laurie St
Maryville, TN 37803-6731, USA

Spradlin, G D (Actor)
La Familia Ranch
PO Box 1294
San Luis Obispo, CA 93406-1294, USA

Spradlin, Jerry (Baseball Player)
Cincinnati Reds
2824 E Diana Ave
Anaheim, CA 92806-4412, USA

Spragan, Donnie (Football Player)
Denver Broncos
312 Riviera Dr
Union City, CA 94587-3722, USA

Sprague, Ed (Baseball Player)
Toronto Blue Jays
4677 Pine Valley Cir
Stockton, CA 95219-1881, USA

Sprague, Ed (Baseball Player)
Oakland A's
19015 N Davis Rd
Lodi, CA 95242-9203, USA

Spratlan, Lewis (Composer)
Amherst College
Music Dept
Amherst, MA 01002, USA

Sprayberry, James M (War Hero)
426 Holiday Dr
Titus, AL 36080-2520, USA

Sprewell, Latrell (Basketball Player)
4340 Purchase St
Purchase, NY 10577-1112, USA

Spriggs, George (Baseball Player)
Pittsburgh Pirates
77 W Bay Front Rd # A
Lothian, MD 20711-9711, USA

Spring, Jack (Baseball Player)
Philadelphia Phillies
PO Box 118
Colbert, WA 99005-0118, USA

Spring, Sherwood C (Astronaut)
8244 Native Violet Dr
Lorton, VA 22079-5664, USA

Springer, Dennis (Baseball Player)
Philadelphia Phillies
1060 W Windsor Ct
Hanford, CA 93230-6572, USA

Springer, Jerry (Talk Show Host)
Jerry Springer Show
454 N Columbus Dr Fl 2
Chicago, IL 60611-5807, USA

Springer, Michael (Golfer)
1482 E Forest Oaks Dr
Fresno, CA 93730-3443, USA

Springer, Robert C (Astronaut)
202 Village Cir
Sheffield, AL 35660-5632, USA

Springer, Russ (Baseball Player)
New York Yankees
PO Box 185
Pollock, LA 71467-0185, USA

Springer, Steve (Baseball Player)
Cleveland Indians
6962 Caria Cir
Huntington Beach, CA 92647, USA

Springfield, Rick (Actor, Musician)
c/o Todd Neville *Agency for the Performing Arts (APA-LA)*
405 S Beverly Dr
Beverly Hills, CA 90212-4416, USA

Springgs, Marcus (Football Player)
Buffalo Bills
830 Regal St
Houston, TX 77034-1231, USA

Springs, Alice (Photographer)
7 Ave Saint-Ramon #T1008
Monte Carlo, MONACO

Springs, Kirk (Football Player)
New York Jets
4925 Paddock Rd
Cincinnati, OH 45237-5548, USA

Springs, Ron (Football Player)
Dallas Cowboys
128 Ron Springs Dr
Williamsburg, VA 23185-6014, USA

Springs, Shawn (Football Player)
Washington Redskins
21300 Redskin Park Dr
Ashburn, VA 20147-6100, USA

Springstead, Marty (Baseball Player)
5164 Flicker Field Cir
Sarasota, FL 34231-3242, USA

Springsteen, Bruce (Musician, Songwriter)
c/o Barbara Carr *Creative Artists Agency LCC (CAA-LA)*
2000 Avenue Of The Stars
Los Angeles, CA 90067-4700, USA

Springsteen, Pamela (Actor, Photographer)
c/o Caryn Weiss *Weiss Artists*
6311 Romaine St # 7234
Los Angeles, CA 90038-2617, USA

Sprinkel, Beryl W (Government Official)
20140 Saint Andrews Dr
Olympia Fields, IL 60461-1169, USA

Sprinkle, Edward A (Ed) (Football Player)
Chicago Bears
3 Saint Moritz Dr
Palos Park, IL 60464-3057, USA

Sprotte, Jimmy (Football Player)
Cincinnati Bengals
2163 E Palmcroft Dr
Tempe, AZ 85282-3062, USA

Sproul, Bob (Baseball Player)
Los Angeles Angels
213 Glenwood Ln Apt D
Enterprise, AL 36330-3595, USA

Sprouse, Cole (Actor)
c/o Josh Werkman *Merimark Entertainment*
5737 Kanan Rd # 597
Agoura Hills, CA 91301-1601, USA

Sprouse, Dylan (Actor)
c/o Josh Werkman *Merimark Entertainment*
5737 Kanan Rd # 597
Agoura Hills, CA 91301-1601, USA

Sprouse, James M (Judge)
US Court of Appeals
PO Box 401
122 N Court St
Lewisburg, WV 24901-0401, USA

Sprowl, Bobby (Baseball Player)
Boston Red Sox
4711 Leonard Avenue
Northport, AL 35476, USA

Spruill, Jim (Football Player)
Baltimore Colts
710 9th St
Levelland, TX 79336-4512, USA

Spurlock, Morgan (Actor)
Warrior Poets
407 Broome St Rm 7B
4th Fl
New York, NY 10013-3213, USA

Spurrier, Paul
Beccles Rd. 47
Lowestoft/Norfolk, ENGLAND, UNITED KINGDOM (UK)

Spurrier, Stephen O (Steve) (Coach, Football Coach, Football Player)
San Francisco 49ers
126 Beaver Ridge Dr
Elgin, SC 29045-8210, USA

Spurrior, Stephen O (Steve) (Coach, Football Player)
17050 Silver Charm Pl
Leesburg, VA 20176-7152, USA

Spuzich, Sandra (Golfer)
Ladies Pro Golf Assn
100 International Golf Dr
Daytona Beach, FL 32124-1082, USA

Spyro Gyro
200 W Superior St Ste 202
Chicago, IL 60610-3554, USA

Squierek, Jack (Football Player)
4051 Vezber Dr
Seven Hills, OH 44131-6233, USA

Squirek, Jack (Football Player)
Los Angeles Raiders
4051 Vezber Dr
Seven Hills, OH 44131-6233, USA

Squires, Mike (Baseball Player)
Chicago White Sox
9548 Autumnwood Cir
Kalamazoo, MI 49009-9385, USA

Squirrel Nut Zippers
2756 N Green Valley Pkwy # 449
Henderson, NV 89014-2120, USA

Squyres, Steven W (Scientist)
Comell University
Planetary Science Dept
Ithaca, NY 14853, USA

SR-71 (Music Group)
c/o Staff Member *Jeff Hanson Management & Promotions*
2813 S Hiawassee Rd Ste 307
Orlando, FL 32835-6690, USA

Sranowski, Wally
Mill Rd.
Toronto, ON M9C 1Y, CANADA

Srb, Adrian M (Misc)
411 Cayuga Heights Rd
Ithaca, NY 14850-1401, USA

Sri Chinmoy (Religious Leader)
85-45 Sri Chinmoy St
Jamaica, NY 11432, USA

Sridevi (Actor, Bollywood)
1 Bishop Wallers South Avenue
C I T Colony
Chennai, TN 600004, INDIA

Sridevi (Actor, Bollywood)
Green Acres
7 Bungalows Lokhandwala Complex
Andheri(W)
Mumbai, 400058 MS, INDIA

Sripriya (Actor, Bollywood)
10 Muthu Pandian Avenue
Santhome
Chennai, TN 600004, INDIA

Srividhya (Actor, Bollywood)
22 North Street
Sriram Nagar
Chennai, TN 600018, INDIA

St, Clair Carl
Pacific Symphony Orchestra
1231 E Dyer Rd
Santa Ana, CA 92705-5606, USA

St Clair, Bob (Football Player)
San Francisco 49ers
3312 Parker Hill Rd
Santa Rosa, CA 95404-1733, USA

St Clair, Mike (Football Player)
Cleveland Browns
1606 Birchwood Ave
Cincinnati, OH 45224-2002, USA

St Clair, Robert B (Bob) (Football Player)
Clover Stornetta Farms
PO Box 750369
Petaluma, CA 94975-0369, USA

St Claire, Randy (Baseball Player)
Montreal Expos
7117 State Route 8
Brant Lake, NY 12815-2234, USA

St Florian, Friedrich G (Architect)
Rhode Island School of Design
Architecture Dept
Providence, RI 02903, USA

St George, William R (Admiral)
862 San Antonio Pl
San Diego, CA 92106-3057, USA

St James, James (Jimmy) (Actor, Radio
Personality)
The Real Jimmy Hollywood
7510 W Sunset Blvd # 333
Los Angeles, CA 90046-3408, USA

St James, Lyn (Race Car Driver)
LSJ Racing
PO Box 2246
Indianapolis, IN 46206-2246, USA

St James, Rebecca (Musician)
Smallbone Management
317 Main St Ste 205
Franklin, TN 37064-2648, USA

St Jean, Garry (Basketball Player, Coach)
Golden State Warriors
1001 Broadway
Oakland, CA 94607-4019, USA

St Jean, Len (Football Player)
Boston Patriots
32 Ledgebrook Ave
Stoughton, MA 02072-1054, USA

St John, Jill (Actor)
Borinstein Oreck Bogart
3172 Dona Susana Dr
Studio City, CA 91604-4356, USA

St John, Kristoff (Actor)
8743 Hanna Ave
Canoga Park, CA 91304-1351, USA

St John, Lara (Musician)
Columbia Artists Mgmt Inc
1790 Broadway Fl 6
New York, NY 10019-1412, USA

St John, Mia (Boxer)
c/o Staff Member *Amsel Eisenstadt &
Frazier Inc*
5055 Wilshire Blvd Ste 865
Los Angeles, CA 90036-6109, USA

St John of Fawsley, Norman A F
(Government Official)
Old Rectory Preston Capes
Daventry
Northants NN11 6TE, UNITED
KINGDOM (UK)

St Laurent, Yves
5 Ave du Marceau
Paris 75016, FRANCE

St Louis, Martin (Hockey Player)
Tampa Bay Lighting
401 Channelside Dr
Ice Palace
Tampa, FL 33602-5400, USA

St Patrick, Mathew (Actor)
c/o Todd Eisner *Agency for the
Performing Arts (APA-LA)*
405 S Beverly Dr
Beverly Hills, CA 90212-4416, USA

St Patrick, Matthew (Actor)
c/o Staff Member *Untitled Entertainment
(LA)*
331 N Maple Dr Fl 3
Beverly Hills, CA 90210-3827, USA

Staab, Rebecca (Actor)
Don Buchwald
6500 Wilshire Blvd Ste 2200
Los Angeles, CA 90048-4942, USA

Staats, Dewayne (Baseball Player,
Sportscaster)
Tampa Bay Devil Rays
1170 Gulf Blvd Apt 1601
Clearwater Beach, FL 33767-2785, USA

Staats, Elmer B (Government Official)
Truman Scholarship Foundation
712 Jackson Pl NW
Washington, DC 20006-4901, USA

Stabile, Nick
c/o Staff Member *Diverse Talent Group*
1875 Century Park E Ste 2250
Los Angeles, CA 90067-2563, USA

Stablein, George (Baseball Player)
San Diego Padres
2903 Penman
Tustin, CA 92782-3314, USA

Stabler, Ken
260 N Joachim St
Mobile, AL 36603-6472, USA

Stacco, Ed (Football Player)
Detroit Lions
1909 Hudson Ct
Oldsmar, FL 34677-2505, USA

Stacey, Caitlin (Actor)
21 Esmond Rd
London W4 1JG, UNITED KINGDOM
(UK)

Stacey, Siran (Football Player)
Philadelphia Eagles
PO Box 131
Hartford, AL 36344-0131, USA

Stacey Q (Actor, Music Group, Musician)
641 S Palm St Ste D
La Habra, CA 90631-5758, USA

Stack, Brian (Writer)
c/o Staff Member *3 Arts Entertainment Inc*
9460 Wilshire Blvd Fl 7
Beverly Hills, CA 90212-2713, USA

Stack, Timothy
10635 Santa Monica Blvd Ste 130
Los Angeles, CA 90025-8306, USA

Stackhouse, Charles (Football Player)
New York Giants
240 Shady Grove St
Marion, AR 72364-9412, USA

Stackhouse, Jerry (Basketball Player)
c/o Staff Member *Dallas Mavericks*
2909 Taylor St
Dallas, TX 75226-1909, USA

Stackpole, H C (Hank) (General)
Asia-Pacific Security Studies Center
2058 Maluhia Rd
Honolulu, HI 96815-1949, USA

Stacomb, Kevin (Basketball Player)
14 Florida Ave
Jamestown, RI 02835-1548, USA

Stacy, Billy (Football Player)
Chicago Cardinals
400 Colonial Cir
Starkville, MS 39759-4214, USA

Stacy, Hollis (Golfer)
9400 W 10th Ave
Lakewood, CO 80215-4700, USA

Stacy, James (Actor)
478 Severn Ave
Tampa, FL 33606-3842, USA

Stadlen, Lewis J. (Actor)
c/o Staff Member *Access Talent*
37 E 28th St Rm 500
New York, NY 10016-7919, USA

Stadler, Craig (Golfer)
113 Elk Xing
Evergreen, CO 80439-4114, USA

Stadler, Sergei V (Musician)
Kaiserstr 43
Munich 80801, GERMANY

Stadtman, Earl R (Misc)
16907 Redland Rd
Derwood, MD 20855-1954, USA

Stadtman, Thressa C (Misc)
16907 Redland Rd
Derwood, MD 20855-1954, USA

Staehle, Marv (Baseball Player)
Chicago White Sox
19421 Cromwell Ct Apt 208
Fort Myers, FL 33912-0386, USA

Staff, Kathy
17 Maple Mews
London, ENGLAND NW6, UNITED
KINGDOM (UK)

Staffieri, Joe (Football Player)
Philadelphia Eagles
6825 Polo Fields Pkwy
Cumming, GA 30040-5731, USA

Stafford, Harrison (Football Player)
New York Giants
RR 1 Box 216
Edna, TX 77957, USA

Stafford, James Francis Cardinal
(Religious Leader)
Pontifical Council for the Laity
Piazza S Calisto 16
Rome 00153, ITALY

Stafford, Jerry (Baseball Player)
2316 Catalina Cir Apt 276
Oceanside, CA 92056-5395, USA

Stafford, Jim (Music Group, Musician,
Songwriter, Writer)
PO Box 6366
Branson, MO 65615-6366, USA

Stafford, Jimmy (Musician)
Jon Landau
158 Rowayton Ave
Norwalk, CT 06853-1442, USA

Stafford, Jo (Musician)
2339 Century Hl
Los Angeles, CA 90067-3543, USA

Stafford, John R (Business Person)
American Home Products
5 Giralda Farms
Madison, NJ 07940-1027, USA

Stafford, Michelle (Actor)
c/o Darryl Marshak *Marshak/Zachary
Company, The*
8840 Wilshire Blvd Fl 1
Beverly Hills, CA 90211-2606, USA

Stafford, Nancy (Actor)
PO Box 11807
Marina Del Rey, CA 90295-2807, USA

Stafford, Robert T (Governor, Senator)
1 Sugarwood Hill Rd
RR 1 Box 3954
Rutland, VT 05701, USA

Stafford, Thomas
1006 Cameron St
Alexandria, VA 22314-2427, USA

Stafford, Thomas P (Astronaut, General)
AVD
PO Box 604
Glenn Dale, MD 20769-0604, USA

Stageman-Roberts, Donna (Baseball
Player)
1831 Jerome Pl
Helena, MT 59601-4735, USA

Staggers, Jon (Football Player)
Pittsburgh Steelers
3835 Oakes Dr
Hayward, CA 94542-1720, USA

Staggs, Jeff (Football Player)
San Diego Chargers
4641 Jeri Way
El Cajon, CA 92020-8329, USA

Staggs, Steve (Baseball Player)
Toronto Blue Jays
4021 Kent St
Norman, OK 73072-2222, USA

Stagliano, John
14141 Covello St
Van Nuys, CA 91405-1491, USA

Stagus, Gus (Coach, Swimmer)
University of Michigan
Athletic Dept
Ann Arbor, MI 48104, USA

Stahl, Jerry (Actor, Writer)
c/o Staff Member *United Talent Agency
(UTA)*
9560 Wilshire Blvd Ste 500
Beverly Hills, CA 90212-2401, USA

Stahl, Larry (Baseball Player)
Kansas City A's
1506 E Main St # A
Belleville, IL 62221-5436, USA

Stahl, Lesley (Correspondent)
c/o Staff Member *60 Minutes*
524 W 57th St
Cbs News
New York, NY 10019-2930, USA

Stahl, Leslie (Actor)
c/o Staff Member *William Morris Agency
(WMA-LA)*
1 William Morris Pl
Beverly Hills, CA 90212-4261, USA

Stahl, Lisa (Actor)
Don Buchwald
6500 Wilshire Blvd Ste 2200
Los Angeles, CA 90048-4942, USA

Stahl, Nick (Actor)
c/o Sean Fay *Imparato Fay Management*
1126 Roxbury Dr
Los Angeles, CA 90035-1031, USA

Stahl, Norman H (Judge)
US Appeals Court
McCormack Federal Building
Boston, MA 02109, USA

Stahler, Jeff (Cartoonist, Editor)
Cincinnati Post
125 E Court St
Editorial Dept
Cincinnati, OH 45202-1214, USA

Stahley, Adele (Baseball Player)
3700 SE Jennings Rd Apt 214W
Port St Lucie, FL 34952-7780, USA

Stahoviak, Scott (Baseball Player)
Minnesota Twins
507 Balmoral Ct
Grayslake, IL 60030-9303, USA

Stai, Brendon (Football Player)
Pittsburgh Steelers
1431 Teal Trce
Pittsburgh, PA 15237-3848, USA

Staiger, Roy (Baseball Player)
New York Mets
1233 Tyler Dr
Lebanon, MO 65536-4121, USA

Staind (Music Group)
c/o Staff Member *William Morris Agency (WMA-LA)*
1 William Morris Pl
Beverly Hills, CA 90212-4261, USA

Stairs, Matt (Baseball Player)
Montreal Expos
79 Skyline Rd
Bangor, ME 04401-2156, USA

Staite, Jewel (Actor)
c/o Nils Larsen *Elements Entertainment*
1635 N Cahuenga Blvd Fl 5
Los Angeles, CA 90028-6201, USA

Stajola, Enzo
Piazza Augusto Albini 5
Rome I-00154, ITALY

Stalcup, Jerry (Football Player)
Los Angeles Rams
1023 Westchester Dr
Rockford, IL 61107-3442, USA

Staley, Bill (Football Player)
Cincinnati Bengals
9210 Todd Rd
Potter Valley, CA 95469-9727, USA

Staley, Dawn M (Basketball Player, Coach)
1228 Callowhill St # 603
Philadelphia, PA 19123, USA

Staley, Gerald A (Gerry) (Baseball Player)
St Louis Cardinals
2517 NE 100th St
Vancouver, WA 98686-5744, USA

Staley, Jerry (Athlete)
2517 NE 100th St
Vancouver, WA 98686-5744, USA

Staley, Joan (Actor)
24516 Windsor Dr Unit B
Valencia, CA 91355-4430, USA

Staley, Lex (Radio Personality)
c/o Staff Member *The Lex & Terry Morning Radio Network*
11700 Central Pkwy
Jacksonville, FL 32224-2600, USA

Staley, Matthew R (Actor, Musician)
PO Box 590
New York, NY 10108-0590, USA

Staley, Walter (Hockey Player)
214 Teal Lake Rd
Mexico, MO 65265-3705, USA

Stallard, Tracy (Baseball Player)
Boston Red Sox
PO Box 905
Wise, VA 24293-0905, USA

Staller, Ilona
Via Cassia 1818
Rome I-00123, ITALY

Stallings, George (Religious Leader)
African American Catholic Congregation
1015 St NE
Washington, DC 20002, USA

Stallings, Larry (Football Player)
St Louis Cardinals
207 S Mason Rd
Saint Louis, MO 63141-8026, USA

Stallone, Frank
10668 Eastborne Ave Apt 206
Los Angeles, CA 90024-5979, USA

Stallone, Jackie
323 San Vicente Blvd Unit 8
Santa Monica, CA 90402-1630, USA

Stallone, Sasha
9 Beverly Park
Beverly Hills, CA 90210-1540, USA

Stallone, Sylvester (Actor, Director, Producer, Writer)
c/o Brian Gersh *Blue Train Entertainment*
798 Brooktree Rd
Pacific Palisades, CA 90272-3901, USA

Stalls, David (Football Player)
Dallas Cowboys
2100 Stout St
Denver, CO 80205-2827, USA

Stallworth, Johnny L (John) (Football Player)
Pittsburgh Steelers
302 Osman Dr
Madison, AL 35756-3499, USA

Stallworth, Ron (Football Player)
New York Jets
1834 Parkview Dr S
Montgomery, AL 36117-7701, USA

Stalmaster, Lynn
12400 Wilshire Blvd Ste 920
Los Angeles, CA 90025-1040, USA

Stamatopoulos, Dino (Writer)
c/o Greg Cavic *Creative Artists Agency LCC (CAA-LA)*
2000 Avenue Of The Stars
Los Angeles, CA 90067-4700, USA

Stamler, Jonathan (Misc)
Duke University
Medical Center
Hematology Dept
Durham, NC 27708-0001, USA

Stamm, Michael (Mike) (Swimmer)
23 Wildwood Rd
Orinda, CA 94563-3323, USA

Stamos, John (Actor, Musician)
c/o Daniel (Danny) Sussman *Brillstein-Grey Entertainment*
9150 Wilshire Blvd Ste 350
Beverly Hills, CA 90212-3453, USA

Stamos, Theodoros (Artist)
37 W 83rd St
New York, NY 10024-5201, USA

Stamp, Terence (Actor)
Markham & Froggatt
Julian House
4 Windmill St
London W1P 1HF, UNITED KINGDOM (UK)

Stamps, Sylvester (Football Player)
Atlanta Falcons
1831 Eisenhower Dr
Vicksburg, MS 39180-3757, USA

Stams, Frank (Football Player)
Los Angeles Rams
2870 Marcia Blvd
Cuyahoga Falls, OH 44223-1146, USA

Stan, Jason (Musician)
Visions Casting Agency Pty Ltd
Level 6/3 Bowen Crs
Victoria, Melbourne 3000, AUSTRALIA

Stan, Sebastian (Actor)
c/o Emily Gerson Saines *Brookside Artists Management (NY)*
250 W 57th St Ste 2303
New York, NY 10107-2399, USA

Stanat, Dug (Artist)
46828 Bradley St
Fremont, CA 94539-7104, USA

Stanback, Haskel (Football Player)
Atlanta Falcons
1530 Kingston Dr
Kannapolis, NC 28083-9280, USA

Standhardt, Kenneth (Artist)
620 Elmwood Dr
Eugene, OR 97401, USA

Standing, John (Actor)
International Creative Mgmt
76 Oxford St
London W1N 0AX, UNITED KINGDOM (UK)

Standly, Mike (Golfer)
2306 Columbia Cir
League City, TX 77573-7622, USA

Stanek, Al (Baseball Player)
San Francisco Giants
96 Allyn St
Holyoke, MA 01040-2549, USA

Stanfel, Richard (Dick) (Coach, Football Player)
Detroit Lions
1104 Juniper Pkwy
Libertyville, IL 60048-3543, USA

Stanfield, Kevin (Baseball Player)
Minnesota Twins
7565 Newcomb St
San Bernardino, CA 92410-4333, USA

Stanfill, Dennis
908 Oak Grove Ave
San Marino, CA 91108-1022, USA

Stanfill, William T (Bill) (Football Player)
Miami Dolphins
3117 Wisteria Ct
Albany, GA 31721-2988, USA

Stanford, Aaron (Actor)
c/o Cyrena Esposito *Cyrena Esposito Management*
437 W 48th St Apt D
New York, NY 10036-1285, USA

Stang, Arnold (Actor)
PO Box 920386
Needham, MA 02492-0005, USA

Stang, Peter J (Misc)
University of Utah
Chemistry Dept
Salt Lake City, UT 84112, USA

Stangassinger, Thomas (Skier)
Hofgasse 19
Durenberg-Hallein 5422, AUSTRIA

Stange, Lee (Baseball Player)
Minnesota Twins
436 Dolphin St
Melbourne Beach, FL 32951-2916, USA

Stange, Maya (Actor)
c/o Lindy King *Peters Fraser & Dunlop (PFD - UK)*
Drury House
34-43 Russell St
London WC2B 5HA, UNITED KINGDOM (UK)

Stangel, Eric (Producer, Writer)
c/o Staff Member *3 Arts Entertainment Inc*
9460 Wilshire Blvd Fl 7
Beverly Hills, CA 90212-2713, USA

Stangel, Justin (Producer, Writer)
c/o Staff Member *3 Arts Entertainment Inc*
9460 Wilshire Blvd Fl 7
Beverly Hills, CA 90212-2713, USA

Stanhope, Doug (Comedian)
c/o Staff Member *Agency for the Performing Arts (APA-LA)*
405 S Beverly Dr
Beverly Hills, CA 90212-4416, USA

Stanhouse, Don (Baseball Player)
Texas Rangers
4 Creekmere Dr
Roanoke, TX 76262-9755, USA

Stanicek, Pete (Baseball Player)
Baltimore Orioles
525 Wilson St
Downers Grove, IL 60515-3845, USA

Stanicek, Steve (Baseball Player)
Milwaukee Brewers
525 Wilson St
Downers Grove, IL 60515-3845, USA

Stanifer, Rob (Baseball Player)
Florida Marlins
189 Quarry Rd
Liberty, SC 29657-3834, USA

Stanis, Bernadette (Actor)
Sheba Media Group
11152 Westheimer Rd # 299
C/O Vanessa Morman
Houston, TX 77042-3208, USA

Stanka, Joe (Baseball Player)
Chicago Cubs
1718 Fry Rd Ste 240
Gulf Coast
Houston, TX 77084-5847, USA

Stankalla, Stefan (Skier)
Furstenstr 14
Gramisch-Partenkirchen 82467, GERMANY

Stankavage, Scott (Football Player)
Denver Broncos
3843 Somerset Dr
Durham, NC 27707-5016, USA

Stankovic, Borislav (Boris) (Basketball Player, Misc)
PO Box 7005
Munich 81479, GERMANY

Stankowski, Paul (Golfer)
4713 Rangewood Dr
Flower Mound, TX 75028-1695, USA

Stanlch, George (Athlete, Basketball Player, Track Athlete)
15816 Marigold Ave
Gardena, CA 90249-4837, USA

Stanler, John W (Misc)
Coutts & Co
440 Strand
London SC2R 0QS, UNITED KINGDOM (UK)

Stanley, Allan H (Hockey Player)
RR 3
Fennelon Falls, ON K0M 1N0, CANADA

Stanley, Frank (Cinematographer)
PO Box 2230
Los Angeles, CA 90078-2230, USA

Stanley, Israel (Football Player)
New Orleans Saints
3850 S Miner St
Milwaukee, WI 53221-1250, USA

Stanley, James (Producer)
c/o Staff Member *United Talent Agency (UTA)*
9560 Wilshire Blvd Ste 500
Beverly Hills, CA 90212-2401, USA

Stanley, Marianne Crawford (Coach)
New York Liberty
2 Penn Plz
Madison Square Garden
New York, NY 10121-1703, USA

Stanley, Marianne Crawford (Basketball Player, Coach)
Washington Mystics
601 F St NW
Mci Center
Washington, DC 20004-1605, USA

Stanley, Mitchell J (Mickey) (Baseball Player)
5319 Timber Bend Dr
Brighton, MI 48116-4796, USA

Stanley, Paul (Musician)
McGhee Entertainment
8730 W Sunset Blvd Ste 200
Los Angeles, CA 90069-2275, USA

Stanley, Ralph (Music Group, Musician)
Press Office
PO Box 159006
Nashville, TN 37215-9006, USA

Stanley, Steven M (Misc)
4308 Folly Quarter Rd
Ellicott City, MD 21042-1424, USA

Stanley, Walter (Football Player)
Green Bay Packers
23977 E Alamo Pl
Aurora, CO 80016-4247, USA

Stansfield, Claire
9300 Wilshire Blvd Ste 555
Beverly Hills, CA 90212-3211, USA

Stansfield, Lisa (Music Group, Musician, Songwriter, Writer)
PO Box 59
Ashwell
Herts SG7 5NG, UNITED KINGDOM (UK)

Stansfield Smith, Colin (Architect)
Three Ministers House
76 High St Winchester
Hants SO23 8UL, UNITED KINGDOM (UK)

Stansky, Peter D L (Historian)
375 Pinehill Rd
Hillsborough, CA 94010-6612, USA

Stantis, Scott (Cartoonist, Editor)
Birmingham News
2201 4th Ave N
Editorial Dept
Birmingham, AL 35203-3863, USA

Stanton, Andrew (Animator, Director, Writer)
Pixar
1200 Park Ave
Emeryville, CA 94608-3677, USA

Stanton, Frank N (Misc)
25 W 52nd St
New York, NY 10019-6104, USA

Stanton, Harry Dean (Actor)
14527 Mulholland Dr
Los Angeles, CA 90077-1713, USA

Stanton, Jeff (Race Car Driver)
1137 Athens Rd
Sherwood, MI 49089-9721, USA

Stanton, Molly (Actor)
c/o Staff Member *Stone Manners Talent & Literary (LA)*
6500 Wilshire Blvd Ste 550
Los Angeles, CA 90048-4950, USA

Stanton, Paul (Hockey Player)
39 Phillips St
Marblehead, MA 01945, USA

Stanton, Phil (Entertainer)
Blue Man Group
3900 Las Vegas Blvd S
Luxor Hotel
Las Vegas, NV 89119-1004, USA

Stapinski, Helene (Writer)
Saint Martin's Press
175 5th Ave
New York, NY 10010-7848, USA

Staple Singers, The
PO Box 170429
San Francisco, CA 94117-0429, USA

Staples, Mavis (Music Group, Musician)
PO Box 498360
Chicago, IL 60649-8360, USA

Stapleton, Jean (Actor)
Bauman-Hiller
5757 Wilshire Blvd # 512
Los Angeles, CA 90036-5810, USA

Stapleton, Kevin (Actor)
Gersh Agency
232 N Canon Dr
Beverly Hills, CA 90210-5302, USA

Stapleton, Oliver (Cinematographer)
MacCorkindale & Holton
1640 5th St Ste 205
Santa Monica, CA 90401-3325, USA

Stapleton, Walter K (Judge)
US Court of Appeals
844 N King St
Federal Building
Wilmington, DE 19801-3519, USA

Stapp, Scott (Musician)
c/o Staff Member *Wind-up Records*
72 Madison Ave Fl 8
New York, NY 10016-8731, USA

Star, Darren (Doctor, Producer, Writer)
c/o Staff Member *Darren Star Productions*
10202 Washington Blvd
Fred Astaire Building #2210
Culver City, CA 90232-3119, USA

Star Sailor (Musician)
c/o Staff Member *Solo Agency Ltd (UK)*
55 Fulham High St
London SW6 3JJ, UNITED KINGDOM (UK)

Starbird, Kate (Basketball Player)
Indiana Fever
125 S Pennsylvania St
Conseco Fieldhouse
Indianapolis, IN 46204-3610, USA

Starbuck, Jo Jo (Figure Skater)
33 Pomeroy Rd
Madison, NJ 07940-2638, USA

Starch, Ken (Football Player)
Green Bay Packers
603 E Hillcrest Dr
Verona, WI 53593-1517, USA

Starck, Philippe (Architect, Designer)
3 Rue Faisans
Shiltigheim 67300, FRANCE

Starfield, Barbara H (Doctor)
Johns Hopkins University
624 N Broadway
Hygiene School
Baltimore, MD 21205-1900, USA

Stargell, Tony (Football Player)
New York Jets
131 Jenny Rd
Grantville, GA 30220-2134, USA

Stark, Chad (Football Player)
Seattle Seahawks
3316 46th Ave SW
Fargo, ND 58104-6655, USA

Stark, Collin (Actor)
c/o Peter Kluge *Impact Artists Group LLC*
244 N California St
Burbank, CA 91505-3505, USA

Stark, Don (Actor)
c/o Tom Harrison *Diverse Talent Group*
1875 Century Park E Ste 2250
Los Angeles, CA 90067-2563, USA

Stark, Freya M (Misc, Writer)
Via Canova
Asolo
Treviso, ITALY

Stark, Graham (Actor)
International Creative Mgmt
76 Oxford St
London W1N 0AX, UNITED KINGDOM (UK)

Stark, Koo (Actor)
Rebecca Blond
52 Shaftesbury Ave
London W1V 7DE, UNITED KINGDOM (UK)

Stark, Melissa (Correspondent, Sportscaster)
NBC-TV
30 Rockefeller Plz Ste 270E
News Dept
New York, NY 10112-0299, USA

Stark, Nathan J (Lawyer)
4000 Cathedral Ave NW # 132
Washington, DC 20016-5249, USA

Stark, Rohn T (Football Player)
Baltimore Colts
PO Box 10067
Lahaina, HI 96761-0067, USA

Starke, Anthony (Actor)
c/o Staff Member *Paradigm (LA)*
360 N Crescent Dr
North Bldg
Beverly Hills, CA 90210-6820, USA

Starker, James
1241 S Winfield Rd
Bloomington, IN 47401-6147, USA

Starker, Janos (Musician)
1241 S Winfield Rd
Bloomington, IN 47401-6147, USA

Starkey, Jason (Football Player)
Arizona Cardinals
1525 Washington Ave # 1
Huntington, WV 25704-1520, USA

Starks, Duane (Football Player)
Baltimore Ravens
811 NW 199th St
Miami, FL 33169, USA

Starling, James D (General)
3581 Joshua Rd
Shingle Springs, CA 95682-9478, USA

Starn, Douglas (Photographer)
Stux Gallery
163 Mercer St # 1
New York, NY 10012-3203, USA

Starn, Mike (Photographer)
Stux Gallery
163 Mercer St # 1
New York, NY 10012-3203, USA

Starner, Shelby (Music Group, Musician)
Morebam Music
30 Hillcrest Ave
Morristown, NJ 07960-5090, USA

Starnes, John G (Football Player)
Atlanta Falcons
8826 Shade Tree
San Antonio, TX 78254-6821, USA

Staroba, Paul (Football Player)
Cleveland Browns
9235 McWain Rd
Grand Blanc, MI 48439-8006, USA

Starr, Albert (Doctor)
5050 SW Patton Rd
Portland, OR 97221-2263, USA

Starr, B Bartlett (Bart) (Football Player)
2065 Royal Fern Ln
Birmingham, AL 35244-1464, USA

Starr, Bart (Football Player)
Green Bay Packers
2647 Rocky Ridge Ln
Birmingham, AL 35216-4809, USA

Starr, Beau (Actor)
c/o Geneva Bray *GVA Talent Agency Inc*
9229 W Sunset Blvd Ste 320
Los Angeles, CA 90069-3403, USA

Starr, Brenda K (Music Group, Musician)
Brothers Mgmt
141 Dunbar Ave
Fords, NJ 08863-1551, USA

Starr, Fredro (Actor, Artist, Musician)
Writers & Artists
360 N Crescent Dr Bldg North
Beverly Hills, CA 90210-6818, USA

Starr, Kay (Music Group, Musician)
Ira Okun Entertainment
708 Palisades Dr
Pacific Palisades, CA 90272-2800, USA

Starr, Kenneth (Government Official, Judge)
Pepperdine Law School
24255 Pacific Coast Hwy
Malibu, CA 90263-3999, USA

Starr, Leonard (Cartoonist)
Tribune Media Services
435 N Michigan Ave Ste 1500
Chicago, IL 60611-4012, USA

Starr, Martin (Actor)
Paradigm Agency
10100 Santa Monica Blvd Ste 2500
Los Angeles, CA 90067-4116, USA

Starr, Mike (Artist)
1505 10th St
Santa Monica, CA 90401-2805, USA

Starr, Paul E (Misc)
Princeton University
Sociology Dept
Green Hall
Princeton, NJ 08544-0001, USA

Starr, Randy (Music Group, Musician, Songwriter, Writer)
DDS
230 Park Ave
New York, NY 10169-0005, USA

Starr, Ringo (Actor, Music Group, Musician)
c/o Staff Member *Special Artists Agency*
9465 Wilshire Blvd Ste 890
Beverly Hills, CA 90212-2607, USA

Starr, Ryan (Musician)
c/o Michael (Mike) Esterman *Esterman Entertainment*
214 Park Rd
Riva, MD 21140-1224, USA

Starr, Steve (Journalist, Photographer)
720 Arcadia Pl
Colorado Springs, CO 80903-2813, USA

Starring, Stephen (Football Player)
New England Patriots
6120 W Tropicana Ave Ste A 16
Las Vegas, NV 89103-4489, USA

Starsailor (Music Group)
c/o Staff Member *Paradigm (Monterey)*
509 Hartnell St
Monterey, CA 93940-2825, USA

Starship
9850 Sandalfoot Blvd # 458
Boca Raton, FL 33428-6645, USA

Starting Line (Music Group)
c/o Staff Member *Virgin Records (NY)*
304 Park Ave S Fl 5
New York, NY 10010-4316, USA

Starzewski, Tomasz (Designer, Fashion Designer)
House of Tomasz Trarzewski
15-17 Pont St
London SW1X 9EH, UNITED KINGDOM (UK)

Starzl, Thomas E (Doctor)
University of Pittsburgh
Medical School
Surgery Dept
Pittsburgh, PA 15261-0001, USA

Stashwick, Todd (Actor)
c/o Megan Schumacher *Himber Entertainment Inc*
15760 Ventura Blvd Ste 700
Encino, CA 91436-3016, USA

Stastny, Anton (Hockey Player)
Montoileu 11
Bussigney-Lausanne 1030,
SWITZERLAND

Stastny, Peter (Hockey Player)
465 S Mason Rd
Saint Louis, MO 63141-8519, USA

Stata, Raymond S (Business Person)
Analog Devices Inc
1 Technology Way
Norwood, MA 02062-2666, USA

Statham, Jason (Actor)
c/o Steve Chasman *Ace Media*
9200 W Sunset Blvd Ph
Los Angeles, CA 90069-3502, USA

Static, Wayne (Musician)
Andy Gould Mgmt
9100 Wilshire Blvd Ste 400W
Beverly Hills, CA 90212-3464, USA

Statler Brothers (Music Group)
The Statler Brothers, LLC
PO Box 2703
Staunton, VA 24402-2703, USA

Staton, Candi (Music Group, Musician)
Capital Entertainment
1201 N St NW # A5
Washington, DC 20005-5115, USA

Status Quo
Pinewood Rd. Ivor
Buckinghamshire, ENGLAND, UNITED KINGDOM (UK)

Statuto, Art (Football Player)
Buffalo Bills
4 Schuyler Rd
Allendale, NJ 07401-1807, USA

Staub, Daniel J (Rusty) (Baseball Player)
WWOR-Radio
9 Broadcast Plz
Secaucus, NJ 07094, USA

Staubach, Roger T (Football Player)
Dallas Cowboys
5242 Ravine Dr
Dallas, TX 75220-2260, USA

Staubach, Scott (Football Player)
New Orleans Saints
6701 Miwok Ct
Bakersfield, CA 93309-3436, USA

Stauber, Liz (Actor)
Creative Artists Agency
9830 Wilshire Blvd
Beverly Hills, CA 90212-1804, USA

Stauffer, William A (Bill) (Basketball Player)
913 Shoalcreek Pl
Wilmington, NC 28405-5211, USA

Staunton, Imelda (Actor)
P F D
Drury House
34-43 Russell St
London WC2B 5HA, UNITED KINGDOM (UK)

Staurovsky, Jason (Football Player)
St Louis Cardinals
4822 E 87th Pl
Tulsa, OK 74137-2825, USA

Stautberg, Gerald (Football Player)
Chicago Bears
3200 Park Road
Monkton, MD 21111, USA

Staveley, William D M (Admiral)
Thames Health Authority
40 Eastbourne Terrace
London W2 3QR, UNITED KINGDOM (UK)

Stavropoulos, William S (Business Person)
Dow Chemical
2030 Dow Center
Midland, MI 48674-0001, USA

Stayskal, Wayne (Cartoonist, Editor)
Tampa Tribune
200 S Parker St
Editorial Dept
Tampa, FL 33606-2308, USA

Staysniak, Joseph A (Joe) (Football Player)
Buffalo Bills
4094 Forest Dr
Brownsburg, IN 46112-8672, USA

Stead, Eugene A Jr (Doctor)
5113 Townsville Rd
Bullock, NC 27507-9438, USA

Steadman, Alison (Actor)
P F D
Drury House
34-43 Russell St
London WC2B 5HA, UNITED KINGDOM (UK)

Steadman, J Richard (Doctor)
Steadman Hawkins Clinic
181 W Meadow Dr Ste 400
Vail, CO 81657-5058, USA

Steadman, Mark (Writer)
450 Pin Du Lac Dr
Central, SC 29630-9435, USA

Steadman, Ralph I (Cartoonist)
Old Loose Court
Loose Valley Maidstone
Kent ME15 9SE, UNITED KINGDOM (UK)

Steadman, Robert L (Cinematographer)
15925 Temecula St
Pacific Palisades, CA 90272-4239, USA

Stearns, Cheryl (Misc)
613 Saddlebred Ln
Raeford, NC 28376-5535, USA

Stearns, Jeff
9200 W Sunset Blvd Ste 1130
Los Angeles, CA 90069-3606, USA

Stecher, Renate Meissner- (Athlete, Track Athlete)
Haydnstr 11
#526/38
Jena 07749, GERMANY

Steck-Weiss, Elma (Baseball Player)
7555 W Kimberly Way
Glendale, AZ 85308-5954, USA

Steckler, Ray Dennis (Director)
2375 E Tropicana Ave
Las Vegas, NV 89119-6564, USA

Steding, Katy (Basketball Player)
Warner Pacific College
2219 SE 68th Ave
Athletic Dept
Portland, OR 97215-4026, USA

Steeb, Carl-Uwe
18 chemin des Jardillets
Hauterive CH-2068, SWITZERLAND

Steed, Joel (Football Player)
Pittsburgh Steelers
2639 Holly St
Denver, CO 80207-3229, USA

Steel, Amy (Actor)
Innovative Artists
1505 10th St
Santa Monica, CA 90401-2805, USA

Steel, David M S (Government Official)
Aikwood Tower
Ettrick Bridge
Selkirkshire, SCOTLAND

Steel, John (Musician)
Lustig Talent
PO Box 770850
Orlando, FL 32877-0850, USA

Steele, Allan
1640 S Sepulveda Blvd Ste 218
Los Angeles, CA 90025-7535, USA

Steele, Barbara (Actor)
2460 Benedict Canyon Dr
Beverly Hills, CA 90210-1433, USA

Steele, Billy (DJ)
c/o Len Evans *Project Publicity*
312 W 53rd St
New York, NY 10019-5743, USA

Steele, Cassie (Actor)
c/o Staff Member *Noble Kaplan Agency*
1260 Yonge St Fl 2
Toronto, ON M4T 1W6, CANADA

Steele, Danielle (Writer)
c/o Staff Member *Doubleday/ RandomHouse*
1745 Broadway
New York, NY 10019-4305, USA

Steele, Ernie (Football Player)
Philadelphia Eagles
4407 244th St SE
Woodinville, WA 98072-8623, USA

Steele, Glen (Football Player)
Cincinnati Bengals
303 E 5th St
Ligonier, IN 46767-2205, USA

Steele, Joyce (Baseball Player)
RR 2 Box 258
Mehoopany, PA 18629-9665, USA

Steele, Larry (Basketball Player)
6901 SE Oaks Park Way Slip 25
Portland, OR 97202-6491, USA

Steele, Michael (Musician)
Bangles Mall
1341 W Fullerton Ave
Box 180
Chicago, IL 60614-2362, USA

Steele, Richard (Boxer, Referee)
2438 Antler Point Dr
Henderson, NV 89074-6269, USA

Steele, Robert (Football Player)
Dallas Cowboys
813 Burning Tree Ct SE
Marietta, GA 30067-4719, USA

Steele, Shelby (Writer)
San Jose State University
English Dept
San Jose, CA 95192-0001, USA

Steele, Tommy (Actor, Musician)
IMG
Media House
3 Burlington Lane
London W4 2TH, UNITED KINGDOM (UK)

Steele, William M (Mike) (General)
Commanding General
Combined Arms Center
Fort Leavenworth, KS 66207, USA

Steele-Perkins, Christopher H (Photographer)
5 Saint John's Buildings
Canterbury St
London SW9 7QB, UNITED KINGDOM (UK)

Steely Dan (Music Group)
c/o Howard Rose *Howard Rose Agency Ltd, The*
9460 Wilshire Blvd Ste 310
Beverly Hills, CA 90212-2710, USA

Steen, Jessica (Actor)
Innovative Artists
1505 10th St
Santa Monica, CA 90401-2805, USA

Steenburgen, Mary (Actor)
165 Copper Cliffs Ln
Sedona, AZ 86336-6215, USA

Steere, Richard (Football Player)
Philadelphia Eagles
1810 Fox Bridge Ct
Fallbrook, CA 92028-8745, USA

Stefan, Greg (Hockey Player)
37648 Baywood Dr # 33
Farmington Hills, MI 48335-3604, USA

Stefani, Gwen (Fashion Designer, Musician, Songwriter)
c/o David Schiff *Schiff Company*
9465 Wilshire Blvd Ste 480
Beverly Hills, CA 90212-2603, USA

Stefanich, Jim (Bowler)
1444 Coral Bell Dr
Joliet, IL 60435-3979, USA

Stefanson, Leslie (Actor)
9271 1/2 W Norton Ave
West Hollywood, CA 90046, USA

Stefanyshyn-Piper, Heidemarie M (Astronaut)
3722 W Pine Brook Way
Houston, TX 77059-3105, USA

Steffen, Dave (Baseball Player)
30531 Maple View Ln
Flat Rock, MI 48134-2744, USA

Steffen, Jim (Football Player)
Detroit Lions
1440 Westway
Arnold, MD 21012-2428, USA

Steffes, Kent (Volleyball Player)
11106 Ave De Cortez
Pacific Palisades, CA 90272, USA

Steffy, Joseph B (Joe) Jr (Football Player)
25 Water Way
Newburgh, NY 12550-1989, USA

Stefy (Music Group)
Wind-up Records
72 Madison Ave Fl 8
New York, NY 10016-8731, USA

Stegent, Larry (Football Player)
St Louis Cardinals
1177 West Loop S # 525
Houston, TX 77027-9006, USA

Steger, Joseph A (Educator)
University of Cincinnati
President's Office
Cincinnati, OH 45221-0001, USA

Steger, Will (Misc)
International Arctic Project
990 3rd St E
Saint Paul, MN 55106-5243, USA

Stegman, Millie (Actor)
c/o Staff Member *Telefe - Argentina*
Pavon 2444 (C1248AAT)
Buenos Aires, ARGENTINA

Stehlin, Savannah (Actor)
c/o Sharon Lane *Lane Management Group*
13017 Woodbridge St
Studio City, CA 91604-1431, USA

Steiger, Ueli (Cinematographer)
2222 Kenilworth Ave
Los Angeles, CA 90039-3010, USA

Stein, Ben (Actor, Comedian)
4549 Via Vienta St
Malibu, CA 90265, USA

Stein, Bob (Basketball Player, Misc)
Minnesota Timberwolves
600 1st Ave N
Target Center
Minneapolis, MN 55403-1416, USA

Stein, Chris (Musician)
Shore Fire Media
32 Court St Ste 1600
Brooklyn, NY 11201-4441, USA

Stein, Ed (Cartoonist, Editor)
Rocky Mountain News
101 W Colfax Ave # 500
Editorial Dept
Denver, CO 80202-5315, USA

Stein, Gilbert (Gil) (Hockey Player, Misc)
National Hockey League
650 5th Ave # 3300
New York, NY 10019-6108, USA

Stein, Horst (Conductor)
Mariedi Anders Artists
535 El Camino Del Mar
San Francisco, CA 94121-1099, USA

Stein, Howard (Financier)
Dreyfus Corp
200 Park Ave
New York, NY 10166-0039, USA

Stein, James (Business Person)
Fluor Corp
3353 Michelson Dr
Irvine, CA 92612-7622, USA

Stein, Joseph (Writer)
1130 Park Ave
New York, NY 10128-1255, USA

Stein, Mark (Music Group, Musician)
Future Vision
280 Riverside Dr Apt 12L
New York, NY 10025-9032, USA

Stein, Pamela Jean
2112 Broadway
Santa Monica, CA 90404-2912, USA

Stein, Robert (Editor)
McCall's Magazine
375 Lexington Ave
Editorial Dept
New York, NY 10017-5644, USA

Steinbach, Alice (Journalist)
Baltimore Sun
501 N Calvert St
Editorial Dept
Baltimore, MD 21202-3604, USA

Steinberg, Leigh (Attorney, Attorney General, General)
Steinberg Moorad Dunn
500 Newport Center Dr Ste 800
Newport Beach, CA 92660-7008, USA

Steinberg, Leo (Historian)
165 W 66th St
New York, NY 10023-6508, USA

Steinberg, Paul (Cartoonist)
New Yorker Magazine
4 Times Sq
Editorial Dept
New York, NY 10036-6592, USA

Steinberg, Saul P (Business Person)
Reliance Group Holdings
5 Hanover Sq Rm 1401
New York, NY 10004-2697, USA

Steinberger, Jack (Nobel Prize Laureate)
25 Chemin des Merles
1213 Onex
Geneva, SWITZERLAND

Steinbrenner, George (Baseball Player, Misc)
New York Yankees
1012 S Frankland Rd
Tampa, FL 33629-5106, USA

Steindorff, Scott (Producer, Writer)
c/o Staff Member *Stone Village Entertainment*
9200 W Sunset Blvd Ste 520
Los Angeles, CA 90069-3507, USA

Steinem, Gloria (Activist, Editor)
118 E 73rd St
New York, NY 10021-4238, USA

Steiner, Andre (Athlete)
Bismarckstr 4
Berlin 14109, GERMANY

Steiner, George (Writer)
32 Barrow Road
Cambridge, UNITED KINGDOM (UK)

Steiner, Mel (Baseball Player)
11296 Linda Way
Los Alamitos, CA 90720-3918, USA

Steiner, Paul (Cartoonist)
Washington Times
3600 New York Ave NE
Washington, DC 20002-1996, USA

Steiner, Peter (Cartoonist)
New Yorker Magazine
4 Times Sq
Editorial Dept
New York, NY 10036-6592, USA

Steiner, Rebel (Football Player)
Green Bay Packers
112 Aaronvale Cir
Birmingham, AL 35242-7353, USA

Steiner, Reed (Producer)
c/o Staff Member *William Morris Agency (WMA-LA)*
1 William Morris Pl
Beverly Hills, CA 90212-4261, USA

Steiner, Tommy
Ettenbergstr. 20
Aalen D-73432, GERMANY

Steiner, Tommy Shane (Music Group, Musician)
Collinsworth
50 Music Sq W # 702
Nashville, TN 37203-3212, USA

Steines, Mark (Television Host)
c/o Staff Member *Entertainment Tonight (ET)*
5555 Melrose Ave
Mae West Bldg Fl 2
Los Angeles, CA 90038-3989, USA

Steinfeld, Jake
622 Toyopa Dr
Pacific Palisades, CA 90272-4471, USA

Steinfort, Fred (Football Player)
Oakland Raiders
PO Box 24981
Denver, CO 80224-0981, USA

Steinhardt, Arnold (Musician)
Herbert Barrett
266 W 37th St Fl 20
New York, NY 10018-6648, USA

Steinhardt, Paul J (Physicist)
1000 Cedar Grove Rd
Wynnewood, PA 19096-2006, USA

Steinhauer, Sherri (Golfer)
5010 Hammersley Rd
Madison, WI 53711-2616, USA

Steinkraus, William (Bill) (Horse Racer)
PO Box 3038
Darien, CT 06820, USA

Steinkuhler, Dean E (Football Player)
Houston Oilers
1135 Oak St
Syracuse, NE 68446, USA

Steinman, Jim (Songwriter, Writer)
DAS Communications
83 Riverside Dr
New York, NY 10024-5713, USA

Steinmetz, Richard (Actor)
c/o Staff Member *Personal Management Company*
425 N Robertson Blvd
West Hollywood, CA 90048-1735, USA

Steinsaltz, Adin (Religious Leader)
Israel Talmudic Publications Institute
PO Box 1458
Jerusalem, ISRAEL

Steinseifer Bates, Carrie (Swimmer)
9309 Benzon Dr
Pleasanton, CA 94588-4767, USA

Steitz, Joan A (Misc)
45 Prospect Hill Rd
Branford, CT 06405-5711, USA

Stela, Annie (Musician)
c/o Staff Member *Paradigm (Monterey)*
509 Hartnell St
Monterey, CA 93940-2825, USA

Stella, Frank P (Artist, Misc)
17 Jones St
New York, NY 10014-4131, USA

Stella, Martina (Actor)
c/o Daniela di Santo *Moviement*
Via P Cavallini 24
Rome 00193, ITALY

Stelle, Kellogg S (Physicist)
Imperial College
Prince Consort Road
London SW7 2BZ, UNITED KINGDOM (UK)

Stempel, Robert C (Business Person)
Energy Conversion Devices
1647 W Maple Rd
Troy, MI 48084, USA

Stemrick, Greg (Football Player)
Houston Oilers
1012 Matthews Dr
Cincinnati, OH 45215-1804, USA

Stenberg, Brigitta
11484th St. #116
Santa Monica, CA 90403, USA

Stenerud, Jan (Football Player)
Kansas City Chiefs
3180 Sheiks Pl
Colorado Springs, CO 80904-1141, USA

Stenger, Brian (Football Player)
Pittsburgh Steelers
7921 Kellogg Creek Dr
Mentor, OH 44060-7111, USA

Stenko, Paul (Football Player)
New York Giants
414 Martzville Rd
Berwick, PA 18603-5642, USA

Stenmark, Ingemar (Skier)
Residence l'Annonciade
17 Av de l'Anncenciade
Monte Carlo 98000, MONACO

Stensrud, Mike (Football Player)
Houston Oilers
304 S Winnebago St
Lake Mills, IA 50450-1637, USA

Stepanova, Maria (Basketball Player)
Phoenix Mercury
201 E Jefferson St
American West Arena
Phoenix, AZ 85004-2412, USA

Stepashin, Sergei V (General, Prime Minister)
Government of Russia
Kasnopresneskaya Embankment 2
Moscow 103274, RUSSIA

Stephanie (Royalty)
Maison Clos St Martin
Saint Remy de Provence, FRANCE

Stephanopolous, Constantine (Costis) (President)
Presidential Palace
7 Vas Georgiou B
Odos Zalokosta 10
Athens, GREECE

Stephanopolous, George R (Journalist, Television Host)
c/o Staff Member *ABC News*
7 W 66th St
New York, NY 10023-6201, USA

Stephens, Darryl (Actor)
c/o Staff Member *Noah's Arc*
75 Charles Rowen House
Merlin Street
London WC1X OEJ, UNITED KINGDOM (UK)

Stephens, Hal (Football Player)
Detroit Lions
221 W Virginia St
Rocky Mount, NC 27804-4940, USA

Stephens, Jamain (Football Player)
Pittsburgh Steelers
200 Wind Rd Apt E
Greensboro, NC 27405-2677, USA

Stephens, James
8271 Melrose Ave Ste 110
Los Angeles, CA 90046-6800, USA

Stephens, Janaya (Actor)
c/o Penny Noble *Noble Kaplan Agency*
1260 Yonge St Fl 2
Toronto, ON M4T 1W6, CANADA

Stephens, John (Football Player)
New England Patriots
PO Box 496
Cullen, LA 71021-0496, USA

Stephens, Laraine
10800 Chalon Rd
Los Angeles, CA 90077-3220, USA

Stephens, Olin James II (Architect, Designer, Yachtsman)
80 Lyme Rd Apt 160
Hanover, NH 03755-1229, USA

Stephens, Robert (Business Person)
Adaptec Inc
691 S Milpitas Blvd
Milpitas, CA 95035-5484, USA

Stephens, Santo (Football Player)
Kansas City Chiefs
1205 Winding Meadows Rd
Rockledge, FL 32955-8404, USA

Stephens, Scott (Football Player)
Green Bay Packers
4132 Palm Tree Ct
La Mesa, CA 91941-7238, USA

Stephens, Stanley G (Stan) (Governor)
4 Capitol Ct
Helena, MT 59601, USA

Stephens, Toby (Actor)
c/o Staff Member *Endeavor Agency LLC (LA)*
9601 Wilshire Blvd Fl 3
Beverly Hills, CA 90210-5204, USA

Stephens, Tom (Football Player)
Boston Patriots
69 Orchard Rd
Swampscott, MA 01907-2349, USA

Stephenson, Debra
2 Henrietta St.
London, ENGLAND WC2E 8PS, UNITED KINGDOM (UK)

Stephenson, Dwight E (Football Player)
Miami Dolphins
4785 Tree Fern Dr
Delray Beach, FL 33445-7025, USA

Stephenson, Garrett (Baseball Player)
503 Gem Dr
Kimberly, ID 83341-1907, USA

Stephenson, Gordon (Architect)
55/14 Albert St
Claremont, WA 6010, AUSTRALIA

Stephenson, Kay (Football Player)
San Diego Chargers
2739 Sanibel Pl
Gulf Breeze, FL 32563-2598, USA

Stepp, Craig
6310 San Vicente Blvd Ste 520
Los Angeles, CA 90048-5421, USA

Steppenwolf (John Kay)
108 E Matilija St
Ojai, CA 93023-2639, USA

Steppling, John (Writer)
William Morris Agency
151 El Camino Dr
Beverly Hills, CA 90212-2775, USA

Steptoe, Jack (Football Player)
San Francisco 49ers
40855 Sandy Gale Ln Unit C
Palm Desert, CA 92211-7232, USA

Steranko, Jim (Cartoonist)
PO Box 974
Reading, PA 19603-0974, USA

Stereo Fuse (Music Group)
c/o Staff Member *Wind-up Records*
72 Madison Ave Fl 8
New York, NY 10016-8731, USA

Stereo MC's (Music Group)
c/o Staff Member *Paradigm (Monterey)*
509 Hartnell St
Monterey, CA 93940-2825, USA

Stereophonics (Music Group)
c/o Staff Member *Nettwerk Management (Canada)*
1850 W Second Ave
Vancouver, BC V6J 4R3, CANADA

Sterkel, Jill (Swimmer)
3025 S Snoddy Rd
Bloomington, IN 47401-9671, USA

Sterling, Annette (Music Group, Musician)
Soundedge Personal Mgmt
332 Southdown Rd
Lloyd Harbor, NY 11743-1053, USA

Sterling, Mindy (Actor)
7307 Melrose Ave
Los Angeles, CA 90046-7512, USA

Sterling, Nici (Adult Film Star)
c/o Staff Member *Atlas Multimedia Inc*
9035 Independence Ave
Canoga Park, CA 91304-1743, USA

Sterling, Tisha (Actor)
PO Box 788
Ketchum, ID 83340-0788, USA

Stern, Andrew L (Misc)
Service Employees International Union
1800 Massachusetts Ave NW Lbby
Washington, DC 20036-1222, USA

Stern, Bert (Photographer)
330 E 39th St
New York, NY 10016-2187, USA

Stern, Daniel (Actor)
PO Box 6788
Malibu, CA 90264-6788, USA

Stern, David J (Basketball Player, Misc)
National Basketball Assn
122 E 55th St
Olympic Tower
New York, NY 10022-4535, USA

Stern, Dawn
400 S Beverly Dr Ste 101
Beverly Hills, CA 90212-4403, USA

Stern, Fritz R (Historian)
15 Claremont Ave
New York, NY 10027-6809, USA

Stern, Gardner (Producer, Writer)
c/o Rick Rosen *Endeavor Agency LLC (LA)*
9601 Wilshire Blvd Fl 3
Beverly Hills, CA 90210-5204, USA

Stern, Gary H (Financier, Government Official)
Federal Reserve Bank
PO Box 291
Minneapolis, MN 55480-0291, USA

Stern, Howard (Radio Personality, Talk Show Host)
c/o Staff Member *Howard Stern Production Company, The*
10 E 44th St
New York, NY 10017-3601, USA

Stern, Joseph (Actor, Producer)
c/o Chris Simonian *Creative Artists Agency LCC (CAA-LA)*
2000 Avenue Of The Stars
Los Angeles, CA 90067-4700, USA

Stern, Leonard B (Producer)
1709 Angelo Dr
Beverly Hills, CA 90210-2721, USA

Stern, Michael (Mike) (Musician)
Tropix International
163 3rd Ave # 206
New York, NY 10003-2523, USA

Stern, Richard G (Writer)
University of Chicago
English Dept
Chicago, IL 60637, USA

Stern, Robert A M (Architect)
Robert A M Stern Architects
460 W 34th St
New York, NY 10001-2341, USA

Stern, Shoshannah (Actor)
c/o Staff Member *Perception Public Relations LLC*
3940 Laurel Public Relations
Pmb 169
Studio City, CA 91604, USA

Sternberg, Thomas (Business Person)
Staples Inc
PO Box 9265
Framingham, MA 01701-9265, USA

Sternecky, Neal (Cartoonist)
52 Bluebird Ln
Naperville, IL 60565-1347, USA

Sternfeld, Reuben (Financier)
Inter-American Development Bank
1300 New York Ave NW
Washington, DC 20577-0006, USA

Sternhagen, Frances (Actor)
152 Sutton Manor Rd
New Rochelle, NY 10801-5756, USA

Sternin, Joshua (Actor)
c/o Staff Member *International Creative Management (ICM-LA)*
10250 Constellation Blvd
Los Angeles, CA 90067-6200, USA

Sterrett, Samuel B (Judge)
US Tax Court
400 2nd St NW
Washington, DC 20217-0002, USA

Sterzinsky, Georg Maximilian Cardinal (Religious Leader)
Archdiocese of Berlin
Wundstr 48/50
Berlin 14057, GERMANY

Stetson, Mark (Designer, Special Effects Designer)
c/o Staff Member *International Creative Management (ICM-LA)*
10250 Constellation Blvd
Los Angeles, CA 90067-6200, USA

Steuert-Armstrong, Beverly (Baseball Player)
211 Cathi Ln
Kernersville, NC 27284-9363, USA

Steussie, Todd (Football Player)
Minnesota Vikings
PO Box 410089
Saint Louis, MO 63141-0089, USA

Steussie, Todd E (Football Player)
34535 Emigrant Trl
Shingletown, CA 96088-9342, USA

Steve Miller Band (Music Group)
c/o Staff Member *Paradigm (Nashville)*
124 12th Ave S Ste 410
Nashville, TN 37203-3170, USA

Stevens, Andrew (Actor)
Irv Schechter
9300 Wilshire Blvd # 410
Beverly Hills, CA 90212-3213, USA

Stevens, April (Music Group, Musician)
19530 Superior St
Northridge, CA 91324-1648, USA

Stevens, Bob (Producer)
c/o Staff Member *United Talent Agency (UTA)*
9560 Wilshire Blvd Ste 500
Beverly Hills, CA 90212-2401, USA

Stevens, Brinke (Actor)
PO Box 7112
Van Nuys, CA 91409-7112, USA

Stevens, Cat
Steinhauser Str. 3
Munich 81677, GERMANY

Stevens, Cat (Yusef Islam) (Music Group, Musician, Songwriter, Writer)
Ariola Steinhauser Str 3
Munich 81667, GERMANY

Stevens, Chuck (Photographer)
PO Box 422782
San Francisco, CA 94142-2782, USA

Stevens, Connie (Actor, Music Group, Musician)
Forever Spring
426 S Robertson Blvd
Los Angeles, CA 90048-3908, USA

Stevens, Courtenay J (Actor)
c/o Caldwell Jeffery
943 Queen St E2nd fl
Toronto, ON M4M 1J6, CANADA

Stevens, Dodie (Musician)
c/o Jim Wagner *American Management*
19948 Mayall St
Chatsworth, CA 91311-3522, USA

Stevens, Dorit (Actor, Model)
206 S Brand Blvd
Glendale, CA 91204-1310, USA

Stevens, Eileen (Activist)
126 Marion St
Sayville, NY 11782-1806, USA

Stevens, Fisher (Actor)
329 N Orange Grove Ave
Los Angeles, CA 90036-2135, USA

Stevens, George Jr (Producer)
New Liberty Productions
John F Kennedy Center
Washington, DC 20566-0001, USA

Stevens, Howard (Football Player)
New Orleans Saints
102 Galewood Rd
Lutherville Timonium, MD 21093-2511, USA

Stevens, Jeremy (Actor, Producer, Writer)
c/o Staff Member *William Morris Agency (WMA-LA)*
1 William Morris Pl
Beverly Hills, CA 90212-4261, USA

Stevens, John Paul (Judge)
US Supreme Court
1 1st St NE
Washington, DC 20543-0002, USA

Stevens, Kaye (Actor, Music Group, Musician)
Ruth Webb
10580 Des Moines Ave
Northridge, CA 91326-2926, USA

Stevens, Kevin M (Hockey Player)
38 Bay Pond Rd
Duxbury, MA 02332-3911, USA

Stevens, Laraine
10800 Chalon Rd
Los Angeles, CA 90077-3220, USA

Stevens, Mick
PO Box 344
West Tisbury, MA 02575-0344, USA

Stevens, R C (Baseball Player)
Pittsburgh Pirates
1405 Mound St
Davenport, IA 52803-3333, USA

Stevens, Rachel (Actor, Musician)
c/o Staff Member *S Club 7*
9830 Wilshire Blvd
Creative Artists Agency Lcc (Caa-La)
Beverly Hills, CA 90212-1804, USA

Stevens, Ray (Music Group, Musician, Songwriter, Writer)
c/o Staff Member *William Morris Agency (WMA-TN)*
1600 Division St Ste 300
Nashville, TN 37203-2755, USA

Stevens, Richard (Football Player)
Philadelphia Eagles
4100 Cimmaron Trl
Granbury, TX 76049-5252, USA

Stevens, Rise (Opera Singer)
930 5th Ave
New York, NY 10021-2651, USA

Stevens, Robert B (Educator)
Covington/Burling
Leconfield House
Curzon St
London W1Y 8AS, UNITED KINGDOM (UK)

Stevens, Robert J (Business Person)
Lockheed Martin Corp
6801 Rockledge Dr
Bethesda, MD 20817-1877, USA

Stevens, Robert M (Cinematographer)
1920 S Beverly Glen Blvd Apt 106
Los Angeles, CA 90025-5161, USA

Stevens, Rogers (Musician)
Shapiro Co
9229 W Sunset Blvd Ste 607
Los Angeles, CA 90069-3406, USA

Stevens, Ronnie (Actor)
Caroline Dawson
125 Gloucester Road
London SW7 4IE, UNITED KINGDOM (UK)

Stevens, Scott (Hockey Player)
102 Oval Rd
Essex Fells, NJ 07021-1521, USA

Stevens, Shadoe (Radio Personality)
2934 N Beverly Glen Cir # 399
Los Angeles, CA 90077-1724, USA

Stevens, Shakin' (Music Group, Musician, Songwriter, Writer)
Mgmt Gerd Kehren
Postfach 1455
Erkelenz 41804, GERMANY

Stevens, Stella (Actor, Model)
Stella Visions
1608 N Cahuenga Blvd # 649
Los Angeles, CA 90028-6202, USA

Stevens, Steve (Musician)
c/o Staff Member *J H Cohn LLP*
720 E Palisade Ave
Englewood Cliffs, NJ 07632-3053, USA

Stevens, Steven (Actor)
Stevens Group
3518 Cahuenga Blvd W
Los Angeles, CA 90068, USA

Stevens, Tabitha (Adult Film Star)
c/o Staff Member *Atlas Multimedia Inc*
9035 Independence Ave
Canoga Park, CA 91304-1743, USA

Stevens, Tony (Musician)
Lustig Talent
PO Box 770850
Orlando, FL 32877-0850, USA

Stevens, Warren (Actor)
14155 Magnolia Blvd Apt 27
Sherman Oaks, CA 91423-1143, USA

Stevens, William S (Football Player)
Green Bay Packers
PO Box 221320
El Paso, TX 79913-4320, USA

Stevenson, Cynthia (Actor)
c/o Jonathan Howard *Innovative Artists (LA)*
1505 10th St
Santa Monica, CA 90401-2805, USA

Stevenson, DeShawn (Basketball Player)
Utah Jazz
301 W South Temple
Delta Center
Salt Lake City, UT 84101-1216, USA

Stevenson, James (Actor)
c/o Melissa Prophet *Melissa Prophet Management*
4321 Matilija Ave Apt 21
Sherman Oaks, CA 91423-3672, USA

Stevenson, Juliet (Actor)
68 Pall Mall
London SW1Y 5ES, UNITED KINGDOM (UK)

Stevenson, Parker (Actor)
c/o Bob Alcorn *Metropolitan*
4500 Wilshire Blvd Fl 2
Los Angeles, CA 90010-3858, USA

Stevenson, Ray (Actor)
c/o John Grant *Conway Van Gelder Ltd*
18-21 Jermyn St Fl 3
London SW1Y 6HP, UNITED KINGDOM (UK)

Stevenson, Rosemary (Baseball Player)
19123 120th Ave
Nunica, MI 49448-9460, USA

Stevenson, Teofilo
Hotel Havana Libre
Havana, CUBA

Stevenson Lorenzo, Teofilo (Boxer)
Comite Olimppicu
Hotel Havana
Libre
Havana, CUBA

Stever, H Guyford (Educator, Engineer)
59 Randolph Hill Rd
Randolph, NH 03593-5138, USA

Steverson, Todd (Baseball Player)
Detroit Tigers
109 W Glenhaven Dr
Phoenix, AZ 85045-0717, USA

Steward, Emanuel (Boxer, Misc)
19244 Bretton Dr
Detroit, MI 48223-1364, USA

Steward, Robert L
2864 S Circle Dr Ste 800
Colorado Springs, CO 80906-4163, USA

Stewart, Al (Music Group, Musician, Songwriter, Writer)
Chapman & Co
14011 Ventura Blvd Ste 405
Sherman Oaks, CA 91423-5230, USA

Stewart, Alana (Actor)
13480 Firth Dr
Beverly Hills, CA 90210-1119, USA

Stewart, Alec (Cricketer)
Surrey County Cricket Club
Kennington Oval
London SE11 5SS, UNITED KINGDOM (UK)

Stewart, Alexandra
37 Ave. de la Dame Blanche
Fontenay-Bois 94120, FRANCE

Stewart, Amy (Actor)
c/o Staff Member *Burstein Company, The*
15304 W Sunset Blvd Ste 208
Pacific Palisades, CA 90272-3656, USA

Stewart, Andy (Baseball Player)
Kansas City Royals
641 Geddes St
Wilmington, DE 19805-3718, USA

Stewart, Bill (Baseball Player)
Kansas City A's
44842 Aspen Ridge Dr
Northville, MI 48168-4435, USA

Stewart, Bill (Musician)
Blue Note Records
6920 W Sunset Blvd
Los Angeles, CA 90028-7010, USA

Stewart, Boo Boo (Actor)
c/o Staff Member *Osbrink Talent Agency*
4343 Lankershim Blvd # 100
North Hollywood, CA 91602-2705, USA

Stewart, Bunky (Baseball Player)
Washington Senators
200 S Carolina Ave
Carolina Beach, NC 28428, USA

Stewart, Catherine Mary (Actor)
350 DuPont St
Toronto, ON M5R 1Z9, CANADA

Stewart, Curtis (Football Player)
Dallas Cowboys
873 April Ct
Montgomery, AL 36105-2430, USA

Stewart, Danica (Actor)
c/o Terrance Hines *Hines and Hunt Entertainment*
1213 W Magnolia Blvd
Burbank, CA 91506-1829, USA

Stewart, David A (Dave) (Musician)
Arista Records
8750 Wilshire Blvd # 300
Beverly Hills, CA 90211-2713, USA

Stewart, David K (Dave) (Baseball Player)
Los Angeles Dodgers
17762 Vineyard Ln
Poway, CA 92064-1061, USA

Stewart, Freddie
4862 Excelente Dr
Woodland Hills, CA 91364-4011, USA

Stewart, French (Actor)
United Talent Agency
9560 Wilshire Blvd Ste 500
Beverly Hills, CA 90212-2401, USA

Stewart, Ian (Government Official)
House of Commons
Westminster
London SW1A 0AA, UNITED KINGDOM (UK)

Stewart, Jackie
24 Rte. de Divonne
Nyon 1260, SWITZERLAND

Stewart, James B (Journalist)
Wall Street Journal
200 Liberty St
Editorial Dept
New York, NY 10281-0084, USA

Stewart, James C (War Hero)
8793 Grape Wagon Cir
San Jose, CA 95135-2161, USA

Stewart, Jermaine (Music Group, Musician)
Richard Walters
1800 Argyle Ave # 408
Los Angeles, CA 90028-5253, USA

Stewart, Jimmy (Baseball Player)
Chicago Cubs
15644 Eastbourn Dr
Odessa, FL 33556-2850, USA

Stewart, Jimmy (Football Player)
New Orleans Saints
3609 Tartan Dr
Metairie, LA 70003-1637, USA

Stewart, John (Musician)
Fuji Productions
2480 Williston Dr
Charlottesville, VA 22901-7738, USA

Stewart, John Y (Jackie) (Race Car Driver)
Stewart GP
16 Tanners Dr
Blakelands
Milton Keynes MK14 5BW, UNITED
KINGDOM (UK)

Stewart, Jon (Actor, Comedian, Television
Host)
The Daily Show with Jon Stewart
604 W 52nd St
New York, NY 10019-5013, USA

Stewart, Josh (Actor)
c/o Lena Roklin *Roklin Management*
8530 Wilshire Blvd Ste 550
Beverly Hills, CA 90211-3133, USA

Stewart, Kimberly (Actor, Model)
c/o Kenya Knight *Nous Model
Management*
117 N Robertson Blvd
Los Angeles, CA 90048-3101, USA

Stewart, Kordell (Football Player)
Pittsburgh Steelers
14755 Preston Rd Ste 830
Dallas, TX 75254-7864, USA

Stewart, Kristen (Actor)
c/o Staff Member *Gersh Agency, The (LA)*
232 N Canon Dr
Beverly Hills, CA 90210-5302, USA

Stewart, Lisa (Actor, Producer)
c/o Staff Member *Vinyl Films*
5555 Melrose Ave
Los Angeles, CA 90038-3989, USA

Stewart, Lisa (Musician)
1344 Lexington Ave
Friedman & Larosa
New York, NY 10128-1507, USA

Stewart, Martha K (Business Person, Talk
Show Host)
Martha Stewart Living Omnimedia
11 W 42nd St Fl 25
New York, NY 10036-8002, USA

Stewart, Mary (Writer)
House of Letterawe
Lock Awe
Argyll PA33 1AH, SCOTLAND

Stewart, Maxine
180 Comanche
Topanga, CA 90290-4426, USA

Stewart, Melvin Jr (Swimmer)
c/o Scott Karp *Immortal Entertainment*
11965 Venice Blvd Ste 204
Los Angeles, CA 90066-3954, USA

Stewart, Michael (Football Player)
Los Angeles Rams
717 Palo Verde St
Bakersfield, CA 93309-1863, USA

Stewart, Natalie (Musician, Songwriter,
Writer)
DreamWorks Records
9268 W 3rd St
Beverly Hills, CA 90210-3713, USA

Stewart, Nick
1285 S La Brea Ave Ste 203
Los Angeles, CA 90019-1657, USA

Stewart, Patrick (Actor)
c/o Staff Member *Flying Freehold
Productions*
233 Wilshire Blvd Ste 600
Santa Monica, CA 90401-1218, USA

Stewart, Paul Anthony
10635 Santa Monica Blvd Ste 130
Los Angeles, CA 90025-8306, USA

Stewart, Peggy (Actor)
PO Box 2468
Cathedral City, CA 92235-2468, USA

Stewart, Potter (Judge)
US Court of Appeals
100 E 5th St
US Courthouse
Cincinnati, OH 45202-3988, USA

Stewart, Ray (Golfer)
2777 Dehavilland Place
Abbotsford, BC V2T 5E2, CANADA

Stewart, Robert L (Astronaut, General)
815 Sun Valley Dr
Woodland Park, CO 80863-7729, USA

Stewart, Roderick D (Rod) (Actor,
Musician)
RCA Records
69-79 Fulham High St
Bedford House, London SW6 3JW,
UNITED KINGDOM (UK)

Stewart, Ronald G (Ron) (Hockey Player)
4010 N 11th St Apt 3
Phoenix, AZ 85014-4835, USA

Stewart, Ryan (Football Player)
Detroit Lions
2715 Owens Ave SW
Marietta, GA 30064-4253, USA

Stewart, Sammy (Baseball Player)
Baltimore Orioles
107 Scenic View Dr
Swannanoa, NC 28778-2625, USA

Stewart, Shannon H (Baseball Player)
Toronto Blue Jays
14348 SW 156th Ave
Miami, FL 33196-6072, USA

Stewart, Steve (Football Player)
Atlanta Falcons
1161 Jeans Ln
Amery, WI 54001-5109, USA

Stewart, Thomas J Jr (Opera Singer)
Columbia Artists Mgmt Inc
1790 Broadway Fl 6
New York, NY 10019-1412, USA

Stewart, Tonea (Actor)
Alabama State University
Theater Arts Dept
Montgomery, AL 36101, USA

Stewart, Tony (Race Car Driver)
Tony Stewart Racing
5644 W 74th St
Indianapolis, IN 46278-1752, USA

Stewart, Tyler (Musician)
Nettwerk Mgmt
8730 Wilshire Blvd # 304
Beverly Hills, CA 90211-2716, USA

Stewart, Will Foster (Actor)
8730 Santa Monica Blvd # 1
Los Angeles, CA 90069-4547, USA

Stewart-Hardway, Donna (Actor)
PO Box 777
Pinch, WV 25156-0777, USA

Stezer, Philip (Musician)
I M G Artists
3 Burlington Lane
Chiswick
London W4 2TH, UNITED KINGDOM
(UK)

Stich, Michael (Tennis Player)
Ernst-Barlach-Str 44
Elmshom 25336, GERMANY

Sticht, J Paul (Business Person)
11732 Lake House Ct
North Palm Beach, FL 33408-3320, USA

Stickel, Fred A (Publisher)
Portland Oregonian
1320 SW Broadway
Portland, OR 97201-3411, USA

Stickler, Alfons M Cardinal (Religious
Leader)
Piazza del S Uffizio 11
Rome 00193, ITALY

Stickles, Montford (Monty) (Football
Player)
San Francisco 49ers
1363 3rd Ave
San Francisco, CA 94122-2718, USA

Stickles, Ted (Swimmer)
1142 Sharynwood Dr
Baton Rouge, LA 70808-6069, USA

Sticky, Fingaz (Artist, Musician)
International Creative Mgmt
8942 Wilshire Blvd # 219
Beverly Hills, CA 90211-1908, USA

Stidham, Howard (Football Player)
San Francisco 49ers
185 Bell Dr W
Winchester, TN 37398-5401, USA

Stidham, Phil (Baseball Player)
Detroit Tigers
5025 Malabar Blvd
Melbourne Beach, FL 32951-3268, USA

Stieb, David (Dave) A (Baseball Player)
Toronto Blue Jays
10860 Shay Ln
Reno, NV 89511-9505, USA

Stieber, Tamar (Journalist)
Albuquerque Journal
7777 Jefferson St NE
Editorial Dept
Albuquerque, NM 87109-4360, USA

Stief, Dave (Football Player)
St Louis Cardinals
PO Box 343
Corbett, OR 97019-0343, USA

Stiefel, Ethan (Ballerina)
American Ballet Theatre
890 Broadway
New York, NY 10003-1278, USA

Stiegler, Josef (Pepi) (Skier)
PO Box 290
Teton Village, WY 83025-0290, USA

Stielike, Uli
Case Postale 78
Neuchatel CH-2000, SWITZERLAND

Stienke, Jim (Football Player)
Cleveland Browns
4707 Interlachen Ln
Austin, TX 78747, USA

Stiers, David Ogden (Actor)
Stubbs
8675 Washington Blvd Ste 203
Culver City, CA 90232-7486, USA

Stieve, Terry (Football Player)
New Orleans Saints
230 Blackmer Pl
Saint Louis, MO 63119-3622, USA

Stigers, Curtis (Actor, Musician)
Shore Fire Media
32 Court St Fl 16
Brooklyn, NY 11201-4441, USA

Stiglitz, Joseph E (Nobel Prize Laureate)
Columbia University
International Affairs Building
New York, NY 10027, USA

Stigman, Dick (Baseball Player)
Cleveland Indians
12914 5th Ave S
Burnsville, MN 55337-3504, USA

Stigwood, Robert
122 E 42nd St
New York, NY 10168-0002, USA

Stigwood, Robert C (Producer)
Barton Manor
Whippingham
East Cowes
Isle of Wight PO32 6LB, UNITED
KINGDOM (UK)

Stiles, Jackie (Basketball Player)
Patrick J Stiles
115 E Hamilton
Claflin, KS 67525, USA

Stiles, Julia (Actor)
c/o Rick Kurtzman *Creative Artists Agency
LCC (CAA-LA)*
2000 Avenue Of The Stars
Los Angeles, CA 90067-4700, USA

Stiles, Rollie (Baseball Player)
St Louis Browns
4811 Kamp Dr
Arnold, MO 63010-4669, USA

Stiles, Ryan (Actor, Comedian)
c/o Kay Liberman *Liberman/Zerman
Management*
252 N Larchmont Blvd Ste 200
Los Angeles, CA 90004-3754, USA

Stilgoe, Richard (Songwriter, Writer)
Noel Gray Artists
24 Denmark St
London WC2H 8NJ, UNITED KINGDOM
(UK)

Still, Arthur B (Art) (Football Player)
Kansas City Chiefs
9813 Betsy Ross Ct
Liberty, MO 64068-8418, USA

Still, Bryan (Football Player)
San Diego Chargers
3812 Brennen Robert Pl
Glen Allen, VA 23060-2505, USA

Still, Ken (Golfer)
1210 Princeton St
Fircrest, WA 98466-6035, USA

Still, Ray (Conductor, Musician)
7101 Bay Front Dr Apt 514
Annapolis, MD 21403-3753, USA

Still, Susan L (Astronaut)
NASA
2101 Nasa Pkwy
Johnson Space Center
Houston, TX 77058-3691, USA

Still, William C Jr (Misc)
Columbia University
Chemistry Dept
New York, NY 10027, USA

Stiller, Ben (Actor, Comedian, Director)
c/o Staff Member *Red Hour Films*
629 N La Brea Ave
Los Angeles, CA 90036-2013, USA

Stiller, Jerry (Actor, Comedian)
c/o Pearl Wexler *Kohner Agency, The*
9300 Wilshire Blvd Ste 555
Beverly Hills, CA 90212-3211, USA

Stiller, Stephen (Music Group, Musician)
17525 Ventura Blvd Ste 210
Encino, CA 91316-5111, USA

Stillman, Royle (Baseball Player)
Baltimore Orioles
580 Jb Ct
Glenwood Springs, CO 81601-8733, USA

Stillman, Whit (Director)
International Creative Mgmt
8942 Wilshire Blvd # 219
Beverly Hills, CA 90211-1908, USA

Stills, Chris (Musician)
Atlantic Records
9229 W Sunset Blvd Ste 900
Los Angeles, CA 90069-3410, USA

Stills, Ken (Football Player)
Green Bay Packers
647 Michael St
Oceanside, CA 92057-3505, USA

Stills, Stephen
c/o Staff Member *William Morris Agency (WMA-LA)*
1 William Morris Pl
Beverly Hills, CA 90212-4261, USA

Stills, The (Music Group)
c/o Staff Member *Paradigm (Monterey)*
509 Hartnell St
Monterey, CA 93940-2825, USA

Stillwagon, Jim R (Football Player)
3999 Parkway Ln
Hilliard, OH 43026-1252, USA

Stillwell, Kurt (Baseball Player)
Cincinnati Reds
1105 Lassen View Dr
Lake Almanor, CA 96137-9537, USA

Stillwell, Richard D (Opera Singer)
1969 Rockingham St
McLean, VA 22101-4923, USA

Stillwell, Roger (Football Player)
Chicago Bears
25 Woodland Ct
Novato, CA 94947-7504, USA

Stillwell, Ron (Baseball Player)
Washington Senators
1105 Lassen View Dr
Lake Almanor, CA 96137-9537, USA

Stilson, Jeff (Producer)
c/o Staff Member *Creative Artists Agency LCC (CAA-LA)*
2000 Avenue Of The Stars
Los Angeles, CA 90067-4700, USA

Stinchcomb, Matt (Football Player)
Oakland Raiders
312 Bradford Way
Peachtree City, GA 30269-2311, USA

Stincic, Thomas (Football Player)
Dallas Cowboys
2121 E Oasis St
Mesa, AZ 85213-9743, USA

Stine, Lee (Baseball Player)
Chicago White Sox
108 Santa Fe Dr
Pueblo, CO 81006-1139, USA

Stine, R L (Writer)
Prachute Press
156 5th Ave
New York, NY 10010-7002, USA

Stine, Richard (Cartoonist, Editor)
PO Box 4699
Rollingbay, WA 98061-0699, USA

Stine, Robert L (R L) (Writer)
Scholastic Book Services
555 Broadway
New York, NY 10012-3919, USA

Sting (Actor, Musician)
c/o Rob Light *Creative Artists Agency LCC (CAA-LA)*
2000 Avenue Of The Stars
Los Angeles, CA 90067-4700, USA

Stingley, Darryl (Football Player)
New England Patriots
400 E Randolph St # K125
Chicago, IL 60601-7329, USA

Stinnett, Kelly (Baseball Player)
New York Mets
PO Box 21736
Mesa, AZ 85277-1736, USA

Stinson, Bob (Baseball Player)
Los Angeles Dodgers
1309 Bando Ln
Lady Lake, FL 32162-0115, USA

Stipe, Michael (Musician)
Single Cell Pictures
1016 Palm Ave
West Hollywood, CA 90069-4059, USA

Stiritz, William P (Business Person)
Ralston Purina Co
Checkerboard Square
Saint Louis, MO 63164-0001, USA

Stirling, Rachel (Actor)
c/o Staff Member *Management Inc*
2032 Pinehurst Rd
Los Angeles, CA 90068-3732, USA

Stirling, Steve (Coach, Hockey Player)
New York Islanders
Nassau Coliseum
Hempstead Trunpike
Uniondate, NY 11553, USA

Stitch, Stephen P (Misc)
Rutgers University
Philosophy Dept
New Brunswick, NJ 08901, USA

Stith, Bryant (Basketball Player)
20697 Governor Harrison Pkwy
Freeman, VA 23856-2451, USA

Stits, Bill (Football Player)
Detroit Lions
74880 Borrego Dr
Palm Desert, CA 92260-4508, USA

Stobart, John (Artist)
613/4 Bat Club Dr
Fort Lauderdale, FL 33308, USA

Stobbs, Charles K (Chuck) (Baseball Player)
Boston Red Sox
1731 Riviera Cir
Sarasota, FL 34232-3509, USA

Stock, Barbara (Actor)
22532 Margarita Dr
Woodland Hills, CA 91364-4030, USA

Stock, Mark (Football Player)
Pittsburgh Steelers
9344 Crest Hill Rd
Marshall, VA 20115-3017, USA

Stock, Wes (Baseball Player)
Baltimore Orioles
PO Box 1309
Allyn, WA 98524-1309, USA

Stock-Poynton, Amy (Actor)
Artists Group
1650 Broadway Ste 610
New York, NY 10019-6833, USA

Stockdale, Gretchen
520 Washington Blvd # 248
Marina Del Rey, CA 90292, USA

Stockdale, James
Hoover Inst
Stanford, CA 94305, USA

Stockemer, Ralph (Football Player)
Kansas City Chiefs
4001 Madison Cir
Plano, TX 75023-5910, USA

Stocker, Kevin (Baseball Player)
Philadelphia Phillies
1204 N Murray Ln
Liberty Lake, WA 99019-7555, USA

Stocker-Bottazzi, Jeanette (Baseball Player)
1440 W Walnut St Apt 811
Allentown, PA 18102-4444, USA

Stockhausen, Karl-Heinz
Stockhausen-Verlag
Kuerten D-51515, GERMANY

Stockhausen, Karlheinz (Composer)
Stockhausen-Vertag
Kurten 51515, GERMANY

Stockman, David A (Financier, Government Official)
Blackstone Group
345 Park Ave
New York, NY 10154-0191, USA

Stockman, Shawn (Music Group, Musician)
c/o Staff Member *Creative Artists Agency LCC (CAA-LA)*
2000 Avenue Of The Stars
Los Angeles, CA 90067-4700, USA

Stockmayer, Walter H (Doctor, Misc)
Willey Hill
Norwich, VT 05055, USA

Stockton, Dave K (Golfer)
222 Escondido Dr
Redlands, CA 92373-7215, USA

Stockton, David Jr (Golfer)
10 Carrera Pl
Rancho Mirage, CA 92270-3227, USA

Stockton, Dick (Sportscaster)
2519 NW 59th St
Boca Raton, FL 33496-2224, USA

Stockton, John H (Basketball Player)
c/o Staff Member *Utah Jazz*
301 W South Temple
Delta Center
Salt Lake City, UT 84101-1216, USA

Stockton, Richard L (Dick) (Tennis Player)
715 Stadium Dr
San Antonio, TX 78212, USA

Stockwell, Dean (Actor)
95723 Highway 99 W
Junction City, OR 97448-9395, USA

Stockwell, Jeff (Writer)
c/o Staff Member *United Talent Agency (UTA)*
9560 Wilshire Blvd Ste 500
Beverly Hills, CA 90212-2401, USA

Stockwell, John (Actor)
United Talent Agency
9560 Wilshire Blvd Ste 500
Beverly Hills, CA 90212-2401, USA

Stoddard, Bob (Baseball Player)
Seattle Mariners
15760 Sunnyside Ave
Morgan Hill, CA 95037-5331, USA

Stoddard, Brandon
241 N Glenroy Ave
Los Angeles, CA 90049, USA

Stoddard, Tim (Baseball Player)
Chicago White Sox
3928 Butternut St
East Chicago, IN 46312-2402, USA

Stofa, John (Football Player)
Miami Dolphins
7344 Jefferson Meadows Dr
Blacklick, OH 43004-9813, USA

Stofer, Ken (Football Player)
Buffalo Bisons
311 N State St
Howell, MI 48843-1845, USA

Stoicheff, Boris P (Physicist)
66 Collier St #6B
Toronto, ON M4W 1L9, CANADA

Stoilov, Nickolai (Actor)
c/o Monique Moss *Warren Cowan & Associates PR*
8899 Beverly Blvd Ste 919
Los Angeles, CA 90048-2436, USA

Stoitchkov, Hristo (Soccer Player)
DC United
14120 Newbrook Dr
Chantilly, VA 20151-2273, USA

Stojko, Elvis (Figure Skater)
Mentor Marketing
2 Saint Clair Ave E
Toronto, ON M4T 2T, CANADA

Stokes, Chris (Business Person, Director, Musician)
c/o Staff Member *Tobin & Associates PR*
4929 Wilshire Blvd Ste 245
Los Angeles, CA 90010-3859, USA

Stokes, Fred (Football Player)
Los Angeles Rams
735 Mosleytown Rd
Tarrytown, GA 30470-4052, USA

Stokes, Jesse (Football Player)
Denver Broncos
5810 Cayuga Dr
San Antonio, TX 78228-4325, USA

Stokes, Sims (Football Player)
Dallas Cowboys
1011 Wind Ridge Cir
Duncanville, TX 75137-3741, USA

Stokes of Leyland, Donald G (Business Person)
2 Branksome Cliff
Westminster Road Poole
Dorset BH13 6JW, UNITED KINGDOM (UK)

Stokkan, Bill (Race Car Driver)
Championship Auto Racing
5350 Lakeview Parkway South Dr
Indianapolis, IN 46268-5129, USA

Stokley, Brandon (Football Player)
c/o Staff Member *Indianapolis Colts*
7001 W 56th St
Indianapolis, IN 46254-9698, USA

Stoklos, Randy (Volleyball Player)
Assn of Volleyball Pros
330 Washington Blvd # 400
Marina Del Rey, CA 90292-5141, USA

Stole, Mink (Actor)
635 Colorado Ave Apt 3B
Baltimore, MD 21210-2135, USA

Stolhandske, Tom (Football Player)
San Francisco 49ers
2531 Old Orchard Ln
San Antonio, TX 78230-4610, USA

Stolhanske, Erik (Comedian)
c/o Staff Member *United Talent Agency
(UTA)*
9560 Wilshire Blvd Ste 500
Beverly Hills, CA 90212-2401, USA

Stolle, Frederick S (Tennis Player)
Turnberry Isle Yacht & Racquet Club
19735 Turnberry Way
Miami, FL 33180-2512, USA

Stoller, Mike (Composer)
Leiber/Stoller Entertainment
9000 W Sunset Blvd
West Hollywood, CA 90069-5801, USA

Stollery, David (Actor)
3203 Bern Ct
Laguna Beach, CA 92651-2007, USA

Stolley, Paul D (Doctor)
10205 Wincopin Cir Apt 312
Columbia, MD 21044-3435, USA

Stolley, Richard B (Editor)
Time Inc
Rockefeller Center
Time-Life Building
New York, NY 10020, USA

Stolojan, Theodor (Prime Minister)
World Bank
1818 H St NW
Washington, DC 20433-0002, USA

Stolper, Pinchas (Religious Leader)
Orthodox Jewish Congregations Union
11 Broadway
New York, NY 10004-1303, USA

Stoltenberg, Bryan (Football Player)
San Diego Chargers
3207 W Farmington Ln
Sugar Land, TX 77479-1883, USA

Stoltz, Eric (Actor, Director, Producer)
c/o Helen Sugland *Landmark Artists*
4116 W Magnolia Blvd Ste 101
Burbank, CA 91505-2700, USA

Stoltzman, Richard L (Musician)
Frank Salomon
201 W 54th St Apt 1C
New York, NY 10019-5520, USA

Stolze, Lena (Actor)
Agentur Carola Studlar
Neuroeder Str 1C
Planegg 82152, GERMANY

Stomare, Peter
1129 N Poinsettia Pl
West Hollywood, CA 90046-5715, USA

Stone, Albert L (Race Car Driver)
700 Central Ave
PO Box 8427
Louisville, KY 40208-1212, USA

Stone, Andrew L (Director)
2132 Century Park Ln Apt 212
Los Angeles, CA 90067-3320, USA

Stone, Angie (Musician)
c/o Reina King *Paradigm (LA)*
360 N Crescent Dr
North Bldg
Beverly Hills, CA 90210-6820, USA

Stone, Dean (Baseball Player)
Washington Senators
256 7th St
Silvis, IL 61282-1124, USA

Stone, Dee Wallace (Actor)
23035 Cumorah Crest Dr
Woodland Hills, CA 91364-3709, USA

Stone, Eddie (Adult Film Star)
c/o Staff Member *Diva Central Inc*
7510 W Sunset Blvd Ste 1445
Los Angeles, CA 90046-3408, USA

Stone, Edward C Jr (Physicist)
Jet Propulsion Laboratory
4800 Oak Grove Dr # 180-904
Pasadena, CA 91109-8001, USA

Stone, Gene (Baseball Player)
Philadelphia Phillies
10195 Chapita Park
Green Mountain Falls, CO 80819, USA

Stone, George H (Baseball Player)
Atlanta Braves
1206 Eastland Ave
Ruston, LA 71270-4724, USA

Stone, Jack (Football Player)
Dallas Texans
16125 Crestridge Ave
Sonora, CA 95370-8752, USA

Stone, Jack (Religious Leader)
Church of Nazarene
6401 Paseo Blvd
Kansas City, MO 64131-1213, USA

Stone, James L (War Hero)
3102 Avon Dr
Arlington, TX 76015-2001, USA

Stone, Jeff (Baseball Player)
Philadelphia Phillies
RR 2 Box 392
Portageville, MO 63873, USA

Stone, Joss (Musician, Songwriter, Writer)
c/o Staff Member *Nine Yards
Entertainment*
8530 Wilshire Blvd Fl 5
Beverly Hills, CA 90211-3102, USA

Stone, Ken (Football Player)
Buffalo Bills
1158 Jason Way
West Palm Beach, FL 33406-5255, USA

Stone, Leonard (Actor)
Capital Artists
6404 Wilshire Blvd Ste 950
Los Angeles, CA 90048-5529, USA

Stone, Matt (Animator, Writer)
c/o Mike Simpson *William Morris Agency
(WMA-LA)*
1 William Morris Pl
Beverly Hills, CA 90212-4261, USA

Stone, Michael (Football Player)
Arizona Cardinals
23162 Coventry Woods Ln
Southfield, MI 48034-5163, USA

Stone, Nikki (Skier)
Podium Enterprises
PO Box 680-332
Park City, UT 84068, USA

Stone, Oliver (Actor, Director, Producer,
Writer)
c/o Bryan Lourd *Creative Artists Agency
LCC (CAA-LA)*
2000 Avenue Of The Stars
Los Angeles, CA 90067-4700, USA

Stone, Ricky (Baseball Player)
Houston Astros
56 Bristol Ct
Hamilton, OH 45013-2038, USA

Stone, Rob
8033 W Sunset Blvd # 450
West Hollywood, CA 90046-2401, USA

Stone, Robert A (Writer)
Donadio & Ashworth
121 W 27th St Ste 704
New York, NY 10001-6262, USA

Stone, Roger D (Politician)
34 W 88th St
New York, NY 10024-2558, USA

Stone, Ron (Baseball Player)
Kansas City A's
11720 NW Lovejoy St
Portland, OR 97229-5028, USA

Stone, Sammy
PO Box 2825
Port Arthur, TX 77643-2825, USA

Stone, Sharon (Actor)
15030 Ventura Blvd # 710
Sherman Oaks, CA 91403-5470, USA

Stone, Steven M (Steve) (Baseball Player,
Sportscaster)
San Francisco Giants
9261 N 128th Way
Scottsdale, AZ 85259-6233, USA

Stone, William J (Football Player)
Baltimore Colts
618 Woodland Knolls Rd
Metamora, IL 61548-9429, USA

Stone III, Charles (Actor, Director, Writer)
c/o Barbara Dreyfus *United Talent Agency
(UTA)*
9560 Wilshire Blvd Ste 500
Beverly Hills, CA 90212-2401, USA

Stone-Richards, Lucille (Baseball Player)
65 Anchor Ct
Marco Island, FL 34145-4703, USA

Stone Temple Pilots (Music Group)
c/o Staff Member *William Morris Agency
(WMA-LA)*
1 William Morris Pl
Beverly Hills, CA 90212-4261, USA

Stonebreaker, Mike (Football Player)
Chicago Bears
3300 Delaware Ave Apt A
Kenner, LA 70065-3689, USA

Stonecipher, David A (Financier)
Jefferson-Pilot Corp
100 N Greene St Ste M
Greensboro, NC 27401-2530, USA

Stonecipher, Harry C (Business Person)
Boeing Co
PO Box 3707
Seattle, WA 98124-2207, USA

Stoneham, John (Baseball Player)
Chicago White Sox
12509 E 83rd St N
Owasso, OK 74055-6234, USA

Stoneman, Bill (Baseball Player)
Chicago Cubs
2519 N San Miguel Dr
Orange, CA 92867-8604, USA

Stoneman, Ronl (Musician)
111 Red Berry Rd
Smyrna, TN 37167-2630, USA

Stoner, Alyson (Musician)
c/o Cindy Osbrink *Osbrink Talent Agency*
4343 Lankershim Blvd # 100
North Hollywood, CA 91602-2705, USA

Stoner, Sherri (Actor, Producer, Writer)
c/o Tom Strickler *Endeavor Agency LLC
(LA)*
9601 Wilshire Blvd Fl 3
Beverly Hills, CA 90210-5204, USA

Stones
4790 Irvine Blvd Ste 105
Irvine, CA 92620-1998, USA

Stones, Rolling (Music Group)
c/o Alix Gucovsky *Special Artists Agency*
9465 Wilshire Blvd Ste 890
Beverly Hills, CA 90212-2607, USA

Stones People Europe
1217 JT
Hilversum, THE NETHERLANDS

Stonesifer, Don (Football Player)
Chicago Cardinals
1502 Canbury Ct Apt C1
Wheeling, IL 60090-6974, USA

Stonestreet, Eric (Actor)
c/o Suzanne (Sue) Wohl *TalentWorks (LA)*
3500 W Olive Ave Ste 1400
Burbank, CA 91505-5512, USA

Stookey, Paul (Music Group, Musician,
Songwriter, Writer)
Newworld
RR 175
South Blue Hill Falls, ME 04615, USA

Stoops, Bob (Coach, Football Coach)
University of Oklahoma
108 E Brooks St
Athletic Dept
Norman, OK 73069, USA

Stoops, Jim (Baseball Player)
Colorado Rockles
160 Woodbridge Ave
Highland Park, NJ 08904-3548, USA

Stoops, Mike (Coach, Football Coach)
Arizona State University
Athletic Dept
Tempe, AZ 85287-0001, USA

Stopel, Terry (Football Player)
Chicago Bears
804 Saddlebrook Dr S
Bedford, TX 76021-5360, USA

Stoppard, Tom S (Writer)
P F D
Drury House
34-43 Russell St
London WC2B 5HA, UNITED KINGDOM
(UK)

Storaro, Vittorio (Cinematographer)
Via Divino Amore 2
Frattocchie Merino 00040, ITALY

Storch, Larry (Actor)
330 W End Ave # 17F
New York, NY 10023-8171, USA

Storch, Scott (Producer)
c/o Tracy Christian *Don Buchwald &
Associates Inc (LA)*
6500 Wilshire Blvd Ste 2200
Los Angeles, CA 90048-4942, USA

Storey, David M (Writer)
2 Lyndhurst Gardens
London NW3, UNITED KINGDOM (UK)

Storey, June
338 Morgan Pl
Vista, CA 92083-8018, USA

Stori, Moneca (Actor)
c/o Elena Kirschner *Lucas Talent Inc*
Sun Tower Floor 7
100 W Pender St
Vancouver, BC V6B 1R8, CANADA

Stork, Gilbert (Misc)
188 Chestnut St
Englewood Cliffs, NJ 07632-1908, USA

Stork, Jeff (Volleyball Player)
Pepperdine University
24255 Pacific Coast Hwy
Athletic Dept
Malibu, CA 90263-0002, USA

Storke, Adam (Actor)
c/o Marc Epstein *Marc Epstein Entertainment*
4539 Mary Ellen Ave
Sherman Oaks, CA 91423-3319, USA

Storm, Crystal
2139 N University Dr # 297
Coral Springs, FL 33071-6134, USA

Storm, Gale (Actor, Musician)
23831 Bluehill Bay
Dana Point, CA 92629-4402, USA

Storm, Hannah (Correspondent, Sportscaster)
CBS-TV
51 W 52nd St
News Dept
New York, NY 10019-6119, USA

Storm, Jim
13576 Cheltenham Dr
Sherman Oaks, CA 91423-4818, USA

Storm, Tempest (Dancer)
3350 E Saint Louis Ave Apt 1012
Las Vegas, NV 89104-4539, USA

Stormer, Horst L (Nobel Prize Laureate)
20 E 9th St # 14P
New York, NY 10003-5944, USA

Storms, Kirsten (Actor)
c/o Nils Larsen *Elements Entertainment*
1635 N Cahuenga Blvd Fl 5
Los Angeles, CA 90028-6201, USA

Storraro, Vittorio (Cinematographer)
c/o Paul Hook *International Creative Management (ICM-LA)*
10250 Constellation Blvd
Los Angeles, CA 90067-6200, USA

Story, Tim (Director)
c/o Staff Member *William Morris Agency (WMA-LA)*
1 William Morris Pl
Beverly Hills, CA 90212-4261, USA

Story, Winston (Actor)
c/o Brian McCabe *The McCabe Group*
8285 W Sunset Blvd Ste 1
West Hollywood, CA 90046-2420, USA

Storz, Erik (Football Player)
Jacksonville Jaguars
114 Andrea Dr
Rockaway, NJ 07866-3702, USA

Stossel, John (Television Host)
c/o Staff Member *20/20*
147 Columbus Ave
Abc
New York, NY 10023-6503, USA

Stott, Kathryn L (Musician)
Mire House
West Martor near Skipton
Yorks BD23 3UQ, UNITED KINGDOM (UK)

Stott, Nicole P (Astronaut)
NASA
2101 Nasa Pkwy
Johnson Space Center
Houston, TX 77058-3691, USA

Stottlemyre, Mel (Baseball Player)
New York Yankees
26004 SE 27th St
Sammamish, WA 98075-9140, USA

Stottlemyre, Melvin L (Mel) (Baseball Player)
1007 Tower Dr
Edgewater, NJ 07020-2204, USA

Stottlemyre, Todd (Baseball Player)
Toronto Blue Jays
26004 SE 27th St
Sammamish, WA 98075-9140, USA

Stottlemyre Jr, Mel (Baseball Player)
Kansas City Royals
3314 Meadowlark Dr
Lewiston, ID 83501-8609, USA

Stotts, Terry (Coach)
Golden State Warriors
1001 Broadway
Oakland, CA 94607-4019, USA

Stoudamire, Damon (Basketball Player)
PO Box 17151
Portland, OR 97217-0151, USA

Stoudemire, Amare (Basketball Player)
Phoenix Suns
201 E Jefferson St
Phoenix, AZ 85004-2412, USA

Stouder, Sharon M (Swimmer)
144 Loucks Ave
Los Altos, CA 94022-1045, USA

Stoudt, Bud (Bowler)
431 Lehman St
Lebanon, PA 17046-3639, USA

Stoudt, Cliff (Football Player)
Pittsburgh Steelers
326 Doe Run Cir
Henderson, NV 89012-2701, USA

Stouffer, Kelly (Football Player)
Seattle Seahawks
7430 370th Trl
Rushville, NE 69360-5150, USA

Stovall, Darond (Baseball Player)
Montreal Expos
1107 Goelz Dr
East Saint Louis, IL 62203-1917, USA

Stovall, Jerry L (Football Player)
St Louis Cardinals
417 Highland Trace Dr # D
Baton Rouge, LA 70810-5062, USA

Stove, Betty (Tennis Player)
Advantage International
1025 Thomas Jefferson St NW # 450
Washington, DC 20007-5201, USA

Stover, George (Actor)
PO Box 10005
Baltimore, MD 21285-0005, USA

Stover, Irwin Russ Juno (Misc, Swimmer)
512 Lanai Cir
Union City, CA 94587-4113, USA

Stover, Jeff (Football Player)
San Francisco 49ers
260 Cohasset Rd Ste 190
Chico, CA 95926-2282, USA

Stover, Matt (Football Player)
Cleveland Browns
10024 Rustleleaf Dr
Dallas, TX 75238-2143, USA

Stover, Stewart (Football Player)
Dallas Texans
9334 La Highway 82
Abbeville, LA 70510-2356, USA

Stowe, David H Jr (Business Person)
Deere Co
John Deere Road
Moline, IL 61265, USA

Stowe, Hal (Baseball Player)
New York Yankees
1361 Union New Hope Rd
Gastonia, NC 28056-8574, USA

Stowe, Madeleine (Actor)
c/o David Schiff *Schiff Company*
9465 Wilshire Blvd Ste 480
Beverly Hills, CA 90212-2603, USA

Stowe, Medeleine (Actor)
United Talent Agency
9560 Wilshire Blvd Ste 500
Beverly Hills, CA 90212-2401, USA

Stowe, Otto (Football Player)
Miami Dolphins
546 Mills Way
Goleta, CA 93117-4021, USA

Stowers, Tommie (Football Player)
New Orleans Saints
2435 NW Valley View Dr
Lees Summit, MO 64081-1977, USA

Stowres, Chris (Baseball Player)
Montreal Expos
3633 High Green Dr
Marietta, GA 30068-2530, USA

Stoyanov, Krasimir M (Misc)
Potchta Kosmonavtov
Moskovskoi Oblasti
Syvisdny Goroduk 141160, RUSSIA

Stoyanovich, Peter (Pete) (Football Player)
Miami Dolphins
18185 Parkshore Dr
Northville, MI 48168-8591, USA

Stracey, John (Boxer)
Van Laeken 4
Norsey Road Billericay
Essex CM11 2AD, UNITED KINGDOM (UK)

Strachan, Mike (Football Player)
New Orleans Saints
PO Box 642007
Kenner, LA 70064-2007, USA

Strachan, Rod (Swimmer)
11632 Ranch Hl
Santa Ana, CA 92705-3130, USA

Strachan, Steve (Football Player)
Oakland Raiders
46 Crimson Rd
Billerica, MA 01821-5420, USA

Strader, Cam (Race Car Driver)
10974 Heritage Green Dr
Cornelius, NC 28031-7407, USA

Stradford, Troy (Football Player)
Miami Dolphins
20636 NE 7th Ct
Miami, FL 33179-2434, USA

Stradlin, Izzy (Musician)
Big FD Entertainment
301 Arizona Ave Ste 200
Santa Monica, CA 90401-1364, USA

Stradling, Harry A Jr (Cinematographer)
3664 Avenida Callada
Calabasas, CA 91302-3030, USA

Strahan, Michael A (Football Player)
New York Giants
99 Lloyd Rd
Montclair, NJ 07042-1731, USA

Strahler, Mike (Baseball Player)
Los Angeles Dodgers
8 Canyon Draw
Alamogordo, NM 88310-3613, USA

Straight, Bering (Music Group)
c/o Staff Member *Creative Artists Agency (CAA-Nashville)*
3310 W End Ave Fl 5
Nashville, TN 37203-1028, USA

Strain, Joe (Baseball Player)
San Francisco Giants
8668 E Otero Cir
Centennial, CO 80112-3351, USA

Strain, Julie (Actor, Model)
c/o Amy Godsick *Candy Entertainment Management*
8981 W Sunset Blvd Ste 310
West Hollywood, CA 90069-1848, USA

Strain, Sammy (Music Group, Musician)
Associated Booking Corp
PO Box 2055
New York, NY 10021-0051, USA

Strait, Donald (War Hero)
6 Burning Tree Pl
Jackson Springs, NC 27281-9756, USA

Strait, George (Musician)
c/o Staff Member *Erv Woolsey Agency, The*
1000 18th Ave S
Nashville, TN 37212-2105, USA

Strait, Steven (Actor)
c/o Nick Frenkel *3 Arts Entertainment (NY)*
9460 Wilshire Blvd Ste 700
Beverly Hills, CA 90212-2713, USA

Straka, Martin (Hockey Player)
Pittsburgh Penguins
66 Mario Lemieux Pl
Mellon Arena
Pittsburgh, PA 15219-3504, USA

Stram, Hank
194 Belle Terre Blvd
Covington, LA 70433-4758, USA

Strampe, Bob (Baseball Player)
Detroit Tigers
24720 W Lance Hill Rd
Cheney, WA 99004, USA

Strampe, Bob (Bowler)
5875 W Michigan Ave
Saginaw, MI 48638-5989, USA

Strand, Eli (Football Player)
Pittsburgh Steelers
35 Rogers St
Tuckahoe, NY 10707-3411, USA

Strand, Robin (Actor)
4118 Elmer Ave
North Hollywood, CA 91602-3312, USA

Strane, John (War Hero)
18230 Mirasol Dr
San Diego, CA 92128-1226, USA

Strang, Deborah (Actor)
Henderson/Hogan
8285 W Sunset Blvd Ste 1
West Hollywood, CA 90046-2420, USA

Strange, Doug (Baseball Player)
Detroit Tigers
7 Pebble Creek Way
Taylors, SC 29687-6628, USA

Strange, Sarah (Actor)
c/o Ryan Martin *Agency for the Performing Arts (APA-LA)*
405 S Beverly Dr
Beverly Hills, CA 90212-4416, USA

Strange Boys, The (Music Group)
c/o Staff Member *Paradigm (Monterey)*
509 Hartnell St
Monterey, CA 93940-2825, USA

Strange-Hansen, Martin (Actor)
c/o Staff Member *Gersh Agency, The (LA)*
232 N Canon Dr
Beverly Hills, CA 90210-5302, USA

Stransky, Bob (Football Player)
Denver Broncos
5970 W Colgate Pl
Denver, CO 80227-3814, USA

Strasser, Teresa (Comedian, Television Host)
c/o Staff Member *OmniPop Inc (LA)*
4605 Lankershim Blvd Ste 201
North Hollywood, CA 91602-1874, USA

Strassman, Marcia (Actor)
c/o Staff Member *Bette Smith Management*
499 N Canon Dr
Beverly Hills, CA 90210-4842, USA

Stratas, Teresa (Opera Singer)
Vincent Farrell Assoc
481 8th Ave # 340
New York, NY 10001-1809, USA

Strathairn, David (Actor)
c/o David DeCamillo *Gersh Agency, The (LA)*
232 N Canon Dr
Beverly Hills, CA 90210-5302, USA

Stratham, Jason (Actor)
International Creative Mgmt
8942 Wilshire Blvd # 219
Beverly Hills, CA 90211-1908, USA

Strathiam, David (Actor)
United Talent Agency
9560 Wilshire Blvd Ste 500
Beverly Hills, CA 90212-2401, USA

Stratton, Frederick P Jr (Business Person)
Briggs & Stratton
PO Box 702
Milwaukee, WI 53201-0702, USA

Stratton, Gil
4227 Colfax Ave Unit B
Studio City, CA 91604-2953, USA

Stratton, Mike (Football Player)
Buffalo Bills
2611 Shore Line Rd
Knoxville, TN 37932-1724, USA

Stratus, Trish (Wrestler)
Stratus Enterprises, Inc
5468 Dundas St West
#579
Toronto, ON M9B 6E3, CANADA

Straub, Peter
53 W 85th St
New York, NY 10024-4132, USA

Straus, Robert (Scientist)
656 Raintree Rd
Lexington, KY 40502-2874, USA

Strauss, Neil (Writer)
8491 W Sunset Blvd # 348
West Hollywood, CA 90069-1911, USA

Strauss, Peter (Actor)
Wolf/Kasteller
335 N Maple Dr Ste 351
Beverly Hills, CA 90210-3860, USA

Strauss, Robert S (Diplomat, Politician)
Akin Gump Strauss Hauer Feld
1700 Pacific Ave Ste 4100
Dallas, TX 75201-4675, USA

Straw, John W (Jack) (Government Official)
House of Commons
Westminster
London SW1A 0AA, UNITED KINGDOM (UK)

Straw, Syd (Musician)
Agency Group Ltd
1775 Broadway Ste 515
New York, NY 10019-1903, USA

Strawberry, Darryl E (Baseball Player)
c/o Team Member *New York Yankees*
Yankee Stadium
161st St & River Ave
Bronx, NY 10451, USA

Strawberry Blondes
Box 33 Pontypool
Gwent, ENGLAND NP4 6YU, UNITED KINGDOM (UK)

Strayhorn, Les (Football Player)
Dallas Cowboys
109 Sir Richard Ln
Chapel Hill, NC 27517-5531, USA

Streep, Meryl (Actor)
c/o Kevin Huvane *Creative Artists Agency LCC (CAA-LA)*
2000 Avenue Of The Stars
Los Angeles, CA 90067-4700, USA

Street, John (Politician)
Mayor's Office
23 N Juniper St
City Hall
Philadelphia, PA 19107, USA

Street, Picabo (Skier)
PO Box 321
Hailey, ID 83333-0321, USA

Street, Rebecca (Actor)
19 W 69th St Apt 1001
New York, NY 10023-4751, USA

Streeter, George (Football Player)
Chicago Bears
35 Brentwood Pl
Fort Thomas, KY 41075-2446, USA

Streisand, Barbra (Actor, Director, Musician, Producer)
c/o Staff Member *Barwood Films*
321 W 78th St Apt 1A
New York, NY 10024-6514, USA

Streit, Clarence K (Journalist)
2853 Ontario Rd NW
Washington, DC 20009-2224, USA

Streitwieser Jr, Andrew (Misc)
University of California
Chemistry Dept
Berkeley, CA 94720-0001, USA

Strekalov, Gennadi M (Cosmonaut)
Federation Peace Committee
36 Mira Prospekt
Moscow 129090, RUSSIA

Strenger, Rich (Football Player)
Detroit Lions
1064 Arbroak Way
Lake Orion, MI 48362-2500, USA

Streuli, Wait (Baseball Player)
Detroit Tigers
1107 Westminster Dr
Greensboro, NC 27410-4545, USA

Stribling, Bill (Football Player)
New York Giants
PO Box 1934
Madison, MS 39130-1934, USA

Stricker, Steve (Golfer)
5804 N Sherman Ave
Madison, WI 53704-2147, USA

Strickland, Gail (Actor)
14732 Oracle Pl
Pacific Palisades, CA 90272-2642, USA

Strickland, George (Baseball Player)
Pittsburgh Pirates
6328 Constance St
New Orleans, LA 70118-5813, USA

Strickland, Jim (Baseball Player)
Minnesota Twins
2139 Equestrian Rd
Paso Robles, CA 93446-4149, USA

Strickland, KaDee (Actor)
c/o Staff Member *United Talent Agency (UTA)*
9560 Wilshire Blvd Ste 500
Beverly Hills, CA 90212-2401, USA

Strickland, Scott (Baseball Player)
Montreal Expos
415 Enchanted River Dr
Spring, TX 77388-5981, USA

Striker, Jake (Baseball Player)
Cleveland Indians
1963 SE Gregory Dr
Dallas, OR 97338-2746, USA

Stringer, C Vivian (Coach)
Rutgers University
Athletic Dept
New Brunswick, NJ 08903, USA

Stringer, Howard (Business Person)
Sony Corporation of America
Sony Drive
Park Ridge, NJ 07656, USA

Stringert, Hal (Football Player)
San Diego Chargers
1711 Dole St Apt 603
Honolulu, HI 96822-4946, USA

Stringfield, Sherry (Actor)
c/o Staff Member *United Talent Agency (UTA)*
9560 Wilshire Blvd Ste 500
Beverly Hills, CA 90212-2401, USA

Stritch, Elaine (Actor, Musician)
Michael Whitehall
125 Gloucester Road
London SW7 4TE, UNITED KINGDOM (UK)

Strobel, Eric (Hockey Player)
6617 129th St W
Apple Valley, MN 55124-7967, USA

Stroble, Bobby (Golfer)
526 W 2nd Ave
Albany, GA 31701-2205, USA

Strock, Donald J (Don) (Coach, Football Coach, Football Player)
Miami Dolphins
1512 Passion Vine Cir
Weston, FL 33326-3656, USA

Strolz, Hubert (Skier)
6767 Warth 19
AUSTRIA

Strom, Brock T (Football Player)
4301 W 110th St
Leawood, KS 66211-1424, USA

Strom, Rick (Football Player)
Pittsburgh Steelers
8905 Moor Park Run
Duluth, GA 30097-6622, USA

Stromberg, Mike (Football Player)
New York Jets
PO Box 1510
Shelter Island, NY 11964-1510, USA

Strominger, Jack L (Misc)
Dana Faber Cancer Institute
44 Binney St
Biochemistry Dept
Boston, MA 02115-6084, USA

Strong, Brenda (Actor)
c/o Kay Liberman *Liberman/Zerman Management*
252 N Larchmont Blvd Ste 200
Los Angeles, CA 90004-3754, USA

Strong, Danny (Actor)
c/o Trice Koopman *Koopman Management*
PO Box 1317
Pacific Palisades, CA 90272-1317, USA

Strong, Jim (Football Player)
San Francisco 49ers
9303 Oxted Ln
Spring, TX 77379-6621, USA

Strong, Johnny (Actor)
c/o Beverly Strong *Anonymous Content (CA)*
9350 Wilshire Blvd Ste 224
Beverly Hills, CA 90212-3204, USA

Strong, Mack (Football Player)
Seattle Seahawks
14343 SE 92nd St
Newcastle, WA 98059-3477, USA

Strong, Maurice F (Government Official)
255 Consummers Road
#401
Toronto, ON M2J 5B6, CANADA

Strong, Rider (Actor)
c/o Ellen Meyer *Ellen Meyer Entertainment*
8899 Beverly Blvd Ste 612
Los Angeles, CA 90048-2429, USA

Strong, Tara (Actor)
c/o Jeff Danis *International Creative Management (ICM-LA)*
10250 Constellation Blvd
Los Angeles, CA 90067-6200, USA

Strongbow, Jay (Wrestler)
707 Matlack Ave Apt 103
Lewisburg, PA 17837-1063, USA

Strossen, Nadine (Lawyer)
57 Worth St
New York, NY 10013-2926, USA

Stroud, Carlos (Misc)
Rockefeller University
Physics Dept
1230 York Ave
Cambridge, MA 02138, USA

Stroud, Don (Actor)
500 Lunalilo Home Rd Apt 16A
Honolulu, HI 96825-1718, USA

Stroud, Morris (Football Player)
Kansas City Chiefs
8744 Old Santa Fe Rd
Kansas City, MO 64138-3920, USA

Stroup Jr, Theodore G (Ted) (General)
2085 Hopewood Dr
Falls Church, VA 22043-1820, USA

Strouse, Charles (Composer)
171 W 57th St
New York, NY 10019-2203, USA

Strube, Juergen F (Business Person)
BASF Corp
Carl-Bosch Str 38
Ludwigshafen 67063, GERMANY

Struber, Larry (Producer)
c/o Staff Member *William Morris Agency (WMA-LA)*
1 William Morris Pl
Beverly Hills, CA 90212-4261, USA

Struchkova, Raisa S (Ballerina)
Sovetskiy Ballet
Tverskaya 22B
Moscow 103050, RUSSIA

Strudwick, Suzanne (Golfer)
5500 Crestwood Dr
Knoxville, TN 37914-5108, USA

Struever, Stuart M (Misc)
200 Sheridan Road
Evanston, IL 60208-0001, USA

Strug, Kerri (Athlete, Gymnast)
2801 N Camino Principal
Tucson, AZ 85715-3112, USA

Strugnell, John (Misc)
Harvard University
45 Francis Ave
Divinity School
Cambridge, MA 02138-1911, USA

Strus, Lusia (Actor)
c/o Staff Member *Himber Entertainment Inc*
15760 Ventura Blvd Ste 700
Encino, CA 91436-3016, USA

Struthers, Sally (Actor)
c/o Staff Member *Vincent Cirrincione Associates*
1516 N Fairfax Ave
Los Angeles, CA 90046-2608, USA

Struycken, Carel (Actor)
1665 E Mountain St
Pasadena, CA 91104-3936, USA

Stryker, Bradley (Actor)
c/o Staff Member *The House of Representatives*
211 S Beverly Dr Ste 208
Beverly Hills, CA 90212-3879, USA

Strykert, Ron (Musician)
TPA
PO Box 124
Round Corner, NSW 2158, AUSTRALIA

Strzelczyk, Justin (Football Player)
Pittsburgh Steelers
420 Fort Duquesne Blvd
Pittsburgh, PA 15222-1435, USA

Stuart, Barbara (Actor)
11156 Valley Spring Ln
North Hollywood, CA 91602-2615, USA

Stuart, Eric (Actor, Musician)
330 Carroll St
Brooklyn, NY 11231-5008, USA

Stuart, Gloria (Actor)
c/o Jeff Hunter *William Morris Agency (WMA-NY)*
1325 Avenue Of The Americas
New York, NY 10019-6026, USA

Stuart, Jason (Actor, Comedian)
c/o Bonny Dore *Bonny Dore Management*
8530 Wilshire Blvd Ste 400
Beverly Hills, CA 90211-3131, USA

Stuart, Katie (Actor)
c/o Russ Mortensen *Pacific Artists Management*
1404-510 W Hastings St
Vancouver, BC V6B 1L8, CANADA

Stuart, Katie (Actor)
c/o Blaine Greenberg *Speak Softly Legal Management*
13540 Ventura Blvd
Sherman Oaks, CA 91423-3826, USA

Stuart, Lyle (Publisher)
1530 Palisade Ave Apt 6L
Fort Lee, NJ 07024-5402, USA

Stuart, Marty (Musician, Songwriter)
c/o Staff Member *Paradigm (Monterey)*
509 Hartnell St
Monterey, CA 93940-2825, USA

Stuart, Maxine (Actor)
S D B Partners
1801 Avenue Of Stars Ste 902
Los Angeles, CA 90067-5981, USA

Stuart, Roy (Football Player)
Cleveland Rams
6800 S Granite Ave Apt 339
Tulsa, OK 74136-7043, USA

Stubbins Jr, Hugh Asher (Architect)
6110 N Ocean Blvd
Boynton Beach, FL 33435-5248, USA

Stubblefield, Dana W (Football Player)
San Francisco 49ers
5226 Pisa Ct
San Jose, CA 95138-2122, USA

Stubblefield, Mickey (Baseball Player)
Kansas City Monarchs
304 S 17th St
Mayfield, KY 42066-2015, USA

Stubbs, Imogen M (Actor)
International Creative Mgmt
76 Oxford St
London W1N 0AX, UNITED KINGDOM (UK)

Stubbs, Levi (Musician)
William Morris Agency
151 El Camino Dr
Beverly Hills, CA 90212-2775, USA

Stuck, Hans-Joachim (Race Car Driver)
Harmstatt 3
Ellmau/Tirol 6352, AUSTRIA

Stuckey, Henry (Football Player)
Miami Dolphins
2005 W Riverside Dr Apt 10
Atlantic City, NJ 08401-1434, USA

Stuckey, James (Jim) (Football Player)
San Francisco 49ers
2044 Egret Ln
Charleston, SC 29414-5302, USA

Studaway, Mark (Football Player)
Houston Oilers
4524 Saint Honore Dr
Memphis, TN 38116-2012, USA

Studdard, Ruben (Musician)
c/o Cara Lewis *William Morris Agency (WMA-NY)*
1325 Avenue Of The Americas
New York, NY 10019-6026, USA

Studdard, Vern (Football Player)
New York Jets
11449 Tara Blvd
Lovejoy, GA 30250, USA

Studer, Cheryl (Opera Singer)
Columbia Artists Mgmt Inc
1790 Broadway Fl 6
New York, NY 10019-1412, USA

Studi, Wes (Actor)
c/o Staff Member *Michael Black Management*
9701 Wilshire Blvd Ste 1000
Beverly Hills, CA 90212-2010, USA

Studnicki-Caden, Mary Lou (Baseball Player)
29 Mazarron Dr
Hot Springs Village, AR 71909-5827, USA

Studstill, Patrick L (Pat) (Football Player)
Detroit Lions
2235 Linda Flora Dr
Los Angeles, CA 90077-1410, USA

Studt, Amy (Musician)
c/o Kelsey Parmley *19 Management Ltd*
33 Ransomes Dock
35-37 Parkgate Rd
London SW11 4NP, UNITED KINGDOM (UK)

Studwell, Scott (Football Player)
Minnesota Vikings
10415 Brown Farm Cir
Eden Prairie, MN 55347-4926, USA

Stuhr, Jerzy (Actor, Director)
Graffutu Ltd
Ul SW Gertrudy 5
Cracow 31-107, POLAND

Stuhr-Thompson, Beverly (Baseball Player)
6379 N Muscatel Ave
San Gabriel, CA 91775-1843, USA

Stukes, Charles (Football Player)
Baltimore Colts
2040 Bishop St
Petersburg, VA 23805-2220, USA

Stults, Geoff (Actor)
c/o Jeff Golenberg *The Collective*
9100 Wilshire Blvd # 700 W
Beverly Hills, CA 90212-3401, USA

Stults, George (Actor)
c/o Liza Anderson *Warren Cowan & Associates PR*
8899 Beverly Blvd Ste 919
Los Angeles, CA 90048-2436, USA

Stump, David (Cinematographer)
HFWD Creative Representation
394 E Glaucus St
Encinitas, CA 92024-1734, USA

Stumpf, Kenneth E (War Hero)
16528 State Highway 131
Tomah, WI 54660-6803, USA

Stumpf, Paul K (Misc)
1515 Shasta Dr Apt 2219
Davis, CA 95616-6683, USA

Stumps, Kathy (Actor)
c/o Staff Member *Gersh Agency, The (LA)*
232 N Canon Dr
Beverly Hills, CA 90210-5302, USA

Sturckow, Frederick W (Rick) (Astronaut)
RR 2 Box 14
Dickinson, TX 77539-9338, USA

Sturdivant, John N (Misc)
American Government Employees Federation
80 F St NW Fl 7
Washington, DC 20001-1528, USA

Sturdivant, Tom
1324 SW 71st St
Oklahoma City, OK 73159-3438, USA

Sturgeon, Bob
3903 Lewis Ave
Long Beach, CA 90807-3617, USA

Sturgess, Jim (Actor)
c/o Jodi Gottlieb *I/D PR (LA)*
8409 Santa Monica Blvd
West Hollywood, CA 90069-4209, USA

Sturgess, Shannon (Actor)
1223 Wilshire Blvd # 577
Santa Monica, CA 90403-5400, USA

Sturm, Jerry (Football Player)
Denver Broncos
3 Niblick Ln
Littleton, CO 80123-6621, USA

Sturm, John F (Misc)
Newspaper Assn of America
1921 Gallows Rd # 4
Vienna, VA 22182-3900, USA

Sturm, Yfke (Model)
Elite Model Mgmt
111 E 22nd St Rm 200
New York, NY 10010-5414, USA

Sturman, Eugene (Artist)
1108 W Washington Blvd
Venice, CA 90291, USA

Sturr, Jimmy (Musician)
United Polka Artists
PO Box 1
Florida, NY 10921-0001, USA

Sturridge, Charles (Director)
PFD
Drury House
34-43 Russell St
London WC2B 5HA, UNITED KINGDOM (UK)

Sturt, Fred (Football Player)
Washington Redskins
120 N Berkey Southern Rd
Swanton, OH 43558-8907, USA

Sturtevant, Julian M (Misc)
14025 3rd Ave NW
Seattle, WA 98177-3923, USA

Sturza, Ion (Prime Minister)
Premier's Office
Piaca Maril Atuner Nacional
Chishinev 277033, MOLDOVA

Stuttering John (Radio Personality)
c/o Staff Member *Howard Stern Show WXRK (K-Rock)*
40 W 57th St Fl 14
New York, NY 10019-4001, USA

Stutzmann, Nathalie (Opera Singer)
Herbert Breslin
119 W 57th St Ste 1505
New York, NY 10019-2401, USA

Styler, Kara
PO Box 8002
Honolulu, HI 96830-0002, USA

Styler, Trudie (Actor, Director, Producer)
c/o Staff Member *Xingu Films*
12 Cleveland Row
St James
London SW1A 1DH, UNITED KINGDOM
(UK)

Styx (Musician)
c/o Sterling Bacon *TBA Artist Management (Atlanta)*
1111 Alderman Dr Ste 285
Alpharetta, GA 30005-5433, USA

Suarez, Carlos (Actor)
c/o Staff Member *Televisa*
Blvd Adolfo Lopez Mateos 232
Colonia San Angel INN
DF CP 01060, MEXICO

Suarez Gomez, Hector (Actor)
c/o Gabriel Blanco *Gabriel Blanco Iglesias (Mexico)*
Rio Balsas 35-32
Colonia Cuauhtemoc
DF 06500, MEXICO

Suarez Gonzalez, Adolfo (Prime Minister)
Sagasta
33
Madrid 4, SPAIN

Suarez Rivera, Adolfo A Cardinal (Religious Leader)
Apartado Postal 7
Loma Larga 2429 Sierra Madre
Monterrey 64000, MEXICO

Suau, Anthony (Journalist)
Denver Post
PO Box 1709
Denver, CO 80201-1709, USA

Suazo, Chloe (Actor)
c/o Cindy Osbrink *Osbrink Talent Agency*
4343 Lankershim Blvd # 100
North Hollywood, CA 91602-2705, USA

Subhash, B (Actor, Bollywood)
1 Coelho House
Juhu Tara Road Juhu
Mumbai, MS 400049, INDIA

Subotnick, Morton L (Composer)
25 Minetta Ln Apt 4B
New York, NY 10012-1253, USA

Subways, The (Music Group)
c/o Staff Member *Paradigm (Monterey)*
509 Hartnell St
Monterey, CA 93940-2825, USA

Such, Alec John (Musician)
Bon Jovi Mgmt
248 W 17th St Apt 501
New York, NY 10011-5330, USA

Sucherman, Todd (Musician)
c/o Sterling Bacon *TBA Artist Management (Atlanta)*
1111 Alderman Dr Ste 285
Alpharetta, GA 30005-5433, USA

Suchet, David (Actor)
Ken McReddie
91 Regent St
London W1R 7TB, UNITED KINGDOM
(UK)

Suchocka, Hanna (Prime Minister)
Urzad Rady Ministrow
Al Ujazdowskie 1/3
Warsaw 00-567, POLAND

Suci, Robert (Football Player)
Houston Oilers
2341 Morton Ave
Flint, MI 48507-4445, USA

Sudakis, Bill
16641 Algonquin St
Huntington Beach, CA 92649-3270, USA

Sudan, Madhu (Scientist)
81 Benton Rd
Somerville, MA 02143-1104, USA

Sudduth, Skip (Actor)
c/o Staff Member *Writers and Artists Group Intl (LA)*
8383 Wilshire Blvd Ste 550
Beverly Hills, CA 90211-2417, USA

Sudduth, Skipp (Actor)
Writers & Artists
360 N Crescent Dr Bldg North
Beverly Hills, CA 90210-6818, USA

Sudersham, Ennackel (Physicist)
University of Texas
Physics Dept
Austin, TX 78713, USA

Sudharmono (General, Government Official)
Senopati St 44B
Jakarta Selatan, INDONESIA

Suede
PO Box 3431
London, ENGLAND N1 7LW, UNITED
KINGDOM (UK)

Sues, Alan (Actor)
9014 Dorrington Ave
West Hollywood, CA 90048-1713, USA

Suess, Hans E (Misc)
University of California
Chemistry Dept
La Jolla, CA 92093, USA

Suganya (Actor, Bollywood)
4/5 Oorur Alcot
5thAvenue Besant Nagar
Chennai, TN 600090, INDIA

Sugar, Bert Randolph (Writer)
6 Southview Rd
Chappaqua, NY 10514-1708, USA

Sugar, Leo T (Football Player)
Chicago Cardinals
7161 Golden Eagle Ct Apt 1012
Fort Myers, FL 33912-1708, USA

Sugarcult (Actor)
Kio Novina Management & Booking
545 N Rossmore Ave Apt 3
Los Angeles, CA 90004-2440, USA

Sugarland (Music Group)
c/o Staff Member *Gail Gellman Management*
23852 Pch #920
Malibu, CA 90265, USA

Sugarman, Burt (Producer)
Giant Group
9440 Santa Monica Blvd Ste 407
Beverly Hills, CA 90210-4607, USA

Sugarman, Joseph (Joe) (Business Person, Writer)
Blublocker Corp
3350 Palm Center Dr
Las Vegas, NV 89103-5668, USA

Sugarman, Josh (Activist)
1650 Harvard St NW
Washington, DC 20009-3740, USA

Sugden, Mollie
Hazel Cottage Wheeler End Commons
Lane End
Bucks, ENGLAND HP14 3NL, UNITED
KINGDOM (UK)

Sugg, Diana K (Journalist)
Baltimore Sun
501 N Calvert St
Editorial Dept
Baltimore, MD 21202-3604, USA

Suggs, M Louise (Golfer)
424 Royal Crescent Ct
Saint Augustine, FL 32092-2786, USA

Suggs, Shafer (Football Player)
New York Jets
12849 Barrow Ln
Plainfield, IL 60585-4214, USA

Suggs, Terrell (Football Player)
Baltimore Ravens
Ravens Stadium
11001 Russell St
Baltimore, MD 21230, USA

Suggs, Walt (Football Player)
Houston Oilers
11105 Bradyville Pike
Readyville, TN 37149-4513, USA

Suharto, Mohamed (General, President)
8 Jalan Cendana
Jakarta, INDONESIA

Suhey, Matthew J (Matt) (Football Player)
Chicago Bears
550 Carriage Way
Deerfield, IL 60015-4535, USA

Suhl, Harry (Physicist)
University of California
9500 Gilman Dr
Physics Dept
La Jolla, CA 92093-5004, USA

Suhonen, Alpo (Coach)
Chicago Blackhawks
1901 W Madison St
United Center
Chicago, IL 60612-2459, USA

Suhor, Yvonne (Actor)
J Michael Bloom
233 Park Ave S # 1000
New York, NY 10003-1606, USA

Suhr, August R (Gus) (Baseball Player)
4516 E Marion Way
Phoenix, AZ 85018-1252, USA

Suhrheinrich, Richard F (Judge)
US Court of Appeals
315 W Allegan St Rm 210
Lansing, MI 48933-1514, USA

Suhrstedt, Timothy (Cinematographer)
Gersh Agency
232 N Canon Dr
Beverly Hills, CA 90210-5302, USA

Sui, Anna (Designer, Fashion Designer)
Anna Sui Corp
275 W 39th St
New York, NY 10018-3107, USA

Suitner, Otmar
Platanestr 13
Berlin-Niederschonhausen 13156,
GERMANY

Suits, Julia (Cartoonist)
Creators Syndicate
5777 W Century Blvd Ste 700
Los Angeles, CA 90045-9023, USA

Suk, Josef (Musician)
Karlovo Namesti 5
Prague 2 12000, CZECH REPUBLIC

Sukawaty, Andrew (Business Person)
Sprint PCS Group
PO Box 11315
Kansas City, KS 66111, USA

Sukova, Helena (Tennis Player)
1 Ave Grande Bretagne
Monte Carlo, MONACO

Sukowa, Barbara (Actor)
Artmedia
20 Ave Rapp
Paris 75007, FRANCE

Sukselainen, Vieno J (Prime Minister)
Palvattarenpolku 2
Tapiola 02100, FINLAND

Sulaiman, Jose (Misc)
World Boxing Council
Genova 33
Colonia Juarez
Cuahtetemoc 0660, MEXICO

Suleymanoglu, Naim (Wrestler)
Olympic Committee
Sisli
Buyukdere Cad 18 Tankaya
Istanbul, TURKEY

Suliotis, Elena (Opera Singer)
Villa il Poderino
Via Incontri
Florence 38, ITALY

Sullivan, Chip (Golfer)
49 Homestead Cir
Troutville, VA 24175-6995, USA

Sullivan, CHris (Football Player)
New England Patriots
64 Wagon Wheel Rd
North Attleboro, MA 02760-3576, USA

Sullivan, Dan (Football Player)
Baltimore Colts
25 Algonquin Ave
Andover, MA 01810-5527, USA

Sullivan, Daniel (Producer, Writer)
c/o Alan Wertheimer *Jackoway Tyerman Wertheimer Austen Mandelbaum & Morris*
1888 Century Park E Fl 18
Los Angeles, CA 90067-1702, USA

Sullivan, Erik Per (Actor)
c/o Jodi Peikoff *Jodi Peikoff Law Office*
145 Avenue Of The Americas Ste 6A
New York, NY 10013-1548, USA

Sullivan, Frank (Athlete)
PO Box 1873
Lihue, HI 96766-5873, USA

Sullivan, Franklin L (Frank) (Baseball Player)
PO Box 1873
Lihue, HI 96766-5873, USA

Sullivan, George (Football Player)
Boston Yanks
41 Howard St
Norwood, MA 02062-2323, USA

Sullivan, Greg (Musician)
David Levin Mgmt
200 W 57th St Ste 308
New York, NY 10019-3211, USA

Sullivan, Kathleen (Correspondent)
1025 N Kings Rd Apt 202
West Hollywood, CA 90069-6008, USA

Sullivan, Kathryn D (Astronaut)
795 Old Oak Trce
Columbus, OH 43235-1761, USA

Sullivan, Kevin (Journalist)
Washington Post
Editorial Dept
1150 15th St NW
Washington, DC 20071-0001, USA

Sullivan, Kevin Rodney (Actor, Director, Producer, Writer)
c/o Steve Rabineau *William Morris Agency (WMA-LA)*
9601 Wilshire Blvd Fl 3
Beverly Hills, CA 90210-5204, USA

Sullivan, Louis W (Secretary)
Morehouse College
720 Westview Dr SW
Medical School
Atlanta, GA 30310-1458, USA

Sullivan, Michael J (Mike) (Governor)
1124 S Durbin St
Casper, WY 82601-4328, USA

Sullivan, Mike (Coach, Hockey Player)
9106 Woodridge Run Dr
Tampa, FL 33647-2282, USA

Sullivan, Mike (Golfer)
130 Browns Cir
Greeneville, TN 37743-8208, USA

Sullivan, Nicole (Actor)
c/o Jonathan Howard *Innovative Artists (LA)*
1505 10th St
Santa Monica, CA 90401-2805, USA

Sullivan, Pattrick J (Pat) (Coach, Football Coach, Football Player)
1717 Indian Creek Dr
Birmingham, AL 35243-1745, USA

Sullivan, Phil (Football Player)
New York Jets
4113 Rollingwood Ct
Jacksonville, FL 32257-7665, USA

Sullivan, Susan (Actor)
c/o Staff Member *Paradigm (LA)*
360 N Crescent Dr
North Bldg
Beverly Hills, CA 90210-6820, USA

Sullivan, Tim (Director)
Agency for Performing Arts
405 S Beverly Dr Ste 500
Beverly Hills, CA 90212-4425, USA

Sullivan, Timothy J (Educator)
College of William & Mary
President's Office
Williamsburg, VA 23188, USA

Sullivan, Tom (Actor, Writer)
c/o Chris Ridenhour *Evolution Entertainment (LA)*
901 N Highland Ave
Los Angeles, CA 90038-2412, USA

Sullivan, William J (Educator)
Seattle University
President's Office
Seattle, WA 98122, USA

Sullivan Jr, Brendon V
725 12th St NW
Washington, DC 20005-3901, USA

Sulston, John E (Nobel Prize Laureate)
39 Mingle Lane
Stapleford
Cambridge CB2 5BG, UNITED KINGDOM (UK)

Sultan, Altoon (Artist)
PO Box 2
Groton, VT 05046-0002, USA

Sultan, Donald K (Artist)
19 E 70th St
New York, NY 10021-4907, USA

Sultan of Brunei
Bandar Seri
Begawan, BRUNEI

Sultan Salman, Abdulaziz Al-Saud (Astronaut)
PO Box 18368
Riyadh 11415, SAUDI ARABIA

Sultanov, Alexel (Musician)
Columbia Artists Mgmt Inc
1790 Broadway Fl 6
New York, NY 10019-1412, USA

Sultonov, Outkir T (Prime Minister)
Prime Minister's Office
Mustarilik 5
Tashkent 70008, UZBEKISTAN

Sulzberger, Arthur Ochs
229 W 43rd St
New York, NY 10036-3913, USA

Sum 41 (Music Group)
c/o Staff Member *Nettwerk Management (LA)*
8730 Wilshire Blvd # 304
Beverly Hills, CA 90211-2716, USA

Sumac, Yma (Musician)
Absolute Artists
8490 W Sunset Blvd Ste 403
West Hollywood, CA 90069-1926, USA

Suman, Shekhar (Actor, Bollywood, Comedian, Talk Show Host)
1 Krishna Apartments 168 Sher-E-Punjab Colony
Mahakali Caves Road Andheri (E)
Bombay, MS 400 093, INDIA

Sumaye, Frederick T (Prime Minister)
Prime Minister's Office
PO Box 980
Dodoma, TANZANIA

Sumerfelt, Josh
6550 Yucca St Apt 310
Los Angeles, CA 90028-4226, USA

Sumino, Naoko (Astronaut)
NASDA
Tsukuba Space Center
2-1-1 Sengen Tukubashi
Ibaraka 305, JAPAN

Suminski, Dave (Football Player)
Washington Redskins
16755 Badger Rd
Mason, WI 54856-9493, USA

Summer, Cree (Actor)
Monterey Peninsula Artists
509 Hartnell St
Monterey, CA 93940-2825, USA

Summer, Donna (Musician)
c/o Staff Member *Richard De La Font Agency*
4845 S Sheridan Rd Ste 505
Tulsa, OK 74145-5719, USA

Summer-Francks, Cree
PO Box 5617
Beverly Hills, CA 90209-5617, USA

Summerall, Pat (Football Player)
Detroit Lions
710 S White Chapel Blvd
Southlake, TX 76092-7319, USA

Summerhays, Bob (Football Player)
Green Bay Packers
12345 SE 91st Ave
Summerfield, FL 34491-8251, USA

Summerhays, Boyd (Golfer)
297 Frontier Rd
Farmington, UT 84025-2616, USA

Summerleigh, George A (Pat) (Football Player)
710 S White Chapel Blvd
Southlake, TX 76092-7319, USA

Summers, Andy (Musician)
21A Noel St
London W1V 3PD, UNITED KINGDOM (UK)

Summers, Carol (Artist)
2817 Smith Grade
Santa Cruz, CA 95060-9764, USA

Summers, Dana (Cartoonist)
Orlando Sentinel
633 N Orange Ave
Editorial Dept
Orlando, FL 32801-1349, USA

Summers, Jerry (Musician)
American Promotions
2011 Ferry Ave Apt U19
Camden, NJ 08104-1900, USA

Summers, Lawrence H (Larry) (Educator, Secretary)
Harvard University
President's Office
Cambridge, MA 02138, USA

Summers, Marc (Chef, Television Host)
c/o Staff Member *Food Network, The*
75 9th Ave
New York, NY 10011-7006, USA

Summers, Wilbur (Football Player)
Detroit Lions
PO Box 72734
Louisville, KY 40272-0734, USA

Summers, Yale (Actor)
c/o Staff Member *Screen Actors Guild (SAG-LA)*
5757 Wilshire Blvd
Los Angeles, CA 90036-5810, USA

Summitt, Pat Head (Coach)
3720 River Trace Ln
Knoxville, TN 37920-7118, USA

Sumner, Walt (Football Player)
Cleveland Browns
PO Box 112
Ocilla, GA 31774-0112, USA

Sumners, Rosalynn (Figure Skater)
International Management Group
420 W 45th St
New York, NY 10036-3503, USA

Sumpter, Jeremy (Actor)
c/o Mark Robert *Mark Robert Management*
14014 Moorpark St Apt 316
Sherman Oaks, CA 91423-3494, USA

Sumpter, Tony (Football Player)
Chicago Rockets
702 S Gray St
Stillwater, OK 74074-4331, USA

Sun Dao Lin (Actor, Director)
Shanghai Film Studio
595 Tsao Hsi North Road
Shanghai 200030, CHINA

Sundance, Robert (Activist)
California Indian Alcoholism Commission
225 W 8th St
Los Angeles, CA 90014-3209, USA

Sunday, Gabriel (Actor)
c/o Judy Savage *Savage Agency*
6212 Banner Ave
Los Angeles, CA 90038-2802, USA

Sunde, Milt (Football Player)
Minnesota Vikings
6008 W 104th St
Bloomington, MN 55438-1826, USA

Sundin, Mats (Hockey Player)
Int'l Management Group
801 6th St SW
#235
Calgary, AB T2P 3V8, CANADA

Sundlun, Bruce G (Governor)
Seawood Cliff Way
Newport, RI 02840, USA

Sundvold, Jon (Basketball Player)
2700 Westbrook Way
Columbia, MO 65203-5221, USA

Sung, Elizabeth (Actor)
GVA Talent
9229 W Sunset Blvd Ste 320
Los Angeles, CA 90069-3403, USA

Sunjata, Daniel (Actor)
c/o Meg Mortimer *Principal Entertainment (LA)*
1964 Westwood Blvd Ste 400
Los Angeles, CA 90025-4695, USA

Sunshine Underground, The (Music Group)
c/o Staff Member *Paradigm (Monterey)*
509 Hartnell St
Monterey, CA 93940-2825, USA

Sununu, John H (Ex-Governor, Government Official, Governor)
49 Linden Rd
Hampton Falls, NH 03844-2035, USA

Superdrag (Music Group)
c/o Staff Member *Paradigm (Monterey)*
509 Hartnell St
Monterey, CA 93940-2825, USA

Supergrass (Music Group)
c/o Staff Member *Paradigm (Monterey)*
509 Hartnell St
Monterey, CA 93940-2825, USA

Supernaw, Kywin (Football Player)
Detroit Lions
1123 Clairborne Ct
Indianapolis, IN 46280-1100, USA

Supertramp
16530 Ventura Blvd Ste 201
Encino, CA 91436-4586, USA

Suplee, Ethan (Actor)
Don Buchwald
6500 Wilshire Blvd Ste 2200
Los Angeles, CA 90048-4942, USA

Suppes, Patrick (Psychic)
678 Mirada Ave
Stanford, CA 94305-8475, USA

Supremes, The (Music Group)
PO Box 1821
Ojai, CA 93024-1821, USA

Suquia Goicoechea, Angel Cardinal (Religious Leader)
El Cardenal Arxobispo
San Justo 2
Madrid 28074, SPAIN

Sura, Bob (Basketball Player)
Atlanta Hawks
190 Marietta St NW
Atlanta, GA 30303-2717, USA

Sure, Al B (Musician)
c/o Staff Member *International Creative Management (ICM-LA)*
10250 Constellation Blvd
Los Angeles, CA 90067-6200, USA

The Celebrity Black Book 2008

Surhoff, William J (BJ) (Baseball Player)
221 Oakland Beach Ave
Rye, NY 10580-2619, USA

Surin, Bruny (Athlete, Track Athlete)
PO Box 2
Succ Saint Michel
Montreal, PQ H2A 3L8, CANADA

Surkowski-Delmonico, Lee (Baseball Player)
10 Via Las Colinas Apt 1
Rancho Mirage, CA 92270-6015, USA

Surkowski-Deyotte, Anne (Baseball Player)
632 Southwind Dr
Kelowna, BC V1W 3G1, CANADA

Surovy, Nicolas (Actor)
Susan Smith
1344 N Wetherly Dr
Los Angeles, CA 90069-1817, USA

Surratt, Al (Baseball Player)
Kansas City Monarchs
3448 E 54th St
Kansas City, MO 64130-4027, USA

Sursok, Tammin (Actor)
Channel Seven
Mobbs Lane
Epping 2121, AUSTRALIA

Surtain, Patrick (Football Player)
Miami Dolphins
14557 Sherwood Rd
Overland Park, KS 66224-9807, USA

Surtees, Bruce (Cinematographer)
36 Linda Vista Pl
Monterey, CA 93940-4345, USA

Surtees, John (Race Car Driver)
Team Surtees
Fircroft Way
Edenbridge
Kent TN8 6EJ, UNITED KINGDOM (UK)

Survivor
PO Box 1821
Ojai, CA 93024-1821, USA

Susa, Conrad (Composer)
433 Eureka St
San Francisco, CA 94114-2714, USA

Susana, Marta (Actor)
c/o Staff Member *Univision*
605 3rd Ave Fl 12
New York, NY 10158-1299, USA

Suschitzky, J Peter (Cinematographer)
13 priory Road
London NW6 4NN, UNITED KINGDOM (UK)

Suschitzky, Wolfgang (Cinematographer)
Douglas House
6 Maida Ave #11
London W2 1TG, UNITED KINGDOM (UK)

Susclick, Kenneth S (Misc)
University of Illinois
Chemistry Dept
Champaign, IL 61820, USA

Susco, Stephen (Producer, Writer)
c/o Chris Ridenhour *Evolution Entertainment (LA)*
901 N Highland Ave
Los Angeles, CA 90038-2412, USA

Susi, Carol Ann (Actor)
846 N Sweetzer Ave
Los Angeles, CA 90069-5942, USA

Susman, Todd (Actor)
Pakula/King
9229 W Sunset Blvd Ste 315
Los Angeles, CA 90069-3403, USA

Sussman, Adam (Writer)
c/o Brian Lutz *Brian Lutz Management*
6565 W Sunset Blvd Ste 416
Hollywood, CA 90028-7218, USA

Sussman, Kevin (Actor)
c/o Jill McGrath *Abrams Artists Agency (NY)*
275 7th Ave Fl 26
New York, NY 10001-6708, USA

Sussman, Susan
927 Noyes St
Evanston, IL 60201-6206, USA

Sutcliffe, David (Actor)
c/o Staff Member *Innovative Artists (LA)*
1505 10th St
Santa Monica, CA 90401-2805, USA

Sutcliffe, Rick
616 NE Seabrook Ct
Lees Summit, MO 64064-1261, USA

Suter, Bob (Hockey Player)
4332 McConnell St
Fitchburg, WI 53711-5928, USA

Suter, Gary (Hockey Player)
2128 County Road D
Lac Du Flambu, WI 54538-9726, USA

Sutera, Paul
11365 Ventura Blvd Ste 100
Studio City, CA 91604-3148, USA

Sutherland, Bill (Actor)
c/o Staff Member *Select Artists Ltd (CA-Westside Office)*
1138 12th St Apt 1
Santa Monica, CA 90403-5459, USA

Sutherland, Dame Joan (Opera Singer)
Chalet Monet Rt De Son
Les Avants ICH-18, SWITZERLAND

Sutherland, David (Golfer)
5431 Tree Side Dr
Carmichael, CA 95608-5958, USA

Sutherland, Donald (Actor, Musician, Producer, Writer)
Creative Artists Agency
9830 Wilshire Blvd
Beverly Hills, CA 90212-1804, USA

Sutherland, Doug (Football Player)
New Orleans Saints
511 Kenilworth Ave
Duluth, MN 55803-2113, USA

Sutherland, Kevin (Golfer)
1230 Carter Rd
Sacramento, CA 95864-5328, USA

Sutherland, Kiefer (Actor)
c/o Suzan Bymel *Management 360*
9111 Wilshire Blvd
Beverly Hills, CA 90210-5508, USA

Sutherland, Kristine (Actor)
c/o Staff Member *SMS Talent Inc*
8730 W Sunset Blvd Ste 440
Los Angeles, CA 90069-2277, USA

Sutherland, Peter D (Government Official)
68 Eglinton Road
Dublin 4, IRELAND

Sutherland, Shirley (Baseball Player)
9613 Ritter Dr
Machesney Park, IL 61115-1759, USA

Sutherland, Thomas
229 Columbine Ct
Fort Collins, CO 80521-1715, USA

Sutorius, James
14014 Milbank St Unit 1
Sherman Oaks, CA 91423-2983, USA

Sutter, Brent (Hockey Player)
2551 Thaddeus Circle #S
Glen Ellyn, IL 60137, USA

Sutter, Brian (Coach, Hockey Player)
Chicago Blackhawks
1901 W Madison St
United Center
Chicago, IL 60612-2459, USA

Sutter, Darryl (Coach, Hockey Player)
Calgary Flames
PO Box 1540
Station M
Calgary, AB T2P 3B9, CANADA

Sutter, Duane (Hockey Player)
3703 High Plne Dr
Coral Springs, FL 33065, USA

Sutter, Eddie (Football Player)
Cleveland Browns
5104 N Bevalon Pl
Peoria, IL 61614-4606, USA

Sutter, Ryan (Football Player)
Carolina Panthers
2405 Rollingwood Dr
Fort Collins, CO 80525-1943, USA

Sutterluty, Elizabeth (Actor)
Cineart
36 Rue de Ponthleu
Paris 75008, FRANCE

Sutton, Ed (Football Player)
Washington Redskins
7471 N Van Ness Blvd
Fresno, CA 93711-0445, USA

Sutton, Eddie (Coach)
Oklahoma State University
Athletic Dept
Stillwater, OK 74078-0001, USA

Sutton, Hal (Golfer)
909 Trabue St
Shreveport, LA 71106-1114, USA

Sutton, Joe (Football Player)
Philadelphia Eagles
508 44th Ave E Lot K48
Bradenton, FL 34203-7526, USA

Sutton, Michael (Actor)
Somers Teitelbaum David
8840 Wilshire Blvd # 200
Beverly Hills, CA 90211-2606, USA

Sutton, Percy E (Politician)
10 W 135th St
New York, NY 10037-2602, USA

Sutton, Ricky (Football Player)
Pittsburgh Steelers
1112 To Lani Farm Rd
Stone Mountain, GA 30083-5364, USA

Suvalatsumi (Actor)
58 2nd Street Venkatesh Nagar
Virugambakkam
Chennai, TN 600 092, INDIA

Suvaluxmi (Actor, Bollywood)
Matri Aasis 22/1/1/1 Monohar Pukur Road
PO Rash Behari Avenue
Kolkata, WB 700029, INDIA

Suvari, Mena (Actor)
c/o Chuck James *Gersh Agency, The (LA)*
232 N Canon Dr
Beverly Hills, CA 90210-5302, USA

Suwa, Gen (Misc)
University of California
Human Evolutionary Science Lab
Berkeley, CA 94720-0001, USA

Suwyn, Mark A (Business Person)
Louisiana-Pacific Corp
111 SW 5th Ave
Portland, OR 97204-3604, USA

Suzman, Janet (Actor)
Faircroft
11 Keats Grove
Hampstead
London NW3, UNITED KINGDOM (UK)

Suzuki, David (Correspondent, Scientist, Writer)
211-3905 Springtree Dr
Vancouver, BC V6L 2E2, CANADA

Suzuki, Ichiro (Baseball Player)
Seattle Mariners
PO Box 4100
Safeco Field
Seattle, WA 98194-0100, USA

Suzuki, Pat
343 E 30th St
New York, NY 10016-6417, USA

Suzuki, Robert (Educator)
California State University
President's Office
Bakersfield, CA 93311, USA

Suzy (Writer)
18 E 68th St Apt 1B
New York, NY 10065-5800, USA

Svankmajer, Jan (Director)
Ceminska 5
Prague 1 118 00, CZECH REPUBLIC

Svare, Harland (Coach, Football Coach, Football Player)
Los Angeles Rams
6127 Paseo Jaquita
Carlsbad, CA 92009-2206, USA

Svenden, Birgitta (Musician)
Ulf Tomqvist
Sankt Eriksgatan 100
Stockholm 113 31, SWEDEN

Svendsen, George (Football Player)
163 Wayzata Blvd W Apt 315
Wayzata, MN 55391-1566, USA

Svendsen, Louise A (Misc)
16 Park Ave
New York, NY 10016-4329, USA

Sveningsson, Magnus (Musician)
Motor SE
Gotabergs Gatan 2
Gothenburg 400 14, SWEDEN

Svenson, Bo (Actor)
247 S Beverly Dr # 102
Beverly Hills, CA 90212-3830, USA

Svensson, Peter (Musician, Songwriter, Writer)
Motor SE
Gotabergs Gatan 2
Gothenburg 400 14, SWEDEN

Sverak, Jan (Director)
PO Box 33
Prague 515 155 00, CZECH REPUBLIC

Svihus, Bob (Football Player)
Oakland Raiders
23000 Guidotti Dr
Salinas, CA 93908-1022, USA

Svoboda, Petr (Hockey Player)
1119 S Jefferson St
Allentown, PA 18103-3026, USA

Swaby, Don (Actor)
c/o Staff Member *Stone Manners Talent & Literary (LA)*
6500 Wilshire Blvd Ste 550
Los Angeles, CA 90048-4950, USA

Swados, Elizabeth A (Composer, Writer)
360 Central Park W Apt 16G
New York, NY 10025-6588, USA

Swagerty, Jane (Swimmer)
9128 N 70th St
Paradise Valley, AZ 85253-1960, USA

Swaggart, Jimmy L (Misc)
8919 World Ministry Ave
Baton Rouge, LA 70810-9000, USA

Swaggert, Jimmy
8912 World Ministry Ave
Baton Rouge, LA 70810, USA

Swail, Julie (Athlete, Coach)
University of California
Athletic Dept
Irvine, CA 92697-0001, USA

Swaim, Caskey
1605 N Cahuenga Blvd Ste 202
Los Angeles, CA 90028-6288, USA

Swain, Brennan (Athlete)
c/o Jerry Shandrew *Shandrew Public Relations*
1050 S Stanley Ave
Los Angeles, CA 90019-6634, USA

Swain, Chelse (Actor)
c/o Staff Member *Identity Talent Agency (ID)*
9107 Wilshire Blvd Ste 450
Beverly Hills, CA 90210-5535, USA

Swain, Dominique (Actor)
c/o Stephen (Steve) Levinson *Leverage Management*
1610 Broadway
Santa Monica, CA 90404-2792, USA

Swain, John (Football Player)
Minnesota Vikings
409 E 135th St
Burnsville, MN 55337-4019, USA

Swaminathan, Monkombu S (Scientist)
MS Swaminathan Foundation
3 Cross St
Taramani
Chennai, TN 600113, INDIA

Swan, Billy (Musician, Songwriter, Writer)
Muirhead Mgmt
202 Fulham Road
Chelsea
London SW10 9PJ, UNITED KINGDOM (UK)

Swan, John W D (President)
Swan Building
26 Victoria St
Hamilton HM12, BERMUDA

Swan, Michael (Actor)
13576 Cheltenham Dr
Sherman Oaks, CA 91423-4818, USA

Swanagon, Mary Lou (Baseball Player)
2193 E Amarillo Way
Palm Springs, CA 92264-8637, USA

Swank, Hilary (Actor)
c/o Jason Weinberg *Untitled Entertainment (LA)*
331 N Maple Dr Fl 3
Beverly Hills, CA 90210-3827, USA

Swanke, Karl (Football Player)
Green Bay Packers
4 Butternut Ct
Essex Junction, VT 05452-3959, USA

Swann, Lynn C (Football Player, Sportscaster)
Pittsburgh Steelers
1 Merriman Rd
Sewickley, PA 15143-2466, USA

Swanson, August G (Physicist)
3146 Portage Bay Pl E Apt H
Seattle, WA 98102-3847, USA

Swanson, Jackie (Actor)
15155 Albright St
Pacific Palisades, CA 90272-2511, USA

Swanson, Judith (Actor)
Persona Mgmt
40 E 9th St
New York, NY 10003-6421, USA

Swanson, Kristy (Actor, Model)
c/o Rob Jones *Integrated Artist Management*
532 Colorado Ave
Santa Monica, CA 90401-2408, USA

Swanson, Red (Baseball Player)
Pittsburgh Pirates
1139 Chippenham Dr
Baton Rouge, LA 70808-5694, USA

Swanson, Stan (Baseball Player)
Montreal Expos
3216 Page Rd
Longview, TX 75605-6200, USA

Sward, Melinda (Actor)
c/o Staff Member *Osbrink Talent Agency*
4343 Lankershim Blvd # 100
North Hollywood, CA 91602-2705, USA

Swardson, Nick (Actor, Musician)
c/o Staff Member *Brillstein-Grey Entertainment*
9150 Wilshire Blvd Ste 350
Beverly Hills, CA 90212-3453, USA

Swarn, George (Football Player)
Cleveland Browns
442 Daisy St
Mansfield, OH 44903-1305, USA

Swaroop, Shikha (Actor, Bollywood)
13/14 Atmanand Saraswat Colony
Santacruz
Mumbai, MS 400054, INDIA

Swartwoudt, Gregg (Football Player)
New York Giants
202 Anderson Rd
Esko, MN 55733-9413, USA

Swartz, Jacob T (Scientist)
251 Mercer St
New York University
New York, NY 10012-1110, USA

Swartzbaugh, Dave (Baseball Player)
Chicago Cubs
113 Orchard St
Middletown, OH 45044-4920, USA

Swatek, Barret (Actor)
c/o Tammy Rosen *Melanie Greene Management & Productions*
425 N Robertson Blvd
West Hollywood, CA 90048-1735, USA

Swathi (Actor, Bollywood)
Flat No 4-42
47th Street 9thAvenue Ashok Nagar
Chennai, TN 600083, INDIA

Swatland, Richard (Football Player)
Houston Oilers
178 Club Rd
Stamford, CT 06905-2120, USA

Sway (Television Host)
c/o Staff Member *MTV Networks (NY)*
1515 Broadway Fl 31L
New York, NY 10036-8901, USA

Swayne, Harry (Football Player)
Tampa Bay Buccaneers
956 Cheswick Dr
Gurnee, IL 60031-5600, USA

Swayze, Don
247 S Beverly Dr # 102
Beverly Hills, CA 90212-3830, USA

Swayze, Patrick (Actor)
c/o Jenny Delaney *Forster-Delaney Entertainment*
12533 Woodgreen St
Los Angeles, CA 90066-2723, USA

Swe, U Ba (Prime Minister)
84 Innes Road
Yangon, MYANMAR

Swearingen, John E Jr (Business Person)
1420 N Lake Shore Dr
Chicago, IL 60610-6657, USA

Sweat, Keith (Musician, Songwriter, Writer)
PO Box 1002
Bronx, NY 10466-0241, USA

Swedberg, Heidi (Actor)
Writers & Artists
360 N Crescent Dr Bldg North
Beverly Hills, CA 90210-6818, USA

Swedlin, Rosalie (Producer)
c/o Staff Member *Jackoway Tyerman Wertheimer Austen Mandelbaum & Morris*
1888 Century Park E Fl 18
Los Angeles, CA 90067-1702, USA

Sweeney, Alison (Actor)
c/o Staff Member *Days of Our Lives*
3000 W Alameda Ave
Burbank, CA 91523-0001, USA

Sweeney, Brian (Baseball Player)
Seattle Mariners
199 Morsemere Ave
Yonkers, NY 10703-2007, USA

Sweeney, Calvin (Football Player)
Pittsburgh Steelers
4120 Olympiad Dr
Los Angeles, CA 90043-1632, USA

Sweeney, D B (Actor)
c/o Staff Member *Lighthouse Entertainment*
409 N Camden Dr Ste 202
Beverly Hills, CA 90210-4423, USA

Sweeney, James (Jim) (Coach, Football Coach)
New York Jets
119 Justabout Rd
Venetia, PA 15367-1230, USA

Sweeney, John J (Politician)
AFL-CIO
1750 New York Ave NW
Washington, DC 20006-5301, USA

Sweeney, Julia (Comedian)
187 N Larchmont Blvd # 214
Los Angeles, CA 90004, USA

Sweeney, Kevin (Football Player)
Dallas Cowboys
12401 N Via Tuscania Ave
Clovis, CA 93619-8382, USA

Sweeney, Mark (Baseball Player)
St Louis Cardinals
9299 E Hillery Way
Scottsdale, AZ 85260-2854, USA

Sweeney, Michael J (Mike) (Baseball Player)
Kansas City Royals
2802 E Tam O Shanter Ct
Ontario, CA 91761-7423, USA

Sweeney, Pepper
1930 Century Park W # 403
Los Angeles, CA 90067-6802, USA

Sweeney, Walter F (Walt) (Football Player)
Boston Patriots
5832 Kantor Ct
San Diego, CA 92122-3832, USA

Sweet, Joe (Football Player)
Los Angeles Rams
1503 NE 89th Ct
Vancouver, WA 98664-6413, USA

Sweet, Matthew (Musician, Songwriter, Writer)
Russell Carter Artists Mgmt
567 Ralph McGill Blvd NE
Atlanta, GA 30312-1110, USA

Sweet, Rachel (Producer)
c/o Staff Member *Endeavor Agency LLC (LA)*
9601 Wilshire Blvd Fl 3
Beverly Hills, CA 90210-5204, USA

Sweet, Rick (Baseball Player)
San Diego Padres
1503 NE 89th Ct
Vancouver, WA 98664-6413, USA

Sweet, Sharon (Opera Singer)
Columbia Artists Mgmt Inc
1790 Broadway Fl 6
New York, NY 10019-1412, USA

Sweet, Shay (Adult Film Star)
c/o Staff Member *Atlas Multimedia Inc*
9035 Independence Ave
Canoga Park, CA 91304-1743, USA

Sweeten, Madylin (Actor)
c/o Staff Member *Innovative Artists (LA)*
1505 10th St
Santa Monica, CA 90401-2805, USA

Sweethearts of the Rodeo
5101 Overton Rd
Nashville, TN 37220-1920, USA

Sweetlin, Jodie
6212 Banner Ave
Los Angeles, CA 90038-2802, USA

Sweetney, Mike (Basketball Player)
New York Knicks
2 Penn Plz
Madison Square Garden
New York, NY 10121-1703, USA

Swensen, Joseph A (Composer, Conductor)
Van Walsum Mgmt
4 Addison Bridge Place
London W14 8XP, UNITED KINGDOM (UK)

Swenson, August
1702 Azores Dr.
Pflurgerville, TX 78880, USA

Swenson, Eliza (Actor, Musician)
Ad Astra Management
5118 Vineland Ave # 102
North Hollywood, CA 91601-3814, USA

Swenson, Inga (Actor, Musician)
3351 Halderman St
Los Angeles, CA 90066-1719, USA

Swenson, Rick (Dog Sled Racer)
PO Box 16205
Two Rivers, AK 99716-0205, USA

Swenson, Robert C (Bob) (Football Player)
Denver Broncos
910 Cypress Ln
Louisville, CO 80027-9428, USA

Swenson, Ruth Ann (Opera Singer)
165 W 57th St
Columbia Artists Mgmt Inc
New York, NY 10019-2201, USA

Swensson, Earl S (Architect)
Earl Swensson Assoc
2100 W End Ave Ste 1200
Nashville, TN 37203-5239, USA

Swerling Jr, Jo
25745 Vista Verde Dr
Calabasas, CA 91302-2165, USA

Swett, James E (War Hero)
PO Box 327
Trinity Center, CA 96091-0327, USA

Swiatek, Kazimierz Cardinal (Religious Leader)
Pl Swobody 9
Minsk 220030, BELARUS

Swiczinsky, Helmut (Architect)
Coop Himmelblau
Seilerstatte 16/11A
Vienna 81010, AUSTRIA

Swider, Larry (Football Player)
Detroit Lions
1903 W 93rd Ave
Crown Point, IN 46307-1809, USA

Swienton, Gregory T (Business Person)
Ryder System Inc
11690 NW 105th St
Medley, FL 33178-1103, USA

Swift, Clive (Actor)
Roxane Vacca Mgmt
8 Silver Place
London W1R 3LJ, UNITED KINGDOM
(UK)

Swift, Doug (Football Player)
Miami Dolphins
265 S 25th St
Philadelphia, PA 19103-5551, USA

Swift, Graham C (Writer)
AP Watt
20 John St
London WC1N 2DR, UNITED KINGDOM
(UK)

Swift, Staphanie
PO Box 9818
Canoga Park, CA 91309-0818, USA

Swift, Stephen J (Judge)
US Tax Court
400 2nd St NW
Washington, DC 20217-0002, USA

Swift, Stromile (Basketball Player)
Memphis Grizziles
191 Beale St
Memphis, TN 38103-3715, USA

Swift, Taylor (Musician)
Taylor Swift Entertainment
242 W Main St
PO Box 412
Hendersonville, TN 37075-3318, USA

Swift, William C (Bill) (Baseball Player)
Seattle Mariners
5880 E Sapphire Ln
Paradise Valley, AZ 85253-2200, USA

Swilley, Dennis (Football Player)
Minnesota Vikings
1020 Gruene River Dr
New Braunfels, TX 78132-3298, USA

Swilling, Patrick T (Pat) (Football Player)
New Orleans Saints
6780 Bundy Rd
Patrick's Place East
New Orleans, LA 70127-2564, USA

Swindell, F Gregory (Greg) (Baseball Player)
Cleveland Indians
5639 E Sanna St
Paradise Valley, AZ 85253-1757, USA

Swindells, William Jr (Business Person)
Williamette Industries
1300 SW 5th Ave
Portland, OR 97201-5671, USA

Swindle, Orson
500 University Ave Apt 309
Honolulu, HI 96826-4903, USA

Swindoll, Luci (Writer)
Thomas Nelson, Inc
PO Box 141000
Nashville, TN 37214-1000, USA

Swinford, Wayne (Football Player)
San Francisco 49ers
100 Beacham Dr
Athens, GA 30606-4004, USA

Swing Out Sister
132 Liverpool Rd Islington
London, ENGLAND N1 1LA, UNITED
KINGDOM (UK)

Swingle, Paul (Baseball Player)
California Angels
6844 S Whetstone Pl
Chandler, AZ 85249-9149, USA

Swingley, Doug (Dog Sled Racer)
General Delivery
Lincoln, MT 59639-9999, USA

Swink, James E (Jim) (Football Player)
Dallas Texans
723 Euclid Ave
Rusk, TX 75785-1919, USA

Swinny, Wayne (Musician)
Helter Skelter Plaza
535 Kings Road
London SW10 0S, UNITED KINGDOM
(UK)

Swinton, Tilda (Actor)
Lorraine Hamilton
76 Oxford St
London W1N 0AT, UNITED KINGDOM
(UK)

Swisher, Carl C (Misc)
Institute of Human Origins
1288 9th St
Berkeley, CA 94710-1501, USA

Swisher, Nick (Baseball Player)
c/o Staff Member Oakland Athletics
7000 Coliseum Way
Oakland, CA 94621-1992, USA

Swisher, Steve (Baseball Player)
Chicago Cubs
1905 Washington Ave
Parkersburg, WV 26101-3607, USA

Swisten, Amanda (Actor)
c/o Staff Member Xposure Public
Relations
8271 Melrose Ave Ste 110
Los Angeles, CA 90046-6800, USA

Swistowicz, Mike (Football Player)
New York Yankees
2519 S Drake Ave
Chicago, IL 60623-3919, USA

Swit, Loretta (Actor)
23852 Pacific Coast Hwy
Malibu, CA 90265-4876, USA

Switchfoot (Music Group)
c/o Staff Member William Morris Agency
(WMA-LA)
1 William Morris Pl
Beverly Hills, CA 90212-4261, USA

Switzer, Barry (Basketball Player)
PO Box 43021
Lubbock, TX 79409-3021, USA

Switzer, Barry (Coach, Football Player)
700 W Timberdell Rd
Norman, OK 73072-6323, USA

Switzer, Jon (Baseball Player)
Tampa Bay Devil Rays
15722 Stonehaven Dr
Houston, TX 77059-4635, USA

Switzer, Veryl (Football Player)
Green Bay Packers
1412 Wreath Ave
Manhattan, KS 66503-2402, USA

Swoboda, Ron (Baseball Player)
New York Mets
315 Alonzo St
New Orleans, LA 70115-2119, USA

Swoopes, Sheryl (Basketball Player)
PO Box 43021
Lubbock, TX 79409-3021, USA

Swope, Tracy Brooks
8730 W Sunset Blvd Ste 480
Los Angeles, CA 90069-2277, USA

Sword, Sam (Football Player)
Oakland Raiders
2781 San Leandro Blvd
San Leandro, CA 94578-2583, USA

SWV
6464 W Sunset Blvd Ste 610
Hollywood, CA 90028-7527, USA

Swygert, H Patrick (Educator)
Howard University
President's Office
Washington, DC 20059-0001, USA

Syal, Meera (Actor)
c/o Dallas Smith Peters Fraser & Dunlop
(PFD - UK)
Drury House
34-43 Russell St
London WC2B 5HA, UNITED KINGDOM
(UK)

Syberberg, Hans-Jurgen (Director)
Genter Str 15A
Munich 80805, GERMANY

Sybil (Musician)
Mission Control
Business Center
Lower Road
London SE16 2XB, UNITED KINGDOM
(UK)

Sydney, Harry (Football Player)
San Francisco 49ers
2025 Argonne St
Green Bay, WI 54304-4007, USA

Sykes, Bob (Baseball Player)
Detroit Tigers
509 W Main St
Carmi, IL 62821-1429, USA

Sykes, Eric (Actor)
Norma Farnes
9 Orme Court
London W2 4RL, UNITED KINGDOM
(UK)

Sykes, Eugene (Football Player)
Buffalo Bills
15809 Council Ave
Baton Rouge, LA 70817-5506, USA

Sykes, Lynn R (Geophysicist, Physicist)
100 Washington Spring Rd
RR 1 Box 248
Palisades, NY 10964-1612, USA

Sykes, Peter (Director)
International Creative Mgmt
76 Oxford St
London W1N 0AX, UNITED KINGDOM
(UK)

Sykes, Phil (Hockey Player)
2312 Hill Ln
Redondo Beach, CA 90278-5218, USA

Sykes, Wanda (Comedian)
c/o Stacey Mark William Morris Agency
(WMA-LA)
1 William Morris Pl
Beverly Hills, CA 90212-4261, USA

Sykora, Petr (Hockey Player)
c/o Staff Member The Mighty Ducks of
Anaheim
2695 E Katella Ave
Anaheim, CA 92806-5904, USA

Sylbert, Anthea (Designer)
13949 Ventura Blvd Ste 309
Sherman Oaks, CA 91423-3570, USA

Sylvester, George H (General)
4571 Conicville Rd
Mount Jackson, VA 22842-2713, USA

Sylvester, Harold (Actor)
International Creative Mgmt
8942 Wilshire Blvd # 219
Beverly Hills, CA 90211-1908, USA

Sylvester, Michael (Opera Singer)
Columbia Artists Mgmt Inc
1790 Broadway Fl 6
New York, NY 10019-1412, USA

Sylvester, Steven P (Football Player)
Oakland Raiders
10425 Londonderry Ct
Cincinnati, OH 45242-5029, USA

Sylvia (Musician)
So Much More Media
PO Box 120426
Nashville, TN 37212-0426, USA

Symington, J Fife III (Governor)
1700 W Washington St
Phoenix, AZ 85007-2812, USA

Symms, Steven D (Senator)
127 S Fairfax St # 137
Alexandria, VA 22314-3301, USA

Symonds, Anthony (Designer, Fashion Designer)
c/o Staff Member *Anthony Symonds*
17B Clerkenwell Road
London, England EC1M 5RD, UNITED KINGDOM (UK)

Symone, Raven (Actor)
c/o Jessica (Pilch) Samuel *Sanders/ Armstrong Management*
2120 Colorado Ave Ste 120
Santa Monica, CA 90404-3561, USA

Symonette, Josh (Football Player)
Washington Redskins
4923 Forrest Run
Lithonia, GA 30038-2794, USA

Syms, Sylvia (Actor)
Barry Brown
47 West Square
London SE11 4SP, UNITED KINGDOM (UK)

Sypek, Ryan (Actor)
c/o Rich Hueners *Paradigm (LA)*
360 N Crescent Dr
North Bldg
Beverly Hills, CA 90210-6820, USA

Syreeta
6255 W Sunset Blvd # 1800
Los Angeles, CA 90028-7403, USA

Syron, Richard F (Financier, Government Official)
American Stock Exchange
86 Trinity Pl
New York, NY 10006-1872, USA

Sytsma, John F (Politician)
Locomotive Engineers Brotherhood
1370 Ontario St
Cleveland, OH 44113-1702, USA

Szabo, Istvan (Director)
Objektiv Fil Studio-MAFILM
Rona Utca 174
Budapest 1149, HUNGARY

Szajda, Pawel (Actor)
c/o Staff Member *Stone Manners Talent & Literary (LA)*
6500 Wilshire Blvd Ste 550
Los Angeles, CA 90048-4950, USA

Szarabajka, Keith (Actor)
Talent Group Inc
6300 Wilshire Blvd Ste 900
Los Angeles, CA 90048-5202, USA

Szasz, Thomas S (Doctor)
4739 Limberlost Ln
Manlius, NY 13104-1405, USA

Szczerbiak, Wally (Basketball Player)
26 Peabody Rd
Cold Spring Harbor, NY 11724-1714, USA

Szekely, Eva (Swimmer)
Szepvolgyi Utca 4/B
Budapest 1025, HUNGARY

Szekessy, Karen (Photographer)
Haynstr 2
Hamburg 20249, GERMANY

Szewczenki, Tanya (Figure Skater)
Niederbeerbacher Str 10
Muhital 64367, GERMANY

Szigmond, Vilmos (Cinematographer)
PO Box 2230
Los Angeles, CA 90078-2230, USA

Szmanda, Eric (Actor)
c/o David Gersh *Gersh Agency, The (LA)*
232 N Canon Dr
Beverly Hills, CA 90210-5302, USA

Szoka, Edmund C Cardinal (Religious Leader)
Prefecture for Economic Affairs
Vatican City 00120, VATICAN CITY

Szotkiewicz, Ken (Baseball Player)
Detroit Tigers
133 Hazelwood Dr
Statesboro, GA 30458-9141, USA

Szott, David (Football Player)
Kansas City Chiefs
11 Manor Dr
Morristown, NJ 07960-2600, USA

Szymanski, Richard (Dick) (Football Player)
Baltimore Colts
5270 Forest Edge Ct
Sanford, FL 32771-7160, USA

Szymborska, Wislawa (Nobel Prize Laureate)
Stowarzyszenie Pissarzy Polskich
Ul Kanonicza 7
Cracow 31-002, POLAND

T, Mr (Actor)
15203 La Maida St
Sherman Oaks, CA 91403-1921, USA

T Hooft, Gerardus (Nobel Prize Laureate)
Leuvenlaan 4
Postbus 80.195
Utrecht 3508, THE NETHERLANDS

T Pain (Musician)
c/o Staff Member *Jive Records*
137 W 25th St
New York, NY 10001-7216, USA

T Rajendar (Actor)
33 Hindi Prachar Sabha Road
T Nagar
Chennai, TN 600 017, INDIA

Tabachnik, Michel (Composer, Conductor)
Garvey & Ivor
59 Lansdowne Place
Hove BN3 1FL, UNITED KINGDOM (UK)

Tabackin, Lewis B (Lew) (Musician)
38 W 94th St
New York, NY 10025-7123, USA

Tabai, Ieremia T (President)
South Pacific Forum Secretariat
Ratu Su Kuna Rd
GPO Box 856
Suva, FIJI

Tabaka, Jeff (Baseball Player)
Pittsburgh Pirates
1481 Norview Dr
Clinton, OH 44216-8804, USA

Tabakov, Oleg P (Actor, Director)
Chemysherskogo 39
#3
Moscow 103062, RUSSIA

Tabaksblat, Morris (Business Person)
Unilever NV
Weena 455
Rotterdam, DK 3000, THE NETHERLANDS

Tabassum (Actor, Bollywood, Talk Show Host, Television Host)
11A Pooja Apartments Master Vinayak Road
Bandra
Bombay, MS 400 050, INDIA

Tabb, Jerry (Baseball Player)
Chicago Cubs
18 E Elm St Apt 612
Chicago, IL 60611-1840, USA

Tabitha, Masentle (Royalty)
Royal Palace
PO Box 524
Maseru, LESOTHO

Tabler, Pat (Baseball Player)
Chicago Cubs
8715 Blome Rd
Cincinnati, OH 45243-1007, USA

Tabone, Anton (President)
33 Carmel St
Slierna, MALTA

Tabor, David (Physicist)
8 Rutherford Road
Cambridge CB2 2HH, UNITED KINGDOM (UK)

Tabor, Greg (Baseball Player)
Texas Rangers
29317 Whalebone Way
Hayward, CA 94544-6427, USA

Tabor, Herbert (Scientist)
National Institute of Health
8 Center Dr
Bethesda, MD 20892-0001, USA

Tabor, Paul (Football Player)
Chicago Bears
3308 Riverwalk Dr
Norman, OK 73072-4852, USA

Tabor, Phil (Football Player)
New York Giants
806 Wood N Creek Rd
Ardmore, OK 73401-2940, USA

Tabori, Kristoffer (Actor)
International Artists
235 Regent St
London W1R 8AX, UNITED KINGDOM (UK)

Tabori, Laszlo (Athlete, Track Athlete)
2221 W Olive Ave
Burbank, CA 91506-2659, USA

Tabu (Actor, Bollywood)
Anukool 2nd Floor
7 Bungalows Versova Andheri (W)
Mumbai, MS 400058, INDIA

Tacha, Deanell R (Judge)
US Court of Appeals
4830 Bob Billings Pkwy
Lawrence, KS 66049-4091, USA

Tackett, Jeffrey (Baseball Player)
Baltimore Orioles
1574 Frazier St
Camarillo, CA 93012-4431, USA

Taco (Musician)
8124 W 3rd St Ste 204
Los Angeles, CA 90048-4341, USA

Tada, Joni Eareckson (Writer)
Joni And Friends headquarters
PO Box 3333
Agoura Hills, CA 91376-3333, USA

Taddei, Giuseppe (Opera Singer)
Metropolitan Opera Assn
Lincoln Center Plaza
New York, NY 10023, USA

Tadic, Boris (President)
President's Office
Nemanjina 11
Belgrade 11000, SERBIA

Taeger, Ralph
5619 Mother Lode Dr
Placerville, CA 95667-8232, USA

Taff, Russ
PO Box 570815
Tarzana, CA 91357-0815, USA

Taffoni, Joe (Football Player)
Cleveland Browns
103 Pine Valley Dr
Medford, NJ 08055-9210, USA

Tafoya, Michele (Sportscaster)
CBS-TV
51 W 52nd St
Sports Dept
New York, NY 10019-6119, USA

Tafoya, Michele (Sportscaster)
c/o Staff Member *ESPN (Main)*
935 Middle St
Espn Plaza
Bristol, CT 06010-1000, USA

Taft, Robert
4300 Drake Rd
Cincinnati, OH 45243-4210, USA

Taft, William H IV (Government Official)
1001 Pennsylvania Ave NW
Washington, DC 20004-2505, USA

Tagawa, Cary Hiroyuki (Actor)
c/o Joseph (Joe) Rice *Abrams Artists Agency (LA)*
9200 W Sunset Blvd Ph 11
Los Angeles, CA 90069-3601, USA

Tagge, Jerry (Football Player)
Green Bay Packers
15033 Patterson Cir
Omaha, NE 68137-5127, USA

Taghmaoui, Said (Actor)
c/o Staff Member *Lee Daniels Entertainment*
39 W 131st St
New York, NY 10037-3502, USA

Tagliabue, Paul (Football Executive)
National Football League
280 Park Ave Fl 12W
New York, NY 10017-1206, USA

Taglianetti, Peter (Hockey Player)
67 Merion Ct
Bridgeville, PA 15017-1088, USA

Tahil, Dalip (Actor, Bollywood)
19 Deepali St Cyril Road
Bandra
Mumbai, MS 400050, INDIA

Tahir, Faran (Actor)
c/o Michael Greene *Greene & Associates*
190 N Canon Dr Ste 200
Beverly Hills, CA 90210-5319, USA

Tai, Kobe (Adult Film Star)
c/o Staff Member *Atlas Multimedia Inc*
9035 Independence Ave
Canoga Park, CA 91304-1743, USA

Taillibert, Roger R (Architect)
163 Rue de la Ponpe
Paris 75116, FRANCE

Taimak (Actor)
c/o Staff Member *Chasin Agency, The*
8899 Beverly Blvd Ste 716
Los Angeles, CA 90048-2449, USA

Tait, John (Football Player)
Kansas City Chiefs
876 E Tyson Ct
Gilbert, AZ 85295-5456, USA

Tait, John E (Business Person)
Penn Mutual Life
Independence Square
Philadelphia, PA 19172-0001, USA

Tait, Tristan (Actor)
Paradigm Agency
10100 Santa Monica Blvd Ste 2500
Los Angeles, CA 90067-4116, USA

Taittinger, Jean (Business Person)
58 Blvd Gouvion
Saint-Cyr
Paris 75017, FRANCE

Tak, Saawan Kumar (Bollywood, Director, Filmmaker, Producer)
A/11 Dakshina Park 10th Road
Juhu
Bombay, MS 400 049, INDIA

Taka, Miiko
14560 Round Valley Dr
Sherman Oaks, CA 91403-4631, USA

Takac, Robby (Musician)
Atlas/Third Rail Entertainment
9200 W Sunset Blvd
West Hollywood, CA 90069-3502, USA

Takacs, Tibor (Director)
IP
104 Richview Ave
Toronto, ON M5P 3E9, CANADA

Takacs-Nagy, Gabor (Musician)
Case Postale 196
Collonge-Bellerive 1245, SWITZERLAND

Takahashi, Joseph S (Scientist)
Northwestern University
Neurobiology Dept
2153 N Campus Dr
Evanston, IL 60208-0001, USA

Takahashi, Michiaki (Scientist)
Osaka University
Microbe Diseases Research Institute
Osaka, JAPAN

Takamatsu, Shin (Architect)
Shin Takamatsu Assoc
195 Jobodaiincho Takeda
Kyoto, JAPAN

Take Six
89 5th Ave Ste 700
New York, NY 10003-3020, USA

Take That
69-79 Fulham High St.
London, ENGLAND SW6 3JW, UNITED
KINGDOM (UK)

Takei, George (Actor)
c/o Michael Greenwald *Don Buchwald &
Associates Inc (LA)*
6500 Wilshire Blvd Ste 2200
Los Angeles, CA 90048-4942, USA

Takenouchi, Naoko (Artist)
Kathleen Gaffney
PO Box 58922
Art Glass Int'l
Renton, WA 98058-1922, USA

Takezawa, Kyoko (Musician)
I C M Artists
40 W 57th St
New York, NY 10019-4001, USA

Tal, Josef (Composer, Musician)
3 Dvira Haneviyah St
Jerusalem, ISRAEL

Talalay, Paul (Scientist)
5512 Boxhill Ln
Baltimore, MD 21210-2039, USA

Talalay, Rachel (Director)
1047 Grant St
Santa Monica, CA 90405-1411, USA

Talamini, Robert (Football Player)
Houston Oilers
3577 Cave Creek Mnr
Las Cruces, NM 88011-4015, USA

Talancon, Ana Claudia (Actor)
c/o Staff Member *Creative Artists Agency
LCC (CAA-LA)*
2000 Avenue Of The Stars
Los Angeles, CA 90067-4700, USA

Talavera, Tracee (Gymnast)
106 Mandala Ct
Walnut Creek, CA 94596-5830, USA

Talbert, Billy (Athlete)
194 Bellevue Ave
Newport, RI 02840-3515, USA

Talbert, Diron (Football Player)
Los Angeles Rams
3803 B F Terry Blvd
Rosenberg, TX 77471-5657, USA

Talbert, Don (Football Player)
Dallas Cowboys
PO Box 261
3027 Highway 123
Richmond, TX 77406-0007, USA

Talbot, Dale (Baseball Player)
Chicago Cubs
608 W Kaweah Ave
Visalia, CA 93277-2510, USA

Talbot, Diron V (Football Player)
3803 B F Terry Blvd
Rosenberg, TX 77471-5657, USA

Talbot, Don (Coach, Swimmer)
Sports Federation
333 River Road
Vanier
Ottawa, ON K1L 8B9, CANADA

Talbot, Fred (Baseball Player)
Chicago White Sox
7701 Lunceford Ln
Falls Church, VA 22043-1207, USA

Talbot, Nita (Actor)
3420 Merrimac Rd
Los Angeles, CA 90049-1034, USA

Talbot, Susan (Actor)
Media Artists Group
6300 Wilshire Blvd Ste 1470
Los Angeles, CA 90048-5200, USA

Talbott, Gloria (Actor)
2066 Montecito Dr
Glendale, CA 91208-1824, USA

Talbott, John H (Doctor)
Commodore Club
177 Ocean Lane Dr
Key Biscayne, FL 33149-1437, USA

Talbott, Michael (Actor)
10340 Santa Monica Blvd
Los Angeles, CA 90025-6904, USA

Talbott, Strobe (Journalist)
State Department
2201 C St NW
Washington, DC 20520-0099, USA

Talese, Gay (Writer)
154 E Atlantic Blvd
Ocean City, NJ 08226-4511, USA

Taliaferro, George (Football Player)
New York Yankees
2708 Olcott Blvd
Bloomington, IN 47401-4417, USA

Taliaferro, Mike (Football Player)
New York Jets
7332 Oakbluff Dr
Dallas, TX 75254-2739, USA

Talking Back Sunday (Music Group)
c/o Staff Member *Kenmore Agency, The*
59 Park St Ste 2
Beverly, MA 01915-4255, USA

Talla (DJ)
c/o Staff Member *Diva Central Inc*
7510 W Sunset Blvd Ste 1445
Los Angeles, CA 90046-3408, USA

Tallchief, Maria (Dancer)
48 Prospect Ave
Highland Park, IL 60035-3329, USA

Tallet, Brian (Baseball Player)
Cleveland Indians
4206 N Donald Ave
Bethany, OK 73008-2724, USA

Talley, Darryl V (Football Player)
Buffalo Bills
8713 Lake Tibet Ct
Orlando, FL 32836-5481, USA

Talley, Gary (Musician)
Horizon Mgmt
PO Box 8770
Endwell, NY 13762-8770, USA

Talley, Joel E (War Hero)
20 Lakeshore Dr
Shalimar, FL 32579-2210, USA

Talley, Stan (Football Player)
Oakland Raiders
24241 Porto Cristo
Dana Point, CA 92629-4511, USA

Tallman, Patricia (Actor)
PMB 2161
1801 E Tropicana Ave Ste 9
Las Vegas, NV 89119-6559, USA

Tallman, Richard C (Judge)
US Court of Appeals
1010 5th Ave
US Courthouse
Seattle, WA 98104-1195, USA

Talor, Vanessa
11271 Ventura Blvd # 396
Studio City, CA 91604-3136, USA

Talsania, Tiku (Actor, Bollywood)
22-A Shruti Yashudham Enclave
Filmcity Rd Goregaon (E)
Mumbai, MS 400053, INDIA

Talton, Tim (Baseball Player)
Kansas City A's
130 Hardy Talton Rd NW
Pikeville, NC 27863-8601, USA

Tam, Jeffrey (Baseball Player)
New York Mets
8535 Bass Ave
Palm Bay, FL 32909-1139, USA

Tam, Vivienne (Designer, Fashion
Designer)
550 Fashion Ave
New York, NY 10018-3203, USA

Tamahori, Lee W (Director)
International Creative Mgmt
8942 Wilshire Blvd # 219
Beverly Hills, CA 90211-1908, USA

Tamargo, John (Baseball Player)
St Louis Cardinals
208 Furse Lakes Cir Apt 11
Naples, FL 34104-6439, USA

Tamaro, Janet (Journalist)
c/o Staff Member *Endeavor Agency LLC
(LA)*
9601 Wilshire Blvd Fl 3
Beverly Hills, CA 90210-5204, USA

Tamayo, Mendez Amaldo (Cosmonaut)
Calle 16
#504 C/5A y 7MA
Miramar, Ciudad Havana 11300, CUBA

Tambellini, Roger (Golfer)
32531 N Scottsdale Rd Ste 105
Scottsdale, AZ 85266-1519, USA

Tamberino, Paul (Referee)
349 Homeland Southway
Baltimore, MD 21212-4153, USA

Tambiah, Stanley J (Misc)
Harvard University
Anthropology Dept
Cambridge, MA 02138, USA

Tamblyn, Amber (Actor)
c/o Staff Member *Endeavor Agency LLC
(LA)*
9601 Wilshire Blvd Fl 3
Beverly Hills, CA 90210-5204, USA

Tamblyn, Russ (Actor, Dancer)
c/o Phil Gittelman *Phillip B Gittelman
Personal Management*
1221 N Kings Rd # Ph405
W Hollywood, CA 90069-2846, USA

Tambor, Jeffrey (Actor)
c/o Amy Zvi *Bragman/Nyman/Cafarelli
(BNC)*
8687 Melrose Ave Fl 8
Pacific Design Center
Los Angeles, CA 90069-5701, USA

Tambor, Jeffrey (Actor)
Brillstein/Grey
9150 Wilshire Blvd Ste 350
Beverly Hills, CA 90212-3453, USA

Tamburello, Ben (Football Player)
Philadelphia Eagles
4385 Milner Rd W
Birmingham, AL 35242-7355, USA

Tamke, George W (Business Person)
Emerson Electric Co
PO Box 4100
Saint Louis, MO 63136-8506, USA

Tamm, Peter (Publisher)
Elbchaussee 277
Hamburg 22605, GERMANY

Tamm, Ralph (Football Player)
Cleveland Browns
2670 Atlantic Ave
Bensalem, PA 19020-3507, USA

Tan, Amy (Writer)
c/o Staff Member *Steven Barclay Agency*
12 Western Ave
Petaluma, CA 94952-2907, USA

Tan, Dun (Composer)
Columbia University
Dodge Hall
Arts School
New York, NY 10027, USA

Tan, Elaine (Actor)
CAM
19 Denmark Street
London WC2H 8NA, UNITED KINGDOM
(UK)

Tan, Melvyn (Musician)
Valerie Barber Mgmt
4 Winsley St
#305
London W1N 7AR, UNITED KINGDOM
(UK)

Tanaev, Nikoly (Prime Minister)
Prime Minister's Office
Ul Perromayskaya 57
Bishkek, KYRGYZSTAN

Tanaka, Koichi (Nobel Prize Laureate)
Shimadzu Corp
1 Nishinokyo-Kuwabaracho
Nakagoku
Kyoto 604-8511, JAPAN

Tanaka, Shoji (Physicist)
Superconductivity Laboratory
1-10-13 Shinonome
Kotoku
Tokyo 135, JAPAN

Tanana, Frank D (Baseball Player)
California Angels
28492 S Harwich Dr
Farmington Hills, MI 48334-4281, USA

Tandon, Raveena (Actor, Bollywood)
Tandon House Nippon Society
Juhu Church
Mumbai, MS 400049, INDIA

Tandon, Ravi (Bollywood, Director,
Filmmaker, Producer)
B/58 Ravi Kiran
New Linking Road
Bombay, MS 400 058, INDIA

Tanford, Charles (Doctor)
Tarlswood
Back Lane
Easingwold, York YO6 3BG, UNITED
KINGDOM (UK)

Tang, David (Designer)
Shanghai Tang
Guangdong Investment Tower 23rd Floor
148 Connaught Road Central
Central Hong Kong, HONG KONG

Tangerine Dream
PO Box 29242
Oakland, CA 94604-9242, USA

Tani, Daniel M (Astronaut)
3703 Montvale Dr
Houston, TX 77059-6038, USA

Tankersley, Dennis (Baseball Player)
San Diego Padres
6 Briarmist Ct
O Fallon, MO 63366-6318, USA

Tankian, Serj (Musician)
Velvet Hammer
9911 W Pico Blvd # 350
Los Angeles, CA 90035-2703, USA

Tanksley, Steven D (Scientist)
Cornell University
Emerson Hall
Plant Genetics Dept
Ithaca, NY 14853, USA

Tannen, Steve (Football Player)
New York Jets
735 N Niagara St
Burbank, CA 91505-3006, USA

Tannenwald, Theodore Jr (Judge)
US Tax Court
400 2nd St NW
Washington, DC 20217-0002, USA

Tanner, Alain (Director)
Chemin Point-du-Jour 12
Geneva 1202, SWITZERLAND

Tanner, Barron (Football Player)
Minnesota Vikings
7556 W Oregon Ave
Glendale, AZ 85303-5685, USA

Tanner, Bruce (Baseball Player)
Chicago White Sox
324 Hearthstone Dr
New Castle, PA 16105-1374, USA

Tanner, Charles W (Chuck) (Baseball
Player)
34 E Maitland Ln
New Castle, PA 16105-1204, USA

Tanner, Hamp (Football Player)
San Francisco 49ers
5960 Cherokee Trce
Cumming, GA 30041-5478, USA

Tanner, John (Football Player)
San Diego Chargers
235 Ash Dr
Merritt Island, FL 32953-4361, USA

Tanner, Joseph R (Astronaut)
1519 Seaget Lane
Houston, TX 77062, USA

Tannous, Afif I (Government Official)
6912 Oak Ct
Annandale, VA 22003-5929, USA

Tanuja (Actor, Bollywood)
14 Usha Kiran 15
M L Dhahanukar Marg
Mumbai, MS 400026, INDIA

Tanumafili, Malietoa II (President)
Government House
Valima, Apia, SAMOA

Tanzi, Vito (Economist)
5912 Walhondine Road
Bethesda, MD 20816, USA

Tapani, Kevin (Baseball Player)
New York Mets
781 Ferndale Rd N
Wayzata, MN 55391-1010, USA

Tape, Gerald F (Physicist)
9707 Old Georgetown Rd Apt 2518
Bethesda, MD 20814-1761, USA

Tapert, Robert (Director, Producer,
Writer)
c/o Staff Member *Renaissance Pictures*
315 S Beverly Dr Ste 216
Beverly Hills, CA 90212-4310, USA

Tapes N Tapes (Music Group)
c/o Staff Member *Paradigm (Monterey)*
509 Hartnell St
Monterey, CA 93940-2825, USA

Tapia, Johnny (Boxer)
2405 Janet Ann Ln
Las Cruces, NM 88007-5119, USA

Tappan V, Alfredo (Director)
c/o Gabriel Blanco *Gabriel Blanco
Iglesias (Mexico)*
Rio Balsas 35-32
Colonia Cuauhtemoc
DF 06500, MEXICO

Tappe, Ted (Baseball Player)
Cincinnati Reds
1415 Koetters Ln
Quincy, IL 62305-1149, USA

Tapping, Amanda (Actor)
c/o Staff Member *Stargate SG-1*
10250 Constellation Blvd
Mgm
Los Angeles, CA 90067-6200, USA

Tapscott, Mark
5663 Ruthwood Dr
Calabasas, CA 91302-1053, USA

Tarand, Andres (Prime Minister)
Riigikogu
Lossi Plats 1A
Tallinn 10130, ESTONIA

Tarantina, Brian (Actor)
c/o Staff Member *HWA Talent*
3500 W Olive Ave Ste 1400
Burbank, CA 91505-5512, USA

Tarantino, Quentin (Actor, Director,
Producer, Writer)
c/o Staff Member *A Band Apart*
5700 Wilshire Blvd
Los Angeles, CA 90036-3659, USA

Taranu, Cornel (Composer, Conductor)
Str Nicolae Iorga
Ckuj-Napoca 3400, ROMANIA

Tarasco, Tony (Baseball Player)
Atlanta Braves
3528 Maplewood Ave
Los Angeles, CA 90066-3020, USA

Tarasova, Tatiana (Coach, Figure Skater)
Connecticut Skating Center
300 Alumni Rd
Newington, CT 06111-1865, USA

Tarasovic, George (Football Player)
Pittsburgh Steelers
1503 Michael Dr
Pittsburgh, PA 15227-3958, USA

Tarbuck, Jimmy
118 Beaufort St.
London, ENGLAND SW3 6BU, UNITED
KINGDOM (UK)

Tardiff, Marc (Hockey Player)
6070 Boul du Jardin
Charlesbourg Toyota
Charlesbourg, PQ G1G 3Z8, CANADA

Tardits, Richard (Football Player)
New England Patriots
3590 Round Bottom Rd
Cincinnati, OH 45244-3026, USA

Tarkan (Musician)
c/o Staff Member *Mydonose Productions*
No 22 K 14
Park Plaza Eski Buyukdere Cad
Maslak, Istanbul, TURKEY

Tarkenton, Francis A (Fran) (Business
Person, Football Player)
Minnesota Vikings
3340 Peachtree Rd NE Ste 1100
Atlanta, GA 30326-1043, USA

Tarle, Jim (Football Player)
Jacksonville Jaguars
2125 Willesdon Dr E
Jacksonville, FL 32246-0549, USA

Tarpey, Erin
77 W 66th St
New York, NY 10023-6201, USA

Tarr, Curtis W (Business Person,
Government Official)
Intermet Corp
301 Commerce St Ste 2901
Fort Worth, TX 76102-4122, USA

Tarr, Robert J Jr (Publisher)
58 River Marsh Ln
Johns Island, SC 29455-5202, USA

Tarrant, Chris (Game Show Host)
c/o Staff Member *Who Wants to Be a
Millionaire*
30 W 67th St
New York, NY 10023-6204, USA

Tarrant, Jim (Football Player)
Miami Seahawks
528 North Dr
Birmingham, AL 35206-2207, USA

Tarses, Matt (Producer)
c/o Staff Member *Endeavor Agency LLC
(LA)*
9601 Wilshire Blvd Fl 3
Beverly Hills, CA 90210-5204, USA

Tartabull, Danilio (Dan) (Baseball Player)
16840 NW 79th Pl
Hialeah, FL 33016-3493, USA

Tartabull, Jose (Baseball Player)
Kansas City A's
6805 Winfield Blvd Apt 32
Margate, FL 33063, USA

Tartakovsky, Genndy (Director, Producer,
Writer)
c/o Staff Member *William Morris Agency
(WMA-LA)*
1 William Morris Pl
Beverly Hills, CA 90212-4261, USA

Tarter, Jill (Astronomer, Physicist)
Seti Institute Research Center
2035 Mountain View
Mountain View, CA 94043, USA

Tarver, John (Football Player)
New England Patriots
PO Box 11961
Portland, OR 97211-0961, USA

Tarver, Laschelle (Baseball Player)
Boston Red Sox
4410 N Emerson Ave
Fresno, CA 93705-1203, USA

Tarzier, Carol (Artist)
1217 32nd St
Oakland, CA 94608-4201, USA

Tasby, Willie (Baseball Player)
Baltimore Orioles
PO Box 623
San Leandro, CA 94577-0062, USA

Taseff, Carl (Football Player)
Cleveland Browns
2548 Bay Pointe Dr
Weston, FL 33327-1421, USA

Tashima, A Wallace (Judge)
US Court of Appeals
125 S Grand Ave
Pasadena, CA 91105-1652, USA

Tasker, Steven J (Steve) (Football Player,
Sportscaster)
16 Gypsy Ln
East Aurora, NY 14052-2108, USA

Tata, Terry (Baseball Player)
23 Stonegate Cir
Cheshire, CT 06410-3461, USA

Tatar, Jerome F (Business Person)
Mead Corp
Courthouse Plaza N
Dayton, OH 45463-0001, USA

Tatarek, Bob (Football Player)
Buffalo Bills
5829 Southhall Rd
Birmingham, AL 35213-1017, USA

Tataurangi, Phil (Golfer)
5204 Glen Heather Dr
Flower Mound, TX 75028-6035, USA

Tate, Albert Jr (Judge)
US Court of Appeals
600 Camp St
New Orleans, LA 70130-3425, USA

Tate, Bruce (Musician)
David Harris Enterprises
24210 E East Fork Rd Spc 9
Azusa, CA 91702-6249, USA

Tate, David (Football Player)
Chicago Bears
3481 S Blackhawk Way
Aurora, CO 80014-3984, USA

Tate, Frank (Boxer)
12731 Water Oak Dr
Missouri City, TX 77489-3903, USA

Tate, James V (Writer)
16 Jones Rd
Pelham, MA 01002-9715, USA

Tate, Jeffrey P
English Chamber Orchestra
2 Coningsby Road
London W5 4HR, UNITED KINGDOM
(UK)

Tate, Kevin
6834 Hollywood Blvd # 303
Hollywood, CA 90028-6116, USA

Tate, Lahmard (Actor)
c/o Rob D'Avola Identity Talent Agency
(ID)
9107 Wilshire Blvd Ste 450
Beverly Hills, CA 90210-5535, USA

Tate, Larena
4116 W Magnolia Blvd Ste 101
Burbank, CA 91505-2700, USA

Tate, Larenz (Actor)
c/o Staff Member Sanders/Armstrong
Management
2120 Colorado Ave Ste 120
Santa Monica, CA 90404-3561, USA

Tate, Lee (Baseball Player)
St Louis Cardinals
32338 Oak Park Dr
Leesburg, FL 34748-8760, USA

Tate, randy (Baseball Player)
New York Mets
106 King St
Muscle Shoals, AL 35661-3698, USA

Tate, Randy (Politician)
Chrsitian Coalition
100 Centerville Tumpike
Virginia Beach, VA 23463-0001, USA

Tate, Stu (Baseball Player)
San Francisco Giants
695 Liberty Hill Rd
Toney, AL 35773-9799, USA

Tatel, David S (Judge)
US Court of Appeals
333 Constitution Ave NW
Washington, DC 20001-2866, USA

Tatiana (Model)
Ford Model Agency
142 Greene St # 400
New York, NY 10012-3236, USA

Tatrai, Vilmos (Musician)
R Wallenberg Utca 4
Budapest XIII 1136, HUNGARY

Tattersall, David (Cinematographer)
Lucasfilm
PO Box 2459
San Rafael, CA 94912-2459, USA

TATU (Music Group)
c/o Robert Hayes Sound Management
1525 S Winchester Blvd
San Jose, CA 95128-4335, USA

Tatum, Bradford
1505 10th St
Santa Monica, CA 90401-2805, USA

Tatum, Channing (Actor)
c/o Craig Shapiro Innovative Artists (LA)
1505 10th St
Santa Monica, CA 90401-2805, USA

Tatum, Earl
6915 W Fond Du Lac Ave
Milwaukee, WI 53218-3919, USA

Tatum, Jim (Baseball Player)
Milwaukee Brewers
7433 Indian Wells Cv
Lone Tree, CO 80124-4207, USA

Tatum, John D (Jack) (Football Player)
Oakland Raiders
10620 Mark St
Oakland, CA 94605-5340, USA

Tatum, Ken (Baseball Player)
California Angels
19 Oakdale Dr
Montevallo, AL 35115-5435, USA

Tatum, Kinnon (Football Player)
Carolina Panthers
4109 Knollwood Dr
Fayetteville, NC 28304-5208, USA

Tatupu, Mosi (Football Player)
New England Patriots
71 Walnut St
Plainville, MA 02762-1413, USA

Taube, Sven-Bertil
113Cheyne Walk
London, ENGLAND SWl0 OES, UNITED
KINGDOM (UK)

Taubensee, Ed (Baseball Player)
Cleveland Indians
2234 Fountain Key Cir
Windermere, FL 34786-5804, USA

Taubman, A Alfred (Business Person)
Taubman Co
200 E Long Lake Rd Ste 300
Bloomfield Hills, MI 48304-2324, USA

Taupin, Bernie (Musician, Songwriter,
Writer)
2905 Roundup Rd
Santa Ynez, CA 93460-9558, USA

Tauran, Jean-Louis Cardinal (Religious
Leader)
Palazzo Apostolico
Vatican City 00120, VATICAN CITY

Taurasi, Diana (Basketball Player)
c/o Staff Member Phoenix Mercury
201 E Jefferson St
Phoenix, AZ 85004-2412, USA

Taurel, Sidney (Business Person)
Eli Lilly Co
Lilly Corporate Center
Indianapolis, IN 46285-0001, USA

Tausch, Terry (Football Player)
Minnesota Vikings
2804 Ryder Ct
Plano, TX 75093-3426, USA

Tauscher, Hansjorg (Skier)
Schwand 7
Oberstdorf 87561, GERMANY

Tauscher, Mark (Football Player)
Green Bay Packers
2245 Red Tail Gln
De Pere, WI 54115-1631, USA

Taussig, Don (Baseball Player)
San Francisco Giants
1111 Ocean Dunes Cir
Jupiter, FL 33477-9128, USA

Tautalatasi, Junior (Football Player)
Philadelphia Eagles
1032 Eagle Ave # A
Alameda, CA 94501-1111, USA

Tautolo, Terry (Football Player)
Philadelphia Eagles
5713 E Huntdale St
Long Beach, CA 90808-2717, USA

Tautou, Audrey (Actor)
c/o Claire Blondel ArtMedia
20 av Rapp
Paris 75007, FRANCE

Tauziat, Nathalie (Tennis Player)
Federation de Tennis
1 Ave Gordon Bennett
Paris 75016, FRANCE

Tavard, Georges H (Misc)
330 Market St
Brighton, MA 02135-2131, USA

Tavare, Jay (Actor)
c/o Paul Greenstone Paul Greenstone
Entertainment
1227 Union St
San Francisco, CA 94109-1922, USA

Tavares, Alex (Baseball Player)
Houston Astros
Calle 7B #18
Reparto Perello Santiago, DOMINICAN
REPUBLIC

Tavarez, Julian (Baseball Player)
Cleveland Indians
1108 Fireside Trl
Broadview Heights, OH 44147-3625,
USA

Tavener, John H (Football Player)
241 N Oregon St
Johnstown, OH 43031-1024, USA

Tavener, John K (Composer)
Chester Music
8-9 Firth St
London W1V 5TZ, UNITED KINGDOM
(UK)

Taverner, Sonia (Ballerina)
PO Box 129
Stony Plain, AB, CANADA

Tavernier, Bertrand R M (Director)
Little Bear Productions
7-9 Rue Arthur Groussler
Paris 75010, FRANCE

Taviani, Paolo (Director)
Instituto Luce SPA
Via Tuscolana 1055
Rome 00173, ITALY

Taviani, Vittorio (Director)
Instituto Luce SPA
Via Tuscolana 1055
Rome 00173, ITALY

Taxier, Arthur (Actor)
Pakula/King
9229 W Sunset Blvd Ste 315
Los Angeles, CA 90069-3403, USA

Taya, Maawiya Ould Sid'Ahmed
(President)
President's Office
Boite Postale 184
Nouakchott, MAURITANIA

Taylor, Aaron (Baseball Player)
Seattle Mariners
6484 Val Del Rd
Hahira, GA 31632-3304, USA

Taylor, Alphonso (Football Player)
Denver Broncos
254 W Trenton Ave Apt 314B
Morrisville, PA 19067-2077, USA

Taylor, Altie (Football Player)
Detroit Lions
5349 Whitehaven Way
Antelope, CA 95843-5992, USA

Taylor, Andy (Musician)
DD Productions
93A Westbourne Park Villas
London W2 5ED, UNITED KINGDOM
(UK)

Taylor, Arthur R (Business Person,
Educator)
Muhlenburg College
President's Office
Allentown, PA 18104, USA

Taylor, Benedict
4 Great Queen St.
London, ENGLAND WC28 5DG, UNITED
KINGDOM (UK)

Taylor, Bill (Baseball Player)
New York Giants
PO Box 146
Acton, CA 93510-0146, USA

Taylor, Billy (Baseball Player)
Oakland A's
201 Washington Pl
Thomasville, GA 31792-4785, USA

Taylor, Billy (Football Player)
New York Giants
3 Greenwich Dr Apt 86
Jersey City, NJ 07305-1158, USA

Taylor, Bob 'Hawk' (Athlete)
136 Skyway Dr
Murray, KY 42071-5401, USA

Taylor, Brian (Basketball Player)
3622 Green Vista Dr
Encino, CA 91436-4038, USA

Taylor, Brien (Baseball Player)
147 Brien Taylor Ln
Beaufort, NC 28516, USA

Taylor, Bruce L (Football Player)
San Francisco 49ers
10324 Pontofino Cir
Trinity, FL 34655-7056, USA

Taylor, Buck (Actor)
1305 Clyde Dr
Marrero, LA 70072-3609, USA

Taylor, Carl E (Physicist)
1201 Hollins Ln
Bittersweet Acres
Baltimore, MD 21209-2209, USA

Taylor, Cecil P (Composer, Musician)
Joel Chriss
300 Mercer St Apt 3J
New York, NY 10003-6732, USA

Taylor, Chad (Musician)
Freedman & Smith
1790 Broadway # 131
New York, NY 10019-1412, USA

Taylor, Charles R (Charley) (Football Executive, Football Player)
Washington Redskins
12023 Canter Ln
Reston, VA 20191-2129, USA

Taylor, Chester (Football Player)
Baltimore Ravens
1625 S Ethel St
Detroit, MI 48217-1671, USA

Taylor, Christian (Actor)
c/o Staff Member *KST Productions*
5543 Edmondson Pike # 1
Nashville, TN 37211-5808, USA

Taylor, Christine (Actor)
c/o David Guillod *United Talent Agency*
(UTA)
9560 Wilshire Blvd Ste 500
Beverly Hills, CA 90212-2401, USA

Taylor, Christy (Actor)
10990 Massachusetts Ave Apt 3
Los Angeles, CA 90024-5530, USA

Taylor, Chuck
242 S Oak Grove Ave
Atherton, CA 94027-2218, USA

Taylor, Clarice (Actor)
380 Elkwood Ter
Englewood, NJ 07631-1935, USA

Taylor, Cordell (Football Player)
Jacksonville Jaguars
1825 Chasewood Park Dr
Marietta, GA 30066-4298, USA

Taylor, Corey (Musician)
c/o Staff Member *Agency Group Ltd, The*
(LA)
1880 Century Park E Ste 711
Los Angeles, CA 90067-1618, USA

Taylor, Dana (Actor)
100 S Sunrise Way # 468
Palm Springs, CA 92262-6778, USA

Taylor, Dave (Hockey Player)
18920 Pasadero Dr
Tarzana, CA 91356-5122, USA

Taylor, David (Football Player)
Baltimore Colts
304 Paddington Rd
Baltimore, MD 21212-3812, USA

Taylor, Delores (Actor)
PO Box 840
Moorpark, CA 93020-0840, USA

Taylor, Ed (Football Player)
New York Jets
2901 Clarke Rd
Memphis, TN 38115-2402, USA

Taylor, Elizabeth (Actor, Producer)
c/o Dick Guttman *Guttman Associates*
118 S Beverly Dr Ste 201
Beverly Hills, CA 90212-3016, USA

Taylor, Eric (Artist)
13 Tredgold Ave
Branhope near Leeds
West Yorkshire LS16 9BS, UNITED
KINGDOM (UK)

Taylor, Eunice (Baseball Player)
955 Carroll Ln
Mount Dora, FL 32757-3726, USA

Taylor, Femi (Actor)
Paul Telford Mgmt
23 Noel St
London W1V 3RD, UNITED KINGDOM
(UK)

Taylor, Fred (Football Player)
Jacksonville Jaguars
7975 Monterey Bay Dr
Jacksonville, FL 32256-2927, USA

Taylor, Gilbert (Cinematographer)
Cinematography Society
11 Croft
Gerrards Cross
Bucks SL9 9E, UNITED KINGDOM (UK)

Taylor, Glen (Basketball Player)
Minnesota Timberwolves
600 1st Ave N
Target Center
Minneapolis, MN 55403-1416, USA

Taylor, Henry S (Writer)
1120 Aqua Vista Dr NW
Gig Harbor, WA 98335-1536, USA

Taylor, Holland (Actor)
1757 N Curson Ave
Los Angeles, CA 90046-2203, USA

Taylor, Hosea (Football Player)
Baltimore Colts
208 Bobby St
Longview, TX 75602-3804, USA

Taylor, J T (Musician)
Famous Artists Agency
250 W 57th St
New York, NY 10107-0001, USA

Taylor, Jackie Lynn (Actor)
PO Box 3182
Citrus Heights, CA 95611-3182, USA

Taylor, James (Musician, Songwriter, Writer)
Borman Entertainment
1250 6th St Ste 401
Santa Monica, CA 90401-1638, USA

Taylor, James A (War Hero)
PO Box 284
Trinity Center, CA 96091-0284, USA

Taylor, James C (Jim) (Football Player)
Green Bay Packers
7840 Walden Rd
Baton Rouge, LA 70808-5939, USA

Taylor, Jason (Football Player)
Miami Dolphins
2980 Paddock Rd
Weston, FL 33331-3604, USA

Taylor, Jason (Rugby Player)
Parramatta Eels
PO BOX 2666
North Parramatta, NSW 1750,
AUSTRALIA

Taylor, Jay (Business Person)
Placer Dorne Inc
1600-1055 Dunsmuir St
Vancouver, BC V7X 1P1, CANADA

Taylor, Jim (Writer)
c/o Staff Member *William Morris Agency*
(WMA-LA)
1 William Morris Pl
Beverly Hills, CA 90212-4261, USA

Taylor, John (Actor)
Left Bank Mgmt
9255 W Sunset Blvd # 200
West Hollywood, CA 90069-3309, USA

Taylor, John (Football Player)
San Francisco 49ers
5682 E Shepherd Ave
Clovis, CA 93619-4210, USA

Taylor, Jonathan (Producer)
c/o Staff Member *United Talent Agency*
(UTA)
9560 Wilshire Blvd Ste 500
Beverly Hills, CA 90212-2401, USA

Taylor, Joseph H Jr (Nobel Prize Laureate)
272 Hartley Ave
Princeton, NJ 08540-5656, USA

Taylor, Josh
422 S California St
Burbank, CA 91505-4707, USA

Taylor, Judson H (Educator)
State University of New York College
President's Office
Cortland, NY 13045, USA

Taylor, Karen (Comedian)
c/o Staff Member *Avalon Management*
4A Exmoor St
London W10 6BD, UNITED KINGDOM
(UK)

Taylor, Kim (Musician)
c/o Staff Member *Paradigm (Monterey)*
509 Hartnell St
Monterey, CA 93940-2825, USA

Taylor, Kitrick L (Football Player)
Kansas City Chiefs
18215 Foothill Blvd Apt 94
Fontana, CA 92335-8512, USA

Taylor, Koko (Musician)
PO Box 60234
Chicago, IL 60660-0234, USA

Taylor, Lance J (Economist)
PO Box 378
Old County Road
Washington, ME 04574-0378, USA

Taylor, Lauriston S (Physicist)
10450 Lottsford Rd # 1-5
Bowie, MD 20721-2734, USA

Taylor, Lawrence (Football Player)
New York Giants
122 Canterbury Pl
Williamsburg, VA 23188-1902, USA

Taylor, Lili (Actor)
William Morris Agency
1325 Avenue Of The Americas
New York, NY 10019-6091, USA

Taylor, Lionel (Coach, Football Coach, Football Player)
Chicago Bears
201 Pinnacle Dr SE Apt 3614
Rio Rancho, NM 87124-0458, USA

Taylor, Livingston (Musician)
Fat City Artists
1906 Chet Atkins Blvd Apt 502
Nashville, TN 37212-2122, USA

Taylor, Marianne (Actor)
Jack Scagnatti
5118 Vineland Ave # 102
North Hollywood, CA 91601-3814, USA

Taylor, Mark L (Actor)
7919 Norton Ave
West Hollywood, CA 90046-5204, USA

Taylor, Maurice (Basketball Player)
Houston Rockets
2 Greenway Plz
Toyota Center
Houston, TX 77046-0297, USA

Taylor, Meshach (Actor)
6300 Wilshire Blvd Ste 900
Los Angeles, CA 90048-5202, USA

Taylor, Michael (Football Player)
New York Jets
5014 Crane St
Detroit, MI 48213-2917, USA

Taylor, Mick (Musician)
Jacobson & Colin
60 Madison Ave Ste 1026
New York, NY 10010-1666, USA

Taylor, Mike (Football Player)
Pittsburgh Steelers
19632 Quiet Bay Ln
Huntington Beach, CA 92648-2614, USA

Taylor, Nancy (Golfer)
3205 Tallia Ct
Charlotte, NC 28269-2193, USA

Taylor, Natascha (Actor)
c/o Staff Member *International Creative Management (ICM-LA)*
10250 Constellation Blvd
Los Angeles, CA 90067-6200, USA

Taylor, Niki (Actor, Model)
Tri Star Sports
215 Ward Cir Ste 200
Brentwood, TN 37027-2306, USA

Taylor, Noah (Actor)
June Cann Mgmt
110 Quenn St
Woolahra, NSW 2025, AUSTRALIA

Taylor, Otis (Football Player)
Kansas City Chiefs
6608 Woodson Rd
Raytown, MO 64133-5400, USA

Taylor, Paul B (Choreographer, Dancer)
Paul Taylor Dance Co
552 Broadway Fl 2
New York, NY 10012-3947, USA

Taylor, Penny (Basketball Player)
Cleveland Rockers
1 Center Ct
Gund Arena
Cleveland, OH 44115-4001, USA

Taylor, Priscilla Lee (Actor, Model)
c/o Dianne Hooper *Starcraft Talent Agency*
1516 N Formosa Ave
Los Angeles, CA 90046, USA

Taylor, Regina (Actor)
8048 Dusenberg Ct
Sacramento, CA 95828-5834, USA

Taylor, Renee (Actor)
Judy Schoen
606 N Larchmont Blvd Ste 309
Los Angeles, CA 90004-1309, USA

Taylor, Richard E (Nobel Prize Laureate)
757 Mayfield Ave
Stanford, CA 94305-1043, USA

Taylor, Rip (Actor, Comedian)
1133 N Clark St
Los Angeles, CA 90069-2073, USA

Taylor, Robert (Athlete, Track Athlete)
1010 S Glenwood Blvd
Tyler, TX 75701-2734, USA

Taylor, Rod (Actor)
2375 Bowmont Dr
Beverly Hills, CA 90210-1808, USA

Taylor, Roger (Musician)
c/o Staff Member *DD Productions*
93A Westbourne Park Villas
London W2 5ED, UNITED KINGDOM
(UK)

The Celebrity Black Book 2008

Taylor, Roger (Tennis Player)
39 Newstead Way
Wimbledon SW19, UNITED KINGDOM
(UK)

Taylor, Roger M (Musician)
Neil Levin
15260 Ventura Blvd Ste 1700
Sherman Oaks, CA 91403-5349, USA

Taylor, Roosevelt (Football Player)
Chicago Bears
7331 Ebbtide Dr
New Orleans, LA 70126-2057, USA

Taylor, Sam (Baseball Player)
Kansas City Monarchs
248 N 74th St
Centreville, IL 62203-2411, USA

Taylor, Sandra (Actor, Model)
IPA Network
231 E Alessandro Blvd # A355
Riverside, CA 92508-6039, USA

Taylor, Stephen Monroe (Actor)
c/o Judy Cosgrove MC Talent
Management
4821 Lankershim Blvd # F329
N Hollywood, CA 91601-4538, USA

Taylor, Susan (Editor)
ESSENCE
1500 Broadway Fl 6
New York, NY 10036-4055, USA

Taylor, Tamara (Actor)
c/o Brit Reece PMK/HBH Public Relations
(PMK-LA)
700 N San Vicente Blvd Ste G910
West Hollywood, CA 90069-5061, USA

Taylor, Tommy (Baseball Player)
Kansas City Monarchs
524 Whitehall St
Jackson, TN 38301-5535, USA

Taylor, Vaughn (Golfer)
2536 Queens Ct
Grovetown, GA 30813-4520, USA

Taylor, William O (Publisher)
Affiliated Publications
135 William Morrissey Blvd
Dorchester, MA 02125, USA

Taylor, Wilson H (Business Person)
CIGNA Corp
1 Liberty Place
1650 Market St
Philadelphia, PA 19192-0001, USA

Taylor-Cotter, Eliza (Actor)
c/o Staff Member Nickelodeon UK
PO Box 6425
LONDON W1A 6UR, UNITED
KINGDOM (UK)

Taylor-Grauman, Joan
9920 Robin Dr.
Los Angeles, CA 90069, USA

Taylor Jr, William (Billy) (Composer,
Musician)
555 Kappock St
Bronx, NY 10463-6420, USA

Taylor-Lukin, Norna (Baseball Player)
7934 W Maple Grove Rd
Andrews, IN 46702-9518, USA

Taylor-Taylor, Courtney (Musician)
Monqui Records
PO Box 5908
Portland, OR 97228-5908, USA

Taylor-Young, Leigh (Actor)
11300 W Olympic Blvd Ste 610
Los Angeles, CA 90064-1643, USA

Taymor, Julie (Director)
International Creative Mgmt
40 W 57th St Ste 1800
New York, NY 10019-4001, USA

Tchaikovsky, Aleksandr V (Composer,
Musician)
Leningradsky Prosp 14
#4
Moscow 125040, RUSSIA

Tcherkassky, Marianna (Ballerina)
American Ballet Theatre
890 Broadway
New York, NY 10003-1278, USA

Te Kanawa, Kiri (Opera Singer)
Jules Haelliger Impressario
Postfach 4113
Lucerne 6002, SWITZERLAND

Tea Leaf Green (Music Group)
c/o Staff Member Paradigm (Monterey)
509 Hartnell St
Monterey, CA 93940-2825, USA

Teaff, Grant (Coach, Football Coach)
8265 Forest Ridge Dr
Waco, TX 76712-2405, USA

Teagle, Terry (Basketball Player)
2111 Heatherwood Dr
Missouri City, TX 77489-3277, USA

Teague, George (Football Player)
Green Bay Packers
6561 Meadow Lark Dr
Montgomery, AL 36116-4227, USA

Teague, Lewis
2190 N Beverly Glen Blvd
Los Angeles, CA 90077-2404, USA

Teague, Marshall (Actor)
c/o Staff Member Pinnacle Commercial
Talent
5757 Wilshire Blvd Ste 510
Los Angeles, CA 90036-3629, USA

Teal, Jim F (Football Player)
Detroit Lions
38444 Kingsway Ct
Farmington Hills, MI 48331-1651, USA

Teal, Jimmy D (Football Player)
Buffalo Bills
2636 Spring Branch Rd
Mesquite, TX 75181-2668, USA

Teal, Willie (Football Player)
Minnesota Vikings
1322 Westchester Dr
Baton Rouge, LA 70810-5234, USA

Teannaki, Teatao (President)
President's Office
PO Box 68
Bairiki
Tarawa Atoll, KIRIBATI

Tear, Robert (Opera Singer)
11 Ravenscourt Court
London W6, UNITED KINGDOM (UK)

Tearry, Larry (Football Player)
Detroit Lions
1334 Kienast Dr
Fayetteville, NC 28314-5422, USA

Tears For Fears (Music Group)
c/o Staff Member Creative Artists Agency
LCC (CAA-LA)
2000 Avenue Of The Stars
Los Angeles, CA 90067-4700, USA

Teasdale, Joseph P (Governor)
911 Main St # 1210
Commerce Tower
Kansas City, MO 64105-2009, USA

Teasley, Nikki (Basketball Player)
Los Angeles Sparks
1111 S Figueroa St
Staples Center
Los Angeles, CA 90015-1300, USA

Teasley, Ron (Baseball Player)
New York Cubans
19317 Coyle St
Detroit, MI 48235-2039, USA

Tebbets, Birdie
229 Oak Ave.
Anna Maria, FL 33501, USA

Tebbit of Chingford, Norman B
(Government Official)
House of Lords
Westminister
London SW1A 0PW, UNITED KINGDOM
(UK)

Techine, Andre J F (Director)
Artmedia
20 Ave Rapp
Paris 75007, FRANCE

Technotronic
89 5th Ave Fl 7
New York, NY 10003-3020, USA

Tedeschi, Susan (Musician)
Blue Sky Artists
761 Washington Ave N
Minneapolis, MN 55401-1101, USA

Tedford, Travis (Actor)
c/o Staff Member Acme Talent & Literary
(LA)
4727 Wilshire Blvd Ste 333
Los Angeles, CA 90010-3874, USA

Teen, Tiffany (Actor, Adult Film Star,
Model)
Phil-Flash Media
352 N Birch St Apt 1
Manteno, IL 60950-1301, USA

Teerlinck, John (Football Player)
San Diego Chargers
9713 Bay Hill Dr
Lone Tree, CO 80124-3182, USA

Teeter, Mike (Football Player)
Minnesota Vikings
4393 E Mount Garfield Rd
Fruitport, MI 49415-9782, USA

Teeuws, Len (Football Player)
Los Angeles Rams
1314 Selkirk Ln
Indianapolis, IN 46260-1230, USA

Teevens, Buddy (Coach, Football Coach)
Stanford University
Athletic Dept
Stanford, CA 94395, USA

Tefkin, Blair (Actor)
Lucie Gamelon
8022 Sunset Blvd #4049
Los Angeles, CA 90046, USA

Tegan and Sara (Music Group)
c/o Staff Member Paquin Entertainment
Agency
110 Bond St
Toronto, ON M5B 1X8, CANADA

Tegart Dalton, Judy (Tennis Player)
72 Grange Road
Toorak, VIC 3412, AUSTRALIA

Teicher, Louis (Lou) (Musician)
Avant-Grade Records
12224 Avila Dr
Kansas City, MO 64145-1750, USA

Teichner, Helmut (Skier)
4250 N Marine Dr Apt 2101
Chicago, IL 60613-1733, USA

Teillet-Schick, Yolande (Baseball Player)
1016 Chevrier Blvd Ft Garry
Winnipeg, MB R3T 1X9, CANADA

Teitel, Robert (Producer)
c/o Staff Member Creative Artists Agency
LCC (CAA-LA)
2000 Avenue Of The Stars
Los Angeles, CA 90067-4700, USA

Teitelbaum, Philip (Doctor)
University of Florida
Psychology Dept
Gainesville, FL 32611, USA

Teitell, Conrad L (Lawyer)
16 Marlow Ct
Riverside, CT 06878-2614, USA

Teitler, William (Producer)
c/o Staff Member International Creative
Management (ICM-LA)
10250 Constellation Blvd
Los Angeles, CA 90067-6200, USA

Tejada, Miguel O M (Baseball Player)
Oakland Athletics
7000 Coliseum Way
NA Coliseum
Oakland, CA 94621-1992, USA

Tejera, Michael (Baseball Player)
c/o Staff Member Florida Marlins
2269 Dan Marino Blvd
Miami Gardens, FL 33056-2600, USA

Tekulve, Kenton C (Kent) (Baseball
Player)
1531 Sequoia Dr
Pittsburgh, PA 15241-3223, USA

Telfer, Paul (Actor)
c/o Michael Greenwald Don Buchwald &
Associates Inc (LA)
6500 Wilshire Blvd Ste 2200
Los Angeles, CA 90048-4942, USA

Telgdi, Valentine L (Physicist)
Eidgenossosche Technische Hochschule
Houggerberg
Zurich, SWITZERLAND

Tellep, Daniel M (Business Person)
Lockheed Corp
PO Box 5118
Thousand Oaks, CA 91359, USA

Teller (Musician)
William Morris Agency
151 El Camino Dr
Beverly Hills, CA 90212-2775, USA

Teller, Edward (Doctor)
PO Box 808
Livermore, CA 94551-0808, USA

Telles, Rick
2934 1/2 S. Beverly Glen Circle #107
Los Angeles, CA 90077, USA

Telnaes, Ann (Cartoonist)
Tribune Media Services
435 N Michigan Ave Ste 1500
Chicago, IL 60611-4012, USA

Teltscher, Eliot (Coach, Tennis Player)
Pepperdine University
Athletic Dept
Malibu, CA 90265, USA

Teltschik, John (Football Player)
Philadelphia Eagles
18 Canyon Crest Ct
Frisco, TX 75034-6846, USA

Temchen, Sybil (Actor)
c/o Staff Member *Untitled Entertainment (LA)*
331 N Maple Dr Fl 3
Beverly Hills, CA 90210-3827, USA

Temesvari, Andrea (Tennis Player)
ProServe
1101 Woodrow Wilson Blvd #1800
Arlington, VA 22209, USA

Temirkanov, Yuri K
State Philharmonia
Mikhailovskaya 2
Saint Petersburg, RUSSIA

Temko, Allan B (Journalist)
San Francisco Chronicle
901 Mission St
Editorial Dept
San Francisco, CA 94103-2934, USA

Temp, Jim (Football Player)
Green Bay Packers
311 Roselawn Blvd
Green Bay, WI 54301-1305, USA

Temple, Lew (Actor)
c/o Peter Young *Don Buchwald & Associates Inc (LA)*
1902 Coldwater Canyon Dr
Beverly Hills, CA 90210-1731, USA

Templeman of White Lackington, Sydney W (Judge)
Manor Heath
Know Hill Woking
Surrey GU22 7HL, UNITED KINGDOM (UK)

Templesman, Maurice
529 5th Ave
New York, NY 10017-4608, USA

Templeton, Ben (Cartoonist)
Tribune Media Services
435 N Michigan Ave Ste 1500
Chicago, IL 60611-4012, USA

Templeton, Christopher
11333 Moor Park St
N Hollywood, CA 91602-2618, USA

Templeton, Garry L (Baseball Player)
13552 Del Poniente Rd
Poway, CA 92064-2230, USA

Templeton, John M (Financier)
Lyford Cay Club
Box N7776
Nassau, BAHAMAS

Temptations, The (Music Group)
c/o Mark Cheatham *International Creative Management (ICM-LA)*
10250 Constellation Blvd
Los Angeles, CA 90067-6200, USA

Ten Napel, Garth (Football Player)
Detroit Lions
PO Box 26
Carmen, ID 83462-0026, USA

Ten Thousand Maniacs
509 Hartnell St
Monterey, CA 93940-2825, USA

Tenace, F Gene (Baseball Player)
2650 Cliff Hawk Ct
Redmond, OR 97756-7301, USA

Tendulkar, Priya (Actor, Bollywood)
1 Anookul Apartments Harminder Singh Marg
Seven Bangalows Versova Andheri
Bombay, MS 400 061, INDIA

Teng-Hui, Lee (President)
Chaehshou Hall Chung King South Rd.
Taipei 10728, TAIWAN

Tengbom, Anders (Architect)
Kornhaminstorg 6
Stockholm 11127, SWEDEN

Tenison, Renee (Actor, Model)
Tension Group
171 Pier Ave # 403
Santa Monica, CA 90405-5311, USA

Tennant, Andy (Actor, Director, Producer, Writer)
c/o Staff Member *Creative Artists Agency LCC (CAA-LA)*
2000 Avenue Of The Stars
Los Angeles, CA 90067-4700, USA

Tennant, Stella (Model)
Select Model Mgmt
Archer House
43 King St
London WC2E 8RJ, UNITED KINGDOM (UK)

Tennant, Veronica (Ballerina)
National Ballet of Canada
157 King St E
Toronto, ON M5C 1G9, CANADA

Tennant, Victoria (Actor)
PO Box 929
Beverly Hills, CA 90213-0929, USA

Tenner, Judge Jack
218 Glenroy Pl
Los Angeles, CA 90049-2420, USA

Tenney, Jon (Actor)
United Talent Agency
9560 Wilshire Blvd Ste 500
Beverly Hills, CA 90212-2401, USA

Tennille, Toni (Musician)
7123 Franktown Rd
Carson City, NV 89704-8531, USA

Tennison, Chalee (Musician)
Tanasi Entertainment
1204 17th Ave S
Nashville, TN 37212-2802, USA

Tennon, Julius (Actor)
c/o Jim Kelly *Charles Talent Agency*
11950 Ventura Blvd Ste 3
Studio City, CA 91604-2635, USA

Tenorio, Pedro P (Governor)
Governor's Office
Capitol Hill
Chalan Kanoa
Saipan, MP 96950, USA

Tensi, Steve (Football Player)
San Diego Chargers
300 Flannery Fork Rd
Blowing Rock, NC 28605-9333, USA

Tenuta, Judy (Actor, Comedian)
c/o Monique Moss *Warren Cowan & Associates PR*
8899 Beverly Blvd Ste 919
Los Angeles, CA 90048-2436, USA

Tepper, Lou (Coach, Football Coach)
University of Illinois
Assembly Hall
Champaign, IL 61820, USA

Tequila Sunrise
4630 Deepdale Dr
Corpus Christi, TX 78413-3108, USA

Ter Horst, Jerald F (Government Official, Journalist)
7815 Evening Ln
Alexandria, VA 22306-2755, USA

Ter-Petrosyan, Levon A (President)
Marshal Baghramjan Prospect 19
Yerevan 375016, ARMENIA

Teran, Arlet (Actor)
c/o Gabriel Blanco *Gabriel Blanco Iglesias (Mexico)*
Rio Balsas 35-32
Colonia Cuauhtemoc
DF 06500, MEXICO

Teraoka, Masami (Artist)
41-048 Kaulu St
Waimanalo, HI 96795-1612, USA

TerBlanche, Esta (Actor)
c/o Chris Schmidt *Paradigm (LA)*
360 N Crescent Dr
North Bldg
Beverly Hills, CA 90210-6820, USA

Terekhova, Margarita B (Actor)
Bolshaya Gruzinskaya Str 57
#92
Moscow 123056, RUSSIA

Terentyeva, Nina N (Opera Singer)
Bolshoi Theater
Teatralnaya Pl 1
Moscow 103009, RUSSIA

Tereschenko, Sergei A (Prime Minister)
Prime Minister's Office
Dom Pravieelstra
Alma-Ata 148008, KAZAKHSTAN

Tereshinski, Joe (Football Player)
Washington Redskins
6508 Millwood Rd
Bethesda, MD 20817-6056, USA

Tereshkova, Valentina V (Cosmonaut)
Int'l Co-operation Assn
Vozdvizhenka Str 14-18
Moscow 103885, RUSSIA

Tergesen, Lee (Actor)
Gersh Agency
232 N Canon Dr
Beverly Hills, CA 90210-5302, USA

Terkel, Studs L (Writer)
850 W Castlewood Ter
Chicago, IL 60640-4217, USA

Terlep, George (Football Player)
Buffalo Bisons
4524 Golf Club Ln
Brooksville, FL 34609-0303, USA

Terlesky, John (Actor)
14239 Dickens St Apt 5
Sherman Oaks, CA 91423-4107, USA

Termeer, Henricus A (Business Person)
Genzyme Corp
1 Kendall Sq Ste 113
Cambridge, MA 02139-1562, USA

Terminator X (Musician)
William Morris Agency
151 El Camino Dr
Beverly Hills, CA 90212-2775, USA

Termo, Leonard (Actor)
Baumgarten/Prophet
1041 N Formosa Ave # 200
West Hollywood, CA 90046-6703, USA

Terra, Scott (Actor)
c/o Mike Cutler *DMG*
505 N Robertson Blvd
West Hollywood, CA 90048-1730, USA

Terrace, Herbert S (Misc)
17 Campfire Rd
Chappaqua, NY 10514-2405, USA

Terrani, Lucia Valenti
Via Venti Settembre 72
Padova I-35122, ITALY

Terranova, Joe (Musician)
Joe Taylor Mgmt
PO Box 279
Williamstown, NJ 08094-0279, USA

Terranova, Phil (Boxer)
30 Bogardus Pl
New York, NY 10040-2320, USA

Terrasson, Jacky (Musician)
Joel Chriss
300 Mercer St Apt 3J
New York, NY 10003-6732, USA

Terrazas Sandoval, Julio Cardinal (Religious Leader)
Arzobispado Casilla 25
Calle Ingavi 49
Santa Cruz, BOLIVIA

Terrell, David (Football Player)
Washington Redskins
196 N Main St
Roanoke, IN 46783, USA

Terrell, Ernie
11136 S Parnell Ave
Chicago, IL 60628-4012, USA

Terrell, Pat (Football Player)
Los Angeles Rams
40 Hidden Lake Dr
Burr Ridge, IL 60527-8371, USA

Terreri, Chris (Hockey Player)
170 Dezenzo Ln
West Orange, NJ 07052-4125, USA

Terrero, Jessy (Director, Producer)
c/o Charles King *William Morris Agency (WMA-LA)*
1 William Morris Pl
Beverly Hills, CA 90212-4261, USA

Terrio, Deney (Dancer, Entertainer)
Paramount Entertainment
PO Box 12
Far Hills, NJ 07931-0012, USA

Terrio, Denny
1560 Broadway # 1308
New York, NY 10036-1518, USA

Terris, Malcolm
14 England's Lane
London, ENGLAND NW3, UNITED KINGDOM (UK)

Terry, Clark (Musician)
4720 S Beech St
Pine Bluff, AR 71603-7327, USA

Terry, Hilda (Cartoonist)
8 Henderson Pl
New York, NY 10028-7557, USA

Terry, Jason (Basketball Player)
Atlanta Hawks
190 Marietta St NW
Atlanta, GA 30303-2717, USA

Terry, John (Actor)
c/o Darren Goldberg *1 Management*
9000 W Sunset Blvd Ph 1550
West Hollywood, CA 90069-1838, USA

Terry, John (Soccer Player)
The FA
25 Soho Square
London W1D 4FA, UNITED KINGDOM (UK)

Terry, John Q (Architect)
Old Exchange Dedham
Colchester
Essex CO7 6HA, UNITED KINGDOM
(UK)

Terry, Megan D (Writer)
2309 Hansom Blvd
Omaha, NE 68105, USA

Terry, Nat (Football Player)
Pittsburgh Steelers
3003 W Palmetto St
Tampa, FL 33607-2936, USA

Terry, Nigel (Actor)
c/o Staff Member *BBC Artist Mail*
PO Box 1116
Belfast BT2 7AJ, UNITED KINGDOM
(UK)

Terry, Ralph W (Baseball Player)
801 Park St
Larned, KS 67550-2632, USA

Terry, Randall A (Activist)
Operation Rescue National
PO Box 360221
Melbourne, FL 32936-0221, USA

Terry, Richard E (Business Person)
Peoples Energy Corp
130 E Randolph St
Chicago, IL 60601-6302, USA

Terry, Rick (Football Player)
New York Jets
109 Highgate Ln
Lexington, NC 27292-5372, USA

Terry, Ruth (Actor, Musician)
622 Hospitality Dr
Rancho Mirage, CA 92270-1312, USA

Terry, Tony (Musician)
Richard Walters
1800 Argyle Ave # 408
Los Angeles, CA 90028-5253, USA

Terzian, Jacques (Artist)
PO Box 883753
San Francisco, CA 94188-3753, USA

Terzieff, Laurent D A (Actor, Director)
8 Rue du Dragon
Paris 75006, FRANCE

Tesh, John (Composer, Entertainer,
Musician)
PO Box 6010
Sherman Oaks, CA 91413-6010, USA

Teske, Rachel (Golfer)
c/o Staff Member *Pro Golfers Association
(PGA) Tour*
112 Tpc Blvd
Ponte Vedra Beach, FL 32082, USA

Tess, John (Business Person)
Heritage
123 NW 2nd Ave Ste 200
Portland, OR 97209-3927, USA

Tessler-Lavigne, Marc (Doctor)
361 Ridgeway Rd
Woodside, CA 94062-2343, USA

Testa, M David (Financier)
T Rowe Price Assoc
100 E Pratt St
Baltimore, MD 21202-1090, USA

Testaverde, Vincent F (Vinny) (Football
Player)
Tampa Bay Buccaneers
15 Tall Oaks Ct
Syosset, NY 11791-1126, USA

Tester, Hans
6310 San Vicente Blvd Ste 401
Los Angeles, CA 90048-5427, USA

Testerman, Don (Football Player)
Seattle Seahawks
3101 Bridges St
Morehead City, NC 28557-3365, USA

Testi, Fabio
Via Francesco Siacci 38
Rome I-00197, ITALY

Testl, Fabio (Actor)
Via Siacci 38
Rome 00197, ITALY

Teteak, Deral (Football Player)
Green Bay Packers
9458 S County Road G
Suring, WI 54174-9689, USA

Tetley, Glen (Choreographer, Director)
15 W 9th St
New York, NY 10011-8918, USA

Tetrault, Roger E (Business Person)
McDermott International
1450 Polydras St
New Orleans, LA 70112, USA

Tetro-Atkinson, Barbara (Baseball Player)
2824 Forest Ln
Waukegan, IL 60087-2835, USA

Tettamanzi, Dlonigi Cardinal (Religious
Leader)
Arclvescovado
Plazza Matteotti 4
Genoa 16123, ITALY

Tetzlaff, Christian (Musician)
Shuman Assoc
120 W 58th St # 80
New York, NY 10019-2141, USA

Teutul Sr, Paul (Reality TV Star,
Television Host)
c/o Staff Member *Endeavor Agency LLC
(LA)*
9601 Wilshire Blvd Fl 3
Beverly Hills, CA 90210-5204, USA

Tewell, Doug (Golfer)
11414 Waters Welling Way
Edmond, OK 73013-0455, USA

Tewes, Lauren (Actor)
c/o Staff Member *The Actor's Group
Talent and Literary Agency*
3400 Beacon Ave S
Seattle, WA 98144-6702, USA

Tewkesbury, Joan F (Director, Writer)
501 S Beverly Dr
Beverly Hills, CA 90212-4562, USA

Tewksbury, Mark
2380 Pierre Depuy Ave
Montreal, PQ H3C 3R4, CANADA

Tews, Andreas (Boxer)
Hamburger Allee 1
Schwerin 19063, GERMANY

Texada, Tia (Actor)
c/o Ben Levine *Evolution Entertainment
(LA)*
10585 Santa Monica Blvd Ste 120
Los Angeles, CA 90025-4984, USA

Tezak-Papesh, Virginia (Baseball Player)
1400 Clement St
Joliet, IL 60435-4209, USA

Thabu (Actor, Bollywood)
Ankul II Floor
7 Bungalows Andheri West
Mumbai, MS 400054, INDIA

Thacker, Brian M (War Hero)
11413 Monterrey Dr
Wheaton, MD 20902-2657, USA

Thackery, Jimmy (Musician)
Mongrel Music
743 Center Blvd
Fairfax, CA 94930-1764, USA

Thaddeus, Patrick (Physicist)
58 Garfield St
Cambridge, MA 02138-1802, USA

Thagard, Norman E (Astronaut, Physicist)
502 N Ride
Tallahassee, FL 32303-5127, USA

Thain, John (Financier)
New York Stock Exchange
11 Wall St
New York, NY 10005-1974, USA

Thaksin, Shinawatra (Prime Minister)
Premier's Office
Govt House
Luke Road
Bangkok 10300/2, THAILAND

Thalia (Actor, Musician)
c/o Staff Member *William Morris Agency
(WMA-LA)*
1 William Morris Pl
Beverly Hills, CA 90212-4261, USA

Than, Shwe (General, Prime Minister)
Prime Minister's Office
Theinbyu Road
Botahtaung
Yangon, MYANMAR

Thani, Sheikh Abdul Aziz Ibn Khalifa al
(Prime Minister)
Prime Minister's Office
Dohar, QATAR

Thani, Sheikh Hamad bin Khalifa al
(Royalty)
Royal Palace
PO Box 923
Dohar, QATAR

Thapa, Surya Bahadur (Prime Minister)
Tangal
Kathmandu, NEPAL

Tharp, Twyla (Choreographer, Dancer)
Twyla Tharp Productions
336 Central Park W Apt 17B
New York, NY 10025-7127, USA

Tharpe, Larry (Football Player)
Detroit Lions
3665 Greenbriar Rd E
Macon, GA 31204-4228, USA

Thatcher, Baroness Margaret
Chester Sq Belgravia
London, ENGLAND, UNITED KINGDOM
(UK)

Thatcher, Roland (Golfer)
18 Flowertuft Ct
Spring, TX 77380-1529, USA

Thatcher of Lincolnshire, Margaret H
(Prime Minister)
11 Dutwich Gate
Dulwich
London SE12, UNITED KINGDOM (UK)

Thaxton, Galand (Football Player)
Atlanta Falcons
1571 N 22nd St
Laramie, WY 82072-2387, USA

Thaxton, James (Football Player)
San Diego Chargers
4319 Deergrove Rd
Memphis, TN 38141-7021, USA

Thayer, Bill (Misc)
PO Box 233
Snohomish, WA 98291-0233, USA

Thayer, Brynn (Actor)
House of Representatives
211 S Beverly Dr Ste 208
Beverly Hills, CA 90212-3879, USA

Thayer, Bryn
400 S Beverly Dr Ste 101
Beverly Hills, CA 90212-4403, USA

Thayer, Helen (Skier)
PO Box 233
Snohomish, WA 98291-0233, USA

Thayer, Maria (Actor)
c/o Barry McPherson *Agency for the
Performing Arts (APA-LA)*
405 S Beverly Dr
Beverly Hills, CA 90212-4416, USA

Thayer, Tom (Football Player)
Chicago Bears
330 W Diversey Pkwy Apt 2303
Chicago, IL 60657-6204, USA

Thayer, W Paul (Business Person,
Government Official)
10200 Hollow Way Rd
Dallas, TX 75229-6635, USA

The Darkness (Music Group)
c/o Sue Whitehouse *Whitehouse
Management*
PO Box 43829
London NW6 3PJ, UNITED KINGDOM
(UK)

The Fray (Music Group)
c/o Staff Member *Paradigm (Monterey)*
509 Hartnell St
Monterey, CA 93940-2825, USA

The Game (Musician)
c/o Staff Member *Interscope Records (LA)
- Main*
2220 Colorado Ave
Santa Monica, CA 90404-3506, USA

The Good The Bad & The Queen (Music
Group)
c/o Staff Member *Paradigm (Monterey)*
509 Hartnell St
Monterey, CA 93940-2825, USA

The Killers (Music Group)
c/o Staff Member *Island Records*
825 8th Ave
New York, NY 10019-7472, USA

The Pretenders (Music Group)
c/o Staff Member *William Morris Agency
(WMA-LA)*
1 William Morris Pl
Beverly Hills, CA 90212-4261, USA

The Rasmus (Music Group)
c/o Staff Member *Playground Music
Scandinavia*
Box 3171
Malmý s-200 22, SWEDEN

The Rockers
PO Box 3859
Stamford, CT 06905, USA

The Saw Doctors (Music Group)
Saw Doctors Office
3 St Mary's Terrace
Galway, IRELAND

The The (Music Group)
c/o Staff Member *Paradigm (Monterey)*
509 Hartnell St
Monterey, CA 93940-2825, USA

The Who (Musician)
c/o Staff Member *William Morris Agency (WMA-LA)*
1 William Morris Pl
Beverly Hills, CA 90212-4261, USA

The Yellowjackets (Music Group)
Axis Artist Management Inc
9715 Belmar Ave
Northridge, CA 91324-1606, USA

Theberge, James D (Diplomat)
4462 Cathedral Ave NW
Washington, DC 20016, USA

Thedford, Marcello (Actor)
c/o Staff Member *Overview Management*
11634 Victory Blvd Unit 3
N Hollywood, CA 91606-3574, USA

Theile, David (Swimmer)
84 Woodville St
Hendea
Brisbane, QLD 4011, AUSTRALIA

Theismann, Joseph R (Joe) (Football Player, Sportscaster)
703-739-0777
1800 Diagonal Rd
Alexandria, VA 22314-2840, USA

Thelan, Jodi
8428 Melrose Pl Ste C
Los Angeles, CA 90069-5300, USA

Theodorakis, Mikis (Composer)
Epifanous 1
Akropolis
Athens, GREECE

Theodore, Donna
10000 Santa Monica Blvd # 305
Los Angeles, CA 90067, USA

Theodore, Jose (Hockey Player)
Montreal Canadiens
1260 de la Gauchetiere W
Montreal, PQ H3B 5EB, CANADA

Theodorescu, Monica (Athlete)
Gestit Lindenhof
Sassenberg 48336, GERMANY

Theodosakis, Jason (Doctor, Writer)
Saint Martin's Press
175 5th Ave
New York, NY 10010-7848, USA

Theodosius, Primate Metropolitian
(Religious Leader)
Orthodox Church in America
PO Box 675
RR 25 A
Syosset, NY 11791-0675, USA

Theofiledes, Harry (Football Player)
Washington Redskins
17806 Carrollwood Dr
Dallas, TX 75252-6357, USA

Theron, Charlize (Actor, Model)
c/o JJ Harris *One Entertainment (LA)*
12 W 57th St Ph
New York, NY 10019-3900, USA

Theroux, Justin (Actor)
c/o Erwin Stoff *3 Arts Entertainment Inc*
9460 Wilshire Blvd Fl 7
Beverly Hills, CA 90212-2713, USA

Theroux, Louis (Television Host)
c/o Staff Member *BBC Artist Mail*
PO Box 1116
Belfast BT2 7AJ, UNITED KINGDOM
(UK)

Theroux, Paul E (Writer)
35 Elsynge Road
London SW18 2NR, UNITED KINGDOM
(UK)

Theuriau, Melissa (Television Host)
Beaugard
4 Sente Des Robertines
Chanteloup-les-Vignes 78570, FRANCE

Theus, Reggie (Basketball Player)
Sanders Agency
241 Avenue Of The Americas Apt 11H
New York, NY 10014-7522, USA

Thewlis, David (Actor)
c/o Steve Dontanville *D/F Management*
1 William Morris Pl
Beverly Hills, CA 90212-4261, USA

Thiandoum, Hyacinthe Cardinal
(Religious Leader)
Archeveche
Ave Jean XXIII
Dakar 1908, SENEGAL

Thibaud, Todd (Musician)
c/o Staff Member *Paradigm (Monterey)*
509 Hartnell St
Monterey, CA 93940-2825, USA

Thibaudet, Jean-Yves (Musician)
3601 Griffith Park Blvd
Los Angeles, CA 90027-1406, USA

Thibault, Charles (Doctor)
4 Place Jussieu
Paris 75005, FRANCE

Thibaut, Jim (Football Player)
Buffalo Bisons
PO Box 251
Kenner, LA 70063-0251, USA

Thibert, Jim (Football Player)
Denver Broncos
1365 County Road L
Swanton, OH 43558-9791, USA

Thibiant, Aida (Designer, Fashion Designer)
Institut de Beaute
449 N Canon Dr
Beverly Hills, CA 90210-4819, USA

Thibodeaux, Keith (Actor)
5372 Jamaica Dr
Jackson, MS 39211-4057, USA

Thicke, Alan (Actor)
c/o Harry Gold *TalentWorks (LA)*
3500 W Olive Ave Ste 1400
Burbank, CA 91505-5512, USA

Thicke, Robin (Musician)
c/o Miguel Melendez *Overbrook Entertainment*
450 N Roxbury Dr Fl 4
Beverly Hills, CA 90210-4232, USA

Thiedemann, Fritz (Misc)
Ostreherweg 28
Heide 25746, GERMANY

Thiele, Gerhard P J (Astronaut)
ESA/EAC
Linder Hohe
Cologne 51147, GERMANY

Thielemann, Ray C (R C) (Football Player)
Atlanta Falcons
210 Rose Meadow Ln
Alpharetta, GA 30005-8339, USA

Thielemans, Jean B (Toots) (Musician)
Peter Levinson Communications
2575 Palisade Ave Apt 11H
Bronx, NY 10463-6149, USA

Thielen, Gunter (Business Person)
Bertelsmann AG
Carl-Bertelsmann-Str 270
Guetersloh 33311, GERMANY

Thiemann, Charles Lee (Financier)
Federal Home Loan Bank
PO Box 598
Cincinnati, OH 45201-0598, USA

Thieme, Paul (Misc)
Tubingen University
Wilhelmstr 7
Tubingen 72074, GERMANY

Thier, Samuel O (Educator, Physicist)
99-20 Florence St Apt 4B
Chestnut Hill, MA 02467-1927, USA

Thieriot, Max (Actor)
Gersh Agency, The
232 N Canon Dr
Beverly Hills, CA 90210-5302, USA

Thierry, John F (Football Player)
Chicago Bears
1431 Federal Rd
Opelousas, LA 70570-1172, USA

Thiess, Ursula (Actor)
1940 Bel Air Rd
Los Angeles, CA 90077-2727, USA

Thiessen, Tiffani (Actor)
c/o Christopher Barrett *Metropolitan*
4500 Wilshire Blvd Fl 2
Los Angeles, CA 90010-3858, USA

Thimmesch, Nicholas (Journalist)
6301 Broad Branch Rd
Chevy Chase, MD 20815-3343, USA

Thinnes, Roy (Actor)
Phoenix Artists
321 W 44th St Ste 400
New York, NY 10036-5461, USA

Third Day (Music Group)
c/o Staff Member *Creative Artists Agency LCC (CAA-LA)*
2000 Avenue Of The Stars
Los Angeles, CA 90067-4700, USA

Third Eye Blind (Music Group)
c/o Eric Godtland *Eric Godtland Management*
1040 Mariposa St # 200
San Francisco, CA 94107-2520, USA

Third World
151 El Camino Dr
Beverly Hills, CA 90212-2704, USA

Thirsk, Robert B (Astronaut)
Space Agency
6767 Route de Aeroport
Saint-Hubert, PQ J3Y 8Y9, CANADA

Thode, Henry G (Scientist)
McMaster University
Nuclear Research Dept
Hamilton, ON L8S 4M1, CANADA

Thoenen, Dick (Baseball Player)
Philadelphia Phillies
PO Box 364
Harrisburg, OR 97446-0364, USA

Thom, Sandi (Musician)
c/o Staff Member *Paradigm (Monterey)*
509 Hartnell St
Monterey, CA 93940-2825, USA

Thoma, Dieter (Skier)
Am Rossleberg 35
Hinterzarten 79856, GERMANY

Thoma, Georg (Skier)
Bisten 6
Hinterzarten 79856, GERMANY

Thomalla, Georg (Actor)
Hans Nefer
Bad Gastein 5640, AUSTRIA

Thomas, Aaron (Football Player)
San Francisco 49ers
2906 NW Golf Course Dr S
Bend, OR 97701-5504, USA

Thomas, Adalius (Football Player)
Baltimore Ravens
1 Willow Bend Dr
Hattiesburg, MS 39402-8552, USA

Thomas, Alex (Actor)
c/o Staff Member *Identity Talent Agency (ID)*
9107 Wilshire Blvd Ste 450
Beverly Hills, CA 90210-5535, USA

Thomas, Andrew S W (Andy) (Astronaut)
NASA
2101 Nasa Pkwy
Johnson Space Center
Houston, TX 77058-3691, USA

Thomas, Aurelius (Football Player)
PO Box 91157
Columbus, OH 43209-7157, USA

Thomas, B J (Musician, Songwriter, Writer)
Gloria Thomas
1324 Crownhill Ct
Arlington, TX 76012, USA

Thomas, Barbara S (Government Official)
News International
1 Virginia St
London E1 9XY, UNITED KINGDOM
(UK)

Thomas, Ben (Football Player)
New England Patriots
2155 Herndon St
Auburn, AL 36830-6603, USA

Thomas, Betty (Actor, Director)
Creative Artists Agency
9830 Wilshire Blvd
Beverly Hills, CA 90212-1804, USA

Thomas, Billy M (General)
2387 Spanish Oak Ter
Colorado Springs, CO 80920-1206, USA

Thomas, BJ (Musician)
c/o Staff Member *Gloria Thomas Inc*
1424 Crownhill Dr
Arlington, TX 76012-2816, USA

Thomas, Blair (Football Player)
New York Jets
401 Gulph Ridge Dr
King Of Prussia, PA 19406-3213, USA

Thomas, Broderick (Football Player)
Tampa Bay Buccaneers
3619 La Costa Rd
Missouri City, TX 77459-2406, USA

Thomas, Bruce (Actor)
c/o Jerry Shandrew *Shandrew Public Relations*
1050 S Stanley Ave
Los Angeles, CA 90019-6634, USA

Thomas, Bud (Baseball Player)
St Louis Browns
2475 Woodland Dr
Sedalia, MO 65301-8915, USA

Thomas, Calvin (Football Player)
Chicago Bears
908 Manchester Ave
Westchester, IL 60154-2719, USA

Thomas, Carl (Baseball Player)
Cleveland Indians
4525 N 66th St Unit 99
Scottsdale, AZ 85251-1020, USA

Thomas, Carl (Musician)
c/o Staff Member *William Morris Agency (WMA-LA)*
1 William Morris Pl
Beverly Hills, CA 90212-4261, USA

Thomas, Carla (Musician)
Talent Consultants International
105 Shad Row Ste B
Piermont, NY 10968-3001, USA

Thomas, Carotine Bedell (Physicist)
2401 Calvert St NW Apt 504
Washington, DC 20008-2669, USA

Thomas, Chris (Musician)
Associated Booking Corp
PO Box 2055
New York, NY 10021-0051, USA

Thomas, Chuck (Football Player)
Atlanta Falcons
2201 Purple Majesty Ct
Las Vegas, NV 89117-2747, USA

Thomas, Clendon (Football Player)
Los Angeles Rams
7508 Rumsey Rd
Oklahoma City, OK 73132-5335, USA

Thomas, Craig (Actor)
Granada Television
Quay Street
Manchester M60 9EA, UNITED KINGDOM (UK)

Thomas, Damien
31 Kensington Church St.
London, ENGLAND W8 4LL, UNITED KINGDOM (UK)

Thomas, Dave (Comedian)
c/o Staff Member *MBST Entertainment*
345 N Maple Dr Ste 200
Beverly Hills, CA 90210-3860, USA

Thomas, Dave G (Football Player)
Dallas Cowboys
2127 Brickell Ave Apt 3404
Miami, FL 33129-2105, USA

Thomas, David (Business Person)
Thomson Corp
1 Station Pl
Metro Center
Stamford, CT 06902-6800, USA

Thomas, David (Musician)
74 Hyde Vale
Greenwich
London SE10 8HP, UNITED KINGDOM (UK)

Thomas, Debi
22 E 71st St
New York, NY 10021-4975, USA

Thomas, Debra J (Deb) (Figure Skater)
Mentor Mgmt
202 S Michigan St Ste 810
South Bend, IN 46601-2012, USA

Thomas, Dennis (D T) (Musician)
Pyramid Entertainment
89 5th Ave Ste 700
New York, NY 10003-3020, USA

Thomas, Derrel (Baseball Player)
Houston Astros
7908 Wisteria Ct
Highland, CA 92346-5744, USA

Thomas, Dominic R (Religious Leader)
Church of Jesus Christ
6th & Lincoln Sts
Monongahela, PA 15063, USA

Thomas, Donald A (Astronaut)
1029 Hart Rd
Towson, MD 21286-1630, USA

Thomas, Donald Michael (D M) (Writer)
Coach House
Rashleigh Vale Tregolls Rd
Truro, Cornwall TR1 1TJ, UNITED KINGDOM (UK)

Thomas, Doug (Football Player)
Seattle Seahawks
11220 NE 53rd St
Kirkland, WA 98033-7595, USA

Thomas, Duane (Football Player)
Dallas Cowboys
PO Box 862
Del Mar, CA 92014-0862, USA

Thomas, E Donnall (Nobel Prize Laureate)
Hutchinson Cancer Research Center
PO Box 19024
Seattle, WA 98109-1024, USA

Thomas, Earl (Football Player)
Chicago Bears
4202 Clearwater Ct
Missouri City, TX 77459-1668, USA

Thomas, Earlie (Football Player)
New York Jets
PO Box 1445
Laporte, CO 80535-1445, USA

Thomas, Eddie Kaye (Actor)
c/o David (Dave) Becky *3 Arts Entertainment Inc*
9460 Wilshire Blvd Fl 7
Beverly Hills, CA 90212-2713, USA

Thomas, Elizabeth Marshall (Writer)
80 E Mountain Rd
Peterborough, NH 03458-2318, USA

Thomas, Emmitt (Football Player)
Kansas City Chiefs
5318 Harbury Cv
Suwanee, GA 30024-7544, USA

Thomas, Ernest (Actor)
Coast to Coast Talent
3350 Barham Blvd
Los Angeles, CA 90068-1404, USA

Thomas, Etan (Basketball Player)
c/o Staff Member *Washington Wizards*
601 F St NW
Mci Center
Washington, DC 20004-1605, USA

Thomas, Frank E (Baseball Player)
Chicago White Sox
3649 Dunhill Dr
Columbus, GA 31906-2714, USA

Thomas, Frank J (Baseball Player)
Pittsburgh Pirates
118 Doray Dr
Pittsburgh, PA 15237-3681, USA

Thomas, Fred (Government Official, Lawyer)
Metropolitan Police Dept
300 Indiana Ave NW
Washington, DC 20001-2175, USA

Thomas, Gareth (Actor)
c/o Staff Member *Julian Belfrage & Associates*
Adam House
14 New Burlington St
London W1S 3BQ, UNITED KINGDOM (UK)

Thomas, George (Baseball Player)
c/o Staff Member *Detroit Tigers*
2100 Woodward Ave
Comerica Park
Detroit, MI 48201-3474, USA

Thomas, Gorman (Baseball Player)
Milwaukee Brewers
W331S5179 Hood Pkwy
North Prairie, WI 53153-9719, USA

Thomas, Heather (Actor)
c/o Larry Kennar *Code Entertainment*
9229 W Sunset Blvd Ste 615
Los Angeles, CA 90069-3406, USA

Thomas, Heidi (Actor)
Lichtman/Salners
15865 Royal Haven Pl
Sherman Oaks, CA 91403-4724, USA

Thomas, Helen A (Journalist)
2501 Calvert St NW
Washington, DC 20008-2620, USA

Thomas, Henry (Actor)
c/o Colton Gramm *Brillstein-Grey Entertainment*
9150 Wilshire Blvd Ste 350
Beverly Hills, CA 90212-3453, USA

Thomas, Henry L Jr (Football Player)
Minnesota Vikings
16811 Southern Oaks Dr
Houston, TX 77068-1509, USA

Thomas, Henry W (Writer)
3214 Warder St NW
Washington, DC 20010-2521, USA

Thomas, Hollis (Football Player)
Philadelphia Eagles
920 Yeadon Ave
Lansdowne, PA 19050-3713, USA

Thomas, Irma (Musician)
Emile Jackson
PO Box 26126
New Orleans, LA 70186-6126, USA

Thomas, Isaac (Football Player)
Dallas Cowboys
510 Grady Ln
Cedar Hill, TX 75104-4212, USA

Thomas, J T (Football Player)
Pittsburgh Steelers
408 Arden Dr
Monroeville, PA 15146-4855, USA

Thomas, Jake (Actor)
c/o Connie Tavel *Forward Entertainment*
9255 W Sunset Blvd Ste 805
Los Angeles, CA 90069-3305, USA

Thomas, Jay (Actor)
Gersh Agency
232 N Canon Dr
Beverly Hills, CA 90210-5302, USA

Thomas, Jean (Artist)
1427 Summit Rd
Berkeley, CA 94708-2214, USA

Thomas, Jeremy (Filmmaker, Producer)
Recorded Picture Co
8-12 Broadwick St
London W1V 1FH, UNITED KINGDOM (UK)

Thomas, Jesse (Football Player)
Baltimore Colts
4955 Woodward Gdns
Columbia, MD 21044-1525, USA

Thomas, John (Basketball Player)
Toronto Raptors
Air Canada Center
40 Bay St
Toronto, ON M5J 2N8, CANADA

Thomas, John C (Athlete, Track Athlete)
51 Mulberry St
Brockton, MA 02302-2327, USA

Thomas, John M (Scientist)
Royal Institution
21 Albemarle St
London W1X 4BS, UNITED KINGDOM (UK)

Thomas, Johnny (Football Player)
Washington Redskins
1818 Darby Ln
Fresno, TX 77545-9233, USA

Thomas, Jonathan Taylor (Actor)
c/o Staff Member *International Creative Management (ICM-LA)*
10250 Constellation Blvd
Los Angeles, CA 90067-6200, USA

Thomas, Justice Clarence (Judge)
US Supreme Court
1 1st St NE
Washington, DC 20543-0002, USA

Thomas, Khleo
c/o Staff Member *Beverly Hecht Agency*
3500 W Olive Ave Ste 1180
Burbank, CA 91505-4651, USA

Thomas, Kleo (Musician)
c/o Staff Member *American Idol*
7800 Beverly Blvd # 251
Los Angeles, CA 90036-2112, USA

Thomas, Kurt (Basketball Player)
1826 Brook Terrace Trl
Dallas, TX 75232-3708, USA

Thomas, Lamar (Football Player)
Tampa Bay Buccaneers
2907 NW 9th Pl
Gainesville, FL 32605-5056, USA

Thomas, Larry (Actor)
c/o Staff Member *Whitaker Agency, The*
4924 Vineland Ave
N Hollywood, CA 91601-3847, USA

Thomas, Larry (Baseball Player)
Chicago White Sox
3825 Graham Ln
Eight Mile, AL 36613-2306, USA

Thomas, LaToya (Basketball Player)
San Antonio Silver Stars
1 Sbc Center Pkwy
San Antonio, TX 78219-3604, USA

Thomas, Lavale (Football Player)
Green Bay Packers
2626 Northwoods Lake Ct
Duluth, GA 30096-7997, USA

Thomas, Lee (Baseball Player)
New York Yankees
14260 Manderieigh Woods Dr
Chesterfield, MO 63017, USA

Thomas, Mark A (Football Player)
San Francisco 49ers
556 Hillsboro St
Monticello, GA 31064-1046, USA

Thomas, Marlo (Actor)
c/o Bruce Vinokour *Creative Artists Agency LCC (CAA-LA)*
2000 Avenue Of The Stars
Los Angeles, CA 90067-4700, USA

Thomas, Mary (Musician)
Superstars Unlimited
PO Box 371371
Las Vegas, NV 89137-1371, USA

Thomas, Mava Lee (Baseball Player)
3447 E Fort King St Apt 112
Ocala, FL 34470-7201, USA

Thomas, Michael Tilson (Conductor, Musician)
San Francisco Symphony
Davies Symphony Hall
San Francisco, CA 94102, USA

Thomas, Michelle Rene (Actor)
Agency for Performing Arts
405 S Beverly Dr Ste 500
Beverly Hills, CA 90212-4425, USA

Thomas, Mike (Baseball Player)
Milwaukee Brewers
904 Linda Ln
Cabot, AR 72023-3919, USA

Thomas, Mike (Football Player)
Washington Redskins
PO Box 446
Missouri City, TX 77459-0446, USA

Thomas, Norris (Football Player)
Miami Dolphins
3202 Boston Ave
Pascagoula, MS 39581-4242, USA

Thomas, Pamela (Business Person)
c/o Staff Member *CNBC*
900 Sylvan Ave
Englewood Cliffs, NJ 07632-3312, USA

Thomas, Pat (Football Player)
Los Angeles Rams
612 Middle Cove Dr
Plano, TX 75023-4802, USA

Thomas, Philip Michael (Actor)
PO Box 3714
Brooklyn, NY 11202-3714, USA

Thomas, Ralph (Football Player)
Chicago Cardinals
3270 Alum Creek Ct
Reno, NV 89509-7117, USA

Thomas, Randy (Football Player)
New York Jets
2945 Jones St Apt 4
Atlanta, GA 30344-4130, USA

Thomas, Ray (Nobel Prize Laureate)
Insight Mgmt
1222 16th Ave S # 300
Nashville, TN 37212-2926, USA

Thomas, Reginald
18 Belgrave Mews West
London, ENGLAND SW1X 8HT, UNITED KINGDOM (UK)

Thomas, Richard (Actor)
c/o Steve Tellez *Creative Artists Agency LCC (CAA-LA)*
2000 Avenue Of The Stars
Los Angeles, CA 90067-4700, USA

Thomas, Ricky (Football Player)
Seattle Seahawks
4621 Melbourne Rd
Indianapolis, IN 46228-2773, USA

Thomas, Rob (Director, Producer, Writer)
c/o Ari Greenburg *Endeavor Agency LLC (LA)*
9601 Wilshire Blvd Fl 3
Beverly Hills, CA 90210-5204, USA

Thomas, Rob (Musician, Songwriter, Writer)
c/o Rob Light *Creative Artists Agency LCC (CAA-LA)*
2000 Avenue Of The Stars
Los Angeles, CA 90067-4700, USA

Thomas, Robert D (Publisher)
223 Mariomi Rd
New Canaan, CT 06840-3315, USA

Thomas, Robert L (Football Player)
Los Angeles Rams
2810 W Slauson Ave Apt 5
Los Angeles, CA 90043-2583, USA

Thomas, Robert R (Football Player)
Chicago Bears
970 Ridgewood Dr
West Chicago, IL 60185-5007, USA

Thomas, Robin (Actor)
c/o Staff Member *Marshak/Zachary Company, The*
8840 Wilshire Blvd Fl 1
Beverly Hills, CA 90211-2606, USA

Thomas, Ross (Actor)
c/o Bryan Bukowski *Simmons & Scott Entertainment*
4110 W Burbank Blvd
Burbank, CA 91505-2121, USA

Thomas, Roy (Baseball Player)
Houston Astros
3825 Tribute Cir E
Fife, WA 98424-3797, USA

Thomas, Rozonda (Chili) (Music Group)
c/o Staff Member *William Morris Agency (WMA-LA)*
1 William Morris Pl
Beverly Hills, CA 90212-4261, USA

Thomas, Sean Patrick (Actor)
c/o Scott Melrose *Endeavor Agency LLC (LA)*
9601 Wilshire Blvd Fl 3
Beverly Hills, CA 90210-5204, USA

Thomas, Serena Scott (Actor)
S M S Talent
8730 W Sunset Blvd Ste 440
Los Angeles, CA 90069-2277, USA

Thomas, Skip (Football Player)
Oakland Raiders
3021 N 63rd St
Kansas City, KS 66104-1935, USA

Thomas, Speedy (Football Player)
Cincinnati Bengals
7534 Weyburn St
Houston, TX 77028-2418, USA

Thomas, Stan (Baseball Player)
Texas Rangers
10827 159th Ct NE
Redmond, WA 98052-2691, USA

Thomas, Steve (Entertainer)
This Old House Show
PO Box 2284
South Burlington, VT 05407-2284, USA

Thomas, Sue (Golfer)
7601 Rialto Blvd Apt 2611
Austin, TX 78735-7450, USA

Thomas, Taylor Lea (Designer)
c/o Staff Member *Elite Soiree*
1221 Brickell Ave Ste 500
Miami, FL 33131-3228, USA

Thomas, Thurman L (Football Player)
240 Pound Rd
Elma, NY 14059-9681, USA

Thomas, Tony (Actor, Producer)
Witt/Thomas/Harris Productions
11901 Santa Monica Blvd # 596
West Los Angeles, CA 90025-2767, USA

Thomas, Tra (Football Player)
Philadelphia Eagles
1 Novacare Way
Philadelphia, PA 19145-5996, USA

Thomas, Valmy (Baseball Player)
New York Giants
PO Box 811
Christiansted, VI 00821-0811, USA

Thomas, Wayne (Hockey Player)
Cleveland Barons
200 Hudson Road E
Cleveland, OH 44115, USA

Thomas, William H Jr (Football Player)
Philadelphia Eagles
2401 Echo Dr
Amarillo, TX 79107-6405, USA

Thomas, William J (Football Player)
Dallas Cowboys
16 Russell St
Waltham, MA 02453-8505, USA

Thomas, Zach (Football Player)
Miami Dolphins
1051 NW 122nd Ave
Plantation, FL 33323-2529, USA

Thomas III, Isiah L (Athlete, Basketball Player, Business Person, Coach)
38505 Woodward Ave Ste 1700
Bloomfield Hills, MI 48304-5205, USA

Thomas of Swynnerton, Hugh S (Historian)
Well House
Sudbourne, Suffolk, UNITED KINGDOM (UK)

Thomaselli, Rich (Football Player)
Houston Oilers
96A Seneca St
Weirton, WV 26062-2627, USA

Thomason, Bob (Football Player)
Los Angeles Rams
2645 Bucknell Ave
Charlotte, NC 28207-2649, USA

Thomason, Erskine (Baseball Player)
Philadelphia Phillies
932 Dial Pl
Laurens, SC 29360-8850, USA

Thomason, Harry (Producer)
c/o Staff Member *Mozark Productions*
4024 Radford Ave Bldg 5 # 104
Studio City, CA 91604-2101, USA

Thomason, Harry Z (Producer)
10732 Riverside Dr
North Hollywood, CA 91602-2313, USA

Thomason, Marsha (Actor)
c/o Tammy Rosen *Melanie Greene Management & Productions*
425 N Robertson Blvd
West Hollywood, CA 90048-1735, USA

Thomassin, Florence (Actor)
Artmedia
20 Ave Rapp
Paris 75007, FRANCE

Thomasson, Gary (Baseball Player)
San Francisco Giants
8300 N 53rd St
Paradise Valley, AZ 85253-2512, USA

Thome, James H (Jim) (Baseball Player)
Cleveland Indians
125 E 8th St
Hinsdale, IL 60521-4520, USA

Thomerson, Tim (Actor)
2635 28th St Apt 14
Santa Monica, CA 90405-2960, USA

Thomlinson, John (Baseball Player)
Negro Baseball Leagues
2351 Beach Way SW
Atlanta, GA 30310-1005, USA

Thomopoulos, Anthony (Business Person)
10727 Wilshire Blvd Apt 1602
Los Angeles, CA 90024-7334, USA

Thomopoulos, Tony
1280 Stone Canyon Rd
Los Angeles, CA 90077-2920, USA

Thompson, Andrea (Actor)
Dayton Milrad Cho Management
8306 Wilshire Blvd # 56
Beverly Hills, CA 90211-2304, USA

Thompson, Andy (Baseball Player)
Toronto Blue Jays
18701 Chopin Dr
Lutz, FL 33558-2875, USA

Thompson, Anthony (Coach, Football Coach, Football Player)
Indiana University
Athletic Dept
Bloomington, IN 47405, USA

Thompson, Arland (Football Player)
Denver Broncos
6692 S Routt St
Littleton, CO 80127-4962, USA

Thompson, Aundra (Football Player)
Green Bay Packers
12060 Galva Dr
Dallas, TX 75243-3702, USA

Thompson, Barbara (Baseball Player)
1721 Edgebrook Dr
Rockford, IL 61107-1320, USA

Thompson, Bennie (Football Player)
Baltimore Ravens
Ravens Stadium
11001 Russell St
Baltimore, MD 21230, USA

Thompson, Bobby (Baseball Player)
Texas Rangers
7006 Hunters Glen Dr
Charlotte, NC 28214-2271, USA

Thompson, Bobby (Football Player)
Detroit Lions
23600 Lahser Rd
Southfield, MI 48033-3202, USA

Thompson, Brian
1010 Olive Ln
La Canada, CA 91011-2367, USA

Thompson, Brooks (Basketball Player)
Orlando Magic
8701 Maitland Summit Blvd
Waterhouse Center
Orlando, FL 32810-5915, USA

Thompson, Caroline W (Director, Producer, Writer)
c/o Brian Sher *International Creative Management (ICM-LA)*
10250 Constellation Blvd
Los Angeles, CA 90067-6200, USA

Thompson, Clifford (Coach, Hockey Player)
3 Summit Dr Apt 16
Reading, MA 01867-4025, USA

Thompson, Craig (Football Player)
Cincinnati Bengals
913 C St
Hartsville, SC 29550-3166, USA

Thompson, Daley (Athlete)
1 Church Row Wandsworth Plain
London, ENGLAND SW18 1ES, UNITED KINGDOM (UK)

Thompson, Darrell (Football Player)
Green Bay Packers
4220 Oakview Ln N
Plymouth, MN 55442-2773, USA

Thompson, David O (Basketball Player)
5114 Berkeley Creek Ln
Charlotte, NC 28277-8716, USA

Thompson, David R (Judge)
US Court of Appeals
940 Front St Ste 5140
San Diego, CA 92101-8949, USA

Thompson, David W (Scientist)
Orbital Science Corp
21839 Atlantic Blvd
Sterling, VA 20166-6850, USA

Thompson, Don (Baseball Player)
Boston Braves
PO Box 8218
Asheville, NC 28814-8218, USA

Thompson, Donnell (Football Player)
Baltimore Colts
PO Box 1146
Durham, NC 27702-1146, USA

Thompson, Edward K (Editor)
Rock Ledge Farm
RR 8 Box 350 Union Valley Road
Mahopac, NY 10541, USA

Thompson, Edward T (Editor)
11 Cotswold Dr
North Salem, NY 10560-2708, USA

Thompson, Emma (Actor)
c/o Staff Member *Hamilton Hodell Ltd*
66 - 68 Margaret St 5th Fl
London W1W 8SR, UNITED KINGDOM (UK)

Thompson, Ernest
RR 1 Box 3248
Ashland, NH 03217, USA

Thompson, F M (Daley) (Athlete, Track Athlete)
Olympic Assn
1 Wadsworth Plain
London SW18 1EH, UNITED KINGDOM (UK)

Thompson, Fred Dalton (Actor)
c/o Staff Member *Abrams Artists Agency (LA)*
9200 W Sunset Blvd Ph 11
Los Angeles, CA 90069-3601, USA

Thompson, G Kennedy (Financier)
First Union Corp
1 First Union Center
Charlotte, NC 28288-0001, USA

Thompson, G Ralph (Religious Leader)
Seventh-Day Adventists
12501 Old Columbia Pike
Silver Spring, MD 20904-6600, USA

Thompson, Gary (Basketball Player)
2531 Park Vista Cir
Ames, IA 50014-4568, USA

Thompson, Gary Scott (Producer, Writer)
c/o Rob Carlson *William Morris Agency (WMA-LA)*
1 William Morris Pl
Beverly Hills, CA 90212-4261, USA

Thompson, Gina (Musician)
Richard Walters
1800 Argyle Ave # 408
Los Angeles, CA 90028-5253, USA

Thompson, Hank (Musician, Songwriter, Writer)
2000 Vista Rd
Roanoke, TX 76262-8803, USA

Thompson, Hilarie
13202 Weddington St
Sherman Oaks, CA 91401-6034, USA

Thompson, Hugh L (Educator)
Washburn University
President's Office
Topeka, KS 66621, USA

Thompson, Ian
44 Perryn Rd
London, ENGLAND W3 7NA, UNITED KINGDOM (UK)

Thompson, J Lee
9595 Lime Orchard Rd
Beverly Hills, CA 90210-1315, USA

Thompson, Jack (Actor)
June Cann Mgmt
110 Queen St
Woollahra, NSW 2025, AUSTRALIA

Thompson, Jack (Football Player)
2507 29th Ave W
Seattle, WA 98199-3323, USA

Thompson, Jack E (Business Person)
Homestake Mining Co
650 California St
San Francisco, CA 94108-2702, USA

Thompson, James B Jr (Misc)
1010 Waltham St Apt F1
Lexington, MA 02421-8061, USA

Thompson, James R (Jim) Jr (Governor)
Winston & Strawn
25 N Wacker Dr
Chicago, IL 60606-2800, USA

Thompson, James R Jr (Misc)
416 Randolph Ave SE
Huntsville, AL 35801-4120, USA

Thompson, Jason (Actor)
c/o Ryan Daly *Kazarian/Spencer & Assoc (LA)*
11969 Ventura Blvd
Box 7409 Fl 3
Studio City, CA 91604-2630, USA

Thompson, Jason (Baseball Player)
San Diego Padres
10636 Esk Dr
Las Vegas, NV 89144-4272, USA

Thompson, Jason D (Baseball Player)
Detroit Tigers
4056 Summerfield Dr
Troy, MI 48085-7033, USA

Thompson, Jennifer (Jenny) (Swimmer)
USA Swimming
1 Olympia Plaza
Colorado Springs, CO 80909, USA

Thompson, Jenny
1 Olympic Plz
Colorado Springs, CO 80909-5780, USA

Thompson, Jill (Cartoonist)
DC Comics
1700 Broadway
New York, NY 10019-5914, USA

Thompson, John B (Basketball Player, Coach, Sportscaster)
3636 16th St NW Apt B1161
Washington, DC 20010-4108, USA

Thompson, John M (Business Person)
IBM Corp
1 N Castle Dr
Armonk, NY 10504-1784, USA

Thompson, Junior (Baseball Player)
Cincinnati Reds
8325 E Hazelwood St
Scottsdale, AZ 85251-1751, USA

Thompson, Justin (Baseball Player)
Detroit Tigers
510 Enchanted Hollow Dr
Spring, TX 77388-6108, USA

Thompson, Kenan (Actor)
c/o Staff Member *Endeavor Agency LLC (LA)*
9601 Wilshire Blvd Fl 3
Beverly Hills, CA 90210-5204, USA

Thompson, Kenneth L (Scientist)
AT & T Bell Lucent Laboratory
600 Mountain Ave
New Providence, NJ 07974-2008, USA

Thompson, Lea (Actor, Director, Musician, Producer)
c/o Ben Press *Innovative Artists (LA)*
1505 10th St
Santa Monica, CA 90401-2805, USA

Thompson, Leonard (Football Player)
Detroit Lions
5534 W Glenrosa Ave
Phoenix, AZ 85031-2220, USA

Thompson, Leonard (Golfer)
9010 Marsh View Ct
Ponte Vedra Beach, FL 32082-1928, USA

Thompson, Leroy (Football Player)
Pittsburgh Steelers
5005 Princess Ann Ct
Knoxville, TN 37918-9274, USA

Thompson, Linda (Actor)
25254 Eldorado Meadow Rd
Hidden Hills, CA 91302-1242, USA

Thompson, Linda (Musician)
High Road
751 Bridgeway # 300
Sausalito, CA 94965-2165, USA

Thompson, Lonnie (Scientist)
Ohio State University
Geology Dept
Columbus, OH 43210, USA

Thompson, Mark (Baseball Player)
Colorado Rockies
131 Iroquois Cir
Russellville, KY 42276-8887, USA

Thompson, Marty (Football Player)
Detroit Lions
1822 E Fir Ave Apt 205
Fresno, CA 93720-2721, USA

Thompson, Mike (Baseball Player)
Washington Senators
7565 Turner Dr
Denver, CO 80221-3432, USA

Thompson, Mike (Cartoonist, Editor)
Detroit Free Press
600 W Fort St
Editorial Dept
Detroit, MI 48226-3198, USA

Thompson, Milt (Baseball Player)
Atlanta Braves
PO Box 663
Williamstown, NJ 08094-0663, USA

Thompson, Norm (Football Player)
St Louis Cardinals
PO Box 4552
Hayward, CA 94540-4552, USA

Thompson, Obadele (Athlete, Track Athlete)
Amateur Athletics Assn
PO Box 46
Bridgetown, BARBADOS

Thompson, Paul H (Educator)
Weber State University
President's Office
Ogden, UT 84408-0001, USA

Thompson, Raynoch (Football Player)
Arizona Cardinals
1739 2nd St
New Orleans, LA 70113-1657, USA

Thompson, Reyna (Football Player)
Miami Dolphins
1502 NW 183rd Ter
Pembroke Pines, FL 33029-3095, USA

Thompson, Rich (Baseball Player)
Cleveland Indians
7 Chambers Ct
Huntington Station, NY 11746-2620, USA

Thompson, Richard (Musician, Songwriter, Writer)
Elizabeth Rush Agency
82 Cumberland Ave
Verona, NJ 07044-2105, USA

Thompson, Richard K (Religious Leader)
African Methodist Episcopal Zion Church
PO Box 32843
Charlotte, NC 28232-2843, USA

Thompson, Ricky (Football Player)
Baltimore Colts
815 Woodland West Dr
Waco, TX 76712-3415, USA

Thompson, Robert (Football Player)
Denver Broncos
Deerfield Beach High School 910 SW 15th St
Deerfield Beach, FL 33441, USA

Thompson, Robert G K (General)
Pitcott House
Winsford Minehead
Somerset, UNITED KINGDOM (UK)

Thompson, Robert L (Football Player)
Detroit Lions
10712 S 7th Ave
Inglewood, CA 90303-1510, USA

Thompson, Robert R (Robby) (Baseball Player)
San Francisco Giants
4438 Gun Club Rd
West Palm Beach, FL 33406-2961, USA

Thompson, Ryan (Baseball Player)
New York Mets
2153 Fullerton Dr
Indianapolis, IN 46214-2130, USA

Thompson, Sada (Actor)
PO Box 490
Southbury, CT 06488-0490, USA

Thompson, Sarah (Actor)
c/o Gerry Harrington *Brillstein-Grey Entertainment*
9150 Wilshire Blvd Ste 350
Beverly Hills, CA 90212-3453, USA

Thompson, Scot (Baseball Player)
Chicago Cubs
110 Beacon Rd
Renfrew, PA 16053-1202, USA

Thompson, Scott
9150 Wilshire Blvd Ste 350
Beverly Hills, CA 90212-3453, USA

Thompson, Shawn
5319 Biloxi Ave
N Hollywood, CA 91601-3514, USA

Thompson, Sophie (Actor)
Jonathan Altaras
13 Shorts Gardens
London WC2H 9AT, UNITED KINGDOM (UK)

Thompson, Starley L (Scientist)
National Atmospheric Research Center
PO Box 3000
Boulder, CO 80307-3000, USA

Thompson, Steve M (Football Player)
New York Jets
11115 Vernon Rd
Lake Stevens, WA 98258-8541, USA

Thompson, Sue (Musician)
Curb Entertainment
3907 W Alameda Ave Ste 200
Burbank, CA 91505-4359, USA

Thompson, Susanna
PO Box 15717
Beverly Hills, CA 90209-1717, USA

Thompson, Tara (Actor)
c/o Staff Member *Innovative Artists (LA)*
1505 10th St
Santa Monica, CA 90401-2805, USA

Thompson, Ted (Football Player)
Houston Oilers
Green Bay Packers PO Box 10628
Director Of Player Personnel
Green Bay, WI 54307-0628, USA

Thompson, Tessa (Actor)
c/o Eric Black *Anonymous Content (CA)*
3532 Hayden Ave
Culver City, CA 90232-2413, USA

Thompson, Tim (Baseball Player)
Brooklyn Dodgers
536 Summit Dr
Lewistown, PA 17044-1252, USA

Thompson, Tina (Basketball Player)
c/o Staff Member *Houston Comets*
1510 Polk St
Houston, TX 77002-1099, USA

Thompson, Tommy (Football Player)
San Francisco 49ers
PO Box 687
Calico Rock, AR 72519-0687, USA

Thompson, Tommy (Politician)
1313 Manassas Trl
Madison, WI 53718-8243, USA

Thompson, Tommy G (Secretary)
Health/Human Service Department
200 Independence Ave SW
Washington, DC 20201-0004, USA

Thompson, Weegie (Football Player)
Pittsburgh Steelers
14501 Felbridge Way
Midlothian, VA 23113-6721, USA

Thompson, Wilbur (Moose) (Athlete, Track Athlete)
11372 Martha Ann Dr
Los Alamitos, CA 90720-3856, USA

Thompson, William A (Football Player)
Denver Broncos
14616 E Hawaii Pl
Aurora, CO 80012-5747, USA

Thompson, William P (Religious Leader)
World Council of Churches
475 Riverside Dr
New York, NY 10115-0697, USA

Thompson-Griffin, Viola (Baseball Player)
200 Edgewood Dr
Belton, SC 29627-1615, USA

Thompson Twins
9 Eccleston St.
London, ENGLAND SW1W 9LX, UNITED KINGDOM (UK)

Thoms, Art (Football Player)
Oakland Raiders
90 Goodfellow Dr
Moraga, CA 94556-1584, USA

Thoms, Tracie (Actor)
c/o Ted Schachter *Schachter Entertainment*
1157 S Beverly Dr Fl 2
Los Angeles, CA 90035-1119, USA

Thomsen, Cecilie (Actor)
c/o Staff Member *Special Artists Agency*
9465 Wilshire Blvd Ste 890
Beverly Hills, CA 90212-2607, USA

Thomsen, Ulrich (Actor)
Paradigm Agency
10100 Santa Monica Blvd Ste 2500
Los Angeles, CA 90067-4116, USA

Thomson, Anna (Actor)
Innovative Artists
1505 10th St
Santa Monica, CA 90401-2805, USA

Thomson, Brian E (Designer)
5 Little Dowling St
Paddington, NSW 2021, AUSTRALIA

Thomson, Cyndi (Musician)
The Firm
9100 Wilshire Blvd Ste 100W
Beverly Hills, CA 90212-3435, USA

Thomson, David (Business Person)
The Thomson Corporation
1 Station Pl
Metro Center
Stamford, CT 06902-6800, USA

Thomson, Dorrie
3349 Cahuenga Blvd W Ste 2
Los Angeles, CA 90068-1379, USA

Thomson, Gordon (Actor)
3914 Fredonia Dr
Los Angeles, CA 90068-1214, USA

Thomson, H C (Hank) (Misc)
PO Box 38
Mullett Lake, MI 49761-0038, USA

Thomson, John (Baseball Player)
Colorado Rockies
1414 E Kent Dr
Sulphur, LA 70663-5017, USA

Thomson, June (Correspondent)
KNBC-TV
News Dept
3000 W Alameda Ave
Burbank, CA 91523-0001, USA

Thomson, Peter (Golfer)
44 Mathoura Street
Toorak, VIC 3142, AUSTRALIA

Thomson, Robert B (Bobby) (Baseball Player)
New York Giants
95 Skidaway Island Park Rd Unit 7
Savannah, GA 31411-1106, USA

Thomson, Scotty (DJ)
c/o Len Evans *Project Publicity*
312 W 53rd St
New York, NY 10019-5743, USA

Thon, Dickie (Baseball Player)
California Angels
C17 Calle Lirio Del Mar
Dorado, PR 00646-2126, USA

Thon, Olaf (Activist)
FC Schalke 04
Postfach 200861
Gelsenkirchen 45843, GERMANY

Thone, Charles (Governor)
Erickson & Sederstrom
301 S 13th St Ste 400
Lincoln, NE 68508-2532, USA

Thoni, Gustav (Coach, Skier)
39026 Prato Allo
Stelvio-Prao, BZ, ITALY

Thora (Actor)
CunninghamEscottDipene
10635 Santa Monica Blvd Ste 130
Los Angeles, CA 90025-8306, USA

Thorell, Clarke (Actor)
c/o Staff Member *Bauman Redanty & Shaul Agency*
5757 Wilshire Blvd Ste 473
Los Angeles, CA 90036-3632, USA

Thorin, Christopher (Musician)
Shapiro Co
9229 W Sunset Blvd Ste 607
Los Angeles, CA 90069-3406, USA

Thormodsgard, Paul (Baseball Player)
Minnesota Twins
7752 E Rose Ln
Scottsdale, AZ 85250-4724, USA

Thorn, Gaston (Prime Minister)
1 Rue de la Forge
Luxembourg, LUXEMBOURG

Thorn, Paul (Musician)
c/o Staff Member *Paradigm (Monterey)*
509 Hartnell St
Monterey, CA 93940-2825, USA

Thorn, Rod (Basketball Player)
20 Loewen Ct
Rye, NY 10580-2823, USA

Thorn, Tracey (Musician)
JFD Mgmt
Acklam Worshops
10 Acklam Road
London W10 5QZ, UNITED KINGDOM (UK)

Thornbladh, Robert (Football Player)
Kansas City Chiefs
3775 Bradford Square Dr
Ann Arbor, MI 48103-6317, USA

Thornburgh, Richard (Ex-Governor, Governor)
2540 Massachusetts Ave NW # 405
Washington, DC 20008-2843, USA

Thornburgh, Richard L (Dick) (Attorney, Attorney General, General, Governor)
Kirkpatrick & Lockhart
1800 Massachusetts Ave NW # 900
Washington, DC 20036-1806, USA

Thorne, Callie (Actor)
c/o Elise Konialian *Untitled Entertainment (NY)*
322 8th Ave Ste 601
New York, NY 10001-6715, USA

Thorne, Dyanne (Actor)
8721 W Sunset Blvd Ste 101
Los Angeles, CA 90069-2271, USA

Thorne, Frank (Cartoonist)
1967 Grenville Rd
Scotch Plains, NJ 07076-2907, USA

Thorne, Gary (Correspondent)
ABC-TV
77 W 66th St
Sports Dept
New York, NY 10023-6201, USA

Thorne, Kip S (Physicist)
California Institute of Technology
Physics Dept
Pasadena, CA 91125-0001, USA

Thorne, Remy (Actor)
c/o Mitchell Gossett *Cunningham Escott Slevin & Doherty (LA)*
10635 Santa Monica Blvd Ste 130
Los Angeles, CA 90025-8306, USA

Thorne-Smith, Courtney (Actor, Model)
c/o Joel Rudnick *Paradigm (LA)*
360 N Crescent Dr
North Bldg
Beverly Hills, CA 90210-6820, USA

Thornell, Jack R (Journalist, Photographer)
6815 Madewood Dr
Metairie, LA 70003-4529, USA

Thornhill, Arthur H Jr (Publisher)
50 S School St
Portsmouth, NH 03801-5258, USA

Thornhill, Josh (Football Player)
Detroit Lions
1580 Haddon Hall Dr
Holt, MI 48842-8688, USA

Thornhill, Leeroy (Dancer)
Midi Mgmt
Jenkins Lane
Great Hallinsburry, Essex CM22 9QL, UNITED KINGDOM (UK)

Thornhill, Lisa (Actor)
208-11 Anin St
Bedford, NS B4A 4E3, CANADA

Thornton, Andre (Baseball Player)
Chicago Cubs
PO Box 395
Chagrin Falls, OH 44022-0395, USA

Thornton, Bill (Football Player)
St Louis Cardinals
2709 Poppy Way
Columbia, MO 65202-1264, USA

Thornton, Billy Bob (Actor, Director)
c/o Geyer Kosinski *Media Talent Group*
9200 W Sunset Blvd Ste 810
W Hollywood, CA 90069-3603, USA

Thornton, Bruce (Football Player)
Dallas Cowboys
3117 Hazlewood Ct
Bedford, TX 76021-2953, USA

Thornton, Frank (Actor)
David Daly
586A King Road
London SW6 2DX, UNITED KINGDOM
(UK)

Thornton, George (Football Player)
San Diego Chargers
2830 Marti Ln
Montgomery, AL 36116-3139, USA

Thornton, James (Football Player)
Chicago Bears
1010 Fuller Rd
Gurnee, IL 60031-1834, USA

Thornton, Joe (Hockey Player)
c/o Pat Brisson *Creative Artists Agency*
LCC (CAA-LA)
2000 Avenue Of The Stars
Los Angeles, CA 90067-4700, USA

Thornton, John (Football Player)
Cleveland Browns
6192 Otoole Ln
Mount Morris, MI 48458-2628, USA

Thornton, John (Football Player)
Tennessee Titans
7340 Indian Hill Rd
Cincinnati, OH 45243-4022, USA

Thornton, Kathryn C (Astronaut)
100 Bedford Pl
Charlottesville, VA 22903-4622, USA

Thornton, Lou (Baseball Player)
Toronto Blue Jays
725 Henderson Rd
Hope Hull, AL 36043-4429, USA

Thornton, Otis (Baseball Player)
Houston Astros
4312 Avenue L
Birmingham, AL 35208-1812, USA

Thornton, Sidney (Football Player)
Pittsburgh Steelers
748 Royal St
Natchitoches, LA 71457-5741, USA

Thornton, Sigrid (Actor)
International Casting Services
147 King St
Sydney, NSW 2000, AUSTRALIA

Thornton, William E (Astronaut)
7640 Pimlico Ln
Boerne, TX 78015-4820, USA

Thornton, Zach (Soccer Player)
Chicago Fire
7000 S Harlem Ave
Bridgeview, IL 60455-1160, USA

Thorogood, George (Musician)
Michael Donahue Mgmt
PO Box 807
Lewisburg, WV 24901-0807, USA

Thorpe, Alexis (Actor)
c/o Marv Dauer *Marv Dauer Management*
11661 San Vicente Blvd Ste 104
Los Angeles, CA 90049-5150, USA

Thorpe, Ian (Swimmer)
PO Box 427
Milsons Point, NSW 2061, AUSTRALIA

Thorpe, James (Director)
20 Loeffler Rd Apt T320
Bloomfield, CT 06002-2277, USA

Thorpe, Jeremy J (Government Official)
2 Orme Square
Bayswater
London W2, UNITED KINGDOM (UK)

Thorpe, Otis H (Basketball Player)
PO Box 400
Canfield, OH 44406-0400, USA

Thorsell, William (Editor)
Toronto Globe & Mail
444 Front St W
Toronto, ON M5V 2S9, CANADA

Thorsness, Leo K (War Hero)
64915 E Brassie Dr
Tucson, AZ 85739-1649, USA

Thorson, Linda (Actor)
S M S Talent
8730 W Sunset Blvd Ste 440
Los Angeles, CA 90069-2277, USA

Thout, Pierre
6606 Patrick Ct
Centreville, VA 20120-3754, USA

Thranhardt, Carlo
Brauweilerstr. 14
Koln D-50859, GERMANY

Thrash, James (Football Player)
Washington Redskins
16005 Hampton Rd
Hamilton, VA 20158-3311, USA

Threadgill, Henry L (Composer, Musician)
Joel Chriss
300 Mercer St Apt 3J
New York, NY 10003-6732, USA

Threats, Jabbar (Football Player)
Jacksonville Jaguars
2015 Miracle Mile
Springfield, OH 45503-2836, USA

Threatt, Sedale (Basketball Player)
5359 Newcastle Ln
Calabasas, CA 91302-3119, USA

Three Days Grace (Music Group)
2239 Dundas St West #2
Toronto, ON M6R 1X6, CANADA

Three Degrees
19 The Willows Maidenhead Rd.
Windsor Berkshire, ENGLAND, UNITED
KINGDOM (UK)

Three Dog Night
c/o Robert Norman *Creative Artists*
Agency LCC (CAA-LA)
2000 Avenue Of The Stars
Los Angeles, CA 90067-4700, USA

Threlfall, David (Actor)
c/o Staff Member *James Sharkey Assoc*
15 Golden Sq Fl 3
London W1R 3PA, UNITED KINGDOM
(UK)

Threlkeld, Richard D (Correspondent)
CBS-TV
51 W 52nd St
News Dept
New York, NY 10019-6119, USA

Threshie, R David Jr (Publisher)
Orange County Register
625 N Grand Ave
Santa Ana, CA 92701-4347, USA

Thrice (Music Group)
c/o Staff Member *Nick Ben-Meir CPA*
652 N Doheny Dr
West Hollywood, CA 90069-5526, USA

Thrift, Cliff (Football Player)
San Diego Chargers
705 Trisha Ln
Norman, OK 73072-3718, USA

Throne, Malachi (Actor)
11805 Mayfield Ave Apt 306
Los Angeles, CA 90049-5748, USA

Throop, George (Baseball Player)
Kansas City Royals
239 Windwood Ln
Sierra Madre, CA 91024-2677, USA

Thrower, Jim (Football Player)
Philadelphia Eagles
17421 Pontchartrain Blvd
Detroit, MI 48203-1720, USA

Thumann, Chad (Writer)
c/o Josh Kesselman *Jericho Entertainment*
2121 Avenue Of The Stars Ste 2900
Los Angeles, CA 90067-5057, USA

Thunman, Nils R (Admiral)
1516 S Willemore Ave
Springfield, IL 62704-3374, USA

Thuot, Pierre
21700 Atlantic Blvd
Dulles, VA 20166-6860, USA

Thurlow, Steve (Football Player)
New York Giants
198 Shore Rd
Old Greenwich, CT 06870-2421, USA

Thurm, Maren (Actor)
ZBF Agentur
Ordensmeisterstr 15-16
Berlin 12099, GERMANY

Thurman, Corey (Baseball Player)
Toronto Blue Jays
27317 Thomas Ave
Warren, MI 48092-3588, USA

Thurman, Dennis L (Football Player)
Dallas Cowboys
3447 W 59th Pl
Los Angeles, CA 90043-3009, USA

Thurman, Gary (Baseball Player)
Kansas City Royals
PO Box 7464
Appleton, WI 54912-7073, USA

Thurman, Mike (Baseball Player)
Montreal Expos
894 SW Lost River Shores Dr
Stuart, FL 34997-7449, USA

Thurman, Uma (Actor, Producer)
c/o Kevin Huvane *Creative Artists Agency*
LCC (CAA-LA)
2000 Avenue Of The Stars
Los Angeles, CA 90067-4700, USA

Thurman, William E (General)
10 Firestone Dr
Pinehurst, NC 28374-7091, USA

Thurmond, Mark (Baseball Player)
San Diego Padres
1614 Kings Castle Dr
Katy, TX 77450-4300, USA

Thurmond, Nate (Basketball Player)
5094 Diamond Heights Blvd # B
San Francisco, CA 94131-1653, USA

Thurow, Lester C (Economist)
Massachusetts Institute of Technology
Economics Dept
Cambridge, MA 02139, USA

Thursday (Music Group)
c/o Staff Member *Island Records*
825 8th Ave
New York, NY 10019-7472, USA

Thurston, Frederick C (Fuzzy) (Football
Player)
Green Bay Packers
E1462 Grandview Rd
Waupaca, WI 54981-9136, USA

Thurston, Joe (Baseball Player)
Los Angeles Dodgers
331 Atlantic Ave
Fairfield, CA 94533-1540, USA

Thyssen, Greta (Actor)
444 E 82nd St
New York, NY 10028-5903, USA

T.I. (Musician)
c/o Staff Member *Atlantic Records (NY)*
1290 Avenue Of The Americas
New York, NY 10104-0184, USA

Tian, Jiyun (Government Official)
Vice President's Office
State Council
Beijing, CHINA

Tibbets, Paul W
5574 Knollwood Dr
Columbus, OH 43232-1543, USA

Tibbs, Jay (Baseball Player)
Cincinnati Reds
905 Smith Rd
Oneonta, AL 35121-7181, USA

Tice, George A (Photographer)
581 Kings Hwy E
Atlantic Hlds, NJ 07716-2326, USA

Tice, John (Football Player)
New Orleans Saints
1004 Bartlett Loop # B
West Point, NY 10996-1201, USA

Tice, Michael P (Mike) (Football Player)
Seattle Seahawks
2114 Gail Ave Apt A
Jacksonville Beach, FL 32250-6170, USA

Tichmarsh, Alan (Actor, Writer)
c/o Staff Member *Arlington Enterprises Ltd*
1-3 Charlotte St
London W1P 1HD, UNITED KINGDOM
(UK)

Tichnor, Alan (Religious Leader)
United Synagogues of Conservative
Judaism
155 5th Ave
New York, NY 10010-6802, USA

Tickner, Charles (Charlie) (Figure Skater)
5410 Sunset Dr
Littleton, CO 80123-1422, USA

Ticotin, Rachel (Actor)
c/o Steve Dontanville *D/F Management*
1 William Morris Pl
Beverly Hills, CA 90212-4261, USA

Tiddy, Kim (Actor)
Bosun House
1 Deer Park Rd
Merton
London SW19 9TL, ENGLAND

Tidrow, Dick (Baseball Player)
Cleveland Indians
324 NE Warrington Ct
Lees Summit, MO 64064-1605, USA

Tidwell, Moody R III (Judge)
US Claims Court
717 Madison Pl NW
Washington, DC 20439-0001, USA

Tidwell, Travis (Football Player)
New York Giants
3300 Caseys Xing
Birmingham, AL 35215-1072, USA

Tiefenbach, Dov (Actor)
c/o Staff Member *The Firm*
9465 Wilshire Blvd Fl 6
Beverly Hills, CA 90212-2605, USA

Tiefenthaler, Verle (Baseball Player)
Chicago White Sox
1852 Quint Ave
Carroll, IA 51401-3567, USA

Tiegs, Cheryl (Model, Television Host)
c/o Staff Member *Ford Models (LA)*
8826 Burton Way
Beverly Hills, CA 90211-1715, USA

Tiemann, Norbert T (Governor)
7511 Pebbiestone Dr
Dallas, TX 75230, USA

Tierney, Maura (Actor)
c/o Raelle Koota *Anonymous Content (NY)*
8522 National Blvd Ste 101
Culver City, CA 90232-2454, USA

Tiffany (Musician)
c/o Charlie Davis *Paradise Artists*
108 E Matilija St
Ojai, CA 93023-2639, USA

Tiffin, Pamela (Actor)
15 W 67th St
New York, NY 10023-6226, USA

Tigar, Kenneth (Actor)
640 Stratford Ave
Stratford, CT 06615-6348, USA

Tiger, Lionel (Scientist)
248 W 23rd St # 400
New York, NY 10011-2304, USA

Tigerman, Stanley (Architect)
Tigerman McCurry Architect
444 N Wells St Ste 206
Chicago, IL 60610-4522, USA

Tighe, Kevin (Actor)
PO Box 453
Sedro Woolley, WA 98284-0453, USA

Tikkanen, Esa (Hockey Player)
New York Rangers
2 Penn Plz
Madison Square Garden
New York, NY 10121-1703, USA

Tilberg, Tasha (Model)
c/o Staff Member *Next (LA)*
8447 Wilshire Blvd Ste 301
Beverly Hills, CA 90211-3206, USA

Tilford, Terrell (Actor)
c/o Staff Member *SMS Talent Inc*
8730 W Sunset Blvd Ste 440
Los Angeles, CA 90069-2277, USA

Tilker, Ewald (Athlete)
2767 40th Ave
San Francisco, CA 94116-2707, USA

Tilleman, Mike (Football Player)
Minnesota Vikings
180 County Road 800 NW
Havre, MT 59501, USA

Tiller, Joe (Coach, Football Coach)
Purdue University
Athletic Dept
W Lafayette, IN 47907, USA

Tiller, Nadja (Actor)
Via Tamporiva 26
Castagnola 6976, SWITZERLAND

Tilley, Patrick L (Pat) (Coach, Football Coach, Football Player)
St Louis Cardinals
5729 Lakefront Dr
Shreveport, LA 71119-3913, USA

Tillis, Mel (Musician, Songwriter, Writer)
Mel Tillis Enterprises
PO Box 305
Silver Springs, FL 34489-0305, USA

Tillis, Pam (Musician, Songwriter, Writer)
Fitzgerald Hartley Co
1908 Wedgewood Ave
Nashville, TN 37212-3733, USA

Tillison, Ed (Football Player)
Detroit Lions
38504 James Crosby Rd
Pearl River, LA 70452-3431, USA

Tillman, Lewis (Football Player)
New York Giants
PO Box 166
Madison, MS 39130-0166, USA

Tillman, Robert L (Business Person)
Lowe's Companies
1605 Curtis Bridge Rd
Wilkesboro, NC 28697-2231, USA

Tillman, Rusty (Baseball Player)
New York Mets
7541 Jana Ln S
Jacksonville, FL 32210-4723, USA

Tillman Jr, George (Director, Producer)
Creative Artists Agency
9830 Wilshire Blvd
Beverly Hills, CA 90212-1804, USA

Tillotson, Johnny (Musician)
American Mgmt
19948 Mayall St
Chatsworth, CA 91311-3522, USA

Tilly, Jennifer (Actor)
c/o Chuck Binder *Binder & Associates*
1465 Lindacrest Dr
Beverly Hills, CA 90210-2519, USA

Tilly, Meg (Actor)
c/o Staff Member *Gersh Agency, The (LA)*
232 N Canon Dr
Beverly Hills, CA 90210-5302, USA

Tilson, Joseph (Joe) (Artist)
2 Brook Street Mansions
41 Davies St
London W1Y 1FJ, UNITED KINGDOM (UK)

Tilton, Charlene (Actor)
c/o Staff Member *Bohemia Entertainment Group*
8170 Beverly Blvd Ste 102
Los Angeles, CA 90048-4533, USA

Tilton, Glenn F (Business Person)
UAL Corp
1200 E Algonquin Rd
Arlington Heights, IL 60005-4712, USA

Tilton, Robert (Misc)
Robert Tilton Ministries
PO Box 819000
Dallas, TX 75381-9000, USA

Timbaland (Musician)
c/o Staff Member *Interscope Records (LA) - Main*
2220 Colorado Ave
Santa Monica, CA 90404-3506, USA

Timberlake, George (Football Player)
Green Bay Packers
13880 Canoe Brook Dr Apt 4D
Seal Beach, CA 90740-3856, USA

Timberlake, Justin (Musician)
Just-in-Time
66 Riverwalk Pl
Memphis, TN 38103-0844, USA

Timberlake, Robert W (Bob) (Football Player)
New York Giants
2219 E Jarvis St
Milwaukee, WI 53211-2149, USA

Timchal, Cindy (Coach)
University of Maryland
Athletic Dept
College Park, MD 20742-0001, USA

Times, Ken (Football Player)
San Francisco 49ers
2603 S Sanford Ave
Sanford, FL 32773-5298, USA

Timken, William R Jr (Business Person)
Timken Co
1835 Dueber Ave SW
Canton, OH 44706-2798, USA

Timlin, Mike (Baseball Player)
2734 Meadowview Ct
Tarpon Springs, FL 34688-7363, USA

Timm, Bruce (Animator)
c/o Staff Member *Peter Strain & Associates Inc (LA)*
5455 Wilshire Blvd Ste 1812
Los Angeles, CA 90036-4268, USA

Timme, Robert (Architect)
Taft Architects
2370 Rice Blvd Ste 112
Houston, TX 77005-2644, USA

Timmermann, Ulf (Athlete, Track Athlete)
Conrad Blenkle Str 34
Berlin 1055, GERMANY

Timmins, Call (Actor)
The Agency
1800 Avenue Of Stars Ste 400
Los Angeles, CA 90067-4206, USA

Timmons, Harold
PO Box 140571
Nashville, TN 37214-0571, USA

Timmons, Jeff (Musician)
DAS Communications
83 Riverside Dr
New York, NY 10024-5713, USA

Timmons, Margo (Musician)
Macklam Feldman Mgmt
1505 W 2nd Ave
#200
Vancouver, BC V6H 3Y4, CANADA

Timmons, Michael (Musician, Songwriter, Writer)
Macklam Feldman Mgmt
1505 W 2nd Ave
#200
Vancouver, BC V6H 3Y4, CANADA

Timmons, Peter (Musician)
Macklam Feldman Mgmt
1505 W 2nd Ave
#200
Vancouver, BC V6H 3Y4, CANADA

Timmons, Tim (Baseball Player)
PO Box 574
New Albany, OH 43054-0574, USA

Timofeev, Valeri (Artist)
464 Blue Mountain Lk
East Stroudsburg, PA 18301-8654, USA

Timofeyeva, Nina V (Ballerina)
Bolshoi Theater
Teatralnaya Pl 1
Moscow 103009, RUSSIA

Timpson, Michael D (Football Player)
New England Patriots
4722 Saint Simon Dr
Coconut Creek, FL 33073-5115, USA

Tin Tin, Rin
PO Box 27
Crockett, TX 75835-0027, USA

Tindermans, Leo (Prime Minister)
Jan Verbertiel 24
Edegem 2520, BELGIUM

Tindle, David (Astronaut)
Redfern Gallery
20 Cork St
London W1, UNITED KINGDOM (UK)

Ting, Samuel C C (Nobel Prize Laureate)
2 Eliot Pl
Jamaica Plain, MA 02130-4021, USA

Ting, Walasse (Artist)
100 W 25th St
New York, NY 10001, USA

Tingelhoff, Mick (Football Player)
Minnesota Vikings
20517 Kalmeadow Ct
Lakeville, MN 55044-6705, USA

Tinglehoff, H Michael (Mick) (Football Player)
19288 Judicial Rd
Prior Lake, MN 55372, USA

Tinker, Grant (Business Person)
541 Perugia Way
Los Angeles, CA 90077-3708, USA

Tinkham, Michael (Physicist)
98 Rutledge Rd
Belmont, MA 02478-2633, USA

Tinoco, Joe
118 N Keeler St
Olathe, KS 66061-3716, USA

Tinsley, Bruce (Cartoonist, Editor)
King Features Syndicate
888 7th Ave Ste 201
New York, NY 10106-0201, USA

Tinsley, Buddy (Football Player)
Los Angeles Dons
10-6645 Roblin Blvd
Winnipeg, MB R3R 3S4, CANADA

Tinsley, Jackson B (Jack) (Editor)
Fort Worth Star-Telegram
400 W 7th St
Editorial Dept
Fort Worth, TX 76102-4793, USA

Tinsley, Jamaal (Basketball Player)
Indiana Pacers
125 S Pennsylvania St
Conseco Fieldhouse
Indianapolis, IN 46204-3610, USA

Tinsley, Scott (Football Player)
Philadelphia Eagles
26852 Sommerset Ln
Lake Forest, CA 92630-5800, USA

Tippet, Andre B (Football Player)
17 Knob Hill St
Sharon, MA 02067-3119, USA

Tippett, Dave (Coach, Hockey Player)
260 Breakers Ln
Stratford, CT 06615-7571, USA

Tippett, Sir Michael
48 Great Marborough St.
London, ENGLAND W1V 2BN, UNITED
KINGDOM (UK)

Tippin, Aaron (Musician, Songwriter,
Writer)
Tip Top Mgmt
PO Box 41689
Nashville, TN 37204-1689, USA

Tippins, Ken (Football Player)
Dallas Cowboys
RR 2 Box 173
Adel, GA 31620, USA

Tipton, Daniel (Religious Leader)
Churches of Christ in Christian Union
PO Box 30
Circleville, OH 43113-0030, USA

Tipton, Dave L (Football Player)
New York Giants
915 Bonneville Way
Sunnyvale, CA 94087-3038, USA

Tiriac, Ion (Coach, Tennis Player)
Blvd. D'Italie 44
Monte Carlo, MONACO

Tirico, Mike (Sportscaster)
ABC-TV
77 W 66th St
Sports Dept
New York, NY 10023-6201, USA

Tirimo, Martino (Musician)
1 Romeyn Road
London SW16 2NU, UNITED KINGDOM
(UK)

Tirole, Jean M (Economist)
Institut D'Economie Industrielle
Toulouse, FRANCE

Tisch, James S (Business Person)
Loews Corp
667 Madison Ave
New York, NY 10065-8087, USA

Tisch, Preston R (Business Person,
Government Official)
Loews Corp
667 Madison Ave
New York, NY 10065-8087, USA

Tisch, Steve (Writer)
1162 Tower Rd
Beverly Hills, CA 90210-2131, USA

Tisdale, Ashley (Actor)
c/o Bill Perlman *New Talent Management*
PO Box 2939
Beverly Hills, CA 90213-2939, USA

Tisdale, Wayman (Basketball Player)
4710 S Wheeling Ave
Tulsa, OK 74105-4928, USA

Tishby, Noa (Actor)
c/o Bob McGowan *McGowan
Management*
8733 W Sunset Blvd Ste 103
W Hollywood, CA 90069-2241, USA

Tishchenko, Boris I (Composer)
79 Rimsky-Korsakoff Ave
#10
Saint Petersburg 190121, RUSSIA

Titanic Historical Society
PO Box 51053
Indian Orchard, MA 01151-5053, USA

Titchenal, Bob (Football Player)
Washington Redskins
2310 Lakeview Dr
Santa Rosa, CA 95405-8654, USA

Titchmarsh, Alan (Talk Show Host)
Alan Titchmarsh Products
New Mills
Slad Rd
Stroud, Gloucestershire Engl GL5 1RN,
UNITED KINGDOM (UK)

Titensor, Glen (Football Player)
Dallas Cowboys
729 Montrose Ct
Flower Mound, TX 75022-8000, USA

Tito, Dennis (Astronaut)
1800 Alta Mura Rd
Pacific Palisades, CA 90272-2700, USA

Tito, Teburoro (President)
President's Office
Tarawa, KIRIBATI

Titone, Jackie (Actor)
c/o Staff Member *Endeavor Agency LLC
(LA)*
9601 Wilshire Blvd Fl 3
Beverly Hills, CA 90210-5204, USA

Titov, German (Hockey Player)
Anaheim Mighty Ducks
2000 E Gene Autry Way
Anaheim, CA 92806-6143, USA

Titov, Vladimir
3 Hovanskaya Str. 8
Moscow 129515, RUSSIA

Titov, Vladimir G (Cosmonaut)
Potcha Kosmonavtov
Moskovskoi Oblasti
Syvisdny Goroduk 141160, RUSSIA

Titov, Yuri E (Gymnast)
Kolokolnikov Per 6
#19
Moscow 103045, RUSSIA

Tittle, Y A
PO Box 571
Lebanon, IN 46052-0571, USA

Tittle, Yelberton A (Y A) (Football Player)
San Francisco 49ers
2500 E Camino Real
Palo Alto, CA 94306, USA

Titus, Christopher (Writer)
c/o Staff Member *OmniPop Inc (LA)*
4605 Lankershim Blvd Ste 201
North Hollywood, CA 91602-1874, USA

Titus-Carmel, Gerard (Artist)
La Grand Maison
Oulchy Le Chateau 02210, FRANCE

Tixby, Dexter (Musician)
David Harris Enterprises
24210 E East Fork Rd Spc 9
Azusa, CA 91702-6249, USA

Tizard, Catherine A (Governor)
12A Wallace St
Herne Bay
Auckland 1, NEW ZEALAND

Tizon, Albert (Journalist)
Seattle Times
1120 John St
Editorial Dept
Seattle, WA 98109-5321, USA

Tizzio, Thomas R Sr (Business Person)
American Int'l Group
70 Pine St
New York, NY 10270-0094, USA

Tjeknavorian, Loris-Zare (Composer,
Conductor)
State Philharmonia
Mashtotsi Prospekt 46
Yerevan, ARMENIA

Tjoflat, Gerald B (Judge)
US Court of Appeals
311 W Monroe St
Jacksonville, FL 32202-4242, USA

Tkachuk, Keith (Hockey Player)
11243 Hunters Pond Rd
Creve Coeur, MO 63141-7672, USA

Tkaczuk, Ivan (Religious Leader)
Ukrainian Orthodox Church
3 Davenport Ave Apt 2A
New Rochelle, NY 10805-3438, USA

Tkaczuk, Walter R (Walt) (Hockey Player)
River Valley Golf & Country Club
RR 3
Saint Mary's, On N0M 2G0, CANADA

TLC (Music Group)
c/o Staff Member *Creative Artists Agency
LCC (CAA-LA)*
2000 Avenue Of The Stars
Los Angeles, CA 90067-4700, USA

TNA Wrestling (Wrestler)
c/o Staff Member *Paradigm (Monterey)*
509 Hartnell St
Monterey, CA 93940-2825, USA

To, Tony (Director)
CAA
9830 Wilshire Blvd
Beverly Hills, CA 90212-1804, USA

Toale, Will (Actor)
c/o Jennifer Wiley *Framework
Entertainment (NY)*
129 W 27th St Fl 12
New York, NY 10001-6206, USA

Toback, James (Director)
International Creative Mgmt
8942 Wilshire Blvd # 219
Beverly Hills, CA 90211-1908, USA

Tobeck, Robbie (Football Player)
Atlanta Falcons
2018 Newport Way NW
Issaquah, WA 98027-5392, USA

Tober, Barbara D (Editor)
Bride Magazine
4 W 42nd St
Editorial Dept
New York, NY 10036, USA

Tobey, David (Dave) (Basketball Player,
Coach, Referee)
Naismith Basketball Hall of Fame
1150 W Columbus Ave
Springfield, MA 01105-2514, USA

Tobey, James (Actor)
Paradigm Agency
10100 Santa Monica Blvd Ste 2500
Los Angeles, CA 90067-4116, USA

Tobian, GAry M (Misc)
9171 Belted Kingfisher Rd
Blaine, WA 98230-5701, USA

Tobias, Andrew (Writer)
787 NE 71st St
Miami, FL 33138-5717, USA

Tobias, Oliver (Actor)
Gavin Barker Assoc
2D Wimpole St
London W1G 0EB, UNITED KINGDOM
(UK)

Tobias, Phillip V (Scientist)
Witwatersrand University
7 York Road
Johannesburg 2193, SOUTH AFRICA

Tobias, Randall L (Business Person)
Eli Lilly Co
Lilly Corporate Center
Indianapolis, IN 46285-0001, USA

Tobias, Robert M (Misc)
National Treasury Employees Union
901 E St NW
Washington, DC 20004-2037, USA

Tobias, Stephen C (Business Person)
Norfolk Southern Corp
3 Commercial Pl
Norfolk, VA 23510-2108, USA

Tobin, Don (Cartoonist)
12312 Ranchwood Rd
Santa Ana, CA 92705-3349, USA

Tobin, Vince (Coach, Football Coach)
15997 W Monterey Way
Goodyear, AZ 85395-8054, USA

Tobolowsky, Stephen (Actor)
William Morris Agency
151 El Camino Dr
Beverly Hills, CA 90212-2775, USA

Toburen, Nelson (Football Player)
Green Bay Packers
1007 Village Dr
Pittsburg, KS 66762-3552, USA

Tobymac (Musician)
c/o Staff Member *Creative Artists Agency
(CAA-Nashville)*
3310 W End Ave Fl 5
Nashville, TN 37203-1028, USA

Tocchet, Rick (Hockey Player)
682 Osage Rd
Pittsburgh, PA 15243-1038, USA

Toczyska, Stefania (Opera Singer)
Columbia Artists Mgmt Inc
1790 Broadway Fl 6
New York, NY 10019-1412, USA

Todd, Hallie (Actor)
Ann Morgan Guilbert
550 Erskine Dr
Pacific Palisades, CA 90272-4247, USA

Todd, James R (Jim) (Baseball Player)
21639 Hill Gail Way
Parker, CO 80138-7249, USA

Todd, Josh (Musician)
The Firm
9100 Wilshire Blvd Ste 100W
Beverly Hills, CA 90212-3435, USA

Todd, Kendra (Business Person, Reality
TV Star)
c/o Staff Member *The Apprentice*
725 5th Ave
The Trump Co
New York, NY 10022-2519, USA

Todd, Mark (Horse Racer)
PO Box 507
Cambridge, NEW ZEALAND

Todd, Rachel (Actor)
6310 San Vicente Blvd Ste 520
Los Angeles, CA 90048-5421, USA

Todd, Richard (Actor)
Chinham Farm
Faringdon
Oxon SN7 8EZ, UNITED KINGDOM (UK)

Todd, Richard (Football Player)
New York Jets
PO Box 471
Sheffield, AL 35660-0471, USA

Todd, Tony (Actor)
Innovative Artists
1505 10th St
Santa Monica, CA 90401-2805, USA

Todd, Trisha (Actor)
c/o Staff Member *Henry Downey Talent Management*
4045 Vineland Ave Ph 538
Studio City, CA 91604-4481, USA

Todd, Virgil H (Religious Leader)
Memphis Theological
168 E Parkway S
Memphis, TN 38104-4340, USA

Todorov, Stanko (Prime Minister)
Narodno Sobranie
Sofia, BULGARIA

Todorovsky, Piotr Y (Director)
Vernadskogo Prospect 70A
#23
Moscow 117454, RUSSIA

Toennies, Jan Peter (Physicist)
Ewaldstr 7
Gottingen 37075, GERMANY

Toerzs, Gregor (Actor)
c/o Staff Member *Richard Schwartz Management*
2934 1/2 N Beverly Glen Cir # 107
Los Angeles, CA 90077-1724, USA

Toews, Jeffrey M (Jeff) (Football Player)
Miami Dolphins
11924 SW 44th St
Davie, FL 33330-1911, USA

Toews, Loren (Football Player)
Pittsburgh Steelers
165 Hawthorne Ave
Los Altos, CA 94022-3704, USA

Tofani, Loretta A (Journalist)
Philadelphia Inquirer
400 N Broad St
Editorial Dept
Philadelphia, PA 19130-4099, USA

Tofflemire, Joe (Football Player)
Seattle Seahawks
2482 196th Ave SE
Sammamish, WA 98075-7448, USA

Toffler, Alvin (Writer)
Randon House
1745 Broadway # B1
New York, NY 10019-4305, USA

Toft, Rod (Bowler)
11350 12th St N
Lake Elmo, MN 55042-8621, USA

Tognini, Gina (Actor)
c/o Staff Member *Innovative Artists (LA)*
1505 10th St
Santa Monica, CA 90401-2805, USA

Tognini, Michel (Cosmonaut)
5413 Newcastle St
Bellaire, TX 77401-2713, USA

Togo, Jonathan (Actor)
c/o Cynthia Shelton-Droke *Sweet Mud Group*
648 Broadway # 1002
New York, NY 10012-2301, USA

Togunde, Victor (Actor)
c/o Staff Member *GVA Talent Agency Inc*
9229 W Sunset Blvd Ste 320
Los Angeles, CA 90069-3403, USA

Tokarev, Valeri I (Cosmonaut)
Potcha Kosmonavtov
Moskovskoi Oblasti
Syvisdny Goroduk 141160, RUSSIA

Tokes, Laszlo (Politician, Religious Leader)
Calvin Str 1
Oradea 3700, ROMANIA

Tokody, Ilona (Opera Singer)
Hungarian State Opera
Andrassy Utca 22
Budapest 1062, HUNGARY

Tolan, Peter (Actor, Director, Producer, Writer)
c/o Michael Wimer *Creative Artists Agency LCC (CAA-LA)*
2000 Avenue Of The Stars
Los Angeles, CA 90067-4700, USA

Tolan, Robert (Bobby) (Baseball Player)
804 Woodstock St
Bellaire, TX 77401-4716, USA

Tolar, Kevin (Baseball Player)
PO Box 2365
Pawtucket, RI 02861-0365, USA

Tolbert, Berlinda (Actor)
c/o Staff Member *Pallas Management*
12535 Chandler Blvd Apt 1
Valley Village, CA 91607-1934, USA

Tolbert, Jim (Football Player)
San Diego Chargers
2435 Corinna Ct
San Diego, CA 92105-5303, USA

Tolbert, Tony L (Football Player)
Dallas Cowboys
475 S White Chapel Blvd
Southlake, TX 76092-7314, USA

Toldeo, Esteban (Golfer)
135 Spring Vly
Irvine, CA 92602-0919, USA

Toledo, Alejandro (President)
Palacio de Gobierno S/N
Plaza de Armas S/N
Lima 1, PERU

Toler, Ken (Football Player)
New England Patriots
2064 Brecon Dr
Jackson, MS 39211-5838, USA

Toles, Alvin (Football Player)
New Orleans Saints
106 Todd Creek Pl
Forsyth, GA 31029, USA

Toles, Thomas G (Tom) (Cartoonist, Editor)
4625 46th St NW
Washington, DC 20016-4477, USA

Tolkan, James (Actor)
Paradigm Agency
10100 Santa Monica Blvd Ste 2500
Los Angeles, CA 90067-4116, USA

Tolles, Tommy (Golfer)
c/o Staff Member *Pro Golfers Association (PGA) Tour*
112 Tpc Blvd
Ponte Vedra Beach, FL 32082, USA

Tolliver, Billy Joe (Football Player)
San Diego Chargers
9837 Neesonwood Dr
Shreveport, LA 71106-7738, USA

Tolsky, Susan (Actor)
10815 Acama St
North Hollywood, CA 91602-3204, USA

Tolson, Billy
2710 N Stemmons Fwy Ste 700
Dallas, TX 75207-2208, USA

Tom, Braatz (Football Player)
Washington Redskins
3131 NE 55th Ct
Fort Lauderdale, FL 33308-3428, USA

Tom, David
3033 Vista Crest Dr
Los Angeles, CA 90068-1824, USA

Tom, Heather (Actor)
c/o Thomas De Lorenzo *SmartPR*
8033 W Sunset Blvd # 1033
West Hollywood, CA 90046-2401, USA

Tom, Kiana (Model)
PO Box 1111
Sunset Beach, CA 90742-1111, USA

Tom, Lauren (Actor)
Gersh Agency
232 N Canon Dr
Beverly Hills, CA 90210-5302, USA

Tom, Mel (Football Player)
Philadelphia Eagles
1118 Via Grande Apt 255
Cathedral City, CA 92234-4300, USA

Tom, Nicolle
3033 Vista Crest Dr
Los Angeles, CA 90068-1824, USA

Toma, David
PO Box 854
Clark, NJ 07066-0854, USA

Tomaini, Amadeo (Football Player)
New York Giants
3750 Oakhill Dr
Titusville, FL 32780-3521, USA

Tomanovich, Dara
8016 Willow Glen Rd
Los Angeles, CA 90046-1617, USA

Tomas, Hildi Santo (Actor, Television Host)
741 Parkside Trl NW
Marietta, GA 30064-4714, USA

Tomasetti, Louis (Football Player)
Pittsburgh Steelers
100 Powell St
Old Forge, PA 18518-1728, USA

Tomasic, Andrew J (Andy) (Baseball Player, Football Player)
Pittsburgh Steelers
677 Maryland St
Whitehall, PA 18052-6517, USA

Tomasson, Helgi (Ballerina, Director)
San Francisco Ballet
455 Franklin St
San Francisco, CA 94102-4471, USA

Tomba, Alberto (Skier)
Castel dei Britti
Bologna 40100, ITALY

Tomberlin, Pat (Football Player)
Indianapolis Colts
891 Arthur Moore Dr
Green Cove Springs, FL 32043-9510, USA

Tombs, Tina (Golfer)
Advantage International
1751 Pinnacle Dr Ste 1500
Mc Lean, VA 22102-3833, USA

Tomczak, Michael J (Mike) (Football Player)
Chicago Bears
139 Witherow Rd
Sewickley, PA 15143-8315, USA

Tomei, Concetta (Actor)
765 Linda Flora Dr
Los Angeles, CA 90049-1626, USA

Tomei, Marisa (Actor)
c/o Sue Leibman *Barking Dog Entertainment*
9 Desbrosses St Fl 2
New York, NY 10013-1701, USA

Tomei, Marisa (Actor)
Three Arts Entertainment
9460 Wilshire Blvd Ste 700
Beverly Hills, CA 90212-2713, USA

Tomey, Dick (Coach, Football Coach)
San Francisco 49ers
4949 Centennial Blvd
Santa Clara, CA 95054-1229, USA

Tomfohrde, Heinn F (Business Person)
GAF Corp
1361 Alps Rd
Wayne, NJ 07470-3687, USA

Tomich, Jared (Football Player)
New Orleans Saints
2222 Red River Dr
Schererville, IN 46375-4492, USA

Tomita, Stan (Photographer)
2439 Saint Louis Dr
Honolulu, HI 96816-2030, USA

Tomita, Tamlyn (Actor)
c/o Staff Member *The Artists Group Ltd (LA)*
1650 Broadway Ste 610
New York, NY 10019-6833, USA

Tomjanovich, Rudolph (Rudy) (Basketball Player, Coach)
3142 Canterbury Ln
Montgomery, TX 77356-8939, USA

Tomko, Jozef Cardinal (Religious Leader)
Villa Betania
Via Urbano VIII-16
Rome 00165, ITALY

Tomlin, Lily (Actor, Comedian)
c/o Scott Henderson *William Morris Agency (WMA-LA)*
1 William Morris Pl
Beverly Hills, CA 90212-4261, USA

Tomlinson, Charles (Writer)
Bristol University
English Dept
Bristol BS8 1TH, UNITED KINGDOM (UK)

Tomlinson, John (Opera Singer)
Music International
13 Ardilaun Road
Highbury
London N5 2QR, UNITED KINGDOM (UK)

Tomlinson, LaDainian (Football Player)
c/o Tom Condon *Creative Artists Agency LCC (CAA-LA)*
2000 Avenue Of The Stars
Los Angeles, CA 90067-4700, USA

Tomlinson, Mel A (Ballerina)
790 Riverside Dr Apt 6B
New York, NY 10032-7445, USA

Tomowa-Sintow, Anna (Opera Singer)
Columbia Artists Mgmt Inc
1790 Broadway Fl 6
New York, NY 10019-1412, USA

Tompkins, Allie (Baseball Player)
Pittsburgh Crawfords
931 1/2 Clarissa St
Pittsburgh, PA 15219-5770, USA

Tompkins, Angel (Actor)
Hurkos
11935 Kling St Apt 10
Valley Village, CA 91607-5406, USA

Tompkins, Dariene (Actor)
15413 Hall Rd # 230
Macomb, MI 48044-3840, USA

Tompkins, Susie (Designer, Fashion
Designer)
2500 Steiner St Ph
San Francisco, CA 94115-1100, USA

Toms, David (Golfer)
6606 Gilbert Dr
Shreveport, LA 71106-2300, USA

Tomsco, George (Musician)
Fireballs Entertainment
1224 Cottonwood St
Raton, NM 87740-3513, USA

Tomsic, Dubravka (Musician)
Trawick Artists
1926 Broadway
New York, NY 10023-6915, USA

Tomsic, Ronald (Ron) (Basketball Player)
448 Isabella Ter
Corona Del Mar, CA 92625-2610, USA

Tone Loc (Musician)
c/o Bobby Bessone *Entertainment Artists*
2409 21st Ave S Ste 100
Nashville, TN 37212-5317, USA

Toneff, Robert (Bob) (Football Player)
San Francisco 49ers
18 Dutch Valley Ln
San Anselmo, CA 94960-1016, USA

Tonegawa, Susumu (Nobel Prize Laureate)
Massachusetts Institute of Technology
Biology Dept
Cambridge, MA 02139, USA

Toner, Mike (Journalist)
Atlanta Journal-Constitution
72 Marietta St NW
Editorial Dept
Atlanta, GA 30303-2899, USA

Toner Jr, Ed (Football Player)
Indianapolis Colts
12 Preston Ct
Swampscott, MA 01907-1650, USA

Toner Sr, Ed (Football Player)
Boston Patriots
225 Ocean St
Lynn, MA 01902-3269, USA

Toney, Andrew (Basketball Player)
Philadelphia 76ers
3601 S Broad St
1st Union Center
Philadelphia, PA 19148-5287, USA

Toney, James
6305 Wellesley Dr
West Bloomfield, MI 48322-2407, USA

Toney, Sedric (Basketball Player)
3831 Sweetwater Dr
Cleveland, OH 44141-4102, USA

Tong, Jian (Figure Skater)
c/o Staff Member *Champions on Ice*
3500 W 80th St
Tom Collins Enterprises Inc
Minneapolis, MN 55431-1068, USA

Tong, Stanley (Director)
c/o Ramses Ishak *William Morris Agency
(WMA-LA)*
1 William Morris Pl
Beverly Hills, CA 90212-4261, USA

Tongue, Marco (Football Player)
Baltimore Colts
8051 Winding Wood Rd
Glen Burnie, MD 21061-5020, USA

Tonic (Music Group)
Tonic Tonic
652 N Doheny Dr
Los Angeles, CA 90069-5526, USA

Tonini, Ersilio Cardinal (Religious Leader)
Via Santa Teresa 8
Ravenna 48100, ITALY

Tony! Toni! Tone!
1995 Broadway Ste 501
New York, NY 10023-5882, USA

Too, Short (Artist)
Pyramid Entertainment
89 5th Ave Ste 700
New York, NY 10003-3020, USA

Too, Slim (Musician)
New Frontier Mgmt
1921 Broadway
Nashville, TN 37203-2719, USA

Tooker, George (Artist)
PO Box 385
Hartland, VT 05048-0385, USA

Tool (Music Group)
Tool Dissectional
2311 W Empire Ave
Burbank, CA 91504-3318, USA

Toomay, Pat (Football Player)
Dallas Cowboys
213 Alameda Rd NW
Albuquerque, NM 87114-2221, USA

Toomer, Amani (Football Player)
New York Giants
25 Regency Pl
Weehawken, NJ 07086-6600, USA

Toomey, Bill
2227 Del Mar Scenic Pkwy
Del Mar, CA 92014-3633, USA

Toomey, Toomey (Cartoonist, Writer)
Andrews & McMeel
4520 Main St Ste 700
Kansas City, MO 64111-7705, USA

Toomey, William A (Bill) (Athlete, Track
Athlete)
4360 Park Terrace Dr Ste 160
Westlake Village, CA 91361-4452, USA

Toomin Straus, Amy (Writer)
c/o Staff Member *United Talent Agency
(UTA)*
9560 Wilshire Blvd Ste 500
Beverly Hills, CA 90212-2401, USA

Toon, Al (Football Player)
New York Jets
4915 Champions Run
Middleton, WI 53562-4078, USA

Toon, Malcolm (Diplomat)
375 Pee Dee Rd
Southern Pines, NC 28387-2118, USA

Toots & The Maytals
151 El Camino Dr
Beverly Hills, CA 90212-2704, USA

Top, Carrot (Actor, Comedian)
Carrot Top Inc
420 Sylvan Dr
Winter Park, FL 32789-3975, USA

Topfer, Morton L (Business Person)
Dell Computer Corp
1 Dell Way
Round Rock, TX 78682-0001, USA

Toploader (Music Group)
c/o Staff Member *Helter Skelter (UK)*
535 Kings Rd
The Plaza
London SW10 0SZ, UNITED KINGDOM
(UK)

Topol, Chaim (Actor)
22 Vale Court Maidville
London W9 1RT, UNITED KINGDOM
(UK)

Topor, Ted (Football Player)
Detroit Lions
2840 Condit St
Highland, IN 46322-1605, USA

Topp, Robert (Football Player)
New York Giants
10351 Douglas Ave
Plainwell, MI 49080-9664, USA

Topper, John (Musician)
Monterey Peninsula Artists
509 Hartnell St
Monterey, CA 93940-2825, USA

Topping, Seymour (Editor)
5 Heathcote Rd
Scarsdale, NY 10583-4413, USA

Toppo, Telesphore P Cardinal (Religious
Leader)
Archdiocese
PO Box 5
Purulia Road
Ranchi, Jharkhand 834001, INDIA

Toradze, Alexander (Musician)
Columbia Artists Mgmt Inc
1790 Broadway Fl 6
New York, NY 10019-1412, USA

Torborg, Jeffrey A (Jeff) (Baseball Player)
5208 Siesta Cove Dr
Sarasota, FL 34242-1709, USA

Torczon, Laverne J (Football Player)
Buffalo Bills
6472 Country Club Dr
Columbus, NE 68601-8338, USA

Torgensen, Paul E (Educator)
Virginia Polytechnic Institute
President's Office
Blacksburg, VA 24061-0001, USA

Torgeson, Lavern (Football Player)
Detroit Lions
17672 Gainsford Ln
Huntington Beach, CA 92649-4723, USA

Tork, Peter (Musician)
524 Anselmo Ave #102
San Anselmo, CA 94960, USA

Torkelson, Eric (Football Player)
Green Bay Packers
1196 Pleasant Valley Dr
Oneida, WI 54155-8634, USA

Torkildsen, Justin
7800 Beverly Blvd # 3371
Los Angeles, CA 90036-2112, USA

Torn, Rip (Actor)
118 S Beverly Dr # 504
Beverly Hills, CA 90212-3016, USA

Torp, Niels A (Architect)
Industrigaten 59
PO Box 5387
Oslo 0304, NORWAY

Torrance, Sam (Golfer)
Carnegie Sports
The Glassmill
Battersea Bridge Rd
London SW11 3BZ, UNITED KINGDOM
(UK)

Torrance, Thomas F (Educator, Religious
Leader)
37 Braid Farm Road
Edinburgh EH10 6LE, SCOTLAND

Torre, Arath de la (Actor)
c/o Staff Member *Televisa*
Blvd Adolfo Lopez Mateos 232
Colonia San Angel INN
DF CP 01060, MEXICO

Torre, Joe (Athlete)
20 Lawrence Ln
Harrison, NY 10528-1108, USA

Torre, Jose Maria (Actor)
c/o Staff Member *Televisa*
Blvd Adolfo Lopez Mateos 232
Colonia San Angel INN
DF CP 01060, MEXICO

Torrence, Gwendolyn (Gwen) (Athlete,
Track Athlete)
Gold Medal Mgmt
1750 14th St
Boulder, CO 80302-6332, USA

Torrens, David (Actor)
c/o Gabriel Blanco *Gabriel Blanco
Iglesias (Mexico)*
Rio Balsas 35-32
Colonia Cuauhtemoc
DF 06500, MEXICO

Torres, Dara (Model, Swimmer)
c/o Evan Morgenstein *PMG Sports*
700 Evanvale Ct
Cary, NC 27518-2806, USA

Torres, Diego (Musician)
Fenix Prod
Av Figueroa Alcorta 3221
Buenos Aires 1215, ARGENTINA

Torres, Gina (Actor)
c/o Christopher Barrett *Metropolitan*
4500 Wilshire Blvd Fl 2
Los Angeles, CA 90010-3858, USA

Torres, Harold (Musician)
Brothers Mgmt
141 Dunbar Ave
Fords, NJ 08863-1551, USA

Torres, Jacques (Chef, Television Host)
c/o Staff Member *Food Network, The*
75 9th Ave
New York, NY 10011-7006, USA

Torres, Jose (Boxer)
364B Greenwich St #B
New York, NY 10013, USA

Torres, Liz (Actor, Musician)
Siegel
1680 Vine St Ste 617
Hollywood, CA 90028-8833, USA

Torres, Oscar (Basketball Player)
c/o Staff Member *Houston Rockets*
1510 Polk St
Houston, TX 77002-1099, USA

Torres, Raffi (Hockey Player)
Edmonton Oilers
11230 110th St
Edmonton, AB T5G 3H7, CANADA

Torres, Tico (Musician)
Bon Jovi Mgmt
248 W 17th St Apt 501
New York, NY 10011-5330, USA

Torres, Tommy (Musician)
c/o Staff Member *Sony Music Miami*
605 Lincoln Rd Fl 7
Miami Beach, FL 33139-2900, USA

Torretta, Gino L (Football Player)
Seattle Seahawks
7322 SW 54th Ct
Miami, FL 33143-5702, USA

Torrey, Bill (Misc)
2740 Clubhouse Pointe
West Palm Beach, FL 33409-2018, USA

Torrey, Rich (Cartoonist)
King Features Syndicate
888 7th Ave Ste 201
New York, NY 10106-0201, USA

Torrijos, Martin (President)
Palaclo Presidencial
Valija 50
Panama City 1, PANAMA

Torrini, Emiliana (Musician)
c/o Staff Member *Paradigm (Monterey)*
509 Hartnell St
Monterey, CA 93940-2825, USA

Torrissen, Birger (Skier)
PO Box 216
Lakeville, CT 06039-0216, USA

Torruella, Juan R (Judge)
US Court of Appeals
150 Ave Cartos Chardon #119
San Juan, PR 00918, USA

Torry, Guy (Actor, Comedian)
c/o Staff Member *William Morris Agency (WMA-LA)*
1 William Morris Pl
Beverly Hills, CA 90212-4261, USA

Torry, Joe (Comedian)
c/o Staff Member *William Morris Agency (WMA-LA)*
1 William Morris Pl
Beverly Hills, CA 90212-4261, USA

Torteller, Yan Pascal (Musician)
MA de Valmalete
Building Gaceau
11 Ave Delcasse
Paris 75635, FRANCE

Torti, Robert (Actor)
5722 Ranchito Ave
Van Nuys, CA 91401-4343, USA

Tortorella, John (Coach)
2801 Northwood Hills Dr
Valrico, FL 33594, USA

Torvaids, Linus (Designer)
Transmeta Corp
3990 Freedom Cir
Santa Clara, CA 95054-1204, USA

Torvalds, Linus (Designer, Engineer)
Open Source Development Labs
12725 SW Millikan Way
Beaverton, OR 97005-1678, USA

Torvill, Jayne (Dancer)
Sue Young
PO Box 32
Heathfield, East Sussex TN21 0BW,
UNITED KINGDOM (UK)

Tory, Guy (Actor)
William Morris Agency
151 El Camino Dr
Beverly Hills, CA 90212-2775, USA

Tosca, Carlos (Misc)
2831 Timber Knoll Dr
Valrico, FL 33596-5665, USA

Toscano, Harry (Golfer)
3209 Mercer St
New Castle, PA 16105-5311, USA

Tosh, Daniel (Comedian)
c/o Staff Member *William Morris Agency (WMA-LA)*
1 William Morris Pl
Beverly Hills, CA 90212-4261, USA

Toski, Bob (Golfer)
20914 Hamaca Ct
Boca Raton, FL 33433-2716, USA

Totenberg, Nina (Correspondent)
National Public Radio
News Dept
615 Main Ave NW
Washington, DC 20024, USA

Toth, Nick (Football Player)
Buffalo Tigers
1 Diaz Ave
San Francisco, CA 94132-2434, USA

Toth, Tom (Football Player)
Miami Dolphins
13723 Lindsay Dr
Orland Park, IL 60462-7011, USA

Toth, Zollie (Football Player)
New York Yankees
1612 Hideaway Ct
Baton Rouge, LA 70806-7674, USA

Totmianina, Tatyana (Figure Skater)
c/o Staff Member *Champions on Ice*
3500 W 80th St
Tom Collins Enterprises Inc
Minneapolis, MN 55431-1068, USA

Toto
50 W Main St
Ventura, CA 93001-4525, USA

Totten, Robert (Director)
PO Box 7180
Big Bear Lake, CA 92315-7180, USA

Totter, Audrey (Actor)
Motion Picture Country Home
23388 Mulholland Dr
Woodland Hills, CA 91364-2733, USA

Totushek, John B (Admiral)
Commander
Naval Reserve Force Hqusn
Pentagon
Washington, DC 20350-0001, USA

Toulouse, Gerard (Physicist)
Laboratoire de Physique de l'ENS
24 Rue Lhomond
Paris 75231, FRANCE

Tountas, Pete (Bowler)
10100 N Calle Del Camero
Tucson, AZ 85737, USA

Toure, Younoussi (Prime Minister)
Union Economique/Monetaire
01 BP 543
Quagadougou 01, Burkina Faso, MALI

Tournier, Michel (Writer)
Le Presbytree Choisel
Chevreuse 78460, FRANCE

Toussaint, Allen (Composer, Musician)
272 Abalon Ct
New Orleans, LA 70114-1374, USA

Toussaint, Beth
11333 Moor Park St Pmb 156
Studio City, CA 91602-2618, USA

Toussaint, Coleman Beth (Actor)
Don Buchwald
6500 Wilshire Blvd Ste 2200
Los Angeles, CA 90048-4942, USA

Toussaint, Lorraine (Actor)
c/o Jonathan Howard *Innovative Artists (LA)*
1505 10th St
Santa Monica, CA 90401-2805, USA

Tovar, Lupita
1527 N Tigertail Rd
Los Angeles, CA 90049-1430, USA

Tovar, Steven E (Steve) (Football Player)
Cincinnati Bengals
1026 Brower Rd
Lima, OH 45801-2316, USA

Tovoli, Luciano (Cinematographer)
United Talent Agency
9560 Wilshire Blvd Ste 500
Beverly Hills, CA 90212-2401, USA

Towe, Monte (Basketball Player, Coach)
3616 Dade St
Raleigh, NC 27612-4606, USA

Tower, Joan P (Composer)
Bard College
Music Dept
Annandale-On-Hudson, NY 12504, USA

Tower of Power
654 N Sepulveda Blvd Ste 14
Los Angeles, CA 90049-2171, USA

Towers, Constance (Actor)
2100 Century Park W # 10263
Los Angeles, CA 90067-6900, USA

Towers, Kenneth (Editor)
Chicago Sun-Times
350 N Orleans St Ste 1270
Editorial Dept
Chicago, IL 60654-2148, USA

Towle, Stephen R (Steve) (Football Player)
Miami Dolphins
609 NE Lake Pointe Dr
Lees Summit, MO 64064-1193, USA

Towles, Tom (Actor)
c/o Craig Dorfman *Blueprint Management*
5670 Wilshire Blvd Ste 2525
Los Angeles, CA 90036-5647, USA

Town, Crazy (Musician)
c/o Staff Member *Creative Artists Agency LCC (CAA-LA)*
2000 Avenue Of The Stars
Los Angeles, CA 90067-4700, USA

Towne, Katharine (Actor)
United Talent Agency
9560 Wilshire Blvd Ste 500
Beverly Hills, CA 90212-2401, USA

Towne, Robert (Director, Writer)
1417 San Remo Dr
Pacific Palisades, CA 90272, USA

Towner, Ralph N (Musician)
Ted Kurtland
173 Brighton Ave
Boston, MA 02134-2003, USA

Townes, Charles H (Nobel Prize Laureate)
1988 San Antonio Ave
Berkeley, CA 94707-1620, USA

Townes, Willie (Football Player)
Dallas Cowboys
5714 Logancraft Dr
Dallas, TX 75227-2847, USA

Towns, Bobby (Football Player)
St Louis Cardinals
1351 Jennings Mill Rd Unit A
Bogart, GA 30622-2537, USA

Towns, Morris (Football Player)
Houston Oilers
127 S Defiance St
West Unity, OH 43570, USA

Townsell, Jo Jo (Football Player)
New York Jets
1857 Borda Way
Gardnerville, NV 89410-6679, USA

Townsend, Andre (Football Player)
Denver Broncos
6206 Providence Club Dr
Mableton, GA 30126-3697, USA

Townsend, Colleen (Actor)
National Presbyterian Church
4101 Nebraska Ave NW
Washington, DC 20016-2793, USA

Townsend, John W Jr (Scientist)
6532 79th St
Cabin John, MD 20818-1201, USA

Townsend, Robert (Actor, Director, Producer, Writer)
c/o Staff Member *Black Family Television Network*
800 Forrest St NW
Atlanta, GA 30318-7620, USA

Townsend, Roscoe (Religious Leader)
Evangelical Friends
2018 Maple St
Wichita, KS 67213-3314, USA

Townsend, Stuart (Actor)
c/o Vanessa Pereira *Artists Independent Management (LA)*
825 Nowita Pl
Venice, CA 90291-3836, USA

Townsend, Tammy (Actor)
c/o Marni Goldman *Abrams Artists Agency (LA)*
9200 W Sunset Blvd Ph 11
Los Angeles, CA 90069-3601, USA

Townshend, Pete
The Boathouse Ranelagh Dr.
Twickenham, ENGLAND TW1 1Q2,
UNITED KINGDOM (UK)

Townshend, Peter D B (Musician, Songwriter, Writer)
Boathouse
Ranelagh Dr
Twickenham, Middx TW1 1QZ, UNITED
KINGDOM (UK)

Toya (Musician)
c/o Staff Member *CEG*
485 Madison Ave Fl 21
New York, NY 10022-5812, USA

Toye, Wendy (Ballerina, Choreographer)
London Mgmt
2-4 Noel St
London W1V 3RB, UNITED KINGDOM
(UK)

Toyoda, Shoichiro (Business Person)
Keidanren
1-9-4 Ohtemachi
Chuyodaku
Tokyo 100, JAPAN

Tozzi, Giorgio (Opera Singer)
BMG Ricordi SpA
Via Berchet 2
Milan 20100, ITALY

Tozzi, Umberto
Heussweg 25
Hamburg D-20255, GERMANY

Traa (Musician)
East West America Records
75 Rockefeller Plz
New York, NY 10019-6908, USA

Trabert, M Anthony (Tony) (Tennis Player)
115 Knotty Pine Trl
Ponte Vedra Beach, FL 32082-3024, USA

Trabert, Tony
115 Knotty Pine Trl
Ponte Vedra, FL 32082-3024, USA

Tracey, Margaret (Ballerina)
New York City Ballet
Lincoln Center Plaza
New York, NY 10023, USA

Trachsel, Stephen P (Steve) (Baseball Player)
4141 Ricardo Dr
Yorba Linda, CA 92886-1924, USA

Trachta, Jeff (Actor)
PO Box 124
Skyforest, CA 92385-0124, USA

Trachte, Don (Cartoonist)
King Features Syndicate
888 7th Ave Ste 201
New York, NY 10106-0201, USA

Trachtenberg, Lyle
18619 Collins St Apt F7
Tarzana, CA 91356-2169, USA

Trachtenberg, Michelle (Actor)
c/o Maryellen Mulcahy *Framework Entertainment (LA)*
9057 Nemo St # C
W Hollywood, CA 90069-5511, USA

Trachtenberg, Stephen J (Educator)
George Washington University
President's Office
Washington, DC 20052-0001, USA

Tracy, Brian (Business Person, Writer)
Brian Tracy International
462 Stevens Ave Ste 202
Solana Beach, CA 92075-2065, USA

Tracy, James E (Jim) (Baseball Player)
4785 Celadon Ave
Fairfield, OH 45014-1709, USA

Tracy, Jeanie (Musician)
c/o Staff Member *Diva Central Inc*
7510 W Sunset Blvd Ste 1445
Los Angeles, CA 90046-3408, USA

Tracy, Keegan Connor (Actor)
SMS Talent
8730 W Sunset Blvd Ste 440
Los Angeles, CA 90069-2277, USA

Tracy, Michael C (Dancer, Director)
Pilobolus Dance Theater
PO Box 388
Washington Depot, CT 06794-0388, USA

Tracy, Paul (Race Car Driver)
Hogan Penske Racing
PO Box 500
Mooresville, NC 28115-0500, USA

Trafficant, James (Politician)
125 Market St
Youngstown, OH 44503-1780, USA

Trager, Milton (Doctor)
Trager Institute
3800 Park East Dr Ste 100
Beachwood, OH 44122-4322, USA

Train (Musician)
c/o Staff Member *Creative Artists Agency LCC (CAA-LA)*
2000 Avenue Of The Stars
Los Angeles, CA 90067-4700, USA

Train, Harry D II (Admiral)
401 College Pl Apt 10
Norfolk, VA 23510-1130, USA

Train, Russell E (Government Official)
World Wildlife Fund
1250 24th St NW
Washington, DC 20037-1193, USA

Trainor, Bernard E (General)
46874 Grissom St
Sterling, VA 20165-3574, USA

Trainor, Mary Ellen (Actor)
c/o Peg Donegan *Framework Entertainment (LA)*
9057 Nemo St # C
W Hollywood, CA 90069-5511, USA

Trammell, Alan S (Baseball Player)
191 22nd St
Del Mar, CA 92014, USA

Trammell, Terry (Doctor)
Orthopedics-Indianapolis
1801 N Senate Blvd Ste 200
Indianapolis, IN 46202-1230, USA

Tramps, The
102 Ryders Ln
East Brunswick, NJ 08816-1328, USA

Tran, Duc Luong (President)
President's Office
Hoang Hoa Tham St
St Hanoi, VIETNAM

Tranelli, Deborah (Actor, Musician)
c/o Staff Member *Image Entertainment*
20525 Nordhoff St Ste 200
Chatsworth, CA 91311-6104, USA

Trang, Thuy
209 N Kenilworth Ave
Glendale, CA 91203-2418, USA

Trani, Eugene P (Educator)
Virginia Commonwealth University
President's Office
Richmond, VA 23228, USA

Trapilo, Steve (Football Player)
New Orleans Saints
879 Main St
Norwell, MA 02061-2317, USA

Trapt (Music Group)
c/o Staff Member *Zig Zag Communications*
5631 Keokuk Ave
Woodland Hills, CA 91367-5523, USA

Trask, Stephen (Composer)
c/o Brice Gaeta *Broder Webb Chervin Silbermann Agency, The (BWCS)*
10250 Constellation Blvd Ste P
Los Angeles, CA 90067-6213, USA

Trask, Thomas E (Religious Leader)
Assemblies of God
1445 N Boonville Ave
Springfield, MO 65802-1894, USA

Traub, Charles (Photographer)
39 E 10th St
New York, NY 10003-6154, USA

Trauth, AJ (Actor)
c/o Aron Giannini *The Collective*
9100 Wilshire Blvd # 700 W
Beverly Hills, CA 90212-3401, USA

Trautmann, Richard (Athlete)
Horemansstr 29
Munich 80636, GERMANY

Trautwig, Al (Sportscaster)
ABC-TV
77 W 66th St
Sports Dept
New York, NY 10023-6201, USA

Travalena, Fred (Actor, Comedian)
4515 White Oak Pl
Encino, CA 91316-4334, USA

Travanti, Daniel J (Actor)
1077 Mellody Rd
Lake Forest, IL 60045-1547, USA

Travers, Mary (Musician)
Fritz/Byers Mgmt
1455 N Doheny Dr
Los Angeles, CA 90069-1109, USA

Travers, Pat (Musician)
ARM
1257 Arcade St
Saint Paul, MN 55106-2022, USA

Travis (Music Group)
c/o Staff Member *Helter Skelter (UK)*
535 Kings Rd
The Plaza
London SW10 0SZ, UNITED KINGDOM (UK)

Travis, Cecil H (Baseball Player)
201 Big Meadows Ct
Canton, GA 30114-4352, USA

Travis, Kylie (Actor, Model)
1196 Summit Dr
Beverly Hills, CA 90210-2248, USA

Travis, Mack (Football Player)
Detroit Lions
605 Holland Ave
Las Vegas, NV 89106-2651, USA

Travis, Nancy (Actor)
231 S Cliffwood Ave
Los Angeles, CA 90049-3823, USA

Travis, Randy (Director, Musical Director, Songwriter, Writer)
Elizabeth Travis Mgmt
1610 16th Ave S
Nashville, TN 37212-2908, USA

Travis, Stacey (Actor)
c/o Brian Alexander *Essential Talent Management*
6399 Wilshire Blvd Ste 400
Los Angeles, CA 90048-5716, USA

Travis-Visich, Gene (Baseball Player)
777 Wearimus Road
Westwood, NJ 07675, USA

Travolta, Ellen (Actor)
6470 E Sunnyside Rd
Coeur D Alene, ID 83814-9503, USA

Travolta, Joey
4975 Chimineas Ave
Tarzana, CA 91356-4301, USA

Travolta, John (Actor)
c/o Randi Michel *William Morris Agency (WMA-LA)*
1 William Morris Pl
Beverly Hills, CA 90212-4261, USA

Traxier, Brian (Baseball Player)
Los Angeles Dodgers
363 Sutton Dr
San Antonio, TX 78228-3122, USA

Traya, Misti (Actor)
c/o Holly Lebed *Himber Entertainment Inc*
15760 Ventura Blvd Ste 700
Encino, CA 91436-3016, USA

Trayham, Jerry (Football Player)
Denver Broncos
6606 S Tomaker Ln
Spokane, WA 99223-6202, USA

Traylor, B Keith (Football Player)
Chicago Bears
1000 Football Dr
Lake Forest, IL 60045-4829, USA

Traylor, Keith (Football Player)
Denver Broncos
11043 S 4317
Chouteau, OK 74337-6063, USA

Traylor, Robert (Basketball Player)
New Orleans Hornets
1250 Poydras St # 19
New Orleans Arena
New Orleans, LA 70113-1804, USA

Traylor, Susan (Actor)
Propaganda Films Mgmt
1741 Ivar Ave
Los Angeles, CA 90028-5105, USA

Traynham, Wade (Football Player)
Atlanta Falcons
PO Box 176
Wake, VA 23176-0176, USA

Traynor, Jay (Musician)
Jet Music
17 Pauline Ct
Rensselaer, NY 12144-9780, USA

Traynowicz, Mark (Football Player)
Buffalo Bills
8000 Alimark Ln
Lincoln, NE 68516-4095, USA

Traywick, Joel
10100 Santa Monica Blvd Ste 2490
Los Angeles, CA 90067-4144, USA

Treach (Musician)
International Creative Mgmt
8942 Wilshire Blvd # 219
Beverly Hills, CA 90211-1908, USA

Treacy, Philip (Designer, Fashion Designer)
Philip Treacy Ltd
69 Elizabeth St
London SW1W 9PJ, UNITED KINGDOM (UK)

Treadaway, John (Football Player)
New York Giants
3140 N 83rd Ave
Phoenix, AZ 85033-4724, USA

Treadway, Edward A (Politician)
Elevator Constructors Union
5565 Sterrett Pl
Columbia, MD 21044-2665, USA

Treadway, James C Jr (Government Official)
Laurel Ledge Farm
Croton Lake Road
RR 4
Mount Kisco, NY 10549, USA

Treadway, Jeff (Baseball Player)
Cincinnati Reds
345 West Rd
Williamson, GA 30292, USA

Treadway, Kenneth (Misc)
Phillips Petroleum Co
Adams Building
Bartlesville, OK 74003, USA

Treadway, Nick (Baseball Player)
1442 Bishop Dr
Troy, MO 63379-3336, USA

Treadway, Ty (Actor)
c/o Frank Gonzales *The Agency (CA)*
3711 Ocean Front Walk # 1
Marina Del Rey, CA 90292-5705, USA

Treadwell, David (Football Player)
Denver Broncos
5445 Dtc Pkey Ste 800
Greenwood Village, CO 80111, USA

Trebek, Alex (Entertainer)
3405 Fryman Rd
Studio City, CA 91604-4119, USA

Trebelhorn, Thomas L (Tom) (Baseball Player)
333 W Camden St
Baltimore, MD 21201-2435, USA

Trebunskaya, Anna (Dancer, Reality TV Star)
c/o Staff Member *ABC Television Network (LA)*
500 S Buena Vista St
Burbank, CA 91521-0001, USA

Tree, Michael (Musician)
45 E 89th St
New York, NY 10128-1251, USA

Treen, David C (Governor)
Deutsch Kerrigan Stile
755 Magazine St
New Orleans, LA 70130-3629, USA

Trefilov, Andrei
Calgary Flames
PO Box 1540
Station M
Calgary, AB T2P 3B9, CANADA

Trejo, Danny (Actor)
Amsel Eisenstadt & Frazier
5055 Wilshire Blvd Ste 860
Los Angeles, CA 90036-6108, USA

Trejos, Fernandez Jose J (President)
Apartado 10 096
San Jose 1000, COSTA RICA

Trelford, Donald G (Editor)
15 Fowler Road
London N1 2EA, UNITED KINGDOM (UK)

Tremblay, Mario (Coach, Hockey Player)
714 Mistassini
Lachenaie, PQ J6W 5H2, CANADA

Tremblay, Michel (Writer)
294 Carre Saint Louis
#5E
Montreal, PQ H2X 1A4, CANADA

Tremel, Bill (Baseball Player)
Chicago Cubs
315 E 23rd Ave
Altoona, PA 16601-4002, USA

Tremie, Chris (Baseball Player)
Chicago White Sox
PO Box 1357
New Waverly, TX 77358-1357, USA

Tremko, Anne
10100 Santa Monica Blvd Ste 2500
Los Angeles, CA 90067-4116, USA

Tremlett, David R (Artist)
Broadlawns
Chipperfield Road
Bovingdon, Herts, UNITED KINGDOM (UK)

Tremont, Ray C (Religious Leader)
Volunteers of America
3939 N Causeway Blvd Ste 400
Metairie, LA 70002-1777, USA

Trendy, Bobby (Designer)
c/o Darryl Marshak *Marshak/Zachary Company, The*
8840 Wilshire Blvd Fl 1
Beverly Hills, CA 90211-2606, USA

Trenhaile, John
4 Wailands Crescent Lewes
E. Sussex, ENGLAND BNT 2QT, UNITED KINGDOM (UK)

Treniers, The
520 N Camden Dr
Beverly Hills, CA 90210-3202, USA

Trent, Buck (Musician)
Buck Trent Breakfast Theater
118 Hampshire Dr
Branson, MO 65616-3765, USA

Trenyce (Reality TV Star)
c/o Staff Member *Diva Central Inc*
7510 W Sunset Blvd Ste 1445
Los Angeles, CA 90046-3408, USA

Treschev, Sergei Y (Cosmonaut)
Potchta Kosmonavtov
Moskovskoi Oblasti
Syvisdny Goroduk 141160, RUSSIA

Trese, Adam
8912 Burton Way
Beverly Hills, CA 90211-1707, USA

Tresh, Tom (Baseball Player)
New York Yankees
1751 Waxwing Cir
Venice, FL 34293-1461, USA

Tressel, Jim (Coach, Football Coach)
Ohio State University
Athletic Dept
Columbus, OH 43210, USA

Trestman, Marc (Football Player)
Minnesota Vikings
PO Box 888
Arizona Cardinals Attn Coaching Staff
Phoenix, AZ 85001-0888, USA

Tretlak, Vladislav (Coach, Hockey Player)
Transglobal Sports
94 Festival Dr
Toronto, ON M2R 3V1, CANADA

Tretyak, Ivan (General)
Ministry of Defense
34 Manerezhnaya M Thoreza
Moscow, RUSSIA

Treu, Adam (Football Player)
Oakland Raiders
556 Creedon Cir
Alameda, CA 94502-7794, USA

Trevanian (Writer)
Jove Books
375 Hudson St
Berkeley Publishing Group
New York, NY 10014-3658, USA

Trever, John (Cartoonist, Editor)
Albuquerque Journal
717 Silver Ave SW
Editorial Dept
Albuquerque, NM 87102, USA

Treves, Frederick
5 St. Catherine's Mews Milner St.
London, ENGLAND SW3 2PX, UNITED KINGDOM (UK)

Trevi, Gloria (Musician)
Leisil Entertainment
Avenida Parque 67 Napoles
Mexico City, DF 03810, MEXICO

Trevino, Alex (Baseball Player)
New York Mets
PO Box 288
Houston, TX 77001-0288, USA

Trevino, Lee B (Golfer)
1901 W 47th Pl Ste 200
Westwood, KS 66205-1834, USA

Trevino, Rick (Musician)
William Morris Agency
1600 Division St Ste 300
Nashville, TN 37203-2755, USA

Trevor, William (Writer)
P F D
Drury House
34-43 Russell St
London WC2B 5HA, UNITED KINGDOM (UK)

Trezza, Betty (Baseball Player)
31 Orient Ave
Brooklyn, NY 11211-2502, USA

Triandos, C Gus (Baseball Player)
New York Yankees
PO Box 5642
San Jose, CA 95150-5642, USA

Trias, Jasmine (Musician)
c/o Staff Member *American Idol*
7800 Beverly Blvd # 251
Los Angeles, CA 90036-2112, USA

Tribbett, Tye (Musician)
c/o Staff Member *Sony Music International*
550 Madison Ave Fl 6
New York, NY 10022-3211, USA

Tribbitt, Sherman W (Governor)
11 Stockley St
Rehoboth Beach, DE 19971-2921, USA

Tribe, Laurence H (Attorney, Attorney General, Educator, General)
Harvard University
Law School
Griswold Hall
Cambridge, MA 02138, USA

Trible, Paul S Jr (Educator, Senator)
Christopher Newport University
50 University Pl
Newport News, VA 23606-2949, USA

Trichter, Judd
10264 Rochester Ave
Los Angeles, CA 90024-5331, USA

Trick, Cheap (Musician)
c/o Staff Member *Paradigm (Monterey)*
509 Hartnell St
Monterey, CA 93940-2825, USA

Trick Daddy (Music Group)
c/o Staff Member *Atlantic Recording Corporation*
1290 Avenue Of The Americas
New York, NY 10104-0184, USA

Trickey, Paula
PO Box 261098
Encino, CA 91426-1098, USA

Trickle, Dick (Race Car Driver)
c/o Donlavey Racing
5011 Old Midlothian Tpke
Richmond, VA 23224-1119, USA

Trickle, Dick (Race Car Driver)
PO Box 645
Skyland, NC 28776-0645, USA

Trickside (Music Group)
c/o Staff Member *Wind-up Records*
72 Madison Ave Fl 8
New York, NY 10016-8731, USA

Triffle, Carol (Director)
Imago Theater
PO Box 15182
Portland, OR 97293-5182, USA

Trigg, Alex (Baseball Player)
Detroit Stars
900 Turner Ln
Shreveport, LA 71106-4528, USA

Trigger, Sarah (Actor)
Paradigm Agency
10100 Santa Monica Blvd Ste 2500
Los Angeles, CA 90067-4116, USA

Triggs, Trini
3178 Allen Marthaville Rd
Robeline, LA 71469-4528, USA

Trillin, Calvin M (Writer)
New Yorker Magazine
4 Times Sq
Editorial Dept
New York, NY 10036-6592, USA

Trimble, David (Nobel Prize Laureate)
2 Queen St
Lurgen
County Arnagh BT66 8BQ, NORTHERN IRELAND

Trimble, Joe (Baseball Player)
Boston Red Sox
14 Fair Oaks Dr
Lincoln, RI 02865-4520, USA

Trimble, Vance H (Editor)
25 Oakhurst St
Wewoka, OK 74884-3714, USA

Trimble, Vivian (Musician)
Metropolitan Entertainment
2 Penn Plz # 2600
New York, NY 10121-0101, USA

Trina (Musician)
c/o Staff Member *Pyramid Entertainment Group*
377 Rector Pl Apt 21A
New York, NY 10280-1439, USA

Trineer, Connor (Actor)
c/o Gregg A Klein *Abrams Artists Agency (LA)*
9200 W Sunset Blvd Ph 11
Los Angeles, CA 90069-3601, USA

Trinh, Eugene (Astronaut)
NASA Headquarters
300 E St SW
Washington, DC 20546-0005, USA

Trinidad, Felix (Tito) (Boxer)
RR 6 Box 11479
Rio Piedras, PR 00926-9505, USA

Trintignant, Jean-Louis (Actor)
Artmedia
20 Ave Rapp
Paris 75007, FRANCE

Triola, Michelle
23215 Mariposa De Oro St
Malibu, CA 90265-4909, USA

Triple H (Wrestler)
c/o Staff Member *Braverman/Bloom Company*
6399 Wilshire Blvd Ste 901
Los Angeles, CA 90048-5712, USA

Triplet, Kirk (Golfer)
8141 E Overlook Dr
Scottsdale, AZ 85255-6481, USA

Triplett, Wally (Football Player)
Detroit Lions
4250 Fullerton St
Detroit, MI 48238-3235, USA

Tripp, Linda
27285 Boyce Mill Rd
Greensboro, MD 21639-1332, USA

Tripp, Valerie (Writer)
Pleasant Company Publications
PO Box 620991
Middleton, WI 53562-0991, USA

Trippi, Charles L (Charlie) (Football Player)
125 Riverhill Ct
Athens, GA 30606-4034, USA

Tripplehorn, Jeanne (Actor)
c/o Cynthia Pett-Dante *Brillstein-Grey Entertainment*
9150 Wilshire Blvd Ste 350
Beverly Hills, CA 90212-3453, USA

Tripplett, Larry (Football Player)
Indianapolis Colts
5324 Overdale Dr
Los Angeles, CA 90043-2023, USA

Tripucka, Frank (Football Player)
Philadelphia Eagles
23 Avon Dr
Essex Fells, NJ 07021-1717, USA

Tripucka, Kelly (Basketball Player)
14 Devon Rd
Boonton, NJ 07005-9305, USA

Tritt, Travis (Actor, Musician)
c/o Bobby Cudd *Paradigm (Nashville)*
124 12th Ave S Ste 410
Nashville, TN 37203-3170, USA

Trivium (Music Group)
c/o Staff Member *Roadrunner Records Inc*
902 Broadway Fl 8
New York, NY 10010-6037, USA

Trixter
210 Westfield Ave
Clark, NJ 07066-1539, USA

Trlicek, Rick (Baseball Player)
Toronto Blue Jays
PO Box 1109
La Grange, TX 78945-1109, USA

Troccoll, Kathy (Musician, Songwriter, Writer)
William Morris Agency
1600 Division St Ste 300
Nashville, TN 37203-2755, USA

Troche, Rose (Actor, Director, Producer, Writer)
c/o Staff Member *Gersh Agency, The (NY)*
41 Madison Ave Fl 33
New York, NY 10010-2202, USA

Troedson, Rich (Baseball Player)
San Diego Padres
899 Bowen Ave
San Jose, CA 95123-5303, USA

Troger, Christian-Alexander (Swimmer)
I Muncher SC
Josefstr 26
Deisenhofen 82941, GERMANY

Troisgros, Pierre E R (Business Person)
Place Jean Troisgros
Roanne 42300, FRANCE

Troitskaya, Natalia L (Opera Singer)
Klostergasse 37
Vienna 1170, AUSTRIA

Troliope, Joanna (Writer)
P F D
Drury House
34-43 Russell St
London WC2B 5HA, UNITED KINGDOM (UK)

Trombley, Mike (Baseball Player)
Minnesota Twins
15800 Glenisle Way
Fort Myers, FL 33912-3923, USA

Trondheim, Lewis (Artist)
c/o Staff Member *Fantagraphics Books*
7563 Lake City Way NE
Seattle, WA 98115-4218, USA

Trone, Roland (Don) (Musician)
Mars Talent
27 L Ambiance Ct
Bardonia, NY 10954-1421, USA

Tronnier, Ellen (Baseball Player)
328 Anemone Ave
Palmyra, WI 53156-9326, USA

Trosch, Gene (Football Player)
Kansas City Chiefs
6393 Oak Tree Dr
Mc Calla, AL 35111-3926, USA

Trosky Jr, Hal (Baseball Player)
Cleveland Indians
1414 Curtis Bridge Rd NE
Swisher, IA 52338-9588, USA

Trosper, Jennifer Harris (Scientist)
Jet Propulsion Laboratory
4800 Oak Grove Dr
Pasadena, CA 91109-8001, USA

Trost, Barry M (Scientist)
24510 Amigos Ct
Los Altos Hills, CA 94024-4773, USA

Trost, Carlisle A H (Admiral)
11 Compromise St
Annapolis, MD 21401-1806, USA

Trott, Stephen S (Judge)
US Court of Appeals
US Courthouse
550 W Fort St
Boise, ID 83724-0001, USA

Trotter, Jeremiah (Football Player)
Philadelphia Eagles
1299 Route 38 Ste 2
Hainesport, NJ 08036-2791, USA

Trottier, Bryan
3868 Forest Dr
Doylestown, PA 18902-8100, USA

Trottier, Bryan J (Coach, Hockey Player)
356 Birdsong Way
Doylestown, PA 18901-4885, USA

Trouble, Valli (Musician)
Q Prime
729 7th Ave Rm 1600
New York, NY 10019-6880, USA

Troup, Bill (Football Player)
Baltimore Colts
4 Quail Wood Ct
Parkton, MD 21120-9444, USA

Troup, Tom
8829 Ashcroft Ave
West Hollywood, CA 90048-2401, USA

Trousdale, Chris (Actor, Musician)
c/o Staff Member *Adonis Productions*
175 Skillman St
Brooklyn, NY 11205-3901, USA

Trout, David (Football Player)
Pittsburgh Steelers
408 Paddock Ct
Sewell, NJ 08080-2509, USA

Trout, Steve (Baseball Player)
Chicago White Sox
PO Box 1155
Tinley Park, IL 60477-7955, USA

Troutt, William E (Educator)
Belmont University
President's Office
Nashville, TN 37212, USA

Trova, Ernest T (Artist)
6 Laylon Terrace
Saint Louis, MO 63124, USA

Trowbridge, Alexander B Jr (Secretary)
1823 23rd St NW
Washington, DC 20008-4030, USA

Trower, Robin (Musician)
Stardust Enterprises
4600 Franklin Ave
Los Angeles, CA 90027-4202, USA

Troxel, Gary
11471 Earle Dr
Mount Vernon, WA 98273-7261, USA

Troy, Donald (Baseball Player)
Baltimore Elite Giants
2603 Kinoole St
Hilo, HI 96720-5744, USA

Troyat, Henri (Writer)
Academie Francaise
23 Quai de Conti
Paris 75006, FRANCE

Troyer, Verne (Actor)
c/o Elaina Bertnolli *Fonolli Management*
11218 Osborne St
Lake View Terrace, CA 91342-6604, USA

Truax, Billy (Football Player)
Los Angeles Rams
735 Ruth Ave
Gulfport, MS 39501-1056, USA

Truax, Dalton (Football Player)
Oakland Raiders
77 Chateau Magdelaine Dr
Kenner, LA 70065-2026, USA

Truby, Chris (Baseball Player)
Houston Astros
12244 Silverado Dr
Fishers, IN 46037-8328, USA

Trucco, Micheal (Actor)
c/o Staff Member *Abrams Artists Agency (LA)*
9200 W Sunset Blvd Ph 11
Los Angeles, CA 90069-3601, USA

Trucks, Virgil O (Fire) (Baseball Player)
Detroit Tigers
1016 Waterford Trl
Calera, AL 35040-7613, USA

Trudeau, Garry (Cartoonist)
459 Columbus Ave # 200
New York, NY 10024-5129, USA

Trudeau, Jack F (Football Player)
Indianapolis Colts
9150 Timberwolf Ln
Zionsville, IN 46077-8320, USA

Trudeau, Kevin (Writer)
PO Box 342
Elk Grove Village, IL 60009-0342, USA

True, Rachel (Actor)
c/o Lorrie Bartlett *Gersh Agency, The (LA)*
232 N Canon Dr
Beverly Hills, CA 90210-5302, USA

True Vibe (Music Group)
c/o Staff Member *Creative Artists Agency LCC (CAA-LA)*
2000 Avenue Of The Stars
Los Angeles, CA 90067-4700, USA

Trueco, Michael (Actor)
c/o Staff Member *Raw Talent Management*
9615 Brighton Way Ste 300
Beverly Hills, CA 90210-5118, USA

Truesdale, Yanic (Actor)
c/o Nancy Iannios *Nancy Iannios PR*
PO Box 430
Signal Mountain, TN 37377-0430, USA

Trufant, Marcus (Football Player)
Seattle Seahawks
11220 NE 53rd St
Kirkland, WA 98033-7595, USA

Truhitte, Dan
4630 Sapp Rd
Concord, NC 28025-1567, USA

Truitt, Anne D (Artist)
29 Boutonville Rd
South Salem, NY 10590-1517, USA

Truitt, Olanda (Football Player)
Minnesota Vikings
1901 16th Way N
Bessemer, AL 35020-3930, USA

Trujillo, Mike (Baseball Player)
Boston Red Sox
2019 S Townsend Ave
Montrose, CO 81401-5444, USA

Trujillo, Solomon D (Business Person)
US West Inc
1801 California St
Denver, CO 80202-2658, USA

Trull, Don (Football Player)
Houston Oilers
8706 Bloomfield Turn
Missouri City, TX 77459-6042, USA

Truly, Richard N (Admiral, Astronaut)
2340 Juniper Ct
Golden, CO 80401-8087, USA

Truman, Dan (Musician)
Dreamcatcher Artists Mgmt
2908 Poston Ave
Nashville, TN 37203-1312, USA

Truman, James (Editor)
Conde Nast Publications
4 Times Sq
Editorial Dept
New York, NY 10036-6561, USA

Trumbo, Karen (Actor)
c/o Staff Member *Creative Artists Management (OR)*
909 SW Saint Clair Ave
Portland, OR 97205-1300, USA

Trumka, Richard L (Politician)
AFL-CIO
1750 New York Ave NW
Washington, DC 20006-5301, USA

Trump, Blaine
166 Avenue Of The Americas
New York, NY 10013-1207, USA

Trump, Donald J (Business Person, Reality TV Star)
c/o Staff Member *Trump Organization*
725 5th Ave
New York, NY 10022-2519, USA

Trump, Ivana (Business Person, Model)
c/o Staff Member *William Morris Agency (WMA-LA)*
1 William Morris Pl
Beverly Hills, CA 90212-4261, USA

Trump, Ivanka (Business Person, Heir/Heiress)
c/o *The Trump Corp*
725 5th Ave Ste 2401
New York, NY 10022-2564, USA

Trump, Melania (Model)
c/o Marc Beckman *Designers Management Agency*
446 Broadway Fl 4
New York, NY 10013-2546, USA

Trumpy, Robert T (Bob) Jr (Football Player, Sportscaster)
Cincinnati Bengals
75 Oak St
Cincinnati, OH 45246-4437, USA

Trundy, Natalie (Actor)
2109 S Wilbur Ave
Walla Walla, WA 99362-9048, USA

Truran, James W Jr (Physicist)
210 Wysteria Dr
Olympia Fields, IL 60461-1202, USA

Truscott, Lucian K IV (Writer)
Avon/William Morrow
1350 Avenue Of The Americas
New York, NY 10019-4702, USA

Truth, Hurts (Actor, Songwriter, Writer)
Aftermath/Interscope Records
2220 Colorado Ave
Santa Monica, CA 90404-3506, USA

Truvillion, Eric (Football Player)
Detroit Lions
10436 Saint Tropez Pl
Tampa, FL 33615-4213, USA

Tryba, Ted (Golfer)
6321 Cheryl St
Orlando, FL 32819-7511, USA

Tryon, Ty (Golfer)
c/o Staff Member *Pro Golfers Association (PGA) Tour*
112 Tpc Blvd
Ponte Vedra Beach, FL 32082, USA

Tsai, Cheryl (Actor)
c/o Gloria Hinojosa *Amsel Eisenstadt & Frazier Inc*
5055 Wilshire Blvd Ste 865
Los Angeles, CA 90036-6109, USA

Tsakalidis, Iakovos (Jake) (Basketball Player)
Memphis Grizzlies
191 Beale St
Memphis, TN 38103-3715, USA

Tsamis, George (Baseball Player)
Minnesota Twins
12 Sweetbriar Ct
Colchester, CT 06415-1887, USA

Tsang, Bion (Musician)
Columbia Artists Mgmt Inc
1790 Broadway Fl 6
New York, NY 10019-1412, USA

Tsantiris, Len (Football Player)
University of Connecticut
Athletic Dept
Storrs Mansfield, CT, USA

Tschechowa, Vera
Gosslerstr 2
Berlin D-12161, GERMANY

Tschida, Tim (Baseball Player)
274 15 1/2 Ave
Turtle Lake, WI 54889-8825, USA

Tschumi, Bernard (Architect)
7 Rue Pecquay
Paris 75004, FRANCE

Tsibliyev, Vasili V (Cosmonaut)
Potchta Kosmonavtov
Moskovskoi Oblasti
Syvisdny Goroduk 141160, RUSSIA

Tsitouris, John (Baseball Player)
Detroit Tigers
5207 Austin Rd
Monroe, NC 28112-7948, USA

Tskitishvili, Nikoloz (Basketball Player)
Denver Nuggets
1000 Chopper Cir
Pepsi Center
Denver, CO 80204-5805, USA

Tsoucalas, Nicholas (Judge)
US Court of International Trade
1 Federal Plz
New York, NY 10278-0001, USA

Tsu, Irene
3349 Cahuenga Blvd W Ste 1
Los Angeles, CA 90068-1379, USA

Tsui, Daniel C (Nobel Prize Laureate)
53 College Rd W
Princeton, NJ 08540-5049, USA

Tu, Francesa
Beethovenstr. 48
Sarstedt D-31157, GERMANY

Tuanku, Salehuddin Abdul Aziz Shah (King, Royalty)
Sultan's Palace
Istana Bukit Serene
Kuala Lumpur 50502, MALAYSIA

Tuaolo, Esera (Football Player)
6520 Promontory Dr
Eden Prairie, MN 55346-1915, USA

Tubbs, Billy (Coach)
Lamar University
Athletic Dept
Beaumont, TX 77710, USA

Tubbs, Gerald J (Jerry) (Football Player)
Chicago Cardinals
3813 Centenary Ave
Dallas, TX 75225-5226, USA

Tubbs, Greg (Baseball Player)
Cincinnati Reds
114 Hunter Ave
Cookeville, TN 38501-2236, USA

Tubbs, Winfred (Football Player)
New Orleans Saints
RR 1 Box 800
Oakwood, TX 75855, USA

Tubert, Marcelo (Actor)
c/o Staff Member *Richard Schwartz Management*
2934 1/2 N Beverly Glen Cir # 107
Los Angeles, CA 90077-1724, USA

Tuberville, Tommy (Coach, Football Coach)
Auburn University
Athletic Dept
Auburn University, AL 36849-0001, USA

Tubes, The
903 10th Ave. So.
Nashville, TN 37212, USA

Tucci, Michael (Actor)
1425 Irving Ave
Glendale, CA 91201-1274, USA

Tucci, Roberto Cardinal (Religious Leader)
Palazzo Pio
Piazza Pia 3
Rome 00193, ITALY

Tucci, Stanley (Actor, Director)
Creative Artists Agency
9830 Wilshire Blvd
Beverly Hills, CA 90212-1804, USA

Tuchman, Maurice (Misc)
150 E 57th St Ph 1A
New York, NY 10022-2783, USA

Tuck, Jessica (Actor)
Brett Adams
448 W 44th St
New York, NY 10036-5220, USA

Tucker, Barbara (Musician)
c/o Staff Member *Diva Central Inc*
7510 W Sunset Blvd Ste 1445
Los Angeles, CA 90046-3408, USA

Tucker, Bill (Boxer)
26126 Meadowcrest Blvd
Huntington Woods, MI 48070-1534, USA

Tucker, Chris (Actor, Comedian)
c/o Tracy Krammer *Toltec Artists*
6353 W Sunset Blvd
Hollywood, CA 90028-7317, USA

Tucker, Corin (Musician)
Legends of 21st Century
7 Trinity Row
Florence, MA 01062-1931, USA

Tucker, Eddie (Baseball Player)
Houston Astros
PO Box 283
Boyle, MS 38730-0283, USA

Tucker, Elizabeth (Baseball Player)
4037 N Fremont Ave
Tucson, AZ 85719-1065, USA

Tucker, Ira Sr (Musician)
Thrill Entertainment Group
10809 Dapple Way
Bakersfield, CA 93312-4148, USA

Tucker, Jason (Football Player)
Dallas Cowboys
620 Remington Park
Robinson, TX 76706-7255, USA

Tucker, Marcia (Misc)
New Museum of Contemporary Art
583 Broadway
New York, NY 10012-3211, USA

Tucker, Marshall Band
315 S Beverly Dr Ste 206
Beverly Hills, CA 90212-4310, USA

Tucker, Michael (Actor)
PO Box 843
Santa Ynez, CA 93460-0843, USA

Tucker, Michael (Baseball Player)
Kansas City Royals
407 Maple Ave N
Lehigh Acres, FL 33972-4001, USA

Tucker, Rex (Football Player)
Chicago Bears
2300 Culpeper Dr
Midland, TX 79705-6314, USA

Tucker, Robert L (Bob) Jr (Football Player)
New York Giants
8 Hunter Rd
Hazleton, PA 18201-6817, USA

Tucker, Tanya (Musician)
c/o Staff Member *William Morris Agency (WMA-LA)*
1 William Morris Pl
Beverly Hills, CA 90212-4261, USA

Tucker, Tony (Boxer)
Club Prana
1619 E 7th Ave
Ybor City
Tampa, FL 33605-3705, USA

Tucker, Travis (Football Player)
Cleveland Browns
964 Lloyd Rd
Wickliffe, OH 44092-2353, USA

Tucker, Wendell (Football Player)
Los Angeles Rams
2042 E 171st Pl
South Holland, IL 60473-3718, USA

Tucker, William E (Educator)
Texas Christian University
Chancellor's Office
Fort Worth, TX 76129-0001, USA

Tucker, Y Arnold (Football Player)
PO Box 514
Hilbert, WI 54129-0514, USA

Tuckwell, Barry E
13140 Fountain Head Rd
Hagerstown, MD 21742-2839, USA

Tudor, John T (Baseball Player)
Boston Red Sox
5 Nathan Ln
Middleton, MA 01949-1531, USA

Tudyk, Alan (Actor)
c/o Leanne Coronel *Endeavor Agency LLC (LA)*
9601 Wilshire Blvd Fl 3
Beverly Hills, CA 90210-5204, USA

Tueting, Sarah (Hockey Player)
488 Ash St
Winnetka, IL 60093-2604, USA

Tufeld, Dick
11020 Wrightwood Pl
Studio City, CA 91604-3960, USA

Tufts, Bob (Baseball Player)
San Francisco Giants
6738 108th St Apt A27
Forest Hills, NY 11375-2358, USA

Tuggle, Anthony (Football Player)
Pittsburgh Steelers
12345 Plymouth Dr
Baton Rouge, LA 70807-1961, USA

Tuggle, Jessie (Football Player)
Atlanta Falcons
540 Avala Ct
Alpharetta, GA 30022-5576, USA

Tuiasosopo, Marques (Football Player)
Oakland Raiders
5569 Gold Creek Dr
Castro Valley, CA 94552-5442, USA

Tuiasosopo, Peter Navy (Actor)
c/o Harold Gray *Shirley Wilson Agency*
5410 Wilshire Blvd Ste 806
Los Angeles, CA 90036-4267, USA

Tuibahadur, Pun (War Hero)
Victoria Cross Assn
Old Admiralty Building
London SW1A 2BL, UNITED KINGDOM
(UK)

Tuilaepa, Sailele Maljelegaio (Prime
Minister)
Prime Minister's Office
PO Box 193
Apia, SAMOA

Tuinei, Tom (Football Player)
Detroit Lions
714 Kihapai Pl Apt B2
Kailua, HI 96734-2677, USA

Tuipala, Joe (Football Player)
New Orleans Saints
43845 Thornberry Sq Unit 103
Leesburg, VA 20176-3403, USA

Tullis, Willie (Football Player)
Houston Oilers
10018 Knoboak Dr Apt 4
Houston, TX 77080-6445, USA

Tully, Darrow (Publisher)
9862 Bridgeton Dr
Tampa, FL 33626-1802, USA

Tully, Susan
265 Liverpool Rd.
London, ENGLAND N1 1LX, UNITED
KINGDOM (UK)

Tulving, Endel (Misc)
45 Baby Point Crescent
York, ON M6S 2B7, CANADA

Tuman, Jerame (Football Player)
Pittsburgh Steelers
1618 Norman Dr
Sewickley, PA 15143-8557, USA

Tumi, Christian W Cardinal (Religious
Leader)
Archeveche
BP 179
Douala, CAMEROON

Tumulty, Tom (Football Player)
Cincinnati Bengals
167 Woodside Ln
Verona, PA 15147-3425, USA

Tune, Thomas J (Tommy) (Actor, Dancer)
1501 Broadway Ste 1508
New York, NY 10036-5505, USA

Tune, Tommy
222 Park Ave S Apt 12C
New York, NY 10003-1508, USA

Tung, Chee-Hwa (Misc)
Asia Pacific Finance Tower
3 Garden Road
Hong Kong, CHINA

Tunie, Tamara (Actor)
c/o Staff Member *Paradigm (LA)*
360 N Crescent Dr
North Bldg
Beverly Hills, CA 90210-6820, USA

Tunnell, Lee (Baseball Player)
Pittsburgh Pirates
6000 Kingsbridge Dr
Oklahoma City, OK 73162-3208, USA

Tunney, John V (Senator)
304 Chautauqua Blvd
Pacific Palisades, CA 90272-4405, USA

Tunney, Robin (Actor)
Borinstein Oreck Bogart
3172 Dona Susana Dr
Studio City, CA 91604-4356, USA

Tunnick, George (Misc)
National Assn of Female Executives
127 W 24th St
New York, NY 10011-1914, USA

Tupa, Thomas J (Tom) (Football Player)
Phoenix Cardinals
6761 Rivercrest Dr
Brecksville, OH 44141-1072, USA

Tupouto'a (Prince)
Royal Palace
PO Box 6
Nuku'alofa, TONGA

Tupper, James (Actor)
c/o Kelly Duncan *Chasin Agency, The*
8899 Beverly Blvd Ste 716
Los Angeles, CA 90048-2449, USA

Tupper, Jeff (Football Player)
Philadelphia Eagles
3263 W 164th Ter
Stilwell, KS 66085-8822, USA

Turang, Brian (Baseball Player)
Seattle Mariners
3014 McNab Ave
Long Beach, CA 90808-4002, USA

Turco, Marty (Hockey Player)
841 Shorewood Dr
Coppell, TX 75019-5665, USA

Turco, Paige (Actor)
c/o Rhonda Price *Gersh Agency, The (NY)*
41 Madison Ave Fl 33
New York, NY 10010-2202, USA

Turco, Richard P (Scientist)
R&D Assoc
4340 Admiralty Way
Marina Del Rey, CA 90292, USA

Turcotte, Donald L (Don) (Geophysicist,
Physicist)
27104 Middle Golf Dr
El Macero, CA 95618-1054, USA

Turcotte, Jean-Claude Cardinal (Religious
Leader)
1071 Rue de la Cathedrale
Montreal, PQ H2B 2V4, CANADA

Turcotte, Ron (Jockey)
82 Seattle Slew Dr
Howell, NJ 07731-3106, USA

Turgeon, Pierre (Hockey Player)
1075 E Oxford Ln
Englewood, CO 80113-4822, USA

Turin Brakes (Music Group)
c/o Staff Member *Paradigm (Monterey)*
509 Hartnell St
Monterey, CA 93940-2825, USA

Turk, Brian (Actor)
c/o Staff Member *The House of
Representatives*
211 S Beverly Dr Ste 208
Beverly Hills, CA 90212-3879, USA

Turk, Godwin (Football Player)
New York Jets
4309 Memorial Dr
Orange, TX 77632-4420, USA

Turk, Stephen (Cartoonist)
927 Westbourne Dr
Los Angeles, CA 90069-4113, USA

Turkel, Ann (Actor)
10701 Wilshire Blvd Apt 2001
Los Angeles, CA 90024-4445, USA

Turkoglu, Hidayet (Basketball Player)
San Antonio Spurs
1 Sbc Center Pkwy
Alamodome
San Antonio, TX 78219-3604, USA

Turkson, Peter K A Cardinal (Religious
Leader)
Archdiocese
PO Box 112
Cape Coast, GHANA

Turley, Bob (Baseball Player)
St Louis Browns
3327 Duluth Highway 120 Ste 101
Duluth, GA 30096-3334, USA

Turley, Kyle (Football Player)
c/o Staff Member *Saint Louis Rams*
1 Rams Way
Earth City, MO 63045-1525, USA

Turley, Robert L (Bob) (Baseball Player)
11053 Big Canoe
Big Canoe, GA 30143-5142, USA

Turlington, Christy (Model)
15030 Ventura Blvd # 710
Sherman Oaks, CA 91403-5470, USA

Turman, Glynn (Actor, Director,
Musician)
c/o Staff Member *Elkins Management*
8306 Wilshire Blvd # 438
Beverly Hills, CA 90211-2304, USA

Turnage, Mark-Anthony (Composer)
Schott Co
Great Marlborough St
London W1V 2BN, UNITED KINGDOM
(UK)

Turnbow, Scot (Baseball Player)
Anaheim Angels
404 Newbary Ct
Franklin, TN 37069-1848, USA

Turnbull, David (Physicist)
4012 Virgilia St
Chevy Chase, MD 20815-5024, USA

Turnbull, Wendy (Tennis Player)
822 Boylston Dt #203
Chestnut Hill, MA 02467, USA

Turnbull, William (Artist)
Waddington Galleries
11 Cork St
London W1, UNITED KINGDOM (UK)

Turner, Bake (Football Player)
Baltimore Colts
PO Box 277
Alpine, TX 79831-0277, USA

Turner, Bree (Actor)
Osbrink
4343 Lankershim Blvd # 100
North Hollywood, CA 91602-2705, USA

Turner, Cathy (Speed Skater)
251 East Ave
Hilton, NY 14468-1333, USA

Turner, Cecil (Football Player)
Chicago Bears
4820 Scott St
Houston, TX 77004-6417, USA

Turner, Debbye (Doctor)
PO Box 12450
Saint Louis, MO 63132-0150, USA

Turner, Edwin L (Physicist)
Princeton University
Astrophysical Sciences Dept
Princeton, NJ 08544-0001, USA

Turner, Floyd (Football Player)
New Orleans Saints
9626 Garden Row Dr
Sugar Land, TX 77478-1033, USA

Turner, Fred L (Business Person)
McDonald Corp
1 Kroc Dr
McDonald's Plaza
Oak Brook, IL 60523-2275, USA

Turner, Glenn (Business Person)
3801 Wimbledon Dr
Lake Mary, FL 32746-4043, USA

Turner, Grant
PO Box 414
Brentwood, TN 37024-0414, USA

Turner, Guinevere (Actor)
Gersh Agency
41 Madison Ave Ste 3301
New York, NY 10010-2210, USA

Turner, Hamp (Football Player)
430172 Milledge Terrace
Athens, GA 30605, USA

Turner, Herschel (Football Player)
St Louis Cardinals
16622 Equestrian Ln
Chesterfield, MO 63005-4880, USA

Turner, Ike (Musician, Songwriter, Writer)
905 Viewpoint Dr
San Marcos, CA 92078-5414, USA

Turner, James A (Jim) (Football Player)
New York Jets
14155 W 59th Pl
Arvada, CO 80004-3724, USA

Turner, James Jr (Business Person)
General Dynamics
3190 Fairview Park Dr Ste 100
Falls Church, VA 22042-4545, USA

Turner, James T (Judge)
US Claims Court
717 Madison Pl NW
Washington, DC 20439-0001, USA

Turner, Janine (Actor, Model)
c/o Greg Clark *Untitled Entertainment
(LA)*
331 N Maple Dr Fl 3
Beverly Hills, CA 90210-3827, USA

Turner, Jerry (Baseball Player)
San Diego Padres
1935 18th St Apt B
Santa Monica, CA 90404-4732, USA

Turner, Jesse
1502 N 5th St
Boise, ID 83702-3703, USA

Turner, Jim (Actor)
c/o Matt Shapira *David Shapira &
Associates*
193 N Robertson Blvd
Beverly Hills, CA 90211-2103, USA

Turner, John (Football Player)
Minnesota Vikings
3217 Cedar Ave S
Minneapolis, MN 55407-3802, USA

Turner, John N (Prime Minister)
27 Dunice Road
Toronto, ON M4V 2W4, CANADA

Turner, Josh (Musician)
c/o Staff Member *Paradigm (Nashville)*
124 12th Ave S Ste 410
Nashville, TN 37203-3170, USA

Turner, Karri (Actor)
Premiere Artists Agency
1875 Century Park E Ste 2250
Los Angeles, CA 90067-2563, USA

Turner, Kathleen (Actor)
c/o Alan Nierob *Rogers & Cowan PR*
8687 Melrose Ave Ste G700
Pacific Design Center
Los Angeles, CA 90069-5721, USA

Turner, Keena (Coach, Football Coach,
Football Player)
San Francisco 49ers
8200 W Erb Way
Tracy, CA 95304-8896, USA

Turner, Ken (Baseball Player)
California Angels
PO Box 252
San Marcos, CA 92079-0252, USA

Turner, Kevin (Football Player)
New England Patriots
4390 Galen Ct
Birmingham, AL 35242-7466, USA

Turner, Kriss (Producer)
c/o Staff Member *William Morris Agency
(WMA-LA)*
1 William Morris Pl
Beverly Hills, CA 90212-4261, USA

Turner, Kristopher (Actor)
c/o Staff Member *Characters Talent
Agency, The (Toronto)*
8 Elm St 3rd Fl
Toronto, ON M5G 1G7, CANADA

Turner, Lane (Musician)
c/o Staff Member *Paradigm (Monterey)*
509 Hartnell St
Monterey, CA 93940-2825, USA

Turner, Lowri (Actor)
c/o Staff Member *Noel Gay Artists*
19 Denmark St
London WC2H 8NA, UNITED KINGDOM
(UK)

Turner, Marcus (Football Player)
Phoenix Cardinals
5032 Meadow Wood Ave
Lakewood, CA 90712-2855, USA

Turner, Matt (Baseball Player)
Florida Marlins
829 Della Dr
Lexington, KY 40504-2319, USA

Turner, Maurice (Football Player)
Minnesota Vikings
3558 Tiffany Ln
Shoreview, MN 55126-3072, USA

Turner, Michael (Artist)
Top Cow Productions Inc
10390 Santa Monica Blvd Ste 110
Los Angeles, CA 90025-5093, USA

Turner, Morrie (Cartoonist)
PO Box 3004
Berkeley, CA 94703-0004, USA

Turner, Norv (Coach, Football Coach)
Oakland Raiders
1220 Harbor Bay Pkwy
Alameda, CA 94502-6570, USA

Turner, Odessa (Football Player)
New York Giants
1416 Perry Ave
Bastrop, LA 71220-4213, USA

Turner, Richard (Football Player)
Green Bay Packers
408 Piney Oak Dr
Norman, OK 73072-4603, USA

Turner, Ryan (Baseball Player)
1221 Shafter St
San Mateo, CA 94402-2901, USA

Turner, Shane (Baseball Player)
Philadelphia Phillies
13104 Glen Ct Unit 20
Chino Hills, CA 91709-1125, USA

Turner, Sherri (Golfer)
PO Box 26
Yale, OK 74085-0026, USA

Turner, Stansfield
600 New Hampshire Ave NW # 800
Washington, DC 20037-2403, USA

Turner, Ted (Business Person)
c/o Staff Member *Ted Turner Pictures*
133 Luckie St NW Fl 7
Atlanta, GA 30303-2038, USA

Turner, Thomas (Baseball Player)
Chicago American Giants
4817 Delhi Arnheim Rd
Georgetown, OH 45121-8229, USA

Turner, Tina (Musician)
c/o Roger Davies *RD Worldwide
Management*
1158 26th St # 564
Santa Monica, CA 90403-4698, USA

Turner, Tyrin (Actor)
c/o David Saunders *Agency for the
Performing Arts (APA-LA)*
405 S Beverly Dr
Beverly Hills, CA 90212-4416, USA

Turner, Vernon (Football Player)
Buffalo Bills
86 Crosshill St
Staten Island, NY 10301-3308, USA

Turnesa, Jim (Golfer)
24 Poplar St
Elmsford, NY 10523-3726, USA

Turnesa, Mike (Golfer)
c/o Staff Member *Pro Golfers Association
(PGA) Tour*
112 Tpc Blvd
Ponte Vedra Beach, FL 32082, USA

Turnesa, Willie (Golfer)
41 Sheraton Dr
Poughkeepsie, NY 12601-5629, USA

Turney, Maura
PO Box 5617
Beverly Hills, CA 90209-5617, USA

Turow, Scott (Writer)
c/o Gail Hochman *Brandt & Hochman
Literary Agent*
1501 Broadway Ste 2310
New York, NY 10036-5600, USA

Turpin, Miles (Football Player)
Green Bay Packers
8444 Wildflower Pl
Lone Tree, CO 80124-3022, USA

Turteltaub, Jon (Director)
Junction Entertainment
500 S Buena Vista St
Animation Building Ste 1B
Burbank, CA 91521-0001, USA

Turtles, The
PO Box 1821
Ojai, CA 93024-1821, USA

Turturro, Aida
9057C Nemo St
W Hollywood, CA 90069, USA

Turturro, John (Actor)
c/o Bart Walker *Creative Artists Agency
(CAA-NY)*
162 5th Ave Fl 6
New York, NY 10010-6047, USA

Turturro, Nicholas (Actor)
c/o Staff Member *Agency for the
Performing Arts (APA-LA)*
405 S Beverly Dr
Beverly Hills, CA 90212-4416, USA

Turturro, Nick (Actor)
c/o Staff Member *Writers and Artists
Group Intl (LA)*
8383 Wilshire Blvd Ste 550
Beverly Hills, CA 90211-2417, USA

Tush, Bill
1 City Cnn Center Box 105366
Atlanta, GA 30348, USA

Tushingham, Rita
4 Kingly St
London, ENGLAND W1R 5LF, UNITED
KINGDOM (UK)

Tuten, Rick (Football Player)
Philadelphia Eagles
1146 SE 15th St
Ocala, FL 34471-4514, USA

Tutin, Dame Dorothy
13 St. Martin's Rd.
London, ENGLAND SW9 0SP, UNITED
KINGDOM (UK)

Tutson, Tom (Football Player)
Atlanta Falcons
6655 Poplar Grove Way
Stone Mountain, GA 30087-4791, USA

Tuttle, Perry (Football Player)
Buffalo Bills
14224 King Eider Dr
Charlotte, NC 28273-6714, USA

Tutu, Desmond (Religious Leader)
7981 Orlando West Box 1131
Johannesburg, SOUTH AFRICA

Twain, Shania (Actor, Musician)
c/o Jason Owen *MCA Records (Nashville)*
60 Music Sq E
Nashville, TN 37203-4325, USA

Tway, Bob (Golfer)
6300 Oak Heritage Trl
Edmond, OK 73025-2766, USA

Tweed, Shannon (Actor)
c/o Danielle Allman *Allman/Rea
Management*
141 S Barrington Ave Ste E
Los Angeles, CA 90049-3314, USA

Tweeden, Leeann (Actor, Model,
Sportscaster)
c/o Jon Orlando *Xposure Public Relations*
8271 Melrose Ave Ste 110
Los Angeles, CA 90046-6800, USA

Tweet, Rodney (Football Player)
Cincinnati Bengals
2096 Placita De Vida
Santa Fe, NM 87505-5489, USA

Twiggs, Greg (Golfer)
c/o Staff Member *Pro Golfers Association
(PGA) Tour*
112 Tpc Blvd
Ponte Vedra Beach, FL 32082, USA

Twilight Singers (Music Group)
c/o Staff Member *Paradigm (Monterey)*
509 Hartnell St
Monterey, CA 93940-2825, USA

Twilley, Howard J Jr (Football Player)
Miami Dolphins
3109 S Columbia Cir
Tulsa, OK 74105-2329, USA

Twilly, Dwight
PO Box 1821
Ojai, CA 93024-1821, USA

Twista (Actor, Musician)
c/o Staff Member *Paradigm (Monterey)*
509 Hartnell St
Monterey, CA 93940-2825, USA

Twitchell, Wayne (Baseball Player)
Milwaukee Brewers
5719 SW Brugger St
Portland, OR 97219-4905, USA

Twitty, Howard (Golfer)
8007 E Mercer Ln
Scottsdale, AZ 85260-6563, USA

Twitty, Jeff (Baseball Player)
Kansas City Royals
812 Willow Cove Rd
Chapin, SC 29036-8733, USA

Twohy, David (Actor)
c/o John Burnham *International Creative
Management (ICM-LA)*
10250 Constellation Blvd
Los Angeles, CA 90067-6200, USA

Twohy, Mike (Cartoonist)
605 Beloit Ave
Kensington, CA 94708-1117, USA

Twohy, Robert (Cartoonist)
New Yorker Magazine
4 Times Sq
Editorial Dept
New York, NY 10036-6592, USA

Twombly, Cy (Artist)
Gagosian Gallery
980 Madison Ave
New York, NY 10075-1848, USA

Twyman, John K (Jack) (Basketball Player,
Business Person)
8955 Indian Ridge Ln
Cincinnati, OH 45243-3740, USA

Tydings, Alexandra (Actor)
Writers & Artists
360 N Crescent Dr Bldg North
Beverly Hills, CA 90210-6818, USA

Tydings, Joseph D (Senator)
2705 Pocock Rd
Monkton, MD 21111-2311, USA

Tyers, Kathy (Writer)
Martha Millard Agency
204 Park Ave
Madison, NJ 07940-1128, USA

Tykwer, Tom (Actor, Director, Writer)
Creative Artists Agency
9830 Wilshire Blvd
Beverly Hills, CA 90212-1804, USA

Tyler, Aisha (Actor, Comedian)
c/o Will Ward *ROAR LLC*
9701 Wilshire Blvd Fl 8
Beverly Hills, CA 90212-2008, USA

Tyler, Anne (Writer)
222 Tunbridge Rd
Baltimore, MD 21212-3422, USA

Tyler, Bonnie (Musician, Songwriter,
Writer)
c/o Joe Smith *International Creative
Management (ICM-LA)*
10250 Constellation Blvd
Los Angeles, CA 90067-6200, USA

Tyler, Cory
9955 Balboa Blvd
Northridge, CA 91325-1610, USA

Tyler, Harold R Jr (Attorney, Attorney General, General)
Patterson Belknap Webb Tyler
30 Rockefeller Plz
New York, NY 10112-0015, USA

Tyler, James Michael (Actor)
c/o Craig Mobbs *AKA Talent Agency*
6310 San Vicente Blvd Ste 200
Los Angeles, CA 90048-5488, USA

Tyler, Jess (Radio Personality)
c/o Staff Member *WPKX*
1331 Main St Ste 4
Springfield, MA 01103-1621, USA

Tyler, Karmyn (Actor, Musician)
c/o Staff Member *BMI (LA)*
8730 W Sunset Blvd Fl 3
Los Angeles, CA 90069-2210, USA

Tyler, Liv (Actor)
c/o David Schiff *Schiff Company*
9465 Wilshire Blvd Ste 480
Beverly Hills, CA 90212-2603, USA

Tyler, Maurice (Football Player)
Buffalo Bills
7066 Whitfield Dr
Riverdale, GA 30296-2161, USA

Tyler, Nikki
4F S Main St Pmb 307
West Bridgewater, MA 02379-1766, USA

Tyler, Richard (Designer, Fashion Designer)
c/o Staff Member *Richard Tyler*
525 Mission St
South Pasadena, CA 91030-3035, USA

Tyler, Robert (Actor)
Innovative Artists
1505 10th St
Santa Monica, CA 90401-2805, USA

Tyler, Steven (Musician, Songwriter, Writer)
c/o Dan Weiner *Paradigm (Monterey)*
509 Hartnell St
Monterey, CA 93940-2825, USA

Tyler, Wendell A (Football Player)
Los Angeles Rams
2541 Still Meadow Ln
Lancaster, CA 93536-5363, USA

Tyler, Willie
1650 Broadway Ste 705
New York, NY 10019-6833, USA

Tylo, Hunter (Actor)
11684 Ventura Blvd # 910
Studio City, CA 91604-2699, USA

Tylo, Michael (Actor)
11684 Ventura Blvd # 910
Studio City, CA 91604-2699, USA

Tylo, Noa (DJ)
c/o Len Evans *Project Publicity*
312 W 53rd St
New York, NY 10019-5743, USA

Tylski, Richard (Football Player)
Jacksonville Jaguars
5456 Tierra Verde Ln
Jacksonville, FL 32258-2281, USA

Tynan, Ronan
c/o Daniel A (Dan) Strone *Trident Media Group LLC*
41 Madison Ave Fl 36
New York, NY 10010-2257, USA

Tyne, George
1449 Benedict Canyon Dr
Beverly Hills, CA 90210-2021, USA

Tyner, Charles (Actor)
Dade/Schultz
6442 Coldwater Canyon Ave Ste 206
North Hollywood, CA 91606-1137, USA

Tyner, Jason (Baseball Player)
New York Mets
5535 Sul Ross Ln
Beaumont, TX 77706-3435, USA

Tyner, Tray (Golfer)
208 Plantation Path
Boerne, TX 78006-3879, USA

Type O Negative (Music Group)
c/o Staff Member *Helter Skelter (UK)*
535 Kings Rd
The Plaza
London SW10 0SZ, UNITED KINGDOM (UK)

Tyra, Charles (Charlie) (Basketball Player)
10812 Glenway Pl
Louisville, KY 40291-3686, USA

Tyree, Jim (Football Player)
Boston Yanks
PO Box 701295
Tulsa, OK 74170-1295, USA

Tyrell, Steve (Musician)
c/o Staff Member *William Morris Agency (WMA-LA)*
1 William Morris Pl
Beverly Hills, CA 90212-4261, USA

Tyrell, Susan
1489 Scott Ave
Los Angeles, CA 90026-2671, USA

Tyrone, Jim (Baseball Player)
Chicago Cubs
107 Encinal St
Alice, TX 78332, USA

Tyrone, Wayne (Baseball Player)
Chicago Cubs
505 Tish Cir Apt 404
Arlington, TX 76006-3549, USA

Tyrrell, Susan (Actor)
Abrams Artists
9200 W Sunset Blvd Ste 1125
Los Angeles, CA 90069-3610, USA

Tyrrell, Tim (Football Player)
Atlanta Falcons
17 Fallstone Dr
Streamwood, IL 60107-1071, USA

Tysoe, Ronald W (Business Person)
Federated Department Stores
151 W 34th St
New York, NY 10001-2101, USA

Tyson, Cathy (Actor)
P F D Drury House
34-43 Russell St
London WC2B 5HA, UNITED KINGDOM (UK)

Tyson, Cicely (Actor)
c/o Staff Member *William Morris Agency (WMA-LA)*
1 William Morris Pl
Beverly Hills, CA 90212-4261, USA

Tyson, Dick (Football Player)
Oakland Raiders
3835 N 67th St
Kansas City, KS 66104-1023, USA

Tyson, Ian (Musician)
Richard Flohil Assoc
60 McGill St
Toronto, ON M5B 1H2, CANADA

Tyson, Mike (Baseball Player)
St Louis Cardinals
479 Thunderhead Canyon Dr
Ballwin, MO 63011-1736, USA

Tyson, Mike (Boxer)
c/o Harlan Werner *Sports Placement Service*
6671 W Sunset Blvd Ste 1521
Los Angeles, CA 90028-7123, USA

Tyson, Neil de Grasse (Physicist)
Hayden Planetarium
W 81st St & Central Park
New York, NY 10024, USA

Tyson, Richard (Actor)
Kritzer
12200 W Olympic Blvd Ste 400
Los Angeles, CA 90064-1047, USA

Tyurin, Mikhail (Cosmonaut)
Potcha Kosmonavtov
Moskovskoi Oblasti
Syvisdny Goroduk 141160, RUSSIA

Tyus, Wyomia (Athlete, Track Athlete)
1102 Keniston Ave
Los Angeles, CA 90019-1709, USA

Tyzack, Margaret (Actor)
Joyce Edwards
275 Kennington Road
London SE1 6BY, UNITED KINGDOM (UK)

Tzadua, Paulos Cardinal (Religious Leader)
PO Box 2141
Addis Abeba, ETHIOPIA

Tzekova, Polina (Basketball Player)
c/o Staff Member *Houston Comets*
1510 Polk St
Houston, TX 77002-1099, USA

U-God (Artist)
Famous Artists Agency
250 W 57th St
New York, NY 10107-0001, USA

U2 (Musician)
30-32 Sir John Rogerson's Quarry
Dublin, IRELAND

UB 40
Kensal House 553-579 Harrow Rd.
London, ENGLAND W10 4RH, UNITED KINGDOM (UK)

UB40 (Music Group)
c/o Staff Member *International Talent Booking (ITB - UK)*
27A Floral St Fl 3
Covent Garden
London WC2E 9, UNITED KINGDOM (UK)

Ubriaco, Gene (Coach)
Chicago Wolves
2301 Ravine Way
Glenview, IL 60025-7627, USA

Uchida, Irene A (Scientist)
20 North Shore Blvd W
Burlington, ON L7T 1A1, CANADA

Uchida, Mitsuko (Musician)
Arts Management Group
1133 Broadway Ste 1025
New York, NY 10010-7985, USA

Udenio, Fabiana (Actor)
Michael Slessinger
8730 W Sunset Blvd Ste 220W
Los Angeles, CA 90069-2275, USA

Uderzo, Albert
26 av. Victor Hugo
Paris F-75116, FRANCE

Udvari, Frank (Referee)
2-379 Gage Ave
Kitchener, ON N2M 5E1, CANADA

Udy, Helene (Actor)
Sterling/Winters
10877 Wilshire Blvd # 15
Los Angeles, CA 90024-4341, USA

Ueberroth, John A (Business Person)
Carlson Cos Inc
12755 State Highway 55
Minneapolis, MN 55441, USA

Ueberroth, Peter
184 Emerald Bay
Laguna Beach, CA 92651-1209, USA

Ueberroth, Peter V (Misc)
Doubletree Hotels Corp
755 Crossover Ln
Memphis, TN 38117-4906, USA

Uecker, Gunther (Artist)
Dusseldorfer Str 29A
Dusseldorf 40545, GERMANY

Uecker, Keith (Football Player)
Denver Broncos
169 Dorchester Rd
Akron, OH 44313-7806, USA

Uelses, John (Athlete, Track Athlete)
30660 Rolling Hills Dr
Valley Center, CA 92082-3351, USA

Uelsmann, Jerry N (Photographer)
5701 SW 17th Dr
Gainesville, FL 32608-5365, USA

Ueltschi, Albert L (Business Person)
Flight Safety Int'l
Marine Air Terminal
Laguardia Airport
Flushing, NY 11371, USA

Ufland, Len (Actor, Director)
4400 Hillcreat Dr #901
Hollywood, FL 33021, USA

UFO
10 Sutherland
London, ENGLAND W9 24Q, UNITED KINGDOM (UK)

Uggams, Leslie (Actor, Musician)
Entertainment Unlimited
72 N Village Ave
Rockville Centre, NY 11570-4600, USA

Ughi, Uto (Musician)
Cannareggio 4990/E
Venice 30121, ITALY

Uh Huh Her (Music Group)
c/o Staff Member *Paradigm (Monterey)*
509 Hartnell St
Monterey, CA 93940-2825, USA

Uhalt, Frenchy (Baseball Player)
Chicago White Sox
1164 Crescenta Ct
Lafayette, CA 94549-3105, USA

Uhl, Petr (Activist)
Anglicka 8
Prague 2 120 00, CZECH REPUBLIC

Uhlaender, Ted (Baseball Player)
Minnesota Twins
60 County Road 3080
Parshall, CO 80468-8600, USA

Uhlenhake, Jeffrey A (Jeff) (Football Player)
Miami Dolphins
1304 Normandy Dr
Newark, OH 43055-9201, USA

Uhlig, Anneliese
1519 Escalona Dr
Santa Cruz, CA 95060-3311, USA

Uhry, Alfred F (Writer)
Marshall Purdy
226 W 47th St Ste 900
New York, NY 10036-1413, USA

Ujdur, Jerry (Baseball Player)
Detroit Tigers
112 Riveness Rd
Duluth, MN 55811-2873, USA

Ujiie, Junichi (Financier)
Normura Securities
2 World Financial Ctr
200 Liberty
New York, NY 10281-1705, USA

Ukropina, James R (Attorney, Attorney General, Business Person, General)
O'Melveny & Myers
400 S Hope St
Los Angeles, CA 90071-2899, USA

Ulene, Art (Doctor)
6511 Moore Dr
Los Angeles, CA 90048-5325, USA

Ulevich, Neal (Journalist, Photographer)
2841 Perry St
Iowa City, IA 52245, USA

Ulf, Gunnar Ekberg
Ace of Base
9975 Santa Monica Blvd
Beverly Hills, CA 90212-1606, USA

Ulinski, Ed (Football Player)
Cleveland Rams
2860 Lander Rd
Cleveland, OH 44124-4820, USA

Ulion, Gretchen (Hockey Player)
22181 Toro Hills Dr
Salinas, CA 93908-1132, USA

Ulisney, Mike (Baseball Player)
Boston Braves
1481 Puritan St
Deltona, FL 32725-8411, USA

Ullger, Scott (Baseball Player)
Minnesota Twins
4149 W Russell Ave
Visalia, CA 93277-5127, USA

Ulliel, Gaspard (Actor)
c/o Brinda Bhatt *United Talent Agency (UTA)*
9560 Wilshire Blvd Ste 500
Beverly Hills, CA 90212-2401, USA

Ullman, Norman V A (Norm) (Hockey Player)
819-25 Austin Dr
Unionville, ON L3R 8H4, CANADA

Ullman, Ricky (Actor)
c/o Itay Reiss *United Talent Agency (UTA)*
9560 Wilshire Blvd Ste 500
Beverly Hills, CA 90212-2401, USA

Ullman, Tracey (Actor, Comedian)
c/o Ilene Feldman *IFA Talent Agency*
8730 W Sunset Blvd Ste 490
Los Angeles, CA 90069-2248, USA

Ullmann, Liv J (Actor)
101 W 79th St Apt 8F
New York, NY 10024-6475, USA

Ulloa, Christina (Actor)
c/o Michael Greenwald *Don Buchwald & Associates Inc (LA)*
6500 Wilshire Blvd Ste 2200
Los Angeles, CA 90048-4942, USA

Ullsten, Ola (Prime Minister)
Folkpartiet
PO Box 6508
Stockholm 11383, SWEDEN

Ulmar, Bin Hassan (Musician)
Agency Group
1775 Broadway Ste 433
New York, NY 10019-1903, USA

Ulmer, Arthur (Football Player)
Denver Broncos
1133 Lloyd Dr
Forest Park, GA 30297-1516, USA

Ulmer, Kristen (Athlete)
3671 Willow Canyon Dr
Salt Lake City, UT 84121-6184, USA

Ulrich, Chuck (Football Player)
Chicago Cardinals
53 Hampton Ln
Bluffton, SC 29910, USA

Ulrich, Henry (Admiral)
Commander
Naval Striking Force Central Europe & 6th Fleet
FPO, AE 09609, USA

Ulrich, Kim Johnston (Actor)
S D B Partners
1801 Avenue Of Stars Ste 902
Los Angeles, CA 90067-5981, USA

Ulrich, Lars (Musician)
Q Prime Inc
729 7th Ave Rm 1600
New York, NY 10019-6880, USA

Ulrich, Laurel T (Historian)
University of New Hampshire
History Dept
Durham, NH 03824, USA

Ulrich, Robert (Business Person)
Target Corporation
1000 Nicollet Mall
Minneapolis, MN 55403-2467, USA

Ulrich, Skeet (Actor)
c/o Geyer Kosinski *Media Talent Group*
9200 W Sunset Blvd Ste 810
W Hollywood, CA 90069-3603, USA

Ulrich, Thomas (Boxer)
Brunsbutteler Damm 29
Berlin 13581, GERMANY

Ultang, Don (Journalist, Photographer)
3500 Lower West Branch Rd # 121
Iowa City, IA 52245-4106, USA

Ultra, Nate (Musician)
Peach Bisquit
963C Kent Ave
Brooklyn, NY 11205, USA

Ulufa'alu, Bartholomew (Prime Minister)
Premier's Office
Legakiki Ridge
Honiara
Guadacanal, SOLOMON ISLANDS

Ulusu, Bulent (Admiral, Prime Minister)
Ciftehavuzlar Yesilbahar 50K 8/27
Kadikoy/Istanbul, TURKEY

Ulvaeus, Bjorn (Composer, Musician)
Gorel Hanser
Sodra Brobanken 41A
Skeppsholmen
Stockholm 11149, SWEDEN

Ulvang, Vegard (Skier)
Fiellveien 53
Kirkenes 9900, NORWAY

Ulyanov, Mikhail A (Actor, Director)
Theater Vakhtango
26 Arbat
Moscow 121002, RUSSIA

Umana, Christina (Actor)
c/o Staff Member *TV Caracol*
Calle 76 #11 - 35
Piso 10AA
Bogota DC 26484, COLOMBIA

Umbach, Arnie (Baseball Player)
Milwaukee Braves
760 Moores Mill Rd
Auburn, AL 36830-6032, USA

Umbarger, Jim (Baseball Player)
Texas Rangers
1140 Ploneer Cir
Watkinsville, GA 30677, USA

Umberger, Andy (Actor)
c/o Claire Miller *Bauman Redanty & Shaul Agency*
5757 Wilshire Blvd Ste 473
Los Angeles, CA 90036-3632, USA

Umermoto, Nanako (Architect)
118 E 59th St
New York, NY 10022-1310, USA

Umphlett, Tommy (Baseball Player)
Boston Red Sox
104 Berkley Rd
Ahoskie, NC 27910-9575, USA

Umphrey's McGee (Music Group)
c/o Staff Member *Paradigm (Monterey)*
509 Hartnell St
Monterey, CA 93940-2825, USA

Umrao, Singh (War Hero)
Victoria Cross Assn
Old Admiralty Building
London SW1A 2BL, UNITED KINGDOM (UK)

Unanue, Emil R (Misc)
Washington University
Medical School
Pathology Dept
Saint Louis, MO 63110, USA

Uncle Kracker (Music Group)
c/o Staff Member *Paradigm (Monterey)*
509 Hartnell St
Monterey, CA 93940-2825, USA

Underwood, Blair (Actor)
c/o JB Roberts *Thruline Entertainment*
9250 Wilshire Blvd Ground Fl
Beverly Hills, CA 90210, USA

Underwood, Carrie (Musician)
c/o Jeff Frasco *Creative Artists Agency LCC (CAA-LA)*
2000 Avenue Of The Stars
Los Angeles, CA 90067-4700, USA

Underwood, Jacob (Musician)
Trans Continental Records
7380 W Sand Lake Rd # 350
Orlando, FL 32819-5248, USA

Underwood, Jay (Actor)
6100 Wilshire Blvd Ste 1170
Los Angeles, CA 90048-5116, USA

Underwood, Olen (Football Player)
New York Giants
302 N Main St
Conroe, TX 77301-2810, USA

Underwood, Pat (Baseball Player)
Detroit Tigers
708 Riverview Dr
Kokomo, IN 46901-7024, USA

Underwood, Ron (Director)
United Talent Agency
9560 Wilshire Blvd Ste 500
Beverly Hills, CA 90212-2401, USA

Underwood, Scott (Musician)
Jon Landua
80 Mason St
Greenwich, CT 06830-5515, USA

Underwood, Tom (Baseball Player)
Philadelphia Phillies
13595 83rd Ln N
West Palm Beach, FL 33412-2331, USA

Ungaro, Emanuel M (Designer, Fashion Designer)
2 Ave du Montaigne
Paris 75008, FRANCE

Ungaro, Susan Kelliher (Editor)
Family Circle Magazine
375 Lexington Ave Bsmt 3
Editorial Dept
New York, NY 10017-5644, USA

Unger, Brian
5750 Wilshire Blvd
Los Angeles, CA 90036-3697, USA

Unger, Brian (Television Host)
c/o Staff Member *Extra (LA)*
1840 Victory Blvd
Telepictures Productions
Glendale, CA 91201-2558, USA

Unger, Deborah Kara (Actor)
c/o Staff Member *I/D PR (LA)*
8409 Santa Monica Blvd
West Hollywood, CA 90069-4209, USA

Unger, Garry D (Hockey Player)
5315 E 93rd St
Tulsa, OK 74137-4415, USA

Unger, Jim (Cartoonist)
Universal Press Syndicate
4520 Main St
Kansas City, MO 64111-1876, USA

Unger, Kay (Designer, Fashion Designer)
Saint Gillian Sportswear
498 Fashion Ave
New York, NY 10018-6798, USA

Unger, Leonard (Diplomat)
31 Amherst Rd
Belmont, MA 02478-2102, USA

Ungers, Oswald M (Architect)
Belvederestr 60
Cologne 50933, GERMANY

Union, Gabrielle (Actor)
c/o Jeff Morrone *Jeff Morrone Management*
9350 Wilshire Blvd Ste 224
Beverly Hills, CA 90212-3204, USA

Union, Sarah (Actor)
c/o Jason Barrett *Alchemy Entertainment*
1401 Ocean Ave # 301
Santa Monica, CA 90401-2106, USA

Unkefer, Ronald A (Business Person)
Good Guys Inc
1600 Harbor Bay Pkwy
Alameda, CA 94502-3085, USA

Uno, Osamu (Business Person)
1-46 Showacho
Hamadera Sakai
Osaka 592, JAPAN

Unroe, Tim (Baseball Player)
Milwaukee Brewers
2719 S Joplin
Mesa, AZ 85209-2508, USA

Unruh, James A (Business Person)
5426 E Morrison Ln
Paradise Valley, AZ 85253-3017, USA

Unseld, Westley S (Wes) (Basketball
Player, Coach)
2210 Cedar Circle Dr
Baltimore, MD 21228, USA

Unser, Alfred (Al) Jr (Race Car Driver)
PO Box 56696
Albuquerque, NM 87187-6696, USA

Unser, Robert W (Bobby) (Race Car
Driver)
7700 Central Ave SW
Albuquerque, NM 87121-2113, USA

Unser Sr, Alfred (Al) (Race Car Driver)
7625 Central Ave NW
Albuquerque, NM 87121-2115, USA

Unutoa, Morris (Football Player)
Philadelphia Eagles
821B Country Club Pkwy
Mount Laurel, NJ 08054-2714, USA

Upchurch, Rickie (Rick) (Football Player)
Denver Broncos
463 Hagens Aly
Mesquite, NV 89027-5815, USA

Updike, John H (Writer)
675 Hale St
Beverly, MA 01915-2179, USA

Upham, Dr Steadman (Educator)
University of Tulsa
President's Office
Tulsa, OK 74104, USA

Uphoff-Becker, Nicole (Horse Racer)
Freiherr-von-Lanen-Str 15
Warendorf 48231, GERMANY

Upshaw, Dawn (Opera Singer)
Columbia Artists Mgmt Inc
1790 Broadway Fl 6
New York, NY 10019-1412, USA

Upshaw, Eugene (Gene) (Football Player)
Oakland Raiders
1102 Peppertree Dr
Great Falls, VA 22066-2205, USA

Upshaw, Marv (Football Player)
Cleveland Browns
3851 Madrone Ave
Oakland, CA 94619-2731, USA

Upshaw, Regan (Football Player)
Washington Redskins
21300 Redskin Park Dr
Ashburn, VA 20147-6100, USA

Upton, Arthur C (Physicist)
250 E Alameda St Apt 636
Santa Fe, NM 87501-6205, USA

Urb, Johann (Actor)
c/o Staff Member *3 Arts Entertainment Inc*
9460 Wilshire Blvd Fl 7
Beverly Hills, CA 90212-2713, USA

Urban, Alex (Football Player)
Green Bay Packers
4341 289th St
Toledo, OH 43611-2908, USA

Urban, Amanda
ICM
40 W 57th St
New York, NY 10019-4001, USA

Urban, Karl (Actor)
Auckland Actors
PO Box 56460
Dominion Road
Auckland 1030, NEW ZEALAND

Urban, Keith (Musician)
c/o Gary Borman *Borman Entertainment*
1250 6th St Ste 401
Santa Monica, CA 90401-1638, USA

Urban, Thomas N (Business Person)
Pioneer Hi-Bred Int'l
PO Box 14454
Capital Square
Des Moines, IA 50306-3454, USA

Urbanchek, Jon (Coach)
University of Michigan
Athletic Dept
Ann Arbor, MI 48109, USA

Urbanek, Karel (President)
Kvetna 54
Brno, CZECH REPUBLIC

Urbano, Mike (Musician)
Creative Artists Agency
9830 Wilshire Blvd
Beverly Hills, CA 90212-1804, USA

Urbanova, Eva (Opera Singer)
National Theater
Narodni Divadlo
Prague 1, CZECH REPUBLIC

Urbanski, Douglas (Writer)
Creative Artists Agency
9830 Wilshire Blvd
Beverly Hills, CA 90212-1804, USA

Urbina, Ugueth U (Baseball Player)
Rojas Conj Res Las Aca Lias 2
Ocumare Del Troy, VENEZUELA

Urch, Scott (Football Player)
New York Giants
645 Foxboro Dr
Avon, IN 46123-7185, USA

Ure, Midge (Musician)
#8 Glenthome 115A Glenhome
Hammersm
London W6 0LJ, UNITED KINGDOM
(UK)

Uremovich, Emil P (Football Player)
2935 S County Road 210
Knox, IN 46534-7968, USA

Urenda, Herman (Football Player)
Oakland Raiders
225 Upton Pyne Dr
Brentwood, CA 94513-6425, USA

Uresti, Omar (Golfer)
2503 Pebble Beach Dr
Austin, TX 78747-1618, USA

Urguhart, Lawrence M (Business Person)
English China Clays
Business Park
Theale
Reading RG7 4SA, UNITED KINGDOM
(UK)

Uribe, Diane (Actor)
23874 Via Jacara
Valencia, CA 91355-2520, USA

Urich, Justin (Actor)
Talent Group
5670 Wilshire Blvd Ste 820
Los Angeles, CA 90036-5613, USA

Urie, Michael (Actor)
c/o Jennifer Craig *Gersh Agency, The (LA)*
232 N Canon Dr
Beverly Hills, CA 90210-5302, USA

Urkal, Oklay (Boxer)
Bautzener Str 4
Berlin 10829, GERMANY

Urlacher, Brian (Football Player)
c/o Staff Member *Chicago Bears*
1000 Football Dr
Lake Forest, IL 60045-4829, USA

Urmanov, Aleksei (Figure Skater)
Union of Skaters
Luzhnetskaya Nab 8
Moscow 119871, RUSSIA

Urmanov, Alexei
Luzhnetskaya nab. 8
Moscow 119871, RUSSIA

Urmson, Claire (Model)
Ford Model Agency
142 Greene St # 400
New York, NY 10012-3236, USA

Urquhart, Brian E (Diplomat)
Howard Farms
Jerusalem Road
Tyringham, MA 01264, USA

Urseth, Bonnie (Actor)
Gage Group
14724 Ventura Blvd Ste 505
Sherman Oaks, CA 91403-3505, USA

Urshan, Nathaniel A (Religious Leader)
United Pentecostal Church International
8855 Dunn Rd
Hazelwood, MO 63042-2212, USA

Ursi, Corrado Cardinal (Religious Leader)
Via Capodimonte 13
Naples 80136, ITALY

Usachyov, Yuri V (Cosmonaut)
Potcha Kosmonavtov
Moskovskoi Oblasti
Syvisdny Goroduk 141160, RUSSIA

Usaher (Actor, Artist)
J Pat Mgmt
3996 Pleasantville Road #104A
Dovaville, GA 30340, USA

Used, The (Music Group)
c/o Staff Member *Freeze Artist
Management*
27783 Hidden Trail Rd
Laguna Hills, CA 92653-7821, USA

Usery, William J Jr (Secretary)
1101 S Arlington Ridge Rd
Arlington, VA 22202-1951, USA

Usgaonkar, Varsha (Actor, Bollywood)
2C-24 Wild Wood Park Yari Road
Versova Andheri (W)
Bombay, MS 400 061, INDIA

Usher, Paul (Actor)
c/o Staff Member *Qdos Entertainment*
8 King St
Covent Garden
London WC2 8HN, UNITED KINGDOM
(UK)

Usher, Thomas J (Business Person)
USX Corp
600 Grant St
Pittsburgh, PA 15219-2800, USA

Uslan, Michael (Producer, Writer)
Branded Entertainment
333 Crestmont Rd
Cedar Grove, NJ 07009-1907, USA

Usova, Maya (Figure Skater)
Connecticut Skating Center
300 Alumni Rd
Newington, CT 06111-1865, USA

Ustvolskaya, Galina I (Composer)
Prospect Gagarina 27
#72
Saint Petersburg 196135, RUSSIA

Ut, Nick (Photographer)
Associated Press
221 S Figueroa St Ste 300
Photo Dept
Los Angeles, CA 90012-2553, USA

Utay, William (Actor)
c/o Staff Member *Days of Our Lives*
3000 W Alameda Ave
Burbank, CA 91523-0001, USA

Uteem, Cassam (President)
President's Office
Le Redult
Port Louis, MAURITIUS

Utley, Adrian (Musician)
Fruit
Saga Centre
326 Kensal Road
London W10 5BZ, UNITED KINGDOM
(UK)

Utley, Garrick (Correspondent)
ABC-TV
News Dept
8 Carburton St
London W1P 7DT, UNITED KINGDOM
(UK)

Utley, Mike (Football Player)
Detroit Lions
PO Box 349
Orondo, WA 98843-0349, USA

Utley, Stan (Golfer)
20701 N Scottsdale Rd # 107-619
Scottsdale, AZ 85255-6413, USA

Utt, Ben (Football Player)
Baltimore Colts
3378 Habersham Rd NW
Atlanta, GA 30305-1171, USA

Utzon, Jorn (Architect)
General Delivery
Hellebaek 3150, DENMARK

Uyeda, Seiya (Geophysicist, Physicist)
2-39-6 Daizawa
Setagayaku
Tokyo 113, JAPAN

Uzawa, Hirofumi (Economist)
Higashi 1-3-6 Hoya
Tokyo, JAPAN

V Gopalakrishnan (Actor)
11D4 Habibullah Road
T Nagar
Chennai, TN 600 017, INDIA

V M T Chaarllee (Actor)
Plot No 11 Kamarajar Nagar
II Street Sathya Gardens Saligramam
Chennai, TN 600 093, INDIA

Vaca, Joselito (Soccer Player)
Dallas Burn
14800 Quorum Dr Ste 300
Dallas, TX 75254-1442, USA

Vacano, Jost (Cinematographer)
Leoprechtingstr 18
Munich 81739, GERMANY

Vacanti, Charles A (Doctor)
Massachusetts University Med Center
Anesthesiology Dept
Worcester, MA 02139, USA

Vacariou, Nicolae (Prime Minister)
Romanian Senate
Piata Revolutiei
Bucharest 71243, ROMANIA

Vaccaro, Brenda (Actor)
c/o Amy De Souza *Niad Management*
15030 Ventura Blvd Ste 19 Ste 860
Sherman Oaks, CA 91403-2444, USA

Vachon, Christine (Producer)
c/o Staff Member *Killer Films*
380 Lafayette St Rm 202
New York, NY 10003-6933, USA

Vachon, Louis-Albert Cardinal (Religious
Leader)
Seminaire de Quebec
1 Rue des Remparts
Quebec, PQ G1R 5LY, CANADA

Vachon, Paul (Wrestler)
RR 4
Mansonville, PQ J0E 1X0, CANADA

Vachon, Rogatien R (Rogie) (Coach,
Hockey Player)
648 Oxford Ave
Venice, CA 90291-4725, USA

Vactor, Ted (Football Player)
Washington Redskins
11504 Channing Dr
Wheaton, MD 20902-2908, USA

Vadivukkarasi (Actor, Bollywood)
49/1A Sadulla Street
Chennai, TN 600017, INDIA

Vaduva, Leontina (Opera Singer)
Luisa Petrov
Glaburgstr 95
Frankfurt 60318, GERMANY

Vaea of Houma, Baron (Prime Minister)
Prime Minister's Office
Nuku'alofa, TONGA

Vago, Constantin (Misc)
University of Sciences
Place Eugene Bataillon
Montpellier 34095, FRANCE

Vahi, Tiit (Prime Minister)
Coalition Party Eesti Koonderakond
Kuhlbarsi 1
Tallinn 0104, ESTONIA

Vai, Steve (Musician)
Septys Entertainment
1223 Wilshire Blvd # 804
Santa Monica, CA 90403-5400, USA

Vaidyanathan, Aparna (Actor, Bollywood)
520 19th Cross 14th Main
Benasankari 2nd Stage
Bangalore, KA 560070, INDIA

Vail, Justina (Actor)
651 N Kilkea Dr
Los Angeles, CA 90048-2213, USA

Vail, Thomas (Editor)
Cleveland Plain Dealer
1801 Superior Ave E
Editorial Dept
Cleveland, OH 44114-2198, USA

Vaishnavi (Actor, Bollywood)
2 Sambandam Street
G N Chetty Road
Chennai, TN 600017, INDIA

Vajiralongkorn (Prince)
Royal Residence
Chirtalad a Villa
Bangkok, THAILAND

Vajna, Andrew (Filmmaker, Producer)
Cinergi Productions
2308 Broadway
Santa Monica, CA 90404-2916, USA

Vajna, Andy (Producer)
c/o Staff Member *Bumble Ward &
Associates*
8383 Wilshire Blvd Ste 102
Beverly Hills, CA 90211-2402, USA

Vajpayee, Atal Bihari (Prime Minister)
6 Raisina Road
New Delhi, Delhi 110011, INDIA

Valabik, Boris (Hockey Player)
Atlanta Thrashers
13 South Ave SE
Philips Arena
Atlanta, GA 30315, USA

Valance, Holly (Musician)
Valance Corporation Ltd
141 Charmon Rd
3193, AUSTRALIA

Valandrey, Charlotte (Actor)
c/o Staff Member *ArtMedia*
20 av Rapp
Paris 75007, FRANCE

Valar, Paul (Skier)
34 Hubertus Ring
Franconia, NH 03580-5114, USA

Valasquez, Nadine (Actor)
c/o Staff Member *Don Buchwald &
Associates Inc (LA)*
6500 Wilshire Blvd Ste 2200
Los Angeles, CA 90048-4942, USA

Valderrama, Carlos (Soccer Player)
Colorado Rapids
1000 Chopper Cir
Denver, CO 80204-5805, USA

Valderrama, Wilmer (Actor)
c/o Glenn Rigberg *Rigberg-Rugolo
Entertainment*
1180 S Beverly Dr Ste 601
Los Angeles, CA 90035-1158, USA

Valdes, Ismael (Baseball Player)
c/o Staff Member *Texas Rangers*
1000 Ballpark Way Ste 306
Arlington, TX 76011-5169, USA

Valdes, Jesus (Chucho) (Musician)
IMN
278 Main St
Gloucester, MA 01930-6022, USA

Valdes, Maximiano (Conductor)
Cramer/Marder Artists
3436 Springhill Rd
Lafayette, CA 94549-2535, USA

Valdez, Luis (Writer)
El Teatro Capesino
705 4th St
San Juan Bautista, CA 95045, USA

Vale, Angelica (Actor)
c/o Staff Member *Televisa*
Blvd Adolfo Lopez Mateos 232
Colonia San Angel INN
DF CP 01060, MEXICO

Vale, Jerry (Musician)
40960 Glenmore Dr
Palm Desert, CA 92260-1665, USA

Vale, Tina (Musician)
DreamWorks Records
9268 W 3rd St
Beverly Hills, CA 90210-3713, USA

Vale, Virginia (Actor)
4039 Edenhurst Ave
Los Angeles, CA 90039-1469, USA

Valek, Vladimir (Conductor)
Na Vapennem 6
Prague 4 140 00, CZECH REPUBLIC

Valen, Nancy (Actor)
Metropolitan Talent Agency
4500 Wilshire Blvd Fl 2
Los Angeles, CA 90010-3858, USA

Valensi, Nick (Musician)
c/o Staff Member *MVO Ltd*
307 7th Ave Rm 807
New York, NY 10001-6066, USA

Valente, Benita (Opera Singer)
Maurice Mayer
201 W 54th St Apt 1C
New York, NY 10019-5520, USA

Valente, Catarina (Musician)
Villa Corallo Via ai Ronci
Bissone 6816, SWITZERLAND

Valente, Caterina (Musician)
ERAKI Entertainment
Casella Postale 91
6976 Castagnola
SWITZERLAND

Valenti, Carl M (Publisher)
Information Services
200 Liberty St
Dow Jones Telerate
New York, NY 10281-1003, USA

Valentin, Barbara (Actor)
Hans-Sachs-Str 22
Munich 80469, GERMANY

Valentin, Dave (Musician)
Turi's Music Enterprises
103 Westwood Dr
Miami Springs, FL 33166, USA

Valentine, Bill (Baseball Player)
15 Blue Ridge Cir
Little Rock, AR 72207-1901, USA

Valentine, Brooke (Musician)
c/o Staff Member *Virgin Records (NY)*
304 Park Ave S Fl 5
New York, NY 10010-4316, USA

Valentine, Dan (Business Person)
C-Cube Microsystems
1551 McCarthy Blvd
Milpitas, CA 95035-7437, USA

Valentine, Darnell (Basketball Player)
7546 SW Ashford St
Tigard, OR 97224-7143, USA

Valentine, Donald T (Business Person)
Network Appliance Inc
495 E Java Dr
Sunnyvale, CA 94089-1125, USA

Valentine, Gary (Actor, Comedian)
c/o Stacey Mark *William Morris Agency
(WMA-LA)*
1 William Morris Pl
Beverly Hills, CA 90212-4261, USA

Valentine, Gary (Musician)
Shore Fire Media
32 Court St Ste 1600
Brooklyn, NY 11201-4441, USA

Valentine, James (Musician)
c/o Staff Member *Creative Artists Agency
LCC (CAA-LA)*
2000 Avenue Of The Stars
Los Angeles, CA 90067-4700, USA

Valentine, Karen (Actor)
PO Box 1410
Washington Depot, CT 06793-0410, USA

Valentine, Raymond C (Misc)
University of California
Plant Growth Laboratory
Davis, CA 95616, USA

Valentine, Robert J (Bobby) (Baseball
Player)
71 Wynnewood Ln
Stamford, CT 06903-1931, USA

Valentine, Scott (Actor)
17465 Flanders St
Granada Hills, CA 91344-2211, USA

Valentine, Stacy (Adult Film Star)
200 W Houston St
New York, NY 10014-4828, USA

Valentine, Steve (Actor)
Craig Wyckoff and Associates
11350 Ventura Blvd Ste 100
Studio City, CA 91604-3140, USA

Valentine, Victoria
PO Box 12324
La Crescenta, CA 91224-5324, USA

Valentine, William N (Doctor)
2128 Quail Point Cir
Medford, OR 97504-4523, USA

Valentine, Zack (Football Player)
Pittsburgh Steelers
162 Harvest Rd
Swedesboro, NJ 08085-1427, USA

Valentino (Designer, Fashion Designer)
Palazzo Mignanelli
Piazza Mignanelli 22
Rome 00187, ITALY

Valentino, Bobby (Musician)
c/o Staff Member *Island Def Jam Music
Group*
825 8th Ave Fl 28
New York, NY 10019-7416, USA

Valenza, Tasia (Actor)
Artists Group
1650 Broadway Ste 610
New York, NY 10019-6833, USA

Valenzuela, Fernando (Baseball Player)
2123 N Beachwood Dr
Los Angeles, CA 90068-3403, USA

Valeriani, Richard G (Correspondent)
23 Island View Dr
Sherman, CT 06784-2036, USA

Valetta, Amber (Model)
c/o Daniel (Dan) Spilo *Artistry
Management*
525 Westbourne Dr
West Hollywood, CA 90048-1913, USA

Valiant, Leslie G (Scientist)
50 Tyler Rd
Belmont, MA 02478-2023, USA

Valiee, Bert L (Doctor)
300 Boyksti St #712
Boston, MA 02116, USA

Valle, Aurora (Actor)
c/o Staff Member *TV Azteca*
Periferico Sur 4121
Colonia Fuentes del Pedregal
DF CP 14141, MEXICO

Vallely, James (Jim) (Writer)
c/o Staff Member *Creative Artists Agency LCC (CAA-LA)*
2000 Avenue Of The Stars
Los Angeles, CA 90067-4700, USA

Valletta, Amber (Actor, Model)
Boss Models
80 8th Ave
New York, NY 10011-5126, USA

Valley, Mark (Actor)
c/o Alisa Adler *Paradigm (LA)*
360 N Crescent Dr
North Bldg
Beverly Hills, CA 90210-6820, USA

Vallez, Emilio (Football Player)
Chicago Bears
General Delivery
Polvadera, NM 87828-9999, USA

Valli, Frankie (Musician)
c/o Michael Eisenstadt *Amsel Eisenstadt & Frazier Inc*
5055 Wilshire Blvd Ste 865
Los Angeles, CA 90036-6109, USA

Vallien, Bertil (Artist)
Roleks Vall
93 Visby
621, SWEDEN

Vallone, Raf
Viale R. Bacone 14
Rome, ITALY

Valot, Daniel L (Business Person)
Total Petroleum
900 19th St
Denver, CO 80202, USA

Valtman, Edmund S (Cartoonist, Editor)
9 Rundelane
Bloomfield, CT 06002-1522, USA

Valverde, Rawley
15207 Magnolia Blvd Unit 106
Sherman Oaks, CA 91403-1105, USA

Van, Allen (Hockey Player)
4890 Ashley Ln Apt 206
Inver Grove Heights, MN 55077-1234, USA

Van, Joey
48607 Presidential Dr # 2
Macomb, MI 48044-1985, USA

Van Allan, Richard
18 Octavia St.
London, ENGLAND SW11 3DN, UNITED KINGDOM (UK)

Van Allsburg, Chris (Writer)
222 Berkeley St Fl 8
C/O Houghton Mifflin Children's Books
Boston, MA 02116-3748, USA

Van Ark, Joan (Actor)
c/o Jason Winters *Sterling/Winters Company, The*
10900 Wilshire Blvd Ste 1550
Los Angeles, CA 90024-6525, USA

Van Buren, Bill (Baseball Player)
Kansas City Monarchs
7006 Kenny Dr
Fulton, MO 65251-6271, USA

Van Buren, Ebert (Football Player)
Philadelphia Eagles
2100 Highway 165 S
Monroe, LA 71202-8219, USA

Van Buren, Steve (Football Player)
Philadelphia Eagles
Professional Football H O F 2121 George Halas Dr NW
Canton, OH 44708, USA

Van Dam, Rob (Actor)
c/o Staff Member *Coast to Coast Talent Group*
3350 Barham Blvd
Los Angeles, CA 90068-1404, USA

Van Damme, Jean-Claude (Actor)
c/o Staff Member *Long Road Productions*
1801 Avenue Of The Stars Fl 6
Los Angeles, CA 90067-5902, USA

van den Hoogenband, Pieter (Swimmer)
PO Box 302
Arnhem 6800 AH, THE NETHERLANDS

Van Der Beek, James (Actor)
c/o Leslie Siebert *Gersh Agency, The (LA)*
232 N Canon Dr
Beverly Hills, CA 90210-5302, USA

Van Der Meer, Johnny
4005 W Leona St
Tampa, FL 33629-8506, USA

Van Der Perren, Kevin (Figure Skater)
Emily Bruines
Dr W Drees laan 35
Goes 4463 XE, THE NETHERLANDS

Van der Pol, Anneliese (Actor, Musician)
c/o Alan Iezman *Shelter Entertainment*
9255 W Sunset Blvd Ste 1010
Los Angeles, CA 90069-3307, USA

Van Derbur-Alter, Marilyn
1401 17th St Ste 600
Denver, CO 80202-1485, USA

Van Devere, Trish
7036 Grasswood Ave
Malibu, CA 90265-4247, USA

Van Dien, Casper (Actor)
c/o Staff Member *Agency for the Performing Arts (APA-LA)*
405 S Beverly Dr
Beverly Hills, CA 90212-4416, USA

Van Doren, Mamie (Actor)
3419 Via Lido # 184
Newport Beach, CA 92663-3908, USA

Van Dusen, Granville
10974 Alta View Dr
Studio City, CA 91604-3903, USA

Van Dyke, Barry (Actor)
27800 Blythedale Rd
Agoura, CA 91301-1824, USA

Van Dyke, Bruce (Football Player)
Philadelphia Eagles
143 Lakeview Dr
Mc Murray, PA 15317-2747, USA

Van Dyke, Dick (Actor)
c/o Staff Member *William Morris Agency (WMA-LA)*
1 William Morris Pl
Beverly Hills, CA 90212-4261, USA

Van Dyke, Jerry
c/o Staff Member *J Cast Productions*
2550 Greenvalley Rd
Los Angeles, CA 90046-1438, USA

Van Dyke, Leroy
29000 Highway V
Smithton, MO 65350-3629, USA

Van Eeghen, Mark (Football Player)
Oakland Raiders
90 Woodstock Ln
Cranston, RI 02920-4639, USA

Van Eman, Charles
12304 Santa Monica Blvd Ste 104
Los Angeles, CA 90025-2586, USA

Van Every, Hal (Football Player)
Green Bay Packers
2700 W 54th St
Minneapolis, MN 55410-2510, USA

Van Exel, Nick (Basketball Player)
c/o Staff Member *San Antonio Spurs*
100 Montana St
Alamodome
San Antonio, TX 78203-1031, USA

Van Galder, Tim (Football Player)
St Louis Cardinals
11851 Charlemagne Dr
Maryland Heights, MO 63043-1505, USA

Van Gorkum, Harry (Actor)
2552 Dearborn Dr
Los Angeles, CA 90068-2240, USA

Van Halen (Music Group)
c/o Jonny (Jon) Podell *Podell Talent Agency LLC*
22 W 21st St Fl 9
New York, NY 10010-7095, USA

Van Halen, Alex
12024 Summit Cir
Beverly Hills, CA 90210-1322, USA

Van Halen, Eddie (Musician)
c/o Staff Member *Azoffmusic Management*
1100 Glendon Ave Ste 2000
Los Angeles, CA 90024-3524, USA

Van Heusen, Billy (Football Player)
Denver Broncos
835 Hudson St
Denver, CO 80220-4436, USA

Van Holt, Brian (Actor)
c/o Brad Schenck *Thruline Entertainment*
9250 Wilshire Blvd Ground Fl
Beverly Hills, CA 90210, USA

Van Horn, Doug (Football Player)
New York Giants
149 Feronia Way
Rutherford, NJ 07070-2437, USA

Van Horn, Kelly (Producer, Writer)
c/o Staff Member *Mirisch Agency*
1801 Century Park E Ste 1801
Los Angeles, CA 90067-2320, USA

Van Horn, Patrick
9200 W Sunset Blvd Ste 1130
Los Angeles, CA 90069-3606, USA

Van Horne, Keith (Football Player)
c/o Staff Member *Dallas Mavericks*
2909 Taylor St
Dallas, TX 75226-1909, USA

Van Houten, Leslie
#W13378 Bed #1B314U Ca Inst. For Women16756 Chino Corona Frontera, CA 91720, USA

van Johnson, Rodney (Actor)
c/o Staff Member *Passions*
4024 Radford Ave
Studio City, CA 91604-2101, USA

Van Kemp, Merete
10000 Santa Monica Blvd # 305
Los Angeles, CA 90067, USA

Van Keulen, Isabelle (Musician)
c/o Staff Member *Columbia Artists Mgmt Inc*
1790 Broadway Fl 6
New York, NY 10019-1412, USA

Van Lowe, Ehrich (Producer, Writer)
c/o Staff Member *Sweet Lorraine Productions*
8060 Melrose Ave Fl 4
Los Angeles, CA 90046-7017, USA

van Nistelrooy, Ruud (Soccer Player)
c/o Staff Member *Manchester United PLC*
Sir Matt Busby Way
Old Trafford
Manchester M160RA, UNITED KINGDOM (UK)

Van Note, Jeff (Football Player)
Atlanta Falcons
345 Hollyberry Dr
Roswell, GA 30076-1215, USA

Van Patten, Dick
13920 Magnolia Blvd
Sherman Oaks, CA 91423-1230, USA

Van Patten, James
14411 Riverside Dr Apt 15
Sherman Oaks, CA 91423-1739, USA

Van Patten, Joyce
c/o Staff Member *SMS Talent Inc*
8730 W Sunset Blvd Ste 440
Los Angeles, CA 90069-2277, USA

Van Patten, Nels
14411 Riverside Dr Apt 18
Sherman Oaks, CA 91423-1740, USA

Van Patten, Tim (Director)
CAA
9830 Wilshire Blvd
Beverly Hills, CA 90212-1804, USA

Van Patten, Timothy
13920 Magnolia Blvd
Sherman Oaks, CA 91423-1230, USA

Van Patten, Vincent
13926 Magnolia Blvd
Sherman Oaks, CA 91423-1230, USA

Van Peebles, Mario (Actor)
c/o Tobie Haggerty *Vincent Cirrincione Associates*
1516 N Fairfax Ave
Los Angeles, CA 90046-2608, USA

Van Pelt, Alex (Football Player)
Buffalo Bills
7209 Quaker Rd
Orchard Park, NY 14127-2008, USA

Van Pelt, Bo (Golfer)
c/o Staff Member *James Management Group*
3411 Preston Rd # C-13
Box 209
Frisco, TX 75034-9010, USA

Van Pelt, Brad (Football Player)
New York Giants
4130 Forest Rd
Harrison, MI 48625-8787, USA

Van Praagh, James (Actor, Producer, Writer)
c/o Suzanne Gluck *William Morris Agency (WMA-NY)*
1325 Avenue Of The Americas
New York, NY 10019-6026, USA

Van Raaphorst, Dick (Football Player)
Dallas Cowboys
720 Devon Ct
San Diego, CA 92109-8005, USA

Van Sant, Doug G (Director)
c/o Gabrielle (Gaby) Morgerman *William Morris Agency (WMA-LA)*
1 William Morris Pl
Beverly Hills, CA 90212-4261, USA

Van Sant, Gus (Actor, Director, Producer, Writer)
c/o Staff Member *Sawtooth*
1300 NW Northrup St Fl 3
Portland, OR 97209-2808, USA

Van Sant-Machado, Helene (Baseball Player)
1221 Marlon Ave
San Bernardino, CA 92407, USA

Van Susteren, Greta (Television Host)
c/o Staff Member *Fox News Channel (NY)*
1211 Avenue Of The Americas
Level C1
New York, NY 10036-8701, USA

Van Valkenberg, Pete (Football Player)
Buffalo Bills
3072 Ninebark Cir
Saint George, UT 84790-8226, USA

Van Valkenburgh, Deborah
2025 Stanley Hills Dr
Los Angeles, CA 90046-7752, USA

Van Varenberg, Kristopher (Actor)
c/o Jack Gilardi *International Creative Management (ICM-LA)*
10250 Constellation Blvd
Los Angeles, CA 90067-6200, USA

Van Vleet, Michael (Baseball Player)
118 Dreamfield Dr
Battle Creek, MI 49014-7846, USA

Van Vooren, Monique
165 E 66th St
New York, NY 10065-6132, USA

Van Wageningen, Yorick (Actor)
c/o Staff Member *Nine Yards Entertainment*
8530 Wilshire Blvd Fl 5
Beverly Hills, CA 90211-3102, USA

Van Wagner, James (Football Player)
New Orleans Saints
5246 N Royal Dr
Traverse City, MI 49684-6984, USA

Van Winkle, Robert 'Vanilla Ice' (Musician)
QT Management
2412 Piedra Dr
Plano, TX 75023-5329, USA

Van Wormer, Steve (Actor)
c/o Staff Member *Innovative Artists (LA)*
1505 10th St
Santa Monica, CA 90401-2805, USA

Van Zandt, Steven (Actor)
c/o Ariel (Ari) Emanuel *Endeavor Agency LLC (LA)*
9601 Wilshire Blvd Fl 3
Beverly Hills, CA 90210-5204, USA

Van Zant, Donnie (Musician)
c/o Staff Member *Vector Management*
1607 17th Ave S
Nashville, TN 37212-2812, USA

VanAllen, James A (Physicist)
5 Woodland Mounds Rd
Rfd 6
Iowa City, IA 52245-1558, USA

VanAllen, Richard (Opera Singer)
18 Octavia St
London SW11 3DN, UNITED KINGDOM (UK)

VanAlmsick, Franziska (Franzi) (Swimmer)
Eichhom
Bizetstr 1
Berlin 13088, GERMANY

VanAmerongen, Jerry (Cartoonist)
10926 Owensmouth Ave
Chatsworth, CA 91311-1342, USA

VanArsdale, Dick (Basketball Player)
5816 N Dragoon Ln
Paradise Valley, AZ 85253-5210, USA

VanArsdale, Tom (Basketball Player)
3930 E Camelback Rd
Phoenix, AZ 85018-2617, USA

VanAuken, John A (Misc)
Canadian Tennis Technology
PO Box 1538
Sydney, NS B1P 6R7, CANADA

VanBasten, Marco (Soccer Player)
AC Milan
Via Turati 3
Milan 20121, ITALY

VanBerg, John C (Jack) (Coach)
420 Fair Hill Dr # 1
Elkton, MD 21921-2573, USA

VanBreda, Kolff Jan (Basketball Player, Coach)
New Orleans Hornets
1250 Poydras St # 19
New Orleans Arena
New Orleans, LA 70113-1804, USA

VanBreda, Kolff Willem (Butch) (Basketball Player, Coach)
1005 Warwick Ct
Sun City Center, FL 33573-5415, USA

VanCamp, Emily (Actor)
International Creative Management (ICM-LA)
10250 Constellation Blvd
Los Angeles, CA 90067-6200, USA

Vance, Courtney B (Actor)
c/o Nicole Nassar *Nicole Nassar PR*
1111 10th St Unit 104
Santa Monica, CA 90403-5363, USA

Vance, Cyrus
425 Lexington Ave
New York, NY 10017-3903, USA

Vance, Eric (Football Player)
Carolina Panthers
17613 Archland Pass Rd
Lutz, FL 33558-8034, USA

Vance, Kenny (Musician)
PO Box 950116
Fort Tilden, NY 11695-0116, USA

Vance, Robert S (Judge)
US Court of Appeals
1800 5th Ave N
Birmingham, AL 35203-2111, USA

VanCitters, Robert L (Psychic)
University of Washington
Medical School
Physiology Dept
Seattle, WA 98815, USA

VanClief, D G (Race Car Driver)
Breeders Cup Ltd
2525 Harrodsburg Rd Ste 500
Lexington, KY 40504-3359, USA

VanCulin, Samuel (Religious Leader)
All Hallows Church
43 Trinity Square
London EC3N 4DJ, UNITED KINGDOM (UK)

VanDam, Jose (Opera Singer)
Zurich Artists
Rutistr 52
Zurich, Gockhausen 8044, SWITZERLAND

VanDantzig, Rudi (Choreographer)
Emma-Straat 27
Amsterdam, THE NETHERLANDS

Vandeman, George
1600 Waverly Rd
San Marino, CA 91108-2038, USA

Vanden Bosch, Kyle (Football Player)
Arizona Cardinals
25 Governors Way
Brentwood, TN 37027-8926, USA

VandenBerg, Lodewijk (Astronaut)
Constellation Technology Corp
7887 Bryan Dairy Rd Ste 100
Largo, FL 33777-1498, USA

VandenBergh, M A (Business Person)
Royal Dutch Petroleum
30 Van Bylandtlaan
Hague, HR 2596, THE NETHERLANDS

Vander, Jagt Guy (Misc)
Baker & Hostetler
1050 Connecticut Ave NW
Washington, DC 20036-5304, USA

Vander, Musetta (Actor)
c/o Richard Kerner *KMA*
311 N Robertson Blvd # 288
Beverly Hills, CA 90211-1705, USA

Vanderbeek, Matt (Football Player)
Indianapolis Colts
4 Monstad St
Aliso Viejo, CA 92656-6246, USA

Vanderberg Shaw, Helen (Coach)
Heaven's Fitness
301 14th St NW
Calgary, AB T2N 2A1, CANADA

Vanderbundt, Skip (Football Player)
San Francisco 49ers
4225 Los Coches Way
Sacramento, CA 95864-5241, USA

Vanderhoef, Larry N (Educator)
University of California
President's Office
Davis, CA 95616, USA

Vanderkelen, Ron (Football Player)
Minnesota Vikings
5300 Vernon Ave S Apt 102
Edina, MN 55436-2328, USA

Vanderlip-Ozburn, Dolly (Baseball Player)
N2844 Smith Valley Rd # Rr2
La Crosse, WI 54601-2935, USA

Vanderloo, Mark (Model)
Wilhelmina Models
300 Park Ave S Fl 2
New York, NY 10010-5398, USA

VanDerMeer, Simon (Nobel Prize Laureate)
4 Chemin des Corbillettes
Saconnex, GD 1218, SWITZERLAND

Vandermeersch, Bernard (Misc)
University of Bordeaux
Anthropology Dept
Bordeaux, FRANCE

Vandersea, Phil (Football Player)
Green Bay Packers
34 Hunting Ave
Shrewsbury, MA 01545-3177, USA

Vanderveen, Loet (Artist)
Lime Creek 5
Big Sur, CA 93920, USA

VanDerveer, Tara (Coach)
1036 Cascade Dr
Menlo Park, CA 94025-6629, USA

Vandervoort, Laura (Actor)
c/o Staff Member *Noble Caplan Abrams*
1260 Yonge St 2nd Fl
Toronto, ON M4T 1W6, CANADA

VandeSande, Theo A (Cinematographer)
2337 High Oak Dr
Los Angeles, CA 90068-2515, USA

VandeWetering, John E (Educator)
17 Cricket Hill Dr
Pittsford, NY 14534-2152, USA

Vandis, Titos
1930 Century Park W # 303
Los Angeles, CA 90067-6802, USA

VanDyke, Philip (Actor)
1464 Madera Rd # 108N
Simi Valley, CA 93065-3077, USA

Vaneck, Pierre (Actor)
c/o Staff Member *Cineart*
36 Rue de Ponthieu
Paris 75008, FRANCE

Vangelis (Musician)
c/o Staff Member *Robert M Urband & Associates*
8981 W Sunset Blvd Ste 311
West Hollywood, CA 90069-1881, USA

VanGundy, Stan (Coach)
c/o Staff Member *Miami Heat*
601 Biscayne Blvd
American Airlines Arena
Miami, FL 33132-1801, USA

VanHorn, Buddy (Director)
4409 Ponca Ave
Toluca Lake, CA 91602-2513, USA

Vanilla Fudge
141 Dunbar Ave
Fords, NJ 08863-1551, USA

Vann, Marc (Actor)
c/o Staff Member *The McCabe Group*
8285 W Sunset Blvd Ste 1
West Hollywood, CA 90046-2420, USA

Vannelli, Gino
28205 Agoura Rd
Agoura Hills, CA 91301-2482, USA

Vanner, Sue
26 Wellesley Rd. Cheswick
London, ENGLAND W4 4BN, UNITED KINGDOM (UK)

Vanous, Lucky (Actor, Model)
28345 La Calenta Mission
Vlejo, CA 92692, USA

Vanover, Larry (Baseball Player)
3037 Sterling Ct
Owensboro, KY 42303-6393, USA

Vanover, Tamarick (Football Player)
Kansas City Chiefs
703 NW Wilson St
Lake City, FL 32055-1863, USA

Vanoy, Vern (Football Player)
New York Giants
3710 E 51st St Apt 409
Kansas City, MO 64130-3061, USA

Vansina, Jan M J (Historian)
2810 Ridge Rd
Madison, WI 53705-5224, USA

Vansittart, Peter (Writer)
Little Manor
Church Hill
Kersey
Ipswich, Suffolk 1P7 6DZ, UNITED
KINGDOM (UK)

Vanska, Osmo
Minnesota Symphony
1111 Nicollet Ave
Orchestra Hall
Minneapolis, MN 55403-2406, USA

VanValkenburgh, Deborah (Actor)
Gaye West
PO Box 1515
Studio City, CA 91614-0515, USA

Vanvieren, Pete (Baseball Player,
Sportscaster)
Atlanta Braves
12260 Magnolia Cir
Alpharetta, GA 30005-7234, USA

Vanzant, Iyanla (Reality TV Star, Writer)
c/o Staff Member *Starting Over*
6007 Sepulveda Blvd
Van Nuys, CA 91411-2502, USA

Vapors, The
44 Valmoral Dr. Woking
Surrey, ENGLAND, UNITED KINGDOM
(UK)

Varda, Agnes (Director)
Cine-Tamaris
86 Rue Daguerre
Paris 75014, FRANCE

Vardalos, Nia (Actor)
c/o Staff Member *Creative Artists Agency
LCC (CAA-LA)*
2000 Avenue Of The Stars
Los Angeles, CA 90067-4700, USA

Vardell, Tommy (Football Player)
Cleveland Browns
2424 E Ruby Hill Dr
Pleasanton, CA 94566-5100, USA

Varga, Imre (Artist)
Bartha Utca 1
Budapest XII, HUNGARY

Vargas, Elizabeth (Television Host)
c/o Staff Member *20/20*
147 Columbus Ave
Abc
New York, NY 10023-6503, USA

Vargas, Jacob (Actor)
c/o Aaron Ray *Nine Yards Entertainment*
8530 Wilshire Blvd Fl 5
Beverly Hills, CA 90211-3102, USA

Vargas, Jay R (War Hero)
12466 Thombrush Court
San Diego, CA 92131, USA

Vargas, Ramon (Opera Singer)
Columbia Artists Mgmt Inc
1790 Broadway Fl 6
New York, NY 10019-1412, USA

Vargas, Roberto (Baseball Player)
Chicago American Giants
24 Calle Brizaida
Urb Runoz Rivera
Guaynabo, PR 00969-3529, USA

Vargas, Valentina (Actor)
5 Rue Norvins
Paris 75018, FRANCE

Vargo, Ed (Baseball Player)
101 Freedom Rd
Butler, PA 16001-1304, USA

Vargo, Larry (Football Player)
Detroit Lions
23337 S Colonial Ct
Saint Clair Shores, MI 48080-2605, USA

Vargo, Tim (Business Person)
AutoZone Inc
123 S Front St
Memphis, TN 38103-3618, USA

Varian, Hal R (Economist)
576 Del Amigo Rd
Danville, CA 94526-3215, USA

Varitek, Jason (Baseball Player)
321 Cypress Landing Dr
Longwood, FL 32779-2602, USA

Varley of Chesterfield, Eric G
(Government Official)
Coalite Group
Buttermilk Lane
Bolsover, Derbyshire S44 6AB, UNITED
KINGDOM (UK)

Varmus, Harold E (Nobel Prize Laureate)
Memorial Sloan-Kettering Cancer Center
1275 York Ave
New York, NY 10065-6007, USA

Varnado, Victor (Actor, Comedian)
New York Comedy Consultants
1600 Broadway # 410
New York, NY 10019-7413, USA

Varo, Marton (Artist)
Phillips Gallery
PO Box 5807
Carmel, CA 93921-5807, USA

Varona, Clemente (Baseball Player)
Memphis Red Sox
1103 E Florida St
Greensboro, NC 27406-3220, USA

Varoni, Miguel (Director)
c/o Staff Member *TV Caracol*
Calle 76 #11 - 35
Piso 10AA
Bogota DC 26484, COLOMBIA

Varrela, Leonor (Actor)
c/o Mimi DiTrani *Untitled Entertainment
(LA)*
331 N Maple Dr Fl 3
Beverly Hills, CA 90210-3827, USA

Varrichione, Frank
55 Dinsmore Ave Apt 103
Framingham, MA 01702-6054, USA

Varrichone, Frank (Football Player)
PO Box 319
RR 72
Alton, NH 03809, USA

Vartan, Michael (Actor)
c/o Stephen Hanks *Stephen Hanks
Management*
252 N Larchmont Blvd Ste 200
Los Angeles, CA 90004-3754, USA

Vartan, Sylvie (Musician)
Scotti
706 N Beverly Dr
Beverly Hills, CA 90210-3322, USA

Varty, Keith (Designer, Fashion Designer)
Bosco di San Francesco #6
Sirolo, ITALY

Varvatos, John (Designer, Fashion
Designer)
Soho New York
149 Mercer St
New York, NY 10012-3240, USA

Vasarely, Victor
83 rue aux Religues
Annet-sur-Marne F-77410, FRANCE

Vasary, Tamas (Musician)
9 Village Road
London N3, UNITED KINGDOM (UK)

Vasicek, Victor (Football Player)
Los Angeles Rams
1502 Douglas Ave
Midland, TX 79701-4056, USA

Vasile, Radu (Prime Minister)
Premier's Office
Piata Vicotriel 1
Bucharest 71201, ROMANIA

Vasilyev, Vladimir V (Ballerina, Dancer)
Bolshoi Theater
Teatralnaya Pl 1
Moscow 103009, RUSSIA

Vasquez, Juan F (Judge)
US Tax Court
400 2nd St NW
Washington, DC 20217-0002, USA

Vasquez, Junior (DJ, Musician)
Junior Vasquez Music
647 9th Ave Apt 3
New York, NY 10036-3661, USA

Vasquez, LaLa (Television Host)
c/o Michael (Mike) Esterman *Esterman
Entertainment*
214 Park Rd
Riva, MD 21140-1224, USA

Vasquez, Rana Mario (Publisher)
El Sol de Mexico
Guillermo Prieto 7
Mexico City, DF, MEXICO

Vasquez, Randy
10600 Holman Ave Apt 1
Los Angeles, CA 90024-5931, USA

Vass, Joan (Designer, Fashion Designer)
Joan Vass Inc
36 E 31st St
New York, NY 10016-6821, USA

Vasser, Jimmy (Race Car Driver)
2398 Broadway St
San Francisco, CA 94115-1234, USA

Vassey, Liz (Actor)
c/o Staff Member *Endeavor Agency LLC
(LA)*
9601 Wilshire Blvd Fl 3
Beverly Hills, CA 90210-5204, USA

Vassilieva, Sofia (Actor)
c/o Staff Member *William Morris Agency
(WMA-LA)*
1 William Morris Pl
Beverly Hills, CA 90212-4261, USA

Vassillou, George V (President)
PO Box 874
21 Academiou Ave
Aglandjia, Nicosia, CYPRUS

Vasu, P (Actor, Bollywood)
25 D Tilak Street
T Nagar
Chennai, TN 600017, INDIA

Vaswani, Vivek (Actor, Bollywood)
141 142 Dalamal Park
Cuffe Parade
Bombay, MS 400 005, INDIA

Vasys, Arunas (Football Player)
Philadelphia Eagles
2525 Hanford Ln
Aurora, IL 60502-6971, USA

Vasyuchenko, Yuri (Ballerina, Dancer)
Bolshoi Theater
Teatralnaya Pl 1
Moscow 103009, RUSSIA

Vasyutin, Vladimir V (Cricketer)
Potcha Kosmonavtov
Moskovskoi Oblasti
Syvisdny Goroduk 141160, RUSSIA

Vataha, Randy (Football Player)
New England Patriots
36 Longmeadow Rd
Lincoln, MA 01773-4810, USA

Vatterott, Charles (Football Player)
St Louis Cardinals
3708 W Pine Orchard Dr
Pearland, TX 77581-8814, USA

Vaughan, Denis E (Musician)
c/o Staff Member *Schofer/Gold Agency*
51 Riverside Dr
New York, NY 10024, USA

Vaughan, Greg
c/o Staff Member *William Morris Agency
(WMA-LA)*
1 William Morris Pl
Beverly Hills, CA 90212-4261, USA

Vaughan, Jimmie (Musician)
2300 S 3rd St
Austin, TX 78704-5087, USA

Vaughan, Peter (Actor)
International Creative Mgmt
76 Oxford St
London W1N 0AX, UNITED KINGDOM
(UK)

Vaughan, Porter (Baseball Player)
Philadelphia Athletics
2931 Polo Pkwy
Midlothian, VA 23113-1453, USA

Vaughan, Stoll (Musician)
c/o Staff Member *Paradigm (Monterey)*
509 Hartnell St
Monterey, CA 93940-2825, USA

Vaughn, Bruce (Golfer)
5615 N Monroe St
Hutchinson, KS 67502-3251, USA

Vaughn, Countess (Actor)
c/o Staff Member *Amsel Eisenstadt &
Frazier Inc*
5055 Wilshire Blvd Ste 865
Los Angeles, CA 90036-6109, USA

Vaughn, Damian (Football Player)
Tampa Bay Buccaneers
10250 E Mountain View Rd Apt 266
Scottsdale, AZ 85258-5307, USA

Vaughn, David (Basketball Player)
New Jersey Nets
390 Murray Hill Pkwy
East Rutherford, NJ 07073-2109, USA

Vaughn, Dewayne (Baseball Player)
Texas Rangers
5501 NW 37th St
Warr Acres, OK 73122-2210, USA

Vaughn, Gregory L (Greg) (Baseball Player)
Milwaukee Brewers
6309 Thresher Ct
Elk Grove, CA 95758-4259, USA

Vaughn, Jacque (Basketball Player)
Atlanta Hawks
190 Marietta St NW
Atlanta, GA 30303-2717, USA

Vaughn, Jimmie (Musician)
Mark I Mgmt
PO Box 29480
Austin, TX 78755-6480, USA

Vaughn, John H (Johnny) (Coach, Football Player)
Highway 6 W
Oxford, MS 38655, USA

Vaughn, Jonathan S (Jon) (Football Player)
New England Patriots
224 N US Highway 67
Florissant, MO 63031-5904, USA

Vaughn, Kip (Baseball Player)
1820 Wildbrook Ct Apt C
Concord, CA 94521-1464, USA

Vaughn, Linda (Race Car Driver)
PO Box 352
Newville, PA 17241-0352, USA

Vaughn, Matthew (Actor)
c/o Cynthia Pett-Dante *Brillstein-Grey Entertainment*
9150 Wilshire Blvd Ste 350
Beverly Hills, CA 90212-3453, USA

Vaughn, Maurice S (Mo) (Baseball Player)
Boston Red Sox
5050 Squirrel Bnd
Columbus, OH 43220-2278, USA

Vaughn, Ned (Actor)
James/Levy/Jacobson
3500 W Olive Ave Ste 920
Burbank, CA 91505-5514, USA

Vaughn, Robert (Actor)
PO Box 2071
Los Angeles, CA 90028, USA

Vaughn, Terri J (Actor)
c/o Sandra Siegal *Siegal Company, The*
9025 Wilshire Blvd Ste 400
Beverly Hills, CA 90211-1828, USA

Vaughn, Thomas R (Football Player)
Detroit Lions
860 E Linda Ln
Gilbert, AZ 85234-5969, USA

Vaughn, Vince (Actor)
c/o Nick Stevens *United Talent Agency (UTA)*
9560 Wilshire Blvd Ste 500
Beverly Hills, CA 90212-2401, USA

Vaugier, Emmanuelle (Actor)
c/o Staff Member *Innovative Artists (LA)*
1505 10th St
Santa Monica, CA 90401-2805, USA

Vavra, Otakar (Director, Writer)
Music & Arts Academy
Smetanova Nabrezo 2
Prague 1 11000, CZECH REPUBLIC

Vazquez, Armondo (Baseball Player)
Indianapolis Clowns
160 W 85th St Apt 1K
New York, NY 10024-4410, USA

Vazquez, Javier (Baseball Player)
c/o Staff Member *Montreal Expos*
4549 Avenue Pierre de Coubertin
Montreal, PQ H1V 3N7, CANADA

Vazquez, Yul (Actor)
c/o Sarah Fargo *Paradigm (NY)*
360 Park Ave S Fl 16
New York, NY 10010-1716, USA

Veal, Coot (Baseball Player)
Detroit Tigers
238 Stone Gables Dr
Gray, GA 31032-5526, USA

Veale, Robert A (Bob) (Baseball Player)
Pittsburgh Pirates
2833 Bush Blvd
Birmingham, AL 35208-2227, USA

Veals, Elton (Football Player)
Pittsburgh Steelers
2981 Joyce Dr
Baton Rouge, LA 70814-2568, USA

Veasey, Josephine (Opera Singer)
5 Meadow Biew
Whitechurch
Hunts RG28 7BL, UNITED KINGDOM (UK)

Vecchione, Mike (Scientist)
Nat'l Oceanic/Atmospheric Admin
14th & Constitution
Washington, DC 20230-0001, USA

Vecsei, Eva H (Architect)
Vecsei Architects
1425 Rue du Fort
Montreal, PQ H3H 2C2, CANADA

Vecsey, George S (Sportscaster, Writer)
New York Times
229 W 43rd St
Editorial Dept
New York, NY 10036-3959, USA

Vedder, Eddie (Musician)
c/o Staff Member *Creative Artists Agency LCC (CAA-LA)*
2000 Avenue Of The Stars
Los Angeles, CA 90067-4700, USA

Vee, Bobby (Musician, Songwriter, Writer)
The Bobby Vee Connection
St Ives
Eden Road
Gordon, Berwickshire TD3 6JT, SCOTLAND

Veerapha, P S (Actor, Bollywood)
Porur
Chennai, TN 600116, INDIA

Vega, Alexa (Actor, Musician)
S D B Partners
1801 Avenue Of Stars Ste 902
Los Angeles, CA 90067-5981, USA

Vega, Paz (Actor)
c/o Jorge Insua *Creative Artists Agency LCC (CAA-LA)*
2000 Avenue Of The Stars
Los Angeles, CA 90067-4700, USA

Vega, Suzanne (Musician)
c/o Staff Member *William Morris Agency (WMA-NY)*
1325 Avenue Of The Americas
New York, NY 10019-6026, USA

Vega 4 (Music Group)
c/o Staff Member *Paradigm (Monterey)*
509 Hartnell St
Monterey, CA 93940-2825, USA

Vegas, Dirty (Music Group)
c/o Staff Member *Creative Artists Agency LCC (CAA-LA)*
2000 Avenue Of The Stars
Los Angeles, CA 90067-4700, USA

Veigel, Al (Baseball Player)
Boston Bees
1907 Dover Ave
Dover, OH 44622-2426, USA

Veil, Simone (Government Official)
11 Place Vauban
Paris 75007, FRANCE

Veils, The (Music Group)
c/o Staff Member *Paradigm (Monterey)*
509 Hartnell St
Monterey, CA 93940-2825, USA

Veingrad, Alan (Football Player)
Green Bay Packers
614 SE 26th Ave
Fort Lauderdale, FL 33301-2708, USA

Vejar, Chico (Boxer)
56 Glenbrook Rd # 3214
Stamford, CT 06902, USA

Vejtasa, Stanley W (Swede) (War Hero)
1649 Summit Ln
Escondido, CA 92025-7535, USA

Vel Johnson, Reginald (Actor)
DGRW
1501 Broadway Ste 703
New York, NY 10036-5505, USA

Velarde, Randy (Baseball Player)
New York Yankees
4902 Thames Ct
Midland, TX 79705-1796, USA

Velasquez, Guillermo (Baseball Player)
San Diego Padres
13577 Fern Pine Rd
Victorville, CA 92392-1265, USA

Velasquez, Jaci (Musician)
Jaci Inc
PO Box 3568
Brentwood, TN 37024-3568, USA

Velasquez, Jorge
770 Allerton Ave
Bronx, NY 10467-8819, USA

Velasquez, Patricia (Actor, Model)
Lasher McManus Robinson
1964 Westwood Blvd Ste 400
Los Angeles, CA 90025-4695, USA

Velazquez, Nadine (Actor, Model)
c/o Ivan De Paz *Arenas Entertainment*
100 N Crescent Dr
Garden Level
Beverly Hills, CA 90210-5408, USA

Velazquez, Patricia (Actor)
c/o Eric Gold *Mosaic Media Group*
24 Music Sq W Fl 1
Nashville, TN 37203-6661, USA

Velez, Eddie (Actor)
c/o Staff Member *Stone Manners Talent & Literary (LA)*
6500 Wilshire Blvd Ste 550
Los Angeles, CA 90048-4950, USA

Velez, Gloria (Model)
c/o Michael (Mike) Esterman *Esterman Entertainment*
214 Park Rd
Riva, MD 21140-1224, USA

Velez, Lauren (Actor)
c/o Staff Member *Gersh Agency, The (LA)*
232 N Canon Dr
Beverly Hills, CA 90210-5302, USA

Velez, Otto (Baseball Player)
33 Villas De Cambalache
Rio Grande, PR 00966, USA

Velga, Carlos A Wahnon de C (Prime Minister)
Prime Minister's Office
Varzea CP 16
Praia, Santiago, CAPE VERDE

Velgos, Alicia (Actor)
William Morris Agency
151 El Camino Dr
Beverly Hills, CA 90212-2775, USA

Velikhov, Yevgeni P (Physicist)
Kurchatovskiy Institute
Kurchatova Pl 1
Moscow 12182, RUSSIA

Veljohnson, Reginald (Actor)
9637 Allenwood Dr
Los Angeles, CA 90046, USA

Vella, John (Football Player)
Oakland Raiders
1890 Saint George Rd
Danville, CA 94526-6253, USA

Veloso, Caetano (Musician, Songwriter, Writer)
Natasha Records/Shows
Rua Marquis Sao Vincente
Rio de Janiero, BRAZIL

Veltman, Martinus J G (Nobel Prize Laureate)
Sachubertiaan 15
Bilthoven 3723, THE NETHERLANDS

Velvet, Jimmy
PO Box 808
Lititz, PA 17543-0538, USA

Velvet Revolver (Music Group)
c/o Staff Member *RCA Records (LA)*
8750 Wilshire Blvd Fl 2
Beverly Hills, CA 90211-2715, USA

Venable, Mac (Baseball Player)
San Francisco Giants
107 Clark St
San Rafael, CA 94901-3604, USA

Venables, Terry F (Coach, Football Coach)
Terry Venables Holdings
213 Putney Bridge Road
London SW15 2NY, UNITED KINGDOM (UK)

Venafro, Mike (Baseball Player)
Texas Rangers
16841 Sanibel Sunset Ct Apt 102
Fort Myers, FL 33908-2999, USA

Venditti, Antonello
Via Zara 12
Rome, ITALY

Venet, Bernar (Artist)
533 Canal St
New York, NY 10013-1328, USA

Veneziale, Mike (Baseball Player)
110 Cloverdale Ln
Williamstown, NJ 08094-2341, USA

Vengerov, Maxim (Musician)
Lies Askonas
6 Henrietta St
London WC2E 8LA, UNITED KINGDOM (UK)

Venitucci, Michele (Actor)
Carol Levi Co
Vla Giuseppe Pisanelli
Rome 00196, ITALY

Venkataraman, Ramaswamy (Ex-President, President)
Pothigal
Greenways Road
Chennai, TN 600028, INDIA

Venniraadai, Murthy (Actor, Bollywood)
44 4th Main Road
Kottur Garden
Chennai, TN 600085, INDIA

Venora, Diane (Actor)
Innovative Artists
1505 10th St
Santa Monica, CA 90401-2805, USA

Ventimiglia, John
9150 Wilshire Blvd Ste 350
Beverly Hills, CA 90212-3453, USA

Ventimiglia, Jon (Actor)
c/o Staff Member *Gersh Agency, The (NY)*
41 Madison Ave Fl 33
New York, NY 10010-2202, USA

Ventimiglia, Milo (Actor)
c/o Rodney Omanoff *Creative Management Group (CMG)*
8522 National Blvd Ste 108
Culver City, CA 90232-2454, USA

Ventimilia, Jeffrey (Actor)
c/o Staff Member *International Creative Management (ICM-LA)*
10250 Constellation Blvd
Los Angeles, CA 90067-6200, USA

Ventresca, Vincent (Actor)
Mindel/Donigan
9057 Nemo St # C
West Hollywood, CA 90069-5511, USA

Ventura, Jesse (Politician)
c/o Mark Itkin *William Morris Agency (WMA-LA)*
1 William Morris Pl
Beverly Hills, CA 90212-4261, USA

Ventura, Robin (Baseball Player)
c/o Staff Member *Los Angeles Dodgers (LA Dodgers)*
1000 Elysian Park Ave
Los Angeles, CA 90012-1112, USA

Ventura, Robin M (Baseball Player)
106 Dingletown Rd
Greenwich, CT 06830-3540, USA

Ventura-Manina, Virginia (Baseball Player)
PO Box 2306
Garfield, NJ 07026-4306, USA

Ventures, The (Music Group)
11761 E Speedway Blvd
Tucson, AZ 85748-2017, USA

Venturi, Ken (Golfer)
161 Waterford Cir
Rancho Mirage, CA 92270-3100, USA

Venus Hum (Music Group)
c/o Staff Member *Paradigm (Monterey)*
509 Hartnell St
Monterey, CA 93940-2825, USA

Vera, Audry (Actor)
c/o Staff Member *Televisa*
Blvd Adolfo Lopez Mateos 232
Colonia San Angel INN
DF CP 01060, MEXICO

Veras, Qullvio (Baseball Player)
Florida Marlins
8014 Wiles Rd # 8A
Coral Springs, FL 33067-2072, USA

Verastegui, Eduardo (Actor)
The Firm
9465 Wilshire Blvd
Beverly Hills, CA 90212-2612, USA

Verba, Ross (Football Player)
Green Bay Packers
13505 4th St N
Stillwater, MN 55082-1921, USA

Verbanic, Joe (Baseball Player)
Philadelphia Phillies
85462 Lorane Hwy
Eugene, OR 97405-9409, USA

Verbinski, Gore (Director, Producer)
c/o Philip Raskind *Endeavor Agency LLC (LA)*
9601 Wilshire Blvd Fl 3
Beverly Hills, CA 90210-5204, USA

Verble, Gene (Baseball Player)
Washington Senators
633 Camrose Cir NE
Concord, NC 28025-3280, USA

Verdi, Frank (Baseball Player)
New York Yankees
10961 Peppertree Ln
Port Richey, FL 34668-2420, USA

Verdin, Clarence (Football Player)
Washington Redskins
6221 Eastover Dr
New Orleans, LA 70128-3619, USA

Verdugo, Elena
PO Box 2048
Chula Vista, CA 91912-2048, USA

Vereen, Ben (Actor, Dancer, Musician)
c/o Bernard Carneol *Progressive Artists Agency*
400 S Beverly Dr Ste 216
Beverly Hills, CA 90212-4404, USA

Vereen, Carl (Football Player)
Green Bay Packers
140 Connemara Rd
Roswell, GA 30075-4883, USA

Veres, Dave (Baseball Player)
Houston Astros
1922 Hollys Way
Sugar Land, TX 77479-5574, USA

Veres, Randy (Baseball Player)
Milwaukee Brewers
9213 W Frank Ave
Peoria, AZ 85382-5364, USA

Vergara, Sofia (Actor, Musician)
Latin World Entertainment Agency
2800 Biscayne Blvd
Miami, FL 33137-4528, USA

Verhoeven, John (Baseball Player)
California Angels
8401 Tepic Dr
Paramount, CA 90723-4450, USA

Verhoeven, Lis
Merzstrasse 14
Munich D-81679, GERMANY

Verhoeven, Paul (Director, Writer)
c/o Staff Member *The Marion Rosenberg Office*
PO Box 69826
Los Angeles, CA 90069-0826, USA

Verica, Tom (Actor)
20 Ironsides St Apt 18
Marina Del Rey, CA 90292-5958, USA

Veris, Garin (Football Player)
New England Patriots
29 Cedar Ave
Stoneham, MA 02180-2420, USA

Verma, Deven (Actor, Bollywood)
7B Todiwala Road
Pune, MS 400041, INDIA

Vermeil, Dick (Coach)
c/o Staff Member *Kansas City Chiefs*
1 Arrowhead Dr
Kansas City, MO 64129-1651, USA

Vernon, Kate
1505 10th St
Santa Monica, CA 90401-2805, USA

Vernon, Mickey (Baseball Player)
Washington Senators
1343 W Baltimore Pike
Media, PA 19063-5519, USA

Veronica (Musician)
c/o Staff Member *Diva Central Inc*
7510 W Sunset Blvd Ste 1445
Los Angeles, CA 90046-3408, USA

Verplank, Scott (Golfer)
1850 W Waterloo Rd
Edmond, OK 73025-1801, USA

Verraros, Jim (Musician)
c/o Staff Member *Fox Television Studios*
10201 W Pico Blvd Bldg 41
Los Angeles, CA 90064-2606, USA

Versace, Donatella (Designer, Fashion Designer)
Gianni Versace SPA
Via Manzoni 38
Milan 20121, ITALY

Verser, David (Football Player)
Cincinnati Bengals
2600 SW Arvonia Pl
Topeka, KS 66614-5294, USA

Versini, Marie
23 res. Elysses 78170 La Celle-St Cloud, FRANCE

Vertical Horizon (Music Group)
c/o Staff Member *Paradigm (Monterey)*
509 Hartnell St
Monterey, CA 93940-2825, USA

Veruca Salt (Music Group)
Veruca Salt/Louise Post
PO Box 291105
Los Angeles, CA 90029-9105, USA

Verve Pipe, The (Music Group)
c/o Staff Member *Paradigm (Monterey)*
509 Hartnell St
Monterey, CA 93940-2825, USA

Verve, The (Music Group)
c/o Staff Member *Paradigm (Monterey)*
509 Hartnell St
Monterey, CA 93940-2825, USA

Verveen, Arie (Actor)
c/o Staff Member *Stone Meyer & Genow*
9665 Wilshire Blvd Ste 510
Beverly Hills, CA 90212-2312, USA

Verwey, Bob (Golfer)
I M G
1360 E 9th St Ste 100
Cleveland, OH 44114-1730, USA

Veryzer, Tom (Baseball Player)
Detroit Tigers
41 Union Ave
Islip, NY 11751-3919, USA

Vessey, Tricia (Actor)
c/o Staff Member *Brillstein-Grey Entertainment*
9150 Wilshire Blvd Ste 350
Beverly Hills, CA 90212-3453, USA

Vest, R Lamar (Religious Leader)
Church of God
PO Box 2430
Cleveland, TN 37320-2430, USA

Vetri, Victoria (Actor)
7045 Hawthorn Ave Apt 206
Los Angeles, CA 90028-6942, USA

Vetrov, Aleksandr (Ballerina, Dancer)
Bolshoi Theater
Teatralnaya Pl 1
Moscow 103009, RUSSIA

Vetter, Jack (Football Player)
Brooklyn Dodgers
312 N Grand St
McPherson, KS 67460-4428, USA

Vettori, Ernst (Skier)
Fohrenweg 1
Absam, Eichat 6060, AUSTRIA

Vez, El
3322 Hamilton Way
Los Angeles, CA 90026-2112, USA

Viaene, David (Football Player)
New England Patriots
W9859 School Rd
Hortonville, WI 54944-9630, USA

Viardo, Vladimir V (Musician)
457 Piedmont Rd
Cresskill, NJ 07626, USA

Vicario, Arantxa Sanchez
22 E 71st St
New York, NY 10021-4975, USA

Vichitra (Actor, Bollywood)
821 Jeevanandam Salai
Chennai, TN 600078, INDIA

Vick, Michael (Football Player)
Atlanta Falcons
5108 W Creek Ct
Suffolk, VA 23435-3523, USA

Vick, Roger (Football Player)
New York Jets
21015 Harvest Terrace Ln
Spring, TX 77379-3080, USA

Vickaryous, Scott (Actor)
c/o Brady McKay *Saffron Management*
9171 Wilshire Blvd Ste 441
Beverly Hills, CA 90210-5516, USA

Vickers, Brian (Race Car Driver)
27 High Tech Blvd
Thomasville, NC 27360-5560, USA

Vickers, Jonathan S (Jon) (Opera Singer)
Collingtree
18 Riddlells Bay Road
Warwick WK 04, BERMUDA

Vickers, Kipp (Football Player)
Indianapolis Colts
3626 Mill Run Cir Apt 1718
Indianapolis, IN 46214-5066, USA

Vickers, Steve (Hockey Player)
209 Washington Ave
Batavia, NY 14020-2211, USA

Vickers, Yvette
10021 Westwanda Dr
Beverly Hills, CA 90210-1428, USA

Victor, James
1944 Whitley Ave Apt 306
Los Angeles, CA 90068-4100, USA

Victoria (Royalty)
Royal Palace
Kung Slottet
Stottsbacken
Stockholm 11130, SWEDEN

Victorin (Ursache), Archbishop (Religious Leader)
Romanian Orthodox Church
19959 Riopelle St
Detroit, MI 48203-1249, USA

Victorino, Shane (Baseball Player)
San Diego Padres
498 S Alu Rd
Wailuku, HI 96793-1508, USA

Vida Blue (Music Group)
c/o Staff Member *Paradigm (Monterey)*
509 Hartnell St
Monterey, CA 93940-2825, USA

Vidal, Christina (Actor)
c/o Bob McGowan *McGowan Management*
8733 W Sunset Blvd Ste 103
W Hollywood, CA 90069-2241, USA

Vidal, Deborah (Golfer)
2033 Paramount Dr
Los Angeles, CA 90068-3120, USA

Vidal, Gore (Writer)
c/o Robert (Bob) Bookman *Creative Artists Agency LCC (CAA-LA)*
2000 Avenue Of The Stars
Los Angeles, CA 90067-4700, USA

Vidal, Jean-Pierre (Skier)
Ski Federation
50 Rue de Marquisats
BP 51
Annecy Cedex 74011, FRANCE

Vidal, Lisa (Actor)
c/o Bob McGowan *McGowan Management*
8733 W Sunset Blvd Ste 103
W Hollywood, CA 90069-2241, USA

Vidal, Ricardo J Cardinal (Religious Leader)
Chancery
PO Box 52
Cebu City 6401, PHILIPPINES

Vidal, Rodrigo (Actor)
c/o Staff Member *Televisa*
Blvd Adolfo Lopez Mateos 232
Colonia San Angel INN
DF CP 01060, MEXICO

Vidali, Lynn (Swimmer)
14750 Mosegard Ln
Morgan Hill, CA 95037-9604, USA

Vidmar, Peter (Gymnast)
23832 Via Roble
Coto De Caza, CA 92679-4011, USA

Vidro, Jose A C (Baseball Player)
Montreal Expos
Olympic Stadium
Montreal, PQ H1V 3N7, CANADA

Vie, Richard C (Business Person)
PO Box 191
Lake Forest, IL 60045-0191, USA

Viehboeck, Franz (Cosmonaut)
Brunnerbergstr 3021
Perchtoldsdorf 2380, AUSTRIA

Vieillard, Roger (Artist)
7 Rue de l'Estrapade
Paris 75005, FRANCE

Vieira, Meredith (Game Show Host, Television Host)
c/o Staff Member *Today Show, The*
30 Rockefeller Plz # 374E
New York, NY 10112-0015, USA

Vieira, Patrick (Soccer Player)
Juventus FC
Corso Galileo Ferraris 32
Turin 10128, ITALY

Vieluf, Vince (Actor)
c/o Staff Member *Endeavor Agency LLC (LA)*
9601 Wilshire Blvd Fl 3
Beverly Hills, CA 90210-5204, USA

Viener, John (Actor)
c/o Staff Member *Don Buchwald & Associates Inc (LA)*
6500 Wilshire Blvd Ste 2200
Los Angeles, CA 90048-4942, USA

Viera, Joey
4253 Navajo Ave
Toluca Lake, CA 91602-2913, USA

Viereck, Peter (Writer)
1346 Murrell Ave
Columbus, OH 43212-3558, USA

Viertel, Peter Wyhergut
7250 Klosters
Grisons, SWITZERLAND

Vieth, Michelle (Actor)
c/o Staff Member *Televisa*
Blvd Adolfo Lopez Mateos 232
Colonia San Angel INN
DF CP 01060, MEXICO

View, The (Music Group)
c/o Staff Member *Paradigm (Monterey)*
509 Hartnell St
Monterey, CA 93940-2825, USA

Vieyra, Veronica (Actor)
c/o Staff Member *Telefe - Argentina*
Pavon 2444 (C1248AAT)
Buenos Aires, ARGENTINA

Vig, Butch (Musician)
c/o Staff Member *Borman Entertainment*
1250 6th St Ste 401
Santa Monica, CA 90401-1638, USA

Vigman, Gillian (Actor)
c/o Jeanne Newman *Hansen, Jacobson, Teller, Hoberman, Newman, Warren, Sloane & Richman, LLP*
450 N Roxbury Dr Fl 8
Beverly Hills, CA 90210-4222, USA

Vigneault, Alain (Coach, Hockey Player)
Saint Louis Blues
1401 Clark Ave
Sawis Center
Saint Louis, MO 63103-2700, USA

Vigneron, Thierry (Athlete, Track Athlete)
Adidas USA
5675 N Blackstock Rd
Spartanburg, SC 29303-6329, USA

Vignesh (Actor, Bollywood)
AP 210 9th Street
2nd Sector
Chennai, TN 600078, INDIA

Vigoda, Abe (Actor)
Scott Sandler
13701 Riverside Dr Ste 201
Sherman Oaks, CA 91423-2447, USA

Vigorito, Tommy (Football Player)
Miami Dolphins
131 Rock Rd
Wayne, NJ 07470-1919, USA

Viguerie, Richard
7777 Leesburg Pike
Falls Church, VA 22043-2411, USA

Vijay, S A (Actor, Bollywood)
64 Kaveri Street
Saligramam
Chennai, TN 600093, INDIA

Vijaya K R (Actor, Bollywood)
9 Raman Street
Chennai, TN 600018, INDIA

Vijayakanth (Actor, Bollywood)
54 Kannambal Street
Kannapiran Colony Saligramam
Chennai, TN 600093, INDIA

Vijayakumar, Manjula (Actor, Bollywood)
236 & 237 8th Street
Asthalakshmi Nagar
Chennai, TN 600116, INDIA

Vila, Bob (Actor, Producer, Television Host)
115 Kingston St # 300
Boston, MA 02111-2132, USA

Vilanch, Bruce (Writer)
c/o Brad Cafarelli *Bragman/Nyman/ Cafarelli (BNC)*
8687 Melrose Ave Fl 8
Pacific Design Center
Los Angeles, CA 90069-5701, USA

Vilanich, Bruce (Comedian)
c/o Staff Member *William Morris Agency (WMA-LA)*
1 William Morris Pl
Beverly Hills, CA 90212-4261, USA

Vilar, Tracy
9200 W Sunset Blvd Ste 1130
Los Angeles, CA 90069-3606, USA

Vilas, Guillermo
86 av. Foch F-75116
Paris, FRANCE

Vilasuso, Jordi (Actor)
c/o Staff Member *Innovative Artists (LA)*
1505 10th St
Santa Monica, CA 90401-2805, USA

Vilella, Edward
905 Lincoln Rd
Miami, FL 33139, USA

Viljoen, Marais (President)
PO Box 5555
Pretoria 0001, SOUTH AFRICA

Villa-Cryan, Marge (Baseball Player)
16305 Summershade Dr
La Mirada, CA 90638-2742, USA

Villano, Mike (Baseball Player)
Bowman
1041 South Dr
Mt Pleasant, MI 48858-2856, USA

Villanueva, Danny (Football Player)
Los Angeles Rams
PO Box 258
Somis, CA 93066-0258, USA

Villapiano, Phillip J (Phil) (Football Player)
Oakland Raiders
21 Riverside Dr
Rumson, NJ 07760-1026, USA

Villaraigosa, Antonio (Politician)
Mayor's Office
200 N Spring St
City Hall
Los Angeles, CA 90012-4801, USA

Villari, Guy (Musician)
293 Airport Rd
Liberty, NY 12754-2613, USA

Villarrial, Chris (Football Player)
Chicago Bears
254 Hidden Meadow Ln
Ebensburg, PA 15931-7511, USA

Villarroel, Vernoica (Opera Singer)
Columbia Artists Mgmt Inc
1790 Broadway Fl 6
New York, NY 10019-1412, USA

Villegas, Camilo (Golfer)
c/o Staff Member *Pro Golfers Assoc of America (PGA)*
100 Avenue Of The Champions
Palm Beach Gardens, FL 33418-3653, USA

Villella, Edward J (Ballerina, Choreographer)
Miami City Ballet
2200 Liberty Ave
Miami Beach, FL 33139-1641, USA

Villeneuve, Jacques (Race Car Driver)
BAR Team
PO Box 5014
Brackley
Northants NN13 7YY, UNITED KINGDOM (UK)

Villiers, Christopher (Actor)
Hillman Trelfall
33 Brookfield
Highgate W Hill
London N6 6AT, UNITED KINGDOM (UK)

Villiers, James (Actor)
International Creative Mgmt
76 Oxford St
London W1N 0AX, UNITED KINGDOM (UK)

Villone, Ron (Baseball Player)
Seattle Mariners
596 Colonial Rd
Rivervale, NJ 07675-6165, USA

Viltz, Theo (Football Player)
Houston Oilers
2729 E De Soto St
Long Beach, CA 90814-2337, USA

Vimond, Paul M (Architect)
91 Ave Niel
Paris 75017, FRANCE

Vina, Fernando (Baseball Player)
Seattle Mariners
PO Box 6723
Stateline, NV 89449-6723, USA

Vinatieri, Adam (Football Player)
New England Patriots
12850 Horseferry Rd
Carmel, IN 46032-7266, USA

Vince, Pruitt Taylor (Actor)
520 Salemo Dr
Pacific Palisades, CA 90272, USA

Vince, Taylor (Misc)
20160 NW 9th Dr
Pembroke Pines, FL 33029-3422, USA

Vincent, Amy (Cinematographer)
5932 Graciosa Dr
Los Angeles, CA 90068-3031, USA

Vincent, Cerina (Actor)
c/o Adam Seid *Bohemia Entertainment Group*
8170 Beverly Blvd Ste 102
Los Angeles, CA 90048-4533, USA

Vincent, Christian (Actor)
c/o Staff Member *Noah's Arc*
75 Charles Rowen House
Merlin Street
London WC1X OEJ, UNITED KINGDOM
(UK)

Vincent, Fay (Baseball Player)
Baseball Commissioner's Office
290 Harbor Dr
Stamford, CT 06902-8700, USA

Vincent, Jay (Basketball Player)
PO Box 27459
Lansing, MI 48909-0459, USA

Vincent, June
1541 Via Entrada Del Lago
San Marcos, CA 92078-5254, USA

Vincent, Marjorie
1325 Boardwalk
Atlantic City, NJ 08401-7240, USA

Vincent, Rhonda (Musician)
c/o Scott Clayton *Creative Artists Agency
(CAA-Nashville)*
3310 W End Ave Fl 5
Nashville, TN 37203-1028, USA

Vincent, Richard F (Misc)
House of Lords
Westminster
London SW1A 0PW, UNITED KINGDOM
(UK)

Vincent, Rick (Musician, Songwriter,
Writer)
Carter Career Mgmt
1028 18th Ave S # B
Nashville, TN 37212-2105, USA

Vincent, Sam (Basketball Player)
PO Box 27459
Lansing, MI 48909-0459, USA

Vincent, Troy (Football Player)
Miami Dolphins
460 Roeloffs Rd
Yardley, PA 19067-4513, USA

Vincent, Virginia (Actor)
1001 Hammond St
Los Angeles, CA 90069-3829, USA

Vincz, Melanie (Actor)
2212 Earle Ct
Redondo Beach, CA 90278-5003, USA

Vineetha (Actor, Bollywood)
Flat No 3B Chandrika Apartments
5 & 6 Ashok Avenue Directors Colony
Kodambakkam
Chennai, TN 600024, INDIA

Vines, C Jerry (Religious Leader)
First Baptist Church
124 W Ashley St
Jacksonville, FL 32202-3189, USA

Vines, Ellsworth
4680 Irvine Blvd. #203
Irvine, CA 92620, USA

Vines, The (Music Group)
c/o Rick Roskin *Creative Artists Agency
LCC (CAA-LA)*
2000 Avenue Of The Stars
Los Angeles, CA 90067-4700, USA

Vineyard, Dave (Baseball Player)
Baltimore Orioles
1850 Tariff Rd
Left Hand, WV 25251-9542, USA

Vining, David (Doctor, Scientist)
1955 Greenberry Rd
Baltimore, MD 21209-4555, USA

Vining, Ken (Baseball Player)
Chicago White Sox
1819 Lela Ave
Charlotte, NC 28208-4874, USA

Vinith, R (Actor, Bollywood)
Flat G 1
68 Halls Road Kilpauk
Chennai, TN 600010, INDIA

Vinnie (Artist, Music Group)
International Creative Mgmt
8942 Wilshire Blvd # 219
Beverly Hills, CA 90211-1908, USA

Vinogradov, Oleg M (Ballerina)
Mariinsky Theater
Teatralnaya Square 1
Saint Petersburg 190000, RUSSIA

Vinoly, Rafael (Architect)
1016 5th Ave
New York, NY 10028-0132, USA

Vinothini (Actor, Bollywood)
3 Alagar Perumal Koil Street
Chennai, TN 600026, INDIA

Vinson, Charlie (Baseball Player)
California Angels
3821 Walters Ln
Forestville, MD 20747-3943, USA

Vinson, Fernandus (Football Player)
Cincinnati Bengals
6572 Glenwood Ave # 221
Raleigh, NC 27612-7156, USA

Vinson, Fred (Football Player)
Green Bay Packers
11220 NE 53rd St
Kirkland, WA 98033-7505, USA

Vinson, James S (Educator)
University of Evansville
President's Office
Evansville, IN 47722-0001, USA

Vint, Jesse
10637 Burbank Blvd
N Hollywood, CA 91601-2512, USA

Vint, Jesse Lee III (Actor)
Film Artists
13563 1/2 Ventura Blvd # 200
Sherman Oaks, CA 91423-3825, USA

Vintas, Gustavo (Actor)
c/o Hal Stalmaster *The Artists Group Ltd
(LA)*
1650 Broadway Ste 610
New York, NY 10019-6833, USA

Vinton, Bobby (Musician)
MPI Talent Agency
9255 W Sunset Blvd Ste 804
Los Angeles, CA 90069-3305, USA

Vinton, Will (Animator)
William Morris Agency
151 El Camino Dr
Beverly Hills, CA 90212-2775, USA

Viola, Bill (Artist)
282 Granada Ave
Long Beach, CA 90803-5520, USA

Viola, Frank
844 Sweetwater Island Cir
Longwood, FL 32779-2345, USA

Viola, Frank J Jr (Baseball Player)
Minnesota Twins
9868 Kilgore Rd
Orlando, FL 32836-5708, USA

Viola, Lisa (Dancer)
Paul Taylor Dance Co
552 Broadway Fl 2
New York, NY 10012-3947, USA

Violent Femmes (Music Group)
15030 Ventura Blvd # 710
Sherman Oaks, CA 91403-5470, USA

Violette, Chris (Actor)
c/o Staff Member *Power Rangers SPD*
500 S Buena Vista St
Burbank, CA 91521-0001, USA

Virata, Cesar E (Prime Minister)
63 E Maya Dr
Quezon City, PHILIPPINES

Virdon, William C (Bill) (Baseball Player)
St Louis Cardinals
1311 E River Rd
Springfield, MO 65804-7901, USA

Viren, Lasse (Athlete, Track Athlete)
Suomen Urhellulirto Ry
Box 25202
Helsinki 25 00250, FINLAND

Virgil Jr, Ozzie (Baseball Player)
Philadelphia Phillies
5444 W Creedance Blvd
Glendale, AZ 85310-3724, USA

Virgil Sr, Ozzie (Baseball Player)
New York Giants
4316 W Mescal St
Glendale, AZ 85304-4132, USA

Virgins, The (Music Group)
c/o Staff Member *Paradigm (Monterey)*
509 Hartnell St
Monterey, CA 93940-2825, USA

Virts, Terry W Jr (Astronaut)
1904 Edgewater Dr
Friendswood, TX 77546-7845, USA

Virtue, Doreen (Writer)
Angel Therapy
PO Box 5100
Carlsbad, CA 92018-5100, USA

Virtue, Frank (Musician)
8309 Rising Sun Ave
Philadelphia, PA 19111, USA

Virtue, Thomas (Tom) (Actor)
c/o Staff Member *Gage Group, The (LA)*
14724 Ventura Blvd Ste 505
Sherman Oaks, CA 91403-3505, USA

Virzaladze, Elizo K (Music Group,
Musician)
Moscow Conservatory
Bolshaya Nikitskaya Str 13
Moscow, RUSSIA

Vis, Anthony (Religious Leader)
Reformed Church in America
475 Riverside Dr
New York, NY 10115-0101, USA

Viscardi, Johnston Catherine (Publisher)
Mirabella Magazine
200 Madison Ave
New York, NY 10016-3903, USA

Visconti, Tony (Musician, Producer)
c/o Joe D'Ambrosio *Joe D'Ambrosio
Management Inc*
1311 Mamaroneck Ave Ste 220
Star Mgmt. Group
White Plains, NY 10605-5222, USA

Visculo, Sal
6491 Ivarene Ave
Los Angeles, CA 90068-2823, USA

Vise, David A (Journalist)
Washington Post
Editorial Dept
1150 15th St NW
Washington, DC 20071-0001, USA

Vishnevskaya, Galina P (Opera Singer)
Gazetny Per 13 #79
Moscow 103009, RUSSIA

Vishnyova, Diana V (Ballerina)
Maninsky Theater
Teatralnaya Square 1
Saint Petersburg 190000, RUSSIA

Visitor, Nana (Actor)
c/o Staff Member *William Morris Agency
(WMA-LA)*
1 William Morris Pl
Beverly Hills, CA 90212-4261, USA

Visnic, Larry (Football Player)
New York Giants
471 Buena Vista Ave
Columbus, OH 43228-1105, USA

Visnjic, Goran (Actor)
c/o Elyse Scherz *Endeavor Agency LLC
(LA)*
9601 Wilshire Blvd Fl 3
Beverly Hills, CA 90210-5204, USA

Viso, Michel (Misc)
7 Domaine Chateau-Gaillard
Maison-d' Alfort 94700, FRANCE

Visscher, Maurice B (Doctor)
120 Melbourne Ave SE
Minneapolis, MN 55414-3516, USA

Visser, Lesley (Sportscaster)
c/o Staff Member *CBS Television*
51 W 52nd St
New York, NY 10019-6119, USA

Visu (Actor, Bollywood)
11 Agastheya Nagar
Kilpaul Garden
Chennai, TN 600012, INDIA

Vitale, Carol (Actor, Model)
1516 S Bundy Dr Ste 309
Los Angeles, CA 90025-2676, USA

Vitale, Dick (Basketball Player, Coach,
Sportscaster)
ESPN-TV
935 Middle St
Sports Department Espn Plaza
Bristol, CT 06010-1000, USA

Vitale, Joe (Business Person, Writer)
The Vitale Estate
121 Canyon Gap Rd
Wimberley, TX 78676-6314, USA

Vitale, Tony (Actor, Director, Writer)
Hung Entertainment Group
8489 W 3rd St
Los Angeles, CA 90048-4124, USA

Vitamin-C (Actor, Musician)
c/o Carter Cohn *International Creative
Management (ICM-LA)*
10250 Constellation Blvd
Los Angeles, CA 90067-6200, USA

Viterbi, Andrew J (Engineer, Scientist)
QUALCOMM Inc
5775 Morehouse Dr
San Diego, CA 92121-1714, USA

Vitez, Michael (Journalist)
Philadelphia Inquirer
400 N Broad St
Editorial Dept
Philadelphia, PA 19130-4099, USA

Vithayathil, Varkey Cardinal (Religious Leader)
Syro-Malabar Archiepiscopal Curia
Bharath Matha College
Kerala, INDIA

Vitiello, Joe (Baseball Player)
Kansas City Royals
4 Waverly St
Stoneham, MA 02180-1615, USA

Vitiello, Sandro (Football Player)
Cincinnati Bengals
9 Dwight Cir
Commack, NY 11725-3313, USA

Vitko, Joe (Baseball Player)
New York Mets
463 Stone St
Johnstown, PA 15906-1666, USA

Vitolo, Dennis (Race Car Driver)
2130 Intracoastal Dr
Fort Lauderdale, FL 33305-3638, USA

Vitousek, Peter M (Misc)
Stanford University
Biological Science Dept
Stanford, CT 94305, USA

Vittadini, Adrienne (Designer, Fashion Designer)
Adrienne Vittadini Inc
575 Fashion Ave
New York, NY 10018-1805, USA

Vitti, Monica (Actor)
IPC
Via F Siacci 38
Rome 00197, ITALY

Vittori, Roberto (Astronaut)
Europe Astronaut Center
Linder Hole
Box 906096
Cologne 51127, GERMANY

Vitukhnovskaya, Alina A (Writer)
Leningradskoye Shosse 80 #89
Moscow 125565, RUSSIA

Vivas, Juan Carlos (Actor)
c/o Gabriel Blanco *Gabriel Blanco Iglesias (Mexico)*
Rio Balsas 35-32
Colonia Cuauhtemoc
DF 06500, MEXICO

Vivek (Actor, Bollywood)
9 Subhiksha Apts
5 Tank Street U.I. Colony
Chennai, TN 600024, INDIA

Viviano, Joseph P (Business Person)
Hershey Foods Corp
100 Crystal A Dr
Hershey, PA 17033-9702, USA

Vizcaino, Jose (Baseball Player)
Los Angeles Dodgers
2150 Chardon Ln
El Cajon, CA 92019-3884, USA

Vizquel, Omar E (Baseball Player)
Seattle Mariners
26630 SE Issaquah Fall City Rd
Issaquah, WA 98029-9183, USA

Vlacil, Frantisek (Director)
Cinska 5
Prague 6 160 00, CZECH REPUBLIC

Vladeck, Judith P (Attorney, Attorney General, General)
Vladeck Waldman Elias Engelhard
1501 Broadway
New York, NY 10036-5601, USA

Vlady, Marina (Actor)
10 Ave de Marivaux
Mission Lafitte 78800, FRANCE

Vlasic, Mark (Football Player)
San Diego Chargers
12809 Catalina St
Leawood, KS 66209-3327, USA

Vlassic, Robert
1910 Rathmor Rd
Bloomfield, MI 48304-2149, USA

Vlk, Miloslav Cardinal (Religious Leader)
Arcibiskupstvi
Hradcanske Nam 16/56
Prague 1 119 02, CZECH REPUBLIC

Vo Nguyen Giap (General)
Dang Cong San Vietnam
1C Blvd Hoang Van Thu
Hanoi, VIETNAM

Vo Van Kiet (Prime Minister)
Prime Minister's Office
Hoang Hoa Thum
Hanoi, VIETNAM

Vogel, Bob (Football Player)
Baltimore Colts
2065 N Galena Rd
Sunbury, OH 43074-9588, USA

Vogel, Dariene (Actor)
Michael Slessinger
8730 W Sunset Blvd Ste 220W
Los Angeles, CA 90069-2275, USA

Vogel, Hans-Jochen (Government Official)
Stresemanstr 6
Bonn-Bad Godesberg 53123, GERMANY

Vogel, Mark (Composer)
c/o Staff Member *Gorfaine/Schwartz Agency Inc*
4111 W Alameda Ave Ste 509
Burbank, CA 91505-4171, USA

Vogel, Mike (Actor, Skateboarder)
c/o Alex Yarosh *Gersh Agency, The (LA)*
232 N Canon Dr
Beverly Hills, CA 90210-5302, USA

Vogel, Mitch (Actor)
3335 Honeysuckle Ave
Palmdale, CA 93550-1305, USA

Vogelsong, Ryan (Baseball Player)
San Francisco Giants
1120 Redwood Dr
Carlisle, PA 17013-1378, USA

Vogelstein, Bert (Doctor, Scientist)
Johns Hopkins University
Medical School
Oncology Center
Baltimore, MD 21218, USA

Vogler, Karl Michael
Auweg 8
Seehausen D-82418, GERMANY

Vogler, Tim (Football Player)
Buffalo Bills
6710 Woodland Dr
Hamburg, NY 14075-6521, USA

Vogt, Lars (Musician)
c/o Staff Member *International Creative Management (ICM-NY)*
40 W 57th St
New York, NY 10019-4001, USA

Vogt, Paul (Actor)
c/o Judy Coppage *Coppage Company, The*
5411 Camellia Ave
N Hollywood, CA 91601-2615, USA

Vogt, Peter K (Misc, Scientist)
LA County/USC Medical School
2011 Zonal Ave
Los Angeles, CA 90089-0110, USA

Vogt, Rochus E (Astronomer, Physicist)
California Institute of Technology
Bridge Laboratory
Pasadena, CA 91125-0001, USA

Vogts, Hans-Hubert (Berti) (Soccer Player)
Mozartweg 2
Korschenbroich 41352, GERMANY

Voight, Jack (Baseball Player)
Baltimore Orioles
1274 Reserve Dr
Venice, FL 34285-5655, USA

Voight, Jon (Actor)
c/o Steven Paul *Crystal Sky Entertainment*
10203 Santa Monica Blvd Fl 5
Los Angeles, CA 90067-6405, USA

Voight, Karen (Fitness Expert)
Entertaining Fitness, Inc
827 Chautauqua Blvd
Pacific Palisades, CA 90272-3802, USA

Voight, Stu (Football Player)
Minnesota Vikings
8832 Hunters Way
Apple Valley, MN 55124-9478, USA

Voigt, Deborah (Opera Singer)
Columbia Artists Mgmt Inc
1790 Broadway Fl 6
New York, NY 10019-1412, USA

Voinovich, George V (Governor, Senator)
601 Lakeside Ave E
Cleveland, OH 44114-1027, USA

Voisard, Mark (Baseball Player)
2524 Harding Ave
Dayton, OH 45414-3214, USA

Voiselle, William S (Bill) (Baseball Player)
New York Giants
105 Lowell St
Ninety Six, SC 29666-1232, USA

Voisine, Rich
1505 W. 2nd Ave. #200
Vancouver, BC V6H 3Y4, CANADA

Volberding, Paul (Scientist)
General Hospital AIDS Activities Dept
995 Potrero Ave
San Francisco, CA 94110-2859, USA

Volcker, Paul (Government Official)
151 E 79th St
New York, NY 10075-0417, USA

Voldstad, John (Actor)
24812 Van Owen St
West Hills, CA 91300, USA

Volibracht, Michaele (Artist, Designer, Fashion Designer)
General Delivery
Safety Harbor, FL 34695-9999, USA

Volk, Igor P (Misc)
Potchta Kosmonavtov
Moskovskoi Oblasti
Syvisdny Goroduk 141160, RUSSIA

Volk, Patricia (Writer)
Gloria Loomis
133 E 35th St
New York, NY 10016-3886, USA

Volk, Phil (Musician)
Paradise Artists
108 E Matilija St
Ojai, CA 93023-2639, USA

Volk, Richard R (Rick) (Football Player)
Baltimore Colts
15860 Irish Ave
Monkton, MD 21111-2120, USA

Volker, Sandra (Swimmer)
DESG
Mensingen Str 68
Munich 80992, GERMANY

Volkert, Stephan (Athlete)
Semmelweisstr 42
Cologne 51061, GERMANY

Volkmann, Elisabeth (Opera Singer)
Sonnenstr 20
Munich 80331, GERMANY

Volkov, Aleksandr A (Misc)
Potchta Kosmonavtov
Moskovskoi Oblasti
Syvisdny Goroduk 141160, RUSSIA

Voll, Rich (Actor)
c/o Steven Fenton *Fenton-Kritzer Entertainment*
8840 Wilshire Blvd Fl 3
Beverly Hills, CA 90211-2606, USA

Vollebak, Knut (Government Official)
Royal Norwegian Embassy
2720 34th St NW
Washington, DC 20008-2705, USA

Vollenweider, Andreas (Musician)
Sempacher Str 16
Zurich 8032, SWITZERLAND

Vollmer, Clyde (Baseball Player)
Cincinnati Reds
1397 Boone Aire Rd
Florence, KY 41042-1201, USA

Volodos, Arcadl (Musician)
Columbia Artists Mgmt Inc
1790 Broadway Fl 6
New York, NY 10019-1412, USA

Voloshin, Valeri (Cosmonaut)
Potchta Kosmonavtov
Moskovskoi Oblasti
Syvisdny Goroduk 141160, RUSSIA

Volpe, Joseph (Joe) (Misc, Opera Singer)
Metropolitan Opera Assn
Lincoln Center Plaza
New York, NY 10023, USA

Volstad, John
15924 Leadwell St
Van Nuys, CA 91406-3030, USA

Voltaggio, Vic (Baseball Player)
1049 Florian Way
Spring Hill, FL 34609-9021, USA

Volynov, Boris V (Misc)
Potchta Kosmonavtov
Moskovskoi Oblasti
Syvisdny Goroduk 141160, RUSSIA

Volz, Nedra
5606 E Fairfield St
Mesa, AZ 85205-5522, USA

Volz, Wilbur (Football Player)
Buffalo Bills
35 Seminary Hi # C-31
West Lebanon, NH 03784, USA

Volz, Wolfgang
Konstanzer Str. 8
Berlin D-10707, GERMANY

Von Bargen, Daniel (Actor)
c/o Mitchell Stubbs *Mitchell K Stubbs & Assoc (MKS)*
8695 Washington Blvd Ste 204
Culver City, CA 90232-7419, USA

Von Bulow, Claus
960 5th Ave
New York, NY 10075-1708, USA

von Damm-Gurtler, Helene
Hotel Sacher bei der Oper
Vienna 1010, AUSTRIA

von Daniken, Eric
CH-Baselstr. 1
Feldbrunnen 4532, SWITZERLAND

von Detten, Erik (Actor)
c/o Elissa Leeds-Fickman *Reel Talent Management*
438 Tuallitan Rd
Los Angeles, CA 90049-1941, USA

von Dohlen, Lenny
121 N San Vicente Blvd
Beverly Hills, CA 90211-2303, USA

Von Drachenberg, Katherine (Reality TV Star)
6756 E Mockingbird Ln
Santa Monica, TX 90405, USA

Von Erich, Jaret (Actor, Musician)
c/o Linda Kordek *Agency Group Ltd, The (LA)*
1880 Century Park E Ste 711
Los Angeles, CA 90067-1618, USA

Von Erick's, The
145 Columbia St. W #9
Waterloo, ON N2L 3, CANADA

Von Frankenstein, Clement (Actor)
c/o Staff Member *Matt Sherman Management*
7510 W Sunset Blvd # 1413
Los Angeles, CA 90046-3408, USA

Von Furstenberg, Betsy
230 Central Park W
New York, NY 10024-6029, USA

Von Furstenberg, Diane (Business Person, Fashion Designer)
444 W 14th St
New York, NY 10014-1004, USA

von Habsburg, Otto
Hindenburgstr. 15
Pocking D-82343, GERMANY

Von Hoff, Bruce (Baseball Player)
Houston Astros
423 S Riverhills Dr
Temple Terrace, FL 33617-7861, USA

Von Hohenzollern, Maja Synke (Prince, Princess)
c/o Joerg Bobsin
11605 W Pico Blvd # 200
Los Angeles, CA 90064-2908, USA

von Kusserow, Ingeborg
16-D Avercorn Pl.
London, ENGLAND NW8, UNITED KINGDOM (UK)

Von Ohlen, Dave (Baseball Player)
St Louis Cardinals
653 Windmill Ave
West Babylon, NY 11704-4403, USA

von Oy, Jenna (Actor)
19 Saddle Ridge Rd
Newtown, CT 06470-2417, USA

Von Schamann, Uwe (Football Player)
Miami Dolphins
PO Box 5562
Norman, OK 73070-5562, USA

Von Scherler Mayer, Daisy (Director)
c/o Tom Strickler *Endeavor Agency LLC (LA)*
9601 Wilshire Blvd Fl 3
Beverly Hills, CA 90210-5204, USA

Von Stade, Frederica (Opera Singer)
1200 San Antonio Ave
Alameda, CA 94501-3932, USA

Von Sydow, Max (Actor)
c/o Staff Member *United Talent Agency (UTA)*
9560 Wilshire Blvd Ste 500
Beverly Hills, CA 90212-2401, USA

Von Teese, Dita (Actor, Model)
Dishell Multimedia Group
8306 Wilshire Blvd Pmb 833
Beverly Hills, CA 90211-2304, USA

von Trier, Lars (Director, Writer)
c/o Staff Member *Jeff Morrone Management*
9350 Wilshire Blvd Ste 224
Beverly Hills, CA 90212-3204, USA

von Weizsacker, Carl
Alpenstr. 1
Socking D-82319, GERMANY

von Weizsacker, Richard (Ex-President, President)
Meisenstr 6
Berlin D-14195, GERMANY

von Wietersheim, Sharon
Leopoldstr. 19
Munich D-80802, GERMANY

VonAroldingen, Karin (Ballerina)
New York City Ballet
Lincoln Center Plaza
New York, NY 10023, USA

VonBulow, Vicco (Loriot) (Actor)
Hohenweg 19
Munsing-Ammerland 82451, GERMANY

Vonderau, Kathryn (Baseball Player)
7224 Hawthorn Ave NE
Albuquerque, NM 87113-2084, USA

VonDerHeyden, Karl I M (Business Person)
PepsiCo Inc
700 Anderson Hill Rd
Purchase, NY 10577-1444, USA

VonDetten, Erik (Actor)
William Morris Agency
151 El Camino Dr
Beverly Hills, CA 90212-2775, USA

VonDohnanyi, Christoph (Conductor)
Cleveland Orchestra
Severance Hall
Cleveland, OH 44106, USA

VonErich, Waldo (Wrestler)
Columbia Sports Med Center
9-145 Columbia W
Waterloo, ON N2L 3L2, CANADA

VonEschenbach, Andrew (Doctor)
National Cancer Institute
9000 Rockville Pike
Bethesda, MD 20892-0001, USA

VonFurstenberg, Egon (Designer, Fashion Designer)
50 E 72nd St
New York, NY 10021-4246, USA

VonGarnier, Katja (Director)
Creative Artists Agency
9830 Wilshire Blvd
Beverly Hills, CA 90212-1804, USA

Vongerichten, Jean-Geoges (Chef)
Jean-Georges Enterprises, LLC
19 Greene St
New York, NY 10013-2535, USA

VonGerkan, Manon (Model)
Shamballa Jewels
92 Thompson St
New York, NY 10012-3713, USA

VonGerkan, Meinhard (Architect)
Elbchaussee 139
Hamburg 22763, GERMANY

VonGrunigen, Michael (Skier)
Chalet Sunneblick
Schonried 3778, SWITZERLAND

VonHabsburg-Lothringem, Otto (Government Official)
Hindenburgstr 14
Pocking 82343, GERMANY

VonHippel, Peter H (Misc)
1900 Crest Dr
Eugene, OR 97405-1753, USA

VonKlitzing, Klaus (Nobel Prize Laureate)
Max Planck Institute
Heisenbergstr 1
Stuttgart 70569, GERMANY

VonMehren, Arthur T (Attorney, Attorney General, Educator, General)
68 Sparks St
Cambridge, MA 02138-2238, USA

VonMehren, Arthur T (Attorney, Attorney General, General)
925 Park Ave
New York, NY 10028-0210, USA

Vonoelhoffen, Kimo (Football Player)
Cincinnati Bengals
1503 Scarlet Oak Dr
Wexford, PA 15090-6931, USA

Vonohlen, Dave (Baseball Player)
St Louis Cardinals
74 Elizabeth St
Floral Park, NY 11001-2129, USA

Vonoimoana, Eric
715 S Circle Dr
Colorado Springs, CO 80910-2324, USA

VonOtter, Anne Sofie (Opera Singer)
I C M Aritsts
40 W 57th St
New York, NY 10019-4001, USA

VonPierer, Heinrich (Business Person)
Seimens AG
Wittelsbacherplatz 2
Munich 80333, GERMANY

VonQuast, Veronika (Actor)
ZBF Agentur
Leopoldstr 19
Munich 80802, GERMANY

VonRunkle, Theodora (Designer, Fashion Designer)
8805 Lookout Mountain Ave
Los Angeles, CA 90046-1819, USA

VonSaltza Olmstead, S Christine (Chris) (Swimmer)
7060 Fairway Pl
Carmel, CA 93923-9586, USA

Vonsonn, Andrew (Football Player)
Los Angeles Rams
PO Box 791538
Paia, HI 96779-1538, USA

VonStrateen, Frans (Artist)
Samuel Muller Plein 17C
Rotterdam 3023, DENMARK

VonWeizsacker, Carl Friedrich (Misc)
Aplenstr 15
Socking 82319, GERMANY

Voog, Ana (Music Group, Musician, Songwriter, Writer)
MCA Records
1755 Broadway
New York, NY 10019-3793, USA

Voorhees, John J (Doctor)
3965 Waldenwood Dr
Ann Arbor, MI 48105-3008, USA

Voorhies, Lark (Actor)
10635 Santa Monica Blvd Ste 130
Los Angeles, CA 90025-8306, USA

Vorgan, Gigi (Actor)
3637 Stone Canyon Ave
Sherman Oaks, CA 91403, USA

Vorhies, Lark (Actor)
c/o Geoff Cheddy *Brillstein-Grey Entertainment*
9150 Wilshire Blvd Ste 350
Beverly Hills, CA 90212-3453, USA

Voris, Roy M (Butch) (Misc)
14563 Fruitvale Ave
Saratoga, CA 95070-6152, USA

Voronin, Vladimir (President)
President's Office
23 Nicolae Iorge Str
Chishinev 277033, MOLDOVA

Vos, Rich (Actor, Comedian)
c/o Jason Steinberg *Steinberg Talent Management Group*
1560 Broadway # 405
New York, NY 10036-1518, USA

Vosberg, Ed (Baseball Player)
San Diego Padres
7839 E Marquise Dr
Tucson, AZ 85715-3774, USA

Vosloo, Arnold (Actor)
c/o Jim Gosnell *Agency for the Performing Arts (APA-LA)*
405 S Beverly Dr
Beverly Hills, CA 90212-4416, USA

Voss, Bill (Baseball Player)
Chicago White Sox
10625 E Oak Creek Tri
Cornville, AZ 86325, USA

Voss, Brian (Bowler)
340 Banyon Brook Pt
Roswell, GA 30076-3672, USA

Voss, James S (Astronaut)
4207 Indian Sunrise Ct
Houston, TX 77059-5533, USA

Voss, Janice E (Astronaut)
587 Kirk Ave
Sunnyvale, CA 94085-3650, USA

Voss, Lloyd (Football Player)
Green Bay Packers
1127 Greentree Rd
Pittsburgh, PA 15220-3130, USA

Votaw, Ty (Golfer)
Ladies Pro Golf Assn
100 International Golf Dr
Daytona Beach, FL 32124-1082, USA

Vowell, Sarah (Actor, Writer)
c/o Staff Member *Steven Barclay Agency*
12 Western Ave
Petaluma, CA 94952-2907, USA

Voyce, Inez (Baseball Player)
2107 Ashland Ave
Santa Monica, CA 90405-6025, USA

Voyles, Brad (Baseball Player)
Kansas City Royals
314 East Ave
Casco, WI 54205-9679, USA

Voytek, Edward (Football Player)
Washington Redskins
2111 NW 13th St
Blue Springs, MO 64015-7734, USA

Voznesensky, Andrei A (Writer)
Kotelnicheskaya Nab 1/15
Bl W #62
Moscow 109240, RUSSIA

Vraa, Sanna (Actor, Model)
Irv Schechter
9300 Wilshire Blvd # 410
Beverly Hills, CA 90212-3213, USA

Vrabel, Mike (Football Player)
Pittsburgh Steelers
8552 Misty Woods Cir
Powell, OH 43065-8356, USA

Vraciu, Alexander (Alex) (War Hero)
309 Merrilee Pl
Danville, CA 94526-4315, USA

Vranes, Danny (Basketball Player)
7105 Highland Dr
Salt Lake City, UT 84121-3753, USA

Vranes, Slavko (Basketball Player)
c/o Staff Member Portland Trail Blazers
1 Center Ct Ste 200
Rose Garden
Portland, OR 97227-2103, USA

Vranitzky, Franz
Ballhausplatz 2
Vienna 1015, AUSTRIA

Vuarnet, Jean (Skier)
Chalet Squaw Peak
Auoriaz 74110, FRANCE

Vucinich, Milt (Football Player)
Chicago Bears
23 Belford Way
San Mateo, CA 94402-1205, USA

Vuckovich, Peter D (Pete) (Baseball Player)
Chicago White Sox
309 Keiper Ln
Johnstown, PA 15909-1725, USA

Vujtek, Vladimir (Hockey Player)
Pittsburgh Penguins
66 Mario Lemieux Pl
Mellon Arena
Pittsburgh, PA 15219-3504, USA

Vukovich, George (Baseball Player)
Philadelphia Phillies
6060 Foxberry Ln
Roswell, GA 30075-6210, USA

Vukovich, John (Baseball Player)
Philadelphia Phillies
6 Knottingham Dr
Voorhees, NJ 08043-3932, USA

Vulkovich, Frances (Baseball Player)
2172 Smithdale Rd
West Newton, PA 15089-9603, USA

Vuono, Carl E (General)
5796 Westchester St
Alexandria, VA 22310-1146, USA

Vyent, Louise (Model)
Pauline's Talent Corp
379 W Broadway # 502
New York, NY 10012-5121, USA

W

W, Kristine (Musician)
c/o Staff Member Diva Central Inc
7510 W Sunset Blvd Ste 1445
Los Angeles, CA 90046-3408, USA

Waadataar, Paar (Musician)
Banada Mgmt
11 Elvaston Place #300
London SW 7 5QC, UNITED KINGDOM (UK)

Waalkes, Otto
Papenhuder Str. 61
Hamburg D-22087, GERMANY

Wach, Caitlin (Actor)
c/o David Brownstein Art Work Entertainment
5900 Wilshire Blvd Ste 2150
Los Angeles, CA 90036-5021, USA

Wachowski, Andy (Director, Producer, Writer)
c/o David Wirtschafter William Morris Agency (WMA-LA)
1 William Morris Pl
Beverly Hills, CA 90212-4261, USA

Wachowski, Larry (Director, Producer, Writer)
c/o Lawrence Mattis Circle of Confusion LLC (NY)
10723 71st Rd # 300
Forest Hills, NY 11375-4707, USA

Wachs, Caitlin (Actor)
c/o Shelly Browning Magnolia Entertainment
9595 Wilshire Blvd Ste 601
Beverly Hills, CA 90212-2506, USA

Wachtel, Christine (Athlete, Track Athlete)
Rostock Sports Club
Rostock
Mecklenburg-Vorpommoem, GERMANY

Wachter, Anita (Skier)
Gantschierstr 579
Schruns 6780, AUSTRIA

Waddell, Charles (Football Player)
Tampa Bay Buccaneers
3600 Bon Rea Dr
Charlotte, NC 28226-3146, USA

Waddell, Ernest (Actor)
c/o Bob McGowan McGowan Management
8733 W Sunset Blvd Ste 103
W Hollywood, CA 90069-2241, USA

Waddell, John Henry (Artist)
Oak Creek Village Road Star Route 2273
Cornville, AZ 86325, USA

Waddell, Justine (Actor)
International Creative Mgmt
8942 Wilshire Blvd # 219
Beverly Hills, CA 90211-1908, USA

Waddell-Wyatt, Helen (Baseball Player)
7714 Deerfield Rd
Loves Park, IL 61111-3218, USA

Waddington, Steven (Actor)
Julian Belfrage Associates
Adam House
14 New Burlington Street
London W1S 3BQ, UNITED KINGDOM (UK)

Waddington of Read, David (General, Governor)
Stable House Sabden
Clitheroe
Lanc BB7 9HP, UNITED KINGDOM (UK)

Waddle, Tom (Football Player)
Chicago Bears
1260 W Kennicott Dr
Lake Forest, IL 60045-1551, USA

Waddy, Billy (Football Player)
Los Angeles Rams
2838 Highway 88
Minneapolis, MN 55418-3243, USA

Wade, Abdoulaye (President)
President's Office
Ave Roume
Dakar BPI 168, SENEGAL

Wade, Adam (Musician)
118 E 25th St # 600
New York, NY 10010-2915, USA

Wade, Charlie (Football Player)
Chicago Bears
3109 E Raines Rd
Memphis, TN 38118-6756, USA

Wade, Dwayne (Basketball Player)
c/o Staff Member Miami Heat
601 Biscayne Blvd
American Airlines Arena
Miami, FL 33132-1801, USA

Wade, Ed (Football Player)
Chicago Bears
436 SW 50th Ave
Pratt, KS 67124-7731, USA

Wade, Edgar L (Religious Leader)
4466 Elvis Presley Blvd Ste 222
Memphis, TN 38116-7100, USA

Wade, Gale (Baseball Player)
Chicago Cubs
10240 Nc 226 S
Nebo, NC 28761-5810, USA

Wade, Jason (Musician)
DreamWorks Records
9268 W 3rd St
Beverly Hills, CA 90210-3713, USA

Wade, Kevin (Writer)
c/o David Lonner William Morris Agency (WMA-LA)
1 William Morris Pl
Beverly Hills, CA 90212-4261, USA

Wade, Russell
47287 W Eldorado Dr
Indian Wells, CA 92210-8654, USA

Wade, Todd (Football Player)
Miami Dolphins
217 Hendricks Isle Apt 302
Fort Lauderdale, FL 33301-5753, USA

Wade, Tom (Football Player)
Pittsburgh Steelers
3309 Oak Knoll Dr
Tyler, TX 75707-1619, USA

Wade, Virginia (Tennis Player)
Sharstead Court
Sittingbourne
Kent, UNITED KINGDOM (UK)

Wade, William J (Bill) Jr (Football Player)
Los Angeles Rams
7740 Buffalo Rd
Nashville, TN 37221-5501, USA

Wadhams, Wayne (Musician)
73 Hemenway St
Boston, MA 02115-2941, USA

Wadhawan, Avinash (Actor, Bollywood)
305 Skyway Shastri Nagar
Off J P Road Andheri
Mumbai, MS 400058, INDIA

Wadkins, Bobby (Golfer)
204 Kinloch Rd
Manakin Sabot, VA 23103-2911, USA

Wadkins, Lanny (Golfer)
6002 Kettering Ct
Dallas, TX 75248-2137, USA

Wadsworth, Andre (Football Player)
Arizona Cardinals
14003 N 99th Way
Scottsdale, AZ 85260-8851, USA

Wadsworth, Charles W (Musician)
PO Box 157
Charleston, SC 29402-0157, USA

Wadsworth, Fred (Golfer)
823 Bryon Rd
Columbia, SC 29209, USA

Waelsch, Salome G (Doctor, Scientist)
90 Morningside Dr
New York, NY 10027-7124, USA

Wages, Harmon (Football Player)
Atlanta Falcons
1846 Margaret St Apt 3C
Jacksonville, FL 32204-4423, USA

Wages, Robert E (Misc)
Oil Chemical Atomic Workers International Union
PO Box 2812
Denver, CO 80201-2812, USA

Wages, William (Cinematographer)
Innovative Artists
1505 10th St
Santa Monica, CA 90401-2805, USA

Waggoner, Lyle (Actor)
1124 Oak Mirage Pl
Westlake Village, CA 91362-5622, USA

Waggoner, Paul E (Misc)
314 Vineyard Point Rd
Guilford, CT 06437-3255, USA

Wagner, Amanda
PO Box 1294
Los Alamos, NM 87544-1294, USA

Wagner, Bret (Baseball Player)
US Olympic Team Bowman
489 Ridge Rd
Lewisberry, PA 17339-9308, USA

Wagner, Bruce (Writer)
United Talent Agency
9560 Wilshire Blvd Ste 500
Beverly Hills, CA 90212-2401, USA

Wagner, Bryan (Football Player)
Chicago Bears
6020 Arlyne Ln
Medina, OH 44256-6852, USA

Wagner, Chuck (Actor, Musician)
1200 Maldonado Dr
Pensacola Beach, FL 32561-2244, USA

Wagner, Dajuan (Basketball Player)
Cleveland Cavaliers
1 Center Ct
Gund Arena
Cleveland, OH 44115-4001, USA

Wagner, Fred (Cartoonist)
King Features Syndicate
888 7th Ave Ste 201
New York, NY 10106-0201, USA

Wagner, Harold A (Business Person)
Air Products & Chemicals
7201 Hamilton Blvd
Allentown, PA 18195-9642, USA

Wagner, Helen (Actor)
c/o Staff Member *As The World Turns*
1268 E 14th St
Jc Studios
Brooklyn, NY 11230-5241, USA

Wagner, Jack (Actor, Musician)
314 Waverly Place Ct
Chesterfield, MO 63017-7819, USA

Wagner, Jane
PO Box 27700
Los Angeles, CA 90027-0700, USA

Wagner, Jill (Actor)
c/o David (Dave) Becky *3 Arts Entertainment Inc*
9460 Wilshire Blvd Fl 7
Beverly Hills, CA 90212-2713, USA

Wagner, John (Cartoonist)
Hallmark Cards
101 McDonald Dr
Shoebox Division
Lawrence, KS 66044-1056, USA

Wagner, Katey (Actor)
1500 Old Oak Rd
Los Angeles, CA 90049-2504, USA

Wagner, Katie (Actor, Television Host)
c/o Staff Member *TV Guide Channel*
7140 S Lewis Ave
Tulsa, OK 74136-5401, USA

Wagner, Lindsay (Actor)
Bartels Co
PO Box 57593
Sherman Oaks, CA 91413-2593, USA

Wagner, Lou (Actor)
21224 Celtic St
Chatsworth, CA 91311-1468, USA

Wagner, Louis C Jr (General)
6336 Manchester Way
Alexandria, VA 22304-3534, USA

Wagner, Lowell (Football Player)
San Francisco 49ers
3013 254th Ave SE
Sammamish, WA 98075-9435, USA

Wagner, Maggie (Actor)
Stephany Hurkos Management
11935 Kling St Apt 10
Valley Village, CA 91607-5406, USA

Wagner, Matt (Cartoonist)
DC Comics
1700 Broadway
New York, NY 10019-5914, USA

Wagner, Melinda (Composer)
Theodore Presser
588 N Gulph Rd
King Of Prussia, PA 19406-2831, USA

Wagner, Michael R (Mike) (Football Player)
Pittsburgh Steelers
203 E Wild Cherry Dr
Mars, PA 16046-4053, USA

Wagner, Paula (Producer)
c/o Staff Member *Cruise/Wagner Productions (C/W)*
10250 Constellation Blvd # 11007
Los Angeles, CA 90067-6200, USA

Wagner, Philip M (Writer)
32 Montgomery St
Boston, MA 02116-6111, USA

Wagner, Robert J (Actor)
c/o Chuck Binder *Binder & Associates*
1465 Lindacrest Dr
Beverly Hills, CA 90210-2519, USA

Wagner, Robert T (Educator)
24497 Playhouse Rd
Keystone, SD 57751-6653, USA

Wagner, Robin S A (Designer)
Robin Wagner Studio
890 Broadway
New York, NY 10003-1211, USA

Wagner, Roy H (Actor, Director)
c/o Lisa Helsing Lenhoff *Lenhoff & Lenhoff*
830 Palm Ave
West Hollywood, CA 90069-4009, USA

Wagner, William E (Billy) (Baseball Player)
5066 Jones Mill Rd
Crozet, VA 22932-2610, USA

Wagner, Wolfgang M M (Director, Opera Singer)
Bayreuth Festival
Postfach 100262
Bayreuth 95402, GERMANY

Wagoner, Betty (Baseball Player)
4830 Rivertree Ln
Spring, TX 77388-4333, USA

Wagoner, Dan (Choreographer, Dancer)
Contemporary Dance Theater
17 Duke's Road
London WC1H 9AB, UNITED KINGDOM (UK)

Wagoner, Dan (Football Player)
Detroit Lions
714 Carriage Hill Rd
Simpsonville, SC 29681-5281, USA

Wagoner, David R (Writer)
5416 154th Pl SW
Edmonds, WA 98026-4348, USA

Wagoner, G Richard (Business Person)
General Motors Corp
100 Renaissance Ctr
Detroit, MI 48243-1114, USA

Wagoner, Harold E (Architect)
331 Lindsey Dr
Berwyn, PA 19312-1822, USA

Wagoner, Porter (Musician, Songwriter, Writer)
Porter Wagoner Enterprises
PO Box 290785
Nashville, TN 37229-0785, USA

Wahl, Ken (Actor)
Sherry Salerno Management
9654 W 131st St # 206
Palos Park, IL 60464-1640, USA

Wahlberg, Donnie (Actor, Musician)
5894 Spirit Lake Ct
Simi Valley, CA 93063-5780, USA

Wahlberg, Mark (Actor, Model, Musician)
c/o Stephen (Steve) Levinson *Leverage Management*
3030 Pennsylvania Ave
Santa Monica, CA 90404-4112, USA

Wahle, Mike (Football Player)
Green Bay Packers
914 Laurie Dr
Madison, WI 53711-2417, USA

Wahlen, George E (War Hero)
1764 Grove Hideaway
Roy, UT 84067-3659, USA

Wahler, Jason (Reality TV Star)
c/o Staff Member *MTV Networks (LA)*
2600 Colorado Blvd
Los Angeles, CA 90041, USA

Wahlgren, Olof G C (Editor)
Nicoloviusgatan 5B
Malmo 217 57, SWEDEN

Wahlquist, Heather (Actor)
c/o Troy Begnaud *Evolution Entertainment (LA)*
901 N Highland Ave
Los Angeles, CA 90038-2412, USA

Wahlstrom, Becky (Actor)
c/o Rob D'Avola *Identity Talent Agency (ID)*
9107 Wilshire Blvd Ste 450
Beverly Hills, CA 90210-5535, USA

Wahlstrom, Jarl H (Religious Leader)
Borgstrominkuja 1A10
Helsinki 84 00840, FINLAND

Waigel, Theodor (Government Official)
Oberrohr
Ursberg 86513, GERMANY

Waihee, John D III (Governor)
745 Fort Street Mall Ste 600
Honolulu, HI 96813-3805, USA

Wain, Bea (Musician)
9955 Durant Dr Unit 305
Beverly Hills, CA 90212-1601, USA

Wainscott, Loyd (Football Player)
Houston Oilers
401 Tarpey Rd
Texas City, TX 77591-3159, USA

Wainwright, James (Actor)
Lew Sherrell
937 N Sinova
Mesa, AZ 85205-5438, USA

Wainwright, Loudon (Actor)
c/o Harriet Sternberg *Harriet Sternberg Management*
4530 Gloria Ave
Encino, CA 91436-2718, USA

Wainwright, Loudon III (Musician, Songwriter, Writer)
Teddy Wainwright
521 SW Halpatiokee St
Stuart, FL 34994-2815, USA

Wainwright, Rufus (Musician)
c/o Staff Member *MCT Management*
333 W 52nd St
New York, NY 10019-6238, USA

Wainwright, Rupert (Director)
c/o Staff Member *United Talent Agency (UTA)*
9560 Wilshire Blvd Ste 500
Beverly Hills, CA 90212-2401, USA

Waite, John (Musician, Songwriter, Writer)
506 Walt Whitman Rd
Melville, NY 11747-2109, USA

Waite, Liam
c/o Staff Member *Gersh Agency, The (LA)*
232 N Canon Dr
Beverly Hills, CA 90210-5302, USA

Waite, Ralph (Actor)
PO Box 810
Palm Desert, CA 92261-0810, USA

Waite, Terence H (Terry) (Religious Leader)
Wheelrights Green Harvest
Bury Saint Demunds
Suffolk IP29 4DH, UNITED KINGDOM (UK)

Waite, Terry
The Green Harvest Bury St. Edmunds
Suffolk, ENGLAND 1P29 4DH, UNITED KINGDOM (UK)

Waiters, Van (Football Player)
Cleveland Browns
6021 NW 201st Ln
Hialeah, FL 33015-4865, USA

Waits, Tom (Music Group, Musician, Songwriter, Writer)
Mitch Schneider Organization
14724 Ventura Blvd Ste 710
Sherman Oaks, CA 91403-3520, USA

Waitt, Theodore W (Ted) (Business Person)
Gateway Inc
7565 Irvine Center Dr
Irvine, CA 92618-2930, USA

Waitz, Grete (Athlete, Track Athlete)
Birgitte Hammers Vei 15G
Oslo 1169, NORWAY

Waitz, Richard H (Cinematographer)
405 Zenith Ave
Lafayette, CO 80026-3104, USA

Wajda, Andrezei
u1 Jezefa Hauke Boska 14
Warsaw 01-540, POLAND

Wajda, Andrzej (Director)
Ul Konopnickiej 26
Cracow 30-302, POLAND

Wakasugi, Hiroshi
Astrid Schoerke
Monckebergallee 41
Hanover 30453, GERMANY

Wakata, Koichi (Astronaut)
NASA
2101 Nasa Pkwy
Johnson Space Center
Houston, TX 77058-3691, USA

Wakeham of Maldon, John (Government Official)
House of Lords
Westminster
London SW1A 0PW, UNITED KINGDOM (UK)

Wakeley, Amanda (Designer, Fashion Designer)
79-91 New Kings Road
London SW6 4SQ, UNITED KINGDOM (UK)

Wakeman, Frederic E Jr (Historian)
702 Gonzalez Dr
San Francisco, CA 94132-2234, USA

Wakeman, Rick (Musician, Songwriter, Writer)
Bajonor House
2 Bridge St Peel
Isle of Man, UNITED KINGDOM (UK)

Wako, Gabriel Zubeir Cardinal (Religious Leader)
Archdiocese
PO Box 49
Khartoum, SUDAN

Wakoski, Diane (Writer)
607 Division St
East Lansing, MI 48823-3428, USA

Waks, Aisha (Actor)
Writers & Artists
360 N Crescent Dr Bldg North
Beverly Hills, CA 90210-6818, USA

Walcott, Gregory (Actor)
22246 Saticoy St
Canoga Park, CA 91303-1043, USA

Walcott, Jennifer (Model)
4400 N Scottsdale Rd Ste 9
Scottsdale, AZ 85251-3331, USA

Walcutt, John (Actor)
c/o Staff Member *MC Talent Management*
4821 Lankershim Blvd # F329
N Hollywood, CA 91601-4538, USA

Walczak, Mark (Football Player)
Buffalo Bills
PO Box 372
Scottsdale, AZ 85252-0372, USA

Wald, Charles F (General)
Deputy Cofs For Air/Space Operations
Hqusaf Pentaton
Washington, DC 20330-0001, USA

Wald, Jeff (Producer)
c/o Jeff Wald *Jeff Wald Entertainment*
3000 Olympic Blvd Bldg 2 # 1400
Santa Monica, CA 90404-5073, USA

Wald, Patricia M (Judge)
US Court of Appeals
3rd & Constitution NW
Washington, DC 20001, USA

Waldegrave, William (Government Official)
66 Palace Gardens Terrace
London W8 4RR, UNITED KINGDOM (UK)

Waldemore, Stan (Football Player)
New York Jets
PO Box 611
New Vernon, NJ 07976-0611, USA

Walden, Lynette (Actor)
Metropolitan Talent Agency
4500 Wilshire Blvd Fl 2
Los Angeles, CA 90010-3858, USA

Walden, Robert (Actor)
1450 Arroyo View Dr
Pasadena, CA 91103-1901, USA

Walden, Robert E (Bobby) (Football Player)
Minnesota Vikings
107 Springfield Dr
Bainbridge, GA 39819-7885, USA

Walden, Ronnie (Baseball Player)
1007 Autumn Way
Blanchard, OK 73010-8961, USA

Waldheim, Kurt (President)
1 Lobkowitz Platz
Vienna 1010, AUSTRIA

Waldhorn, Gary (Actor)
London Mgmt
2-4 Noel St
London W1V 3RB, UNITED KINGDOM (UK)

Waldie, Marc (Volleyball Player)
4990 Almondwood Way
San Diego, CA 92130-2762, USA

Waldner, Jan-Ove (Athlete, Tennis Player)
Banda
Skiulstagatan 1O
Eskilstuna 632 29, SWEDEN

Waldo, Janet
15735 Royal Oak Rd
Encino, CA 91436, USA

Waldorf, Duffy (Golfer)
17100 Halsted St
Northridge, CA 91325-1960, USA

Waldron, Jeremy J (Educator)
1061 Keith Ave
Berkeley, CA 94708-1604, USA

Wales, Ross (Swimmer)
2233 Riverside Dr Unit 1B
Cincinnati, OH 45202-1855, USA

Walesa, Lech (Nobel Prize Laureate, President)
Ul Polanki 54
Gdansk-Oliwa 80-308, POLAND

Walheim, Rex J (Astronaut)
142 Hidden Lake Dr
League City, TX 77573-6976, USA

Walia, Sonu (Actor, Bollywood)
20 The Anchorage Juhu-Versova Link Road
Andheri(W)
Bombay, MS 400 058, INDIA

Walik, Billy (Football Player)
Philadelphia Eagles
PO Box 10712
Bainbridge Island, WA 98110-0712, USA

Walkabouts, The
PO Box 360524
Berlin 10975, GERMANY

Walken, Christopher (Actor)
c/o Toni Howard *International Creative Management (ICM-LA)*
10250 Constellation Blvd
Los Angeles, CA 90067-6200, USA

Walker, Adam (Football Player)
San Francisco 49ers
923 Bucknell Ave
Johnstown, PA 15905-2215, USA

Walker, Alan (Misc)
Johns Hopkins
Medical School
Cell Biology/Anatomy Dept
Baltimore, MD 21205, USA

Walker, Alice M (Activist, Writer)
670 San Luis Rd
Berkeley, CA 94707-1744, USA

Walker, Ally (Actor)
c/o Joel Rudnick *Paradigm (LA)*
360 N Crescent Dr
North Bldg
Beverly Hills, CA 90210-6820, USA

Walker, Anetia
19551 Turtle Ridge Ln
Northridge, CA 91326-3808, USA

Walker, Antoine (Basketball Player)
c/o Staff Member *Boston Celtics*
151 Merrimac St # 1
Boston, MA 02114-4714, USA

Walker, B J (Financier)
First Union Corp
1 First Union Center
Charlotte, NC 28288-0001, USA

Walker, Bree
3347 Tareco Dr
Los Angeles, CA 90068-1527, USA

Walker, Brian (Cartoonist)
King Features Syndicate
888 7th Ave Ste 201
New York, NY 10106-0201, USA

Walker, Bruce (Football Player)
New England Patriots
279 Eastlawn St
Detroit, MI 48215-3072, USA

Walker, Butch (Musician)
Progressive Global Agency
103 W Tyne Dr
Nashville, TN 37205-4428, USA

Walker, Catherine (Designer, Fashion Designer)
65 Sydney St
Chelsea
London SW3 6PX, UNITED KINGDOM (UK)

Walker, Charles D (Astronaut)
Boeing Co
1200 Wilson Blvd
Mc Rs00
Arlington, VA 22209-2305, USA

Walker, Charlie (Musician)
c/o Staff Member *Tessier-Marsh Talent*
505 Canton Pass
Madison, TN 37115-5449, USA

Walker, Charls E (Economist)
9426 Thrush Ln
Potomac, MD 20854-3991, USA

Walker, Chet (Basketball Player)
124 Fleet St
Marina Del Rey, CA 90292-7849, USA

Walker, Chris (Actor)
Roll Kruger
121 Gloucester Place
London W1H 3PJ, UNITED KINGDOM (UK)

Walker, Chuck (Football Player)
St Louis Cardinals
1613 Tradd Ct
Chesterfield, MO 63017-5627, USA

Walker, Cleo (Football Player)
Green Bay Packers
2512 Saint Xavier St
Louisville, KY 40212-1433, USA

Walker, Clint (Actor)
101 W McKnight Way Ste B 303
Grass Valley, CA 95949-9613, USA

Walker, Colleen (Golfer)
3612 Sugar Loaf Ln
Valrico, FL 33596-6062, USA

Walker, Darnell (Football Player)
Atlanta Falcons
2636 Columbus St
Muskogee, OK 74401-5129, USA

Walker, Darrell (Basketball Player, Coach)
16122 Patriot Dr
Little Rock, AR 72212-2669, USA

Walker, David (Government Official)
General Accounting Office
441 G St NW
Washington, DC 20548-0002, USA

Walker, Denard (Football Player)
Tennessee Oilers
17214 Lechlade Ln
Dallas, TX 75252-4208, USA

Walker, Derek (Architect)
2 General Sage Dr
Santa Fe, NM 87505-6333, USA

Walker, Derrick (Misc, Race Car Driver)
Walker Racing
147 Midland Rd Royston
Bamsley
S York S71 4B1, UNITED KINGDOM (UK)

Walker, Dwight (Football Player)
Cleveland Browns
221 N Laurel St Apt B
Metairie, LA 70003-6268, USA

Walker, Eamonn (Actor)
c/o Scott Schachter *International Creative Management (ICM-LA)*
10250 Constellation Blvd
Los Angeles, CA 90067-6200, USA

Walker, Fiona
13 Despard Rd.
London, ENGLAND 5NP, UNITED KINGDOM (UK)

Walker, George T Jr (Composer)
323 Grove St
Montclair, NJ 07042-4223, USA

Walker, Glen (Football Player)
Los Angeles Rams
5592 Nelson St
Cypress, CA 90630-3147, USA

Walker, Greg (Cartoonist)
King Features Syndicate
888 7th Ave Ste 201
New York, NY 10106-0201, USA

Walker, Harry
2120 Montevallo Rd
Leeds, AL 35094-3738, USA

Walker, Herschel J (Football Player)
3000 Blackburn St Apt 1901
Dallas, TX 75204-2211, USA

Walker, Hershell
19 West St
New York, NY 10004, USA

Walker, Hezekiah (Musician)
Covenant Agency
123 California Ave Apt 116
Santa Monica, CA 90403-3560, USA

Walker, Hugh (Baseball Player)
Bowman
24 Georgeann Dr
Jacksonville, AR 72076-5352, USA

Walker, Jackie (Football Player)
Tampa Bay Buccaneers
13014 N Dale Mabry Hwy # 120
Tampa, FL 33618-2808, USA

Walker, James E (Educator)
Middle Tennessee State University
President's Office
Murfreesboro, TN 37132-0001, USA

Walker, James L (Jimmy) (Misc)
Fireman & Oilers Brotherhood
1100 Cir 75 Pkwy
Atlanta, GA 30339-3064, USA

Walker, Jason (Musician)
c/o Len Evans *Project Publicity*
312 W 53rd St
New York, NY 10019-5743, USA

Walker, Jeff (Football Player)
San Diego Chargers
3712 Ringgold Rd # 204
Chattanooga, TN 37412-1638, USA

Walker, Jerry Jeff (Musician, Songwriter)
Tried & True Music
PO Box 39
Austin, TX 78767-0039, USA

Walker, Jimmie (J J) (Actor, Comedian)
c/o Wes Stevens *VOX Inc*
5670 Wilshire Blvd Ste 820
Los Angeles, CA 90036-5613, USA

Walker, Joe Louis (Musician)
Rick Bates Mgmt
714 Brookside Ln
Sierra Madre, CA 91024-1426, USA

Walker, John (Athlete, Track Athlete)
Jeffs Road
RD Papatoetoe, NEW ZEALAND

Walker, John E (Nobel Prize Laureate)
MRC Molecular Biology Laboratory
Hills Road
Cambridge CB2 2QH, UNITED
KINGDOM (UK)

Walker, Johnny (Baseball Player)
Raleigh Tigers
718 Franklin St SE
Grand Rapids, MI 49507-1307, USA

Walker, Junior
141 Dunbar Ave
Fords, NJ 08863-1551, USA

Walker, Kenny (Basketball Player)
2252 Terrace Woods Park
Lexington, KY 40513-1611, USA

Walker, Kenyatta (Football Player)
Tampa Bay Buccaneers
14813 Tudor Chase Dr
Tampa, FL 33626-3353, USA

Walker, LeRoy T (Coach, Educator)
PO Box 110105
Durham, NC 27709-5105, USA

Walker, Malcolm (Football Player)
Dallas Cowboys
7140 Winterwood Ln
Dallas, TX 75248-5246, USA

Walker, Marcy (Actor)
c/o David Shapira *David Shapira &
Associates*
193 N Robertson Blvd
Beverly Hills, CA 90211-2103, USA

Walker, Marquis (Football Player)
St Louis Rams
17576 Cherrylawn St
Detroit, MI 48221-2508, USA

Walker, Mickey (Football Player)
New York Giants
22828 S Maple Point Rd
Pickford, MI 49774-9145, USA

Walker, Mort (Cartoonist)
61 Studio Rd
Stamford, CT 06903-4724, USA

Walker, Nicholas
1900 Avenue Of The Stars Ste 1640
Los Angeles, CA 90067-4407, USA

Walker, Paul (Actor)
c/o Matt Luber *Nine Yards Entertainment*
8530 Wilshire Blvd Fl 5
Beverly Hills, CA 90211-3102, USA

Walker, Paul L (Religious Leader)
Church of God
PO Box 2430
Cleveland, TN 37320-2430, USA

Walker, Peter (Director)
23 Bentick St
London W1, UNITED KINGDOM (UK)

Walker, Polly (Actor)
Markham & Froggatt
Julian House
4 Windmill St
London W1P 1HF, UNITED KINGDOM
(UK)

Walker, Rick (Football Player)
Cincinnati Bengals
906 Winstead St
Great Falls, VA 22066-2546, USA

Walker, Robert M (Physicist)
1 Brookings Dr # Cb1105
Saint Louis, MO 63130-4862, USA

Walker, Roger N (Architect)
8 Brougham St
Mount Victoria
Wellington, NEW ZEALAND

Walker, Ronald C (Publisher)
Smithsonian Magazine
900 Jefferson Dr SW
Washington, DC 20560-0004, USA

Walker, Sammy (Football Player)
Pittsburgh Steelers
1031 Kings Row
Mc Kinney, TX 75069-6207, USA

Walker, Sandra (Opera Singer)
Columbia Artists Mgmt Inc
1790 Broadway Fl 6
New York, NY 10019-1412, USA

Walker, Sarah E B (Opera Singer)
152 Inchmery Road
London SE6 1DF, UNITED KINGDOM
(UK)

Walker, Val Joe (Football Player)
Green Bay Packers
3857 S Versailles Ave
Dallas, TX 75209-5927, USA

Walker, Wally (Basketball Player)
154 Lombard St Apt 58
San Francisco, CA 94111-1125, USA

Walker, Wayne (Football Player)
Detroit Lions
2033 White Pine Ln
Boise, ID 83706-4048, USA

Walker, Wesley D (Football Player)
New York Jets
PO Box 20438
Huntington Station, NY 11746-0857, USA

Walker, William D (Business Person)
Tektronix Inc
26600 Sourtwest Parkway
Wilsonville, OR 97070, USA

Walker Jr, Robert (Actor)
TOPS
23410 Civic Center Way Ste C1
Malibu, CA 90265-5925, USA

Walker of Worchester, Peter E
(Government Official)
Abbots Morton Manor
Grooms Hill Abbots Morton
Worc WR7 4LT, UNITED KINGDOM
(UK)

Wall, Brian A (Artist)
306 Lombard St
San Francisco, CA 94133-2415, USA

Wall, Carolyn (Publisher)
Newsweek Magazine
251 W 57th St
New York, NY 10019-1802, USA

Wall, David (Ballerina)
Royal Ballet
Covent Garden
Bow St
London WC2E 9DD, UNITED KINGDOM
(UK)

Wall, Frederick T (Misc)
8515 Costa Verde Blvd Unit 606
San Diego, CA 92122-1140, USA

Wall, John F (General)
507 Hanover St
Fredericksburg, VA 22401-5711, USA

Wall, Lindsay (Hockey Player)
University of Minnesota
Athletic Dept
Minneapolis, MN 55455, USA

Wall, Paul (Musician)
c/o Staff Member *Rebel Entertainment
Partners Inc*
5700 Wilshire Blvd Ste 456
Los Angeles, CA 90036-3648, USA

Wallace, Aaron (Football Player)
Oakland Raiders
612 Gardenia St
Desoto, TX 75115-1449, USA

Wallace, Anthony F C (Misc)
University of Pennsylvania
Anthropology Dept
Philadelphia, PA 19014, USA

Wallace, Aria (Actor)
c/o DebraLynn Findon *Discover Inc
Management*
11425 Moorpark St
Studio City, CA 91602-2009, USA

Wallace, B J (Baseball Player)
US Olympic Team
12775 River Creek Dr
Fairhope, AL 36532-6501, USA

Wallace, B Steven (Steve) (Football
Player)
San Francisco 49ers
4455 Harris Trl NW
Atlanta, GA 30327-3813, USA

Wallace, Ben (Basketball Player)
c/o Staff Member *Chicago Bulls*
1901 W Madison St
United Center
Chicago, IL 60612-2459, USA

Wallace, Bob (Football Player)
Chicago Bears
44111 N 43rd Dr
New River, AZ 85087-5956, USA

Wallace, Bruce (Doctor, Scientist)
940 McBryde Ln
Blacksburg, VA 24060-3221, USA

Wallace, Carol (Editor)
People Magazine
Editorial Dept
Time-Life Building
New York, NY 10020, USA

Wallace, Chris (Correspondent)
c/o Staff Member *20/20*
147 Columbus Ave
Abc
New York, NY 10023-6503, USA

Wallace, Christopher (Chris)
(Correspondent)
Fox-TV
205 E 67th St
News Dept
New York, NY 10065-6050, USA

Wallace, Clifford J (Judge)
US Court of Appeals
940 Front St Ste 5140
San Diego, CA 92101-8949, USA

Wallace, Craig K (Doctor)
National Institutes of Health
9000 Rockville Pike
Bethesda, MD 20892-0002, USA

Wallace, David Foster (Writer)
Illinois State University
English Dept
Normal, IL 61761, USA

Wallace, Don (Actor)
c/o Staff Member *SMS Talent Inc*
8730 W Sunset Blvd Ste 440
Los Angeles, CA 90069-2277, USA

Wallace, George (Musician)
c/o Staff Member *Paradigm (Monterey)*
509 Hartnell St
Monterey, CA 93940-2825, USA

Wallace, Gerald (Basketball Player)
Sacramento Kings
1 Sports Pkwy
Arco Arena
Sacramento, CA 95834-2301, USA

Wallace, Jane (Entertainer)
Cosgrove-Meurer Productions
4303 W Verdugo Ave
Burbank, CA 91505-3358, USA

Wallace, Jerry
1161 NW 76th Ave
Plantation, FL 33322-5120, USA

Wallace, Julie T (Actor)
Annette Stone
9 Newburgh St
London W1V 1LH, UNITED KINGDOM
(UK)

Wallace, Kenny (Race Car Driver)
8929 Harris Rd
Concord, NC 28027, USA

Wallace, Laurie
PO Box 3023
Guttenberg, NJ 07093-6023, USA

Wallace, Marcia (Actor)
Artists Group
1650 Broadway Ste 610
New York, NY 10019-6833, USA

Wallace, Mike (Correspondent)
c/o Staff Member *60 Minutes*
524 W 57th St
Cbs News
New York, NY 10019-2930, USA

Wallace, Randall (Actor, Director,
Producer, Writer)
c/o Staff Member *Wheelhouse, The*
15464 Ventura Blvd
Sherman Oaks, CA 91403-3002, USA

Wallace, Rasheed (Basketball Player)
01905 SW Greenwood Rd
Portland, OR 97219-8367, USA

Wallace, Ray (Football Player)
Houston Oilers
2480 Port Kembla Dr
Mount Juliet, TN 37122-7512, USA

Wallace, Rheagan (Actor)
c/o Staff Member *Abrams Artists Agency
(LA)*
9200 W Sunset Blvd Ph 11
Los Angeles, CA 90069-3601, USA

Wallace, Rodney (Football Player)
Dallas Cowboys
20566 E Maplewood Pl
Centennial, CO 80016-1264, USA

Wallace, Roger (Football Player)
New York Giants
408 N Oakland St
Urbana, OH 43078-1521, USA

Wallace, Rusty (Race Car Driver)
Penske Racing
149 Knob Hill Rd
Mooresville, NC 28117-6847, USA

Wallace, Tommy Lee (Director)
Innovative Artists
1505 10th St
Santa Monica, CA 90401-2805, USA

Wallace, Will (Actor)
c/o Andrew Stawiarski *ADS Management*
269 S Beverly Dr # 441
Beverly Hills, CA 90212-3851, USA

Wallace, William (General)
Commanding General
V Corps
APO, AE 09079, USA

Wallach, Eli (Actor)
90 Riverside Dr
New York, NY 10024-5306, USA

Wallach, Evan J (Judge)
US International Trade Court
1 Federal Plz
New York, NY 10278-0001, USA

Wallenberg, Raoul Committee
823 Union Plz Fl 8
New York, NY 10017-3543, USA

Wallendas, The Great
138 Frog Hollow Rd
Churchville, PA 18966-1031, USA

Waller, Gordon (Musician)
7 Passage St
Powey
Cornwall PL23 1DE, UNITED KINGDOM
(UK)

Waller, Michael (Editor)
Hartford Courant Co
285 Broad St
Hartford, CT 06115-2510, USA

Waller, Peter
7 Passage St. owley
Cornwall, ENGLAND PL23 IDE, UNITED
KINGDOM (UK)

Waller, Rik (Musician)
c/o Staff Member *Pop Idol (Fremantle Media)*
2700 Colorado Ave Ste 450
Santa Monica, CA 90404-3599, USA

Waller, Robert James (Writer)
Aaron Priest Literary Agency
708 3rd Ave Rm 2300
New York, NY 10017-4211, USA

Waller, Ron (Football Player)
Los Angeles Rams
900 Concord Rd
Seaford, DE 19973, USA

Waller, William L (Governor)
220 S President St
Jackson, MS 39201-4307, USA

Wallerstein, Ralph G (Misc)
3447 Clay St
San Francisco, CA 94118-2008, USA

Wallflowers, The (Music Group)
c/o Rick Roskin *Creative Artists Agency LCC (CAA-LA)*
2000 Avenue Of The Stars
Los Angeles, CA 90067-4700, USA

Walliams, David (Actor, Writer)
TROIKA
74 Clerkenwell Rd 3rd Fl
London EC1M52A, UNITED KINGDOM
(UK)

Walling, Camryn (Actor)
c/o TJ Stein *Stein Entertainment Group*
11271 Ventura Blvd # 477
Studio City, CA 91604-3136, USA

Walling, Cheves T (Misc)
214 Rivermead Rd
Peterborough, NH 03458-1745, USA

Wallis, Shani (Actor)
15460 Vista Haven Pl
Sherman Oaks, CA 91403-4327, USA

Walliser, Maria (Skier)
Selfwingert
Malans 7208, SWITZERLAND

Wallop, Malcolm (Senator)
58 Canyon Ranch Road
Big Horn, WY 82833, USA

Walls, Denise (Nee-C) (Musician, Songwriter, Writer)
2113 South Ave
Youngstown, OH 44502-2255, USA

Walls, Everson C (Football Player)
Dallas Cowboys
4812 Portrait Ln
Plano, TX 75024-3803, USA

Walls, Herkie (Football Player)
Houston Oilers
1002 Cherrywood Dr
Garland, TX 75040-7437, USA

Walls, Lenny (Football Player)
Denver Broncos
2800 Bush St
San Francisco, CA 94115-2905, USA

Walls, Wesley (Football Player)
San Francisco 49ers
8711 Lake Challis Ln
Charlotte, NC 28226-2666, USA

Walmsley, Jon (Actor)
13810 Magnolia Blvd
Sherman Oaks, CA 91423-1202, USA

Walpot, Heike (Astronaut)
DLR
Abt Raumflugbetrieb
Cologne 51170, GERMANY

Walser, Don (Musician, Songwriter, Writer)
Nancy Fly Agency
6618 Wolfcreek Pass
Austin, TX 78749-1744, USA

Walser, Martin
Zum Hecht 36
Uberlingen D-88662, GERMANY

Walsh, Addie (Writer)
c/o Staff Member *William Morris Agency (WMA-LA)*
1 William Morris Pl
Beverly Hills, CA 90212-4261, USA

Walsh, Amanda (Actor)
c/o Staff Member *Relativity Management*
8899 Beverly Blvd Ste 510
Los Angeles, CA 90048-2449, USA

Walsh, Arthur
12360 Riverside Dr
N Hollywood, CA 91607-3644, USA

Walsh, Chris (Football Player)
Buffalo Bills
1850 Bryant St
Palo Alto, CA 94301-3709, USA

Walsh, David M (Cinematographer)
15436 Valley Vista Blvd
Sherman Oaks, CA 91403-3812, USA

Walsh, Diana Chapman (Educator)
Wellesley College
President's Office
Wellesley, MA 02181, USA

Walsh, Don (Misc, Swimmer)
International Maritime Inc
14758 Sitkum Ln
Myrtle Point, OR 97458-9692, USA

Walsh, Donnie (Basketball Player, Coach)
Indiana Pacers
125 Pennsylvania
Conseco Fieldhouse
Indianapolis, IN 46204, USA

Walsh, Dylan (Actor)
c/o Bob McGowan *McGowan Management*
8733 W Sunset Blvd Ste 103
W Hollywood, CA 90069-2241, USA

Walsh, Frances (Fran) (Producer, Writer)
c/o Staff Member *WingNut Films*
PO Box 15208
Miramar
Wellington 6003, NEW ZEALAND

Walsh, Gwynyth (Actor)
c/o Staff Member *Characters Talent Agency, The (Toronto)*
8 Elm St 3rd FL
Toronto, ON M5G 1G7, CANADA

Walsh, Joe (Musician, Songwriter, Writer)
PO Box 1188
Easton, PA 18044-1188, USA

Walsh, John (Television Host)
c/o Sean Perry *Endeavor Agency LLC (LA)*
9601 Wilshire Blvd Fl 3
Beverly Hills, CA 90210-5204, USA

Walsh, John Jr (Misc)
J Paul Getty Museum
1200 Getty Center Dr
Getty Center
Los Angeles, CA 90049-1687, USA

Walsh, Kate (Actor)
c/o Tiffany Kuzon *Evolution Entertainment (LA)*
901 N Highland Ave
Los Angeles, CA 90038-2412, USA

Walsh, Kerri (Volleyball Player)
Assoc of Volleyball Pros
6100 Center Dr Ste 900
Los Angeles, CA 90045-9207, USA

Walsh, Lawrence E (Attorney, Attorney General, General, Government Official)
1902 Bedford Dr
Nichols Hills, OK 73116-5306, USA

Walsh, M Emmet (Actor)
4173 Motor Ave
Culver City, CA 90232-3414, USA

Walsh, Martin (Misc)
National Organization on Disability
910 16th St NW Ste 600
Washington, DC 20006-2916, USA

Walsh, Matt (Comedian)
c/o Staff Member *United Talent Agency (UTA)*
9560 Wilshire Blvd Ste 500
Beverly Hills, CA 90212-2401, USA

Walsh, Patrick C (Doctor)
Johns Hopkins University
Brady Urological Institute
Baltimore, MD 21205, USA

Walsh, Peter (Actor)
c/o Staff Member *The Learning Channel (TLC)*
7700 Wisconsin Ave
Bethesda, MD 20814-3578, USA

Walsh, Sheila (Musician, Writer)
PO Box 1516
Celina, TX 75009-1516, USA

Walsh, Stephen J (Steve) (Football Player)
Dallas Cowboys
339 Flamingo Dr
West Palm Beach, FL 33401-7721, USA

Walsh, Steve
Box 6 Wickford
Essex, ENGLAND SS12 9D0, UNITED
KINGDOM (UK)

Walsh, Sydney (Actor)
Innovative Artists
1505 10th St
Santa Monica, CA 90401-2805, USA

Walsh, Tom (Artist)
PO Box 133
Philomath, OR 97370-0133, USA

Walsh, Ward (Football Player)
Houston Oilers
1658 W Carson St Ste C
Torrance, CA 90501-2897, USA

Walshe, Tommy (Actor, Television Host)
c/o Staff Member *Arlington Enterprises Ltd*
1-3 Charlotte St
London W1P 1HD, UNITED KINGDOM
(UK)

Walske, Steven (Business Person)
Parametric Technology
140 Kendrick St
Needham Heights, MA 02494-2739, USA

Walsman, Leanna (Actor)
c/o Chris Andrews *Creative Artists Agency LCC (CAA-LA)*
2000 Avenue Of The Stars
Los Angeles, CA 90067-4700, USA

Walte, Grant (Golfer)
9380 S Magnolia Ave
Ocala, FL 34476-7535, USA

Walter, Jessica (Actor)
27 W 87th St # 2
New York, NY 10024-3005, USA

Walter, Joe (Football Player)
Cincinnati Bengals
4136 Binley Dr
Richardson, TX 75082-3723, USA

Walter, Lisa Ann (Actor, Comedian)
United Talent Agency
9560 Wilshire Blvd Ste 500
Beverly Hills, CA 90212-2401, USA

Walter, Mike (Football Player)
Dallas Cowboys
6900 SW Knollwood St
Tualatin, OR 97062-7717, USA

Walter, Paul H L (Misc)
3 Benedictine Retreat
Savannah, GA 31411-1624, USA

Walter, Robert D (Business Person)
Cardinal Health
7000 Cardinal Pl
Dublin, OH 43017-1092, USA

Walter, Tracey (Actor)
257 N Rexford Dr
Beverly Hills, CA 90210-4907, USA

Walter, Ulrich (Astronaut)
IBM Germany
Schonaicherstr 220
Boblingen 71032, GERMANY

Walters, Barbara (Journalist, Talk Show Host)
c/o Staff Member *Barwall Productions*
320 W 66th St Fl 2
New York, NY 10023-6304, USA

Walters, Charles (Director)
23922 De Ville Way Apt A
Malibu, CA 90265-4844, USA

Walters, David L (Governor)
RR 2
Watts, OK 74964, USA

Walters, Harry N (Government Official)
DHC Holdings Corp
125 Thomas Dale
Williamsburg, VA 23185-6576, USA

Walters, Hugh
15 Christchurch Ave
London, ENGLAND NW6 7QP, UNITED KINGDOM (UK)

Walters, Jamie (Actor, Musician)
4702 Ethel Ave
Sherman Oaks, CA 91423-3315, USA

Walters, Julie (Actor)
International Creative Mgmt
76 Oxford St
London W1N 0AX, UNITED KINGDOM (UK)

Walters, Lisa (Golfer)
211 S Westland Ave Unit 2
Tampa, FL 33606-1721, USA

Walters, Melora (Actor)
United Talent Agency
9560 Wilshire Blvd Ste 500
Beverly Hills, CA 90212-2401, USA

Walters, Mike (Baseball Player)
Minnesota Twins
79070 Desert Stream Dr
La Quinta, CA 92253-4295, USA

Walters, Peter I (Business Person)
22 Hill St
London W1X 7FU, UNITED KINGDOM (UK)

Walters, Roger T (Architect)
46 Princess Road
London NW1 8JL, UNITED KINGDOM (UK)

Walters, Stan (Football Player)
Cincinnati Bengals
10 Lcklingham Wood
Sewell, NJ 08080, USA

Walters, Susan (Actor)
c/o Gabrielle Krengel *Domain*
4526 Wilshire Blvd
Los Angeles, CA 90010-3801, USA

Walters, Tom (Football Player)
Washington Redskins
8 Heritage Ln
Magnolia, TX 77354-1337, USA

Walters, Tome H Jr (General)
Defense Security Cooperation Agency
1111 Davis Highway
Arlington, VA 22202, USA

Walterscheild, Len (Football Player)
Chicago Bears
2312 I Rd
Grand Junction, CO 81505-9646, USA

Walthall, Romy (Actor)
c/o Dede Binder-Goldsmith *Defining Artists*
10 Universal City Plz Ste 2000
Universal City, CA 91608-1074, USA

Walther, Herbert (Physicist)
Egenhoferstr 7A
Munich 81243, GERMANY

Walton, Anthony J (Tony) (Designer)
International Creative Mgmt
40 W 57th St Ste 1800
New York, NY 10019-4001, USA

Walton, Bennie (Baseball Player)
188 S Palm Villas Way
Palm Springs, FL 33461-1084, USA

Walton, Bill
1010 Myrtle Way
San Diego, CA 92103-5123, USA

Walton, Bruce (Baseball Player)
Oakland A's
10625 Tivoli Ct
Bakersfield, CA 93311-2217, USA

Walton, Cedar A Jr (Musician)
Bridge Agency
35 Clark St Apt A5
Brooklyn, NY 11201-2374, USA

Walton, Danny (Baseball Player)
Houston Astros
PO Box 296
Huntsville, UT 84317-0296, USA

Walton, David (Actor)
c/o Eric Black *Anonymous Content (CA)*
3532 Hayden Ave
Culver City, CA 90232-2413, USA

Walton, Helen R (Business Person)
Wal-Mart Stores
702 SW 8th St
Bentonville, AR 72716-6209, USA

Walton, Jess (Actor)
15030 Ventura Blvd # 710
Sherman Oaks, CA 91403-5470, USA

Walton, John (Football Player)
Philadelphia Eagles
401 New York Ave
Elizabeth City, NC 27909-5939, USA

Walton, Joseph (Joe) (Coach, Football Coach, Football Player)
Washington Redskins
8 Windycrest Dr
Beaver Falls, PA 15010-3041, USA

Walton, Lawrence (Football Player)
Detroit Lions
438 W Tierra Buena Ln
Phoenix, AZ 85023-7414, USA

Walton, Reggie (Baseball Player)
Seattle Mariners
1142 S Curson Ave
Los Angeles, CA 90019-6611, USA

Walton, Robin (Golfer)
8404 SW 50th Ln
Gainesville, FL 32608-4307, USA

Walton, S Robson (Rob) (Business Person)
Wal-Mart Stores
702 SW 8th St
Bentonville, AR 72716-6209, USA

Walton, Whip (Football Player)
New York Giants
5662 Weatherstone Ct
San Diego, CA 92130-4826, USA

Waltrip, Darrell L (Race Car Driver)
PO Box 381
Harrisburg, NC 28075-0381, USA

Waltrip, Robert L (Business Person)
Service Corp International
1929 Allen Pkwy
Houston, TX 77019-2500, USA

Waltz, Lisa (Actor)
Writers & Artists
360 N Crescent Dr Bldg North
Beverly Hills, CA 90210-6818, USA

Walulik-Kiely, Helen (Baseball Player)
493 W Hill Rd
Glen Gardner, NJ 08826-3265, USA

Walz, Carl E (Astronaut)
129 Lake Point Dr
League City, TX 77573-6973, USA

Walz, Zach (Football Player)
Arizona Cardinals
6270 E Wilshire Dr
Scottsdale, AZ 85257-1114, USA

Wamala, Emmanuel Cardinal (Religious Leader)
PO Box 14125
Mengo
Kampala, UGANDA

Wambach, Abby (Soccer Player)
Patrick Wambach
1600 Parkwood Cir SE Ste 600
Powerplan Consultants Inc
Atlanta, GA 30339-2147, USA

Wambaugh, Joseph (Writer)
3520 Kellogg Way
San Diego, CA 92106-3346, USA

Wambold, Richard L (Business Person)
Pactiv Corp
1900 W Field Ct
Lake Forest, IL 60045-4828, USA

Wan, Li (Government Official)
State Council
People's Congress
Tian An Men Square
Beijing, CHINA

Wanamaker, Zoe (Actor)
Conway Van Gelder Robinson
18-21 Jermyn St
London SW1Y 6NB, UNITED KINGDOM (UK)

Wang, Garrett (Actor)
501 E Del Mar Blvd Apt 310
Pasadena, CA 91101-3613, USA

Wang, Hannah
c/o Staff Member *Nickelodeon UK*
PO Box 6425
LONDON W1A 6UR, UNITED KINGDOM (UK)

Wang, Jida (Artist)
7612 35th Ave Apt 3E
Jackson Heights, NY 11372-4612, USA

Wang, Junxia (Athlete, Track Athlete)
Athletic Assn
9 Tlyuguan Road
Chongwen District
Beijing 10061, CHINA

Wang, Taylor G (Astronaut, Physicist)
1224 Amo Dr
Sierra Madre, CA 91024, USA

Wang, Tian-Ren (Artist)
Shaanxi Sculpture Institute
Longshoucun
Xi'am
Shaanxi 710016, CHINA

Wang, Vera (Designer, Fashion Designer)
Vera Wang Bridal House
225 W 39th St # 1000
New York, NY 10018-3103, USA

Wang, Wayne (Director)
1888 Century Park E Ste 1888
Los Angeles, CA 90067-1722, USA

Wang, Zhen-Yi (Doctor, Scientist)
Hopital de Shanghai
Rul Jin Road 11
Shanghai 200025, CHINA

Wang Zhl Zhi (Basketball Player)
Miami Heat
601 Biscayne Blvd
American Airlines Arena
Miami, FL 33132-1801, USA

Wangchuck, Dasho Jigme Khesar Namgyal (Prince)
Royal Palace
Tashichhodzong
Thimpu, BHUTAN

Wangchuck, Jigme Singye (King)
Royal Palace
Tashichhodzong
Thimpu, BHUTAN

Wanner, H Eric (Misc)
Russell Sage Foundation
112 E 64th St
New York, NY 10065-7383, USA

Wannsdedt, David R (Dave) (Coach, Football Coach)
12600 N Stonebrook Cir
Davie, FL 33330-1288, USA

Wannstedt, David R (Dave) (Coach, Football Coach)
University of Pittsburgh
Athletic Dept
Pittsburgh, PA 15260, USA

Wansel, Dexter (Musician)
Walt Reeder Productions
PO Box 27641
Philadelphia, PA 19118-0641, USA

Wantland, Hal (Football Player)
Miami Dolphins
825 W Woodchase Rd
Knoxville, TN 37934-1629, USA

Wanzer, Robert F (Bobby) (Basketball Player)
28 Greenwood Park
Pittsford, NY 14534-2965, USA

Waples, Keith (Horse Racer)
PO Box 632
Durham, ON N0G 1R0, CANADA

Wapner, Joseph A (Actor, Judge)
2388 Century Hl
Los Angeles, CA 90067-3514, USA

Wapnick, Steve (Baseball Player)
Detroit Tigers
4401 Picadilly Dr
Fort Collins, CO 80526-5255, USA

War
250 W 57th St # 407
New York, NY 10107-0001, USA

Warbeck, Stephen (Composer)
c/o Staff Member *Soundtrack Music Assoc*
2229 Cloverfield Blvd
Santa Monica, CA 90405-1820, USA

Warburton, Patrick (Actor)
c/o Dolores Robinson *Dolores Robinson Entertainment*
3815 Hughes Ave # 3
Culver City, CA 90232-2715, USA

Ward, Anita (Musician)
c/o Staff Member *Diva Central Inc*
7510 W Sunset Blvd Ste 1445
Los Angeles, CA 90046-3408, USA

Ward, Burt (Actor)
Gentle Giants & Adoptions
PO Box 6005
Norco, CA 92860-8033, USA

Ward, Charlie (Basketball Player, Football Player)
109 Heisman Way
Thomasville, GA 31792-7104, USA

Ward, Chris (Baseball Player)
Chicago Cubs
12858 Williams Ranch Rd # 13
Moorpark, CA 93021-2109, USA

Ward, Chris (Football Player)
Baltimore Ravens
1920 Sylvan Ridge Dr SW
Atlanta, GA 30310-4945, USA

Ward, Christopher L (Chris) (Football Player)
New York Jets
PO Box 1365
Inglewood, CA 90308-1365, USA

Ward, Colby (Baseball Player)
Cleveland Indians
1508 Hobble Creek Dr
Springville, UT 84663-2890, USA

Ward, Colin (Baseball Player)
San Francisco Giants
10558 E Carol Ave
Mesa, AZ 85208-7427, USA

Ward, Dale (Musician)
A Crosse the World
PO Box 23066
London W11 3FR, UNITED KINGDOM (UK)

Ward, Daryle (Baseball Player)
Houston Astros
18073 Granite Ave
Riverside, CA 92508-9777, USA

Ward, David (Opera Singer)
1 Kennedy Crescent
Lake Wanaka, NEW ZEALAND

Ward, Fred (Actor)
1215 Cabrillo Ave
Venice, CA 90291-3773, USA

Ward, Gary (Baseball Player)
Minnesota Twins
18073 Granite Ave
Riverside, CA 92508-9777, USA

Ward, Gemma (Actor)
c/o Jack Heller *Schiff Company*
9465 Wilshire Blvd Ste 480
Beverly Hills, CA 90212-2603, USA

Ward, Hines (Football Player)
805 City Park Dr
McDonough, GA 30252-1027, USA

Ward, Jay (Baseball Player)
Minnesota Twins
PO Box 184
Libby, MT 59923-0184, USA

Ward, John (Football Player)
Minnesota Vikings
9501 Silver Lake Dr
Oklahoma City, OK 73162-7547, USA

Ward, John F (Business Person)
Russell Corp
755 Lee St
Alexander City, AL 35010-2638, USA

Ward, John Milton (Educator)
20 Follen St
Cambridge, MA 02138-3503, USA

Ward, Jon P (Business Person)
RR Donnelley & Sons
77 W Wacker Dr
Chicago, IL 60601-1604, USA

Ward, Jonathan (Actor)
Auckland Actors
Po Box 56460
Dominion Road
Auckland 1030, NEW ZEALAND

Ward, Kevin (Baseball Player)
San Diego Padres
160 F Ave
Coronado, CA 92118-1212, USA

Ward, Lala (Actor)
London Mgmt
2-4 Noel St
London W1V 3RB, UNITED KINGDOM (UK)

Ward, Maitland (Actor)
Shelter Entertainment
9255 W Sunset Blvd Ste 1010
Los Angeles, CA 90069-3307, USA

Ward, Mary (Actor)
Melbourne Artists
643 Saint Kilda Road
Melbourne, VIC 3004, AUSTRALIA

Ward, Mary B (Actor)
Innovative Artists
1505 10th St
Santa Monica, CA 90401-2805, USA

Ward, Megan (Actor)
PO Box 481219
Los Angeles, CA 90036, USA

Ward, Michael P (Doctor, Mountaineer)
Saint Andrews's Hospital
Bow St
London E3 3NT, UNITED KINGDOM (UK)

Ward, Pete (Baseball Player)
Baltimore Orioles
575 G Ave
Lake Oswego, OR 97034-2272, USA

Ward, Preston (Baseball Player)
Brooklyn Dodgers
4371 De Silva Pl
Las Vegas, NV 89121-5347, USA

Ward, R Duane (Baseball Player)
1660 City View Ct
Las Vegas, NV 89117-1333, USA

Ward, Rachel (Actor)
c/o Staff Member *Himber Entertainment Inc*
15760 Ventura Blvd Ste 700
Encino, CA 91436-3016, USA

Ward, Robert (Composer)
2701 Pickett Rd Apt 4022
Durham, NC 27705-5652, USA

Ward, Ronald L (Ron) (Hockey Player)
3178 W 140th St
Cleveland, OH 44111-1442, USA

Ward, Sela (Actor)
c/o Michelle Bohan *Endeavor Agency LLC (LA)*
9601 Wilshire Blvd Fl 3
Beverly Hills, CA 90210-5204, USA

Ward, Simon (Actor)
Shepherd & Ford
13 Radner Walk
London SW3 4BP, UNITED KINGDOM (UK)

Ward, Sterling (Religious Leader)
Brethren Church
524 College Ave
Ashland, OH 44805-3703, USA

Ward, Susan (Actor)
c/o Staff Member *Agency Group Ltd, The (LA)*
1880 Century Park E Ste 711
Los Angeles, CA 90067-1618, USA

Ward, Turner M (Baseball Player)
Cleveland Indians
232 Autumn Dr
Saraland, AL 36571-2619, USA

Ward, Vincent (Director)
PO Box 423
Kings Cross
Sydney, NSW 2011, AUSTRALIA

Ward, Wendy (Golfer)
12845 Sassin Station Rd N
Edwall, WA 99008-9564, USA

Ward, Zach (Actor)
Diverse Talent Group
1875 Century Park E Ste 2250
Los Angeles, CA 90067-2563, USA

Warden, John (Attorney, Attorney General, General)
Sullivan & Cromwell
125 Broad St
New York, NY 10004-2498, USA

Warden, Jon (Baseball Player)
Detroit Tigers
6575 Oasis Dr
Loveland, OH 45140-5817, USA

Wardlaw, Kim McLane (Judge)
US Court of Appeals
125 S Grand Ave
Pasadena, CA 91105-1652, USA

Wardle, Curt (Baseball Player)
Minnesota Twins
13900 Pheasant Knoll Ln
Moreno Valley, CA 92553-5330, USA

Ware, Andre (Football Player)
Detroit Lions
3910 Wood Park
Sugar Land, TX 77479-2838, USA

Ware, Chris (Artist)
c/o Staff Member *Fantagraphics Books*
7563 Lake City Way NE
Seattle, WA 98115-4218, USA

Ware, Clyde
5142 Clinton St
Los Angeles, CA 90004-1661, USA

Ware, Derek (Football Player)
Phoenix Cardinals
4426 E Desert Willow Rd
Phoenix, AZ 85044-6064, USA

Ware, Jeff (Baseball Player)
Toronto Blue Jays
2560 Mulberry Loop
Virginia Beach, VA 23456-7818, USA

Warfield, Eric (Football Player)
Kansas City Chiefs
718 Meadows Rd
Texarkana, AR 71854-8341, USA

Warfield, Paul D (Football Player)
Cleveland Browns
16 Normandy Way
Rancho Mirage, CA 92270-1635, USA

Wargo, Tom (Golfer)
2801 Putter Dr
Centralia, IL 62801-6183, USA

Warhols, James (Writer)
PO Box 748
Rhinebeck, NY 12572-0748, USA

Wariner, Steve (Musician, Songwriter, Writer)
Steve Wariner Productions
PO Box 1647
Franklin, TN 37065-1647, USA

Waring, Amanda
8 Chester Close Queens Ride
Barnes, ENGLAND, UNITED KINGDOM (UK)

Waring, Richard
1 Chester Close Queens Ride
London, ENGLAND SW13 OJE, UNITED KINGDOM (UK)

Waring, Todd (Actor)
Artists Agency
1180 S Beverly Dr Ste 301
Los Angeles, CA 90035-1154, USA

Wark, Robert R (Misc)
Huntington Library & Art Gallery
1151 Oxford Rd
San Marino, CA 91108-1218, USA

Warlick, Ernie (Football Player)
Buffalo Bills
121 Presidents Walk
Buffalo, NY 14221-2447, USA

Warlock, Billy (Actor)
c/o Staff Member *Peter Strain & Associates Inc (LA)*
5455 Wilshire Blvd Ste 1812
Los Angeles, CA 90036-4268, USA

Warmenhoven, Daniel (Business Person)
Network Appliance Inc
495 E Java Dr
Sunnyvale, CA 94089-1125, USA

Warmerdam, Cornelius
3976 N 1st St
Fresno, CA 93726-4304, USA

Warne, Jim (Football Player)
Detroit Lions
5850 Hardy Ave # 112
San Diego, CA 92115, USA

Warnecke, John Carl (Architect)
300 Broadway St
San Francisco, CA 94133-4587, USA

Warnecke, Mark (Swimmer)
Am Schichtmeister 100
Witten 58453, GERMANY

Warner, Amelia (Actor)
c/o Staff Member *Handprint Entertainment*
1100 Glendon Ave Ste 1000
Los Angeles, CA 90024-3514, USA

Warner, Charley (Football Player)
Kansas City Chiefs
1890 Rena St
Beaumont, TX 77705-4729, USA

Warner, Chris (Cartoonist)
Dark House Publishing
10956 SE Main St
Portland, OR 97216, USA

Warner, Curt (Football Player)
Seattle Seahawks
10811 SE Mill Plain Blvd
Vancouver, WA 98664-4533, USA

Warner, Dan (Actor)
c/o Staff Member *Players Talent Agency*
7700 W Sunset Blvd # 1
Los Angeles, CA 90046-3913, USA

Warner, David (Actor)
Julian Belfarge
46 Albermarle St
London W1X 4PP, UNITED KINGDOM
(UK)

Warner, Douglas A III (Financier)
JP Morgan Chase
270 Park Ave Fl 12
New York, NY 10017-7924, USA

Warner, Jack (Baseball Player)
Chicago Cubs
5938 W Calle Lejos
Glendale, AZ 85310-3505, USA

Warner, Jackie (Baseball Player)
California Angels
19136 US Highway 18
Apple Valley, CA 92307-2507, USA

Warner, Jackie (Fitness Expert, Reality TV Star)
Sky Sport & Spa
8500 Wilshire Blvd Ph
Beverly Hills, CA 90211-3109, USA

Warner, Jane
166 Ditching Rd.
Brighton, CA BN1 6JA, UNITED KINGDOM (UK)

Warner, John (Senator)
PO Box 1320
Atoka Farms
Middleburg, VA 20118-1320, USA

Warner, Julie (Actor)
c/o Molly Madden *3 Arts Entertainment Inc*
9460 Wilshire Blvd Fl 7
Beverly Hills, CA 90212-2713, USA

Warner, Kirk (Football Player)
New England Patriots
110 S 5th St
Cochran, GA 31014-6632, USA

Warner, Kurt (Football Player)
c/o Staff Member *Arizona Cardinals*
PO Box 888
Phoenix, AZ 85001-0888, USA

Warner, Malcolm-Jamal (Actor)
PO Box 69646
Los Angeles, CA 90069-0646, USA

Warner, Margaret (Correspondent)
News Hour Show
2700 S Quincy St Ste 250
Arlington, VA 22206-2222, USA

Warner, T C (Actor)
S D B Partners
1801 Avenue Of Stars Ste 902
Los Angeles, CA 90067-5981, USA

Warner, Todd (Artist)
8799 Boyne City Rd
Charlevoix, MI 49720-9102, USA

Warner, Tom (Producer)
Carsey-Warner Productions
4024 Radford Ave Bldg 3
Studio City, CA 91604-2101, USA

Warner, Ty (Designer)
Ty Inc
PO Box 5377
Oak Brook, IL 60522-5377, USA

Warner, William W (Writer)
2243 47th St NW
Washington, DC 20007-1034, USA

Warnes, Jennifer (Musician, Songwriter, Writer)
Donald Miller
12746 Kling St
Studio City, CA 91604-1125, USA

Warnke, Paul
5037 Garfield St NW
Washington, DC 20016-3465, USA

Warnock, John (Business Person)
Adobe Systems
345 Park Ave
San Jose, CA 95110-2704, USA

Warrant
15216 Burbank Blvd Ste 103
Sherman Oaks, CA 91411-3561, USA

Warren, Chris (Football Player)
Seattle Seahawks
13707 Black Spruce Way
Chantilly, VA 20151-2346, USA

Warren, Cicero (Baseball Player)
Homestead Grays
3820 Saratoga Dr
Raleigh, NC 27604-3445, USA

Warren, Diane (Musician)
Realsongs
6363 W Sunset Blvd # 810
Los Angeles, CA 90028-7318, USA

Warren, Don (Football Player)
Washington Redskins
6001 Union Mill Rd
Centerville High School Attn: Athletic Dept
Clifton, VA 20124-1128, USA

Warren, Estalia (Actor, Model)
AGS
200 Park Ave # 800
New York, NY 10166-0005, USA

Warren, Estella (Actor, Model)
c/o Stephanie Simon *Untitled Entertainment (LA)*
331 N Maple Dr Fl 3
Beverly Hills, CA 90210-3827, USA

Warren, Fran (Musician)
Richard Barz
21 Cobble Creek Dr
Tannersville, PA 18372-9681, USA

Warren, Frederick M (Architect)
65 Cambridge Terrace
Christchurch 1, NEW ZEALAND

Warren, Gerard (Football Player)
c/o Staff Member *Denver Broncos*
13655 Broncos Pkwy
Englewood, CO 80112-4150, USA

Warren, Gloria (Actor, Musician)
16872 Bosque Dr
Encino, CA 91436-3531, USA

Warren, Jennifer (Actor)
1675 Old Oak Rd
Los Angeles, CA 90049-2505, USA

Warren, Jim (Football Player)
San Diego Chargers
2200 Riverfront Dr Apt 3113
Little Rock, AR 72202-2242, USA

Warren, Karle (Actor)
c/o Justine Hunt *Hines and Hunt Entertainment*
1213 W Magnolia Blvd
Burbank, CA 91506-1829, USA

Warren, Kenneth S (Doctor, Scientist)
Picower Medical Research Institute
350 Community Dr
Manhasset, NY 11030-3816, USA

Warren, Kiersten (Actor)
Stubbs
8675 Washington Blvd Ste 203
Culver City, CA 90232-7486, USA

Warren, L D (Cartoonist, Editor)
1815 William Howard Taft Rd Apt 203
Cincinnati, OH 45206-1842, USA

Warren, Lesley Ann (Actor)
c/o Mimi DiTrani *Untitled Entertainment (LA)*
331 N Maple Dr Fl 3
Beverly Hills, CA 90210-3827, USA

Warren, Michael
11500 W Olympic Blvd Ste 510
Los Angeles, CA 90064-1527, USA

Warren, Michael (Mike) (Actor, Basketball Player)
21216 Escondido St
Woodland Hills, CA 91364-5905, USA

Warren, Mike (Baseball Player)
Oakland A's
12281 Diane St
Garden Grove, CA 92840-3224, USA

Warren, Rick (Religious Leader, Writer)
1 Saddleback Pkwy
Lake Forest, CA 92630-8700, USA

Warren, Ron (Baseball Player)
Detroit Stars
4025 Paddock Rd Apt 401
Cincinnati, OH 45229-1635, USA

Warren, Rosanna (Writer)
11 Robinwood Ave
Needham, MA 02492-2112, USA

Warren, Sahron (Actor)
c/o Kathryn Boole *Studio Talent Group*
1328 12th St
Santa Monica, CA 90401-2051, USA

Warren, Thomas L (Misc)
National Wildlife Federation
11100 Wildlife Center Dr
Reston, VA 20190-5362, USA

Warren, Tom (Athlete)
2393 La Marque St
San Diego, CA 92109-2342, USA

Warren, Ty (Football Player)
New England Patriots
Gillette Stadium
Rr1 60 Washington
Foxboro, MA 02035, USA

Warren Brothers
PO Box 120479
Nashville, TN 37212-0479, USA

Warren Brothers, The (Music Group)
c/o Staff Member *Creative Artists Agency (CAA-Nashville)*
3310 W End Ave Fl 5
Nashville, TN 37203-1028, USA

Warren G (Artist, Music Group, Musician)
Richard Walters
1800 Argyle Ave # 408
Los Angeles, CA 90028-5253, USA

Warren-Green, Christopher (Conductor, Musician)
Columbia Artists Mgmt Inc
1790 Broadway Fl 6
New York, NY 10019-1412, USA

Warren Jr, Christopher C (Chris) (Football Player)
1020 W Casino Rd
Everett, WA 98204-7900, USA

Warrenskjold, Dorothy
165 W 57th St
New York, NY 10019-2201, USA

Warrick, Peter (Football Player)
Cincinnati Bengals
4305 17th St E
Ellenton, FL 34222-2688, USA

Warsi, Arshad (Actor, Bollywood)
Kohinoor Apartments 503 Yari Road
Versova Andheri
Mumbai, MS 400061, INDIA

Warthen, Dan (Baseball Player)
Montreal Expos
3933 SW Wapato Ave
Portland, OR 97239-1412, USA

Warwick, Carl (Baseball Player)
Los Angeles Dodgers
14102 Bonney Brier Dr
Houston, TX 77069-1324, USA

Warwick, Lonnie (Football Player)
Minnesota Vikings
828 Main St
Mount Hope, WV 25880-1321, USA

Warwick-McAuley, Mildred (Baseball Player)
9407 62 St NW
Edmonton, AB T6B 1P3, CANADA

Warzeka, Ron (Football Player)
Oakland Raiders
424 McEwen Dr
Belgrade, MT 59714-3125, USA

Was, Don (Composer, Musician)
10984 Bellagio Rd
Los Angeles, CA 90077, USA

Wasdin, John (Baseball Player)
Oakland A's
1897 Shady Oaks Dr
Tallahassee, FL 32303-7361, USA

Wash, Martha (Musician)
c/o Staff Member *Diva Central Inc*
7510 W Sunset Blvd Ste 1445
Los Angeles, CA 90046-3408, USA

Washburn, Abigail (Musician)
c/o Staff Member *Paradigm (Monterey)*
509 Hartnell St
Monterey, CA 93940-2825, USA

Washburn, Barbara (Misc)
1010 Waltham St Apt D327
Lexington, MA 02421-8063, USA

Washburn, Beverly (Actor)
2561 Olivia Heights Ave
Henderson, NV 89052-7130, USA

Washburn, Greg (Baseball Player)
California Angels
1685 E Stellon St
Diamond, IL 60416-6028, USA

Washburn, Jarod (Baseball Player)
10003 Olinger Rd
Webster, WI 54893-7435, USA

Washburn, Ray C (Baseball Player)
St Louis Cardinals
19001 131st Dr SE
Snohomish, WA 98296-7844, USA

Washburn Jr, H Bradford (Misc)
1010 Waltham St Apt D327
Lexington, MA 02421-8063, USA

Washington, Alonzo (Cartoonist)
Omega 7
PO Box 171046
Kansas City, KS 66117-0046, USA

Washington, Baby (Musician)
Headline Talent
1650 Broadway Ste 508
New York, NY 10019-6833, USA

Washington, Chris (Football Player)
Tampa Bay Buccaneers
2917 Via Asoleado
Alpine, CA 91901-3183, USA

Washington, Claudell (Baseball Player)
Oakland A's
4067 Hardwick St
Lakewood, CA 90712-2350, USA

Washington, Denzel (Actor)
c/o Ed Limato *International Creative Management (ICM-LA)*
10250 Constellation Blvd
Los Angeles, CA 90067-6200, USA

Washington, Dewayne (Football Player)
Minnesota Vikings
6205 Rocky Creek Way
Wake Forest, NC 27587-6267, USA

Washington, Dwayne (Pearl) (Basketball Player)
206 Grenadier Dr # 206C
Liverpool, NY 13090-2744, USA

Washington, Eugene (Gene) (Football Player)
2725 Jewel Ln N
Plymouth, MN 55447-1737, USA

Washington, Gene A (Football Player)
San Francisco 49ers
10521 Bellagio Rd
Los Angeles, CA 90077-3820, USA

Washington, Hayma (Producer)
c/o Staff Member *Innovative Artists (LA)*
1505 10th St
Santa Monica, CA 90401-2805, USA

Washington, Herb (Baseball Player)
Oakland A's
640 Saddlebrook Dr
Youngstown, OH 44512-4781, USA

Washington, Isaiah (Actor)
c/o Ben Press *Innovative Artists (LA)*
1505 10th St
Santa Monica, CA 90401-2805, USA

Washington, Joe (Football Player)
Atlanta Falcons
434 E 42nd Pl
Chicago, IL 60653-2916, USA

Washington, Joe (Football Player)
San Diego Chargers
4 Treadwell Ct
Lutherville Timonium, MD 21093-3716, USA

Washington, Joe D (Football Player)
First Union Securities
2350 W Joppa Rd
Lutherville, MD 21093-4616, USA

Washington, Keith (Football Player)
Minnesota Vikings
548 Parkview Dr
Grand Prairie, TX 75052-3168, USA

Washington, Kermit (Basketball Player)
16740 SW Estuary Dr
Beaverton, OR 97006-7959, USA

Washington, Kerry (Actor)
c/o Kathy Atkinson *Washington Square Arts (LA)*
1041 N Formosa Ave
Writers Bldg #305
West Hollywood, CA 90046-6703, USA

Washington, Larue (Baseball Player)
Texas Rangers
6323 Reseda Blvd Unit 16
Tarzana, CA 91335-6981, USA

Washington, Lionel (Football Player)
Los Angeles Rams
1873 Horseshoe Ln
De Pere, WI 54115-7943, USA

Washington, MaliVai (Tennis Player)
5 S Roscoe Blvd
Ponte Vedra Beach, FL 32082-3813, USA

Washington, Mickey (Football Player)
New England Patriots
9420 Riggs St
Beaumont, TX 77707-1164, USA

Washington, Mike L (Football Player)
Tampa Bay Buccaneers
3235 Hernon Road
Montgomery, AL 36106, USA

Washington, Ron (Baseball Player)
Los Angeles Dodgers
7365 Perth St
New Orleans, LA 70126-1753, USA

Washington, Ronnie (Football Player)
Atlanta Falcons
2204 Burg Jones Ln
Monroe, LA 71202-4411, USA

Washington, Russ (Football Player)
San Diego Chargers
9060 Gramercy Dr
San Diego, CA 92123-2395, USA

Washington, Sam (Football Player)
Pittsburgh Steelers
7111 Cumberland Pl
Tampa, FL 33617-8423, USA

Washington, Tamia (Actor, Musician)
c/o Dennis Ashley *Creative Artists Agency LCC (CAA-LA)*
2000 Avenue Of The Stars
Los Angeles, CA 90067-4700, USA

Washington, Ted (Football Player)
Buffalo Bills.
PO Box 434
Waxhaw, NC 28173-1047, USA

Washington, Theodore (Ted) (Football Player)
San Francisco 49ers
3522 E 26th Ave
Tampa, FL 33605-1602, USA

Washington, U L (Baseball Player)
Kansas City Royals
PO Box 164
Stringtown, OK 74569-0164, USA

Washington, Vic (Football Player)
San Francisco 49ers
4850 E Desert Cove Ave Unit 241
Scottsdale, AZ 85254-7405, USA

Wasilewski, Paul (Actor)
c/o Susan Calogerakis *Thruline Entertainment*
9250 Wilshire Blvd Ground Fl
Beverly Hills, CA 90210, USA

Wasim, Akram (Cricketer)
Lancashire Cricket Club
Old Trafford
Manchester M16 0PX, UNITED KINGDOM (UK)

Wasinger, Mark (Baseball Player)
San Diego Padres
18021 Carson Dr
Horizon City, TX 79928-6402, USA

Waskiewicz, Jim (Football Player)
New York Jets
4360 Nelson Dr
Broomfield, CO 80023-9598, USA

Waskow, Thomas C (General)
Unit 5068
APO, AP 96328-5068, USA

Waslewski, Gary (Baseball Player)
Boston Red Sox
1799 E Terrestrial Pl
Tucson, AZ 85737-3469, USA

Wasmeier, Markus (Skier)
Breitensteinstr 14B
Schliersee-Neuhaus 83727, GERMANY

Wass, Ted (Actor)
3825 Longridge Ave
Sherman Oaks, CA 91423-4921, USA

Wasserburg, Gerald J (Geophysicist, Physicist)
PO Box 2959
Florence, OR 97439-0167, USA

Wasserman, Dale (Writer)
Casa Blanca Estates #37
Paradise Valley, AZ 85253, USA

Wasserman, Dan (Cartoonist, Editor)
Boston Globe
Editorial Dept
135 William Morrissey Blvd
Dorchester, MA 02125, USA

Wasserman, Lew
911 Foothill Rd
Beverly Hills, CA 90210-2925, USA

Wasserman, Rob (Musician)
Leslie Wiener Financial Services
PO Box 245
Sausalito, CA 94966-0245, USA

Wasserman, Robert H (Doctor)
Cornell University
Veterinary Medicine College
Ithaca, NY 14853, USA

Wasserstein, Bruce (Business Person)
Lazard
30 Rockefeller Plz Fl 59
New York, NY 10112-5999, USA

Wasserstein, Wendy (Writer)
c/o Robert (Bob) Bookman *Creative Artists Agency LCC (CAA-LA)*
2000 Avenue Of The Stars
Los Angeles, CA 90067-4700, USA

Wasson, Erin (Model)
I M G Models
304 Park Ave S # 1200
New York, NY 10010-4301, USA

Waszgis, B J (Baseball Player)
Texas Rangers
2708 Dover Ln
Albany, GA 31721-1583, USA

Watanabe, Gedde
1632 Westerly Ter
Los Angeles, CA 90026-1234, USA

Watanabe, Ken (Actor)
c/o Will Ward *ROAR LLC*
9701 Wilshire Blvd Fl 8
Beverly Hills, CA 90212-2008, USA

Watanabe, Milio (Scientist)
Nippon Electric Co
Computer Labs
5-33-1 Shiba
Tokyo, JAPAN

Watanabe, Sadao (Musician)
International Music Network
278 S Main St #400
Gloucester, MA 01930, USA

Watanabe, Youji (Architect)
1-6-13 Hirakawacho
Chiyodaku
Tokyo, JAPAN

Waterboys
3 Monmouth Rd.
London, ENGLAND W2, UNITED KINGDOM (UK)

Waterbury, Steve (Baseball Player)
St Louis Cardinals
710 N Garfield St
Marion, IL 62959-3429, USA

Waterhouse, Matthew (Actor)
Boyce
1 Kingsway House
Albion Rd
London N16 0TA, UNITED KINGDOM (UK)

Waterman, Denis
D&J Arlon
Pinewood Studios
Iverheath
Iver SL0 0NH, UNITED KINGDOM (UK)

Waterman, Felicity (Actor)
PO Box 20
Elk, CA 95432-0020, USA

Waterman, Pete (Actor)
c/o Staff Member *Pop Idol (Fremantle Media)*
2700 Colorado Ave Ste 450
Santa Monica, CA 90404-3599, USA

Waters, Alice (Chef)
Chez Panisse
1517 Shattuck Ave
Berkeley, CA 94709-1598, USA

Waters, Andre (Football Player)
Philadelphia Eagles
7715 Carriage Pointe Dr
Gibsonton, FL 33534-3004, USA

Waters, Charles T (Charlie) (Coach, Football Coach, Football Player)
Dallas Cowboys
9305 Moss Trl
Dallas, TX 75231-1409, USA

Waters, Crystal (Musician)
270 Lafayette St Ste 602
New York, NY 10012-3327, USA

Waters, Derek (Actor)
c/o Naomi Odenkirk *Odenkirk Talent Management*
650 N Bronson Ave Bldg B145
Raleigh Studios
Los Angeles, CA 90004-1404, USA

Waters, Frank (Muddy) (Coach, Football Coach)
4850 Gratiot Rd # 2D
Saginaw, MI 48638-6202, USA

Waters, John (Director)
c/o Staff Member *Atomic Books*
1100 W 36th St
Baltimore, MD 21211-2409, USA

Waters, John B (Government Official)
405 Burridge Waters Edge
Sevierville, TN 37862, USA

Waters, Lou (Correspondent)
Cable News Network
1050 Techwood Dr NW
News Dept
Atlanta, GA 30318-5604, USA

Waters, Mark (Director)
Miramax Films
11 Beach St
New York, NY 10013-2429, USA

Waters, Richard (Publisher)
20 Somerset Downs
Saint Louis, MO 63124-1007, USA

Waters, Roger (Musician)
Agency Group
370 City Road
London EC1V 2QA, UNITED KINGDOM (UK)

Waterston, James (Actor)
c/o Beth Colt *Gateway Management Partners*
5225 Wilshire Blvd Ste 702
Los Angeles, CA 90036-4351, USA

Waterston, Sam (Actor)
c/o Sandra Chang *Industry Entertainment*
955 Carrillo Dr Ste 300
Los Angeles, CA 90048-5400, USA

Wathan, Dusty (Baseball Player)
Kansas City Royals
1132 Turnbridge Rd
Charlotte, NC 28226-5862, USA

Wathan, John D (Baseball Player)
Kansas City Royals
1354 NE Todd George Rd
Lees Summit, MO 64086-5337, USA

Watkin, David (Cinematographer)
6 Sussex Mews
Brighton BN2 1GZ, UNITED KINGDOM (UK)

Watkins, Bob (Baseball Player)
Houston Astros
4417 W 58th Pl
Los Angeles, CA 90043-3409, USA

Watkins, Bobby (Football Player)
Detroit Lions
1112 Devonshire Dr
Desoto, TX 75115-3756, USA

Watkins, Carlene (Actor)
104 Fremont Pl
Los Angeles, CA 90005-3867, USA

Watkins, Dave (Baseball Player)
Philadelphia Phillies
506 Ridgewood Rd
Louisville, KY 40207-1325, USA

Watkins, Dean A (Business Person, Inventor)
Watkins-Johnson Co
401 River Oaks Pkwy
San Jose, CA 95134-1916, USA

Watkins, James D (Admiral, Secretary)
2021 Indian Cir
Saint Leonard, MD 20685-2400, USA

Watkins, Lloyd I (Economist)
PO Box 111
Bloomington, IL 61702-0111, USA

Watkins, Marilyn
217 N San Marino Ave
San Gabriel, CA 91775-2909, USA

Watkins, Michelle (Actor)
Capital Artists
6404 Wilshire Blvd Ste 950
Los Angeles, CA 90048-5529, USA

Watkins, Pat (Baseball Player)
Cincinnati Reds
1205 Fowler Dr
Garner, NC 27529-4420, USA

Watkins, Robert A (Football Player)
Chicago Bears
6 White Alder Way
South Dartmouth, MA 02748-1429, USA

Watkins, Scott (Baseball Player)
Minnesota Twins
14577 W 19th St
Sand Springs, OK 74063-4428, USA

Watkins, Tasker (Judge, War Hero)
5 Pump Court
Middle Temple
London EC4, UNITED KINGDOM (UK)

Watkins, Tionne (T-Boz) (Artist, Musician)
c/o Staff Member *William Morris Agency (WMA-LA)*
1 William Morris Pl
Beverly Hills, CA 90212-4261, USA

Watkins, Tom (Football Player)
Cleveland Browns
40 Lawrence St
Detroit, MI 48202-1015, USA

Watkins, Tuc
9229 W Sunset Blvd Ste 311
Los Angeles, CA 90069-3403, USA

Watkins, William D (Business Person)
Seagate Technology
920 Disc Dr
Scotts Valley, CA 95066-4542, USA

Watkinson of Working, Harold A (Government Official)
Tyma House
Bosham near Chichester
Sussex, UNITED KINGDOM (UK)

Watley, Jody (Musician)
Baker Winokur Rider
9100 Wilshire Blvd # 600
Beverly Hills, CA 90212-3401, USA

Watling, Deborah
183 Trevelyan Rd
London, ENGLAND SW17 9LW, UNITED KINGDOM (UK)

Watling, Leonor (Actor)
c/o Staff Member *Endeavor Agency LLC (LA)*
9601 Wilshire Blvd Fl 3
Beverly Hills, CA 90210-5204, USA

Watros, Cynthia (Actor)
c/o Marsha McManus *Principal Entertainment (LA)*
1964 Westwood Blvd Ste 400
Los Angeles, CA 90025-4695, USA

Watrous, Cynthia (Actor)
c/o Staff Member *Innovative Artists (LA)*
1505 10th St
Santa Monica, CA 90401-2805, USA

Watrous Jr, William R (Bill) (Musician)
GNP/Crescendo Records
8271 Melrose Ave Ste 104
Los Angeles, CA 90046-6800, USA

Watson, A J (Engineer, Race Car Driver)
5420 Crawfordsville Rd
Indianapolis, IN 46224-5407, USA

Watson, Albert M (Photographer)
777 Washington St
New York, NY 10014-1748, USA

Watson, Alberta (Actor)
c/o Staff Member *Cathy Atkinson*
2629 Main St
Pmb 129
Santa Monica, CA 90405-4001, USA

Watson, Alexander F (Diplomat)
Nature Conservancy International
4245 Fairfax Dr Ste 100
Arlington, VA 22203-1637, USA

Watson, Allen (Baseball Player)
St Louis Cardinals
6144 65th St
Flushing, NY 11379-1027, USA

Watson, Angela (Actor)
c/o Tom Chasin *Chasin Agency, The*
8899 Beverly Blvd Ste 716
Los Angeles, CA 90048-2449, USA

Watson, Barry (Actor)
15030 Ventura Blvd # 710
Sherman Oaks, CA 91403-5470, USA

Watson, Bob (Baseball Player)
Houston Astros
6110 W Pleasant Ridge Road
Houston, TX 77055, USA

Watson, Cecil J (Doctor)
Abbott Northwestern Hospital
2727 Chicago Ave
Minneapolis, MN 55407-3707, USA

Watson, Dale (Musician)
Crowley Artist Mgmt
602 Wayside Dr
Wimberley, TX 78676-5151, USA

Watson, Dennis
420 San Marco Dr
Ft Lauderdale, FL 33301-2544, USA

Watson, Doc (Musician)
CM Mgmt
5479 Larryon Dr
Woodland Hills, CA 91367, USA

Watson, Elizabeth M (Judge)
Houston Police Department
1200 Travis St
Chief's Office
Houston, TX 77002-6001, USA

Watson, Emily (Actor)
William Morris Agency
151 El Camino Dr
Beverly Hills, CA 90212-2775, USA

Watson, Emma (Actor)
c/o Staff Member *Special Artists Agency*
9465 Wilshire Blvd Ste 890
Beverly Hills, CA 90212-2607, USA

Watson, Gene (Musician)
Bobby Roberts
3050 Business Park Cir Ste 303
Goodlettsville, TN 37072-3588, USA

Watson, James D (Nobel Prize Laureate)
Bungtown Road
Cold Spring Harbor, NY 11724, USA

Watson, Joe (Football Player)
Detroit Lions
112 Baldwin Rd
Hillsborough, NC 27278-7389, USA

Watson, Kenneth M (Oceanographer, Physicist)
8515 Costa Verde Blvd Unit 2008
San Diego, CA 92122-1150, USA

Watson, Mark (Baseball Player)
Cleveland Indians
555 Spender Trce
Atlanta, GA 30350-5017, USA

Watson, Martha (Athlete, Track Athlete)
5509 Royal Vista Ln
Las Vegas, NV 89149-6644, USA

Watson, Max P Jr (Business Person)
BMC Software
2101 Citywest Blvd
Houston, TX 77042-2829, USA

Watson, Mills (Actor)
2824 Dell Ave
Venice, CA 90291-4547, USA

Watson, Paul (Journalist, Photographer)
Toronto Star
Editorial Dept
1 Yonge St
Toronto, ON M5E 1E6, CANADA

Watson, Paul (Misc)
Sea Shepherd Conservation Society
PO Box 2616
Friday Harbor, WA 98250-2616, USA

Watson, Polly Jo (Misc)
Washington University
Anthropology Dept
Saint Louis, MO 63130, USA

Watson, Robert A (Religious Leader)
Salvation Army
615 Slaters Ln
Alexandria, VA 22314-1112, USA

Watson, Robert M (Bobby) Jr (Musician)
Split Second Timing
11 Ridge Rd
Chappaqua, NY 10514-2508, USA

Watson, Russell (Musician)
Box 806
Manchester M60 2XS, UNITED KINGDOM (UK)

Watson, Sid (Football Player)
Pittsburgh Steelers
3150 Binnacle Dr Apt 212
Naples, FL 34103-2712, USA

Watson, Stephen E (Business Person)
Dayton Hudson
1000 Nicollet Mall
Minneapolis, MN 55403-2542, USA

Watson, Stephen R (Football Player)
Denver Broncos
4675 S Vine Way
Englewood, CO 80113-6044, USA

Watson, Thomas S (Tom) (Golfer)
1901 W 47th Pl Ste 200
Mission, KS 66205-1834, USA

Watson, Tim (Football Player)
Kansas City Chiefs
113 Crestwood Dr RR 13
Fort Valley, GA 31030, USA

Watson, Wayne (Musician)
TBA Artist Mgmt
PO Box 331189
Nashville, TN 37203-7511, USA

Watson-Johnson, Vernee (Actor)
Gage Group
14724 Ventura Blvd Ste 505
Sherman Oaks, CA 91403-3505, USA

Watson Jr, Jack H (Government Official)
Long Aldridge Norman
1900 K St NW
Washington, DC 20006-1110, USA

Watson Richardson, Lillian (Pockey)
(Swimmer)
4960 Maunalani Cir
Honolulu, HI 96816-4016, USA

Watt, Ben (Musician, Songwriter, Writer)
JFD Mgmt
Acklam Workshops
10 Acklam Road
London W10 5QZ, UNITED KINGDOM
(UK)

Watt, Eddie (Baseball Player)
Baltimore Orioles
PO Box 7
North Bend, NE 68649-0007, USA

Watt, James G (Designer, Secretary)
PO Box 3705
Jackson Hole, WY 83001-3705, USA

Watt, Mike (Musician)
c/o Staff Member *Agency Group Ltd, The (NY)*
1775 Broadway Ste 515
New York, NY 10019-1903, USA

Watt, Tom (Coach, Hockey Player)
Calgary Flames
PO Box 1540
Station M
Calgary, AB T2P 3B9, CANADA

Wattelet, Frank (Football Player)
New Orleans Saints
4 Deer Run Dr
Joplin, MO 64804-5832, USA

Wattenberg, Ben J (Television Host)
Think Tank with Ben Wattenberg
4455 Connecticut Ave NW Ste C100
Washington, DC 20008-2372, USA

Watters, Richard J (Rickie) (Football
Player)
11100 NE 8th St Ste 600
Bellevue, WA 98004-4402, USA

Watters, Ricky (Football Player)
San Francisco 49ers
6107 Springford Dr Apt S3
Harrisburg, PA 17111-4941, USA

Watters, Tim (Hockey Player)
804 Oak Grove Pkwy
Houghton, MI 49931-2707, USA

Watterson, John B (Brett) (Astronaut)
2508 Via Anacapa
Palos Verdes Estates, CA 90274-4333,
USA

Wattleton, A Faye (Entertainer)
Fischer-Ross Agency
250 W 57th St
New York, NY 10107-0001, USA

Wattlington, Neal (Baseball Player)
Philadelphia Athletics
PO Box 418
Yanceyville, NC 27379-0418, USA

Watts, Andre (Musician)
205 W 57th St
New York, NY 10019-2105, USA

Watts, Brian (Golfer)
1701 Wisteria Way
Westlake, TX 76262-9083, USA

Watts, Charles R (Charlie) (Musician)
Rupert Lowenstein
2 King St
London SW1Y 6QL, UNITED KINGDOM
(UK)

Watts, Charlie
Half Moon Chambers Chapel Walks
Manchester, ENGLAND M2 1HN,
UNITED KINGDOM (UK)

Watts, D Henry (Business Person)
Norfolk Southern Corp
3 Commercial Pl
Norfolk, VA 23510-2108, USA

Watts, Ernest J (Ernie) (Musician)
DeLeon Artists
4031 Panama Ct
Piedmont, CA 94611-4930, USA

Watts, Ernie (Designer, Director)
International Creative Mgmt
40 W 57th St Ste 1800
New York, NY 10019-4001, USA

Watts, Heather (Ballerina)
New York City Ballet
Lincoln Center Plaza
New York, NY 10023, USA

Watts, Helen J (Opera Singer)
Rock House Wallis
Ambleston Haverford-West
Dyfed, WALES SA62 5RA, UNITED
KINGDOM (UK)

Watts, Kristi (Religious Leader, Television
Host)
c/o Staff Member *700 Club*
Christian Broadcasting Network
977 Centerville Turnpike
Virginia Beach, VT 23463, USA

Watts, Naomi (Actor)
c/o Jason Weinberg *Untitled
Entertainment (LA)*
331 N Maple Dr Fl 3
Beverly Hills, CA 90210-3827, USA

Watts, Quincy (Athlete, Track Athlete)
First Team Marketing
PO Box 67581
Los Angeles, CA 90067-0581, USA

Watts, Robert (Football Player)
Oakland Raiders
99 Villa Dr
San Pablo, CA 94806-3736, USA

Watts III, Claudius E (Educator, General)
Citadel
President's Office
Charleston, SC 29409-0001, USA

Waugh, Jim (Baseball Player)
Pittsburgh Pirates
501 Bourland Rd Apt 3106
Keller, TX 76248-3578, USA

Waugh, John S (Misc)
Massachusetts Institute of Technology
Chemistry Dept
Cambridge, MA 02139, USA

Waugh, Stephen (Steve) (Cricketer)
Octagon
1751 Pinnacle Dr Ste 1500
McLean, VA 22102-3833, USA

Wawryshyn-Moroz, Evelyn (Baseball
Player)
139 Royal Ave
Winnipeg, MB R2V 1H5, CANADA

Wax, Ruby (Actor, Comedian)
c/o Staff Member *International Artistes
Limited*
Holborn Hall - 4th Floor
193-7 High Holborn
London WC1V 7BD, UNITED KINGDOM
(UK)

Waxenberg, Alan M (Publisher)
Good Housekeeping Magazine
959 8th Ave
New York, NY 10019-3737, USA

Waxman, Henry (Politician)
6913 Ayr Ln
Bethesda, MD 20817-4901, USA

Waxman, Keoni (Director, Writer)
c/o Jeff Okin *Paradigm (LA)*
360 N Crescent Dr
North Bldg
Beverly Hills, CA 90210-6820, USA

Wayans, Damien Dante (Actor, Director,
Producer, Writer)
c/o Aaron Kaplan *Kaplan/Perrone
Entertainment*
1 William Morris Pl
Beverly Hills, CA 90212-4261, USA

Wayans, Damon (Actor)
c/o Staff Member *Wayans Brothers
Entertainment*
110 S Fairfax Ave Ste 250
Los Angeles, CA 90036-2100, USA

Wayans, Keenan Ivory (Actor, Director,
Producer, Writer)
c/o Staff Member *Wayans Brothers
Entertainment*
110 S Fairfax Ave Ste 250
Los Angeles, CA 90036-2100, USA

Wayans, Kim (Actor)
1742 Granville Ave Apt 2
Los Angeles, CA 90025-1899, USA

Wayans, Marlon (Actor, Comedian)
c/o Staff Member *Wayans Brothers
Entertainment*
110 S Fairfax Ave Ste 250
Los Angeles, CA 90036-2100, USA

Wayans, Shawn (Actor)
c/o Lisa Suzanne Blum *Modus
Entertainment*
110 S Fairfax Ave Ste 250
Los Angeles, CA 90036-2100, USA

Wayda, Stephen (Photographer)
Playboy Magazine
680 N Lake Shore Dr
Reader Service
Chicago, IL 60611-4546, USA

Wayne, Fredd
117 Strand St
Santa Monica, CA 90405-2293, USA

Wayne, Jimmy (Musician)
c/o Staff Member *William Morris Agency
(WMA-TN)*
1600 Division St Ste 300
Nashville, TN 37203-2755, USA

Wayne, John (Bowler)
5018 S Barley Ct
Gilbert, AZ 85298-8633, USA

Wayne, June (Artist)
1108 Tamarind Ave
Los Angeles, CA 90038-1906, USA

Wayne, Lil (Musician)
Troy Carter
9100 Wilshire Blvd Ste 520 E
The Coalition
Beverly Hills, CA 90212-3401, USA

Wayne, Nathaniel (Football Player)
Denver Broncos
2878 Grey Moss Pass
Duluth, GA 30097-5226, USA

Wayne, Patrick (Actor)
10502 Whipple St
Toluca Lake, CA 91602-2838, USA

Wayne, Reggie (Football Player)
Indianapolis Colts
7001 W 56th St
Indianapolis, IN 46254-9698, USA

Wayt, Russell (Football Player)
Dallas Cowboys
600 E Tuttle Rd
White Oak, TX 75693-1354, USA

Wazed, Sheik Hasina (Prime Minister)
Sere-e Bangla Nagar
Gono Bhaban
Sher-e-Banglanagar
Dakar, BANGLADESH

Weah, George (Soccer Player)
AC Milan
Via Turati 3
Milan 20221, ITALY

Weatherill, B Bruce (Government
Official)
Emmets House
Ide Hill
Kent TN14 6BA, UNITED KINGDOM
(UK)

Weatherly, Gerald (Football Player)
Chicago Bears
506 1/2 E Clayton St
Cuero, TX 77954-2820, USA

Weatherly, Jim (Football Player)
Atlanta Falcons
23679 Calabasas Rd # 558
Calabasas, CA 91302-1502, USA

Weatherly, Michael (Actor)
c/o Nancy Gates *United Talent Agency
(UTA)*
9560 Wilshire Blvd Ste 500
Beverly Hills, CA 90212-2401, USA

Weatherly, Shwan (Actor, Beauty Pageant
Winner)
135 N Westgate Ave
Los Angeles, CA 90049-2916, USA

Weathers, Carl (Actor)
13701 Marina Pointe Dr Apt 239
Marina Del Rey, CA 90292-9242, USA

Weathers, Carl (Football Player)
Oakland Raiders
10960 Wilshire Blvd Fl 11
Los Angeles, CA 90024-3702, USA

Weatherspoon, Cephus (Football Player)
New Orleans Saints
5322 W Henderson Pl
Santa Ana, CA 92704-1036, USA

Weatherspoon, Clarence (Basketball
Player)
PO Box 117
Crawford, MS 39743-0117, USA

Weatherspoon, Teresa G (Basketball
Player)
Los Angeles Sparks
1111 S Figueroa St
Staples Center
Los Angeles, CA 90015-1300, USA

Weatherwax, Bob
16133 Soledad Canyon Rd
Canyon Country, CA 91387-1821, USA

Weatherwax, Jim (Football Player)
Green Bay Packers
636 Cucharas Mountain Dr
Livermore, CO 80536-8609, USA

Weaver, Fritz (Actor)
161 W 75th St
New York, NY 10023-1801, USA

Weaver, Gary (Football Player)
Oakland Raiders
3496 Arden Rd
Hayward, CA 94545-3906, USA

Weaver, Herman (Football Player)
Detroit Lions
8105 Hamilton Mill Dr
Chattanooga, TN 37421-2766, USA

Weaver, Jason (Actor)
c/o Lisa Chance *Kyle Avery Public Relations*
1107 Fair Oaks Ave # 321
S Pasadena, CA 91030-3311, USA

Weaver, Jean (Baseball Player)
4960 Illinois 145 Rd
Metropolis, IL 62960-3609, USA

Weaver, Jed (Football Player)
Philadelphia Eagles
696 E 16th Ave
Eugene, OR 97401, USA

Weaver, John (Football Player)
New York Bulldogs
520 E Ward St
Versailles, OH 45380-1436, USA

Weaver, Reg (Misc)
National Education Assn
1201 16th St NW
Washington, DC 20036-3290, USA

Weaver, Robby (Actor)
Artists Group
1650 Broadway Ste 610
New York, NY 10019-6833, USA

Weaver, Rufus (Inventor)
77 Adelaide St
New London, CT 06320-6522, USA

Weaver, Sigourney (Actor)
c/o Jeremy Zimmer *United Talent Agency (UTA)*
9560 Wilshire Blvd Ste 500
Beverly Hills, CA 90212-2401, USA

Weaver, Warren E (Misc)
7607 Horsepen Road
Richmond, VA 23229, USA

Weaver, Wayne (Football Executive)
Jacksonville Jaguars
1 Alltel Stadium Pl
Jacksonville, FL 32202-1917, USA

Weaving, Hugo (Actor)
c/o Ann Churchill-Brown *Shanahan Management*
PO Box 1509
Darlinghurst 1300, AUSTRALIA

Webb, Chloe (Actor)
PO Box 2824
Venice, CA 90294-2824, USA

Webb, Christiaan (Musician, Songwriter, Writer)
SuperVision Mgmt
109B Regents Park Road
London NW1 8UR, UNITED KINGDOM (UK)

Webb, James R (Jimmy) (Football Player)
1319 S Prairie Flower Rd
Turlock, CA 95380-9367, USA

Webb, Jimmy (Musician, Songwriter, Writer)
1560 N Laurel Ave Apt 109
Los Angeles, CA 90046-2533, USA

Webb, Justin (Musician, Songwriter, Writer)
SuperVision Mgmt
109B Regents Park Road
London NW1 8UR, UNITED KINGDOM (UK)

Webb, Karrie (Golfer)
725 Presidential Dr
Boynton Beach, FL 33435-2431, USA

Webb, Lee (Religious Leader, Television Host)
c/o Staff Member *700 Club*
Christian Broadcasting Network
977 Centerville Turnpike
Virginia Beach, VT 23463, USA

Webb, Lucy (Actor, Comedian)
1360 N Crescent Heights Blvd # 38
West Hollywood, CA 90046-4553, USA

Webb, Richmond J (Football Player)
Miami Dolphins
4120 Humphrey Dr
Dallas, TX 75216-4908, USA

Webb, Russell (Russ) (Athlete, Misc)
611 Knob Hill Ave
Redondo Beach, CA 90277-4255, USA

Webb, Sonny (Baseball Player)
Negro Baseball Leagues
3194 Jordan Rd
Pleasant Plain, OH 45162-9238, USA

Webb, Tamilee (Physicist)
7031 Calle Portone
Rancho Santa Fe, CA 92091-0262, USA

Webb, Veronica (Actor, Model)
c/o Staff Member *United Talent Agency (UTA)*
9560 Wilshire Blvd Ste 500
Beverly Hills, CA 90212-2401, USA

Webb, Wayne (Bowler)
4413 McGuire St
North Las Vegas, NV 89081-2709, USA

Webb, Wellington E (Misc)
Mayor's Office
1437 Bannock St
City-County Building
Denver, CO 80202-5337, USA

Webb, William H (Business Person)
Altria Group
120 Park Ave
New York, NY 10017-5577, USA

Webber, Chris (Basketball Player)
c/o Staff Member *Philadelphia 76ers*
3601 S Broad St
1st Union Center
Philadelphia, PA 19148-5287, USA

Webber, Julian Lloyd (Musician)
Columbia Artists Mgmt Inc
1790 Broadway Fl 6
New York, NY 10019-1412, USA

Webber, Lord Andrew Lloyd (Director, Musician, Producer, Writer)
c/o Staff Member *Really Useful Picture Company*
22 Tower St
London WCH2 H9NS, UNITED KINGDOM (UK)

Webber, Mark (Actor)
Handprint Entertainment
1100 Glendon Ave Ste 1000
Los Angeles, CA 90024-3514, USA

Webber, Tristan (Designer, Fashion Designer)
Brower Lewis
74 Gloucester Place
London W1H 3HN, UNITED KINGDOM (UK)

Weber, Amy (Actor)
c/o Staff Member *Select Artists Ltd (CA-Westside Office)*
1138 12th St Apt 1
Santa Monica, CA 90403-5459, USA

Weber, Arnold R (Educator)
Northwestern University
Chancellor's Office
Evanston, IL 60208-0001, USA

Weber, Ben (Actor)
c/o Amy Guenther *Gateway Management Partners*
5225 Wilshire Blvd Ste 702
Los Angeles, CA 90036-4351, USA

Weber, Bruce (Coach)
University of Illinois
Athletic Dept
Assembly Hall
Champaign, IL 61820, USA

Weber, Bruce (Photographer)
Robert Miller Gallery
526 W 26th St Rm 10A
New York, NY 10001-5541, USA

Weber, Charlie (Actor)
c/o Liza Anderson *Warren Cowan & Associates PR*
8899 Beverly Blvd Ste 919
Los Angeles, CA 90048-2436, USA

Weber, Chuck (Football Player)
Cleveland Browns
26433 S Moonshadow Dr
Sun Lakes, AZ 85248-9219, USA

Weber, Eberhard (Composer, Musician)
Ted Kurland
173 Brighton Ave
Boston, MA 02134-2003, USA

Weber, Eugen J (Historian)
11579 W Sunset Blvd
Los Angeles, CA 90049-2048, USA

Weber, George B (Misc)
Chemin Moise-Duboule 19
Geneva 1209, SWITZERLAND

Weber, Jack (Actor)
Gersh Agency
232 N Canon Dr
Beverly Hills, CA 90210-5302, USA

Weber, Jake (Actor)
Gersh Agency
232 N Canon Dr
Beverly Hills, CA 90210-5302, USA

Weber, Leyna Juliet
c/o Staff Member *Atlas Talent Agency Inc*
36 W 44th St Ste 1000
New York, NY 10036-8106, USA

Weber, Mary E (Astronaut)
14 Hawkview St
Portola Valley, CA 94028-8037, USA

Weber, Peter D (Pete) (Bowler)
10500 Saint Xavier Ln
Saint Ann, MO 63074-2607, USA

Weber, Robert M (Bob) (Cartoonist)
New Yorker Magazine
4 Times Sq
Editorial Dept
New York, NY 10036-6592, USA

Weber, Stephen L (Educator)
State University of New York
President's Office
Oswego, NY 13126, USA

Weber, Steven (Actor)
c/o Edward (Eddie) Yablans *International Creative Management (ICM-LA)*
10250 Constellation Blvd
Los Angeles, CA 90067-6200, USA

Weber, Vin (Misc)
Empower America
1776 I St NW
Washington, DC 20006-3700, USA

Weber Jr, Bob (Cartoonist)
King Features Syndicate
888 7th Ave Ste 201
New York, NY 10106-0201, USA

Webre, Septime (Choreographer)
Washington Ballet
3515 Wisconsin Ave NW
Washington, DC 20016-3085, USA

Webster, Alexander (Alex) (Coach, Football Coach, Football Player)
New York Giants
8461 SE Palm Hammock Ln
Hobe Sound, FL 33455-8227, USA

Webster, Cornell (Football Player)
Seattle Seahawks
4575 Palm Ave Apt H
Riverside, CA 92501-3966, USA

Webster, George D (Football Player)
Houston Oilers
6215 E Lake Dr
Haslett, MI 48840-8990, USA

Webster, Larry (Football Player)
Miami Dolphins
12 Oakridge Ct
Elkton, MD 21921-3928, USA

Webster, Marvin (Basketball Player)
8819 Stonehaven Rd
Randallstown, MD 21133-4223, USA

Webster, Nikki (Actor, Musician)
Baseline StudioSystems
3415 S Sepulveda Blvd Ste 200
Los Angeles, CA 90034-6016, USA

Webster, R Howard (Baseball Player, Publisher)
Toronto Globe & Mail
444 Front St W
Toronto, ON M5V 2S9, CANADA

Webster, Robert D (Bob) (Misc, Swimmer)
269 Hacienda Carmel
Carmel, CA 93923-7947, USA

Webster, Tom (Coach, Hockey Player)
1750 Longfellow Dr
Canton, MI 48187-2995, USA

Webster, Victor (Actor)
c/o Courtney Kivowitz *Benderspink*
110 S Fairfax Ave Ste 350
Los Angeles, CA 90036-2179, USA

Webster, William H (Government Official)
4777 Dexter St NW
Washington, DC 20007-1060, USA

Wechsler, Nick (Actor)
c/o Staff Member *BBA*
4605 Lankershim Blvd Ste 721
North Hollywood, CA 91602-1878, USA

Wecht, Cyril H
5420 Darlington Rd
Pittsburgh, PA 15217-1506, USA

Weck, Peter
Bambauer Keplerstr. 2
Munich D-81679, GERMANY

Wecker, Andreas (Gymnast)
Am Dorfplatz 1
Klein-Ziethen 16766, GERMANY

Weddington, Mike (Football Player)
Green Bay Packers
237 Sycamore Grove St
Simi Valley, CA 93065-7342, USA

Weddington, Sarah R (Attorney, Attorney
General, General)
709 W 14th St
Austin, TX 78701-1707, USA

Weddle-Hines, Mary (Baseball Player)
329 Park Hills Rd
Corbin, KY 40701-2583, USA

Wedeen, Kelsey (Actor)
c/o Staff Member *Select Artists Ltd (CA-
Westside Office)*
1138 12th St Apt 1
Santa Monica, CA 90403-5459, USA

Wedel, Dieter (Director)
Tonndorfer Strand 2
Hamburg 22045, GERMANY

Weder, Gustav (Athlete)
Haltenstr 2
Stachen/TG, SWITZERLAND

Wedge, Chris (Actor, Director, Writer)
c/o Staff Member *Blue Sky Studios*
44 S Broadway Fl 17
White Plains, NY 10601-4411, USA

Wedge, Eric M (Baseball Player)
31 Abington Rd
Danvers, MA 01923-3665, USA

Wedgeworth, Ann (Actor)
70 Riverside Dr
New York, NY 10024-5714, USA

Wedman, Scott (Basketball Player)
7912 NW Scenic Dr
Kansas City, MO 64152-1645, USA

Weed, Kent (Director, Producer, Writer)
c/o Staff Member *Arthur Smith & Co*
1811 Centinela Ave
Santa Monica, CA 90404-4203, USA

Weed, Maurice James (Composer)
308 Overlook Rd # 55
Asheville, NC 28803-3319, USA

Weege, Reinhold (Producer)
2035 Via Don Berito
La Jolla, CA 92037, USA

Weekend Players (Music Group)
c/o Staff Member *Paradigm (Monterey)*
509 Hartnell St
Monterey, CA 93940-2825, USA

Weeks, Claire
11048 Chimineas Ave
Northridge, CA 91326-2820, USA

Weeks, John D (Misc)
15301 Watergate Rd
Silver Spring, MD 20905-5779, USA

Weeks, John R (Architect)
39 Jackson's Lane
Highgate
London N6 5SR, UNITED KINGDOM
(UK)

Weeks, Michelle
c/o Staff Member *Diva Central Inc*
7510 W Sunset Blvd Ste 1445
Los Angeles, CA 90046-3408, USA

Weeks, Rollo (Actor)
Artists Independent Network
825 Nowita Pl
Venice, CA 90291-3836, USA

Weeks, Rosey (Baseball Player)
1290 Menna St
Jacksonville, FL 32205-8330, USA

Weese, Miranda (Ballerina)
New York City Ballet
Lincoln Center Plaza
New York, NY 10023, USA

Weezer (Music Group)
c/o Donald (Don) Muller *Creative Artists
Agency LCC (CAA-LA)*
2000 Avenue Of The Stars
Los Angeles, CA 90067-4700, USA

Wefald, Jon (Educator)
Kansas State University
President's Office
Manhattan, KS 66506, USA

Weger, Mike (Football Player)
Detroit Lions
825 Markwood Dr
Oxford, MI 48370-2929, USA

Wegman, Marie (Baseball Player)
4158 Westwood Northern Blvd
Cincinnati, OH 45211-2444, USA

Wegman, William G (Artist,
Photographer)
239 W 18th St
New York, NY 10011-4502, USA

Wegner, Hans J (Designer)
Tinglevej 17
Gentoftte 2820, DENMARK

Wegner, Mark (Baseball Player)
2607 Lakeview Way
Plant City, FL 33566-6774, USA

Wehba, Ray (Football Player)
Brooklyn Dodgers
10312 Sunrise Blvd
Oklahoma City, OK 73120-2329, USA

Wehling, Ulrich (Athlete)
Skiverband
Hubertusstr 1
Munich 81477, GERMANY

Wehrli, Roger R (Football Player)
St Louis Cardinals
46 Fox Meadows Ct
Saint Charles, MO 63303-1701, USA

Wei, Dan-Wen (Musician)
Columbia Artists Mgmt Inc
1790 Broadway Fl 6
New York, NY 10019-1412, USA

Weibel, Robert (Doctor)
University of Pennsylvania
Med School
Pediatrics Dept
Philadelphia, PA 19104, USA

Weibring, D A (Golfer)
5865 Versailles Ave
Frisco, TX 75034-5957, USA

Weich, Gillian (Musician)
DS Mgmt
1017 16th Ave S Ste A
Nashville, TN 37212-2324, USA

Weicker, Lowell P Jr (Governor, Senator)
PO Box 357
Earlysville, VA 22936-0357, USA

Weida, Johnny (Educator, General)
Superintendent
US Air Force Academy
Colorado Springs, CO 80840, USA

Weide, Bob (Director)
CAA
9830 Wilshire Blvd
Beverly Hills, CA 90212-1804, USA

Weide, Robert B (Director, Producer)
c/o Jonathan Brandstein *MBST
Entertainment*
345 N Maple Dr Ste 200
Beverly Hills, CA 90210-3860, USA

Weidemann, Jakob (Artist)
Ringsveen
Lillehammer 2600, NORWAY

Weidenbaum, Murray L (Economist,
Government Official)
6231 Rosebury Ave
Saint Louis, MO 63105-3243, USA

Weidenfeld of Chelsea, Arthur G
(Publisher)
9 Chelsea Embankment
London SW3 4LE, UNITED KINGDOM
(UK)

Weider, Joe (Publisher)
Weider Health & Fitness
21100 Erwin St
Woodland Hills, CA 91367-3772, USA

Weidinger, Christine (Opera Singer)
John J Miller
801 W 181st St Apt 20
New York, NY 10033-4518, USA

Weidner, Bert (Football Player)
Miami Dolphins
517 NW 106th Ave
Plantation, FL 33324-1629, USA

Weigel, Teri (Actor, Model)
6433 Topanga Canyon Blvd # 103
Woodland Hills, CA 91303-2621, USA

Weigert, Robin (Actor)
c/o Staff Member *Bauman Redanty &
Shaul Agency*
5757 Wilshire Blvd Ste 473
Los Angeles, CA 90036-3632, USA

Weight, Doug (Hockey Player)
Saint Louis Blues
1401 Clark Ave
Sawis Center
Saint Louis, MO 63103-2700, USA

Weihenmayer, Erik (Mountaineer)
682 Partridge Cir
Golden, CO 80403-1548, USA

Weikel, M Keith (Business Person)
Manor Care Inc
333 N Summit St Ste 100
Toledo, OH 43604-2617, USA

Weikl, Bernd (Opera Singer)
Ulf Torgvist
Sankt Eriksgatan 100
Stockholm 113 31, SWEDEN

Weil, Andrew (Doctor)
University of Arizona
Medical Center
1501 N Campbell Ave
Tucson, AZ 85724-0001, USA

Weil, Bruno (Composer, Conductor)
Kaylor Mgmt
130 W 57th St Apt 8G
New York, NY 10019-3311, USA

Weil, Cynthia (Songwriter, Writer)
Gorfaine/Schwartz
4111 W Alameda Ave Ste 509
Burbank, CA 91505-4171, USA

Weil, Frank A (Misc)
Smithsonian Institution
900 Jefferson Dr SW
Washington, DC 20560-0005, USA

Weil, Liza (Actor)
c/o Kim Hodgert *Creative Artists Agency
LCC (CAA-LA)*
2000 Avenue Of The Stars
Los Angeles, CA 90067-4700, USA

Weiland, Scott (Musician, Songwriter,
Writer)
Q Prime
729 7th Ave Rm 1600
New York, NY 10019-6880, USA

Weill, Claudia B (Director)
2800 Seattle Dr
Los Angeles, CA 90046-1209, USA

Weill, David (Dave) (Athlete, Track
Athlete)
120 Mountain Spring Ave
San Francisco, CA 94114-2120, USA

Weill, Sanford I (Sandy) (Business Person)
Citigroup Inc
399 Park Ave
New York, NY 10022-4699, USA

Wein, George (Producer)
Festival Productions
30 Irving Pl Fl 6
New York, NY 10003-2303, USA

Weinbach, Arthur F (Business Person)
Automatic Data Processing
1 Adp Blvd Ste 1
Roseland, NJ 07068-1728, USA

Weinbach, Lawrence A (Business Person)
Unisys Corp
Unisys Way
Blue Bell, PA 19424-0001, USA

Weinberg, Max (Musician)
c/o Staff Member *Cunningham Escott
Slevin & Doherty (LA)*
10635 Santa Monica Blvd Ste 130
Los Angeles, CA 90025-8306, USA

Weinberg, Mike (Actor)
c/o Elissa Leeds-Fickman *Reel Talent
Management*
438 Tuallitan Rd
Los Angeles, CA 90049-1941, USA

Weinberg, Robert A (Doctor, Scientist)
Whitehead Institute
9 Cambridge Ctr
Cambridge, MA 02142-1479, USA

Weinberg, Steven (Nobel Prize Laureate)
University of Texas
2613 Wichita St
Physics Dept
Austin, TX 78712, USA

Weinberger, Caspar (Publisher, Secretary)
Rogers & Wells
2001 K St NW
Washington, DC 20006-1037, USA

Weinbrecht, Donna (Skier)
General Delivery
West Milford, NJ 07480-9999, USA

Weiner, Art E (Football Player)
New York Yankees
404 Kimberly Dr
Greensboro, NC 27408-5020, USA

Weiner, Eric (Producer, Writer)
c/o Staff Member *Writers and Artists Group Intl (LA)*
8383 Wilshire Blvd Ste 550
Beverly Hills, CA 90211-2417, USA

Weiner, Gerry (Government Official)
40 Fredmir St
Dollard-des-Ormeaux, PQ H9A 2R3, CANADA

Weiner, Timothy E (Tim) (Journalist)
New York Times
1627 I St NW
Editorial Dept
Washington, DC 20006-4085, USA

Weingarten, David M (Architect)
Ace Architects
330 2nd St
Oakland, CA 94607-4149, USA

Weingarten, Reid (Attorney, Attorney General, General)
Steptoe & Johnson
4603 Harrison St
Chevy Chase, MD 20815-3721, USA

Weinger, Scott (Actor)
9255 W Sunset Blvd Ste 1010
West Hollywood, CA 90069-3307, USA

Weinke, Chris (Football Player)
Carolina Panthers
5718 Providence Country Club Dr
Charlotte, NC 28277-2621, USA

Weinman, Roz (Producer)
c/o Staff Member *Wolf Films Inc (LA)*
100 Universal City Plz Bldg 2252
Universal City, CA 91608-1002, USA

Weinstein, Bob (Business Person, Producer)
c/o Staff Member *Miramax Films (LA)*
8439 W Sunset Blvd Fl 4th
West Hollywood, CA 90069-1951, USA

Weinstein, Diane Gilbert (Judge)
US Court of Claims
717 Madison Pl NW
Washington, DC 20439-0001, USA

Weinstein, Harvey (Actor, Business Person, Director, Producer)
c/o Staff Member *The Weinstein Company*
345 Hudson St Fl 13
New York, NY 10014-4502, USA

Weinstein, Jack B (Judge)
US District Court
225 Cadman Plz E
US Courthouse
Brooklyn, NY 11201-1818, USA

Weinstein, Sidney T (General)
11936 Holly Branch Ct
Great Falls, VA 22066-1216, USA

Weintraub, Carl
10390 Santa Monica Blvd Ste 300
Los Angeles, CA 90025-5091, USA

Weintraub, Jerry (Producer)
27740 Pacific Coast Hwy
Malibu, CA 90265-4341, USA

Weir, Arabella (Actor)
c/o Staff Member *Lip Service Casting Ltd*
4 Kingly St, Soho
London W1B 5PE, UNITED KINGDOM (UK)

Weir, Bill (Correspondent)
c/o Staff Member *Good Morning America (NY)*
147 Columbus Ave Fl 6
Abc
New York, NY 10023-6503, USA

Weir, Bob (Musician)
Grateful Dead
PO Box 1073
San Rafael, CA 94915-1073, USA

Weir, Gillian C (Musician)
78 Robin Way
Tilehurst
Berks RG3 5SW, UNITED KINGDOM (UK)

Weir, Johnny (Figure Skater)
c/o Staff Member *Champions on Ice*
3500 W 80th St
Tom Collins Enterprises Inc
Minneapolis, MN 55431-1068, USA

Weir, Judith (Composer)
Chester Music
8/9 Frith St
London W1V 5TZ, UNITED KINGDOM (UK)

Weir, Mike (Golfer)
744 Draper Heights Way
Draper, UT 84020-7630, USA

Weir, Peter (Director)
Salt Pan Films
PO Box 29
Palm Beach, NSW 2108, AUSTRALIA

Weir, Stephanie (Actor)
c/o Dan Baron *Agency for the Performing Arts (APA-LA)*
405 S Beverly Dr
Beverly Hills, CA 90212-4416, USA

Weis, Charlie (Coach, Football Coach)
University of Notre Dame
PO Box 518
Athletic Dept
Notre Dame, IN 46556-0518, USA

Weis, Heidelinde
Schleissheimer Str. 207
Munich D-80809, GERMANY

Weis, Joseph F Jr (Judge)
US Court of Appeals
700 Grant St
US Courthouse
Pittsburgh, PA 15219-1906, USA

Weisacosky, Ed (Football Player)
New York Giants
15321 Lawrence 2090
Mount Vernon, MO 65712-7281, USA

Weisberg, Ruth (Artist)
11452 W Washington Blvd
Los Angeles, CA 90066-6013, USA

Weisberg, Tim (Musician)
Pyramid Entertainment
89 5th Ave Ste 700
New York, NY 10003-3020, USA

Weisel, Heidi (Designer, Fashion Designer)
202 W 40th St
New York, NY 10018-1504, USA

Weiser-Most, Franz (Conductor)
Van Walsum Mgmt
4 Addison Bridge Place
London W14 8XP, UNITED KINGDOM (UK)

Weishoff, Paula (Volleyball Player)
20021 Colgate Cir
Huntington Beach, CA 92646-4913, USA

Weishuhn, Clayton (Football Player)
New England Patriots
4521 Kropala Rd
San Angelo, TX 76905-7412, USA

Weiskopf, Tom (Golfer)
7580 E Gray Rd Ste 204
Scottsdale, AZ 85260-3408, USA

Weiskrantz, Lawrence (Doctor)
Oxford University
Experimental Psychology Dept
Oxford OX1 3UD, UNITED KINGDOM (UK)

Weisman, Annie (Comedian)
c/o Staff Member *Gersh Agency, The (LA)*
232 N Canon Dr
Beverly Hills, CA 90210-5302, USA

Weisman, Kevin (Actor)
c/o Holly Lebed *Holly Lebed Personal Management*
10535 Wilshire Blvd Apt 808
Los Angeles, CA 90024-4556, USA

Weisman, Sam (Actor, Director)
United Talent Agency
9560 Wilshire Blvd Ste 500
Beverly Hills, CA 90212-2401, USA

Weisner, Maurice F (Admiral)
3000 Steeplechase
Alpharetta, GA 30004-1443, USA

Weiss, Barry (Business Person)
Zomba Recording Corporation
137 W 25th St # 139
New York, NY 10001-7200, USA

Weiss, Brian L (Writer)
c/o Staff Member *William Morris Agency (WMA-LA)*
1 William Morris Pl
Beverly Hills, CA 90212-4261, USA

Weiss, Eric (Actor)
c/o Staff Member *Brant Rose Agency, The*
10537 Santa Monica Blvd # 305
Los Angeles, CA 90025-4952, USA

Weiss, Frank (Football Player)
Washington Redskins
729 Fairfax Dr
Salinas, CA 93901-1250, USA

Weiss, Glenn (Director)
c/o Staff Member *William Morris Agency (WMA-LA)*
1 William Morris Pl
Beverly Hills, CA 90212-4261, USA

Weiss, Heinz
Rosskopfstr. 10
Grunwald D-82031, GERMANY

Weiss, Janet (Musician)
Legends of 21st Century
7 Trinity Row
Florence, MA 01062-1931, USA

Weiss, Julie (Designer)
International Creative Mgmt
8942 Wilshire Blvd # 219
Beverly Hills, CA 90211-1908, USA

Weiss, Karen (Golfer)
1135 Raymond Ave
Saint Paul, MN 55108-1922, USA

Weiss, Melvyn I (Attorney, Attorney General, General)
Milberg Weiss Bershad
1 Pennsylvania Plaza
New York, NY 10119, USA

Weiss, Michael (Figure Skater)
PO Box 12311
Burke, VA 22009-2311, USA

Weiss, Michael T. (Actor, Director)
c/o Staff Member *Endeavor Agency LLC (LA)*
9601 Wilshire Blvd Fl 3
Beverly Hills, CA 90210-5204, USA

Weiss, Morry (Business Person)
American Greetings Corp
1 American Rd
Cleveland, OH 44144-2398, USA

Weiss, Robert W (Bob) (Basketball Player, Coach)
1600 Windermere Dr E
Seattle, WA 98112-3738, USA

Weiss, Roberta (Actor)
Sarnoff Co
3500 W Olive Ave Ste 300
Burbank, CA 91505-4647, USA

Weiss, Walter W (Baseball Player)
1275 Castlepoint Cir
Castle Rock, CO 80108, USA

Weissenberg, Alexis (Musician)
Michael Schmidt
59 E 54th St Rm 83
New York, NY 10022-9206, USA

Weissenhofer, Ron (Football Player)
New Orleans Saints
16156 Seneca Lake Cir
Crest Hill, IL 60403-1500, USA

Weisser, Morgan (Actor)
c/o Jeri Scott *Jeri Scott Management*
211 S Beverly Dr
Beverly Hills, CA 90212-3828, USA

Weissflog, Jens (Skier)
Markt 2
Kurort Oberweisenthal 09484, GERMANY

Weissman, Robert (Business Person)
IMS Health Inc
1499 Post Rd
Fairfield, CT 06824-5936, USA

Weissman, Steven (Artist)
c/o Staff Member *Fantagraphics Books*
7563 Lake City Way NE
Seattle, WA 98115-4218, USA

Weisz, Paul B (Engineer, Physicist)
University of Pennsylvania
Bio-Engineering Dept
Philadelphia, PA 19104, USA

Weisz, Rachel (Actor)
c/o Stacy Boniello *The Firm*
9465 Wilshire Blvd Fl 6
Beverly Hills, CA 90212-2605, USA

Weithaas, Antje (Musician)
Harrison/Parrott
12 Penzance Place
London W11 4PA, UNITED KINGDOM (UK)

Weitz, Bruce (Actor)
18826 Erwin St
Tarzana, CA 91335-6827, USA

Weitz, Chris (Actor, Director, Writer)
c/o Staff Member *William Morris Agency
(WMA-LA)*
1 William Morris Pl
Beverly Hills, CA 90212-4261, USA

Weitz, Paul (Writer)
c/o Staff Member *William Morris Agency
(WMA-LA)*
1 William Morris Pl
Beverly Hills, CA 90212-4261, USA

Weitz, Paul J (Astronaut)
3086 N Tam Oshanter Dr
Flagstaff, AZ 86004-7405, USA

Weitzman, Howard (Attorney, Attorney
General, General)
Katten Muchin Zavis Weitzman
1999 Avenue Of Stars Ste 1400
Los Angeles, CA 90067-6047, USA

Wejbe, Jolean (Actor)
c/o Bob McGowan *McGowan
Management*
8733 W Sunset Blvd Ste 103
W Hollywood, CA 90069-2241, USA

Wek, Alek (Model)
c/o Staff Member *IMG Models*
304 Park Ave S Fl 12
New York, NY 10010-4301, USA

Welbourn, John (Football Player)
Philadelphia Eagles
3301 Palos Verdes Dr N
Palos Verdes Estates, CA 90274-1030,
USA

Welbring, D A (Golfer)
c/o Staff Member *Pro Golfers Association
(PGA) Tour*
112 Tpc Blvd
Ponte Vedra Beach, FL 32082, USA

Welch, Claxton (Football Player)
Dallas Cowboys
9721 SE Ankeny St
Portland, OR 97216-2311, USA

Welch, Herb (Football Player)
New York Giants
999 La Senda
Santa Barbara, CA 93105-4512, USA

Welch, Justin (Musician)
CMO Mgmt
Ransomes Dock
35037 Parkgate Road
London SW11 4NP, UNITED KINGDOM
(UK)

Welch, Lenny (Musician)
Brothers Mgmt
141 Dunbar Ave
Fords, NJ 08863-1551, USA

Welch, Michael (Actor)
c/o Susan Curtis *Curtis Talent
Management*
9607 Arby Dr
Beverly Hills, CA 90210-1202, USA

Welch, Mike (Baseball Player)
3 Inca Dr
Nashua, NH 03063-3544, USA

Welch, Raquel (Actor)
c/o Steve Sauer *Media Four*
8840 Wilshire Blvd Fl 2
Beverly Hills, CA 90211-2606, USA

Welch, Robert L (Bob) (Baseball Player)
11055 E Gold Dust Ave
Scottsdale, AZ 85259-4801, USA

Welch, Tahnee (Actor, Model)
PO Box 823
Beverly Hills, CA 90213-0823, USA

Welch Jr, John F (Business Person)
General Electric Co
3135 Easton Tpke
Fairfield, CT 06828-0001, USA

Weld, Tuesday (Actor)
c/o Staff Member *TalentWorks (LA)*
3500 W Olive Ave Ste 1400
Burbank, CA 91505-5512, USA

Weld, William F (Governor)
Hale & Dorr
60 State St
Boston, MA 02109-1816, USA

Weldon, Fay (Writer)
Casorotto Ramsay
National House
62/66 Wardour
London W1V 3HP, UNITED KINGDOM
(UK)

Weldon, Joan (Actor)
67 E 78th St
New York, NY 10075-0204, USA

Weldon, W Casey (Football Player)
Washington Redskins
21300 Redskin Park Dr
Ashburn, VA 20147-6100, USA

Welk, Lawrence (All Stars)
901 Winding River Rd
Vero Beach, FL 32963-2548, USA

Welke, Tim (Baseball Player)
7790 Doubletree Ct
Kalamazoo, MI 49009-9771, USA

Welke, William (Baseball Player)
54 Country Hls
Marshall, MI 49068-9674, USA

Welker, Frank
10635 Santa Monica Blvd Ste 130
Los Angeles, CA 90025-8306, USA

Welland, Colin (Actor, Writer)
Peter Charlesworth
68 Old Brompton Road
London SW7 3LQ, UNITED KINGDOM
(UK)

Wellborn, Joe (Football Player)
New York Giants
803 Paulus St
Schulenburg, TX 78956-1424, USA

Weller, Freddie (Musician, Songwriter,
Writer)
Ace Productions
PO Box 428
Portland, TN 37148-0428, USA

Weller, Paul (Musician)
c/o Staff Member *Variety Artists
International Inc*
793 Higuera St Ste 6
San Luis Obispo, CA 93401-0500, USA

Weller, Peter (Actor)
c/o Bill Treusch *Bill Treusch Management*
853 7th Ave Apt 9A
New York, NY 10019-5222, USA

Weller, Rene
Kelterstr. 18 Grafenhausen
Birkenfeld D-75217, GERMANY

Weller, Robb
4249 Beck Ave
Studio City, CA 91604-2913, USA

Weller, Thomas H (Nobel Prize Laureate)
56 Winding River Rd
Needham, MA 02492-1025, USA

Weller, Watter (Musician)
Doblinger Hauptstr 40
Vienna 1190, AUSTRIA

Welles, Terri (Actor, Model)
PO Box 2549
Del Mar, CA 92014-1849, USA

Wellford, Harry W (Judge)
US Court of Appeals
167 N Main St
Federal Building
Memphis, TN 38103-1816, USA

Welling, Tom (Actor)
c/o Jimmy Darmody *Creative Artists
Agency LCC (CAA-LA)*
2000 Avenue Of The Stars
Los Angeles, CA 90067-4700, USA

Wellings, Bob
40 Kent Gardens Ealing
London, ENGLAND W13 8BW, UNITED
KINGDOM (UK)

Wellington, Harry H (Educator)
New York Law School
57 Worth St
New York, NY 10013-2926, USA

Welliver, Titus (Actor)
c/o Staff Member *Fenton-Kritzer
Entertainment*
8840 Wilshire Blvd Fl 3
Beverly Hills, CA 90211-2606, USA

Wellman, Gary (Football Player)
Houston Oilers
1638 Wellington Pl
Westlake Village, CA 91361-1535, USA

Wellman Jr, William (Actor)
410 N Barrington Ave
Los Angeles, CA 90049-2002, USA

Wells, Annie (Journalist, Photographer)
Press Democrat
427 Mendocino Ave
Editorial Dept
Santa Rosa, CA 95401-6385, USA

Wells, Audrey (Director, Writer)
c/o David Lonner *William Morris Agency
(WMA-LA)*
1 William Morris Pl
Beverly Hills, CA 90212-4261, USA

Wells, Carole (Actor)
Burton Moss
8827 Beverly Blvd # L
Los Angeles, CA 90048-2405, USA

Wells, Charles (Baseball Player)
Philadelphia Stars
1035 Beaver Creek Dr
Duncanville, TX 75137-3731, USA

Wells, Claudia (Actor)
c/o Staff Member *Privilege Talent Agency*
PO Box 260860
Encino, CA 91426-0860, USA

Wells, Cory (Musician)
Three Dog Night
PO Box 96597
Business Office
Las Vegas, NV 89193-6597, USA

Wells, David (Dave) (Baseball Player)
2519 N McMullen Booth Rd # 510-198
Clearwater, FL 33761-4173, USA

Wells, Dawn (Actor)
c/o Wes Stevens *VOX Inc*
5670 Wilshire Blvd Ste 820
Los Angeles, CA 90036-5613, USA

Wells, Dean (Football Player)
Seattle Seahawks
1146 Copperfield Dr
Georgetown, IN 47122-9082, USA

Wells, Gawen D (Bonzi) (Basketball
Player)
c/o Staff Member *Sacramento Kings*
1 Sports Pkwy
Arco Arena
Sacramento, CA 95834-2301, USA

Wells, Harold (Football Player)
Philadelphia Eagles
2315 New Bern Ave
Raleigh, NC 27610-2434, USA

Wells, Joel (Football Player)
New York Giants
11 Flicker Pt
Greenville, SC 29609-6646, USA

Wells, John (Producer)
c/o Staff Member *John Wells Productions*
4000 Warner Blvd Bldg 1
Burbank, CA 91522-0001, USA

Wells, Kitty (Musician)
Midnight Special Productions
PO Box 916
Hendersonville, TN 37077-0916, USA

Wells, LLewellyn (Producer)
c/o Wayne Fitterman *United Talent
Agency (UTA)*
9560 Wilshire Blvd Ste 500
Beverly Hills, CA 90212-2401, USA

Wells, Mark (Hockey Player)
27619 Harrison Woods Ln
Harrison Township, MI 48045-3545, USA

Wells, Norman (Football Player)
Dallas Cowboys
600 Lakes Edge Dr
Oxford, MI 48371-5229, USA

Wells, Patricia (Journalist)
Harper Collins Publishers
10 E 53rd St Fl Cellar2
New York, NY 10022-5076, USA

Wells, Terry (Football Player)
Houston Oilers
25036 Polktown Rd
Lucedale, MS 39452, USA

Wells, Thelma (Writer)
PO Box 398020
Dallas, TX 75339-8020, USA

Wells, Thomas B (Judge)
US Tax Court
400 2nd St NW
Washington, DC 20217-0002, USA

Wells, Warren (Football Player)
Detroit Lions
1399 Pipkin St
Beaumont, TX 77705-2056, USA

Wells-Hawkes, Sharlene
24 Maria Ave Apt C
Southbridge, MA 01550-3055, USA

Welser-Most, Franz (Conductor)
Cleveland Symphony
11001 Euclid Ave
Severance Hall
Cleveland, OH 44106-1713, USA

Welsh, Moray M (Musician)
28 Somerfield Ave
Queens Park
London NW6 6JY, UNITED KINGDOM
(UK)

Welsh, Stephanie (Journalist, Photographer)
PO Box 277
Wayne, ME 04284-0277, USA

Welsom, Elleen (Journalist)
Albuquerque Tribune
7777 Jefferson St NE
Editorial Dept
Albuquerque, NM 87109-4343, USA

Welti, Lisa (Actor)
c/o Staff Member *Select Artists Ltd (CA-Westside Office)*
1138 12th St Apt 1
Santa Monica, CA 90403-5459, USA

Welty, John D (Educator)
4411 N Van Ness Blvd
Fresno, CA 93704-3725, USA

Wen, Jinbao (Misc, Prime Minister)
Premier's Office
Zhonganahai
Beijing, CHINA

Wendell, Krissy (Hockey Player)
University of Minnesota
Athletic Dept
Minneapolis, MN 55455, USA

Wendell, Martin (Football Player)
Chicago Rockets
405 W Olive Ave
Prospect Heights, IL 60070-1430, USA

Wendelstedt, Hunter (Baseball Player)
88 S Saint Andrews Dr
Ormond Beach, FL 32174-3857, USA

Wendelstedt Jr, Harry H (Baseball Player, Referee)
88 S Saint Andrews Dr
Ormond Beach, FL 32174-3857, USA

Wenden, Michael (Swimmer)
Palm Beach Currmbin Center
Thrower Dr
Palm Beach Queens, AUSTRALIA

Wenders, Wim (Director)
Road Movies Filmprodution
Clausewitzstra 4
Berlin 10629, GERMANY

Wendkos, Gina (Writer)
c/o Staff Member *Industry Entertainment*
955 Carrillo Dr Ste 300
Los Angeles, CA 90048-5400, USA

Wendryhoski, Joe (Football Player)
Los Angeles Rams
312 Williams Blvd
Nfl Players Association
Kenner, LA 70062-7630, USA

Wendt, George (Actor)
3856 Vantage Ave
Studio City, CA 91604-3636, USA

Wenge, Ralph (Correspondent)
Cable News Network
1050 Techwood Dr NW
News Dept
Atlanta, GA 30318-5604, USA

Wenger, Arsene (Coach)
Arsenal Football Club
Highbury House
75 Drayton Park
London N5 1BU, UNITED KINGDOM
(UK)

Wenglikowski, Alan (Football Player)
Buffalo Bills
7168 Weidner Rd
Springboro, OH 45066-7779, USA

Wengren, Mike (Musician)
Mitch Scneider Organization
14724 Ventura Blvd Ste 710
Sherman Oaks, CA 91403-3520, USA

Wenham, David (Actor)
c/o Vanessa Pereira *Artists Independent Management (LA)*
825 Nowita Pl
Venice, CA 90291-3836, USA

Wenner, Jann S (Publisher)
Wenner Media
1290 Avenue Of The Americas
New York, NY 10104-0295, USA

Went, Joseph J (General)
9204 Kristin Ln
Fairfax, VA 22032-1809, USA

Wente, Jean R (Business Person)
California State Automobile Assn
PO Box 422940
San Francisco, CA 94142-2940, USA

Wentworth, Alexandra (Actor, Comedian)
Gersh Agency
232 N Canon Dr
Beverly Hills, CA 90210-5302, USA

Wenzel, Andreas (Skier)
Oberhul 151
Liechtenstein-Gamprin, LIECHTENSTEIN

Wenzel, Hanni Weirather- (Skier)
Fanalwegle 4
Schaan 9494, LIECHTENSTEIN

Wenzel, Ralph M (Football Player)
Pittsburgh Steelers
2432 Pebble Beach Dr
League City, TX 77573-6417, USA

Wenzel, Ralph R (Football Player)
Pittsburgh Steelers
921 Creek Dr
Annapolis, MD 21403-2309, USA

Wenzell, Marge (Baseball Player)
78287 Brookhaven Ln
Palm Desert, CA 92211-2735, USA

Wepner, Chuck (Boxer)
153 Avenue E
Bayonne, NJ 07002-4434, USA

Wepper, Fritz
Lamonstr. 9
Munich D-81679, GERMANY

Werbach, Adam (Misc)
Sierra Club
85 2nd St Ste 200
San Francisco, CA 94105-3488, USA

Werber, William M (Bill) (Baseball Player)
5800 Old Providence Rd Apt 5117
Charlotte, NC 28226-6880, USA

Werkheiser, Devon (Actor)
c/o Meredith Fine *Coast to Coast Talent Group*
3350 Barham Blvd
Los Angeles, CA 90068-1404, USA

Werner, Anna (Correspondent)
KHOU
1945 Allen Pkwy
News Department
Houston, TX 77019-2506, USA

Werner, Clyde (Football Player)
Kansas City Chiefs
3009 Islandview Ct
Gig Harbor, WA 98335-1258, USA

Werner, Marianne (Athlete, Track Athlete)
Gauseland 2A
Dortmund 44227, GERMANY

Werner, Michael (Misc)
Michael Werner Ltd
21 E 67th St
New York, NY 10065-5817, USA

Werner, Roger L Jr (Misc, Television Host)
Prime Sports Ventures
10000 Santa Monica Blvd
Los Angeles, CA 90067, USA

Wersching, Raimund (Ray) (Football Player)
San Diego Chargers
18 Buttercup Ln
San Carlos, CA 94070-1528, USA

Werth, Isabell (Horse Racer)
Winterswicker Feld 4
Rheinberg 47495, GERMANY

Wertheim, Jorge (Misc)
UNESCO
Un Plaza
Director's Office
New York, NY 10017, USA

Wertheimer, Fredric M (Misc)
3502 Macomb St NW
Washington, DC 20016-3162, USA

Wertheimer, Linda (Correspondent)
National Public Radio
2025 M St NW
News Dept
Washington, DC 20036-3309, USA

Werthein, Julio
c/o Staff Member *United Nations Educational, Scientific and Cultural Organization (UNESCO)*
7, place de Fontenoy
75352
Paris 07 SP, FRANCE

Wertimer, Ned (Actor)
Acme Talent
4727 Wilshire Blvd Ste 333
Los Angeles, CA 90010-3874, USA

Wertmuller, Lina (Director)
Piazza Clotilde
Rome 00196, ITALY

Wesker, Arnold (Writer)
37 Ashley Road
London N19 3AG, UNITED KINGDOM
(UK)

Wesley, David (Basketball Player)
c/o Staff Member *Houston Rockets*
1510 Polk St
Houston, TX 77002-1099, USA

Wesley, Norman (Business Person)
Fortune Brands Inc
300 Tower Pkwy
Lincolnshire, IL 60069-3665, USA

Wesley, Paul (Actor)
c/o Susan Calogerakis *Thruline Entertainment*
9250 Wilshire Blvd Ground Fl
Beverly Hills, CA 90210, USA

WesleySmith, Michael (Actor)
c/o Staff Member *Sharon Power Management*
PO Box 54 049
Wellington, NEW ZEALAND

Wessling, John (Actor, Comedian)
c/o Nick Nuciforo *Creative Artists Agency LCC (CAA-LA)*
2000 Avenue Of The Stars
Los Angeles, CA 90067-4700, USA

West, Adam (Actor)
c/o Tom Chasin *Chasin Agency, The*
8899 Beverly Blvd Ste 716
Los Angeles, CA 90048-2449, USA

West, Billy (Artist, Voice Over Artist)
c/o Jeff Danis *International Creative Management (ICM-LA)*
10250 Constellation Blvd
Los Angeles, CA 90067-6200, USA

West, Bob (Football Player)
Kansas City Chiefs
3915 Boston Ave
San Diego, CA 92113-3318, USA

West, Chandra
c/o Staff Member *Industry Entertainment*
955 Carrillo Dr Ste 300
Los Angeles, CA 90048-5400, USA

West, Cornel (Activist, Misc)
Harvard University
Afro American Studies Dept
Cambridge, MA 02138, USA

West, David (Baseball Player)
New York Mets
1571 Crossing Dr
Horn Lake, MS 38637-8553, USA

West, David (Basketball Player)
New Orleans Hornets
1250 Poydras St # 19
New Orleans Arena
New Orleans, LA 70113-1804, USA

West, Dominic (Actor)
c/o Staff Member *Creative Artists Agency LCC (CAA-LA)*
2000 Avenue Of The Stars
Los Angeles, CA 90067-4700, USA

West, Doug (Basketball Player)
15 Holly Rd
Wheeling, WV 26003-5656, USA

West, Ed (Football Player)
Green Bay Packers
1930 Ma Lee Dr
Moody, AL 35004-2813, USA

West, Ernest E (War Hero)
912 Adams Ave
Wurtland, KY 41144-1504, USA

West, Jake (Misc)
International Assn of Iron Workers
1750 New York Ave NW Ste 400
Washington, DC 20006-5301, USA

West, James E (Inventor)
724 Berkeley Ave
Plainfield, NJ 07062-2010, USA

West, Jeff (Football Player)
St Louis Cardinals
12376 Adair Creek Way NE
Redmond, WA 98053-5686, USA

West, Jerome A (Jerry) (Basketball Player)
Memphis Grizzlies
191 Beale St
Memphis, TN 38103-3715, USA

West, Jerry
Memphis Grizzlies
191 Beale St
Memphis, TN 38103-3715, USA

West, Joe (Baseball Player)
114 N Eastern St
Greenville, NC 27858-2137, USA

West, Joel (Model)
William Morris Agency
1325 Avenue Of The Americas
New York, NY 10019-6091, USA

West, John B (Scientist)
9626 Blackgold Rd
La Jolla, CA 92037-1110, USA

West, Jon Fredric (Opera Singer)
Opera et Concert
Maximilianstr 22
Munich 80539, GERMANY

West, Kanye (Actor, Musician)
c/o Staff Member *William Morris Agency
(WMA-LA)*
1 William Morris Pl
Beverly Hills, CA 90212-4261, USA

West, Leslie (Musician)
James Faith Entertainment
318 Wynn Ln
Port Jefferson, NY 11777-1670, USA

West, Lizzie (Musician)
Warner Bors Records
3300 Warner Blvd
Burbank, CA 91505-4694, USA

West, Lori (Golfer)
2110 Augusta Dr SE
Marietta, GA 30067-8215, USA

West, Lyle (Football Player)
New York Giants
719 1st St SE
Moultrie, GA 31768-5509, USA

West, Mark (Basketball Player)
1659 E Sharon Dr
Phoenix, AZ 85022-5035, USA

West, Max (Baseball Player)
Boston Bees
4040 Piedmont Dr Spc 125
Highland, CA 92346-4834, USA

West, Nathan (Actor)
c/o Jeff Morrone *Jeff Morrone
Management*
9350 Wilshire Blvd Ste 224
Beverly Hills, CA 90212-3204, USA

West, Paula (Musician)
PO Box 2142
San Francisco, CA 94126-2142, USA

West, Peter
4708 Largo Way
Las Vegas, NV 89121-2836, USA

West, Price (Baseball Player)
Raleigh Tigers
3540 Mill Point Dr SE
Grand Rapids, MI 49512-9337, USA

West, Red (Actor)
6676 Memphis Arlington Rd
Bartlett, TN 38135, USA

West, Richard L (War Hero)
6341 Crosswoods Dr
Falls Church, VA 22044-1209, USA

West, Ronnie (Football Player)
Minnesota Vikings
PO Box 110
Pineview, GA 31071-0110, USA

West, Sam
34-43 Russell
London, ENGLAND WC2B 5HA, UNITED
KINGDOM (UK)

West, Samuel (Actor)
P F D
Drury House
34-43 Russell St
London WC2B 5HA, UNITED KINGDOM
(UK)

West, Shane (Actor)
c/o Jeff Morrone *Jeff Morrone
Management*
9350 Wilshire Blvd Ste 224
Beverly Hills, CA 90212-3204, USA

West, Simon (Director)
c/o Staff Member *Simon West Productions*
5555 Melrose Ave
Dressing Room Building 109
Los Angeles, CA 90038-3989, USA

West, Stan (Football Player)
Los Angeles Rams
2455 Manchester Dr Unit 3
Oklahoma City, OK 73120-3771, USA

West, Timothy L (Actor)
Gavin Barker Assoc
2D Wimpote St
London W1G 0EB, UNITED KINGDOM
(UK)

West, Troy (Football Player)
Philadelphia Eagles
725 N Greenberry Ave
West Covina, CA 91790-1331, USA

West, Willie (Football Player)
St Louis Cardinals
PO Box 50430
Eugene, OR 97405-0980, USA

West Jr, Togo D (Secretary)
922 N Cameron Ave
Winston Salem, NC 27101-3316, USA

Westbrook, Bryant (Football Player)
Detroit Lions
3501 Link Valley Dr Apt 1104
Houston, TX 77025-5105, USA

Westbrook, Jake (Baseball Player)
New York Yankees
PO Box 574
Danielsville, GA 30633-0574, USA

Westbrook, Michael (Football Player)
Donald Lucki
1585 Oregon Trl
Garden Suite
Elk Grove Village, IL 60007-2853, USA

Westbrooks, Greg (Football Player)
New Orleans Saints
3832 10th Avenue Pl
Moline, IL 61265-2429, USA

Westenra, Hayley (Actor)
c/o Staff Member *Decca Music Group
Limited*
347-353 Chiswick High Rd
London W4 4HS, UNITED KINGDOM
(UK)

Westerberg, Paul (Musician, Songwriter,
Writer)
Mitch Scneider Organization
14724 Ventura Blvd Ste 710
Sherman Oaks, CA 91403-3520, USA

Westerfield, Putney (Publisher)
10 Greenview Ln
Hillsborough, CA 94010-6424, USA

Westerman, Floyd (Red Crow) (Actor)
c/o Staff Member *Red Crow Creations*
3440 Wilshire Blvd Ste 904
Los Angeles, CA 90010-2123, USA

Westerman-Austin, Helen (Baseball
Player)
1837 Stonehenge Rd
Springfield, IL 62702-3244, USA

Western Underground (Music Group)
c/o Staff Member *Paradigm (Monterey)*
509 Hartnell St
Monterey, CA 93940-2825, USA

Westfall, Ed
PO Box 39
Locust Valley, NY 11560-0039, USA

Westfall, V Edward (Ed) (Hockey Player)
699 Hillside Ave
New Hyde Park, NY 11040-2512, USA

Westfeldt, Jennifer (Actor)
c/o Tammy Rosen *Melanie Greene
Management & Productions*
425 N Robertson Blvd
West Hollywood, CA 90048-1735, USA

Westhead, Barb (Golfer)
9820 E Thompson Peak Pkwy Unit 707
Scottsdale, AZ 85255-6656, USA

Westhead, Paul (Basketball Player, Coach)
2217 Via Alamitos
Palos Verdes Estates, CA 90274-1652,
USA

Westheimer, Frank H (Misc)
33 Timothy Ln
Carlisle, MA 01741-1619, USA

Westheimer, Gerald (Doctor, Misc)
582 Santa Barbara Rd
Berkeley, CA 94707-1746, USA

Westheimer, Ruth S (Doctor)
c/o *King Features*
888 7th Ave Ste 201
New York, NY 10106-0201, USA

Westlake, Wally (Baseball Player)
Pittsburgh Pirates
3800 61st St
Sacramento, CA 95820-2421, USA

Westlife (Music Group)
c/o Staff Member *BMG (UK)*
Bedford House
6979 Fulham High Street
London SW6 3JW, UNITED KINGDOM
(UK)

Westling, Jon (Educator)
285 Goddard Ave
Brookline, MA 02445-7411, USA

Westmore, McKenzie (Actor)
3904 Laurel Canyon Blvd # 766
Studio City, CA 91604, USA

Westmoreland, Dick (Football Player)
San Diego Chargers
5601 Sea Reef Pl
San Diego, CA 92154, USA

Westmoreland, James (Actor)
8019 1/2 Norton Ave
West Hollywood, CA 90046-5002, USA

Weston, Celia (Actor)
Innovative Artists
1505 10th St
Santa Monica, CA 90401-2805, USA

Weston, David
123-A Grosvenor Rd.
London, ENGLAND SW1, UNITED
KINGDOM (UK)

Weston, J Fred (Educator)
258 Tavistock Ave
Los Angeles, CA 90049-3229, USA

Weston, Jeff (Football Player)
New York Giants
7235 Alakoko St
Honolulu, HI 96825-2712, USA

Weston, Kim (Musician)
Powerplay
5434 W Sample Rd
Pmb 533
Margate, FL 33073-3453, USA

Weston, Mickey (Baseball Player)
Baltimore Orioles
819 Lydia Dr
Warsaw, IN 46582-1949, USA

Weston, P John (Government Official)
13 Denbigh Gardens
Richmond
Surrey TW10 6EN, UNITED KINGDOM
(UK)

Weston, Randolph (Randy) (Musician)
PO Box 749
Maplewood, NJ 07040-0749, USA

Weston, Wesley (Lil' Flip) (Musician)
c/o Staff Member *Sony Music
Entertainment*
555 Madison Ave
New York, NY 10022-3301, USA

Westphal, Paul D (Basketball Player,
Coach)
1424 Granvia Altamira
Palos Verdes Estates, CA 90274-2131,
USA

Westwood, Vivienne (Designer, Fashion
Designer)
Westwood Studios
9-15 Elcho St
London SW11 4AU, UNITED KINGDOM
(UK)

Wetherbee, James D (Astronaut)
710 Huntercrest St
Seabrook, TX 77586-5933, USA

Wetherby, Jeff (Baseball Player)
Atlanta Braves
28410 Great Bend Pl
Wesley Chapel, FL 33543-5726, USA

Wetherell, T R (Educator)
Florida State University
Athletic Dept
Tallahassee, FL 32306, USA

Wetherill, George W (Geophysicist,
Physicist)
Camergie Institution
Terrestrial Magnetism Dept
Washington, DC 20015, USA

Wethington, Charles T Jr (Educator)
2926 Four Pines Dr
Lexington, KY 40502-2969, USA

Wetnight, Ryan S (Football Player)
Chicago Bears
3156 Griffon Ct
Simi Valley, CA 93065-0500, USA

Wetoska, Robert (Football Player)
Chicago Bears
1295 Forest Glen Dr S
Winnetka, IL 60093-1427, USA

Wetteland, John (Baseball Player)
Los Angeles Dodgers
1229 Kentucky Derby Dr
Argyle, TX 76226-7005, USA

Wetter, Friedrich Cardinal (Religious Leader)
Kardinal-Faulhaber-Str 7
Munich 80333, GERMANY

Wetton, John (Musician)
Entourage Talent
133 W 25th St # 500
New York, NY 10001-7206, USA

Wetzel, Gary G (War Hero)
PO Box 84
Oak Creek, WI 53154-0084, USA

Wetzel, John (Basketball Player, Coach)
13011 N Sunrise Canyon Ln
Marana, AZ 85658-4035, USA

Wetzel, Robert L (General)
1425 Dartmouth Rd
Columbus, GA 31904-1902, USA

Wetzel, Rosemarie
111 E 22nd St Rm 200
New York, NY 10010-5414, USA

Wever, Stefan (Baseball Player)
New York Yankees
7 Corte Los Sombras
Greenbrae, CA 94904-1149, USA

Wexler, Anne (Government Official)
1317 F St NW Ste 600
Washington, DC 20004-1105, USA

Wexler, Haskell (Cinematographer)
1247 Lincoln Blvd # 585
Santa Monica, CA 90401-1700, USA

Wexler, Jacqueline G (Educator)
222 Park Ave S
New York, NY 10003-1504, USA

Wexner, Leslie H (Business Person)
Limited Inc
3 Limited Pkwy
PO Box 16000
Columbus, OH 43230-1467, USA

Weyand, Frederick C (General)
4389 Malia St Apt 317
Honolulu, HI 96821-1167, USA

Weyerhaeuser, George (Business Person)
Weyerhaeuser Co
33663 32nd Ave SW
Federal Way, WA 98023, USA

Weymouth, Tina (Musician)
Premier Talent
3 E 54th St # 1100
New York, NY 10022-3108, USA

Whalen, Dorothy (Baseball Player)
8315 125th St
Kew Gardens, NY 11415-2705, USA

Whalen, Jim (Football Player)
Boston Patriots
9 Wauketa Rd
Gloucester, MA 01930-1423, USA

Whalen, Laurence J (Judge)
US Tax Court
400 2nd St NW
Washington, DC 20217-0002, USA

Whalen, Lindsay (Basketball Player)
Connecticut Sun
Mohegan Sun Arena
Uncasville, CT 06382, USA

Whaley, Frank (Actor)
c/o Staff Member *Shelter Entertainment*
9255 W Sunset Blvd Ste 1010
Los Angeles, CA 90069-3307, USA

Whaley, Joanne
9830 Wilshire Blvd
Beverly Hills, CA 90212-1804, USA

Whalin, Justin
3604 Holboro Dr
Los Angeles, CA 90027-1432, USA

Whalley, Joanne (Actor)
1435 Lindacrest Dr
Beverly Hills, CA 90210-2519, USA

Whalum, Kirk (Musician)
Cole Classic Mgmt
PO Box 231
Canoga Park, CA 91305-0231, USA

Wham, Tom (Football Player)
Chicago Cardinals
415 John St
Greer, SC 29651-1412, USA

Whang, Suzanne (Actor)
c/o Staff Member *Kragen & Company*
14039 Aubrey Rd
Beverly Hills, CA 90210-1062, USA

Whannell, Leigh (Actor, Writer)
c/o Stacey Testro *Stacey Testro International*
8265 W Sunset Blvd Ste 100
West Hollywood, CA 90046-2433, USA

Wharton, Bernard (Architect)
Shope Reno Wharton
18 W Putnam Ave
Greenwich, CT 06830-5341, USA

Wharton, Hogan (Football Player)
Houston Oilers
5736 W Airport Blvd
Houston, TX 77035-4314, USA

Whatmore, Sarah (Musician)
c/o Staff Member *Pop Idol (Fremantle Media)*
2700 Colorado Ave Ste 450
Santa Monica, CA 90404-3599, USA

Wheat, Lee (Baseball Player)
Philadelphia Athletics
4010 Galt Ocean Dr Apt 1406
Ft Lauderdale, FL 33308-6519, USA

Wheatley, E H (Publisher)
Vancouver Sun
2250 Granville St
Vancouver, BC V6H 3G2, CANADA

Wheatley, Tyrone (Football Player)
New York Giants
20730 Westhampton St
Oak Park, MI 48237-2710, USA

Wheaton, David (Tennis Player)
20045 Cottagewood Ave
Excelsior, MN 55331-9239, USA

Wheaton, Kenny (Football Player)
Dallas Cowboys
6427 S 21st Pl
Phoenix, AZ 85042-4652, USA

Wheaton, Wil (Actor)
2603 Sea Pine Ln
La Crescenta, CA 91214-1443, USA

Wheatus (Music Group)
c/o Robert Hollingsworth *So Called Management*
1055 Homer St #1006
Vancouver, BC V6B 1G3, CANADA

Whedon, Joss (Director, Producer, Writer)
c/o Chris Harbert *Creative Artists Agency LCC (CAA-LA)*
2000 Avenue Of The Stars
Los Angeles, CA 90067-4700, USA

Wheeler, Blake (Hockey Player)
Philadelphia Flyers
3601 S Broad St
1st Union Center
Philadelphia, PA 19148-5297, USA

Wheeler, Charles F (Cinematographer)
79125 Jack Rabbit Trl
La Quinta, CA 92253-4514, USA

Wheeler, Cheryl (Musician, Songwriter, Writer)
Morningstar Mgmt
PO Box 1770
Hendersonville, TN 37077-1770, USA

Wheeler, Daniel (Baseball Player)
Tampa Bay Devil Rays
254 Milton Rd
Warwick, RI 02888-1830, USA

Wheeler, Daniel S (Editor)
American Legion Magazine
700 N Pennsylvania St
Indianapolis, IN 46204-1129, USA

Wheeler, Dwight (Football Player)
New England Patriots
2124 Blair Blvd
Nashville, TN 37212-4902, USA

Wheeler, Ellen
13576 Cheltenham Dr
Sherman Oaks, CA 91423-4818, USA

Wheeler, H Anthony (Architect)
Hawthombank House
Dean Village
Edinburgh EH4 3BH, SCOTLAND

Wheeler, John (Actor)
Levin Agency
8484 Wilshire Blvd Ste 745
Beverly Hills, CA 90211-3235, USA

Wheeler, John A (Physicist)
1904 Meadow Lane
Highstown, NJ 08542, USA

Wheeler, Maggie (Actor)
c/o Belle Zwerdling *Progressive Artists Agency*
400 S Beverly Dr Ste 216
Beverly Hills, CA 90212-4404, USA

Wheeler, Margaret
4950 Cahuenga Blvd
N Hollywood, CA 91601-4706, USA

Wheeler, Mark (Football Player)
Tampa Bay Buccaneers
101 Meadowridge Cv
San Marcos, TX 78666-2251, USA

Wheelock, Gary (Baseball Player)
California Angels
12151 Dale Ave Apt D205
Stanton, CA 90680-3848, USA

Whelan, Bill (Composer)
Sony Records
2100 Colorado Ave
Santa Monica, CA 90404-3504, USA

Whelan, Jill (Actor)
c/o Staff Member *Scott Stander & Associates*
13701 Riverside Dr Ste 201
Sherman Oaks, CA 91423-2447, USA

Whelan, Julia (Actor)
c/o Tracy Brennan *Creative Artists Agency LCC (CAA-LA)*
2000 Avenue Of The Stars
Los Angeles, CA 90067-4700, USA

Whelan, Wendy (Ballerina)
New York City Ballet
Lincoln Center Plaza
New York, NY 10023, USA

Whelchel, Lisa (Actor)
8221 Navisota Dr
Lantana, TX 76226-7342, USA

Wheless, Jamy (Animator)
405 Fair St
Petaluma, CA 94952-2519, USA

Whelpley, John (Actor)
c/o Staff Member *Lenhoff & Lenhoff*
830 Palm Ave
West Hollywood, CA 90069-4009, USA

Whibley, Deryck (Musician)
c/o Staff Member *Nettwerk Management (LA)*
8730 Wilshire Blvd # 304
Beverly Hills, CA 90211-2716, USA

Whicker, Alan D (Correspondent)
Le Gallais Chambers
Saint Helier
Jersey, UNITED KINGDOM (UK)

Whigham, Larry (Football Player)
New England Patriots
6110 Midway Rd
Raymond, MS 39154-8357, USA

Whigham, Shea (Actor)
c/o Colton Gramm *Original Film*
284 N Saltair Ave
Los Angeles, CA 90049-2913, USA

Whillock, Jack (Baseball Player)
Detroit Tigers
2118 River Ridge Rd
Arlington, TX 76017-2758, USA

Whinnery, Barbara (Actor)
Baier/Kleinman
3575 Cahuenga Blvd W Ste 500
Los Angeles, CA 90068-1344, USA

Whirry, Shannon (Actor)
Shapiro-Lichtman
1333 Beverly Green Dr
Los Angeles, CA 90035-1018, USA

Whisenant, Matt (Baseball Player)
Florida Marlins
1035 Fairview Dr
La Canada Flintridge, CA 91011-2351, USA

Whisenhunt, Ken (Football Player)
Atlanta Falcons
1511 W Grand Canyon Dr
Chandler, AZ 85248-4816, USA

Whisenton, Larry (Baseball Player)
Atlanta Braves
1453 Beecher St SW
Atlanta, GA 30310-2563, USA

Whishaw, Anthony (Artist)
7A Albert Place
Victoria Road
London W8 5PD, UNITED KINGDOM (UK)

Whisler, J Steven (Business Person)
Phelps Dodge Corp
1 N Central Ave
Phoenix, AZ 85004-4464, USA

Whiston, Don (Hockey Player)
2 Jeffreys Neck Rd
Ipswich, MA 01938-1328, USA

Whitacre, Edward E Jr (Business Person)
SBC Communications
175 E Houston
San Antonio, TX 78205-2255, USA

Whitaker, Forest (Actor, Director, Producer)
15030 Ventura Blvd # 710
Sherman Oaks, CA 91403-5470, USA

Whitaker, Jack (Golfer)
Int'l Golf Partners
3300 Pga Blvd Ste 820
West Palm Beach, FL 33410-2811, USA

Whitaker, Jack (Sportscaster)
500 Berwyn Baptist Rd # L-Fleur
Devon, PA 19333-1038, USA

Whitaker, Johnny
4924 Vineland Ave
N Hollywood, CA 91601-3847, USA

Whitaker, Louis R (Lou) Jr (Baseball Player)
4798 S Florida Ave # 406
Lakeland, FL 33813-2181, USA

Whitaker, Mark (Editor)
Newsweek Magazine
251 W 57th St
Editorial Dept
New York, NY 10019-1802, USA

Whitaker, Meade (Judge)
US Tax Court
400 2nd St NW
Washington, DC 20217-0002, USA

Whitaker, Pernell (Boxer)
3808 Cranberry Ct
Virginia Beach, VA 23456-8109, USA

Whitaker, Roger
1730 Tree Blvd Ste 2
St Augustine, FL 32084-4193, USA

Whitaker, Steve (Baseball Player)
New York Yankees
250 S Gordon Rd
Fort Lauderdale, FL 33301-3742, USA

Whitaker, William (Football Player)
Green Bay Packers
Lake Road 135 12
Gravois Mills, MO 65037, USA

Whitbank, Ben (Baseball Player)
203 Apollo Ln
Milton, DE 19968-9781, USA

Whitbread, Fatima (Athlete, Track Athlete)
Chafford Information Ctr
Elozabeth Road
Grays
Essex RM16 6QZ, UNITED KINGDOM (UK)

Whitby, Bill (Baseball Player)
Minnesota Twins
13926 Huntersville Concord Rd
Huntersville, NC 28078-6262, USA

Whitcomb, Bob (Race Car Driver)
Whitcomb Racing
9201 Garrison Rd
Charlotte, NC 28278, USA

Whitcomb, Edgar D (Governor)
15415 Rome Rd
Rome, IN 47574, USA

Whitcomb, Ian (Musician, Songwriter, Writer)
PO Box 451
Altadena, CA 91003-0451, USA

Whitcomb, Richard T (Inventor)
119 Tide Mill Ln
Hampton, VA 23666-5204, USA

White, Adrian (Football Player)
New York Giants
686 Allen Ln
Orange Park, FL 32073-3986, USA

White, Alan (Musician)
Ignition Mgmt
54 Linhope St
London NW1 6HL, UNITED KINGDOM (UK)

White, Albert (Baseball Player)
St Louis Browns
32 Jessana Hts
Colorado Springs, CO 80906-7902, USA

White, Andre (Football Player)
Denver Broncos
5122 Hunters Luck
Stone Mountain, GA 30088-3123, USA

White, Anna
9950 Durant Dr Unit 402
Beverly Hills, CA 90212-1610, USA

White, Betty (Actor, Comedian)
PO Box 491965
Los Angeles, CA 90049-8965, USA

White, Bob W (Football Player)
San Francisco 49ers
763D Espada Dr
El Paso, TX 79912-1913, USA

White, Bradley
8730 W Sunset Blvd Ste 480
Los Angeles, CA 90069-2277, USA

White, Brian (Actor)
c/o Staff Member *United Talent Agency (UTA)*
9560 Wilshire Blvd Ste 500
Beverly Hills, CA 90212-2401, USA

White, Bryan (Musician, Songwriter, Writer)
Holly Co
3415 W End Ave Ste 101G
Nashville, TN 37203-6878, USA

White, Charles R (Football Player)
University of Southern California
Heritage Hall
Los Angeles, CA 90089-0001, USA

White, Charles R (Football Player)
Cleveland Browns
51 Foxtail Ln
Trabuco Canyon, CA 92679-3805, USA

White, Cheryl (Musician)
Hallmark Direction
713 18th Ave S
Nashville, TN 37203-3214, USA

White, Chris (Musician)
Lustig Talent
PO Box 770850
Orlando, FL 32877-0850, USA

White, Danny (Coach, Football Player)
Utah Blaze
405 S Main St Ste 1100
Salt Lake City, UT 84111-3411, USA

White, Derrick (Baseball Player)
Montreal Expos
161 Laurelwood Dr
Novato, CA 94949-8427, USA

White, Devon M (Baseball Player)
California Angels
6440 E Sierra Vista Dr
Paradise Valley, AZ 85253-4351, USA

White, DeVoreaux
4505 Santa Rosalia Dr
Los Angeles, CA 90008-1571, USA

White, Diz (Actor)
203 N Plymouth Blvd
Los Angeles, CA 90004-3833, USA

White, Dwayne (Football Player)
New York Jets
1916 Dickinson St
Philadelphia, PA 19146-4662, USA

White, Dwight (Financier, Football Player)
406 Landon Gate
Pittsburgh, PA 15238-1523, USA

White, Dwight (Football Player)
Pittsburgh Steelers
PO Box 614
Pro Athlete Marketing
Beaver Falls, PA 15010-0614, USA

White, Ed
1225 Grand View Dr
Berkeley, CA 94705-1629, USA

White, Ed (Football Player)
Minnesota Vikings
PO Box 1437
Julian, CA 92036-1437, USA

White, Edmund (Writer)
185 Nassau St Rm 224
Princeton, NJ 08544-2003, USA

White, Elder (Baseball Player)
Chicago Cubs
919 Colony Ave N
Ahoskie, NC 27910-2107, USA

White, Eugene (Baseball Player)
Chicago American Giants
4166 Lockhart Dr N
Jacksonville, FL 32209-1928, USA

White, Frank (Baseball Player)
Kansas City Royals
412 NE Parks Edge Dr
Lees Summit, MO 64064-1270, USA

White, Gabe (Baseball Player)
Montreal Expos
911 SE Lakeview Dr
Sebring, FL 33870, USA

White, Gene C (Football Player)
Green Bay Packers
180 National Dr
Pinehurst, NC 28374-8165, USA

White, Gerald (Football Player)
Dallas Cowboys
1501 Halo Dr
Halo Creative Concepts
Troy, MI 48084, USA

White, Gilbert F (Misc)
624 Pearl St Apt 302
Boulder, CO 80302-5072, USA

White, Jahidi (Athlete, Basketball Player)
c/o Staff Member *Washington Wizards*
601 F St NW
Mci Center
Washington, DC 20004-1605, USA

White, Jai (Actor)
c/o Craig Baumgarten *Baumgarten Merims Entertainment*
1640 S Sepulveda Blvd Ste 216
Los Angeles, CA 90025-7535, USA

White, Jaleel (Actor)
8916 Ashcroft Ave
West Hollywood, CA 90048-2404, USA

White, James
7529 Franklin Ave
Los Angeles, CA 90046-2241, USA

White, James B (Attorney, Attorney General, Educator, General)
1606 Morton Ave
Ann Arbor, MI 48104-4441, USA

White, James C (Football Player)
Minnesota Vikings
14430 Andrea Way Ln
Houston, TX 77083-7712, USA

White, Jamie (Radio Personality)
c/o Staff Member *Star 98.7 FM*
3400 W Olive Ave Ste 550
Burbank, CA 91505-5544, USA

White, Jan (Football Player)
Buffalo Bills
6507 Burkwood Dr
Clayton, OH 45315-9602, USA

White, Jeris (Football Player)
Miami Dolphins
PO Box 3031
Frederick, MD 21705-3031, USA

White, Jerry (Baseball Player)
Montreal Expos
581 Glen Dr # 1D
San Leandro, CA 94577-2900, USA

White, John H (Journalist, Photographer)
Chicago Sun-Times
350 N Orleans St Ste 1270
Editorial Dept
Chicago, IL 60654-2148, USA

White, John Patrick (Actor)
Metropolitan Talent Agency
4500 Wilshire Blvd Fl 2
Los Angeles, CA 90010-3858, USA

White, Jordie (Musician)
Marilyn Manson
83 Riverside Dr
New York, NY 10024-5713, USA

White, Joseph (Jo Jo) (Basketball Player)
2 Mansfield Rd
Middleton, MA 01949-1515, USA

White, Joy Lynn (Musician)
Buddy Lee
38 Music Sq E Ste 200
Nashville, TN 37203-4304, USA

White, Julie (Actor)
4129 Laurelgrove Ave
Studio City, CA 91604-1622, USA

White, Karyn (Musician)
Warner Bors Records
3300 Warner Blvd
Burbank, CA 91505-4694, USA

White, Kate (Editor)
Cosmopolitan Magazine
224 W 57th St
Editorial Dept
New York, NY 10019-3200, USA

White, L Robert (Bob) (Football Player)
Houston Oilers
1044 Grouse Way
Venice, FL 34285-6613, USA

White, Lari (Actor)
c/o Staff Member *William Morris Agency (WMA-LA)*
1 William Morris Pl
Beverly Hills, CA 90212-4261, USA

White, Larri (Musician, Songwriter, Writer)
Carter Career Mgmt
1028 18th Ave S # B
Nashville, TN 37212-2105, USA

White, Larry (Baseball Player)
Los Angeles Dodgers
19053 N 37th Pl
Phoenix, AZ 85050-2699, USA

White, Lee (Football Player)
New York Jets
600 Langtry Dr
Las Vegas, NV 89107-2019, USA

White, Leon (Football Player)
Cincinnati Bengals
11033 Paseo Castanada
La Mesa, CA 91941-7330, USA

White, Lorenzo (Football Player)
Houston Oilers
3450 NW 7th St
Fort Lauderdale, FL 33311-6505, USA

White, Marco P (Chef)
The Restaurant
66 Knightsbridge
London SW1X 7LA, UNITED KINGDOM
(UK)

White, Marilyn (Athlete, Track Athlete)
9605 S 6th Ave
Inglewood, CA 90305-3207, USA

White, Mark (Musician)
DAS Communications
84 Riverside Dr
New York, NY 10024-5723, USA

White, Marsh (Football Player)
New York Giants
7502 Bayhill Dr
Rowlett, TX 75088-5465, USA

White, Martha G (Publisher)
London Free Press
369 York St
London, ON N6A 4G1, CANADA

White, Matt (Baseball Player)
Boston Red Sox
1853 Old Route 9
Windsor, MA 01270-9397, USA

White, Meg (Music Group, Musician)
Jack White Productions
Muenchner Str 45
Unterfoehring 85774, GERMANY

White, Michael Jai (Actor)
Baumgarten
1640 S Sepulveda Blvd Ste 216
Los Angeles, CA 90025-7535, USA

White, Michael R (Misc)
11794 Blue Ridge Rd
Newcomerstown, OH 43832-9172, USA

White, Michael S (Producer)
48 Dean St
London W1V 5HL, UNITED KINGDOM
(UK)

White, Mike (Actor)
c/o Staff Member *Black and White
Productions*
100 Universal City Plz Bldg 4113
Universal City, CA 91608-1002, USA

White, Mike (Baseball Player)
Houston Colt .45's
26438 S Jardin Dr
Sun Lakes, AZ 85248-7114, USA

White, Mike (Coach, Football Coach)
Kansas City Chiefs
1 Arrowhead Dr
Kansas City, MO 64129-1651, USA

White, Miles D (Business Person)
Abbott Laboratories
100 Abbott Park Rd
Abbott Park, IL 60064-3500, USA

White, Myron (Baseball Player)
Los Angeles Dodgers
3201 S Deegan Dr
Santa Ana, CA 92704-6614, USA

White, Nera D (Basketball Player)
RR 3 Box 165
Lafayette, TN 37083, USA

White, Persia (Actor)
c/o Staff Member *Acme Talent & Literary
(LA)*
4727 Wilshire Blvd Ste 333
Los Angeles, CA 90010-3874, USA

White, Peter (Actor)
S M S Talant
8730 W Sunset Blvd Ste 440
Los Angeles, CA 90069-2277, USA

White, Randy L (Football Player)
Dallas Cowboys
1360 E Frontier Pkwy
Prosper, TX 75078-9181, USA

White, Raymond P Jr (Doctor)
1506 Velma Rd
Chapel Hill, NC 27514-7601, USA

White, Reggie (Football Player)
Philadelphia Eagles
17325 Connor Quay Ct
Cornelius, NC 28031-6502, USA

White, Reggie (Football Player)
San Diego Chargers
3631 Washington Ave
Baltimore, MD 21244-3776, USA

White, Rick (Baseball Player)
Pittsburgh Pirates
2007 Teal Trce
Pittsburgh, PA 15237-3828, USA

White, Robert A (Football Player)
Dallas Cowboys
11 Jackson St
Jefferson, MA 01522-1429, USA

White, Robert M (General)
PO Box 2488
APO, AE 09063, USA

White, Robert M (Misc)
5610 Wisconsin Ave Apt 1506
Somerset House II
Bethesda, MD 20815-4439, USA

White, Robert M II (Journalist)
4871 Glenbrook Rd NW
Washington, DC 20016-3245, USA

White, Rodney (Basketball Player)
Denver Nuggets
1000 Chopper Cir
Pepsi Center
Denver, CO 80204-5805, USA

White, Ron (Actor, Comedian, Producer,
Writer)
c/o John MacDonald *Parallel
Entertainment*
9229 W Sunset Blvd Ste 311
West Hollywood, CA 90069-3403, USA

White, Rondell (Baseball Player)
Montreal Expos
407 Creekside Dr
Gray, GA 31032-6213, USA

White, RoseDenville Hall
62 Ducks Hill Rd. Northwood
Middlesex, ENGLAND HA6 2SB, UNITED
KINGDOM (UK)

White, Roy (Baseball Player)
New York Yankees
306 Green View Way
Toms River, NJ 08753-7306, USA

White, Roy H (Baseball Player)
1001 2nd St
Sacramento, CA 95814-3201, USA

White, Russell (Football Player)
Los Angeles Rams
17450 Vanowen St Unit 4
Van Nuys, CA 91406-4312, USA

White, Sammy (Football Player)
Minnesota Vikings
102 Margaret Dr
Monroe, LA 71203-9588, USA

White, Sharon
380 Forest Retreat Rd
Hendersonville, TN 37075, USA

White, Sheldon (Football Player)
New York Giants
PO Box 622
Novi, MI 48376-0622, USA

White, Sherman (Football Player)
Cincinnati Bengals
2710 Summerland Rd
Aromas, CA 95004-9117, USA

White, Shernan E (Sherm) (Football
Player)
PO Box 1856
Pebble Beach, CA 93953-1856, USA

White, Stan (Football Player)
New York Giants
10716 Pot Spring Rd
Cockeysville, MD 21030-3021, USA

White, Stephen (Writer)
Penguin Books
375 Hudson St
New York, NY 10014-3672, USA

White, Steve (Football Player)
Tampa Bay Buccaneers
11928 Middlebury Dr
Tampa, FL 33626-2520, USA

White, Steven A (Admiral, Business
Person)
Stone & Webster Engineering Corp
4 Mount Royal Ave Ste 420
Marlborough, MA 01752-1961, USA

White, Timothy D (Misc)
University of California
Hiuman Evolutionary Studies Lab
Berkeley, CA 94720-0001, USA

White, Tony L (Business Person)
PE Corp
710 Bridgeport Ave
Shelton, CT 06484-4750, USA

White, Vanna (Entertainer, Model)
Wheel of Fortune' Show
10202 Washington Blvd # 5300
Culver City, CA 90232-3119, USA

White, Verdine (Musician)
Atlas Rail Entertainment
9200 W Sunset Blvd
West Hollywood, CA 90069-3502, USA

White, Walter (Football Player)
Kansas City Chiefs
504 NW 44th Ter
Kansas City, MO 64116-1580, USA

White, Wilford (Football Player)
Chicago Bears
30A S Macdonald
Mesa, AZ 85210-1322, USA

White, Willard W (Opera Singer)
10 Montague Ave
London SE4 1YP, UNITED KINGDOM
(UK)

White, William (Football Player)
Detroit Lions
2323 Woodland Hall Dr
Powell, OH 43065-7141, USA

White, William B (Bill) (Baseball Player)
8517 Bam Owl
San Antonio, TX 78255, USA

White, Willye B (Athlete, Track Athlete)
5882 S Ensenada St
Aurora, CO 80015-5110, USA

White Jr, Josh (Musician)
23625 Ripple Crk
Novi, MI 48375-3546, USA

White of Rhymney, Eirene L (Government
Official)
64 Vandon Court
Petty France
London SW1H 9HF, UNITED KINGDOM
(UK)

White Stripes, The (Music Group)
c/o Staff Member *Agency Group Ltd, The
(NY)*
1775 Broadway Ste 515
New York, NY 10019-1903, USA

Whited, Ed (Baseball Player)
Atlanta Braves
209 Silver Ct
Trenton, NJ 08690-3514, USA

Whitefield, A D (Football Player)
Dallas Cowboys
807 Tangle Way Ct
Cedar Hill, TX 75104-7817, USA

Whitehead, Alfred K (Misc)
International Assn of Fire Fighters
1750 New York Ave NW
Washington, DC 20006-5395, USA

Whitehead, Bud (Football Player)
San Diego Chargers
5438 N Brooks Ave
Fresno, CA 93711-2913, USA

Whitehead, Geoffrey
81 Shaftesbury Ave.
London, ENGLAND W1, UNITED
KINGDOM (UK)

Whitehead, Jerome (Basketball Player)
1543 Merritt Dr
El Cajon, CA 92020-7847, USA

Whitehead, John C (Financier,
Government Official)
131 Old Chester Rd
Essex Fells, NJ 07021-1625, USA

Whitehead, John C (Scientist)
Brookings Institute
1775 Massachusetts Ave NW
Washington, DC 20036-2103, USA

Whitehead, Lorne (Inventor)
3015 12th Ave W
Vancouver, BC V6K 2R4, CANADA

Whitehead, Paxton (Actor)
Abrams Artists
9200 W Sunset Blvd Ste 1125
Los Angeles, CA 90069-3610, USA

Whitehead, Richard F (Admiral)
American Cage & Machine Co
135 S La Salle St
Chicago, IL 60674-1000, USA

Whitehouse, Len (Baseball Player)
Texas Rangers
300 Shore Rd
Burlington, VT 05408-2632, USA

Whitehurst, C David (Football Player)
Green Bay Packers
11010 Linbrook Ln
Duluth, GA 30097-1772, USA

Whitehurst, Wally (Baseball Player)
New York Mets
186 Ardmore Ave
Shreveport, LA 71105-2108, USA

Whitelaw, Billie (Actor)
Rose Cottage Plum St
Glensford
Suffolk C010 7PX, UNITED KINGDOM
(UK)

Whitemore, Hugh (Writer)
c/o Staff Member *Creative Artists Agency
LCC (CAA-LA)*
2000 Avenue Of The Stars
Los Angeles, CA 90067-4700, USA

Whitemore, Willet F Jr (Doctor, Scientist)
2 Hawthorne Ln
Plandome, NY 11030-1505, USA

Whiten, Mark (Baseball Player)
Toronto Blue Jays
5810 Jefferson Park Dr
Tampa, FL 33625-3313, USA

Whiten, Richard (Actor)
247 S Beverly Dr # 102
Beverly Hills, CA 90212-3830, USA

Whiteread, Rachel (Artist)
Anthony d'Offay
22 Dering St
London W1R 9AA, UNITED KINGDOM
(UK)

White's
PO Box 2158
Hendersonville, TN 37077-2158, USA

Whitesell, Emily (Producer, Writer)
c/o Staff Member *Endeavor Agency LLC
(LA)*
9601 Wilshire Blvd Fl 3
Beverly Hills, CA 90210-5204, USA

Whitesell, Sean (Actor)
c/o Staff Member *United Talent Agency
(UTA)*
9560 Wilshire Blvd Ste 500
Beverly Hills, CA 90212-2401, USA

Whiteside, Matt (Baseball Player)
Texas Rangers
255 Palisades Ridge Ct
Eureka, MO 63025-3706, USA

Whiteside, Sean (Baseball Player)
Detroit Tigers
22447 Inverness Way
Foley, AL 36535-9387, USA

Whitesides, George M (Misc)
124 Grasmere St
Newton, MA 02458-2235, USA

Whitesnake (Music Group)
c/o Staff Member *International Talent
Booking (ITB - UK)*
27A Floral St Fl 3
Covent Garden
London WC2E 9, UNITED KINGDOM
(UK)

Whitfield, Annelie (Actor)
c/o Catriona Ribon *Peters Fraser &
Dunlop (PFD - UK)*
Drury House
34-43 Russell St
London WC2B 5HA, UNITED KINGDOM
(UK)

Whitfield, Dondre T (Actor)
Writers & Artists
360 N Crescent Dr Bldg North
Beverly Hills, CA 90210-6818, USA

Whitfield, Fred (Baseball Player)
St Louis Cardinals
RR 1 Box 91
Vandiver, AL 35176, USA

Whitfield, Lynn (Actor)
c/o Staff Member *Innovative Artists (LA)*
1505 10th St
Santa Monica, CA 90401-2805, USA

Whitfield, Mal
1 Hoosier Dome
Indianapolis, IN 46225-1052, USA

Whitfield, Terry (Baseball Player)
New York Yankees
849 Clearfield Dr
Millbrae, CA 94030-2148, USA

Whitford, Brad (Musician)
12811 Ninebark Trl
Charlotte, NC 28278-6837, USA

Whitford, Bradley (Actor)
c/o Adena Chawke *Greenlight
Management*
1505 10th St
Santa Monica, CA 90401-2805, USA

Whiting, Leonard
7 Leicester Pl.
London, ENGLAND WC2H 7BP, UNITED
KINGDOM (UK)

Whiting, Margaret (Musician)
41 W 58th St # 5A
New York, NY 10019-1617, USA

Whitlam, Gough (Prime Minister)
Westfiel Towers
100 William St
Sydney, NSW 2001, AUSTRALIA

Whitley, Curtis (Football Player)
San Diego Chargers
1290 Whitley Farm Rd
Smithfield, NC 27577-9463, USA

Whitley, Keith Society
PO Box 222
Sandy Hook, KY 41171-0222, USA

Whitlow, Bob (Football Player)
Washington Redskins
315 W Gordon Pike Trir 154
Bloomington, IN 47403, USA

Whitman, Kari (Actor, Model)
1155 N La Cienega Blvd Apt 104
West Hollywood, CA 90069-2430, USA

Whitman, Mae (Actor)
CunninghamEscottDipene
10635 Santa Monica Blvd Ste 130
Los Angeles, CA 90025-8306, USA

Whitman, Marina Von Neumann
(Economist)
University of Michigan
Public Policy School
Ann Arbor, MI 48109, USA

Whitman, Meg (Business Person)
eBay
2145 Hamilton Ave
San Jose, CA 95125-5905, USA

Whitman, Ryan (Baseball Player)
9788 Jonquil Cir S
Palm Beach Gardens, FL 33410-5535,
USA

Whitman, Slim (Musician)
3830 Old Jennings Rd
Middleburg, FL 32068-3738, USA

Whitman, Stuart (Actor)
749 San Ysidro Rd
Santa Barbara, CA 93108-1328, USA

Whitmer, Dan (Baseball Player)
California Angels
823 Robinhood Ln
Redlands, CA 92373-6665, USA

Whitmire, Steve (Actor)
c/o Staff Member *Jim Henson Company
(LA)*
1416 N La Brea Ave
Hollywood, CA 90028-7506, USA

Whitmore, Darrell (Baseball Player)
Florida Marlins
301 E 15th St
Front Royal, VA 22630-4112, USA

Whitmore, James (Actor)
4990 Puesta Del Sol St
Malibu, CA 90265-2512, USA

Whitmore, Kay (Hockey Player)
16 Springwood Rd
Farmington, CT 06032-1105, USA

Whitmore Jr, James (Actor)
1284 La Brea Dr
Thousand Oaks, CA 91362-2216, USA

Whitmyer, Nat (Football Player)
Los Angeles Rams
5305 W Goldenwood Dr
Inglewood, CA 90302-1037, USA

Whitney, Ashley (Swimmer)
125 Villa View Ct
Brentwood, TN 37027-3919, USA

Whitney, CeCe (Actor)
1145 E Barham Dr Spc 217
San Marcos, CA 92078-4547, USA

Whitney, David (Baseball Player)
Kansas City Monarchs
2178 Popps Ferry Rd
Biloxi, MS 39532-4233, USA

Whitney, Jane (Entertainer)
5 TV Pl
Needham, MA 02494-2302, USA

Whitney, Russ (Business Person, Misc)
Whitney Education Group Inc
1612 Cape Coral Pkwy E
Cape Coral, FL 33904-9618, USA

Whitney-Dearfield, Norma (Baseball
Player)
786 Camp Hollow Rd
West Mifflin, PA 15122-3387, USA

Whitney-Lee, Grace (Actor)
PO Box 79
Coarsegold, CA 93614, USA

Whitsett, Vivicca (Actor)
c/o Karin Olsen *Amazon PR*
269 S Beverly Dr # 750
Beverly Hills, CA 90212-3851, USA

Whitson, Ed (Baseball Player)
Pittsburgh Pirates
10473 Mackenzie Way
Dublin, OH 43017-8775, USA

Whitson, Peggy A (Astronaut)
306 Lakeview Cir
Seabrook, TX 77586-5846, USA

Whitt, Ernie (Baseball Player)
Boston Red Sox
37370 Moravian Dr
Clinton Township, MI 48036-3604, USA

Whittaker, James (Jim) (Mountaineer)
2023 E Sims Way # 277
Port Townsend, WA 98368-6905, USA

Whittaker, Roger (Musician, Songwriter,
Writer)
BML Mgmt
426 Marsh Point Cir
Saint Augustine, FL 32080-5863, USA

Whitted, Alvis (Football Player)
Jacksonville Jaguars
6107 Bent Oak Dr
Durham, NC 27705-9115, USA

Whittenton, Jesse (Football Player)
Los Angeles Rams
PO Box 1626
204 Moon Silver
Santa Teresa, NM 88008-1626, USA

Whittingham, Charles A (Publisher)
11 Woodmill Rd
Chappaqua, NY 10514-1128, USA

Whittinghill, Dick
11310 Valley Spring Ln
Toluca Lake, CA 91602-2613, USA

Whittington, Art (Football Player)
Oakland Raiders
6709 La Tijera Blvd # 190
Los Angeles, CA 90045-2017, USA

Whittington, C L (Football Player)
Houston Oilers
2332 Galilee Rd # 121
Hallsville, TX 75650-6189, USA

Whittington, Michael S (Football Player)
New York Giants
4246 Turtle Mound Rd
Melbourne, FL 32934-8505, USA

Whittle, Ricky (Football Player)
New Orleans Saints
514 Tulare St
Fresno, CA 93706-3723, USA

Whitton, Margaret (Actor)
William Morris Agency
151 El Camino Dr
Beverly Hills, CA 90212-2775, USA

Whitwam, David R (Business Person)
Whirlpool Corp
2000 N State St
RR 63
Benton Harbor, MI 49022, USA

Whitwell, Mike (Football Player)
Cleveland Browns
PO Box 6
Cotulla, TX 78014-0006, USA

Whitworth, Kathy
5990 Lindenshire Ln Apt 101
Dallas, TX 75230-2726, USA

Wholey, Dennis (Television Host)
Dennis Wholey Enterprises
1333 H St NW
Washington, DC 20005-4707, USA

Whoppers, Wendy (Actor)
c/o Staff Member *Wow Entertainment Inc*
8362 Pines Blvd # 296
Pembroke Pines, FL 33024-6600, USA

Whyte, Sandra (Hockey Player)
81 Golden Hills Rd
Saugus, MA 01906-4010, USA

Wiberg, Kenneth B (Misc)
160 Carmalt Rd
Hamden, CT 06517-1904, USA

Wiberg, Pernilla (Skier)
Katterunsvagen 32
Norrkopping 60 210, SWEDEN

Wick, Charles Z (Government Official)
US Information Agency
400 C St SW
Washington, DC 20024-2800, USA

Wickander, Kevin (Baseball Player)
Cleveland Indians
4319 W Banff Ln
Glendale, AZ 85306-3601, USA

Wicker, Floyd (Baseball Player)
St Louis Cardinals
1758 West G Bro Chapel Hill Rd
Snow Camp, NC 27349, USA

Wicker, Thomas G (Tom) (Journalist, Writer)
PO Box 361
Rochester, VT 05767-0361, USA

Wicker, Tom
229 W 43rd St
New York, NY 10036-3913, USA

Wickersham, Dave (Baseball Player)
Kansas City A's
9118 W 104th Ter
Shawnee Mission, KS 66212-5517, USA

Wickert, Tom (Football Player)
Miami Dolphins
3717 Beach Dr SW
Seattle, WA 98116-3060, USA

Wickham, Daniel (Baseball Player)
3221 E Mountain Vista Dr
Phoenix, AZ 85048-5802, USA

Wickham, John A Jr (General)
13590 N Fawnbrooke Dr
Tucson, AZ 85737, USA

Wicki-Fink, Agnes (Actor)
Weisgerberstr 2
Munich 80805, GERMANY

Wickman, Robert J (Bob) (Baseball Player)
New York Yankees
PO Box 161
Plain, WI 53577-0161, USA

Wicks, Ben (Cartoonist, Editor)
38 Yorkville Ave
Toronto, ON M4W 1L5, CANADA

Wicks, Sidney (Basketball Player)
1030 S La Jolla Ave
Los Angeles, CA 90035-2523, USA

Wicks, Sue (Basketball Player)
New York Liberty
2 Penn Plz
Madison Square Garden
New York, NY 10121-1703, USA

Wicoff, Erika (Golfer)
7815 Four Leaf Dr
Greenville, IN 47124-9524, USA

Widby, G Ronald (Ron) (Basketball Player, Football Player)
Dallas Cowboys
542 Mahler Rd
Wichita Falls, TX 76310-0326, USA

Widdoes, Kathleen (Actor)
24 E 11th St
New York, NY 10003-4402, USA

Widdoes, Kathleen (Actor)
As the World Turns' Show
524 W 57th St # 5330
Cbs-Tv
New York, NY 10019-2930, USA

Widdrington, Peter N T (Business Person)
Laidlaw Inc
3221 N Service Road
Burlington, ON L7R 3Y8, CANADA

Widell, Dave (Football Player)
Dallas Cowboys
13050 Wexford Hollow Rd N
Jacksonville, FL 32224-9625, USA

Widell, Doug (Football Player)
Denver Broncos
870 21st St
Vero Beach, FL 32960-5314, USA

Wideman, John Edgar (Writer)
University of Massachusetts
Englesh Dept
Amherst, MA 01003, USA

Widener, H Emroy Jr (Judge)
US Court of Appeals
PO Box 1689
Bristol, VA 24203-1689, USA

Widger, Chris (Baseball Player)
Seattle Mariners
95 Fort Mott Rd
Pennsville, NJ 08070-2839, USA

Widman, Herbert (Herb) (Athlete, Swimmer)
844 Monarch Cir
San Jose, CA 95138-1343, USA

Widmark, Richard (Actor)
c/o Jack Gilardi *International Creative Management (ICM-LA)*
10250 Constellation Blvd
Los Angeles, CA 90067-6200, USA

Widmer, Corey (Football Player)
New York Giants
2640 Lake Shore Dr Unit 2508
West Palm Beach, FL 33404-4674, USA

Widom, Benjamin (Misc)
204 The Pkwy
Ithaca, NY 14850-2247, USA

Wie, Michelle (Golfer)
c/o Staff Member *William Morris Agency (WMA-LA)*
1 William Morris Pl
Beverly Hills, CA 90212-4261, USA

Wiebe, Mark (Golfer)
4123 S Elkhart St
Aurora, CO 80014-8100, USA

Wiebe, Susanne (Designer, Fashion Designer)
Amalienstr 39
Munich 80799, GERMANY

Wiedemann, Josef (Architect)
Im Eichgeholz 11
Munich 80997, GERMANY

Wiedlin, Jane (Musician)
c/o Staff Member *William Morris Agency (WMA-LA)*
1 William Morris Pl
Beverly Hills, CA 90212-4261, USA

Wiedorfer, Paul J (War Hero)
2506 Moore Ave
Baltimore, MD 21234-7531, USA

Wiegart, Zach (Football Player)
3747 Saltmeadow Ct S
Jacksonville, FL 32224-9652, USA

Wiegmann, Casey (Football Player)
Indianapolis Colts
30051 N Waukegan Road
North Chicago, IL 60064, USA

Wiehl, Christopher (Actor)
c/o Staff Member *Gersh Agency, The (LA)*
232 N Canon Dr
Beverly Hills, CA 90210-5302, USA

Wielicki, Krzysztof (Mountaineer)
Ul A Frycza Modrzewskiego 21
Tychy 43-100, POLAND

Wieman, Carl E (Nobel Prize Laureate)
University of Colorado
440 Physics Campus Box
Boulder, CO 80309-0001, USA

Wiener, Jacques L Jr (Judge)
US Court of Appeals
500 Fannin St
Federal Buliding
Shreveport, LA 71101-3023, USA

Wier, Murray (Basketball Player, Coach)
118 Goodwater St
Georgetown, TX 78633-4505, USA

Wiese, John P (Judge)
US Claims Court
717 Madison Pl NW
Washington, DC 20439-0001, USA

Wiesel, Elie (Nobel Prize Laureate, Writer)
555 Madison Ave Ste 2000
New York, NY 10022-3308, USA

Wiesen, Bernard (Director)
Weisgerberstr 2
Munich 80805, GERMANY

Wiesner, Kenneth (Ken) (Athlete, Track Athlete)
3601 Meta Lake Rd
Eagle River, WI 54521-9119, USA

Wiest, Dianne (Actor)
59 E 54th St Rm 22
New York, NY 10022-9222, USA

Wiggin, Paul (Coach, Football Coach, Football Player)
Cleveland Browns
5013 Ridge Rd
Edina, MN 55436-1013, USA

Wiggins, Audrey (Musician)
William Morris Agency
1600 Division St Ste 300
Nashville, TN 37203-2755, USA

Wiggins, Jermaine (Football Player)
New York Jets
403 Overlook Dr
Beckley, WV 25801-9255, USA

Wiggins, John (Musician)
William Morris Agency
1600 Division St Ste 300
Nashville, TN 37203-2755, USA

Wigglesworth, Marian McKean (Skier)
General Delivery
Wilson, WY 83014-9999, USA

Wiggs, Susan (Writer)
PO Box 4469
Rollingbay, WA 98061-0469, USA

Wight, Paul (Wrestler)
c/o Staff Member *World Wrestling Entertainment (WWE)*
1241 E Main St
Stamford, CT 06902-3520, USA

Wightman, Donald E (Misc)
Utility Workers Union
815 16th St NW
Washington, DC 20006-4101, USA

Wigiser, Margaret (Baseball Player)
7101 SE Quincy Ter
Hobe Sound, FL 33455-7357, USA

Wigle, Ernest D (Doctor)
101 College St
Toronto, ON M56 1L7, CANADA

Wiig, Kristen (Actor)
c/o Naomi Odenkirk *Odenkirk Talent Management*
650 N Bronson Ave Bldg B145
Raleigh Studios
Los Angeles, CA 90004-1404, USA

Wiik, Sven (Skier)
PO Box 774484
Steamboat Springs, CO 80477-4484, USA

Wijdenbosch, Jules A (President)
Presidential Palace
Onafhankelikheidsplein 1
Paramaribo, SURINAME

Wilander, Mats (Tennis Player)
Einar Wilander
Vickervagen 2
Vaxjo 352 53, SWEDEN

Wilber, Doreen V H (Athlete)
1401 W Lincolnway St
Jefferson, IA 50129-1675, USA

Wilbraham, John H G (Musician)
9 D Cuthbert St
Wells
Somerset BA5 2AW, UNITED KINGDOM (UK)

Wilbur, John (Football Player)
Dallas Cowboys
PO Box 10002
Honolulu, HI 96816-0002, USA

Wilbur, Richard C (Judge)
US Tax Court
400 2nd St NW
Washington, DC 20217-0002, USA

Wilbur, Richard P (Writer)
88 Dodswell Road
Cummington, MA 01026, USA

Wilbur, Richard S (Doctor)
985 Hawthome Place
Lake Forest, IL 60045, USA

Wilburn, J R (Football Player)
Pittsburgh Steelers
2211 Chalkwell Dr
Midlothian, VA 23113-3897, USA

Wilburn Brothers
PO Box 50
Goodlettsville, TN 37070-0050, USA

Wilby, James (Actor)
William Morris Agency
52/53 Poland Place
London W1F 7KX, UNITED KINGDOM (UK)

Wilcher, Mary (Actor)
c/o Staff Member *Levine Management*
9028 W Sunset Blvd # Ph1
Los Angeles, CA 90069-1846, USA

Wilcox, Chris (Basketball Player)
Los Angeles Clippers
1111 S Figueroa St
Staples Center
Los Angeles, CA 90015-1300, USA

Wilcox, Christopher (Editor)
Reader's Digest Magazine
Readers Digest Rd
Pleasantville, NY 10570-7001, USA

Wilcox, Collin
121 N San Vicente Blvd
Beverly Hills, CA 90211-2303, USA

Wilcox, David (Music Group, Musician, Songwriter, Writer)
Elizabeth Rush Agency
82 Cumberland Ave
Verona, NJ 07044-2105, USA

Wilcox, Davie (Dave) (Football Player)
San Francisco 49ers
94471 Willamette Dr
Junction City, OR 97448-9606, USA

Wilcox, John (Football Player)
Philadelphia Eagles
82038 S Fork Walla Walla River Rd
Milton Frwtr, OR 97862-7025, USA

Wilcox, Larry (Actor)
10 Appaloosa Ln
Bell Canyon, CA 91307-1002, USA

Wilcox, Lisa (Actor)
Stone Manners
6500 Wilshire Blvd Ste 550
Los Angeles, CA 90048-4950, USA

Wilcox, Shannon (Actor)
20518 Pacific Coast Hwy
Malibu, CA 90265-5402, USA

Wilcutt, Terence W (Terry) (Astronaut)
1216 Red Wing Dr
Friendswood, TX 77546-5888, USA

Wild, Earl (Composer, Musician)
2233 Femleaf Lane
Columbus, OH 43235, USA

Wild Orchid
PO Box 90370
City Of Industry, CA 91715-0370, USA

Wild Orchid (Music Group)
c/o Staff Member Diva Central Inc
7510 W Sunset Blvd Ste 1445
Los Angeles, CA 90046-3408, USA

Wilde, Kim (Musician, Songwriter, Writer)
Dance Crazy Mgmt
294-296 Nether St
Finchley
Lake Forest N31 RJ, UNITED KINGDOM (UK)

Wilde, Olivia (Actor)
c/o Robbie Kass Kass & Stokes Management
9229 W Sunset Blvd Ste 504
Los Angeles, CA 90069-3405, USA

Wilde, Patricia (Artist, Ballerina, Director)
Pittsburgh Ballet Theater
2900 Liberty Ave
Pittsburgh, PA 15201-1511, USA

Wilder, Alan (Musician)
Reach Media
295 Greenwich St # 109
New York, NY 10007-1049, USA

Wilder, Bert (Football Player)
New York Jets
501 Willow View Dr
Greensboro, NC 27455-1379, USA

Wilder, Don (Cartoonist)
North American Syndicate
235 E 45th St
New York, NY 10017-3305, USA

Wilder, Gene (Actor, Director, Writer)
c/o Andrew Hersh Lovett Management
1327 Brinkley Ave
Los Angeles, CA 90049-3619, USA

Wilder, James (Actor)
Stone Manners
6500 Wilshire Blvd Ste 550
Los Angeles, CA 90048-4950, USA

Wilder, Yvonne
11836 Hesby St
N Hollywood, CA 91607-3218, USA

Wilding, Anna (Actor)
c/o Staff Member Carpe Diem Films LLC
9663 Santa Monica Blvd # 557
Beverly Hills, CA 90210-4303, USA

Wilding Jr, Michael
34 Ellis Ranch Rd
Santa Fe, NM 87505-1415, USA

Wildman, George (Cartoonist)
1640 Shepard Ave
Hamden, CT 06518-2036, USA

Wildman, Valerie (Actor)
110 Hurricane St Apt 305
Marina Del Rey, CA 90292-5935, USA

Wildmon, Donald (Activist)
National Federation of Decency
PO Box 1398
Tupelo, MS 38802-1398, USA

Wildung, Richard K (Dick) (Football Player)
Green Bay Packers
10368 Rich Rd
Bloomington, MN 55437-2505, USA

Wiles, Jason (Actor)
c/o Joanne Wiles William Morris Agency (WMA-LA)
1 William Morris Pl
Beverly Hills, CA 90212-4261, USA

Wiley, Enloe Steve (Baseball Player)
Negro Baseball Leagues
1222 Cedar St
Clarksville, TN 37040-3515, USA

Wiley, Lee (Musician)
Country Crossroads
7787 Monterey St
Gilroy, CA 95020-5217, USA

Wiley, Marcellus (Football Player)
San Diego Chargers
4020 Murphy Canyon Rd
San Diego, CA 92123-4407, USA

Wiley, Marcellus (Football Player)
Buffalo Bills
PO Box 83070
Los Angeles, CA 90083-0070, USA

Wiley, Michael E (Business Person)
Atlantic Richfield Co
333 S Hope St
Los Angeles, CA 90071-1406, USA

Wiley, William T (Artist)
PO Box 661
Forest Knolls, CA 94933-0661, USA

Wiley-Sears, Janet (Baseball Player)
19629 Gilmer St
South Bend, IN 46614-5605, USA

Wilford, John Noble Jr (Journalist)
232 W 10th St
New York, NY 10014-2976, USA

Wilhelm, Erik (Football Player)
Cincinnati Bengals
6452 SE Division St
Portland, OR 97206-1278, USA

Wilhelm, John W (Misc)
Hotel & Restaurant Employees Union
1219 28th St NW
Washington, DC 20007-3362, USA

Wilhelm, Kati (Athlete)
SC Motor Zella-Mehlis
Bierbachstr 68
Zella-Mehlis 98544, GERMANY

Wilhoite, Kathleen
PO Box 5617
Beverly Hills, CA 90209-5617, USA

Wilk, Brad (Musician)
GAS Entertainment
8935 Lindblade St
Culver City, CA 90232-2438, USA

Wilk, Vic (Golfer)
9160 Umberland Ave
Las Vegas, NV 89149-3029, USA

Wilkening, Laurel L (Educator)
University of California
Chancellor's Office
Irvine, CA 92717, USA

Wilkens, Lanny
2660 Peachtree Rd NW Apt 39F
Atlanta, GA 30305-3683, USA

Wilkens, Leonard R (Lenny) Jr (Basketball Player, Coach)
3429 Evergreen Point Rd
Medina, WA 98039-1022, USA

Wilkerson, Bobby (Basketball Player)
4012 Zinfadel Way
Indianapolis, IN 46254, USA

Wilkerson, Brad (Baseball Player)
c/o Staff Member Washington Nationals
2400 East Capitol Street SE
Rfk Stadium
Washington, DC 20003, USA

Wilkerson, Bruce (Football Player)
Oakland Raiders
2013 Breakers Pt
Knoxville, TN 37922-5676, USA

Wilkerson, Doug (Football Player)
Houston Oilers
PO Box 7090
Rancho Santa Fe, CA 92067-7090, USA

Wilkerson, Isabel (Journalist)
New York Times
229 W 43rd St
Editorial Dept
New York, NY 10036-3959, USA

Wilkes, Donna
16228 Maplegrove St
La Puente, CA 91744-1348, USA

Wilkes, Glenn (Basketball Player, Coach)
Stetson University
Athletic Dept
Campus Box 8359
Deland, FL 32720, USA

Wilkes, Jamaal (Basketball Player)
7846 W 81st St
Playa Del Rey, CA 90293-7911, USA

Wilkes, Jimmy (Baseball Player)
Newark Eagles
26-C Oakhill Drive
Brantford, ON N3T 1R1, CANADA

Wilkes, Reggie (Football Player)
Philadelphia Eagles
6912 Wissahickon Ave
Philadelphia, PA 19119-3728, USA

Wilkie, Chris (Musician)
Primary Talent Int'l
2-12 Petonville Road
London N1 9PL, UNITED KINGDOM (UK)

Wilkie, David (Swimmer)
Oaklands Queens Hill
Ascot
Berkshire, UNITED KINGDOM (UK)

Wilkin, Richard E (Religious Leader)
Winebrenner Theological Seminary
950 N Main St
Findlay, OH 45840-3652, USA

Wilkins, Donna (Golfer)
3617 Bancroft Main NW
Kennesaw, GA 30144-6011, USA

Wilkins, J Dominique (Basketball Player)
c/o Staff Member Atlanta Hawks
101 Marietta St NW Ste 1900
Centennial Tower
Atlanta, GA 30303-2771, USA

Wilkins, Laisha (Actor)
c/o Staff Member Televisa
Blvd Adolfo Lopez Mateos 232
Colonia San Angel INN
DF CP 01060, MEXICO

Wilkins, Maurice (Mac) (Athlete, Track Athlete)
PO Box 1058
328 Coldbrook Lane
Soquel, CA 95073-1058, USA

Wilkins, Roger (Journalist)
George Mason University
207 East Building
Fairfax, VA 22030, USA

Wilkins, William W Jr (Judge)
US Court of Appeals
PO Box 10857
Greenville, SC 29603-0857, USA

Wilkinson, Adrienne (Actor)
9157 W Sunset Blvd Ste 215
W Hollywood, CA 90069-3167, USA

Wilkinson, Amanda (Music Group, Musician)
Fitzgerald-Hartley
1908 Wedgewood Ave
Nashville, TN 37212-3733, USA

Wilkinson, Dan (Football Player)
Detroit Lions
222 Republic Dr
Allen Park, MI 48101-3650, USA

Wilkinson, Geoffrey (Nobel Prize Laureate)
Imperial College
Chemistry Dept
London SW7 2AY, UNITED KINGDOM (UK)

Wilkinson, J Harvie III (Judge)
US Court of Appeals
255 W Main St
Charlottesville, VA 22902-5058, USA

Wilkinson, Johnny (Soccer Player)
c/o Staff Member Newcastle United FC
Saint James Park
Newcastle-Tyne NE1 4ST, UNITED KINGDOM (UK)

Wilkinson, Joseph B Jr (Admiral)
340 Chesapeake Dr
Great Falls, VA 22066-3815, USA

Wilkinson, June (Actor, Model)
1025 N Howard St
Glendale, CA 91207-1720, USA

Wilkinson, Kendra (Model, Reality TV Star)
Playboy Mansion
10236 Charing Cross Rd
Los Angeles, CA 90024-1815, USA

Wilkinson, Laura (Misc, Swimmer)
201 S Capitol Ave Ste 300
Indianapolis, IN 46225-1058, USA

Wilkinson, Leon (Musician)
Alliance Artists
6025 Corners Parkway #202
Norcross, GA 30092, USA

Wilkinson, Signe (Cartoonist, Editor)
Philadelphia Daily News
400 N Broad St
Editorial Dept
Philadelphia, PA 19130-4015, USA

Wilkinson, Steve (Musician)
Fitzgerald Hartley
1908 Wedgewood Ave
Nashville, TN 37212-3733, USA

Wilkinson, Tom (Actor)
Lou Coulson
37 Berwick St
London W1V 3RF, UNITED KINGDOM
(UK)

Wilkinson, Tyler (Musician)
Fritzgerald Hartley
1908 Wedgewood Ave
Nashville, TN 37212-3733, USA

Wilks, Jim (Football Player)
New Orleans Saints
4314 Leaflock Ln
Katy, TX 77450-8251, USA

Will, George (Writer)
9 Grafton St
Chevy Chase, MD 20815-3427, USA

Will-Halpin, Maggie (Golfer)
178 Tall Trees Ct
Sarasota, FL 34232-1961, USA

Will to Power (Music Group)
c/o Staff Member Diva Central Inc
7510 W Sunset Blvd Ste 1445
Los Angeles, CA 90046-3408, USA

Willard, Fred (Actor, Comedian)
c/o Staff Member Amsel Eisenstadt &
Frazier Inc
5055 Wilshire Blvd Ste 865
Los Angeles, CA 90036-6109, USA

Willard, Kenneth H (Ken) (Football
Player)
San Francisco 49ers
3071 Viewpoint Road
Midlothian, VA 23113, USA

Willcocks, David V (Musician)
13 Grange Road
Cambridge CB3 9AS, UNITED KINGDOM
(UK)

Willcox, Toyah (Actor)
c/o Staff Member Roseman Organisation,
The
51 Queen Anne St
London W1G 9HS, UNITED KINGDOM
(UK)

Willebrands, Johannes Cardinal (Religious
Leader)
Council for Promoting Christian Unity
Via dell'Erba I
Rome 00120, ITALY

Willem-Alexander (Prince)
Huis ten Bosch
Hague, THE NETHERLANDS

Willerth, Jeffrey
6615 W. Tamarack Ave.
Sun Valley, CA 91352, USA

Willet, E Crosby (Artist)
Willet Stained Glass Studios
10 E Moreland Ave
Philadelphia, PA 19118-3539, USA

Willets, Kathy
3251 Spanish River Dr
Pompano Beach, FL 33062-6809, USA

Willett, Chad
PO Box 5617
Beverly Hills, CA 90209-5617, USA

Willett, Malcolm (Cartoonist)
Universal Press Syndicate
4520 Main St
Kansas City, MO 64111-1876, USA

Willett, Walter (Doctor, Scientist)
Harvard Medical School
25 Shattuck St
Boston, MA 02115-6092, USA

Willette, Jo Ann
9300 Wilshire Blvd Ste 400
Beverly Hills, CA 90212-3210, USA

Willey, Kathleen
2642 New Timer Way
Powhattan, VA 23139, USA

Willey, Norm (Football Player)
Philadelphia Eagles
133 Netherlands Dr
Middletown, DE 19709-9679, USA

Willhite, Gerald (Football Player)
Denver Broncos
10464 Lliff Court
Rancho Cordova, CA 95670, USA

Willhite, Kevin (Football Player)
Green Bay Packers
2316 Moorhen Ct
Elk Grove, CA 95757-8142, USA

Will.I.Am (Musician)
c/o Staff Member Paradigm (LA)
360 N Crescent Dr
North Bldg
Beverly Hills, CA 90210-6820, USA

William (Prince)
Clarence House
Stable Yard Gate
London SW1, UNITED KINGDOM (UK)

William, David (Actor, Director)
194 Langarth St E
London, ON N6C 1Z5, CANADA

William, Edward (Religious Leader)
Bible Way Church
5118 Clarendon Rd
Brooklyn, NY 11203-5329, USA

Williams, Adrian (Basketball Player)
Phoenix Mercury
201 E Jefferson St
American West Arena
Phoenix, AZ 85004-2412, USA

Williams, Aeneas D (Football Player)
Phoenix Cardinals
746 High Hampton Rd
Saint Louis, MO 63124-1018, USA

Williams, Alvin (Basketball Player)
Toronto Raptors
Air Canada Center
40 Bay St
Toronto, ON M5J 2N8, CANADA

Williams, Andy (Musician)
161 Berms Cir Apt 3
Branson, MO 65616-3932, USA

Williams, Anson (Actor)
24612 Skyline View Dr
Malibu, CA 90265-4720, USA

Williams, Anthony A (Politician)
Mayor's Office
District Building
14th & E Sts NW
Washington, DC 20004, USA

Williams, Ashley (Actor)
c/o Andrea Pett-Joseph Brillstein-Grey
Entertainment
9150 Wilshire Blvd Ste 350
Beverly Hills, CA 90212-3453, USA

Williams, Barbara (Actor)
Innovative Artists
1505 10th St
Santa Monica, CA 90401-2805, USA

Williams, Barry (Actor, Musician)
2337 Roscomare Rd # 2-242
Los Angeles, CA 90077-1854, USA

Williams, Bernabe (Bernie) (Baseball
Player)
5 Hallock Pl
Armonk, NY 10504-1131, USA

Williams, Bernard (Football Player)
Philadelphia Eagles
1570 Waverly Ave
Memphis, TN 38106-2424, USA

Williams, Bert (Actor)
Susan Nathe
8281 Melrose Ave Ste 200
Los Angeles, CA 90046-6890, USA

Williams, Betty (Nobel Prize Laureate)
Orchardville Gardens
Finaghy
Belfast 10, NORTHERN IRELAND

Williams, Billy (Cinematographer)
Coah House
Hawkshill Place Esher
Surrey KT10 9HY, UNITED KINGDOM
(UK)

Williams, Billy Dee (Actor)
18411 Hatteras St Unit 204
Tarzana, CA 91356-1989, USA

Williams, Billy Dee (Actor)
c/o Staff Member Artist Agency, THE (NY)
230 W 55th St Apt 29D
New York, NY 10019-5206, USA

Williams, Bob A (Football Player)
602 Stone Bam Road
Towson, MD 21286, USA

Williams, Branden (Actor)
c/o Edward G (Eddie) Horowitz Creative
Management Group (CMG)
8522 National Blvd Ste 108
Culver City, CA 90232-2454, USA

Williams, Brian (Correspondent,
Television Host)
c/o Staff Member NBC Nightly News
30 Rockefeller Plz # 300S
New York, NY 10112-0015, USA

Williams, Brian (Football Player)
New York Giants
1725 Charleston Ln
Waconia, MN 55387-4539, USA

Williams, Brian (Football Player)
Green Bay Packers
1133 Ashington Pl
Desoto, TX 75115-7419, USA

Williams, Bruce (Entertainer)
PO Box 2095
Elfers, FL 34680-2095, USA

Williams, Bryan (Baby) (Musician)
c/o Staff Member Universal Music Group
(UMG - LA)
2220 Colorado Ave
Santa Monica, CA 90404-3506, USA

Williams, C K (Writer)
Princeton University
English Dept
Princeton, NJ 08544-0001, USA

Williams, Calvin (Football Player)
Philadelphia Eagles
5032 Yellowwood Ave
Baltimore, MD 21209-4602, USA

Williams, Cara (Actor)
Dann
9903 Santa Monica Blvd # 606
Beverly Hills, CA 90212-1606, USA

Williams, Carlton (Football Player)
San Francisco 49ers
5 Pinegate Ct
Peachtree City, GA 30269-1144, USA

Williams, Carnell 'Cadillac' (Football
Player)
c/o Ben Dogra Creative Artists Agency
LCC (CAA-LA)
2000 Avenue Of The Stars
Los Angeles, CA 90067-4700, USA

Williams, Charlie (Football Player)
Dallas Cowboys
2607 Encina
Irving, TX 75038-5559, USA

Williams, Chris (Actor)
c/o Carolyn Govers Artist Management
1118 15th St Apt 1
Santa Monica, CA 90403-5580, USA

Williams, Chris (Football Player)
Phoenix Cardinals
2851 E Nunneley Rd
Gilbert, AZ 85296-8887, USA

Williams, Chris A (Football Player)
Buffalo Bills
2800 Christopher Blvd
Hamburg, NY 14075-3456, USA

Williams, Christy (Artist)
PO Box 849
Lopez Island, WA 98261-0849, USA

Williams, Cindy (Actor)
Sterling/Winters
10877 Wilshire Blvd # 15
Los Angeles, CA 90024-4341, USA

Williams, Clarence (Football Player)
Green Bay Packers
4724 Vine St
Cincinnati, OH 45217-1254, USA

Williams, Clarence (Journalist)
Los Angeles Times
202 W 1st St
Editorial Dept
Los Angeles, CA 90012-4105, USA

Williams, Cliff (Musician)
11 Leominster Road
Morden
Surrey SA4 6HN, UNITED KINGDOM
(UK)

Williams, Clyde (Baseball Player)
Cleveland Buckeyes
17135 San Juan Dr
Detroit, MI 48221-2622, USA

Williams, Clyde (Football Player)
St Louis Cardinals
9754 Highway 79
Bethany, LA 71007, USA

Williams, Colleen (Correspondent)
KNBC-TV
News Dept
3000 W Alameda Ave
Burbank, CA 91523-0001, USA

Williams, Cress (Actor)
c/o Staff Member *William Morris Agency (WMA-LA)*
1 William Morris Pl
Beverly Hills, CA 90212-4261, USA

Williams, Curtis (Musician)
Neal Hollander Agency
9966 Majorca Pl
Boca Raton, FL 33434-3714, USA

Williams, Cynda (Actor)
Innovative Artists
1505 10th St
Santa Monica, CA 90401-2805, USA

Williams, Dafydd R (David) (Astronaut)
NASA
2101 Nasa Pkwy
Johnson Space Center
Houston, TX 77058-3691, USA

Williams, Dana (Musician)
Dreamcatcher Artists Mgmt
2908 Poston Ave
Nashville, TN 37203-1312, USA

Williams, Daniel (General)
Governor General's Office
Botanical Gardens
Saint George's, GRENADA

Williams, Danny (Boxer)
c/o Frank Warren *Sports Network*
Centurion House
Bircherley Green
Hertford HERTS SG14 1AP, UNITED KINGDOM (UK)

Williams, Darnell (Actor)
Stone Manners
6500 Wilshire Blvd Ste 550
Los Angeles, CA 90048-4950, USA

Williams, Darryl (Football Player)
Cincinnati Bengals
7351 Peppertree Cir S
Davie, FL 33314-6922, USA

Williams, David (Athlete, Football Player)
109 E Oxford St
Valley Stream, NY 11580-4622, USA

Williams, David (Football Player)
Houston Oilers
30201 Redtree Dr
Leesburg, FL 34748-9584, USA

Williams, David (Football Player)
St Louis Cardinals
30826 Tanoa Rd
Evergreen, CO 80439-7963, USA

Williams, David G T (Educator)
Emmanuel College
Cambridge CB2 3AP, UNITED KINGDOM (UK)

Williams, David W (Football Player)
108 E Oxford St
Valley Stream, NY 11580, USA

Williams, Delvin (Football Player)
San Francisco 49ers
173 Sierra Vista Ave Apt 11
Mountain View, CA 94043-4468, USA

Williams, Deniece (Musician)
Green Light Talent Agency
PO Box 3172
Beverly Hills, CA 90212-0172, USA

Williams, Deron (Basketball Player)
c/o Staff Member *Utah Jazz*
301 W South Temple
Delta Center
Salt Lake City, UT 84101-1216, USA

Williams, Derwin (Football Player)
New England Patriots
12014 Windermere Crossing Cir
Winter Garden, FL 34787-5518, USA

Williams, Dick
3680 Madrid St
Las Vegas, NV 89121-3415, USA

Williams, Dick Anthony (Actor)
Abrams Artists
9200 W Sunset Blvd Ste 1125
Los Angeles, CA 90069-3610, USA

Williams, Don (Musician, Songwriter, Writer)
Kathy Gangwisch
5100 Harris Ave
Kansas City, MO 64133-2331, USA

Williams, Donald E (Astronaut)
Science Applications Int'l
2200 Space Park Dr Ste 200
Houston, TX 77058-3678, USA

Williams, Doug (Comedian)
c/o James Kellem *JKA Talent & Literary Agency*
12725 Ventura Blvd Ste H
Studio City, CA 91604-2437, USA

Williams, Douglas L (Doug) (Coach, Football Coach, Football Player)
Tampa Bay Buccaneers
10120 Lemon Rd
Zachary, LA 70791-6407, USA

Williams, Dudley (Dancer)
Alvin Alley American Dance Foundation
211 W 61st St # 300
New York, NY 10023-7832, USA

Williams, E Virginia (Choreographer, Director)
Boston Ballet
19 Clarendon St
Boston, MA 02116-6100, USA

Williams, Easy (Actor)
Judy Schoen
606 N Larchmont Blvd Ste 309
Los Angeles, CA 90004-1309, USA

Williams, Ed (Football Player)
Cincinnati Bengals
521 Royal Ave
Oklahoma City, OK 73130-2719, USA

Williams, Edy (Actor, Model)
PO Box 6325
Woodland Hills, CA 91365-6325, USA

Williams, Eli (Baseball Player)
St Louis Stars
214 Thomas Ct NW
Fort Walton Beach, FL 32548-4139, USA

Williams, Ellery (Football Player)
New York Giants
1987 Wimbledon Pl
Los Altos, CA 94024-7062, USA

Williams, Elmo (Director, Producer)
1249 Iris St
Brookings, OR 97415-9643, USA

Williams, Eric (Basketball Player)
c/o Staff Member *Toronto Raptors*
20 Bay St #1702
Toronto, ON M5J 2N8, CANADA

Williams, Eric (Football Player)
c/o Staff Member *Pittsburgh Steelers*
3400 S Water St
Pittsburgh, PA 15203-2349, USA

Williams, Eric (Football Player)
c/o Staff Member *Saint Louis Cardinals (St Louis Cardinals)*
250 Stadium Plz
Saint Louis, MO 63102, USA

Williams, Eric M (Football Player)
Detroit Lions
13330 Noel Rd Apt 825
Dallas, TX 75240-5092, USA

Williams, Erik (Football Player)
Dallas Cowboys
1 Wortham Ct
Bear, DE 19701-2060, USA

Williams, Ernie (Football Player)
Washington Redskins
45 Oakwood Dr
Chapel Hill, NC 27517-5650, USA

Williams, Esther (Actor, Swimmer)
9377 Readcrest Dr
Beverly Hills, CA 90210-2532, USA

Williams, Eugene (Baseball Player)
Memphis Red Sox
110 Townsend Rd
Oak Ridge, TN 37830-5566, USA

Williams, Frank (Baseball Player)
Memphis Red Sox
9283 Medallion Way
Sacramento, CA 95826-4643, USA

Williams, Frank (Basketball Player)
New York Knicks
2 Penn Plz
Madison Square Garden
New York, NY 10121-1703, USA

Williams, Freeman (Basketball Player)
450 W 41st Pl
Los Angeles, CA 90037-2119, USA

Williams, Gary (Basketball Player, Coach)
University of Maryland
Athletic Dept
College Park, MD 20742-0001, USA

Williams, Gary Anthony (Actor)
c/o Staff Member *Innovative Artists (LA)*
1505 10th St
Santa Monica, CA 90401-2805, USA

Williams, Gerald (Football Player)
Pittsburgh Steelers
9613 Callis Ct
Harrisburg, NC 28075-9619, USA

Williams, Gluyas (Cartoonist)
New Yorker Magazine
4 Times Sq
Editorial Dept
New York, NY 10036-6592, USA

Williams, Greg (Actor)
1680 Vine St Ste 604
Los Angeles, CA 90028-8833, USA

Williams, Gregg (Coach, Football Coach)
Buffalo Bills
1 Bills Dr
Orchard Park, NY 14127-2237, USA

Williams, Gregory Alan (Actor)
c/o Staff Member *Pakula/King & Associates*
9229 W Sunset Blvd Ste 315
Los Angeles, CA 90069-3403, USA

Williams, Hal (Actor)
Marter
PO Box 14227
Palm Desert, CA 92255-4227, USA

Williams, Harland (Actor)
Brillstein/Grey
9150 Wilshire Blvd Ste 350
Beverly Hills, CA 90212-3453, USA

Williams, Harold M (Misc)
J Paul Getty Museum
1200 Getty Center Dr
Getty Center
Los Angeles, CA 90049-1687, USA

Williams, Herb (Basketball Player)
4500 Bentley Dr
Plano, TX 75093-7149, USA

Williams, Hershel W (War Hero)
3450 Wire Branch Rd
Ona, WV 25545-9513, USA

Williams, Howard E (Howie) (Basketball Player)
1940 Hamilton Ln
Carmel, IN 46032-3521, USA

Williams, Howard L (Howie) (Football Player)
Green Bay Packers
4731 Proctor Ave
Oakland, CA 94618-2540, USA

Williams, Hype (Director, Producer)
Creative Artists Agency
9830 Wilshire Blvd
Beverly Hills, CA 90212-1804, USA

Williams, Ivy (Writer)
Mediachase
834 N Harper Ave
Los Angeles, CA 90046-6804, USA

Williams, Jaimie (Actor)
1019 Kane Concourse Ste 202
Bay Harbor Islands, FL 33154-2138, USA

Williams, Jamal (Football Player)
San Diego Chargers
4020 Murphy Canyon Rd
San Diego, CA 92123-4407, USA

Williams, James A (General)
8928 Maurice Ln
Annandale, VA 22003-3914, USA

Williams, James A (Froggy) (Football Player)
296 Sugarberry Cir
Houston, TX 77024-7248, USA

Williams, James D (Admiral)
1111A N Stuart St
Arlington, VA 22201-4781, USA

Williams, James F (Jimmy) (Baseball Player)
1401 Olde Post Rd
Palm Harbor, FL 34683-1470, USA

Williams, James O (Football Player)
Chicago Bears
330 S Western Ave
Lake Forest, IL 60045-3245, USA

Williams, Jay (Basketball Player)
Chicago Bulls
1901 W Madison St
United Center
Chicago, IL 60612-2459, USA

Williams, Jay (Football Player)
Los Angeles Rams
1503 Alydar Ct
Waxhaw, NC 28173-6672, USA

Williams, Jayson (Basketball Player, Sportscaster)
NBC-TV
30 Rockefeller Plz Ste 270E
Sports Dept
New York, NY 10112-0299, USA

Williams, Jeff (Football Player)
Los Angeles Rams
9710 15th Ave NW
Seattle, WA 98117-2314, USA

Williams, Jeffrey N (Astronaut)
17303 Saturn Ln
Houston, TX 77058-2295, USA

Williams, Jerome (Basketball Player)
Toronto Raptors
Air Canada Center
40 Bay St
Toronto, ON M5J 2N8, CANADA

Williams, Jerrol (Football Player)
Pittsburgh Steelers
2562 Mizzoni Cir
Henderson, NV 89052-4926, USA

Williams, Jerry (Football Player)
941 W Oden Bay Rd
Sandpoint, ID 83864-8615, USA

Williams, Jessica (Musician)
c/o Staff Member *Diva Central Inc*
7510 W Sunset Blvd Ste 1445
Los Angeles, CA 90046-3408, USA

Williams, Jimy (Baseball Player)
1401 Olde Post Rd
Palm Harbor, FL 34683-1470, USA

Williams, JoBeth (Actor)
c/o Staff Member *Innovative Artists (LA)*
1505 10th St
Santa Monica, CA 90401-2805, USA

Williams, Jody (Nobel Prize Laureate)
663 Lancaster St
Fredericksburg, VA 22405-2447, USA

Williams, Joel (Football Player)
Atlanta Falcons
PO Box 311802
Atlanta, GA 31131-1802, USA

Williams, Joel (Football Player)
Miami Dolphins
1515 Penn Ave Apt 305
Wilkinsburg, PA 15221-2659, USA

Williams, John (Composer, Musician)
Askonas Holt Ltd
27 Chancery Lane
London WC2A 1PF, UNITED KINGDOM
(UK)

Williams, John A (Writer)
693 Forest Ave
Teaneck, NJ 07666-2042, USA

Williams, John C (Athlete)
718 David Rd
Santa Maria, CA 93455-4931, USA

Williams, John E (Football Player)
Washington Redskins
33211 Blue Fin Dr
Dana Point, CA 92629-1416, USA

Williams, John L (Football Player)
Seattle Seahawks
1709 Husson Ave
Palatka, FL 32177-5809, USA

Williams, John M (Football Player)
Baltimore Colts
2222 Victory Memorial Dr
Minneapolis, MN 55412-1116, USA

Williams, John T (Actor, Composer)
c/o Staff Member *Gorfaine/Schwartz Agency Inc*
4111 W Alameda Ave Ste 509
Burbank, CA 91505-4171, USA

Williams, John T (Composer, Conductor, Musician)
333 Loring Ave
Los Angeles, CA 90024-2640, USA

Williams, Joseph R (Publisher)
Memphis Commercial Appeal
495 Union Ave
Memphis, TN 38103-3217, USA

Williams, Kameelah (Musician)
Creative Artists Agency
9830 Wilshire Blvd
Beverly Hills, CA 90212-1804, USA

Williams, Karl (Football Player)
Tampa Bay Buccaneers
6502 Falcon St
Rowlett, TX 75089-8260, USA

Williams, Katt (Actor, Comedian)
c/o Staff Member *William Morris Agency (WMA-LA)*
1 William Morris Pl
Beverly Hills, CA 90212-4261, USA

Williams, Kelli (Actor, Musician)
c/o Beth Colt *Gateway Management Partners*
5225 Wilshire Blvd Ste 702
Los Angeles, CA 90036-4351, USA

Williams, Kevin (Football Player)
Washington Redskins
5715 Baltimore Dr Unit 148
La Mesa, CA 91942-4246, USA

Williams, Kevin (Football Player)
Dallas Cowboys
2201 Long Prairie Rd # 107-384
Flower Mound, TX 75022-4832, USA

Williams, Kevin (Football Player)
Minnesota Vikings
9520 Viking Dr
Eden Prairie, MN 55344-3898, USA

Williams, Kiely Alexis (Actor, Musician)
c/o Dina Shapiro *Wright-Crear Management*
3815 Hughes Ave
Culver City, CA 90232-2715, USA

Williams, Kimberly (Actor, Producer)
c/o Michael Nilon *Creative Artists Agency LCC (CAA-LA)*
2000 Avenue Of The Stars
Los Angeles, CA 90067-4700, USA

Williams, Kimberly Kevon (Actor)
c/o TJ Stein *Stein Entertainment Group*
11271 Ventura Blvd # 477
Studio City, CA 91604-3136, USA

Williams, Lee E (Football Player)
11651 NW 4th St
Plantation, FL 33325-2509, USA

Williams, Lewis T (Scientist)
Howard Hughes Medical Institute
5323 Harry Hines Blvd
Dallas, TX 75390-7208, USA

Williams, Lorenzo (Basketball Player)
2731 Via Capri Unit 924
Clearwater, FL 33764-3993, USA

Williams, Lucinda (Musician, Songwriter, Writer)
Azoff Music
1100 Glendon Ave Ste 2000
Los Angeles, CA 90024-3524, USA

Williams, Lynn R (Misc)
Harvard University
79 Jfk St
Politics Institute
Cambridge, MA 02138-5801, USA

Williams, Maiya (Producer)
c/o Staff Member *Principal Entertainment (LA)*
1964 Westwood Blvd Ste 400
Los Angeles, CA 90025-4695, USA

Williams, Malinda (Actor)
c/o Staff Member *Leverage Management*
1610 Broadway
Santa Monica, CA 90404-2792, USA

Williams, Mark (Bowler)
Professional Bowlers Assn
719 2nd Ave Ste 701
Seattle, WA 98104-1747, USA

Williams, Mary Alice (Correspondent)
NYNEX Corp
1113 Westchester Ave
Public Relations Dept
White Plains, NY 10604, USA

Williams, Mason (Composer, Musician)
13479 SE Lost Lake Dr
Prineville, OR 97754-8487, USA

Williams, Matt (Writer)
Zeiderman
211 E 48th St
New York, NY 10017-1538, USA

Williams, Maurice (Musician)
Willis Blume Agency, The
PO Box 509
Orangeburg, SC 29116-0509, USA

Williams, Maurice J (Misc)
Overseas Development Council
1875 Connecticut Ave NW
Washington, DC 20009-5728, USA

Williams, Maxie (Football Player)
Houston Oilers
624 Squaw Run Rd
Ellwood City, PA 16117-6958, USA

Williams, Merriwether (Artist)
c/o Staff Member *Endeavor Agency LLC (LA)*
9601 Wilshire Blvd Fl 3
Beverly Hills, CA 90210-5204, USA

Williams, Michael (Actor)
Michael Whitehall
125 Gloucester Road
London SW7 4TE, UNITED KINGDOM (UK)

Williams, Michael D (Mike) (Baseball Player)
240 Horseshoe Farm Rd
Pembroke, VA 24136-3480, USA

Williams, Michael J (General)
Assistant Commander In Chief
Hqsmc 2 Navy St
Washington, DC 20380-0001, USA

Williams, Michael L (Actor)
Julian Belfarge
46 Albermarle St
London W1X 4PP, UNITED KINGDOM (UK)

Williams, Micheal (Basketball Player)
1415 Reynoldston Ln
Dallas, TX 75232-2411, USA

Williams, Michelle (Actor, Director, Producer, Writer)
c/o Hylda Queally *Creative Artists Agency LCC (CAA-LA)*
2000 Avenue Of The Stars
Los Angeles, CA 90067-4700, USA

Williams, Mike (Football Player)
Detroit Lions
2152 NW 74th Ave
Hollywood, FL 33024-1058, USA

Williams, Mike (Football Player)
Buffalo Bills
1 Bills Dr
Orchard Park, NY 14127-2237, USA

Williams, Mikell (Football Player)
San Diego Chargers
222 W Edwards St
Covington, LA 70433-1626, USA

Williams, Mitch (Baseball Player)
Texas Rangers
67 Highbridge Blvd
Medford, NJ 08055-3341, USA

Williams, Montel B (Actor, Director, Producer, Talk Show Host)
The Montel Williams Show
433 W 53rd St Fl 2
New York, NY 10019-5603, USA

Williams, Natalie (Basketball Player)
Indiana Fever
125 S Pennsylvania St
Conseco Fieldhouse
Indianapolis, IN 46204-3610, USA

Williams, Natashia (Actor)
c/o Teresa Valente *Beverly Hecht Agency*
3500 W Olive Ave Ste 1180
Burbank, CA 91505-4651, USA

Williams, Nick (Football Player)
Cincinnati Bengals
21760 Parklane St
Farmington Hills, MI 48335-4221, USA

Williams, O L (Religious Leader)
United Free Will Baptist Church
1101 J E Reddick Cir
Kinston, NC 28501, USA

Williams, Oliver (Football Player)
Indianapolis Colts
11924 Daleside Ave
Hawthorne, CA 90250-1925, USA

Williams, Olivia (Actor)
c/o Risa Shapiro *International Creative Management (ICM-LA)*
10250 Constellation Blvd
Los Angeles, CA 90067-6200, USA

Williams, Otis (Musician)
Barry Pollock Associates
9255 W Sunset Blvd Ste 404
Los Angeles, CA 90069-3364, USA

Williams, Parker (Adult Film Star)
c/o Staff Member *Diva Central Inc*
7510 W Sunset Blvd Ste 1445
Los Angeles, CA 90046-3408, USA

Williams, Pat (Football Player)
DVA Brand Communications
1968 W Adams Blvd Ste 205
C/O Danielle Gibbs
Los Angeles, CA 90018-3510, USA

Williams, Patrick (Musician)
3156 Mandeville Canyon Rd
Los Angeles, CA 90049-1014, USA

Williams, Perry (Football Player)
New York Giants
273 Old Laurinburg Rd
Hamlet, NC 28345-8069, USA

Williams, Perry (Football Player)
Green Bay Packers
480 Canyon Oaks Dr Apt A
Oakland, CA 94605-3858, USA

Williams, Pharell (Actor, Composer)
c/o Staff Member Brillstein-Grey Entertainment
9150 Wilshire Blvd Ste 350
Beverly Hills, CA 90212-3453, USA

Williams, Pharrell (Musician)
c/o David Schiff Schiff Company
9465 Wilshire Blvd Ste 480
Beverly Hills, CA 90212-2603, USA

Williams, Phillip L (Publisher)
Los Angeles Times
202 W 1st St
Editorial Dept
Los Angeles, CA 90012-4105, USA

Williams, Prince Charles (Boxer)
Boxing Ministry
3675 Polley Dr
Austintown, OH 44515-3349, USA

Williams, R J
1505 10th St
Santa Monica, CA 90401-2805, USA

Williams, Randy (Athlete, Track Athlete)
5655 N Marty Ave Apt 204
Fresno, CA 93711-1575, USA

Williams, Reggie (Baseball Player)
Los Angeles Dodgers
9300 Clearstone Cv
Collierville, TN 38017-9414, USA

Williams, Reggie (Baseball Player)
California Angels
10 Percy St
Charleston, SC 29403-5312, USA

Williams, Reggie (Basketball Player)
2016 Callaway St
Temple Hills, MD 20748-4354, USA

Williams, Reginald (Reggie) (Football Player)
Cincinnati Bengals
503 Jennifer Ln
Windermere, FL 34786-8400, USA

Williams, Reuben (Baseball Player)
Chicago American Giants
PO Box 3982
Winter Haven, FL 33885-3982, USA

Williams, Richard H (Dick) (Baseball Player)
PO Box 778057
Henderson, NV 89077-8057, USA

Williams, Rick (Baseball Player)
Houston Astros
1217 Wessmith Way
Madera, CA 93638-1854, USA

Williams, Robert (Artist)
c/o Staff Member Fantagraphics Books
7563 Lake City Way NE
Seattle, WA 98115-4218, USA

Williams, Robert (Baseball Player)
Newark Eagles
6233 Delancey St
Philadelphia, PA 19143-1019, USA

Williams, Robert A (Football Player)
Chicago Bears
602 Stone Barn Rd
Towson, MD 21286-1418, USA

Williams, Robert C (Football Player)
Dallas Cowboys
347 Walnut Grove Ln
Coppell, TX 75019-5342, USA

Williams, Robert Cary
c/o Staff Member Robert Cary Williams
5 Claremont Villas, Southampton Way
Camberwell
London, England 8E4 96W, UNITED KINGDOM (UK)

Williams, Robert J (Ben) (Football Player)
Buffalo Bills
5961 Huntview Dr
Jackson, MS 39206-2128, USA

Williams, Robert (Robbie) (Musician)
c/o Jeff Frasco Creative Artists Agency LCC (CAA-LA)
2000 Avenue Of The Stars
Los Angeles, CA 90067-4700, USA

Williams, Robin (Actor, Comedian)
c/o Staff Member Blue Wolf Productions
3145 Geary Blvd # 524
San Francisco, CA 94118-3316, USA

Williams, Roderick (Opera Singer)
Van Walsum Mgmt
4 Addison Bridge Place
London W14 8XP, UNITED KINGDOM (UK)

Williams, Rodney (Football Player)
St Louis Rams
44520 15th St E Unit 3
Lancaster, CA 93535-6321, USA

Williams, Roger (Musician)
16150 Clear Valley Pl
Encino, CA 91436-3312, USA

Williams, Roland (Football Player)
St Louis Rams
305 Elmdorf Ave
Rochester, NY 14619-1823, USA

Williams, Rosel (Baseball Player)
Birmingham Black Barons
204 Little Mountain Rd
Ninety Six, SC 29666-9253, USA

Williams, Roshumba (Model)
c/o Gail Parenteau Parenteau Guidance
132 E 35th St # 3J
New York, NY 10016-3892, USA

Williams, Rowan (Religious Leader)
Lambert Palace
London SE1 9JU, UNITED KINGDOM (UK)

Williams, Roy (Coach)
University of North Carlonia
PO Box 2126
Chapel Hill, NC 27515-2126, USA

Williams, Roy (Football Player)
Dallas Cowboys
1 Cowboys Pkwy
Irving, TX 75063-4999, USA

Williams, Sam (Baseball Player)
Birmingham Black Barons
3314 Coldwater Dr
San Jose, CA 95148-1211, USA

Williams, Sam (Football Player)
Los Angeles Rams
28960 Westfield St
Livonia, MI 48150-3137, USA

Williams, Sam B (Inventor)
Williams International
2280 E West Maple Rd
Commerce Township, MI 48390-3828, USA

Williams, Scott (Basketball Player)
Phoenix Suns
201 E Jefferson St
Phoenix, AZ 85004-2412, USA

Williams, Scott (Football Player)
Detroit Lions
284 Heathrow Dr
Riverdale, GA 30274-2729, USA

Williams, Serena (Tennis Player)
c/o Staff Member Women's Tennis Association (WTA (US))
1 Progress Plz Ste 1500
St Petersburg, FL 33701-4335, USA

Williams, Shad (Baseball Player)
California Angels
4682 E Cornell Ave
Fresno, CA 93703-1607, USA

Williams, Shaun (Football Player)
New York Giants
11738 Gruen St
Lake View Terrace, CA 91342-6117, USA

Williams, Sherman (Football Player)
Dallas Cowboys
119 Patricia Ave
Prichard, AL 36610-2114, USA

Williams, Sidney (Football Player)
Cleveland Browns
1044 W 82nd St
Los Angeles, CA 90044-3518, USA

Williams, Simon (Actor)
Rebecca Blond Assoc
69A Kings Road
London SW3 4NX, UNITED KINGDOM (UK)

Williams, Stanley W (Stan) (Baseball Player)
Los Angeles Dodgers
4702 Hayter Ave
Lakewood, CA 90712-3509, USA

Williams, Stepfret (Football Player)
Dallas Cowboys
913 S Talton St
Minden, LA 71055-5448, USA

Williams, Stephanie E (Actor)
S M S Talent
8730 W Sunset Blvd Ste 440
Los Angeles, CA 90069-2277, USA

Williams, Stephen (Misc)
1017 Foothills Trl
Santa Fe, NM 87505-4537, USA

Williams, Stephen F (Judge)
US Court of Appeals
333 Constitution Ave NW
Washington, DC 20001-2866, USA

Williams, Steven (Actor)
Geddes Agency
8430 Santa Monica Blvd Ste 200
West Hollywood, CA 90069-4253, USA

Williams, T Franklin (Doctor)
Monroe Community Hospital
Director's Office
Rochester, NY 14620, USA

Williams, Tamika (Basketball Player)
Minnesota Lunx
600 1st Ave N
Target Center
Minneapolis, MN 55403-1400, USA

Williams, Terry (Musician)
Damage Mgmt
16 Lambton Place
London W11 2SH, UNITED KINGDOM (UK)

Williams, Terry Tempest
Brandt & Brandt Literary Agency
1501 Broadway
New York, NY 10036-5601, USA

Williams, Thomas S Cardinal (Religious Leader)
Viard
21 Eccleston Hill Po Box 198
Wellington 1, NEW ZEALAND

Williams, Todd (Baseball Player)
Los Angeles Dodgers
6244 Fly Rd
East Syracuse, NY 13057-9337, USA

Williams, Tonya Lee (Actor)
Artists Agency
1180 S Beverly Dr Ste 301
Los Angeles, CA 90035-1154, USA

Williams, Treat (Actor)
c/o Josh Katz United Talent Agency (UTA)
9560 Wilshire Blvd Ste 500
Beverly Hills, CA 90212-2401, USA

Williams, Tyrone (Football Player)
Dallas Cowboys
9516 Valley Ranch Pkwy E Apt 1024
Irving, TX 75063-7851, USA

Williams, Ulis (Athlete, Track Athlete)
2511 29th St
Santa Monica, CA 90405-2913, USA

Williams, Van (Actor)
Pierce & Shelly
612 Lighthouse Ave # 220
Pacific Grove, CA 93950-2615, USA

Williams, Van (Football Player)
Buffalo Bills
1804 Parkwood Ln Apt 26
Johnson City, TN 37604-7784, USA

Williams, Vanessa L (Actor, Musician)
c/o Brad Cafarelli Bragman/Nyman/Cafarelli (BNC)
8687 Melrose Ave Fl 8
Pacific Design Center
Los Angeles, CA 90069-5701, USA

Williams, Vanessa P (Actor)
c/o Melisa Spamer Domain
9229 W Sunset Blvd Ste 415
West Hollywood, CA 90069-3404, USA

Williams, Venus (Athlete, Tennis Player)
c/o Lisa Sorensen LSPR
12198 Ventura Blvd Ste 210
Studio City, CA 91604-2542, USA

Williams, Victor L (Actor, Musician)
c/o Matt Altman Creative Artists Agency LCC (CAA-LA)
2000 Avenue Of The Stars
Los Angeles, CA 90067-4700, USA

Williams, Victoria (Musician, Songwriter, Writer)
PO Box 342
Joshua Tree, CA 92252-0342, USA

Williams, W Clyde (Religious Leader)
Christian Methodist Episcopal Church
4466 E Presley Blvd
Memphis, TN 38116, USA

Williams, Wade (Actor, Director, Producer, Writer)
c/o Stacey Bock-McLaughlin Principal Entertainment (LA)
1964 Westwood Blvd Ste 400
Los Angeles, CA 90025-4695, USA

Williams, Wallace (Baseball Player)
Pittsburgh Crawfords
213 Yosemite Dr
Pittsburgh, PA 15235-2045, USA

Williams, Walt (Baseball Player)
Houston Colt .45's
2417 Monterey St
Brownwood, TX 76801-7808, USA

Williams, Walt (Basketball Player)
3240 Beaumont St
Temple Hills, MD 20748-4541, USA

Williams, Walter (Baseball Player)
Newark Eagles
15700 Good Hope Rd
Silver Spring, MD 20905-4034, USA

Williams, Walter (Musician)
Associated Booking Corp
PO Box 2055
New York, NY 10021-0051, USA

Williams, Wendy (Radio Personality)
WBLS
3 Park Ave Fl 41
New York, NY 10016-5902, USA

Williams, Wendy Lian (Swimmer)
Advantage International
1025 Thomas Jefferson St NW # 450
Washington, DC 20007-5201, USA

Williams, William A (Astronaut)
Environmental Protection Agency
200 SW 35th St
Corvallis, OR 97333-4902, USA

Williams, Willie (Baseball Player)
Newark Eagles
2729 20th St
Sarasota, FL 34234-7807, USA

Williams, Willie (Football Player)
New York Giants
4928 Country Club Dr
Mesquite, TX 75150-1169, USA

Williams, Willie (Football Player)
Pittsburgh Steelers
1402 Forest Edge Ct
Wexford, PA 15090-9598, USA

Williams, Woody (Baseball Player)
Toronto Blue Jays
1180 County Road 136A
Alvin, TX 77511-1584, USA

Williams & Ree
PO Box 163
Hendersonville, TN 37077-0163, USA

Williams III, Clarence (Actor)
Flick East-West
9057 Nemo St # A
West Hollywood, CA 90069-5511, USA

Williams III, Clearance (Actor)
c/o Staff Member *Abrams Artists Agency (LA)*
9200 W Sunset Blvd Ph 11
Los Angeles, CA 90069-3601, USA

Williams Jr, Hank (Musician, Songwriter, Writer)
c/o Greg Oswald *William Morris Agency (WMA-TN)*
1600 Division St Ste 300
Nashville, TN 37203-2755, USA

Williams Jr, Redford B (Misc)
Duke University
Medical School
Box 3708
Durham, NC 27706, USA

Williams Jr, Robin M (Scientist)
414 Oak Ave
Ithaca, NY 14850-4822, USA

Williams Jr, Walter Ray (Bowler)
6503 NW 223rd St
Micanopy, FL 32667-7539, USA

Williams Jr, Warren (Football Player)
Pittsburgh Steelers
1935 Pauldo St
Fort Myers, FL 33916-4122, USA

Williams of Crosby, Shirley V T B (Government Official)
House of Lords
Westminster
London SW1A 0PW, UNITED KINGDOM (UK)

Williams of Elvel, Charles C P (Government Official)
48 Thurloe Square
London SW7 2SX, UNITED KINGDOM (UK)

Williamson, Antone (Baseball Player)
Milwaukee Brewers
9419 S Stanley Pl
Tempe, AZ 85284-4109, USA

Williamson, Corliss (Basketball Player)
c/o Staff Member *Sacramento Kings*
1 Sports Pkwy
Arco Arena
Sacramento, CA 95834-2301, USA

Williamson, Fred (Actor, Football Player)
H David Moss
733 Seward St Ph
Los Angeles, CA 90038-3503, USA

Williamson, Jay (Golfer)
24 Clermont Ln
Saint Louis, MO 63124-1346, USA

Williamson, Keith A (Misc)
National Westminster Bank
Fakenham
Norfolk, UNITED KINGDOM (UK)

Williamson, Kevin (Director, Producer, Writer)
c/o Staff Member *Outerbanks Entertainment*
9000 W Sunset Blvd Ste 1001
Los Angeles, CA 90069-5810, USA

Williamson, Marianne (Doctor)
Los Angeles Center for Living
8265 W Sunset Blvd
West Hollywood, CA 90046-2429, USA

Williamson, Mark (Baseball Player)
Baltimore Orioles
9321 Carmichael Dr
La Mesa, CA 91941-5629, USA

Williamson, Martha (Producer)
c/o Bob Broder *Broder Webb Chervin Silbermann Agency, The (BWCS)*
10250 Constellation Blvd Ste P
Los Angeles, CA 90067-6213, USA

Williamson, Matthew (Designer, Fashion Designer)
Beverly Cable
11 Saint Christopher's Place
London W1M 5HB, UNITED KINGDOM (UK)

Williamson, Michael (Journalist)
Washington Post
Editorial Dept
1150 15th St NW
Washington, DC 20071-0001, USA

Williamson, Michael (Writer)
10400 Hutting Pl
Silver Spring, MD 20902-4952, USA

Williamson, Mykelti (Actor)
c/o Jim Hess *Paradigm (LA)*
360 N Crescent Dr
North Bldg
Beverly Hills, CA 90210-6820, USA

Williamson, Nicol (Actor)
Jonathan Altaras
13 Shorts Gardens
London WC2H 9AT, UNITED KINGDOM (UK)

Williamson, Oliver E (Economist)
University of California
Economics Dept
Berkeley, CA 94720-0001, USA

Williamson, Scott (Baseball Player)
c/o Staff Member *Chicago Cubs*
1060 W Addison St
Wrigley Field
Chicago, IL 60613-4397, USA

Williamson, Shaun (Actor)
McIntosh Rae Management
Thornton House
Thornton Road
London SW19 4NG, ENGLAND

Williamson Jr, Samuel R (Educator)
University of the South
President's Office
Sewanee, TN 37375, USA

Willig, Matt (Football Player)
New York Jets
4241 Prado De Los Pajaros
Calabasas, CA 91302-3619, USA

Willingham, Larry (Football Player)
St Louis Cardinals
983 W Lagoon Ave
Gulf Shores, AL 36542-6301, USA

Willingham, Tyrone (Coach, Football Coach)
University of Washington
Athletic Dept
Seattle, WA 98195-0001, USA

Willis, Bruce W (Actor)
c/o Richard Lovett *Creative Artists Agency LCC (CAA-LA)*
2000 Avenue Of The Stars
Los Angeles, CA 90067-4700, USA

Willis, Carl (Baseball Player)
Detroit Tigers
6811 Lipscomb Dr
Durham, NC 27712-9292, USA

Willis, Dale (Baseball Player)
Kansas City A's
3415 Hayes Bayou Dr
Ruskin, FL 33570-6157, USA

Willis, Dave (Writer)
c/o Staff Member *William Morris Agency (WMA-LA)*
1 William Morris Pl
Beverly Hills, CA 90212-4261, USA

Willis, Dontrelle (Baseball Player)
c/o Staff Member *Florida Marlins*
2269 Dan Marino Blvd
Miami Gardens, FL 33056-2600, USA

Willis, Dontrelle (Baseball Player)
Florida Marlins
8110 Cedar Brush Cir
Spring, TX 77379-3508, USA

Willis, Fred (Football Player)
Cincinnati Bengals
31 Blithewood Ave Apt 601
Worcester, MA 01604-3558, USA

Willis, Garrett (Golfer)
211 Coyatee Shrs
Loudon, TN 37774-3177, USA

Willis, Gordon (Cinematographer)
11849 W Olympic Blvd # 100
Los Angeles, CA 90064-1155, USA

Willis, Jim (Artist)
5323 SW 53rd Ct
Portland, OR 97221-1937, USA

Willis, Jim (Baseball Player)
Chicago Cubs
PO Box 35
Boyce, LA 71409-0035, USA

Willis, Katherine (Actor)
c/o Heather Collier *Collier Talent Agency*
2313 Lake Austin Blvd # 103
Austin, TX 78703-4545, USA

Willis, Keith (Football Player)
Pittsburgh Steelers
116 Coffeeberry Ct
Garner, NC 27529-5934, USA

Willis, Kevin A (Basketball Player)
4970 Carriage Lakes Dr NE
Roswell, GA 30075-3159, USA

Willis, Mark (Musician)
c/o Staff Member *William Morris Agency (WMA-TN)*
1600 Division St Ste 300
Nashville, TN 37203-2755, USA

Willis, Mike (Baseball Player)
Toronto Blue Jays
6234 Taggart St
Houston, TX 77007-2051, USA

Willis, Mitch (Football Player)
Oakland Raiders
1398 Fairhaven Dr
Mansfield, TX 76063-3765, USA

Willis, Pete (Musician)
Q Prime Mgmt
729 7th Ave Rm 1400
New York, NY 10019-6889, USA

Willis, Peter Tom (Football Player)
Chicago Bears
PO Box 237
Morris, AL 35116-0237, USA

Willis, Rumer (Actor)
c/o Staff Member *Untitled Entertainment (LA)*
331 N Maple Dr Fl 3
Beverly Hills, CA 90210-3827, USA

Willis, William K (Bill) (Football Player)
Cleveland Rams
1715 Franklin Park S
Columbus, OH 43205-2217, USA

Willison, Mike (Musician)
Metropolitan Entertainment Group
2 Penn Plz Rm 1500
New York, NY 10121-1590, USA

Willman, David (Journalist)
Los Angeles Times
202 W 1st St
Editorial Dept
Los Angeles, CA 90012-4105, USA

Willmon, Trent (Musician)
Hallmark Direction Company
713 18th Ave S
C/O Shelia Shipley Biddy
Nashville, TN 37203-3214, USA

Willms, Andre (Athlete)
Rennebogen 94
Magdeburg 39130, GERMANY

Willoch, Kare I (Prime Minister)
Fr Nansens V 17
Lysaker 1324, NORWAY

Willoughby, Bill (Basketball Player)
350 W Englewood Ave
Englewood, NJ 07631-3239, USA

Willoughby, Jim (Baseball Player)
San Francisco Giants
PO Box 707
Eufaula, OK 74432-0707, USA

Wills, Bump (Baseball Player)
Texas Rangers
12118 E 25th Ave
Spokane Valley, WA 99206-5729, USA

Wills, Frank (Baseball Player)
Kansas City Royals
733 General Pershing St
New Orleans, LA 70115-1448, USA

Wills, Garry (Historian, Writer)
Northwestern University
History Dept
Evanston, IL 60201, USA

Wills, Maurice M (Maury) (Athlete, Baseball Player)
Los Angeles Dodgers
5 Dalton Valley Dr
M And R Sports Marketing
Saint Peters, MO 63376-7720, USA

Wills, Rick (Musician)
Hard to Handle Mgmt
16501 Ventura Blvd Ste 602
Encino, CA 91436-2072, USA

Wills, Ted (Baseball Player)
Boston Red Sox
10585 E Duckpoint Way
Clovis, CA 93619-4629, USA

Willson, John (Business Person)
Placer Dome Inc
1600-1055 Dunsmuir St
Vancouver, BC V7X 1P1, CANADA

Willson-Piper, Marty (Musician)
Globeshine
101 Chamberlayne Road
London NW10 3ND, UNITED KINGDOM (UK)

Willumstad, Robert (Financier)
Citigroup Inc
399 Park Ave
New York, NY 10022-4699, USA

Wilmarth, Dick (Misc)
1111 F St
Anchorage, AK 99501-4344, USA

Wilmer, Douglas (Actor)
Julian Belfarge
46 Albermarle St
London W1X 4PP, UNITED KINGDOM (UK)

Wilmer, Harry A (Psychic)
Texas Health Science Center
Psychiatric Dept
San Antonio, TX 78284, USA

Wilmet, Paul (Baseball Player)
Texas Rangers
PO Box 330074
Nashville, TN 37203-7500, USA

Wilmore, Barry E (Astronaut)
3002 Bryant Ln
Webster, TX 77598-6011, USA

Wilmsmeyer, Klaus (Football Player)
San Francisco 49ers
8209 Paddington Dr
Louisville, KY 40222-5542, USA

Wilmut, Ian (Misc)
Roslin Institute
Roslin Bio Centre
Midlothian EH25 9PS, SCOTLAND

Wilpon, Fred (Baseball Player)
New York Mets
100 Sheep Ln
Locust Valley, NY 11560-1115, USA

Wilson, A N (Writer)
21 Arlington Road
London NW1 7ER, UNITED KINGDOM (UK)

Wilson, Al (Musician)
Talent Consultants International
105 Shad Row Ste B
Piermont, NY 10968-3001, USA

Wilson, Al (Football Player)
Denver Broncos
11561 Warrington Ct
Parker, CO 80138-8735, USA

Wilson, Alexander G (Sandy) (Composer, Writer)
2 Southwell Gardens
#4
London SW7 4SB, UNITED KINGDOM (UK)

Wilson, Alexandra (Actor)
c/o Staff Member *GVA Talent Agency Inc*
9229 W Sunset Blvd Ste 320
Los Angeles, CA 90069-3403, USA

Wilson, Ann (Musician)
H K Mgmt
9200 W Sunset Blvd Ste 530
Los Angeles, CA 90069-3509, USA

Wilson, Archie (Baseball Player)
New York Yankees
1620 Woodland St SE
Decatur, AL 35601-5242, USA

Wilson, Artie (Baseball Player)
New York Giants
2226 NE 10th Ave
Portland, OR 97212-4018, USA

Wilson, Ben (Football Player)
Los Angeles Rams
702 Maple St
Crossett, AR 71635-3520, USA

Wilson, Bill (Baseball Player)
Chicago White Sox
64245 Doral Dr
Desert Hot Springs, CA 92240-1143, USA

Wilson, Billy (Football Player)
San Francisco 49ers
PO Box 84
Whitehawk Ranch
Clio, CA 96106-0084, USA

Wilson, Blaine (Gymnast)
2660 Carters Corner Rd
Sunbury, OH 43074-8962, USA

Wilson, Blenda J (Educator)
California State University
President's Office
Northridge, CA 91330-0001, USA

Wilson, Bob (Baseball Player)
806 Cabot Ln
Madison, WI 53711-2810, USA

Wilson, Brian (Musician, Songwriter, Writer)
15030 Ventura Blvd # 710
Sherman Oaks, CA 91403-5470, USA

Wilson, Brian Anthony (Actor)
Bernard Liebhaber
352 7th Ave
New York, NY 10001-5012, USA

Wilson, C A S John (Architect)
John Wilson Assoc
27 Horsell Road
London N5 1XL, UNITED KINGDOM (UK)

Wilson, Carnie (Musician)
c/o Tim Curtis *William Morris Agency (WMA-LA)*
1 William Morris Pl
Beverly Hills, CA 90212-4261, USA

Wilson, Cassandra (Musician)
Dream Street Mgmt
4346 Redwood Ave Apt 307
Marina Del Rey, CA 90292-6495, USA

Wilson, Chandra (Actor)
c/o Richard Fisher *Abrams Artists Agency (NY)*
275 7th Ave Fl 26
New York, NY 10001-6708, USA

Wilson, Charles (Football Player)
Green Bay Packers
5444 Calder Dr
Tallahassee, FL 32317-1429, USA

Wilson, Chris (Musician)
c/o Staff Member *Fein Music*
81 Pondfield Rd
Bronxville, NY 10708-3818, USA

Wilson, Cindy (Musician)
Direct Management Group
947 N La Cienega Blvd # 2
Los Angeles, CA 90069-4782, USA

Wilson, Colin H (Writer)
Tetherdown Trewallock Lane
Gorran Haven
Cornwall, UNITED KINGDOM (UK)

Wilson, Craig (Baseball Player)
St Louis Cardinals
22 Parole St
Annapolis, MD 21401-3917, USA

Wilson, Craig (Baseball Player)
Chicago White Sox
3427 E Tere St
Phoenix, AZ 85044-3625, USA

Wilson, Craig (Misc)
1423 Lake Blvd
Davis, CA 95616-2620, USA

Wilson, Dan (Musician, Songwriter, Writer)
Monterey Peninsula Artists
509 Hartnell St
Monterey, CA 93940-2825, USA

Wilson, Daniel A (Dan) (Baseball Player)
Cincinnati Reds
2161 E Interlaken Blvd
Seattle, WA 98112-3432, USA

Wilson, Dave (Football Player)
New Orleans Saints
4301 San Rufino Cir
Yorba Linda, CA 92886-2351, USA

Wilson, David (Actor)
Susan Smith
1344 N Wetherly Dr
Los Angeles, CA 90069-1817, USA

Wilson, Dean (Golfer)
10914 Iris Canyon Ln
Las Vegas, NV 89135-1719, USA

Wilson, De'Angelo (Actor)
c/o Staff Member *Overbrook Entertainment*
450 N Roxbury Dr Fl 4
Beverly Hills, CA 90210-4232, USA

Wilson, Debra (Actor)
c/o Joan Rosenberg *Joan Rosenberg & Assoc Ltd*
3 Adam St
New York, NY 11001, USA

Wilson, Dick
2705 Cricket Hollow Ct
Henderson, NV 89074-1924, USA

Wilson, Don The Dragon
178 S Victory Blvd Ste 205
Burbank, CA 91502-2881, USA

Wilson, Dorien (Actor)
c/o Staff Member *Innovative Artists (LA)*
1505 10th St
Santa Monica, CA 90401-2805, USA

Wilson, Doug (Hockey Player)
18580 Petunia Ct
Saratoga, CA 95070-5390, USA

Wilson, Duane (Baseball Player)
Boston Red Sox
1945 N Porter Ave Apt A54
Wichita, KS 67203-2293, USA

Wilson, Earl (Football Player)
San Diego Chargers
1510 W Riverside Dr
Atlantic City, NJ 08401-1630, USA

Wilson, Earle L (Religious Leader)
Wesleyan Church
PO Box 50434
Indianapolis, IN 46250-0434, USA

Wilson, Edward O (Writer)
1010 Waltham St # A208
Lexington, MA 02421-8044, USA

Wilson, Elizabeth
200 W 57th St Ste 900
New York, NY 10019-3211, USA

Wilson, Eric C T (War Hero)
Woodside Cottage
Stowell Sherborne
Dorset, UNITED KINGDOM (UK)

Wilson, Eugene (Skier)
25775 Ranchview Lane N #1
Plymouth, MN 55447, USA

Wilson, F Paul (Writer)
PO Box 33
Allenwood, NJ 08720-0033, USA

Wilson, Frank (Race Car Driver)
North Carlonia Motor Speedway
PO Box 500
Rockingham, NC 28380, USA

Wilson, Gary (Baseball Player)
Pittsburgh Pirates
1021 Glendale Dr Spc 9
McKinleyville, CA 95519-9763, USA

Wilson, Gary (Baseball Player)
Houston Astros
713 Ouachita 64 Rd
Camden, AR 71701-9616, USA

Wilson, Georges (Director)
Moulin de Vilgris
Rambouillet 78120, FRANCE

Wilson, Gerald S (Composer, Musician)
4625 Brynhurst Ave
Los Angeles, CA 90043-1205, USA

Wilson, Glenn (Baseball Player)
Detroit Tigers
11 Wedgewood Blvd
Conroe, TX 77304-1349, USA

Wilson, Grandy (Baseball Player)
Pittsburgh Pirates
311 Chapelwood Dr
Dothan, AL 36305-1077, USA

Wilson, Gretchen (Musician)
c/o Dale Morris *Dale Morris & Associates Inc*
818 19th Ave S
Nashville, TN 37203-3202, USA

Wilson, Harry (Football Player)
Philadelphia Eagles
2600 N Lawrence St Apt 307
Philadelphia, PA 19133-3140, USA

Wilson, Harry C (Religious Leader)
Wesleyan Church Int'l Center
6060 Castleway West Dr
Indianapolis, IN 46250-1930, USA

Wilson, Hugh (Director)
William Morris Agency
151 El Camino Dr
Beverly Hills, CA 90212-2775, USA

Wilson, J C (Football Player)
Houston Oilers
4785 Young Rd
Waldorf, MD 20601-4483, USA

Wilson, J Tylee (Business Person)
PO Box 2057
Ponte Vedra Beach, FL 32004-2057, USA

Wilson, James (Football Player)
Cincinnati Bengals
4688 NW Falling Creek Rd
Lake City, FL 32055-5348, USA

Wilson, James B (Admiral)
321 Crosslands Dr
Kennett Square, PA 19348-2007, USA

Wilson, James M (Misc)
University of Pennsylvania
Med Center
Genetics Dept
Philadelphia, PA 19104, USA

Wilson, James Q (Educator)
University of California
Graduate Management School
Los Angeles, CA 90024, USA

Wilson, Jean D (Doctor)
Texas Southwestern Medical Center
5323 Harry Hines Blvd
Dallas, TX 75390-7200, USA

Wilson, Jeannie (Actor)
General Delivery
Ketchum, ID 83340-9999, USA

Wilson, Jennifer
1947 Lake Shore Dr
Branson, MO 65616-9476, USA

Wilson, Jerrel (Football Player)
Kansas City Chiefs
13860 W Main St
Larose, LA 70345-3006, USA

Wilson, Jerry (Football Player)
Philadelphia Eagles
2117 Mountain View Dr
Birmingham, AL 35216-2023, USA

Wilson, Jerry (Football Player)
Miami Dolphins
4272 Ironwood Ct
Weston, FL 33331-3827, USA

Wilson, Jim (Baseball Player)
Cleveland Indians
8112 NW Bacon Rd
Vancouver, WA 98665-6634, USA

Wilson, Jim M (Football Player)
San Francisco 49ers
PO Box 52
Evans, GA 30809-0052, USA

Wilson, Joe (Football Player)
Cincinnati Bengals
328 Valley View Ln
Chester Springs, PA 19425-9605, USA

Wilson, John (Baseball Player)
Chicago American Giants
8 Hillcrest Dr
Lock Haven, PA 17745-1014, USA

Wilson, Julie (Actor, Musician)
Stan Scotland Entertainment
157 E 57th St # 188
New York, NY 10022-2104, USA

Wilson, Justin (Musician)
David Levin Mgmt
200 W 57th St Ste 308
New York, NY 10019-3211, USA

Wilson, Kenneth G (Nobel Prize Laureate)
Ohio State University
174 W 18th Ave
Physics Dept
Columbus, OH 43210-1106, USA

Wilson, Kim (Musician)
Ricci Assoc
28205 Agoura Rd
Agoura Hills, CA 91301-2482, USA

Wilson, Kristen (Actor)
c/o Norman Aladjem *Paradigm (LA)*
360 N Crescent Dr
North Bldg
Beverly Hills, CA 90210-6820, USA

Wilson, Lambert (Actor)
c/o Estelle Lasher *Principal Entertainment (LA)*
1964 Westwood Blvd Ste 400
Los Angeles, CA 90025-4695, USA

Wilson, Lanford (Writer)
PO Box 891
Sag Harbor, NY 11963-0023, USA

Wilson, Lawrence F (Larry) (Football Player)
St Louis Cardinals
11834 N Blackheath Rd
Scottsdale, AZ 85254-4809, USA

Wilson, Luke (Actor)
c/o David Styne *Creative Artists Agency LCC (CAA-LA)*
2000 Avenue Of The Stars
Los Angeles, CA 90067-4700, USA

Wilson, Mara (Actor)
c/o Bonnie Liedtke *William Morris Agency (WMA-LA)*
3500 W Olive Ave Ste 1400
Burbank, CA 91505-5512, USA

Wilson, Marc (Football Player)
Oakland Raiders
18020 157th Ave NE
Woodinville, WA 98072-9238, USA

Wilson, Marc D (Football Player)
113113 Mount Wallace Court
Alta Loma, CA 91737, USA

Wilson, Marie
6 Oakdale
Irvine, CA 92604-3221, USA

Wilson, Mark (Golfer)
N41W27751 Ishnala Trl
Pewaukee, WI 53072-2140, USA

Wilson, Melanie (Actor)
Irv Schechter
9300 Wilshire Blvd # 410
Beverly Hills, CA 90212-3213, USA

Wilson, Michael (Baseball Player)
Minnesota Twins
1623 Schnell Dr
Arabi, LA 70032-1660, USA

Wilson, Michael H (Government Official)
Industry & Science Dept
235 Queen's St
Ottawa, ON K1A OH5, CANADA

Wilson, Mike D (Football Player)
Cincinnati Bengals
1967 Litchfield Ave
Dayton, OH 45406-3811, USA

Wilson, Mike R (Football Player)
San Francisco 49ers
2908 N Poinsettia Ave
Manhattan Beach, CA 90266-2405, USA

Wilson, Mookie (Baseball Player)
New York Mets
1111 Heyward Wilson Rd
Eastover, SC 29044-9627, USA

Wilson, Nancy (Musician)
c/o Staff Member *Shore Fire Media*
32 Court St Ste 1600
Brooklyn, NY 11201-4441, USA

Wilson, Neal C (Religious Leader)
Seventh-Day Adventists
12501 Old Columbia Pike
Silver Spring, MD 20904-6600, USA

Wilson, Neil (Baseball Player)
Florida Marlins
4300 Highway 412 W
Lexington, TN 38351-5423, USA

Wilson, Nemiah (Football Player)
Denver Broncos
11000 E Idaho Pl
Aurora, CO 80012-4118, USA

Wilson, Nigel (Baseball Player)
Florida Marlins
35 Sabbe Cres
Ajax, ON L1T 4E3, CANADA

Wilson, Otis (Football Player)
Chicago Bears
7B W 15th St
Chicago, IL 60605-2723, USA

Wilson, Owen C (Actor)
c/o Lisa Hallerman *United Talent Agency (UTA)*
9560 Wilshire Blvd Ste 500
Beverly Hills, CA 90212-2401, USA

Wilson, Patrick (Actor, Musician)
c/o Staff Member *Creative Artists Agency LCC (CAA-LA)*
2000 Avenue Of The Stars
Los Angeles, CA 90067-4700, USA

Wilson, Paul (Baseball Player)
New York Mets
4114 SW Gleneagle Cir
Palm City, FL 34990-4460, USA

Wilson, Peta (Actor)
June Cann Mgmt
73 Jersey Road
Woollahra, NSW 2025, AUSTRALIA

Wilson, Preston (Baseball Player)
New York Mets
130 S Bemiston Ave Ste 508
Saint Louis, MO 63105-1913, USA

Wilson, Rainn (Actor)
c/o Staff Member *3 Arts Entertainment Inc*
9460 Wilshire Blvd Fl 7
Beverly Hills, CA 90212-2713, USA

Wilson, Ralph C Jr (Misc)
Buffalo Bills
1 Bills Dr
Orchard Park, NY 14127-2237, USA

Wilson, Red (Baseball Player)
Chicago White Sox
806 Cabot Ln
Madison, WI 53711-2810, USA

Wilson, Reinard (Football Player)
Cincinnati Bengals
2595 NW 49th Ave Apt 108
Laud Lakes, FL 33313-3354, USA

Wilson, Rick (Coach, Hockey Player)
166 E Bethel Rd
Coppell, TX 75019-4085, USA

Wilson, Rick (Race Car Driver)
PO Box 304
Mulberry, FL 33860-0304, USA

Wilson, Rita (Actor)
c/o Staff Member *Playtone Productions*
PO Box 7340
Santa Monica, CA 90406-7340, USA

Wilson, Robert E (Bobby) (Football Player)
1034 Liberty Park Dr Apt 408R
Austin, TX 78746-6854, USA

Wilson, Robert M (Actor)
RW Work
131 Varick St Ste 908
New York, NY 10013-1418, USA

Wilson, Robert N (Business Person)
Johnson & Johnson
1 Johnson And Johnson Plz
New Brunswick, NJ 08933-0002, USA

Wilson, Robert W (Nobel Prize Laureate)
94 Lucille Ave
Dumont, NJ 07628-2034, USA

Wilson, Robin (Musician)
William Morris Agency
1600 Division St Ste 300
Nashville, TN 37203-2755, USA

Wilson, Roger (Actor)
c/o Staff Member *Joel Stevens Entertainment*
206 S Brand Blvd
Glendale, CA 91204-1310, USA

Wilson, Ron (Coach, Hockey Player)
San Jose Sharks
525 W Santa Clara St
San Jose Arena
San Jose, CA 95113-1500, USA

Wilson, Ryan (Actor)
c/o Staff Member *Osbrink Talent Agency*
4343 Lankershim Blvd # 100
North Hollywood, CA 91602-2705, USA

Wilson, Samuel W (Educator, General)
Hampden-Sydney College
President's Office
Hampden-Sydney, VA 23943, USA

Wilson, Sarah (Religious Leader)
Friends United Meeting
101 Quaker Hill Dr
Richmond, IN 47374-1926, USA

Wilson, Scott
PO Box 5617
Beverly Hills, CA 90209-5617, USA

Wilson, Sheree J (Actor)
c/o Joanna (Joanie) Burstein *Burstein Company, The*
15304 W Sunset Blvd Ste 208
Pacific Palisades, CA 90272-3656, USA

Wilson, Stephanie D (Astronaut)
14910 Hollydale Dr
Houston, TX 77062-2907, USA

Wilson, Steve (Baseball Player)
Texas Rangers
1888 Caminito De La Montana
Glendale, CA 91208-3043, USA

Wilson, Steve (Football Player)
Dallas Cowboys
3503 Brymoor Ct
Pearland, TX 77584-4810, USA

Wilson, Stuart (Actor)
c/o Staff Member *International Creative Management (ICM-UK)*
Oxford House
76 Oxford St
London W1N OAX, UNITED KINGDOM (UK)

Wilson, Thomas L (Football Player)
Los Angeles Rams
4342 Oakdale Pl
Pittsburg, CA 94565-6256, USA

Wilson, Tom (Cartoonist)
Universal Press Syndicate
PO Box 419149
Kansas City, MO 64141-6149, USA

Wilson, Torrie (Model, Wrestler)
c/o Staff Member *World Wrestling Entertainment (WWE)*
1241 E Main St
Stamford, CT 06902-3520, USA

Wilson, Trevor (Baseball Player)
San Francisco Giants
8045 E Camelback Rd
Scottsdale, AZ 85251-2777, USA

Wilson, Vance (Baseball Player)
New York Mets
6368 Elizabeth Ave
Springdale, AR 72762-4234, USA

Wilson, Wade (Football Player)
Minnesota Vikings
6126 Mimosa Ln
Dallas, TX 75230-5042, USA

Wilson, Wayne (Football Player)
New Orleans Saints
5430 Lynx Ln Apt 152
Columbia, MD 21044-2319, USA

Wilson, William (Football Player)
Baltimore Colts
130 Belmont St
Englewood, NJ 07631-1502, USA

Wilson, William J (Activist)
Harvard University
Kennedy Government School
Cambridge, MA 02138, USA

Wilson, Willie (Baseball Player)
Kansas City Royals
14 Pengelly Crt
Scarborough, ON M1L 4L9, CANADA

Wilson, Woody (Cartoonist)
King Features Syndicate
888 7th Ave Ste 201
New York, NY 10106-0201, USA

Wilson David, Mackenzie (Director)
Lifeboat House
Castletown
Isle of Man IM9 1LD, UNITED KINGDOM (UK)

Wilson-Johnson, David R (Opera Singer)
28 Englefield Road
London N1 4ET, UNITED KINGDOM (UK)

Wilson Jr, George B (Mike) (Football Player, General)
1062 E Lancaster Ave
Bryn Mawr, PA 19010-1552, USA

Wilson Jr, Louis H (General, War Hero)
100 University Park Dr
Birmingham, AL 35209-6766, USA

Wilson of Tillyorn, David C (Government Official)
House of Lords
Westminster
London SW1A 0PW, UNITED KINGDOM (UK)

Wilson Phillips
1290 Avenue Of The Americas # 4200
New York, NY 10104-0101, USA

Wilson-Sampras, Bridgette (Actor)
c/o Andrea Pett-Joseph *Brillstein-Grey Entertainment*
9150 Wilshire Blvd Ste 350
Beverly Hills, CA 90212-3453, USA

Wiltse-Collins, Dottie (Baseball Player)
4726 Caballero Ct
Fort Wayne, IN 46835-3700, USA

Wimmer, Brian (Actor)
c/o Jean-Pierre (JP) Henraux *Shelter Entertainment*
1041 N Formosa Ave
Santa Monica Bldg W #17
W Hollywood, CA 90046-6703, USA

Wimmer, Kurt (Actor, Director, Producer, Writer)
c/o Tom Strickler *Endeavor Agency LLC (LA)*
9601 Wilshire Blvd Fl 3
Beverly Hills, CA 90210-5204, USA

Winans
1420 Coleman Rd
Franklin, TN 37064-7452, USA

Winans, BeBe (Musician)
Covenant Agency
123 California Ave Apt 116
Santa Monica, CA 90403-3560, USA

Winans, CeCe (Musician)
Wellspring Mgmt
2300 Franklin Road #2B
Franklin, TN 37064, USA

Winans, Jeff (Football Player)
Buffalo Bills
175 21st Ave SE
Saint Petersburg, FL 33705-2826, USA

Winans, Mario (Musician)
c/o Staff Member *Bad Boy Worldwide Entertainment*
1710 Broadway
New York, NY 10019-5254, USA

Winans, Matthew (Baseball Player)
21 Saint George Pl
Sandy Hook, CT 06482-1089, USA

Winans, Vicki (Musician)
Convenant Agency
123 California Ave Apt 116
Santa Monica, CA 90403-3560, USA

Winborne, Jamie (Football Player)
San Francisco 49ers
195 Roscoe Lee Cir
Wetumpka, AL 36092-3681, USA

Winbush, Angela (Musician, Songwriter, Writer)
Joyce Agency
370 Harrison Ave
Harrison, NY 10528-2714, USA

Winbush, Camille (Actor)
c/o Staff Member *Innovative Artists (LA)*
1505 10th St
Santa Monica, CA 90401-2805, USA

Winbush, Troy (Actor)
c/o Staff Member *Paradigm (LA)*
360 N Crescent Dr
North Bldg
Beverly Hills, CA 90210-6820, USA

Winceniak, Ed (Baseball Player)
Chicago Cubs
10828 S Avenue O
Chicago, IL 60617-6543, USA

Wincer, Simon (Director, Producer)
c/o Glen Bickel *Creative Artists Agency LCC (CAA-LA)*
2000 Avenue Of The Stars
Los Angeles, CA 90067-4700, USA

Wincer, Simon G (Director)
PO Box 241
Toorak, VIC 3142, AUSTRALIA

Winchester, Jesse (Musician, Songwriter, Writer)
Keith Case Assoc
1025 17th Ave S Fl 2
Nashville, TN 37212-2211, USA

Winchester, Scott (Baseball Player)
Cincinnati Reds
4705 Oakridge Dr
Midland, MI 48640-7409, USA

Wincott, Jeff P (Actor)
Judy Shane & Associates
606 N Larchmont Blvd
Los Angeles, CA 90004-1321, USA

Winder, Sammy (Football Player)
Denver Broncos
Winder Construction 4823 Greens Crossing Rd
Ridgeland, MS 39157, USA

Winders, Rich (Bowler)
720 Augusta St
Racine, WI 53402-4412, USA

Winders, Wim (Director)
Paul Kohner
9300 Wilshire Blvd Ste 555
Beverly Hills, CA 90212-3211, USA

Windhorn, Gordie (Baseball Player)
New York Yankees
145 Bent Creek Rd
Danville, VA 24540-5213, USA

Windle, William F (Misc)
229 Cherry St
Granville, OH 43023-1165, USA

Windom, William (Actor)
House of Representatives
211 S Beverly Dr Ste 208
Beverly Hills, CA 90212-3879, USA

Windon, Stephen (Cinematographer)
PO Box 659
Northbridge
Sydney, NSW 2063, AUSTRALIA

Windsor, Barbara (Actor, Comedian)
104 Crouch Hill
London NB 9EA, UNITED KINGDOM (UK)

Windsor, Robert E (Football Player)
San Francisco 49ers
2625 Legends Way
Ellicott City, MD 21042-2257, USA

Windsor-Smith, Barry (Artist)
c/o Staff Member *Fantagraphics Books*
7563 Lake City Way NE
Seattle, WA 98115-4218, USA

Wine, David M (Religious Leader)
Church of Brethren
1451 Dundee Ave
Elgin, IL 60120-1694, USA

Winegardner, Mark (Writer)
Random House
1745 Broadway
New York, NY 10019-4343, USA

Winfield, Antoine (Football Player)
Buffalo Bills
10451 White Tail Xing
Eden Prairie, MN 55347-5026, USA

Winfield, David (Dave) (Baseball Player)
2235 Stratford Cir
Los Angeles, CA 90077-1316, USA

Winfield, Peter (Actor)
c/o Staff Member *Screen Actors Guild (SAG-LA)*
5757 Wilshire Blvd
Los Angeles, CA 90036-5810, USA

Winfrey, Oprah (Actor, Producer, Talk Show Host)
c/o Staff Member *Harpo Productions*
110 N Carpenter St
Harpo Studios
Chicago, IL 60607-2146, USA

Winfrey, W C (Bill) (Misc)
7802 Sierra Trl
Spring Lake, NC 28390, USA

Wing-Merrill, Toby
PO Box 889
Mathews, VA 23109-0889, USA

Wingate, Elmer (Football Player)
Baltimore Colts
807 Wellington Rd
Baltimore, MD 21212-1931, USA

Wingate, J W (Baseball Player)
Kansas City Monarchs
3215 Case St
Beaumont, TX 77703-3607, USA

Winger, Debra (Actor)
c/o Johnnie Planco *Untitled Entertainment (NY)*
322 8th Ave Ste 601
New York, NY 10001-6715, USA

Winger, Kip (Musician)
Joseph Minkes Assoc
2740 W Magnolia Blvd Unit 204
Burbank, CA 91505-3051, USA

Wingle, Blake (Football Player)
Pittsburgh Steelers
8200 Stockdale Hwy Apt 10
Bakersfield, CA 93311-1091, USA

Wingreen, Jason
4224 Teesdale Ave
N Hollywood, CA 91604-1544, USA

Wingrove-Earl, Elsie (Baseball Player)
PO Box 61
N Portal, SK S0C 1W0, CANADA

Winkleman, Sophie (Actor)
c/o Staff Member *Creative Artists Agency LCC (CAA-LA)*
2000 Avenue Of The Stars
Los Angeles, CA 90067-4700, USA

Winkler, David (Director)
Rigberg Roberts Rugoto
1180 S Beverly Dr Ste 604
Los Angeles, CA 90035-1158, USA

Winkler, Francis M (Football Player)
Green Bay Packers
8223 Creekside Hwy Apt 10
Cordova, TN 38016, USA

Winkler, Gerard (Actor)
Alsertra 26-3A
Vienna 1090, AUSTRIA

Winkler, Hans-Gunter (Misc)
Dr Rau Allee 48
Warendorf 48231, GERMANY

Winkler, Henry (Actor, Producer)
c/o Staff Member *Wolf Kasteler Van Iden & Associates (LA)*
335 N Maple Dr Ste 351
Beverly Hills, CA 90210-3860, USA

Winkler, Irwin (Director, Producer)
Irwin Winkler Productions
211 S Beverly Dr # 220
Beverly Hills, CA 90212-3828, USA

Winkles, Bobby B (Misc)
78452 Calle Huerta
La Quinta, CA 92253-2372, USA

Winn, D Randolph (Randy) (Baseball Player)
59 Leeds Ct E
Danville, CA 94526-4348, USA

Winner, Michael R (Director, Producer)
31 Melbury Road
London W14 8AB, UNITED KINGDOM (UK)

Winningham, Mare (Actor)
United Talent Agency
9560 Wilshire Blvd Ste 500
Beverly Hills, CA 90212-2401, USA

Winokur, Marissa Jaret (Actor)
c/o Michael Valeo *McKeon-Valeo-Myones Management*
9100 Wilshire Blvd Ste 350W
Beverly Hills, CA 90212-3437, USA

Winslet, Kate (Actor)
c/o Hylda Queally *Creative Artists Agency LCC (CAA-LA)*
2000 Avenue Of The Stars
Los Angeles, CA 90067-4700, USA

Winslow, Dan (Musician)
3807 114th Ln NE
Minneapolis, MN 55449-7031, USA

Winslow, George (Football Player)
Cleveland Browns
14 Daisy Ln
Maple Glen, PA 19002-2326, USA

Winslow, Kellen B (Football Player)
San Diego Chargers
5173 Waring Rd # 312
San Diego, CA 92120-2705, USA

Winslow, Michael (Actor, Comedian)
1327 Ocean Ave Ste J
Santa Monica, CA 90401-1033, USA

Winsor, Jackie (Artist)
Paula Cooper Gallery
534 W 21st St
New York, NY 10011-2812, USA

Winstead, Mary Elizabeth (Actor)
c/o Staff Member *Jeff Morrone Management*
9350 Wilshire Blvd Ste 224
Beverly Hills, CA 90212-3204, USA

Winston, George (Composer, Musician)
Dancing Cat Productions
PO Box 4287
Santa Cruz, CA 95063-4287, USA

Winston, Hattie (Actor)
13025 Jarvis Ave
Los Angeles, CA 90061-2247, USA

Winston, Patrick H (Engineer, Scientist)
Massachusetts Institute of Technology
Technology Square
Cambridge, MA 02139, USA

Winston, Roland (Physicist)
3384 Locksley Ct
Merced, CA 95340-0751, USA

Winston, Roy C (Football Player)
Minnesota Vikings
708 Highway 401
Napoleonville, LA 70390-3205, USA

Winston, Stan (Artist, Director, Producer, Writer)
7032 Valiean Ave
Van Nuys, CA 91406, USA

Winstone, Ray (Actor)
c/o Staff Member *IFA Talent Agency*
8730 W Sunset Blvd Ste 490
Los Angeles, CA 90069-2248, USA

Winter, Alex (Actor)
c/o Chris Ridenhour *Tavel Entertainment*
9255 W Sunset Blvd Ste 805
West Hollywood, CA 90069-3305, USA

Winter, Blaise (Football Player)
Indianapolis Colts
W5837 Royaltroon Dr
Menasha, WI 54952-9712, USA

Winter, Edgar
26033 Mulholland Hwy
Calabasas, CA 91302-1946, USA

Winter, Edward D (Actor)
32070 Waterside Ln
Westlake Village, CA 91361-3622, USA

Winter, Eric (Actor)
c/o Staff Member *Days of Our Lives*
3000 W Alameda Ave
Burbank, CA 91523-0001, USA

Winter, Fred (Tex) (Coach)
Los Angeles Lakers
1111 S Figueroa St
Staples Center
Los Angeles, CA 90015-1300, USA

Winter, Harrison L (Judge)
US Court of Appeals
101 W Lombard St
Baltimore, MD 21201-2605, USA

Winter, Johnny (Musician)
Slatus Mgmt
35 Hayward Ave
Colchester, CT 06415-1221, USA

Winter, Judy
Merzstr. 14
Munich D-81679, GERMANY

Winter, Olaf (Athlete)
An der Pirschheide 28
Potsdam 14471, GERMANY

Winter, Paul T (Musician)
Living Music Records
PO Box 72
Litchfield, CT 06759-0072, USA

Winter, Ralph (Producer)
c/o Staff Member *Ralph Winter Productions*
10201 W Pico Blvd Bldg 6 # 101
Los Angeles, CA 90064-2606, USA

Winter, Terence (Producer)
c/o Staff Member *Creative Artists Agency LCC (CAA-LA)*
2000 Avenue Of The Stars
Los Angeles, CA 90067-4700, USA

Winter, William F (Governor)
633 N State St
Jackson, MS 39202-3306, USA

Winter Jr, Ralph K (Judge)
US Court of Appeals
55 Whitney Ave
New Haven, CT 06510-1300, USA

Winterbottom, Michael (Director, Producer, Writer)
c/o Staff Member *Revolution Films*
9A Dallington St
London EC1V 0BQ, UNITED KINGDOM (UK)

Winters, Dean (Actor)
c/o Bill Butler *Gersh Agency, The (NY)*
41 Madison Ave Fl 33
New York, NY 10010-2202, USA

Winters, Dean (Actor)
c/o Staff Member *Gersh Agency, The (LA)*
232 N Canon Dr
Beverly Hills, CA 90210-5302, USA

Winters, Frank (Football Player)
Cleveland Browns
820 17th St
Union City, NJ 07087-1928, USA

Winters, Jonathan (Actor, Comedian)
c/o Staff Member *Abrams Artists Agency (LA)*
9200 W Sunset Blvd Ph 11
Los Angeles, CA 90069-3601, USA

Winters, Mike (Baseball Player)
8008 Paseo Aliso
Carlsbad, CA 92009-9025, USA

Winters, Scott William (Actor)
c/o Staff Member *Abrams Artists Agency (LA)*
9200 W Sunset Blvd Ph 11
Los Angeles, CA 90069-3601, USA

Winther, Richard (Football Player)
Green Bay Packers
1620 6th Way NW
Birmingham, AL 35215-5374, USA

Winwood, Steve (Musician)
Trinley Cottage
Tirley
Gloucs GL19 4EU, UNITED KINGDOM (UK)

Winzenried, Jesse D (Financier)
Securities Investor Protection
805 15th St NW
Washington, DC 20005-2215, USA

Wire II, William S (Business Person)
706 Overton Park
Nashville, TN 37215-2452, USA

Wirgowski, Dennis (Football Player)
Boston Patriots
1127 Brissette Beach Rd
Kawkawlin, MI 48631-9454, USA

Wirth, Billy (Actor, Director)
c/o Edward G (Eddie) Horowitz *Creative Management Group (CMG)*
8522 National Blvd Ste 108
Culver City, CA 90232-2454, USA

Wirth, Timothy E (Senator)
United Nations Foundation
1301 Connecticut Ave NW
Washington, DC 20036-1815, USA

Wirtz, W Willard (Secretary)
1211 Connecticut Ave NW
Washington, DC 20036-2701, USA

Wirtz, William W (Bill) (Misc)
181 De Windt Rd
Winnetka, IL 60093-3708, USA

Wisdom, Norman (Actor, Comedian)
Ballalaugh
Lhen Andreas Ramsey
Isle of Man IM7 3EH, UNITED KINGDOM (UK)

Wisdom, Robert (Actor)
c/o Ben Levine *Evolution Entertainment (LA)*
10585 Santa Monica Blvd Ste 120
Los Angeles, CA 90025-4984, USA

Wisdom, Sir Norman
The Lhen
Andreas Ramsay ISLE OF MAN 1M7 3EH, UNITED KINGDOM (UK)

Wise, Ray (Actor)
Gold Marshak Liedtke
3500 W Olive Ave Ste 1400
Burbank, CA 91505-5512, USA

Wise, Richard C (Rick) (Baseball Player)
5302 W Baseline Rd Apt 117
Hillsboro, OR 97123-6413, USA

Wise, William A (Business Person)
El Paso Energy Corp
1001 Louisiana St
Houston, TX 77002-5083, USA

Wise, Willie (Basketball Player)
5232 215th St SE
Woodinville, WA 98072-8355, USA

Wisecarver, Ellsworth (Sonny)
305 Mill Creek Rd
Mentone, CA 92359, USA

Wiseman, Frederick (Producer)
Zipporah Films
1 Richdale Ave Unit 4
Cambridge, MA 02140-2610, USA

Wiseman, Joseph (Actor)
382 Central Park W
New York, NY 10025-6054, USA

Wiseman, Len (Director, Writer)
c/o Nick Reed *International Creative Management (ICM-LA)*
10250 Constellation Blvd
Los Angeles, CA 90067-6200, USA

Wiseman, Mac (Musician)
PO Box 17028
Nashville, TN 37217-0028, USA

Wisener, Gary (Football Player)
Dallas Cowboys
10 Encantado Way
Hot Springs Village, AR 71909-7405, USA

Wish Bone (Musician)
Creative Artists Agency
9830 Wilshire Blvd
Beverly Hills, CA 90212-1804, USA

Wishart III, Leonard P (General)
19360 Magnolia Grove Sq Unit 315
Leesburg, VA 20176-6896, USA

Wiska, Jeffrey R (Football Player)
Cleveland Browns
18579 Fox Hollow Ct
Northville, MI 48168-8848, USA

Wismann, Pete (Football Player)
San Francisco 49ers
7923 Caledonia Dr
San Jose, CA 95135-2112, USA

Wisner, Frank G (Diplomat)
American International Group
70 Pine St # 1800
New York, NY 10270-0002, USA

Wisniewski, Andreas (Actor)
Gage Group
14724 Ventura Blvd Ste 505
Sherman Oaks, CA 91403-3505, USA

Wisniewski, Leo (Football Player)
Baltimore Colts
8036 Woodcreek Dr
Bridgeville, PA 15017-3610, USA

Wisniewski, Stephen A (Steve) (Football
Player)
Los Angeles Raiders
36 El Alamo Ct
Danville, CA 94526-1455, USA

Wisoff, Peter J K (Jeff) (Astronaut)
4268 Brindisi Pl
Pleasanton, CA 94566-2238, USA

Wistert, Albert A (Ox) (Football Player)
Philadelphia Eagles
256 Gunnell Rd
Grants Pass, OR 97526-9621, USA

Wistert, Alvin L (Moose) (Football Player)
10250 7 Mile Rd
Northville, MI 48167-9107, USA

Wistrom, Grant (Football Player)
St Louis Rams
5769 S Fox Hollow Ave
Springfield, MO 65810-2326, USA

**with Spencer Davis, Strawberry Alarm
Clock** (Music Group)
c/o Geoffrey Blumenauer *Geoffrey
Blumenauer Artists*
PO Box 343
Burbank, CA 91503-0343, USA

Withers, Bill (Musician, Songwriter,
Writer)
PO Box 16698
Beverly Hills, CA 90209-2698, USA

Withers, Googie (Actor)
Larry Dalzall
17 Broad Court
London WC2B 5QN, UNITED KINGDOM
(UK)

Withers, Jane (Actor)
Scott Stander
13701 Riverside Dr Ste 201
Sherman Oaks, CA 91423-2447, USA

Withers, Pick (Musician)
Damage Mgmt
16 Lambton Place
London W11 2SH, UNITED KINGDOM
(UK)

Witherspoon, Jimmy
223 1/2 E 48th St
New York, NY 10017, USA

Witherspoon, John (Actor)
T-Boyds Boy Inc
12400 Ventura Blvd
Box 354
Studio City, CA 91604-2406, USA

Witherspoon, Reese (Actor, Producer)
c/o Evelyn O'Neill *Management 360*
9111 Wilshire Blvd
Beverly Hills, CA 90210-5508, USA

Withrow, Phil (Football Player)
San Diego Chargers
730 Oakland Hills Cir Apt 106
Lake Mary, FL 32746-5833, USA

Witiuk, Doris (Baseball Player)
11821 N Hemlock St
Spokane, WA 99218-2718, USA

Witkin, Isaac (Artist)
Bennington College
Art Dept
Bennington, VT 05201, USA

Witkin, Joel-Peter (Photographer)
1707 Five Points Rd SW
Albuquerque, NM 87105-3017, USA

Witkop, Bernhard (Misc)
3807 Montrose Driveway
Chevy Chase, MD 20815, USA

Witman, Jon (Football Player)
Pittsburgh Steelers
568 Woodsview Ln
Hellam, PA 17406-9344, USA

Witt, Alicia (Actor)
c/o Daniel (Danny) Sussman *Brillstein-
Grey Entertainment*
9150 Wilshire Blvd Ste 350
Beverly Hills, CA 90212-3453, USA

Witt, Katarina (Figure Skater)
c/o Gail Parenteau *Parenteau Guidance*
132 E 35th St # 3J
New York, NY 10016-3892, USA

Witt, Michael A (Mike) (Baseball Player)
37 Poppy Hills Rd
Laguna Niguel, CA 92677-1010, USA

Witt, Robert E (Educator)
University of Alabama
President's Office
Tuscaloosa, AL 35487-0001, USA

Witten, Edward (Physicist)
Institute for Advanced Study
Einstein Lane
Princeton, NJ 08540, USA

Witter, Karen (Actor, Model)
H/H/M
247 S Beverly Dr # 102
Beverly Hills, CA 90212-3830, USA

Wittman, Randy (Basketball Player,
Coach)
8646 French Curv
Eden Prairie, MN 55347-5359, USA

Wittum, Tom (Football Player)
San Francisco 49ers
6704 Johnsburg Rd
Spring Grove, IL 60081-9364, USA

Witucki, Casimir (Football Player)
Washington Redskins
3909 Spring Ter
Temple Hills, MD 20748-3439, USA

Wixted, Kevin
101001 Santa Monica Blvd. #700
Los Angeles, CA 90067, USA

Wizbicki, Alex (Football Player)
Green Bay Packers
10B Hayes Ct
Superior, WI 54880-2939, USA

Wobst, Frank (Financier)
Huntington Bancshares
Huntington Center
41 S High St
Columbus, OH 43287-0001, USA

Wockenfuss, Anett (Model)
c/o *Chadwick model management*
Private Bag 38
Darlinghurst NSW 2010, AUSTRALIA

Wocket-Eckert, Barbel (Athlete)
Im Bangert 61
Lutzelbach 64750, GERMANY

Woerner, Scott (Football Player)
Atlanta Falcons
11268 Turner Rd
Hampton, GA 30228-1534, USA

Woessner, Mark M (Business Person,
Publisher)
Erich-Kastner-Str 25
Gutersloh 33332, GERMANY

Woetzel, Damian (Choreographer,
Dancer)
New York City Ballet
Lincoln Center Plaza
New York, NY 10023, USA

Wofford, Harris L (Senator)
260 Burch Dr
Coraopolis, PA 15108-3153, USA

Wogan, Gerald N (Misc)
Massachusetts Institute of Technology
Toxicology Div
Cambridge, MA 02139, USA

Woggon, Bill (Cartoonist)
2724 Cabot Ct
Thousand Oaks, CA 91360-1640, USA

Wohl, Dave (Basketball Player, Coach)
23 Tompkins Rd
East Brunswick, NJ 08816-1710, USA

Wohlers, Mark E (Baseball Player)
135 Old Cedar Ln
Alpharetta, GA 30004-3795, USA

Wohlhuter, Richard C (Rick) (Athlete,
Track Athlete)
175 Dickinson Dr
Wheaton, IL 60187-7473, USA

Wohlwender-Fricker, Marian (Baseball
Player)
15210 Portside Dr Apt 401
Fort Myers, FL 33908-6827, USA

Woit, Dick (Misc)
Lehmann Sports Center
2700 N Lehmann Ct
Chicago, IL 60614, USA

Woiwode, Larry (Writer)
State University of New York
English Dept
Binghamton, NY 13901, USA

Wojciechowski, John (Football Player)
Chicago Bears
13317 Clyde Rd
Holly, MI 48442-9010, USA

Wojciehowicz, Alex
105 Silway Dr.
Forked River, NJ 08731, USA

Wojtowicz, R P (Misc)
Railway Carmen Union
3 Research Pl
Rockville, MD 20850-3279, USA

Wolaner, Robin P (Publisher)
Sunset Publishing Corp
80 Willow Rd
Menlo Park, CA 94025-3691, USA

Wolcott, Charles
Box 155
Haifa, ISRAEL

Wolf, David A (Astronaut)
1714 Neptune Ln
Houston, TX 77062-6108, USA

Wolf, Frank (Publisher)
Seventeen Magazine
850 3rd Ave
New York, NY 10022-6222, USA

Wolf, Jim (Baseball Player)
1507 E Glenhaven Dr
Phoenix, AZ 85048-9446, USA

Wolf, Joe (Football Player)
Phoenix Cardinals
2324 Lehigh Pkwy N
Allentown, PA 18103-3748, USA

Wolf, Naomi (Writer)
Random House
1745 Broadway # B1
New York, NY 10019-4305, USA

Wolf, Peter (Musician)
c/o Irving Azoff *Azoffmusic Management*
1100 Glendon Ave Ste 2000
Los Angeles, CA 90024-3524, USA

Wolf, Randall C (Randy) (Baseball Player)
7266 Angela Ave
West Hills, CA 91307-1406, USA

Wolf, Scott (Actor)
c/o Ken Sunshine *Ken Sunshine
Consultants Inc*
149 5th Ave Fl 7
New York, NY 10010-6824, USA

Wolf, Sigrid (Skier)
Elbigenalp 45 A
6652, AUSTRIA

Wolf, Stephen M (Business Person)
US Airways Group
4000 E Sky Harbor Blvd
Phoenix, AZ 85034-3802, USA

Wolfe, Dick (Actor, Director, Producer,
Writer)
c/o Staff Member *United Talent Agency
(UTA)*
9560 Wilshire Blvd Ste 500
Beverly Hills, CA 90212-2401, USA

Wolfe, George C (Director)
Shakespeare Festival
425 Lafayette St
New York, NY 10003-7021, USA

Wolfe, Kenneth L (Business Person)
Hershey Foods Corp
100 Crystal A Dr
Hershey, PA 17033-9702, USA

Wolfe, Michael
41 Lansdowne Rd.
London, ENGLAND W11 26Q, UNITED
KINGDOM (UK)

Wolfe, Sterling (Actor)
2609 W Wyoming Ave Ste A
Burbank, CA 91505-1950, USA

Wolfe, Thad A (General)
4790 Longwood Pt
Colorado Springs, CO 80906-8609, USA

Wolfe, Tom
21 E 79th St
New York, NY 10075-0125, USA

Wolfe, Traci (Actor)
c/o Staff Member *AM Productions & Management*
8899 Beverly Blvd Ste 713
Los Angeles, CA 90048-2450, USA

Wolfenden of Westcott, John F (Educator)
White House
Guildford Road Westcott near Dorking
Surrey, UNITED KINGDOM (UK)

Wolfenstein, Lincoln (Physicist)
Carnegie-Mellon University
Physics Dept
Pittsburgh, PA 15213, USA

Wolfermann, Klaus (Athlete, Track Athlete)
Fasenenweg 13A
Herzogenaurach 91074, GERMANY

Wolff, Christian
Zinnkopfstr. 6
Aschau/Chiemsee D-83229, GERMANY

Wolff, Christoph J (Educator)
182 Washington St
Belmont, MA 02478-3560, USA

Wolff, Hugh (Conductor)
Van Walsun Mgmt
4 Addison Bridge Place
London W14 8XP, UNITED KINGDOM (UK)

Wolff, Jon A (Misc)
1122 University Bay Dr
Madison, WI 53705-2252, USA

Wolff, Jonathan (Composer, Musician)
Music Consultants Group
531 Fairfield Dr
Louisville, KY 40206-2931, USA

Wolff, Sanford I (Misc)
8141 Broadway
New York, NY 10023, USA

Wolff, Tobias J A (Writer)
Stanford University
English Dept
Stanford, CA 94305, USA

Wolfley, Craig (Football Player)
Pittsburgh Steelers
1767 Robson Dr
Pittsburgh, PA 15241-2617, USA

Wolford, Will (Football Player)
Buffalo Bills
205 Waterleaf Way
Louisville, KY 40207-5720, USA

Wolfowitz, Paul D (Financier, Government Official)
World Bank
1818 H St NW
Washington, DC 20433-0002, USA

Wolfson, Louis E (Business Person)
10205 Collins Ave
Bal Harbour, FL 33154-1403, USA

Wolken, Jonathan (Artist, Dancer, Director)
Pilobolus Dance Theater
PO Box 388
Washington Depot, CT 06794-0388, USA

Wolkowyski, Ruben (Basketball Player)
c/o Staff Member *Seattle Supersonics*
1201 3rd Ave Ste 1000
Seattle, WA 98101-3038, USA

Wollman, Harvey L (Governor)
RR 1 Box 43
Hitchcock, SD 57348, USA

Wollman, Roger L (Judge)
US Court of Appeals
400 S Phillips Ave Rm 104
Federal Building
Sioux Falls, SD 57104-6851, USA

Wolman, M Gordon (Geophysicist, Physicist)
2104 W Rogers Ave
Baltimore, MD 21209-4553, USA

Wolpe, Lenny (Actor)
c/o Staff Member *Gage Group, The (LA)*
14724 Ventura Blvd Ste 505
Sherman Oaks, CA 91403-3505, USA

Wolper, David L (Producer)
617 N Rodeo Dr
Beverly Hills, CA 90210-3207, USA

Wolpert, Julian (Geophysicist, Physicist)
188 E 64th St Apt 2304
New York, NY 10065-7467, USA

Wolski, Bill (Football Player)
Atlanta Falcons
14435 Freemanville Rd
Alpharetta, GA 30004-3176, USA

Wolski, Dariusz (Director)
The Mack Agency
5726 Woodman Ave Apt 4
Van Nuys, CA 91401-4410, USA

Wolter, Sherilyn (Actor)
128 Old Topanga Canyon Rd
Topanga, CA 90290-3807, USA

Wolters, Kara (Basketball Player)
137 Westfield Dr
Holliston, MA 01746-1256, USA

Womack, Bruce L (Football Player)
Detroit Lions
2834 Triway Ln
Houston, TX 77043-1809, USA

Womack, James E (Scientist)
2105 Farley
College Station, TX 77845-5601, USA

Womack, Lee Ann (Actor, Musician)
c/o Staff Member *Buddy Lee Attractions Inc*
38 Music Sq E Ste 200
Nashville, TN 37203-4304, USA

Woman, Nancy
PO Box 3601
Torrance, CA 90510-3601, USA

Wombats, The (Music Group)
c/o Staff Member *Paradigm (Monterey)*
509 Hartnell St
Monterey, CA 93940-2825, USA

Womble, Royce (Football Player)
Baltimore Colts
6350 Newt Patterson Rd
Mansfield, TX 76063-6157, USA

Wonder, Stevie (Musician, Songwriter, Writer)
c/o Robert Norman *Creative Artists Agency LCC (CAA-LA)*
2000 Avenue Of The Stars
Los Angeles, CA 90067-4700, USA

Wong, B D (Actor)
c/o Staff Member *Innovative Artists (LA)*
1505 10th St
Santa Monica, CA 90401-2805, USA

Wong, James (Director, Producer, Writer)
c/o Marty Adelstein *Original Film*
284 N Saltair Ave
Los Angeles, CA 90049-2913, USA

Wong, Kailee (Football Player)
Minnesota Vikings
5003 Mimosa Dr
Bellaire, TX 77401-5736, USA

Wong, Russell (Actor)
International Creative Mgmt
8942 Wilshire Blvd # 219
Beverly Hills, CA 90211-1908, USA

Wonsley, George (Football Player)
Indianapolis Colts
6418 Amblewood Pl
Jackson, MS 39213-7803, USA

Woo, John (Director, Producer)
c/o Staff Member *Tiger Hill Entertainment*
2120 Colorado Ave Ste 225
Santa Monica, CA 90404-5520, USA

Wood, Brenton (Musician)
PO Box 4127
Inglewood, CA 90309-4127, USA

Wood, C Norman (General)
5440 Mount Corcoran Pl
Burke, VA 22015-2147, USA

Wood, Carolyn (Swimmer)
4380 SW 86th Ave
Portland, OR 97225-2428, USA

Wood, Carri (Golfer)
2001 Sabal Ridge Ct Apt H
Palm Beach Gardens, FL 33418-8922, USA

Wood, Charles G (Writer)
London Mgmt
2-4 Noel St
London W1V 3RB, UNITED KINGDOM (UK)

Wood, Danny
496 Adams St
Dorchester, MA 02122-1954, USA

Wood, Dick (Football Player)
San Diego Chargers
41 Audubon Pl
Newnan, GA 30265-2003, USA

Wood, Duane (Football Player)
Dallas Texans
407 W Caddo Ave
Wilburton, OK 74578-3431, USA

Wood, Elijah (Actor)
15030 Ventura Blvd # 710
Sherman Oaks, CA 91403-5470, USA

Wood, Evan Rachel (Actor)
c/o Toni Howard *International Creative Management (ICM-LA)*
10250 Constellation Blvd
Los Angeles, CA 90067-6200, USA

Wood, Gene
PO Box 805
Culver City, CA 90232-0805, USA

Wood, Glen (Race Car Driver)
57 Rhody Creek Loop
Stuart, VA 24171-3011, USA

Wood, Gordon S (Historian)
77 Keene St
Providence, RI 02906-1507, USA

Wood, James (Business Person)
Great A & P Tea Co
2 Paragon Dr
Montvale, NJ 07645-1718, USA

Wood, James N (Director)
Art Institute of Chicago
111 S Michigan Ave
Chicago, IL 60603-6488, USA

Wood, Janet (Actor)
Acme Talent
4727 Wilshire Blvd Ste 333
Los Angeles, CA 90010-3874, USA

Wood, John (Actor)
Royal Shakespeare Co
Stratford-on-Avon
Warwickshire CV37 6BB, UNITED KINGDOM (UK)

Wood, John A (Geophysicist, Physicist)
1716 Cambridge St Apt 16
Cambridge, MA 02138-4343, USA

Wood, Jon (Race Car Driver)
Hendrick Motorsports
4400 Papa Joe Hendrick Blvd
Charlotte, NC 28262-5703, USA

Wood, Kimba M (Judge)
US District Court House
40 Foley Sq Ste 104
New York, NY 10007-1507, USA

Wood, Lana (Actor)
868 Masterson Dr
Thousand Oaks, CA 91360-5949, USA

Wood, Leon (Basketball Player)
4217 Faculty Ave
Long Beach, CA 90808-1601, USA

Wood, Maurice (Doctor)
RR 2 Box 543B
Hot Springs, VA 24445, USA

Wood, Mike (Football Player)
Minnesota Vikings
630 N Geyer Rd
Saint Louis, MO 63122-2756, USA

Wood, Oliver (Cinematographer)
1549 N Gardner St
Los Angeles, CA 90046-2807, USA

Wood, Rachel Hurd (Actor)
c/o Michael Lazo *Paradigm (LA)*
360 N Crescent Dr
North Bldg
Beverly Hills, CA 90210-6820, USA

Wood, Richard (Football Player)
New York Jets
5413 Windbrush Dr
Tampa, FL 33625-4051, USA

Wood, Robert E (Publisher)
Peninsula Times Tribune
435 N Michigan Ave # 1609
Chicago, IL 60611-4066, USA

Wood, Robert J (Astronaut)
McDonnell Douglas Corp
PO Box 516
Saint Louis, MO 63166-0516, USA

Wood, Ron
Sandy Mount House
County Kildare S., IRELAND

Wood, Ronald (Ron) (Musician)
c/o Staff Member *Monroe Sounds*
5 Church Row
Wandsworth Plain
London SW18 1ES, UNITED KINGDOM (UK)

Wood, Sharon (Misc)
PO Box 1482
Canmore, AB T0L 0M0, CANADA

Wood, Sidney B B (Tennis Player)
170 Chilean Ave Apt 5C
Palm Beach, FL 33480-4402, USA

Wood, Stuart (Woody) (Musician)
27 Preston Grange Road
Preston Pans E
Lothlan, SCOTLAND

Wood, Thomas H (Publisher)
Atlanta Constitution
72 Marietta St NW
Atlanta, GA 30303-2899, USA

Wood, Tom
6310 San Vicente Blvd Ste 520
Los Angeles, CA 90048-5421, USA

Wood, Wilbur F (Baseball Player)
3 Elmbrook Rd
Bedford, MA 01730-1810, USA

Wood, William V (Football Player)
Green Bay Packers
7941 16th St NW
Washington, DC 20012-1230, USA

Wood, Willie (Golfer)
6120 Stonegate Pl
Edmond, OK 73025-2526, USA

Wood Brothers, The (Music Group)
c/o Staff Member *Paradigm (Monterey)*
509 Hartnell St
Monterey, CA 93940-2825, USA

Wood Jr, Harlington (Judge)
US Court of Appeals
600 E Monroe St Ste 324
Springfield, IL 62701-1672, USA

Woodall, Al (Football Player)
New York Jets
131 Field Crest Rd
New Canaan, CT 06840-6331, USA

Woodall, Jerry M (Engineer, Inventor)
Yale University
105 Wall St
Microelectronic Materials Ctr
New Haven, CT 06511-8917, USA

Woodard, Alfre (Actor)
602 Bay St
Santa Monica, CA 90405-1215, USA

Woodard, Charlayne (Actor, Writer)
Agency for Performing Arts
405 S Beverly Dr Ste 500
Beverly Hills, CA 90212-4425, USA

Woodard, Lynette (Basketball Player)
University of Kansas
Allen Fieldhouse
Lawrence, KS 66045-0001, USA

Woodard, Ray (Football Player)
Denver Broncos
RR 1 Box 208
Corrigan, TX 75939-9750, USA

Woodard, Rickey (Musician)
JVC Music
3800 Barham Blvd Ste 409
Los Angeles, CA 90068-1042, USA

Woodard, Steven L (Steve) (Baseball Player)
800 Frost Ct SW
Hartselle, AL 35640-2714, USA

Woodbine, Bokeem (Actor)
19351 Ventura Blvd
Tarzana, CA 91356-3028, USA

Woodbridge, Todd (Tennis Player)
Advantage International
PO Box 3297
North Burnley, VIC 3121, AUSTRALIA

Woodburn, Danny (Actor)
c/o Staff Member *TalentWorks (LA)*
3500 W Olive Ave Ste 1400
Burbank, CA 91505-5512, USA

Woodcock, Leonard
140 Matthew Dr
Hendersonville, NC 28739-9325, USA

Wooden, John (Basketball Player, Coach)
17711 Margate St Apt 102
Encino, CA 91316-3208, USA

Wooden, Shawn (Football Player)
Miami Dolphins
17741 SW 12th St
Pembroke Pines, FL 33029-4811, USA

Woodeshivk, Tom (Football Player)
Philadelphia Eagles
PO Box 716
Blakeslee, PA 18610-0716, USA

Woodforde, Mark (Tennis Player)
Octagon
1751 Pinnacle Dr Ste 1500
McLean, VA 22102-3833, USA

Woodhead, Cynthia (Swimmer)
PO Box 1193
Riverside, CA 92502-1193, USA

Wooding, Michelle (Golfer)
c/o Staff Member *Pro Golfers Association (PGA) Tour*
112 Tpc Blvd
Ponte Vedra Beach, FL 32082, USA

Woodland, Lauren
c/o Jerry Shandrew *Shandrew Public Relations*
1050 S Stanley Ave
Los Angeles, CA 90019-6634, USA

Woodlawn, Holly
PO Box 27766
Los Angeles, CA 90027-0766, USA

Woodlief, Doug (Football Player)
Los Angeles Rams
7928 Wilkinson Ave
N Hollywood, CA 91605-2209, USA

Woodmansee Jr, John W (General)
6609 Shady Creek Cir
Plano, TX 75024-7439, USA

Woodring, Jim (Artist)
c/o Staff Member *Fantagraphics Books*
7563 Lake City Way NE
Seattle, WA 98115-4218, USA

Woodring, Wendell P (Misc)
6647 El Colegio Rd
Goleta, CA 93117-4203, USA

Woodruff, Billie (Actor)
c/o Joe Gatta *Gersh Agency, The (NY)*
41 Madison Ave Fl 33
New York, NY 10010-2202, USA

Woodruff, Blake (Actor)
c/o Justine Hunt *Hines and Hunt Entertainment*
1213 W Magnolia Blvd
Burbank, CA 91506-1829, USA

Woodruff, Bob (Journalist)
c/o Staff Member *ABC News*
7 W 66th St
New York, NY 10023-6201, USA

Woodruff, Dwayne (Football Player)
Pittsburgh Steelers
10382 Grubbs Rd
Wexford, PA 15090-9420, USA

Woodruff, Frank
170 N Crescent Dr
Beverly Hills, CA 90210-5423, USA

Woodruff, John Y (Athlete, Track Athlete)
9 Dennison Dr # J
East Windsor, NJ 08520-5307, USA

Woodruff, Judy C (Correspondent, Television Host)
Cable News Network
820 1st St NE
News Dept
Washington, DC 20002-4243, USA

Woods, Aubrey (Actor)
James Sharkey
21 Golden Square
London W1R 3PA, UNITED KINGDOM (UK)

Woods, Barbara Alyn (Actor)
Honey Prod
2930 Falaise Ave SW
#H1
Calgary, AL T3E 7J2, CANADA

Woods, Chris (Football Player)
Oakland Raiders
202 Stone Ridge Trl
Birmingham, AL 35210-1730, USA

Woods, Dan (Actor)
The Core Group Talent Agencies
89 Bloor St W 3rd Fl
Toronto, ON M5S 1M1, CANADA

Woods, Don (Football Player)
San Diego Chargers
10415 Johncock Ave SW
Albuquerque, NM 87121-9414, USA

Woods, Elbert (Ickey) (Football Player)
Cincinnati Bengals
916 Surrey Trl
Cincinnati, OH 45245-1137, USA

Woods, George (Athlete, Track Athlete)
7631 Green Hedge Rd
Edwardsville, IL 62025-6135, USA

Woods, James (Actor)
c/o Chris Andrews *Creative Artists Agency LCC (CAA-LA)*
2000 Avenue Of The Stars
Los Angeles, CA 90067-4700, USA

Woods, Jerome (Football Player)
c/o Staff Member *Kansas City Chiefs*
1 Arrowhead Dr
Kansas City, MO 64129-1651, USA

Woods, Jerry L (Football Player)
Detroit Lions
8976 Stratford Ct
Minneapolis, MN 55443-2976, USA

Woods, Michael (Actor)
1346 Havenhurst Dr
West Hollywood, CA 90046-4511, USA

Woods, Paul (Hockey Player)
4276 S Shore St
Waterford, MI 48328-1157, USA

Woods, Philip (Phil) (Composer, Musician)
PO Box 278
Delaware Water Gap, PA 18327-0278, USA

Woods, Qyntel (Basketball Player)
Portland Trail Blazers
1 N Center Court St
Rose Garden
Portland, OR 97227-2102, USA

Woods, Rick (Football Player)
Pittsburgh Steelers
713 Baldwin St
Meadville, PA 16335-1959, USA

Woods, Robert E (Football Player)
New York Jets
2002 Arden Landing Dr
Germantown, TN 38139-5709, USA

Woods, Robert S (Actor)
ITA
227 Central Park W Apt 5A
New York, NY 10024-6057, USA

Woods, Simon (Actor)
c/o Staff Member *International Creative Management (ICM-LA)*
10250 Constellation Blvd
Los Angeles, CA 90067-6200, USA

Woods, Stuart (Writer)
Harper Collins Publishers
10 E 53rd St Fl Cellar2
New York, NY 10022-5076, USA

Woods, Tiger (Golfer)
c/o Sandy Montag *International Management Group (IMG Sports)*
1360 E 9th St Ste 100
Cleveland, OH 44114-1730, USA

Woods, Victoria (Musician)
c/o John Elias *Three Twins Entertainment, Inc*
PO Box 100210
Staten Island, NY 10310-0210, USA

Woodside, DB (Actor)
Paradigm Agency
10100 Santa Monica Blvd Ste 2500
Los Angeles, CA 90067-4116, USA

Woodside, Keith (Football Player)
Green Bay Packers
1903 Laura Anne Dr
Houston, TX 77049-3832, USA

Woodson, Abraham B (Abe) (Football Player)
San Francisco 49ers
3680 Waynesvill St
Las Vegas, NV 89122-4111, USA

Woodson, Alli (Musician)
Superstars Unlimited
PO Box 371371
Las Vegas, NV 89137-1371, USA

Woodson, Charles (Football Player)
Oakland Raiders
9080 Great Heron Cir
Orlando, FL 32836-5483, USA

Woodson, Darren R (Football Player)
Dallas Cowboys
5315 Ambergate Ln
Dallas, TX 75287-5514, USA

Woodson, Dick (Baseball Player)
Minnesota Twins
27879 Panorama Hills Dr
Menifee, CA 92584-7401, USA

Woodson, Kerry (Baseball Player)
Seattle Mariners
19392 La Serena Dr
Fort Myers, FL 33967-0525, USA

Woodson, Michael (Mike) (Basketball Player)
19918 Parsons Green Ct
Katy, TX 77450-5214, USA

Woodson, Robert L (Activist)
National Neighborhood Enterprise Center
1424 16th St NW
Washington, DC 20036-2211, USA

Woodson, Roderick K (Rod) (Football Player)
c/o Team Member *Oakland Raiders*
1220 Harbor Bay Pkwy
Alameda, CA 94502-6570, USA

Woodson, Sean (Football Player)
Philadelphia Eagles
753 Glencross Dr
Jackson, MS 39206-2557, USA

Woodson, Tracy (Baseball Player)
Los Angeles Dodgers
1559 Byfield Pkwy
Valparaiso, IN 46385-9115, USA

Woodson, Warren V (Coach, Football Coach)
12680 Hillcrest Rd Apt 1106
Dallas, TX 75230-2019, USA

Woodville, Kate (Actor)
PO Box 6613
Malibu, CA 90264-6613, USA

Woodward, Bob
2907 Q St NW
Washington, DC 20007-3010, USA

Woodward, Chris (Baseball Player)
Toronto Blue Jays
15049 Howellhurst Dr
Baldwin Park, CA 91706-5625, USA

Woodward, Edward (Actor, Musician)
Ravens Court Calstock
Cornwall PL18 9ST, UNITED KINGDOM
(UK)

Woodward, Joanne (Actor)
c/o Toni Howard *International Creative Management (ICM-LA)*
10250 Constellation Blvd
Los Angeles, CA 90067-6200, USA

Woodward, Kenneth L (Writer)
Simon & Schuster/Pocket/Summit
1230 Avenue Of The Americas
New York, NY 10020-1513, USA

Woodward, Kirsten (Designer, Fashion Designer)
Kirsten Woodward Hats
26 Portobello Green Arcade
London W10, UNITED KINGDOM (UK)

Woodward, Louise
Elton, ENGLAND, UNITED KINGDOM
(UK)

Woodward, Morgan (Actor)
2111 Rockledge Rd
Los Angeles, CA 90068-3135, USA

Woodward, Peter
84 Park Rd Kingston Gate
Surrey, ENGLAND KT2 5JZ, UNITED
KINGDOM (UK)

Woodward, Rob (Baseball Player)
Boston Red Sox
HC 63 Box 43A
Lebanon, NH 03765, USA

Woodward, Roger R (Composer, Conductor, Musician)
LH Productions
2/37 Hendy Ave
Coogee, NSW 2034, AUSTRALIA

Woodward, Woody (Baseball Player)
Milwaukee Braves
10 San Marco Ct
Palm Coast, FL 32137-2104, USA

Woodward III, Neil W (Astronaut)
5701 Ridgefield Rd
Bethesda, MD 20816-1250, USA

Woodwell, George M (Scientist)
Woods Hole Research Center
13 Church St
Woods Hole, MA 02543-1007, USA

Woody, Damien (Football Player)
New England Patriots
12170 Ashland Heights Rd
Ashland, VA 23005-7634, USA

Woody, Paul (Misc)
New Frontier Mgmt
1921 Broadway
Nashville, TN 37203-2719, USA

Wool, Christopher (Artist)
Luhring Augustine Gallery
531 W 24th St
New York, NY 10011-1104, USA

Wooldridge, Dean E (Business Person)
355 S Grand Ave Ste 2600
Los Angeles, CA 90071-1505, USA

Wooldridge, Floyd (Baseball Player)
St Louis Cardinals
214 Barber St
Greenfield, MO 65661-1110, USA

Woolery, Chuck (Television Host)
2555 Silver Cloud Dr
Park City, UT 84060-7040, USA

Woolfolk, Andre (Football Player)
Tennessee Titans
460 Great Circle Rd
Nashville, TN 37228-1404, USA

Woolfolk, Harold (Butch) (Football Player)
New York Giants
4519 Magnolia Ln
Sugar Land, TX 77478-5457, USA

Woolford, Donnell (Football Player)
Chicago Bears
2925 Spur Ave
Fayetteville, NC 28306-8387, USA

Woolford, Gary (Football Player)
New York Giants
6321 S Four Peaks Pl
Chandler, AZ 85249-3946, USA

Woolley, Catherine (Writer)
PO Box 67
Higgins Hollow Road
Orleans, MA 02653-0067, USA

Woolley, Kenneth F (Architect)
790 George St
LV 5
Sydney, NSW 2000, AUSTRALIA

Woolley, Sheb
123 Walton Ferry Rd # 200
Hendersonville, TN 37075-3616, USA

Woolridge, Susan
4 Windmill St.
London, ENGLAND W1P 1HF, UNITED
KINGDOM (UK)

Woolsey, Elizabeth D (Skier)
Trail Creek Ranch
Wilson, WY 83014, USA

Woolsey, R James (Lawyer)
Shea & Gardner
901 New York Ave NW
Washington, DC 20001-4432, USA

Woolsey, Ralph A (Cinematographer)
23388 Mulholland Dr # 109
Woodland Hills, CA 91364-2733, USA

Woolsey, Roland (Football Player)
Dallas Cowboys
10499 W Sultana Ln
Boise, ID 83714-3661, USA

Woolstenhulme, Rick (Musician)
c/o Staff Member *Untitled Entertainment (LA)*
331 N Maple Dr Fl 3
Beverly Hills, CA 90210-3827, USA

Woomble, Roddy (Musician)
Agency Group Ltd
370 City Road
London EC1V 2QA, UNITED KINGDOM
(UK)

Woosnam, Ian H (Golfer)
I M G
1360 E 9th St Ste 100
Cleveland, OH 44114-1730, USA

Woosnam, Phil (Misc)
2211 Mainsail Dr
Marietta, GA 30062-1765, USA

Wooten, Earl (Baseball Player)
Washington Senators
702 Williams St
Williamston, SC 29697-1922, USA

Wooten, Jim (Correspondent)
ABC-TV
5010 Creston St
News Dept
Hyattsville, MD 20781-1216, USA

Wooten, John (Football Player)
Cleveland Browns
505 Boronia Rd
Arlington, TX 76002-4515, USA

Wooten, Morgan (Coach)
De Matha High School
Athletic Dept
Hyattsville, MD 20781, USA

Wooten, Nicholas (Producer)
c/o Staff Member *Endeavor Agency LLC (LA)*
9601 Wilshire Blvd Fl 3
Beverly Hills, CA 90210-5204, USA

Wooten, Ron (Football Player)
New England Patriots
2401 Lewis Grove Ln
Raleigh, NC 27608-1380, USA

Wooten, Shawn (Baseball Player)
Anaheim Angels
7966 Leucite Ave
Rancho Cucamonga, CA 91730-2727,
USA

Wooten, Victor (Musician)
c/o Staff Member *Skyline Music*
PO Box 38
Jefferson, NH 03583-0038, USA

Wooton, John (Football Player)
Cleveland Browns
13520 Darley Ave
Cleveland, OH 44110-2122, USA

Wootton, Charles G (Diplomat)
Chevron Corp
555 Market St
San Francisco, CA 94105-2800, USA

Wopat, Tom (Actor, Musician)
c/o Staff Member *Brokaw Company, The*
9255 W Sunset Blvd Ste 804
Los Angeles, CA 90069-3305, USA

Word, Barry (Football Player)
New Orleans Saints
5746 Janneys Mill Cir
Haymarket, VA 20169-6196, USA

Word, Roscoe (Football Player)
New York Jets
175 Richardson Rd
Ridgeland, MS 39157-9781, USA

Worden, Alfred M (Astronaut)
PO Box 8065
Vero Beach, FL 32963-8065, USA

Worden, Marc (Actor)
c/o Joanna (Joanie) Burstein *Burstein Company, The*
15304 W Sunset Blvd Ste 208
Pacific Palisades, CA 90272-3656, USA

Worden, Neil (Football Player)
Philadelphia Eagles
2 Indian Camp Trl
Portage, IN 46368-1001, USA

Worgull, David (Religious Leader)
Wisconsin Evangelical Lutheran Synod
1270N N Dobson Rd
Chandler, AZ 85224, USA

Working Title, The (Music Group)
c/o Staff Member *Paradigm (Monterey)*
509 Hartnell St
Monterey, CA 93940-2825, USA

Workman, Hank (Baseball Player)
New York Yankees
307 19th St
Santa Monica, CA 90402-2409, USA

Workman, Vincent (Football Player)
Green Bay Packers
1116 Pilgrim Way Apt D
Green Bay, WI 54304-5832, USA

World Party (Music Group)
c/o Staff Member *Paradigm (Monterey)*
509 Hartnell St
Monterey, CA 93940-2825, USA

World Wrestling Entertainment (WWE)
1241 E Main St
Stamford, CT 06902-3520, USA

Worlds Apart
PO Box 21
London, ENGLAND W10 6BR, UNITED
KINGDOM (UK)

Worley, Darryl (Musician)
c/o Rendy Lovelady
1102 17th Ave S # 402
Rlm / Mission Management
Nashville, TN 37212-2208, USA

Worley, Jo Anne (Actor)
9720 Wilshire Blvd Fl 3
Beverly Hills, CA 90212-2015, USA

Worndl, Frank (Skier)
Burgsiedlung 19C
Sonthofen 87527, GERMANY

Woronov, Mary (Actor)
4350 1/4 Beverly Blvd
Los Angeles, CA 90004, USA

Worrell, Tim (Baseball Player)
San Diego Padres
4719 W El Cortez Pl
Phoenix, AZ 85083-2206, USA

Worrell, Todd (Baseball Player)
St Louis Cardinals
13320 Buckland Hall Rd
Saint Louis, MO 63131-1214, USA

Worsley, Lorne J (Gump) (Hockey Player)
421 Bonaire Ave
Beloeil, PQ H3G L1L, CANADA

Worth, Maurice (Business Person)
Della Air Lines
Hartsfield International Airport
Atlanta, GA 30320, USA

Wortham, Barron (Football Player)
Houston Oilers
8608 Busch Gardens Dr
Fort Worth, TX 76123-1445, USA

Wortham, Rich (Baseball Player)
Chicago White Sox
10247 Missel Thrush Dr
Austin, TX 78750-2136, USA

Worthen, John E (Educator)
Ball State University
President's Office
Muncie, IN 47306-0001, USA

Worthington, Al (Baseball Player)
New York Giants
12070 Highway 55
Sterrett, AL 35147-9601, USA

Worthington, Cal
3815 Florin Rd
Sacramento, CA 95823-1801, USA

Worthington, Craig (Baseball Player)
Baltimore Orioles
10019 Mattock Ave
Downey, CA 90240-3528, USA

Worthington, Melvin L (Religious Leader)
Free Will Baptists
PO Box 5002
Antioch, TN 37011-5002, USA

Worthington, Sam
9830 Wilshire Blvd
Beverly Hills, CA 90212-1804, USA

Worthy, James (Basketball Player, Sportscaster)
11821 Henley Ln
Los Angeles, CA 90077-1368, USA

Worthy, Rick (Richard) (Actor)
c/o Charles Silver *SMS Talent Inc*
8730 W Sunset Blvd Ste 440
Los Angeles, CA 90069-2277, USA

Wortman, Keith (Football Player)
Green Bay Packers
240 Big Sky Dr
Saint Charles, MO 63304-7170, USA

Wottle, Dave
9245 Forest Hill Ln
Germantown, TN 38139-7906, USA

Wotus, Ron (Baseball Player)
Pittsburgh Pirates
1902 Strayhorn Rd
Pleasant Hill, CA 94523-1600, USA

Woudenberg, John (Football Player)
Pittsburgh Steelers
3116 S Roosevelt St
Tempe, AZ 85282-2008, USA

Wouk, Herman (Writer)
303 W Crestview Dr
Palm Springs, CA 92264-8920, USA

Woytowicz-Rudnicka, Stefania (Musician)
Al Przyiaciol 2 m
Warsaw 00-565, POLAND

Wozniak, Steve (Designer, Inventor)
c/o Staff Member *Beverly Hecht Agency*
3500 W Olive Ave Ste 1180
Burbank, CA 91505-4651, USA

Wragg, John (Artist)
6 Castle Lane
Devizes
Wilts SN10 1HJ, UNITED KINGDOM (UK)

Wrangler, Jack
41 W 58th St # 5A
New York, NY 10019-1617, USA

Wray, Gordon R (Designer, Engineer)
Stonestack Rempstone
Loughborough
Leics LE12 6RH, UNITED KINGDOM (UK)

Wreckers, The (Music Group)
c/o Jeff Rabhan *The Firm*
9465 Wilshire Blvd Fl 6
Beverly Hills, CA 90212-2605, USA

Wregget, Ken (Hockey Player)
120 Devon Rd
Bloomfield Hills, MI 48302-1123, USA

Wren, Claire
5757 Wilshire Blvd Ste 473
Los Angeles, CA 90036-3632, USA

Wren, Darryl (Football Player)
New England Patriots
1418 Skipjack Dr
Fort Washington, MD 20744-4216, USA

Wrenn, Robert (Golfer)
8911 Alendale Rd
Richmond, VA 23229-7701, USA

Wright, Alexander (Football Player)
Dallas Cowboys
501 S Mississippi St
Amarillo, TX 79106-8735, USA

Wright, Ben (Sportscaster)
CBS-TV
51 W 52nd St
Sports Dept
New York, NY 10019-6119, USA

Wright, Betty (Musician)
Rodgers Redding
1048 Tattnall St
Macon, GA 31201-1537, USA

Wright, Bob (Business Person)
c/o Staff Member *NBC Universal*
100 Universal City Plz
Universal City, CA 91608-1002, USA

Wright, Bonnie (Actor)
P F D Drury House
34-43 Russell St
London WC2B 5HA, UNITED KINGDOM (UK)

Wright, Bracey (Basketball Player)
c/o Staff Member *Minnesota Timberwolves*
600 1st Ave N
Target Center
Minneapolis, MN 55403-1416, USA

Wright, Bruce A (General)
Vice Commander
Air Combat Command
Langley Air Force Base, VA 23665, USA

Wright, Charles (Football Player)
St Louis Cardinals
2698 Wakefield Ln
Westlake, OH 44145-3837, USA

Wright, Chely (Musician)
c/o Staff Member *Paradigm (Monterey)*
509 Hartnell St
Monterey, CA 93940-2825, USA

Wright, Clyde (Baseball Player)
California Angels
528 S Jeanine St
Anaheim, CA 92806-4415, USA

Wright, Craig M (Architect)
C M Wright Inc
706 N La Cienega Blvd
West Hollywood, CA 90069-5204, USA

Wright, David (Baseball Player)
c/o Staff Member *New York Mets*
12301 Roosevelt Ave
Shea Stadium
Flushing, NY 11368-1699, USA

Wright, Dick (Cartoonist)
Columbus Dispatch
34 S 3rd St
Editorial Dept
Columbus, OH 43215-4241, USA

Wright, Donald C (Don) (Cartoonist)
PO Box 1176
Palm Beach, FL 33480-1176, USA

Wright, Doug (Writer)
c/o Staff Member *International Creative Management (ICM-NY)*
40 W 57th St
New York, NY 10019-4001, USA

Wright, Elmo (Football Player)
Kansas City Chiefs
11419 Olympia Dr
Houston, TX 77077-6419, USA

Wright, Eric (Football Player)
Chicago Bears
PO Box 804
Pittsburg, TX 75686-0804, USA

Wright, Ernie H (Football Player)
Los Angeles Chargers
1414 Lauren Ct
Encinitas, CA 92024-6214, USA

Wright, Felix (Football Player)
Cleveland Browns
2698 Wakefield Ln
Westlake, OH 44145-3837, USA

Wright, Felix E (Business Person)
Leggett & Platt Inc
1 Leggett Rd
Carthage, MO 64836-9649, USA

Wright, Geoffrey (Actor)
Innovative Artists
1505 10th St
Santa Monica, CA 90401-2805, USA

Wright, George (Baseball Player)
Texas Rangers
4228 NE 18th St
Oklahoma City, OK 73121-7210, USA

Wright, George (Football Player)
Baltimore Colts
10627 Seaford Dr
Houston, TX 77089-1425, USA

Wright, Gerald (Director)
Guthrie Theatre
725 Vineland Pl
Minneapolis, MN 55403-1139, USA

Wright, Heather
1 Sunnyside Wimbledon
London, ENGLAND SW19, UNITED KINGDOM (UK)

Wright, Hugh (Musician)
William Morris Agency
1600 Division St Ste 300
Nashville, TN 37203-2755, USA

Wright, Ian (Television Host)
c/o Staff Member *Public Broadcasting Service (PBS)*
1320 Braddock Pl
Alexandria, VA 22314-1692, USA

Wright, Irving S (Doctor)
25 E End Ave
New York, NY 10028-7052, USA

Wright, J Oliver (Diplomat)
Burstow Hall
Hortey
Surrey H6 9SR, UNITED KINGDOM (UK)

Wright, James E (Historian)
7 Quail Dr
Etna, NH 03750-4404, USA

Wright, Jamey (Baseball Player)
Colorado Rockies
12801 Lorien Way
Oklahoma City, OK 73170-0407, USA

Wright, Jaret (Baseball Player)
Cleveland Indians
528 S Jeanine St
Anaheim, CA 92806-4415, USA

Wright, Jay (Writer)
General Delivery
Piermont, NH 03779-9999, USA

Wright, Jeff (Football Player)
Minnesota Vikings
6341 Rolf Ave
Edina, MN 55439-1434, USA

Wright, Jeff (Football Player)
Buffalo Bills
23426 N 21st Pl
Phoenix, AZ 85024-8631, USA

Wright, Jeffrey (Actor)
c/o Jimmy Darmody *Creative Artists Agency LCC (CAA-LA)*
2000 Avenue Of The Stars
Los Angeles, CA 90067-4700, USA

Wright, Jenny (Actor)
Paul Kohner
9300 Wilshire Blvd Ste 555
Beverly Hills, CA 90212-3211, USA

Wright, Jim (Baseball Player)
Kansas City Royals
2822 S 29th St
Saint Joseph, MO 64503-1114, USA

Wright, Jim (Baseball Player)
Boston Red Sox
549 E Randall St
Coopersville, MI 49404-9649, USA

Wright, John (Football Player)
Atlanta Falcons
1673 County Road 2500 E
Saint Joseph, IL 61873-9704, USA

Wright, Johnny (Actor, Producer)
Wright Entertainment Group
7680 Universal Blvd Ste 500
Orlando, FL 32819-8998, USA

Wright, Judith A (Writer)
17 Devonport St
#1
Lyons, ACT 2060, AUSTRALIA

Wright, Keith (Football Player)
Cleveland Browns
17750 County Road 605
Farmersville, TX 75442-6895, USA

Wright, Ken (Baseball Player)
Kansas City Royals
1651 Ora Dr
Pensacola, FL 32506-8250, USA

Wright, Laura (Actor)
c/o Staff Member *Stone Manners Talent & Literary (NY)*
900 Broadway Ste 803
New York, NY 10003-1229, USA

Wright, Lawrence A (Judge)
US Tax Court
400 2nd St NW
Washington, DC 20217-0002, USA

Wright, Louie (Football Player)
Denver Broncos
2263 S Quentin Way # 301
Aurora, CO 80014-7316, USA

Wright, Louis B (Historian)
3702 Leland St
Chevy Chase, MD 20815-4904, USA

Wright, Louis D (Football Player)
Digi-Tec
3140 S Peoria St # K274
Seismic Corp
Aurora, CO 80014-3178, USA

Wright, Max (Actor)
Bresler Kelly Assoc
11500 W Olympic Blvd Ste 510
Los Angeles, CA 90064-1527, USA

Wright, Michael (Actor)
c/o Steven Arcieri *Arcieri & Associates Inc*
305 Madison Ave Ste 2315
New York, NY 10165-5015, USA

Wright, Michael W (Business Person)
Super Valu Inc
11840 Valley View Rd
Eden Prairie, MN 55344-3643, USA

Wright, Michelle (Musician)
Savannah Music
205 Powell Pl # 214
Brentwood, TN 37027-7522, USA

Wright, Mickey
2972 SE Treasure Island Rd
Port St Lucie, FL 34952-5773, USA

Wright, Nathaniel (Nate) (Football Player)
Atlanta Falcons
11247 Zorita Ct
San Diego, CA 92124-2207, USA

Wright, N'Bushe
1505 10th St
Santa Monica, CA 90401-2805, USA

Wright, Pat (Musician)
Superstars Unlimited
PO Box 371371
Las Vegas, NV 89137-1371, USA

Wright, Peter R (Choreographer, Dancer)
10 Chiswick Wharf
London W4 2SR, UNITED KINGDOM (UK)

Wright, Petra (Actor)
c/o Bob Glennon *One Entertainment (LA)*
12 W 57th St Ph
New York, NY 10019-3900, USA

Wright, Randy (Football Player)
Green Bay Packers
3591 Richie Rd
Verona, WI 53593-9649, USA

Wright, Raymond R (War Hero)
10 Holt Cir
Fletcher, NC 28732-8427, USA

Wright, Rick (Musician)
Agency Group
370 City Road
London EC1V 2QA, UNITED KINGDOM (UK)

Wright, Ricky (Baseball Player)
Los Angeles Dodgers
2502 Clark Ln
Paris, TX 75460-6220, USA

Wright, Ron (Baseball Player)
Seattle Mariners
310 S 2100 E
Saint George, UT 84790-1465, USA

Wright, Ronald (Winkie) (Boxer)
c/o James Prince *Prince Boxing Enterprises*
3030 Jensen Dr
Houston, TX 77026, USA

Wright, Roy (Baseball Player)
New York Giants
331 Pinehurst Cir
Chickamauga, GA 30707-1459, USA

Wright, Samuel E (Actor)
c/o Marvin Josephson *Gilla Roos Ltd*
16 W 22nd St Ste 303
New York, NY 10010-5825, USA

Wright, Stephen T (Football Player)
Green Bay Packers
14 Conifer Sq
Augusta, GA 30909-4505, USA

Wright, Steve (Football Player)
Dallas Cowboys
15 Camel Point Dr
Laguna Beach, CA 92651-6988, USA

Wright, Steven (Actor)
c/o Staff Member *United Talent Agency (UTA)*
9560 Wilshire Blvd Ste 500
Beverly Hills, CA 90212-2401, USA

Wright, Tom (Actor)
c/o Steven Siebert *Lighthouse Entertainment*
409 N Camden Dr Ste 202
Beverly Hills, CA 90210-4423, USA

Wright, Tom (Baseball Player)
Boston Red Sox
1116 Poplar Springs Church Rd
Shelby, NC 28152-8071, USA

Wright, Trevor (Actor)
c/o Wendi Green *Abrams Artists Agency (LA)*
9200 W Sunset Blvd Ph 11
Los Angeles, CA 90069-3601, USA

Wright, Van Earl (Actor)
c/o Jill Smoller *William Morris Agency (WMA-LA)*
1 William Morris Pl
Beverly Hills, CA 90212-4261, USA

Wright, Weldon (Football Player)
Brooklyn Dodgers
701 E Bluff St Apt 6406
Fort Worth, TX 76102-2372, USA

Wright, Willie (Football Player)
Phoenix Cardinals
13456 Dry Gulch Rd
Paonia, CO 81428-7119, USA

Wright Jr, Charles P (Writer)
940 Locust Ave
Charlottesville, VA 22901-4030, USA

Wright Jr, Cobina (Actor)
1326 Dove Meadow Rd
Solvang, CA 93463-9621, USA

Wright Jr, John M (General)
21227 George Brown Ave
Riverside, CA 92518-2881, USA

Wright-Mason, Sarah (Actor)
c/o Michael Baum *Handprint Entertainment*
1100 Glendon Ave Ste 1000
Los Angeles, CA 90024-3514, USA

Wright Penn, Robin (Actor)
Creative Artists Agency
9830 Wilshire Blvd
Beverly Hills, CA 90212-1804, USA

Wrightman, Tim (Football Player)
Chicago Bears
3505 S Denison Ave
San Pedro, CA 90731-6803, USA

Wrightson, Bernard (Bernie) (Swimmer)
924 Birch Ave
Escondido, CA 92027-3903, USA

Wrigley, Edward A (Historian)
13 Sedley Taylor Rd
Cambridge CB2 2PW, UNITED KINGDOM (UK)

Wrigley Jr, William (Business Person)
William Wrigley Jr Co
410 N Michigan Ave
Chicago, IL 60611-4287, USA

Wrona, Rick (Baseball Player)
Chicago Cubs
2946 E 57th St
Tulsa, OK 74105-7404, USA

Wszola, Jacek (Athlete, Track Athlete)
Ul Chrzanowskiego 7 m 70
Warsaw 04-381, POLAND

Wu, Alice (Writer)
c/o Staff Member *Creative Artists Agency LCC (CAA-LA)*
2000 Avenue Of The Stars
Los Angeles, CA 90067-4700, USA

Wu, Gordon Y S (Business Person)
Hopewell Holdings
Hopewell Center
183 Queen Road East
Hong Kong, CHINA

Wu, Kristy (Actor)
c/o Staff Member *Abrams Artists Agency (LA)*
9200 W Sunset Blvd Ph 11
Los Angeles, CA 90069-3601, USA

Wu, Madame Sylvia
1515 Capri Dr
Pacific Palisades, CA 90272-2709, USA

Wu, Sau Lan (Physicist)
35 Robinson St
Cambridge, MA 02138-1403, USA

Wu, Tai Tsun (Physicist)
35 Robinson St
Cambridge, MA 02138-1403, USA

Wu, Vivian (Actor)
McKeon-Myones Management
9100 Wilshire Blvd Ste 350W
C/O Laura Myones
Beverly Hills, CA 90212-3437, USA

Wu-Tang
BMG/RCA
1540 Broadway # 3500
New York, NY 10036-4039, USA

Wu Yigong (Director)
52 Yong Fu Road
Shanghai, CHINA

WuDunn, Sheryl (Journalist)
New York Times
229 W 43rd St
Editorial Dept
New York, NY 10036-3959, USA

Wuethrich, Kurt (Nobel Prize Laureate)
Federal Institute of Technology
ETH Zentrum
Zurich 8092, SWITZERLAND

Wuhl, Robert (Actor)
Paradigm Agency
10100 Santa Monica Blvd Ste 2500
Los Angeles, CA 90067-4116, USA

Wuhrer, Kari (Actor)
PO Box 69188
Los Angeles, CA 90069-0188, USA

Wunderlich, Paul (Artist)
Haynstr 2
Hamburg 20949, GERMANY

Wunsch, Carl I (Oceanographer)
78 Washington Ave
Cambridge, MA 02140-2708, USA

Wunsch, Jerry (Football Player)
Tampa Bay Buccaneers
2601 Red Maple Rd
Wausau, WI 54401-9151, USA

Wunsch, Kelly (Baseball Player)
Chicago White Sox
11613 Hunters Green Trl
Austin, TX 78732-2055, USA

Wuorinen, Charles P (Composer)
Howard Stokar Mgmt
870 W End Ave
New York, NY 10025-4918, USA

Wurtzel, Elizabeth (Actor, Writer)
c/o Staff Member *Artist Agency, THE (NY)*
230 W 55th St Apt 29D
New York, NY 10019-5206, USA

Wurz, Alexander (Race Car Driver)
McLaren Int'l Working Park
Albert Dr
Woking
Surrey GU21 5JY, UNITED KINGDOM (UK)

Wuycik, Dennis (Basketball Player)
31 Rogerson Dr
Chapel Hill, NC 27517-4037, USA

Wyant, Fred (Football Player)
Washington Redskins
516 Westwood Ave
Morgantown, WV 26505-2125, USA

Wyatt, Alvin (Football Player)
Oakland Raiders
PO Box 244
Daytona Beach, FL 32115-0244, USA

Wyatt, Doug (Football Player)
New Orleans Saints
23 Andante Trail Pl
Shenandoah, TX 77381-2775, USA

Wyatt, Jane (Actor)
16 Sotelo Ave
Piedmont, CA 94611-3535, USA

Wyatt, Jennifer (Golfer)
Carolina Group
2321 Devine St Ste A
Columbia, SC 29205-2428, USA

Wyatt, Keke (Musician)
Universal Attractions
145 W 57th St # 1500
New York, NY 10019-2220, USA

Wyatt, Leslie (Educator)
Arkansas State University
President's Office
State University, AR 72467, USA

Wyatt, Shannon (Actor)
8949 Falling Creek Ct
Annandale, VA 22003-4108, USA

Wyatt, Sharon (Actor)
16830 Ventura Blvd Ste 300
Encino, CA 91436-1715, USA

Wyatt Jr, Oscar S (Business Person)
Coastal Corp
6955 Union Park Ctr Ste 540
Midvale, UT 84047-6520, USA

Wyche, Samuel D (Sam) (Coach, Football Coach, Sportscaster)
Cincinnati Bengals
PO Box 1570
Pickens, SC 29671-1570, USA

Wycheck, Frank (Football Player)
4674 Sunrise Ave
Bensalem, PA 19020-1112, USA

Wycinsky, Craig (Football Player)
Cleveland Browns
6890 E Sunrise Dr Ste 120
Tucson, AZ 85750-0739, USA

Wycoff, Brooks (Athlete)
1 Mohegan Sun Blvd
Uncasville, CT 06382-1355, USA

Wyeth, James Browning (Artist)
701 Smiths Bridge Rd
Lookout Farm
Wilmington, DE 19807-1325, USA

Wylde, Chris
3313 1/2 Barham Blvd
Los Angeles, CA 90068-1450, USA

Wylde, Zakk (Musician)
c/o Jamie Adler *Agency Group Ltd, The (LA)*
1880 Century Park E Ste 711
Los Angeles, CA 90067-1618, USA

Wylde Bunch, The (Music Group)
c/o Staff Member *Paradigm (Monterey)*
509 Hartnell St
Monterey, CA 93940-2825, USA

Wyle, Noah (Actor, Producer)
c/o Staff Member *Wyle/Katz Company, The*
1041 N Formosa Ave
Writers Bldg #311
West Hollywood, CA 90046-6703, USA

Wyler, Gretchen (Actor)
2711 Patricia Ave
Los Angeles, CA 90064-4422, USA

Wylie, Adam
14011 Ventura Blvd # 202
Sherman Oaks, CA 91423-3533, USA

Wyludda, Ilke (Athlete, Track Athlete)
LAC Chemnitz
Relchengainer Str 154
Chemnitz 09125, GERMANY

Wyman, Bill (Musician)
Ripple Productions
344 Kings Road
London SW3 5UR, UNITED KINGDOM (UK)

Wyman, David (Football Player)
Seattle Seahawks
2114 204th Pl NE
Sammamish, WA 98074-4390, USA

Wyman, Joel (Producer, Writer)
c/o Staff Member *Creative Artists Agency (CAA-LA)*
2000 Avenue Of The Stars
Los Angeles, CA 90067-4700, USA

Wymore, Patrice (Actor)
Port Antonio
JAMAICA BWI, WEST INDIES

Wyn-Davies, Geraint (Actor)
Oscars Abrams Zimel
438 Queen St E
Toronto, ON M5A 1T4, CANADA

Wynalda, Eric (Soccer Player)
2313 Stomcroft Court
Westlake Village, CA 91361, USA

Wynant, H M
300 S Raymond Ave Ste 11
Pasadena, CA 91105-2639, USA

Wynegar, Butch (Baseball Player)
Minnesota Twins
PO Box 915811
Longwood, FL 32791-5811, USA

Wyner, George (Actor)
3450 Laurie Pl
Studio City, CA 91604-3881, USA

Wyngaarden, James B (Doctor)
NAS
2101 Columbus Ave NW
Washington, DC 20418-0001, USA

Wyngarde, Peter (Actor)
41
4 Acre Lane
Clock Face Saint Helen's
Lancash WA9 4DZ, UNITED KINGDOM (UK)

Wynn, Bob (Golfer)
78455 Calle Orense
La Quinta, CA 92253-2370, USA

Wynn, Jimmy (Baseball Player)
Houston Colt .45's
5507 Sandy Field Ct
Rosharon, TX 77583-2040, USA

Wynn, Renaldo (Football Player)
Jacksonville Jaguars
19805 Rothschild Ct
Ashburn, VA 20147-4124, USA

Wynn, Spergon (Football Player)
Cleveland Browns
614 32nd St
Galveston, TX 77550, USA

Wynn, Stephen A (Business Person)
Desert Inn Hotel
3245 Las Vegas Blvd S
Las Vegas, NV 89109, USA

Wynn, Steve (Business Person)
Wynn Las Vegas
3131 Las Vegas Blvd S
Las Vegas, NV 89109-1967, USA

Wynn, Tracy Keenan
700 W 3rd St
Los Angeles, CA 90071, USA

Wynne, Billy (Baseball Player)
New York Mets
7722 Greenwich Ct W
Jacksonville, FL 32277-0924, USA

Wynne, Marvell (Baseball Player)
Pittsburgh Pirates
39640 Del Val Dr
Murrieta, CA 92562-4038, USA

Wynter, Dana (Actor)
Contemporary Artists
610 Santa Monica Blvd Ste 202
Santa Monica, CA 90401-1645, USA

Wynter, Sarah (Actor)
c/o David (Dave) Fleming *Mosaic Media Group*
24 Music Sq W Fl 1
Nashville, TN 37203-6661, USA

Wyss, Amanda (Actor)
Badgley Connor Talent
1680 Vine St Ste 1016
Los Angeles, CA 90028-8800, USA

Xiaoshuang, Li
Rue Tiyukuan 9
Beijing, PEOPLES REPUBLIC OF CHINA

Xie Bingxin (Writer)
Central Nationalities Institute
Residential Qtrs
Beijing 100081, CHINA

Xie Jin (Director)
Shanghai Film Studio
595 Caoxi Beilu
Shanghai, CHINA

Xscape (Musician)
c/o Staff Member *So So Def Recordings Inc*
1350 Spring St NW Ste 750
Atlanta, GA 30309-2870, USA

Xu Bing (Artist)
540 Metropolitan Ave
Brooklyn, NY 11211-3554, USA

Xu Shuyang (Artist)
Zheijang Academy of Fine Arts
PO Box 169
Hangzhou, CHINA

Xue Wei (Musician)
134 Sheaveshill Ave
London NW9, UNITED KINGDOM (UK)

Xuereb, Emanuel (Actor)
c/o Staff Member *The Artists Group Ltd (LA)*
1650 Broadway Ste 610
New York, NY 10019-6833, USA

Xuereb, Salvator (Actor)
Metropolitan Talent Agency
4500 Wilshire Blvd Fl 2
Los Angeles, CA 90010-3858, USA

Xzibit (Musician)
c/o John Boyle *Sanctuary Artist Management (LA)*
9255 W Sunset Blvd # 200
Los Angeles, CA 90069-3309, USA

Yabians, Frank (Producer)
88 Bull Path
East Hampton, NY 11937-4622, USA

Yablans, Frank
100 Bull Path
East Hampton, NY 11937-4601, USA

Yablonski, Ventan (Football Player)
Chicago Cardinals
1049 W Douglas Ave
Naperville, IL 60540-4356, USA

Yaeger, Andrea (Tennis Player)
1490 S Ute Ave
Aspen, CO 81611-2814, USA

Yaffe, Martin (Physicist)
University of Toronto
Biophysics Dept
Toronto, ON M4W 1J3, CANADA

Yager, Faye (Activist)
Children of the Underground
902 Curlew Ct NW
Atlanta, GA 30327, USA

Yager, Rick (Cartoonist)
North American Syndicate
235 E 45th St
New York, NY 10017-3305, USA

Yagher, Jeff
15057 Sherview Pl
Sherman Oaks, CA 91403-5037, USA

Yago, Gideon (Journalist, Television Host)
c/o Staff Member *MTV Networks (NY)*
1515 Broadway Fl 31L
New York, NY 10036-8901, USA

Yaguda, Stan (Musician)
Joyce Agency
370 Harrison Ave
Harrison, NY 10528-2714, USA

Yagudin, Alexei (Figure Skater)
Connecticut Skating Center
300 Alumni Rd
Newington, CT 06111-1865, USA

Yahr, Betty (Baseball Player)
10360 Timber Ridge Dr
Milan, MI 48160-8929, USA

Yakavonis, Ray (Football Player)
Minnesota Vikings
8 Strand St
Hanover Township, PA 18706-4011, USA

Yake, Terry (Hockey Player)
3 Stratford Park
Bloomfield, CT 06002-2143, USA

Yakovlev, Aleksandr N (Government Official)
Prisoner Rehabilitation Commission
Ul Iljinka 8/4
Moscow 103132, RUSSIA

Yale, Brian (Musician)
c/o Staff Member *Creative Artists Agency LCC (CAA-LA)*
2000 Avenue Of The Stars
Los Angeles, CA 90067-4700, USA

Yallop, Frank (Coach)
San Jose Earthquakes
100 N Almaden Ave
San Jose, CA 95110-2437, USA

Yalow, Roslyn
3242 Tibbett Ave
Bronx, NY 10463-3801, USA

Yamagata, Hiro (Artist)
1080 Avenue D
Redondo Beach, CA 90277, USA

Yamagata, Rachel (Musician)
c/o Staff Member *Paradigm (Monterey)*
509 Hartnell St
Monterey, CA 93940-2825, USA

Yamaguchi, Kristi T (Figure Skater)
Always Dream Foundation
1203 Preservation Park Way Ste 102
Oakland, CA 94612-1246, USA

Yamaguchi, Roy (Business Person)
Roy's Restaurant
Kai Corporate Plaza
6600 Kalaniaole Hwy
Honolulu, HI 96825, USA

Yamame, Marlene Mitsuko (Actor)
Herb Tannen
10801 National Blvd Ste 101
Los Angeles, CA 90064-4140, USA

Yamamoto, Kansai (Designer, Fashion Designer)
103 Grand St
New York, NY 10013-2685, USA

Yamamoto, Kenichi (Business Person)
Mazda Motor Corp
4-6-19 Funairi-Minami
Minamiku
Hiroshima, JAPAN

Yamamoto, Takuma (Business Person)
Fujitsu Ltd
1-6-1 Marunouchi
Chiyodaku
Tokyo 100, JAPAN

Yamamoto, Yohji (Designer, Fashion Designer)
14-15 Conduit St
London W1R 9TG, UNITED KINGDOM (UK)

Yamanaka, Tsuyoshi (Swimmer)
6-10-33-212 Akasaka
Minatoku
Tokyo, JAPAN

Yamani, Sheikh Ahmed Zaki (Government Official)
Chermignon near Crans-Montana
Valais, SWITZERLAND

Yamaoka, Seigen H (Religious Leader)
Buddhist Churches of America
1710 Octavia St
San Francisco, CA 94109-4341, USA

Yamasaki, Taro M (Journalist)
People Magazine Editorial Dept
Time-Life Building
New York, NY 10020, USA

Yamashita, Yasuhiro (Athlete, Coach)
1117 Kitakaname
Hitatsuka Kanagawa 259-1207, JAPAN

Yan, Romina (Actor)
c/o Staff Member Telefe - Argentina
Pavon 2444 (C1248AAT)
Buenos Aires, ARGENTINA

Yancey, Emily
247 S Beverly Dr # 102
Beverly Hills, CA 90212-3830, USA

Yanchar, William (Football Player)
Cleveland Browns
PO Box 460141
Aurora, CO 80046-0141, USA

Yancy, Emily (Actor)
Henderson/Hogan
8285 W Sunset Blvd Ste 1
West Hollywood, CA 90046-2420, USA

Yancy, Hugh (Baseball Player)
Chicago White Sox
2743 18th St
Sarasota, FL 34234-7844, USA

Yanez, Edwardo (Actor)
c/o Dolores Robinson Dolores Robinson Entertainment
3815 Hughes Ave # 3
Culver City, CA 90232-2715, USA

Yang, C K
PO Box 7855-39 Tsoying
Kaoshking, TAIWAN R.O.C., TAIWAN

Yang, Chuan-Kwang (C K) (Athlete, Track Athlete)
PO Box 7855-39
Tsoying
Kaohsking, TAIWAN

Yang, Jerry (Business Person, Engineer)
Yahoo!
701 First Ave
Sunnyvale, CA 94089-1019, USA

Yang, Liwei (Misc)
Satellite Launch Center
Jiuquan
Gansu Province, CHINA

Yang, Shang-Fa (Misc)
118 Villanova Dr
Davis, CA 95616, USA

Yankelovich, Daniel (Scientist)
Public Agenda Foundation
6 E 39th St Ste 900
New York, NY 10016-0112, USA

Yankovic, Al (Weird Al) (Actor, Comedian, Musician, Songwriter, Writer)
c/o Michael Eisenstadt Amsel Eisenstadt & Frazier Inc
5055 Wilshire Blvd Ste 865
Los Angeles, CA 90036-6109, USA

Yankovsky, Oleg I (Actor)
Komsomolsky Prospekt 41
#10
Moscow 119270, RUSSIA

Yankowski, George (Baseball Player)
Philadelphia Athletics
12 Porter Ln
Lexington, MA 02420, USA

Yankowski, Ron (Football Player)
St Louis Cardinals
1318 Saint Paul Rd
Ballwin, MO 63021-8208, USA

Yannas, I V (Engineer, Scientist)
Massachusetts Institute of Technology
Engineering School
Cambridge, MA 02139, USA

Yanni (Musician, Songwriter, Writer)
PO Box 46996
Eden Prairie, MN 55344-6996, USA

Yao, Ming (Basketball Player)
Houston Rockets
1510 Polk St
Houston, TX 77002-1099, USA

Yaralian, Zaven (Football Player)
Green Bay Packers
7770 S Peoria St
Englewood, CO 80112-4138, USA

Yarber, Eric (Football Player)
Washington Redskins
325 Valley Football Ctr
Oregon State University Attn Football Program
Corvallis, OR 97331-8544, USA

Yarborough, Cale
2723 W Palmetto St
Florence, SC 29501-5929, USA

Yarborough, Glenn
PO Box 158
Malibu, CA 90265-0158, USA

Yarborough, W Caleb (Cale) (Race Car Driver)
Yarborough Racing
2723 W Palmetto St
Florence, SC 29501-5929, USA

Yarborough, William P (General)
3525 Slade Run Dr
Falls Church, VA 22042-3923, USA

Yarbrough, Curtis (Religious Leader)
General Baptists Assn
100 Stinson Dr
Poplar Bluff, MO 63901-8736, USA

Yarbrough, Glenn (Musician, Songwriter, Writer)
150 Avenida Presidio
San Clemente, CA 92672-3170, USA

Yarbrough, Jim (Football Player)
Detroit Lions
720 N Phelps Ave
Winter Park, FL 32789-2757, USA

Yarbrough, Jim (Football Player)
New York Giants
440 Capricorn St
Cedar Hill, TX 75104-8106, USA

Yard, Mollie
1000 16th St. W
Washington, DC, USA

Yardbirds, The
PO Box 1821
Ojai, CA 93024-1821, USA

Yared, Gabriel (Composer)
c/o Staff Member Evolution Music Partners
9100 Wilshire Blvd
East Tower #201
Beverly Hills, CA 90212-3401, USA

Yarkin, Cori (Musician)
GreeneHouse Management
PO Box 151234
C/O Allan Greene
Altamonte Springs, FL 32715-1234, USA

Yarlett, Claire (Actor)
1540 Skylark Ln
Los Angeles, CA 90069-1233, USA

Yarnall, Celeste (Actor)
2899 Agoura Rd # 315
Westlake Village, CA 91361-3218, USA

Yarnell, Lorene (Misc)
Arthur Shafman International
PO Box 352
Pawling, NY 12564-0352, USA

Yarno, George (Football Player)
Tampa Bay Buccaneers
1081 White Pine Flats Rd
Troy, ID 83871-9674, USA

Yarno, John (Football Player)
Seattle Seahawks
10535 158th Ave NE
Redmond, WA 98052-2659, USA

Yarrow, Peter (Musician, Songwriter, Writer)
27 W 67th St # 5E
New York, NY 10023-6258, USA

Yary, A Ronald (Ron) (Football Player)
Minnesota Vikings
38886 Calle De Companero
Murrieta, CA 92562-8877, USA

Yasbeck, Amy (Actor)
c/o Jonathan Howard Innovative Artists (LA)
1505 10th St
Santa Monica, CA 90401-2805, USA

Yashin, Alexei (Hockey Player)
New York Islanders
Hempstead Turnpike
Nassau Coliseum
Uniondale, NY 11553, USA

Yasutake, Patti
145 S Fairfax Ave Ste 310
Los Angeles, CA 90036-2176, USA

Yates, Al (Baseball Player)
Milwaukee Brewers
11613 W Yuma Ct
New Berlin, WI 53146, USA

Yates, Albert C (Educator)
Colorado State University System
President's Office
Denver, CO 80202, USA

Yates, Bill (Cartoonist)
King Features Syndicate
888 7th Ave Ste 201
New York, NY 10106-0201, USA

Yates, Bob (Football Player)
Boston Patriots
391 Bentwood Dr
Spring Branch, TX 78070-6016, USA

Yates, Cassie (Actor)
260 S Beverly Dr Ste 210
Beverly Hills, CA 90212-3812, USA

Yates, Jim (Race Car Driver)
Commonwealth Service & Supply
PO Box 510
Occoquan, VA 22125-0510, USA

Yates, Peter
3340 Caroline Ave
Culver City, CA 90232, USA

Yates, Peter J (Director)
334 Caroline Ave
Culver City, CA 90232, USA

Yates, Ronald W (Ron) (General)
525 Silhourette Way
Monument, CO 80132, USA

Yauch, Adam (MCA) (Artist)
GAS Entertainment
8935 Lindblade St
Culver City, CA 90232-2438, USA

Yavneh, Cyrus (Producer)
c/o Staff Member International Creative Management (ICM-LA)
10250 Constellation Blvd
Los Angeles, CA 90067-6200, USA

Yayo, Tony (Musician)
c/o Staff Member Interscope Records (NY)
1790 Broadway
New York, NY 10019-1412, USA

Ybarra y Churruca, Emilio de (Financier)
Banco Bilbao-Vizcaya
Plaza de San Nicolas 4
Bilboa 48005, SPAIN

Yeager, Andrea
3137 Devlin Dr.
Grand Junction, CO 81504, USA

Yeager, Bunny (Model, Photographer)
9165 Park Dr Ste 9
Miami Shores, FL 33138-3163, USA

Yeager, Charles E (Chuck) (General)
PO Box 579
Penn Valley, CA 95946-0579, USA

Yeager, Jeana (Misc)
3695 Highway 50
Campbell, TX 75422, USA

Yeager, Stephen W (Steve) (Baseball Player)
Los Angeles Dodgers
PO Box 34184
Granada Hills, CA 91394-4184, USA

Yeagley, Jerry (Coach)
1418 S Sare Rd
Bloomington, IN 47401-4431, USA

Yeagley, Susan (Actor)
c/o Staff Member *OmniPop Inc (LA)*
4605 Lankershim Blvd Ste 201
North Hollywood, CA 91602-1874, USA

Yeah Yeah Yeahs (Music Group)
249 Metropolitan Ave
Brooklyn, NY 11211-4009, USA

Yeakel, G Scott (Astronaut)
14224 E Kalil Dr
Scottsdale, AZ 85259-4624, USA

Yearley, Douglas C (Business Person)
Phelps Dodge Corp
1 N Central Ave
Phoenix, AZ 85004-4464, USA

Yearwood, Trisha (Musician)
c/o Keith Miller *William Morris Agency (WMA-TN)*
1600 Division St Ste 300
Nashville, TN 37203-2755, USA

Yeates, Jeff (Football Player)
Buffalo Bills
3793 Club Dr NE
Atlanta, GA 30319-1107, USA

Yeghiayan, Lori (Actor)
c/o Staff Member *Kyle Fritz Management*
6325 Heather Dr
Los Angeles, CA 90068-1633, USA

Yelchin, Anton (Actor)
c/o Staff Member *International Creative Management (ICM-LA)*
10250 Constellation Blvd
Los Angeles, CA 90067-6200, USA

Yelding, Eric (Baseball Player)
Houston Astros
PO Box 325
Montrose, AL 36559-0325, USA

Yeliseyev, Aleksei S (Cosmonaut)
Bauman Higher Technical School
Baumanskaya Ul 5
Moscow 107005, RUSSIA

Yellen, Janet L (Financier, Government Official)
683 San Luis Rd
Berkeley, CA 94707-1725, USA

Yellen, Larry (Baseball Player)
Houston Colt .45's
3886 Toccoa Falls Dr
Duluth, GA 30097-8105, USA

Yellen, Linda B (Director, Producer)
3 Sheridan Sq
New York, NY 10014-6828, USA

Yellowcard (Musician)
Capitol Records
1750 Vine St # T-06
Hollywood, CA 90028-5209, USA

Yellowjackets
9220 W Sunset Blvd # 320
Los Angeles, CA 90069-3501, USA

Yeltsin, Boris N (Ex-President, President)
Belji Don
Krascnopresneskaj Nab 2
Moscow 103274, RUSSIA

Yelvington, Richard J (Football Player)
New York Giants
2105 Barbe St
Lake Charles, LA 70601-9017, USA

Yen, Donnie (Actor)
c/o Staff Member *Paradigm (LA)*
360 N Crescent Dr
North Bldg
Beverly Hills, CA 90210-6820, USA

Yeo, Gwendoline (Actor)
c/o Ann Geddes *Geddes Agency, The*
8430 Santa Monica Blvd Ste 200
Los Angeles, CA 90069-4253, USA

Yeoh, Michelle (Actor)
c/o Lee Stollman *Endeavor Agency LLC (LA)*
9601 Wilshire Blvd Fl 3
Beverly Hills, CA 90210-5204, USA

Yeohlee (Designer, Fashion Designer)
Yeohlee Designs
530 Fashion Ave
New York, NY 10018-4878, USA

Yeoman, William F (Bill) (Coach, Football Coach, Football Player)
3030 Country Club Blvd
Sugar Land, TX 77478-3630, USA

Yeosock, John J (General)
223 Newport Dr
Peachtree City, GA 30269-4277, USA

Yepremian, Garabed S (Garo) (Football Player)
Detroit Lions
613 Martin Dr
Avondale, PA 19311-1316, USA

Yerby, Frank
Avenida del America 37
Madrid E-28002, SPAIN

Yerman, Jack (Athlete, Track Athlete)
753 Camellia Dr
Paradise, CA 95969-3817, USA

Yes (Music Group)
c/o Staff Member *10th Street Entertainment*
700 N San Vicente Blvd # G410
W Hollywood, CA 90069-5060, USA

Yeston, Maury (Composer)
Yale University
Music Dept
New Haven, CT 06520, USA

Yetnikoff, Walter
c/o Daniel A (Dan) Strone *Trident Media Group LLC*
41 Madison Ave Fl 36
New York, NY 10010-2257, USA

Yett, Rich (Baseball Player)
Minnesota Twins
5840 E Fairbrook Cir
Mesa, AZ 85205-5559, USA

Yeutter, Clayton K (Secretary)
10955 Martingale Ct
Potomac, MD 20854-1500, USA

Yevtushenko, Yevgeny A (Writer)
Kutuzovski Prospekt 2/1
#101
Moscow 121248, RUSSIA

Yewcic, Thomas (Tom) (Baseball Player, Football Player)
Detroit Tigers
31 Cherokee Rd
Arlington, MA 02474-1946, USA

Yilmaz, A Mesut (Prime Minister)
Basbakanlik
Bakanliklar
Ankara, TURKEY

Yimou, Zhang (Actor, Director, Producer, Writer)
c/o William (Bill) Kong *Edko Films*
1212 Tower 2
Admiralty Centre
Hong Kong, CHINA

Ying Yang Twins (Music Group)
TVT Records
23 E 4th St Fl 3
A&R Dept
New York, NY 10003-7028, USA

Yip, David
15 Golden Square #315
London, ENGLAND W1R 3AG, UNITED KINGDOM (UK)

Yip, Francoise (Actor)
Infinite Artists
10 - 206 East 6th Ave
Vancouver, BC V5T 1J8, CANADA

Yip, Vern (Designer)
c/o Staff Member *Trading Spaces*
7700 Wisconsin Ave
The Learning Channel
Bethesda, MD 20814-3578, USA

Ylonen, Juha (Hockey Player)
Ottawa Senators
1000 Palladium Dr
Kanata, ON K2V 1A4, CANADA

Ylonen, Lauri Johannes (Musician)
c/o Staff Member *Rasmus, The*
Playground Music Scandinavia
Box 3171
Malmý s-200 22, SWEDEN

Yo-Yo (Musician)
William Morris Agency
1325 Avenue Of The Americas
New York, NY 10019-6091, USA

Yo Yo Ma (Actor, Musician)
c/o Staff Member *International Creative Management (ICM-LA)*
10250 Constellation Blvd
Los Angeles, CA 90067-6200, USA

Yoakam, Dwight (Musician, Songwriter, Writer)
Fitzgerald Hartley
1908 Wedgewood Ave
Nashville, TN 37212-3733, USA

Yoakum, Dwight (Musician)
Borman Entertainment
1250 6th St Ste 401
Santa Monica, CA 90401-1638, USA

Yoba, Malik (Actor)
c/o Matt Luber *Nine Yards Entertainment*
8530 Wilshire Blvd Fl 5
Beverly Hills, CA 90211-3102, USA

Yochim, Len (Baseball Player)
Pittsburgh Pirates
316 Nelson Dr
New Orleans, LA 70123-1958, USA

Yock, Robert J (Judge)
US Claims Court
717 Madison Pl NW
Washington, DC 20439-0001, USA

Yodoyman, Joseph (Prime Minister)
Prime Minister's Office
N'Djamena, CHAD

Yogaraj (Actor, Bollywood)
18 34th Street
Ashok Nagar
Chennai, TN 600083, INDIA

Yohn, John (Football Player)
Baltimore Colts
12 Riverview Dr
Middletown, PA 17057-3433, USA

Yoho, Mack (Football Player)
Buffalo Bills
2205 Sacramento St Apt 304
San Francisco, CA 94115-2316, USA

Yoken, Mel B (Writer)
261 Carroll St
New Bedford, MA 02740-1412, USA

Yonaker, John (Football Player)
20450 Lake Shore Blvd
Cleveland, OH 44123-1845, USA

Yonamine, Wally (Football Player)
San Francisco 49ers
4389 Malia St Apt 454
Honolulu, HI 96821-1172, USA

Yonder Mountain String Band (Music Group)
c/o Staff Member *Paradigm (Monterey)*
509 Hartnell St
Monterey, CA 93940-2825, USA

Yoo, Paula (Writer)
c/o Nancy Etz *International Creative Management (ICM-LA)*
10250 Constellation Blvd
Los Angeles, CA 90067-6200, USA

Yore, Jim (Football Player)
San Francisco 49ers
1084 Westlake Woods Dr
Springfield, MI 49037-7665, USA

York, Francine (Actor)
6430 W Sunset Blvd Ste 1205
Los Angeles, CA 90028-8002, USA

York, Glen P (War Hero)
1620 E Driftwood Dr
Tempe, AZ 85283-2168, USA

York, Herbert F (Physicist)
6110 Camino De La Costa
La Jolla, CA 92037-6520, USA

York, Jim (Baseball Player)
Kansas City Royals
31262 Via Del Verde
San Juan Capistrano, CA 92675-6315, USA

York, John J (Actor)
4804 Laurel Canyon Blvd # 212
Valley Village, CA 91607-3717, USA

York, Kathleen (Actor)
Bresler Kelly Assoc
11500 W Olympic Blvd Ste 510
Los Angeles, CA 90064-1527, USA

York, Michael (Actor)
c/o Christopher Barrett *Metropolitan*
4500 Wilshire Blvd Fl 2
Los Angeles, CA 90010-3858, USA

York, Michael M (Journalist)
Lexington Herald-Leader
Editorial Dept
Main & Midland
Lexington, KY 40507, USA

York, Michael (Mike) (Hockey Player)
Edmonton Oilers
11230 110th St
Edmonton, AB T5G 3H7, CANADA

York, Mike (Baseball Player)
Pittsburgh Pirates
8001 S 84th Ct
Justice, IL 60458-1420, USA

York, Morgan (Actor)
c/o Meredith Fine *Coast to Coast Talent Group*
3350 Barham Blvd
Los Angeles, CA 90068-1404, USA

York, Ray (Jockey)
27918 Taft Hwy
Taft, CA 93268-9612, USA

York, Susannah (Actor)
P F D Drury House
34-43 Russell St
London WC2B 5HA, UNITED KINGDOM (UK)

Yorke, Thom (Musician)
c/o Staff Member *Creative Artists Agency LCC (CAA-LA)*
2000 Avenue Of The Stars
Los Angeles, CA 90067-4700, USA

Yorkin, Alan (Bud) (Director, Producer)
Bud Yorkin Productions
250 Delfem Dr
Los Angeles, CA 90077, USA

Yorkin, Bud
250 Delfern Dr
Los Angeles, CA 90077-3543, USA

Yorkin, Peg (Politician)
Fund for Feminist Majority
1600 Wilson Blvd Ste 704
Arlington, VA 22209-2505, USA

Yorn, Pete (Musician)
c/o Staff Member *William Morris Agency (WMA-LA)*
1 William Morris Pl
Beverly Hills, CA 90212-4261, USA

Yorn, Peter (Musician, Songwriter, Writer)
The Firm
9100 Wilshire Blvd Ste 100W
Beverly Hills, CA 90212-3435, USA

Yorzyk, William A (Bill) (Swimmer)
162 W Sturbridge Rd # 7
East Brookfield, MA 01515-2017, USA

Yoseliani, Otar D (Director)
Mitskewitch 1 Korp
1 #38
Tbilisi 380060, GEORGIA

Yost, Dennis
PO Box 8770
Endwell, NY 13762-8770, USA

Yost, Edward F J (Eddie) (Baseball Player)
Washington Senators
48 Oakridge Rd
Wellesley, MA 02481-2504, USA

Yost, Paul A Jr (Admiral)
James Medison Memorial Foundation
200 K St NW
Washington, DC 20001-5500, USA

Yothers, Tina (Actor, Musician)
12368 Apple Dr
Chino, CA 91710-2706, USA

Youel, Jim (Football Player)
Washington Redskins
1102 Avenue F
Fort Madison, IA 52627-2743, USA

Youmans, Floyd (Baseball Player)
Montreal Expos
1915 E Noel St
Tampa, FL 33610-6157, USA

Youmans, Maury (Football Player)
Chicago Bears
300 Beach Dr NE Apt 2104
Saint Petersburg, FL 33701-3461, USA

Young, Ace (Musician)
Anderson, Buchanan, & Gillum
1239 Gordon St
Los Angeles, CA 90038-1909, USA

Young, Aden (Actor)
June Cann Mgmt
110 Queen St
Woollahra, NSW 2025, AUSTRALIA

Young, Adrian (Musician)
Rebel Waltz Inc
31652 2nd Ave
Laguna Beach, CA 92651-8244, USA

Young, Al (Football Player)
Pittsburgh Steelers
1947 Green Forest Dr
North Augusta, SC 29841-2174, USA

Young, Alan (Actor)
c/o Staff Member *Tisherman Agency Inc*
6767 Forest Lawn Dr Ste 101
Los Angeles, CA 90068-1050, USA

Young, Almon (Football Player)
Houston Oilers
PO Box 983
Mc Crory, AR 72101-0983, USA

Young, Andre (Dr. Dre) (Actor, Musician)
c/o Staff Member *Aftermath Entertainment*
2220 Colorado Ave
Santa Monica, CA 90404-3506, USA

Young, Angus (Musician, Songwriter, Writer)
East-West Records
46 Kensington Court St
London W8 5DP, UNITED KINGDOM (UK)

Young, Anthony (Baseball Player)
New York Mets
13107 Ellesmere Dr
Houston, TX 77015-2111, USA

Young, Anthony (Football Player)
Indianapolis Colts
914 Colonial Ct
Coatesville, PA 19320-1685, USA

Young, Archie (Baseball Player)
Birmingham Black Barons
1804 Ethel Ave SW
Birmingham, AL 35211-4914, USA

Young, Barbara
23-B Deodar Rd.
London, ENGLAND SWl5- 2NP, UNITED KINGDOM (UK)

Young, Bellamy (Actor)
c/o Katie Rhodes *Untitled Entertainment (LA)*
331 N Maple Dr Fl 3
Beverly Hills, CA 90210-3827, USA

Young, Bob (Cartoonist)
King Features Syndicate
888 7th Ave Ste 201
New York, NY 10106-0201, USA

Young, Boyd (Misc)
United Paperworkers Union
3340 Perimeter Hill Dr
Nashville, TN 37211-4123, USA

Young, Brian (Musician)
MOB Agency
6404 Wilshire Blvd Ste 505
Los Angeles, CA 90048-5507, USA

Young, Bryant C (Football Player)
San Francisco 49ers
5802 Country Club Pkwy
San Jose, CA 95138-2223, USA

Young, Burt (Actor)
c/o Denny Sevier *The House of Representatives*
211 S Beverly Dr Ste 208
Beverly Hills, CA 90212-3879, USA

Young, Charle E (Football Player)
16035 Mink Rd NE
Woodinville, WA 98077-9460, USA

Young, Charles L (Football Player)
Dallas Cowboys
2120 Daufuskie Dr
Raleigh, NC 27604-2074, USA

Young, Chris T
5959 Triumph St
Commerce, CA 90040-1609, USA

Young, Christoper (Composer)
Kraft-Benjamin-Engel
15233 Ventura Blvd Ste 200
Sherman Oaks, CA 91403-2244, USA

Young, Colville N (General, Governor)
Governor General's Office
Belize House
Belnopan, BELIZE

Young, Corey
11553 Sunshine Ter
Studio City, CA 91604-3835, USA

Young, Curt (Baseball Player)
Oakland A's
10800 E Cactus Rd Unit 2
Scottsdale, AZ 85259-2503, USA

Young, Dean (Cartoonist)
King Features Syndicate
888 7th Ave Ste 201
New York, NY 10106-0201, USA

Young, Dey (Actor, Producer)
c/o Devon Jackson *Trademark Talent*
4758 Allott Ave
Sherman Oaks, CA 91423-2403, USA

Young, Duane (Football Player)
San Diego Chargers
2255 River Run Dr
San Diego, CA 92108-5888, USA

Young, Earl (Athlete, Track Athlete)
4344 Livingston Ave
Dallas, TX 75205-2608, USA

Young, Eric O (Baseball Player)
28 Regina Dr
Hattiesburg, MS 39402-8353, USA

Young, Frank E (Government Official, Scientist)
Food & Drug Administration
5600 Fishers Ln
Rockville, MD 20852-1750, USA

Young, Fred (Musician)
Mitchell Fox Mgmt
212 3rd Ave N Ste 301
Nashville, TN 37201-1632, USA

Young, Fredd (Football Player)
Seattle Seahawks
4200 Real Del Sur
Las Cruces, NM 88011-7204, USA

Young, George L (Athlete, Track Athlete)
8926 N Cox Rd
Casa Grande, AZ 85294-7230, USA

Young, Glenn (Football Player)
Green Bay Packers
8035 Burchmore Rd
Three Lakes, WI 54562-9264, USA

Young, H Edwin (Religious Leader)
Southern Baptist Convention
901 Commerce St Ste 400
Nashville, TN 37203-3628, USA

Young, Howard (Howie) (Hockey Player)
5527 N 22nd Dr
Phoenix, AZ 85015-2316, USA

Young, J Warren (Publisher)
Boys Life Magazine
1325 W Walnut Hill Ln
Irving, TX 75038-3008, USA

Young, Jacob (Actor)
c/o Staff Member *International Creative Management (ICM-LA)*
10250 Constellation Blvd
Los Angeles, CA 90067-6200, USA

Young, James (Musician)
c/o Sterling Bacon *TBA Artist Management (Atlanta)*
1111 Alderman Dr Ste 285
Alpharetta, GA 30005-5433, USA

Young, Jerry (Religious Leader)
Grace Brethren Church Fellowship
855 Tumbull St
Deltona, FL 32725, USA

Young, Jesse Colin (Musician, Songwriter, Writer)
Skyline Music
PO Box 38
Jefferson, NH 03583-0038, USA

Young, Jewell L (Basketball Player)
4480 Fairways Blvd Bldg 8 # 203
Bradenton, FL 34209-8059, USA

Young, Jim (Coach, Football Coach)
US Military Academy
Athletic Dept
West Point, NY 10966, USA

Young, Joe (Football Player)
Denver Broncos
33261 Windtree Ave
Wildomar, CA 92595-8235, USA

Young, John A (Business Person)
Norvell Inc
122 E 1700 S
Provo, UT 84606-6194, USA

Young, John W (Astronaut)
NASA
2101 Nasa Pkwy
Johnson Space Center
Houston, TX 77058-3691, USA

Young, John Zachary (Misc)
1 Crossroads
Brill
Bucks HP18 9TL, UNITED KINGDOM (UK)

Young, Judith Knight (Actor)
Ann Steel
330 W 42nd St Ste 1800
New York, NY 10036-6902, USA

Young, Kathy (Musician)
Cape Entertainment
8432 NW 31st Ct
Sunrise, FL 33351-8901, USA

Young, Keone (Actor)
Gage Group
14724 Ventura Blvd Ste 505
Sherman Oaks, CA 91403-3505, USA

Young, Kevin (Athlete, Track Athlete)
8860 Corbin Ave
Northridge, CA 91324-3309, USA

Young, Larry (Baseball Player)
PO Box 255
Roscoe, IL 61073-0255, USA

Young, Laurence Retman (Astronaut)
217 Thorndike St Apt 108
Cambridge, MA 02141-1504, USA

Young, Lee Thompson (Actor)
c/o Staff Member *William Morris Agency (WMA-LA)*
1 William Morris Pl
Beverly Hills, CA 90212-4261, USA

Young, Lonnie (Football Player)
St Louis Cardinals
6437 S Cedar St
Express Personnel Services
Lansing, MI 48911-5960, USA

Young, M Adrian (Football Player)
Philadelphia Eagles
10300 4th St Ste 100
Rancho Cucamonga, CA 91730-5808, USA

Young, Martin D (Misc)
1110 Marshall Rd # 2007
Greenwood, SC 29646-4216, USA

Young, Melissa (Actor)
Badgley Connor Talent
1680 Vine St Ste 1016
Los Angeles, CA 90028-8800, USA

Young, Mighty Joe (Musician)
Jay Reil
3430 Bayberry Dr
Northbrook, IL 60062-2217, USA

Young, Mike (Football Player)
Los Angeles Rams
20 Cherry Hills Farm Dr
Englewood, CO 80113-7165, USA

Young, Neil (Musician)
c/o Elliot Roberts *Lookout Management*
1460 4th St Ste 300
Santa Monica, CA 90401-3415, USA

Young, Nina (Actor)
c/o Staff Member *BBC Television Centre*
Incoming Mail
Wood Lane
London W12 7RJ, UNITED KINGDOM (UK)

Young, Paul (Musician)
What Mgmt
PO Box 1463
Culver City, CA 90232-1463, USA

Young, Ray (Misc)
3360 Barham Blvd
Los Angeles, CA 90068-1473, USA

Young, Raymond
7 Church St.
Littlehampton, ENGLAND BN1Y 5EL, UNITED KINGDOM (UK)

Young, Ric (Actor)
c/o Staff Member *Coast to Coast Talent Group*
3350 Barham Blvd
Los Angeles, CA 90068-1404, USA

Young, Richard
1275 Westwood Blvd
Los Angeles, CA 90024-4811, USA

Young, Richard E (Scientist)
Jet Propulsion Laboratory
4800 Oak Grove Dr
Pasadena, CA 91109-8001, USA

Young, Richard S (Educator)
137 Saint Croix Ave
Cocoa Beach, FL 32931-3334, USA

Young, Richard S (Photographer)
110 Highlever Road
London W10 6PL, UNITED KINGDOM (UK)

Young, Rickey (Football Player)
San Diego Chargers
13670 Valley View Rd Apt 116
Eden Prairie, MN 55344-1977, USA

Young, Robert (Football Player)
Los Angeles Rams
RR 7 Box 306
Carthage, MS 39051, USA

Young, Robert (Bob) (Athlete, Track Athlete)
8705 Fairfield Dr
Bakersfield, CA 93311-1593, USA

Young, Ron Jr (War Hero)
c/o Staff Member *Premiere Speakers Bureau*
1000 Corporate Centre Dr Ste 120
Franklin, TN 37067-6209, USA

Young, Roynell (Football Player)
Philadelphia Eagles
11823 Beinhorn Dr
Houston, TX 77065-1607, USA

Young, Sean (Actor)
c/o Staff Member *Cathy Atkinson*
2629 Main St
Pmb 129
Santa Monica, CA 90405-4001, USA

Young, Steve (Football Player)
Tampa Bay Buccaneers
3780 Edgewood Dr
Provo, UT 84604, USA

Young, Steve (Football Player, Sportscaster)
c/o Staff Member *ESPN (Main)*
935 Middle St
Espn Plaza
Bristol, CT 06010-1000, USA

Young, Steve (Misc)
American Federation of Musicians
1501 Broadway Ste 800
New York, NY 10036-5505, USA

Young, Tom (Coach)
Washington Wizards
601 F St NW
Mci Centre
Washington, DC 20004-1605, USA

Young, Tracy (DJ)
c/o Len Evans *Project Publicity*
312 W 53rd St
New York, NY 10019-5743, USA

Young, Vince (Football Player)
c/o Team Member *Tennessee Titans*
460 Great Circle Rd
Baptist Sports Park
Nashville, TN 37228-1404, USA

Young, Vincent (Actor)
c/o Alan Ellsweig *Metropolitan*
4500 Wilshire Blvd Fl 2
Los Angeles, CA 90010-3858, USA

Young, Wilbur (Football Player)
Kansas City Chiefs
121 W Bannister Rd
Kansas City, MO 64114-4010, USA

Young, Will (Musician)
c/o Staff Member *Pop Idol (Fremantle Media)*
2700 Colorado Ave Ste 450
Santa Monica, CA 90404-3599, USA

Young, William Allen (Actor)
5519 S Holt Ave
Los Angeles, CA 90056-1312, USA

Young, Willie (Football Player)
New York Giants
134 Lewis St
Grambling, LA 71245-3227, USA

Young, Wise (Scientist)
Rutgers University
Collaborative Neuroscience Center
New Brunswick, NJ 08901, USA

Young Jr, Walter R (Business Person)
Champion Enterprises
2710 University Dr
Auburn Hills, MI 48326, USA

Young Knives, The (Music Group)
c/o Staff Member *Paradigm (Monterey)*
509 Hartnell St
Monterey, CA 93940-2825, USA

Young MC (Musician)
Universal Attractions
145 W 57th St # 1500
New York, NY 10019-2220, USA

Youngberg, Renae (Baseball Player)
2001 Gasparilla Rd # 25
Placida, FL 33946-2603, USA

Youngblood, George (Football Player)
Los Angeles Rams
16429 Lazare Ln
Huntington Beach, CA 92649-1862, USA

Youngblood, H Jackson (Jack) (Football Player, Sportscaster)
Los Angeles Rams
4377 Steed Ter
Winter Park, FL 32792-7630, USA

Youngblood, Jimmy L (Jim) (Football Player)
Los Angeles Rams
534 N Manhattan Pl
Los Angeles, CA 90004-2513, USA

Youngblood, Rob
1604 N Vista St
Los Angeles, CA 90046-2818, USA

Youngblood, Sydney
Postfach 20 13 43
Hamburg D-29243, GERMANY

Youngen, Lois (Baseball Player)
45 Prall Ln
Eugene, OR 97405-3335, USA

Younger, Ben (Director, Writer)
c/o Staff Member *Creative Artists Agency LCC (CAA-LA)*
2000 Avenue Of The Stars
Los Angeles, CA 90067-4700, USA

Youngerman, Jack (Artist)
PO Box 508
Bridgehampton, NY 11932-0508, USA

Youngfellow, Barrie (Actor)
c/o Staff Member *Gage Group, The (LA)*
14724 Ventura Blvd Ste 505
Sherman Oaks, CA 91403-3505, USA

Younis, Waqar (Cricketer)
Surrey County Cricket Club
Kennington Oval
London SE11 5SS, UNITED KINGDOM (UK)

Yount, Robin R (Baseball Player)
5001 E Arabian Way
Paradise Valley, AZ 85253-1501, USA

Youso, Frank (Football Player)
New York Giants
PO Box 1046
International Falls, MN 56649-1046, USA

Youssoufi, Abdderrahmane El (Prime Minister)
Prime Minister's Office
Rabat, MOROCCO

Yowarsky, Walt (Football Player)
Washington Redskins
395 Dogwood Pl NW
Cleveland, TN 37312-4414, USA

Yu, Ronnie (Director, Producer, Writer)
c/o Richard Arlook *Gersh Agency, The (LA)*
232 N Canon Dr
Beverly Hills, CA 90210-5302, USA

Yu Chuan Yong (Architect)
Urban/Rural Construction Committee
149 Guangming Road
Weihai PR, CHINA

Yuan, Ron (Actor)
c/o Staff Member *Amsel Eisenstadt & Frazier Inc*
5055 Wilshire Blvd Ste 865
Los Angeles, CA 90036-6109, USA

Yuan Enfeng (Musician)
Provincial Broadcasting/TV Station
Xian, Shaanxi, CHINA

Yuan Zhongyi (Archaeologist, Misc)
Qin Shi Huang's Terracotta Army Museum
Lintong, Xi'an, CHINA

Yuasa, Joji (Composer)
1517 Shields Ave
Encinitas, CA 92024-2911, USA

Yudof, Mark G (Educator)
University of Minnesota
President's Office
Minneapolis, MN 55434, USA

Yue Jingyu (Swimmer)
Physical Culture/Sports Bureau
9 Tiyuguan Road
Beijing, CHINA

Yuen, Corey (Actor, Director)
c/o Steve Chasman *Ace Media*
1411 5th St Ste 405
Santa Monica, CA 90401-2417, USA

Yulin, Harris (Actor)
40 W 86th St # 5C
New York, NY 10024-3605, USA

Yun-Fat, Chow (Actor)
c/o Lee Stollman *Endeavor Agency LLC (LA)*
9601 Wilshire Blvd Fl 3
Beverly Hills, CA 90210-5204, USA

Yune, Johnny
1921 Scenic Sunrise Dr
Las Vegas, NV 89117-7237, USA

Yune, Rick (Actor)
Innovative Artists
1505 10th St
Santa Monica, CA 90401-2805, USA

Yunis, Jorge J (Misc)
Thomas Jefferson University
Jefferson Medical College
Philadelphia, PA 19107, USA

Yunus, Muhammad (Nobel Prize Laureate)
Grameen America
500 W Cummings Park Ste 5200
Woburn, MA 01801-6503, USA

Yurchikhin, Fyodor N (Cosmonaut)
NASA
2101 Nasa Pkwy
Johnson Space Center
Houston, TX 77058-3691, USA

Yushchenko, Victor (President)
President's Office
Bankova Str 11
Kiev 01220, UKRAINE

Yushkevich, Dmitri (Hockey Player)
International Sports Advisors
878 Ridge View Way
Franklin Lakes, NJ 07417-1524, USA

Yuvarani (Actor, Bollywood)
Plot No 28 Annamalai Colony
Virugambakkam
Chennai, TN 600092, INDIA

Yzaguirre, Raul (Activist)
National Council of La Raza
1126 16th St NW Ste 500
Washington, DC 20036-4826, USA

Yzerman, Steve (Hockey Player)
PO Box 488
Bloomfield Hills, MI 48303-0488, USA

Z

Z, Jenna (Model)
PO Box 39624
N Ridgeville, OH 44039-0624, USA

Zaa, Charlie (Musician)
c/o Staff Member *Sony Music Miami*
605 Lincoln Rd Fl 7
Miami Beach, FL 33139-2900, USA

Zabaleta, Nicanor (Musician)
Villa Izar
Aldapeta
San Sebasatian 20009, SPAIN

Zabarain, Ines (Actor)
c/o Staff Member *TV Caracol*
Calle 76 #11 - 35
Piso 10AA
Bogota DC 26484, COLOMBIA

Zabel, Mark (Athlete)
Grosse Fischerei 18A
Calbe/Saale 39240, GERMANY

Zabel, Steven G (Steve) (Football Player)
Philadelphia Eagles
6000 Oak Tree Rd
Edmond, OK 73025-2625, USA

Zaborowski, Robert R J M (Religious Leader)
Mariavite Old Catholic Church
2803 10th St
Wyandotte, MI 48192-4994, USA

Zabriski, Bruce (Golfer)
6228 Winding Lake Dr
Jupiter, FL 33458-3787, USA

Zabriskie, Grace (Actor)
c/o David Rose *Innovative Artists (LA)*
1505 10th St
Santa Monica, CA 90401-2805, USA

Zachara, Jan (Boxer)
Sladkovicova 13
Nova Dubnica 01851, CZECH REPUBLIC

Zacharius, Walter (Publisher)
475 Park Ave S
New York, NY 10016-6901, USA

Zachary, Ken (Football Player)
San Diego Chargers
General Delivery
Newalla, OK 74857-9999, USA

Zacherle, John (Actor)
125 W 96th St Apt 4B
New York, NY 10025-6423, USA

Zadan, Craig (Producer)
c/o Staff Member *William Morris Agency (WMA-LA)*
1 William Morris Pl
Beverly Hills, CA 90212-4261, USA

Zadeh, Lofti A (Scientist)
904 Mendocino Ave
Berkeley, CA 94707-1925, USA

Zadel, C William (Business Person)
Millipore Corp
80 Ashby Rd
Bedford, MA 01730-2271, USA

Zaentz, Saul (Producer)
Saul Zaentz Co
2600 10th St
Berkeley, CA 94710-2597, USA

Zaeske, Paul (Football Player)
Houston Oilers
12250 S Kirkwood Rd Apt 1818
Stafford, TX 77477-2129, USA

Zaffaroni, Alejandro C (Misc)
Alza Corp
1950 Charleston Rd
Mountain View, CA 94043-1218, USA

Zafferani, Rosa (Misc)
Co-Regent's Office
Government Palace
47031, SAN MARINO

Zagaria, Anita (Actor)
Carol Levi Co
Via Giuseppe Pisanelli
Rome 00196, ITALY

Zaglmann-Willinger, Cornelia (Director)
Siegfriedstr 9
Munich 80802, GERMANY

Zagorin, Perez (Historian)
2990 Beaumont Farm Rd
Charlottesville, VA 22901-8717, USA

Zahn, Geoffrey C (geof) (Baseball Player)
6536 Walsh Rd
Dexter, MI 48130-9656, USA

Zahn, Paula (Television Host)
Paula Zahn Now
1 Time Warner Ctr Fl 7
Cnn
New York, NY 10019-6038, USA

Zahn, Steve (Actor)
c/o Marsha McManus *Principal Entertainment (LA)*
1964 Westwood Blvd Ste 400
Los Angeles, CA 90025-4695, USA

Zahn, Wayne (Bowler)
2143 E Center Ln
Tempe, AZ 85281-7719, USA

Zaklinsky, Konstantin (Dancer)
Mariinsky Theater
Teatralnaya Square 1
Saint Petersburg 190000, RUSSIA

Zaks, Jerry (Director)
Helen Merrill
337 W 22nd St
New York, NY 10011-2607, USA

Zal, Roxana (Actor)
P M K Public Relations
700 N San Vicente Blvd Ste G910
West Hollywood, CA 90069-5061, USA

Zalapski, Zarley (Hockey Player)
308 Kingsberry Cir
Pittsburgh, PA 15234-1069, USA

Zale, Richard N (Misc)
724 Santa Ynez St
Stanford, CA 94305-8441, USA

Zalejski, Ernie (Football Player)
Baltimore Colts
427 S Grant St
South Bend, IN 46619-3533, USA

Zalyotin, Sergei V (Cosmonaut)
Potchta Kosmonavtov
Moskovskoi Oblasti
Syvisdny Goroduk 141160, RUSSIA

Zamba, Frieda (Misc)
2706 S Central Ave
Flagler Beach, FL 32136-4037, USA

Zambri, Chris (Golfer)
1329 La Culebra Cir
Camarillo, CA 93012-5551, USA

Zamecnik, Paul (Misc)
101 Chestnut St
Boston, MA 02108-1032, USA

Zamecnik, Paul C (Doctor)
Worcester Experimental Biology Foundation
222 Maple Ave
Shrewsbury, MA 01545-2732, USA

Zamka, George D (Astronaut)
144 Lake Point Dr
League City, TX 77573-6970, USA

Zampini, Carina (Actor)
c/o Staff Member *Telefe - Argentina*
Pavon 2444 (C1248AAT)
Buenos Aires, ARGENTINA

Zamprogna, Dominic (Actor)
Margie Weiner Management
8205 Santa Monica Blvd
C/O Margie Weiner
West Hollywood, CA 90046-5977, USA

Zander, Carl (Football Player)
Cincinnati Bengals
2536 W Palomino Dr
Chandler, AZ 85224-1639, USA

Zander, Robin (Musician)
Monterey Peninsula Artists
509 Hartnell St
Monterey, CA 93940-2825, USA

Zander, Thomas (Wrestler)
Grundfeldstr 23
Aalen 73432, GERMANY

Zanders, Emanuel (Football Player)
New Orleans Saints
11015 Goodwood Blvd
Baton Rouge, LA 70815-5222, USA

Zane, Billy (Actor)
15030 Ventura Blvd # 710
Sherman Oaks, CA 91403-5470, USA

Zane, Lil (Musician)
c/o Staff Member *JL Entertainment Inc*
18653 Ventura Blvd # 340
Tarzana, CA 91356-4103, USA

Zane, Lisa (Actor)
505 N Lake Shore Dr Apt 5407
Chicago, IL 60611-6446, USA

Zanes, Dan (Musician, Songwriter, Writer)
c/o Harriet Sternberg *Harriet Sternberg Management*
4530 Gloria Ave
Encino, CA 91436-2718, USA

Zanetti, Eugenio (Actor, Director)
c/o Frank Wuliger *Gersh Agency, The (LA)*
232 N Canon Dr
Beverly Hills, CA 90210-5302, USA

Zano, Nick (Actor)
c/o Staff Member *3 Arts Entertainment Inc*
9460 Wilshire Blvd Fl 7
Beverly Hills, CA 90212-2713, USA

Zanuck, Lili Fini (Director, Producer)
Zanuck Co
9465 Wilshire Blvd Ste 308
Beverly Hills, CA 90212-2602, USA

Zanuck, Richard D (Producer)
Zanuck Co
9465 Wilshire Blvd Ste 308
Beverly Hills, CA 90212-2602, USA

Zanussi, Krzysztof (Director)
Ul Kaniowska 114
Warsaw 01-529, POLAND

Zapalac, Willie (Football Player)
New York Jets
1400 Shannon Oaks Trl
Austin, TX 78746-7345, USA

Zapata, Carmen (Actor)
6107 Ethel Ave
Van Nuys, CA 91401-3218, USA

Zapata, Laura (Actor)
c/o Staff Member *Televisa*
Blvd Adolfo Lopez Mateos 232
Colonia San Angel INN
DF CP 01060, MEXICO

Zapp, Jim (Baseball Player)
Baltimore Elite Giants
820 Youngs Ln
Nashville, TN 37207-4828, USA

Zappa, Dweezil (Actor, Musician)
7885 Woodrow Wilson Dr
Los Angeles, CA 90046-1213, USA

Zappa, Moon
PO Box 5265
N Hollywood, CA 91616-5265, USA

Zappa, Moon Unit (Actor, Musician)
10377 Oletha Ln
Los Angeles, CA 90077-2417, USA

Zara, Lucy (Actor, Model)
c/o Staff Member *Don Capo Entertainment*
Ste 5 South Bank Terrace
Surbiton
Surrey KT6 6DG, UNITED KINGDOM (UK)

Zarate, Carlos (Boxer)
Gene Aguilera
PO Box 113
Montebello, CA 90640-0113, USA

Zarley, Kermit (Golfer)
16600 N Thompson Peak Pkwy Unit 2081
Scottsdale, AZ 85260-2185, USA

Zarnas, August C (Gust) (Football Player)
850 Jennings St
Bethlehem, PA 18017-7010, USA

Zatkoff, Roger (Football Player)
Green Bay Packers
5726 Woodwind Dr
Bloomfield Hills, MI 48301-1068, USA

Zatopkova, Dana (Athlete, Track Athlete)
Nad Kazankov 3
Prague 7 171 00, CZECH REPUBLIC

Zaunbrecher, Godfrey (Football Player)
Minnesota Vikings
532 Pacific St
Elkhorn, NE 68022-3357, USA

Zaveri, Anjala (Actor, Bollywood)
604 Jupiter Apts Yari Road
Andheri (W)
Mumbai, MS 400058, INDIA

Zaveri, Anjali (Actor, Bollywood)
604 Jupiter Apartments
Yari Road
Andheri, Mumbai 400058, INDIA

Zawadzkas, Gerald (Football Player)
Detroit Lions
2712 Alcazar St NE
Albuquerque, NM 87110-3514, USA

Zawoluk, Robert (Zeke) (Basketball Player)
325 W 17th St
New York, NY 10011, USA

Zdrok, Victoria (Model)
PO Box 332
Pompton Lakes, NJ 07442-0332, USA

Zea, Natalie (Actor)
c/o Robert Semon *Imparato Fay Management*
1126 Roxbury Dr
Los Angeles, CA 90035-1031, USA

Zeal, Meredith (Actor)
c/o Marv Dauer *Marv Dauer Management*
11661 San Vicente Blvd Ste 104
Los Angeles, CA 90049-5150, USA

Zeamer Jr, Jay (War Hero)
108 Emery Ln
Boothbay Harbor, ME 04538-1966, USA

Zech, Rosel
Agensstr. 47
Munich 80798, GERMANY

Zecher, Rich (Football Player)
Oakland Raiders
PO Box 1859
Eureka, MT 59917-1859, USA

Zeckendorf Jr, William (Business Person)
502 Park Ave
New York, NY 10022-1108, USA

Zeckhauser, Richard J (Economist)
138 Irving St
Cambridge, MA 02138-1929, USA

Zedillo Ponce de Leon, Ernesto (Politician, President)
Institutional Revolutionary
Insurges N 61
Mexico City, DF 06350, MEXICO

Zedlitz, Jean (Golfer)
4587 Gatetree Cir
Pleasanton, CA 94566-6031, USA

Zeffirelli, G Franco (Director)
c/o Johnnie Planco *Untitled Entertainment (NY)*
322 8th Ave Ste 601
New York, NY 10001-6715, USA

Zegers, Kevin (Actor)
c/o Paul Nicholls *Artistry Management*
525 Westbourne Dr
West Hollywood, CA 90048-1913, USA

Zeglis, John D (Business Person)
AT & T Corp
32 Avenue Of The Americas
New York, NY 10013-2473, USA

Zeh, Geoffrey N (Misc)
Maintenance of Way Employees Brotherhood
12050 Woodward Ave
Detroit, MI 48203-3578, USA

Zehetner, Nora (Actor)
c/o Paul Nelson *Mosaic Media Group*
24 Music Sq W Fl 1
Nashville, TN 37203-6661, USA

Zeidel, Larry (Hockey Player)
101 Millcreek Rd
Ardmore, PA 19003-1537, USA

Zeidler, Eberard H (Architect)
Zeidler Roberts Architects
315 Queen St W
Toronto, ON M5V 2X2, CANADA

Zeier, Eric (Football Player)
Cleveland Browns
PO Box 327
Nashville, GA 31639-0327, USA

Zeigler, Alma (Baseball Player)
1245 Del Mar Dr
Los Osos, CA 93402-4018, USA

Zeigler, Dusty (Football Player)
Buffalo Bills
440 Hodgeville Rd
Guyton, GA 31312-7103, USA

Zeigler, Heidi (Actor)
c/o Staff Member *Mary Grady Agency (MGA)*
4400 Coldwater Canyon Ave Ste 135
The Landmark Bldg
Studio City, CA 91604-5038, USA

Zeigler, Larry
10620 Woodchase Cir
Orlando, FL 32836-5885, USA

Zeigler, Marie (Baseball Player)
2502 N 22nd Ave
Phoenix, AZ 85009-1926, USA

Zeile, Todd E (Baseball Player)
c/o Staff Member *New York Mets*
12301 Roosevelt Ave
Shea Stadium
Flushing, NY 11368-1699, USA

Zeilic, Mauricio (Actor)
c/o Staff Member *Telemundo*
2470 W 8th Ave
Hialeah, FL 33010-2000, USA

Zeitlin, Zvi (Musician)
204 Warren Ave
Rochester, NY 14618-4316, USA

Zelensky, Igor (Dancer)
New York City Ballet
Lincoln Center Plaza
New York, NY 10023, USA

Zelepukin, Valeri (Hockey Player)
Chicago Blackhawks
1901 W Madison St
United Center
Chicago, IL 60612-2459, USA

Zelezny, Jan (Athlete, Track Athlete)
Rue Armady 683
Boleslav, CZECH REPUBLIC

Zell, Samuel (Business Person)
Itel Corp
2 N Riverside Plz
Chicago, IL 60606-2600, USA

Zellars, Ray (Football Player)
New Orleans Saints
1327 Island Ave
Pittsburgh, PA 15212-2845, USA

Zeller, Hank
2120 Greentree Rd Apt 100E
Pittsburgh, PA 15220-6405, USA

Zellner, Peppi (Football Player)
Dallas Cowboys
31 Dew Pl
Forsyth, GA 31029-3302, USA

Zellweger, Renee (Actor, Musician, Producer)
c/o John Carrabino *John Carrabino Management*
5900 Wilshire Blvd Ste 406
Los Angeles, CA 90036-5015, USA

Zelman, Aaron (Writer)
c/o Staff Member *International Creative Management (ICM-LA)*
10250 Constellation Blvd
Los Angeles, CA 90067-6200, USA

Zelmani, Sophie (Musician)
United Stage Artists
PO Box 11029
Stockholm 100 61, SWEDEN

Zeman, E Robert (Football Player)
Los Angeles Chargers
PO Box 132907
Big Bear Lake, CA 92315-8998, USA

Zeman, Ed (Football Player)
Los Angeles Rams
3002 Jeffrey Dr # C
Costa Mesa, CA 92626-2929, USA

Zeman, Jacklyn (Actor)
STone Manners
6500 Wilshire Blvd Ste 550
Los Angeles, CA 90048-4950, USA

Zeman, Milos (Prime Minister)
Premier's Office
Nabrezi E Benese 4
Prague 1 118 01, CZECH REPUBLIC

Zemanova, Veronica (Model)
Veronica Zemanova Management
G Noodtstr 12 SW
Nijmegen 6511, THE NETHERLANDS

Zembriski, Walter (Golfer)
6507 Doubletrace Ln
Orlando, FL 32819-4653, USA

Zemeckis, Robert L (Director, Producer, Writer)
100 Universal City Plz
#Building 484
Universal City, CA 91608-1002, USA

Zenawi, Hailu (Prime Minister)
Prime Minister's Office
PO Box 1013
Addis Ababa, ETHIOPIA

Zenawi, Meles (President)
President's Office
PO Box 5707
Addis Ababa, ETHIOPIA

Zendejas, Luis (Football Player)
Dallas Cowboys
6609 S 47th Pl
Phoenix, AZ 85042-5352, USA

Zender, Hans (Composer)
Am Rosenheck
Bad Soden 65812, GERMANY

Zender, Stuart (Musician)
Searles
Chapel
26A Munster St
London SW6 4EN, UNITED KINGDOM (UK)

Zeno, Coleman (Football Player)
New York Giants
PO Box 202
Banner Elk, NC 28604-0202, USA

Zeno, Lance (Football Player)
Cleveland Browns
530 Landfair Ave
Los Angeles, CA 90024-2104, USA

Zentmyer Jr, George A (Misc)
955 S El Camino Real # 216
San Mateo, CA 94402-2346, USA

Zentner, Sy
4825 Fairfax Ave
Las Vegas, NV 89120-1739, USA

Zepeda, David (Actor)
c/o Staff Member *Osbrink Talent Agency*
4343 Lankershim Blvd # 100
North Hollywood, CA 91602-2705, USA

Zephaniah, Benjamin (Actor, Writer)
18 Fountain Street
Ulverston LA12 7EQ, UNITED KINGDOM (UK)

Zeppelin, Dread (Musician)
The M.O.B Agency
6404 Wilshire Blvd Ste 700
Los Angeles, CA 90048-5509, USA

Zeppelin, Led (Musician)
46 Kensington Ct St
London, ENGLAND W8 5DP, UNITED KINGDOM (UK)

Zerbe, Anthony (Actor)
411 W 115th St Apt 51
New York, NY 10025-1730, USA

Zereoue, Amos (Football Player)
Pittsburgh Steelers
116 Tanglewood Dr
Wexford, PA 15090-8692, USA

Zerhouni, Elias A (Doctor, Government Official)
National Institutes of Health
9000 Rockville Pike
Bethesda, MD 20892-0002, USA

Zernial, Gus E (Baseball Player)
687 Coventry Ave
Clovis, CA 93611-8526, USA

Zero, Mark (Musician)
PO Box 656507
Fresh Meadows, NY 11365-6507, USA

Zervas, Nicholas T (Doctor)
100 Canton Ave
Milton, MA 02186-3507, USA

Zeta-Jones, Catherine (Actor)
c/o Cary Berman *William Morris Agency (WMA-LA)*
1 William Morris Pl
Beverly Hills, CA 90212-4261, USA

Zetsche, Dieter (Business Person)
Daimler-Chrysler AG
Plieningstr
Stuttgart 70546, GERMANY

Zettler, Michael E (General)
Deputy Chief Of Staff For Logistics
Hqusa Pentagon
Washington, DC 20310-0001, USA

Zettler, Rob (Hockey Player)
31 Tadcaster Place
Saulte Sainte Marie, ON P6B 5E3,
CANADA

Zewail, Ahmed H (Nobel Prize Laureate)
871 Winston Ave
San Marino, CA 91108-1430, USA

Zgonina, Jeff (Football Player)
41 Hawthorne Ln
Barrington, IL 60010-5109, USA

Zhamnov, Alexei (Hockey Player)
1950 N Orchard St
Chicago, IL 60614-5130, USA

Zhang, Aiping (General, Government
Official)
Ministry of Defense
State Council
Beijing, CHINA

Zhang, Xianliang (Writer)
Ningxia Writers Assn
Yinchuan City, CHINA

Zhang, Ziyi (Actor)
c/o Kelly Bush I/D PR (LA)
8409 Santa Monica Blvd
West Hollywood, CA 90069-4209, USA

Zhang, Ziyl (Actor)
William Morris Agency
151 El Camino Dr
Beverly Hills, CA 90212-2775, USA

Zhe-Xi Lo (Misc)
Camegie Natural History Museum
4400 Forbes Ave
Pittsburgh, PA 15213-4007, USA

Zhenan, Bao (Inventor)
AT & T Bell Lucent Laboratory
600 Mountain Ave
New Providence, NJ 07974-2008, USA

Zhirinovsky, Vladimir V (Government
Official)
Liberal Democratic Party
1st Basmanny Per 3
Moscow 103045, RUSSIA

Zhislin, Grigory Y (Musician)
25 Whiteball Gardens
London W3 9RD, UNITED KINGDOM
(UK)

Zhitnik, Alexel (Hockey Player)
Buffalo Sabres
1 Seymour St
Hsbc Arena
Buffalo, NY 14210, USA

Zholobov, Vitall M (Cosmonaut)
Ul Yanvarskovo Vostaniya D 12
Klev 252010, UKRAINE

Zhou Long (Composer)
University of Missouri
Music Dept
Kansas City, MO 64110, USA

Zhudov, Vyacheslav D (Cosmonaut)
Potchta Kosmonavtov
Moskovskoi Oblasti
Syvisdny Goroduk 141160, RUSSIA

...maliyev, Kubanychbek M
...ent Buildings
...7200003, KYRGYZSTAN

Zhvanetsky, Mikhail M (Actor, Writer)
Lesnaya Str 4
#63
Moscow 125047, RUSSIA

Zia, B Khaleda (Prime Minister)
Sere-e Bangla Nagar
Gono
Bhaban Sher-e-Banglanagar
Dakah, BANGLADESH

Ziblijew, Wassili (Cosmonaut)
Potchta Kosmonavtov
Moskovskoi Oblasti
Syvisdny Goroduk 141160, RUSSIA

Zidane, Zinedine (Soccer Player)
Real Madrid FC
Avda Concha Espina 1
Madrid 28036, SPAIN

Ziegler, Dolorea (Opera Singer)
Lynda Kay
2702 Crestworth Ln
Buford, GA 30519-6483, USA

Ziegler, Jack (Cartoonist)
New Yorker Magazine
4 Times Sq
Editorial Dept
New York, NY 10036-6592, USA

Ziegler, Larry (Golfer)
10315 Luton Ct
Orlando, FL 32836-3733, USA

Ziegler, Ron
413 N Lee St # 1417-D49
Alexandria, VA 22314-2301, USA

Ziegler Jr, John A (Misc)
Dickinson Wright
38525 Woodward Ave Ste 2000
Bloomfield, MI 48304-5092, USA

Ziemann, Sonia (Actor)
Via del Alp Dorf
Saint Moritz 7500, SWITZERLAND

Ziemann, Sonja
Neherstr. 7
Munich D-81675, GERMANY

Zien, Chip (Actor)
c/o Staff Member Gersh Agency, The (LA)
232 N Canon Dr
Beverly Hills, CA 90210-5302, USA

Ziering, Ian (Actor)
c/o Monica Barkett Global Artists Agency
1648 Wilcox Ave Ste 3
Los Angeles, CA 90028-6898, USA

Ziering, Nikki Schieler (Actor)
c/o Brady McKay Saffron Management
9171 Wilshire Blvd Ste 441
Beverly Hills, CA 90210-5516, USA

Ziffren, Kenneth (Lawyer)
Ziffren Brittenham Branca
1801 Century Park W
Los Angeles, CA 90067-6409, USA

Ziglar, Zig (Business Person)
Ziglar Training Systems
15303 Dallas Pkwy Ste 550
Addison, TX 75001-6480, USA

Zigler, Edward F (Educator)
Yale University
Bush Child Development Center
New Haven, CT 06520, USA

Zikarsky, Bengt (Swimmer)
SV Wurzburg 05
Oberer Bogenweg 1
Wurzburg 97074, GERMANY

Zikarsky, Bjorn (Swimmer)
555 California St Ste 2600
San Francisco, CA 94104-1602, USA

Zikes, Les (Bowler)
424 S Stuart Ln
Palatine, IL 60067-6730, USA

Zilinskas, Annette (Musician)
Creative Artists Agency
9830 Wilshire Blvd
Beverly Hills, CA 90212-1804, USA

Zilly, Jack (Football Player)
Los Angeles Rams
68 Lakewood Dr
Narragansett, RI 02882-3508, USA

Zim Zum (Musician)
Mitch Schneider Organization
14724 Ventura Blvd Ste 710
Sherman Oaks, CA 91403-3520, USA

Zima, Madeline (Actor)
c/o Sheila Wenzel Innovative Artists (LA)
1505 10th St
Santa Monica, CA 90401-2805, USA

Zimbalist, Stephanie (Actor)
c/o Staff Member The Blake Agency
1333 Ocean Ave
Santa Monica, CA 90401-1023, USA

Zimbalist III, Efrem (Business Person)
Times Mirror Co
Times Mirror Square
Los Angeles, CA 90053, USA

Zimbalist Jr, Efrem (Actor)
1448 Holsted Dr
Solvang, CA 93463-2054, USA

Zimerman, Krystian (Musician)
Columbia Artists Mgmt Inc
1790 Broadway Fl 6
New York, NY 10019-1412, USA

Zimm, Bruno H (Misc)
2522 Horizon Way
La Jolla, CA 92037-1122, USA

Zimmer, Constance (Actor)
c/o David Sweeney Sweeney
Management
8755 Lookout Mountain Ave
Los Angeles, CA 90046-1861, USA

Zimmer, Don
7069 Key Haven Rd Apt 201
Seminole, FL 33777-3870, USA

Zimmer, Hans (Composer)
1547 14th St
Santa Monica, CA 90404-3302, USA

Zimmer, Norma
661 Wood Lake Dr
Brea, CA 92821-2828, USA

Zimmerer, Wolfgang (Athlete)
Schwaigangerstr 22
Mumau 82418, GERMANY

Zimmerlink, Geno (Football Player)
Atlanta Falcons
318 Crestwood Dr
Milltown, NJ 08850-1849, USA

Zimmerman, Don (Football Player)
Philadelphia Eagles
107 Coretta St
Monroe, LA 71202-6901, USA

Zimmerman, Gary W (Football Player)
Minnesota Vikings
17450 Skyliners Rd
Bend, OR 97701-5203, USA

Zimmerman, H Leroy (Football Player)
808 Willis Ace
Madera, CA 93637, USA

Zimmerman, Howard E (Misc)
7813 Westchester Dr
Middleton, WI 53562-3671, USA

Zimmerman, James M (Business Person)
Federated Department Stores
151 W 34th St
New York, NY 10001-2101, USA

Zimmerman, John T (Scientist)
University of Colorado
Medical School
Neurology Dept
Denver, CO 80202, USA

Zimmerman, Kent (Publisher)
Friendly Exchange Magazine
1999 Shepard Rd
Saint Paul, MN 55116-3210, USA

Zimmerman, Mary Beth (Golfer)
2403 Bonshaw Ln
Marietta, GA 30064-5756, USA

Zimmerman, Matt
562 Eastern Ave. lford
Essex, ENGLAND 1G2 6PH, UNITED
KINGDOM (UK)

Zimmerman, Philip (Phil) (Designer)
Network Assoc
4677 Old Ironsides Dr
Santa Clara, CA 95054-1809, USA

Zimmerman, Ryan (Athlete, Baseball
Player)
c/o Staff Member Washington Nationals
2400 East Capitol Street SE
Rfk Stadium
Washington, DC 20003, USA

Zimmermann, Egon (Skier)
Hotel Krisberg
Am Arlberg 67644, AUSTRIA

Zimmermann, Frank P (Musician)
Riaskoff Mgmt
Concertgebouwplein 15
Amsterdam 1071 LL, THE NETHERLANDS

Zimmermann, Markus (Athlete)
Waldhauserstr 51-33
Schonau am Konigsee 83471, GERMANY

Zimmermann, Udo (Composer)
Operhaus Leipzig
Augustusptatz
Leipzig 04109, GERMANY

Zimny, Bob (Football Player)
Chicago Cardinals
1205 Maple Dr
Shelbyville, IN 46176-3209, USA

Zinder, Norton D (Misc)
450 E 63rd St
New York, NY 10065-7928, USA

Zinke, Olaf (Speed Skater)
Johannes Bobrowski Str 22
Berlin 12627, GERMANY

Zinkernagel, Rolf M (Nobel Prize
Laureate)
Rebhusstr 47
Zumikon 8126, SWITZERLAND

Zinman, David J (Conductor)
1212 Cathedral St
Baltimore Symphony
Baltimore, MD 21201-5556, USA

Zinner, Nick (Musician)
Yeah Yeah Yeahs
249 Metropolitan Ave
Brooklyn, NY 11211-4009, USA

Zinta, Preity (Actor, Bollywood)
C-10/A Ranwar Wadora Road
Off Hill Road Bandra (W)
Mumbai, MS 400050, INDIA

Zippel, David (Musician)
Kraft-Benjamin-Engel
15233 Ventura Blvd Ste 200
Sherman Oaks, CA 91403-2244, USA

Zisk, Richard W (Richie) (Baseball Player)
4231 NE 26th Ter
Lighthouse Point, FL 33064-8053, USA

Ziskin, Laura
c/o Staff Member *William Morris Agency (WMA-LA)*
1 William Morris Pl
Beverly Hills, CA 90212-4261, USA

Zito, Barry (Baseball Player)
c/o Team Member *San Francisco Giants*
24 Willie Mays Plz
Sbc Park
San Francisco, CA 94107-2199, USA

Zito, Chuck (Actor, Boxer)
c/o Darren Prince *Prince Marketing Group*
454 Prospect Ave # 74
West Orange, NJ 07052, USA

Zivkovic, Zoran (Prime Minister)
Prime Minister's Office
Nemanjina 11
Belgrade 11000, SERBIA

Ziyi, Zhang (Actor)
c/o Ling Lucas *Nine Muses and Apollo Inc*
525 Broadway Rm 201
New York, NY 10012-4482, USA

Zlatoper, Ronald J (Zap) (Admiral)
1001 Kamokila Blvd
Kapolei, HI 96707-2014, USA

Zlotoff, Lee (Director)
c/o Wendi Niad *Niad Management*
15030 Ventura Blvd Ste 19 Ste 860
Sherman Oaks, CA 91403-2244, USA

Zmed, Adrian (Actor)
c/o Staff Member *Tisherman Agency Inc*
6767 Forest Lawn Dr Ste 101
Los Angeles, CA 90068-1050, USA

Zmeskal, Kim (Gymnast)
Cincinnati Gymnastics Academy
3635 Woodridge Blvd
Fairfield, OH 45014-8521, USA

Zmievskaya Petrenko, Galina (Nina) (Coach)
International Skating Center
PO Box 577
Simsbury, CT 06070-0577, USA

Zmuda, Bob (Actor, Comedian)
c/o Monique Moss *Warren Cowan & Associates PR*
8899 Beverly Blvd Ste 919
Los Angeles, CA 90048-2436, USA

ZoeGirl (Music Group)
EMI Christian Music Group
101 Winners Cir N
Brentwood, TN 37027-5017, USA

Zoeller, Frank (Fuzzy) (Golfer)
Fuzzy Zoeller Productions Inc
12701 Covered Bridge Rd
Sellersburg, IN 47172-9699, USA

Zoeller, Fuzzy
418 Deer Run Trce
Floyds Knobs, IN 47119-8505, USA

Zoffinger, George R (Financier)
CoreStates (NJ) Bank
370 Scotch Rd
Pennington, NJ 08534, USA

Zofko, Mickey (Football Player)
Detroit Lions
321 W Fern Ave
Foley, AL 36535-2128, USA

Zokol, Richard (Golfer)
Contemporary Communication
1663 7th Ave W
Vancouver, BC V6J 1S4, CANADA

Zolak, Scott (Football Player)
New England Patriots
40 Comstock Dr
Wrentham, MA 02093-1852, USA

Zolotow, Charlotte (Writer)
29 Elm Pl
Hastings On Hudson, NY 10706-1703, USA

Zomalt, Eric (Football Player)
Philadelphia Eagles
25387 Delphinium Ave
Moreno Valley, CA 92553-7153, USA

Zombie, Rob
c/o Staff Member *The Firm*
9465 Wilshire Blvd Fl 6
Beverly Hills, CA 90212-2605, USA

Zombo, Rick (Hockey Player)
557 Vista Hills Ct
Eureka, MO 63025, USA

Zook, John E (Football Player)
Atlanta Falcons
9425 Riviera Rd
Roswell, GA 30075-5025, USA

Zook, Ron (Coach, Football Coach)
University of Illinois
Athletic Dept
Champaign, IL 61820, USA

Zophres, Mary (Designer)
c/o Staff Member *United Talent Agency (UTA)*
9560 Wilshire Blvd Ste 500
Beverly Hills, CA 90212-2401, USA

Zoran (Designer, Fashion Designer)
157 Chambers St # 1200
New York, NY 10007-1015, USA

Zordich, Mike (Football Player)
New York Jets
373 S Hazelwood Ave
Youngstown, OH 44509-2228, USA

Zorich, Christopher R (Chris) (Football Player)
Chicago Bears
47 W Polk St Ste 100
Chicago, IL 60605-2085, USA

Zorich, Louis (Actor)
c/o Staff Member *Susan Smith Company, The*
1344 N Wetherly Dr
Los Angeles, CA 90069-1817, USA

Zorn, James A (Jim) (Coach, Football Coach)
Seattle Seahawks
2006 W Mercer Way
Mercer Island, WA 98040-2020, USA

Zorrilla, Alberto (Swimmer)
580 Park Ave
New York, NY 10065-7313, USA

Zorrilla, China (Actor)
c/o Staff Member *Telefe - Argentina*
Pavon 2444 (C1248AAT)
Buenos Aires, ARGENTINA

Zsigmond, Vilmos (Cinematographer)
c/o Shari Shankewitz *Innovative Artists (LA)*
1505 10th St
Santa Monica, CA 90401-2805, USA

Zubak, Kresimir (President)
Presidency
Marsala Titz 7A
Sarajevo 71000, BOSNIA-HERZEGOVINA

Zuber, Maria (Geophysicist, Physicist)
Massachusetts Institute of Technology
Geophysics Dept
Cambridge, MA 02139, USA

Zucco, Victor (Football Player)
Chicago Bears
2276 Wulfert Rd
Sanibel, FL 33957-2209, USA

Zucker, David (Director, Producer)
c/o Staff Member *Zucker/Netter Productions*
1411 5th St Ste 402
Santa Monica, CA 90401-2417, USA

Zucker, Jerry (Director, Producer)
c/o Staff Member *Zucker Productions*
1250 6th St Ste 201
Santa Monica, CA 90401-1637, USA

Zuckerman, Josh (Actor)
c/o Anne Woodward *Saffron Management*
9171 Wilshire Blvd Ste 441
Beverly Hills, CA 90210-5516, USA

Zuckerman, Mortimer (Publisher)
Boston Properties
599 Lexington Ave
New York, NY 10022-7661, USA

Zuckerman, Pinchas (Conductor, Musician)
Shirley Kirshbaum Assoc
711 W End Ave Apt 5kn
New York, NY 10025-6843, USA

Zugsmith, Albert (Director)
23388 Mulholland Dr
Woodland Hills, CA 91364-2733, USA

Zuiker, Anthony E (Producer)
c/o Staff Member *Creative Artists Agency LCC (CAA-LA)*
2000 Avenue Of The Stars
Los Angeles, CA 90067-4700, USA

Zukav, Gary (Writer)
Fireside/Simon & Schuster
1230 Avenue Of The Americas Fl Conc1
New York, NY 10020-1513, USA

Zuker, Danny (Producer, Writer)
c/o Staff Member *Creative Artists Agency LCC (CAA-LA)*
2000 Avenue Of The Stars
Los Angeles, CA 90067-4700, USA

Zukerman, Eugenia (Musician)
Brooklyn College of Music
Bedford & H Aves
Brooklyn, NY 11210, USA

Zullo, Alan (Cartoonist)
Tribune Media Services
435 N Michigan Ave Ste 1500
Chicago, IL 60611-4012, USA

Zuniga, Daphne (Actor)
Murphy
2401 Main St
Santa Monica, CA 90405-3515, USA

Zuniga, Jose (Actor)
c/o Nancy Sanders *Sanders/Armstrong Management*
2120 Colorado Ave Ste 120
Santa Monica, CA 90404-3561, USA

Zuniga, Miles (Musician)
c/o Staff Member *Russell Carter Artist Management*
567 Ralph McGill Blvd NE
Atlanta, GA 30312-1110, USA

Zurbriggen, Pirmin (Skier)
Hotel Larchenhof
3905 Saas-Almagell
SWITZERLAND

Zurkowski-Holmes, Agnes (Baseball Player)
206-2339 Lorne St
Regina, SK S4P 2N2, CANADA

Zuverink, George (Baseball Player)
Cleveland Indians
1027 E McNair Dr
Tempe, AZ 85283-4733, USA

Zuvic, Daniella (Actor)
c/o Lani Lively *LA Entertainment*
1317 N San Fernando Blvd # 155
Burbank, CA 91504-4236, USA

Zvereva, Natalya (Tennis Player)
c/o Staff Member *Women's Tennis Association (WTA (US))*
133 1st St NE
St Petersburg, FL 33701-3307, USA

Zwanzig, Robert (Scientist)
5314 Sangamore Rd
Bethesda, MD 20816-2355, USA

Zweig, George (Physicist)
Los Alamos National Laboratory
PO Box 1663
Ms B276
Los Alamos, NM 87544-0600, USA

Zweig, Ivan (Baseball Player)
US Olympic Team
6502 Duffield Dr
Dallas, TX 75248-1314, USA

Zwerling, Darrell (Actor)
c/o Staff Member *CLInc Talent*
843 N Sycamore Ave
Los Angeles, CA 90038-3316, USA

Zwick, Charles J (Financier)
626 Coral Way Apt 1603
Coral Gables, FL 33134-7509, USA

Zwick, Edward M (Actor, Director, Producer, Writer)
c/o Staff Member *Bedford Falls Company, The*
409 Santa Monica Blvd Ph
Santa Monica, CA 90401-2232, USA

Zwick, Joel (Director)
c/o Staff Member *Irv Schechter Company*
9460 Wilshire Blvd Ste 300
Beverly Hills, CA 90212-2710, USA

Zwilich, Ellen Taaffe (Composer)
c/o Staff Member *Music Association of America*
224 King St
Englewood, NJ 07631-3026, USA

Zycinski, Jozef (Religious Leader)
Ul Prumasa St Wyszynskiego 2
Skr Poczt 198
Lublin 20-950, POLAND

Zydeco, Buckwheat (Musician)
c/o Staff Member *Concerted Efforts*
59 Parsons St
West Newton, MA 02465-2137, USA

Zykina, Lyudmila G (Musician)
Kotelnicheskaya Nab Y15 Korp B #64
Moscow, RUSSIA

Zylberstein, Elsa (Actor)
c/o Staff Member *Agence Intertalent*
5 Rue Clement Marot
Paris 75008, FRANCE

Zylis-Gara, Teresa (Opera Singer)
16A Blvd de Belgique
Monaco-Ville, MONACO

ZZ Top (Musician)
c/o Staff Member *Creative Artists Agency
LCC (CAA-LA)*
2000 Avenue Of The Stars
Los Angeles, CA 90067-4700, USA

Printed in the United States
129900LV00001BB/1-8/P

9 781604 870022